OUTSTANDING
ALA
RUSA
REFERENCE SOURCE

Acronyms, Initialisms
& Abbreviations
Dictionary
was named an
***"Outstanding
Reference Source,"***
*the highest honor
given by the
American Library
Association Reference
and User Services
Association.*

Acronyms, Initialisms & Abbreviations Dictionary

ISSN 0270-4404

Acronyms, Initialisms & Abbreviations Dictionary

A Guide to Acronyms, Abbreviations, Contractions, Alphabetic Symbols, and Similar Condensed Appellations

Covering: Aerospace, Associations, Banking, Biochemistry, Business, Data Processing, Domestic and International Affairs, Economics, Education, Electronics, Genetics, Government, Information Technology, Internet, Investment, Labor, Language, Law, Medicine, Military Affairs, Pharmacy, Physiology, Politics, Religion, Science, Societies, Sports, Technical Drawings and Specifications, Telecommunications, Trade, Transportation, and Other Fields

32nd Edition

Volume 1

Part 2

D-I

Mary Rose Bonk,
Project Editor

GALE®

THOMSON
GALE™

Detroit • New York • San Diego • San Francisco • Cleveland • New Haven, Conn. • Waterville, Maine • London • Munich

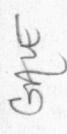

THOMSON
GALE

Acronyms, Initialisms and Abbreviations Dictionary
Volume 1

Project Editor
Mary Rose Bonk

Editorial
Pamela A. Dear

Data Capture
Katrina Coach
Cynthia Jones
Elizabeth Pilette
Ron Montgomery

Technical Support Services
Charlene Lewis

Product Design
Cynthia Baldwin

Manufacturing
Nekita McKee

For more information, contact
The Gale Group, Inc.
27500 Drake Road
Farmington Hills, MI 48331-3535
Or you can visit our Internet site at
http://www.gale.com

LIBRARY OF CONGRESS CATALOG CARD NUMBER 84-643188

ISBN 0-7876-4107-3 (Volume 1 Complete)
ISBN 0-7876-4108-1 (Part 1: A-C only)
ISBN 0-7876-4109-X (Part 2: D-I only)
ISBN 0-7876-4110-3 (Part 3: J-P only)
ISBN 0-7876-5804-9 (Part 4: Q-Z only)
ISSN 0270-4404

Printed in the United States of America
10 9 8 7 6 5 4 3 2 1

Contents

Volume 1
Part 1 A-C

Volume 1
Part 2 D-I

Volume 1
Part 3 J-P

Volume 1
Part 4 Q-Z

Gale's publications in the acronyms and abbreviations field include:

Acronyms, Initialisms & Abbreviations Dictionary series:

Acronyms, Initialisms & Abbreviations Dictionary (Volume 1). A guide to acronyms, initialisms, abbreviations, and similar contractions, arranged alphabetically by abbreviation.

Reverse Acronyms, Initialisms & Abbreviations Dictionary (Volume 3). A companion to Volume 1 in which terms are arranged alphabetically by meaning of the acronym, initialism, or abbreviation.

Acronyms, Initialisms & Abbreviations Dictionary Subject Guide series:

Computer & Telecommunications Acronyms (Volume 1). A guide to acronyms, initialisms, abbreviations, and similar contractions used in the field of computers and telecommunications in which terms are arranged alphabetically both by abbreviation and by meaning.

Business Acronyms (Volume 2). A guide to business-oriented acronyms, initialisms, abbreviations, and similar contractions in which terms are arranged alphabetically both by abbreviation and by meaning.

International Acronyms, Initialisms & Abbreviations Dictionary series:

International Acronyms, Initialisms & Abbreviations Dictionary (Volume 1). A guide to foreign and international acronyms, initialisms, abbreviations, and similar contractions, arranged alphabetically by abbreviation.

Reverse International Acronyms, Initialisms & Abbreviations Dictionary (Volume 2). A companion to Volume 1, in which terms are arranged alphabetically by meaning of the acronym, initialism, or abbreviation.

Periodical Title Abbreviations series:

Periodical Title Abbreviations: By Abbreviation (Volume 1). A guide to abbreviations commonly used for periodical titles, arranged alphabetically by abbreviation.

Periodical Title Abbreviations: By Title (Volume 2). A guide to abbreviations commonly used for periodical titles, arranged alphabetically by title.

User's Guide

The following examples illustrate possible elements of entries in *AIAD*:

①	②	③	④	⑤

FATAC...Force Aeirienne Tactique [Tactical Air Force] [French] (NATG)

⑥ ⑦

MMT...Multiple-Mirror Telescope [Mount Hopkins, AZ] [Jointly operated by Smithsonian Institution and the University of Arizona] [Astronomy]

⑧

① Acronym, Initialism, or Abbreviation

② Meaning or Phrase

③ English Translation

④ Language (for non-English entries)

⑤ Source code (Allows you to verify entries or find additional information. Decoded in the List of Selected Sources)

⑥ Location or Country of origin (Provides geographic identifiers for airports, colleges and universities, libraries, military bases, political parties, radio and television stations, and others)

⑦ Sponsoring organization

⑧ Subject category (Clarifies entries by providing appropriate context)

The completeness of a listing is dependent upon both the nature of the term and the amount of information provided by the source. If additional information becomes available during future research, an entry is revised.

Arrangement of Entries

Acronyms, initialisms, and abbreviations are arranged alphabetically in letter-by-letter sequence. Spacing, punctuation, and capitalization are not considered. If the same term has more than one meaning, the various meanings are subarranged in word-by-word sequence.

Should you wish to eliminate the guesswork from acronym formation and usage, a companion volume could help. *Reverse Acronyms, Initialisms and Abbreviations Dictionary* contains essentially the same entries as *AIAD*, but arranges them alphabetically by meaning, rather than by acronym or initialism.

List of Selected Sources

Each of the sources included in the following list contributed at least 50 terms. It would be impossible to cite a source for every entry because the majority of terms are sent by outside contributors, are uncovered through independent research by the editorial staff, or surface as miscellaneous broadcast or print media references.

For sources used on an ongoing basis, only the latest edition is listed. For most of the remaining sources, the edition that was used is cited. The editors will provide further information about these sources upon request.

(AABC) *Catalog of Abbreviations and Brevity Codes.* Washington, DC: U.S. Department of the Army, 1981. [Use of source began in 1969]

(ABAC) "Abbreviations, Acronyms, and Initialisms." <http://www.pnl.gov/ag/usage/acroel.html> (27 January 2000).

(AAEL) "Common Abbreviations and Acronyms in Electronics." By Gunham Kaytaz. <http://www.seas.smu.edu/~kaytaz/menu.html> (27 April 1999).

(AAG) *Aerospace Abbreviations Glossary.* Report Number AG60-0014. Prepared by General Dynamics/Astronautics. San Diego, CA: 1962.

(AAGC) *Acronyms and Abbreviations in Government Contracting.* 2d ed. By Patricia A. Tobin and Joan Nelson Phillips. Washington, DC: George Washington University, 1997.

(AAMN) *Abbreviations and Acronyms in Medicine and Nursing.* By Solomon Garb, Eleanor Krakauer, and Carson Justice. New York, NY: Springer Publishing Co., 1976.

(ABAR) "Abbreviations." American Journal of Archaeology. <http://www.ajaonline.org> (4 May 2002).

(ABBR) *Abbreviations: The Comprehensive Dictionary of Abbreviations and Letter Symbols.* Vol. 1 C. By Edward Wall. Ann Arbor, MI: The Pierian Press, 1984.

(AC) *Associations Canada* 1995/96. Edited by Ward McBurney. Toronto: Canadian Almanac & Directory Publishing Co. Ltd., 1995.

(ACAE) *Aerospace and Defense Acronyms.* 2d ed. Compiled by Fernando B. Morinigo. Washington,DC: American Institute of Aeronautics and Astronautics, 1992

(ACII) "Acronym and Initials Index." <http://www.ioi.ie/~readout/cl.html> (7 November 1996).

(AD) *Abbreviations Dictionary.* 8th ed. By Ralph De Sola. Boca Raton, FL: CRC Press, 1992.

(ADA) *The Australian Dictionary of Acronyms and Abbreviations.* 2d ed. Compiled by David J. Jones. Leura, NSW, Australia: Second Back Row Press Pty. Ltd., 1981.

(ADDR) *Army Dictionary and Desk Reference.* By Tim Zurick. Harrisburg, PA: Stackpole Books, 1992.

(ADWA) *Abbreviations Dictionary; A Practical Compilation of Today's Acronyms and Abbreviations.* By Robert S. Wachal. Boston: Houghton Mifflin Co., 1999.

(AEBE) *Acronyms in Electronics Business and Engineering.* By Ken Westover. Boulder, CO: Cliff Canyon Publishing Co., 1998.

(AEBS) *Acronyms in Education and the Behavioral Sciences.* By Toyo S. Kawakami. Chicago, IL: American Library Association, 1971.

(AEE) *American Educators' Encyclopedia.* By Edward L. Dejnozka and David E. Kapel. Westport, CT: Greenwood Press, 1991.

(AEPA) *U.S. Environmental Protection Agency.* ACCESS EPA. 1995/96 ed. Washington, DC: Office of Information Resources Management, 1996.

(AF) *Reference Aid: Abbreviations in the African Press.* Arlington, VA: Joint Publications Research Service, 1979.

(AFIT) *Compendium of Authenticated Systems and Logistics.* Washington, DC: Air Force Institute of Technology, 1984.

(AFM) *Air Force Manual of Abbreviations.* Washington, DC: U.S. Department of the Air Force, 1975. [Use of source began in 1969]

(AG) "Acronym Glossary." <http://www.disa.org/apps/acrolook.cfm?acronym=> (23 October 2002).

(AGLO) *Abbreviations, Acronyms, Glossary for American Readers.* 13th ed. San Jose, CA: American Readers Publishing Co., 2001.

(AIA) *Aviation Insurance Abbreviations, Organisations and Institutions.* By M.J. Spurway. London, England: Witherby & Co. Ltd., 1983.

(AIE) *Acronyms and Initialisms in Education.* 6th ed. Compiled by John Hutchins. Norwich, England: Librarians of Institutes and Schools of Education, 1995.

(AL) "Acronyms & Abbreviations." American Library Association. <http://www.ala.org/> (2 December 1997).

(ALHF) "Alaska Housing Finance Corporation Glossary." <http://www.ahfc.state.ak.us.index.htm> 18 October 1999).

(AMHC) *Glossary of Managed Care Medical Terms, Abbreviations and Acronyms.* By Margaret D. Bischel, M.D. Santa Barbara, CA: Apollo Managed Care Consultants, 1998.

(ANA) "Abbreviations" - U.S. Navy Dictionary. 3rd revision. Washington, DC: DCP, 1989.

(ANEX) *American Novel Explication 1969-1980.* Compiled by Catherine Glitsch. New Haven, CT: Archon Books, 2000.

(APTA) *Australian Periodical Title Abbreviations.* Compiled by David J. Jones. Leura, NSW, Australia: Second Back Row Press Pty. Ltd., 1985.

(ARC) *Agricultural Research Centres: A World Directory of Organizations and Programmes.* 2 vols. Edited by Nigel Harvey. Harlow, Essex, England: Longman Group, 1983.

(ARCH) *Dictionary of Architecture and Construction.* Edited by Cyril M. Harris. New York, NY: McGraw-Hill, Inc., 1975.

(ARMP) "Global Change Acronyms and Abbreviations." <http://www.arm.gov/docs/index/html> (8 February 2000).

(ASC) *Associations Canada 1995/96.* Edited by Ward McBurney. Toronto: Canadian Almanac & Directory Publishing Co Ltd., 1995.

(ASF) *Guide to Names and Acronyms of Organizations, Activities, and Projects.* By Food and Agriculture Organization of the United Nations. Fishery Information, Data, and Statistics Service and U.S. National Oceanic and Atmospheric Administration. Aquatic Sciences and Fisheries Information System Reference Series, Number 10, 1982. n.p.

(AUEG) "Acronyms Used by Environmental Groups and Agencies." <http://www.etd.ameslab.gov/etd/library/acronyms/acronym.html> (2000).

(AUER) "Abbreviations Used for Navy Enlisted Ratings." <http://www.history.navy.mil/faq78.2html> (19 October 2000).

(AVGL) "Aircraft Owners and Pilots Association Aviation Glossary." <http://www.aopa.ch/xgloss.htm> (20 October 1999).

(BABM) *Bailliere's Abbreviations in Medicine.* 5th ed. By Edwin B. Steen. London, England: Bailliere Tindall, 1984.

(BARN) *The Barnhart Abbreviations Dictionary.* Edited by Robert K. Barnhart. New York, NY: John Wiley & Sons, Inc., 1995.

(BB) "Acronyms Finder: Acronyms for Training, Business and Communication." <http://www.business-balls.com/acronyms.htm> (23 October 2002).

(BCP) "BCP Guidebook." <http://www.dtic.dla.mil/environdod/> (Fall 1995).

(BEE) "The Beeline." <http://www.bton.com/tb17/abbr/a.html> (17 November 1999).

(BI) *British Initials and Abbreviations.* 3rd ed. By Ian H. Wilkes. London, England: Leonard Hill Books, 1971.

(BIB) *Bibliotech.* Ottawa: National Library of Canada, 1988-89.

(BIBA) "North American 4 Letter Codes to Identify Birds." <http://www.birding.about/library/weekly/aa0011601b.htm> (23 October 2001).

(BJA) *Biblical and Judaic Acronyms.* By Lawrence Marwick. New York, NY: Ktav Publishing House, Inc., 1979.

(BRI) *Book Review Index.* 1997 Cumulation. Edited by Beverly Baer. Detroit, MI: Gale Research, 1998.

(BROA) *Broadcasting & Cable Yearbook 2002-2003.* New York, NY: Reed Elsevier Inc., 2002.

(BTTJ) *Breaking Through Technical Jargon: A Dictionary of Computer and Automation Acronyms.* By Mark S. Merkow. New York, NY: Van Nostrand Reinhold, 1990.

(BUAC) *Buttress's World Guide to Abbreviations of Organizations.* 11th ed. Revised by L.M. Pitman. London, England: Blackie Academic and Professional, 1997.

(BUR) *Computer Acronyms and Abbreviations Handbook.* Tokyo, Japan: Burroughs Co. Ltd., 1978.

(BYTE) *Byte: The Small Systems Journal.* Peterborough, NH: McGraw-Hill Information Systems, Inc., 1987-89.

(CAAL) *CAAL COMOPTEVFOR Acronym and Abbreviation List.* Norfolk, VA: (CAAL-U) Operational Test and Evaluation Force, 1981.

(CABS) "Serials Source List for Computer and Information Systems Abstracts." Internet Database Service. <http://www.csa.com/htbin/sjldisp.cgi?filename=/wais/data/srcjnl/comp001> (12 March 2002).

(CARB) "Carbon Dioxide Information Analysis Center-Acronyms and Abbreviations." <http://www.cdiac.esd.oorni.gov/cdiac/pns/acronyms.html> (18 July 1996).

(CARL) *The International Dictionary of Intelligence.* By Leo D. Carl. McLean, VA: International Defense Consultant Services, Inc., 1990.

(CB) *Centres & Bureaux: A Directory of Concentrations of Effort, Information and Expertise.* Edited by Lindsay Sellar. Beckenham, Kent, England: CBD Research Ltd., 1987.

(CCCA) *ABC Pocket Guide for the Field on C3 Acronyms; An Anthology of Command, Control, and Communications Acronyms and Abbreviations.* 2d. ed. Edited by Charles R. Wolfson. Geneva, IL: ABC Tele-Training, Inc., 1986.

(CDAI) *Concise Dictionary of Acronyms and Initialisms.* By Stuart W. Miller. New York, NY: Facts on File Publications, 1988.

(CDE) *The Computer Desktop Encyclopedia.* By Alan Freedman. New York, NY: AMACOM, 1996.

(CDI) *The Cancer Dictionary.* By Roberta Altman and Michael Sarg, M.D. New York, NY: Facts on File, 1992.

(CED) *Current European Directories.* 2d ed. Edited by G.P. Henderson. Beckenham, Kent, England: CBD Research, 1981.

(CET) *Communications-Electronics Terminology.* AFM 11-1. Vol. 3. U.S. Department of the Air Force, 1973.

(CGWS) *The Comprehensive Guide to Wireless Resources; Definitions and Acronyms, and National Trade Shows, Association and Publication Listings.* By Lawrence Harte and Steven Kellogg. Fuquay-Varina, NC: APDG Publishing, 1998.

(CINC) *A CINCPAC Glossary of Commonly Used Abbreviations and Short Titles.* By Ltc. J.R. Johnson. Washington, DC: 1968.

(CIST) *Computer & Information Science & Technology Abbreviations & Acronyms Dictionary.* Edited by David W. South. Boca Raton, FL: CRC Press, Inc., 1994.

(CMD) *Complete Multilingual Dictionary of Computer Terminology.* Compiled by Georges Nania. Chicago, IL: National Textbook Co., 1984.

(CNC) *American National Standard Codes for the Representation of Names of Countries, Dependencies, and Areas of Special Sovereignty for Information Interchange.* U.S. National Bureau of Standards. Washington, DC: Government Printing Office, 1986. [Use of source began in 1977]

(COBU) "Common Business and Professional Abbreviations and Acronyms." <http://www.instantaccess.co.uk/infozone/abbreviations.html> (27 January 2000).

(COE) *Cooper's Comprehensive Environmental Desk Reference.* Edited by Andre R. Cooper. New York, NY: John Wiley & Sons, 1990.

(COMM) *Common Stock Newspaper Abbreviations and Trading Symbols.* By Howard R. Jarrell. Metuchen, NJ: Scarecrow Press, 1989.

(CPGU) *Canadian Parliamentary Guide, Parlementaire Canadien, 1998-1999.* Edited by Kathryn O'Handley. Farmington Hills, MI: Gale Group, Inc., 1999.

(CPH) *The Charles Press Handbook of Current Medical Abbreviations.* 3rd ed. Philadelphia, PA: The Charles Press Publishers, Inc., 1991.

(CRD) *Computer-Readable Databases: A Directory and Data Sourcebook.* 6th ed. Edited by Kathleen Young Marcaccio. Detroit, MI: Gale Research, 1990.

(CROSS) *Cross-Border Links: A Directory of Organizations in Canada, Mexico, and the United States,.* Edited by Ricardo Hernandez and Edith Sanchez. Albuquerque, NM: Inter-Hemispheric Education Resource Center, 1992.

(CSR) *Computer Science Resources: A Guide to Professional Literature.* Edited by Darlene Myers. White Plains, NY: Knowledge Industry Publications, Inc., 1981.

(CTAA) *Common Terminology, Abbreviations and Symbols for Terapeutic Recreation and Other Activity Therapies.* By David L. Jewell. Springfield, IL: Charles C. Thomas Publisher, Ltd., 2002.

(CTAS) "CTAS Acronym Dictionary." <http://www.ctas.arc.nase.gov/acronyms> (10 October 2000).

(CTT) *Corporate TrendTrac.* Edited by A. Dale Timpe. Detroit, MI: Gale Research, 1988-89.

(CWA) "Civil War Acronyms." <http://www.antiqueresources.com/articles/cwacronyms.html> (1998).

(DA) *Dictionary of Aviation.* By R. J. Hall and R. D. Campbell. Chicago, IL: St. James Press, 1991.

(DAS) *Dictionary of Abbreviations and Symbols.* By Edward Frank Allen. London, England: Cassell and Co. Ltd., 1949.

(DAVI) *Medical Abbreviations; 14,000 Conveniences at the Expense of Communications and Safety.* 9th ed. By Neil M. Davis. Huntingdon Valley, PA: Neil M. Davis Associates, 1999.

(DB) *Dictionary of Biomedical Acronyms and Abbreviations.* 2d ed. By Jacques Dupayrat. New York, NY: John Wiley & Sons, 1990.

(DBA) *Directory of British Associations.* Edited by G.P. Henderson and S.P.A. Henderson. Beckenham, Kent, England: CBD Research, Ltd., 1990.

(DBQ) *A Dictionary of British Qualifications.* London, England: Kogan Page Ltd., 1985.

(DCDG) *The Dictionary of Computing & Digital Media; Terms & Acronyms.* Edited by Brad Hansen. Wilsonville, OR: Franklin, Beedle & Associates, Inc., 1999.

(DCOM) *The Dictionary of Computing & Digital Media; Terms and Acronyms.* By Brad Hansen. Wilsonville, OR: ABF Content, 1999.

(DCT) *Dictionary of Communications Technology.* 3rd ed. By Gilbert Held. New York, NY: John Wiley & Sons Ltd., 1998.

(DCTA) *Dictionary of Commercial Terms and Abbreviations.* By Alan E. Branch. London, England: Witherby & Co. Ltd., 1984.

(DD) *The Financial Post Directory of Directors 1997.* Toronto, Canada: The Financial Post, 1996.

(DDC) *The International Dictionary of Data Communications.* By Robert A. Saigh. Chicago, IL: The Glenlake Publishing Company, Ltd., 1998.

(DDSO) *D & D Standard Oil Abbreviator.* 4th ed. Compiled by the Association of Desk and Derrick Clubs. Tulsa, OK: PennWell Books, 1994.

(DEMM) "Department of Emergency Management Master List of Acronyms." <http://bcem.co.bay.fl.us/dem/htm> (27 January 2000).

(DEN) *Dictionary of Electronics and Nucleonics.* By L.E.C. Hughes, R.W.B. Stephens, and L. D. Brown. New York, NY: Barnes & Noble, 1969.

(DET) *Dictionary of Educational Terms.* Edited by David Blake and Vincent Hanley. Brookfield, VT: Ashgate Publishing Co., 1995.

(DFIT) *Dictionary of Finance and Investment Terms.* 4th ed. Edited by John Downes and Jordan Elliot Goodman. Hauppauge, NY: Barron's Educational Series, 1995.

(DGA) *Dictionary of Graphic Arts Abbreviations.* By L. W. Wallis. Rockport, MA: Rockport Publishers, Inc., 1986.

(DHP) *Dictionary of Abbreviations and Acronyms in Helping Professions.* By John W. Hollis. Muncie, IN: Accelerated Development, Inc., 1987.

(DHSM) *Dictionary of Health Services Management.* 2d ed. By Thomas C. Timmreck. Owings Mills, MD: Rynd Communications, 1987.

(DI) *The Dictionary of Initials-What They Mean.* Compiled and edited by Harriette Lewis. Kingswood, Surrey, England: Paper Fronts Elliot Right Way Books, 1983.

(DIAR) *The Dictionary of Art.* Edited by Jane Turner. London, England: MacMillan Publishers Limited, 1996.

(DICI) *The Dictionary of Initials.* By Betsy M. Parks. Secaucus, NJ: Citadel Press, 1981.

(DINT) *Dictionary of Internetworking Terms and Acronyms.* San Jose, CA: Cisco Press for Cisco Systems, 2001.

(DIPS) *The Dictionary of Psychology.* By Raymond J. Corsini. Philadelphia: Taylor and Francis, 1999.

(DIT) *Dictionary of Informatics Terms in Russian and English.* By G.S. Zhdanov, E.S. Kolobrodov, V.A. Polushkin, and A.I. Cherny. Moscow: Nauka, 1971.

(DLA) *Bieber's Dictionary of Legal Abbreviations.* 3rd ed. By Mary Miles Prince. Buffalo, NY: William S. Hein & Co., 1988.

(DMA) *Dictionary of Military Abbreviations: British, Empire, Commonwealth.* By B.K.C. Scott. Hastings, East Sussex, England: Tamarisk Books, 1982.

(DMAA) *Dictionary of Medical Acronyms and Abbreviations.* 3rd ed. Edited by Stanley Jablonski. Philadelphia, PA: Hanley & Belfus, Inc., 1998.

(DMC) *Webster's New World Dictionary of Media and Communications.* Revised ed. By Richard Weiner. New York, NY: Macmillan, 1996.

(DNAB) *Dictionary of Naval Abbreviations.* 3rd ed. Compiled and edited by Bill Wedertz. Annapolis, MD: Naval Institute Press, 1984.

(DOAD) *The Dictionary of Advertising.* Edited by Laurence Urdang. Lincolnwood, IL: NTC Business Books, 1986.

(DOG) *A Dictionary of Genetics.* 5th ed. By Robert C. King and William D. Stansfield. New York, NY: Oxford University Press, 1997.

(DOGT) "List of Acronyms." <http://www.em.doe.gov/rtc1994/loa.html> (5 March 1997).

(DOM) *The Dictionary of Multimedia: Terms & Acronyms.* By Brad Hansen. Wilsonville, OR: Franklin, Beedle & Associates, 1997.

(DOMA) *Dictionary of Military Abbreviations.* By Norman Polmar, Mark Warren, and Eric Wertheim. Annapolis, MD: Naval Institute Press, 1994.

(DS) *Dictionary of Shipping International Trade Terms and Abbreviations.* 3rd ed. By Alan E. Branch. London, England: Witherby & Co. Ltd., 1986.

(DSA) *Dictionary of Sigla and Abbreviations to and in Law Books before 1607.* By William Hamilton Bryson. Charlottesville: University Press of Virginia, 1975.

(DSUE) *A Dictionary of Slang and Unconventional English.* 8th ed. By Eric Partridge. New York, NY: Macmillan Publishing Co., 1984.

(DUND) *Directory of United Nations Databases and Information Services.* 4th ed. Compiled by the Advisory Committee for the Coordination of Information Systems. New York, NY: United Nations, 1990.

(DWSG) *Defense Weapon Systems Glossary.* By David Trotz. Piscataway, NJ: Target Marketing, 1992.

(EA) *Encyclopedia of Associations.* 34th ed. Vol. 1, National Organizations of the U.S. Edited by Christine Maurer and Tara E. Sheets. Farmington Hills, MI: Gale Group, 1999. [Use of source began in 1960]

(EAAP) *Encyclopedia of Associations: Association Periodicals.* 3 vols. Edited by Denise M. Allard and Robert C. Thomas. Detroit, MI: Gale Research, 1987.

(EAGT) *Environmental Acronyms, Abbreviations, and Glossary of Terms.* United States Environmental Protection Agency, Information Resources Directory, Spring 1989 (OPA 003-89).

(EAIO) *Encyclopedia of Associations: International Organizations.* 29th ed. Edited by Linda Irvin. Detroit, MI: Gale Research, 1995. [Use of source began in 1985]

(EBF) *Encyclopedia of Banking and Finance.* 10th ed. Edited by Charles J. Woelfel. Chicago, IL: Probus Publishing Co., 1994.

(ECED) *The European Communities Encyclopedia and Directory* 1992. London, England: Europa Publications Ltd., 1991; distributed in U.S. by Gale Research, Detroit, MI.

(ECII) *Electronics, Computers and Industrial Instrumentation Abbreviations and Acronyms.* Edited by Sergio Sobredo. Miami, FL: Sergio Sobredo Technical Services, 1986.

(ECON) *The Economist.* London, England: The Economist Newspaper Ltd., 2001. [Use of source began in 1988]

(EDAA) *Elsevier's Dictionary of Abbreviations, Acronyms, Synonyms and Symbols Used in Medicine.* Compiled by Dr. Samuel A. Tsur (Mansoor). New York, NY: Elsevier Science, 1999.

(EDAC) *Dictionary of Educational Acronyms, Abbreviations, and Initialisms.* 2d ed. Edited by James C. Palmer and Anita Y. Colby. Phoenix, AZ: Oryx Press, 1985.

(EDCT) *Encyclopedic Dictionary of Chemical Technology.* By Dorit Noether and Herman Noether. New York, NY: VCH Publishers, Inc., 1993.

(EE) *Eastern Europe and the Commonwealth of Independent States 1992.* London, England: Europa Publications Ltd., 1992; distributed in U.S. by Gale Research, Detroit, MI.

(EECA) *Dictionary of Electrical, Electronics, and Computer Abbreviations.* By Phil Brown. London, England: Buttersworth, 1985.

(EES) *A Dictionary of Ecology, Evolution and Systematics.* 2d ed. Edited by Roger Lincoln, Geoff Boxshall and Paul Clark. New York, NY: Cambridge University Press, 1998.

(EEVL) *Environmental Engineering Dictionary.* 3rd ed. Edited by C.C. Lee. Rockville, MD: Government Institutes, 1998.

(EFIS) *Corporate Acronym Resource Guide, 1800s-1995.* Seattle, WA: Environmental Financial Information Services, Inc. (EFIS), 1996.

(EG) *Environmental Glossary.* 4th ed. Edited by G. William Frick and Thomas F.P. Sullivan. Rockville, MD: Government Institutes, Inc., 1986.

(EGA) "Acronyms Used by Environment Groups and Agencies." <http://www.epsci.aimeslab.gov/etd/library/acronyms/acronym.html> (23 October 2002).

(EGAO) *Encyclopedia of Governmental Advisory Organizations.* 9th ed. Edited by Donna Batten. Detroit, MI: Gale Research, 1994-95 (and supplement, 1995). [Use of source began in 1975]

(EMRF) *The St. James Encyclopedia of Mortgage & Real Estate Finance.* By James Newell, Albert Santi, and Chip Mitchell. Chicago, IL: St. James Press, 1991.

(ELAL) *Computer Acronyms & Abbreviations; Over 4,000 Entries and What They Stand For.* Compiled by Elie Albala. Quebec, Canada: Alpel Publishing, 1992.

(EOSA) "Earth Observing System (EOS) Acronyms and Abbreviations." <http://eospso.gsfc.nasa/eos_homepage/misc> (5 October 1999).

(EPA) *Glossary of EPA Acronyms.* Washington, DC: Environmental Protection Agency, 1987.

(EPAT) "Terms of Environment." <http://www.epa.gov/OCEPAterms/aaad.html> (3 November 1999).

(ERG) *Environmental Regulatory Glossary.* 5th ed. Edited by G. William Frick and Thomas F.P. Sullivan. Rockville, MD: Government Institutes, Inc., 1990.

(EURO) *Eurojargon; A Dictionary of European Union Acronyms, Abbreviations, and Sobriquets.* 6th ed. Edited by Anne Ramsay. Chicago: Fitzroy Dearborn Publishers, 2000.

(EY) *The Europa World Year Book 1992.* London: Europa Publications Ltd., 1992. distributed in U.S. by Gale Research, Detroit, MI.

(FAAC) *Contractions Handbook.* Changes. U.S. Department of Transportation. Federal Aviation Administration, 1993. [Use of source began in 1969]

(FAAL) *Location Identifiers.* U.S. Department of Transportation. Federal Aviation Administration. Air Traffic Service, 1982.

(FEA) *The Far East and Australasia 1987.* 18th ed. London, England: Europa Publications Ltd., 1986; distributed in U.S. by Gale Research, Detroit, MI.

(FFDE) *The Facts on File Dictionary of Environmental Science.* By L. Harold Stevenson and Bruce Wyman. New York, NY: Facts on File, 1991.

(FOTI) *Acrobuster: Dictionary of Canadian English Acronyms, Initialisms, and Abbreviations.* Edited by Vadim Fotinov and Svetlana Fotinov. Ottawa, Canada: Fotinov and Fotinov, 2000.

(FUCW) *"Frequently Used Contractions in National Weather Service Products."* <http://www.awc-kc.noaa.gov/info/domestic_contractions.html>

(GA) *Countries of the World and Their Leaders 2003.* Farmington Hills, MI: Gale, 2002.

(GAAI) *"Glossary of Abbreviations, Acronyms, and Initialisms."* <http://www.em.doe.gov/idb97/acropdf.html> (17 February 1998).

(GART) *The Gartner Glossary of Information Technology Acronyms and Terms.* 4th ed. Stamford, CT: Gartner Group, Inc., 2000.

(GAVI) "Glossary of Aviation Acronyms and Abbreviations." <http://olias.arc.nasa.gov/AFO_Acronyms_html> (5 March 1997).

(GEA) *Government Economic Agencies of the World: An International Directory of Governmental Organisations Concerned with Economic Development and Planning.* A Keesing's Reference Publication. Edited by Alan J. Day. Harlow, Essex, England: Longman Group Ltd., 1985.

(GEAB) "Genealogy Abbreviations." <http://www.genweb.net/~samcasey/abbre.html> (17 November 1999).

(GEOI) "Dictionary of Abbreviations and Acronyms in Geographic Information Systems, Cartography, and Remote Sensing." By Philip Hoehn and Mary Lynette Larsgaard. <http://www.lib.berkeley.edu/EART/abbrev.html> (June 1999).

(GFGA) *Guide to Federal Government Acronyms.* Edited by William R. Evinger. Phoenix, AZ: The Oryx Press, 1989.

(GOBB) *The Gobbledygook Book; Dictionary of Acronyms, Abbreviations, Initializations & Esoteric Terminology.* Compiled by Franklin W. Fox, III. Troy, MI: Momentum Books, Ltd., 1996.

(GNE) *The Green Encyclopedia.* By Irene Franck and David Brownstone. New York, NY: Prentice Hall General Reference, 1992.

(GPO) *Style Manual.* Washington, DC: Government Printing Office, 1984. [Terms are Included in Chapter 24, Foreign Languages]

(GRD) *Government Research Directory.* 8th ed. Edited by Joseph M. Palmisano. Detroit, MI: Gale Research, 1994. (and supplement, 1994).

(GROV) "Abbreviation List." <http://www.grovemusic.com/grovemusic/az/general00.html> (16 January 2001).

(GRST) "Glossary of Remote Sensing Terms." <http://ceo1409.ceo.sai.jrc.it:8080...2/tutorials/glossary> (5 October 1999).

(GVA) "Glossary of Veterinary Acronyms." <http://www/spvs.org.uk/glossary.htm> (October 1999).

(HAWK) "Hawkman's Automotive Abbreviations." <http://www3.sympatico.ca/dhaughey/index2.htm> (19 October 2000).

(HCT) *Health Care Terms.* 2d ed. By Vergil N. Slee and Debora A. Slee. St. Paul, MN: Tringa Press, 1991.

(HEAS) "Acronyms and Abbreviations Used in Health and Safety Executive Information Services." <http://www.healthandsafety.co.uk/acronyms.html> (26 September 2000).

(HGAA) *The Handy Guide to Abbreviations and Acronyms for the Automated Office.* By Mark W. Greenia. Seattle, WA: Self-Counsel Press, Inc., 1986.

(HGEN) "Human Genome Acronym List." <http://www.ornl.gov/hgmis/acronym.html> (2 December 1998).

(HLLA) "Honeywell Abbreviation and Acronym Dictionary." <http://www.cas.honeywell.com/ats/acronym.html> (27 January 2000).

(HODG) *Computers: Systems, Terms and Acronyms.* 12th ed. By M. Susan Hodges. Winter Park, FL: SemCo Enterprises, Inc., 2000.

(HRG) *The Human Resources Glossary: The Complete Desk Reference for HR Executives, Managers, and Practitioners.* 2d ed. By William R. Tracey. Boca Raton, FL: St. Lucie Press, 1998.

(HRNC) *How to Read a Nautical Chart: A Complete Guide to the Symbols, Abbreviations, and Data Displayed on Nautical Charts.* By Nigel Calder. Camden, ME: International Marine/McGraw-Hill, 2003.

(HVTR) "HIV Vaccine Trials Network, Abbreviations & Acronms: Medical Abbreviations" <http://www.scharp.org/hvtn/resources/abbrev.other.html> (12 March 2002).

(IAA) *Index of Acronyms and Abbreviations in Electrical and Electronic Engineering.* Compiled by Buro Scientia. New York, NY: VCH Publishers, 1989.

(IAS) “International Arctic Science Committee.” <http://www.iasc.no/acronyms.htm> (20 October 1999).

(IBMDP) *IBM Data Processing Glossary*. 6th ed. White Plains, NY: IBM Corp., 1977.

(ICAO) *Aircraft Type Designators*. 13th ed. International Civil Aviation Organization, August, 1981.

(ICDA) *Designators for Aircraft Operating Agencies, Aeronautical Authorities and Services*. 49th ed. International Civil Aviation Organization, June, 1982.

(ICLI) *Location Indicators*. 51st ed. International Civil Aviation Organization, February, 1987.

(IDAI) *The International Dictionary of Artificial Intelligence*. By William Raynor. Chicago: Glenlake Publishing Co., Ltd., 1999.

(IDOE) *The Illustrated Dictionary of Electronics*. 6th ed. By Stan Gibilisco. New York, NY: TAB Books, 1994.

(IDYL) *Medical Abbreviations for the Health Professions*. Edited by Thomas K. Skalko. Ravensdale, WA: Idyll Arbor, Inc., 1998.

(IEEE) *IEEE Standard Dictionary of Electrical and Electronics Terms*. Edited by Frank Jay. New York, NY: The Institute of Electrical and Electronics Engineers, Inc., 1977, 1984.

(IGQR) *The Internet Glossary & Quick Reference Guide*. By Alan Freedman, Alfred Glossbrenner and Emily Glossbrenner. New York, NY: AMACOM, 1998.

(IGSL) *International Reference Guide to Space Launch Systems*. 3rd ed. Edited by Steven J. Isakowitz, Joseph P. Hopkins, Jr., Joshua B. Hopkins. Reston, VA: American Institute of Aeronautics and Astronautics, 1999.

(IIA) *Index of Initials and Acronyms*. Compiled by Richard Kleiner. New York, NY: Auerbach Publishers, 1971.

(IID) *Information Industry Directory*. 15th ed. Edited by Annette Novallo. Detroit, MI: Gale Research, 1995. (and supplement, 1995).

(ILCA) *Index to Legal Citations and Abbreviations*. By Donald Raistrick. Abingdon, Oxfordshire, England: Professional Books Ltd., 1981.

(IMH) *International Marketing Handbook*. 2d ed. Edited by Frank Bair. Detroit, MI: Gale Research, 1985.

(INF) *Infantry*. Fort Benning, GA: U.S. Army Infantry Training School, 1996. [Use of source began in 1983]

(IOWA) “Iowa Department of Natural Resources Quick Facts.” <http://www.state.ia.us/government/dnr/part1.htm> (19 October 1999).

(IRC) *International Research Centers Directory 1992-93*. 6th ed. Edited by Annette Piccirelli. Detroit, MI: Gale Research, 1991.

(IRUK) *Industrial Research in the United Kingdom*. 12th ed. Harlow, Essex, England: Longman Group UK Ltd., 1987.

(ISAK) *International Reference Guide to Space Launch Systems*. 3rd ed. Edited by Steven J. Isakowitz, Joseph P. Hopkins, Jr., and Joshua B. Hopkins. Reston, VA: American Institute of Aeronautics and Astronautics, 1999.

(IT) *Information Today: The Newspaper for Users and Producers of Electronic Information Services*. Medford, NJ: Learned Information, Inc., 1988-89.

(ITCA) *Internet Terms and Computer Acronyms, A Useful Guide*. By Mary Brookhart. Charlotte, NC: Southeast Consulting, Inc., 1998.

(ITD) *International Tradeshow Directory*. 5th ed. Frankfurt, Germany: M + A Publishers for Fairs, Exhibitions and Conventions Ltd., 1989.

(IUSS) “IUSS Acronyms.” <http://206.239.241.41/Acronym/1.html> (12 October 1999).

(IYR) *The 1989-92 International Yacht Racing Rules.* London, England: International Yacht Racing Union, 1989.

(JAGO) *Export Terms and Acronyms: Glossary of the Export Sales and Marketing Manual.* By. John R. Jagoe. Minneapolis, MN: Export Institute, 2000.

(JLIT) "Journal of Economic Literature, Journal Abbreviation List." <http://www.aeaweb.org/journal/abbrev.html> (12 March 2002).

(KSC) *A Selective List of Acronyms and Abbreviations.* Compiled by the Documents Department, Kennedy Space Center Library, 1971, 1973.

(LAIN) *Latest Intelligence: An International Directory of Codes Used by Government, Law Enforcement, Military, and Surveillance Agencies.* By James E. Tunnell. Blue Ridge Summit, PA: TAB BOOKS, 1990.

(LCCP) *MARC Formats for Bibliographic Data. Appendix II.* Washington, DC: Library of Congress, 1982.

(LCLS) *Symbols of American Libraries.* 14th ed. Edited by the Enhanced Cataloging Division. Washington, DC: Library of Congress, 1992. [Use of source began in 1980]

(LDOE) *Lewis' Dictionary of Occupational and Environmental Safety and Health.* By Jeffrey W. Vinvoli. Boca Raton, FL: Lewis Publishers, 2000.

(LPT) "Learning, Performance, and Training Acronyms." <http://www.nwlink.com/~donclark/hrd/acron.html> (23 October 2002).

(LWAP) *Legal Words and Phrases: Speed Abbreviations.* By Joel Larus. Boston, MA: Aurico Publishing, 1965.

(MAE) *Medical Abbreviations and Eponyms.* By Sheila B. Sloane. Philadelphia, PA: W.B. Saunders Co., 1985.

(MARI) "Glossary of Marine Abbreviations." <http://www.royalsunalliance.ca/rsa.arine/glossabbrevdisp.html> (26 September 2000).

(MAH) *Medical Abbreviations Handbook.* 2d ed. Oradell, NJ: Medical Economics Co., Inc., 1983.

(MCD) *Acronyms, Abbreviations, and Initialisms.* Compiled by Carl Lauer. St. Louis, MO: McDonnell Douglas Corp., 1989. [Use of source began in 1969]

(MDG) *Microcomputer Dictionary and Guide.* By Charles J. Sippl. Champaign, IL: Matrix Publishers, Inc., 1975.

(ME) *The Marine Encyclopaedic Dictionary.* 5th ed. By Eric Sullivan. London, England: LLP Ltd., *1996.*

(MEC) *Macmillan Encyclopedia of Chemistry.* Vol. 1. Edited by Joseph J. Lagowski. New York, NY: Macmillan Reference USA, 1997.

(MED) *McGraw-Hill Electronic Dictionary.* 5th ed. Edited by John Markus and Neil Sclater. New York, NY: McGraw-Hill, Inc., 1994.

(MEDA) *Medical Acronyms.* 2d ed. By Marilyn Fuller Delong. Oradell, NJ: Medical Economic Books, 1989.

(MELL) *Melloni's Illustrated Dictionary of Medical Abbreviations.* By John Melloni and Ida G. Dox. Pearl River, NY: Parthenon Publishing Group, Inc., 1998.

(MENA) *The Middle East and North Africa 1987.* 33rd ed. London, England: Europa Publications Ltd., 1986; distributed in U.S. by Gale Research, Detroit, MI.

(MGMA) "Medical Group Management Associations Book of Acronyms for Medical Practice Executives." <http://www.mgma.com/library/acronyms.html> (19 October 1999).

(MHCS) *Managed Health Care Simplified: A Glossary of Terms.* By Michael S. Austrin. Albany, NY: Delmar, 1999.

(MHDB) *McGraw-Hill Dictionary of Business Acronyms, Initials, and Abbreviations.* By Jerry M. Rosenberg. New York, NY: McGraw-Hill, Inc., 1992.

(MHDI) *McGraw-Hill Dictionary of Information Technology and Computer Acronyms, Initials, and Abbreviations.* By Jerry M. Rosenberg. New York, NY: McGraw-Hill, Inc., 1992.

(MHDW) *McGraw-Hill Dictionary of Wall Street Acronyms, Initials, and Abbreviations.* By Jerry M. Rosenberg. New York, NY: McGraw-Hill, Inc., 1992.

(MILB) *The Military Balance 1998/99.* London: Oxford University Press for the International Institute for Strategic Studies, 1998.

(MIST) *Means Illustrated Construction Dictionary.* 3rd ed. Kingston, MA: R.S. Means Co., 2000.

(MLOA) "Marconi-List of Acronyms." <http://www.fore.com/atm-edu/acronyms.html> (1999).

(MSA) *Military Standard Abbreviations for Use on Drawings, and in Specifications, Standards, and Technical Documents.* MIL-STD-12D. U.S. Department of Defense, 1981. [Use of source began in 1975]

(MSC) *Annotated Acronyms and Abbreviations of Marine Science Related Activities.* 3rd ed. Revised by Charlotte M. Ashby and Alan R. Flesh. Washington, DC: U.S. Department of Commerce. National Oceanographic and Atmospheric Administration. Environmental Data Service. National Oceanographic Data Center, 1976, 1981.

(MTAA) *Medical Terms & Abbreviations.* 2nd ed. Edited by Juliet McCleery. Springhouse, PA: Lippincott Williams & Wilkins, 2002.

(MUGU) *The Mugu Book of Acronyms and Abbreviations.* Missile Range, CA: Management Engineering Office, 1963, 1964.

(MUSM) *Dictionary of Modern United States Military.* By S.F. Tomajczyk. Jefferson, NC: McFarland and *Co., Inc., 1996.*

(MVRD) *The MVR Decoder Digest.* Edited by Michael L. Sankey. Tempe, AZ: BRB Publications, 2001.

(MWOL) "Commonly Used Acronyms." <http://www.microsoft.com/hwdev/acronym.htm> (20 November 2001).

(NADA) *The New American Dictionary of Abbreviations.* By Mary A. De Vries. New York, NY: Signet, 1991.

(NAKS) "NASA/KSC Acronym List." <http://www.ksc.nasa.gov/facts/acronyms.html> (27 May 1999).

(NASA) *Space Transportation System and Associated Payloads: Glossary, Acronyms, and Abbreviations.* Washington, DC: U.S. National Aeronautics and Space Administration, 1985.

(NASQ) *1999 Nasdaq-AMEX Fact Book and Company Directory.* Washington, DC: Nasdaq-MAEX Market Group, 2000.

(NATG) *Glossary of Abbreviations Used in NATO Documents.* AAP 15 (B), n.p., 1979. [Use of source began in 1976]

(NAU) "The Nautical Institute: Acronyms & Abbreviations." <http://www.nautinst.org/Acronyms.htm> (20 October 1999).

(NAV) "Navoceano Acronym List." <http://www.navo.hpc.mil> (12 November 1993).

(NCC) *NCC The National Centre for Information Technology. Guide to Computer Aided Engineering, Manufacturing and Construction Software.* Manchester, England: NCC Publications, The National Computing Centre Ltd., 1985.

(NDBD) *The New Dickson Baseball Dictionary.* By Paul Dickson. San Diego, CA: Harcourt, Brace, and Co., 1999.

(NFD) *The NSFRE Fund-Raising Dictionary.* Edited by Barbara R. Levy. New York, NY: John Wiley & Sons, Inc., 1996.

(NFLA) "National Football League Abbreviations and Team Histories." <http://maxwell.uhh.hawaii.edu/football/archive/nflAbbreviations.html> (1998).

(NFPA) *Standard for Fire Safety Symbols*/NFPA170. Quincy, MA: National Fire Protection Association, 1994.

(NG) *NAVAIR Glossary of Unclassified Common-Use Abbreviated Titles and Phrases.* NAVAIRNOTE 5216 AIR-6031, n.p., July, 1969.

(NGC) *Catalogue of the National Gallery of Canada.* Compiled by National Gallery of Canada. Ottawa: National Gallery of Canada, 1998.

(NHD) *The New Hacker's Dictionary.* Edited by Eric Raymond. Cambridge, MA: MIT Press, 1991.

(NITA) *Dictionary of New Information Technology Acronyms.* 2d ed. By Michael Gordon, Alan Singleton, and Clarence Rickards. London, England: Kogan Page, Ltd., 1986.

(NLC) *Symbols of Canadian Libraries.* 12th ed. National Library of Canada. Minister of Supply and Services Canada, 1987.

(NOAA) *NOAA Directives Manual.* 66-13 Acronyms. 1977.

(NQ) *NASDAQ Company Directory.* New York, NY: National Association of Securities Dealers, Inc., 1990. [Use of source began in 1983]

(NRCH) *A Handbook of Acronyms and Initialisms.* Washington, DC: U.S. Nuclear Regulatory Commission. Division of Technical Information and Document Control, 1985.

(NRGU) *NORD Resource Guide.* 4th ed. New Fairfield, CT: National Organization for Rare Disorders, Inc., 2000.

(NTA) *The Boat Book's Nautical Terms and Abbreviations: The Language of Boats and Boating.* Compiled and edited by Helene Gaillet de Neergaard. Roslyn Harbor, NY: The Near Field Press, 1994.

(NTCM) *NTC's Mass Media Dictionary.* R. Terry Ellmore. Lincolnwood, IL: National Textbook Co., 1991.

(NTIO) *NTC's Dictionary of Acronyms and Abbreviations.* Compiled by Steven R. Kleinedler. Edited by Richard A. Spears. Lincolnwood, IL: NTC Publishing Group, 1996.

(NTPA) *NTPA '97: National Trade and Professional Associations of the United States.* 32d ed. Edited by John J. Russell. Washington, DC: Columbia Books, Inc., 1997.

(NUCP) *A Dictionary of Nuclear Power and Waste Management with Abbreviations and Acronyms.* Foo-Sun Lau. Letchworth, England: Research Studies Press Ltd., 1987.

(NUJO) "Initials, Credentials, Abbreviations Found on Medical Resumes." <http://www.nursesearch.net/initials.html> (1 February 2000).

(NUMA) "The Numa Dictionary of Derivatives Acronyms." <http://www.numa.com/ref/acronym.html> (24 February 1999).

(NVT) *Naval Terminology.* NWP3. Rev. B. U.S. Department of the Navy. Office of the Chief of Naval Operations, 1980. [Use of source began in 1974]

(OA) *Ocran's Acronyms: A Dictionary of Abbreviations and Acronyms Used in Scientific and Technical Writing.* By Emanuel Benjamin Ocran. London, England: Routledge & Kegan Paul Ltd., 1978.

(OAG) *Official Airline Guide Worldwide Edition.* Oak Brook, IL: Official Airlines Guide, Inc., 1984. [Use of source began in 1975]

(OCD) *Oxford Classical Dictionary.* 2d ed. Edited by N.G. Hammond and H.H. Scullard. London, England: Oxford University Press, 1970.

(OCLC) *OCLC Participating Institutions Arranged by OCLC Symbol.* Dublin, OH: OCLC, 1981.

(ODA) *The Oxford Dictionary of Abbreviations.* Edited by Fran Alexander, et. al. New York, NY: Oxford University Press, 1998.

(ODBW) *The Oxford Dictionary for the Business World.* New York, NY: Oxford University Press, Inc., 1993.

(ODCC) *The Oxford Dictionary of the Christian Church.* Edited by F.L. Cross and E.A. Livingstone. New York, NY: Oxford University Press, 1997.

(OHS) *Occupational Health and Safety: Terms, Definitions, and Abbreviations.* 2nd ed. By Robert G. Confer and Thomas R. Confer. Boca Raton, FL: Lewis Publishers, 1999.

(OICC) *Abbreviations and Acronyms.* Des Moines: Iowa State Occupational Information Coordinating Committee, 1986.

(OLDSS) *Online Database Search Services Directory.* 2d ed. Edited by Doris Morris Maxfield. Detroit, MI: Gale Research, 1988.

(OPSA) *"Official Postal Service Abbreviations."* <http://www.usps.gov/ncsc/lookups/abbr_suffix.txt> (17 December 1996).

(OSI) *OSI Standards and Acronyms.* 3rd ed. Compiled by Adrian V. Stokes. United Kingdom: Stokes, 1991.

(OTD) *Official Telecommunications Dictionary.* Edited by Thomas F.P. Sullivan. Rockille, MD: Government Institutes, Inc., 1997.

(PA) "Planning Acronyms." <http://www.planning.org/info/acronyms/html> (24 February 1999).

(PABS) "Serials Source List for Pollution Abstracts." Internet Database Service. <http://www.csa.com/htbin/sjldisp.cgi?filename=/wais/data/srcjnl/polu001> (12 March 2002).

(PALA) *Stedman's Pathology & Lab Medicine Words.* 2nd ed. Edited by Christa Scott. Baltimore, MD: Lippincott Williams and Wilkins, 1993.

(PAZ) *Parenting A to Z.* By Irene M. Franck and David M. Brownstone. New York, NY: HarperCollins Publishers, Inc., 1996.

(PCM) *PC Magazine.* New York, NY: Ziff-Davis Publishing Co., 1997. [Use of source began in 1987]

(PD) *Political Dissent: An International Guide to Dissident, Extra-Parliamentary, Guerrilla and Illegal Political Movements. A Keesing's Reference Publication.* Compiled by Henry W. Degenhardt. Edited by Alan J. Day. Harlow, Essex, England: Longman Group, 1983.

(PDAA) *Pugh's Dictionary of Acronyms and Abbreviations: Abbreviations in Management, Technology and Information Science.* 5th ed. By Eric Pugh. Chicago, IL: American Library Association, 1987.

(PGP) *Peterson's Graduate Programs in the Humanities, Arts & Social Sciences.* 31st ed. Princeton, NJ: Peterson's 1997.

(PHSD) *1998/1999 Public Human Services Directory.* Vol 59. Washington, DC: American Public Human Services Association, 1998.

(PIAV) "Pilot's Magazine's A to Z Aviation Jargon." Compiled by James Allan and Mike Jerran. <http://web1.hiway.co.uk/aviation/pterms.html> (10 October 2000).

(PIPO) *Pilot's Pocket Handbook.* 4th ed. N.p.: Flight Time Publishing, 1999.

(POLM) *Dictionary of Military Abbreviations.* By Norman Polmar, Mark Warren, and Eric Wertheim. Anapolis, MD: Naval Institute Press, 1994.

(PPE) *Political Parties of Europe.* 2 vols. Edited by Vincent E. McHale. The Greenwood Historical Encyclopedia of the World's Political Parties. Westport, CT: Greenwood Press, 1983.

(PPW) *Political Parties of the World.* 2d ed. A Keesing's Reference Publication. Compiled and edited by Alan J. Day and Henry W. Degenhardt. Harlow, Essex, England: Longman Group, 1980, 1984.

(PROS) *Prospector's Choice. User's Guide.* Detroit: The Taft Group, 1997.

(PS) *Popular Science.* New York, NY: Times-Mirror Magazines, Inc., 2001. [Use of source began in 1992]

(PSAP) *World Encyclopedia of Political Systems and Parties.* 3rd ed. Edited by George E. Delury and Deborah A. Kaple. New York, NY: Facts on File, Inc., 1999.

(PSS) *Peterson's Sports Scholarships & College Athletic Programs.* 3rd ed. Edited by Ron Walker. Princeton, NJ: Peterson's, 1998.

(QUAC) "Dictionary of Quaternary Acronyms." <http://www.ualberta.ca/abeaudoi/cap/diction/atoc.html> (12 October 1999).

(QSUL) Quantities, Symbols, Units, & Abbreviations in the Life Sciences. By Arnost Kotyk. Totowa, NJ: Humana Press, 1995.

(RALS) *Encyclopedia of Computer Science.* 4th ed. Edited by Anthony Ralston, Edwin E. Reilly, and David Hemmendinger. London: Nature Publishing Group, 2000.

(RAWO) *Stedman's Radiology Words.* Edited by Kathryn Mason. 3rd ed. Baltimore, MD: Lippincott Williams and Wilkins, 2000.

(RCD) *Research Centers Directory.* 19th ed. Edited by Thomas J. Cichonski. Detroit, MI: Gale Research, 1994. [Use of source began in 1986]

(RDA) *Army RD and A Magazine.* Alexandria, VA: Development, Engineering, and Acquisition Directorate, Army Materiel Command, 1997. [Use of source began in 1979]

(REAL) "Abbreviations." <http://www.reboc.on.ca/abbreviations.html> (24 February 1999).

(RIMS) "Rimship AS Forkortelser." <http://www.rimship.no/sider/liste.html> (26 September 2000).

(RION) *Religion Index One: Periodicals; a Subject Index to Periodical Literature including an Author/Editor Index and a Scripture Index.* Semiannual edition 1999. Edited by Carolyn K. Coates. Evanston, IL: American Theological Library Association, 1999.

(ROAS) "Acronym and Abbreviation Server Results." <http://www.ucc.ie/cgi-bin/acronym> (20 September 1999).

(ROG) *Dictionary of Abbreviations.* By Walter T. Rogers. London, England: George Allen & Co. Ltd., 1913; reprinted by Gale Research, 1969.

(SAA) *Space-Age Acronyms, Abbreviations and Designations.* 2d ed. By Reta C. Moser. New York, NY: IFI/Plenum, 1969.

(SAFN) *South African Legal Abbreviations.* By Nico M. Ferreira and Karen E. Breckon. Buffalo, NY: William S. Hein and Co., 1999.

(SAG) *Stock Abbreviation Guide.* New York, NY: Associated Press. [Database]

(SARE) "Safety and Related Acronyms." <http://www.labsafety.org/acro.htm> (1999).

(SAUO) *International Encyclopedia of Abbreviations and Acronyms of Organizations.* 3rd ed. Compiled by Paul Spillner and Peter Wennrich. 6 vol. set. Munich, Germany: K. G. Saur, 1990.

(SAUS) *International Encyclopedia of Abbreviations and Acronyms in Science and Technology.* Compiled by Michael Peschke. 8 vol. set. Munich, Germany: K.G. Saur, 1996.

(SDI) *Report to the Congress on the Strategic Defense Initiative.* U.S. Department of Defense. Strategic Defense Initiative Organization, April, 1987.

(SEAT) "Dictionary of Initials, Acronyms, and Abbreviations Used by Counselors and Social Workers." <http://www.counselingseattle.com/initials.htm> (12 March 2002).

(SEIS) *Seismograph Station Codes and Characteristics.* Geological Survey. Circular 791. By Barbara B. Poppe, Debbi A. Naab, and John S. Derr. Washington, DC: U.S. Department of the Interior, 1978.

(SEWL) "Space and Electronic Warfare Lexicon." <http://www.sew-lexicon.com> (10 October 2000).

(SG) *Standard & Poor's Stock Guide.* New York, NY: Standard & Poor's, 2001.

(SHCU) *Short Cuts; The Dictionary of Useful Abbreviations.* Edited by Steven Kleinedler. Lincolnwood, IL: NTC Publishing Group, 1997.

(SLS) *World Guide to Scientific Associations and Learned Societies/Internationales Verzeichnis Wissenschaftlicher Verbande und Gesellschaften.* 4th ed. Edited by Barbara Verrel. New York, NY: K.G. Saur, 1984.

(SPSG) *Security Owner's Stock Guide.* New York, NY: Standard & Poor's Corp., 1994. [Use of source began in 1988]

(SPST) "Space Station Acronyms." <http://www.spacefllight.nasa.gov/cgi-bi> (1999).

(SPVS) "SPVS: Glossary of Veterinary Clinical Abbreviations and Acronyms." <http://www.spvs.org.uk/clinglos.htm> (23 October 2002).

(SRA) *State and Regional Associations of the United States.* 9th ed. Edited by Tracey E. Chirico, Buck J. Downs and John J. Russell. Washington, DC: Columbia Books, Inc., 1997.

(SSD) *Space Station Directory and Program Guide.* Edited and compiled by Melinda Gipson, Jane Glass, and Mary Linden. Arlington, VA: Pasha Publications, Inc., 1988.

(STAH) *Abbreviations Dictionary.* 10th ed. Edited by Dean Stahl and Karen Kerchelich. Originated by Ralph DeSola. Boca Raton, FL: CRC Press, 2001.

(STED) *Stedman's Abbreviations, Acronyms and Symbols.* Edited by William R. Hensyl. Baltimore, MD: Williams & Wilkins, 1992.

(TAD) *The AIDS Dictionary.* By Sarah Barbara Watstein and Karen Chandler. New York, NY: Facts on File, Inc., 1998.

(TAG) *Transportation Acronym Guide 1996.* U.S. Department of Transportation. Washington, DC: Bureau of Transportation Statistics, 1996.

(TBD) *Thomson Bank Directory.* Skokie, IL: Thomson Financial Publishing, 1991.

(TDOB) *The Dictionary of Banking.* By Charles J. Woelfel. Chicago, IL: Probus Publishing Company, 1994.

(TED) *The Equine Dictionary: An Ultimate Reference Book for the Horse Owner.* By Maria Ann Belknap. North Pomfret, VT: Trafalgar Square Publishing, 1997.

(TEL) *Telephony's Dictionary.* 2d ed. By Graham Langley. Chicago, IL: Telephony Publishing Corp., 1986.

(TELE) "List of Libraries Abbreviations Encountered in the Context of EU R&D." <http://www2.echo.lu/libraries/en/acronym.html> (24 February 1999).

(TES) *Tests: A Comprehensive Reference for Assessments in Psychology, Education, and Business.* 3rd ed. Austin, TX: PRO-ED, Inc., 1991.

(TIMI) "Texas Instruments Military Acronym List." <http://www.ti.com/sc/docs/military/millprdov/acroindx.htm> (28 September 2000).

(TIR) "Indian Railways FAQ: Acronyms and Abbreviations." <http://www.irfca.org/faq/faq-acronym.html> (23 October 2002).

(TMMY) *The Thirteenth Mental Measurements Yearbook.* Edited by James C. Impara and Barbara S. Plake. Lincoln: NE: The Buros Institute of Mental Measurements of the University of Nebraska-Lincoln, 1998.

(TNIG) *Telecommunications, Networking and Internet Glossary.* By George S. Machovec. Chicago, IL: American Library Association, 1993.

(TOCD) *The Official Catholic Directory 1997.* New Providence, NJ: P.J. Kennedy & Sons, 1997.

(TRID) "Travel Industry Dictionary." <http://www.hometravelagency.com/dictionary/itra/html> (15 August 2000).

(TSPED) *Trade Shows and Professional Exhibits Directory.* 2d ed. Edited by Robert J. Elster. Detroit, MI: Gale Research, 1987. [Use of source began in 1986]

(TSSD) *Telecommunications Systems and Services Directory.* 4th ed. (and supplement). Edited by John Krol. Detroit, MI: Gale Research, 1989. [Use of source began in 1985]

(TVEL) *The Travel Dictionary.* By Claudine Dervaes. Tampa, FL: Solitaire Publishing, 1998.

(USCA) "U.S. Census Bureau Abbreviations and Acronyms." <http://www.census.gov/cgi-bin/main/allacro.pl> (20 October 1999).

(USDC) "Glossary of Acronyms." U.S. Department of Commerce. <http://www.pmel.noaa.gov/pubs/acronym.html> (5 March 1997).

(USGC) "U.S. Government Commonly Used Abbreviations and Acronyms." <http://www.fed.gov/hptext/info-hwy/gov_acro.html> (5 March 1997).

(USMO) *The Military Online: A Directory for Internet Access to the Development of Defense.* Edited by William M. Arkin. Washington, DC: Brassey's, 1997.

(UWER) *Scientific and Technical Acronyms, Symbols, and Abbreviations.* By Uwe Erb and Harald Keller. New York: John Wiley and Sons, Inc., 2001.

(VERA) "VERA-Virtual Entity of Relevant Acronyms." <http://www/thphy.uni~duesseldorf. de/~gnu/info/VERA/vera_2.html>#SEC3> (1 December 1998).

(VLIE) *Dictionary of Acronyms and Technical Abbreviations: For Information and Communication Technologies and Related Areas.* 2d ed. By Jakob Vliestra. London, England: Springer, 2001.

(VNW) *Words of the Vietnam War.* By Gregory R. Clark. Jefferson, NC: McFarland and Co., Inc., 1990.

(VRA) *VRA Special Bulletin.* No. 2, 1987: Standard Abbreviations for Image Descriptions for Use in Fine Arts Visual Resources Collections. Compiled by Nancy S. Schuller. Austin, TX: Visual Resources Association, 1987.

(WA) *Whitakers Almanack 1998.* London: The Stationery Office, Ltd., 1997.

(WDAA) *Webster's New World Dictionary of Acronyms and Abbreviations.* By Auriel Douglas and Michael Strumpf. New York, NY: Webster's New World, 1989.

(WDMC) *Webster's New World Dictionary of Media and Communications.* Revised and updated ed. By Richard Weiner. New York, NY: Webster's New World, 1996.

(WEAT) "Weather Abbreviations." <http://www.ukweather.freeserve.co.uk/abbrev.html> (16 November 1999).

(WGA) *Webster's Guide to Abbreviations.* Springfield, MA: Merriam-Webster, Inc., 1985.

(WORL) *World Guide to Libraries.* Edited by Willemina van der Meer. 14th ed. Munich, Germany: Saur, 1999.

(WPI) "Selected Acronyms and Abbreviations for Wood Products, Forest Industry and Governmental Affairs." <http://www.ari.net/awpi/acronyms.html> (3 March 1999).

(WYGK) *HR Words You Gotta Know!* By William R. Tracey. New York, NY: AMACOM, 1994.

D

By Acronym

D........ Absorbed Dose [*Environmental science*] (COE)
D........ Air-Cushion Vehicle built by Denny Brothers [*England*] [*Usually used in combination with numerals*]
D........ Air Force Training Category [*Inactive duty training periods and 15 days active duty training per year*]
D........ Ancient Order of Druids (SAUO)
d........ Angular Deformation (SAUS)
D........ Anisotropy Constant [*Solid-state physics*] (UWER)
D........ Application for Writ of Error Dismissed for Want of Jurisdiction [*Legal term*] (DLA)
D........ Arithmetic Factor Register [*Computer science*]
D........ Aspartic Acid [*One-letter symbol; see Asp*]
D........ Bond Dissociation Energy (UWER)
d........ British Penny [*Derived from Latin "denarius"*]
D........ Chemiewerke Homburg [*Germany*] [*Research code symbol*]
D........ Cholecalciferol [*Organic chemistry*] (DAVI)
D........ Cleveland [*Branch in the Federal Reserve regional banking system*] (BARN)
D........ Codex Bezae (BJA)
D........ Cold Snow Forest Climate (UWER)
d........ Collision Diameter of a Molecule [*Symbol*] [*IUPAC*]
D........ Combustible Metals [*Fire classification*]
D........ Court of Divorce and Matrimonial Causes [*England*] (DLA)
D........ Da [*Give*] [*Pharmacy*]
D........ Dacryon (STED)
D........ Dagga [*Marijuana*] [*Medicine*] (EDAA)
D........ Dahlonega [*Georgia*] [*Mint mark, when appearing on US coins*]
d........ Daily (WDMC)
D........ Daily
D........ Daler [*Numismatics*]
D........ Dallas' Pennsylvania and United States Reports [*A publication*] (DLA)
D........ Dallas' United States Supreme Court Reports [*A publication*] (DLA)
D........ Dalton (MELL)
D........ Dam
D........ Damasus [*Flourished, 13th century*] [*Authority cited in pre-1607 legal work*] (DSA)
D........ Dame
D........ Damn
D........ Dance Halls (Commercial) [*Public-performance tariff class*] [*British*]
D........ Danger Area [*ICAO*] (FAAC)
d........ Dangling, at Bedside [*Medicine*]
D........ Daphnia [*Genus of water fleas*] (UWER)
D........ Darcy [*Physics*]
d........ Dare [*To Give*] [*Latin*] (MAE)
d........ dark (SAUS)
D........ Darkness [*or Darktime*] [*Endocrinology*]
d........ Data (WDMC)
D........ Data
D........ Date
D........ Dative (ROG)
D........ Datum
D........ Daughter
D........ Daunorubicin [*Daunomycin, Rubidomycin*] [*Also, DNR, DRB, R*] [*Antineoplastic drug*]
D........ Day [*Approach and landing charts*] [*Aviation*]
D........ Day [*Broadcasting term*]
d........ Day [*SI symbol*]
D........ Day Return [*Round trip fare within one calendar day*] [*British*]
D........ Daytime (NTCM)
D........ Deacon
d........ Dead (DMAA)
D........ Dead [*or Deceased*]
D........ Dead Air Space
D........ Dead Space [*Medicine*] (DAVI)
D........ Dead Space Gas (SAUS)
D........ Dead Time (UWER)
D........ Dean
D........ Dear (ROG)
D........ Death
D........ Debenture [*Type of bond*] [*Investment term*]
D........ Debye [*Unit of electric moment or movement*]
D........ Debys (SAUS)
D........ Decagonal [*Materials science*] (UWER)
D........ Decalin [*A trademark*]
D........ Decamethonium (MELL)
D........ Decca [*Record label*] [*Great Britain, Europe, Australia, etc.*]
d........ Deceased (DMAA)
D........ Deceased
D........ December
D........ Decessit [*Died*] [*Latin*]
d........ Deci [*A prefix meaning divided by ten*] [*SI symbol*]
D........ Deciduous
D........ Decimal (BUR)
D........ Decimal Reduction Time (DAVI)
D........ Decision (ADA)
D........ Decision Table Language [*Ace Microsystems*] [*A programming language*] (NITA)
D........ Deck (NASA)
D........ Declination
D........ Decodon (UWER)
d........ Decomposition
D........ Decoy [*Missile mission symbol*]
d........ Decrease (MELL)
D........ Decrease (STED)
D........ Decree (ADA)
D........ Decret [*Decree*] [*French*] (ILCA)
D........ Decreto [*Decree*] [*Italian*] (ILCA)
D........ Decretum [*Decree*] [*Latin*]
D........ Deed (ROG)
D........ Deep (MSA)
d........ Deepwell Pump [*Liquid gas carriers*]
D........ Defeated
D........ Defendant [*Legal shorthand*] (LWAP)
D........ Defense [*Basketball; lacrosse*]
D........ Defense Department [*US government*]
D........ Defense Notice [*Classification given to British news items which are considered harmful to national security and which are voluntarily censored by the press*]
D........ Deferred [*Finance*]
D........ Deflection (IAA)
D........ Defocussing (SAUS)
D........ Degeneracy (SAUS)
d........ Degree (IDOE)
D........ Degree
D........ Degree of Curve (SAUS)
D........ Dehydration (UWER)
d........ Deictic [*Linguistics*]
D........ Delaware Reports [*A publication*] (DLA)
D........ Delay [*Electronics*]
D........ Deleted
D........ Delivery [*or Delivered*]
D........ Delivery Dollar (EBF)
D........ Delta [*Phonetic alphabet*] [*International*] (DSUE)
D........ Demagnetization Factor (UWER)
D........ Demagnification (UWER)
D........ Demand Curve [*Economics*]
D........ Democrat [*or Democratic*]
D........ Demolish (UWER)
D........ Demonstration (ACAE)
D........ Demy [*Half*] [*Size of paper*] (ADA)
D........ Denarii [*Pence*] [*Monetary unit*] [*British*]
d........ Denarius [*Penny*] (WA)
D........ Denarius [*or Denarii*] [*Silver coin in Ancient Rome; gold coin in Roman Empire*]
D........ Dendrite [*Anatomy*] (UWER)
D........ Denied [*Legal term*] (DLA)
D........ Denio's New York Reports [*A publication*] (DLA)
D........ Denison's English Crown Cases [*1844-52*] [*A publication*] (DLA)
D........ Denmark [*IYRU nationality code*]
D........ Denominator [*In formulas for life annuities and life insurance premiums*]
d........ Density (IDOE)
D........ Density
D........ Dental
D........ Dental Surgery Attendant [*Ranking title*] [*British Royal Navy*]
d........ dented (SAUS)
D........ Dentes [*Applied to Teeth*] (ROG)
D........ Dentin (UWER)
D........ Dentur [*Give*] [*Pharmacy*]
D........ Denver [*Colorado*] [*Mint mark, when appearing on US coins*]
d........ Deoxy [*or Desoxy*] [*Biochemistry*]
d........ Deoxyribose [*Biochemistry*] (MAE)

D ... Depart
D ... Department
D ... Dependence (UWER)
D ... Dependent (IDYL)
D ... Depeptidase (UWER)
D ... Deplacement (SAUS)
d ... deposit (SAUS)
D ... Depositus [*Laid to Rest*] [*Latin*]
d ... Depot (SAUS)
D ... Depot [*DoD*]
D ... Depreciation
D ... Depression
D ... Depth
D ... Depth of Ship
D ... Deputy
D ... Derated (GAVI)
D ... Derivation [*or Derivative*] (IAA)
D ... Derivative (WGA)
D ... Dermacentor [*Genus of ticks*] (UWER)
D ... Dermatologic (STED)
D ... Dermatologist [*or Dermatology*]
D ... Dermis [*Anatomy*] (UWER)
d ... Desert (ODA)
D ... Deserter [*Military*]
D ... Design (AAG)
D ... Destination
D ... Destra [*Right*] [*Italian*]
D ... Destroyed
D ... Destroyer [*Navy*] [*British*]
D ... Detail (AAG)
D ... Detective
D ... Detector (NFPA)
D ... Detergent (UWER)
D ... determinant (SAUS)
D ... Deterministic (IAA)
d ... Detonation (SAUS)
D ... Detritus [*Geology*] (UWER)
D ... Detroit (SAUS)
d ... Detur [*Give*] [*Pharmacy*] (MAE)
D ... Deus [*God*] [*Latin*] (GPO)
D ... Deuterium [*Also, H^2*] [*Radioisotope of hydrogen*]
d ... Deuteron (ADWA)
D ... Deuteron [*Nuclear physics*] (WGA)
D ... Deuteronomist Source of the Pentateuch (BJA)
D ... Deutschland [*Germany*] [*German*]
D ... Developed [*Medicine*] (DAVI)
D ... Developer [*Photography*] (DGA)
D ... Development
d ... Deviation (DIPS)
D ... Deviation
D ... Devonian Period [*Geology*]
d ... Devteron [*A nuclear particle*]
D ... Dew (UWER)
D ... Dewoitine [*French aircraft type*] [*World War II*]
D ... Dexamethasone [*Also, DEX, DXM*] [*Antineoplastic drug*]
D ... Dexter [*Right*] [*Latin*]
D ... Dextro [*Configuration in chemical structure*]
d ... Dextro(rotatory) [*Chemistry*]
D ... Dextrose [*Medicine*] (MAE)
D ... Diagnosis
D ... Diagonal Engines (DS)
D ... Diagonal Polarization [*Physics*] (ECON)
D ... Diagram
D ... Dialyser (UWER)
D ... Diameter
d ... Diameter [*Symbol*] [*IUPAC*]
D ... Diametric (SAUS)
D ... Diamond (ADA)
D ... Diaphragm
D ... Diarrhea [*Medicine*]
D- ... Diarrhoea Absent [*or diminished*] (SPVS)
d ... Diastasis (DMAA)
D ... Diastolic (MELL)
D ... Diathermy [*Medicine*]
D ... Diatom [*Botany*] (UWER)
D ... Diatomite [*Geology*] (UWER)
D ... Diazepam [*Also, DAP, DZ*] [*A sedative*]
D ... Dickenvektor (SAUS)
D ... Dicta (DLA)
D ... Dictum (DLA)
D ... Didymium [*Mixture of rare-earth elements*] [*Chemistry*] (ROG)
d ... Died (VRA)
D ... Died
D ... Dielectric
D ... dielectric flux density (SAUS)
D ... Dies [*Day*] [*Latin*]
D ... Diesel [*British Waterways Board sign*]
D ... Diesel Oil
D ... Dietitian
d ... Difference (VLIE)
D ... Difference
d ... Differential (IDOE)
D ... Differential Coefficient
D ... Differential (of)
D ... Differentiation
D ... Diffractometer (UWER)
D ... Diffuse [*Immunology*]
D ... Diffuse Line (UWER)
D ... Diffusing Capacity
D ... dif fusing capacity (SAUS)
D ... Diffusion (VLIE)
D ... Diffusion Coefficient [*Symbol*] [*IUPAC*]
D ... Diffusion Constant [*Medicine*] (DAVI)
D ... dif fusion constant (SAUS)
D ... Diffusivity (UWER)
D ... Digest
D ... Digesta of the Corpus Juris Civilis of Justinian (SAFN)
D ... Digest of Justinian [*A publication*] (DLA)
D ... Digest of Public General Bills [*Library of Congress*] [*A publication*]
D ... Digit [*or Digital*] (MDG)
D ... Digital (SAUS)
D ... Dihydrotestosterone [*Also, DHT*] [*Endocrinology*]
D ... Dihydrouridine [*One-letter symbol; see H_2Urd*]
D ... Dilated (MELL)
D ... Dilution (MELL)
D ... Dimanche [*French*] (ASC)
D ... Dime [*Monetry unit*]
D ... Dimension (SHCU)
D ... Dimensional
D ... Dinar [*Monetary unit*] [*Tunisia*]
D ... Diode (MDG)
D ... Diopter [*Also, DIOPT*] [*Optics*]
D ... dioptric power (SAUS)
D ... Dip
D ... Diphyllobothrium [*Genus of tapeworms*] (UWER)
D ... Diploid
D ... Diplom (SAUS)
D ... Diplomat [*License plate code assigned to foreign diplomats in the US*]
D ... Diplomate (MAE)
D ... Dipole moment unit of measure [*Chemistry*] (MEC)
D ... Direct (VLIE)
D ... Direction [*Computer science*]
D ... Directivity (SAUS)
D ... Director [*Films, television, etc.*]
D ... Director aircraft capable of controlling drones or missiles [*Designation for all US military aircraft*]
D ... Directorate (SAUS)
D ... Dirt [*Gossip*] [*Slang*]
D ... Disaster (SAUS)
D ... Disc (SAUS)
D ... Discharge (MIST)
D ... Discharged
D ... Disc Issuer and Assistant [*Sports*]
D ... Disconnect (SAUS)
D ... Discount
D ... Discriminator (ACAE)
D ... Disease
D ... Disinfect (UWER)
D ... Disintegrator (UWER)
D ... Dislocation [*Materials science*] (UWER)
D ... Dismissed [*Legal term*] (DLA)
D ... Disney's Ohio Superior Court Reports [*A publication*] (DLA)
D ... Dispense [*Prescription*] [*Medicine*] (EDAA)
D ... Dispenser (MCD)
D ... Dispersion [*Physics*] (ODA)
D ... Displacement
d ... Displacement
D ... Display (MDG)
D ... Dispose [*or Destroy*] [*Routing slip*]
D ... Disqualified [*Horse racing*]
D ... Dissertation (BJA)
D ... Dissipated Energy (UWER)
D ... Dissipation (IAA)
d ... Dissipation (IDOE)
D ... dissipation factordose (SAUS)
D ... Dissolve (NTCM)
d ... Distal (DMAA)
D ... Distal [*Medicine*]
d ... Distance (IDOE)
D ... Distance
D ... Distance Winner [*Horse racing*]
D ... Distant (SAUS)
D ... Distinctio [*Decretum Gratiani*] [*A publication*] (DSA)
D ... Distinction
D ... Distinguished (ADA)
d ... Distinguished [*Case at bar different either in law or fact from case cited for reasons given*] [*Used in Shepard's Citations*] [*Legal term*] (DLA)
D ... Distortion (IAA)
D ... Distortion Factor (UWER)
D ... District
D ... District Court [*Federal*] (DLA)
D ... Disturb (UWER)
d ... disturbed site (SAUS)
d ... Diurnal (MAE)
D ... Diver [*British military*] (DMA)
D ... Diversity [*Genetics*]
D ... Diverticulum [*Anatomy*] (AAMN)
d ... Divide (SAUS)

D — Dividend [*Investment term*]
D — Division
D — Divorced
D — Divus [*The Late*] [*Latin*]
D — Doctor
D — Document
D — Dog [*Veterinary science*] (DAVI)
D — Dog [*Phonetic alphabet*] [*World War II*] (DSUE)
d — Dollar (EBF)
D — Dollar [*Monetary unit*]
D — Dom [*Port*] [*Latin*] (ROG)
D — Domain [*Telecommunications*]
D — Dome
D — Domestic
D — Dominant [*Applied to a species*]
D — Dominion Resources [*NYSE symbol*] (TTSB)
D — Dominion Resources, Inc. [*NYSE symbol*] (SPSG)
D — Dominion Rubber Co. [*Canada*] [*Research code symbol*]
D — Dominus [*The Lord*] [*Latin*] (GPO)
D — Don [*Phonetic alphabet*] [*Pre-World War II*] (DSUE)
D — Don [*Sir*] [*Spanish*]
D — Donative (ROG)
D — Dong [*Monetary unit*] [*Vietnam*] (BARN)
D — Donor
D — Dopamine [*Pharmacology*] (DAVI)
D — Doriden [*Glutethimide*] [*Sedative*]
D — Dormant (UWER)
d — Dorsal (DMAA)
D — Dorsal
D — Dorsal Spine [*Anatomy*] (DAVI)
D — Dorsal Vertebra [*Anatomy*] (DAVI)
d — Dose [*Medicine*] (DMAA)
D — Dosis [*Dose*] [*Pharmacy*]
D — Douane [*Customs*] [*French*]
D — Double
d — Doubled (SAUS)
D — Doubler (SAUS)
D — Doublet
d — Doubtful (DMAA)
D — Doubtful
D — Douglas (SAUS)
D — Douglas Aircraft Co., Inc. (SAUO)
D — Dowager
D — Down (ADWA)
D — Download [*Computer science*] [*Telecommunications*]
d — Down (Quark) [*Atomic physics*]
D — Downrange Distance during Launch [*NASA*]
D — Doxorubicin [*Also, DOX, DXR*] [*Formerly, ADR, Adriamycin*] [*Antineoplastic drug*]
d — Drachma (ADWA)
D — Drachma [*Monetary unit in Greece*]
D — Draft [*or Drafting*] (ROG)
D — Drafting Program [*Association of Independent Colleges and Schools specialization code*]
D — Drag (MCD)
D — Dragoons [*Military unit*] [*British*]
d — Drain (IDOE)
D — Drain [*Electron device*] (MSA)
D — Drama
D — Draperies [*Astronomy*] (BARN)
D — Draught (SAUS)
D — Draw
D — Drawing (SAUS)
D — Dream (UWER)
D — Dream Time [*Neurology and psychiatry*] (DAVI)
D — Dressing [*Medicine*]
D — Drift (SAUS)
D — Drill (UWER)
D++ — Drinking Increased (SPVS)
D — Drip (UWER)
d — Drive (IDOE)
D — Drive [*State*] [*Psychology*]
D — Driver [*British military*] (DMA)
d — Drive Stimuli (DIPS)
D — Drive Strength (DIPS)
D — Driving
D — Drizzle (SAUS)
D — Drizzling [*Meteorology*]
D — Drogue (UWER)
D — Droit [*Right*] [*French*]
D — drone-control version (SAUS)
D — Drone Plane [*Navy symbol*]
D — Drop
D — Droppable Fuel Tank [*Suffix to plane designation*]
D — Drug
D — Druids [*Freemasonry*]
D — Drum (MDG)
D — Dry (NFPA)
D — Dry-Bulk Container [*Packaging*] (DCTA)
D — Dual Capacity [*London Stock Exchange*]
D — Dublett (SAUS)
D — Dublin (SAUS)
D — Duchess
D — Duchy
D — Duct (NFPA)
D — Ducture (SAUS)
D — Ductwork (UWER)
D — Dues
D — Duff [*Phonetic alphabet*] [*Royal Navy*] [*World War I*] (DSUE)
D — Duke
D — Dulcis [*Dear One*] [*Latin*]
D — Dull
D — Dummy [*in game of bridge*]
D — Dump
D — Dun [*Thoroughbred racing*]
D — Dunlop, Bell, and Murray's Scotch Court of Session Cases, Second Series [*1838-62*] [*A publication*] (DLA)
D — Duodecimo [*Book up to 20 centimeters in height*]
D — Duodenum [*Anatomy*]
D — Duplex
d — Duration (DMAA)
D — Duration
D — Duration of treatment (SAUO)
D — Dusio [*In Cisitalia car model "D46"*]
D — Dust [*Meteorology*]
D — Dutch
D — Duty [*Navy*]
D — Duxbury's High Court Reports [*South African Republic*] [*A publication*] (DLA)
D — Dwarf
D — Dwelling (GEOI)
D — Dye [*Classification key in textile printing*]
D — Dyer's Edition of Valiant's English King's Bench Reports [*1513-82*] [*A publication*] (DLA)
D — Dynamic Capital Corp. [*Toronto Stock Exchange symbol*]
D — Dynamotor (IAA)
d — Dyne (DMAA)
D — Dyne [*Unit of force*] [*Also, Dy, dyn*] [*Preferred unit is N, Newton*]
D — Electric Displacement [*Symbol*]
D — Electric Flux Density [*Symbol*]
D — electrostatic flux density (SAUS)
D — Faulty Diction [*Used in correcting manuscripts, etc.*]
D — Five Hundred [*Roman numeral*]
D — Fraunhofer lines caused by sodium (SAUS)
D — Grade for Below-Average Work (UWER)
D — High-Carbon, High-Chromium Type Cold-Work Tool Steels (UWER)
D — Humid Cold Climates [*Classification symbol*] (UWER)
D — Intermediate Dialing Center on a Toll Ticket [*Telecommunications*] (TEL)
D — Knoll AG [*Germany*] [*Research code symbol*]
D — Labs. Dr. J. Auclair [*France*] [*Research code symbol*]
D — License Class [*Motor vehicle violation code used in state of Maryland*] (MVRD)
D++ — Marked Diarrhoea (SPVS)
D — Mean Dose [*Pharmacology*] (DAVI)
D — Medium [*Men's shoe width*]
D — Morison's Dictionary of Scotch Session Cases [*A publication*] (DLA)
D — Naturally Aspirated [*Automotive engineering*]
D — Optical Density (UWER)
D — Penny [*Nail size*]
D — Pilotless Carrier [*Communications term*] (DCT)
D — Pitch Diameter (UWER)
D — Radiac [*Communications term*] (DCT)
d — Relative Density [*Symbol*] [*IUPAC*]
D — Response to Detail [*Rorschach*] [*Psychology*]
d — Response to Small Detail [*Rorschach*] [*Psychology*]
D — Restoring Torque (UWER)
D — Royal Dragoons (SAUO)
D — Selection Index [*H. J. Eysenck*] (DIPS)
D+++ — Severe Diarrhoea (SPVS)
D — Shoe Width Greater than C and Less than E (BARN)
D — Siegfried AG [*Switzerland*] [*Research code symbol*]
D — Sound Energy Density (UWER)
D — Spin-Wave Stiffness [*Solid-state physics*] (UWER)
D — Symbol for Electrostatic Flux Density (VLIE)
D — Transmission Density [*Optics*] (UWER)
D — Troponwerke Dinklage & Co. [*Germany*] [*Research code symbol*]
D — United States District Court [*Used citation*] (AAGC)
D — Usually Reliable Source of Intelligence [*Military*]
D — Wide [*Women's shoe width*]
D0 — Day Zero (UWER)
D0i — Bezugsdicke der i-ten Farbglasschicht (SAUS)
D1 — Day One [*First day seen for treatment*] [*Medicine*] (MELL)
D1 — Double First Class
D1 — First Coast Guard District [*Boston, MA*] [*USCG*] (TAG)
D_1 — First Dorsal Nerve [*Second dorsal nerve is D_2, etc., through D12*] [*Medicine*] (DAVI)
D_1 — First Dorsal Vertebra [*Second dorsal vertebra is D_2, etc.*] [*Medicine*]
D1A — Dickey [*Maine*] [*Seismograph station code, US Geological Survey*] (SEIS)
D1S — Dressed One Side [*Lumber*] (DAC)
D2 — Angola [*Aircraft nationality and registration mark*] (FAAC)
D-2 — Armys Special Operations Unit (SAUS)
D2 — Data Distribution (SAUS)
D2 — Dicke des zweiten Farbfilters (SAUS)
D2 — Dud Disposer (SAUS)
D-2 — National Interest Lands, Section D-2, Alaska Native Claims Settlement Act (SAUO)
D2 — Second Coast Guard District [*St. Louis, MO*] [*USCG*] (TAG)

D2A Dickey [*Maine*] [*Seismograph station code, US Geological Survey*] (SEIS)
D2A Digital-to-Analog (AEBE)
D2B Deceptive Deployment Basing [*Military*]
D2B Digital Data Base [*Computer science*] (PDAA)
D2B digital data bus (SAUS)
D2C Decimal to Character (SAUS)
D2D Discovery to Delivery
D2D Display 2-Dimensional (SAUS)
D2EHPA di-2-ethyl-hexyl phosphoric acid (SAUS)
D2M Diethylene Glycol Dimethyl Ether (SAUS)
D2 MOS Double diffused metal oxide semiconductor (SAUS)
D2S Dressed Two Sides [*Lumber*] (DAC)
D2S & CM Dressed Two Sides and Center Matched [*Lumber*] (DAC)
D2S & M Dressed Tow Sides and Matched (SAUS)
D2S & M Dressed Two Sides and Matched [*Lumber*] (DAC)
D2S & SM Dressed Two Sides and Standard Matched [*Lumber*] (DAC)
D2T2 Dye Diffusion Thermal Transfer [*Printer technology*] (PCM)
D2X Decimal to Hexadecimal (SAUS)
D3 Cholecalciferol [*Medicine*] (MELL)
D^3 Detection, Discrimination, and Designation
D/3 Distal Third [*Medicine*] (MELL)
D3A Dickey [*Maine*] [*Seismograph station code, US Geological Survey*] (SEIS)
D3M Domain Distributed Data Management System [*Computer science*] (HODG)
D3WCA Davis 3-Wheel Club of America (EA)
D4 Cape Verde [*Aircraft nationality and registration mark*] (FAAC)
D4 Cape Verde Islands [*International civil aircraft marking*] (ODBW)
D4 Design Data Dictionary and Directory (SAUO)
D4 Fourth Digit [*Medicine*] (EDAA)
D4S Dressed Four Sides [*Lumber*] (DAC)
d4T AIDS drug Zerit (SAUS)
D5 Dextrose Five Percent [*Pharmacology*] (DAVI)
D5 Fifth Coast Guard District [*Portsmouth, VA*] [*USCG*] (TAG)
D/5HS Dextrose (5%) in Hartman's Solution [*Medicine*]
D5LR Dextrose (5%) in Lactated Ringer's Solution [*Medicine*]
D5MTD Dipentamethylene Thiuram Disulfide (SAUS)
D5/NS Dextrose 5% in Normal Saline [*Pharmacology*] (DAVI)
D5/NSS Dextrose (5%) in Normal Saline Solution [*Medicine*]
D5/S Dextrose (5%) in Saline [*Medicine*]
D-5-S dextrose 5 percent in saline (SAUS)
D5/W Dextrose (5%) in Water [*Medicine*]
D6 Airline Flight Code for Inter Air (ODA)
D6 Comoros [*International civil aircraft marking*] (ODBW)
D7 Seventh Coast Guard District [*Miami, FL*] [*USCG*] (TAG)
D8 Eighth Coast Guard District [*New Orleans, LA*] [*USCG*] (TAG)
D9 Ninth Coast Guard District [*Cleveland, OH*] [*USCG*] (TAG)
D10 Decagonal [*Crystallographic symmetry group symbol*] (UWER)
D11 Eleventh Coast Guard District [*Los Angeles, CA*] [*USCG*] (TAG)
D12 Dodecagonal [*Crystallographic symmetry group symbol*] (UWER)
d 1/2 d despatch half demurrage (SAUS)
d 1/2 dbe despatch half demurrage at both ends (SAUS)
d 1/2 ddo despatch half demurrage discharging only (SAUS)
d 1/2 dlo despatch half demurrage loading only (SAUS)
D13 Thirteenth Coast Guard District [*Seattle, WA*] [*USCG*] (TAG)
D14 Fourteenth Coast Guard District [*Honolulu, HI*] [*USCG*] (TAG)
D17 Seventeenth Coast Guard District [*Juneau, AK*] [*USCG*] (TAG)
D-66 Democraten '66 [*Democrats '66*] [*Netherlands*] (PPW)
D 860 Tolbutamide [*Pharmacology*] (DAVI)
D-1 Duplicate License [*Motor vehicle violation code used in state of Maryland*] (MVRD)
DA Airline Flight Code for Air Georgia (ODA)
DA Arm Data Archive (SAUS)
DA CRS Sirrine, Inc. [*NYSE symbol*] (COMM)
DA Dacryoadenitis [*Medicine*] (MELL)
DA Daily (AFIT)
DA Daily Abstract [*Tea trade*] (ROG)
DA Daily Allowance
Da Dakota Territory Reports [*A publication*] (DLA)
Da Dalton [*Physics*] [*Chemistry*] (DOG)
DA Damage Assessment [*Environmental science*] (COE)
DA Damage Assessment [*Military*] (MUSM)
DA Damaged (CINC)
Da Damasus [*Flourished, 13th century*] [*Authority cited in pre-1607 legal work*] (DSA)
Da Damkoehler Number of Fluid Flow (UWER)
DA Dan-Air Services [*ICAO designator*] (AD)
DA Danger Area (DA)
Da Danish (ADWA)
DA Danish
DA Danish Army (NATG)
DA Dansylaspartate [*Biochemistry*]
Da Darcy Number of Fluid Flow (UWER)
DA Dark Adaptation [*Medicine*] (EDAA)
DA Dark Agouti [*Rat strain*]
DA Dassault-Breguet [*Avions Marcel Dassault*] [*France*] [*ICAO aircraft manufacturer identifier*] (ICAO)
DA Data Acquisition (MDG)
DA Data Adapter (MCD)
DA Data Address (SAUS)
DA Data Administration [*Computer science*] (GART)
DA Data Administrator
DA Data Analysis (AFM)
DA Data Analyzer (SAUS)
DA Data Area (UWER)
DA Data Array (SAUS)
DA Data Assembler
DA Data Automation (AFM)
DA Data Available
DA Date [*Online database field identifier*]
D/A Date of Accident (DMAA)
D/A Date of Admission [*Medicine*] (AAMN)
da Datolite (SAUS)
da Daughter (DMAA)
DA Daughter
DA Daughter Atom [*Physics*] (UWER)
DA Daunomycin and Cytosine (STED)
DA Daunomycin and Cytosine Arabinoside [*Antineoplastic drug regimen*] (DAVI)
DA Daunorubicin, ara-C [*Cytarabine*] [*Antineoplastic drug regimen*]
da Day (DMAA)
DA Day
d/A Day of Admission [*Medicine*] (DAVI)
d/a Days After Acceptance (EBF)
DA Days after Acceptance [*Business term*]
DA Dayton Area Office (SAUO)
DA Deacon-Arrow (SAA)
DA Deactivated for Acidic Compounds (UWER)
DA Deaerator (NRCH)
DA Dealers Alliance (EA)
DA Debtors Anonymous (EA)
D/A Debt to Asset Ratio [*Economics*]
DA Debye Approximation [*Physics*] (UWER)
da Deca [*A prefix meaning multiplied by 10*] [*SI symbol*]
DA Decarburization Anneal (UWER)
DA Decimal Add
DA Decimal Addition (SAUS)
DA Decimal Association (SAUO)
DA Decimal-to-Analog (CET)
DA Decision Altitude [*Aviation*] (DA)
DA Decision Analysis [*Military*] (DOMA)
DA Decision Area (MCD)
DA Decoded Address (SAUS)
DA Decontaminating Agent (UWER)
DA Decubitus Angina [*Cardiology*] (DAVI)
DA Decylamine (UWER)
D/A Deductible Average [*Business term*]
DA Defect Analysis (UWER)
DA Defence Act (DLA)
DA Defence Adviser [*British*]
DA Defence Attache [*British*] (DS)
DA Defence of Airfields [*British*] [*World War II*]
DA Defense Agency (SAUS)
DA Defense Aid [*Lend-Lease*] [*World War II*]
DA Deferred Annuity [*Insurance*] (ADA)
DA Define Address (UWER)
DA Define Area
DA Defined Adult (SAUS)
DA Deformation Acoustic (SAUS)
DA Degenerative Arthritis
DA Degree of Analgesia [*Medicine*] (EDAA)
DA Degree of Anisotropy (UWER)
da Deka (IDOE)
DA Delay Amplifier [*Electronics*] (OA)
DA Delayed Action [*Pharmacy*]
DA Delayed Alternation (SAUS)
DA Delayed Answer (SAUS)
DA Delayed Arming [*of explosive device*]
DA Delivery Awareness (STED)
DA Delta Air Lines, Inc. (AAG)
DA Delta Amplitude (AAG)
DA Deluxe Paint Animation [*Electronic art*]
DA Demand Assignment [*Telecommunications*] (TEL)
DA Democratic Agenda (EA)
DA Democratic Alliance [*Philippines*] [*Political party*] (FEA)
DA Democratic Alternative (Macedonia) [*Political party*] (PSAP)
DA Democratic Renewal (Greece) [*Political party*] (PSAP)
DA Democrats Abroad (EA)
DA Demokratischer Aufbruch [*Democratic Awakening*] [*Later, Christian Democratic Union*] [*Germany*] (EAIO)
DA Denmark [*Message traffic*] [*Military*] (DNAB)
Da Denmark (MILB)
DA Density Altitude [*Navigation*]
DA Dental Anesthetic [*Medicine*]
DA Dental Apprentice
DA Dental Assistant
DA Deoxyadenosine (MELL)
DA Departmental Approval (FOTI)
DA Department of Agriculture
DA Department of the Army
DA Departure Approved [*Aviation*] (FAAC)
DA Depletion Allowance [*Business term*]
DA Deployment Assembly [*Skylab*] [*NASA*]
d/a Deposit Account (EBF)
DA Deposit Account [*Banking*]
DA Deposit Administration
DA Depth Appearing [*Typography*] (DGA)
DA Deputy Administrator (COE)
DA Deputy Advocate [*Legal term*] (DLA)

DA.............. Deputy Assistant (DAS)
DA.............. Dermatology Associates (SAUS)
DA.............. Descending Aorta [*Anatomy*]
DA.............. Descent Advisor [*FAA*] (TAG)
DA.............. Design administration (SAUS)
DA.............. Design Agent (CAAL)
DA.............. Design Allowables (UWER)
DA.............. Design analysis (SAUS)
DA.............. Designated Adult [*Most serious person in a group of flippant people*]
DA.............. Designated Agent [*Environmental science*] (COE)
DA.............. Design Authorization
DA.............. Design Automation (BUR)
DA.............. Desk Accessory [*Computer science*] (BYTE)
da.............. Desk Assistant [*Broadcasting*] (WDMC)
DA.............. Destination Address
DA.............. Detector Amplifier (IAA)
DA.............. Detector Assembly
DA.............. Detergent Aid
DA.............. Detroit Arsenal [*Michigan*] [*Army*] (MCD)
DA.............. Developing Activity [*Military*] (DOMA)
DA.............. Developing Agency (CAAL)
DA.............. Developmental Age
DA.............. Development Assistance
DA.............. Development Authorisation (SAUS)
DA.............. Deviation Authorization
DA.............. Device Adapter (IAA)
DA.............. Device Address (ACRL)
DA.............. Devil's Advocate
DA.............. Devonshire Association for the Advancement of Science, Literature and the Arts (SAUO)
DA.............. Dextrose Agar [*Microbiology*]
DA.............. Diabetes Australia
DA.............. Diabetic Acidosis [*Medicine*] (STED)
DA.............. Diacetamide (UWER)
DA.............. Diacetylene (UWER)
DA.............. Diagnostic Aid
DA.............. Diagnostic Analyzer
DA.............. Diagnostic Arthroscopy [*Medicine*] (STED)
DA.............. Dianhydride (UWER)
DA.............. Dicti Anni [*Of the Said Year*] [*Latin*]
DA.............. Dictionary of Americanisms [*A publication*]
DA.............. Did Not Answer (IIA)
DA.............. Dielectric Absorption (UWER)
DA.............. Diels-Alder [*Chemistry*] (UWER)
DA.............. Difference Amplifier (SAUS)
DA.............. Difference Answering (SAUS)
DA.............. Differential Address (SAUS)
DA.............. Differential Amplifier
DA.............. Differential Analyzer (IEEE)
dA.............. differential of amplification (SAUS)
dA.............. differential of area (SAUS)
DA.............. Differentiation Antigen [*Medicine*] (STED)
DA.............. Diffused Base Alloy (IAA)
DA.............. Diffused-base Alloy (SAUS)
DA.............. Digestive Anlage
DA.............. Digit Absorbing (SAUS)
DA.............. Digit Absorption (SAUS)
DA.............. Digital Access (SAUS)
DA.............. Digital Alternator
D/A.............. Digital/Analog (SAUS)
DA.............. Digital Audio (VLIE)
D/A.............. Digital to Analog (SHCU)
d/a.............. Digital-to-Analog (IDOE)
D-A.............. Digital-to-Analog [*Converter*] [*Computer science*]
D/A.............. Digital to Analog conversion (SAUS)
D/A.............. Digital to Analog converter (SAUS)
DA.............. Dilution Air (EEVL)
DA.............. Dinar [*Monetary unit*] [*Algeria*]
DA.............. Dining Area (ADWA)
DA.............. Dinner Ale [*British*] (ADA)
DA.............. Diphenylchlorarsine (SAUS)
da.............. diphenylchlorasine (SAUS)
DA.............. Diphenylchloroarsine [*Tear gas*] [*Army symbol*]
DA.............. Diploma in Aesthetics (SAUS)
DA.............. Diploma in Anaesthetics [*British*]
DA.............. Diploma in Anesthetics (SAUS)
DA.............. Diploma in Art
DA.............. Direct Access (BUR)
DA.............. Direct Acting (SAUS)
DA.............. Direct Action [*Bomb or shell fuze*]
DA.............. Direct Address [*Telecommunications*] (NITA)
DA.............. Direct Admission [*Medicine*] (DAVI)
DA.............. Direct Agglutination [*Clinical chemistry*]
DA.............. Direct Analog (SEWL)
DA.............. Direct Answer (HGAA)
DA.............. Direct Ascent (AAG)
DA.............. Direction Action [*Bomb fuze*]
DA.............. Directional Aerial (SAUS)
da.............. Directional Antenna (WDMC)
DA.............. Directional Antenna
DA.............. Direction Finding [*JETDS nomenclature*]
DA.............. Directive authorization (SAUS)
DA.............. Director Angle (SAUS)
DA.............. Directorate of Administration (SAUO)
DA.............. Director of Administration (SAUS)
DA.............. Director of Aircraft (MUGU)
DA.............. Director of Army (SAUO)
DA.............. Director of Artillery (SAUO)
da.............. Director's Assistant (WDMC)
DA.............. Directory Assistance [*Telecommunications*] (TEL)
DA.............. Disability Assistance
DA.............. Disaggregated (MAE)
DA.............. Disassemble
D/A.............. Disbursement Account (RIMS)
DA.............. Disbursements Account (SAUS)
d/a.............. Discharge Afloat (EBF)
DA.............. Discharge Afloat
D/A.............. Discharge and Advise [*Medicine*]
DA.............. Discharged Alive (SAUS)
DA.............. Disclosure Avoidance (SAUS)
DA.............. Discontinuous action (SAUS)
DA.............. Discrete Address
DA.............. Discretionary Account [*Investment term*]
da.............. discriminant analysis (SAUS)
DA.............. Discrimination Acuity
DA.............. Discrimination Analysis [*Agronomy*]
DA.............. Disk Access (SAUS)
DA.............. Disk Action (VLIE)
DA.............. Disk Address (SAUS)
DA.............. Dislocation Allowance [*Military*] (AFM)
DA.............. Dispense as Directed [*Medicine*] (MEDA)
DA.............. Dispensing Allowance [*British military*] (DMA)
DA.............. Dispersal Airfield (SAUS)
DA.............. Display Adapter
DA.............. Dissecting Aneurysm [*Medicine*] (MELL)
D/A.............. Dissemin/Action [*Defunct*] (EA)
DA.............. Dissertation Abstracts (SAUS)
DA.............. Dissolved Acetylene
DA.............. Distended Abdomen (MELL)
DA.............. Distributed Application [*Automotive engineering*]
DA.............. Distributing Agency (SAUO)
DA.............. Distributing Authority (SAUS)
DA.............. Distribution-Abundance [*Ecology*]
DA.............. Distribution Amplifier
DA.............. Distribution Assembly [*Ground Communications Facility, NASA*]
DA.............. Distribution Automation (ACII)
DA.............. District Administrator
DA.............. District Agent [*Insurance*]
DA.............. District Assembly [*British*]
DA.............. District Attorney
DA.............. District Authorities [*British*]
DA.............. Divisional Artillery (SAUO)
DA.............. Division Artillery [*Army*]
DA.............. Divorce Anonymous [*Defunct*] (EA)
DA.............. Docking Adapter [*Aerospace*] (MCD)
DA.............. Doctor of Accounting (PGP)
DA.............. Doctor of Administration (UWER)
DA.............. Doctor of Archaeology
DA.............. Doctor of Arts
DA.............. Document Analyst (UWER)
DA.............. Documentary Bill for Acceptance
DA.............. Documentation Abstracts (journ.) (SAUS)
DA.............. Documentation Aids (SAUS)
DA.............. Documentation Associates Information Services, Inc. (IID)
D/A.............. Documenti Contro Accettazione [*Documents Against Acceptance*] [*Italian*] [*Business term*]
D/A.............. Documentos Contra Aceptacion [*Documents Against Acceptance*] [*Spanish*] [*Business term*]
DA.............. Documents against Acceptance [*Investment term*] (DFIT)
DA.............. Documents Attached
D/A.............. Documents Contre Acceptation [*Documents Against Acceptance*] [*French*] [*Banking*]
D/A.............. Documents for Acceptance [*Banking*] (ROG)
DA.............. Dodecanedioic Acid (UWER)
DA.............. Does not Answer (SAUS)
DA.............. Doesn't Answer (ADA)
da.............. Doesn't Answer [*Telephone marketing*] (WDMC)
D/A.............. Dokumente Gegen Akzept [*Documents Against Acceptance*] [*German*] [*Banking*]
DA.............. Dollar Averaging Cost [*Investment term*]
DA.............. Domain Analysis (VLIE)
DA.............. Domestic Android [*Quasar Industries*]
DA.............. Dominion Arsenal [*World War I*] [*Canada*]
DA.............. Dominion Atlantic Railway Co. [*Absorbed into CP Rail*] [*AAR code*]
DA.............. Donor-Acceptor
DA.............. Do Not Answer
DA.............. Dont Answer (SAUS)
DA.............. Dopamine [*Biochemistry*]
DA.............. Dopamine Agonist [*Medicine*] (MELL)
DA.............. Dormant Account [*Banking*]
DA.............. Dorsal Aorta [*Anatomy*]
DA.............. Dorsal Area [*Anatomy*]
DA.............. Dose Assessment [*Nuclear energy*] (NRCH)
DA.............. Dosieraerosol (SAUS)
DA.............. Double-Acting
da.............. double acting (SAUS)
DA.............. Double Action [*Gunnery*]
DA.............. Double-Action [*Gun*] (GOBB)
DA.............. Double Aged [*Metals*]
DA.............. Double Amplitude (KSC)

DA .... Double Armor [*Telecommunications*] (TEL)
DA .... Draft Action [*Defunct*] (EA)
DA .... Dragon Airways Ltd.
DA .... Drainage Area (UWER)
DA .... Drift Angle [*Navigation*]
DA .... Drive by Air-Side (UWER)
DA .... Drop Address (SAUS)
DA .... Drug Abuse (MELL)
DA .... Drug Addict
DA .... Drugs Anonymous (EA)
DA .... Drum Address (SAUS)
DA .... Dry air (SAUS)
DA .... Dual Action
DA .... Ducktail [*Hair style*] [*Bowdlerized version*]
DA .... Ductus Arteriosus [*Anatomy*]
DA .... Dummy Address (SAUS)
DA .... Dummy Aerial (SAUS)
DA .... Dummy Antenna
DA .... Dummy Argument (SAUS)
DA .... Dummy Load [*JETDS nomenclature*] [*Military*] (CET)
DA .... Dunlap & Associates, Inc. (MCD)
DA .... Duodenal Atresia [*Medicine*] (MELL)
DA .... Dust Analyzer (ACAE)
DA .... DUSTOFF [*Dedicated Unhesitating Service to Our Fighting Forces*] Association (EA)
DA .... Dynamic Analysis Branch [*Redstone Arsenal*]
Da .... [*The*] "Holy Scriptures" (1881) [*J. N. Darby*] [*A publication*] (BJA)
DA .... Istituto de Angeli [*Italy*] [*Research code symbol*]
DA .... National Council, Daughters of America [*Harrisburg, OH*] (EA)
d/a .... Commerce Days after Acceptance (ODA)
d/a .... Commerce Documents against Acceptance (ODA)
DA .... Daughters of America (ODA)
DA .... Deed of Arrangement (ODA)
DA .... Design Automation (ODA)
DA .... Destructive Analysis (ODA)
DA-1 .... Directional Antenna Day and Night [*Broadcasting term*]
DA-2 .... Directional Antenna with Changing Patterns, Day and Night [*Broadcasting term*]
DA-3 .... Directional Antenna with Changing Patterns, Day and Night with Additional Pattern Change [*Broadcasting term*]
DA '91 .... Democratisch Alternatief 1991 [*Democratic Alternative 1991*] [*Suriname*] [*Political party*] (EY)
DAA .... Danish Atlantic Association (SAUO)
DAA .... Data Access Arrangement [*Telecommunications*] [*Obsolete*]
DAA .... Data Authentication Algorithm (HGAA)
DAA .... Data Automation Activity (AFM)
DAA .... Data Availability Acknowledgment (ADWA)
DAA .... Days after Anthesis [*Botany*]
DAA .... Deadlock Avoidance Algorithm (VLIE)
DAA .... Deaf Artists of America (EA)
DAA .... Decatur Aviation, Inc. [*ICAO designator*] (FAAC)
DAA .... Decimal Adjust Accumulator
DAA .... Decimal Adjust for Addition (VLIE)
DAA .... Defense Acquisition Agency (SAUS)
DAA .... Dehydroascorbic Acid [*Also, DHA*] [*Oxidized form of Vitamin C*] [*Biochemistry*]
DAA .... Dementia Associated with Alcoholism (MELL)
DAA .... Dental Assistants Association (SAUO)
DAA .... Department of Aeronautics and Astronautics [*MIT*] (MCD)
DAA .... Dependents Assistance Act
DAA .... Deposit Administration Arrangement (WYGK)
DAA .... Deputy Assistant Adjutant [*Military*] [*British*] (ROG)
DAA .... Deputy Assistant Administrator (GFGA)
DAA .... Derivative Activation Analysis [*Analytical chemistry*]
DAA .... Desaparagine Insulin [*Pharmacology*]
DAA .... Designated Accrediting Authority (SAUS)
DAA .... Designated Approval Authority (MCD)
DAA .... Designated Approving Authority (SAUO)
DAA .... Diacetone Acrylamide [*Organic chemistry*]
DAA .... Diacetone Alcohol [*Organic chemistry*]
DAA .... Diaminoacetanilide [*Organic chemistry*]
DAA .... Diaminoanisole [*A dye*] [*Organic chemistry*]
DAA .... Dictionary of Architectural Abbreviations (SAUS)
DAA .... Diesel Automobile Association [*Defunct*] (EA)
DAA .... Dietitians Association of Australia (SAUO)
DAA .... Digest Access Authentication (VERA)
DAA .... Digital/Analog Adapter (SAUS)
DAA .... Digital Automatic Acquisition (MCD)
DAA .... Diploma of the Advertising Association (DGA)
DAA .... Direct Access Acknowledge (ACAE)
DAA .... Direct Access Arrangement [*Telecommunications*]
DAA .... Director of Army Automation
DAA .... Director of Army Aviation (UWER)
DAA .... Discharge Always Afloat (SAUS)
DAA .... Distributed Applications Architecture [*Computer science*] (BTTJ)
DAA .... Division Administrative Assistant
DAA .... Divisional Administrative Area [*Military*] [*British*]
DAA .... Divisional Assistance Authorization (ACAE)
DAA .... DNA Amplification Assay
DAA .... Doctor of Applied Arts
DAA .... Documents Against Acceptance [*Banking*]
DAA .... Doubly Asymptotic Approximation (MCD)
DAA .... Dream Anxiety Attack (MELL)
DAA .... Drug Amendments Act (BARN)
DAA .... Drug and Alcohol Abuse (OICC)
DAA .... Drugs Available Abroad [*A publication*]
DAA .... Dual Access Array (MCD)
DAA .... Dual Address Adapter (VLIE)
DAA .... Dual and Associates (SAUS)
DAA .... Durene Association of America (EA)
DAA .... Fort Belvoir, VA [*Location identifier*] [*FAA*] (FAAL)
DAAA .... Alger [*Algeria*] [*ICAO location identifier*] (ICLI)
DAAA .... Department of the Army Administrative Area
DAA & AM ... Defense Aid [*Lend-Lease*] Aircraft and Aeronautical Material [*World War II*]
DAA and QMG ... Deputy Assistant Adjutant and Quarter-Master-General (SAUO)
DAA & QMG ... Deputy Assistant-Adjutant and Quartermaster-General [*British*]
DAAAS .... American Association for the Advancement of Science, Washington, DC [*Library symbol*] [*Library of Congress*] (LCLS)
DAAB .... 4-Dimethylaminoazobenzene (UWER)
DAAB .... Blida [*Algeria*] [*ICAO location identifier*] (ICLI)
DAAB .... Diazoaminobenzene (UWER)
DAAC .... Data Acquisition and Analysis Complex [*Computer science*] (VLIE)
DAAC .... Data Active Archive Center (CARB)
DAAC .... Dental Alliance for AIDS/HIV Care (SAUO)
DAAC .... Digital Adaptive Area Correlation
DAAC .... Director of Allied Air Cooperation [*World War II*]
DAAC .... Distributed Active Archive Center [*NASA*]
DAACA .... Delegation for Afro-American and Caribbean Cultural Affairs
DAACA .... Department of the Army Allocation Committee, Ammunition (AABC)
DAACC .... Drug/Alcohol Abuse Control Committee (SAUO)
DAACCE .... Department of the Army Alternate Command and Control Element (AABC)
DAACM .... Direct Airfield Attack Combined Munition [*Air Force*] (DOMA)
DAACT .... Diabetes Association of the Australian Capital Territory
DAAD .... Bou Saada [*Algeria*] [*ICAO location identifier*] (ICLI)
DAAD .... Deutscher Akademischer Austauschdienst [*German Academic Exchange Service*] (EA)
DAAD .... Diazaanthracenedione [*Organic chemistry*]
DAAD .... Direct Action Against Drugs (SAUO)
DAAD .... Drug and Alcohol Abuse Division (SAUO)
DAADB .... Department of the Army Active Duty Board
DAAE .... Bejaia/Soummam [*Algeria*] [*ICAO location identifier*] (ICLI)
DAAE .... Defense Aid [*Lend-Lease*] Administration Expenses [*World War II*]
DAAE .... Diethylamine Analog of Ethmozine [*Biochemistry*]
DAAF .... Aoulef [*Algeria*] [*ICAO location identifier*] (ICLI)
DAAG .... Alger/Houari Boumediene [*Algeria*] [*ICAO location identifier*] (ICLI)
DAAG .... Deputy Assistant Adjutant-General [*British*]
DAAG .... Diode AND-AND Gate (SAUS)
DAAG .... Dose Assessment Advisory Group [*Department of Energy*] [*Las Vegas, NV*] (EGAO)
DA AGO .... Department of the Army Adjutant General Office (SAUO)
DA-AHEW .... Department of the Army Plan for Assistance in Department of Health, Education, and Welfare (AABC)
DA-AHEW .... Department of the Army Plan for Assistance to Department of Health, Education and Welfare (SAUO)
DAAI & OC ... Defense Aid [*Lend-Lease*] Agricultural, Industrial, and Other Commodities [*World War II*]
DAAIS .... Danger Area Activity Information Service (PIAV)
DAAIUGM .... Disaster Aid Association of the International Union of Gospel Missions (EA)
DAAJ .... Djanet [*Algeria*] [*ICAO location identifier*] (ICLI)
DAAK .... Boufarik [*Algeria*] [*ICAO location identifier*] (ICLI)
DAAL .... Alger [*Algeria*] [*ICAO location identifier*] (ICLI)
DAAM .... Dynamic Associative Random Access Memory [*Computer science*] (VLIE)
DAAM .... Telergma [*Algeria*] [*ICAO location identifier*] (ICLI)
DAAMP .... Department of the Army Avionics Master Plan (AABC)
DAAMRA .... Department of the Army Acquisition Management Review Agency (MCD)
DAAN .... Reggan [*Algeria*] [*ICAO location identifier*] (ICLI)
DA & A .... Drug Addiction and Alcoholism [*Title XVI*] [*Social Security Administration*] (OICC)
Da & Bos ..... Darby and Bosanquet's Statutes of Limitation [*2nd ed.*] [*1893*] [*A publication*] (DLA)
DA & D .... Data Acquisition and Distribution
DA & M .... Director of Administration and Management [*DoD*] (DOMA)
DA & P .... Data Acquisition and Processing
DA & P .... Data Analysis and Processing (SAA)
DA & QMG ... Deputy Adjutant and Quartermaster General [*British*]
DA&SM .... Data Acquisitions and Systems Maintenance (GEOI)
DAAO .... D-Amino Acid Oxidase [*An enzyme*]
DAAO .... Diaminoacid Oxidase (DB)
DAAP .... Department of the Army Audiovisual Program
DAAP .... Illizi [*Algeria*] [*ICAO location identifier*] (ICLI)
DAAPM .... Diploma, American Academy of Pain Management [*Medical degree*] (CMD)
DAAPP .... Department of the Army Audiovisual Production Program (MCD)
DAAPPP .... Data Archive on Adolescent Pregnancy and Pregnancy Prevention [*Sociometrics Corp.*] [*Information service or system*] (IID)
DAAPS .... Division of Advanced Automotive Power Systems [*Energy Research and Development Administration*]
DAAQ .... Ain Oussera [*Algeria*] [*ICAO location identifier*] (ICLI)
DAAR .... Daily Air Activity Report (CINC)
DAAR .... Day Air-to-Air Refueling (SAUS)
DAAR .... Department of the Army, Office of the Chief, Army Reserve
DAAR .... Deviation Approved as Requested [*Aviation*] (FAAC)
DA architecture ... Distributed-Arithmetic architecture (SAUS)
DAARL .... Directory of Australian Academic and Research Libraries [*Australia*] [*A publication*]

DAARP......... American Association of Retired Persons, Washington, DC [*Library symbol*] [*Library of Congress*] (LCLS)
DAAS.......... Data Acquisition and Analysis System (ODA)
DAAS.......... Defense Activity Address System (MCD)
DAAS.......... Defense Automated Addressing System (AAGC)
DAAS.......... Defense Automatic Addressing System (AFIT)
DAAS.......... Demonstration Advanced Avionics System (MCD)
DAAS.......... Diamineanisole Sulfate [*Organic chemistry*]
DAAS.......... Discrete Automatic Address System
DAAS.......... Distribution Adjustment Assistance Scheme (SAUO)
DAAS.......... DoD [*Department of Defense*] Automatic Addressing System (NG)
DAAS.......... Drilling Activity Analysis System [*Petroleum Information Corp.*] [*Information service or system*] (NITA)
DAAS.......... Setif/Ain-Arnat [*Algeria*] [*ICAO location identifier*] (ICLI)
DAASC......... Defense Automated Addressing System Center (GEOI)
DAASC......... Defense Automated Addressing System Center laboratory (SAUO)
DAASE......... Director of Avionics and Armament Sub-System Engineering (SAUO)
DAASM......... Doppler Arrival Angle Spectral Measurement System [*Geophysics*]
DAASO......... Defense Automatic Addressing System Office (NATG)
DAAT.......... Digital Angle of Attack Transmitter (SAUS)
DAAT.......... Draughtsmen and Allied Technicians (SAUO)
DAAT.......... Tamanrasset [*Algeria*] [*ICAO location identifier*] (ICLI)
DAATA......... Dictionary of Aeronautics and Aerospace Technology Abbreviations (SAUS)
DAATCO........ Department of the Army Air Traffic Coordinating Officer
DAATS......... Digital Analog Automatic Test System (ACAE)
DAAUW......... American Association of University Women Educational Foundation, Washington, DC [*Library symbol*] [*Library of Congress*] (LCLS)
DAAV.......... Jijell/Taher [*Algeria*] [*ICAO location identifier*] (ICLI)
DAAVMPP....... Department of the Army Audiovisual Media Production Program
DAAW.......... Bordj Omar Driss [*Algeria*] [*ICAO location identifier*] (ICLI)
DAAWA......... Dental Assistants' Association of Western Australia
DAA w/o OP... Driving Away Auto without Owner's Permission [*FBI standardized term*]
DAAX.......... Cheragas [*Algeria*] [*ICAO location identifier*] (ICLI)
DAAY.......... Mecheria [*Algeria*] [*ICAO location identifier*] (ICLI)
DAAZ.......... Relizane [*Algeria*] [*ICAO location identifier*] (ICLI)
DAB........... Daily Audience Barometer [*British*] (ADA)
DAB........... Data Acquisition Bus (NASA)
DAB........... Data Announcement Bulletin (ACAE)
DAB........... Daten-Autobahn (SAUS)
DAB........... Dave and Buster's [*NYSE symbol*]
DAB........... Days after Birth (MELL)
DAB........... Daytona Beach [*Florida*] [*Airport symbol*] (OAG)
DAB........... Deacon Air Ballistic (MUGU)
DAB........... Defense Acquisition Board [*DoD*]
DAB........... Delayed Accessory Bus [*Automotive engineering*]
DAB........... Delayed Action Bomb
DAB........... Demand Access Buffer (SAUS)
DAB........... Demand Adjustment Bucket (VLIE)
DAB........... Demand Assigned Bus [*Communications term*] (DCT)
DAB........... Democratic Alliance of Burma [*Myanmar*] [*Political party*] (EY)
DAB........... Design Appraisal Board (SAUO)
DAB........... Designated Audit Body (AAEL)
DAB........... Destroyer Advisory Board [*Navy*]
DAB........... Detroit Aluminum & Brass Corp. (EFIS)
DAB........... Deutsches Arzneibuch [*German Medical Book*] [*Medicine*]
DAB........... Devereux Adolescent Behavior [*Rating scale*] [*Also, ABRS*] [*Psychology*]
DAB........... Diabrasive International Ltd. [*Toronto Stock Exchange symbol*]
DAB........... Diagnostic Achievement Battery
DAB........... Dial-a-Bus [*TRB*] (TAG)
DAB........... Diaminobenzene [*Organic chemistry*]
DAB........... Diaminobenzidine [*Organic chemistry*]
DAB........... Diaminobutanoic Acid [*An amino acid*]
dab........... diamlinobenzidine (SAUS)
DAB........... Diazabutadiene [*Organic chemistry*]
DAB........... Dictionary of American Biography [*A publication*] (GEAB)
DAB........... Dictionary of Assyrian Botany [*A publication*] (BJA)
DAB........... Digital Audio Broadcast [*or Broadcasting*] (IAA)
DAB........... Digital Audio Broadcasting
DAB........... Digital Audio Broadcasting System (SAUO)
DAB........... Dimethylaminoazobenzene [*Organic chemistry*]
dab........... dimetylaminoazobenzene (SAUS)
DAB........... Directly Authorised Body [*Securities and Investments Board*] [*British*]
DAB........... Director of the Army Budget
DAB........... Disbursing Accounting Branch (SAUO)
DAB........... Display Arrangement Bits (NITA)
DAB........... Display Assignment BITS [*Binary Digits*]
DAB........... Display Attention BITS [*Binary Digits*] [*Computer science*]
DAb........... Dissertation Abstracts (journ.) (SAUS)
DAB........... Divisional Administration Bulletin (SAUS)
DAB........... Driver Air Bag [*Automotive safety systems*]
DAB........... Dual Access Buffer (SAUS)
DAB........... Dysrhythmic Aggressive Behavior
DAB-2......... Diagnostic Achievement Battery-2 [*P. Newcomer*] (TES)
DABA.......... Diaminobenzanilide [*Organic chemistry*]
DABA.......... Diaminobenzoic Acid [*Organic chemistry*]
DABA.......... Diaminobutyric Acid [*Biochemistry*] (DB)
DABA.......... Diploma, American Board of Anesthesia [*Medical degree*] (CMD)
DABA & CI... Diploma, American Board of Allergy & Clinical Immunology [*Medical degree*] (CMD)
DAB Acid..... Diaminobutyric Acid (SAUS)
DABAL......... Data Bank Language (SAUS)
DABAS......... Data Base Access Service [*Computer science*] (VLIE)
DABAS......... Data Base System (SAUS)
DABAWAS....... Datenbank fuer Wassergefahrdende Stoffe [*Data Bank on Substances Harmful to Water*] [*Information service or system*] [*Germany*] (IID)
DABB.......... Annaba/El Mellah [*Algeria*] [*ICAO location identifier*] (ICLI)
DABBLE........ Definitive Atmospheric Buoyant Boundary Layer Experiments (SAUS)
DABC.......... African Bibliographic Center, Washington, DC [*Library symbol*] [*Library of Congress*] (LCLS)
DABC.......... Constantine/Ain El Bey [*Algeria*] [*ICAO location identifier*] (ICLI)
DABCC......... Diploma, American Board of Clinical Chemists [*Medical degree*] (CMD)
DABCO......... Diazabicyclooctane [*Organic chemistry*]
DABD.......... Diploma, American Board of Dermatology [*Medical degree*] (CMD)
DABDS......... Diploma, American Board of Dermatology and Syphilology [*Medical degree*] (CMD)
DABEM......... Diploma, American Board of Emergency Medicine [*Medical degree*] (CMD)
DABFP......... Diploma, American Board of Family Practice [*Medical degree*] (CMD)
DABI.......... Del Greco Assertive Behavior Inventory [*Psychology*] (EDAC)
DABIA......... (Dimethylaminoazobenzene)iodoacetamide [*Organic chemistry*]
DABIM......... Diploma, American Board of Internal Medicine [*Medical degree*] (CMD)
DABITC........ (Dimethylaminoazobenzene)isothiocyanate [*Organic chemistry*]
DABL.......... Daisy Behavioural Language [*Computer science*] (NITA)
DABLC......... Director, Advanced Base Logistics Control [*Navy*]
DABM.......... Defense Against Ballistic Missiles (ACAE)
DABN.......... Diploma, American Board of Neurology [*Medical degree*] (CMD)
DABN.......... Med. Diffuse Acute Bacterial Nephritis (ODA)
DABNS......... Diploma, American Board of Neurosurgery [*Medical degree*] (CMD)
DABOA......... Director, Advanced Base Office, Atlantic [*Navy*]
DABOG......... Diploma, American Board of Obstetrics and Gynecology [*Medical degree*] (CMD)
DABOP......... Director, Advanced Base Office, Pacific [*Navy*]
DABOph........ Diploma, American Board of Opthalmology [*Medical degree*] (CMD)
DABOS......... Diploma, American Board of Orthopedic Surgery [*Medical degree*] (CMD)
DABOtol....... Diploma, American Board of Otolaryngology [*Medical degree*] (CMD)
DABP.......... Skikda [*Algeria*] [*ICAO location identifier*] (ICLI)
DABPath....... Diploma, American Board of Patholgoy [*Medical degree*] (CMD)
DABPathAnat... Diploma, American Board of Pathological Anatomy [*Medical degree*] (CMD)
DABPath & MA... Diploma, American Board of Pathology and Morbid Anatomy [*Medical degree*] (CMD)
DABPed........ Diploma, American Board of Pediatrics [*Medical degree*] (CMD)
DABPH......... Diploma, American Board of Public Health [*Medical degree*] (CMD)
DABPM......... Diploma, American Board of Physical Medicine [*Medical degree*] (CMD)
DABPMR........ Diploma, American Board of Physical Medicine and Rehabilitation [*Medical degree*] (CMD)
DABPN......... Diploma, American Board of Psychiatry and Neurology [*Medical degree*] (CMD)
DABPrevMed... Diploma, American Board, Preventive Medicine [*Medical degree*] (CMD)
DABPS......... Diploma, American Board of Plastic Surgery [*Medical degree*] (CMD)
D Abr......... D'Anvers' General Abridgment of the Common Law [*A publication*] (DLA)
DABR.......... David's Bridal [*NASDAQ symbol*] (SG)
DABR.......... Diploma, American Board of Radiology [*Medical degree*] (CMD)
DABRK......... Daybreak
DABS.......... Decennial Automated Budget System (SAUS)
DABS.......... Diploma, American Board of Surgery [*Medical degree*] (CMD)
DABS.......... Direct Access Beacon System (MCD)
DABS.......... Director, Air Battle Staff (ACAE)
DABS.......... Discrete Address Beacon SSR (Secondary Surveillance Radar) (SAUS)
DABS.......... Discrete Address Beacon System
DABS.......... Discretely Addressed Beacon System (SAUS)
DABS.......... Dynamic Air Blast Simulator (MCD)
DABS.......... Tebessa [*Algeria*] [*ICAO location identifier*] (ICLI)
DABSCI........ Dimethylamino Azobenzene Sulfonyl Chloride [*Organic chemistry*]
DABS-IPC...... Discrete Address Beacon System with Intermittent Positive Control (PDAA)
DABSIPCS...... Discrete Address Beacon System with Intermittent Positive Control System (SAUS)
DABT.......... Batna [*Algeria*] [*ICAO location identifier*] (ICLI)
DABT.......... Diamino(tribromopropyl)triazine [*Flame retardant*] [*Organic chemistry*]
DABTH......... Dimethylaminobenzenethiohydantoin [*Organic chemistry*]
DABTR......... Diploma, American Board of Therapeutic Radiology [*Medical degree*] (CMD)
DABTS......... Diploma, American Board of Thoracic Surgery [*Medical degree*] (CMD)
DABU.......... Diploma, American Board of Urology [*Medical degree*] (CMD)
DABUL......... Depolarization and Backscatter Lidar (SAUS)
DABW.......... Directory of American Book Workers [*A publication*]
DABXT......... Deep Airborne Expendable Bathythermograph (SAUS)
DAC........... Dacca [*Bangladesh*] [*Airport symbol*]
DAC........... Dachiardite [*A zeolite*]
dac........... Dacryon [*Medicine*] (EDAA)
DAC........... Daily Administrative Check (SAUS)
DAC........... Dalby Agricultural College [*Australia*]
DAC........... Damage Assessment Center (SAUO)
DAC........... Dangerous Air Cargo (SAUS)
DAC........... Danish Army Command (SAUO)
DAC........... Darwin [*California*] [*Seismograph station code, US Geological Survey*] (SEIS)

DAC .... Data Acceptance Check [*Bureau of the Census*] (GFGA)
DAC .... Data Accepted (ELAL)
DAC .... Data Acquisition (ACAE)
DAC .... Data Acquisition and Control (NASA)
DAC .... Data Acquisition Camera
DAC .... Data Acquisition Card (SAUS)
DAC .... Data Acquisition Center (ACAE)
DAC .... Data Acquisition Chassis (AAG)
DAC .... Data Acquisition Computer
DAC .... Data Acquisition Controller
DAC .... Data Analysis and Control (SAUS)
DAC .... Data Analysis Center (SAUS)
DAC .... Data Analysis Computer
DAC .... Data Analysis Console (AFM)
DAC .... Data Analysis Control (MCD)
DAC .... Data and Computation Center [*University of Wisconsin, Madison*] [*Research center*] (RCD)
DAC .... Data Assembly Center (or Centre) (SAUO)
DAC .... Data Assembly Centers [*Marine science*] (OSRA)
DAC .... Data Assistance and Control (SAUS)
DAC .... Data Authentication Code [*Telecommunications*] (OSI)
DAC .... Data Automation Corporation (SAUO)
DAC .... Date after Award of Contract (SAUO)
DAC .... Day Activity Center
DAC .... Days after Contact
DAC .... Days after Contract [*Business term*] (MCD)
DAC .... Decimal Arithmetic Carry (SAUS)
DAC .... Decrement Accumulator
DAC .... Deductible Average Clause [*Insurance*]
DAC .... Defect Action Sheet [*A publication*]
DAC .... Defence Audit Centre (SAUS)
DAC .... Defenders of the American Constitution (EA)
DAC .... Defense Acquisition Circular [*DoD*] (RDA)
DAC .... Delay, Attenuate, and Compare (UWER)
DAC .... Delayed Action Command (SAUO)
DAC .... Delayed Atomization Cuvette [*Laboratory analysis*]
DAC .... Delivery Against Cost [*Business term*]
DAC .... Demand Assignment Controller
DAC .... Democratic Action Committee [*Pakistan*] [*Political party*]
DAC .... Democratic Action Congress [*Trinidad and Tobago*] [*Political party*] (PPW)
DAC .... Democratic Advisory Committee (SAUO)
DAC .... Dental Association of Canada (FOTI)
DAC .... Department of the Army Civilian
DAC .... Deployable ACCS Component (SAUS)
DAC .... Deputate for Avionics Control (SAUS)
DAC .... Derived Air Concentration (MCD)
DAC .... Derived Air Conservation [*Environmental science*] (COE)
DAC .... Derived air contamination (SAUS)
DAC .... Design Analysis Cycle (SPST)
DAC .... Designated Acquisition Commander (SAUS)
DAC .... Design Augmented by Computer [*General Motors Corp.*]
DAC .... Design Automation Conference (TIMI)
DAC .... Detroit Athletic Club (SAUO)
DAC .... Development Advisory Committee (SAUO)
DAC .... Developmental Activity Center
DAC .... Development Assistance Committee [*Organization for Economic Cooperation and Development*] [*Paris, France*] (EAIO)
DAC .... Diabetes Association of Greater Cleveland (SAUO)
DAC .... Diallyl Chlorendate [*Fire retardant*]
DAC .... Diamond Anvil Cell [*Spectrometry*]
DAC .... Dictionary of the Apostolic Church [*A publication*] (BJA)
DAC .... Differential Aeration Corrosion (SAUS)
DAC .... Differentiated Adenomatous Carcinoma [*Medicine*] (MELL)
DAC .... Diffuse Alveolar Consolidation [*Medicine*] (MELL)
DAC .... Digital Analog Converter (SAUS)
DAC .... Digital Analysis Converter (NITA)
DAC .... Digital Area Correlator
DAC .... Digital Arithmetic Center
DAC .... Digital Associates Corporation (SAUO)
DAC .... Digital Audio Cassette (SAUS)
DAC .... Digital Autopilot Control (SAUS)
DAC .... Digital Azimuth Control
DAC .... Digital-to-Analog Circuit [*Computer science*] (IAA)
DAC .... Digital-to-Analog Computer (ELAL)
DAC .... Digital-to-Analog Control [*Computer science*] (IAA)
DAC .... Digital-to-Analog Conversion
DAC .... Digital to Analog Converter (SAUS)
DAC .... Digital-to-Analog Converter [*Computer science*]
DAC .... Digital-to-analog converters (SAUS)
DAC .... Digital to Analogue Converter (SAUS)
DAC .... Digital to Analytical Conversion (SAUS)
DAC .... Digital-to-Audio Converter [*Communications term*] (DCT)
DAC .... Diocesan Advisory Committee [*Church of England*]
DAC .... Diode-Assisted Commutation (PDAA)
DAC .... Direct Access Capability (MCD)
DAC .... Direct Access Communications (MCD)
DAC .... Direct Access Computing (MCD)
DAC .... Direct Access Control (MCD)
DAC .... Direct-Acting Carcinogen [*Medicine*] (MELL)
DAC .... Direct Air Cycle
DAC .... Director Assignment Console (NVT)
DAC .... Director of Army Contracts (SAUO)
DAC .... Directors Advisory Committee [*National Institutes of Health*]
DAC .... Directory of Associations in Canada [*Micromedia, Ltd.*] [*Information service or system*] [*A publication*] (IID)
DAC .... Disabilities Aids Collective [*Australia*]
DAC .... Disability Advisory Council (DHP)
DAC .... Disabled Adult Child [*Social Security Administration*] (OICC)
DAC .... Disablement Advisory Committee [*Department of Employment*] [*British*]
DAC .... Disassemble Communications Pool (SAUS)
DAC .... Disaster Aid Centre (SAUO)
DAC .... Disaster Application Center [*Department of Emergency Management*] (DEMM)
DAC .... Disaster Assistance Center [*Federal Emergency Management Agency*]
DAC .... Discretionary Access Control (CDE)
DAC .... Discriminative Avoidance Conditioning [*Biochemistry*]
DAC .... Disk Access Control (SAUS)
DAC .... Disk array controller (SAUS)
DAC .... Disk Attachment Control (SAUS)
DAC .... Display Analysis Console
DAC .... Distance Amplitude Correction (OA)
DAC .... Distributed Academic (SAUO)
DAC .... Distributed Academic Computing (SAUS)
DAC .... Distribution Automation and Control (MCD)
DAC .... District Advisory Committee (SAUO)
DAC .... Division Administrative Center (SAUO)
DAC .... Divisional Ammunition Column (ADA)
DAC .... Divisional Artillery Commander (SAUO)
DAC .... Division Ammunition Column (SAUO)
DAC .... Division of Adult Corrections (OICC)
DAC .... Division of Ambulatory Care [*Later, DACHP*] (EA)
D Ac............ Doctor of Accounts
DAc............ Doctor of Acupuncture (ODA)
DAC .... Document Availability Code (MCD)
DAC .... Domestic Affairs Council [*Replaced Urban Affairs Council, Rural Affairs Council, and Cabinet Committee on Environment*] [*White House*]
DAC .... Domestic Annual Fishing Capacity [*Fishery management*] (MSC)
DAC .... Donor Activity Coefficient (SAUS)
DAC .... Double Action Cylinder (SAUS)
DAC .... Double-Action Cylinder
DAC .... Double Average Comparison (SAUS)
DAC .... Douglas Aircraft Co. [*of McDonnell Douglas Corp.*]
DAC .... Douglas Aircraft Corporation (AAGC)
DAC .... Downed Aircraft (NVT)
DAC .... Drug Abuse Council [*Defunct*]
DAC .... Drugs Advisory Committee [*Australian Capital Territory, South Australia*]
DAC .... Dual Attached Concentrator (SAUS)
DAC .... Dual Attachment Concentrator [*Telecommunications*] (ACRL)
DAC .... Duplicate Aperture Card
DAC .... Durex Abrasives Corp. [*Defunct*] (EA)
DAC .... Durex Abrasives Corporation (SAUO)
DAC .... Dynamic Accelerated Cooling [*Sumitomo Metals*]
dac............ dynamic amplitude control (SAUS)
DAC .... McDonnell Douglas Corp. [*ICAO designator*] (FAAC)
DAC .... National Society, Daughters of the American Colonists (EA)
DAC .... Yuma, AZ [*Location identifier*] [*FAA*] (FAAL)
DACA .... Days after Contract Award [*Business term*] (MCD)
DACA .... Department of the Army Certificate of Achievement
DACA .... Department of the Army Corps of Engineers [*Military Project*] (AAGC)
DACA .... Design Accreditation and Certification Advisers (AIE)
DACA .... Digital-to-Analog Control Apparatus [*Computer science*] (IAA)
DACA .... Dimethylaminocarbamoyloxyacetophenon (SAUS)
daca............ diphenylaminochloroarsine (SAUS)
DACA .... Drug Abuse Control Amendment (DAVI)
DACA .... Institute for the Development of Agricultural Cooperation in Asia (SAUO)
DACAB .... Dutch-Australian Community Assistance Bureau
DACAC .... Digital-to-Analog Converter, Alternating Current [*Computer science*] (IAA)
DACAD .... Dansylcadaverine [*Biochemistry*]
DACAN .... Data Acquisition and Analysis (NOAA)
DACAN .... Douglas Aircraft Co. of Canada [*of McDonnell Douglas Corp.*] (MCD)
DACAN .... Military Committee Distribution and Accounting Agency, NATO (SAUO)
DACAN .... Military Committee Standing Group Distribution and Accounting Agency, NATO
DACAPS .... Data Collection and Processing System (IAA)
DACAR .... Damage Assessment and Casualty Report [*Military*]
DACAR .... Data Acquisition and Communication Techniques and their Assessment for Road Transport (SAUO)
DACARY .... Decoustics/ACS Centre for Acoustical Research [*York University*] [*Research center*] (RCD)
DACAS .... Damage Assessment and Casualty Report [*Military*] (AFM)
DACB .... Data Acquisition and Control Buffer (MCD)
DACB .... Data Adapter Control Block (COE)
DACB .... Diaminochlorobenzene [*Organic chemistry*]
DACBU .... Data Acquisition and Control Buffer Unit (NASA)
DACBU .... Data Acquisition Control and Buffer Unit (SAUS)
DACC .... Dangerous Air Cargoes Committee (SAUO)
DACC .... Danish American Chamber of Commerce (EA)
DACC .... Data Acquisition and Checkout Computer (SAUS)
DACC .... Data and Computation Center (SAUO)
DACC .... De Havilland Aircraft Co., Canada
DACC .... Department of the Army Communications Center (AABC)

DACC .... Design Assertion Consistency Checker (SAUS)
DACC .... Direct Access Communications Channels
DACC .... Direct Access Computing Corporation (SAUO)
DACC .... Directory Assistance Call Completion (CGWS)
DaCC .... Display and Computer Console (SAUS)
DACC .... Display and Control Card (SAUS)
D Acc .... Doctor of Accountancy [*or Accounting*]
Dacca .... All India Reporter, Dacca Series [*1949-50*] [*A publication*] (DLA)
DACCA .... Deflect Amplifier Circuit Card (DWSG)
Dacca .... Pakistan Law Reports, Dacca Series [*A publication*] (DLA)
DACCC .... Defense Area Communications Control Center
DACCC .... Detroit Area Consortium of Catholic Colleges [*Library network*]
DACCC-AL.... Defense Area Communications Control Center, Alaska
DACCC-CON... Defense Area Communications Control Center, CONUS
DACCCEUR... Defence Area Communications Control Centre Europe (SAUO)
DACCC-EUR... Defense Area Communications Control Center, Europe (SAUS)
DACCC-PAC... Defense Area Communications Control Center, Pacific (SAUO)
DACCEUR .... Defense Area Communications Control Center, Europe (NATG)
DAC Computer... Divide and Conquer Computer (SAUS)
DACCP .... Diaminocyclohexane(carboxyphthalato)platinum [*Antineoplastic drug*]
DACCS .... Department of the Army Command and Control System (AABC)
DACCS .... Digital Access Cross Connect System (SAUS)
DACD .... Delaware Association of Conservation Districts (SRA)
DACDIC.......... Digital-to-Analog Converter, Direct Current [*Computer science*] (IAA)
DACE .... Data Acquisition and Control Executive [*Hewlett-Packard Co.*]
DACE .... Data Administration Center Equipment [*Telecommunications*] (TEL)
DACE .... Data and Command Equipment (ACAE)
DACE .... Department of the Army Alternate Command and Control Element (AABC)
DACE .... Design and Computational Experiments
DACE .... Doctor of Air Conditioning Engineering
DACE .... United States Army, Corps of Engineers, Office of the Chief of Engineers Library, Washington, DC [*Library symbol*] [*Library of Congress*] (LCLS)
DACEC .... Digital Azimuth Control / Environmental Control
DACEMS ...... Data Communications Equipment Monitoring and Switching (MCD)
DAC Eng ...... Doctor of Air Conditioning Engineering
DACFC .... David Allan Coe Fan Club (EA)
DACG .... DA Consulting Group, Inc. [*NASDAQ symbol*] (NASQ)
DACG .... Departure Airfield Control Group [*Military*] (AABC)
DACG .... Deputy Assistant and Chaplain General (SAUO)
DACG .... Deputy Assistant Chaplain-General [*British*]
DACG .... Deputy Assistant Commissary-General [*Military*] [*British*] (ROG)
DACH .... Department of Arts and Cultural Heritage [*Australia*]
DACH .... Deputy Assistant Chief Hydrologist (GEOI)
DACH .... Diaminocyclohexane [*Organic chemistry*]
DA Chem ..... Doctor of Applied Chemistry
DACHP .... Division of Ambulatory Care and Health Promotion [*of the American Hospital Association*] (EA)
DACI .... Direct Adjacent Channel Interference
DACI .... Dual Audio Cassette Interface
DACIL .... Department of the Army Critical Items List
DACIS .... Department of Agriculture Corporate Information System (SAUO)
DACL .... Depression Adjective Check Lists [*Psychology*]
DACL .... Diablo Application Compiler Language [*Computer science*] (MHDI)
DACL .... Dictionnaire d'Archeologie Chretienne et de Liturgie [*A publication*] (ODCC)
DACL .... Discretionary Access Control List (SAUS)
DACL .... Dynamic Analysis and Control Laboratory [*MIT*] (MCD)
DACM .... Data Adapter Control Mode (COE)
DACM .... Defensive Air Combat Maneuvering [*Military*]
DACM .... (Dimethylamino(methyl)coumarinyl)maleimide [*Organic chemistry*]
DACM .... Direct Addressable Core Memory (SAUS)
DACM .... Director of Acquisition Career Mangement [*DoD*]
DACM .... Dissimilar Air Combat Maneuvering (SAUS)
DACM .... Dissimilar Air Combat Maneuvers
DACMD .... Deputy Associate Chief Medical Director (DMAA)
DACMIS .... Development and Configuration Management Information System (MCD)
DACNOS ...... Distributed Academic Computing Network Operating System [*Computer science*] (VERA)
DACO .... Data Consistency Orbit
DACO .... Departure Airfield Control Officer [*Army*]
DACO .... Departure Airfield Group [*Army*] (ADDR)
DACO .... Deputy Assistant Chief Officer (WDAA)
DACO .... Divisional Administrative Contracting Officer [*Military*]
DACO .... Douglas Aircraft Company (SAUO)
DACO .... Douglas Aircraft Company (or Corporation) Overseas (SAUO)
DACO .... Douglas Aircraft Co. Overseas [*Obsolete*]
DACOM.......... Data and Configuration Management (SAUS)
DACOM.......... Data Communications Corp. of Korea [*Seoul, South Korea*] [*Telecommunications service*] (TSSD)
Da-Com .... Data Communications, Inc. [*Information service or system*] (IID)
DACOM.......... Datascope Computer Output Microfilmer [*Eastman Kodak Co.*]
DACOM.......... Differential-Absorption Carbon Monoxide Monitor (MCD)
DACOM.......... Differential Absorption CO Measurement (SAUS)
DACOM.......... Digital Data Communication System (ACAE)
DACOM.......... Double Average Comparison (SAUS)
DACOMP...... Damage Assessment Computer Program [*Military*]
DACOMP...... Data Compressor (MCD)
DACON.......... Dac Cong [*North Vietnamese combat engineers*] (VNW)
DACON.......... Data Controller
DACON.......... Digital-to-Analog Converter [*Computer science*]
dacon.......... digital to analog converter (SAUS)
D/A converter... Digital-to-Analog Converter [*Computer science*] (DDC)
DACOR.......... Data Correction [*IBM Corp.*]
DACOR.......... Data Correlation (SAUS)
DACOR.......... Data Correlator
DACOR.......... Diplomatic and Consular Officers, Retired (EA)
DACOS.......... Data Communication Operating System
DACOS.......... Deputy Assistant Chief of Staff (NATG)
DACOWITS... Defense Advisory Committee on Women in the Services [*DoD*] [*Washington, DC*]
DA Coy .... Divisional Ammunition Company (SAUO)
DA/CP .... Data Acquisition and Control Processor [*Computer science*] (NITA)
DACP .... Deserving Airman Commissioning Program [*Military*]
DACPO.......... Data Count Printout [*Computer science*]
DACQ.......... Data Acquisition (IAA)
dacr .... Dacron [*Fabric*] (ODA)
DACR.......... Delete and Complete Reinstall [*Computer science*] (VLIE)
DACR.......... Diploma, American College of Radiology [*Medical degree*] (CMD)
DACR.......... Director of Airfield and Carrier Requirements [*British*]
DACRB.......... Department of the Army Compassionate Review Board
DACRP.......... Department of the Army Communication Resources Plan (AABC)
DACRS.......... Department of the Army Classification Review Committee (MCD)
DACRYLON... Dacron and Nylon
DACS .... American Chemical Society, Washington, DC [*Library symbol*] [*Library of Congress*] (LCLS)
DACS .... Danger Area Crossing Service (PIAV)
DACS .... Data Access and Control System (SAUS)
DACS .... Data Access Control System [*Computer science*] (CIST)
DACS .... Data Acquisition and Computer System (SAUS)
DACS .... Data Acquisition and Control Subsystems (ADWA)
DACS .... Data Acquisition and Conversion System [*Computer science*] (CIST)
DACS .... Data Acquisition and Correction System (SAUS)
DACS .... Data Acquisition, Control, and Simulation Centre [*University of Alberta*] [*Research center*] (RCD)
DACS .... Data Acquisition Control System (IEEE)
DACS .... Data and Analysis Center for Software [*Air Force*] [*Information service or system*] (IID)
DACS .... Dataset Control System (SAUS)
DACS .... DCSOPS [*Deputy Chief of Staff for Operations and Plans*]/ACSI Computer System [*Assistant Chief of Staff for Intelligence*] [*Army*]
DACS .... De La Rue Automatic Cash System [*Banknote-disbursing equipment*] [*British*]
DACS .... Department of Agriculture and Consumer Services (DEMM)
DACS .... Deployable Acoustic Calibration System (SAUS)
DACS .... Design Aided by Computer System (VLIE)
DACS .... Design and Artists Copyright Society Ltd. [*British*]
DACS .... Design Automation Control System (TIMI)
DACS .... Designers and Artists Copyright Society
DACS .... Digital Access and Crossconnect System [*Telecommunications*] (TEL)
DACS .... Digital Access Control System [*Computer science*] (VERA)
DACS .... Digital Access Cross connect System (SAUS)
DACS .... Digital Access Cross-Current System [*Telecommunications*] (NITA)
DACS .... Digital Acquisition and Control System (MCD)
DACS .... Digital acquisition control system (SAUS)
dACs .... Digital AC Servos (SAUS)
DACS .... Digital Aeronautical Chart Supplement (CTAS)
DACS .... Digital Animated Control System
DACS .... Digital Avionics Control System (MCD)
DACS .... Digital-to-Analog Converter [*Electronics*] (ECII)
DACS .... Direct Access Communications System (SAUS)
DACS .... Directorate of Aerospace Combat Systems (SAUO)
DACS .... Director of Ambulatory Care Services [*Medicine*] (EDAA)
DACS .... Directory Assistance Charging System (SAUS)
DACS .... Discrete Address Communications System
DACS .... Divert and Attitude Control System (SEWL)
DACS .... Dot Addressable Channel Set (SAUS)
DACS/CCR ... Digital Access Cross-Connect System/Customer Controlled Rerouting [*Communications term*] (DCT)
DACSS .... Deployable AWACS Computer Support Systems (SAUS)
DACST .... Department of Arts, Culture, Science, and Technology [*South Africa*] [*Research center*]
DACT .... Dactinomycin (Actinomycin-D) [*Also, act-D, AMD*] [*Antineoplastic drug*]
dact .... dactylus (SAUS)
DACT .... Data Compression Technology (SAUS)
DACT .... Deactivate (KSC)
DACT .... Digital Automated Communications Terminal (SEWL)
DACT .... Direct Acting
DACT .... Disposable Absorption Collection Trunk (MCD)
DACT .... Dissimilar Aerial Combat Tactics (SAUS)
DACT .... Dissimilar Air Combat Tactics [*Navy*] (MCD)
DACT .... Dissimilar Air Combat Training (MCD)
DACT .... United States ACTION Library, Washington, DC [*Library symbol*] [*Library of Congress*] (LCLS)
DACTION...... Derivative Action (SAUS)
DACTL .... Declarative Alvey Compiler Target Language [*Computer science*] (NITA)
DACTS .... Dispersion Against Concealed Targets [*Experiment*] [*Army*] (RDA)
dacty.......... dactyloscopy (SAUS)
dactygram ... dactylogram (SAUS)
DACU .... Data Acquisition and Control Unit
DACU .... Defence Arms Control Unit (SAUS)
DACU .... Device Attachment Control Unit [*IBM Corp.*]
DACU .... Digital Azimuth Control Unit
DACU .... Digital-to-Analog Converter Unit [*Computer science*]

DACU .... Digitizing and Control Unit
DACU/AT ...... Device Attachment Control Unit for Asynchronous Terminals [*Computer science*] (VLIE)
DACVR .... Digital Analog Convertera (NITA)
DACW .... Department of the Army Corps of Engineers (Civil Works Project) (AAGC)
DACX .... VIP Tank Car Service [*Private rail car owner code*]
DAD .... Dads Against Discrimination [*An association*] (EA)
DAD .... Damage Assessment Department (SAA)
DAD .... Danang [*Vietnam*] [*Airport symbol*] (OAG)
DAD .... Data Acquisition Device (SAUS)
DAD .... Data Acquisition Division (SAUO)
DAD .... Data Automation Digest (journ.) (SAUS)
DAD .... Database Action Diagram (CDE)
DAD .... Data Description Language [*Computer science*]
DAD .... Davis Distributing Ltd. [*Toronto Stock Exchange symbol*]
DAD .... Days after Deployment
DAD .... Days After Draining (SAUO)
DAD .... Decimal Accumulating Device (SAUS)
DAD .... Deep Air Defence (SAUS)
DAD .... Delayed Afterdepolarization (DMAA)
DAD .... Depression after Delivery (EA)
DAD .... Deputy Assistant Director
DAD .... Design and Development (ADA)
DAD .... Design Approval Data
DAD .... Designated Alert Detachment [*Military*] (MCD)
DAD .... Design Automation Division (TIMI)
DAD .... Desktop Application Director [*Computer science*] (PCM)
DAD .... Desktop Application Driver (SAUS)
DAD .... Development activity description (SAUS)
DAD .... Device for Automated Desensitization (DIPS)
DAD .... Dial-a-Design [*Computer-based design service*]
DAD .... Diaminodurene (SAUS)
DAD .... Differential Amplitude Discriminator (PDAA)
DAD .... Diffuse Alveolar Damage [*Medicine*]
DAD .... Digital Address
DAD .... Digital Angle Data
DAD .... Digital Animation Dream (VLIE)
DAD .... Digital Animation Dreammachine (SAUS)
DAD .... Digital-Assisted Dispatching (UWER)
dad .... digital audio definition (SAUS)
DAD .... Digital Audio Disc [*Audio/video technology*]
DAD .... Digital Audio Disk (SAUS)
DAD .... Dignity after Death (EA)
DAD .... Diode Array Detector (UWER)
DAD .... Direct Access Desktop [*Fifth Generation Systems*] (PCM)
DAD .... Direct Access Device (SAUS)
DAD .... Directional Aerial Disposal [*Insecticide spray*]
DA-D .... Directional Antenna Daytime Only [*Broadcasting term*]
DAD .... Directorate of Armament Development [*British*] (MCD)
DAD .... Directory of Australian Directories [*A publication*]
DAD .... Discharged Area Development (UWER)
DAD .... Dispense as Directed [*Pharmacy*]
DAD .... Divisional Ammunition Dump (SAUO)
DAD .... Dockyard Armament Depot (SAUO)
DAD .... Document Access Definition [*Computer science*] (VLIE)
DAD .... Documents Against Discretion [*Banking*]
DAD .... Documents Against Discretion (or Disposition) (SAUS)
DAD .... Dogs Against Drugs (SAUO)
DAD .... Domestic Animal Diversity (SAUS)
DAD .... Donor-Acceptor-Donor [*Physiology*]
DAD .... Doppler Analyzer Display (SAUS)
DAD .... Doppler Azimuth Discrimination (MCD)
DAD .... Dorado Air [*Dominican Republic*] [*ICAO designator*] (FAAC)
DAD .... Double-Acting Door [*Technical drawings*]
DAD .... Double Amplitude Displacement (SAUS)
DAD .... Double-Amplitude Displacement (MCD)
DAD .... Double Atmospheric Density (SAUS)
DAD .... Douglas County Public Library, Castle Rock, CO [*OCLC symbol*] (OCLC)
DAD .... Draft Addendum (OSI)
DAD .... Drug Administration Device [*Pharmacology*] (DAVI)
DAD .... Drug and Alcohol Directorate [*New South Wales*] [*Australia*]
DAD .... Drum and Display [*Computer science*] (ADA)
DAD .... Dual Air Density [*Explorer satellite*] [*NASA*]
DAD .... Vulcan Air Defense (SAUO)
DADA .... Deputy Assistant Director of Artillery [*British*]
DADA .... Designers and Art Directors Association [*British*] (BI)
D-ADA .... Deuterated Ammonium Dihydrogen Arsenate (UWER)
DADA .... Dichloroacetic Acid Diisopropylammonium [*Salt*] (DMAA)
DADA .... Diisopropylamine [*or Diisopropylammonium*] Dichloroacetate [*Pharmacology*]
DADA .... Director of Army Dental Services (SAUO)
DADAC .... Department of the Army Distribution/Allocation Committee (AABC)
DADAC .... Digital-to-Analog Deck Angle Converter [*Computer science*] [*Navy*]
DADADS ...... Deputy Assistant Director of Army Dental Service (SAUO)
DADADS ...... Deputy Assistant Director of Army Dental Services [*British*]
DADAG .... Diacetyldianhydrogalacitol [*Antineoplastic drug*]
DADAH .... Deputy Assistant Director of Army Health [*British*]
DADAP .... Department of Assistant Director of Army Psychiatry (SAUO)
DAD Assembler... Data Dictionary Assembler (SAUS)
DADAVS .... Deputy Assistant Director, Army Veterinary Services
DADB .... Data Analysis Database
d ADC .... Absolute Unsicherheit bei der Erfas-sung der Grauwerte durch den Ana-log-Digital-Wandler der Kamera (SAUS)
DADC .... Digital Air Data Computer
DADC .... Digital Audio Disc Corp. [*Sony Corp.*]
DADC .... Direct Access Data Channel (IAA)
DAD-C2 .... Division Air Defense Command and Control (MCD)
DAD-C3 .... Division Air Defense Command, Control, and Communications [*Study*] (MCD)
DADCAD ...... Dawn and Dusk Combat Air Patrol (SAUO)
DADCAP .... Dawn and Dusk Combat Air Patrol
DADCMI .... Department of the Army Policy for Disclosure of Classified Military Information [*to foreign government*] (AABC)
DADCOK ...... Digital Air Data Computer Status
DADCSLOG... Department of the Army, Deputy Chief of Staff for Logistics
DADCTS .... Digital Air Data Computer Test Set
DADDS .... Deputy Assistant Director of Dental Services (SAUO)
DADDS .... Diacetyldiaminodiphenylsulfone [*Antibacterial compound*]
DADDTC .... Diethylammonium Diethyldithiocarbamate [*Organic chemistry*]
DADE .... Data Acquisition and Decommutation Equipment
DADE .... Department of Army Directed Effort
DADE .... Digital Acquisition and Documentation Equipment (KSC)
DADE .... Dual Air Density Explorer [*Satellite*] [*NASA*]
DADEAC .... Diallyldiethylammonium Chloride [*Organic chemistry*]
DADEC .... Design and Demonstration Electronic Computer (MHDB)
DADEE .... Dynamic Analog Differential Equation Equalizer
DADEMS .... Department of the Army Data Elements Management System (MCD)
DADF .... Diacetyldihydrofluorescein [*Organic chemistry*]
DADG .... Deputy Assistant Director General (SAUS)
DADG .... Deputy Assistant Director-General (SAUO)
DADGMS .... Deputy Assistant Director-General of Medical Services [*British*] (ADA)
DADH .... Deputy Assistant Director of Hygiene (SAUO)
DADHT .... Diacetyldioxohexahydrotriazine [*Laundry bleach activator*]
DAdI .... Adas Israel Congregation, Washington, DC [*Library symbol*] [*Library of Congress*] (LCLS)
DADI .... Dianisidine Diisocyanate (DICI)
DADI .... Directly Addressable Device Interface [*Computer science*] (GART)
DADIC .... Data Dictionary [*Computer science*]
DADIOS .... Direct Analog-to-Digital Input-Output System [*Computer science*] (MHDB)
DAD-IS .... Domestic Animal Diversity Information System (SAUS)
DADiSP .... Data Acquisition and Digital Signal Processing
DADISP .... Data Analysis and Display [*Computer science*]
DADIT .... Daystrom Analog-to-Digital Integrating Translator
DADIWT .... Deputy Assistant Director of Inland Water Transport [*British military*] (DMA)
DADIWT .... Deputy Assistant Director of Inland Water Transport Service (SAUO)
DADL .... (D-Ala, D-Leu) Enkephalin [*Biochemistry*]
DADL .... Deputy Assistant Director of Labor [*Allied Control Commission*] [*World War II*]
DADLE .... (D-Ala, D-Leu) Enkephalin [*Biochemistry*]
DADM .... Data Acquisition and Data Management
DADM .... Decision Authority, Decision Memorandum [*Military*] (MCD)
DADM .... Deductively Augmented Data Management [*Computer science*]
DADM .... Deputy Assistant Director of Movements (SAUO)
DADM .... Detailed Air Defense Model (SAUS)
D Adm .... Doctor of Administration
DADMAC .... Diallyldimethylammonium Chloride [*Organic chemistry*]
DADMC .... Defense Advanced Disposal Management Course [*Army*]
DADMCS .... Department of the Army Decoration for Meritorious Civilian Service
DADME .... Deputy Assistant Director of Mechanical Engineering [*British military*] (DMA)
DADME .... Deputy Assistant Director of Military Engineering (SAUS)
D Adm Eng... Doctor of Administrative Engineering
DADMS .... Defense Automated Document Management System (MCD)
DADMS .... Defense Mapping Agency Automated Distribution Management System (DNAB)
DADMS .... Deputy Assistant Director of Medical Services [*Military*]
DAD/MSD .... Deputy Assistant Director for Management Support Division [*Vietnam*]
DADO .... Data Automation Design Office [*Air Force*] (AFM)
dAdo .... Deoxyadenosine (ADWA)
DADO .... Director of Air Defence Operations (SAUS)
DAD of S&T... Deputy Assistant Director of Supplies and Trasport (SAUO)
DAD of ST ... Deputy Assistant Director of Supplies and Transport (SAUS)
DAD of W .... Deputy Assistant Direcor of Works (SAUO)
DAD of W .... Deputy Assistant Director of Works (SAUS)
DADOS .... Deputy Assistant Director of Ordnance Services (SAUO)
DADOS .... Deputy Assistant Director of Ordnance Stores [*Military*]
DADOS(E) .... Deputy Assistant Director of Ordnance Services (Engineering) [*British*]
DADOTA .... Drug and Alcohol Dependent Offenders' Treatment Act of 1986
dADP .... Deoxyadenosine Diphosphate [*Biochemistry*]
DADP .... Dialkyl Dithiophosphate (SAUS)
DADP .... Directorate of Air Defence Plans (SAUO)
DAD/PE .... Deputy Assistant Director for Plans and Evaluation [*Vietnam*]
DADPE .... Diaminodiphenyl Ether [*Organic chemistry*]
DADPM .... Diaminodiphenylmethane [*Organic chemistry*]
DAD/POD .... Deputy Assistant Director for the Psychological Operations Division [*Vietnam*]
DADPR .... Deputy Assistant Director of Public Relations [*British military*] (DMA)
DADPS .... Diaminodiphenyl Sulfone [*Also, DAPSONE, DDS*] [*Pharmacology*]
DADPS .... Diamino Diphenyl Sulphone (SAUS)
DADPTC .... Defence ADP Training Centre (SAUS)
DADPTC .... Defence Automatic Data Processing Training Centre [*British military*] (DMA)
DADQ .... Deputy Assistant Director of Quartering [*British*]
DADR .... Deputy Assistant Director of Remounts [*British*]

DADR .... Digital Angle Data Recorder
DADRT .... Deputy Assistant Director of Railway Transport [*British military*] (DMA)
DADRT .... Deputy Assistant Director of Railway Trasport (SAUO)
DADRy .... Deputy Assistant Director of Railway Transport (SAUS)
DADS .... Dads Advising Dads
DADS .... Dads Against Discrimination [*An association*] (EA)
DADS .... DARCOM [*Development and Readiness Command, Army*] Announcement DistributionSystem (RDA)
DADS .... Data Access and Dissemination System (AAGC)
DADS .... Data Acquisition and Display System [*or Subsystem*]
DADS .... Defense Acquisition and Display System (AAGC)
DADS .... Defense Acquisition Data System (AAGC)
DADS .... Defense Audiovisual Depository System
DADS .... Defense Automated Depot System (MCD)
DADS .... Deficiency Analysis Data System (DNAB)
DADS .... Digital Air Data-Computer System (SAUS)
DADS .... Digital Air Data System
DADS .... Digital Analog Data System (CAAL)
DADS .... Digital Assisted Data Base System (GEOI)
DADS .... Digital Audio Distribution System
DADS .... Direct Access Data Set (SAUS)
DADS .... Direct Application Decontamination System (SAUS)
DADS .... Director of Army Dental Services [*British*]
DADS .... Dittler Airline Data Systems [*Information service or system*] (IID)
DADS .... Division Air Defense System [*Military*]
DADS .... Document Availability and Distribution Services (ACAE)
DADS .... Dosimetry Acquisition and Display System
DADS .... Dual Air Density Satellite [*NASA*] (NASA)
DADS .... Dynamic Allocation/Deallocation Subsystem [*Computer science*] (HODG)
DADS .... Dynamic Analysis and Design of Systems (RDA)
DADS .... Dynamic Analysis and Design Software
DAD Satellite... Dual Air Density Satellite (SAUS)
DADSI .... Director of Air Defence Systems Integration (SAUO)
DADSM .... Direct Access Device Space Management (MCD)
DADSOT .... Digital/Analog Daily System Operability Tests (MCD)
DADST .... Deputy Assistant Director of Supplies and Transport [*British*]
DADT .... Deputy Assistant Director of Transportation [*British*]
DADTA .... Durability and Damage Tolerance Analysis [*Air Force*]
DADT-M .... Diaminobenzene-Dithiol-Containing Transition Metal Polymer (UWER)
DADTn .... Deputy Assistant Director of Transportation (SAUS)
DADU .... Data Accumulation and Distribution Units [*Navy*] (MCD)
DADVRS .... Deputy Assistant Director of Veterinary and Remount Services [*British military*] (DMA)
DADVS .... Deputy Assistant Director of Veterinary Services (DMA)
DADW .... Deputy Assistant Director of Welfare (SAUO)
Dady .... Dadyburjar. Small Court Appeals [*India*] [*A publication*] (DLA)
DAE .... Danish Air Force [*ICAO designator*] (FAAC)
DAE .... Data Acquisition Equipment (KSC)
DAE .... Data Automation Equipment
DAE .... Days after Emergence [*Botany*]
DAE .... Dealers Art Exchange (EA)
DAE .... Defense Acquisition Executive (MCD)
DAE .... Department of Aerospace Engineering (UWER)
DAE .... Department of Atomic Energy [*India*]
DAE .... Design, Analysis, and Engineering (ACAE)
DAE .... Design and Analysis of Experiments (SAUO)
DAE .... Diacetic Acid (UWER)
DAE .... Diacetylethylene (SAUS)
DAE .... Differential-Algebraic Equations [*Mathematics*]
DAE .... Digital Audio Extraction (SAUS)
DAE .... Diphenylanthracene Endoperoxide [*Organic chemistry*]
DAE .... Diploma in Advanced Education (ADA)
DAE .... Diploma in Advanced Engineering [*British*]
DAE .... Direction Aerial (SAUS)
DAE .... Directorate of Aircraft Engineering (SAUO)
DAE .... Director of Aircraft Equipment [*Ministry of Aircraft Production*] [*British*]
DAE .... Director of Air Equipment (SAUS)
DAE .... Director of Air Equipment and Naval Photography (SAUO)
DAE .... Director of Army Education [*British*]
DAE .... Disaster Assistance Employee (SAUO)
DAE .... Distributed Applications Environment (TIMI)
DAE .... Distributed Automation Edition [*Computer science*] (BTTJ)
DAE .... Distribution of Adsorption Energies (UWER)
DAE .... District Airport Engineer
DAE .... Diving Air Embolism [*Medicine*] (DAVI)
DAE .... Division of Adult Education [*Office of Education*]
D Ae .... Doctor of Aeronautics
DAE .... Doctor of Art Education
DAE .... Dry Air Equivalent [*Engineering*]
DAE .... DSA [*Defense Supply Agency*] Augmentation Element
DAE .... Dual Acquisition Equipment (SAUS)
DAE .... Dynamic Asian Economy (UWER)
DAE .... Dynamic Augmentation Experiment (SAUS)
DAE .... Dynamics Augmentation Experiment (MCD)
DAE .... Dictionary of American English (ODA)
DAEA .... Dimethyl Aminoethyl Acetate [*Organic chemistry*]
DAEA .... Drug Abuse Education Act (OICC)
DAEC .... Danish Atomic Energy Commission
DAEC .... Diethyl Aminoethyl Cellulose (UWER)
DAEC .... Duane Arnold Energy Center (NRCH)
DA Ed .... Doctor of Arts in Education (PGP)
DAEDAC .... Drug Abuse Epidemiology Data Center [*Ceased operation*] [*Texas Christian University*] (IID)
DAEDALUS .... Documenting Aerosol Electromagnetics, Defining Aerosol Lifetimes, and Understanding Sources [*Research station*] (CARB)
DAEDARC .... Department of the Army Equipment Data Review Committee (AABC)
DAEDR .... Delimitation, Alignment and Error Detection in Receive Direction (VLIE)
DAEDR .... Delimitation, Alignment, Error Detection, Reception (SAUS)
DAEDT .... Delimitation, Alignment, Error Detection, Transmitting (SAUS)
D Ae E .... Doctor of Aeronautical Engineering
DAeEng .... Doctor of Aeronautical Engineenng (SAUS)
D Ae Eng .... Doctor of Aeronautical Engineering
DAEEP .... Division of Applied Experimental and Engineering Psychologists (EA)
DAEL .... Division of Adult Education and Literacy (SAUO)
DAEM .... Department of Agriculture, Energy and Minerals (SAUS)
DAEM .... Digital Acoustic Emission Monitor (PDAA)
DAEM .... Directorate of Aircraft Engineering and Maintenance (MCD)
DAEM .... Draper Aden Environmental Modeling
DAEMON .... Data Adaptive Evaluator and Monitor
DAEMON .... Disk and Execution Monitor [*Unix*] (VERA)
DAEng .... Director of Aircraft Engineering (SAUO)
DAEO .... Designated Agency Ethics Official [*Telecommunications*] (OTD)
DAEP .... Department of the Army Equipment Publication
DAEP .... Diamino(adamantyl)ethylpyrimidine [*Biochemistry*]
DAEP .... Director of Army Equipment Policy (SAUO)
DAEP .... Division of Atomic Energy Production (ODA)
DAE/PE .... Defense Acquisition Executive/Procurement Executive (AAGC)
DAER .... Daily Ammunition Expenditure Rate (SAUS)
DAER .... Department of Aeronautical and Engineering Research (SAUO)
DAER .... Department of Aeronautical Engineering Research (SAUS)
DAERA .... Disability Alliance Educational and Research Association [*British*]
D Aero E .... Doctor of Aeronautical Engineering
DAES .... Defense Acquisition Executive Summary
DAES .... Diploma in Advanced Educational Studies, University of Newcastle [*British*] (DBQ)
DAES .... Direct Access Education System (AEBS)
DAES .... Division of Adult Education Service [*of NEA*]
D Ae S .... Doctor of Aeronautical Science
DAES .... Drug Abuse Education Specialist (DNAB)
DAEs .... Dynamic Asian Economies (SAUO)
D Ae Sc .... Doctor of Aeronautical Science
DAESRA .... Denver Area Employees Service and Recreation Association (SAUO)
DAF .... Dafare [*Djibouti*] [*Seismograph station code, US Geological Survey*] (SEIS)
DAF .... Danish Air Force [*Denmark*] [*FAA designator*] (FAAC)
DAF .... Data Acquisition Facility [*of STADAN*]
DAF .... Data Analysis Facility
DAF .... Days after Flowering [*Botany*]
DAF .... Decay-Accelerating Factor [*Biochemistry*]
DAF .... Dedicated Access Facility [*Library science*]
DAF .... Deferred Annuity Fund
DAF .... Delay Amplification Factor (IAA)
DAF .... Delay Auditory Feedback (SAUS)
DAF .... Delayed Action Fuse
DAF .... Delayed Auditory Feedback [*Audiology*]
DAF .... Delivered at Frontier [*Seller's responsibility is fulfilled when goods have arrived at frontier, but before "customs border," of country named*] [*"INCOTERM," International Chamber of Commerce official code*]
DAF .... Demographic Adjustment Factor (NTCM)
DAF .... Demonstration Air Force
DAF .... Denmark-America Foundation (EA)
DAF .... Department of Agriculture and Fisheries [*New South Wales*] [*Australia*]
DAF .... Department of the Air Force
DAF .... Departure Airfield (AABC)
DAF .... Desalkylflurazepam [*Sedative*]
daf .... described as follows (SAUS)
DAF .... Desert Air Force [*British*]
DAF .... Design Action to Follow
DAF .... Destination Address Field [*Computer science*] (IBMDP)
DAF .... Deutsche Arbeitsfront [*German Workers Front*] [*Post-World War II*]
DAF .... Development Assistance Fund (SAUO)
DAF .... Device Address Field (SAUS)
DAF .... Device Assembly Facility
DAF .... Diacetyl Ferrocene (SAUS)
DAF .... Diacetylferrocene [*Organic chemistry*]
DAF .... Diacetylfluorescein [*Organic chemistry*]
DAF .... Diallyl Fumarate (EDCT)
DAF .... Differentiation-Activating Factor (DB)
DAF .... Dilutin Attenuation Factor [*Metallurgy*]
DAF .... Direct Access Facility [*Communications term*] (DCT)
DAF .... Direct Access File [*Computer science*] (VLIE)
DAF .... Directory Authentication Framework (VLIE)
DAF .... Discard at Failure (MCD)
daf .... discharge afloat (SAUS)
DAF .... Dispersion Attenuation Factor (VLIE)
DAF .... Dissolved Air Flotation
DAF .... Distributed Acquisition Facility (NITA)
DAF .... Distributed Application Framework [*Computer science*] (VERA)
DAF .... Divorced Asian Female (ADWA)
DAF .... Document Acquisition File (DNAB)
DAF .... Dominium Aluminum Fabricating (SAUO)
DAF .... Double Apron Fence (SAUS)
DAF .... Draw-a-Family [*Test*] [*Psychology*] (DAVI)

DAF Dressing after Finish [*Manufacturing term*]
DAF Dry and Ash-Free [*Coal*]
DAF Dual Access Feature (IAA)
DAF Due and Ancient Form [*Freemasonry*]
DAF Dynamic amplification factor (SAUS)
DAF Dynamic Axial Fatigue (PDAA)
DAF Framework for Distributed Application [*Telecommunications*] (OSI)
DAF Van Doorn's Automobile Fabrieken [*Dutch automobile manufacturer; acronym used as name of its cars*]
DAFA American Forestry Association, Washington, DC [*Library symbol*] [*Library of Congress*] (LCLS)
DAFA Data Accounting Flow Assessment (MHDB)
DAF & E Defense Aid [*Lend-Lease*] Facilities and Equipment [*World War II*]
DAFB Dyess Air Force Base [*Texas*] (AAG)
DAF Basis Dry Ash Free Basis (SAUS)
DAFC Departure Airfield Control (AABC)
DAFC Dictionnaire Apologetique de la Foi Catholique [*A publication*] (BJA)
DAFC Digital Automatic Frequency Control
DAFCCS Department of the Air Force Command and Control System
DAFCG Departure Airfield Control Group [*Military*] (AABC)
DAFCS Digital Automated Flight Control System (SAUS)
DAFCS Digital Automatic Flight Control System
DAFD Dayton Air Force Depot
DAFD Department of the Army Forward Depot (AABC)
DAFDS Digital Autopilot Flight Director System (MCD)
DAFDTA Dipole Antenna with Feed-Points Displaced Transverse to Its Axis (PDAA)
DAFE Designated Acronym Free Environment (SAUO)
DAFF Daffodil (DSUE)
DAFF Department of Agriculture, Fisheries and Forestry (SAUO)
DAFFA Delicatessen and Fine Food Association [*British*] (DBA)
DAFFD Department of the Army Forward-Floating Depot (AABC)
DAFFS Design of Advanced Fossil Fuel System
DAFFY Direct Aid for Full Yaw
DAFG Deutsch-Albanische Freundschaftsgesellschaft EV [*German Albanian Friendship Society*] [*Germany*] (EAIO)
DAFGD Drag and File Gold Desktop [*Computer science*] (VLIE)
DAFH Tilrempt/Hassi R'Mel [*Algeria*] [*ICAO location identifier*] (ICLI)
DAFH United States Air Force, Headquarters U.S. Air Force, Office of Air Force History, Bolling Air Force Base, Washington, DC [*Library symbol*] [*Library of Congress*] (LCLS)
DAFI Djelfa/Tletsi [*Algeria*] [*ICAO location identifier*] (ICLI)
DAFICCS Department of the Air Force Integrated Command and Control Systems (MCD)
DAFIE Directorate for Armed Forces Information and Education [*Military*]
DAFL American Federation of Labor and Congress of Industrial Organizations Library, Washington, DC [*Library symbol*] [*Library of Congress*] (LCLS)
DAFL Differential Area Force Law (MCD)
DAFL Digital Automatic Frequency Lock (SAUS)
DAFM Department of the Army Field Manuals
DAFM Direct Access File Manager
DAFM Discard-at-Failure Maintenance (IEEE)
DAFM Distal Accessory Flexor Muscle [*of a lobster*]
DAFNE Double Annular Factory for Nice Experiments
DAFO Division Accounting and Finance Office [*Air Force*] (AFIT)
DAFOSR United States Air Force, Office of Scientific Research, Washington, DC [*Library symbol*] [*Library of Congress*] (LCLS)
DAFS Damage Analysis and Fundamental Studies (MCD)
DAFS Deepwater Actively Frozen Seabed (UWER)
D/AFS Department of Administrative and Financial Services (SAUO)
DAFS Department of Agriculture and Fisheries for Scotland
DAFS Developments in Aquaculture and Fishery Science (SAUS)
DAFS Diffraction Anomalous Fine Structure (SAUS)
DAFS Direct Aerial Fire Support [*Military*] (AABC)
DAFS Director of Air Force Security (SAUO)
DAFS Director of Army Fire Services [*British*]
DAFS Duty Air Force Specialty
DAFSC Duty Air Force Specialty Code
DAFSO Department of the Air Force Special Order (AFM)
DAFT Data Acquisition Frequency Table (MCD)
daft digital/analog function table (SAUS)
DAFT Digital Analogic Function Table [*Electronics*] (ECII)
DAFT Digital-to-Analog Function Table [*Packard Bell Computer Corp.*]
DAFT Dissolved Air Flotation Thickener (LDOE)
DAFT Draw-A-Family Test (MEDA)
DAFW Directorate of Air Force Welfare [*British*]
DAFX U.S. Department of Defense [*Private rail car owner code*]
DAFZ Dawn Foods [*Federal Railroad Administration identification code*]
DAFZ Dubai Airport Free Zone
DAG Agriculture Canada Library [*UTLAS symbol*]
DAG Aquadag [*Graphite coating*] (NTCM)
DAG Daggett, CA [*Location identifier*] [*FAA*] (FAAL)
DAG Danmarkshavn [*Greenland*] [*Seismograph station code, US Geological Survey*] (SEIS)
DAG Data Acquisition Glove
DAG Data Analysis Group [*Military*]
DAG Data Authentication Group (SAUO)
DAG Debendox Action Group [*British*] (DBA)
dag Decagram (ADWA)
DAG Defence Against Gas (SAUS)
DAG Defense Aerial Gunner
DAG Defense Special Security Communications System Address Group (MCD)
DAG Deflocculated Acheson Graphite (SAUS)
dag Dekagram (NTIO)
DAG Dekagram [*Unit of measure*]
DAG Department of the Attorney-General [*Commonwealth, Queensland*] [*Australia*]
DAG Deputy Adjutant-General [*Military*]
DAG Deputy Advocate-General [*Military*] [*British*] (ROG)
DAG Deputy Assistant General (UWER)
DAG Design Advisory Group (IAA)
DAG Development Assistance Group
DAG Diacylglycerol [*Organic chemistry*]
DAG Dianhydrogalacitol [*Antineoplastic drug*] (DAVI)
DAG Dianilinogossypol [*Organic chemistry*]
DAG Digital Address Group (ACAE)
DAG Diode AND Gate (SAUS)
DAG Directed Acyclic Graph (MCD)
DAG Directorate of Geographic Affairs (SAUS)
DAG Division Advisory Group (MCD)
DAG Division Artillery Group [*Military*] (AABC)
D Ag Doctor of Agriculture
DAG Doll Artisan Guild (EA)
dag dysproslum aluminum garnet (SAUS)
DAG Dystrophin-Associated Glycoprotein [*Biochemistry*]
DAGAS Dangerous Goods Advisory Service [*British*] (NITA)
DAGC Delayed Automatic Gain Control (MSA)
DAGC Digital Automatic Gain Control (MCD)
Dag Cr L Dagge's Criminal Law [*A publication*] (DLA)
Dag Ct M D'Aguilar on Courts-Martial [*A publication*] (DLA)
DAGDL Diacetyl(glucarodilactone) [*Biochemistry*]
DAGE UCD Ag Econ (SAUS)
DAGET Daggett, CA [*American Association of Railroads railroad junction routing code*]
DAGK Diacylglycerol Kinase (DMAA)
DAGMAR Defining Advertising Goals for Measured Advertising Results [*Title of book written by Russell Colley and published by the Association of National Advertisers*]
DAGMAR Drift and Ground-Speed Measuring Airborne RADAR
dagmar drift-and-groundspeed-measuring radar (SAUS)
DAGN Diaminoguanidine Nitrate [*Organic chemistry*]
DAGNA Association of the German Nobility in North America (EA)
DAGNA Deutsche Adels-Gesellschaft in Nord Amerika [*Association of the German Nobility in North America*] (EA)
DAGO District Aviation Gas Office [*Navy*]
DAGR Dictionnaire des Antiquites Grecques et Romaines d'Appres les Textes et les Monuments [*A publication*] (BJA)
D Agr Doctor of Agriculture
DAGR Green [*Daniel*] Co. [*NASDAQ symbol*] (NQ)
DAGRA Deputy Adjutant-General, Royal Artillery [*British military*] (DMA)
D Agr E Doctor of Agricultural Engineering
D Agr Eng Doctor of Agricultural Engineering
D Agric Doctor of Agriculture
D Agr S Doctor of Agricultural Science
D Agr Sc Doctor of Agricultural Science
DAGSA Dangerous Goods Advisory Serive (SAUO)
DAgSc Doctor of Agricultural Science (ADA)
DAGT Direct Antiglobulin Test [*Clinical chemistry*] (MAE)
DAGUERR Daguerrotype [*Photography*] (ROG)
Daguet French participation in the 1991 Gulf War against Iraq. (SAUS)
D'Agu Oeuv D'Aguesseau. Oeuvres [*A publication*] (DLA)
DAH Air Algerie [*Algeria*] [*ICAO designator*] (FAAC)
DAH Dahomey (ROG)
Dah Dahomy (VRA)
DAH Dathina [*Yemen*] [*Airport symbol*] (AD)
DAH Days After Harvest (SAUO)
DAH Dictionary of American History [*A publication*]
DAH Dictionary of American Hymnology [*Database*] [*Hymn Society of America, Inc.*] [*Information service or system*] (IID)
DAH Diffuse Alveolar Hemorrhage [*Medicine*] (MELL)
DAH Director of Army Hygiene (SAUO)
DAH Disarticulation of Hip (MELL)
DAH Disordered Action of the Heart [*Medicine*]
DAH Domestic Annual Harvest
DaH Dopamine-a-Hydoxylase (SAUS)
DAH National Society Women Descendants of the Ancient and Honorable Artillery Company (EA)
DAHA Data Acquisition, Handling and Analysis Plan (ACAE)
DAHAC Department of the Army Historical Advisory Committee [*Washington, DC*] (EGAO)
DAHC Dutch-American Historical Commission (EA)
DAHE Department of Allied Health Evaluation [*AMA*]
DAHE Department of the Arts, Heritage & Environment (SAUO)
DAHEA Department of Allied Health Education and Accreditation [*AMA*] (DAVI)
DAHL Dahlen [*Saxony*] (ROG)
Dahl Mar Int L Dahlgren's Maritime International Law [*A publication*] (DLA)
DAHM Division of Allied Health Manpower [*Bureau of Health Professions Education and Manpower Training, HEW*]
DAHM Division of Allied Health Monpower (SAUO)
DAHP 3-Deoxy-D-Arabino-Heptulosonate-7-Phosphate
DAHP Diaminohydroxypirimidin (SAUS)
DAHP Division of Associated Health Professions [*DHHS*]
DAHQ Di-tert-amylhydroquinone [*Organic chemistry*]
DAHR Director for Administration and Human Resources
DAHRS Doppler Attitude Heading Reference System (MCD)
DAHRT Dual-Axis Radiographic Hydrotest [*For evaluating nuclear weapons*]

DAHRT......... Dual-Axis Radiographic Hydrotest Facility [*For simulation of nuclear weapons*]
DAHS........... Danish American Heritage Society (EA)
DAI.............. Daimler-Benz AG [*NYSE symbol*] (SPSG)
DAI.............. Daimler-Benz Aktieng ADS [*NYSE symbol*] (TTSB)
DAI.............. Dairen [*Republic of China*] [*Seismograph station code, US Geological Survey*] [*Closed*] (SEIS)
DAI.............. Dan' Air [*Benin*] [*FAA designator*] (FAAC)
DAI.............. Days After Inoculation (SAUO)
DAI.............. Days After Installation (SAUS)
DAI.............. Death Attitude Indicator
DAI.............. Death from Accidental Injuries [*Military*]
DAI.............. Demonstrators Association of Illinois (EA)
DAI.............. Detroit Adjustment Inventory [*Psychology*]
DAI.............. Development Alternatives, Incorporated (SAUO)
DAI.............. Device Application Interface [*Computer science*] (VERA)
DAI.............. Diamidinoindole [*Organic chemistry*]
DAI.............. Diarthrodial Joint (MELL)
DAi.............. Diffues Axonal Injury [*Neurology*] (DAVI)
DAI.............. Diffuse Axonal Injury [*Medicine*] (STED)
DAI.............. Digital Applications International [*Commercial firm*] [*British*] (NITA)
DAI.............. Digital Audio Interface (SEWL)
D-AI............ Diplomate, American Board of Allergy and Immunology (DHSM)
DAI.............. Direct Access Information
DAI.............. Direct Access Interface (SAUS)
DAI.............. Direct Aqueous Injection (ABAC)
DAI.............. Director of Aeronautical Inspection [*British*]
DAI.............. Director of Air Intelligence (SAUO)
DAI.............. Director of Army Instruction
DAI.............. Discrete Activity Indicator [*NASA*] (KSC)
DAI.............. Disease Activity Index [*Medicine*]
DAI.............. Distributed Artificial Intelligence [*Computer science*]
DAI.............. Dittberner Associates, Inc. [*Bethesda, MD*] [*Information service or system*] [*Telecommunications*] (TSSD)
DAI.............. Doubly Auto-Ionizing (PDAA)
DAI.............. Drift Angle Indicator [*Navigation*]
DAI.............. Drug Abuse Information (SAUS)
DAI.............. Dynamic Application Integration [*Computer science*] (PCM)
DAIA............ American Institute of Architects, Washington, DC [*Library symbol*] [*Library of Congress*] (LCLS)
D/AIA.......... DoD [*Department of Defense*]/Army Information Architecture (RDA)
DAIB............ (Dimethylamino)isoborneol [*Organic chemistry*]
DAIC............ Danish Association For International Cooperation (SAUO)
DAIC............ United States Industrial College of the Armed Forces [*Fort McNair*], Washington, DC [*Library symbol*] [*Library of Congress*] (LCLS)
DAICS.......... Data-Acquisition and Instrument-Control System (SAUS)
DAICS.......... Data Inventory Control System (MCD)
DAID............ Data Applications and Interactive Display (SAUS)
DAID............ Delayed Action Incendiary Device
DAID............ United States Agency for International Development, Office of Population, Washington, DC [*Library symbol*] [*Library of Congress*] (LCLS)
DAIDS.......... Division of AIDS (SAUS)
DAIDS.......... Division of the AIDS [*Acquired Immune Deficiency Syndrome*] [*National Institutes of Health*] (EGAO)
DAIE............ Dai'ei, Inc. [*NASDAQ symbol*] (NQ)
Dai Ei.......... Dai'ei, Inc. [*Associated Press*] (SAG)
DAIEY.......... Daiei Inc.ADS [*NASDAQ symbol*] (TTSB)
DAI/FLO....... Directorate of Air Intelligence (SAUO)
DAIG............ Daig Corp. [*NASDAQ symbol*] (SAG)
DAIG............ Department of the Army Inspector General
DAIG............ Deputy Assistant Inspector General (GFGA)
DAI/GC........ Direct Aqueous Injection/Gas Chromatography (ABAC)
DaigCp......... Daig Corp. [*Associated Press*] (SAG)
DAIL............ Data Information Link (SAUS)
Daily Leg News (PA)... Daily Legal News (Pennsylvania) [*A publication*] (DLA)
Daily Leg (PA)... Daily Legal Record [*Pennsylvania*] [*A publication*] (DLA)
Daily L N..... Daily Legal News [*Pennsylvania*] [*A publication*] (DLA)
Daily L R..... Daily Legal Record [*Pennsylvania*] [*A publication*] (DLA)
Daily Trans... New York Daily Transcript, Old and New Series [*A publication*] (DLA)
Daily Transc... New York Daily Transcript [*A publication*] (DLA)
DAIM............ Data Analysis Information Memorandum
DAIM............ Dynamic Active Index Matrix (BUR)
DAIMC.......... Defense Advanced Inventory Management Course [*Army*]
DAIMS.......... Department of the Army Integrated Materiel Support
DAIN............ Director of Action Information and Navigation (SAUO)
DAING.......... Daingerfield, TX [*American Association of Railroads railroad junction routing code*]
DAIO............ Data I/O [*NASDAQ symbol*] (TTSB)
DAIO............ Data I/O Corp. [*NASDAQ symbol*] (NQ)
DAIO............ Divisional Artillery Intelligence Officer [*British*]
DAIP............ Defense Acquisition Improvement Program [*DoD*]
DAIP............ Deliquency Account Inventory Profile [*IRS*]
DAIP............ Department of the Army Intelligence Plan
DAIP............ Diallyl Isophthalate [*Organic chemistry*]
DAIP............ Diploma, American Institute of Psychoanalysis [*Medical degree*] (CMD)
DAIPR.......... Department of the Army in Process Review (MCD)
DAIPs.......... Diallyl Isophthalates (SAUS)
DAIR............ D & I Railroad [*Federal Railroad Administration identification code*]
DAIR............ Debit Accounting Information Retrieval
DAIR............ Dial Access Information Retrieval (SAUS)
DAIR............ Direct Altitude and Identification Readout [*Aviation*] (MCD)
DAIR............ Driver Aid, Information, and Routing [*Computer science*]
DAIR............ Driver Air, Information, and Routing (SAUS)
DAIR............ Dynamic Allocation Interface Routine [*Computer science*] (BUR)
DAIR............ Dynamic Assignation Interface Routine [*Electronics*] (ECII)
DAIRE.......... Direct Altitude and Identification Readout Equipment [*Aviation*] (FAAC)
Dai Reg........ New York Daily Register [*A publication*] (DLA)
DAIRI........... Dissertation Abstracts International Retrospective Index (SAUS)
DAIRO.......... Department of the Army International Rationalization Office (RDA)
DAIRS.......... Dial Access Information Retrieval System [*Shippensburg State College, Shippensburg, PA*]
DAIRS.......... Differential Absorption Infrared Sensor (SAUS)
DAIRS.......... Distributed Aperture Infrared System (SEWL)
DAIR System... Driver Aid Information and Routing System (SAUS)
Dairy........... Dairy Mart Convenience Stores, Inc. [*Associated Press*] (SAG)
Dairy Counc Dig... Dairy Council Digest [*A publication*] (UWER)
Dairy Ind Int... Dairy Industry International [*A publication*] (UWER)
Dairy Prod I... Dairy Products Journal [*A publication*] (UWER)
Dairy Res Dig... Dairy Research Digest [*A publication*] (UWER)
Dairy Sci Technol... Dairy Science and Technology [*A publication*] (UWER)
DAIS............ Data Acquisition and Information System [*Telecommunications*] (NITA)
DAIS............ Data Avionics Information System (MCD)
DAIS............ Dealer Association Information Service [*Association of Free Newspapers*] [*British*]
DAIS............ Defense Automatic Integrated Switch (SAUS)
DAIS............ Defense Automatic Integrated Switching [*Army communications system*]
DAIS............ Digital Avionics Information System [*Air Force*]
DAIS............ Digital Avionics Integration System
DAIS............ Direct Access Intelligence System (PDAA)
DAIS............ Directorate of Aeronautical Inspection Services [*British*]
DAIS............ Director of Aeronautical Inspection Services (SAUS)
DAIS............ Director of Automatic Information Service (SAUO)
DAIS............ Directory of Automated Information Systems (MCD)
DAIS............ Distributed Ada Interface Set (SSD)
DAIS............ Distributed Application Integration System (SAUS)
DAIS............ Distributed Automatic Intercept System (SAUS)
DAIS............ District Agricultural Improvement Station (SAUO)
DAIS............ Doctor of Arts in Information Science (GAGS)
DAISEY........ Development Assessment and Instruction for Success in the Early Years [*Education*] (AIE)
DAISO.......... Directorate Automated Information Security Official (SAUS)
DAISS.......... Digital Airborne Intercommunication and Switching System (ACAE)
DAISY.......... Daily Summary (MCD)
DAISY.......... Dairy Information System [*British*] (NITA)
DAISY.......... Data Acquisition and Interpretation System
DAISY.......... Data Analysis of the Interpreter System (IAA)
DAISY.......... Decision Aided Information System (SAUS)
DAISY.......... Decision Aiding Information System
DAISY.......... Digital Acoustic Imaging System (UWER)
DAISY.......... Digital Action Information System (SAUS)
DAISY.......... Digital Audio-Based Information System
DAISY.......... Displacement Automated Integrated System (SAUS)
DAISY.......... Disposal Automated Information System (SAUS)
DAISY.......... Domestic Appliances Information System (SAUS)
DAISY.......... Double-Precision Automatic Interpretive System
DAISY 201... Double-Precision Automatic Interpretive System (SAUS)
DAISys......... Developer's Assistant for Information Systems [*Computer science*] (HODG)
Daisytk......... Daisytek International Corp. [*Associated Press*] (SAG)
DAIT............ Division of Allergy, Immunology, and Transplantation (SAUS)
DAITA.......... Database of Antiviral and Immunomodulatory Therapies for AIDS [*Acquired Immune Deficiency Syndrome*]
DAITDM....... Department of the Army Integrated Technical Document Manual (MCD)
DAIU............ Digital-to-Analog Interface Unit [*Computer science*]
DAIV............ Data Area Initializer and Verifier [*Telecommunications*] (TEL)
DAJ.............. Daimler-Benz 5.75% Sub Notes [*NYSE symbol*] (SG)
DAJ.............. Direct Air [*British*] [*ICAO designator*] (FAAC)
DAJAG.......... Deputy Assistant Judge Advocate General [*Legal term*] (DLA)
DAJAG.......... Deputy Assistant Judge Advocate-General (SAUO)
DAJS............ Distributed Area Jamming System [*Air Force*]
DAK.............. Dakair [*France*] [*ICAO designator*] (FAAC)
DAK.............. Dakar [*Senegal*] [*Seismograph station code, US Geological Survey*] [*Closed*] (SEIS)
dak.............. Dakota [*MARC language code*] [*Library of Congress*] (LCCP)
Dak.............. Dakota (ODBW)
Dak.............. Dakotan (SAUS)
Dak.............. Dakota Territory Reports [*A publication*] (DLA)
DAK.............. Data Acknowledge [*Computer science*] (VLIE)
DAK.............. Data Authentication Key (SAUS)
DAK.............. Decision Acknowledge (BUR)
DAK.............. Deny All Knowledge [*Telecommunications*] (TEL)
DAK.............. Deutsches Afrika Korps [*World War II*]
DAK.............. Director of Army Kinematography (SAUO)
DAK.............. Disarticulation of Knee (MELL)
DAK.............. Fayetteville, AR [*Location identifier*] [*FAA*] (FAAL)
Daka............ Daka International, Inc. [*Associated Press*] (SAG)
Dakota......... Dakota Reports [*A publication*] (DLA)
Dakotah....... Dakotah, Inc. [*Associated Press*] (SAG)
DakotaM....... Dakota Mining Corp. [*Associated Press*] (SAG)
DAKR........... Dakota Railroad [*Federal Railroad Administration identification code*]
DAKT........... Daktronics, Inc. [*NASDAQ symbol*] (SAG)
Daktron........ Daktronics, Inc. [*Associated Press*] (SAG)
Dak Zoo........ Dakota Zoo (SAUS)

Dal .... Benloe and Dalison's English Common Pleas Reports [*A publication*] (DLA)
DAL .... Dalhousie University (SAUO)
DAL .... Dalhousie University Library [*UTLAS symbol*]
Dal .... Dalison's English Common Pleas Reports [*A publication*] (DLA)
DAL .... Dallas [*Texas*] [*Seismograph station code, US Geological Survey*] (SEIS)
Dal .... Dallas Cowboys [*National Football League*] [*1960-present*] (NFLA)
DAL .... Dallas [*Texas*] Love Field [*Airport symbol*]
Dal .... Dallas' Pennsylvania Reports [*A publication*] (DLA)
Dal .... Dallas' United States Reports [*A publication*] (DLA)
Dal .... Dalrymple. Scotch Court of Session Cases [*A publication*] (DLA)
Dal .... Daly's New York Common Pleas Reports [*A publication*] (DLA)
DAL .... Dash Lake Resources [*Vancouver Stock Exchange symbol*]
DAL .... Data Accession List (NASA)
DAL .... Data Access Language [*Apple, Inc.*] (PCM)
DAL .... Data Access Line
DAL .... Data Access List (ACAE)
DAL .... Data Acquisition Language [*Computer science*] (CSR)
DAL .... Data Acquisition List (MCD)
DAL .... Data Address Line
DAL .... Data/Address Line (SAUS)
DAL .... Data Aided Loop (SAUS)
DAL .... Data-Aided Loop [*NASA*]
DAL .... Data Analysis Laboratory [*Temple University*] [*Research center*]
daL .... Decaliter (STED)
dal .... decaliter (or decalitre) (SAUS)
DAL .... Dedicated Access Line [*Telecommunications*] (ITD)
DAL .... Defect Action Level [*FDA*]
DAL .... Defence Analysts Ltd. [*British*]
DAL .... Defended Assets List (SAUS)
DAL .... Defender Australia Ltd.
DAL .... Dekaliter [*Unit of measure*]
DAL .... Delhi Avoiding Line [*Indian Railway*] (TIR)
DAL .... Delta Air Lines [*NYSE symbol*] (TTSB)
DAL .... Delta Air Lines, Inc. [*NYSE symbol*] [*Air carrier designation symbol*] (SPSG)
DAL .... Democratic Action League (SAUS)
DAL .... Department of Agriculture Library (SAUS)
DAL .... Design Analysis Language [*Programming language*]
DAL .... Design Approval Layout (SAA)
DAL .... Destructive Action Link (ECON)
DAL .... Digital Access Line (IAA)
DAL .... Digital Analysis Library [*Computer Design*] [*Software package*] (NCC)
DAL .... Direct Access Line (SAUS)
DAL .... Direct Address Line [*Telecommunications*] (NITA)
DAL .... Direct Attached Drop (VLIE)
DAL .... Directional Arm Lock
DAL .... Disk Access Lockout [*Computer science*] (VLIE)
DAL .... Distribution Authority List (MCD)
DAL .... Divisional Administration List (SAUS)
DAL .... Document Address Lister (VLIE)
DAL .... Dog at Large [*Humorous notation put on letters that cannot be delivered*] [*British postmen's slang*]
DAL .... Downed Aircraft Locator [*Military*] (PDAA)
DAL .... Drawing Assembly List (MCD)
DAL .... Drug Analysis Laboratory (DAVI)
DAL .... United States Army Library, Pentagon Building, Arlington, VA [*Library symbol*] [*Library of Congress*] (LCLS)
DAL .... Direct Acid Leaching (ODA)
DALA .... (D-Ala^2)-Met-enkephalinamide [*Analgesic peptide*]
DALA .... Delta-Aminolevulinic Acid [*Biochemistry*]
DALAS .... Deck Approach & Landing Aid System (SAUS)
D Alaska .... United States District Court for the District of Alaska (DLA)
DALATS .... Data Logging and Transmission System (MCD)
DALB .... Dictionary of American Literary Biography [*A publication*]
DALC .... Danquah. Akan Laws and Customs [*Ghana*] [*A publication*] (DLA)
DALC .... Deployment Area Location Code [*Army*] (AABC)
DALC .... Divided Access Line Circuit
DALC .... Dubuque Area Library Consortium [*Library network*]
DALC .... Dynamic Asynchronous Logic Circuit
Dal Coop .... Dallas' Report of Cooper's Opinion on the Sentence of a Foreign Court of Admiralty [*A publication*] (DLA)
DALCOS .... Digital Advanced Lead-Computing Optical Signature (MCD)
Dal C P .... Dalison's English Common Pleas Reports [*A publication*] (DLA)
DALDO .... Disposite d'Aide a la Designation d'Objectif [*Target Designation Aid System*] [*French*]
DALE .... Dale [*Commonly used*] (OPSA)
Dale .... Dale's Judgments [*1868-71*] [*England*] [*A publication*] (DLA)
Dale .... Dale's Reports [*2-4 Oklahoma*] [*A publication*] (DLA)
DALE .... Developmental Assessment of Life Experiences [*Test*]
DALE .... Digital Anemograph Logging Equipment (SAUS)
DALE .... Drug Abuse Law Enforcement [*Department of Justice*]
DALE .... Drug Abuse Law Enforcement Agency (SAUO)
Dale Cl HB .... Dale's Clergyman's Legal Handbook [*A publication*] (DLA)
Daleco .... Daleco Resources Corp. [*Associated Press*] (SAG)
Dale Ecc .... Dale's Ecclesiastical Reports [*England*] [*A publication*] (DLA)
Dale Eccl .... Dale's Ecclesiastical Reports [*England*] [*A publication*] (DLA)
Dale Leg Rit .... Dale's Legal Ritual [*Ecclesiastical Reports*] [*1868-71*] [*England*] [*A publication*] (DLA)
Dale Par Ch .... Dale's Law of the Parish Church [*5th ed.*] [*1975*] [*A publication*] (DLA)
DALFA .... Directorate of Air Land Forces Application (SAUO)
DALG .... D-Algorithm (SAUS)
DALGT .... Daylight (FAAC)
DALHT .... Dalhart, TX [*American Association of Railroads railroad junction routing code*]
DALI .... Delivery and Access to Local Information and Services (EURO)
DALI .... Digitally Archived Library Images
DALI .... Document and Library Integration (TELE)
DALIB .... Direct Access Library [*Computer science*] (VLIE)
Dal in Keil .... Dalison's Reports in Keilway [*1533-64*] [*England*] [*A publication*] (DLA)
DALIS .... Disaster Assistance Logistics Information System
DALIS .... Documentation and location identification system (SAUS)
Dalison .... Dalison's English Common Pleas Reports [*Bound with Benloe*] [*123 English Reprint*] [*A publication*] (DLA)
DALK .... Data Link Controller [*Computer science*] (NITA)
Dall .... Dallam's Texas Supreme Court Decisions [*A publication*] (DLA)
Dall .... Dallas' Laws of Pennsylvania [*A publication*] (DLA)
Dall .... Dallas' Pennsylvania and United States Reports [*A publication*] (DLA)
Dall .... Dallas' Styles of Writs [*Scotland*] [*A publication*] (DLA)
Dallam Dig (Tex) .... Dallam's Digest [*Texas*] [*A publication*] (DLA)
Dallas .... Dallas' Pennsylvania and United States Reports [*A publication*] (DLA)
Dall Coop .... Dallas' Report of Cooper's Opinion on the Sentence of a Foreign Court of Admiralty [*A publication*] (DLA)
Dall Dec .... Dallam's Texas Decisions, from Dallam's Digest [*A publication*] (DLA)
Dall Dig .... Dallam's Digest and Opinions [*Texas*] [*A publication*] (DLA)
DallG .... Dallas Gold & Silver Exchange, Inc. [*Associated Press*] (SAG)
Dall in Keil .... Dallison [*or Dalison*] in Keilway's Reports, English King's Bench [*A publication*] (DLA)
Dall L .... Dallas' Laws of Pennsylvania [*A publication*] (DLA)
Dall Laws .... Dallas' Laws of Pennsylvania [*A publication*] (DLA)
Dall (PA) .... Dallas' Pennsylvania Reports [*4*] [*A publication*] (DLA)
Dall S C .... Dallas' United States Supreme Court Reports [*A publication*] (DLA)
Dall Sty .... Dallas' Styles of Writs [*Scotland*] [*A publication*] (DLA)
Dall Tex .... Dallas' Supreme Court Decisions [*Texas*] [*A publication*] (DLA)
DALM .... Dysplasia-Associated Lesion or Mass [*Medicine*]
Dalmat .... Dalmatian (DIAR)
DALO .... Defense Attache Liaison Officer (AFM)
DALO .... Disaster Area Liaison Officer (SAUO)
DALO .... Disconnect at Lift-Off [*NASA*] (KSC)
DALO .... Divisional Air Liaison Officer (SAUS)
DALO .... Office of the Deputy Chief of Staff for Logistics (SAUS)
DALP .... Defence Advanced Lithography Program (SAUS)
DALPrC .... Delta Air Lines Cv Dep Pfd [*NYSE symbol*] (TTSB)
Dal R .... Dalhousie Review [*A publication*] (BRI)
Dalr .... Dalrymple. Decisions of the Scotch Court of Session [*A publication*] (DLA)
Dalr .... (Dalrymple of) Stair's Decisions of the Scotch Court of Session [*A publication*] (DLA)
DALR .... Dry Adiabatic Lapse Rate [*Heat transfer*]
Dalr Dec .... Dalrymple. Decisions of the Scotch Court of Session [*A publication*] (DLA)
Dalr Ent .... Dalrymple on the Polity of Entails [*A publication*] (DLA)
Dalr Feud Prop .... Dalrymple on Feudal Property [*A publication*] (DLA)
Dalr Feu Pr .... Dalrymple on Feudal Property [*A publication*] (DLA)
DALRLV .... Department of the Army Logistics Readiness Liaison Visits (AABC)
DALRO .... Dramatic, Artistic, and Literary Rights Organization (DGA)
Dalr Ten .... Dalrymple on Tenures [*A publication*] (DLA)
DALRTF .... Department of the Army Long-Range Technological Forecast
DAL S .... Dal Segno [*Repeat from the Sign*] [*Music*]
DALS .... Data Acquisition Logging System
DALS .... Digital Approach and Landing System [*Aviation*] (IAA)
DALS .... Director [*or Directorate*] of Army Legal Services [*British*]
DALS .... Distress Alerting and Locating System
DALS .... Dive Auditory Location System (MCD)
DALS .... Diver Auditory Localization System (SAUS)
DALS .... Double-Acting Limit Switch
DALS .... Downed Aircrew Locator System (SAUS)
DALSCOM .... DoD [*Department of Defense*] ATE Language Standardization Committee
DAL SEG .... Dal Segno [*Repeat from the Sign*] [*Music*]
DalSem .... Dallas Semiconductor [*Associated Press*] (SAG)
Dal Sh .... Dalton on Sheriffs [*A publication*] (DLA)
DALSO .... Department of Army Logistics Support Officer
Dalt .... Dalton's Justices of the Peace [*Many eds.*] [*1618-1746*] [*A publication*] (DLA)
DALT .... Department of the Army Liaison Team (AABC)
DALT .... Drop Altitude
DALTA .... Dramatic and Lyric Theatres Association [*British*] (BI)
Dalt Just .... Dalton's Justices of the Peace [*Many eds.*] [*1618-1746*] [*A publication*] (DLA)
DALTN .... Dalton, GA [*American Association of Railroads railroad junction routing code*]
DALTS .... Data Link Test Set
Dalt Sh .... Dalton's Sheriff [*A publication*] (DLA)
DALU-SMUSPG .... Domestic Animal Luteolytic Uterine Smooth Muscle Prostaglandin (DB)
DALVP .... Delay Enroute Authorized as Ordinary Leave Provided It Does Not Interfere with Reporting Date [*Military*]
Daly .... Daly's New York Common Pleas Reports [*A publication*] (DLA)
DALY .... Disability-Adjusted Life Year [*Public health*] (ECON)
Daly May Ct .... Daly's Hand-Book on Practice in the Lord Mayor's Court [*A publication*] (DLA)
Daly's R .... Daly's New York Common Pleas Reports [*A publication*] (DLA)
Daly Sur .... Daly's Nature of Surrogate's Courts [*New York*] [*A publication*] (DLA)
DAM .... Dam [*Commonly used*] (OPSA)
DAM .... Damage (AABC)
DAM .... Damaged (SAUS)

DAM............ Damascus [*Syria*] [*Airport symbol*] (OAG)
DAM............ Damocles [*Greek courtier, c.300BC*] (ROG)
DAM............ Data Access Management (SAUS)
DAM............ Data Access Manager [*Computer science*] (VLIE)
DAM............ Data Access Method (SAUS)
DAM............ Data Acquisition and Monitoring [*Computer science*] (VLIE)
DAM............ Data Acquisition Module (SAUS)
DAM............ Data Addressed Memory [*Computer science*]
DAM............ Data Association Manager (UWER)
DAM............ Data Association Message
DAM............ Database Access Manager [*Computer science*] (BTTJ)
DAM............ Days after Manufacture (SAUS)
DAM............ Dayton Art Museum (SAUS)
dam............ Decameter (STED)
DAM............ Decametric Radio Emission
DAM............ Decontaminating Agent, Multipurpose [*Military*] (DOMA)
DAM............ Defended Area Model [*Army*] (AABC)
DAM............ Definition, Analysis, and Mechanization
DAM............ Degraded Amyloid [*Medicine*]
DAM............ Dekameter
DAM............ Delayed Action Mine (SAUS)
DAM............ Dental Amalgam Mercury (UWER)
DAM............ Denver Art Museum (SAUS)
DAM............ Department of Astronomy and Meteorology (UWER)
DAM............ Descriptor Attribute Matrix
DAM............ Detection and Mapping [*Package*] [*NASA*]
DAM............ Detection And Mapping Package (SAUS)
DAM............ Device Adapter Modules (SAUS)
DAM............ Diacetyl Monooxine [*Organic chemistry*]
DAM............ Diacetylmonoxide (SAUS)
DAM............ Diacetylmonoxime (STED)
dam............ diacetyl monoxime (SAUS)
DAM............ Diacetylmorphine [*Pharmacology*]
DAM............ Diaethylaminomethyl (SAUS)
DAM............ Diagnostic Abilities in Math [*Educational test*]
DAM............ Diagnostic Acceptability Measure (PDAA)
DAM............ Diallyl Maleate [*Organic chemistry*]
DAM............ Diallylmelamine [*Organic chemistry*]
DAM............ Diaminomesitylene (UWER)
DAM............ Diamond Abrasive Machining (SAUS)
DAM............ Dictionary of Abbreviations in Medicine [*A publication*]
DAM............ Digital acquisition module (SAUS)
DAM............ Digital Answering Machine (SAUS)
DAM............ Digital Automatic Machine (SAUS)
DAM............ Digital-to-Analog Multiplier (IEEE)
DAM............ Diploma in Ayurvedic Medicine (SAUS)
DAM............ Direct Access Memory [*Computer science*] (BUR)
DAM............ Direct Access Method [*Sperry UNIVAC*] [*Computer science*]
DAM............ Direct Access Mode [*Computer science*] (VERA)
DAM............ Direct Action Mission (SAUS)
DAM............ Direction des Applications Militaries [*France*]
DAM............ Directly Addressable Memory (SAUS)
DAM............ Director Attack Mine [*Air Force*] (MCD)
DAM............ Director of Air Material [*Navy*] [*British*]
DAM............ Discrete Atom Method (UWER)
DAM............ Discriminant Analytic Model (STED)
DAM............ Display Aided Maintenance [*Army*]
DAM............ Distributed Abstract Machine (VERA)
DAM............ Divorced Asian Male (ADWA)
DAM............ DNA [*Deoxyribonucleic Acid*] Adenine Methylation [*Biochemistry*]
DAM............ Doctor of Applied Management (UWER)
DAM............ Double Aluminized Mylar (NASA)
dam............ down-range antimissile (SAUS)
DAM............ Downrange Antimissile Program [*Army*]
DAM............ Draft Amendment (OSI)
DAM............ Driver Amplifier Module (NASA)
DAM............ Dual Absorption Model [*Nuclear physics*] (OA)
DAM............ Dummy Average Machine (VLIE)
DAM............ Dummy Average Memory (SAUS)
DAM............ Duplex Adding Machine (SAUS)
DAM............ United States Army Topographic Command, Washington, DC [*Library symbol*] [*Library of Congress*] (LCLS)
DAM²........... Square Dekameter
DAM³........... Cubic Dekameter
DAM³/D........ Cubic Decameters per Day
DAMA.......... American Medical Association, Washington Office, Washington, DC [*Library symbol*] [*Library of Congress*] (LCLS)
DAMA.......... Dairy Appliance Manufacturers Association (SAUO)
DAMA.......... Dark Matter (SAUS)
DAMA.......... Data Administration Management Association (SAUO)
DAMA.......... Data Administration Management Association International (EA)
DAMA.......... Data Assigned Multiple Access [*Computer science*] (VLIE)
DAMA.......... Demand Access Multiple Assignment (SAUS)
DAMA.......... Demand Assigned Multiple Access (COE)
DAMA.......... Demand Assignment Multiple Access [*Telecommunications*]
DAMA.......... Department of the Army Materiel Annex (AABC)
DAMA.......... Diode Array Multichannel Analyzer [*Instrumentation*]
DAMA.......... Discharge Against Medical Advice [*Medicine*] (STED)
DAMA.......... Discharged against Medical Advice (MELL)
Damark........ Damark International, Inc. [*Associated Press*] (SAG)
Damas......... Damasus [*Flourished, 13th century*] [*Authority cited in pre-1607 legal work*] (DSA)
DAMASK...... Direct Attack Munition Affordable Seeker [*Military*] (SEWL)
DAMBED...... Dialphamethylbenzylethylenediamine (SAUS)
DAMC.......... Digital Automatic Map Compilation (SAUS)
DAMC.......... Digital Automation Map Compilation [*Computer science*] (VLIE)
DAMC.......... Dimethylaminomethylcoumarin [*Organic chemistry*]
DAMCONINSTGP... Damage Control Instruction Group (SAUO)
Dam Cont.... Damage Control (SAUS)
DAMCONTRACEN... Damage Control Training Center [*Military*] (DNAB)
DAMCS........ Display Aided Maintenance Control System [*Army*]
DAMD.......... Duct air monitor device (SAUS)
DAMDA........ Dairy Appliance Manufacturers' and Distributors' Association Ltd. (BI)
DAMDF........ Durham Air Monitoring Demonstration Facility [*Environmental Protection Agency*] (GFGA)
DAME.......... Dark Avenger Mutation Engine [*A polymorphic encryption engine*] (PCM)
DAME.......... Data Acquisition and Monitoring Equipment [*Electronics*]
DAME.......... Defense Against Methods of Entry [*Military intelligence*]
DAME.......... Determination of Air-Launched Missile Environment (MCD)
DAME.......... Developments in Agricultural and Managed-forest Ecology (SAUS)
DAME.......... Dictionary of American English [*A publication*]
DAME.......... Digital Automatic Measuring Equipment (MHDB)
DAME.......... Director Area Mechanical Estimating (SAUS)
DAME.......... Distance and Angularity Measurement Equipment [*Navy*] (MCD)
DAME.......... Distance Azimuth Measuring Equipment [*Navy*] (MCD)
DAME.......... Division Airspace Management Element [*Military*] (INF)
DAMEC........ Drug and Alcohol Multicultural Education Centre [*Medicine*] [*Australia*]
DAMed......... Director of Aviation Medicine (SAUO)
DA Memory... Direct Access Memory (SAUS)
DameMr...... Dames & Moore, Inc. [*Associated Press*] (SAG)
Damen......... Damen Financial Corp. [*Associated Press*] (SAG)
DAMES........ Defense Automated Message Exchange Service (GEOI)
DAMES........ Defense Automated Message Exchange Service Laboratory (SAUO)
DAMES........ Demonstration of Avionics Module Exchangeability via Simulation [*Communications term*] (DCT)
DAMES........ Division Airspace Management Element System (SAUO)
DAMES........ Dynamic Airlift Management and Execution System (SAUS)
DAMF.......... Director of Air Ministry Factories [*British*] [*World War II*]
DAMG.......... Damages [*Legal term*] (DLA)
DAM-Geog.... United States Army Topographic Command, Office of Geography, Washington, DC [*Library symbol*] [*Library of Congress*] (LCLS)
DAMGO........ Deputy Assistant Master-General of Ordnance [*British*]
DAMH.......... United States Army, U.S. Army Center for Military History, Washington, DC [*Library symbol*] [*Library of Congress*] (LCLS)
DAMHB........ Directorate of Ancient Monuments and Historic Buildings [*Department of the Environment*] [*British*] (DI)
DAMI........... Designated Aircraft Maintenance Inspector
DAMID......... Discounting Analysis Model for Investment Decisions (PDAA)
DAM II-EE.... Defended Area Model II Engagement Evaluation [*Army*] (AABC)
DAM II-EP.... Defended Area Model II Engagement Planning [*Army*] (AABC)
DAMIS......... Defense Analysis Modeling Information System (SAUO)
DAMIS......... Department of the Army Management Information System (AABC)
DAMIT......... Data Analysis Computer Program by Massachusetts Institute of Technology (SAUS)
DAMIT......... Data Analysis [*Program*] of Massachusetts Institute of Technology
DAmL.......... AMTRAK Library, Washington, DC [*Library symbol*] [*Library of Congress*] (LCLS)
DAML........... Digital Added Main Line (SAUS)
DAML........... Directorate, Army MAP [*Military Assistance Program*] Logistics
DAMLG........ Dental Amalgamator
DAMM.......... Alger [*Algeria*] [*ICAO location identifier*] (ICLI)
DAMM.......... Direct Access Memory Management (SAUS)
DAMM.......... Drinkers Against Mad Mothers (EA)
DAMMO........ Directorate of Ammunition [*Canada*] [*Military*]
DAMMS........ Department of the Army Movements Management System (MCD)
DAMMS-R.... Department of the Army Movements Management System-Redesign (GFGA)
DAMN.......... Diaminomaleonitrile [*Organic chemistry*]
DAMN.......... Dynamic Analysis of Mechanical Networks (PDAA)
DAMO.......... Department of Army Military Operations (SAUO)
DAMO.......... Office of the Deputy Chief of Staff for Operations & Plans (SAUS)
DA MOB C2S... Department of the Army Mobilization Command and Control System (MCD)
DAMOC........ Director Autopilot Mode Organization Computer (SAUS)
DAMOD........ Direct Access Module (SAUS)
DA-MON-YR... Day-Month-Year (DNAB)
DAMOS........ Data Moving System (PDAA)
DAMOS........ Disposal Area Monitoring System
DAMOS........ Drug Application Methodology with Optical Storage (GART)
DAMO-ZS..... Army Simulation Strategic Planning Office (SAUS)
DAMP.......... Dallas Area Media Project [*Library network*]
DAMP.......... Databank of Atomic and Molecular Physics [*Queen's University Belfast*] [*British*] (NITA)
dAMP.......... Deoxyadenosine Monophosphate [*Biochemistry*]
dAMP.......... Deoxyadenylic Acid (STED)
DAMP.......... Department of the Air Member for Personnel [*British*]
DAMP.......... Department of the Army Materiel Program
DAMP.......... Diacetoxydiphenylmethylpyridine [*Pharmacology*]
DAMP.......... Dibutyryl CAMP [*Cyclic Adenosine Monophosphate*] [*Biochemistry*]
DAMP.......... Dinitroanilino Amino-Methylpropylamine
DAMP.......... Distribution Amplifier (MSA)
DAMP.......... Dockyard Assisted Maintenance Period (SAUS)
DAMP.......... Downrange Antimissile Measurement Program [*RADAR*]
DAMP.......... Down-Range Anti-Missile Measurement Project (SAUS)
DAMP.......... Downrange Anti-Missile Measuring Project [*Army*] (UWER)
DAMP.......... Downrange Anti-Missile Program [*Army*] (UWER)
DAM-PACKAGE... Detection and mapping package (SAUS)
Dampier MSS... Dampier's Paper Book, Lincoln's Inn Library [*A publication*] (DLA)

DAMPIP .... Department of the Army Productivity Improvement Program
DAMPL .... Department of the Army Master Priority List (AABC)
DAMPL .... Department of the Army Material Priority List
DAMPMT ..... Department of the Army Military Personnel Management Team (AABC)
DAMPR .... Digital Automatic Multiple Pressure Recorder [*Lewis Research Center*]
DAMPRE ...... Drill Attendance Monitoring Procedure and Report [*National Guard*]
DAM Program... Down-range Anti-Missile Program (SAUS)
DAMPS .... Dairy Market Policy Simulator (SAUO)
DAMPS .... Data Acquisition Multiprogramming System [*IBM Corp.*] [*Computer science*]
DAMPS .... DDN Automated Message Processing System (SAUS)
DAMPS .... Department of Allied Medical Professions and Services [*Medicine*] (EDAA)
DAMPS .... Digital Advanced Mobile Phone Service (UWER)
D-AMPS .... Digital-Advanced Mobile Phone Service (SAUS)
D-AMPS .... Digital Advanced Mobile Phone System (SAUS)
D-AMPS .... Digital AMPS (SAUS)
D-AMPS .... Dual-Mode Advanced Mobile Phone System (CGWS)
DAMP/TVPB... Department of the Army Motion Picture/Television Production Board (AABC)
DAMP/TVPP... Department of the Army Motion Picture/Television Production Program
DAMQAM ..... Dynamically Adaptive Multicarrier Quadrative Amplitude Modulation [*Computer science*]
DAMR .... Director of Aircraft Maintenance and Repair [*Navy*] [*British*]
DAMR .... Division of Adult and Management Review [*United Nations*] (ECON)
DAMR .... Duct Assignment and Manhole Racking (SAUS)
DAMRC .... Department of the Army Material Readiness Command (MCD)
DAMRIP .... Department of the Army Management Review and Improvement Program (AABC)
DAMR(N) ..... Director of Aircraft Maintenance and Repair (Naval) [*British*]
DAMR(W) .... Director of Aircraft Maintenance and Repair (Washington) [*Navy*]
DAMs .... Data Addressed Memories (SAUS)
DAMS .... Deductive Analysis of Missile Systems (MCD)
DAMS .... Defencively Armed Merchant Ship [*World War I*] [*British*]
DAMS .... Defense Against Missiles Systems
DAMS .... Defense Antimissile System (SAUS)
DAMS .... Defensively Armed Merchant Ship (SAUS)
DAMS .... Dental Amalgam Mercury Syndrome (UWER)
DAMS .... Deployable Automated Maintenance System (SAUS)
D/AMS .... Deputy Air Member for Technical (SAUO)
DAMS .... Deputy Assistant Military Secretary [*British*]
DAMS .... Differential Amplification Magnetic Sensor (UWER)
DAMS .... Direct Access Management System
DAMS .... Disposal Accounting Management System [*DoD*]
DAMS .... Drum Auxiliary Memory Sub-Unit (SAUS)
DAMS .... Dynamically Adaptable Multi-Service System (EURO)
DAMSO .... Department of the Air Member for Supply and Organization [*British*]
DAMSO .... Deputy of the Air Member for Supply and Organization [*British*]
DAMSU .... Digital Automanual Switching Unit [*Telecommunications*] (TEL)
DAMT .... Department of the Air Member for Training [*British*]
D/AMTS .... Deputy Air Member for Technical Services (SAUO)
DAMUS .... Data Management and User Services (SAUS)
DAMUS .... Data Management and User Services System [*National Oceanic and Atmospheric Administration*] (GFGA)
DAMUSC ...... Direct Access, Multi-User, Synchrocyclotron Computer (PDAA)
DAMUT .... Ducted-Air Medium Underground Transmission (PDAA)
DAMV .... Dasheen Mosaic Virus [*Plant pathology*]
DAMV .... Destruction of Aircraft or Motor Vehicles
DAMV .... Double-Air Movement Valve
DAMWO .... Department of the Army Modification Work Order
DAN .... Army and Navy Club, Washington, DC [*Library symbol*] [*Library of Congress*] (LCLS)
DAN .... Dana College, C. A. Dana-Life Library, Blair, NE [*OCLC symbol*] (OCLC)
DAN .... Danair AS [*Denmark*] [*ICAO designator*] (FAAC)
Dan .... Dana's Reports [*31-39 Kentucky*] [*A publication*] (DLA)
DAN .... Dane [*Ontario*] [*Seismograph station code, US Geological Survey*] [*Closed*] (SEIS)
Dan .... Daniel [*Old Testament book*]
DAN .... Daniel Indus [*NYSE symbol*] (TTSB)
DAN .... Daniel Industries, Inc. [*NYSE symbol*] (SPSG)
Dan .... Daniell's Exchequer and Equity Reports [*159 English Reprint*] [*1817-23*] [*A publication*] (DLA)
Dan .... Daniels' Compendium Compensation Cases [*England*] [*A publication*] (DLA)
Dan .... Danish (ADWA)
DAN .... Danish
dan .... Danish [*MARC language code*] [*Library of Congress*] (LCCP)
Dan .... Danner's Reports [*42 Alabama*] [*A publication*] (DLA)
DAN .... Danube [*River in central Europe*]
D'An .... D'Anvers' General Abridgment of the Common Law [*A publication*] (DLA)
DAN .... Danville [*Virginia*] [*Airport symbol*] (OAG)
DAN .... Danville, VA [*Location identifier*] [*FAA*] (FAAL)
DAN .... Deacon and Nike [*Research rocket*]
DAN .... Defense Activity North Carolina (MCD)
daN .... Dekanewton [*Unit of force*]
DAN .... Deployment Adjustment Notification [*Military*] (CINC)
DAN .... Deposit Account Number (NG)
DAN .... Desk Area Network (SAUS)
DAN .... Diaminonaphthalene (SAUS)
D-AN .... Diplomate, American Board of Anesthesiology (DHSM)
DA-N .... Directional Antenna Nighttime Only [*Broadcasting term*]
DAN .... Disciplinary Action Notice (DNAB)
DAN .... Distant Area Networking (SAUS)
DAN .... Distributed Audio Network [*Sound Apprentice*]
DAN .... Distribution Analysis (UWER)
DAN .... District Anglers Notice (SAUS)
DAN .... Divers Alert Network [*Marine science*] (OSRA)
DAN .... Document Accession Number (IAA)
DAN .... Domestic Area Network (SAUO)
DAN .... Dual Area Nozzle (KSC)
DAN .... Duration Mines Ltd. [*Toronto Stock Exchange symbol*] [*Vancouver Stock Exchange symbol*]
Dana .... Dana's Kentucky Supreme Court Reports [*1833-40*] [*A publication*] (DLA)
DANA .... Delaware Association of Nonprofit Agencies (SRA)
DANA .... Deutsche Allgemeine Nachrichten Agentur [*German general news agency, sponsored by US newspapermen as a successor to the NAZI-controlled DNB*] [*Post-World War II*]
DANA .... Diffraction Analysis System (SAUS)
DANA .... Drug and Alcohol Nursing Association (EA)
DANA .... Drug-Induced Antinuclear Antibodies [*Immunology*] (DAVI)
Dan Abr .... Dane's Abridgment of American Law [*A publication*] (DLA)
DANAC .... Data Analysis and Classification (SAUS)
DanaCp .... Dana Corp. [*Associated Press*] (SAG)
DANAGRO .... Danish Agricultural Organizations (ECON)
DANAIR .... Danish Airlines (SAUO)
DANAK .... Danish Accreditation, National Agency of Industry & Trade (SAUS)
Dana (KY) .... Dana's Reports [*31-39 Kentucky*] [*A publication*] (DLA)
Dan & L .... Danson and Lloyd's English Mercantile Cases [*A publication*] (DLA)
Dan & Ll ...... Danson and Lloyd's English Mercantile Cases [*A publication*] (DLA)
Dan & Lld .... Danson and Lloyd's English Mercantile Cases [*A publication*] (DLA)
DANAS .... Deposit Account Name and Address System (SAUS)
DANASAT ..... Direct Ascent Nuclear Antisatellite
Dan Att .... Daniel's Law of Attachment [*A publication*] (DLA)
Dana Wh ..... Dana's Edition of Wheaton's International Law [*A publication*] (DLA)
DANB .... Danbury [*England*]
DANB .... Dave & Buster's [*NASDAQ symbol*] (TTSB)
DANB .... Dave & Busters, Inc. [*NASDAQ symbol*] (SAG)
DANB .... Dental Assisting National Board (EA)
DANBIB .... Cooperation project for all libraries (SAUS)
DanBib .... Danish national library system (SAUS)
DANC .... Decontaminating Agent, Noncorrosive
DANCA .... Dimethylamino(naphthoyl)cyclohexanoic Acid [*Organic chemistry*]
Dance .... Dance Magazine [*A publication*] (BRI)
DANCED ...... Danish Cooperation for Environment and Development (SAUO)
Dance RJ ..... Dance Research Journal [*A publication*] (BRI)
Dan Ch .... Daniell's Chancery Practice [*A publication*] (DLA)
Dan Ch Pr .... Daniell's Chancery Practice [*A publication*] (DLA)
DANCOM ...... Danube Commission (BARN)
DAND .... Dandus [*To Be Given*] [*Pharmacy*]
D & A .... Dear and Anderson's Scotch Session Cases [*1829-32*] [*A publication*] (DLA)
D and A .... Detail and Assembly (SAUS)
D & A .... Dialling and Answering (SAUS)
D&A .... Dilatation and Aspiration [*Medicine*] (DMAA)
D & A .... Discharge and Advise [*Medicine*] (MELL)
D & A .... Drawn and Annealed (SAUS)
D&A .... Drugs and Allergy [*Medicine*] (DMAA)
D & A .... International Defense and Aid Fund for Southern Africa, US Committee (EA)
D&AD .... Designers and Art Directors Association (ODA)
D&B .... Dead and Burried (SAUS)
D & B .... Deals and Boards [*Business term*] (ROG)
D & B .... Dearsley and Bell's English Crown Cases [*1856-58*] [*A publication*] (DLA)
D & B .... Design-and-Build (ECON)
D & B .... Devereux and Battle's North Carolina Equity Reports [*A publication*] (DLA)
D & B .... Devereux and Battle's North Carolina Law Reports [*A publication*] (DLA)
D & B .... Docking and Berthing (SSD)
D&B .... Dun & Bradstreet (AAGC)
D & B .... Dun & Bradstreet, Inc.
D & B CC ..... Dearsley and Bell's English Crown Cases [*1856-58*] [*A publication*] (DLA)
D & BCS ...... D & B Computing Services [*Information service or system*] (IID)
D & B Pr Pr... Dodd and Brook. Probate Practice [*A publication*] (ILCA)
D & C .... David & Charles [*Commercial firm*] [*British*]
D & C .... Deacon and Chitty's English Bankruptcy Reports [*1832-35*] [*A publication*] (DLA)
D & C .... Dean and Chapter [*Anglican Church*]
D&C .... Deep & Clear (SAUS)
D&C .... Demand and Coverage (SAUS)
D&C .... Democrat and Chronicle (SAUS)
D & C .... Development & Commercial Bank [*Malaysia*]
D & C .... Dilation [*or Dilatation*] and Curettage [*of the uterus*] [*Obstetrics*]
D & C .... Direct and Consensual (MELL)
D&C .... Discipline & Complaints (WDAA)
D & C .... Display and Control (KSC)
D & C .... District and County Reports [*Pennsylvania*] [*A publication*] (DLA)
D&C .... Doctrine and Covenants (SAUS)
D & C .... Dow and Clark's English House of Lords Cases [*A publication*] (DLA)
D&C .... Drill and Ceremonies [*Army*]
D & C .... Drill and Ceremony [*Military*] (ADDR)
D & C .... Drug and Cosmetic Colors

D & C .... Drugs and Cosmetics [*Pharmacology*] (DAVI)
D&C .... Duck and cover. (SAUS)
D & C2d .... District and County, Second Series [*A publication*] (DLA)
D & CB .... Debt and Correspondence Branch [*BUPERS*]
D & CC .... Pennsylvania District and County Reports [*A publication*] (DLA)
D & C Dyes... Drugs and Cosmetics Dyes (SAUS)
D & Ch .... Deacon and Chitty's English Bankruptcy Reports [*1832-35*] [*A publication*] (DLA)
D & Chit ...... Deacon and Chitty's English Bankruptcy Reports [*1832-35*] [*A publication*] (DLA)
D & Cl .... Dow and Clark's Reports [*A publication*] (DLA)
D & CM .... Dressed and Center Matched [*Lumber*] (DAC)
D & COH ...... Daughter and Co-Heiress [*Genealogy*]
D&CS .... Data and Computer Systems (SAUS)
D & CS .... Display and Control Subsystem (NASA)
D & CT .... Docking and Crew Transfer [*Aerospace*]
D&D .... Deaf and Damp (SAUS)
D&D .... Death and Decay (SAUS)
D & D .... Death and Dignity (MELL)
D & D .... Death and Dying [*Medical course*]
D & D .... Decontaminate and Decommission [*Nuclear energy*]
D&D .... Decontamination and Decommissioning [*Environment term*] (EGA)
D & D .... Decoration and Design [*Building*] [*New York City*]
d&d .... defiled and deflowered (SAUS)
D & D .... Degaussing and Deperming [*Navy*]
D & D .... Deposit and Difference [*Tea trade*] (ROG)
D & D .... Design and Development (SSD)
D & D .... Desk and Derrick [*Oil industry*]
D&D .... Destroy and Disposal (SPVS)
D & D .... Detection and Discrimination
D&D .... Detention and Deportation (SAUS)
D and D ...... Development and Design (SAUS)
D & D .... Devonshire and Dorset Regiment [*British military*] (DMA)
D&D .... Dial and Deliver [*Environmental science*] (COE)
D & D .... Diarrhea and Dehydration [*Gastroenterology*] (DAVI)
D & D .... Direct and Distribution [*Postal Service*]
D & D .... Distress and Diversion Cells at Air Traffic Control Centres [*British*] (PIAV)
D&D .... Drug and Disease (SAUS)
D&D .... Drug and Disease Free (ADWA)
D & D .... Drunk and Dirty [*Military*]
D & D .... Drunk and Disorderly
D & D .... Dungeons and Dragons [*Game*]
D & D .... Dysphagia and Dysphonia [*Medicine*] (MELL)
D & DC .... Drunk and Disorderly Conduct
D & DS .... Dictatorships and Double Standards [*Title of an article written by Jeane Kirkpatrick in 1979 that became basis of conservative foreign policy*]
D and E ...... Davis and Elkins College (SAUO)
D & E .... Diet and Elimination [*Gastroenterology*] (DAVI)
D & E .... Diet and Excretion [*Gastroenterology*] (DAVI)
D & E .... Dilatation and Evacuation [*Medicine*]
D & E .... Dilation and Evacuation [*Medicine*] (STED)
D&E .... Dilation and Extraction (ADWA)
D&E .... Discharge and Exit [*Environmental science*] (COE)
D & E .... Durnford and East's (Term) Reports, English King's Bench [*1785-1800*] [*A publication*] (DLA)
D & E Cm ...... D & E Communications [*Associated Press*] (SAG)
D and F ...... Determination and Finding (SAUS)
D & F .... Determination and Findings
D & F .... Disposition and Findings (AAG)
D & F .... Judgments of Divisional and Full Courts, Gold Coast [*A publication*] (DLA)
D & F 11-16... Divisional and Full Court Judgments [*1911-1916*] [*A publication*] (DLA)
D and FS ...... Discharge and Final Statement (SAUS)
D & G .... Deafness and Goiter (MELL)
D & G .... Diprose and Gammon's Reports of Law Affecting Friendly Societies [*1801-97*] [*England*] [*A publication*] (DLA)
D & G .... Doom and Gloom
D&H .... Dangerous and Hazardous [*MARAD*] (TAG)
D & H .... Daughter and Heiress [*Genealogy*]
D & H .... Delaware & Hudson Railway Co. [*Nickname: Delay and Hesitate*]
D&H .... Delivery and Handling (GOBB)
D & H .... Dressed and Headed [*Lumber*]
D & HAA ...... Dock and Harbour Authorities' Association [*British*] (ODBW)
D&HRR .... Delaware & Hudson Railroad Co. (SAUO)
D&I .... Development and Implementation (SAUO)
D & I .... Disassembly and Inspection (DNAB)
D & I .... Drawn and Ironed
D&I .... Drop and Insert [*Communications term*] (DCT)
D & IC .... Dependency and Indemnity Compensation [*Military*] (AFM)
D & IR .... Duluth & Iron Range Railway Co.
D & J .... December and June [*Denotes semiannual payment of interest or dividends in these months*] [*Business term*]
D & J .... De Gex and Jones' English Chancery Reports [*A publication*] (DLA)
D&J .... Semiannual Payments of Interest or Dividends in December and June (EBF)
D & JB .... De Gex and Jones' English Bankruptcy Reports [*1857-59*] [*A publication*] (DLA)
D & K Int Rev... Davidge and Kimball's Internal Revenue Laws [*A publication*] (DLA)
D & K Whl... D & K Wholesale Drug, Inc. [*Associated Press*] (SAG)
D & L .... Distillate plus Loss
D & L .... Dowling and Lowndes' English Bail Court Reports [*A publication*] (DLA)
D & M .... Davison and Merivale's English Queen's Bench Reports [*A publication*] (DLA)
D & M .... Deep and Meaningful
D & M .... Detroit & Mackinac Railway Co.
D & M .... Doctor and Martyr (ROG)
D & M .... Dressed and Matched [*Technical drawings*]
D&MB .... Dressed and Matched Beaded [*Construction term*] (MIST)
D & Mer ...... Davison and Merivale's English Queen's Bench Reports [*A publication*] (DLA)
D&MRR .... Detroit and Mackinac Railroad (SAUO)
D & MRR ...... Detroit & Mackinac Railway Co.
D & N .... Dekker & Nordemann [*Publisher*]
d & n .... dumb and numb (SAUS)
D & NF .... D & N Financial Corp. [*Associated Press*] (SAG)
D & N Fn ...... D & N Financial Corp. [*Associated Press*] (SAG)
D & O .... Description and Operations (NASA)
D&O .... Director's and Officer's (LDOE)
D & O .... Directors' and Officers' [*Liability insurance*]
DANDOK ...... Danish Committee for Scientific and Technical Information and Documentation [*Information service or system*] (IID)
D & P .... Damon and Pythias [*Fourth-century BC Greek philosophers renowned for their loyalty to one another*]
D & P .... Deberny and Peignot (DGA)
D & P .... Denison and Pearce's English Crown Cases [*1844-52*] [*A publication*] (DLA)
D&P .... Design and Performance (ACAE)
D & P .... Design and Production
D & P .... Developing and Printing
D & P .... Drain and Purge (NASA)
D & P .... Drunk and Proud
D & PD .... Definition and Preliminary Design (SSD)
D & PS .... Design and Performance Specification (MCD)
D & PS .... Dog and Pony Show
D&Q .... Deep and Quiet (SAUS)
D&R .... Decontamination and Repair (SAUS)
D&R .... Definition and Requirement (SAUS)
D & R .... Desquamation and Regeneration [*Medicine*] (MELL)
D and R ...... Diagnostic and Repair (SAUS)
D and R ...... Discharge and Release (SAUS)
D & R .... Distiller and Rectifier
D & R .... Dowling and Ryland's English King's Bench Reports [*A publication*] (DLA)
D & RG .... Denver & Rio Grande Railroad
D & RGW ...... [*The*] Denver & Rio Grande Western Railroad Co.
D & R Mag Cas... Dowling and Ryland's English Magistrates' Cases [*A publication*] (DLA)
D & RMC ...... Dowling and Ryland's English Magistrates' Cases [*A publication*] (DLA)
D & RNP ...... Dowling and Ryland's English Nisi Prius Cases [*A publication*] (DLA)
D & RNPC ... Dowling and Ryland's English Nisi Prius Cases [*A publication*] (DLA)
D&R ROD ...... Disposal and Reuse Record of Decision [*Environmental science*] (BCP)
D & S .... Dangerous and Suspicious
D & S .... Deane and Swabey's English Ecclesiastical Reports [*A publication*] (DLA)
D & S .... De Gex and Smale's English Chancery Reports [*63-64 English Reprint*] [*1846-52*] [*A publication*] (DLA)
D & S .... Demand and Supply (WDAA)
D & S .... Deployment and Support [*Military*]
D & S .... Dermatology and Syphilology [*Medicine*] (MAE)
D & S .... Display and Storage (MSA)
d & s .... distribution and supply (SAUS)
D & S .... Doctor and Student [*A publication*] (DLA)
D & S .... Documentation and Status (AAG)
D & S .... Dollars & Sense [*Economic Affairs Bureau*] [*A publication*]
D & S .... Dominance and Submission
D&S .... Domination and Submission (ADWA)
D & S .... Drewry and Smale's English Chancery Reports [*A publication*] (DLA)
D&SE .... Dublin & South-Eastern Railway (SAUO)
D & SF .... Denver & Santa Fe Railway
D & SL .... Denver & Salt Lake Railroad
D&SL .... Denver & Salt Lake Railroad Co. (SAUO)
D & Sm .... De Gex and Smale's Reports Tempore Knight-Bruce and Parker, Vice-Chancellor's Court [*1846-52*] [*England*] [*A publication*] (DLA)
D&SM .... Dressed and Single Matched [*Wood industry*] (WPI)
D & SM .... Dressed and Standard Matched [*Lumber*] (DAC)
D & Sm .... Drewry and Smale's English Chancery Reports [*A publication*] (DLA)
D & SU .... Daughters and Sons United (EA)
D & Sw .... Deane and Swabey's English Ecclesiastical Reports [*A publication*] (DLA)
D&T .... Deloitte & Touche (SAUO)
D & T .... Demonstration and Training
D & T .... Dependence and Tolerance (MELL)
D & T .... Development and Technology
D and T ...... Double and Twist (SAUS)
D & TSL ...... [*The*] Detroit & Toledo Shore Line Railroad Co.
D&V .... Demonstration & Validation programme (SAUS)
D&V .... Design and Validation (SAUS)
D & V .... Diarrhea and Vomiting [*Medicine*]
D & W .... Danville & Western Railroad (IIA)
D & W .... Detection and Warning

D & W .... Drury and Walsh's Irish Chancery Reports [*1837-40*] [*A publication*] (DLA)
D & W .... Drury and Warren's Irish Chancery Reports [*1841-43*] [*A publication*] (DLA)
D & Wal ...... Drury and Walsh's Irish Chancery Reports [*1837-40*] [*A publication*] (DLA)
D & War ...... Drury and Warren's Irish Chancery Reports [*1841-43*] [*A publication*] (DLA)
D & WTF ..... Daily and Weekly till Forbidden [*Advertising*]
D&X .... Dilation and Extraction (ADWA)
D & YE .... Diabetes and Your Eyes [*National Eye Institute*] [*A publication*]
DANE .... Defense Activity for Nontraditional Education Support [*Military*] (MCD)
DANE .... Departamento Administrativo Nacional de Estadstica [*Colombia*] (GEOI)
Dane Abr ..... Dane's Abridgment of American Law [*A publication*] (DLA)
Dane's Abr... Dane's Abridgment of American Law [*A publication*] (DLA)
Dan Exch ..... Daniell's Exchequer and Equity Reports [*159 English Reprint*] [*1817-23*] [*A publication*] (DLA)
Dan Exch (Eng)... Daniell's Exchequer and Equity Reports [*159 English Reprint*] [*1817-23*] [*A publication*] (DLA)
Dan Forms... Daniell. Forms and Precedents in Chancery [*7th ed.*] [*1932*] [*A publication*] (DLA)
DANFS .... Dictionary of American Naval Fighting Ships [*A publication*]
DANG .... Dangerous [*FBI standardized term*]
DANG .... Director of the Army National Guard
DANGER ...... Divisionalized Analytical Ground Rule Exception Report
Dang Mod.... Dangling Modifier (SAUS)
Danher .... Danaher Corp. [*Associated Press*] (SAG)
DANHORS.... Danish Farmers and Horsedealers Export Union (SAUO)
Dani .... Daniel [*Old Testament book*] (DSA)
DANI .... Department of Agriculture for Northern Ireland [*British*] (IRUK)
DANIDA........ Danish Agency for International Development (SAUS)
DANIDA........ Danish International Development Agency
DANIDA........ Danish International Development Authority (SAUS)
Daniel.......... Daniel Industries, Inc. [*Associated Press*] (SAG)
Daniell Ch Pl & Prac... Daniell's Chancery Pleading and Practice [*A publication*] (DLA)
Daniell Ch Pr... Daniell's Chancery Pleading and Practice [*A publication*] (DLA)
Daniell Ch Prac... Daniell's Chancery Pleading and Practice [*A publication*] (DLA)
Daniel Neg Inst... Daniel's Negotiable Instruments [*A publication*] (DLA)
DANIS .... Datennachweis Informationssystem [*Arbeitsgemeinschaft Sozialwissenschaftlicher Institut*] [*Germany*] [*Information service or system*] [*Defunct*] (CRD)
DANK .... Danka Business Systems [*NASDAQ symbol*] (SAG)
DANK .... Danka Business Systems PLC [*NASDAQ symbol*] (NASQ)
DANK .... Deutsch-Amerikanischer National-Kongress [*German-American National Congress*] (EA)
Danka .... Danka Business Systems [*Associated Press*] (SAG)
DANKY.......... Danka Business Systems ADR [*NASDAQ symbol*] (TTSB)
Danl.............. Daniel [*Old Testament book*]
DanlHd .... Danielson Holding Corp. [*Associated Press*] (SAG)
DANMARC ... Danish Machine-Readable Catalogue (NITA)
DANMARC ... Danish MARC (SAUS)
Dan Moll ..... Daniel Moller [*Deceased, 1600*] [*Authority cited in pre-1607 legal work*] (DSA)
Dann............. Danner's Reports [*42 Alabama*] [*A publication*] (DLA)
DANN............ Danninger Medical Technology [*NASDAQ symbol*] (SAG)
DANN............ Danninger Med Tech [*NASDAQ symbol*] (TTSB)
Dann............. Dann's Reports [*22 California*] [*2nd ed.*] [*1871*] [*A publication*] (DLA)
Dann............. Dann's Reports [*1 Arizona*] [*A publication*] (DLA)
DANN............ Deoxyribonucleic Acid (SAUS)
DANN............ Dermatology Nurses Association (SAUO)
DANN............ Designated National Agency (SAUS)
DANN............ Digital Network Architecture (SAUS)
DANN............ Djiboutian National Army (SAUS)
DANN............ Document Enabled Network (SAUS)
DANNASAT... Direct Ascent Nonnuclear Antisatellite
Dan Neg Ins... Daniel's Negotiable Instruments [*A publication*] (DLA)
Danner.......... Danner's Reports [*42 Alabama*] [*A publication*] (DLA)
Danngr.......... Danninger Medical Technology, Inc. [*Associated Press*] (SAG)
DAN-NY .... Disposal Analysis Network for New York [*U.S. Army Corps of Engineers*]
Dan Ord....... Danish Ordinances [*A publication*] (DLA)
Dan P .... Danish Patent (SAUS)
DANP .... Deleted Active Neighbourhood Pattern (SAUS)
Danquah...... Cases in Gold Coast Law [*A publication*] (DLA)
DANRIC........ Department of Agriculture and National Resources Information Council (SAUO)
DAN Rocket... Deacon and Nike Rocket (SAUS)
DANS .... Danskin, Inc. [*NASDAQ symbol*] (SAG)
Dans .... Dansyl Chloride (SAUS)
DANS .... Dimethylaminonaphthalenesulfonyl Chloride [*Also, DNSC*] [*Fluorescent reagent*]
DANS .... Director of Army Nursing Services [*British military*] (DMA)
DANS .... Distributed Access Node System (SAUS)
Dans & L...... Danson and Lloyd's English Mercantile Cases [*A publication*] (DLA)
Dans & LL.... Danson and Lloyd's English Mercantile Cases [*A publication*] (DLA)
DANSE......... Dance Artists' Nationwide Space Emergency [*In association name, DANSE Coalition*] (EA)
DaNSHC....... Cambridge Military Library, Halifax, NS, Canada [*Library symbol*] [*Library of Congress*] (LCLS)
Danskin .... Danskin, Inc. [*Associated Press*] (SAG)
DANSW........ Diabetes Australia - New South Wales [*Medicine*] [*Australia*]
Dansyl .... Dimethylaminonaphthalenesulfonyl [*Also, Dns, DNS*] [*Biochemical analysis*]
DANT .... Diallyl-Nor-Toxiferin (SAUS)
DANTAN....... Detection Avoidance Navigation/Threat Avoidance Navigation [*Military*] (SEWL)
DANTE .... Delays Alternating with Nutations for Tailored Excitation (SAUS)
DANTE .... Delivery of Advanced Network Technologies in Europe (SAUS)
DANTE .... Delivery of Advanced Network Technologies (or Technology) in/to Europe Ltd. (SAUO)
DANTE .... Delivery of Advanced Network Technology for Europe (ECON)
DANTERM.... Danish Terminological Data Bank (SAUO)
DANTES .... Defense Activities (or Activity) for Non-Traditional Education Support (SAUO)
DANTES .... Defense Activity for Non-Traditional Educational Service (SAUS)
DANTES .... Defense Activity for Nontraditional Education Support [*Military*]
DANTISC...... Dantiscum [*Dantzig*] (ROG)
Dan T M .... Daniel. Trade Marks [*1876*] [*A publication*] (DLA)
DANTS .... Day and Night Television System [*Army*] (MCD)
Danv .... D'Anvers' General Abridgment of the Common Law [*A publication*] (DLA)
Danv Abr ..... D'Anvers' General Abridgment of the Common Law [*A publication*] (DLA)
DANVJ .... Danville Junction, ME [*American Association of Railroads railroad junction routing code*]
DANVL .... Danville, IL [*American Association of Railroads railroad junction routing code*]
DANY........... Dannemora [*New York*] [*Seismograph station code, US Geological Survey*] (SEIS)
DAO .... Daallo Airlines [*Djibouti*] [*FAA designator*] (FAAC)
DAO .... Data Access Objects [*Microsoft Corp.*] (PCM)
DAO .... Data Assimilation Office (SAUS)
DAO .... Data Automation Officer [*Air Force*]
DAO .... Dayton Area Office [*Energy Research and Development Administration*]
DAO .... Deasphalted Oil [*Petroleum refining*]
DAO .... Defense Administration Office (SAUS)
DAO .... Defense Attache Office (AFM)
DAO .... Department Administrative Order [*Department of Commerce*] (NOAA)
DAO .... Departmental Administrative Order (SAUO)
DAo.............. Descending Aorta [*Medicine*] (EDAA)
DAO .... Destination Address Omitted [*Computer science*] (VERA)
DAO .... Dial Assist Operator (CET)
DAO .... Diamine Oxidase [*Also, DO*] [*An enzyme*]
DAO .... Directory of Amateur Observers (SAUS)
DAO .... Disability Adviser's Officer (South Australia) [*Medicine*]
DAO .... Disc at once (SAUS)
DAO .... Disk-At-Once (SAUS)
DAO .... District Accounting Office [*or Officer*] [*Navy*]
DAO .... District Adjudications Officer (SAUS)
DAO .... District Advisory Officer (SAUS)
DAO .... District Aviation Office [*or Officer*] [*Navy*]
DAO .... Division Air Officer
DAO .... Divisional Agricultural Officer [*Ministry of Agriculture, Fisheries, and Food*] [*British*]
DAO .... Division Ammunition Office [*or Officer*] [*Army*]
DAO .... Doctor of Art of Oratory
DAO .... Dominion Astrophysical Observatory (SAUO)
DAO .... Dorsal Accessory Olive [*Neuroanatomy*]
DAO .... Double Action Only [*Gun*] (GOBB)
DAO .... Duly Authorized Officer
DAO .... Fort Huachuca, AZ [*Location identifier*] [*FAA*] (FAAL)
DAO & OS ... Defense Aid [*Lend-Lease*] Ordnance and Ordnance Stores [*World War II*]
DAOB .... Daily Average Occupied Beds [*Medicine*]
DAOB .... Tiaret [*Algeria*] [*ICAO location identifier*] (ICLI)
DAOC .... Bechar/Ouakda [*Algeria*] [*ICAO location identifier*] (ICLI)
DAOC .... Deputy Air Officer Commanding [*British military*] (DMA)
DAOC-in-C ... Deputy Air Officer Commanding-in-Chief [*British military*] (DMA)
DAOCS.......... Deacetoxycephalosporin C Synthase [*An enzyme*]
DAOE .... Bou Sfer [*Algeria*] [*ICAO location identifier*] (ICLI)
DAOF .... Tindouf [*Algeria*] [*ICAO location identifier*] (ICLI)
DAOI .... Ech-Cheliff [*Algeria*] [*ICAO location identifier*] (ICLI)
DAOL .... Oran/Tafaroui [*Algeria*] [*ICAO location identifier*] (ICLI)
DAOMIS........ Division Ammunition Office Management Information System (SAUO)
DAON........... Tlemcen/Zenata [*Algeria*] [*ICAO location identifier*] (ICLI)
DAOO........... Oran/Es Senia [*Algeria*] [*ICAO location identifier*] (ICLI)
DA-OPRR..... Department of the Army Plan for [*Possession, Control, and*] Operation of Railroads (AABC)
DAOR........... Bechar/Ouakda [*Algeria*] [*ICAO location identifier*] (ICLI)
DAOR........... Discriminator Average Output Rate (SAUS)
DAOS........... Dynamically Adaptive Operating System (SAUS)
DAOS........... Sidi Bel Abbes [*Algeria*] [*ICAO location identifier*] (ICLI)
DAOSR......... Director Army Operational Science and Research (SAUO)
DAOSR......... Director of Army Operational Science and Research (SAUS)
DAOT .... Director of Air Organisation and Training [*British military*] (DMA)
DAOT .... Director of Air Organization and Training (SAUS)
DAOU........... DAOU Systems, Inc. [*NASDAQ symbol*] (NASQ)
DAOV .... Ghriss [*Algeria*] [*ICAO location identifier*] (ICLI)
DAP .... Aerovias Dap [*Chile*] [*ICAO designator*] (FAAC)
DAP .... Application for Writ of Error Dismissed by Agreement of Parties [*Legal term*] (DLA)
DAP .... Data Access Page
DAP .... Data Access Point (SAUS)
DAP .... Data Access Processor (SAUS)
DAP .... Data Access Protocol [*Telecommunications*]
DAP .... Data Acquisition and Processing (FOTI)
DAP .... Data Acquisition Package (IAA)

DAP .... Data Acquisition Plan (MCD)
DAP .... Data Acquisition Platform (SAUS)
DAP .... Data Acquisition Processor (STED)
DAP .... Data Analysis and Processing (FOTI)
DAP .... Data Analysis Package (SAUS)
DAP .... Data Analysis Program
DAP .... Data Automation Panel (MCD)
DAP .... Data Automation Proposal (AFM)
DAP .... Days After Planting (SAUO)
DAP .... Days after Pollination [*Botany*]
DAP .... Days All Purposes (RIMS)
DAP .... Deaf Anthropology Page (SAUO)
DAP .... Death Associated Protein (UWER)
DAP .... Declines Appointment (NOAA)
DAP .... Decontamination Apparatus, Portable
DAP .... Defense Acquisition Package [*DoD*]
DAP .... Defense Acquisition Program
DAP .... Defensive Armed Penetrator (SAUS)
DAP .... Deformation Alignment Phase (SAUS)
DAP .... Deformation of Aligned Phase (MCD)
DAP .... Delayed-Action Preparation [*Medicine*] (MELL)
DAP .... Delayed after Depolarization [*Medicine*] (MELL)
DAP .... Delayed After Polarization (STED)
DAP .... Delayed Alpha Particle
DAP .... Democratic Action Party [*Malta*] [*Political party*] (PPE)
DAP .... Democratic Action Party [*Malaysia*] [*Political party*] (PPW)
DAP .... Department of Applied Physics (UWER)
DAP .... Department of the Army Pamphlet
DAP .... Department of the Army Publication (DOMA)
DAP .... Depolarizing After-Potential [*Neurochemistry*]
DAP .... Depot Acceptance Procedures
DAP .... Derived Attainable Performance [*Industrial engineering*]
DAP .... Design Analysis Phase (SAUS)
DAP .... Designated Acquisition Program
DAP .... Detail Assembly Panel
DAP .... Developers Assistance Program [*IBM Corp*] (VERA)
DAP .... Developmental Articulation Profile [*Speech evaluation test*]
DAP .... Dextroamphetamine Phosphate [*Medicine*] (MELL)
DAP .... Diabetes-Associated Peptide [*Biochemistry*]
DAP .... Diagnostic Accreditation Program (ADWA)
DAP .... Diagnostic Assistance Program (VLIE)
DAP .... Diallyl Phthalate [*Organic chemistry*]
DAP .... Diaminopimelate (SAUS)
DAP .... Diaminopimelic Acid [*Also, DAPA, DPM*] [*An amino acid*]
DAP .... Diaminopurine [*Biochemistry*]
DAP .... Diaminopyridine [*Organic chemistry*]
DAP .... Diammonium Phosphate [*Inorganic chemistry*]
DAP .... Diammonium Phosphate Plant (UWER)
DAP .... Diastolic Aortic Pressure (SAUS)
DAP .... Diastolic Arterial Pressure [*Medicine*] (MELL)
DAP .... Diazepam [*Also, D, DZ*] [*A sedative*]
DAP .... Dibasic Ammonium Phosphate (UWER)
DAP .... Diffused Alloy Power
DAP .... Digital Access Point (SAUS)
DAP .... Digital Assembly Program (MCD)
dap .... digital audio processor (SAUS)
DAP .... Digital Autopilot (MCD)
DAP .... Digital Avionics Processor [*Northrop Corp.*]
DAP .... Dihydroxyacetone Phosphate [*Also, DHAP*] [*Organic chemistry*]
DAP .... Dipeptidyl Aminopeptidase [*An enzyme*]
DAP .... Direct Access Photomemory (SAUS)
DAP .... Direct Access Processing [*Computer science*] (VLIE)
dap .... direct-agglutination pregnancy (SAUS)
DAP .... Direct Aid Program
DAP .... Directed Audit Program (AFM)
DAP .... Direct Latex Agglutination Pregnancy [*Test*] [*Medicine*]
DAP .... Director Assign Panel (MCD)
DAP .... Directorate of Accident Prevention [*RAF*] [*British*]
DAP .... Directorate of Armament Projects (SAUO)
DAP .... Directorate of Army Psychiatry (SAUO)
DAP .... Director of Aeroplane Production [*Air Ministry*] [*British*] [*World War II*]
DAP .... Director of Air Personnel [*Air Force*] [*British*]
DAP .... Director of Ammunition Production [*Ministry of Supply*] [*British*] [*World War II*]
DAP .... Director of Army Programs (AABC)
DAP .... Director of Army Psychiatry [*British*]
DAP .... Directory Access Protocol [*Telecommunications*] (OSI)
DAP .... Directory Application Protocol [*Computer science*] (VERA)
DAP .... Disaster Assistance Programs (DEMM)
DAP .... Discount Auto Parts [*NYSE symbol*] (SPSG)
DAP .... Dispatch Applications Processor (CGWS)
DAP .... Display Adjust Panel (MCD)
DAP .... Distant Aiming Point
DAP .... Distributed Analysis Program (MCD)
DAP .... Distributed Application Processing (SAUS)
DAP .... Distributed Array Processor [*Sperry UNIVAC*] [*Telecommunications*]
DAP .... Division Advisory Panel (SAUO)
DAP .... Division of Air Pollution [*Public Health Service*] [*Obsolete*]
DAP .... Do All Possible
DAP .... Do Anything Possible (SAUS)
DAP .... Doctorat en Administration Publique [*French*] (CPGU)
DAP .... Document Against Payment (SAUS)
DAP .... Document Application Profile [*Computer science*] (VERA)
DAP .... Documentation & analysis of packaging (SAUS)
DAP .... Documents Against Payment [*Banking*] (ADA)
DAP .... Dodecylammonium Propionate [*Organic chemistry*]
DAP .... Domestic Action Program [*Army*] (INF)
DAP .... Domestic Annual Processing
DAP .... Donor Acceptor Pairs [*Electronics*] (AAEL)
DAP .... Dorsal Artery of Penis [*Medicine*] (MELL)
dap .... Double Amplitude Peak (SAUS)
DAP .... Double-Amplitude Peak (DEN)
DAP .... Double Amplitude Peak-value (SAUS)
DAP .... Double Antiparallel [*Molecular biology*]
DAP .... Downlink Aircraft Parameter (SAUS)
DAP .... Draft Assembly Point (SAUO)
D-A-P .... Draw-a-Person [*Psychology*]
d-a-p .... draw-a-person (psychological test) (SAUS)
DAP .... Drug Abuse Program [*Medicine*] (EDAA)
DAP .... Dynamic Aortic Patch [*Medicine*] (STED)
DAP .... Dynamic Assertion Processor [*Computer science*]
DAP .... Dystrophin-Associated Protein [*Biochemistry*]
DAP .... Parents Against Dyslexia (SAUS)
DAP .... WHO Action Programme on Essential Drugs (SAUO)
DAP .... Director of Administrative Planning (ODA)
DAPA .... Diaminopimelic Acid [*Also, DAP, DPM*] [*An amino acid*]
DAPA .... Drug Abuse Program Adviser (SAUO)
DAPA .... Drug and Alcohol Abuse Program Advisor [*Navy*] (NVT)
DAPA .... Drug and Alcohol Program Adviser (SAUO)
DAPAC .... Danger Areas in the Pacific
DAPAF .... Data Processing And Analysis Facility (SAUS)
DAPAL .... Daystrom Powerplant Automation Language (SAUS)
DA PAM .... Department of the Army Pamphlet
DAP & E .... Diploma in Applied Parasitology and Entomology [*British*]
DAP&SS .... Director of Army Printing and Stationery Services (SAUO)
DAPAS .... Diamond Abrasive Performance Analysis System (SAUS)
DAPATF .... Department of the Army Accountability Task Force (SAUO)
DAPATF .... Department of the Army Property Accountability Task Force (MCD)
DAPB .... Diallylpentobarbital [*Sedative*]
DAPC .... Diarachidoylphosphatidylcholine [*Biochemistry*]
DAPCA .... Development and Procurement Costs of Aircraft (MCD)
DAPCA .... Development and Production Costs for Aircraft (SAA)
DAP Computer... Distributed Array Processor Computer (SAUS)
DAPCS .... Data Acquisition and Process Control System (SAUS)
DAPD .... AEERL Dual Alkali FGD Process Demonstration (SAUS)
DAPD .... Descend at Pilot's Discretion [*Aviation*] (FAAC)
DAPD .... Directorate of Aircraft Production and Development (SAUO)
DAPD .... Directorate of Aircraft Production Development [*British*] (DEN)
DAPE .... Days After Panicle Emergence (SAUO)
DAPE .... Developed Armament Probable Error (SAA)
DAPE .... Direct Addressable Peripheral Equipment (SAUS)
DAPE .... Distributed Application Programming Environment (SAUS)
DAPEP .... Department of the Army Panel on Environmental Physiology
DAPEP .... Department of the Army Panel on Environmental Psychology (SAUO)
DAPF .... Data Analysis and Processing Facility
DAPF .... Divorced Asian Professional Female (SAUO)
DAPFS .... Direct Ascent Powered Flight Simulation (SAUS)
DAPFS .... Direct-Ascent Powered-Flight Simulation [*NASA*]
DAPG .... Deutsch-Amerikanische Petroleum Gesellschaft [*German-American Petroleum Society*]
DAPG .... Drug and Allied Products Guild [*Later, NAPM*]
DAPGIR .... Defense Advisory Panel on Government Industry Relations [*DoD*]
DAPh .... American Pharmaceutical Association, Washington, DC [*Library symbol*] [*Library of Congress*] (LCLS)
DAPHNE .... Dido and Pluto Handmaiden for Nuclear Experiments [*Nuclear reactor at Harwell, England*]
DAPHNE .... Document Application Processing in a Heterogeneous Network Environment [*Computer science*] (VERA)
DAPI .... American Petroleum Institute, Washington, DC [*Library symbol*] [*Library of Congress*] (LCLS)
DAPI .... Days After Panicle Initiation (SAUO)
DAP I .... Diahydrogalacititol, Adriamycin, Cisplatin [*Antineoplastic drug regimen*] (DAVI)
DAPI .... Diamidinophenylindole [*A dye*] [*Organic chemistry*]
DAPIA .... Design Approval Primary Inspection Agency [*Department of Housing and Urban Development*] (GFGA)
DAPIE .... Developers Application Programming Interface Extensions (SAUS)
DAP-II .... Dianhydrogalactitol, Adriamycin, Platinol [*Cisplatin*] [*Antineoplastic drug regimen*]
DAPL .... Direct Access Programming Language [*Computer science*] (VLIE)
DAPL .... Directory of Australian Public Libraries [*Australia*] [*A publication*]
DAPLARCH... Data Plan for Land Use and Land Cover Research (SAUS)
DAPM .... Deputy Assistant Provost-Marshall [*British*]
DAPM .... Diaminodiphenylmethane [*Organic chemistry*]
DAPM .... District Assistant Provost Marshal (SAUO)
DAPM .... Divorced Asian Professional Male (SAUO)
DAPMC .... Defense Advanced Procurement Management Course [*Army*]
DAP/MIS .... Deficiency Abatement Program/Management Information System [*Navy*]
DAPN .... Dauphin Deposit [*NASDAQ symbol*] (TTSB)
DAPN .... Dauphin Deposit Corp. [*NASDAQ symbol*] (NQ)
DAPN .... Directional Aerial Phasing Network (SAUS)
DAPN .... Directional Antenna Phasing Network
DAPO .... Deep Attack Programs Office [*Army*]
DAPO .... Digital Advance Production Order [*Telecommunications*] (TEL)
DAPO .... Do All Possible [*Travel industry*] (TRID)
DAPP .... Daily Ambient Photophase [*Biochronometry*]
DAPP .... Data Acquisition and Processing Program [*Later, DMSP*] [*Air Force*]
DAPP .... Data Acquisition and Processing Program Satellite (SAUS)
DAPP .... Defense Acquisition Pilot Program [*Army*] (RDA)

DAPP .... Department of Army Productivity (Improvement) Program
DAPP .... Design Aid for Post-Processors [*IBM Corp.*]
DAPP .... Development Aid from People to People (EAIO)
DAPPER .... Distribution Analysis for Power Planning, Evaluation, and Reporting [*Computer science*]
DAPPL .... Department of the Army Programming Priority List
DAPPO .... Device and Program Performance Optimization (VLIE)
DAppSc .... Doctor of Applied Science (ADA)
DAppSci .... Doctor of Applied Science (SAUS)
DAPR .... Data Processing (SAUS)
DAPR .... Department of the Army Program Report
DAPR .... Department of the Army Program Review (RDA)
DAPR .... Digital Automatic Pattern Recognition (IEEE)
DAPR .... Digital Automatic Pattern Recognizer (SAUS)
DAPRE .... Daily Adjustable Progressive Resistance Exercise
DA Press ..... Double Acting Press (SAUS)
DAPRO Description System... Data and Program Description System (SAUS)
DAPRU .... Drug Abuse Prevention Resource Unit [*National Institute on Drug Abuse*] [*Databank*]
DAPS .... Data Acquisition and Processing System
DAPS .... Data Processing Automatic Publication Service
DAPS .... DC-AC-Power-System (SAUS)
DAPS .... DCS Automated Processing System (SAUS)
DAPS .... Defence Administrative Planning Staff (SAUO)
DAPS .... Defence & Aerospace Publishing Services SA (SAUS)
DAPS .... Department of Applied Physical Science (UWER)
DAPS .... Deployable Aircraft Planning System (SAUS)
DAPS .... Direct Access Performance Software (IAA)
DAPS .... Direct Access Programming System [*Computer science*]
DAPS .... Direct Automatic Publication Service (SAUS)
DAPS .... Director of Army Postal Services [*British*]
DAPS .... Disappearance Potential Spectroscopy (SAUS)
DAPS .... Distributed Application Processing System
DAPs .... Distributed Array Processors (SAUS)
DAPS .... Double Absorption Photofragment Spectroscopy
DAPS .... Downed Airman Power Source [*Navy*]
DAPSONE .... Diaminodiphenyl Sulfone [*Also, DADPS, DDS*] [*Pharmacology*]
DAPSRB .... Department of the Army Physical Security Review Board (MCD)
DAPSS .... Document and Personnel Security System (COE)
DAPST .... Denver Auditory Phoneme Sequencing Test [*Speech and language therapy*] (DAVI)
Dapt .... Daptazole (MAE)
DAPT .... Diamino(diethoxyphosphinyl)triazine [*Organic chemistry*]
DAPT .... Diaminophenylthiazole [*Pharmacology*]
DAPT .... Direct Agglutination Pregnancy Test [*Clinical chemistry*]
dapt .... direct-agglutination pregnancy test (SAUS)
DAPT .... Direct Latex Agglutination Pregnancy Test (SAUS)
DAPT .... Draw-A-Person Test (MEDA)
DAP Test ..... Draw A Person Test (SAUS)
DAPTF .... Declining Amphibian Populations Task Force (SAUO)
DAPTRA .... Drug Abuse Prevention, Treatment, and Rehabilitation Act [*1972*]
DAP Transistor... Diffused-Alloy Power Transistor (SAUS)
DAPU .... Data Acquisition and Processing Unit [*Viking orbiter system*] [*NASA*]
D-APV .... D-Amino Phosphonovaleric Acid
DAQ .... Data Acquisition
DAQ .... Develop and Qualify
DAQ .... Diabetes Association of Queensland [*Medicine*] [*Australia*]
DAQ .... Diagnostic Assessment Questionnaire [*Medicine*] (DMAA)
DAQ .... Distributor Auto Quote (TIMI)
DAQC .... Data Acquisition Card (UWER)
DAQC .... Data Acquisition Center (KSC)
D/AQD .... Director of Aeronautical Quality Assurance Directorate (SAUO)
DAQMG .... Deputy Assistant Quartermaster General
DAR .... Biology Branch Herbarium, Biological and Chemical Research Institute (SAUS)
DAR .... Daily Activity Report [*Military*]
DAR .... Daily Affective Rhythm [*Medicine*] (EDAA)
DAR .... Damage Assessment Routines (MDG)
DAR .... Damned Average Raiser [*A diligent student*] [*Slang*]
DAR .... Danish Army [*ICAO designator*] (FAAC)
DAR .... Dar Es Salaam [*Tanzania*] [*Airport symbol*] (OAG)
DAR .... Darien Library [*UTLAS symbol*]
DAR .... Darling International [*AMEX symbol*] (SG)
DAR .... Darwin [*Australia*] [*Seismograph station code, US Geological Survey*] [*Closed*] (SEIS)
DAR .... Data Access Register [*Computer science*] (MDG)
DAR .... Data Acquisition Recorder
DAR .... Data Acquisition Report (SAUS)
DAR .... Data Acquisition Request (SAUS)
DAR .... Data Acquisition Requirements (ACAE)
DAR .... Data Aided Receiver (SAUS)
DAR .... Data-Aided Receiver [*NASA*]
DAR .... Data Aided Review (SAUS)
DAR .... Data Archaeology and Rescue (SAUS)
DAR .... Data Article Requirements (AAG)
DAR .... Data Assembly Register (ACAE)
DAR .... Data Automation Request (SAUS)
DAR .... Data Automation Requirement
DAR .... Day-After Recall [*Advertising*]
DAR .... Days Awaiting Repair (ACAE)
DAR .... Dead Animal Removal (SAUS)
DAR .... Death after Resuscitation (MELL)
DAR .... Debrett Ancestry Research [*British*]
DAR .... Defense Acquisition RADAR
DAR .... Defense Acquisition Regulation [*or Requirement*]
DAR .... Defense Aid Report (IIA)
DAR .... Defense Aquisition Regulation (SAUO)
DAR .... Deficiency Action Report (NATG)
DAR .... Delaware Association of Realtors (SRA)
DAR .... Delay Address Register (VLIE)
DAR .... Delayed Allergic Response [*Medicine*] (BARN)
DAR .... Delayed Automatic Reclose (IAA)
DAR .... Delayed Auto-Reclose (PDAA)
DAR .... Delinquent Accounts and Returns [*IRS*]
DAR .... Department of Animal Regulation (SAUS)
DAR .... Department of Applied Research (UWER)
DAR .... Department of Audience Research (SAUO)
DAR .... Departure Approval Request [*Aviation*] (DNAB)
DAR .... Depletion-Approximation Replacement (MCD)
DAR .... Deployment Adjustment Request [*Military*] (CINC)
DAR .... Design Action Request (MCD)
DAR .... Design Approval Request (ACAE)
DAR .... Design Assessment Report [*Nuclear energy*] (NRCH)
DAR .... Designated Agency Representative [*Communications term*] (DCT)
DAR .... Destination Access Register [*Computer science*] (NITA)
DAR .... Destination Address Register (SAUS)
DAR .... Detroit Arsenal [*Michigan*] [*Army*] (NATG)
DAR .... Developed Area Ratio [*Propellers*] (DNAB)
DAR .... Development-Accelerator-Releasing Couplers [*Photography*]
DAR .... Deviation Approval Request [*NASA*] (KSC)
DAR .... Device Address Register (SAUS)
DAR .... Diacereine [*Medicine*] (EDAA)
DAR .... Dial-a-Ride [*TRB*] (TAG)
DAR .... Differential Absorption Ratio (IAA)
DAR .... Differentiation with Asymmetrical Reinforcement
DAR .... Digital AIDS (Aircraft Integrated Data System) Recorder (SAUS)
DAR .... Digital Angle Recorder
DAR .... Digital Audio Radio (SAUS)
DAR .... Digital Autopilot Requirements (NASA)
DAR .... Direct Access Request (ACAE)
DAR .... Direct Assistance Request (COE)
DAR .... Direct-Axis Regulator (SAUS)
DAR .... Directorate of Armament Requirements [*RAF*] [*British*]
DAR .... Directorate of Army Research (GRD)
DAR .... Directorate of Atomic Research [*Canada*] (BARN)
DAR .... Director of Army Recruiting (SAUO)
DAR .... Director of Army Requirements [*British*]
DAR .... Director of Army Research (SAUO)
DAR .... Director of Atomic Research (SAUS)
DAR .... Distal Absolute Reabsorption [*Medicine*] (EDAA)
DAR .... Distortion Adaptive Receiver (COE)
DAR .... Distributed Array RADAR (MCD)
DAr .... District of Columbia Archives, Washington, DC [*Library symbol*] [*Library of Congress*] (LCLS)
DAR .... Division of Applied Research (SAUO)
DAR .... Division of Atmospheric Research (SAUO)
DAR .... Drawing Analysis Record (MCD)
DAR .... Driver Augmented Readout [*Computer science*]
DAR .... Drivers accident report (SAUS)
DAR .... Drone Anti-RADAR [*German military - World War II*]
DAR .... Drug-Abuse Reporting (MELL)
DAR .... Drug-Appropriate Responding [*Biochemistry*]
DAR .... Dynamic Address Register [*Computer science*] (VLIE)
DAR .... National Society, Daughters of the American Revolution (SAUO)
DAR .... Daughters of the American Revolution (ODA)
DAR .... Direct Absorption Receiver (ODA)
DARA .... Department of Agriculture and Rural Affairs (SAUO)
DARA .... Deputy Associate Regional Administrator
DARA .... Deutsche Agentur fur Raumfahrtangelegenheiten [*Germany*] (EOSA)
DARA .... Deutsche Arbeitsgemeinschaft fuer Rechen-Anlagen [*German Working Committee for Computing Machines*]
DARA .... German Space Agency (SAUS)
DARAC .... Damped Aerodynamic Righting Attitude Control
DARACS ...... Damped Aerodynamic Righting Attitude Control System
daraf .... Farad backwards (Unit of Elastance) (SAUS)
DARAS .... Direction and Range Acquisition System (MCD)
DARB .... Data Access Request Block [*Computer science*] (VLIE)
DARB .... Distressed Airman Recovery Beacon (IAA)
Darb & B Lim... Darby and Bosanquet's Statutes of Limitations [*2nd ed.*] [*1893*] [*A publication*] (DLA)
DARC .... American National Red Cross, Washington, DC [*Library symbol*] [*Library of Congress*] (LCLS)
DARC .... Data Acquisition and Reduction Center (IAA)
DARC .... Data Acquisition and Reports Control [*Army*] (AABC)
DARC .... Data Radio Channel
DARC .... Defense Acquisition Regulatory Council (MCD)
DARC .... Delayed-Action Radar Calibrator (SAUS)
DARC .... Description, Acquisition, Restitution, Correlation (SAUS)
DARC .... Description, Acquisition, Retrieval, Conception [*Computer science*]
DARC .... Description, Acquisition, Retrieval, Correlation (SAUS)
DARC .... Device for Automatic Remote Data Collection [*Marine science*] (OSRA)
DARC .... Direct Access Radar Channel (SAUS)
DARC .... Direct-Access RADAR Channel [*System*] [*Aviation*]
DARC .... Division Alarm Recording Center (SAUO)
DARC .... Documentation and Automatization of Researches for Correlations [*For molecular structure*] [*Chemical physics*]
DARCEE .... Demonstration and Research Center for Early Education [*George Peabody College, Nashville*]
D Arch .... Diploma in Architecture [*British*]

D Arch .... Doctor of Architecture
D Arch C .... Directorate of Architectural Construction (SAUO)
D Arch Des... Doctor of Architectural Design
D Arch E .... Doctor of Architectural Engineering
D Arch Eng... Doctor of Architectural Engineering
DARCIMC..... Development and Readiness Command Installation Management Course [*Military*]
DarColl .... Royal Naval College Dartmouth (SAUO)
DARCOM...... Army Materiel Development and Readiness Command [*Now AMC*] (AAGC)
DARCOM...... Development and Readiness Command [*Formerly, AMC*] [*See also MDRC*] [*Alexandria, VA*] [*Army*]
DARCOM...... United States Army Material Development and Readiness Command (SAUO)
DARCOMALMSA... Development and Readiness Command Automated Logistics Management Systems Agency [*Army*] (AABC)
DARCOM-C... Development and Readiness Command Circular [*Army*]
DARCOMFASC... Development and Readiness Command Facilities and Services Center [*Army*] (AABC)
DARCOMFSA... Development and Readiness Command Field Safety Agency [*Army*] (AABC)
DARCOMI & SA... Development and Readiness Command Installations and Service Agency [*Army*] (AABC)
DARCOMLDC... Development and Readiness Command Logistics Data Center [*Army*] (AABC)
DARCOMLSSA... Development and Readiness Command Logistics Systems Support Agency [*Army*] (AABC)
DARCOMPI... Development and Readiness Command Procurement Instruction [*Army*] (MCD)
DAR Council... Defense Acquisition Regulatory Council [*Also DARC*] (AAGC)
DARD.......... Data Acquisition Requirements Document (KSC)
DARD.......... Data Reduction (SAUS)
DARD.......... Depressives Anonymous: Recovery from Depression (EA)
DARD.......... Directorate of Aircraft Research and Development (SAUO)
DARDC......... Device for Automatic Remote Data Collection [*National Weather Service*]
Darden......... Darden Restaurants, Inc. [*Associated Press*] (SAG)
DARD Method... Data Reduction Method (SAUS)
DARDO .... Direct Access to Remote Data Bases Overseas [*Italy*] [*Telecommunications*]
DARE .... Computerized Data Retrieval System for Documentation in the Social and Human Siences (SAUO)
DARE .... Damage Assessment Reduction and Evaluation (SAA)
DARE .... Data Analysis and Reduction [*Computer science*] (VLIE)
DARE .... Data Automatic Reduction Equipment (CET)
DARE .... Data Automation Research and Experimentation (CET)
DARE .... Database of Abstracts of Reviews of Effectiveness (SAUO)
DARE .... Data Retrieval Area (MCD)
DARE .... Data Retrieval System (SAUO)
DARE .... Decision Aids for Resource Expenditure (MCD)
DARE .... Delay Asymptotic Relative Efficiency (IAA)
DARE .... Demand and Resource Evaluation (ODBW)
DARE .... Denver AWIPS [*Advanced Weather Interactive Processing System*] Risk Reduction and Requirements Evaluation [*Workstation*] [*Marine science*] (OSRA)
DARE .... Department of Agricultural Research and Education (SAUO)
dare .... destination arrival research engineering (SAUS)
DARE .... Developing Agricultural Resources Effectively (SAUO)
DARE .... Diagnostic Analysis of Reading Errors [*Educational test*]
DARE .... Diagnostic and Repair Expert [*Computer-aided tank maintenance program*] [*Army*] (RDA)
DARE .... Dictionary of American Regional English [*A publication*]
DARE .... Dictionary of American Regional English Project [*University of Wisconsin - Madison*] [*Research center*] (RCD)
DARE .... Differential Analyzer Replacement [*Programming language*] [*1967*] (CSR)
DARE .... Digital Avionics Research System (MCD)
DARE .... Director Action for Rehabilitation and Employment [*Ex-offenders*] (OICC)
DARE .... Disabled Adults Residential Establishments [*Australian Capital Territory*]
DARE .... Document Abstract Retrieval Equipment (IEEE)
DARE .... Documentation Automated Retrieval Equipment [*System*] [*Army*]
DARE .... Doppler and Range Evaluation
DARE .... Doppler Automatic Reduction Equipment (MCD)
DARE .... DOVAP [*Doppler Velocity and Position*] Automatic Reduction Equipment (AAG)
DARE .... DOVAP (Doppler Velocity and Position) Automatic Reduction Equipment (SAUS)
DARE .... Drug Abuse Research and Education (SAUS)
DARE .... Drug Abuse Resistance Education
DARE .... Drug Addiction Rehabilitation Enterprise (EA)
DARE .... Drug Assistance, Rehabilitation, and Education (SAUS)
DARES .... Data Analysis and Reduction System
DARE System... Data Retrieval System (SAUS)
DARF .... Defense Atomic Research Facility (MCD)
DARF .... Direct Aerosol Radiative Forcing (QUAC)
DARF .... Document acceptance review form (SAUS)
DARFAX....... Department of the Army Secure Facsimile (AABC)
DARFD......... Depressives Anonymous: Recovery from Depression (EA)
DARFIS......... Department of Army Financial Information System
DARG.......... Discourse Analysis Research Group [*University of Calgary*] [*Research center*] (RCD)
DARHT......... Dual Axis Radiographic Hydrodynamic Test (SAUS)
DARHT......... Dual Axis Radiographic Hydro-Test (SAUS)
DArI .... Arab Information Center, Arab League Office, Washington, DC [*Library symbol*] [*Library of Congress*] (LCLS)
DARI .... Center for Applied Research in the Apostolate [*CARA*], African Research andInformation Center, Washington, DC [*Library symbol*] [*Library of Congress*] (LCLS)
DARI .... Database Application Remote Interface [*Computer science*] (VERA)
DARI .... Digital Angular Readout by LASER Interferometry (MCD)
DARIAS......... Digico Automated Radio-Immunoassay Analytical System (PDAA)
DARIC .... Data Reduction in Columns (VLIE)
DARIC .... Defense Automation Resources Information Center (SAUS)
DARIS .... Detroit Art Registration Information System [*Detroit Institute of Arts*] [*Information service or system*] (IID)
D Ariz .... United States District Court for the District of Arizona (DLA)
DARK .... Discrimination Analysis Technique Adapted and Refined at Kwajalein [*Army*] (AABC)
D Ark .... Doctor of Archaeology
DARL .... Darling [*Correspondence*] (DSUE)
DARL .... Darling International [*NASDAQ symbol*] (TTSB)
DARL .... Darling International, Inc. [*NASDAQ symbol*] (SAG)
DARL .... Douglas Advanced Research Laboratories [*Obsolete*] (KSC)
DARLI .... Digital Angular Readout by LASER Interferometry (MCD)
Darling .... Darling International, Inc. [*Associated Press*] (SAG)
Darlistor ...... Darlington-Transistor (SAUS)
Darl Pr Ct Sess... Darling. Practice of the Scotch Court of Session [*A publication*] (DLA)
DARM .... Data Acquisition Room (SAUS)
DARMA......... Defense against Rocket and Mortar Attack Fires [*Military*] (VNW)
DARMA......... Discrete Autoregressive-Moving Average Model [*Statistics*]
DArmD......... Directorate of Armament Development [*Ministry of Aircraft Production*] [*British*] [*World War II*]
D Armd........ Directorate of Royal Canadian Armoured Corps (SAUO)
D Arm D ...... Director of Armament Development (SAUO)
DARME......... Director, Armament Engineering [*Canada*] [*Military*]
DARMP......... Defense Automation Resources Management Program (SAUS)
DARMS......... Data Automation Resource Management System (SAUS)
DARMS......... Developmental Army Mobilization System (DOMA)
DARMS......... Digital Alternate Realization of Musical Symbols (SAUS)
DARMS......... Digital Alternate Representation of Musical Symbols
DARMS......... Digital Alternate Representation of Music Scores (SAUS)
DARMS......... Drifting Automatic Radiometeorological Station
DARNG .... Director of the Army National Guard
DARO........... Days after Receipt of Order (MCD)
DARO........... Defense ADPE [*Automatic Data Processing Equipment*] Reutilization Office
DARO........... Defense Airborne Reconnaissance Office
DARP........... DAAS ADPE Replacement Program (SAUS)
DARP........... Drug Abuse Rehabilitation Program (DMAA)
DARP........... Drug Abuse Reporting Program (EDAC)
DARPA......... Defense Advanced Research Projects Administration [*DoD*] (CIST)
DARPA......... Defense Advanced Research Projects Agency [*Arlington, VA*] [*DoD*]
DARPA......... Defense Applied Research Projects Agency (SAUS)
DARPA......... US Defense Advanced Research Projects Agency (SAUS)
DARPP......... Dopamine- and Cyclic AMP-Regulated Phosphoprotein [*Biochemistry*]
DARR........... Delft Atmospheric Research RADAR (MCD)
DARR........... Department of the Army Regional Representative (AABC)
DARR........... Drawing and Assembly Release Record (AAG)
DARRIS......... Department of the Army Requisitioning, Receipt, and Issue System
DARS........... Daily Aerial Reconnaissance and Surveillance [*Military*] (DOMA)
DARS........... Data Accounting and Reporting Sheet (SAUS)
DARS........... Data Accumulating and Reporting Sheet
DARS........... Data Acquisition and Reduction System
DARS........... Data Acquisition and Reporting System [*Data processing*]
DARS........... Data Acquisition Recording System
DARS........... Decommutation and Readout System [*Computer science*]
DARS........... Defense Acquisition Regulatory System [*DoD*] (RDA)
DARS........... Defense Aquisition Regulatory System (SAUO)
DARS........... Degree Audit Reporting System (SAUS)
DARS........... Department of the Army Relocation Sites (AABC)
DARs........... Design Assist Reports (SAUS)
DARS........... Design of Advanced Robotics Systems [*Computer science*] (VLIE)
DARS........... Dial Access Retrieval System (SAUS)
DARS........... Differential-Absorption Remote Sensing [*LASER*]
dars........... differential absorption remote sensing (SAUS)
DARS........... Digital Acoustic Receiver System (SAUS)
DARS........... Digital Adaptive Recording System
DARS........... Digital Archival Repositories
DARS........... Digital Attitude and Rate System (IEEE)
DARS........... Digital Attitude Reference System
DARS........... Digital Audio Radio Service
DARS........... Distributed Autonomous Robotic Systems (SAUS)
D Ar Sc......... Doctor of Arts and Sciences
DARSS......... Diode Array Rapid Scan Spectrometer
darss........... diode-array rapid-scan spectrometer (SAUS)
DART........... Daily Automatic Rescheduling Technique [*Computer science*]
DART........... Dallas Area Rapid Transit [*FHWA*] (TAG)
DART........... Damage Analysis in Rapid Time (MCD)
DART........... Damage Assessment Reporting Team (SAUO)
DART........... Dart Drug Corp. [*NASDAQ symbol*] (SAG)
Dart........... Dart on Vendors and Purchasers [*A publication*] (DLA)
DART........... Data Accumulation and Retrieval of Time (UWER)
DART........... Data Acquisition and Recording Terminal (SAUS)
DART........... Data Acquisition, Real-Time (SAUS)
DART........... Data Analysis Real-Time [*Southwest Research Institute*]
DART........... Data Analysis Recording Tape

DART .... Data Analysis Reduction Tape (SAA)
DART .... Data and Remote control Terminal (SAUS)
DART .... Datagraphix Automated Retrieval Technique (SAUS)
DART .... Data Reduction Translation (SAUS)
DART .... Data Reduction Translator
DART .... Data Research and Technology (SAUS)
DART .... Debug AN/UYS-2 Run-time Tester (SAUS)
DART .... Decentralized Advanced Replenishment Technique (AFIT)
DART .... Decomposed Ammonia Radioisotope Thruster [*Aerospace*]
DART .... Defect Area Revisit Technology (UWER)
DART .... Defense Acquisition Review Team (ACAE)
DART .... Defense Assistance Response Team (UWER)
DART .... Delay and Retransmit
DART .... Demand Actuated Road Transit
DART .... Dependable and Reliable Transit (UWER)
DART .... Deployable Automatic Relay Terminal [*Air Force*]
DART .... Depot Automatic Rescheduling Technique
DART .... Depression: Awareness, Recognition, and Treatment [*National Institute of Mental Health program*]
DART .... Design Automation Routing Tool (IAA)
DART .... Detection, Action, and Response Technique
DART .... Development Advanced Rate Technique (SAUS)
dart .... development advanced rate techniques (SAUS)
DART .... Developmental And Reproductive Toxicology (SAUO)
DART .... Development and Reproductive Toxicology [*Database*] [*Environmental Protection Agency*]
DART .... Development of Advanced Rate Techniques
DART .... Diagnostic-Assistance Reference Tool
DART .... Dial-a-Ride Transportation
DART .... Digital Audio Reconstruction Technology (SAUS)
DART .... Digital Automatic Readout Tracker [*Computer science*] (IAA)
DART .... Digital Auto-Ranging Tester (SAUS)
DART .... Diode Automatic Reliability Tester (IAA)
DART .... Direct-Access Radio Transceiver (UWER)
DART .... Direct Advisory of Recorded Transactions (AABC)
DART .... Direct Airline Reservations Ticketing
DART .... Directional Automatic Realignment of Trajectory (NG)
DART .... Director and Response Tester (KSC)
DART .... Directorate of Ranges and Targets [*Army*]
DART .... Director of Army Research and Technology [*Washington, DC*] (GRD)
DART .... Directory of American Research and Technology [*R. R. Bowker Co.*] [*Information service or system*] [*A publication*]
dart .... disappearing automatic retaliation target (SAUS)
DART .... Disappearing Automatic Retaliatory Target [*Military*] (RDA)
DART .... Disaster Area Relief Team (SAUO)
DART .... Disaster Assistance Recovery Teams [*Military*]
DART .... Disaster Assistance Response Team [*Office of U.S. Foreign Disaster Assistance*]
DART .... Discovery Activities Related to Science
DART .... Distant Area Reduced Toll [*Telecommunications*] (TSSD)
DART .... Dive and Release Trajectory (MCD)
DART .... Downed Aircraft Recovery Team [*Army*] (DOMA)
DART .... Drill Attendance Reporting Test [*National Guard*]
DART .... Drug & Alcohol Registry of Treatment (SAUS)
DART .... Dual Axis Rate Transducer [*A gyroscope*]
DART .... Dublin Area Rapid Transit [*Ireland*]
DART .... Dublin Area Rapid Transport (SAUS)
DART .... Duplex Army Radio/Radar Targeting (ACAE)
DART .... Dynamic Acoustic Response Trigger (IEEE)
DART .... Dynamic Advertising Reporting & Targeting (SAUS)
DART .... Dynamically Adaptive Receiver Transmitter (CAAL)
DART .... Dynamic Analysis and Replanning Tool
DART .... Dynamic Analytic Replanning Tool (SAUS)
DART .... Dynamic Automatic RADAR Tester (SAA)
DART .... Dynamic Response of the Forest-Tundra Ecotone to Environmental Change (SAUS)
DART .... Dynamic Simulation of Auto and Passenger Rail Transports
DArt .... Doctor of Art (ODA)
DARTA .... Dart Group Cl'A' [*NASDAQ symbol*] (TTSB)
DARTAB .... Dose and Risk Assessment Tabulation (SAUS)
Dart Col Ca... Dartmouth College Case [*A publication*] (DLA)
Dart Coll .... Dartmouth College [*Hanover, NH*]
DARTE .... Discrete Angle Radiative Transfer Equation (SAUS)
DartGp .... Dart Drug Corp. [*Associated Press*] (SAG)
DARTM .... Dartmouth [*Municipal borough in England*]
DARTM .... Defeat Armor Road Target Mine
Dartmouth C... Dartmouth College (GAGS)
DARTS .... Data Analysis, Recovery, and Training Systems (MCD)
DARTS .... Deployable Acoustic Readiness Training System (MCD)
DARTS .... Design Aids for Real-Time Systems [*Computer science*] (MCD)
DARTS .... Design Approach for Real-Time Systems (SEWL)
DARTS .... Diagnostic Analysis and Repair Tool Set
DARTS .... Digital Airborne Radar Threat Simulator (SAUS)
DARTS .... Digital Antijam Radio Teletype System (MCD)
DARTS .... Digital Automated RADAR Tracking System (MCD)
DARTS .... Digital Azimuth Range Tracking System
DARTS .... Distributed Architecture Robust Tactical System (SAUS)
DARTS .... Distributors Automated Real-Time System (SAUS)
DARTS .... DOE Audit Report Tracking System (SAUS)
DARTS .... Drug and Alcohol Rehabilitation Testing System [*Navy*] (NVT)
DARTS .... Dutch-Auction-Rate Transferable Securities [*Investment term*]
DARTS .... Dynamically Actuated Road Transit System (SAUS)
DARTS .... Dynamic Analytic Replanning Tools [*DoD*]
Dart Vend .... Dart on Vendors and Purchasers [*A publication*] (DLA)
D Arty .... Director of Artillery (SAUO)
D Arty .... Director of Royal Canadian Artillery (SAUO)
DARU .... Distributed automatic intercept system Audio Response Unit (SAUO)
Darw .... Darwin College, Cambridge (SAUS)
Darw Cr L .... Darwin's Criminal Law [*A publication*] (DLA)
DARYL .... Data Analysing Robot Youth Lifeform [*From the movie entitled "D.A.R.Y.L."*]
DARZ .... Delta Rail [*Federal Railroad Administration identification code*]
Das .... Common Law Reports, Volume 3 [*England*] [*A publication*] (DLA)
DAS .... Daisetta, TX [*Location identifier*] [*FAA*] (FAAL)
DAS .... Damage Assessment Strike (ACAE)
DAS .... Danish Acoustical Society (SAUO)
DAS .... Dante Alighieri Society [*Australia*]
Das .... Dasent's Bankruptcy and Insolvency Reports [*1853-55*] [*England*] [*A publication*] (DLA)
DAS .... DAS Legal Expenses Insurance Co. Ltd. (SAUO)
DAS .... Dassen Gold Resources Ltd. [*Vancouver Stock Exchange symbol*]
DAS .... Data Access Security
DAS .... Data Accountability System
DAS .... Data Acquisition and Signal conditioning (SAUS)
DAS .... Data Acquisition Station
DAS .... Data Acquisition Subsystem (SAUS)
DAS .... Data Acquisition System
DAS .... Data Administration Section (MCD)
DAS .... Data Administration System (SAUS)
DAS .... Data Administrative Services
DAS .... Data Amplification Sheet (KSC)
DAS .... Data Analysis Software [*Telecommunications*] (TEL)
DAS .... Data Analysis Station (NASA)
DAS .... Data Analysis System [*Computer science*] (NITA)
DAS .... Data Analysis System Information System (SAUS)
DAS .... Data-Assimilation System (CARB)
DAS .... Data Automation Subsystem (SAUS)
DAS .... Data Automation System [*or Subsystem*] [*NASA*]
DAS .... Data Auxiliary Set [*Telecommunications*] (TEL)
DAS .... Datatron Assembly System [*Burroughs Corp.*]
DAS .... Date Arrived Station [*Military*] (AFM)
DAS .... Days After Seeding (or Sowing) (SAUO)
DAS .... Days at Sea (USDC)
DAS .... Dead Air Space [*Medicine*] (EDAA)
DAS .... Dead-Arm Syndrome [*Medicine*] (MELL)
DAS .... Death Anxiety Scale
DAS .... Decimal Adjust for Subtraction (SAUS)
DAS .... Decision Assist System (SAA)
DAS .... Decorative Arts Show
DAS .... Defect and Analysis Section (SAUO)
DAS .... Defense Against Self-Defense [*Suggested program against falling missiles*]
DAS .... Defense Analysis Seminar [*Military*]
DAS .... Defense Attache System [*Department of State*]
DAS .... Defense Audit Service [*Abolished 1982, functions transferred to Office of the Inspector General (DoD)*]
DAS .... Defensive Aids Suite (SAUS)
DAS .... Defensive Aids System [*Military*] (SEWL)
DAS .... Defensive Aid System
DAS .... Defensive Avionics System (ACAE)
DAS .... Deficiency Analysis Summary
DAS .... Delaware Assocation of Surveyors (GEOI)
DAS .... Delayed Anovulatory Syndrome [*Medicine*] (DMAA)
DAS .... Delivered Alongside Ship
DAS .... Delivery Alongside Ship (SAUS)
DAS .... Demand Access System (SAUS)
DAS .... Demand-Assignment Signaling (MCD)
DAS .... Dendrite Arm Spacing (RDA)
DAS .... Department of Aboriginal Sites [*Australia*]
DAS .... Department of Applied Science (SAUO)
DAS .... Deputy Assistant Secretary (ABAC)
DAS .... Design Analysis System (MCD)
DAS .... Design Automation System (SAUS)
DAS .... Detector Angular Subtense [*Instrumentation*]
DAS .... Development Advisory Service (ODBW)
DAS .... Developmental Apraxia of Speech
DAs .... Development Areas (SAUS)
DAS .... Developments in Atmospheric Science (SAUS)
DAS .... Device Analysis System (SAUS)
DAS .... Devon Archaeological Society (SAUO)
DAS .... Dextroamphetamine Sulfate [*CNS stimulant*]
DAS .... Diacetoxyscirpenol [*Fungal toxin*]
DAS .... Dial Assistance Switchboard (CET)
DAS .... Dialdehyde Starch [*Wet-strength agent*]
DAS .... Diallyl Sulfide
DAS .... Diaminostilbenedisulfonic Acid [*Also, DASD, DASDS*] [*Organic chemistry*]
DAS .... Dictionary of American Slang [*A publication*]
DAS .... Differential Ability Scales [*C. D. Elliott*] (DIPS)
DAS .... Differential-Absorption and Scattering [*Remote sensing technique*]
DAS .... Digital Address System (MCD)
DAS .... Digital Aircraft Simulator (MCD)
DAS .... Digital Altimeter Scanner
DAS .... Digital Analog Simulator [*Computer science*]
DAS .... Digital Analog System [*Computer science*] (IAA)
DAS .... Digital Annunciator System [*Automotive engineering*]
DAS .... Digital Attenuator System
DAS .... Digital Attitude Simulation (SAUS)
DAS .... Digital Audio System (SAUS)
DAS .... Digital Autopilot System (SAUS)

DAS .... Digital Avionics System (MCD)
DAS .... Digital Signature Algorithm (SAUS)
DAS .... Digital Storage Architecture (SAUS)
DAS .... Digit Analysis [*Communications term*] (DCT)
DAS .... Dimer-Adatom Stacking (SAUS)
DAS .... Dimer-Adatom-Stacking [*Fault model*]
DAS .... Dimethoxyanthracene Sulfonate [*Organic chemistry*]
DAS .... Dipole Antenna System
DAS .... direct absorption spectroscopy (SAUS)
DAS .... Direct Access SAAIF (SAUS)
DAS .... Direct Access Storage (SAUS)
DAS .... Direct Access Store [*Computer science*] (IAA)
DAS .... Direct Access Subscriber (COE)
DAS .... Direct Access System (CARB)
DAS .... Direct Acting Steam (MSA)
DAS .... Direct Air Support [*Military*] (AFM)
DAS .... Direct Analog Storage [*Computer science*] (CIST)
DAS .... Direct Automotive Support
DAS .... Directly Addressable Storage (SAUS)
DAS .... Director Aiming Sight (SAUS)
DAS .... Director Aiming System (SAUS)
DAS .... Directorate for Advanced Systems [*Army*] (RDA)
DAS .... Directorate of Aerodrome Standards (SAUO)
DAS .... Directorate of Aerospace Safety (SAUO)
DAS .... Directorate of Aerospace Studies [*Kirtland Air Force Base, NM*]
DAS .... Directorate of Armament Supply (SAUO)
DAS .... Director of Administrative Services [*US Military Government, Germany*]
DAS .... Director of Administrative Support (SAUO)
DAS .... Director of Armament Supplies [*British*] [*World War II*]
DAS .... Director of the Army Staff
DAS .... Directory Access Service (SAUS)
DAS .... Directory Allocation Sector (SAUS)
DAS .... Directory Assistance Service [*Computer science*] (VERA)
DAS .... Directory Assistance System [*Telecommunications*] (TEL)
DAS .... Directory System Agent (SAUS)
DAS .... Discount Access Services (UWER)
DAS .... Discrete Algebraic Structures (UWER)
DAS .... Disk Array Subsystem (SAUS)
DAS .... Disk Auxiliary Storage [*Computer science*] (ECII)
DAS .... display system activity (SAUS)
DAS .... Distance Aids School (SAA)
DAS .... Distant Air Superiority (ACAE)
DAS .... Distributed Systems Architecture (SAUS)
DAS .... Distributor And Scanner (SAUS)
DAS .... District Auditors Society (SAUO)
DAS .... Disturbance Analysis System [*Nuclear energy*] (NRCH)
DAS .... Division of Administrative Support (SAUO)
DAS .... Division of Applied Sciences [*Harvard University*] [*Research center*] (RCD)
DAS .... Division of Assistance to States [*Department of Education*]
DAS .... Division of Atmospheric Surveillance [*Environmental Protection Agency*]
DAS .... Doctor-Assisted Suicide (MELL)
DAS .... Doctor of Applied Science
D As............ Doctor of Astronomy
DAS .... Document Aids System (SAUS)
DAS .... Document Analysis Sheet (MCD)
DAS .... Documentation Accountability Sheet (MCD)
DAS .... Documentation Aid System (IAA)
DAS .... Dollar Air Services Ltd. [*British*] [*ICAO designator*] (FAAC)
DA's............ Domestic Afflictions [*Menstruation*] [*Slang*] (DSUE)
DAS .... Doppler Acoustic Sounder (SAUS)
DAS .... double attached station (SAUS)
DAS .... Dramatic Authors' Society [*British*]
DAS .... Draw-a-Story: Screening for Depression and Age or Gender Differences [*Test*] (TMMY)
DAS .... Dreaded Abbreviation Syndrome
DAS .... Drive Authorization System [*Automotive engineering*]
DAS .... Drug Addiction Service [*Medicine*] (EDAA)
DAS .... Dual Address Space [*Computer science*] (ITCA)
DAS .... Dual Attached Station [*Computer science*] (TNIG)
DAS .... Dual Attachment Station [*Computer science*] (VERA)
DAS .... Dual Attach Station (SAUS)
DAS .... Dutch Australian Society
DAS .... Dyadic Adjustment Scale [*Psychology*] (EDAC)
DAS .... Dynamic Alert System (SAUS)
DAS .... Dynamic Allocation Scheme [*Computer science*] (VERA)
DAS .... Dynamically Assigned Sockets (VLIE)
DAS .... Dynamic Angle Spinning [*Spectroscopy*]
DAS .... Dynamiclly Alterable System (PDAA)
DAS .... Dynamic Scalable Architecture (SAUS)
DAS .... Dynamo Alert System (AAG)
DAS .... United States Department of Commerce, National Oceanic and Atmospheric Administration, Atmospheric Sciences Library, Silver Spring, MD [*Library symbol*] [*Library of Congress*] (LCLS)
DAS .... Double Algebraic Sum (ODA)
DAS3 .... Decentralize ADP [*Automatic Data Processing*] Service Support System
DAS3 .... Decentralized Automated Service Support System [*Army*] (RDA)
DASA .... Daimler-Benz-Aerospace (SAUO)
DASA .... Daimler Chrysler Aerospace
DASA .... Data Acquisition Signal Analysis [*Computer science*] (NITA)
DASA .... Days After Straw Application (SAUO)
DASA .... Defense Atomic Support Agency [*Later, DNA*]
DASA .... Delaware Association of School Administrators (SRA)
DASA .... Department of the Army Security Agency (MCD)
DASA .... Department of the Army Staff Agencies (COE)
DASA .... Deutsche Aerospace (ECON)
DASA .... Deutsche Aerospace Administration (SAUO)
DASA .... Distal Articular Set Angle [*Orthopedics*] (DAVI)
DASA .... Domestic Appliance Service Association [*British*] (DBA)
DA/SA .... Double-Action/Single-Action [*Gunnery*]
DASA .... Dual Aerospace Servo Amplifier (NASA)
dasa .... dual aerospace servoamplifier (SAUS)
DASA .... Dumping at Sea Act [*1974*]
DASA-DC .... Defense Atomic Support Agency Data Center
DASADD .... Defense Atomic Support Agency Data Division (SAA)
DAS & E .... Defense Aid [*Lend-Lease*] Services and Expenses [*World War II*]
DASA(P) .... Deputy Assistant Secretary, Army (Procurement) (AAGC)
DASAT .... Data Selector and Tagger (MUGU)
DASA-TP .... Defense Atomic Support Agency Technical Publications
DASC .... DA System Coordination (MCD)
DASC .... Data Aquisition and Signal Conditioning (SAUS)
DASC .... Defence Aid Supply Committee [*Later, ISC*] [*World War II*]
DASC .... Defense Automotive Supply Center
DASC .... Defense Logistics Agency Administrative Support Center (SAUS)
DASC .... Department of the Army System Coordinator (RDA)
DASC .... Department of the Army Systems Coordinator (SAUS)
DASC .... Design Automation Standard Subcommittee (VLIE)
DASC .... Design Automation Steering Committee (TIMI)
DASC .... Direct Air Support Center [*Later, ASOC*]
DAS/C .... Directory Assistance Sytem/Computer [*Communications term*] (DCT)
DASC .... District Air Support Center (MCD)
DASC .... Division of Advanced Scientific Computing (SAUS)
DASc .... Doctor in Agricultural Sciences
DASc .... Doctor of Agricultural Science (SAUS)
DA Sc .... Doctor of Applied Science
DASC .... Double-Aperture Speckle Camera
DASC-A .... Direct Air Support Center-Airborne (DOMA)
DASCAR .... Data Acquisition System for Crash Avoidance Research [*NHTSA*] (TAG)
DASCH .... Disk Automation Storage Control Hardware [*Macintosh computer*]
DASci .... Doctor of Agricultural Science (SAUS)
DAS/CM .... Directory Assistance Systems / Computer and Microfilm [*Bell System*]
DASCO .... Data Switching Computer (SAUS)
DASCO .... Digital-to-Analog Synchro Converter (DNAB)
DASCO .... Discriminant Analysis with Shrunken Coveriances [*Mathematics*]
DASCOTAR .... Data Acquisition System, Correlation Tracking and Ranging [*Air Force*]
DASCS .... Direct Air Support Center Squadron [*Air Force*]
DASD .... Data Access Storage Device [*Communications term*] (DCT)
DASD .... Data Acquisition Support Document (KSC)
DASD .... Department of the Army Shipping Document
DASD .... Deputy Assistant Secretary of Defense
DASD .... Diaminostilbenedisulfonic Acid [*Also, DAS, DASDS*] [*Organic chemistry*]
DASD .... Direct Access Storage Device [*Pronounced "daz-dee"*] [*Computer science*]
DASD .... Direct Access Storage (or Store) Device (SAUS)
DASD .... Direct Access Storage (or Store) Drive (SAUS)
DASD .... Directly Accessible Storage Device (SAUS)
DASD .... Director, Anti-Submarine Division [*British military*] (DMA)
DASD .... Director of Army Staff Duties [*British*] (RDA)
DASD(CP) .... Deputy Assistant Secretary of Defense (Civilian Personnel) (DNAB)
DASDDR .... Direct Access Storage Device Dump Restore (SAUS)
DASDDR .... Direct Access Storage Device Dump/Restore [*Computer science*] (VLIE)
DASD(EO) .... Deputy Assistant Secretary of Defense (Equal Opportunity) (DNAB)
DASDI .... Direct Access Storage Device Initialization (SAUS)
DASDI .... Direct Access Storage Device Initialization Program [*Computer science*] (IAA)
DASDI .... Direct Access Store Disk Initialization (SAUS)
DASDL .... Data and Structure Definition Language [*Computer science*] (BUR)
DASDM .... Direct Access Storage Data Management [*Computer science*] (VLIE)
DASD(MP) .... Deputy Assistant Secretary of Defense (Military Personnel Policy) (DNAB)
DASDP .... Deputy Assistant Secretary for Defense Program (SAUO)
DASDR .... Direct Access Storage Dump Restore
DASDS .... Diaminostilbenedisulfonic Acid [*Also, DAS, DASD*] [*Organic chemistry*]
DASDs .... Direct Access Storage (or Store) Devices (SAUS)
DASE .... Data Adaptive Signal Estimator (MCD)
DASE .... Defense Against Sound Equipment [*Military intelligence*]
DASE .... Denver Articulation Screening Exam [*Speech evaluation test*]
DASE .... Department of Army Scientific & Engineering Cooperative (SAUO)
DASE .... Differential Absorption of Scattered Energy (SAUS)
DASE .... Digital Automatic Stabilization Equipment (MCD)
DASE .... Diploma in Advanced Studies in Education [*British*] (DI)
DASE .... Directory Access Service Element [*Telecommunications*] (OSI)
DASE .... Distributed Application Support Environment [*Computer science*] (VLIE)
DASE .... Dutch Association of Safety Experts
DASEB .... Department of the Army Suitability Evaluation Board (AABC)
DASEC .... Digital Automatic Stabilization Equipment Computer (MCD)
DAS/EE .... Deputy Assistant Secretary/Energy Emergency (COE)
DASEL .... Data Analysis and Statistical Experimental Language [*Computer science*] (MHDI)
Dasent .... Acts of the Privy Council (Dasent) [*England*] [*A publication*] (DLA)

Dasent .... Dasent's Bankruptcy and Insolvency Reports [*1853-55*] [*England*] [*A publication*] (DLA)
DASES .... Digital Automatic Stabilization Equipment System [*or Subsystem*] (MCD)
DASET .... Deputy Assistant Secretary for Employment and Training [*Department of Labor*]
DASETT .... Department of the Arts, Sport, the Environment, Tourism and Territories (SAUS)
DASF .... Defense Aid [*Lend-Lease*] Special Fund [*World War II*]
DASF .... Direct Access Storage Facility [*Computer science*]
DASF .... Direct Air Support Flight [*Military*] (AFM)
DASFAA .... Database Systems for Advanced Applications [*Computer science*] (VLIE)
DASG .... Data Acquisition Subsystem Group (ACAE)
DASG .... Developmental Assessment of Spanish Grammar (EDAC)
DASH .... Data Acquisition Sequential Histogram [*Computer science*] (VLIE)
DASH .... Database Acquisition for Student Health
DASH .... Delta Airlines Special Handling (SAUS)
DASH .... Deputy Assistant Secretary for Health [*U.S. Department of Health and Human Services*]
DASH .... Destroyer, Antisubmarine Helicopter
DASH .... Developmental Assessment for the Severely Handicapped [*Test*]
DASH .... Dietary Approaches to Stop Hypertension
DASH .... Differential Air-Speed Hold (PDAA)
DASH .... Digital Audio Stationary Head [*Recording*] (NTCM)
DASH .... Direct Access Storage Handler [*Telecommunications*] (TEL)
DASH .... Display and Sight Helmet (SAUS)
DASH .... Display and Sight Helmet System (MCD)
DASH .... Distress Alarm for Severely Handicapped [*British*]
DASH .... Division of Adolescent and School Health (SAUO)
DASH .... Downtown Area Short Hops [*Battery-powered bus service in Long Beach, California*]
DASH .... Drishat Shalom [*Best Regards*] [*Hebrew*]
DASH .... Drone Antisubmarine Helicopter [*Air Force, Navy*]
DASH .... Dual Access Storage Handling
DASH .... Dynamic ALGOL [*Algorithmic Language*] String Handling [*Computer science*] (IAA)
DASHER .... Dynamic Analysis of Shells of Revolution (SAUS)
DASHO .... Designed Agency Safety and Health Official (ERG)
DASI .... Degree Angular Scale Interferometer (SAUS)
DASI .... Deputy Assistant Secretary for Intelligence (SAUO)
DASI .... Developing Anti-Sexist Innovations (AIE)
DASI .... Developmental Activities Screening Inventory [*Psychology*]
DASI .... Dial Access Signaling Interface [*Computer science*] (VERA)
DASI .... Diffusion of Arsenic in Silicon (PDAA)
DASI .... Digital Altimeter Setting Indicator [*FAA*] (TAG)
DASIAC .... Defense Atomic Support Agency Information and Analysis Center (SAUO)
DASIAC .... Department of Defense Information & Analysis Center (SAUS)
DASIAC .... DoD [*Department of Defense*] Nuclear Information and Analysis Center [*Defense Atomic Support Agency Information and Analysis Center*] [*Kaman Tempo*] [*Acronym is based on former name,*] [*Information service or system*] (IID)
DASIQ .... Distributed Automated System for Inspection and Quality Control (EURO)
DASIS .... Drug and Alcohol Services Information System (SAUS)
DASL .... Data Access System Language
DASL .... Department of the Army Strategic Logistics [*Study*]
DASL .... Digital Adapter for Subscriber Loops [*Telecommunications*] (NITA)
DASL .... Direct Access System Language [*Computer science*] (VLIE)
DASL .... Directory of Special Libraries in Australia [*A publication*]
DASM .... Data Acquisition System Manual (ACAE)
DASM .... Deep Attack Smart Munition (SAUS)
DASM .... Delayed Action Space Missile (SAUS)
DASM .... Design and Analysis Support Model (SAUS)
DASM .... Direct Access Storage Media [*Computer science*]
DASM .... Director of Advanced Systems Management
DA/SM .... Director of Antisubmarine Material [*British*]
DAS/M .... Directory Assistance System/Microfilm [*Bell System*]
DASMA .... Deputy Assistant Secretary for Millitary Applications (SAUO)
DASMAI .... Door and Access Systems Manufacturers' Association, International (NTPA)
DASNET .... Data Switching Network (SAUS)
DASNM .... Deputy Assistant Secretary for Nuclear Materials (SAUO)
DASO .... Demonstration and Shakedown Operations [*Military*] (AFM)
DASO .... Department of the Army Special Order
DASO .... Deputy (or District) Armament Supply Officer (SAUS)
DASO .... Development and Shakedown Operations (SAUS)
DASO .... District Armament Supply Officer [*British*]
DASOC .... Disturbance Accommodation Standard-Deviation Optimal Controller [*Space telescope*] [*NASA*]
DASOP .... Demonstration and Shakedown Operation Piggyback [*Kit*] [*Military*]
DASP .... Datapoint Attached Support (SAUS)
DASP .... Datapoint Attached Support Processor [*Computer science*] (VLIE)
DASP .... Defense Acquisition Scholarship Program [*DoD*] (RDA)
DASP .... Direct Air Support Center (ACAE)
DASP .... Director of Advanced Systems Planning
DASP .... Discrete Analog Signal Processing
DASP .... Double Antibody Solid-Phase [*Clinical chemistry*] (AAMN)
DASP .... Double Antibody Solid-Phase Radioimmunoassay [*Clinical chemistry*]
DASP .... Double Arm Magnetic Spectrometer
dasp .... double-arm magnetic spectrometer (SAUS)
DASP .... Double Arm Spectrometer (SAUS)
DASP .... Drive Active. Slave Present [*Computer science*] (VERA)
DASP .... Dynamic Adaptive Speculative Pre-Processor
DASPA .... Defense Attache System Property Accounting (MCD)
DASPAC .... Defense Audit Service, Pacific (DNAB)
DASPAN .... Data Spanning (IAA)
DASPAN .... Data-Spanning (SAUS)
DASPO .... Department of Army Special Photographic Office (SAUO)
DASPO .... Department of the Army Special Photographic Office (AABC)
DASPS .... Department of the Army Standard Port System
DASPS-E .... Department of the Army Standard Port System - Enhanced (MCD)
DASPS-E-SDG ... Department of the Army Standard Port System - Enhanced - System Development Group (MCD)
DASPS-E SDG ... Department of the Army Standard Port System-Enhanced, System Development Group (SAUO)
DAS-PSG ..... Department of Administrative Services - Purchasing and Sales Group [*Australia*]
DASq .... Direct Air Support Squadron [*Military*] (AFM)
DASR .... Data Acquisition Statistical Recorder
DASR .... Defense Analysis Special Report (MCD)
DASR .... Design Audit Status Report (SAUS)
DASR .... Directorate of Aviation Safety Regulation [*Australia*]
DASS .... Data Access Security System (IAA)
DASS .... Defensive Aids Subsystem [*Military*] (SEWL)
DASS .... Defined Antigen Substrate Sphere [*Medicine*] (PDAA)
DASS .... Demand-Assignment Signaling and Switching Unit
DASS .... Design Automation Standards Subcommittee (CIST)
DASS .... Diesel Air Start System (IEEE)
DASS .... Digital Access Signaling System [*Telecommunications*] (OSI)
DASS .... Digital Access Signalling System
DASS .... Digital Acoustic Sensor Simulation (MCD)
DASS .... Digital Acoustic Simulation System (MCD)
DASS .... Digital-Analog Servo System [*Computer science*] (SAA)
DASS .... Direct Access Secondary Storage [*Computer science*] (AGLO)
DASS .... Direct Access Signalling System
DASS .... Direct Air Support Squadron [*Air Force*]
DASS .... Direct Air Support System (ACAE)
DASS .... Director of Air Staff Services (SAUO)
DASS .... Distributed Authentication Security Service [*Computer science*] (VERA)
DASS .... Disturbance Analysis and Surveillance System [*NRC*]
D As S .... Doctor of Association Science
DASS 2 .... Digital Access Signaling System 2 (SAUS)
DASSA .... Deputy Assistant Secretary for Security Affairs (SAUO)
DASSA .... Direct Access Storage Space Allocation (SAUS)
DASSC .... Dante Alighieri Society of Southern California [*Defunct*] (EA)
D As Sc .... Doctor of Association Science
DASSC .... Double-Aperture Speckle Shearing Camera (PDAA)
Dass Dig ...... Dassler's Kansas Digest [*A publication*] (DLA)
Dass Ed .... Dassler's Edition, Kansas Reports [*A publication*] (DLA)
Dass Ed (Kan) ... Dassler's Edition, Kansas Reports [*A publication*] (DLA)
DASSH .... Dean of Arts, Social Sciences and Humanities
DASSL .... Differential Algebraic System Solver (AAEL)
DASSO .... Data Systems Support Office (MCD)
DASSO .... Department of the Army Systems Staff Officer (AABC)
DASSO/FMSO ... Data Systems Support Office/Fleet Material Support Office (SAUO)
DASSq .... Direct Air Support Squadron [*Air Force*]
DASSS .... Decentralized Automated Service Support System (COE)
DASSS .... Demand-Assignment Signaling and Switching Subsystem [*Telecommunications*] (IAA)
Dass Stat ..... Dassler's Kansas Statutes [*A publication*] (DLA)
DAST .... Dassault Systemes, S.A. [*NASDAQ symbol*] (NASQ)
DAST .... Denver Audiometric Screening Test
DAST .... Design, Architecture, Software, and Testing (MCD)
DAST .... Detective - Agents - Science Fiction - Thriller [*Acronym used as title of magazine*]
DAST .... Device Assignment Table
DAST .... Diethylaminosulfur Trifluoride [*Organic chemistry*]
DAST .... Digital Aircraft Systems Trainer (SAUS)
DAST .... Diploma of Advanced Studies in Teaching (PGP)
DAST .... Direct Air Support Team [*Military*] (CINC)
DAST .... Directorate of Advanced Systems Technology
DAST .... Director of Army Supply and Transport (SAUO)
DAST .... Division for Advanced Systems Technology (SAA)
DAST .... Division of Advanced Systems Technology (SAUO)
DAST .... Division of Supplied Science and Technology (SAUO)
DAST .... DoD AUTODIN Subscriber Terminal (SAUS)
DAST .... Drones for Aerodynamic and Structural Testing (MCD)
DAST .... Drug Abuse Screening Test (MELL)
DAST-20 ...... Drug Use Questionnaire (TMMY)
DA Staff ...... Department of the Army Staff (SAUO)
DASTARD .... Destroyer Antisubmarine Transportable Array Detector
DASTL .... Defense Atomic Support Agency Technical Letters
DASTM .... Double-Acting Steam
DASTOR .... Data Storage and Retrieval (SAUS)
DASTY .... Dassault Systemes
DASTY .... Dassault Systems ADS [*NASDAQ symbol*] (SG)
DASV .... Differential Anodic Stripping Voltammetry [*Electronics*]
DASVA .... Defense Attache System Vehicle Accounting (MCD)
DA/SW .... Director of Antisubmarine Warfare [*British*]
DASWE .... Director, Admiralty Surface Weapons Establishment [*Navy*] [*British*]
DASWZ .... Data Switch Wrrt [*NASDAQ symbol*] (TTSB)
DASY .... Data Analysis System
DASY .... Design Automation System [*Computer science*] (VLIE)
DASYS .... Data System Environment Simulator (SAUS)
DASYS .... Data System Simulator (SAUS)
DAT .... Daily Activity Team (SAUO)
DaT .... Dallas Texans [*National Football League*] [*1952*] (NFLA)

DAT............ Dangerous Articles Tariff
DAT............ Data Abstract Tape [*Computer science*]
DAT............ Data Acceptance Tests
DAT............ Data Acquisition Test [*Later, DST*]
DAT............ Data File [*Computer science*]
DAT............ Data General Corp., Westboro, MA [*OCLC symbol*] (OCLC)
DAT............ Date After Tomorrow (SAUS)
dat............ Dative (SHCU)
DAT............ Dative
DAT............ Datum (MSA)
DAT............ Datumone Petroleum [*Vancouver Stock Exchange symbol*]
DAT............ Daunomycin, ara-C [*Cytarabine*], Thioguanine [*Antineoplastic drug regimen*]
DAT............ Day Applied Tactics (SAUS)
DAT............ Days After Transplanting (SAUO)
DAT............ Days after Treatment [*Agriculture*]
DAT............ Decorative Arts Trust (EA)
DAT............ Defense Attache
DAT............ Delayed Action Tablet [*Pharmacy*]
DAT............ Delta Air Transport [*Belgium*] [*ICAO designator*] (FAAC)
DAT............ Demand Access Technology (SAUS)
DAT............ Dementia Alzheimer Type [*Medicine*]
dAt............ dementia of the Alzheimer type (SAUS)
DAT............ Den, Aoyama, and Takemake [*Early investors in automobile manufacturer Nissan*] [*Initials used in creating automobile name DATSUN*] [*Japan*]
DAT............ Dental Admission Test [*Education*]
DAT............ Dental Aptitude Test [*Education*] (AEE)
DAT............ Deoxyaconitine [*Biochemistry*]
DAT............ Department Approved Training (OICC)
DAT............ Department of Acoustic Technology (SAUS)
DAT............ Department of Science and Technology (SAUO)
DAT............ Dependents Assistance Team [*Military*] (DNAB)
DAT............ Deployment Action Team [*Army*] (DOMA)
DAT............ Design Acceptance [*or Approval*] Test
DAT............ Design Approval Test (DNAB)
DAT............ Designation Acquisition Track (IAA)
DAT............ Design Automation (SAUS)
DAT............ Desktop Analysis Tool [*A publication*]
DAT............ Detail Assembly Template
DAT............ Development Acceptance Test [*Army*]
DAT............ Development Assist Team (SAUO)
DAT............ Development Assist Test
DAT............ Device Assignment Table (MCD)
DAT............ Diacetylthiamine (SAUS)
DAT............ Diaminotropolone [*Biochemistry*]
DAT............ Diet as Tolerated [*Medicine*]
DAT............ Differential Agglutination Test (SAUS)
DAT............ Differential Agglutination Titer [*Hematology*]
DAT............ Differential Antibody Titer [*Immunology*] (DAVI)
DAT............ Differential Aptitude Test [*Psychology*]
DAT............ Diffused-Alloy Transistor [*Electronics*] (ECII)
DAT............ Digital Acoustic Target
DAT............ Digital Archival Tape (UWER)
DAT............ Digital Audio Broadcast (SAUS)
DAT............ Digital Audio Tape [*Also facetiously translated as Damn the Artist and Talent*]
DAT............ Di(isoamyloxy)thiocarbanilide [*Pharmacology*]
DAT............ Diphtheria Antitoxin [*Immunology*]
DAT............ Dipole Array Telescope (UWER)
DAT............ Direct Action Team (MCD)
DAT............ Direct Agglutination Test [*Clinical chemistry*] (MAE)
DAT............ Direct Amylase Test [*Clinical chemistry*]
DAT............ Direct Antiglobulin Test [*Clinical chemistry*]
DAT............ Direct Ascent Threat (ACAE)
DAT............ Director [*or Directorate*] of Advanced Technology [*Air Force*]
DAT............ Director of Air Training (SAUS)
DAT............ Director of Army Telegraph (SAUS)
DAT............ Director of Army Telegraphs (SAUO)
DAT............ Director of Army Telegraphy (SAUO)
DAT............ Director of Army Training [*British*]
DAT............ Director of Army Transportation
DAT............ Disassembly actuating tool (SAUS)
DAT............ Disaster Action Team [*Red Cross*]
DAT............ Disconnect Actuating Tools [*Nuclear energy*] (NRCH)
DAT............ Disk Access Time (UWER)
DAT............ Disk Allocation Table [*Computer science*] (IBMDP)
DAT............ Disk Array Technology (SAUS)
DAT............ Distillate Assistance/Advisory Team [*Military*] (DNAB)
DAT............ District Advisory Team [*Military*] (VNW)
DAT............ Division of Applied Technology [*Coast Guard*]
DAT............ Docking Alignment Target [*NASA*] (MCD)
DAT............ Docking Alignment Test (SAUS)
DAT............ Documentation Analysis Technique (ACAE)
DAT............ Dopamine Transporter [*Biochemistry*]
DAT............ Drone Assisted Torpedo
DAT............ Drug Abuse Team [*Military*] (DNAB)
DAT............ Drum Access Time (SAUS)
DAT............ Duration Adjusting Type
DAT............ Dynamic Address Table [*Computer science*] (IAA)
DAT............ Dynamic Address Translation [*Computer science*]
DAT............ Dynamic Address Translator (SAUS)
DAT............ Dynamic Allocation Translator [*Computer science*] (IAA)
DAT............ Dynamic Area Telethermometry (SAUS)
DATA.......... Babystar, Inc. [*NASDAQ symbol*] (SAG)
DATA.......... Data Acquisition and Technical Analysis (SAUS)
DATA.......... Datamation (journ.) (SAUS)
DATA.......... DataTRAK International, Inc. [*NASDAQ symbol*] (NASQ)
DATA.......... Datatrend Services [*NASDAQ symbol*] (TTSB)
DATA.......... Decision Aids for Target Aggregation (MCD)
DATA.......... Defense Air Transport Administration (SAUS)
DATA.......... Defense Air Transportation Administration [*Abolished 1962, functions transferred to Office of the Under Secretary of Commerce for Transportation*]
DATA.......... Department of Agriculture Technicians Association (SAUO)
DATA.......... Derivation & Tabulation Associates, Inc. [*Information service or system*] (IID)
DATA.......... Derivation and Tabulation Associates, Incorporated (SAUS)
DATA.......... Design and Technology Association (AIE)
DATA.......... Development and Technical Assistance
DATA.......... Development and Technical Assistance International (SAUO)
DATA.......... Dial a Teacher Assistance [*Telephone service*]
DATA.......... Digital Automatic Tape Adaption (SAUS)
DATA.......... Direct Access Terminal Application [*Computer science*] (BUR)
DATA.......... Display Automated Telemetry Analyzer (MCD)
DATA.......... Draughtsmen's and Allied Technicians' Association [*British*] (DI)
DATA.......... Drawing for Army Training Aids
DATA-2........ Diagnostic Achievement Test for Adolescents, Second Edition (TMMY)
DATABNK..... Data Bank (SAUS)
DATABUS Language... Datapoint Business Language (SAUS)
DATAC......... Data Acquisition Division [*National Weather Service*]
DATAC......... Data Analog Computer
DATAC......... Database Access (SAUS)
DATAC......... Defense and Tactical Armament Control
DATAC......... Design Authority Technical Assistance Contract (SAUS)
DATAC......... Development Areas Treasury Advisory Committee (SAUO)
DATAC......... Digital Automatic Tester and Classifier
DATAC......... Digital Autonomous Terminal Access Communication [*Data Bus*]
DATACOL..... Data Collection
DATACOL System... Data Collection System (SAUS)
DATACOM.... Data Communications
DATACOM.... Data Communication Service (NITA)
DATACOM.... Data Communications Network [*Air Force*] (NITA)
DATACOM System... Data Communications System (SAUS)
DATACORTS... Data Correlation and Transfer System
DATA/DAT.... Data Digital Audio Tape (CDE)
DATAEASE... Fourth Generation Language Data Base (SAUS)
DATA FUNNEL... Data Fusion Using Neural Network Learning (SAUS)
DATAG......... Department of the Army, The Adjutant General (SAUO)
DATAG......... Department of the Army, The Adjutant-General (SAUS)
DATAGEN.... Data File Generator (MCD)
DATAGEN.... Data Generator (SAUS)
DataGn........ Data General Corp. [*Associated Press*] (SAG)
Data IO........ Data I-O [*Associated Press*] (SAG)
Data Knowl Eng... Data & Knowledge Engineering [*A publication*] (CABS)
DATALEED... LEED w/ extremely fast data acquisition & computer processing (SAUS)
Datalgx........ Datalogix International, Inc. [*Associated Press*] (SAG)
DATALIBRIS... An integrated PC package from Datapoint (SAUS)
DATALINK.... Digitized Information Transfer [*Air/ground*] (GAVI)
DATAM......... Data Attribute Modification (SAUS)
DATAMAN.... Data Management System [*Computer science*] (MCD)
DATAMAP.... Data from Aeromechanics' Test and Analytics-Management and Analysis Package (RDA)
Datamation... Data Automation (SAUS)
Datamet........ Datametrics Corp. [*Associated Press*] (SAG)
DATAN......... Data Analysis (IEEE)
DAT & OV.... Defense Aid [*Lend-Lease*] Tanks and Other Vehicles [*World War II*]
DATANET.... Data Network (CET)
DATAP......... Data Transmission and Processing (NATG)
DATAPAC..... Data Packet (SAUS)
DATAPHONE... Data Transmission via Telephon Lines (SAUS)
DATAPRO.... DATAPRO Research Corp. (SAUO)
Datapt.......... Datapoint Corp. [*Associated Press*] (SAG)
DATAR......... Detection and Tactical Alert of Radar (SAUS)
DATAR......... Digital Automatic Tracking and Ranging [*or Remoting*] [*Air Force*]
DATAR......... Digital Automatic Tracking and Remoting (SAUS)
DATAR......... Digital Auto Transducer and Recorder (SAUS)
DATAR......... Digital Autotransducer and Recorder (IEEE)
Dataram....... Dataram Corp. [*Associated Press*] (SAG)
DataRce....... Date Race, Inc. [*Associated Press*] (SAG)
Data Record Engr... Data Recording Engineer (SAUS)
Data Rep...... Data Report (journ.) (SAUS)
DATAS......... Data in Associative Storage [*Computer science*] (MHDB)
DATAS......... Data Link and Transponder Analysis System (DA)
Datascpe..... Dastascope Corp. [*Associated Press*] (SAG)
Datastr........ Datastream Systems, Inc. [*Associated Press*] (SAG)
DataSysN..... Data Systems Network Corp. [*Associated Press*] (SAG)
DataSyst...... Data Systems & Software, Inc. [*Associated Press*] (SAG)
DATATELEX... DATA Processing Telecommunication Exchange (SAUS)
DATATERM... Data Terminal (SAUS)
DATATOP..... Deprenyl and Tocopherol Antioxidative Therapy of Parkinsonism [*Medicine*]
DATA-tronix... DATA-tronix Corp. (SAUO)
DATAW......... Datatrend Svcs Wrrt [*NASDAQ symbol*] (TTSB)
Dataware..... Dataware Technologies, Inc. [*Associated Press*] (SAG)
DATB........... Department of the Army Technical Bulletin (MCD)
DATB........... Diaminotrinitrobenzene [*An explosive*]
DATBP......... Diallyl Tetrabromophthalate [*Organic chemistry*]

Dat C .... Datum Centre (SAUS)
DATC .... Design Automation Technical Committee [*Electronics*] (AAEL)
DATC .... Development and Training Center [*Navy*] (NVT)
DATC .... Dichloroallyl Diisopropylthiocarbamate [*Di-allate*] [*Herbicide*]
DATC .... Direct Assistance and Training Command [*Navy*] (NVT)
DATC .... Director of Air Training Corps [*British*]
DATC .... Drake Authorized Testing Center (SAUO)
D/Atchd .... Documents Attached (EBF)
DATCIG .... Deferred Adverse Tax Consequences Implementation Group [*IRS*]
DATCO .... Coordinating Committee on the Standardization of the Writing of Dates (SAUO)
DATCO .... Data Coordinating Committee (SAUS)
DATCO .... Duty Air Traffic Control Officer (DA)
DATCOL .... Data Collection (IAA)
DATCOM .... Data Compendium (MCD)
DATCOM .... Data Support Command [*Army*]
DATD .... Diallyltartardiamide [*Also, DATDA*] [*Organic chemistry*]
DATDA .... Diallyltartardiamide [*Also, DATD*] [*Organic chemistry*]
datda .... diallyltartardiamide (SAUS)
DATDC .... Data Analysis and Technique Development Center
DA-TDMA .... Demand Assigned Time Division Multiple Access (SAUS)
DA/TDMA .... Demand Assigned/Time Division Multiple Access
DATE .... Dash Automatic Test Equipment
DATE .... Data Exchange Service (IAA)
DATE .... Data for Allotments Transmitted Electronically (MCD)
DATE .... DATICO [*Digital Automatic Tape Intelligence Checkout*] Acceptance Test Evaluation (MCD)
DATE .... Decision Aids Test Environment (ACAE)
DATE .... Dedicated Access to X.25 Transport Extension (SAUS)
DATE .... Dental Auxiliary Teacher Education [*Medicine*] (DMAA)
DATE .... Designation Accuracy Test Equipment
DATE .... Design Automation and Test in Europe (VLIE)
DATE .... Dial Access Technical Education [*Telecommunications*] (PDAA)
DATE .... Digital Angular Torquing Equipment
DATE .... Digital Audio for Television [*System to improve sound*] [*Public Broadcasting Service*]
DATE .... Dynamic, Acoustic, Thermal Environment (MCD)
DATE .... Dynamics, Acoustics, and Thermal Environment (NASA)
DATE .... Dynamics, Acoustics and Thermal Experiment (SAUS)
DATEC .... Data and Telecommunications
DATEC .... Data Technical Support Group [*Telecommunications*] (TEL)
DATEC .... Design and Art Technician Education Council (AIE)
DATEC .... Differential and Alignment Unit and Total Error Corrector (PDAA)
DATEC .... Digital Adaptive Technique for Communications (SAUS)
DATEC .... Digital Adaptive Technique for Efficient Communications
datel .... Data and Telecommunication (SAUS)
Datel .... Data Telecommunication (SAUO)
DATEL .... Data Telecommunications [*RCA Global Communications Data Transmission Service over Telephone Circuits*] [*Telecommunications*] (TEL)
Datem .... Diacetyl Tartaric Acid Esters of Mono/Diglycerides
DATEP .... Department of the Army Telecommunications Plan (MCD)
DATEPLAN .... Data Tabulation and Editing Program Language (IAA)
DATEX .... Data and Telex Network (VLIE)
DATEX .... Data Exchange (IAA)
DATEX .... Data-Telegraph-Exchange (SAUS)
Datex-J .... Data Exchange for Jedermann (SAUO)
Datex-L .... Data Exchange by Lines (SAUS)
Datex-M .... Data Exchange Multi-Megabit (SAUO)
Datex-P .... Data Exchange in Packages (SAUO)
DATEXP .... Data Exchange-Packetized (SAUS)
Datflx .... Dataflex Corp. [*Associated Press*] (SAG)
DATGEN Routines .... Data Generator Routines (SAUS)
DATHF .... Dideazatetrahydrofolic Acid [*Antineoplastic drug*]
DATI .... Department of Agriculture and Technical Instumentation for Ireland (SAUO)
DATI .... Director of Army Technical Information (AABC)
DATI .... Drill Artwork Test Information (SAUS)
DATICO .... Data Analysis and Technique Development Center [*Alexandria, VA*]
DATICO .... Digital Automatic Tape Intelligence Checkout
DATICS .... Data Inventory Control System
DATIME .... Date and Time (VLIE)
DATIMTEX .... Data, Images, and Text [*European Patent Office*]
DATIN .... Data Inserter
DATIS .... Digital Airborne Topographic Imaging System (GEOI)
Datkey .... Datakey, Inc. [*Associated Press*] (SAG)
DATL .... Doctor of Arts in Training and Learning (GAGS)
DATM .... Bordj Mokhtar [*Algeria*] [*ICAO location identifier*] (ICLI)
DATM .... Datum, Inc. [*NASDAQ symbol*] (NQ)
DATM .... Department of the Army Technical Manual (NATG)
DATM .... Dual Approach Temperatures Method [*Heat exchange design*]
Datmar .... Datamarine International, Inc. [*Associated Press*] (SAG)
DATMOBAS .... David W. Taylor Model Basin [*Also, DTMB, TMB*] [*Later, DTNSRDC, NSRDC*] (MUGU)
DATMP .... Diethylaluminum Tetramethylpiperidide [*Organic chemistry*]
DATMRPSTL .... Department of the Army Technical Manual Repair Parts Special Tool List
DATN .... Defence Automatic Telephone Network (SAUS)
DATO .... Disbursing and Transportation Office
DATO .... Discover America Travel Organizations, Inc. [*Later, TIA*]
DATOC .... Division Artillery Tactical Operations Center (MCD)
DATOM .... Data Aids for Training, Operations, and Maintenance
DATOM .... Direct Access to Members [*Trade union membership database*] [*British*]
DATOR .... Data Operational Requirements Board [*NATO Military Committee*] (NATG)
DATOR .... Digital Auxiliary Track Output Recording [*Computer science*] (VLIE)
DATOR .... Digital Data, Auxiliary Storage, Track Display, Outputs, and RADAR Display
DATOS .... Detection and Tracking of Satellites (CINC)
DATOS .... Drug Abuse Treatment Outcome Study [*National Institute on Drug Abuse*]
datotek .... datotek, inc., communications security (SAUO)
dATP .... Deoxyadenosine Triphosphate [*Biochemistry*]
DATP .... Detailed Acceptance Test Procedure (KSC)
DATP .... Detroit Arsenal Tank Plant [*Army*]
DATP .... Dissolved Adenosine Triphosphate [*Oceanography*]
DATP .... Dominion Air Training Plan (SAUS)
DATP .... Drug Abuse Testing Program (SAUO)
DATPE .... Direction de l'Amernagement du Territoire et de la Protection de l'Environnement [*Haiti*] (GEOI)
DATPG .... Digital Automatic Test Program Generation (ACAE)
Datpt .... Datapoint Corp. [*Associated Press*] (SAG)
DATR .... Design Acceptance [*or Approval*] Test Report
DATR .... Design Approval Test Report (SAUS)
DATR .... Disconnect actuating tool redesign (SAUS)
DaTran .... Data Transmission (VLIE)
DATRAN .... Data Transmission Co. (SAUO)
DATRDA .... Defense Aid [*Lend-Lease*] Testing, Reconditioning, etc., of Defense Articles [*World War II*]
DATREC .... Data Recording (CET)
DATRI .... Direct Access to Reference Information (SAUS)
DATRI .... Division of AIDS Treatment Research Initiative (SAUS)
DATRIX .... Direct Access to Reference Information [*Xerox Corp.*]
Datron .... Datron Systems, Inc. [*Associated Press*] (SAG)
Datronics .... Datronics, Inc. (SAUO)
DATRs .... Design Approval Test Reports (SAUS)
DAtS .... Atonement Seminary of the Holy Ghost, Washington, DC [*Library symbol*] [*Library of Congress*] (LCLS)
DATS .... Data Accumulation and Transfer Sheet
DATS .... Data Accumulation/Transmittal Sheet (SAUS)
DATS .... Data Acquisition and Transmission System (MCD)
DA/TS .... Data Acquisition/Transmittal Sheet
DATS .... Data Automated Tower Simulator [*Army, Air Force*]
DATS .... Data Transmission System
DATS .... Despun Antenna Test Satellite [*Air Force*]
DATS .... Detailed Acceptance Test Specification (KSC)
DATS .... Developing Area Transportation System (SAUS)
DATS .... Digital Access Timeslot Selector (MCD)
DATS .... Digital Avionics Transmission System (SAUS)
DATS .... Digital Avionic Transmission System (IAA)
DATS .... Director, Auxiliary Territorial Service [*British military*] (DMA)
DATS .... Drill and Transfer System
DATS .... Dynamic Accuracy Test Set [*or System*]
DATS .... Dynamic Accuracy Test System (SAUS)
DATSA .... Depot Automatic Test System for Avionics (DWSG)
DATSC .... Department of the Army Training and Support Committee (AABC)
Datscp .... Datascope Corp. [*Associated Press*] (SAG)
DatSN .... Data Systems Network Corp. [*Associated Press*] (SAG)
DATST .... Datura stramonium [*Jimsonweed*]
DATT .... Defense Attache (AFM)
DATTA .... Diagnostic and Therapeutic Technology Assessment [*Medicine*]
DATTS .... Data Acquisition, Telecommand, and Tracking Station (UWER)
DATTS .... Data Acquisition, Telemetry and Tracking System (SAUS)
DATTS .... Data Acquisition, Tracking and Telecommand Station (SAUS)
DATU .... Direct-Access Test Unit [*Computer science*]
Datum .... Datum, Inc. [*Associated Press*] (SAG)
DATUM .... Dokumentations- und Ausbildungszentrum fuer Theorie und Methode der Regionalforschung [*Documentation and Training Center for Theory and Methods of Regional Research*] [*Germany*]
DATV .... Digital Advanced Television
DATV .... Digital Amateur Television (SAUS)
DATV .... Digital Assisted Television (VLIE)
DATV .... Digitally-Assisted Television (SAUS)
DAT-VR .... Differential Aptitude Test-Verbal Reasoning [*Psychology*] (EDAC)
DATX .... Data Translation [*NASDAQ symbol*] (TTSB)
DATX .... Data Translation, Inc. [*NASDAQ symbol*] (NQ)
DATZ .... Datsun [*Federal Railroad Administration identification code*]
DAU .... American University, Washington, DC [*Library symbol*] [*Library of Congress*] (LCLS)
DAU .... Daniels Canyon [*Utah*] [*Seismograph station code, US Geological Survey*] (SEIS)
DAU .... Daru [*Papua New Guinea*] [*Airport symbol*] (OAG)
DAU .... Data Access Unit [*Computer science*] (CIST)
DAU .... Data Acquisition Unit
DAU .... Data Adapter Unit
DAU .... Data Archive Utility (SAUS)
DAU .... Data Arithmetic Unit [*Computer science*]
dau .... Daughter (STED)
Dau .... Daughter (UWER)
DAU .... Daughter
DAU .... Deazauridine (DB)
DAU .... Declaration of Atlantic Unity [*Defunct*]
DAU .... Decryption Authentication Unit (ADWA)
DAU .... Defense Acquisition University [*DoD*] (RDA)
DAU .... Dental Auxiliary Utilization
DAU .... Digital Adapter Unit (MCD)
DAU .... Digital Amplifier Unit (DWSG)
DAU .... Digital Announcement Unit (SAUS)

DAU .... Digital Applique Unit (MCD)
DAU .... Disc Adapter Unit (SAUS)
DAU .... Display Adapter Unit (SAUS)
DAU .... Display Assembly Unit (MCD)
DAU .... Disposable Adsorbent Unit (UWER)
DAU .... Distributed Access Unit [*Computer science*]
DAU .... Drugs of Abuse in Urine [*Toxicology*]
DAUA .... Adrar/Touat [*Algeria*] [*ICAO location identifier*] (ICLI)
DAU & COH... Daughter and Co-Heir [*Genealogy*] (ROG)
DAU & H...... Daughter and Heir [*Genealogy*] (ROG)
DAUB .... Biskra [*Algeria*] [*ICAO location identifier*] (ICLI)
Dau Co Rep... Dauphin County Reports [*Pennsylvania*] [*A publication*] (DLA)
DAUD .... Director of Anti-U-Boat Division [*British*] [*World War II*]
D Au E .... Diploma in Automobile Engineering [*British*]
D Au E .... Doctor of Automobile Engineering
DAUE .... El Golea [*Algeria*] [*ICAO location identifier*] (ICLI)
D Au Eng ..... Doctor of Automobile Engineering
DAUG .... Ghardaia/Noumerate [*Algeria*] [*ICAO location identifier*] (ICLI)
Daughters of St Paul DSP... Pious Society of the Daughters of St Paul (SAUO)
DAUGR .... Daughter
DAUH .... Hassi-Messaoud/Oued Irara [*Algeria*] [*ICAO location identifier*] (ICLI)
DAUHS .... Daughters (ROG)
DAUI .... In Salah [*Algeria*] [*ICAO location identifier*] (ICLI)
DAUK .... Touggourt/Sidi Mahdi [*Algeria*] [*ICAO location identifier*] (ICLI)
DAU-L .... American University, Washington College of Law, Washington, DC [*Library symbol*] [*Library of Congress*] (LCLS)
DAUL .... Laghouat [*Algeria*] [*ICAO location identifier*] (ICLI)
Daun .... Daunorubicin [*Antineoplastic drug*] (DAVI)
DAUNO .... Daunorubicin (STED)
DAUO .... El Oued/Guemar [*Algeria*] [*ICAO location identifier*] (ICLI)
Dauph .... Dauphin County Reporter [*Pennsylvania*] [*A publication*] (DLA)
Dauph Co Rep... Dauphin County Reporter [*Pennsylvania*] [*A publication*] (DLA)
Dauphn .... Dauphin Deposit Corp. [*Associated Press*] (SAG)
DAUS .... Defense Against Underwater Swimmers [*Military*] (MCD)
DAusE .... Australian Embassy, Washington, DC [*Library symbol*] [*Library of Congress*] (LCLS)
DAUT .... Timimoun [*Algeria*] [*ICAO location identifier*] (ICLI)
DAUU .... Ouargla [*Algeria*] [*ICAO location identifier*] (ICLI)
DAUWE .... Director, Admiralty Underwater Weapons Establishment [*Navy*] [*British*]
DAUZ .... Zarzaitine/In Amenas [*Algeria*] [*ICAO location identifier*] (ICLI)
DAV .... Dapple Apple Virus (SAUS)
DAV .... Data above Voice [*Telecommunications*] (TEL)
DAV .... Data Available (MCD)
DAV .... Data Valid (IEEE)
DAV .... Davao [*Philippines*] [*Seismograph station code, US Geological Survey*] (SEIS)
DAV .... Davenport [*Diocesan abbreviation*] [*Iowa*] (TOCD)
DAV .... David [*Panama*] [*Airport symbol*] (OAG)
DAV .... David Minerals Ltd. [*Vancouver Stock Exchange symbol*]
Dav .... Davies' English Patent Cases [*1785-1816*] [*A publication*] (DLA)
Dav .... Davies' Irish King's Bench and Exchequer Reports [*1604-12*] [*A publication*] (DLA)
Dav .... Davies' United States District Court Reports [*Republished as 2 Ware*] [*A publication*] (DLA)
Dav .... Davis' Hawaiian Reports [*A publication*] (DLA)
Dav .... Davis' Reports [*Abridgment of Sir Edward Coke's Reports*] [*A publication*] (DLA)
Dav .... Davis' United States Supreme Court Reports [*A publication*] (DLA)
DAV .... Delayed Automatic Volume (IAA)
DAV .... Delta-Aminovaleric Acid [*Organic chemistry*]
DAV .... Diaminovaleric Acid [*Biochemistry*]
DAV .... Digital Analyzing Voltmeter [*Electricity*] (NITA)
DAV .... Digital Audio Video (VERA)
DAV .... Dirac Aviation [*France*] [*ICAO designator*] (FAAC)
DAV .... Direct Access Volume (SAUS)
DAV .... Disabled American Veterans (EA)
DAV .... Disabled Vehicle
DAV .... Domestic Abuse and Violence (MELL)
DAV .... Domestic Added Value (JAGO)
DAV .... Duck Adenovirus (DMAA)
Dav .... Reports of Irish Cases, by Sir John Davis [*1604-11*] [*A publication*] (DLA)
DAVA .... Defense Audiovisual Agency [*DoD*]
DAVA .... Diaminovaleric Acid
DAVA .... Directorate for Audiovisual Activities (SAUO)
DAVA .... Director [*or Directorate*] of Audiovisual Activities [*Army*]
DAVA .... Disabled American Veterans Auxiliary (EA)
DAVA .... DoD [*Department of Defense*] Audiovisual Activities
Dav & Dic Pr... Davidson and Dicey's Concise Precedents in Conveyancing [*A publication*] (DLA)
Dav & Kim IRL... Davidge and Kimball's Internal Revenue Laws [*A publication*] (DLA)
Dav & M...... Davison and Merivale's English Queen's Bench Reports [*A publication*] (DLA)
Dav & M (Eng)... Davison and Merivale's English Queen's Bench Reports [*A publication*] (DLA)
Dav & Mer... Davison and Merivale's English Queen's Bench Reports [*A publication*] (DLA)
DAV & OW... Defense Aid [*Lend-Lease*] Vessels and Other Watercraft [*World War II*]
DAV and RS... Director of Army Veterinary and Remount Services (SAUO)
Dav Ann .... Davies on Annuities [*A publication*] (DLA)
DAVAR .... Dealer-Authorized Value-Added Retailer (HGAA)
DAVB .... Digital Audio and Video Broadcasting (VLIE)
DAVB .... Digital Audio Video Broadcasting
DAVBADS .... Defense Audiovisual Booking and Distribution System
Dav B & B... Davidson on Banks and Banking [*Canada*] [*A publication*] (DLA)
Dav Bdg Soc... David on Building Societies [*A publication*] (DLA)
DAVC .... Delayed Automatic Volume Control
Dav Can .... Davis' English Church Canons [*A publication*] (DLA)
DAVCI .... David City, NE [*American Association of Railroads railroad junction routing code*]
Davco .... Davco Restaurants, Inc. [*Associated Press*] (SAG)
Dav Coke ...... Davis' Abridgment of Coke's Reports [*A publication*] (DLA)
Dav Conv ..... Davidson's Conveyancing [*A publication*] (DLA)
Dav Cr Cons... Davis' Criminal Law Consolidation Acts [*A publication*] (DLA)
Dav Cr Law... Davis' Criminal Law [*A publication*] (DLA)
DAVD .... Davidson & Associates, Inc. [*NASDAQ symbol*] (SAG)
Dav Dig .... Davis' Indiana Digest [*A publication*] (DLA)
DAVDS .... Data Acquisition and Visual Display System (NRCH)
Davdsn .... Davidson & Associates, Inc. [*Associated Press*] (SAG)
DAVE .... Data Addition, Verification, and Editing [*Lotus 1-2-3*]
DAVE .... Distributed Audio Video Environment (SAUO)
DAVE .... Do Anything Very Easily [*Computer science*] (PCM)
DAVE .... Famous Daves of America, Inc. [*NASDAQ symbol*] (SAG)
Dave&B .... Dave & Busters, Inc. [*Associated Press*] (SAG)
Davel .... Davel Communications Corp. [*Associated Press*] (SAG)
Dav Elec ...... Davis' Law of Registration and Election [*A publication*] (DLA)
DAVEN .... Davenport, IA [*American Association of Railroads railroad junction routing code*]
Dav Eng Ch Can... Davis' English Church Canons [*A publication*] (DLA)
DAVF .... Dural Arteriovenous Fistula [*Medicine*] (DMAA)
Dav Fr Merc Law... Davies on French Mercantile Law [*A publication*] (DLA)
Dav Fr Soc... Davis on Friendly Societies and Trade Unions [*A publication*] (DLA)
DAVFU .... Direct Access Vertical Format Unit (SAUS)
DAVH .... Dibromodulcitol, Adriamycin, Vincristine, Halotestin [*Fluxoymesterone*] [*Antineoplastic drug regimen*]
DAVI .... Department of Audiovisual Instruction [*of NEA*] [*Later, AECT*] (EA)
DAVI .... Dynamic Antiresonant Vibration Isolator
DAVIC .... Digital Audio Visual Council (DCOM)
DAVIC .... Digital Audio Visual Interoperability Council [*Switzerland*] (DDC)
DAVIC .... Digital Audio Visual Interoperatibility Council (SAUO)
DAVID .... Data Above Video System (NITA)
DAVID .... Defense of Airborne Vehicles in Depth
DAVID .... Digital and Video Interactive Device (EDAC)
DAVID .... Digital Audio/Video Interactive Decoder [*Computer science*]
DAVID .... Distributed Access View Integrated Database (ACAE)
DAVID .... Dynamic Audio Video Interactive Device [*Hearing aid*]
Davidson ..... Davidson's Reports [*92-111 North Carolina*] [*A publication*] (DLA)
DAVIE .... Department of the Army Vocabulary of Information Elements (AABC)
DAVIE .... Digital Alphanumeric Video Insertion Equipment [*Aviation*] (OA)
Davies .... Davies' Patent Cases [*1785-1816*] [*A publication*] (DLA)
Davies .... Davies' United States District Court Reports [*Republished as 2 Ware*] [*A publication*] (DLA)
Davies (Eng)... Davies' English Patent Cases [*1785-1816*] [*A publication*] (DLA)
Davies (US)... Davies' District Court Reports [*2 Ware*] [*United States*] [*A publication*] (DLA)
Dav Ind Dig... Davis' Indiana Digest [*A publication*] (DLA)
Dav Ind Soc... Davis on Industrial and Provident Societies [*A publication*] (DLA)
DAVIPP .... Department of the Army Visual Information Production Program
Davis .... Davis' Hawaiian Reports [*A publication*] (DLA)
Davis .... Davis' United States Supreme Court Reports [*A publication*] (DLA)
DAVIS .... Defense Audiovisual Information System [*DoD*]
DAVIS .... Defense Automated Visual Information System [*Database*] (IID)
DAVIS .... Digital-Audio-Visual Interactive Media Society (AGLO)
Davis Admin Law... Davis' Administrative Law Treatise [*A publication*] (DLA)
Davis Bdg... Davis' Law of Building Societies [*A publication*] (DLA)
Davis Bldg Soc... Davis' Law of Building Societies [*A publication*] (DLA)
Davis Cr Law... Davis' Criminal Law [*A publication*] (DLA)
Davis (JCB)... Davis' United States Supreme Court Reports [*A publication*] (DLA)
Davis Land Ct Dec (Mass)... Davis' Land Court Decisions (Massachusetts) [*1898-1908*] [*A publication*] (ILCA)
Davis L Ct Cas... Davis' Land Court Decisions [*1898-1908*] [*A publication*] (DLA)
Davis Mass Convey Hdbk... Davis' Massachusetts Conveyancer's Handbook [*A publication*] (DLA)
Davis Rep.... Davis' Hawaiian Reports [*A publication*] (DLA)
DAVIT .... Danish Verapamil Infarction Trial [*Medicine*] (DMAA)
DAVJC .... Davis Junction, IL [*American Association of Railroads railroad junction routing code*]
Dav Jus .... Davis' Justice of the Peace [*A publication*] (DLA)
DAVL .... Data Available - Low (MCD)
DAVL .... Davel Communications Corp. [*NASDAQ symbol*] (SAG)
DAVL .... Davel Communications Grp [*NASDAQ symbol*] (TTSB)
Dav Lab L.... Davis on the Labor Laws [*A publication*] (DLA)
Dav Land Ct Cas... Davis' Land Court Decisions [*1898-1908*] [*A publication*] (DLA)
DAVLB .... Desacetylvincaleukoblastine
DAVM .... Dural Arteriovenous Malformation [*Medicine*] (DMAA)
Dav M & S... Davis' Law of Master and Servant [*A publication*] (DLA)
D Av Med .... Diploma in Aviation Medicine [*British*]
DAvn .... Divisional Aviation (SAUO)
DAVNO .... Division Aviation Officer
DAVO .... Daylight Visual Observation (MCD)
DAVO .... Dynamic Analog of Vocal Tract
DAVO .... Dynamic Vocal (SAUS)
DAVOR .... Datenbank fuer Forderungsvorhaben [*Ongoing Research Project Data Bank*] [*Ministry for Research and Technology*] [*Information service or system*] (IID)
Davos Rev... Davoser Revue (SAUS)
Davox .... Davox Corp. [*Associated Press*] (SAG)

DAVP .... Deamino-Agrinine Vasopressin [*Medicine*] (DMAA)
DAVP .... Doctrinal Audio-Visual Program [*Military*]
Dav Pat Cas... Davies' English Patent Cases [*1785-1816*] [*A publication*] (DLA)
Dav P C .... Davies' English Patent Cases [*1785-1816*] [*A publication*] (DLA)
Dav Prec Conv... Davidson's Precedents in Conveyancing [*A publication*] (DLA)
Dav Prec Ind... Davis' Precedents of Indictment [*A publication*] (DLA)
DAVR .... Division of Adult and Vocational Research [*Office of Education*]
Dav Reg .... Davison on Registration and Elections [*A publication*] (DLA)
DAVRS .... Director of Army Veterinary and Remount Services [*British*]
DAVSA .... Defense Audiovisual Support Activity
DAVSC .... Defense Audiovisual Steering Committee (SAUO)
DAVSF .... Disabled American Veterans Service Foundation (SAUO)
DAVSS .... Doppler Acoustic Vortec Sensing System [*FAA*] (MCD)
DAVSS .... Doppler Acoustic Vortex Sensing Equipment [*Meteorology*] (DA)
Dav Tr Un... Davis' Trade Unions [*A publication*] (DLA)
Dav (US)... Davies' District Court Reports [*2 Ware*] [*United States*] [*A publication*] (DLA)
DavWht .... David White, Inc. [*Associated Press*] (SAG)
DavWtr .... Davis Water & Waste Industries, Inc. [*Associated Press*] (SAG)
DAVX .... Davox Corp. [*NASDAQ symbol*] (NQ)
Davys .... Davys' English King's Bench Reports [*A publication*] (DLA)
Davys (Eng)... Davys' English King's Bench Reports [*A publication*] (DLA)
DAW .... Data Address Word (ACAE)
DAW .... Daw [*New Britain*] [*Seismograph station code, US Geological Survey*] [*Closed*] (SEIS)
DAW .... Dawson College Library [*UTLAS symbol*]
DAW .... Days a Week [*Classified advertising*]
DAW .... Dedicated All-Weather aircraft (SAUS)
DAW .... Dienstanweisung [*Service regulations*] [*German military - World War II*]
DAW .... Directorate of Atomic Warfare
DAW .... Director of Naval Air Warfare [*British military*] (DMA)
DAW .... Director of Naval Air Warfare, Naval Staff (SAUO)
DAW .... Disk Address Word (SAUS)
DAW .... Dispense as Written [*Prescription cannot be filled using a generic equivalent*] [*Pharmacy*]
DAW .... Dry Active Waste [*Nuclear energy*] (NUCP)
DAW .... Dubai Air Wing (SAUS)
DAWA .... Danish American Women's Association [*Defunct*] (EA)
DAWA .... Department of Agriculture Western Australia (SAUO)
DAWA .... Diabetes Association of Western Australia
DAWA .... Divinatory Arts World Association [*See also AMAD*] [*Rillieux-La-Pape, France*] (EAIO)
Daw Ar .... Dawe on Arrest in Civil Cases [*A publication*] (DLA)
Daw Att .... Dawson's Attorney's [*A publication*] (DLA)
DAWCLM .... Data Automation Workload Control and Library Maintenance (SAUO)
Daw Cr & Pun... Dawe on Crimes and Punishments [*A publication*] (DLA)
DAWG .... Data Assimilation Working Group (SAUO)
DAWG .... Deployable Array Working Group (DWSG)
DAWG .... Directed Acyclic Word Graph (SAUS)
DAWG .... Dynamic Air War Game [*Military*]
DAWGS .... Difference Acoustic Wave Generation System (SEWL)
DAWH .... White [*David*], Inc. [*NASDAQ symbol*] (SAG)
DAWI .... Driving While Ability Impaired (SAUS)
DAWIA .... Defense Acquisition Workforce Improvement Act (RDA)
DAWID .... Device for Automatic Word Identification and Discrimination [*Computer science*]
DAWK .... Daw Technologies [*NASDAQ symbol*] (TTSB)
DAWK .... Daw Technologies, Inc. [*NASDAQ symbol*] (SAG)
DAWK .... Dove and Hawk [*One who took a moderate position on the Vietnam War*]
Daw Land Pr... Dawe's Epitome of the Law of Landed Property [*A publication*] (DLA)
DAWMR .... Disabled Association for Welfare of Mentally Retarded (SAUS)
DAWN .... Data Acquisition with a Network
DAWN .... Defense Attache Worldwide Network (SAUS)
DAWN .... Development Alternatives with Women for a New era (SAUS)
DAWN .... Digital Access to Wide Area Network [*Telemax Corp.*]
DAWN .... Digital Automatic Weather Network
DAWN .... Drug Abuse Warning Network [*Public Health Service*] [*Rockville, MD*]
DAWNS .... Design of Aircraft Wing Structures [*Computer program*]
DAWNS .... Digital Automatic Weather and NOTAM System (SAUO)
DAWN SET... Defence & Early Warning Network, Southeastern Turkey (SAUS)
Daw Or Leg... Dawson's Origo Legum [*A publication*] (DLA)
Daw Real Pr... Dawe's Real Estate Law [*A publication*] (DLA)
DAWS .... Defense Automated Warning System (ADWA)
DAWS .... Digital Advanced Wireless Service (SEWL)
DAWS .... Director of Army Welfare Services [*British*]
DAWS .... Diver Alternative Work System
DAWSN .... Dawson, GA [*American Association of Railroads railroad junction routing code*]
DawsnP .... Dawson Production Services, Inc. [*Associated Press*] (SAG)
Dawson .... Dawson Geophysical Co. [*Associated Press*] (SAG)
Dawson's Code... Dawson's Code of Civil Procedure [*Colorado*] [*A publication*] (DLA)
DAWT .... Diffuser Augmented Wind Turbine (SAUS)
DAWT .... Director of Naval Air Warfare and Flying Training [*British*]
Daw Tch .... Daw Technologies, Inc. [*Associated Press*] (SAG)
DAX .... Aalborg Airtaxi [*Denmark*] [*ICAO designator*] (FAAC)
DAX .... Data Acquisition and Control
DAX .... Data Exchange
DAX .... Deutscher Aktien Index [*German Index of Stock Prices*] [*A publication*] (BARN)
DAX .... Developper API Extension (SAUS)
DAX .... Digital Access Exchange (ACAE)
DAX .... Digital Art Exchange (SAUS)
DAXBT .... Deep Airborne Expendable Bathythermograph [*Naval Oceanographic Office*]
Dax Exch Pr... Dax's Exchequer Precedents [*A publication*] (DLA)
DAXI .... Digital Auxiliary Information Code [*Computer science*]
Dax Mast Pr... Dax's Practice in the Offices of the Masters [*A publication*] (DLA)
Daxor .... Daxor Corp. [*Associated Press*] (SAG)
DAXREP .... Department of the Army Command and Control Reporting System (AABC)
DAXWT .... Drive Axle Weight [*Automotive emissions*]
DAXX .... Diamond Alkali [*Private rail car owner code*]
DAY .... Benday [*Engraving*] (NTCM)
DAY .... Dayco Corp. (SAUO)
DAY .... Daylight (NTCM)
Day .... Day's Connecticut Reports [*A publication*] (DLA)
Day .... Day's Election Cases [*1892-93*] [*England*] [*A publication*] (DLA)
DAY .... Dayton [*Ohio*] [*Airport symbol*] (OAG)
DAY .... Dayton-James Cox Airport, DC (SAUO)
DAY .... Dayton Mining [*AMEX symbol*] (TTSB)
DAY .... Dayton Mining Corp. [*AMEX symbol*] (SAG)
DAY .... Dayton, OH [*Location identifier*] [*FAA*] (FAAL)
DAY .... Development Aid for You (SAUS)
DAY .... Dialysis and You [*of the DAY Association*] [*Defunct*] (EA)
DAY .... Dwarf Aster Yellows [*Plant pathology*]
DAY .... University of Dayton, Dayton, OH [*OCLC symbol*] (OCLC)
DAYCO .... Dayflex Co. (EFIS)
Dayco .... Dayton Rubber Company (SAUO)
Day(Conn) ... Connecticut Reports, by Day [*1802-13*] [*A publication*] (DLA)
Day Elect Cas... Day's Election Cases [*1892-93*] [*England*] [*A publication*] (DLA)
DAyM .... Doctor of Ayurvedic Medicine
DAYR .... Day Runner [*NASDAQ symbol*] (TTSB)
DAYR .... Day Runner, Inc. [*NASDAQ symbol*] (SAG)
DayRun .... Day Runner, Inc. [*Associated Press*] (SAG)
DAYS .... Depression and Anxiety in Youth Scale [*Test*] (TMMY)
Day's Ca .... Day's Connecticut Reports [*A publication*] (DLA)
Day's Ca Er... Day's Connecticut Reports [*A publication*] (DLA)
Day's Cases... Day's Connecticut Reports [*A publication*] (DLA)
Day's Conn Rep... Day's Connecticut Reports [*A publication*] (DLA)
Day Sur .... Dayton's Law of Surrogates [*A publication*] (DLA)
DaytHd .... Dayton-Hudson Corp. [*Associated Press*] (SAG)
DaytMn .... Dayton Mining Group [*Associated Press*] (SAG)
DAYTN .... Dayton, OH [*American Association of Railroads railroad junction routing code*]
Dayton .... Dayton Superior and Common Pleas Reports [*Ohio*] [*A publication*] (DLA)
Dayton .... University of Dayton. Intramural Law Review [*A publication*] (DLA)
DaytonMn .... Dayton Mining Corp. [*Associated Press*] (SAG)
Dayton (Ohio)... Dayton Reports (Ohio) [*A publication*] (DLA)
Dayton Rep... Dayton Reports [*Ohio*] [*A publication*] (DLA)
DAYTOP .... Drug Addicts Yield to Persuasion [*of Daytop Village, Inc., a narcotics-addiction rehabilitation facility*]
Dayt Sur .... Dayton's Law of Surrogates [*A publication*] (DLA)
Dayt Term Rep... Dayton Term Reports [*Ohio*] [*A publication*] (DLA)
DAZ .... Deleted in Azoospermia [*Genetics*]
DAZAS .... Digitally Adjustable Zero and Span (SAUS)
DAZD .... Double Anode Zener Diode
DAZZ .... Danceable Jazz [*In music group name Dazz Band*]
DB .... Bachelor of Divinity
Db .... Base Diameter [*Manufacturing term*]
DB .... Baudeloeque's Diameter [*External conjugate diameter of pelvis*] [*Obstetrics*] (DAVI)
DB .... Bomber [*Russian aircraft symbol*]
DB .... Brittany Air International [*ICAO designator*] (AD)
DB .... Daily Bulletin [*Military*] (AABC)
DB .... Daimler-Benz [*Name of German engine factory*] [*World War II*]
DB .... Damned Bad
DB .... Damp Basement (ADWA)
DB .... Dancing Baby
DB .... Dangling Bond [*Surface chemistry*]
DB .... Dark Blue (SAUS)
DB .... Data Band (SAUS)
DB .... Data Bank
DB .... Databank (SAUS)
DB .... Database [*Computer science*]
DB .... Data Base Data Buffer (SAUS)
DB .... Data Bit (VLIE)
DB .... Data Booth (SAUS)
DB .... Data Bus [*Computer science*] (MCD)
DB .... Data Byte (SAUS)
DB .... Datebook (WDMC)
DB .... Datenbank (SAUS)
DB .... Datenbestand (SAUS)
db .... Date of Birth (MELL)
DB .... Date of Birth
DB .... David Brown [*Prefix designation on Aston-Martin cars*] [*British*]
D-B .... Davis-Bacon Act (SAUS)
DB .... Davis-Bacon Act Decision [*DOL*] (AAGC)
DB .... Day Book [*Accounting*]
DB .... Dead Band
DB .... Dead Beat (SAUS)
DB .... Dead Body (IIA)
DB .... Deaf/Blind
D/B .... Deals and Batten (SAUS)
DB .... Deals and Battens [*Business term*]
D/B .... Deals and Boards (SAUS)

DB............... Debenture [*Type of bond*] [*Investment term*]
DB............... Debit
Db............... Decibel (DIPS)
DB............... Decibel (EAGT)
db............... Decibel (WDMC)
dB............... Decibel [*Symbol*] [*SI unit of sound level*]
DB............... Decimal Base (SAUS)
D/B............... Decimal to Binary [*Computer science*] (KSC)
DB............... Declining Balance (SAUS)
DB............... Deep Basing [*Underground placement of missiles*]
DB............... Deep Breath [*or Breathe*] [*Medicine*]
DB............... Defensive Back [*Football*]
DB............... Deficit Budget
DB............... Define Byte [*Computer science*] (PCM)
DB............... Defined Benefit retirement plan (SAUS)
DB............... Delayed Boiling (SAUS)
DB............... Delayed Broadcast [*Television*]
DB............... Demand Base (DNAB)
DB............... Dense Body [*Medicine*] (DB)
DB............... Dental Board (SAUO)
DB............... Dental Branch [*British military*] (DMA)
DB............... Departmentalized Billing
D/B............... Deposit Book
DB............... Depth Bomb [*Military*]
DB............... Der Betrieb-Data Bank [*Handelsblatt GmbH*] [*Germany*] [*Information service or system*] (IID)
DB............... Desert Biome [*Ecological biogeographic study*]
DB............... Design Baseline (NASA)
DB............... Design basis (SAUS)
DB............... Design Burst (KSC)
DB............... Detection Bit (SAUS)
DB............... Detective Bureau
DB............... Deutsche Bank (EFIS)
DB............... Deutsche Bibliothek [*Database producer*]
DB............... Deutsche Bundesbahn [*German Federal Railway*] [*Since 1949*] [*Germany*]
DB............... Developmental Bulletin (MCD)
DB............... Device Bay (SAUS)
DB............... Device Busy (VLIE)
DB............... Dextran Blue [*Organic chemistry*] (MAE)
db............... Diabetes (STED)
Db............... Diabetic [*Medicine*] (DAVI)
DB............... Diagonal Band (STED)
DB............... Dial Box (VLIE)
DB............... Diamant Bore (SAUS)
DB............... Diamond-Blackfan [*Disease*] [*Medicine*] (DB)
DB............... Dibromodifluoromethane [*Fire extinguishing agent*] [*Organic chemistry*] (ADA)
DB............... Dichlorophenoxybutyric Acid (SAUS)
DB............... Diconjugate Bilirubin [*Biochemistry*]
DB............... Dictionary of Biochemistry (SAUS)
DB............... Dictionary of the Bible [*A publication*] (BJA)
DB............... Dictionnaire de la Bible [*A publication*] (BJA)
DB............... Die Bahn [*Tourist card for rail travel*] [*Germany*]
D/B............... Die Bonding (AAEL)
DB............... Dielectric Breakdown (SAUS)
DB............... Diet Beverage
dB............... differential of susceptance (SAUS)
DB............... Diffused (SAUS)
DB............... Diffused Base
DB............... Diffusion Bonding
DB............... Digital Block [*Computer science*]
DB............... Digital Bridge (ACAE)
D/B............... Digital-to-Binary (NTCM)
DB............... Dignity Battalion [*Paramilitary group formed to bolster the regime of Panamanian strongman, Manuel Noriega*]
db............... diode block (SAUS)
DB............... Dip Brazing
DB............... direct-beam (SAUS)
DB............... Direct Bilirubin [*Medicine*] (DMAA)
DB............... Direct Billing
DB............... Direct Broadcast (CARB)
DB............... Direct Bronchoscopy [*Medicine*] (MELL)
DB............... Director Bomber [*Air Force*]
DB............... Dirty Book
DB............... Disability (MAE)
DB............... Disc Brakes [*Automotive engineering*]
DB............... Disciplinary Barracks
DB............... Dispersal Base [*Military*] (AFM)
DB............... Display Buffer [*Computer science*]
DB............... Display Bytes [*Pascal programming*] (UWER)
DB............... Distobuccal [*Dentistry*]
db............... distribution board (SAUS)
DB............... Distribution Box [*Technical drawings*]
DB............... Distributor Board (SAUS)
DB............... Dive Bank
DB............... Dive Bomb
DB............... Dive Bomber (SAUS)
DB............... Dive Bomber Aircraft
DB............... Dive Bombing (SAUS)
DB............... Divergent Beam (UWER)
DB............... Division Base [*Army*]
DB............... Division Burden (SAUS)
DB............... Division of Botany (SAUS)
Db............... Dobra [*Monetary unit*] (ODBW)
DB............... Dock Brief [*British*] (ADA)
D/B............... Documentary Bill (ADA)
DB............... Dodge Brothers (SAUS)
DB............... Dollinger-Bielschowsky [*Syndrome*] [*Medicine*] (DB)
DB............... Dolly Back [*Films, television, etc.*]
DB............... Domain Boundary (UWER)
DB............... Domesday Book [*Census-like record of the lands of England, 1085-86*]
db............... domestic boiler (SAUS)
DB............... Dominion Breweries (SAUS)
DB............... Doppler-Broadening (SAUS)
DB............... Double-Barreled (ADA)
DB............... Double Barrier (UWER)
DB............... Double Base [*Rocket propellant*] (MUSM)
db............... Double Bass (GROV)
db............... Doublebass
DB............... Double Bass [*Music*]
DB............... Double Bayonet (SAUS)
DB............... Double Bayonet Base [*Electronics*] (IAA)
DB............... Double Beam (UWER)
db............... Double Bed
DB............... Double Biased (CET)
DB............... Double Blind Study [*Medicine*] (DMAA)
DB............... Double Bond (UWER)
DB............... Double Bottom (MSA)
DB............... Double Bounce [*Electronics*] (IAA)
DB............... Double Braid (AAG)
DB............... Double Break
DB............... Double Breasted [*Clothing industry*]
DB............... Double-Ended Boiler [*Shipping*] (DS)
DB............... Doubler Biased (SAUS)
db............... Drab [*Philately*]
DB............... Draw Bar (ADA)
DB............... Drawbar Pull
DB............... Drifting Buoy (SAUS)
DB............... Drill Box (UWER)
DB............... Drilling Barge (SAUS)
DB............... Drive barrel (SAUS)
DB............... Driving Band (UWER)
DB............... Drop Box (LAIN)
DB............... Drop-By [*Brief social appearance*]
db............... drop by for a few minutes (SAUS)
DB............... Dry Basis
DB............... Dry Bath [*Instrumentation*]
DB............... Dry Bulb [*Thermometer, of a psychrometer*] [*Meteorology*]
DB............... Dry Bulk (SAUS)
Db............... dubhium (SAUS)
Db............... Dubnium [*Chemistry*] (MEC)
DB............... Duke of Buccleuch [*British*] (ROG)
DB............... Dumbbell (SAUS)
DB............... Dunnage Board
DB............... Duodenal Bulb (STED)
DB............... Duplex Bearing [*Military*]
DB............... Dutch Belted [*Rabbits*]
DB............... Dutch Borneo (SAUO)
DB............... Dynamic Backtracking (SAUS)
db............... dynamic brake (SAUS)
DB............... Dynamic Braking
DB............... Dynamic Breaking (SAUS)
DB2............... Database Two [*Computer science*] (HGAA)
DB2CS............... DataBase 2 Client/Server (SAUS)
DB2SDK............... DataBase 2 Software Development Toolkit (SAUS)
dBa............... Adjusted Decibel (AAEL)
DBA............... Air Alpha, Inc. [*ICAO designator*] (FAAC)
DBA............... Bar Association of the District of Columbia, Washington, DC [*Library symbol*] [*Library of Congress*] (LCLS)
DBA............... Danish Brotherhood in America (EA)
DBA............... Data Bank Access (SAUS)
DBA............... Database Access (SAUS)
DBA............... Data Base Administration (SAUS)
DBA............... Database Administration [*or Administrator*] [*Computer science*] (BUR)
DBA............... Data Base Administrator (SAUO)
DBA............... Database Agent (SAUS)
DBA............... Data Base Analyst (SAUO)
DBA............... Data Block Address (SAUS)
DBA............... Davis-Bacon Act [*1921*]
DBA............... Days before Anthesis [*Botany*]
DBA............... Daytime Broadcasters Association [*Defunct*] (EA)
dBa............... dB adjusted (SAUS)
DBA............... DBA Systems, Inc. [*Associated Press*] (SAG)
DBA............... Dead before Arrival [*Term used by some members of Congress to describe 1986 federal budget proposals*]
DBA............... Dealer Bank Association [*Washington, DC*] (EA)
DBA............... De Bonis Asportatis [*Trespass to Personalty*] [*Latin*] [*Legal term*] (DLA)
dBA............... Decibel Adjusted (SAUS)
dBA............... Decibel A-Weighted
dBA............... Decibel referred to one Anything (SAUS)
DBA............... Decibel Related to Amperage (SAUS)
dBA............... Decibels, Adjusted
dba............... Decibels on the A Scale
DBA............... Deep Battle Area (INF)
DBA............... Default Basis Accident [*Environmental science*] (COE)
DBA............... Default Bounding Accident [*Environmental science*] (COE)

DBA .... Defense Base Act
DBA .... Demonstration and Briefing Auditorium (ACAE)
DBA .... Dense Blasting Agent (MCD)
DBA .... Design Basis Accident [*Nuclear energy*]
DBA .... Design-basis accident (SAUS)
DBA .... Design-basis analysis (SAUS)
DBA .... Design Business Association (COBU)
DBA .... Diamond-Blackfan Anemia [*Medicine*] (DMAA)
DBA .... Dibasic Acid [*Waste from adipic acid production*]
DBA .... Dibenzanthracene [*Carcinogen*]
DBA .... Dibenzoylacetylene [*Organic chemistry*]
DBA .... Dibenzylamine [*Organic chemistry*]
DBA .... Diffused Base Alloy (SAUS)
DBA .... Digital Broadcasting Alliance (SAUS)
DBA .... Dihydro-Dimethyl-Benzopyranbutyric Acid
dba .... dihydro-dimethyl-benzopyran butyric acid (SAUS)
DBA .... Direct Budget Authority (ACAE)
DBA .... Directory of British Associations [*A publication*]
DBA .... Disabled Businesspersons Association (EA)
DBA .... Doctor of Business Administration
DBA .... Dog Bite Abscess (SPVS)
dba .... Doing Business As (EBF)
d/b/a .... Doing Business As (SHCU)
DBA .... Doing Business As [*Followed by company name*]
dba .... Doing Business At (SAUS)
DBA .... Dolichos biflorus Agglutinin [*Immunology*]
DBA .... Dominant Battlefield Awareness [*Military*] (SEWL)
DBA .... Donor-Bridge-Acceptor [*Physical chemistry*]
Dba .... Dubai (SAUS)
DBA .... Ducellier-Bendix-Air-Equipment (SAUS)
DBA .... Duct Burner Augmentation
DBA .... Duke Bar Association (SAUO)
DBA .... Dynamic Bandwidth Allocation [*Computer science*]
DBA .... Dynamic Boolean Algebra (SAUS)
dBaO .... dBa at zero transmission level (SAUS)
DBAAM .... Disk Buffer Area Access Method
DBAAU .... Dail Backup Auto Answer Unit (SAUS)
DBAAU .... Dial backup auto answer unit (SAUS)
DBAC .... Data Base Administration Center (SAUS)
DBAC .... DataBase Administration Center (SAUO)
DBAC .... Distributed Budget at Completion
DBA Conditions... Design Basis Accident Conditions (SAUS)
DBACS .... Database Administrator Control System
DBACS .... Drawback Accounting and Computing System [*Australia*]
DBACT .... Dental Board of the Australian Capital Territory
DB Ad .... Doctor of Business Administration
DB Adm .... Doctor of Business Administration
DBAE .... Dihydroxyborylaminoethyl [*Organic chemistry*]
DBAE .... Discipline-Based Art Education (SAUS)
DBAF .... Data Base Access Facility (SAUS)
DBAF .... Database Access Facility
DBAG .... Daimler-Benz AG [*Manufacturer of Mercedes-Benz cars and trucks*] [*German*]
DBA-GK .... Supreme Commands Long Range Bomber Arm (SAUS)
DBAH .... Diisobutylaluminum Hydride [*Also, DIBAH*] [*Organic chemistry*]
DBAM .... Data Base Access Method (SAUS)
DBAM .... Database Access Method
DBAM .... Database Access Module (NITA)
DBA/M .... Data Base Administrator/Manager [*Army*]
DB&B .... Deals, Battens and Boards (SAUS)
DB & C .... Deep Breathing and Coughing [*Medicine*] (DAVI)
DB&C .... Dwelling, Building, and Contents
DB&C .... Dwelling, Buildings, and Contents [*Insurance*]
DB & M .... Dunlop, Bell, and Murray's Scotch Court of Session Cases, Second Series [*1838-62*] [*A publication*] (DLA)
D (Bank) .... Data Bank
dBaO .... Circuit Noise Power Referred to Zero Transmission Level (SAUS)
DBAO .... Digital Block AND-OR (SAUS)
DBAO .... Digital Block And-Or Gate [*Computer science*] (IEEE)
DBAO Gate... Digital Block AND-OR Gate (SAUS)
DBAP .... Darien Book Aid Plan (SAUS)
DBAR .... Diamond Blackfan Anemia Registry (NRGU)
d/bar .... draw bar (SAUS)
DBAS .... Database Administration System (SAUO)
DBAS .... DBA Systems [*NASDAQ symbol*] (TTSB)
DBAS .... DBA Systems, Inc. [*NASDAQ symbol*] (NQ)
DBAS .... Delaware Business Advisory Service (SAUO)
DBAS .... Delmarva Business Advisory Service (SAUS)
DBAS .... Development Bank of American Samoa (SAUS)
DBAS .... Division of Biometry and Applied Sciences [*Department of Health and Human Services*] (GFGA)
DBASI .... Digital Bar and Altitude Setting Indicator (DWSG)
DBASI .... Digital Barometer Altimeter Setting Indicator [*Aviation*] (FAAC)
DBAT .... Data Base Access Facility (SAUS)
DBAT .... Dating Behavior Assessment Test (SAUS)
DBATS .... Dynamic Balancing and Tracking System (MCD)
DBA UK .... Ducellier-Bendix-Air-Equipment United Kingdom (SAUS)
DBAWG .... Database Administration Working Group [*CODASYL*]
DBB .... Bethune-Cookman College, Daytona Beach, FL [*OCLC symbol*] (OCLC)
DBB .... Deals, Battens, and Boards [*Business term*]
DBB .... Delayed Blowback (SAUS)
DBB .... Detector Back Bias
DBB .... Detector Balanced Bias
DBB .... Deutsche Bundesbahn [*German Federal Railway*] [*Since 1949*] [*Germany*]
DBB .... Dibenzoylbenzene [*Organic chemistry*]
DBB .... Dinner, Bed, and Breakfast
dbb .... dinner, bed, breakfast (SAUS)
DBB .... Director of the Bureau of Budget (SAUO)
dbb .... distance between bends (SAUS)
dBB .... Sound Level in Decibels as Determined on the B Scale of a Sound-Level Meter [*Industrial hygiene term*] (OHS)
DBB .... United States Office of Management and Budget, Washington, DC [*Library symbol*] [*Library of Congress*] (LCLS)
DBBA .... Danny Boy Breeders Association (EA)
DBBAL .... Debit Balance (SAUS)
DB Base .... Double-Bayonet Base (SAUS)
DBBB .... Cotonou/Cadjehoun [*Benin*] [*ICAO location identifier*] (ICLI)
DBBC .... Cana/Bohicon [*Benin*] [*ICAO location identifier*] (ICLI)
DBBD .... Djougou [*Benin*] [*ICAO location identifier*] (ICLI)
DBBK .... Kandi [*Benin*] [*ICAO location identifier*] (ICLI)
DBBL .... Decimal Base Binary Logic (SAUS)
DBBL .... Dismounted Battlespace Battle Lab [*Army*] (INF)
DBBN .... Natitingou [*Benin*] [*ICAO location identifier*] (ICLI)
DBBO .... Porga [*Benin*] [*ICAO location identifier*] (ICLI)
DBBOL .... Digital Building Block Oriented Language (SAUS)
DBBOR .... Digital Building Block Oriented (SAUS)
DBBP .... dibutyl butyl phosphate (SAUS)
DBBP .... Dibutyl Butylphosphonate [*Organic chemistry*]
DBBP .... Parakou [*Benin*] [*ICAO location identifier*] (ICLI)
DBBR .... Bimbereke [*Benin*] [*ICAO location identifier*] (ICLI)
DBBS .... Save [*Benin*] [*ICAO location identifier*] (ICLI)
DBBTZ .... Dibutylaminomethyl Benzotriazole (SAUS)
DBBV .... Cotonou [*Benin*] [*ICAO location identifier*] (ICLI)
dBC .... C-Scale sound level in decibels (SAUS)
DBC .... Dairy Bureau of Canada (FOTI)
DBC .... Darwin Bushwalking Club [*Australia*]
DBC .... Databank COMECON (SAUS)
DBC .... Data Base Computer (SAUS)
DBC .... Database Computer (MCD)
DBC .... Data Base Configuration [*Computer science*] (ECII)
DBC .... Database Container (SAUS)
DBC .... Data Base Controller (SAUS)
DBC .... Database Creation [*Computer science*] (TIMI)
DBC .... Data Bibliography Card
DBC .... Data Bridging Capability (SAUS)
DBC .... Data Bridging Capacity (SAUS)
DBC .... Data Bus Control [*Computer science*] (MCD)
DBC .... Data Bus Controller (SAUS)
DBC .... Data Bus Coupler [*Computer science*] (MCD)
DBC .... D. B. Communications, Inc. [*Bethesda, MD*] [*Telecommunications service*] (TSSD)
DBC .... Deaf Broadcasting Campaign [*British*]
DBC .... Decatur Baptist College [*Iowa*]
DBC .... Decibel Relative to the Carrier (SAUS)
dBc .... Decibels above One Carrier
dBc .... Decibels Referred to Carrier (IDOE)
DBC .... Decimal to Binary Conversion [*Computer science*] (IAA)
DBC .... Decimal-to-Binary Conversion (or Converter) (SAUS)
DBC .... Decomposed Block Code (IAA)
DBC .... Delamination, Bond, Crack [*Plastics technology*]
DBC .... Delaware Business Connection
DBC .... Demerara Bauxite Company (SAUO)
DBC .... Democratic Business Council (EA)
DBC .... Denied-Boarding Compensation [*Airlines*]
DBC .... Dense Barium Crown (SAUS)
DBC .... Deputy Brigade Commander [*Army*]
DBC .... Desert Bighorn Council (EA)
DBC .... Detective Book Club (SAUS)
DBC .... Developmental Biology Center [*Case Western Reserve University*] [*Research center*] (RCD)
DBC .... Device Bay Controller (SAUS)
DBC .... Diameter Bolt Circle [*Technical drawings*]
DBC .... Diamond Baseball Conference (PSS)
DBC .... Dibencozide [*Medicine*] (EDAA)
DBC .... Dictionnaire Biographique du Canada [*A publication*]
DBC .... Digital Battlefield Communications [*Military*] (SEWL)
DBC .... Digital-Binary Converter (SAUS)
DBC .... Digital Business Center (SAUS)
DBC .... Digital-to-Binary Converter [*Computer science*]
DBC .... Dimethylbenzimidazolylcobamide [*Biochemistry*]
DBC .... Direct Bond Copper [*Electronics*]
DBC .... Director of Barrack Construction [*British military*] (DMA)
DBC .... Display Blocks Configuration [*Computer science*] (ECII)
DBC .... District Base Commandant (SAUO)
DBC .... Disturbing Behavior Checklist [*Psychology*] (EDAC)
DBC .... Doctor of Beauty Culture
DBC .... Dodge Brothers Club (EA)
DBC .... Don Bosco College [*Newton, NJ*]
DBC .... Double Bottom Center [*of a ship*] (DS)
DBC .... Dries Below a Century [*Ink*] (DGA)
DBC .... Drums and Bugle Corps (SAUS)
dbc .... dry breast care (SAUS)
DBC .... Duck Book Communications Ltd. [*Vancouver Stock Exchange symbol*]
DBC .... Dye-Binding Capacity
DBC .... Dynamic-Breaking Contactor (SAUS)

dBC .... Sound Level in Decibels as Determined on the C Scale of a Sound-Level Meter [*Industrial hygiene term*] (OHS)
DBC .... United States Bureau of the Census, Suitland, MD [*Library symbol*] [*Library of Congress*] (LCLS)
DBCA .... Deaf-Blind Care Association [*Australia*]
DBCA .... Du Bois Clubs of America (SAUS)
DBCAA .... Dutch Belted Cattle Association of America (EA)
DBCATA .... Disposable Barrel Cartridge Area Target Ammunition [*Weapon launcher*]
DBCB .... Database Control Block
DBCC .... Data Broadcasting [*NASDAQ symbol*] (TTSB)
DBCC .... Data Broadcasting Corp. [*NASDAQ symbol*] (SAG)
DBCC .... Decrement, Test, Branch if Condition True [*Computer science*]
DBCC .... District Business Conduct Committee [*of the National Association of Securities Dealers*]
DBCCP .... Data Base Command and Control Processor (SAUS)
DBCCP .... Database Command and Control Processor (SAUS)
DBCD .... Differential Base Current Drift
DBCE .... Division of Building, Construction and Engineering (SAUO)
DBCES .... Dynamic Bandwidth Utilization in 64 kBit/s Time Slot Trunking over ATM Using Circuit Emulation Services (SAUS)
DBCI .... DB with Respect to a Circular Polarized Antenna (GFGA)
DBCL .... Database Command Language
dbcl .... dilute blood clot lysis (SAUS)
DBCL .... Dilute Blood Clot Lysis Method [*Hematology*] (MAE)
DB Clg .... Double-Headed Ceiling (DAC)
DBCLOB .... Double-Byte Character Large Object [*Computer science*] (VLIE)
DBCM .... De Beers Consolidated Mines (SAUS)
DBCO .... Digital Block Clock Oscillator [*Computer science*]
DBCO .... Dunbar Brothers Company (SAUO)
D/B Comd .... Deputy Base Commander (SAUO)
DB COMECON ... Databank Council for Mutual Economic Assistance (SAUO)
DBCP .... Data Bank Control Project (SAUS)
DBCP .... Data Buoy Cooperation Council [*Marine science*] (OSRA)
DBCP .... Data Buoy Cooperation Panel (SAUO)
DBCP .... Dibromochloropropane [*Pesticide*]
DBCP .... Double Bounce, Circularly Polarized
DBCR .... Data Base Change Request (SAUS)
DBCRC .... Defense Base Closure & Realignment Commission (SAUS)
DBCS .... Data Base Control System (SAUS)
DBCS .... Database Control System
DBCS .... Delivery Bar Code Sorter (SAUS)
DBCS .... Deterministic Bounded Cellular Space (PDAA)
DBCS .... Double-Byte Character Set [*Computer science*] (PCM)
DBCTG .... Data Base Concepts Task Group [*Computer science*] (VLIE)
DBCU .... Data Bus Control Unit [*Computer science*] (KSC)
DBD .... Air Niagara Express, Inc. [*Canada*] [*ICAO designator*] (FAAC)
DBD .... Dashboard
DBD .... dashboard/dash (SAUS)
DBD .... Database Definition (BYTE)
DBD .... Database Description [*Computer science*] (BUR)
DBD .... Data Base Descriptor (SAUS)
DBD .... Database Design Document
DBD .... Database Diagnostics (NITA)
DBD .... Database Directory (IAA)
DBD .... Data Base Document (SAUS)
DBD .... Death by Drugs (SAUS)
DBD .... Definite Brain Damage (MELL)
DBD .... Demokratische Bauernpartei Deutschlands [*Democratic Farmers' Party of Germany*] (PPW)
dbd .... Depth Below Datum (QUAC)
DBD .... Design-basis documents (SAUS)
DBD .... Detailed Budget Decision (AFM)
DBD .... Dibromodulcitol [*Mitolactol*] [*Antineoplastic drug*]
DBD .... Diebold, Inc. [*NYSE symbol*] (SPSG)
DBD .... Diesel Belt Drive (MSA)
DBD .... Diffuse Brain Damage (MELL)
DBD .... Digital Bargraph Display
DBD .... Digital Bearing Discrimination (SEWL)
DBD .... Digoxigenin Bisdigitoxoside [*Biochemistry*]
DBD .... Director of Bomb Disposal (SAUO)
DBD .... Director of Boom Defence (SAUO)
DBD .... Disruptive Behavior Disorder (MELL)
DBD .... Distribution Board (VLIE)
DBD .... DNA [*Deoxyribonucleic Acid*] Binding Domain [*Genetics*]
DBD .... Don't Bait Deer (GOBB)
DBD .... Double Backscattering Diffractometer Double-Base Diode (SAUS)
DBD .... Double-Base Diode
DBD .... Double Beta Decay
D Bd .... Drug Board (SAUS)
DBD .... dry-bulk density (SAUS)
DBDA .... Database Design Aid [*Computer science*] (BUR)
DBDA .... Design Basis Depressurization Accident [*Nuclear energy*] (NRCH)
DBDA .... Dibenzyldodecylamine (SAUS)
DBDB .... Digital Bathymetry Data Base (GEOI)
DB/DC .... Data Bank/Data Communication (SAUS)
DB/DC .... Database/Data Communications [*IBM Corp.*]
DBDC .... Dennis Brutus Defense Committee (EA)
DBDD .... Database Design Document (MCD)
DBDDD .... Division of Birth Defects and Developmental Disabilities (SAUO)
DBDE .... Data Base Design Evaluator [*Computer science*] (VLIE)
DBDG .... Distobuccal Developmental Groove [*Medicine*] (DMAA)
DBDGEN .... Data Base Description Generator [*Computer science*] (VLIE)
DBDK .... DataBlade Developer's Kit [*Computer science*] (HODG)
DBDL .... Database Definition Language
DB/DM .... Data Base/Data Management [*Computer science*] (VLIE)
DBDM .... Data Base Development Methodology [*Computer science*] (VLIE)
DBDMA .... Database Direct Memory Access (SAUS)
DBDNAME .... Data Base Description Name [*Computer science*] (VLIE)
DBDO .... Decabromodiphenyl Oxide (LDT)
DBDPO .... Decabromodiphenyl Oxide [*Flame retardant*] [*Organic chemistry*]
DBD Process ... Dry-Blanch-Dry Process (SAUS)
DBDQ .... Distributed Queue Dual Bus (SAUS)
DBDS .... Data Base Definition Subsystem (SAUS)
DBDS .... Data Base Directory Service [*Formerly, Data Base User Service*] [*Knowledge Industry Publications, Inc.*] [*Database*]
DBDS .... Duffel Bag Delivery System [*Military*] (INF)
DBDU .... Desert Battle Dress Uniform [*Military*] (INF)
DBDU .... Digital Bargraph Display Unit
DBE .... British Embassy, Washington, DC [*Library symbol*] [*Library of Congress*] (LCLS)
DBE .... Dame Commander of the [*Order of the*] British Empire
DBE .... Danube-Air Ltd. [*Hungary*] [*ICAO designator*] (FAAC)
DBE .... Databank Eurocontrol (SAUS)
DBE .... Database Engine (SAUS)
DBE .... Data Base Environment (SAUS)
DBE .... Database Environment [*Computer science*] (TIMI)
DBE .... Data Bus Element [*Computer science*]
DBE .... Data Bus Enable [*Computer science*]
DBE .... Daughters of the British Empire (SAUO)
DBE .... De Bene Esse [*Conditionally*] [*Latin*] [*Legal term*] (DLA)
DBE .... Deep Basin Experiment (SAUS)
DBE .... Deep Breathing Exercise [*Medicine*] (DAVI)
DBE .... Default Boundary Effect [*Environmental science*] (COE)
DBE .... Design Basis Earthquake [*Nuclear energy*] (NRCH)
DBE .... Design Basis Event [*Nuclear energy*] (NRCH)
DBE .... Develpoment Bank of Ethiopia (SAUS)
DBE .... Dibasic Ester [*DuPont organic solvent*]
DBE .... Dibenzyl Ether [*Organic chemistry*]
DBE .... Dibromoethane [*Same as EB, EDB*] [*Organic chemistry*]
DBE .... Digital-Based Exciter (SEWL)
DBE .... Disadvantaged Business Enterprise [*Business term*]
DBE .... Dispatch Payable Both Ends [*Shipping*] (DS)
DBE .... Division of Biological Effects [*Bureau of Radiological Effects*]
DBE .... Division of Biometry and Epidemiology [*Department of Health and Human Services*] (GFGA)
DBE .... Donor Bound Exciton [*Process*] [*Electronics*] (AAEL)
dbe .... doublebell euphonium (SAUS)
DBE .... Double Bond Equivalent [*Analytical chemistry*]
DBE .... Dribromoethane [*Medicine*] (EDAA)
DBE .... Droplet Burning Experiment (SAUS)
DBE .... Dynamic Balancing Equipment
DBE .... National Society, Daughters of the British Empire in the United States of America (EA)
DBEATS .... Dispatch Payable Both Ends All Time Saved [*Shipping*] (DS)
DBED .... Dibenzylethylenediamine [*Organic chemistry*]
DB Ed .... Doctor of Business Education
DbED .... Double b-adjacent Error Detecting (SAUS)
DBED .... Penicillin G Benzathine [*Pharmacology*] (DAVI)
DBED Code ... Double Byte Error Detecting Code (SAUS)
DBeer .... DeBeers Consolidated Mines [*Associated Press*] (SAG)
DBeer .... DeBeers Consolidated Mines Ltd. [*Associated Press*] (SAG)
DBEHO .... Deputy Borough Environmental Health Officer (HEAS)
DBELTS .... Dispatch Payable Both Ends on Laytime Saved [*Shipping*] (DS)
DBenz .... Daimler-Benz AG [*Associated Press*] (SAG)
DBEP .... Dibutoxyethyl Phthalate (EDCT)
DBER .... Division of Biomedical and Environmental Research [*Later, Office of Health and Environmental Research*] [*Department of Energy*]
DBER .... ERDA: Division of Biomedical and Environmental Research (SAUS)
DBES .... Date Based Export Scheme (SAUS)
dBEST .... Database of Expressed Sequence Tags [*Genetics*]
DBF .... Dashboard Fracture [*Medicine*] (MELL)
DBF .... Data Base Facility [*Computer science*] (CIST)
DBF .... Data Base File [*Military*] (AABC)
dbf .... Database File [*Computer science*] (VLIE)
DBF .... Data Base Format [*Computer science*] (CIST)
DBF .... DBase Format (SAUS)
dBf .... Decibel Femtowatt (SAUS)
dBf .... Decibels above 1 Femtowatt [*Electronics*] (MED)
DBF .... Demodulator Band Filter (MSA)
DBF .... Department of Banking and Finance (DEMM)
DBF .... Design Basis Fault [*Nuclear energy*] (NRCH)
DBF .... Design Basis Fire [*Environmental science*] (COE)
dbf .... design basis flood (SAUS)
DBF .... Digital Beam Former (SAUS)
DBF .... Digital Beam-Forming (PDAA)
DBF .... Digital Block Flop [*Computer science*] (IAA)
DBF .... Discrete Block Format (SAUS)
DBF .... Disturbed Bowel Function [*Medicine*] (MEDA)
DBF .... Divorced Black Female [*Classified advertising*] (CDAI)
DBF .... Domestic Bought Funds (EBF)
DBF .... Dominant Bubble Frequency [*Nuclear energy*] (NRCH)
DBF .... Double Book Form [*Photography*] (ROG)
DBF .... Dressing before Finish [*Manufacturing term*]
DBF .... Drexel Bond Fund (SAUO)
DBF .... Dual Bowl Feeder
DBF .... Dynamic Beam Focus (SAUS)
DBF .... Dynamic Beam Forming (SAUS)
DBFAS .... Digital Beam-Focusing Array Signal (SAUS)
DBFB .... Deep-Bed Filter and Blower Building [*Nuclear energy*] (NRCH)

DBFC .... David Birney Fan Club (EA)
DBFC .... Debby Boone Fan Club [*Defunct*] (EA)
DBFF .... Digital Block Flip-Flop [*Computer science*]
DBFL .... Design Basis Flood [*Environmental science*] (COE)
DBFL .... Design Basis Flooding Level [*Nuclear energy*] (NRCH)
DBFM .... Defensive Basic Flight Manoeuvres (SAUS)
DBFM .... Dun & Bradstreet France Marketing [*Dun & Bradstreet France*] [*Database*]
DBFN .... Database File Numbers (MCD)
DBFN .... Data Bus File Number (NASA)
DBFN .... Digital Beam Forming Network (ACAE)
DBFO .... Design, Build, Finance & Operate (WDAA)
DBFR .... Domestic Base Factor Report [*Army*]
DBFS .... Deep Bed Farming Society (EA)
DBFS .... Department of Bush Fire Services [*New South Wales*] [*Australia*]
DBFS .... Dull Black Finish Slate (KSC)
DBFU .... Digital Beam Former Unit (SAUS)
DBF Unit .... Digital Beam Former Unit (SAUS)
DBG .... Data Base Generation (COE)
DBG .... Database Generator
DBG .... Data Bus Group [*Computer science*] (MCD)
DBG .... David Ben-Gurion (BJA)
DBG .... Desert Botanical Garden [*An association*] (EA)
DBG .... Design Business Group [*British*] (DBA)
DBG .... Dextrose/Barbital/Gelatin [*Biochemistry*] (DB)
DBG .... Distance between Guides [*Construction term*] (MIST)
DBG .... Division of Basic Grants [*Office of Education*]
DBG .... Dyersburg Corp. [*NYSE symbol*] (SPSG)
DBGCM .... Dun & Bradstreet Guide to Canadian Manufacturers [*Information service or system*] (IID)
DBGEN .... Database Generation [*Computer science*]
DBGF .... Database Generation Facilities (SAUS)
DBGLS .... Development Bank of the Great Lake States [*Zaire*] (EAIO)
DBGMP .... Data Bus Generation and Maintenance Package [*Computer science*] (MCD)
DBGS .... Database Generation System (MCD)
DBGZ .... Debruce Grain [*Federal Railroad Administration identification code*]
DBH .... Data Base Handler (SAUS)
DBH .... Database Handler (SAUS)
DBH .... Days Before Harvest (SAUO)
DBH .... Days Before Heading (SAUO)
DBH .... Developmental Big Hydrofoil (SAUS)
DBH .... Development Big Hydrofoil [*Also, DEH*] (MCD)
DBH .... Diameter at Breast Height [*Of trees*]
dbh .... diameter breast high (SAUS)
DBH .... Diazabicycloheptene [*Organic chemistry*]
DBH .... Divisional Beachhead (SAUS)
DBH .... Division Beachhead [*Army*]
DBH .... Dopamine-a-Hydroxylase (SAUS)
DBH .... Dopamine Beta-Hydroxylase [*An enzyme*]
DBH .... Dopamine Hydroxylase (LDT)
DBH .... DTIC [*Dacarbazine*], BCNU , and Hydroxyurea [*Carmustine*] [*Antineoplastic drug regimen*] (DAVI)
DBHI .... DBH [*Dopamine Beta-Hydroxylase*] Index
DBHI .... Dopamine Beta-Hydroxylase Inhibitor (SAUS)
DBHN .... Dibutyl Hyponitrite [*Organic chemistry*]
DBHNT .... Detective Bureau Hostage Negotiating Team (SAUS)
DBHOB .... Diameter at Breast Height of a Tree [*Forestry*] (EES)
DBHOB .... Diameter at Breast Height over Bark
DBHP .... Drawbar Horsepower
DBHR .... Debrett's Business History Research [*British*]
DBHS .... Database Handling System
DBHS .... Dissolver Basket Handling System (SAUS)
DBHUB .... Diameter at Breast Height of a Tree Under the Bark [*Forestry*] (EES)
DBHUB .... Diameter at Breast Height under Bark
DBI .... Brookings Institution, Washington, DC [*Library symbol*] [*Library of Congress*] (LCLS)
DBI .... Data Based Interactive (SAUS)
DBI .... Data Base Index [*SDC Information Services*]
DBI .... Database Index (SAUS)
DBI .... Database Integrity (SAUS)
DBI .... Data Base Interactive [*Computer science*] (VLIE)
DBI .... Data Base Interface (SAUS)
DBI .... Database Interface (SAUS)
DBI .... Data Bus Interface (SAUS)
DBI .... Data Bus Interface Unit-Launch [*Computer science*] (MCD)
DBI .... Days Before Inoculation (SAUO)
DBI .... Decibels (Isotropic) (MCD)
dBI .... Decibels Referenced to Isotropic Gain (ADWA)
DBI .... Defense Budget Issue (COE)
DBI .... Design Basis Incident [*Nuclear energy*] (NRCH)
DBI .... Deutsches Bibliotheksinstitut [*German Library Institute*] [*Information service or system*] (IID)
DBI .... Development at Birth Index [*Medicine*]
DBI .... Diazepam Binding Inhibitor [*Biochemistry*]
DBI .... Dibi Resources, Inc. [*Vancouver Stock Exchange symbol*]
DBi .... Dictionary of the Bible [*A publication*] (BJA)
DBI .... Differential Bearing Indicator
DBI .... Dittler Brothers, Inc [*Printer of U.S. postage stamps*] (BARN)
DBI .... Diver Biographical Inventory [*Navy*]
DBI .... Diversified Builders Incorporated (SAUO)
DBI .... Double Byte Interleaved
DBI .... Double dyte Interleaved (SAUS)
Dbi .... Dubai (SAUS)
DBI .... Duct/Bundle interaction (SAUS)
DBI .... Duct/Bundle interference (SAUS)
DBI .... Dull but Important [*Wall Street Journal slang*] (WDMC)
DBI .... Phenethylbiguanide [*or Phenformin*] [*Pharmacology*] (DAVI)
DBIA .... Danish Brotherhood in America (EA)
DBIA .... Data Bus Interface Adapter [*Computer science*] (MCD)
DBIA .... Data Bus Isolation Amplifier [*Computer science*] (MCD)
DBIA .... Design-Build Institute of America (NTPA)
DBIA .... Digital Block Inverter Amplifier [*Computer science*]
DBIA .... Digital Block Inverting Amplifier (SAUS)
D Bib .... Douay Bible
DBIC .... Dibutylindolocarbazole [*Organic chemistry*]
D Bi Ch .... Doctor of Biochemistry
D Bi Chem .... Doctor of Biochemistry
DBiChem .... Doctor of Biological Chemistry (NADA)
DBID .... Data Bank and Information Division (SAUS)
DBIDI .... Database Imagery Derived Information (MCD)
DBIDI .... DoD DB of Imagery Derived Information (SAUS)
D Bi E .... Doctor of Biological Engineering
D Bi Eng .... Doctor of Biological Engineering
DBIFC .... David Birney International Fan Club (EA)
DBII .... Digital Biometrics [*NASDAQ symbol*] (TTSB)
DBII .... Digital Biometrics, Inc. [*NASDAQ symbol*] (SAG)
DBII .... Dunserve II [*Canada Systems Group*] [*Information service or system*] (IID)
DBIL .... Database Input Languages [*Computer science*]
DBIL .... Digital Block Inverting Amplifier (SAUS)
DBIL .... Direct Bilirubin [*Also, DBili*] [*Clinical chemistry*]
DBili .... Direct Bilirubin [*Also, DBIL*] [*Clinical chemistry*]
DBIN .... Data Bus In [*Computer science*]
DBIOC .... Database Input/Output Control
DB/IP .... Database/Information Provider (SAUS)
DBIP .... Discrimination by Identification of Pictures [*Psychiatry*] (DAVI)
D Bi Phy .... Doctor of Biological Physics
DBI-PT .... Long Acting (Prolonged Time) Capsule of DBI [*Medicine*] (EDAA)
DBIR .... Directory of Biotechnology Information/Resources [*American Type Culture Collection*] [*Information service or system*] (CRD)
DBIR .... Directory of Biotechnology Resources (ADWA)
DBIRD .... Department of Business, Industry, and Regional Development [*Queensland*] [*Australia*]
DBIS .... Data Base Information System (ACAE)
D Bi S .... Doctor of Biological Sciences
DBIS .... Document-Based Indexing System (ADA)
DBIS .... Dun & Bradstreet Information Services (SAUO)
D Bi Sc .... Doctor of Biological Sciences
DBIU .... Data Bus Interface Unit [*Computer science*] (MCD)
DBIU .... DFIRS Bus Interface Unit (SAUS)
DBIU .... Dominion Board of Insurance Underwriters [*Canada*] (ODBW)
DBJ .... Duchess of Brittany (Jersey) Ltd. [*British*] [*ICAO designator*] (FAAC)
DBJC .... Daytona Beach Junior College (SAUS)
dBj/s .... Decibels of jamming power over signal power (SAUS)
DBK .... Data Bank (AABC)
DBK .... Decarboxylase Base Moeller [*Biochemistry*] (DAVI)
dBK .... Decibels above One Kilowatt (DEN)
dB/K .... Decibels per degree Kelvin (SAUS)
DBK .... Diabetic Management [*Medicine*] (DAVI)
DBK .... Dibromomannitol [*or Mitobronitol*] [*Antineoplastic drug*] (DAVI)
dBK .... Dobeckmun (SAUS)
DBK .... Drawback [*Business term*]
DBK .... N.B. MacDonald Services Ltd. [*New Zealand*] [*FAA designator*] (FAAC)
dbk .... Debark (ODA)
DBKN .... Debarkation (SAUS)
DBL .... Damage before Launch (CINC)
DBL .... Dantrolene Blood Level [*Clinical chemistry*]
DBL .... Database Language [*Computer science*]
DBL .... Database List (CINC)
DBL .... Database Load [*Computer science*]
DBL .... Database Locking (SAUS)
DBL .... Data Block Length (SAUS)
DBL .... Data Bus Line (SAUS)
DBL .... Debarred Bidder's List
DBL .... Desbromoleptophos [*Insecticide*]
DBL .... Detail Billing (SAUS)
DBL .... Detailed Billing (SAUS)
DBL .... Deutsche Biologische Literatur [*German Biological Literature*] [*Also, DT BIOL*] [*Database*] [*Forschungsinstitut Senckenberg*] [*Information service or system*] (CRD)
DBL .... Diffusive Boundary Layer [*Physical chemistry*]
DBL .... Direct Broadcasting Ltd. [*British*]
DBL .... Direct Burdenable Labor (ACAE)
DBL .... Direct Business Lines [*Telecom Canada*] [*Telecommunications service*] (TSSD)
DBL .... Disability Benefit Law [*Insurance*]
DBL .... Displaced Business Loan [*Small Business Administration*]
DBL .... distance between lenses (SAUS)
DBL .... Double (AAG)
dbl .... Double (VRA)
Dbl .... Double
DBL .... Drawing Breakdown List
DBLACT .... Double-Acting (IAA)
dbl act .... double acting (SAUS)
DBLB .... Doubler (SAUS)
DBLB .... Double Room with Bath (TRID)
DBL CH .... Double Check [*Chess*] (GOBB)
DBLCN .... Double Contact Switch (IAA)

DBLCNT .... Double Contact (SAUS)
dbl cnt .... double contract (SAUS)
dbld .... doubled (SAUS)
dble .... Double (ADWA)
DBLE .... Double (ROG)
DBLE .... Double Eagle Pete & Mng [*NASDAQ symbol*] (TTSB)
DBLE .... Double Eagle Petroleum & Mining Co. [*NASDAQ symbol*] (NQ)
dble bsn ...... double bassoon (SAUS)
DblEgl .... Double Eagle Petroleum & Mining Co. [*Associated Press*] (SAG)
dbl eleph fol... double elephant folio-books about 50 inches high (SAUS)
Dbletree ...... Doubletree Corp. [*Associated Press*] (SAG)
DBLF .... Double Face
DBLIB .... Database Library (GART)
DBLN .... Double Room without Bath/Shower [*Travel industry*] (TVEL)
dB-loss .... Decibel-Loss (SAUS)
Dbl Pch .... Double Punch (SAUS)
DBLR .... Database Log/Restore Kit [*Computer science*] (TIMI)
DBLR .... Doubler (KSC)
DBLS .... Debarred Bidders List System [*GSA bulletin board*] [*Now EPL*] (AAGC)
DBLS .... Double Room with Shower [*Travel industry*] (TVEL)
DBLSA .... Defense Basic Logistics Support Analysis [*DoD*] (RDA)
DBL SKIN..... Double Skinned (RIMS)
DBLT .... Dynamic Back Link Technology [*Computer science*] (VERA)
DBLTG .... Database Language Task Group [*CODASYL*]
DBLW .... Double Wall
DBM .... Database Machine (SAUS)
DBM .... Database Management [*or Manager*] [*Computer science*] (NVT)
DBM .... Data Base Manager (COE)
DBM .... Database Marketing (GART)
DBM .... Database Model (SAUS)
DBM .... Data Base Module (SAUS)
DBM .... Data Buffer Module (IEEE)
DBM .... Data Bus Memory (SAUS)
DBM .... Data Bus Monitor [*Computer science*]
DBM .... Debra Markos [*Ethiopia*] [*Airport symbol*] (AD)
DBM .... Decarboxylase Base Moeller [*Medium*] [*Microbiology*]
dBM .... Decibel Based on Milliwatt (SAUS)
DBM .... Decibel Meter (KSC)
DBM .... Decibel referred to one Milliwatt (SAUS)
dBM .... Decibels above One Milliwatt
dBm .... Decibels Above or Below 1 Milliwatt (AEBE)
DBM .... Decibels below One Milliwatt
dBm .... Decibels per Meter (SAUS)
dBm .... Decibels per Milliwatt (ADWA)
DBM .... Decibels to One Milliwatt [*Unit of signal strength*] [*Telecommunications*] (NITA)
DBM .... Demineralized Bone Matrix [*Substance which, when surgically implanted, stimulates development of new bone*]
DBM .... Dense-Branching Morphology [*Physical chemistry*]
DBM .... Deputy Base Manager (MUGU)
DBM .... Deterministic Boltzmann Machine (SAUS)
DBM .... Diabetic Management [*Medicine*]
DBM .... Diazobenzyloxymethol [*Organic chemistry*]
DBM .... Dibenzyl Mercaptane (SAUS)
DBM .... Dibromomannitol [*Mitobronitol*] [*Antineoplastic drug*]
DBM .... Dibutylmagnesium [*Organic chemistry*]
DBM .... Dibutyl Maleate [*Organic chemistry*]
DBM .... Dielectric Breakdown Model [*Physics*]
DBM .... Diploma in Business Management (NADA)
DBM .... Direct Bombardment Mode (SAUS)
DBM .... Direct Branch Mode
D/BM .... Directorate of Ballistic Missiles
DBM .... Director Brent Manning (SAUO)
DBM .... Director of Bureau of Mines (SAUO)
DBM .... Division Battle Model (MCD)
DBM .... Division of Biology and Medicine (SAUS)
DBM .... Divorced Black Male [*Classified advertising*] (CDAI)
DBM .... Doctor of Business Management
DBM .... Double Balanced Mixer
DBM .... Drake Beam Morin, Inc.
DBM .... Dry Bulk Material
DBM .... Dual-Bed Monolith [*Automotive engineering*]
DBM .... Dynamic Balance Mechanism (ACAE)
DBM .... Dynamic Battle Management [*Military*] (SEWL)
dBm0 .... dBm at zero transmisson level (SAUS)
dBm0p .... Decibels above One Milliwatt, Referred to or Measured at a Point of Zero Transmission Level, Psophometrically Weighted
DB/M² .... Decibels above Milliwatt per Square Meter (MCD)
DBMA .... Dibenzylmethylamine [*Organic chemistry*]
DBMA .... Dibutylmalonic Acid [*Organic chemistry*]
DBMA .... Distillate Burner Manufacturers Association (EA)
DBMC .... Data Base Management Computer (SAUS)
DBMC .... Di-tert-butyl-m-cresol [*Organic chemistry*]
DBMC .... Di-tert-Butyl-Methylphenol (SAUS)
DBMCS .... Database Management and Control System (MCD)
DBME .... Data Base Management Element (SSD)
DBME .... Database Management Environment
DBME .... Database Managment Environment (SAUS)
dB meter ..... Decibel Meter [*Electronics*] (MED)
DB Mgr .... Database Manager (SAUS)
DBMI .... Data Base Management, Inc. (SAUS)
DBMI .... Data Base Management Incorporated (SAUO)
DBMI .... Data Base Management Intrinsic (SAUS)
dB/mi .... Decibels per mile (SAUS)
DBMI .... drill-bit motion indicator (SAUS)
DBMIB .... Dibromomethyl(isopropyl)benzoquinone [*Organic chemistry*]
DBMIRS .... Data Base Management and Information Retrieval System (SAUS)
DBML .... Data Base Management Language [*Computer science*] (CIST)
DBML .... Data Base Manipulation Language (SAUS)
DBML .... Data Base Markup Language (SAUS)
DBMM .... Database Mismanager (SAUS)
dBm my .... dbm per square meter (SAUS)
dBm my Mhz... dBm per square meter per megahertz (SAUS)
DBMN .... Data Base Management Network (SAUS)
DBMOP .... DBMO and Psophometrically Weighted for Telephony [*Telecommunications*] (NITA)
DBMOP .... DBMO and psophometrically weighted signal strength (SAUS)
DBMOPS ...... DBMO and Psophometrically Weighted for Sound Programme Transmission [*Telecommunications*] (NITA)
DBMOPS ...... DBMO and psophometrically weighted for sound transmission (SAUS)
DBMP .... Data Base Management Plan (SAUS)
DBM paper... Diazobenzyloxymethyl Paper [*Genetics*] (DOG)
DBMPS .... Directorate of Engineering and Maintenance Planning Standardization (SAUS)
DBMS .... Data Based Management Software (SAUS)
DBMS .... Database Management Software [*Computer science*]
DBMS .... Database Management System [*or Subsystem*] [*Computer science*] (BUR)
DBMS .... Data Base Managing System (SAUS)
DBMS .... Director of Base Medical Services
DBMS .... Director of Boom Defence and Marine Salvage (SAUO)
DBMS-OS ..... Data Based Management System/ Operating System (SAUS)
DBMS-OS ..... Data Base Management System/ Operating System (SAUS)
DBMSPSM... Database Management System Problem Specification Model
DBMT .... Displacement Bone-Marrow Transplantation (ODA)
DBmV .... Decibel-Millivolt (SAUS)
dBmV .... Decibels Relative to 1 Millivolt (VLIE)
DBMV .... Digital Block Multivibrator [*Computer science*]
DBMW .... Decibels above One Milliwatt (IAA)
DBN .... Database Network
DBN .... Data Bus Network [*Computer science*] (MCD)
DBN .... Day Beacon [*USCG*] (TAG)
DBN .... De Bilt [*Netherlands*] [*Later, WIT*] [*Geomagnetic observatory code*]
DBN .... De Bonis Non [*Of the Goods Not Yet Administered*]
DBN .... DEC Business Network (SAUS)
DBN .... Diazobicyclononene [*Organic chemistry*]
DBN .... Dibutylnitrosamine [*Also, DBNA*] [*Organic chemistry*]
DBN .... Doing Business, NOT (SAUS)
dbn .... Double Bassoon (GROV)
DBN .... Double Bassoon [*Music*]
DBN .... Dublin, GA [*Location identifier*] [*FAA*] (FAAL)
Dbn .... Durban [*South Africa*] (ILCA)
DBNA .... Dibutylnitrosamine [*Also, DBN*] [*Organic chemistry*]
DBNA .... Digital Block Noninverting Amplifier [*Computer science*]
DBNK .... Command Supply Management Data Bank (SAUS)
DBNK .... Data Bank
DBNMA .... Disposable Baby Napkin Manufacturers Association [*British*] (DBA)
DBNPA .... Dibromonitrilopropionamide [*Organic chemistry*]
DBNPG .... Dibromoneopentyl Glycol [*Flame retardant*] [*Organic chemistry*]
DBNPS .... Davis-Besse Nuclear Power Station (NRCH)
DBNS .... Digital Bombing-Navigation System
DBNS .... Doppler Bombing / Navigation System (SAUS)
DBNSW .... Dental Board of New South Wales [*Australia*]
DBNUSSE .... Dual Binary Non-Uniform Simple Surface Evaporation Model [*US Army Chemical Research, Development, and Engineering Center*] (RDA)
DBO .... Data Buoy Office [*National Oceanic and Atmospheric Administration*] (DNAB)
DBO .... Data Bus Out (VLIE)
DBO .... Dawn Battle Order [*British military*] (DMA)
DBO .... Dead Blackout (IIA)
DBO .... Design-Build-Operate (AAGC)
DBO .... Design By Objective (SAUS)
DBO .... Diploma of British Orthoptics
DBO .... Diploma of the British Orthoptic Board (SAUS)
DBO .... Directorate of Biological Operations [*Pine Bluff Arsenal, AR*]
dbo .... disassembled by owner (SAUS)
DBO .... Distobucco-Occlusal [*Dentistry*]
DBO .... Distobusso-Occlusal (SAUS)
DBO .... District Barrack Officer [*British military*] (DMA)
DBO .... District Building Officer [*National Health Service*] [*British*] (DI)
DBO .... Dopamine-Beta-Oxidase (SAUS)
dbo .... dreadful body odor (SAUS)
DBO .... Drop Build Out (SAUS)
DBO .... Drop Build-Out Capacitor [*Telecommunications*] (TEL)
DBO .... Dual Beam Oscilloscope
DBO .... Dubbo [*New South Wales*] [*Airport symbol*] (AD)
DBO .... Dubbo [*Australia*] [*Airport symbol*] (OAG)
DBO .... Royal Phoenix Airlines [*Nigeria*] [*ICAO designator*] (FAAC)
DBOA .... Delayed Breeder or Alternative [*Nuclear energy*] (NRCH)
db/ob .... diabetic obese [*Medicine*] (EDAA)
DBO Carrier... different bulk oil carrier (SAUS)
DBOE .... Data Base Operating Environment [*Computer science*] (VLIE)
DBOEP .... Di(butoxyethyl) Phthalate [*Organic chemistry*]
DBOF .... Defense Business Operating Fund [*Military*] (DOMA)
DBOF .... Defense Business Operations Fund (SAUS)
DBOF-T .... Defense Business Operations Fund-Transportation (COE)
DBOI .... Developmental Basis of Issue [*Military*] (AABC)

DBOM .... Design, Build, Operate, Maintain
DBOM .... Driver Block Output Mode [*Computer science*] (VLIE)
DBOMB .... Data Base Organisation and Maintenance Processor (SAUS)
D Bomb .... Depth Bomb (SAUS)
DBOMP .... Database Organization and Maintenance [*or Management*] Processor
DBOMP .... DOS Bill of Materials Processor [*Computer science*] (HODG)
DBON .... Driver Block Output Node (SAUS)
DBOO .... Design-Build-Own-Operate (AAGC)
DBOps .... Director of Bombing Operations [*Air Ministry*] [*British*] [*World War II*]
DBOS .... Data-Based Operating System (SAUS)
DBOS .... Data Base Operating System (SAUS)
DBOS .... Database Operating System (IAA)
DBOS .... Disc based operating system (SAUS)
DBOS .... Disk Based Operating System (SAUS)
DBOS .... Disk-Based Operating System [*Computer science*] (IEEE)
DBOT .... Design-Build-Operate-Transfer (AAGC)
DBot .... Dictionary of Botany (SAUS)
D Box .... Distribution Box (SAUS)
DBP .... Darband [*Pakistan*] [*Seismograph station code, US Geological Survey*] (SEIS)
DBP .... Database Preparation (SAUS)
DBP .... Data Base Processor (SAUS)
DBP .... Database Processor
DBP .... Database Publishing (SAUS)
DBP .... Data Buoy Project [*Navy*] [*Coast Guard*] (DNAB)
dBp .... Decibel/Picowatt (VLIE)
dBP .... Decibels above One Picowatt (DEN)
DBP .... Defense Budget Project (EA)
DBP .... Defensive Beating Posture (SAUS)
DBP .... Defined Benefit Plan [*Human resources*] (WYGK)
DBP .... Demineralized Bone Powder [*Medicine*]
DBP .... Dense Random-Packed (SAUS)
DBP .... Dense Random Packing (SAUS)
DBP .... Descent Battery Pack (KSC)
DBP .... Design Baseline Program (MCD)
dbp .... design-basis probability, diastolic blood pressure (SAUS)
DbP .... Dewan Bahasa Dan Pustaka, Kuala Lumpur, Malaysia [*Library symbol*] [*Library of Congress*] (LCLS)
DBP .... Diastolic Blood Pressure [*Medicine*]
DBP .... Dibromophenol [*Organic chemistry*]
DBP .... Dibutyl Phosphate [*Organic chemistry*] (NUCP)
DBP .... Dibutylphosphoric Acid [*Organic chemistry*]
DBP .... Dibutyl Phthalate [*Also, DBPh*] [*Organic chemistry*]
DBP .... Dibutylphthlatat (SAUS)
DBP .... Dichlorobenzophenone [*Also, DCBP*] [*Organic chemistry*]
DBP .... Dicionario Bibliografico Portugues [*A bibliographic publication*] [*Portugal*]
DBP .... Digital Recording Process (SAUS)
DBP .... Directional Radiated Power (SAUS)
DBP .... Disinfection By-Product [*Enviromental chemistry*]
DBP .... Distobuccopulpal [*Dentistry*]
DBP .... Distribution Requirements Planning (SAUS)
DBP .... Distribution Resource Planning (SAUS)
DBP .... Distributor Buy Price (TIMI)
DBP .... Diversity Best Practices
DBP .... Division of Beaches and Parks (SAUS)
DBP .... DNA [*Deoxyribonucleic Acid*]-Binding Protein [*Genetics*]
DBP .... Dohle Body Panmyelopathy [*Medicine*] (DMAA)
DBP .... Double Base Propellant (SAUS)
DBP .... Double-Base Propellant (AAG)
DBP .... Drawbar Pull
DBP .... Dried Bakery Products [*An animal feed*]
DBP .... Dynamic transaction Backout Program (SAUS)
DBPA .... Decanediylbis(phosphonic acid) [*Organic chemistry*]
DBP Absorption ... Dibutyl Phthalate Absorption (SAUS)
DB Part .... Double Beaded Partition (SAUS)
DBPB .... Design Basis Pipe Break [*Nuclear energy*] (NRCH)
DBPC .... Data Base Processing Center (SAUS)
DBPC .... Database Processing Center (SAUS)
DBPC .... Diteritary-Butyl-Para-Cresol (SAUS)
DBPC .... Di-tert-butyl-p-cresol [*Also, BHT*] [*Antioxidant*]
DBPC .... Ditertiary-Butyl-Para-Cresol (SAUS)
DB-PCB .... Data Base Program Communication Block [*Computer science*] (VLIE)
DBPCB .... Database Program Communication Block (SAUS)
DBPCl .... Dibenzylphosphoryl Chloride [*Organic chemistry*]
DBPE .... Days Before Panicle Emergence (SAUO)
DBPF .... Design-basis power failure (SAUS)
DBPF .... Divorced Black Professional Female (SAUO)
DBPh .... Dibutyl Phthalate [*Also, DBP*] [*Organic chemistry*]
DBPH .... Division for the Blind and Physically Handicapped [*Later, NLS*] [*Library of Congress*]
DBPH .... Divsion for the Blind and Physically Handicapped (SAUS)
DBPI .... Days Before Panicle Initiation (SAUO)
DBPL .... Database Programming Language (SAUS)
DBPM .... Divorced Black Professional Male (SAUO)
dB(PN) .... Perceived Noise Decibels (SAUS)
DBPO .... Data Buoy Project Office [*Later, NDBC*] [*National Oceanic and Atmospheric Administration*]
DBPPEE .... Diisobutylphenoxypolyethoxyethanol (DB)
DBPPWG .... Data Base Population Planning Working Group (GEOI)
DBPR .... DB - Panhard Registry (EA)
DBPR .... Department of Business and Professional Regulation (DEMM)
DBPROTOTYPE ... Data Base Prototype (SAUS)
DBPRS .... Database Performance Reporting System (TIMI)
DBPSL .... Document-Based Problem Statement Language (SAUS)
DBPW .... Decibels above One Picowatt (IAA)
DBPWG .... Data Base Population Working Group (GEOI)
DBQ .... Data Base for Quality [*Computer science*] (VLIE)
DBQ .... Database Query (MCD)
DBQ .... Debrisoquin [*Pharmacology*] (DAVI)
DBQ .... Decibels measured with a quasi-peak noise meter (SAUS)
DBQ .... Dental Board of Queensland [*Australia*]
DBQ .... [*The*] Dictionary of Biographical Quotation [*A publication*]
DBQ .... Dubuque [*Iowa*] [*Airport symbol*] (OAG)
DBQ .... Dubuque [*Iowa*] [*Seismograph station code, US Geological Survey*] (SEIS)
DBQS .... Data Base Query Subsystem (SAUS)
DBR .... Data Base Recovery [*Computer science*] (VLIE)
DBR .... Database Report (SAUS)
DBR .... Data Base Representation (SAUS)
DBR .... Data Base Retrieval (SAUS)
DBR .... Database Retrieval
DBR .... Data Block Reader [*Computer science*] (SAA)
DBR .... Data Buffer Register (ACAE)
DBR .... Data Bus Reguest (SAUS)
DBR .... David Brown Racing [*Prefix designation on Aston-Martin racing cars*] [*British*]
DBR .... Decibel Relative Level (SAUS)
dBr .... Decibels Above Reference Noise (MWOL)
D Br .... Defendants Brief (SAUS)
DBR .... Descriptor Base Register [*Computer science*] (IAA)
DBR .... Descriptor Oase Register (SAUS)
DBR .... Detail Billing Record (ACAE)
DBR .... Direct Bilirubin [*Also, DBIL, DBili*] [*Clinical chemistry*] (DAVI)
DBR .... Director of Biological Research [*Military*] [*British*]
DBR .... Disk, Balls, and Roller
DBR .... Disordered Breathing Rate [*Medicine*] (STED)
DBR .... Distorted Breathing Rate [*Medicine*] (DMAA)
DBR .... Distributed Bragg Reflector [*LASER*]
DBR .... Doppler Beam Rider (MCD)
DBR .... Double Book Rack (SAUS)
DBR .... Doubly Buffered Ringer [*Physiology*]
DBR .... Dubrovnik [*Yugoslavia*] [*Seismograph station code, US Geological Survey*] [*Closed*] (SEIS)
DBR .... Dynamic Base Relocation (VLIE)
DBR .... National Society, Daughters of the Barons of Runnemede (EA)
DBRAD .... Data Base Relational Application Dictionary [*IBM Corp.*] (CIST)
DBRAD .... Data Base Relational Application Directory [*Computer science*] (VERA)
dBrap .... Decibels Above Reference Acoustical Power (SAUS)
dBRAP .... Decibels above Reference Acoustic Power (DEN)
DBRB .... Data Base Review Board (ACAE)
DBRC .... Dairy Breeding Research Center [*Pennsylvania State University*] [*Research center*] (RCD)
DBRC .... Database Recovery Control [*Computer science*] (HGAA)
DBRC .... Data Base Recovery Control Feature [*Computer science*] (HODG)
DBRC .... Defense Base Closure and Realignment Commission [*Military*] (SEWL)
DBRE .... Association of American Railroads, Economics and Finance Department Library, Washington, DC [*Library symbol*] [*Library of Congress*] (LCLS)
DB Relay .... Double-Biased Relay (SAUS)
DBRF .... Dog Bite-Related Fatality
DBRI .... Danish Building Research Institute
DBRI .... Dysfunctional Behavior Rating Instrument [*Medicine*] (DMAA)
DBRITE .... Digital Bright RADAR Indicator Tower Equipment [*Air traffic control*]
DBRITE .... Digital Bright Radar Tower Equipment (SAUS)
DBRL .... DeBeers Research Laboratory (SAUS)
DBRL .... Dibrell Brothers, Inc. [*NASDAQ symbol*] (NQ)
DBRM .... Data Base Request Module [*Computer science*] (VERA)
DBRN .... Data Bank Release Notice (NASA)
dBRN .... Decibels above Reference Noise
DBRN .... Dress Barn [*NASDAQ symbol*] (SAG)
dBrnC .... Decibel Reference Noise C-Message Weighted [*Communications term*] (DCT)
dBRNC .... Decibels above Reference Noise, C-Message Weighted (IEEE)
dBrnCO .... Decibels Above Reference Noise, C-message weighted, at zero transmission level (SAUS)
DBRS .... De Beers Consolidated Mines [*NASDAQ symbol*] (NQ)
dbrs .... Debris (VRA)
DBRS .... Dominion Bond Rating Service (SAUS)
DBR Solution ... Doubly Buffered Ringer Solution (SAUS)
DBRSY .... DeBeers Cons Mns ADR [*NASDAQ symbol*] (TTSB)
DBRT .... Delay Before Repeat Time (CIST)
DBRT .... Direct Beam Refresh Terminal (SAUS)
DBRT .... Direct Beam Refresh Tube (SAUS)
DBRT .... Directed Beam Refresh Terminal (SAUS)
DBRT .... Double Barrier Resonant Tunneling (AAEL)
DB RTS .... Debenture Rights [*Investment term*] (MHDW)
DBRTS .... Double-Barrier Resonant Tunneling Structure [*Physics*]
DBS .... Danbus Resources, Inc. [*Vancouver Stock Exchange symbol*]
DBS .... Data Bank System (SAUS)
DBS .... Database Access Service [*Eastern Telecommunications Philippines, Inc.*] [*Information service or system*] (IID)
DBS .... Data Base Server (SAUS)
DBS .... Database Server (SAUS)
DBS .... Data Base Service (SAUS)
DBS .... Database Software (IAA)
DBS .... Data Base Specifications (GEOI)
DBS .... Data Base Supplier (NITA)

DBS .... Database Supplier (SAUS)
DBS .... Data Base System (SAUS)
DBS .... Database System (MCD)
DBS .... Data Bridging Service (SAUS)
DBS .... Days Before Seeding (SAUO)
DBS .... Deep Brain Stimulation [*Neurology*] (DAVI)
DBS .... Demand Broadcast System (SAUS)
DBS .... Demodulator BIT [*Binary Digit*] Synchronizer (MCD)
DBS .... Denis Browne Splint [*Orthopedics*] (DAVI)
dbs .... Depth Below Surface (QUAC)
DBS .... Despeciated Bovine Serum
DBS .... Diamond-Blackfan Syndrome [*Medicine*] (MELL)
DBS .... Dibromosalicil [*Germicide*]
DBS .... Dibromostyrene [*Organic chemistry*]
DBS .... Dibutyl Sebacate [*Organic chemistry*]
DBS .... Dibutyl Sulfate [*Organic chemistry*]
DBS .... Dictionary of Biological Sciences (SAUS)
DBS .... Dictionnaire de la Bible. Supplement [*A publication*] (BJA)
DBS .... Digital Beacon Simulator (MCD)
DBS .... Digital Book System (TELE)
DBS .... Diminshed Breath Sound [*Medicine*] (DAVI)
DBS .... Diploma in Buddhist Studies
DBS .... Direct Binary Search (SAUS)
DBS .... Direct Bonding System (STED)
DBS .... Direct Broadcast by Satellite (SAUS)
DBS .... Direct Broadcasting Satellite (SAUS)
DBS .... Direct Broadcasting System (SAUS)
DBS .... Direct Broadcast Satellite [*Television transmission system in which signals are transmitted by satellite directly to individual locations*] (MCD)
DBS .... Direct Broadcast Service (SAUO)
DBS .... Direct Broadcast System
DBS .... Discount Brokerage Services, Inc. (EFIS)
DBS .... Distressed British Seaman [*Granted a free passage home*]
DBS .... Distributor Buffer Storage (SAUS)
DBs .... Distributor Bus (SAUS)
DBS .... Division Battle Simulation
DBS .... Division of Biological Sciences (SAUO)
DBS .... Division of Biological Standards (STED)
DBS .... Division of Biologics Standards [*FDA*]
DBS .... Doctor at Bedside (MELL)
DBS .... Doctor of Business Science
DBS .... Dodecyl Benzene Sulfonate (SAUS)
DBS .... Dodecyl Benzenesulfonate [*Organic chemistry*]
DBS .... Dominion Bureau of Statistics [*Canada*]
DBS .... Dominion Bureau of Statistics, Ottawa (SAUO)
DBS .... Donkey Breed Society [*British*] (DBA)
DBS .... Doppler Beam Sampling [*Air navigation*]
DBS .... Doppler Beam Shaping
DBS .... Doppler Beam Sharpened (ACAE)
DBS .... Doppler Beam Sharpener
DBS .... Doppler Beam Sharpening (SAUS)
DBS .... Doppler beam swinging (SAUS)
DBS .... Doppler Broadening Spectroscopy
DBS .... Double Barrier Structure (SAUS)
DBS .... Double Bass [*Music*]
DBS .... Double Beam Spectrophotometer
DBS .... Double Blind Study
DBS .... Drama Book Specialists
DBS .... Draw Bead Simulator [*Metal Stamping*]
DBS .... Drill/Bolt/Screening Head (SAUS)
DBS .... Drinking Behavior Scale [*Test*]
DBS .... Drinking Behaviour Scale (SAUS)
DBS .... Dual-Beam-Sputtering [*Coating technology*]
DBS .... Dubois, ID [*Location identifier*] [*FAA*] (FAAL)
DBS .... Duck-Billed Speculum [*Medicine*] (MELL)
DBS .... Duplex Bus Selector (VERA)
DBS .... Duplication Buffer Storage (SAUS)
DBS .... Library Association of Slovenia (SAUO)
DBS .... United States National Bureau of Standards, Gaithersburg, MD [*Library symbol*] [*Library of Congress*] (LCLS)
DBS .... Physics Diffraction Back-Scattering (ODA)
DBSA .... Daniel B. Stephen Associates (SAUO)
DBSA .... Dawn Bible Students Association (EA)
DBSA .... Dental Board of South Australia
DBSA .... Direct Broadcast Satellite Association [*Later, SBCA*] (EA)
DBSC .... (Dibutylaminosulfenyl)methylcarbamate [*Insecticide*]
DBSC .... Digital Block Slave Clock [*Computer science*]
DBSC .... Direct Broadcast Satellite Corp. [*Bethesda, MD*] [*Telecommunications*] (TSSD)
DB Sc .... Doctor of Business Science
DBSC .... Dynamic Beam Spot Control (SAUS)
DBSD .... Double Backscattering Diffractometer (SAUS)
DBSE .... Distance between Shaft Ends [*Mechanical engineering*]
DBSFTT .... Doppler Beam Sharpening Fixed Target Tracking (ACAE)
DBSH .... Benzene- 1,3-Disulfohydrazide (SAUS)
DBSI .... Development Bank of the Solomon Islands (SAUS)
DBSI .... Direct Broadcasting System Inc. (SAUS)
DBSI .... Direct Broadcasting System Incorporated (SAUO)
DBSM .... Decibels per Square Meter
DBSO .... District Base Service Office
DBSO .... District Base Services Office (SAUO)
DB Sonnd Eng Mag... DB, The Sound Engineering Magazine (journ.) (SAUS)
DBSP .... Double Based Solid Propellant (SAUS)
DBSP .... Double-Base Solid Propellant (MSA)
DBSP .... Drug Bioequivalence Study Panel [*Medicine*] (EDAA)
dB SPL .... Decibel Sound Pressure Level (SAUS)
DB Sqn .... Day Bomber Squadron (SAUO)
dbsr .... double bed sitting room (SAUS)
DBSR .... Double Bituminous Surface Treatment (SAUS)
DBSR/SQL ... Database System Relational/Structured Query Language [*NCR Corp.*]
DBSS .... Direct Broadcast Satellite Service (SAUS)
DBSS .... Doppler Beam Sharpening Sector (ACAE)
DBSSG .... Database Systems Study Group (SAUS)
DBSSS .... Double Bowl Stainless Steel Sink [*Classified advertising*] (ADA)
DBST .... Digital Block Schmitt Trigger [*Computer science*]
DBST .... Double Bituminous Surface Treatment
DBST .... Double British Standard Time (IAA)
DBST .... Double British Summer Time
DBT .... Data Base Task Group (SAUO)
DBT .... Data Base Transmission (SAUS)
DBT .... Data Bulk Transmission (SAUS)
DBT .... David Brown Tractors (SAUS)
DBT .... Days Before Transplanting (SAUO)
DBT .... DBT Online [*NYSE symbol*] (SG)
DBT .... Deballasted Test Vehicle
DBT .... Debit (ROG)
DBT .... Debra Tabor [*Ethiopia*] [*Airport symbol*] (AD)
DBT .... Deck Board Tie Connector [*Simpson Strong-Tie*] [*Construction*]
DBT .... Department of Biotechnology [*Medicine*]
DBT .... Depleted Base Transistor (IAA)
DBT .... Design Basis Tornado [*Nuclear energy*] (NRCH)
dbt .... design-bassis tornado (SAUS)
DBT .... Dialectical Behavior Therapy [*Medicine*] (MELL)
DBT .... Dibenzothiophene [*Organic chemistry*]
DBT .... Dibenzoylthiamine (SAUS)
DBT .... Dibutyltin [*Organic chemistry*]
DBT .... Dictionary of Biblical Theology [*A publication*] (BJA)
DBT .... Diffused Base Transistor (SAUS)
DBT .... Disordered Breathing Time [*Medicine*] (STED)
DBT .... (Dodecylbenzyl)trimethylammonium Chloride [*Organic chemistry*]
DBT .... Doppler Bearing Tracker [*Military*] (CAAL)
DBT .... Double Base Transistor (SAUS)
DBT .... Double-Base Transistor
DBT .... Double-Blind Test [*Medicine*] (MELL)
DBT .... Double-Blind Trial [*Medicine*] (MELL)
Dbt .... Downbeat [*A publication*] (BRI)
DBT .... Dry Bed Training [*Medicine*]
DBT .... Dry Blood Temperature (MAE)
DBT .... Dry Bulb Temperature
DBT .... Dry Bulb Thermometer (SAUS)
DBT .... Ductile-to-Brittle Transition (SAUS)
DBT .... Dumbbell Tumor [*Medicine*] (MELL)
DBT .... Dual-Buffer Titration [*Chemistry*] (ODA)
DBTAC .... Pacific Disability and Business Technical Assistance Center (SAUO)
DB-TBS .... Deceptively Based-Terminal Defense System (ACAE)
DBTC .... Data Base Task Force (SAUS)
DBTC .... Data Base Task-force Contact (SAUS)
DBTC .... Department of Business, Technology, and Communications [*Northern Territory*] [*Australia*]
dbtd .... debited (SAUS)
dbtd .... Doubted (SAFN)
DBTDL .... Dibutylin Dilaurate (SAUS)
DBTDL .... Dibutyltin Dilaurate [*Organic chemistry*]
DBTF .... Doubtful (FAAC)
dbtfl .... doubtful (SAUS)
DBTG .... Data Base Task Group (SAUO)
DBTG .... Database Task Group [*CODASYL*]
dbtg .... debiting (SAUS)
DB Thermometer... Dry Bulb Thermometer (SAUS)
DBTL .... Dibutyltin Dilaurate [*Organic chemistry*]
DBTL .... Dibutyltinmlaurat (SAUS)
dbtl .... doubtful (SAUS)
DBTO .... DBT Online, Inc. [*NASDAQ symbol*] (SAG)
DBTO .... Di(benzotriazolyl)oxalate [*Organic chemistry*]
DBT Onl .... DBT Online, Inc. [*Associated Press*] (SAG)
DB Transistor... Diffused Base Transistor (SAUS)
DBTS .... Defence Blood Transfusion Services (SAUS)
DBTT .... Ductile-brittle transition temperature (SAUS)
dbtt .... ductile-brittle transmission temperature (SAUS)
DBTT .... Ductile to Brittle Transition Temperature
DBTT .... ductile-to-brittle transition temperatures (SAUS)
DBTT .... Ductile-to-Brittle Transition Transformation (SAUS)
DBTU .... dibutylthiourea (SAUS)
dbtw .... design-basis tornado and windstorm (SAUS)
DBU .... Days Before Use (ACAE)
dBU .... Decibel Unit
DBU .... Dial Back Up [*Communications term*] (DCT)
DBU .... Diaminobutyric acid (SAUS)
DBU .... Diazabicycloundecene [*Biochemistry*]
DBU .... Diazobicycloundecane [*Organic chemistry*]
DBU .... Digital Back-Up (SAUS)
DBU .... Digital Buffer Unit
DBU .... Disadvantaged Business Utilization (MCD)
DBU Acid ..... Diaminobutyric Acid (SAUS)
DBuE&B .... Double Bottom Under Engines and Boilers (SAUS)
dbuf .... dry-buffed (SAUS)
d-bug .... debugged (SAUS)
d-bug .... debugging (SAUS)

DBUK .... Dental Board of the United Kingdom (SAUO)
DBUR .... Data Bank Update Request (SAUS)
DBUR .... Databank Update Request (NASA)
DBUR .... Data Base Update Request (SAUS)
DBus .... Doctor of Business (ADA)
DBUS .... Dun & Bradstreet United States [*STM Systems Corp.*] [*Canada*] [*Information service or system*] (CRD)
DBUT .... Data Base Update Time (SAUS)
DBUT .... Database Update Time
DBV .... De Badande Vannerna [*Sweden*]
dBV .... Decibels above One Volt
dBV .... Decibels Relative to 1 Volt (VLIE)
DBV .... Dental Board of Victoria [*Australia*]
DBV .... Deutsches Bucherverzeichnis [*A bibliographic publication*] [*German*]
DBV .... Diagonal Bracked Vehicle (SAUS)
DBV .... Diagonal Braked Vehicle [*FAA*]
DBV .... Dieticians' Board of Victoria [*Australia*]
DBV .... Digital Broadcast Video (SAUS)
DBV .... Distributed Budget Variance (MCD)
DBV .... Doppler Broadening Velocity [*Spectroscopy*] (OA)
DBV .... DTIC [*Dacarbazine*], BCNU , and Vincristine [*Carmustine*] [*Antineoplastic drug regimen*] (DAVI)
DBV .... Dubrovnik [*Former Yugoslavia*] [*Airport symbol*] (OAG)
DBVF .... Dual Bowl Vibratory Feeder
DBW .... Data Bus Wire [*Computer science*] (MCD)
dBW .... Decibels above One Watt
dBW .... Decibels Referenced to One Watt (ADWA)
dBW .... Decibels Relative to 1 Watt (VLIE)
DBW .... Decibel-Watt (SAUS)
dBW .... Decibel Watts [*Ratio of the power received to the transmission of one watt, expressed in decibels*] [*Communications term*] (DCT)
DBW .... Design Bandwidth
DBW .... desirabie body weight (SAUS)
DBW .... Desirable Body Weight [*Medicine*]
DBW .... Differential Ballistic Wind
DBW .... Drive by Wire [*Electronics*] [*Automotive engineering*]
DBWC .... Differential Ballistic Wind Computer
DBWI .... Disc Brake Wear Indicator [*Automotive engineering*]
DBWO .... Differential Ballistic Wind Offset
DBWP .... Double Braid Weatherproof [*Wire insulation*] (IAA)
DBWR .... development boiling water reactor (SAUS)
DBWZ .... DB Western [*Federal Railroad Administration identification code*]
DBX .... Debugger for UNIX (SAUS)
DBX .... Decibel Above the Reference Coupling (MCD)
dBx .... Decibels Above Reference Coupling (SAUS)
dbx .... Decibels Expanded [*Initialism is name of electronics company and brand name of its products*]
dbx .... design-basis explosion (SAUS)
DBX .... Digital Branch Exchange (CIST)
DBX .... Digital Business Exchange (SAUS)
DBX .... Distributed Branch Exchange (SAUS)
DBX .... Dive Bombing Exercise (SAUS)
DBY .... Dalby [*Australia*] [*Airport symbol*] (OAG)
DBZ .... Dibenzamine [*Pharmacology*] (DAVI)
DBZ .... Driscoll Brothers [*Federal Railroad Administration identification code*]
DC .... Cancrizans of the Duration series (SAUS)
DC .... Christian Democracy (Spain) [*Political party*] (PSAP)
DC .... Christian Democratic Party (Italy) [*Political party*] (PSAP)
DC .... Committee for Documentary and Legal Problems (SAUS)
DC .... Company of the Daughters of Charity of St Vincent-de-Paul (SAUO)
DC .... Complete Depolarization
Dc .... Critical Dilution Rate [*Medicine*] (EDAA)
DC .... Cuba [*License plate code assigned to foreign diplomats in the US*]
DC .... Current Loop [*Communications term*] (DCT)
dc .... Da Capo [*From the Head*] [*Italian*] [*Music*] (WDAA)
DC .... Da Capo [*Return to Beginning*] [*Music*]
DC .... Daily Census [*Medicine*]
DC .... Dairy Cattle (SAUS)
DC .... Dairylea Cooperative (EA)
DC .... Daisy Chains [*Oil industry term*]
DC .... "Daisy Cutter" [*A type of World War II bomb*]
DC .... Damage Control [*or Controlman*] [*Navy*]
DC .... Dana College (SAUS)
DC .... Dana Corporation (SAUO)
dc .... Daniel Construction Company, Inc. (SAUO)
DC .... DANSE Coalition (EA)
DC .... Danube Commission (EA)
DC .... Dartmouth College (SAUO)
DC .... Data Call
DC .... Data Camera
DC .... Data Capacity (SAUS)
DC .... Data Card (SAUS)
DC .... Data Carrier (SAUS)
DC .... Data Cartridge
DC .... Data Cassette (ELAL)
DC .... Data Cell [*Computer science*]
DC .... Data Center (EA)
DC .... Data Center (or Centre) (SAUS)
DC .... Data Channel [*Computer science*]
DC .... Data Check (BUR)
DC .... Data Classifier (IEEE)
DC .... Data Code
DC .... Data Collection
DC .... Data Communication [*Computer science*] (BUR)
DC .... Datacommunication (SAUS)
DC .... Data Communications (SAUS)
DC .... Data Compatible (SAUS)
DC .... Data Compression [*Modem status information light*] [*Computer science*] (IGQR)
DC .... Data Concentrator [*Computer science*] (BUR)
DC .... Data Content (SAUS)
DC .... Data Control (AFM)
DC .... Data Controlled (SAUS)
DC .... Data Controller
D/C .... Data Conversion [*Computer science*] (KSC)
DC .... Data Coordinator (MCD)
DC .... Data Counter [*Computer science*] (IAA)
DC .... Data Courier, Inc. (SAUO)
DC .... Datametrics Corp. [*AMEX symbol*] (SPSG)
DC .... Daughters of Charity [*Australia*]
DC .... Daughters of Charity of St. Vincent de Paul [*Roman Catholic religious order*]
DC .... Daughters of the Cincinnati (EA)
DC .... Daughters of the Cross [*Roman Catholic religious order*]
DC .... Daunomycin, Cytarabine [*Antineoplastic drug*] (CDI)
DC .... Daunorubicin and Cytarabine (STED)
DC .... Davidson College (SAUS)
DC .... Davy Crockett [*A tactical atomic weapon*] [*Army*]
DC .... Dawson's Creek [*Television program title*]
DC .... Dayco Corporation (SAUO)
DC .... Dead Center
DC .... Dead Center (or Centre) (SAUS)
DC .... Death Cell (SAUS)
DC .... Death Certificate
DC .... Debit Collection
DC .... Decade Counter
DC .... Decagram [*Unit of issue*] [*Military*] (DNAB)
DC .... De Candolle [*Botanist, 1778-1841*] (ROG)
DC .... Decertify
DC .... Decimal Classification
DC .... Decimal Code (SAUS)
DC .... Decimal Counter (SAUS)
DC .... Deck Cargo
DC .... Deck Count
DC .... Deck Court
DC .... Decoder Connector
DC .... Decontamination
DC .... Decorators Club (EA)
DC .... Decrease
DC .... Dedicated Circuit (SAUS)
DC .... Deep Compartment [*Pharmacokinetics*] (DB)
DC .... Deep Discount Issue [*In bond listings of newspapers*] [*Investment term*]
DC .... Defect Control (SAUS)
DC .... Defence Committee (SAUO)
DC .... Defence Council (SAUO)
DC .... Defense Command (SAUO)
DC .... Defense Committee (NATG)
DC .... Defense Counseil (SAUO)
DC .... Defense Counsel
DC .... Defiance College (SAUS)
DC .... Define Constant (MDG)
DC .... Define Contrast (SAUS)
DC .... Defined Contribution (SAUS)
DC .... Definition Card (SAUS)
DC .... Definition of a Constant (SAUS)
DC .... Definitive Constract (SAUS)
DC .... Definitive Contract
DC .... Deflector Coil (SAUS)
DC .... Degenerating Cell (STED)
DC .... Degree of Conjugation [*Analytical biochemistry*]
DC .... Degrees Celsius (KSC)
DC .... Deiters' Cell [*Anatomy*]
DC .... Delay Cable (SAUS)
DC .... Delay Code
DC .... Delayed Coker [*Chemical engineering*]
DC .... Deleted Unpostable from Cards [*IRS*]
DC .... Delivered Capacity
D/C .... Delivery Clause (FOTI)
DC .... Delray Connecting Railroad Co. [*AAR code*]
DC .... Delta Clipper
DC .... Demobilization Centre (SAUO)
DC .... Democracia Cristiana [*Christian Democratic Party*] [*Paraguay*] [*Political party*] (PD)
DC .... Democratic Arrangement (Dominican Rep.) [*Political party*] (PSAP)
DC .... Democratic Convergence (Guatemala) [*Political party*] (PSAP)
DC .... Dendritic Cell [*Cytology*]
DC .... Dense Concrete (SAUS)
DC .... Density Controller
DC .... Dental Caries (MELL)
DC .... Dental Corp. (SAUS)
DC .... Dental Corporation (SAUO)
DC .... Dental Corps [*Navy*]
D-C .... Denver-Chicago (SAUS)
DC .... Deoxycholate [*Biochemistry*] (MAE)
DC .... Deoxycytidine (SAUS)
dC .... Deoxycytidylate [*Biochemistry*]
DC .... Departmental Circulars
DC .... Departmental Cluster (SAUS)
DC .... Departmental Computing

DC Department of Command (SAUO)
DC Department of Commerce
DC Department of Commerces (SAUS)
DC Dependent Coverage Rider [*Health insurance*] (GHCT)
DC Depolarization Current (SAUS)
DC Deposited Carbon
DC Depth Charge [*Aerial*] [*Navy*]
DC Deputy Captain [*Military*] [*British*] (ROG)
DC Deputy Charge (SAUS)
DC Deputy Chief
DC Deputy Clerk (GEAB)
DC Deputy Commandant
DC Deputy [*Police*] Commissioner (LAIN)
DC Deputy Commissioner [*British*] (ADA)
DC Deputy Consul
DC Deputy Counsel [*British*] (ADA)
DC Dermoid Cyst [*Medicine*] (MELL)
DC Descending Colon [*Medicine*] (STED)
DC Descriptor Code [*Database terminology*] (NITA)
DC Design calculations (SAUS)
DC Design Change (AAG)
DC Design Concept
D/C Design/construct (SAUS)
DC Design Contractor (NRCH)
DC Design Cooperative [*British*]
DC Design Council [*British*] (DI)
DC Designs for Change [*An association*] (EA)
DC Desk Calculator (SAUS)
DC Desk Checking (IAA)
DC Destination Code (SAUS)
DC Destruct Charge
DC Detail Condition (MDG)
DC Detection Coil [*Magneto-encephalography*]
DC Detective Constable [*Scotland Yard*]
DC Detention Center (WDAA)
D/C Detention Clause [*Insurance*]
DC Deterioration Control
DC Detroit Cooperative Cataloging Center (SAUS)
DC Deuterocanonicals
DC Deutz Corporation (SAUO)
DC Developed Country
DC Developing Countries (FOTI)
DC Developing Country
DC Development Center (MCD)
DC Development Centre (SAUS)
DC Development Characteristic
DC Development Commission [*British*]
DC Development Committee
DC Development Costs
DC Deviation Clause [*Business term*]
DC Device Clear (SAUS)
DC Device Code (SAUS)
DC Device Configuration (SAUS)
DC Device Context (PCM)
DC Device Control
DC Device Controller (ELAL)
DC Device Coordinate
DC Device Coordinates (SAUS)
DC deviee control (SAUS)
DC Dewey Decimal Classification [*Also, DDC*]
DC Diagnostic Center
DC Diagnostic Center (or Centre) (SAUO)
DC Diagnostic Centre (SAUS)
DC Diagnostic Code [*Medicine*]
DC Diagonal Conjugate [*Medicine*]
D/C Diarrhea/Constipation (MEDA)
dc Dick Cavett (SAUS)
DC Dickinson College (SAUS)
DC Dictaphone Corporation (SAUO)
DC Dielectric Constant
dc diesel car (SAUS)
DC Dietary Chaos (MELL)
DC Dieticians of Canada (FOTI)
DC Difference, Center
DC Different Coupling [*Music*]
DC Differential Calculus (AAG)
DC Differential Correction
DC Differential Cross Talk (IAA)
DC Differential Crosstalk (SAUS)
DC Differentiated Cell (DB)
DC Difficult Communication
DC Digestibility Coefficient (OA)
DC Digital Card (SAUS)
DC Digital Clock
DC Digital Clubbing (MELL)
DC Digital Code (AAG)
DC Digital Communication (SAUS)
DC Digital Comparator
DC Digital Computation (SAUS)
DC Digital Computer
DC Digital Computing (SAUS)
DC Digital Control (IAA)
DC Digital Controller (SAUS)
DC Digital Counter (SAUS)
DC digitale Steuerung (SAUS)
DC Digit Control (SAUS)
DC Digit Copying [*Psychiatry*]
DC Dihydrocodeine [*An analgesic*]
DC Dilatation Catheter [*Medicine*] (MELL)
DC Dilated Cardiomyopathy [*Cardiology*]
DC Dilute complex (SAUS)
DC Dimensional Coordination (SAUS)
DC Dinero Contante [*Cash*] [*Spanish*] [*Business term*]
DC Diners Club (SAUO)
DC Diners Club, Inc. (ADA)
DC Dining Car (SAUS)
DC Diode Cathode (IAA)
DC Dip Coating
DC Diphenylarsine Cyanide
DC Diphenylarsinzyanid (SAUS)
DC Diphenylcyanoarsine [*A war gas*]
DC Diplomatic Corps
DC Direct and Consensual [*Neurology and ophthalmology*] (DAVI)
DC Direct Chill (HEAS)
DC Direct Code (SAUS)
DC Direct Command
DC Direct Connection [*Telecommunications*] (OA)
DC Direct Control (IAA)
DC Direct Coombs [*Test*] [*Medicine*] (MELL)
DC Direct Cost
DC Direct Costs (MARI)
DC Direct Coupled
dc Direct Coupling (SAUS)
dc direct credit (SAUS)
dc Direct Current (IDOE)
DC Direct Current
DC Direct Cycle
DC Directed Change (MCD)
DC Directional Control [*Rocket*] (RDA)
DC Directional Coupler
DC Direction Center [*SAGE*] [*RADAR*]
DC Direction Center (or Centre) (SAUO)
DC Direction Commerciale (SAUS)
DC Direction Cosine (KSC)
DC Direction Cycle (MDG)
DC Directives Control [*Employment and Training Administration*] [*Department of Labor*]
DC Direct Operating Cost (DA)
DC Director Deputy of Communications-Electronics (AFIT)
DC Director of Ceremonies [*Freemasonry*] (ROG)
DC Directory Clearinghouse [*Defunct*] (EA)
DC Dirt [*or Dust*] Collector (AAG)
DC Disabled Child [*Title XVI*] [*Social Security Administration*] (OICC)
DC Disarmament Commission [*Also, DC (UN), UNDC*]
DC Disarmament Conference (ACAE)
DC Disaster Control (AAG)
DC Disc Ceramic (SAUS)
DC Disc Controller [*Computer science*] (HGAA)
d/c Discharge (ADWA)
DC Discharge [*or Discharged*]
DC Discharge Capacity (RIMS)
DC Disciples of Christ
DC Discommensurate Model [*Physics*]
DC Disconnect (NTCM)
DC Disconnect Confirm (VLIE)
DC Disconnect switch (SAUS)
dc Discontinue (ADWA)
d/c Discontinue [*Therapy term*] (CTAA)
DC Discontinue
d/c discount (SAUS)
DC Discrepancy Check (KSC)
DC Discrete (IAA)
DC Discrete Command
DC Discriminator (SAUS)
DC Disc to Card (SAUS)
DC Dishonored Check [*IRS*]
DC Disk Cartridge (SAUS)
DC Disk Controller [*Computer science*] (IEEE)
DC Disk to Card [*Computer science*] (IAA)
DC Dislocated Civilian
DC Disorderly Conduct
DC Dispatcher Console (SAUS)
DC Dispersion Coefficient
DC Displaced Civilian [*Military*] (INF)
DC Display Code
DC Display Compartments [*Freight*]
DC Display Computer
DC Display Console (KSC)
DC Display Context (SAUS)
DC Display Control (SAUS)
DC Display Controller (SAUS)
DC Display Coupler (MCD)
D/C Displays/Controls (SAUS)
D/C Disseminated Intravascular Coagulation [*Hematology*] (DAVI)
DC Dissimilarity Coefficient [*Numerical taxonomy*]
DC Dissolved Organic Carbon (FOTI)
DC Distance (IAA)
DC Distance-Controlled (SAUS)
DC Distillation Column (SAUS)
DC Distocervical [*Dentistry*]

DC .... Distorted Communication (IAA)
DC .... Distorted Communications (SAUS)
DC .... Distributed Computing (GART)
DC .... Distribution Center (SAUO)
DC .... Distribution Centers
DC .... Distribution Code
DC .... Distribution Coefficient
DC .... District Chief (GEOI)
DC .... District Colombia (SAUS)
DC .... District Commissioner [*British government*]
DC .... District Council [*British*]
DC .... District Court
DC .... District of Columbia [*Postal code*]
DC .... District of Columbia Reports [*A publication*] (DLA)
DC .... Divisional Commander (WDAA)
DC .... Divisional Court [*Legal term*] (DLA)
DC .... Division Chief (SAUS)
DC .... Division of Classification [*Energy Research and Development Administration*]
DC .... Division of Contracts
D/C .... DLCI/Control (SAUS)
DC .... Doane College (SAUS)
DC .... Docking Compartment [*NASA*] (SPST)
DC .... Doctor of Chiropractic
DC .... Doctor of Chiropraxis
DC .... document (SAUS)
DC .... Document Code [*Computer science*]
DC .... Document Control
D/C .... documents against cash (SAUS)
DC .... Domain Control (SAUS)
DC .... Domain Controller [*Computer science*] (MWOL)
DC .... Domestic Council [*Executive Office of the President*] [*Abolished 1978, functions transferred to the President*]
DC .... Dominican College (SAUS)
DC .... Donnelly College (SAUS)
DC .... Donor's Cells [*Medicine*]
DC .... Door Closer (AAG)
DC .... Dopo Cristo [*After Christ*] [*Italian*]
DC .... Dor Chemical (SAUS)
DC .... Dordt College (SAUS)
DC .... Dorsal Cortex [*Neuroanatomy*]
DC .... Dot Cycle [*Telecommunications*] (IAA)
DC .... Double Cap [*or Crown*] [*Paper size*]
dc .... double certifcated (SAUS)
DC .... Double Channel (SAUS)
DC .... Double Column [*Publishing*] (NTCM)
dc .... Double Column (WDAA)
DC .... Double Concentric (SAUS)
DC .... Double-Concentric
DC .... Double Conductor
DC .... Double Contact [*Lamp base type*] (NTCM)
DC .... Double Cotton [*Wire insulation*] (AAG)
DC .... Double Crank (SAUS)
DC .... Double Crochet
DC .... Double Cropped [*Agriculture*]
dc .... Double Crown (WDAA)
DC .... Double Crown [*Monetary unit*] [*British*]
DC .... Double-Crucible [*Optics*] (EECA)
DC .... Double Current (IAA)
DC .... Double Cylinder (SAUS)
dc .... Double-Cylinder Tank [*Liquid gas carriers*]
DC .... Douglas Aircraft Company, Inc. (SAUO)
DC .... Douglas Commercial [*Airplane*] (IIA)
DC .... Dow Center (SAUS)
D-C .... Dow-Coniing (SAUS)
DC .... Down Center [*Theater*] (WDMC)
DC .... Down Centre (SAUS)
D/C .... Down Converter [*Environmental science*] (COE)
DC .... Downconverter [*Satellite communications*]
DC .... downcore (SAUS)
DC .... downcurrent (SAUS)
DC .... Downing College (SAUS)
DC .... Downtime Costs [*Quality control*]
DC .... Downward Coefficient (SAUS)
DC .... Downward Compatible (VLIE)
DC .... Dracula and Co. [*An association*] (EA)
dc .... draft card (SAUS)
DC .... Drafting Committee (SAUO)
DC .... Drag Coefficient
DC .... Drain Channel (NRCH)
DC .... Drama Criticism [*A publication*]
DC .... Drawing Center (EA)
DC .... Drawing Change (AAG)
DC .... Dressing Change [*Medicine*] (MELL)
DC .... Drift Chamber (MCD)
D/C .... Drift Correction
dc .... drill collar (SAUS)
DC .... Driver Cell (IAA)
DC .... Driver Control (SAUS)
DC .... Drought Code (SAUS)
DC .... Drug Combination [*Medicine*] (MELL)
DC .... Drury College (SAUS)
DC .... Dry Cargo (SAUS)
DC .... Dry Chemical (PIPO)
DC .... Dry Chemical System [*NFPA pre-fire planning symbol*] (NFPA)
dc .... dry coniferous (SAUS)
DC .... Dual Capable (NATG)
DC .... Dual Channel
DC .... Dual Choice
DC .... Dublic Core (SAUS)
DC .... Dublin Castle
DC .... Dublin Core (SAUO)
DC .... Duchesne College (SAUS)
DC .... Duchy of Cornwall [*British*] (ROG)
dc .... Duck (VRA)
DC .... Duct Carcinoma [*Oncology*]
DC .... Dumbarton College (SAUS)
DC .... Dump condenser (SAUS)
DC .... Dump Core (SAUS)
DC .... Duplicate Copy
DC .... Dust Collector (SAUS)
DC .... Dust Core (SAUS)
DC .... Dutton Cars Ltd. (SAUO)
DC .... Duty Controller [*Tactical Air Command*]
DC .... Duty Cycle [*Engineering*]
DC .... Dyke College (SAUS)
DC .... Dynamic Computer (SAUS)
DC .... Dyskeratosis Congenita [*Medicine*] (DMAA)
DC .... generator direct-current generator (SAUS)
DC .... I/S Datacentralen [*Information service or system*] (IID)
DC .... McDonnell-Douglas Aircraft Co., Inc. [*ICAO aircraft manufacturer identifier*] (ICAO)
DC .... Partito della Democrazia Cristiana [*Christian Democrat Party*] [*Italy*] [*Political party*] (EY)
DC .... Pennsylvania District and County Reports [*A publication*] (DLA)
DC .... Trans Catalina Airlines [*ICAO designator*] (AD)
DC .... Treasury Department Circular [*United States*] [*A publication*] (DLA)
DC .... United States Department of Commerce, Washington, DC [*Library symbol*] [*Library of Congress*] (LCLS)
DC .... United States District Court (DLA)
DC .... Decimal Currency (ODA)
DC1 .... Damage Controlman, First Class [*Navy*] (DNAB)
DC1 .... Device Control 1 [*Computer science*] (DCDG)
DC1 .... Device Control One (SAUS)
DC2 .... Damage Controlman, Second Class [*Navy*] (DNAB)
DC2 .... Device Control 2 [*Computer science*] (DCDG)
DC2 .... Device Control Two (SAUS)
DC2 .... Distrbuted Command and Control [*Army*]
DC 2d .... Pennsylvania District and County Reports, Second Series [*A publication*] (DLA)
DC3 .... Damage Controlman, Third Class [*Navy*] (DNAB)
DC3 .... Device Control 3 [*Computer science*] (DCDG)
DC3 .... Device Control Three (SAUS)
DC^3 .... Distributed Command, Control, and Communications [*Army*]
DC-3 .... Douglas 21 -passenger twin-engine transport aircraft also known as the C-47, Dakota, or Skytrain (SAUS)
DC^3I .... Distributed Command, Control, Communications, and Intelligence [*Army*] (RDA)
DC4 .... Device Control Four (SAUS)
DC-4 .... Douglas 44-passenger four-engine transport aircraft also called C-54 or Skymaster (SAUS)
DC-6 .... Douglas 64 to 92-passenger transport also known as C-118 Liftmaster because of its cargo-carrying capacity (SAUS)
DC-8 .... Douglas DC8 jet airplane (SAUS)
DC63 .... Darvon Compound 63 [*Eli Lilly & Co.*] (DAVI)
DC 65 .... Darvon Compound 65 [*Medicine*] (EDAA)
DCA .... Corcoran Art Gallery, Washington, DC [*Library symbol*] [*Library of Congress*] (LCLS)
DCA .... Dachshund Club of America (EA)
DCA .... Dacono-Air [*Former USSR*] [*FAA designator*] (FAAC)
DCA .... Daewoo Campus Advisor [*Automotive marketing*]
DCA .... Dalmatian Club of America (EA)
DCA .... Damage Control Assessment (MCD)
DCA .... Damage Control Assistant [*Military*] (NVT)
DCA .... Dance Critics Association (EA)
DCA .... Data Center Administration (SAUO)
DCA .... Data Collection Assignment (SAUS)
DCA .... Data Communications Administrator
DCA .... Data Concentration Adapter [*Computer science*] (VLIE)
DCA .... Data Corporation of America (SAUO)
DCA .... Data Correction Amplifier
DCA .... Debt Collection Agency (DCTA)
DCA .... Decade Counting Assembly (IEEE)
DCA .... Decimal Classification of Astronautics (SAUS)
DCA .... Defelection Coil Amplifier (SAUS)
DCA .... Defence Codification Authority (SAUS)
DCA .... Defence Communications Agency (SAUO)
DCA .... Defence Co-operation Agreement (SAUS)
DCA .... Defence Costs Agreement (SAUS)
DCA .... Defense Cataloging Agency (SAUO)
DCA .... Defense Communications Agency [*Arlington, VA*] [*DoD*]
DCA .... Defense Contract Administrator (MCD)
DCA .... Defense Contre Aeronefs [*Antiaircraft Defense*] [*French*]
DCA .... Defense Control Administration
DCA .... Defense Cooperation Account (POLM)
DCA .... Defense Cooperation Agreement (MCD)
DCA .... Defensive Counter Air (SAUS)
DCA .... Defensive Counterair [*Army*] (ADDR)
DCA .... Deferred Commercial Annuity [*Insurance*]
DCA .... Deferred Compensation Administrator

DCA .... Deflection Coil Amplifier
DCA .... Delahaye Club of America (EA)
DCA .... Democratic Congress Alliance [*Gambia*]
DCA .... Denmark Cheese Association [*Defunct*] (EA)
DCA .... Deoxycholate-Citrate Agar [*Microbiology*]
DCA .... Deoxycholate Citrate Sugar (SAUS)
DCA .... Deoxycholic Acid [*Biochemistry*]
DCA .... Deoxycorticosterone [*or Desoxycorticosterone*] Acetate [*Also, DOCA*] [*Endocrinology*]
DCA .... Department of Civil Aviation
DCA .... Department of Community Affairs (DEMM)
DCA .... Department of Courts Administration [*New South Wales*] [*Australia*]
DCA .... Department of Covered Activities (SAUO)
DCA .... Deputy Chief Architect [*British*]
DCA .... Deputy Chief of Staff for Administration
DCA .... Deputy County Architect [*British*]
DCA .... Designated Conservation Area [*Forest industry*] (WPI)
DCA .... Design calculations and analyses (SAUS)
DCA .... Design Change Authorization (KSC)
DCA .... DeSoto Club of America (EA)
DCa .... Desoxycorticorticosterone Acetate (LDT)
DCA .... Desoxycorticosteron-Acetat (SAUS)
DCA .... Desoxycorticosterone Acetate [*Endocrinology*] (MAH)
DCA .... Detachable Container Association [*Defunct*] (EA)
DCA .... Detrended Correspondence Analysis [*Mathematics*]
DC-A .... Development Center-Atlanta (SAUO)
DCA .... Development Corp. of America (EFIS)
DCA .... Development Credit Authority (SAUO)
DCA .... Device Cluster Adapter (SAUS)
DCA .... Device Control Area (IAA)
DCA .... Devon Cattle Association (EA)
DCA .... Diagnostic Connector Assembly (RDA)
Dca .... Dialysate Calcium [*Medicine*] (EDAA)
DCA .... Diamond Council of America (EA)
DCA .... Diapulse Corporation of America (SAUO)
DCA .... Diastematic Club of America [*Later, IDC*] (EA)
DCA .... Dicarboxylic Aciduria [*Medicine*]
DCA .... Dichloroacetate [*Organic chemistry*]
DCA .... Dichloroacethylene (SAUS)
DCA .... Dichloroacetic Acid [*Pharmacology*] (DAVI)
DCA .... Dichloroanilin (SAUS)
DCA .... Dichloroaniline [*Dye intermediate*]
DCA .... Dictionary of Christian Antiquities [*A publication*] (BJA)
DCA .... Dicyanoanthracene [*Organic chemistry*]
DCA .... Digital Command Assembly [*NASA*] (KSC)
DCA .... Digital Communications Associates (SAUS)
DCA .... Digital Communications Associates, Inc. [*Alpharetta, GA*] (CDE)
DCA .... Digital Computer Association (MUGU)
DCA .... Digital Computers Association (SAUS)
DCA .... Digital Controlled Amplifier (VERA)
DCA .... Digitally Controlled Attenuator (SAUS)
DCA .... DiLucia Chinese Alphabet [*57-character Chinese type font created for typewriter keyboards*]
DCA .... Diploma Centro America (SAUS)
DCA .... Diploma in Computer Application (SAUS)
DCA .... Direct Calorimetric Analysis (OA)
DCA .... Direct Chip Attachment (AAEL)
DCA .... Direct Colorimetric Analysis (SAUS)
DCA .... Direct-Contact Aftercooler [*Engineering*]
DCA .... Direct Current Ampere (SAUS)
DCA .... Direct Current Amplifier (SAUS)
DCA .... Direct-Current Amplifier
DCA .... Direct Current Arc (SAUS)
DCA .... Direct-Current Arc
DCA .... Direct Customer Access (SAUS)
DCA .... Direct Grate of Civil Aviation (SAUS)
DCA .... Direction Center Active [*SAGE*] [*RADAR*]
DCA .... Directorate of Civil Aviation
DCA .... Director of Civil Affairs [*Military*] [*British*]
DCA .... Directory Client Agent
DCA .... Directory of Corporate Affiliations
DCA .... Disassembly Compliance and Analysis (SAUS)
DCA .... Disc Company of America (SAUO)
DCA .... Discrepancy Control Area (SAA)
DCA .... Dispatch Control Area (SAUS)
DCA .... Displacement Contour Analyzer (MCD)
DCA .... Distributed Communication Architecture (SAUS)
DCA .... Distributed Communications Architecture (BUR)
DCA .... Distribution Contractors Association [*Tulsa, OK*] (EA)
DCA .... Distribution Control Agency (SAUS)
DCA .... Distribution Control Assembly (MCD)
DCA .... District Court of Appeals (SAUS)
DCA .... Divisional Court of Appeal [*Legal term*] (ILCA)
DCA .... Division of Consumer Affairs (SAUS)
DCA .... Doctor of Commercial Arts
DCA .... Doctor of Creative Arts
DCA .... Document Center Architecture [*Computer science*] (VERA)
DCA .... Document Change Analysis (SAA)
DCA .... Document Change Authorization (SAA)
DCA .... Document Composition Architecture (SAUS)
DCA .... Document Content (SAUS)
DCA .... Document Content Architecture [*IBM Corp.*]
DCA .... Document Control and Approval (SAUS)
DCA .... Document Control Architecture (SAUS)
DCA .... Document Control Assistant [*Environmental Protection Agency*] (EPA)
DCA .... Dollar Cost Averaging (AGLO)
DCA .... Doll Collectors of America (EA)
DCA .... Dominion Curling Association (SAUO)
DCA .... Doppler Count Accumulator (IAA)
DCA .... Dorion's Queen's Bench Reports [*Canada*] [*A publication*] (DLA)
DCA .... Dosimeter Corp. of America [*Nuclear energy*] (NRCH)
DCA .... Double Conversion Adapter
DCA .... Downlink Channel Assignment (CAAL)
DCA .... Drafting Contractors Association (SAUO)
DCA .... Drawing Change Authority (SAUS)
DCA .... Dredging Contractors of America (NTPA)
DCA .... Drift Correction Angle
DCA .... Driver Control Area [*Computer science*] (BUR)
DCA .... Drug Control Agency (SAUS)
DCA .... Dual-Capable Aircraft (MCD)
DCA .... Dynamic Channel Allocation (PDAA)
DCA .... Dynamic Contact Analyzer (SAUS)
DCA .... Dynamics Corporation of America (SAUO)
DCA .... Washington International Airport (SAUS)
DCA .... Washington [*DC*] National Airport [*Airport symbol*]
DCAA .... Debon Country Agricultural Association (SAUO)
DCAA .... Defense Contract Audit Agency [*DoD*]
DCAA .... Defense Contracting Audit Agency (SAUO)
DCAA .... Dichloroacetic Acid [*Organic chemistry*]
DCA-A .... Disassembly Compliance and Analysis - Abbreviated (SAUS)
DCAA .... Dissolved Combined Amino Acid [*Marine biology*]
DCAA .... Dual-Call Auto Answer (HGAA)
DCAA CAM... Defense Contract Audit Agency Contract Audit Manual [*A publication*] (AAGC)
DCAAI .... Defense Contract Audit Agency Instruction (AAGC)
DCAAM .... Defense Contract Audit Agency Manual [*A publication*] (AAGC)
DCAAO .... Defense Contract Audit Agency Office (ACAE)
DCAAP .... Defense Contract Audit Agency Pamphlets [*DoD*]
DCAAR .... Defense Contract Audit Agency Regulation [*A publication*] (AAGC)
DCAB .... Defense Contract Adjustment Board (AAGC)
DCAB .... Department of Commerce Appeals Board (AAGC)
DCAB .... United States Civil Aeronautics Board, Washington, DC [*Library symbol*] [*Library of Congress*] (LCLS)
DCABC .... Dance Collection Automated Book Catalog (SAUS)
DCABG .... Double Coronary Artery Bypass Graft [*Medicine*]
DC/AC .... Allstrom (SAUS)
DCAC .... Defense Communications Agency Circular
DCAC .... Design Change Approval Committee (SAA)
DCAC .... Dichloroacetyl Chloride [*Organic chemistry*]
d-c a-c .... Direct Current / Alternating Current (SAUS)
DCAC .... Direct-Current / Alternating-Current (IAA)
DC-AC .... Direct Current to Alternating Current (VLIE)
DCAC .... Division Control and Analysis Center (SAUO)
DCACA .... Data Collection, Analysis, and Corrective Action (CAAL)
DCA/CCCCS... Defense Communications Agency Center for Command, Control, and Communications Systems [*Arlington, VA*]
dc-ac: chopper... direct-current alternating-current chopper (SAUS)
dc-ac converter... direct-current alternating-current converter (SAUS)
DCA/CCSO ... Defense Communications Agency Command and Control Systems Organization [*Washington, DC*]
dc-ac inverter... direct-current alternating-current inverter (SAUS)
DCACOC .... DCA Operations Center [*Communications term*] (DCT)
DCAD .... Dichlorobenzaldehyde (SAUS)
DCAD .... Digital Computer-Aided Design (TIMI)
DCAD .... documented coronary artery disease (SAUS)
DCADA .... District of Columbia Alley Dwelling Authority (SAUO)
D Cadets .... Director of Army (SAUS)
D Cadets .... Director of Army Cadets (SAUO)
DCA/DIA .... Document Content Architecture/Document Interchange Architecture (SAUS)
DCADS .... Defense Contract Action Data System (AAGC)
DCaE .... Canadian Embassy, Washington, DC [*Library symbol*] [*Library of Congress*] (LCLS)
DCAe .... Diploma of the College of Aeronautics [*British*]
DCAEUR .... Defence (or Defense) Communications Agency Europe (SAUO)
DCAEUR .... Defense Communications Agency, Europe (NATG)
DCAF .... Design Corrective Action Form
DCAF .... Distributed Console Access Facility [*Computer science*] (VLIE)
DCAG .... Deputy Air Wing Commander [*No longer used*] [*Navy*] (DOMA)
DCAI .... Defense Communications Agency Instruction
DCAI .... Defense Contract Audit Institute (AAGC)
DCAI .... Dialysis Corp. Amer [*NASDAQ symbol*] (TTSB)
DCAI .... Dialysis Corp. of America [*NASDAQ symbol*] (SAG)
DCAI .... Digital Consulting Associates, Inc. [*Andover, MA*] [*Later, DCI*] [*Telecommunications*] (TSSD)
DCAI .... Direct-Current Analog Input (MCD)
DCAIU .... Dialysis Corp. Amer Unit [*NASDAQ symbol*] (TTSB)
DCAIW .... Dialysis Corp. Amer Wrrt [*NASDAQ symbol*] (TTSB)
DCAJ .... Dixie Council of Authors and Journalists (EA)
DCA/JDSSC... Defense Communications Agency Joint Data Systems Support Center [*Washington, DC*]
DCAL .... Center for Applied Linguistics, Washington, DC [*Library symbol*] [*Library of Congress*] (LCLS)
DCAL .... Danquah. Cases in Akan Law [*Ghana*] [*A publication*] (DLA)
DCAL .... Detroit Community AIDS Library (SAUO)
DCALC .... Calculated D-spacing (SAUS)
DCAM .... Data Collection Access Method
DCAM .... Data Communication Access Method (IAA)

DCAM Defense Contract Audit Agency Manual [*A publication*] (AAGC)
DCAM Digital Camera (VLIE)
DCAM Direct Chip Attach Module (VLIE)
DCAM Director of Craft and Amphibious Material [*British military*] (DMA)
DCAM Discriminating Content Addressable Memory (SAUS)
DCAMIP Data Center for Atomic and Molecular Ionization Processes
DCAMP Dibutyryl Cyclic Adenosine Monophosphate [*Organic chemistry*] (DAVI)
DCAMPS Deployable Computer Aided Mission Planning System (SAUS)
DCAMS Deployable Core Automated Maintenance System (SAUO)
DCAMS DOE Contracts and Assistance Management System (SAUS)
DCA/MSO Defense Communications Agency/MILSATCOM [*Military Satellite Communications*] Systems Office [*Arlington, VA*]
DCAN Defense Communications Agency Note [*or Notice*]
DCan Director of Canteen Service (SAUO)
DC&A Data Collection and Analysis (GEOI)
DC&AS Digital Control and Automation System [*Computer science*] (VLIE)
DC & B Dilation, Curettage, and Biopsy [*Gynecology*] (DAVI)
DC & C Diabetes Control and Complications [*Medicine*]
DC&P Data Collection and Processing (SAUS)
DC&R Diseases of the Colon & Rectum (SAUS)
DC & S Detroit, Caro & Sandusky Railroad (IIA)
DC & T Detection, Classification, and Targeting [*or Tracking*]
DC & TSC Defense Clothing and Textile Supply Center [*Later, Defense Personnel Support Center*] [*DoD*]
DCANG District of Columbia Air National Guard (MUSM)
D Can L Doctor of Canon Law
DCAO Digital Card and-or Gate [*Computer science*]
DCAO Deputy County Advisory Officer (ODA)
DCAOC Defence Communications Agency Operations Center (SAUS)
DCAOC Defense Communications Agency Operations Center
DCap Capitol [*Record label*] [*Great Britain*]
DCAP Data link switching Client Access Protocol (SAUS)
DCAP Decompression Computation and Analysis Program
DCAP Deficiency Corrective Action Program [*Surface missile systems*]
DCAP Dependent Care Assistance Plan [*Insurance*] (WYGK)
DCAP Dihydrocapaicin [*Biochemistry*]
DCAP Double Foolscap [*Paper*] (ADA)
DCAP Draft Conventional Armaments Plan (SAUS)
DCAP Dynamic Checkout Assistance Program (VLIE)
DCAPAC Defense Communications Agency Pacific (SAUO)
DCAPP Deutz Corporation Advanced Power Products (SAUO)
DC App District of Columbia Appeals Reports [*A publication*] (DLA)
DCAPT Discrepancy & Corrective Action Tracking (SAUS)
DCAR Danish Centre for Atmospheric Research (SAUO)
DCAR Data Collection Analysis Request (SAUS)
DCAR Design Corrective Action Report (NASA)
DCAR Disassembly Compliance and Analysis Report (SAUS)
DCAR Discrepancy and Corrective Action Report
DCARE Driver Control Area Region Extension [*Computer science*] (BUR)
DCA-RFT Document Content Architecture-Revisable Form Text (SAUS)
DCART Disease-Controlling Antirheumatic Therapy [*Medicine*]
DCAS Corcoran School of Art, Washington, DC [*Library symbol*] [*Library of Congress*] (LCLS)
D/CAS Data Cassette (CDE)
DCAS Data Collection and Analysis System [*NASA*]
DCAS Defense Contract Administration Services [*DoD*]
DCAS Defense Contract Audit Service (SAUO)
DCAS Defense Control Administration Services (ACAE)
DCAS Deputy Chief of the Air Staff [*British*]
DCAS Deputy Commander of Aerospace Systems [*Inglewood, CA*] [*Air Force*]
DCAS Digital Control and Automation System (NITA)
DCAS Digital Core Avionics System (ACAE)
DCAS Director of Civil Air Service (SAUO)
DCAS Director of Costing and Accounting Services (SAUO)
DCAS Distribution Cost Analysis System (MCD)
DCAS Division of Central Administration Services (SAUO)
DCASA Defense Contract Administration Services Agency (AAGC)
DCASD Defense Contract Administration Services District [*DoD*] (AABC)
DCASEF Defense Communications Agency Systems Engineering Facility [*Reston, VA*]
DCASMA Defense Contract Administration Services Management Area [*DoD*] (MCD)
DCASMARO Defense Contract Administration Services Management Area Regional Office (AAGC)
DCASO Defense Contract Administration Services Office [*DoD*] (AABC)
DCASPO Defense Contract Administration Services Plant Office [*DoD*] (DNAB)
DCASPRO Defense Contract Administration Service Representatives Office (SAUS)
DCASPRO Defense Contract Administration Services Plant Representative Office [*DoD*] (AABC)
DCASQ Defense Contract Administration Services Quarters (SAUO)
DCASR Defence Contract Administration Services Representative (SAUS)
DCASR Defense Contract Administration Services Region [*DoD*]
DCASR Department of the Controller of American Supplies and Repair (SAUO)
DCASS Defense Communications and Army Switched System (RDA)
DCASS Digital Cartographic Software System (GEOI)
DCAT Developing Cognitive Abilities Test [*Canadian Comprehensive Assessment Program*]
DCAT Device Class Access Type (SAUS)
DCAT Directional Control Antitank [*Missile*]
D Cat Directorate of Cataloguing (SAUO)
DCAT Discourse Comprehension Abilities Test (EDAC)
DCAT Drug, Chemical and Allied Trades (SAUS)
DCAT Drug, Chemical, and Allied Trades Association (EA)
DCAT Drug, Chemical and Allied Trades Association, Inc. (SAUO)
DCAT Dry Contact Acoustic Transmission [*Automotive engineering*]
DCATR Decatur, IL [*American Association of Railroads railroad junction routing code*]
DCATS Data Communication Applications Test System [*Computer science*] (HODG)
DCATS Data Communication Application Test System (SAUS)
DCATS Defense Communications and Army Transmissions System [*DoD*]
DCATS Double-Contained Acid Transfer System (AAEL)
DC-AUTOMET Directional Controlled-Automatic Meteorological Compensation (DNAB)
DCAVU Clear or Scattered Clouds and Visibility Greater than Ten, Remainder of Report Missing [*NWS*] (FAAC)
DCB Damage Control Booklet (DNAB)
DCB Dame Commander of the Most Honourable Order of the Bath (SAUS)
DCB Dame Commander of the Order of the Bath [*British*] (ADA)
DCB Data and Control Bus (SAUS)
DCB Data Communication Bank [*Computer science*] (VLIE)
DCB Data Communications Bureau (GART)
DCB Data Control Block [*Computer science*]
DCB Data Control Board (SAUO)
DCB Data Control Bus [*Computer science*] (NITA)
Dcb December (CDAI)
DCB Decimal Code Binaire [*Binary Coded Decimal*] [*French*] [*Computer science*]
DCB Defense Communications Board
DCB Define Control Block [*Computer science*] (OA)
DCB Design Certificate Board
DCB Design Change Board (ACAE)
DCB Design Control Board (SAUO)
DCB Destination Code Base
DCB Devereux Child Behavior [*Rating scale*] [*Psychology*]
DCB Device Code Byte (SAUS)
DCB Device Control Block [*Computer science*] (PCM)
DCB diamond core barrel (SAUS)
DCB Dichlorobenzene (SAUS)
DCB Dichlorobenzidine [*Organic chemistry*]
DCB Dichlorobenzoate [*Organic chemistry*]
DCB Dichlorobiphenyl [*Organic chemistry*]
DCB Dichlorobutane (SAUS)
DCB Dictionary of Canadian Biography [*A publication*]
DCB Dictionary of Christian Biography [*A publication*] (ODCC)
DCB Dictionary of Christian Biography and Literature [*A publication*] (OCD)
DCB Dicyanobenzene [*Also, DCNB*] [*Organic chemistry*]
DCB Digital Camera Back (SAUS)
DCB Dilutional Cardiopulmonary Bypass [*Cardiology*] (AAMN)
DCB Diocesan Chaplains Board (SAUO)
DCB Direct Copper Bonding (SAUS)
DCB Directed Cyclic Biologic (SAUS)
DCB Disciplinary Control Board [*Air Force*]
DCB Disk Control Block (ROAS)
DCB Disk Coprocessor Board [*Computer science*] (VERA)
DCB Distance Controlled Boat (SAUS)
DCB Distant-Control Boat
DCB District Contracts Board [*Australia*]
DCB Dithionite-Citrate-Bicarbonate [*Extractive chemistry*]
DCB Division Crime Buffer
DCB Document Control Book (MCD)
DCB Double Cantilever Beam [*Stress condition of aluminum alloy*]
DCB Double Current Branch (SAUS)
DCB Drawout Circuit Breaker [*Electronics*] (OA)
DCB O-Dichlorobenzene (SAUS)
DCB O-Dichlorobenzol (SAUS)
DCB United States Bureau of Customs, Washington, DC [*Library symbol*] [*Library of Congress*] (LCLS)
DCBA Damage Control Breathing Apparatus (PDAA)
DCBA Deer Breeders' Co-operative Association [*Australia*]
DCBA Dichlorobenzaldehyde (SAUS)
DCBA Dichlorobenzoic Acid (SAUS)
DCBA Differential Cost Benefit Analysis (COE)
DCBay double-contact bayonet cap (SAUS)
DCBC Daily Child Behavior Checklist [*Psychology*] (EDAC)
DCBC Dichlorobenzyl Chloride [*Organic chemistry*]
DCBC digital geobailistic computer (SAUS)
DCBD Define Control Block Dummy [*Computer science*] (OA)
DCBD Division for Children with Behavioral Disorders [*of Council for Exceptional Children*] (EA)
DCBD Division of Cancer Biology and Diagnosis [*National Cancer Institute*]
DCB/DBC Dictionary of Canadian Biography / Dictionnaire Biographique du Canada (SAUS)
DCBDC Division of Cancer Biology, Diagnosis and Centers (SAUS)
DCBE Double Contrast Barium Enema [*X-ray procedure*] (CPH)
DCBF Dynamic Cardiac Blood Flow [*Medicine*] (DMAA)
DCBI Delphos Citizens Bancorp, Inc. [*NASDAQ symbol*] (SAG)
DCBJ District of Columbia Bar Journal (SAUS)
DCBK Desert Community Bank [*NASDAQ symbol*] (SAG)
DCBP Decachlorobiphenyl (SAUS)
DCBP Dichlorobenzophenone [*Also, DBP*] [*Organic chemistry*]
DCBP Dissemination Capacity Building Project (EDAC)
DCBR Descriptive Cataloging of Rare Books [*Library of Congress*]
DCBRE Defence Chemical, Biological, and Radiation Establishment [*Canada*]
DCBRE Defense Chemical, Biological and Radiation Establishment (SAUS)
DCBRL Defence Chemical, Biological, and Radiation Laboratories [*Canada*]

DCBRL .... Defense Chemical, Biological and Radiation Laboratories (SAUS)
DCBS .... Dual Combined Brake System [*Motorcycle engineering*]
DCBTF .... Dichlorobenzotrifluoride [*Organic chemistry*]
DCBX .... Degussa [*Private rail car owner code*]
DCBX .... distributed computerized branch exchange (SAUS)
DCC .... Caribbean Air Cargo [*Barbados*] [*ICAO designator*] (FAAC)
DCC .... Caribbean Development and Cooperation Committee (SAUO)
DCC .... Chamber of Commerce of the United States, Washington, DC [*Library symbol*] [*Library of Congress*] (LCLS)
DCC .... Chief Damage Controlman [*Navy*]
DCC .... Daily Calibration Check [*Automotive emissions*]
DCC .... Daimler-Chrysler Corporation
DCC .... Dairy Council of California (SRA)
DCC .... Dale Carnegie Course
DCC .... Dallas Cowboys Cheerleaders
DCC .... Damage Control Center (NATG)
DCC .... Damage Controlman, Chief [*Navy*] (DNAB)
DCC .... Dark Curtain Closed (SAUS)
DCC .... Darmstadt Career Center (SAUO)
DCC .... Database Control Center [*Computer science*] (HODG)
DCC .... Data Carrier Conversion (SAUS)
DCC .... Data Change Code (ACAE)
DCC .... Data Channel Converter (NITA)
DCC .... Data Circuit Concentration
DCC .... Data Circuit Concentrator (SAUS)
DCC .... Data Collecting Card (SAUS)
DCC .... Data Collection Center [*Army Infantry Board*] (RDA)
DCC .... Data Collection Center (or Centre) (SAUS)
DCC .... Data Communication Channel (DOM)
DCC .... Datacommunication Channel (SAUS)
DCC .... Data Communications Channel
DCC .... Data Communications Computer (VERA)
DCC .... Data Communications Controller [*Computer science*]
DCC .... Data Communications Corp. [*Information service or system*] (IID)
DCC .... Data Communications Corporation (SAUO)
DCC .... Data Computation Complex [*NASA*] (NASA)
DCC .... Data Condition Code
DCC .... Data Control Center (SAUO)
DCC .... Data Control Characters (CMD)
DCC .... Data Converter Check (SAUS)
DCC .... Data Country Code [*Telecommunications*] (OSI)
DCC .... Day Care Center
DCC .... Dean and Chapter of Canterbury [*Anglican Church*] (ROG)
DCC .... Debarkation Control Center [*Navy*] (CAAL)
DCC .... Debarkation Control Centre (SAUO)
DCC .... Deck Compression Chamber (PDAA)
DCC .... Deep Catalytic Crack [*Chemical engineering*]
DCC .... Defence Construction Canada
DCC .... Defense Command Center (ACAE)
DCC .... Defense Concessions Committee
DCC .... Defense Construction Canada (SAUS)
DCC .... Defense Control Center (AABC)
DCC .... Delayed Contact Closure
DCC .... Delcommune [*Zaire*] [*Seismograph station code, US Geological Survey*] (SEIS)
DCC .... Delegation Catholique pour la Cooperation (EA)
DCC .... Deleted from Colorectal Carcinoma (SAUS)
DCC .... Deleted in Colon Cancer [*Gene*]
DCC .... Deleted in Colorectal Carcinomas [*A gene*]
DCC .... Dental Charity Commission (SAUO)
DCC .... Dental Charity Committee (SAUO)
DCC .... Department of Culture and Communications (SAUS)
DCC .... Dependent Care Connection (ADWA)
DCC .... Deputy Chief Constable
DCC .... Descriptive Cataloging Committee (SAUS)
DCC .... Design Change Control
DCC .... Design Change Coordination (ACAE)
DCC .... Design Concept Change (AAG)
DCC .... Destination Code Cancel (SAUS)
DCC .... Destination Code Cancelled (SAUS)
DCC .... Development Capital Corp. [*British*]
DCC .... Development Control Center
DCC .... Development Coordination Committee (SAUO)
DCC .... Device Cluster Controller
DCC .... Device Control Character [*Computer science*] (IEEE)
DCC .... Devis de Construction Canada [*Construction Specifications Canada*] [*Formerly, Association des Redacteurs de Devis du Canada - ARDC*]
DCC .... Dextran-Coated Charcoal
DCC .... Dick Clark Companies
DCC .... Dictionary Catalog Code (SAUS)
DCC .... Dicyclohexylcarbodiimide [*Also, DCCD, DCCI*] [*Organic chemistry*]
DCC .... Dielectric Constant Change [*Analytical chemistry*]
DCC .... Differential Chain Code (SAUS)
DCC .... Differential Chain Coding (SAUS)
DCC .... Digital Command Control (SAUS)
DCC .... Digital Communication Console (IAA)
DCC .... Digital Communications Corp. (CCCA)
DCC .... Digital Compact Cassette [*Audio technology*]
DCC .... Digital Computer Complex (SAUS)
DCC .... Digital Computer Control (SAUS)
DCC .... Digital Computer Controls, Inc. (SAUO)
DCC .... Digital Computer Controls, Incorporated (SAUS)
DCC .... Digital Content Creation
DCC .... Digital Control Computer
DCC .... Digital Cross Connect (VLIE)
DCC .... Digital Cross Correct (SAUS)
DCC .... Digital Cross Current
DCC .... Diocesan Consistory Club (SAUO)
DCC .... Diocesan Consistory Court [*Legal term*] (DLA)
DCC .... Diploma of Chelsea College [*British*] (DI)
DCC .... Direct Cable Connection [*Computer science*] (IGQR)
DCC .... Direct Calculating Capability (VLIE)
DCC .... Direct Calculating Capacility (SAUS)
DCC .... Direct Client Connection (VLIE)
DCC .... Direct Client-to-Client [*A feature of Internet Relay Chat*] (DCDG)
DCC .... Direct Commercial Contracts (AAGC)
DCC .... Direct Computer Control
DCC .... Direct Conductor-to-Circuit [*Advanced Circuit Technology, Inc.*] [*Electronics*]
DCC .... Direct Connect Service (SAUS)
DCC .... Direct Contact Condensation (SAUS)
DCC .... Direct Control Channel
DCC .... Direct Coupled System (VLIE)
DCC .... Direct Current Clamp (IAA)
DCC .... Directorate of Covert Collection [*South African secret military-intelligence unit*] (ECON)
DCC .... Disaster Control Center (AAG)
DCC .... Disburse Control Code (SAUS)
DCC .... Disconnect Command Chaining (SAUS)
DCC .... Disconnected Command Chain (SAUS)
DCC .... Discrimination and Control Computer (MUGU)
DCC .... Disease Control Center (SAUS)
DCC .... Disk Controller Channel (VLIE)
DCC .... Diskette Controller Chip (SAUS)
DCC .... Dispatch Center Console (SAUS)
DCC .... Displal Control Console (SAUS)
DCC .... Display Channel Complex [*FAA*] (TAG)
DCC .... Display Combination Code [*Computer science*] (VERA)
DCC .... Display Control Computer (SAUS)
DCC .... Display Control Console (KSC)
DCC .... Distant Control Cutter (SAUS)
DCC .... Distributed Call Center [*Telecommunications*]
DCC .... Distributed Computing Consultants (SAUS)
DCC .... Distribution Control Center (AAG)
DCC .... District Communications Center [*Navy*]
DCC .... Division of Cataloging and Classification [*Later, CCS, RTSD*] [*American Library Association*]
DCC .... Division of Consumer Credit [*Federal Trade Commission*]
DCC .... Documentation Consulative Committee (SAUS)
DCC .... Documentation Coordinating Committee (SAUS)
DCC .... Document Control Center
DCC .... Document Control Chief [*NASA*]
DCC .... Dodge City College [*Kansas*]
DCC .... Dorsal Cell Column (MELL)
DCC .... DOS Command Center (SAUS)
DCC .... Double Call Club (SAUO)
dcc .... Double Clothes Closet (REAL)
DCC .... Double Coax Conversion [*Communications term*] (DCT)
DCc .... Double Concave [*Medicine*]
DCC .... Double Cotton Covered [*Wire insulation*]
DCC .... Double-Current Catheter [*Medicine*] (MELL)
DCC .... Dow Chemical Co.
DCC .... Downtown Copy Center [*Washington, DC*] [*Telecommunications*] (TSSD)
DCC .... Drill, Command, and Ceremony [*Military*] (DNAB)
DCC .... Drone Control Center [*Military*] (MCD)
DCC .... Droplet Counter-Current Chromatograph (SAUS)
DCC .... Dry-Column Chromatography
DCC .... Dual Cam Clutch
DCC .... Dual Constant Composition (SAUS)
DCC .... Dupont Chemical [*Federal Railroad Administration identification code*]
DCC .... Dutchess Community College (SAUS)
DCC .... Dynamic Color Control (SAUS)
DCC .... Dynamic Command Center (SAUS)
DCC .... Dynamic Component Change (MCD)
DCC .... Dynamic Contour Control (SAUS)
DCC .... Dynamic Control Contour (SAUS)
DCC .... Dynamic Controls Corp. (SAUS)
DCC .... dynamic crispening circuit (SAUS)
DCC .... Dystrophic Cardiac Calcinosis [*Medicine*] (MELL)
DCCA .... Department of Commerce and Community Affairs
DCCA .... Dependable Computing for Critical Applications [*Conference*] (VERA)
DCCA .... Design Change Cost Analysis (PDAA)
DCCA .... Dextran-Coated Charcoal Analysis [*Analytical biochemistry*]
DCCA .... dextran-coated charcoal assay (SAUS)
DCCA .... Dichloroisocyanuric Acid [*Organic chemistry*]
DCCA .... Direct Current Capacitive Accelerometer [*Electronics*]
DCCA .... Directional Crossing Contractors Association (NTPA)
DCCA .... Distributed Component Computing Architecture [*Computer science*] (VERA)
DCCA .... District of Columbia Compensation Act (DLA)
DCCA .... Drying Control Chemical Additive [*Ceramic technology*]
DCCAB .... District of Columbia Contract Appeals Board (AAGC)
DCCAH .... District of Columbia Commission on the Arts and Humanities (SAUS)
DCCAO .... Deputy Chief Civil Affairs Officer [*US and Britain*]
DC Casting ... Direct Chill Casting (SAUS)
DCCB .... Data Carrier Control Block (SAUS)
DCCB .... Defense Center Control Building [*Army*] (AABC)
DCCB .... Digital Connectivity Control Bus (VLIE)

DCCC .... Data Communication Control Character (IEEE)
DCCC .... Defense Collection Coordination Center (COE)
DCCC .... Defense Communications Control Center
DCCC .... Defense Communications Control Complex (IAA)
DCCC .... Democratic Congressional Campaign Committee (EA)
DCCC .... Design Change Coordination Committee (SAA)
DCCC .... Digital Command Communications Channel (SAUS)
DCCC .... Disabled Collectors' Correspondence Club (EA)
DCCC .... Division Central Computer Center (SAUO)
DCCC .... Domestic Coal Consumers' Council [*British*] (DI)
DCCC .... Double Current Cable Code [*Telecommunications*]
DCCC .... Droplet Countercurrent Chromatography
DCCCIC .... Drug Command Coordination Control and Intelligence Center (CARL)
DCCCs .... Double Current Cable Codes (SAUS)
DCCD .... Deputy Commissioner for Civil Defence (SAUO)
DCCD .... Dicyclohexylcarbodiimide [*Also, DCC, DCCI*] [*Organic chemistry*]
DCCD .... digital charge-coupled device (SAUS)
DCCD .... Division for Children with Communication Disorders [*Council for Exceptional Children*]
DCCDCA .... Day Care and Child Development Council of America (SAUO)
DCCE .... Department of Chemistry and Chemical Engineering (SAUS)
DCCE .... Department of the Controller of Communications Equipment (SAUO)
DCCE .... District of Columbia Code Encyclopedia [*A publication*] (DLA)
DCCEAS .... District of Columbia Council of Engineering and Architectural Societies (SAUO)
DCCEAS .... District of Columbia Council of Engineering and Architecture (SRA)
DCCEP .... Developing Country Combined Exercise Program [*Environmental science*] (COE)
DCCF .... Discounted Cumulative Cash Flow (AAEL)
DCCF .... Dural Carotid-Cavernous Fistula [*Medicine*] (STED)
DCCG .... Digital Check Character Generator (PDAA)
DCCH .... Commerce Clearing House, Washington, DC [*Library symbol*] [*Library of Congress*] (LCLS)
DCCH .... Dedicated Control Channel [*Computer science*] (VERA)
DCCH .... Digital Control Channel (SEWL)
DCCH .... Disk Cartridge Channel (VLIE)
DC Chromatography... Dual Column Chromatography (SAUS)
DCCI .... Data Converter-Control Indicator (DNAB)
DCCI .... Dichlorohexylcarbodiimide (SAUS)
DCCI .... Dicyclohexylcarbodiimide [*Also, DCC, DCCD*] [*Organic chemistry*]
DC Cir .... [*Court of Appeals for the*] District of Columbia Circuit (AAGC)
DC Cir .... District of Columbia Court of Appeals Cases [*A publication*] (DLA)
DC Cir R .... District of Columbia Circuit Court Rules [*A publication*] (DLA)
DCCL .... digital charge-coupled device (SAUS)
DCCL .... Digital Charge Coupled Logic (SAUS)
DCCL .... Digital Charge-Coupled Logic (MCD)
DCCM .... Master Chief Damage Controlman [*Navy rating*]
DCCMP .... Daunomycin Cyclocytidine, 6-Mercaptopurine, and Prednisolone (STED)
DCCMP .... Daunorubicin, Cyclocytidine [*Ancitabine*], Mercaptopurine, Prednisone [*Antineoplastic drug regimen*]
DCC-MSF .... Direct Contact Condensation-Multistage Flash (SAUS)
DCCO .... Defense Commercial Communications Office (SAUO)
DC_{CO} .... Diffusing Capacity for Carbon Dioxide [*Medicine*] (DAVI)
DCCO .... Diffusing Capacity of Carbon Monoxide (MELL)
DCCO .... Digital Card Clock Oscillator [*Computer science*]
DCCO .... Double-Crested Cormorant [*North American bird banding code*] (BIBA)
DC Code .... District of Columbia Code [*A publication*] (DLA)
DC Code Ann... District of Columbia Code, Annotated [*A publication*] (DLA)
DC Code Encycl... District of Columbia Code Encyclopedia [*A publication*] (DLA)
DC Code Legis & Admin Serv... District of Columbia Code Legislative and Administrative Service (West) [*A publication*] (DLA)
DCCP .... Design Change Control Program
DCCP .... Digital Computer Control Panel
DCCP .... Direct Current Common Point (SAUS)
DCCP .... Directorate of Communication Components Production (SAUS)
DCCP .... Directorate of Communications Components Production (SAUO)
DCCP .... Dump condenser condensate pump (SAUS)
DCCP .... Dump condenser coolant pump (SAUS)
DCCPS .... Division of Cancer Control and Population Sciences (ADWA)
DCCR .... Destination Control Chain Record (SAUS)
DCCR .... Documentation Change Control Report
DCCRM .... Center for Chinese Research Materials, Washington, DC [*Library symbol*] [*Library of Congress*] (LCLS)
DCCRP .... Domestic Council Committee on the Right of Privacy (SAUO)
DCCS .... Data Collection and Control Subsystem [*Computer science*] (TIMI)
DCCS .... Data Communications Control System (SAUS)
DCCS .... Defense Case Control System (DNAB)
DCCS .... Defense Communications Control System [*Air Force*]
DCCS .... Deputy Chief of Staff, Support (SAUS)
DCCS .... Design Change Clearance Sheet (MCD)
DCCS .... Digital Camera Control System
DCCS .... Digital Command Communications System (MCD)
DCCS .... Digital Comparator Correlator System (SAUS)
DCCS .... Discontiguous Shared Segments (SAUS)
DCCS .... Distributed Capability Computing System (SAUS)
DCCS .... Distributed Capacity Computing System (NITA)
DCCS .... Distributed Command and Control System
DCCS .... Distributed Computer Control System (VLIE)
DCCS .... Downrange Computer Output System (SAUS)
DCCS .... Dynamic Cell Culture System (SAUS)
DCCS .... Senior Chief Damage Controlman [*Navy rating*]
DCCSA .... Dictionary of Computer and Control Systems Abbreviations, Signs, and Symbols [*New York: Odyssey Press, 1965*] [*A publication*]
DCCSA .... Dictionary of Computer und Control Systems Abbreviations (SAUS)
DCCT .... Design Center of Connecticut Technology
DCCT .... Diabetes Control and Complications Trial
DCCT .... Direct Current-Current Transformer (IAA)
DCCT .... Durham County Conservation Trust (SAUO)
DCCTC .... United States Department of Defense, Command and Control Technical Center, the Pentagon, Washington, DC [*Library symbol*] [*Library of Congress*] (LCLS)
DCCU .... Data Communication Control Unit (SAUS)
DCCU .... Data Communications Control Unit (DEN)
DCCU .... Data Correlation Control Unit
DCCU .... Decommutator Conditioning Unit (KSC)
DCCU .... Digital Command and Control Unit (NASA)
DCCU .... Digital Communications and Control Unit (MCD)
DCCU .... Digital Television Equipment Cluster Control Unit (MCD)
DCCU .... Display Computer Control Unit (MCD)
DCCU .... Displays and Controls Control Unit (VLIE)
DCCUS .... Dominican Chamber of Commerce of the United States (SAUO)
DCCV .... Direct Current Cardioversion [*Medicine*] (DMAA)
DCCVS .... Domestic Council Committee on Veterans Services [*Veterans Administration*]
DCCWS .... Deputy Chief, Chemical Warfare Service [*Army*]
DCCZ .... Decatur County Co-Operative [*Federal Railroad Administration identification code*]
DCD .... Congressional Digest, Washington, DC [*Library symbol*] [*Library of Congress*] (LCLS)
DCD .... Daitch Crystal Dairies (SAUS)
DCD .... Damage Control Diagrams [*Naval Ship Systems Command*]
DCD .... Data Carrier Detect [*or Detector*] [*Data communication signal*] [*Telecommunications*] (TEL)
DCD .... Data Cell Drive [*Computer science*] (VLIE)
DCD .... Data Collecting Device (IAA)
DCD .... Data Collection Device (SAUS)
DCD .... Data Correlation and Documentation (SAUS)
DCD .... Data Correlation and Documentation System (IAA)
DCD .... DC Demagnitization (SAUS)
DCD .... Deceased (ADA)
DCD .... Decennial Census Division [*Census*] (OICC)
DCD .... Decode (MSA)
DCD .... Decomposition Diagramer [*Computer science*]
DCD .... Defecation-Collection Device [*Apollo*] [*NASA*]
DCD .... Defense Communications Department (IAA)
DCD .... Deflection Coil Drive
DCD .... Delco Chassis Division [*General Motors Corp.*]
DCD .... Dennis Test of Child Development (STED)
DCD .... Department of Community Development [*Proposed government department*]
DCD .... Design Change Document
DCD .... Design Control Document (ACAE)
DCD .... Design Control Drawing
DCD .... Design Criteria Document (ACAE)
DCD .... Desired Completion Date (SAUS)
DCD .... Detector-Cooling Dewar (SAUS)
DCD .... Dicyandiamide [*or Dicyanodiamide*] [*Also, DICY*] [*Organic chemistry*]
DCD .... dielectric constant detection (SAUS)
DCD .... Differential Current Density
DCD .... Digital Capture Device [*Computer science*] (MWOL)
DCD .... Digital Coherent Detector (OA)
DCD .... Digital Compact Disk
DCD .... Digital Computing Densitometer [*Medicine*] (EDAA)
DCD .... Digital Correlation Detector (SAUS)
DCD .... Digital Countdown Display [*Computer science*]
DCD .... Dimensional Control Drawing
DCD .... Diode-Capacitor- Diode (SAUS)
DCD .... Diode-Capacitor-Diode
DCD .... Diploma in Chest Diseases [*British*]
DCD .... Direct Contact Desulfation
DCD .... Direct Current Demagnitization [*Electronics*] (AAEL)
dcd .... Direct Current Dialing (SAUS)
DCD .... Direct-Current Dialing (IAA)
DCD .... Direct-Current Dump
DCD .... Directorate of Civil Disturbance (SAUS)
DCD .... Directorate of Combat Developments [*Army*]
DCD .... Director of Civil Defense (SAUO)
DCD .... Director of Combat Development [*British*] (RDA)
DCD .... Director of Communications Development [*Ministry of Aircraft Production*] [*British*]
DCD .... Director of Compass Department [*British military*] (DMA)
DCD .... Document Content Description [*Computer science*] (GART)
DCD .... domestic collections division (SAUS)
DCD .... Don't-Care-a-Damn [*British naval slang term for torpedo-boat destroyer*] [*World War I*]
DCD .... Double Channel Duplex
DCD .... double crystal diffraction (SAUS)
DCD .... Double Crystal Diffractometer (SAUS)
DCD .... Dual Center Distance (SAUS)
DCD .... Dynamically-Correlated Domain [*Physics*]
DCD .... Dynamic Computer Display (IEEE)
DCD .... NAVSHIPS [*Naval Ship Systems Command*] Damage Control Diagrams
DCD .... Drain-Current Drift [*Electronics*] (ODA)
DCDA .... Data Communication Dealers Association (EA)
DCDA .... Delyn Cooperative Development Agency [*British*]
DCDA .... Deuterium With Cesium Dihydrogen Arsenate (STED)
DCDA .... Dicyanodiamine (SAUS)

DCDAS......... Dicyanodiamine Sulfate (SAUS)
DCDB.......... Data Centre for Digital Bathymetry (SAUS)
DCDB.......... digital cadastral database (SAUS)
DCDB.......... Digital Cartographic Database [*Computer science*]
DCDB.......... Domain Control DataBase (SAUS)
DC/DC.......... Data Communication to Disk Control
DCDC.......... Decennial Census Decision Conference (SAUS)
DC/DC.......... Direct Current/Direct Current (SAUS)
DC/DC.......... Direct Current to Direct Current [*Telecommunications*]
DC/DC Converter... Direct Current to Direct Current Converter (SAUS)
DCDCEC....... Division on Career Development of the Council for Exceptional Children (EA)
DCDCR......... Definition of Control, Display, and Communications Requirement (DNAB)
DCDD.......... Dichlorodibenzodioxin [*Also, DDD*] [*Organic chemistry*]
DCDES......... Dichlorodiethyl Sulfide (SAUS)
DCDFL......... Defense Civil Disturbance Facility List
DCDFM........ Dichlorodifluoromethane (SAUS)
DCDG.......... Data Computation Subsystem Group (SAUO)
DCDG.......... Diode-Capacitor-Diode Gate
DCDH.......... Diploma in Child Dental Health [*British*] (DBQ)
DC Dist Col... United States District Court for the District of Columbia (DLA)
DCDL.......... Digital Control Design Language [*1968*] [*Computer science*] (CSR)
DCDL.......... Double Cylinder Deadlock
DCD Logic... Diode-Capacitor-Diode Logic (SAUS)
DCD-LPR..... Digital Clock Distribution - Local Primary Reference [*Navigation systems*]
DCDM.......... Digital Controlled Delta Modulation (SAUS)
DCDM.......... Digitally Controlled Delta Modulation (SAUS)
DCDM.......... Digitally Controlled Delta Modulator (MCD)
DCDMA........ Diamond Core Drill Manufacturers Association (EA)
DC-dot......... Dublin Core metadata creation program (SAUS)
DCDP.......... Defense Center Data Processing [*Army*] (AABC)
dCDP.......... Deoxycytidine Diphosphate [*Biochemistry*]
DCDPC......... Defense Command and Data Processing Center (ACAE)
DCDPO......... Directorate for Civil Disturbance Planning and Operations [*Army*] (AABC)
DCDPS......... Dichlorodiphenylsulfone [*Organic chemistry*]
DCDR.......... Data Collection and Data Relay [*Telecommunications*] (TEL)
DCDR.......... Decoder (AAG)
D-CDR......... Deputy Commander (DNAB)
DCDR.......... Direct Cycle Diphenyl Reactor
DCDRS......... Drone Control and Data Retrieval System [*Later, CDRS*] [*Air Force*] (MCD)
DCDS.......... Deceased Confirmed Dead at Scene [*Criminology*] (LAIN)
DCDS.......... Deputy Chief of Defence Staff [*British*]
DCDS.......... Digital Cartographic Data Standard (SAUO)
DCDS.......... Digital Control Design System (IEEE)
DCDS.......... Digital Countdown Display System [*Computer science*]
DCDS.......... Distributed Computer Design System (SDI)
DCDS.......... Double Cotton Double Silk [*Wire insulation*]
DCDS.......... Dual Channel Dual Speed
DCDS(OR).... Deputy Chief of Defence Staff (Operational Requirements) [*British*]
DCDSTF....... Digital Cartographic Data Standards Task Force (GEOI)
DCDT.......... Decedent [*Legal shorthand*] (LWAP)
DCDT.......... Direct-Current Differential Transformer
DCDT.......... Direct Current Displacement Transducer (SAUS)
DCDT.......... Direct-Current Displacement Transducer (IAA)
DCDT.......... Direct Current Distribution Terminal (SAUS)
DCDT.......... Division on Career Development and Transition [*Council for Exceptional Children*] (PAZ)
DCDTs......... Direct Current Distribution Terminals (SAUS)
DCDU.......... Data Collection and Distribution Units [*Military*] (AABC)
DCDU.......... Digital Cassette Data Unit (SAUS)
DC-DVM....... Direct Current - Digital Voltmeter (SAUS)
DCE............. Dairy Cow Equivalent (SAUS)
DCE............. Dallas Cotton Exchange (EA)
DCE............. Data Carrier End (SAUS)
DCE............. Data Circuit Equipment (SAUS)
DCE............. Data Circuit-Terminating Equipment [*Computer science*] (BUR)
DCE............. Data Collecting Equipment (SAUS)
DCE............. Data Collection Engine (SAUS)
DCE............. Data Communication Equipment
DCE............. Data Communication Equipment, Distributed (SAUO)
DCE............. Data Communications Equipment (DOM)
DCE............. Data Communications Exchange (SAUO)
DCE............. Data Concentrating Equipment [*Computer science*] (DGA)
DCE............. Data Consultants of Europe (NITA)
DCE............. Data Control Equipment (IAA)
DCE............. Data Conversion Equipment [*Computer science*]
DCE............. Defense Combat Evaluation (AABC)
DCE............. Defense Coordinating Executive [*Department of Defense*] (DEMM)
DCE............. Definitive Design Cost Estimate (SAUS)
DCE............. Department of Ceramic Engineering (SAUS)
DCE............. Department of Chemical Engineering (SAUS)
DCE............. Department of Civil Engineering (SAUS)
DCE............. Department of Conservation and Environment [*Proposed name for US Department of the Interior*]
DCE............. Department of Continuing Education (AIE)
DCE............. Designated Compensable Event (STED)
DCE............. Desmosterol-to-Cholesterol Enzyme (DMAA)
DCE............. Despin Control Electronics [*Aerospace*]
DCE............. Device Control Entry [*Computer science*]
DCE............. Dichloroethane [*Organic chemistry*]
DCE............. Dichloroethylene (SAUS)
DCE............. Dictionary of Christian Ethics (SAUS)
DCE............. Dictionary of Contemporary English (SAUS)
DCE............. Dicyanoethylene [*Organic chemistry*]
DCE............. Die Casting Engineer (SAUS)
DCE............. Differential Compound Engine (PDAA)
DCE............. Digital Communications Equipment (ELAL)
DCE............. Digital Computer Equipment (SAUS)
DCE............. Digital Control Element (NITA)
DCE............. Diploma in Chemical Engineering (SAUS)
DCE............. Diploma of Curative Education [*British*]
DCE............. Direct Computing Environment (SAUS)
DCE............. Direct Contact Evaporator [*Chemical engineering*]
DCE............. Directorate of Conservation and Environment (SAUS)
DCE............. Director [*or Directorate*] of Civil Engineering [*Air Force*]
DCE............. Director [*or Directorate*] of Communications - Electronics [*ADC*]
DCE............. Discounted Cash Equivalent (ADA)
DCE............. Discrete Control Equipment (SAUS)
DCE............. Display Common Equipment (SAUS)
DCE............. Display Control Equipment (SAUS)
DCE............. Displays Common Equipment (SAUS)
DCE............. Distributed Computer Environment (SAUO)
DCE............. Distributed Computing Environment
DCE............. Distributed Computing Equipment (SAUS)
DCE............. Division of Cancer Etiology (SAUS)
DCE............. Division of Career Education [*Office of Education*]
DCE............. Division of Coal and Energy (SAUO)
DCE............. Division of Compensatory Education (SAUS)
DCE............. Dnepropetrovsk Commodity Exchange [*Ukraine*] (EY)
DCE............. Doctor of Civil Engineering
DCE............. Domestic Credit Expansion
DCE............. Drive Command Electronics (ACAE)
DCE............. Drive Control Equipment
DCE............. Dust Control Equipment (SAUS)
DCE............. Design and Construction Error (ODA)
DCEA.......... Democratic Council on Ethnic Americans [*Defunct*] (EA)
DCEA.......... Dictionary of Civil Engineering Abbreviations (SAUS)
DCEA.......... Distributed Computing Environment Architecture (CIST)
DCEC.......... Defense Communications Engineering Center [*Reston, VA*] [*DoD*] (GRD)
DCEC.......... Direct Current Electroconversion [*Medicine*] (EDAA)
DCEC.......... Directorate of Construction Engineering Control (SAUO)
DCED.......... Distributed Computing Environment Daemon (SAUO)
DC Ed.......... Doctor of Commercial Education
DCEDCMA.... Data Communication Equipment (SAUO)
DCEE.......... Defence Components and Equipment Exhibition [*British*] (ITD)
DCEE.......... Defense Components and Equipment Exposition
DCEE.......... Department of Civil and Environmental Engineering (SAUS)
DCEE.......... Dichloroethyl Ether [*Organic chemistry*]
DCEE.......... Documentation Centre for Education in Europe (SAUS)
D Ce Eng..... Doctor of Cement Engineering
DCEF.......... Discounted Cash Equivalent Flow (ADA)
DCEG.......... Division of Cancer Epidemiology and Genetics (ADWA)
DCEHO........ Deputy Chief Environmental Health Officer (HEAS)
DCEL.......... DC Electroluminescent displays (SAUS)
DCEL.......... Direct-Current Electroluminescence
DCEL.......... Direct Current Electroluminescent (SAUS)
DCEL.......... Dobson Communic. 'A' [*NASDAQ symbol*] (SG)
DCEM.......... Directorate of Construction Engineering Maintenance (SAUO)
DCEM.......... Drilling Cost Estimates Model [*Department of Energy*] (GFGA)
DCEMS........ depth selective CEMS (SAUS)
DCEN.......... Direct Current Electrode Negative (SAUS)
DCEO.......... Defense Communications Engineering Office [*Army*]
DCEO.......... Director of Control Environment Operations (SAUO)
DCEO.......... Division Communications-Electronics Officer [*Military*] (AABC)
DCEP.......... Diploma of Child and Educational Psychology (ADA)
DCEP.......... Direct Current Electrode Positive (SAUS)
DCEPC........ Decimal Classification Editorial Pulicy Committee (SAUS)
DCER.......... Data Circuit-Terminating Equipment Ready [*Computer science*] (ACRL)
DCER.......... Directorate of Cataloguing and Equipment Requirements (SAUO)
DCER.......... United States Army, Corps of Engineers, Coastal Engineering Research Center, Fort Belvoir, VA [*Library symbol*] [*Library of Congress*] (LCLS)
D Cer E........ Doctor of Ceramic Engineering
D Cer Eng.... Doctor of Ceramic Engineering
DCERPC....... Distributed Computing Environment/Remote Procedure Call (VERA)
DCERR......... Depot Component/Equipment Rework Report [*Navy*] (NG)
DCES.......... Data Collection and Evaluation System (NVT)
DCES.......... Delaware Council of Engineering Societies (SAUO)
DCES.......... Dermal Clinical Evaluation Society
DCES.......... Direct Current Electrical Stimulation (MELL)
DCES.......... Discretionary Capital Expenditure System [*Bell System*]
DCES.......... DSS [*Deep Space Station*] Communications Equipment Subsystem
DCESA........ Department of Commerce Economics and Statistics Administration (SAUO)
DCET.......... Dicarbethoxythiamine [*Pharmacology*]
DCEU.......... Dictionary of Carribean English Usage [*A publication*]
DCEV.......... Diabetes Center of Eastern Virginia [*Eastern Virginia Medical School*]
DCF............. Claretian Fathers Library, Washington, DC [*Library symbol*] [*Library of Congress*] (LCLS)
DCF............. Daniell. Forms and Precedents in Chancery [*7th ed.*] [*1932*] [*A publication*] (ILCA)
DCF............. Data Capture Facility (ADWA)
DCF............. Data Capture File (SAUS)
DCF............. Data Channel Filter [*Computer science*]

DCF .... Data Collection Form [*Civil Defense*]
DCF .... Data Communication Facility (SAUO)
DCF .... Data Communication Functions (SAUS)
DCF .... Data Communications Formatter (IAA)
DCF .... Data Compression Facility (SAUO)
DCF .... Data Connector/Formatter [*Computer science*] (TIMI)
DCF .... Data Control Facility [*Computer science*] (HODG)
DCF .... Data Conversion File [*Bureau of the Census*] (GFGA)
DCF .... Data Correlation Facility
DCF .... Data Count Field [*Computer science*] (ACRL)
DCF .... DCEC Computer Facility (SAUS)
DCF .... Deal-Cased Frame [*Carpentry*]
DCF .... DeCarb-Free Product (SAUS)
DCF .... Defenders of the Christian Faith [*Later, CCI*] (EA)
DCF .... Degradation Conversion Factor (MCD)
DCF .... Democratic Candidate Fund (EA)
DCF .... Democratie Chretienne Francaise [*French Christian Democracy*] [*Political party*] (PPE)
DCF .... Denomination Commune Francaise (DB)
DCF .... Deoxycoformycin [*Also, dCF*] [*Antileukemia drug*]
DCF .... Department of Children and Families (DEMM)
DCF .... Dependency Certificate Filed
DCF .... Deputy Chief (SAUS)
DCF .... Deputy for Contract Financing [*Air Force*]
DCF .... Developing Countries Foundation of 1962 [*Denmark*] (EAIO)
DCF .... Dicarboxyfluorescein [*A biological stain*]
DCF .... Die Casting Federation [*Defunct*] (EA)
DCF .... Digestible Crude Fibre (SAUS)
DCF .... Digital Cartographic File (GEOI)
DCF .... Digital Communications Facility (ELAL)
DCF .... Digital Controlled Filter (SAUS)
DCF .... Dilution Correction Factor [*Automotive emissions*]
DCF .... Direct Centrifugal Flotation [*Parasitology*]
DCF .... Direct Contrifugal Flotation (STED)
DCF .... Direct Control Feature (CMD)
DCF .... Directed Chopped Fiber [*Plastics technology*]
DCF .... Disaster Control Force
DCF .... Disc controller formatter (SAUS)
DCF .... Discounted Cash Flow
DCF .... Discrete Correlation Function [*Mathematics*]
DCF .... Dishonored Check File [*IRS*]
DCF .... Disk Control Field (SAUS)
DCF .... Disk Control Field: Disk Controller Formatter (SAUS)
DCF .... Disk Controller/Formatter [*Computer science*]
DCF .... Dispersion Coated Fabric [*Plastics technology*]
DCF .... Distributing Center Facility (SAUS)
DCF .... Distribution Chart File
DCF .... Division Counterattack Force (SAUO)
DCF .... Divorced Christian Female (SAUO)
DCF .... Doctor of City Forestry
DCF .... Document Composition Facility [*IBM Corp.*]
DCF .... Document Control File
DCF .... Dollar Credit & Financing (SAUO)
DCF .... Dominica-Cane [*West Indies*] [*Airport symbol*] (OAG)
DCF .... Donner Canadian Foundation (SAUO)
DCF .... Dopachrome Conversion Factor [*Medicine*] (DMAA)
DCF .... Dose Commitment Factor [*Radioactivity calculations*]
DCF .... Dose Conversion Factor [*Radioactivity calculations*] (NRCH)
DCF .... Driver Configuration File (SAUS)
DCF .... Drone Control Facility (ACAE)
DCF .... Droplet Combustion Facility
dcf .... Dry Cubic Feet (COE)
DCF .... Dry Cubic Feet (ERG)
DCF .... Dynamic Coercive Force
DCF .... Dynamic Coupling Factor (SAUS)
DCF77 .... Digital Code Frequency 77,5 kHz (SAUS)
DCFA .... Damage Controlman, Fireman Apprentice [*Navy*]
DCFA .... Device Capacity-selection and File Assignment (SAUS)
DCFB .... Dichlorotetrafluorobenzene [*Organic chemistry*]
DCFB .... Dodge City, Ford & Bucklin Railroad [*Federal Railroad Administration identification code*]
DCFC .... Dale Chapp Fan Club [*Defunct*] (EA)
DCFC .... Danny Cooksey Fan Club (EA)
DCFC .... David Copperfield Fan Club (EA)
DCFC .... Dehydrated and Convenience Foods Council [*Defunct*] (EA)
DCFC .... Desiree Coleman Fan Club (EA)
DCFC .... Dick Curless Fan Club (EA)
DCFE .... Device Control Functional Element (SAUS)
DCFEL .... Direct Current Film Electroluminescence (SAUS)
DCFEM .... Dynamic Crossed-Field Electron Multiplication
DCFEM .... Dynamic Crossed Field Electron Multiplier (SAUS)
DCFEM .... Dynamic Crossed Fields, Electric and Magnetic (SAUS)
DCFETL .... directly coupled FET logic (SAUS)
DCFF .... Digital Card Flip-Flop [*Computer science*]
DCFF .... Direct Current Flip-Flop (SAUS)
DCFF .... Direct-Current Flip-Flop [*Electronics*] (IAA)
DCFG .... Digital Controlled Function Generator (SAUS)
DCFG .... Direct Curent Free Gyro (SAUS)
DCFG .... Direct-Current Free Gyro
DCFL .... Department of Conservation, Forests, and Lands [*Victoria*] [*Australia*]
DCFL .... Direct-Coupled FET [*Field Effect Transistor*] Logic [*Integrated circuitry*]
DCFL .... direct-coupled field effect transistor logic (SAUS)
DCFL .... Dusky-Capped Flycatcher [*North American bird banding code*] (BIBA)
DCFLOS .... Dynamic Cloud Free Line of Sight (MCD)
DCFM .... Discounted Cash Flow Method
DCFM .... Doppler Color Flow Mapping [*Cardiology*] (DAVI)
DCFMD .... Director of Coastal Forces Material Department [*British*]
DCFN .... Damage Controlman, Fireman [*Navy*]
DCFN .... Developing Countries Farm Radio Network (SAUS)
DCFO .... Defence Communications Field Office (SAUS)
DCFO .... Defense Communications Field Office (SAUO)
DCFO .... Direct Current Fan-Out (SAUS)
DCFP .... Dynamic Crossed-Field Photomultiplier
dcfp .... dynamic cross-feld photomultiplier (SAUS)
DCFR .... Demonstration Commercial Fast Reactor (SAUS)
DCFRN .... Developing Countries Farm Radio Network (EAIO)
DCFROR .... Discounted Cash Flow Rate of Return (SAUS)
DCFRR .... Discounted Cash Flow Rate of Return [*Business term*]
DCFS .... Data Communications Functional Support (SAUS)
DCFT .... Commodity Futures Trading Commission, Washington, DC [*Library symbol*] [*Library of Congress*] (LCLS)
DCFT .... Double-Coated Foam Tape
DCG .... Christian Democrats (Guatemala) [*Political party*] (PSAP)
DCG .... Dacryocystography [*Ophthalmology*] (CPH)
DCG .... Damage Control Group [*Military*] (DNAB)
DCG .... Damage Controlman (Shipboard) [*U.S. Navy enlisted rating*] (AUER)
DCG .... Dancing (ADA)
DCG .... Data Control Group (MCD)
DCG .... Data Element Coordination Group (of TAG 7 of ISO) (AG)
DCG .... Decigram [*Unit of measure*]
DCG .... Decisions of the Comptroller General
DCG .... Decoupled Gun (MCD)
DCG .... Definite Clause Grammar [*Computer programming*] (BYTE)
DCG .... Deoxycorticosterone Glucoside [*Also, DOCG*] [*Endocrinology*]
DCG .... Department of the Controller-General (SAUO)
DCG .... Dependent Charge Group [*Telecommunications*] (TEL)
DCG .... Deputy Chaplain-General [*British*]
DCG .... Deputy Commanding General
DCG .... Deputy Commissary-General
DCG .... Deputy Comptroller General (FOTI)
DCG .... Derived Concentration Guide [*Environmental science*] (COE)
DCG .... Derived or design concentration guide (SAUS)
DCG .... Descendants of Colonial Governors (GEAB)
DCG .... Design Coordination Group (SAUO)
DCG .... Designs Coordination Group [*Telecommunications*] (TEL)
DCG .... Diagnostic Cost Group
DCG .... Diagonostic Cost Group [*Medicine*] (HCT)
DCG .... Dichromated Gelatin
DCG .... Dictionary of Christ and the Gospels [*A publication*] (BJA)
DCG .... Diode-Capacitor Gate
DCG .... Diploma in Careers Guidance [*British*] (DI)
DCG .... Direct-Current Generator
DCG .... Disaster Control Group
DCG .... Disodium Cromoglycate [*Pharmacology*] (MAE)
DCG .... Displacement Cardiograph [*Medicine*]
DCG .... Divisional Controls Group [*British*] (NITA)
DCG .... Documentation Control Group (SAUO)
DCG .... Domain Coordination Group (AAEL)
DCG .... Doppler Control Gain (IAA)
DCG .... Doppler Controlled Gain (SAUS)
DCG .... Double Current Generator
DCG .... Dynamic Cardiogram
DCG .... Hereditary Order of the Descendants of Colonial Governors (EA)
DCG .... San Diego, CA [*Location identifier*] [*FAA*] (FAAL)
DCG .... Direct Coal Gasification (ODA)
DC/GCI .... Direction Center-Ground Control Intercept (SAUO)
DC/GCI .... Direction Center - Ground Controlled Intercept [*SAGE*] [*RADAR*] (CINC)
DCG/CONARC .... Deputy Commanding General, Continental Army Command [*Later, DCG/T*] [*Army*]
DCGD .... Direct-Current Glow Discharge (SAUS)
DCGE .... Department of Civil and Geological Engineering (SAUO)
DCGE .... Dicresyl Glycerin Ether (SAUS)
DCGEM .... Directorate of Clothing, General Engineering and Maintenance (SAUS)
DCGFF .... Diode-Coupled Gated Flip-Flop (SAUS)
DCGFF .... Diode-Coupled Gate Flip-Flop
DCGG .... Display Character and Graphics Generator (SAUS)
DCGICP .... Deputy Commanding General for International Cooperative Programs [*Army*]
DCGM .... Decorticated Groundnut Meal (SAUS)
DCGMD .... Deputy Commanding General for Materiel Development [*Army*]
DCGMR .... Deputy Commanding General for Materiel Readiness [*Army*]
DCGN .... Distributed Communications Grid Network (CCCA)
DCGO .... District Coast Guard Officer
DCGP .... Direct Current Ground Point (SAUS)
DCGRDA .... Deputy Commanding General for Research, Development, and Acquisition [*Army*]
DCGS .... Deputy Chief of the General Staff (SAUS)
DCGS .... Deputy Chief of the General Staff in the Field [*Military*] [*British*]
DCG/T .... Deputy Commanding General, Training [*Formerly, DCG/CONARC*] [*Army*]
DCH .... 1st County of London Yeomanry (SAUO)
D Ch .... Chirurgiae Doctor [*Doctor of Surgery*]
DCH .... Damage Control Hulk (DNAB)
DCH .... Data Channel [*Computer science*]
DCH .... Data Chief
DCH .... Data Communication Handbook [*Computer science*] (VLIE)
DCH .... Data Communications Handler (DNAB)

DCH .... Day-Care Home (MELL)
DCH .... D Channel Handler (SAUS)
DCH .... Deep Case Hardened
DCH .... Defendant's Case History (SEAT)
D Ch .... Delaware Chancery Reports [*A publication*] (DLA)
DCH .... Delayed Cutaneous Hypersensitivity [*Medicine*] (AAMN)
DCH .... Denote Chassis
DCH .... Department of Community Health [*Australia*]
DCH .... Dichlorohydrin (SAUS)
DCH .... Dicyclohexyl [*Organic chemistry*]
DCH .... Diploma in Child Health [*British*]
DCH .... Direct Containment Heating [*Environmental science*] (COE)
DCH .... District Chaplain [*Navy*]
DCH .... Drain Collection Header [*Nuclear energy*] (NRCH)
DCH .... Dual-Circuit Hydraulic [*Automotive brakes*]
DCH .... Reports of the United States District Court of Hawaii [*A publication*] (DLA)
DCh .... Doctor of Surgery [*Latin*] [*Doctor Chirurgiae*] (ODA)
DCHA .... Dicyclohexylamine [*Organic chemistry*]
DCHA .... Docosahexaenoic Acid (DMAA)
DCHAN .... Difference Channel (MSA)
D-channel .... Data Channel (PCM)
D-channel .... Delta Channel [*Used for communicating between the phone company switch and an ISDN adapter*] [*Computer science*]
DCHBH .... Dicyclohexylborane [*Organic chemistry*]
DCHC .... Dunbarton College of Holy Cross [*Closed, 1973*] [*Washington, DC*]
DCHCL .... Dropsie College for Hebrew and Cognate Learning (SAUS)
DCHD .... Di(N-carbazoly)hexadiyne [*Organic chemistry*]
DChD .... Doctor Chirurgiae Dentalis [*Doctor of Dental Surgery*] [*British*]
D Ch E .... Doctor of Chemical Engineering
DCHEB .... Dichlorohexafluorobutane (DMAA)
D Che E .... Doctor of Chemical Engineering
DChem .... Doctor of Chemistry (GAGS)
DCHEM .... Dry Chemical
D Chem E .... Doctor of Chemical Engineering
DCHEMT ...... Doped-Channel High Electron Mobility Transistor (SAUS)
D Ch Eng ..... Doctor of Chemical Engineering
DCHFB .... Dichlorohexafluorobutane [*Organic chemistry*] (MAE)
DCHi .... Columbia Historical Society, Washington, DC [*Library symbol*] [*Library of Congress*] (LCLS)
DCHIDCH ..... Diploma in Child Health (SAUS)
dchn .... dicyclohexylamine nitrate (SAUS)
DCHN .... Dicyclohexylamine Nitrite [*Organic chemistry*] (MAE)
DChO .... Diploma in Ophthalmic Surgery (SAUS)
D Ch O .... Diploma in Opthalmic Surgery [*British*]
DChO .... Doctor of Ophthalmic Surgery (DMAA)
DCHP .... Dicyclohexyl Phthalate [*Organic chemistry*]
DCHQ .... Damage Control Headquarters [*Military*] [*British*]
D Chr Ed ..... Doctor of Christian Education
DCHS .... Center for Hellenic Studies, Harvard University, Washington, DC [*Library symbol*] [*Library of Congress*] (LCLS)
DCHS .... Department of Community & Health Services, Tasmania (SAUS)
DCHS .... Disciples of Christ Historical Society (EA)
DCHSS .... Duchess
DCHT .... Diploma in Community Health in Tropical Countries [*British*] (DBQ)
DCHT .... Direct-Contact Heat Transfer [*Chemical engineering*]
DCHT .... Dual-channel Heterostructure Transistor (SAUS)
DCHUM .... Digital Chart Update Manual (GEOI)
DCHUM .... Digital Chart Update Manual Laboratory (SAUO)
DCHV .... Domiciliary Care for Homeless Veterans [*Department of Veterans Affairs*]
DCI .... Carnegie Institution of Washington, Washington, DC [*Library symbol*] [*Library of Congress*] (LCLS)
DCI .... Daily Call-In
DCI .... Damage Control Instructor [*Navy*] (DNAB)
DCI .... Daniel Construction Company International (SAUO)
DCI .... DARCOM [*Development and Readiness Command, Army*] Career/Control Inventory (MCD)
DCI .... Data Call-In (EEVL)
DCI .... Data Capture Interface [*Computer science*] (VERA)
DCI .... Data Carrier Input (SAUS)
DCI .... Data Channel Interface (SAUS)
DCI .... Data Collection Interface [*Computer science*] (VLIE)
DCI .... Data Communication Interlock (SAUS)
DCI .... Data Communication Interrogate (OA)
DCI .... Data Communications, Inc.
DCI .... Data Communications Incorporated (SAUO)
DCI .... Data Communications Interface
DCI .... Data Communications Interrogate (HGAA)
DCI .... Data Composition, Inc. [*Information service or system*] (IID)
DCI .... Data Courier, Inc. (IID)
DCI .... Dayco Corporation International Division (SAUO)
DCI .... Deaf Communications Institute [*Defunct*] (EA)
DCI .... Decided Cases Index (HEAS)
DCI .... Decision Concepts Incorporated (SAUO)
DCI .... Decompression Illness
DCI .... Defence Council Instructions [*Military*] [*British*]
DCI .... Defence Counter-Proliferation Initiative (ECON)
DCI .... Defence for Children International Movement [*See also DEI*] [*Database producer*] (EAIO)
DCI .... Defense Computer Institute
DCI .... Defense for Children International (SAUO)
DCI .... Deliverable Contract Item (KSC)
DCI .... DeLorean Club International (EA)
DCI .... Denomination Commune Internationale (DB)
DCI .... Department of Central Index [*Computer center*] [*Department of Health and Social Security*] [*British*]
DCI .... Department of Central Intelligence [*Thailand*] (CINC)
DCI .... Department of Citizenship and Immigration (SAUS)
DCI .... Deputy Chief for Intelligence (AAG)
DCI .... Deputy Chief Inspector (HEAS)
DCI .... Design Change Information (SAA)
DCI .... Desktop Color Imaging (VLIE)
DCI .... Des Moines and Central Iowa (SAUS)
DCI .... Des Moines & Central Iowa Railway [*Federal Railroad Administration identification code*]
DCI .... Des Moines & Central Iowa Railway Co. [*AAR code*]
DCI .... Desorption Chemical Ionization
DCI .... Detective Chief Inspector [*British*] (WDAA)
DCI .... Device Control Interface [*Computer science*] (VERA)
DCI .... Dialing Code Information [*Telecommunications*] [*British*]
DCI .... Dichloroisocoumarin [*Organic chemistry*]
DCI .... Dichloroisoprenaline
DCI .... Dichloroisoproterenol [*Pharmacology*]
DCI .... Dielectric Constant Indicator
DCI .... Differential Corrections, Inc. (GEOI)
DCI .... Differential Corrections, Incorporated (SAUO)
DCI .... Differential Current Integrator (IAA)
DCI .... Digital Clock Indicator
DCI .... Digital Consulting, Inc. [*Andover, MA*] (TSSD)
DCI .... Digital Control Interface [*Computer science*] (PCM)
DCI .... Direct Carrier Injection
DCI .... Direct Channel Interface
DCI .... Direct Computer Input (MCD)
DCI .... Direct Coupled Inverter (SAUS)
DCI .... Direct-Coupled Inverter (IAA)
DCI .... Direct-Current Ionization (SAUS)
DCI .... Direct Cylinder Injection [*Engine design*]
DCI .... Directorate of Cataloging & Identification (SAUS)
DCI .... Director of Central Intelligence
DCI .... Director of Chemical Inspectorate (SAUS)
DCI .... Director of Combat Intelligence (MCD)
DCI .... Director of Corporate Information
dci .... dischloroisoproterenol (SAUS)
DCI .... Disk Core Image (CMD)
DCI .... Dispersive Corrosion Inhibitor (SAUS)
DCI .... Display Control Interface [*Computer science*] (PCM)
DCI .... Disseminated Cryptococcus Neoformans Infection [*Medicine*]
DCI .... Distribution Codes Institute [*Defunct*] (EA)
DCI .... Division of Chemical Information [*American Chemical Society*] [*Information service or system*] (IID)
DCI .... Documentation Change Instruction (KSC)
DCI .... Donaldson Co. [*NYSE symbol*] (TTSB)
DCI .... Donaldson Co., Inc. [*NYSE symbol*] (SPSG)
DCI .... Doppler Compensation Inhibit (SAUS)
DCI .... Double Column Inch [*Typography*] (DGA)
dci .... doublecolumn inch (SAUS)
DCI .... Dramatic Criticism Index [*A publication*]
DCI .... Driving Car Intoxicated
DCI .... Driving Control Indicator
DCI .... Drum Corps International (EA)
DCI .... Dry Creek [*Idaho*] [*Seismograph station code, US Geological Survey*] (SEIS)
DCI .... Ductile Cast Iron
DCI .... Duplicate Coverage Inquiry [*Insurance*]
DCI .... Direct Computer Interviewing (ODA)
DCIA .... Digital Card Inverting Amplifier [*Computer science*]
DCIA .... Direction Center Initial Appearance (SAA)
DCIB .... Data Communication Input Buffer
DCIB .... Defense Counterintelligence Board (MCD)
DCIC .... Defense Ceramic Information Center [*Later, MCIC*] [*Battelle Memorial Institute*] (MCD)
DCIC .... Defense Ceramics Information Center (SAUS)
DCIC .... Double Column Ion Chromotography
dcid .... decide (SAUS)
DCID .... Department of Commercial and Industrial Development (SAUS)
DCID .... Development Change in Design (SAUS)
DCID .... Director Central Intelligence Directive (SAUS)
DCID .... Director of Central Intelligence Directive
DCID .... Director of Central Intelligence Document
DCID 1/2 .... Director of Central Intelligence directive of 21 January 1972 that was a five-year plan for planning and programming (CARL)
DCIEM .... Canadian Defence Civil Institute of Environmental Medicine (SAUS)
DCIEM .... Defence and Civil Institute of Environmental Medicine [*Canada*]
DCIEM .... Defence (or Defense) and Civil Institute of Environmental Medicine (SAUO)
DCIF .... Deputy Chief Inspector of Factories (HEAS)
DCIFC .... David Copperfield International Fan Club (EA)
DCI-G .... Carnegie Institution of Washington, Geophysical Laboratory, Washington, DC [*Library symbol*] [*Library of Congress*] (LCLS)
DC ignition ... Dead Center ignition (SAUS)
DCIGS .... Deputy Chief of the Imperial General Staff [*Military*] [*British*]
DCII .... Defense Central Index of Information (SAUS)
DCII .... Defense Central Index of Investigations (AFM)
DCILM .... Direct Computer Input Load Module (MCD)
DCIM .... Display System Computer Input Multiplexer (MCD)
DCIM .... Documentation Centre of International Music (SAUS)
DCIMI .... Defense Council of Integrity in Management and Improvement [*DoD*]
DC-in-C .... Deputy Commander-in-Chief (SAUO)
DCINO .... Deputy Chief Inspector of Naval Ordnance (SAUO)

DCIO .... Deputy Chief Inspecting Officer (HEAS)
DCIO .... Direct Channel Interface Option
DCIOO .... Import Opportunities Office for Developing Countries (SAUO)
DCIP .... Data Correction Indicator Panel (MUGU)
DCIP .... Dichlorophenolindophenol [*Also, DCPI, DCPIP, DPIP*] [*Analytical reagent*]
DCIP .... Disk Cartridge Initialization Program (CMD)
DCIP .... Display and Controls Input Processor
DCIPT .... Damage Control In-Port Training (NVT)
DCIR .... Daily Cadweld Inspection Report [*Nuclear energy*] (NRCH)
DCIRC .... Defense Contracting for Information Resources Course [*DoD*] (RDA)
DCIS .... Dartmouth College Information System [*Library network*] (IT)
DCIS .... Data Call-In Staff (SAUS)
DCIS .... Defense Criminal Investigation Service
DCIS .... Delta Computec [*NASDAQ symbol*] (TTSB)
DCIS .... Department of Commercial and Intelligence Statistics (SAUO)
DCIS .... Department of Computing and Information Science (SAUS)
DCIS .... Digital Computer Interface System (MCD)
DCIS .... Distribution Construction Information System [*IBM Corp.*]
DCIS .... Downrange Computer Input System (MUGU)
DCIS .... Ductal Carcinoma in Situ [*Medicine*] (ADWA)
DCIS .... Duct Carcinoma In Situ [*Oncology*]
DCIST .... Directory of Computerized Information in Science and Technology [*Leonard Cohen, ed., New York: Science Associates International, 1968*] [*A publication*]
DCI-T .... Carnegie Institution of Washington, Department of Terrestrial Magnetism, Washington, DC [*Library symbol*] [*Library of Congress*] (LCLS)
DCITY .... Dodge City, KS [*American Association of Railroads railroad junction routing code*]
DCIU .... Data Channel Interface Unit (SAUS)
DCIU .... Data Communications Interface Unit [*Computer science*] (VLIE)
DCIU .... Digital Control and Interface Unit (MCD)
DCI-USA ...... Defense for Children International - United States of America (EA)
DCivL .... Doctor of Civil Law (NADA)
DCIX .... Danella Construction [*Private rail car owner code*]
DClyL .... Direct Coupled Integrated Injection Logic (SAUS)
DCJ .... Carmelitae Divini Cordis Jesu [*Carmelite Sisters of the Divine Heart of Jesus*] [*Roman Catholic religious order*]
DCJ .... Dade County Jail (SAUS)
DCJ .... Department of Criminal Justice (SAUS)
DCJ .... DISCovering Careers and Jobs [*Database*]
DCJ .... District Court Judge
DCJ .... Doctor of Criminal Jurisprudence
DCJC .... Dawson County Junior College [*Montana*]
DCK .... Dahl Creek, AK [*Location identifier*] [*FAA*] (FAAL)
DCK .... Data Check (VLIE)
DCK .... Deoxycytidine Kinase (DMAA)
Dck .... Duck [*Medicine*] (EDAA)
DCKG .... Docking (MSA)
DCKNG .... Docking [*Aerospace*] (NASA)
DCKP .... Direct-Current Key Pulsing (IEEE)
DCL .... Clear Daylight (SAUS)
DCL .... Danish Container Line (SAUS)
DCL .... Dartmouth College Library (SAUS)
DCL .... Data Capture Link (SAUS)
DCL .... Data Checklist
DCL .... Data Command Language [*Computer science*] (VLIE)
DCL .... Data Communications Language (SAUS)
DCL .... Data Communications Link (ACAE)
DCL .... Data Compression Library (CDE)
DCL .... Data Control Language [*NCR Corp.*]
DCL .... Data Control List (IAA)
DCL .... Data Conversion Languages (SAUS)
DCL .... Data Coordination Logic (SAUS)
DCL .... Data Coupled Logic (SAUS)
DCL .... Daylight Clear (SAUS)
dcl .... decaliter (or decalitre) (SAUS)
DCL .... Decalitre
DCL .... DEC Command Language (SAUS)
DCL .... DEC Control Language (SAUS)
DCL .... Declaration (ADA)
dcl .... declarative (SAUS)
DCL .... Declare (VLIE)
DCL .... Decline (WDAA)
DCL .... Defence Construction [*1951*] Ltd. [*Canada*]
DCL .... Defense Contractors List (SAUS)
DCL .... Delay Calculator Language (SAUS)
DCL .... Delayed Call Limited [*Telecommunications*] (TEL)
DCL .... Delete Character Line (SAUS)
DCL .... Demountable Cathode Lamp
DCL .... Depth of Cut Line (MCD)
DCL .... Deputy Commander for Logistics (MCD)
DCL .... Designate Command Line [*Computer science*]
DCL .... Design Capability Line [*Army*] (AABC)
DCL .... Design Change Listing
DCL .... Design Choice Logic (SAUS)
DCL .... Designer Choice Logic
DCL .... Detailed Checklist
DCL .... Detailed Configuration List (MCD)
DCL .... Detection, Classification and Localization (SAUS)
Dcl .... Detention clause (SAUS)
DCL .... Detroit College of Law [*Michigan*]
DCL .... Deuterium of Canada, Limited (SAUS)
Dcl .... Deviation clause (SAUS)
DCL .... Device Clear (SAUS)
DCL .... Devices Clear [*Computer science*] (CIST)
DCL .... Diagnostic Chemicals Ltd.
DCL .... Dialog Control/Command Language [*Computer science*] (VLIE)
DCL .... Diamond Cut Lug (DICI)
DCL .... Diebold Computer Leasing, Inc. (SAUO)
DCL .... Die Card Lever (SAUS)
DCL .... Diffuse [*or Disseminated*] Cutaneous Leishmaniasis [*Medicine*] (DMAA)
DCL .... Digital Channel Link
DCL .... Digital Command Language [*Digital Equipment Corp.*] (NITA)
DCL .... Digital Computer Laboratory [*Massachusetts Institute of Technology*] (MCD)
DCL .... Digital Computer Language (SAUS)
DCL .... Digital configuration line (SAUS)
DCL .... Digital Control Laboratory (SAUS)
DCL .... Digital Control Language [*Computer science*] (AGLO)
DCL .... Digital Control Loading [*System*] (MCD)
DCL .... Digital Control Logic [*Computer science*] (CIST)
DCL .... Digital Counter/Locator [*Medical dictation and transcription equipment*] (DAVI)
DCL .... Diners Club, Inc. (SAUO)
DCL .... Diode-Less Core Logic (VLIE)
DCL .... Direct Coal Liquefaction [*Fuel science*]
DCL .... Direct Communications Link [*US/USSR*]
DCL .... Direct-Coupled Logic
DCL .... Directly Controlled Link (SAUS)
DCL .... Director of Contract Labour [*Admiralty*] [*British*]
DCL .... Discretionary Credit Limit [*Business term*] (MHDB)
DCL .... Display Communication Log (AAEL)
DCL .... Distillers Company Limited (SAUO)
DCL .... Division of Chemical Literature [*ACS*]
DCL .... Doctor of Canon Law
DCL .... Doctor of Civil Law
DCL .... Doctor of Classical Literature
DCL .... Doctor of Commercial Law
DCL .... Doctor of Common Law (CPGU)
DCL .... Doctor of Comparative Law (DLA)
DCL .... Document Change List (MCD)
DCL .... Door Closer
DCL .... Drawing Change List
DCL .... Dual Current Layer (OA)
DCL .... Dynamic Characteristic Load
DCL .... United States Department of Commerce, Washington, DC [*OCLC symbol*] (OCLC)
DCL1 .... Region 1 Library Document Control System (SAUS)
DCLA .... Deputy Chief of Staff, Logistics and Administration [*NATO*] (NATG)
DCLA .... District of Columbia Library Association (SAUO)
DCLA .... District of Columbia Libray Association (SAUS)
DC Lab S ..... Dominion of Canada Labour Service [*Commerce Clearing House*] [*A publication*] (DLA)
DClark .... Dick Clark Productions, Inc. [*Associated Press*] (SAG)
DCLAS .... Department of the Controller of Labour Allocation and Supply (SAUO)
DCLC .... Drift Cyclotron Loss Cone [*Plasma physics*]
DCLC .... RLIN [*Research Libraries Information Netword*] code for the Library of Congress
DClChem ..... Doctor of Clinical Chemistry (SAUS)
DCLCO .... Diffusing Capacity of Lung for Carbon Monoxide (MELL)
DCLCS .... Data Conversion and Limit Check Submodule [*Computer science*] (IAA)
DCLD .... Digital Communications Section (SAUO)
DCLD .... Division of Clinical Laboratory Devices [*Center for Devices and Radiological Health*]
DCL/DCS ...... Delay Calculation Language/Delay Calculation System (VLIE)
DCLE .... Department of Criminal Law Enforcement (SAUS)
DCLE .... Designated Centre of Library Excellence (SAUS)
DCLF .... Diploma in Contact Lens Fitting [*British*] (DBQ)
dclg .... declining (SAUS)
DCLI .... Duke of Cornwall's Light Infantry [*Military unit*] [*British*]
DCLIR .... Dead Cat Lying in the Road [*Traffic report*]
DCLK .... DoubleClick, Inc. [*NASDAQ symbol*] (SG)
DCLM .... Department of Command, Leadership, and Management [*DoD*]
DCLM .... Department of Conservation and Land Management (SAUO)
DCLM .... Division of Concessions and Lease Management (SAUO)
DCLN .... Direct Coupled Loop Network [*Computer science*]
DCLO .... Deputy Congressional Liaison Officer (SAUO)
DCLP .... Diploma in Contact Lens Practice [*British*] (DBQ)
DCL PI .... Delay Calculator Language Procedural Interface (SAUS)
DCLPT .... In-Port Damage Control Training [*Navy*] (NVT)
DCLR .... Decelerate (MSA)
DCLR .... Defense Contract Litigation Reporter [*Shepard's McGraw-Hill*] [*A publication*] (AAGC)
DCLR .... Delaware Coast Line [*Federal Railroad Administration identification code*]
DCLR .... District Court Law Reports [*Hong Kong*] [*A publication*] (ILCA)
DCLR(Can)... Dominion Companies Law Reports [*Canada*] [*A publication*] (DLA)
DCLRT .... Decelerate [*Aviation*] (FAAC)
DCLS .... Data Collection and Location System [*Telecommunications*]
DCLS .... Deoxycholate Citrate Lactose Saccharose (SAUS)
DCLS .... Deoxycholate-Citrate-Lactose-Sucrose [*Agar*] [*Microbiology*]
dcls .... disclose (SAUS)
DCLS .... Dual Channel Line Scanner (SAUS)
DClSc .... Doctor of Clinical Science (ADA)
DCLSc .... Doctor of Clinical Science (ODA)
DClSci .... Doctor of Clinical Science (NADA)

dclsd........... disclosed (SAUS)
dclsg........... disclosing (SAUS)
DCLSO........ DLA CALS Support Office (SAUO)
dclsr........... disclosure (SAUS)
DCLTC........ Dry Cargo Loading Technical Committee [*NATO*] (NATG)
DCLTR........ Declines Transfer (SAUS)
DCLTR........ Decline Transfer (NOAA)
DCLTS........ Dry Cargo Loading Technical Committee (SAUO)
DCLU........... Declutch
DCLU........... Developing Countries Liaison Unit (SAUS)
DCLU........... Digital Carrier Line Unit (VERA)
DCLX........... Dow Chemical [*Private rail car owner code*]
DCLZ........... Data Compression Lempel Ziv (SAUS)
DCLZ........... Data Compression Lempel-Ziv [*Computer science*]
DCLZ........... Derby City Lumber [*Federal Railroad Administration identification code*]
DCM............ Chester, SC [*Location identifier*] [*FAA*] (FAAL)
DCM............ Dangerous Cargo Manifest [*RSPA*] (TAG)
DCM............ Data Channel Module [*Computer science*] (NOAA)
DCM............ Data Circuit Module (SAUS)
DCM............ Data Communication Multiplexer (or Multiplexor) (SAUS)
DCM............ Data Communications Methods (SAUS)
DCM............ Data Communications Modem (SAUS)
DCM............ Data Communications Multiplexer
DCM............ Data Compression Module [*Computer science*] (AGLO)
DCM............ Data Conversion Machine (MCD)
DCM............ Day Care Mother (ADA)
DCM............ DC Noise Margin (MCD)
DCM............ Decameter
DCM............ DECOM Control Memory (SAUS)
DCM............ Decommutator Control Memory (MCD)
DCM............ Deep Chlorophyll Maximum [*Oceanography*]
DCM............ Deep Convection Model (SAUS)
DCM............ Defence Common Market (SAUS)
DCM............ Defense Combat Maneuvers (SAUS)
DCM............ Defense Common Market (MCD)
DCM............ Defensive Countermaneuvering
DCM............ Defined Culture Medium [*For blastoderms*]
DCM............ Demand Chain Management (GART)
DCM............ Department of Coins and Medals (SAUO)
DCM............ Department of the Chief Minister [*Northern Territory*] [*Australia*]
DCM............ Deputy Chief of Maintenance (MCD)
DCM............ Deputy Chief of Mission [*Diplomatic corps*]
DCM............ Deputy Commander for Maintenance (SAUO)
DCM............ Deputy Commander for Material (SAUS)
DCM............ Design criteria manual (SAUS)
DCM............ Diagnostic Controlled MODEM [*Computer science*] (BUR)
DCM............ Diagnostic Control Module (SAUS)
DCM............ Dichloromaleic Acid [*Organic chemistry*]
DCM............ Dichloromethane [*Anesthetic*] [*Organic chemistry*]
DCM............ Dichloromethotrexate [*Also, DCMTX*] [*Antineoplastic drug*]
DCM............ Die Casting Mold (MCD)
DCM............ Diffused Current Mode (SAUS)
DCM............ Digital Capacitance Meter (IDOE)
DCM............ Digital Carrier Module (VERA)
DCM............ digital cartographic model (SAUS)
DCM............ Digital Circuit Module [*Computer science*]
DCM............ Digital Circuit Multiplication [*Computer science*] (ACRL)
DCM............ Digital Command Language (SAUS)
DCM............ Digital Conference Module [*Telecommunications*] (NITA)
DCM............ Dilated Cardiomyopathy [*Cardiology*]
DCM............ Dimension Control Memory
DCM............ Diocesan Carmelites of Maine (TOCD)
DCM............ Direct Connection Module [*Computer science*]
DCM............ Direct Control Module (SAUS)
DCM............ Direct-Current, Main (IAA)
DCM............ Direct Current Mains (SAUS)
DCM............ Direct Current Motor (SAUS)
DCM............ Direct Current Noise Margin (SAUS)
DCM............ Direction Cosine Matrix (MCD)
DCM............ Directorate for Classification Management [*DoD*]
DCM............ Directorate of Classified Management (SAUS)
DCM............ Director of Civilian Marksmanship [*Army*]
DCM............ Directory Control Module [*Computer science*] (HGAA)
DCM............ Disability Case Management [*Insurance*] (WYGK)
DCM............ Display and Control Module (MCD)
DCM............ Display Control Module (SAUS)
DCM............ Distinguished Conduct Medal [*British*]
DCM............ Distributed Computing Model (SAUS)
DCM............ Distributed Control Module (SAUS)
DCM............ District Court-Martial [*Facetious translation: "Don't Come Monday," in reference to a one-day suspension*] [*British*]
DCM............ District Cub Master [*Scouting*]
DCM............ distuted control modul (SAUS)
DCM............ Diversified Composite Material (PDAA)
DCM............ Division of Civilian Marksmanship [*Army*]
DCM............ Divorced Christian Male (SAUO)
DCM............ Doctor of Church Music (PGP)
DCM............ Doctor of Comparative Medicine
DCM............ Document Component Management (GART)
DCM............ Dominican Campaign Medal
DCM............ Double Common Meter [*Music*]
DCM............ Double Common Multiple [*Mathematics*] (ROG)
DCM............ Double Crystal Monochromator
DCM............ Drawing Control Manual (MCD)
DCM............ Dreyfus California Municipal Income, Inc. [*AMEX symbol*] (CTT)
DCM............ Dreyfus Cal Muni Income [*AMEX symbol*] (TTSB)
DCM............ Drumhead Court-Martial (SAUO)
DCM............ Dry Cell Mass
dcm............ Dry Cubic Meter (COE)
DCM............ Dry Cubic Meter (EG)
DCM............ Duty Committee Member (SAUO)
DCM............ Dynamic Connection Management [*Communications term*] (DCT)
DCM............ Dyssynergia Cerebellaris Myoclonica [*Medicine*] (DMAA)
DCMA.......... Defence Combined Material Agency (SAUS)
DCMA.......... Defense Contract Management Agency
DCMA.......... Defense Contract Management Association (SAUO)
DCMA.......... Dichloromaleic Acid [*Organic chemistry*]
DCMA.......... Digital Millennium Copyright Act
DCMA.......... Direct-Current Milliamp (IAA)
DCMA.......... District of Columbia Manpower Administration
DCMA.......... double-pauss CMA (SAUS)
DCMA.......... Dry Color Manufacturers Association (EA)
DCMA.......... Duty Cycle Modulation Alternator
DCMA.......... Duty Cycle Modulation Attenator (SAUS)
DCMAILSUB... Discharge Certificate Mailed Subsequent to Separation [*Navy*] (DNAB)
DCM & G..... Direct Current Motor and Generator Facility [*General Electric Co.*]
DCMAO........ Defense Contract Management Area Operation (DOMA)
DCMAO........ Defense Contract Management Area Operations (RDA)
DC mark...... Dead Center mark (SAUS)
DCMAS........ Debt Collection and Management Assistance Service [*Department of Education*] (GFGA)
DC-MAW...... Directionally-Controlled-Medium Anti-Tank Assault Weapon (SAA)
DCMB.......... Development Configuration Management Board (MCD)
DCMBA........ Dairy, Confectionery and Mixed Business Association (SAUO)
DCMC.......... Defense Contract Management Command [*DoD*]
DCMD.......... Defense Contract Management District [*Replaced DCASR*] (AAGC)
DCMD.......... Demonstration Cities and Metropolitan Development Act (COE)
DCMD.......... District of Columbia Military District (AABC)
DCMDA........ Demonstration Cities and Metropolitan Development Act
DCMDE........ Defense Contract Management District East
DCMDI......... Defense Contract Management District International
DCME.......... Dichloromethyl Ether (SAUS)
DCME.......... Dichloromethyl Methyl Ether [*Organic chemistry*]
DCME.......... Digital Circuit Multiplication Equipment [*Telecommunications*]
DCMFM........ Dichloromonofluoromethane (SAUS)
DCMG.......... Dame Commander of the Order of St. Michael and St. George [*British*]
DCMG.......... Data Center for Marine Geology (SAUO)
DCMH.......... Data Collection Module, High Speed
DCMHQ........ Denver Community Mental Health Questionnaire (DB)
DCMI........... Disclosure of Classified Military Information [*to foreign governments*] (AFM)
DC/MIP........ Dynamic Computer/Multipurpose Information Processor (SAUS)
DCML........... Data Collection Module, Low Speed
DCML........... Decimal (SAUS)
DCML........... Differential Current Mode Logic [*Computer science*] (NITA)
DCML........... Diplomatic Conference of International Maritime Law
DCML........... Dorsal Column Medial Lemniscal (DB)
DCML........... Dorsal Column Medial Lemniscus [*Medicine*] (DMAA)
DCMNTN...... Documentation
DCMO.......... Dairy, Cowshed, and Milk Shop Order [*1885-1886*] [*Legal*] [*British*] (ROG)
DCMO.......... DLA Civilian Personnel Management Support Office (SAUO)
DCMO.......... Documentation and Configuration Management Office (SSD)
DC motor..... direct current motor (SAUS)
DCMP.......... Daunorubicin, Cytarabine, Mercaptopurine, Prednisone [*Antineoplastic drug regimen*]
dCMP........... Deoxycytidine Monophosphate [*Biochemistry*]
dCMP........... Deoxycytidine-Phosphate [*Biochemistry*] (DAVI)
dCMP........... Deoxycytidylic Acid (ADWA)
DCMPO........ Deputy Chief of the Military Planning Office
DCMPS........ Degaussing Compass
DCMPTR...... Degaussing Computer
DCMR.......... Defense Contract Management Regions (DOMA)
DCMR.......... District Of Columbia Municipal Regulations [*A publication*]
DCMRS........ DC Metropolitan Radiological Society (SAUO)
DCMS.......... Dannebrog Container and Marine Services (SAUS)
DCMS.......... Data Capture and Management System (IAA)
DCMS.......... Data Control Multiplex System
DCMS.......... Dedicated Computer Message (SAUS)
DCMS.......... Dedicated Computer Message Switching
DCMS.......... Depot Command Management System
DCMs.......... Deputy Chiefs of Missions (SAUS)
DCMS.......... Deputy Commissioner Medical Services [*British*] (DAS)
DCMS.......... Deputy Commissioner of Medical Services (SAUO)
DCMS.......... Digital Capacitance Measuring System (MCD)
DCMS.......... Digital Circuit Multiplication System (SAUS)
DCMS.......... Digital Communications Management System [*Navy*]
DCMS.......... Director Communications Material Security (MCD)
DCMS.......... Director, COMSEC Material System (SAUO)
DCMS.......... Distributed Call Measurement System
DCMS.......... Distribution Center Management and Control System (SAUS)
DCMSN........ Decommission (FAAC)
DCMSND...... Decommissioned
DCMT.......... Decrement (EECA)
DCMT.......... Diploma in Clinical Medicine of the Tropics [*British*]
DCMT.......... Diploma in Clinical Medicine of Tropics (SAUS)
DCMT.......... Doctor of Clinical Medicine of the Tropics [*British*] (DAVI)

dcmt .... document (SAUS)
DCMTX .... Dichloromethotrexate [*Also, DCM*] [*Antineoplastic drug*]
DCMU .... (Dichlorophenyl)dimethylurea [*Herbicide*]
DCMU .... Digital Colour Map Unit (SAUO)
DCMU .... Digital Concentrator Measurement Unit (SAUS)
DC Mun App... Municipal Court of Appeals for the District of Columbia (DLA)
DCMV .... Digital Card Multivibrator [*Computer science*]
dCMV .... Disseminated Cytomegalovirus [*Infection*] [*Medicine*] (DB)
DCMX .... Dichloro-meta-Xylenol [*Organic chemistry*]
DCMXT .... Dichloromethotrexate [*Antineoplastic drug*] (DAVI)
DCN .... Daily Consumer News [*Consumers' Association*] [*Information service or system*] (IID)
DCN .... Dana Corp. [*NYSE symbol*] (SAG)
DCN .... Darvocet N [*Medicine*] (EDAA)
DCN .... Databases in Computer Networks (SAUS)
DCN .... Data Change Notice (KSC)
DCN .... Data Communications Network [*Computer science*] (ACRL)
DCN .... Deacon
DCN .... Debt Crisis Network [*Defunct*] (EA)
DCN .... Deep Cerebellar Nuclei [*Brain anatomy*]
DCN .... Defence Communication Network [*British*] (NATG)
DCN .... Delayed Conditional Necrosis (MAE)
DCN .... Delayed Conditioned Necrosis (SAUS)
DCN .... Dental Care Network [*Blue Cross and Blue Shield*] [*Insurance*]
DCN .... Dental Computer Newsletter (SAUO)
DCN .... Depot Control Number
DCN .... Depressed, Cognitively Normal [*Medicine*] (MELL)
DCN .... Design Change Notice
DCN .... Deuterated Hydrocyanic Acid (SAUS)
DCN .... Development Change Notice [*Aerospace*]
DCN .... Dichloronaphthalene (SAUS)
DCN .... Dichloronitrosalicylanilide [*Economic poison*] [*Organic chemistry*]
DCN .... Dicyanonaphthalene [*Organic chemistry*]
DCN .... Digital Computer Newsletter [*A publication*] (DNAB)
DCN .... Direct change notice (SAUS)
DCN .... Discalced Carmelite Nuns [*Italy*] (EAIO)
DCN .... Disconnect
DCN .... Distributed Computer Network
DCN .... Documentation Change Notice
DCN .... Document Change Notice
DCN .... Document Control Number (AFM)
DCN .... Dorsal Cardiac Nerve [*Anatomy*]
DCN .... Dorsal Column Nucleus (DB)
DCN .... Dorsal Cutaneous Nerve
DCN .... Double Check Negotiation (SAUS)
DCN .... Double Crown [*Monetary unit*] [*British*] (ADA)
DCN .... Draft Change Notice (MCD)
DCN .... Drawing Change Notice
DCN .... Dual-Coded Number (SAUS)
DCN .... Federal Armed Forces of Germany [*ICAO designator*] (FAAC)
DCN1 .... Data Communication Methods (SAUS)
DCNA .... Data Communication Network Architecture (BUR)
DCNA .... Deputy Chief Naval Adviser [*British*]
DCNA .... Dichloronitroaniline [*Also, DICHLORAN*] [*Fungicide*]
DCNA .... Digital Card Noninverting Amplifier [*Computer science*]
DCNA .... District of Columbia Nurses Association
DCNB .... Dicyanobenzene [*Also, DCB*] [*Organic chemistry*]
DCNEO .... Deputy Chief Naval Engineering Officer [*British*]
DCNET .... Direct Current Network [*Solutions for resistive components and voltage sources*]
DCNF .... Dishonored Check Name File [*IRS*]
DCNG .... District of Columbia National Guard (AABC)
DCNI .... Department of the Chief of Naval Information [*British military*] (DMA)
D Cn L .... Doctor of Canon Law
DCNM .... Deputy Chief of Naval Management (SAUO)
DCNM .... Deputy Chief of Naval Material
DCNM(A) ..... Deputy Chief of Naval Material (Acquisition) (MCD)
DCNM(D) ..... Deputy Chief of Naval Material, Development
DCNM(L) ...... Deputy Chief of Naval Material (Logistics) (MCD)
DCNM(M & F)... Deputy Chief of Naval Material, Material and Facilities
DCNM(M & O)... Deputy Chief of Naval Material, Management and Organization
DCNM(P & FM)... Deputy Chief of Naval Material, Programs and Financial Management
DCNO .... Deputy Chief of Naval Operations
DCNOA .... Deputy Chief of Naval Operations, Administration
DCNO(AIR)... Deputy Chief of Naval Operations (Air)
DCNO(D) ...... Deputy Chief of Naval Operations (Development)
DCNOFOR .... Deputy Chief of Naval Operations, Fleet Operations and Readiness
DCNOFOR .... Deputy Chief of Naval Operations for Fleet Operations and Readiness (SAUS)
DCNO/L .... Deputy Chief of Naval Operations (SAUS)
DCNO(L) ...... Deputy Chief of Naval Operations (Logistics)
DCNO(M & NR)... Deputy Chief of Naval Operations (Manpower and Naval Reserve)
DCNO(MPT)... Deputy Chief of Naval Operations (Manpower, Personnel, and Training) (DNAB)
DCNOP&NR... Deputy Chief of Naval Operations for Personnel and Naval Reserve (SAUS)
DCNO(P & P)... Deputy Chief of Naval Operations (Plans and Policies)
DCNO(P & R)... Deputy Chief of Naval Operations (Personnel and Naval Reserve)
DCNO(R) ...... Deputy Chief of Naval Operations (Readiness) [*British*]
DCNOR&D ... Deputy Chief of Naval Operations for Research and Development (SAUS)
DCNO(SW)... Deputy Chief of Naval Operations (Submarine Warfare) (DNAB)
DCNOTEMAILSUB... Discharge Certificate/Notification Mailed Subsequent to Separation [*Navy*] (DNAB)
DCNP .... Deputy Chief of Naval Personnel (SAUO)
DCNP .... Diploma in Clinical Neuropsychology [*Medical degree*] (CMD)
DCNP .... Document Change Notice Proposal (MCD)
DCNP .... Donald C. Cook Nuclear Power Plant (NRCH)
DCNPP .... Diablo Canyon Nuclear Power Plant (NRCH)
DCNR .... Dental Corps, Naval Reserve (SAUO)
DCNR .... Department of Conservation and Natural Resources [*Victoria*] [*Australia*]
DCNS .... Deputy Chief of Naval Staff [*Marine Corps; also, British Navy*]
DCNSW .... Disability Council of New South Wales [*Australia*]
DCNSW .... District Court of New South Wales [*Australia*]
DCNT .... Docent, Inc. [*NASDAQ symbol*]
DCNU .... Chlorozotocin [*Organic chemistry*] (DAVI)
DCO .... Covington & Burling, Washington, DC [*OCLC symbol*] (OCLC)
DCO .... Dallas Civic Opera (SAUS)
DCO .... Data Carrier Output (SAUS)
DCO .... Data Category Option (ACAE)
DCO .... Data Center Operations [*Social Security Administration*]
DCO .... Data Change Order (SAUS)
DCO .... Data Collection Order (MCD)
DCO .... Data-Controlled Oscillator (SAUS)
DCO .... Data Control Office (AAG)
DCO .... Debt Collection Order (DCTA)
DCO .... Deco Plantminder [*Vancouver Stock Exchange symbol*]
DCO .... Defence Communications Office (SAUS)
DCO .... Defense Coordinating Officer [*Department of Defense*] (DEMM)
DCO .... Dehydrated Castor Oil [*Organic chemistry*]
DCO .... Delayed Compliance Order [*Compliance Assurance Agreement*] [*Environmental Protection Agency*] (EPA)
DCO .... Depth Cut Out [*Navy*] (NG)
DCO .... Deputy Censorship Office [*London*] [*World War II*]
DCO .... Deputy Chief Officer (WDAA)
DCO .... Deputy Chief of Staff, Operations [*NATO*] (NATG)
DCO .... Deputy Commander of Operations
DCO .... Deputy Commanding Officer
DCO .... Deputy Commissioner for Operations (SAUS)
DCO .... Design Change Order (SAUS)
DCO .... Detailed Checkout
DCO .... Development Contract Office (SAUO)
DCO .... Development Contract Officer (MUGU)
DCO .... Dial Central Office (MCD)
DCO .... Dial Control Office (SAUO)
Dco .... Diffusing Capacity for Carbon Monoxide (MAE)
DCO .... Digital Central Office [*Trademark of the Stromberg-Carlson Corp.*] [*Telecommunications*]
DCO .... digital central office telecommunications (SAUS)
DCO .... Digital-Controlled Oscillator (SAUS)
DCO .... Digital Dial Control Office (SAUS)
DCO .... Digitally-Controlled Oscillator [*Electronics*]
DCO .... Diploma of the College of Optics [*British*] (EY)
DCO .... Direct Clinical Observation [*Psychology*]
DCO .... Directional Coupler Oscillator (IAA)
DCO .... Director Control Officer (SAUO)
DCO .... Director of Combat Operations
DCO .... Director of Combined Operations [*British Army*] [*World War II*]
DCO .... Disaster Control Officer (AAG)
DCO .... District Camouflage Office [*or Officer*]
DCO .... District Capacity Office (SAUO)
DCO .... District Clothing Office [*or Officer*]
DCO .... District Communication Officer
DCO .... District Council Office [*British*] (ROG)
DCO .... Divco-Wayne Corporation (SAUO)
DCO .... Division Classification Officer
D Co .... Doctor of Cosmology
DCO .... Document Change Order (SAUS)
DCO .... Document Control Officer [*Environmental Protection Agency*] (EPA)
DCO .... Dominion, Colonial, and Overseas (SAUS)
DCO .... Dominions, Colonies, and Overseas [*British*] (DI)
dco .... doppler cutoff (SAUS)
dco .... double crossover (SAUS)
DCO .... Draft Collection Only [*Business term*]
DCO .... Drawing Change Order (MUGU)
DCO .... Dry Carbon Monoxide
DCO .... Ducommun, Inc. [*AMEX symbol*] (SPSG)
DCO .... Dukcy of Cornwall Office (SAUO)
DCO .... Duke of Cambridge's Own [*Military unit*] [*British*]
DCO .... Duke of Connaught's Own [*Military unit*] [*British*]
DCO .... Duty Cypher Officer [*Military*] [*British*]
DCO .... Dynamic Checkout [*Aerospace*] (IAA)
D_{CO} .... Pulmonary Diffusion Capacity for Carbon Monoxide [*Medicine*] (DAVI)
DCO2 .... Dry Carbon Dioxide
DCOA .... Direct-Current Operational Amplifier [*Electronics*]
DCOBE .... Darne Commander Order of the British Empire (SAUS)
DCOC .... Drain Cutoff Current
DC of S .... Deputy Chief of Staff
DCOFS .... Deputy Chief of Staff
DC of SA ...... Deputy Chief of Staff, Army
DCOFSADMIN... Deputy Chief of Staff for Administration (SAUO)
DCOFSPCO... Deputy Chief of Staff for Plans and Combat Operations (SAUO)
DCOG .... Diploma of College of Obstetricians and Gynecologists
DCO(I) .... Director of Combined Operations (India)
DCOL .... Direct Control Oriented Language [*Computer science*]

DCOL .... Discovery Channel Online [*Computer science*]
DCoL .... Doctor of Canon Law (SAUS)
D-COL .... Double Column (ADA)
d col .... Double Column [*Advertising*] (ODBW)
D Colo .... United States District Court for the District of Colorado (DLA)
DColU .... Columbia Union College, Takoma Park, MD [*Library symbol*] [*Library of Congress*] (LCLS)
DCOM .... Data Center Operations Management (SAUS)
DCOM .... Departmental Coordinating Committee on Ocean Minings [*Canada*]
DCOM .... Department of Command (SAUO)
DCOM .... Dime Community Bancshares [*NASDAQ symbol*] [*Formerly, Dime Community Bancorp*]
D Com .... Directorate of Communications (SAUO)
DCOM .... Disk Communications Area (CMD)
DCOM .... Distributed COM (SAUS)
DCOM .... Distributed Common/Component Object Model (SAUS)
DCOM .... Distributed Common Object Model (SAUS)
DCOM .... Distributed Component Object Model [*Computer science*]
D Com .... Doctor of Commerce
D Com Adm... Doctor of Commercial Administration
DCOMD .... Director Combined Operations Material Department (SAUO)
DCO(ME) .... Director of Combined Operations (Middle East)
DCOME .... Dworkin/Culatta Oral Mechanism Examination [*Speech and language therapy*] (DAVI)
DComL .... Doctor of Commercial Law (ADA)
D Comm .... Director of Communications (SAUO)
DComm .... Doctor of Commerce
DCOMP .... Data Center Operations Management Plan [*Social Security Administration*]
D Comp L .... Doctor of Comparative Law
D Com Sc .... Doctor of Commercial Science
DCON .... UCD Preserva (SAUS)
D Conn .... United States District Court for the District of Connecticut (DLA)
DCOO .... Deputy Chief Ordnance Officer (SAUO)
DCOP .... Detailed Checkout Procedures (MCD)
DCOP .... Director Combined Operations Personnel (SAUO)
DCOP .... Displays, Controls, and Operation Procedures (NASA)
DCOPA .... Dichloropropyl Acrylate [*Organic chemistry*]
DCOPO .... Deputy Chief of Personnel Operations (AABC)
DCOR .... Decor Corp. [*NASDAQ symbol*] (COMM)
DCOR .... Defense Committee on Research [*Air Force*]
DCOR .... Departmental Committee On Range (SAUO)
DCos .... Cosmos Club, Washington, DC [*Library symbol*] [*Library of Congress*] (LCLS)
DCOS .... Data Collection Operating System
DCOS .... Data Communication Output Selector (KSC)
DCOS .... Department of the Controller of Ordnance Services (SAUO)
DCOS .... Deputy Chief of Staff (NATG)
DCOS .... Direct Couple Operating System
DCOS .... Downrange Computer Output System (MUGU)
DCOSS .... Defense Communications Operational Support System (SAUO)
DC/OSx .... DataCenter/OSx (CDE)
DCOT .... Distant Central Office Transceivers
DCOTFP .... Deputy Commander, Operational Test and Evaluation Force, Pacific [*Navy*]
DCov .... Covington & Burling, Washington, DC [*Library symbol*] [*Library of Congress*] (LCLS)
DCOV .... Discharge Cut-Off Voltage [*Automotive engineering*]
D coy .... D company (SAUO)
DCOZ .... Dover Co-Op [*Federal Railroad Administration identification code*]
DCP .... Daily Cumulative Persistence [*Environmental science*]
DCP .... Damage Controlman (Painter) [*U.S. Navy enlisted rating*] (AUER)
DCP .... Dangerous Contact Premises (SAUO)
DCP .... Daniell's Chancery Practice [*A publication*] (DLA)
DCP .... Data Carrier Production (SAUS)
DCP .... Data Change Proposal
DCP .... Data Ciphering Processor [*Computer science*] (VLIE)
DCP .... Data Collecting Platform (SAUS)
DCP .... Data Collecting Position (SAUS)
DCP .... Data Collection Package (SAUS)
DCP .... Data Collection Plan (MCD)
DCP .... Data Collection Platform [*National Weather Service*] [*Weather satellite system*]
DCP .... Data Collection Program [*Computer science*] (VLIE)
DCP .... Data Collector Processor [*Computer science*] (TIMI)
DCP .... Data Communication Processor [*Computer science*] (BUR)
DCP .... Data Compression Protocol [*Computer science*] (VERA)
DCP .... Data Connection Platform (SAUS)
DCP .... Data Control Processor (IAA)
DCP .... Data Coordinating Point (SAUS)
DCP .... Dean and Chapter of St. Paul's [*Anglican Church*] (ROG)
DCP .... Decentralized Pharmacy (DAVI)
DCP .... Decision Coordinating Paper
DCP .... Decision Coordinating Plan (SAUO)
DCP .... Defense Concept Paper [*Military*] (RDA)
DCP .... Defense Concept Plan (SAUO)
DCP .... Defined Contribution Plan [*Insurance*] (WYGK)
DCP .... Degree Completion Program [*Army*] (INF)
DCP .... Deluge Control Panel (SAUS)
DCP .... Democratic Convergence Party (SAUO)
DCP .... Dental Capitation Plan [*Insurance*] (WYGK)
DCP .... Dental Care Plan [*Insurance*] (WYGK)
DCP .... Dental Continuation Pay [*Military*] (AABC)
DCP .... Department of City Planning (SAUO)
DCP .... Department of Consumer Protection (SAUS)
DCP .... Dependent Care Program [*Insurance*] (WYGK)
DCP .... Depot Condemnation Percent (NASA)
DCP .... Depth-Charge Projector
DCP .... Deputy Controller of Property [*World War II*]
DC(P) .... Deputy Controller (Polaris) [*Navy*] [*British*]
DCP .... Desen Computer Industries, Inc. [*Vancouver Stock Exchange symbol*]
DCP .... Design Change Package (IEEE)
DCP .... Design Change Proposal
DCP .... Design Competition Phase (AAGC)
DCP .... Design Criteria Plan (IEEE)
DCP .... Desktop Color Proofer (SAUS)
DCP .... DEU [*Display Electronics Unit*] Control Program [*NASA*] (NASA)
DCP .... Development Concept Paper (MCD)
DCP .... Development Concept Plan (ACAE)
DCP .... Development Control Program (SAA)
DCP .... Development Cost Plan (NASA)
DCP .... Diagnostic Control Program (IAA)
DCP .... Dicalcium Phosphate [*Inorganic chemistry*]
DCP .... Dicapryl Phthalate [*Organic chemistry*]
DCP .... Dicetylphosphat (SAUS)
DCP .... Dicetyl Phosphate [*Organic chemistry*]
DCP .... Dichloropentane (SAUS)
DCP .... Dichlorophenol [*Organic chemistry*]
DCP .... Dichloropropane [*Pesticide*]
DCP .... Dicumyl Peroxide [*Organic chemistry*]
DCP .... Dicyclopentadiene [*Also, DCPD*] [*Organic chemistry*]
DCP .... Differential Computing Potentiometer
DCP .... Diffusion Controlled Pellistor (SAUS)
DCP .... Digestible Crude Protein (SAUS)
DCP .... Digital California Project
DCP .... Digital Cartographic Production (GEOI)
DCP .... Digital Clock Pulse
DCP .... Digital Command Processor (SAUS)
DCP .... Digital Communications Protocol [*Computer science*] (NITA)
DCP .... Digital Computer Processor (IEEE)
DCP .... Digital Computer Programming [*Computer science*] (BUR)
DCP .... Digital Contour Processing (SAUO)
DCP .... Digital Contour Processor (VLIE)
DCP .... Digital Controller Programmer (SAUS)
DCP .... Digital Control Programmer (SAUS)
DCP .... Digital Cursor Positioner (SAUS)
DCP .... Digital Light Processing (SAUS)
DCP .... Digital Light Protocol [*Computer science*] (AGLO)
DCP .... Dipeptidyl Carboxypeptidase [*An enzyme*]
DCP .... Diphencyprone [*Medicine*]
DCP .... Diploma in Clinical Pathology [*British*]
DCP .... Diploma in Clinical Psychology [*British*]
DCP .... Direct Current Panel
DCP .... Direct-Current Plasma [*Spectrometry*]
DCP .... direct-current plasma spectrometry (SAUS)
DCP .... direct currentpolarography (SAUS)
DCP .... Directives Control Point (SAUS)
DCP .... Directly-Coupled Plasma (SAUS)
DCP .... Directorate Controlled Project
DCP .... Director of [*Air*] Campaign Plans [*Central Command*] [*Military*] (DOMA)
DCP .... Director of Civilian Personnel [*Navy*]
DCP .... Director of Convict Prisons (SAUO)
DCP .... Disaster Control Panel (SAUS)
DCP .... Disaster Control Plan (AFM)
DCP .... Discharge Plan (MEDA)
DCP .... Discrete Component Part
DCP .... Discrimination Complaints Program (COE)
DCP .... Display Control Panel
DCP .... Display Control Program (NTCM)
DCP .... Distributed Collaborative Planning (SAUS)
DCP .... Distributed Communications Processor [*Sperry UNIVAC*]
DCP .... Distribution Common Point [*Telecommunications*] (TEL)
DCP .... Distributor Communication Processor (SAUS)
DCP .... District Community Physician
DCP .... Division de Chimie Physique [*Division of Physical Chemistry - DPC*] (EAIO)
DCP .... Division of Cancer Prevention (ADWA)
DCP .... Division of Capital Police (DEMM)
DCP .... Division of Commissioned Personnel [*U.S. Department of Health and Human Services*]
DCP .... Division of Consumer Protection (SAUS)
DCP .... Doctor in Clinical Pathology
DCP .... Doctor of City Planning
DCP .... Doctor of Clinical Pathology (SAUS)
DCP .... Document control plan (SAUS)
DCP .... Domain Control Point (SAUS)
DCP .... Dominion Res [*NYSE symbol*]
DCP .... Donald C. Cook Plant [*Nuclear energy*] (NRCH)
DCP .... Doped Conjugated Polymer [*Materials science*]
DCP .... Draft Concept Paper
DCP .... Drill Cluster Plate (MCD)
DCP .... Dry Chemical Powder (PDAA)
DCP .... Dual Circularly Polarized (SEWL)
DCP .... Dump Control Program (SAUS)
DCP .... Duplex Central Processor (VLIE)
DCP .... Dynamic Compression-Plate
DCP .... Dyskinetic Cerebral Palsy [*Medicine*] (EDAA)
DCP .... freight/carriage paid to (SAUS)

DCP .... Freight or Carriage Paid To _____ [*"INCOTERM," International Chamber of Commerce official code*]
DCP .... United States Patent Office, Washington, DC [*OCLC symbol*] (OCLC)
DCP .... Diploma in Conservation of Paintings (ODA)
DCP-40 .... Distributed Communications Processor, Model 40 (SAUS)
DCPA .... Defense Civil Preparedness Agency [*FEMA*] [*Washington, DC*]
DCPA .... DEU [*Display Electronics Unit*] Control Program [*End Item*]
DCPA .... Dichloropropionanilide [*Also, DPA*] [*Herbicide*]
DCPA .... dicylcopentenyl acrylate (SAUS)
DCPA .... Dimethyl Tetrachloroterephthalate [*Herbicide*]
DCPADB .... Dichloropropionaniline (SAUS)
DCPADB .... Dimethyl Tetrachloroterephthalate (SAUS)
DCPADB .... Distribution Common Point (SAUS)
DCPANDP .... Deputy Chief of Staff, Plans and Policy [*NATO*] (NATG)
DCPath .... Diploma of College of Pathologists (SAUS)
DC Path .... Diploma of the College of Pathologists [*British*]
DCPB .... Daughters of Charity of Most Precious Blood (TOCD)
DCPB .... Departmental Civilian Personnel Branch
DCPBH .... Double Channel Planar Buried Heterostructure (SAUS)
DC-PBH .... Double-Channel Planar Buried Heterostructure
DC-PBH-LD .... Double Channel Planar-Buried-Heterostructure Laser-Diode (SAUS)
DCPBX .... Digitally Connected Private Branch Exchange [*Telecommunications*] (ROAS)
DCPC .... Dichlorodiphenylmethylcarbinol [*Also, DMC*] [*Insecticide*]
DCPC .... Digital Clock Pulse Generator (SAUS)
DCPC .... Division of Cancer Prevention and Control [*National Cancer Institute*]
DCPC .... Dual Channel Port Controller [*Computer science*] (NITA)
DC-PCB .... Data Communication Program Communication Block [*Computer science*] (VLIE)
DCPCD .... Dicyclopentadine
DCPCM .... Differentially Coherent Pulse Code Modulation
DCPC Modulation .... Differentially Coherent Pulse Code Modulation (SAUS)
DCPD .... Defense Contract Property Disposition [*DoD*] (RDA)
DCPD .... Dense Cytoplasmic Protoplast Derivative (SAUS)
DCPD .... Dicalcium Phosphate Dihydrate [*Inorganic chemistry*]
DCPD .... Dicyclopentadiene [*Also, DCP*] [*Organic chemistry*]
DCPD .... Direct-Current Potential Drop (MCD)
DCPDA .... Deoxycytidylyl Deoxyadenosine (SAUS)
DCPDC .... Dual Chamber Preliminary Design Code (MCD)
Dcpdg .... Deoxycytidylyl Deoxyguanosine (SAUS)
DCPE .... Documentacion y Comunicacion Publicitaria Espanola [*Database*] [*Universidad Complutense de Madrid*] [*Spanish*] [*Information service or system*] (CRD)
DCPEI .... DEU [*Display Electronics Unit*] Control Program End Item [*NASA*] (NASA)
DCPEL .... Direct Current Powder Electroluminescence (SAUS)
DCPES .... Direct Current Plasma Emission Spectroscopy (MEC)
DCPF .... Displaced Cosine Pulse Function (IAA)
DCPF .... Divorced Christian Professional Female (SAUO)
DCPG .... Defense Communications Planning Group (KSC)
DCPG .... Digital Clock Pulse Generator
DCPG .... Direction Center Programming Group [*Semiautomatic Ground Environment*] (IAA)
DCPI .... Data Collection Platform Interrogation (ACAE)
DCPI .... Data Collection Platform Interrupt (ACAE)
DCPI .... Deputy Chief Patrol Inspector [*Immigration and Naturalization Service*]
DCPI .... Deputy Police Commissioner for Public Information (LAIN)
DCPI .... Dichlorophenolindophenol [*Also, DCIP, DCPIP, DPIP*] [*Analytical reagent*]
DCPI .... dick clark productions [*NASDAQ symbol*] (TTSB)
DCPI .... Dick Clark Productions, Inc. [*NASDAQ symbol*] (NQ)
DCPIF .... Distributed Communications Processor Interface [*Computer science*] (TIMI)
DCPIP .... Dichlorophenolindophenol [*Also, DCIP, DCPI, DPIP*] [*Analytical reagent*]
DCPL .... Demonstrated Compliance Parameter Limits [*Environmental science*] [*Environmental Protection Agency*]
DCPL .... Distributed Control Programming Language [*Computer science*] (CSR)
DCPL .... District of Columbia Public Library
DCP-LA .... Direct-Current Plasma-LASER Ablation
DCPLS .... Data Collection and Platform Location System [*National Weather Service*] [*Weather satellite system*] (NOAA)
DCPM .... Daunomycin Cytarabine, Prednisolone, Mercaptopurine [*Antineoplastic drug*] (CDI)
DCPM .... Daunorubicin, Cytarabine, Prednisolone, and Mercaptopurine (STED)
DCPM .... Decision Critical Path Method
DCPM .... Di(chlorophenoxy)methane (IIA)
DCPM .... Divorced Christian Professional Male (SAUO)
DCPMAS .... Double Cross-Polarization, Magic Angle Spinning [*Spectroscopy*]
DCPMU .... (Dichlorophenyl)methylurea [*Organic chemistry*]
DCPMWG .... Dryland Catchments Program Management Working Group (SAUS)
DCPN .... Direction-Changing Positional Nystagmus (STED)
DCPO .... Damage Control Petty Officer [*Navy*] (DNAB)
DCPO .... Deputy Chief of Staff, Personnel and Organization [*NATO*] (NATG)
DCPO .... Deputy Chief of Staff, Plans and Operations (MCD)
DCPO .... Deputy Chief Political Officer [*British Military Administration*]
DCPO .... Director of Civilian Personnel Office (SAUO)
DCPO .... District Civilian Personnel Office [*or Officer*]
DCPO .... DSA [*Defense Supply Agency*] Civil Preparedness Office
DCPOC .... Document Center of the Patent Office of China [*Library*]
DCP-OES .... direct coupled plasma--optical emission spectroscopy (SAUS)
DCPolaris .... Deputy Controller (Polaris) [*Navy*] [*British*]
DCPP .... Data Communication Preprocessor
DCPR .... Data Collection Platform Radio (ACAE)
DCPR .... Data Collection Platform Response (ACAE)
DCPR .... Data Collection Platform Retransmission (SAUS)
DCPR .... Defense Contractor Planning Report
DCPR .... Deputy Chief of Staff for Plans and Research
DCPR .... Detailed Continuing Property Record (SAUS)
DCPR .... Detailed Contuing Property Record (SAUS)
DCPR .... Direction Center Processor for Remote Combat Center (SAA)
DCPR .... Dry Cleaning Plant Registration (SAUS)
DCPRS .... Data Collection Platform Radio Sets [*National Weather Service*] [*Weather satellite system*] (NOAA)
DCPS .... Data Collection & Processing System (SAUS)
DCPs .... Data Collection Platforms (SAUS)
DCPS .... Data Collection Platform System (ACAE)
DCPS .... Data Communication Processing System
DCPS .... Data Communications Protocol Standards (SAUS)
DCPS .... Data Compression Processing System (SAUS)
DCPS .... Data Control Panel Submodule
DCPS .... Digital Cartographic Production Segment (GEOI)
DC/PS .... Digital Computer / Power Supply
DCPS .... Digitally Controlled Power Source (IEEE)
DCPS .... Dynamic Crew Procedures Simulator
DCPSA .... District of Columbia Political Science Association (SAUO)
DCPSC .... Dynamic Contact Patch Stress Compensation [*Tire design*]
DCPSK .... Differential [*or Differentially*] Coherent Phase Shift Keyed [*or Keying*] [*System*] [*Computer science*]
DCPSK .... Differentially Coherent Phase Shift Keyed (SAUS)
DCPSK .... Differentially Coherent Phase Shift Keying (SAUS)
DCPSK .... Differentially-Coherent Phase-Shut-Keyed (SAUS)
DCPSP .... Direct-Current Power Supply Panel (AAG)
DCPT .... DCP Tapes (SAUS)
DCPT .... Direct-Current Plasma Torch
DCPT .... Doctor of Chiropractic and Physiological Therapeutics
DCPTA .... (Dichlorophenoxy)triethylamine [*Herbicide*]
dcpta .... dichlorophenoxy triethylamine (SAUS)
DCPU .... Dacryocystorhinostomy (STED)
DCPU .... Data Center Policy and Usage [*Environmental science*] (COE)
DCPU .... Data Communication Protocol Unit (SAUO)
DCPU .... Display Control Power Unit (SAUS)
DCPV .... Direct-Current Peak Voltage (IAA)
DCPX .... Dacar Chemical Products [*Private rail car owner code*]
DCQ .... Double-Cascade-Quench (SAUS)
DCQM .... Deputy Chief Quartermaster
DCQM .... Digital Circuit Quality Monitor [*Computer science*]
DCQM .... Digital Circuit Quality Motor (SAUS)
DCR .... Dacro-Cysto-Rhinostomy [*Medicine*]
DCR .... Daily Communication Report
DCR .... Data Carrier Recognition (SAUS)
DC/R .... Data Collection/Relay (MCD)
DCR .... Data Collection Request (SAUS)
DCR .... Data Collection Routine (VLIE)
DCR .... Data Communication Read (OA)
DCR .... Data Communication Ready (SAUS)
DCR .... Data Conversion Receiver [*Computer science*]
DCR .... Data Coordinator and Retriever [*Computer science*]
DCR .... Debt Coverage Ratio [*Business term*]
DCR .... Decatur, IN [*Location identifier*] [*FAA*] (FAAL)
DCR .... Decision Circuit Reception
DCR .... Decor
DCR .... Decoration (AABC)
DCR .... Decrease (KSC)
DCR .... Decreasing (SAUS)
DCR .... Decrement Register (SAUS)
DCR .... Degradation Category Rating (SAUS)
DCR .... Degree of Cell Rupture
DCR .... Delayed Cutaneous Reaction [*Dermatology*] (DAVI)
DCR .... Delray Connecting Railroad (MHDB)
DCR .... Democratic Constitutional Rally [*Tunisia*] [*Political party*] (BARN)
DCR .... Dental Corps, General Service [*USNR officer designation*]
DCR .... Dependent-Care Reimbursement [*Insurance*] (WYGK)
DCR .... Deputy Commander for Resources [*Air Force*] (DOMA)
DCR .... Design calculation reports (SAUS)
DCR .... Design Certification Review [*NASA*] (KSC)
DCR .... Design Change Recommendation [*or Request*]
DCR .... Design Change Request [*Computer science*] (VERA)
DCR .... Design Characteristic Review (AAG)
DCR .... Design Concept Review (GEOI)
DCR .... Design Concern Report (NASA)
DCR .... Destruct Command Receiver (KSC)
DCR .... Detail Condition Register
DCR .... Development Council for Research (MUGU)
DCR .... Dewar Cryogenic Refrigerator
DCR .... Diaphragm-Controlled Restrictor (SAUS)
DCR .... Dichlororesorcine (SAUS)
DCR .... Dielectric Card Reading (SAUS)
DCR .... Differential Correlation Radiometer (MCD)
DCR .... Digital Cable Radio (SAUS)
DCR .... Digital Cassette Recorder
DCR .... Digital Coded RADAR
DCR .... Digital Communications Readout (SAUS)
DCR .... Digital Concentration Readout [*Computer science*]
DCR .... Digital Condition Register (NITA)
DCR .... Digital Conversion Receiver
DCR .... Diocesan Chancellor and Registrar (SAUO)
DCR .... Direct Connecting Receptacle (SAUS)

DCR .... Direct Conversion Reactor
DCR .... Direct Conversion Reactor Study (SAUS)
DCR .... Direct Cortical Response
DCR .... Direct Critical Response (MEDA)
dcr .... Direct Current Resistance (SAUS)
DCR .... Direct Current Restorer (SAUS)
DCR .... Direct-Current Restorer
DCR .... Directed Change Request (SAUS)
DCR .... Directorate of Central Registries (SAUO)
DCR .... Directorate of Collateral Responsibility (SAUS)
DCR .... Discretionary Conditional Release [*Legal term*] (WDAA)
DCR .... Disk Capture Restore (SAUS)
DCR .... Disk Capture/Restore [*Computer science*] (VLIE)
DCR .... Disposition of Contract Request (SAA)
DCR .... District Chief Ranger [*Ancient Order of Foresters*]
DCR .... divided clock receiver (SAUS)
dcr .... division credit rebate (SAUS)
DCR .... Division of Clinical Research [*Medicine*] (EDAA)
DCR .... Division of Computer Research [*Formerly, OCA*] [*National Science Foundation*]
DCR .... Doctor of Comparative Religion
D Cr .... Doctor of Criminology
DCR .... Documentation Change Request (SAUS)
DCR .... Document Change Record (NASA)
DCR .... Document Change Release
DCR .... Document change request (SAUS)
DCR .... Document Change Review (SAUS)
DCR .... Document Control Register (COE)
DCR .... Dominant Control Region [*Genetics*]
DCR .... Double Cold Reducing (SAUS)
DCR .... Downstream Control Region [*Biochemistry*]
DCR .... Drawing Change Request
DCR .... Drawing Copy Request (MCD)
DCR .... Drayage Carriers Inc., Fort Wayne IN [*STAC*]
DCR .... Dried Coffee Residue
DCR .... Dual Channel Radiometer
DCR .... Dual Channel Receiver (MCD)
DCR .... Dual Combustor Ramjet (MCD)
DCR .... dual cycle reactor (SAUS)
DCR .... Dual Cycle Rifle
DCR .... Duff and Phelps Credit Rating [*NYSE symbol*] (TTSB)
DCR .... Duff & Phelps Credit Rating Co. [*NYSE symbol*] (SAG)
DCR .... Dynamic Color Rendition [*Computer science*]
DCRA .... DCASR [*Defense Contract Administration Services Region*], Atlanta
DCRA .... Department of Community & Regional Affairs (SAUO)
DCRA .... Dominion of Canada Rifle Association
DCRA .... Dry Crease Recovery Angle [*Textile technology*]
DCRA .... Dyers' and Cleaners' Research Association (BI)
DCRABS .... Disk Copy Restore and Backup System
DCR & Regs ... District of Columbia Rules and Regulations [*A publication*] (DLA)
DCRB .... DCASR [*Defense Contract Administration Services Region*], Boston
DCRB .... Descriptive Cataloging of Rare Books [*American Library Association*]
DCRB .... Design Change Review Board
DCRB .... Drawn Cup Roller Bearing
DCRC .... DCASR [*Defense Contract Administration Services Region*], San Francisco
DCRC .... Digital Cellular Radio Conference (VERA)
DCRCH .... Duke of Connaught's Royal Canadian Hussars [*British military*] (DMA)
DCRD .... DCASR [*Defense Contract Administration Services Region*], Detroit
DCRD .... Department of the Controller of Research and Development (SAUO)
DCRDR .... Detailed Control Room Design Review [*Nuclear energy*] (NRCH)
DCRE .... Decree [*Legal shorthand*] (LWAP)
DCRE .... Deputy Commandant Royal Engineers [*British*]
DCREO .... Design Change Request Engineering Order
DCREO .... Drawing Change Request Engineering Order (SAUS)
DCREOS .... Department of the Controller of Repair, Equipment and Overseas Supplies (SAUO)
DCRESMAILSUB ... Discharge Certificate/Naval Reserve Appointment Mailed Subsequent to Separation [*Navy*] (DNAB)
DCRF .... Die Casting Research Foundation (EA)
DCRF .... Disabled Children's Relief Fund (NRGU)
DCRI .... DCASR [*Defense Contract Administration Services Region*], Chicago
DCrim .... Doctor of Criminology (GAGS)
DC Rim .... Drop Centre Rim (SAUS)
DCRK .... Democratic Confederate Republic of Koryo [*Reunified Korean state*] [*Proposed*]
DCRL .... DCASR [*Defense Contract Administration Services Region*], Los Angeles
DCRLA .... District of Columbia Redevelopment Land Agency (SAUS)
DCRM .... Discrepancy Check Request Memorandum (SAA)
DCR (MU) .... Diploma-College of Radiographers (SAUS)
DCR MU .... Diploma of the College of Radiographers in Medical Ultra Sound [*British*] (DBQ)
DCRN .... Dashpot Cup Retention Nut [*Nuclear energy*] (NRCH)
DCRN .... DCASR [*Defense Contract Administration Services Region*], New York
DCRN .... Diacrin, Inc. [*NASDAQ symbol*] (NASQ)
DCRND .... Division of Cardiovascular, Respiratory, and Neurological Devices [*Center for Devices and Radiological Health*]
DCR (NM) .... Diploma-College of Radiographers (SAUS)
DCRNM .... Diploma of the College of Radiographers in Nuclear Medicine [*British*] (DI)
DCRNZ .... Diacrin Inc. Unit [*NASDAQ symbol*] (TTSB)
DCRO .... DCASR [*Defense Contract Administration Services Region*], Cleveland
DCRO .... Deputy Chief, Royal Ordnance (SAUO)
DCRO .... District Civil Readjustment Office [*or Officer*]
DCRO .... Dyers and Cleaners Research Organization (SAUS)
DCRP .... DCASR [*Defense Contract Administration Services Region*], Philadelphia
DCRP .... Department of City and Regional Planning [*MIT*] (MCD)
DCRP .... Design Controlled Repair Parts (MCD)
DCRP .... Developmental Cycle Research Plan
DCRP .... Deviation Change Request Proposal (SAUS)
DCRP .... Direct-Current Reverse Polarity [*Electronics*]
DCRP .... Disaster Control Recovery Plan
DCR (R) .... Diploma-College of Radiography (SAUS)
DCRR .... District of Colu8mbia Rules and Regulations [*A publication*] (AAGC)
DCRR .... Drawing Change Recorder Request (SAUS)
DCRR .... Dubois County Railroad [*Federal Railroad Administration identification code*]
DCR REG5 ... Document Control (SAUS)
DCR RNI .... Diploma of the College of Radiographers in Radionuclide Imaging [*British*] (DBQ)
DCRS .... Data Collection and Reduction System
DCRS .... DCASR [*Defense Contract Administration Services Region*], St. Louis
DCRS .... Decrease (VLIE)
DCRS .... Design Change Request Serial Engineering Order (SAUS)
DCRS .... Devon and Cornwall Record Society (SAUO)
D-CRS .... Diplomate, American Board of Colon and Rectal Surgery (DHSM)
DCRS .... Document Control Remote Station
DCRS .... Document Control Remote Station DCRSEO (SAUS)
DCRSEO .... Design Change Request Serial Engineering Order (MCD)
DCRT .... Data Collection Receive Terminal (SAUS)
DCRT .... DCASR [*Defense Contract Administration Services Region*], Dallas
DCR (T) .... Diploma-College of Radiotgraphers (SAUS)
DCRT .... Division of Computer Research and Technology [*Bethesda, MD*] [*National Institutes of Health*]
DCRT .... Double-contained receiver tank (SAUS)
DCRTO .... DSA [*Defense Supply Agency*] Central Regional Telecommunications Office
DCRTR .... Decorator
DCRV .... Double-contained receiver vessel (SAUS)
DCRX .... Deadwood Central Railroad [*Federal Railroad Administration identification code*]
DCRZ .... Descend to and Cruise [*Aviation*] (FAAC)
DCS .... ARGOS/Data Collection System (SAUS)
DCS .... Dalton Computer Services, Inc. [*Information service or system*] (IID)
DCS .... Damage Control School [*Navy*]
DCS .... Damage Control Suit [*Navy*]
DCS .... Damage Control System (KSC)
DCS .... Dartmouth Computing Services
DCS .... Data Capture Subsystem (MCD)
DCS .... Data Carrier Store (SAUS)
DCS .... Data Carrier System [*Teltone Corp.*] [*Kirkland, WA*] (TSSD)
DCS .... Data Cell Store (SAUS)
DCS .... Data Center Scheduler (VLIE)
DCS .... Data Center Service (SAUS)
DCS .... Data Channel Selection (SAUS)
DCS .... Data Checking System (SAUS)
DCS .... Data Clarification System (SAUS)
DCS .... Data Classification System (IAA)
DCS .... Data Collecting System (SAUS)
DCS .... Data Collection Subsystem (SAUS)
DCS .... Data Collection System [*or Subsystem*] [*Computer science*]
DCS .... Data Communication Services [*Regie des Telegraphes et des Telephones*] [*Brussels, Belgium*]
DCS .... Data Communications Server (SAUS)
DCS .... Data Communications Service (SAUS)
DCS .... Data Communications Subsystem (SAUS)
DCS .... Data Communication System [*or Subsystem*]
DCS .... Data Conditioning System [*NASA*]
DCS .... Data Consolidation Simulation (SAUS)
DCS .... Data Control Services (BUR)
DCS .... Data Control System [*Burroughs Corp.*] (AAG)
DCS .... Data Conversion System [*Computer science*]
DCS .... Data Correction System (SAUS)
DCS .... Data Sharing Control System [*Computer science*] (VERA)
DCS .... Davis Computer Systems, Inc.
DCS .... Deaf Community Services (SAUS)
DCS .... Dealer Communication System [*Automotive service*]
DCS .... Decision Communications System (ACAE)
DCS .... Deck Cooling System (MCD)
DCS .... Decommissioning Conceptual Study (SAUS)
DCS .... Decompression Sickness [*Deep-sea diving*]
DCS .... Dedicated Computer System (SAUS)
DCS .... Defect Control System [*The Software Edge, Inc.*] [*Computer science*] (PCM)
DCS .... Defence and Control System (SAUS)
DCS .... Defence Communications System (SAUS)
DCS .... Defence Construction Service (SAUO)
DCS .... Defense Communications System [*DoD*]
DCS .... Defense Construction Service (NATG)
DCS .... Defense Courier Service [*DoD*]
DCS .... Defined Context Set [*Telecommunications*] (OSI)
DCS .... Deflection Coil Set
DCS .... Delayed Coincidence Spectroscopy
DCS .... Del Castillo Syndrome [*Medicine*] (MELL)

DCS .... Deleage-Curschmann-Steinert [*Syndrome*] [*Medicine*] (DB)
DCS .... Delerium/Confusional State [*Medicine*] (MELL)
DCS .... Dense Canalicular System [*Medicine*] (DMAA)
DCS .... Department of Computer Science [*University of Illinois*] [*Research center*] (RCD)
DCS .... Department of Computing Service [*University of Waterloo*] [*Research center*] (RCD)
DCS .... Department of Corporate Services (SAUO)
DCS .... Department of Correctional Services [*Northern Territory, South Australia*]
DCS .... Department of Corrective Services [*New South Wales, Western Australia*]
DCS .... Departure Control System [*IATA*] (DS)
DCS .... Deputy Chief of Staff
DCS .... Deputy Clerk of Session [*British*]
DCS .... Deputy Crown Solicitor (ADA)
DCS .... Design Capture System (SAUS)
DCS .... Design Change Schedule
DCS .... Design Change Summary (AAG)
DCS .... Design Communication System (MCD)
DCS .... Design Control Specification (KSC)
DCS .... Design Criteria Specification (NASA)
DCS .... Desktop Color Separation [*Quark, Inc.*] (PCM)
DCS .... Desktop Color Standard (AGLO)
DCS .... Despin Control Subsystem [*Aerospace*]
DCS .... Destination Control Statement Form (JAGO)
DCS .... Destruct Command System (MUGU)
DCS .... Detail Checkout Specifications (MCD)
DCS .... Developing Countries Staff (COE)
DCS .... Development & Consulting Services (SAUS)
DCS .... Diagnostic Communications System (SAUS)
DCS .... Diagnostic Compiler System (SAUS)
DCS .... Diagnostic Control Software
DCS .... Diagnostic Control Store
DCS .... diamond coring system (SAUS)
DCS .... Dichlorosilane [*Photovoltaic energy systems*]
DCS .... Diecasting Society [*British*] (DBA)
DCS .... Dielectric Card Scanning (SAUS)
DCS .... Differential Cross Section [*Chemistry*]
DCS .... Differential Current Switch (SAUS)
DCS .... Diffuse Cerebral Sclerosis [*Medicine*] (DB)
DCS .... Diffuse Cortical Sclerosis [*Medicine*] (DMAA)
DCS .... Diffuse Cutaneous Scleroderma [*Medicine*] (MELL)
DCS .... Digital Camera System [*Eastman Kodak Co.*]
DCS .... Digital Cartography Section (GEOI)
DCS .... Digital Cellular System [*Telecommunications*] (DDC)
DCS .... Digital Classified Software (NITA)
DCS .... Digital Coded Squelch (SAUS)
DCS .... Digital Color Separate (SAUS)
DCS .... Digital Color System (VERA)
DCS .... Digital Command Signal [*Telecommunications*] (OSI)
DCS .... Digital Command Subsystem (SAUS)
DCS .... Digital Command System [*or Subsystem*]
DCS .... Digital Communications Services (SAUS)
DCS .... Digital Communications System (SAUS)
DCS .... Digital Communication System [*Computer science*]
DCS .... Digital Computer Speed (SAUS)
DCS .... Digital Computer System [*Vancouver Stock Exchange symbol*]
DCS .... Digital Control Signal (SAUS)
DCS .... Digital Control Station [*Computer science*]
DCS .... Digital Control System
DCS .... Digital Cordless Standard [*Telecommunications*] (ACRL)
DCS .... Digital Countdown System [*Computer science*]
DCS .... Digital Crosconnect System (SAUS)
DCS .... Digital Cross-Connect System [*Telecommunications*]
DCS .... Digitally Controlled System (SAUS)
DCS .... Digit Selector Common (SAUS)
DCS .... Dimensional Control Standard (MCD)
DCS .... Diode Capacitor Store (SAUS)
DCS .... Direct Commercial Sales (SEWL)
DCS .... Direct coupled system (SAUS)
DCS .... Direct-Coupled System (IAA)
DCS .... Direct Coupler System (SAUS)
DCS .... Direct Couple System
DCS .... Direct Credits Society (ADWA)
DCS .... Direct Current Sensor (SAUS)
DCS .... Direct-Current Sensor
DCS .... Direction Center Standby [*SAGE*] [*RADAR*]
DCS .... Directorate of Colonial Surveys (SAUS)
DCS .... Director Comptroller Systems (AABC)
DCS .... Director of Clothing and Stores [*Military*] [*British*]
DCS .... Director of Community Services (SAUS)
DCS .... Disadvantaged Children Series [*A publication*]
DCS .... Discount Communications Services [*Telecommunications service*] (TSSD)
DCS .... Discrete Continuous System (SAUS)
DCS .... Disease Control Serum (STED)
DCS .... Dispatch Critical System (MCD)
DCS .... Displaced Child Syndrome (MELL)
DCS .... Display and Control Station
DCS .... Display and Control System (SAUS)
DCS .... distal coronary sinus electrogramm (SAUS)
DCS .... Distillers Corporation-Seagrams (SAUO)
DC/S .... Distributed Client Server (SAUS)
DCS .... Distributed Commercial System (IAA)
DCS .... Distributed Communications Software (SAUS)
DCS .... Distributed Communications System [*Telecommunications*] (CDE)
DCS .... Distributed Computer System (SAUS)
DCS .... Distributed Computer Systems (MDG)
DCS .... Distributed Computing Services
DCS .... Distributed Computing System (SAUS)
DCS .... Distributed Control System [*Engineering*]
DCS .... Distributed Customer Service (SAUS)
DCS .... Distribution Control System (SAUS)
DCS .... Distributive Control System (SAUS)
DCS .... Diversity Combiner System
DCS .... Divisional Chief Superintendent [*British police*]
DCS .... Division Clearing Station [*Medicine*] [*Army*]
DCS .... Division of Constituency Services (SAUO)
DCS .... Division of Constituent Services (SAUO)
DCS .... Doctor of Christian Science
DCS .... Doctor of Christian Service
DCS .... Doctor of Commercial Science
DCS .... Doctor of Computer Science (PGP)
DCS .... Doctrine and Command Systems [*Army*] (RDA)
DCS .... Document Control Services
DCS .... Document Control Sheet (SAUS)
DCS .... Document Control Software (CDE)
DCS .... Document Control Station (SAUS)
DCS .... Document Control System [*Computer science*]
DCS .... Document cover sheet (SAUS)
DCS .... Domestic Contact Service (SAUS)
DCS .... DONCASTERS plc ADS [*NYSE symbol*] (SG)
DCS .... Dorsal Column Stimulator [*Pain killer*]
DCS .... Dorsal Cord Stimulation (DB)
DCS .... Double Channel Simplex
DCS .... Double Compton Scattering
DCS .... Double-Contrast Study (MELL)
dcs............ double cotton silk (SAUS)
DCS .... Double Cotton Single Silk [*Wire insulation*] (AAG)
dcs............ Double Cotton Single-silk (SAUS)
DCS .... Double-Current System (SAUS)
DCs............ Douglas Commercial-type airplanes (SAUS)
DCS .... downward-coarsening sandstone (SAUS)
DCS .... Drawing Change Summary
DCS .... Drone Control System [*Military*]
DCS .... Dry Clamp Selector (SAUS)
DCS .... Dual Catalyst System [*Automotive engineering*]
DCS .... Dual Checkout Station (MCD)
DCS .... Dummy Control Section (SAUS)
DCS .... Dummy Control Selection (SAUS)
DCS .... Dynamic Computer System (SAUS)
DCS .... Dynamic Control Store (SAUS)
DCS .... Region 10 Library Document Control (SAUS)
DCS .... United States Civil Service Commission, Washington, DC [*Library symbol*] [*Library of Congress*] (LCLS)
DCS .... University of South Carolina, College of Librarianship, Columbia, SC [*OCLC symbol*] (OCLC)
DCS 1800 .... Digital Cellular Standard for 1800 MHz band (SAUS)
DCS-1800 .... Digital Communications System on 1800 MHz Band (CGWS)
DCS-1800 .... Digital Cordless Standard (SAUS)
DCSA .... Department and Chain Store Association (SAUO)
DCSA .... Direct Current Servo Amplifier (SAUS)
DCSA .... Direct-Current Servo Amplifier
DCSA .... Double Contrast Shoulder Arthrography [*Radiology*] (DAVI)
DCSA .... Dual Chamber Shock Absorbers (MCD)
DCSAB .... Distinguished Civilian Service Awards Board (SAUS)
DCSADN ...... Defense Communications System Automatic Digital Network [*DoD*]
DC/SAF .... Deputy Chief of Staff, Air Force
DCSAIROPNET... Defense Communications System Air Operational Network (AFM)
DCS&H .... Department of Community Services and Health (SAUS)
DCSAO .... Defense Customer Supply Assistance Office [*DoD*]
DCSAR .... Defense Contract Services Administration Region
DCSAS .... Deputy Chief Superintendent of Armament Supply (SAUO)
DCS/AUTODIN... Defense Communications System Automatic Digital Information Network [*DoD*]
DCSB .... Data Check Sense Bit (SAUS)
DCSC .... Defense Construction Supply Center [*Defense Supply Agency*]
DCS/C .... Deputy Chief of Staff, Comptroller
DCSC .... Digital Card Slave Clock [*Computer science*]
DC Sc .... Doctor of Commercial Science
DC Sc .... Doctor of Commercial Sience (SAUS)
DCSCD .... Deputy Chief of Staff for Combat Developments (AABC)
DCSC-E .... Deputy Chief of Staff, Communications-Electronics [*Army*] (AABC)
DCSCI .... Defense Communications Systems Configuration Items (MCD)
DCSCOMMEL... Deputy Chief of Staff Communications-Electronics (SAUS)
DCSCOMPT... Deputy Chief of Staff, Comptroller (AABC)
DCSCS .... Data Code and Speed Conversion Subsystem [*Computer science*] (NITA)
DCSCU .... Dual Capability Servo Control Unit (COE)
DCS/D .... Deputy Chief of Staff, Development
DCSD .... Doctrine and Command Systems Directorate [*Army*] (RDA)
DCSDATANET... Defense Communications System Data Network (NG)
DCSDOC ...... Deputy Chief of Staff for Doctrine
DCSE .... Department of Computer Science and Engineering (SAUO)
DCSE .... Diba Consulting Software Engineers (SAUS)
DC Se .... Doctor of Commercial Service
DCSF .... Data Communications Services Functions (SAUO)
DCSF .... Diba Consulting Software Engineers (GEOI)
DCSF .... Digital Cockpit Simulation Facility (MCD)

DCSF .... Downton Castle Sandstone Formation [*England*] [*Geology*]
DCSF .... Dry Caisson Storage Facility (SAUS)
DCS/FF .... Deputy Chief of Staff / Flight Facilities (SAA)
DCSFOR....... Deputy Chief of Staff, Force Development (AABC)
DCSG .... Data Computation Subsystem Group
DCSG .... David Cassidy Support Group (EA)
DC shaft ...... Downcast shaft (SAUS)
DCSHG......... DC-Induced Second Harmonic Generation (MCD)
DC shock...... direct current shock (SAUS)
DCSI .... Data and Control Signal Interface (NASA)
DCSI .... Defense Satellite Communication Systems Installation (RDA)
DCSI .... Deputy Chief of Staff for Intelligence [*Army*] (AABC)
DC/S(I & L)... Deputy Chief of Staff, Installations and Logistics [*Marine Corps*] (DOMA)
dc-Signal..... direct candle signal (SAUS)
DCSigO........ Deputy Chief Signal Officer (SAUS)
DCSIM .... Deputy Chief of Staff for Information Management [*Army*]
DCSIM .... District of Columbia Society of Internal Medicine (SRA)
DCSINT........ Deputy Chief of Staff for Intelligence (SAUS)
DCSINT........ Deputy Chief of Staff for Intellingence (SAUS)
DCS/INT....... Deputy Chief of Staff, Intelligence [*Air Force*] (MCD)
DCSIRM........ Deputy Chief of Staff for Information Resource Management (SAUO)
DCSJS & L.... Deputy Chief of Staff for Systems and Logistics (SAUS)
DCSL .... Deputy Chief of Staff, Logistics [*Army*] (KSC)
DCSL .... Deterministic Context Sensitive Language [*Computer science*] (MHDI)
DCSL .... Distributed CSL (SAUS)
DCSL .... District Cub Scout Leader (SAUS)
DCS/L/A....... Deputy Chief of Staff, Logistics & Administration (SAUO)
DCSLAM .... Development of a Corps Logistics Analysis Methodology
DCS/LE .... Deputy Chief of Staff for Logistics and Engineering [*See also AF/LE*] [*Air Force*] (DOMA)
DCSLOG....... Deputy Chief of Staff, Logistics [*Army*]
DCSLOG-MR... Deputy Chief of Staff, Logistics - Material Readiness (SAUO)
DCS/M .... Deputy Chief of Staff/Material (ACAE)
DCSM .... Deputy Chief of Staff, Materiel
DCSM .... Deterministic Complete Sequential Machine (PDAA)
DCS(M & RA)... Deputy Chief of Staff (for Manpower and Reserve Affairs) (RDA)
DCSMAT .... Deputy Chief of Staff, Materiel (SAUS)
DCSMG......... Deputy Chief of Staff for Military Government [*World War II*]
DCSMIS........ Deputy Chief of Staff, Management Information Systems (AABC)
DCS/MIP....... Dynamic Computer System/Multipurpose Information Processor (SAUS)
DC/SMO....... Deputy Chief of Staff, Military Operations [*Army*]
DCSN........... Data Carrier Sequence Number (SAUS)
DCSN........... Decision
DCSN........... Decision Systems, Inc. [*NASDAQ symbol*] (COMM)
DCSO........... Defense Communications System Office (SAUO)
DCSO........... Defense Communications System Organization
DCSO........... Deputy Chief of Staff, Operations
DCS/O.......... Deputy Chief of Staff/Operations (ACAE)
DCSO........... Deputy Chief Scientific Officer [*British*]
DCSO........... Deputy Chief Signal Officer [*British military*] (DMA)
DCSO........... Deputy Commander for Space Operations (ACAE)
DCSO........... DSA [*Defense Supply Agency*] Command Security Support Office
DCSOA......... Deputy Chief of Staff, Operations and Administration
DCSO & T.... Deputy Chief of Staff, Operations and Training (AABC)
DCSOC......... Defense Communications System Operations Center (RDA)
DCSocPE..... District of Columbia Society of Professional Engineers (SAUO)
DCSOI.......... Deputy Chief of Staff for Operations and Intelligence (AABC)
DCSOP......... Deputy Chief of Staff for Military Operations (SAUO)
DCSOP......... Deputy Chief of Staff, Military Operations (SAUS)
DCSOPS....... Deputy Chief of Staff for Operations [*Army*]
DCSOPS....... Deputy Chief of Staff for Operations and Plans [*Army*]
DCSOPS....... Deputy Chief of Staff, military Operations (SAUS)
DCSOPS-FD... Deputy Chief of Staff for Operations - Force Development [*Army*]
DCSOR......... Deputy Chief-of-Staff Operational Requirements [*Army*]
DCSOT......... Deputy Chief of Staff for Operations and Intelligence [*Army*]
DCSP .... Defense (SAUS)
DCSP .... Defense Communications Satellite Program (SAUO)
DCSP .... Defense Communications Satellite Project [*or Program*]
DCS/P .... Deputy Chief of Staff, Personnel
DCSP .... Digital Control Signal Processor (NASA)
DCSP .... Direct-Current Straight Polarity (MCD)
DCSP .... Director of Corporate Strategic Planning
DCSP .... Dynamic Constraint Satisfaction Problem (SAUS)
DCSPA......... Deputy Chief of Staff, Personnel and Administration (AABC)
DCSPAL........ Deputy Chief of Staff for Personnel, Administration, and Logistics
DCS/P & O... Deputy Chief of Staff for Plans and Operations (AFM)
DCSP&O...... Deputy Chief of Staff, Plans and Operations (SAUS)
DCS/P & P... Deputy Chief of Staff for Plans and Programs
DCS/P & R... Deputy Chief of Staff for Programs and Resources (AFM)
DCS/PEAB.... Defense Communications System - Personnel Emergency Actions Book
DCS/PEAB.... Defense Communications System-Personnel Emergency Actions Book (SAUS)
DCS/PEAB.... Display Control/Storage and Retrieval (SAUS)
DCSPER....... Deputy Chief of Staff, Personnel [*Army*]
DCSPERS..... Deputy Chief of Staff, Personnel (SAUS)
DCSPR......... Deputy Chief of Staff for Plans and Research [*Army*]
DCSPR......... Deputy Chief of Staff, Plans and Research (SAUS)
DCSPS......... Defense Communications System Performance Simulator (SAUS)
DC SQUID.... Direct Current Superconducting Quantum Interference Device (SAUS)
DCSR........... Da Capo Senza Replica [*From the Beginning, Playing Only Once the Parts Marked with Repeats*] [*Music*]
DCSR........... Daily Combat Supply Rate (SAUS)
DCSR........... Digitally Corrected SubRanging (SAUS)
DCSR........... DISC Inc. [*NASDAQ symbol*] (TTSB)
DC/SR.......... Display and Control/Storage and Retrieval
DC/SR.......... Display and Control/Storage and Retrieval System (SAUS)
DC/SR.......... Display Control/Storage and Retrieval (SAUS)
DCSR........... Document Imaging Systems Corp. [*NASDAQ symbol*] (SAG)
DCSR........... Dominican College of San Rafael [*California*]
DCS/R & D... Deputy Chief of Staff for Research and Development (SAUS)
DCS/R&D..... Deputy Chief of Staff, Research and Development (SAUS)
DCSR & D... Deputy Chief of Staff, Research and Development [*Army*]
DCS/R & T... Deputy Chief of Staff, Research and Technology
DCS/RC........ Deputy Chief of Staff, Reserve Components [*Army*]
DCS/RD........ Deputy Chief of Staff for Research and Development (ACAE)
DCSRDA....... Deputy Chief of Staff for Research, Development, and Acquisition [*Army*]
DCSRDA....... Deputy Chief of Staff Research, Development and Acquisition (SAUS)
DCS RD & S... Deputy Chief of Staff for Research, Development, and Studies [*Marine Corps*] (DOMA)
DCS(RDL).... Deputy Chief-of-Staff (Research Development and Logistics) [*Air Force*]
DCSRM......... Deputy Chief of Staff for Resource Management (AABC)
DCSROTC.... Deputy Chief of Staff for Reserve Officers' Training Corps (AABC)
DCS/RSE...... Data Collection System Receiving Site Equipment (GEOI)
DCSRW........ DISC Inc. Wrrt [*NASDAQ symbol*] (TTSB)
DCSS........... Damage Control Suit System [*Navy*]
DCSS........... Defense Communications Satellite System [*Telecommunications*] (TEL)
DCSS........... Defense Communication Terminal System (SAUS)
DCSS........... Deployable Combat Support System (SAUS)
DCSS........... Deputy Chief of Staff, Support (SAUS)
DCSS........... Digital Communications Satellite Subsystem (MCD)
DCSS........... Digital Communications Subsystem (SAUS)
DCSS........... Digital Conferencing & Switching System (SAUS)
DCSS........... Double-Cotton Single-Silk (SAUS)
DCSS&L...... Deputy Chief of Staff, Systems and Logistics (SAUS)
DCS/S & L... Deputy Chief of Staff, Systems and Logistics
DCSSC......... Data Center Services and Support Center (VLIE)
DCSSI.......... Development Commissioner, Small Scale Industries (SAUO)
DCSSPO....... Deputy Chief of Staff, Security, Plans and Operations (SAUO)
DCSST......... Deputy Chief of Staff, Supplies and Transport (SAUS)
DCSSVC....... Deputy Chief of Staff, Services (SAUO)
DCST........... Data Collection System Tape (GEOI)
DCST........... Data Collection System Transponder (SAUS)
DCST........... Deputy Chief of Staff for Training [*Army*]
DCST........... Digital Card Schmitt Trigger [*Computer science*]
DCST........... Dynamic Combat System Test [*Military*] (CAAL)
DCST........... Deputy Chief of Supplies and Transport (ODA)
DCSTC......... Defense Communications Station Technical Control (DNAB)
DCSTE......... Deputy Chief of Staff for Test and Evaluation [*Army*]
DCSTS......... Deputy Chief of Staff for Training and Schools (AABC)
DCSTTYNET... Defense Communications System Teletype Network (AFM)
DCSU........... Differential Corrected Spectral Unit [*Spectrometry*]
DCSU........... Digital Computer Switching Unit (MCD)
DCSW.......... Diplomate in Clinical Social Work (SEAT)
DCT............. Damage Control Texts [*Naval Ship Systems Command*]
DCT............. Data Channel Transfer (SAUS)
DCT............. Data Collection Terminal [*Computer science*] (VLIE)
DCT............. Data Collection Terminator [*Computer science*] (VERA)
DCT............. Data Communications Terminal
DCT............. Data Conversion Transmitter [*Computer science*]
DCT............. Daunomycin Cytarabine, Thioguanine [*Antineoplastic drug*] (CDI)
DCT............. Deaf Communicating Terminal [*Telephone for the deaf*]
DCT............. Decceleration Time
DCT............. Decimal Code Translator
DCT............. Decoding Part (IAA)
DCT............. Dedicated Carbon Tax (SAUS)
DCT............. Deep Chest Therapy [*Medicine*] (DAVI)
DCT............. Department of Classroom Teachers [*of NEA*] (EA)
DCT............. Department of Commerce and Trade (SAUS)
DCT............. Depot Chassis Testers (ACAE)
DCT............. Depth Charges Track (SAUS)
DCT............. Depth-Charges Track
DCT............. Depth-Charge Thrower
DCT............. Depth Control Tank
dct.............. depth-control tank (SAUS)
DCT............. Destination Control Table [*Computer science*] (IAA)
DCT............. Detection, Classification, and Targeting [*or Tracking*] (MCD)
DCT............. Device Characteristics Table [*Computer science*] (IBMDP)
DCT............. Diastolic Control Team [*Cardiology*] (DAVI)
DCT............. Dichlorotoluene [*Organic chemistry*]
dct.............. Dictionary (VLIE)
DCT............. Digital Carrier Trunk (VLIE)
DCT............. Digital Comm Tech [*AMEX symbol*] (TTSB)
DCT............. Digital Communications Technology Corp. [*AMEX symbol*] (SAG)
DCT............. Digital Communications Terminal (MCD)
DCT............. Digital Computer Trainer (IAA)
DCT............. Digital Conversion Terminal [*Computer science*] (VLIE)
DCT............. Digital Cordless Telephone (CGWS)
DCT............. Digital Curve Tracer (IAA)
DCT............. Dihydrotestosterone, Corticosterone, and Thyroxine [*Endocrinology*]
DCT............. Diode Curve Tracer
DCT............. Direct [*In relation to flight plan clearances and type of approach*] [*Aviation*]

DCT.......... Direct Antiglobulin Coombs' Test [*Medicine*]
DCT.......... Direct Carbon Transfer
DCT.......... Direct Coombs Test (DB)
DCT.......... Direct Cosine Transform (SSD)
DCT.......... Direct Coupled Transistor (SAUS)
DCT.......... Direct-Coupled Transistor (IAA)
DCT.......... Direct Current Test (SAUS)
DCT.......... Direct Flight Ltd. [*British*] [*ICAO designator*] (FAAC)
DCT.......... Direction Topographique et du Cadastre [*Congo*] (GEOI)
DCT.......... Director, Control Tower [*British military*] (DMA)
DCT.......... Disaster Control Team (AFM)
DCT.......... Discourse Comprehension Test (TMMY)
DCT.......... Discrete Cosine Transform [*Telecommunications*]
DCT.......... Discrete Cosine Transformation compression (SAUS)
DCT.......... Discrete Cosinus Tranformation (SAUS)
DCT.......... Discrete Cosinus Transformation [*Computer science*] (VERA)
DCT.......... Dispatcher Control Table [*Computer science*] (ELAL)
DCT.......... Dissector Camera Tube
DCT.......... Distal Convoluted Tubule [*Nephrology*]
DCT.......... Distributed Computer Telephony
D Ct.......... District Court [*Usually federal*] (DLA)
DCT.......... Diurnal Cortisol Test [*Medicine*] (DMAA)
DCT.......... Diversified Computer Technology, Inc. (MCD)
DCT.......... Diversified Cooperative Training (SAUO)
DCT.......... Divide Check Test [*Computer science*] (IAA)
DCT.......... Divided Clock Transmitter (SAUS)
DCT.......... Division of Cancer Treatment [*Department of Health and Human Services*] (GFGA)
DCT.......... Docked Configuration Transfer (MCD)
DCT.......... Doctor of Christian Theology
DCT.......... Doctor of Christian Training
DCT.......... Document (ADA)
dct.......... documentation (SAUS)
DCT.......... Dodrill, Charles T., Hurricane WV [*STAC*]
DCT.......... Doklady Chemical Technology
DCT.......... Domestic Container Terminal [*Indian Railway*] (TIR)
DCT.......... double crystal topography (SAUS)
DCT.......... DSS [*Deep Space Station*] Communications Terminal Subsystem
DCT.......... Dynamic Computed Tomography [*Medicine*] (DMAA)
DCT.......... NAVSHIPS [*Naval Ship Systems Command*] Damage Control Texts
D Ct.......... Selected Judgments of the Divisional Courts [*Ghana*] [*A publication*] (DLA)
DCT2L.......... direct-coupled transistor-transistor logic (SAUS)
DCT-1800.... Digital Cellular Communications-1800 (CGWS)
DCTA.......... Diaminocyclohexanetetraacetic Acid [*Also, OCTA*] [*Organic chemistry*]
DCTA.......... Documentation Control Testing Application (VLIE)
DCTAF.......... (Dichlorotriazinyl)aminofluorescein [*Also, DTAF*] [*Analytical biochemistry*]
DCTB.......... Data Communications Testing Branch [*Social Security Administration*]
DCTBatt...... Diploma of the College of Technology, Battersea (SAUS)
DCTC.......... Dependent Care Tax Credit
DCTC.......... Dew Cycle Test Chamber
DCTC.......... Digital Centroid Terminal Correlation
DCTC.......... District of Columbia Teachers College [*Later, University of the District of Columbia*]
DCTC.......... Documentation Control Testing Center (VLIE)
DCTC.......... Dodge County Teachers College (SAUS)
DCTD.......... Diploma in Chest and Tuberculous Diseases (SAUS)
DCTD.......... Directors of Commodity and Technical Divisions (SAUO)
DCTDP.......... Disparity-Compensated Transform-Domain Predictive coding (SAUS)
DCTE.......... Data Circuit Terminating Equipment (VLIE)
DCTE.......... Data Collection and Terrain Evaluation (SAUS)
DC Technology... Double-coated Cup Technology (SAUS)
DCTED.......... Department of Community, Trade and Economic Development (SAUO)
DCTF.......... Danger Coefficient Test Facility (SAUS)
DCTF.......... Direct Currant Thick Film (SAUS)
DCTFE.......... Dichlorotetrafluoroethane (SAUS)
DCTG.......... Decorating (SAUS)
DCTG.......... Dihydrotestosterone, Corticosterone, Thyroxine, and Growth Hormone [*Endocrinology*]
DCTI.......... Digital Courier Technologies, Inc. [*NASDAQ symbol*] (NASQ)
DCTL.......... Data Control (VLIE)
DCTL.......... Diode-Capacitor-Transistor Logic [*Electronics*] (ECII)
DCTL.......... Direct-Coupled Transistor Logic
DCTLC.......... Direct-Coupling Transistor Logic Circuit
DCTM.......... DC Technology Missile (MCD)
DCTM.......... Delay Computer Tomographic Myelography [*Radiology*] (DAVI)
DCTM.......... Direct-Current Torque Motor
DCTM.......... Directional Control Test Missile (SAUS)
DCTM.......... Documentum, Inc. [*NASDAQ symbol*] (SAG)
DCTMA.......... Desoxycorticosterone Trimethylacetate [*Endocrinology*]
DCTN.......... Decoration
DCTN.......... Defense Commercial Telecommunications Network (DOMA)
DCTN.......... Defense Commercial Telephone Network (SAUO)
DCTN.......... Defense Commercial Television Network (SAUS)
DCTN.......... Defense Communications Telecommunications Network (SAUO)
dc-to-ac converter... direct-current alternating-current converter (SAUS)
dCTP.......... Deoxycytidine Triphospate (DB)
DCTP.......... Deoxycytidinetriphosphate [*Organic chemistry*]
DCTP.......... Duct Type
DCTPA.......... Desoxycorticosterone Triphenylacetate [*Endocrinology*] (AAMN)
dCTPase...... Deoxycytidinetriphosphatase [*An enzyme*]
DCTR.......... Device Controller (SAUS)
DCTR.......... Division of Controlled Thermonuclear Research [*Energy Research and Development Administration*]
DCT Recording... Direct Carbon Transfer Recording (SAUS)
DCTS.......... Data Communication Terminal System [*Computer science*] (DA)
DCTS.......... Digital Coordinate Transformation System
DCTS.......... Dimension Custom Telephone Service (SAUS)
DCTS.......... Document Control and Testing System (SAUS)
DCTS.......... DOE Concurrence Tracking System (SAUS)
DCTS.......... Double-Charge-Transfer Spectroscopy (MCD)
DCTS.......... Dynamic Carpal Tunnel Syndrome [*Medicine*] (DMAA)
DCTSC.......... Defense Clothing and Textile Supply Center [*Later, Defense Personnel Support Center*] [*DoD*]
DCTT.......... Damage Control Training Team (SAUS)
DCTT.......... Division Contract Termination Team (AAG)
DCTTL.......... Direct Coupled Transistor Transistor Logic (SAUS)
DCTU.......... Directly Corrected Test Unit (SAUS)
DCTUR.......... Decatur, AL [*American Association of Railroads railroad junction routing code*]
DCTV.......... Digital Color Television
DCTyL.......... Direct Coupled Transistor Transistor Logic (SAUS)
DCTyL.......... direct-coupled transistor transistor logic (SAUS)
DCU.......... Catholic University of America, Washington, DC [*Library symbol*] [*Library of Congress*] (LCLS)
DCU.......... Damage Control Unit (WDAA)
DCU.......... Data Cache Unit (SAUS)
DCU.......... Data-Cache Unit [*Computer science*]
DCU.......... Data Capture Unit (AIE)
DCU.......... Data Coding Unit (SAUS)
DCU.......... Data Collection Unit
DCU.......... Data Command Unit (MCD)
DCU.......... Data Communications Unit
DCU.......... Data Communications Utility [*Social Security Administration*]
DCU.......... Data Computation Unit (SAUS)
DCU.......... Data Computer Unit (SAUS)
DCU.......... Data Control Unit
DCU.......... Decade Counting Unit
DCU.......... Decatur, AL [*Location identifier*] [*FAA*] (FAAL)
dcu.......... Decimal Counting Unit (IDOE)
DCU.......... Decimal Counting Unit
DCU.......... Deck Calibration Unit (SAUS)
DCU.......... Dedicated Control Unit (SSD)
DCU.......... Deer Creek Reservoir [*Utah*] [*Seismograph station code, US Geological Survey*] (SEIS)
DCU.......... Demodulator/Computer Unit (ACAE)
DCU.......... Dental Care Unit [*Medicine*] (EDAA)
DCU.......... Deployment Control Unit [*Army*] (DOMA)
DCU.......... Desert Camouflage Uniform [*Military*]
DCU.......... Deskewing Control Unit (SAUS)
DCU.......... Detection and Control Unit (MCD)
DCU.......... Device Control Unit
DCU.......... Diagnostic Control Unit (SAUS)
DCU.......... Dichloral Urea [*Medicine*] (MAE)
DCU.......... Dichlorourethane (SAUS)
DCU.......... Digital Coefficient Unit [*Computer science*] (RDA)
DCU.......... Digital Communication Unit (SAUS)
DCU.......... Digital Computer Unit (MCD)
DCU.......... Digital Conference Unit (CCCA)
DCU.......... Digital Control Unit (KSC)
DCU.......... Digital Counting Unit
DCU.......... direct coefficient of utilization (SAUS)
DCU.......... Disbandment Control Unit [*Allied Military Government of Occupied Territory*] [*Post-World War II*]
DCU.......... Disc control unit (SAUS)
DCU.......... Discrete Control Unit [*American Solenoid Co.*] [*Somerset, NJ*]
DCU.......... Disk Cartridge Unit [*Computer science*] (ECII)
DCU.......... Disk Control Unit [*Computer science*] (IAA)
DCU.......... Dispenser Control Unit (RDA)
DCU.......... Display and Command Unit [*Military*]
DCU.......... Display and Control Unit (CET)
DCU.......... Display Central Unit (SAUS)
DCU.......... Display/Controller Unit (SAUS)
DCU.......... Distributed Control Unit (SAUS)
DCU.......... Distribution Control Unit
dcu.......... District of Columbia [*MARC country of publication code*] [*Library of Congress*] (LCCP)
DCU.......... Divide and Concatenate Unit (SAUS)
DCU.......... Drum Control Unit (AABC)
DCU.......... Dublin City University (ACII)
DCU.......... Dynamic Checkout Unit [*Aerospace*] (AAG)
DCU.......... Dynamic Component Upgrade (SAUS)
DCUA.......... Division of College and University Assistance [*HEW*]
DCU-C.......... Catholic University of America, Clementine Library, Washington, DC [*Library symbol*] [*Library of Congress*] (LCLS)
DCUC.......... Defense Credit Union Council (EA)
DCUG.......... Datamac Computer Users Group (HGAA)
DCU-H.......... Catholic University of America, Hyvernat Collection, Washington, DC [*Library symbol*] [*Library of Congress*] (LCLS)
DCU-IA.......... Catholic University of America, Ibero-American Collection, Washington, DC [*Library symbol*] [*Library of Congress*] (LCLS)
DCUL.......... Delaware Credit Union League (SRA)
DC (UN)....... Disarmament Commission of the United Nations [*Also, DC, UNDC*]
DCU-R.......... Data Control Unit-Receiver (MCD)
DCUTL.......... Direct-Coupled Unipolar Transistor Logic

DCV .... Dacarbazine, CCNU [*Lomustine*], Vincristine [*Antineoplastic drug regimen*]
dcv .... DC Voltage (IDOE)
dcv .... DC Volts (IDOE)
DCV .... Dense-Cored Vesicles [*Anatomy*]
DCV .... Derivative Cyclic Voltammetry [*Analytical electrochemistry*]
DCV .... Design Change Verification
DCV .... Destination Coded Vehicle (SAUS)
DCV .... Digital Coded Voice (IAA)
DCV .... Digital Compressed Video [*Telecommunications*] (ITD)
DCV .... Digitally Coded Voice (SAUS)
DCV .... Direct Current Voltage (SAUS)
DCV .... Direct Current Voltmeter (ACAE)
DCV .... Direct-Current Volts
DCV .... Directional Control Valve
DCV .... Distribution of Conduction Velocities (DMAA)
DCV .... double check val (SAUS)
DCV .... Double Check Valve (SAUS)
DCV .... Double-Check Valve
DCV .... Double Cotton Varnish [*Wire insulation*] (AAG)
DCV .... DTIC [*Dacarbazine*], CCNU , Vincristine [*Lomustine*] [*Antineoplastic drug regimen*] (DAVI)
DCV .... Direct Charge Voucher [*Accounting*] (ODA)
DCVA .... Double Check Valve Assembly [*Environmental science*] (COE)
DCVC .... Dichlorovinylcysteine [*Biochemistry*]
DCVD .... Dielectric Chemical Vapor Deposition (SAUS)
DCVD .... Directorate Co-ordinated Valve Development (SAUO)
DCVG .... Dichlorovinylglutathione [*Biochemistry*]
DCVG .... Digital Control and Vector Generator
DCVG .... Display Control and Vector Generator (SAUS)
DCVGLA ...... Digital Control Variable Gain Linear Amplifier (IAA)
DCVGLA ...... Digitally Controlled Variable-Gain Linear Amplifier (SAUS)
DCVH .... Democratic Community of Vojvodina Hungarians [*Former Yugoslavia*] [*Political party*]
DCVM .... Direct Current Voltmeter (SAUS)
DCVMA .... District of Columbia Veterinary Medical Association (GVA)
DCVN .... Directorate Co-ordinated Valve Development (SAUS)
DCVO .... Dame Commander of the Royal Victorian Order [*British*]
DCVO .... Deputy Chief Veterinary Officer (DAVI)
DCVO .... Deputy Chief Veterinary Officr (BABM)
DCVR .... Direct-Current Voltage Reference
DCVR .... Direct-Current Voltage Regulator
D/CVR .... Dust Cover [*Automotive engineering*]
DCVT .... Distillerie Cooperative Viticole (SAUS)
DCVZ .... Denver Convergence Vorticity Zone (SAUO)
DCW .... Damage Controlman (Carpenter) [*U.S. Navy enlisted rating*] (AUER)
DCW .... Data Communication Write [*Computer science*] (HGAA)
DCW .... Data Control Word (CMD)
DCW .... Data Control Work [*Computer science*] (ELAL)
DCW .... Dead Carcass Weight (SAUS)
DCW .... Dean and Chapter of Westminster [*Anglican Church*] (ROG)
DCW .... Define Constant with Wordmark
DCW .... Dependent Coverage Waiver [*Insurance*] (WYGK)
DCW .... Detroit Chemical Works (SAUS)
DCW .... Diagonal Conducting Wall (MCD)
DCW .... Diesel Component Works [*Patiala*] [*Indian Railway*] (TIR)
DCW .... Differentially Compound-Wound (SAUS)
DCW .... Digital Chart of the World [*Database*] [*Army*]
DCW .... Digital Chart of the World Laboratory (SAUO)
DCW .... Digital display Control and Warning light (SAUS)
DCW .... Display Call Waiting (SAUS)
DCW .... Dynamic Channel Exchange (NITA)
DCW .... National Society, Daughters of Colonial Wars
DCW .... Domestic Cold Water (ODA)
DCW&S .... Director of Chemical Warfare and Smoke (SAUO)
DCWC .... Diocesan Child Welfare Committee (SAUO)
DCWCS .... Directional Control and Warning Communications System (MCD)
DCWG .... Data Collection Working Group (ACAE)
DCW Light .... Digital-display Control and Warning Light (SAUS)
DCWM .... Differentially Compound-Wound Motor (SAUS)
DCWO .... Design Change Work Order
DCWOS .... Deaerating Cold Weather Oil System
DCWS .... Debris Collision Warning Sensor [*NASA*] (CIST)
DCWS .... Division of Church World Service [*Later, CWSW*] (EA)
DCWV .... Direct Current Working Voltage (SAUS)
DCWV .... Direct-Current Working Volts
DCWX .... WR Grace [*Private rail car owner code*]
DCX .... DaimlerChryler AG [*NYSE symbol*] (SG)
DCX .... Data Communication Exchange (SAUS)
DC-X .... DC Experimental (SAUS)
DCX .... DCX, Inc. [*Associated Press*] (SAG)
DC-X .... Delta Clipper-Experiment (SAUS)
DCX .... Delta Clipper Experimental
DCX .... Device Control Character [*Computer science*] (CMD)
DCX .... Digital Equipment Corp., Colorado Springs, Colorado Springs, CO [*OCLC symbol*] (OCLC)
DCX .... Direct Current Experiment (SAUS)
DCX .... direct-current experimental device (SAUS)
DCX .... Direct-Current Experiments [*Nuclear energy*] (NRCH)
DCX .... Double-Charge Exchange
DCx .... Double Convex
DCX .... Miami, FL [*Location identifier*] [*FAA*] (FAAL)
DCX .... Zsoft multipage Paintbrush image format (SAUS)
DC-XA .... Delta Clipper Experimental Advanced [*Rocket*] [*An experimental rocket that takes off and lands on its tail*] [*NASA*]
DCXI .... DCX, Inc. [*NASDAQ symbol*] (NQ)
DCX(RD) ...... double crystal XRD (SAUS)
DCY .... Dicon Systems Ltd. [*Toronto Stock Exchange symbol*]
DCY .... Washington, IN [*Location identifier*] [*FAA*] (FAAL)
DCYRA .... Duster Class Yacht Racing Association (EA)
DCYS .... Department of Children and Youth Services (SAUO)
DCZ .... Davidson Chemical [*Federal Railroad Administration identification code*]
DCZ .... Dichloro Analog of Zomepirac [*Biochemistry*]
DCZ .... Die Cast Zinc
DCZ .... District of the Canal Zone (SAUS)
DD .... Associate Directorate for Design [*Kennedy Space Center*] [*NASA*] (NASA)
DD .... Association Internationale: Donnees pour le Developpement [*Data for Development International Association - DFD*] (EA)
DD .... Command Airways [*ICAO designator*] (AD)
DD .... Continuous Drizzle (SAUS)
DD .... Daily Docket [*Costing*] (DGA)
DD .... Daily Double [*Horse racing*]
DD .... Damage Done [*Insurance*] (ODBW)
DD .... Dandruff (MELL)
DD .... Dangerous Deck (SAUS)
DD .... Dangerous Defective [*British*]
DD .... Dangerous Drug
DD .... Dangerous goods, Deck shipment only (SAUS)
DD .... Daredevils (SAUS)
DD .... Dark Detail (ELAL)
DD .... Database Description (ACRL)
DD .... Data Decoding (SAUS)
DD .... Data Definition [*Computer science*] (BUR)
DD .... Data Definition Statement (NITA)
DD .... Data Demand
DD .... Data Density (SAUS)
DD .... Data Depository (MCD)
DD .... Data Description (MCD)
DD .... Data Descriptor (SAUS)
DD .... Data Dictionary [*Computer science*]
DD .... Data Directory [*Computer science*] (IAA)
DD .... Data Display (NASA)
DD .... Data Division [*Computer science*]
DD .... Dated (FOTI)
D/D .... Date of Draft [*Business term*]
DD .... Day (SAUS)
DD .... Day of Delivery [*Medicine*] (MELL)
d/D .... Day of Discharge (DAVI)
d/d .... Days After Date (EBF)
DD .... Days after Date [*Business term*]
D/D .... Days after Days (SAUS)
DD .... Days after Delivery
DD .... Day's Date
DD .... Dayton Development Corp. [*Vancouver Stock Exchange symbol*]
DD .... Deadline Data [*Computer science*] [*Database terminology*] (NITA)
DD .... Deadline Date
DD .... Deaf and Dumb (IIA)
DD .... Death from Disease [*Military*]
DD .... Decimal Data (SAUS)
DD .... Decimal Decode (SAUS)
DD .... Decimal Degrees (SAUS)
DD .... Decimal Device (ECII)
DD .... Decimal Devide (SAUS)
DD .... Decimal Digit (SAUS)
DD .... Decimal Display
DD .... Decimal Divide
DD .... Decision Data [*Computer science*] (NITA)
DD .... Decision-to-Decision (SAUS)
DD .... Declaration Date [*of dividend payment*] [*Investment term*]
DD .... Decoder Driver (MCD)
DD .... Decreased Desire (SAUS)
DD .... De Dato [*Of Today's Date*] [*Latin*]
DD .... Dederunt [*They Gave*] [*Latin*]
DD .... Dedicated Displays (MCD)
DD .... De Die [*Daily*] [*Pharmacy*]
DD .... Dedit [*or Dedicavit*] [*Gave, Dedicated*] [*Latin*]
DD .... Deep Drawing (SAUS)
DD .... Deep-Drawn [*Metals*]
DD .... Defect Density (SAUS)
DD .... Defence (or Defense) Department (SAUO)
DD .... Defense Department [*US government*] (MCD)
DD .... Defense Depot [*DoD*]
DD .... Deferent Duct [*Medicine*] (MELL)
DD .... Deferred Delivery [*Especially, of securities*]
DD .... Deferred Development
DD .... Deficiency Disorder (FOTI)
DD .... Define Double-Word [*Computer science*] (PCM)
DD .... Definite Decoding
DD .... Definitely Dull [*Medicine*]
DD .... Definition Description (SAUS)
DD .... Definition Direction (SAUS)
DD .... Definitive Design (ABAC)
DD .... Deflection Difference (SAUS)
DD .... Deformation Dipole (SAUS)
DD .... Deformation Donor (AAEL)
DD .... Degenerated Disk [*Medicine*] (MELL)
DD .... Degenerative Disease (DAVI)
DD .... Degree Day (SAUS)

DD .... Degree Days
DD .... Degree of Difficulty [*Diving*]
DD .... Delay Driver (MCD)
DD .... Delayed Delivery [*Especially, of Securities*]
D/D .... Deletions/Deferments [*Military*]
Dd .... Delivered (MARI)
dd .... Delivered (WDMC)
DD .... Delivered
D/D .... Delivered at Destination (SAUS)
DD .... Delivered at Docks
d/d .... Delivered Docks (EBF)
DD .... Delivery Date [*Medicine*] (MELL)
DD .... Delusional Disorder [*Medicine*] (MELL)
DD .... Demand Deposits
DD .... Demand Draft [*Business term*]
d/d .... Demand Drafts (EBF)
DD .... Demonstration Division [*Forecast Systems Laboratory*] (USDC)
DD .... Density Dependent (OA)
DD .... Dental Decay (MELL)
DD .... Dental Discomfort (SAUS)
DD .... Deny and Deception (ACAE)
DD .... Deo Dedit [*He Gave to God*] [*Latin*]
DD .... Depacketization Delay (VERA)
DD .... Department of Defence (or Defense) (SAUO)
DD .... Department of Defense
DD .... Departure Date
DD .... Dependent Drainage [*Medicine*]
DD .... Depth Dose (SAUS)
DD .... Deputy Director
DD .... Deputy for Development (SAUO)
DD .... Desconnecting Device (SAUS)
DD .... Design and Development (SAUS)
DD .... Designator Detector (MCD)
DD .... Design Data (SAUS)
DD .... Design Deviation [*Aerospace*] (AAG)
DD .... Designer Drug [*Medicine*] (MELL)
DD .... Desmethyldiazepam [*Biochemistry*]
DD .... Destination/Destination [*Inspection/Acceptance point*] (MCD)
DD .... Destination Determination (SAUS)
DD .... Destroyer [*Navy symbol*]
DD .... Destroyer Division (SAUO)
DD .... Destructive Dilemma [*Rule of inference*] [*Logic*]
DD .... Detailed Design [*Phase*]
D-D .... Detail to Detail (SAUS)
DD .... Detective District (SAUS)
DD .... Detective Division (SAUS)
d/d .... detergent dispersant (SAUS)
DD .... Detergents Dispersants (SAUS)
DD .... Determination of Dependency
DD .... Detur Ad [*Let It Be Given To*] [*Pharmacy*]
D-D .... Deuterium-Deuterium Reaction [*Nuclear energy*] (NRCH)
DD .... deuteron-deuteron (SAUS)
DD .... Developer Demonstrator
DD .... Developer's Digest [*Australia*] [*A publication*]
DD .... Developmental Disability [*Medicine*]
DD .... Developmental Dyslexia [*Medicine*] (MELL)
DD .... Developmentally Delayed
dd .... developmentally disabled (SAUS)
DD .... Development Decade [*Ten-year plan designed to bring about self-sufficiency in developing countries*] [*United Nations*]
DD .... Development Department (SAUS)
DD .... Development Directive
DD .... Development Disorder
DD .... Deviation Difficulty [*Aerospace*] (AAG)
DD .... Deviation Drawing (MCD)
DD .... Device Data (SAUS)
DD .... Device Description (ACII)
DD .... Device Driver (VLIE)
DD .... Dewey Decimal (GEOI)
DD .... Dewey Decimal Number [*Online database field identifier*]
DD .... Diamond drilling (SAUS)
DD .... diastolic diameter (SAUS)
DD .... dichloropropane dicholoropropylene (SAUS)
DD .... Dichloropropene-Dichloropropane [*Pesticide*]
DD .... Died of Disease (MAE)
DD .... Diesel Direct (MSA)
DD .... Differential Detection (CCCA)
DD .... Differential Diagnosis [*Medicine*]
DD .... Differential Doppler
dD .... differential of electric displacement (SAUS)
DD .... Diffused Device (ELAL)
DD .... Diffusion Destainer [*Electrophoresis*]
DD .... Diffusionn Destainer (SAUS)
DD .... Digestive Disorder (MELL)
DD .... Digital Data (CET)
DD .... Digital Device (ELAL)
DD .... Digital Differential Analyzer [*Algorithm*] [*Computer science*] (IAA)
DD .... Digital Display
DD .... digital-to-digital (SAUS)
DD .... digital-to-digital converter (SAUS)
DD .... Digit Display (SAUS)
DD .... Dignified Dying (MELL)
DD .... DiGuglielmo's Disease [*Medicine*] (AAMN)
DD .... Diploma in Dermatology [*British*] (DI)
D-D .... Diplomate, American Board of Dermatology (DHSM)
DD .... Direct Debit [*Banking*]
dd .... direct deposit (SAUS)
DD .... Direct Development [*Phylogeny*]
DD .... Direct Diagnosis [*Medicine*] (MELL)
dd .... direct dial (SAUS)
DD .... Direct Dialing [*or Dialed*] [*Telecommunications*] (TEL)
DD .... direct discharging (SAUS)
DD .... Direct Distance Dialling (SAUS)
DD .... Direct Drive
DD .... direct drivs (SAUS)
DD .... Directives Documentation [*NASA*] (NASA)
DD .... Direct Vessel Discharge (SAUS)
DD .... Disability Determination [*Social Security Administration*] (OICC)
DD .... Disagreement Detector (SAUS)
DD .... Disc Diameter (BABM)
DD .... Discharged Dead [*On a serviceman's papers*]
DD .... Discharge Diagnosis [*Medicine*] (MELL)
DD .... Disconnecting Device (MSA)
DD .... Discontinued Design [*Tire design*]
DD .... Discriminating Digit [*Telecommunications*] (TEL)
DD .... Discrimination Difficulty [*Psychometrics*]
DD .... Dishonorable Discharge
DD .... Disjunctive Data (SAUS)
DD .... Disk Defender trademark (SAUS)
dd .... Disk Diameter [*Ophthalmology*]
DD .... Disk Doubler (SAUS)
DD .... Disk Drive (VLIE)
DD .... Disk-to-Disk (IAA)
DD .... Dislocation Density (AAEL)
dd .... dispatch days (SAUS)
DD .... Display Description (VLIE)
DD .... Display Driver
DD .... Disthymic Disorder (SAUS)
DD .... Distribution Depot (SAUO)
DD .... District Director
DD .... Divide Decimal (SAUS)
DD .... Dividend [*Investment term*] (IAA)
DD .... Divinitatis Doctor [*Doctor of Divinity*] [*Latin*]
D/D .... Divorce Division (SAUO)
DD .... Dockyard Department [*Navy*] [*British*]
Dd .... doctorandus (SAUS)
DD .... Doctor Divinitatis [*Doctor of Divinity*] [*Latin*]
DD .... Doctor of Divinity (DD)
DD .... Doctor of Divinity in Metaphysics
D/D .... Documentary Draft (ADA)
DD .... Document Delivery [*Computer science*] (NITA)
DD .... Document Distribution (SAA)
DD .... Dog Dander [*Test*] [*Medicine*] (DB)
DD .... Dogs for the Deaf (EA)
DD .... Domain Decomposition (SAUS)
DD .... Domain Directory (ACRL)
DD .... Domestic Duties (ADA)
D/D .... Domicile to Domicile (SAUS)
DD .... Dominick & Dominick (SAUO)
D/D .... Donation on Discharge
DD .... Donum Dedit [*Gave, Dedicated*] [*Latin*]
dD .... Dorsomandibular Dilator (SAUS)
DD .... Dot and Dash (IAA)
D-D .... Doty-Dayton Productions (SAUO)
DD .... Doubled
DD .... Double Dacron Braid Lacquered (MDG)
DD .... Double Dark [*Photography*] (ROG)
DD .... Double Deck
DD .... Double-Decker (SAUS)
DD .... Double Definition (SAUS)
DD .... Double Demy [*Paper*] (DGA)
DD .... Double Density
DD .... Double Diamond (MSA)
DD .... Double Diffused (SAUS)
DD .... Double Diffusion [*Test*]
DD .... Double Diode
DD .... Double-Dipper [*Retired military-government employee*]
DD .... Double-Distilled (SAUS)
DD .... Double Dominance [*Ethology*]
DD .... Double Donor (AAEL)
DD .... Double Draft [*Banking*] (ROG)
DD .... Double Drift [*As used in a navigator's log*]
DD .... downdepth (SAUS)
DD .... downdip (SAUS)
DD .... Down Drain [*Medicine*] (DAVI)
DD .... Draft for Development (OSI)
DD .... Draft on Demand (SAUS)
DD .... Drama Desk (EA)
DD .... Drawing Deviation (MCD)
DD .... Drift-Diffusion (SAUS)
D/D .... Drift Down (GAVI)
DD .... Drilled (WDAA)
DD .... Drop Dead
DD .... Drug Dependence (MELL)
DD .... Drug Discrimination [*Psychopharmacology*]
DD .... Drum Demand
DD .... Drunk and Disorderly [*Military*] (MUSM)
DD .... Dry Days [*Ecology*]
DD .... Dry Dock (SAUS)
DD .... Drydock

DD .... Dry Dressing [*Medicine*]
DD .... Dual Damping (SAUS)
DD .... Dual Diagnosis [*Medicine*] (MELL)
DD .... Dual Diaphragm [*Automotive engineering*]
DD .... Dual Disorder [*Medicine*] (MELL)
DD .... Duct Detector [*NFPA pre-fire planning symbol*] (NFPA)
DD .... Duct dilation (SAUS)
DD .... Due Date
DD .... Dumb Driver [*Auto-racing*]
d-d .... dumb-dumb (SAUS)
d-d .... dum-dum (SAUS)
DD .... Dump Diode (SAUS)
DD .... Duplex Drive (SAUS)
DD .... Duplex-Drive [*Amphibious tank*]
DD .... Du Pont [*E. I.*] De Nemours & Co., Inc. [*NYSE symbol*] (SPSG)
DD .... duPont(EI)deNemours [*NYSE symbol*] (TTSB)
DD .... Dupuytren's Disease [*Medicine*] (DB)
DD .... Dutch Door [*Technical drawings*]
DD .... Duty Driver [*Military*]
DD .... Dynein Defective Cilia [*Medicine*]
DD .... dyspeptic disease (SAUS)
DD .... E. I. du Pont de Nemours & Co. (SAUO)
DD .... E.I. du Pont de Nemours & Company (SAUS)
DD .... German Democratic Republic [*ANSI two-letter standard code*] (CNC)
DD .... Mechanical and Facilities Engineering (SAUS)
Dd .... Response to Very Small Detail [*Rorschach*] [*Also written dd*] [*Psychology*]
DD .... D Dimer [*Chemistry*] (ODA)
dd .... Dedicated (ODA)
D/D .... Dock Dues (ODA)
dd .... [*Today's*] Date (ODA)
DD .... Duchenne Dystrophy [*Medicine*] (ODA)
DD-2 .... Second United Nations Development Decade (SAUO)
DD214 .... Department of Defense Form 214 [*U.S. military discharge certificate*] (TAD)
DD-214 .... Department of Defense Honorable Discharge (SAUS)
DDA .... Acetic Derivation of DDT (SAUS)
DDA .... Dallas, TX [*Location identifier*] [*FAA*] (FAAL)
DDA .... Dangerous Drugs Act [*British*]
DDA .... Data Delivery Acknowledgment (ADWA)
DDA .... Data Descriptive Area (GEOI)
DDA .... Data Differential Analyzer (OA)
DDA .... Decentralized Data Acquisition (SAUS)
DDA .... De Dion Axle [*Automotive engineering*]
DDA .... Defence Diversification Agency (SAUS)
DDA .... Defined Display Area (SAUS)
DDA .... Dell Drive Array [*Computer science*]
DDA .... Demand Deposit Account (TDOB)
DDA .... Demand Deposit Accounting [*Banking*] (MDG)
DDA .... Dementia Associated with Alcoholism [*Medicine*] (MELL)
DDA .... Dental Dealers of America (EA)
DDA .... Depth-Duration-Area
DDA .... Depth-Duration-Area Value (SAUS)
DDA .... Deputy Director for Administration [*National Security Agency*]
DDA .... Deputy Director of Administration (SAUS)
DDA .... Deputy Director of Armaments [*British*]
DDA .... Deputy Director of Artillery (SAUO)
DDA .... Designated Deployment Area
DDA .... Designated Development Activity (COE)
DDA .... Designated Development Agency (MCD)
DDA .... Design Data Administration (SAUS)
DDA .... Design Decision Analysis (VLIE)
DDA .... Design Direction Approval [*Automotive project management*]
DDA .... Designed Deployment Area (SAUS)
DDA .... Detroit Diesel Allison (SAUS)
DDA .... Detroit Diesel Allison Division [*of General Motors Corp.*]
DDA .... Development Display Assembly
DDA .... Dezentralized Data Acquisition (SAUS)
DDA .... Dichloro-Diphenyl Acetate/Acetic Acid [*Acetic metabolite of DDT excreted in the urine*] [*Medicine*] (EDAA)
DDA .... Didecyldimethylammonium (SAUS)
DDA .... Dideoxyadenosine (DB)
ddA .... Dideoxyadenosine [*Biochemistry*] [*Medicine*]
DDA .... Die Makers and Die Cutters Association (SAUO)
DDA .... Diemakers and Diecutters Association [*Later, NADD*] (EA)
DDA .... Diemaking and Diecutting Association (SAUO)
DDA .... Digital Data Acquisition [*Computer science*] (VLIE)
DDA .... Digital Dealers Association (EA)
DDA .... Digital Design Automation (RALS)
DDA .... Digital Differantial Analyzer (SAUS)
DDA .... Digital Differential Analysis (DMAA)
DDA .... Digital Differential Analyzer [*Algorithm*] [*Computer science*]
DDA .... Digital Directory Assistance, Inc. [*Information service or system*] (IID)
DDA .... Digital Display Alarm
DDA .... Digital Drive Amplifier (AABC)
DDA .... Digitally Directed Analog (MSA)
DDA .... Direct Data Attachment
DDA .... Direct Deposit Account (SAUS)
DDA .... Direct Device Attachment (NITA)
DDA .... Direct Differential Analyzer (SAUS)
DDA .... Direct Digital Analysis (IAA)
DDA .... Direct Disk Attachment
DDA .... Directed Duty Assignment [*Military*] (AFM)
DDA .... Directory Database Administration [*Communications term*] (DCT)
DDA .... Disabled Drivers' Association [*British*]
DDA .... Discrete Dipole Approximation [*Physics*]
DDA .... discrete-dipole approximation (SAUS)
DDA .... Display and Decision Area
DDA .... Display Distributors Association (NTPA)
DDA .... Distributed Data Access [*Computer science*] (VLIE)
DDA .... Distributed Database Architecture (SAUS)
DDA .... Dividend Disbursing Agent (DLA)
DDA .... Division of Drug Advertising [*FDA*]
DDA .... Doctor of Dramatic Art
DDA .... Dodecenyl Acetate [*Pheromone*] [*Organic chemistry*]
DDA .... Dodecylamine [*Organic chemistry*]
DDA .... Dodecyldimethylamine [*or Dimethyldodecylamine*] [*Organic chemistry*]
DDA .... Domain Defined Attribute (VLIE)
DDA .... Dominica Democratic Alliance [*Political party*] (PPW)
DDA .... Double-Displacement Amplitude (SAUS)
DDA .... DRAM Development Alliance (SAUS)
DDA .... Drawing Departure Authorization (KSC)
DDA .... Dr. Dvorkovitz & Associates [*Information service or system*] (IID)
DDA .... Duty Deferment Account [*Customs*] (DS)
DDA .... Duty Deposit Account [*Customs*] (DS)
DDA .... Dynamic Demand Assignment [*Army*] (MCD)
DDA .... Dynamic Dielectric Analysis (SAUS)
DDA .... Dynamic Differential Analyzer (SAUS)
DDA .... Dynamics Differential Analyzer (IEEE)
DDA .... ICD [*Interface Control Document*] Departure Authorization [*NASA*] (NASA)
DDA .... International Dairy-Dell Association (SAUO)
DD(A & HR) ... Deputy Director (Attaches and Human Resources) [*Defense Intelligence Agency*] (DNAB)
DDAB .... Didodecyldimethyl Ammonium Bromide [*Inorganic chemistry*]
DDACM .... Deputy Director for Acquisition Career Management [*Army*]
DDACS .... Dandenong and District Aborigines Cooperative Society [*Australia*]
DDAD .... Detroit Diesel Allison Division [*of General Motors Corp.*]
DD-Additive ... Detergents-Dispersants-Additive (SAUS)
DDAE .... Deputy Director of Army Education (SAUO)
DDAFP .... Diesel Driven Auxiliary Feedwater Pump (SAUS)
DDAFP .... Diesel-Driven Auxiliary Feed Water Pump (IEEE)
DDAG .... Disabled Drivers' Action Group [*British*] (DI)
DDAH .... Deputy Director of Army Health (SAUO)
DDAL .... Doris Day Animal League (EA)
DDALV .... Days Delay Enroute Authorized Chargeable as Leave [*Military*]
DDALVAHP ... Days Delay at Address within CONUS [*Continental United States*] Authorized Chargeable as Leave [*Military*]
DDAM .... Diploma, Direction & Administration Medicine [*Medical degree*] (CMD)
DDAM .... Dynamic Design Analysis Method [*Navy*]
DDAMP .... Dideoxyadenosine Monophosphate [*Biochemistry*]
DDAMS .... Dynamic Design Analysis Method System [*Navy*]
DD & A .... Depreciation, Depletion, and Amortization
DD&A .... Dr. Dvorkovitz & Associates (SAUO)
DD&BD .... Design disclosure and base document (SAUS)
DD & CS .... Dedicated Display and Control Subsystem (NASA)
DD&J .... Deacons for Defense and Justice (SAUS)
DD&M .... Dockyards and Maintenance Department (SAUO)
DD & RB .... Document Distribution and Reproduction Branch [*NTIS*]
DD&Shpg .... Dock Dues & Shipping (WDAA)
DD & T .... Detection, Discrimination, and Tracking
DDANS .... Deputy Director of Army Nursing Services [*British military*] (DMA)
DD-Anweisung ... Datendefinitionsanweisung (SAUS)
DDAP .... Deutsche Demokratische Arbeiterpartei [*German Democratic Workers' Party*] [*Germany*] [*Political party*] (PPW)
DDAP .... Digital Distribution of Advertising for Publications (NTPA)
DDAPS .... Deputy Director of Army Postal Services (SAUO)
DDAPS .... Digital Data Acquisition and Processing System
DDAR .... Department of Disarmament and Arms Regulation [*United Nations*]
DDAR .... Division of Defense Aid Reports [*Abolished, 1941*] [*Military*]
DDAR .... Division of Defense Air Reports (SAUO)
DDARS .... Digital Data Acquisition and Reduction System (MCD)
DDAS .... Dedicated Demand Assignment Signaling (MCD)
DDAS .... Design of Data Acquisition Subsystem (NOAA)
DDAS .... Digital Data Acquisition System
DDAS .... Digital Data Archives System
DDAS .... Dosimetry Data Acquisition System (SAUS)
DDAS (ET) ... Deputy Director of Armament Supply (Eastern Theater)
DDASL .... Dowty Defence & Air Systems Ltd. (SAUS)
DDAT .... Depot Design Assistance Task (ACAE)
DDATS .... Deputy Director, Auxiliary Territorial Service [*British military*] (DMA)
DDATS .... Deputy Director of Auxiliary Territorial Service (SAUO)
DDAU .... Doctoral Dissertations Accepted by American Universities [*A bibliographic publication*]
DDAVP .... Deamino-D-arginine Vasopressin [*Antidiuretic*]
DDAVP .... Decamino-Darginine Vasopressin (SAUS)
ddavp .... desmopressin acetate (SAUS)
DDAY .... Date of Commencement of Hostilities (SAUS)
D-Day .... Day of Attack (SAUS)
D day .... Debarkation day (SAUS)
D (Day) .... Decimalisation Day [*February 15, 1971, day English money was decimalized*]
DDB .... Colorado State Publications Depository and Distribution Center, Denver, CO [*OCLC symbol*] (OCLC)
DDB .... Data Display Board
DDB .... Data Display Buffer
DDB .... Dead Band Setting [*Electronics*] (ECII)
DDB .... Decentralized Data Bank (SAUS)

DDB .... De Dion-Bouton [*Automobile*] [*French*]
DDB .... Deductive Database (IDAI)
DDB .... Defined Dollar Benefit
DDB .... Delayed Direct Broadcast (SAUS)
DDB .... Design Data Book
DDB .... Device Data Block [*Computer science*] (CIST)
DDB .... Device Dependent Bitmap (SAUS)
DDB .... Device-Dependent Bitmap [*Computer science*] (PCM)
DDB .... Device Description Block [*Computer science*] (CIST)
DDB .... Device Descriptor Block [*Computer science*] (VLIE)
DDB .... Diagnostic Development Branch [*National Institutes of Health*]
DDB .... Dial Drive Belt
DDB .... Digital Data Bank [*Computer science*] (CIST)
DDB .... Digital Database (MCD)
DDB .... Digital Data Buffer
DDB .... Digital Data Bus (SAUS)
DDB .... Directory of Data Bases in the Social and Behavioral Sciences (SAUS)
DDB .... Distributed Database
DDB .... Distribution Disk Builder [*Computer science*]
DDB .... Division of Drug Biology [*Department of Health and Human Services*] (GRD)
DDB .... Djiboutian Democratic Bureau (SAUS)
DDB .... Document Data Base (SAUS)
DDB .... Dodecylbenzene [*Organic chemistry*]
DDB .... Don't Ditch a Buddy [*Promise made by members of the Junior Woodchucks, organization to which comic strip character Donald Duck's nephews belonged*]
DDB .... Dortmund Data Bank [*University of Dortmund*] [*Germany*] [*Information service or system*] (IID)
DDB .... Double Declining Balance [*Depreciation method*] [*Accounting*]
DDB .... Double-Declining-Balance Depreciation Method [*Finance*] (DFIT)
DDB .... Doyle Dane Bernbach, Inc. [*Advertising agency*]
DDB .... Driller Down Buffer (SAUS)
DDB .... Dutch Dairy Bureau (EA)
DDB .... Dynamic Database (SEWL)
DDBA .... Digioxigenin(dibromoacetate) [*Biochemistry*]
DDBA .... Dodecylbenzenesulfonate (SAUS)
DDBDBFC .... Dave Durham and the Bull Durham Band Fan Club (EA)
DDBF .... Damaged DNA [*Deoxyribonucleic Acid*] Binding Factor [*Biochemistry*]
DDBG .... DIMDI [*Deutsches Institut fuer Medizinische Dokumentation und Information*] Database Generator [*Index to Scientific Reviews*] (NITA)
DDBG .... DIMDI Data Base Generator (SAUS)
DDBJ .... DNA [*Deoxyribonucleic Acid*] Data Bank of Japan
DDBMS .... DDB Management System (SAUS)
DDBMS .... Distributed Database Management System [*Computer science*]
DDBOps .... Deputy Director of Bomber Operations [*Air Ministry*] [*British*] [*World War II*]
DDBP .... Dance Data Bank Project [*University of California*] [*Los Angeles*] [*Information service or system*] (IID)
D/DBP .... Disinfectant and Disinfection Byproduct (ADWA)
D/DBP .... Disinfectants & Disinfection By-Products Rule (ACII)
DDB-P .... Distinguished Pistol Shot Badge [*Military decoration*] (GFGA)
DDBP .... Distributed Data Base Processor (SAUS)
D/DBPS .... Disinfection and Disinfection By-Products (SAUS)
DDB-R .... Distinguished Rifleman Badge [*Military decoration*] (GFGA)
DDBS .... Descriptor Database System
DDBS .... Development Data Bases Service (VLIE)
DDBS .... Digital Data Broadcast System (SAUS)
DDBS .... Display Data Base Subs (SAUS)
DDBS .... Distributed Data Base System (SAUS)
DDBS .... Dodecyl Benzenesulfonate [*Organic chemistry*]
DDBSA .... Dodecylbenzenesulfonic Acid [*Organic chemistry*]
DDBTP .... Digital Database Transformation Program (MCD)
ddC .... AIDS drug Hivid (SAUS)
DDC .... Corvette [*Navy symbol*] [*Obsolete*]
DDC .... Dairy Development Corp. (SAUO)
DDC .... Dangerous Drug Cabinet [*Lockable auxiliary to bathroom medicine chest*]
DDC .... Data Description Committee (SAUS)
DDC .... Data Device Corporation (SAUO)
DDC .... Data Display Center (SAUO)
DDC .... Data Display Central
DDC .... Data Display Controller
DDC .... Data Dissemination Center (or Centre) (SAUS)
DDC .... Data Distribution Center
DDC .... Data Distribution Center (or Centre) (SAUS)
DDC .... Data Documentation Costs
DDC .... Date Due Calibration [*Military*] (AFIT)
DDC .... Decision, Design, and the Computer [*Symposium*]
DDC .... Decision Difficulty Checklist (SAUS)
DDC .... Deck Decompression Chamber [*Undersea technology*]
DDC .... Defence Documentation Center (SAUS)
DDC .... Defense Distribution Center
DDC .... Defense Documentation Center [*for Scientific and Technical Information*] [*Later, DTIC*] [*Alexandria, VA*]
DDC .... Defensive Driving Course [*National Safety Council*]
DDC .... Degree Day, Celsius (SAUS)
DDC .... Departmental Data Coordinator (MCD)
DD(C) .... Deputy Director for Collection [*Defense Intelligence Agency*] (DNAB)
DDC .... Deputy Directory Comerio (SAUO)
DDC .... Deputy Divisional Commander (WDAA)
DDC .... Design and Development Contract (SAUS)
DDC .... Design Development Center (ACAE)
DDC .... Designed Data [*Vancouver Stock Exchange symbol*]
DDC .... Desk-type Digital Computer (SAUS)
DDC .... Detection Data Converter (SEWL)
DDC .... Detroit Data Center [*IRS*]
DDC .... Detroit Diesel [*NYSE symbol*] (SPSG)
DDC .... Detroit Diesel Corp. [*Automotive industry supplier*]
DDC .... Developmental Disability Center [*Columbia University*] [*Research center*] (RCD)
DDC .... Device Color Characterization (VERA)
DDC .... Dewey Decimal Classification [*Also, DC*]
DDC .... Diamond Dealers Club (EA)
DDC .... Dicarbethoxydihydrocollidine [*Biochemistry*]
DDC .... Diccionario de Citas [*A publication*]
DDC .... Dictionnaire de Droit Canonique [*A publication*] (ODCC)
ddC .... Dideoxycytidine (TAD)
DDC .... Dideoxycytidine [*Biochemistry*]
DDC .... Diecasting Development Council (EA)
DDC .... Diethyldithiocarbamate [*Also, DDTC, DEDC*] [*Organic chemistry*]
DDC .... Diethyldithiocarbamic Acid [*Organic chemistry*] (AAMN)
DDC .... Differential Chain Code (SAUS)
DDC .... Differential Dynamic Calorimetry (SAUS)
DDC .... Digital Data Cell (NASA)
DDC .... Digital Data Channel (SAUS)
DDC .... Digital Data Conversion [*Computer science*] (NITA)
DDC .... Digital Data Converter
DDC .... Digital Development Corporated (SAUS)
DDC .... Digital Development Corporation (SAUO)
DDC .... Digital Display Console (SAUS)
DDC .... Digital Display Conversion [*Computer science*] (NITA)
DDC .... Digital Display Converter (BUR)
DDC .... Digital Document Connection (SAUS)
DDC .... Digital Dynamic Convergence (SAUS)
DDC .... Digitally Directed Control (MSA)
DDC .... Digital-to-Digital Conversion (SAUS)
DDC .... Digital-to-Digital Converter [*Electronics*] (IAA)
DDC .... Dihydrocollidine [*Organic chemistry*] (DAVI)
DDC .... Direct Data Channel
DDC .... Direct Data Collection (SAUS)
DDC .... Direct Data Command (ACAE)
DDC .... Direct Data Connection (ACAE)
DDC .... Direct Department Calling (SAUO)
DDC .... Direct Digital Computer (IAA)
DDC .... Direct Digital Control
DDC .... Direct Digital Controller (MIST)
DDC .... Direct Displacement Controller
DDC .... Direct Display Console (MAE)
DDC .... Direct Distance Dialling (SAUS)
DDC .... Direct Drawing Change (AAG)
DDC .... Direct Drive Cylinder (AGLO)
DDC .... Director Digital Control (SAUS)
DDC .... Display Data Channel [*Computer science*] (PCM)
DDC .... Display Data Control (SAUS)
DDC .... Display Data Controller (IAA)
DDC .... Disruptive Discharge Cleaning (SAUS)
DDC .... Distributed Data Coupling (SAUS)
DDC .... Distributed Digital Control [*Computer science*]
DDC .... District Court, District of Columbia (DLA)
DDC .... District Development Communities (SAUO)
DDC .... Diverticular Disease of the Colon [*Medicine*] (DMAA)
DDC .... Division Data Center [*Army*] (RDA)
DDC .... Division Directors Council (SAUO)
DDC .... Division of Drug Chemistry [*Department of Health and Human Services*] (GRD)
DDC .... Docteur en Droit Canonique [*Doctor of Canon Law*] [*French*] (ILCA)
DDC .... Document Control Center (SAUS)
DDC .... Dodge City [*Kansas*] [*Airport symbol*] (OAG)
DDC .... Dodge City Weather Forecast Office (SAUS)
DDC .... Dominican House of Studies, Immaculate Conception Convent Library, Washington, DC [*Library symbol*] [*Library of Congress*] [*OCLC symbol*] (LCLS)
DDC .... Dopa Decarboxylase [*An enzyme*]
DDC .... Doris Day Collectors (EA)
DDc .... Double Concave (STED)
DDC .... Double-Doped Crystal
DDC .... Drifter Data Center (SAUO)
DDC .... Driver Development Centre [*South Australia*]
DDC .... Dual Data Collection (SAUS)
DDC .... Dual Dielectric Charge (SAUS)
DDC .... dual dielectric charge storage (SAUS)
DDC .... Dual Directional Coupler (SAUS)
DDC .... Dual Diversity Comparator
DD/C .... Dual Down-Converter (SAUS)
DDC .... Duration of Disease Control
DDC .... Dynamic Deformation and Characterization (UWER)
DDC .... Dynamic Differential Calorimetry (UWER)
DDC1 .... Display Data Channel (PCM)
DDC1 .... Display Data Channel One (SAUS)
DDC2B .... Display Data Channel Standard, Level 2B [*Computer science*] (MWOL)
DDCA .... Defense Communications Agency, Technical Library, Washington, DC [*Library symbol*] [*Library of Congress*] (LCLS)
DDCA .... Deputy Director of Civil Affairs [*War Office*] [*British*] [*World War II*]
DDCA .... Diethyldithio Carbamic Acid [*Organic chemistry*]
DDCA .... Director, Defense Communications Agency (CINC)
DDCAS .... Deputy Director, Contract Administration Services [*DoD*]

DDCASM...... Deputy Director, Contract Administration Services Memorandum [*DoD*]
DDCC.......... Developmental Disability Center for Children [*Louisiana State University*] [*Research center*] (RCD)
DDC Cells.... Dual-Dielectric Charge-storage Cells (SAUS)
DDCDM........ Didemethylchlordimeform [*A pesticide*]
DDCE.......... Digital Data Conversion Equipment
DDCFG......... Data Display & Control Functional Group (SAUO)
DDCFG......... Display Data Control Functional Group (SAUO)
DDCFSO....... Defense Documentation Center Field Services Office (SAUO)
DDCI............ Deputy Director of Central Intelligence [*CIA*] (ECON)
DDCI............ Douglas Development Co. - Irvine [*California*]
DDCIP.......... Dipolar-Decoupled Composite Inversion Pulse (UWER)
DD Circuit.... Double-Diode Circuit (SAUS)
DDCMP........ Digital Data Communications Message Protocol [*Digital Equipment Corp.*]
DDCMPs...... Digital Data Communications Message Protocols (SAUS)
DD-Code...... Document Description Code (SAUS)
D-D Code..... dot-and-dash code (SAUS)
DDCO (I)...... Deputy Director of Combined Operations (India)
DDCONUS.... Date Departed Continental United States [*Military*] (AFM)
DD Converter... Digital to Digital Converter (SAUS)
DD-COR....... Division Director-Contracting Officers Representative (SAUS)
DD Corp....... Delrose Development Corporation (SAUO)
DDCP.......... Definitive Design Change Proposal (ACAE)
DDCP.......... Department of Defense Claimant Program
DDCP.......... Direct Digital Color Proofing [*Graphic arts*] (DGA)
DDCP.......... Draft Development Concept Paper (RDA)
DDCPO........ Division Damage Control Petty Officer [*Navy*] (DNAB)
DDCS.......... Data Definition Control System
DDCS.......... Data Distribution and Command System (SAUS)
DDCS.......... Dedicated Data Calibration System
DDCS.......... Defense Diamond Development (SAUS)
DDCs.......... Desk and Derrick Club members (SAUS)
DDCS.......... Dichlorodiphenyl-1,1 Dichloroethane (SAUS)
DDCS.......... Digital Data Calibration System (KSC)
DDCS.......... Digital Data Collection System (TIMI)
DDCS.......... Digital Display and Control Set (MCD)
DDCS.......... Direct Digital Control System
DDCS.......... Direct Distance Dialing (SAUS)
DDCS.......... Display Decoder Driver (SAUS)
DDCS.......... Distributed Database Connection Service [*IBM Corp.*] (PCM)
DDCs.......... District Development Councils (Sri Lanka) [*Political party*] (PSAP)
DDCS.......... Double-Density Disk Drive (SAUS)
DDCS.......... Double Differential Cross Section
DDCS.......... Double Differential Cross-Section (SAUS)
DDCS2......... Distributed Database Connection Services /2 (SAUS)
DDCS/2........ Distributed Database Connection Services/2 (AGLO)
DDCSD......... Dual Dielectric Charge Storage Device (SAUS)
DDCSTI........ Defense Documentation Center for Scientific and Technical Information [*DoD*] (DNAB)
DDC Storage... Dual Dielectric Charge Storage (SAUS)
DDCT.......... Derby and District College of Technology (SAUO)
ddCTP.......... Dideoxycytidine Triphosphate [*Biochemistry*]
DDCU.......... DC to DC Converter Unit (SAUS)
DDD............ Chequemate, Intl. [*AMEX symbol*]
DDD............ Comprehensive Dishonesty, Disappearance, and Destruction Policy [*Insurance*]
DDD............ Dangerous, Difficult, and Dirty [*Tundish maintenance*] (UWER)
DDD............ Darling Discipline of the Decade (SAUS)
DDD............ Data Description Document (SAUS)
DD/D........... Data Dictionary/Directory [*Computer science*]
DDD............ Data Display Debugger (SAUS)
DDD............ Data Display Device (SAUS)
DDD............ Dat, Dicat, Dedicat [*He Gives, Devotes, and Dedicates*] [*Latin*]
DDD............ Date Deficiency [*or Discrepancy*] Discovered (MCD)
DDD............ Deadline Delivery Date
DDD............ Debility, Dependency, and Dread [*Factors producing compliance in hostages, prisoners, etc.*]
DDD............ Dedicated Display Device (MCD)
DDD............ Defense, Description, and Designation (UWER)
DDD............ Defense Diamond Development (UWER)
DDD............ Defined Daily Dose [*Medicine*] (DB)
DDD............ Degenerative Disc Disease [*Medicine*]
DDD............ Den Danske Dyrlaegeforening [*Danish Veterinary Association*] (GVA)
DDD............ Dense Deposit Disease (MAE)
DDD............ Denver Dialysis Disease [*Medicine*] (DB)
DDD............ Department of Decentralization and Development (SAUS)
DDD............ Deputy Director of Design [*British*]
DDD............ Deputy District Director (SAUS)
DDD............ Design Definition Document [*NASA*] (NASA)
DDD............ Design, Development, and Delivery (ACAE)
DDD............ Design Disclosure Data
DDD............ Desired Delivery Date (AFM)
DDD............ Desired Deposit of Dividends [*Investment term*] (MHDW)
ddd............. detail data display (SAUS)
DDD............ Detailed Data Display
DDD............ Detailed-Design Document (SAUS)
DDD............ Detection, Discrimination, and Designation (ACAE)
DDD............ Deutscher Depeschen-Dienst [*Press agency*] [*Germany*]
DDD............ Diarrhoe/Douleur/Diabetes mellitus (SAUS)
DDD............ Dichlorodibenzodioxin [*Also, DCDD*] [*Organic chemistry*]
DDD............ Dichlorodiphenyldichloroethane [*Also, TDE*] [*Insecticide*]
DDD............ Diesel Direct Drive
DDD............ Digital Data Distributor (CET)
DDD............ Digital Depth Detector (DNAB)
DDD............ Digital Diagnostic Diskette [*Computer science*] (NITA)
DDD............ Digital-Digital-Digital (SAUS)
DDD............ Digital Display Detection (SAUS)
DDD............ Digital Display Driver (KSC)
DDD............ Dihydroxydinaphthyl Disulfide [*Analytical chemistry*]
DDD............ Dildo Detonation Division (SAUO)
DDD............ Direct Deposit of Dividends
DDD............ Direct Digital Dialling (SAUS)
DDD............ Direct Distance Dial (SAUS)
DDD............ Direct Distance Dialing [*of telephone numbers for toll calls*]
DDD............ Disability Determination Division [*Social Security Administration*] (DHP)
DDD............ Display Decoder Drive (MCD)
DDD............ Display Decoder Driver (SAUS)
D/DD........... Display/Display Driver (ACAE)
DDD............ Domestic Door-to-Door [*Personal property*]
DDD............ Dono Dedit Dedicavit [*He Gave and Dedicated as a Gift*] [*Latin*]
DDD............ Double-Diode Detector (SAUS)
ddd............. drink, drank, drunk (SAUS)
DDD............ Drug Detection Dog (DNAB)
DDD............ Drug Distribution Data [*Medicine*] (DB)
DDD............ Dual Diaphragm Distributor [*Automotive engineering*]
DDD............ Duplexed Display Distributor
DDD............ Dynamic Dummy Director
ddd............. dynamic dummy dlrector (SAUS)
DDD............ Three Dimensional [*Also, 3D*] (DAVI)
DDD............ Wind Direction (SAUS)
DDDA.......... Decimal Digital Differential Analyzer
DDDA.......... Decimal-to-Digit Differential Analyzer (SAUS)
DDDA.......... Dodecadienyl Acetate [*Pheromone*] [*Organic chemistry*]
DDDA.......... Dodecanedioic Acid [*Organic chemistry*]
dd/dc........... diamond differential direct current (SAUS)
DDDC.......... Didehydrodideoxycytidine [*Antiviral*]
DDDC.......... Diethylammonium Diethyldithiocarbamate (SAUS)
DDDC.......... Disk Drive Dry Cleaner (NITA)
DDD CT....... Double-Dose-Delay Computed Tomography [*Medicine*] (EDAA)
DDDD.......... Dignum Deo Donum Dedit [*Latin*] (DLA)
DDDD.......... Fourth Dimension Software [*NASDAQ symbol*] (SAG)
DDDDF........ New Dimension Software [*NASDAQ symbol*] (TTSB)
DDDEP......... Defense Development Data Exchange Program (MCD)
DDDI........... Downey Designs International, Inc. [*NASDAQ symbol*] (COMM)
DDDIC......... Department of Defense Disease and Injury Code (SAUS)
DDDL.......... Data Dictionary Definition Language (SAUS)
DDDL.......... Dedicated Digital Data Link (SAUS)
DDDL.......... Dictionary Data Definition Language [*Computer science*] (ELAL)
DDDL.......... Digital Data Down Link [*Computer science*] (MCD)
DDDL.......... Double Diffused Diode Logic (SAUS)
DDDM.......... Dihydroxydichlorodiphenylmethane [*Fungicide*]
DDD network... Direct Distance Dialing (DDD) Telephone Network [*Communications term*] (DCT)
DDDOL......... Dodecandienol [*Pheromone*] [*Organic chemistry*]
DDDP.......... Detail Data Display Processor (ACAE)
DDDP.......... Detailed Design Data Package (ABAC)
DDDP.......... Discrete Differential Dynamic Programming [*Computer science*]
DDDR & E (T & E)... Deputy Director, Defense Research and Engineering (Test and Evaluation) [*DoD*] (DOMA)
DDDRE......... Deputy Director, Defense Research and Engineering [*Army*]
DD/DS......... Data Dictionary/Directory System [*Computer science*]
DDDS.......... Defense Data Dictionary System (SAUS)
DDDS.......... Deputy Director of Dental Services [*Military*] [*British*]
DDDS.......... Dichlorodiphenyl Disulfide [*Insecticide*]
DDDS.......... Digital Data Display System
DDDS.......... Directorate of Documentation and Drawing Services (MCD)
DDDT.......... Didehydrodideoxythymidine [*Antiviral*]
DDDU.......... Digital Decoder Driver Unit (MCD)
DDDU.......... Display Data Distribution Unit (SAUS)
DDDU.......... Drug Detector Dog Unit
DDE............ Decentralized Data Entry (IEEE)
DDE............ Department of Defense Education (SAUO)
DDE............ Deputy Director of Equipment [*Air Force*] [*British*]
DDE............ Designated Destroyer Escort (SAUS)
DDE............ Dichlordiphenyltrichlorethylen (SAUS)
DDE............ Dichlorodiphenyl-1,1-Dichloroethylene (SAUS)
DDE............ Dichlorodiphenyldichloroethylene [*Pesticide residue*]
DDE............ Dichlorodiphenylethane (SAUS)
DDE............ Difference-Differential Equation (SAUS)
DDE............ Differential Difference Equation [*Mathematics*] (IAA)
DDE............ Diospyrin Dimethyl Ether [*Biochemistry*]
DDE............ Direct Data Entry [*Computer science*] (BUR)
DDE............ Direct Data Exchange (SAUS)
DDE............ Direct Design Engineering (SAUS)
DDE............ Direct Digital Encoder
DDE............ Director Design Engineering (KSC)
DDE............ Distributed Data Entry
DDE............ Distributed Debugging Environment (SAUS)
DDE............ Distributive Data Environment
DDE............ Diversified Entertainment [*Vancouver Stock Exchange symbol*]
DDE............ Double Diffused Epitaxial (SAUS)
DDE............ double diffused epitaxial processs (SAUS)
DDE............ Double Diffusion Epitaxial Process (IAA)
DDE............ Drift-Diffusion Equations (SAUS)
DDE............ Dry-Dot Etching (SAUS)
DDE............ Dual Displacement Engine
dde............. dual-displacement engine (SAUS)

DDE .... Dwight David Eisenhower [*US general and president, 1890-1969*]
DDE .... Dynamic Data Evaluation (ACAE)
DDE .... Dynamic Data Exchange [*Message protocol*] [*Computer science*] (BYTE)
DDE .... Escort Destroyer [*Navy symbol*]
DDEA .... Defense Dependents Education Act of 1978 (COE)
DDEAMC ...... Dwight D. Eisenhower Army Medical Center [*Fort Gordon, GA*]
DDEC .... Death with Dignity Education Center (EA)
DDEC .... Detroit Diesel Electronic [*or Engine*] Control [*Automotive engineering*]
D Dec .... Dix's School Law Decisions [*New York*] [*A publication*] (DLA)
DDEDS .... Defense Disposal Executive Development Seminar [*DoD*]
DDEE .... Dramatic Developments in Eastern Europe (CARL)
DDEF .... Department of Defence (SAUO)
DD/EFT .... Direct Deposit / Electronic Fund Transfer
d de JC .... Despues de Jesucristo [*After Jesus Christ*] [*Spanish*] (GPO)
DDEL .... Danube Direct Express Line (SAUS)
DDEL .... Defense Development and Engineering Laboratories [*Military*]
DDEL .... Dwight D. Eisenhower Library
D Del .... United States District Court for the District of Delaware (DLA)
DDEM .... Dwight David Eisenhower Museum (SAUS)
DDEM .... Dwight D. Eisenhower Museum (SAUS)
DDEML .... Dynamic Data Exchange Management Library [*Microsoft, Inc.*] (PCM)
DDEML .... Dynamic Data Exchange Manager Library (SAUS)
DDEOC .... Destroyer Engineered Operating Cycle (MCD)
DDEP .... Defense Development Data Exchange Program (AAGC)
DDEP .... Defense Development Exchange Program (AFM)
DDEP .... Dicarbethoxy(dimethyl)(ethyl)dihydropyridine [*Biochemistry*]
DDEP .... Double Diffusion Epitaxial Plane
DDEPHS .... Dwight D. Eisenhower Philatelic and Historical Society (EA)
DDE Process... Double Diffused Epitaxial Process (SAUS)
DDERS .... Direct Data Entry Replacement System
DDES .... Digital Data Editing System (GEOI)
DDES .... Digital Data Exchange Specification (SAUS)
DDES .... Digital Data Exchange Specifications [*Computer science*] (VLIE)
DDES .... Digital Data Exchange Standards [*Telecommunications*] (DGA)
DDES .... Digital Data Exchange System [*Computer science*] (VERA)
DDES .... Direct Data Entry Station (NITA)
DDES .... Direct Data Entry System
D Des .... Doctor of Design
DDES .... Double Data Encryption Standard (SAUS)
DDESB .... Department of Defense Explosives Safety Board [*Alexandria, VA*]
DDF .... Database Definition File (NITA)
DDF .... Database Description File (SAUS)
DDF .... Data Decryption Field [*Computer science*] (MWOL)
DDF .... Data Description Facility (PDAA)
DDF .... Data Descriptive File (GEOI)
DDF .... Data Dictionary Facility (VLIE)
DDF .... Data Dictionary File [*Computer science*] (PCM)
DDF .... Data Distribution Facility (ADWA)
DDF .... Defense Department Form (AAG)
DDF .... Degree Day, Fahrenheit (SAUS)
DDF .... Delaware Group Dividend Income [*NYSE symbol*] (SPSG)
DDF .... Delaware Grp Dividend Income [*NYSE symbol*] (TTSB)
DDF .... Dental Documentary Foundation
DDF .... Deputy Director for Field Management and Evaluation [*National Security Agency*]
DDF .... descriptive data file (SAUS)
DDF .... Design Discharge Format
DDF .... Design Disclosure Formats [*Naval Applied Science Laboratory*]
DDF .... Dideoxy Finger-Printing (MELL)
DDF .... Dielectric Dissipation Factor
DDF .... difference distribution function (SAUS)
DDF .... Digital Data Formatter (SAUS)
DDF .... Digital Decimation Filter (SAUS)
DDF .... Digital Display Format (ACAE)
DDF .... Digital Distribution Frame [*Telecommunications*] (TEL)
DDF .... Director's Discretionary Fund
DDF .... Discontinued Depreciation Function
DDF .... Display & Debriefing Facility (SAUS)
DDF .... Display Data Channel (SAUS)
DDF .... Display Data File [*Computer science*] (VLIE)
DDF .... Distribution of Deposit Form (SAUS)
DDF .... Dominion Drama Festival [*Canada*]
DDF .... Dose Distribution Factor (UWER)
ddf .... double defruit (SAUS)
DDF .... Downtown Development Foundation [*Washington, DC*] [*Defunct*] (EA)
D/DF .... Drug and Disease Free (ADWA)
DDF .... Dual Doctor Families (EA)
DDF .... Due-In - Due-Out File (AFIT)
DDF .... Dump Display Facility (CIST)
DDF .... Dynamic Data Format (SAUS)
DDF .... Dynamic Data Formatting [*Computer science*] (VLIE)
DDF .... Food and Drug Administration Medical Library, Rockville, MD [*OCLC symbol*] (OCLC)
DDF .... Military Order, Devil Dog Fleas (EA)
DDFA .... Data Communications and Terminal Controller Device File Access (SAUS)
DDFC .... Dave Durham Fan Club (EA)
DDFC .... Deoxydifluorocytidine [*Antineoplastic drug*]
DDFF .... Distributed Disk File Facility [*Computer science*] (VLIE)
DDFF .... Distributed Document Formatting Facility (VLIE)
DDFII .... Data Description File for Information Interchange [*Computer science*] (VLIE)
DDFO .... Deputy Director of Fighter Operations (SAUO)
DDFs .... Design Discharge Formats (SAUS)
DDFs .... Design Disclosure Formats (SAUS)
DDFS .... Distant-Disease Free Survival (STED)
DDFT .... Design, Development, Fabrication, Testing
DDG .... Data Dependence Graph (VLIE)
DDG .... Data Display Generator
DDG .... Data Display Group (SAUO)
DDG .... Davis Department of Geology (SAUO)
DDG .... Decoy Discrimination Group (AAG)
DDG .... Deer Lodge, MT [*Location identifier*] [*FAA*] (FAAL)
DDG .... Deoxy-D-Glucose [*Also, DG, DOG*] [*Biochemistry*]
DDG .... Deputy Director-General [*British*]
DDG .... Destroyer Development Group (SAUO)
DDG .... Destroyer with missiles (SAUS)
DDG .... Deutsche Dermatologische Gesellschaft [*German Dermatological Society*] (EAIO)
DDG .... Development and Discretionary Grants Bureau
DDG .... Dial Depth Gauge
DDG .... Didecyl Glutarate [*Organic chemistry*]
DDG .... Dideoxyguanosine [*Antiviral*]
DDG .... Digital Data Generator (IEEE)
DDG .... Digital Data Group
DDG .... Digital Delay Generator (SAUS)
DDG .... Digital Display Generator
DDG .... Distillers Dried Grain
DDG .... Dodge
DDG .... Double Derivatized Guar [*Chemical technology*]
DDG .... Guided Missile Destroyer [*Navy symbol*]
DDGAMS .... Deputy Director-General, Army Medical Services (ODA)
DDGB .... Double-Dose Gallbladder [*Medicine*] (MEDA)
DDGC .... Dishonorable Discharge, General Court-Martial, after Confinement in Prison [*Navy*]
DDGCA .... Department of Director-General of Civil Aviation (SAUO)
DDGE .... Digital Display Generator Element
DDGI .... Dishonorable Discharge, General Court-Martial, Immediate [*Navy*]
DDGL .... Device Dependent Graphics Layer (VLIE)
DDGM .... District Deputy Grand Master [*Freemasonry*] (ROG)
DDGMP .... Department of Director-General of Munitons Production (SAUO)
DDGMR .... Deputy Director-General of Military Railways [*British military*] (DMA)
DDGMS .... Deputy Director General of Medical Service (SAUS)
DDGMS .... Deputy Director-General of Royal Air Force Medical Service (SAUO)
DDGN .... Nuclear Powered Guided Missile Destroyer [*Navy symbol*]
DDGOF .... Deputy Director-General of Ordnance Factories [*Ministry of Supply*] [*British*] [*World War II*]
DDGOF(E) .... Deputy Director-General of Ordnance Factories, Engineering Factories [*Ministry of Supply*] [*British*] [*World War II*]
DDGOF(F) .... Deputy Director-General of Ordnance Factories, Filling Factories [*Ministry of Supply*] [*British*] [*World War II*]
DDGOS .... Deep-Diving Submarines, General Overhaul Specifications (DNAB)
DDGP .... Deputy Director-General of Production [*Ministry of Aircraft Production*] [*British*] [*World War II*]
DDGP .... Dishonorable Discharge, General Court-Martial, after Violation of Probation [*Navy*]
DDGP .... Dubbo Division of General Practice (SAUS)
DDGS .... Distillers' Dried Grain with Solubles [*Feedstuff*]
DDGSE .... Deputy Director General of Signal Equipment (SAUS)
DDGSE .... Deputy Director-General of Signals Equipment (SAUO)
DDGSE .... Deputy Director Genera-Signals Equipment (SAUS)
DDGSR .... Deputy Director General of Signals Equipment (SAUS)
DDGSR .... Division of the Director-General of Scientific Research (SAUO)
DDGT .... Deputy Director-General of Transportation [*British military*] (DMA)
DDGTA .... Deputy Director-General of the Territorial Army (SAUO)
DDGTA .... Deputy Director General of the Territorial Army (SAUS)
DDGTP .... Dideoxyguanosine Triphosphate [*Biochemistry*]
DDGX .... Guided Missile Destroyer
DDH .... Danish Land Development Service (SAUO)
DDH .... Departed Deadheading - Empty (SAUS)
DDH .... Destroyer, Antisubmarine Helicopter [*NATO*]
DDH .... Development Dysplasia of Hip [*Medicine*] (MELL)
ddh .... diamond drill hole (SAUS)
DDH .... Dibromodimethylhydantoin (SAUS)
DDH .... Dichlorodimethylhydantoin [*Organic chemistry*]
DDH .... Digital Data Handling
DDH .... Diploma in Dental Health [*British*]
DDH .... Director, Division of Health [*New Zealand*]
DDH .... Dissociated Double Hypertropia [*Ophthalmology*]
DDH .... Distributed Document Handling (SAUS)
DDH .... Division of Dental Health [*Bureau of Health Professions Education and Manpower Training, HEW*]
DDH .... Dodecahedron [*Golf ball design*]
DDHA .... Detective Division Homicide Assault Squad (SAUS)
DDHA .... Digital Data Handling Assembly (MCD)
DDHADS ...... Digital Data Handling and Display System (SAUS)
DDH & DS ... Digital Data Handling and Display System (NRCH)
DDHBirm ...... Diploma in Dental Health, University of Birmingham [*British*] (DI)
DDHC .... Division of Defense Housing Coordination (SAUO)
DDHEALTH... Health Issues for People with Developmental Disabilities
DDHG .... Deputy Director, Home Guard [*British military*] (DMA)
DDHG .... Guided Missile Aviation Destroyer [*Navy symbol*]
DDHGN .... Nuclear-Powered Guided Aviation Destroyer [*Navy symbol*]
DD/HH:MM:SS... Day/Hour:Minute:Second (NASA)
DDHO .... Deputy Director of Home Operations [*Air Ministry*] [*British*] [*World War II*]
DDHP .... Deputy Director of Hygiene and Pathology [*Military*] [*British*]
DDHP .... Deringer Duell Head Process

DDHS .... Decimp Data Line Switch [*Computer science*]
DDHS .... Digital Data Handling System (NOAA)
DDHSF .... Darling Downs Health Services Foundation [*Australia*]
DDHT .... Double Dissociated Hypertropia [*Medicine*] (STED)
ddI .... AIDS drug Videx (SAUS)
DDI .... Data and Dimensions Interface
DDI .... Data Development, Inc. [*Database producer*] (IID)
DDI .... Data Dimensions, Incorporated (SAUO)
DDI .... Data Display Indicator
DDI .... Data Dynamics, Incorporated (SAUO)
DDI .... Daydream Island [*Australia*] [*Airport symbol*] (OAG)
DDI .... Decoy and Defensive Integration [*Military*] (SEWL)
DDI .... Dedicated Display Indicator (NASA)
DDI .... Dehra Dun [*India*] [*Later, SAB*] [*Geomagnetic observatory code*]
DDI .... Delivery Distribution Indicator (MCD)
DDI .... Demand Development Interval (MCD)
DDI .... Demographic Data for Development, International Statistical Program Center [*Bureau of the Census*] (GFGA)
DDI .... Density Dependent Inhibition [*of cell growth*]
DDI .... Depression Deviation Indicator
DDI .... Depth Deviation Indicator
DDI .... Deputy Director for Intelligence [*CIA*] (DOMA)
DDI .... Deputy Director of Intelligence [*Air Ministry*] [*British*] [*World War II*]
DDI .... Design Data, Inc. (GEOI)
DDI .... Design Data Incorporated (SAUO)
DDI .... Developing Defence Industry (SAUS)
DDI .... Device-Driver Interface [*Computer science*]
DDI .... Diazodicyanoimidazole [*Organic chemistry*]
DDI .... Dibasic Diisocyanate (SAUS)
DDI .... Didanosine [*Drug used in the treatment of AIDS*]
DDI .... Dideoxyinosine (ADWA)
ddI .... Dideoxyinosine [*Medicine*]
DDI .... Dideoxyinosine Videx [*An AIDS treatment drug*] (CDI)
DDI .... Diethyl Dicarbocyanine Iodide [*Organic chemistry*]
DDI .... Digital Databases of Illinois (SAUO)
DDI .... Digital Data Indicator (MCD)
DDI .... Digital Display Indicator (MCD)
DDI .... Digital Document Interchange (SAUS)
DDI .... Direct Data Input (SAUS)
DDI .... Direct Dial In (BUR)
DDI .... Direct Digital Interface
DDI .... Directed Drawing Instrument
DDI .... Director of Defense Information (DNAB)
DDI .... Discrete Data Input (MCD)
DDI .... Discrete Digital Input (NASA)
DDI .... Dislocation-Dislocation Interaction (SAUS)
DDI .... Distilled Deionized [*Chemistry*]
DDI .... Distributed Data Interface (SAUS)
DDI .... Divisional Detective Inspector [*British police*]
DDI .... Document Disposal Indicator
DDI .... Dodecylimidazole [*Antifungal*]
DDI .... Downwelling Diffuse Irradiance (SAUS)
DDI .... Dressing Dry and Intact [*Medicine*] (DAVI)
DDI .... Drug Didanosine (SAUS)
DDI .... Drug Dynamics Institute [*University of Texas at Austin*] [*Research center*] (RCD)
DDI .... Durg-Dependency Insomnia [*Medicine*] (EDAA)
DDI .... Dynamic-Link Library (AGLO)
DDI .... FAO Industry Cooperative Programme (SAUS)
D(DIA) .... Director (Defense Intelligence Agency) [*DoD*]
DDIB .... Disease Detection Information Bureau [*Medicine*] (DMAA)
DDIC .... DDi Corp. [*NASDAQ symbol*] (SG)
DDIC .... Department of Defense Disease and Injury Codes (DNAB)
DDIC .... Depository Institutions Deregulation Committee (EBF)
DDIC .... Digital Data Input Converter [*Computer science*] (VLIE)
D Did .... Doctor of Didactics
DDIE .... Digital Display Indicator Element (SAUS)
DDIE .... Direct Digital Interface Equipment [*Telecommunications*] (TEL)
D Di E .... Doctor of Diesel Engineering
D Di Eng .... Doctor of Diesel Engineering
DDIF .... Digital Document Interchange File (SAUS)
DDIF .... Digital Document Interchange Format
DDIFC .... Dick Damron International Fan Club [*Defunct*] [*Defunct*] (EA)
DDI Form .... Drawing Data Input Form (SAUS)
DDII .... Data Documents [*NASDAQ symbol*] (TTSB)
DDII .... Data Documents, Inc. [*NASDAQ symbol*] (SAG)
DDIL .... Drugs & Devices Information Line (SAUS)
DDIM .... Data Dimensions [*NASDAQ symbol*] (TTSB)
DDIM .... Data Dimensions, Inc. [*NASDAQ symbol*] (SAG)
DDIM .... Dry Deposition Inferential Method [*Marine science*] (OSRA)
DDIMP .... Dideoxyinosine Monophosphate [*Biochemistry*]
DD in D .... De Die in Diem [*From Day to Day*] [*Latin*]
dd-ing .... double dipping (SAUS)
DDIP .... Darling Downs Institute Press (DGA)
DDIP .... Digital Design Input Processor (TIMI)
D Dipl .... Doctor of Diplomacy
DDIR .... District Directors of Internal Revenue [*IRS*]
DDIR .... Division of Drug Information Resources [*Public Health Service*] [*Information service or system*] (IID)
D/DIRNSA .... Deputy Director, National Security Agency
DDIS .... Data Depository Index System (SAUS)
DDIS .... Data Display
DDIS .... Depository Distribution Information System (GEOI)
DD(IS) .... Deputy Director (Information Systems) [*Defense Intelligence Agency*] (DNAB)
DDIS .... Development Drilling Incentive System (SAUS)
DDIS .... Digital Display Indicator Section (SAUS)
DDIS .... Document Data Indexing Set
DDIS .... Document Depository Index System (MCD)
DDIS .... Dover Downs International Speedway [*Auto racing facility*]
DDIT .... Diagnostic Data Interface Tape (SAUS)
DDiv .... Doctor of Divinity
DDIWT .... Deputy Director of Inland Water Transport [*British military*] (DMA)
DDJ .... Digital Differencing Junction
DDJ .... Dr. Dobb's Journal [*M & T Publishing, Inc.*] [*Information service or system*] (CRD)
DDJC .... Deputy Director John Comerio (SAUO)
DDK .... Daini Denden Kikaku
DDK .... Data Decimal Keyboard (SAUS)
DDK .... Designer's Developer Kit [*Microsoft*] (AGLO)
DDK .... Device Development Kit [*Microsoft Corp.*]
DDK .... Device Driver Kit [*Computer science*] (PCM)
DDK .... Driver Development Kit (TIMI)
DDK .... Drivers Developers Kit (SAUS)
DDK .... Dunsink Observatory [*Ireland*] [*Seismograph station code, US Geological Survey*] (SEIS)
DDK .... Hunter-Killer Destroyer [*Navy ship symbol*] [*Navy*] [*Obsolete*]
DDK .... Windows Device Driver Kit (SAUS)
DDL .... Data Definition Language [*NCR Corp.*]
DDL .... Data Description Language [*Computer science*]
DDL .... Data Dialog
DDL .... Data Disclosure List (SAUS)
DDL .... Data Distribution List
DDL .... Data Down Link [*Computer science*] (MCD)
DDL .... Data Downlink (SAUS)
DDL .... Data Drawing List
DDL .... Dated Drawing List (MCD)
DDL .... DDL Electronics [*Formerly, Data-Design Laboratories*] [*NYSE symbol*] (SPSG)
DDL .... DDL Foodshow [*Food emporium which derives its name from its creator, movie producer Dino DeLaurentiis*]
DDL .... Dedicated Discipline Laboratory (SAUS)
DDL .... Delegation of Disclosure Authority Letters [*Military*] (AFIT)
DDL .... Deputy Director of Labour [*British*]
DDL .... Descriptive Design Language (SAUS)
DDL .... Detailed Data List (MCD)
DDL .... Device Description Language (ACII)
DDL .... Devices and Diagnostics Letter [*Center for Devices and Radiological Health*] [*Also known as The Orange Sheet*] [*A publication*]
DDL .... Differential Distribution Law [*Meteorology*]
DDL .... Digital Data Line (SAUS)
DDL .... Digital Data Link
DDL .... Digital Data Logger
DDL .... Digital debugging tape (SAUS)
DDL .... Digital Delay Line [*Electronic musical instruments*]
DDL .... Digital Design Language [*Air Force*] [*Computer science*]
DDL .... Digital system Design Language (SAUS)
DDL .... Digital Uata Logger (SAUS)
DDL .... Diode-Diode Logic [*Physics*]
DDL .... Direct Data Link (CDE)
DDL .... direct downlink (SAUS)
DDL .... Dispersive Delay Line
DDL .... Display Description (SAUS)
DDL .... Display Description Language (SAUS)
DDL .... Distortion Detection Loop (SAUS)
DDL .... Doctor of Divine Literature
DDL .... Documentation Distribution List (KSC)
DDL .... Document Description Language [*Computer science*]
DDL .... Dodollo [*Ethiopia*] [*Airport symbol*] (AD)
DDL .... Domain Dynamics Ltd.
DDL .... Dynamic Data Link (RALS)
DDL .... Dynamic debugging technique (SAUS)
DDL .... Dynamic Down-Loading (SAUS)
DDL .... Light Destroyer (ADA)
DDLA .... Department of Documentation, Libraries and Archives (SAUS)
DDLC .... Data Description Language Committee [*CODASYL*]
DDLC .... Data Description Language Computer (IAA)
DDLCN .... Distributed Double Loop Computer Network (MCD)
DDLDS .... Date Departed Last Duty Station [*Military*] (AFM)
DDLE .... Disseminated Discoid Lupus Erythematosus [*Medicine*]
DDL Elc .... DDL Electronics [*Associated Press*] (SAG)
DDLG .... Data Definition Language Group (SAUO)
DDLM .... Digital Data Link Monitor
DDLP .... Database Definition Language Processor (BYTE)
DDLP .... Data Definition Language Processor (SAUS)
DDL-P .... Digital Design Language-PASCAL (MCD)
DDLP .... Dominican Democratic Labor Party (Dominica) [*Political party*] (PSAP)
DDLS .... Dump Data Line Switch (MCD)
DDLT .... Diagnostic Decision Logic Table [*Computer science*]
DDLT .... Direct Detector Laser Transceiver (ACAE)
DDM .... Data Demand Module (IEEE)
DDM .... Data Description Modification (SAUS)
DDM .... Data Description Module (SAUS)
DDM .... Data Diffusion Machine [*Computer science*]
DDM .... Data Display Module (MCD)
DDM .... Data Display Monitoring (MCD)
DDM .... Decision Direct Measurement (IAA)
DDM .... Defense Disposal Manual [*DoD*] (AFIT)
DDM .... Deformable-Disk Model (SAUS)

DDM .... Department of Data Management [*Veterans Administration*]
DDM .... Deputy Director of Military Survey (SAUS)
DDM .... Derived Delta Modulation
DDM .... Design Decision Memo (MCD)
DDM .... Design, Drafting and Manufacturing (SAUS)
DDM .... Design Drafting Manufacture (SAUS)
DDM .... Device Descriptor Module [*Computer science*] (ELAL)
DDM .... Dialkyl Dihexadecylmalonate [*Organic chemistry*]
DDM .... Diaminodiphenylmethane [*Organic chemistry*]
DDM .... Dichlorodiphenylmethane [*Organic chemistry*]
DDM .... Difference in Depth of Modulation (IEEE)
DDM .... difterence depth of modulation (SAUS)
DDM .... Digital Database Maps (MCD)
DDM .... Digital Data Modem (COE)
DDM .... Digital Data Multiplexer [*Telecommunications*] (ACRL)
DDM .... Digital Dimmer Memory (SAUS)
DDM .... Digital Display Machine
DDM .... Digital Display Makeup
ddm .... digital drawing monitoring (SAUS)
DDM .... Dihydroxydichlorodiphenylmethane (SAUS)
DDM .... Diphenyldiazomethane [*Organic chemistry*]
DDM .... Diploma in Dermatological Medicine [*British*]
DDM .... Direct Drive Motor (SAUS)
DDM .... Discrete Data Management (MCD)
DDM .... Distributed Data Management [*IBM Corp.*] (VERA)
DDM .... Distributed Data Manager
DDM .... Distributed Disk Manager [*Computer science*] (HODG)
DDM .... Dividend Discount Model (EBF)
DDM .... Doctor of Dental Medicine
DDM .... Documents Data Miner (GEOI)
DDM .... Dodecyl Mercaptan (SAUS)
DDM .... Dodecylmorpholine [*Antifungal*]
DDM .... Donnely Dome [*Alaska*] [*Seismograph station code, US Geological Survey*] (SEIS)
DDM .... Doppler-Difference Method (SAUS)
DDM .... Double Diffused Mesa
DDM .... Driver's Door Module [*Automotive electronics*]
DDM .... Drop Dynamics Module (MCD)
DDM .... Dynamic Depletion Mode (IAA)
DDM .... Master of Dental Medicine
DDMA .... Disc direct memory access (SAUS)
DDMA .... Discette Direct Memory Access (SAUS)
DDMA .... Disk Direct Memory Access
DDMAC .... Division of Drug Marketing, Advertising, and Communications [*Food and Drug Administration*]
DDMC .... Design and Drafting Management Council [*Defunct*] (EA)
DDMC .... Directed Deployable Maintenance Concept (MCD)
DDMC .... Disabled Drivers' Motor Club [*British*]
DDMC .... Distributed Diagnostics and Machine Control [*Machine tools*]
DDMD .... Digital Data Message Devices (SAUS)
DDME .... Deputy Director of Mechanical Engineering [*British*]
DDMI .... Deputy Director of Military Intelligence [*British*]
DDMIIS .... David Davies Memorial Institute of International Studies (MSC)
DDML .... Display Driver Management Layer [*Computer science*] (MWOL)
DDMO .... Defense Data Management Office (SAUO)
DDMO .... Deputy Director of Military Operations (SAUO)
DDMO .... Divisions Data Management Office (ACAE)
DDMOI .... Deputy Director of Military Operations and Intelligence [*British*]
DDMOW .... Deputy Director of Medical Organization for War [*Military*] [*British*]
DDMP .... Deep-Drawn Metal Part
DDMP .... Defense Depot - Mechanicsburg, Pennsylvania [*DoD*]
DDMP .... Deputy Director of Manpower Planning [*Military*] [*British*]
DDMP .... domain-decomposition-message-passing (SAUS)
DDMQ .... Deputy Director of Movements and Quartering [*Military*] [*British*]
DDMS .... Defect Data Management System (AAEL)
DDMS .... Department of Defense Manned Space Flight
DDMS .... Deputy Director Medical Services (SAUS)
DDMS .... Deputy Director of Medical Services [*Military*] [*British*]
DDMS .... Dictionary and Dictionary Management System (SAUS)
DDMS .... Dictionary and Directory Management Subsystem (SAUS)
DDMS .... Digital Data Measuring System
DDMS .... Digital Desertification Monitoring System (SAUS)
DDMS .... Distributed Data Management System (ACAE)
DDMS .... DoD [*Department of Defense*] Manager for Space Shuttle Support (MCD)
DDMT .... Defense Depot - Memphis, Tennessee [*DoD*]
DDMT .... Deputy Director of Military Training [*British*]
DDMTMA .... Department of Defense Military Traffic Management Agency (AAG)
DDMWG .... Data Distribution And Marketing Working Group (SAUO)
DDN .... Data Defense Network (SAUS)
DDN .... Data Delivery Notice (ADWA)
DDN .... Documentation Development Notification (SAUS)
DDN .... Deep Draft Navigation [*Type of water project*]
DDN .... Defense Data Network
DDN .... Defense Department Network (SAUS)
DDN .... Defense Digital Network (ACAE)
DDN .... Defuse Data Network (SAUS)
DDN .... Delta Downs [*Australia*] [*Airport symbol*] [*Obsolete*] (OAG)
DDN .... Design Decision Notice (MCD)
DDN .... Design-Drafting-Numerical Control [*Automotive engineering*]
DDN .... Devis Directeurs Nationaux [*Canada*] (DD)
DDN .... Digital Data Network
DDN .... Diploma de Droit Notarial [*Canada*] (DD)
DDN .... Distributed Data Node (ACAE)
D Dn .... Doctor of Design
DDN .... Documentation Development Notification (KSC)
DDN .... Documented Discount Notes [*Banking*]
Ddn .... Dunedin (SAUS)
DDN .... Dynamex, Inc. [*AMEX symbol*] (SG)
dDNA .... Denatured Deoxyribonucleic Acid [*Medicine*] (EDAA)
DDNA .... Developmental Disabilities Nurses Association (NTPA)
D(DNA) .... Director (Defense Nuclear Agency) [*DoD*]
DDNAME .... Data Definition Name (ECII)
DDNAME .... Define Data Name (SAUS)
DDNC .... Deputy Director of Naval Construction [*British*]
DDNC .... Digestive Disease National Coalition (EA)
DDNC .... Direct Digital Numerical Controller
DDNI .... Deputy Director of Naval Intelligence [*British*]
DDNIA .... Defense Data Network Interface Adapter (SAUS)
DDNJ FDC ... Food and Drug Administration, Notices of Judgment [*A publication*] (DLA)
DDNN .... Dominis Nostris [*To Our Lords*] [*Latin*]
DDN NIC .... Defense Data Network Network Information Center (IGQR)
DDNO .... Dodecyldimethylamine [*or Dimethyldodecylamine*] N-Oxide [*Organic chemistry*]
DDNP .... Diazodinitrophenol [*Organic chemistry*]
DDNS .... Distributed Domain Naming Service (VERA)
DDNS .... Dynamic DNS (SAUS)
DDN SCC .... Defense Data Network Security Coordination Center
DDNTP .... Dideoxynucleoside Triphosphate (DMAA)
ddNTP .... Dideoxyribonucleotide Triphosphate [*Organic chemistry*]
DDNTP .... Didicyclohexylammonium Naphthylthiolphosphate [*Organic chemistry*]
DDO .... Dansyl Derivative of Oligothymidilate [*Biochemistry*]
DDO .... David Dunlap Observatory (SAUS)
DDO .... Defensive Duty Officer (SAUO)
DDO .... Deputy Director for Operations (SAUS)
DDO .... Deputy Director of Operations [*Air Force*]
DDO .... Deputy Director of Organisation [*Air Ministry*] [*British*]
DDO .... Deputy Director of Organization (SAUO)
DDO .... Deputy Disbursing Officer (DNAB)
DDO .... Despatch Discharging Only (SAUS)
DDO .... Destroyers, Disbursing Office [*Navy*]
DDO .... Developmental Disabilities Office [*Department of Health and Human Services*]
DDO .... Diocesan Director of Ordinands [*Church of England*]
DDO .... Diploma in Dental Only (SAUS)
DDO .... Diploma in Dental Orthopaedics [*British*]
DDO .... Diploma in Dental Orthopedics (SAUS)
DDO .... Direct Data Output (SAUS)
DDO .... Direct Deposit Option (FOTI)
DDO .... Direct Dialing Overseas (SAUS)
DDO .... Director, Development and Operations (MUGU)
DDO .... Discrete Data Output (MCD)
DDO .... Discrete Digital Output (MCD)
DDO .... Dispatch Discharging Only [*Shipping*] (DS)
DDO .... Dispute Decision Official (EEVL)
DDO .... District Dental Office [*or Officer*] [*Navy*]
DDO .... District Dental Officer (SAUS)
DDO .... Document Development Organization (SAUS)
DDO .... Double Draw-Off [*Crystallizer*] [*Chemical engineering*]
DDO .... Dumbarton Oaks Research Library of Harvard University, Washington, DC [*Library symbol*] [*Library of Congress*] [*OCLC symbol*] (LCLS)
DDO .... Dummy Delivery Order (DNAB)
DDO .... Dynamic Data Object (SAUS)
DDO .... Dynamic Drive Overlay (SAUS)
DDOA .... Deputy Director of Operations and Administration (DNAB)
DDOA .... District Director of Operations and Administration (SAUO)
DDOA .... Doctoral Dissertations on Asia (SAUS)
DDOATS .... Deputy Director of Organisation, Auxiliary Territorial Service [*British military*] (DMA)
DDOCE .... Digital Data Output Conversion Element [*or Equipment*]
DDOCE .... Digital Data Output Conversion Equipment (SAUS)
DDOCE .... Digital Data Output Converter Equipment (SAUS)
DDOCS .... UCD Docs (SAUS)
DDOD .... Deputy Director of Operations Division [*Air Ministry*] [*British*]
DDOE .... United States Department of Energy, Washington, DC [*Library symbol*] [*Library of Congress*] (LCLS)
DD of D .... Deputy Director of Dockyards (SAUO)
DD of P .... Deputy Director of Plans (SAUO)
DD of S .... Deputy Director of Naval Store Department (SAUO)
DD of S .... Deputy Director of Supplies (SAUO)
DD of ST .... Deputy Director of Sea Transport (SAUO)
DD of T .... Director, Division of Traffic
DDOF(X) .... Deputy Director of Ordnance Factories, Explosives Factories [*Ministry of Supply*] [*British*] [*World War II*]
D-dog .... detector dog (SAUS)
DDOI .... Deputy Director of Operations and Intelligence [*Air Ministry*] [*British*]
DDOL .... Data Dictionary Online (SAUS)
DDOL .... Dodecenol (SAUS)
DDOM .... Depth Domain (TIMI)
DDOMC .... Defense Depot Operations Management Course [*DoD*]
DDOP .... DSA [*Defense Supply Agency*] Disposal Operating Procedures
D-DOPA .... D-3,4-Dihydroxyphenylalanine (SAUS)
DDORCPS Glas... Diplomate in Dental Orthoptics of the Royal College of Physicians and Surgeons of Glasgow [*British*]
DDOrthRCPS(Glas)... Diploma in Dental Orthopaedics of the Royal College of Physicians and Surgeons (Glasgow) (DI)
DDOS .... Deputy Director of Ordinance Services (SAUS)
DDOS .... Deputy Director of Ordnance Services [*British*]

DDOT .... Delaware Department of Transportation [*Federal Railroad Administration identification code*]
DDOT .... United States Department of Transportation, Washington, DC [*Library symbol*] [*Library of Congress*] (LCLS)
DDOU .... Defense Depot - Ogden, Utah [*DoD*]
DDOU .... Defense Distribution Depot Ogden
DDP .... Cisplatin [*Antineoplastic drug*] (DAVI)
DDP .... Daily Delinquency Penalty [*IRS*]
DDP .... Database Definition Processor (SAUS)
DDP .... Data Description Print (SAUS)
DDP .... Data Display Panel (SAUS)
DDP .... Data Display Parameter
DDP .... Data Distribution Panel (KSC)
DDP .... Data Distribution Point [*NATO*] (NATG)
DDP .... Datagram Delivery Protocol
DDP .... Debriefing Display Program (SAA)
DDP .... Decentralized Data Processing (SAUS)
DDP .... Declaration of Design and Performance (SAUS)
DDP .... Declaration of Design Performance [*British*]
DDP .... Defense Dissemination Plan (SAUO)
DDP .... Defense Dissemination Program (MCD)
DDP .... Defense Diversification Program (SAUS)
DDP .... Deferred Development Program [*Military*]
DDP .... Deliverable Data Package (SSD)
DDP .... Delivered Duty Paid [*"INCOTERM," International Chamber of Commerce official code*]
DDP .... Delivery Distribution Point (MCD)
DDP .... Delta Dental Plan
DDP .... Demand Data Processing (SAUS)
DDP .... Demand Development Period (MCD)
DDP .... Density-Dependent Phosphoprotein [*Medicine*] (DMAA)
DDP .... Department of Defense Production
DDP .... Dependents' Dental Plan [*DoD*]
DDP .... Deployment Detailed Planning (SAUS)
DDP .... Deputy Director of Personnel (SAUS)
DDP .... Deputy Director of Plans [*CIA*]
DDP .... Derecha Democratica Espanola [*Spanish Right-Wing Democratic Party*] (PPW)
DDP .... Design Data Package
DDP .... Design Data Printing (SAUS)
DDP .... Design Development Plan (NASA)
DDP .... Deutsche Demokratische Partei [*German Democratic Party*] [*Political party*] (PPE)
DDP .... Devalued Dollar Planning (SAUS)
DDP .... Diagnostic Disk Pack (SAUS)
DDP .... Diamminodichloroplatinum [*Cisplatin*] [*Also, CDDP, cis-DDP, CPDD, CPT, P*] [*Antineoplastic drug*]
DDP .... Dichlorodiammineplatinum [*Organic chemistry*]
DDP .... Didecyl Phthalate [*Organic chemistry*]
DDP .... Differential Dynamic Programming (MCD)
DDP .... Digital Data Processing (SAUS)
DDP .... Digital Data Processor
DDP .... Digital data recorder (SAUS)
DDP .... Digital Display Processor (CMD)
DDP .... Dipole Disk Pack (SAUS)
DDP .... Direct Data Processing (SAUS)
DDP .... Direct Deposit of Payroll
DDP .... Director [*or Directorate*] of Development Planning [*Air Force*]
DDP .... discrete dynamic programming (SAUS)
DDP .... Distributed Data Path (SAUS)
DDP .... Distributed Data Processing [*Computer science*] [*Telecommunications*]
DDP .... Distributed Data Processor (RALS)
DDP .... Distribution Data Processing (ACAE)
DDP .... Distribution Drop Point (AABC)
DDP .... Distributive Data Path (SAUS)
DDP .... Doctors for Disaster Preparedness (EA)
DDP .... Dodecyl Phthalate (EDCT)
ddp .... dodecyl phthalte (SAUS)
DDP .... Dodecylpyrene [*Organic chemistry*]
DDP .... Dorado [*Puerto Rico*] [*Airport symbol*] (OAG)
DDP .... Double Diffusion Precipitin (SAUS)
DDP .... Double Diode-Pentode
DDp .... Drug Dependence [*Medicine*] (EDAA)
DDP .... Dry Discharge Pump
DDP .... Erato (Discophiles de Paris Series) [*Record label*] [*France*]
DDP .... San Juan, PR [*Location identifier*] [*FAA*] (FAAL)
DDPA .... Delta Dental Plans Association (EA)
DDPA .... Deputy Director of Personnel Administration (SAUO)
DDPC .... DCSLOG [*Deputy Chief of Staff for Logistics*] Data Processing Center [*Military*] (AABC)
DDPC .... Departmental Data Processing Center [*Department of Labor*]
DDPC .... Digital Data Processing Center [*or Complex*] (MCD)
DDPC .... Digital Data Processing Complex (SAUS)
DD(PCD & T)... Deputy Director (Personnel, Career Development, and Training) [*Defense Intelligence Agency*] (DNAB)
DD-PCR .... Differential Display PCR (SAUS)
DDPE .... Digital Data Processing Equipment
DDPEX .... Device Dependent Packet Exchange (VLIE)
DDPEX .... Device Dependent PEX (SAUS)
DDPF .... Dedicated Display Processing Function (NASA)
DDPH .... Deputy Director of Public Health (HEAS)
DDPH .... Diploma in Dental Public Health [*British*]
DDPHP .... Deputy Director of Post-Hostilities Plans [*Military*] [*British*]
DDPHRCS Eng... Diploma in Dental Public Health, Royal College of Surgeons of England
DDPL .... Data Drawing and Parts List
DDPL .... Demand Deposit Program Library [*Computer science*] (OA)
DDPLO .... Designated Disabled Persons Liaison Officer (AIE)
ddpm .... Dial Divisions per Minute
DDPM .... Distributed Data Processing Management (SAUS)
DDPM .... Distributed Data Processing Model (MCD)
DDPN .... Deafness, Diabetes, Photomyoclonus and Nephropathy [*Medicine*] (MELL)
DDPO .... Defense Dissemination Program Office (GEOI)
DDPOW .... Deputy Director of Prisoners of War [*British*]
DDPP .... Deputy Director for Plans and Policy [*National Security Agency*]
DDPP .... Detailed design data package (SAUS)
DDPP .... Direct Digital Printing Plate (VLIE)
DDPR .... Deputy Director for Programs and Resources [*National Security Agency*]
DDPR .... Deputy Director of Public Relations [*Military*] [*British*]
DDPR .... Digital Data Processing Request (ACAE)
DDPrA .... du Pont(E.I.),$3.50 Pfd [*NYSE symbol*] (TTSB)
DDPrB .... du Pont(E.I.),$4.50 Pfd [*NYSE symbol*] (TTSB)
DDPREP .... Device Dependent Parameter conversion and Replacement (SAUS)
DDPREP .... Device-Dependent Parameter Conversion and Replacement (VLIE)
DDPS .... Data Directed Programming System [*British*] (DIT)
DDPS .... Department of Defense Project Specification (MCD)
DDPS .... Deputy Director of Personal Services [*Navy*] [*British*]
DDPS .... Deputy Director of Personnal Services (SAUO)
DDPS .... Deputy Director of Postal Service (SAUO)
DDPS .... Deputy Director of Postal Services (SAUS)
DDPS .... Desktop Digital Photogrammetry System (GEOI)
DDPS .... Dichlorodiphenylsulfone Monomer (EDCT)
DDPS .... Digital Data Processing System
DDPS .... Discrete Depth Plankton Sampler
DDPS .... Discrimination Data Processing System (AABC)
DDPS .... Distributive Document Processing System (SAUS)
DDPS .... Dual Driver Protective Service [*MTMC*] (TAG)
DDPU .... Digital Data Processing Unit (IEEE)
DDQ .... Deep Drawing Quality (SAUS)
DDQ .... Deputy Director of Quartering [*Military*] [*British*]
DDQ .... Dichlorodicyanobenzoquinone [*Organic chemistry*]
DDQ .... Dimensions Description Questionnaire
DDQ .... Dynmaic Data Queuing (SAUS)
DDQ .... Minot, ND [*Location identifier*] [*FAA*] (FAAL)
DDR .... Daily Demand Rate
DDR .... Damage-to-Dose Ratio [*Physics*] (UWER)
DDR .... DASD [*Direct Access Storage Device*] Dump Restore [*Computer science*] (IBMDP)
DDR .... Data Dependent Routing (VLIE)
DDR .... Data Descriptive Record (GEOI)
DDR .... Data Dictionary Reporter (SAUS)
DDR .... Data Direction Register [*Microcomputer*]
DDR .... Data Discrepancy Report (MCD)
DDR .... Daughters of the Defenders of the Republic, USA (EA)
DDR .... Daughters of the Divine Redeemer [*Roman Catholic religious order*]
DDR .... Decision-Directed Receiver (SAUS)
DDR .... Decoy Discrimination RADAR
DDR .... Deficiency and Disposition Report [*Nuclear energy*] (NRCH)
DDR .... Definitive Design Review (SAUS)
DDR .... Delayed Disposition Record (MCD)
DDR .... Delinquency Delivery Report (MCD)
DDR .... Density Dependent Recruitment [*Pisciculture*]
DDR .... Deputy Director of Research (CARL)
DDR .... Design Development Record (MCD)
DDR .... Detail Design Review (MCD)
DDR .... Detector Dependent Response [*Measurement*]
DDR .... Deutsche Demokratische Republik [*German Democratic Republic (East Germany)*]
DDR .... Developers Diversified Realty [*NYSE symbol*] (SPSG)
DDR .... Development Discrepancy Report
DDR .... Device Dependent Routine
DDR .... Dialectic Data Reader (SAUS)
DDR .... Dialed Digit Receiver [*Telecommunications*] (TEL)
DDR .... Dialled Digit Receiver (SAUS)
DDR .... Dial-on-Demand Routing [*Telecommunications*] (PCM)
DDR .... Digital Data Receiver
DDR .... Digital Data Recorder (MCD)
DDR .... Digital Data Recording (SAUS)
DDR .... Digital Demand Recorder (IAA)
DDR .... Digital Disk Recorder (DOM)
DDR .... Digital Display and Recorder (ACAE)
DDR .... Digroup Data Reduction [*Telecommunications*] (MCD)
DDR .... Diploma in Diagnostic Radiology [*British*]
DDR .... Direct Data Reading (SAUS)
DDR .... Direct Data Recording (SAUS)
DDR .... Direct Debit [*Banking*] (DCTA)
DDR .... Direct Drive
DDR .... Discharged During Referral [*Medicine*] (MEDA)
DDR .... Discontinuous Dynamic Recrystallization [*Metallurgy*] (UWER)
DDr .... Doctor of Divinity (EY)
DDR .... Dodaira [*Japan*] [*Seismograph station code, US Geological Survey*] (SEIS)
DDR .... Double Data Rate [*Computer science*]
DDR .... Double Drift Region (IEEE)
DDR .... Downrange Data Report
DDR .... Drawing Data Requirement (IAA)

DDR............ Drunk Driving Defense (LAIN)
DDR............ Dual Dial Restore [*Communications term*] (DCT)
DDR............ Dual Discrimination Ratio (IAA)
DDR............ Dynamic Desktop Router [*Computer science*] (VERA)
DDR............ Dynamic Device Reallocation (SAUS)
DDR............ Dynamic Device Reconfiguration [*IBM Corp.*] [*Computer science*] (MDG)
DDR............ Dynamic Document Review (SAUS)
DDR............ RADAR Picket Destroyer [*Navy symbol*] [*Navy*]
DDRA........... Dead Despite Resuscitation Attempt [*Medicine*] (CPH)
DDRA........... Decimal Divide Restore Answer (VLIE)
DDRA........... Deputy Director of Royal Artillery [*Military*] [*British*]
DDRA........... Deputy Director, Royal Artillery (SAUO)
DDRA........... Deputy DirectorRoyal Artillery (SAUS)
DDRA........... Didehydroretinoic Acid [*Biochemistry*]
DDRAE.......... Directorate for Defense Research and Engineering (SAUS)
DD R & D.... Department of Defense Research and Development (SAUS)
DDR & E...... Defense Development Research and Engineering (MCD)
DDR&E........ Deputy Director, Defense Research and Engineering [*OSD*] (AAGC)
DDR&E........ Deputy Director of Research and Engineering (SAUS)
DDR & E...... Detailed Design Review and Evaluation (MCD)
DDR&E........ Directorate for Defense Research and Engineering (SAUO)
DDR&E........ Directorate of Defense Research and Engineering (SAUS)
DDR&E........ Director, Defense Research and Engineering (SAUS)
DDR & E...... Director [*or Directorate*] of Defense Research and Engineering [*DoD*]
DDR&F........ Deputy Director, Research and Engineering (ACAE)
DDRB........... Danish Defense Research Board
DDRB........... Design Data Review Board (ACAE)
DDRB........... Doctors' and Dentists' Review Body [*British*] (DI)
DDRC........... Drawing Data Required for Change (KSC)
DDRC........... Drug Dependence Research Center (SAUO)
DDRC........... Drug Dose-Response Curve [*Medicine*] (MELL)
DDRD........... Deputy Directorate of Research and Development (SAUS)
DDRD........... Deputy Director of Recruiting and Demobilization [*Military*] [*British*]
DDRD........... Direct Data Recording Device (SAUS)
DDR Diode... Double Drift Region Diode (SAUS)
DDRE........... Danish Defense Research Establishment (NATG)
DDRE........... Director [*or Directorate*] of Defense Research and Engineering [*DoD*]
DDRF........... Degenerative Deseases Research Foundation (SAUO)
DDRF........... Degenerative Diseases Research Foundation (EA)
DDRF........... Dose and Dose-Rate Reduction Factor [*Environmental Protection Agency*]
DDRH........... Digital Data Recording Head
DDRI........... Design Drafting Reference Information
DDRI........... Diversified Data Resources, Inc. [*Information service or system*] (IID)
DDRM........... Data, Document, and Records Management (SSD)
DDRM........... Deputy Directorate of Repair and Maintenance (SAUO)
DDRM........... Deputy Director of Repair and Maintenance (SAUS)
DDRM........... Device driver interface/Driver kernel interface Reference Manual (SAUS)
DDRM........... Direct Dial Response Marketing, Inc. [*Information service or system*] (IID)
DDRMI......... Digital Distance Radio Magnetic Indicator (HLLA)
DDRO........... Dual Dielectric Resonator Oscillator (SAUS)
DDRP........... Dial Dictation Relay Panel (HGAA)
DDRP........... Direct/Delayed Response Project (SAUS)
DDRPrA....... Developers Div Rlty 9.50% Pfd [*NYSE symbol*] (TTSB)
DDRPrB....... Developers Div Rlty 9.44% Pfd [*NYSE symbol*] (TTSB)
DDR Press... Deep Drawing Press (SAUS)
DDRR........... Digital Data Recorder Reproducer (DWSG)
DDRR........... Digital Data Regenerative Repeater (DNAB)
DDRR........... Directional Discontinuity Ring Radiator
DDRR Antenna... Directional Discontinuity Ring Radiator Antenna (SAUS)
DDRS........... Declassified Documents Reference System [*Research Publications, Inc.*] [*Woodbridge, CT*]
DDRS........... Defense Data Repository System [*DoD*]
DDRS........... Demographic Data Retrieval System [*Census Bureau*] [*Information service or system*] (IID)
DDRS........... Digital Data Recording System
DDRSDRAM... Double-Data-Rate Synchronous Dynamic Random Access Memory (AEBE)
DDR System... Digital Data Recording System (SAUS)
DDRT........... Diseases, Disorders, and Related Topics [*Medicine*] (DMAA)
DDRW........... Defense Distribution Region West
DDRX........... Diedrich Coffee [*NASDAQ symbol*] (NASQ)
DDS............. Damaged Disc Syndrome [*Medicine*] (DMAA)
DDS............. Damien-Dutton Society (SAUO)
DDS............. Damien Dutton Society for Leprosy Aid (EA)
DDS............. Dapsone [*Antimalarial medication*] (VNW)
DDS............. Data Delivery Services (SAUS)
DDS............. Data Dependent System (VLIE)
DDS............. Data Description Specification (VLIE)
DDS............. Data Dialog System (MCD)
DDS............. Data Dictionary System [*Computer science*]
DDS............. Data Display Set (MCD)
DDS............. Data Display System [*or Subsystem*]
DDS............. Data Dissemination System [*European Space Agency - Information Retrieval Service*] [*Rome, Italy*]
DDS............. Data Distribution System [*or Subsystem*]
DDS............. Data Documentation System (SAUS)
DDS............. Data-Phone Digital Service [*Trademark of the American Telephone & Telegraph Co.*]
DDS............. Dataphone Digital System [*AT&T*] (NITA)
DDS............. Dataption Digital Service (SAUS)
DDS............. Data Telephone Digital Service (SAUS)
DDS............. Deaf and Dumb Society (SAUO)
DDS............. Decision Support System (VLIE)
DDS............. Decoy Dispensing Set (MCD)
DDS............. Deep-Diving System
DDS............. Defense Dissemination System (MCD)
DDS............. Deflection Detection System [*Automotive tires*]
DD/S........... Delivered Sound [*Shipping*]
dds............. delivered sound (SAUS)
DDS............. Demos D Scale [*Psychology*]
DDS............. Dendrodendritic Synaptosome [*Medicine*] (DMAA)
DDS............. Dental Data System (SAUS)
DDS............. Dental Distress Syndrome [*Medicine*] (DMAA)
DDS............. Dentaurum Data Service (SAUS)
DDS............. Dentist
DDS............. Denys-Drash Syndrome [*Medicine*]
DDS............. Department of Defense Support (SAUS)
DDS............. Department of Developmental Services (SAUS)
DDS............. Deployable Defence System (SAUS)
DDS............. Deployable Defense System (IEEE)
DDS............. Depressed DNA Synthesis [*Medicine*] (DMAA)
DDS............. Deputy Defense Secretary (SAUO)
DD(S).......... Deputy Director for Support [*Defense Intelligence Agency*] (DNAB)
DDS............. Deputy Director of Science [*Military*] [*British*]
DDS............. Deputy Director of Support (SAUS)
DDS............. Descriptor Differential Scale [*Medicine*] (MELL)
DDS............. Designator Detection System (MCD)
DDS............. Design Data Sheet [*Naval Ship Engineering Center*]
DDS............. Design Disclosure Standard
DDS............. Design Disclosure System (SAUS)
DDS............. Detailed Design Specification (MCD)
DDS............. Developmental Disabilities Service
DDS............. Development Data Sheet (MCD)
DDS............. Development Documentation System (SAUS)
DDS............. Deviation Dependent Sensitivity [*Navigation*] (IAA)
DDS............. Device Dependent Section (SAUS)
DDS............. Dewey Decimal System (SAUS)
DDS............. Dialysis Disequilibrium Syndrome
DDS............. Diaminodiphenyl Sulfone [*Also, DADPS, DAPSONE*] [*Pharmacology*]
dds............. diaminodiphenylsulfone (SAUS)
DDS............. Differential and Derivative Spectrophotometry (SAUS)
DDS............. Digital Dataphone Service [*Telecommunications*] (DOM)
DDS............. Digital Data Secure (DWSG)
DDS............. Digital Data Service [*Telecommunications*] (ADA)
DDS............. Digital Data Servo
DDS............. Digital Data Set (SAUS)
DDS............. Digital Data Storage [*Computer science*]
DDS............. Digital Data Stream (SAUS)
DDS............. Digital Data System
DDS............. Digital Dental Society (SAUS)
DDS............. Digital Design Studio
DDS............. Digital Differences Summator (SAUS)
DDS............. Digital Display Scope
DDS............. Digital Drafting System
DDS............. Digital Dynamics Simulator (IEEE)
D/DS........... Digitizing Drafting System (SAUS)
DDS............. Dillard Department Stores, Inc. Class A [*NYSE symbol*] (SPSG)
DDS............. Dillard Dept Str'A' [*NYSE symbol*] (TTSB)
DDS............. Dillard's Inc.'A' [*NYSE symbol*] (SG)
DDS............. Direct Data Service (SAUS)
DDS............. Direct Data Set [*Computer science*] (VLIE)
DDS............. Direct Delivery by Satellite (SAUS)
DDS............. Direct Dial Service [*Telecommunications*] (HGAA)
DDS............. Direct Digital Sampling (SAUS)
DDS............. Direct Digital Service (AGLO)
DDS............. Direct Digital Synthesis (SEWL)
DDS............. Direct Digital Synthesizer (MCD)
DDS............. Direct Distance Service
DDS............. Directional Doppler Sonography [*Medicine*] (DMAA)
DDS............. Director of Dental Services [*British*]
DDS............. Directory Development Study
DDS............. Disability Determination Service [*Social Security Administration*] (GFGA)
DDS............. Discarded Data Storage (SAUS)
DDS............. Discrete Depth Sampler
DDS............. Disease-Disability Scale [*Medicine*] (MELL)
DDS............. Disk Data Storage (SAUS)
DDS............. Disk Definition Structure (SAUS)
DDS............. Display and Debriefing Subsystem (MCD)
DDS............. Display & Debriefing System (SAUS)
DDS............. Display Data Subsystem (SAUS)
DDS............. Distillation Desalination System
DDS............. Distillers Dried Solubles (OA)
DDS............. Distributed Database Services (SAUS)
DDS............. Distributed Database System (SAUS)
DDS............. Distributed Data Server [*Computer science*] (MWOL)
DDS............. Distributed Data Services (SAUS)
DDS............. Distributed Data Storage (SAUS)
DDS............. Distributed Defense Study [*DoD*]
DDS............. Distributed Directory Service [*Computer science*] (VERA)
DDS............. Diversified Data Systems, Incorporated (SAUS)
DDS............. Diving Dentists Society (EA)
DDS............. Doctor of Dental Science
DDS............. Doctor of Dental Surgery
DDS............. Documentation Distribution System (NASA)
DDS............. Document Delivery Services (TELE)

DDS .... Document Development Services (COE)
DDS .... Document Distribution Services (SAUS)
DDS .... Dodecenylsuccinic Anhydride (SAUS)
DDS .... Dodecyl Sulfate [*Medicine*] (DMAA)
DDS .... Domestic Data Service
DDS .... Domestic Disclosure Spreadsheet (SAUS)
DDS .... Donovan Data Systems [*A company*] [*New York, NY*] (WDMC)
DDS .... Doped Deposited Silica (SAUS)
DDS .... Doped Deposited Silical [*Corning process*]
DDS .... Doppler Detection Station [*Detection station on the Mid-Canada Line*]
DDS .... Doppler Detection System
DDS .... Dose Detector System
DDS .... Double Decidual Sac [*Medicine*] (DMAA)
DDS .... double dispersive spectrometer (SAUS)
DDS .... Dow Dividend Strategy
DDS .... Drastically Disturbed Sites (SAUO)
DDS .... Driver decay storage (SAUS)
DDS .... Drug Delivery System [*Pharmacy*]
DDS .... Drug Development (Scotland) Ltd. [*British*] (IRUK)
DDS .... Dry Deck Shelter [*Navy*] (DOMA)
DDS .... Dry Dock Shelter (MILB)
DDS .... Dummy Data Set (SAUS)
DDS .... Dummy Director Set
DDS .... Dust Detector Subsystem (ACAE)
DDS .... Dynamically Decoupled Steering [*Automotive engineering*]
DDS .... Dynamic Debugging Source (SAUS)
DDS .... Dynamic Diagnostic System (MCD)
DDS .... Dynamic Dispatch System [*Computer science*] (ELAL)
DDS .... Dystrophy-Dystocia Syndrome [*Medicine*] (MAE)
DDSA .... Digital Data Service Adapter [*Computer science*] (VERA)
DDSA .... Dodecenylsuccinic Anhydride [*Organic chemistry*]
DDSA .... Dodecylsuccinic Anhydride (SAUS)
DDS & T ...... Deputy Director of Science and Technology (SAUS)
DD:S & T ...... Diamond Depositions: Science and Technology [*A publication*]
DDS&T .... Directorate of Science and Technology [*CIA*] (LAIN)
DDSC .... Design and Drafting Standards Committee (ACAE)
DDSC .... Dewey Decimal System of Classification (SAUS)
DD Sc .... Doctor of Dental Science
DDSD .... Deputy Director of Staff Duties [*Military*] [*British*]
DDSD .... DFN Directory Services Deutschland (SAUO)
DDS-DC .... Digital Data Storage - Data Compression (SAUS)
DDSDC .... Digital Data Storage-Data Compression [*Computer science*] (VERA)
DDSE .... Design Disclosure for Systems and Equipment
DDSF .... Digital Data Surveillance Facility (SAUS)
DDSG .... Digital Data Switching Group (CAAL)
DDSI .... Data Dissemination Systems, Incorporated (SAUO)
DDSI .... Digital Damage Severity Index (DMAA)
DDSI .... Digital Descriptor Systems [*NASDAQ symbol*] (SAG)
DDS II .... Dataphone Digital Service with Secondary Channel [*Communications term*] (DCT)
DDSIU .... Digital Descriptor Sys Unit [*NASDAQ symbol*] (TTSB)
DDSIW .... Digital Descriptor Sys Wrrt'A' [*NASDAQ symbol*] (TTSB)
DDSIZ .... Digital Descriptor Sys Wrrt'B' [*NASDAQ symbol*] (TTSB)
DDSLA .... Damien Dutton Society for Leprosy Aid (EA)
DDSM .... Decontrolled Defense Supply Material
DDSM .... Defense Distinguished Service Medal [*Military decoration*]
DDSM .... Digital Data Switching Matrix
DDSMS .... Department for Development Support and Management Services (SAUO)
DDSMS .... Digital Dispatch Security Monitoring System (SAUS)
DDSN .... Digital Derived Services Network [*Computer science*] (CIST)
DDSN .... Distributed Decision Support Network (SAUS)
DDSN .... Distributed Diagnostics and Service Network (DINT)
DDSN .... Parkfield Downhole Digital Seismic Network [*Seismology*]
DDSO .... Developmentally Disabled Service Office
DDSO .... Diaminodiphenyl Sulfoxide [*Pharmacology*] (MAE)
ddso .... diamino-diphenyl sulphoxide (SAUS)
DDSOT .... Digital Daily System Operability Test
DDSP .... Defense Development Sharing Program [*US and Canada*] (RDA)
DDSP .... Deputy Director of Selection of Personnel [*Military*] [*British*]
DDSP .... Digital Doppler Signal Processor (ACAE)
DDSR .... Demand Delivery System Regulator [*Automotive emissions*]
DDSR .... Deputy Director of Scientifc Research (SAUS)
DDSS .... Developmental Disabilities Special Interest Section [*American Occupational Therapy Association*]
DDSS .... Diffusion Dependence Shell Structure (SAUS)
DDSS .... Digital Data Storage System (SAUS)
DDSS .... Distributed Decision Support Server (SAUS)
DDSS .... Diversified Data Services and Sciences, Inc. (SAUO)
DDSS .... Double Dynamic Suspension System (SAUS)
DDSS .... DS Decision Support System (SAUS)
DDSSA .... Digital Distributed System Security Architecture trademark (SAUS)
DDS-SC .... Dataphone Digital Service with Secondary Channel [*Communications term*] (DCT)
DDS S/C ...... DDS with Secondary Channel [*Communications term*] (DCT)
DDSSF .... Dilute double-shell slurry feed (SAUS)
DDSSJ .... Drone Deceptive Self-Screening Jammer [*Military*] (MCD)
DDST .... Denver Developmental Screening Test [*For mental development of infants*]
DDST .... Deputy Director for Science and Technology (SAUO)
DDST .... Deputy Director of Supply and Transport [*British*]
DDST .... Deputy Director of Surface Transport (SAUO)
DDST .... Double Daylight Saving Time (SAUS)
DDSTS .... Double-door sealed transfer system (SAUS)
DDSU .... Digital Data Storage Unit
DDSUBEX .... Destroyer-Submarine Exercise (SAUO)
DD Sur .... Doctor of Dental Surgery
DDT .... Data Debugging Tool
DDT .... Data Description Table (BUR)
DDT .... Davidson Tisdale Mines Ltd. [*Toronto Stock Exchange symbol*]
DDT .... Debye Dipole Theory [*Physics*]
DDT .... Deduct
DDT .... Defect Detection Trial (SAUS)
DDT .... Deferent Duct Tumor [*Medicine*] (MELL)
DDT .... Define Device Table (MCD)
DDT .... Deflagration to Detonation Transition (IEEE)
DDT .... Degos-Delort-Tricot [*Syndrome*] [*Medicine*] (DB)
DDT .... Delayed Dialing Tone [*Telecommunications*] (TEL)
DDT .... Department of Development and Technology (SAUO)
DDT .... Department of Development and Tourism (SAUS)
DDT .... Deputy Director for Tourism (SAUO)
DDT .... Design and Debug Tool (SAUS)
DDT .... Design and Drafting Techniques
DDT .... Design Data Transmittal (NRCH)
DDT .... Design, Development and Testing (SAUS)
DDT .... Design Development Test
DDT .... Device Descriptor Table (SAUS)
DDT .... Diagnostic Decision Table [*Computer science*]
DDT .... DIBOL Debugging Technique [*Digital Equipment Corp.*]
DDT .... Dichlorodiphenyltrichloroethane [*Insecticide*]
DDT .... Dideoxythymidine [*Biochemistry*]
DDT .... Differential die-away technique (SAUS)
DDT .... Digital Data Terminal (MCD)
DDT .... Digital Data Transceiver
DDT .... Digital Data Transmission (SAUS)
DDT .... Digital Data Transmitter
DDT .... Digital Debugging Tape
DDT .... Digital Debugging Technique (SAUS)
DDT .... Digital Decoding Technique (SAUS)
DDT .... Digital Demodulation Technique
DDT .... Digital Diagnostic Tool [*Automotive engineering*]
DDT .... Digital tape transmitter (SAUS)
DDT .... Dillard's Cap Tr 7.50% Cap Sec [*NYSE symbol*] (SG)
ddt .... direct-decision therapy (SAUS)
DDT .... Direct Digital Targeting (SAUS)
DDT .... Display Date (SAUS)
DDT .... Dithiotreitol (SAUS)
DDT .... Doctor of Drugless Therapy
DDT .... Document Delivery Test
DDT .... Dodecanethiolate [*Organic chemistry*]
DDT .... Doppler Data Translator
DDT .... Double Deflection Tube (BUR)
DDT .... Double Diffusion Test [*Medicine*] (MELL)
DDT .... Double Diode-Triode
DDT .... Double Dual Tandem [*Aviation*] (DA)
DDT .... Driver Dispatch Table [*Computer science*] (CIST)
ddt .... drop dead twice (SAUS)
DDT .... Dual Deflection Tube (IAA)
DDT .... Dual-Double Tandem Axle (PIPO)
DDT .... Ductus Deferens Tumor [*Type of cell line*]
DDT .... Duplex-Drive Tank
DDT .... Dye Disappearance Test (SAUS)
DDT .... Dynamic Debugging Tape (IAA)
DDT .... Dynamic Debugging Technique (DEN)
DDT .... Dynamic Debugging Tool [*Computer science*] (VERA)
DDT .... Dynamic Display Tester
DDT .... Dyslexia Determination Test [*Educational test*]
DDT .... Training Destroyer [*Navy symbol*]
DDTA .... Deputy Director of Technical Administration [*Ministry of Supply*] [*British*]
DDTA .... Derivative Differential Thermal Analysis (PDAA)
DDTA .... Digital Distributed Transaction Architecture (SAUS)
DDTA .... Displayed Data Video Recorder
D/DTA .... Durability/Damage Tolerance Analysis [*Air Force*]
DD-T & E ..... Deputy Director for Test and Evaluation [*NASA*]
DDT&E .... Design, Development, Test and Engineering (SAUS)
DDT & E ...... Design, Development, Test, and Evaluation
DDT & E ...... Director, Defense Test and Evaluation (DOMA)
DDTC .... Defense Depot - Tracy, California [*DoD*]
DDTC .... Diethyldithiocarbamate [*Also, DDC, DEDC*] [*Organic chemistry*]
DDTC .... Drug Dependence Treatment Center (MELL)
DDTCA .... Dandie Dinmont Terrier Club of America (EA)
DDT/DDS ..... Digital Data Throughout/Dataphone Digital Service [*Communications term*] (DCT)
DDTE .... Deputy Director, Test and Evaluation (SAUS)
DDTE .... Design, Development, Test, and Evaluation (ADWA)
DDTE .... Digital Data Terminal Equipment
DDTE .... Director, Defense Test and Evaluation [*Army*] (RDA)
DDTE .... OSD [*Office of the Secretary of Defense*] Developmental Test and Evaluation (RDA)
DDTESM ...... Digital Data Terminal Equipment Service Module
DDTESS ...... Digital Data Terminal Equipment Service Submodule (IAA)
DDTF .... Dynamic Docking Test Facility [*NASA*] (NASA)
DDTI .... Deputy Director of Tactical Investigation [*Military*] [*British*]
DD-time ...... Decision-Delivery time (SAUS)
DDTL .... Diffused Diode Transistor Logic (SAUS)
DDTL .... Diode-Diode Transistor Logic [*Electronics*] (IAA)
DDTL .... Double Diffused Transistor Logic [*Electronics*] (IAA)
DDTL .... Double Diode Transistor Logic (SAUS)
ddtl .... dreary desk-top lunch (SAUS)

DDTN .... Dideoxy-Didehydrothymidine (DMAA)
DDto .... Delayed Due to (SAUS)
DDTO .... Demonstration Detail Test Objectives (AAG)
DDTO .... District Domestic Transportation Office [*or Officer*]
DDTP .... Drug Dependence Treatment Program (MELL)
DDTS .... Digital Data Test Set (MCD)
DDTS .... Digital Data Transmission System (KSC)
DDTS .... Direct Dial Telephone System
DDTS .... Distributed Data and Telecommunications System (SAUS)
DDTS .... Distributed Database Testbed System (MCD)
DDTS .... Double Door Transfer System (SAUS)
DDTS .... Dynamic Docking Test System [*NASA*] (NASA)
ddTTP .... Dideoxythymidine Triphosphate [*Biochemistry*]
DDTU .... Digital Data Transfer Unit (SAUS)
DDTU .... Discrimination, Designation, and Track Unit (ACAE)
DDTV .... Dry Diver Transport Vehicle [*Navy*]
DDTX .... Detroit Department of Transportation [*Federal Railroad Administration identification code*]
DDU .... Dadu [*Pakistan*] [*Airport symbol*] (AD)
DDU .... Data Diagnostic Unit (SAUS)
DDU .... Data Display Unit (NASA)
DDU .... Data Distribution Unit (SAUS)
DDU .... Data Drum Unit (SAUS)
DDU .... Decommutator Distribution Unit (MCD)
DDU .... Delivered Duty Unpaid
DDU .... Delivery Duty Unpaid (FOTI)
DDU .... Dermo-Distortive Urticaria [*Medicine*] (DMAA)
ddu .... design diagnostic unit (SAUS)
DDU .... Diagnostic Display Unit (MCD)
DDU .... Dialog Data Unit [*Computer science*] (VERA)
DDU .... Digital Data Unit (MUGU)
DDU .... Digital Display Unit
DDU .... Digital Distributing Unit
DDU .... Digital Distribution Unit (SAUS)
DDU .... Diploma in Diagnostic Ultrasound
DDU .... Disk Data Unit
DDU .... Disk Drive Unit (SAUS)
DDU .... Display and Debug Unit [*Computer science*] (MDG)
DDU .... Display Driver Unit (NASA)
ddu .... distribution data unit (SAUS)
DDU .... Driver Display Unit (SAUS)
DDU .... Drug Dependency Unit (WDAA)
DDU .... Dual Diversity Unit
DDU .... Duplex Doppler Ultrasound [*Medicine*] (DMAA)
DDU .... University of District of Columbia, Van Ness Campus, Washington, DC [*OCLC symbol*] (OCLC)
DDU-KB .... Data Display Unit and Keyboard (SAUS)
DDUMP .... Disk Dump [*Computer science*] (VLIE)
DDUS .... Date Departed United States [*Military*]
DDV .... Columbus, OH [*Location identifier*] [*FAA*] (FAAL)
DDV .... Deck Drain Valve
DDV .... Deep-Diving Vehicle [*Navy*]
DDV .... Destroyer Variant [*Surface warfare study*] [*Navy*] (DOMA)
DDV .... Dialog Data Validation [*Computer science*] (VERA)
DDV .... Direct Drive Valvetrain [*Automotive engines*]
DDV .... Displacement Ducted Vessel [*Marine architecture*]
DDV .... Durability Data Vehicle [*Automotive emissions*]
DDVN .... Direct Dedicated Voice Network (SAUO)
DDVP .... Dichlorvos (GNE)
DDVP .... Dimethyl Dichlorovinyl Phosphate [*An insecticide*]
DDVRS .... Deputy Director, Veterinary Remount Service [*British military*] (DMA)
DDVS .... Daimler-Benz Datenverbundsystem (SAUO)
DDVS .... Deputy Director of Veterinary Services [*British military*] (DMA)
DDVT .... Dialog Data Validation (SAUS)
DDVT .... Dynamic Dispatch Virtual Tables [*Computer science*] (VERA)
DDW .... Deionized-Distilled Water
DDW .... Dense Dislocation Wall (SAUS)
DDW .... Diffuse Domain Wall (SAUS)
DDW .... Digestive Disease Week (ADWA)
DDW .... Direct Digital Writer
DDW .... Discrete Data Word (ACAE)
ddw .... displaying a deadly weapon (SAUS)
DDW .... Distributed Data Warehouse [*Computer science*] (GART)
DDWE & M ... Deputy Director of Works, Electrical and Mechanical [*British*]
DDWG .... Digital Display Working Group (SAUS)
DDWO .... Deputy Director of War Organisation (SAUO)
DDWO .... Deputy Director of War Organization (SAUS)
DDWP .... Deputy Directorate of Weapons, Polaris [*Navy*] [*British*]
DDWS .... Drowsy Driver Warning System
DDX .... Dedenkosha Digital Data Exchange (SAUS)
DDX .... Dendenkosha Digital Data Exchange (SAUS)
DDX .... Device-Dependent X-windows (SAUS)
DDX .... Dialog Data eXchange (SAUS)
DDx .... Differential Diagnosis [*Medicine*] (CPH)
DDX .... Differential Diagnosis [*Medicine*] (STED)
DDX .... Digital Data Exchange [*Telecommunications*] (TEL)
DDX .... Distributed Data Exchange (SAUS)
DDX .... Goldsboro, NC [*Location identifier*] [*FAA*] (FAAL)
DDX-C .... A Circuit Switched Network Operated by NTT in Japan [*Communications term*] (DCT)
DDXF .... DISSOS [*Distributed Office Support System*] Document Exchange Facility [*IBM Corp.*] (NITA)
DDX-P .... Digital Data Exchange-Packet [*Telecommunications*] (TSSD)
DDX-P .... Digital Data Exchange, Packet-switching Network (SAUO)
DDxx .... Differential Diagnosis (SPVS)
DDY .... Dynayoke Deflection Yoke
DDZ .... Dedza [*Malawi*] [*Airport symbol*] (AD)
DDZ .... Dimethyl-3,5-Dimethoxybenzyloxycarbonyl (SAUS)
DE .... Assistant Vice Director for Estimates (MCD)
DE .... Dail Eireann [*House of Representatives*] [*Ireland*] (ILCA)
DE .... Damage Equivalent
DE .... Damage Estimation (SAUS)
DE .... Damage Expectancy (NATG)
DE .... Data Element [*Computer science*]
DE .... Data Encoder
DE .... Data Encoder (or Encoding) (SAUS)
DE .... Data Encryption [*Computer science*] (UWER)
DE .... Data Engineering (SAUS)
DE .... Data Entry
DE .... Data Error (SAUS)
DE .... Data Extraction (GEOI)
D/E .... Data of Establishment (WDAA)
DE .... Date of Entry [*Military*]
DE .... Date of Extension [*Military*]
DE .... Daughter Element [*Physics*] (UWER)
DE .... Daughters of Evrytania (EA)
DE .... Days After Emergence (SAUO)
DE .... Debye Effect [*Physics*] (UWER)
DE .... Debye Equation [*Solid-state physics*] (UWER)
DE .... Decay (SAUS)
DE .... Decelerating Electrode (UWER)
DE .... Deceleration Enleanment [*Automotive fuel systems*]
DE .... December (ADA)
DE .... Decimal Exponent (SAUS)
DE .... Decimeter [*Unit of measure*]
DE .... Decision Element
DE .... Decision Error
D/E .... Decision Estimator (SAUS)
DE .... Deck and Engineering Duties, General Service [*USNR officer designation*]
DE .... Deckle-Edged [*Paper*]
DE .... Declared Excess [*Military*]
DE .... Decommissioning Engineering (SAUS)
DE .... Deemphasis
DE .... Deep Etch [*Lithography term*]
DE .... Deere & Co. [*NYSE symbol*] (SPSG)
DE .... Defect Engineering (SAUS)
DE .... Defence Emergency (SAUS)
DE .... Defense Electronics [*A publication*] (DOMA)
DE .... Defense Emergency (AABC)
DE .... Defense Engineer (UWER)
DE .... Defensive End [*Football*]
DE .... Defensive Expenditures (SAUS)
DE .... Deflection Error [*Military*]
DE .... Degree of Elasticity (IAA)
DE .... Delaware [*Postal code*]
De .... Delaware. Department of Community Affairs and Economic Development, Division of Libraries, Dover, DE [*Library symbol*] [*Library of Congress*] (LCLS)
DE .... Delayed Early (SAUS)
DE .... Delivered Energy
DE .... Delta Echo [*Radio engineering*] (UWER)
DE .... Demokratiki Enosis [*Democratic Union*] [*Greek*] (PPE)
DE .... Dendritic Expansion (STED)
DE .... Denmark (NATG)
DE .... Densimeter (DNAB)
DE .... Dentistry (DAVI)
DE .... Departmental Estimate (AAG)
DE .... Department of Economics (SAUO)
DE .... Department of Education [*Generic*]
DE .... Department of Employment [*Formerly, DEP, MOL*] [*British*]
DE .... Department of Energy (ILCA)
DE .... Department of the Environment (SAUS)
DE .... Dependent Edema [*Medicine*] (MELL)
DE .... Deposition Efficiency [*Industrial hygiene term*] (OHS)
D/E .... Depression/Elevation (CAAL)
DE .... Deprived Eye [*Optics*]
DE .... Deputy Chief of Staff/Engineering and Services (SAUO)
DE .... Descent Engine [*NASA*] (KSC)
DE .... Description Entry (SAUS)
DE .... Descriptor [*Online database field identifier*]
DE .... Descriptor Entry Version [*Database terminology*] (NITA)
DE .... designational expression (SAUS)
DE .... Designation Equipment
DE .... Design Engineer (SAUS)
DE .... Design Engineering (KSC)
DE .... Design Evaluation
DE .... Desktop Engineering
DE .... Destination Exchange (SAUS)
DE .... Destroyer Escort [*Navy symbol*]
DE .... Destruction Efficiency [*Environmental science*] (COE)
DE .... Destructive examination (SAUS)
DE .... Detailed Event (SAUS)
DE .... Detector (NFPA)
DE .... Detector Efficiency (SAUS)
DE .... Deterministic Equivalent (PDAA)
DE .... Detroit Edison [*Federal Railroad Administration identification code*]
DE .... Developer Evaluation
DE .... Development Engineering
DE .... Development Ephemeris

DE............... Development Estimate
DE............... Device End
DE............... Devonshire Regiment (SAUO)
DE............... Dexreose Equivalent (SAUS)
DE............... Dextrose Equivalency (SAUS)
DE............... Dextrose Equivalent [*Food technology*]
DE............... Diabetic Extemity [*Medicine*] (EDAA)
DE............... Diagnostic Emulator (SEWL)
DE............... Diagnostic Error [*Medicine*] (STED)
DE............... Diagnostic Evaluation [*Medicine*] (EDAA)
DE............... Dialysis Encephalopathy [*Medicine*] (EDAA)
DE............... Diameter, External (SAUS)
DE............... Diatomaceous Earth (PDAA)
DE............... Dictating Equipment (ELAL)
DE............... Dictation Equipment
DE............... Die Deborah (BJA)
DE............... Dielectric (SAUS)
DE............... Diesel Electric
DE............... Diesel Engine (UWER)
DE............... Differential Equation
dE............... differential of voltage (SAUS)
DE............... Digestible Energy (OA)
DE............... Digestive Energy [*Medicine*] (MAE)
DE............... Digital Electronics (SAUS)
DE............... Digital Element (IEEE)
DE............... Digital Encoder (MSA)
DE............... Digital Enhancement (UWER)
DE............... Digital Equipment [*Electronics*] (IAA)
DE............... digital exchange (SAUS)
DE............... Dimensional Engineering (UWER)
DE............... Diotamaceous Earth (SAUS)
DE............... Directed Energy [*Weaponry*] (INF)
DE............... Direct Electrolysis (ODA)
de............... direct elimination (SAUS)
DE............... Direct Encounter (KSC)
DE............... Direct Entry (SAUS)
DE............... Direct Escort (ACAE)
DE............... Directorate of Design Engineering [*NASA*] (KSC)
DE............... Director Error [*Military*] (AFM)
DE............... Director of Engineering [*Navy*] [*British*]
DE............... Director of Engineering Services (SAUO)
DE............... Director of Equipment (SAUO)
DE............... Directory Element (SAUS)
DE............... Disability Examiners [*Social Security Administration*] (DHP)
DE............... Discard Eligibility (SAUS)
DE............... Discard-Eligibility [*Computer science*]
DE............... Discard Eligible (SAUS)
DE............... Disintegration Energy (UWER)
DE............... Disk Electrophoresis
DE............... Disk Enclosure [*Computer science*] (VLIE)
DE............... Dispersed Emission [*Spectroscopy*]
DE............... Displacement Energy (UWER)
DE............... Display Electronics (KSC)
DE............... Display Element
DE............... Display Equipment
DE............... Display Erase (SAUS)
DE............... Disposable Element [*Automotive engineering*]
DE............... Dissociation Energy (UWER)
DE............... Distant Element (MDG)
DE............... Distant End (SAUS)
DE............... Distributed Executive (SSD)
DE............... Distributive Education
DE............... District Engineer [*Army*]
DE............... District Establishment (SAUO)
DE............... District Executive [*Boy Scouts of America*]
DE............... District of Europe [*Proposed location of an EEC federal capital*]
DE............... Division Entry (BUR)
DE............... Division Equivalent (MCD)
DE............... Division of Engineering (UWER)
DE............... Doctor of Economics (NADA)
DE............... Doctor of Engineering
DE............... Doctor of Entomology
DE............... Documentary Evidence (SAUS)
DE............... Document Engineering (SAUS)
DE............... Domestic Engineer (SAUS)
DE............... Domestic Engineering (SAUS)
DE............... Donor Eggs [*Medicine*]
DE............... Doppler Effect (MELL)
DE............... Doppler Extractor (MCD)
DE............... dose efficace (SAUS)
DE............... Dose Equivalent [*Radioactivity calculations*]
DE............... Double Elephant [*Paper*] (ADA)
DE............... Double Enamel [*Insulation*] (MSA)
DE............... Double End [*Technical drawings*]
de............... Double Entry [*Bookkeeping*] (ODBW)
DE............... Double Entry [*Bookkeeping*]
DE............... Double Error (SAUS)
DE............... Double Extension [*Camera stand*] (ROG)
DE............... Downeast Airlines [*ICAO designator*] (AD)
DE............... Dream Element [*Psychology*] (MAE)
de............... dream elements (SAUS)
de............... Drift Error, Individual [*Environmental science*] (COE)
De............... Drift Error, Total [*Environmental science*] (COE)
DE............... Drive End (MSA)
DE............... Driver evaluation (SAUS)
DE............... Driver experiment (SAUS)
DE............... Drop Electrode (SAUS)
DE............... Drug Evaluation
DE............... Drum equivalent (SAUS)
DE............... Dry Etching (SAUS)
DE............... Dual Camshafts and Electronic Management [*Automotive engineering*]
DE............... Duchenne-Erb [*Syndrome*] [*Medicine*] (DB)
DE............... Duck Embryo [*Medicine*] (EDAA)
DE............... Duke of Edinburgh's Wiltshire Regiment [*Military unit*] [*British*] (ROG)
DE............... Duodendal Exclusion [*Medicine*] (STED)
DE............... Duration of Ejection (MAE)
DE............... Dynamic Energy [*Foglight*] [*Hella, Inc.*] [*Automotive engineering*]
DE............... Dynamic Engineer
DE............... Dynamic Equation (SAUS)
DE............... Dynamics Explorer [*NASA*]
DE............... Escort Destroyer (SAUS)
DE............... Escort Ship [*Destroyer Escort*] [*Navy symbol*]
DE............... Federal Republic of Germany [*ANSI two-letter standard code*] (CNC)
DE............... Germany [*Internet country code*]
DE............... Sub-committee on Ship Design and Equipment (SAUO)
DE............... Diesel Engine (ODA)
DE08............... designation for an ice core drilled in 1977 at Law Dome, Antarctica (SAUS)
DEA............... ANSA [*Agenzia Nazionale Stampa Associata*]'s Electronic Documentation Service [*ANSA Agency*] (IID)
DEA............... Daily Equivalent Amplitude (UWER)
DEA............... Dairy Engineers' Association [*British*] (BI)
DEA............... Dairy Equipment Association (SAUO)
DEA............... Dance Educators of America (EA)
DEA............... Dark Etching Area (SAUS)
DEA............... Data Encryption Algorithm
DEA............... Data Exchange Agreement
DEA............... Data Exchange Annex (AABC)
DEA............... Davis Escape Apparatus [*British military*] (DMA)
dea............... Deacon (GEAB)
DEA............... Deacon
Dea............... Deady's United States Circuit and District Court Reports [*A publication*] (DLA)
DEA............... Deak International Resources Corp. [*Toronto Stock Exchange symbol*]
DEA............... Dean (ROG)
DEA............... Defense Exchange Agreement (MCD)
DEA............... Deflection Error Average [*Military*] (MUGU)
DEA............... Dehydroepiandrosterone [*Also, DHA, DHEA, DHIA*] [*Endocrinology*] (AAMN)
DEA............... Delta Aerotaxi [*Italy*] [*ICAO designator*] (FAAC)
DEA............... Department of Economic Affairs [*Department of Agriculture*]
DEA............... Department of External Affairs (UWER)
DEA............... Deployed Electronics Assembly (MCD)
DEA............... Desethylamiodarone [*Biochemistry*]
DEA............... Design Engineering Analysis [*Army*]
DEA............... Detectives Endowment Association (SAUO)
DEA............... Dethanolamin (SAUS)
DEA............... Development Education Association (WDAA)
DEA............... Development, Engineering, and Acquisition [*Directorate*] [*Army*] (RDA)
DEA............... Dictionary of Electronics Abbreviation (SAUS)
DEA............... Dictionary of Electronics Abbreviations, Signs, and Symbols [*A publication*]
DEA............... Dielectric Absorption (SAUS)
DEA............... Dielectric Analysis (SAUS)
DEA............... Dielectric Analyzer
DEA............... Diethanolamine [*Also, DIOLAMINE*] [*Organic chemistry*]
DEA............... Diethoxyanthracene [*Organic chemistry*]
DEA............... Diethylamine [*Organic chemistry*]
DEA............... Diethylaniline (SAUS)
DEA............... Digital Equipment Australia (SAUS)
DEA............... Dimethylaniline [*Organic chemistry*]
DEA............... Director of Expenses and Accounts (SAUO)
DEA............... Directory of European Associations [*A publication*]
DEA............... Display Electronics Assemblies (KSC)
DEA............... Division of Ecumenical Affairs [*Church of England*]
DEA............... Division of Extramural Activities (SAUS)
DEA............... Dominican Educational Association [*Defunct*] (EA)
DEA............... Double-Ended Amplifier (VLIE)
dea............... Drift Error, Aerospace [*Environmental science*] (COE)
DEA............... Driver Evaluation Assembly [*Nuclear energy*] (NRCH)
DEA............... Drug Enforcement Administration [*Formerly, Bureau of Narcotics and Dangerous Drugs*]
DEA............... Drug EnForcement Agency (STED)
DEA............... Dynamo Electric Amplifier
DEA............... Data Encryption Algorithm [*Computing*] (ODA)
DEA-1............... Data Encryption Algorithm--1 [*Communications term*] (DCT)
DEAA............... Department of Egyptian and Assyrian Antiquities (SAUO)
DEAA............... Diethylacetoacetamide [*Organic chemistry*]
Dea & Ch............... Deacon and Chitty's English Bankruptcy Reports [*1832-35*] [*A publication*] (DLA)
Dea & Chit............... Deacon and Chitty's English Bankruptcy Reports [*1832-35*] [*A publication*] (DLA)
Dea & Sw............... Deane and Swabey's English Ecclesiastical Reports [*A publication*] (DLA)
DEAB............... Diethylamine Borane (SAUS)
DEAC............... Data Exchange Auxiliary Console (CAAL)
deac............... Deaccentuator (IDOE)

DEAC .... Deacon
Deac .... Deacon's English Bankruptcy Reports [*1835-40*] [*A publication*] (DLA)
DEAC .... Dealer Election Action Committee [*Campaign funding*]
DEAC .... Defense Economic Analysis Council (MCD)
DEAC .... Delta Environmental Advisory Committee (SAUS)
DEAC .... Diethylaluminum Chloride [*Organic chemistry*]
Deac & C..... Deacon and Chitty's English Bankruptcy Reports [*1832-35*] [*A publication*] (DLA)
Deac & Ch... Deacon and Chitty's English Bankruptcy Reports [*1832-35*] [*A publication*] (DLA)
Deac & Chit... Deacon and Chitty's English Bankruptcy Reports [*1832-35*] [*A publication*] (DLA)
Deac Bank Pr... Deacon's Bankruptcy Law and Practice [*3rd ed.*] [*1864*] [*A publication*] (DLA)
Deac Cr Law... Deacon on Criminal Law of England [*A publication*] (DLA)
Deac Dig ..... Deacon's Digest of the Criminal Law [*A publication*] (DLA)
DEACON....... Defense Estimates Analytical Computer On-Line Network (MCD)
DEACON....... Definitions Abbreviations and Conventions [*Handbook*]
DEACON....... Direct English Access and Control [*Computer science*]
Deacon & C... Deacon and Chitty's English Bankruptcy Reports [*1832-35*] [*A publication*] (DLA)
Deacon & C Bankr Cas... Deacon and Chitty's English Bankruptcy Records [*1832-35*] [*A publication*] (DLA)
Deacon & C Bankr Cas (Eng)... Deacon and Chitty's English Bankruptcy Cases [*A publication*] (DLA)
Deacon Bankr Cas... Deacon's English Bankruptcy Cases [*A publication*] (DLA)
Deacon Bankr (Eng)... Deacon's English Bankruptcy Cases [*A publication*] (DLA)
DEACONS .... Direct English Access and Control System (SAUS)
DEACT .... Deactivation (KSC)
DEACTLH ..... Deactivate Line Halt [*Computer science*] (VLIE)
DEACTLO ..... Deactivate Line Orderly [*Computer science*] (VLIE)
DEACTLO ..... Deactivitate Line Orderly (SAUS)
DEAD .... Dallas Encephalopathic and Abortifactive Disease [*Acronym used as title of novel*]
DEAD .... Dedicated to Eliminating Acronymic Designations [*An association*]
dead .... destruction-entrusted automatic devices (SAUS)
DEAD .... Destruction of Enemy Air Defenses [*Military*] (SEWL)
DEA-D .... Diethylaminoethyl Dextran (STED)
DEAD .... Diethyl Azodicarboxylate [*Organic chemistry*]
DEAD .... Doppler Evaluated Attack Depth [*Navy*] (CAAL)
Deadfrt .... Dead Freight (SAUS)
Dead Or Laws... Deady and Lane's Oregon General Laws [*A publication*] (DLA)
DEADS .... Detroit Air Defense Sector [*ADS*]
Deady .... Deady's United States Circuit and District Court Reports [*A publication*] (DLA)
DEAE........... Diethylaminoethanol [*Organic chemistry*]
DEAE........... Diethylaminoethyl [*Organic radical*]
DEAE........... Diethylaminoethyl Cellulose [*Organic chemistry*] (MAE)
DEAE........... Division of Eligibility and Agency Evaluation [*OE*]
DEAE-C .... Diethylaminoethyl Cellulose (SAUS)
DEAE-cellulose... Diethylaminoethyl-Cellulose (DOG)
DEAE-D .... Diethylaminoethyl Dextran [*Organic chemistry*]
DEAE-D .... Diethylaminoethyl Ether of Dextran (SAUS)
DEAEM......... Diethylaminoethyl Mercaptan [*Organic chemistry*]
DEAEMA .... Diethylaminoethyl Methacrylate [*Organic chemistry*]
DEAE-RNA ... Ribonucleic Acid, DEAE Salt (SAUS)
DEAF........... Deaf Passenger [*Travel industry*] (TRID)
DEAFWATCH... Demanding Equal Access to Facts and Warnings Aired on TV for Citizens Who are Hearing-Impaired [*Student legal action organization*] (EA)
DEAG .... Data Extraction und Analysis Group (SAUO)
DEAG .... Distance Education Action Group (SAUO)
DEAH .... Diethylaluminum Hydride [*Organic chemistry*]
DEAI........... Diethylaluminum Iodide [*Organic chemistry*]
DEAL........... Data Entry Application Language
DEAL........... Decision Evaluation and Logic
DEAL........... Design and Logistics (VLIE)
DEAL........... Detachment Equipment Authorization List [*Military*]
DEAL........... Documentation East European Agricultural Literature (SAUS)
DEALE......... Declining Exponential Approximation of Life Expectancy [*Method*] (DMAA)
Dealer Prep... Dealer Preparation (SAUS)
De Alex Fort... De Fortuna Alexandri [*of Plutarch*] [*Classical studies*] (OCD)
DEAL-MCH... Data Enhancement for Accountability and Leadership in Maternal and Child Health (SAUO)
DEALS .... Demountable Externally Anchored Low-Stress Magnet (MCD)
Deamino DPN... Deaminodiphosphopyridine Nucleotide [*Biochemistry*] (UWER)
Deamino DPNH... Deaminodiphosphopyridine Nucleotide, Reduced Form [*Biochemistry*] (UWER)
Deamino NAD... Nicotinamide Hypoxanthine Dinucleotide [*Biochemistry*] (UWER)
Deamino NAD... Nicotinic Acid Adenine Dinucleotide [*Biochemistry*] (UWER)
Deamino NADH... Nicotinamide Hypoxanthine Dinucleotide, Reduced Form [*Biochemistry*] (UWER)
DEAMS .... Defence Equipment Acquisition & Material Support (SAUS)
De An .... De Anima [*of Aristotle*] [*Classical studies*] (OCD)
DEAN .... Deputy Educators Against Narcotics [*Defunct*]
DE&CD......... Directorate of Electrical and Communications Development (SAUO)
Deane.......... Deane and Swabey's English Ecclesiastical Reports [*A publication*] (DLA)
Deane.......... Deane and Swabey's English Probate and Divorce Reports [*A publication*] (DLA)
DEANE .... Deane, KY [*American Association of Railroads railroad junction routing code*]
Deane.......... Deane's English Blockade Cases [*A publication*] (DLA)
Deane.......... Deane's Reports [*24-26 Vermont*] [*A publication*] (DLA)
Deane & S Eccl... Deane and Swabey's English Ecclesiastical Reports [*A publication*] (DLA)
Deane & S Eccl (Eng)... Deane and Swabey's English Ecclesiastical Reports [*A publication*] (DLA)
Deane & S Eccl Rep... Deane and Swabey's English Ecclesiastical Reports [*A publication*] (DLA)
Deane & Sw... Deane and Swabey's English Ecclesiastical Reports [*A publication*] (DLA)
Deane Bl ..... Deane's English Blockade Cases [*A publication*] (DLA)
Deane Ecc ... Deane and Swabey's English Ecclesiastical Reports [*A publication*] (DLA)
Deane Ecc Rep... Deane and Swabey's English Ecclesiastical Reports [*A publication*] (DLA)
Deane Ecc Rep B... Deane and Swabey's English Ecclesiastical Reports [*A publication*] (DLA)
Deane Neut... Deane on the Effect of War as to Neutrals [*A publication*] (DLA)
DeanFd........ Dean Foods Co. [*Associated Press*] (SAG)
De Anim ...... De Testimonio Animae [*of Tertullian*] [*Classical studies*] (OCD)
Dean Med Jur... Dean's Medical Jurisprudence [*A publication*] (DLA)
DEANOL....... Dimethylaminoethanol (SAUS)
DEANOL....... Dimethylethanolamine (SAUS)
De Antr Nymph... De Antro Nympharum [*of Porphyry*] [*Classical studies*] (OCD)
DEANZ .... Distance Education Association of New Zealand (SAUO)
DEAP .... Diethoxyacetophenone [*Organic chemistry*]
DEAP .... Differential Equation Analyzer Program (MCD)
DEAP .... diffused eutectic aluminium process (SAUS)
DEAP .... Diffused Eutectic Aluminum Process (IEEE)
DEAP .... Division of Engineering and Applied Physics [*Harvard University*] (MCD)
DEAPA .... Diethylaminopropylamine [*Organic chemistry*]
DEAPA .... Downeast Association of Physician Assistants (SRA)
DEAPS .... Department of Earth Atmospheric and Planetary Sciences (SAUO)
DEAPSIE ...... Department of Economic, Administrative, and Policy Studies (AIE)
De-Ar.......... Delaware Department of State, Division of Historical and Cultural Affairs, Hall of Records, Dover, DE [*Library symbol*] [*Library of Congress*] (LCLS)
DEAR .... Department of Energy Acquisition Regulation [*A publication*] (AAGC)
DEAR .... Diamonds, Emeralds, Amethysts, and Rubies
DEAR .... Disease and Environmental Alert Report [*Army*] [*A publication*] (INF)
DEAR .... Drop Everything and Read
DEARAS....... Department of Defense Emergency Authorities Retrieval and Analysis System (COE)
De Arch .... De Architectura [*of Vitruvius*] [*Classical studies*] (OCD)
DEAR DAD... Decision Tree for Exploration Applications of Remote Sensing by Dekker and Dams (SAUS)
DEARG PIL... Deargentur Pilulae [*Let The Pills Be Silverized*] [*Pharmacy*]
Dears.......... Dearsley's English Crown Cases Reserved [*169 English Reprint*] [*1852-56*] [*A publication*] (DLA)
Dears & B ... Dearsley and Bell's English Crown Cases [*1856-58*] [*A publication*] (DLA)
Dears & BCC... Dearsley and Bell's English Crown Cases [*1856-58*] [*A publication*] (DLA)
Dears & B Crown Cas... Dearsley and Bell's English Crown Cases [*1856-58*] [*A publication*] (DLA)
Dears C C.... Dearsley's English Crown Cases [*1852-56*] [*A publication*] (DLA)
Dears Cr Pr... Dearsley's Criminal Process [*1853*] [*A publication*] (DLA)
Dearsl Cr Pr... Dearsley's Criminal Process [*1853*] [*A publication*] (ILCA)
DEARTG....... Deaerating
DEAS .... Data Entry Aboard Ship [*Navy*] (NVT)
DEAS .... Delaware Education Accountability System (EDAC)
DEAS .... Directorate of Engineering, Aeronautical Systems (SAA)
DEAS .... Duke of Edinburgh Award Scheme [*Australia*]
DEASA .... Diethylanilinesulfonic Acid [*Organic chemistry*]
Deas & A..... Deas and Anderson's Decisions [*1829-33*] [*Scotland*] [*A publication*] (DLA)
Deas & And... Deas and Anderson's Decisions [*1829-33*] [*Scotland*] [*A publication*] (DLA)
DEA-SOG ..... Drug Enforcement Administration - Special Operations Group
Deas Ry........ Deas on the Law of Railways in Scotland [*A publication*] (DLA)
DEAUA .... Diesel Engineers and Users Association (SAUO)
Deaug Pil .... Deaurentur Pilulae [*Let the Pills Be Gilded*] [*Pharmacology*] (DAVI)
DEAUR......... Deauretur [*Let It Be Gilded*] [*Pharmacy*]
DEAUR PIL... Deaurentur Pilulae [*Let The Pills Be Gilded*] [*Pharmacy*]
DEB............. Data Event Block [*Computer science*] (EECA)
DEB............. Data Extend Block (SAUS)
DEB............. Data Extension Block (SAUS)
DEB............. Data Extent Block (MCD)
DEB............. De Baca Resources, Inc. [*Vancouver Stock Exchange symbol*]
DEB............. Debate [*Legal shorthand*] (LWAP)
deb .... Debenture [*Investment term*] (ODBW)
Deb .... Debenture (WDAA)
DEB............. Debenture [*Type of bond*] [*Investment term*]
DEB............. Debit
DEB............. Debrecen [*Hungary*] [*Seismograph station code, US Geological Survey*] [*Closed*] (SEIS)
deb .... Debridement [*Medicine*] (DAVI)
DEB............. Debut (WDAA)
deb .... Debutante (ADWA)
DEB............. Debutante
DEB............. Decaying Extrastellar Body [*Astronomy*]
DEB............. Defense Estimative Brief (MCD)
DEB............. Dental Estimates Board [*British*] (DI)
DEB............. Dental Examining Board
DEB............. Departure End of Runway (SAUS)

DEB.......... Derivation (SAUS)
DEB.......... Derivative (SAUS)
DEB.......... Diesel Engine Reduction-Drive (SAUS)
DEB.......... Diethylbutanediol [*Organic chemistry*] (AAMN)
DEB.......... Diethylstilbestrol (SAUS)
DEB.......... Digital European Backbone [*System*] (MCD)
DEB.......... Directory Entry Block [*Computer science*] (VLIE)
DEB.......... Division of Environmental Biology [*National Science Foundation*]
DEB.......... Downward Ejection Bomblet (MCD)
DEB.......... Drug Evaluation Branch [*Therapeutic Goods Administration*] [*Australia*]
DEB.......... Dynamic Ephemeral Bodies [*Planetary science*]
DEB.......... Dystrophic Epidermolysis Bullosa [*Medicine*]
DEBA.......... Diethylbarbituric Acid (MAE)
DEBA.......... Dynamically-Loaded Engineering Bearing Analysis (PDAA)
De Bapt.......... De Baptismo [*of Tertullian*] [*Classical studies*] (OCD)
DEBASS.......... Debug Assembler (VLIE)
DEBC.......... Directional Electron Ballistic Coupler (SAUS)
DEBE.......... Does Everything but Eat [*Superseded by DITTO*] [*Computer science*]
DEBHS.......... Dr. Edward Bach Healing Society [*Defunct*] (EA)
DEBI.......... Direct memory access Extended Bus Interface (SAUS)
DEBI.......... DMA Extended Bus Interface (SAUS)
debil.......... debilitating (SAUS)
debil.......... debilitation (SAUS)
Debil.......... Debility (AAMN)
DEBIS.......... Distributed Expert-Based Information System (SAUS)
DEBITS.......... Deposition of Biogeochemically Important Trace Species (SAUO)
Deb Jud.......... Debates on the Judiciary [*A publication*] (DLA)
DEBK.......... Debark (AABC)
DEBK.......... Debarkation (SAUS)
DEBM.......... Directorate of Engineering, Ballistic Missiles (SAA)
DeB Mar Int L... DeBurgh's Maritime International Laws [*A publication*] (DLA)
DEBNA.......... Digital Ethernet BI Network Adapter (SAUS)
DEBR.......... Division of Economic and Business Research [*University of Arizona*] [*Tucson*] [*Information service or system*] (IID)
DEBRA.......... Dystrophic Epidermolysis Bullosa Research Association (ADWA)
DEBRA.......... Dystrophic Epidermolysis Bullosa Research Association of America (EA)
DEBRE.......... Debenture [*Investment term*] (ROG)
DEBS.......... Deb Shops [*NASDAQ symbol*] (TTSB)
DEBS.......... Deb Shops, Inc. [*NASDAQ symbol*] (NQ)
DEBS.......... Deoxyerythronolide B Synthase [*An enzyme*]
DEBS.......... Digital Electron Beam Scanner
DEBS.......... Display Exercise for Battle Staff (SAA)
DEBS.......... Dominant Epidermolysis Bullosa Simplex [*Medicine*] (EDAA)
DEBSA.......... Doctor Edward Bach Society of Australia
DebShp.......... Deb Shops, Inc. [*Associated Press*] (SAG)
DEB SPIS.......... Debita Spissitudo [*Proper Consistency*] [*Pharmacy*] (MAH)
DEB SPISS.......... Debita Spissitudo [*Proper Consistence*] [*Pharmacy*]
DEB STK.......... Debenture Stock (SAUS)
Debt & Cred... Debtor and Creditor (DLA)
debug.......... debugging (SAUS)
DEBUT.......... Daughters of the Elderly Bridging the Unknown Together (EA)
DEBUT.......... Delay Buffered Terminal [*Computer science*] (VLIE)
DeC.......... Claymont Public Library, Claymont, DE [*Library symbol*] [*Library of Congress*] (LCLS)
DEC.......... Control Escort Ship (SAUS)
DEC.......... Control Escort Vessel [*Navy symbol*]
DEC.......... Daily Effective Circulation [*Advertising*] (WDMC)
DEC.......... Dairy Equipment Co. (EFIS)
DEC.......... Danish Employers Confederation (SAUO)
DEC.......... Data Encryption Circuit (SAUS)
DEC.......... Data Entry Console (ACAE)
DEC.......... Data Equipment Company (SAUO)
DEC.......... Data Evaluation Center (VLIE)
DEC.......... Data Evaluation Center (or Centre) (SAUS)
DEC.......... Data Exchange Control (SAUS)
DEC.......... Date of Estimated Closing (AAGC)
DEC.......... Davis and Elkins College [*West Virginia*]
DEC.......... Deaf Broadcasting Campaign [*England*]
DEC.......... Decade (WGA)
DEC.......... Decal
DEC.......... Decani [*Of the Dean*] [*Music*]
DEC.......... Decanta [*Pour Off*] [*Pharmacy*]
Dec.......... Decanus [*Dean*] [*Latin*] (ILCA)
DEC.......... Decatur [*Illinois*] [*Airport symbol*] (OAG)
Dec.......... Decatur Staleys [*National Football League*] [*1920*] (NFLA)
dec.......... Decayed [*Quality of the bottom*] [*Nautical charts*]
DEC.......... Decca
dec.......... Deceased (WDMC)
DEC.......... Deceased
Dec.......... December (ASC)
DEC.......... December (EY)
dec.......... Decembre [*December*] [*French*] (ASC)
DEC.......... Decentration (SAUS)
DEC.......... Deception Island [*Antarctica*] [*Seismograph station code, US Geological Survey*] [*Closed*] (SEIS)
dec.......... Deciduous (MAE)
Dec.......... Decile [*Statistics*] (BARN)
DEC.......... Decimal (KSC)
DEC.......... Decimal Equivalent Chart
DEC.......... Decimal Error Correcting Code (VLIE)
DEC.......... Decimate (ROG)
DEC.......... Decimeter [*Unit of measure*] (ROG)
DEC.......... Decision
dec.......... Declaration (ADWA)
DEC.......... Declaration
DEC.......... Declared [*Cricket*] (ROG)
DEC.......... Declension (ROG)
dec.......... Declination (GEOI)
DEC.......... Declination
Dec.......... Declination of the sun (SAUS)
DEC.......... Decoder
DEC.......... Decompose
DEC.......... Decorated [*or Decoration*] (ROG)
dec.......... Decoration (ADWA)
Dec.......... Decorative (DIAR)
DEC.......... Decorative
dec.......... Decorative (VRA)
DEC.......... Decorator (SAUS)
DEC.......... Decrease (AAG)
dec.......... Decrease (WDMC)
DEC.......... Decreasing (SAUS)
DEC.......... Decrement
DEC.......... Decrement Device Clear (SAUS)
DEC.......... Decrescendo [*Decreasing in Loudness*] [*Music*] (ROG)
DEC.......... Deductible Employee Contribution [*IRS*]
DEC.......... Defence Emergency Committee (SAUO)
DEC.......... Defense Electronics Center (SAUS)
DEC.......... Deltec Resources Ltd. [*Vancouver Stock Exchange symbol*]
DEC.......... Dendritic Epidermal Cell [*Cytology*]
DEC.......... Dental Education Center [*Veterans Administration*] (GFGA)
DEC.......... Dental Examination Centre (SAUS)
DEC.......... Department of Environmental Conservation (COE)
DEC.......... Dependents Educational Committee (SAUO)
DEC.......... Detached Experiment Carrier (MCD)
DEC.......... Determination of Exceptional Circumstances (SAUS)
DEC.......... Detroit Edison Company (SAUO)
DEC.......... Developing Economies [*A publication*]
DEC.......... Developmental Education Center (SAUS)
DEC.......... Development and Education Command
DEC.......... Development Education Center (SAUS)
DEC.......... Development Engineering Change (SAUS)
DEC.......... Device Clear (SAUS)
DEC.......... Dickson Electronics Corporation (SAUO)
DEC.......... Diecast Exchange Club (EA)
DEC.......... Dielectric Current (SAUS)
DEC.......... Diethanol Cocoamide [*Surfactants*]
DEC.......... Diethylaminoethyl Chloride [*Organic chemistry*]
DEC.......... Diethylcarbamazine [*Anthelmintic drug*]
DEC.......... Diethylcarbinol (SAUS)
DEC.......... Digital Electric Corporation (SAUO)
DEC.......... Digital Electronic Circuit (SAUS)
DEC.......... Digital Electronic Control (SAUS)
DEC.......... Digital Electronic Controller (HAWK)
DEC.......... Digital Equipment [*NYSE symbol*] (TTSB)
DEC.......... Digital Equipment Company (SAUO)
DEC.......... Digital Equipment Corp. [*Maynard, MA*] [*NYSE symbol*] (SPSG)
DEC.......... Digital Equipment Corp. Australia Proprietary Ltd.
DEC.......... Digital Equipment Corp., Corporate Library, Maynard, MA [*OCLC symbol*] (OCLC)
DEC.......... Digital Equipment Corporarion (SAUS)
DEC.......... Digital Evaluation Computer
DEC.......... Diplome d'Etudes Collegiales [*Canada*]
DEC.......... Direct Energy Conversion
DEC.......... Direct-Shell Evacuation Control (EEVL)
DEC.......... Disaster Emergency Commitee (SAUS)
DEC.......... Disposable Extraction Column
DEC.......... Distance Education Council (SAUO)
DEC.......... Distance Electric Control (SAUS)
DEC.......... Distant Electric Control (IAA)
DEC.......... Distributor Electronic Control
DEC.......... District Economic Council (SAUO)
DEC.......... District Election Committee (SAUS)
DEC.......... Diver Escape Capsule (MCD)
DEC.......... Division for Early Childhood (EA)
D Ec.......... Doctor of Economics
DEC.......... Documentation European Ceramic (SAUS)
DEC.......... Document Effected Code (IAA)
DEC.......... Document Evaluation Center (IAA)
DEC.......... DOE Environmental Checklist (SAUS)
DEC.......... Dollar Export Council (SAUO)
DEC.......... Dominion Executive Council (SAUO)
DEC.......... Double Error Correction (SAUS)
DEC.......... Drug Evaluation and Classification [*NHTSA*] (TAG)
DEC.......... Drug Evaluation Center
DEC.......... Dry Electrolytic Capacitor
DEC.......... Dual-Engine Centaur [*Space launch term*] (ISAK)
DEC.......... Dynamic Emission Control (SAUS)
DEC.......... Dynamic Energy Conversion
DEC.......... Dynamic Environmental Conditioning [*Cycling*] [*Medicine*] (DAVI)
DEC.......... Dynamic Equilibrium Cycling (IAA)
DEC 1st.......... First Detector (SAUS)
DECA.......... Decathalon Association [*Acronym is used as name of association*] (EA)
DECA.......... Decoma International, Inc. [*NASDAQ symbol*] (NASQ)
DECA.......... Defense & Economic Co-operation Agreement (SAUS)
DeCA.......... Defense Commissary Agency [*DoD*]
DECA.......... Defense Economic Cooperation Agreements (MUSM)
DECA.......... Department of Economic Affairs (SAUO)

DECA .... Descent Engine Control Assembly [*Apollo*] [*NASA*]
DECA .... Design Expression and Confirmation (SAUS)
DECA .... Development of counterintelligence awareness (SAUS)
DECA .... Digital Electronic Countermeasures Analyzer (MCD)
DE(CA)........ Director of Economics, Civil Affairs [*War Office*] [*British*] [*World War II*]
DECA .... Director of Evaluation and Curriculum Analysis (SAUO)
DECA .... Display/AGAP [*Attitude Gyro Accelerometer Package*] Electronic Control Assembly (KSC)
DECA .... Display Electronic Control Assembly (SAUS)
DECA .... Distributive Education Clubs of America (EA)
DECA .... Driver Employer Council of America (NTPA)
DECACC .... Decimal Accumulator (SAUS)
DECACCN..... Decimal Accumulation (SAUS)
decad.......... decadence (SAUS)
decad.......... decadency (SAUS)
decad.......... decadently (SAUS)
DECADE .... DEC [*Digital Equipment Corp.*] Automatic Design (NITA)
DECADE System... Digital Equipment Corporation's Automatic Design System (SAUS)
DECAF .... Decaffeinated (WDAA)
decaf .... Decaffeinated Coffee (ADWA)
DECAF .... Distribution Control Analysis File [*NASA*] (MCD)
decal .... Decalcomania [*An adhesive paper*] (WDMC)
DECAL .... Decalcomania
Decal .... De Decalogo [*Philo*] (BJA)
DECAL .... Design Communication Algorithm (MCD)
DECAL .... Desk Calculator (IAA)
DECAL .... Detailed Experimental Computer-Assisted Language
DECAL .... Detection and Classification of Acoustic Lens (IAA)
DECAL .... Digital Equipment CAI Author Language (SAUS)
DECAL .... Digital Equipment Corporation Author Language [*Computer science*] (CSR)
DEC Alpha ... Digital Equipment Corporation Alpha (DCOM)
DECAN .... Distance Measuring Equipment Command and Navigation
DE C Ann..... Delaware Code, Annotated [*A publication*] (DLA)
DECAP .... De-Encapsulation [*Electronics*]
DECAP-CHUTE... Decontamination Capabilities - Chemical Units and Teams (MCD)
DECARB....... Decarburization (MSA)
DECARP....... Desert Encroachment Control And Rehabilitation Programme (SAUO)
decasyl....... decasyllabic (SAUS)
decasyl....... decasyllable (SAUS)
DECAT .... Driver Energy Conservation Awareness Training [*US government program*]
DECB .... Data Event Control Block [*Computer science*] (BUR)
DECC .... D & E Communications [*NASDAQ symbol*] (SAG)
DECC .... Defense Commercial Communications Center (SAUO)
DECC .... Diethylcarbamazine Citrate [*Biochemistry*]
DECC .... Diethylcarbamoyl Chloride [*Organic chemistry*]
DECC .... Disciples Ecumenical Consultative Council (EA)
Decca .... Decca Navigation System (SAUS)
DECCA .... Defense Commercial Communications Activity [*Military*]
Deccan .... Deccan Plain of southern India (SAUS)
DECCC .... Defense Commercial Communications Center [*Military*]
DecCen........ Decadal-to-Centennial [*Marine science*] (OSRA)
DEC-CEN...... Decadal to Centennial time-scale variability (SAUS)
Dec Ch......... Decisions from the Chair (Parliamentary) [*England*] [*A publication*] (DLA)
DECCO .... Defence Communication Contracting Office (SAUS)
DECCO .... Defense Commercial Communications Office [*Military*]
DECCO .... Defense Commercial Contracting Office (DOMA)
DEC Code .... Double Error-Correcting Code (SAUS)
Dec Comm'r Pat... Patents, Decisions of the Commissioner and of United States Courts [*A publication*] (DLA)
Dec Com Pat... Decisions of the Commissioner of Patents [*A publication*] (DLA)
DEC Comput... DEC Computing (journ.) (SAUS)
decd............ dec'd [*Medicine*] (EDAA)
decd............ Deceased (ADWA)
DECD .... Deceased (AFM)
DECD .... Deceased, Dead (SAUS)
DECD .... Declared
DECD .... Decreased (MUGU)
DECd........... Diethyl Cadmium (SAUS)
DECD EST.... Deceased Estate (SAUS)
Dec Dig .... American Digest System, Decennial Digests [*A publication*] (DLA)
DECDR......... Decoder (NITA)
DECDR......... Decorder (SAUS)
DECE........... Decease (ROG)
DECE........... Denominational Executives of Christian Education (EA)
DECEA .... Defense Communication Engineering Agency (AABC)
DECED .... Deceased (ROG)
Decel .... Deceleration [*Therapy term*] (CTAA)
DECEL.......... Deceleration (NVT)
DECELERON... Decelerator and Aileron [*NASA*]
DE CELL ...... Destructive examination cell (SAUS)
Decen Dig ... American Digest (Decennial Edition) [*A publication*] (ILCA)
DECENT .... Distribution of Exact Classical Energy Transfer [*Physics*]
DECEO .... Defense Communications Engineering Office [*Army*] (AABC)
DeCeTe........ Duisburg Container Terminal (SAUS)
DECFA .... Distributed Emission Crossed Field Amplifier (IAA)
Dec-FB......... Decrease Feedback
Dec Fed Mar Comm'n... Decisions of the Federal Maritime Commission [*United States*] [*A publication*] (DLA)
DE CH........... Delaware Chancery Reports [*A publication*] (DLA)
DECH .... Dictionary of English Church History [*A publication*] (ODCC)
DECH .... Diethylcyclohexane [*Organic chemistry*]
DECH .... Diploma, Epidemiology & Community Health [*Medical degree*] (CMD)
DE Ch E........ Doctor of Electro-Chemical Engineering
DECHEMA.... Dechema Chemical Engineering and Biotechnology Abstracts Database (SAUS)
DECHEMA.... Deutsche Gesellschaft fuer Chemisches Apparatewesen, Chemische Technik, und Biotechnologie eV [*Database producer*] (IID)
DE Ch Eng ... Doctor of Electro-Chemical Engineering
DECHIP........ Data Flow Chip [*Computer science*] (VLIE)
DECI............ Defense Employment Cost Index [*DoD*]
DE-CI .... Dose equivalent curie (SAUS)
DECID .... Deciduous
DECIDE .... Darmstadt Enterprise for Career and Individual Development (SAUO)
DECIDE .... Decide the problem precisely, Enumerate two groups of decision factors, Collect relevant information, Identify the best (SAUO)
DECIDE .... Decision Support Models for DSS (SAUS)
DECIDE .... Deployable Capability for Information Dissemination and Exchange (SEWL)
DECIM .... Decimeter [*Unit of measure*]
DECIM .... Defense Environmental Corporate Information Management [*DoD*]
DECIMAL ..... Decision Making in Libraries (TELE)
decis........... Decision (GEAB)
DECIS .... Decision
Decis Support Syst... Decision Support Systems [*A publication*] (PABS)
DECIT........... Decimal Digit (DIT)
De Civ D...... De Civitate Dei [*of Augustine*] [*Classical studies*] (OCD)
DECIX .... Deutscher Commercial Internet Exchange (VERA)
Dec Jt Com... Decisions of Joint Commission [*A publication*] (DLA)
DECK .... Deckers Outdoor [*NASDAQ symbol*] (TTSB)
DECK .... Deckers Outdoor Corp. [*NASDAQ symbol*] (SAG)
DECkit......... Digital Kit (SAUS)
DeckOut....... Deckers Outdoor Corp. [*Associated Press*] (SAG)
Decl............ Declaration (EBF)
decl .... Declaration (EBF)
DECL............ Declaration (ROG)
DECL............ Declaration of War/National Emergency (SAUO)
DECL............ Declare
Decl............ Declared (EBF)
decl .... Declared (EBF)
DECL............ Declassify [*Military*] (NVT)
decl .... Declension (SHCU)
DECL............ Declension
DECL............ Decline
D-ECL .... Dielectrically-isolated Emitter Coupled Logic (SAUS)
DECL............ Diode-Emitter-Coupled Logic
DECL............ Direct Energy Conversion Laboratory [*Johnson Space Center*] [*NASA*] (NASA)
decl .... Grammar Declension (ODA)
DECLAB .... Digital Equipment Corp. Laboratory
DECLAN .... Declaration (ROG)
DECLG .... Double-Ended Cold Leg Guillotine [*Nuclear energy*] (NRCH)
Decl J.......... Declaratory Judgements [*A publication*] (DLA)
DECLN......... Declaration [*Legal shorthand*] (LWAP)
DECLON....... Declaration (ROG)
DECM.......... Deceptive Electronic Countermeasure [*Military*] (CAAL)
DECM.......... Defense Electronic Countermeasure
DECM.......... Digital Electronic Countermeasure (LAIN)
DECmcc .... DEC [*Digital Equipment Corporation*] Managment Control Center (CDE)
DECMD .... Detroit Contract Management District (SAUS)
DECMOV...... Decimal Move (SAUS)
DECMS .... Digital Eastern Caribbean Microwave System (SAUO)
DECMSN...... Decommission (DNAB)
DECMSND.... Decommissioned (DNAB)
decn........... Decision (ADWA)
DECN .... Decision (AFM)
DECN .... Declaration (ADA)
DECN .... Declension
DECN .... Decontamination
DECNET .... DEC [*Digital Equipment Corp.*] Network (NITA)
DECnet........ Digital Equipment Corporation Network (SAUO)
DECNET .... Digital Equipment Corporation Networking (SAUO)
DECNET .... Digital Equipment Corporations proprietary network architecture (SAUS)
DECNET .... Digital Equipment Corporation Telecommunications Network
DECnet........ Digital Equipment Corporation trademark (SAUS)
DECnet........ Digital Equipment Network (SAUS)
DECNET E-net... DEC Engineering Network [*Communications term*] (DCT)
Dec No Sys... Decimal Number System (SAUS)
DECO .... Deconvolution [*Computer program*] (MCD)
DECO .... Decora Industries [*NASDAQ symbol*] (TTSB)
DECO .... Decora Industries, Inc. [*NASDAQ symbol*] (SAG)
DECO .... Decreasing Consumption of Oxygen [*Endocrinology*]
Deco .... Denver Equipment Company (SAUO)
DECo........... Detroit Edicon Company (SAUO)
DECO .... Detroit Edison Company (SAUO)
DECO .... Direct Energy Conversion Operation
DECO .... Document Engineering Co., Inc. [*Information service or system*] (IID)
Dec O .... Ohio Decisions [*A publication*] (DLA)
DECOCT....... Decoctum [*Decoction*] [*Pharmacy*]
DECOD......... Decodage (SAUS)
DECOD......... Dental Education in Care of the Disabled (SAUO)
Dec of Ind Acc Com... Decisions of the Industrial Accident Commission of California [*A publication*] (DLA)

De Col .... De Colyar's English County Court Cases [*1867-82*] [*A publication*] (DLA)
DECOL .... Descriptive Cataloguing On-Line (SAUS)
De Col Guar... De Colyar's Law of Guaranty [*A publication*] (DLA)
De Coly........ De Colyar's English County Court Cases [*1867-82*] [*A publication*] (DLA)
DECOM .... Decommissioned (AFM)
DECOM .... Decommutator
DECOM .... Delay Cost Model
DECOM .... Low-Rate Engineering Decommutator Executive [*Computer program*] [*NASA Viking Mission*]
DECOMATE... Delivery of Copyright Materials to End-Users (TELE)
DECOMD....... Decommissioned (DNAB)
DECOMG...... Decommissioning [*Date*] [*Navy*] (NVT)
DECOMM ..... Decommissioning [*Date*] [*Navy*] (NVT)
DECOMM ..... Decommutation
DECOMNET... Dedicated Communications Network (MCD)
decomp......... Decompensation [*Cardiology*]
DECOMP...... Decompose [*or Decomposition*]
DECOMP...... Decomposition Mathematical Programming (SAUS)
DECOMP...... Decomposition Mathematical Programming System
Decompg ..... Decomposing (SAUS)
DECOMPN.... Decompression (MSA)
DECOMPR.... Decompression
DECON......... Decontaminate (AABC)
DECON......... Decontamination
decon........... Decontamination
D Econ......... Doctor of Economics (EY)
DECON EQ ... Decontamination Equipment (SAUS)
D Econ Sc.... Doctor of Economic Science
DECONTIC.... Decentral Control Automatic (SAUS)
DECONTN .... Decontamination (KSC)
Decon U ...... Decotamination Unit (WDAA)
DECOR......... DECHEMA [*Deutsche Gesellschaft fuer Chemisches Apparatewesen, Chemische Technik, und Biotechnologie eV*] Corrosion Data Base [*Germany*] [*Information service or system*] (CRD)
DECOR......... Decorating
DECOR......... Decorative (ROG)
De Cor......... De Corona [*of Demosthenes*] [*Classical studies*] (OCD)
DECOR......... Digital Electronic Continuous Ranging
Decora......... Decora Industries, Inc. [*Associated Press*] (SAG)
Decorat........ Decorator Industries, Inc. [*Associated Press*] (SAG)
DECPrA........ Digital Equip 8.875% Dep'A'Pfd [*NYSE symbol*] (TTSB)
DEC Prof...... DEC Professional (journ.) (SAUS)
DECPSK....... Differentially Encoded Coherent Phase Shift Keying [*Telecommunications*] (TEL)
Dec Pt......... Decimal Point (SAUS)
DECPT MAN... Deceptive Maneuver (MCD)
DECR........... December (ROG)
DECR........... Decimation Register (SAUS)
DECR........... Decrease [*or Decrement*] (MSA)
dec (R)........ Decrease, Relative (DAVI)
DECR........... Decrement (GAVI)
DECR........... Document Error/Clarification Request (SAA)
Dec R.......... Ohio Decisions Reprint [*A publication*] (DLA)
Dec Re........ Ohio Decisions Reprint [*A publication*] (DLA)
Dec Rep...... Ohio Decisions Reprint [*A publication*] (DLA)
Dec Repr..... Ohio Decisions Reprint [*A publication*] (DLA)
DECRES....... Decrescendo [*Decreasing in Loudness*] [*Music*]
DECRESC..... Decrescendo [*Decreasing in Loudness*] [*Music*]
Decretal....... Decretalia of the Canon Law [*A publication*] (DLA)
Decret Greg IX... Decretales Gregorii IX [*A publication*] (DSA)
decrg........... Decreasing [*Nautical term*] (HRNC)
DECRT......... Decrement (MSA)
DECRTN....... Decoration
DECS........... Civil Engineering Office at Vandenberg (SAUS)
DECS........... Data Entry Control System
DECS........... Deceased (DAVI)
DECS........... Decoration for Exceptional Civilian Service [*Army civilian employee award*]
DECS........... Defense Electronics Control Service (ACAE)
DECS........... Digital Engine Control System (SAUS)
DECS........... Digital Excitation System [*Electrical engineering*]
DECS........... Direct Evacuation Control System (SAUS)
DECs........... Distance Education Centres (SAUO)
DECS........... Distributed Electronic Control System (SAUS)
DECS........... Dual Employed Coping Scale [*Psychology*] (EDAC)
DECS........... Dutch Exporters of Computer Service (SAUS)
Dec SDA...... Bengal Sadr Diwani Adalat Decisions [*A publication*] (DLA)
DECSE......... Diesel Engine Control Sulfur Effects [*Automotive emissions*]
DEC Station... Digital Equipment Corporation Station (SAUO)
dec stories... detective stories (SAUS)
Dec Sw........ Decade Switch (SAUS)
DECT........... Digital Enhanced Cordless Telecommunications (SEWL)
DECT........... Digital Enhanced Cordless Telephone (AAEL)
DECT........... Digital European Cordless Telecommunications [*or Telephone*]
DECT........... Digital European Cordless Telephone (ACRL)
DECT........... Distant-End Crosstalk (SAUS)
DECTAT....... Decision Table Translator (SAUS)
Dec T H & M... Admiralty Decisions Tempore Hay and Marriott [*England*] [*A publication*] (DLA)
DECTP......... Diethylchlorothiophosphate [*Ethyl Chemical Co.*] [*Organic chemistry*]
DECTRA....... Decca Track and Range (SAUS)
DECTRA....... Decca Track-guide and Ranging (SAUS)
DECTRA....... Decca Tracking and Ranging (MCD)
DECU........... Data Exchange Control Unit (NASA)
DECU........... Decontamination Unit (SAUS)
DECU........... Developmental & Educational Communications Unit (SAUS)
DECU........... Digital Engine Control Unit (MCD)
Decuary....... December and January (SAUS)
Decub.......... Decubitus [*Medicine*] (AMHC)
DECUB......... Decubitus [*Lying Down*] [*By extension, the medical term for bedsores*]
DECUF......... Defense Capability Under Fallout (SAA)
DECUK......... Duane Eddy Circle, United Kingdom (EAIO)
DECUS......... Digital Equipment Computer Users Society (EA)
DECUS......... Duane Eddy Circle, USA (EA)
Dec US Comp Gen... Decisions of the Comptroller General of the United States [*A publication*] (DLA)
Dec US Compt Gen... Decisions of the United States Comptroller General [*A publication*] (DLA)
Decus Europe... Digital Equipment Computer Users Society Europe (SAUO)
Dec US Mar Comm'n... Decisions of the United States Maritime Commission [*A publication*] (DLA)
DEC Writer... Digital Equipment Corporation Character Writer (SAUO)
DECZ........... Decker Coal [*Federal Railroad Administration identification code*]
DED............. Darkness Emitting Diode (AEBE)
DED............. Data Element Definition [*DoD*]
DED............. Data Element Definitions (SAUS)
DED............. Data Element Descriptor [*Computer science*] (IAA)
DED............. Data Element Dictionary [*A publication*] [*Army*]
DED............. Data Element Directory (SAUS)
DED............. Data Encryption and Decryption (SAUS)
DED............. Data End Device (SAUS)
DED............. Data Entry Device (SAUS)
DED............. Data Entry Display (SAUS)
DED............. Date Expected Delivery [*Medicine*]
DED............. Death-Effector Domain
DED............. Debrancher Enzyme Deficiency [*Medicine*] (MELL)
DED............. Deceased [*Motor vehicle violation status code used in state of Arkansas*] (MVRD)
DED............. Declared Dead [*Military*]
DED............. Dedendum [*Design engineering*]
ded............. dedicate (SAUS)
DED............. Dedicated [*or Dedication*] (ROG)
ded............. Dedicated (VRA)
ded............. Dedication (WDAA)
DED............. Deduct [*or Deductible*] (AABC)
ded............. Deduct (ADWA)
DED............. Deducted (SAUS)
Ded............. Deductible (SAUS)
DED............. Defect-Enhanced Diffusion (SAUS)
DED............. Defense Electronics Division (SAA)
DED............. Defense Engine Division (SAUO)
DED............. Deferred Enforced Departure (SAUS)
DED............. Defined Exposure Dose [*Medicine*] (DMAA)
DED............. Deland, FL [*Location identifier*] [*FAA*] (FAAL)
DED............. Delayed Erythema Dose [*Medicine*] (DMAA)
DED............. Dell Embedded Diagnostics [*Computer science*] (PCM)
DED............. Design Engineering Directorate (KSC)
DED............. Development Engineering Division (SAA)
DED............. Diesel Engine, Direct Drive (SAUS)
DED............. Diesel Engine Driven (NATG)
DED............. Digital Evaluation Device (SAUS)
DED............. Directorate of Engineer Development (SAUO)
DED............. Director of Engine Development [*Ministry of Aircraft Production*] [*British*]
DED............. Director of Engineering Development (SAUO)
DED............. Director of the Education Department [*Navy*] [*British*]
DED............. Distant End Disconnect [*Telecommunications*] (TEL)
DED............. Docking & rectification of Essential Defects (SAUS)
DEd............. Doctor of Education (AIE)
DED............. Doctor of English Divinity
DED............. Doctor of Environmental Design (GAGS)
DED............. Double Error Detection
DED............. duodenal erosive disease (SAUS)
DED............. Dutch Elm Disease
DED............. Dynamically Established Data Link [*Communications term*] (DCT)
DED............. Emergeny Preparedness and Disaster Relief Coordination Unit (SAUO)
ded............. Deduce (ODA)
DEDA........... Data Entry and Display Assembly [*Apollo*] [*NASA*]
DEDAAS....... Digital Electrophysiological Data Acquisition and Analysis System [*Neurometrics*]
DE DARHT... Dual Axis Radiographic Hydrodynamic Test (SAUS)
DEDAS......... Decontamination Emulsion Direct Application System (SAUS)
D Ed AS....... Diploma in Education Administration and Supervision
DEDAS......... Direct Entry Dispatching Audio System (SAUS)
DEDB........... Data Entry Data Base [*Computer science*] (ELAL)
DEDB........... Digital Elevation Database (RDA)
DEDC........... Diethyl Dicarbonate [*Fungistatic agent*]
DEDC........... Diethyldithiocarbamate [*Also, DDC, DDTC*] [*Organic chemistry*]
DED/D......... Data Element Dictionary/Directory [*A publication*]
DEDD........... Diesel-Electric Direct Drive
DEDE........... Density-Depth
DEDEC......... Detroit Deere Corp. [*Proposed trademark*]
De Def Or.... De Defectu Oraculorum [*of Plutarch*] [*Classical studies*] (OCD)
De Deo Soc... De Deo Socratico [*of Apuleius*] [*Classical studies*] (OCD)
dedic........... dedicating (SAUS)
DEDIC......... Dedication

dedic .... dedicative (SAUS)
DEDICATE .... Distance Education Information Courses through Networks (TELE)
DE D in D .... De Die in Diem [*From Day to Day*] [*Latin*]
DEDIP .... Department of Environmental and Drug-Induced Pathology [*Later, DETP*] (EA)
DEDL .... Data Element Description List [*Computer science*]
DEDM .... Diethyl Diazomalonate [*Organic chemistry*]
DEdn .... Director of Education (SAUO)
DEDO .... Defense Engineering Data Office
DEDOC System ... Design and Documentation System (SAUS)
De Dog Plat ... De Dogmate Platonis [*of Apuleius*] [*Classical studies*] (OCD)
DEDP .... Data Entry and Display Panel (MCD)
DEDP .... Detailed Emergency Defense Plan (SAUO)
DEDP .... Director of Executive Development Programs (SAUS)
DEDPU .... Diethyldiphenylurea (SAUS)
DEDS .... Data Entry and Display Subsystem
DeDS .... Delaware State College, Dover, DE [*Library symbol*] [*Library of Congress*] (LCLS)
DEDS .... Digital Enhancement Database System (SAUS)
DEDS .... Digital Error Detection Subsystem [*Computer science*] (AABC)
DEDS .... Directory of Engineering Document Services [*A publication*]
DEDS .... Discrete Event Dynamic Simulation (AAEL)
DEDS .... Dual Exchangeable Disc Storage (NITA)
DEDS .... Dual Exchangeable Disk Storage (SAUS)
DEdStudies ... Doctor of Educational Studies
DEDT .... Data Set Definition Table (SAUS)
DeDT .... Delaware Technical and Community College, Dover, DE [*Library symbol*] [*Library of Congress*] (LCLS)
DEDT .... Department of Economic Development and Tourism (SAUS)
DEDTX .... Delaware: Decatur Total Return Cl.A [*Mutual fund ticker symbol*] (SG)
DEDU .... Data Encryption and Decryption Unit (SAUS)
DEduc .... Doctor of Education (ADA)
DEDUCOM .... Deductive Communicator (IEEE)
DEDUCT .... Deduction (SAUS)
DEE .... Daily Energy Expenditure [*Physiology*]
DEE .... Data Encryption Equipment [*Telecommunications*] (OSI)
DEE .... Dee Corp. PLC [*NYSE symbol*] (COMM)
DEE .... Del Norte Chrome [*Vancouver Stock Exchange symbol*]
DEE .... Department of Electrical Engineering (SAUS)
DEE .... Diethoxyethylene [*Organic chemistry*]
DEE .... Diethyl Ether (PDAA)
DEE .... Digital Electronic Exchange (VLIE)
DEE .... Digital Encryption Equipment (SAUS)
DEE .... Digital Evaluation Equipment
DEE .... Digital Events Evaluator (MCD)
dee .... digital events recorder (SAUS)
DEE .... Digited Evaluation Equipment (SAUS)
DEE .... Diploma in Electrical Engineering (ADA)
DEE .... Direct Engineering Estimate (MCD)
DEE .... Direct Entry Equipment (VLIE)
DEE .... Directorate of Electrical Engineering (SAUO)
DEE .... Discrete Event Evaluator (KSC)
DEE .... Division of Electrical Engineering (SAUS)
DEE .... Division of Energy Engineering (SAUO)
DEE .... Doctor of Electrical Engineering
DEE .... Transportation America Corp. [*ICAO designator*] (FAAC)
DEE .... Diploma in Electrical Engineering (ODA)
DEEA .... Division of Energy and Environmental Assessment (SAUO)
DEEB .... Development and Economy in Educational Building (SAUS)
DEEC .... Digital Electronic Engine Control (MCD)
DEECS .... Digital Electronic Engine Control System (ADWA)
DEED .... [*USA*] Department of Energy and Economic Development (ODA)
Deedee .... Dorothy (SAUS)
DEEDS .... Documents of Essex England Data Set [*System for the analysis of medieval charters*] [*Canada*] (NITA)
DEEG .... Depth Electroencephalogram [*or Electroencephalography*] [*Neurology*] (DAVI)
DEEG .... Depth Electrography [*Neurology*] (DAVI)
Dee High ..... Doctor of Hygiene (SAUS)
dee jay .... disc jockey (SAUS)
deeks .... duck decoys (SAUS)
DE Eng .... Doctor of Electrical Engineering
DEEO .... Director of Equal Employment Opportunity [*Department of Labor*]
DEEP .... Dairy Export Enhancement Program [*Department of Agriculture*]
DEEP .... Dangerous Environment Electrical Protection system (SAUS)
DEEP .... Data Exception Error Protection
DEEP .... Deep Tech International [*NASDAQ symbol*] (TTSB)
DEEP .... DeepTech International, Inc. [*NASDAQ symbol*] (SAG)
DEEP .... Describe Each Element in the Procedure (PDAA)
DEEP .... Developmental Economic Education Program
DEEP .... Development Economic Education Program (SAUS)
DEEP .... Development Education Exchange Papers [*FAO*] [*Information service or system*] [*United Nations*] (DUND)
DEEP .... Diffusion of Exemplary Educational Practices (EDAC)
DEEP .... Direct Elected European Parliament (SAUS)
DEEP .... Dyer EEG Evoked Potential (SAUS)
deep 6 .... disposing of anything unwanted in at least six fathoms of water (SAUS)
DEEPDET ..... Double Exposure Endpoint Detection Technique (IAA)
Dee Pee ...... Doctor of Pharmacy (SAUS)
Deep-Sea Bes A ... Deep-Sea Research, Part A (journ.) (SAUS)
Deep-Sea Res ... Deep-Sea Research (SAUS)
Deep-Sea Res B ... Deep-Sea Research, Part B (journ.) (SAUS)
Deep-Sea Res Oceanogr Abstr ... Deep-Sea Research and Oceanographic Abstracts (journ.) (SAUS)
DEEPSEAT ... Deep-Sea System for Evaluating Acoustic Transducers [*Navy*] (MCD)
DEEPSUBSYS ... Deep Submergence Systems [*Navy*]
DEEPSUBSYSPROJO ... Deep Submergence Systems Project Office [*Navy*]
DeepTech .... DeepTech International, Inc. [*Associated Press*] (SAG)
DEER .... Deer Environment Ecology and Resources [*An association*]
DEER .... Diet and Exercise for Elevated Risk [*Medicine*] (EDAA)
DEER .... Directed Energy Experimental Range (ACAE)
DEER .... Directional Explosive Echo Ranging
Dee R .... doctor (SAUS)
Deere .... Deere & Co. [*Associated Press*] (SAG)
Deering's Cal Adv Legis Serv ... Deering's California Advance Legislative Service [*A publication*] (DLA)
Deering's Cal Code Ann ... Deering's Annotated California Code [*A publication*] (DLA)
Deering's Cal Gen Laws Ann ... Deering's California General Laws, Annotated [*A publication*] (DLA)
DEERS .... Defense Enrollment Eligibility Reporting System [*DoD*]
DEES .... Department of Earth and Environmental Sciences (SAUO)
DEES .... Development Education Exchange Service (SAUO)
DEES .... Dynamic Electromagnetic Environment Simulator
DEES .... Dynamic Electronic Environment Simulator (SAUS)
DEESC .... Deescalate (ABBR)
DEESCD .... Deescalated (ABBR)
DEESCG .... Deescalating (ABBR)
DEESCN .... Deescalation (ABBR)
Deeside .... River Dee valley around Aberdeen (SAUS)
Dees Ins .... Dees on the Law of Insolvent Debtors [*A publication*] (DLA)
DEET .... Department of Employment, Education and Training (SAUO)
DEET .... Diethyl-m-toluamide [*Insect repellent*]
DEET .... Diethyltoluamide (STED)
deet .... diethyl toluamide (SAUS)
DEEVAL .... Detailed European Evaluation (MCD)
DEEVE .... Dynamically Equivalent Equal-Volume Ellipsoid
De Exil .... De Exilio [*of Plutarch*] [*Classical studies*] (OCD)
DEF .... Daily Electronic Feed [*ABC news service*] (WDMC)
DEF .... Data Encryption Facility [*Computer science*] (HODG)
DEF .... Data Entry Facility
DEF .... Data Exchange Format (ACAE)
DEF .... Data Extension Frame [*Computer science*] (NITA)
DEF .... Deaf
DEF .... Decayed, Extracted, or Filled [*Dentistry*]
Def .... Default (EBF)
def .... Default (EBF)
DEF .... Default [*Business term*]
DEF .... Defaults (SAUS)
DEF .... Defeated
def .... defecate (SAUS)
def .... Defecation (STED)
DEF .... Defecation
DEF .... Defect (SAUS)
DEF .... Defection [*or Defector*] (ABBR)
DEF .... Defective (MSA)
Def .... Defector (SAUS)
DEF .... Defence (SAUS)
DEF .... Defendant
DEF .... Defense (AFM)
def .... Defense (MILB)
DEF .... Defense Specifications (SAUS)
Def .... Defensive (SAUS)
DEF .... Defensive Systems (SAUS)
DEF .... Defensor [*Defender*] [*Coin inscription*] [*Latin*] (ROG)
def .... defer (SAUS)
Def .... Deferred (EBF)
def .... Deferred (EBF)
DEF .... Deferred
DEF .... Defiance College, Defiance, OH [*OCLC symbol*] (OCLC)
DEF .... Deficiency (STED)
def .... Deficiency [*or Deficient*]
Def .... Deficit (EBF)
def .... Deficit (EBF)
DEF .... Deficit
DEF .... Define [*or Definite*] (KSC)
DEF .... Defined (SAUS)
def .... Definite (ADWA)
def .... Definitely (ADWA)
DEF .... Definition
def .... Definitions (VLIE)
Def .... Definitive (EBF)
def .... Definitive (EBF)
DEF .... Definitive (ROG)
DEF .... Deflagrate (ABBR)
def .... deflagration (SAUS)
DEF .... Deflect (ABBR)
Def .... Deflecting (SAUS)
def .... defoliate (SAUS)
def .... defoliating (SAUS)
DEF .... Defoliation
def .... deformans (SAUS)
DEF .... Defrost
DEF .... Defroster (SAUS)
DEF .... Defrosting (SAUS)
def .... defunct (SAUS)
def .... defunction (SAUS)

def ..... defunctive (SAUS)
DEF ..... Defunctus [*Deceased*] [*Latin*] (ADA)
DEF ..... Delay Equalizer, Fixed Set (IAA)
DEF ..... Desktop Functional Equivalent (VLIE)
DEF ..... Destination Element Field [*Computer science*] (ELAL)
def ..... detlagrating (SAUS)
DEF ..... Development and Evaluation Facility (SAUS)
DEF ..... Development Evaluation Facility (LAIN)
DEF ..... Dielectric Foil (IAA)
DEF ..... Diethylfluorene. (SAUS)
DEF ..... Direct Equipment Failure (VLIE)
DEF ..... Disarmed Enemy Forces (SAUO)
DEF ..... Disarm Education Fund (EA)
DEF ..... Display Evaluation Form (SAUS)
DEF ..... Duck Embryo Fibroblasts (PDAA)
DEF ..... Ministry of Defence (SAUO)
DEFA ..... Daily Express Film Award [*British*]
DEFA ..... Driver-enriched fuel assemblies (SAUS)
De Fac ..... De Facie in Orbe Lunae [*of Plutarch*] [*Classical studies*] (OCD)
DEFAIR ..... Defense Air (MCD)
DEFAR ..... Department of Defence, Army [*Australia*]
DEF ART ..... Definite Article (WDAA)
DEFBA ..... Domestic European Ferret Breeders Association (EA)
DEFC ..... Danish Export Credit Finance Corporation
DEFCE ..... Defence (ROG)
DEFCLOTH & TEXSUPCEN ... Defense Clothing and Textile Supply Center [*Later, Defense Personnel Support Center*] [*DoD*]
DEFCOM ..... Defense Command
DEFCOMARS ... Defence Communications Automatic Relay Station
DEFCOMMNET ... Defence Force Communications Network [*Australia*]
DEFCOMMSYS ... Defense Communications System [*DoD*] (DNAB)
DEFCOMNON ... Defense Command, North Norway (SAUS)
DEFCOMNOR ... Defense Command, Norway (SAUS)
DEFCOMSONOR ... Defense Command, South Norway (SAUS)
DEFCON ..... Defense Condition [*The higher number indicates a higher state of military readiness*] [*Numbered from 1 through 5*] [*Military*] (DOMA)
DEFCON ..... Defense Readiness Condition [*Army*]
DEFCON ..... Defensive Concentration
DEFCON ..... Defensive Contact [*Artillery fire*] [*Military*] (VNW)
DEFCONSTSUPCEN ... Defense Construction Supply Center (SAUO)
DEFCONTRSUPCEN ... Defense Construction Supply Center [*Defense Supply Agency*]
DEFCORD ..... Defense Coordination Network (SAUO)
DEFCS ..... Digital Electronic Flight Control System (MCD)
DEFEC ..... Defective (IAA)
DEFECT ..... Defective Verb [*Grammar*] (ROG)
DEFEL ..... Deferred Delivery
DEFELECSUPCEN ... Defense Electric Supply Center
DEFELECSUPCEN ... Defense Electronics Supply Center (SAUO)
Def Electron ... Defense Electronics (journ.) (SAUS)
Defense ..... Department of Defense (SAUS)
DEFENSIVE ... General Counsel Defense Docket System (SAUO)
DEFEW ..... Defensive Electronic Warfare (SEWL)
DEFEWS ..... Design Engineers Field Experience with Soldiers [*Army*] (RDA)
DEFFC ..... Defence Forces Charter [*Australia*]
DefFor ..... Defense Forces (SAUO)
DEFGAN ..... Desensitized Fertilizer-Grade Ammonium Nitrate [*Nonexplosive*]
DEFGENSUPCEN ... Defense General Supply Center
DEFGR ..... Defogger [*Automotive engineering*]
Def Grp ..... Defense Group (SAUO)
DEFI ..... Defiance Inc. [*NASDAQ symbol*] (TTSB)
DEFI ..... Defiance Precision Products [*NASDAQ symbol*] (NQ)
DEFI ..... Defibrillator (SAUS)
DEFI ..... Deficiency (ABBR)
DEFI ..... Digital Electronic Fuel Injection [*Automotive engineering*]
DEFIA ..... Defiance, OH [*American Association of Railroads railroad junction routing code*]
DEFIB ..... Defibrillate [*Cardiology*]
defib ..... Defibrillation [*Medicine*] (STED)
Defib ..... Defibrillator [*Medicine*] (AMHC)
DEFIC ..... Deficiency (ROG)
defic ..... Deficiency (STED)
defic ..... Deficit (CPH)
DEFINDPLANTEQUIPCEN ... Defense Industrial Plant Equipment Center [*DoD*]
DEFINDSUPCEN ... Defense Industrial Supply Center
DEFINDSUPDEP ... Defense Industrial Supply Depot
DEFINTELAGCY ... Defense Intelligence Agency [*Formerly, JJ-2*]
DEFL ..... Deflate (ABBR)
Defl ..... Deflation (SAUS)
DEFL ..... Deflect [*or Deflection*] (MSA)
DEFL ..... Deflector [*Automotive engineering*]
DEFL ..... Diode Emitter Follower Logic
DEFL ..... Direct Effective Fire Line [*Military*] (INF)
DeflcShd ..... Deflecta Shield Corp. [*Associated Press*] (SAG)
DEFLOR ..... Defloration (ABBR)
DEFLOWH ..... Defense Liaison Officer to the White House (AABC)
DEFLT ..... Deflect (AAG)
deflt ..... dynamic error free transmission (SAUS)
DEFLTN ..... Deflection (AAG)
DEFLTR ..... Deflector (AAG)
DEFM ..... Demographic and Economic Forecasting Model (SAUO)
DeF Min ..... De Fooz on Mines [*A publication*] (DLA)
DEFMT ..... Deafmute (ABBR)
DEFN ..... Danubian Endemic Familial Nephropathy [*Medicine*] (DMAA)
DEFN ..... Deafen (ABBR)
DEFN ..... Deficiency (AABC)
defn ..... Definition (MILB)
DEFNAV ..... Department of Defence, Navy [*Australia*]
DEFNC ..... Defence
DEFND ..... Deafened (ABBR)
DEFNG ..... Deafening (ABBR)
DEFNGY ..... Deafeningly (ABBR)
DefnInc ..... Defiance Precision Products [*Associated Press*] (SAG)
DEFNS ..... Deafness (ABBR)
DEFNS ..... Defense
DEFOG ..... Deterministic Factory Operation Game (SAUS)
DEFOL ..... Defoliation (CINC)
DEFORM ..... Deformation [*National Highway Traffic Safety Administration Fatal Accident Recording System code*]
deform ..... Deformity
DEForm ..... Department of Education Form (SAUO)
Deformat ..... Deformation (SAUS)
De Fort Rom ... De Fortuna Romanorum [*of Plutarch*] [*Classical studies*] (OCD)
Defo Value ... Deformation Value (SAUS)
DEFPA ..... Defence of Ports & Anchorages (SAUS)
DEFPERSUPPCEN ... Defense Personnel Support Center
DEFPLAN ..... Defense Plan (SAUS)
DEFPO ..... Hanford Defense Program Planning Office (SAUS)
DEF PROS ... Deferred Prosecution [*Motor vehicle term used in state of Washington*] (MVRD)
DEFR ..... Deafer (ABBR)
DEFR ..... Defrauding [*FBI standardized term*]
DEFR ..... Defroster [*Automotive engineering*]
DEFRA ..... Deficit Reduction Act [*1984*]
DEFRAG ..... Defragment (SAUS)
De Frat Amor ... De Fraterno Amore [*of Plutarch*] [*Classical studies*] (OCD)
DEFREP ..... Defense Readiness Posture [*Army*] (AABC)
DEFREP ..... Defense Response Status (SAUS)
DEFREPNAMA ... Defense Representative, North Atlantic and Mediterranean Area
DEFREPNAMA/USRO ... Defense Representative North Atlantic and Mediterranean Areas / United States Regional Office (SAA)
Def Res Abs Contractors Ed ... Defense Research Abstracts-Contractors Edition (journ.) (SAUS)
DEFSATCOM ... Defense Satellite Communications System [*Military*]
DEFSCAP ..... Defense Standard Contract Administration Procedure
DEFSCE ..... Defeasance (ROG)
Def Sci J ..... Defence Science Journal [*A publication*] (CABS)
DEFSEC ..... Defense Section (SAUO)
DEFSEC ..... Defense Sector [*Navy*]
DEF SEG ..... Definition Segment (SAUS)
DEFSIM ..... Defense Simulation (ACAE)
DEFSIP ..... Defense Scientists Immigration Program (AFM)
DEFSIP ..... Design Effect (SAUS)
DEFSIP ..... Driven Equilibrium Fourier Transform (SAUS)
DEFSIP ..... Dynamic Error-Free Transmission (SAUS)
DEFSMAC ..... Defense Special Missile and Astronautics Center [*Pronounced "deff-smack"*] [*National Security Agency*]
DEFSMAC ..... Defense Status Military Alert Center (ACAE)
DEFSMAC ..... Department Special Missile and Astronautic Center (SAUO)
DEFST ..... Deafest (ABBR)
DEFSTAN ..... Defence Standard (SAUS)
DEF STD ..... Defence Standard (SAUS)
DEFSUBSUPCEN ... Defense Subsistence Supply Center [*Later, Defense Personnel Support Center*]
DEFT ..... Defendant
DEFT ..... Definite-Time [*Relay*]
DEFT ..... Deflection (ADA)
DEFT ..... Design Effect [*Ratio used in statistics*]
DEFT ..... Development and Evaluation of a Firearms Training Facility
DEFT ..... Diagnostic Expert-Final Test [*IBM Corp.*]
DEFT ..... Direct Electronic Fourier Transform [*Camera*]
DEFT ..... Direct Epifluorescence Filter Technique [*Microbiology*]
DEFT ..... Director Evaluation Feasibility [*or Flight*] Test (MCD)
DEFT ..... Display Evaluation Flight Testing (MCD)
DEFT ..... Driven Equilibrium Fourier Transform [*Mathematics*]
DEFT ..... Dynamic Error-Free Transmission
DEFTNS ..... Deftness (ABBR)
DEFT-SENSOR ... Discrete Electronic Fourier Transform Sensor (SAUS)
DEFT System ... Dynamic Error-Free Transmission System (SAUS)
DEFUNCT ..... Desirability Function
DEFWEAPSYSMGMTCEN ... Defense Weapons Systems Management Center (SAUO)
DEFWEAPSYSMGTCEN ... Defense Weapons System Management Center
Def Wg ..... Defense Wing (SAUO)
DEFY ..... Deafly (ABBR)
DEFY ..... Drug Education for Youth (SAUO)
DEG ..... Dawson Eldorado Gold [*Vancouver Stock Exchange symbol*]
DEG ..... Degaussing Calibration (NVT)
deg ..... degenerate (SAUS)
DEG ..... Degenerated Electron Gas (SAUS)
DEG ..... Degenerate Electron Gas
deg ..... Degeneration (STED)
DEG ..... Degeneration
De G ..... De Gex's English Bankruptcy Reports [*A publication*] (DLA)
DEG ..... Degrade
DEG ..... Degree (AFM)
deg ..... Degree (NTIO)
deg ..... Degrees (IDOE)

Deg............ DeGroot, Dr. A. T., Texas Christian University, Fort Worth, TX [*Library symbol*] [*Library of Congress*] (LCLS)
DEG............ Delay Error Generator (SAUS)
DEG............ Destroyer Escort, Guided Missile [*British military*] (DMA)
DEG............ Developing Economies Group (SAUO)
DEG............ Development Economics Group
DEG............ Diagnostic Educational Grouping
DEG............ Diethanolglycine (EDCT)
DEG............ Diethylene Glycol [*Organic chemistry*]
DEG............ Diethylglycine [*Biochemistry*]
DEG............ Dimensional Electron Gas (AAEL)
DEG............ Directorate of Environmental Geology (SAUO)
DEG............ Divisional Engineering Guide (SAUS)
DEG............ Double-Ended Guillotine [*Nuclear energy*] (NRCH)
DEG............ Guided Missile Escort Ship [*Navy symbol*]
de ga.......... depth gage (SAUS)
DEGA.......... Depth Gauge
DEGA.......... Diethylene Glycol Adipate [*Organic chemistry*]
DEGA.......... Diethylene Glycolamine [*Organic chemistry*]
DEGaCl........ Diethylgallium Chloride (SAUS)
DEGADEP..... Degaussing and Deperming (SAUS)
DEGADIS...... Dense Gas Dispersion [*Computer model*]
DEG & DEP... Degaussing and Deperming [*Navy*]
De G & J..... De Gex and Jones' English Chancery Reports [*A publication*] (ILCA)
De G & JB... De Gex and Jones' English Bankruptcy Appeals [*1857-59*] [*A publication*] (DLA)
De G & J By... De Gex and Jones' English Bankruptcy Appeals [*1857-59*] [*A publication*] (ILCA)
De G & S..... De Gex and Smale's English Chancery Reports [*63-64 English Reprint*] [*1846-52*] [*A publication*] (DLA)
De G & Sm... De Gex and Smale's English Chancery Reports [*63-64 English Reprint*] [*1846-52*] [*A publication*] (ILCA)
De Garr........ De Garrulitate [*of Plutarch*] [*Classical studies*] (OCD)
DEGB........... Diethylene Glycol Benzoate (SAUS)
DEGB........... Double-Ended Guillotine Break [*Nuclear energy*] (NRCH)
De G Bankr... De Gex's English Bankruptcy Reports [*A publication*] (DLA)
De G Bankr (Eng)... De Gex's English Bankruptcy Reports [*A publication*] (DLA)
degC........... Degree Celsius [*British Standards Institution*]
DegC........... Degrees Celsius (SAUS)
DEGCAL........ Degaussing Calibration (SAUS)
DEGCALB..... Degaussing Calibration (NVT)
DEGCENT..... Degree Centigrade (IAA)
DEGE........... DeGeorge Financial Corp. [*NASDAQ symbol*] (SAG)
DeGE........... Eleutherian Mills Historical Library, Greenville, DE [*Library symbol*] [*Library of Congress*] (LCLS)
degen.......... Degeneration
De Gen........ De Genio Socratis [*of Plutarch*] [*Classical studies*] (OCD)
DeGeT......... Delaware Technical and Community College, Southern Campus, Georgetown, DE [*Library symbol*] [*Library of Congress*] (LCLS)
De Gex........ De Gex's English Bankruptcy Reports [*A publication*] (DLA)
De Gex F & J... De Gex, Fisher, and Jones' English Chancery Reports [*A publication*] (DLA)
De Gex J & S... De Gex, Jones, and Smith's English Chancery Reports [*A publication*] (DLA)
De Gex M & G... De Gex, Macnaghten, and Gordon's English Reports [*A publication*] (DLA)
De Gex M & GB... De Gex, Macnaghten, and Gordon's English Bankruptcy Reports [*A publication*] (DLA)
degF........... Degree Fahrenheit [*British Standards Institution*]
De G F & J... De Gex, Fisher, and Jones' English Chancery Reports [*A publication*] (DLA)
Degge.......... Degge's Parson's Counsellor and Law of Tithes [*A publication*] (DLA)
DEGGX......... Delaware: U.S. Govt. Fund Cl.A [*Mutual fund ticker symbol*] (SG)
DeGH........... Hagley Museum and Library, Greenville, DE [*Library symbol*] [*Library of Congress*] (LCLS)
DEGIX.......... Delaware: Intl. Equity Fund Cl.A [*Mutual fund ticker symbol*] (SG)
De G J & S... De Gex, Jones, and Smith's English Chancery Reports [*A publication*] (DLA)
De G J & S By... De Gex, Jones, and Smith's English Bankruptcy Appeals [*1862-65*] [*A publication*] (DLA)
De G J & S (Eng)... De Gex, Jones, and Smith's English Chancery Reports [*A publication*] (DLA)
De G J & Sm... De Gex, Jones, and Smith's English Chancery Reports [*A publication*] (DLA)
degK........... Degree Kelvin [*British Standards Institution*]
De Glor Ath... De Gloria Atheniensium [*of Plutarch*] [*Classical studies*] (OCD)
DEGLUT....... Deglutiatur [*Swallow*] [*Pharmacy*]
DEGLUTIEND... Deglutiendus [*To be Taken or Swallowed*] [*Pharmacy*] (ROG)
DEGM.......... Dynamic End Game Model (ACAE)
De G M & G... De Gex, Macnaghten, and Gordon's English Bankruptcy Reports [*A publication*] (DLA)
De G M & G... De Gex, Macnaghten, and Gordon's English Chancery Reports [*A publication*] (DLA)
De G M & G By... De Gex, Macnaghten, and Gordon's English Bankruptcy Appeals [*1837-55*] [*A publication*] (DLA)
DEGMBE...... Diethylene Glycol Monobutyl Ether (SAUS)
DEGMEE...... Diethylene Glycol Monoethyl Ether (SAUS)
DEGN.......... Diethylene Glycol Dinitrate [*Explosive*]
DEGN.......... Diethylene Glycol Nitrate (EDCT)
DEGpGl........ Delaware Group Global Dividend Fund [*Associated Press*] (SAG)
DEGpGlb...... Delaware Group Global Dividend Fund [*Associated Press*] (SAG)
degr............ Degree (GEAB)
degR........... Degree Rankine [*British Standards Institution*]
DEGRA......... Degradation (DSUE)
DEGRAD...... Degradable (ABBR)
DEGREE....... Diversity Effects in Grassland Ecosystems of Europe (EURO)
DeGrgeFnl.... DeGeorge Financial Corp. [*Associated Press*] (SAG)
DEGROSS.... Degross Aerial Mapping (SAUS)
DEGS........... Department of Environmental and Geographical Sciences (SAUO)
DEGS........... Diethylene Glycol Succinate [*Organic chemistry*]
DEG/SEC...... Degrees per Second
DEGSVC...... Degaussing Services [*Navy*] (NVT)
DEGUSG...... Degaussing
degust......... degustation (SAUS)
DEH............ Dallas Enviro-Health Systems Ltd. [*Vancouver Stock Exchange symbol*]
DEH............ Decorah, IA [*Location identifier*] [*FAA*] (FAAL)
DEH............ Deepwater Escort Hydrofoil [*Also, DBH*] (MCD)
DEH............ Department of Education & Health (WDAA)
DEH............ Department of Environment and Heritage [*Queensland*]
DEH............ Destroyer Escort Hydrofoil (SAUS)
DEH............ Diethylhydroxylamine [*Also, DEHA*] [*Organic chemistry*]
DEH............ Digital Electrohydraulic (NRCH)
DEH............ Digital Encoder Handbook
DEH............ Direct Electrical Heating (PDAA)
DEH............ Direct Engineering Hours (MCD)
DEH............ Directorate of Engineering and Housing [*Army*] (RDA)
DEH............ Director of Engineering & Housing (SAUO)
DEH............ Director of Environmental Health (HEAS)
DEH............ Double Exposure Holography (SAUS)
DEH............ Drifting Electron Hole
DEH............ dual elevator handler (SAUS)
DEH............ Dysplasia Epiphysealis Hemimelica [*Medicine*] (DMAA)
DEHA.......... Di(ethylhexyl) Adipate [*Also, DOA*] [*Organic chemistry*]
DEHA.......... Diethylhydroxylamine [*Also, DEH*] [*Organic chemistry*]
DeHa........... Harrington Public Library, Harrington, DE [*Library symbol*] [*Library of Congress*] (LCLS)
DEHAA......... Department of Environment, Heritage and Aboriginal Affairs (SAUO)
De Hart Mil Law... DeHart on Military Law [*A publication*] (DLA)
DEHB........... Digital Encoder Handbook
DEHB........... Double Extra Hard Black [*Pencil leads*] (ROG)
DEHCD......... Department of Environment, Housing, and Community Development (SAUS)
DEHFT......... Developmental Hand Function Test
DeHi............ Historical Society of Delaware, Wilmington, DE [*Library symbol*] [*Library of Congress*] (LCLS)
DeH ML........ DeHart on Military Law [*A publication*] (DLA)
DEHNR........ Department of Environment, Health, and Natural Resources (BCP)
DEHO........... District Environmental Health Officer (HEAS)
DeHoCo....... Detroit House of Correction (SAUS)
DEHP........... Di(ethylhexyl)phthalate [*Also, DOP, DHP*] [*Organic chemistry*]
DEHP........... Diethyl Hydrogen Phosphite [*Organic chemistry*]
DEHPA......... Di(ethylhexyl)phosphoric Acid [*Organic chemistry*]
DEHS........... Director of Environmental Health Services (HEAS)
DEHS........... Division of Emergency Health Services (SAUS)
DEHT........... Deep-Etched Halftone [*Engraving*] (DGA)
DEHT........... Developmental Hand Function Test [*Medicine*] (DMAA)
DEHYD......... Dehydrated
DEI.............. Data Export/Import (SAUS)
DEI.............. Declaration of European Interest (EURO)
DEI.............. Defense des Enfants - International [*Defence for Children International Movement - DCI*] (EAIO)
DEI.............. Defense Electronics, Inc.
DEI.............. Denis Island [*Seychelles Islands*] [*Airport symbol*] (OAG)
DEI.............. Dent [*Idaho*] [*Seismograph station code, US Geological Survey*] [*Closed*] (SEIS)
DEI.............. Design Engineering Identification (NASA)
DEI.............. Design Engine Inspection (AFM)
DEI.............. Development Engineering Inspection (MCD)
DEI.............. Development Exchange, Incorporated (SAUO)
DEI.............. Digital Electronics Incorporated (SAUO)
DEI.............. Director of Electrical Inspection (SAUO)
DEI.............. Display Evaluation Index
DEI.............. Diversified Energies, Inc. (EFIS)
DEI.............. Dose Equivalent Iodine [*Nuclear energy*] (NRCH)
DEI.............. Double Electrically Insulated (SAUS)
dei............... double electrically isolated (SAUS)
DEI.............. Dutch East Indies
DEI.............. Dynamic Effect Induction [*Automotive engineering*]
DEI.............. Dynamic Engineering Incorporated (SAUO)
DEI.............. Export-Import Bank of the United States, Washington, DC [*Library symbol*] [*Library of Congress*] (LCLS)
DEIA............ Division of Environmental Impact Analysis (SAUO)
DEIA............ Division of Environment Information and Assessment of UNEP (SAUO)
DEIB............ Developmental Engineering Inspection Board (AAG)
DEIC............ Diver Equipment Information Center [*Battelle Memorial Institute*] [*Information service or system*] (IID)
DEID............ EI Dupont de Nemours [*Federal Railroad Administration identification code*]
DEIDP.......... Department of Engraving, Illustration, Design and Painting (SAUO)
DEIFCN........ Deification (ABBR)
DEIFD.......... Deified (ABBR)
DEIFG.......... Deifying (ABBR)
DEIFR.......... Deifier (ABBR)
DEIIS........... Detailed Experiment Integration Interface Specification (ACAE)
De Imit......... De Imitatione [*of Dionysius Halicarnassensis*] [*Classical studies*] (OCD)
DEIMOS....... Development Investigations in Military Orbiting Systems
DEIMOS....... Diesel Engine Intelligent Monitoring System [*Automotive engineering*]

DEIMOS...... Discrete Element Idealization Model of Solar (ACAE)
DEIMS......... Defense Economic Impact Modeling System
DEIMS......... Dendenkosha Information Management System (SAUS)
DEION......... Deionized (SAUS)
DEION......... Deionizer (SAUS)
Deiot........... Pro Rege Deiotaro [*of Cicero*] [*Classical studies*] (OCD)
DEIP............ Dairy Export Incentive Program
DEIR............ Department of Employment and Industrial Relations (SAUS)
DEIS............ Defense Energy Information System [*DoD*] [*Washington, DC*] (AFM)
DEIS............ Defense Enterprise Integration Services [*Military*] (SEWL)
DEIS............ Design Engineering Inspection Simulation (NASA)
deis............ design engineering inspection simulator (SAUS)
DEIS............ Design Evaluation Inspection Simulator (NASA)
DEIS............ Dielectrics and Electrical Insulation Society (SAUO)
DEIS............ Digital Electronic Image Stabilization (PS)
DEIS............ Director of Engineering and Industrial Services [*Edgewood Arsenal, MD*]
DEIS............ DoD [*Department of Defense*] Worldwide Energy Information System (MCD)
DEIS............ Draft Environmental Impact Statement [*NRC*] (MSC)
DEIS............ Dual Electron Injector Structure (MCD)
D E I S DOD... Worldwide Energy Information System (SAUS)
De Is et Os... De Iside et Osiride [*of Plutarch*] [*Classical studies*] (OCD)
DEI Technique... Display Evaluation Index Technique (SAUS)
DEJ............ Albany, NY [*Location identifier*] [*FAA*] (FAAL)
DEJ............ David Ezekiel Joshua [*Shanghai*] (BJA)
DEJ............ Dejour Mines Ltd. [*Toronto Stock Exchange symbol*]
DEJ............ Delta Jet SA [*Spain*] [*ICAO designator*] (FAAC)
DEJ............ Dento-Enamel Junction [*Dentistry*]
DEJ............ Dermoepidermal Junction [*Anatomy*]
DEJ ALVI..... Dejectiones Alvi [*Discharge from the Bowels*] [*Pharmacy*] (ROG)
DEJF........... Double End Jig Feet (SAUS)
De Jure Mar... Hale's De Jure Maris, Appendix to Hall on the Sea Shore [*A publication*] (DLA)
DEK............ Data Encryption Key [*Computer science*] (DCDG)
DEK............ Data Entry Keyboard [*Computer science*] (MCD)
Dek............ Dekameter (SAUS)
DEK............ Dekeleia [*Greece*] [*Later, PEN*] [*Geomagnetic observatory code*]
DEK............ Demokratiki Enosis Kyprou [*Democratic Union of Cyprus*] [*Political party*] (PPE)
DEK............ Devtek Corp. [*Toronto Stock Exchange symbol*]
DEK............ Diethyl Ketone [*Organic chemistry*]
DEKAG......... Dekagram [*Unit of measure*]
DEKAL......... Dekaliter [*Unit of measure*] (ROG)
Dekal........... Dekalitre (SAUS)
DEKAM......... Dekameter [*Unit of measure*] (ROG)
Dekam......... Dekametre (SAUS)
Deke........... Donald (SAUS)
DEKE........... Doppler Ekelund Ranging [*Navy*] (CAAL)
DEKJT.......... De Kalb Junction, NY [*American Association of Railroads railroad junction routing code*]
DEKO........... Demokratiko Komma [*Democratic Party*] [*Greek Cyprus*] [*Political party*] (PPE)
dekon.......... economic declaration (SAUS)
Dekont......... Dekontamination (SAUS)
De Krets...... DeKretser's Matara Appeals [*Ceylon*] [*A publication*] (DLA)
DEL............ Carib Aviation Ltd. [*Antigua and Barbuda*] [*FAA designator*] (FAAC)
DEL............ Data Entry Language
DEL............ Data Entry Library (SAUS)
DEL............ Data Evaluation Laboratory (ACAE)
DEL............ Decode Encode Language (SAUS)
DEL............ Defence Electric Light [*British military*] (DMA)
Del............ Delane's English Revision Cases [*1832-35*] [*A publication*] (DLA)
DEL............ Delary [*Sweden*] [*Seismograph station code, US Geological Survey*] (SEIS)
DEL............ De Laval Separator Co. (SAUO)
DEL............ Delaware (AFM)
del............ Delaware [*MARC language code*] [*Library of Congress*] (LCCP)
Del............ Delaware (ODBW)
Del............ Delawarean (SAUS)
Del............ Delaware County Reports [*Pennsylvania*] [*A publication*] (DLA)
Del............ Delaware Reports [*A publication*] (DLA)
Del............ Delaware Supreme Court Reports [*1832-*] [*A publication*] (ILCA)
del............ Delay (WDMC)
DEL............ Delay
DEL............ Delegacy (ROG)
DEL............ Delegate [*or Delegation*] (ADA)
del............ Delegate (PROS)
del............ Delegation (ADWA)
DEL............ Del Electronics Corp. [*AMEX symbol*] (SPSG)
DEL............ Delete [*Code used in some instances to delete transmitted characters or to exit modes of operation*] [*Communications term*] (DCT)
Del............ Delete (SHCU)
del............ Delete (WDMC)
DEL............ Delete Character [*Keyboard*] (CMD)
Del............ Deletion (QSUL)
del............ Deletion (QSUL)
DEL............ Delft Hydraulics Laboratory (SAUS)
DEL............ Del Global Technologies [*AMEX symbol*] [*Formerly, Del Electronics Corp.*] (SG)
DEL............ Delhi [*India*] [*Airport symbol*] (OAG)
DEL............ Deliberate (ABBR)
del............ delineate (SAUS)
del............ delineated (SAUS)
del............ Delineation (GEOI)
DEL............ Delineation (MSA)
del............ delineator (SAUS)
DEL............ Delineavit [*He (or She) Drew It*] [*Latin*] (ROG)
del............ Delineavit [*He/She Drew It*] (WA)
DEL............ Delinquent
Del............ Delitzsch (BJA)
DEL............ Deliver [*or Delivery*] (KSC)
del............ delivered (SAUS)
DEL............ Dellaterra Resources Ltd. [*Vancouver Stock Exchange symbol*]
DEL............ Del Monte Corp. (SAUO)
Del............ Delphinus [*Constellation*]
DEL............ Deltic Timber [*NYSE symbol*] (SG)
DEL............ Delusion
DEL............ Denver Engineering Laboratories (ACAE)
DEL............ Deorbit, Entry, and Landing [*Aerospace*] (MCD)
DEL............ Diesel-Electric Locomotive (SAUS)
DEL............ Diode Electroluminescente (SAUS)
DEL............ Direct Electrical Linkage
DEL............ Direct Electronic Library (SAUS)
DEL............ Direct Exchange Line [*Telecommunications*]
DEL............ Directly Employed Labour [*British*]
DEL............ Directly Executable Language (MCD)
DEL............ Directly Executed Language (SAUS)
DEL............ Divisional Engineering List (SAUS)
D El........... Doctor of Elements
DEL............ Doctor of English Literature
DEL............ Dollar Error Limit (DICI)
DEL............ Donor Energy Level
DEL............ Duck Egg Lysozyme [*Biochemistry*]
DEI............ Dutch East Indies (SAUS)
Del............ Hymnus in Delum [*of Callimachus*] [*Classical studies*] (OCD)
DELA........... Delactonized Ascorbate [*Biochemistry*]
DELA........... Del Paint Corp. [*NASDAQ symbol*] (COMM)
DEIA........... Dictionary of Electrical Abbreviations, Signs, and Symbols [*A publication*]
DEL AC........ Delayed Action (SAUS)
DELACCT..... Delinquent Account
DelaGP......... Delaware Group Dividend & Income Fund [*Associated Press*] (SAG)
Delane......... Delane's Revision Courts Decisions [*England*] [*A publication*] (DLA)
DelaOts........ Delaware Ostego Corp. [*Associated Press*] (SAG)
DELARF....... Delaware Association of Rehabilitation Facilities (SRA)
DELASEM.... Delegation for Assistance to Jewish Emigrants [*World War II organization*]
De Lat Viv... De Latenter Vivendo [*of Plutarch*] [*Classical studies*] (OCD)
DELAW........ Delaware, OH [*American Association of Railroads railroad junction routing code*]
Delaware Co Reps... Delaware County Reports [*Pennsylvania*] [*A publication*] (DLA)
Delaware J Corp L... Delaware Journal of Corporate Law [*A publication*] (DLA)
Del C Ann.... Delaware Code, Annotated [*A publication*] (ILCA)
delcap......... Delay Capacity (SAUS)
DELCAP....... Delay/Capacity [*Airport terminal*] [*FAA*]
Del Cas....... Delaware Cases [*1792-1830*] [*A publication*] (DLA)
DELCD......... Declared (ROG)
Del Ch......... Delaware Chancery Reports [*A publication*] (DLA)
Delchm........ Delchamps, Inc. [*Associated Press*] (SAG)
DEL CHRG... Delivery Charge (SAUS)
Del Civ Dec... Delaware Chancery Reports [*A publication*] (DLA)
Del Civ Dec... Delhi Civil Decisions [*India*] [*A publication*] (DLA)
DELCL......... Delete Clause (SAUS)
DELCO......... Dayton Engineering Laboratories Co.
Delco.......... Dayton Engineering Laboratories Company (SAUO)
Del Co......... Delaware County Reports [*Pennsylvania*] [*A publication*] (DLA)
Delco.......... Dielectronics (SAUS)
Del Code..... Delaware Code (DLA)
Del Code Ann... Delaware Code, Annotated [*A publication*] (DLA)
Del Co L J (PA)... Delaware County Law Journal [*Pennsylvania*] [*A publication*] (DLA)
DELCOMBI.... Command Delivering Orders Initiate Background Investigation [*Military*] (DNAB)
Del Const..... Delaware Constitution [*A publication*] (DLA)
Del Co (PA)... Delaware County Reports [*Pennsylvania*] [*A publication*] (DLA)
Del Co R...... Delaware County Reports [*Pennsylvania*] [*A publication*] (DLA)
Del Co Reps... Delaware County Reports [*Pennsylvania*] [*A publication*] (DLA)
Del County... Delaware County Reports [*Pennsylvania*] [*A publication*] (DLA)
Del County Rep... Delaware County Reports [*Pennsylvania*] [*A publication*] (DLA)
Del Cr Cas.... Delaware Criminal Cases [*A publication*] (DLA)
Del Ct M...... Delafon on Naval Courts Martial [*A publication*] (DLA)
DELCY......... Delinquency (ABBR)
deld............ Delivered (WDAA)
DELD........... Delivered
DELDT......... Delivery Date (SAUS)
DELDX......... Delaware: Decatur Income Cl.A [*Mutual fund ticker symbol*] (SG)
DELE........... Copyeditors instruction: Delete (SAUS)
Dele............ Deleatur [*Delete*] [*Latin*] (DLA)
DELE........... Delete (ABBR)
dele............ Delete (WDMC)
DELEA......... Digest of Environmental Law and Environmental Assessment [*A publication*] (SAFN)
D El Ed....... Diploma in Elementary Education
DELEG......... Delegate
DELEG......... Delegation (ROG)
Delehanty.... New York Miscellaneous Reports [*A publication*] (DLA)
DelElc......... Del Electronics Corp. [*Associated Press*] (SAG)

Del El Cas ... Delane's Election Revision Cases [*England*] [*A publication*] (DLA)
Del Ent ... Delete Entirely (SAUS)
DELENT ... Delete in Its Entirety (AAG)
DELEX ... Data Elements Lexicon (SAUS)
DELEX ... Destroyer Life Extension [*Canadian Navy program*]
DELFIA ... Dissociation Enhanced Lanthanide Fluoroimmunoassay [*Clinical chemistry*]
DELFIC ... Defense Land Fallout Interpretive Code (MCD)
delfwr ... Delftware (VRA)
DELFX ... Delaware: Delaware Fund Cl.A [*Mutual fund ticker symbol*] (SG)
DELG ... Dealing (ABBR)
DELG ... Delgratia Mining Corp. [*NASDAQ symbol*] (SAG)
delg ... delivering (SAUS)
Del GCL ... Delaware General Corporation Law [*A publication*] (DLA)
DELGF ... Delgratia Mining [*NASDAQ symbol*] (TTSB)
DelGlobal ... Del Global Technologies Corp. [*Associated Press*] (SAG)
Delgn ... Delegation
Delgrt ... Delgratia Mining Corp. [*Associated Press*] (SAG)
DELGRU ... Delaware Group (SAUO)
Delhi Alum Patrika ... Delhi Aluminium Patrika (journ.) (SAUS)
deli ... Delicatessen (ADWA)
DELI ... Delicatessen
DELI ... Desertification Library [*Database*] [*UNEP*] [*United Nations*] (DUND)
DELI ... Jerry's Famous Deli [*NASDAQ symbol*] (TTSB)
DELI ... Jerry's Famous Deli, Inc. [*NASDAQ symbol*] (SAG)
DELIB ... Deliberation (ROG)
DELIC ... Delicatamente [*Delicately*] [*Music*]
delic ... Delicious
DELICAT ... Data Enhancement of Library Catalogues (TELE)
DELICAT ... Delicatamente [*Delicately*] [*Music*] (ROG)
DELICATISS ... Delicatissimo [*Very Delicately*] [*Music*] (ROG)
DELILAH ... Duck Experiment on Low-Frequency and Incident-Band Longshore and Across-Shore Hydrodynamics [*Coastal Engineering Research Center*]
DELIMCO ... German-Liberian Mining Company (SAUO)
DELIMITER ... Definite Limit Evaluator (SAUS)
DELIMITER ... Definitive Limit Evaluator (SAUS)
delin ... delineating (SAUS)
delin ... delineative (SAUS)
delin ... delineator (SAUS)
delin ... delineatrix (SAUS)
DELIN ... Delineavit [*He (or She) Drew It*] [*Latin*] (WGA)
delin ... delinquencies (SAUS)
DELIN ... Delinquency (ABBR)
delin ... delinquently (SAUS)
delin ... delinquents (SAUS)
DELIND ... Delineated (ROG)
DELINQ ... Delinquent (MUGU)
DELINUS ... Authorized to Delay [*Number of Days*], Any Portion of Which May Be Taken inCONUS [*Navy*]
DELIQ ... Deliquescence (SAUS)
DELIQ ... Deliquescent
De L Isls ... De Long Islands (SAUS)
DELIX ... Delaware: Tax Free DMC Pa Fund Cl.A [*Mutual fund ticker symbol*] (SG)
DELJC ... Delta Junction, OH [*American Association of Railroads railroad junction routing code*]
DEL key ... Delete Key (CDE)
DELL ... Dell Computer Corp. [*NASDAQ symbol*] (NQ)
Dell ... Dell Publishing Co. (SAUO)
DelLabs ... Del Laboratories, Inc. [*Associated Press*] (SAG)
Del Law ... Delaware Lawyer [*A publication*] (DLA)
Del Laws ... Laws of Delaware [*A publication*] (DLA)
DellCpt ... Dell Computer Corp. [*Associated Press*] (SAG)
DEL LN ... Delay Line (SAUS)
DEL LN MEM ... Delay Line Memory (SAUS)
DELM ... Department of Environment & Land Management, Tasmania (SAUS)
DELM ... Department of the Environment and Land Management (SAUO)
DELMAR ... Data Element Management Accounting and Reporting
DELMARVA ... Delaware, Maryland, Virginia [*Peninsula*]
DELMES ... Delay Message (SAUS)
DelmPL ... Delmarva Power & Light Co. [*Associated Press*] (SAG)
Delmrv ... Delmarva Power Financing I [*Associated Press*] (SAG)
Del Mus Nat Hist ... Delaware Museum of Natural History (SAUS)
DelNG ... Delaware National Guard (SAUO)
DELNI ... Digital Ethernet Local Network Interface (SAUS)
DELNI ... Digital Ethernet Local Network Interconnect (VERA)
DELNQY ... Delinquency
DELO ... Delicato [*Delicately*] [*Music*] (ROG)
D Elo ... Doctor of Elocution
D-E Loco Repm ... Diesel-Electric Locomotive Repairman (SAUS)
De Lolme Eng Const ... De Lolme on the English Constitution [*A publication*] (DLA)
Del Order ... Delegation Order (DLA)
DELOS ... Division for Experimentation and Laboratory-Oriented Studies (SAUS)
DELP ... Department of Environment, Lands, and Planning [*Australian Capital Territory*]
DELPARTURE ... Authorized to Delay [*Number of Days*], Any Portion of Which May Be Taken Prior to or after Departure [*Navy*]
DelpFin ... Delphi Financial Group, Inc. [*Associated Press*] (SAG)
DELPH ... Delphi, IN [*American Association of Railroads railroad junction routing code*]
Delph ... Delphinus [*Constellation*]
DelphCt ... Delphos Citizens Bancorp, Inc. [*Associated Press*] (SAG)
DELPHO ... Deliver by Telephone [*Message handling*]
DelpInf ... Delphi Information Systems [*Associated Press*] (SAG)
Del PM Ex ... Delafield on Post Mortem Examinations [*A publication*] (DLA)
DELPRO ... Delegated Procurement System [*Science*]
DELQ ... Delinquent
DELQA ... Digital Ethernet Lowpower Q-Bus Network Adapter [*Computer science*] (VERA)
DELR ... Dealer (ABBR)
DELR ... Delaware River Basin (SAUS)
DELR ... Deliver (ROG)
DELRAC ... DECCA Long-Range Area Coverage (MCD)
Del Reg of Regs ... Delaware Register of Regulations [*A publication*] (DLA)
DELREP ... Authorized to Delay [*Number of Days*], in Reporting [*Navy*]
DELREPANY ... Authorized to Delay [*Number of Days*], in Reporting, Any Portion of Which May Be Taken Prior to or after Reporting at Temporary Duty Station [*Navy*]
DELREPARUS ... Authorized to Delay [*Number of Days*], Any Portion of Which May Be Taken Prior to or after Arrival in United States [*Navy*]
DELREPGRAD ... Authorized to Delay [*Number of Days*], in Reporting, to Count as GraduationLeave [*Navy*]
DELREPVAN ... Authorized to Delay [*Number of Days*], in Reporting, Keep New Station Advised Address [*Navy*]
DELRIBACO ... Delaware River Basin Commission [*Successor to INCODEL*]
Delrina ... Delrina Corp. [*Associated Press*] (SAG)
DELRIVEPOE ... Delay in Arriving at Port of Embarkation [*Navy*]
dels ... deliveries (SAUS)
DELS ... Diagnostics through Error and Logic Simulation (VLIE)
DELS ... Direct Electrical Linkage System (MCD)
DELSA ... Doppler Electrophoretic Light Scanning Analyzer
DELSI ... Delta Modulation Speech Interpretation (SAUS)
DELSN ... Delson, PQ [*American Association of Railroads railroad junction routing code*]
DELSTR ... Delete String (VLIE)
DELT ... Deck Edge Light (AAG)
DELT ... Delete (AAG)
Delt ... Deletion (SAUS)
delt ... Delineator (GEOI)
DELT ... Delineavit [*He (or She) Drew It*] [*Latin*]
DELT ... Delta Galil Industries, Ltd. [*NASDAQ symbol*] (NASQ)
DELT ... Dynamic Environmental Laboratory Test
DELTA ... Decision Box, Event Box, Logic Box, Time Arrow, and Activity Box (PDAA)
DELTA ... Dedication and Everlasting Love to Animals [*An association*]
DELTA ... DELTA Air Lines, Inc. (SAUO)
DELTA ... Delta, MO [*American Association of Railroads railroad junction routing code*]
DELTA ... Descriptive Language for Taxonomy (SAUO)
DELTA ... Detailed Labor and Time Analysis [*PERT*]
DELTA ... Determination Effective Levels of Task Automation [*Computer science*]
DELTA ... Developing European Learning through Technological Advance [*EC*] (ECED)
DELTA ... Development of European Learning through Technological Advance [*British*]
DELTA ... Development of European Learning through Technological Advance Exploratory Action (SAUO)
DELTA ... Development of Learning and Teaching in the Arts (AIE)
DELTA ... Development of Learning through Technological Advance [*European Community*] (MHDB)
DELTA ... Differential Electronically-Locking Test Accessory
DELTA ... Diploma in English Language Teaching for Adults
DELTA ... Distributed Electronic Library with Terminal Assistance (SAUS)
DELTA ... Distributed Electronic Test and Analysis
DeltaA ... Delta Air Lines, Inc. [*Associated Press*] (SAG)
DeltaAir ... Delta Air Lines, Inc. [*Associated Press*] (SAG)
DELTABANK ... Drug Effects on Laboratory Tests: Attention [*Worldwide Medical Information Ltd.*] [*Database*]
Delta M ... Delta Modulation (SAUS)
Delta St U ... Delta State University (GAGS)
DeltaW ... Delta Woodside Industries, Inc. [*Associated Press*] (SAG)
Del Term R ... Delaware Term Reports [*A publication*] (DLA)
DELTIC ... Delay Line Time Compression
DELTIC Correlator ... Delay Line Time Compressor Correlator (SAUS)
DeltNG ... Delta Natural Gas Co. [*Associated Press*] (SAG)
DeltPine ... Delta & Pine Land Co. [*Associated Press*] (SAG)
DeltPnt ... DeltaPoint, Inc. [*Associated Press*] (SAG)
DELTRAC ... Delay Line Transmission Converter (SAUS)
delts ... Deltoid Muscles (ADWA)
DELTX ... Delaware: Trend Fund Cl.A [*Mutual fund ticker symbol*] (SG)
DELU ... Delusion (ABBR)
DELUA ... Digital Ethernet Lowpower Unibus Network Adapter [*Computer science*] (VERA)
DELUG ... Deutsche Linux User Group (VERA)
Del Univ ... University of Delaware (SAUO)
DELURN ... Delay in Returning to Duty Station [*Military*] (DNAB)
Deluxe ... Deluxe Corp. [*Associated Press*] (SAG)
DELV ... Deliver (ADA)
Delv ... Delivered (DLA)
DEL V ... Deluge Valve (DAC)
DELV'D ... Delivered
DELVRNC ... Deliverance
DELWD ... Dellwood, PA [*American Association of Railroads railroad junction routing code*]
DELWU ... Delegate [*or Delegation*] to Western Union [*NATO*] (NATG)
DELX ... Delcora [*Federal Railroad Administration identification code*]
DELX ... De Luxe Transport [*Private rail car owner code*]
DELXO ... Delivery Ex Option [*Shares*]

dely .... Delivery (EBF)
DELY .... Delivery
Dely .... Delyse [*Record label*] [*Great Britain*]
Dely&Redely... Delivery and Redelivery (SAUS)
DEM .... Data Energy Modernization (SAUS)
DEM .... Data Entry Manager (SAUS)
DEM .... Data Entry Mode (MCD)
DEM .... Decoy Ejection Mechanism
Dem .... De Demosthene [*of Dionysius Halicarnassensis*] [*Classical studies*] (OCD)
DEM .... Delta Modulation [*Telecommunications*] (TEL)
DEM .... Demagogue (ROG)
Dem .... Dema'i (BJA)
Dem .... Demand (EBF)
dem .... Demand (ELAL)
DEM .... Demand
Dem .... Demarest's New York Surrogate's Court Reports [*A publication*] (DLA)
DEM .... Dembidollo [*Ethiopia*] [*Airport symbol*] (OAG)
De M .... De Mello's Extradition Cases [*1877-1913*] [*Malaya*] [*A publication*] (DLA)
dem .... dementia (SAUS)
DEM .... Demerol [*Medicine*] (DMAA)
Dem .... Demerol [*Meperidine hydrochloride*] [*Analgesic compound*] [*Trademark*]
DEM .... Demijohn [*Freight*]
DEM .... Democrat [*or Democratic*] (EY)
Dem .... Democrat (WDAA)
Dem .... Democratic (NTIO)
DEM .... Democratic
Dem .... Democratic Party (SAUO)
DEM .... Democritus Greek Nuclear Center, near Athens Greece (SAUS)
dem .... demodulate (SAUS)
DEM .... Demodulation Electronic Modules (SAUS)
dem .... Demodulator (ADWA)
DEM .... Demodulator [*Telecommunications*] (KSC)
DEM .... Demolish [*Technical drawings*]
DEM .... Demonstration
DEM .... Demonstration Account [*For messages to and from UTLAS*]
Dem .... Demonstrative (BJA)
dem .... Demonstrative (NTIO)
Dem .... Demonstrator (CMD)
DeM .... DeMorgans Theorems [*Rules of replacement*] [*Logic*]
Dem .... Demosthenes [*Greek orator, 384-322BC*] [*Classical studies*] (OCD)
DEM .... Demote (AABC)
dem .... demotion (SAUS)
DEM .... Demulator (SAUS)
DEM .... Demulcent [*Softening, Lubricating*] [*Pharmacy*] (ROG)
DEM .... Demur (ABBR)
dem .... Demurrage (ADWA)
Dem .... Demurrage (EBF)
DEM .... Demurrage [*Shipping*]
DEM .... Demy [*Half*] [*Size of paper*]
DEM .... Department Engineering Materials (SAUS)
DEM .... Department of Emergency Management (SAUS)
DEM .... Department of Emergency Medicine (MEDA)
DEM .... Department of Environmental Management (SAUS)
DEM .... Detective, Enigma, and Mystery [*Publisher*] [*Former USSR*] (ECON)
DeM .... Deus Misereatur [*67th Psalm*] [*Music*]
DEM .... Development Engineering Memorandum (SAUS)
DEM .... Diethyl Maleate [*Biochemistry*]
DEM .... Diethyl Malonate [*Organic chemistry*]
DEM .... Diethylmandelamide [*Organic chemistry*]
dem .... differential element movement (SAUS)
DEM .... Digital Echo Modulation (VLIE)
DEM .... Digital Electronic Modules (SAUS)
DEM .... Digital Elevation Map (SAUS)
DEM .... Digital Elevation Matrix (GEOI)
DEM .... Digital Elevation Model [*For study of topography*]
D Em .... Digit Emitter (SAUS)
DEM .... Digitized Elevation Models (SAUS)
DEM .... Directional Emittance Measurement
DEM .... Director of Extramural Department (SAUO)
DEM .... Distribution, Excretion, and Metabolism [*Environmental chemistry*]
DEM .... Division of Emergency Management (DEMM)
DEM .... Division of Energy and Minerals (SAUO)
DEM .... Dynamic Effect Model (SAUS)
DEM .... Dynode Electron Multiplier (SAUS)
DEM .... Dysplasia Epiphysalis Multiplex [*Medicine*] (MELL)
DEM .... ERL-Athens Dynamic Estuary Model (SAUS)
dem .... Demerara (ODA)
dem .... Democracy (ODA)
DEMA .... Danish Emergency Management Agency (SAUO)
DEMA .... Data Entry Management Association (EA)
DEMA .... Diesel Engine Manufacturers Association [*Defunct*] (EA)
DEMA .... Distributed Emission Magnetron Amplifier (MSA)
DEMA .... Diving Equipment Manufacturers Association (EA)
DEMAC .... Deck and Engine Mechanic (SAUS)
DEMAC .... Diesel Engine Monitoring and Control [*ASMAP Electronics Ltd.*] [*Software package*] (NCC)
demacs .... Emacs for DOS (SAUS)
Dem Adj ...... Demonstrative Adjective (SAUS)
DEM-AMPL... Demodulator-Amplifier (SAUS)
DEMAND ...... Digitalized Electronics MARC [*Machine-Readable Cataloging*] and Non-MARC Display [*Machine-Readable Cataloging*] [*Library of Congress*]
DEMAND ...... Digitized Electronics Marc and NonMarc Display (SAUS)
DEMANDS .... Depicts Each Months Averages and New Demand (SAUS)
DEMAR .... Data Element Management Accounting and Reporting (MCD)
DEMARC ...... Demarcation (COE)
DEMARC ...... Distributed Enterprise Management Architecture (SAUS)
Demarest ..... Demarest's New York Surrogate's Court Reports [*A publication*] (DLA)
DEMAT .... Department of Educational Media and Technology (SAUS)
DEMATRON... Distributed Emission Magnetron Amplifier
Demba .... Demarara bauxite (SAUS)
DEMBA .... Demarara Bauxite Company (SAUO)
DEMBOMB ... Demolition Bomb
DEMC .... Defense Electronics Management Center (DNAB)
Dem Cap ..... Democratic Capitalism (SAUS)
DEMCE .... Design, Engineering, Manufacturing Collaborative Environment [*Army*]
DEMCO .... DEMCO Library Supplies, Inc. (SAUO)
DEMD .... Demised (ROG)
DEMD .... Digital Engine Monitor Display (PDAA)
dem/des ...... demurrage/despach (SAUS)
DE/ME .... Decoding Memory (SAUS)
DEME .... Director of Electrical and Mechanical Engineering [*Military*] [*British*]
DEMED .... Depletion Etch Method (SAUS)
DE-ME-DRIVE... Decoding Memory Drive [*Computer science*] (MDG)
DEMERIL ..... Demerol [*Trademark of Winthrop Pharmaceuticals*] [*Analgesic compound*] (DAVI)
DEMETER .... deuterium moderated materials testing reactor (SAUS)
DEMETER .... Digital Electronic Mapping of European Territory
Demetr .... Demetrius [*of Plutarch*] [*Classical studies*] (OCD)
DEMF .... Display Exception Monitoring Facility (VLIE)
DEM-G .... Digital Elevation Model-Graphic (GEOI)
DEMI .... Deliverable, Executable Machine Instructions
DEMI .... DEM Inc. [*NASDAQ symbol*] (TTSB)
demij .... demijohn (SAUS)
DEMIL .... Demilitarize (AABC)
demimond ... demimondaine (SAUS)
demimond ... demimonde (SAUS)
demirep ...... demireputation (SAUS)
DEMIS .... Defense Environmental Management Information System [*Navy*]
DEMIST .... Design Methodology Incorporating Self Test (SAUS)
DEMIZ .... DEW [*Distant Early Warning*] East Military Identification Zone
DEMJ .... Demijohn [*Freight*] (WGA)
DEML .... Detached Enlisted Men's List [*Army*]
DEM/LAB ..... Demographics Laboratory [*Information service or system*] (IID)
DEML(CIC).... Enlisted Men on Duty with the Counter Intelligence Corps [*Army*]
DEML(NG) ... Enlisted Men on Duty with the National Guard [*Army*]
DEML(OR) ... Enlisted Men on Duty with the Organized Reserves [*Army*]
DEML(ROTC)... Enlisted Men on Duty with the Reserve Officers' Training Corps [*Army*]
DEMLTN ...... Demolition
DEMM .... Division of Educational Media Management (SAUS)
DEMMA .... Direct Electronic Mail Marketing Association
DEMNG .... Deming, NM [*American Association of Railroads railroad junction routing code*]
DemNPN ...... Democratic Non-Party Nationalist Party [*British*]
DEMNS .... Distributed Explosive Mine Neutralization System (DOMA)
Dem (NY) .... Demarest's New York Surrogate's Court Reports [*A publication*] (DLA)
Demo .... Demolition [*Construction term*] (MIST)
DEMO .... Demolition
demo .... Demonstration (ADWA)
DEMO .... Demonstration (WDAA)
DEMO .... Demonstrator (KSC)
Demob .... Demobilization (SAUS)
DEMOB .... Demobilize (AABC)
demob .... Demobilize (ADWA)
DEMOBED .... Demobilized (ABBR)
DEMOC .... Democracy (ABBR)
Democ .... Democratic (DIAR)
democ .... democratization (SAUS)
democ .... democratize (SAUS)
democ .... democratizer (SAUS)
DEMOCATE... Project to provide end users with access to copyright materials in electronic form run by a consortium of Tilburg university (SAUO)
Democr .... Democritus [*Fifth century BC*] [*Classical studies*] (OCD)
DEMOD .... Deletion Etch Method (SAUS)
DEMOD .... Demodulate (SAUS)
DEMOD .... Demodulation (SAUS)
DEMOD .... Demodulator [*Telecommunications*] (AAG)
DEMOD .... Depletion Etch Method (IAA)
DEMOD .... Deployment Model [*Army*] (AABC)
Demog .... Demography (DIAR)
DEMOG .... Demography
Demogr .... Demographer (SAUS)
DEMOL .... Demolition
Demol .... Demolombe's Code Napoleon [*A publication*] (DLA)
Demol C N... Demolombe's Code Napoleon [*A publication*] (DLA)
DEMON .... Decision Mapping via Optimum Go-No Networks
DEMON .... Decision Mapping via Optimum Network (SAUS)
DEMON .... Demodulated Noise (CAAL)
Demon .... Demonax [*of Lucian*] [*Classical studies*] (OCD)
DEMON .... Demonology (ABBR)

demon .... Demonstrative (ADWA)
DEMON .... Demonstrative
DEMON .... Digital Electric Monitor
DEMON .... Diminishing Error Method for Optimization of Networks (SAUS)
DEMON .... Diminishing Error Method of Optimization for Networks [*Computer science*] (RDA)
demon .... Demonstrate (ODA)
De Monog .... De Monogamia [*of Tertullian*] [*Classical studies*] (OCD)
DEMONOL .... Demonologic (ABBR)
DEMONS ...... Demonstrative (ROG)
DEMONST .... Demonstrator
demonstr ..... Demonstrative (ADWA)
DEMONSTR ... Demonstrative (Pronoun) [*Linguistics*]
DEMOP .... Demopolis, AL [*American Association of Railroads railroad junction routing code*]
DEMOS .... Democratic Opposition of Slovenia [*Political party*] (EY)
Demos .... Democrats (SAUS)
demos .... Demographics [*The external characteristics of a population*] (WDMC)
DEMOS .... Demonstrations (ACAE)
DEMOS .... Dendenkosha Multi-access Online System (SAUS)
DEMOS .... Directorate of Estate Management Overseas (SAUO)
DemoWad .... Wadden Sea Project (SAUS)
DEMP .... Democratic Party [*Slang*]
DEM-P .... Digital Elevation Model-Planar (GEOI)
DEMP .... Dispersed Electro-Magnetic Pulse (PDAA)
DEMP .... Drug Emporium [*NASDAQ symbol*] (TTSB)
DEMP .... Drug Emporium, Inc. [*NASDAQ symbol*] (NQ)
DEMPAQ ...... Developing and Evaluating Methods to Promote Ambulatory Care Quality (IDYL)
DEMPR .... Digital Ethernet Multi-Port Repeater [*Computer science*] (VERA)
Dem Pro ...... Demonstrative Pronoun (SAUS)
DEMPS .... Dispersed Electromagnetic Pulse Simulator (ACAE)
DEMPT .... Diethylmethylphosphorothionate (SAUS)
DEMR .... Department of Energy, Mines, and Resources [*Canada*]
DEMR .... Division of Energy and Mineral Resources (SAUO)
DEMRO .... DEMRO Products, Inc. (SAUO)
DEMS .... Defense and Electronics Management System (TIMI)
DEMS .... Defensively-Equipped Merchant Ship
Dems .... Democrats (SAUO)
DEMS .... Denomination System (SAUS)
DEMS .... Development Engineering Management System [*Air Force*]
DEMS .... Differential Electrochemistry/Mass Spectrometry
DEMS .... Digital Electronic Message Service (CIST)
DEMS .... Digital Electronic Message Systems
DEMS .... Digital Error Monitoring Subsystem (SAUS)
DEMS .... Digital Error Monitoring System (MCD)
DEMS .... Diver Equivalent Manipulator System [*General Electric*]
DEMS .... Dormant Equipping of Merchant Ships [*Organization*] (MCD)
DEMS .... Dynamic Effectiveness Model Study (SAUS)
DEMS .... Dynamics Environment Measurement System (SAUS)
DEMS Org .... Defensively Equipped Merchant Ships Organization (SAUO)
DEMSS .... Defensively-Equipped Merchant Ship School
DEMSTAT .... Deployment/Employment/Mobilization Status System [*MTMC*] (TAG)
Dem Surr ..... Demarest's New York Surrogate's Court Reports [*A publication*] (DLA)
DEMTR .... Demmler Transfer, PA [*American Association of Railroads railroad junction routing code*]
DEMU .... Diesel Electric Multiple Unit (ADA)
De Mul Vir ... De Mulierum Virtutibus [*of Plutarch*] [*Classical studies*] (OCD)
DEMUR .... Demurrer (ROG)
DEMUR .... Double Electron Muon Resonance (MCD)
demur .... Demurrage (ODA)
De Mus .... De Musica [*of Plutarch*] [*Classical studies*] (OCD)
DEMUX .... Demultiplex (SAUS)
DEMUX .... Demultiplexer [*Computer science*]
DEMUX .... Demultiplexing (SAUS)
DEMVAL ...... Demonstration and Evaluation (SAUS)
DEM/VAL ..... Demonstration/Validation (MCD)
DEM/VAL ..... Demonstration/Validation Phase (AAGC)
DEMVFY ...... Digital Elevation Model Verify (GEOI)
DEMVPI ...... Department of Engineering Mechanics, Virginia Polytechnic Institute (SAUO)
DEMX .... Demeter [*Private rail car owner code*]
DEMYC .... Democrat Youth Community of Europe [*Formerly, Conservative and Christian Democrat Youth Community of Europe*] (EA)
DEN .... Data Element Number (MCD)
DEN .... DenAmerica Corp. [*AMEX symbol*] [*Formerly, American Family Restaurants*] (SG)
DEN .... Denbighshire [*County in Wales*] (ROG)
DEN .... Dengue [*Virus*]
den .... Denied (AAGC)
Den .... Denied [*Legal term*] (DLA)
DEN .... Denied [*Motor vehicle violation status code used in state of Arkansas*] (MVRD)
den .... Denier [*Later, tex*]
Den .... Denio's New York Reports [*A publication*] (DLA)
Den .... Denison and Pearce's English Crown Cases Reserved [*169 English Reprint*] [*1844-52*] [*A publication*] (DLA)
DEN .... Denison Mines Ltd. [*Toronto Stock Exchange symbol*] [*Vancouver Stock Exchange symbol*]
DEN .... Denison, TX [*American Association of Railroads railroad junction routing code*]
Den .... Denis' Reports [*32-46 Louisiana*] [*A publication*] (DLA)
Den .... Denmark (VRA)
DEN .... Denmark
den .... Denotation (ADWA)
DEN .... Denote (MSA)
DEN .... Denouement (ROG)
DEN .... Density
DEN .... Dental (AABC)
DEN .... Dentist (WDAA)
DEN .... Denver [*Colorado*] [*Seismograph station code, US Geological Survey*] (SEIS)
DEN .... Denver [*Colorado*] [*Airport symbol*]
Den .... Denver Broncos [*National Football League*] [*1960-present*] (NFLA)
DEn .... Department of Energy [*British*]
DEN .... Design engineers notebook (SAUS)
DEN .... Device Evaluation Network [*FDA*] [*Information service or system*]
DEN .... Device Experience Network (DB)
DEN .... Diethylnitrosamine [*Also, DENA*] [*Carcinogen*]
DE(N) .... Director of Engineering (Naval) [*British military*] (DMA)
DEN .... Directory Enabled Network [*Computer science*] (DCDG)
DEN .... Directory-Enabled Networks (GART)
DEN .... Distribution Element Name (SAUS)
DEN .... District Enrolled Nurse [*British*]
D En .... Doctor of English
DEN .... Document Enabled Networking [*Computer science*]
DEN .... Double Edge Notched (SAUS)
DEN .... Dow Epoxy Novolac
DeN .... Newark Free Library, Newark, DE [*Library symbol*] [*Library of Congress*] (LCLS)
DEN .... Stapleton International Airport [*FAA*] (TAG)
DENA .... Delrina Corp. [*NASDAQ symbol*] (SAG)
DENA .... Diethylnitrosamine [*Also, DEN*] [*Carcinogen*]
DENALT .... Density Altitude [*Computer*]
DenAmer ..... DenAmerica Corp. [*Associated Press*] (SAG)
Den & P ...... Denison and Pearce's English Crown Cases [*1844-52*] [*A publication*] (DLA)
Den & PCC ... Denison and Pearce's English Crown Cases [*1844-52*] [*A publication*] (DLA)
Den & Sc Pr ... Denison and Scott's House of Lords Appeal Practice [*A publication*] (DLA)
Den App ...... Denying Appeal (DLA)
DENAS .... Daily European Naval Activity Summary (MCD)
denat .... Denatured [*Medicine*] (EDAA)
DENAT .... Denatured
DENB .... Denbighshire [*County in Wales*]
Den BA Rec ... Denver Bar Association. Record [*A publication*] (DLA)
DENBIGHS ... Denbighshire [*County in Wales*]
DENBN .... Dental Battalion (DNAB)
Denbs .... Denbighshire (DIAR)
DENBS .... Denbighshire [*County in Wales*]
DENC .... Divergent Exhaust Nozzle Control (MCD)
Den C C ...... Denison's English Crown Cases [*1844-52*] [*A publication*] (DLA)
DeNcD .... Delaware State Hospital, New Castle, DE [*Library symbol*] [*Library of Congress*] (LCLS)
DENCO .... Dental Co. [*Marine Corps*]
DEND .... Dendrology (ABBR)
DEND .... Dividend (SAUS)
D en D .... Docteur en Droit [*Doctor of Law*] [*French*]
DeND .... E. I. Du Pont de Nemours & Co., Stine Laboratory, Newark, DE [*Library symbol*] [*Library of Congress*] (LCLS)
DENDRAL .... Dendritic Algorithm [*Organic molecules*]
DENDRO ...... Dendrometer (ABBR)
DENDROL .... Dendrology (ABBR)
Dendrte .... Dendrite International, Inc. [*Associated Press*] (SAG)
Den ED .... Dental Equipment Depot (SAUO)
DENet .... [*The*] Danish Ethernet Network [*Computer science*] (TNIG)
DENG .... Diesel Engine (SAUS)
DEng .... Doctor of Engineering (ASC)
DEngC .... Directorate of Engineering Construction (SAUO)
DEngg .... Doctor of Engineering
D Eng P .... Doctor of Engineering Physics
D Eng Sc ..... Doctor of Engineering Science
DENH .... Denison International plc [*NASDAQ symbol*] (NASQ)
DENI .... Damage Equivalent of Normally Incident (IAA)
DENI .... Department of Education of Northern Ireland [*British*]
DENIC .... Deutsches Network Information Center (VERA)
DENIM .... Detector Enhancement, Integration and Multiplexing (ACAE)
DENIM .... Directory-Enabled Network Infrastructure Model [*Computer science*] (HODG)
Denio .... Denio's New York Supreme Court Reports [*1845-48*] [*A publication*] (DLA)
Denio R .... Denio's New York Reports [*A publication*] (DLA)
DENIS .... Deep Near-Infrared Survey
Denis .... Denis' Reports [*32-46 Louisiana*] [*A publication*] (DLA)
DENIS .... Display Entry for INES (SAUS)
DENISE .... Dense Negative Ion-Beam Surface Experiment (SAUS)
Denison Cr Cas ... Denison's English Crown Cases [*1844-52*] [*A publication*] (DLA)
DENIX .... Defense Environmental Network and Information Exchange (BCP)
DENK .... Dual Employed, No Kids [*Lifestyle classification*]
Den L N .... Denver Legal News [*A publication*] (DLA)
DENM .... Denmark
DENMARK .... Demarcation [*Communications term*] (DCT)
DenMedVet ... Docteur en Medicine Veterinaire [*Doctor of Veterinary Medicine*] [*French*] (ASC)
DENMK .... Denmark, SC [*American Association of Railroads railroad junction routing code*]
DENN .... Denomination (ROG)
Denny .... Denis (SAUS)

denom .... denominate (SAUS)
Denom .... Denomination (EBF)
denom .... Denomination (SHCU)
DENOM .... Denomination
denom .... Denominative [*or Denominator*] (BJA)
denom .... denominator (SAUS)
DENOT .... Denotation (ABBR)
Denot .... Denotement (SAUS)
de novo .... Arising Anew [*Latin*] (EES)
DENPA .... Density Phenomena [*Japan*]
DENPAY .... Dental Pay
DENPRE .... Density Probe (MUGU)
DENR .... Denominator (ROG)
DENR .... Department of Energy and Natural Resources
Den Rearg ... Denying Reargument [*Legal term*] (DLA)
Den Reh ...... Denying Rehearing [*Legal term*] (DLA)
DENRF .... Denbury Resources [*NASDAQ symbol*] (TTSB)
DENS .... Density (AFM)
dens .... Density (IDOE)
Dens .... Denslow's Notes to Second Edition [*1-3 Michigan*] [*A publication*] (DLA)
DENS .... Diffuse Elastic Neutron Scattering (MCD)
DENS .... Directory and Equipment Number Status System (MCD)
DENSP .... Deanship (ABBR)
DENT .... Dental (ROG)
dent .... Dental (SHCU)
DENT .... Dental Civic Action Program (SAUO)
DENT .... Dental Exposure Normalization Technique [*Medicine*] (DMAA)
dent .... Dentistry (ADWA)
DENT .... Dentistry
DENT .... Dentition [*Medicine*]
DENT .... Dentur [*Give*] [*Pharmacy*]
DENT .... Denture (ABBR)
DENT .... Directions for Education in Nursing Via Teaching (SAUS)
DENT .... Directions for Education in Nursing via Technology
D Ent .... Doctor of Ent"mology (SAUS)
D Ent .... Doctor of Entomology
Dent .... JM Dent & Sons Ltd (SAUS)
DENTAC .... Dental Accounting (SAUS)
DENTAC .... Dental Activity (AABC)
DENTAL .... Dental Service Report (SAUS)
DENTALPROJ... Dental Research Projects (DMAA)
Dent C .... Dental Corps (SAUO)
DENTCAP ...... Dental Civic Action Program [*Vietnam*]
Dent Clin N Amer... Dental Clinics of North America (journ.) (SAUS)
DENTCORPS... Dental Corps [*Air Force*]
Dent Hyg ..... Dental Hygienist (SAUS)
Denticare ..... Dental Care (SAUS)
DENTL .... Dental
DENTN .... Denton, TX [*American Association of Railroads railroad junction routing code*]
DENTR .... Denture
Dent Res ..... Dental Corps Reserve (SAUO)
DENTS .... Director of Naval Education and Training Support
Dentsply ...... Dentsply International [*Associated Press*] (SAG)
Dentsply ...... Dentsply International, Inc. (SAUO)
Dent Surv .... Dental Survey (journ.) (SAUS)
DENT TAL DOS... Dentur Tales Doses [*Give in Such Doses*] [*Pharmacy*]
DE-NUM .... Data Element Dictionary Number
Den Univ ..... Denison University (SAUO)
DENV .... Denver [*Colorado*] (ROG)
D Env .... Doctor of Environment (PGP)
DEnvDes ...... Doctor of Environmental Design (GAGS)
Denver J Int L & Policy... Denver Journal of International Law and Policy [*A publication*] (DLA)
Denver J Int'l L... Denver Journal of International Law [*A publication*] (DLA)
Denver L N... Denver Legal News [*A publication*] (DLA)
DeNvo .... DeNovo [*Associated Press*] (SAG)
DENVR .... Denver, CO [*American Association of Railroads railroad junction routing code*]
Denv Univ .... Denver University (SAUO)
DENYG .... Denying
DEO .... Data Entry Operator (SAUS)
DEO .... Deck Edge Outlet [*Navy*]
Deo .... De Deo [*Philo*] (BJA)
DEO .... Deobstruent [*Removing Obstructions*] [*Pharmacy*] (ROG)
DEO .... Department of Executive Officer
DEO .... Diageo Plc ADS [*NYSE symbol*] [*Formerly, Grand Metropolitan ADS*] (SG)
DEO .... Diesel Engine Oil
DEO .... Digital End Office [*Telecommunications*]
DEO .... Directed Energy Office (ACAE)
DEO .... Director of Emergency Operations (COE)
DEO .... District Engineering Office (SAUS)
DEO .... District Engineer Officer [*Army*]
DEO .... District Engineers Office (SAUS)
DEO .... Divisional Education Officer [*British*]
DEO .... Divisional Entertainments Officer [*British*]
DEO .... Divisional Executive Officer [*British*]
DEO .... Doped Erbium Oxide
DEO .... Duke of Edinburgh's Own [*Military unit*] [*British*]
DEOA .... Department of Education Organization Act (GFGA)
DEOA .... Department of Energy Organization Act of 1977 (COE)
DEO(A) .... Dependents' Education Office (Atlantic) (DNAB)
DEOB .... Dental Explanation of Benefits [*Army*]
DEOC .... District Emergency Operations Controller [*Australia*]
DEOD .... Deodorant (ABBR)
DEODS .... Defence Explosive Ordnance Disposal School (SAUO)
DEODZ .... Deodorize (ABBR)
DEODZD .... Deodorized (ABBR)
DEODZG .... Deodorizing (ABBR)
DEODZN .... Deodorization (ABBR)
DEODZR .... Deodorizer (ABBR)
DEOMI .... Defense Equal Opportunity Management Institute
DEO(P) .... Dependents' Education Office (Pacific) (DNAB)
De Or .... De Oratore [*of Cicero*] [*Classical studies*] (OCD)
De Orat .... Cicero's De Oratore [*A publication*] (DLA)
DEORB .... Deorbit (NASA)
DEOS .... Data Exchange Optimization Study [*DoD*] (MCD)
DEOS .... Director of Equipment and Ordnance Stores [*British military*] (DMA)
DEOT .... Disconnect, End of Transmission
DE/OVD .... Digitally Encoded Optical Video Disc (SAUS)
DE/OVD .... Digitally Encoded Optical Video Disk (SAUS)
DEOVR .... Duke of Edinburgh's Own Volunteer Rifles [*Military unit*] [*British*]
DEOWRB ...... Dictionaries, Encyclopedias, and Other Word-Related Books [*A publication*]
DEP .... Data Element Profile (SAUS)
DEP .... Data Entry Panel (MCD)
DEP .... Data Exchange Program
DEP .... Decorated End-Papers [*Publishing*]
DEP .... Dedicated Experiment Processor [*Spacelab mission*]
DEP .... Deep External Pudendal Artery [*Anatomy*]
DEP .... Defence and Ex-Services Party of Australia [*Political party*]
DEP .... Defended Post (SAUS)
DEP .... Defense Electronic Products
DEP .... Defense Enterprise Program [*DoD*]
DEP .... Defense Estimate for Production (MCD)
DEP .... Deflection Error Probable [*Military*] (AFM)
DEP .... Degraduation Effects Program
DEP .... Delayed Enlistment [*or Entry*] Program [*Military*] (AFM)
DEP .... Delayed Entry Program (SAUS)
DEP .... Dense Electronic Population
Dep .... Density Dependent [*Biology*]
DEP .... Depart (AFM)
dep .... Department [*Also dept or dpt*] (WDMC)
DEP .... Department
DEP .... Department of Employment and Production (SAUS)
DEP .... Department of Employment and Productivity [*Later, DE*] [*British*]
DEP .... Department of Environmental Protection (AUEG)
DEP .... Department of Export Promotion (SAUS)
DEP .... Departure (GOBB)
dep .... Departure (NTIO)
DEP .... Departure Message [*Aviation code*]
DEP .... DEP Corp. [*Associated Press*] (SAG)
DEP .... Dependencies (ROG)
Dep .... Dependency (SAUS)
Dep .... Dependent (AMHC)
DEP .... Dependent
DEP .... Depilate (ABBR)
DEP .... Depilatory (ABBR)
DEP .... Deployment
DEP .... Deponent
DEP .... Deport (ROG)
DEP .... Deportation [*FBI standardized term*]
dep .... depose (SAUS)
dep .... Deposed (ADWA)
DEP .... Deposed
Dep .... Deposit (EBF)
DEP .... Deposit [*or Depositor*] (EY)
dep .... Deposit (WDMC)
Dep .... Depositary (EBF)
DEP .... Depositary [*Banking*]
Dep .... Depositary Receipts (SG)
DEP .... Deposit Guaranty Corp. [*NYSE symbol*] (SAG)
DEP .... Deposition (ADA)
dep .... Deposition [*Legal term*] (WDAA)
dep .... depositor (SAUS)
DEP .... Depository
DEP .... Depository Library (SAUS)
DEP .... Depot (AFM)
dep .... Depot (GEAB)
DEP .... Depot Element Profile (SAUS)
dep .... depotize (SAUS)
dep .... Depreciation
DEP .... Depressed [*Technical drawings*]
DEP .... Depth
DEP .... Depuratus [*Purified*] [*Pharmacy*]
DEP .... Deputy (AFM)
Dep .... Deputy (PHSD)
dep .... Deputy (WDMC)
DEP .... Design Engineering Program [*Military*]
DEP .... Design External Pressure (NRCH)
DEP .... Design Eye Point [*Cockpit visibility*]
DEP .... Detailed Experiment Plan (MCD)
DEP .... Diabetes Education Program [*Medicine*] (EDAA)
DEP .... Diabetic Encephalopathy [*Medicine*] (MELL)
DEP .... Diagnostic Execution Program (NOAA)
DEP .... Diagnostic Executive Program (NITA)
DEP .... Dielectrophoresis
DEP .... Dielectrophoretic (SAUS)

DEP............. Diesel Exhaust Particulates [*Medicine*] (MELL)
DEP............. Diethyl Phthalate [*Organic chemistry*]
DEP............. Diethylpropanediol [*Biochemistry*]
DEP............. Diethyl Pyrocarbonate [*Chemical preservative*] [*Also, DEPC*] [*Organic chemistry*]
DEP............. Dilution End Point [*Medicine*] (DMAA)
DEP............. Direct Electrophotographic Paper (SAUS)
DEP............. Directional Error Probable (SAUS)
DEP............. Displaced Employee Program [*Department of Labor*]
DEP............. Division of Environmental Protection (SAUO)
dep............. do everything possible (SAUS)
DEP............. Domestic Emergency Plan (AAG)
DEP............. Doppler Enhancement Processor (SAUS)
DEP............. Double-Ended Pivot
DEP............. Double-Exposure Prevention [*Advanced photo system*]
DEP............. Draft Equipment Publications (ACAE)
DEP............. Draft Experiment Publication (MCD)
DEP............. Driver evaluation program (SAUS)
DEP............. Dry Electrostatic Precipitator (SAUS)
DEP............. dual-element packer (SAUS)
DEP............. Dual Element Pump
DEP............. European Depository Library (SAUO)
DEP............. Unit of Descriptive Epidemiology (SAUO)
DEPA.......... Defense Electric Power Administration [*Terminated, 1977*] [*Department of the Interior*]
DEPA.......... Defense Entry and Departure Act [*1918*]
DEPA.......... Demonstrably Effective Program Aid
DEPA.......... Diethylene Phosphoramide [*Organic chemistry*] (BABM)
DEPA.......... Diversified Economic and Planning Associates
DEPA.......... Dual Energy Photon Absorptiometry (MELL)
DEPA.......... United States Environmental Protection Agency, Headquarters Library, Washington,DC [*Library symbol*] [*Library of Congress*] (LCLS)
DEPACK....... Deployment Package System (SAUS)
DEPACTV..... Depot Activity
dep agt........ depot agreement (SAUS)
DEPAIR........ Air Deputy [*NATO*] (NATG)
DEPA-NA...... United States Environmental Protection Agency, Office of Noise Abatement and Control, Washington, DC [*Library symbol*] [*Library of Congress*] (LCLS)
DEPART....... Department
DEPART....... Departure (SAUS)
DePaul U..... DePaul University (GAGS)
Dep Bn......... Depot Battalion (SAUO)
DEPC........... Defence Equipment Policy Committee [*British*] (RDA)
DEPC........... Defence Equipment Procurement Council [*British*]
DEPC........... Defence Expenditure Procurement Committee (SAUS)
DEPC........... DEP Corp. [*NASDAQ symbol*] (NQ)
DEPC........... Diethylaminopropyl Chloride Hydrochloride (SAUS)
DEPC........... Diethyl Pyrocarbonate [*Chemical preservative*] [*Also, DEP*] [*Organic chemistry*]
DEPCA......... Digital Ethernet Personal Computer Adapter
DEPCA......... International Study Group for the Detection and Prevention of Cancer (SAUO)
DEPCDR(R & D)... Deputy Commander for Research and Development [*Navy*]
DEPCDR(SA)... Deputy Commander for Ship Acquisitions [*Navy*]
Dep CFO....... Deputy Chief Fire Officer (SAUS)
DEPCH......... Deputy Chief (CINC)
DEPCHNAVMAT... Deputy Chief of Naval Material (DNAB)
DEPCHNAVMAT(MAT & FAC)... Deputy Chief of Naval Material (Material and Facilities) (DNAB)
DepCofS....... Deputy Chief of Staff (SAUO)
DEPCOM...... Deputy Commander (DNAB)
DEPCOMFEWSG... Deputy Commander, Fleet Electronic Warfare Support Group [*Navy*] (DNAB)
depcomgen... deputy commissary general (SAUO)
DEPCOMLANTNAVFACENGCOM... Deputy Commander, Atlantic Naval Facilities Engineering Command (DNAB)
DEPCOMOPTEVFORLANT... Deputy Commander, Operational Test and Evaluation Force, Atlantic [*Navy*] (DNAB)
DEPCOMOPTEVFORPAC... Deputy Commander, Operational Test and Evaluation Force, Pacific [*Navy*]
DEPCOMPACNAVFACENGCOM... Deputy Commander, Pacific Naval Facilities Engineering Command (DNAB)
DEPCOMPT... Deputy Comptroller (DNAB)
DEPCOMSTRIKFORSOUTH... Deputy Commander, Naval Striking and Support Forces, Southern Europe (NATG)
DEPCOMSTS... Deputy Commander, Military Sea Transport Service [*Obsolete*] [*Navy*]
DEPCOMUSMACTHAI... Deputy Commander, United States Military Assistance Command, Thailand
DEPCOMUSMACV... Deputy Commander, United States Military Assistance Command, Vietnam
dep con........ departmental control (SAUS)
DEPCON....... Departure Control
DEPCOS........ Departure Coordination System (SAUS)
DEPCOS........ Deputy Chief of Staff [*Military*] (CAAL)
DEPCRU........ Dependents' Daylight Cruise [*Navy*] (NVT)
Dep Ctf......... Deposit Certificate [*Banking*] (MHDW)
DEPD........... Departed (ABBR)
DEPD........... Dislocation Etch Pit Density (SAUS)
DEPD........... Division Engineering Planning Document
DEPDA......... Deployment Data File
DEPDATE..... Departure Date from POE (SAUS)
DepDefRep... Department of Defense Representative (SAUO)
DEPDIR........ Deputy Director
DEPDIRPACDOCKS... Deputy Director Pacific Division, Bureau of Yards and Docks [*Later, NFEC*] [*Navy*]
DepDirPers... Deputy Director, Personnel (SAUO)
DEPE............ Double Escape Peak Efficiency [*Nuclear science*] (OA)
DEPECH....... Deployment Echelon (SAUS)
DEPEND....... Dependency (ABBR)
depend........ dependent (SAUS)
DEPENDS..... Detail Part Engineering Drawing System (SAUS)
depen-undepen... dependably undependable (SAUS)
DEPERM...... Deperming [*Navy*] (ANA)
DEPERMSTA... Deperming and Flashing Station [*Navy*]
DEPES......... Development Environment for Pronunciation Expert Systems [*Computer science*]
DEPEST........ Deployment Package Estimation System (SAUO)
DEPEVACPAY... Dependents' Evacuation Pay [*Military*]
DEPEX......... Deployment Exercise [*Military*] (ADDR)
DEPEX......... Deployment on NIKE/X Study [*Military*]
DepFonMin... Deputy Foreign Minister
DEPG........... Departing (ABBR)
DepGty......... Deposit Guaranty Corp. [*Associated Press*] (SAG)
DEPGUIDE... Deployment Guide (SAUS)
DE Phy......... Doctor of Engineering Physics
DEPI............. Differential Equations Pseudocode Interpreter [*Jet Propulsion Laboratory, NASA*]
DEPIC.......... Dual-Expanded Plastic-Insulated Conductor [*Telecommunications*] (TEL)
DEPICT........ Defense Electronics Products Integrated Control Technique (PDAA)
depict.......... Depicting (VRA)
DEPID.......... Deployment Indicator Code
DEPILAT...... Depilatorium [*Depilatory*] [*Pharmacy*]
DEP in CT.... Deposits in Court [*Legal term*] (DLA)
Dep Insp...... Deputy Inspector (SAUS)
DEP INST..... Depot Installed (SAA)
DEPL........... Depilation (ABBR)
depl............ deplete (SAUS)
DEPL........... Depletion (KSC)
DEPL........... Deploy (KSC)
depl............ deployment (SAUS)
Dep-L.......... Depotleitung (SAUS)
deplab......... depilatory laboratory (SAUS)
DEPLADIS.... Development Planning Documents Information System (SAUS)
DEPLAN....... Deployment Plan (SAUS)
DepLIS......... Department of Library and Information Services (TELE)
DEPL-MAN... Deployment Manifest [*Army*]
DEPLOC....... Daily Estimated Position Location [*Navy*] (NVT)
DEPLOC....... Depot-Location (SAUS)
DEP LOG..... Deputy Chief of Staff for Logistics (SAUO)
DEPMAS...... Deployment Management System (SAUO)
DEPMED...... Deployable Medical [*Equipment*] [*Military*]
DEPMEDS.... Deployable Medical System [*Military*]
DEPMIS....... Depot Management Information System [*Army*]
depn........... dependency (SAUS)
DEPN........... Dependent (AFM)
DEPNAV....... Department of the Navy (SAUO)
DEPNAV....... Naval Deputy [*NATO*] (NATG)
DEPNAVSCI... Department of Naval Science (DNAB)
DEPNOTAUTH... Dependents Not Authorized Overseas Duty Station [*Military*]
Dep N Sec.... Deputy Naval Secretary (SAUO)
DEPO........... Deportee (TVEL)
depo............ Deposit
DEPO........... Deposition [*Legal shorthand*] (LWAP)
DEPO........... DepoTech Corp. [*NASDAQ symbol*] (SAG)
DEPO........... Depo Tech Inc. [*NASDAQ symbol*] (TTSB)
DEPO........... Devils Postpile National Monument
depod.......... deposited (SAUS)
depog.......... depositing (SAUS)
DEPOL......... Depolarization
DEPOL......... Police Department (SAUO)
DEPON......... Deponent (ABBR)
DEPOPSDEP... Deputy Operations Deputy [*In JCS system*] [*Military*]
depor........... depositor (SAUS)
DEPOS......... Democratic Coalition of Serbia (Yugoslavia) [*Political party*] (PSAP)
DEPOS......... Depositary [*Banking*] (EY)
DEPOS......... Didier Engineering Project Operation System (SAUS)
DEPOS & D... Deposition and Discovery [*Legal term*] (DLA)
DEPOSN....... Deposition
DEPOT......... Desktop and Electronic Publishing Online Terminal
DEPP........... Daily Encephalic Photophase [*Biochronometry*]
DEPP........... Deep Earth Penetrating Projectile (MCD)
DEPPC......... Declared Excess Personal Property Catalog [*Military*]
Depr............ Depreciation (EBF)
DEPR........... Depreciation [*Accounting, Economics*]
depr............ Depreciation
depr............ depreciative (SAUS)
Depr............ Depress (SAUS)
depr............ Depressed [*Psychiatry*] (DAVI)
DEPR........... Depression [*Board on Geographic Names*] (MSA)
DEPR........... Division of Epidemiology and Prevention Research (SAUO)
DEPRA......... Defense European and Pacific Redistribution Activity [*DoD*] (AFIT)
DEPRA......... Defense Excess Property Redistribution Agency (SAUO)
De Praescr Haeret... De Praescriptione Haereticorum [*of Tertullian*] [*Classical studies*] (OCD)
DEPREC....... Depreciation
DEPREP....... Deployment Reporting System

DEPREP System... Deployment Reporting System (SAUS)
DEPRESS..... Depressurize (NASA)
depr neur..... Depressive Neurosis [*Psychiatry*] (DAVI)
De Prof Virt... De Profectu in Virtute [*of Plutarch*] [*Classical studies*] (OCD)
DEPS.......... Council Deputies (SAUO)
DEPS.......... Data Entry and Payment System (SAUS)
DEPS.......... Departmental Entry Processing Systems [*Customs processing for sea and airports*] [*October, 1981*] [*British*] (DCTA)
DEPS.......... Deposit Guaranty [*NASDAQ symbol*] (TTSB)
DEPS.......... Deposit Guaranty Corp. [*NASDAQ symbol*] (NQ)
DEPS.......... Depots (SAUO)
DEPS.......... Development Engineering Prototype Site (ACAE)
DEPS.......... Diploma in Economics and Political Science (SAUS)
Deps.......... direct entry processing system (SAUS)
DEPS.......... Distal Effective Potassium Secretion [*Medicine*] (DMAA)
DEPS.......... Double-Ended Pump Suction [*Nuclear energy*] (NRCH)
DEPs.......... Dry Electrostatic Precipitators (SAUS)
DEPSAC....... Deputy Supreme Air Commander (SAUS)
DEPSAC....... Deputy Supreme Air Commander, Europe (SAUO)
DEPSACLANT... Deputy Supreme Allied Commander, Atlantic (NATG)
DEPSCoR..... Defense Experimental Program to Stimulate Competitive Research (RDA)
DEP seat..... Deposited seat (SAUS)
DEPSEC....... Deputy Secretary (ADA)
DEPSECDEF... Deputy Secretary of Defense (AABC)
DEPSECLANTFAP... Deputy Secretary ACLANT Frequency Allocation Panel (SAUO)
DEPSK......... Differential Encoding Phase Shift Keying (MCD)
DepSO......... Departmental Standardization Office (SAUO)
DEPSO......... Department Standardization Office [*Navy*]
DEPSTAR..... Deployment Status of Army Units (AABC)
DEPSUBSYSPROJTECHO... Deep Submergency Systems Project Technical Office (SAUO)
DEPSUM...... Daily Estimated Position Summary [*Navy*]
DEPSUM...... Deployment Summary Report [*Air Force*]
Dep Sup Bn... Depot Supply Battalion (SAUO)
DEPT.......... Depart
DEPT.......... Department (EY)
Dept.......... Department (PHSD)
Dept.......... Departmental (DIAR)
DEPT.......... Departure (ABBR)
DEPT.......... Deponent [*Legal term*] (ROG)
DEPT.......... Deposit (ROG)
dept.......... depot (SAUS)
dept.......... Deputy (ADWA)
DEPT.......... Deputy
DEPT.......... Distortionless Enhancement by Polarization Transfer [*Spectroscopy*]
Dept56......... Department 56, Inc. [*Associated Press*] (SAG)
Dept AE....... Department for Atomic Energy (SAUS)
Dept Ag....... Department of Agriculture (SAUS)
Dept Agr...... Department of Agriculture (SAUO)
DEPTAR....... Department of the Army
DEPTAR/MAIN... Department of the Army/Main (AABC)
DeptCom...... Department of Commerce (SAUO)
DEPTD......... Division of Electric Power Transmission and Distribution [*Energy Research and Development Administration*]
Deptel.......... Department of State Telegram
DEPTEL........ State Department Telegram (NATG)
DEPTH......... Design Analysis for Personnel Training and Human Factors [*Military*] (SEWL)
Dept Hd........ Department Head (SAUS)
DeptInt......... Department of the Interior (SAUO)
DEPTL.......... Departmental (ABBR)
DeptLab........ Department of Labor (SAUO)
DEPTM......... Draft Equipment Publication Technical Manual (MCD)
DEPTNAVINSTR... Department of Naval Instruction (DNAB)
Dept of A..... Department of Agriculture (SAUO)
Dept R......... Department Reports, State Department [*New York*] [*A publication*] (DLA)
deptr........... departure (SAUS)
Dept R Un... New York State Department Reports, Unofficial [*A publication*] (DLA)
Dept State Bul... Department of State Bulletin (journ.) (SAUS)
Dept State Bull... Department of State Bulletin (SAUS)
DEPU........... Departure (ABBR)
DEPU........... De Paul University [*Chicago, IL*]
DEPU........... Diethylphenylurea (SAUS)
DEPUS......... Departmental User (SAUS)
DEPUTN....... Deputation
deputn......... deputation (SAUS)
Depuy.......... Depuy, Inc. [*Associated Press*] (SAG)
DEPV........... Air-Cushion Vehicle built by Research Vehicle Department [*Brazil*] [*Usually used in combination with numerals*]
DEPV........... Diesel-electric paddle vessel (SAUS)
DEPY........... Deputy
De Pyth Or... De Pythiae Oraculis [*of Plutarch*] [*Classical studies*] (OCD)
DEQ............ Daydream Island [*Queensland*] [*Airport symbol*] (AD)
DEQ............ Delivered Ex Quay (RIMS)
DEQ............ Department of Environment Quality
DEQ............ Depression Experiences Questionnaire [*Medicine*] (DMAA)
DEQ............ DeQueen, AR [*Location identifier*] [*FAA*] (FAAL)
DEQ............ Dequeue [*Computer science*]
DE/Q........... Design Evaluation/Qualification (KSC)
DEQ............ Dose Equivalent [*Radioactivity calculations*] (IEEE)
DEQ............ Doubled-Ended Queue (SAUS)
DEQ............ Double-Ended Queue (VLIE)
DEQ............ Idaho Department of Health and Welfare [*Division of Environmental Quality*] (DOGT)
DEQCT......... double energy quantitative Computertomography (SAUS)
D/EQD.......... Director of the Electrical Quality Assurance Directorate (SAUO)
DEQMAR...... Determining Economic Quantities of Maintenance Resources (PDAA)
DEQNA......... Digital Ethernet Q-Bus Network Adapter [*Computer science*] (VERA)
DEQPPM...... Defnse Environmental Quality Program Policy Memorandum (SAUO)
DEQUE......... Double-Ended Queue (RALS)
DEQUIP........ DECHEMA [*Deutsche Gesellschaft fuer Chemisches Apparatewesen, Chemische Technik, und Biotechnologie eV*] Equipment Suppliers Databank [*Database*]
DEQUISA...... Desarrollo Quimico Industrial, SA [*Spain*]
DER............. Daily Report for Executives (SAUO)
DER............. Data Evaluation Record (SAUS)
DER............. Declining Error Rate
DER............. Defective Equipment Report (SAUS)
DER............. Defective Equipment Review (MCD)
DER............. Delegated Engineering Representative
DER............. Demonstration and Evaluation Report (MCD)
DER............. Denar Mines Ltd. [*Vancouver Stock Exchange symbol*]
DER............. Department of Environmental Regulation (SAUS)
DER............. Department of Environmental Resources (COE)
DER............. Departure End of Runway [*Aviation*] (DA)
DER............. Derby [*Colorado*] [*Seismograph station code, US Geological Survey*] [*Closed*] (SEIS)
DER............. Dereco, Inc. (SAUO)
DER............. Derekh Erets Rabbah [*or Derek Erez Rabbah*] (BJA)
DER............. De Rigo ADS [*NYSE symbol*] (TTSB)
DER............. DeRigo SPA [*NYSE symbol*] (SAG)
DER............. Derim [*Papua New Guinea*] [*Airport symbol*] (OAG)
DER............. Derivation [*or Derivative*]
der............. Derivative (ADWA)
der............. Derivative of Chromosome [*Genetics*] (DAVI)
DER............. Derived (ROG)
DER............. Dermatine
DER............. Dermatology (DAVI)
der............. derrick (SAUS)
DER............. Derricks (DS)
Der............. Derringer (SAUS)
DER............. Designated Engineer Representative [*FAA title*] (AFM)
DER............. Design Electrical Rating [*Nuclear energy*] (NRCH)
DER............. Design Error Rate (SAUS)
DER............. Destination Resources (SAUS)
DER............. Destroyer Escort RADAR (IAA)
DER............. destruction removal efficiency (SAUS)
DER............. Development Engineering Review (AAG)
DER............. Diesel Engine, Reduction Drive
DER............. Digital Event Recorder (VLIE)
DER............. Directly Executable Representation
DER............. Directory of Environmental Resources (SAUO)
DER............. Disk Entry Record [*Computer science*] (VLIE)
DER............. Distinguished Encoding Rules [*Computer science*] (VLIE)
DER............. Distributed Energy Release [*Computer program*]
DER............. Disulfiram-Ethanol Reaction [*Medicine*] (DMAA)
DER............. Division of Economic Research [*Social Security Administration*] [*Washington, DC*] (GRD)
DER............. Division of Engineering Research [*Michigan State University*] [*Research center*] (RCD)
DER............. Division of Environmental Radiation (SAUO)
DER............. Division of Evaluation and Research [*Department of Labor*] (GRD)
DER............. Document Error Report
DER............. Doll's Eyes Reflex [*Positive in total coma*] [*Medicine*] (EDAA)
DER............. Double Edge Receiver (MCD)
DER............. Double Ended Receiver (ACAE)
DER............. Double-Ended Rupture [*Nuclear energy*] (NRCH)
DER............. Draft environmental report (SAUS)
DER............. Drawing Error Report (NASA)
DER............. Dual Energy Radiography [*Medicine*] (DMAA)
DER............. Dunn-Erwin Railway [*Federal Railroad Administration identification code*]
DER............. External Developer Release (SAUS)
DER............. Out of Order [*International telex abbreviation*] (WDMC)
DER............. RADAR Picket Escort Ship [*Navy symbol*]
DeR............. Reaction of Degeneration [*Physiology*]
DER............. United States Army Engineer Research and Development Laboratory, Technical Documents Center, Fort Belvoir, VA [*Library symbol*] [*Library of Congress*] (LCLS)
DERA........... Defence Evaluation and Research Agency [*British*]
DERA........... Defense Eastern Regional Audit Office [*DoD*]
DERA........... Defense Environmental Restoration Account [*DoD*]
DERA........... Defense European Redistribution Activity [*DoD*] (MCD)
DERA........... Deference Experimental Research Agency [*British*] (WDAA)
DERA........... Direction de l'Analyse Economique et Regionale [*Economic and Regional Analysis Branch*] [*Transport Canada*]
DERA........... Directory of Education and Research in Australia (SAUS)
DERA........... Directory of Education Research and Researchers in Australia (NITA)
DERAL......... Distance Education in Rural Areas via Libraries (TELE)
DERAP......... Development Economics Research and Advisory Service (SAUS)
DERAX......... Detection and Range [*Early name for RADAR*]
DERB........... Derby (ROG)
DERB........... Derbyshire [*County in England*]
Derbs........... Derbyshire [*County in England*] (DAS)
DERBSH....... Derbyshire [*County in England*] (ROG)
DERBY......... Derby Aviation (SAUS)
Derby.......... Derbyshire [*County in England*] (ODBW)

DERBY .... Derbyshire [*County in England*]
Derbys .... Derbyshire (GROV)
DERBYS .... Derbyshire [*County in England*]
DERBY YEO ... Derbyshire Yeomanry, Royal Artillery Corps, Territorial Army (SAUO)
DERC .... Development Economics Research Centre [*University of Warwick*] [*British*] (CB)
DERC .... Directory of Executive Recruitment Consultants [*A publication*]
DERC .... Drill and Exercise Review Committee [*Environmental science*] (COE)
DERCCA .... Derbyshire England Red Cap Club of America (EA)
DERD .... Diesel Electric Reduction Drive
DERD .... Directorate of Engine Research and Development (SAUO)
DERD .... Directory of Engine Research and Development (SAUS)
DERD .... Display of Extracted RADAR Data (DA)
DERDA .... United States Energy Research and Development Administration, Washington, DC [*Library symbol*] [*Library of Congress*] (LCLS)
DERE .... Dounreay Experimental Reactor Establishment [*British*]
DEREC .... Definitive Election Results Evaluation Computer (DI)
dereg .... deregulation (SAUS)
DEREK .... Deductive Estimation of Risk from Existing Knowledge [*Data analysis*]
DEREP .... Digital Ethernet Repeater [*Computer science*] (VERA)
DERES .... DECHEMA [*Deutsche Gesellschaft fuer Chemisches Apparatewesen, Chemische Technik, und Biotechnologie eV*] Research and Education Databank [*Frankfurt Am Main, Federal Republic of Germany*] [*Information service or system*] (IID)
DERF .... Division of Educational and Research Facilities [*Bureau of Health Professions Education and Manpower Training, HEW*]
DERF .... Dynamical Extended Range Forecasting [*Meteorology*]
DERG .... Deferred Exchange-Rate Guarantee [*Investment term*] (ECON)
DERI .... Deep Electric Research Investigation [*Navy*]
DERI .... Diethyl(ribityl)isoalloxazine [*Biochemistry*]
DERIC .... De Ea Re Ita Censuere [*Concerning That Matter Have So Decreed*] [*Latin*] [*Legal term*] (DLA)
DERIGID .... Derigidize (NASA)
DeRigo .... DeRigo SPA [*Associated Press*] (SAG)
DERIPS .... Doppler-Enhanced RADAR Intensity Profiling System (MCD)
deriv .... Derivation (ADWA)
DERIV .... Derivation [*or Derivative*]
deriv .... derivative (SAUS)
DERIV .... Derived (ROG)
DERIVB .... Derivable (ABBR)
DERIVD .... Derived (ABBR)
DERIVG .... Deriving (ABBR)
DERIVN .... Derivation (ABBR)
DERIVP .... Derivative Program (MCD)
DERIVV .... Derivative (ABBR)
DERL .... Defense Electronics Research Laboratory (SAUS)
DERL .... Denmark's Electronic Research Library (TELE)
DERL .... Derived Emergency Reference Level [*of radiation*]
DERM .... Delayed Echo RADAR Marker
DERM .... Department of Environmental Resources Management (SAUO)
DERM .... Derma [*Skin*] [*Medicine*] (ROG)
DERM .... Derma-Lock Medical Corp. [*Norway*] (NQ)
DERM .... Dermatitis [*Medicine*]
derm .... Dermatology (ADWA)
Derm .... Dermatology [*Medicine*] (AMHC)
DERM .... Dermatology [*or Dermatologist*]
DERM .... Dermatophyte (ABBR)
DERM .... Diagnostic Energy Reserve Module [*Airbags and safety systems*]
DERM .... Digital Elevation And Radiometry Model (SAUS)
DERM .... Dynamic Econometric Retention Model (MCD)
DERM .... Penederm, Inc. [*NASDAQ symbol*] (SAG)
DermaSci .... Derma Sciences, Inc. [*Associated Press*] (SAG)
DERMAT .... Dermatology (ABBR)
DERMATOL ... Dermatology
dermatol .... dermatotogy (SAUS)
DermIS .... Dermatology Internet Service. Dermatologie Internet Service (SAUO)
DERMTLGST ... Dermatologist
DERN .... Dermatology
Derniers .... Dernieres Islands (SAUS)
DERNS .... Dearness (ABBR)
derog .... Derogatory (ADWA)
DEROG .... Derogatory (DCTA)
DEROS .... Date Eligible for Return from Overseas [*Military*]
DEROS .... Date of Estimated Return from Overseas [*Military*]
DEROS .... Date of Expected Return from Overseas (SAUS)
DEROS .... Departing Roster (DNAB)
DERP .... Defective Equipment Repair Program [*Telephone company*]
DERP .... Defective Equipment Replacement Program (SAUS)
DERP .... Defense Environmental Restoration Program [*DoD*]
DERP .... Defense Environmental Restriction Program (SAUS)
DERP .... Deficient Equippage Reporting Procedures
DERP .... Disposable Eye Respiratory Protection (SAUS)
DERP .... Drug Evaluation Rating Program (SAUS)
DERPMIS .... Defense Environmental Restoration Information System (SAUO)
DERR .... Daily Effective Repair Rate (MCD)
DERR .... Duke of Edinburgh's Royal Regiment [*Military unit*] [*British*]
Derry .... County of Londonderry (SAUO)
DERRY .... Londonderry [*County in Ireland*] (ROG)
DERS .... Data Entry Reporting System
DERS .... Digital Emergency Response System [*Environmental science*] (COE)
DERS .... Division of Educational Research Services [*University of Alberta*] [*Research center*] (RCD)
DERTF .... Defense Environmental Response Task Force
DERTO .... DSA [*Defense Supply Agency*] Eastern Regional Telecommunications Office
DERV .... Diesel Engined Road Vehicle
derv .... diesel-engined road vehicle (SAUS)
DERV .... Duck Embryo Rabies Vaccine (MELL)
DERWeb .... Dental Education Resources on the Web (ADWA)
DES .... Chilcotin Caribou Aviation [*Canada*] [*ICAO designator*] (FAAC)
DES .... Dalhousie Earth Sciences (SAUO)
DES .... Data Elements Standardization Requirements (MCD)
DES .... Data Encoding System (ACAE)
DES .... Data Encryption Standard (ACAE)
DES .... Data Encryption System (SAUS)
DES .... Data Engineering Section
DES .... Data Entry Scan (SAUS)
DE/S .... Data Entry/Separation (MCD)
DES .... Data Entry Sheet [*Computer science*] (VLIE)
DES .... Data Entry Station (SAUS)
DES .... Data Entry System
DES .... Data Exchange System (NASA)
DE/S .... Data Extraction Segment (GEOI)
DES .... Dead-End Shaft
DES .... Defence Engineering Service (SAUS)
DES .... Defense Encryption Standard (SAUS)
DES .... Delivered Ex Ship (RIMS)
DES .... Delta Epsilon Sigma (EA)
DES .... Demag Programmier- System (SAUS)
DES .... Department of Earth Sciences (SAUS)
DES .... Department of Education and Science [*British*]
DES .... Department of Emergency Services (SAUO)
DES .... Department of Employment Security (SAUS)
DES .... Dermal-Epidermal Separation [*Medicine*] (STED)
Des .... Desaussure. South Carolina Equity Reports [*1784-1816*] [*A publication*] (DLA)
DES .... Descend (SAUS)
DES .... Descending (VLIE)
DES .... Descend To [*Aviation*]
DES .... Descent (KSC)
des .... Description (VLIE)
DES .... Descriptor (NITA)
DES .... Desc S.A. ADS [*NYSE symbol*] (TTSB)
DES .... Desc SA de CV [*NYSE symbol*] (SAG)
DES .... Desert [*Hawaii*] [*Seismograph station code, US Geological Survey*] (SEIS)
des .... desert (SAUS)
Des .... Desert (SHCU)
DES .... Desert Botanical Garden [*An association*] (EA)
DES .... Desertion
DES .... Desferrioxamine [*Also, Deferoxamine*] [*A chelating agent*]
Des .... Design (DIAR)
des .... Design (VRA)
DES .... Design (NASA)
DES .... Design and Evaluation System (VLIE)
des .... designate (SAUS)
des .... Designation (ADWA)
Des .... Designation Strip [*Telecommunications*] (ITD)
DES .... Designator (KSC)
DES .... Designatus [*Named*] [*Latin*]
DES .... Designavit [*He, or She, Drew It*] [*Latin*] (ROG)
DES .... Design Engineering Show and Conference (ITD)
DES .... Design Engineering Support (MCD)
DES .... Design Environmental Simulator (SAUS)
DES .... Designer (WDAA)
DES .... Design Expansion System
DES .... Desire (AABC)
DES .... Desmethylsertraline (SAUS)
Des .... Des Moines (SAUS)
Des .... Desmond (SAUS)
des .... Desorb (SAUS)
DES .... Desoxycholate (SAUS)
DES .... Dessert (WDAA)
DES .... Destination End System [*Telecommunications*] (MLOA)
DES .... Destroyer [*Navy*]
DES .... Detroit Steel Corp. (SAUO)
DES .... Development Enquiry Service (SAUS)
DES .... Dialysis Encephalopathy Syndrome [*Medicine*] (DMAA)
DES .... Diccionario Enciclopedico Salvat [*A publication*]
DES .... Diesel Electric Ship (IAA)
DES .... Diesel Electronic Submarine (MCD)
DES .... Diethylstilbesterol (EEVL)
DES .... Diethyl Stilbestrol (SAUS)
DES .... Diethylstilbestrol [*Endocrinology*]
DES .... Diethyl Succinate [*Organic chemistry*]
DES .... Diethyl Sulfate [*Organic chemistry*]
DES .... Differential Emotional Scale [*Medicine*] (EDAA)
DES .... Differential Energy Spectrum
DES .... Differential Equation Solver
DES .... Diffuse Esophageal Spasm [*Medicine*]
DES .... Digital Echo Suppressor (NITA)
DES .... Digital Editing Station (GEOI)
DES .... Digital Encryption Standard [*Computer science*] (PCM)
DES .... Digital Exchange System (MCD)
DES .... Digital Expansion System
DES .... Diplome d'Etudes Superieures [*Canada*] (DD)
DES .... Direct Entry System (SAUS)
DES .... Directorate of Engineering Standardization (SAUS)

DES............ Director of Educational Services [*Air Force*] [*British*]
DES............ Director of Engineering Stores (SAUO)
DES............ Director of Engineer Services (SAUO)
DES............ Director of Engineer Stores Service [*British*]
DES............ Disc Edges Sharp (SAUS)
DES............ Discrete Elastic System
DES............ Disequilibrium Syndrome [*Medicine*]
DES............ Dismounted Entry Switch [*Military*]
DES............ Dismounted Extension Switch (SAUS)
DES............ Dispersed Emergency Station (NATG)
DES............ Display Editing System (VLIE)
DES............ Display Equipment Status (AAEL)
DES............ Distilling Experimental Station (SAUO)
DES............ Distributed End System (VLIE)
DES............ Divers' Environmental Survey
DES............ Division Engineering Standards (SAUS)
DES............ Division for Exceptional Students (SAUO)
DES............ Division of Earth Sciences [*National Research Council*] (USDC)
DES............ Division of Educational Services [*Department of Education*]
DES............ Division of Energy Storage [*Energy Research and Development Administration*]
DES............ Division of Environmental Science [*Marine science*] (OSRA)
DES............ Division of Environmental Sciences [*National Science Foundation*] (USDC)
DES............ Doctor of Engineering Science
DES............ Doctor of Environmental Studies (DD)
DES............ Doctors Emergency Service [*New York City*]
DES............ Document Entry Subsystem (SAUS)
DES............ Doppler Error Sensor (ACAE)
DES............ Douglas Equipment Specification
DES............ Dow Education Systems [*Dow Chemical Corp.*]
DES............ Draft Environmental Statement [*Bureau of Outdoor Recreation*]
DES............ Drug Education Specialist [*Military*] (AABC)
DES............ Dry Eye Syndrome (SAUS)
DES............ dual-elevator stool (SAUS)
DES............ dual elevator system (SAUS)
DES............ Dual Exciter System
DES............ Dual Exhaust System [*Automotive emissions*]
DES............ Ducosyn Excitation Switch
DES............ Duke Engineering & Services, Inc. (SAUO)
DES............ Dynamic Electrospeaker
DES............ Dynamic Environment Simulator [*Air Force*]
DES............ Office of Economic Security, Department of Economic Security, St. Paul, MN [*OCLC symbol*] (OCLC)
DES............ Washington State Department of Energy Services (SAUS)
Des............ Deaconess (ODA)
DESA.......... Data Entry Services of America (SAUS)
DESA.......... Department of Economic and Social Affairs
DESA.......... Division of Epidemiology and Statistical Analysis [*Department of Health and Human Services*] (GFGA)
DESAC........ Destroyer SONAR Analysis Center [*Navy*] (NVT)
DESAD........ Diethylstilbestrol Adenosis [*Oncology*]
DESAF........ Destroyers, Asiatic Fleet [*Navy*]
Desai.......... Handbook of Criminal Cases [*India*] [*A publication*] (DLA)
DESAIRDEX... Destroyer and Submarine Forces Air Defense Exercise (SAUO)
DESAIRDEX... Destroyer and Submarine-forces Air Defense Exercise (SAUS)
DESAL.......... Desalinization (ABBR)
De Sanctis Stor Rom... De Sanctis, Storia dei Romani [*1907-1966*] [*A publication*] (OCD)
DESAT......... Defense Small Advanced Technology (SAUS)
DESAT......... Defense Small Business Advanced Technology Program
DESAT......... Desaturated (NASA)
desat.......... Desaturated (STED)
DESAT......... Desaturation (SAUS)
Desaus........ Desaussure. South Carolina Equity Reports [*A publication*] (DLA)
Desaus Eq... Desaussure. South Carolina Equity Reports [*A publication*] (DLA)
DESB.......... Delta Epsilon Sigma Bulletin (journ.) (SAUS)
DESB.......... Desborough [*England*]
DESB.......... Devereux Elementary School Behavior [*Rating scale*] [*Psychology*]
Des Base..... Destroyer Base (SAUS)
DESBATFOR... Destroyer Battle Force [*Navy*]
DESC.......... Data Entry Station Cluster (SAUS)
DESC.......... Data Entry System Controller
DESC.......... Defense Electronics Supply [*or Support*] Center [*DSA*]
DESC.......... Defense Electronic Supply Center (MED)
DESC.......... Defense Energy Support Center
DESC.......... Dependency Selection Criterion (SAUS)
DESC.......... Descend
desc........... Descendant (STED)
DESC.......... Descendant (WDAA)
desc........... descendens (SAUS)
desc........... Descending (ADWA)
DESC.......... Descent (NASA)
DESC.......... Description (MCD)
DESC.......... Digital Equation-Solving Computer (IEEE)
DESc.......... Doctor of Economic Science (DD)
DE Sc.......... Doctor of Engineering Science
DESC.......... Dry Etching Station Computerized [*Graphic arts*] (DGA)
desc........... Describe (ODA)
DESC & D.... Descent and Distribution [*Legal term*] (DLA)
Desc Ao...... Descending Aorta [*Medicine*] (EDAA)
DESCARTES... Debugging and Specification of ADA Real Time Embedded Systems (SAUS)
DESCBC....... Data Encryption Standard/Cipher Block Chaining [*Computer science*] (VERA)
DESCDT....... Descendant
DESCF......... Dependency Selection Criterion Flag (SAUS)
DESCG......... Descending (SAUS)
DESCHA....... Destination Change [*Military*] (NVT)
DESCIM....... Defense Environmental Security Corporate Information Management (BCP)
DESCNET..... Data Network on Environmentally Significant Chemicals (DCTA)
Descodiv...... Destroyer Scouting Division (SAUO)
Descoflot..... Destroyer Scouting Flotilla (SAUO)
DESCOFOR... Destroyer Scouting Force [*Navy*]
DESCOM...... Depot Systems Command [*Army*] (RDA)
DESCOM...... Detainees Support Committee (SAUS)
DESCON....... Consultative Group for Desertification Control (SAUO)
DESCONAP... Research and Training Centres on Desertification Control in Asia and the Pacific (SAUO)
Descoron..... Destroyer Scouting Squadron (SAUO)
DESCP......... Description (MSA)
Descr........... Descrambler (SAUS)
DESCR......... Describe (KSC)
DESCR......... Description (SAUS)
DESCR......... Descriptor (SAUS)
DESCR......... Other Abnormal Morphology [*On differential*] [*Biochemistry*] (DAVI)
DESCRD....... Described (ROG)
DESCRIP...... description (SAUS)
De Script Eccles Proleg... De Scriptoribus Ecclesiasticis Prolegomena [*of St. Jerome*] [*Classical studies*] (OCD)
DESCRON..... Description
DESCRPN.... Description (ABBR)
DESCRUPAC... Destroyers/Cruisers, Pacific Fleet [*Navy*]
DescSA........ Desc SA de CV [*Associated Press*] (SAG)
DESCSD....... Directorate of Evaluation, Standardization, Concepts, Studies and Doctrine [*Army*]
desd............ Desorbed (SAUS)
DES(D)......... Diplome des Etudes Superieures en Droit [*French*] (CPGU)
DESDATA..... Descriptive Data (SAUS)
DESDEVDIV... Destroyer Development Division [*Navy*] (DNAB)
DESDEVGRU... Destroyer Development Group [*Navy*]
DESDEVRON... Destroyer Development Squadron [*Navy*] (DNAB)
desdg........... descending (SAUS)
DESDIV........ Destroyer Division [*Navy*]
DESDMM..... Diethylsulfone Dimethyl Methane (SAUS)
Desdorpt..... Desorption (SAUS)
DESE........... Data Encryption Standard Encryption protocol (SAUS)
DESE........... DES Encryption Algorithm [*Computer science*] (HODG)
DeSEA......... Delaware Society of Enrolled Agents (SAUO)
DESEB......... Defence Shipping Executive Board (SAUO)
DESEFF....... Deserter's Effects [*Military*]
DesEng........ Design Engineer (SAUS)
DES ENG...... Design Engineering (SAUS)
Des Engr...... Design Engineer (SAUS)
De Sera....... De Sera Numinis Vindicta [*of Plutarch*] [*Classical studies*] (OCD)
Desert......... Desert Community Bank [*Associated Press*] (SAG)
DESEX......... Deployment Staff Exercise (MCD)
DESFEX....... Desert Field Exercise [*Military*] (NVT)
DESFEX....... Destroyer Force Exercise (SAUO)
DESFIREX.... Desert Firing Exercise [*Military*] (NVT)
DESFLOT..... Destroyer Flotilla [*Navy*]
DESFLTSURG... Designated Student and Naval Flight Surgeon (DNAB)
DESFTD....... Department of Employment, Small Firms and Tourism Division [*British*]
DESG.......... Defence Engineering and Science Group
DESG.......... Design (SAUS)
DESG.......... Designate (AFM)
desg........... designation (SAUS)
DesgnF........ Designer Finance Trust [*Associated Press*] (SAG)
desgnr........ designer (SAUS)
Des Gp Ldr... Design Group Leader (SAUO)
DESGR........ Designer (SAUS)
DESH.......... DE&S Hanford, Inc. (SAUO)
DESI........... Designated Hitter [*Formerly, DPH*] [*Also, DH*] [*Baseball*]
DESI........... Designs, Inc. [*NASDAQ symbol*] (NQ)
DESI........... Diversified Energy Services, Inc. (GEOI)
DESI........... Division for Economic and Social Information (SAUS)
DESI........... Drug Efficacy Study Implementation (STED)
DESI........... Drug Efficacy Study Implementation Notice [*Food and Drug Administration*]
DESI........... Drug efficiency study (SAUS)
DESI........... Duke Engineering & Services Hanford Inc. (SAUO)
DESID......... Desiderata (ABBR)
DESID......... Desideratum [*Wanted*] [*Latin*] (ADA)
DESID......... Desired (ABBR)
DESIDER...... Desiderative (ABBR)
DESIDOC..... Defence Scientific Information and Documentation Centre (SAUO)
DESIDOC..... Deference Scientific Information and Documentation Centre (SAUS)
DESIG......... Designate [*or Designation*] (KSC)
DESIG......... Designation (SAUS)
DESIG......... Designer (ABBR)
DESIGDISBAGENT... Designated Special Disbursing Agent
DESIGNAP... Designated as Naval Aviation Pilot [*Marine Corps*]
DesignH....... Designer Holdings Ltd. [*Associated Press*] (SAG)
Designs....... Designs, Inc. [*Associated Press*] (SAG)
DESILU........ Desi-Lucille Arnaz Co.
DESIPA........ Department for Economic and Social Information and Policy Analysis (SAUS)
DESIR......... Department of Science and Industrial Research (SAUO)

DESIR Direct English Statement Information Retrieval [*Military*]
DESIRE Development of a European Service for Information on Research and Education (SAUO)
DESIRE Direct English Statement Information Retrieval Extraction (SAUS)
DESIS Desertification Information System [*UNEP*] [*United Nations*] (DUND)
DESK FAX Desk-top Facsimile (SAUS)
DeskTopDt Desktop Data, Inc. [*Associated Press*] (SAG)
Desktop Publ Today Desktop Pub1ishingToday (journ.) (SAUS)
Des L Desired Length (SAUS)
DESL Diesel (ABBR)
DesL Docteur es Lettres [*French*] [*Doctor of Literature*] (CPGU)
DESL Double-Ended Suction Leg Slot [*Nuclear energy*] (NRCH)
DESLANT Destroyer Force, Atlantic Fleet [*Navy symbol*]
desload Design Load (SAUS)
DESM Drainage Evaluation Spreadsheet Model (SAUS)
DESMC Department of Defense Systems Management Center (MCD)
DESMO DoD [*Department of Defense*] Logistics Data Element Standardization and Management Office
desn Desorption (SAUS)
DESNAVAV Designated Student Naval Aviator
Des News Design News (SAUS)
DESNS Directorate of Engineering Standards and Naval Specifications (SAUO)
DESNW Duke Engineering Services Northwest Inc. (SAUO)
DESO Defence Export Services Organization (SAUO)
DESO De Soto National Memorial
DESO District Educational Services Officer [*Navy*]
DESO Double End Shut-Off (SAUS)
DESOIL Diesel Oil
De Soll An De Sollertia Animalium [*of Plutarch*] [*Classical studies*] (OCD)
DESOMS Deaf Sons of Master Masons
Desorpt Desorption (SAUS)
DeSoto DeSoto, Inc. [*Associated Press*] (SAG)
DESP Data Element Standardization Program (SAUS)
DESP Department of Elementary School Principals [*of NEA*] (EA)
DESP Despatch
desp Despatched (SAUS)
desp despatch money (SAUS)
DESP Directorate of Equipment and Spare Parts (SAUO)
DESP Primeros Puestos del Deporte Espanol [*Ministerio de Cultura*] [*Spain*] [*Information service or system*] (CRD)
DESPAC Destroyer Force, Pacific Fleet [*Navy symbol*]
despd despatched (SAUS)
De Spect De Spectaculis [*of Tertullian*] [*Classical studies*] (OCD)
despg despatching (SAUS)
DESPORT Daily Equipment Status Report [*Army*] (AABC)
DESPOT Design Performance Optimization (NASA)
DESPR Digital Ethernet Single Port Repeater [*Computer science*] (VERA)
Desq View trademark of Quarterdeck International of Santa Monica (SAUS)
DESR Daily Effective Supply Rate (MCD)
desr Designer (SAUS)
DESRAD Desiccant-Enhanced Radiative Cooling [*Solar-cooling concept*]
DesRCA Designer of the Royal College of Art (SAUS)
Des RCA Diploma of Designer, Royal College of Art [*British*]
DESREP Destroyer Repair [*Navy*]
DESREP Destroyer Representative [*Navy*]
DESROC Destroyer Rocket
DESRON Destroyer Squadron [*Navy*]
DESRT Demonstration of Site Remediation Technology [*Environmental science*]
DESRT Development and Demonstration of Site Remediation Technology (SAUS)
DESS Defective Equipment Sorting Section (SAUO)
DESS Department of Earth and Space Sciences (SAUO)
DESS Department of Economics and Social Science [*MIT*] (MCD)
Dess Dessaussure's Equity [*South Carolina*] [*A publication*] (DLA)
dess dessiatine (SAUS)
DESS Destroyer Schoolship [*Navy*] (NVT)
DESS Digital Electronic Switching System (SAUS)
DESS Dual Environment Safety Switch (SAUS)
Dessaus Dessaussure's Equity [*South Carolina*] [*A publication*] (DLA)
DesScApp Docteur es Science Appliquee [*Doctor of Applied Science*] [*French*] (ASC)
DesScEco Docteur es Sciences Economiques (DD)
DESSIM Defense System Simulator
DESSIM Design Simulator
D Es S LJ Dar Es Salaam Law Journal [*A publication*] (DLA)
DESSOWESPAC Destroyers, Southwest Pacific Fleet [*Navy*]
des spd Designed Speed (SAUS)
Des Spec Design Specialist (SAUS)
DESSQDN Destroyer Squadron (SAUO)
D Es S ULJ Dar Es Salaam University. Law Journal [*A publication*] (DLA)
DeST Delaware Technical and Community College, Stanton Campus, Newark, DE [*Library symbol*] [*Library of Congress*] (LCLS)
DEST Denver Eye Screening Test
DEST Department of the Environment, Sport and Territories (SAUO)
Des T Desired Thickness (SAUS)
DEST Destia Communications, Inc. [*NASDAQ symbol*] (NASQ)
DEST Destillata [*Distilled*] [*Pharmacy*]
DEST Destination (AABC)
DEST Destra [*Right*] [*Italian*]
DEST Destroy (AABC)
DEST Destroyer [*Navy*] [*British*]
DEST Destruct (KSC)
DEST Dichotic Environmental Sounds Test [*Medicine*] (DMAA)
DEST Directed Energy Science & Technology (SAUS)
DEST Domestic Emergency Support Team [*Federal Bureau of Investigation*] (DEMM)
DESTA Digital Ethernet Thin-Wire Station Adapter [*Computer science*] (VERA)
Dest Cal Dig Desty's California Digest [*A publication*] (DLA)
Dest Com & Nav Desty on Commerce and Navigation [*A publication*] (DLA)
Dest d destroyed (SAUS)
destdist destructive distillation (SAUS)
DEST-DIST Destructively Distilled
Destec Destec Energy [*Associated Press*] (SAG)
DESTECH Design and Technology in Education (AIE)
Dest Fed Cit Desty's Federal Citations [*A publication*] (DLA)
Dest Fed Cons Desty on the Federal Constitution [*A publication*] (DLA)
Dest Fed Proc Desty's Federal Procedure [*A publication*] (DLA)
DESTIL Destilla [*Distill*] [*Pharmacy*] (ROG)
DESTIN Destination (DNAB)
destination SPPK destination Singapore, Penang, and Port Klang (SAUS)
destn Destination (ADWA)
DESTN Destination
DEST PT Destination Point (SAUS)
DESTR Desires to Transfer (NOAA)
DESTR Destroyed [*or Destructor*] (AAG)
destr Destroyed (VRA)
destr Destructor (SAUS)
DESTR FIR Destructive Firing (SAA)
Dest Sh & Adm Desty on Shipping and Admiralty [*A publication*] (DLA)
Desty Tax'n Desty on Taxation [*A publication*] (DLA)
DESUBEX Destroyer/Submarine Antisubmarine Warfare Exercise [*Military*] (NVT)
De Superst De Superstitione [*of Plutarch*] [*Classical studies*] (OCD)
DESUS Destroyers, United States Fleet (SAUO)
Deswell Deswell Industries, Inc. [*Associated Press*] (SAG)
Deswll Deswell Industries, Inc. [*Associated Press*] (SAG)
DET Damage Evaluation Team (SAA)
DET Data Evaluation Team (SAUS)
DET DECS Trust 8.50% 2000 [*NYSE symbol*] (SG)
DET Delta Aviation SA [*Spain*] [*ICAO designator*] (FAAC)
DET Department of Employment and Training [*Victoria*] [*Australia*]
DET Design Evaluation Test
DET Design Evaluation Testing (SAUS)
DET Detach
Det Detachable (DLA)
DET detached (SAUS)
det Detachment (MILB)
DET Detachment
det Detail (VRA)
DET Detail
Det detained (SAUS)
DET Detainee
DET Detection [*or Detector*] (AFM)
DET Detective
DET Detector (SAUS)
DET Detent [*Mechanical Engineering*] (NASA)
det detention (SAUS)
DET Detergent (ROG)
det determinant (SAUS)
det determinant of (SAUS)
DET Determination [*or Determine*] (KSC)
det Determination
Det Determinativ (SAUS)
DET Determinative (ROG)
DET Determine (SAUS)
DET Determiner [*Linguistics*]
DET Detonate (SAUS)
DET Detonation (SAUS)
DET Detonator (MSA)
DET Detroit [*City in Michigan*] (ROG)
DET Detroit [*Michigan*] City Airport [*Airport symbol*] (OAG)
Det Detroit Lions [*National Football League*] [*1934-present*] (NFLA)
DET Detur [*Give*] [*Pharmacy*]
DET Device Error Tabulation [*Computer science*] (IAA)
DET Device Execute Trigger (SAUS)
DET Dielectric Testing (SAUS)
DET Diesel Electric Tandem Motor Drive
DET Diesel Electric Trawler (IAA)
DET Diethyltartarate [*Organic chemistry*]
DET Diethyl Tartrate (SAUS)
DET Diethyl Telluride (SAUS)
DET Diethyltoluamide [*Also, DETA*] [*Insect repellant*] [*Organic chemistry*]
DET Diethyltryptamine (STED)
det diethyltryptanmine (SAUS)
DET Diffusive Equilibration in a Thin-Film [*Physical chemistry*]
DET Digital Event Timer (KSC)
DET Dimethyltryptamine [*A hallucinogenic drug*]
DET Direct Energy Transfer
DET Directory Entry Table (AGLO)
DET Displaced Equipment Training [*DoD*]
DET Distributed Explosive Technologies [*Military*] (DOMA)
DET Division of Educational Technology (SAUS)
DET Divorced Eutectic Transformation (SAUS)
DET Domestic Escorted Tour [*Travel*]
DET Double Eagle Energy [*Vancouver Stock Exchange symbol*]
DET Double Electron Transfer (MCD)
DET Double End Trimmed (DAC)

DET............ Double Exposure Technique (SAUS)
DET............ Dust Erosion Tunnel (MCD)
Det............ Quod Deterius Potiori Insidiari Soleat [*Philo*] (BJA)
Det 4.......... Big Safari Detachment four, Ontario, California (SAUS)
Det 6.......... Special Activity Squadron (SAUO)
DE/TA.......... Department of Employment / Training Agency [*British*]
DETA........... Dielectric Thermal Analysis
DETA........... Diethylenetriamine [*Also, DTA*] [*Organic chemistry*]
DETA........... Diethyltoluamide [*Also, DET*] [*Insect repellant*] [*Organic chemistry*]
DETA........... Divisao de Exploracao dos Transportes Aereos [*Angolan airline*]
DETAB.......... Decision Table [*Computer science*]
DETAB.......... Design Table (SAUS)
DETABGT........ Decision Table General Translator [*Computer science*] (IAA)
DETAB-GT....... Decision Table/General Translator (SAUS)
DETAB-X........ Decision Table, Experimental [*Computer science*]
DETAB-X........ Design Table, Experimental (SAUS)
DETAC.......... Digital Equipment Technology Analysis Center (MCD)
DETALL......... Detached from Duty Indicated and from All Other Duty Assigned
DETAP.......... Decision Table Processor [*IBM Corp.*]
DETAPAC........ Diethylenetriaminepentaacetic Acid (SAUS)
DETAPS......... Decision Table Processing System (SAUS)
DETASAD........ Detecon Al Saudia Ltd. (SAUO)
Det BJ......... Detroit Bar Journal [*A publication*] (DLA)
DETC........... Dendritic Epidermal T Cell [*Biochemistry*]
DETC........... Detection Systems [*NASDAQ symbol*] (TTSB)
DETC........... Detection Systems, Inc. [*NASDAQ symbol*] (NQ)
DETC........... Diesel-Electric Tower Car [*Indian Railway*] (TIR)
DETC........... Diethylthiacarbocyanine [*Organic chemistry*]
DETC........... Digital Element Tester Console (MCD)
DETC........... Distance Education and Training Counsel [*Formerly National Home Study Council (NHSC)*] (PAZ)
DetCan......... Detroit & Canada Tunnel Corp. [*Associated Press*] (SAG)
DET CDR CO... Determine FA Commander Concept of Operation (SAUS)
detch.......... Detached (VRA)
det chg........ detention charge (SAUS)
det cl......... Detention clause (SAUS)
DET CON........ Detective Constable [*Scotland Yard*] [*British*] (ADA)
DETD........... Detached Duty (DNAB)
DETD........... Detected (SAUS)
DETD........... Determined
DETD........... Drift Equivalent Temperature Difference (ACAE)
DETDA.......... Diethyl Toluene Diamine (SAUS)
DetDiesl....... Detroit Diesel Corp. [*Associated Press*] (SAG)
DetE........... Detroit Edison Co. [*Associated Press*] (SAG)
DETe........... Diethyltelluride
DETE........... Distributed Electronic Telephone Exchange [*Telecommunications*] (PDAA)
DetE25......... Detroit Edison Co. [*Associated Press*] (SAG)
DetE26......... Detroit Edison Co. [*Associated Press*] (SAG)
DETEC.......... Defense Technology Evaluation Code (SAUS)
DETEC.......... Detection (KSC)
detec.......... Detrection (SAUS)
detectionary... dictionary of detectives (SAUS)
DETED.......... Determined (ROG)
DetEd.......... Detroit Edison Co. [*Associated Press*] (SAG)
DETEN.......... Detention (DSUE)
DETEQ.......... DECHEMA [*Deutsche Gesellschaft fuer Chemisches Apparatewesen, Chemische Technik, und Biotechnologie eV*] Environmental Technology Equipment Databank [*Information service or system*] [*Germany*] (IID)
DETER.......... Detection, Enforcement, and Tutoring for Driver Error Reduction (EURO)
deter.......... Determinate (SAUS)
DETER.......... Determination (KSC)
DETERMD........ Determined (ROG)
DETERME........ Determine (ROG)
determin....... Determination
DETERMN........ Determination [*Legal term*] (ROG)
DETERS......... Damage Tolerant/Easy Repair Structures (MCD)
DETES.......... Deep-Towed Explosive Source [*Seismology*]
DETEST......... Demystify the Established Standardized Tests [*Project*]
DE TF.......... Data Engineering Technical Framework (SAUS)
DETF........... Data Exchange Test Facility (DA)
DETF........... Double-End Tuning Fork (SAUS)
DET-FFs........ Double Edge Triggered Flip-Flops (SAUS)
DETG........... Defense Energy Task Group (DNAB)
detg........... Determining (SAUS)
det gar........ detached garage (SAUS)
DETHERM........ DECHEMA [*Deutsche Gesellschaft fuer Chemisches Apparatewesen, Chemische Technik, und Biotechnologie eV*] Thermophysical Property Data Bank [*Germany*] [*Information service or system*] (CRD)
DETHERM-SDC... DECHEMA [*Deutsche Gesellschaft fuer Chemisches Apparatewesen, Chemische Technik, und Biotechnologie eV*] Thermophysical Property Data Bank - Data Evaluation System [*Database*]
DETHERM-SDR... DECHEMA [*Deutsche Gesellschaft fuer Chemisches Apparatewesen, Chemische Technik, und Biotechnologie eV*] Thermophysical Property Data Bank - Data RetrievalSystem [*Database*]
DETHERM-SDR... DECHEMA Thermophysical Property Data Base-Substance Retrieval System (SAUS)
Det in 2 Plo... Detur in Duplo [*Let Twice as Much Be Given*] [*Pharmacy*] (DAVI)
Det in Dup... Detur in Duplo [*Let Twice as Much Be Given*] [*Pharmacy*] (DAVI)
DET INSP....... Detective Inspector [*Scotland Yard*] [*British*] (ADA)
DETIR.......... Defense Technology Information Repository (MCD)
detl........... detail (SAUS)
DETLA.......... Detroit Lakes, MN [*American Association of Railroads railroad junction routing code*]
DETLA.......... Double Extended Three-Letter Abbreviation (ADWA)
Det Leg N...... Detroit Legal News [*A publication*] (DLA)
Det LJ......... Detroit Law Journal [*A publication*] (DLA)
Det L Rev...... Detroit Law Review [*A publication*] (DLA)
DETM........... Determine (AABC)
Detmt.......... Detachment [*British military*] (DMA)
DETN........... Detection (NASA)
detn........... Detention [*Medicine*] (EDAA)
DETN........... Detention (MSA)
detn........... Determination (ADWA)
DETN........... Determination
DETO........... Devils Tower National Monument
DETO........... Dyestuffs Environmental and Toxicology Organization
DETOC.......... Decision Table to COBOL [*Common Business-Oriented Language*] Processor [*Computer science*]
DETOL.......... Directly Executable Test-Oriented Language [*1968*] [*Computer science*] (CSR)
DE-TO PR....... Derated Takeoff Engine Pressure Ratio (GAVI)
DETOX.......... Detoxification (DSUE)
detox.......... detoxification center (SAUS)
DETOX.......... Wet Oxidation Waste Treatment Technology (DOGT)
detoxcen....... detoxification center (SAUS)
DETP........... Data Entry and Teleprocessing (SAUS)
DETP........... Department of Environmental and Toxicologic Pathology [*An association*] (EA)
DETP........... Diethylenetriaminepentaacetic Acid [*Also, DETPA, DTPA*] [*Chelating agent*]
DETP........... Displaced Equipment Training Plan [*DoD*]
DETPA.......... Diethylenetriaminepentaacetic Acid [*Also, DETP, DTPA*] [*Chelating agent*]
DETR........... Department of Environment, Transport, and the Regions
DETR........... Detector
DETR........... Detrimental (AABC)
DETRAH......... Detrahatur [*Let It, or Them, Be Drawn*] [*Pharmacy*] (ROG)
DETRAHAT....... Detrahatur [*Let It, or Them, Be Drawn*] [*Pharmacy*] (ROG)
DETRAN......... Decision Table Translator [*Computer science*]
DETRAN......... Decision Translator (NITA)
De Tranq Anim... De Tranquillitate Animi [*of Plutarch*] [*Classical studies*] (OCD)
DETRESFA....... Distress Phase [*Aviation*]
DETRINS........ Detailed Routing Instructions (NATG)
Detroit BQ..... Detroit Bar Quarterly [*A publication*] (DLA)
Detroit C Law... Detroit College of Law (GAGS)
Detroit Coll L... Detroit College of Law [*Michigan*] (DLA)
Detroit Inst... Detroit Institute of Arts (SAUS)
Detroit L...... Detroit Lawyer [*A publication*] (DLA)
Detroit Leg N... Detroit Legal News [*A publication*] (DLA)
Detroit L J.... Detroit Law Journal [*A publication*] (DLA)
Detroit L Rev... Detroit Law Review [*A publication*] (DLA)
DetrxC......... Detrex Corp. [*Associated Press*] (SAG)
dets........... details (SAUS)
D et S......... Detur et Signatur [*Let It Be Given and Labeled*] [*Pharmacy*]
D et S......... Detur et Signetur [*Let It Be Given and Labeled*] [*Pharmacy*] (DAVI)
DETS........... Diesel Engine Tuning System (SAUS)
DETS........... Digital Element Test Set
DET SGT........ Detective Sergeant [*Scotland Yard*] [*British*] (ADA)
Det Sup........ Detective Superintendent (SAUS)
Det Sym Orch... Detroit Symphony Orchestra (SAUS)
DET SYNC....... Detector Synchronization (SAUS)
DetSys......... Detection Systems, Inc. [*Associated Press*] (SAG)
D'ETTE......... Dinette [*Classified advertising*] (ADA)
Det-Tronics... Detector Electronics Corp. (SAUS)
DETU........... Diethylthiourea [*Organic chemistry*]
DETW........... Detroit & Western [*Later, DW*] [*AAR code*]
DETWAD......... Divorced Eutectic Transformation With Associated Deformation (SAUS)
DETWX.......... Delaware: Delchester Income Cl.A [*Mutual fund ticker symbol*] (SG)
DETX........... Detroit Edison [*Private rail car owner code*]
DEU............ Data Encoder Unit
DEU............ Data Encryption Unit
DEU............ Data Entry Unit
DEU............ Data Exchange Union (SAUO)
DEU............ Data Exchange Unit
DEU............ Dead-End User (ADWA)
deu............ Delaware [*MARC country of publication code*] [*Library of Congress*] (LCCP)
DEU............ Detector Electronics Unit (ACAE)
DEU............ Digital Evaluation Unit
DEU............ Direct Entry Unit (SAUS)
DEU............ Disk Electronics Unit (SAUS)
DEU............ Display Electronics Unit (NASA)
DEU............ Drug Epidemiology Unit (SAUS)
DEU............ Dumb End User (SAUS)
DEU............ Duplicates Exchange Union (EA)
DEU............ Federal Republic of Germany [*ANSI three-letter standard code*] (CNC)
DeU............ University of Delaware, Newark, DE [*Library symbol*] [*Library of Congress*] (LCLS)
DEUA........... Diesel Engines and Users Association (SAUS)
DEUA........... Diesel Engine Users Association (SAUS)
DEUA........... Digitronics Equipment Users Association

DeU-Ag........ University of Delaware, Agricultural Experiment Station, Newark, DE [*Library symbol*] [*Library of Congress*] (LCLS)
DEUC.......... Division of End Use Conservation [*Energy Research and Development Administration*]
DEUCE........ Deployable Universal Combat Earthmover (RDA)
DEUCE........ Design Unique Coupe Extension [*Concept vehicle*]
DEUCE........ Digital Electronic Universal Calculating [*or Computing*] Engine
DEUNA........ Digital Ethernet Unibus Network Adapter [*Computer science*] (VERA)
DEurL.......... Doctor of European Law (DD)
DEUS.......... Data Entry, University of Saskatchewan (SAUO)
DEUS.......... Dual Energy Use System
Deus........... Quod Deus Immutabilis Sit [*Philo*] (BJA)
DEUT.......... Data Encoder Unit Transmitter
Deut........... Deuteronomy [*Old Testament book*]
DeutR.......... Deuteronomy Rabba (BJA)
Deut Tel...... Deutsche Telekom AG [*Associated Press*] (SAG)
DEV............ Deep Epithelial Volume (SAUS)
DEV............ Delay Equalizer, Variable (IAA)
DEV............ Denver Silver [*Vancouver Stock Exchange symbol*]
DEV............ Derecha Emergente de Venezuela [*Political party*] (EY)
DEV............ Design Evaluation Vehicle
DEV............ Deva [*Romania*] [*Seismograph station code, US Geological Survey*] (SEIS)
dev............. Devant [*Front*] (BARN)
DEV............ Develop [*or Development*] (AFM)
DEV............ Developer (SAUS)
Dev............ Development (AAGC)
DEV............ Development Well (SAUS)
Dev............ Devereux's North Carolina Law Reports [*A publication*] (DLA)
Dev............ Devereux's Reports, United States Court of Claims [*A publication*] (DLA)
dev............. deviate (SAUS)
DEV............ Deviation (AAG)
DEV............ Deviator (SAUS)
DEV............ Device (KSC)
De V........... De Vilbiss (SAUS)
DEV............ Devilbiss Co. (SAUO)
dev............. devition (SAUS)
DEV............ Devjo Industries, Inc. [*Toronto Stock Exchange symbol*]
Dev............ Devon (SAUS)
DEV............ Devonian [*Geology*]
Dev............ Devonshire County [*England*] (BARN)
DEV............ Diesel electro vessel (SAUS)
DEV............ Director [*or Directorate*] of Evaluation [*Army*]
DEV............ Duck Egg Virus [*or Duck Embryo Vaccine*] [*Immunology*]
DEV............ Duck Embryo Origin Vaccine (ADWA)
DEV............ Duck Embryo Vaccine [*Medicine*] (DB)
Dev............ Eamon De Valera (SAUS)
DEV............ Red Devils Parachute Display Team [*British*] [*ICAO designator*] (FAAC)
DEVA.......... Death Valley National Monument
DEVA.......... Develop Address (SAUS)
DEVA.......... Development Acceptance (AABC)
DEVA.......... Development Validation Acceptance
DEVA.......... Document-Enabled Vertical Application [*Computer science*] (GART)
DEVA.......... Drone Employment Value Analysis (MCD)
DEVA IPR.... Demonstration and Validation In-Process Review
DEVAIPR..... Development Acceptance in Process Review (RDA)
Dev & B....... Devereux and Battle's North Carolina Equity Reports [*A publication*] (DLA)
Dev & B....... Devereux and Battle's North Carolina Law Reports [*A publication*] (DLA)
Dev & Bat.... Devereux and Battle's North Carolina Law Reports [*A publication*] (DLA)
Dev & Bat Eq... Devereux and Battle's North Carolina Equity Reports [*A publication*] (DLA)
Dev & B Eq... Devereux and Battle's North Carolina Equity Reports [*A publication*] (DLA)
Dev & BL (NC)... Devereux and Battle's North Carolina Law Reports [*A publication*] (DLA)
DEVAR......... Device Address Register (SAUS)
DEVAT......... Depot Vehicle Automatic Tester
Dev Biol...... Developmental Biology (journ.) (SAUS)
DeVBul........ DeVlieg Bullard, Inc. [*Associated Press*] (SAG)
DEVC.......... Devcon International [*NASDAQ symbol*] (TTSB)
DEVC.......... Devcon International Corp. [*NASDAQ symbol*] (NQ)
DEVC.......... Development Change [*Aerospace*] (AAG)
Dev CC........ Devereux's Reports, United States Court of Claims [*A publication*] (DLA)
DEVCENTRE... Development Centre (SAUS)
Dev Change... Development and Change [*A publication*] (PABS)
DEVCO........ Development Committee [*ISO*] (DS)
DEVCOM...... Device Communications [*Computer science*]
Devcon........ Devcon International Corp. [*Associated Press*] (SAG)
DEVCONF..... Conference on the Problems of Standardization in the Developing Countries (SAUO)
Dev Ct Cl..... Devereux's Reports, United States Court of Claims [*A publication*] (DLA)
DEVCTR....... Development Center (MCD)
DevD........... Developers Diversified Realty Corp. [*Associated Press*] (SAG)
devd........... device data set residence (SAUS)
DEVD.......... Device Description (SAUS)
DEVD.......... Devilled [*Culinary*] (ROG)
DEVD.......... Devised (ROG)
Dev Deeds... Devlin on Deeds and Real Estate [*A publication*] (DLA)
DEVE........... Data Entry and Validation Equipment (SAUS)
DEVE........... Devise (ROG)
devel.......... developer (SAUS)
Devel.......... Development (AL)
devel.......... Development (DD)
DEVEL......... Development
Devel Change... Development and Change [*A publication*] (JLIT)
Develop....... Development
Develop Cen... Development Center (SAUS)
Developing Ed... Developing Education [*A publication*]
Development Committee... Joint Ministerial Committee of the Boards of Governors of the Bank and the Fund of/on the Transfer of Real Resources to Developing Countries (SAUO)
Dev Engr...... Development Engineer (SAUS)
Dev Eq......... Devereux's North Carolina Equity Reports [*A publication*] (DLA)
DEV EQL...... Deviation Equalizer (SAUS)
DEV FA LOG SPT... Develop FA Logistics Support Plan (SAUS)
DEV FA SPT PLAN... Develop FA Support Plan (SAUS)
DevG........... Devisengesetz [*Law on Exchange Control*] [*German*] (DLA)
DEV GENC... Federation of Turkish Revolutionary Youth
DEV HGT...... Developed Height (MSA)
Dev Hydrobiol... Developments in Hydrobiology [*A publication*] (PABS)
DEVIC.......... Delaware Valley Information Consortium (SAUS)
DEVIL.......... Development of Integrated Logistics (NATG)
DEVIL.......... Diary on Events in Leicester (SAUS)
DEVIL.......... Direct Evaluation of Indexed Language (IAA)
Devils Postpile... Devils Postpile National Monument (SAUS)
Dev Immunol... Developmental Immunology (SAUS)
Devin.......... Devin-Adair (SAUS)
De Vir Ill..... De Viris Illustribus [*of St. Jerome*] [*Classical studies*] (OCD)
DEVIS.......... development science information system (SAUS)
devis........... Devised (GEAB)
Dev Kin Bl... Devereux's Kinne's Blackstone [*A publication*] (DLA)
Dev Kin Kent... Devereux's Kinne's Kent [*A publication*] (DLA)
Dev L.......... Devereux's North Carolina Law Reports [*A publication*] (DLA)
DEVLA......... Devils Lake, ND [*American Association of Railroads railroad junction routing code*]
Devl Deeds... Devlin on Deeds [*A publication*] (DLA)
DevlDv........ Developers Diversified Realty Corp. [*Associated Press*] (SAG)
DEV LG........ Developed Length (SAUS)
DEV LGTH.... Developed Length (SAUS)
devlp.......... develop (SAUS)
devlpd........ developed (SAUS)
devlpg........ developing (SAUS)
DEVLPMNTL... Developmental
DEVLPMT.... Development
DEVLPMTL.... Developmental
DEVLX......... Delaware: Value Fund Cl.A [*Mutual fund ticker symbol*] (SG)
DEVMIS........ Development Management Information System (SAUS)
DEVN.......... Deviation (MSA)
DEVN.......... Devon Group [*NASDAQ symbol*] (TTSB)
DEVN.......... Devon Group, Inc. [*NASDAQ symbol*] (NQ)
DEVNAME.... Device Name (SAUS)
DevnE.......... Devon Energy Corp. [*Associated Press*] (SAG)
DEVNET....... Development Information Network [*United Nations*] (NITA)
DEVNO......... Deviation Request Number (DNAB)
DEVO.......... Data Entry Validation Option [*Computer science*] (TIMI)
DEVO.......... De-Evolution [*Acronym is name of musical group*]
Devon......... Devon Group, Inc. [*Associated Press*] (SAG)
DEVON........ Devonshire [*County in England*]
DEVON........ Devonshire Regiment (SAUO)
Devons........ Devonshire [*County in England*]
Devot.......... Devotionalien (SAUS)
devp........... develop (SAUS)
DEVPRO....... Standing Co-ordinating Bureau for the Promotion of Standardization in the Developing Countries (SAUO)
Devpt.......... Development
DevR........... Development of Amnesty International (SAUO)
DEVR.......... Distortion-Eliminating Voltage Regulator
DEVR.......... Dominant Exudative Vitreoretinopathy [*Ophthalmology*] (DAVI)
DeVry.......... DeVry, Inc. [*Associated Press*] (SAG)
devs........... developers (SAUS)
DEVS.......... Devotions
DEVS.......... DODAAC [*Department of Defense Activity Address Code*] Edit/Validation System [*Military*]
DEVSIS........ Development of Science Information Systems (SAUS)
DEVSIS........ Development Sciences Information System [*Information service or system*] [*Canada*] (IID)
DEVSIS........ International Information System for the Development Sciences (SAUO)
DEVT.......... Data-Entry Virtual Terminal [*Computer science*]
DEVT.......... Developed Technology Resource [*NASDAQ symbol*] (TTSB)
DEVT.......... Development
Devt Assoc Bull... Development Association. Bulletin [*A publication*]
DEVTOS....... Developmental Tactical Operations Systems (MCD)
Devts Mfuring Ind... Developments in Manufacturing Industry [*A publication*]
DEVTYPE..... Device Type (SAUS)
DEV W......... Developed Width (SAUS)
DEV WD....... Developed Width (MSA)
DEW............ Deep Early Warning (SAUS)
DEW............ Delmarva Power & Light Co. [*NYSE symbol*] (SPSG)
DEW............ Delmarva Power Financing I [*NYSE symbol*] (SAG)
DEW............ Delmarva Pwr & Lt [*NYSE symbol*] (TTSB)
DEW............ Demineralization Water (SAUS)
Dew............ Dewey's Kansas Court of Appeals Reports [*A publication*] (DLA)

Dew .... Dewey's Reports [*60-70 Kansas*] [*A publication*] (DLA)
dew .... dewpoint (SAUS)
DEW .... Digital Electronic Watch (SAUS)
DEW .... Digital Encyclopedia Workstation [*Medinfo 86*]
DEW .... Directed Energy Warfare [*Army*] (INF)
DEW .... Directed Energy Weapon
DEW .... Director of Electronic Warfare (SAUO)
DEW .... Distant Early Warning [*North American RADAR system*] [*Obsolete*]
DEW .... Division Early Warning [*Army*] (INF)
DEWA .... Defence Wall (SAUS)
DEWA .... Delaware Water Gap National Recreation Area
DeWAt .... Atlas Chemical Industries, Inc., Wilmington, DE [*Library symbol*] [*Library of Congress*] (LCLS)
DEWAT .... Deactivated War Trophy (DICI)
DeWB .... Brandywine College, Wilmington, DE [*Library symbol*] [*Library of Congress*] (LCLS)
DEWCOM .... Divisional Electronic Warfare Combat (MCD)
DEWCOM T & E ... Divisional Electronic Warfare Combat Model Test and Evaluation
DEWD .... Detailed Elementary Wiring Diagrams
Dew Div .... Dewey on Divorce Law [*A publication*] (DLA)
DeWDJ .... E. I. Du Pont de Nemours & Co., Jackson Laboratory, Wilmington, DE [*Library symbol*] [*Library of Congress*] (LCLS)
DeWDL .... E. I. Du Pont de Nemours & Co., Lavoisier Library, Wilmington, DE [*Library symbol*] [*Library of Congress*] (LCLS)
DeWDT .... E. I. Du Pont de Nemours & Co., Technical Library, Wilmington, DE [*Library symbol*] [*Library of Congress*] (LCLS)
DE-Wert .... dextrose equivalent (SAUS)
D'Ewes J .... D'Ewes' Journal and Parliamentary Collection [*A publication*] (DLA)
DEWEY .... Dewey, OK [*American Association of Railroads railroad junction routing code*]
DEWG .... Directed Energy Weapon Ground (ACAE)
DeWH .... Hercules Powder Co. [*Later, Hercules, Inc.*], Experiment Station, Wilmington,DE [*Library symbol*] [*Library of Congress*] (LCLS)
DeWHI .... Hercules, Inc., Wilmington, DE [*Library symbol*] [*Library of Congress*] (LCLS)
DEWI .... Direct Environmental Warming Impact
DeWI .... Wilmington Institute Free Library and the New Castle County Free Library, Wilmington, DE [*Library symbol*] [*Library of Congress*] (LCLS)
DEWIDZ .... Distant Early Warning Identification Zone (SAUS)
DEWIFAS .... Divisional Electronic Warfare Intelligence Functional Analysis (MCD)
DeWint .... Henry Francis DuPont Winterthur Museum, Winterthur, DE [*Library symbol*] [*Library of Congress*] (LCLS)
DeWint-M .... Henry Francis DuPont Winterthur Museum, Joseph Downs Manuscript and Microfilm Collection, Winterthur, DE [*Library symbol*] [*Library of Congress*] (LCLS)
DeWitt .... DeWitt's Reports [*24-42 Ohio State*] [*A publication*] (DLA)
DEWIZ .... Distant Early Warning Identification Zone [*North American RADAR system*] [*Obsolete*]
DEWK .... Dual Employed, with Kids [*Lifestyle classification*]
DEWKS .... Dual Employed With Kids (DFIT)
DEWL .... Directed Energy Weapon, Laser (ACAE)
DEW line .... Distant Early Warning Line (WDAA)
DEW LINE .... Distant Early Warning Line [*North American RADAR system*] [*Obsolete*]
DEWLINE .... Distant Early Warning Viewing Line (FOTI)
DEWO .... Directed Energy Weapon, Orbital (ACAE)
DeWolfe .... [*The*] DeWolfe Cos., Inc. [*Associated Press*] (SAG)
DEWP .... Directed Energy Weapon, Particle-Beam (ACAE)
DEWPO .... Distant Early Warning Project Office [*North American RADAR System*] [*Obsolete*] (IAA)
DEW Radar ... Distant Early Warning Radar (SAUS)
DEWS .... Diagnostic Evaluation of Writing Skills (SAUS)
DEWS .... Digital EW Simulator (SAUS)
DEWS .... Distant Early Warning System (CCCA)
DEWS .... Doppler Electronic Weather Sensor (SAUS)
Dew St .... Dewey's Compiled Statutes of Michigan [*A publication*] (DLA)
DEWSUM .... Distant Early Warning Summary (MCD)
DeWT .... Delaware Technical and Community College, Northern Campus, Wilmington, DE [*Library symbol*] [*Library of Congress*] (LCLS)
DEWT .... Dimensional and Excessive Weight (SAUS)
DeWTC .... Third Circuit Court of Appeals, Wilmington, DE [*Library symbol*] [*Library of Congress*] (LCLS)
DEWTRG .... Dewatering (MSA)
DEW-V .... Directed Energy Warfare Vehicle (SEWL)
DEW-V .... Directed Energy Weapons - Vehicle [*Army*]
DeWV .... United States Veterans Administration Center, Wilmington, DE [*Library symbol*] [*Library of Congress*] (LCLS)
DEWY .... Dewey Electronic Corp. [*NASDAQ symbol*] (COMM)
DEX .... Data Exchange
DEX .... Decision Expediting [*Graphic Sciences, Inc., copying machine*]
DEX .... Deferred Execution
DEX .... Departed for Export (SAUS)
DEX .... Destroyer Escort Experimental (MCD)
DEX .... Dexamethasone [*Also, D, DXM*] [*Antineoplastic drug*]
DEX .... Dexamphetamine Sulfate Tablet [*Slang*] (DSUE)
DEX .... Dexedrine
DEX .... Dexter [*Right*] [*Latin*] (ROG)
DEX .... [*The*] Dexter Corp. [*NYSE symbol*] (SPSG)
DEX .... Dextran [*Organic chemistry*]
dex .... dextroamphetamine tablet (SAUS)
dex .... Dextrorotatory (DOG)
dex .... Dextrose [*Pharmacology*] (DAVI)
dex .... Dextro-Stix [*Pharmacology*] (DAVI)
DEX .... Direct Exempt (TIMI)
D Ex .... Doctor of Expression
DEX .... Double Exposure
DEX .... Interflight, Inc. [*ICAO designator*] (FAAC)
DEXA .... Dual Energy X-Ray Absorptiometry [*Analytical chemistry*]
DEXAN .... Digital Experimental Airborne Navigator
dexe .... dexedrine (SAUS)
DEXEC .... Diagnostic EXEc software (SAUS)
DEXGAL .... Dexamethasonyl Galactoside [*Biochemistry*]
DEXGLU .... Dexamthasonyl Glucopyranoside [*Biochemistry*]
D/EXH .... Dual Exhaust [*Automotive engineering*]
DEXIE .... Dexedrine
dexies .... dexedrine tablets (SAUS)
DEXO .... Dexon, Inc. [*NASDAQ symbol*] (COMM)
DEXOIL .... Diesel-Engine-Expert-Oil (SAUS)
DEXPO .... DEC Exposition (SAUS)
DEXT .... Dexter [*Right*] [*Latin*]
DEXT .... Dexter Carpenter Coal [*Federal Railroad Administration identification code*]
DEXT .... Distant End Cross-Talk [*Telecommunications*] (NITA)
DEXTER .... Dental X-Ray Teaching and Training Replica
Dexter .... [*The*] Dexter Corp. [*Associated Press*] (SAG)
DEXTOR .... Deep Experimental Torpedo [*Also, DSWS*] [*Later, EXTOR*] (MCD)
DEXTR .... Dexter, MO [*American Association of Railroads railroad junction routing code*]
DEXTRO .... Dextrorotatory (SAUS)
DEZ .... Deir Ez Zor [*Syria*] [*Airport symbol*] (OAG)
DEZ .... Derekh 'Erets Zuta [*or Derek Erez Zuta*] (BJA)
DEZ .... Diethyl Zinc [*Used for deacidification of paper to arrest book decay*]
DEZ .... Docklands Enterprise Zone [*British*]
DF .... Air Nebraska [*ICAO designator*] (AD)
DF .... Associate Directorate for Facilities and Systems Management [*Kennedy Space Center*] [*NASA*] (NASA)
DF .... Daae-Finsen [*Disease*] [*Medicine*] (DB)
DF .... Daedalian Foundation (EA)
DF .... Dairy Farmer (journ.) (SAUS)
DF .... Damage Free [*Business term*]
DF .... Damping Factor
DF .... Danish People's Party [*Political party*] (PSAP)
DF .... Danmarks (SAUS)
DF .... Danny Foundation (EA)
DF .... Darkfield (AAEL)
DF .... Data Fetch (SAUS)
DF .... Data Field [*Computer science*]
DF .... Data Flag (VLIE)
DF .... Data Folder
DF .... Date Filed [*IRS*]
DF .... Day Fighter (SAUS)
DF .... Day Frequency (IAA)
DF .... Daylight Factor (DAC)
d/f .... Dead Freight (EBF)
DF .... Dead Freight [*Shipping*]
D/F .... Deadfreight (SAUS)
DF .... Dean Foods [*NYSE symbol*] (TTSB)
DF .... Dean Foods Co. [*NYSE symbol*] (SPSG)
DF .... Dean of the Faculty
DF .... Debre-Fibiger [*Syndrome*] [*Medicine*] (DB)
DF .... Decal Film
DF .... Decapacitation Factor [*with reference to sperm*] [*Medicine*]
DF .... Decayed and Filled [*Dentistry*] (DAVI)
DF .... Decimal Factor (MCD)
DF .... Decimal Fraction (MDG)
DF .... Decision Feature (SAUS)
DF .... Decision Feedback (SAUS)
DF .... Decision Function (SAUS)
DF .... Decontamination Facility
DF .... Decontamination Factor
DF .... Deep Freezing (SAUS)
DF .... Deere Funk [*Automotive industry supplier*]
DF .... Default [*Automotive emissions*]
DF .... Defence Fellowship [*British*]
DF .... Defender of the Faith (WDAA)
DF .... Defensive Fire
DF .... Defensor Fidei [*Defender of the Faith*] [*Latin*]
DF .... Deferoxamine [*Also, Desferrioxamine*] [*Chelating agent*]
Df .... Deficiency (QSUL)
DF .... Deficiency Factor (MAE)
DF .... Defined Flora Animal [*Medicine*] (DMAA)
DF .... Definition
df .... deflect (SAUS)
df .... Deflection (SAUS)
DF .... Deflection Factor (IEEE)
DF .... Defluorination (SAUS)
DF .... Defogging (AAG)
DF .... Degrees Fahrenheit (KSC)
DF .... Degrees of Freedom [*of movement*]
df .... Degrees of Freedom
DF .... Deionization-Filtration
DF .... Delay Fuse
DF .... Demagnetization Factor (SAUS)
DF .... Democracy Fund [*Defunct*] (EA)
DF .... Dengue Fever [*Medicine*] (MELL)
DF .... Dense Film (SAUS)
DF .... Dense Flint (AAG)
DF .... Department of Forestry (SAUS)
DF .... Deposition Form [*Army*] (ADDR)

DF............... Depot Fixed (AAG)
DF............... Depreciation Factor (IAA)
DF............... Depressed Fracture [*Medicine*] (MELL)
DF............... Depth of Field [*or Focus*] [*Photography*]
DF............... Derating Factor
DF............... Derivation of Frequency with Respect to Time (IAA)
DF............... Dermatofibroma [*Medicine*] (MELL)
DF............... Dermatology Foundation (EA)
df............... derrick floor (SAUS)
DF............... Describing Function
DF............... Desferrioxamine [*Deferoxamine*] [*Pharmacology*] (DAVI)
DF-.............. Design For (SAUS)
DF............... Design Formula
DF............... Destination Field
DF............... Destroyer Flotilla [*Navy*]
DF............... Detailed Forecast (MCD)
DF............... Deterioration Factor [*Automotive engineering*]
DF............... Deutereium Fluoride (IEEE)
DF............... Development Fixture (MCD)
DF............... Development Flight (NASA)
DF............... Development-Forward (MCD)
DF............... Development Fund
DF............... Device Flag [*Computer science*]
DF............... Device Function [*Computer science*] (IAA)
DF............... Diabetic Father [*Medicine*]
DF............... Diagnostic Flag (SAUS)
DF............... Dialogue Foundation (EA)
DF............... Dialysis Fluid [*Physiology*]
DF............... Dialyzable Fraction
DF............... Diamond Flap [*Envelopes*]
DF............... Diastolic Filling [*Medicine*] (EDAA)
DF............... Dicke-Fix [*Electronics*]
DF............... Dickens Fellowship (SAUO)
DF............... Die Forming (SAUS)
DF............... Dierk's Forest [*Federal Railroad Administration identification code*]
DF............... Diesel Fuel [*or Fueled*] (CINC)
DF............... Dietary Fiber [*Nutrition*]
DF............... Difference Frequency (SAUS)
DF............... Differential Flotation (SAUS)
DF............... Differential Frequency (IAA)
dF............... differential of field intensity (SAUS)
dF............... differential of force (SAUS)
DF............... Differentiation Factor [*Biochemistry*]
DF............... Digital Filter (SAUS)
DF............... Digital Fluoroscopy (SAUS)
DF............... Dilution Factor [*Also, Fd*] [*Nuclear energy*] (NRCH)
DF............... Dimensional Flowcharting [*Computer science*]
DF............... Dirac-Fock Theory [*Electrodynamics*]
DF............... Direct File (SAUS)
DF............... Direct Flight (MCD)
DF............... Direct Flow
DF............... Direct Fluorescence
DF............... Direct Frequency (ACAE)
DF............... Direction Finder [*or Finding*] [*Radio aid to navigation*]
df............... Direction Finding (IDOE)
DF............... Direction-Finding (PIAV)
DF............... Direction Flag [*Computer science*] (VERA)
DF............... Disaccommodation Factor
DF............... Disappearing Filament (SAUS)
DF............... Disassembly Facility [*NASA*] (NASA)
DF............... disc file (SAUS)
DF............... Discharge Flow [*Chemical kinetics*]
DF............... Discriminant Function [*Physiology*]
DF............... Discrimination Factor (SAUS)
DF............... Discrimination Filter (AAG)
DF............... Discripteur de Fichier (SAUS)
DF............... Disk File [*Computer science*] (BUR)
DF............... Disk Free [*Computer science*] (VERA)
DF............... Dislocated Farmer [*Job Training and Partnership Act*] (OICC)
DF............... Dispersion Factor [*Environmental science*] (COE)
DF............... display format facility (SAUS)
DF............... Disposition Form [*Army*]
DF............... Disseminated Foci [*Medicine*]
DF............... Dissipation Factor
DF............... distorrion factor (SAUS)
DF............... Distortion Factor [*Telecommunications*] (IAA)
DF............... Distributing Frame (SAUS)
DF............... Distribution Factor
DF............... Distribution Feeder [*Telecommunications*] (OA)
DF............... Distribution Frame (KSC)
DF............... Distribution From (CCCA)
DF............... Distribution Function [*Statistics*]
DF............... Ditchley Foundation (EA)
DF............... Diva Foundation (EA)
DF............... Diversity Factor
DF............... Diverted Force (CINC)
DF............... Doctor of Forestry
DF............... Document Feeding (SAUS)
DF............... Dodge Foundation (SAUO)
DF............... Dog Fight (ACAE)
DF............... domestic or foreign recipient. (SAUS)
DF............... Dominance Factor (VLIE)
DF............... Dong Feng [*East Wind*] [*Chinese missile*]
DF............... Don't Fragment [*Telecommunications jargon*] (ACRL)
DF............... Door in Flat [*Theater*]
DF............... Dorsal Fold
DF............... Dorsiflexion [*Medicine*]
DF............... Dose Factor [*Radioactivity calculations*]
d/f.............. double Deece (SAUS)
DF............... Double Feeder [*Line*] [*Technical drawings*]
DF............... Double Flag (SAUS)
DF............... Double Focusing (SAUS)
DF............... Double Foolscap [*Paper*] (ADA)
DF............... Double Frequency
DF............... Double Fronted (SAUS)
D-F.............. Double-Fronted
DF............... Douglas Fir (MSA)
DF............... downflow (SAUS)
DF............... Draft (ADA)
DF............... Draft Printer (SAUS)
DF............... Drag Factor (VLIE)
DF............... Drag Friction
DF............... Drainage Free (MIST)
DF............... Dream Factory (EA)
DF............... Drift Flux (SAUS)
DF............... Drinking Fountain (AAG)
Df............... Drittfach (SAUS)
DF............... Drive Fit [*Technical drawings*]
DF............... Drop Forge (KSC)
DF............... Drop Forging (SAUS)
DF............... Drug Free (MELL)
DF............... Drum File (SAUS)
DF............... Dual Facility
DF............... Dual filter (SAUS)
df............... dummy fuse (SAUS)
df............... dunnage free (SAUS)
DF............... Duodenal Flexure [*Medicine*] (MELL)
DF............... Duplex filter (SAUS)
DF............... Duty Factor [*Military*] (CAAL)
DF............... Duty Free [*Customs*]
DF............... Dye-Free [*Pharmacy*]
DF............... Dynamic Fermenter [*Microbiology*]
DF............... Dysautonomia Foundation (EA)
DF............... Dysgonic Fermenter (DB)
DF............... Fallout Forecast Data [*Civil Defense*]
DF............... Methylphosphonic Difluoride (SAUS)
DF............... Project Management (SAUS)
DF-1............. Digitales Fernsehen 1 (SAUS)
DF31............. Dong Feng 31 [*Chinese missile system*]
DFA.............. Aero Coach Aviation International, Inc. [*ICAO designator*] (FAAC)
DFA.............. Dairy Farmers Association (SAUO)
DFA.............. Dance Films Association (EA)
DFA.............. Data Flow Analyzer (ACAE)
DFA.............. Defense Fisheries Administration [*Abolished, 1953*]
DFA.............. Defense Fisheries Association (SAUO)
DFA.............. Department for the Arts [*Western Australia*] [*Australia*]
DFA.............. Department of Food and Agriculture [*Victoria*] [*Australia*]
DFA.............. Department of Foreign Affairs (CINC)
DFA.............. Deposit Fund Account
DFA.............. Describing Function Analyzer [*NASA*]
DFA.............. Designated Field Activity [*DoD*]
DFA.............. Design Fabrication Assembly
DFA.............. Design for Assembly [*Automotive engineering*]
DFA.............. Design for Automation [*Manufacturing technology*]
DFA.............. Deterministic Finite Automation (MCD)
DFA.............. Detonation Fragmentation and Air Blast (SAA)
DFA.............. Development Fund for Africa (SAUO)
DFA.............. Diamonds Fields Artillery [*British military*] (DMA)
DFA.............. Dick Family Association (EA)
DFA.............. Die Forged Aluminum
DFA.............. Diesel Fuel with an Antarctic Additive
DFA.............. Diet for Age [*Medicine*] (DAVI)
DFA.............. Difficulty Falling Asleep (MELL)
DFA.............. Diffuse fibrosing alveolitis (SAUS)
DFA.............. Digital Fault Analysis
DFA.............. Digital Frequency Analyzer
DFA.............. Dimensional Fund Advisors [*Fund-management firm*] (ECON)
DFA.............. Diploma in Foreign Affairs (ADA)
DFA.............. Diploma of Fine Art [*British*]
DFA.............. Direct Fluorescent Antibody (Stain) [*Clinical medicine*]
DFA.............. Direct Immunofluorescent Assay [*Analytical biochemistry*]
DFA.............. Direction Finding Aerial (SAUS)
DFA.............. Direction Finding Antenna
DFA.............. Discriminant Function Analysis (DMAA)
DFA.............. Distributed Function Architecture
DFA.............. Dividend Franking Account
DFA.............. Division Final Appearance (SAA)
DFA.............. Division Freight Agent
DFA.............. Doctor of Fine Arts
DFA.............. Doctors for Artists (EA)
DFA.............. Document Format Architecture (SAUS)
DFA.............. Domestic Field Allowance (ACAE)
DFA.............. Dominant Feature Analysis
DFA.............. Dorsiflexion Assistance (DMAA)
DFA.............. Dried Fruit Association of California [*Later, DFA of California*] (EA)
DFA.............. Drive Front Axle
DFA.............. Driver Fuel Assembly [*Nuclear energy*] (NRCH)
DFA.............. Drop Forging Association [*Later, FIA*] (EA)
DFA.............. Dummy Fuel Assembly [*Nuclear energy*] (NRCH)
DFA.............. DXI Frame Address (SAUS)

DFA Dynamic Force Analysis
DFA National Association of Drop Forgers and Stampers (SAUO)
DFA Partnership for a Drug Free America (EA)
DFAA Dissolved Free Amino Acids
DFAA United States Federal Aviation Administration, Washington, DC [*Library symbol*] [*Library of Congress*] (LCLS)
DFAAS Dissolved Free Amino Acids (SAUS)
DFAC Dining Facilities Administration Center (MCD)
DFAC Dried Fruit Association of California [*Later, DFA of California*]
DFACS Distributed Factory Automated Control System (TIMI)
DFAD Digital Feature Analysis Data [*Military*]
DFADL developmental functional activities of daily living score (SAUS)
DFA/DM Driver fuel assembly/dismantling machine (SAUS)
DFADS Destroyer/Frigate Air Defence System (SAUS)
DFAE Director of Facilities and Engineering [*Military*] (AABC)
DFAED Dated Forecast Authorization Equipment Data (MCD)
DFAG Double-Frequency Amplitude Grating (SAUS)
DFAI Department of Foreign Affairs and Information [*South Africa*]
DFAIR Defense Financial and Investment Review [*Pronounced "dee-fair"*] [*DoD*]
DFAIT Department of Foreign Affairs & International Trade [*Canada*]
DFAM Derived File Access Method [*Computer science*] (PDAA)
DFAMS Defense Fuels Automated Management System [*DoD*]
DFAN Dean of the Faculty, Aeronautics [*Air Force Academy*]
DFAn Discriminate Function Analysis
DF & J De Gex, Fisher, and Jones' English Chancery Reports [*A publication*] (DLA)
DF & JB De Gex, Fisher, and Jones' English Bankruptcy Reports [*A publication*] (DLA)
DFAO Food and Agricultural Organization of the United Nations, North American Regional Office, Washington, DC [*Library symbol*] [*Library of Congress*] (LCLS)
DFAR Daily Field Activity Report
DFAR Defense Federal Acquisition Regulations
DFARS Defense Federal Acquisition Regulation Supplement (RDA)
DFARS Department of Defense FAR Supplement [*A publication*] (AAGC)
DFAS Defense Finance and Accounting Service [*DoD*]
DFAS Detailed Functional Application Sub-System (SAUS)
DFAS Direct Fire Artillery System (SAUS)
DFAS Distributed Financial Accounting System (SAUS)
DFASC Deployable Force Automated Service Center (SAUO)
DFAST Dynamic File Allocation System
DFAT Destination Final Acceptance Test (LAIN)
DFAT Direct Fluorescent Antibody Technique [*Clinical chemistry*]
DFAW Direct Fire Antitank Weapon
DFAWS Direct Fire Antitank Weapon System (SAA)
DFAX Diversifax, Inc. [*NASDAQ symbol*] (SAG)
DFB Data Flag Branch [*Computer science*] (NITA)
DFB Deutsche Frauenbewegung [*German Women's Movement*] [*Germany*] (PPW)
DFB Diffusion Brazing
DFB Digital Filter Bank (ACAE)
DFB Dinitrofluorobenzene [*Also, DNFB, FDNB*] [*Organic chemistry*]
DFB Distributed Feedback (AAEL)
DFB Distributed Feedback semiconductor (SAUS)
DFB Distribution Fuse Board (IEEE)
DFB Dried Fruits Board [*New South Wales, South Australia, Western Australia*]
DFB Dry Film Binder
dfb dunnagefree bulkheads (SAUS)
DFB Dysfunctional Uterine Bleeding [*Gynecology*] (DAVI)
DFB South African Deciduous Fruit Board (SAUO)
DFBI Depth First Begin Index (SAUS)
DFB Laser Distributed Feedback Laser (SAUS)
DFB-LD Distributed Feedback LASER Diode
DFBM Data Flag Branch Manager [*Computer science*] (NITA)
D-FBM Declarative Feature Based Modeller (VLIE)
DFBPT Digital Force Balance Pressure Transducer
DFBR Data Flag Branch Register [*Computer science*] (NITA)
DFBR Disc file optimiser (SAUS)
DFBS Daily Finish Build Schedule (VLIE)
DFBT Dynamic Functional Board Tester (SAUS)
DFBW Digital Fly by Wire [*Aviation*]
DFC Dairy Farmers of Canada (SAUO)
DFC Data Flow Chart (SAUS)
DFC Data Flow Control [*Computer science*] [*Telecommunications*] (IBMDP)
DFC Data Format Converter
DFC De Facto Cases [*Australia*] [*A publication*]
DFC Defect (VLIE)
DFC Delta Financial [*NYSE symbol*] (SG)
DFC Department Frequency Coordinator (SAUS)
DFC Desert Fishes Council (EA)
DFC Design Field Change (NRCH)
DFC Designs for Change (EA)
DFC Developmental Field Complex (DMAA)
DFC Development Finance Company [*Generic term*] [*Banking*]
DFC Devils Fan Club (EA)
DFC Devo Fan Club (EA)
DFC Diagnostic Flow Chart [*Computer science*] (IEEE)
DFC Dial Financial Corporation (SAUO)
DFC Di'anno Fan Club (EA)
DFC Diesel Fuel and Coolant [*Nuclear energy*]
DFC Diffusion Formed Coating
DFC Digital-Automatic Flight Control (SAUS)
DFC Digital Fire Control [*Military*] (CAAL)
DFC Digital Flight Control (SAUS)
DFC Digital Flight Controller (AAG)
DFC digital frequency control (SAUS)
DFC Digital Fuel Controller (SAUS)
DFC Digital function code (SAUS)
DFC Digital Future Coalition
DFC Direct Field Costs (SAUS)
DFC Directorate of Fire Control (SAUO)
DFC Disaster Finance Center (SAUO)
DFC Disc file check (SAUS)
DFC Disc File Control (SAUS)
DFC Disc File Controller [*Computer science*] (NITA)
dfc discriminant function coeffcient (SAUS)
DFC Disk File Check [*Computer science*]
DFC Disk File Control [*Computer science*]
DFC Disk File Controller (SAUS)
DFC Display Formatting and Control (SAUS)
DFC Distinguished Flying Cross [*US and British*] [*Military decoration*]
DFC Distributed Coordination Function (SAUS)
DFC Divisional Field Code (SAUS)
DFC Division Forms Control (AAG)
DFC Divisions Forms Control (SAUS)
DFC Document Flow Component [*Computer science*] (IAA)
DFC Dondino Fan Club (EA)
DFC Doppler Frequency Converter (MCD)
DFC Double Frequency Change (IAA)
DFC Double Frequency Changer (SAUS)
DFC Double Frequency Changing (SAUS)
DFC Double Front Contact [*Photovoltaic energy systems*]
DFC Downflow cooling (SAUS)
DFC Drop Forged Clamp
DFC Dry-Filled Capsules [*Pharmacy*]
DFC Dual-Feed Carriage (IAA)
DFC Dual-Feed Channel (IAA)
DFC Dual-Feed Coupler
DFC Dust-Free Chamber
DFC dynamic focusing (SAUS)
DFC Dynasty Fan Club (EA)
DFC Federal City College [*Later, UDC*], Washington, DC [*Library symbol*] [*Library of Congress*] [*Obsolete*] (LCLS)
DFC Headquarters Defense Communications Agency, Washington, DC [*OCLC symbol*] (OCLC)
DFCA Dual Fault Correction Actuator
DFCA National Fire Prevention and Control Administration, Washington, DC [*Library symbol*] [*Library of Congress*] (LCLS)
DFC/ADM Digital Fuel Controller/Advanced Development Model (SAUS)
DFCC Development Finance Cooperative Committee (EURO)
DFCC Digital Fire Control Computer [*Military*] (MCD)
DFCC Dual Frame Cross Coupling (SAUS)
DFCC United States Federal Communications Commission, Washington, DC [*Library symbol*] [*Library of Congress*] (LCLS)
DFCD Data Format Control Documents (ADWA)
DFCE Defense Control Element (SAUS)
DFCHIP Data Flow Chip (SAUS)
DFCI Dana-Farber Cancer Institute [*Harvard Medical School*] [*Research center*] (RCD)
DFCI Device Function Controller Interface (SAUS)
DFCIX Delaware: Delcap Fund Cl.A [*Mutual fund ticker symbol*] (SG)
DFCLS Digital Flight Control and Landing System
DFCLT Difficult (FAAC)
DFCMA Dalton Floor Covering Market Association (NTPA)
DFCNV Disc data file conversion program (SAUS)
DFCNV Disk Data File Conversion Program [*IBM Corp.*]
DFCNVP Data File Conversion Program (SAUS)
DFCO Deputy Federal Coordinating Officer (DEMM)
DFCO Destron Fearing [*NASDAQ symbol*] (TTSB)
DFCO Destron Fearing Corp. [*NASDAQ symbol*] (SAG)
DFCO Duty Flying Control Officer [*Navy*]
DFCOFP Digital Flight Control Operational Flight Program (MCD)
DFCO-M Deputy Federal Coordinating Officer for Mitigation (SAUO)
DFCP Division Funding Control Point
DFCR Denver Federal Center [*Federal Railroad Administration identification code*]
DFCR Directorate of Flying Control and Reserve (SAUO)
DFCS Defensive Fire Control System (ACAE)
DFCS Department of Family and Children Services (SAUO)
DFCS Department of Family and Community Services [*South Australia*]
DFCS Deployment Flow Computer System (SAUS)
dFCS Dialyzed Fetal Calf Serum
DFCS Digital-Automatic Flight Control System (SAUS)
DFCS Digital Fire Control System [*Military*] (CAAL)
DFCS Digital Flight Control Software [*NASA*] (NASA)
dfcs digital flight-control software (SAUS)
DFCS Digital Flight Control System
DF/CS Direction Finding Control Station (MCD)
DFCS Director Fire Control System [*Air Force*] (MCD)
DFCS Distinguished Federal Civilian Service [*Award*] (RDA)
DFCS Distributed Factory Control System (TIMI)
DFCS Drone Formation Control System [*Military*]
dfct Deflection (MIST)
DFCT Deputy Federal Commissioner of Taxation (SAUS)
dfcty difficulty (SAUS)
DFCU Disk File Control Unit [*Computer science*]
DFCU Dynamic Flow Control Unit [*Chromatography*]

DFCZ .... Davis Farms [*Federal Railroad Administration identification code*]
DFD .... Damages for Detention (SAUS)
DFD .... Dancers for Disarmament [*Defunct*] (EA)
DFD .... Dark, Firm, Dry (SAUS)
DFD .... Data Field Description (SAUS)
DFD .... Data File Documents (SAUS)
DFD .... Data Final Device (SAUS)
DFD .... Data Flow Diagram
DFD .... Dataflow-Diagramm (SAUS)
DFD .... Data for Development International Association [*See also DD*] [*Marseille, France*] (EAIO)
DFD .... Data Functional Diagram (MCD)
DFD .... Data Function Diagram (SAUS)
DFD .... Deadly Frequency Distortion (VLIE)
dfd .... defended (SAUS)
DFD .... Defined Formula Diets [*Dietetics*] (DAVI)
DFD .... Degenerative Facet Disease [*Medicine*] (STED)
DFD .... Demolition Firing Device
DFD .... Designed for Disassembly [*Product design*]
DFD .... Design-for-Discard [*Engineering*]
DFD .... Digital Flight Display
DFD .... Digital Frequency Discrimination [*Military*] (CAAL)
DFD .... Digital Frequency Discriminator (SAUS)
DFD .... Digital Frequency Display
DFD .... Di-Isopropyl Phosphorofluoridate [*Organic chemistry*] (DAVI)
DFD .... Dogs for Defense [*Organization which trained dogs for armed services*] [*World War II*]
DFD .... Dogs for the Deaf [*An association*] (EA)
DFDA .... United States Food and Drug Administration, Bureau of Food, Washington, DC [*Library symbol*] [*Library of Congress*] (LCLS)
DFDAT .... Defence Force Discipline Appeal Tribunal [*Australia*]
DFDAU .... Digital Flight Data Acquisition Unit [*Aviation*]
DFDC .... Defence Force Development Committee [*Australia*]
DFDC .... Difluorodeoxycytidine [*Biochemistry*]
DFDC .... Disk File Descriptor Control [*Computer science*]
DFDCM .... Difluorodichloromethane (SAUS)
DFDD .... Difluoro-Diphenyl-Dichloroethane [*Organic chemistry*] (DAVI)
DFDEL .... Deferred Delivery
DFDHIDWA ... Die Furcht des Herrn Ist der Weisheit Anfang [*Fear of the Lord Is the Beginning of Wisdom*] [*(Ps., CXI. 10) Motto of Dorothee Hedwig, Princess of Anhalt (1587-1608); Johann Sigismund, Elector of Brandenburg (1572-1619)*]
DFDI .... Diffuse Downward Irradiance (SAUS)
DFDL .... Dorsal Fin, Depressed Length [*Pisciculture*]
DFDL .... Dual Frequency Doppler Lidar (SAUS)
DFDL .... Dual-Frequency Dye Laser (ODA)
DFDNB .... Difluoro(dinitro)benzene [*Organic chemistry*]
DFDP .... Defense Facilities Decommissioning Program (SAUO)
DFDP .... Defense Facility Decommissioning Program (COE)
DFDP .... Distribution-Free Doppler Processor (PDAA)
DFDPSAR .... Dual Frequency Dual Polarization SAR (SAUS)
DFDR .... Digital Flight-Data Recorder (MCD)
DFDRs .... Digital Flight Data Recorders (SAUS)
DFDRS .... Digital Flight Data Recording System (MCD)
DFDS .... Data Facility Device Support (VLIE)
DF/DS .... Data Facility/Device Support (SAUS)
DFDSE .... Design for Disassembly, Service, and the Environment
DFDSG .... Direct-Fired Downhole Steam Generator (SAUS)
DFDSM .... Data Facility Distributed Storage Management [*IBM Corp.*] (VERA)
DFDSS .... Data Facility Data Set Services
DFDT .... Difluorodiphenyltrichloroethane [*Insecticide*]
DFDT .... Dynamic Fault Diagnosis Technique (MCD)
DFDV .... Department of Training and Veterinarian information Dissemination (SAUO)
DFE .... Data Facility Extended
DFE .... Data Flow Editor [*Computer science*] (VLIE)
DFE .... Data Flow Emulator (SAUS)
DFE .... Data Flow Engineer (MCD)
DFE .... Debye-Falkenhagen Effect [*Physics*]
DFE .... Decision Feedback Equalization (AEBE)
DFE .... Decision Feedback Equalizer (IAA)
DFE .... Departed from Export for Emptying (SAUS)
DFE .... Department for Education [*British*]
DFE .... Department of Further Education (SAUS)
DFE .... Derivative Fighter Engine
DFE .... Design for Engineering
DfE .... Design for Environment
DFE .... Desktop Functional Equivalent [*Computer science*]
DFE .... Diffuse Fasciitis With Eosinophilia (STED)
DFE .... Directed Fan Engine
DFE .... Direction Fan Engine (SAUS)
DFE .... Direction Finding Equipment
DFE .... Directorate of Facilities Engineering [*Military*]
DFE .... Distal Femoral Epiphysis [*Orthopedics*] (DAVI)
DFE .... Division Force Equivalents [*Army*] (AABC)
DFE .... Doctor of Forest Engineering
dfe .... double fish eye (SAUS)
DFEC .... Defense Finance Economic Committee (NATG)
DFEC .... Douglas Fir Export Co. [*Defunct*] (EA)
DFECT .... Dense Fibroelastic Connective Tissue [*Medicine*] (STED)
DfEE .... Department for Education & Employment (WDAA)
DFEE .... Department for Education and Employment (WA)
DFEI .... Depth First End Index (SAUS)
DFELL .... Duke Free-Electron LASER Laboratory
DF Eng .... Doctor of Forest Engineering
DFES .... Doctor of Forestry and Environmental Studies (PGP)
DFES .... Doctor of Forestry and Environmental Systems (GAGS)
DFESH .... Design for Environment, Safety, and Health (AAEL)
D-FET .... Depletion (NITA)
D-FET .... depletion FET (SAUS)
DFET .... Depletion Field-Effect Transistor (SAUS)
DFET .... Depletion-mode Field-Effect Transistor (SAUS)
DFET .... Drift Field-Effect Transistor [*Electronics*]
DFEU .... Disk File Electronics Unit [*Computer science*]
DFF .... Debbie Fox Foundation [*Later, NACH*] (EA)
DFF .... Delay Flip-Flop [*Computer science*] (IAA)
DFF .... Directorate of Fire Fighting (SAUO)
DFF .... Display Format Facility
DFF .... Division Final Fade
DFF .... Downward Flux Fraction (SAUS)
DFFC .... David Frizzell Fan Club (EA)
DFFC .... Donna Fargo Fan Club [*Later, DFIFC*] (EA)
DFFF .... Demokratiska Foerbundet av Finlands Folk [*Finnish People's Democratic League*] (PPE)
DFFME .... Direction Finding Frequency Measuring Equipment (IAA)
DFFR .... Dynamic Forcing Function [*Information*] Report [*Nuclear energy*] (NRCH)
DF Frame .... Direction Finder Frame (SAUS)
DFFT .... Dry-Fat-Free-Tissue (SAUS)
DFFX .... Glidden [*Private rail car owner code*]
DFG .... Data Flow Graph
DFG .... Delphi Fin'l Group 'A' [*NYSE symbol*] (SG)
DFG .... Department of Fish and Game (GEOI)
DFG .... Difference Frequency Generator (MCD)
DFG .... Digital Frequency Generator (SAUS)
DFG .... Digital Function Generator
DFG .... Diode Function Generator
DFG .... Direct Forward Gaze (DMAA)
DFG .... Discrete Frequency Generator
DFG .... Dispensed Foam Gasket
DFG .... Display Format Generator (MCD)
DFG .... Freer Gallery of Art, Washington, DC [*Library symbol*] [*Library of Congress*] (LCLS)
DF/GA .... Day Fighter/Ground Attack [*British military*] (DMA)
DFGA .... Distributed Floating Gate Amplifier (MCD)
DFGC .... Digital Flight Guidance Computer (HLLA)
DFGJPC .... Daniel and Florence Guggenheim Jet Propulsion Center (SAUS)
DFGM .... Degenerate Fermi Gas Model (SAUS)
DFGO .... Damn Fool Ground Officer [*Military slang*] (DNAB)
DFGR .... Dual Frequency GPS Receiver
DFGS .... Digital Flight Guidance System (IEEE)
DFGS/C .... Digital Flight Guidance System/Computer (GAVI)
DFGZ .... Dewey Fisher Grain [*Federal Railroad Administration identification code*]
DFH .... Decorative Fabrics Institute (SAUS)
DFH .... Defense Family Housing [*Army*] (AABC)
DFH .... Deployable Field Headquarters
DFH .... Developmental Fast Hydrofoil (MCD)
DFH .... Diploma of the Faraday House (SAUS)
DFH .... Direct Flame Impingement (SAUS)
DFH .... Dollars per Flight Hour (MCD)
DFH .... Dual Filter Hybrid
DFHL .... United States Federal Home Loan Bank Board, Research Library, Washington, DC [*Library symbol*] [*Library of Congress*] (LCLS)
DFHMA .... Defense Family-Housing Management Account (DNAB)
DFHom .... Diploma of the Faculty of Homeopathy (SAUS)
DF Hom .... Diploma of the Faculty of Homoeopathy [*British*]
DFHP .... Dislocation-Free High-Purity (SAUS)
DFHS .... Dutch Family Heritage Society (EA)
DFHSM .... Data Facility Hierarchical Storage Manager [*IBM Corp.*] (NITA)
DFI .... Dark Field Illumination
DFI .... Data Field Identifier (SAUS)
DFI .... Data File Interrogate (SAUS)
DFI .... Decorative Fabrics Institute [*Defunct*] (EA)
DFI .... Decreased Fuel Ingestion
DFI .... Deep Foundations Institute (EA)
DFI .... Defiance, OH [*Location identifier*] [*FAA*] (FAAL)
DFI .... Definite (SAUS)
DFI .... Delegationen for Vetenskaplig och Teknisk Informationsforsorjning [*Swedish Delegation for Scientific and Technical Information*] [*Information service or system*] [*Defunct*] (IID)
DFI .... Delegation for Scientific and Technical Information (SAUO)
DFI .... Design, Fabricate, and Install (SAUS)
DFI .... Designs for Information
DFI .... Developmental Flight Instrumentation [*NASA*]
DFI .... Development finance institute (SAUS)
DFI .... Diabetes Foundation, Inc. [*Later, JDC*]
DFI .... Dialogue with People of Living Faith and Ideologies [*A publication*] (BJA)
DFI .... Diesel Fuel Injection (SAUS)
DFI .... Differential Fluorescence Induction [*Analytical biochemistry*]
DFI .... Digital Facility Interface (SAUS)
DFI .... Digitally Fuel-Injected [*Automotive engineering*]
DFI .... Direct-Firs-Ignition (SAUS)
D F I .... Direct Flame Impingement (SAUS)
DFI .... Direct-Flame Incineration (SAUS)
DFI .... Direct Foreign Investment
DFI .... Direct Fourier Inversion [*Mathematics*]
DFI .... Direct Fuel Injection [*Automotive engineering*]
DF I .... Direction Finding, Phase I [*Course*] [*Military*] (DNAB)

DFI.............. Directorate for the Freedom of Information [*Formerly, Directorate for Security Review*] [*DoD*]
DFI.............. Directorate of Food Investigation, Cambridge (SAUO)
DFI.............. Directory of Foreign Investors in the US [*A publication*]
DFI.............. disc file interrogate (SAUS)
DFI.............. Discrete Input High (SAUS)
DFI.............. Disease-Free Intervals
DFI.............. Disk File Interrogate [*Computer science*]
DFI.............. Domain Specific Part Format Identifier [*Telecommunications*] (ACRL)
DFI.............. Duty Free International, Inc. [*NYSE symbol*] (SPSG)
DFI.............. Duty Free Intl. [*NYSE symbol*] (TTSB)
DFI.............. Duty, Freight, and Insurance (TIMI)
DFI.............. Dynamic Functional Interaction (EDAC)
DFIB.............. Data Function Information Book
DFib.............. Defibrillator [*Medicine*] (WDAA)
DFIC.............. Dairy Foods Information Center (SAUS)
DFIC.............. Dehydrated Foods Industry Council [*Later, DCFC*]
DFID.............. Department for International Development
DFIFC.............. Donna Fargo International Fan Club (EA)
DF II.............. Direction Finding, Phase II [*Course*] [*Military*] (DNAB)
DFILS.............. Day Fighter Leaders School (SAUS)
DFIN.............. Damen Financial [*NASDAQ symbol*] (TTSB)
DFIN.............. Damen Financial Corp. [*NASDAQ symbol*] (SAG)
DFIN.............. Finance Directorate (SAUO)
DFING.............. Direction Finding [*Radio*] [*Military*]
DFIP-D.............. Diesel Fuel Injection Pump-Distributor
DFIP-IL.............. Diesel Fuel Injection Pump-Inline
DFIS.............. Digital Facsimile Interface System
DFIS.............. Dual Filament Ion Source
DFISA.............. Dairy and Food Industries Supply Association (EA)
DFIST.............. Duty-Free Into-Store Cost
DFITW.............. Dead Flat In The Water (SAUS)
dfiy.............. definitely (SAUS)
DFJ.............. Draper Fisher Jurvetson
DFJ.............. Dual Function Jammer
DFJ.............. New Bedford, MA [*Location identifier*] [*FAA*] (FAAL)
DFK.............. Direct Free Kick [*Soccer*]
DFL.............. Daily Flight Log [*Aviation*] (FAAC)
DFL.............. Deflating (MSA)
DFL.............. Deflect (KSC)
DFL.............. Degree of Financial Leverage
DFL.............. Democrat-Farmer-Labor [*Party*] [*Minnesota*]
DFL.............. Dental Fillings Limited (SAUO)
DFL.............. Department of Family Life [*Later, Commission on Marriage and Family Life*] [*of NCC*] (EA)
DFL.............. Department of Foreign Languages [*National Education Association*] (AEBS)
DFL.............. Design for Logistics (GART)
DFL.............. Deviation for Failure Location
DFL.............. Digital Film Library (DMAA)
DFL.............. Display Formatting Language
DFL.............. Divisional Facilities List (SAUS)
DFL.............. Doctor of Family Life
DFL.............. Doctor of Forest Engineering (SAUS)
DFL.............. Donauflug Bedarfsfluggesellschaft GmbH [*Austria*] [*ICAO designator*] (FAAC)
DFL.............. Double Four-Valve Long Distance [*Cosworth racing engines*]
dfl.............. Douglas Fir-Larch [*Softwood*] (MIST)
DFL.............. downward-fining layers (SAUS)
DFL.............. Dry Film Lubricant
Dfl.............. Dutch Florin [*Monetary unit*] (IMH)
D fl.............. Dutch florins (SAUS)
Dfl.............. Dutch guilder (SAUO)
DFL.............. Dynamic Function Language (SAUS)
DFLC.............. Division of Foreign Labor Conditions [*Department of Labor*]
DFLCE.............. DFL Container Express (SAUS)
Dflct.............. Deflection (DAC)
dfld.............. defiled (SAUS)
DFLD.............. Definitely Loaded (SAUS)
dfld.............. deflated (SAUS)
DFLD.............. Device Field (SAUS)
DFLD.............. Distribution-Free Logic Design
DFLE.............. Dog Fight Lock-On Enable (ACAE)
D flip-flop.............. Delay Flip Flop (SAUS)
DFLP.............. Defense Foreign Language Program (SAUS)
DFLP.............. Democratic Front for the Liberation of Palestine (PD)
DFLP.............. Design for Low Power (AAEL)
DFLS.............. Day Fighter Leaders School [*British military*] (DMA)
DFLS.............. Direction Finding & Location System (SAUS)
DFLX.............. Dataflex Corp. [*NASDAQ symbol*] (NQ)
DFM.............. Data Flow Manager (SAUS)
DFM.............. Decorative Furniture Manufacturers Association [*Defunct*] (EA)
DFM.............. Decreased Fetal Movement [*Obstetrics*] (DMAA)
DFM.............. Defect-Free Manufacturing (SAUS)
DFM.............. Defiant Minerals [*Vancouver Stock Exchange symbol*]
DFM.............. Design for Maintainability (RDA)
DFM.............. Design for Manufacturability (GART)
DFM.............. Design for Manufacturing
DFM.............. Diesel Fuel, Marine (NVT)
DFM.............. Dietary Food Management
DFM.............. Difference Frequency Mixing (SAUS)
DFM.............. Digital Forecast Matrix (SAUS)
DFM.............. Digital Frequency Meter [*or Monitor*]
DFM.............. Digital Frequency Monitor (SAUS)
DFM.............. Diploma in Forensic Medicine (ADA)
DFM.............. Direct Flight Mode
DFM.............. Director, Food Management [*Army*] (AABC)
DFM.............. Director of Fleet Maintenance [*Navy*] [*British*]
DFM.............. Directory/File Manager (TIMI)
DFM.............. Distinguished Flying Medal [*British*]
DFM.............. Distortion Factor Meter [*Telecommunications*] (IAA)
DFM.............. Division of Financial Management (SAUO)
DFM.............. Dog Fight Mode (ACAE)
DFM.............. Double Failure Matrix [*Hazard quantification method*]
DFM.............. Douglas Furnished Material [*DAC*]
DFM.............. Dual-Frequency Method
DFM.............. Dust, Fume and Mist (HEAS)
DFM.............. Dynamic File Manager (SAUS)
DFM.............. Franciscan Monastery, Washington, DC [*Library symbol*] [*Library of Congress*] (LCLS)
DFMA.............. Design Failure-Mode Analysis
DFMA.............. Design for Manufacture and Assembly (RDA)
DFMA.............. Design for Manufacturing and Assembly
DFMA.............. Difluoromethylarginine [*Organic chemistry*]
DFMA.............. Director for Military Assistance (NATG)
DFMACH.............. Drafting Machine
DFManS.............. Director of Fleet Management Services [*Navy*] [*British*]
DFMC.............. Daily Fetal Movement Count [*Obstetrics*] (DAVI)
DFMD.............. DifluoromethylDOPA (DB)
DFMEA.............. Design Failure-Mode Effects Analysis [*Automotive engineering*]
DFMFG.............. Department of Forest Management and Forest Geodesy (SAUO)
DFML.............. Dictionary of Folklore, Mythology, and Legend [*A publication*]
DFMMS.............. Data File/Media Management System
DFMO.............. Difluoromethylornithine [*Organic chemistry*]
DFMO.............. Doppler Filter Mixer-Oscillator [*Electronics*] (AABC)
DFMR.............. Daily Fetal Movements Record
DFMR.............. Dazian Foundation for Medical Research (SAUO)
DFmr.............. Deputy Firemaster (WDAA)
DFMR.............. Dual Frequency Microwave Radar (SAUS)
DFMS.............. Digital Facility Management System (SAUS)
DFMS.............. Domestic and Foreign Missionary Society [*British*]
DFMSR.............. Directorate of Flight and Missile Safety Research [*Air Force*]
DFN.............. Data File Number
DFN.............. Defined (SAUS)
DFN.............. Deutsches Foerschungsnetz [*German*] [*Computer science*] (TNIG)
dfn.............. distance from noise (SAUS)
DFN.............. Distance from Nose (SAUS)
DFN.............. German research network (SAUS)
DFN-CERT.............. DFN Computer Emergency Response Team (SAUS)
dfndt.............. Defendant (ODA)
DFNJ.............. Descendants of Founders of New Jersey (EA)
DFN-NOC.............. DFN Network Operation Center (SAUS)
DFNS.............. Debt-for-Nature Swap (SAUO)
DFNT.............. Definite (FAAC)
DFNTN.............. Definition
DFNWR.............. Deer Flat National Wildlife Refuge (SAUS)
DFO.............. Dairy Farmers of Ontario [*Canada*] (FOTI)
DFO.............. Danube Field Organization (SAUO)
DFO.............. Decade Frequency Oscillator (IAA)
DFO.............. Defense Food Order [*Production and Marketing Administration*] [*Department of Agriculture*] (DLA)
DFO.............. Deferoxamine [*Pharmacology*] (DAVI)
DFO.............. Department of Fisheries and Oceans [*Canada*] (OSRA)
DFO.............. Deputy for Flight Operations [*NASA*] (KSC)
DFO.............. Desferrioxamine [*Also, Deferoxamine*] [*A chelating agent*] (AAMN)
DFO.............. Design for Ownership (SEWL)
DFO.............. Diazafluorenone [*Organic chemistry*]
DFO.............. Directed Format Option [*Rapid access management information system*]
DFO.............. Direct Format Option (SAUS)
DFO.............. Director, Flight Operations [*NASA*] (KSC)
DFO.............. Disaster Field Office [*Federal Emergency Management Agency*] (GFGA)
DFO.............. Disk File Optimizer [*Computer science*] (BUR)
DFO.............. Disk File Organization (SAUS)
DFO.............. Distilled Fuel Oil
DFO.............. District Finance Officer
DFO.............. Divisional Food Office (SAUO)
DFO.............. Division Follow-On
DFO.............. Dorsal Fold (Oesophagus)
DFo.............. Folger Shakespeare Library, Washington, DC [*Library symbol*] [*Library of Congress*] (LCLS)
DFOA.............. Deferoxamine [*Also, Desferrioxamine*] [*Chelating agent*]
DFOD.............. Defense Field Operations Department (SAA)
DF-ODMR.............. Delayed-Fluorescence Optically Detected Magnetic Resonance [*Physics*]
DFOIS.............. Depth of Flash Optical Landing System (SAUS)
DFOLS.............. Depth of Flash Optical Landing System [*Navy*]
DFOM.............. Deferoxamine (STED)
DFOM.............. Deferoxamine Methanesulfonate [*or Desferrioxamine Mesylate*] [*Pharmacology*]
DFOM.............. Difference Figure of Merit (MCD)
DFOP.............. Direction Finder Operator (IAA)
DFOR.............. Disk File Organization Routine (SAUS)
D forg.............. Drop Forging (SAUS)
DForSc.............. Doctor of Forest Science (ADA)
DFOS.............. Diesel Fuel Oil System [*Nuclear energy*] (NRCH)
DFOV.............. Dual Field-of-View
DFP.............. Data Facilities Program (SAUS)
DFP.............. Data Facility Product

DFP............ Data Fast Printer (SAUS)
DFP............ Davidon-Fletcher-Powell [*Method*]
DFP............ Decimal Floating Point (SAUS)
DFP............ Dedicated Function Pushbutton
DFP............ Define File Processor [*Computer science*]
DFP............ Demand Forecasting Program (BUR)
DFP............ Democratic Freedom Party (Dominica) [*Political party*] (PSAP)
DFP............ Demokratische Fortschrittliche Partei [*Democratic Progressive Party*] [*Austria*] (PPE)
DFP............ Department of Family Practice (SAUO)
DFP............ Designated Force Potential [*Military*]
DFP............ Design for Producibility
DFP............ Detroit Free Press [*A publication*]
DFP............ Deviant Flight Plan
DFP............ Diastolic Femoralis Pressure (SAUS)
DFP............ Diastolic Filling Period [*Medicine*]
DFP............ Diesel Fire Pump [*Nuclear energy*] (NRCH)
DFP............ Difluorophosphate [*Inorganic chemistry*]
DFP............ Digital Flat Panel [*Computer science*]
DFP............ Digital Flat Panel group (SAUO)
DFP............ Digital Fuzzy Processor (SAUS)
DFP............ Diisopropyl Fluorophosphate [*or Diisopropyl Fluorophosphonate*] [*Also, DIFP*] [*Ophthalmic drug*]
dfp............ diisopropyl phosphofluoridate (SAUS)
DFP............ Diode Flat Pack
DFP............ Diploma in Family Practice (SAUS)
DFP............ Diploma of Financial Planning
D-FP............ Diplomate, American Board of Family Practice (DHSM)
DFP............ Dipole Flat Plate
DFP............ Directed Fiber Preform (SAUS)
DFP............ Direct Fire Plan [*Army*] (INF)
DFP............ Disappearing Filament Pyrometer (SAUS)
DFP............ disproportion foeto-pelvienne (SAUS)
DFP............ Distributed Functional Plane (VERA)
DFP............ Distribution Fuse Panel
DFP............ Divisional Facilities Practice (SAUS)
DFP............ Divisional Field Park (SAUO)
DFP............ Divisional Foot-Police (SAUO)
DFP............ Division of Fairs and Promotions (SAUO)
DFP............ Domestic Floating Pool (EBF)
DFP............ Dominica Freedom Party [*Political party*] (PPW)
DFP............ Drawing File Processor (MCD)
DFP............ Dry Film Processor
DFP............ Dry Filter Processing
DFP............ Ductile Fracture Propagation [*Engineering*]
DFP............ Duns Financial Profile (SAUS)
DFP............ Dun's Financial Profiles Report [*Dun & Bradstreet Credit Services*] [*Information service or system*] (CRD)
DFP............ Dyflos [*Medicine*] (EDAA)
DFP............ Dynamic Flow Parameter
DFPA............ Douglas Fir Plywood Association [*Later, APA*] (EA)
DFPA............ National Society, Daughters of Founders and Patriots of America (EA)
DFP Aerial... Dipole Flat Plate Aerial (SAUS)
DFP Antenna... Dipole Flat Plate Antenna (SAUS)
DFPase............ Di-isopropyl Phosphorofluoridase [*An enzyme*]
DFPC............ United States Federal Power Commission, Washington, DC [*Library symbol*] [*Library of Congress*] (LCLS)
DFPE............ Deflection Probable Errors (MCD)
DFPE............ Democratic Front for Peace and Equality (Israel) [*Political party*] (PSAP)
DFPG............ Double-Frequency Phase Grating (SAUS)
DFPL............ Data Flow Programming Language
DFPM............ Disappearing Filament Pyrometer (SAUS)
DFP Method... Davidon, Fletcher and Powell Method (SAUS)
DFPP............ Demonstration Fusion Power Plant (SAUS)
DFPP............ Double Filtration Plasmapheresis [*Medicine*] (DMAA)
DFPP............ Dredge and Fill Permit Program (EEVL)
DFPS............ Digital Ferrite Phase Shifter
DFPT............ Disk File Protection Table [*Computer science*] (IAA)
DF/Q............ Design Evaluation/Qualification (SAUS)
DFQAO............ Defense Fuel Quality Assurance Office [*DoD*]
DFQAR............ Defense Fuel Quality Assurance Residency [*DoD*] (DNAB)
DFQIS............ Dual Fuel Quantity Indicating System (MCD)
DFR............ Board of Governors, Federal Reserve System, Washington, DC [*Library symbol*] [*Library of Congress*] (LCLS)
DFR............ Data File Recovery System [*Computer science*] (HODG)
DFR............ Data Flow Rate (SAUS)
DFR............ Data Freight Receipt (SAUS)
DFR............ Declining Failure Rate [*Quality management*]
DFR............ Decreasing Failure Rate
DFR............ Defence Force Reserves [*Australia*]
DFR............ Defense Fuel Region [*DoD*]
DFR............ Defer (AABC)
DFR............ Defrost (MSA)
DFR............ Defrosting (SAUS)
DFR............ Degradation Failure Rate
DFR............ Delayed Free Recall
DFR............ Departmental Forecast Report (SAUS)
DFR............ Department of Fisheries Research (HEAS)
DFR............ Design for Reliability (RDA)
DFR............ Diabetic Floor Routine [*Medicine*] (DMAA)
DFR............ Diesel-Fuel Program Foreign Refiner [*Automotive emissions*]
DFR............ Digital Filter Replacement (SEWL)
DFR............ Dihydroflavonol Reductase [*An enzyme*]
DFR............ Direct Fire Rocket (SAUS)
DFR............ Direction Finding Receiver
DFR............ Director of Fuel Research (SAUO)
DFr............ Discophiles Francais [*Record label*] [*France*]
DFR............ Disk File Read [*Computer science*] (OA)
DFR............ Distal Functional Reabsorption [*Medicine*] (EDAA)
DFR............ Distance - Force - Resistance [*Instrumentation*]
DFR............ Document Filing and Retrieval [*Computer science*] (TELE)
DFR............ Dofor Inc. [*Toronto Stock Exchange symbol*]
DFR............ Doppler Frequency Rate (MCD)
DFR............ Double Frequency Recording (HGAA)
DFR............ Dounreay Fast Reactor [*British*]
DFR............ Dropped from Rolls
DFR............ Dual Free Room (SAUS)
DFR............ Dual-Frequency Receiver
DFR............ Dun's Financial Records [*Dun's Marketing Services*] [*Parsippany, NJ*] [*Information service or system*] (IID)
DFR+............ Dun's Financial Records Plus [*Dun's Marketing Services*] [*Information service or system*] (IID)
DFR............ Durant Family Registry (EA)
DFR............ Dust-Free Room
DFRA............ Decreasing Failure Rate Average
DFRA............ Drop Forging Research Association [*British*]
DFRC............ Dairy Forage Research Center [*Department of Agriculture*] [*Madison, WI*] (GRD)
DFRC............ Deglycerolized Frozen Red Cells [*Medicine*] (EDAA)
DFRC............ Distillers Feed Research Council (EA)
DFRC............ Dryden Flight Research Center [*Astronomy term*]
DFRDBA...... Defence Forces Retirement and Death Benefits Authority (SAUS)
DFRDBS...... Defence Force Retirement and Death Benefits Scheme [*Australia*]
DFRDC...... Dried Fruits Research and Development Council [*Australia*]
DFRDP...... Dairy Farmers for Responsible Dairy Policy (EA)
DFR/E............ Defense Fuel Region/Europe [*Military*] (DOMA)
DFR-E............ Defense Fuels Region, Europe (SAUO)
DFRF............ Dryden Flight Research Facility (SAUO)
DFRIF............ Defense Freight Railway Interchange Fleet [*Army*] (AABC)
DFRL............ Differential Relay (KSC)
DFRM............ Department of Forest Resource Management (SAUO)
DFR/ME...... Defense Fuel Region/Middle East [*Military*] (DOMA)
DFRN............ Data File Reference Number (ACAE)
DFRN............ Differential
DFRN............ Differential Velocity (NASA)
DFRP............ Deficiency and Replacement
DFRP............ Downcomer Flow Resistance Plate [*Nuclear energy*] (NRCH)
DFRR............ Detailed Functional Requirements Review (SSD)
DFRRI............ Directorate of Food, Road and Rural Infrastructure (SAUS)
DFRS............ Differs (FAAC)
DFRT............ Demonstration Flight Rating Test (MCD)
DFS............ Daily Flow System [*Environmental Protection Agency*] (AEPA)
DFS............ Daisy Fault Simulator [*On Daisy CAD work station*] (NITA)
DFS............ Dancer-Fitzgerald-Sample [*Advertising agency*]
DfS............ Dataflow Systems, Inc. [*Information service or system*] (IID)
DFS............ Dead Fetus Syndrome (MELL)
DFS............ Defense Facsimile System (MCD)
DFS............ Defense Fuel Support [*DoD*] (DNAB)
DFS............ Demonstration Flight Satellite (MCD)
DFS............ Denali Fault System [*Geology*]
DFS............ Dental Fear Syndrome
DFS............ Deoxyfructoserotonin [*Antibacterial*]
DFS............ Department 56 [*NYSE symbol*] (TTSB)
DFS............ Department 56, Inc. [*NYSE symbol*] (SPSG)
DFS............ Department of Food Science (SAUS)
DFS............ Department of Forest Sciences (SAUO)
DFS............ Departure from Specifications (DNAB)
DFS............ Depth-First Search
DFS............ Detailed Functional Specification (DA)
DFS............ Detail Finish Specification (MCD)
DFS............ [*A*] Dictionary of Forces' Slang [*A publication*]
DFS............ Differential Fluorescent Staining [*Medicine*] (EDAA)
DFS............ Digital Facsimile System (MCD)
DFS............ Digital Field System
DFS............ Digital Formatting System (ACAE)
DFS............ Digital Frequency Synthesizer
DFS............ Direct File System [*Computer science*] (VERA)
DFS............ Direct Fire Simulator
DFS............ Direct Fire System
DFS............ Direct Flow Sampler [*Meteorology*]
DFS............ Direct Forces Support [*Military*]
DFS............ Direct Function Search (PDAA)
DFS............ Direction Finding Set [*or System*]
DFS............ Director of Flight Safety [*Air Force*]
DFS............ Disease-Free Survival (MEDA)
DFS............ Disk Filing System (SAUS)
DFS............ Dispersive Fourier Spectroscopy (PDAA)
DFS............ Display Formatting System
DFS............ Distance Finding Station
DFS............ Distributed File System [*Computer science*] (VERA)
Dfs............ Distributed File System [*Computer science*]
DFS............ Dividends from Space [*Defunct*] (EA)
DFS............ Divisional Facilities Standard (SAUS)
DFS............ Doctor of Foreign Science
DFS............ Doctor of Foreign Service
DFS............ Doctor of Forest Science
DFS............ Document Finding System (SAUS)
DFS............ Dofasco, Inc. [*Toronto Stock Exchange symbol*]

DFS............ Down Feeding Spindle
DFS............ Dragon Flight Simulator [*Military*] (MCD)
DFS............ Drain and Fill Stand (ACAE)
DFS............ Drop Foot Splint (MELL)
DFS............ Dual Frequency Scatterometer (SAUS)
DFs............ Duty Frees (SAUS)
DFS............ Duty Free Shopper (SAUO)
DFS............ Dwyer Aircraft Sales, Inc. [*ICAO designator*] (FAAC)
DFS............ Dynamic Flight Simulator
DFSA........... Defense Atomic Support Agency (SAUS)
DFSB........... Defense Force Section Base [*Navy*]
DFSC........... Defence Force Structure Committee (SAUO)
DFSC........... Defense Fuel Supply Center [*Alexandria, VA*] (MCD)
DFSc........... Doctor of Financial Science
DFSD........... Directorate of Fleet Supply Duties [*Navy*] [*British*]
DFSF........... digital fine Sun sensor (SAUS)
DFSG........... Data Flow Sub-Graph [*Computer science*] (VLIE)
DFSG........... Direct Formed Supergroup [*Telecommunications*] (TEL)
DFSG........... Disaster Financial Services Group (SAUO)
DFSHW.......... Department of Family Services and Housing Welfare [*Queensland*] [*Australia*]
DFSI........... Dice Fanual Similarity and Index [*Ecology*]
DFSK........... Differential Frequency Shift Keying (VLIE)
DFSK........... Double Frequency Shift Keying [*Radio*]
DFS Laser...... Direct Fire Simulation Laser (SAUS)
DFSM........... Deterministic Finite-State Machine (PDAA)
DFSM........... Dispersion Flattened Single Mode (IAA)
DFSM........... Distinguished Fire Service Medal (SAUS)
DFSMS.......... Data Facility Storage Management Subsystem [*Computer science*] (VLIE)
DFSORT......... Data Facility Sort [*Computer science*] (VLIE)
DFSP........... Data Flow Signal Processor (MCD)
DFSP........... Defense Fuel Support Point [*DoD*]
DFSP........... Dermatofibrosarcoma Protuberans [*Oncology*]
DF-SPE-A....... Shuttle Project Engineering Office (SAUS)
DFSR........... Detailed Function System Requirement
DFSR........... Diffuser (AAG)
DFSR........... Director [*or Directorate*] of Flight Safety Research [*Air Force*]
DFSS........... Democratic Front for the Salvation of Somalia (PD)
DFSs........... Distance Finding Stations (SAUS)
DFST........... Division of Food Science and Technology (SAUS)
DFST........... Division of Forest Science and Technology (SAUO)
DFSTN.......... Direction Finding Station [*Aviation*] (FAAC)
DFSU........... Disk File Storage Unit [*Computer science*]
DFSU........... Dual Frequency Signaling Units (MCD)
DFSWO.......... Department of the Financial Secretary of the War Office [*British*]
DFT............ Air Direct Ltd. [*British*] [*ICAO designator*] (FAAC)
DFT............ Deaerating Feed Tank
DFT............ Default Value (SAUS)
DFT............ Defect and Fault Tolerance (VLIE)
dft............ Defendant (ADWA)
DFT............ Defendant
DFT............ Defibrillation Threshold [*Medicine*] (DB)
DFT............ Degree of Fiber Treatment (SAUS)
DFT............ Density Functional Theory [*Quantum chemistry*]
DFT............ Department of Fire Technology (SAUS)
DFT............ Deployment for Training
DFT............ Design Feasibility Test
DFT............ design for test (SAUS)
DFT............ Design for Testability [*Military*]
DFT............ Destination Fetch Trigger (VLIE)
DFT............ Development Flight Test [*Military*] (CAAL)
DFT............ Diagnostic Fault Test (SAUS)
DFT............ Diagnostic Function Test [*Computer science*]
DFT............ Diagnostic Funtion Test (SAUS)
DFT............ Dictionary of Foreign Trade (SAUS)
DFT............ Digital Facility Terminal [*Telecommunications*] (TEL)
DFT............ Digital Filtering Technique
DFT............ Digital Fourier Transform [*or Transformation*] [*Computer science*]
DFT............ Direct Flight Test (KSC)
DFT............ Director, Fleet Training
DFT............ Discrete Fourier Theorem (SAUS)
DFT............ Discrete Fourier Transform
DFT............ Distributed Function Terminal (ACRL)
DFT............ Distributed Transaction Facility (SAUS)
DFT............ Distribution Function Terminal [*Computer science*]
DFT............ Document File Transfer [*Computer science*]
DFT............ Downdraft (DA)
dft............ Draft (WDMC)
DFT............ Draft
DFT............ Draught (SAUS)
DFT............ Drift (MSA)
DFT............ Drive Fitness Test (SAUS)
DFT............ Dry Film Thickness (LDOE)
DFT............ Dry-Film Thickness (LDOE)
DFT............ Dual Function Terminal (SEWL)
DFT............ United States Federal Trade Commission, Washington, DC [*Library symbol*] [*Library of Congress*] (LCLS)
DFT............ Dual-Flow Turbine (ODA)
DFTA........... Department For The Aging (SAUS)
DFT/a.......... Draft Attached (EBF)
dft/a.......... Draft Attached (EBF)
DFT/A.......... Draft Attached [*Business term*]
DFTA........... Dwarf Fruit Trees Association [*Later, International Dwarf Fruit Trees Association*] (EA)
DFTAC.......... Distributing Frame Test Access Controller [*Communications term*] (DCT)
DFT/c.......... Clean Draft (EBF)
dft/c.......... Clean Draft (EBF)
DFT/C.......... Clean Draft [*Business term*]
DFTC........... doped face trench capacitor (SAUS)
DFTDS.......... Data Fusion Technology Demonstration System project (SAUS)
DFTEM.......... Dark Field TEM (SAUS)
DFTFACE........ Direction Finding and Tracking of Frequency Agile Communications Emitter (MCD)
DFTG........... Drafting (KSC)
DFTI........... Dansk Fiskeriteknologisk Institut [*Danish Fisheries Technology Institute*] [*Also, an information service or system*] (IID)
DFTI........... Distance from Threshold Indicator (PDAA)
DFTI........... Distance from Touchdown Indicator [*Aviation*] (DA)
DFTI Radar..... Distasnce-from-Threshold Indicator Radar (SAUS)
DFTM........... Direction Finder Team (IAA)
DFTM........... Douglas-Fir Tussock Moth
DFTMN.......... Draftsman (AFM)
DFT-Mode....... Distributed-Function Terminal-Mode (SAUS)
DFTPP.......... Decaflucrotriphenylphosphine
DFTR........... Deflector (MSA)
DFTS........... Defence Fixed Telecommunications System (SAUS)
DFTS........... Dispersive Fourier Transform Spectroscopy (MCD)
DFTS........... Doppler Filter Test Station (ACAE)
DFTSMN......... Draftsman (KSC)
d-f tube....... double-flare tube (SAUS)
DFU............ Data File Utility [*Computer science*] (IBMDP)
DFU............ Dead Fetus in Uterus
DFU............ Diabetic Foot Ulcer [*Medicine*] (MELL)
DFU............ Dideoxyfluorouridine [*Medicine*] (DMAA)
DFU............ Difluorourea [*Organic chemistry*]
DFU............ Directions For Use [*Packaging*]
DFU............ Disk File Unit (SAUS)
DFU............ Disposable Filter Unit (SAUS)
DFU............ Drainage Fixture Unit (DNAB)
dfu............ Drainage Fixture Unit [*Construction term*] (MIST)
DFU............ Dummy Firing Unit
dfu............ dummy flying unit (SAUS)
DFUS........... Diffuse (FAAC)
DF(V).......... Deafness Foundation [*Victoria*] [*Australia*]
DFV............ Deep Freeze Vacuum (SAUS)
DFV............ Designed for Victory [*Auto racing engine designation*]
DFV............ Device Function (SAUS)
DFV............ Diarrhea with Fever and Vomiting [*Medicine*] (DMAA)
DFV............ Double Four Valve [*Cosworth racing engines*]
DFV............ Dual Camshaft Four-Valve [*Engine*] [*Automotive engineering*]
DFVLR.......... Deutsche Forschungs und Versuchsanstalt fuer Luft und Raumfahrt [*German Research Institute for Air and Space Travel*] [*An association*]
DFVR........... Defense Visual Flight Rule [*Military*] (DA)
DFW............ Dallas/Fort Worth [*Texas*] [*Airport symbol*]
DFW............ Data Field Width (SAUS)
DFW............ Delegation for Friendship among Women (EA)
DFW............ Department of Fish and Wildlife (GEOI)
DFW............ Dexide Face Wash [*Medicine*] (EDAA)
DFW............ Diesel Fuel Waiver (DNAB)
DFW............ Diffusion Welding
DFW............ Director of Fortifications and Works [*British*]
DFW............ Disk File Write [*Computer science*] (OA)
DFW............ Drug-Free Workplace (MELL)
DFWA........... Drug-Free Workplace Act of 1988 (WYGK)
DFW Airport.... Dallas Fort Worth Airport (SAUS)
DFWES.......... Direct Fire Weapon Engagement System (SAUS)
DFWES.......... Direct Fire Weapons Effect Simulator [*Military*] (PDAA)
DFWM........... Degenerate Four-Wave Mixing [*Optical reflection*]
DFWMAC......... Distributed Foundation Wireless Media Access Control [*Computer science*]
DFWMP.......... Difficult waste management plan (SAUS)
DFWT........... Dallas Fort Worth Teleport Ltd. [*Irving, TX*] [*Telecommunications*] (TSSD)
dfwt........... Distribution Function of Waiting Times (SAUS)
DFWU........... Detroit Fast Food Workers' Union [*Defunct*] (EA)
DFX............ Design For X (SAUS)
DFX............ Dicke-Fix [*Electronics*] (CET)
DFX............ Dylan Flight Service SA [*Switzerland*] [*ICAO designator*] (FAAC)
DFX............ Faximile Datafax (SAUS)
DFXI........... Direct Focus, Inc. [*NASDAQ symbol*] (NASQ)
DFY............ Dafrey Resources, Inc. [*Vancouver Stock Exchange symbol*]
DFYS........... Division of Family & Youth Services (SAUO)
DFZ............ Dislocation-Free Zone (SAUS)
DFZ............ Drug-Free Zone (MELL)
DG............. Associated Dry Goods Corp. (SAUO)
DG............. Daily Guardian [*A publication*]
DG............. Dallas Group (SAUO)
DG............. Damaged Goods
DG............. Damianus Gulianus [*Authority cited in pre-1607 legal work*] (DSA)
DG............. Dangerous Goods [*Shipping*]
DG............. Dansyl Glutamate [*Biochemistry*]
DG............. Danygraig [*Welsh depot code*]
DG............. Darien Airlines [*ICAO designator*] (AD)
DG............. Dark Green
DG............. Dark Ground (SAUS)
DG............. Data Gathering (SAUS)
DG............. Data General Corp. [*Computer manufacturer*]

DG .... Data Generator (MCD)
DG .... Datagram [*Telecommunications*]
DG .... Data Group (SPST)
DG .... Decigram [*Unit of measure*] (GPO)
dg .... deci gram (SAUS)
dg .... Decigram (IDOE)
DG .... Decimal Gauge (SAUS)
DG .... Declaration de Guerre [*Declaration of War*] [*French*] (ILCA)
DG .... Decomposed Granite (SAUS)
DG .... Decreto Governatoriale [*Governor's Decree*] [*Italian*] (ILCA)
DG .... Defense Grouping (DNAB)
DG .... Defense Guidance
DG .... Defensive Guard [*Football*]
DG .... Degaussing
dg .... degenerated (SAUS)
DG .... De Gex's English Bankruptcy Reports [*A publication*] (DLA)
DG .... Degree (IAA)
DG .... Degree Year [*Database terminology*] (NITA)
DG .... Dei Gratia [*By the Grace of God*] [*Latin*] (GPO)
DG .... Dekagram [*Unit of measure*] (ROG)
DG .... Delay Generator (SAUS)
DG .... Democracy and Governance (SAUO)
DG .... Dense Granules (SAUS)
DG .... Density Gradient
DG .... Dentate Granule Cell
DG .... Dentate Gyrus [*Neuroanatomy*]
DG .... Deo Gratias [*Thanks Be to God*] [*Latin*] (GPO)
DG .... Deoxy-D-glucose [*Also, DDG, DOG*] [*Biochemistry*]
DG .... Deoxyglucose [*Biochemistry*] (DAVI)
DG .... Deoxyguanosine [*Biochemistry*]
dG .... Deoxyguanylate [*Biochemistry*]
DG .... Dependency Graph and Control [*Computer science*]
DG .... Descriptive Graphs (SAUS)
DG .... Design Guide [*Army Corps of Engineers*] (AAGC)
DG .... Destroyer, Guided Missile [*Surface-to-air*] [*NATO*]
DG .... Detonation Gun (SAUS)
DG .... Deutsche Genossenschaftsbank [*Germany*]
DG .... Diagnosis (AABC)
DG .... Diastolic Gallop [*Medicine*]
dg .... diastolic gallup (SAUS)
DG .... Dictionary of Genetics (SAUS)
DG .... Diesel General [*Service*] [*Automotive engineering*]
DG .... Diesel Generator (NRCH)
DG .... Differential Gain
DG .... Differential Generator
DG .... Differential Geometry (SAUO)
DG .... Differentially (Expressed) Gastrula [*Genetics*]
dG .... differential of conductance (SAUS)
DG .... Digestive Gland
DG .... Di Giorgio Corp. (EFIS)
DG .... Digital Group (NITA)
DG .... Diglyceride [*Clinical chemistry*]
DG .... Diglyme (SAUS)
DG .... Digoxigenin [*Biochemistry*]
DG .... Dimensional Graphics [*Automotive design*]
DG .... Diode Gate
DG .... Direct Grant
DG .... Directional Grid (IAA)
D/G .... Directional Gyro (PIPO)
DG .... Directorate General (HEAS)
DG .... Directorate-General (SAUO)
D-G .... Director General (JAGO)
DG .... disability grant (SAUS)
DG .... Disc Grind [*Technical drawings*]
DG .... Discussion Group
dg .... disk grind (SAUS)
DG .... Displacement Gyro [*Aerospace*]
DG .... Displacement Gyroscope (SAUS)
DG .... Display Gate (VLIE)
DG .... Display Generator (NASA)
DG .... Distinguished Graduate [*Military*]
DG .... Distinguished Guest [*Hotel term*]
DG .... Distogingival [*Dentistry*]
DG .... District Guard [*British military*] (DMA)
DG .... Disturbed Gum [*Philately*]
Dg .... Diving [*British military*] (DMA)
D-G .... Divisional-General [*British*]
DG .... Documentation Group [*Range Commanders Council*] [*NASA*]
DG .... Dogged
DG .... Dollar General [*NYSE symbol*] (TTSB)
DG .... Dollar General Corp. [*NYSE symbol*] (SAG)
DG .... Dorothy Gray (SAUO)
DG .... Double Gear [*Engineering*] (ROG)
DG .... Double Girder (SAUS)
DG .... Double Glass (AAG)
DG .... Double Groove [*Insulators*]
DG .... Double-Gummed [*Envelopes*]
DG .... downgoing (SAUS)
DG .... Downgrade (NVT)
DG .... Dragoon Guards [*Military unit*] [*British*]
DG .... Dramatists Guild (EA)
DG .... Dramatists Guild of the Authors League of America (SAUO)
DG .... Drill Gauge (SAUS)
DG .... Drive Gate (SAUS)
DG .... Dry Goods (SAUS)
dg .... dry grassland (SAUS)
DG .... Duchenne-Griesinger [*Disease*] [*Medicine*] (DB)
DG .... Dump Gate (SAUS)
dg .... durable gum (SAUS)
DG .... Dutch Guilder [*Monetary unit*] (NATG)
DG .... Duty Group (SAUO)
DG .... Dynamogram
DG .... General Aviation Services Ltd. [*British*] [*ICAO designator*] (ICDA)
Dg .... Grain Density (SAUS)
DGA .... Damned Good Airplane
DGA .... Dangerous Good Anchorage (SAUS)
DGA .... Dangerous Goods Advisor (SAUS)
DGA .... Dangerous Goods Anchorage (SAUS)
DGA .... Dangriga [*Belize*] [*Airport symbol*] (OAG)
DGA .... Delegation General pour l'Armament [*General Armaments Delegation*] [*France*]
DGA .... Democratic Governors Association (EA)
DGA .... Dense Grade Aggregate
DGA .... Department of Geophysics and Astronomy (SAUO)
DGA .... Deutsche Gesellschaft fuer Amerikastudien [*German Association for American Studies*] (EA)
DGA .... Differential Gravimetric Analysis (SAUS)
DGA .... Diglycolamine [*Organic chemistry*]
DGA .... Diploma in Government Administration [*British*]
DGA .... Direct Graphics Access [*Computer science*] (VLIE)
DGA .... Director General Aircraft (SAUS)
DGA .... Directors Guild of America (EA)
DGA .... Displacement Gyro Assembly (SAUS)
DGA .... Dummy Guide Assembly [*Nuclear energy*] (NRCH)
DGA .... Durum Growers Association of the United States (EA)
DGA .... German Association for Asian Studies (SAUO)
DGAA .... Accra/Kotoka International [*Ghana*] [*ICAO location identifier*] (ICLI)
DGAA .... Distressed Gentlefolks' Aid Association [*British*] (DI)
DGAC .... Accra [*Ghana*] [*ICAO location identifier*] (ICLI)
DGAD .... Ada [*Ghana*] [*ICAO location identifier*] (ICLI)
DGAE .... Director-General of Aircraft Equipment [*Ministry of Aircraft Production*] [*British*]
DGAE .... Director-General of Army Education [*British*]
DGAE .... Kete-Krachi [*Ghana*] [*ICAO location identifier*] (ICLI)
DGAEM .... Director-General of Aerospace and Engineering Maintenance (MCD)
DGAH .... Ho [*Ghana*] [*ICAO location identifier*] (ICLI)
DGAK .... Akuse [*Ghana*] [*ICAO location identifier*] (ICLI)
DGALA .... Dramatists Guild of the Authors League of America (SAUO)
DGAMS .... Director-General, Army Medical Services (SAUO)
DGAMS .... Director-General of Army Medical Services [*British*]
DGA(N) .... Director-General of Aircraft (Naval) [*British military*] (DMA)
DG & J .... De Gex and Jones' English Chancery Reports [*A publication*] (DLA)
DG & JB .... De Gex and Jones' English Bankruptcy Reports [*1857-59*] [*A publication*] (DLA)
DGANL .... Digital to Analog (MCD)
DGAO .... United States General Accounting Office, Washington, DC [*Library symbol*] [*Library of Congress*] (LCLS)
DGAP .... Akatsi [*Ghana*] [*ICAO location identifier*] (ICLI)
DGAP .... Development Group for Alternative Policies (EA)
DGAP .... Director General of Aircraft Production (SAUS)
DGAP .... Director-General of Aircraft Production (SAUO)
DGAR .... Director-General of Army Requirements [*British*]
DG Arm .... Directorate-General of Armament (SAUO)
DGAS .... Delta Natural Gas [*NASDAQ symbol*] (TTSB)
DGAS .... Delta Natural Gas Co., Inc. [*NASDAQ symbol*] (NQ)
DGAS .... Diesel Generator Auxiliary System [*Nuclear energy*] (NRCH)
DGAS .... Director General of Aircraft Safety (SAUS)
DGAS .... Director-General of Aircraft Safety (SAUO)
DGAS .... Saltpond [*Ghana*] [*ICAO location identifier*] (ICLI)
DGASP .... Dye 3 Gas and Aerosol Sampling Programme (SAUS)
DGAT .... Tema [*Ghana*] [*ICAO location identifier*] (ICLI)
DGAV .... Director-General of Armoured Vehicles [*British*]
DGAVP .... Desglycinamide-Arginine-Vasopressin [*Antidiuretic*]
DGAVS .... Director-General of the Army Veterinary Service [*British military*] (DMA)
DGB .... Dangerous Goods Board [*IATA*] (DS)
DGB .... Deutscher Gewerkschaftsbund [*Confederation of German Trade Unions*] [*Germany*] (DCTA)
DGB .... Diesel Generator Building [*Nuclear energy*] (NRCH)
DGB .... Disk Gap Band [*Parachute*]
DGB .... Doppler Gravity Bias (ACAE)
DGBA .... Diethylene Glycol Butyl Acetate [*Organic chemistry*]
DGBAS .... Directorate General of Budget, Accounting and Statistics (SAUS)
DGBAS .... Directorate-General of Budgets, Accounts and Statistics (SAUO)
DGBAS .... Director General of Budget, Accounting and Statistics (SAUS)
DGBAW .... Der Grosse Baumeister aller Welten [*The Grand Architect of the Universe*] [*Freemasonry*] [*German*]
DGBC .... Digital Geoballistic Computer
DGBE .... Diethylene Glycol Butyl Ether [*Organic chemistry*]
DGBG .... Dimethylglyoxal Bisguanyl-Hydrazone (DMAA)
DGBIT .... Disagreement Bit (VLIE)
DG BRIT REG FD ... Dei Gratia Britanniarum Regina, Fidei Defensor [*By the Grace of God, Queen of England, Defender of the Faith*] [*Latin*] (ROG)
DGBUS .... Digital Ground Bus
DGC .... Dangerous Goods Classification (SAUS)
DGC .... Data General Corp. [*Computer manufacturer*]
DGC .... Data Graphics Corp.
DGC .... Democratic Governors Conference (EA)
DGC .... Departement Grand Clients (SAUO)
DGC .... Diagnostic (VLIE)

DGC .... Diamond Grain Configuration
DGC .... Digicon, Inc. [*AMEX symbol*] (SPSG)
DGC .... Digital Geoballistic Computer
DGC .... Diploma in Guidance and Counseling (SAUS)
DGC .... Diploma in Guidance and Counselling (ADA)
DGC .... Direct Geodetic Constraint (GEOI)
DGC .... Directors Guild of Canada
DGC .... Distance Gain Control (SAUS)
DGC .... Distributed Garbage Collection (SAUS)
DGC .... Durango [*Colorado*] [*Seismograph station code, US Geological Survey*] [*Closed*] (SEIS)
DGC .... Duty Group Captain (SAUO)
DGC .... Dystrophin-Glycoprotein Complex [*Biochemistry*]
DGC .... Gallaudet College, Washington, DC [*Library symbol*] [*Library of Congress*] (LCLS)
DGC .... Density-Gradient Centrifugation [*Biology*] (ODA)
DGCA .... Director-General of Civil Aviation [*British*]
DGCAIES ...... Diesel Generator Combustion Air Intake and Exhaust System [*Nuclear energy*] (NRCH)
DGCB .... Diocesan Guild of Church Bellringers (SAUO)
DGCC .... Director-General of Civilian Clothing [*British*]
DGCC .... DISA Global Control Center (SAUS)
DGCCP .... Dental Guidance Council for Cerebral Palsy (EA)
DGCE .... Directorate-General of Communications Equipment (SAUO)
DGCE .... Director General of Communications Equipment (SAUS)
DGCGO .... Dangerous Cargo (FAAC)
DGC-K .... Gallaudet College, Kendall Demonstration School, Washington, DC [*Library symbol*] [*Library of Congress*] (LCLS)
DGCI&S .... Directorate General of Commercial Intelligence and Statistics (SAUS)
DGCM .... Direct Geodetic Constraint Method (SAUS)
DGCM .... Division of Grants and Contracts Management (MELL)
DGCM .... Dynamic Global Vegetation Model (SAUO)
DGC-M .... Gallaudet College, Model Secondary School for the Deaf, Washington, DC [*Library symbol*] [*Library of Congress*] (LCLS)
DGCMA .... Defense and Government Contracts Management Association (SAUO)
DG Coil .... Degaussing Coil (SAUS)
DGCR .... Defective Glucose Counterregulation [*Medicine*] (MELL)
DG/CS .... Data General/Communications System [*Data General Corp.*] (NITA)
DGCStJ .... Dame Grand Cross of the Order of Saint John of Jerusalem [*British*] (ADA)
DGCWS .... Diesel Generator Cooling Water System [*Nuclear energy*] (NRCH)
DGCWS .... Digicon Inc. Wrrt [*AMEX symbol*] (TTSB)
DGCX .... Dakota Gasification [*Private rail car owner code*]
DGD .... Decision Guidance Documents (SAUS)
DGD .... Deutsche Gesellschaft fuer Dokumentation [*German Society for Documentation*] [*Information service or system*] (IID)
DGD .... Dialkylglycine Decarboxylase [*An enzyme*]
DGD .... Diesel Geared Drive
DGD .... Director, Gunnery Division [*British military*] (DMA)
DGD .... Director of Ground Defence [*Military*] [*British*]
DGD .... Dogwood, MO [*Location identifier*] [*FAA*] (FAAL)
DGD .... Double Glass Door [*Classified advertising*] (ADA)
dgd .... double glass doors (SAUS)
DGD .... Dynamic Gas Disengagement [*Chemical engineering*]
DGD .... Dynamic Gravity Detector
DGD&M .... Director-General, Dockyards and Maintenance (SAUO)
DGDB .... Dipropylene Glycol Dibenzoate [*Organic chemistry*]
DGDC .... Deputy Grand Director of Ceremonies [*Freemasonry*]
DGDC .... Direct Current to Direct Current (SAUS)
DGDG .... Digalactosyl Diacyl Glycerol [*Organic chemistry*]
DGDG .... Distributor-to-Group Display Generator
DGDGE .... Distributor-to-Group Display Generator Electronics (IAA)
DGDME .... Diethyleneglycol Dimethylether (SAUS)
DGDO .... Director of Ground Defence Operations (SAUS)
DG Docks Admy... Director-General of Docks, Admiralty (SAUO)
dGDP .... Deoxyguanosine Diphosphate [*Biochemistry*]
DGDP .... Double Groove, Double Petticoat [*Insulators*]
DGDS .... Director General, Dental Services (SAUS)
DGDS .... Director-General, Dental Services (SAUO)
DGE .... Data Gathering Equipment (SAUS)
DGE .... Davisson-Germer Experiment [*Physics*]
DGE .... Delayed Gastric Emptying [*Medicine*] (DMAA)
DGE .... Density Gradient Electrophoresis
DGE .... Department of Geothermal Energy (SAUO)
DGE .... Design Engineer
DGE .... Diglycidyl Ether (SAUS)
DGE .... Directorate General of Equipment (SAUS)
DGE .... Director-General of Equipment [*Air Force*] [*British*]
DGE .... Division of General Education (SAUO)
DGE .... Dual Gauge Expander
DGE .... Dusty Gas Enveloped [*Astronomy*]
DGE .... Mudgee [*Australia*] [*Airport symbol*] (OAG)
DGEBA .... Diglycidyl Ether of Bisphenol A [*Monomer*] [*Organic chemistry*]
DGEC .... Direccion General de Estadistica y Censos [*Costa Rica*] (GEOI)
D Ge E .... Doctor of Geological Engineering
D Ge Eng ..... Doctor of Geological Engineering
DGEIS .... Draft Generic Environmental Impact Statement (SAUS)
DGEL .... Director-General Engineering, Land [*Canada*]
DGEME .... Director-General, Electrical and Mechanical Engineering (ODA)
DGEMER .... Diglycidyl Ether of Methylolresorcinol [*Organic chemistry*] (MCD)
DGEMS .... Director General of Emergency Medical Service (SAUS)
DGEN .... Data Generation
DG Eng .... Directorate-General of Engineering (SAUO)
DGeogr .... Dictionary of Geography (SAUS)
DGeol .... Dictionary of Geology (SAUS)
DGEP .... Director-General of Engine Production [*British*]
DGES .... Director General of Equipment and Stores (SAUS)
DGES .... Director-General of Equipment and Stores (SAUO)
DGES .... Division of Graduate Education in Science [*National Science Foundation*]
DGF .... Degrees Fahrenheit (AAG)
DGF .... Delaware Group Global Dividend Fund [*NYSE symbol*] (SAG)
DGF .... Delaware Grp Global Div & Inc. [*NYSE symbol*] (TTSB)
DGF .... Demountable Growth Flange (SAUS)
DGF .... Department of Game and Fish (GEOI)
DGF .... Dinan, Galbraith, and Fischer (SAUS)
DGF .... disability glare factor (SAUS)
DGF .... Discomfort Glare Factor (SAUS)
DGF .... Dragonfly Distillers [*Vancouver Stock Exchange symbol*]
DGF .... Duct Growth Factor [*Medicine*] (DMAA)
DGF .... Dynamic Gradient Freeze (AAEL)
DG F & J ..... De Gex, Fisher, and Jones' English Chancery Reports [*A publication*] (DLA)
DG F & JB ... De Gex, Fisher, and Jones' English Bankruptcy Reports [*A publication*] (DLA)
DGFC .... Accra [*Ghana*] [*ICAO location identifier*] (ICLI)
DGFC .... Del Gray Fan Club (EA)
DGFF .... Director-General of Filling Factories [*Formerly, DGOF(F)*] [*Ministry of Supply*] [*British*] [*World War II*]
DGFOSTS ..... Diesel Generator Fuel Oil Storage and Transfer System [*Nuclear energy*] (NRCH)
DGFV .... Director-General of Fighting Vehicles [*British military*] (DMA)
DGFVE .... Director-General of Fighting Vehicles and Engineer Equipment [*British*] (RDA)
DGG .... Department of Geology and Geography (SAUO)
DGG .... Department of Geology and Geophysics [*MIT*] (MCD)
DGG .... Deutsche Grammophon Gesellschaft [*Phonograph recording company*]
DGG .... D-Glutamylglycine [*Biochemistry*]
DGG .... Dynamic Gravity Generator
DGGB .... Directors Guild of Great Britain
DGGD .... Director-General of Ground Defence [*Military*] [*British*]
DGGE .... Denaturing Gradient-Gel Electrophoresis [*Analytical Biochemistry*]
DGGE .... Department of Geodesy and Geomatics Engineering (SAUO)
DGGHP .... Deputy General Grand High Priest [*Freemasonry*]
DGGM .... Direccion General de Geologia y Minas [*Colombia*] (GEOI)
DGGRE .... Director General of Graves Registration and Enquiries (SAUS)
DGGRE .... Director-General of Graves Registration and Enquiries (SAUO)
DGGS .... Directorate General of Geological Surveys (SAUS)
DGGS .... Division of Geological and Geophysical Surveys (SAUS)
DGGWL .... Director-General of Guided Weapons and Electronics [*British*] (RDA)
DGH .... Diameter at Ground Height [*Botany*]
DGH .... Director General of Housing (SAUS)
DGH .... Director-General of Housing (SAUO)
DGH .... District General Hospital
DGhE .... Embassy of Ghana, Washington, DC [*Library symbol*] [*Library of Congress*] (LCLS)
DGHG .... Director-General, Home Guard [*British military*] (DMA)
DGHG .... Director-General of the Home Guard (SAUO)
DGH Mode ... Dory-Guest-Harris Mode (SAUS)
DGHP .... Deputy Grand High Priest [*Freemasonry*]
DGHP .... Drive-Gearhead Package
Dghtie .... Doughtie's Foods, Inc. [*Associated Press*] (SAG)
DGHTR .... Daughter
DGI .... Date Growers' Institute [*Defunct*] (EA)
DGI .... Decision Graphics, Inc.
DGI .... Dental Gold Institute (EA)
DGI .... Deoxyglucose Imaging [*Medicine*] (CPH)
DGI .... Department of Geographic Information (SAUO)
DGI .... Direccion General de la Inteligencia [*Intelligence agency*] [*Cuba*]
DGI .... Direct Gasoline Injection
DGI .... Directorate of General Intelligence (SAUS)
DGI .... Director General, Infantry (SAUS)
DGI .... Director General of Information (SAUS)
DGI .... Director-General of Information (SAUO)
DGI .... Director General of Inspection (SAUS)
DGI .... Director-General of Inspection (SAUO)
DGI .... Direktorat Geologi [*Indonesia*] (GEOI)
DGI .... Disc Graphics, Inc. [*AMEX symbol*] (SAG)
DGI .... Disseminated Gonococcal Infection [*Clinical chemistry*]
DGI .... Duncan Gold Resources [*Vancouver Stock Exchange symbol*]
DGIA .... Director-General of Internal Audit [*British*] (RDA)
DGIAB .... Durable Goods Industries Advisory Board [*New Deal*]
DGIAI .... Direccion General de Integracion y Analisis de la Informacion [*Mexico*] (GEOI)
DGIAX .... Davis Growth & Income Fund Cl.A [*Mutual fund ticker symbol*] (SG)
DGIC .... Donegal Group [*NASDAQ symbol*] (TTSB)
DGIC .... Donegal Group, Inc. [*NASDAQ symbol*] (NQ)
DGID .... Division of Grazing, Interior Department (SAUO)
DGIES .... Digital Geographic Information Exchange Standard (SAUO)
DGIF .... Delta GIF (SAUS)
DGII .... Digi International [*NASDAQ symbol*] (SG)
DGII .... Digi International, Inc. [*NASDAQ symbol*] (NQ)
DG III-E1 ...... Foodstuffs:- Legislation and scientific and technical aspects (SAUS)
DGIL .... Durga Container India Ltd (SAUS)
DGILLO .... Downgrade in Lieu of Layoff
DG Insulator... Double Groove Insulator (SAUS)
DGIP .... Division of General Information Programme (SAUS)
DGIP .... Division of Global and Interregional Projects (SAUS)

DGIR .... Department of Scientific and Industrial Research (SAUS)
DGIS .... Direct Graphics Interface Specification
DGIS .... Direct Graphics Interface Standard (CDE)
DGIS .... Director-General of Intelligence and Security (MCD)
DGIS .... DoD [*Department of Defense*] Gateway Information System [*Defense Technical Information Center*] (TSSD)
DGISD .... Director General of the Intelligence Service Department (SAUS)
DGISD .... Director-General of the Intelligence Service Department (SAUO)
DGISP .... Danish Government Institute of Seed Pathology (SAUO)
DGIT .... Digital Generation Systems [*NASDAQ symbol*] (TTSB)
DGIWG .... Ditigal Geographic Information Working Group (GEOI)
DGIX .... Dyna Group International, Inc. [*NASDAQ symbol*] (NQ)
DGIX .... Dyna Group Intl. [*NASDAQ symbol*] (TTSB)
DGJ .... Donovan, Gerard J., Co., Inc., North Attleboro MA [*STAC*]
DG J & S .... De Gex, Jones, and Smith's English Chancery Reports [*A publication*] (DLA)
DG J & SB ... De Gex, Jones, and Smith's English Bankruptcy Reports [*A publication*] (DLA)
DGJMS .... Director General, Joint Medical Services (SAUS)
DGJMS .... Director-General, Joint Medical Services (SAUO)
DGK .... Diacylglycerol Kinase [*An enzyme*]
DGKA .... Akim Oda [*Ghana*] [*ICAO location identifier*] (ICLI)
DGKK .... Koforidua [*Ghana*] [*ICAO location identifier*] (ICLI)
dgl .... Dangling Construction (ADWA)
DGL .... Dangling Construction [*Used in correcting manuscripts, etc.*]
DG/L .... Data General's System Programming Language
DGL .... Descriptive Geometry Language (SAUS)
DGL .... Device-independent Graphics Library (SAUS)
DGL .... Diagonal European Airways Link [*France*] [*FAA designator*] (FAAC)
DGL .... Diffuse Galactic Light
DGL .... Distinguished Guest Lecturer (DOMA)
DGL .... Doped Glass LASER
DGL .... Douglas, AZ [*Location identifier*] [*FAA*] (FAAL)
Dgl .... Douglasie (SAUS)
DGL .... Douglas [*Arizona*] Municipal [*Airport symbol*] (OAG)
DGLA .... dihomo-gamma linolenic acid (SAUS)
DGLAS .... Douglas, AZ [*American Association of Railroads railroad junction routing code*]
DGLB .... Bole [*Ghana*] [*ICAO location identifier*] (ICLI)
DGLD .... Diaphragm Gland
DGLE .... Tamale [*Ghana*] [*ICAO location identifier*] (ICLI)
DGLF .... Dark Green Leafy Vegetable (DI)
DGLN .... Navrongo [*Ghana*] [*ICAO location identifier*] (ICLI)
DGLP(A) .... Director-General, Logistic Policy (Army) (ODA)
DGLS .... Diesel Generator Lubrication System [*Nuclear energy*] (NRCH)
DGLS .... Division of Geology and Land Survey (SAUO)
Dgls .... Douglas (SAUS)
DGLS .... Missouri Division of Geology and Land Survey [*State of Missouri Department of Natural Resources*] [*Research center*] (RCD)
Dglsh .... Daglish (SAUS)
DglsLom .... Douglas & Lomason Co. [*Associated Press*] (SAG)
D-glucose ... Rhesus Antigen (ODA)
DGLW .... Wa [*Ghana*] [*ICAO location identifier*] (ICLI)
DGLY .... Yendi [*Ghana*] [*ICAO location identifier*] (ICLI)
DGM .... Data Gathering Monitoring [*System*]
DGM .... Data-Grade Media (SAUS)
dgm .... Decigram [*Unit of measure*]
DGM .... Defense Guidance Memorandum
DGM .... Deputy General Manager [*AEC*]
DGM .... Deputy Grand Marshal (ROG)
DGM .... Deputy Grand Master [*Freemasonry*]
DGM .... Destroyer, Guided Missile [*Surface-to-air/Surface-to-surface*] [*NATO*]
DGM .... Differential Galvanometer (SAUS)
DGM .... Digital Geospatial Metadata (SAUO)
DGM .... Digital Group Multiplexer (MCD)
DGM .... Diploma in General Medicine (SAUS)
DGM .... Directional Gyro Mode
DGM .... Directorate of Guided Missiles (SAUO)
DGM .... Director General of Maintenance (SAUS)
DGM .... Director-General of Maintenance (SAUO)
DGM .... Director-General of Manpower [*Ministry of Labour*] [*British*]
DGM .... Dissolved Gaseous Mercury [*Environmental chemistry*]
DGM .... Division General Manager (WDAA)
DGM .... Draco Gold Mines [*Vancouver Stock Exchange symbol*]
DGM .... Drawing Generating Mode (SAUS)
DGM .... Ductal Glandular Mastectomy [*Medicine*] (DAVI)
DGM .... Dummy Guided Missile
DGM .... Durable Goods Manufacturer [*DoD*]
DGMA .... Dental Group Management Association (EA)
DGMA .... German Society for Measuring Technique and Automation (SAUS)
DG M & G ... De Gex, Macnaghten, and Gordon's English Chancery Reports [*A publication*] (DLA)
DG M & GB... De Gex, Macnaghten, and Gordon's English Bankruptcy Reports [*A publication*] (DLA)
DGMD .... Director, Guided Missiles Division (SAUO)
DGME .... Director General of Military Education (SAUS)
dgme .... Director-General of Military Education (SAUO)
DGMechE(S)... Director-General of Mechanical Engineering, Supply [*Ministry of Supply*] [*British*]
DG-MG .... Diesel Geared - Motor Geared
DGMG .... Direccion General de Minas y Geologia [*Venezuela*] (GEOI)
dGMP .... Deoxyguanosine Monophosphate [*Biochemistry*]
dGMP .... Deoxyguanylic Acid (ADWA)
DGMP .... Direccion de Geologia, Minas y Petrolio [*Costa Rica*] (GEOI)
DGMP .... Director-General of Munitions Production [*Ministry of Supply*] [*British*] [*World War II*]
DGMR .... Directorate of Petroleum and Mineral Resources (SAUS)
DGMR .... Director-General of Military Railways [*British military*] (DMA)
DGMS .... Director-General of Medical Services [*British*]
DGMS .... Division of General Medical Sciences [*National Institutes of Health*]
DGMT .... Director-General of Military Training [*British*]
DGMV .... Dark Green Mottle Virus (SAUS)
DGMV .... Peach Dark Green Mottle Virus (SAUS)
DGMW .... Director-General of Military Works [*British military*] (DMA)
DGMW .... Director-General or Military Works (SAUO)
DGMW .... Double-Gimbaled Momentum Wheel
dgmw .... double-gimbal momentum wheel (SAUS)
DGN .... Dangerous Goods Note [*Shipping*] (DCTA)
DGN .... Data General [*NYSE symbol*] (TTSB)
DGN .... Data General Corp. [*NYSE symbol*] (SPSG)
DGN .... Design
DGN .... Diffuse Glomerulonephritis (DB)
DGN .... Direccion General de Normas [*National Standards Organization*] [*Mexico*]
DGN .... Distributed Graphics Network (SAUS)
DGN .... Distribution Group Name (SAUO)
DGN .... Domestic Geographic Name (GEOI)
DGN .... Dragoon Resources Ltd. [*Vancouver Stock Exchange symbol*]
DGNAST .... Design Assist (SAUS)
DGND .... Digital Ground (SAUS)
DGNL .... Diagonal (FAAC)
DGNMT .... Director-General of Naval Manpower and Training [*British*]
DGNO .... Dallas, Garland & Northeastern Railroad [*Federal Railroad Administration identification code*]
DGNO .... Director General of Naval Ordnance (SAUS)
DGNO .... Director-General of Naval Ordnance (SAUO)
DGNPS .... Director-General of Naval Personnel Services [*British*]
DGNSTC .... Diagnostic
DGO .... Daily General Order (SAUS)
DGO .... Degaussing Officer [*Navy*]
DGO .... Delay Generated Offset (SAUS)
DGO .... Diploma in Gynecology and Obstetrics [*British*]
DGO .... Direccion General de Oceanografia [*Mexico*] (GEOI)
DGO .... Directional Gyro Operation
DGO .... Director General of Organization (SAUS)
DGO .... Director-General of Organization [*RAF*] [*British*]
DGO .... Domego Resources Ltd. [*Toronto Stock Exchange symbol*]
DGO .... Durango [*Mexico*] [*Airport symbol*] (OAG)
DGOA .... Director-General of [*Quality*] Assurance
DGOF .... Director-General of Ordnance Factories [*Ministry of Supply*] [*British*] [*World War II*]
DGOF(F) .... Director-General of Ordnance Factories (Filling) [*Later, DGFF*] [*Ministry of Supply*] [*British*] [*World War II*]
DG of S .... Directorate-General of Signals (SAUO)
DGOH .... Directorate General of Highways [*Vietnam*]
DGOR .... Deutsche Gesellschaft fuer Operations Research [*German Society for Operational Research*] [*Germany*]
DGOS .... Director General of Ordnance Survey (SAUS)
DGOS .... Director-General of Ordnance Survey (SAUO)
DGOS .... Director-General, Ordnance Systems [*Canada*]
DGOS .... Dublin Grand Opera Society (SAUO)
DGP .... Dabrowa Gornicza [*Poland*] [*Seismograph station code, US Geological Survey*] (SEIS)
DGP .... Dangerous Goods Panel [*ICAO*] (DA)
DGP .... Data Generating Program
DGP .... Dean's Grant Project (EDAC)
DGP .... Deoxyglucose-Phosphate [*Biochemistry*]
DGP .... Design Guidance Package [*Military*] (CAAL)
DGP .... Destruction of Government Property
DGP .... Digital Graphic Product (GEOI)
DGP .... Diploma in Graduate and Professional Studies (PGP)
DGP .... Directional Gyroscope Position (SAUS)
DGP .... Director-General of Personnel [*British*]
DGP .... Director-General of Production [*British Air Ministry*]
DGP .... Dissimilar Gateway Protocol [*Computer science*] (VERA)
DGP .... Drive-Gearhead Package
DGP .... Dry Gas Pump
DGP .... USX-Delhi Group [*NYSE symbol*] (SPSG)
DGPA .... Deputy General Purchasing Agent [*Military*]
DGPA .... Direccion General de la Produccion Agraria [*Spain*] (GEOI)
DGPCSAHS... Division of General Practice Central Sydney Area Health Service (SAUS)
DGPG .... Department of Geology and Petroleum Geology (SAUO)
DGPH .... Data/Graphics Processor Hybrid (SAUS)
DGPL .... Downers Grove Public Library [*Illinois*]
DGPM of S... Directorate of Guided Projectiles, Ministry of Supply (SAUO)
DGPNRNSW... Division of General Practice Norther Rivers, New South Wales (SAUS)
DGPNT .... Division of General Practice Northern Tasmania (SAUS)
DGPO .... United States Government Printing Office, Washington, DC [*Library symbol*] [*Library of Congress*] (LCLS)
DGPO-S .... United States Government Printing Office, Serials Library, Alexandria, VA [*Library symbol*] [*Library of Congress*] (LCLS)
DGPS .... Department of Geology and Planetary Sciences (SAUO)
DGPS .... Differential Global Positioning Satellite (GEOI)
DGPS .... Differential Global Positioning System
DGPS .... Director General of Personnel Services (SAUS)
DGPS(N) .... Director-General, Personal Services (Naval) [*British military*] (DMA)
DGQA .... Director-General of Quality Assurance [*British*]

DGR .... Daily Going Rate (SAUS)
DGR .... Danger
Dgr .... Dangerous (SAUS)
DGR .... Dangerous Goods Regulations (SAUO)
DGR .... Degrease
DGR .... Denver & Rio Grande Western Railroad Co. (SAUO)
DGR .... Directorate of Geophysics Research [*Air Research and Development Command*] (AAG)
DGR .... Director of Graves Registration [*British*]
DGR .... Discomfort Glare Rating (SAUS)
DGR .... Division of Geothermal Research [*Energy Research and Development Administration*]
DGR .... Division of Government Research [*University of New Mexico*] [*Research center*] (RCD)
DGR .... Door Gunner [*Military*]
DGRA .... Diamond and Gemstone Remarketing Association [*Defunct*] (EA)
DGRAFMS .... Director-General of Royal Air Force Medical Services [*British*]
DG Range .... Degaussing Range (SAUS)
DGRBX .... Mgn. Stanley D. Witter Develop. Growth [*Mutual fund ticker symbol*] (SG)
DGRC .... Digital Geographic Research Corporation (SAUO)
DGRD .... Director General of Research Department (SAUS)
DGRD .... Director-General, Research and Development Policy [*Military*] [*Canada*]
DGRD .... Division of General and Restorative Devices [*Center for Devices and Radiological Health*]
DGRDS .... Director-General, Research and Development Services [*Military*] [*Canada*]
DG Rev .... DG Review (journ.) (SAUS)
DGRM .... Direccion General de Recursos Minerales [*Panama*] (GEOI)
DGRM .... Director-General of Raw Materials [*Ministry of Supply*] [*British*]
DGRM .... Director General of Repair and Maintenance (SAUS)
DGRO .... Degaussing Range Officer [*Navy*]
DGROUP .... Data Group (SAUO)
DGRTP .... Death Gratuity Payment [*Army*] (AABC)
DGS .... Data Gathering System (MCD)
DGS .... Data Generation System (SAUS)
DGS .... Datagram Service (SAUS)
DGS .... Data Ground Station [*NASA*] (KSC)
DGS .... Degaussing System
DGS .... Delaware Geological Survey (GEOI)
DGS .... Density Gradient Sedimentation [*Analytical biochemistry*]
DGS .... Department of General Services (WPI)
DGS .... Department of Geodetic Science (SAUO)
DGS .... Department of Geological Sciences (SAUS)
DGS .... Department of Geological Survey (SAUS)
DGS .... Deputy General Secretary (DCTA)
DGS .... Destroyer, Guided Missile (Surface-to-Surface) [*NATO*]
DGS .... Diabetic Glomerulosclerosis [*Endocrinology*] (DAVI)
DGS .... DiGeorge Syndrome [*Medicine*]
DGS .... Digital Ground System
DGS .... Digital Group Selector (SAUO)
DGS .... Diploma, General Surgery [*Medical degree*] (CMD)
DGS .... Diploma in General Surgery (SAUS)
DGS .... Diploma in Graduate Studies [*British*]
DGS .... Directorate-General of Signals (SAUO)
DGs .... Directorates General of the European Commission (SAUO)
DGS .... Director General of Ships (SAUS)
DGS .... Director-General Ships (SAUO)
DGS .... Director of Ground Safety [*Air Force*]
DGS .... Display Generating Software (SAUS)
DGS .... display generating system (SAUS)
DGS .... Display Generation System
DGS .... Display GhostScript [*Computer science*] (VERA)
DGS .... Distance Gain Size (SAUS)
DGS .... Distributed Graphics System (MCD)
DGS .... Doctor of Geological Sciences (SAUS)
DGS .... Dollar Gen'l 8.50%'STRYPES' [*NYSE symbol*] (SG)
DGS .... Dominion Government Survey [*Canada*]
DGS .... Don't Give a Spit [*Slang*] [*Bowdlerized version*]
DGS .... Double Green Silk (SAUS)
DGS .... Double Green Silk Covered [*Wire insulation*]
DGS .... Drill Guidance System
DGS .... Drone Generation Squadron
DGS .... Durham Geological Sciences (SAUO)
DGS .... University of Denver, Graduate School of Librarianship, Denver, CO [*OCLC symbol*] (OCLC)
DGSA .... Dairy Goat Society of Australia
DGSA .... Defense Goal Security Architecture (SAUO)
DGSAA .... Director-General of Small Arms Ammunition Production [*Ministry of Supply*] [*British*] [*World War II*]
DGSB .... Sefwi-Bekwai [*Ghana*] [*ICAO location identifier*] (ICLI)
DGSC .... Defense General Supply Center
DGSC .... Defense General Support Center (SAUO)
DGSD .... Digital Sound Corp. [*NASDAQ symbol*] (SAG)
DGSD .... Director-General, Supply and Secretariat Department (SAUO)
DGSD .... Double Glass Sliding Doors [*Classified advertising*] (ADA)
DGSE .... Dallas Gold and Silver Exchange [*NYSE symbol*]
DGSE .... Department of Geological Survey and Exploration (SAUS)
DGSE .... Developmental Ground Support Equipment (DNAB)
DGSE .... Direction Generale de la Securite Exterieure [*Formerly, SDECE*] [*French intelligence agency*]
DGSE .... Dual Gate Storage Element (SAUS)
DGSF .... Department of Geological Survey and Exploration [*Burma*] (GEOI)
DGSFR .... Degasifier
DGShips .... Director-General, Ships [*Navy*] [*British*]
DGSI .... Digital Solutions [*NASDAQ symbol*] (TTSB)
DGSI .... Digital Solutions, Inc. [*NASDAQ symbol*] (NQ)
DGSI .... Don't Get Sucked In
DGSI .... Kumasi [*Ghana*] [*ICAO location identifier*] (ICLI)
DGSIS .... Danish Government Ships Inspection Service (SAUS)
DGSIS .... Director General, Secret Intelligence Service [*British*] (CARL)
DGSJ .... Druggist's Guild of St. James [*Defunct*] (EA)
DGSM .... Directorate-General of Servicing and Maintenance (SAUO)
DGSM .... Director-General of Servicing and Maintenance [*RAF*] [*British*]
DGSM .... Director General, Submarines (SAUS)
DGSN .... Sunyani [*Ghana*] [*ICAO location identifier*] (ICLI)
DGSO .... Director-General of Safety Operations (SAUO)
DGSP .... Director-General of Statistics and Planning [*Ministry of Supply*] [*British*]
DGSR .... Director-General, Ship Refitting [*Ministry of Defence*] [*British*]
DGSRD .... Directorate-General of Scientific Reserach and Development (SAUO)
DGSRD .... Director-General of Scientific Research and Development [*Ministry of Supply*] [*British*]
DGSS .... Diesel Generator Starting System [*Nuclear energy*] (NRCH)
DGSS .... Director General Secret Service (SAUS)
DGSS .... Director General, Security Service [*British*] (CARL)
DGSS .... Distributed Graphics Support Subroutines [*Tektronix, Inc.*] (NITA)
DGST .... Digest
DGST .... Director-General, Supply and Transport [*British military*] (DMA)
DG/STAGE .... Data General's Standard Applications and Graphics Environment [*Engineering software*]
DGStJ .... Dame of Grace, Order of St. John of Jerusalem [*Later, D St J*] [*British*]
DGST(N) .... Director-General of Supplies and Transport (Naval) [*British*]
DGSW .... Wenchi [*Ghana*] [*ICAO location identifier*] (ICLI)
DGSWS .... Department of Geological Sciences Web Server (SAUO)
DGT .... Database Graphics Toolkit [*Blackhawk Data Corp.*]
DGT .... Daughter (WGA)
DGT .... Defence Technology Group (SAUO)
DGT .... Deterministic Grammar Tree (SAUS)
DGT .... Dictionary of Geological Terms (SAUS)
dgt .... Digit (ADWA)
DGT .... Digit
DGT .... Digital Equipment Corp. [*ICAO designator*] (FAAC)
DGT .... Digitech Ltd. [*Toronto Stock Exchange symbol*]
DGT .... Direction Generale des Telecommunications [*Government of Quebec*] [*Canada*] (TSSD)
DGT .... Direction Generale des Telecommunications [*Telecommunications administration*] [*France*]
DGT .... Directorate General of Telecommunications [*Taipei, Taiwan*]
DGT .... Director-General of Training [*British military*] (DMA)
DGT .... Director General of Transportation (SAUS)
DGT .... Director-General of Transportation [*British military*] (DMA)
DGT .... Director of Ground Training (SAUS)
DGT .... Dragon Gunnery Trainer (SAUS)
DGT .... Dumaguete [*Philippines*] [*Airport symbol*] (OAG)
Dgt .... Dumaguette (SAUS)
DGT .... Large German Telescope [*Acronym is based on German phrase*]
DGTA .... Director-General of the Territorial Army [*British*]
DGTA .... Director-General of the Territorial Army Branch, War Office (SAUO)
DGTB .... Data Generating Technology Base (ACAE)
DGTC .... Del Global Technologies Corp. [*NASDAQ symbol*] (SAG)
DGTC .... Digitech, Inc. [*NASDAQ symbol*] (COMM)
DGTD .... Directorate-General of Technical Development (SAUO)
DGTF .... Director-General of the Territorial Force [*British military*] (DMA)
DGTK .... Takoradi [*Ghana*] [*ICAO location identifier*] (ICLI)
DGTL .... Digital (MSA)
DGTL .... Digital Systems International, Inc. [*NASDAQ symbol*] (SAG)
DGTL .... Digital Systems Intl. [*NASDAQ symbol*] (TTSB)
DgtlLnk .... Digital Link Corp. [*Associated Press*] (SAG)
DGTn .... Director General of Transportation (SAUS)
DG Tn .... Director-General of Transportation Services [*British*]
DGTn .... Director-General of Transportation Servies (SAUO)
DGTO .... Degaussing Technical Officer [*Navy*]
dGTP .... Deoxyguanosine Triphosphate (DB)
DGTP .... Deoxyguanosine Triphosphate [*Biochemistry*]
DG/TPMS .... Data General/Transaction Processing Management System [*Data General Corp.*] (NITA)
DgTrns .... Digital Transmission Systems, Inc. [*Associated Press*] (SAG)
DGTS .... Director General of Technical Services (SAUS)
DGTS .... Director-General of Technical Services (SAUO)
DGTS .... Dynamic Ground Target Simulator (ACAE)
DGTX .... Axim [*Ghana*] [*ICAO location identifier*] (ICLI)
DGTZR .... Digitizer (MSA)
DGU .... Boston, MA [*Location identifier*] [*FAA*] (FAAL)
DGU .... Danmarks Geologiske Undersogelse (GEOI)
DGU .... Dedougu [*Upper Volta*] [*Airport symbol*] (AD)
DGU .... Digital Grid Unit (SAUS)
DGU .... Directional Gyro Unit
DGU .... Display Generator Unit (DNAB)
DGU .... Downgrade to Unclassified [*Military*] (MCD)
DGU .... Georgetown University, Washington, DC [*Library symbol*] [*Library of Congress*] [*OCLC symbol*] (LCLS)
D Guam .... United States District Court for the District of Guam (DLA)
DGU-KIE .... Georgetown University, Kennedy Institute, Center for Bioethics, Washington, DC [*Library symbol*] [*Library of Congress*] (LCLS)
DGU-L .... Georgetown University, Law Library, Washington, DC [*Library symbol*] [*Library of Congress*] (LCLS)

DGU-M........ Georgetown University, Medical, Dental, and Nursing Library, Washington, DC [*Library symbol*] [*Library of Congress*] (LCLS)
DGU-Pop...... Georgetown University, Kennedy Institute, Center for Population Research, Washington, DC [*Library symbol*] [*Library of Congress*] (LCLS)
DGU-S......... Georgetown University, Science Library, Washington, DC [*Library symbol*] [*Library of Congress*] (LCLS)
DGU-W........ Georgetown University, Woodstock Theological Center, Washington, DC [*Library symbol*] [*Library of Congress*] (LCLS)
DG/UX.......... Data General UNIX (CDE)
DGV............ Degaussing Vessel [*British military*] (DMA)
DGV............ Dextrose-Gelatin-Veronal [*Solution*] [*Microbiology*]
DGV............ Dienst Grondwaterverkenning [*TNO Institute of Applied Geoscience*] [*Information service or system*] [*Netherlands*] (IID)
DGV............ Digital Generator Video (DNAB)
DGV............ Digital Lava [*AMEX symbol*] (SG)
DGV............ Double Glass Varnish (SAUS)
DG V............ Employment, Industrial Relations and Social Affairs (SAUS)
DGVA.......... Delta-Guanidinovaleric Acid [*Biochemistry*]
DGVB.......... Dextrose-Gelatin-Veronal Buffer [*Microbiology*] (MAE)
DGVC.......... Georgetown Visitation Preparatory School, Washington, DC [*Library symbol*] [*Library of Congress*] (LCLS)
DG VI........... Agriculture (SAUS)
DGVM.......... Dynamic Global Vegetation Model (SAUO)
DGVS.......... Director General of Veterinary Services (SAUS)
DGVS.......... Director-General of Veterinary Services (SAUO)
DGVS.......... Doppler Ground Velocity System (SAUS)
DGVT.......... Director General for Vocational Training (AIE)
DGVX.......... Durbin & Greenbrier Valley Scenic Railroad [*Federal Railroad Administration identification code*]
DGW............ Director-General of Weapons [*British military*] (DMA)
DGW............ Director-General of Works [*RAF*] [*British*]
DGW............ Double Gypsy Winch
DGW............ Douglas, WY [*Location identifier*] [*FAA*] (FAAL)
DGW............ George Washington University, Washington, DC [*Library symbol*] [*Library of Congress*] [*OCLC symbol*] (LCLS)
DGW(A)....... Director-General of Weapons (Army) [*British military*] (RDA)
DGW-C......... George Washington University, Carnegie Endowment for International Peace Collection, Washington, DC [*Library symbol*] [*Library of Congress*] (LCLS)
DGWE.......... Director General of Water Engineering (DCTA)
DGWIP......... Director-General of Weapons and Instruments Production [*Military*] [*British*]
DGW-L.......... George Washington University, Law Library, Washington, DC [*Library symbol*] [*Library of Congress*] (LCLS)
DGW-M......... George Washington University, Medical Library, Washington, DC [*Library symbol*] [*Library of Congress*] (LCLS)
DGW(N)....... Director-General of Weapons Department (Naval) [*British*]
DGWO.......... Degaussing Wiping Officer [*Navy*]
DGW-PIP..... George Washington University, Medical Center, Population Information Program, Washington, DC [*Library symbol*] [*Library of Congress*] (LCLS)
DGWRD....... Directorate of Guided Weapons Research and Development (SAUO)
DGWS.......... Division for Girls' and Women's Sports [*of American Association for Health, Physical Education, and Recreation; also used in a book title*] [*Later, NAGUS*]
DGWT.......... Digital Guided Weapon Technology (MCD)
DGX............ Director-General of Explosives Production [*Ministry of Supply*] [*British*] [*World War II*]
DGX............ Dungannon Explorations Ltd. [*Vancouver Stock Exchange symbol*]
DGX............ Quest Diagnostics, Inc. [*NYSE symbol*] (SAG)
DG XI........... Environment, Nuclear Safety and Civil Protection (SAUS)
DG XI-D....... Environment quality and natural resources (SAUS)
DG XI-D3..... Air quality, urban environment, noise, transport and energy (SAUS)
DG XIII......... Directorate-General (Section XIII) [*Council of European Communities*] (NITA)
DG XXI......... Customs and Indirect Taxation (SAUS)
DGZ............ Designated Ground Zero (MSA)
DGZ............ Desired Ground Zero [*Bombing*]
DGZ............ Deutsche Girozentrale - Deutsche Kommunalbank [*West German bank*]
DGZ............ Dorchester Grain [*Federal Railroad Administration identification code*]
DGZ............ Drop Ground Zone (SAUS)
DGZPRO...... Desired Ground Zero Program [*Military*] (IAA)
DGZPRO...... Desired Ground Zero Tape Prepare Program [*Bombing*] (SAA)
DH.............. Chromosome-Doubled Haploid (SAUS)
DH.............. Daihatsu [*Society of Automotive Engineers auto manufacturer code for service information interchange*]
DH.............. Daily Habits (STED)
DH.............. Darling Husband (ADWA)
DH.............. Das Heisst [*That Is*] [*German*]
DH.............. Data Handbook (MCD)
DH.............. Day Hospital
DH.............. Dayton Hudson Corp. [*NYSE symbol*] (SAG)
dh.............. Deadhead (ELAL)
DH.............. Deadhead [*Freight*]
DH.............. Dead Heat
DH.............. Dear Husband
DH.............. Decay Heat [*Nuclear energy*] (NRCH)
DH.............. Deccan Horse [*British military*] (DMA)
D-H............ Decimal to Hexadecimal (IEEE)
DH.............. Decision Height [*Aviation*]
DH.............. Declaration of Homestead (SAUS)
DH.............. Decoherent Histories
DH.............. Definitive Host (MELL)
DH.............. De Havilland Aircraft Co.
DH.............. De Havilland Aircraft of Canada Ltd. [*ICAO aircraft manufacturer identifier*] (ICAO)
DH.............. Dehumidifier (SAUS)
DH.............. Dehydratase [*An enzyme*]
DH.............. Dehydrocholic Acid [*Organic chemistry*] (MAE)
DH.............. Dehydrogenase [*An enzyme*]
DH.............. Delaware & Hudson Railway Co. (SAUO)
DH.............. Delayed Hypersensitivity [*Immunology*]
DH.............. Deliquescence Humidity
DH.............. Demeure Historique [*An association*] [*France*] (EAIO)
DH.............. Denavit-Hartenberg Process (SAUS)
DH.............. Dental Habits (STED)
DH.............. Dental Hygienist [*British military*] (DMA)
DH.............. Department of Health (WDAA)
DH.............. Department of Hygiene (SAUO)
DH.............. Dermatitis Herpetiformis [*Medicine*]
DH.............. Designated Hitter [*Formerly, DPH*] [*Also, DESI*] [*Baseball*]
DH.............. Design Handbook
DH.............. Destination Hospital [*Aeromedical evacuation*]
D-H............ Detail of Heading (SAUS)
DH.............. Detention Home
D/H............ deuterium/hydrogen (SAUS)
D/H............ Deuterium/Hydrogen Ratio
D/H............ deuterium-hydrogen ratio diameter (SAUS)
DH.............. Developmental History [*Medicine*] (DMAA)
DH.............. Developmentally Handicapped
DH.............. Device Handler
DH.............. Diapause Hormone [*In insects*] [*Endocrinology*]
DH.............. Diaphragmatic Hernia [*Gastroenterology*] (DAVI)
DH.............. Difference in Height
dh.............. differential of height (SAUS)
dH.............. differential of magnetic field intensity (SAUS)
DH.............. Diffuse Histiocytic [*Lymphoma*] [*Oncology*] (DAVI)
DH.............. Dignitatis Humanae [*Declaration on Religious Freedom*] [*Vatican II document*]
dh.............. Direct Heating (SAUS)
D/H............ Direct Hit
DH.............. Directly Heated (DEN)
DH.............. Director of Hygiene [*British military*] (DMA)
DH.............. Dirham [*Monetary unit*] [*Morocco*]
DH.............. Disc Harrowing [*Agriculture*]
DH.............. Discovery Airlines [*ICAO designator*] (AD)
DH.............. Dislocated Homemaker [*Job Training and Partnership Act*] (OICC)
DH.............. Disorderly House
DH.............. Display Hold
DH.............. Disseminated Histoplasmosis [*Medicine*]
DH.............. Dissociative Hysteria [*Medicine*] (MELL)
DH.............. District Heating (SAUS)
DH.............. Diuretic Hormone [*Endocrinology*]
DH.............. Divided Hatch (SAUS)
DH.............. Dividing Head (SAUS)
DH.............. Doctor of Humanics
DH.............. Doctor of Humanities
DH.............. Document Handling (IAA)
DH.............. Dominant Hand [*Psychometrics*]
DH.............. Doors of Hope [*An association*] (EA)
DH.............. Dopamine-a-Hydroxylase (SAUS)
DH.............. Dorsal Horn (STED)
DH.............. Doubleheader [*Baseball term*] (NDBD)
DH.............. Double Helix [*Cytology, genetics*]
DH.............. Double Heterojunction (SAUS)
DH.............. Double Heterostructure [*Physics*]
DH.............. Double Homology [*Biochemistry*]
DH.............. Double-Hung [*Construction*]
dh.............. double hung (SAUS)
DH.............. Double Hydrant [*On fire insurance maps*]
DH.............. Dowager's Hump [*Medicine*] (MELL)
DH.............. Dow Chemical Co. [*Research code symbol*]
DH.............. Downhill [*Bicycle handlebars*]
DH.............. downhole (SAUS)
DH.............. Drill Hole (GEOI)
D/H............ Drug History
DH.............. Drug Hypersensitivity [*Medicine*] (DAVI)
DH.............. Dry Heaves [*Medicine*] (MELL)
DH.............. Dual Hopper (SAUS)
D-H............ Duane-Hunt (SAUS)
DH.............. Ductal Hyperplasia [*Medicine*] (DMAA)
DH.............. Duct heater (SAUS)
DH.............. Dynamic Head (SAUS)
DH.............. Tonga Air Service [*ICAO designator*] (AD)
Dh8............ Boeing Canada Dash-8 [*Airplane code*]
DHA............ Dairy Husbandry Adviser [*Ministry of Agriculture, Fisheries, and Food*] [*British*]
DHA............ Defense Health Agency (SAUS)
DHA............ Dehydrated Humulinic Acid (OA)
DHA............ Dehydroabietic Acid (SAUS)
DHA............ Dehydroacetic Acid [*Pharmacology*]
DHA............ Dehydroandrosterone (SAUS)
DHA............ Dehydroascorbic Acid [*Also, DAA*] [*Oxidized form of Vitamin C*] [*Biochemistry*]
DHA............ Dehydroepiandrosterone [*Also, DEA, DHEA, DHIA*] [*Endocrinology*]
DHA............ Denver Handwriting Analysis [*Educational test*]
DHA............ Department of Health Regulations (SAUS)
DHA............ Department of Humanitarian Affairs [*United Nations*]

DHA .... Dependent Housing Area [*Army*] (AABC)
DHA .... Design Hazard Analysis (MCD)
DHA .... Dhahran [*Saudi Arabia*] [*Airport symbol*] (OAG)
DHA .... Dhahran, Saudi Arabia (SAUS)
DHA .... Dihydroacetic Acid (STED)
DHA .... Dihydroacetone (EDCT)
DHA .... Dihydroactinidiolide [*Organic chemistry*]
DHA .... Dihydroalprenolol [*Pharmacochemistry*]
DHA .... Dihydroanthracene [*Organic chemistry*]
DHA .... Dihydroxyacetone [*Organic chemistry*]
dha .... dihydroxyacetone phosphate (SAUS)
DHA .... Diploma, Hospital Administration [*Medical degree*] (CMD)
DHA .... District Health Authority [*British*]
DHA .... District Heating Association [*British*]
DHA .... Docosahexaenoic Acid [*Organic chemistry*]
DHA .... Doctor of Hospital Administration
DHA .... Double Heave Amplitude
DHA .... Duck Head Apparel [*AMEX symbol*]
DHA .... Dutch Harbor [*Alaska*] [*Seismograph station code, US Geological Survey*] [*Closed*] (SEIS)
DHAA .... Dehydroabietic Acid [*Organic chemistry*]
DHAA .... Dock and Harbour Authorities Association (SAUO)
DHAC .... Derry Housing Action Committee (SAUO)
DHAC .... Division of Health Assessment and Consultation (SAUS)
DHAD .... Dihydroxyanthracenedione [*Quinazarin*] [*Organic chemistry*]
DH Adm .... Doctor of Hospital Administration
DHAE .... Dihydrogentad Alkaloids of Ergotamine [*Medicine*] (EDAA)
DHAEMAE .... Disposable Hypodermic and Allied Equipment Manufacturers Association of Europe (EAIO)
DHAN .... Dihaloacetonitrile [*Organic chemistry*]
DH&FS .... Department of Health and Family Services (SAUS)
DHANP .... Diplomate of Homeopathic Academy of Naturopathic Physicians [*Medicine*]
DHAP .... Dehydroxyacetone Phosphate (SAUS)
DHAP .... Dihydroxyacetone Phosphate [*Also, DAP*] [*Organic chemistry*]
dhard .... dehaired (SAUS)
DHARS .... Doppler Heading, Attitude, and Reference System (ACAE)
DHAS .... Daily Herd Analysis Service (SAUS)
DHAS .... Deborah Harry Appreciation Society (EA)
DHAS .... Dehydroandrostenedione (DMAA)
DHAS .... Dehydroepiandrosterone Sulfate [*Biochemistry*]
DHAS .... Doctors Health Advisory Service [*Australia*]
DHAT .... Dental Hygiene Aptitude Test (EDAC)
DHA(T) .... District Health Authority (Teaching) [*National Health Service*] [*British*] (DI)
DHA Timber ... Dhaman Timber (SAUS)
D Hawaii .... United States District Court, District of Hawaii (DLA)
DHB .... Damp Heat Bias (AGLO)
DHB .... Daniel Hudson Burnham [*Architect and urban planner, 1846-1912*]
DHB .... Defended Hard Basing (ACAE)
DHB .... Defense Halfback [*Football*] (GOBB)
DHB .... Dihydroxibenzene (SAUS)
DHB .... Dihydroxybenzoic Acid [*Organic chemistry*]
DHB .... District Health Board (FOTI)
DHB .... Duck Hepatitis B (DMAA)
DHBA .... Dihydroxybenzylamine [*Organic chemistry*]
DHBD .... Dihydroxybiphenyl Dioxygenase [*An enzyme*]
DHBE .... Dihydroxybutyl Ether (DMAA)
DHBG .... (Dihydroxybutyl)guanine [*Biochemistry*]
DHBP .... Dihydroxybenzophenone [*Organic chemistry*]
DHBS .... Dihydrobiopterin Synthetase (DMAA)
DHBS .... Dihydroxybenzoylserine [*Organic chemistry*]
DHBT .... Double Heterostructure Bipolar Transistor [*Electronics*] (AAEL)
DHBT .... Dual-channel Heterojunction Bipolar Transistor (SAUS)
DHBV .... Duck Hepatic B Virus
DHC .... Air-Cushion Vehicle built by DeHavilland Aircraft Co. of Canada [*Usual ly used in combination with numerals*] [*Canada*]
DHC .... Boeing Dehavilland Canada [*ICAO designator*] (FAAC)
DHC .... Danielson Holding Corp. [*AMEX symbol*] (SPSG)
DHC .... Data Handling Center (KSC)
DHC .... Defence Housing Committee [*Australia*]
DHC .... Defense Homes Corp. [*World War II*]
DHC .... De Havilland, Inc. [*Canada*] [*FAA designator*] (FAAC)
DHC .... Dehydrocholesterol [*Organic chemistry*]
DHC .... Dehydrocholic Acid [*Organic chemistry*]
DHC .... Delayed Hydrogen Cracking (SAUS)
DHC .... Department of Housing and Construction (SAUS)
DHC .... Detroit House of Correction (SAUS)
DHC .... Diamond High Council (SAUO)
DHC .... Dihydrochalcone [*Sweetening agent*]
DHC .... Dihydrocodeine [*An analgesic*] [*Pharmacology*]
DHC .... Dilute Homogeneous Charge
DHC .... Direct Hydrophilic Conjugation
DHC .... District Health Committee (SAUO)
DHC .... District Health Council [*Australia*]
DHC .... District Hetring & Cooling (SAUO)
DHC .... Doctorat Honoris Causa [*Canada*] (DD)
DHC .... Donner-Hanna Coke [*Federal Railroad Administration identification code*]
DHC .... Donohue, Inc. [*Toronto Stock Exchange symbol*]
DHC .... Dorsal Horn Cell [*Medicine*] (EDAA)
DHC .... Drop Head Coupe [*Convertible automobile*] [*British*]
DHC .... Dry Hydrocarbon
DHCA .... Deep Hypothermia and Circulatory Arrest [*Medicine*] (DMAA)
DHCA .... Dihydroxycholestanoic Acid [*Biochemistry*]
DHCA .... Kaya [*Burkina Faso*] [*ICAO location identifier*] (ICLI)
DHCB .... Barsalogho [*Burkina Faso*] [*ICAO location identifier*] (ICLI)
DHCC .... Decay Heat Closed Cooling [*Nuclear energy*] (IEEE)
DHCC .... Dehydroxycholecalciferol (DMAA)
DHCC .... Dihydroxycholecalciferol [*Vitamin D_3*]
DHCC .... Ouahigouya [*Burkina Faso*] [*ICAO location identifier*] (ICLI)
DHCD .... Department of Housing and Community Development (OICC)
DHCD .... Didyr [*Burkina Faso*] [*ICAO location identifier*] (ICLI)
DHCE .... Batie [*Burkina Faso*] [*ICAO location identifier*] (ICLI)
DHCE .... Dynamic helium charging experiment (SAUS)
DHCF .... Distributed Host Command Facility (NITA)
DHCF .... Holy Cross Foreign Mission Seminary, Washington, DC [*Library symbol*] [*Library of Congress*] (LCLS)
DHCG .... Kongoussi [*Burkina Faso*] [*ICAO location identifier*] (ICLI)
DHCHST .... Downey Hand Center Hand Sensitivity Test
DHCI .... Titao [*Burkina Faso*] [*ICAO location identifier*] (ICLI)
DHCJ .... Djibo [*Burkina Faso*] [*ICAO location identifier*] (ICLI)
DHCK .... Koudougou [*Burkina Faso*] [*ICAO location identifier*] (ICLI)
DHCL .... Leo [*Burkina Faso*] [*ICAO location identifier*] (ICLI)
DHCM .... Manga [*Burkina Faso*] [*ICAO location identifier*] (ICLI)
DHCN .... Daily Historical Climate Network (CARB)
DHC News ... District Health Committee News (journ.) (SAUS)
DHCO .... Boromo [*Burkina Faso*] [*ICAO location identifier*] (ICLI)
DHCP .... Decentralized Hospital Computer Program [*Veterans Administration*]
DHCP .... Double Hexagonal Close-Packed [*Metallography*]
DHCP .... Dynamic Host Configuration Program [*Computer science*]
DHCP .... Dynamic Host Configuration Protocol [*Computer science*]
DHCP .... Dynamic Host Control Protocol [*Computer science*]
DHCP .... Po [*Burkina Faso*] [*ICAO location identifier*] (ICLI)
DHCR .... Poura [*Burkina Faso*] [*ICAO location identifier*] (ICLI)
DHCS .... Debbie Harry Collector's Society (EA)
DHCS .... Seguenega [*Burkina Faso*] [*ICAO location identifier*] (ICLI)
DHCT .... Tenado [*Burkina Faso*] [*ICAO location identifier*] (ICLI)
DHCU .... Data Handling and Control Unit
DHCU .... Gourcy [*Burkina Faso*] [*ICAO location identifier*] (ICLI)
DHCY .... Division of Handicapped Children and Youth [*HEW*]
DHCY .... Yako [*Burkina Faso*] [*ICAO location identifier*] (ICLI)
dhd .... despatch half demurrage (SAUS)
DHD .... Dihydrodigoxin [*Biochemistry*]
DHD .... Distillate Hydrosulfurization (SAUS)
DHD .... District Health Department (DMAA)
DHD .... Doghouse Disease (MELL)
DHD .... Double Heat-Sink Diode (CET)
DHD .... Double High Density (SAUS)
DHD .... Drop-Hammer Die (MSA)
DHD .... Durham Downs [*Australia*] [*Airport symbol*] (OAG)
DHDAA .... Dihexadecyldimethylammonium Acetate [*Organic chemistry*]
dhdats .... despatch halfdemurrage on all time saved (SAUS)
dhdatsbe .... despatch half demurrage on all time saved at both ends (SAUS)
DHDATSBE ... Despatch Half Demurrage on All Time Saved Both Ends (RIMS)
dhdawtsbe ... despatch half demurrage on all working time saved at both ends (SAUS)
dhdbe .... despatch half demurrage at both ends (SAUS)
DHDD .... Digital High-Definition Display (KSC)
dhddo .... despatch half demurrage discharging only (SAUS)
DHDEE .... Dihydroxydiethyl Ether (SAUS)
DHDI .... Drop-Hammer Die
dhdlo .... despatch half demurrage loading only (SAUS)
DHDMI .... Dihydroxy(dimethyl)imidazolidinone [*Organic chemistry*]
DH-DOC .... Dihydrodeoxycorticosterone [*Endocrinology*]
DHDS .... Data Handling and Display Subsystem
DHDSC .... Dayton Hudson Department Store Co. [*Division of Dayton-Hudson Corp.*]
dhdws .... despatch half demurrage on working time saved (SAUS)
dhdwtsbe .... despatch half demurrage on working time saved at both ends (SAUS)
DHDWTSBE ... Despatch Half Demurrage on Working Time Saved Both Ends (RIMS)
DHE .... Data Handling Electronics (SAUS)
DHE .... Data Handling Equipment
DHE .... Debye-Hueckel Equation [*Physics*]
DHE .... Dehydroepiandrosterone (DB)
DHE .... Dehydroergotamin (SAUS)
DHE .... Department of Home Economics [*of NEA*] [*Later, HEEA*] (EA)
DHE .... Dielectric Heating Equipment
DHE .... Dihematoporphyrin Ether [*Pharmacology*]
DHE .... Dihydroergocornine [*Endocrinology*]
DHE .... Dihydroergotamine [*Pharmacology*]
DHE .... Diploma in Horticulture, Royal Botanic Garden, Edinburgh [*British*] (DBQ)
DHE .... Doctor of Church History
DHE .... DOE-HQ Environmental (SAUS)
DHE .... Down-Hole Emulsification (SAUS)
DHE .... Dump Heat Exchanger [*Nuclear energy*] (OA)
DHEA .... Boulsa [*Burkina Faso*] [*ICAO location identifier*] (ICLI)
DHEA .... Dehydroepiandrosterone [*Also, DEA, DHA, DHIA*] [*Endocrinology*]
DHEA .... UCD Health (SAUS)
DHEAS .... Dehydroepiandrosterone Sulfate [*Biochemistry*]
DHEAS .... Dihydroeplandrosterone (ADWA)
DHEB .... Bogande [*Burkina Faso*] [*ICAO location identifier*] (ICLI)
DHEBA .... (Dihydroxyethylene)bisacrylamide [*Organic chemistry*]
DHEC .... Department of Health and Environmental Control (SAUO)
DHEC .... Dihydroergocryptine [*Organic chemistry*]
DH Ec .... Doctor of Home Economics
DH Ec .... Doctor of Household Economy
DHEC .... Komin-Yanga [*Burkina Faso*] [*ICAO location identifier*] (ICLI)

DHED .... Diapaga [*Burkina Faso*] [*ICAO location identifier*] (ICLI)
DHEE .... Dori [*Burkina Faso*] [*ICAO location identifier*] (ICLI)
DHEF .... Fada N'Gourma [*Burkina Faso*] [*ICAO location identifier*] (ICLI)
DHEG .... Di(hydroxyethyl)glycine [*Organic chemistry*]
DHEG .... Gorom-Gorom [*Burkina Faso*] [*ICAO location identifier*] (ICLI)
DHEK .... Koupela [*Burkina Faso*] [*ICAO location identifier*] (ICLI)
DHEL .... Kantchari [*Burkina Faso*] [*ICAO location identifier*] (ICLI)
DHEM .... Tambao [*Burkina Faso*] [*ICAO location identifier*] (ICLI)
D-HEMT .... Depletion-Mode High-Electron Mobility Transistor (SAUS)
DHEN .... Garango [*Burkina Faso*] [*ICAO location identifier*] (ICLI)
DHEO .... Zorgo [*Burkina Faso*] [*ICAO location identifier*] (ICLI)
DHEP .... Detailed Human Engineering Plan
DHEP .... Pama [*Burkina Faso*] [*ICAO location identifier*] (ICLI)
DHER .... Arli [*Burkina Faso*] [*ICAO location identifier*] (ICLI)
DHERF .... Dental Health Education and Research Foundation [*Australia*]
DHES .... Department of Health and Environmental Science (SAUO)
DHES .... Division of Health Examination Statistics [*HEW*]
DHES .... Sebba [*Burkina Faso*] [*ICAO location identifier*] (ICLI)
DHESN .... Dihydroergosine [*Biochemistry*]
DHET .... Dihydroergotoxine [*Organic chemistry*]
DHET .... Tenkodogo [*Burkina Faso*] [*ICAO location identifier*] (ICLI)
DHEW .... Department of Health, Education, and Welfare [*Later, DHHS*]
DHEW .... United States Department of Health, Education, and Welfare, Washington, DC [*Library symbol*] [*Library of Congress*] (LCLS)
DHEY .... Ouargaye [*Burkina Faso*] [*ICAO location identifier*] (ICLI)
DHEZ .... Zabre [*Burkina Faso*] [*ICAO location identifier*] (ICLI)
DHF .... Dag Hammarskjold Foundation [*Sweden*] (EAIO)
DHF .... Data Handling Function (SSD)
DHF .... Demand History File [*DoD*]
DHF .... Dengue Hemorrhagic Fever [*Medicine*]
DHF .... Diastolic Heart Failure [*Medicine*] (MELL)
DHF .... Dihydrofolate [*Biochemistry*]
DHF .... Dihydrofolic Acid (ADWA)
DHF .... Dihydroxyflavone [*Organic chemistry*]
DHF .... Dilute Hydrofluoric Acid (AAEL)
DHF .... Dirac-Hartree-Fock (SAUS)
DHF .... Divorced Hispanic Female (SAUO)
DHF .... Document History File (MCD)
DHF .... Dorsi-Hyperflexion [*Medicine*] (EDAA)
DHF .... Double Hollow Fork [*Bicycle part or a fool*] [*Slang*] [*British*] (DSUE)
DHFA .... Dominion High Fidelity Association (SAUO)
DHFA .... Double-Conductor, Heat and Flame-Resistant, Armored [*Cable*]
DHFB .... Dihydrofolate Reductase (SAUS)
DHFC .... David Hasselhoff Fan Club (EA)
DHFC .... David Heavener Fan Club (EA)
DHFC .... David Hedison Fan Club [*Defunct*] (EA)
DHFC .... Deidre Hall Fan Club (EA)
DHF/DSS .... Dengue Hemorrhagic Fever/Dengue Shock Syndrome [*Medicine*] (EDAA)
DHFR .... Dihydrofolate Reductase [*An enzyme*]
DHFS .... Dengue Hemorrhagic Fever Syndrome [*Medicine*]
DHFS .... Department of Health & Family Services (SAUO)
DHG .... Di(hydroxyethyl)glycinate [*Organic chemistry*]
DHg .... Doctor of Hygiene
DHG .... Double Helical Gear (SAUS)
DHGE .... Dictionnaire d'Histoire et de Geographie Ecclesiastique [*A publication*] (BJA)
DHGG .... Deaggregated Human Gammaglobulin [*Medicine*] (DMAA)
DHH .... Deaf and Hard of Hearing
DHH .... Department of Health and Hospitals (SAUO)
DHH .... Doctor of Honorary Humanities
DHHEC .... Deaf and Hard of Hearing Entrepreneurs Council (EA)
DHHH .... Ouagadougou (Airport) [*Burkina Faso*] [*ICAO location identifier*] (ICLI)
DHHR .... Department of Health & Human Resources (SAUO)
DHHS .... Department of Health and Human Services
DHHS .... United States Department of Health and Human Services, Washington, DC [*Library symbol*] [*Library of Congress*] (LCLS)
DHHV .... Ouagadougou [*Burkina Faso*] [*ICAO location identifier*] (ICLI)
DHI .... Dairy Herd Improvement (OA)
DHI .... Deafness, Hyperprolinuria, and Ichthyosis [*Medicine*] (MELL)
DHI .... Defense Hydrographic Initiative (GEOI)
DHI .... Defense Hydrographic Initiative Laboratory (SAUO)
DHI .... Dental Health International (EA)
DHI .... Department Head Instruction (NRCH)
DHI .... Dhangarhi [*Nepal*] [*Airport symbol*] (OAG)
DHI .... Dictionary of the History of Ideas [*A publication*]
DHI .... Dihydroxyindol
DHI .... Directional Horizon Indicator
DHI .... Disk Head Interference (SAUS)
DHI .... Door and Hardware Institute (EA)
DHI .... D.R.Horton [*NYSE symbol*] (TTSB)
DHI .... DR Horton, Inc. [*NYSE symbol*] (SAG)
DHI .... Dunhill International Inc. (SAUO)
DHIA .... Dairy Herd Improvement Association [*Later, AIPL*] (EA)
DHIA .... Dehydroisoandrosterone [*Also, DEA, DHA, DHEA*] [*Endocrinology*]
DHIC .... Dihydroisocodeine [*Pharmacology*]
DHIFC .... Doyle Holly International Fan Club [*Defunct*] (EA)
DHIR .... Dairy Herd Improvement Registry
DHIRS .... District Headquarters Induction and Recruiting Station [*Marine Corps*]
DHIS .... Distributed Heterogeneous Information Systems (SAUS)
DHIS .... Division of Health Interview Statistics [*Department of Health and Human Services*] (GFGA)
DHISF .... Document Handling and Information Services Facility [*General Accounting Office*] (IID)
DHist .... Director of Historical Section (SAUO)
DHIY .... Devonshire Hussar Imperial Yeomanry [*Military*] [*British*] (ROG)
DHJ .... Doing His Job (ADWA)
DHK .... Diet/Health Knowledge Survey [*Department of Agriculture*] (GFGA)
DHK .... Dihydrokaempferol [*Botany*]
DHKP/C .... Revolutionary People's Liberation Party/Front [*Government term*] (GA)
DHL .... Dag Hammarskjold Library [*United Nations*] (DUND)
DHL .... David Herbert Lawrence [*British novelist, 1885-1930*]
DHL .... Davies Herbarium, University of Louisville [*Kentucky*]
DHL .... Degenerescence Hepato-Lenticulaire (SAUS)
DHL .... Dhala [*Aden*] [*Airport symbol*] (AD)
DHL .... DHL Airways, Inc. [*FAA designator*] (FAAC)
DHL .... Diffuse Histiocytic Lyphoma [*Medicine*]
DHL .... Digital Equipment Corp., Hudson, Westboro, MA [*OCLC symbol*] (OCLC)
dhl .... distemper, hepatitis, leptospirosis (SAUS)
DHL .... Division of Hospital Libraries (SAUS)
DHL .... Doctor of Hebrew Letters
DHL .... Doctor of Hebrew Literature
DHL .... Doctor of Humane Letters
DHL .... Dynamic Head Loading (SAUS)
DHL .... House of Lords Appeals, in Dunlop's Court of Session Cases, from Vol. 13 [*1851-62*] [*A publication*] (DLA)
DHLB .... Dihydrolevobunolol [*Biochemistry*]
DH Lett .... Doctor of Hebrew Letters (SAUS)
DHLG .... Department of Housing and Local Government [*Queensland*] [*Australia*]
DH Lit .... Doctor of Hebrew Literature
DH Litt .... Doctor of Hebrew Letters [*or Literature*]
DHLLP .... Direct High-Level Language Processor
DHLNL .... Dihydroxylysinonorleucine [*Biochemistry*]
dhl-p .... distemper, hepatitis, leptospirosis-parainfluenza (SAUS)
dhlpp .... distemper, hepatitis, leptospirosis, parainfluenza, parvovirus (SAUS)
DHLPPi .... Distemper, Hepatitis, Leptospirosis, Parvovirus and Parainfluenza [*Dog vaccine covering these diseases*] (SPVS)
DHlthSc .... Diploma in Health Science
DHLW .... Defense High-Level Radioactive Waste [*Nuclear energy*]
DHLWTP .... Defense High-Level Waste Technology Program (SAUS)
DHM .... Daughters of the Heart of Mary [*Roman Catholic religious order*]
DHM .... Debye-Huckel-Manning [*Theory*] [*Physical chemistry*]
DHM .... Detroit Historical Museum (SAUS)
DHM .... Dexterous Hand Master [*Robotics*]
DHM .... Dihydromorphine [*Analgesic compound*] [*Organic chemistry*]
DHM .... Dihydromuscimol [*Biochemistry*]
DHM .... Dillingham Corp. (SAUO)
DHM .... Diocesan Home Missionary
DHM .... Divorced Hispanic Male (ADWA)
DHM .... Dry Honing Machine
DHM .... Duct hardfacing material (SAUS)
DHM .... Mokuleia, Oahu, HI [*Location identifier*] [*FAA*] (FAAL)
DHMA .... Dehydroxymandelic Acid (SAUS)
DHMA .... Dihydroxymandelic Acid [*Also, DMA, DOMA*] [*Organic chemistry*]
DHMA .... Drapery Hardware Manufacturers Association [*Defunct*] (EA)
DHMAA .... Draft Horse and Mule Association of America (EA)
DHMES .... Division of Health Manpower Educational Services (SAUO)
DHM Fur .... Diloxanide Furoate [*Medicine*] (EDAA)
DHMH .... Maryland Department of Health and Mental Hygiene (SAUO)
DHMM .... Director of Hazardous Materials Management (SARE)
DHMPA .... Dihydromycoplanecin A [*Biochemistry*]
DHMPA .... Dihydroxymethoxyphenylalanine [*Biochemistry*]
DHMS .... Dense Hydrous Magnesium Silicate [*Geochemistry*]
DHMS .... Diamond Home Services, Inc. [*NASDAQ symbol*] (NASQ)
DHMSA .... Diploma in the History of Medicine, Society of Apothecaries [*Medical degree*] (CMD)
DHMSA .... Diploma in the History of Medicine, Society of Apothecaries of London [*British*] (DBQ)
DHMT .... Deuterated Hexamethylenetetramine (SAUS)
DHMU .... Diesel Hydraulic Multiple Unit [*Indian Railway*] (TIR)
DHMY .... Dehumidify (MSA)
DHN .... Decahydronaphthalene (SAUS)
DHN .... Department of Hospital Nursing (SAUS)
DHN .... Dihydronaphthacene [*Organic chemistry*]
DHN .... Directorate of Hydrography and Navigation (SAUS)
DHN .... Displaced Homemakers Network (EA)
DHN .... Dothan [*Alabama*] [*Airport symbol*] (OAG)
DHN .... Dynamic Hardness Number
DHNR .... Dynamically Hierarchical Network Routing [*Communications term*] (DCT)
DHO .... Department of Highways, Ontario (SAUS)
DHO .... Deuterium Hydrogen [*Protium*] Oxide [*Organic chemistry*] (DAVI)
DHO .... Dihydroouabain [*Biochemistry*]
DHO .... Director of Home Operations [*Air Ministry*] [*British*] [*World War II*]
DHO .... District Historical Office [*or Officer*] [*Navy*]
DHO .... Downhill Only Ski Club (SAUO)
DHO .... Damped Harmonic Oscillator [*Electronics*] (ODA)
DHO 180 .... Dihydroergocomine (STED)
DHOA .... Dano [*Burkina Faso*] [*ICAO location identifier*] (ICLI)
DHOB .... Banfora [*Burkina Faso*] [*ICAO location identifier*] (ICLI)
DHOD .... Dedougou [*Burkina Faso*] [*ICAO location identifier*] (ICLI)
DHODH .... Dihydroorotate Dehydrogenase (STED)
DHOF .... Safane [*Burkina Faso*] [*ICAO location identifier*] (ICLI)
DHOF Wire .... Two-conductor, Heat-Oil-, and Flame-Resistant Wire (SAUS)
DHOG .... Gaoua [*Burkina Faso*] [*ICAO location identifier*] (ICLI)
DH/OH .... Down Hours to Operating Hours Ratio [*Quality control*]

DHOH Hounde [*Burkina Faso*] [*ICAO location identifier*] (ICLI)

DHOL Loumana [*Burkina Faso*] [*ICAO location identifier*] (ICLI)

DHOM Diploma, Hospital Organization & Management [*Medical degree*] (CMD)

DHOM Dominion Homes, Inc. [*NASDAQ symbol*] (NASQ)

DHON Nouna [*Burkina Faso*] [*ICAO location identifier*] (ICLI)

DHOO Bobo-Dioulasso [*Burkina Faso*] [*ICAO location identifier*] (ICLI)

D Hor Doctor of Horticulture

DHOR Orodara [*Burkina Faso*] [*ICAO location identifier*] (ICLI)

DHOS Sideradougou [*Burkina Faso*] [*ICAO location identifier*] (ICLI)

D Ho Sc Doctor of Household Science

DHOT Tougan [*Burkina Faso*] [*ICAO location identifier*] (ICLI)

DHOU Diebougou [*Burkina Faso*] [*ICAO location identifier*] (ICLI)

DHOY Aribinda [*Burkina Faso*] [*ICAO location identifier*] (ICLI)

DHP Dehydrogenated Polymer (STED)

DHP Dehydrogenative Polymerization [*Biology*]

DHP Dehydroproline [*Biochemistry*]

DHP Delivered Horse-Power (SAUS)

DHP Delivered Horsepower to Propeller (IAA)

DHP Demokratik Halk Partisi [*Democratic People's Party*] [*Turkish Cyprus*] [*Political party*] (PPE)

DHP Dense High Purity (SAUS)

DHP Deoxidized High-Residual Phosphorus [*Copper*]

DHP Department Head Procedures (NRCH)

DHP Designed Horsepower (IAA)

DHP Deutsche Hannover Partei [*German Hanover Party*] (PPE)

DHP Developed Horsepower

DHP Diheptyl Phthalate [*Organic chemistry*]

DHP Dihexadecyl Phosphate [*Organic chemistry*]

DHP Dihexyl Phthalate (EDCT)

DHP Dihydric Phenol (SAUS)

DHP Dihydroheptaprenol [*Biochemistry*]

DHP Dihydroprogesterone (STED)

DHP Dihydropyrane [*Organic chemistry*]

DHP Dihydropyridine [*Organic chemistry*]

DHP Dihydroxyacetone Phosphate (STED)

DHP Dihydroxyphenol [*Organic chemistry*]

DHP Dihydroxypropyl (SAUS)

DHP Diploma in Hypnosis and Psychotherapy [*British*] (DBQ)

DHP Directed Hamiltonian Path (RALS)

DHP Direct High Power (ADWA)

DHP Document Handler Processor

DHP Drawbar Horsepower

DHP Dr. Halo PIC (SAUS)

DHP Drum Head Plug (VLIE)

DHPA Degree of Honor Protective Association [*St. Paul, MN*] (EA)

DHPA Dihydroxypropyladenine [*Biochemistry*]

DHPc Dorsal Hippocampus (STED)

DHPC Dorsal Hippocampus [*Neuroanatomy*]

DHPE Data Hardware Project Engineer [*NASA*]

DHPE Dihydroxyphenylethanol [*Organic chemistry*]

DHPF Divorced Hispanic Professional Female (SAUO)

DHPG Dehydroxyphenylglycol [*Also, DOPEG*] [*Organic chemistry*]

DHPG Dihydroxyphenethyleneglycol [*Organic chemistry*]

DHPG Dihydroxyphenylethylene Glycol (STED)

DHPG Dihydroxyphenylglycol (STED)

DHPG (Dihydroxypropoxymethyl)guanine [*Biochemistry*]

DHPGTP (Dihydroxypropoxymethyl)guanine Triphosphate [*Antiviral compound*]

DHPh Diploma in Homeopathic Pharmacy [*Medicine*] (EDAA)

DHPM Divorced Hispanic Professional Male (SAUO)

DHPMA Dihydroxypropyl Methacrylate [*Organic chemistry*]

DHP-MP Dihydroxypropyl Methylpiperazine (SAUS)

DHPR Dihydropteridine Reductase [*An enzyme*]

DHPR Dihydropyridine Receptor [*Biochemistry*]

dhPRL Decidual Proclactin (BABM)

dhPRL Decidual Prolactin [*Medicine*] (DAVI)

DHPTA Diaminohydroxypropanetetraacetic Acid [*Also, DTA, DPTA*] [*Organic chemistry*]

dHpuA Deoxyheptulosonic Acid [*Biochemistry*]

DHPX Degussa [*Private rail car owner code*]

DHQ Dihydroquercetin [*Botany*]

DHQ Dihydroquinidine [*Organic chemistry*]

DHQ District Headquarters

DHQ Division Headquarters [*Military*]

DHQ Mean Diurnal High-Water Inequality

DHQHS Dihydroqinghaosu [*Organic chemistry*]

DHQS Dehydroquinate Synthase [*An enzyme*]

DHR Danaher Corp. [*NYSE symbol*] (SPSG)

DHR Darjeeling Himalayan Railway [*Indian Railway*] (TIR)

DHR Decay Heat Removal [*Nuclear energy*] (NRCH)

DHR Delayed Hypersensitivity Reaction [*Medicine*]

DHR Delivery History Report (AFIT)

DHR Department of Human Resources (IAA)

DHR Department of Human Rights (SAUO)

DHR Director of Human Resources (SAUS)

DHR Division of Housing Research (SAUO)

DHR Double High-Resolution File [*Computer science*]

DHR Holy Redeemer College, Washington, DC [*Library symbol*] [*Library of Congress*] (LCLS)

DHRA Delta Houseboat Rental Association (EA)

DHRBT Decreased Hot Rolling Reduction Treatment (SAUS)

DHRC Douglas Hospital Research Centre [*McGill University, Douglas Hospital*] [*Canada*] [*Research center*] (RCD)

DHRF Democracy and Human Rights Fund (SAUO)

DHRS Data Handling Recording System [*Computer science*] (PDAA)

DHRS Decay Heat Removal Service [*or System*] [*Nuclear energy*] (NRCH)

DHRS Direct Heat Removal Service [*or System*] [*Nuclear energy*] (IEEE)

DHRS Direct Heat Removal System (SAUS)

DHRVVF Ducking, Hiding and Running Very Very Fast (SAUS)

DHS Dance History Scholars (EA)

DHS Data Handling System

DHS Daughters of the Holy Spirit [*Roman Catholic religious order*]

DHS Decontamination Hot Shop [*Nuclear energy*] (NRCH)

DHS Delayed Hypersensitivity [*Medicine*] (MELL)

DHS Demographic and Health Survey [*Agency for International Development*]

DHS Demographic Health Survey (SAUO)

DHS Department of Health for Scotland (SAUO)

DHS Department of Health Services (DOGT)

DHS Department of Human Services (SAUO)

DHS Department of Hypertension and Stress (SAUS)

DHS Desert Hot Springs [*California*] [*Seismograph station code, US Geological Survey*] [*Closed*] (SEIS)

DHS Designated Health Services (MHCS)

DHS Design History Society [*British*] (DBA)

DHS Despun Heat Shield

DHS Destroyer Helicopter System (MCD)

DHS Detroit, Hillsdale & South Western Railway Co. (SAUO)

DHS Dextrose in Hartman's Solution [*Medicine*] (EDAA)

DHS Diabetic Hyperosmolar State [*Medicine*] (MELL)

DHS Digital Handshaking Speed (SAUS)

DHS Dihydrostreptomycin [*Also, DHSM, DST*] [*Antimicrobial agent*]

DHS Dinshah Health Society (EA)

DHS Diploma in Horticultural Science (ADA)

DHS Director Historical Section [*World War I*] [*Canada*]

DHS Director of Health Services [*Army*] (AABC)

DHS Discrete Horizon Sensor (MCD)

DHS Division of Health Studies (SAUS)

DHS Division of HIV Services (SAUO)

DHS Divorce Help Sourcebook [*A publication*]

DHS Doctor of Health Science

DHS Doctor of Hebrew Studies (BJA)

DHS Doctor of Humanitarian Service

DHS Doctor of Human Services (GAGS)

DHS Domestic Heating Society [*British*] (DBA)

DHS Donor Horse Serum [*Pharmaceutical manufacture*]

DHS Doppler Hover System (MCD)

DHS Dried Human Serum [*Medicine*] (EDAA)

DHS Dry Heat Sterilization

DHS Dual-Hardness Steel

DHS Dublin High School (SAUS)

DHS Duration of Hospital Stay

DHS Durham High School (SAUO)

DHS Dynamic Hip Screw [*System*] [*Orthopedics*] (DAVI)

DHSA Diploma-Health Service Administration (SAUS)

DHSC Department of Health and Social Security (SAUS)

DHSD Diesel Hybrid System Design (SAUS)

DHSD Duplex High Speed Data (SAUS)

DHS Device Double Heterostructure Device (SAUS)

DHSF Dublin Hospital Sunday Fund (SAUO)

DHSFT Dynamic High-Speed Functional Tester (MCD)

DHSH Department of Human Services and Health [*Australia*]

DHSM Diagnostic Health Services, Inc. [*NASDAQ symbol*] (SAG)

DHSM Diagnostic Health Svcs [*NASDAQ symbol*] (TTSB)

DHSM Dihydrostreptomycin [*Also, DHS, DST*] [*Antimicrobial agent*]

DHSMV Department of Highway Safety & Motor Vehicles (DEMM)

DHSP Data High Speed Printer (SAUS)

DHSRU Dental Health Services Research Unit (SAUO)

DHSS Alaska Department of Health & Social Services (SAUO)

DHSS British Department of Health and Social Security (SAUS)

DHSS Data Handling Subsystem (NATG)

DHSS Data Highway Services System (SAUS)

DHSS Delaware Health and Social Services (SAUO)

DHSS Department of Health and Social Security [*British*]

DHSS Dihydrostreptomycin Sulfate [*Antimicrobial agent*]

DHSSi Department of Health and Social Security (SAUS)

DHSV Down-Hole Safety Valve

DHT Dalhart, TX [*Location identifier*] [*FAA*] (FAAL)

DHT Dehydrotestosterone [*A banned performance-enhancng drug*] (ECON)

DHT Delayed Hypersensitivity to Tuberculin [*Medicine*]

DHT Delayed-Type Hypersensitivity [*Medicine*] (TAD)

DHT Dihydrotachysterol [*Same as ATL-IO*] [*Biochemistry*]

DHT Dihydrotestosterone [*Also, D*] [*Endocrinology*]

DHT Dihydrothymine (MAE)

DHT Dihydroxytryptamine [*Biochemistry*]

DHT Discrete Hartley Transform (BYTE)

DHT Discrete Hilbert Transform (IEEE)

DHT Distillate Hydrotreating (SAUS)

DHT Drilled Hole Tester (SAUS)

Dht Twin Otter [*Airplane code*]

DHTB Dihydroteleocidin B [*Biochemistry*]

DH Tch DH Technology, Inc. [*Associated Press*] (SAG)

DHTDMAC Dihydrogenated Tallow Dimethylammonium Chloride [*Fabric softener*] [*Organic chemistry*]

DHT Filter Discrete Hilbert Transform Filter (SAUS)

DHTI Dynamic Healthcare Tech [*NASDAQ symbol*] (TTSB)

DHTI Dynamic Healthcare Technologies, Inc. [*NASDAQ symbol*] (SAG)

DHTK DH Technology [*NASDAQ symbol*] (TTSB)

DHTK DH Technology, Inc. [*NASDAQ symbol*] (NQ)

DHTML .... Dynamic HTML [*Hyper Text Markup Language*] [*Computer science*]
dHTML .... Dynamic HTML [*HyperText Markup Language*] [*Computer science*]
DHTML .... Dynamic Hypertext Markup Language [*Computer science*]
DHTP .... Dihydrotestosterone Propionate [*Endocrinology*]
DHTR .... Delayed Hemolytic Transfusion Reaction [*Medicine*]
dhtv .... downhole television (SAUS)
DHU .... Data Handling Unit (ACAE)
DHU .... Deck Hand Uncertified [*Shipping*] (DS)
DHU .... Disability Hearings Unit [*Social Security Administration*] (OICC)
D Hu .... Doctor of Humanities
DHU .... Document Handler Unit
DHU .... Howard University, Washington, DC [*Library symbol*] [*Library of Congress*] [*OCLC symbol*] (LCLS)
DHUD .... Department of Housing and Urban Development
DHUD .... United States Department of Housing and Urban Development, Washington, DC [*Library symbol*] [*Library of Congress*] (LCLS)
D Hu L .... Doctor of Humane Letters
DHUL .... Dorchester Hugoton Ltd. [*NASDAQ symbol*] (NQ)
DHU-L .... Howard University, School of Law, Washington, DC [*Library symbol*] [*Library of Congress*] (LCLS)
DHULZ .... Dorchester Hugoton [*NASDAQ symbol*] (TTSB)
D Hum .... Doctor of Humanities
DHumL .... Doctor of Humane Letters (NADA)
DHumLitt ..... Doctor of Humane Letters
DHV .... Design Hourly Volume [*Transportation*]
DHV .... Duck Hepatitis Virus
DHVA .... De Haas-van Alphen [*Effect*]
DHVM .... Digital Hardware Voter Monitor (MCD)
DHW .... Domestic Hot Water
DHW .... Double-Hung Windows [*Technical drawings*]
DHW .... Dyer Hill [*Washington*] [*Seismograph station code, US Geological Survey*] (SEIS)
DHWS .... Defense Health and Welfare Service (SAUO)
DHX .... Dependable Hawaiian Express (SAUS)
DHX .... Dump Heat Exchanger [*Nuclear energy*] (NRCH)
DHXCS .... Dump Heat Exchanger Control System [*Nuclear energy*] (NRCH)
DHY .... Deuterated Hydrogen Y [*Type of zeolite*]
DHY .... Develet Hava Yollari [*Airline*]
DHY .... Dhoney [*Ship's rigging*] (ROG)
D Hy .... Doctor of Hygiene
D Hyg .... Doctor of Hygiene
DHZ .... Dihydralazine [*Antihypertensive agent*]
DI .... American Dental Institute [*Formerly, Dental Information*] (EA)
DI .... Argo, SA [*Dominican Republic*] [*ICAO designator*] (ICDA)
D-I .... Dai-Ichi (SAUS)
DI .... Daily Inspection [*Military*] (MCD)
DI .... Dakota & Iowa Railroad [*Federal Railroad Administration identification code*]
DI .... Dalanated Insulin [*Medicine*] (EDAA)
DI .... Dark Ignition
DI .... Das Ist [*That Is*] [*German*]
DI .... Data Identifier (VLIE)
DI .... Data In [*Computer science*] (VLIE)
DI .... Data Information (SAUS)
DI .... Data Input [*Computer science*] (IEEE)
DI .... Data Integration (or Integrator) (SAUS)
DI .... Data Integrator (MCD)
DI .... Data Integrity (SAUS)
DI .... Data Interchange
DI .... Data Interface
DI .... Data Item
DI .... Data Logic (SAUS)
DI .... Date of Injury [*Medicine*] (HGAA)
DI .... Daylight Impression [*Psychical research*]
DI .... Dead Indian [*Careless man*] [*Army slang*]
DI .... Deciliter [*NHTSA*] (TAG)
DI .... Decision Instruction (SAUS)
DI .... Decoder Identification (SAUS)
DI .... Decoder Information (SAUS)
DI .... Deep Interdiction
DI .... Defective-Interfering [*Virology*]
DI .... Defence Intelligence [*British*]
DI .... Defense Industry
DI .... Defense Information (AFM)
DI .... Defense Instruction (ADA)
DI .... Defense Intelligence (SAUS)
DI .... Definite Integral (UWER)
DI .... Deformability Index
DI .... Degradation Increase (UWER)
DI .... Deicer (UWER)
DI .... Deicing
DI .... Deionization
DI .... De-Ionized (AAEL)
DI .... Delay Indefinite (FAAC)
DI .... Delete Inhibit [*Computer science*] (VLIE)
DI .... Deliverable Item (UWER)
DI .... Delta Air [*ICAO designator*] (AD)
DI .... Demand Indicator (KSC)
DI .... [*The*] Democracy International (EA)
DI .... Densely Inhabited (UWER)
DI .... Density Indicator
DI .... Dental Implant [*Medicine*] (EDAA)
DI .... Dental Information (EA)
DI .... Dent In (SAUS)
DI .... Dentinogenesis Imperfecta [*Medicine*] (DMAA)
DI .... Deoxyinosin (SAUS)
DI .... Departmental Instruction (AAG)
DI .... Department of Industry [*British*] (DCTA)
DI .... Department of the Interior (MCD)
DI .... Deputy for Intelligence
DI .... Deputy Inspector [*British*] (ROG)
DI .... Description and Instructions
DI .... Desert Inn
DI .... Designation Indicator
DI .... Design Integration (DNAB)
DI .... Design International (EA)
DI .... Desk instructions (SAUS)
DI .... Desorption Ionization
DI .... Destination Index [*Computer science*]
DI .... Destroyed Information (SAUS)
DI .... Detective Inspector [*Scotland Yard*]
DI .... Detergent Inhibitor [*Lubricants*]
DI .... Deterioration Index [*Index of intellectual impairment on intelligence test*]
DI .... Detrusor Instability [*Urology*] (DAVI)
DI .... Developed Item (SAUS)
D/I .... Develop Inspect (AAEL)
DI .... Development Integrated (MCD)
DI .... Development International [*Defunct*] (EA)
DI .... Deviation Generator (SAUS)
DI .... Deviation Indicator
DI .... Device Independence
DI .... Device Independent (SAUS)
DI .... Device Interface [*Electronics*] (ECII)
DI .... Diabetes Insipidus
DI .... Diagnostician (SAUS)
DI .... Diagnostic Imaging [*Radiology*] (DAVI)
DI .... Diagnostic Inspection [*Clean Water Act*] [*Environmental Protection Agency*] (EPA)
DI .... Diagnostic Instruction (SAUS)
DI .... Diagnostic Isotopes (SAUS)
DI .... dialysis index (SAUS)
DI .... Diameter
DI .... Diameter, Internal (SAUS)
di .... Diatomic (SAUS)
di .... Diatomite (SAUS)
Di .... Diatoms [*Quality of the bottom*] [*Nautical charts*]
Di .... Didymium (ADWA)
Di .... Didymium [*Mixture of rare-earth elements*] [*Chemistry*] (ROG)
Di .... Diego [*Blood group*]
DI .... dielectrically insulated (SAUS)
DI .... Dielectric Insulation (SAUS)
DI .... Dielectric Isolation
DI .... dielektrische Isolierung (SAUS)
Di .... Diesel (SAUS)
DI .... Difference Index [*Protein calculation*] [*Biochemistry*]
dI .... differential of current (SAUS)
DI .... Differentiated Infiltrating Tumor [*Oncology*]
DI .... differentiation index (SAUS)
DI .... Difficulty Index (AEE)
DI .... Diffusion Index [*Economics*]
DI .... Digital Image (GEOI)
DI .... Digital Input [*Computer science*]
DI .... Digital Integrator [*Computer science*] (ELAL)
DI .... Digitalis Intoxication [*Medicine*] (MELL)
DI .... Digit Impulse (SAUS)
Di .... Dinorah (SAUS)
Di .... Dinus de Mugello [*Flourished, 1278-98*] [*Authority cited in pre-1607 legal work*] (DSA)
DI .... Diode (IAA)
di .... Diopside [*CIPW classification*] [*Geology*]
DI .... Diploid Index
DI .... Diplomatic Immunity (ADA)
DI .... direct ignition (SAUS)
DI .... Direct Image (SAUS)
DI .... Direct Imaging (SAUS)
DI .... Direct Impact (SAUS)
DI .... Direct Impulse (DNAB)
DI .... Direct-Indirect
DI .... Direct Injection [*Automotive engineering*]
DI .... Direct Investor
DI .... Direction Indicator
DI .... Direct Issue (VLIE)
DI .... Directivity Index
DI .... Directivity Indicator (SAUS)
DI .... Directorate (SAUO)
D/I .... Director/Illuminator (CAAL)
DI .... Director of Infantry [*Military*] [*British*]
DI .... Director of Installation (SAUS)
DI .... Director [*or Directorate*] of Installations [*Abolished 1953, functions transferred to Department of Defense*] [*Air Force*]
DI .... Directory Information [*Newsletter*]
DI .... Disability Income [*Insurance*]
DI .... Disability Insurance (AAG)
DI .... Disabled Individual [*Title XVI*] [*Social Security Administration*] (OICC)
DI .... Disable Interrupts (SAUS)
D/I .... Disassembly and Inspection (ACAE)
DI .... Disc Harrowing and Ridging [*Agriculture*]
DI .... Discomfiture Index [*Weather*]
DI .... Discomfort Index (SAUS)

DI .... Discrete Input [*Computer science*] (KSC)
DI .... Disease Index [*Botany*]
DI .... Dispenser [*Unit of issue*] [*Military*] (DNAB)
DI .... Display (SAUS)
di .... display indicators (SAUS)
DI .... Display Instruction (SAUS)
DI .... Display Interface (NASA)
DI .... Disposition Instructions
Di .... Distal [*Medicine*]
DI .... Distillation [*Calorimetry*]
Di .... Distinctio [*Decretum Gratiani*] [*A publication*] (DSA)
DI .... Distinctive Insignia [*Military*]
D/I .... Distinctness of Image (SAUS)
DI .... Distoincisal [*Dentistry*]
DI .... Distorted (SAUS)
DI .... Distributed Intelligence (VLIE)
DI .... Distribution Intsruction
DI .... Distribution of Industry [*British*]
DI .... Distributor Ignition [*Automotive term*] (HAWK)
DI .... District Inspector [*Navy*]
DI .... District Liaison (SAUO)
DI .... Diverting Ileostomy [*Medicine*]
DI .... Divisional Inspector [*Education*] (AIE)
DI .... Division Increment [*DoD*]
DI .... Division Instruction (ACAE)
DI .... DOCARE International (EA)
DI .... Document Identifier [*Military*] (AFM)
di .... document identifier double imperial (SAUS)
DI .... Dolly In [*Films, television, etc.*]
DI .... Dominance Index [*Neurology*]
DI .... Don Internati Ltd. (SAUO)
DI .... Donor Insemination [*Medicine*]
DI .... Doppler Inertial
DI .... Dosage Index [*Equine term*] (TED)
DI .... Double Imperial [*Paper*] (ADA)
DI .... Double Impulse (SAUS)
DI .... Double Indemnity [*Insurance*]
DI .... Double Indexing (VLIE)
DI .... Double Injection
DI .... Double Integer (SAUS)
DI .... Dresser Industries [*NYSE symbol*] (TTSB)
DI .... Dresser Industries, Inc. [*NYSE symbol*] (SPSG)
DI .... Drifters, Inc. (EA)
DI .... Drillers, Inc. (EFIS)
DI .... Drill Instructor [*Marine Corps*]
DI .... Driveability Index
DI .... driver improvement (SAUS)
DI .... Driving Issue (ACAE)
DI .... Drug-Induced (MELL)
DI .... Drug Information
DI .... Drug Interactions
DI .... Drug Intoxication (MELL)
DI .... Dry Ice (MELL)
DI .... Dry Injection (EEVL)
DI .... Due In
DI .... Dummy Information (SAUS)
DI .... Dummy Instruction (SAUS)
DI .... durability index (SAUS)
DI .... Dvorak International (EAIO)
DI .... Dynamic Impedance (SAUS)
DI .... Dyskaryosis, Index of [*Cytopathology*]
DI .... Dyspnea Index [*Medicine*] (DAVI)
DI .... Fighter [*Russian aircraft symbol*]
DI .... Flight Path Deviation Indicator [*Navigation*]
D$_I$ .... Insulin Dialysance [*Endocrinology*] (DAVI)
Di .... Inulin Dialysance [*Medicine*] (MAE)
DI .... Inversion of the Duration series (SAUS)
DI .... United States Department of the Interior, Washington, DC [*Library symbol*] [*Library of Congress*] (LCLS)
DIA .... Dar es Salaam International Airport (SAUS)
DIA .... Date of Initial Appointment
DIA .... Death in Action (SAUS)
DIA .... Decentralized Information Acquisition (SAUS)
DIA .... Defense Intelligence Agency [*Formerly, JJ-2*] [*DoD*] [*Washington, DC*]
DIA .... Defense Intelligence Agency, Washington, DC [*OCLC symbol*] (OCLC)
DIA .... Defense Investigative Agency (SAUS)
DIA .... Deficiency in Allowance [*Military*] (MSA)
DIA .... Denmarks Academy for Engineering (SAUS)
DIA .... Denver International Airport [*Facetious translation: Delay It Again*] (ECON)
DIA .... Department of Indian Affairs (GEOI)
DIA .... Department of Institutions and Agencies (SAUS)
DIA .... Department of International Affairs (GEOI)
DIA .... Design and Industries Association [*British*]
DIA .... Designated International Accounts (SAUS)
DIA .... Design Institute of America
DIA .... Design Institute of Australia
DIA .... Desirability Index Array (SAUS)
DIA .... Development Information Abstracts (SAUS)
DIA .... Device Interface Adaptor (SAUS)
DIA .... Diabetes [*Medicine*] (DHSM)
DIA .... Diagram (ADA)
DIA .... Dialect (ADA)
DIA .... Dialectic (WDAA)
DIA .... Dialogue (NTCM)
dia .... Diameter (VRA)
DIA .... Diameter
DIA .... Diamond
DIA .... Diamond Alkali Co. (SAUO)
DIA .... Diamond Shamrock Corp. (SAUO)
DIA .... DIAMONDS Trust, Series 1 [*AMEX symbol*] (SG)
Dia .... Diaphon [*Record label*] [*Australia*]
DIA .... Diaphone [*Fog signal*]
DIA .... Diaphoretic [*Inducing Perspiration*] [*Pharmacy*] (ROG)
DIA .... Diaphragm (NTCM)
DIA .... Diathermy [*Medicine*]
DIA .... Diego Antigen [*Medicine*] (DMAA)
DIA .... Differentiation Inhibitory Activity [*Cytology*]
DIA .... Dig-In Angle
DIA .... Digital Input Adaptor [*Computer science*] (NITA)
DIA .... Digital Interface Adapter [*Computer science*] (MCD)
DIA .... Digital Isolation Amplifier
DIA .... Dimethylindoaniline [*Organic chemistry*]
DIA .... Diploma in International Affairs (ADA)
DIA .... Direct Air, Inc. [*Germany*] [*ICAO designator*] (FAAC)
DIA .... Direct-Interaction Approximation (SAUS)
DIA .... Direct Interface Adapter
DIA .... Disabled in Action National [*Defunct*] (EA)
DIA .... Display Industry (SAUS)
DIA .... Display Industry Architecture (SAUS)
DIA .... Display Industry Association (SAUO)
DIA .... Division of International Affairs [*An association*] (EA)
DIA .... Doctor of Industrial Arts
DIA .... Documentation et Information Africaines [*African Documentation and Information*] [*Catholic News Agency*]
DIA .... Document Filing and Retrieval [*Telecommunications*] (OSI)
DIA .... Document Interchange Architecture [*Telecommunications*] (OSI)
DIA .... Document Interface Architecture (SAUS)
DIA .... Documents Information Accessing (BUR)
DIA .... Donaldson International Airways (SAUO)
DIA .... Dow Jones Industrial Average
DIA .... Driving Instructors Association [*British*] (DBA)
DIA .... Drug Induced Agranulocytosis [*Medicine*]
DIA .... Drug Information Association (EA)
DIA .... Dual Interface Adapter
DIA .... Dubai International Airport
DIA .... Due in Assets
DIA .... Dulles International Airport [*FAA*]
DIA .... Dutch Interchurch Aid and Service to Refugees [*Netherlands*]
DIA .... Dyadic Interaction Analysis
DIA .... Dying in Action (SAUS)
DIAA .... Dairy Industry Association of Australia
DIAA .... Drug-Induced Aplastic Anemia [*Medicine*] (MELL)
DIAB .... Defense Internal Audit Board (SAUS)
Diab .... Diabetes [*Medicine*] (AMHC)
DIAB .... Diabetes [*or Diabetic*]
diab .... Diabetic (ADWA)
DIAC .... Dairy Industry Advisory Committee [*Australia*]
DIAC .... Data Interpretation and Analysis Center [*Canadian Navy*]
DIAC .... Defence Industry Advisory Committee (SAUS)
DIAC .... Defense Industry Advisory Control (SAUS)
DIAC .... Defense Industry Advisory Council [*Later, IAC*] (AFM)
DIAC .... Defense Information Analysis Center [*DoD*]
DIAC .... Defense Intelligence Analysis Center (COE)
DIAC .... Digital Applications International Club (SAUO)
DIAC .... Diiodothyroacetic Acid [*Biochemistry*]
DIAC .... Diode, Alternating Current (IAA)
DIAC .... Diode Alternating Current switch (SAUS)
DIAC .... Directorate of Internal Affairs and Communications [*Allied German Occupation Forces*]
DIAC .... Distributed Intelligence Acquisition and Control (PDAA)
DIAC .... Dixie Intercollegiate Athletic Conference (PSS)
DIACS .... Documentation Information and Control System [*Military*]
DIAC Switch ... Diode, Alternating-Current Switch (SAUS)
DIACTOR .... Direct-Acting Regulator (SAUS)
DIAD .... Adiake [*Ivory Coast*] [*ICAO location identifier*] (ICLI)
DIAD .... Data Immediate Access Diagram
DIAD .... Dennis Infra-communication Analysis Device (SAUS)
DIAD .... Diademed [*Numismatics*]
di ad .... die adapter (SAUS)
DIAD .... Digital Image Analysis and Display [*Computer science*] (NITA)
DIAD .... Digital Interferometric Analyzer and Display (MCD)
DIAD .... Diisopropyl Azodicarboxylate (SAUS)
DIAD .... Donor-Insulator-Acceptor Device [*Electronics*]
DIAD .... Drum Information Assembler and Dispatcher
DIAD .... Drum Information Assembler/Dispatcher (SAUS)
DIAD .... Inter-American Defense College, Fort McNair, Washington, DC [*Library symbol*] [*Library of Congress*] (LCLS)
DIADC .... Defense Intelligence Agency Dissemination Center (SAUO)
DIA/DCA .... Document Interchange Architecture/Document Content Architecture [*Computer science*] (VLIE)
DIADEM .... Dynamic International Access to Databases and Economic Models [*Economic Models Ltd.*] [*British*] (NITA)
DIADS .... Digital Image Analysis and Display System [*Computer science*]
DIADS .... Digital Integrated Air Defense System [*Military*] (SEWL)
DIAE .... Agboville [*Ivory Coast*] [*ICAO location identifier*] (ICLI)
DIA-FS .... Design Institute of Australia Federal Secretariat
DIAG .... Diagnosis

DIAG .... Diagnostic (VLIE)
diag .... diagnostician (SAUS)
Diag .... Diagnostic/Retrieval Systems, Inc. [*Associated Press*] (SAG)
Diag .... Diagonal [*Medicine*] (AMHC)
diag .... Diagonal (WDMC)
DIAG .... Diagonal
Diag .... Diagonal Bands [*Navigation markers*]
diag .... Diagonally (ADWA)
diag .... Diagram (NTIO)
DIAG .... Diagram (VLIE)
DIAG .... Spectral Diagnostics, Inc. [*NASDAQ symbol*] (SAG)
DIAGE .... Defense Industry Advisory Group Europe [*Terminated, 1977*]
DIAGF .... Spectral Diagnostics [*NASDAQ symbol*] (TTSB)
DiagH .... Diagnostic Health Services, Inc. [*Associated Press*] (SAG)
DiagHlt .... Diagnostic Health Services, Inc. [*Associated Press*] (SAG)
DIAGL .... Defense Intelligence Agency Guidance Letter (MCD)
DIAGN .... Diagnose (NASA)
diagn .... Diagnostic (BJA)
Diagn Imaging Clin Med ... Diagnostic Imaging in Clinical Medicine (journ.) (SAUS)
DIAGNO .... Diagnosis (SAUS)
DiagPd .... Diagnostic Products Corp. [*Associated Press*] (SAG)
DIAGR .... Diagrammatic
DiagRet .... Diagnostic Retrieval Systems [*Associated Press*] (SAG)
Diags .... Diagnostics
DIAGS .... Diagonals (SAUS)
DIAGS .... Diagrams (SAUS)
DIAI .... Defense Intelligence Agency Instruction (MCD)
DIAKONIA .... World Federation of Diaconal Associations and Sisterhoods [*Germany*] (EAIO)
DIAL .... Databank Inquiry Answering Link (SAUS)
DIAL .... Data for Interchange at the Application Level (SAUS)
DIAL .... Data Independent Analysis Library (CAAL)
DIAL .... Data Information Accession List (MCD)
DIAL .... Data Information Access Link [*Computer science*]
DIAL .... Data Interchange Application Level [*Computer science*] (ELAL)
DIAL .... Decimal Index of Art in the Lowlands [*A publication*]
DIAL .... Decimal Index to Artin the Law Countries (SAUS)
DIAL .... Deficiencies in Allowance List [*Military*] (NVT)
DIAL .... Developmental Indicators for the Assessment of Learning [*Education*]
DIAL .... Device Independent Access Level [*Telecommunications*] (OSI)
dial .... Dialect (WDMC)
DIAL .... Dialect [*or Dialectal*]
dial .... Dialectal (ADWA)
dial .... dialectical (SAUS)
dial .... dialectician (SAUS)
dial .... dialectics (SAUS)
DIAL .... Dialog Corp. ADS [*NASDAQ symbol*] (SG)
Dial .... Dialogi [*of Seneca the Younger*] [*Classical studies*] (OCD)
dial .... Dialogue (WDMC)
DIAL .... Dialogue
Dial .... Dialogus de Oratoribus [*of Tacitus*] [*Classical studies*] (OCD)
DIAL .... Differential Absorption Laser (SAUS)
DIAL .... Differential-Absorption LIDAR [*Spectroscopy*]
DIAL .... differential infrared absorption lidar (SAUS)
DIAL .... Digital Image Analysis Laboratory [*University of Arizona*] [*Research center*] (RCD)
DIAL .... Digital Information Access Line (SAUS)
DIAL .... Direct Information Access Line (SAUS)
DIAL .... Direct Information Access Link [*Computer science*]
DIAL .... Disablement Information Advice Lines [*British*]
DIAL .... Disk Interrogation Alternation and Loading (IAA)
DIAL .... Display Interactive Assembly Language [*Computer science*] (IEEE)
DIAL .... Display Interface Assembly Language (SAUS)
DIAL .... Distance Instruction for Adult Learning [*New School for Social Research, New York*]
DIAL .... Documentacion Iglesial America Latina [*France*]
DIAL .... Draper Industrial Assembly Language [*Computer science*]
DIAL .... Drum Interrogation, Alteration, and Loading System [*Honeywell, Inc.*] (IEEE)
DIA-LAB .... Digital Image Analysis Laboratory (SAUS)
DIAL-A-LOG ... Air Force On-Line Bulletin Board Systems (SAUS)
dial-a-mation ... dial-a-cremation (SAUS)
DIALATOR .... Diagnostic Logic Simulator (SAUS)
DIALCOM .... Dialed Communications (SAUS)
DialCp .... Dial Corp. [*Associated Press*] (SAG)
DialCp .... Dialysis Corp. of America [*Associated Press*] (SAG)
DialCpA .... Dialysis Corp. of America [*Associated Press*] (SAG)
Dial D .... Dialogi Deorum [*of Lucian*] [*Classical studies*] (OCD)
dialec .... dialectics (SAUS)
dialec .... dialectology (SAUS)
DIALGOL .... Dialect of Algorithmic Language
DIALID .... Differential Absorption Lidar (SAUS)
DIALINDEX ... DIALOG On-line Index (SAUS)
Dial Meret ... Dialogi Meretricii [*of Lucian*] [*Classical studies*] (OCD)
Dial Mort .... Dialogi Mortuorum [*of Lucian*] [*Classical studies*] (OCD)
DIALOG .... Direction for Army Logistic (MCD)
DIALOG .... On-Line Search Service [*Lockheed*] (DLA)
Dialogic .... Dialogic Corp. [*Associated Press*] (SAG)
DIA-LOGICS ... Document Indexing and Listing of Graphic Information Codes System [*Jet Propulsion Laboratory, NASA*]
DIA-LOGICS ... Document Indexing And Listing Of Graphic Information Codes System (SAUS)
Dialogue .... Dialogue: Canadian Philosophical Review [*A publication*] (BRI)
DIALORDER ... DIALOG On-line Ordering (SAUS)
Dialorder .... document delivery system (SAUS)
DialPge .... Dial Page, Inc. [*Associated Press*] (SAG)
DIAL-R .... Developmental Indicators for the Assessment of Learning - Revised [*Child development test*]
DIALS .... Defense Information Automated Locator System (AABC)
DIALS .... Digital Integrated Automatic Landing System [*Aviation*]
DIAL System ... Drum Interrogation Alteration and Loading System (SAUS)
DIAL-UK .... National Association of Disablement Information and Advice Lines (SAUO)
DIALY .... Dialog Corp. ADS [*NASDAQ symbol*] [*Formerly, MAID ADS*] (SG)
DIAM .... Data Independent Architecture Model
DIAM .... Defense Intelligence Acquisition Manual (MCD)
DIAM .... Defense Intelligence Agency Manual (MCD)
DIAM .... Defense Intelligence Agency Memorandum (MCD)
Diam .... Diameter [*Medicine*] (EDAA)
diam .... Diameter (IDOE)
DIAM .... Diameter
diamat .... dialectical materialism diamond carbon (SAUS)
DIAMAT .... Dialektischer Materialismus
DiaMet .... Dia Met Minerals Ltd. [*Associated Press*] (SAG)
Diametrc .... Diametrics Medical, Inc. [*Associated Press*] (SAG)
DiamM .... Diamond Multimedia Systems, Inc. [*Associated Press*] (SAG)
DIAMON .... Diagnostic Monitor [*Computer science*]
DIAMOND .... Data Information Access for Modified On-Line Network Delivery (SAUS)
DIAMOND .... Development and Integration of Accurate Mathematical Operations in Numerical Data-Processing (VERA)
DIAMOND .... Dielectrically Isolated Arrays of Monolithic Devices (MCD)
Diamond Relat Mater ... Diamond and Related Materials [*A publication*] (CABS)
DIAN .... Decca Integrated Airborne Navigation (or Navigator) (SAUS)
DIAN .... DECCA Integrated Airborne Navigator
DIAN .... Dianon Systems [*NASDAQ symbol*] (TTSB)
DIAN .... Dianon Systems, Inc. [*NASDAQ symbol*] (SPSG)
DIAN .... Digital Analog [*Computer science*] (IEEE)
DIAN .... Digital Analog Simulator (NITA)
DIAN .... Doppler Inertial Airdata Navigation (ACAE)
Dian .... Hymmus in Dianam [*of Callimachus*] [*Classical studies*] (OCD)
DIANA .... Data and Information Available now in Africa (SAUS)
DIANA .... Descriptive Intermediate Attributed Notation for ADA [*Computer science*] (NITA)
DIANA .... Diagnostic Analyzer (SAUS)
DIANA .... Digital Image Analysis (SAUS)
DIANA .... Dimokratiki Ananeossi [*Greece*] [*Political party*] (ECED)
DIANA .... Direct Information Access Network for Africa (SAUS)
DIANA .... Dusseldorf's Institution Art Network Application (IID)
DianaCp .... Diana Corp. [*Associated Press*] (SAG)
DIAND .... Department of Indian Affairs and Northern Development [*Canada*]
DIANE .... Development of an Automat Integrated System of Neutronography (SAUO)
DIANE .... Digital Integrated Attack and Navigation Equipment
DIANE .... Direct Access Network for Europe (SAUS)
DIANE .... Direct Information Access Network for Europe [*Commission of the European Communities*] [*Information service or system*] [*Defunct*] (IID)
DIANE .... Disque pour l'Analyse Economique (IID)
DIANE .... Distance Indicating Automatic Navigation Equipment
DIANE .... Duct Integrity and Nozzle Efficiency (MCD)
DIANM .... Defense Intelligence Analytical Memorandum (MCD)
DIANN .... Diann, MI [*American Association of Railroads railroad junction routing code*]
Dianon .... Dianon Systems, Inc. [*Associated Press*] (SAG)
DIANS .... Digital Integrated Attack Navigation System (SAUS)
DIAO .... Aboisso [*Ivory Coast*] [*ICAO location identifier*] (ICLI)
DIAOB .... Defense Intelligence Air Order of Battle (MCD)
DIAOBS .... DIA Order of Battle (SAUS)
DiaOff .... Diamond Offshore Drilling, Inc. [*Associated Press*] (SAG)
DIAOLS .... Defense Intelligence Agency On-Line Information System (MCD)
DIAOLS .... DIA On-line Intelligence System (SAUS)
DIAP .... Abidjan/Port Bouet [*Ivory Coast*] [*ICAO location identifier*] (ICLI)
DIAP .... Defense-Wide Information Assurance Program [*Military*] (SEWL)
DIAP .... Diapason [*Octave*] [*Music*]
DIAP .... Digitally-Implemented Analogue Processing (IAA)
DIAP .... Drug Interdiction Assistance Program [*FHWA*] (TAG)
DIAPAS .... Diabetes Personalized Alerting Service
DIAPAT .... Diagonal Pattern (SAUS)
DIAPER .... Division Adaptation Personnel (SAA)
DIAPH .... Diaphony (SAUS)
DIAPH .... Diaphragm (MSA)
diaph .... Diaphragmatic (MAE)
diaph .... Diaphram [*Medicine*] (EDAA)
diaphor .... diaphoresis (SAUS)
DIAPPERS .... Delirium, Infection, Atrophic Urethritis, Pharmaceuticals, Psychologic Depressi on, Excessive Urination, Restricted Mobility, and Stool Impaction [*Causes of transient urinary incontinence*] [*Medicine*] (MELL)
DIAR .... Defense Intelligence Agency Regulation
DIAR .... Department of the Interior Acquisition Regulation [*A publication*] (AAGC)
DIAR .... Development-Inhibitor Anchimeric Releasing [*Photography*]
DIAR .... Drew Institute for Archaeological Research [*Drew University*] [*Research center*] (RCD)
DIARAD .... Dual Irradiance Absolute Radiometer (ADWA)
DI Arch .... Doctor of Interior Architecture
DI Arch E .... Doctor of Interior Architectural Engineering
DI Arch Eng ... Doctor of Interior Architectural Engineering
DIARD .... Diabetes Insipidus and Related Disorders Network (NRGU)

DI Arm......... Director of Inspection of Armaments (SAUO)
diars.......... O-Phenylenebis (Dimethylarsine) [*Used in formulae*] (ODA)
DIAS........... Defense Automatic Integrated System (SAUS)
DIAS........... Defense Integrated Automatic Switch (SAUS)
DIAS........... Delivery and Impact Analysis System (MCD)
DIAS........... Diastolic [*Medicine*]
DIAS........... Digital Image Analysis System (SAUS)
DIAS........... Digital Integrated Avionics System (MCD)
DIAS........... DIMDI's [*Deutsches Institut fuer Medizinische Dokumentation und Information*] Administration System (NITA)
DIAS........... Distributed Information Architecture for Ships (SAUS)
DIAS........... Distributed Intelligent Actuators and Sensors (ACII)
DIAS........... Double Isobaric Analogue State [*Physics*]
DIAS........... Drug Information Analysis Service (SAUS)
DIAS........... Drug Information and Assistance Service (SAUS)
DIAS........... Dublin Institute for Advanced Studies
DIAS........... DUNS [*Data Universal Numbering System*] Industrial Affiliations Service (IID)
DIAS........... Dynamic Inventory Analysis System [*Computer science*]
DIAS BH...... Diastolic Blood Pressure [*Medicine*] (EDAA)
DiaShm........ Diamond Shamrock R & M, Inc. [*Associated Press*] (SAG)
DIASIM........ DIALOG Simulator (SAUS)
diast........... Diastolic [*Therapy term*] (CTAA)
DIAST.......... Diastolic [*Medicine*] (WDAA)
DIA SW........ Short Wave Diathermy (SAUS)
DiaSys......... DiaSys Corp. [*Associated Press*] (SAG)
DIAT............ Dairy Industry Appeals Tribunal [*Queensland*] [*Australia*]
diat............. diathermy (SAUS)
DIAT............ Do-it-yourself Investment Analysis Tables (SAUS)
DIAT............ Dundee Institute of Art and Technology (SAUS)
diath........... Diathermy (STED)
DIATH.......... Diathermy [*Medicine*]
Diath SW..... Diathermy Short Wave [*Physical therapy*] (DAVI)
DIATH SW... Diathermy Short Wave (STED)
DIAU........... Abengourou [*Ivory Coast*] [*ICAO location identifier*] (ICLI)
DIAV........... Abidjan [*Ivory Coast*] [*ICAO location identifier*] (ICLI)
DIAVID........ Discussion with Audio Visual Equipment between Interactive and Distant Partners (SAUS)
DIAWA........ Dairy Industry Authority of Western Australia
DIAZ............ Diazepam (STED)
DIB.............. Butyl Di-Iodohydroxybenzoate [*Organic chemistry*] (DAVI)
DIB.............. Daily Intelligence Bulletin [*British*] [*A publication*] (NITA)
DIB.............. Data Input Bus [*Computer science*] (MDG)
DIB.............. Data Integrity Block [*Computer science*] (ELAL)
DIB.............. Decency in Broadcasting (NTCM)
DIB.............. Defence Information Bulletin [*A publication*]
DIB.............. Defense Industrial Base [*DoD*]
DIB.............. Defense Information Base (SAUO)
DIB.............. Defense Intelligence Board (MCD)
DIB.............. Department Information Bulletin
DIB.............. Department of Information and Broadcasting
DIB.............. Design Information Bulletin
DIB.............. Device-Independent Bitmap [*Microsoft, Inc.*] (PCM)
DIB.............. Device Information Block (TIMI)
DIB.............. Diagnostic Interview for Borderlines [*Medicine*] (DMAA)
dib.............. diameter inside bark (SAUS)
DIB.............. Dibrugarh [*India*] [*Airport symbol*] (OAG)
DIB.............. Dictionary of International Biography [*A publication*]
DIB.............. Dielectric Infrared Beamsplitter
DIB.............. Difficulty in Breathing [*Medicine*] (DMAA)
DIB.............. Diffuse Interstellar Band [*Astrophysics*]
DIB.............. Digital Interconnecting Box (DWSG)
DIB.............. Diiodobutane (SAUS)
DIB.............. Diphenylisobenzofuran [*Organic chemistry*]
DIB.............. Directory Information Base [*Computer science*] (TNIG)
DIB.............. Disability Insurance Benefits [*Social Security Administration*] (OICC)
DIB.............. Disk Brakes
DIB.............. Disk Information Block (SAUS)
DIB.............. DL/I Interface Block (SAUS)
DIB.............. Domestic and International Business (MCD)
DIB.............. DOS Info Block (SAUS)
DIB.............. Dot Immunobinding [*Medicine*] (DMAA)
DIB.............. Dot Immunobinding Assay [*Immunology*]
DIB.............. Dry Cleaning Information Bureau [*British*] (CB)
DIB.............. Dual Independent Bus [*Computer science*] (IGQR)
DIB.............. Duodenoileal Bypass [*Medicine*] (DMAA)
DIB.............. Windows or OS/2 DIB image format (SAUS)
DIBA........... Digital Integral Ballistic Analyzer (NG)
DIBA........... Diisobutyl Adipate [*Organic chemistry*]
DIBA........... Diisobutyladipinat (SAUS)
DIBA........... Diisobutylamine [*Organic chemistry*]
DIBA........... Doctor of International Business Administration (GAGS)
DIBA........... Domestic and Internal Business Administration (SAUS)
DIBA........... Domestic and International Business Administration [*Terminated 1977, functions assumed by Industry and Trade Administration*] [*Department of Commerce*]
DIBA........... Dominion Investment and Banking Association (SAUO)
DIBAC......... Diisobutylaluminum Chloride [*Organic chemistry*]
DIBAH......... Diisobutylaluminum Hydride [*Also, DBAH*] [*Organic chemistry*]
DIBAL.......... Diisobutylaluminum (SAUS)
DIBALH....... Diisobutylaluminum Hydride (EDCT)
dibas........... Dibasic (SAUS)
DIBASE........ Drug Information Base (SAUS)
dibb............ double-income baby boomers (SAUS)
DIBBL.......... Dismounted Infantry Battle Space Battle Lab [*Army*] (RDA)
DIBC........... Bocanda [*Ivory Coast*] [*ICAO location identifier*] (ICLI)
DIBF........... Domestic International Banking Facilities (SAUO)
DI-BHA........ drill-in bottom-hole assembly (SAUS)
DIBHP......... Diisopropylbenzene Hydroperoxide [*Organic chemistry*]
DIBI............ Boundiali [*Ivory Coast*] [*ICAO location identifier*] (ICLI)
Dibid........... Dublin Interbank Bid Rate [*Ireland*] (NUMA)
DIBIT.......... Di-Binary Digit [*Two consecutive binary digits*] (TEL)
DI-BIT......... Two Bits (SAUS)
DIBITS........ Di-Binaly Digits (SAUS)
DIBITS........ di-binary digits (SAUS)
DIBK........... Bouake [*Ivory Coast*] [*ICAO location identifier*] (ICLI)
DIBK........... Diisobutyl Ketone [*Organic chemistry*]
DIBK........... Dime Financial Corp. [*NASDAQ symbol*] (NQ)
DIBK........... Dime Finl (CT) [*NASDAQ symbol*] (TTSB)
DIBL........... Drain-Induced Barrier Lowering (IAA)
DIBN........... Bouna/Tehini [*Ivory Coast*] [*ICAO location identifier*] (ICLI)
DIBOA......... Dihydroxy Benoxazin One [*Organic chemistry*]
DIBOL......... Diboll, TX [*American Association of Railroads railroad junction routing code*]
DIBOL......... Digital Business Oriented Language [*Digital Equipment Corp.*] (NITA)
DIBOL......... Digital Equipment's Business-Oriented Language [*Computer science*]
DIBOL......... Digital Interactive Business Oriented Language [*Computer science*] (ITCA)
DIBOSWA..... Diamond Board of South-West Africa (SAUS)
DI-Box......... Direct Injection Box (SAUS)
DIBP........... Diisobutyl Phthalate
DIBR........... Dartnell Institute of Business Research (SAUS)
DIBRAC....... Direct Broadcast Access (MCD)
DIBS........... Digital Integrated Business System [*Digital Equipment Corp.*]
DIBU........... Bondoukou/Soko [*Ivory Coast*] [*ICAO location identifier*] (ICLI)
DIBUA......... Defence in Built-Up Areas (SAUS)
DIC.............. Automatic Door Isolating Cock [*British railroad term*]
DIC.............. Dai Nippon Ink and Chemicals (SAUS)
DIC.............. Dairy Industry Committee (EA)
DIC.............. Dairy Institute of California (SRA)
DIC.............. Danish Isotope Center, Copenhagen (SAUO)
DIC.............. Data Input Check (HGAA)
DIC.............. Data Input Clerk [*Computer science*]
DIC.............. Data Input Consoles [*Computer science*] (NVT)
DIC.............. Data Insertion Converter
DIC.............. Data Interchange Code (IAA)
DIC.............. Data Item Catalog (IAA)
DIC.............. Data Item Category
DIC.............. Datcon Instrument Company (SAUO)
DIC.............. Days in Culture [*of cells*]
DIC.............. Death and Indemnity Compensation [*Veterans Administration*] (GFGA)
DIC.............. Defence Intelligence Centre (SAUS)
DIC.............. Defense Identification Code (NATG)
DIC.............. Defense Industrial Cooperation (ACAE)
DIC.............. Defense Intelligence College (CARL)
DIC.............. Defense Intelligence Commentary (MCD)
DIC.............. Demand-Increasing Costs [*Economics*]
DIC.............. Democratie Integrale au Cameroun [*Political party*] (EY)
DIC.............. Department of Industrial Cooperation [*University of Maine*] [*Research center*] (RCD)
DIC.............. Dependency and Indemnity Compensation [*Military*]
DIC.............. Designers d'Interieur du Canada [*Interior Designers of Canada - IDC*]
DIC.............. Detailed Interrogation Center [*Navy*]
DIC.............. Detection in Clutter (SEWL)
DIC.............. Detroit Institute for Children
DIC.............. Deviation Indicating Controller (IAA)
DIC.............. Dicarbazine (DMAA)
dic.............. Dicentric (MAE)
Dic.............. Dicta (DLA)
DIC.............. Dictionary
DIC.............. diesel cargo vessel (SAUS)
DIC.............. Difference in Conditions
DIC.............. Differential Input Chopper (SAUS)
DIC.............. Differential Interference Contrast [*Microscope*]
DIC.............. Diffuse Intravascular Clotting [*Medicine*] (STED)
DIC.............. Diffuse Intravascular Coagulation [*or Coagulopathy*] [*Hematology*]
DIC.............. Digital Concentrator (SAUS)
DIC.............. Digital Incremental Computer (SAUS)
DIC.............. Digital Input Channel (SAUS)
DIC.............. Digital Input [*or Integrating*] Computer [*Computer science*]
DIC.............. Digital Input Contact (SAUS)
DIC.............. Digital Input Control [*Computer science*] (IAA)
DIC.............. Digital Input group Contact (SAUO)
DIC.............. Digital Integrated Circuit [*Computer science*]
DIC.............. Digital Integrated Computer (SAUS)
dic.............. digital integrating computer (SAUS)
DIC.............. Digital Interchange Code (NITA)
DIC.............. Digital Interface Component (MCD)
DIC.............. Digital Interface Controller [*Computer science*] (VERA)
DIC.............. Digital Interface Converter (ACAE)
DIC.............. Diisopropylaminoethyl Chloride [*Organic chemistry*]
DIC.............. Diisopropylaminoethyl Chloride Hydrochloride (SAUS)
DIC.............. Dili [*Zaire*] [*Airport symbol*] (AD)
DIC.............. Dimethylamino Isopropyl Chloride [*Organic chemistry*]
DIC.............. (Dimethyltriazenyl)imidazolecarboxamide [*Dacarbazine*] [*Also, DTIC*] [*Antineoplastic drug*]
DIC.............. Diploma in Industrial Chemistry
DIC.............. Diploma of Membership of Imperial College of Science and Technology, University of London [*British*]

DIC.............. Diplomate of the Imperial College (SAUS)
DIC.............. Diplom of Membership of the Imperial College (SAUO)
DIC.............. Direct Illumination Component (MELL)
DIC.............. Direct Importing Company (SAUO)
DIC.............. Direct Inter-LATA Connecting trunk (SAUS)
DIC.............. Direct Isotope Cystography (DMAA)
DIC.............. Director of Infestation Control (SAUO)
DIC.............. Discrete Integrated Circuit (IAA)
DIC.............. Disregard Incoming Call (SAUS)
DIC.............. Disseminated Intravascular Coagulation [*Hematology*]
DIC.............. Disseminated Intravascular Coagulopathy [*Medicine*] (STED)
DIC.............. Disseminating Intravascular Coagulation (SAUS)
DIC.............. Dissolved Inorganic Carbon [*Also, DIOC*]
DIC.............. Divestiture Implementation Committee [*Ghana*]
DIC.............. Diving Information Center [*Navy*]
DIC.............. Division of Industrial Cooperation [*MIT*] (MCD)
DIC.............. Division of Inorganic Chemistry (SAUO)
DIC.............. Documentacion Internacional de Carreteras [*International Road Research Documentation*] [*Database*] [*Ministerio de Obras Publicas y Urbanismo*] [*Spanish*] [*Information service or system*] (CRD)
DIC.............. Document and Information Center (SAUS)
DIC.............. Documentation and Information Centre (SAUS)
DIC.............. Documentation Internationale Contemporaine (SAUS)
DIC.............. Document identification codes (SAUS)
DIC.............. Document Identifier Code [*Military*] (AFM)
DIC.............. Double Index Control (VLIE)
DIC.............. drill-in casing (SAUS)
DIC.............. Drip Infusion Cholangiography [*Medicine*] (MELL)
DIC.............. Driver Information Center [*Automotive engineering*]
DIC.............. Drug-Induced Constipation [*Medicine*] (MELL)
DIC.............. Drug Information Center (DMAA)
DIC.............. Drug Interaction Center (SAUS)
DIC.............. Drunk in Charge
DIC.............. Dual In-Line Case [*Computer science*] (IAA)
DIC.............. Dual Inline Package (SAUS)
DIC.............. Inverted Cancrizans of the Duration series (SAUS)
DIC.............. Radioisotopes Laboratory, Dicar Corporation (SAUO)
DIC.............. United States Interstate Commerce Commission, Washington, DC [*Library symbol*] [*Library of Congress*] (LCLS)
DICA............ Daily Interest Checking Account (SAUS)
DICA............ Dance in Canada Association
DICA............ Defense Industry Cooperation Agreement [*Military*]
DICA............ Derecho de Importacion Centroamericano [*Central American Import Right*] [*Central American Common Market*] (EY)
DICA............ Diagnostic Interview for Children and Adolescents
DICA............ Diagnostic Inventory for Children and Adolescents [*For depression and other psychiatric disorders*] (SEAT)
DICAB.......... Directive Coordinated and Approved by Budget Director [*Air Force*]
DICACE........ Detailed Interrogation Center Allied Command Europe (SAUO)
DICAM.......... Datasystem Interactive Communications Access Method [*Digital Equipment Corp.*]
DICANNE...... Digital Interference Cancelling Adaptive Null Network Equipment (SAUS)
DICAP.......... Direct-Current Circuit Analysis Program [*Computer science*]
DICARWS...... Division of Inter-Church Aid, Refugees and World Service (SAUO)
DICAS.......... Directional Command Activated Sonobuoy [*System*] [*Navy*] (NVT)
DICASS........ Directional Command Activated Sonobuoy System [*Navy*]
DICASS........ Directional Command Active Sonobuoy System (SAUS)
DICAS System... Directional Command Activated Sonobuoy System (SAUS)
DICAUTOM... Automatic Dictionary Look-up (SAUS)
DICB............ Demolition Industry Conciliation Board (SAUO)
DICBM.......... Defense Intercontinental Ballistic Missile
DICBM.......... Depressed-Trajectory Intercontinental Ballistic Missile (MCD)
DICBM.......... Detection of Intercontinental Ballistic Missile (IAA)
DICC............ Digital Interface Code Converter [*Computer science*]
DICCAP........ Distributed Impressed Current Cathodic Protection [*Anticorrosion system*]
DICCASS...... Document and Information Center of the Chinese Academy of Social Sciences
DICCS.......... Demurrage Inventory Control Card System (SAUS)
DICD............ Dispersion-Induced Circular Dichroism [*Medicine*] (STED)
Dic Dom...... Dicey. Law of Domicil [*A publication*] (DLA)
DICE............ Crown Casino [*NASDAQ symbol*] (TTSB)
DICE............ Crown Casino Corp. [*NASDAQ symbol*] (SAG)
DICE............ Dairy and Ice Crem Equipment Association (SAUS)
DICE............ DARPA [*Defense Advanced Research Projects Agency*] Initiatives in Concurrent Engineering [*DoD*]
DICE............ Data Integration and Collection Environment (ADWA)
DICE............ Delivering Information in a Cellular Environment [*Software*]
DICE............ dephasing-induced coherent emission (SAUS)
DICE............ Development Interim Control Equipment (IAA)
Dice............ Dice's Reports [*79-91 Indiana*] [*A publication*] (DLA)
DICE............ Digital Integrated Circuit Element [*Computer science*]
DICE............ Digital Integrated Circuit Exerciser (SAUS)
DICE............ Digital Intercontinental Conversion Equipment (MCD)
DICE............ Digital Interface Countermeasures Equipment [*Air Force*]
dice............ digital-intertace countermeasure equipment (SAUS)
DICE............ Digitally Implemented Communications Experiment (MCD)
DICE............ Digitally Interlaced Countermeasures Equipment (SAUS)
DICE............ Directed information communications environment (SAUS)
dice............ direct-installation coaxial equipment (SAUS)
DICE............ Division of Improved Conversion Efficiency [*Energy Research and Development Administration*]
Dice............ Double [*or Dual*] Income, Children, and Everything [*Term coined by William F. Doescher, publisher of "D & B Reports"*] [*Lifestyle classification*]
DICE............ Dynamic Input to Control Center Equipment (IAA)
DICE............ Dynamic Integrated Climate Economy (CARB)
DICEA.......... Division for the Investigation of Cartels and External Assets (SAUO)
DICEF.......... Digital Communications Experimental Facility [*Air Force*]
Dicey & Morris... Dicey. Conflict of Laws [*A publication*] (DLA)
Dicey Confl Laws... Dicey. Conflict of Laws [*A publication*] (DLA)
Dicey Const... Dicey's Lectures Introductory to the Study of the Law of the English Constitution [*A publication*] (DLA)
Dicey Dom... Dicey. Law of Domicil [*A publication*] (DLA)
Dicey Domicil... Dicey. Law of Domicil [*A publication*] (DLA)
DIChem........ Diploma of Industrial Chemistry (ADA)
DICHLORAN... Dichloronitroaniline [*Also, DCNA*] [*Fungicide*]
dichlorvos.... dimethyldichlorovinyl phosphate (SAUS)
DICI............ Direct Intracytoplasmic Injection [*Medicine*] (WDAA)
DICIFER....... Digital Image Complex for Image Feature Extraction and Recognition System (MCD)
DICIFER....... Digital Interactive Complex for Image Feature Extraction and Recognition [*Air Force*]
DICIS.......... Duane Information Center Indexing Service [*Database compilers*] (NITA)
dick............ detective (SAUS)
DICK............ Dickcissel [*North American bird banding code*] (BIBA)
Dick............ Dickens' English Chancery Reports [*A publication*] (DLA)
Dick............ Dickinson's New Jersey Equity Precedents [*A publication*] (DLA)
dick............ Ethyldichloroarsine [*Organic chemistry*] (DAVI)
Dick Black... Dickson's Analysis of Blackstone's Commentaries [*A publication*] (DLA)
Dick Ch........ Dickens' English Chancery Reports [*A publication*] (DLA)
Dick Ch (Eng)... Dickens' English Chancery Reports [*A publication*] (DLA)
dickel.......... dime and nickel (SAUS)
Dickens........ Dickens' English Chancery Reports [*A publication*] (DLA)
Dick Eq Pr... Dickinson's New Jersey Equity Precedents [*A publication*] (DLA)
Dick Ev........ Dickson's Law of Evidence in Scotland [*A publication*] (DLA)
Dickie.......... Dickman (SAUS)
Dickinson Sch Law... [*The*] Dickinson School of Law (GAGS)
Dick Int'l L Ann... Dickinson's International Law Annual [*A publication*] (DLA)
Dick Just..... Dickinson's Justice [*A publication*] (DLA)
Dick Kent..... Dickson's Analysis of Kent's Commentaries [*A publication*] (DLA)
Dick (NJ)...... Dickinson's New Jersey Equity Precedents [*A publication*] (DLA)
Dick Quar Ses... Dickinson's Practical Guide to the Quarter Sessions [*A publication*] (DLA)
diclox.......... Dicloxacillin (STED)
DICM............ Differential Interference Contrast Microscope
DICM............ Diffusing Capacity of Carbon Monoxide (DMAA)
DICN............ Digital Computer Newsletter (SAUS)
DICNAVAB... Dictionary of Naval Abbreviations [*A publication*]
DICO............ Committee on Directives (SAUO)
DICO............ Data Information and Coordination Office (SAUO)
DICO............ Data Information Coordination Office (COE)
DICODE........ Digital Correlation Demonstrator
DIC of WA... Defence Industries Council of Western Australia (SAUO)
DICOM.......... Digital Imaging and Communications in Medicine
DICOMED..... Online graphics recorder used at NCAR for producing microfilm and microfiche output (SAUS)
DICOMNET... Defense Intelligence Teletypewriter Network (SAUO)
DICOMSS..... Direct Commissary Support System [*DoD*]
DICOMTA..... Documentation Informatisee pour les Comptables [*CEDIC*] [*Database*]
DICON.......... Digital Communication through Orbiting Needle (IAA)
DICOR.......... Directional Control Rocket (ACAE)
DICORAP..... Directional Controlled Rocket-Assisted Projectile (MCD)
DICORS........ Diver Communication Research System (PDAA)
DICORTS...... Digital Compare Recirculating Test System [*Computer science*] (VLIE)
DICOS.......... Digital Communications System Evaluator (MCD)
DICOSE........ Digital Communications System Evaluator (MCD)
DICOST........ Diagnostic Control System (VLIE)
DICOSY........ Directional Coupler Synthesis (MCD)
DICOT.......... Dicotyledon (SAUS)
Dicots.......... Dicotyledonous Plants
DICP............ Drop-In Care Partners (EA)
DIC Package... Dual Inline Ceramic Package (SAUS)
Dic Par........ Dicey on Parties to Actions [*A publication*] (DLA)
DICR............ Daily Inspection Call Record (MCD)
DICS............ Digital Channel Selection (IAA)
DICS............ Digital Image Correction System (ACAE)
DICS............ Display Interface Computer System (MCD)
DICS............ Double Image Concentric System (ACAE)
DICS............ Down-Island Communication System [*Taiwan*] (CINC)
DIC Syndrome... Disseminated Intravascular Coagulation Syndrome (SAUS)
DICT............ Dictaphone
dict............ Dictation (ADWA)
DICT............ Dictation
DICT............ Dictator
dict............ Diction (WDMC)
Dict............ Dictionary [*Medicine*] (EDAA)
dict............ Dictionary (WDMC)
DICT............ Dictionary
Dicta............ Dicta of Denver Bar Association [*A publication*] (DLA)
DICTA.......... Dictaphone (IAA)
DICTA.......... Digital Integrated Circuit Training Aid [*Computer science*] (IAA)
DICTA.......... Diploma of the Imperial College of Tropical Agriculture (SAUS)

DiCTA.......... District Council Technical Association (SAUO)
Dict Amer Biog... Dictionary of American Biography [*A publication*] (ODCC)
Dict Amer Slang... Dictionary of American Slang (SAUS)
Dict Bibl...... Dictionnaire de la Bible [*A publication*] (ODCC)
Dictn.......... Dictation (UWER)
dictsort........ dictionary sorter (SAUS)
Dict Sp........ Dictionnaire de Spiritualite [*A publication*] (ODCC)
Dicty.......... Dictionary (UWER)
DICU.......... Digital Interface and Control Unit
DICU.......... Display Interface Control Unit (SAUS)
DICUP.......... Dicumyl Peroxide (SAUS)
DICWA.......... Defence Industries Council of Western Australia
DICY.......... Dicyanodiamide [*Also, DCD*] [*Organic chemistry*]
DID.......... Daily Intelligence Digest
DID.......... Dangerous Infectious Disease [*British*] (ROG)
DID.......... Data Identification [*or Identifier*]
DID.......... Data Information Delivery (GEOI)
DID.......... Data Information Description (GEOI)
DID.......... Data Input Device (SAUS)
DID.......... Data Input Display [*Computer science*]
DID.......... Data Item Description
DID.......... Datamation Industrial Directory (SAUS)
DID.......... Datamation Industry Directory (MCD)
DID.......... Dead of Intercurrent Disease [*Medicine*] (MAE)
DID.......... Defence in Depth (SAUS)
DID.......... Defence Industry Department (SAUS)
DID.......... Defence Industry Development (SAUS)
DID.......... Defence Industry Directorate (SAUS)
DID.......... Defense in Depth (ACAE)
DID.......... Delayed-Interval Delivery [*Medicine*] (EDAA)
DID.......... Delayed Ischemic Deficit [*Medicine*]
DID.......... Densely Inhabited District (UWER)
DID.......... Department of Industrial Development (SAUS)
DID.......... Department of Industries and Development [*Northern Territory*] [*Australia*]
DID.......... Destination Identification/Identifier (VLIE)
DID.......... Destron/Idi, Inc. [*Vancouver Stock Exchange symbol*]
DID.......... Detailed Issue Depot [*Military supply organization for Allied armies in Europe*] [*World War II*]
DID.......... Detailed Issuing Depot (SAUO)
DID.......... Detergent Ingredients Database (UWER)
DID.......... Development Information Dissemination (SAUS)
DID.......... Device Identifier
DID.......... Device-Independent Display (SAUS)
Did.......... Didache (BJA)
did.......... Didactic (VRA)
DID.......... Didactic
DID.......... Didactics (SAUS)
DID.......... Didcot [*British depot code*]
Did.......... Didot (SAUS)
DID.......... Digital Image Data (GEOI)
DID.......... Digital Image Design [*Computer science*] (VERA)
DID.......... Digital Image Document (SAUO)
DID.......... Digital Information Detection [*Computer science*] (IAA)
DID.......... Digital Information Director (SAUS)
DID.......... Digital Information Display [*Computer science*]
DID.......... Dimethylphthalate Indalone Dimethylcarbonate [*Insect repellant*] (IIA)
did.......... direct in dialing (SAUS)
DID.......... direct in dialling (SAUS)
DID.......... Direct Injection Diesel [*Automotive engineering*]
DID.......... Direct Inward Dial (SAUS)
DID.......... Direct Inward Dialing [*Telecommunications*]
DID.......... Direct Inward Dialling
DID.......... Directorate of Interservice Development (SAUO)
DID.......... Director of the Intelligence Division [*British military*] (DMA)
DID.......... Discharge Ionization Detector
DID.......... Disodium Iminodiacetate [*Organic chemistry*]
DID.......... Display Interface Device [*Telecommunications*] (TEL)
DID.......... Divisional Intelligence Detachment (SAUO)
DID.......... Division of Innovation and Development [*Department of Education*]
DID.......... Division of Institutional Development [*Office of Education*]
DID.......... Division of Isotopes Development [*AEC*]
DID.......... Double Immunodiffusion (DB)
DID.......... Double Isotope Derivative
DID.......... Drivers Integrated Display [*Military*] (RDA)
DID.......... Drum Information Display
DID.......... Dust Impact Detection System [*Astrophysics*]
DID.......... dust impact detector (SAUS)
DID.......... Dynamic identification (SAUS)
DIDA.......... Defense Industry Development and Support Administration [*Turkey*]
DIDA.......... Depository Institutions Deregulation and Monetary Control Act of 1980
DIDA.......... Differential In-Depth Analysis (PDAA)
DIDA.......... Digital Data Network [*NASDAQ symbol*] (TTSB)
DIDA.......... Dignity in Death Alliance [*British*]
DIDA.......... Diisodecyl Adipate [*Organic chemistry*]
DIDA.......... Director of Intelligence, Division of the Admiralty [*British*]
DIDA.......... Dynamic Instrumentation Digital Analyzer
DIDAC.......... Defense Intelligence Agency Dissemination Center (DNAB)
didac.......... didacticism (SAUS)
didac.......... didactics (SAUS)
DIDAC.......... digital data acquisition system (SAUS)
DIDAC.......... Digital Data Communication (IAA)
DIDAC.......... Digital Data Computer
DIDACS.......... Digital Data Communications System (MCD)
DIDAD.......... Digital Data Display
Dida de Segu... Didacus de Segura [*Flourished, 16th century*] [*Authority cited in pre-1607 legal work*] (DSA)
D Idaho.......... United States District Court for the District of Idaho (DLA)
DIDAK.......... Digital Image Data Analysis System Karlsruhe (SAUS)
DIDAMES.......... Distributed Industrial Design and Manufacturing of Electronic Subassemblies (SAUO)
DIDAP.......... Digital Data Processor
DIDAS.......... Digital Data Acquisition System [*Computer science*] (VLIE)
DIDAS.......... Digital Data System (IAA)
DIDAS.......... Dynamic Instrumentation Data Automobile System [*Telemetering system for auto test tracks*]
DIDAW.......... Digital Data Network Wrrt [*NASDAQ symbol*] (TTSB)
DIDB.......... Dabou [*Ivory Coast*] [*ICAO location identifier*] (ICLI)
DIDB.......... Digital Input/Output Buffer (SAUS)
DIDB.......... DLA Inventory Data Base (SAUS)
DIDB.......... Inter-American Development Bank, Washington, DC [*Library symbol*] [*Library of Congress*] (LCLS)
DIDC.......... Data Input Display Console [*Computer science*]
DIDC.......... Depository Institutions Deregulation Committee [*Department of the Treasury*] [*Terminated, 1986*]
DIDC.......... Digital Input Data Channel (SAUS)
DIDD.......... Dense Intramembranous Deposit Disease [*Medicine*] (DMAA)
DIDD.......... Dynamic Integrated Data Display
DIDDF.......... Dual Input Discrete Describing Function [*Computer science*] (IAA)
DID/DOD.......... Direct inward dialing/direct outward dialing (SAUS)
DIDDS.......... Dynamic Integrated Data Display System
DIDEG.......... Decartelization and Industrial Deconcentration Group (SAUO)
DID engine... direct-injection Diesel engine (SAUS)
dident.......... distortion identity (SAUS)
DIDENT.......... Distortion Indentity (SAUS)
DI/DES.......... Vessels Disposed of by Sinking, Burning, Abandoning, or Other Means of Destruction [*Navy*]
DIDEX.......... Distributed Database Experiment (SAUS)
DIDF.......... Dual Input Describing Function [*Computer science*]
DIDG.......... Diisodecyl Glutarate [*Organic chemistry*]
DIDHS.......... Deployable Intelligence Data Handling System (COE)
DI Diesel engine... direct-injection Diesel engine (SAUS)
Did Iul.......... Didius Iulianus [*of Scriptores Historiae Augustae*] [*Classical studies*] (OCD)
DIDK.......... Dimbokro [*Ivory Coast*] [*ICAO location identifier*] (ICLI)
DIDL.......... Daloa [*Ivory Coast*] [*ICAO location identifier*] (ICLI)
DIDL.......... Digital Integrated Design Language [*Computer science*] (CSR)
DIDM.......... Document Identification and Description Macros [*IBM Corp.*]
DIDMCA.......... Deposit Insurance Deregulation and Monetary Control Act (EBF)
DIDMCA.......... Depository Institutions Deregulation and Monetary Decontrol Act [*1980*]
DIDMOA.......... Diabetes Insipidus-Diabetes Mellitus-Optic Atrophy [*Syndrome*] [*Medicine*] (DMAA)
DIDMOAD.... Diabetes Insipidus, Diabetes Mellitus, Optic Atrophy, Deafness Syndrome [*Medicine*] (DMAA)
DIDMSNJ.......... Dying In Dignity Mensa Special-interest-group News Journal (SAUS)
DI/DO.......... Data Input/Data Output [*Computer science*]
DIDO.......... Device Independent Disk Open (SAUS)
DIDO.......... Device Independent Disk Operation [*Computer science*] (IAA)
DIDO.......... Digital Input/Digital Output [*Computer science*]
DIDO.......... Directional Doppler (MCD)
DIDOC.......... Desired Image Distribution Using Orthogonal Constraints [*Illinois Institute of Technology*]
DIDOCS.......... Device-Independent Display Operator Console Support (BUR)
DIDOL.......... Division of Information, Department of Lands (SAUO)
DIDOS.......... Distributed Data processing Operating System (SAUS)
dIDP.......... Deoxyinosine Diphosphate [*Biochemistry*]
DIDP.......... Diisodecyl Phthalate [*Organic chemistry*]
DIDS.......... Data Item Description System (MCD)
DIDS.......... Decision Information Distribution System (VLIE)
DIDS.......... Defense Information Distribution System [*Proposed in-home disaster warning system*]
DIDS.......... Defense Integrated Data System (AFM)
DIDS.......... Digital Display System (SAUS)
DIDS.......... Digital Information Display System [*Computer science*]
DIDS.......... Diisothiocyanatostilbene Disulfonic Acid (SAUS)
DIDS.......... Diisothiocyano (Disulfonic Acid) Stilbene [*Organic chemistry*]
DIDS.......... DISC Integrated Data Systems (SAUS)
DIDS.......... Distributed Information Delivery System (SAUS)
DIDS.......... Distributed Intrusion Detection System (SAUS)
DIDS.......... DLSC [*Defense Logistics Services Center*] Integrated Data System [*Military*]
DIDS.......... Document Information Directory System [*NIOSH*] [*Database*]
DIDS.......... Domestic Information Dispatching System (SAUS)
DIDS.......... Domestic Information Display System [*Computer graphics*]
DIDS.......... Donor-Impurity Density of States [*Electronics*] (ODA)
DIDS-CD.......... Decision Information Distribution System - Civil Defense [*Military*] (AABC)
DIDSIM.......... Defense In-Depth Simulation
DIDSO.......... Defense Integrated Data System Program Management Office [*DoD*]
DIDSRS.......... Defense Intelligence Dissemination, Storage, and Retrieval System (MCD)
DIDSY.......... Dust Impact Detection System [*Astrophysics*]
DID System... Development Information Dissemination System (SAUS)
DID Timber... Didu Timber (SAUS)
DIDU.......... Defense Item Data Utilization
DIDU.......... Disaster Dump (VLIE)
DIDV.......... Divo [*Ivory Coast*] [*ICAO location identifier*] (ICLI)
DIE.......... Defense Intelligence Estimate (MCD)

DIE Designated Investment Exchange [*British*] (NUMA)
DIE Deuterium Isotope Effect (MCD)
DIE Developmental Independent Evaluator [*Army*]
DIE Died in Emergency Room (MAE)
DIE Diego Suarez [*Madagascar*] [*Airport symbol*] (OAG)
DIE Digital Image Enhancement [*Microscopy*]
DIE Diploma in Industrial Engineering (ADA)
DIE Diploma of the Institute of Engineering [*British*]
DI/E Direct Import/Export (VLIE)
DIE Direct Injection Enthalpimetry
DIE Directors-in-Exile [*British*]
DIE Dissipation Inequality (SAUS)
DIE Distance in Error
DIE Division of International Education [*Office of Education*]
DIE Doctor of Industrial Engineering
DIE Document of Industrial Engineering (KSC)
DIE Double Injection Effect
D/IEA Data/Information Exchange Annex (SAUS)
DIEA Dictionary of Industrial Engineering Abbreviations [*A publication*] (KSC)
DIEA (Diisopropyl)ethylamine [*Organic chemistry*]
DIE (ACE) Division of International Education (of the American Council on Education) (EA)
DIEAG Defense Industry Export Advisory Group
DIEB Department of the Interior Energy Board (USDC)
DIEB ALT Diebus Alternis [*Every Other Day*] [*Pharmacy*]
Diebold Diebold, Inc. [*Associated Press*] (SAG)
DIEBRA Digital Image Enlarging Balanced Reconstruction Algorithm (SAUS)
DIEB SECUND Diebus Secundis [*Every Second Day*] [*Pharmacy*]
DIEB TERT Diebus Tertiis [*Every Third Day*] [*Pharmacy*]
DIEC Defense Item Entry Control (AFIT)
DIECA Diethyldithiocarbonate [*Analytical chemistry*]
DIECAST Display Interaction Enhancing Computer-Aided Shape Technique (PDAA)
Die Cast Eng Die Casting Engineer [*A publication*] (CABS)
Diecast Met Mould Diecasting and Metal Moulding (journ.) (SAUS)
DIECO Defense Item Entry Control Office [*Military*]
DIECP Defense Item Entry Control Program [*Military*] (AABC)
DIED Department of Industrial and Economic Development
DIED Died in Emergency Department (MELL)
DIEDA Diethyl-Iminodiacetic Acid [*Biochemistry*] (DAVI)
DIEEng/TAD Directorate of Instrument and Electrical Engineering, Training Aid Devices (SAUO)
DIEFng Director of Instrument and Electrical Engineering (SAUO)
DIEG Diehl Graphsoft [*NASDAQ symbol*] (TTSB)
DIEG Diehl Graphsoft, Inc. [*NASDAQ symbol*] (SAG)
DIEGME Diethylene Glycol Monomethyl Ether (SAUS)
Diehl Diehl Graphsoft, Inc. [*Associated Press*] (SAG)
DiehlG Diehl Graphsoft, Inc. [*Associated Press*] (SAG)
DIEL Advisory Committee on Telecommunications for Disabled and Elderly People (SAUO)
DIEL Dielectric (IAA)
DIEL Diesel Electric
DIELEC Dielectric
DIELGUIDE Dielectric Waveguide (MCD)
DIELOG DAASC Integrated E-Mail Logistics System (SAUS)
DIELOG DAASC Integrated E-Mail Logistics System Laboratory (SAUO)
DIEM Control Chief Hldgs [*NASDAQ symbol*] (TTSB)
DIEME Directorate of Inspection of Electrical and Mechanical Equipment (SAUO)
DIEMN Dust-Induced Electromagnetic Noise
DIEN Data Input Enable (SAUS)
DIEN Data Input Ensemble (NITA)
dien Diethylenediamine [*Organic chemistry*]
DIEN Diethylenetriamine (SAUS)
DI Eng Doctor of Industrial Engineering
DI engine direct-injection engine (SAUS)
DIEO Decennie Internationale d'Exploration des Oceans [*International Decade of Ocean Exploration*] (MSC)
DIEOB Defense Intelligence Electronic Order of Battle (MCD)
DIEP Department of Industry and Economic Planning
DIEP Diabetes in Early Pregnancy [*Medicine*]
DIE Part Die Parting (SAUS)
DIEPER Digitised European Periodicals (SAUS)
DIEPO Dieterich-Post (SAUS)
DIEPS Digital Image Exploitation and Production System (SEWL)
DIER Departmental Industrial Equipment Reserve (AAGC)
DIER Department Instrument Equipment Reserve
DIER Died in Emergency Room (MELL)
DIER diesel-electric caterpillar swing crane (SAUS)
DIERS Design Institute for Emergency Relief Systems (SAUO)
DIES Data Interpretation and Evaluation System (SAUS)
DIES Design Information Exchange System (SAUS)
DIES Diesel
DIES Digital Image Enhancement System (GEOI)
DIES Distributed Illuminated Electronic System (DWSG)
DIESA Department of International Economic and Social Affairs [*United Nations*] [*Information service or system*] (IID)
DIESEL Dumb Interpretatively Evaluated String Expression Language [*Computer science*] (VERA)
Diesel Gas Turbine Prog Diesel and Gas Turbine Prngress (journ.) (SAUS)
Diesel Gas Turbine Prog World Diesel and Gas Turrbine Progress Worldwide (journ.) (SAUS)
Diesel Gas Turbine Worldw Diesel and Gas Turbine Worldwide (journ.) (SAUS)
Diesel Prog Engines Drives Diesel Progress Engines and Drives (journ.) (SAUS)
Diesel Prog North Am Diesel Progress North America (journ.) (SAUS)
DIESO Diesel Oil (SAUS)
DIET Desorption Induced by Electronic Transition [*Physics*]
diet Dietary (ADWA)
DIET Dietary (WDAA)
diet Dietetic (SAUS)
DIET Dietetics
DIET Dietician (WDAA)
Diet Dietics (SAUS)
Diet Dietitian (ADWA)
DIET Division of Integration and Environmental Testing [*Social Security Administration*]
DIET Drug Information and Education Team (SAUO)
DIETC Dietetic
Diet Tech Dietetic Technician (DAVI)
DIF Dairy Industry Federation (GVA)
DIF Dakota Indian Foundation
DIF Data Integration Function (SAUS)
DIF Data Interchange Facility (SAUS)
DIF Data Interchange Format
DIF Data Interface Facility (SSD)
DIF Death in Family (GOBB)
DIF Decay in Flight [*Nuclear physics*]
DIF Decimation In Frequency (SAUS)
DIF Defense Industrial Fund
DIF Deposit Insurance Fund [*Pronounced "diff"*]
DIF Descriptive Item File
DIF Device Independent File (SAUS)
DIF Device Input Format
dif differ (SAUS)
DIF Difference (AFM)
dif Difference (NTIO)
dif Different (VRA)
DIF Differential (AFM)
DIF Differential Interference Microscopy (SAUS)
dif differentiation-inducing factor (SAUS)
DIF Differentiation Inducting Factor [*Immunology*]
DIF Difficulty-Importance-Frequency
DIF Diffuse
DIF Diffuse Interstitial Fibrosis [*Medicine*] (AAMN)
DIF Diffuser [*Freight*] [*Microbiology*]
DIF Digital Interface Frame [*Computer science*] (VLIE)
DIF Diiodofluorescein [*Organic chemistry*]
DIF Direct Immunofluorescence [*Analytical biochemistry*] (CPH)
DIF Direction Finder [*or Finding*] [*Radio aid to navigation*]
DIF Directory Interchange Format (VLIE)
DIF Directory Interoperability Forum (GART)
DIF Discrete Increment Filter (NASA)
dif discriminant function (SAUS)
DIF Discriminate Function [*Physiology*]
DIF Display Information Facility (CDE)
DIF District Inspector of Fisheries (SAUO)
DIF Division of International Finance [*of FRS*]
DIF Document Interchange Facility (IAA)
DIF Document Interchange Format
DIF DOMSAT [*Domestic Satellite*] Interface Facility (MCD)
DIF Dose Increase Factor [*Medicine*] (DB)
DIF Dreyfus Intercontinental Investment Fund N.V. (SAUO)
DIF Drug Information Fulltext [*American Society of Hospital Pharmacists*] [*Bethesda, MD*] [*Database*]
DIF Dual In-Line Flatpack (CDE)
DIF Dutch Internationals Fund (SAUO)
DIF Duty Involving Flying [*Military*]
DIF Dvorak International Federation (EA)
DIFA Deposit Insurance Flexibility Act [*1982*]
DIFA Differential Amplifier (MSA)
DIFA Difurfurylideneacetone [*Organic chemistry*]
DIFA Digital Interface Assembly (ACAE)
DIFA Diploma, International Fertility Association [*Medical degree*] (CMD)
DIFAD Digitally Integrated Fleet Air Defense
DIF AMP Difference Amplifier (SAUS)
DIF AMP Differential Amplifier (SAUS)
dif amps Differential Amplifiers (SAUS)
difar directional frequency analysis and recording (SAUS)
DIFAR Directional Frequency Analysis and Recording System (MCD)
DIFAR Directional Low Frequency Analyzer Recorder (SAUS)
DIFAR Direction-Finding and Ranging
DIFAR Direction Frequency Analysis and Recording (SAUS)
DIFAS Digial Ice Forecast and Analysis System (SAUS)
DIFAS Digital Ice Forecasting & Analysis System (SAUO)
DIFAX Defense Intelligence Facsimile Network (SAUO)
DIFC Decommutator Interface Controller (MCD)
DIFCE Difference
DIFCLT Difficult
DIFCLTY Difficulty
DIFCREW Duty Involving Flying Crewman [*Military*] (NVT)
DIFCT Difficult (ROG)
DIFCTY Difficulty (ROG)
DIFDEN Duty in a Flying Status Not Involving Flying [*Air Force*] (NVT)
DIFDENIS Duty under Instruction in a Flying Status Not Involving Flying [*Military*] (DNAB)
DIFDENRELAS Duty in a Flying Status Not Involving Flying as His Relief [*Military*] (DNAB)
DIFDENREPT Detailed to Duty in a Flying Status Not Involving Flying Effective upon Reporting [*Military*] (DNAB)

DIFET.......... Dielectrically Isolated FET (SAUS)
DIFET.......... Double Injection Field Effect Transistor [*Electronics*]
DIFET.......... Dual-Injection Field-Effect Transistor (SAUS)
DIFF.......... Development Import Finance Facility [*Australia*] [*Defunct*]
diff.......... Difference (ADWA)
DIFF.......... Difference (KSC)
DIFF.......... Different
DIFF.......... Differential (AABC)
diff.......... Differential (IDYL)
DIFF.......... Differential Blood Count
diff.......... differential white blood count (SAUS)
diff.......... Difficult (DAVI)
Diff.......... Diffusion (DIAR)
diff.......... Differ (ODA)
DIFFA.......... Design Industries Foundation Fighting AIDS (EA)
DIFFA.......... Design Industries Foundation for AIDS [*Acquired Immune Deficiency Syndrome*] (EA)
DIFF AMP.... Difference Amplifier (SAUS)
DIFFAMP..... Differential Amplifier (IAA)
DIFF BAL..... Differential Balance (SAUS)
DIFFCALC.... Differential Calculus (IAA)
DIFFCE.......... Difference (ROG)
Diff Diag...... Differential Diagnosis (AAMN)
DIFFEQ........ Differential Equations numerical integration (SAUS)
DIFFER........ Difference (DSUE)
Differ Equations... Differential Equations (journ.) (SAUS)
difff.......... differential (SAUS)
DIFFFT.......... Decimation-In-Frequency Fast Fourier Tranform (SAUS)
DIFFFWR..... Differential and Full Wave Rectifier (IAA)
DIFF G.......... Difference Gauge (SAUS)
DIFF H.......... Difference Height (SAUS)
diffn.......... Diffusion (SAUS)
DIFFR.......... Diffraction (MSA)
DIFF SENS... Differential Sense [*Computer science*]
DIFFSN.......... Diffusion
DIFFTECH.... Differential Technology Ltd. (SAUS)
DIFFTR.......... Differential Time Relay (IEEE)
DIFFTRAP.... Digital Fast Fourier Transform Processor (PDAA)
DIFFU.......... Diffusion (WDAA)
DIFFUS........ Diffusing
DIFI.......... Dierk Filmer (SAUS)
difi calc...... differential calculus (SAUS)
DIFID.......... Disposal from an Instantaneous Dump [*US Army Corps of Engineers*]
DIFINSOPS... Duty under Instruction in a Flying Status Involving Operational or Training Flights [*Military*] (DNAB)
DIFINSPRO... Duty under Instruction in a Flying Status Involving Proficiency Flying [*Military*] (DNAB)
DIFK.......... Ferkessedougou [*Ivory Coast*] [*ICAO location identifier*] (ICLI)
DIFKIN.......... Diifusion Kinetics (SAUS)
DI/FLC.......... Vessels in Forward Areas Transferred to State Department Foreign Liquidation Corporation [*Navy*]
DIFM.......... Do It for Me [*Automotive repair*]
DIFM.......... Due-In from Maintenance [*Military*] (AFM)
DIFMA.......... Dresdner International Financial Markets (Australia) Ltd.
DIFMOS.......... Dual-Injection Floating-Gate Metal Oxide Semiconductor (PDAA)
DIFO.......... Due-In from Overhaul [*Military*] (MCD)
DIFOPS.......... Duty in a Flying Status Involving Operational or Training Flights [*Air Force*] (NVT)
DIFOPSDORSE... Duty in a Flying Status Involving Operational or Training Flights Effective SuchDate as Endorsed [*Military*] (DNAB)
DIFOT.......... Duty Involving Flight Operations & Training (SAUS)
DIFOT.......... Duty Involving Operational or Training Flights [*Air Force*]
DIFOTDORSE... Duty in a Flying Status Involving Operational or Training Flights Effective Such Date as Endorsed [*Military*] (DNAB)
DIFOTECH.... Duty in a Flying Status Involving Operational or Training Flights as a TechnicalObserver [*Air Force*]
DIFOTINS..... Duty in a Flying Status Involving Operational or Training Flights under Instruction [*Air Force*]
DIFOTRELAS... Duty in a Flying Status Involving Operational or Training Flights as His Relief [*Air Force*]
DIFOTRVK.... Duty in a Flying Status Involving Operational or Training Flights Revoked [*Air Force*]
DI Foundation... Diabetes Insipidus Foundation, Inc. (NRGU)
DIFP.......... Diffuse Interstitial Fibrosing Pneumonitis [*Medicine*] (STED)
DIFP.......... Diisopropyl Fluorophosphonate [*Also, DFP*] [*Toxic compound*]
DIFP.......... Diphenyliodonium Hexafluorophosphate [*Biochemistry*]
DIFP.......... International Food Policy Research Institute, Washington, DC [*Library symbol*] [*Library of Congress*] (LCLS)
DIFPEC.......... Differentially Pumped Environmental Chamber (SAUS)
DIFPP.......... Defense Industrial Facilities Protection Program [*DoD*]
DIFPRO.......... Duty in a Flying Status Involving Proficiency Flying [*Air Force*] (NVT)
DIFr.......... diesel fruit vessel (SAUS)
DIFR.......... Diesel Fuel Vessel (SAUS)
DIFR.......... Difference Register (SAUS)
DIFRACC..... Digital Fractional Count Computer (SAUS)
DIFS.......... Defense Integrated Financial System (AAGC)
DIFS.......... Deployable Intelligence Fusion System (SAUS)
DIFS.......... Distributed coordination function Interframe Space (SAUS)
DIFS.......... Distributed Inter Frame Space (SAUS)
DIFSD.......... Diversified Foods, Inc. (MHDW)
DIFT.......... Dartford International Freight Terminal [*British*] (DS)
DIFT.......... Dartford International Ferry Terminal (SAUS)
DIFT.......... Different
DIFTECH...... Duty as Technical Observer in a Flying Status Involving Operational or Training Flights [*Military*] (DNAB)
diftl.......... differential (SAUS)
DI-FTMS...... Desorption Ionization Fourier Transform Mass Spectrometry
DIFU.......... Deutsches Institut fuer Urbanistik [*Vereins fuer Kommunalwissenschaften eV*] [*Database producer*]
DIFU.......... Digital Interface Unit (ACAE)
DIFV.......... Diesel Fuel Vessel (SAUS)
DIG.......... Delivery Indicator Group (NATG)
DIG.......... Delphi International Group (EA)
DIG.......... Departement Documentation et Information Geologique [*Geological Information and Documentation Department*] [*Bureau of Geological and Mining Research*] [*Information service or system*] (IID)
DIG.......... Deputy Inspector-General
DIG.......... Designated Industry Group (AAGC)
DIG.......... Design Implementation Guide [*Telecommunications*] (TEL)
DIG.......... Detonator Inspection Gauge
DIG.......... Developers/Implementors Group (SAUO)
DIG.......... Diffuse Ionized Gas [*Astrophysics*]
dig.......... digamist (SAUS)
dig.......... digamy (SAUS)
DiG.......... DiGeorge Syndrome [*Medicine*]
Dig.......... Digeratur [*Let It Be Digested*] [*Pharmacy*]
Dig.......... Digest [*1901-06*] [*Lahore, India*] [*A publication*] (DLA)
DIG.......... Digest
Dig.......... Digesta [*Latin*] (OCD)
Dig.......... Digestion (SAUS)
dig.......... Digestive (SAUS)
Dig.......... Digest of Justinian [*A publication*] (DLA)
Dig.......... Digest of Writs [*A publication*] (DLA)
Dig.......... Digger [*Military*] (WDAA)
DIG.......... DiGiorgio Corp. (SAUO)
DIG.......... Digit (SAUS)
DIG.......... Digital (AFM)
dig.......... Digital (ELAL)
DIG.......... Digital Image Generated (SAUS)
DIG.......... Digital-Image-Generated [*Computer science*] (IEEE)
DIG.......... Digital Image Generation (SAUS)
DIG.......... Digital Imaging Group (SAUO)
DIG.......... Digital Imposition Geometry (SAUS)
DIG.......... Digital Input Gate
DIG.......... Digitalis [*Foxglove*] [*Pharmacy*]
DIG.......... Digitoxin
DIG.......... Digoxin
DIG.......... Direct Injection-Gasoline
DIG.......... Disablement Income Group [*British*]
DIG.......... Discussion in Groups
DIG.......... Discussion Interest Groups (SAUO)
DIG.......... Distinctness of Image Gloss (SAUS)
DIG.......... Distributed Infinite Gain (SAUS)
DIG.......... DOE Interaction Group (SAUS)
DIG.......... Doppler-Inertial Gyrocompass (PDAA)
DIG.......... Justinian Digesta [*Libri Pandectarum*] [*Legal*] (ROG)
DIGA.......... Department of Infrastructure and Government Assets [*Western Australia*]
DIGA.......... Dynamics International Gardening Association (EA)
DIGA.......... Gagnoa [*Ivory Coast*] [*ICAO location identifier*] (ICLI)
DIGAC.......... Digital Avionics Control
DIGACC........ Digital Guidance and Control Computer
DIGACE........ Digital Guidance and Control Equipment (IAA)
digas.......... digastric (SAUS)
DIGATEC...... Digital Gas Turbine Engine Control (MCD)
DIGBAT........ Dignity Battalion [*Military*] (CARL)
Digby RP..... Digby's History of the Law of Real Property [*A publication*] (DLA)
DIGCAT........ Digital Catalog (GEOI)
DIGCIRENGR... Digital Circuit Engineer (IAA)
Dig Cir Engr... Digital Circuits Engineer (SAUS)
Dig CLW....... Digest of Commercial Law of the World [*A publication*] (DLA)
DIGCOM........ Digital Computer (IEEE)
DIGCOMP...... Digital Computer (IAA)
Dig Crim Proc... Stephen's Digest of Criminal Procedure [*9th ed.*] [*1950*] [*A publication*] (DLA)
DigDs.......... Digital Descriptor Systems [*Associated Press*] (SAG)
DigDsc.......... Digital Descriptor Systems [*Associated Press*] (SAG)
DIGE.......... Digene Corp. [*NASDAQ symbol*] (TTSB)
Dig Em.......... Digit Emitter (SAUS)
DIGENI.......... Digit Emitter (SAUS)
DIGEST........ Diebold Generator for Statistical Tabulation (MUGU)
Digest.......... Digest of Justinian [*A publication*] (DLA)
DIGEST........ Digital Geographic Exchange Standard (SAUO)
DIGEST........ Digital Geographic Information Exchange Standards (SAUS)
Digestion..... Digestion (SAUS)
Digex.......... Digex Incorp. [*Associated Press*] (SAG)
DIGEX.......... Disabled Interest Group Electronic Exchange (HGAA)
Dig Fla.......... Thompson's Digest of Laws [*Florida*] [*A publication*] (DLA)
DIGI.......... Digital
DIGI.......... DSC Communications [*NASDAQ symbol*] (TTSB)
DIGI.......... DSC Communications Corp. [*NASDAQ symbol*] (NQ)
Digic.......... Digicon, Inc. [*Associated Press*] (SAG)
DIGICOM...... Digital Communications
DIGICOM...... Digital Communications System (NITA)
DIGICOM System... Digital Communication System (SAUS)
Digicon........ Digicon, Inc. [*Associated Press*] (SAG)
DIGICULT..... Digital Heritage and Cultural Content (EURO)

DIGIDOPS.... Digital Doppler System (MCD)
DIGIFON..... Digitales Telefon (SAUS)
DigiIntl....... Digi International, Inc. [*Associated Press*] (SAG)
Digijet......... Digital Injection (SAUS)
DIGILIN........ Digital Linear (IAA)
Digimap....... Digital Map (SAUS)
Digimet........ Digimetrics, Inc. [*Associated Press*] (SAG)
Dig Imp....... Digital Impulse (SAUS)
DIGINESS.... Digital Network Simulation System (MCD)
Dig Int Conf Sens Actuators... Digest of International Conference on Sensors and Actuators (SAUS)
DIGIPLOT..... Digital Plotter (SAUS)
DIGIPLOT..... Digital Plotting (SAUS)
DIGIPLOT..... Digital Plotting System (SAUS)
DIGIPLOT System... Digital Plotting System (SAUS)
DIGIRAD...... Digital RADIAC
DIGIRALT..... Digital RADAR Altimeter (MUGU)
DIGISAT...... Digital Data Satellite Service [*Communications Satellite Corp.*]
DIGISMAC.... Digital Scene Matching Area Correlator [*Military*] (MCD)
DIGISPLAY... Digitally Scanned Image Display (MCD)
DIGIT.......... Digitalis [*Foxglove*] [*Pharmacy*] (ROG)
DIGIT.......... Digitally Integrated Geographic Information Technologies laboratory (SAUO)
DIG-IT......... Dramatic Interpretation of the Ghetto through Improvisational Theater [*Washington, DC*]
DIGITAC....... Digital Airborne Computer (SAUS)
DIGITAC....... Digital Tactical Airborne Computer (SAUS)
DIGITAC....... Digital Tactical Aircraft Control (SAUS)
DIGITAC....... Digital Tactical Automatic Control (IEEE)
Digital......... Digital Equipment Corp. [*Associated Press*] (SAG)
DIGITAL....... Digitalis [*Foxglove*] [*Pharmacy*] (ROG)
digital IC...... digital integrated circuit (SAUS)
DIGITALIS.... Discussion Group on Information Technology in Library and Information Studies Schools (AIE)
DIGITAR....... Digital Airborne Computer (IEEE)
DigitBio....... Digital Biometrics, Inc. [*Associated Press*] (SAG)
DigitCT........ Digital Communications Technology Corp. [*Associated Press*] (SAG)
Digitonics.... Digitronics Corporation (SAUO)
Digit Process... Digital Processes (journ.) (SAUS)
DigitR.......... Digital Recorders, Inc. [*Associated Press*] (SAG)
DigitRec....... Digital Recorders, Inc. [*Associated Press*] (SAG)
Digit Rev....... Digital Review (journ.) (SAUS)
DigitTel....... Digitale Telekable AG [*Associated Press*] (SAG)
digiverse..... Digital Universe (ADWA)
DIGIVISION... Digital Television (NITA)
Dig Jpn Ind Technol... Digest of Japanese Industry and Technology (journ.) (SAUS)
DIGL............ Digital Lightwave [*NASDAQ symbol*] (SG)
DIGL............ Guiglo [*Ivory Coast*] [*ICAO location identifier*] (ICLI)
Dig LL.......... Digest Law of Libels [*A publication*] (DLA)
DIGLYME..... Diethylene Glycol Dimethyl Ether [*Organic chemistry*]
DIGM........... Control Chief Holdings [*NASDAQ symbol*] (SAG)
DIGM........... Diffusion-Induced Grain Boundary Migration (SAUS)
DIGM........... Digimetrics, Inc. [*NASDAQ symbol*] (NQ)
DigMic......... Digital Microwave Corp. [*Associated Press*] (SAG)
DIGN........... Diagnostic (MSA)
DIGN........... Grand Bereby/Nero Mer [*Ivory Coast*] [*ICAO location identifier*] (ICLI)
Dignity......... Dignity Partners, Inc. [*Associated Press*] (SAG)
DIGOPS........ Digest of Operations (DNAB)
Dig Ops JAG... Digest of Opinions of Judge Advocate General, United States [*A publication*] (DLA)
DIGOXN....... Digoxin [*Pharmacology*] (DAVI)
Dig Proem... Digest of Justinian, Proem [*A publication*] (DLA)
Dig Pu......... Digit Pickup (SAUS)
digraph....... Directed Graph [*Computing*] (ODA)
digres.......... digressionary (SAUS)
digres.......... digressiveness (SAUS)
DIGRM......... Digit/Record Mark [*Computer science*] (MDG)
DIGRMGM... Digit/Record Mark Group/Mark [*Computer science*] (MDG)
DIGRO......... Digital Readout [*Computer science*] (AAG)
Dig R Pr...... Digby's Introduction to the History of Real Property [*A publication*] (DLA)
Digs............ Archeological Excavation (SAUS)
DIGS............ Dairy Industries Golfing Society (SAUO)
DIGS............ Data and Information Gathering System (SAUS)
DIGS............ Defense Information Guidance Series [*A publication*] (DNAB)
DIGS............ Delta [*or Digital*] Inertial Guidance System [*NASA*]
DIGS............ Deputy Inspector-General for Safety [*Air Force*]
DIGs............ Development Import Grants (SAUS)
DIGS............ Diagnostic Interview for Genetic Studies
DIGS............ Diggings [*i.e., Lodgings*] [*British*] (ROG)
DIGS............ Digital Image Generation System (ACAE)
DIGS............ Digital Inertial Guidance System
DIGS............ Disorder-Induced Gap States (SAUS)
DI-GS........... United States Geological Survey, Reston, VA [*Library symbol*] [*Library of Congress*] (LCLS)
Dig Sel........ Digital Selection (SAUS)
Dig Sel........ Digit Selector (SAUS)
Dig Sel Com... Digit Selector Common (SAUS)
Dig Shares... Digby's Sales and Transfer of Shares [*A publication*] (DLA)
DIGSIGPROC... Digital Signal Processor [*Computer science*] (IAA)
Dig Sig Prog... Digital Signal Processing (SAUS)
Dig St.......... English's Digest of the Statutes [*Arkansas*] [*A publication*] (DLA)
DIGT............ Digitext, Inc. [*NASDAQ symbol*] (COMM)
DIGTL.......... Digital (KSC)
DigtlSol....... Digital Solutions, Inc. [*Associated Press*] (SAG)
DigtlSy........ Digital Systems International, Inc. [*Associated Press*] (SAG)
Dig Tox........ Digitalis Toxicity [*Medicine*] (DAVI)
DigtSd......... Digital Sound Corp. [*Associated Press*] (SAG)
DigVd........... Digital Video Systems, Inc. [*Associated Press*] (SAG)
Dig Vet........ Digestum Vetus [*A publication*] (DSA)
DigVid......... Digital Video Systems, Inc. [*Associated Press*] (SAG)
DigVideo...... Digital Video Systems, Inc. [*Associated Press*] (SAG)
DIGX............ Digex Inc.'A' [*NASDAQ symbol*] (SG)
DIGX............ Digex Incorp. [*NASDAQ symbol*] (SAG)
DIGYRAC..... Digital Gyro Accelerometer (SAUS)
Dig Zr Tr...... Digit Zero Trigger (SAUS)
DIH............. Deputy Inspector-General of Hospitals (SAUO)
DIH............. Deputy Inspector-General of Hospitals and Fleet [*Navy*] [*British*] (ROG)
DIH............. Died in Hospital (STED)
DIH............. Differential in Hours [*Environmental science*] (COE)
Di-H............ Di-Hydrogen (SAUS)
DIH............. Diploma, Industrial Health [*Medical degree*] (CMD)
DIH............. Diploma in Industrial Health [*British*]
DIH............. Discrete Input High (MCD)
DIH............. Division of Indian Health (SAUS)
DIH............. Drug-Induced Headache [*Medicine*] (MELL)
DIHE........... Drug-Induced Hepatic Encephalopathy [*Medicine*] (MELL)
DIHEST........ Direct-Induced High-Explosive Simulation Technique (MCD)
diHETE........ Dihydroxyeicosatetraenoic Acid [*Medicine*] (EDAA)
Di-HETE...... Dihydroxyeicosatetraenoic Acid (SAUS)
DIHJHU....... Department of International Health-Johns Hopkins University (SAUO)
DIHL........... Declaration of Independence House and Library [*An association*] (EA)
DIHom........ Diploma of the Institute of Homeopathy [*Medicine*] (EDAA)
Di-HP.......... Dihexylphthalat (SAUS)
DIHP........... Diisoheptylphthalat (SAUS)
DIHP........... Diisoheptyl Phthalate
DIHPPA....... Diiodo(Hydroxyphenyl)pyruvic Acid [*Organic chemistry*]
DIHY........... Dihydrate
DII.............. Decorator Indus [*AMEX symbol*] (TTSB)
DII.............. Decorator Industries, Inc. [*AMEX symbol*] (SPSG)
DII.............. Defense Industry Initiative (AAGC)
DII.............. Defense Information Infrastructure [*Military*]
DII.............. Diesel Ignition Improver (SAUS)
DII.............. Diode Ion Injector
DII.............. Dynamic Input Indicator (UWER)
DII.............. Dynamic Invocation Interface (RALS)
DIIA............ Daily Industrial Index Analyzer [*News-a-tron Corp.*] [*Information service or system*] (CRD)
DIIB............ Dorel Industries, Inc. [*NASDAQ symbol*] (NASQ)
DIIBF.......... Dorel Industries'B' [*NASDAQ symbol*] (SG)
DIIC............ Daughters of Isabella, International Circle (EA)
DIIC............ Dielectrically Insulated Integrated Circuit (SAUS)
DIIC............ Dielectrically Isolated Integration Circuit
diic............. dielectric-isolated integrated circuit (SAUS)
DIICC.......... Defense Information Infrastructure Control Concept (SAUO)
DIICOE........ Defense Information Infrastructure Common Operating Environment [*Military*] (SEWL)
DIIG............ Digital Information Infrastructure Guide (SAUS)
DIIG............ DII Group [*NASDAQ symbol*] [*Formerly, DOVatron International*] (SG)
DIII............. Abidjan [*Ivory Coast*] [*ICAO location identifier*] (ICLI)
DI Ind......... Defence Intelligence Industries (SAUS)
DI Ind......... DI Industries [*Associated Press*] (SAG)
DI/INT......... Disposition of Vessel by Department of the Interior (DNAB)
DIIO............ District Industrial Incentive Office [*or Officer*] [*Navy*]
DIIP............ Defense Inactive Item Program (NG)
DIIP............ Defense Intelligence Interoperability Panel
DIIP............ Delinquency Investigation Inventory Profile [*IRS*]
DIIP............ Direct Interrupt Identification Port (UWER)
DIIPS.......... Digital Interactive Image Processing System (SAUS)
DIIR............ Digital Infared Image Reformatter
DIIR............ Digital Image-Intensifier Radiography (ODA)
DIIS............ DCAA [*Defense Contract Audit Agency*] Integrated Information System [*DoD*] (GFGA)
DIIS............ DIA [*Defense Intelligence Agency*] Integrated Intelligence System
DIIS............ Diatomics in Ionic Systems (UWER)
DIIS............ Direct Inversion in the Iterative Subspace (UWER)
DIIVS.......... Defense Intransit Item Visibility System (MCD)
DIJ............. Dijon [*France*] [*Airport symbol*] (AD)
di ji............ drill rig (SAUS)
DIJIT........... direct imaging by jet ink transfer (SAUS)
DIJOA......... Dominantly Inherited Juvenile Optic Atrophy [*Ophthalmology*] (DAVI)
DIK............. Dickinson [*North Dakota*] [*Airport symbol*] [*Obsolete*] (OAG)
DIK............. Direct Input Keyboard (SAUS)
DIK............. Dixon [*Former USSR*] [*Geomagnetic observatory code*]
Dik............. Double [*or Dual*] Income, Kids [*Lifestyle classification*]
dik.............. drug-identifcation kit (SAUS)
DIK............. Drug Identification Kit
DIKB........... Dai-Ichi Kangyo Bank (SAUS)
DIKKI.......... Democratic Social Movement (Greece) [*Political party*] (PSAP)
DIKO........... Demokratiko Komma [*Democratic Party*] [*Cyprus*] [*Political party*] (EY)
DIKO........... Korhogo [*Ivory Coast*] [*ICAO location identifier*] (ICLI)
diks............ double income, kids (SAUS)
DIL............. Daily Instruction Logs [*Environmental science*] (COE)
DIL............. Danube Interlighter (SAUS)
DIL............. Data In-Line [*Computer science*] (IAA)

DIL.............. Daughter in Law (SAUS)
DIL.............. Deliverable Items List (NASA)
DIL.............. Digital Integrated Laboratory (SAUS)
DIL.............. Digital Integrated Logic (SAUS)
Dil.............. Dilantin [*Diphenylhydantoin*] [*Anticonvulsant*]
Dil.............. Dilation [*Medicine*] (AMHC)
DIL.............. Dilatus [*Dissolve*] [*Pharmacy*] (DHSM)
DIL.............. Dili [*Indonesia*] [*Airport symbol*] (OAG)
DIL.............. Dillard University, New Orleans, LA [*OCLC symbol*] (OCLC)
DIL.............. Dillon (ROG)
DIL.............. Dillon Ranch [*California*] [*Seismograph station code, US Geological Survey*] (SEIS)
Dil.............. Dillon's United States Circuit Court Reports [*A publication*] (DLA)
DIL.............. Dilloway (ROG)
DIL.............. Dilly [*Portuguese Timor*] [*Airport symbol*] (AD)
DIL.............. Diltiazem [*Pharmacology*]
dil.............. Dilute (ADWA)
DIL.............. Dilute
DIL.............. Dilution (SAUS)
DIL.............. Director of International Logistics [*Military*]
DIL.............. Disability Insurance Letter [*Social Security Administration*] (OICC)
DIL.............. Discrete Input Low (MCD)
DIL.............. Dispatch Inoperative List (MCD)
DIL.............. Displayed Impact Line (MCD)
dil.............. dissolve (SAUS)
DIL.............. Diversity Interfacility Link (LAIN)
DIL.............. Division of Insured Loans [*Office of Education*]
DIL.............. Doctor of International Law
DIL.............. Doppler Inertial LORAN
DIL.............. Double Injection Luminescence
DIL.............. dual induction log (SAUS)
DIL.............. Dual In-Line [*Electronic components*]
DIL.............. Dual In Line package (SAUS)
DILAG.......... Differential LASER Gyro (MCD)
DILAN.......... Dilantin [*Parke, Davis & Co.*] [*Pharmacology*] (DAVI)
DILAPD........ Dilapidated (ROG)
DILAPIDN.... Dilapidation (ROG)
dilat............ dilate (SAUS)
DILAT.......... Dilation [*Medicine*]
DILC............ Dedicated Intelligence Loop Circuits (SAUS)
DILC............ Defense Intelligence Loop Circuit (SAUS)
DILC............ Display Interface Processor (SAUS)
Dil Cir Court Rep... Dillon's United States Circuit Court Reports [*A publication*] (DLA)
DILCS.......... Dedicated Intelligence Loop Circuit (SAUS)
DILD............ Diffuse Infiltrative Lung Disease [*Medicine*]
DILD............ Diluted
dild soln...... Diluted Solution (SAUS)
DILE............ Drug-Induced Lupus Erythematosus [*Rheumatology*] (DAVI)
DILEP.......... Digital Line Engineering Program [*Telecommunications*] (TEL)
DILET.......... Dilettante (ROG)
dilg............. Diluting (SAUS)
DILGEA........ Department of Immigration Local Government and Ethnic Affairs (SAUO)
DIL (Hack)... Digest of International Law (Hackworth) [*A publication*] (DLA)
DILIC........... Dual In-Line Integrated Circuit [*Electronics*] (IAA)
DILIC........... dual inline pinned integrated circuit (SAUS)
DI-List........ Dangerously Ill List (SAUS)
Di-litho........ direct lithographic printing (SAUS)
DILK............ Double [*or Dual*] Income, Lots of Kids [*Lifestyle classification*]
Dill.............. Dillon's United States Circuit Court Reports [*A publication*] (DLA)
Dillard......... Dillard Department Stores [*Associated Press*] (SAG)
DILIC........... Dual inline pinned integrated circuit (SAUS)
Dill Ir Jud A... Dillon on the Irish Judicature Act [*A publication*] (DLA)
Dill Laws Eng & Am... Dillon's Laws and Jurisprudence of England and America [*A publication*] (DLA)
Dill Mun Bonds... Dillon on Municipal Bonds [*A publication*] (DLA)
Dill Mun Cor... Dillon on Municipal Corporations [*A publication*] (DLA)
Dill Mun Corp... Dillon on Municipal Corporations [*A publication*] (DLA)
Dillon........... Dillon's United States Circuit Court Reports [*A publication*] (DLA)
Dillon CC...... Dillon's United States Circuit Court Reports [*A publication*] (DLA)
Dillon Cir Court Rep... Dillon's United States Circuit Court Reports [*A publication*] (DLA)
Dillon Mun Corp... Dillon on Municipal Corporations [*A publication*] (DLA)
Dill Rem Caus... Dillon on the Removal of Causes [*A publication*] (DLA)
Dill Rep........ Dillon's United States Circuit Court Reports [*A publication*] (DLA)
DILM............ Dartmouth Intensive Language Model (EDAC)
DILMC.......... Defense International Logistics Management Course [*DoD*]
DIL (Moore)... Digest of International Law (Moore) [*A publication*] (DLA)
DILN............ Dilution
DILOG.......... DIstributed LOGic (SAUS)
DILOG.......... Distributed Logik Corporation (SAUO)
DILOT.......... [*An*] Introduction to the Literature of the Old Testament [*S. R. Driver*] [*A publication*] (BJA)
DILP............ Dual In-Line Package [*Computer science*]
DIL Package... Dual In-Line Package (SAUS)
DILS............ Dataskil Integrated Library System [*International Computers Ltd.*] [*British*] (NITA)
DILS............ Departmental Information Locator System [*Department of Agriculture*] (GFGA)
DILS............ Doppler Inertial LORAN System
DILS............ Doppler Instrument Landing System (SAUS)
DIL Skt........ Dual-In-Line Socket (SAUS)
DILSUP........ Disposal List Ship Unit Portsmouth [*Navy*] [*British*]
DIL Sw.......... Dual-In-Line Switch (SAUS)
DIL Timber... Dilienia Timber (SAUS)
DILUC.......... Diluculo [*At Daybreak*] [*Pharmacy*]
Dil Univ....... Dillard University (SAUO)
DILUT.......... Dilutus [*Dilute*] [*Pharmacy*]
DILVA.......... Dillonvale, OH [*American Association of Railroads railroad junction routing code*]
DIL (White)... Digest of International Law (Whiteman) [*A publication*] (DLA)
DIM.............. Data and Instruction Management Machine (NITA)
DIM.............. Data Information Record (AAEL)
DIM.............. Data Interpretation Module
DIM.............. Data In the Middle (SAUS)
dim.............. Defense Information Memo (SAUS)
DIM.............. Defense Information Memorandum (NATG)
DIM.............. Dense Ionized Medium [*Astrophysics*]
DIM.............. Denver and Intermountain Railroad Co. (SAUO)
DIM.............. Departed for Import (SAUS)
DIM.............. Description, Installation, and Maintenance
DIM.............. Design Information Manual (KSC)
DIM.............. Design Interface Meeting (NASA)
DIM.............. Device Interface Module
DIM.............. Dialogue Inter-Monasteries (SAUS)
DIM.............. Differential Interference Microscopy (PDAA)
DIM.............. Differential Inversion Method (SAUS)
dim.............. digital dimmer memory (SAUS)
DIM.............. Digital Ignorant Mechanism [*Pocket calculator facetiously described by T. R. Reid in his book, "The Chip"*]
DIM.............. Digital Image Matching (GEOI)
DIM.............. Digital Image Model (ACAE)
DIM.............. Digital Imaging Microscope
DIM.............. Digital Input Module [*Computer science*]
DIM.............. Digital Input Multiplexer (CAAL)
DIM.............. Digital Interface Module (SAUS)
dim.............. dimensioinal (SAUS)
DIM.............. Dimension (KSC)
dim.............. Dimension (VRA)
Dim.............. Dimension [*Wood industry*] (WPI)
dim.............. dimensional (SAUS)
DIM.............. Dimidius [*One-Half*] [*Pharmacy*]
dim.............. Diminished (WDMC)
DIM.............. Diminished
DIM.............. Diminuendo [*Getting Softer*] [*Music*]
Dim.............. Diminution (SAUS)
dim.............. Diminutive (SHCU)
DIM.............. Diminutive
DIM.............. Dimissory [*Ecclesiastical*] (ROG)
DIM.............. Dimitrovgrad [*Bulgaria*] [*Seismograph station code, US Geological Survey*] (SEIS)
DIM.............. Dimmer
DIM.............. Diploma in Industrial Management (ADA)
DIM.............. Direct Interaction Mechanism (SAUS)
DIM.............. Directory of International Mail [*A publication*]
DIM.............. Display Image Manipulation (IAA)
DIM.............. Display Image Manipulator (SAUS)
DIM.............. District Industrial Manager [*Navy*]
DIM.............. District Inspector of Musketry [*Military*] [*British*] (ROG)
DIM.............. Divalent Ion Metabolism (MAE)
DIM.............. Dmitry Ivanovich Mendeleyev (SAUS)
DIM.............. Dorsal Intersegmental Muscles [*Anatomy*]
DIM.............. Dosis Infectiosa Media (SAUS)
DIM.............. Driver Interface Module
DIM.............. Drop-In-Maintenance (MCD)
DIM.............. Dynamic Impedance Measurement
DIM-3C........ Diatomics-in-Molecules plus Three-Center Terms (UWER)
DIMA............ Device for Multi-Analysis [*Medicine*] (EDAA)
DIMA............ Digital Image Analysis (SAUS)
DIMA............ Direct Imaging Mass Analysis (SAUS)
DIMA............ Direct Imaging Mass Analyzer
DIMA............ Drilling Individual Mobilization Augmentation [*Army*] (DOMA)
DIMAC.......... DIMAC Corp. [*Associated Press*] (SAG)
DIMACE........ Digital Monitor and Control Equipment (SAUS)
DIMACS........ Center for Discrete Mathematics and Theoretical Computer Science [*Rutgers University*] [*Research center*] (RCD)
DIMADC........ Diffusion in Metals and Alloys Data Center [*National Institute of Standards and Technology*]
DIMAP.......... Digital/Modular Avionics Program [*Aerospace*] (MCD)
DIMAP.......... Distributed Image Management And Projection (SAUS)
DIMAPA........ Dimethylaminopropylamine [*Also, DMAPA*] [*Organic chemistry*]
DIMAPS........ Digital Image Manipulation, Analysis and Processing System (SAUS)
Dimark......... DiMark, Inc. [*Associated Press*] (SAG)
DIMARSI...... Disaster Management and Refugee Studies Institute (SAUO)
DIMASZ........ Dimension of Arrowhead Size (VLIE)
DIMATE........ Depot-Installed Maintenance Automatic Equipment (SAUS)
DIMATE........ Depot-Installed Maintenance Automatic Test Equipment
DIMBOA........ Dihydroxymethoxybenzoxazinone [*Organic chemistry*]
DIMC............ Defense Inventory Management Course [*DoD*]
DIMC............ Division of Information Management and Compliance [*Department of Education*] (GFGA)
DIMCH.......... Diesel Mechanics
DIMCP.......... Defense Item Management Coding Program (ACAE)
DIMD............ Diamond Multimedia Systems [*NASDAQ symbol*] (TTSB)
DIMD............ Diamond Multimedia Systems, Inc. [*NASDAQ symbol*] (SAG)
DIMD............ Drug-Induced Movement Disorder [*Medicine*] (MELL)

DIMDI .... Deutsches Institut fuer Medizinische Dokumentation und Information [*German Institute for Medical Documentation and Information*] [*Ministry for Youth, Family, and Health Affairs*] [*Database producer*] [*Information service or system*] (IID)
DIMDINET .... DIMDI Network (SAUS)
DIME .... Desktop Integrated Media Environment [*Computer science*] (VERA)
DIME .... Development of Integrated Monetary Electronics [*EC*] (ECED)
DIME .... Digital Map Editor (TIMI)
DIME .... Dime Community Bancorp, Inc. [*NASDAQ symbol*] (SAG)
DIME .... Disk Management Environment (SAUS)
DIME .... Division of International Medical Education [*Association of American Medical Colleges*]
DIME .... Dual Incidence Matrix Encoding
DIME .... Dual Independent Map Encoder (SAUS)
DIME .... Dual Independent Map Encoding [*Transportation*]
DIME .... Dynamic Infrared Missile Evaluator (ACAE)
DimeBcp .... Dime Bancorp, Inc. [*Formerly, Dime Savings Bank NY*] [*Associated Press*] (SAG)
DimeCo .... Dime Community Bancorp, Inc. [*Associated Press*] (SAG)
DIMECO .... Dual Independent Map Encoding File of Countries [*Harvard University*] [*A databank*] (NITA)
DIMECO .... Dual Independent Map Encoding-file of the Counties of the United States (SAUS)
DIMEDONE ... Dimethylcyclohexanedione [*Analytical chemistry*]
DimeFn .... Dime Financial Corp. [*Associated Press*] (SAG)
DIMEN .... Dimension
DIMEO .... Defense Industrial and Management Engineering Office [*DoD*]
DIMES .... Defense Improved Management Engineering System [*Military*]
DIMES .... Defense Integrated Management Engineering System [*Military*] (AFM)
DIMES .... Development of Improved Management Engineering Systems [*Military*] (AABC)
DIMES .... Development of Integrated Management Engineering Systems [*Military*]
DIMES .... Digital Image Manipulation and Enhancement Systems
DIMHRS .... Defense Integrated Military Human Resources System
DIMIA .... Depository Institution Management Interlocks Act [*1978*]
DIMIAS .... Digital Interactive Multi-Image Analysis System (SAUS)
DIMID .... Dimidius [*One-Half*] [*Pharmacy*]
DIMIG .... Disintegrations per Minute per Gram [*Environmental science*] (COE)
dimin .... diminish (SAUS)
DIMIN .... Diminuendo [*Getting Softer*] [*Music*] (WGA)
dimin .... diminution (SAUS)
DIMIN .... Diminutive (WDAA)
DIMINCO ...... National Diamond Mining Company (SAUO)
DIMIS .... Depot Installation Management Information System [*Army*]
DIML .... Dimensional
DIMM .... Defense Integrated Material Management (MCD)
DIMM .... Dual Inline Memory Module [*Computer science*]
dimn .... dimension (SAUS)
DIMN .... Man [*Ivory Coast*] [*ICAO location identifier*] (ICLI)
DIMOAD .... Diabetes Insipidus, Diabetes Mellitus, Optic Atrophy, and Deafness [*Medicine*]
DIMOB .... Defense Intelligence Missile Order of Battle (MCD)
DIMODE .... Discontinuity Modulation Effect (ACAE)
DIMOH .... Diploma, Industrial Medicine & Occupational Health [*Medical degree*] (CMD)
DIMON .... Dimension (ROG)
Dimon .... Dimon, Inc. [*Associated Press*] (SAG)
DIMOND ...... Dual Interconnecting Modular Network Device (SAUS)
dimorph .... Dimorphous (SAUS)
dimorph .... Dimorphus (SAUS)
DIMOS .... double implanted metal-oxide semiconductor (SAUS)
DIMOS .... Double Implanted MOS (SAUS)
DIMOS .... Double-Implanted Metal-Oxide Semiconductor (SAUS)
DIMOTF .... Digital Module Tester (ACAE)
DIMOX .... Directed Metal Oxidation (SAUS)
DIMP .... Data and Information Management Panel (SAUS)
dIMP .... Deoxyinosine Monophosphate [*Biochemistry*]
DIMP .... Diisopropyl Methylphosphonate [*Organic chemistry*]
DIMPC .... Defense Item Management Coding Program [*DoD*] (AFIT)
DIMPE .... Distributed Integrated Multimedia Publishing Environment (SAUO)
DIMPEA .... (Dimethoxyphenyl)ethylamine [*Also, DMPE, DMPEA*] [*Psychomimetic compound*]
DIMPLE .... Deuterium Moderated Pile Low Energy [*Reactor*]
DIMPLE Reactor ... Deuterium Moderated Pile Low Energy Reactor (SAUS)
DIMPS .... Distributed Message Processing System (SAUS)
Dimps .... Dual Income, Money Problems [*Lifestyle Classification*]
DIMR .... Denver & Intermountain Railroad [*Federal Railroad Administration identification code*]
DIMS .... Data and Information Management System [*Computer science*] (ODBW)
DIMS .... Data Information and Manufacturing System (PDAA)
DIMS .... Data Information Management System (SAUS)
DIMS .... Data Input Management System (SAUS)
DIMS .... Democratic Indicators Monitoring System (SAUO)
DIMS .... Digital Imaging Medical System
dims .... dimensions (SAUS)
DIMS .... Director, International Military Staff Memorandum [*NATO*] (NATG)
DIMS .... Disorder of Initiating and Maintaining Sleep [*Medicine*]
DIMS .... Distributed Intelligence Microcomputer System
DIMS .... Document-and-Image Management System [*Computer science*] (PCM)
DIMS .... Dynamic Inertial Measurement Systems (ACAE)
DIMSA .... Depot Integrated Maintenance Support Agreement [*Air Force*]
DIMSA .... Distribuidora de Impresos, Sociedad Anonima [*Mexico*]
DIMSCALE ... Dimension of Overall Scale (VLIE)
DIMSS .... DSN Integrated Management Support System (SAUS)
DIM System ... Distributed Intelligence Microcomputer System (SAUS)
DIMT .... Deputy Inspector of Mechanized Troops (SAUO)
DIMTXT .... Dimension of Text Height (VLIE)
DIMUN .... Distributed International Manufacturing (SAUO)
DIMUS .... Digital Multibeam Steering
DIMUS .... Directional Multibeam Steering
DIMZ .... DIM Associates Railroad [*Federal Railroad Administration identification code*]
DIN .... Aerodin SA de CV [*Mexico*] [*ICAO designator*] (FAAC)
DIN .... AUTODIN Data Identification Number (SAUS)
DIN .... Consorcio G. Grupo Dina [*NYSE symbol*] (SPSG)
DIN .... Consorcio G Grupo Dina ADS [*NYSE symbol*] (TTSB)
din .... Damage Inducible [*Gene*] [*Medicine*] (EDAA)
DIN .... Data Identification Number (AFM)
DIN .... Data In (VLIE)
DIN .... Data-in-Line (SAUS)
DIN .... Dedicated Intelligence Network (MCD)
DIN .... Defense Intelligence Notice (MCD)
DIN .... Deutsche Industrie Normen [*International system for trimmed printing paper sizes*] (EES)
DIN .... Deutsches Institut fuer Normung [*German Institute for Standardization*] (IID)
DIN .... Device Initialize [*Computer science*] (IAA)
DIN .... Diana Stores Corp. (SAUO)
DIN .... Digital Input [*Computer science*] (KSC)
DIN .... Dinar [*Monetary unit*] [*Former Yugoslavia*]
DIN .... Dinghy [*Coast Guard*] (DNAB)
din .... Dining Room (ADWA)
din .... Dinka [*MARC language code*] [*Library of Congress*] (LCCP)
DIN .... Dinner (ADA)
DIN .... Dinuclear (IAA)
DIN .... Direct Injection Nebulization [*For spectrometry*]
DIN .... Discrete Input (SAUS)
DIN .... Dissolved Inorganic Nitrogen [*Chemistry*]
DIN .... Document Identification Number (NG)
DIN .... Do It Now [*Category of service call for maintenance or repair work*] [*Air Force*]
DIN .... Do It Now Foundation [*An association*]
DIN .... Drug Indentification Number [*Medicine*] (DB)
DIN .... International Industrial Standard Designator (SAUS)
DIN .... Digital Imaging Network (ODA)
DIN.L .... Consorcio G Grupo Dina'L'ADS [*NYSE symbol*] (TTSB)
D in 2PLO .... Detur in Duplo [*Let Twice as Much Be Given*] [*Pharmacy*] (ROG)
DINA .... Chilean Directorate of National Intelligence (SAUS)
DINA .... Database Industry Association (SAUO)
DINA .... Departamento de Inteligencia Nacional [*National Intelligence Department*] [*Chilean secret police*] [*Superseded by CNI*]
DINA .... Digital Network Analyzer
DINA .... Diisononyl Adipate
DINA .... Dioxyethylnitramine Dinitrate (EDCT)
DINA .... Direct Internal Noise Amplification (NG)
DINA .... Direct Noise Amplification (VLIE)
DINA .... Direct Noise Amplifier (SAUS)
DINA .... Distributed Information Processing Network Architecture
DINA .... Japan Database Industry Association [*Tokyo*] [*Information service or system*] (IID)
DINABOC ..... Digital Navigation And Bombing Computer (SAUS)
DINADE .... Diode Interrogation, Navigation, and Detection (IAA)
DINAH .... Desktop Interface to AUTODIN Host (SAUO)
DINAP .... Digital Network Analysis Program (SAUS)
DINAS .... Digital Inertial Navigation/Attack System (SAUS)
DINATUR ..... Direccion Nacional de Turismo [*National Direction of Tourism*] [*Bolivia*] (EAIO)
DINBX .... Mgn. Stanley D. Witter Diversified Inc. Cl.B [*Mutual fund ticker symbol*] (SG)
Dinc .... Double [*or Dual*] Income, No Children [*Lifestyle classification*]
DInd .... Doctor of Industrial Engineering
D Ind .... Doctor of Industry
DINDAC .... Digital Access Direct Access (SAUS)
DIN/DCSS .... Digital Network-Defense Special Security Communications System [*National Security Agency*]
DIN/DSSCS ... Digital Information Network/Defense Special Security Communications System (SAUS)
D in DUP ...... Detur in Duplo [*Let Twice as Much Be Given*] [*Pharmacy*]
diner .... dining car (SAUS)
DINET .... Defense Industrial-Base Network (POLM)
DINET .... Defense Industrial Net (COE)
DINET .... Defense Industrial Network [*DoD*]
DINET .... Defense Information Network [*DoD*]
DINF .... Advantica Restaurant Group, Inc. [*NASDAQ symbol*] (NASQ)
D Inf .... Directorate of Infantry (SAUO)
D-INF .... Director of Infantry [*Military*] [*British*]
DINF .... Do It Now Foundation (EA)
DINFOS .... Defense Information School
DING .... Directory of Item Names for the Gas Industry [*A publication*]
D Ing .... Doctor Ingeniariae [*Doctor of Engineering*]
DINGO .... Discounted Investment in Negotiated Government Obligations (EBF)
DINJ .... DIN Jack (SAUS)
Dink .... Double [*or Dual*] Income, No Kids [*Lifestyle classification*]
DINK .... Dual Income, No Kids (TAG)
DINKS .... Dual-Income, No Kids (DFIT)
Dinky .... Double [*or Dual*] Income, No Kids Yet [*Lifestyle classification*]

DINN .... Dual Input Null Network
DINO .... Deputy Inspector of Naval Ordnance
DINO .... Dinosaur National Monument
DINOB .... Defense Intelligence Naval Order of Battle (MCD)
DINOS .... Distributed Interactive Operating System (IAA)
Dinosaur .... Dinosaur National Monument, Colorado and Utah (SAUS)
DINOSEB .... Dinitro-sec-Butyl-Phenol (SAUS)
DINP .... Diisononyl Phthalate [*Organic chemistry*]
DINP .... DIN Plug (SAUS)
DINP .... Dunk Island National Park (SAUS)
D in P AEQ ... Dividatur in Partes Aequales [*Divide into Equal Parts*] [*Pharmacy*]
din paeq .... divide in partes aequales (SAUS)
dinrm .... Dining Room (REAL)
DINS .... Digital Inertial Navigation System (SAUS)
DINS .... Directorate for Inspection Services [*Assistant Secretary of Defense for Administration*] (CINC)
DINS .... Dormant Inertial Navigation System (MCD)
DINS .... Dual Inertial Navigation System (SEWL)
DINSA .... Disability Information Network of South Australia
DInstPA .... Diploma of the Institute of Park Administration (SAUS)
DINSUM .... Defense Intelligence Summary (WPI)
DINUPS .... DIMDI's [*Deutsches Institut fuer Medizinische Dokumentation und Information*] Input and Updata System (NITA)
DIO .... Data Input/Output [*Computer science*]
DIO .... Defence Arrangements for Indian Ocean [*British*] [*World War II*]
DIO .... Defense Intelligence Officer [*Defense Intelligence Agency*] (MCD)
DIO .... Diet-Induced Obese [*Mice*]
DIO .... Digital Input/Output [*Computer science*]
dio .... Diocese (GEAB)
DIO .... Diocese
DIO .... Diode (KSC)
DIO .... Diodes, Inc. [*AMEX symbol*] (SPSG)
Dio .... Dionysius [*Authority cited in pre-1607 legal work*] (DSA)
DIO .... Direct Input/Output [*Telecommunications*] (TEL)
DI(O) .... Directorate of Intelligence (Operations) [*RAF*] [*British*]
DIO .... Director of Industrial Operations [*Military*] (AABC)
DIO .... Disk Input/Output (ACAE)
DIO .... District Intelligence Officer
DIO .... Divisional Intelligence Officer (SAUO)
DIO .... Do It Ourselves (VLIE)
DIO .... Dominion International Opera (WDAA)
DIO .... Doppler Inertial Omega (IAA)
DIO .... Duty Intelligence Officer [*Air Force*]
DIOA .... Differential Input Operational Amplifier [*Electronics*]
DIOA .... Diisooctyl Adipate [*Organic chemistry*]
DIOA .... Dynamic Input-Output Analysis [*Economics*]
DIOB .... Data Input/Output Buffer (SAUS)
DIOB .... Digital Input/Output Buffer [*Computer science*]
DIOBS .... Defense Intelligence Order of Battle Systems (MCD)
DIOBS .... DIA Order of Battle (SAUS)
DIOC .... Digital Input/Output Control [*Computer science*]
DIOC .... Dimethyloxacarbocyanine [*Organic chemistry*]
dioc .... Diocesan (ADWA)
DIOC .... Diocese [*or Diocesean*]
DIOC .... Displayed Independent of Computer (ACAE)
DIOC .... Dissolved Inorganic Carbon [*Also, DIC*]
DIOC .... District Intelligence Operations Centers [*Vietnam*]
DIOC .... Ducati International Owners Club (EA)
Dio Cass .... Dio Cassius [*Third century AD*] [*Classical studies*] (OCD)
DIOCB .... Device Input/Output Control Block [*Computer science*] (ELAL)
DIOCC .... District Intelligence and Operations Coordination Center [*Vietnam*] (VNW)
Dio Chrys .... Dio Chrysostomus [*First century AD*] [*Classical studies*] (OCD)
DIOCN .... Diocesan (ROG)
dioc syn .... Diocesan Synod (ODA)
DIOD .... Digital Input/Output Device (ACAE)
DIOD .... Digital Input/Output Display (SAUS)
DIOD .... Digital Inward/Outward Dialling (SAUS)
DIOD .... Diode
Diod .... Diodorus Siculus [*First century BC*] [*Classical studies*] (OCD)
DIOD .... Odienne [*Ivory Coast*] [*ICAO location identifier*] (ICLI)
DIODE .... Digital Input/Output Display Equipment
Diodes .... Diodes, Inc. [*Associated Press*] (SAG)
Diod Sic .... Diodorus Siculus [*First century BC*] [*Classical studies*] (OCD)
DIOF .... Display Input/Output Facility [*Computer science*] (VLIE)
DIOF .... Ouango Fitini [*Ivory Coast*] [*ICAO location identifier*] (ICLI)
DIOG .... Decylidenimino(octyl)guanidine [*Organic chemistry*]
Diog Laert ... Diogenes Laertius [*Third century AD*] [*Classical studies*] (OCD)
DIOH .... Due in from Overhaul (AFIT)
DIOI .... Digital Input/Output Interface [*Computer science*] (KSC)
DIOL .... Dihydric Alcohol (SAUS)
DIOLAMINE ... Diethanolamine [*Also, DEA*] [*USAN*] [*Organic chemistry*]
DIOM .... Device I/O Manager (SAUS)
DIOM .... Digital Input/Output Module (SAUS)
Diomed Mari ... Diomedes Mariconda [*Deceased, 1511*] [*Authority cited in pre-1607 legal work*] (DSA)
DION .... Dionics, Inc. [*NASDAQ symbol*] (COMM)
Dion .... Dionisio (SAUS)
DION .... Division (SAUO)
Dionex .... Dionex Corp. [*Associated Press*] (SAG)
Dion Hal .... Dionysius Halicarnassensis [*First century BC*] [*Classical studies*] (OCD)
DIOP .... Defense Intelligence Objectives and Priorities (MCD)
DIOP .... Digital Input/Output Package [*Computer science*]
DIOP .... Diisooctyl Phthalate [*Organic chemistry*]
DIOP .... Dimethyldioxolane (SAUS)
Diop .... Diopter [*Medicine*] (EDAA)
diop .... diopter (SAUS)
DIOP .... Dioptrics (SAUS)
DIOP .... Directorate for Information, Operation, and Patents (AAGC)
DIOP .... Double-Density Disk Drive Input/Output Processor [*Computer science*] (NITA)
DIOPEN .... Device Independence Open (SAUS)
DIOPT .... Diopter [*Also, D*] [*Optics*]
dior .... diorama (SAUS)
DIOR .... Directorate for Information Operations and Reports [*Washington, DC*] [*DoD*]
DIOS .... Digital Input/Output System (SAUS)
DIOS .... Diisooctyl Sebacate [*Organic chemistry*]
Dios .... Dionysius [*Authority cited in pre-1607 legal work*] (DSA)
DIOS .... Direct Memory Access Input/Output Subsystem (MCD)
DIOS .... Direct Memory Access Input/Output System [*Computer science*] (NITA)
DIOS .... Distributed Input/Output System
DIOS .... Distribution, Information, and Optimizing System (OA)
dios .... diver lockout submersible (SAUS)
DIOSS .... Distributed Interface Object Server System [*Computer science*] (HODG)
DIOSS .... Distributed Office Support System (SAUS)
DIOX .... Dioxide [*Freight*]
Diox .... Dioxygen (SAUS)
DIOZ .... Diisooctyl Azelate (EDCT)
DIP .... Data Input Processor [*Computer science*]
DIP .... Data Input Programming (SAUS)
DIP .... Data Integration Program (GEOI)
DIP .... Data Interchange Program (SAUS)
DIP .... Dead Item Purge [*Military*] (AFIT)
DIP .... Debtor-in-Possession (TDOB)
DIP .... Decentralized Information Processing (SAUS)
DIP .... Defamation, Identification, and Publication
DIP .... Defence Industry Productivity Program (SAUS)
DIP .... Defense Improvement Project (COE)
DIP .... Defense Industry Productivity (SAUS)
DIP .... Defense Intelligence Plan (MCD)
DIP .... Defense Investigative Program (SAUO)
DIP .... De-Inking Pulp [*Process*] [*Paper recycling*]
DIP .... Department of Information and Propaganda (SAUS)
DIP .... Depth Image Processing (SAUS)
DIP .... Designated Inspection Points (MCD)
DIP .... Design Improvement Program
DIP .... Design Internal Pressure [*Nuclear energy*] (NRCH)
DIP .... Desirability Index Plan (SAUS)
DIP .... Desquamative Interstitial Pneumonia [*Medicine*]
DIP .... Destruction of Interstate Property
DIP .... Detached Issue Park (SAUO)
DIP .... Detailed Inspection Procedure (MCD)
DIP .... Device Interface Processor (TIMI)
DIP .... Diagnostic Interrogation Program (VLIE)
DIP .... Dial Pulse (SAUS)
DIP .... Dial-Up Internet Protocol [*Computer science*] (VLIE)
dip .... Dial up IP (SAUS)
DIP .... Difference in Perils (MARI)
DIP .... Digital Image Processor or Processing (SAUS)
DIP .... Digital Impact Predictor
DIP .... Digital Incremental Plotter
DIP .... Digital Information Processing (SAUS)
dip .... digital inline pins (SAUS)
DIP .... Digital Instrumentation Programmer
DIP .... Digital Interface Processor (SAUS)
DIP .... Digitizer Input (SAUS)
DIP .... Diisopropyl (UWER)
DIP .... Diisopropylphenol [*Anesthetic*]
DIP .... Di-Isopropyl Phosphate [*Organic chemistry*] (DAVI)
DIP .... Dimethylaminoisopropyl (SAUS)
dip .... dipeptide (SAUS)
DIP .... Diphtheria [*Medicine*]
dip .... diphthong (SAUS)
dip .... diplex (SAUS)
dip .... diplococcus (SAUS)
DIP .... Diploid
dip .... Diploma (SHCU)
Dip .... Diploma (WDAA)
DIP .... Diploma
dip .... diplomacy (SAUS)
DIP .... Diplomat (WDAA)
DIP .... Diplomat Resources [*Vancouver Stock Exchange symbol*]
dip .... Diplotene (QSUL)
Dip .... Diptera [*Entomology*]
DIP .... Dipyridyl [*Also, DIPY*] [*Organic chemistry*]
DIP .... Direct Immunoperoxidase [*Clinical medicine*]
DIP .... Direct Insertion Probe
DIP .... Direct Intraperitoneal Insemination [*Alternative to traditional in-vitro fertilization (IVF)*] (PAZ)
DIP .... Directories in Print [*Formerly, DOD*] [*A publication*]
DIP .... Director of Industrial Planning [*War Office*] [*British*] [*World War II*]
DIP .... Disbursement In Process (SAUS)
DIP .... Displayed Impact Point (MCD)
DIP .... Display Information Processing (SAUS)
DIP .... Display Information Processor [*Air Force*]
DIP .... Display Input Processor (NASA)

DIP............. Display Interface Processing (MCD)
DIP............. Display Interface Processing (or Processor) (SAUS)
DIP............. Disposition of Inactive Parts List
dip............. dissemination and improvement of practice (SAUS)
DIP............. Dissolved Inorganic Phosphate
DIP............. Dissolved Inorganic Phosphorus [*Chemistry*]
DIP............. Distal Interphalangeal [*Joint*] [*Anatomy*]
DIP............. Distributed Information Processing
DIP............. Distribution Information Processing (SAUS)
DIP............. Dividend Investment Plan [*Stock purchase*] [*Investment term*]
DIP............. Division of Industrial Participation [*AEC*]
DIP............. Dizionario Italiano di Perfezione [*A publication*] (ODCC)
DIP............. Doctrine Improvement Program
DIP............. Document Image Processing [*Computer science*]
DIP............. Dokumentations- und Informationssystem fuer Parlamentsmaterial [*Documentation and Information System for Parliamentary Materials*] [*German Federal Diet Division of Scientific Documentation*] [*Information service or system*] (IID)
DIP............. Dormit in Pace [*Sleeps in Peace*] [*Latin*]
DIP............. Double In-Line Package [*Computer science*]
DIP............. Drip Infusion Pyelography [*Radiography*]
DIP............. Driver Improvement Program [*American Automobile Association*]
DIP............. Droit International Prive [*Private International Law*] [*French*] (DLA)
dip............. dropping inward pilot (SAUS)
DIP............. Drug-Induced Pneumonitis [*Medicine*]
DIP............. Dual In-Line Package [*Computer science*]
DIP............. Dual In-Line Pin
DIP............. Dual-Inline Plastic (SAUS)
DIP............. Ductile Iron Pipe (PDAA)
DIP............. Dust Infall Predominant (AAG)
DIP............. Dynamic Inclined Plane (PDAA)
DIP .... Deep Inelastic Processes (ODA)
DIPA........... Diamond Industrial Products Association [*British*] (DBA)
DIPA........... Diisopropanolamine [*Organic chemistry*]
DIPA........... Diisopropylamine [*Also, DIPAM*] [*Organic chemistry*]
DipA........... Diploma in Analytical Chemistry
DipA........... Diploma in Aquaculture (SAUS)
DIPA........... Diploma of the Institute of Park Administration (SAUS)
DIPA........... Ductile Iron Pipe Association (SAUO)
DIPA........... Interacting Protein A [*Biochemistry*]
DipAc.......... Diplomate of Acupuncture [*Medicine*]
DipAcc......... Diploma in Accounting
DipAcctgFin... Diploma in Accounting and Finance
Dip AD......... Diploma in Art and Design
DipAdmin(Nursing)... Diploma in Administration (Nursing)
DipAdminSc... Diploma in Administrative Science (ADA)
DipAdStudEd... Diploma in Advanced Studies in Education
DipAdvAcc... Diploma in Advanced Accounting (ADA)
DipAdvEd..... Diploma of Advanced Education (ADA)
DipAE.......... Diploma in Adult Education [*British*] (DI)
DipAe.......... Diploma in Aeronautics (ODA)
DipAg.......... Diploma in Agriculture (ADA)
DipAgE........ Diploma in Agricultural Economics
DipAgEc...... Diploma in Agricultural Economics (ADA)
DipAgExt..... Diploma in Agricultural Extension
DipAgr........ Diploma in Agriculture
DipAgrChem... Diploma in Agricultural Chemistry (ADA)
DipAgrEc...... Diploma in Agricultural Economics (ADA)
DipAgrEnt.... Diploma in Agricultural Entomology (ADA)
DipAgrExt.... Diploma in Agricultural Extension (ADA)
DipAgrExtn... Diploma in Agricultural Extension (ADA)
DipAgrGen... Diploma in Agricultural Genetics (ADA)
DipAgr(ic).... Diploma in Agriculture (CPGU)
DipAgrMicro... Diploma in Agricultural Microbiology (ADA)
DipAgrSc..... Diploma in Agricultural Science (ADA)
DipAK.......... Diploma in Applied Kinesiology
DipALing...... Diploma in Applied Linguistics (ADA)
DIPAM......... Diisopropylamine [*Also, DIPA*] [*Organic chemistry*]
Dip AM........ Diploma in Applied Mechanics [*British*]
DipAmerBd P&N... Diploma American Board of Psychiatry and Neurology (SAUS)
Dip Amer Bd P & N... Diploma of the American Board of Psychiatry and Neurology (SAUS)
DipAmerBdP & N... Diplomate, American Board of Psychiatry and Neurology (DAVI)
Dip Amer Bd P & N... Diplomate of the American Board of Psychiatry and Neurology (SAUS)
Dip AMS...... Diploma in Ayurvedic Medicine and Surgery (SAUS)
DipAnat........ Diploma in Anatomy
Dip Anch...... Diploma in Architecture (SAUS)
DipAnHus..... Diploma in Animal Husbandry (ADA)
DipAnth........ Diploma in Anthropology (ADA)
DipAnthr...... Diploma in Anthropology
DipAnthrop... Diploma in Anthropology (ADA)
DipAppChem... Diploma in Applied Chemistry
DipAppChildPsych... Diploma in Applied Child Psychology
DipAppFarmMgmt... Diploma in Applied Farm Management
DipAppLing... Diploma in Applied Linguistics
DipAppMath... Diploma in Applicable Mathematics
DipAppPhys... Diploma of Applied Physics
DipAppPsych... Diploma in Applied Psychology (ADA)
DipAppSc..... Diploma of Applied Science (ADA)
DipAppSci.... Diploma in Applied Science (NADA)
DipAppSc(Nursing)... Diploma in Applied Science (Nursing)
DipAppSt...... Diploma in Applied Statistics
Dip Arch...... Diploma in Architecture [*British*]
DipArch........ Diploma of Architecture (SAUS)
DipArchAdm... Diploma in Architectural Administration
DipArchComp... Diploma in Architectural Computing
DipArchDes... Diploma in Architectural Design (ADA)
DipArchivAdmin... Diploma in Archives Administration (ADA)
Dip ARM...... Diploma, Australian Risk Management
DipArs......... Diploma in Arts (NADA)
DipArt.......... Diploma in Art
DipArtEd...... Diploma in Art Education
DipArtFilmTV... Diploma in Art Film and Television
DipArts........ Diploma in Arts (ADA)
DIPAS.......... Defence Institute of Physiology and Allied Sciences [*New Delhi, India*]
DipAse(CofP)... Graduate Level Specialist Diplomas in Advanced Study in Education, College of Preceptors [*British*] (DBQ)
DipAssSc..... Diploma in Association Science (SAUO)
DipAst.......... Diploma in Astrology
DipAud......... Diploma in Audiology
DipAvMed.... Diploma in Avian Medicine
DipAvMed.... Diploma in Aviation Medicine (ADA)
DIPB........... Deep Infrapatellar Bursa [*Medicine*] (MELL)
DIPB........... Diisopropylbenzene [*Organic chemistry*]
DipBA......... Diploma in Business Administration (ODA)
DipBac......... Diploma in Bacteriology (NADA)
Dip Bact...... Diploma in Bacteriology [*British*]
DipBact........ Diploma in Bateriology (SAUS)
DipBdgSc..... Diploma in Building Science
DipBdgSc(ECD)... Diploma in Building Science (Energy-Conservative Design) (ADA)
DipBiom...... Diploma in Biometry (ADA)
DipBM......... Diploma in Business Management (ADA)
DipBMS....... Diploma in Basic Medical Sciences (ADA)
DipBS.......... Diploma in Fine Art, Byam Shaw School (ODA)
DipBuildSc... Diploma of Building Science
DipBus........ Diploma in Business (ADA)
DipBusAdmin... Diploma in Business Administration
DipBusMangt... Diploma in Business Management (ADA)
DipBusStud... Diploma in Business Studies (ADA)
DipBusStudies... Diploma in Business Studies (ADA)
DIPC........... Defense Industrial Plant/Equipment Center (COE)
DIPC........... Diffuse Interstitial Pulmonary Calcification [*Medicine*] (AAMN)
DIPC........... Diisopropyl Carbodiimide [*Organic chemistry*]
Dip CAM...... Diploma in Communications, Advertising, and Marketing (SAUS)
DipCAM....... Diploma of the Communication Advertising and Marketing Education Foundation [*British*] (DBQ)
DipCard....... Diploma in Cardiology (ADA)
DipCareers... Diploma in Careers
DipCC.......... Diploma of the Central College (ODA)
DIPCd.......... Diisopropyl Cadmium (SAUS)
DipCD.......... Diploma in Civic Design [*British*]
DipCD.......... Diploma in Child Development (ODA)
DIPCDI......... Diisopropylcarbodiimide (SAUS)
DipCE........... Diploma of Civil Engineering (ADA)
DipCEpi........ Diploma in Clinical Epidemiology
DipCH.......... Diploma in Clinical Hypnotherapy (ADA)
DipChD......... Diploma in Chest Diseases
Dip Chem..... Diploma in Chemistry [*Medicine*] (DMAA)
DipChemE.... Diploma of Chemical Engineering
DipChemEng... Diploma in Chemical Engineering [*Academic degree*] (WDAA)
DipChemInd... Diploma of Chemistry in Industry
DipChiLit..... Diploma in Children's Literature
DipClinHyp... Diploma in Clinical Hypnosis
DipClinHypno... Diploma in Clinical Hypnotherapy
DipClinNut... Diploma in Clinical Nutrition
Dip Clin Path... Diploma in Clinical Pathology [*British*]
DipClinPharm... Diploma in Clinical Pharmacology
DipClinPsych... Diploma in Clinical Psychology
DipClinSc.... Diploma in Clinical Science (ADA)
DipCM......... Diploma in Community Medicine
DipCoalGeol... Diploma in Coal Geology
Dip Com...... Diploma in Commerce (SAUS)
DipCom........ Diploma of Commerce (ADA)
DipCom & Con... Diploma in Computers and Control
DipComDP... Diploma in Commercial Data Processing
DipComm.... Diploma in Commerce (ADA)
DipComm(Acc)... Diploma in Commerce (Accounting)
DipCommArt... Diploma in Commercial Art
DipCommChildHealth... Diploma in Community Child Health
DipCommSc... Diploma in Community Science
DipCommun... Diploma in Communications
DipCommunityMgmt... Diploma of Community Management
DipComp...... Diploma in Computer Studies
DipCompEd... Diploma in Computer Education
DipCompSc... Diploma in Computer Science (ADA)
DipCompSt... Diploma in Computer Studies
DipConsStud... Diploma in Conservation Studies
DipContEd.... Diploma in Continuing Education (ADA)
Dip Cor........ Diplomatic Correspondence of the United States [*A publication*] (DLA)
DipCOT........ Diploma of the College of Occupational Therapists [*British*] (DBQ)
DipCoun....... Diploma in Counselling
DipCPsy....... Diploma in Child Psychiatry
DipCrim........ Diploma in Criminology (ADA)
Dip CS......... Diploma in Christian Studies (PGP)
DipCS.......... Diploma of the Chamber of Shipping [*Australia*]

DipCultSt...... Diploma in Cultural Studies
DipCVD........ Diploma in Cardiovascular Disease
DIPD........... Diagnostic Interview for Personality Disorders (MELL)
DIPD........... Double Inverse Pinch Device [*Physics*] (OA)
DipDDCP...... Diploma in Drug Development and Clinical Pharmacology
DipDentTherapy... Diploma in Dental Therapy
DipDermat... Diploma in Dermatology
DipDes........ Diploma in Design
DipDesCra ... Diploma in Design and Crafts
DipDevDis ... Diploma in Developmental Disabilities
DipDHus...... Diploma in Dairy Husbandry (ADA)
DipDiet........ Diploma in Dietetics (ADA)
DipDistEd .... Diploma in Distance Education
DipDiv .... Diploma in Divinity
DipDN.......... Diplome en Droit Civil (DD)
DipDomArts... Diploma in Domestic Arts
DipDomSc ... Diploma in Domestic Science
DIPDOP....... Disc and Drum Input/Output Routines [*Honeywell, Inc.*]
DipDP.......... Diploma in Drawing and Painting (NADA)
DipDramArt... Diploma in Dramatic Art
DipDramEd... Diploma in Drama Education
DipDS.......... Diploma in Dental Surgery (NADA)
DIPE............ Diisopropyl Ether [*Gasoline*] [*Organic chemistry*]
DIPE............ Distributed Interactive Processing Environment (SAUS)
DIPEC .... Defense Industrial Plant (USGC)
DIPEC .... Defense Industrial Plant Equipment Center [*DoD*] (AFM)
DIPEC .... Defense Industrial Production Equipment Center
DipEc.......... Diploma in Economics (ADA)
DipEco .... Diploma in Economics (NADA)
Dip Econ...... Diploma of Economics (ADA)
DipEconGeog... Diploma of Economic Geography (ADA)
DipEconStats... Diploma in Economic Statistics (ADA)
DipEcStud.... Diploma in Economic Studies
DIPED .... Diisopropylethanediol [*Organic chemistry*]
Dip Ed .... Diploma in Education (SAUS)
DipEd.......... Diploma of Education [*British*] (EY)
DipEdAdm.... Diploma in Education Administration
DipEdAdmin... Diploma in Educational Administration (ADA)
DipEdMan.... Diploma in Educational Management
DipEdPsych... Diploma in Educational Psychology (ADA)
DipEdRes..... Diploma in Education Research
DipEdSt....... Diploma in Education Studies
DipEdStud.... Diploma in Education Studies
DipEdTech ... Diploma in Education Technology
DipEEng....... Diploma of Electrical Engineering (ADA)
DIPEF.......... Defense Industrial Plant Equipment Facility [*DoD*]
DipEF.......... Diploma in Executive Finance [*British*] (DBQ)
DipEH.......... Diploma in Environmental Health [*British*] (DBQ)
DipEl .... Diploma in Electronics (ODA)
DipElecEng... Diploma of Electrical Engineering (ADA)
DipEMA........ Diploma in Executive Finance for Non-Accountants [*British*] (DBQ)
Dip Eng........ Diploma in Engineering [*British*]
DipEngGeol... Diploma in Engineering Geology
DipEngMgt... Diploma in Engineering Management (ADA)
DipEngTech... Diploma in Engineering Technology (SAUS)
DipEnvHlth... Diploma in Environmental Health
DipEnvIA..... Diploma in Environmental Impact Assessment
DipEnvironEng... Diploma in Environmental Engineering
DipEnvironStud... Diploma in Environmental Studies (ADA)
DipEnvSc..... Diploma in Environmental Science
DipEnvSt...... Diploma in Environmental Studies
DipEnvStud... Diploma in Environmental Studies
DipEpid........ Diploma in Epidemiology
DipESL .... Diploma in English as a Second Language (ODA)
DipEth .... Diploma in Ethnology (ODA)
DIPF........... Diffuse Interstitial Pulmonary Fibrosis [*Medicine*] (MELL)
DIPF........... Diisopropylphosphofluordate (LDT)
DIPF........... Diisopropylphosphofluoridate (DMAA)
DipFA.......... Diploma in Fine Arts (ADA)
DipFamMed... Diploma in Family Medicine
DipFamT...... Diploma in Family Therapy
DipFashArt... Diploma in Fashion Art
DipFD .... Diploma in Funeral Directing, National Association of Funeral Directors [*British*] (DBQ)
DipFDA .... Diploma in Food and Drug Analysis (ADA)
DipFIA .... Diploma in Furniture and Interior Architecture
DipFinMan... Diploma in Financial Management
DipFinMangt... Diploma in Financial Management (ADA)
DipFM.......... Diploma in Financial Management
Dip For .... Diploma in Forestry (SAUS)
DipFor .... Diploma of Forestry (ADA)
DipFP........... Diploma in Family Planning
DipFP........... Diploma in Financial Planning
DipFrenchStud... Diploma in French Studies
DipFSt .... Diploma in Film Studies
DipFTV........ Diploma in Film and Television
DIPG .... Port Gauthier [*Ivory Coast*] [*ICAO location identifier*] (ICLI)
DipGA .... Diploma in Graphic Arts
DipG&O .... Diploma in Gynaecology and Obstetrics (NADA)
DipGD .... Diploma in Graphic Design
DipGem .... Diploma in Gemmology
DipGenLing... Diploma in General Linguistics
DipGeog ...... Diploma in Geography
DipGeotEng... Diploma in Geotechnical Engineering
DipGerm...... Diploma in German
DipGraphicDes... Diploma of Graphic Design
DipGSM ...... Diploma in Music, Guildhall School of Music and Drama (ODA)
DipGT .... Diploma in Glass Technology (ADA)
DipGUM....... Diploma in Genito-Urinary Medicine
DIPH........... Diaphragm (SAUS)
diph .... Diphtheria (ADWA)
DIPH .... Diphtheria [*Medicine*]
DIPH .... Diphthong [*Linguistics*]
DipHA .... Diploma in Health Administration (ADA)
Dip HA........ Diploma in Hospital Administration (SAUS)
DipHCM .... Diploma in Hotel and Catering Management
Dip HE .... Diploma in Higher Education (SAUS)
DipHE .... Diploma in Highway Engineering (ADA)
DipHE .... Diploma in Hydraulic Engineering
DipHE .... Diploma of Higher Education
DipHealthSc... Diploma in Health Science
DipHEd .... Diploma in Higher Education
DipHHRE...... Diploma in Health and Human Relations Education
DipHigherEd... Diploma in Higher Education (ADA)
DipHistStud... Diploma in History Studies
DipHlthE...... Diploma in Health Education
DipHlthSc.... Diploma in Health Science
DipHMS....... Diploma in Human Movement Studies
DipHom .... Diploma in Homeopathy
DipHomEc.... Diploma in Home Economics
DipHortSc.... Diploma in Horticultural Science (ADA)
DIPHOS....... Diphenylphosphinoethane (SAUS)
DipHospAdm... Diploma in Hospital Administration
DipHospAdmin... Diploma in Hospital Administration (ADA)
DipHPharm... Diploma in Hospital Pharmacy (ADA)
DipHS .... Diploma in Health Sciences
DipHSc .... Diploma in Home Science (ADA)
DIPH/TET .... Diphtheria/Tetanus [*Immunology*]
diph tet........ diphtheria tetanus (SAUS)
DIPHTH........ Diphthong (WDAA)
diph tox .... diphtheria toxin (SAUS)
DIPH TOX .... Diphtheria Toxoid [*Immunology*]
diph tox ap... diphtheria toxin alum precipitated (SAUS)
DIPH TOX AP... Diphtheria Toxoid, Alum Precipitated [*Immunology*]
DipHum .... Diploma in Humanities
DipHumBiol... Diploma in Human Biology
DipHumNut... Diploma in Human Nutrition
DipHumRelEd... Diploma in Human Relations Education
DipHus......... Diploma in Husbandry (NADA)
DipH-WU ..... Diploma of Heriot-Watt University [*British*] (DI)
DipHyp......... Diploma in Hypnosis
DIPI .... Defective Interfering Particle Induction (DMAA)
DIPI .... Diimidazolinophenylindole [*Biochemistry*]
DIPI .... Direct Intra-Peritoneal Insemination [*Medicine*]
DipIB(Scot)... Diplomate of the Institute of Bankers in Scotland [*British*] (DBQ)
DIPIC .... Drug Information to Patient Care via Television (SAUS)
DipIllumDes... Diploma in Illumination Design
DipIllus........ Diploma in Illustration
DipIM-ArchivAd... Diploma in Information Management - Archives Administration (ADA)
DipIM-Lib .... Diploma in Information Management - Librarianship (ADA)
DipImm........ Diploma in Immunology
Dip Ind Chem... Diploma in Industrial Chemistry [*British*]
DipInfMan.... Diploma in Information Management
DipInfmProcessing... Diploma in Information Processing (ADA)
DipIng.......... Diploma in Engineering [*Canada*] (ASC)
DipIntAffs .... Diploma in International Affairs
DipIntDes .... Diploma of Interior Design (ADA)
DipIntMed.... Diploma in Internal Medicine
DipIPharm ... Diploma in Industrial Pharmacy (ADA)
Dip J............ Diploma in Journalism (SAUS)
DipJ............. Diploma of Journalism (ADA)
DipJ............. Diploma of Jurisprudence
DIPJ............. Distal Interphalangeal Joint [*Anatomy*]
DipJewDes... Diploma of Jewellery Design
DipJour........ Diploma in Journalism (ADA)
DipJourn...... Diploma in Journalism (ADA)
DipJur.......... Diploma in Jurisprudence
DipJuris........ Diploma of Jurisprudence (ADA)
DipKindT...... Diploma in Kindergarten Teaching
dipl .... Diploma (ADWA)
DIPL............. Diploma (EY)
Dipl.............. Diploma (PGP)
dipl .... diplomacy (SAUS)
DipL............. Diploma in Language (NADA)
Dip L .... Diploma in Languages (SAUS)
DipL............. Diploma of Law
dipl .... Diplomat [*or Diplomacy*]
DIPL............. Diplomat Corp. [*NASDAQ symbol*] (SAG)
DIPL............. Diplomatic (ADA)
dipl .... Diplomatic (SHCU)
DIPL............. Diplomatist (WDAA)
DIPL............. Display Initial Program Load (MCD)
DipLA........... Diploma in Landscape Architecture
DipLabAnimSc... Diploma in Laboratory Animal Science
DipLabRel ... Diploma in Labour Relations
DipLabRelations and the Law... Diploma in Labour Relations and the Law
DipLaw .... Diploma in Law
DipL(BAB).... Diploma of Law (Barristers' Admission Board)
Dipl Chem ... Diploma in Chemistry [*British*]

DipLD .... Diploma of Landscape Design (ADA)
DipLDes....... Diploma in Landscape Design
DipLE.......... Diploma in Land Economy
DipLegStud... Diploma in Legal Studies
Dipl Eng ...... Diploma in Engineering [*British*]
DipLib.......... Diploma in Librarianship (ADA)
DipLibSc....... Diploma in Library Science
DipLibSci..... Diploma in Library Science (NADA)
DipLibStud... Diploma in Library Studies (ADA)
DipLibTech... Diploma in Library Technology (SAUS)
DipLing........ Diploma in Linguistics
DipLIS .... Diploma in Library and Information Studies
DipLitLangEd... Diploma in Literacy and Language Education
Dipl Kaufm... Diploma in Commerce [*German*]
Dipl Kfm ...... Diploma in Commerce [*German*]
DipLLIRel .... Diploma in Labor Law and Industrial Relations
Diplm........... Diplomat Corp. [*Associated Press*] (SAG)
Dipl Math .... Diploma in Mathematics [*British*]
diplo .... diploma (SAUS)
diplo .... diplomacy (SAUS)
diplo .... diplomat (SAUS)
diplo .... diplomatic (SAUS)
diplo .... diplomatics (SAUS)
diplo .... diplomatism (SAUS)
diplo .... diplomatist (SAUS)
DipLocGovt... Diploma in Local Government
DipLocGovtAdmin... Diploma in Local Government Administration
DIPLOM .... Diploma (ROG)
Diplomat...... Diplomat Corp. [*Associated Press*] (SAG)
DIPLOMAT... Diplomatic Service [*Communications term*] (DCT)
Dipl PA......... Diploma in Public Administration [*British*]
Dipl Phys..... Diploma in Physics [*British*]
DipLS........... Diploma of Legal Studies
DipL(SAB).... Diploma of Law (Solicitors' Admission Board)
DipLSc......... Diploma in Library Science (ADA)
DIPLW .... Diplomat Corp. Wrrt [*NASDAQ symbol*] (TTSB)
DIPLXR......... Diplexer [*Electronics*]
DipM............ Diploma in Marketing, Institute of Marketing [*British*] (DBQ)
DIPM .... Distorted Independent Particle Model (SAUS)
DipMA .... Diploma in Marine Affairs (SAUS)
DipMan......... Diploma in Management
DipManTech... Diploma in Manufacturing Technology
DipMark....... Diploma in Marketing
DipMatEng... Diploma in Materials Engineering
DipMathsEd... Diploma in Mathematics Education
DipMathStud... Diploma in Mathematical Studies
DipME.......... Diploma in Mechanical Engineering (NADA)
DipMechE .... Diploma of Mechanical Engineering (ADA)
DipMed .... Diploma in Medicine
DipMedAc..... Diploma in Medical Acupuncture
DipMedHyp... Diploma in Medical Hypnosis
DipMedia..... Diploma in Media
DipMedRad... Diploma in Medical Radiography
DipMedSurg... Diploma in Medical Surgery (ADA)
DipMEE........ Diploma in Mechanical and Electrical Engineering
DipMet......... Diploma in Metallurgy
DipMFOS ..... Diploma in Maxial, Facial, and Oral Surgery (ADA)
Dip Mgmnt... Diploma of Management (SAUS)
DipMgmt...... Diploma in Management (NADA)
DipMH .... Diploma in Mental Health
DipMic .... Diploma in Microbiology
DipMicr........ Diploma in Microbiology (SAUS)
DipMicro...... Diploma in Microbiology
Dip Microbiol... Diploma in Microbiology [*British*]
DipMid......... Diploma in Midwifery
DipMigStud... Diploma in Migrant Studies
DipMigTeach... Diploma in Migrant Teaching
DipMilStudies... Diploma in Military Studies
DipMinSc..... Diploma in Mineral Science
DipMJ(Clin)... Diploma in Medical Jurisprudence (Clinical)
DipMLT .... Diploma in Medical Laboratory Technology
DipMRT .... Diploma in Medical Radiation Therapy
DipMS .... Diploma in Museum Studies
DipMT.......... Diploma of Medical Technology (ADA)
DipMus........ Diploma in Music (ADA)
DipMusComp... Diploma in Musical Composition
Dip (Mus Ed) RSAM... Diploma in Musical Education, Royal Scottish Academy of Music and Drama
DipMusEdu... Diploma in Musical Education (NADA)
DipMuseumStud... Diploma in Museum Studies
DIPN .... Diisopropylnaphthalene [*Organic chemistry*]
DipN .... Diploma in Nursing (ODA)
DipNA .... Diploma in Nursing Administration
DipNA & AC... Diploma in Numerical Analysis and Automatic Computing (ADA)
DipNAdmin... Diploma of Nursing Administration (ADA)
DipNatRes ... Diploma in Natural Resources (ADA)
DipNatTh ..... Diploma in Natural Therapies
DipND .... Diploma in Nutrition and Dietetics (ADA)
DipNE .... Diploma in Nursing Education
DipNEd .... Diploma in Nursery School Education (ADA)
DipNEd .... Diploma in Nursing Education
DipNSEdu .... Diploma in Nursery School Education (NADA)
DipNSTC ...... Diploma of the Nursery School Teachers' College [*Australia*]
DipNucEng.... Diploma in Nuclear Engineering (ADA)
DipNucSc..... Diploma in Nuclear Science (ADA)
DipNurs....... Diploma in Nursing
DipNut & Diet... Diploma in Nutrition and Dietetics
DipNutrDiet... Diploma in Nutrition and Dietetics
Dip NZLS..... Diploma of the New Zealand Library Service (SAUS)
DipNZLS ...... Diploma of the New Zealand Library Society (SAUO)
DIPO .... Defense Investigative Program Office (CARL)
Dip O & G .. Diploma in Obstetrics and Gynaecology (ADA)
DipOccHazMan... Diploma in Occupational Hazard Management
DipOccHlth... Diploma in Occupational Health
DipOccHyg... Diploma of Professional Competence in Comprehensive Ocupational Hygiene [*British*] (DBQ)
DipOccMed... Diploma in Occupational Medicine
DipOccThy ... Diploma in Occupational Therapy (ADA)
Dip of N....... Diploma of Nursing (ADA)
DipOHS........ Diploma in Occupational Health and Safety
DIPOL.......... Development of Polar Industries (SAUS)
DipOL .... Diploma in Oriental Learning (ADA)
DIPOL.......... French group for the Development of Polar industries (SAUO)
DIPOLES ...... Defense Intelligence Photoreconnaissance On-Line Exploitation System (MCD)
DipOpArt ...... Diploma in Operatic Art
DipOpsRes... Diploma in Operations Research
DIPORS........ Digital Image Processing Of Remotely Sensed Data (SAUS)
DipOrth .... Diploma in Orthodontics (ADA)
DipOS .... Diploma in Operational Salesmanship [*British*] (DI)
DipOS .... Diploma in Oral Surgery
DIPOS.......... Distributed Processing Operating System (SAUS)
DipOsteo...... Diploma in Osteopathy
DipOT .... Diploma in Occupational Therapy
DipOutEd ..... Diploma in Outdoor Education
DIPP .... Dairy Indemnity Payment Program [*Department of Agriculture*]
DIPP .... Defence Industry Productivity Program [*Canada*]
DIPP .... Defense Industrial Procurement Program [*Canada*]
DIPP .... Defense Intelligence Planning Projection (SAUS)
DIPP .... Defense Intelligence Projection for Planning (MCD)
DIPP .... Diisopentylphthalat (SAUS)
DIPP .... Diisopropyl Percarbonate [*Organic chemistry*]
DIPP .... Dual Inline Pin Package [*Communications term*] (DCT)
DIPPA .... Digital Parallel Processing Array
DipPA .... Diploma in Public Administration (SAUS)
DipPA .... Diploma in Public Affairs (SAUS)
DipPA .... Diploma of Practitioners in Advertising [*British*]
DIP Package... Dual Inline Plastic Package (SAUS)
DipPaed....... Diploma in Paediatrics
DipPall .... Diploma in Palliative Care
DipP&OT...... Diploma in Physical and Occupational Therapy (NADA)
Dip PE .... Diploma in Physical Education [*British*]
DipPerfArt.... Diploma in Performing Arts
DipPersMan... Diploma in Personnel Management
DipPetResEng... Diploma in Petroleum and Reservoir Engineering
DipPH .... Diploma in Poultry Husbandry (SAUS)
DipPH .... Diploma in Public Health
DipPhar .... Diploma in Pharmacology (NADA)
DipPharm .... Diploma in Pharmacy (ADA)
DipPharmMed... Diploma in Pharmaceutical Medicine [*British*] (DBQ)
DipPhilMed... Diploma in Philosophy of Medicine
DipPhot........ Diploma in Photogrammetry (ADA)
DipPhty........ Diploma in Physiotherapy (ADA)
DipPHus ...... Diploma in Poultry Husbandry (ADA)
DipPhysAnth... Diploma in Physical Anthropology
DipPhysEd ... Diploma in Physical Education (ADA)
DipPhysEdu... Diploma in Physical Education (NADA)
DipPhysio .... Diploma of Physiotherapy (ADA)
DipPlPath .... Diploma in Plant Pathology (ADA)
DipPM .... Diploma in Medical Practice Management
DipPM .... Diploma in Professional Management
DipPowEng... Diploma in Power Engineering
DipPPS .... Diploma in Public Policy Studies
DIPPR.......... Design Institute for Physical Property Data [*AIChE*]
DipPrDerm... Diploma in Practical Dermatology
DipPrehistArch... Diploma of Prehistoric Archaeology (ADA)
DipPrimEd .... Diploma in Primary Education
DipPrimT ..... Diploma in Primary Teaching
DipPrivSec... Diploma of the Institute of Private Secretaries [*Australia*]
DipProArtS... Diploma in Professional Art Studies
DipProcessSystemsEng... Diploma in Process Systems Engineering
DipProd .... Diploma in Production
DipPSA .... Diploma in Public and Social Administration
DipPsy .... Diploma in Psychiatry
DipPsy .... Diploma in Psychotherapy
DipPsych ...... Diploma in Psychiatry
Dip Psych .... Diploma in Psychology [*British*]
DipPsychol... Diploma in Psychology
DipPsyMed... Diploma in Psychological Medicine (ADA)
DipPT........... Diploma in Psychotherapy
DipPubAd .... Diploma in Public Administration (ADA)
DipPubAdm... Diploma in Public Administration (NADA)
DipPubAdmin... Diploma in Public Administration (ADA)
DipPubPol ... Diploma in Public Policy
DipQS .... Diploma in Quantity Surveying (ADA)
DIPR .... Defence Institute of Psychological Research (SAUS)
DIPR .... Departmental Industrial Plant Reserve [*DoD*] (AFIT)
DIPR .... Detailed In-Process Review (MCD)
DIPR .... Device Interface Processor (TIMI)
DIPR .... Direct Interaction with Product Repulsion [*Chemical kinetics*]

DIPRA......... Ductile Iron Pipe Research Association (EA)
DipRADA...... Diploma of Royal Academy of Dramatic Art [*British*] (EY)
Dip RADA.... Diploma of the Royal Academy of Dramatic Art (SAUS)
DipRadDiagnostic... Diploma in Diagnostic Radiography
DipRadEng... Diploma in Radio Engineering
DipRadTVProd... Diploma in Radio and Television Production
DipRAM....... Diploma of the Royal Academy of Music [*British*] (DBQ)
DIP RAM...... Dual-in-Line Package Random-Access Memory (SAUS)
DIPRC......... Drug Information and Pharmacy Resource Center (SAUS)
DipRCM........ Diploma of the Royal College of Music [*British*] (DBQ)
DipRE......... Diploma in Religious Education
DipRectMan... Diploma in Recreation Management
DipREd........ Diploma of Religious Education
DipRehabStud... Diploma in Rehabilitation Studies
DipRelStud... Diploma in Religious Studies
DipREM...... Diploma in Rural Estate Management (ODA)
DipRemEd... Diploma of Remedial Education
DIPRES........ Direct press spheroidized (SAUS)
DipResGeol... Diploma in Resource Geology
DipRMS........ Diploma of the Royal Microscopical Society [*British*] (DBQ)
DIPROG....... Request Diagnosis, Prognosis, Present Condition [*Army*] (AABC)
Dip RSAM.... Diploma from the Royal Scottish Academy of Music (WDAA)
Dip RSAM.... Diploma of the Royal Scottish Academy of Music (SAUS)
diprt............ discharge printed (SAUS)
DipRTA......... Diploma in Radio and Television Arts (CPGU)
DipRTC........ Diploma of the Royal Technical College (SAUS)
DipRTP........ Diploma in Regional and Town Planning (ADA)
DipRurAcc... Diploma in Rural Accounting (ADA)
DIPS............ Defection, Intercept-Passive Submarine (MCD)
DIPS............ Defense Instantanee Position Strategique (SAUS)
DIPS............ Defense Intelligence Production Schedule (MCD)
DIPS............ Denden Information Processing Service (SAUS)
DIPS............ Dendenkosha Information Processing System (SAUS)
DIPS............ Department of Interior Payroll System (SAUO)
DIPS............ Development Information Processing System
DIPS............ Diagnostic Inventory of Personality and Symptoms [*Personality development test*] [*Psychology*]
DIPS............ Dietary Information Processing System (SAA)
DIPS............ Digital Image Processing System of DMAHTC (SAUS)
DIPS............ Digital Imagery Processing System (MCD)
DIPS............ Digital Information Processing System (SAUS)
DIPS............ Digital Photogrammetric Station (SAUS)
DIPS............ Digital Program Selection (IAA)
dips............ dipeptides (SAUS)
dips............ diphtheria patients (SAUS)
dips............ diphthongs (SAUS)
DIPS............ Dipix Image Processing System (SAUS)
dips............ diplexes (SAUS)
dips............ diplomats (SAUS)
dips............ dipsomaniacs (SAUS)
DIPS............ Display Image Processing System (SAUS)
DIPS............ Display Information Processor System (SAUS)
DIPS............ Dual Impact Prediction System [*Aerospace*] (IAA)
DIPS............ Dual-Inline Packages (SAUS)
DIPs............ Dynamic Inclined Planes (SAUS)
DIPS............ Dynamic Isotope Power System
DIPSA......... Democratic Initiative of Portuguese in South Africa (SAUS)
DipS & PA... Diploma in Social and Public Administration (ADA)
DipScAg...... Diploma in Science in Agriculture (ADA)
DIPSCAM..... Diploma Scam [*FBI investigation of mail-order colleges*]
DipSchoolAdmin... Diploma in School Administration
DipSecEd..... Diploma in Secondary Education (ADA)
DipSecStud... Diploma in Secretarial Studies
Dipsey......... Deep-Sea Lead (SAUS)
DipSKTC...... Diploma of the Sydney Kindergarten Teachers' College [*Australia*]
DipSM......... Diploma in Sports Medicine
Dip SMS...... Diploma in School Management Studies (SAUS)
Dipso.......... Dipsomania (SAUS)
dipso.......... drunkard (SAUS)
DipSObC...... Diploma in Shared Obstetric Care
DipSoc......... Diploma in Sociology (ADA)
Dip Soc Ad... Diploma in Social Administration [*British*]
DipSocAdmin... Diploma of Social Administration (ADA)
DipSocCommun... Diploma in Social Communication
DipSociol..... Diploma in Sociology
Dip Soc Med... Diploma in Social Medicine [*British*]
DipSocSc..... Diploma in Social Science
DipSocSci.... Diploma of Social Science (ADA)
DipSocStud... Diploma in Social Studies (ADA)
Dip Soc Studies... Diploma in Social Studies [*British*]
DipSocWk.... Diploma of Social Work
DipSoilSc.... Diploma in Soil Science
DipSP......... Diploma in Sound Preservation
DipSpecEd... Diploma in Special Education
DipSpecSubjTeach... Diploma of Special Subject Teaching
Dip Sp Ed.... Diploma in Special Education (SAUS)
DipSpEd....... Diploma of Special Education
DipSpSc....... Diploma in Sport Science
DipSpSci...... Diploma in Sports Science
DipSpThy..... Diploma in Speech Therapy (ADA)
DIPSS.......... Department of Integrated Personnel Service System (COE)
DipSS.......... Diploma in Social Studies (ADA)
DipStats...... Diploma in Statistics
DipStructEng... Diploma in Structural Engineering
DipStructFoundEng... Diploma in Structural and Foundation Engineering
DipSurvSc.... Diploma in Surveying Science (ADA)
DipSW......... Diploma in Social Work (ADA)
DIP switch... Dual In-Line Package Switch [*Electronics*] (DOM)
DIPT............ Diisopropyl Tartrate [*Organic chemistry*]
DipT............ Diploma in Teaching (ADA)
DIPT............ Diplomate
DIPT............ Direct Intraperitoneal Insemination [*Medicine*] (ADWA)
Dip T.......... Teachers Diploma (SAUS)
DIPTA......... Defense Intelligence Project for Threat Analysis (SAUO)
DIPTAC........ DIFAR [*Directional Frequency Analyzing and Recording*] Pointing Tactic [*Military*] (CAAL)
Dip T & CP... Diploma in Town and Country Planning (SAUS)
DipT & CP... Diploma of Town and Country Planning (ADA)
DipTaxLaw... Diploma in Tax Law
DipTCD........ Diploma in Tuberculosis and Chest Diseases
DipTchg........ Diploma of Teaching
DipTChM...... Diploma in Traditional Chinese Medicine
DipTchrLib... Diploma in Teacher Librarianship (ADA)
DipTCP........ Diploma in Town and Country Planning (ADA)
DIPTe.......... Diisopropyl Telluride (SAUS)
DipTE.......... Diploma in Transportation Engineering [*British*] (DBQ)
DipTeach..... Diploma in Teaching
DipTeach(ECE)... Diploma in Teaching (Early Childhood Education)
DipTeachLib... Diploma in Teacher Librarianship
DipTeach(Nursing)... Diploma in Teaching (Nursing)
DipTeach(Primary)... Diploma in Teaching (Primary)
DipTeach(Tert)... Diploma of Teaching (Tertiary)
DipTec......... Diploma in Technology (NADA)
Dip Tech...... Diploma in Technology [*British*]
DipTech(Arch)... Diploma in Technology (Architecture) (ADA)
DipTech(Buil)... Diploma in Technology (Building) (ADA)
DipTechBusAdmin... Diploma in Technical Business Administration
DipTech(Comm)... Diploma in Technology (Commerce) (ADA)
Dip Tech (Eng)... Diploma of Technology (Engineering) [*British*]
DipTech(InfProc)... Diploma in Technology (Information Processing) (ADA)
DipTech(Mgt)... Diploma in Technology (Management) (ADA)
DipTech(PubAdm)... Diploma in Technology (Public Administration) (ADA)
DipTech(PubRel)... Diploma in Technology (Public Relations) (ADA)
DipTech(Sci)... Diploma in Technology (Science) (ADA)
DipTechT..... Diploma in Technical Teaching
Dip TEFL..... Diploma in Teaching English as a Foreign Language (SAUS)
DipTEFL....... Diploma in Teaching of English as a Foreign Language (ADA)
DipTelecomm... Diploma in Telecommunications
DipTEM........ Diploma in Teaching English to the Migrant (ADA)
DipTertEd.... Diploma in Tertiary Education
DipTertiary Ed... Diploma in Tertiary Education (ADA)
DipTertStud... Diploma in Tertiary Studies
DipTESL........ Diploma of Teaching English as a Second Language (ADA)
DipTexInd.... Diploma of Textile Industry
DipTG.......... Diploma of the Teachers Guild (ADA)
DipTh.......... Diploma in Theology (ADA)
DipThe......... Diploma in Theology (NADA)
Dip Theol..... Diploma of Theology (ADA)
DipTLiB........ Diploma in Teachers Librarianship (ADA)
DipTM.......... Diploma in Training Management, the Institute of Training and Development [*British*] (DBQ)
DipTP........... Diploma in Town Planning [*British*]
DipTP........... Diploma of Teacher of Physiotherapy
DipTPT......... Diploma in Theory and Practice of Teaching [*British*]
DipTropAgron... Diploma in Tropical Agronomy (ADA)
DipTRP........ Diploma in Town and Regional Planning (ADA)
DipUEMan... Diploma in Urban Estate Management
DipUrbDes(Arch)... Diploma in Urban Design
DipUrbRegSt... Diploma in Urban and Regional Studies
DipUrbSoc... Diploma in Urban Sociology
DipUrbStud... Diploma in Urban Studies
DipUSP........ Diploma in Urban and Social Planning
DipVA.......... Diploma of Visual Arts
Dip Ven....... Diploma in Venereology [*British*]
DipVetAn..... Diploma in Veterinary Anaesthesia
DipVetClinStud... Diploma in Veterinary Clinical Studies
DipVetPath... Diploma in Veterinary Pathology (ADA)
DipVetRad... Diploma in Veterinary Radiology
DipVFM........ Diploma in Valuation and Farm Management (ADA)
DipVisArt..... Diploma in Visual Arts
DipWCF....... Diploma of the Worshipful Company of Farriers [*British*] (DI)
DipWildlifeMed & Hus... Diploma in Wildlife Medicine and Husbandry
DipWomSt... Diploma in Women's Studies
DIPX........... Diplex [*Electronics*] (MSA)
DIPY........... Dipyridyl [*Also, DIP*] [*Organic chemistry*]
DIQ............. Deviation Intelligence Quotient [*Education*]
dIQ............. deviation IQ (SAUS)
DIQ............. Due-In Quantity
DIQ............. Las Vegas, NV [*Location identifier*] [*FAA*] (FAAL)
DIQAP......... Defence Industries Quality Assurance Panel (SAUO)
DIQD........... Disk-Insulated Quad [*Telecommunications*] (TEL)
DIR............. Daiwa Institute of Research Ltd. [*Database producer*] (IID)
DIR............. Darlington International Raceway [*Auto racing*]
DIR............. Data Input Rate (SAUS)
DIR............. Data Input Register [*Computer science*]
DIR............. Data Item Requirement
DIR............. Daytime Infrared (SAUS)
DIR............. Deep Inguinal Ring [*Medicine*] (MELL)
DIR............. Defect Introduction Rate
DIR............. Defense Industrial Research (SAUS)

DIR .... Defense Industrial Reserve [*DoD*]
DIR .... Defense Intelligence Report (MCD)
DIR .... Delayed Impulse Response [*Psychology*] (DHP)
DIR .... Delivered in Room [*Obstetrics*] (CPH)
DIR .... Delivery and Installation Request (SAUS)
DIR .... Departmentally-Initiated Review
DIR .... Department of Industrial Relations (SAUO)
DIR .... Department of Information Resources (SAUS)
DIR .... Depot Inspection and Repair
DIR .... Design Information Release
DIR .... Desired Impulse Response (SAUS)
DIR .... Detailed Inspection Report (SAUS)
DIR .... Development-Inhibitor-Releasing [*Photography*]
DIR .... diagnose Responder (SAUS)
DIR .... Diamond Ranch [*California*] [*Seismograph station code, US Geological Survey*] (SEIS)
DIR .... Dielectric Information Reading (SAUS)
DIR .... Diffusion-Induced Recrystallization (SAUS)
DIR .... Digital Instrumentation RADAR
dir .... Direct (QSUL)
DIR .... Direct
DIR .... Directed (SAUS)
DIR .... Directed Investigation Report (ACAE)
DIR .... Direct Information Reading (SAUS)
DIR .... Direct Information Recording (SAUS)
dir .... Direction (ADWA)
Dir .... Direction (DIAR)
dir .... Directional (SAUS)
dir .... Directione [*Directions*] [*Latin*] (DAVI)
DIR .... Directive
DIR .... Directly Interpretable Representation (SAUS)
DIR .... Director [*or Directorate*] (AFM)
Dir .... Director (PHSD)
dir .... Director (DD)
Dir .... Directorate (SAUO)
DI(R) .... Directorate of Intelligence (Research) [*RAF*] [*British*]
DIR .... Directory
DIR .... Dire Dawa [*Ethiopia*] [*Airport symbol*] (OAG)
DIR .... Dirgantara Air Service PT [*Indonesia*] [*ICAO designator*] (FAAC)
DIR .... Dirigo [*I Guide*] [*Latin*] (ROG)
DIR .... Disassembly Inspection Report
DIR .... Discipline Oriented Information Retrieval (NITA)
dir .... discrimination (SAUS)
DIR .... Dispersive Infrared [*Automotive engineering*]
DIR .... Diurnal Insulin Resistance [*Medicine*] (MELL)
dir .... divergence (SAUS)
DIR .... Division of Intramural Research (SAUS)
DIR .... Doctrine of Incremental Reduction
DIR .... Document Information Record (KSC)
DIR .... Document Information Retrieval (NITA)
DIR .... Donald, Luf & Jen-DLJdirect [*NYSE symbol*] (SG)
DIR .... Double Isomorphous Replacement [*Medicine*] (DMAA)
DIR .... Dynamic Inducer Rotor (MCD)
DIRAC .... Database for Reliability Calculations (SAUO)
DIRAC .... Direct Access [*Computer science*] (MHDB)
DIRAC .... Direct Access Project (SAUS)
DIRAFIED ..... Director, Armed Forces Information and Education Division (DNAB)
DIRAM .... Digital Range Machine
DIRARFCOS... Director, Armed Forces Courier Service (DNAB)
DIRB .... Diffuse Isotropic Infrared Background [*Galactic spectrum*]
DIRB .... Dissimilar Iron Reducing Bacteria (ABAC)
DIRBE .... Diffuse Infrared Background Experiment [*Spectral instrumentation*]
DIRBY .... When Directed By
DIRC .... Defense Intelligence Relay Center (MCD)
DIRC .... Defense Investigative Review Council
DIRC .... Detection of Internally Reflected Cerenkov Light (SAUS)
DIRC .... Digital Inter Relay Communication (SAUS)
DIRC .... Disability Information & Referral Centre Eastern Sydney (SAUO)
DIRC .... Disability Information & Resource Centre South Australia (SAUO)
DIRC .... Dithered Infrared Configuration
DIRC .... Drug Information Research Center [*Medicine*] (EDAA)
DIRCARIBDOCKS... Caribbean Division Naval Facilities Engineering Command
DIRCHESDOCKS... Chesapeake Division Naval Facilities Engineering Command
DIRCM .... Directional Infrared Countermeasures (SEWL)
DIRCOL .... Direction Cosine Linkage
dir conn .... direct-connect (SAUS)
DIR Conn ..... Direct Connected (SAUS)
DIRCONN ..... Direct-Connected [*Mechanical engineering*] (IAA)
DIRCONN ..... Direct Connection (SAUS)
DIRCORAP .... Directionally Controlled Rocket-Assisted Projectile (SAUS)
DIRCOUP ..... Directional Coupler (IAA)
DIRCSA .... Disability Information & Resource Centre South Australia (SAUS)
DIRCTN .... Direction
DIRCTNL ...... Directional
DIRCTRT ...... Directorate
DIRCTRY ...... Directory
dircty .... directly (SAUS)
Dir Cut .... Director's Cut
DIRD .... Data and Information Resource Directory [*Navy*] (GFGA)
DIRD .... Director, International Research and Development [*Military*] [*Canada*]
DIRD .... Drug-Induced Renal Disease [*Medicine*] (DMAA)
DIRDET .... When Directed, Detach Duty Indicated
DIRE .... Dire Is Really Emacs (SAUS)
DIRE .... Divertor in Torus Experiment (SAUS)
D Ir E .... Doctor of Irrigation Engineering
DIREC .... Digital Rate Error Computer (SAUS)
DIREC .... Direct Instant Response Electronic Composition
DIREC .... Director (ROG)
DIRECT .... Digital Rectifier (SAUS)
DIRECT .... Directory (SAUS)
DIR/ECT .... Directory Project [*Bell Laboratories*]
DIRECT .... Driver Information Experimenting with Communication Technology [*FHWA*] (TAG)
Direct Midrex... Direct from Midrex (journ.) (SAUS)
Directrt .... Directorate (DIAR)
D Ir Eng .... Doctor of Irrigation Engineering
DIRENT .... Direct Entry (SAUS)
DIREP .... Difficulty Report (AFIT)
DIREURDOCKS... European Division Naval Facilities Engineering Command
DIRF .... Delinquent Investigation Research File [*IRS*]
DIRFLDSUPPACT... Director, Field Support Activity
DIR FLT .... Directional Filter (SAUS)
DIRFM .... Director Field Maintenance [*Army*] (AABC)
Dir Gen .... Director General (SAUS)
DIR-GEN ...... Director-General (WDAA)
Dir-Genl .... Director-General (SAUS)
DIRGULFDOCKS... Gulf Division Naval Facilities Engineering Command
DIRH .... Dirham [*Monetary unit*] [*Iraq*]
DIRID .... Directional Infrared Intrusion Detector (MCD)
DIR/INTC .... Direct Intercept (GAVI)
DIRJOAP ...... Director, Joint Oil Analysis Program [*Military*] (DNAB)
DIRJOAPTSC... Director, Joint Oil Analysis Program Technical Support Center [*Military*] (DNAB)
DIRK .... Dosemeter Issue and Record Keeping
DIRK .... Dual Independent Ranging Kit (ACAE)
Dirk .... Everett McKinley Dirksen (SAUS)
Dirl .... Dirleton's Decisions, Court of Sessions [*Scotland*] [*A publication*] (DLA)
Dir L&R .... Director of Light Railways and Roads (SAUO)
DIRLANTDOCKS... Director, Atlantic Division, Bureau of Yards and Docks [*Obsolete*]
Dirlar .... Director of Light Railways and Roads (SAUO)
DIRLAUTH ... Direct Liaison Authorized [*Military*] (NVT)
Dirl D .... Dirleton's Doubts and Questions in the Law [*A publication*] (DLA)
Dirl Dec .... Dirleton's Decisions, Court of Sessions [*Scotland*] [*A publication*] (DLA)
DIRLINE .... Directory of Information Sources Online [*National Library of Medicine*] [*Database*]
DirLog .... Director of Logistics (SAUS)
Dir Log Plans Div... Director, Logistics Planning Division (SAUO)
DirLt .... Direction Light [*Navigation*]
DIRM .... Data Item Responsibility Matrix (SAUS)
DIRM .... Defense Intelligence Requirement Manual (AFM)
DIRM .... Directorate for Information and Resource Management (COE)
DIRM .... Director, Information Resource Management (SAUO)
dir max .... directional maximum (SAUS)
DIRMIDWESTDOCKS... Midwest Division Naval Facilities Engineering Command
dir min .... directional minimum (SAUS)
DIRMOBFOR... Director of Mobility Forces (SAUS)
DIRNAVCOM... Director of Naval Communications (SAUS)
DIRNAVCURSERV... Director, Naval Courier Service (DNAB)
DIRNAVHIS... Director of Naval History (DNAB)
DIRNAVHIST... Director of Naval History
DIRNAVINSERV... Director, Naval Investigative Service (DNAB)
DIRNAVINVSERV... Director, Naval Investigative Service (SAUO)
DIRNAVMARCORMARS... Director, Navy-Marine Corps Military Affiliate Radio Service (DNAB)
DIRNAVPUBPRINTSERV... Director, Navy Publication and Printing Service
DIRNAVRESINTPRO... Director, Naval Reserve Intelligence Program (DNAB)
DIRNAVSCOL... Director, Naval School (SAUO)
DIRNAVSECGRUEUR... Director, Naval Security Group, Europe (DNAB)
DIRNAVSECGRULANT... Director, Naval Security Group, Atlantic (DNAB)
DIRNAVSECGRUPAC... Director, Naval Security Group, Pacific (DNAB)
DIRNCPB ...... Director, Naval Council of Personnel Boards (DNAB)
DIRNCPBDET... Director, Naval Council of Personnel Boards Detachment (DNAB)
DIRNRL .... Director, Naval Research Laboratory (SAA)
DIRNSA .... Director, National Security Agency [*Pronounced "dern-za"*]
DIRNSA/CHCSS... Director National Security Agency / Chief Central Security Service
DIRNSCPO ... Director, Navy Secretariat Civilian Personnel Office (DNAB)
DIRO .... Deionization Reverse Osmosis [*Water treatment*]
DIRO .... Director, Industrial Relations Office (SAUO)
DIRO .... District Industrial Relations Officer [*Navy*]
DIROCD .... Director, Office of Civil Defense (AABC)
Dir of Engrg... Director of Engineering (SAUS)
Dir of R&D... Director of Research & Development (SAUS)
DIRON .... Direction
DIR OP .... Directie Overheids-Personeelsbeleid [*Netherlands*]
DIROR .... Director (ROG)
DIRP .... Defense Industrial Research Program (SAUS)
DIRPA .... Director of Personnel and Administration [*Army*] (AABC)
DIRPACALDOCKS... Director, Pacific and Alaskan Divisions, Bureau of Yards and Docks [*Obsolete*]
DIRPACDOCKS... Director, Pacific Division, Bureau of Yards and Docks [*Obsolete*]
DIRPOSTALS... Director of Postal Services (SAUO)
Dir Pref .... Direction Preferred (SAUS)
DIRPRO .... When Directed Proceed
DIR Program... Defence Industrial Research Program (SAUS)
DIR PROP .... Directione Propria [*With Proper Direction*] [*Pharmacy*]
DIRR .... Documentation Internationale de Recherche RoutiSre (SAUS)

DIRS .... Damage Information Recording System (ACAE)
DIRS .... Damage Information Reporting System [*Military*] (MCD)
DIRS .... Data Information Requirements System [*Military*]
DIRS .... Departmental Industrial Reserve System
DIRS .... Dialog-Information-Retrieval-System (SAUS)
DIRS .... Digital Image Rectification System (MCD)
DIRS .... DIM Data Input Information Retrieval System (SAUS)
DIRS .... DIMDI Information Retrieval System (NITA)
DIRS .... Directors (SAUS)
DIRS .... Division Integrated Record System (SAA)
DIRSDIMA ... Director, San Diego [*California*] Intermediate Maintenance Activity [*Military*] (DNAB)
DIRSO .... Defense Industrial Resources Support Office (ACAE)
DIRSOEASTDOCKS... Southeast Division Naval Facilities Engineering Command
DIRSOWESTDOCKS... Southwest Division Naval Facilities Engineering Command
DIRSP/PROJMGRFBM... Director, Special Projects/Project Manager, Fleet Ballistic Missile (MCD)
DIRSSP .... Director of Strategic Systems Project (SAUO)
DIRSSP .... Director, Strategic Systems Project Office [*Navy*]
DirSWDUSCONARC... Director of Special Weapons Division, United States Continental Army Command (SAUO)
DIRT .... Data in Real Time
DIRT .... Defense Infrared Test (MCD)
DIRT .... Department of Industrial Relations and Technology (SAUS)
DIRT .... Deposit Interest Retention Tax [*Ireland*]
DIRT .... Design In Real Time (SAUS)
DIRT .... Director's Instant Reversible Talkback [*Device enabling contact between director in control room and crew in studio*]
DIRT .... Drivers' Independent Race Tracks [*An association*]
DIRT .... Dust Infrared Test (MCD)
Dirte .... Directorate (TBD)
DIRTFT .... Do It Right the First Time (TIMI)
DIRTMAP ..... Dust Indicators and Records from Terrestrial and Marine Paleoenvironments (SAUS)
DIRTY .... Darned Insulting, Rotten, Terrible Yarns [*Book title*]
DIRUS .... Directory of Information Resources in the United States (SAUS)
DIRVIR .... Directory Verification Processor [*Computer science*]
DIRW .... Director of Women Marines
DIRWESTDOCKS... Western Division Naval Facilities Engineering Command
DIRWSEG .... Director, Weapons Systems Evaluation Group (CINC)
DIRZ .... Diamond Shamrock Refinery [*Federal Railroad Administration identification code*]
DIS .... Daily Issue Store [*British military*] (DMA)
DIS .... Dairy Industry School (SAUO)
DIS .... Dairy Industry Society (SAUO)
DIS .... Danish International Shipping Register (SAUS)
DIS .... Database Information Services (NITA)
DIS .... Database Information System
DIS .... Data Initialization Statement (SAUS)
DIS .... Data Input Station (SAUS)
DIS .... Data Input Supervisor [*Computer science*] (IAA)
DIS .... Data Input System [*Computer science*]
DIS .... Data Inspection Station
DIS .... Data Interface System (SAUS)
DIS .... Data Interpretation System (BTTJ)
DIS .... Days in Shop (ACAE)
DIS .... Daytona International Corporation (SAUS)
DIS .... Daytona International Speedway [*Auto racing*]
DIS .... Decision Information Services Ltd. [*Information service or system*] (IID)
DIS .... Decreasing Index Sequence (SAUS)
DIS .... Dedicated Information System (SAUS)
DIS .... Deep Inelastic Scattering [*Particle physics*]
DIS .... Defence Intelligence Staff [*British*]
DIS .... Defense Information System (SAUO)
DIS .... Defense Institute of Security Assistance Management, Wright-Patterson AFB, OH [*OCLC symbol*] (OCLC)
DIS .... Defense Intelligence School
DIS .... Defense Intelligence Service (ACAE)
DIS .... Defense Intelligence Staff (MCD)
DIS .... Defense Intelligence Summary (MCD)
DIS .... Defense Investigative Service [*DoD*]
dis .... delivered into store (SAUS)
DIS .... Department of Defense Index of Specifications and Standards
DIS .... Department of Industrial Services (SAUS)
DIS .... Department of Intelligence and Security (SAUS)
DIS .... Department of Internal Security
DIS .... Design Improvement Study
DIS .... Design Integration Sheet (MCD)
DIS .... Design Integration Subsystem
DIS .... Development Information System [*United Nations*] [*Information service or system*] (IID)
DIS .... Diagnostic Interview Schedule [*Psychology*]
DIS .... Dialectic Information System (PDAA)
DIS .... DIALOG Information Services (SAUS)
DIS .... Dialog Terminal System (IAA)
DIS .... Digalactosyl Diglycerideafta [*Organic chemistry*]
DIS .... Digital Identification Signal [*Computer science*]
DIS .... Digital Image Stabilizer (SAUS)
DIS .... Digital Image System (SAUS)
DIS .... Digital Imaging Spectrophotometer [*or Spectroscopy*]
DIS .... Digital Imaging System (SAUS)
DIS .... Digital Instrumentation Subsystem
DIS .... Digital Instrumentation System (SAUS)
DIS .... Digital Instrument System (SAUS)
DIS .... Digital Integration System (IEEE)
DIS .... Digital Interface Subsystem (SAUS)
DIS .... Digitized Imaging System (SAUS)
DIS .... Diploma in Industrial Studies, Loughborough University of Technology [*British*] (DBQ)
DIS .... Direct Ignition System [*Automotive engineering*]
DIS .... Direct Information Service (SAUS)
DIS .... Directorate of Installation Services (MCD)
DI(S) .... Directorate of Intelligence (Security) [*RAF*] [*British*]
DIS .... Directory Information Service [*A publication*]
dis .... Disability (MELL)
DIS .... Disability
DIS .... Disabled (ECII)
DIS .... Disabled-in-Service (SAUO)
DIS .... Disagree (NASA)
dis .... Discharge (GEAB)
DIS .... Discharge
Dis .... Discharge (MIST)
DIS .... Disciple
DIS .... Discipline
dis .... disclosure (SAUS)
DIS .... Disconnect (DEN)
Dis .... Disconnection (SAUS)
DIS .... Discontinued
dis .... Discontinuity [*Geology*] (BARN)
dis .... Discount (WDAA)
DIS .... Discount
DIS .... Discrete (AAG)
DIS .... Discutient [*Dissolving*] [*Pharmacy*] (ROG)
dis .... Disease (MELL)
DIS .... Disease
DIS .... Disease Intervention Specialist [*Medicine*]
dis .... Disintegration (ABAC)
DIS .... Disintegration
dis .... Dislocation (DAVI)
DIS .... Disney Channel (ADWA)
DIS .... [*The*] Disney [*Walt*] Co. [*Wall Street slang name: "Mickey Mouse"*] [*NYSE symbol*] (SPSG)
Dis .... Disney's Ohio Superior Court Reports [*A publication*] (DLA)
DIS .... Disorderly [*FBI standardized term*]
DIS .... Dispatch (SAUS)
dis .... dispensary (SAUS)
DIS .... Dispensed (ADA)
DIS .... Dispensing (SAUS)
DIS .... Display (KSC)
DIS .... Displaying [*Motor vehicle violation code used in state of Maryland*] (MVRD)
DIS .... Disposition System (SAUS)
DIS .... Disqualified [*Motor vehicle violation status code used in state of Arkansas*] (MVRD)
dis .... disrespect (SAUS)
DIS .... Disrotatory [*Chemistry*]
dis .... Dissaying [*Slang*] (WDMC)
DIS .... Disseminated Intravascular Coagulation [*Medicine*] (BARN)
Dis .... Dissent [*A publication*] (BRI)
DIS .... Dissertation Inquiry Service [*Xerox Corp.*]
DIS .... Dissolve [*Optical technique*] [*Filmmaking*] (WDMC)
Dis .... Dissolved
dis .... distal (SAUS)
DIS .... Distance (MUGU)
DIS .... Distanced [*Horse racing*]
dis .... Distant (ADWA)
DIS .... Distant
Dis .... Distinctio [*Decretum Gratiani*] [*A publication*] (DSA)
DIS .... Distribute (ROG)
DIS .... Distributed Information System [*Computer science*]
DIS .... Distributed Instructional System [*Military*]
DIS .... Distributed Intelligence System (SAUS)
DIS .... Distributed Interactive Simulation [*Army*] (RDA)
DIS .... Distributed Interface Simulation (SEWL)
dis .... distribution (SAUS)
DIS .... Distribution Advisory Service (SAUS)
DIS .... Distribution Information System
DIS .... Distributor Gasket [*Automotive engineering*]
DIS .... Distributorless Ignition System [*Automotive engineering*]
DIS .... District
DIS .... Divisional Information System (SAUS)
DIS .... Division of Information Services [*Council for Scientific and Industrial Research*] [*South Africa*] (IID)
DIS .... Division of Information Services [*Council of State Governments*] [*Information service or system*] (IID)
DIS .... Documentary Information System (FOTI)
DIS .... Documentation Index System (MCD)
DIS .... Documentation Inventory System (SAUS)
DIS .... Document Inquiry and Storage (SAUS)
DIS .... Document Inquiry System (SAUS)
DIS .... DoD Investigative Service (SAUO)
DIS .... Doppler Imaging System [*Physics*]
DIS .... Doppler Inertial System (AAG)
DIS .... Double Index Selection (SAUS)
DIS .... Douglas Inspection Standard (SAA)
DIS .... Dow Industrial Service (SAUS)
DIS .... Draft International Standard [*International Standards Organization*]
DIS .... Drilling Information Services [*Adams Engineering, Inc.*] [*Information service or system*] (IID)

DIS .... Drosophila Information Service [*Genetics*]
DIS .... Drug Information Service [*Memorial Medical Center of Long Beach*] [*Information service or system*] (IID)
DIS .... Drug Information Services [*University of Minnesota, Minneapolis*] (IID)
DIS .... Drug Information Sources (SAUS)
DIS .... Drug Instruction Service (SAUS)
DIS .... Druse-Immunoserum (SAUS)
DIS .... Dual Image System
DIS .... Ductile Iron Society (EA)
DIS .... Dwarf Iris Society (SAUO)
DIS .... Dynamic Impedance Stabilization (VLIE)
DIS .... Dynamic Impedance Standard (SAUS)
DIS .... Dynamic Independance Stabilization (SAUS)
DIS .... Dynamic Information Systems (SAUS)
DIS .... General District Court [*Court type found in state of Virginia*] (MVRD)
DIS .... Loubomo [*Congo*] [*Airport symbol*] (OAG)
DIS .... Walt Disney Productions (SAUO)
DIS 9041 .... draft international standard for VTP (SAUS)
DISA .... Dairy Industries Supply Association [*Later, DFISA*]
DISA .... Dansk Industri Syndikat A/S [*Danish manufacturer of a machine gun mount being tested by US Army*] (RDA)
DISA .... Data Interchange Standards Association, Inc (SAUO)
DISA .... Defense Information Services Activity (USGC)
DISA .... Defense Information Services Agency (DOMA)
DISA .... Defense Information Systems Agency [*Formerly, DSA*] [*DoD*]
DISA .... Defense Institute of Security Assistance (MCD)
DISA .... Deployable Information Systems Architecture (SAUS)
DISA .... Digital Intravenous Subtraction Angiography [*Medicine*] (MELL)
DISA .... Direct Inward System Access (HGAA)
DISA .... Directorate of Intelligence and Security of Angola (SAUS)
DisA .... Dissertation Abstracts (journ.) (SAUS)
DISA .... Division of International Security Affairs [*Energy Research and Development Administration*]
DISA .... Division of Security Affairs [*ERDA*] (AAGC)
DISA .... Dwarf Iris Society of America (EA)
DISAB .... Disability (ADA)
disab .... Disability (ADWA)
disab .... disable (SAUS)
disab .... disabled (SAUS)
DISAB .... DoD [*Department of Defense*] Information Security Advisory Board
disabl .... Disability (SAUS)
DISABLD .... Disabled (FAAC)
DISAC .... Digital Simulator and Computer (IEEE)
DISACET .... Dissolution of Acetaminophen [*Clinical chemistry*]
DISAE .... Development of Implementation Strategies for Approximation in Environment (SAUO)
DISAF .... Delinquency Item Summary and Forecast (MCD)
DISAIS .... DISA Information System (SAUS)
DI/SAL .... Vessels Disposed of by Sale through Navy Material Redistribution Agency [*Navy*]
DISALLCE .... Disallowance [*Legal*] [*British*] (ROG)
DISALLD .... Disallowed [*Legal*] [*British*] (ROG)
DISAM .... Defense Institute of Security Assistance Management [*Air Force*]
DISAM .... Direct and Index Sequential Access Method (SAUS)
DISAM .... Direct and index sequential access system (SAUS)
DISAM .... Direct Indexed Sequential Access Method (SAUS)
DISAM .... Direct Indexed-Sequential Access Method (VLIE)
DISANET .... DISA Information Network (SAUS)
DISAO .... Designated Independent Senior Acquisition Official (AAGC)
Disap .... Disappointment (SAUS)
DISAP .... Disapprove (AABC)
DISAPG .... Disappearing
DISAPPD .... Disapproved (SAUS)
Disappr .... Disapproved In [*or Disapproving*] [*Legal term*] (DLA)
disarm .... Disarmament (SAUS)
DISAS .... disassemble (SAUS)
disas .... disaster (SAUS)
DISASM .... Disassemble (VLIE)
disassem .... disassemble (SAUS)
DISASSM .... Disassemble
DISASSY .... Disassembly (KSC)
DISB .... Disburse (AABC)
disb .... disbursement (SAUS)
DISBL .... Disable (VLIE)
DISBMT .... Disbursement (AFM)
DISBN .... Disband (SAUS)
DISBN .... Distribution (DCTA)
DISBO .... Disbursing Officer [*Military*] (DNAB)
DISBOFF .... Disbursing Officer
DISBOFFCOP .... Disbursing Officer Making Payment on These Orders Forward Copy [*Military*] (DNAB)
disbon .... dishonest (SAUS)
disbon .... dishonesty (SAUS)
disbon .... dishonorable (SAUS)
disbon .... dishonorably (SAUS)
Disbs .... Disbursements (EBF)
DISBS .... Disbursements [*Business term*]
DISBSUBREPT .... Disbursing Officer Making Payment Submit Monthly Letter Reports [*Military*] (DNAB)
disbt .... disbursement (SAUS)
DISBX .... Disable Receive (SAUS)
DISC .... Daily Intelligence Summary Cable (MCD)
DISC .... Dakota Information Service to the Community (IID)
DISC .... Data Index for Software Configuration (MCD)
DISC .... Data Index for Software Control (MCD)
DISC .... Data, Information, and System Control
DISC .... Data Information System for Management Control [*Military*]
DISC .... Data Input Sample Control (SAUS)
DISC .... Data Processing and Information Science Contents [*BRS Information Technologies*] [*Online database*] [*Discontinued*]
DISC .... Decision Information Screening Center (MCD)
DISC .... Defect Information and Servicing Control [*Aviation*]
DISC .... Defense Documentation Centre (SAUS)
DISC .... Defense Industrial Supply Center
DISC .... Defense Industrial Support Center (MCD)
DISC .... Defense Information System Council (SAUO)
DISC .... Delay in Separation Code [*Military*] (AABC)
DISC .... Delivering Information Solutions to Customers [*British*]
DISC .... Delivering Information Systems to Customers (SAUS)
DISC .... Developmental Information Science Curriculum (SAUS)
DISC .... Development of Irrigation and Specialty Crops (SAUO)
DISC .... Diagnostic Interview Schedule for Children [*Psychology*]
DISC .... Diagnostic Inventory for Screening Children [*Test*] (TMMY)
DISC .... Differential Isochronous Self-Collimating Counter (SAUS)
DISC .... Differential Scatter [*Remote sensing technique*]
DISC .... digital channel selection (SAUS)
DISC .... Digital Information Storage Corporation (SAUO)
DISC .... Digital International Switching Center [*Telecommunications*] (TEL)
DISC .... Digital Simulation Computer System (SAA)
DISC .... Digital Stereo Correlation System (SAUS)
disc .... dimension of schooling questionnaire (SAUS)
DISC .... Diodes International Sales Corp. (EFIS)
DISC .... Direct-Injected Stratified Charge [*Engine*] (RDA)
disc .... direct-injection stratified charge (SAUS)
DISC .... Director of Information Services Control (SAUO)
DISC .... Director of Inspection of Stores and Clothing (SAUO)
DISC .... Disability Information Services of Canada (SAUS)
DISC .... Disability Insurance Sales Course [*LUTC*]
DISC .... Disaster Information Systems Clearinghouse (SAUO)
disc .... discharge (SAUS)
DISC .... Discharged [*Military*]
DISC .... Disciple (ADA)
DISC .... Discipline (WDAA)
Disc .... Discography (SAUS)
DISC .... Discone (NASA)
DISC .... Disconnect (KSC)
DISC .... Disconnect Command (VLIE)
DISC .... Disconnected (SAUS)
DISC .... Disconnection (SAUS)
DISC .... Disconnector (SAUS)
DISC .... Discontinue (AFM)
disc .... Discontinued (SAUS)
disc .... discophile (SAUS)
Disc .... Discount (EBF)
DISC .... Discount
disc .... Discount (WDMC)
DISC .... Discourse (ROG)
DISC .... Discover [*or Discoverer*]
disc .... Discovered (ADWA)
DISC .... Discovery (SAUS)
DISC .... Discovery Channel [*Cable television channel*]
DISC .... Discrepancy Identification and System Checkout (DNAB)
DISC .... Discrete (KSC)
disc .... Discrimination (SAUS)
DISC .... Discriminator (IAA)
DISC .... Discus Corp. [*NASDAQ symbol*] (COMM)
disc .... Discussed (SAFN)
Disc .... Discussion (AL)
disc .... discus throw (SAUS)
DISC .... Disposition and Information System in Com bined Traffic (SAUS)
DISC .... Dissemination Center (VLIE)
DISC .... Distribution Stock Control System (MHDB)
DISC .... District
DISC .... Divisional Interests Special Committee [*American Library Association*]
DISC .... Documentation and Integration of Software into the Classroom Project (EDAC)
DISC .... Domestic International Sales Corp. [*See also Foreign Sales Corp. - FSC*]
DISC .... DORLS Information Services Committee (SAUS)
DISC .... Drilling Information Service Co. [*Houston, TX*] [*Telecommunications*] (TSSD)
DISC .... Drop-In Skills Centre [*British*] (AIE)
DISC .... Drug Information Service Center (SAUS)
DISC .... Dynamic Intelligent Scheduling [*Computer science*]
DISC4 .... Director of Information Systems for Command, Control, Communications, and Computers [*DoD*]
DISCA .... Dissolution Inhibitor Solubilizable by Chemical Amplification [*Chemistry*]
Discalced Carmelite Fathers .... Order of Discalced Brothers of the Blessed Virgin Mary of Mount Carmel (SAUO)
DISCAN .... Christian Church (Disciples of Christ) in Canada [*Formerly, All-Canada Committee of the Christian Church (Disciples of Christ)*] (AC)
DISCAS .... Defense Intelligence Special Career Automated System (MCD)
DISCAS .... Department Integrated Standardized Core Accounting System (SAUS)
DiscAut .... Discount Auto Parts Co. [*Associated Press*] (SAG)
DISCC .... Director Information Services Control Command (SAUO)
DISCC .... District Information Services Control Command (SAUO)

DISCCNC...... Declaration of Independence Second Centennial Commemorative National Committee (EA)
discd........... discounted (SAUS)
Dis Cert....... Discharge Certificate (SAUS)
discg........... discounting (SAUS)
DiscGph....... Disc Graphics, Inc. [*Associated Press*] (SAG)
DISCH.......... Defense Intelligence School [*Air Force*]
disch........... Discharge (ADWA)
DISCH.......... Discharge (AFM)
Disch........... Discharge (EBF)
DISCH.......... Discharged (SAUS)
Disch........... Discharging (EBF)
DIS CH......... Discovered Check [*Chess*] (GOBB)
dischd.......... discharged (SAUS)
DISCHE......... Discharge (ROG)
dischg.......... discharging (SAUS)
dischge........ discharge (SAUS)
DISCIP......... Disciplinary (DSUE)
discip........... Discipline (GEAB)
Disciples of Christ... Christian Churches, International Convention (SAUO)
DISCIS......... District and Municipal Court Information System (SAUO)
DISCLOSE.... Dunchurch Industrial Staff College Learn Ourselves Exercise (SAUS)
DISCLOSE.... Dunchurch Industrial Staff Training College Learn Ourselves Exercise (SAUO)
DISCO.......... Defense Industrial Security Clearance Office
DISCO.......... Defense Investigative Service Cognizant Office (SAUO)
DISCO.......... Detroit Investigation to Stop Criminal Operations (SAUO)
DISCO.......... Digital Scan Converter (SAUS)
disco............ disc jockey (SAUS)
disco............ Discotheque (ADWA)
DISCO.......... Discotheque (DSUE)
disco............ discotheque music (SAUS)
DISCO.......... Dissertations on Chemical Oceanography
DISCO.......... Distributed Switching with Centralized Optics [*AT&T*] (CIST)
DISCOID...... Direct Scan Operating with Integrated Delay (MCD)
Discol.......... Discolored
DISCOL........ Large Scale Disturbance and Re-colonization Experiment (SAUO)
DISCOLA...... Digital Integrated Solid-State Controller for Low-Cost Automation (PDAA)
Discoldd....... discoloured (SAUS)
DISCOM....... Defense Integrated Secure Communications (SAUS)
DISCOM....... Digital Selective Communications
DISCOM....... District Command (SAUS)
DISCOM....... Division Support Center (SAUO)
DISCOM....... Division Support Command [*Army*] (AABC)
discomb....... discombobulation (SAUS)
DISCOMP..... Diskette Compare (SAUS)
DISCON........ Defence Integrated Secure Communications Network (SAUS)
DISCON........ Disconnect (KSC)
DISCON........ Disconnection (SAUS)
DISCON........ Discontinue
DISCON........ Discrepancy in Shipment Confirmation [*DoD*]
discon.......... disorderly conduct (SAUS)
Discond........ discontinued (SAUS)
DISCONSTAFF... Controlling Directing Staff (SAUO)
discont......... Discontinued (SAUS)
discontd....... Discontinued
DISCOP......... Digital Simulation of Continuous Processes
DISCORAP... Directionally-Controlled Rocket-Assisted Projectile
DISCORS..... Discrepancy in Shipment Cargo Outturn Reporting System [*DoD*] (DNAB)
discort......... Disconnect [*Disorderly Conduct*] (BARN)
discos.......... discotheques (SAUS)
DISCOS........ Disturbance Compensation System [*Navy satellite navigation*]
DISCOVD..... Discovered (ROG)
DISCOVY...... Discovery (ROG)
DISCOY........ Discovery (ROG)
DISC-P......... Diagnostic Interview Schedule for Children - Parents Form [*Psychology*]
DI/SCP......... Disposition of Vessel by Scrapping (DNAB)
DI/SCP......... Vessels Disposed of by Scrapping [*Navy*]
DISCR.......... Directorate of Industrial Security Clearance Review [*DoD*]
DISCR.......... Discrepancy (GAVI)
DISCR.......... Discriminate (AABC)
DISCR.......... Discriminator (SAUS)
Discreet....... Discreet Logic, Inc. [*Associated Press*] (SAG)
DISCREP...... Discrepancy Report
Discrete Comput Geom... Discrete and Computational Geometry (journ.) (SAUS)
discrim......... discriminant (SAUS)
discrim......... Discriminator (SAUS)
DISCRM....... Discriminant (SAUS)
DISCRM....... Discriminate (MUGU)
DISCRM....... Discrimination (SAUS)
Discrom....... Discriminator (SAUS)
DISCRON..... Discretion
DISCRP........ Discrepancy (AABC)
DISCR Review... Directorate for Industrial Security Clearance (AAGC)
discrtn......... discretion (SAUS)
DISCs.......... Domestic International Sales Corporations (SAUO)
DI-SCSI........ Differential SCSI (SAUS)
DISC System... Distribution Stock Control System (SAUS)
DISCT.......... Discount
DISCT.......... District
Discur.......... Discuriosities [*Record label*]
DISCUS........ Data Interchange and Synergistic Collateral Usage System (VLIE)
DISCUS........ Dealer Information System for Customer Satisfaction [*Automotive retailing*]
DISCUS........ Disposal and Collection User Simulation (PDAA)
DISCUS........ Distilled Spirits Council of the United States (EA)
Discuss Faraday Soc... Discussions of the Faraday Society (SAUO)
DiscZone..... Discovery Zone, Inc. [*Associated Press*] (SAG)
DISD............ Data and Information Systems Division [*IT & T*]
DISD............ Defense Industrial Supply Depot
DIS-DATE..... discharge date (SAUS)
DISDEP....... Distant Deployment (DNAB)
DisDGM....... District Deputy Grand Master [*Freemasonry*]
DISDKB........ Descendants of the Illegitimate Sons and Daughters of the Kings of Britain (EA)
DISDOC....... Disarmament Information System - Documents (SAUS)
DISE............ Deployable Intelligence Support Element [*Army*] (SEWL)
DISE............ Development in Science Education [*National Science Foundation*] (GRD)
DISE............ Distribution and Illumination System, Electrical [*Army*] (INF)
DISE Committee... Digital Systems Education Committee (SAUS)
DISECS........ Defense Intelligence Space Exploitation and Correlation System (MCD)
DISEGS........ Diagnostic Segments (VLIE)
DISEM......... Disseminate (AABC)
DISEMB........ Disembark (AABC)
DISENG........ Disengage
DISERF........ Data Interchange Standards Education and Research Foundation (VLIE)
DISESTAB.... Disestablish
DISFP.......... Disc-Indexed Sequential File Package [*Computer science*] (PDAA)
DISFREE...... Distribution-Free Statistics
disg............. disagreeable (SAUS)
DISG............ Seguela [*Ivory Coast*] [*ICAO location identifier*] (ICLI)
DIS GOSC.... Distributed Interactive Simulation General Officer Steering Committee [*Army*] (RDA)
DISGRAT...... Discharge Gratuity [*Military*]
DISH............ Data Interchange for Shipping (SAUS)
DISH............ Data Interchange in the Shipping Industry
DISH............ Design & Implementation of Software in History (SAUS)
DISH............ Differential Integrating Sample and Hold (SAUS)
DISH............ Diffuse Idiopathic Skeletal Hyperostosis [*Medicine*]
DISH............ Digital Sky Highway [*Communications term*] (DCT)
DISH............ Discrete Identifiable Silicone Handler (VLIE)
DISH............ Disseminated Idiopathic Skeletal Hyperostosis [*Medicine*] (DAVI)
Dish............. Double [*or Dual*] Income, Separate Homes [*Lifestyle classification*]
DISH............ EchoStar Communications'A' [*NASDAQ symbol*] (TTSB)
DISH............ EchoStar Communications Corp. [*NASDAQ symbol*] (SAG)
DISHES........ Determined Involved Supermodels Helping to End Suffering [*An association*]
DISHIDROS... Dinas Hidro Oceanografi [*Indonesia*] (GEOI)
DISHON........ Dishonorable (ADA)
dishon.......... Dishonourable (SAUS)
dishon.......... Dishonourably (SAUS)
DISHOND..... Dishonored (ROG)
dishwr.......... Dishwasher (REAL)
DISI............. Dairy Industries (or Industry) Society International (SAUO)
DISI............. Defense Industrial Security Institute [*DoD*]
DISI............. Diode Ion Source Injector
DISI............. Direct Injection Spark-Ignited [*Engine*]
DISI............. Directory Information Services Infrastructure
disi.............. door insulating system Index (SAUS)
DISI............. Door Insulating Systems Index
DISI............. Dorsal Intercalary Segment Instability [*Medicine*]
DISI Bulletin... Dairy Industries Society International Bulletin (SAUO)
DISID........... Disposable Seismic Intrusion Detector (SAUS)
DISIDA......... Diisopropyl Iminodiacetic Acid (ADWA)
DISIDS......... Display and Information Distribution System [*or Subsystem*] (MCD)
DISIM........... Digital Input Simulator [*Computer science*]
DISIMP........ Device Independent Software For Image Processing (SAUS)
DISIN........... Disinfectant (SAUS)
disin............ disinfection (SAUS)
DISINT......... Discrete Integrator (IAA)
DISISS......... Design of Information Systems in the Social Sciences (SAUS)
disj.............. disjunction (SAUS)
DISJ............. Disjunctive (ROG)
DISJUNCT.... Disjunctive [*Linguistics*]
DISK............ Confederation of Revolutionary Workers' Unions (Turkey) [*Political party*] (PSAP)
DISK............ Image Entertainment [*NASDAQ symbol*] (TTSB)
DISK............ Image Entertainment, Inc. [*NASDAQ symbol*] (NQ)
DISKCOMP... Disk Compare [*Computer science*]
DISK-O-TEK... Disk Organization Technique (SAUS)
DISKUS........ Digital Information System for Art and Social History
Disk Watcher... trademark of RG Software Systems (SAUS)
Disl.............. Dislocation (DAVI)
DISLAN........ Display Language [*Computer science*] (MHDB)
DISLIC......... Directory of Special Libraries and Information Centres (SAUS)
disloc........... Dislocation [*Medicine*] (AMHC)
DISLOC........ Dislocation [*Medicine*]
DISLVD........ Dissolved
DISM........... Delayed Impact Space Missile (IAA)
DISM........... Dismantle (MSA)
DISM........... Dismiss (AABC)
dism............ dismissal (SAUS)
DISM........... Display Monitor (SAUS)
DISM........... Dissimilar (SAUS)

DISM .... Documentation and Informtation System for Metallurgy (SAUS)
dismac .... Digital Scene-Matching Area Correlation Sensors [*Military*] (ODA)
Dismals .... Dismal Gardens near Phil Campbell, Alabama (SAUS)
DISMD .... Dismissed [*Legal shorthand*] (LWAP)
DisMD .... Distal Muscular Dystrophy [*Medicine*]
dis/min .... Disintegration per Minute (ABAC)
DIS/MIN ...... Disintegrations per Minute
Dis Mon .... Disease-a-month (SAUS)
DISMS .... Defense Integrated Subsistence Management System (SAUS)
dismtd .... Dismounted (SAUS)
DISN .... Defense Information System Network
DISN .... Diiminosuccinonitrile [*Organic chemistry*]
Disn .... Disney's Superior Court of Cincinnati Reports [*Ohio*] [*A publication*] (DLA)
Dis Nerv Syst... Diseases of the Nervous System (journ.) (SAUS)
DISNET .... Defense Information Systems Network [*Communications term*] (DCT)
DISNET .... Defense Integrated Secure Network (DOMA)
DISNET .... Domain-Independent Information Services Network (SAUO)
DISNET .... Drug Information Systems Network
Disney .... [*The*] Disney [*Walt*] Co. [*Wall Street slang name: "Mickey Mouse"*] [*Associated Press*] (SAG)
Disn Gam ...... Disney. Gaming [*1806*] [*A publication*] (DLA)
DISNNT .... Defense Information Systems Network-Near Term (SAUO)
Disn (Ohio)... Disney's Ohio Superior Court Reports [*A publication*] (DLA)
DISO .... Dictionnaire des Inscriptions Semitiques de l'Ouest [*A publication*] (BJA)
DISO .... Die Shoe (SAUS)
DISO .... Display Inquiry System Online (SAUS)
disod .... Disodium [*Medicine*] (EDAA)
DISOD .... Disodium
DISOP .... Discharge by Operator (DNAB)
Dis Op .... Dissenting Opinion [*Legal term*] (DLA)
DISOPE .... Dynamic Integrated System Optimization and Parameter Estimation (VLIE)
disord .... disorder (SAUS)
DISORD H.... Disorderly House [*Legal term*] (DLA)
disorg .... Disorganized (SAUS)
DISORT .... discrete ordinate (SAUS)
DISORT .... Discrete Ordinate Radiative Transfer (ARMP)
DISOSS .... Distributed Office Support System [*IBM Corp.*]
DISP .... Declassified Intelligence Satellite Photography
DISP .... Defense Industrial Security Program [*DoD*]
DISP .... Defense Industry Studies Program (NG)
DISP .... Directory Information Shadowing Protocol
disp .... discharge port (SAUS)
DISP .... Dispatch
DISP .... Dispatcher (MSA)
disp .... Dispensary (ADWA)
DISP .... Dispensary (AFM)
Disp .... Dispensary [*Medicine*] (EDAA)
DISP .... Dispensation
disp .... Dispensatory (DAVI)
DISP .... Dispenser
DISP .... Dispensetur [*Dispense*] [*Pharmacy*]
Dis P .... Dispersal Point (SAUS)
DISP .... Disperse
disp .... Dispersion (VRA)
DISP .... Dispersion (WDAA)
DISP .... Displacement
DISP .... Displacement Information Shadowing Protocol (SAUS)
DISP .... Display (KSC)
DISP .... Displayed Composition [*Graphic arts*] (DGA)
DISP .... Disposal
DISP .... Disproportionation
DISP .... DoD [*Department of Defense*] Industrial Security Program (AABC)
DISP .... Draft International Standardized Profile [*OSI*] (OSI)
DISP .... Dutch Independent Shareware Programmer (VERA)
DISP .... San Pedro [*Ivory Coast*] [*ICAO location identifier*] (ICLI)
DISPAC .... Domestic and International Scientific Planning and Cooperation
DISPDJC ...... Display Dependent Job Control tables (SAUS)
dispen .... dispensatories (SAUS)
dispen .... dispensatory (SAUS)
DISPENS ...... Dispensary (ADA)
DISPERSE .... Discretionary Population Effects for Riot and Stability Employment [*Crowd control*]
Disp Imaging... Display and Imaging [*A publication*] (CABS)
Disp Imaging Technol... Display and ImagingTechnology (journ.) (SAUS)
DISPL .... Displacement (AAG)
displ .... Displacement (ADWA)
DISPL .... Display (SAUS)
DISPLAN ...... Disaster Plan [*Australia*]
DISPLAY ...... Digital Service Planning Analysis [*Telecommunications*] (TEL)
DISPLY .... Display (SAUS)
DISPN .... Disposition (MSA)
DISPNSG ..... Dispensing
dispo .... Disposition (DAVI)
DISPOSAL.... Developing Improved Sizing Procedures Over Sanitary Area Landfills
DISPOSN ..... Disposition (ROG)
DISPR .... Dispatcher
Disp Technol Appl... Displays, Technology and Applications (journ.) (SAUS)
DISQ .... Disqualified [*Motor vehicle term used in state of Washington*] (MVRD)
disq .... disqualified (SAUS)
DISQ .... Disquisition (ROG)
DISQUAL ...... Disqualify (AABC)
DISR .... Daily Indicator Status Report (MCD)
DISR .... Defense Indications Status Report (MCD)
DISR .... Department of Industrial and Scientific Research (SAUO)
DISR .... Department of Industry, Science and Resources [*Commonwealth*] [*Atmosphere*] (ATR)
DI/SR .... Descent Imager/Spectral Radiometer (ACAE)
DISR .... Discrepant Item - Ships Record
Dis R .... Disney's Superior Court of Cincinnati Reports [*Ohio*] [*A publication*] (DLA)
DISRE .... Disregard (AABC)
DISREP .... Discrepancy in Shipment Report [*DoD*] (AABC)
DISRES .... General Assembly Disarmament Resolution File (SAUS)
DIS RET .... Disability Retirement [*Military*] (DNAB)
DISRP .... Double Index Selection Register Party (SAUO)
DIS RX .... disable receive (SAUS)
DIS RX .... Disable receive status (SAUS)
DISS .... Data Input Subsystem [*Computer science*] (SAA)
DISS .... Diameter Index Safety System (DB)
DISS .... Digest of Intelligence and Security Services (MCD)
DISS .... Digital Interface Switching System
DISS .... Digital Ionospheric Sounding System (SAUS)
DISS .... Directorate of Information Systems and Settlement (SAUO)
diss .... disassembly (SAUS)
DIS/S .... Disintegrations per Second
diss .... dissent (SAUS)
DISS .... Dissenter
diss .... Dissertation (ADWA)
DISS .... Dissertation
diss .... Dissipation (SAUS)
Diss .... Dissociation (SAUS)
Diss .... Dissolution (SAUS)
DISS .... Dissolve
DISS .... Dissolvent (SAUS)
DISS .... Distributed Information Processing Service System (NITA)
DISS .... Sassandra [*Ivory Coast*] [*ICAO location identifier*] (ICLI)
Diss Abs .... Dissertation Abstracts (journ.) (SAUS)
Diss Abstr Int... Dissertation Abstracts International (journ.) (SAUS)
DissadHRP.... Dissertationes ad Historiam Religionum Pertinentes [*A publication*] (BJA)
dissassy .... Disassembly (SAUS)
DIS-SC .... DIS Standing Committee (SAUO)
DISSC .... Dredging Industry Size Standard Committee (EA)
DISSCO .... User Community [*Programming language*] [*Argonne National Laboratory*] [*Argonne, IL*] (CSR)
dissd .... Dissociated (SAUS)
dissd .... Dissolved
dis/sec .... Disintegrations per Second (ABAC)
DIS/SEC .... Disintegrations per Second
dissec .... dissection (SAUS)
dissed .... disrespectful (SAUS)
dissem .... Disseminate (SAUS)
DISSEM .... Disseminated
DISSERT .... Dissertation
DISSIG .... Distress Signal (IAA)
dissim .... dissimilated (SAUS)
dissim .... dissimilation (SAUS)
DISSIP .... Dissipation
DISSIS .... Dissemination of Information in the Social Sciences (SAUS)
DISSOC .... Dissociate
dissocg .... Dissociating (SAUS)
dissocn .... Dissociation (SAUS)
disson .... dissonance (SAUS)
DISSOS .... Distributed Office Support System (SAUS)
DISSP .... Defense Information Systems Security Program [*Military*] (DOMA)
DISSPLA ...... Display Integrated Software System and Plotting Language [*Computer science*]
dissyl .... dissyllable (SAUS)
DISSYS .... Distribution System (IAA)
DIST .... AMCON Distributing [*NASDAQ symbol*] (TTSB)
DIST .... AMOON Distributing [*NASDAQ symbol*] (SAG)
DIST .... Data Input Strobe (NITA)
DIST .... Delegation for Scientific and Technical Information (IID)
DIST .... Department of Industry, Science, and Technology [*Australia*]
DIST .... Discount
DIST .... Distal [*Medicine*]
DIST .... Distance [*or Distant*] (AFM)
dist .... Distance (WDMC)
DIST .... Distanced [*Horse racing*]
dist .... Distant (VRA)
DIST .... Distilla [*Distill*] [*Pharmacy*] (ROG)
Dist .... Distillate
DIST .... Distillation (SAUS)
Dist .... Distilled (AMHC)
DIST .... Distilled [*or Distillery*]
DIST .... Distiller (SAUS)
DIST .... Distillery (SAUS)
Dist .... Distinctio [*Decretum Gratiani*] [*A publication*] (DSA)
DIST .... Distinction (ROG)
DIST .... Distinguish
DIST .... Distort (IAA)
DIST .... Distribute
DIST .... Distributed Time (KSC)
dist .... Distribution (IEEE)
dist .... Distributive (SAUS)
DIST .... Distributor (KSC)
DIST .... District (AFM)

Dist............ District (CMD)
dist............ District (WDMC)
DIST............ Disturbance [*FBI standardized term*]
DIST............ Division of Information Science and Technology [*National Science Foundation*]
DISTA.......... Distributor A (SAUS)
DISTAB........ Disestablish (NVT)
DISTAD........ District Administrator (CINC)
Distads........ Administrative Districts (SAUS)
DISTAFF...... Directing Staff (NATG)
distal........... At a distance (SAUS)
DISTAN........ Distributed Interactive Secure Telecommunications Area Network (MCD)
Dist & Co Rep... Pennsylvania District and County Reports [*A publication*] (DLA)
distar........... direct instruction (SAUS)
DISTAR........ Direct Instructional System for Teaching Arithmetic and Reading
DISTAR........ Direct Instructional Systems to Arithmetic and Reading (AIE)
DistAtt......... District Attorney (SAUO)
Dist Atty...... District Attorney (WGA)
distb........... distillable (SAUS)
DISTBG........ Distributing (SAUS)
distbtr.......... distributor (SAUS)
Dist C.......... District Court (DLA)
Dist Civ Engr... District Civil Engineer (SAUS)
Dist Col App... District of Columbia Court of Appeals (DLA)
Dist Ct......... District Court [*State*] (DLA)
Dist Ct App... District Court of Appeal (DLA)
DISTD.......... Distilled
DISTDAHS... Distributed Satellite Telemetry Data Handling System (GEOI)
DISTDENTALO... District Dental Officer (SAUO)
DISTEL......... Delft Document Delivery Program (SAUS)
DISTENGR... District Engineer [*Army*] (AABC)
DISTEX........ District Relief Exercise [*Military*] (DNAB)
Dist F........... Distinguished From [*Medicine*] (DAVI)
dist f........... Distinguished From [*Medicine*] (EDAA)
distg........... Distilling (SAUS)
distil........... distillation (SAUS)
distil........... Distilled (SAUS)
distil........... distilling (SAUS)
DISTING....... Distinguish
DISTING....... Distinguished (ROG)
DistInsGen... District Inspector General (SAUO)
Dist J........... District Judge (SAUS)
DISTL........... Display Electronics communications (SAUS)
DISTLLRY.... Distillery
DISTLR......... Distiller
DISTMEDO... District Medical Officer [*Military*] (DNAB)
DistMg.......... District Magistrate (SAUO)
distn........... Distillation (ADWA)
DISTN.......... Distillation
DISTN.......... Distortion (MSA)
DISTN.......... Distribution (AAG)
DISTNCTV.... Distinctive
distng.......... distinguish (SAUS)
distng.......... distinguishing (SAUS)
DISTO.......... Defense Industrial Security Education and Training Office (AABC)
Dis TP.......... Distinction in Town Planning (SAUS)
Dist PWO.... District Public Works Officer (SAUO)
Dist R........... Distant Reconnaissance (SAUS)
DISTR.......... Distracted
distr............ Distribute (SAUS)
distr............ distributed (SAUS)
DISTR.......... Distribution [*or Distributor*] (AFM)
distr............ distributiv (SAUS)
distr............ Distributor (ADWA)
Distr............ Distributor (PROS)
Distr............ District (DIAR)
DISTR.......... District (ROG)
distr............ District (VRA)
DistR........... District Railway (SAUO)
Dist R.......... Pennsylvania District Reports [*A publication*] (DLA)
DISTRA........ Distribution Authority [*Army*] (AABC)
DISTRAM...... Digital Space Trajectory Measurement System [*Raytheon Co.*]
DISTRAMS.... Digital Space Trajectory Measurement System (SAUS)
DISTRAM System... Digital Space Trajectory Measurement System (SAUS)
DISTRAN...... Diagnostic FORTRAN [*Formula Translating System*] (IAA)
distrb........... Distribute (VRA)
DISTRB........ Distributes
DISTRB........ Distribution
distrbn......... Distribution (SAUS)
Distr Col BAJ... District of Columbia Bar Association. Journal [*A publication*] (DLA)
DISTREAT.... Upon Discharge Treatment [*Military*]
Dist Rep...... District Reports [*A publication*] (DLA)
Dist Reports... Pennsylvania District Reports [*A publication*] (DLA)
Dist Reps..... Pennsylvania District Reports [*A publication*] (DLA)
DISTRG........ Distributing
Distrib......... Distribution (MIST)
DISTRIB....... Distribution
distrib.......... Distributive (ADWA)
distrib.......... distributor (SAUS)
District......... Pennsylvania District Reports [*A publication*] (DLA)
District Court LR... District Court Law Reports [*Hong Kong*] [*A publication*] (DLA)
District Reps... Pennsylvania District Reports [*A publication*] (DLA)
DISTRIPRESS... Federation Internationale des Distributeurs de Presse [*International Federation of Wholesale Newspaper, Periodical, and Book Distributors*]
DISTRIX....... Distributed UNIX (SAUS)
DISTRO........ Distribution Rotation (SAUS)
Dists........... Districts (SAUS)
DIS TX......... Disable Transmit (NITA)
DIS TX......... Disable transmit status (SAUS)
DISU........... Digital International Switching Unit [*Telecommunications*] (TEL)
DISUB.......... Duty Involving Underway Operations in Submarines
DISUM......... Daily Intelligence Summary [*Air Force*]
DISUS.......... Disused (ROG)
DISVI........... Disarmo e Sviluppo (SAUO)
DISY........... Dimokratikos Synagermos [*Democratic Rally*] [*Political party*] (EAIO)
disy............. disyllabic (SAUS)
DISY........... Disyllable
DISYLL........ Disyllable (ROG)
DISYNDA..... Display of Synoptic Data
DISZ............ Diamond Salt [*Federal Railroad Administration identification code*]
DIT.............. Daido Institute of Technology (SAUS)
DIT.............. Data Identification Table (MCD)
DIT.............. Data ID Table (SAUS)
DIT.............. Data Input Tape (SAUS)
DIT.............. Data Input Technician (SAUS)
DIT.............. Data Inquiry Terminal
DIT.............. Data Insertion Technician (SAUS)
DIT.............. Days in Transit (ACAE)
DIT.............. Decimation In Time (SAUS)
DIT.............. Defense Intelligence Thesaurus (MCD)
DIT.............. Deferoxamine Infusion Test [*Medicine*] (MELL)
DIT.............. Defining Issues Test (EDAC)
DIT.............. Delay Ignition [*or Igniting*] Tracer [*Military*] (MCD)
DIT.............. Delivery Issue Team (MCD)
DIT.............. Department of Information Technology [*Commonwealth of Virginia*] [*Telecommunications service*] (TSSD)
DIT.............. Depth of Inheritance Tree (SAUS)
DIT.............. Detroit Institute of Technology
DIT.............. Development Integration Test (SPST)
dit............... Dictyate (QSUL)
DIT.............. Diet-Induced Thermogenesis [*Medicine*] (WDAA)
DIT.............. Digital Information Transmission (SAUS)
DIT.............. Digital Instrumentation Technology, Inc. (PCM)
DIT.............. Diiodotyrosine [*Biochemistry*]
DIT.............. Director for Individual Training (MCD)
DIT.............. Directory Information Tree (TNIG)
DIT.............. Discrete Trial Training
DIT.............. Dithiothreitol [*Organic chemistry*]
DIT.............. Diversified Techs Inc. [*Vancouver Stock Exchange symbol*]
DIT.............. Division of Information Technology (SAUO)
DIT.............. Doctor of Industrial Technology (GAGS)
DIT.............. Documentation Implementation Team [*Deep Space Network, NASA*]
DIT.............. Documentation Information Transmittal (NVT)
DIT.............. Domestic Independent Tour [*or Travel*]
DIT.............. Dorsal Intermediate Tract [*Anatomy*]
DIT.............. Double Incidence Technique
DIT.............. Double Income Tax (ODBW)
DIT.............. Draft Initiation Time (SAUS)
DIT.............. Dresdner International Research Institute GmbH (SAUS)
DIT.............. Drexel Institute of Technology [*Pennsylvania*] (MCD)
DIT.............. Drug-Induced Thrombocytopenia [*Medicine*] (MELL)
DIT.............. Dual Input Transponder
DIT.............. Dublin Institute of Technology (ACII)
DIT.............. Durham Institute of Technology (SAUS)
DIT.............. Dynamic Integrated Test (MCD)
DITA............ Design-in Test Points and Alarms (SAUS)
DiTa............ diesel tanker vessel (SAUS)
DITA............ Diesel Tank Vessel
DITAC......... Department of Industry, Technology and Commerce (SAUO)
DITAC......... DIFAR [*Directional Frequency Analyzing and Recording*] Tactic [*Military*] (CAAL)
DITACS........ Digital Tactical System (PDAA)
DITAR.......... Digital Telemetry Analog Recording
DITARD........ Department of Industry, Technology and Regional Development (SAUS)
DITA Vessel... Diesel Tanker Vessel (SAUS)
DITB............ Digital Imagery Test Bed (MCD)
DITB............ Distribution Industry Training Board [*Terminated*] [*British*]
DITB............ Tabou [*Ivory Coast*] [*ICAO location identifier*] (ICLI)
DITC............ Department of Industry, Trade and Commerce (SAUO)
DITC............ Diisothiocyanate (SAUS)
DITC............ Disability Insurance Training Council [*Washington, DC*] (EA)
DITC............ Ditech Communications
DITCC.......... Defence Information Technology Co-ordinating Committee (SAUS)
DITCO.......... Defense Information Technology Contracting Office (SAUO)
DITE............ digital dual induction tool (SAUS)
DITE............ Diverter Injection Tokamak [*Toroidal Kamera Magnetic*] Experiment (MCD)
DITEC.......... Digital Television Camera (MCD)
DITEC.......... Digital Television Communications (SAUS)
DITEC.......... Digital Television Communication System (SAUS)
DITEC.......... Digital Television Encoding
Ditech.......... Direct-Injection Technology
DITEG.......... Digital Television Generator (ACAE)
DI/TES......... Vessels Disposed of by Using as Targets and Tests [*Navy*]
DITFFT......... Decimation-In-Time Fast Fourier Transform (SAUS)

dithy .... dithyrambs (SAUS)
DITI .... Diatide, Inc. [*NASDAQ symbol*] (NASQ)
DITL .... [*A*] Day in the Life [*Series*] [*Photojournalism project*]
DITLA .... [*A*] Day in the Life of America [*Photojournalism project*]
DITLOHA .... [*A*] Day in the Life of Hawaii [*Photojournalism project*]
DITM .... Drive-in Theater Machine (SAUS)
DITM .... Touba/Mahana [*Ivory Coast*] [*ICAO location identifier*] (ICLI)
DITMB .... Defence Information Technology Management Board (SAUS)
DITMCO .... Data Information Test Material Checkout
DITN .... Diabetes in the News (SAUS)
Dito .... Ernesto (SAUS)
dITP .... Deoxyinosine Triphosphate [*Biochemistry*]
DITP .... Detailed Individual Test Plan (MCD)
DITR .... Department of Industry, Technology and Resources (SAUO)
DITR .... Deutsches Informationszentrum fuer Technische Regeln [*German Information Center for Technical Rules*] [*German Institute for Standardization*] [*Information service or system*] (IID)
DITRACO .... Diamond Trading Company (SAUO)
DITRAN .... Diagnostic FORTRAN [*Computer science*] (IEEE)
DI/TRN .... Vessels Transferred to Other Government Agencies and Miscellaneous Activities [*Navy*]
DITROFF .... Device Independent Typesetting Run Off [*Typography*] (DGA)
DITS .... Dancing in the Streets
DITS .... Digital Imagery Transmission System (SAUS)
DITS .... Digital Information Transfer Set (CAAL)
DITS .... Digital Information Transfer System
DITS .... Digital Television Spectrometer (NG)
DITS .... Dismounted Infantry Training Strategy (SAUS)
DITSO .... Defense Technology Services Organization [*Military*] (SEWL)
DITT .... Department of Industry, Trade and Technology [*South Australia*]
DIT Theory .... Discrete Integral Transport Theory (SAUS)
DITTL .... Dittlinger, TX [*American Association of Railroads railroad junction routing code*]
DITTO .... Data Interactive Testing and Operations (SAUS)
DITTO .... Data Interfile Transfer, Testing, and Operations Utility [*IBM program product*]
DITTO .... Directory of Independent Training and Tutorial Organisations (AIE)
DITU .... Digital Interface Test Unit [*Computer science*] (KSC)
DITY .... Committee for Do-It-Yourself Household Moving (EA)
DITY .... Do-It-Yourself (MCD)
DIU .... Data Information Unit [*Marine science*] (OSRA)
DIU .... Data Input Unit (SAUS)
DIU .... Data Interchange Utilities (or Utility) (SAUS)
DIU .... Data Interchange Utility (IAA)
DIU .... Data Interface Unit
DIU .... Dedicated Interface Unit
DIU .... Destratification Impeller Unit
DIU .... Destruction Initiation Unit (CAAL)
DIU .... Digital Input Unit [*Computer science*]
DIU .... Digital Insertion Unit [*Computer science*]
DIU .... Digital Interchange Utility (NITA)
DIU .... Digital Interface Unit [*Computer science*] (KSC)
DIU .... Display Interface Unit (ACAE)
DIU .... Diuretic [*Increasing Discharge of Urine*] [*Pharmacy*] (ROG)
DIU .... Diversion Investigative Unit [*Drug Enforcement Administration*]
DIU .... Document Interchange Unit (SAUS)
DIU .... drug induced ulcer (SAUS)
DIU .... Office of Development Information and Utilization [*Agency for International Development*] [*Information service or system*] (IID)
Diu .... Sanol Arzneimittel Dr. Schwarz [*Germany*] [*Research code symbol*]
DIUMCM .... Disaggregate Inter-Urban Mode Choice Model [*Traffic management*]
DIUP .... Diisoundecyl Phthalate
DIUP .... Director, Industry and University Programs [*Military*] [*Canada*]
DIV .... Data in Virtual (SAUS)
DIV .... Data in Voice [*Telecommunications*]
DIV .... Days in Vitro [*Cell culture*]
Div .... De Divinatione [*of Cicero*] [*Classical studies*] (OCD)
DIV .... Defense Intelligence Videocassettes (MCD)
DIV .... Derived Investment Value (SAUS)
DIV .... Desired Intermediate Vertex (IAA)
DIV .... Devon Industries [*Vancouver Stock Exchange symbol*]
DIV .... Differential Interface Velocity [*Engineering*]
DIV .... Digital Input Group Voltage (IAA)
DIV .... Digital Input Voltage (SAUS)
div .... digits in voice (SAUS)
DIV .... Direction de l'Information de la Valorisation [*Information and Valorization Directorate*] [*National Institute of Agronomic Research*] [*Information service or system*] (IID)
DIV .... Divergence
div .... divergence of (SAUS)
DIV .... Diverse (ROG)
div .... Diversion (SAUS)
DIV .... Diverter (KSC)
div .... Divide (IDYL)
DIV .... Divide (MSA)
Div .... Dividend (EBF)
div .... Dividend (WDAA)
DIV .... Dividend [*Investment term*]
DIV .... Divider (SAUS)
DIV .... Divine [*or Divinity*]
DIV .... Diving
Div .... Divinity (BARN)
DIV .... Divisi [*Divide*] [*Music*]
div .... divisibility (SAUS)
Div .... Divisi (It) [*Divided*] [*Italian*] [*Music*] (WDAA)
DIV .... Division (EY)
Div .... Division (PHSD)
div .... Division (WDAA)
Div .... Divisional (EBF)
DIV .... Divisor [*Mathematics*] (ROG)
div .... divorce (SAUS)
div .... Divorced (GEAB)
DIV .... Divorced
Div .... Divorce Proceedings [*Legal term*] (DLA)
DIV .... Double-Inlet Ventricle [*Cardiology*] (DAVI)
DIV .... Dynamic Imagery Viewer
DIV .... Hancock [*John*] Patriot Select Dividend Trust [*NYSE symbol*] (SPSG)
DIV .... John Hancock Patr Sel Div Tr [*NYSE symbol*] (TTSB)
DIV .... PCL Diversifund [*AMEX symbol*] (COMM)
DIVA .... Data Input-Voice Answerback [*Telecommunications*] (EECA)
DIVA .... Data Inquiry Voice Answer (SAUS)
DIVA .... Determination, Integrity, Vitality, and Aspiration [*Self-esteem plan devised by fitness instructor Terri Walsh*]
DIVA .... Digital Input Voice Answerback [*Telecommunications*] (NITA)
DIVA .... Digital Inquiry - Voice Answerback [*Touch-tone*] [*Bell System*] [*Telecommunications*]
DIVA .... Digital Interactive Virtual Acoustics (SAUS)
DIVA .... Digital Intravenous Angiography [*Cardiology*] (DAVI)
DIVA .... Double Interferometer for Visual Astrometry (SAUS)
divab .... digital input/voice answer back (SAUS)
DIVAD .... Division Air Defence Gun (SAUS)
DIVAD .... Division Air Defense
DIVADA .... Division Air Defense Artillery (MCD)
DIVADS .... Division Air Defense Study (MCD)
DIVADS .... Division Air Defense System (ACAE)
DIVADS .... Divisional Air Defense System (AAGC)
Div Ammn Coy ... Divisional Ammunition Company (SAUO)
Div Ammn Sub Pk ... Divisional Ammunition Sub-Park (SAUO)
Div & Mat Ct ... Divorce and Matrimonial Causes Court (DLA)
DIV & S .... Divorce and Separation (DLA)
DIVAR .... Diving Instrumentation Vehicle for Environmental and Acoustic Research (MCD)
DIVART .... Division Artillery [*Army*]
DIVARTY .... Divisionally Artillery Organization (SAUS)
DIVARTY .... Division Artillery [*Army*] (INF)
DIVAS .... Development In-Vehicle Acquisition System
DIVBASE .... Division Base [*Army*]
DIVBC .... Disseminated Intravascular Blood Coagulation [*Medicine*] (DMAA)
DIVBX .... Mgn. Stanley D. Witter Dividend Growth [*Mutual fund ticker symbol*] (SG)
DIVC .... Disseminated Intravascular Coagulation [*Medicine*] (DMAA)
Div C .... Division Court [*Canada*] (DLA)
Div Caec .... Divinatio in Caecilium [*of Cicero*] [*Classical studies*] (OCD)
DIVCAV .... Division Cavalry Squadron [*Army*]
DIV CF .... Divinity Calf [*Bookbinding*] (DGA)
DIVCHK .... Divide Check (SAUS)
DIV CIRC .... Divinity Circuit Edges [*Bookbinding*] (DGA)
DIVCO .... Divisional Council (SAUO)
Div Col Pt .... Division Collecting Point (SAUS)
DIVCOM .... Division Commander [*Navy*]
DIVCON .... Division Concepts and Force Design Study (SAUO)
Div Coy .... Divisional Company (SAUO)
Div CP .... Divisional Command Post (SAUO)
Div Ct .... Divisional Court Selected Judgments, Divisional Courts of the Gold Coast Colony [*A publication*] (DLA)
DIVD .... Decentralized in Vitro Diagnostic [*Medicine*] (DB)
DIVD .... Divided (SAUS)
DIVD .... Dividend [*Investment term*]
Divde .... Dividende [*Dividend*] [*French*] [*Business term*] (ILCA)
Div Dp .... Divisional Depot (SAUO)
DIVDS .... Dividends (SAUS)
DIVE .... American Oilfield Divers, Inc. [*NASDAQ symbol*] (SAG)
DIVE .... Amer Oilfield Divers [*NASDAQ symbol*] (TTSB)
DIVE .... Direct Interface Video Extensions [*IBM Corp.*] (VERA)
DIVE .... Distributed Interactive Virtual Environment (SAUO)
DIV E .... Divinity Edges [*Bookbinding*] (DGA)
DIVE .... Division Engineer (MCD)
DIVEAR .... Diving Instrumentation Vehicle for Environmental and Acoustic Research (SAUS)
DIVEAR .... Driving Instrumentation Vehicle for Environmental and Acoustic Research (SAUS)
DIVEMA .... Divinyl Ether-Maleic Anhydride [*Organic chemistry*]
DIVENGR .... Division Engineer [*Army*] (AABC)
Div Engr Dp ... Divisional Engineer Depot (SAUO)
divers .... Diversion (DD)
DIVERSITAS ... IUBS/SCOPE/UNESCO Programme on Biological Diversity (SAUO)
divertic .... Diverticulum [*Medicine*] (DAVI)
DIVERTORD ... Diversion Order [*Military*] (NVT)
divg .... Diving (SAUS)
DIV-H .... Delta IV Heavy (IGSL)
DIVHED .... Division Headquarters [*Army*]
Div HQ .... Divisional Headquarters (WDAA)
DIVIC .... Digital Variable Increment Computer
divid .... Dividatur [*Let It Be Divided*] [*Latin*] [*Pharmacy*] (BARN)
DIVIDE .... Divide [*Commonly used*] (OPSA)
DIVINFO .... Division of Information [*Marine Corps*]
DIV in PAR AEQ ... Dividatur in Partes Aequales [*Divide into Equal Parts*] [*Pharmacy*]
DIV in PT AEQ ... Dividatur in Partes Aequales [*Divide into Equal Parts*] [*Pharmacy*]
Div JA .... Division Judge Advocate (SAUO)

Divl Comdr... Divisional Commander (SAUO)
DIVLEV........ Division Level [*Combat model*] (MCD)
Div Loc Bty... Divisional Locating Battery (SAUO)
DIVLOGMOD... Division Logistics Model (MCD)
DIV-M........ Delta IV Medium (IGSL)
DIVN........ Division
DIVNL........ Divisional (ADA)
Divnl Sigs.... Divisional Signals (SAUO)
Divns........ Divisions (SAUO)
DIVO........ Digitale Vermittlungsstelle Ortsnetz (SAUO)
DIVOO........ Division Ordnance Officer
Div Ord Off... Divisional Ordnance Officer (SAUO)
DIVOT........ Digital-to-Voice Translation (SAUS)
DIVOT........ Digital-to-Voice Translator
DIVOT........ Digital-to-Voice Transportation (SAUS)
DIVOTS........ Data Input Voice Output Telephone System
DIVPAY........ Diving Pay [*Navy*]
DivPetCoy.... Divisional Petrol Company (SAUO)
DivPetPk...... Divisional Petrol Park (SAUO)
Div Pro Coy... Divisional Provost Company (SAUO)
DIVPRTR...... EMSL-LV Expenditure System (SAUS)
Div Res........ Divisional Reserve (SAUO)
Div Rr Ech.... Divisional Rear Echelon (SAUO)
Divrs........ Diversifax, Inc. [*Associated Press*] (SAG)
Divrsfax........ Diversifax, Inc. [*Associated Press*] (SAG)
divs........ dividends (SAUS)
DIVS........ Signed Division [*Computer science*]
DIVSA........ digital intravenous subtraction angiography (SAUS)
DivSigO........ Division Signal Officer (SAUS)
DIVSNL........ Divisional
Div Somn..... De Divinatione per Somnia [*of Aristotle*] [*Classical studies*] (OCD)
DIVSP........ Division Supply Point
Div Sup Col... Divisional Supply Column (SAUO)
Div Syst........ Divariant System (SAUS)
DIVTAG........ Division through Army Group
DIVTOS........ Division Tactical Operations System (MCD)
Div Tr........ Divisional Train (SAUO)
DIVU........ Unsigned Division [*Computer science*]
divvy........ divide (SAUS)
divvy........ dividend (SAUS)
DIVWAG........ Division War Game (MCD)
DIVWAG........ Division War Game Model (SAUO)
Div Wks O..... Divisional Works Officer (SAUO)
DIVX........ Digital Video Express (RALS)
Divx........ Digital Video Express [*Computer science*]
DIVY........ Discovery Associates, Inc. [*NASDAQ symbol*] (COMM)
DIVYEO........ Diving Yeoman [*British military*] (DMA)
DIW........ Dead in the Water [*Navy*] (NVT)
DIW........ Defensive Information Warfare (SAUS)
DIW........ Deionized Water (ABAC)
DIW........ Department of Industrial Works (SAUO)
DIW........ Design Information Worksheet
DIW........ Deutsches Institut fuer Wirtschaftsforschung [*Data Resources, Inc.*] [*Database*]
DIW........ Diagonal Wear [*Tire maintenance*]
DIW........ D-Inside Wire (SAUS)
DIWAC........ Digital Interface Weapon Aiming Computer (MCD)
DI-water..... De-ionized water (SAUS)
DIWSA........ Digital Imagery Workstation Suites Afloat (SEWL)
DI/WSA........ Vessels Transferred to War Shipping Administration - Maritime Commission for Disposition [*Navy*]
DI-W-SCSI... Differential Wide SCSI (SAUS)
DIWT........ Director of Inland Water Transport Service [*British*]
DIWT........ Dokumentations - und Informationsgesellschaft fuer Wirtschaft und Touristik mbH [*Database producer*]
DIWTM........ Dictionary of Initials - What They Mean [*A publication*]
DIX........ DEC, Intel, Xerox (SAUS)
DIX........ Device-Independent X-windows (SAUS)
DIX........ Digital equipment, Intel and Xerox (SAUS)
DIX........ Digital, Intel, and Xerox [*Telecommunications*] (ACRL)
DIX........ Discount [*Stock exchange*] [*British*] (ROG)
Dix........ Dixie (SAUS)
DIX........ Dixieline Products, Inc. (MHDW)
DIX........ Dixon, CA [*Location identifier*] [*FAA*] (FAAL)
Dix........ Fort Dix, New Jersey (SAUS)
DIX........ Grand Dixence [*Switzerland*] [*Seismograph station code, US Geological Survey*] (SEIS)
Dix Av........ Dixon on General Average [*A publication*] (DLA)
DIXBI........ Diaminotriazine Xanthene Biphenyl Imide [*Biochemistry*]
Dix Dec........ Dix's School Law Decisions [*New York*] [*A publication*] (DLA)
Dix Dec (NY)... Dix's School Law Decisions [*New York*] [*A publication*] (DLA)
Dix Farm..... Dixon's Law of the Farm [*6th ed.*] [*1904*] [*A publication*] (DLA)
DIXIE........ Dixie, NC [*American Association of Railroads railroad junction routing code*]
DixieN........ Dixie National Corp. [*Associated Press*] (SAG)
DixieYr........ Dixie Yarns, Inc. [*Associated Press*] (SAG)
DIXIT........ Delegation for Scientific and Technical Information, Communication, and Culture [*Information service or system*] (IID)
Dix Mar Ins... Dixon's Marine Insurance and Average [*A publication*] (DLA)
Dix Mar Law... Dixon's Abridgment of the Maritime Law [*A publication*] (DLA)
DixnTic........ Dixon Ticonderoga Co. [*Associated Press*] (SAG)
DIXON........ Dixon, IL [*American Association of Railroads railroad junction routing code*]
Dix Part....... Dixon on Partnership [*1866*] [*A publication*] (DLA)
Dix Pr........ Dixon's Probate and Administration Law and Practice [*3rd ed.*] [*1912*] [*A publication*] (DLA)
Dix Ship...... Dixon's Law of Shipping [*A publication*] (DLA)
DIX standard... DEC-[*Digital Equipment Corp.*] Intel-Xerox Standard (CDE)
Dix Subr...... Dixon's Law of Subrogation [*A publication*] (DLA)
DIXT........ Diaminotriazine Xanthene Thymine [*Biochemistry*]
Dix Tit D...... Dixon on Title Deeds [*A publication*] (DLA)
DIXY........ Dipole Xerography
DIY........ Derbyshire Imperial Yeomanry [*British military*] (DMA)
DIY........ Diyarbakir [*Turkey*] [*Airport symbol*] (OAG)
DIY........ Do-It-Yourself
DIYE........ Do-It-Yourself Economics
DIYH........ DIY Home Warehouse [*NASDAQ symbol*] (SAG)
DIY Hme...... DIY Home Warehouse Co [*Associated Press*] (SAG)
D-I-Y- IC...... Do-It-Yourself Integrated Circuit (SAUS)
DIYO........ Yamoussoukro [*Ivory Coast*] [*ICAO location identifier*] (ICLI)
DIYRI........ Do-It-Yourself Research Institute [*Later, HIRI*] (EA)
DIYS........ DiaSys Corp. [*NASDAQ symbol*] (SAG)
DIY Stereo... Do It Yourself Stereo (SAUS)
DIYSW........ DiaSys Corp. Wrrt [*NASDAQ symbol*] (TTSB)
DIZ........ Defense Identification Zone
DIZ........ Description in Zip (VLIE)
DIZ........ Development Impact Zone (SAUS)
DIZ........ Dissolve (NTCM)
Diz Epigr...... Dizionario Epigrafico di Antichita Romana [*A publication*] (OCD)
dizz........ dizziness (SAUS)
DJ........ Air Djibouti [*ICAO designator*] (AD)
DJ........ Daiichi Seiyaku Co. Ltd. [*Japan*] [*Research code symbol*]
DJ........ Dark-Eyed Junco [*Ornithology*]
DJ........ Department of Journalism (SAUO)
DJ........ Department of Justice (SAUO)
DJ........ Diamond Jet (SAUS)
DJ........ Dieses Jahres [*Of This Year*] [*German*] (ROG)
dj........ Diffused Junction (IDOE)
DJ........ Diffused Junction
DJ........ Diffusion Junction (SAUS)
DJ........ Digital Junction [*Telecommunications*] (TEL)
DJ........ Dinner Jacket (ADA)
DJ........ Diploma in Journalism (ADA)
dj........ Disc Jockey (WDMC)
DJ........ Disc Jockey
DJ........ Disc Jockeys (Mobile) [*Public-performance tariff class*] [*British*]
DJ........ Dishonest John [*In TV series "Time for Beany"*]
DJ........ Disjoncteur [*Indian Railway*] (TIR)
DJ........ Disk Jockey (SAUS)
DJ........ Distributed Jamming (MCD)
DJ........ District Judge
DJ........ District Office of Jurisdiction [*IRS*]
DJ........ Diversity-Joining [*Genetics*]
DJ........ Divorce Judge (DAS)
Dj........ Djibouti (MILB)
DJ........ Djibouti [*IYRU nationality code*] [*ANSI two-letter standard code*] (CNC)
DJ........ Doctor Juris [*Doctor of Law*]
DJ........ Doctor of Jurisprudence (ACAE)
DJ........ Don Jail (SAUS)
DJ........ Double Jeopardy
D-J........ Dow-Jones (SAUS)
DJ........ Dow Jones & Co. [*NYSE symbol*] (TTSB)
DJ........ Dow Jones & Co., Inc. [*Also, the stock market averages compiled by this co mpany*] [*NYSE symbol*] (SPSG)
DJ........ Dragon Jump [*Pack*] [*Military*] (MCD)
DJ........ Drill Jig (MSA)
DJ........ Dubin-Johnson [*Syndrome*] [*Medicine*] (DB)
DJ........ Dump job (SAUS)
dj........ Dust Jacket (WDMC)
DJ........ Dust Jacket [*Paper cover for a hardbound book*]
DJ........ United States Department of Justice, Washington, DC [*Library symbol*] [*Library of Congress*] (LCLS)
DJA........ Disabled Journalists of America (EA)
DJA........ Disc Jockey Association (NTCM)
DJA........ Djakarta [*Batavia*] [*Java*] [*Seismograph station code, US Geological Survey*] (SEIS)
DJA........ Dow Jones Averages [*Information retrieval*]
DJAA........ Dog Judges Association of America [*Defunct*] (EA)
DJAD........ Department of Justice Antitrust Division (SAUS)
DJAG........ Deputy Judge Advocate General
DJAG........ Deputy Judge Advocate-General (SAUO)
DJAMA........ Masses (Guinea) [*Political party*] (PSAP)
DJ & S........ De Gex, Jones, and Smith's English Chancery Reports [*A publication*] (DLA)
DJ & SB...... De Gex, Jones, and Smith's English Bankruptcy Reports [*A publication*] (DLA)
DJB........ Air Djibouti [*ICAO designator*] (FAAC)
DJB........ Cleveland, OH [*Location identifier*] [*FAA*] (FAAL)
DJB........ Djambi [*Indonesia*] [*Airport symbol*] (AD)
DjB........ Dow Jones Books, Princeton, NJ [*Library symbol*] [*Library of Congress*] (LCLS)
DJB........ Drill Jig Bushing
DJB........ Jambi [*Indonesia*] [*Airport symbol*] (OAG)
DJB........ Joint Bank-Fund Library, Washington, DC [*OCLC symbol*] (OCLC)
DJBF........ International Monetary Fund and International Bank for Reconstruction and Development, Joint Bank-Fund Library, Washington, DC [*Library symbol*] [*Library of Congress*] (LCLS)

DJC .... Application for Writ of Error Dismissed, Judgment Correct [*Legal term*] (DLA)
DJC .... Danville Junior College [*Illinois*]
DJC .... Dependent Job Control (SAUS)
DJC .... Detroit Jazz Center [*Defunct*] (EA)
DJC .... Dixie Junior College (SAUO)
DJC .... Docklands Joint Committee (SAUO)
DJCB .... Dominican Junior College of Blauvelt [*Later, Dominican College*] [*New York*]
DJCD .... Department of Justice Civil Division (SAUS)
DJCD .... Department of Justice Criminal Division (SAUS)
DJC/JRI .... Detroit Jazz Center/Jazz Research Institute [*Later, DJC*] (EA)
DJCN .... Dow Jones Cable News [*Cable-television system*]
DJCO .... Daily Journal [*NASDAQ symbol*] (TTSB)
DJCO .... Daily Journal Corp. South Carolina [*NASDAQ symbol*] (NQ)
DJCP .... Division of Justice and Crime Prevention (SAUS)
DJCRD .... Department of Justice Civil Rights Division (SAUS)
DJD .... Degenerative Joint Disease
DJDE .... Dynamic Job Description Entity [*For Xerox printer*] (NITA)
DJDR .... Jones, Day, Reavis and Pogue, Law Library, Washington, DC [*Library symbol*] [*Library of Congress*] (LCLS)
DJDS .... Division of Juvenile Delinquency Service [*of SSA*]
DJE .... Deception Jamming Equipment (SAUS)
DJE .... Deflected Jet Exhaust
DJE .... Demokratischer Jugendverband Europas [*Democrat Youth Community of Europe*] [*Political party*] (EAIO)
DJE .... Dictionary of Jamaican English [*A publication*]
DJE .... Djerba [*Tunisia*] [*Airport symbol*] (OAG)
DJ Ed .... Doctor of Jewish Education (PGP)
DJET .... Delayed Jam Exceeds Threshold (ACAE)
DJF .... December-January-February [*Marine science*] (OSRA)
DJF .... Descriptor Justification Form [*ERIC*]
DJF .... Divorced Jewish Female [*Classified advertising*]
DJG .... Djanet [*Algeria*] [*Airport symbol*] (OAG)
DJHi .... Jewish Historical Society of Greater Washington, Washington, DC [*Library symbol*] [*Library of Congress*] (LCLS)
DJI .... Designcraft Industries, Inc. [*AMEX symbol*] (COMM)
DJI .... Dow Jones Index [*Stock market*] [*Investment term*]
DJI .... Dow-Jones Industrials (SAUS)
DJI .... Dow Jones Interactive
DJIA .... Dow Jones Industrial Average [*Stock market*] [*Investment term*]
DJIC .... Dow Jones Index - Composite [*Stock market*] [*Investment term*]
DJII .... Dow Jones Index - Industrials [*Stock market*] [*Investment term*]
DJIN .... Dow Jones Investor Network
DJIRS .... Dow Jones Information Retrieval System (HGAA)
DJIT .... Dow Jones Index - Transport [*Stock market*] [*Investment term*]
DJIU .... Dow Jones Index - Utilities [*Stock market*] [*Investment term*]
DJJ .... Department of Juvenile Justice (SAUS)
DJJ .... Djajapura [*West Irian, Indonesia*] [*Airport symbol*] (AD)
DJJ .... Jayapura [*Indonesia*] [*Airport symbol*] (OAG)
DJJX .... J. Joseph David [*Private rail car owner code*]
DJK .... Daughters of Jesus of Kermaria [*See also FJ*] [*Paris, France*] (EAIO)
DJK Approximation ... Dichtel, Jelitto and Koppe Approximation (SAUS)
Djkta .... Djakarta (SAUS)
DJL .... Doctor of Jewish Literature (BJA)
DJLNRD .... Department of Justice Land and Natural Resources Division (SAUS)
DJLX .... J. Joseph David [*Private rail car owner code*]
DJM .... Director, Joint Staff Memorandum [*Military*]
DJM .... Divorced Jewish Male [*Classified advertising*]
DJM .... Djambala [*Congo*] [*Airport symbol*] (AD)
DJN .... Delta Junction, AK [*Location identifier*] [*FAA*] (FAAL)
DJN .... Demijohn [*Freight*]
DJN .... Dow Jones News [*Dow Jones & Co., Inc.*] [*Information service or system*] (CRD)
DJNET .... Dependent Job control Network name (SAUS)
DJNF .... Dow Jones Newspaper Fund (EA)
DJNR .... Dow Jones News/Retrieval [*Princeton, NJ*] [*Bibliographic database*] [*Information service or system*]
DJNR .... Dow Jones news retrieval service (SAUS)
DJNRS .... Dow Jones News/Retrieval Service (SAUS)
DJO .... Daloa [*Ivory Coast*] [*Airport symbol*] (OAG)
DJO .... Digital Journal of Ophthalmology (SAUO)
DJOA .... Dominant Juvenile Optic Atrophy [*Medicine*] (MELL)
DJOEO .... Development Job Outline Engineering Order [*DAC*]
Djokja .... Djokjakarta Java, Indonesia (SAUS)
DJOT .... Delayed Jam on Target
DJourn .... Doctor of Journalism (SAUS)
DJOWT .... District of Columbia Teachers College [*Later, University of the District of Columbia*], Washington, DC [*Library symbol*] [*Library of Congress*] [*Obsolete*] (LCLS)
DJP .... Democratic Justice Party [*Mauritania*] [*Political party*] (EY)
DJP .... Democratic Justice Party [*South Korea*] [*Political party*] (PPW)
DJP .... Deputy Judge President (SAFN)
DJP .... Doctor of Jewish Pedagogy
DJP .... Dragon Jump Pack [*Military*] (MCD)
DJPC .... Deputy Justice of Peace Clerk [*British*] (ROG)
DJPF .... Divorced Jewish Professional Female (SAUO)
DJPM .... Divorced Jewish Professional Male (SAUO)
DJR .... Dajarra [*Queensland*] [*Airport symbol*] (AD)
DJR .... Marietta, GA [*Location identifier*] [*FAA*] (FAAL)
DJRX .... J. Joseph David [*Private rail car owner code*]
DJS .... David Jones Society [*British*] [*England*] (EAIO)
DJS .... Deception Jamming System
DJs .... Department of Justice investigators (SAUS)
DJS .... Director, Joint Staff [*Military*] (AABC)
DJS .... Doctor of Jewish Studies (PGP)
DJS .... Doctor of Judicial Science
DJS .... Doctor of Juridical Science
DJS .... Dubin-Johnson Syndrome [*Medicine*] (CPH)
DJSC .... Daily Journal of the Supreme Court
DJ Sc .... Doctor of Judicial Science
DJ Sc .... Doctor of Juridical Science (SAUS)
DJSM .... Director, Joint Staff Memorandum [*Military*] (AABC)
DJStJ .... Dame of Justice of St. John of Jerusalem [*Later, D St J*] [*British*]
DJSU .... Digital Junction Switching Unit (IAA)
DJT .... Denver Jet, Inc. [*ICAO designator*] (FAAC)
DJT .... Doctor of Jewish Theology
DJT .... Drill Jig Template (SAUS)
DJT .... Trump Hotels & Casino Resorts [*NYSE symbol*] (TTSB)
DJT .... Trump Hotels & Casino Resorts, Inc. [*NYSE symbol*] (SAG)
DJTA .... Dow Jones Transportation Average [*Information retrieval*]
DJTD .... Department of Justice Tax Division (SAUS)
DJ Th .... Doctor of Jewish Theology
DJUA .... Dow Jones Utility Average [*Information retrieval*]
DJUOL .... Daily JUMPS [*Joint Uniform Military Pay System*] Update Output Listing (AABC)
D Jur .... Doctor of Jurisprudence
D Jur et Rer Pol ... Doctor Juris et Rerum Politicarum [*Doctor of Law and Politics*] [*Latin*]
DJuris .... Doctor of Jurisprudence
D Jur Sc .... Doctor of Juridical Science
DJV .... Dabajuro [*Venezuela*] [*Airport symbol*] (AD)
DJV .... Deshapremi Janatha Viyaparaya [*Patriotic People's Organisation*] [*Sri Lanka*] [*Political party*]
DK .... Dance Kaleidoscope [*Indiana*]
DK .... Danish Krone [*Monetary unit*] (NATG)
dk .... Dark [*Medicine*] (EDAA)
dk .... Dark (VRA)
DK .... Dark
DK .... Daughters of the King (EA)
DK .... David Kaufmann Collection. Hungarian Academy of Sciences [*Budapest*] (BJA)
DK .... Deca [*or Deka*] [*A prefix meaning multiplied by 10*] (KSC)
DK .... Decatur [*ICAO designator*] (AD)
DK .... Decay (MAE)
Dk .... Deck (MIST)
DK .... Deck
DK .... Degrees Kelvin (KSC)
DK .... Dejerine-Klumpke [*Syndrome*] [*Medicine*] (DB)
DK .... Democratic Kampuchea [*Pol Pot's regime in Cambodia*]
DK .... Democratic People's Republic of Korea [*IYRU nationality code*] (IYR)
DK .... Denmark [*ANSI two-letter standard code*] (CNC)
dk .... Denmark [*MARC country of publication code*] [*Library of Congress*] (LCCP)
DK .... Deutscher Kulturbund [*German Cultural Federation*] [*Germany*] (PPE)
DK .... Dezimal Klassifikation [*Netherlands*]
DK .... Diabetic Ketoacidosis [*Medicine*] (MELL)
Dk .... Dielectric Constant (AAEL)
DK .... Diet Kitchen
Dk .... Diffusion Coefficient [*or Permeability constant as described by Krogh*] [*Medicine*] (DAVI)
DK .... Digit Keyboard (SAUS)
DK .... Direct Kinematics (SAUS)
DK .... Disbursing Clerk [*Navy rating*]
DK .... Diseased Kidney [*Medicine*] (MAE)
DK .... Disk [*Computer science*] (IAA)
DK .... Display/Keyboard [*Computer science*] (MCD)
dk .... Dock (ADWA)
DK .... Dock
DK .... Docking
DK .... Dog Kidney (MAE)
dk .... donkey (SAUS)
DK .... Donna Karan Intl. [*NYSE symbol*] (SG)
DK .... Don't Know
DK .... Dorling Kindersley, Ltd. [*British*]
DK .... Dorsal Kidney
D/K .... Downlink
DK .... drop keel (SAUS)
dk .... drop kick (SAUS)
DK .... Duck
DK .... Duct Keel [*of a ship*] (DS)
DK .... Duke (ROG)
dk .... dusky (SAUS)
DK1 .... Disbursing Clerk, First Class [*Navy rating*]
DK2 .... Disbursing Clerk, Second Class [*Navy rating*]
DK3 .... Disbursing Clerk, Third Class [*Navy rating*]
DKA .... Daka [*Kazakhstan*] [*ICAO designator*] (FAAC)
DKA .... Decca Records, Inc. (SAUO)
DKA .... Deutscher Koordinierungsausshuss [*Coordinating European Council*]
DKA .... Diabetic Ketoacidosis [*Medicine*]
DKA .... Did not Keep Appointment (SAUS)
DKA .... Diketogulonic Acid [*Organic chemistry*]
DKAI .... Daka International, Inc. [*NASDAQ symbol*] (CTT)
DKAI .... DAKA Intl. [*NASDAQ symbol*] (TTSB)
DKAM .... Double Known Addition Method [*Analytical electrochemistry*]
D Kan .... United States District Court for the District of Kansas (DLA)
DKAP .... Datakit Application Processor (VLIE)
DKB .... Dai-Ichi Kangyo Bank [*Japan*]
DKB .... Decimal Keyboard [*Computer science*]

DKB .... Deep Knee Bends (DAVI)
DKB .... DeKalb, IL [*Location identifier*] [*FAA*] (FAAL)
DKB .... Diagnostic Knowledge-Based System (VLIE)
DKB .... Distributed Knowledge Base [*Computer science*] (ODBW)
DKBS .... Deep Knowledge Based Systems [*Computer science*]
DKC .... De Kalb College (SAUS)
DKC .... Dickinson College, Carlisle, PA [*OCLC symbol*] (OCLC)
DKC .... Disbursing Clerk, Chief [*Navy rating*]
DKC .... Disk Channel (SAUS)
DK Car......... Dormitory Kitchen Car (SAUS)
DKCM .... Disbursing Clerk, Master Chief [*Navy rating*]
DKCS .... Disbursing Clerk, Senior Chief [*Navy rating*]
DKDI .... Dinking Die [*Tool*] (AAG)
DKDK .... Don't Know That You Don't Know (VLIE)
DKDP .... Deuterated Potassium Dihydrogen Phosphate [*Electronics*] (BARN)
DKE .... Deck Edge
DKE .... Delta Kappa Epsilon [*Society*]
DKE .... Jubilee Airways Ltd. [*British*] [*ICAO designator*] (FAAC)
DKEL .... Demokratikon Komma Ergazomenou Laou [*Democratic Party of Working People*] [*Greek*] (PPE)
DKEY .... Datakey, Inc. [*NASDAQ symbol*] (NQ)
DKF .... Dokumentation Kraftfahrwesen [*Motor Vehicle Documentation*] [*Germany*] [*Information service or system*] (IID)
DKF .... Dudley, Kenneth F., Ottumwa IA [*STAC*]
DKFC .... David Kirchner Fan Club [*Defunct*] (EA)
DKFC .... Dena Kaye Fan Club (EA)
Dkfm .... Diploma in Commerce [*German*]
DKFTCOL ..... Dark Fast Color (SAUS)
dkfz .... Deutsches Krebsforschungszentrum [*Germany*]
DKG .... Columbus, OH [*Location identifier*] [*FAA*] (FAAL)
Dkg .... Decking (DAC)
dkg .... Dekagram (ADWA)
DKG .... Dekagram [*Unit of measure*] (GPO)
DKG .... Delta Kappa Gamma Society, International (AEBS)
DKG .... Diketogluconic Acid [*Organic chemistry*]
DKG .... Docking [*Aerospace*] (KSC)
DKGM .... Dekagram [*Unit of measure*] (ROG)
DKGRCOL .... Dark Ground (SAUS)
DKH .... Dorling Kindersley Holdings
DK HSE .... Deck House (SAUS)
DK HSE .... Deckhouse (SAUS)
DKI .... Daniel K. Inouye [*US Senator from Hawaii*]
DKI .... Dart & Kraft, Inc. [*Toronto Stock Exchange symbol*] (SPSG)
DKI .... Data Key Idle
DKI .... Device Kernel Interface (SAUS)
DKI .... Docking Initiate
DKI .... Don't Knock It [*Slang*]
DKI .... Driver Kernel Interface (SAUS)
DKI .... Dunk Island [*Australia*] [*Airport symbol*] (OAG)
DKIE .... Decontamination Kit Individual Equipment [*Army*] (DOMA)
DKK .... Disaster Preparedness Plan (SAUO)
DKK .... Don't Know That You Know (VLIE)
DKK .... Dunkirk, NY [*Location identifier*] [*FAA*] (FAAL)
DkL .... Deck Load (SAUS)
DkL .... Deck Loss (SAUS)
dkl .... Dekaliter (ADWA)
DKL .... Dekaliter [*Unit of measure*] (GPO)
DKL .... Dickinson School of Law, Sheeley-Lee Law Library, Carlisle, PA [*OCLC symbol*] (OCLC)
DKL .... Dielectro-Kinetic Laboratories, LLC
DklbGn .... DeKalb Genetics [*Associated Press*] (SAG)
DK Lndg ...... Deck Landing (SAUS)
Dk LR .... Dickinson Law Review [*A publication*] (DLA)
DKM .... Dakomat [*Poland*] [*ICAO designator*] (FAAC)
dkm .... Dekameter (ADWA)
DKM .... Dekameter [*Unit of measure*] (GPO)
Dkm .... Dekametre (SAUS)
DKM .... Duke Minerals Ltd. [*Vancouver Stock Exchange symbol*]
DKM .... Dyson-Kissner-Moran Corp. (EFIS)
Dkm^2 .... Square Dekameter
Dkm^3 .... Cubic Dekameter
dkm3 .... Cubic Dekameter (or Dekametre) (SAUS)
dkmy .... square dekameter (SAUS)
dkmy .... square dekametre (SAUS)
DKMZ .... Dotiki Mine [*Federal Railroad Administration identification code*]
DKN .... Dakon Metals, Inc. [*Vancouver Stock Exchange symbol*]
dkN .... Dekanewton (SAUS)
DKNF .... Domain-Key Normal Form (SAUS)
DKNY .... Donna Karan New York [*Sportswear*]
DKO .... Ayer, Ft. Devens, MA [*Location identifier*] [*FAA*] (FAAL)
DKO .... Dankoe Mines Ltd. [*Vancouver Stock Exchange symbol*]
DKO .... Delay Key On
DKO .... Die Deutsche Kirche im Orient [*Cairo*] [*A publication*] (BJA)
DKO .... Double Knockout [*Genetics*]
DKP .... Dania Kommunista Partja [*Communist Party of Denmark*] [*Political party*]
DKP .... Danmarks Kommunistiske Parti [*Communist Party of Denmark*] [*Political Party*] (PPW)
DKP .... Decontamination Kit, Personal (SAUS)
DKP .... Democratic Korea Party [*South Korea*] [*Political party*] (PPW)
DKP .... Deutsche Kommunistische Partei [*German Communist Party*] [*Political party*] (PPE)
DKP .... Dikalium Phosphate [*Pharmacology*]
DKP .... Dikaliuphosphat (SAUS)
dkp .... diketopiperazene (SAUS)
DKP .... Diketopiperazine [*Organic chemistry*]
DKP .... Dipotassium Phosphate (SAUS)
DKP .... DK Platinum Corp. [*Vancouver Stock Exchange symbol*]
DKPG .... Depth Keeping
Dk Pltg .... Deck Plating (SAUS)
DKR .... Dakar [*Senegal*] [*Airport symbol*] (OAG)
D KR .... Danish Krone [*Monetary unit*]
Dkr .... Dan Korona [*Danish Crown*] [*Monetary unit*]
DKR .... Decker Resources Ltd. [*Vancouver Stock Exchange symbol*]
DKS .... Data Key Signal (SAUS)
DKS .... Data Key System [*Computer science*] (VLIE)
DKS .... Dekastere [*Unit of measure*]
DKS .... Deoxyketosteroids (MEDA)
DKS .... Deputy Keeper of the Signet (DLA)
DKS .... Direct Keying System
DKS .... Disseminated Kaposi Sarcoma [*Medicine*]
DKS .... Doniphan, Kensett & Searcy Railway [*AAR code*]
DKSA .... Seaman Apprentice, Disbursing Clerk, Striker [*Navy rating*]
Dks Coy RE... Docks Company, Royal Engineers (SAUO)
DKSEN .... Don King Sports and Entertainment Network [*Cable-television system*]
DKSME .... International Conference on Data and Knowledge Systems for Manufacturing and Engineering (SAUS)
DKSN .... Seaman, Disbursing Clerk, Striker [*Navy rating*]
DKSY .... Display and Keyboard System (SAUS)
DKT .... Dahl-Kirkam Telescope
DKT .... Dakota Energy Corp. [*Vancouver Stock Exchange symbol*]
DKT .... Dakota Mining [*Formerly, MinVen Gold Corp.*] [*AMEX symbol*] (SPSG)
DKT .... dipotassium tartrate (SAUS)
dkt .... Docket (ADWA)
DKT .... Docket [*Law, Packaging*]
Dkt .... West Publishing Company's Docket [*1909-41*] [*A publication*] (DLA)
DKTC .... Dog Kidney Tissue Culture
DKTC .... Door-Kewaunee Teachers College (SAUS)
DKTH .... Dakotah, Inc. [*NASDAQ symbol*] (SAG)
DKTS .... Dakotas (FAAC)
DKTS .... Digital Key Telephone System [*Communications term*] (DCT)
DKU .... Display Keyboard Unit (SAUS)
DKUUG .... Danish UNIX Users Group (SAUO)
DKV .... Deer Kidney Virus
DKW .... Dampf-Kraft-Wagen [*Steam-Powered Vehicle*] [*German*]
DKW .... Das Kleine Wunder [*The Little Wonder*] [*Initialism used as name of German automobile, manufactured by Auto Union*]
DKW .... Dresdner Kleinwort Wasserstein
DKWD .... D & K Healthcare Resources, Inc. [*NASDAQ symbol*] (NASQ)
DKWD .... D & K Wholesale Drug [*NASDAQ symbol*] (SAG)
DKWIC .... Double Key Word In Context (SAUS)
DKWT .... De Kalb & Western Transportation R. R. [*AAR code*]
DKX .... Knoxville, TN [*Location identifier*] [*FAA*] (FAAL)
DKY .... Donkey Boiler [*of a ship*] (DS)
Dkyd .... dockyard (SAUS)
DL .... Associate Directorate for LPS [*Launch Processing System*] Development [*Kennedy Space Center*] [*NASA*] (NASA)
DL .... Dacron Braid Lacquered (MDG)
DL .... Dale
DL .... Damage Limitation [*Strategy*] [*Military*]
DL .... Danger List [*Medicine*]
DL .... Danske Lov [*Laws in Force*] [*Denmark*] (ILCA)
DL .... Daresbury Laboratory (SAUO)
DL .... Dark on Light
DL .... Data Laboratories Ltd. (SAUO)
DL .... Data Language
DL .... Data Length (IAA)
DL .... Data Limit (SAUS)
DL .... Data Link
DL .... Data List [*DoD*]
DL .... Data Logger (SAUS)
DL .... Data Logging (GEOI)
DL .... Datum Level
DL .... Davidson Laboratory [*Stevens Institute of Technology*]
DL .... Day Labour (SAUS)
DL .... Day Letter [*Telegraphy*]
DL .... Daylight (MSA)
DL .... Days Lost [*Military*]
DL .... Dead Light (AAG)
dl .... deadlight (SAUS)
DL .... Deadline (AABC)
DL .... Dead Load
DL .... Deadload (SAUS)
DL .... Deadweight Loss [*of grain*] [*Agriculture*]
dl .... Decaliter (AAMN)
DL .... Deciliter [*Unit of measure*] (GPO)
dL .... Deciliter, 1 E-1 L [*Industrial hygiene term*] (OHS)
DL .... Decision Leaflets [*US Patent Office*]
DL .... Deck Log (SAUS)
DL .... Decret-Loi [*Decree-Law*] [*French*] (ILCA)
DL .... Decreto Legge [*Decree-Law*] [*Italian*] (ILCA)
DL .... Dedicated Landline
DL .... Dedicated Line (SAUS)
DL .... Defence Light [*British military*] (DMA)
DL .... Defended Locality (SAUS)
DL .... Definition List (SAUS)
DL .... Dekaliter [*Unit of measure*] (ROG)

DL ... Delaware-Lackawanna Railroad [*Federal Railroad Administration identification code*]

DL ... Delay Line

DL ... D'Eldona Resources Ltd. [*Toronto Stock Exchange symbol*]

DL ... Delete Line (SAUS)

DL ... Delta Air Lines, Inc. [*ICAO designator*]

D/L ... De Luxe (SAUS)

DL ... Demand Loan (FOTI)

D/L ... Demand Loan

DL ... Demarcation Line (SAUS)

DL ... Democratic League (SAUO)

DL ... Den Leader [*Boy Scouts of America*]

DL ... Dentate Line [*Anatomy*]

D/L ... Deorbit/Landing [*Aerospace*] (MCD)

DL ... Departmental Letter [*Air Force*] (AAGC)

DL ... Department of Labor

DL ... Departure Locator

DL ... Deputy Lieutenant [*British*]

DL ... Derived Limit (PDAA)

DL ... Dermal Leishmanoid (SAUS)

DL ... Description Language (SAUS)

DL ... Description Leaf (SAUS)

DL ... Description of Leaf (ROG)

dl ... designer links (SAUS)

DL ... Design Language (SAUS)

DL ... design load (SAUS)

DL ... Destroyer Leader [*Navy*]

DL ... Detection Limit [*Analytical chemistry*]

DL ... Developed Length (AAG)

DL ... Development laboratories (SAUS)

DL ... Development-Left (MCD)

d-l ... dextro-levo (SAUS)

dl ... Dextro-Levo(rotary) [*Also, r, rac*] [*Chemistry*]

DL ... Diagnostic Laparoscopy [*or Laparotomy*] (DAVI)

DL ... Dial Corp. [*NYSE symbol*] (SPSG)

dl ... Diallage (SAUS)

DL ... Dielectric Loading (SAUS)

DL ... Dielectric Loading Factor [*Electronics*] (MDG)

DL ... Diesel (MIST)

DL ... Diesel Locomotive Works (SAUS)

DL ... Difference Limen [*Physiology, psychology*]

DL ... Difference Limit (SAUS)

DL ... Difference Lumen (SAUS)

DL ... Difference of Latitude [*Navigation*] (MUGU)

DL ... difference of longitude (SAUS)

dL ... differential of inductance (SAUS)

DL ... Diffraction Limited (MCD)

DL ... Diffuse Leiomyomatosis [*Medicine*]

DL ... Diffuse Lymphoma [*Oncology*] (DAVI)

DL ... Diffusing Capacity of the Lung (AAMN)

DL ... Diffusion-Limited (SAUS)

DL ... Digital Loop [*Communications term*] (DCT)

DL ... Digital Stimulation [*Of rectal sphincter*] [*Gastroenterology*] (DAVI)

DL ... Digit Line (SAUS)

DL ... Diode LASER (SEWL)

DL ... Diode Limiter (SAUS)

DL ... Diode Logic

DL ... Diogenes Laertius [*Third century AD*] [*Classical studies*] (OCD)

DL ... Direction Layer (SAUS)

DL ... Direct Labor

DL ... Direct Laryngoscopy [*Otorhinolaryngology*] (DAVI)

DL ... Direct Line [*Followed by telephone number*]

DL ... Direct Listening (CAAL)

DI ... Direct Interchange (SAUS)

DL ... Direct Load

DL ... Directorate of Licensing (SAUO)

DL ... Director Layer [*British military*] (DMA)

DL ... Director of Laboratories [*AFSC*]

DL ... Director of Labour [*Military*] [*British*]

DL ... Directory Listing (SAUS)

DL ... Disabled List [*Athletics*]

DL ... Disarm Line (SAUS)

DL ... Discharge Lamp (SAUS)

DL ... Disjunctively Linear

D/L ... Displacement to Length [*Ratio*]

DL ... Display Library (SAUS)

DL ... Distance Learning (HEAS)

DL ... Distolingual [*Dentistry*]

DL ... Distributed Lab (MDG)

DL ... Distributed Learning (SAUS)

DL ... Distribution List

DL ... District Office of Location [*IRS*]

DL ... Disturbance Lines [*Marine science*] (OSRA)

DL ... Dividing Line (SAUS)

DL ... Djakarta Lloyd (SAUS)

DL ... Doctor of Law (SAUS)

DL ... Doctor of Laws

DL ... Doctor of Letters

DL ... Doctor of Literature

DL ... Documentation Library (SAUO)

DL ... Document List (SAUS)

DL ... Document Log (AABC)

DL ... Dog Licence (SAUS)

dl ... dog license (SAUS)

DL ... Dominical Letter

DL ... Donath-Landsteiner [*Antibody*] [*Medicine*] (DB)

DL ... Doppellafette [*Two-barreled mount*] [*German military - World War II*]

DL ... Dorsal Lip

DL ... Dorsal Longitudinal

DL ... Dose Limit (SAUS)

dl ... double acetate (SAUS)

DL ... Double Layer (SAUS)

DL ... Double Ledger [*Accounting*]

DL ... Double Loop (SAUS)

DL ... Dow-Lepetit [*Research code symbol*]

DL ... downlap (SAUS)

DL ... Down Left [*The front left portion of a stage*] [*A stage direction*]

DL ... Down limit (SAUS)

DL ... Down Link [*Computer science*]

D/L ... Downlink (SAUS)

D/L ... Downlist (NASA)

DL ... Download [*Computer science*] (VLIE)

D/L ... Download, transmit to you (SAUS)

DL ... Draft Legislation

D/L ... Drag/Lift (SAUS)

dl ... Drame Lyrique [*Music*] (GROV)

DL ... Drawing List [*Engineering*]

DL ... Drill Leader [*British military*] (DMA)

DL ... Driver's License (SARE)

DL ... Driving Licence [*British*] (ADA)

DL ... Drury Lane (SAUS)

DL ... Dual Language

DL ... Duchenne-Leyden [*Syndrome*] [*Medicine*] (DB)

dl ... Dull [*Philately*]

DL ... Dummy Load [*Military*] (MCD)

DL ... Dunning Leukemia [*Medicine*] (DB)

DL ... Duolateral

DL ... Dynamic Load (SAUS)

DL ... Dynamic Load Characteristic (MDG)

DL ... Dynamic Loader (SAUS)

DL ... Electronics Engineering (SAUS)

DL ... Frigate [*Navy symbol*]

DL ... General Counsel (AAGC)

DL ... Liberal Democracy (France) [*Political party*] (PSAP)

DL ... Most Distal Leaf [*Botany*]

DL ... United States Department of Labor Library, Washington, DC [*Library symbol*] [*Library of Congress*] (LCLS)

DL/1 ... Data Language Version 1 [*Computer science*]

DLA ... Air Dolomiti [*Italy*] [*ICAO designator*] (FAAC)

DLA ... Damaged Lyman-Alpha [*Galaxy*]

DLA ... Data Link Acquisition (MCD)

DLA ... Data Link Adapter

DLA ... Data Link Adapter (or Adaptor) (SAUS)

DLA ... Data Link Address

DLA ... Data Logger/Archiver (SAUS)

DLA ... Data Logging and Archiving (SAUS)

DLA ... Date Last Active (TIMI)

DLA ... Declination of Launch Asymptote [*NASA*] (KSC)

DLA ... Decorative Lighting Association [*British*] (DBA)

DLA ... Defence Land Agent (SAUO)

DLA ... Defense Logistics Agency [*Alexandria, VA*]

DLA ... Defense Logistics Area (MCD)

DLA ... Define user Label Area (SAUS)

DLA ... Delaware [*Ontario*] [*Seismograph station code, US Geological Survey*] (SEIS)

DLA ... Delaware Law School of Widener College, Wilmington, DE [*OCLC symbol*] (OCLC)

DLA ... Delaware Library Association (SAUO)

DLA ... Delay Line Assembly

DLA ... Delay Message [*Aviation code*]

DLA ... Delhi Library Association (SAUO)

DLA ... Democratic Labor Association [*Philippines*]

DLA ... Dental Laboratories Association [*British*] (DBA)

DLA ... Department of Land Administration [*Western Australia*]

DLA ... Department of Landscape Architecture (SAUO)

DLA ... Depot Level Activity (NATG)

DLA ... Deputy Chief of Staff, Logistics and Administration (SAUO)

DLA ... Designated Liability Area (EEVL)

DLA ... Diffusion-Limited Aggregation [*Physical chemistry*]

DLA ... Direct Lift Control (SAUS)

DLA ... Direct Line Attachment (VLIE)

DLA ... Direct-Line Attachment (SAUS)

DLA ... Diseased Leaf Area (SAUO)

DLA ... Disk Label (SAUS)

DLA ... Dislocation Allowance [*Military*]

DLA ... Distolabial [*Dentistry*]

DLA ... Distributed Lumped Active [*Electronics*] (OA)

DLA ... District Licensing Authority (SAUS)

DLA ... Divisional Land Agent [*Ministry of Agriculture, Fisheries, and Food*] [*British*]

DLA ... Division of Land Acquisition (SAUO)

DLA ... Division of Library Automation [*University of California, Berkeley*] [*Information service or system*] (IID)

DLA ... Doctor of Liberal Arts

DLA ... Documentation, Libraries and Archives Department (SAUS)

DLA ... Documentation, Libraries and Archives Directorate (SAUO)

DIA ... document interchange architecture (SAUS)

DLA ... Dog Lymphocytotoxicity

DLA ... Dole Food $2.7475'TRACES' [*AMEX symbol*] (SG)

DLA............. Dole Food Automatic Common Exchange Security Trust [*AMEX symbol*] (NASQ)
DLA............. Dole Food Co. [*AMEX symbol*] (SAG)
DLA............. Douala [*Cameroon*] [*Airport symbol*] (OAG)
DLA............. Dual Launching Adaptor (DNAB)
DLAA........... DARCOM Logistics Assistance Acitivity (SAUO)
DLAA........... DARCOM [*Development and Readiness Command, Army*] Logistics Assistance Activity (MCD)
DLAB........... Defense Language Aptitude Battery [*Army*] (INF)
DLab........... Director of Labour Service (SAUO)
dlab........... disc label (SAUS)
DLAB........... Disk Label (VLIE)
DLAB........... Divisor Latch Access BIT [*Computer science*]
D-L Ab........ Donath-Landsteiner Antibody [*Immunology*] (MAE)
DLABI.......... Disk Label Information (SAUS)
DLAC........... Delay Account Of (FAAC)
DIA/DCA....... Document Interchange And Document Content Architecture (SAUS)
DIA/DCA....... Document Interchange Architecture/Document Content Architecture (SAUS)
DLAH........... Defense Logistics Agency Handbook [*A publication*] (AAGC)
DLA-HSI....... Defense Logistics Agency-Headquarters Staff Instructor (AAGC)
DLaI............ Distolabioincisal (DB)
DLAI............ Distolabioincisal [*Dentistry*]
DLAI............ Documentation, Library, and Archives Infrastructures (SAUS)
D La L......... Doctor of Latin Letters
DLAM........... Defense Logistics Agency Manual [*A publication*] (AAGC)
DLAMP......... Defense Leadership and Management Program [*Army*]
DL & B......... Direct Laryngoscopy and Bronchoscopy [*Medicine*] (DAVI)
DL & E......... Design Limit and Endurance
DL & W........ Delaware, Lackawanna & Western Railroad [*Nicknames: Delay, Linger & Wait; Darn Long & Winding; Dirty, Long & Weary*]
DL & WRR... Delaware, Lackawanna & Western Railroad
DIANE......... direct information access network for europe (SAUS)
DLANET....... Defense Logistics Agency Network (SAUO)
DLA Network... Distributed-Lumped-Active Network (SAUS)
D Lang......... Doctor of Languages
DLANT......... Department of the Legislative Assembly of the Northern Territory [*Australia*]
D-L antibody... Donath-Landsteiner antibody (SAUS)
DLAO........... Defense Logistics Analysis Office (MCD)
DLAOR......... Directorate Land/Air Operation Research (SAUO)
DLAP........... Defense Logistics Agency Pamphlet (AAGC)
DLaP............ Distolabiopulpal [*Dentistry*]
DLAPS......... Defense Logistics Agency Publishing System [*CD-ROM*] (AAGC)
DLAR........... Defense Logistics Acquisition Regulation (AAGC)
DLAR........... Defense Logistics Agency Regulation [*DoD*] (GFGA)
DL Arch....... Doctor of Landscape Architecture
DLAS........... Damped Lyman-Alpha System [*Galactic science*]
DLAS........... Defence of Literature and the Arts Society (SAUO)
DLAS........... Department of Labour and Administrative Services [*Northern Territory*] [*Australia*]
DLAT........... Defense Language Aptitude Test [*Army*] (AABC)
DLAT........... Delayed Alert Velocity Tracker (ACAE)
DLAT........... Delay Time [*Aviation*] (FAAC)
DLAT........... Destructive Lot Acceptance Testing (NASA)
d lat............ difference in latitude (SAUS)
DLAT........... Difference of Latitude [*Navigation*]
DLAT........... Directory Look-Aside Table (ELAL)
DLAT........... Discharge-Line Air Temperature [*Nuclear energy*] (NRCH)
DLATCH....... Display Latch (SAUS)
DL/AW......... Director of Land / Air Warfare (SAUS)
DL/AW......... Director of Land/Air Warfare (SAUO)
D Law.......... Doctor of Law (PGP)
DLAW........... UCD Law (SAUS)
D-Layer....... Day-Timer Layer (SAUS)
DLB............. Brandywine College of Widener University, Wilmington, DE [*OCLC symbol*] (OCLC)
DLB............. d'Albertis [*Australia*] [*Airport symbol*] (AD)
DLB............. Dannemiller, Lawrence B., Columbus OH [*STAC*]
DLB............. Dead Letter Box (BARN)
DLB............. Delbancor Industry [*Vancouver Stock Exchange symbol*]
DLB............. Dementia with Lewy Bodies [*Nerve cell pathology*]
DLB............. Deposit Liquidation Board
DLB............. Depository Library Board (SAUS)
DLB............. Dictionary of Literary Biography [*A publication*]
DLB............. Digital Loopback [*Communications term*] (DCT)
DLB............. Discrete Linear Basis (SAUS)
DLB............. DLB Oil & Gas, Inc. [*NYSE symbol*] (SAG)
DIB.............. documentary bill (SAUS)
DL-BAPNA... Benzoyl-DL-Arginine-p-Nitroanilide (SAUS)
DLBD........... Diffuse Lewy Body Disease [*Medicine*] (DMAA)
DLBI............ Device Level Burn-In (AAEL)
DLBI............ Differential Long-Baseline Interferometer [*Radio interferometry*]
DLBI............ DLB Oil & Gas [*NASDAQ symbol*] (TTSB)
DLBI............ DLB Oil & Gas, Inc. [*NASDAQ symbol*] (SAG)
DLBI............ Double Line Block Instrument [*Indian Railway*] (TIR)
DLBL........... Disk Label (SAUS)
DLB OG....... DLB Oil & Gas, Inc. [*Associated Press*] (SAG)
DIBOL......... Digital Business Oriented Language (SAUS)
DLC............. Dalien [*China*] [*Airport symbol*] (OAG)
DLC............. Data Line Controller (SAUS)
DLC............. Data Link Command (ACAE)
DLC............. Data Link Connection [*Computer science*] (CIST)
DLC............. Data Link Connector [*Electronics*]
DLC............. Data Link Control [*Computer science*] (BUR)
DLC............. David Lipscomb College [*Tennessee*]
DLC............. Dealy Clearance [*Aviation*] (FAAC)
DLC............. Decision Level Concentration (ABAC)
DLC............. Decision Logic Control (SAUS)
DLC............. Defense Logistics Agency (SAUS)
DLC............. Delayed Clearance (SAUS)
DLC............. Delay Line Case
DLC............. Deliverable Link Connections SDH (SAUS)
DLC............. Democratic Leadership Council (EA)
DLC............. Dental Laboratory Conference [*Defunct*] (EA)
DLC............. Develcon Electronics Ltd. [*Toronto Stock Exchange symbol*]
DLC............. Development Loan Committee [*Department of State*]
DLC............. Diamondlike Carbon [*Materials science*]
DIC.............. difference in conditions (SAUS)
DLC............. Differential Leukocyte Count [*Hematology*]
DLC............. Digital Learning Center (SAUS)
DLC............. Digital Light and Color [*Computer science*] (PCM)
DLC............. Digital Line Carrier (SAUS)
DLC............. Digital Logic Circuit
DLC............. Digital Loop Carrier [*Telecommunications*] (OSI)
DLC............. Dillon, SC [*Location identifier*] [*FAA*] (FAAL)
DLC............. Diploma of Loughborough College [*British*]
DLC............. Direct Lift Control
DLC............. Disaster Loan Corp. [*Dissolved 1945, functions transferred to Reconstructi on Finance Corp.*]
DLC............. Distributed Loop Carrier (SAUS)
DLC............. District Library Center (SAUS)
DLC............. Divisional Land Commissioner (SAUO)
DLC............. Doctor of Celtic Literature
DLC............. Dominion Labour Conference (SAUO)
DLC............. Donation Land Claim [*Legal term*] (DLA)
DLC............. Double Lumen Catheter [*Medicine*] (EDAA)
DLC............. Down Left Center (IAA)
DLC............. Down Line Control (SAUS)
DLC............. Downlink Communications (SAUS)
DLC............. Drivers License Compact (SAUS)
DLC............. Drummond Lighterage [*AAR code*]
DLC............. Dual-Lumen Catheter [*Medicine*] (DMAA)
DLC............. Duolateral Coil [*Electromagnetism*] (IAA)
DLC............. Duplex Line Control (BUR)
DLC............. Duquesne Light Company (SAUO)
DLC............. Dymo LASER Composer (DGA)
DLC............. Dynamic Load Characteristic
DLC............. Dynamic Load Control (SAUS)
DLC............. dynamic lung compliance (SAUS)
DLC............. Library of Congress, Washington, DC [*Library symbol*] [*Library of Congress*] [*OCLC symbol*] (OCLC)
DLC............. Osterhout Free Library [*Library network*]
DLC............. United States Library of Congress, Washington, DC [*Library symbol*] [*Library of Congress*] (LCLS)
DLCA........... Dairymen's League Cooperative Association [*Later, DC*] (EA)
DLCA........... Diffusion-Limited Cluster Aggregation [*Physical chemistry*]
DLCA........... Driver Leasing Council of America (EA)
DLCA........... Dynamic Logic Chassis Analyzer
DLCB........... Drifting Limited Capability Buoy (SAUS)
DLCB........... Drifting Low-Capability Buoys [*National Oceanic and Atmospheric Administration*] (MCD)
DLC-B.......... Library of Congress, National Library Service for the Blind and Physically Handicapped, Washington, DC [*Library symbol*] [*Library of Congress*] (LCLS)
DLC-BM....... Library of Congress, National Library Service for the Blind and Physically Handicapped, Music Library, Washington, DC [*Library symbol*] [*Library of Congress*] (LCLS)
DLCC........... Data Link Control Chip [*Computer science*] (HGAA)
DLCC........... Desert Locust Control Committee [*Food and Agriculture Organization*] [*United Nations*] (EA)
DLCC........... Digital Load Cell Comparison (SAUS)
DLCC........... Division Logistics Control Center
DLCCA......... Diffusion-Limited Cluster-Cluster Aggregation (SAUS)
DICE............ Digital Integrated Circuit Exerciser (SAUS)
DLC/EA....... Desert Locust Control Organizations for Eastern Africa (SAUS)
DLC(ESR).... United States Library of Congress, Early State Records Collection, Washington, DC [*Library symbol*] [*Library of Congress*] (LCLS)
DLCF........... Data Link Control Field [*Computer science*]
DLC-GB........ United States Library of Congress, Generalized Bibliography System, Washington, DC [*Library symbol*] [*Library of Congress*] (LCLS)
DLCH........... Delchamps, Inc. [*NASDAQ symbol*] (NQ)
DLCI............ Data Line Connection Identifier (SAUS)
DLCI............ Data Link Connection Identifier [*Computer science*]
DLCL........... Diffuse Large-Cell Lymphoma [*Oncology*]
DLCL........... Doubly-Linked Circular List (RALS)
DLC/LLC...... Data Link Control/Logical Link Control (ADWA)
DLCM........... Drinker Library of Choral Music (EA)
DI/CMOS...... dielectrically insulated complementary metal-oxide semiconductor (SAUS)
DLCN........... Distributed Loop Computer Network (PDAA)
DLC-N.......... United States Library of Congress, National Serials Data Program, Washington, DC [*Library symbol*] [*Library of Congress*] (LCLS)
DLC-NR........ United States Library of Congress, National Resources Program, Washington, DC [*Library symbol*] [*Library of Congress*] (LCLS)
DLCNs......... Distributed Loop Computer Networks (SAUS)
DLC-NTC...... United States Library of Congress, National Translations Center, Washington, DC [*Library symbol*] [*Library of Congress*] (LCLS)
DLCO........... Decade LC Oscillator (SAUS)
DLCO........... Deck Landing Control Officer [*British*]

DLCO .... Desert Locust Control Office (SAUS)
DLCO .... Desert Locust Control Organization (SAUS)
DLCO .... Diffusing Capacity of the Lungs for Carbon Monoxide
DLCO .... Direct Labor Charges by Organization (MCD)
$DLCO_2$ .... Diffusing Capacity for Lung Carbon Dioxide [*Medicine*] (DAVI)
DLCO-EA .... Desert Locust Control Organization-East Africa (SAUS)
DLCO-EA .... Desert Locust Control Organization for East Africa (SAUS)
DLCO-EA .... Desert Locust Control Organization for Eastern Africa (SAUO)
D_LCO/M^2 .... Diffusing Capacity of the Lungs for Carbon Monoxide per Square Meter of Body Su rface [*Medicine*] (DAVI)
DLCO-SB .... Single-Breath Diffusing Capacity of the Lung for Carbon Monoxide [*Medicine*] (MEDA)
D_{LCOSB} .... Single Breath Diffusing Capacity of the Lungs for Carbon Monoxide [*Medicine*] (DAVI)
DLCO-SS .... Steady State Diffusing Lung Capacity for Carbon Monoxide (MAE)
DLCP .... Data Link Controller-Processor [*Automotive engineering*] [*Electronics*]
DLCP .... Data Link Control Panel [*Computer science*] (MCD)
DLC-P4 .... United States Library of Congress, Priority Four Collection, Washington, DC [*Library symbol*] [*Library of Congress*] (LCLS)
DLCPP .... Depository Library Council to the Public Printer (EA)
DLC-R .... United States Library of Congress, Regional and Cooperative Cataloging Division, Washington, DC [*Library symbol*] [*Library of Congress*] (LCLS)
DLCS .... Data-Line Concentration System [*Bell System*]
DLCS .... Data Link Communications System (SAUS)
DLCS .... Data Link Controller Series [*or Serial*] [*Electronics*]
DLC-S .... United States Library of Congress, Serial Record Division, Washington, DC [*Library symbol*] [*Library of Congress*] (LCLS)
DICTA .... District Council Technical Association (SAUO)
DLCTRC .... Dielectric
DLCU .... Digital Line Carrier Unit (SAUS)
DLCW .... Department of Land and Water Conservation (GEOI)
DLCX .... Data Link Control Exchange (SAUS)
DLCX .... Dearborn Leasing [*Private rail car owner code*]
DLCYP .... Division of Libraries for Children and Young People (SAUO)
DLD .... Dark Line Defect (PDAA)
DLD .... Data Link Decoder (MCD)
DLD .... Date of Last Drink [*Medicine*] (MELL)
DLD .... Dead-Letter Drop [*British*] (CARL)
DLD .... Deadline Date [*Air Force*] (AFM)
DLD .... Delaware Technical and Community College, Wilmington, DE [*OCLC symbol*] (OCLC)
DLD .... Delay Line Driver (SAUS)
DLD .... Delivered
DLD .... Destruct Logic Decoder
DLD .... Detailed Level Design (SAUS)
DLD .... Deutsche Linux Distribution [*Computer science*] (VERA)
DLD .... Digital Light Deflection (SAUS)
DLD .... Digital Light Deflector (PDAA)
DLD .... Dihydrolipoamide Dehydrogenase (DMAA)
DLD .... Diplay List Driver (SAUS)
DLD .... Diploma of Landscape Design (ADA)
DLD .... Direction Level Detector (IAA)
DLD .... Direct Link for the Disabled, Inc. (ADWA)
DLD .... Discount Long Distance [*Larose, LA*] [*Telecommunications*] (TSSD)
DLD .... Display List Driver [*Computer science*] (PCM)
DLD .... Division of Learning Disabilities [*Council for Exceptional Children*]
DLD .... Division of Lung Disease [*Medicine*] (EDAA)
DLD .... Dromoland Development [*Vancouver Stock Exchange symbol*]
DLD .... Drug and Laboratory Disposal, Inc. (EFIS)
DLD .... Duck Lethal Dose (SAUS)
DLD .... dynamic linear drive (SAUS)
DIDAII .... Digital Data Display (SAUS)
DLDBS .... Distributed-Loop Database System (PDAA)
DLDED .... Division Level Data Entry Device (MCD)
DL Des .... Doctor of Landscape Design
DLDM .... Distorted Liquid Drop Model (SAUS)
DI/DO .... Digital Input/Digital Output (SAUS)
DL-DOPA .... DL-3,4-Dihydroxyphenylalanine (SAUS)
DL-DOPS .... DL-3,4-Dihydroxyphenylserine (SAUS)
DLDPANSW .... Dental Laboratories and Dental Prosthetists' Association of New South Wales [*Australia*]
DLDR .... Differential Line Driver Receiver (IAA)
DLDS .... Division of Library Development and Services (SAUS)
DLDV .... Differential LASER Doppler Velocimeter (PDAA)
DLE .... Data Length Escape [*Computer science*] (DCDG)
DLE .... Data Link Equipment
DLE .... Data Link Escape [*Computer science*] (NITA)
DLE .... Data Link Escape Character [*Keyboard*] (CMD)
DLE .... Deflected Lamine Electrophoresis
DLE .... Delaware Technical and Community College, Stanton Campus, Newark, DE [*OCLC symbol*] (OCLC)
DLE .... Delayed Light Emission [*Green plant phenomenon*]
DLE .... Department of Law Enforcement (SAUS)
DLE .... Detailed Labor Estimate (MCD)
DLE .... Detailed ledger entry (SAUS)
DLE .... Dialyzable Leukocyte Extract [*Hematology*]
DLE .... Digital Line Equipment (SAUS)
DLE .... Digital Local Exchange (PDAA)
DLE .... Direct Laboratories Estimate (MCD)
DLE .... Direct Line Equipment (SAUS)
DLE .... Discoid Lupus Erythematosus [*Medicine*]
DLE .... diskoider Lupus erythematodes (SAUS)
DLE .... Disseminated Lupus Erythematosus [*Hematology*]
DLE .... Dole [*France*] [*Airport symbol*] [*Obsolete*] (OAG)
DLE .... Down Link Expansion (ACAE)
DLE .... Dreaded Lake Effect [*Weather condition, resulting in increased precipitation, produced by Utah's Great Salt Lake*]
DLE .... Drooped Leading Edge
DLEA .... Double Leg Elbow Amplifier
DLEA .... Drug Law Enforcement Agencies (POLM)
DLEC .... Data Link Escape Character [*Computer science*] (EECA)
DLEC .... Digital Local Exchange Carrier (SEWL)
DL Ec .... Doctor of Library Economics
DLED .... Dedicated Loop Encryption Device (SAUS)
DLED .... Digital Loop Encryption Device (SAUS)
DLEED .... Diffuse Low-Energy Electron Diffraction [*Microscopy*]
DLEG .... Legal Directorate (SAUO)
DLEN .... Display Entry (SAUS)
DL Eng .... Doctor of Landscape Engineering
DLES .... Department of Labor and Employment Security (DEMM)
DLES .... Department of Labour and Employment Services (SAUS)
DLES .... Division of Law Enforcement Sciences [*Bureau of Indian Affairs*] (BARN)
DLES .... Doctor of Letters in Economic Studies
D Let .... Doctor of Letters
Dletd .... Deleted (SAUS)
Dletg .... Deleting (SAUS)
D Level .... Depot Level of Maintenance (AAGC)
D LEVEL .... Depot Level of Maintenance (POLM)
DLEX .... Datalex plc ADS [*NASDAQ symbol*]
DIF .... Data Interchange Facility (SAUS)
DLF .... Data List File
DLF .... Daughters of Our Lady of Fatima (TOCD)
DLF .... Delaware Academy of Medicine, Wilmington, DE [*OCLC symbol*] (OCLC)
DLF .... Del Rio, TX [*Location identifier*] [*FAA*] (FAAL)
DLF .... Designers Lighting Forum
DLF .... Deutschlandfunk [*Radio network*] [*Germany*]
DLF .... Development Loan Fund [*Abolished 1961, functions redelegated to Agency for International Development*]
DLF .... Dhofar Liberation Front [*Oman*]
DLF .... Dielectric Loading Factor [*Electronics*] (IAA)
DLF .... Difference Limens for Frequency [*Medicine*] (EDAA)
DLF .... Diffraction Limited Focusing
DLF .... Digitalis-Like Factor [*Biochemistry*]
DLF .... digitalis like factors (SAUS)
DLF .... Digital Library Federation
DLF .... Digoxin-Like Factor [*Biochemistry*]
DLF .... Direct Line Filter (SAUS)
DLF .... Direct Lytic Factor [*Polypeptide from cobra venom*]
DLF .... Disabled [*or Disability*] Living Foundation [*British*] (DI)
DLF .... Document Library Facility [*Computer science*]
DLF .... Dorsolateral Fascicle [*Muscular anatomy, neuroanatomy*]
DLF .... Dorsolateral Funiculus [*Neuroanatomy*]
DLF .... Downlink Frequency
DLF .... downward longwave flux (SAUS)
DLF .... Drydock Launch Facility
DLF .... Liberal People's Party (Norway) [*Political party*] (PSAP)
DLFDU .... Data Line Flight Direction Unit (MCD)
DLFET .... Depletion-mode Load Field Effect Transistor (SAUS)
DIFF .... Different (SAUS)
DIFF/FWR .... Differentiator and Full Wave Rectifier (SAUS)
DLFI .... Delphi Financial Group, Inc. [*NASDAQ symbol*] (SAG)
DLFI .... Delphi Fin'l Group'A' [*NASDAQ symbol*] (TTSB)
DLFM .... Division Level Financial Management [*System*] (MCD)
DLFs .... Dynamic Load Factors (SAUS)
DLFW .... Department of Lands, Forests and Waters (SAUS)
DLG .... Daddy's Little Girl
DLG .... Dealing
D Lg .... Decreto Legislativo [*Legislative Decree*] [*Italian*] (ILCA)
DLG .... Defense Liaison Group (CINC)
DLG .... Destroyer Leader, Guided Missile (MCD)
DLG .... Devilish Little Grin (SAUS)
DLG .... Digital LASER Gyro (SEWL)
DLG .... Digital Line Graph
DLG .... Dillingham [*Alaska*] [*Airport symbol*] (OAG)
DLG .... Distolingual Groove [*Medicine*] (DMAA)
DLG .... Double-Line-To-Ground (SAUS)
DLG .... Dynamic Lead Guidance (PDAA)
DLG .... Guided Missile Frigate [*Navy symbol*]
DLG .... Large Destroyer, Guided Missile (SAUS)
DLG .... Wilmington Medical Center, Wilmington, DE [*OCLC symbol*] (OCLC)
DLG2DEM .... Digital Line Graph to Digital Elevation Model (GEOI)
DLGA .... Decorative Lighting Guild of America (SAUO)
DLGC .... Dialogic Corp. [*NASDAQ symbol*] (SAG)
DLGCD .... Department of Local Government and Community Development (SAUS)
DLG-E .... Digital Line Graph-Enhanced (CARB)
DLG-E .... Digital Line Graph-Enhanced Maps (PA)
DLGF .... Digital Line Graph-Framework (GEOI)
DLGHT .... Delight
dLGN .... Dorsal Lateral Geniculate Nucleus [*Also, LGd*] [*Anatomy*]
DLGN .... Guided Missile Frigate (Nuclear Propulsion) [*Navy symbol*]
DLGNC .... Diligence
DLG-O .... Digital Line Graph-Optional (GEOI)
DLGS .... Doppler Landing Guidance System
DLGX .... Datalogix International, Inc. [*NASDAQ symbol*] (SAG)
DLGX .... Datalogix Intl. [*NASDAQ symbol*] (TTSB)

DLH .... Dalhousie [*India*] [*Seismograph station code, US Geological Survey*] [*Closed*] (SEIS)
DLH .... Data Link Hardware (IAA)
DLH .... Data Link Layer Header [*Telecommunications*] (ACRL)
DLH .... Data Lower Half Byte (IAA)
DLH .... Department of Lands and Housing [*Northern Territory*] [*Australia*]
DLH .... Deutsche Lufthansa AG [*German Lufthansa*] [*Airline*] (EG)
DIH .... Diploma in Industrial Health (SAUS)
DLH .... Direct Labor Hours (DNAB)
DLH .... Docking Lock Handle
DLH .... Domestic Long Hair [*Non-pedigree cat*] (SPVS)
DLH .... Duluth [*Minnesota-Superior, Wisconsin*] [*Airport symbol*] (AD)
DLH .... Henry Francis DuPont Winterthur Museum, Winterthur, DE [*OCLC symbol*] (OCLC)
DLHC .... Diamondlike Hydrocarbon [*Coating material*]
DLI .... Dalat [*South Vietnam*] [*Airport symbol*] (AD)
DL/I .... Data Language/I [*Computer science*] (HODG)
DLI .... Data Liberation Initiative [*Canada*] (GEOI)
DLI .... Data Line Interface [*Computer science*] (GART)
DLI .... Data Link Interface (ACAE)
DLI .... Data Location Index (SAUO)
DLI .... Deck-Launched Intercept (MCD)
DLI .... Deck Launched Interceptor (ACAE)
DLI .... Defense Language Institute [*DoD*] [*Washington, DC*]
DLI .... Delay Indefinite (DA)
DLI .... Del Laboratories [*AMEX symbol*] (TTSB)
DLI .... Del Laboratories, Inc. [*AMEX symbol*] (SPSG)
DLI .... Depolarized Light Intensity
DLI .... Development and Leadership Initiative
DLI .... Digital Library Initiative (SAUS)
DLI .... Digital Line Interface [*Computer science*] (NITA)
DLI .... Direct Liquid Injection (SAUS)
DLI .... Direct Liquid Inlet [*Interface*] [*Analytical instrumentation*]
DLI .... Distolinguoincisal [*Dentistry*]
DLI .... Distributorless Ignition [*Automotive engineering*]
DLI .... Doctor of Literary Interpretation
DLI .... Do-List Item [*Military*]
DLI .... Double Label Index [*Medicine*] (DMAA)
DLI .... Dual Link Interface (SAUS)
DLI .... Dummy Load In (ACAE)
DLI .... Durham Light Infantry [*Military unit*] [*British*]
DLI .... E. I. Du Pont de Nemours & Co., Haskell Laboratory, Newark, DE [*OCLC symbol*] (OCLC)
DLIA .... dELiAs, Inc. [*NASDAQ symbol*] (SG)
DLIA .... Dental Laboratories Institute of America (SAUS)
DLIA .... Discover Life in America
D-lib .... Electronic Magazine of Digital Library Research Mirrors (SAUS)
D-library .... duplicating library (SAUS)
DLIC .... Detachments Left in Contact [*Military*]
DLIC .... Digital Line Interface Controller [*Telecommunications*] (NITA)
DLIDC .... Defense Logistics Instructor Development Course [*Army*]
DLIEC .... Defense Language Institute, East Coast Center (AABC)
DLIEL .... Defense Language Institute, English Language Center (AABC)
DLIELC .... Defense Language Institute, English Language Center [*Military*]
DLIF .... Design Limit Load Factor
DLIF .... Digoxin-Like Immunoreactive Factor [*Laboratory analysis*]
DLIFC .... Defense Language Institute, Foreign Language Center (SAUO)
DLIFLC .... Defense Language Institute, Foreign Language Center (AABC)
DLILMN .... Dial Illumination
DLIM .... Delimiter (SAUS)
DLIM .... Diploma in Life Insurance Medicine [*Medical degree*] (CMD)
DLIMP .... Descriptive Language for Implementing Macro-Processor (SAUS)
DLIMP .... Descriptive Language Implemented by Macroprocessors
DLIMP .... Descriptive language implemented by microprocessor (SAUS)
DLINDG .... Dial Indicating
D Link .... Diagonal Link (SAUS)
DLIP .... Directory of Library and Information Professionals [*Gale Research, Inc.*] [*Information service or system*] (CRD)
DLIR .... Depot Level Inspection and Repair (SAUS)
DLIR .... Depot Level Inspection Auto Repair (MCD)
DLIR .... Downward-Looking Infrared [*Air Force*]
DLIS .... Defense Logistics Information Service
DLIS .... Digoxin-Like Immunoreactive Substance [*Biochemistry*]
DLIS .... Diploma in Library Information Services
DLIS .... Doctor of Library and Information Sciences (GAGS)
DLIS .... Dowlais Central [*Cardiff*] [*Welsh depot code*]
DLIS .... Downward-Looking Infrared System [*Air Force*] (MCD)
DLISC-EP .... Defense Language Institute, Support Command - El Paso (AABC)
DLISDA .... Defense Language Institute, Systems Development Agency (AABC)
DLISW .... Defense Language Institute, Southwest Branch (AABC)
D Lit .... Doctor of Letters
D Lit .... Doctor of Literature
DLitt .... Doctor of Letters
DLitt .... Doctor of Literature
DLittS .... Doctor of Sacred Letters
DLIWC .... Defense Language Institute, West Coast Branch (AABC)
DLJ .... DLJ Capital Trust I [*NYSE symbol*] (SAG)
DLJ .... Donaldson Lufkin & Jenrette [*NYSE symbol*] (SAG)
DLJ .... Donaldson, Lufkin & Jenrette Securities Corporation (SAUS)
DLJ .... Donaldson, Lufkin & Securities Corporation (SAUO)
DLJ .... Downlink Jamming (ACAE)
DLJC .... Disciples of the Lord Jesus Christ (TOCD)
DLJ Ca .... DLJ Capital Trust I [*Associated Press*] (SAG)
DLK .... Data Link (KSC)
DLK .... Democratic League of Kosovo [*Albania*] [*Political party*] (ECON)
DLK .... Diamond Locking Knurl
DLK .... Downbank Telemetry Processing (SAUS)
DLK .... ICI Americas, Inc., Wilmington, DE [*OCLC symbol*] (OCLC)
DLK .... Salomon, Inc. [*AMEX symbol*] (SAG)
DLL .... Dalhousie University Law Library [*UTLAS symbol*]
DLL .... Dames of the Loyal Legion of the United States of America (EA)
DLL .... Damietta-Latakia Line [*Nile river delta*] [*Geology*]
DLL .... Delay Locked Loop [*Computer science*] (IAA)
DLL .... Dells, WI [*Location identifier*] [*FAA*] (FAAL)
DLL .... Design Limit Load (SAUS)
DLL .... design live load (SAUS)
DLL .... Design Load Limit (MSA)
DLL .... Desing Live Load (SAUS)
DLL .... Dial Long Line [*Bell System*]
DLL .... Dial Long Line equipment (SAUS)
DLL .... Dihomo-Gammalinoleic Acid [*Biochemistry*] (DAVI)
Dll .... Dilation [*Medicine*] (STED)
DLL .... Dillon Companies, Inc. (SAUO)
DLL .... direct load and lock (SAUS)
DLL .... Discharge-Line Length [*Nuclear energy*] (NRCH)
DLL .... Doctor of Late Laws
DLL .... Donaldson Line Limited (SAUS)
DLL .... Double Length Line
dll .... Double-Linked List of (SAUS)
DLL .... Downline Loading
DLL .... dynamically linked library (SAUS)
DLL .... Dynamic Linkage Loader (SAUS)
DLL .... Dynamic Link Library [*Software*] [*Computer science*] (BYTE)
DLL .... Dynamic Link Loader [*Computer science*] (VERA)
DLL .... dynamic load (SAUS)
DLL .... Dynamic Load Libraries (SAUS)
dllat .... Dilatation (STED)
DL/I CHKP ... DL/I Checkpoint (SAUS)
DLLD .... Direct Linear Loop Detector [*Computer science*] (IAA)
DLLE .... Decoy Low-Level Electronics
DL-LEA .... Directed Listening-Language Experience Approach (EDAC)
DLLF .... Design Limit Load Factor (MCD)
DLLI .... Dulcitol Lysine Lactose Iron [*Agar*] [*Microbiology*]
DLLL .... Doubly-Linked Linear List (RALS)
DLLR .... Dollar
DLLRS .... Dollars [*Monetary unit*] (ROG)
DllrTree .... Dollar Tree Stores, Inc. [*Associated Press*] (SAG)
DLLs .... Deleting Important Program Files [*Computer science*]
DLLWTP .... Defense Low-Level Waste Technology Program (SAUS)
DLM .... Daily List of Mail (IAA)
DLM .... Dalaman [*Turkey*] [*Airport symbol*] (OAG)
DLM .... Dalhousie University Health Sciences Library [*UTLAS symbol*]
DLM .... Data Line Monitor
DLM .... Data Linkage Module (SAUS)
DLM .... Data Link Monitor (SAUS)
DLM .... Delay Line Memory
DLM .... Del Monte Foods [*NYSE symbol*] (SG)
DLM .... DeLorme Maps (SAUO)
DLM .... Democratic Labour Movement [*Guyana*] [*Political party*] (PPW)
DLM .... Democratic League Movement (SAUO)
DLM .... Department of Legal Medicine (SAUS)
DLM .... Depolarized Light Mixing (PDAA)
DLM .... Depot Level Maintenance [*Air Force*] (AFM)
DLM .... Deputy Lord Mayor [*British*] (ADA)
DLM .... Designated Location Move (ACAE)
DLM .... Des Laufenden Monats [*Of the Current Month*] [*German*]
DLM .... Destination Load Model (SAA)
DLM .... Developmental Learning Materials (TIMI)
DLM .... digital landscape model (SAUS)
DLM .... Digital Linking Module (NITA)
DLM .... Digital Logic Module
DLM .... Direct Logistics Maintenance (SAUS)
DLM .... Director of Liaison and Munitions [*Military*] [*British*]
DLM .... Distributed LAN Monitoring (SAUS)
DLM .... Distributed Lock Manager (ACRL)
DLM .... Distributed Logic Memory (VLIE)
DLM .... Divine Light Mission [*A cult*]
DLM .... Doctor of Landscape Management
DLM .... Dominica Liberation Movement [*Political party*] (EY)
DLM .... Dorsal Longitudinal Muscle [*Anatomy*]
DLM .... Double-Level Metal [*Electronics*] (MED)
DLM .... Double Long Meter [*Music*]
DLM .... Dwight-Lloyd-McWane (SAUS)
DLM .... Dynamic Link Module (VLIE)
DLM .... University of Delaware, Newark, DE [*OCLC symbol*] (OCLC)
DLMA .... Decorative Lighting Manufacturers Association (SAUS)
DLMA .... Department of Labor, Manpower Administration
DLMA .... Diocesan Lay Ministry Adviser [*Church of England*]
DLMA .... Downtown Lower Manhattan Association (SAUO)
DLMCP .... Distributed Loop Message Communication Protocol
DLMF .... David Livingstone Missionary Foundation
DLMF .... Depot Level Maintenance Facility (MCD)
DLMF .... Drug Literature Microfilm File (NITA)
DLMH .... Direct Labor Man-Hours (RDA)
DLMO .... Dim Light Melatonin Onset [*Physiology*]
DLMP .... Date of Last Menstrual Period [*Medicine*] (DMAA)
DLMP .... Depot Level Maintenance Plant
DLMP .... Double Layer Metal Process (SAUS)
DLMP .... Down-Link Multipath (MCD)

DLMPS .... Division of Logic, Methodology, and Philosophy of Science [*International Council of Scientific Unions*]
DLMRR .... Depot Level Maintenance Requirement Review (AFIT)
DLMS .... Digital Land Mass Simulation (MCD)
DLMS .... Digital Land Mass System [*Directorate of Military Survey*] [*British*]
DLMS .... Digital Landmass System (SAUS)
DLMS .... Digital Level Mass Simulator (ACAE)
DLMS .... Down Link Monitoring System (ACAE)
DLMSFDS .... Digital Landmass System Feature Display System (SAUS)
DLMSS .... Digital Land Mobile Satellite System (SAUS)
DIMS System... distributed-intelligence microprocessor system (SAUS)
DLMTB .... Defense Logistics Management Training Board (AFM)
DLMV .... Delmarva Peninsula (SAUS)
DLN .... Daily Legal News [*Pennsylvania*] [*A publication*] (DLA)
DLN .... Dalton [*Australia*] [*Seismograph station code, US Geological Survey*] [*Closed*] (SEIS)
DLN .... Digital Ladder Network (IAA)
DLN .... Dillon, MT [*Location identifier*] [*FAA*] (FAAL)
DLN .... Document Locator Number [*Computer science*]
DLN .... Dorsolateral Nucleus [*Neuroanatomy*]
DLN .... Double Length Number
DLNC .... Deputy Local Naval Commander
DLNC .... Diamond-Like Nano-Composites (AAEL)
DLNC .... Document Locator Number Counter File [*IRS*]
DLNK .... Digital Link [*NASDAQ symbol*] (TTSB)
DLNK .... Digital Link Corp. [*NASDAQ symbol*] (SAG)
DLNMP .... Date of Last Normal Menstrual Period [*Medicine*] (DMAA)
DLNR .... Department of Land and Natural Resources (GEOI)
DLNS .... Department of Labour and National Service (SAUS)
DLNWR .... Des Lacs National Wildlife Refuge (SAUS)
DLO .... Agricultural Research Department, Ministry of Agriculture, Nature Conservation and Fisheries (SAUO)
DLO .... Daleco Resources Corp. [*Vancouver Stock Exchange symbol*]
DLO .... Data Line Occupied [*Computer science*] (VLIE)
DLO .... Data Link Occupied [*Computer science*] (HGAA)
DLO .... Daylight Opening
DLO .... Dead Letter Office [*US Postal Service*]
DLO .... Dead-Letter Office (SAUO)
DLO .... Decisions de l'Orateur (NITA)
DLO .... Defense Liaison Office (MCD)
DLO .... Defense Logistics Agency, Alexandria, VA [*OCLC symbol*] (OCLC)
DLO .... Delano, CA [*Location identifier*] [*FAA*] (FAAL)
DLO .... Delayed Output [*Computer science*]
DLO .... Dense Linear Ordering (SAUS)
DLO .... Deputy for Launch Operations [*NASA*] (KSC)
DLO .... Desired Learner Outcomes [*Education*]
DLO .... Despatch Loading Only (SAUS)
D Lo .... Difference in Longitude (SAUS)
DLO .... Difference of Longitude [*Navigation*]
DLO .... Diploma in Laryngology and Otolaryngology [*British*]
DLO .... Direct Labor Organization
DLO .... Director, Launch Operations [*NASA*] (KSC)
DLO .... Dirty Lubricating Oil (AAG)
DLO .... Dispatch Loading Only
DLO .... Distolinguo-Occlusal [*Dentistry*]
DLO .... District Legal Office [*or Officer*] [*Navy*]
DLO .... Division Liaison Officer
DLO .... Division Loading Officer (SAUO)
DLO .... Document-Like Objects
DLO .... Double Local Oscillator
DLO .... Drug Licence Opportunity [*Medicine*] (DB)
DLO .... Dual Loop Oscillator
DLO .... Duke of Lancaster's Own [*British military*] (DMA)
D_{LO2} .... Diffusing Capacity of the Lungs for Oxygen [*Medicine*] (DAVI)
DLOA .... Draft Letter of Agreement (MCD)
DLOC .... Daimler and Lanchester Owners' Club (EA)
DLOC .... Delayed Lock-On Command (ACAE)
DLOC .... developed lines of code (SAUS)
DLOC .... Developed Source Lines of Code [*Electronics*] (AAEL)
DLOC .... Division Logistical Operation Center
DLOCA .... Department of Law Office Consumer Affairs (SAUS)
DLOCK .... Dial Lock
D Lock .... Dial-lock (SAUS)
DLOC of NA... Daimler and Lanchester Owners Club of North America (EA)
DLOG .... Distributed Logic Corp. [*NASDAQ symbol*] (COMM)
DLOGS .... Division Logistics System (MCD)
d long .... difference in longitude (SAUS)
DLONG .... Difference of Longitude [*Navigation*]
DLO-NL .... Netherlands Organization for Agricultural Research (GVA)
D loop .... Displacement Loop [*Genetics*] (DOG)
dlop .... dropping last outward pilot (SAUS)
DLOR .... Downward Light Output Ratio (PDAA)
DL or D/L .... Download (SAUS)
DLORL .... Downward Light Output Ratio Luminaire (SAUS)
DLORW .... Downward Light Output Ratio Working (SAUS)
DLOS .... Deep Level Optical Spectroscopy (SAUS)
DLOS .... Dismountable Line-of-Sight (SAUS)
DLOS .... Distributed Loop Operating System
DLOS .... Disturbed Line-of-Sight (SAUS)
DLOS .... Diver Lock-Out Submersible (SAUS)
DLOS .... Division Logistics Organization Structure (MCD)
DLOS .... Dynamic Logic Simulation (VLIE)
DLOSP .... Dropping Last Outwards Sea Pilot (RIMS)
DLOV .... Daleco Resources Corp. [*NASDAQ symbol*] (NQ)
Dlove .... Deficiency Love [*A. Maslow*] (DIPS)
DLOVF .... Daleco Res [*NASDAQ symbol*] (TTSB)
DLOY .... Duke of Lancaster's Own Yeomanry [*Military unit*] [*British*]
DLP .... CenTrust Savings Bank [*AMEX symbol*] (COMM)
DLP .... Damage Limiting Program
DLP .... Data Link and application Processor (SAUS)
DLP .... Data Link Processor [*Burroughs Corp.*] [*Computer science*] (BUR)
DLP .... Data Link Programs (MCD)
DLP .... Data Listing Programs (IEEE)
DLP .... Data Load Partition (SAUS)
DLP .... Date of Last Payment [*Insurance*]
DLP .... Defense Language Program (AFM)
DLP .... Delcorp Resources, Inc. [*Vancouver Stock Exchange symbol*]
DLP .... Delipidized Serum Protein (STED)
DLP .... Delta and Pine Land [*NYSE symbol*] (TTSB)
DLP .... Democratic Labor Party [*Barbados*] [*Political party*] (PPW)
DLP .... Democratic Labor Party [*Trinidad and Tobago*] [*Political party*] (PPW)
DLP .... Democratic Labor Party [*Australia*] [*Political party*]
DLP .... Democratic Left Party [*Turkey*] [*Political party*] (MENA)
DLP .... Democratic Liberal Party [*Taiwan*] [*Political party*] (EY)
DLP .... Democratic Liberal Party [*South Korea*] [*Political party*]
DLP .... Deoxidized, Low-Phosphorus Copper (SAUS)
DLP .... Deoxidized Low-Residual Phosphorus [*Copper*]
DLP .... Developmental Learning Programs (STED)
DLP .... Development Learning Problem(s) [*Medicine*] (EDAA)
DLP .... Diffusing Light Photography [*Imaging Science*]
DLP .... Digital LASER Printer (PDAA)
DLP .... Digital Library Project
DLP .... Digital Light Processing
DLP .... Digital Light Projector
DLP .... Diocesan Labor Priests (TOCD)
dlp .... Diocesan Labor Priests (TOCD)
DLP .... Direct Letter Perfect [*Actors' slang*]
DLP .... Direct Linear Plotting (STED)
DLP .... Director of Laboratory Programs [*Navy*]
DLP .... Discrete Logarithmic Problem (VERA)
DLP .... Discrete Logarithm Problem (SAUS)
DLP .... Discretionary Lifer Panel (WDAA)
DLP .... Dislocation of Patella [*Medicine*] (MELL)
DLP .... Display-List Processor [*Computer science*]
DLP .... Distance Learning Project [*Joint program of the Center for Talented Youth (Johns Hopkins University) and the Education Program for Gifted Youth (Stanford University)*] (PAZ)
DLP .... Distolinguopulpal [*Dentistry*]
DLP .... Distributed Logic Programming (VLIE)
DLP .... Division of Library Programs (SAUO)
DLP .... Doctrinal Literature Program [*Military*]
D/LP .... Dome Lamp [*Automotive engineering*]
DLP .... Dominica Labor Party [*Political party*] (PPW)
DLP .... Dorsal Lithotomy Position [*Medicine*] (MELL)
DLP .... Double Large Post (ADA)
DLP .... Double Layer Polysilicon (IAA)
DLP .... Drone Launch Platform [*Navy*] (CAAL)
DLP .... Dynamic Limit Programming (MHDB)
DLP .... Dynamic Low-Pass (SAUS)
DLP .... Dysharmonic Luteal Phase (STED)
DLP .... Graf und Maresch GmbH, Augsburg [*Germany*] [*FAA designator*] (FAAC)
DLPA .... Decorative Laminate Products Association (EA)
DLPA .... dl-Phenylalanine [*Biochemistry*]
DLPA .... Dry Lining and Partition Association [*British*] (DBA)
DLPC .... Dilauroylphosphatidylcholine [*Biochemistry*]
DLPDU .... Data Link Protocol Data Unit [*Computer science*] (VLIE)
DLPE .... Department of Lands, Planning and Environment (SAUS)
DLPE .... Dilaurylphosphatidylethanolamine [*Biochemistry*]
DLPF .... dynamic low pass filter (SAUS)
DLPFC .... Dorsolateral Prefrontal Cortex [*Brain anatomy*]
dlPFC .... Dorsolateral Prefrontal Cortex [*Brain anatomy*]
DLPG .... DIMDI [*Deutsches Institut fuer Medizinische Dokumentation und Information*] List Program Generator (NITA)
DLPGSE .... Depot Level Peculiar Ground Support Equipment (ACAE)
DLPH .... Delphi Information Sys [*NASDAQ symbol*] (TTSB)
DLPH .... Delphi Information Systems, Inc. [*NASDAQ symbol*] (NQ)
DLPHO .... Delphos, OH [*American Association of Railroads railroad junction routing code*]
DLPI .... Data Link Provider Interaface [*Computer science*] (VERA)
DLPP .... Data Link Pre-Processor [*Ferranti Ltd.*]
DLPR .... Defense Logistics Procurement Regulation (MCD)
DLPr .... Dial Corp. $4.75cmPfd [*NYSE symbol*] (TTSB)
DLPR .... Dual Linear Polarization Radar (SAUS)
DLPRO .... Delpro, AR [*American Association of Railroads railroad junction routing code*]
DLPS .... Data Links Processor System (SAUS)
DLPS .... Deck Landing Projector Sight [*British military*] (DMA)
DLPS .... Department of Law and Public Safety (SAUS)
DLPT .... Defense Language Proficiency Tests [*Military*]
DLPT .... Discretionary Lifer Panel Tribunal (WDAA)
DLPU .... Data Link Processor Unit (DA)
DLPX .... Degussa [*Private rail car owner code*]
DLQ .... Deck Landing Qualification [*Navy*] (DOMA)
DLQ .... Mean Diurnal Low-Water Inequality
DLR .... Data Link Receiver [*Computer science*] (MCD)
DLR .... Data Loader/Reducer (SAUS)
DLR .... Dealer (MSA)
dlr .... Dealer (WDAA)
DLR .... Decision Level Count Rate (SAUS)

DLR .... Delay Line Register
DLR .... Dependent LU Requester (SAUS)
DLR .... Depot Level Repairable (NVT)
DLR .... Depot Logistics Report (MCD)
DLR .... Deutsche Forschungsanstalt fuer Luft-und Raumfahrt [*Germany*]
DLR .... Deutsches Zentrum Fuer Luft- und Raumfahrt
DLR .... Developing Learning Readiness
DLR .... Dickinson Law Review [*A publication*] (DLA)
DLR .... Digital Luminescence Radiography [*Medicine*] (DMAA)
DLR .... Direct Labor Rate
dlr .... discharged, landed, and reshipped (SAUS)
dlr .... discharge, land, and reload (SAUS)
d-l-r .... discharge-load-reposition (SAUS)
DLR .... District Land Registrar (SAUS)
DLR .... Division of Labor Relations [*Energy Research and Development Administration*]
DLR .... Division of Land Reclamation (SAUO)
DLR .... Docklands Light Railway [*British*] (ECON)
DlR .... Dock Receipt (SAUS)
DLR .... Dollar [*Monetary unit*]
DLR .... Dominion Law Reporter [*India*] [*Usually with a province abbreviation, as DLR (AM), Ajmer-Merwara*] [*A publication*] (DLA)
DLR .... Dominion law reports (SAUS)
DLR .... Doppler LASER RADAR
DLR .... DOS LAN Requester [*Computer science*]
DLR .... Double Lens Reflex (SAUS)
dlr .... double lift restow (SAUS)
DLR .... Draft Letter Requirement (MCD)
DLR .... Driving after License Revoked
DLR .... Driving Licences Regulations [*British*] (ILCA)
DLR .... Dynamic Line Regulation
DLR .... Dynamic Link Routine (SAUS)
DLR .... Dynamic Load Regulation
DLR .... German Aerospace Research Establishment (GAVI)
DLRA .... Department of Labor Recreation Association
DLRA .... Divorce Law Reform Association [*British*] (DBA)
DLRA .... Door Lock Rotary Actuator
D/L Ratio ..... Drag/Lift Ratio (SAUS)
DLR Camera... Double Lens Reflex Camera (SAUS)
DLRD .... Design Layout Report Date [*Telecommunications*] (TEL)
DLRF .... Direct Loan Revolving Fund [*Department of Veterans Affairs*]
DLRG .... Design Layout Report Date (SAUS)
DLRI .... Dry Lands Research Institute (SAUO)
DLRL .... Diffraction Limited Raman LASER
DLRM .... Doctors & Lawyers for Responsible Medicine (WDAA)
DLRN .... Distance Learning Resource Network
DLRO .... Director, Labor Relations Office (SAUO)
DLRO .... District Labor Relations Office [*or Officer*] [*Navy*]
DLRP .... Data Link Reference Point (NVT)
DLRP .... Diabetes Literature Retrieval Project (SAUS)
DLRS .... Delaware Learning Resource System (SAUS)
DLRS .... Depot Level Reparables (SAUS)
dlrs .... dollars (SAUS)
DLRs .... Dominion Law Reports (SAUS)
DLRTD .... Dollar Time Group(New) [*NASDAQ symbol*] (TTSB)
DLRU .... Dryland Research Unit [*Washington State University*] [*Research center*] (RCD)
DLRV .... Dual Mode Lunar Roving Vehicle [*NASA*]
DLRWS .... Dirty Liquid Radioactive Waste System [*Nuclear energy*] (NRCH)
DLRX .... Disney Land Railroad [*Federal Railroad Administration identification code*]
DLRy .... Director of Light Railways (SAUO)
DLS .... Daily Living Skills (STED)
DLS .... Dallas [*Texas*] [*Seismograph station code, US Geological Survey*] [*Closed*] (SEIS)
DLS .... Dallas Gold & Silver Exchange, Inc. [*AMEX symbol*] (SAG)
DLS .... [*The*] Dalles [*Oregon*] [*Airport symbol*] (AD)
DLS .... Damped Least Square [*Mathematics*]
DLS .... Data Librarian System (PDAA)
DLS .... Data Link Services [*Computer science*] (VLIE)
DLS .... Data Link Set
DLS .... Data Link Simulator
DLS .... Data Link Software (IAA)
DLS .... Data Link Splitter (DA)
DLS .... Data Link Subsystem (ACAE)
DLS .... Data Link Support
DLS .... Data Link Switching [*Computer science*] (PCM)
DLS .... Data Link System (SEWL)
DLS .... Data Loader System (SAUS)
DLS .... Data Logging System
DLS .... Date Last Seen [*Medicine*]
DLS .... Debt Liquidation Schedule
DLS .... Decision Learning System (ACAE)
DLS .... Decoy Launching System [*Navy*] (CAAL)
DLS .... Deep Look Surveillance (MCD)
DLS .... Defence Light Section [*British military*] (DMA)
DLS .... Defense Legal Services Agency [*DoD*]
DLS .... Delay Line Storage (VLIE)
DLS .... Delay Line Store (SAUS)
DLS .... Delay Line Synthesizer
DLS .... Department of Lands and Survey [*Guyana*] (GEOI)
DLS .... Department of Library Studies (SAUS)
DLS .... Department of Life Sciences (SAUS)
DLS .... Dependent LU Server (SAUS)
DLS .... Depot Level Services (SAUS)
DLS .... Desert Locust Survey (SAUO)
DLS .... Device Level Selection (VLIE)
DLS .... Dictionary of Life Science (SAUS)
DLS .... Differential Light Scattering
DLS .... Differential Load Sensing [*Hydraulics*]
DLS .... Diffused Light Storage (SAUS)
DLS .... Digitalis-Like Substance [*Medicine*] (MELL)
DLS .... Digital Ladder Structure (SAUS)
DLS .... Digital Library Systems, Inc. [*Database producer*] (IID)
DLS .... Digital Line System [*Telecommunications*] (TEL)
DLS .... Digital Link Service [*Computer science*] (VLIE)
DLS .... Digital Logic Simulator (SAUS)
DLS .... Digital Logic System
dL'S .... Dilaudid [*or Hydromorphone*] [*Knoll Pharmaceutical Co.*] [*Chemical dependency*] [*Slang*] (DAVI)
DLS .... Direct Least Squares [*Econometrics*]
DLS .... Direct Logistical Support (RDA)
DLS .... Director of Legal Services [*British military*] (DMA)
DLS .... Disaster Legal Services (DEMM)
DLS .... Discrete Least Squares (SAUS)
DLS .... Display Lot Status (AAEL)
DLS .... Distance Least-Squares [*Mathematics*]
DLS .... Distributed Lighting System
DLS .... Distributed Link Services [*Computer science*] (MWOL)
DLS .... Distributed Load Sharing (SAUS)
DLS .... Distributed Logic Store (SAUS)
DLS .... Distribution and Logistic Services (FOTI)
DLS .... District Law Society (SAUO)
DLS .... Dital Logic Simulator (SAUS)
DLS .... Divergent Lobed Suppressor [*NASA*]
DLS .... Division of Labor Studies [*Indiana University*] [*Research center*] (RCD)
DLS .... Division of Library Services (SAUS)
DLS .... Doctor of Librarian Sciences (SAUS)
DLS .... Doctor of Library Science
DLS .... Doctor of Library Service (SAUS)
DLS .... Document Library Services (SAUS)
DLS .... Documents of Limited Significance (MCD)
DLS .... Dogwood Library System [*Library network*]
dls .... Dolares [*Dollars*] [*Monetary unit*] [*Spanish*]
Dls .... Dollars (EBF)
DLS .... Dollars [*Monetary unit*]
DLS .... Dominion Land Surveyor [*Canada*]
DLS .... Doppler LIDAR Wind Sounder (SAUS)
DLS .... Double Left Shift
DLS .... Double Leg Support (SAUS)
DLS .... Downloadable Sample [*Computer science*]
DLS .... Downloadable Sound [*Computer science*] (DCOM)
DLS .... Driving after License Suspended
DLS .... DuPage Library System [*Library network*]
DLS .... Dynamic LASER Scattering [*Spectroscopy*]
DLS .... Dynamic Light Scattering [*Physics*]
DLS .... Dynamic Limb Sounder (EOSA)
DLS .... Dynamic Load Simulator (NASA)
DLS .... The Dalles, OR [*Location identifier*] [*FAA*] (FAAL)
DLS .... University of Pittsburgh, School of Librarianship and Information Science, Pittsburgh, PA [*OCLC symbol*] (OCLC)
DLSA .... Defense Legal Services Agency [*DoD*]
DLSA .... Digital Linear Slide Switch Assembly
DLSA .... Director, Land Service Ammunition (SAUS)
DLSAP .... Data Link Service Access Point (TNIG)
DLSAP .... Destination Link Service Access Point (SAUS)
DLSC .... Defense Logistics Service Center [*Military*] (AFIT)
DLSC .... Defense Logistics Support Center [*Military*]
DLSC .... Defense Logistics Support Command (SAUO)
DLSC .... Defense Logistics System Center
DLSC .... Differential Logistics Services Center [*AEC*]
DISC .... disconnect (SAUS)
DL Sc .... Doctor of Library Science
D-LSD .... D-Lysergic-acid Diethylamide (SAUS)
D-LSD .... D-Lysergig-acid Diethylamide (SAUS)
DLSDC .... Data Link Signal Data Converter (ACAE)
DLSE .... Device Level Selection Enhanced (SAUS)
DLSEF .... Division of Library Services and Educational Facilities [*Office of Education*]
DLSF .... Dog-Leg Severity Factor [*Well drilling technology*]
DLSG .... Department of Land Surveying and Geoinformatics (SAUO)
DLSHLS .... Dorothy L. Sayers Historical and Literary Society [*British*]
DLSI .... Detectable Least Signal Increment [*Instrumentation*]
DLSIE .... Defense Logistics Studies Information Exchange [*Army*]
DLSLD .... Documents of Limited Significance - Limited Distribution (MCD)
DLSM .... Data Link Summary Message (MCD)
D/LSM .... Directorate of Logistic Support Management [*or Manager*] (AAG)
DIS/min .... disintegration per minute (SAUS)
DLSN .... Dorsolateral Septal Nucleus [*Neuroanatomy*]
DLSO .... Dial Line Service Observing [*Telecommunications*] (TEL)
DLSS .... Defense Logistic Standard Service (ACAE)
DLSS .... Digital Linear Slide Switch (MCD)
DLSS .... Direct Logistic Support System (MCD)
DLSSA .... Digital Linear Slide Switch Assembly (MCD)
DLSSD .... Defense Logistics System Standardisation Division (SAUS)
DLS/SHR .... Dollars per Share [*Investment term*] (MHDW)
DLSSO .... Defense Logistics Agency Standard System Office (ACAE)
DLSSO .... Defense Logistics Standards Systems Office
DLS Soc .... Dorothy L. Sayers Society (EAIO)

DLST........... Dihydrolipoamide S-Succinyltransferase (DMAA)
DLST........... Division Logistics System Test [*Army*] (AABC)
DLST/SEACAPS... Division Logistics System Test/Seventh Army Card Processor System
DLSw........... Data Link Switching [*IBM Co.*] (ACRL)
DL/SWA....... Commission for Controlling the Desert Locust in the Eastern Region of its Distribution Area in/on South West Asia (SAUO)
DLSX........... Diesel Supply [*Private rail car owner code*]
DLT............. Daily Letter Telegram (IAA)
DLT............. Dalton [*California*] [*Seismograph station code, US Geological Survey*] [*Closed*] (SEIS)
DLT............. Darton, Longman & Todd [*Publisher*] [*British*]
DLT............. Data Linear Tape (SAUS)
DLT............. Data Line Terminal (IAA)
DLT............. Data Line Translator (IAA)
DLT............. Data Link Layer Trailer [*Telecommunications*] (ACRL)
DLT............. Data Link Terminal
DLT............. Data Link Transceiver (SAUS)
DLT............. Data Link Translator
DLT............. Data Loop Transceiver [*Computer science*]
dlt............. Daylight (WDMC)
DLT............. Decision Logic Table [*DoD*]
DLT............. Decision Logic Translator
DLT............. Deck Landing Training
DLT............. Deck Landing Trial (SAUS)
DLT............. DECs Linkage Test (SAUS)
DLT............. Delete (FAAC)
DLT............. Delivery Lead Time [*Army*]
DLT............. Delivery Term [*Military*]
DLT............. Delta
DLT............. Delta Air Lines, Inc. (MCD)
DLT............. Deltona Corp. (SAUO)
DLT............. Dental Laboratory Technician [*Medicine*] (EDAA)
DLT............. Depletion Layer Transistor (SAUS)
DLT............. Depletion-Layer Transistor (IEEE)
DLT............. Depletion Load Transistor (SAUS)
DLT............. Developed Layout Template (MCD)
DLT............. Development Land Tax [*British*]
DLT............. Device Level Test [*Electronics*] (AAEL)
DLT............. Digital Linear Tape [*Computer science*] (PCM)
DLT............. Digital Line Tape [*Computer science*] (VERA)
DLT............. Digital Line Termination [*Telecommunications*] (TEL)
DLT............. Digital Line Terminator (SAUS)
DLT............. Dihydroepiandrosterone Loading Test [*Endocrinology*]
DLT............. Dilauryl Thiodipropionate [*Also, DLTDP, DLTP*] [*Food preservative*]
DLT............. Direct Labor Time
DLT............. Direct Linear Transform (SAUS)
DLT............. Direct Linear Transformation (PDAA)
DLT............. Direct Lunar Transport (IIA)
DLT............. Discrimination Learning Test (SAUS)
DLT............. Distributed Language Translation [*Project being developed by BSO, a Dutch computer company*]
DLT............. Dog-Leg Transducer (SAUS)
D-L T........... Donath-Landsteiner Test (SAUS)
DLT............. Dose Limiting Toxicity [*Medicine*]
DLT............. Double Lumen Tube [*Medicine*] (MELL)
DLT............. Double-Lung Transplantation [*Medicine*] (MELL)
DLT............. Double Reduction-Locked Train
dlt............. dry long tons (SAUS)
DLT............. Dual Language Translation [*Chinese University of Hong Kong*] (NITA)
DLTA........... Delta US Corp. [*NASDAQ symbol*] (COMM)
DltaPtr......... Delta Petroleum Corp. [*Associated Press*] (SAG)
DLTD........... Delphi International, Ltd. [*NASDAQ symbol*] (NASQ)
DLTDP......... Dilauryl Thiodipropionate [*Also, DLT, DLTP*] [*Food preservative*]
DLTK........... Deltak Corp. [*NASDAQ symbol*] (COMM)
DLTK........... Deltek Systems, Inc. [*NASDAQ symbol*] (NASQ)
DLTM........... Data Line Terminal Module [*Military*] (RDA)
DLTM........... Data Link Test Message
DLTMA......... Dynamic Load Thermo-Mechanical Analysis [*Thermal analysis*]
DLTO........... Dog-Leg-to-Orbit (SAA)
DLTOE......... Draft Living Table of Organization and Equipment [*Military*] (INF)
DLT/P........... Deck-Landing Training/Practice [*Navy*] [*British*]
DLTP........... Dilauryl Thiodipropionate [*Also, DLT, DLTDP*] [*Food preservative*]
DLTPM......... Date of Last Payment (SAUS)
DLT Procedure... Down-Loading Termination Procedure (SAUS)
DLTR........... Data Link Terminal Repeater (NASA)
DLTR........... Data Link Transmission Repeater (NASA)
DLTR........... Dollar Tree Stores [*NASDAQ symbol*] (SG)
dltr............. Dollar Tree Stores [*NASDAQ symbol*] (TTSB)
DLTR........... Dollar Tree Stores, Inc. [*NASDAQ symbol*] (SAG)
DLTS........... Deck Landing Training School
DLTS........... Deep-Level Tansient Spectrum (SAUS)
DLTS........... Deep Level Transient Spectroscopy (AAEL)
DLTS........... Defraction Limited Thermograph System (MCD)
DLTT........... Down-Link Television Terminal
DLTU........... Digital Line and Trunk Unit (SAUS)
DLTU........... Digital Line Terminating Unit (SAUS)
DLTU........... Digital Line/Trunk Unit (SAUS)
DLU............. Data Line Unit
DLU............. Data Logging Unit [*Electronics*]
DLU............. Destination Logical Unit [*Communications term*] (DCT)
DLU............. Development Laboratory Unit (MCD)
DIU............. Digital input unit (SAUS)
DIU............. Digital interchange utility (SAUS)
DLU............. Digital Line Unit [*Telecommunications*]
DLU............. Digitizer Logic Unit
DLU............. Discharge Load Unit (ACAE)
DLU............. Display Logic Unit
DLU............. Disposable Loading Unit (DB)
DLU............. Dual Logical Units (SAUS)
DLUC........... Digital Line Unit Control (SAUS)
DLUG........... Double Lock Up Garage
DLUR........... Dependent Logical Unit Register (SAUS)
DLUR........... Dependent LU Requester (SAUS)
DLUR/DLUS... Dependent Lu [*Logical Unit*] Requester/Server (CDE)
DLUR/S......... Dependent LU Requester/Server (SAUS)
DLUS........... Dependent Logical Unit Server (SAUS)
DLUS........... Dependent LU Server (SAUS)
DLUs........... Digitizer Logic Units (SAUS)
DLV............. Dandelion Latent Virus [*Plant pathology*]
DLV............. Defective Leukemia Virus [*Medicine*] (DMAA)
DLV............. Demonstration Launch Vehicle [*Space launch term*] (ISAK)
DLV............. Differential Lung Ventilation
DLV............. Direct LASER Vaporization
DLV............. Discharge-Line Volume [*Nuclear energy*] (NRCH)
DLV............. Dominant Logic Value (SAUS)
DLV............. Dorman Long Vanderbijl Corporation (SAUO)
DLV............. Montgomery, AL [*Location identifier*] [*FAA*] (FAAL)
DLV............. US Delivery Systems, Inc. [*NYSE symbol*] (SAG)
DLVA........... Detector Logarithmic Video Amplifier (SAUS)
DLVA........... Detector Log Video Amplifier (TIMI)
DLVD........... Delivered (NATG)
DLVD........... Diastolic Left Ventricular Dysfunction [*Medicine*] (MELL)
DLVL........... Diverted into Low-Velocity Layer (OA)
d-LVN......... Dorsal branch of Lateral Ventricular Nerve (SAUS)
DLVO........... Derjaguin-Landau-Verwey-Overbeek [*Colloid science*]
DLVO Theory... Derjaguin-Landau-Verwey-Overbeek Theory [*Stability of colloidal dispersions*]
DLVR........... Cortecs International Ltd. [*NASDAQ symbol*] (SAG)
DLVR........... Cortecs plc [*NASDAQ symbol*] (NASQ)
DLVR........... Deliver (AABC)
DLVRY......... Contecs Intl Ltd ADS [*NASDAQ symbol*] (TTSB)
DLVRY......... Delivery
DLVX........... Thiokol [*Private rail car owner code*]
dlvy............. Delivery (ADWA)
DLVY........... Delivery (MSA)
DLW............. Delaware, Lackawanna & Western Railroad [*AAR code*]
DLW............. Delaware Resources Corp. [*Vancouver Stock Exchange symbol*]
DLW............. Delta Woodside Ind. [*NYSE symbol*] (TTSB)
DLW............. Delta Woodside Industries, Inc. [*NYSE symbol*] (CTT)
DLW............. Diesel Loco Works [*Indian Railway*] [*Varanasi*] (TIR)
DLW............. Diploma in Labour Welfare (SAUS)
DLW............. Double Loop Whorl [*Fingerprint*] (MELL)
DLW............. Doubly-Labelled Water [*Analytical chemistry*]
DLWC........... Department of Land and Water Conservation [*Australia*] (GEOI)
DLWD........... Delta Woodside Industries, Inc. (MHDW)
DLWD........... Diffuse Lymphocytic Well Differentiated [*Medicine*] (STED)
DLWG........... Daily Weight Gain (SAUS)
DLWL........... Designed Load Waterline [*Technical drawings*] (IAA)
DLWL........... Discharge-Line Water-Leg Length [*Nuclear energy*] (NRCH)
DLWR........... Depew, Lancaster & Western Railroad [*Federal Railroad Administration identification code*]
DLWX........... DL and W [*Private rail car owner code*]
DLX............. Deluxe (MSA)
DLX............. DeLuxe Corp. [*NYSE symbol*] (SPSG)
DLX............. Deluxe Room [*Travel industry*] (TRID)
DLX............. Die Lock
DLX............. Dylex Ltd. [*Toronto Stock Exchange symbol*]
DLX............. Washington, DC [*Location identifier*] [*FAA*] (FAAL)
DLY............. Daily
DLY............. Delay (KSC)
DLY............. Delivery (ROG)
DLY............. Diffusion Linted Yield (SAUS)
DLY............. Dillon Bay [*Vanuatu*] [*Airport symbol*] (OAG)
DLY............. Dolly (MSA)
DLY............. Paine Webber Group [*AMEX symbol*] (SAG)
Dlyd............. Delayed (SAUS)
DlyJour......... Daily Journal Corp. [*Associated Press*] (SAG)
DLZ............. Davidson & Lumber [*Federal Railroad Administration identification code*]
DLZ............. Delaware, OH [*Location identifier*] [*FAA*] (FAAL)
DLZ............. Divine Light Zentrum (SAUO)
DLZ............. Drop Landing Zone [*Air Force*] (AFM)
DLZ............. Dynamic Launch Zone (SAUS)
dm............... Dahomey [*Benin*] [*MARC country of publication code*] [*Library of Congress*] (LCCP)
DM............... Daily Mirror [*A publication*]
DM............... Dam
DM............... Damage Monitor (SAUS)
DM............... Dame
DM............... Dames & Moore Group [*NYSE symbol*] [*Formerly, Dames & Moore, Inc.*] (SG)
DM............... Dames & Moore, Inc. [*NYSE symbol*] (SPSG)
DM............... Damien Ministries (EA)
DM............... Danbury Mint
D/M............. Dance/Movement Therapy
DM............... Dark Matter [*Astrophysics*]
DM............... Dasymeter (SAUS)
DM............... Database Manager (SAUS)

DM .... Data Maintenance Item (ASC X12) (AG)
DM .... Data Management (KSC)
DM .... Data Manager
DM .... Data Mark (SAUS)
DM .... Data Mart (GART)
DM .... Data Master
DM .... Data Memory
DM .... Data Mining (SAUS)
Dm .... Data Mobile Channel (CGWS)
DM .... Data Mode (SAUS)
DM .... Data Module (SAUS)
D/M .... Date and Month (SAUS)
DM .... Daughters of Mary of the Immaculate Conception [*Roman Catholic religious order*]
DM .... Daughters of Our Lady of Mercy [*Roman Catholic religious order*]
DM .... Daunomycin [*Antineoplastic drug*]
DM .... Davison and Merivale's King's Bench Reports [*64 RR*] [*1843-44*] [*A publication*] (DLA)
D/M .... Day and Month (SAUS)
DM .... Deacon and Martyr [*Church calendars*]
DM .... Dead Meat (SAUS)
DM .... Deaf Missions (EA)
DM .... Debit Memo (SAUS)
DM .... Debit Memorandum (MCD)
DM .... Debugging Mode
DM .... Decade Mean (SAUS)
DM .... Decameter
dm .... decametre (SAUS)
DM .... Decamired
DM .... Deception Material (MUSM)
DM .... Deciduous (Primary) Molar [*Dentistry*]
DM .... Decimal Multiply
dM .... decimega (SAUS)
dm .... Decimeter (ABAC)
DM .... Decimeter [*Unit of measure*]
DM .... Decimeter (or Decimetre) (SAUS)
DM .... Decimetric (SAUS)
DM .... Decimilli (SAUS)
dM .... decimorgan (SAUS)
DM .... Decision Maker
DM .... Decision Making (SAUS)
DM .... Decision Mate (SAUS)
DM .... Decision Memorandum (ACAE)
DM .... Decreto Ministeriale [*Ministerial Decree*] [*Italian*] (ILCA)
DM .... Deep Monitoring (CARB)
DM .... Defect Management (AAEL)
DM .... Defensive Medicine (MELL)
DM .... Defensive Missile (ACAE)
DM .... Deflection Modulation (IAA)
DM .... Dekameter [*Unit of measure*]
DM .... Delay Modulation (NITA)
DM .... Deletion Mutant [*Genetics*]
DM .... Delta Ministry [*Later, DMM*] (EA)
DM .... Delta Modulation
DM .... Delta Modulator (SAUS)
DM .... Demand Meter
DM .... Demineralized [*Water*] (NRCH)
DM .... Demister (EEVL)
D/M .... Demodulate/Modulate
D/M .... Demodulation/Modulation (SAUS)
DM .... Density Matrix (SAUS)
DM .... Density Meter [*Instrumentation*]
D/M .... Density/Moisture (SAUS)
DM .... Dental Mechanic [*Ranking title*] [*British Royal Navy*]
DM .... Depot Maintenance (AAGC)
DM .... Depot Manufacture (MCD)
DM .... Deputy for Materiel
DM .... Deputy Master [*Freemasonry*] (ROG)
DM .... Deputy Minister (SAUO)
DM .... Dermatomyositis [*Medicine*]
DM .... Dermorphin [*Biochemistry*]
DM .... Descemet's Membrane [*Medicine*] (MELL)
DM .... Descriptive Method
DM .... Design for Manufacturing
DM .... Design Manual
DM .... Design margin (SAUS)
DM .... Design Memorandum
DM .... Design Modified
DM .... Des Moines [*Diocesan abbreviation*] [*Iowa*] (TOCD)
DM .... despatch money (SAUS)
DM .... Destra Mano [*Right Hand*] [*Music*] [*Italian*]
DM .... Destroyer Minelayer [*Navy symbol*] (MCD)
DM .... Detecting Magnetometer (IAA)
DM .... Detecting Mechanism (IAA)
DM .... Detector Mosaic
DM .... Detroit & Mackinac Railway [*Federal Railroad Administration identification code*]
DM .... Detroit & Mackinac Railway Co. [*AAR code*]
DM .... Deutsche Mark [*Monetary unit*] [*Germany*]
DM .... Developmental instrumentation MDM-Mid (SAUS)
DM .... Development and Maintenance (SAUS)
DM .... Development Machine (SAUS)
DM .... Development Manager
DM .... Development Milestone [*Aerospace*] (AAG)
DM .... Development Module (ACAE)
DM .... Development Motor (MCD)
DM .... Devon Militia [*British military*] (DMA)
DM .... Dextromaltose (DB)
DM .... Dextromethorphan [*Antitussive*] [*Pharmacy*]
DM .... Dextromethorphan Hydrobromide (SAUS)
DM .... Diabetes Mellitus [*Medicine*]
DM .... Diabetic Mother [*Medicine*]
DM .... Diagnostic Message (SAUS)
DM .... Diagnostic Module [*Automotive engineering*]
DM .... Diagnostic Monitor [*Computer science*] (IAA)
DM .... Dialog Manager (SAUS)
DM .... Dialogue Management system (SAUS)
dm .... Diamond (SAUS)
DM .... Diastolic Murmur [*Medicine*]
DM .... Dichroic Mirror
DM .... Dicrete Mathematics (SAUS)
DM .... Die Musik [*A publication*]
DM .... Diesel Mechanic [*or Mechanical*]
DM .... Diesel Mechanical (SAUS)
DM .... Diesel Moderate [*Service*] [*Automotive engineering*]
DM .... Dieses Monats [*Of This Month*] [*German*] (ROG)
DM .... Differential Mechanism (IAA)
DM .... Differential Mode [*Electronics*] (OA)
dM .... differential of mutual inductance (SAUS)
DM .... Differentiating Mechanism (SAUS)
DM .... Diffused Mesa
DM .... Diffuse Mixed [*Lymphoma*] [*Oncology*] (DAVI)
DM .... Diffuse Myalgia [*Medicine*] (MELL)
Dm .... Diffusing Capacity of the Alveolar Capillary Membrane [*Medicine*] (DAVI)
DM .... Digital Memory (SAUS)
DM .... Digital Modelling (SAUS)
DM .... Digital MODEM (SAUS)
DM .... Digital Modulation (ACAE)
DM .... Digital Modulator (SAUS)
DM .... Digital Module [*Telecommunications*] (TEL)
DM .... Digital Monolithic [*Electronics*] (OA)
DM .... Digital Multimeter (IAA)
DM .... Digital Multiplex (LAIN)
DM .... Digital Multiplexer (SAUS)
DM .... Digital Music Tuner [*Cable television*]
DM .... Diis Manibus [*To the Manes, i.e., Departed Souls*] [*Latin*]
Dm .... dimensions (SAUS)
DM .... Diode Matrix (SAUS)
DM .... Diode Memory (SAUS)
DM .... Dioxane-Methanol [*Scintillation solvent*] [*Bray solution*]
dm .... diphenylamine-arsine chloride (SAUS)
DM .... Diphenylamine Chloroarsine (SAUS)
DM .... Diphenylaminechloroarsine [*Tear gas*] [*Military*]
DM .... Diploma in Dermatological Medicine (DAVI)
D-M .... Diplomate, American Board of Internal Medicine (DHSM)
DM .... Directional Microphone (ELAL)
DM .... Direct Mail
DM .... Direct Manipulation (SAUS)
DM .... Direct Marketing
DM .... Direct Match (SAUS)
DM .... Direct Material (TIMI)
DM .... Direct Memory Access (SAUS)
dm .... direct monitoring (SAUS)
DM .... Directorate of ADPS Management (SAUO)
DM .... Directorate of Maintenance (AFIT)
DM .... Director of Management [*Military*]
DM .... Director of Mobilization [*British military*] (DMA)
DM .... Director of Music [*British military*] (DMA)
DM .... Disassembly Manual [*NASA*]
DM .... Discard Message (CET)
DM .... Disc Magnetic (SAUS)
DM .... Disc Monitor (SAUS)
DM .... Disconnected Mode [*Telecommunications*]
DM .... Disconnecting Manhole
DM .... Disconnect Mode (SAUS)
DM .... Discussion Memorandum (SAUO)
DM .... Diseased Mucosa [*Oncology*]
DM .... Disease Management
D/M .... Disintegrations per Minute
DM .... Disk Monitor [*Computer science*] (IAA)
DM .... Dismantling machine (SAUS)
DM .... Dispersion Measure [*Astronomy*]
DM .... Dispersive Medium (SAUS)
DM .... Display Monitor (ACAE)
DM .... Distal Metastases [*Medicine*] (MELL)
DM .... Distance Measurement (SAUS)
DM .... Distance Measuring (SAUS)
dm .... distance multiplier (SAUS)
DM .... Distolic Murmur [*Medicine*] (MELL)
DM .... Distributed Memory (SAUS)
DM .... Distributed Monitor (SAUS)
DM .... Distributing Main (SAUS)
DM .... Distribution Manager (SAUS)
DM .... Distribution Module [*Telecommunications*]
DM .... District Magistrate (SAUO)
DM .... District Manager
DM .... District Members [*Also, EN for secrecy*] [*Fenian Brotherhood*] (ROG)
DM .... District Municipality (SAUS)
DM .... Ditch Mile [*Newmarket Racecourse*] [*Horseracing*] [*British*]

DM............ Docking Mechanism (MCD)
DM............ Docking Module [*NASA*]
DM............ Doctor Martens [*Footwear*]
DM............ Doctor of Dental Medicine (DAVI)
DM............ Doctor of Management (PGP)
DM............ Doctor of Mathematics
DM............ Doctor of Medicine
DM............ Doctor of Music
DM............ Doctor of Musicology (NADA)
DM............ Documenta et Monumenta [*A publication*] (BJA)
DM............ Documentation Manager [*Air Force*] (AFM)
DM............ DodecylMaltoside [*Organic chemistry*]
DM............ Dome Mines, Ltd. (SAUO)
DM............ Dominica [*ANSI two-letter standard code*] (CNC)
DM............ Dopamine [*Biochemistry*] (AAMN)
DM............ Doppler Missile (MUGU)
DM............ Dorne & Margolin Inc. (SAUS)
DM............ Dot Matrix
DM............ Double Make (IAA)
DM............ Double-Make Drum (SAUS)
DM............ Double Master [*LORAN stations*]
DM............ Double Medium (ADA)
DM............ Double Membrane [*Medicine*] (DB)
DM............ Double Minute [*Cytology*]
DM............ Double Monochromator (SAUS)
DM............ Douglas Model (SAA)
DM............ Drafting Manual (AABC)
DM............ Dram (MCD)
D/M............ Dr. & Mrs. (VRA)
DM............ Dredged Material (SAUS)
d/m............ Drips per Minute (COE)
DM............ Drive Magnet
DM............ Driver, Master
DM............ Driver Mechanic [*British military*] (DMA)
DM............ Driving and Maintenance (IAA)
DM............ Drug Monograph [*Medicine*] (DB)
DM............ Drum
dm............ Drum
DM............ Drum Module [*Computer science*] (IAA)
DM............ Dry Mass
DM............ Dry Matter
DM............ Dry Mixed (SAUS)
DM............ Dual Mode (ACAE)
DM............ Dummy Round (MCD)
DM............ Du Mont (SAUS)
DM............ Dungeon Master [*In game Dungeons and Dragons*]
DM............ Dungeon Module (SAUS)
DM............ Dust and Mist (SARE)
DM............ Dynamic Melting [*Chemistry*]
DM............ Dynamic Memory (SAUS)
DM............ Dynamo (IAA)
DM............ Dynamotor (IAA)
DM............ Illustrator Draftsman [*Navy rating*]
DM............ Iran [*License plate code assigned to foreign diplomats in the US*]
DM............ Light Minelayer [*Later, MMD*] [*Navy symbol*]
DM............ Magnetic Drum Module [*Computer science*]
DM............ Master Diver [*Navy*]
DM............ Master of Divinity
DM............ Meersk Air [*ICAO designator*] (AD)
Dm............ Membrane Component of Diffusion [*Cytology*] (MAE)
DM............ Myotonic Dystrophy (SAUS)
DM............ Per cent Design Modified (SAUS)
DM............ Union of Durham Miners (SAUO)
DM............ Vomiting Gas [*US Chemical Corps symbol*]
DM............ Working Group on Data Management (SAUO)
DM............ Daily Mail (ODA)
DM............ Dipole Moment [*Physics*] (ODA)
DM............ Direct Methanation [*Chemistry*] (ODA)
DM1............ Draftsman, First Class, Illustrator [*Navy*] (DNAB)
DM2............ Draftsman, Second Class, Illustrator [*Navy*] (DNAB)
Dm^2............ Square Decimeter (ROG)
Dm^3............ Cubic Decimeter (ROG)
dm3............ Cubic Decimeter (or Decimetre) (SAUS)
DM3............ Draftsman, Third Class, Illustrator [*Navy*] (DNAB)
dm3/h............ Cubic Decimetre per Hour (SAUS)
DM5............ Disk Monitor System (SAUS)
DMA............ Dance Masters of America (EA)
DMA............ Data Management Administrator (SAUO)
DMA............ Data Management Agent (MCD)
DMA............ Data Management Analysis
DMA............ Data Management Association (SAUO)
DMA............ Data-Matching Agency
DMA............ Data Memory Access
DMA............ Dealer Management Association [*Exeter, NH*] [*Commercial firm*] (EA)
DMA............ Dean Martin Association (EAIO)
DMA............ Debt Market Analysis [*MMS International*] [*Information service or system*] (CRD)
DMA............ Decimal Matrix Adder (SAUS)
DMA............ Defence Manufacturers Association [*British*] (DS)
DMA............ Defense Manpower Administration [*Superseded by Office of Manpower Administration, 1953*] [*Department of Labor*]
DMA............ Defense Mapping Agency [*Washington, DC*]
DMA............ Defense Mineral Administration (SAUO)
DMA............ Deferred Maintenance Alarm (SAUS)
DMA............ Degraded Mission Assessment
DMA............ Delay Arming Mechanism (SAUS)
DMA............ Delicatessen Managers Association (SAUO)
DMA............ Denervated Muscle Atrophy [*Medicine*] (MELL)
DMA............ Dental Manufacturers of America (EA)
DMA............ Department of Medical Assistance (SAUO)
DMA............ Department of Memorial Affairs [*Veterans Administration*]
DMA............ Department of Military Aeronautics (SAUO)
DMA............ Department of Military Affairs (DEMM)
DMA............ Department of Municipal Affairs (SAUS)
DMA............ Deployed Mechanical Assembly (MCD)
DMA............ Depot Maintenance Activity (MCD)
DMA............ Depth and Motion Analysis (EURO)
DMA............ Designated Maintenance Activity (MCD)
DMA............ Designated Maintenance Agency (SAUO)
DMA............ Designated Market Area [*Advertising*]
DMA............ Designated Marketing Area (SAUS)
DMA............ Design Management Award [*Financial Times and London Business School*] [*British*]
DMA............ Devil Mountain [*Alaska*] [*Seismograph station code, US Geological Survey*] (SEIS)
DMA............ Diagnosis of Multiple Alarms System [*Environmental science*] (COE)
DMA............ Dietary Managers Association (EA)
DMA............ Differential Mobility Analyzer [*Marine science*] (OSRA)
DMA............ Digital Major Alarm (MCD)
DMA............ Digital Map Analyzer
DMA............ Digital Model Assembly
DMA............ Digraph Matrix Analysis (SPST)
DMA............ Dihydroxymandelic Acid [*Also, DHMA, DOMA*] [*Organic chemistry*]
DMA............ Dimethyl Acetal (SAUS)
DMA............ Dimethylacetamide [*Also, DMAC*] [*Organic chemistry*]
DMA............ Dimethyladenosine [*Organic chemistry*] (MAE)
DMA............ Dimethyl Adipimidate [*Biochemistry*]
DMA............ Dimethylamine [*Organic chemistry*]
DMA............ Dimethylaniline [*Organic chemistry*]
DMA............ Dimethylanisole [*Organic chemistry*]
DMA............ Dimethylarginine [*Biochemistry*]
DMA............ Dimethyl Arsonic Acid [*Organic chemistry*]
DMA............ Dimethylnaphthylamin [*Medicine*] (EDAA)
DMA............ Diploma in Municipal Accounting (ADA)
DMA............ Diploma in Municipal Administration [*British*]
DMA............ Direct Mail Association (SAUO)
DMA............ Direct Marketing Association [*New York, NY*] (EA)
DMA............ Direct Memory Access [*Computing method*]
DMA............ Direct Memory Address [*Computer science*]
DMA............ Direct Memory Addressing (SAUS)
dma............ direct memory asset (SAUS)
DMA............ Direct. Microassembly (SAUS)
DMA............ Director of Maritime Aviation (SAUO)
DMA............ Director of Medical Affairs (HCT)
DMA............ Director of Military Assistance
DMA............ Directory of Military Application (SAUS)
DMA............ Disodium Methyl Arsenate (EDCT)
DMA............ District Manager's Assistant [*British*] (DCTA)
DMA............ Divisional Maintenance Area [*Military*] [*British*]
DMA............ Division Of Military Aeronautics (SAUO)
DMA............ Division of Military Application [*Energy Research and Development Administration*]
DMA............ Doctor of Municipal Administration
DMA............ Doctor of Musical Arts
DMA............ Document Management Alliance
DMA............ Dog Museum of America (SAUS)
DMA............ Dominica [*ANSI three-letter standard code*] (CNC)
DMA............ Dominion Marine of Association (SAUO)
DMA............ Double Motor Alternator
DMA............ Drawing mark as built (SAUS)
DMA............ Drive Motor Assembly (MCD)
DMA............ Drum Memory Adapter (SAUS)
DMA............ Drum Memory Assembly [*Computer science*]
DMA............ Dry Matter Accumulation (OA)
DMA............ Dum Memory Assembly (SAUS)
DMA............ Dynamic Mechanical Analysis
DMA............ Dynamic Memory Access [*Computer science*] (VLIE)
DMA............ Dynamic Microprocessor Associates (PCM)
DMA............ Hospital, Institution and Educational Food Service Society (SAUO)
DMA............ Maersk Air IS [*Denmark*] [*ICAO designator*] (FAAC)
DMA............ Tucson, AZ [*Location identifier*] [*FAA*] (FAAL)
DMA............ United States Maritime Administration, Washington, DC [*Library symbol*] [*Library of Congress*] (LCLS)
DMAA............ Defence Manufacturers Association of Australia Ltd. (SAUO)
DMAA............ Dimethylacetoacetamide [*Organic chemistry*]
DMAA............ Dimethylarsenonic Acid [*Organic chemistry*]
DMAA............ Dimethylarsinic Acid (LDT)
DMAA............ Direct Mail Advertising Association [*Later, DMMA*]
DMAAC............ Defense Mapping Agency Aeronautical Center (ACAE)
DMAAC............ Defense Mapping Agency Aerospace Center [*Formerly, ACIC*]
DMAACK............ Direct Memory Access Acknowledge (SAUS)
DMAAC-ST............ Defense Mapping Agency Aerospace Center Directorate of Systems and Techniques
DMAAC-TC............ Defense Mapping Agency Aerospace Center Technical Library/Translation Section
DMA-AF............ Defense Message System-Air Force (SAUO)
DMAB............ Defended Modular Array Basing [*Military*]
DMAB............ Dimethylaminobenzaldehyde [*Ehrlich's reagent*] [*Analytical chemistry*]
DMAB............ Dimethylaminobenzoic Acid (SAUS)

DMAB .... Dimethylaminoborane [*Organic chemistry*]
DMAB .... P-Dimethylaminobenzaldehyd (SAUS)
DMABA .... Dimethylaminobenzaldehyde [*Analytical chemistry*] (AAMN)
DMABO .... Defense Mapping Agency Branch Office (DNAB)
DMABODET... Defense Mapping Agency Branch Office Detachment (DNAB)
DMAC .... Design and Manufacturing Automation Corporation (SAUO)
DMAC .... Des Moines Art Center (SAUS)
DMAC .... Dimethylacetamide [*Also, DMA*] [*Organic chemistry*]
DMAC .... Direct Memory Access Channel [*Pronounced "DEEmack"*] [*Computer science*]
DMAC .... direct memory-access contro (SAUS)
DMAC .... Direct Memory Access Control [*Computer science*]
DMAC .... Disseminated Mycobacterium Avium Complex [*Medicine*]
DMAC .... Diving Medical Advisory Committee (SAUS)
DMAC .... DMA Controller (SAUS)
DMAC .... duobinary multiplexed analog components (SAUS)
DMAC .... Dusty Mac Oil & Gas Ltd. [*NASDAQ symbol*] (SAG)
DMACC .... Direct Marketing Association Catalog Council [*New York, NY*] (EA)
DMA Controller... Direct Memory Access Controller (SAUS)
DMACP .... Direct Memory Access Communications Processor
DMACS .... Descriptive Macro Code Generation System [*Computer science*]
DMACS .... Distributed Manufacturing Automation and Control Software (VLIE)
DMACSS ...... Distributed Marketing and Customer Service System (TIMI)
DMAD .... Diagnostic Machine Aids/Digital [*Raytheon Co.*] [*Programming language*] (CSR)
DMAD .... Dimethylacetylenedicarboxylate [*Organic chemistry*]
DMAD .... Disease-Modifying Antirheumatic Drug [*Medicine*] (EDAA)
DMADISTRCEN... Defense Mapping Agency Distribution Center (DNAB)
DM Adm ...... Doctor of Municipal Administration
DMAE .... Dimethylaminoethanol [*Antidepressant*]
DMAE .... Dimethylaminoethoxide (SAUS)
D Ma E .... Doctor of Marine Engineering
DMAEC .... Dimethylaminoethylchloride (EDCT)
DMAEMA ..... Dimethylaminoethyl Methacrylate [*Organic chemistry*]
D Ma Eng .... Doctor of Marine Engineering
DMAFB .... Davis Monthanfield Air Force Base (SAUO)
DMAFF .... Defense Mapping Agency Feature File (GEOI)
DMAFF .... Defense Mapping Agency Feature Format (SAUO)
DMAH .... Dimethylaluminum Hydride (SAUS)
DMAHC .... Defense Mapping Agency Hydrographic Center [*Later, DMAHTC*]
DMAHP .... Dystrophia Myotonica-Associated Homeodomain Protein [*Biochemistry*]
DMAHT .... Defense Mapping Agency Hydrographic/Topographic Center (COE)
DMAHTC ...... Defense Mapping Agency Hydrographic/Topographic Center [*Washington, DC*] [*Also, an information service or system*] (IID)
DMAI .... Direct Memory Access Interface
DMAI .... UCD Shiells (SAUS)
DMAIAGS ..... Defense Mapping Agency Inter-American Geodetic Survey (GEOI)
DMAINST ..... Defense Mapping Agency Instruction (COE)
DMAIO .... Direct Memory Access Input/Output (SAUS)
D/Maj .... Drum-Major [*British military*] (DMA)
DMAL .... Dimethylacetal (SAUS)
D/M Allocator... Data/Memory Allocator (SAUS)
DMALO .... Defense Mapping Agency Liaison Office (DNAB)
DMAM .... Dimethyl Aminoethyl Methacrylate [*Organic chemistry*]
DMAM .... Di(methylamyl) Maleate [*Organic chemistry*]
DMAM .... Direct Memory Access Multiplexer (SAUS)
DMaM .... United States Marine Corps Museum, Washington, DC [*Library symbol*] [*Library of Congress*] (LCLS)
DMAMP .... (Dimethylaminomethyl)phenol [*Organic chemistry*]
DMAMP .... Dimethylamino(methyl)propanol [*Organic chemistry*]
DMAN .... Data Manager (KSC)
DMAN .... Differential Manchester (SAUS)
DMan .... Directorate of Manning (SAUO)
D-man .... drug-enforcement officer (SAUS)
DMAN .... Manpower Directorate (SAUO)
DM & CW .... Diploma in Maternity and Child Welfare
DM & E .... Dakota, Minnesota & Eastern Railroad
D M & G ...... De Gex, Macnaghten, and Gordon's English Chancery Reports [*A publication*] (DLA)
D M & GB .... De Gex, Macnaghten, and Gordon's English Bankruptcy Reports [*A publication*] (DLA)
DM & IR ...... Duluth, Missabe & Iron Range Railway Co.
DM & IRR .... Duluth, Missabe & Iron Range Railroad (MHDB)
DM & M ...... D'Arcy-MacManus & Masius [*Advertising agency*]
DM & N .... Duluth, Missabe & Northern Railway
DM & O .... Data Management and Operations (SSD)
DM & S .... Department of Medicare and Surgery [*Veterans Administration*] (GFGA)
DM & T .... Defense Markets & Technology [*Predicasts, Inc.*] [*Database*]
DM & TS ..... Department of Mines and Technical Survey [*Canada*] (DNAB)
DM & V .... Delaware, Maryland & Virginia Railroad
DManEng .... Directorate of Management Engineering (SAUO)
DMANS .... Dimethylamino(nitro)stilbene [*Organic chemistry*]
DManSc ...... Doctor of Management Sciences
DMAO .... Directorate of Military Aid Overseas [*British*]
DMAO .... District Management Assistance Office (SAUO)
DMAODS ..... Defense Mapping Agency Office of Distribution Services (DNAB)
DMAP .... DARCOM [*Development and Readiness Command, Army*] Modification Application Plan (MCD)
DMAP .... Digital Missile Autopilot (MCD)
DMAP .... Dimethylaminopurine [*Organic chemistry*]
DMAP .... Dimethylaminopyridine [*Organic chemistry*]
DMAP .... Direct Matrix Abstraction Process
DMAPA .... Dimethylaminopropylamine [*Also, DIMAPA*] [*Organic chemistry*]
DMAPMA ..... Dimethylaminopropyl Methacrylamide [*Organic chemistry*]
DMAPN .... (Dimethylaminophenyl)phenylnitrone [*Organic chemistry*]
DMAPN .... Dimethylaminopropionitrile [*Organic chemistry*]
DMAPP .... Dimethylallyl Pyrophosphate [*Organic chemistry*]
DMAPS .... Digital Manufacturing Process System (VLIE)
DMAPS .... Digital Marine Acquisition and Processing System (SAUS)
DMAR .... Datamarine International, Inc. [*NASDAQ symbol*] (NQ)
DMAR .... Datamarine Int'l [*NASDAQ symbol*] (TTSB)
DMAR .... Deferred Maintenance and Repair [*DoD*]
DMARA .... Dynamic Multicast Address Relay Agent (VLIE)
Dmarc .... Demarcation Point [*Telecommunications*] (ITD)
DMARC .... DOBIS MARC (SAUS)
DMarC .... Marist College, Washington, DC [*Library symbol*] [*Library of Congress*] (LCLS)
DMARD .... Disease-Modifying Antirheumatic Drug [*Medicine*]
dmards .... disease-modifying anti-rheumatic drugs (SAUS)
DMARQ .... Direct Memory Access Request (SAUS)
DMARS .... Deposit Message Retrieval System (SAUS)
DMarS .... Marist Seminary, Washington, DC [*Library symbol*] [*Library of Congress*] (LCLS)
DMAS .... Defense Manufacturers and Supplies Association of America (AAGC)
DMAS .... Defense Material Allotment System (AFIT)
DMAS .... Digital Modular Avionics System
DMAS .... Digital Multiplexed Audio System (ACAE)
DMAS .... Distribution Management Accounting System (IEEE)
DMAS .... Distributors Management Accounting System (VLIE)
DMASPOEM... Defense Mapping Agency Special Program Office for Exploitation Modernization (GEOI)
DMASS .... Data Management and Automated Storage Strategy (SAUS)
D Mass .... United States District Court for the District of Massachusetts (DLA)
DMAT .... Decision-Making Ability Test [*Psychology*] (BARN)
DMAT .... Digital Module Automatic Tester
DMAT .... Direct Memory Access Transfer (SAUS)
D-MAT .... Directorate of Materials Research and Development [*Aviation*] [*British*]
DMAT .... Disaster Medical Assistance Team (MELL)
DMATC .... Defense Mapping Agency Topographic Center [*Later, DMAHTC*]
DMath .... Doctor of Mathematics (NADA)
DMATS .... Defense Metropolitan Area Telephone Service [*or System*] (MCD)
D-MAT/S ...... Directorate of Materials and Structures Research and Development [*British*]
DMAU .... Dictionary of the Modern American Usage (SAUS)
DMAUSE ...... DMA Utility Software Environment Laboratory (SAUO)
D-Max .... Density Maximum (SAUS)
DMB .... Daily Maximum Benefit [*Insurance*]
DMB .... Dairy Marketing Board (SAUS)
DMB .... Data Management Block
DMB .... Data Management Branch (SAUO)
DMB .... Datum Marker Buoy (COE)
DMB .... Defense Manufacturing Board [*DoD*]
DMB .... Defense Mediation Board (SAUO)
DMB .... Defense Mobilization Board [*Terminated, 1958*]
DMB .... Demineralized Bone [*Medicine*]
DMB .... Dibutanoylmorphine [*An analgesic*]
DMB .... Dichloro (Methyl) Benzhydrol [*Organic chemistry*]
DMB .... Digital Multipoint Bridge (SAUS)
DMB .... Dihydro(methyl)benzodiazepinone [*Biochemistry*]
DMB .... Dimethoxybenzene [*Organic chemistry*]
DMB .... Dimethylbenzamil [*Organic chemistry*]
DMB .... Dimethylbusulfan [*Organic chemistry*]
DMB .... Dimethylmethylene Blue [*Organic chemistry*]
DMB .... Disconnect and Make Busy [*Telecommunications*] (TEL)
DMB .... Distinguished Marksmanship Badge
DMB .... Division Maintenance Battalion (MCD)
DMB .... Domain Master Browser (SAUS)
DMB .... Double Mouldboard [*Ploughing*]
DMB .... Double Mouldboarding (SAUS)
dmb .... dual-mode bus (SAUS)
Dmb .... Dumbarton (SAUS)
DMB .... Duty Motor Boat (SAUS)
DMB .... Dynamic Memory Block (SAUS)
DMB .... Dynamic Multipoint Bridging [*Computer science*] (ACRL)
DMB .... P-Dimethoxybenzene (SAUS)
DMBA .... Dimethylbarbituric Acid [*Organic chemistry*]
DMBA .... Dimethylbenzanthracene [*Carcinogen*]
DMBA .... Dimethyl(butyl)amine [*Organic chemistry*]
DMBAO .... Dimethylbenzanthraceneoxide [*Organic chemistry*]
DMBAS .... Dimethoxy(amino)stilbene [*Organic chemistry*]
DMBC .... Detroit Motor Boat Club (SAUS)
DMBC .... Dimethylbenzylcarbinol [*Organic chemistry*]
DMBC .... Direct Material Balance Control
DMBC .... Double Mark Blank Column (BUR)
DMBCA .... Dimethylbenzylcarbinol Acetate [*Organic chemistry*]
DMBE .... Double Many-Body Expansion [*Kinetics*]
DMBI .... Dmobilize (SAUS)
DM-BilG ...... DM-Bilanzgesetz (SAUS)
Dmbl .... Demobilization (SAUS)
Dmbl .... Demobilize (SAUS)
dmbl .... demobilized (SAUS)
DMBO .... Distance Most Bundles Ordering (SAUS)
DMBP .... Data Management Block Pool (TIMI)
DMBS .... Defense Material Billing System (AFIT)
DMBS .... Digital Measuring Borescope System
DMBZ .... Dimethylbenzimidazole [*Organic chemistry*]
DMC .... Chief Illustrator Draftsman [*Navy rating*]

DMC............ Dactinomycin, Methotrexate, and Cyclophosphamide [*Medicine*] (EDAA)
DMC............ Dactinomycin, Methotrexate, Cytoxan [*Antineoplastic drug*] (CDI)
DMC............ Dairy Mart Convenience Stores, Inc. [*AMEX symbol*] (NASQ)
DMC............ Daniels Manufacturing Corp. (SAUS)
DMC............ Daniels Manufacturing Corporation (SAUO)
DMC............ Darryl McDaniels [*A rap recording artist whose initials appear in the album title, "Run-D.M.C."*]
DMC............ Data Management Center (CAAL)
DMC............ Data Management Channel
DMC............ Data Management Committee (SAUO)
DMC............ Data Management Communication (SAUS)
DMC............ Data Management Component (VLIE)
DMC............ Data Management Computer (KSC)
DMC............ Data Management Control (SAUS)
DMC............ Data Management Coordinator (ACAE)
DMC............ Data Manager Computer (SAUS)
DmC............ Datametrics Corp. (SAUS)
DmC............ Datametrics Corporation (SAUO)
DmC............ Data Microfilming Corp., Whittier, CA [*Library symbol*] [*Library of Congress*] (LCLS)
DMC............ Data Mode Control (COE)
DMC............ Data Multiplexer Control (SAUS)
DMC............ Dead Man Controls (SAA)
DMC............ Decision Module Compiler (DNAB)
DMC............ Deck Motion Compensator (MCD)
DMC............ Defence Manufacturers Council (SAUO)
DMC............ Defence Movement Coordination Committee [*Australia*]
DMC............ Defense Manpower Commission
DMC............ Defense Materiel Council [*DoD*]
DMC............ Defiance Mining Company (SAUO)
DMC............ Degraded Mission Capability
DMC............ Delgratia Mining Corporation (SAUO)
DMC............ Del Mar College (SAUS)
DMC............ DeLorean Motor Co. [*Initials used as name of its cars*]
DMC............ Demeclocycline [*Also, DMCT*] [*Antimicrobial compound*]
DMC............ Democratic Movement for Change [*Political party*] [*Israel*]
DMC............ Department of Mathematics and Computing (SAUO)
DMC............ Depot Maintenance Concept (SAUS)
DMC............ Deputy Chairman, Military Committee (SAUO)
DMC............ Deputy Marshal of Ceremonies (ROG)
DMC............ Design, Manage, Construct
DMC............ Design Manufacturing Change (SAUS)
DMC............ Desktop Multimedia Conferencing (VERA)
DMC............ Destination Digital Media Computers
DMC............ Destination Management Company [*Generic term*]
DMC............ Detroit Medical Center
DMC............ Dichlorodiphenylmethylcarbinol [*Also, DCPC*] [*Insecticide*]
dmc............ dichlorodiphenyl methyl carbinol (SAUS)
DMC............ Dichloromethotrexate [*Antineoplastic drug*] (CDI)
DMC............ Dichlorophenyl Methyl Carbinol (SAUS)
DMC............ Dielectric, Magnetic and Capacitor (IAA)
DMC............ Diffusion Monte Carlo [*Mathematics*]
DMC............ Digital Media Center (SAUO)
DMC............ Digital Microcircuit
DMC............ Digital Monitor Computer
DMC............ Digital Multiplex Control (IAA)
DMC............ DIMAC Corp. [*AMEX symbol*] (SAG)
DMC............ Dimethoxychalcone [*Organic chemistry*]
DMC............ Dimethylaminoethyl Chloride [*Organic chemistry*]
DMC............ Dimethylaminoethyl Chloride Hydrochloride (SAUS)
DMC............ Dimethyl Carbinol [*Organic chemistry*]
DMC............ Dimethyl Carbonate [*Organic chemistry*]
DMC............ Dimethylcysteine (Penicillamine) [*Pharmacology*]
DMC............ Directional Minimum Check [*Travel industry*] (TRID)
DMC............ Direct Maintenance Cost (NASA)
DMC............ Direct Manufacturing Cost [*Marketing*]
DMC............ Direct Memory Channel
DMC............ Direct Memory Controller (SAUS)
DMC............ Direct Microscopic Count [*Biochemistry*] (DAVI)
DMC............ Direct Multiplex Channel (SAUS)
DMC............ Direct Multiplex Control (SAUS)
DMC............ Direct multiplexed channel (SAUS)
DMC............ Direct Multiplexed Control
DMC............ Direct Multiplexor Channel
DMC............ Directorate of Militia and Cadets (SAUO)
DMC............ Discrete Memoryless Channel [*Computer science*]
DMC............ Disk Memory Controller [*Computer science*]
DMC............ Distributed Management Chain (SAUS)
DMC............ Distributed Master Control (SAUS)
DMC............ District Materials Center (SAUS)
DMC............ Diversified Industries, Inc. (SAUO)
DMC............ Diversified Mountaineer Corporation (SAUO)
DMC............ Dough-Molding Compound [*Plastics technology*]
DMC............ Drought Monitoring Centre (SAUS)
DMC............ DSIF [*Deep Space Instrumentation Facility*] Monitor and Control Subsystem [*NASA*]
DMC............ Duff Moisture Code (SAUS)
DMC............ Dull Men's Club (EA)
DMC............ Duration of Muscle Contraction [*Medicine*] (DMAA)
DMC............ Dynamic Markov Coding (SAUS)
DMC............ Dynamic Markov Compression (RALS)
DMC............ Dynamic Matrix Control [*Chemical engineering*] [*Computer science*]
DMC............ Dynamic Memory Control [*Computer science*]
DMC............ Metropolitan Club, Washington, DC [*Library symbol*] [*Library of Congress*] (LCLS)
DMCA.......... DeLorean Motor Club of America [*Defunct*] (EA)
DMCA.......... Dependents' Medical Care Act [*HEW*]
DMCA.......... Digital Millennium Copyright Act
DMCA.......... Direct Marketing Computer Association [*Defunct*] (EA)
DMCA.......... Direct Marketing Credit Association [*Defunct*] (EA)
DMCA.......... DM-Chapter-Award (SAUS)
DMCB.......... Dairy Mart Conven Str'B' [*AMEX symbol*] (SG)
DMCB.......... Data Measurement Corp. [*NASDAQ symbol*] (NQ)
DMCBAC...... Dimethylcetylbenzylammonium Chloride [*Antiseptic*] [*Organic chemistry*]
DMCC.......... Data and Maintenance Control Center (SAUO)
DMCC.......... Dean Martin Collector's Club [*Defunct*] (EA)
DMCC.......... Defence Movements Co-ordinating Committee (SAUO)
DMCC.......... Depot Maintenance Control [*or Coordinator*] Center [*Army*] (AABC)
DMCC.......... Dimethylcarbamoyl Chloride [*Organic chemistry*]
DMCC.......... Direct Microscopic Clump Count
DMCC.......... Division Movement Control Center (SAUO)
DMCC.......... Dual Multiple Column Control (VLIE)
DMCCC........ Deputy Missile Combat Crew Commander
DMCd.......... Dimethylcadmium
DMCD.......... Dimethylcyclohexanedicarboxilate (SAUS)
DMCD.......... Directed Missile Countermeasures Device (SEWL)
DMCE.......... Division of Medicaid Cost Estimates [*Department of Health and Human Services*] (GFGA)
DMCF.......... Deservicing, Maintenance, and Checkout Facility [*NASA*] (NASA)
DMCG.......... Direct Marketing Creative Guild [*New York, NY*] (EA)
DMCGS........ Descriptive Macro-Code Generation System (DNAB)
DMCHA........ Dimethylcyclohexamine [*Organic chemistry*]
DMCHA........ Dimethylcyclohexyladipate (SAUS)
DMCI.......... Dimethylclomipramine (DMAA)
DMCI.......... Direct Memory Communications Interface (SAUS)
DMCL.......... Device Media Control Language [*CODASYL/Honeywell, Inc.*]
DMCL.......... Digital MODEM Command Language [*Computer science*] (BYTE)
DMCM.......... Dimethoxyethylcarboline Carboxylate [*Organic chemistry*] (DAVI)
DMCM.......... Double Density Modular Core Memory (MCD)
DMCM.......... Master Chief Illustrator Draftsman [*Navy rating*]
DMCO.......... Delta Mission Checkout [*Space launch term*] (ISAK)
DMCOD........ Dimethylcyclooctadiene [*Organic chemistry*]
DMCP.......... Dimethylcyclopentene (SAUS)
DMCP.......... DOE Methods Compendium program (SAUS)
DMC/PC...... Drives, Motors, Controls, and Programmable Controllers Exhibition [*British*] (ITD)
DMCR.......... Director, Marine Corps Reserve
DMCS.......... Data Management and Control System (SAUS)
DMC's.......... Dialysis-Related Muscle Cramps [*Medicine*]
DMCS.......... Digital Missile Controller Set
DMCS.......... Digital Mobil Communications System (SAUS)
DMCS.......... Dimethyldichlorosilane [*Organic chemistry*]
DMCS.......... Distributed Manufacturing Control System (SAUS)
DMCS.......... Senior Chief Illustrator Draftsman [*Navy rating*]
DMCT.......... Demethylchlortetracycline [*Obsolete name*] [*Antimicrobial compound*] [*See DMC*]
DMCT.......... Dimethylchlortetracycline (DMAA)
DMCT.......... Directorate of Missile Captive Test (AAG)
DMCTC........ Dimethylchlortetracycline [*Antimicrobial compound*] (DAVI)
DMCU.......... Disk Memory Control Unit (SAUS)
DMCU.......... Display Monitor and Control Unit
DMCu.......... Metropolitan Club, Washington, DC [*Library symbol*] [*Library of Congress*] (LCLS)
DMCV.......... Dairy Mart Convenience Stores [*NASDAQ symbol*] (SAG)
DMCVA........ Dairy Mart Conven Str'A' [*NASDAQ symbol*] (TTSB)
DMCVB........ Dairy Mart Conven Str'B' [*NASDAQ symbol*] (TTSB)
DMCVX........ Dreyfus Midcap Value
DMD............ Carrizo Springs, TX [*Location identifier*] [*FAA*] (FAAL)
DMD............ Dark Mantle Deposit [*Lunar surface*]
DMD............ Data Measuring Device (SAUS)
DMD............ Data Model Diagramer [*Computer science*]
DMD............ Decennial Management Division (SAUS)
DMD............ Defense Manufacturing Board [*DoD*] (EGAO)
DMD............ Deformable Device [*Texas Instruments, Inc.*] [*Computer science*]
DMD............ Deformable Mirror Device (VLIE)
DMD............ Deformable Mirror Display (TIMI)
DMD............ Delmed, Inc. [*AMEX symbol*] (COMM)
dmd............ demand (SAUS)
DMD............ Department of Membership Development [*Medicine*] (EDAA)
DMD............ Deployment Management System (SAUS)
DMD............ Deployment Manning Document (MCD)
DMD............ Depressive Mood Disturbance [*Medicine*] (EDAA)
Dm/d............ Depth Molded (DS)
DMD............ Deputy Managing Director
DMD............ Device Manager Driver [*Computer science*] (VERA)
DMD............ Devices Management Directorate [*Army*]
DMD............ Dextrous Manipulator Demonstration (SAUS)
DMD............ Diamond (MSA)
dmd............ Diamond (VRA)
DMD............ Diamond Resources [*Vancouver Stock Exchange symbol*]
DMD............ Differential Mode Delay (SAUS)
DMD............ Digital Map Display
DMD............ Digital Message Device (AABC)
DMD............ Digital Methods Division (SAUS)
DMD............ Digital Micromirror Device [*Silicon chip*] [*Telecommunications*] (PCM)
DMD............ Digital Micromirror Display [*Electronics*] (PS)
DMD............ Digital Mirror Device (SAUS)

DMD .... Digital Missile Device (MCD)
DMD .... Digital Muirhead Display (NOAA)
DMD .... Digital Multisensor Display (ACAE)
DMD .... Digoxigenin Monodigitoxoside [*Biochemistry*]
DMD .... Dimethadione [*Biochemistry*]
DMD .... Dimethylmetadioxane (EDCT)
DMD .... Dimethyloxozolidinedione (SAUS)
DMD .... Direct Manipulation Device (SAUS)
DMD .... Direct Metallic Deposition (SAUS)
DMD .... Director of Manning Department (SAUO)
DMD .... Director of Mobilization Department (SAUO)
DMD .... Directory Management Domain [*Computer science*] (VERA)
dmd .... disc memory drive (SAUS)
DMD .... Disease-Modifying Drug [*Medicine*] (EDAA)
DMD .... Disk Memory Division (SAUS)
DMD .... Disk Memory Drive (SAUS)
DMD .... Distal Muscular Dystrophy [*Medicine*] (MELL)
DMD .... Doctor of Dental Medicine
DMD .... Doctor of Mathematics and Didactics
DMD .... Doctor of Medical Dentistry
DMD .... Domodossola [*Italy*] [*Seismograph station code, US Geological Survey*] [*Closed*] (SEIS)
DMD .... Doomadgee Mission [*Australia*] [*Airport symbol*] (OAG)
DMD .... Doppler Method of Diagnosis [*Medicine*] (MELL)
DMD .... Double Meridian Distance (PDAA)
DMD .... Dry Matter Disappearance (OA)
DMD .... Dual Mode Display
DMD .... Duchenne Muscular Dystrophy
DMD .... Dynamic Map Display
DMD .... Dystonia Musculorum Deformans [*Medicine*]
DMD .... RST Aviation, NV [*Belgium*] [*ICAO designator*] (FAAC)
D MD .... United States District Court for the District of Maryland (DLA)
DMDAAC...... Dimethyldiallylammonium Chloride [*Organic chemistry*]
DMDB .... Depot Maintenance Data Bank [*DARCOM*] (MCD)
DMDC .... Defense Manpower Data Center [*Alexandria, VA*]
DMDC .... Diffusion in Metals and Alloys Data Center [*National Institute of Standards and Technology*] (IID)
DMDC .... Dimethyl Dicarbonate [*Fungistatic agent*]
DMDC .... Dimethyldithiocarbamate [*Organic chemistry*]
DMDC .... Dual Module Display and Control [*Computer science*] (VLIE)
DMDC/MRB... Defense Manpower Data Center Management [*or Market*] Research Branch [*Arlington, VA*]
DMDCS .... Depot Management Data Collection System (MCD)
DMDCS .... Dimethyldichlorosilane (SAUS)
DMDC/SMAD... Defense Manpower Data Center Survey and Market Analysis Division [*Arlington, VA*]
DMDC Unit... Dual Module Display and Control Unit (SAUS)
dmdd .... demanded (SAUS)
DMDD .... Distributed Multiplexing Distributed Demultiplexing [*Computer science*] (VERA)
DMDEL .... Dimethyldiethyllead [*Organic chemistry*]
DMDF .... Digital Map Data Format (SAUS)
DMDF .... Distributed Management Data Facility [*Computer science*] (VERA)
dmdg .... demanding (SAUS)
DMDG.......... Department of the Medical Director-General [*Navy*] [*British*]
DMDG.......... Digital Message Device Group [*Later, SOICS*] [*Army*] (INF)
DMDGN........ Deputy Medical Director General of the Navy (SAUS)
DMDGN........ Deputy Medical Director-General of the Navy (SAUO)
DMDHEU...... Dimethylol Dihydroxyethyleneurea [*Used to provide durable press finish in fabrics*]
DMDL .... Dot Matrix Display Legibility (ACAE)
DMDM .... Data Management Directives Manual (ACAE)
DMDMH........ Dimethylol dimethylhydantoin [*Organic chemistry*]
DMDP .... Data Maintenance Diagnostic Program
DMD/PACT... Digital Message Device/Processing and Communication Terminal (MCD)
DMDPU......... Dimethyldiphenylurea (SAUS)
DMDR .... (Demethoxy)daunorubicin [*Antineoplastic drug*]
DMDS .... Data Management Display System (SAUS)
DMDS .... Dimethyl Disulfide [*Organic chemistry*]
DMDSAB...... Defence Medical and Dental Services Advisory Board (SAUO)
DMDT .... Dimethoxydiphenyl Trichloroethane [*Organic chemistry*] (DMAA)
DMDT .... Methoxychlor [*An insecticide*] (DAVI)
DMDU.......... Drug Misuse Database Unit (SAUS)
DMDX .... Dominion Dairies [*Private rail car owner code*]
DMDXA........ DM-DX-Club Award (SAUS)
DMDZ .... Desmethyldiazepam (DMAA)
DME............. Dakota, Minnesota & Eastern Railroad [*Federal Railroad Administration identification code*]
DME............. Data Measuring Equipment (SAUS)
DME............. Defense Microelectronics (IIA)
DME............. Delta Modulation, Evolved (SAUS)
DME............. Department of Materials Engineering (SAUS)
DME............. Department of Mechanical Engineering (SAUS)
DME............. Department of Mechanics [*JHU*]
DME............. Department of Medical Education (SAUS)
DME............. Department of Metallurgical Engineering (SAUS)
DME............. Department of Mineral Economics (SAUO)
DME............. Department of Mines and Energy [*Nova Scotia*] (GEOI)
DME............. Department of Mining Engineering (SAUO)
DME............. Depot Maintenance Equipment (SAA)
DME............. Designated Mechanic Examiners
DME............. Designated Medical Examiner (SAUS)
DME............. Design Margin Evaluation (NG)
DME............. Design Mission Effect
DME............. Design Mission Evaluation
DME............. Despin Motor Electronics (ACAE)
DME............. Developing Market Economy (SAUS)
DME............. Dextromethorphan [*Pharmacology*] (DAVI)
DME............. Diabetic Macular Edema (SAUS)
DME............. Diagnostic Monitor Executive [*Computer science*]
D-M-E.......... Dialogue, Music, and Effects [*Film*] (WDMC)
DME............. Digital Measuring Equipment (SAUS)
DME............. Digital Motor Electronics
DME............. Digital Multiplex Equipment [*Telecommunications*]
DME............. Dime Bancorp [*NYSE symbol*] (TTSB)
DME............. Dime Savings Bank of New York [*NYSE symbol*] (SPSG)
DME............. Dimethoxyethane [*Also known as GLYME*] [*Organic chemistry*]
DME............. Dimethylethanolamine [*Organic chemistry*]
DME............. Dimethyl Ether [*Organic chemistry*]
DME............. Diphasic Meningoencephalitis [*Medicine*] (DB)
DME............. Diploma in Mechanical Engineering (ADA)
DME............. Direct Machine Environment
DME............. Direct Maintenance Effort (ACAE)
DME............. Direct Marketing Enterprises Incorporated (SAUO)
DME............. Direct Measurement Explorer (SAUS)
DME............. Direct Measurements Explorer [*Satellite*]
DME............. Direct Medical Education
DME............. Direct Memory Execution [*Computer science*]
DME............. Director of Electrical and Mechanical Engineers (SAUO)
DME............. Director of Mechanical Engineering [*War Office*] [*British*] [*World War II*]
DME............. Director of Medical Education
DME............. Directory of Mining Equipment (SAUO)
DME............. Discharge monitoring report (SAUS)
DME............. distance measuring device (SAUS)
DME............. Distance Measuring Equipment [*Navigation*]
DME............. Distance Monitoring Equipment [*Military*]
DME............. Distributed Management Environment
DME............. Division of Mechanical Engineering [*National Research Council of Canada*]
DME............. Doctor of Mechanical Engineering
D Me .... Doctor of Metaphysics
DME............. Doctor of Music Education (PGP)
DME............. Domestic Medical Equipment (GART)
DME............. Draftsman, Electrical (IAA)
DME............. Drilling Mud Emulsifier (BARN)
DME............. Dropping Mercury Electrode [*Electrochemistry*]
DME............. Drug Metabolizing Enzyme
DME............. Dulbecco's Modified Eagle's Medium [*Also, DMEM, DMM*] [*Medium for cell growth*]
DME............. Durable Medical Equipment
DME............. Dynamic Mission Equivalent (IAA)
DME............. Moscow [*Former USSR*] [*Airport symbol*]
DME............. Moscow Domodedovo Airport [*Former USSR*] [*Airport symbol*] (OAG)
DME............. United States Department of Commerce, National Oceanic and Atmospheric Administration, Marine and Earth Sciences Library, Rockville, MD [*Library symbol*] [*Library of Congress*] (LCLS)
D ME .... United States District Court for the District of Maine (DLA)
DMEA........... Damage Modes and Effects Analysis (MCD)
DMEA........... Defense Minerals Exploration Administration [*Department of the Interior*]
DMEA........... Delaware Music Education Association (SAUO)
DMEA........... Dictionary of Mechanical Engineering Abbreviations (SAUS)
DMEA........... Dimethylethylamine (SAUS)
DME-A .... Direct Measurements Explorer A [*Satellite*]
DMEAA .... Dimethylethylaminealane (SAUS)
DMEC........... Defense Metals Equipment Center (DNAB)
DMecE .... Doctor of Mechanical Engineering (NADA)
D Mech........ Doctor of Mechanics
DMechE .... Doctor of Mechanical Engineering (SAUS)
DME/COTAB... Distance-Measuring Equipment/Correlation Tracking and Ranging (SAUS)
DMECOTAR... Distance Measuring Equipment Correlation Tracking and Ranging (SAUS)
DME/COTAR... Distance Measuring Equipment/Correlation Tracking and Ranging
DMeCP .... Dimethylcarboxypsoralen [*Metabolite of TMeP*]
DMECS .... Dimethl(ethyl)chlorosilane [*Organic chemistry*]
DMED .... Defence Medical Equipment Depot (SAUS)
DMED .... Diametrics Medical [*NASDAQ symbol*] (TTSB)
DMED .... Diametrics Medical, Inc. [*NASDAQ symbol*] (SAG)
DMED .... Digital Message Entrance Device (SAUS)
DMED .... Digital Message Entry Device [*Computer science*]
D Med .... Doctor of Medicine
DM Ed .... Doctor of Musical Education
DMED .... UCD Med Center (SAUS)
DMEDA .... Director of Medical Activities (AABC)
DME/DP .... Dropping Mercury Electrode/Differential Pulse (SAUS)
DMedRehab... Diploma in Medical Rehabilitation [*British*] (DBQ)
DMEDs......... Digital Message Entry Devices (SAUS)
DMEDS .... Distributed Multimedia Electronic Document System (VLIE)
D Med Sc .... Doctor of Medical Science (PGP)
DMedVer ..... Doctor Medicinae Veterinariae [*Doctor of Veterinary Medicine*] [*Latin*]
DMEF........... Dannemiller Memorial Educational Foundation (EA)
DMEF........... Direct Marketing Educational Foundation [*New York, NY*] (EA)
DMEF........... Society of Air Force Anestesiologists (SAUO)
DMEG........... Discharge Multimedia Environmental Goals [*Environmental Protection Agency*]
DMEG .... Distance Measuring Equipment Collocated With Glide Slope [*Aviation*] (FAAC)

DMEK.......... Dimethylethylketone (SAUS)
DMEL.......... Distance Measuring Equipment Collocated With Localizer [*Aviation*] (FAAC)
DMEM.......... Dulbecco's Minimum Essential Medium
DMEM.......... Dulbecco's Modified Eagle's Medium [*Also, DME, DMM*] [*Medium for cell growth*]
D-men.......... drug-enforcement officers (SAUS)
DMEng.......... Director of Maintenance Engineering (SAUO)
DM Eng.......... Doctor of Mechanical Engineering
DMEP.......... Data Network Modified Emulator Program [*Telecommunications*] (TEL)
DMEP.......... Dimethoxyethylphthalate (SAUS)
DME/P.......... Precision Distance Measuring Equipment [*FAA*] (TAG)
DMER.......... Distance Measuring Equipment Tactical Air Navigation With DME Only Commissioned [*Aviation*] (FAAC)
DMERC.......... Durable Medical Equipment Regional Carriers (SAUO)
DMERT.......... Duplex Multi-Environment Real Time (SAUS)
DMERT.......... Duplex Multiple-Environment Real-Time (SAUS)
DMES.......... Deployable Mobility Execution System (SAUS)
DMES.......... Digital Message Entry System
DMESFET.......... Depletion-Mode Metal Semiconductor Field Effect Transistor (IAA)
D-MESFET.......... depletion mode metal-semiconductor field effect transistor (SAUS)
DMET.......... Defense Management Educating and Training [*DoD*] (AFM)
DMet.......... Diploma of Meteorology (SAUS)
DMET.......... Directorate of Marine Engineering Training (SAUO)
dmet.......... distance-measuring equipment and tacan (SAUS)
DMET.......... Distance Measuring Equipment TACAN [*Tactical Air Navigation*] (NG)
DMET.......... Distance Measuring Equipment Terminal (CET)
D Met.......... Doctor of Metallurgy
DMet.......... Doctor of Meteorology (ADA)
DMETB.......... Defense Management Education and Training Board [*DoD*]
D Met E.......... Doctor of Metallurgical Engineering
DMETEG.......... Dimethyl Ether of Tetraethylene Glycol [*Organic chemistry*]
D Met Eng.......... Doctor of Metallurgical Engineering
D Meteor.......... Doctor of Meteorology (SAUS)
DMeteor.......... Doctor of Meterology (NADA)
DMETU.......... Dimethylethyl Thiourea (SAUS)
DMEU.......... Dimethylolethyleneurea [*Organic chemistry*]
DMEW.......... Deterministic Mix Evaluation Worldwide (MCD)
DMF.......... Dance Magazine Foundation (EA)
DMF.......... Data Management Facility
DMF.......... Datamanagement Facility (SAUS)
DMF.......... Data Manipulating Function (SAUS)
DMF.......... Data Migration Facility [*Computer science*]
DMF.......... Decayed, Missing, and Filled Teeth (ADWA)
DMF.......... Decayed, Missing, Filled [*Dentistry*]
DMF.......... Decision Making Framework (SAUS)
DMF.......... Deoxymorpholinofructose [*Biochemistry*]
DMF.......... Depot Maintenance Facility (SAA)
DMF.......... Detail Matching Figures Test [*Psychology*] (EDAC)
DMF.......... Development Master File (SAUS)
DMF.......... Differential Matched Filter (SAUS)
DMF.......... Digest Message Format [*Computer science*] (VERA)
DMF.......... Digital Matched Filter
DMF.......... Digital Multiplexing and Formatting [*Computer science*] (MCD)
DMF.......... Dimethylformamide [*Also, DMFA*] [*Organic chemistry*]
DMF.......... Dimethylfuran (SAUS)
DMF.......... Diphasic Milk Fever (DB)
DMF.......... Disabled Motorists Federation [*British*] (DBA)
DMF.......... Disk Management Facility [*Computer science*]
DMF.......... Distributed Management Facility (SAUS)
DMF.......... Distribution Media Floppy (SAUS)
DMF.......... Distribution Media Format (CDE)
DMF.......... Dominican Mission Foundation (EA)
DMF.......... Dose Modifying Factor [*Medicine*]
DMF.......... Dreyfus Municipal Income Fund [*AMEX symbol*] (CTT)
DMF.......... Dreyfus Muni Income [*AMEX symbol*] (TTSB)
DMF.......... Drug Master File
DMF.......... Dry Material Facility (SAUS)
DMF.......... DSIF [*Deep Space Instrumentation Facility*] Maintenance Facility [*NASA*]
DMF.......... Dual Tone Multifrequency [*AT&T*] (CIST)
DMF.......... Dummy Missile Firing
DMF.......... Dyers of Man-Made Fibre Fabrics Federation [*British*] (BI)
DMF.......... formula of decyed, missing and filled teeth (SAUS)
DMFA.......... Dallas Museum of Fine Arts (SAUO)
DMFA.......... Dimethylformamide [*Also, DMF*] [*Organic chemistry*]
DMFA.......... Direct Mail Fundraisers Association (EA)
DMFAS.......... Debt Management and Financial Analysis (SAUS)
DMFC.......... Daniel McVicar Fan Club (EA)
DMFC.......... Debbie Myers Fan Club (EA)
DMFC.......... Dennis Miller Fan Club (EA)
DMFC.......... Direct Methanol Fuel Cell
DMF-DMA.......... Dimethylformamide Dimethyl Acetal (SAUS)
DMFE.......... Division of Magnetic Fusion Energy (SAUO)
DMFIX.......... Delaware: Tax Free Insur. Fund Cl.A [*Mutual fund ticker symbol*] (SG)
DMFL.......... Dimethylformal [*Organic chemistry*]
DMFO.......... Defense Medical Facilities Office [*DoD*] (GFGA)
DMFOS.......... Diploma in Maxillo-Facial and Oral Surgery (SAUS)
DMFP.......... Draft Materiel Fielding Plan [*Army*]
DMF-R.......... Depot Maintenance Facility - Recycle (SAA)
DMF respirator... Dust, Mist, and Fume Respirator (LDOE)
DMFS.......... Decayed, Missing and Filled Surfaces (SAUS)
DMFS.......... Decayed, Missing, or Filled Surfaces [*Dentistry*]
DMFS.......... destination motor freight station (SAUS)
DMFT.......... Decayed, Missing, and Filled Teeth [*Dentistry*]
DMFT.......... Decayed, Missing or Filled Teeth (SAUS)
DMFT.......... Doctor of Marriage and Family Therapy (PGP)
DMG.......... Damage (AFM)
DMG.......... Damaged (SAUS)
DMG.......... Damaging (SAUS)
DMG.......... Data Management Group (MCD)
DMG.......... Davis Medical Group [*Commercial firm*]
DMG.......... Defense Marketing Group [*AMA*]
DMG.......... Deputy Master-General [*Military*] [*British*]
DMG.......... Deputy-Master-General (SAUO)
DMG.......... Deputy Military Governor [*US Military Government, Germany*]
DMG.......... Deterministic Microgrinding [*Optics manufacturing*] (RDA)
DMG.......... Deutsche Morgan Grenfell [*Germany*] [*Banking*]
DMG.......... Digital Map Generator (MCD)
dmg.......... Dimethylgloxime (SAUS)
DMG.......... Dimethyl Glutarate (EDCT)
DMG.......... Dimethylglycine [*Biochemistry*]
DMG.......... Dimethylglyoxide (ABAC)
DMG.......... Dimethylglyoxime [*Organic chemistry*]
DMG.......... Directed Metalation Group [*Organic chemistry*]
DMG.......... Distinguished Military Graduate
DMG.......... Distress Message Generator (SAUS)
DMG.......... Diversified Mortgage Investors (SAUO)
DMG.......... Division of Mines and Geology (SAUO)
DMGBL.......... Dimethyl-gamma-butyrolactone [*Biochemistry*]
Dmge Code... Damage Code (SAUS)
DMGEN.......... Diffusion Mask Generator (SAUS)
DMGO.......... Department of the Master General of the Ordnance [*British*]
DMGO.......... Deputy Master-General of Ordnance (SAUO)
DMGO.......... Divisional Machine Gun Officer [*British military*] (DMA)
DMGS.......... Digital Map Generation System (SAUS)
DMGS.......... Digital Missile Guidance Set (ACAE)
DMGT.......... Data Management (MSA)
DMGT.......... DNA-Mediated Gene Transfer [*Genetics*] (ODA)
DMGU.......... Dual Mode Guidance Unit (ACAE)
DMGZ.......... Demagnetize
DMH.......... Data Message Handler (CGWS)
DMH.......... Decimeter Height-Finder [*RADAR*]
DMH.......... Department of Marine and Harbours [*South Australia, Western Australia*]
DMH.......... Department of Mental Health [*or Hygiene*]
DMH.......... Device Message Handler [*IBM Corp.*] (NITA)
DMH.......... Dextromethorphan [*Antitussive*] [*Pharmacy*]
DMH.......... Dimension House [*Vancouver Stock Exchange symbol*]
DMH.......... Dimethylhexane [*Organic chemistry*]
DMH.......... Dimethyl Hydantoin (EDCT)
DMH.......... Dimethylhydrazine [*Rocket fuel base, convulsant poison*]
DMH.......... Direct Man-Hours
DMH.......... Director of Mental Hygiene (SAUS)
DMH.......... Display Message Helps (AAEL)
DMH.......... Division of Mental Hygiene (SAUS)
DMH.......... Donald Mitchell Healey [*Designer of Healey sports cars*] [*British*]
DMH.......... Drop Manhole [*Technical drawings*]
DMH.......... Dual Mode Hydrazine
DMH.......... Ducati Motor Hldg ADS [*NYSE symbol*] (SG)
dm/ha.......... dry matter per hectare (SAUS)
DMHDD.......... Division of Mental Health & Developmental Disabilities (SAUO)
DMHDD/LISN... Illinois Department of Mental Health and Developmental Disabilities, Library Services Network (SAUS)
DMHF.......... Dimethylhydantoin Formaldehyde [*Organic chemistry*]
DMHR.......... Daughters of the Most Holy Redeemer [*Roman Catholic religious order*]
DMHS.......... Director of Medical and Health Services [*British*]
DMHS.......... Dolley Madison High School (SAUS)
DMHX.......... Davenport Mahmohet Heavy Transportation [*Private rail car owner code*]
DMI.......... Danish Meteorological Institute
DMI.......... Dartco Manufacturing, Incorporated (SAUO)
DMI.......... Data Machines Incorporated (SAUO)
DMI.......... Data Management Inquiry (SAUS)
DMI.......... Data Memory, Incorporated (SAUO)
DMI.......... Daughters of Mary Immaculate (Chaldean) (TOCD)
D/M/I.......... Decision/Making/Information [*Information service or system*] (IID)
DMI.......... Defense Material Item
DMI.......... Defense Mechanisms Inventory [*Psychology*]
DMI.......... Deferred Maintenance Item (SAUS)
DMI.......... Definition of Management Information [*Computer science*] (VERA)
DMI.......... Department of Microbiology and Immunology (SAUS)
DMI.......... Depomed, Inc. [*AMEX symbol*] (SG)
DMI.......... Depot Maintenance Interservice
DMI.......... Design Management Institute (EA)
DMI.......... Desipramine [*Antidepressant*] (DAVI)
DMI.......... Desktop Management Interface [*Computer science*] (PCM)
DMI.......... Desmethylimipramine [*Antidepressant*]
DMI.......... Des Moines [*Iowa*] [*Seismograph station code, US Geological Survey*] [*Closed*] (SEIS)
DMI.......... Destratification Motor Impeller
DMI.......... Detroit, MI [*Location identifier*] [*FAA*] (FAAL)
DMI.......... Diagnostic Mathematics Inventory
DMI.......... Diagnostic Medical Instruments [*Commercial firm*] (DAVI)
DMI.......... Diagnostic Monitor Interface (ACAE)
DMI.......... Diamond Manufacturers and Importers Association of America

DMI............ Diaphragmatic Myocardial Infarct [*Cardiology*] (MAE)
DMI............ Digital Master Imager (DGA)
DMI............ Digital Measuring Instrument (SAUS)
DMI............ Digital Multiplexed Interface (HGAA)
DMI............ Digital Multiplexing Interface (SAUS)
DMI............ Digital Multiplex Interface (SAUS)
DMI............ Dimethylimidazolidinone [*Organic chemistry*]
DMI............ Dimethylisophthalate (SAUS)
DMI............ Dimethyl Isosorbide [*Organic chemistry*]
DMI............ Direct Material Inventory (DNAB)
DMI............ Direct Member Input [*British*] (NUMA)
DMI............ Direct Memory Interface [*Computer science*] (NITA)
DMI............ Direct Migration Inhibition (DB)
DMI............ Director of Military Intelligence [*US, British*]
DMI............ Director of Missile Intelligence (SAUO)
DMI............ Disable Manual Input (SAUS)
DMI............ Distance Measuring Instrument
DMI............ DiTomasso Methodology Inventory (EDAC)
DMI............ Division of Manpower Intelligence (SAUO)
DMI............ DMI International Airlines [*Ukraine*] [*FAA designator*] (FAAC)
DMI............ Draftsman (Illustrator) [*U.S. Navy enlisted rating*] (AUER)
DMI............ Dreyfus Management International Ltd. (SAUO)
DMI............ Dry Matter Intake (SAUO)
DMI............ Dumagami Mines Ltd. [*Toronto Stock Exchange symbol*]
DMI............ Dun's Market Identifiers [*Dun's Marketing Services*] [*Information service or system*] (CRD)
DMI............ Dwell Mode Inhibit (ACAE)
DMI............ Dynamic Memory Interface [*Computer science*] (NITA)
DMIA.......... Diamond Manufacturers and Importers Association of America (NTPA)
DMIA.......... Document Management Industries Association (NTPA)
DMIA.......... Dual Multiplexer Interface Adapter (NASA)
DMIAA........ Diamond Manufacturers and Importers Association of America (EA)
DMIAAI....... Diamond Manufacturers and Importers Association of America, Incorporated (SAUO)
DMI-BOS...... Digital Multiplexed Interface Bit-Oriented Signaling [*Communications term*] (DCT)
DMIC.......... Defense Metals Information Center [*Later, MCIC*] [*Battelle Memorial Institute*] (MCD)
DMIC.......... Digital Microwave [*NASDAQ symbol*] (TTSB)
DMIC.......... Digital Microwave Corp. [*NASDAQ symbol*] (NQ)
DMIC.......... Direct Marketing Insurance Council [*New York, NY*] (EA)
D Mic.......... Doctor of Microbiology
DMICS........ Distributed Management Information and Control System (SAUS)
DMID.......... Department of Manufacturing and Industry Development [*Victoria*] [*Australia*]
DMID.......... Division of Microbiology and Infectious Diseases (SAUS)
DMIDF........ Depot Master Item Data File [*Army*]
D Mi E......... Doctor of Mining Engineering
D Mi Eng..... Doctor of Mining Engineering
D Mi Eng..... Doctor of Minning Engineering (SAUS)
DMIF........... Depot Maintenance Industrial Fund (MCD)
DMIF........... DMI Furniture [*NASDAQ symbol*] (TTSB)
DMIF........... DMI Furniture, Inc. [*NASDAQ symbol*] (NQ)
DMIFCUS..... Depot Maintenance Industrial Funding Customer (MCD)
DMI Frn....... DMI Furniture, Inc. [*Associated Press*] (SAG)
DMII........... Descriptive Method Item Identification [*DoD*]
DMIL........... Demilitarization
DMIL........... Military Directorate (SAUO)
DMIL/EOD.... Demilitarization / Explosive Ordnance Demolition
D Mil S........ Doctor of Military Science
DMil Sc....... Doctorate of Military Science (DD)
DMIM.......... Double Mannitol Isolation Method [*Microscopy*]
DMIM.......... Dual Mode Imbedded Munitions (MCD)
DMI-MOS..... Digital Multiplexed Interface Message-Oriented Signaling [*Communications term*] (DCT)
D-Min.......... Density Minimum (SAUS)
D/MIN......... Disintegrations per Minute
DMin........... Doctor of Ministry
dmin........... Drift Distance, Minimum [*Environmental science*] (COE)
DMIN.......... United States Bureau of Marine Inspection and Navigation, Washington, DC [*Library symbol*] [*Library of Congress*] [*Obsolete*] (LCLS)
D Minn........ United States District Court for the District of Minnesota (DLA)
DMINS........ Distributed Minicomputer Systems (AAGC)
DMINS........ DLAs Distributed Minicomputer System (SAUS)
DMINS........ Dual Miniature Inertial Navigation Systems (MCD)
DMIP.......... Database Machine for Image Processing (SAUS)
DMIP.......... DCS Mediterranean Improvement Program (SAUS)
DMIP.......... Defense Materiel Interservicing Program [*DoD*]
DMIP.......... Defense Mediterranean Improvement Program (SAUS)
DMIP.......... Democratic Malaysia Indian Party [*Political party*] (FEA)
DMIP.......... Dimethyl Isophthalate [*Organic chemistry*]
DMIR.......... Designated Manufacturing Inspection Representative (MCD)
DMIR.......... Duluth, Missabe & Iron Range Railway Co. [*AAR code*]
DMIRR........ Demand Mode Integral Rocket Ramjet (MCD)
DMIS.......... Data Management Information System [*DoD*]
DMIS.......... DATICO [*Digital Automatic Tape Intelligence Checkout*] Missile Interface Simulator
DMIS.......... Defense Medical Information System (DOMA)
DMIS.......... Director, Management Information Systems [*Later, ADD*] [*Army*] (AABC)
DMIS.......... Directory Management Information System (SAUS)
DMIS.......... Distributed Multimedia Information System (RALS)
DMIS.......... Distribution/Transportation Management Information System [*Computer science*] (PDAA)
DMIS.......... Donnelley Marketing Information Services [*Database producer*] (IID)
DMIS.......... Doppler Microwave Landing System (SAUS)
DMIS.......... Duns Marketing Identification System (COE)
DMISA........ Depot Maintenance Interservice Support Agreement [*Military*]
DMISS........ Division of Management, Information, and Support Services [*Center for Devices and Radiological Health*]
D Miss........ Doctor of Missiology (PGP)
DMIS technique... double-diffused MIS technique (SAUS)
DMIU.......... Destratification Motor Impeller Unit
DMIX.......... Minnesota Corn Processors [*Private rail car owner code*]
DMJ............ Daughters of Mary and Joseph [*Roman Catholic religious order*]
DMJ............ Deus Meumque Jus [*God and My Right*] [*Freemasonry*] [*Latin*]
DMJ............ Diploma in Medical Jurisprudence [*British*]
DMJ (Clin)... Diploma in Medical Jurisprudence (Clinical) [*British*]
DMJM.......... Daniel, Mann, Johnson, & Mendenhall [*A major contributor to architecture in Jakarta, Sidney, Manila, and Seoul*]
DMJO.......... Defense Management Journal Office [*DoD*]
DMJP.......... Door Mounted Junction Panel
DMJP.......... Dragon Missile Jump Pack [*Military*] (MCD)
DMJ (Path)... Diploma in Medical Jurisprudence (Pathological) [*British*]
DMJS.......... December, March, June, September [*Denotes quarterly payments of interest or dividends in these months*] [*Business term*]
DMJS.......... Quarterly Payments of Interest or Dividends in December, March, June and September (EBF)
DMJTC........ Differential Multi-Junction Thermal Converter (PDAA)
DMK............ Demirkoy [*Turkey*] [*Seismograph station code, US Geological Survey*] (SEIS)
DMK............ Dial Marking Kit
DMK............ Digital Equipment Corp., Merrimack, Merrimack, NH [*OCLC symbol*] (OCLC)
DMK............ Dimark, Inc. [*Formerly, Mars Graphic Services, Inc.*] [*AMEX symbol*] (SPSG)
DMK............ Dimethylketone (SAUS)
DMK............ Direct Action Marketing, Inc. [*AMEX symbol*] (COMM)
DMK............ Dominick Fund, Inc. (SAUO)
DMK............ Dravida Munnetra Kazhagam [*India*] [*Political party*] (PPW)
DMKA.......... Diabetes Mellitus Ketoacidosis [*Endocrinology*] (DAVI)
dmkit........... Drum Kit
DMKP.......... Dali-Mazdoor-Kisan Party (SAUO)
DML............ Dan River, Inc. (SAUO)
DML............ Dan River Mills (SAUO)
DML............ Database Management Language [*Computer science*] (CIST)
DML............ Database Manipulation Language (SAUS)
DML............ Data Macro Language (SAUS)
DML............ Data Management Language [*Digital Equipment Corp.*]
DML............ Data Management Logic (SAUS)
DML............ Data Manipulation Language [*Digital Equipment Corp.*] [*Computer science*]
DML............ Data Manipulation Logic [*Computer science*] (VERA)
DML............ Data Mining Laboratory (SAUO)
DML............ Decision & Modelling Language (SAUS)
dml............. demolish (SAUS)
DML............ Demolition
DML............ Depot Maintenance Level
DML............ Depot Maintenance Literature (MCD)
DML............ Describe Macro Language [*Computer science*]
DML............ Developmental Instrumentation MDM-Left (SAUS)
DML............ Developmental Instrumentation Medium-Left
DML............ Developmental [*Instrumentation*] MDM [*Manipulator Deployment Mech anism*] Left
DML............ Development mobile vapor sampling laboratory (SAUS)
DML............ Device Media Language [*Computer science*] (ELAL)
DML............ Devonport Management Ltd. (SAUO)
DML............ Dickenson Mines Ltd. (EFIS)
DML............ Diffuse Mixed Lymphoma [*Oncology*]
DML............ Digital Mapping Laboratory (SAUO)
DML............ Digital Motor Logic (SAUS)
DML............ Digitized Message Link
DML............ Dimensional Metrology Laboratory (SAUS)
DML............ Dimyristoyl-Lecithin [*Biochemistry*]
DML............ Direct Memory Line (IAA)
DML............ Direct Memory Load (ADWA)
DML............ Display Message Log (AAEL)
DML............ Distal Motor Latency (DMAA)
DML............ Distributed Mode Loudspeaker (SAUS)
DML............ Dock Mounted Loader (RDA)
DML............ Doctor Martin Luther College, New Ulm, MN [*OCLC symbol*] (OCLC)
DML............ Doctor of Modern Languages
DML............ Double Mars Loiter
DML............ Draftsman (Lithographic) [*U.S. Navy enlisted rating*] (AUER)
DML............ Dry Matter Loss
DML............ Dual Mode LASER
DML............ N-Dimethyllysine (SAUS)
D Mld.......... Depth Moulded (SAUS)
DML DY....... Demolition Duty (DNAB)
DMLE.......... Democratic Movement for the Liberation of Eritrea (SAUO)
DMLF.......... Descending Medial Longitudinal Fasciculus
DMLIA........ Double-Modified Lysine Iron Agar [*Microorganism medium*]
DMLP.......... Democratic Movement for the Liberation of Eritrea [*Political party*] (PSAP)
DMLQU....... Digital Map Library at Queens University (SAUO)
DMLR.......... Division of Mihed Land Reclamation (SAUO)
DMLRD....... Direct Mail Lists, Rates, and Data

DMLS Doppler Microwave Landing System
Dml Sqd Demolition Squad (SAUO)
DMLT Diploma in Medical Laboratory Technology (ADA)
DMLTG Data Manipulation Language Task Group (SAUO)
DMLX Dresser Minerals [*Federal Railroad Administration identification code*]
DMM [*The*] Dansville & Mount Morris Railroad Co. [*AAR code*]
DMM Dark Mantling Material [*Lunar surface*]
DMM Data Management Module [*Aviation*]
DMM Data Manipulation Mode
DMM Dayton and Montgomery County Public Library, Dayton, OH [*OCLC symbol*] (OCLC)
DMM Dedicated Man/Months [*Jet Propulsion Laboratory, NASA*]
DMM Defence Market Measures (SAUS)
DMM Defense Market Measures [*Database on Department of Defense contracts*] (NITA)
DMM Delta Ministry of Mississippi [*Defunct*] (EA)
dMM Deoxymannojirimycin [*Biochemistry*]
DMM Department of Mines and Minerals (SAUO)
DMM Department of Mining and Metallurgy (SAUS)
DMM Depleted MORB [*Mid-Ocean Ridge Basalt*] Mantle [*Geology*]
DMM Desmethylmetoxuron [*Organic chemistry*]
DMM Dia Met Minerals Ltd. [*Vancouver Stock Exchange symbol*]
DMM Dickson Mounds Museum (SAUO)
DMM Diffuse Mismatch Model (AAEL)
DMM Digital Mass Memory (SAUS)
dmm Digital Multimeter (IDOE)
DMM Digital Multimeter
DMM Digital Multiservice Module [*Telecommunications*]
DMM Dimethoxymethane [*Organic chemistry*]
DMM Dimethylmercury [*Toxicology*]
DMM Dimethylmyleran [*Organic chemistry*] (DAVI)
DMM Diploma in Manufacturing Management [*British*]
DMM Direct Mail Manager [*Software package*]
DMM Direct Memory Management [*Computer science*] (NITA)
DMM direct metal (SAUS)
DMM Direct Metal Mastering [*System for manufacturing phonograph records*]
DMM Directorate of Materiel Management (MCD)
DMM Director of Mechanical Maintenance [*British military*] (DMA)
DMM Doctor of Music Ministry (PGP)
DMM Domestic Mail Manual [*US Postal Service*] [*A publication*]
DMM Draftsman (Mechanical) [*U.S. Navy enlisted rating*] (AUER)
DMM Drawing Measuring Machine (SAUS)
DMM Dulbecco's Modified Eagle's Medium [*Also, DME, DMEM*] [*Medium for cell growth*]
DMM DynaMetric Model (SAUS)
DMM Dynamical Material Modeling (SAUS)
DMM Dynamic Magnetic Memory (SAUS)
DMMA Dimethylmuconic Acid [*Organic chemistry*]
dmma Direct Mail Marketing Association (SAUS)
DMMA Direct Mail/Marketing Association (EA)
DMM & SA Depot Materiel Maintenance and Support Activities [*Army*]
DMMB Defense Medical Material Board (AFM)
DMMBF Delta Modulation Multi Beamformer (ACAE)
DMMC Decentralized Materiel Management Center (SAUO)
DMMC Department of Metallurgy and Metallurgical Chemistry (SAUO)
DMMC Digital Multimeter Control
DMMC Division Materiel Management Center [*Military*] (AABC)
DMMC DM Management [*NASDAQ symbol*] (TTSB)
DMMC DM Management Co. [*NASDAQ symbol*] (SAG)
DMMCS Dimethylmonochlorosilane [*Organic chemistry*]
DMMEF Direct Mail/Marketing Educational Foundation (EA)
DMMF Dry and Mineral Matter Free [*Coal*]
dmmf dry mineral matter free (SAUS)
DMMF Basis Dry Mineral Matter Free Basis (SAUS)
DMMG Direccion Nacional de Mineria y Geologia [*Uruguay*] (GEOI)
DMMG Displacement Method Matrix Generator
DM Mgt DM Management Co. [*Associated Press*] (SAG)
DMMH/FH Direct Maintenance Man-Hours per Flight Hour [*Navy*] (NG)
DMMH/MA Direct Maintenance Man-Hours per Maintenance Action
DMMH/ME Direct Maintenance Man-Hours per Maintenance Event
DM-MIMD distributed memory, multiple instruction, multiple data (SAUS)
DMMIS Depot Maintenance Management Information System [*Air Force*] (GFGA)
DMMM Direct Maintenance Man-Minutes (MCD)
DMMnom Development Manmouths Nominal
DMMO Direct Marketing Minorities Opportunities [*Defunct*] (EA)
DMMO Division Material Management Officer (SAUS)
DMMO Division of Marine Meteorology and Oceanography (SAUO)
DMMP Deferred Monthly Mortgage Payment (FOTI)
DMMP Dimethyl Methylphosphonate [*Organic chemistry*]
DMMP Direct Marketing Market Place [*A publication*]
DMMP Distributed-Memory Multiprocessing System (SAUS)
DMMR Deputy Ministry for Mineral Resources [*Saudi Arabia*] (GEOI)
DMMR Distributed-Memory Microprocessor systems (SAUS)
DMMS Dee-Mack Middle School (SAUO)
DMMS Depot Maintenance Management Subsystem (DNAB)
DMMS Depot Maintenance Management system (SAUS)
DMMs Digital Multimeters (SAUS)
DMMS Dynamic Memory Management System (SAUS)
DMMSS Depot Maintenance Management Support System (SAUS)
DMM technology Direct Metal Mastering (SAUS)
DMMU Discrete Main Memory Unit [*Computer bus*]
DMMV Deutscher Multimedia Verband (SAUS)
DMN Damon Corp. (SAUO)
DMN Data Model Normalizer [*Computer science*]
DMN Data Multiplexing Network [*FAA*] (TAG)
DMN Defective Material Notice (KSC)
DMN Deming, NM [*Location identifier*] [*FAA*] (FAAL)
DMN Differential-Mode Noise [*Electronics*] (IAA)
DMN Dimension (AABC)
dmn Dimensional (SAUS)
DMN Dimethylnaphthalene [*Organic chemistry*]
DMN Dimethylnitrosamine [*Also, DMNA, NDMA*] [*Organic chemistry*]
DMN Dimethynaphthidine [*An indicator*] [*Chemistry*]
DMN Dimon, Inc. [*NYSE symbol*] (SAG)
DMn Dissolved Manganese [*Chemistry*]
DMN Dominion Explorers, Inc. [*Toronto Stock Exchange symbol*]
DMN Dorsal Motor Nucleus [*of the vagus*]
DMN Dorsomedial Nucleus [*Brain anatomy*]
Dmn Drammen (SAUS)
DMN Dysplastic Melanocytic Nevi [*Medicine*]
DMNA Dimethylnitrosamine [*Also, DMN, NDMA*] [*Organic chemistry*]
DMNA Distributed Microcomputer Network for Avionics (MCD)
DMND Diamon
DMNFA Daily Mail National Film Award [*British*]
DMNH Delaware Museum of Natural History (SAUS)
DMNH Denver Museum of Natural History
DMNI Device Multiplexing Nonsynchronized Inputs [*Computer science*]
DMNL Direct Multi Network Link (SAUS)
DMNL Dorsomedial Hypothalamic Nucleus Lesion [*Medicine*] (EDAA)
DMNO Device Multiplexing Nonsynchronized Outputs [*Computer science*] (CET)
DMNPAA Dimethyl(nitrophenylazo)anisole [*Organic chemistry*]
DMNRLZR Demineralizer
DMNSC Digital Main Network Switching Center (SAUS)
DMNSC Digital Main Network Switching Centre (SAUS)
DMNSC Digital main network switching system (SAUS)
Dmnstr Demonstrate (SAUS)
DMNSTR Demonstrator (IAA)
DMNT Dominant (FAAC)
DMO Contract Data Management Officer (SAUO)
DMO Data Management Office [*or Officer*] [*Air Force*] (AFM)
DMO Data Management Operating Plan (ACAE)
DMO Data Management Organization (ACAE)
DMO Decimal Multiply Operation (SAUS)
DMO Decision Making Organizer [*Test*]
DMO Defense Mobilization Order
DMO Demetallized Oil (SAUS)
DMO Demineralized Oil [*Petroleum Refining*]
DMO Dental health Maintenance Organization (SAUS)
DMO Dental Maintenance Organization
DMO Dependent Meteorological Office
DMO Deputy Medical Officer (SAUS)
DMO Destination Marketing Organization (TRID)
DMO Dimethadone [*Pharmacology*] (DAVI)
DMO Dimethyloxazolidin (SAUS)
DMO Dimethyloxazolidinedione [*Pharmacology*]
DMO Diode Microwave Oscillator
DMO Directed Military Overstrength (GFGA)
DMO Directorate Meteorological Office (SAUO)
DMO Directorate of Military Operations (SAUO)
DMO Director Meteorological Officer, Ministry of Defence, London [*British*] (NATG)
DMO Director of Manpower and Organization [*Air Force*]
DMO Director of Maritime Operations [*RAF*] [*British*]
DMO Director [*or Directorate*] of Military Operations
DMO Directory of Mortuary Operations [*Army*] (AABC)
DMO Distributed Management Objects (SAUS)
DMO District Management Office
DMO District Marine Officer [*Navy*]
DMO District Marketing Office (TVEL)
DMO District Material Officer [*Navy*]
DMO District Medical Officer [*Navy*]
DMO Divisional Medical Officer [*British*]
DMO Documentation Management Officer [*Air Force*] (AFM)
DMO Domodedovo Civil Air Production Association [*Former USSR*] [*FAA designator*] (FAAC)
DMO Drug-Misusing Offender (WDAA)
DMO Dymo Industries, Inc. (SAUO)
DMO Practice/Demo Warning [*Telecommunications*] (OTD)
DMO Sedalia [*Missouri*] [*Airport symbol*] [*Obsolete*] (OAG)
DMOA Diabetes Mellitus - Optic Atrophy [*Syndrome*] [*Medicine*] (EDAA)
DMO & I Director of Military Operations and Intelligence (SAUS)
DMO & P Director of Military Operations and Planning (SAUS)
DMOB Defensive Missile Order of Battle (MCD)
DMOC Diabetes Mellitus Out of Control [*Medicine*] (MEDA)
DMOC Distinguished Members of the Corps [*Army*]
DMOC Division Medical Operations Center (SAUS)
DMOD Delta Modulation (NITA)
DMOD Depositors Mutual Oil Development Co. (SAUO)
DMOD Dimethyloctadiene [*Organic chemistry*]
DMOD Displacement Measuring Optical Device (SAUS)
DMOI Director of Military Operations and Intelligence
DMOIN Des Moines, IA [*American Association of Railroads railroad junction routing code*]
DMON Discrete Monitoring (MCD)
DMon Montessori School, Washington, DC [*Library symbol*] [*Library of Congress*] (LCLS)
D Mont United States District Court for the District of Montana (DLA)

DMOOC........ Diabetes Mellitus Out of Control [*Medicine*] (DMAA)
DMOP.......... Digital manual operating panel (SAUS)
DMOR.......... Distinguished Member of the Regiment
DMORT........ Disaster Mortuary Response Team (DEMM)
DMORT........ Disaster Mortuary Team (SAUO)
DMOS.......... Data Management Operating System
DMOS.......... Degradation Mean Opinion Score (SAUS)
DMOs.......... Democratic Mass Organization (Tanzania) [*Political party*] (PSAP)
DMOS.......... Depletion Metal-Oxide Semiconductor (BUR)
DMOS.......... Diffusion Metal-Oxide Semiconductor [*Telecommunications*] (TEL)
DMOS.......... Diffusive Mixing of Organic Solutions [*Materials processing*]
DMOS.......... difiusive mixing of organic solutions (SAUS)
DMOS.......... Discrete Metal-Oxide Semiconductor (HGAA)
DMOS.......... discrete metal oxide semiconductor (SAUS)
DMOS.......... Discrete MOS (SAUS)
DMOS.......... Double-Diffused Metal-Oxide Semiconductor [*Microelectronics*] (MCD)
D/MOS......... Double Diffused MOS (SAUS)
DMOS.......... Double-implanted Metal Oxide Semiconductor (SAUS)
DMOS.......... Duty Military Occupational Specialty
DMOS.......... Dynamic Model Operations Section
DMOSFET.... Depletion Metal Oxide Silicon Field Effect Transistor (VLIE)
DMOS(N)..... Director of Meteorological and Oceanographical Services (Naval) [*British*]
DMOST........ Double-Diffused Medal Oxide Semiconductor Technology [*Microelectronics*] (PDAA)
DMOST........ Double-diffused Metal Oxide Semiconductor Transistor (SAUS)
DMOT.......... Dimethyloctatriene [*Organic chemistry*]
DMov.......... Director of Movements (SAUO)
DMOX.......... Dynamic Modelling Open Extensions (VLIE)
DMP............ Daily Maintenance Pack (SAUS)
DMP............ Data Management Plan [*Jet Propulsion Laboratory, NASA*]
DMP............ Data Management Program
DMP............ Data Manipulation Processor (SAUS)
DMP............ Data Mapping Program (VLIE)
DMP............ Defecation Motor Program [*Physiology*]
DMP............ Defense Manpower Policy
DMP............ Defense Materials Procurement Agency [*Abolished 1953, functions transferred to General Services Administration*] (DLA)
DMP............ Delayed Merge Package (MCD)
DMP............ Demokratik Merkez Partisi [*Democratic Centre Party*] [*Turkey*] [*Political party*] (EY)
DMP............ Demokratik Mucadele Partisi [*Democratic Struggle Party*] [*Turkish Cyprus*] [*Political party*] (EY)
DMP............ De Mortibus Persecutorum (BJA)
DMP............ Demultiplexer (SAUS)
DMP............ Dental Market Place [*Publication*] [*Medicine*] (EDAA)
DMP............ Deployable Maintenance Platform (MCD)
DMP............ Dermatopathology [*Medical specialty*] (DHSM)
DMP............ DEU [*Display Electronics Unit*] Message Processor (NASA)
DMP............ Deutsche Mittelstandspartei [*German Middle Class Party*] (PPW)
DMP............ Developing Mathematical Processes (SAUS)
DMP............ Diagnostic and Maintenance Processor (SAUS)
DMP............ Diagnostic and Monitoring Protocol (VLIE)
dmp............ difference of meridional parts (SAUS)
DMP............ Diffuse Mesangial Proliferation [*Medicine*] (EDAA)
DMP............ Digital Mapping Programme (SAUO)
DMP............ Digital Map Processor
DMP............ Digital Mass Programmer (SAUS)
DMP............ Digital Microprocessor (SAUS)
DMP............ Digital Modification Program (ACAE)
DMP............ Dimercaprol [*Medicine*] (MELL)
DMP............ Dimercaptopropanol [*Also, BAL: British Anti-Lewisite*] [*Detoxicant*] [*Organic chemistry*]
DMP............ Dimethoxypropane [*Organic chemistry*]
DMP............ Dimethylimide Perylene (SAUS)
DMP............ Dimethylphenol [*Organic chemistry*]
DMP............ Dimethylphosphate (SAUS)
DMP............ Dimethyl Phthalate [*Organic chemistry*]
DMP............ Dimethylpiperazine [*Also, DMPP*] [*Organic chemistry*]
DMP............ Dimethylpropanediol [*Organic chemistry*]
DMP............ Dimethyl Pyrocarbonate [*Organic chemistry*]
DMP............ Dimethylpyrrole [*Organic chemistry*]
DMP............ Diploma in Medical Psychology (ADA)
DMP............ Direct Maximum Principle (IAA)
DMP............ Direct Memory Processor
DMP............ Director of Manpower Planning [*British*]
DMP............ Director of Materiel Procurement [*Canada*] (ACAE)
DMP............ Director of Military Personnel [*Air Force*]
DMP............ Disarmed Military Personnel
DMP............ discrete maximum principle (SAUS)
DMP............ Disk Management Program (VLIE)
DMP............ Display Maintenance Program
DMP............ Display Makeup (IAA)
DMP............ Distributed Message Passing [*Computer science*] (GART)
DMP............ Division of Materials Processing (SAUO)
DMP............ Division of Mineral Products (SAUO)
DMP............ Documentation Material Processed (SAUS)
DMP............ Documented Material Processed
DMP............ Doe-Moffitt Project (SAUS)
DMP............ Dorsal Median Pallium [*Neuroanatomy*]
dMP............ Dorsal Midline Precursor [*Neuroanatomy*]
DMP............ Dot Matrix Printer (VLIE)
DMP............ Downhole Measurements Panel (SAUO)
DMP............ Dry Matter Production (SAUO)
DMP............ Dual Mode Phaser (SAUS)
DMP............ Dump [*Computer science*]
DMP............ Pathfinder Regional Library Service System, Montrose, CO [*OCLC symbol*] (OCLC)
DMPA.......... Defense Material Procurement Administration (SAUO)
DMPA.......... Defense Materials Procurement Agency [*Abolished 1953, functions transferred to General Services Administration*]
DMPA.......... Defense Medical Program Activity [*Military*]
dmpa.......... depomedroxyprogesterone (SAUS)
DMPA.......... Depomedroxyprogesterone Acetate [*Contraceptive*]
DMPA.......... (Dichlorophenyl) Methyl Isopropylphosphoramidothioate [*Herbicide*]
DMPA.......... Dichlorophenylmethyl Isopropylphosphoramidothioate (SAUS)
DMPA.......... Digitally-Modulated Power Amplifier (SAUS)
DMPA.......... Dimethoxyphenylacetophenone [*Organic chemistry*]
DMPA.......... Dimethylolpropionic Acid [*Organic chemistry*]
DMPA.......... Dimethylphenoxyaceton (SAUS)
DMPA.......... Dimyristoyl Phosphatidic Acid [*Biochemistry*]
DMPA.......... Direct Mail Producers Association [*British*] (DBA)
DMPA.......... Distal Main Pulmonary Artery [*Anatomy*]
DMPB.......... Diploma in Medical Pathology and Bacteriology (SAUS)
DMPC.......... Data Mining Products Consultancy (SAUO)
DMPC.......... Deep Moored Profiling CTDs (SAUS)
DMPC.......... Dimethylaminopropyl Chloride [*Organic chemistry*]
DMPC.......... Dimyristoyl Phosphatidylcholine [*Biochemistry*]
DMPC.......... Distributed Memory Parallel Computer (VLIE)
DMPD.......... Defense Medical Purchase Description [*Defense Supply Agency*]
DMPD.......... Dimethylphenylenediamine [*Organic chemistry*]
DMPD.......... Director of Dockyard Manpower and Productivity [*Navy*] [*British*]
DMPDT........ Dimethylphosphorodithioate [*Organic chemistry*]
DMPDU........ Derived Medium Access Control Protocol Data Unit (VLIE)
DMPE.......... Depot Maintenance Plant Equipment (MCD)
DMPE.......... Dimethoxphenylethylamine (SAUS)
DMPE.......... (Dimethoxyphenyl)ethylamine [*Also, DIMPEA, DMPEA*] [*Psychomimetic compound*]
DMPE.......... Dimyristoyl Phosphatidylethanolamine
DMPEA........ (Dimethoxyphenyl)ethylamine [*Also, DIMPEA, DMPE*] [*Psychomimetic compound*]
DMPG.......... Dimyristoylphosphatidylglycerol [*Biochemistry*]
DMPG.......... Dumping (MSA)
DMPI........... Designated Mean Point of Impact [*Environmental science*] (COE)
DMPI........... Desired Mean Point of Impact [*Military*]
DMPI........... Dimyristoyl Phosphatidylinositol
DMPI........... dystrophie musculaire progressive infantile (SAUS)
DMPIA......... Dimethoxyphenylisopropylamine [*Organic chemistry*]
DMPK.......... Dystrophia Myotonica Protein Kinase [*An enzyme*]
DMPL.......... Des Moines Public Library (SAUS)
DMPL.......... Digital Microprocessor Plotter Language (CDE)
DMPO.......... Data Management Policy Office [*Army*]
DMPO.......... Dimethylpyrrolineoxide [*Organic chemistry*]
DMPP.......... Dimethyl(phenyl)piperazinium [*Organic chemistry*]
DMPP.......... Dimethylpiperazine [*Also, DMP*] [*Organic chemistry*]
DMPP.......... Display and Multi-Purpose Processor [*Computer science*]
DMPP.......... Distributed Memory Parallel Processor (SAUS)
DMPP.......... Duck Mountain Provincial Park (SAUS)
DMPPD........ Dimethyl-para-phenylenediamine [*Organic chemistry*]
DMPR.......... Damper (KSC)
DMPR.......... Depot Maintenance Production Report
DMPRL........ Defense Master Priority Requirements List
DMPRT........ Dual-Mode Personal Rapid Transport (SAUS)
DMPS.......... Data Management Programming System (VLIE)
DMPS.......... Deepwater Motion Picture System
DMPS.......... Dimercaptopropanesulfonate [*Salt*] [*Organic chemistry*]
DMPS.......... Dimethylpolysiloxane [*Organic chemistry*]
DMPs.......... Dysmyelopoietic Syndrome [*Medicine*] (STED)
DMPT.......... Dimethyl P-toluidine [*Plastics*]
DMPU.......... Dimethylol Propylene Urea (SAUS)
DMPU.......... Dimethylolpropyleneurea [*Organic chemistry*]
DMPU.......... Dimethylpropyleneurea (SAUS)
DMPW.......... Dutch Ministry of Public Works
DMQ............ Dimethylquinoline [*Organic chemistry*]
DMQ............ Direct Memory Queue [*Computer science*]
DMQ............ Director of Movements and Quartering [*British*]
DMQ............ Dominco Industry Corp. [*Vancouver Stock Exchange symbol*]
DMQL.......... Data Mining Query Language (IDAI)
DMQR.......... Douglas Material Qualification Report [*DAC*]
DMQRP........ Division of Mammography Quality and Radiation Programs [*Center for Devices and Radiological Health*]
DMQS.......... Display Mode Query and Set [*Computer science*] (VLIE)
DMR............ DAC Maintainability Representative (MCD)
DMR............ Daily Market Report [*Coffee, Sugar, and Cocoa Exchange*] [*A publication*]
DMR............ Daily Mechanical Report
DMR............ Data Maintenance Request (PAEB) (AG)
DMR............ Data Management Routine
DMR............ Date Material Required
DMR............ Deep Muscle Relaxation [*Medicine*] (DHP)
DMR............ Defective Materiel Report [*Air Force*]
DMR............ Defense Management Report [*DoD*]
DMR............ Defense Management Review [*Army*] (RDA)
DMR............ Demultiplexing/Mixing/Remultiplexing [*Device*] [*Telecommunications*] (TEL)
DMR............ Departmental Materiel Requisition
DMR............ Department of Main Roads (SAUS)
DMR............ Department of Medical Radiology (SAUO)
DMR............ Department of Mineral Resources [*New South Wales*] [*Australia*]

DMR .... Detailed Mission Requirements (ADWA)
DMR .... Detail Mission Requirements (SAUS)
DMR .... Detroit Manufacturers Railroad [*Federal Railroad Administration identification code*]
DMR .... Deutsche Motorrad Register [*German Motorcycle Register*] [*Defunct*] (EA)
DMR .... Developmental Instrumentation Medium-Right (NASA)
DMR .... Diagnostic Reading Scales [*Diagnostic assessment test*] (PAZ)
DMR .... Diebold-Management-Report (SAUS)
DMR .... Differentially Methylated Region [*Genetics*]
DMR .... Differential Material Removal (SAUS)
DMR .... Differential Microwave Radiometer [*Cosmic Background Explorer*] [*NASA*]
DMR .... Digital Equipment Corp., Marlboro, Marlboro, MA [*OCLC symbol*] (OCLC)
DMR .... Digital Master Recording (SAUS)
DMR .... Digital Meter Reader (IAA)
DMR .... Digital Microwave Radio (SAUS)
DMR .... Digital Mobilized Radio (BARN)
DMR .... Dimmer (MSA)
DMR .... Diploma in Medical Radiology [*British*]
DMR .... Diploma in Medical Rehabilitation
DMR .... Direct Magnification Radiography
DMR .... Direct Metal Reaction [*Soap making*]
DMR .... Directorate of Medical Research [*Army*]
DMR .... Director of Materiel Readiness [*Army*]
DMR .... Director of Merchant Ship Repairs (SAUO)
DMR .... Discharge Monitoring Report [*Environmental Protection Agency*] (EG)
DMR .... Display Move Requests (AAEL)
DMR .... Distributed Message Router (NITA)
DMR .... Distributor-Manufacturer-Representative
DMR .... Division Management Review (ACAE)
DMR .... Division of Materials Research [*National Science Foundation*]
DMR .... Division of Mineral Resources (SAUO)
DMR .... Division of Monetary Research (SAUO)
DMR .... Document Modification Request (COE)
DMR .... Downy Mildew Resistant (GNE)
DMR .... Drummer [*Military*] [*British*]
DMR .... Dual-Channel Microwave Radiometer (SAUS)
DMR .... Dual Mode Radar (ACAE)
DMR .... Dual Mode Recognizer (MCD)
DMR .... Dynamic Modular Radio (SEWL)
DMR .... Dynamic Modular Replacement (SAUS)
DMR .... Dynamic Module Replacement
DMR .... NPDES Discharge Monitoring Report (SAUS)
DMRA .... DSA [*Defense Supply Agency*] Central Regional Audit Office
DMRC .... Deering Milliken Research Corporation (SAUO)
DMRC .... Defence Maintenance and Repair Committee (SAUO)
DMRC .... Delhi Metro Rail Corporation [*Indian Railway*] (TIR)
DMRC .... Dynamic Mid-Ride Controls [*Truck seating*]
DMRD .... Davy McKee Research & Development [*British*] (IRUK)
DMRD .... Defense Management Report Decision [*Military*] (SEWL)
DMRD .... Defense Management Review Decision [*Army*] (RDA)
DMRD .... Defense Management Review Directive (AAGC)
DMRD .... Diploma in Medical Radio-Diagnosis [*British*]
DMRD .... Diploma in Medicine, Radio-Diagnostic [*Medical degree*] (CMD)
DMRD .... Directorate of Materials Research and Development (ODA)
DMRE .... Design and Management of Rural Ecosystems (SAUO)
DMRE .... Diploma in Medical Radiology and Electrology [*British*]
DMRE .... Division of Medical Radiation Exposure [*Bureau of Radiological Health*]
DMRF .... Dorsal Medullary Reticular Formation [*Medicine*] (STED)
DMRF .... Dystonia Medical Research Foundation (EA)
DMRHF .... Dry Materials Receiving and Handling Facility (SAUS)
DMRI .... Data Material Required, Increasing Urgency [*Navy*] (NG)
DMRI .... Dynamic Magnetic Resonant Imaging [*Medicine*]
DMRIS .... Defense Medical Regulating Information System (DOMA)
DMRK .... Damark International'A' [*NASDAQ symbol*] (TTSB)
DMRK .... Damark International, Inc. [*NASDAQ symbol*] (SAG)
DMRL .... Decreasing Mean Residual Life
DMRL .... Defense Metallurgical Research Laboratory (SAUS)
DMRLS .... Data Management and Research Liaison Staff [*Environmental Protection Agency*] (GFGA)
DMR(N) .... Director of Materials Research (Naval) [*British*]
DMRP .... Dredged Material Research Program [*Waterways Experiment Station*] [*Army*] (RDA)
DMR-QA .... Discharge Monitoring Report-Quality Assurance Studies (SAUS)
DMRR .... Defense Manpower Requirements Report (DNAB)
DMRS .... Data Management and Retrieval System
DMRS .... Digital Mission Recording System (SAUS)
DmRsBW .... Dominion Resources Black Warrior Trust [*Associated Press*] (SAG)
DmRsEW .... Dominion Resources Black Warrior Trust [*Associated Press*] (SAG)
DMRT .... Department of Mineral Resources of Thailand (GEOI)
DMRT .... Diploma in Medical Radio-Therapy [*British*]
DMS .... Dairy Management Scheme (SAUS)
DmS .... Dakota Microfilm Service, Inc., Denver, CO [*Library symbol*] [*Library of Congress*] (LCLS)
DMS .... Danish Medical Society (SAUO)
DMS .... Dartmouth Medical School [*Medicine*] (EDAA)
DMS .... Database Management System [*Computer science*]
DMS .... Data/Document Management Software (SAUS)
DMS .... Data/Document Management System (SAUS)
DMS .... Data Management Service (IEEE)
DMS .... Data Management Software [*Computer science*] (HODG)
DMS .... Data Management Standard (AAEL)
DMS .... Data Management Subsystem (IGSL)
DMS .... Data Management Supervisor (SAUS)
DMS .... Data Management System [*Computer science*]
DMS .... Data Measuring System
DMS .... Data Mining Services (SAUO)
DMS .... Data Monitoring System
DMS .... Data Multiplexer Sub-unit (SAUS)
DMS .... Data Multiplex Switching (SAUS)
DMS .... Data Multiplex System [*Computer science*]
DMS .... Decision Making System
DMS .... Deep Mine Safety (SAUO)
DMS .... Defence Management System (SAUS)
DMS .... Defence Medical Services (SAUS)
DMS .... Defense Management Simulation (OA)
DMS .... Defense Management System (NATG)
DMS .... Defense Mapping School [*Army*] (AABC)
DMS .... Defense Marketing Service (SAUO)
DMS .... Defense Marketing Survey (MCD)
DMS .... Defense Materials Service [*of GSA*]
DMS .... Defense Materials System
DMS .... Defense Message System (SAUO)
DMS .... Defense Messaging Service [*Military*] (SEWL)
DMS .... Defense Messaging System (DOMA)
DMS .... Defense Meteorological System (COE)
DMS .... Defense Missile Systems (KSC)
DMS .... Defense Mobilization Ship (MILB)
DMS .... Degrees, Minutes, Seconds (TIMI)
DMS .... Delayed Matching-to-Sample [*Psychology*]
DMS .... Delayed Microembolism Syndrome [*Medicine*] (STED)
DMS .... Delayed Muscle Soreness
DMS .... Delta Milliohm Sensor
DMS .... Delta Modulation System
DMS .... Demarcation Membrane System [*Medicine*] (DMAA)
DMS .... Denominational Ministry Strategy [*Later, CSM*] (EA)
DMS .... Dense Media Separation (PDAA)
DMS .... Dense Medium Separating [*Chemical engineering*]
DMS .... Dense Microsphere (STED)
DMS .... Density Manipulation Subsystem (MCD)
DMS .... Departmental Management System [*Department of Labor*]
DMS .... Department of Management Services (DEMM)
DMS .... Department of Materials Science (SAUS)
DMS .... Department of Mathematics and Statistics (SAUS)
DMS .... Department of Medicine and Surgery (STED)
DMS .... Department of the Military Secretary (SAUO)
DMS .... Depot Maintenance Service (AFIT)
DMS .... Depot Maintenance Study [*Army*]
DMS .... Depot Maintenance Support (AAG)
DMS .... Deputy Military Secretary [*British*]
DMS .... Dermatomyositis [*Medicine*]
DMS .... [*The*] Designer Menswear Show [*British*] (ITD)
DMS .... Desktop Management Software (SAUS)
DMS .... Desktop Management Suite [*Computer science*]
DMS .... Desktop Management System (SAUS)
DMS .... Desktop Mapping System
DMS .... Destroyer Minesweeper [*Navy symbol*] [*Obsolete*]
DMS .... Development Management System [*IBM Corp.*]
DMS .... Deviation from Mean Standard (MUGU)
dms .... diacritical marking system (SAUS)
DMS .... Diagnostic Medical Sonographer (DAVI)
DMS .... Diagnostic Methodology Section [*National Institute of Dental Research*]
DMS .... Diagonostic Medical Sonographer (HCT)
DMS .... Difference of Messing Subscription [*British military*] (DMA)
DMS .... Differential Maneuvering Simulator [*Aviation*]
DMS .... Differential Multiple Simulator (MCD)
DMS .... Differentiated Micrographic System (SAUS)
DMS .... Diffuse Mesangial Sclerosis [*Medicine*] (STED)
DMS .... digital management system (SAUS)
DMS .... Digital Mapping System (SAUS)
DMS .... Digital Marketing Service (SAUS)
DMS .... Digital Mass Storage (SAUS)
DMS .... Digital Matrix Switch (MCD)
DMS .... Digital Measuring System (SAUS)
DMS .... Digital Microsystems [*Digital Microsystems Ltd.*] [*Software package*] (NCC)
DMS .... Digital Microwave System (ACAE)
DMS .... Digital Motion System
DMS .... Digital Multimeter System (SAUS)
DMS .... Digital Multiplexed System [*Computer science*] (VERA)
DMS .... Digital Multiplexer Synchronizer (SAUS)
DMS .... Digital Multiplexing Synchronizer [*Computer science*]
DMS .... Digital Multiplex Switch [*Trademark of Northern Telecom Ltd.*]
DMS .... Digital Multiplex Switching (SAUS)
DMS .... Digital Multiplex Switching System (SAUS)
DMS .... Digital Multiplex System (SAUS)
DMS .... Digital MUMPS Standard (SAUS)
DMS .... Diis Manibus Sacrum [*Sacred to the Manes, i.e., Departed Souls*] [*Latin*]
DMS .... Diluted Magnetic Semiconductor [*Materials science*]
DMS .... Dimercaptosuccinic Acid [*Organic chemistry*]
DMS .... Dimethyl Silicone [*Organic chemistry*]
DMS .... Dimethylsilyl (SAUS)
DMS .... Dimethylstilbestrol [*Biochemistry*]
DMS .... Dimethylsuberimidate [*Organic chemistry*]
DMS .... Dimethyl Sulfate (LDT)

DMS .... Dimethyl Sulfide [*Organic chemistry*]
DMS - .... Dimethylsulfide (SAUS)
DMS .... dimethyl sulfide or dimethylsulphide (SAUS)
DMS .... Dimethyl Sulfoxide [*Also, DMSO*] [*Organic chemistry*]
DMS .... DiMethylsulphide (SAUS)
DMS .... Diminishing Manufacturing Service (MCD)
DMS .... Diminishing Manufacturing Sources
DMS .... Diploma in Management Studies [*British*]
DMS .... Direct Match Screening
DMS .... Direct Molded Sole [*Boot*] [*Military*]
DMS .... Directorate of Microgram Services [*RAF*] [*British*]
DMS .... Director for Mutual Security
DMS .... Director of Medical Services [*British*]
DMS .... Director of Mine-Sweeping Division (SAUO)
DMS .... Disc management system (SAUS)
DMS .... disc monitor system (SAUS)
DMS .... Discrete Memoryless Source [*Computer science*] (HGAA)
DMS .... Diskless Management Service [*Computer science*] (AGLO)
DMS .... Diskless Management Services (SAUS)
DMS .... Disk Monitoring System (SAUS)
DMS .... Disk Monitor System [*Computer science*]
DMS .... Display Management Subsystems (SAUS)
DMS .... Display Management System [*IBM Corp.*]
DMS .... Disposables Marketing Services Corp. (SAUO)
DMS .... Distance Measuring System
DMS .... Distinguished Military Students
DMS .... Distributed Maintenance Service (SAUS)
DMS .... Distributed Maintenance Services (NITA)
DMS .... Distributed Management System (SAUS)
DMS .... Distributed Media Services (SAUS)
DMS .... Distributed Memory System (SAUS)
DMS .... Distributed Models and Simulation [*Army*]
DMS .... Distributed Monitoring System (ACII)
DMS .... Distribution and Management Services (SAUS)
DMS .... Distribution Management System (GEOI)
DMS .... Distributor Modulator System [*Automotive engineering*]
DMS .... District Management Services [*Medicine*] (EDAA)
DMS .... Division of Marine Sciences (SAUS)
DMS .... Division of Materials Sciences (SAUS)
DMS .... Division of Medical Standards (SAUS)
DMS .... Docking Mechanism System [*or Subsystem*] [*NASA*] (NASA)
DMS .... Docking Module Subsystem (MCD)
DMs .... Doctor in Missionology
DMS .... Doctor of Mechanical Science
DMS .... Doctor of Medical Science [*or Sciences*]
DMS .... Doctor of Military Science
DMS .... Documentary Management System [*for citations*]
DMS .... Documentation of Molecular Spectroscopy
DMS .... Document Management Software [*Computer science*]
DMS .... Document Management System [*Computer science*] (VERA)
DMS .... Domestic Military Sales (SAUS)
DMS .... Dominion Mutual Securities (SAUS)
DMS .... Domini Sportswear [*Vancouver Stock Exchange symbol*]
DMS .... Doppler Measurement System
dms .... Double Minute Sphere (STED)
DMS .... Draftsman (Structural) [*U.S. Navy enlisted rating*] (AUER)
DMS .... Dragon [*Missile*] Maintenance Set [*Military*]
DMS .... Drawing Management System (SAUS)
DMS .... Drilling Mud Surfactant (BARN)
DMS .... Drone Maintenance Squadron
DMS .... Drum Memory System [*Computer science*]
dms .... Drums (WDAA)
DMS .... Dry Matter Solubles (SAUO)
DMS .... Dual Maneuvering Simulator (MCD)
DMS .... Dual Mechanical Seal [*Engineering*]
DMS .... Dual Mode Seeker (ACAE)
DMS .... Dun's Marketing Services [*Dun & Bradstreet, Inc.*] [*Parsippany, NJ*] [*Information service or system*] (IID)
DMS .... Duplex Microstructure (SAUS)
DMS .... Dynamic Magnetic Store (SAUS)
DMS .... Dynamic Mapping Scheme (SAUS)
DMS .... Dynamic Mapping System [*Hewlett-Packard Co.*]
DMS .... Dynamic Mechanical Spectroscopy
DMS .... Dynamic Missile Simulator
DMS .... Dynamic Modelling System (AIE)
DMS .... Dynamic Motion Simulator (MCD)
DMS .... Dynamo Management System (AAG)
DMS .... Dysmyelopoietic Syndrome [*Medicine*] (STED)
DMS .... High-Speed Minelayer (SAUS)
DMS .... High-Speed Minesweeper [*Navy symbol*] [*Obsolete*]
DMSA .... Defense Manufacturers and Suppliers Association (AAEL)
DMSA .... Defense Medical Activity SL (USGC)
DMSA .... Defense Medical Support Activity (DOMA)
DMSA .... Dimercaptosuccinic Acid [*Organic chemistry*]
DMSA .... Diploma in Medical Services Administration [*British*]
DMSA .... Disodium Monomethanearsonate (DMAA)
DMSA .... Illustrator Draftsman, Seaman Apprentice [*Navy rating*]
DMSAFIF .... Depot Maintenance Service Air Force Industrial Fund (AFIT)
DMSB .... Decimillistilb (SAUS)
DMSB .... Disposable Molecular Sieve Beds (SAUS)
DMSC .... Defence Material Standardization Committee [*British military*] (DMA)
DMSC .... Defense Medical Supply Center [*Later, Defense Personnel Support Center*]
DMSC .... Direct Simulation Monte Carlo Technique [*Statistics*]
DMSC .... Disinfected Mail Study Circle (EA)
DMSC .... Dispatch Management Services Corp. [*NASDAQ symbol*] (NASQ)
DM Sc .... Doctor of Medical Science
DMSc .... Doctor of Missionary Science
DMSCC .... Direct Microscopic Somatic Cell Count (OA)
DMSCMS .... Display Management System/Conversional Monitor System [*Computer science*] (VERA)
DMS/CS .... Data Management System/Computer Subsystem [*Computer science*]
DMSD .... Digital Multi Sensor Display (ACAE)
DMSD .... Digital Multistandard Decoding [*Computer science*]
DMSDS .... Direct Mail Shelter Development System [*Civil Defense*]
DMSE .... Developing Models for Special Education (SAUS)
DMSE .... Direct Mission Support Equipment (MCD)
DMSE .... Director of Mobile Support Equipment (SAUO)
DMSELC .... Diatomic Molecule Spectra and Energy Levels Center
DMSes .... Document-Management Systems
DMSH .... Diminish (FAAC)
DMS-HZ .... Dimethyl Sulfate-Hydrazine [*Organic chemistry*]
DMSI .... Data Management Segment Interface [*Control Document*] (GEOI)
DMSI .... Directorate of Management and Support of Intelligence (SAUS)
DMSIG .... Defense Message System Implementation Group (SAUO)
DMSIG .... DMS Information Group (SAUO)
dmsk .... Damask (VRA)
DMSK .... Differential Minimum Shift Keying (SAUS)
DMSL .... Descriptive Macro Simulation Language [*Computer science*] (PDAA)
DMSLT .... Daytime Multiple Sleep Latency Test [*Neurology*] (DAVI)
DMSM .... Defense Manpower Static Model
DMSM .... Defense Meritorious Service Medal [*Military decoration*]
DMSM .... Diminishing Manufacturing Sources and Material Shortages (MCD)
DMSMART ... Dredged Material Spatial Management Analysis Resolution Tool [*U.S. Army Corps of Engineers*]
DMS/MS .... Diminishing Manufacturing Sources/Material Shortages (MCD)
DMS(N) .... Director of Marine Services (Naval) [*British*]
DMSN .... Illustrator Draftsman, Seaman [*Navy rating*]
DmS-O .... Dakota Microfilm Service, Inc., Orlando, FL [*Library symbol*] [*Library of Congress*] (LCLS)
DMSO .... Defense Mapping School Operations Office (GEOI)
DMSO .... Defense Mapping School Operations Office Laboratory (SAUO)
DMSO .... Defense Materials Systems Office
DMSO .... Defense Modeling and Simulation Office [*Military*]
DMSO .... Dental Management Service Organization (SAUO)
DMSO .... Dimethyl Sulfoxide [*Also, DMS*] [*Organic chemistry*]
DMSO .... Director Major Staff Office (MCD)
DMSO .... Director of Major Staff Offices (SAUO)
DMSO .... Division Medical Supply Office [*Army*]
DMSO2 .... DiMethylsulphone (SAUS)
DMSOG .... Diploma in Medicine, Surgery, Obstetrics and Gynecology
DMSP .... Data Management Summary Processor (KSC)
DMSP .... Defense Meteorological Satellite Program [*Formerly, DAPP*] [*Air Force*]
DMSP .... Defense Meteorological Space Program (SEWL)
DMSP .... Defense Meteorological Support Program [*Air Force*] (MUSM)
DMSP .... Defense Military Satellite Programme (SAUO)
DMSP .... Depot Maintenance Support Plan [*Air Force*] (AFM)
DMSP .... Dichroic Microspectrophotometer
DMSP .... Dimethylsulfoniopropionate [*Organic chemistry*]
DMSP .... Distributed Mail System Protocol [*Computer science*] (VERA)
DMSP .... Dragon Missile Special Jump Pack [*Military*] (MCD)
DMSP .... Dual Mode Speech Processor (SAUS)
DMSPA .... Defense Mobilization and Support Planning Agency (SAUO)
DMSPC .... Defence Material (or Materiel) Standardization Policy Committee (SAUS)
DMSPC .... Defence Materiel Standardization Policy Committee (SAUO)
DMSPSM .... Data Management System Problem Specification Model [*Air Force*]
DMSQ .... Duty Military Occupational Specialty Qualified [*Army*] (DOMA)
DMSR .... Denatured Molten Salt Reactors (SAUS)
DMSR .... Dhond-Manmad State Railway [*Indian Railway*] (TIR)
DMSR .... Director of Missile Safety Research [*Air Force*]
DMSR .... Director of Mission Safety Research [*Air Force*]
DMSR .... Division of Management Survey and Review (SAUO)
DMSRD .... Directorate of Materials and Structures Research and Development [*British*]
DMSS .... Data Management System Simulator [*NASA*] (NASA)
DMSS .... Data Multiplexing Subsystem (SAUS)
DMSS .... Data Multiplex Subsystem [*Computer science*]
DMSS .... Defense Meteorological Satellite System [*Air Force*]
DMSS .... Digital Multibeam Steering System
DMSS .... Digital Multiplex Switching System (SAUS)
DMSS .... Directorate of Medical and Sanitary Services (SAUO)
DMSS .... Directorate of Military Satellite Systems (AAG)
DMSS .... Director of Medical and Sanitary Services [*British*]
DMSS .... Distributed Mass Storage System (SAUS)
DMSS .... Dual Mode Surveillance System (ACAE)
DMSSB .... Defense Material Specifications and Standards Board (DNAB)
DMSSB .... Direct Mail Services Standards Board [*British*]
DMSSC .... Defense Materiel Specifications and Standards Office (ACAE)
DMSSC .... Defense Medical Systems Support Center [*DoD*] (GFGA)
DMSSO .... Defense Material Standards and Specifications Office (SAUO)
DMSSO .... Defense Materiel Specifications and Standards Office (SAUO)
DmS-SP .... Dakota Microfilm Service, Inc., Saint Paul, MN [*Library symbol*] [*Library of Congress*] (LCLS)
DMST .... Demonstrate (AFM)
DMST .... Dynamic Magnetic Storage Technique (SAUS)
DMSTN .... Demonstration (AFM)
dmstr .... Demonstrator (ODA)

DMSTTIAC ... Defense Modeling, Simulation, and Tactical Technology Information Analysis Center [*Military*]
DMSTWG ..... Defense Message System Transition Working Group (SAUO)
DMSU .... Digital Main Network Switching Unit (NITA)
DMT .... Air Dan [*Nigeria*] [*FAA designator*] (FAAC)
DMT .... Daily Maximum Temperature (SAUS)
DMT .... Daily Metabolic Turnover (SAA)
DMT .... Data Management Team (ARMP)
DMT .... Deep Mobile Target
DMT .... Defense Mechanism Test [*Psychometrics*]
DMT .... Demountable [*Technical drawings*]
DMT .... Demycinosyltylosin [*Antibacterial*]
DMT .... Depot Module Tester (ACAE)
DMT .... Dermatophytosis (DB)
DMT .... Des Moines Terminal [*Federal Railroad Administration identification code*]
DMT .... Detailed Maneuver Table
DMT .... Development Management Tool [*Computer science*] (CIST)
DMT .... Device Mask Table (SAUS)
DMT .... Diamantina [*Brazil*] [*Airport symbol*] (AD)
DMT .... Dictaphone Machine Transcriber
DMT .... Digital Magnetic Tape (SAUS)
DMT .... Digital Message Terminal (MCD)
DMT .... Digital Multi-Tone (SAUS)
DMT .... Digital Multi Tone Modulation (SAUS)
DMT .... Dimensional Motion Time
dmt .... Dimethoxytrityl [*As substituent on nucleoside*] [*Biochemistry*]
DMT .... Dimethoxytrityl Chloride (SAUS)
DMT .... Dimethoxytryptamine [*Possible central nervous system neuroregulator*]
DMT .... Dimethylerephthalat (SAUS)
DMT .... Dimethylester of Terephthalate (SAUS)
DMT .... Dimethyl Terephthalate [*Organic chemistry*]
DMT .... Dimethyltryptamine [*Hallucinogenic agent*]
DMT .... Direct Memory Transfer [*Computer science*]
DMT .... Direct Modulation Technique
DMT .... Directorate of Military Technology (SAUO)
DMT .... Director of Machine Tools [*Ministry of Aircraft Production and Ministry of Supply*] [*British*]
DMT .... Director of Mechanical Transport and Marine Craft (SAUO)
DMT .... Director of Military Training
DMT .... Director of Military Transport (SAUS)
DMT .... Director of Mining Technology (SAUO)
DMT .... Disc Operating System Module Tester (SAUS)
DMT .... Discrete Module Tester (ACAE)
DMT .... Discrete Monitor Timings [*Computer science*] (VERA)
DMT .... Discrete Multi-Tone (DCDG)
DMT .... Discrete Multitone Technology (VERA)
DMT .... Disk Operating System - Module Tester [*Computer science*] (IAA)
DMT .... Dismounted Marksmanship Test [*Military*] (INF)
DMT .... Dispersion Modeling and Transport (EEVL)
DMT .... Dispersive Mechanism Test (NRCH)
DMT .... District Management Team (SAUO)
DMT .... Division of Medical Technology (SAUO)
DMT .... Division of Mining Technology (SAUO)
DMT .... Doctor of Medical Technology
DMT .... Doppler Modulated Target (ACAE)
DMT .... Dorsal Median Tract [*Anatomy*]
DMT .... Draftsman (Topographic) [*U.S. Navy enlisted rating*] (AUER)
DMT .... Driver, Motor Transport (SAUS)
DMT .... Dual Mode laser/TV Tracker (SAUS)
DMT .... Dual Mode Tracker (MCD)
DMT .... Dual Mode Transmission
DMT .... Dynamic Mechanical Testing
DMTA .... Dynamic Mechanical Thermal Analysis
DMTA .... Dynamic Mechanical Thermal Analyzer (SAUS)
DMTB .... Deployment Mobilization Troop Basis (AABC)
DMTC .... Digital Magnetic Tape Controller (CAAL)
DMTC .... Digital Message Terminal Computer (IEEE)
DMTC .... Dimethoxytrityl Chloride (SAUS)
DMTCNQ ...... Dimethyl(Tetracyano)Quinodimethane
DMTD .... Dimercaptothiadiazole [*Organic chemistry*]
DMTDL .... Doppler Modulated Target Delay Line (ACAE)
DMTe .... Dimethyl Telluride (SAUS)
DMTF .... Desktop Management Task Force (PCM)
DMTF .... Diffraction Limited Modulation Transfer Function (MCD)
DMTF .... Distributed Management Task Force (MWOL)
DMTFX .... Delaware: Tax Free USA Fund Cl.A [*Mutual fund ticker symbol*] (SG)
DMTG .... Data Manipulation Task Group (SAUO)
DMTG .... Design and Modeling Task Group (SAUO)
DMTI .... Defence Marketing Testing Initiative (SAUS)
DMTI .... Desktop Mapping Technologies, Inc. (GEOI)
DMTI .... Digital Moving Target Indication (SAUS)
DMTI .... Digitized Moving Target Indicator (CET)
DMTI .... Doppler Moving Target Indication (SAUS)
DMTI .... Doppler Moving Target Indicator (IAA)
DMTIK .... Dimethyl Terephthalate [*Organic chemistry*] (NUCP)
DMTM .... Detailed Monthly Trade Monitor [*Database*] [*Data Resources, Inc.*] [*Information service or system*] (CRD)
DMTP .... Disaster Management Training Programme (SAUO)
DMTPS .... Digital Magnetic Tape Plotting System
DMTR .... Deuterium Materials Testing Reactor (SAUS)
DMTR .... Dounreay Materials Testing Reactor [*British*]
DMTS .... Deck-Mounted Torpedo-launch System (SAUS)
DMTS .... Defence Message Transfer System (SAUS)
DMTS .... Delayed Matching to Sample [*Psychology*]
DMTS .... Department of Mines and Technical Survey [*Canada*]
DMTS .... Digital Magnetic Tape System (CAAL)
DMTS .... Digital Module Test Set
DMTS .... Dimethyl Trisulfide [*Organic chemistry*]
DMTS .... Dynamic Multi-Tasking System (DNAB)
DMTSF .... Dimethyl(methylthio)sulfonium Fluoroborate [*Organic chemistry*]
DMTT .... Dimethyltetrahydrothiadiazinethione [*Pesticide*] [*Organic chemistry*]
DMTU .... Default Maximum Transmission Unit (SAUS)
DMTU .... Digital Magnetic Tape Controller Unit
DMTU .... Digital Magnetic Tape Unit (MCD)
DMTU .... Dimethylthiourea [*Organic chemistry*]
DMTU .... Dual Modular Magnetic Tape Unit (CAAL)
DMTZ .... Dundalk Marine Terminal [*Federal Railroad Administration identification code*]
DMTZR .... Demagnetizer
DMU .... Data Management Unit [*Computer science*]
DMU .... Data Manipulation Unit [*Computer science*] (VERA)
DMU .... Data Measurement Unit (SAA)
DMU .... Decision-Making Unit (WDMC)
DMU .... Defense Mapping Unit [*Singapore*] (GEOI)
DMU .... Des Moines Union Railway Co. [*AAR code*]
DMU .... Destratification Motor Unit
DMU .... Device Mount Unit (MCD)
DMU .... Dictionary Management Utility (SAUS)
DMU .... Diesel Multiple Unit [*Indian Railway*] (TIR)
DMU .... Digital Management Unit (MCD)
DMU .... Digital Master Unit (SAUS)
DMU .... Digital Message Unit (MCD)
DMU .... Digital Microfilm Unit (NITA)
DMU .... Digital Mock-Up (SAUS)
DMU .... Digital Monitor Unit
DMU .... Digital Multiplexer Unit [*Electronics*] (ECII)
DMU .... Dimapur [*India*] [*Airport symbol*] (OAG)
DMU .... Dimethylolurea [*Organic chemistry*]
DMU .... Dimethyluracil [*Biochemistry*]
DMU .... Dimethylurea (EDCT)
DMU .... Diploma in Medical Ultrasound
DMU .... Directly Managed Unit [*Hospital administration*]
DMU .... Disk Memory Unit (COE)
DMU .... Distance-Measuring Unit (IAA)
DMU .... Distortion Measuring Unit (SAUS)
DMU .... Distributed Microprocessor Unit
DMU .... Dual Maneuvering Unit [*A spacecraft*]
DMU .... dwarf mouse unit (SAUS)
DMU .... Dynamic Mockup
DMUC .... Decision-Making Under Certainty (FOTI)
DMUP .... Defense Materiel Utilization Program [*DoD*]
DMUR .... Decision-Making Under Risk (FOTI)
DMUS .... Data Management Utility System
D Mus .... Doctor of Music
D Mus A ...... Doctor of Musical Arts
DMusCantuar ... Archbishop of Canterbury's Doctorate in Music [*British*] (DBQ)
D Mus Ed ..... Doctor of Musical Education
DMusEd .... Doctor of Music Education (GAGS)
DMUSX .... Delaware: Tax Free USA Intermed. Fund [*Mutual fund ticker symbol*] (SG)
DMUU .... Decision-Making Under Uncertainty (FOTI)
DMUX .... Demultiplexer [*Computer science*]
DMV .... Dahlia Mosaic Virus [*Plant pathology*]
DMV .... Daisy Mentor Valid (NITA)
DMV .... Delay Multivibrator
DMV .... Delta Multivibrator
DMV .... Department of Motor Vehicles
DMV .... Deserted Medieval Village [*British*]
DMV .... Digital Message Voice [*Device*] (MCD)
DMV .... Discrete Multivibrator (SAUS)
DMV .... Diurnal Mood Variations [*Medicine*] (DMAA)
DMV .... Division of Motor Vehicles (MCD)
DMV .... Doctorat en Medecin Veterinaire (DD)
DMV .... Doctor of Veterinary Medicine (NADA)
DMV .... Dolphin Morbillivirus
DMV .... Dual-Mode Vehicle (PDAA)
DMV .... Mount Vernon College, Washington, DC [*Library symbol*] [*Library of Congress*] (LCLS)
DMVA .... Direct Mechanical Ventricular Actuator [*Medicine*] (MELL)
DMVC .... Dayton-Miami Valley Library Consortium - Library Division [*Library network*]
DMVM .... Dakota, Missouri & Valley Western [*Federal Railroad Administration identification code*]
DMVRG .... Deserted Medieval Village Research Group (SAUO)
DMVS .... Desert Mobility Vehicle System [*Army*]
DMVS .... Deutz Magnetic Valve System [*Diesel engines*]
DMVS .... Dynamic Manned Vehicle Simulator (SAUS)
DMVW .... Dakota, Missouri Valley & Western Railroad [*Federal Railroad Administration identification code*]
DMW .... Daft, McCune, Walker (GEOI)
DMW .... Decimetric Wave [*Electromagnetism*] (IAA)
DMW .... Demineralized Makeup Water [*Nuclear energy*] (NRCH)
DMW .... Demineralized Water
DMW .... Des Moines Western Railway [*Federal Railroad Administration identification code*]
DMW .... Digital Milliwatt [*Telecommunications*] (TEL)
DMW .... Dissimilar-Metal Weld
DMWD .... Director of Miscellaneous Weapons Department (SAUO)

DMWG .... Direct Marketing Writers Guild [*Later, DMCG*] (EA)
DMWP .... Depot Maintenance Workload Plan (MCD)
DMWR .... Depot Maintenance Work Request [*or Requirement*] [*Army*] (AABC)
DMWR .... Depot Maintenance Work Requirement (SAUS)
DMWRO ...... Depot Maintenance Work Requirements Order (ACAE)
DMWS .... Direct Mineral Water Supply (ROG)
DMWV .... Descendants of Mexican War Veterans [*An association*] (EA)
DMX .... Data Multiplex [*Computer*]
DMX .... Data Multiplexer (NITA)
DMX .... Demultiplexer (SAUS)
DMX .... Diathermy, Massage, and Exercise [*Physical therapy*] (DAVI)
DMX .... Digital Musical Express (ECON)
DMX .... Digital Music Express (SAUS)
DMX .... Direct Memory Exchange
DMX .... Document Manager for Microsoft Exchange (GART)
DMX Inc ...... DMX, Inc. [*Associated Press*] (SAG)
DM-XX .... Douglas Missile - Model XX (MCD)
DMY .... Day Month Year (SAUO)
DMY .... Day-Month-Year (ELAL)
DMY .... destination motor yard (SAUS)
DMY .... Dummy (KSC)
DMY .... Merrill Lynch & Co. [*AMEX symbol*] (SAG)
dmy .... square decimetre (SAUS)
DMZ .... Declared Management Zone
DMZ .... Demilitarized Zone
DMZ .... Dorsal-Axial [*Embryology*]
DMZ .... Drug Mending Zone [*Drug abuse center*]
DMZn .... Dimethylzinc
DN .... Daily Nation [*A publication*]
Dn .... Daniel [*Old Testament book*]
DN .... Data Name
DN .... Data Net (MCD)
DN .... Datanet (SAUS)
DN .... Data Node (SAUS)
DN .... Data Number
DN .... Date Number
DN .... Day and Night [*Approach and landing charts*] [*Aviation*]
D/N .... Day-for-Night (WDMC)
DN .... Day Number (SSD)
DN .... Days Notice (SAUS)
DN .... Deacon (ROG)
DN .... Debit Note [*Business term*]
DN .... Decimal Notation (SAUS)
DN .... Decimal Number
DN .... Decimal Numbering (SAUS)
dn .... DeciNEM [*One-tenth of a NEM*] [*See NEM*]
dN .... Decineper [*Physics*] (DEN)
DN .... Decineper [*Reference unit*] (NITA)
DN .... Deci-Nepper (SAUS)
DN .... Decision Notice (WPI)
DN .... Decoder Network (SAUS)
DN .... Decrement (SAUS)
DN .... Deficiency Notice [*Government contracting*]
DN .... Deiter's Nucleus [*Medicine*] (EDAA)
DN .... DekaNEM [*Ten NEM*] [*See NEM*]
DN .... Delayed Neutron
D/N .... Delivery Note (ADA)
DN .... Delivery Notification (SAUS)
DN .... Delphian Node [*Medicine*] (MELL)
D/N .... Demand Note [*Banking*]
DN .... Democrazia Nazionale - Constituente di Destra [*National Democracy - Right Constituent*] [*Italy*] [*Political party*] (PPE)
Dn .... Denial [*Psychology*]
DN .... Density of Negative (SAUS)
DN .... Dentalman [*Nonrated enlisted man*] [*Navy*]
DN .... Departmental Notice (AAG)
DN .... Department of the Navy
DN .... Descending Neuron [*Neurology*]
DN .... Descending Node (SAUS)
DN .... Destination Node (SAUS)
DN .... Destra Nazionale [*National Right*] [*Italy*] [*Political party*] (PPE)
DN .... Detail Networks (MCD)
DN .... developing nation (SAUS)
DN .... Develop Number (SAUS)
d/N .... dextrose/nitrogen (SAUS)
D:N .... Dextrose:Nitrogen Ratio
DN .... Diabetes Neuropathy [*Medicine*] (DB)
DN .... Diabetic Nephropathy [*Medicine*] (MELL)
DN .... Diagnostic (SAUS)
DN .... Dialect Notes [*A publication*]
DN .... diameter nominal (SAUS)
DN .... Diamond International Corp. (SAUO)
DN .... Dibucaine Number [*Anesthesiology*]
DN .... Dicrotic Notch [*Cardiology*]
DN .... Died Near (SAUS)
DN .... Digital node (SAUS)
DN .... Digital Notation (SAUS)
DN .... Digital Number (GEOI)
DN .... Dilute noncomplexed (SAUS)
DN .... Dinitrocresol (LDT)
DN .... Dinitro-ortho-Cresol [*Also, DNOC*] [*Herbicide*]
DN .... Diploma in Nursing
DN .... Diploma in Nutrition [*British*]
DN .... Direct Normalized [*Steel*]
DN .... Directorate Notice (AAG)
DN .... Directory Number [*Computer science*]
DN .... Discipline Node (SAUS)
DN .... Disconnect (SAUS)
DN .... Discrepancy Notice [*NASA*] (NASA)
dn .... Dismine (SAUS)
D/N .... Dispatch Note [*Shipping*]
DN .... Disposition Pennant [*Navy*] [*British*]
D/N .... Distance and at Near (SAUS)
DN .... Distinguished Name (VERA)
DN .... Distribution Network (VERA)
DN .... District Nurse [*British*]
DN .... Divine Name (BJA)
DN .... Division Notice (AAG)
DN .... Division of Nursing (SAUO)
DN .... Doctor of Nursing
DN .... Document Number (NITA)
Dn .... Dolphin [*Mooring post*] [*British*]
DN .... Domain Name [*Computer science*] (AGLO)
DN .... Domino Nostro [*Our Lord*] [*Latin*]
DN .... Dominus [*The Lord*] [*Latin*]
DN .... Dominus Noster [*Our Lord*] [*Latin*]
DN .... Dore-Norbaska Resources, Inc. [*Toronto Stock Exchange symbol*]
DN .... Dorsal Nerve [*Anatomy*]
DN .... Double Negation [*Rule of replacement*] [*Logic*]
dn .... Down (WDMC)
DN .... Down
dn .... downward (SAUS)
DN .... Dozen (ROG)
Dn .... Dragoon [*British military*] (DMA)
DN .... Dublin [*City and county in Ireland*] (ROG)
DN .... Duke of Northumberland [*British*] (ROG)
DN .... Dun (WGA)
DN .... Duplicate Negative (MCD)
DN .... Dystrophic Neurite [*Neurophysiology*]
DN .... Heavenly Bodys Meridian Altitude (SAUS)
Dn .... Kongelige Bibliotek [*Royal Library*], Kobenhavn, Denmark [*Library symbol*] [*Library of Congress*] (LCLS)
DN .... National Directorate (Nicaragua) [*Political party*] (PSAP)
DN .... Skystream Airlines [*ICAO designator*] (AD)
DN .... United States Department of the Navy, Department Library, Washington, DC [*Library symbol*] [*Library of Congress*] (LCLS)
DNA .... Aerodespachos de El Salvador [*ICAO designator*] (FAAC)
DNA .... Copy Deoxyribonucleic Acid
DNA .... Dance Network Australia
DNA .... Data Network Address (SAUS)
DNA .... Data Network Architecture (IAA)
DNA .... Data Not Available (SAUS)
DNA .... DEC Network Architecture (SAUS)
DNA .... Defense Nuclear Agency [*DoD*] [*Washington, DC*]
DNA .... Delayed Neutron Analysis (SAUS)
DNA .... Del Norske Arbeiderparti [*Norwegian Labor Party*] (BARN)
DNA .... Delta Nu Alpha Transportation Fraternity (EA)
DNA .... Deoxyribonucleic Acid [*Biochemistry, genetics*]
DNA .... Deoxyribose Nucleic Acid
DNA .... Deputy for Nuclear Affairs (NATG)
DNA .... Dermatology Nurses' Association (EA)
DNA .... Designated National Agency [*for exchange of oceanographic data*] (MSC)
DNA .... Designated NICSMA Agent (SAUS)
DNA .... Desoxyribonucleicacid (SAUS)
DNA .... Desoxy Ribose Nucleic Acid (SAUS)
DNA .... Det Norske Arbeiderparti [*Norwegian Labor Party*] (PPE)
DNA .... Deutscher Normenausschuss [*German Standards Committee*] [*Later, DIN*] (EG)
DNA .... Diabetes Nutritional Assessment (MELL)
DNA .... Diana Corp. [*NYSE symbol*] (SPSG)
DNA .... Did Not Answer (DMAA)
DNA .... Did Not Arrive [*For no-show hotel reservation*]
DNA .... Did Not Attend
DNA .... Digital Network Architecture [*Digital Equipment Corp.*] [*Computer science*]
DNA .... Digital Networking Architecture (SAUS)
DNA .... DIMUS [*Digital Multibeam Steering*] Narrow-Band Accelerated (NVT)
DNA .... Dinolylaniline (SAUS)
DNA .... Dinonyl Adipate (EDCT)
DNA .... Dioxyribonuclic Acid (SAUS)
DNA .... Directional Neighbourhoods Approach
DNA .... Direct Network attach (VERA)
DNA .... Directorate of Naval Aviation (SAUO)
DNA .... Director of Naval Accounts [*Obsolete*] [*British*]
DNA .... Disposal Notification Area [*Community Land Act*] [*British*] (DI)
DNA .... Distributed interNet Architecture (SAUS)
DNA .... Distributed Network Architecture (IAA)
DNA .... District Nursing Association [*British*] (DBA)
DNA .... DNA Plant Technology Corp. [*Associated Press*] (SAG)
D Na .... Doctor of Navigation
DNA .... Document Enabled Network (SAUS)
DNA .... Does Not Answer [*Telephone operator's designation*]
DNA .... Does Not Apply (MSA)
Dna .... Dona [*Mrs.*] [*Spanish*] (BARN)
DNA .... Do Not Attack (ACAE)
DNA .... Doses Not Answer (SAUS)
DNA .... Downstream Neighbor Address (SAUS)
DNA .... Dynamar Energy Ltd. [*Toronto Stock Exchange symbol*]
DNA .... Herbarium of the Northern Territory, Darwin (SAUS)

DNA .... Herbarium of the Northern Territory, Darwin International Acronym (SAUO)
DNA .... Labor Party (Norway) [*Political party*] (PSAP)
DNA .... United States National Archives and Records Service, National Archives Library, Washington, DC [*Library symbol*] [*Library of Congress*] (LCLS)
DNAA .... Abuja/International [*Nigeria*] [*ICAO location identifier*] (ICLI)
DNAA .... Delayed Neutron Activation Analysis (PDAA)
DNA-AEC ...... Defense Nuclear Agency-Atomic Energy Commission (DNAB)
DNAAS .... Delayed Neutron Activation Analysis System (SAUS)
DNAase .... Deoxyribonuclease [*Preferred form, DNase*] [*An enzyme*]
DNAC .... Division of Numerical Analysis and Computing (SAUO)
DNACC .... Defense National Agency Check Center [*DoD*]
DNA Cell Biol... DNA and Cell Biology (SAUS)
DNAD .... Director of Naval Air Division
DNADA .... Division of Narcotic Addiction and Drug Abuse [*National Institute of Mental Health*]
DNAE .... Dissemination Network for Adult Educators (EDAC)
DN-Aer .... United States Department of the Navy, Naval Air Systems Command, Arlington, VA [*Library symbol*] [*Library of Congress*] (LCLS)
DNAG .... Decade of North American Geology [*Geological Society of America*]
DNAG .... Decade of North American Geology project (SAUO)
DNA/G .... Deoxyribonucleic Acid Content Per Genome [*Medicine*] (EDAA)
DNAL .... United States National Agricultural Library, Beltsville, MD [*Library symbol*] [*Library of Congress*] (LCLS)
DNAM .... Data Network Access Method
DNAM .... Division of Numerical and Applied Mathematics (SAUO)
DNAME .... Department of Naval Architecture and Marine Engineering [*MIT*] (MCD)
DNAN .... Department Number Assignment Notice (SAUS)
DN & D .... Director of Navigation and Direction (SAUS)
DNANR .... Department of Northern Affairs and National Resources (SAUS)
DNAO .... Director of Naval Air Organisation (SAUO)
DNAO .... Director of Naval Air Organization [*British*]
DNA-P .... Deoxyribonucleic Acid-Phosphorus [*Biochemistry*] (DAVI)
DNAp .... Deoxyribonucleic Acid Polymerase [*An enzyme*]
DNAP .... Dinitroaminophenol (SAUS)
DNAP .... (Dinitrophenylazo)phenol [*Organic chemistry*]
DNAP .... Directorate of Naval Administration Planning [*British*]
DNAP .... DNA [*Deoxyribonucleic Acid*] Affinity Precipitation [*Analytical biochemistry*]
DNAP .... DNA Plant Technology [*NASDAQ symbol*] (TTSB)
DNAP .... DNA Plant Technology Corp. [*NASDAQ symbol*] (NQ)
DNAPL .... Defense Non-Aqueous Phase Liquid (SAUO)
DNAPL .... Dense Non-Aqueous Phase Liquid [*Chemical engineering*]
DNAPL .... Dense Non-Aqueous Pollutant Liquid (SAUS)
DNA Pl .... DNA Plant Technology Corp. [*Associated Press*] (SAG)
DNAPP .... DNA Plant Tech $2.25 Cv Ex Pfd [*NASDAQ symbol*] (TTSB)
D/NAPS .... Day/Night Adverse weather Pilotage System (SAUS)
DNAR .... Do Not Attempt Resuscitation [*Medicine*] (HCT)
DNAr .... United States National Arboretum, Washington, DC [*Library symbol*] [*Library of Congress*] (LCLS)
DN Arch .... Doctor of Naval Architecture
D Na S .... Doctor of Naval Science
DNAS .... DODIIS Network Access System (SAUO)
DNASA .... United States National Aeronautics and Space Administration, Washington, DC [*Library symbol*] [*Library of Congress*] (LCLS)
DNASA-G ...... United States National Aeronautics and Space Administration, Goddard Space Flight Center, Greenbelt, MD [*Library symbol*] [*Library of Congress*] (LCLS)
D Na Sc .... Doctor of Naval Science
DNase .... Deoxyribonuclease [*An enzyme*]
DNAS-HRB ... National Academy of Sciences, Highway Research Board Library, Washington, DC [*Library symbol*] [*Library of Congress*] (LCLS)
DNAS-NAE ... National Academy of Sciences, National Academy of Engineering Library, Washington, DC [*Library symbol*] [*Library of Congress*] (LCLS)
D Nat .... Doctor of Naturopathy
DNATO .... Director of North Atlantic Treaty Organization Affairs (SAUO)
DNA-TP .... Defense Nuclear Agency Technical Publications [*DoD*]
DNATS .... Day and Night Airborne Thermal Sensor [*Military*] (SEWL)
DNAU .... Digital Network Access Unit [*Bytex Corp.*]
DnAu .... Statsbiblioteket i Arhus Universitetsbiblioteket [*State and Arhus University Library*], Arhus, Denmark [*Library symbol*] [*Library of Congress*] (LCLS)
DNAV .... Naval Directorate (SAUO)
DNAW .... Directorate of Naval Air Warfare [*British*]
DNAWFT .... Director, Naval Air Warfare and Flying Training (SAUO)
DNAWFT .... Director of Naval Air Warfare and Flying Training (SAUS)
DNAX .... Dana Railcare [*Private rail car owner code*]
DNB .... Dance Notation Bureau (EA)
DNB .... Departure from Nuclear Boiling (SAUS)
DNB .... Departure from Nucleate Boiling (NRCH)
DNB .... Destructive Nerve Block [*Medicine*] (MELL)
DNB .... Deutsche Nachrichtenburo [*German News Bureau*]
DNB .... Dictionary of National Bibliography (SAUS)
DNB .... Dictionary of National Biography [*A publication*] (WA)
DNB .... Did Not Bat [*Cricket*]
DNB .... Dinitrobenzene [*Organic chemistry*]
DNB .... Dinitrobenzidine [*Organic chemistry*]
DNB .... Dinitrobenzoyl (SAUS)
DNB .... Dinitrochlorobenzene [*Organic chemistry*] (DAVI)
DNB .... Diplomate of the National Board of Medical Examiners (AAMN)
DNB .... Distribution Number Bank
DNB .... Dorsal Nonadrenergic Bundle [*Medicine*] (EDAA)
DNB .... Double Non-Return Valve (SAUS)
DNB .... Dun & Bradstreet [*NYSE symbol*] (TTSB)
DNB .... Dun & Bradstreet, Inc. [*NYSE symbol*] (SPSG)
DNB .... Dunbar [*Australia*] [*Airport symbol*] [*Obsolete*] (OAG)
DNB .... Dynamic Noise Reduction (SAUS)
DNBA .... Dinitrobenzoic Acid [*Organic chemistry*]
DNBA .... Di-normal-butylamine [*Organic chemistry*]
DNBC .... Defence Nuclear, Biological and Chemical School (SAUO)
DNBC .... Dinitrobenzoyl Chloride [*Organic chemistry*]
DNBCC .... Defence NBC Centre (SAUS)
DNBE .... Benin [*Nigeria*] [*ICAO location identifier*] (ICLI)
DNBI .... Bida [*Nigeria*] [*ICAO location identifier*] (ICLI)
DNBI .... Disease and Nonbattle Injury [*Military*] (NVT)
DNBJ .... Abuja [*Nigeria*] [*ICAO location identifier*] (ICLI)
DNBM .... Di-normal-Butylmagnesium [*Organic chemistry*]
DNBP .... Dinitrobutyphenol [*Biochemistry*] (DAVI)
DNBP .... Dinitro-ortho-secondary-butylphenol [*Also, DNOSBP, DNSBP*] [*Herbicide*]
DNBPG .... Dinitrobenzoylphenylglycine [*Biochemistry*]
DNBR .... Departure from Nucleate Boiling Ratio (NRCH)
DNBS .... Dinitrobenzenesulfonic [*Organic chemistry*]
DNBSC .... Dinitrobenzenesulfenyl Chloride [*Organic chemistry*]
DNBwi .... Dun & Bradstreet, New [*NYSE symbol*]
DNC .... Dance
DNC .... Daon Centre Ltd. [*Partnership units*] [*Vancouver Stock Exchange symbol*]
DNC .... Data Name Card
DNC .... Data Network Corporation (SAUO)
DNC .... Day-Night Capability [*Aerospace*] (AAG)
DNC .... Delayed Neutron Counter (SAUS)
DNC .... Delayed Neutron Counting
DNC .... Delayed Neutron Coupling (SAUS)
DNC .... Democratic National Committee (EA)
DNC .... Department of the Navy Civilian (DNAB)
DNC .... depreciation of national capital (SAUS)
DNC .... Did Not Come
DNC .... Did Not Compete [*Yacht racing*] (IYR)
DNC .... Digital Nautical Chart (GEOI)
DNC .... Digital Network Control (SAUS)
DNC .... Digital Numeric Control [*Computer science*] (GART)
DNC .... Dinitrocarbanilide [*Organic chemistry*]
DNC .... Dinitrocellulose [*Organic chemistry*]
DNC .... Dinitrocresol (LDT)
DNC .... Direct Notice of Cancellation [*Insurance*]
DNC .... Direct Numerical Control [*Automation method*] [*Computer science*]
DNC .... Direct Numeric Control (SAUS)
DNC .... direct numeric controll (SAUS)
DNC .... Directorate of National Coordination (CINC)
DNC .... Director of Naval Communications (SAUO)
DNC .... Director of Naval Construction [*British*]
DNC .... Director of Navy Communications
DNC .... Disaster Nursing Chairman [*Red Cross*]
DNC .... Distance to New Course (SAUS)
DNC .... Distributed Network Computing (ACAE)
DNC .... Distributed Network Control (VLIE)
DNC .... Distributed Numerical Control [*Computer science*] (ODBW)
DNC .... Domestic National Committee (SAUS)
DNC .... Dynamic Network Controller (VERA)
DNC .... Washington Cathedral, Washington, DC [*Library symbol*] [*Library of Congress*] (LCLS)
DNCA .... Calabar [*Nigeria*] [*ICAO location identifier*] (ICLI)
DNCB .... Dinitrochlorobenzene [*Organic chemistry*]
DNCC .... Data Network Control Center (or Centre) (SAUS)
DNCC .... Data Network Control Centre (NITA)
DNCC .... Domain Network Control Center (SAUS)
DNCC .... Dunn Computer [*NASDAQ symbol*] (SG)
DNCCC .... Defense National Communications Control Center
DNCCC .... Directorate of Naval Command, Control and Communications
DNCCCS .... Defense National Communications Control Center System (IAA)
DNCD .... National Society of Colonial Dames of America, Washington, DC [*Library symbol*] [*Library of Congress*] (LCLS)
DNCDCC .... Democratic National Committee - Department of Constituent Coordination [*Defunct*] (EA)
DNCE .... Directorate of Naval Communications Engineering
DNCG .... Digital Null Command Generator
DNCIAWPRC ... Danish National Committee of the International Association on Water Pollution Research and Control (EAIO)
D/NCIG .... Day/Night Approach Computer Image Generator [*Aviation*]
DNCINST .... Director, Naval Communications Instruction
DNCMD .... Dayton Contract Management Office (SAUS)
DNCNOTE ..... Director, Naval Communications Notice
DNCOM .... Directorate of Naval Communication (SAUO)
DNCRI .... Division of Networking and Communications Research and Information (SAUO)
DNCRI .... Division of Networking and Communications Research and Infrastructure (SAUS)
DNCRI .... Division of Networking and Communic. Research and Infrastructure (SAUS)
DNCS .... Day/Night Camera System (MCD)
DNCS .... Distributed Network Control System
DNCS .... Distribution Network Communication System (SAUS)
DNCSS .... Director, Navy Configuration Survival and Safety
DNCT .... National Cable Television Association, Washington, DC [*Library symbol*] [*Library of Congress*] (LCLS)
DNCTL .... Down Control (IAA)

DNCU .... Data Net Control Unit (NVT)
DNCW .... United States Catholic Conference, Washington, DC [*Library symbol*] [*Library of Congress*] (LCLS)
DNCWAD ..... Democratic National Committee - Women's Affairs Division [*Later, DNCWD*] (EA)
DNCWD .... Democratic National Committee - Women's Division [*Formerly, DNCWAD*] (EA)
DND .... Danra Resources Ltd. [*Vancouver Stock Exchange symbol*]
DND .... Degenerative Neurological Disease [*Medicine*] (EDAA)
DND .... Demodulator Neon Driver
DND .... Department of National Defence [*Canada*]
DND .... Department of National Development (SAUS)
DND .... Deutscher Nachrichten Dienst [*German News Service*] (BARN)
DND .... Died a Natural Death
DND .... Directorate of Navigation and Direction (SAUO)
DND .... Director of Navigation and Direction [*British military*] (DMA)
DND .... Directory of Numerical Databases [*Database*] [*NASA*] [*Information service or system*] (CRD)
DND .... Dislocation Nucleation Diagram (SAUS)
DND .... Disqualification Not Discardable [*Yacht racing*] (IYR)
DND .... Dividend (SAUS)
DND .... Division of Narcotic Drugs (SAUS)
DND .... Dobokuken-Nijuhenpa-Doppler (SAUS)
DND .... Do Not Disturb [*Telecommunications*] (ITD)
DND .... Do Not Duplicate
DND .... Doppler Noise Decoy (SEWL)
DND .... double needle dialysis (SAUS)
DND .... Dundee [*Scotland*] [*Airport symbol*] (OAG)
Dnd .... Dunedin (SAUS)
DND .... Eldinder Aviation [*Sudan*] [*ICAO designator*] (FAAC)
D ND .... United States District Court for the District of North Dakota (DLA)
DNDAR .... Daughters of the American Revolution, Washington, DC [*Library symbol*] [*Library of Congress*] (LCLS)
DNDFT .... Downdraft
DNDG .... Dynamic Network Data Generator (VLIE)
DNDI .... Department of National Defence Intelligence [*Canada*] (CARL)
DNDO .... Do Not Disturb Override (SAUS)
dNDP .... Desoxyribonucleoside Diphosphate (SAUS)
DNDS .... Dinitrodiphenyl Disulfide [*Organic chemistry*]
DNDS .... Dinitrostilbenedisulfonic Acid [*Antimalarial*]
DNDS .... Director, Naval Dental Services [*British*]
DNDS .... Distributed Network Design System (VLIE)
DNDT .... Department of the Navy Declassification Team (DNAB)
DNDU .... National Defense University, Fort Lesley J. McNair, Washington, DC [*Library symbol*] [*Library of Congress*] (LCLS)
DNE .... Department of Nuclear Engineering [*MIT*] (MCD)
DNE .... Diffuse Neuroendocrine System [*Also, DNS*]
DNE .... Diploma in Nursing Education (ADA)
DNE .... Directorate of Naval Education (SAUO)
DNE .... Director of Naval Equipment
DNE .... Director of Nursing Education
DNE .... Dnepa-Air [*Ukraine*] [*FAA designator*] (FAAC)
DNE .... Doctor of Naval Engineering
DNE .... Doctor of Nursing Education (DAVI)
DNE .... Doron Exploration, Inc. [*Vancouver Stock Exchange symbol*]
DNE .... Dounreay Nuclear Establishment (SAUO)
DNE .... Duluth & Northeastern Railroad Co. [*AAR code*]
DNE .... Group D Nonenterococcal Streptococcus [*Bacteriology*] (DAVI)
DNEA .... National Education Association, Washington, DC [*Library symbol*] [*Library of Congress*] (LCLS)
DNEC .... Distribution Navy Enlisted Classification (DNAB)
DNED .... Deputy, Naval Education Development (MCD)
DN Ed .... Doctor of Nursing Education
DNEDS .... Director of Naval Education Service [*British*]
Dneeds .... Deficiency Needs [*A. Maslow*] (DIPS)
DNEN .... Enugu [*Nigeria*] [*ICAO location identifier*] (ICLI)
DN Eng .... Doctor of Naval Engineering
DNES .... Department of Non-conventional Energy Sources (SAUO)
DNES .... Director of Naval Education Service [*British*] (DMA)
DNESYS ...... Drainage Network Extraction System (SAUS)
DNET .... Data-Net [*Data-Net, Inc.*] [*Rochester, NY*] [*Telecommunications*] (TSSD)
DNET .... Director of Naval Engineering Training [*British military*] (DMA)
DNET .... Division of Nuclear Education and Training [*AEC*]
DNET .... Dysembryoplastic Neuroepithelial Tumor [*Medicine*] (DMAA)
D Nev .... United States District Court for the District of Nevada (DLA)
DNEX .... Dionex Corp. [*NASDAQ symbol*] (NQ)
DNEX .... Direct Nonexempt (TIMI)
DNEY .... Da Nang East Yard [*Vietnam*] [*Navy*]
DNF .... Decimal Number Format (SAUS)
DNF .... Defenders of Nature Foundation [*Guatemala*] (EAIO)
DNF .... Det Nye Folkepartiet [*New People's Party*] [*Norway*] (PPE)
DNF .... Did Not Finish
DNF .... Directorate of Naval Finance (SAUO)
DNF .... Disjunctive Normal Form (IDAI)
DNF .... Disjunctive Normal Formula
DNF .... Dissolved Nitrogen Flotation (LDOE)
DNF .... Dominion Naval Forces
DNF .... Do Not Fill (VLIE)
DNF .... Durand-Nicolas-Favre [*Disease*] [*Medicine*] (DB)
DNF .... dynamic noise filter (SAUS)
DNFA .... Dinitrofluoroaniline [*Organic chemistry*]
DNFB .... Dinitrofluorbenzene (SAUS)
DNFB .... Dinitrofluorobenzene [*Also, DFB, FDNB*] [*Organic chemistry*]
DNFC .... D & N Financial Corp. [*NASDAQ symbol*] (SPSG)
DNFC .... D&N Finl Corp. [*NASDAQ symbol*] (TTSB)
DNFCT .... Director of Naval Foreign and Commonwealth Training [*British*]
DNFCW .... D&N Financial Wrrt [*NASDAQ symbol*] (TTSB)
DNFPS .... Director, Naval Future Policy Staff [*British*]
DNFS .... Directorate of Naval Flight Safety (SAUO)
DNFSB .... Defense Nuclear Facilities Safety Board [*Military*] (DOMA)
DNFST .... Department of Nutrition, Food Science, and Technology [*MIT*] (MCD)
DNFST .... Division of Nutrition, Food Science and Technology (SAUO)
dnft .... directional non-force technique (SAUS)
DNFYP .... Department of the Navy Five-Year Program
DNG .... Da Nang [*Vietnam*] (VNW)
DNG .... Danger
DNG .... Danghila [*Ethiopia*] [*Airport symbol*] (AD)
DNG .... Daru [*Papua New Guinea*] [*Seismograph station code, US Geological Survey*] [*Closed*] (SEIS)
DNG .... Diffuse Nontoxic Goiter [*Medicine*] (MELL)
DNG .... Dining
DNG .... Distinguished Naval Graduate
DNG .... District of Columbia National Guard (ACAE)
DNG .... Dorsal (Nephridial Gland)
DNG .... Dutch New Guinea [*Later, Irian Barat*]
DNG .... National Geographic Society, Washington, DC [*Library symbol*] [*Library of Congress*] (LCLS)
DNGA .... National Gallery of Art, Washington, DC [*Library symbol*] [*Library of Congress*] (LCLS)
DN-GF .... United States Department of the Navy, Naval Gun Factory, Washington, DC [*Library symbol*] [*Library of Congress*] [*Obsolete*] (LCLS)
DNGS .... National Genealogical Society, Washington, DC [*Library symbol*] [*Library of Congress*] (LCLS)
DNGU .... Gusau [*Nigeria*] [*ICAO location identifier*] (ICLI)
DNGuA .... National Guard Association of the United States, Washington, DC [*Library symbol*] [*Library of Congress*] (LCLS)
DNGV .... Dedicated Natural Gas Vehicle [*Automotive engineering*]
DNGW .... Director of Naval Guided Weapons [*British*]
DNH .... Department of National Heritage [*British*] (TELE)
DNH .... Directory of Nursing Homes [*A publication*] (MELL)
DNH .... Dunhuang [*China*] [*Airport symbol*] (OAG)
D NH .... United States District Court for the District of New Hampshire (DLA)
DNHAS .... Dorset Natural, Historical, and Archaeological Society (SAUS)
DN-HC .... United States Department of the Navy, Naval Historical Center, Operational Archives, Washington, DC [*Library symbol*] [*Library of Congress*] (LCLS)
DNHL .... Diffuse Non-Hodgkin's Lymphoma [*Medicine*] (MELL)
DNHM .... Di-normal-Hexylmagnesium [*Organic chemistry*]
DN-HO .... United States Department of the Navy, Naval Oceanographic Office, Washington, DC [*Library symbol*] [*Library of Congress*] (LCLS)
DNHR .... Dynamic Non-Hierarchical Routing [*Computer science*] (VERA)
DNHR .... Dynamic Nonhierarchical Structure [*Computer science*] (AGLO)
DNHS .... Di-Normal-Hexyl Sulfide [*Organic chemistry*]
DNHS .... Durham Natural History Society (SAUO)
DNHW .... Department of National Health and Welfare (SAUS)
DNI .... Data Network Interface (SAUS)
DNI .... Desktop Network Interface [*Cabletron Systems, Inc.*] [*Computer science*]
DNI .... Digital Equipment Corp., Salem, Salem, NH [*OCLC symbol*] (OCLC)
DNI .... Digital Non-Interpolated (LAIN)
DNI .... Digital Non-Interpolation (SAUS)
DNI .... Director of National Intelligence (SAUS)
DNI .... Director of Naval Intelligence [*US, British*]
DNI .... Distributable Net Income
DNI .... Division of Naval Intelligence
DNI .... DNI Holdings, Inc. [*Vancouver Stock Exchange symbol*]
DNI .... Do Not Intubate [*Medicine*] (DAVI)
DNI .... Do Not Invite
DNI .... Sherman-Denison, TX [*Location identifier*] [*FAA*] (FAAL)
DNI .... Wad Medani [*Sudan*] [*Airport symbol*] (AD)
DNIAS .... Day-Night Indirect Attack Seeker (DNAB)
DNIB .... Ibadan [*Nigeria*] [*ICAO location identifier*] (ICLI)
DNIC .... Data Net Identification Code (NITA)
DNIC .... Data Network Identification Code [*Telecommunications*] (TEL)
DNIC .... Destination Network Identification Code (VLIE)
DNIC .... Diffuse Noxious Inhibitory Control (PDAA)
DNIC .... Digital Multiplex Control (SAUS)
DNIC .... Digital Network Interface Circuit [*Telecommunications*]
DNIE .... Distance Measuring Equipment (SAUS)
DNIE .... National Institute of Education, Washington, DC [*Library symbol*] [*Library of Congress*] (LCLS)
DNIF .... Duty Not Involving Flying
DNIG .... De Novo Inflammatory Growth [*Medicine*] (MELL)
DNigE .... Nigerian Embassy, Washington, DC [*Library symbol*] [*Library of Congress*] (LCLS)
DNIH .... United States National Institutes of Health, Bethesda, MD [*Library symbol*] [*Library of Congress*] (LCLS)
DNIH-HM ..... United States National Institutes of Health, Bureau of Health Manpower, Bethesda, MD [*Library symbol*] [*Library of Congress*] (LCLS)
DNIL .... Ilorin [*Nigeria*] [*ICAO location identifier*] (ICLI)
DNINF .... Directorate of Naval Information (SAUO)
DNIP .... Dinitroiodophenyl [*Medicine*] (EDAA)
DNIS .... Dataport Network Information System [*California*] [*Bulletin board system*]
DN-IS .... Defense Intelligence School, Washington, DC [*Library symbol*] [*Library of Congress*] (LCLS)
DNIS .... Dialed Number Identification Service [*Telecommunications*] (ACRL)

dnj .... drone noise jammer (SAUS)
DNJ .... Drone Noise Jammers [*Military*]
D NJ .... United States District Court for the District of New Jersey (DLA)
DN-JAG .... United States Department of the Navy, Office of the Judge Advocate General, Law Library, Washington, DC [*Library symbol*] [*Library of Congress*] (LCLS)
DNJC .... Dominus Noster Jesus Christus [*Our Lord Jesus Christ*] [*Latin*]
DNJENER .... Dutch-Norwegian Joint Establishment for Nuclear Energy Research (SAUO)
DNJO .... Jos [*Nigeria*] [*ICAO location identifier*] (ICLI)
DNJS .... Descendants of the New Jersey Settlers (EA)
DNK .... Dam Neck (SAUO)
DNK .... Data Network (SAUS)
DNK .... Denmark [*ANSI three-letter standard code*] (CNC)
DNK .... Did Not Keep Appointment [*Medicine*] (CPH)
DNKA .... Did Not Keep Appointment [*Medicine*]
DNKA .... Kaduna [*Nigeria*] [*ICAO location identifier*] (ICLI)
DnKBO .... Bibliotekernes Oplysningskontor, Centre de Pret International, Kobenhavn, Denmark [*Library symbol*] [*Library of Congress*] (LCLS)
DnKDR .... Center for Development Research, Koobenhavn, Denmark [*Library symbol*] [*Library of Congress*] (LCLS)
DNKK .... Kano [*Nigeria*] [*ICAO location identifier*] (ICLI)
DnKL .... Danmarks Laererhojskole [*Royal Danish School of Educational Studies*], Kobenhavn, Denmark [*Library symbol*] [*Library of Congress*] (LCLS)
DNKN .... Kano/Mallam Aminu International [*Nigeria*] [*ICAO location identifier*] (ICLI)
DnKP .... Danmarks Paedagogiske Bibliotek [*Danish National Library of Education*], Kobenhavn, Denmark [*Library symbol*] [*Library of Congress*] (LCLS)
DnKU .... Kobenhavns Universitetsbibliotekets [*University of Copenhagen*], Afdeling, Norre Alle, Kobenhavn, Denmark [*Library symbol*] [*Library of Congress*] (LCLS)
DnKU-S .... Kobenhavns Universitetsbibliotekets [*University of Copenhagen*], Afdeling, Fiolstraede, Kobenhavn, Denmark [*Library symbol*] [*Library of Congress*] (LCLS)
DNKY .... Donnkenny, Inc. [*NASDAQ symbol*] (SAG)
DNKZ .... Datennetz-Kontrollzentrum (SAUS)
DNL .... Augusta, GA [*Location identifier*] [*FAA*] (FAAL)
DNL .... Day and Night Average Sound Levels
DNL .... Det Norske Luftfartselskap AS [*Norwegian Airlines Ltd.*] (EY)
DNL .... Diack Newsletter [*Database*] [*Diack, Inc.*] [*Information service or system*] (CRD)
DNL .... Differential Non-Linearity (OA)
DNL .... Director of Naval Laboratories
DNL .... Do Not Like
DNL .... Do Not List
DNL .... Do Not Load [*Instruction re a freight car*]
DNL .... Dune Resources Ltd. [*Toronto Stock Exchange symbol*]
DNL .... Dynamic Noise Limiter [*Electronics*] (IAA)
DNLC .... Directory Name Lookup Cache (SAUS)
DNLC .... Dixie National Corp. [*NASDAQ symbol*] (NQ)
DNLC .... Dixie Natl [*NASDAQ symbol*] (TTSB)
DNLCA .... Deoxynorlaudanosolinecarboxylic Acid [*Biochemistry*]
DNLI .... Denali, Inc. [*NASDAQ symbol*] (NASQ)
DNLK .... Downlink (MCD)
DNLL .... Dorsal Nucleus of Lateral Lemniscus [*Medicine*] (MELL)
DNLL .... Lagos App [*Nigeria*] [*ICAO location identifier*] (ICLI)
DNLM .... United States National Library of Medicine, Bethesda, MD [*Library symbol*] [*Library of Congress*] (LCLS)
DNLR .... National Labor Relations Board, Washington, DC [*Library symbol*] [*Library of Congress*] (LCLS)
DNLT .... Downlist (NASA)
DNM .... Delayed Neutron Monitor [*Nuclear energy*] (NRCH)
DNM .... Denham [*Australia*] [*Airport symbol*] (OAG)
dNM .... Deoxynojirimycin [*Biochemistry*]
DNM .... Dilator Naris Muscle [*Medicine*] (MELL)
DNM .... Dinosaur National Monument (SAUS)
DNM .... Director of Naval Manning [*British military*] (DMA)
DNM .... Distance to Nearest Male Plant [*Botany*]
DNM .... Distribution Network Module (SAUS)
DNM .... Dreyfus New York Municipal Income Fund [*AMEX symbol*] (CTT)
DNM .... Dreyfus N.Y. Muni Income [*AMEX symbol*] (TTSB)
DNM .... Dulce [*New Mexico*] [*Seismograph station code, US Geological Survey*] [*Closed*] (SEIS)
D NM .... United States District Court for the District of New Mexico (DLA)
DNMA .... Maiduguri [*Nigeria*] [*ICAO location identifier*] (ICLI)
DNMC .... United States Naval Medical Center, Bethesda, MD [*Library symbol*] [*Library of Congress*] (LCLS)
DNMES .... Dynamic Non-Member Economies (SAUO)
DN-MHi .... United States Department of the Navy, United States Marine Corps Historical Library, Washington, DC [*Library symbol*] [*Library of Congress*] (LCLS)
DNMK .... Makurdi [*Nigeria*] [*ICAO location identifier*] (ICLI)
DNMM .... Division of Nuclear Materials Management [*AEC*]
DNMM .... Lagos/Murtala Muhammed [*Nigeria*] [*ICAO location identifier*] (ICLI)
DNMO .... Director of Naval Management and Organization [*British military*] (DMA)
DNMO .... District Naval Material Office
DNMOV .... Directorate of Naval Movements (SAUO)
DNMP .... Deoxynucleoside Monophosphate [*Biochemistry*]
dNMP .... Desoxyribonucleoside Monophosphate (SAUS)
DNMP .... Director of Naval Manpower Planning [*British*]
DNMP .... Domestic Net Material Product (ACAE)
DNMR .... Deuterium Nuclear Magnetic Resonance (DB)
DNMR .... Director of Naval Manpower Requirements [*or Resources*] [*British*]
DNMR .... Document Number Master Record (ACAE)
DNMR .... Double Nuclear Magnetic Resonance (SAUS)
DNMR .... dynamic NMR (SAUS)
DNMR .... Dynamic Nuclear Magnetic Resonance
DN-MRC .... United States Department of the Navy, Naval Regional Medical Center, San Francisco, CA [*Library symbol*] [*Library of Congress*] (LCLS)
DN-MRI .... United States Department of the Navy, Naval Medical Research Institute, Bethesda, MD [*Library symbol*] [*Library of Congress*] (LCLS)
DNMRT .... Duncan's New Multiple Range Test (OA)
DNMS .... Datennetz-Management-Software (SAUS)
DNMS .... Delayed Neutron Monitoring Subsystem [*Nuclear energy*] (NRCH)
DNMS .... Delayed Nonmatch to Sample [*Test design*]
DNMS .... Dial Network Management System [*Telecommunications*]
DNMS .... Director of Naval Medical Services (SAUO)
DNMS .... Division of Nuclear Materials Safeguards [*AEC*]
DN-MS .... United States Department of the Navy, Naval Medical School, Bethesda, MD [*Library symbol*] [*Library of Congress*] (LCLS)
DNMSP .... Director of Naval Manpower Structure Planning [*British military*] (DMA)
DNMT .... Director of Naval Manning and Training [*British*]
DNMTB .... Drift Nets Mending Trade Board (SAUO)
DNN .... Dalton, GA [*Location identifier*] [*FAA*] (FAAL)
DNN .... Dannevirke [*New Zealand*] [*Seismograph station code, US Geological Survey*] [*Closed*] (SEIS)
DNN .... Dansk Normal Nul [*Oceanography*]
DNN .... Dinitronaphthalene (SAUS)
DN-NPG .... United States Department of the Navy, Naval Weapons Laboratory, Technical Library, Dahlgreen, VA [*Library symbol*] [*Library of Congress*] (LCLS)
DNNS .... Dinitronaphtholsulfonic Acid [*Organic chemistry*]
DNNSA .... Dinonyl Naphthalene Sulfonic Acid (SAUS)
DNO .... Alinord [*Italy*] [*ICAO designator*] (FAAC)
DNO .... Debit Note Only
DNO .... Descending Node Orbit (MCD)
DNO .... Director of Naval Operations
DNO .... Director of Naval Ordnance [*Admiralty*] [*Obsolete*] [*British*]
DNO .... District Naval Officer [*British*] (ADA)
DNO .... District Nursing Officer
DNO .... Do Not Operate (COE)
DNO .... United States Naval Observatory, Washington, DC [*OCLC symbol*] (OCLC)
DNO .... Divisional Nursing Officer (ODA)
DNOA .... Director of Naval Officer Appointments [*British*]
DN-Ob .... United States Department of the Navy, Naval Observatory, Washington, DC [*Library symbol*] [*Library of Congress*] (LCLS)
DNOC .... Dinitro-O-Cresol (SAUS)
DNOC .... Dinitro-ortho-Cresol [*Also, DN*] [*Herbicide*]
DNOCHP .... Dinitrocyclohexylphenol [*Insecticide*]
DNOCHP .... Dinitro-O-Cyclohexylphenol (SAUS)
DNOCP .... Dinocap (LDT)
DN-OGC .... United States Department of the Navy, Office of the General Counsel, Arlington, VA [*Library symbol*] [*Library of Congress*] (LCLS)
DN-OL .... United States Department of the Navy, Naval Ordnance Laboratory, White Oak, MD [*Library symbol*] [*Library of Congress*] (LCLS)
DNOM .... Director of Naval Oceanography and Meteorology [*British*]
DN-ONR .... United States Department of the Navy, Office of Naval Research, Arlington, VA [*Library symbol*] [*Library of Congress*] (LCLS)
DNOP .... Di-n-octylphthalat (SAUS)
DNOP .... Director of Naval Officer Procurement
DNOR .... Directorate of Naval Operational Requirements [*British*]
DNOR .... Directorate of Naval Organization (SAUO)
DN-Ord .... United States Department of the Navy, Naval Ordnance Systems Command, Arlington,VA [*Library symbol*] [*Library of Congress*] (LCLS)
DNOS .... Director of Naval Operational Studies [*British*]
DNOS .... Distributed Network Operating System (TIMI)
DNOS .... Oshogbo [*Nigeria*] [*ICAO location identifier*] (ICLI)
DNOSBP .... Dinitro-ortho-secondary-butylphenol [*Also, DNBP, DNSBP*] [*Herbicide*]
DNOSBP .... Dinitro-O-Sec-Butylphenol (SAUS)
DNOT .... Directorate of Naval Operations and Trade [*British*]
D-Notices .... Defense Notices (SAUS)
D-notice system ... British Defense-notice system for protecting state secrets with the cooperation of the press (SAUS)
DnOU .... Odense Universitet [*Odense University*], Odense, Denmark [*Library symbol*] [*Library of Congress*] (LCLS)
DNOX .... Dry Oxides of Nitrogen
DNP .... Dai Nippon Printing Co. Ltd. [*Publisher*] [*Japan*]
DNP .... Dang [*Nepal*] [*Airport symbol*] (OAG)
DNP .... Declared National Program [*to share oceanographic data with other nations*]
DNP .... Deferred Nesting Program (MCD)
DNP .... Democratic Nationalist Party [*1959-1966*] [*Malta*] [*Political party*] (PPE)
DNP .... Denpasar [*Indonesia*] [*Seismograph station code, US Geological Survey*] (SEIS)
DNP .... Deoxyribonucleoprotamine [*Biochemistry*]
DNP .... Deoxyribonucleoprotein [*Biochemistry*]
DNP .... Dicrotic Notch Pressure (SAUS)
DNP .... Did Not Play

DNP .... Diiodonitrophenol [*Pharmacology*]
DNP .... Dinitrophenol [*Organic chemistry*]
Dnp .... Dinitrophenyl [*Biochemistry*]
DNP .... Dinitrophenylhydrazine [*Also, DNPH*] [*Organic chemistry*]
DNP .... Dinitropyrene (LDT)
DNP .... Dinonyl Phthalate [*Organic chemistry*]
DNP .... Direct Nitride Passivated (SAUS)
DNP .... direct nitride passivated base-surface (SAUS)
DNP .... Distributed Network Processing (VLIE)
DNP .... Division of Nuclear Physics (SAUS)
DNP .... Do Not Publish
DNP .... Drill Nonpay Status [*Naval Reserve*]
DNP .... Dry Non-Polish
DNP .... Duff/Phelps Util Income [*NYSE symbol*] (TTSB)
DNP .... Duff/Phelps Utilities Income [*NYSE symbol*] (SPSG)
DNP .... Dummy Nose Plug
DNP .... Dynamic Nuclear Polarization
DNPA .... Dinitropropyl Acrylate [*An explosive*]
DNPA .... Di-normal-propylamine [*Organic chemistry*]
DNPA .... Directorate of Naval Pay Accounting (SAUO)
DNPA .... Division of Nutrition and Physical Activity (SAUS)
DNPBA .... Dinitroperoxybenzoic Acid [*Organic chemistry*]
DNPC .... Denpac Corp. [*NASDAQ symbol*] (COMM)
DNPC .... Dinitro-p-cresol [*Organic chemistry*]
DNPC .... Directorate of Naval Programme Control (SAUO)
DN-PC .... United States Department of the Navy, Naval Photographic Center, Washington, DC [*Library symbol*] [*Library of Congress*] (LCLS)
DNPCT .... Direction National de Production Cartographique et Topographique [*Mali*] (GEOI)
DNPD .... Di(naphthyl)phenylenediamine [*Organic chemistry*]
DN-Pers .... United States Department of the Navy, Bureau of Naval Personnel, Washington, DC [*Library symbol*] [*Library of Congress*] (LCLS)
DNPG .... Defense Navigation Planning Group [*DoD*]
DNPG .... Digital Networks Product Group (SAUS)
DNPH .... Dinitrophenylhydrazine [*Also, DNP*] [*Organic chemistry*]
DN-PIC .... United States Department of the Navy, Naval Intelligence Support Center, Washington, DC [*Library symbol*] [*Library of Congress*] (LCLS)
DNP-KLK .... Dinitrophenylated Keyhole Limpet Hemocyanin [*Immunology*]
DNPlans .... Directorate of Naval Plans [*British*]
DNPM .... Dinitrophenylmorphine [*Biochemistry*] (AAMN)
DNPO .... Directorate of Naval Plans and Operations (SAUO)
DNPO .... Port Harcourt [*Nigeria*] [*ICAO location identifier*] (ICLI)
DNPP .... Dinitrophenyl Phosphate [*Organic chemistry*]
DNPP .... Director, Navy Program Planning
DNPP .... Dominus Noster Papa Pontifex [*Our Lord the Pope*] [*Latin*]
DN-PP .... United States Department of the Navy, Naval Ordnance Station, Indian Head, MD [*Library symbol*] [*Library of Congress*] (LCLS)
DNPPG .... Department of the Navy Policy and Planning Guidance (MCD)
DNPPS .... Director, Navy Publications and Printing Service (SAUO)
DNPR .... Director, Navy Petroleum Reserves
DNPr .... National Press Club, Washington, DC [*Library symbol*] [*Library of Congress*] (LCLS)
DNPS .... Dresden Nuclear Power Station (NRCH)
DNPS .... United States National Park Service, National Capital Park Library, Washington, DC [*Library symbol*] [*Library of Congress*] (LCLS)
DNPS-NR .... United States National Park Service, National Register Division, Washington, DC [*Library symbol*] [*Library of Congress*] (LCLS)
DNPT .... Dinitrosopentamethylenetetramine [*Organic chemistry*]
DNPTS .... Director of Naval Physical Training and Sport [*British*]
DNPV .... National Paint, Varnish, and Lacquer Association, Inc., Washington, DC [*Library symbol*] [*Library of Congress*] (LCLS)
DNPW .... Directorship of National Parks and Wildlife (SAUO)
DNPyr .... Dinitropyridyl (SAUS)
DNPZ .... Dinitrosopiperazine [*Animal carcinogen*]
DNQ .... Deniliquin [*Australia*] [*Airport symbol*] (OAG)
DNQ .... Diazonaphthoquinone [*Organic chemistry*]
DNQ .... Did Not Qualify [*Automobile racing*]
DNQX .... Dinitroquinoxalinedione [*Organic chemistry*]
DNR .... Daily News Record [*A publication*] [*New York, NY*] (WDMC)
DNR .... Data Network Routing (VLIE)
DNR .... Daunorubicin [*Daunomycin*] [*Also, D, DRB, R*] [*Antineoplastic drug*]
DNR .... Democrats of the New Republic (SAUS)
DNR .... Denbury Resources [*NYSE symbol*] (SG)
DNR .... Department of National Revenue (SAUO)
DNR .... Department of Natural Resources [*Department of Agriculture*] [*Sometimes facetiously referred to as Department of Nuts with Rifles*]
DNR .... Device Not Ready (VLIE)
D/NR .... Dextrose to Nitrogen Ratio (AAMN)
D/N r .... dextrose-to-nitrogen ratio (SAUS)
DNR .... Dialed-Number Recorder (SEWL)
DNR .... Diana Resources Ltd. [*Vancouver Stock Exchange symbol*]
DNR .... Did Not Report (OICC)
DNR .... Did Not Respond
DNR .... Differential Negative Resistance (SAUS)
DNR .... Digital Noise Reduction [*Television*]
DNR .... Digital Number Recorder (SAUS)
DNR .... Dinard [*France*] [*Airport symbol*] (OAG)
DNR .... Diner
DNR .... Director of National Recruiting (SAUS)
DNR .... Director of Naval Recruiting [*British*]
DNR .... Director of the Naval Reserve (DOMA)
DNR .... Division of Natural Resources (SAUO)
DNR .... Division of Naval Reactors [*Energy Research and Development Administration*]
DNR .... Does Not Run
DNR .... Domain Name Resolver (SAUS)
dnr .... Donor [*MARC relator code*] [*Library of Congress*] (LCCP)
DNR .... Do Not Reduce
DNR .... Do Not Renew [*A policy*] [*Insurance*]
DNR .... Do Not Report [*Medicine*] (DAVI)
DNR .... Do Not Resuscitate [*Medicine*] (EDAA)
DNR .... Dorsal Nerve Root [*Medicine*] (MELL)
DNR .... Dovas Nordiske Rad [*Nordic Council for the Deaf - NCD*] (EAIO)
DNR .... Downrange [*NASA*] (KSC)
DNR .... Dynamair Aviation, Inc. [*Canada*] [*ICAO designator*] (FAAC)
DNR .... Dynamic Noise Reduction [*Video technology*]
DNRC .... Democritus Nuclear Research Center [*Greece*]
DNRC .... Department of Natural Resources and Conservation (AUEG)
DNRC .... Domain Name Rights Coalition (SAUS)
DNRC .... United States Nuclear Regulatory Commission, Washington, DC [*Library symbol*] [*Library of Congress*] (LCLS)
DNRE .... Department of Natural Resources and Energy (SAUS)
DNRE .... Department of Natural Resources and Environment (SAUS)
DNREC .... Department of Natural Resources and Environmental Control (SAUO)
DNREP .... Department of Natural Resources and Environmental Protection [*Kentucky*] (GEOI)
DNRH .... Director of Naval Records and History
DNRIU .... Digital Net Radio Interface Unit (MCD)
DN-RL .... United States Department of the Navy, Naval Research Library, Arlington, VA [*Library symbol*] [*Library of Congress*] (LCLS)
DnRoU .... Roskilde Universitet [*Roskilde University*], Roskilde, Denmark [*Library symbol*] [*Library of Congress*] (LCLS)
DNRP .... Department of Natural Resource Protection
DNRQ .... Did Not Receive Questionnaire
DNRS .... Day/Night Range Sight (SAUS)
DNRS .... Day/Night Reflex Sight [*Military*] (INF)
DNRT .... Digital Noise Riding Threshold (SEWL)
DN-RTPC .... United States Department of the Navy, Navy Training Publication Center, Pensacola, FL [*Library symbol*] [*Library of Congress*] (LCLS)
DNRZ .... Delayed Non-Return-to Zero (SAUS)
DNS .... DACOM-Net Service [*A packet-switching public data network*]
dns .... Dansyl [*As substituent on nucleoside*] [*Biochemistry*]
DNS .... Dansyl,5-Dimethylaminonaphthalene-1-Sulfonyl (SAUS)
DNS .... Data Network Service (ACAE)
DNS .... Data Network Signalling (SAUS)
DNS .... Data Network System (ACAE)
DNS .... Decentralized Data Processing Network System (BUR)
DNS .... Decimal Numbering System (SAUS)
DNS .... Decimal Number System (AAG)
DNS .... Deflected Nasal Septum [*Medicine*]
DNS .... Denison, IA [*Location identifier*] [*FAA*] (FAAL)
DNS .... Denniston [*New Zealand*] [*Seismograph station code, US Geological Survey*] [*Closed*] (SEIS)
DNS .... Denoyl Sebacate (SAUS)
DNS .... Dense (FAAC)
DNS .... Department of National Savings [*British*]
DNS .... Development Needs Analysis
DNS .... Deviated Nasal Septum [*Otorhinolaryngology*] (DAVI)
D/NS .... Dextrose in Normal Saline [*Pharmacology*] (DAVI)
DNS .... Dextrose in Normal Solution [*Medicine*] (MELL)
DNS .... Diaphragm Nerve Stimulation
DNS .... Did Not Show [*Medicine*]
DNS .... Did Not Show for appointment (SAUS)
DNS .... Did Not Start [*Racing*] (IYR)
DNS .... Did Not Suit
DNS .... Diffuse Neuroendocrine System [*Also, DNE*]
Dns .... Dimethylaminonaphthalene Sulfonyl (SAUS)
DNS .... Dimethylaminonaphthalenesulfonyl [*Also, Dansyl, dns*] [*Biochemical analysis*]
DNS .... Dinitrosalicylic [*Organic chemistry*]
DNS .... Dinonyl Sebacate [*Organic chemistry*]
D-NS .... Diplomate, American Board of Neurological Surgery (DHSM)
DNS .... Direct Network Subscriber (SAUS)
DNS .... Direct NICS Subscriber (SAUS)
DNS .... Direct Numerical Simulation (AAEL)
DNS .... Directorate of Naval Signals [*British*]
DNS .... Director of Naval Signals [*British military*] (DMA)
DNS .... Director of Nuclear Safety [*Air Force*]
DNS .... Director of Nursing Services (IDYL)
DNS .... Director of the Naval Service [*Canada, 1910-1926*]
DNS .... Discrete Network Simulation
DNS .... Diseases of the Nervous System [*Journal*] [*Medicine*] (EDAA)
DNS .... Dispatch News Service (IIA)
DNS .... Distributed Naming Service [*Computer science*] (GART)
DNS .... Distributed Nesting System (MCD)
DNS .... Distributed Network Software (SAUS)
DNS .... Distributed Network Supervisor (SAUS)
DNS .... Distributed Network System
DNS .... Distributor Nesting System [*Military*]
DNS .... Doctor of Nursing Science
DNS .... Domain Name/Naming Server/Service (SAUS)
DNS .... Domain Name Scheme (SAUS)
DNS .... Domain Name Server [*Computer science*]
DNS .... Domain Name Service
DNS .... Domain Name System [*or Service*] [*Computer science*]
DNS .... Domain Naming Server (SAUS)

DNS .... Domain Naming Service (SAUS)
DNS .... Domain Naming System
DNS .... Do Not Set [*Printing*] (DICI)
DNS .... Dopler Navigation System (SAUS)
DNS .... Doppler Navigation Sensor
DNS .... Doppler Navigation System
DNS .... Dowling's English Bail Court Reports, New Series [*1841-43*] [*A publication*] (DLA)
DNS .... Dow. New Series [*Dow and Clark, English House of Lords Cases*] [*A publication*] (DLA)
DNS .... Downs [*Maps and charts*] (ROG)
DNS .... Dynamic Noise Suppression [*Electronics*]
DNS .... Dysplastic Nevus Syndrome [*Medicine*]
DNSA .... Dimethylaminonaphthalenesulfonamide [*Organic chemistry*]
DNSA .... Dinitrosalicylate [*Organic chemistry*]
DNSA .... Diploma in Nursing Administration (ADA)
DNSA .... Diploma in Nursing Service Administration (SAUS)
DNSA .... Director of National Security Affairs (SAUS)
DN-SA .... United States Department of the Navy, Naval Supply Systems Command, Alexandria, VA [*Library symbol*] [*Library of Congress*] (LCLS)
DNS Acid .... Dimethylamino Naphthalene Sulfonic Acid (SAUS)
DNSAP .... Danmarks Nationalsocialistisk Arbejdersparti [*National Socialist Worker's Party of Denmark (or Danish NAZI Party)*] (PPE)
DNSAR .... Sons of the American Revolution, National Society Library, Washington, DC [*Library symbol*] [*Library of Congress*] (LCLS)
DNSARC .... Department of the Navy System Acquisition Review Council (MCD)
DNS-B .... Daten-Netz-Signalisierung Typ B (SAUS)
DNSBP .... Dinitro-ortho-secondary-butylphenol [*Also, DNBP, DNOSBP*] [*Herbicide*]
DNSC .... Data Network Service Center (or Centre) (SAUS)
DNSC .... Defense National Stockpile Center
DNSC .... Defense Nuclear Facilities Safety Board
DNSC .... Democratic National Strategy Council (EA)
DNSC .... Digital Network Service Centre (NITA)
DNSC .... Dimethylaminonaphthalenesulfonyl Chloride [*Also, DANS*] [*Fluorescent reagent*]
DNSC .... Director of Naval Service Conditions [*British*]
DNSc .... Doctor of Nursing Science (GAGS)
DNSDC .... Defence National Storage and Distribution Centre [*Australia*]
DNSDP .... Defense Navigation Satellite Demonstration Program (ACAE)
DNSDP .... Defense Navigation Satellite Development Program (MCD)
DnsePc .... Dense Pac Microsystems, Inc. [*Associated Press*] (SAG)
DNSF .... Democratic National Salvation Front [*Romania*] [*Political party*] (ECON)
DNSF .... National Science Foundation, Washington, DC [*Library symbol*] [*Library of Congress*] (LCLS)
DN-Sh .... United States Department of the Navy, Naval Ship Systems Command, Washington, DC [*Library symbol*] [*Library of Congress*] (LCLS)
DNSI .... Direct-Normal Solar Irradiance (ARMP)
DNSIX .... Defense Network Security Information Exchange (SEWL)
DNSIX .... DODIIS Network Security for Information Exchange (SAUO)
DNSLP .... Downslope (FAAC)
DNS-MIM .... Distributed Network Server - Media Interface Module [*Cabletron Systems, Inc.*]
DNSO .... Defense Network Systems Organization (VERA)
DNSO .... Domain Name Supporting Organization (SAUS)
DNSO .... Sokoto [*Nigeria*] [*ICAO location identifier*] (ICLI)
DNSP .... Doctor Did Not See Patient [*Medicine*] (EDAA)
DNSPD .... Divisions of Naval Staff Plans Division [*British*]
DNSPRB .... DOC [*Department of Commerce*]/NASA Satellite Program Review Board (NOAA)
DNS-PS .... Dimethylaminonaphthalenesulfonyl Phosphatidylserine [*Biochemistry*]
DNSR .... Directorate of Nuclear Safety Research USAF (SAUS)
DNSR .... Director of Nuclear Safety Research [*Air Force*]
DNSS .... Defense Navigation Satellite System [*Formerly, SSPN*] (MCD)
DNSS .... Doppler Navigation Satellite System (PDAA)
DNST .... Daughters of the Nile, Supreme Temple (EA)
DNST .... Directorate Naval Shore Telecommunications (SAUS)
DNSTAN .... Directorate of Naval Standardization (SAUO)
DNSTRM .... Downstream (FAAC)
DNSVT .... Digital Non-Secure Voice Terminal (ACAE)
DNSW .... Day Night Switching Equipment [*Telecommunications*]
DNSy .... Directorate of Naval Security [*British*]
DNSy .... Director of Naval Security (SAUS)
DNT .... Delta Air Lines 8.125% Nts [*NYSE symbol*] (SG)
Dnt .... Dent (SAUS)
DNT .... Denton [*Texas*] [*Seismograph station code, US Geological Survey*] [*Closed*] (SEIS)
DNT .... Dermonecrotic Toxin [*Immunology*]
DNT .... Desmethylnortriplyline (SAUS)
DNT .... Detent (SAUS)
DNT .... Developing Nations Tractor [*Ford Motor Co.*]
DNT .... Device Name Table (IAA)
DNT .... Did Not Test [*Medicine*]
DNT .... Digital Network Terminator
DNT .... Dinitrotoluene [*Organic chemistry*]
DNT .... Dinitrotrifluoromethyl [*Organic chemistry*]
DNT .... Direccion Nacional de Topografia [*Uruguay*] (GEOI)
DNT .... Directorate of Naval Training (SAUO)
DNT .... Director of Naval Telecommunications
DNT .... Director of Naval Training [*British military*] (DMA)
DNT .... Downtime [*Computer science*] [*Telecommunications*]
DNT .... Dragon Night Tracker [*Military*] (MCD)
DNT .... National Trust for Historic Preservation, Washington, DC [*Library symbol*] [*Library of Congress*] (LCLS)
DNT .... Natitingou [*Dahomey*] [*Airport symbol*] (AD)
DNTA .... Dinitrosoterephthalamide [*Organic chemistry*]
DNTC .... Dimethyl-Amino-Naphthyl Isothio-Cyanate [*Medicine*] (EDAA)
DNTh .... Diploma in Natural Therapeutics [*British*]
DNTKFX .... DownTrack Fix (GAVI)
DNTL .... Dental
DNTM .... Disseminated Nontuberculous Mycobacterial Infection
DN-TMB .... United States Department of the Navy, Naval Ship Research and Development Center, Carderock, MD [*Library symbol*] [*Library of Congress*] (LCLS)
Dntn .... downtown (SAUS)
DNTO .... Danish National Travel Office (SAUS)
DNTO .... District Naval Transport Officer (SAUO)
DNTO .... Divisional Naval Transport Officer [*British military*] (DMA)
DNTP .... Deoxynucleoside Triphosphate [*Biochemistry*]
dNTP .... Deoxyribonucleoside Triphosphate [*Medicine*] (EDAA)
DNTP .... Deoxyribonucleoside Triphosphate (SAUS)
DNTP .... Diethyl Nitrophenyl Phosphorothioate [*Insecticide*]
DNTP .... Parathion (GNE)
DNTPS .... Deoxyribonucleoside Triphosphat (SAUS)
DNTRD .... Denaturated (SAUS)
DNTRD .... Denatured
DNTS .... Digital Data Exchange Network Testing System (SAUS)
DNTS .... Director, Naval Transportation Service [*Later, CNTS*]
DNTSS .... Day/Night Thermal Sight System (SAUS)
DNTSTRY .... Dentistry
DNU .... Democracy Now in Ulster [*Northern Ireland*] [*An association*]
DNU .... Denison University, Granville, OH [*OCLC symbol*] (OCLC)
DNU .... Digital Networking Unit [*Telecommunications*] (ACRL)
DNU .... Directorio Nacional Unido [*Guerrilla forces*] [*Honduras*] (EY)
DNU .... Do Not Use
DNU .... Dundee Resources [*Vancouver Stock Exchange symbol*]
DNUG .... Deutsche Notes User Group (SAUS)
D-NuM .... Diplomate, American Board of Nuclear Medicine (DHSM)
DNV .... Danville [*Illinois*] [*Airport symbol*] (OAG)
DNV .... Detector Number Valid (ACAE)
DNV .... Don Airlines [*Former USSR*] [*FAA designator*] (FAAC)
DNV .... Dorsal Nucleus of Vagus Nerve [*Medicine*] (EDAA)
DNVO .... DeNovo [*NASDAQ symbol*] (SAG)
DNVOF .... De Novo Corp. [*NASDAQ symbol*] (TTSB)
DNVP .... Deutschnationale Volkspartei [*German National People's Party*]
DNVT .... Digital Nonsecure Voice Telephone (DWSG)
DNVT .... Digital Nonsecure Voice Terminal (MCD)
DNW .... Dedicated Network (SAUS)
DNW .... Directorate of Naval Warfare [*British*]
DNW .... Dual Narrow White [*Tire design*]
DNW .... Dunoir, WY [*Location identifier*] [*FAA*] (FAAL)
DNW .... United States National War College, Fort McNair, Washington, DC [*Library symbol*] [*Library of Congress*] (LCLS)
DNWA .... Director, Naval Warfare Analysis (SAUO)
DNWC .... Director of Naval Weapons Contracts [*British*]
dnwind .... downwind (SAUS)
DNWM .... National Museum of Women in the Arts, Washington, DC [*Library symbol*] [*Library of Congress*] (LCLS)
DNWND .... Downwind [*Aviation*] (FAAC)
DNWR .... Darling National Wildlife Refuge (SAUS)
DNWR .... Delta National Wildlife Refuge (SAUS)
DNWR .... Desert National Wildlife Range
DNWR .... Desert National Wildlife Refuge (SAUS)
DNWR .... Desert NWR (SAUS)
DNWS .... Director of Naval Weather Service (SAUS)
DNWS .... Director of Naval Weather Service, Ministry of Defence [*British*] (NATG)
DNWS .... Discrete Network Simulation
DNX .... DNX Corp. [*Associated Press*] (SAG)
DNX .... Dynamic Network X connect (SAUS)
DNXX .... DNX Corp. [*NASDAQ symbol*] (SPSG)
DNY .... Danish Navy [*ICAO designator*] (FAAC)
DNY .... Delancey, NY [*Location identifier*] [*FAA*] (FAAL)
DNY .... Dersam [*New York*] [*Seismograph station code, US Geological Survey*] (SEIS)
DNY .... Destiny Resources Ltd. [*Vancouver Stock Exchange symbol*]
DNY .... Donnelley [*R. R.*] & Sons Co. [*NYSE symbol*] (SPSG)
DNY .... Donnelley(RR)& Sons [*NYSE symbol*] (TTSB)
DN-YD .... United States Department of the Navy, Naval Facilities Engineering Command, Washington, DC [*Library symbol*] [*Library of Congress*] (LCLS)
DNYO .... Yola [*Nigeria*] [*ICAO location identifier*] (ICLI)
DNZ .... Darned Near Zero (SAUS)
DNZA .... Zaria [*Nigeria*] [*ICAO location identifier*] (ICLI)
Do .... Byk-Gulden Lomberg [*Germany*] [*Research code symbol*]
DO .... Compania Dominicana de Aviacion SA [*ICAO designator*] (OAG)
DO .... Dangerous Occurrence (HEAS)
D-O .... Dansgaard-Oeschger [*Climatic cycles*]
D-O .... Dansgaard-Oeschger events (SAUO)
DO .... Dark Operated (SAUS)
DO .... Data Operation (SAUS)
DO .... Data Organization (SAUS)
DO .... Data Output [*Computer science*] (IEEE)
D/O .... Daughter Of [*Genealogy*]
DO .... Day-Old
DO .... Day Order [*Investment term*]
DO .... Decanter Oil [*Petroleum technology*]

D-O .... Decimal to Octal [*Computer science*] (IEEE)
DO .... Defence Operations [*British*] [*World War II*]
DO .... Defense Order
DO .... Deferred Ordinary (ADA)
DO .... Deformation Optical (SAUS)
DO .... Delegation Order [*Legal term*] (DLA)
d/o .... Delivery Order (EBF)
D/O .... Delivery Order [*Business term*]
DO .... Delta Omicron [*An association*] (NTPA)
DO .... Demand Operation (SAUS)
DO .... Demi Official [*Military*] [*British*]
DO .... Demolition Order (ROG)
DO .... Dental Officer
DO .... Dent Out (SAUS)
DO .... Department of Oceanography (SAUS)
D/O .... Depot Overhaul (MCD)
DO .... Depression Obvious [*Psychology*]
DO .... Deputy for Operations
DO .... Derived Operand (MCD)
DO .... Designated Official (NRCH)
DO .... Design fice (SAUS)
DO .... Design Objective (IEEE)
DO .... Design Office (SAUO)
DO .... Design Order (TIMI)
DO .... Desirable Objective (KSC)
DO .... Deuterium Oxide (SAUS)
DO .... Development Officer (SAUO)
DO .... Deviating Oscillator
DO .... Diamine Oxidase [*Also, DAO*] [*An enzyme*]
DO .... Diamond Offshore Drilling [*NYSE symbol*] (TTSB)
DO .... Diamond Offshore Drillings, Inc. [*NYSE symbol*] (SAG)
do .... Dictum [*As Before*] [*Latin*] (DAVI)
d/o .... Died Of (DAVI)
DO .... Diesel Oil
DO .... Digital Ortho (GEOI)
DO .... Digital Output [*Computer science*]
DO .... Digoxin (DB)
DO .... Diode Outline (IAA)
DO .... Diploma in Ophthalmology
DO .... Diploma in Osteopathy [*British*]
D-O .... Directive-Organic [*Designation for biologically oriented, authoritarian psychiatrists*]
DO .... Direct Obligation
DO .... Direct Operand (SAUS)
DO .... Directorate of Operations (SAUO)
DO .... Direct Order
DO .... Director of Operations
DO .... Director's Office
DO .... Direct Oxidation (SAUS)
DO .... Disability Officer
DO .... Disbursing Officer
DO .... Disbursing Order
DO .... Discrete Optimization (SAUO)
DO .... Discrete Output [*Computer science*] (KSC)
D/O .... Disorder (DAVI)
DO .... Disponent Owner (SAUS)
DO .... Dissolved Oxygen
DO .... Disto-Occlusal [*Dentistry*]
DO .... Distributed Objects [*Computer science*] (VERA)
DO .... Distribution Office (DCTA)
DO .... District Office [*or Officer*]
DO .... Ditto (AFM)
Do .... Ditto (MIST)
do .... Ditto (WDMC)
DO .... Diving Officer
DO .... Divisional Officer [*Agricultural Development and Advisory Service*] [*British*]
DO .... Divisional Orders
DO .... Division of Oceanography (SAUO)
DO .... Dock Office (ROG)
DO .... Dock Operations (DS)
DO .... Doctor of Ophthalmology
DO .... Doctor of Optometry
DO .... Doctor of Oratory
DO .... Doctor of Osteopathic Medicine (SAUO)
DO .... Doctor of Osteopathy
DO .... Doctor's Orders
DO .... Dollar [*Monetary unit*]
DO .... Dolly Out [*Cinematography*] (NTCM)
Do .... Dominance [*Psychology*]
DO .... Dominican (SAUS)
DO .... Dominicana de Aviacion [*ICAO designator*] (AD)
DO .... Dominican Republic [*ANSI two-letter standard code*] (CNC)
Do .... Dominicus de Sancto Geminiano [*Flourished, 1407-09*] [*Authority cited in pre-1607 legal work*] (DSA)
DO .... Dominion Observatory (SAUS)
DO .... Dominions Office [*British*]
DO .... Donor [*Searchable field, Dialog*] [*Information service or system*] (NITA)
DO .... Donors' Offspring [*An association*] (EA)
DO .... Doppler (IAA)
DO .... Dora Explorations Ltd. [*Vancouver Stock Exchange symbol*]
DO .... Doric Corp. (SAUO)
DO .... Dornier [*German airplane type*]
DO .... Dornier-Werke GmbH [*Germany*] [*ICAO aircraft manufacturer identifier*] (ICAO)
Do .... Dorsetshire Regiment (SAUO)
DO .... Double Offset [*Engineering*]
D/O .... Drain Out [*Removal of surgical drain*] (SPVS)
DO .... Drawing Office (WDAA)
DO .... Draw Out (KSC)
D/O .... Drop Off
DO .... Drop Out (SAUS)
DO .... Dropout (AAG)
DO .... Drug Overdose (MELL)
DO .... Drug Oxidation (MELL)
DO .... Drugs Only [*Medicine*] (DB)
do .... dual ownership (SAUS)
DO .... Due Out [*Army*]
DO .... Duty Officer [*Military*]
DO .... Dynamic Optimization (AAEL)
DO .... Dysbaric Osteonecrosis (SAUS)
DO .... Grammar Direct Object (ODA)
DO .... Oiselet [*Record label*] [*France*]
Do .... Oligophranic Detail [*Psychology*]
Do8 .... Dornier 228 [*Airplane code*]
DO-27 .... Dornier 6-passenger utility aircraft built in West Germany and also called Skyservant (SAUS)
DOA .... Compania Dominicana de Aviacion SA [*Dominican Republic*] [*ICAO designator*] (FAAC)
DOA .... Dasher Owners of America (EA)
DOA .... Data Origin Authentication (SAUS)
DoA .... Date of Admission [*Medicine*] (EDAA)
DOA .... Date of Admission [*Medicine*]
DOA .... Date of Admittance (SAUS)
DOA .... Date of Announcement (SAUS)
DOA .... Date of Arrival (SAUS)
DOA .... Date of Availability [*Military*] (AFM)
DOA .... Date of Contract Award (DNAB)
DOA .... Day of Admission (SAUS)
DOA .... Day of Ammunition
DOA .... Dead on Admission (SAUS)
DOA .... Dead-On Alignment [*Electronics*] (AAEL)
DOA .... Dead on Arrival [*Rock music group*]
DOA .... Dead on Arrival [*Medicine*]
DOA .... Defeat Opiate Addiction [*An association*]
DOA .... Degree Of Anoxicity [*Biology*]
DOA .... Delegation of Authority (MCD)
DOA .... Department of Agriculture
DoA .... Department of Agronomy (SAUS)
DOA .... Department of Army (SAUS)
DOA .... Department of the Army
DOA .... Depth of Anesthesia [*Medicine*] (DMAA)
DOA .... Dicks of America [*An association*] (EA)
DOA .... Difference of Arrival (ACAE)
DOA .... Differential Operational Amplifier [*Electronics*] (OA)
DOA .... Differential Optical Absorption [*Medicine*] (DMAA)
DOA .... Digital Output Adapter
DOA .... Dioctyl Adipate [*Also, DEHA*] [*Organic chemistry*]
doa .... direction of approach (SAUS)
DOA .... Direction of Arrival
DOA .... Directorate of Officer Appointments (SAUO)
DOA .... Director of Officer Appointments [*British military*] (DMA)
DOA .... Director of Operations and Administration (SAUO)
DOA .... Disabled Officers Association (EA)
doa .... disposal of assets (SAUS)
doa .... dissolved oxygen analysis (SAUS)
DOA .... Dissolved Oxygen Analyzer (DNAB)
DOA .... Distributed Office Application (SAUS)
DOA .... Doany [*Madagascar*] [*Airport symbol*] (OAG)
DOA .... Documents on Acceptance [*Banking*]
DOA .... Dominant Obstacle Allowance (MCD)
DOA .... Dominant Optic Atrophy [*Medicine*] (DMAA)
DOA .... Draft on Arrival (SAUS)
DOA .... Driver of Automobile (MAE)
DOA .... Duty Orbital Analyst (IAA)
DOA .... Organization of American States, Washington, DC [*OCLC symbol*] (OCLC)
DOA&E .... Department of Agriculture and Extension (SAUO)
DOAC .... Dubois Oleic Albumin Complex [*Microbiology*]
DOA-DRA .... Dead on Arrival Despite Resuscitation Attempt (MELL)
DOA-DRA .... Dead On Arrival Despite Resuscitative Attempts [*Emergency medicine*] (DAVI)
DOAE .... Defence Operational Analysis Establishment [*British*]
DOAE .... Department of Oriental Antiquities and Ethnology (SAUO)
DOAG .... Directed Ordered Acyclic Graph (SAUS)
DOAI .... Department of Agriculture (SAUO)
DOAI .... Department of Agriculture, Indonesia (SAUS)
DOAL .... Directorate of Airlift [*Air Force*] (MCD)
DOALOS .... Division for Ocean Affairs and the Law of the Sea [*United Nations*] (OSRA)
DOAM .... Distributed Office Application Model [*Telecommunications*] (OSI)
DOAMS .... Distant Object Attitude Measuring System (MCD)
DO/AO .... District Office/Area Office [*IRS*]
DOAO(FE) .... Defence Operational Analysis Organisation [*Far East*]
DOAP .... Daunorubicin, Oncovin [*Vincristine*], ara-C, Prednisone [*Antineoplastic drug regimen*]
DOAPI .... DOS Open Application Programming Interface (SAUS)
DOARS .... Donnelly Official Airline Reservation Service (SAA)

DOAS.......... Department of Administrative Services (SAUO)
DOAS.......... Department of Agriculture for Scotland (SAUO)
DOAS.......... Diesel Odor Analysis System
DOAS.......... Differential Optical Absorption Spectrometer
DOAS.......... Differential Optical Absorption Spectroscopy (SARE)
DOAS.......... Directorate of Aviation Stores (SAUO)
DOAS.......... Organization of American States, Washington, DC [*Library symbol*] [*Library of Congress*] (LCLS)
DOASL.......... Department of Agriculture, Sri Lanka (SAUO)
DOA/TOA.......... Direction of Arrival/Time of Arrival (MCD)
DOB.......... Data Output Bus [*Computer science*]
DOB.......... Date of Birth (STED)
DOB.......... Daughters of Bilitis [*Superseded by United Sisters*] (EA)
DOB.......... Daughters of Bosses
DOB.......... Day of Birth (SAUS)
DOB.......... Decent Old Buffer [*British*] [*Slang*]
DOB.......... Defense Office Building [*Pentagon*] (DNAB)
DOB.......... Defensive Operations Branch (SAUS)
DOB.......... Department of Energy, Bartlesville Energy Technology Center, Bartlesville, OK [*OCLC symbol*] (OCLC)
DOB.......... Deployed Operating Base (MCD)
DOB.......... Depth of Burial [*of explosives*]
DOB.......... Depth of Burst (NATG)
DOB.......... Detained on Board [*Referring to seamen*]
DOB.......... Diameter Outside Bark (SAUS)
dob.......... diameter overbark (SAUS)
DOB.......... Diesel Oil Bentonite (SAUS)
DOB.......... Dimethoxybromoamphetamine (DB)
DOB.......... Disbursed Operating Base (SAUS)
DOB.......... Discrete Out Blockhouse [*NASA*] (KSC)
DOB.......... Dispersed Operating Base [*Air Force*] (AFM)
DOB.......... Dobrolet Airlines [*Russian Federation*] [*ICAO designator*] (FAAC)
DOB.......... Dobutamine [*Pharmacology*] (DAVI)
DOB.......... Doctor's Order Book
DOB.......... Dombas [*Norway*] [*Geomagnetic observatory code*]
DOB.......... Duplication of Benefits (DEMM)
DOB.......... Dynamically Obtained Buffer (SAUS)
DOB.......... Marietta, GA [*Location identifier*] [*FAA*] (FAAL)
DOBA.......... Diploma of the Orthoptic Board of Australia
DOBANIAN... Descendants of Black African Natives in the American North [*Proposed appellation*]
DOBAS.......... Deployment Operation Bases - Activation and Support (SAUO)
DOBC.......... Diesel Oil, Bentonite, Cement [*Oil well drilling technology*]
DOBCP.......... bis-4-Decyloxybenziliden-2-chloro-1,4-phenylendiamin (SAUS)
dobe.......... Doberman Pinscher (ADWA)
DOBETA.......... Domestic Oil Burning Equipment Testing Association [*British*] (DI)
DOBG.......... Doughtie's Foods [*NASDAQ symbol*] (TTSB)
DOBIN.......... Dobbins, TX [*American Association of Railroads railroad junction routing code*]
DOBIS.......... Dortmunder Bibliothekssystem [*Dortmund Bibliographic Information System*] [*Cataloguing system developed in Germany*]
DOBIS/LIBIS... Dortmund Library System/Leuven Library System (SAUS)
DOBIS/LIBIS... IBM Integrated Library System (SAUS)
DOBP.......... Dodecyloxyhydroxybenzophenone [*Organic chemistry*]
DOBQ.......... Doughtie's Foods, Inc. [*NASDAQ symbol*] (NQ)
DOBRIC.......... Docklands Business Research and Information Centre (SAUS)
DOBRO.......... Dopyera Brothers [*Guitar*] (IIA)
DOBS.......... Disk-On-Bearing System (SAUS)
dobs.......... observed d-spacing (SAUS)
DObst.......... Diploma in Obstetrics
DObstRCOG... Diploma in Obstetrics of the Royal College of Obstetricians and Gynaecologists (SAUS)
D Obst RCOG... Diploma in Obstetrics, Royal College of Obstetricians and Gynaecologists [*British*]
D Obst RCOG... Diplomate of the Royal College of Obstetricians and Gynaecologists (SAUS)
DO Buffer..... Data Out Buffer (SAUS)
DOC.......... Bureau of Documents; Dr. Pepper Company (SAUO)
DOC.......... DARCOM [*Development and Readiness Command, Army*] Operations Center (MCD)
DOC.......... Dartmouth Outing Club (SAUO)
DOC.......... Data and Operations Center (SAUS)
DOC.......... Data Operating Control
DOC.......... Data Operation Center (IAA)
DOC.......... Data, Operations, and Control
DOC.......... Data Optimizing Computer
DOC.......... Data Output Channel (MSA)
DOC.......... Data Output Clock (SAUS)
DOC.......... Date of Change
DOC.......... Date of Commencement
DOC.......... Date of Conception (MELL)
DOC.......... Datsun Owners Club [*Defunct*] (EA)
DoC.......... Deacon of the Chapel (WDAA)
DOC.......... Decimal to Octal Conversion
DOC.......... Deck of Cards (MCD)
DOC.......... Defence Operations Centre (SAUO)
DOC.......... Defense Operations Center
DOC.......... Degree of Control (MCD)
DOC.......... Degree of Cooperation [*Military*] (NVT)
DOC.......... Delayed Opening Chaff
DOC.......... Delay Opening Chaff (SAUS)
DOC.......... Delivery Order Contract (MIST)
DOC.......... Denominazione di Origine Controllata [*Italian wine designation*]
DOC.......... Deoxycholate [*Biochemistry*]
DOC.......... Deoxycorticoid (MAE)
DOC.......... Deoxycorticosterone [*Endocrinology*]
DOC.......... Department of Ceramics (SAUO)
DOC.......... Department of Circulation (SAUO)
DOC.......... Department of Commerce
DOC.......... Department of Communications [*Canada*]
DOC.......... Department of Conservation (SAUO)
D o C.......... Department of Correction (SAUS)
D o C.......... Department of Corrections (SAUS)
DOC.......... Depth of Cut [*Machining*]
DOC.......... Descend on Course [*Aviation*]
DOC.......... Designated Operational Coverage (DA)
DOC.......... Designed Operational Capabilities (SAUS)
DOC.......... Design Office Consortium (SAUS)
DOC.......... Design Operation Capability (MCD)
doc.......... desoxycorticosterone (SAUS)
DOC.......... Desoxycortone (SAUS)
DOC.......... Deterministic Optimal Control (SAUS)
DOC.......... Developmental Optical Correlator (PDAA)
DOC.......... Diabetes Out of Control [*Endocrinology*] (DAVI)
DOC.......... Dichromate Oxygen Consumed (EDCT)
DOC.......... Dictionary on Computer (SAUS)
DOC.......... Died of Other Causes [*Medicine*]
doc.......... diesel oil cement (SAUS)
DOC.......... Diethyloxacarbocyanine (SAUS)
DOC.......... Digital Optical Cassette [*Information retrieval*]
DOC.......... Digital Oscillator Chip [*Apple Computer, Inc.*]
DOC.......... Digital Output Channel (MCD)
DOC.......... Digital Output Control
DOC.......... Direct Operating Cost [*Accounting*]
DOC.......... Directorate of Camouflage (SAUO)
DOC.......... Directorate of Contracting [*Military*] (RDA)
DOC.......... Director of Camouflage [*British*]
DOC.......... Director of Contracts [*Military*] [*British*]
DOC.......... Disaster Operations Center (GNE)
DOC.......... Discipline Operations Center (SAUS)
DOC.......... Disk-Oriented Computer System (SAUS)
DOC.......... Display Operator Console (SAUS)
DOC.......... Dissolved Organic Carbon
DOC.......... Distributed Object Computing (RALS)
DOC.......... Distributed Objects Computing (SAUS)
DOC.......... Distributed Operator Console [*Environmental science*]
DOC.......... District Officer Commanding
DOC.......... District Officer in Command (SAUS)
DOC.......... Divested Operating Company
D o C.......... Division of Corrections (SAUS)
DOC.......... Division Officer Course (SAUS)
DOC.......... DOC (Doctors Ought to Care) (EA)
Doc.......... Docent (SAUS)
DOC.......... Docket
DOC.......... Doctor (EY)
Doc.......... Doctor (SHCU)
doc.......... Doctor (WDAA)
doc.......... doctoral (SAUS)
DOC.......... Doctor Blade [*Photogravure*] (DGA)
Doc.......... Doctores Bononienses [*Latin*] (DSA)
D-o-C.......... Doctors-on-Call (SAUS)
DOC.......... Doctors Opposing Circumcision (SAUO)
DOC.......... Doctors Ought to Care [*An association*] (EA)
DOC.......... Document [*or Documentation*] (AFM)
Doc.......... Document (TBD)
doc.......... Document (WDMC)
doc.......... Documentary (WDMC)
Doc.......... Documentation (AL)
DOC.......... Document of Compliance (SAUS)
DOC.......... Documentor (SAUS)
Doc.......... Documents (AL)
DOC.......... Douglas College Learning Resources Centre [*UTLAS symbol*]
DOC.......... Drawn-on-Cover [*Graphic arts*] (DGA)
DOC.......... Drive Other Car
DOC.......... Drive Other Cars [*Insurance*]
DOC.......... drop-off charge (SAUS)
DOC.......... Dropout Compensation (AGLO)
DOC.......... Dropout Compensator (NTCM)
DOC.......... Dropout Connector
DOC.......... Dr. Pepper Co. (IIA)
DOC.......... Drug of Choice (MELL)
DOC.......... Duchy of Cornwall (SAUO)
DOC.......... Due-Out Cancellation [*Military*] (AFM)
DOC.......... Dynamic Overload Control (SAUS)
DOC.......... Dynamic Overload Controls [*Telecommunications*]
DOC.......... Norsk Luftambulanse AS [*Norway*] [*ICAO designator*] (FAAC)
DOC.......... Oblate College, Washington, DC [*Library symbol*] [*Library of Congress*] (LCLS)
DOC.......... Region 4 Library Tracking System (SAUS)
DOC.......... US Department of Commerce (SAUS)
DOCA.......... Automatic Documentation Section (SAUS)
DOCA.......... Data of Current Appointment (SAUS)
DOCA.......... Date of Change of Accountability [*Military*]
DOCA.......... Date of Current Appointment [*Military*]
DOCA.......... Defense Orientation Conference Association (EA)
DOCA.......... Defense Orientation Conference Organization (SAUO)
DOCA.......... Deoxycorticosterone [*or Desoxycorticosterone*] Acetate [*Also, DCA*] [*Endocrinology*]
DoCA.......... Department of Communications and the Arts [*Australia*]
DOCA.......... Desoxycorticosterone acetate (SAUS)

DOCA .... Director of Overseas Civil Aviation [*British*]
DOCA .... Distributed Object Computing Architecture (GART)
DOCB .... Deep Ocean Cable Burial
Doc Bon .... Doctores Bononienses [*Latin*] (DSA)
DOCC .... Databank of Cancer Control (SAUS)
DOCC .... DCA Operations Control Complex (SAUS)
DOCC .... Deep Operations Command Cell (SAUS)
DOCC .... Defense Communications Agency Operations Center Complex
DOCC .... Digital Optronics Corp. [*NASDAQ symbol*] (COMM)
DOCC .... Director of the Operational Command Committee (SAUS)
DOCC .... DISA Operations Control Complex (SAUS)
DOCC .... DocuCorp International, Inc. [*NASDAQ symbol*] (NASQ)
DOCC .... Ducati Owners' Club of Canada (EA)
DOCC .... Office of the Comptroller of the Currency, Washington, DC [*Library symbol*] [*Library of Congress*] (LCLS)
DOCD .... Department of Community Development - WA State (SAUS)
DOCD .... DOCdata N.V. [*NASDAQ symbol*] (NASQ)
DOCDEL .... Document Delivery [*Information service or system*]
DOCDEL .... Document Delivery and Electronic Publishing Initiative (SAUS)
DOCDEL .... Documents Delivered Electronically (SAUS)
DOCE .... Date of Current Enlistment [*Military*]
DOCED .... Documentation Edition (SAUO)
Doc Eng .... Doctor of Engineering
DOCET .... Differential Orbit Correction and Ephemeris Tables (SAUS)
DOCEX .... Document Exploitation
Doc Faun Helv... Documenta Faunistica Helvetiae (SAUS)
DOCFAX .... Document Facsimile (SAUS)
DOCFAX .... Document Facsimile Transmission (NITA)
DOCFILE ...... United Nations Documents File (SAUS)
DOCG .... Denominazione di Origine Controllata e Garantita [*Italian wine designation*]
DOCG .... Deoxycorticosterone Glucoside [*Also, DCG*] [*Endocrinology*]
DOCGEN ...... Document Generator
DOCHSIN ..... District of Columbia Health Sciences Information Network [*Library network*]
DOCHSINE ... District of Columbia Health Sciences Information Network (SAUS)
DOCI .... DecisionOne Holdings [*NASDAQ symbol*] (TTSB)
DOCID .... Document Identifier [*Military*] (MCD)
DOCILIS .... Documents, Interrogation Libres (SAUS)
DocIm .... Document Imaging Systems Corp. [*Associated Press*] (SAG)
DocImg .... Document Imaging Systems Corp. [*Associated Press*] (SAG)
DOCIP .... Indigenous Populations Center for Documentation, Research and Information (SAUS)
DOCIP .... Indigenous Populations Documentation Research and Information Center (SAUO)
DOCIS .... Documentation des Institutions Sociales (SAUS)
DOCIT .... Directors of Central Institutes of Technology (SAUS)
DOCK .... [*The*] Chicago Dock & Canal Trust [*NASDAQ symbol*] (NQ)
DOCK .... Docket (DLA)
Docket .... Docket and the Barrister [*1889-98*] [*Canada*] [*A publication*] (DLA)
DOCKET .... Enforcement Docket System (SAUS)
Docket .... West Publishing Company's Docket [*1909-41*] [*A publication*] (DLA)
DOCKS .... Chicago Dock & Canal Trust [*NASDAQ symbol*] (TTSB)
DOCKS .... Yards and Docks (SAUO)
DOCL .... Department of Commerce Library (IID)
DOCLINE ...... Docum. Delivery On-Line (SAUS)
DOCLINE ...... Document Delivery On-Line (SAUS)
DOCLINE ...... Document Ordering Online [*Document delivery system, MEDLARS*] (NITA)
DOCLINE ...... Documents On-Line [*Medicine*] (DMAA)
DOCMOD ..... Documentation Modernization [*Program*] [*Army*] (INF)
docn .... documentation (SAUS)
DOCO .... Director to Commissary Operations [*Military*] (AABC)
DOCOLSYS ... Document Ordering Identification and Location System (SAUS)
DOC OSIS .... Documentation Oversea Information Section (SAUO)
DOCP .... Delaware Otsego Corp. [*NASDAQ symbol*] (NQ)
DOCP .... Deterministic Optimal Control Problem (SAUS)
DOCPAL .... Sistema de Documentacion sobre Poblacion en America Latina [*Latin American Population Documentation System*] [*Economic Commission for Latin America and the Caribbean*] [*United Nations*] [*Information service or system*] (IID)
Doc Parl ...... Documents Parlementaires [*A publication*] (DLA)
DocPolSci ... Doctor of Political Science (SAUS)
DOCPR .... Department of Commerce Procurement Regulation [*A publication*] (AAGC)
DOCPREP .... Document Preparation in Support of E-3A (SAUS)
DOCPROC .... Document Processing (SAUS)
DOCR .... Document Optical Character Recognition (SAUS)
DocRerPol ... Doctor Rerum Politicarum [*Doctor of Political Science*] [*Latin*]
DOCS .... Combined Services Directorate (SAUO)
DOCS .... Data Operations Control System (SAUS)
DOCS .... Deoxycorticosteroids [*Medicine*] (DMAA)
DOCS .... Department of Correctional Services (SAUS)
DOCS .... Designated Operational Capability Statement (SAUS)
DOCS .... Design Optimization Codes for Structures (MCD)
DOCS .... Developmental Observation Checklist System [*Test*] (TMMY)
DOCS .... Dictionary of Organic Compounds [*A publication*]
DOCS .... Digital/Optical Control System (SAUS)
DOCS .... Disk-Oriented Computer System (IEEE)
DOCS .... Display Operator Console Support (SAUS)
DOCS .... Display Operator Console System (SAUS)
DOCS .... Distribution Operation Control System (SAUS)
Docs .... Doctores Bononienses [*Latin*] (DSA)
D Oc S .... Doctor of Ocular Science
DOCS .... Document Organization and Control System [*Telecommunications*] (TEL)
Docs .... Documents (EBF)
DOCS .... Documents
docs .... Documents (EBF)
DOCS .... DSCS Operational Control System (SAUO)
DOCS .... DSCS [*Defense Satellite Communication System*] Operations Control System [*DoD*]
DOCS .... Dynamic Operations Control System (SAUS)
DOCS .... PC DOCS Group International [*NASDAQ symbol*] (SAG)
D Oc Sc .... Doctor of Ocular Science
DOCSECO .... Combined Services Directorate and Economic Directorate (SAUO)
DOCSF .... PC DOCS Gp Intl. [*NASDAQ symbol*] (TTSB)
DOCSIS .... Data Over Cable Service Interface Specification [*Telecommunications*]
DOCSIS .... Data Over Cable System Interface Specification (SAUS)
DOC-SR ...... Desoxycorticosterone Secretion Rate [*Endocrinology*] (MAE)
DOCSV .... Data over Circuit-Switched Voice [*Computer science*] (PCM)
DOCSYS ...... Display of Chromosome Statistics System
DOCSYS ...... Documentation System (SAUS)
Doct .... Doctor
Doct .... Doctores Bononienses [*Latin*] (DSA)
DOCT .... Doctrine (ROG)
DOCT .... Document
DoctArch ...... Doctor of Christian Archeology
Doct Dem .... Doctrine of Demurrers [*A publication*] (DLA)
Doc To .... Doctores Tholosani [*Latin*] (DSA)
DOCTOR ...... Dictionary Operation and Control for Thesaurus Organization (PDAA)
DOCTOR ...... Dictionary Operation and Control of Thesaurus Organization (SAUS)
DOCTOR ...... Display Oriented Communication Tool for Online Retrieval (SAUS)
Doct Pl .... Doctrina Placitandi [*A publication*] (DLA)
DOCTRN ...... Doctrine
DOCU .... DocuCon, Inc. [*NASDAQ symbol*] (NQ)
DOCU .... Document (AABC)
docubio .... documentary biographee (SAUS)
docubio .... documentary biographer (SAUS)
docubio .... documentary biography (SAUS)
DocuCn .... DocuCon, Inc. [*Associated Press*] (SAG)
docudrama... documentary drama (SAUS)
DOCUM .... Document (SAUS)
docum .... Documentary (BARN)
docum .... documented (SAUS)
Documnt ...... Documentum, Inc. [*Associated Press*] (SAG)
DOCUS .... Display-Oriented Compiler Usage System (SAUS)
DOCUS .... Display-Oriented Computer Usage System
DocuSci .... Document Sciences Corp. [*Associated Press*] (SAG)
Doc Ve .... Doctores Veteres [*Latin*] (DSA)
DOCX .... Docugraphix, Inc. [*NASDAQ symbol*] (COMM)
DOCX .... Document Sciences Corp. [*NASDAQ symbol*] (SAG)
DOCX .... EI Dupont de Nemours [*Private rail car owner code*]
DOD .... Data Output Device (SAUS)
DOD .... Date and Dock (SAUS)
DoD .... Date of Death [*Medicine*] (EDAA)
DOD .... Date of Death
DOD .... Date of Discharge [*Medicine*] (MELL)
DOD .... Date on Dock (SAUS)
DOD .... Dead [*or Died*] of Disease (DAVI)
DoD .... Dead of Disease [*Medicine*] (EDAA)
DOD .... Dear Old Dad (DICI)
DOD .... Degree of Disorder [*Coatings*]
DOD .... Dementia of Depression [*Syndrome*] [*Medicine*] (EDAA)
DOD .... Dentino-Osseous Dysplasia [*Medicine*] (MELL)
DOD .... Department of Defense (AAGC)
DoD .... Department of Defense [*Washington, DC*]
DOD .... Depth of Discharge [*Electric vehicles*]
DOD .... Depth on Discharge (SAUS)
DOD .... Detroit Ordnance District [*Army*]
DOD .... Development Operations Division [*NASA*] (KSC)
d o d .... diameter over bark (SAUS)
DOD .... Diameter Over the Dielectric (SAUS)
DOD .... Died of Disease
DOD .... Dielectric Outer Diameter (IAA)
DOD .... Digital Omega Dropwindsonde (SAUS)
DOD .... Digital Optical Device (VLIE)
DOD .... Digital Optical Disc [*Storage medium*] (NITA)
DOD .... Dihydroxydiphenyl [*Antioxidant*] [*Organic chemistry*]
DoD .... Director of Development [*Medicine*] (EDAA)
DOD .... Director of Dockyards [*Admiralty*] [*British*]
DOD .... Director of Operations Division [*Navy*] [*British*]
DOD .... Directory of Directories [*Later, DIP*] [*A publication*]
DOD .... Directory of Online Databases [*A publication*]
DOD .... Directory on Disk [*Information service or system*] (IID)
DOD .... Direct Outward Dial [*Telecommunications*] (ITD)
DOD .... Direct Outward Dialing [*Telecommunications*]
DOD .... Dissolved Oxygen Deficit [*Water pollution*]
DoD .... Dissolved Oxygen Demand
DOD .... Divisional Ordnance Depot (SAUO)
DoD .... Division of Dentistry [*Medicine*] (EDAA)
DOD .... Division of Ophthalmic Devices [*Center for Devices and Radiological Health*]
Dod .... Dodecanese (SAUS)
DOD .... Dodge City [*Diocesan*] [*Kansas*] (TOCD)
DOD .... Dodoma [*Tanzania*] [*Airport symbol*] (OAG)
DOD .... Dodoma [*Tanzania*] [*Seismograph station code, US Geological Survey*] [*Closed*] (SEIS)

Dod Dodson's English Admiralty Reports [*A publication*] (DLA)
Dod Dod's Parliamentary Companion. Annual [*A publication*] (DLA)
DOD Dollars On Demand (SAUS)
DOD Domestic Operations Division (SAUS)
DOD Draft on Demand [*Banking*] (ROG)
DOD Drop-on-Demand [*Computer printer*]
DOD Drug Overdose (MELL)
dod dust of desuetude (SAUS)
DOD German Oceanographic Data Centre (SAUS)
DOD United States Department of Energy, Regional Energy Information Center, Dallas, TX [*OCLC symbol*] (OCLC)
DODA Department of Defence, Australia
DODA Department of Defense-Army [*Federal Railroad Administration identification code*]
DODA Door and Operator Dealers Association (EA)
DODAAC Department of Defense Activity Address Code (AABC)
DODAAD Department of Defense Activity Address Designer (MCD)
DODAAD Department of Defense Activity Address Directory (AFM)
DODAAF Department of Defense Activity Address File
DODAAS Department of Defense Automatic Address System (MCD)
DODABMA Development Operations Division, Army Ballistic Missile Agency (SAUO)
DODAC Department of Defense Ammunition Code (AFM)
DODAC Dioctadecyldimethylammonium Chloride [*Organic chemistry*]
DODADL Department of Defense Authorized Data List
Dod Adm Dodson's English Admiralty Reports [*A publication*] (DLA)
DOD-AGFSRS Department of Defense Aircraft Ground Fire Suppression and Rescue Office
Dod Ant Parl Doderidge on the Antiquity and Power of Parliaments [*A publication*] (DLA)
DODAQAC Department of Defense Acquisition Quality Assurance Course (RDA)
DODAQAMC Department of Defense Acquisition Quality Assurance Management Course (RDA)
DODAR Determination of Direction and Range (IAA)
DODAR Director of Drafting and Records [*British military*] (DMA)
DODAS Digital Oceanographic Data Acquisition System (MCD)
DOD C & T Department of Defense Clothing and Textile Board (EGAO)
DODCAPS Department of Defense Central Automated Personnel System (AFM)
DODCCP Department of Defense Central Control Point (AAGC)
DODCI Department of Defense Computer Institute
DODCI Diethyloxadicarbocyanine Iodide [*A dye*]
DODCLIPMI Department of Defense Consolidated List of Principal Military Items
DODCLPMI Department of Defense Consolidated List of Principal Military Items
DOD-CODSIA Department of Defense - Council of Defense and Space Industry Associations (SAUO)
DODCPM Department of Defense Civilian Personnel Manual (MCD)
DODCSC Department of Defense Computer Security Center (GFGA)
DODCSC DoD Computer Security Center (SAUS)
DODD Department of Defense Directive
DODD DoD Directive (SAUS)
Dodd Dodd, Mead (SAUS)
DODD DOD [*Department of Defense*] Document (DOMA)
DODDAC Department of Defense Damage Assessment Center
Dodd & Br Pr Pr Dodd and Brooks' Probate Court Practice [*A publication*] (DLA)
Dodd Bur Fees Dodd on Burial and Other Church Fees [*A publication*] (DLA)
DoDDS Department of Defense Dependent Schools (SAUS)
DODDS Department of Defense Dependents Schools
DODDSEUR Department of Defense Dependents Schools, European Region (SAUO)
DODDSLANT Department of Defense Dependents Schools, Atlantic (DNAB)
DODE Department of Defense-Air Force [*Federal Railroad Administration identification code*]
DODE Development Optical Diagnostic Equipment [*Military*]
DODE Diagnostic Optical Demonstration Equipment (ACAE)
DODEA Department of Defense Education Education Activity [*DoD*]
DODEC Department of Defense Environmental Contamination (SAUO)
Dodec Dodecanese (SAUS)
Dodecanese Dodecanese Islanders (SAUS)
Dodecanese Dodecanese Islands (SAUS)
Dod Eng Law Doderidge's English Lawyer [*A publication*] (DLA)
DODEP Department of Defense Emergency Plans (AABC)
DODEP Department of Defense Exercise Planning (AFM)
Do de Ro Domini de Rota [*Authority cited in pre-1607 legal work*] (DSA)
DODES Department of Disaster and Emergency Services (SAUO)
Do de San Gemi Dominicus de Sancto Geminiano [*Flourished, 1407-09*] [*Authority cited in pre-1607 legal work*] (DSA)
DODEX DOD [*Department of Defense*][*Intelligence Information System*] Extension (DOMA)
DOD(F) Director of Operations Division (Foreign) [*Navy*] [*British*]
DODFCI Department of Defense Foreign Counterintelligence Program
DODFDCO Department of Defense Foreign Disclosure Coordinating Office (AABC)
DODGAR Department of Defense Grant and Agreement Regulation [*A publication*] (AAGC)
DODGE Department of Defense Gradient Experiment (SAUS)
DODGE Department of Defense Gravity Experiment [*Satellite*]
DODGE-M Department of Defense Gravity Experiment, Multipurpose [*Satellite*]
DODGX Dodge & Cox Stock [*Mutual fund ticker symbol*] (SG)
DODH Department of Defense Handbook
DOD(H) Director of Operations Division (Home) [*Navy*] [*British*]
DoD/HA Department of Defense for Health Affairs
DODHBK Department of Defense Handbook
DODHGCSO Department of Defense Household Goods Commercial Storage Office
DODHGFO Department of Defense Household Goods Field Office
DODHSNS Department of Defense High School Newspaper Service
DODI Department of Defense Instruction
DODI District Office Direct Input [*Social Security computerized system*]
DODI DoD Instruction (SAUS)
DODIC Department of Defense Identification Code (AFM)
DODIC Department of Defense Item Code
DODIDENTBAD Department of Defense Identification Badge
DODIEC Department of Defense Item Entry Control
DODIER Department of Defense Industrial Equipment Reserve (AABC)
DODIG Department of Defense Inspector General
DOD IGARTS Department of Defense Inspector General Audit Report Tracking System (AAGC)
DODIIS Department of Defence Intelligence Information System (SAUS)
DoDIIS Department of Defense Intelligence Information System (ADWA)
DODIIS Department of Defense Intelligence Information System (MCD)
DODIM Department of Defense Inventory Manager
DODINST Department of Defense Instruction
DOD INST Department of Defense instructions (SAUS)
DODIP Department of Defense Information Program (SAUO)
DODIPP Department of Defense Intelligence Production Program [*CIA terminology*]
DOD-IR Department of Defense Intelligence Reports (DNAB)
DODIS Distribution of Oceanographic Data at Isentropic Levels System
DODIS Distribution of Oceanographic Data on Isotropic Levels (SAUS)
DODISB Department of Defense Industrial Security Bulletin
DODISC Department of Defense Item Standardization Code
DODISL Department of Defense Industrial Security Letter
DODISM Department of Defense Industrial Security Manual
DODISPR Department of Defense Information Security Program Regulation (MCD)
DODISR Department of Defense Industrial Security Regulation
DODISS Department of Defense Index of Specifications and Standards
DoDISS Index of Specifications and Standards (SAUO)
DODJET Drop on Demand Jet Printing [*Carpet manufacturing*] (ECON)
DOD-JIC DOD [*Department of Defense*] Joint Intelligence Center (DOMA)
Dod Law L Doderidge's The Lawyer's Light [*A publication*] (DLA)
DODLOGPLAN Department of Defense Logistics Systems Plan (MCD)
DODM Department of Defense Manual
DoD-M Department of Defense-Manual (SAUS)
DODMAB Dioctadecyldimethylammonium Bromide (SAUS)
DODMAM Department of Defense Military Assistance Manual
DODMDS Department of Defense Material Distribution System (MCD)
DODMERB Department of Defense Medical Examination Board (SAUS)
DODMERB Department of Defense Medical Examination Review Board
DOD/MIS Department of Defense Management Information System
DODMNL Department of Defense Manual
DODMPAC Department of Defense Military Pay and Allowance Committee
DODMPRC Department of Defense Military Personnel Records Center
DODMUL Department of Defense Master Urgency List (AFM)
DODN Department of Defense-Navy [*Federal Railroad Administration identification code*]
DODNACC Department of Defense National Agency Check Center (AABC)
DODNAF Department of Defense Non Appropriated Fund (ACAE)
Dod Nobility Doderidge's Nobility [*A publication*] (DLA)
DODO Drain on Day One [*Classification for new newspaper*]
DODP Disk Oriented Data Processing (SAUS)
DOD-PEC Department of Defense Program Element Code (AFIT)
DODPM Department of Defense Military Pay and Allowance Entitlements Manual (AABC)
DODPMRP Department of Defense Precious Metals Recovery Program
DOD/POPHM Department of Defense Performance-Oriented Packaging of Hazardous Materials [*Washington, DC*]
DOD-Prinzip droplet-ondemand principle (SAUS)
DODPRO Department of Defense, Pacific Research Office (CINC)
DODPRT Date of Departure [*Military*] (AABC)
DODPSTR Department of Defense Poster
DODR Department of Defense Regulation
DoD-R Department of Defense-Regulation (SAUS)
DODRE Department of Defense Research and Engineering
DODREE Department of Defense Research and Engineering (SAUS)
DODS Definitive Orbit Determination System [*NASA*]
DODS Different Orbitals for Different Spins [*Atomic physics*]
DODS Distributed Ocean Data System
DODS Distributed Oceanographic Data System (SAUS)
Dods Dodson's English Admiralty Reports [*A publication*] (DLA)
DODSASP Department of Defense Small Arms Serialization Program
DODSASP Small Arms Serialization Program (SAUS)
DODSB Data Out Disable (SAUS)
DodSO$_4$ Dodecyl Sulfate [*Organic chemistry*]
Dodson Adm (Eng) Dodson's English Admiralty Reports [*A publication*] (DLA)
DODSPBL Department of Defense Surplus Property Bidders List
DOD-SSP Department of Defense Single Stock Point (MCD)
DoDSSP Department of Defense Single Stock Point for Specifications and Standards (SAUO)
DODT Design Option Decision Tree
DODT Display Octal Debugging Technique
DODTP Deployment Observation Discrimination Technical Program (ACAE)
DODWHS Department of Defense Washington Headquarters Services (ACAE)
DODX Department of Defense Oversized Flatcar (INF)
DODX Department of Defense-Owned Rail Cars [*MTMC*] (TAG)
DODX Military Traffic Management Command (SAUO)
DODX U.S. Department of Defense [*Private rail car owner code*]
DOE Data Origination Event (VLIE)
DOE Date of Enlistment [*Military*]
DOE Date of Examination [*Medicine*] (DAVI)

DOE .... Declaration of Excess (SAUS)
DOE .... Deep Ocean Environment
D-O-E .... Deoxyephedrine [*or Desoxyephedrine*] [*Pharmacology*]
DOE .... Department of Ecology (COE)
DOE .... Department of Education [*Cabinet department*] (CDAI)
DoE .... Department of Employment (WDAA)
DOE .... Department of Energy [*Washington, DC*]
DoE .... Department of Energy
DOE .... Department of Environment (SAUS)
DOE .... Department of Ocean Engineering (SAUO)
DoE .... Department of the Environment (WA)
DOE .... Department of the Environment [*Formerly, MPBW, MT*] [*British*]
DOE .... Depends on Experience [*Employment*] (ODBW)
doe .... Depends on Experience [*Employment*] (ODBW)
DOE .... dept of energy (SAUS)
DOE .... Design of Experiments [*Army*] (RDA)
DOE .... Desoxyephedrine Hydrochloride [*Pharmacy*] (AAMN)
DOE .... Device-Oriented Electronic (IAA)
DOE .... Dictionary of Old English [*University of Toronto*] [*Canada*] [*Information service or system*] (IID)
DOE .... Diffractive Optical Element (SAUS)
DOE .... Direct Observation Evaluation [*Medicine*] (DMAA)
DOE .... Directorate of Organization and Establishment (SAUO)
DOE .... Dissolved Oxygen Electrode
DOE .... Distributed Object Environment (SAUS)
DOE .... Distributed Objects Everywhere [*Computer science*]
DOE .... Djoemoe [*Surinam*] [*Airport symbol*] (OAG)
DOE .... Doctor of Oral English
DOE .... Dyspnea on Exercise [*or Exertion*] [*Medicine*]
DOE .... Dyspnea on Exertion [*Medicine*] (DMAA)
DOE .... United States Department of Energy Library, Washington, DC [*OCLC symbol*] (OCLC)
DOEA .... Department of Elder Affairs (DEMM)
DOE/AES .... Department of Environment/Atmospheric Environment Service (SAUS)
DOE/AL .... DOE [*Department of Engery*] Albuquerque Operations Office, Albuquerque, NM (GAAI)
DOEBCA .... Department of Energy Board of Contract Appeals (AAGC)
DOE/BSO .... Department of Energy/Berkeley Site Office (SAUS)
DOEC .... Department of Ecology/Washington State (SAUS)
DOEC .... Diploma in Economics (SAUO)
D Oec .... Doctor Oeconomiae [*Doctor of Economics*]
DOE/CAO .... DOE [*Department of Energy*] Carlsbad Area Office, Carlsbad, NM (GAAI)
DOE/CH .... DOE [*Department of Energy*] Chicago Operations Office [*Illinois*] (GAAI)
DOE/CH .... DOE Chicago Operations Office, Argonne (SAUS)
DoEd .... Department of Education
DOE-DP .... Department of Energy, Defense Programs (SAUO)
DOE/DP .... DOE [*Department of Energy*] Office of Defense Programs (GAAI)
DOE/DP .... DOE/Office of Defense Programs, Germantown (SAUS)
DOE-EH .... DOE Office of Environmental, Safety and Health (SAUS)
DOE EH-13 .... Department of Energy, Office of Nuclear Science (SAUS)
DOE EH-24 .... Department of Energy, Office of Environmental Audit (SAUS)
DOE/EIA .... DOE [*Department of Energy*] Energy Information Administration (GAAI)
DOE/EM .... DOE [*Department of Energy*] Office of Environmental Management (GAAI)
DOE/EM .... DOE/Office of Environmental Restoration and Waste Management, Germantown (SAUS)
DOE/ER .... Department of Energy, Office of Energy Research [*Washington, DC*]
DOE/ET .... Department of Energy/Assistant Secretary for Energy Technology [*Washington, DC*]
DOE/FN .... DOE [*Department of Energy*] Fernald Area Office [*Ohio*] (GAAI)
DOE-GJPO .... DOE Grand Junction Projects Office (SAUS)
DOE-HQ .... Department of Energy, Headquarters (SAUS)
DOE/HQ .... Department of Energy, Headquarters Office (SAUS)
DOE/HQ .... DOE [*Department of Energy*] Headquarters (GAAI)
DOE/HQ .... DOE Headquarters, Washington and Germantown (SAUS)
DOE-ID .... DOE Idaho (SAUS)
DOE/ID .... DOE [*Department of Energy*] Idaho Operations Office (GAAI)
DOE/ID .... DOE Idaho Operations Office, Idaho Falls (SAUS)
DOELAP .... Department of Energy Laboratory Accreditation Program
DOELAP .... DOE Laboratory Accreditation Program (SAUS)
DOEM .... Designated Officials for Environmental Matters [*Environment term*] (EGA)
DOEN .... Department of Energy (WDAA)
DOE-NE .... DOE - Office of Nuclear Energy (SAUS)
DOE/NV .... Department of Energy Nevada Operations Office [*Marine science*] (OSRA)
DOE/NV .... DOE [*Department of Energy*] Nevada Operations Office (USDC)
DOE/NV .... DOE Nevada Operations Office, Las Vegas (SAUS)
DOEO .... Darwin Office of Equal Opportunity [*Australia*]
DOE/OAK .... Department of Energy/Oakland Operations Office (SAUS)
DOE/OAK .... DOE [*Department of Energy*] Oakland Operations Office [*Oakland, CA*] (GAAI)
DOE/OH .... DOE Ohio Field Office, Miamisburg (SAUS)
DOEOIS .... Design and Operational Evaluation of Distributed Offices Information Servers (SAUO)
DOE/OR .... DOE [*Department of Energy*] Oak Ridge Operations Office [*Oak Park Ridge, TN*] (GAAI)
DOE-OSA .... DOE - Office of Special Applications (SAUS)
DOE/OSTI .... DOE [*Department of Energy*] Office of Scientific and Technical Information [*Tennessee*] (GAAI)
DOE/OSTI .... DOE/Office of Scientific and Technical Information, Oak Ridge (SAUS)
DOE-PI .... DOE Procurement Instruction (SAUS)
DOE-PMR .... Department of Energy Property Management Regulations [*A publication*] (AAGC)
DOE-PR .... Department of Energy Procurement Regulation [*A publication*] (AAGC)
DOE-PR .... DOE Procurement Regulation (SAUS)
DOEPR .... DOE Procurement Regulations (SAUS)
DOE QECPR .... DOE Quarterly Energy Conservation Progress Report (SAUS)
DOEQP .... DOE Qualification Program (SAUS)
DOER .... Dredging Operations and Environmental Research [*U.S. Army Corps of Engineers*]
DOE/RECON .... Department of Energy -- Remote Console (SAUS)
DOE/RECON .... Department of Energy's Remote Console Information System [*Department of Energy*] [*Database*]
DOE/RF .... DOE [*Department of Energy*] Rocky Flats Office [*Colorado*] (GAAI)
DOE/RF .... DOE Rocky Flats Office, Golden (SAUS)
DOE/RF .... DOE Rocky Flats Operations Office (SAUS)
DOERHA .... DOE Record Holding Area (SAUS)
DOE/RI .... DOE [*Department of Energy*] Richland Operations Office [*Richland, WA*] (GAAI)
DOE-RL .... Department of Energy, Richland Operations Office (SAUS)
DOE-RL .... DOE Richland Field Office (SAUS)
DOE/RL .... DOE Richland Operations Office, Richland (SAUS)
DOE RS .... DOE Records Schedules (SAUS)
DOE/RW .... DOE/Office of Civilian Radioactive Waste Management (SAUS)
DOE/RW .... DOE/Office of Civilian Radioactive Waste Management, Washington (SAUS)
DOES .... Decision-Oriented Evaluation System
DOES .... Defense Organization Entity Standards [*DoD*]
DOES .... Defense Organization Entity System [*DoD*] (MCD)
DOES .... Direct Order Entry System [*Computer science*] (MHDB)
DOES .... Directory of Educational Software [*British*] (NITA)
DOES .... Disk-Oriented Engineering System [*Computer science*]
DOES .... Disorders of Excessive Sleepiness [*Medicine*] (DMAA)
DOES .... Disorders of Excessive Somnolence [*Medicine*] (MEDA)
DOES .... Distribution Order Entry System (IAA)
DOE-SR .... DOE - Savannah River (SAUS)
DOE/SR .... DOE [*Department of Energy*] Savannah River Operations Office [*Aiken, South Carolina*] (GAAI)
DOE/SR .... DOE Savannah River Operations Office, Aiken (SAUS)
DOET .... Dimethoxyethyl Amphetamine [*A hallucinogenic drug, more commonly known as STP*] (MAH)
DOE-TIC .... Department of Energy Technical Information Center [*Oak Ridge, TN*] [*Database producer*]
DOE-TN .... DOE - Oakridge, TN (SAUS)
DOETRS .... DOE Transportation Risk Study (SAUS)
DOETS .... Dual-Object Electronic Tracking System
DOE-VPP .... Department of Energys Voluntary Protection Program (SAUS)
DOE/WIPP .... DOE [*Department of Energy*] WIPP [*Waste Isolation Pilot Plant*] Project Office [*Carlsbad, NM*] (GAAI)
DOE/WIPP .... DOE/WIPP Project Office, Carlsbad (SAUS)
DOE/WVAO .... DOE [*Department of Energy*] West Valley Area Office [*West Valley, NY*] (GAAI)
DOE/WVAO .... DOE/West Valley Area Office, West Valley (SAUS)
DOE/WVPO .... DOE/West Valley Project Office, West Valley (SAUS)
DOEZ .... Dorchester Elevator [*Federal Railroad Administration identification code*]
DOF .... Date of Flight (SAUS)
DOF .... Deep Ocean Floor
DOF .... Defenders of Furbearers [*Later, Defenders of Wildlife*]
DOF .... Degree of Freedom
DoF .... Degree(s) of Freedom [*Of movement*] [*Medicine*] (EDAA)
DOF .... Delivery on Field
DOF .... Demonstration of Operational Feasibility
DOF .... Departed for off hire (SAUS)
DoF .... Department of Finance (SAUS)
DOF .... Department of Fisheries [*South Australia*]
DOF .... Department of Forestry [*Queensland*] [*Australia*]
DOF .... Depot Overhaul Factor
DOF .... Depth of Field (MCD)
DOF .... Depth of Focus [*Optics*]
DOF .... Developmental Optics Facility (ACAE)
DOF .... Device Operating Failure (SAUS)
DOF .... Device Output Format
DOF .... Diesel Oil Fuel (SAUS)
DOF .... Dioctyl Fumarate [*Organic chemistry*]
DOF .... Direction of Fire [*Weaponry*] (INF)
DOF .... Direction of Flight (KSC)
DOF .... Director of Fun
DOF .... Director of Ordnance Factories [*Ministry of Supply*] [*British*] [*World War II*]
DOF .... Division of Forestry (DEMM)
DOF .... Divorced Oriental Female (SAUO)
doF .... Dorsal Odontophore Flexor (SAUS)
DOF .... United States Department of Energy NEICA, Albuquerque, NM [*OCLC symbol*] (OCLC)
DOFA .... Date of Full Availability
D of A .... Daughters of America (SAUO)
D of A .... Defenders of Animals (SAUS)
D of A .... Deltiologists of America (EA)
D of A .... Department of Agriculture
D of A .... Department of the Army (SAUO)
DOFA .... Details of Agreement [*NATO*] (NATG)

D of A......... Director of Artillery [*British*]
D of A......... National Council, Daughters of America
DOFAB......... Damned Old Fool About Books [*Acronym created by Eugene Field*]
D of Arty...... Director of Artillery (SAUS)
Dofasco Illus News... Dofasco Illustrated News (journ.) (SAUS)
D of C......... Daughters of the Confederacy
DOFC......... Defense Orthopedic Footwear Clinic [*Military*] (AABC)
D of C......... Department of Commerce (SAUO)
D of C......... Department of Communications (SAUS)
D of C......... Director of Contract and Purchase Department (SAUO)
DOFC......... Donny Osmond Fan Club (EA)
D of CORN LI... Duke of Cornwall's Light Infantry [*Military unit*] [*British*] (ROG)
DOFCOSY.... Double-Quantum Filtered Correlated Spectroscopy [*Medicine*] (DMAA)
DOFD......... Date of First Demand [*Military*] (AFIT)
D of D......... Department of Defence (SAUO)
D of D......... Director of Dockyards [*Admiralty*] [*British*]
D of E......... Department of Energy (SAUS)
D of E......... Department of the Environment (SAUS)
D of E......... Dictionary of Electronics (SAUS)
D of E......... Director of Education (SAUO)
D of E......... Director of Equipment (SAUO)
DOF(E)......... Director of Ordnance Factories, Engineering Factories [*Ministry of Supply*] [*British*] [*World War II*]
D of ESS...... Director of Engineering Stores Service (SAUO)
D of F......... Department of Finance (ADA)
D of F......... Department of Fisheries (SAUS)
D of F......... Director of Farms (SAUO)
D of GD....... Director of Gunnery Division (SAUO)
D of H......... Degree of Honor (SAUS)
D of I......... Declaration of Independence (SAUS)
D of I......... Department of Insurance (SAUS)
D of I......... Department of Interior (SAUO)
D of I......... Department of the Interior
D of I......... Director of Intelligence [*RAF*] [*British*]
D of I......... Division of Intelligence (SAUS)
DOFIC......... Domain-Originated Functional Integrated Circuit (IEEE)
DOFICS........ Domain-Oriented Functional Integrated Circuits (VLIE)
DOFICS........ Domain-Originated Functional Integrated Circuits (SAUS)
D of J......... Department of Justice
D of J......... Dominion of Jamaica (SAUS)
D of L......... Department of Labor
D of L......... Department of Labour (SAUS)
D of L......... Department of Law (SAUS)
DOFL......... Diamond Ordnance Fuze Laboratory [*Later, Harry Diamond Laboratories*] [*AMC*] [*Washington, DC*]
D of L......... Director of Labour Service (SAUO)
D of L......... Duchy of Lancaster [*British*] (ILCA)
DOFLI......... Data of Last Issue (SAUS)
D of L S....... Director of Labour Service (SAUS)
DOFLT......... Date of Last (VLIE)
DOFLT......... Date Of Last issue (SAUS)
D of M......... Dames of Malta (EA)
D of M......... Director of Manning [*British military*] (DMA)
D of M......... Director of Mechanization (SAUO)
D of M......... Supreme Caldron, Daughters of Mokanna (EA)
D of N......... Director of Navigation (SAUO)
D of NR....... Director of Naval Recruiting [*British*]
D of O......... Director of Organization (SAUO)
DOFOS......... Disturbance of Function Occlusion Syndrome [*Medicine*] (DMAA)
D of P......... Degree of Pocahontas
DOFP......... Direct-on-Finish Process (SAUS)
D of P......... Director of Planes [*Admiralty*] [*British*]
D of P......... Director of Planning (SAUS)
D of P......... Director of Plans (SAUS)
D of P......... Director of Postings (SAUO)
D of P......... Director of Press (SAUO)
D of PD(Q).... Director of Plans Division (Quartering) [*Navy*] [*British*]
D of PS........ Director of Public Service
D of Q......... Director of Quartering [*British military*] (DMA)
D of Q(N)..... Directorate of Quartering (Navy) [*British*]
D of R......... Director of Railways (SAUO)
D of R......... Director of Remounts [*Military*] [*British*]
D of Ry........ Director of Railways (SAUS)
D of S......... Daughters of Scotia [*Bayonne, NJ*]
D of S......... Day of Supply [*Military*]
DOFS......... Day of Supply [*Military*]
DOFS......... Department of Organization and Field Services, AFL-CIO (EA)
D of S......... Department of State
D of S......... Depot of Supplies [*Marine Corps*]
D of S......... Director of Signals (SAUS)
D of S......... Director of Stores (SAUS)
DOFS......... Distributed Optical-Fiber Sensing (SAUS)
D of S & T.... Director of Supplies and Transport (SAUS)
D of S D....... Director of Staff Duties (SAUS)
DOFS(W)..... Director of Stores (Washington) [*Navy*] (DNAB)
D of S (W).... Director of Stores (Washington) [*Navy*]
D of T......... Department of the Treasury [*Commonly TD, Treasury Department*]
D of T......... Director of Traffic
D of T......... Director of Training (SAUO)
D of T......... Director of Transport (SAUS)
D of TD........ Director of Tactical Division [*Navy*] [*British*]
D of TT........ Dominion of Trinidad and Tobago (SAUS)
D of V......... Director of Victualling [*British military*] (DMA)
DOFW......... Department of Fish & Wildlife (SAUS)
D of W......... Department of Woodwork (SAUO)
D of W......... Department of Works [*Military*] [*British*]
D of W......... Died of Wounds (SAUS)
D of W......... Directorate of Weapons (SAUO)
D of W......... Director of Works (SAUS)
D of WI........ Director of Office of War Informations (SAUO)
DOF(X)......... Director of Ordnance Factories, Explosives Factories [*Ministry of Supply*] [*British*] [*World War II*]
DOG......... Days of Grace [*for payment*] [*Business term*]
DOG......... Deoxy-D-glucose [*Also, DDG, DG*] [*Biochemistry*]
DOG......... Deoxyglucose (DMAA)
DOG......... Department of Geology (SAUO)
DOG......... Difference of Gaussian (SAUS)
DOG......... Difference of Gaussians [*Image processing*]
DOG......... Dioctanoylglycerol [*Organic chemistry*]
D-OG......... Diplomate, American Board of Obstetrics and Gynecology (DHSM)
DOG......... Directory of Opportunities for Graduates [*A publication*]
DOG......... Disaster Organization Group (TIMI)
DOG......... Disgruntled Old Graduate [*West Point*]
DOG......... Dissolver Off-Gas [*Nuclear energy*] (NRCH)
DOG......... Division Officer's Guide [*A publication*] (DNAB)
DOG......... Division of Oil and Gas (SAUO)
DOG......... Dog Owners' Guild
DOG......... Dongola [*Sudan*] [*Airport symbol*] (OAG)
DOG......... Dot On the Ground (SAUS)
DOG......... Double Chain Branch-Oblong Master Link-Grab Hook
DOG......... Drop Out Generator (NG)
DOG......... Due-Out of Group [*Military*] (MCD)
dog......... frankfurter (SAUS)
DOGDO........ Division of Oil and Gas District Office (SAUO)
DOGE......... Doris Orbitography and Geopotential Evaluation (SAUS)
Dog Fan....... Dog Fancy [*A publication*] (BRI)
DOGG......... Department of Geology and Geophysics (SAUO)
DOGI......... Dottrina Giuridica [*Consiglio Nazionale delle Ricerche*] [*Italy*] [*Information service or system*] (CRD)
DOGIT......... Deed of Grant in Trust
DOGM......... Dogmatic
dogm......... dogmatism (SAUS)
dogm......... dogmatist (SAUS)
DOGMAD..... Dissatisfied Owners of General Motors Automotive Diesels (SAUS)
DOGS......... Department of Geological Sciences (SAUO)
DOGS......... Design Oriented Graphics System (SAUS)
DOGS......... Directorate of General Stores (SAUO)
DOGS......... Drawing Office Graphics System [*Deltacam Systems Ltd.*] [*Software package*] (NCC)
DOGS......... Dwingeloo Obscured Galaxy Survey
DOGSYS...... Display of Chromosome Statistics System (SAUS)
DoH......... Department of Health (AIE)
DOH......... Department of Health [*British*] (ECON)
DOH......... Department of Highways (COE)
DOH......... Department overhead (SAUS)
DoH......... Depatment of Health (SAUS)
DOH......... Deutscher Orden der Harugari [*German Order of Harugari*] (EA)
DOH......... Diploma in Occupational Health
doh......... direct operating hours (SAUS)
DOH......... Discrete Output High (MCD)
DOH......... Doha [*Qatar*] [*Airport symbol*] (OAG)
DOH......... Dorchester Hotels, Inc. [*Vancouver Stock Exchange symbol*]
DOH......... Fort Bragg, NC [*Location identifier*] [*FAA*] (FAAL)
DOHA......... Daughters of Hirsutism Association of America (EA)
DOH&S....... Diploma, Occupational Health & Safety [*Medical degree*] (CMD)
dohc......... double overhead (SAUS)
dohc......... double overhead cam (SAUS)
DOHC......... Double Overhead Camshaft [*Automotive term*]
dohc......... dual overhead cam (SAUS)
DOHG......... Double Overhead Camshaft (SAUS)
DOHL......... Dohle Bodies [*Biochemistry*] (DAVI)
DOHS......... Department of Health Services (SARE)
DOHS......... Diploma of Occupational Health and Safety
DOHS......... Disconnected Operation Handling System (VLIE)
DOHSA........ Death on the High Seas Act
DOHSW....... Department of Health, Safety, and Welfare [*Western Australia*]
DOHSWA..... Department of Occupational Health, Safety and Welfare (SAUO)
DO Hyg....... Diploma in Occupational Hygiene [*British*]
DOI......... Daily Operating Instruction (SAUS)
DOI......... Date of Illness (MELL)
DOI......... Date of Implant (MELL)
DOI......... Date of Information (MCD)
DOI......... Date of Injury [*Medicine*]
DOI......... Date of Inquiry (SAUS)
DOI......... Date of Introduction (ADDR)
DOI......... Date of Investigation (MELL)
DOI......... Dead of Injuries [*Medicine*] (BARN)
DOI......... Decision Oriented Information (SAUS)
DOI......... Declaration of Intent (FOTI)
DOI......... Deep Ocean Installation
DOI......... Defence Oceanology International Exhibition [*British*] (ITD)
DOI......... Department of Industry [*British*] (DS)
DOI......... Department of Injustice (SAUO)
D o I......... Department of Institutions (SAUS)
DOI......... Department of Insurance (DEMM)
DOI......... Department of the Interior (AABC)
DoI......... Department of the Interior
DOI......... Department Operating Instruction
DOI......... Descent Orbit Insertion [*Aerospace*]

DOI .... Died of Injuries [*Military*] (AABC)
DOI .... Differential Orbit Improvement
DOI .... Digital Object Identifier [*Computer science*]
DOI .... Digital Operation Interpreter (SAUS)
DOI .... Directorate Office Instruction
DOI .... Director of Information (ODA)
D o I .... Director of Institutions (SAUS)
DOI .... Distinctiveness of Image (SAUS)
DOI .... Distinctness of Image [*Mobay Corp.*]
D o I .... Division of Institutions (SAUS)
DOI .... Division Operating Instruction [*Air Force*]
DOI .... Document Object Identifier (GEOI)
DOI .... Document-Oriented Interface [*Computer science*]
doi .... Dogri [*MARC language code*] [*Library of Congress*] (LCCP)
DOI .... Domain of Interpretation (DINT)
DOI .... DSSCS Operating Instruction (SAUO)
DOI .... Wing Director of Intelligence
DOIA .... Dermatology Online Atlas (SAUO)
DOIC .... Defence Operations and Intelligence Centre [*Australia*]
DOIG .... Divisional Offices of the Inspector General (COE)
DOIM .... Delivery Order Initiating Meeting Procurement
DOIM .... Director [*or Directorate*] of Information Management [*DoD*]
DOIM .... Directory of International Mail [*A publication*]
DO Imp .... Drop out Impulse (SAUS)
DOIMP .... Drop-Out Impulse (VLIE)
DOIN .... Donny Osmond International Network (EA)
DoInt .... Department of the Interior (SAUS)
DOIO .... Directly Operable Input/Output
DOIP .... Dial Other Internet Providers (SAUS)
DOIP .... Dioctylisophthalat (SAUS)
DOIP .... Dioctyl Isophthalate [*Organic chemistry*]
DOIT .... Database Oriented Interrogation Technique [*Comserv Corp.*]
DOIT .... Development of Onsite Innovative Technologies (BCP)
DO/IT .... Digital Output/Input Translator [*Computer science*]
DO-IT .... Disabilities, Opportunities, Internetworking, and Technology
DOJ .... Department of Justice [*Queensland, Tasmania*] [*Australia*]
DOJ .... Directorate of Combat Employment (SAUO)
DOJ .... Dominican Oblates of Jesus [*Roman Catholic women's religious order*]
DOJ .... United States Department of Justice Library, Washington, DC [*OCLC symbol*] (OCLC)
DOK .... De Odeon Kring [*The Odeon Club, for homosexuals*] [*Holland*]
DOK .... Donetsk [*Former USSR*] [*Airport symbol*] [*Obsolete*] (OAG)
DOK .... Order of the Daughters of the King (EA)
DOKDI .... Documentation Service [*Swiss Academy of Medical Sciences*] [*Information service or system*] (IID)
DOKK .... Dramatic Order Knights of Khorassan (EA)
Dokl Biochem... Doklady Biochemistry (journ.) (SAUS)
Dokl Biol Sci... Doklady Biological Sciences (journ.) (SAUS)
Dokl Biophys... Doklady Biophysics (journ.) (SAUS)
Dokl Bot Sci... Doklady Botanical Sciences (journ.) (SAUS)
Dokl Chem... Doklady Chemistry (journ.) (SAUS)
Dokl Chem Technol... Doklady Chemical Technology (journ.) (SAUS)
Dokl Phys Chem... Doklady Physical Chemistry (journ.) (SAUS)
DOL .... Daily Official List [*London Stock Exchange prices*]
DOL .... Daily Operating Log
DOL .... Data Optimization Language (SAUS)
DOL .... Data Optimizing Language (SAUS)
DOL .... Data Output Line (HAWK)
DOL .... Deauville [*France*] [*Airport symbol*] (AD)
DOL .... Deep Ocean Laboratory (SAUO)
DOL .... Degree of Operating Leverage [*Finance*]
Dol .... Department of Industry (SAUS)
DOL .... Department of Labor
DOL .... Department of Labour [*South Australia, Victoria*]
DOL .... Department of Lands [*Queensland*] [*Australia*]
DOL .... Department of Law [*Northern Territory*] [*Australia*]
DOL .... Design Oriented Language [*Computer science*] (VLIE)
DOL .... Detached Officer's List [*Army*]
DOL .... Direct Object Linking (SAUS)
DOL .... Direct On-Line (SAUS)
DOL .... Directorate of Licensing [*AEC*] (NUCP)
DOL .... Director of Laboratories (MCD)
DOL .... Director [*or Directorate*] of Logistics [*DoD*]
DOL .... Discrete Output Low (MCD)
DOL .... Dispersed Operating Locations (SAUS)
DOL .... Display-Oriented Language [*Computer science*] (IEEE)
DOL .... Distal Occlusal Lingual [*Tooth*] [*Medicine*] (EDAA)
DOL .... Dock Owner's Liability [*Insurance*] (MARI)
DOL .... Doctor of Oriental Languages
DOL .... Doctor of Oriental Learning
DOL .... Documentation Language (SAUS)
dol .... Dolar [*Dollar*] [*Monetary unit*] [*Poland*]
DOL .... Dolce [*Sweet*] [*Music*]
DOL .... Dole Food Co. [*NYSE symbol*] (SAG)
DOL .... Dolichol [*Biochemistry*]
DOL .... Dollar (GOBB)
dol .... Dollar [*Monetary unit*] [*French*]
DOL .... Dolomite [*Lithology*]
dol .... Dolor [*Unit of Pain*] [*Medicine*] (BARN)
Dol .... Dolphin
Dol .... Dorothea (SAUS)
Dol .... Dorothy (SAUS)
DOL .... Dynamic Octal Load
DOL .... Dynamic Oil Ltd. [*Vancouver Stock Exchange symbol*]
DOL .... Ebsco, Inc. [*ICAO designator*] (FAAC)
DOLA .... Department of Land Information (SAUO)
DOLA .... Department of Local Administration (Thailand) [*Political party*] (PSAP)
DOLA .... Department of Local Affairs (COE)
DOLA .... Dog Owners League of America [*Defunct*] (EA)
DOLA .... Downtown Los Angeles (SAUS)
Do Lab .... Department of Labor (SAUS)
DOLA/DOLD... Date of Last Adjustment/Date of Last Demand [*Military*] (AFIT)
DOLAN .... Design Office Language [*Computer science*]
DOLAP .... Desktop On Line Analytical Processing (VLIE)
DOLAR .... Department of Labor Acquisition Regulation [*A publication*] (AAGC)
DOLARS .... Departmental On-Line Accounting and Reporting System (SAUS)
DOLARS .... Departmental On-Line Reporting System [*Military*]
DOLARS .... Digital Offline Automatic Recording System
DOLARS .... Disk On-Line Accounts Receivable System [*Computer science*] (MHDB)
DOLARS .... Doppler Location and Ranging System
DOLARS .... Dynamic Preferential Runway System (SAUS)
DolAutEx .... Dole Food Co. [*Associated Press*] (SAG)
Dolby HX .... Dolby headroom extension (SAUS)
Dolby SR .... Dolby Spectral Recording (SAUS)
DOLCE .... Digital On-Line Cryptographic Equipment (NATG)
DOLCEM .... Dolcemente [*Sweetly, Softly*] [*Music*] (ROG)
DOLCIS .... Dolcissimo [*Very Sweetly*] [*Music*]
DOLCISS .... Dolcissimo [*Very Sweetly*] [*Music*] (ROG)
Dolco .... Dolco Packaging Corp. [*Associated Press*] (SAG)
DOLCO .... Down-Link Communications [*Antisubmarine warfare*] (MCD)
DOLD .... Diffuse Obstructive Lung Disease [*Medicine*] (EDAA)
DOLDIS .... Directory of Online Databases Produced in Sweden [*Database*] [*Royal Institute of Technology Library*] [*Information service or system*] (CRD)
DOLE .... Data On-Line Editing System (SAUS)
DOLE .... Data On-Line Editor (SAUS)
DOLE .... Department of Labor and Employment (SAUO)
DOLE .... Designing Out Labour Electronically (NITA)
DOLE .... Detection of Laser Emissions (SAUS)
DOLE .... Digital On-Line Editing System (SAUS)
DOLE .... Digital On-Line Editor (SAUS)
DOLE .... Distributed Object Linking and Embedding [*Communications term*] (DCT)
DOLE .... Distributed On-Line Editing (SAUS)
DOLE .... Distributed On-Line Editor (SAUS)
Dole .... Dole Food Co. [*Associated Press*] (SAG)
DOLENT PART... Dolenti Parti [*To the Afflicted Part*] [*Pharmacy*]
DOLF .... Date of Last Follow-Up (AFIT)
DOLI .... Date of Last Inventory (AFIT)
DOLICH .... Dolichos [*Plant commonly known as Cowitch*] [*Pharmacology*] (ROG)
dolichocephs... dolichocephalics (SAUS)
DOLIN .... Design On-Line (SAUS)
DOLIOES .... Department of Labor Industry Occupational Matrix (SAUO)
DOLIS .... Department of Library and Information Studies (SAUS)
DOLITAC .... Department of Labor International Technical Assistance Corps
DOLL .... Dollar [*Monetary unit*] (ROG)
DOLLARS .... Dedicated On-Line Logistical Airlift Ratemaking System (SAUS)
dollies .... dolophine pills (SAUS)
DollrGn .... Dollar General Corp. [*Associated Press*] (SAG)
DOLLS .... Delayed Opening Leaflet System [*Military propaganda*]
DOLLUS .... Dames of the Loyal Legion of the United States of America (EA)
DOLLY .... Airborne Data Link Equipment (SAUS)
DOLLY .... Data Link (FAAC)
DOLM .... College of Our Lady of Mount Carmel, Washington, DC [*Library symbol*] [*Library of Congress*] (LCLS)
DOLO .... Disbursing Officers Liaison Office
Dolo .... Dolophine (SAUS)
DOLO .... Doloroso [*Mournfully*] [*Music*] (ROG)
DOLOG .... Do Logic (SAUS)
Dolomites .... Dolomite Alps of northeastern Italy (SAUS)
DOLPHIN .... Deep Ocean Logging Profiler Hydrographic Instrumentation and Navigation (SAUS)
DOLPHIN .... Deep Ocean Long Path Hydrographic Instrument (ECON)
DOLPR .... Department of Labor Procurement Regulation [*A publication*] (AAGC)
DOLPRO .... Designer Oriented Language Program (VLIE)
DOLPRO .... Design Oriented Language Program (SAUS)
DOLPS .... Dual Output Linear Power Supply (DWSG)
DOLR .... Dollar General Corp. [*NASDAQ symbol*] (COMM)
DOLRAM .... Detection of Laser, Radar, and Millimeter (ACAE)
DolrTr .... Dollar Tree Stores, Inc. [*Associated Press*] (SAG)
DOLS .... Directorate of Electrical Stores (SAUO)
dols .... dollars (SAUS)
DOLS .... Domino Off-Line Services (VLIE)
DOLT .... Date of Last Transaction (AFIT)
DOLT .... Delay Oriented Logic Tester (SAUS)
DO/IT .... Digital Output/Input Translator (SAUS)
DOLTN .... Dolton, IL [*American Association of Railroads railroad junction routing code*]
DOL URG .... Dolore Urgente [*When the Pain Is Severe*] [*Pharmacy*]
DOLV .... Double Outlet Left Ventricle [*Cardiology*] (DAVI)
DOLY .... Dynamic Global Phytogeography Model (SAUO)
DOM .... Database Options Menu
DOM .... Data On Master group (SAUO)
DOM .... Data Output Mixer (SAUS)
DOM .... Data Output Multiplexer [*Computer science*] (KSC)
DOM .... Data Quality Message (ADWA)
DOM .... Date of Marriage (SAUS)
DOM .... Datur Omnibus Mori [*It Is Allotted unto All to Die*] [*Latin*]

DOM .... Daughters of Mercy (Croatian) (TOCD)
DOM .... Day of Month (COE)
DOM .... Dealer Operations Manager [*Automotive retailing*]
DOM .... Deaminated-O-Methyl Metabolite [*Biochemistry*] (MAE)
Dom .... De Domo Sua [*of Cicero*] [*Classical studies*] (OCD)
DOM .... Delivery Order Manager [*Army*]
DOM .... Delta Oil Mill [*Federal Railroad Administration identification code*]
DOM .... Deo Optimo Maximo [*To God, Most Good, Most Great*] [*Latin*]
DOM .... Department of Medicine
DOM .... Department of Metalwork (SAUO)
DOM .... Department of Mines [*Tasmania*] [*Australia*]
DOM .... Depth of Modulation
DOM .... Description, Operation, and Maintenance
DOM .... Designing Out Maintenance
DOM .... Design of Maintenance (SAUS)
DOM .... Design-out Maintenance (SAUS)
dom .... digestible organic matter (SAUS)
DOM .... Digital Ohmmeter
DOM .... Digital Output Multiplexer (CAAL)
DOM .... Digit Organized Memory (SAUS)
DOM .... dimethoxyalpha methyl phenethylmine (SAUS)
DOM .... Dimethoxymethylamphetamine [*A hallucinogenic drug, more commonly known as STP*]
DOM .... Diocese Of Melanesia (SAUS)
DOM .... Diocytl Maleate (SAUS)
DOM .... Diploma in Ophthalmic Medicine
DOM .... Dirty Old Man [*Slang*]
DOM .... disc operating monitor (SAUS)
DOM .... Discrete Ordinate Method (SAUS)
DOM .... Disk Operating Monitor [*Computer science*]
DOM .... Dispersed Organic Matter [*Chemistry*]
DOM .... Dissolved Organic Macromolecules (CARB)
DOM .... Dissolved Organic Matter
DOM .... Dissolved Oxygen Monitor (SAUS)
DOM .... Distributed Object Management [*Computer science*]
DOM .... Distributed Operations Master (MWOL)
DOM .... Division of Overseas Ministries [*National Council of Churches*]
DOM .... Divorced Oriental Male (SAUO)
DOM .... Document Object Model [*Computer science*]
DOM .... Document Object Module (RALS)
Dom .... Domain (SAUS)
DOM .... Doman Industries Ltd. [*Toronto Stock Exchange symbol*] [*Vancouver Stock Exchange symbol*]
Dom .... Domenico (SAUS)
DOM .... Domesday [*British*] (ROG)
DOM .... Domestic (AFM)
Dom .... Domestic (TBD)
dom .... Domestic (TRID)
DOM .... Domicile
DOM .... Dominance [*Psychology*]
dom .... Dominant (ADWA)
DOM .... Dominant
Dom .... Domingo [*Sunday*] [*Spanish*]
Dom .... Dominic (SAUS)
DOM .... Dominica [*Leeward Islands*] [*Airport symbol*] (AD)
DOM .... Dominica [*West Indies*] [*Airport symbol*] (OAG)
DOM .... Dominica [*West Indies*] [*Seismograph station code, US Geological Survey*] (SEIS)
Dom .... Dominican (NTIO)
DOM .... Dominican (WDAA)
DOM .... Dominican Republic [*ANSI three-letter standard code*] (CNC)
dom .... Dominion (NTIO)
DOM .... Dominion
DOM .... Dominion Res Black Warrior Tr [*NYSE symbol*] (TTSB)
DOM .... Dominion Resources Black Warrior Trust [*NYSE symbol*] (SAG)
DOM .... Dominus [*The Lord*] [*Latin*]
DOM .... Dominus Omnium Magister [*God the Master, or Lord, of All*] [*Motto of the Benedictine Order*] [*Latin*]
Dom .... Domitianus [*of Suetonius*] [*Classical studies*] (OCD)
DOM .... Dos Mundos [*Dominican Republic*] [*ICAO designator*] (FAAC)
DOM .... Drawn over Mandrel [*Tubes*]
DOM .... Quit for Domestic Reasons [*Unemployment insurance*] (OICC)
DOMA .... Dihydroxymandelic Acid [*Also, DHMA, DMA*] [*Organic chemistry*]
DOMA .... Director, Operation and Maintenance, Army
DOMA .... Dokumentation Maschinenbau [*Mechanical Engineering Documentation*] [*Technical Information Center*] [*Information service or system*]
DOMAC .... Drug Marketing, Advertising, and Communications [*FDA*]
DOMADIZ .... Domestic Air Defense Identification Zone (SAUS)
DOMAIN .... Distributed Operating Multi-Access Interactive Network [*Apollo Computer, Inc.*] [*Chelmsford, MA*] [*Telecommunications*] (TSSD)
DOMAINS .... Deep Ocean Instrumented Station (SAA)
DOMAINS .... Deep Ocean Manned Instrumented Station [*National Oceanic and Atmospheric Administration*] (PDAA)
DOMAPP .... Domestic Appliance (IAA)
DOMAR .... Doppler Martin RADAR [*Air Force*]
Domat Civ Law .... Domat's Civil Law [*A publication*] (DLA)
DOMB .... Dead Old Martian Bacterium [*Humorous biology terminology*]
DOMB .... Deep Ocean Moored Buoy [*Marine science*] (MSC)
DOMB .... Director of the Office of Management and Budget (COE)
Dom Book .... Domesday Book [*Census-like record of the lands of England, 1085-86*] [*A publication*] (DLA)
Dom Can .... Dominion of Canada (SAUS)
Dom Civ Law .... Domat's Civil Law [*A publication*] (DLA)
DOMCO .... Deep Ocean Mining Co. (SAUS)
Domco .... Deep Ocean Mining Co.Ltd. (SAUO)
DOMCO .... Deep Ocean Mining Company (SAUO)
DOMD .... Digestible Organic Matter in Dry (OA)
DOMD .... Digital Oxygen Metering Device [*Aerospace*]
DOME .... Deputy Ordnance Mechanical Engineer (SAUO)
DOME .... Development of Opportunities through Meaningful Education [*Project*]
DOME .... Diagnosis, Objectives, Method, Evaluation [*Formula*] [*LIMRA*]
DOME .... Distributed Object Management Environment [*Computer science*] (BTTJ)
DOME .... District Ordnance Mechanical Engineer (SAUO)
Dome .... Dome Petroleum Ltd. (SAUO)
dom econ .... domestic economy (SAUS)
DOMES .... Deep Ocean Mining and Environmental Study (SAUO)
DOMES .... Deep Ocean Mining Environmental Study [*National Oceanic and Atmospheric Administration*]
DOMES .... Deep Ocean Mining Experimental Study (SAUS)
DOMES .... Digest of Middle East Studies [*A publication*] (BRI)
Domes .... Domesday Book [*Census-like record of the lands of England, 1085-86*] [*A publication*] (DLA)
DOMESA .... Don't Overlook Mature Expertise, South Australia
DOMESD .... Domesday Book [*Census-like record of the lands of England, 1085-86*] (ROG)
Domesday .... Domesday Book [*Census-like record of the lands of England, 1085-86*] [*A publication*] (DLA)
DOMESTIC .... Development of microcomputers in an environment of science and technology inform (SAUS)
DOMESTIC .... Development of Minicomputers Applications in an Environment of Scientific and Technological Information Centers (SAUS)
DOMESTIC .... Development of Minicomputers in an Environment of Scientific and Technological Information Centers [*Computer science*]
DOMEV .... Don't Overlook Mature Expertise, Victoria [*Australia*]
DOMEX .... Display Oriented Macro Expander [*Computer science*] (PDAA)
Dom Ex .... Domestic Exchange (MHDW)
DOMF .... Dibromohydroxymercurifluorescein [*Antiseptic*]
DOMF .... Distributed Object-Management Facility
Dom Fiji .... Dominion of Fiji (SAUS)
DOMFS .... Diploma, Oral & Maxillofacial Surgery [*Medical degree*] (CMD)
domi .... domicile (SAUS)
Domi .... Dominicus de Sancto Geminiano [*Flourished, 1407-09*] [*Authority cited in pre-1607 legal work*] (DSA)
DOM ICE .... Domestic Icebreaking [*USCG*] (TAG)
DOMICS .... Direct Computation of Minimal Cut Sets (SAUS)
Domi de San Gemi .... Dominicus de Sancto Geminiano [*Flourished, 1407-09*] [*Authority cited in pre-1607 legal work*] (DSA)
DOMINA .... Distribution-Oriented Management Information Analyzer [*Computer science*] (MHDI)
Dominican C San Rafael .... [*The*] Dominican College of San Rafael (GAGS)
Dominican Republic .... eastern half of Hispaniola in the West Indies (SAUS)
DOMIS .... Directory of Materials Data Information Services (SAUO)
DOMISAT .... Domestic Satellite (SAUS)
DOMLIB .... Domestic Library Automation Functions [*Computer science*]
DOMMDA .... Drawing Office Material Manufacturers' and Dealers' Association [*British*] (BI)
DOMN .... Domain Technology, Inc. [*NASDAQ symbol*] (COMM)
Domng .... Dominguez Services Corp. [*Associated Press*] (SAG)
DOMNN .... Dominion
DOMO .... Deep Ocean Mining Operations [*Marine science*] (MSC)
DOMO .... Dispensing Opticians Manufacturing Organisation [*British*] (BI)
DOMO .... Dispensing Opticians Manufacturing Organization (SAUO)
domo .... Domingo [*Sunday*] [*Spanish*]
DOMO .... Downwardly Mobile [*Lifestyle classification*]
DOMONIC .... Johnsten Island Experiment (SAUS)
DOMP .... disease of medical progress (SAUS)
DOMP .... Dope and Wimp [*Term used by Ross Thomas in his book, "Briarpatch"*]
Dom Pedro II .... Dom Pedro de Alcantara, emperor and president of Brazil (SAUS)
DOMPRINT .... DOMESTIC [*Development of Microcomputers in an Environment of Scientific and Technological Information Centers*] Print Generator [*Computer science*]
DOM PROC .... Domus Procerum [*The House of Lords*] [*Latin*] (ROG)
DOMREP .... Dominican Republic (AFM)
Dom Rep .... Dominican Republic (VRA)
DomRes .... Dominion Resources, Inc. [*Associated Press*] (SAG)
DOMS .... Defence Operational Movement Staff (SAUO)
DOMS .... Delayed-Onset Muscle Soreness
DOMS .... Depot Operation Management System [*Army*]
DOMS .... Diploma in Ophthalmic Medicine and Surgery [*British*]
DOMS .... Directorate of Military Support (AABC)
DOMS .... Director of Military Support [*Army*] (DEMM)
DOMS .... Distributed Object Management System [*Computer science*] (AGLO)
DOMS .... Doctor of Orthopaedic Medicine and Surgery
domsast .... Domestic Satellite (SAUS)
DOMSAT .... Domestic Communications Satellite (DOAD)
DOMSAT .... Domestic Satellite [*Australia*] (NITA)
domsat .... domestic satellite carrier (SAUS)
DOMSAT .... Domestic Satellite Network (SAUO)
DOMSATCOM System .... Domestic Satellite Communications System (SAUS)
DOMSATS .... Domestic Satellite Systems (SAUS)
DOMSAT System .... Domestic Satellite System (SAUS)
DOM SC .... Domestic Science [*Freight*]
dom sci .... domestic science (SAUS)
Domtar .... Domtar Ltd. [*Associated Press*] (SAG)
DOMZ .... Dominguez Services Corp. [*NASDAQ symbol*] (NQ)
DOMZ .... Dominquez Services [*NASDAQ symbol*] (TTSB)
DON .... Delayed Order Notice [*Telecommunications*] (TEL)

DON............ Demand Order Number [*Army*] (AABC)
DON............ Demyelinating Optic Neuritis (SAUS)
DON............ Deoxynivalenol [*A mycotoxin*]
DON............ Department of the Navy
DON............ Determination of Need (MELL)
DON............ Deuterium-Moderated Organic-Cooled Nuclear Reactor (SAUS)
DON............ Diazooxo-L-norleucine [*Antineoplastic drug*]
DON............ Digital Overlay Network [*Communications term*] (DCT)
DON............ Dimensionality of Nations Project [*Hawaii*]
DON............ Dioxynaphthalene (SAUS)
DON............ Diploma in Orthopaedic Nursing (SAUS)
DON............ Director of Nursing
DON............ Dissolved Organic Nitrogen [*Analytical chemistry*]
DON............ Distribution Octane Number [*Engineering*] (IAA)
DON............ Donair Flying Club Ltd. [*British*] [*ICAO designator*] (FAAC)
DON............ Donative
DON............ Donec [*Until*] [*Pharmacy*] (ROG)
Don............ Donegal (ADWA)
DON............ Donegal [*County in Ireland*]
DON............ Dongola [*Missouri*] [*Seismograph station code, US Geological Survey*] (SEIS)
DON............ Donnelly Corp. [*AMEX symbol*] (SPSG)
DON............ Donnelly Corp.Cl'A' [*NYSE symbol*] (SG)
don............ Donor (PROS)
DON............ Doppler Optical Navigation
DON............ Dysbaric Osteonecrosis [*Scuba diving disorder*]
DONA.......... Decentralized Open Network Architecture (BUR)
DONA.......... Doulas of North America [*An association*] (PAZ)
DONA.......... Dynamic Organizational Network Analysis (SAUS)
DONADPM... Department of the Navy Automatic Data Processing Management (DNAB)
Donaker....... Donaker's Reports [*165 Indiana*] [*A publication*] (DLA)
DONAL......... Department of the Navy Occupational Level (DNAB)
Donalbane... Donald Bane (SAUS)
Donaldsn..... Donaldon Co., Inc. [*Associated Press*] (SAG)
don alv sol fuerit... Donec Alvus Soluta Fuerit [*Until the Bowels Are Opened*] [*Latin*] [*Medicine*] (DAVI)
Donat.......... Aelius Donatus [*Fourth century AD*] [*Classical studies*] (OCD)
DONAU........ domain oriented natural language understanding (SAUS)
Donbas........ Donets Basin in the Ukraine (SAUS)
DONCS......... Director of Operations Narcotics Control Reports [*CIA*]
DONEC ALV BIS DEJ... Donec Alvus Bis Dejiciatur [*Until the Bowels Have Been Twice Evacuated*] [*Pharmacy*] (ROG)
DONEC ALV SOL FUER... Donec Alvus Soluta Fuerit [*Until the Bowels Are Opened*] [*Pharmacy*] (ROG)
DONEC ALV SOL FUERIT... Donec Alvus Soluta Fuerit [*Until the Bowels Are Opened*] [*Pharmacy*]
DONEC DOL NEPH EXULAV... Donec Dolor Nephriticus Exulaverit [*Until the Nephritic Pain Is Removed*] [*Pharmacy*] (ROG)
DONEG......... Donegal [*County in Ireland*] (ROG)
Donegal....... Donegal Group, Inc. [*Associated Press*] (SAG)
Donelly........ Donnelley Corp. [*Associated Press*] (SAG)
Donets......... Donets Basin or Donbas of the Ukraine (SAUS)
DON FEORP... Department of the Navy Federal Equal Opportunity Recruitment Program (DNAB)
Donghwa..... Donghwa News Agency (SAUO)
donk............ donkey (SAUS)
donk............ donkey boy (SAUS)
donk............ donkeycart (SAUS)
donk............ donkey sled (SAUS)
Donkeny...... Donnkenny, Inc. [*Associated Press*] (SAG)
DonLJ.......... Donaldson Lufkin & Jenrette [*Associated Press*] (SAG)
Donlley........ Donnelley [*R.R.*] & Sons Co. [*Associated Press*] (SAG)
DONMICS.... Department of the Navy Management Information Control System
Donn........... Donnell's Irish Land Cases [*1871-76*] [*A publication*] (DLA)
Donn........... Donnelly's English Chancery Reports [*A publication*] (DLA)
Donnelly...... Donnelly's English Chancery Reports [*A publication*] (DLA)
Donnelly (Eng)... Donnelly's English Chancery Reports [*A publication*] (DLA)
Donn Eq....... Donnelly's English Chancery Reports [*A publication*] (DLA)
Donn Ir Land Cas... Donnell's Irish Land Cases [*1871-76*] [*A publication*] (DLA)
DONO.......... Dimethyloctadecanamine N-Oxide [*Organic chemistry*]
DONOACS.... Department of the Navy Office Automation and Communication System (SAUO)
DONOACS.... Department of the Navy Office Automation and Communication Systems (GFGA)
DONPIC........ Department of the Navy Program Information Center
Don Q.......... Don Quixote (SAUS)
DONR.......... Department of Natural Resources (SAUS)
DoNSIR....... Department of the Navy Suicide Incident Report
DonSoc........ Donizetti Society (EA)
DONSS......... Directorate of Naval Survival and Safety
Don Tr......... Donovan's Modern Jury Trials [*A publication*] (DLA)
DONUT......... Digitally Operated Network Using Threshold (SAUS)
DONUT......... Direct Observation of the Nu Tau
DONUT......... Doughnut
DONUTS....... Driver Oriented New Ultimate Tire Science
DOO............ Daily Operations Order (SAUO)
DOO............ Deep Ocean Ordnance
DOO............ Departmental Organization Order [*Marine science*] (OSRA)
DOO............ Department Organization Order [*Department of Commerce*] (NOAA)
doo............ diesel oil odor (SAUS)
DOO............ Directing Ordnance Officer [*Military*] [*British*]
DOO............ Director, Office of Oceanography [*UNESCO*]
DOO............ Director of the Office of Oceanography (SAUS)
DOO............ Disposition One Only (MCD)
DOO............ District Operations Office [*or Officer*] [*Navy*]
DOO............ District Ordnance Office [*or Officer*] [*Navy*]
DOO............ Division Ordnance Officer
DOO............ Doolan Road [*California*] [*Seismograph station code, US Geological Survey*] (SEIS)
DOO............ Dorobisoro [*Papua New Guinea*] [*Airport symbol*] (OAG)
DOO............ Driver-Only Operation [*Railroad*] [*British*]
DOOBE......... Disillusioned, Overcharged, Outraged Buyers Explode [*Computer hacker's terminology*] (PCM)
DOOC.......... Diabetes Out of Control [*Medicine*] (MEDA)
DOOD.......... De Olympiade Onder Dectatuur [*The Olympics Under Dictatorship*] [*An exhibition in 1936 by 150 artists protesting Nazi repression*] [*Reconstructed in 1996 by the Amsterdam Municipal Archives*]
DOODY........ Do-Object-Oriented-Development-Yourself [*Computer science*]
DOOF.......... Driver-Only Operation, Freight [*Railroad*] [*British*]
DOOL.......... Days of Our Lives [*NBC-TV daytime serial*]
DOOLAR...... Deep Ocean Object Location and Recovery [*Navy*]
DOOLEY....... Dooley Foundation (SAUS)
DOOM.......... Decentralised Object Orientated Machine [*Computer science*] (VERA)
DOOM.......... Deep Ocean Optical Measurement
DOOP.......... Driver-Only Operation, Passenger [*Railroad*] [*British*]
DOOPO........ Director of Operations, Operational Plans Officer (MUGU)
DOOR.......... Deafness, Onycho-Osteodystrophy, Mental Retardation Syndrome [*Medicine*] (DMAA)
DOORS........ Data on Occupations Retrieval System [*Great Britain Manpower Services Commission*] [*Information service or system*] (CRD)
DOORS........ Defense Oriented Online Retrieval System (SAUS)
DOORS........ Development of Operational Reasoning Skills
DOORS........ Directory of Outpatient Ostomy Resources and Services [*International Association for Enterostomal Therapy*]
DOORS........ Dynamic Object-Oriented Requirements System [*Computer science*] (HODG)
DOOW.......... Diving Officer-of-the-Watch [*Navy*] (DNAB)
DOP............ Data Out-Port (TIMI)
DOP............ Declaration of Principles (Israel) [*Political party*] (PSAP)
DOP............ Declaration of Principles on Interim Self-Governing Arrangements (SAUO)
DOP............ Degree of Protection
DOP............ Degree of Pyritization [*Geology*]
DOP............ Deliver Documents on Payment of Draft (SAUS)
D o P........... Department of Prisons (SAUS)
DOP............ Department of Productivity (SAUS)
DOP............ Depth of Penetration [*Test*] [*Medicine*] (DB)
DOP............ Dermo-Optical Perception [*Parapsychology*]
DOP............ Designated Overhaul Point
DOP............ Desoctapeptide Insulin [*Medicine*]
DOP............ Detachment of Patients
DOP............ Detailed Observing Plan (SAUS)
DOP............ Detailed Operating Procedure
DOP............ Detection Operational Program [*Military*] (CAAL)
DOP............ Developer Oxidation Product [*Photography*]
DOP............ Developing-Out Paper
DOP............ Development Options Paper (SAUO)
DOP............ Digital Offset Press (SAUS)
DOP............ Dilution of Position (SAUS)
DOP............ Dilution of Precision
DOP............ Dioctyl Phosphate [*Organic chemistry*]
DOP............ Di-Octyl-Phthalat (SAUS)
DOP............ Dioctyl Phthalate [*Also, DEHP*] [*Organic chemistry*]
dop............ diocytl phthalate (SAUS)
D-OP.......... Diplomate, American Board of Ophthalmology (DHSM)
DOP............ Director of Office of Programming [*Military*]
DOP............ Directory Operational Binding Management Protocol (SAUS)
DOP............ Directory Operational Protocol [*Computer science*] (MWOL)
DOP............ Disaster Operations Plan [*Nuclear energy*] (NRCH)
DOP............ Di-Secondary Octyl Phthalate (GFGA)
DOP............ Display Output Processor (SAUS)
DOP............ Dissolved Organic Phosphorus
DOP............ Diver Operated Plug (MCD)
DOP............ Division of Planning (SAUO)
DOP............ Doctor of Philosophy (SAUO)
DOP............ Documents on Payment [*Banking*]
DOP............ Dolpa [*Nepal*] [*Airport symbol*] (OAG)
DOP............ Dopamine [*Pharmacology*] (DAVI)
DOP............ Doppler (KSC)
DOP............ Driver's Open Practice [*Motorsports*]
DOP............ Drop-Off Point (SAUS)
DOP............ Dropping Outward Pilot (RIMS)
DOP............ Dumbarton Oaks Papers [*A publication*] (ABAR)
dopa........... Dihydroxyphenylalanine (ADWA)
DOPA.......... Dihydroxyphenylalanine [*Biochemistry*]
DOPA.......... Disapproval of Permit Applications (SAUO)
DOPA.......... Dopamine [*Pharmacology*] (DAVI)
DOPA.......... Dynamic Output Printer Analyzer (IAA)
DOPAA........ Description of Proposed Actions and Alternatives [*Military*]
DOPAC........ Dihydroxyphenylacetic Acid [*Biochemistry*]
DOPAC Acid... Dihydroxyphenylacetic Acid (SAUS)
DOPACK...... Doppler Software Package (ADA)
dopadic....... dope addict (SAUS)
DOPAMINE... Dihydroxyphenethylamine (SAUS)
DOPASE....... Dihydroxyphenylalanine Oxidase [*Organic chemistry*] (DMAA)
dopase........ dopa oxidase (SAUS)
DOPC.......... Determined Osteogenic Precursor Cell [*Medicine*] (MELL)
DOPC.......... Dioleoylphosphatidylcholine [*Organic chemistry*]
DOPCOM...... Doppler Command Missile Delivery System (ACAE)

DOPDF......... Doppler Direction-Finding (SAUS)
DOPDF Equipment... Doppler Direction-Finding Equipment (SAUS)
DOPE........... Databank of Program Evaluations [*University of California, Los Angeles*] (IID)
DOPE........... Dioleylphosphatidylethanolamine [*Organic chemistry*]
DOPE........... Display, Oral, Printed, and Electronic [*Media*]
DOPE........... Double Odd Pass Even [*System in game of bridge*]
DOPEG......... Dihydroxyphenylglycol [*Also, DHPG*] [*Organic chemistry*]
DOPET......... Dihydroxyphenylethanol [*Organic chemistry*]
DOPF........... Divorced Oriental Professional Female (SAUO)
DOPF........... Duty Directed in Order Is Being Performed For
DOPG........... Duty Officers Procedure Guide [*Department of Emergency Management*] (DEMM)
D OPH......... Doctor of Ophthalmology (WDAA)
DOPHHH...... Division on Physically Handicapped, Homebound, and Hospitalized [*Later, DPH*] (EA)
DOphth........ Doctor of Ophthalmology (NADA)
DOPI............ Delay-On-Pull-In (SAUS)
DOPI............ Overseas Private Investment Corp., Washington, DC [*Library symbol*] [*Library of Congress*] (LCLS)
DOPIC.......... Documentation of Programs in Core [*Computer science*] (IEEE)
DOP/INS...... Doppler/Inertials (SAUS)
DOPLID........ Doppler Lidar (EOSA)
DOPLIGHT... Doppler-Balloon [*Marine science*] (OSRA)
DOPLIGHT... Doppler-Lighting (USDC)
DOPLOC....... Doppler & Lock (SAUS)
DOPLOC....... Doppler Location (IAA)
DOPLOC....... Doppler Phase Lock
DOPLOON.... Doppler-balloon (SAUS)
DOPLR......... Department of Productivity and Labour Relations (SAUO)
DOPM.......... Divorced Oriental Professional Male (SAUO)
DOPMA........ Defense Officer Personnel Management Act [*1980*] (MCD)
DOPMS........ Defense Officer Personnel Management Study (NVT)
DOPO.......... Delivery Order Project Officer (SAUO)
DOPODT...... Doped Polysilicon Diffusion Technology [*Electronics*] (IAA)
DOPOS......... Doped Poly-Silicon (SAUS)
DOPOS......... doped polysilicon diffusion (SAUS)
DOPOS......... Doped Polysilicon Diffusion Source [*Electronics*] (IAA)
DOPOS......... Doped Polysilicon Diffusion Technology (SAUS)
DOPOS technology... doped-polysilicon diffusion technology (SAUS)
DOPOS Technology... Doped Poly-Silicon Technology (SAUS)
DOPP........... Dihydroxyphenylpyruvic Acid [*Biochemistry*] (DB)
DOPP........... Dioctylphenyl Phosphonate [*Organic chemistry*]
DOPP........... Doppler (MUGU)
DOPP PED... Doppio Pedale [*Double Pedal*] [*Music*]
DOPR........... Defense Order Priority Rating [*DoD*] (GFGA)
DOPR........... Dove Prion [*North American bird banding code*] (BIBA)
DOPRT......... Date of Departure [*Army*]
DOPS........... DIA [*Defense Intelligence Agency*] Outline Plotting System
DOPS........... Diffuse Obstructive Pulmonary Syndrome [*Medicine*] (MAE)
DOPS........... Digital Optical Projection System (IEEE)
DOPS........... Dihydroxyphenylserine [*Biochemistry*]
DOPS........... Dioleoylphosphatidylserine [*Biochemistry*]
DOPS........... Direct Optical Position Sensor [*Instrumentation*]
DOPS........... Directorate of Personnel Stores (SAUO)
DOps........... Director of Operations (SAUS)
DOPS........... Display Observer Performance Study (SAUS)
DOPSK......... Differential Offset Phase Shift Keying (SAUS)
DOPSUM...... Daily Operations Summary (SAUS)
d-o psychiatrists... directive-organic psychiatrists (SAUS)
DOPT........... Defence Organisation Project Team (SAUS)
DOpt........... Diploma in Ophthalmics (ADA)
D OPT.......... Doctor of Optometry (WDAA)
DOPTAR....... Doppler Tracking and Ranging [*Military*] (CAAL)
D Opth......... Doctor of Ophthalmology
DOQ............ Digital Orthophoto Quadrangle (GEOI)
DOQ............ Dynamic Order Quantity
DOQQ.......... Digital Orthophoto Quarter Quadrangle (GEOI)
DOR............ Daily Operational Report
DOR............ Daily Operations Report (SAUS)
DOR............ Daily Outage Report (SSD)
DOR............ Dance-Oriented Rock [*Music*] (BARN)
DOR............ Data Output Register [*Computer science*]
DOR............ Date of Rank [*Air Force*]
DOR............ Date of Ratification (SAUS)
DOR............ Date of Request (AFM)
DOR............ Dead on Road (SAUS)
DOR............ Dental Operating Room (SAUS)
DOR............ Department of Offender Rehabilitation (SAUS)
DoR............ Department of Rehabilitation (SAUS)
DOR............ Department of Revenue (DEMM)
DOR............ Design Objective Reliability
DOR............ Deuterium-Moderated and Organic-Cooled Reactor (SAUS)
DOR............ Differenced One-way Range (SAUS)
DOR............ Differential One-Way Ranging (ACAE)
DOR............ Digital - Optical - Reader (SAUS)
DOR............ Digital Optical Record (IAA)
DOR............ Digital Optical Recorder (SAUS)
DOR............ Digital Optical Recording (SAUS)
DOR............ Digital Output Relay
DOR............ diminished ovarian reserve (SAUS)
DOR............ Directorate of Operational Requirements (SAUO)
DOR............ Director of Operational Requirements [*Air Ministry*] [*British*]
DOR............ Directory Overhead Record (TIMI)
DOR............ Disaster Operations Room [*Public safety*]
DOR............ Discharged on Own Recognizance (IIA)
DOR............ Division of Operating Reactors (SAUS)
DOR............ Division of Research [*Indiana University*] [*Research center*] (RCD)
DOR............ Division of responsibility matrix (SAUS)
D Or............ Doctor of Oratory
D Or............ Doctor of Orientation (SAUS)
DOR............ Document Ordres et Reglements Statutaires [*Statutory Orders and Regulations - SOR*] [*Database*] [*Federal Department of Justice*] [*Canada*] [*Information service or system*] (CRD)
Dor............. Dorado [*Constellation*]
DOR............ Dori [*Upper Volta*] [*Airport symbol*] (AD)
DOR............ Dori [*Burkina Faso*] [*Airport symbol*] (OAG)
Dor............. Doric (ADWA)
DOR............ Doric
Dor............. Dorion's Quebec Reports [*A publication*] (DLA)
DOR............ Dormitory
DOR............ Dornier Reparaturwerft GmbH [*Germany*] [*ICAO designator*] (FAAC)
Dor............. Dorothy (SAUS)
DOR............ Dorr-Oliver, Inc. (SAUO)
dor............. Dorsal [*Medicine*] (EDAA)
DOR............ Dorse (SAUS)
DOR............ Double Rotation [*Spectroscopy*]
DOR............ Dropout Rate (DNAB)
DOR............ Dropped Own Request [*Navy*]
DOR............ Due-Out Release (ACAE)
DOR............ Dundarave Resources [*Vancouver Stock Exchange symbol*]
DOR............ Endorex Corp. [*AMEX symbol*] (SG)
DOR............ Graduate School of Business Administration, Division of Research [*University of Michigan*] [*Research center*] (RCD)
D OR.......... United States District Court for the District of Oregon (DLA)
DORA.......... Defence of the Realm Act [*World War I*] [*British*]
DORA.......... Directorate of Operational Research and Analysis (SAUS)
DORA.......... Directory of Rare Analyses [*A publication*]
DORA.......... Disbursing Officers' Relief Act [*1982*]
DORA.......... Dora, AL [*American Association of Railroads railroad junction routing code*]
Dora........... Dorado [*Constellation*]
Dora........... Dorothea (SAUS)
Dora........... Dorothy (SAUS)
DORA.......... Double Roll Out Arrays (MCD)
DORA.......... Dynamic Operator Response Apparatus
dora........... dynamic operators response apparatus (SAUS)
Dora........... Eudora (SAUS)
DORACE...... Design Organization, Record, Analyze, Charge, Estimate (MHDB)
DORAN........ DLAs Operations Research Analysis Network (SAUS)
doran.......... Doppler Range (SAUS)
DORAN........ Doppler Range and Navigation [*Electronics*]
doran.......... Doppler Ranging and Navigation (SAUS)
Dor Bank..... Doria's Law and Practice in Bankruptcy [*2nd ed.*] [*1873*] [*A publication*] (DLA)
DORC.......... Dental Officers Reserve Corps (SAUO)
DORCA........ Dynamic Operational Requirements and Cost Analysis [*Computer program*] [*NASA*]
DORCG........ Date of Rank, Current Grade [*Air Force*] (AFM)
DORCH........ Dorchester [*City in England*] (ROG)
DORCMA..... Door Operator and Remote Controls Manufacturers Association (EA)
DORCSA...... District Officer for Reserve Communication Supplementary Activities
DORD.......... Deep Ocean Resources Development Co. Ltd. (SAUO)
Dord........... Dordogne (SAUS)
DORDEC...... Domestic Refrigeration Development Committee [*British*] (BI)
DORDEC...... Domestic Refrigerator Development Council (SAUO)
DORDISK..... Digital Optic Recording Disk (SAUS)
DORE.......... Defense Operational Research Establishment (SAUS)
DORE.......... DoD [*Department of Defense*] Officer Record Examination
DORE.......... Dynamic Object Rendering Environment (VLIE)
DOR/ER...... Direct oxide reduction/electrorefining (SAUS)
DORF.......... Diamond Ordnance Radiation Facility [*Nuclear reactor*]
DORFA........ Subcommittee on Department Operations, Research, and Foreign Agriculture [*Congress*]
DOrg........... Director of Organization (SAUS)
DORI........... Displace on Order - Replace Installed (SAUS)
DORI........... Displace on Order-Replace Installed (VLIE)
DORIDN....... Doriden [*Rhone-Poulenc Rorer Consumer Pharmaceuticals*] [*Pharmacology*] (DAVI)
Dorie.......... Doris (SAUS)
Dor Ins....... Dorsay's Law of Insolvency [*A publication*] (DLA)
Dorion........ Dorion's Quebec Queen's Bench Reports [*A publication*] (DLA)
Dorion (Can)... Dorion's Quebec Queen's Bench Reports (Canada) [*A publication*] (DLA)
Dorion QB.... Dorion's Quebec Queen's Bench Reports [*A publication*] (DLA)
DORIS......... Dealers' Office Realtime Information System [*London Stock Exchange*] (NITA)
DORIS......... Decision-Oriented Resource Information System [*Ventura County, CA*] (GEOI)
DORIS......... Deck-Operated Remote Inspection Submersible
DORIS......... Demographic Online Retrieval Information System [*CACI, Inc.*]
DORIS......... Designer's Online Realtime Interactive Secretary (SAUS)
DORIS......... Determination d'Orbite et Radiopositionement Integre par Satellite (EOSA)
DORIS......... Development of Reasoning in Science
DORIS......... Diagnostic Oriented Rockwell Intelligent System (SAUS)
DORIS......... Direct Order Recording and Invoicing System [*A computer-based system of British petroleum companies*]
DORIS......... Division of Research Information System (SAA)
DORIS......... Doppler Orbit and Radio Positioning Integration by Satellite (SAUS)

DORIS......... Doppler Orbitography and Radiopositioning Integrated by Satellite [*Marine science*] (OSRA)
DORIS......... Doppler Orbitography Integrated by Satellite
DORIS......... Doppler Ranging and Information System [*Navy*] (MCD)
DORIS......... Dornier Recoverable Instrument Sonde (MCD)
DORIS......... Dornier Recycling Informationssystem (SAUS)
DORIS......... Double-Ring Storage [*Particle accelerator*]
DO-RITE....... Define, Observe, Record, Intervene, Test, Evaluate (SAUS)
DORJC......... Dorchester Junction, VA [*American Association of Railroads railroad junction routing code*]
DORK.......... Diagnostically Optimizable Recursive Keyword [*Program generator*] (NITA)
DORK.......... Direct On-Line Retrievable Knowledge (SAUS)
DORK.......... Direct Order Recording Keyboard (SAUS)
DORL.......... Developmental Orbital Research Laboratory (SAUS)
DORL.......... Diploma in Otorhinolaryngology
DORL.......... Doral Financial Corp. [*NASDAQ symbol*] (NASQ)
DORLS......... Directors of Ontario Regional Library Systems (SAUS)
dorm.......... Dormitory (VRA)
DORM.......... Dormitory
Dor MD Laws... Dorsey's Maryland Laws [*A publication*] (DLA)
dorna.......... desoxyribose nucleic acid (SAUS)
Dorn Bk....... Domesday Book (SAUS)
DORO.......... Displace on Order - Replace on Order (SAUS)
DORO.......... Displace on Order-Replace on Order (VLIE)
DORPG......... Date of Rank, Permanent Grade [*Air Force*] (AFM)
Dor QB........ Dorion's Quebec Queen's Bench Reports [*A publication*] (DLA)
DORRA......... DLA Office of Operations Research and Resource Analysis (SAUO)
DORRI......... Distinction of Retro-Reflected Image [*Metal finishing*]
DORS.......... Davis Online Reference Services [*University of California, Davis*] (OLDSS)
DORS.......... Defence Operational Requirements [*British military*] (DMA)
DORS.......... Defence Operational Requirements Staff (SAUO)
DORS.......... Defense Outplacement Referral System [*DoD*]
DORS.......... Director of Operational Research Section (SAUS)
Dors.......... Dorsal [*Medicine*] (EDAA)
dors.......... Dorsal (SPVS)
Dors.......... Dorset [*County in England*] (ODBW)
DORS.......... Dorsetshire [*County in England*] (ROG)
DORS.......... Dynamic Operator Response System
D Or Sc....... Doctor of the Science of Oratory
DORSET........ Dorsetshire [*County in England*]
DORSET........ Dorsetshire Regiment (SAUO)
DorseyTr...... Dorsey Trailers, Inc. [*Associated Press*] (SAG)
DORT.......... Detroit Objective Reference Test (SAUS)
Dort.......... Dordrecht (SAUS)
DOrth.......... Diploma in Orthodontics [*British*]
DOrth.......... Diploma in Orthopedics
D Orth......... Diploma in Orthoptics [*British*]
D Orth RCS Eng... Diplomate in Orthodontics, Royal College of Surgeons of England
DORTS......... Department of Rapid Transit Systems [*Taipei*] (ECON)
DORV.......... Deep Ocean Research Vehicle (IEEE)
DORV.......... double oulet right ventricle (SAUS)
DORV.......... Double Outlet Right Ventricle [*Cardiology*]
DORx.......... Date of Treatment [*Medicine*] (DAVI)
DOS.......... Data Organization Service (IAA)
DOS.......... Date of Sale (SAUS)
DOS.......... Date of Seeding (SAUO)
DOS.......... Date of Separation [*Military*]
DOS.......... Date of Service
DOS.......... Date of Surgery (DAVI)
DOS.......... Daughters of Scotia
DOS.......... Day of Sale [*Business term*] (ADA)
DOS.......... Day of Supply (SAUS)
DOS.......... Day of Surgery [*Medicine*] (EDAA)
DOS.......... Day Optical Scope
DOS.......... Days of Supply [*Rations*]
DOS.......... Days on Stream (SAUS)
DOS.......... Decentralized Operating System (SAUS)
DOS.......... Decision Outstanding [*Computer science*] (BUR)
DOS.......... Declaration of Support (SAUS)
DOS.......... Deep Ocean Survey (ACAE)
DOS.......... Defense Occupational Specialties [*Army*]
DOS.......... Deferred Organic Supply (MCD)
DOS.......... Defunct Operating System (SAUS)
DOS.......... Degenerate Oscillating System
DOS.......... Degree of Sensitization (ABAC)
DOS.......... Delaware Otsego [*Federal Railroad Administration identification code*]
DOS.......... Deliverer of Services (OICC)
DOS.......... Democratic Opposition of Serbia
DOS.......... Denial of Service (ADWA)
DoS.......... Denial of Service (VLIE)
DOS.......... Densities of States [*Photovoltaic energy systems*]
DOS.......... Density of States [*Physics*]
DOS.......... Deoxystreptamine [*Organic chemistry*]
DOS.......... Department of Space (SAUO)
DOS.......... Department of State
DOS.......... Department of State, Washington, DC [*OCLC symbol*] (OCLC)
DOS.......... Department of Surgery
DOS.......... Dependents Overseas [*Military*]
DOS.......... Depot of Supply (SAUS)
DOS.......... Depth of Seam (SAUO)
DOS.......... Diabetes Opinion Survey [*Child development test*] [*Psychology*]
DOS.......... Dialysis Osteomalacia Syndrome [*Medicine*] (MELL)
DOS.......... Digital Operation System (IEEE)
DOS.......... Digital Orthophoto System (GEOI)
DOS.......... Dioctyl Sebacate [*Organic chemistry*]
DOS.......... Diploma in Orthopaedic Surgery (ADA)
D-OS.......... Diplomate, American Board of Orthopaedic Surgery (DHSM)
DOS.......... Direct Operating System [*Computer technology*]
DOS.......... Directorate of Overseas Surveys [*Overseas Development Administration*] [*British*] (DS)
DOS.......... Director of Ordnance Services [*Military*] [*British*]
DOS.......... Director of Sales
DOS.......... Director of Stores [*Navy*] [*British*]
DOS.......... Director of Studies
DOS.......... Director [*or Directorate*] of Support [*Army*]
DOS.......... disc operating system (SAUS)
DOS.......... Discrete, Open-loop, and Self-paced (SAUS)
DOS.......... Discrete Orthonormal Sequence
DOS.......... Diskette Operating System (SAUS)
DOS.......... Disk Operating System [*Computer science*] (IID)
DOS.......... Disk Oriented System (SAUS)
DOs.......... Disponent Owners (SAUS)
DOS.......... Distal Opener System (SAUS)
DOS.......... Distributed Office System (VLIE)
DOS.......... Distributed Operation System [*Computer science*] (IAA)
DOS.......... Division of Operational Safety [*Energy Research and Development Administration*] (MCD)
DOS.......... Doctor of Dental Surgery (SAUS)
DOS.......... Doctor of Ocular Science
DOS.......... Doctor of Optical Science
DOS.......... Doctor of Optometric Science
DOS.......... Doctyl Sebacate (SAUS)
dos.......... Dosage [*Medicine*] (EDAA)
DOS.......... Dosage [*Medicine*]
DOS.......... Dos Bocas Dam [*Puerto Rico*] [*Seismograph station code, US Geological Survey*] (SEIS)
dos.......... dose (SAUS)
DOS.......... Dosieraerosol (SAUS)
dos.......... Dosimetric (SAUS)
dos.......... dosimetry (SAUS)
dos.......... dosiology (SAUS)
DOS.......... Dosis [*Dose*] [*Pharmacy*] (ROG)
DOS.......... Drum Out of Service (CET)
DOS.......... Dysosteosclerosis [*Medicine*] (MELL)
DOSAAF........ Dobrovol'noe Obshchestvo Sodeistviia Armii, Aviatsii, i Flotu [*Voluntary Society for Cooperation with the Army, Aviation, and the Fleet*] [*Former USSR*]
DOS-A/DCP... Department of State, Office of Diplomatic Contingency Programs (SAUO)
DOSAFF........ Voluntary Society for Cooperation with the Army, Air Force and Navy (SAUO)
DOSAR......... Department of State Acquisition Regulation [*A publication*] (AAGC)
DOSAR......... Dosimetry Applications Research Facility [*AEC*]
DOSC.......... Dimensions of Self-Concept [*Personality test*]
DO Sc.......... Doctor of Optometric Science
DOSC.......... Dubois Oleic Serum Complex [*Bacteriology*]
DOSCA......... Department of State Correspondents Association (EA)
Do Scale....... Dominance Scale [*Psychology*] (DHP)
DOSCIS........ Data Over Cable Service Interface Specification (SAUS)
DOSCO......... Dominion Steel and Coal Corporation (SAUO)
DOSE.......... Capstone Pharmacy Services, Inc. [*NASDAQ symbol*] (SAG)
DOSE.......... Capstone Pharmacy Svc [*NASDAQ symbol*] (TTSB)
DOSE.......... Choice Drug Systems, Inc. [*NASDAQ symbol*] (NQ)
DOSE.......... Dictionary of Substances and their Effects (SAUO)
DOSE.......... Disk Operating System - Enhanced [*Computer science*] (MCD)
DOSE.......... Distributed Office Support Executive [*IBM Corp.*] (IAA)
DOSE.......... Dynamics of the Solid Earth (SAUO)
DOSECC........ Deep Observation and Sampling of the Earth's Continental Crust [*National Science Foundation*]
DOSEM......... Disk Operating System Emulation [*Computer science*] (VLIE)
DOSEM......... DOS Emulation (SAUS)
DOSEM......... DOS Emulator (SAUS)
DoSER......... Dialogue on Science, Ethics, and Religion
DOSES......... Development of Statistical Expert Systems [*Computer science*] (CIST)
DOS/ES........ Disk Operating System/ ESER (SAUS)
DOSEW......... Capstone Pharmacy Svcs Wrrt [*NASDAQ symbol*] (TTSB)
DOSF.......... Deep Ocean Simulation Facility (SAA)
DOSF.......... Distributed Office Support Facility (ELAL)
Doshisha LJ... Doshisha Law Journal. International Edition [*A publication*] (DLA)
Doshisha L Rev... Doshisha Law Review [*A publication*] (DLA)
Dosh Univ...... Doshira University (SAUO)
DOSI.......... Directorate of Operational Services and Intelligence (SAUO)
DOSIM......... Dosimeter (NASA)
dosim.......... dosimetry (SAUS)
DOSK.......... Distributed Operating System Kernel [*Computer science*]
DOSKey........ Disk Operating System Key [*Computer science*] (DCDG)
Dos Let........ Dosis Letalis [*Lethal Dose*] [*Latin*]
DOSLI......... Department of Survey and Land Information [*New Zealand*] (GEOI)
DOS-LV........ Disk Operating System - Large Volumes [*Computer science*]
DOSM.......... Desialylated Ovine Submaxillary Mucin [*Biochemistry*]
DOSN.......... Disbursing Office Serial Number
DOSNS......... DOS Virtual Storage (SAUS)
DOSP.......... Dalhousie Ocean Studies Programme [*Dalhousie University*] [*Canada*] [*Research center*] (RCD)
DOSP.......... Deep Ocean Sediment Probe [*Marine science*] (MSC)
DOS/P......... Disk Cperating System/ Prime (SAUS)

DOSP.......... Disk Operating System Prime [*Computer science*] (VLIE)
DOS/P.......... Disk Operating System/Prime (SAUS)
DOSP.......... Distal Opener System Pulse (SAUS)
Dos Passos Stock-Brok... Dos Passos on Stock-Brokers and Stock Exchanges [*A publication*] (DLA)
DOSPR.......... Department of State Procurement Regulations
DOS prompt... Disk Operating System Prompt [*Computer science*] (DDC)
DOSPT.......... Disk Operating System Performance Tool [*Computer science*] (VLIE)
DOS/RS.......... Disc operating system/real storage (SAUS)
DOS/RS.......... Disk Operating System/ Real Storage (SAUS)
DOSS.......... Ad hoc Study Group on IOC Development, Operations, Structure and Statutes (SAUO)
DOSS.......... Decision-Oriented Scheduling System (MCD)
DOSS.......... Dedicated Office Systems and Services (VERA)
DOSS.......... Deep Ocean Search System [*Marine science*]
DOSS.......... Department of State Services (SAUO)
DOSS.......... Dioctyl Sodium Sulfosuccinate [*Organic chemistry*]
DOSS.......... Disk Operating System-Standard [*Computer science*] (VLIE)
DOS/S.......... Disk Operating System/ Standard (SAUS)
DOSS.......... Disk-Oriented Supply System [*Computer science*] (DNAB)
DOSS.......... Distal Over-Shoulder Strap
DOSS.......... Documentation on Social Security [*ILO*] [*Information service or system*] [*United Nations*] (DUND)
DOSS.......... Docusate Sodium [*Medicine*] (DMAA)
DOSS.......... Doppler Optical Surveillance System
Doss.......... Dossier (DIAR)
DOSS.......... DSCS [*Defense Satellite Communication System*] Operational Support System [*DoD*]
DOSS.......... DSCS Operational Support Systems (SAUS)
DOSS-AF.......... Directorate of Operational Support Services - Air Force
DOSSIER.......... Disk Operated Search System for Information Executed Remotely (SAUS)
DOSSU.......... Dogs on Stamps Study Unit (EA)
DOS-SV.......... Disk Operating System - Small Volumes [*Computer science*]
DOST.......... Data Output Strobe (NITA)
DOST.......... Department of Science and Technology [*Science and Technology Information Institute*] [*Philippines*] (IID)
DOST.......... Dictionary of the Older Scottish Tongue [*A publication*]
DOst.......... Diploma in Osteopathy [*Australia*]
DOST.......... Direct Oocyte-Sperm Transfer [*Medicine*] (ADWA)
DOST.......... Dynamic Offshore Structure Test (SAUS)
DOSTN.......... Departmemt of State Telecommunication Network (ACAE)
DOS/TOS.......... Disk Operating System/Tape Operating System (SAUS)
DOSTOVS.......... DOS to OS/VS (SAUS)
DOSV.......... Deep Oceanographic Survey Vehicle [*Naval Oceanographic Office*]
DOSV.......... Deep Ocean Survey Vehicle (SAUS)
DOS/VM.......... Disc Operating System, Virtual Memory (SAUS)
DOS/VM.......... Disk Operating System/Virtual Memory (SAUS)
DOS/VS.......... Disk Operating System/Virtual Storage [*IBM Corp.*] [*Computer science*] (MCD)
DOS/VSAF.......... Disk Operating System/Virtual Storage Advanced Functions (SAUS)
DOS/VSAF.......... DOS/Virtual Storage (SAUS)
DOS/VS-AF... DOS/VS - advanced functions (SAUS)
DOS/VSE.......... Disk Operating System/Virtaul Storage Extended (SAUS)
DOS/VSE.......... Disk Operating System/ Virtual Storage Extended (SAUS)
DOS/VSE.......... DOS/Virtual Storage Extended (SAUS)
DOS/VSE.......... DOS/VS extended (SAUS)
DOSWL.......... Doswell, VA [*American Association of Railroads railroad junction routing code*]
DOSY.......... Digiset Oriented Setting System [*Siemens-Hell*] (NITA)
DOT.......... Daily Operability Test [*Military*] (CAAL)
DOT.......... Data Organizing Translator (SAUS)
DOT.......... Data Output Tape (SAUS)
DOT.......... Date of Trade [*Investment term*]
DOT.......... Date of Transcription [*Medicine*] (EDAA)
DOT.......... Date of Transfer (SAUS)
DOT.......... Date of Transplanting (SAUO)
DOT.......... Day of Training (SAUS)
DOT.......... Deep Oceanic Turbulence
DOT.......... Deep Ocean Technology
DOT.......... Deep Ocean Transponder
DOT.......... Deep Ocean Trough (SAUS)
DOT.......... Deep Oil Technology , Co. (SAUO)
DOT.......... Deep-Operating Torpedo (MCD)
DoT.......... Defense of the Territory (SAUS)
DOT.......... Delayed on Target
DOT.......... Department of Overseas Trade [*British*]
DOT.......... Department of Textiles (SAUO)
DOT.......... Department of the Treasury (AFM)
DoT.......... Department of Trade [*British*]
DoT.......... Department of Transport (PIAV)
DOT.......... Department of Transport [*Canada*]
DOT.......... Department of Transportation
DOT.......... Department of Treasury [*Victoria*] [*Australia*]
DOT.......... Dependent Overseas Territory
DOT.......... Deployment Operations Team
DOT.......... Designated Order Turnaround [*NYSE term*]
DOT.......... Designating Optical Tracker [*Telescope*]
DOT.......... Dictionary of Occupational Titles [*Department of Labor*] [*A publication*]
DOT.......... Died on [*Operating*] Table [*Medicine*] (DAVI)
DOT.......... Differential Oil Temperature [*Automotive engineering*]
DOT.......... Digital Optical Technology (SAUS)
DOT.......... Digital Optical Technology System (NITA)
DOT.......... Digital Optical Transceiver [*Citifax Corp.*]
DOT.......... Digital Output Timer [*Computer science*]
DOT.......... Digital Overlay Technique (SAUS)
DOT.......... Dioctyltin [*Organic chemistry*]
DOT.......... Diploma of Occupational Therapy
D-OT.......... Diplomate, American Board of Otolaryngology (DHSM)
DOT.......... Direction of Trade (NITA)
DOT.......... Directly-Observed Therapy
DOT.......... Direct Operation Technique (SAUS)
DOT.......... Directorate of Overseas Trade (SAUO)
DOT.......... Director of Operational Training [*RAF*] [*British*]
DOT.......... Director [*or Directorate*] of Training [*Army*]
DOT.......... Director on Target [*Military*] (CAAL)
DOT.......... Directory of Occupational Titles (DNAB)
DOT.......... discrete ordinates transport (SAUS)
DOT.......... Discrete Ordinate Transport
DOT.......... Displacement-Oriented Transducer
DOT.......... Dissolved Oxygen Tension [*Chemistry*]
DOT.......... Division of Organ Transplantation [*Department of Health and Human Services*] (PAZ)
DOT.......... Documents to Think with (SAUS)
DOT.......... Document Template (SAUS)
DOT.......... Domain Tip (PDAA)
DOT.......... Domain-Tip Memory (SAUS)
DOT.......... Domain-Tip Technology [*Computer*] [*Medicine*] (EDAA)
DOT.......... Doppler Ophthalmic Test (CPH)
DOT.......... Dorset Resources Ltd. [*Toronto Stock Exchange symbol*]
Dot.......... Dotation (SAUS)
DOT.......... Double Offset Tactic (SAA)
DOT.......... drilling operations team (SAUS)
DOT.......... Duplex One-Tape (SAUS)
DOT.......... Duplex One-Tape System
DOT.......... Duplex On-Tape (SAUS)
DOT.......... Dutch Open Telescope
DOT.......... Dynamic Operation Test
DOT.......... Kansas City, MO [*Location identifier*] [*FAA*] (FAAL)
DOTA.......... Diakonia of the Americas (EA)
DOTA.......... Diakonia of the Americas and Caribbean [*An association*] (EA)
DOT&E.......... Director, Operational Test and Evaluation [*OSD*] (AAGC)
D o T & T.... Dominion of Trinidad and Tobago (SAUS)
DOTAP.......... Dioleoyl Trimethylammonium Propane [*Organic chemistry*]
DOT BCA.......... Department of Transportation Board of Contract Appeals (AAGC)
DOTC.......... Dameshek's Oval Target Cell (DB)
DOTC.......... Data Observing Testing Console
DOTC.......... Department of Transport (SAUO)
DOTC.......... Department of Transportation Classification (SAUS)
DOTC.......... Diethyl-Oxatricarbo-Cyanine [*Medicine*] (EDAA)
DOTC.......... Director, Office of Transport and Communications [*Department of State*] (AAG)
DOTCAB.......... Department of Transportation Contract Adjustment Board (AAGC)
DOTCAB.......... Department of Transportation Contract Appeals Board
DOTCAP.......... Department of Transportation Contract Assistance Program (AAGC)
DOT-CG-N.... Department of Transportation Coast Guard Office of Navigation [*Washington, DC*]
DOT/CIAP.......... Department of Transportation/Climatic Impact Assessment Program (NASA)
DOT/CIAP.......... DOT Climatic Impact Assessment Program (SAUS)
DOTCOOP.... Department of Transportation Continuity of Operations Plan [*Federal emergency plan*]
DOTD.......... Directorate of Training and Development [*Army*]
DOTD.......... Directorate of Training Doctrine (SAUS)
DOTE.......... Department of the Environment (SAUS)
DOTE.......... OSD [*Office of the Secretary of Defense*] Operational Test and Evaluation (RDA)
DOT EO.......... Department of Transportation Emergency Organization (SAUS)
DOTEO.......... Department of Transportation's Emergency Organization
DOTES.......... Doctrine, Organization, Training, Equipment, and Supporting Facilities [*Military*]
DOT/FAA/AM... Department of Transportation Federal Aviation Administration Office of Aviation Medicine [*Washington, DC*]
DOT/FAA/AP... Department of Transportation Federal Aviation Administration Office of Airports Programs [*Washington, DC*]
DOT/FAA/ASF... Department of Transportation Federal Aviation Administration Office of Aviation Safety [*Washington, DC*]
DOT/FAA/AT... Department of Transportation Federal Aviation Administration Air Traffic Service [*Washington, DC*]
DOT/FAA/CP... Department of Transportation Federal Aviation Administration Airport Capacity Program Office [*Washington, DC*]
DOT/FAA/EE... Department of Transportation Federal Aviation Administration Office of Environment and Energy [*Washington, DC*]
DOT/FAA/EM... Department of Transportation Federal Aviation Administration Office of Systems Engineering Management [*Washington, DC*]
DOT/FAA/ES... Department of Transportation Federal Aviation Administration Systems EngineeringService [*Washington, DC*]
DOT/FAA/PM... Department of Transportation Federal Aviation Administration Program Engineeringand Maintenance Service [*Washington, DC*]
DOT/FAA/PP... Department of Transportation Federal Aviation Administration Office of Airport Planning and Programming [*Washington, DC*]
DOT/FAA/PS... Department of Transportation Federal Aviation Administration Program EngineeringService [*Washington, DC*]
DOT/FAA/RD... Department of Transportation Federal Aviation Administration Systems Research and Development Service [*Washington, DC*]
DOTFAP.......... Department of Transportation Financial Assistance Program (AAGC)
DOTG.......... Di-ortho-toylguanidine [*Organic chemistry*]
DOTH.......... Defense of the Homeland (SEWL)

DOTHA......... Dothan, AL [*American Association of Railroads railroad junction routing code*]
DOT-HS........ Department of Transportation National Highway Traffic Safety Administration [*Washington, DC*]
DOTI............ Department of Trade and Industry [*British*] (NITA)
DOTI............ Director of Operations, Training and Intelligence [*Army*] (AABC)
DOTIC.......... Directory of Title Pages Indexes and Contents Pages [*UK Serials Group*] (NITA)
DOTIG.......... Department of Transportation Inspector General
DOTIPOS...... Deep Ocean Test-in-Place and Observation System [*Navy*]
DOTIPOS...... Deep Ocean Test Instrument Placement and Observation System (SAUS)
DOTLMS...... Doctrine, Organizations, Training, Leaders, Material, and Soldiers [*Military*] (RDA)
DOTM.......... Department of Ordnance, Torpedoes, and Mines (SAUS)
DOTM.......... Director of Naval Ordnance, Torpedoes and Mines (SAUO)
DOTM.......... Due-Out to Maintenance [*Military*] (MCD)
DOT memory... Domain-Tip Memory [*Computer science*] (MED)
DOT memory... domain tip propagation memory (SAUS)
DOTMPL...... Doctrine, Organization, Training, Materiel, Personnel and Leader Development [*Army*]
DOTO.......... Ohio Department of Transportation [*Federal Railroad Administration identification code*]
DOT-OS........ Department of Transportation Office of Assistant Secretary for Systems Development and Technology [*Washington, DC*]
DOTP.......... Deep Ocean Technology Project
DOTP.......... Dental Officer Training Plan [*Canada*]
DOTp.......... Department of Transport [*British*] (DA)
DOTP.......... Dioctyl Terephthalate [*Organic chemistry*]
DOTP.......... Duty Operational Test Director
DOTPF......... Department of Transportation & Public Facilities (SAUO)
DOTPR........ Department of Transportation Procurement Regulations (AAGC)
DOT Propagation... Domain Tip Propagation (SAUS)
DOTr........... Department of Treasury (EEVL)
DotR........... Dramatists of the Restoration [*British*] (ROG)
DOTRAM...... Domain Tip Random Access Memory [*Computer science*]
DOTREX...... Deep Ocean Tracer Experiment [*Marine science*] (OSRA)
Dotrnix........ Dotronics, Inc. [*Associated Press*] (SAG)
DOTS........... Deviation of Temperature and Salinity
DOTS........... Digital Office Timing Supply (SAUS)
DOTS........... Digital Optical Tape System [*Computer science*] (CIST)
DOTS........... Digital Optical Technology System [*3-D television system*]
DOTS........... Dimensions of Temperament Survey [*Psychology*] (DHP)
DOTS........... Diploma of Tertiary Studies
DOTS........... Direction of Trade Statistics [*International Monetary Fund*] [*Information service or system*] (CRD)
DOTS........... Directly Observed Treatment Short-Course [*Therapy regime*]
DOTS........... Division On-Line Tool System [*Allan Collautt Associates, Inc.*] [*Automotive engineering*]
DOTS........... Document tracking system (SAUS)
DOTS........... Dredging Operations Technical Support (RDA)
DOTS........... Dynamic Ocean Track System (DA)
DOTSP......... Distinctive Ovarian Tumor with Sexual Precocity
DOTSP......... Doctrinal and Organization Test Support Package [*Army*]
DOT-SST...... Department of Transportation Office of Supersonic Transportation [*Washington, DC*]
DOTSYS....... Dot System [*Mitre Corp.*] [*Braille translation system*] (NITA)
DOTT........... Decision-Oriented Templating Techniques
DOTT........... Di-o-tolylthiourea [*Organic chemistry*]
DOTT........... Doctrinal and Organizational Training Team [*Army*]
DOTT........... Documentation for Translation and Terminology (SAUS)
DOTT........... Documents from Old Testament Times [*A publication*] (BJA)
DOTT........... Duties Other than Teaching (ADA)
DOT Technology... Domain-Tip Technology (SAUS)
Dott Ing....... Dottore Ingenieur [*Doctor of Engineering*] [*Italian*]
DOT-TSC...... Department of Transportation, Transportation Systems Center (SAUO)
DOTU.......... Diorthotolyl Urea (SAUS)
DOT UK....... Department of Overseas Trade (SAUS)
DOT/UN....... Department ofTransportation/United Nations (SAUS)
DOTX.......... Dotronics, Inc. [*NASDAQ symbol*] (SAG)
DOTX.......... Dotronix, Inc. [*NASDAQ symbol*] (NQ)
DOTX.......... Federal Railroad Administration [*Private rail car owner code*]
DOU............ Definitive Observation Unit [*Medicine*] (MEDA)
DOU............ Dourados [*Brazil*] [*Airport symbol*] (OAG)
DOU............ Dourbes [*Belgium*] [*Seismograph station code, US Geological Survey*] (SEIS)
Douay.......... Douay Version of the Bible (SAUS)
doub........... Double (SAUS)
DOUB.......... Doubler (SAUS)
double-B...... double-backed (SAUS)
double-B...... double-banked (SAUS)
double-B...... double-barreled (SAUS)
double-B...... double-bass (SAUS)
double-B...... double-bedded (SAUS)
double-B...... double-benched (SAUS)
double-B...... double-bonded (SAUS)
double-B...... double-bottomed (SAUS)
double-B...... double-breasted (SAUS)
double-B...... double-brooded (SAUS)
Double D...... Doubleday (SAUS)
double-X...... doublecross (SAUS)
double-X...... double quality (SAUS)
double-X...... double quantity (SAUS)
double-X...... double thickness (SAUS)
double-X...... doubleweight (SAUS)
doublexing... Double-Crossing (ADWA)
doubt.......... doubtful (SAUS)
DOUDDAS.... Deep Ocean Untended Digital Data Acquisition System [*Marine science*] (MSC)
DOUG.......... Department of Urban Geology (SAUO)
DOUG.......... Douglas & Lomason [*NASDAQ symbol*] (TTSB)
DOUG.......... Douglas & Lomason Co. [*NASDAQ symbol*] (NQ)
Doug........... Douglas' English Election Cases [*A publication*] (DLA)
Doug........... Douglas' English King's Bench Reports [*A publication*] (DLA)
Doug........... Douglas' Michigan Supreme Court Reports [*A publication*] (DLA)
Doug........... Douglas' Reports [*A publication*] (DLA)
Doug El Ca... Douglas' English Election Cases [*A publication*] (DLA)
Doug El Cas... Douglas' English Election Cases [*A publication*] (DLA)
Doug fir....... Douglas fir (SAUS)
DOUG FIR-L... Douglas Fir Larch [*Lumber*]
DOUG FIR-L... Douglas Fir-Lumber (SAUS)
Doug KB...... Douglas' English King's Bench Reports [*A publication*] (DLA)
DOUGL........ Douglas, GA [*American Association of Railroads railroad junction routing code*]
Douglas UN... Douglas United Nuclear Inc. (SAUO)
Dougl El Cas... Douglas' English Election Cases [*A publication*] (DLA)
Dougl KB..... Douglas' English King's Bench Reports [*A publication*] (DLA)
Dougl KB (Eng)... Douglas' English King's Bench Reports [*A publication*] (DLA)
Dougl (Mich)... Douglas' Michigan Supreme Court Reports [*A publication*] (DLA)
Doug (Mich)... Douglas' Michigan Supreme Court Reports [*A publication*] (DLA)
DOULT......... Doulton Ware [*Ceramics*] (ROG)
DOUSEB....... Doppler Unbeamed Search Radar (SAUS)
DOUSER...... Doppler Unbeamed Search RADAR
DOUT.......... Data Output Line (SAUS)
DOUT Line... Data Out Line (SAUS)
Dout Pr....... Doutre. Procedure Civile de Bas Canada [*A publication*] (DLA)
DOV............ Data over Voice [*Telecommunications*] (TEL)
DOV............ Defence of Village (SAUS)
DOV............ Degree of Variance (SAUS)
DOV............ Diaphragm Operated Valve
DOV............ Digital-Over-Voice (SAUS)
DOV............ Director of Orbital Verification (SAUS)
DOV............ Disbursing Officer's Voucher
DOV............ Discharged on Visit [*Psychiatry*]
DOV............ Discreet Operational Vehicle (SAUS)
DOV............ Discreet Operations Vehicle [*Military*] (LAIN)
DOV............ Discrete Out Vehicle [*NASA*] (KSC)
DOV............ Distilled Oil of Vitriol
DOV............ Double Oil of Vitriol
DOV............ Dover [*Delaware*] [*Airport symbol*] (AD)
DOV............ Dover Corp. [*NYSE symbol*] (SPSG)
DOV............ Dover, DE [*Location identifier*] [*FAA*] (FAAL)
DOV............ Dover Public Library, Dover, DE [*OCLC symbol*] (OCLC)
DOV............ Doverton Oils Ltd. [*Vancouver Stock Exchange symbol*]
Dov............. Dovid (SAUS)
DOVACK...... Differential, Oral, Visual, Aural, Computerized Kinesthetic
DOVAP........ Doppler, Velocity and Position [*NASA*]
Dovatrn....... DOVatron International [*Associated Press*] (SAG)
DOVE.......... Data on Vocational Education [*Department of Education*] (GFGA)
DOVE.......... Data-Over-Voice Equipment (SAUS)
DOVE.......... Dove Audio [*NASDAQ symbol*] (TTSB)
DOVE.......... Dove Audio, Inc. [*NASDAQ symbol*] (SAG)
DOVE.......... Dovekie [*North American bird banding code*] (BIBA)
DoveAud...... Dove Audio, Inc. [*Associated Press*] (SAG)
Dover.......... Dover Corp. [*Associated Press*] (SAG)
Dover.......... Dover Publications (SAUS)
DoverD........ Dover Downs Entertainment, Inc. [*Associated Press*] (SAG)
DOVETT....... Double Velocity Transit Time [*Physics*]
DOV PULV... Doveri Pulvis [*Dover's Powder*] [*Pharmacy*] (ROG)
DOVR.......... Dover, ID [*American Association of Railroads railroad junction routing code*]
DOVT.......... Dovatron International [*NASDAQ symbol*] (SAG)
DOW........... Date of Withdrawal (SAUS)
DOW........... Day-of-Week (TIMI)
DOW........... Deep Observation Wells (SAUS)
DOW........... Defenders of Wildlife
DOW........... Delivery on Wheels [*Shipping*] (DS)
DOW........... Density of Water
DOW........... Department of Wildlife (GNE)
DOW........... Description of work (SAUS)
DOW........... Died of Wounds [*Military*]
DOW........... Digital Orderwire channel (SAUS)
DOW........... Digital Orthophoto Workstation (SAUS)
DOW........... Direct Overwrite [*Computer science*]
DOW........... Division of Wildlife
DOW........... Doctors of the World (SAUO)
DOW........... Doppler on Wheels [*Instrumentation*]
dow............ dowager (SAUS)
DOW........... Dow Chemical [*NYSE symbol*] (TTSB)
DOW........... Dow Chemical Co. [*NYSE symbol*] [*Toronto Stock Exchange symbol*]
DOW........... Dow Chemical Co., Granville Research Center, Granville, OH [*OCLC symbol*] (OCLC)
DOW........... Dow Chemical Company (SAUO)
DOW........... Dow Chemicals (SAUS)
dow............ dowel (SAUS)
DOW........... Dower [*or Dowager*]
Dow............ Dow Jones Industrial Average (SAUS)
Dow............ Dowling's English Practice Cases [*A publication*] (DLA)
DOW........... Downeast Flying Service, Inc. [*FAA designator*] (FAAC)

Dow .... Dow's House of Lords (Parliamentary) Cases [*Same as Dow's Reports*] [*3 English Reprint*] [*A publication*] (DLA)
DOW .... dry operating weight (SAUS)
DOW .... Dry Organic Weight
DOW .... Duration of War
Dow & C ...... Dow and Clark's English House of Lords Cases [*A publication*] (DLA)
Dow & C (Eng)... Dow and Clark's English House of Lords Cases [*A publication*] (DLA)
Dow & Cl ..... Dow and Clark's English House of Lords Cases [*A publication*] (DLA)
Dow & L ...... Dowling and Lowndes' English Bail Court Reports [*A publication*] (DLA)
Dow & Lownd... Dowling and Lowndes' English Practice Cases [*A publication*] (DLA)
Dow & Ry .... Dowling and Ryland's English King's Bench Reports [*A publication*] (DLA)
Dow & Ry .... Dowling and Ryland's English Nisi Prius Cases [*A publication*] (DLA)
Dow & Ry KB... Dowling and Ryland's English King's Bench Reports [*A publication*] (DLA)
Dow & Ry KB... Dowling and Ryland's English Nisi Prius Cases [*A publication*] (DLA)
Dow & Ry MC... Dowling and Ryland's English Magistrates' Cases [*A publication*] (DLA)
Dow & Ry NP... Dowling and Ryland's English Nisi Prius Cases [*A publication*] (DLA)
DoWaPO ...... Dictionary of Word and Phrase Origins (SAUS)
DOWB .... Deep Ocean Work Boat [*Marine science*] (MSC)
DOWB .... Deep Operating Work Board (IEEE)
DOWB .... Deep Operation Work Boat (SAUS)
DOWB .... Director of Works and Buildings [*British*]
DowCh .... Dow Chemical Co. [*Associated Press*] (SAG)
Dowd Ins ..... Dowdeswell on Life and Fire Insurance [*A publication*] (DLA)
Dow Inc .... Dowell's Income Tax Acts [*9th ed.*] [*1934*] [*A publication*] (DLA)
DowJns .... Dow Jones & Co., Inc. [*Associated Press*] (SAG)
Dowl .... Dowling's English Bail Court (Practice) Cases [*A publication*] (DLA)
Dowl & L ..... Dowling and Lowndes' English Bail Court Reports [*A publication*] (DLA)
Dowl & Lownd... Dowling and Lowndes' English Bail Court Reports [*A publication*] (DLA)
Dowl & R ..... Dowling and Ryland's English King's Bench Reports [*A publication*] (DLA)
Dowl & R (Eng)... Dowling and Ryland's English King's Bench Reports [*A publication*] (DLA)
Dowl & R Mag Cas (Eng)... Dowling and Ryland's English Magistrates' Cases [*A publication*] (DLA)
Dowl & R NP... Dowling and Ryland's English Nisi Prius Cases [*A publication*] (DLA)
Dowl & R NP (Eng)... Dowling and Ryland's English Nisi Prius Cases [*A publication*] (DLA)
Dowl & Ryl... Dowling and Ryland's English King's Bench Reports [*A publication*] (DLA)
Dowl & Ryl MC... Dowling and Ryland's English Magistrates' Cases [*A publication*] (DLA)
Dowl & Ryl NP... Dowling and Ryland's English Nisi Prius Cases [*A publication*] (DLA)
Dowl (Eng)... Dowling's English Bail Court (Practice) Cases [*A publication*] (DLA)
Dowl NS ...... Dowling's English Bail Court Reports, New Series [*1841-43*] [*A publication*] (DLA)
Dowl NS (Eng)... Dowling's English Bail Court Reports, New Series [*1841-43*] [*A publication*] (DLA)
Dowl PC ...... Dowling's English Bail Court (Practice) Cases [*A publication*] (DLA)
Dowl PC (Eng)... Dowling's English Bail Court (Practice) Cases [*A publication*] (DLA)
Dowl PC NS... Dowling's English Practice Cases, New Series [*A publication*] (DLA)
Dowl Pr .... Dowling's Common Law Practice [*A publication*] (DLA)
Dowl PR ...... Dowling's Practice Reports [*A publication*] (DLA)
Dowl Pr Cas... Dowling's English Practice Cases [*A publication*] (DLA)
Dowl Pr C NS... Dowling's English Practice Cases, New Series [*A publication*] (DLA)
DOWM .... Database of Off-Site Waste Management [*Public Data Access, Inc.*] [*No longer available online*] [*Information service or system*]
DOWN .... Downing College [*Cambridge University*] (ROG)
Down .... Downing College, Cambridge (SAUS)
Down & Lud... Downton and Luder's English Election Cases [*A publication*] (DLA)
DowneyF ...... Downey Financial Corp. [*Formerly, Downey S & L Association*] [*Associated Press*] (SAG)
down-h .... Down-Hole (SAUS)
Dow NS .... Dow and Clark's English House of Lords Cases [*A publication*] (DLA)
Dow NS .... Dowling's English Bail Court Reports, New Series [*1841-43*] [*A publication*] (DLA)
DOWO .... Downy Woodpecker [*North American bird banding code*] (BIBA)
DOWP .... Dead Oil Well Permits (SAUO)
Dow PC .... Dowling's English Practice Cases [*A publication*] (DLA)
Dow PC .... Dow's House of Lords (Parliamentary) Cases [*Same as Dow's Reports*] [*3 English Reprint*] [*A publication*] (DLA)
Dow PC (Eng)... Dowling's English Practice Cases [*A publication*] (DLA)
Dow PC (Eng)... Dow's House of Lords (Parliamentary) Cases [*Same as Dow's Reports*] [*3 English Reprint*] [*A publication*] (DLA)
Dow Pr .... Dowling's English Practice Cases [*A publication*] (DLA)
DOWR .... Division of Water Resources (SAUO)
DOWS .... Damped Oscillatory Wave Simulator
DOWS .... Directional Ocean Wave Spectrum (SAUS)
dows .... dowsers (SAUS)
Dow St .... Dowell's Stamp Duties [*1873*] [*A publication*] (DLA)
DOWX .... Dow Chemical [*Private rail car owner code*]
DOWX .... Dow Chemicals [*Federal Railroad Administration identification code*]
DOX .... Amdocs Ltd. [*NYSE symbol*] (SG)
DOX .... Directorate of Operational Plans (SAUO)
DOX .... Dissolved Organic Halogen (LDOE)
DOX .... Dolphin Explorations Ltd. [*Vancouver Stock Exchange symbol*] [*Toronto Stock Exchange symbol*]
DOX .... Dongara [*Australia*] [*Airport symbol*] (OAG)
DOX .... Doxology (ROG)
Dox .... Doxorubicin (DB)
DOX .... Doxorubicin [*Also, D, DXR*] [*Formerly, ADR, Adriamycin*] [*Antineoplastic drug*]
DOXA .... DOXA Watch Co. Inc. (SAUO)
Dox Graec ... Doxographi Graeci [*A publication*] (OCD)
DOXOL .... Doxorubicinol [*Antineoplastic drug*]
DOXYL .... Dimethyloxazolidine-N-Oxyl (SAUS)
DOXYL .... Dimethyloxazolinyloxy (SAUS)
DOY .... Day of Year
DOY .... Deboyne [*Louisiade Archipelago, Papua*] [*Airport symbol*] (AD)
DOZ .... Dioctyl Azelate [*Organic chemistry*]
DOZ .... Dozen (AFM)
doz .... Dozen (MEC)
DP .... By Direction of the President
DP .... Cochise Airlines [*ICAO designator*] (AD)
DP .... Daily Penalty (ROG)
DP .... Damp-Proofing (AAG)
DP .... Dash Pot [*Relay*]
DP .... Data Acquisition Package (IAA)
D/P .... Database Size/Program Size
DP .... Data Package (SSD)
DP .... Data Packet (SAUS)
DP .... Data Path
DP .... Data Phone (SAUS)
DP .... Data Plotter (SAUS)
DP .... Data Pointer [*Computer memory*]
DP .... Data Port (SAUS)
DP .... Data Preparation (SAUS)
DP .... Data Printer
DP .... Data Processing [*Medicine*] (EDAA)
DP .... Data Processing and/or Computer Programming Programs [*Association of Independent Colleges and Schools specialization code*]
DP .... Data Processing Detection Point (SAUS)
DP .... Data Processing Technician [*Navy rating*]
DP .... Data Processor (SAUS)
DP .... Data Production (SAUS)
DP .... Data Products (SAUS)
DP .... Data Protection Act [*1980's*] [*British*]
DP .... Data Pulse (IAA)
DP .... Date of Publication [*Online database field identifier*]
DP .... Datum Point
DP .... Daughters of Penelope (EA)
DP .... Day Parole (FOTI)
DP .... Days Prior (ACAE)
DP .... Days' Purposes [*Shipping*]
DP .... Dead Point
DP .... Decadic Pulsing (SAUS)
DP .... Decimal Place [*Mathematics*] (IAA)
DP .... Decimal Point (SAUS)
dp .... Decipig (SAUS)
DP .... Decision Package [*Military*]
DP .... Decision Point (CAAL)
DP .... Deck Piercing
DP .... Decommissioning Programs Department (SAUS)
DP .... Dedicated Peripherie (SAUS)
DP .... Deed Poll
DP .... Deep (FAAC)
DP .... Deep Penetration [*Air Force*]
DP .... Deep Pulse [*Medicine*]
DP .... Deep-Space Perturbations (ACAE)
DP .... Defence Point (SAUS)
DP .... Defense Paper (SAUO)
DP .... Defense Point
DP .... Defense Program (COE)
D/P .... Deferred Payment [*Business term*] (ADA)
DP .... Deflection Plate [*Technical drawings*]
DP .... Deflector Plate (SAUS)
DP .... Degradation Products [*Hematology*]
DP .... Degree of Polymerization
DP .... Delacorte Press [*Publisher*]
DP .... Delayed Procurement (NASA)
DP .... Deliberate Planning (SAUS)
D/P .... Delivery Against Payment [*Business term*] (ADA)
D/P .... Delivery Papers (SAUS)
DP .... Delivery Point
DP .... Delta Pile (SAUS)
DP .... Deltopectoral [*Anatomy*] (DAVI)
DP .... Demand Meter, Printing
DP .... Demand Pacemaker (MELL)
DP .... Demand Planning (GART)
DP .... Demarcation Point (SAUS)
DP .... Dementia Praecox [*or a patient with this condition*] [*Medical slang*]
DP .... Demi-Pension [*Hotel rate*]
DP .... Democracy Project (EA)
DP .... Democratic Party [*Lithuania*] [*Political party*] (EAIO)
DP .... Democratic Party [*Thailand*] [*Political party*] (PPW)
DP .... Democratic Party [*Cook Island*] [*Political party*] (PPW)

DP............... Democratic Party [*Kenya*] [*Political party*] (EY)
DP............... Democratic Party [*Uganda*] [*Political party*] (PD)
DP............... Democratic Party [*Poland*] [*Political party*] (PPW)
DP............... Democratic Party (Seychelles) [*Political party*] (PSAP)
DP............... Democratic Party (South Africa) [*Political party*] (PSAP)
DP............... Democratic Party (Zimbabwe) [*Political party*] (PSAP)
DP............... Democratische Partij - Bovenwinden [*Democratic Party - Windward Islands*] [*Netherlands Antilles*] [*Political party*] (PPW)
DP............... Democratische Partij van Curacao [*Democratic Party - Curacao*] [*Netherlands Antilles*] [*Political party*] (PPW)
DP............... Democrazia Proletaria [*Proletarian Democracy*] [*Italy*] [*Political party*] (PPE)
DP............... Demokratesch Partei [*Democratic Party*] [*Luxembourg*] [*Political party*] (PPE)
DP............... Demokraticheska Partiia [*Democratic Party*] [*Bulgaria*] [*Political party*] (PPE)
DP............... Demokratiki Parataksis [*Democratic Front*] [*Greek*] (PPE)
DP............... Demolition Proceeding (ADWA)
DP............... Density of Positive (SAUS)
DP............... Dental Plaque (MELL)
DP............... Dental Prosthetics [*Dentistry*] (DAVI)
DP............... Dental Prosthetic Technician
DP............... Denver Post (SAUS)
DP............... Depart (DA)
DP............... Department (IAA)
DP............... Department of the Pacific [*Marine Corps*]
dp............... departure (SAUS)
DP............... Departure Point (AFM)
DP............... Deployment Payload (MCD)
DP............... Deployment Pennant [*Navy*] [*British*]
D-P............... Depo-Provera [*Contraceptive*] [*The Upjohn Co.*]
DP............... Deposit
DP............... Deposited Plan (ADA)
DP............... Depot (SAUO)
DP............... Depreciation Percentage [*Finance*] (WDAA)
dp............... Depression (IDYL)
DP............... De Profundis
Dp............... Depth (MIST)
dp............... Depth (VRA)
DP............... Depth (MSA)
DP............... Depth Perception (PAZ)
DP............... depth profiling (SAUS)
DP............... Der Deutsche Pionier [*A publication*] (BJA)
Dp............... Dermatophagoides pteronyssinus [*House dust*]
DP............... Description Pattern
DP............... Desiderius Pastor [*Pseudonym used by Gerard Moultree*]
DP............... Designated Player [*Baseball term*] (NDBD)
DP............... Designation Punching (SAUS)
DP............... Design Program (SAUS)
DP............... Design Proof (NASA)
DP............... Design Proposal
DP............... Desktop Publishing [*Computer science*]
DP............... Destination Punching (SAUS)
DP............... Detailed Process (ACAE)
DP............... Detail Printing (SAUS)
D/P............... Detained Pay
DP............... Detection Point (VERA)
DP............... Detention of Pay (DNAB)
DP............... Detrucking Point
DP............... Deutsche Partei [*German Party*] [*Political party*] (PPE)
DP............... Developed Pressure [*Cardiology*]
DP............... Developing Proboscis
DP............... Development Phase (NASA)
DP............... Development Plan
DP............... Development Play (EDAC)
DP............... Development Program [*Military*]
DP............... Development project (SAUS)
DP............... Development Proposal (NVT)
DP............... Development Prototype
DP............... Device Pool (SAUS)
DP............... Devil Pups (EA)
DP............... Dew Point
DP............... Diabetes-Prone [*Medicine*]
DP............... Diagnostic Processor (CCCA)
DP............... Diagnostic Products [*NYSE symbol*] (TTSB)
DP............... Diagnostic Products Corp. [*NYSE symbol*] (SPSG)
DP............... Dial Fulsing (SAUS)
DP............... Dial Port [*Communications term*] (DCT)
DP............... Dial Pulse [*Telecommunications*]
DP............... Dial Pulsing (SAUS)
DP............... Diametral Pinch (SAUS)
DP............... Diametral Pitch (SAUS)
DP............... Diametrical Pitch
DP............... Diamond Pin (SAUS)
DP............... Diaphosgene [*A choking agent*] (ADDR)
DP............... Diaphragm (IAA)
DP............... diapirs (SAUS)
DP............... Diastatic Power
DP............... Diastolic Pressure [*Medicine*]
DP............... Dichlorophenoxypropionate (SAUS)
DP............... Diesel Particulate
DP............... Difference in Pressure
DP............... Difference of Potential
DP............... Difference, Port [*Navigation*]
dp............... differential of pressure (SAUS)
DP............... Differential Phase [*Telecommunications*]
dp............... Differential Pressure (ABAC)
DP............... Differential Pressure
DP............... Differential Pulse
DP............... Diffraction Pattern (SAUS)
DP............... Diffused Planar
DP............... Diffusion Pressure
DP............... Diffusion Pump
DP............... digestible pressure (SAUS)
DP............... Digestible Protein [*Medicine*] (MAE)
DP............... Digitally Programmed (IAA)
DP............... Digital Person (SAUS)
DP............... Digital Photogrammetry (GEOI)
DP............... Digital Plotter
DP............... Digital Position (SAUS)
DP............... Digital Processing (SAUS)
DP............... Digital Processor (MCD)
DP............... Digital Product (SAUS)
DP............... Digital Pulser (SAUS)
DP............... Digit Position (SAUS)
DP............... Digit Present
DP............... Digit Pulse (SAUS)
DP............... Digit Punching (SAUS)
DP............... Dilute phosphate (SAUS)
DP............... Dimeric Polymer (SAUS)
DP............... Dining Permit [*Slang*]
DP............... Diode Plate (IAA)
DP............... Diphenyl [*Organic chemistry*]
DP............... Diphosgene [*Poison gas*] [*Army symbol*]
DP............... Diphosphate [*Biochemistry*]
DP............... Diploma in Pediatrics
DP............... Diploma in Psychiatry (SAUS)
D-P............... Diplomate, American Board of Pathology (DHSM)
DP............... Dipole (DEN)
DP............... Dipropionate [*Pharmacology*] (MAE)
DP............... Directed Proliferation
DP............... Directing Point
DP............... Directional Preponderance (MAE)
DP............... Directione Propria [*With Proper Direction*] [*Pharmacy*]
DP............... Direction of President
DP............... Director of Pathology
DP............... Director of Personnel (MCD)
DP............... Director of Photography [*Cinematography*] (WDMC)
DP............... Director of Postings [*RAF*] [*British*]
DP............... Director of Programs [*Air Force, Army*]
DP............... Director of the Port (SAUS)
DP............... Direct Participation (ADA)
DP............... Direct Path (NVT)
DP............... direct playback (SAUS)
DP............... Direct Port [*Transportation*]
DP............... Direct Positive [*Photography*] (WDMC)
DP............... direct potentiometry (SAUS)
DP............... Direct Price
DP............... Direct Program (SAUS)
DP............... Direct Programming (SAUS)
DP............... Disability Pension (MAE)
DP............... Disabled Person (ADA)
DP............... Disadvantaged Person
DP............... Disaster Preparedness (NVT)
DP............... Discharged Patient [*British*]
DP............... Disciple
DP............... Disconnection Pending [*Telecommunications*] (TEL)
DP............... disc pack (SAUS)
DP............... Disc Plowing [*Agriculture*]
DP............... Discretionary Program (OICC)
dp............... discriminatory power (SAUS)
DP............... Disc to Printer (SAUS)
DP............... Discussion Paper
DP............... Disk Pack [*Computer science*] (IEEE)
DP............... Disk to Printer (IAA)
DP............... Disopyramide Phosphate [*Cardiac depressant*] (AAMN)
DP............... Disorderly Person
DP............... Dispatch Point
DP............... Dispensing Precaution
DP............... Dispersal Point
DP............... Dispersed Phase (OA)
DP............... Displaced Person [*Post-World War II*]
DP............... Displaced Personnel [*Military*]
DP............... Displaced Persons (SAUS)
DP............... Displacement
DP............... Display Package
DP............... Display Panel
DP............... Display Postscript (SAUS)
DP............... Display Processor
DP............... Disruptive Pattern (SAUS)
DP............... Dissolution Patterns [*Physics*]
D/P............... Distal Interphalangeal [*Joints*] [*Anatomy*] (DAVI)
DP............... Distal Pancreatectomy [*Medicine*] (AAMN)
DP............... Distal Phalanx [*Medicine*] (MELL)
DP............... Distal Pulses (SAUS)
DP............... Distance Portion (SAUS)
DP............... Distending Pressure
DP............... Distopulpal [*Dentistry*]
DP............... Distributed Pipeline (SAUS)
DP............... Distributed Printing (SAUS)

DP............... Distributing Point (SAUO)
DP............... Distribution Panel [*Communications term*] (DCT)
DP............... Distribution Plan (AFIT)
DP............... Distribution Point
DP............... Distribution Programmer (IAA)
DP............... District Plan (SAUS)
DP............... Disturb Pulse (SAUS)
DP............... Divide decimal Packed (SAUS)
DP............... Divide Packed (SAUS)
DP............... Docking Protein [*Biochemistry*]
DP............... Doctor of Pharmacy
DP............... Doctor of Philosophy
DP............... Doctor of Podiatry (WGA)
D/P............... Documenti Contro Pagamento [*Documents Against Payment*] [*Italian*] [*Business term*]
D/P............... Documentos Contra Pago [*Documents Against Payment*] [*Spanish*] [*Business term*]
DP............... Document Publishing (IAA)
DP............... Documents against Payment (DFIT)
DP............... Documents and Publications service (SAUO)
D/P............... Documents Contre Paiement [*Documents Against Payment*] [*French*] [*Banking*]
dp............... documents for payment (SAUS)
DP............... Documents Presargoniques [*A publication*] (BJA)
DP............... DOE Office of the Assistant Secretary for Defense Programs (SAUS)
D-P............... Dog Pound [*Multistory parking lot*] [*Slang*] [*British*]
DP............... Domestic Prelate
DP............... Dominion Party (SAUO)
DP............... Dom Perignon [*Champagne*]
DP............... Domus Procerum [*The House of Lords*] [*Latin*]
DP............... Donor's Plasma [*Medicine*]
d/p............... door-to-port/port-to-door (SAUS)
DP............... Doppelposten [*Double Sentry*] [*German military - World War II*]
DP............... Dorsalis Pedis [*Pulse*] [*Medicine*]
DP............... Dorsalis pedis Pulse (SAUS)
DP............... Dorsal Pallium [*Neuroanatomy*]
DP............... Dorsal Pioneer Cell [*Cytology*]
DP............... Dorsal Pit (SAUS)
DP............... Dorsal Pitt
DP............... Dot Pattern (SAUS)
dp............... Dot Pitch (ADWA)
DP............... Dot Pitch (CDE)
DP............... Double Paper [*Wire insulation*] (AAG)
DP............... Double Parallel [*Molecular biology*]
DP............... Double-Pass (SAUS)
DP............... Double Petticoat [*Insulators*]
DP............... Double Pitched [*Construction term*] (MIST)
DP............... Double Plasma
DP............... Double Play [*Baseball*]
dp............... double plays (SAUS)
DP............... Double Ply (SAUS)
DP............... Double Pneumonia (MELL)
DP............... Double Pole [*Switch*]
DP............... Double Precision (NASA)
DP............... Double Propellant (SAUS)
DP............... Double Punch (SAUS)
DP............... Double Purpose (SAUS)
DP............... Double-Purpose Gun
DP............... Draft Printer (ELAL)
DP............... Draft Proposal
DP............... Draft Proposed Standard (SAUS)
DP............... Drainage Program (SAUO)
DP............... Drain Panel (AAG)
DP............... Drain Pipe (SAUS)
DP............... Drill Pay
DP............... Drill Pipe (SAUS)
DP............... Drill Plate [*Tool*] (MSA)
DP............... Drill Purposes [*British military*] (DMA)
dp............... Drip Proof (SAUS)
DP............... Drip-Proof (AAG)
DP............... Driving Point (SAUS)
DP............... Driving Power
DP............... Drop Point [*Air Force*] (AFM)
DP............... Drum Processor [*Computer science*] (IEEE)
dp............... dry pint (SAUS)
DP............... Dry Point
DP............... Dual Phase (MCD)
DP............... Dual Pilot (MUGU)
DP............... Dual-Port Bus (SAUS)
DP............... Dual Printing (SAUS)
DP............... Dual Processor (SAUS)
DP............... Dual Property (SAUS)
DP............... Dual Purpose (NG)
DP............... Ducted Propellers [*Aviation*] (AAG)
DP............... Due Point (SAUS)
DP............... Due Process
DP............... Dummy Part (MCD)
DP............... Dummy Procedure (SAUS)
dp............... dump (SAUS)
DP............... Dungpit (ROG)
DP............... Duo Plus (SAUS)
DP............... Duplicate Positive (MCD)
Dp............... Duplication (QSUL)
DP............... Du Pont de Nemours (SAUO)
DP............... Durable Press [*Textile technology*]
DP............... Duty Paid [*International trade*]
DP............... Duty Pay
DP............... Dying Patient (MELL)
DP............... Dynamically Positioned
DP............... Dynamic Party (SAUO)
DP............... Dynamic Planner (CTAS)
DP............... Dynamic Positioning (SAUS)
DP............... Dynamic Pressure (SAUS)
DP............... Dynamic Programming [*Computer science*]
DP............... Dynorphin [*Biochemistry*]
DP............... Office of Defense Programs (SAUS)
DP............... Popular Democracy (Ecuador) [*Political party*] (PSAP)
DP............... Potential Difference [*Electricity*] (ROG)
DP............... Two Pole (MSA)
DP............... United States Patent Office, Arlington, VA [*Library symbol*] [*Library of Congress*] (LCLS)
DP............... Airline Flight Code for Air 2000 (ODA)
D/P............... Delivery on Payment (ODA)
DP-1............... Assistant Secretary for Defense Programs (SAUO)
DP1............... Data Processing Technician, First Class [*Navy rating*]
DP2............... Data Processing Technician, Second Class [*Navy rating*]
DP3............... Data Processing Technician, Third Class [*Navy rating*]
DP3T............... Double-Pole Triple-Throw (SAUS)
DPA............... Black Data Processing Associates (EA)
DPA............... Chicago/West Chicago, IL [*Location identifier*] [*FAA*] (FAAL)
DPA............... Dampier Port Authority [*Australia*]
DPA............... Darwin Port Authority [*Australia*]
DPA............... Data Processing Accounting (SAUS)
DPA............... Data Processing Activities
DPA............... Data Processing Activities (or Activity) (SAUO)
DPA............... Data Processing Agency
DPA............... Data Processing Algorithm
DPA............... Data Processing Area
DPA............... Data Processing Assembly (MCD)
DPA............... Data Processing Authorization (ACAE)
DPA............... Data Processsing Agency (SAUO)
DPA............... Data Protection Act [*British*] (NITA)
DPA............... Data Protection Agency [*British*]
DPA............... Data Protection Authority (SAUO)
DPA............... Decimal Point Alignment (SAUS)
DPA............... Deep Water Ports Act [*1974*] [*Environmental Protection Agency*] (EPA)
DPA............... Deepwater Ports Act (SAUO)
DPA............... Defense Production Act [*Obsolete*] (NG)
DPA............... Defense Production Administration [*Functions transferred to Office of Defense Mobilization*]
DPA............... Deferred Payment Account [*Business term*] (WDAA)
DPA............... Delay Path Analysis (SAUS)
DPA............... Delegation of Procurement Authority
DPA............... Demand Protocol Architecture [*Computer science*] (PCM)
DPA............... Democratic Party of Albania [*Political party*] (EY)
DPA............... Demonstration Programs Administration [*HUD*]
DPA............... Densely Populated Area (SAUS)
DPA............... Deoxidized Phosphorus Copper, Arsenical (SAUS)
DPA............... Department of Physics and Astronomy (SAUS)
DPA............... Department of Political Affairs (SAUO)
DPA............... Department Purpose Analysis (TIMI)
DPA............... Designated Processing Agency (MCD)
DPA............... Designated Procuring Activity (MCD)
DPA............... Design Professionals Association (NTPA)
DPA............... Desktop Publishing Association (EA)
DPA............... Destructive Part Analysis
DPA............... Destructive Physical Analysis
DPA............... Detailed Performance Analysis [*Bell System*]
DPA............... Deutsche Presse Agentur [*German Press Agency*]
DPA............... Dextroposition of Aorta [*Cardiology*] (DAVI)
DPA............... Diabetes Press of America (SAUS)
DPA............... Diagnostic Prescriptive Arithmetic (EDAC)
DPA............... Dial Pulse Acceptor (SAUS)
DPA............... Dial Pulse Access [*Telecommunications*] (TEL)
DPA............... Diary Publishers' Association [*British*] (BI)
DPA............... Dichloropropionanilide [*Also, DCPA*] [*Herbicide*]
DPA............... Dichloropropionic Acid (SAUS)
DPA............... Differential Power Analysis (SAUS)
DPA............... Differential pressure alarm (SAUS)
DPA............... Different Premises Address [*Telecommunications*] (TEL)
DPA............... Digital Precipitation Arrays (SAUS)
DPA............... Digital Processor Assembly (MCD)
DPA............... Digital Pulse Analyzer (SAUS)
DPA............... Dihydroxyprogesterone (DB)
DPA............... Diphenolic Acid [*Organic chemistry*]
DPA............... Diphenylamine [*Organic chemistry*]
DPA............... Diphenylanthracene [*Organic chemistry*]
DPA............... Dipicolinic Acid [*Organic chemistry*]
DPA............... Diploma in Pathological Anatomy (SAUS)
DPA............... Diploma in Public Administration [*British*]
DPA............... Dipropylacetate (MAE)
DPA............... Dipropylacetic Acid [*Also, VPA*] [*Valproic acid*] [*Anticonvulsant compound*]
DPA............... Dipropylamine [*Organic chemistry*]
DPA............... Directorate of Personnel Administration (SAUO)
DPA............... Directorate of Policy [*Air Ministry*] [*British*]
DPA............... Directorate of Presidential Affairs
D/PA............... Director of Personnel and Administration (SAUO)
DPA............... Directory Publishers Alliance (EA)

DPA .... Directory Publishers Association [*British*] [*England*] (EAIO)
DPA .... Direct Processor Adaptor (SAUS)
DPA .... Direct Provider Agreement
DPA .... Disabled Peoples' Association [*Singapore*] (EAIO)
DPA .... Discharged Prisoners' Aid [*British*]
DPA .... Discharged Prisoners Association (SAUO)
dpa .... Displacements per Atom (ABAC)
DPA .... Displacements per Atom (MCD)
DPA .... Display Printer Adapter (ELAL)
DPA .... Display/Printer Adapter (SAUS)
DPA .... Distributed Password Authentication [*Computer science*] (MWOL)
DPA .... Distributed Print Architecture (GART)
DPA .... Distributed Processing Algorithm (SAUS)
DPA .... Distribution Plan Authorization [*Military*] (AFIT)
DPA .... Diversion Path Analysis (PDAA)
DPA .... Division of Performing Arts (SAUS)
DPA .... Division of Public Affairs (SAUO)
DPA .... Division Produits Automobiles (SAUS)
DPA .... Division Property Administrator (ACAE)
D Pa .... Doctor of Painting
DPA .... Doctor of Public Administration
DPA .... Document Printing Application (SAUS)
DPA .... Document Printing Architecture (SAUS)
DPA .... Document Printing Network Signaling System [*Telecommunications*] (OSI)
DPA .... DOD Protocol Architecture (SAUS)
DPA .... Domestic Policy Association [*Later, NIF*] (EA)
DPA .... Double-Precision Arithmetic (AAG)
DPA .... D-Pantothenyl Alcohol [*Biochemistry*]
DPA .... Driving Point Admittance
DPA .... Dual Photon Absorptiometry [*Analytical chemistry*]
DPA .... Dubai Port Authority
DPA .... Duck Producers Association [*British*] (DBA)
DPA .... Duke Papyrus Archive (SAUS)
DPAA .... Data Processing, Analysis, and Archiving (NOAA)
DPAA .... Desktop Publishing Applications Association (EA)
DPAA .... Draught Proofing Advisory Association [*British*] (DBA)
DPA&E .... Director Program Analysis and Evaluation (ACAE)
DPAC .... Data Processing and Control (Unit) (CAAL)
DPAC .... Dedicated Plant Assignment Center (SAUS)
DPAC .... Defense Policy Advisory Committee [*DoD*]
DPAC .... Dense-Pac Microsystems [*NASDAQ symbol*] (TTSB)
DPAC .... Dense-Pac Microsystems, Inc. [*NASDAQ symbol*] (NQ)
DPAC .... Differential Perturbed Angular Correlation (SAUS)
DPAC .... Displaced Persons Assembly Centre (SAUO)
DPAC .... Dizionario Patristico e di Antichita Cristiane [*A publication*] (ODCC)
DPACCS .... Displaced Persons Assembly Center Camp Staffs [*Allied Military Government of Occupied Territory*] [*Post-World War II*]
DPACD .... Data Processing Agreement and Customer Documents (SAUS)
DPACD .... Data Processing Agreements and Customer Documents (SAUS)
DPACT .... Defense Policy Advisory Committee on Trade [*DoD*]
DP Adm .... Doctor of Public Administration
DPAE .... Data Processing Automatic Equipment
DPAE .... Director of Program Analysis and Evaluation (RDA)
DPaed .... Doctor of Paediatrics [*Medicine*]
DPaed .... Doctor of Pedagogy
DPAF .... Dual Payload Attachment Fitting [*Space launch term*] (ISAK)
D-PAF .... German Processing and Archiving Facility (SAUS)
DPAG .... Dangerous Pathogen Advisory Group (HEAS)
DPAGE .... Device Page (SAUS)
DPAH .... Direct Product Actual Hours (MCD)
DPAHC .... Durable Power of Attorney for Health Care
DPAHO .... Pan American Health Organization, Pan American Sanitary Bureau, Washington, DC [*Library symbol*] [*Library of Congress*] (LCLS)
DPAHO-FH .... Pan American Health Organization, Documentation Center, Division of Family Health, Washington, DC [*Library symbol*] [*Library of Congress*] (LCLS)
DPAI .... (Dipropylaminoethyl)indole [*Organic chemistry*]
DPAI .... drug protein activity index (SAUS)
DPAIAI .... Disregard Previous Assignment Instructions and Assign as Indicated [*Army*] (AABC)
DPAM .... Demand Priority Access Method (SAUS)
DPAMMH .... Direct Productive Annual Maintenance Manhours (MCD)
DP & AD .... Depressive Personality and Allied Disorders (MELL)
DP&L .... Dallas Power and Light (SAUS)
DP & L .... Dallas Power & Light Co.
DP & LC .... Dundee (SAUS)
DP & P .... Director of Plans and Programs [*Army*] (RDA)
DP & S .... Data Processing and Software (NASA)
DP & SPA .... Display Producers' and Screen Printers' Association (DGA)
DP & SS .... Data Processing and Software Subsystem (NASA)
D/P & T .... Director of Personnel and Training [*Army*]
DPANS .... Draft Proposal American National Standards (SAUO)
DPANS .... Draft Proposed American National Standard (SAUS)
dpANS .... Draft Proposed ANS (SAUS)
DPANZ .... Decorator and Painter for Australia and New Zealand [*A publication*]
DPAO .... Deputy Public Affairs Officer [*United States Information Service*]
DPAO .... District Public Affairs Officer [*Military*]
DPAP .... Data Processing Administrative Procedure (VLIE)
DPAP .... Data Processing Asset Protection (VLIE)
DPAP .... Dipeptidyl Aminopeptidase [*An enzyme*]
DPAP .... Drought-Prone Area Program (SAUO)
D-PARC .... Daigo Proving Ground and Research Centre [*Japan*]
DPAREN .... Data Parity Enable (VLIE)
DPARS .... Data Processing Automatic Record Standardization
DPAS .... Defense Priorities and Allocations System [*DoD*] (GFGA)
DPAS .... Digital Patch and Access System (ACAE)
DPAS .... Discharged Prisoners' Aid Society [*British*]
DPASV .... differential puls ASV (SAUS)
DPASV .... Differential Pulse Anodic Stripping Voltametry [*Electrochemistry*]
DPAT .... Di-N Propylaminotetraline (DB)
D-PAT .... Drum-Programmed Automatic Tester
D Path .... Diploma in Pathology [*British*]
DPATS .... Detector Packing Assembly Test Station (ACAE)
DPay .... Directorate of Pay (SAUO)
DPB .... Bucks County Free Library, Doylestown, PA [*OCLC symbol*] (OCLC)
DPB .... Dampier's Paper Book, Lincoln's Inn Library [*A publication*] (DLA)
DPB .... Data Path Bus
DPB .... Data Plotting Board
DPB .... Data Processing Branch (IEEE)
DPB .... Days Post-Burn [*Medicine*] (DMAA)
DPB .... Defence (or Defense) Production Board (SAUO)
DPB .... Defence Production Board [*NATO*] (NATG)
DPB .... Defence-Protected Build-Down [*Nuclear arms reduction strategy*] [*British*]
DPB .... Defence Purchasing Board (SAUO)
DPB .... Defense Policy Board (SAUO)
DPB .... Deffects Per Billion (SAUS)
DP-B .... Democratische Partij - Bonaire [*Democratic Party - Bonaire*] [*Netherlands Antilles*] [*Political party*] (EY)
DPB .... Dental Practice Board of England and Wales [*British*]
DPB .... Department of Plant Biology [*Carnegie Institution of Washington*] [*Research center*] (RCD)
DPB .... Deposit Byte [*Computer science*] (NHD)
DPB .... Deposit Pass Book (SAUS)
DPB .... Deposit Passbook [*Banking*]
DPB .... Destruct Package Building (SAA)
DPB .... Device Parameter Block (ACAE)
DPB .... Dibutyl Phosphate [*Organic chemistry*] (NUCP)
DPB .... Diffuse Panbronchiolitis [*Medicine*] (DMAA)
DPB .... Diphenylbutadiene [*Organic chemistry*]
DPB .... Directive Parameter Block (SAUS)
DPB .... Disability Policy Board [*Veterans Administration*]
DPB .... Disabled Persons Bureau [*Northern Territory*] [*Australia*]
DPB .... Disaster Preparedness Bill (DNAB)
DPB .... Discounted Payback (SAUS)
DPB .... Distinguished Pistol Badge
DPB .... Doctor of Physical Biology
DPB .... Document Processing Branch [*NTIS*]
DPB .... Dodecylpyridinium Bromide [*Organic chemistry*]
DPB .... Domestic Purposes Benefit (SAUS)
DPB .... Double Positioning Boundary [*Electronics*] (AAEL)
DPB .... Drive Parameter Block [*Computer science*] (PCM)
DPB .... Dynamic Pool Block [*Computer science*] (ELAL)
Dp BA .... Diploma in Business Administration [*British*]
DPBA .... Dr. Pepper Bottlers Association (EA)
DpBact .... Diploma in Bacteriology [*British*] (DBQ)
DPBAX .... Digital Private Branch Automatic Exchange (ACAE)
DPBC .... Depolarizing Bipolar Cell [*In the retina*]
DPBC .... Double Pole Back Connected (SAUS)
DPBC .... Double-Pole, Back Connected [*Switch*] (MCD)
DPBC .... Double Pole Both Connected (SAUS)
DPBC .... Double-Pole, Both Connected [*Switch*]
DPBG .... Democratic Party for British Gibraltar (PPW)
DPBO .... Division Property Book Officer [*Military*] (AABC)
DPBP .... Diphenylbutylpiperidine (DMAA)
DPBSP .... Drowning Prevention and Beach Safety Program (EA)
DPBX .... Digital Private Branch Exchange [*Communications term*] (DCT)
DPC .... Chief Data Processing Technician [*Formerly, MAC*] [*Navy rating*]
DPC .... Dairyland Power Cooperative (SAUO)
DPC .... Damp-Proof Course [*Civil engineering*] (IAA)
DPC .... Daniel Payne College (SAUS)
DPC .... Database Promotion Center, Japan [*Information service or system*] (IID)
DPC .... Data Path Control [*Computer science*] (IAA)
DPC .... Data Processing Capacity (SAUS)
DPC .... Data Processing Center
DPC .... Data Processing Center (or Centre) (SAUO)
DPC .... Data Processing Central
DPC .... Data Processing Centre (SAUS)
DPC .... Data Processing Circuit (SAUS)
DPC .... Data Processing Computer (CAAL)
DPC .... Data Processing Control (AFM)
DPC .... Data Product Code (ADWA)
DPC .... Data Products Committee (SAUS)
DPC .... Data Protection Commission (SAUS)
DPC .... Data Protection Committee (SAUO)
DPC .... Date Physically Completed (AAGC)
DPC .... Dating Problems Checklist [*Psychology*]
DPC .... Day-Patient Care/Clinic [*Medicine*] (EDAA)
DPC .... Days Post Coitum [*Medicine*] (MELL)
DPC .... Debt Previously Contracted (EBF)
DPC .... Defence (or Defense) Planning Committee (SAUO)
DPC .... Defence (or Defense) Production Committee (SAUO)
DPC .... Defence Planning Committee [*NATO*] (NATG)
DPC .... Defence Production Chief [*British*]
DPC .... Defence Production Committee [*NATO*] (NATG)
DPC .... Defense Planning Committee (SAUS)
DPC .... Defense Planning Council

DPC .... Defense Plant Corp. [*Subsidiary of Reconstruction Finance Corp.*] [*Obsolete*]
DPC .... Defense Plant Corporation (SAUO)
DPC .... Defense Procurement Center (SAUS)
DPC .... Defense Procurement Circular [*DoD*]
DPC .... Defense Production Chief (SAUS)
DPC .... Deferred Procedure Call (VLIE)
DPC .... Delayed Primary Closure [*Medicine*]
DPC .... Delayed Procedure Call (MWOL)
DPC .... Democratic Policy Commission [*Defunct*] (EA)
DPC .... Democratic Policy Committee (SAUO)
DP-C .... Democratische Partij - Curacao [*Democratic Party - Curacao*] [*Netherlands Antilles*] [*Political party*] (EY)
DPC .... Dense Phosphate Crown (SAUS)
DPC .... Department of the Premier and Cabinet [*South Australia, Tasmania, Victoria*] [*Australia*]
DPC .... Departure Control (DA)
DPC .... Deputy Police Commissioner (SAUS)
DPC .... Deputy Port Commander (SAUO)
DPC .... Desaturated Phosphatidylcholine [*Biochemistry*]
DPC .... Desert Protective Council (EA)
DPC .... Destination Point Code [*Telecommunications*] (TEL)
DPC .... Devotional and Practical Commentary [*A publication*]
DPC .... Diagnostic Products Corp.
DPC .... Differential Phase Contrast (SAUS)
DPC .... Differential Photocalorimetry [*Analytical technique*]
DPC .... Differential Pressure Control
DPC .... Digital Phase Comparator
DPC .... Digital Planimetric Compiler [*Computer science*] (PDAA)
DPC .... Digital Preservation Consortium (SAUS)
DPC .... Digital Pressure Converter
DPC .... Digital Printing Computer (SAUS)
DPC .... Digital Process Controller
DPC .... Digital Pulse Converter (SAUS)
DPC .... Diphenylaminecarboxylate [*Organic chemistry*]
DPC .... Diphenylcarbazide [*Organic chemistry*]
DPC .... Diphenylcarbene [*Organic chemistry*]
DPC .... Diphenyl Carbinol (SAUS)
DPC .... Diphenyl Carbonate [*Organic chemistry*]
DPC .... Directive Parental Counseling
DPC .... Director of Postings and Careers (SAUO)
DPC .... Directory for ports and coasts (SAUS)
DPC .... Direct Path Cancellation (SAUS)
DPC .... Direct Patient Care [*Medicine*]
DPC .... Direct Platelet Count [*Medicine*] (MELL)
DPC .... Direct Power Conversion [*Nuclear energy*] (AAG)
DPC .... Direct Program Control (BUR)
DPC .... Direct prograni control (SAUS)
DPC .... Disabled Persons Corporation (SAUO)
DPC .... Discharge Planning Coordinator [*Medicine*] (DMAA)
DPC .... Disc Pack Controller (SAUS)
DPC .... Disk Pack Controller [*Computer science*] (IAA)
DPC .... Displaced Persons' Camps
DPC .... Displaced Persons Center (SAUO)
DPC .... Displaced Persons Commission [*Terminated, 1952*]
DPC .... display code (SAUS)
DPC .... Display Controller (SAUS)
DPC .... Display Pipeline Controller (SAUS)
DPC .... Display Power Control
DPC .... Display Processor Code
DPC .... Dissemination Policy Council (SAUO)
DPC .... Distal Palmar Crease [*Anatomy*]
DPC .... Distributed Processing Computer (VLIE)
DPC .... Distributed Processing Control (SAUS)
DPC .... Distribution Processing Center (MCD)
DPC .... District Police Commissioner (SAUS)
DPC .... Division of Physical Chemistry (EA)
DPC .... Division of Poison Control [*Medicine*] (EDAA)
DPC .... Division Planning Corporation (SAUO)
DPC .... Doctor of Pastoral Counseling (PGP)
DPC .... Documentation Processing Center [*British*]
DPC .... Document Processing Center (SAUS)
DPC .... Document Production Cost (GART)
DPC .... Dodecylpyridinium Chloride [*Also, LPC*] [*Organic chemistry*]
DPC .... Doklady Physical Chemistry
DPC .... Dollar Penny Coalition (EA)
DPC .... Domestic Policy Council [*Executive Office of the President*] (GFGA)
DPC .... Double Paper Covered (SAUS)
DPC .... Double Paper-Covered [*Wire insulation*] (DEN)
dpc .... double paper single cotton (SAUS)
DPC .... Double Precision Constant (SAUS)
DPC .... Dowling's English Practice Cases [*A publication*] (DLA)
DPC .... Driving Power Car [*Indian Railway*] (TIR)
DPC .... Dry-Packed Concrete (SAUS)
DPC .... Dual Punch Card (SAUS)
DPC .... Dual Purpose Card (SAUS)
DPC .... Duke Power Company (SAUO)
DPC .... Duke Primate Center [*North Carolina*]
DPC .... DuPage County (SAUO)
DPC .... Duty Preference Card (DNAB)
DPC .... Dynamic Pressure Control (SAUS)
DPC .... Dynamic Process Controller
DPC .... Dystrophin Protein Complex [*Biochemistry*]
DPC .... Peace Corps, Information Services Division, Washington, DC [*Library symbol*] [*Library of Congress*] (LCLS)
DPCA .... Data Processing Control Area [*Space Flight Operations Facility, NASA*]
DPCA .... Department of Public and Consumer Affairs
DPCA .... Diphenylcyclopentylamine [*Organic chemistry*]
DPCA .... Director of Personnel and Community Activities [*Army*] (AABC)
DPCA .... Displaced Phase Center Antenna
DPCA .... Displaced Phase Centre Aerial (SAUS)
DPCA .... Doberman Pinscher Club of America (EA)
DPCA .... Dual Port Communications Adapter (SAUS)
DPCAQ .... DEP Corp. 'A' [*NASDAQ symbol*] (TTSB)
DP Car .... Dining and Parlor Car (SAUS)
DPCBQ .... DEP Corp.'B' [*NASDAQ symbol*] (TTSB)
DPCC .... Data Processing Control Center [*or Console*] [*Space Flight Operations Facility, NASA*]
DPCC .... Director of Postal and Courier Communications [*British military*] (DMA)
DPCC .... Double Potential Step Chronocoulometry (SAUS)
DPCC .... Duneland Post Card Club [*Defunct*] (EA)
DPCCP .... Defective Parts and Components Control Program
DPCE .... Data Processing Customer Engineering (ADA)
DPCF .... Dorsal Peristomial Collar Fold
DPCF .... Dorsal Peristominal Collar Fold (SAUS)
DPCF .... Dover Patrol Comforts Fund (SAUO)
DPCI .... Distributed Processing Contractual Input [*Computer science*]
DPCLD .... Division of Public Contracts, Labor Department (SAUO)
DPCM .... Delta Pulse Code Modulation [*Electronics*] (IAA)
DPCM .... Delta Pulse Compression Modulation (SAUS)
DPCM .... Difference Pulse Code Modulation (SAUS)
DPCM .... Differential Pulse Code Modulation [*Transmission technique*]
DPCM .... Differenz-PCM (SAUS)
DPCM .... Digital Pulse Code Modulation (ACAE)
DPCM .... Distributed Processing Communications Module
DPCM .... Master Chief Data Processing Technician [*Formerly, MACM*] [*Navy rating*]
DPCMB .... Defense Procurement Career Management Board (SAUO)
DPCN .... D-Penicillamine [*Pharmacology*]
DPCP .... Department of Prices and Consumer Protection [*British*]
DPCR .... Departure Procedure [*Aviation*] (FAAC)
DPCRT .... Double-Blind Placebo-Controlled Randomized Clinical Trial [*Medicine*] (DMAA)
DPCS .... Data Processing and Communications System (VLIE)
DPCS .... Dedham Pottery Collectors Society (EA)
DPCS .... Desktop Page Composition System [*Vision Research*]
DPCS .... Difference Pressure Control Switch
DPCS .... Distributed Process Control System (SAUS)
DPCS .... Senior Chief Data Processing Technician [*Formerly, MACS*] [*Navy rating*]
DPCSMA .... Dry Process Ceramic and Steatite Manufacturers Association [*Later, TECMA*] (EA)
DPCSV .... differential puls CSV (SAUS)
DPCSV .... Differential-Pulse Cathodic Stripping Voltage (SAUS)
DPCT .... Differential Protection Current Transformer
DPCTE .... Data Processor and Computer Test Equipment
DPCTG .... Database Program Conversion Task Group [*CODASYL*]
DPCU .... Digital Processing and Control Unit
DPCX .... Distributed Processing Control Executive [*IBM Corp.*]
DPCX .... Dragon Products [*Private rail car owner code*]
DPCZ .... Deltech Polymers [*Federal Railroad Administration identification code*]
DPD .... Data for Development International Association (SAUO)
DPD .... Data Preparation Division (SAUS)
DPD .... Data Processing Department
DPD .... Data Processing Detachment
DPD .... Data Processing Digest (SAUS)
DPD .... Data Processing Directive (ODBW)
DPD .... Data Processing Division [*IBM Corp.*]
DPD .... Data Procurement Document (SSD)
DPD .... Data Products Division (SAUS)
DPD .... Data Project Directive (AFM)
DPD .... Deaminophenylalaninedehydroproline [*Biochemistry*]
DPD .... Decimal Point Digit (VLIE)
DPD .... Decontamination as Precursor to Decommissioning [*Nuclear energy*] (NRCH)
DPD .... Define the Page Data set (SAUS)
DPD .... Department of Public Dispensary (DMAA)
DPD .... Depression Pure Disease [*Medicine*] (DMAA)
DPD .... Desoxypyridoxine [*or Deoxypyridoxine*] Hydrochloride [*Pharmacology*] (DAVI)
DPD .... Detailed Procedures Description (SAUS)
DPD .... (Diethyl)phenylenediamine [*Organic chemistry*]
DPD .... Diethyl-P-Phenylene Diamine (SAUS)
DPD .... Differential Phase Detection (SAUS)
DPD .... Diffuse Pulmonary Disease [*Medicine*]
DPD .... Diffusion Pressure Deficit
DPD .... Digital Phase Difference
DPD .... digital plane driver (SAUS)
DPD .... Digit Plane Driver [*Computer science*] (IEEE)
DPD .... Dignitary Protective Division [*US Secret Service*]
DPD .... Diphenamid [*or Diphenyl-dimethylacetamide*] [*Organic chemistry*] (DAVI)
DPD .... Diploma in Public Dentistry [*British*]
D-Pd .... Diplomate, American Board of Pediatrics (DHSM)
DPD .... Director of Plans Division [*Navy*] [*British*]
DPD .... Director, Personnel Department [*Marine Corps*]
DPD .... Directory of Portable Databases [*A publication*]

DPD .... Direct Payroll Deposit
DPD .... Disk Pack Data (SAUS)
DPD .... Disk Partition Data (SAUS)
DPD .... Distributor Products Division (SAUO)
DPD .... District Port Director [*Navy*]
DPD .... Division of Program Development (SAUO)
D Pd .... Doctor of Pedagogy
DPD .... Domestic Presidential Directive [*Jimmy Carter Administration*]
DPD .... Double Plug Diode (IAA)
DPD .... Drug Product Database (ADWA)
DPD .... Method of Measuring Chlorine Residual in Water (SAUS)
DPDA .... Deterministic Pushdown Automata (PDAA)
DPDA .... Deterministic Push-Down Automation (SAUS)
DPDA .... Deterministic Pushdown Automaton (SAUS)
DPDA .... Diperoxydodecanedioic Acid (SAUS)
DPDA .... Phosphorodiamidic Anhydride [*Organic chemistry*] (DAVI)
DPDC .... Data Processing and Distribution Center (SAUS)
DPDC .... Double Paper, Double Cotton [*Wire insulation*]
DPDD .... Defense Property Disposal Detachment (AFIT)
DPDI .... Dimple Die
DPDL .... Diffuse Poorly Differentiated Lymphocytic (Lymphoma) [*Oncology*]
DPDL .... Distributed Program Design Language
DPDLL .... Diffuse, Poorly Differentiated, Lymphocytic Lymphoma [*Oncology*] (DAVI)
DPDM .... Dawro Peoples Democratic Movement (SAUO)
DPDM .... Digital Pulse Duration Modulation (SAUS)
DPDM .... Diphenyl Diazomalonate [*Organic chemistry*]
DPDM .... Diphenyldiazomethane [*Organic chemistry*]
DPDM .... DODIIS Protocol Development and Maintenance (SAUS)
DPDM .... Double Pulse Duration Modulation (KSC)
DPDM-R .... Defense Property Disposal Precious Metals Recovery [*DoD*] (AFIT)
DPDO .... Decennial Policy and Design Office (SAUS)
DPDO .... Defense Property Disposal Office [*DoD*]
DPDP .... Data Processing Development Plan (ACAE)
DPDP .... Defense Property Disposal Program [*DoD*] (DNAB)
DPDPMRO-E... Defense Property Disposal Precious Metals Recovery Office - Earle [*New Jersey*] [*DoD*]
DPDR .... Defense Property Disposal Region [*DoD*]
DPDRAM .... Dual-Ported Dynamic Random Access Memory [*Computer science*]
DPDR-E .... Defense Property Disposal Region-Europe (SAUO)
DPDREG .... Defense Property Disposal Region [*DoD*] (DNAB)
DPDRPACDET... Defense Property Disposal Region, Pacific Detachment [*DoD*] (DNAB)
DPDRPACSO... Defense Property Disposal Region, Pacific Sales Office [*DoD*] (DNAB)
DPDS .... DARC [*Description, Acquisition, Retrieval, and Conception*] Pluridata System [*Association for Research and Development of Chemical Informatics*] [*Information service or system*] (IID)
DPDS .... Data Processing Distributed Systems (SAUS)
DPDS .... Defense Property Disposal Service [*DoD*]
DPDSE .... Defense Property Disposal Service in Europe (SAUO)
DPDSSO .... Defense Property Disposal Ship Sales Office (SAUO)
DP/DT .... Delta Pressure/Delta Time (MCD)
DPDT .... Double Pole, Double Throw [*Switch*]
dpdt .... Double-Pole, Double-Throw (IDOE)
DPDTD .... Distributed Processing Design Technology Development (SAUS)
DPDT DB .... Double-Pole, Double-Throw, Double-Break (SAUS)
DPDTSW .... Double-Pole, Double-Throw Switch
DPDT Switch... Double-Pole Double-Throw Switch (SAUS)
DPDU .... Data Link Protocol Data Unit [*Communications term*] (DCT)
DPDU Dund... Diploma in Public Dentistry, University of Dundee [*British*]
DPDZ .... Destor-Porcupine Deformation Zone [*Geology*]
DPE .... Data Path Extender [*Computer science*] (VLIE)
DPE .... Data Processing Element (SAUS)
DPE .... Data Processing Engineer (ADWA)
DPE .... Data Processing Environment (GEOI)
DPE .... Data Processing Equipment
DPE .... Delta Pi Epsilon [*Fraternity*] (AEE)
DPE .... Demande Pour Emettre (SAUS)
DPE .... Demand Processing Unit (SAUS)
DPE .... Demilitarization Protective Ensemble (RDA)
DPE .... Department for Professional Employees [*AFL-CIO*]
DPE .... Department of Plastics Engineering (SAUS)
DPE .... Desktop Publishing Editor [*Computer program*]
DPE .... Detailed Plan Execution (MCD)
DPE .... Deuterated Polyethylene [*Organic chemistry*]
d-p-e .... development-printing-enlargement (SAUS)
DPE .... Development Project Engineer (NRCH)
DPE .... Dieppe [*France*] [*Airport symbol*] [*Obsolete*] (OAG)
DPE .... Differential Paramagnetic Effect [*Low-temperature physics*]
dpe .... digital processing effects (SAUS)
dpe .... digital production effects (SAUS)
DPE .... Diphenylethylene [*Organic chemistry*]
DPE .... Diphenyltrichloroethane [*Also, DPT*] [*Organic chemistry*]
DPE .... Dipiperidinoethane (DMAA)
DPE .... Diploma in Physical Education [*British*]
DPE .... Director of Physical Education (SAUO)
DPE .... Director of Primary Education (SAUS)
DPE .... Director of Public Education (SAUS)
DPE .... Director Program Evaluation [*Navy*] (CAAL)
DPE .... Direct Plate Exposer [*Printing*] (NITA)
DPE .... Direct Plate Exposure (DGA)
DPE .... Disk Processor Enclosure (GART)
DPE .... Distributed Processing Environment
DPE .... Distributor-to-Printer Electronics
DPE .... District Power Equalizer [*Formula for school grants*]
DPE .... Doctor of Physical Education
DPE .... Dual-Porosity Element [*Automotive engineering*]
DPE .... Duration of the Present Emergency [*British*] [*World War II*]
DPE .... Dynamic Phase Error
DPEC .... Diploma in Parent Education and Counselling
DPEc .... Doctor of Political Economy
DPED .... Data Processing Education Department [*Computer science*] (VLIE)
DPED .... Department of Planning and Economic Development (GEOI)
D Ped .... Doctor of Pedagogy
D Pe E .... Doctor of Petroleum Engineering
D Pe Eng .... Doctor of Petroleum Engineering
DPEIS .... Draft programmatic environmental impact statement (SAUS)
DPEK .... Differential Phase Exchange Keying (IEEE)
DPEM .... Depot Purchased Equipment Maintenance (SAUS)
DPEM .... Depot Purchased Equipment Management [*DoD*]
DPEP .... Defense Professionals Exchange Program
DPEP .... Deoxophylloerythroetioporphyrin [*Biochemistry*]
DPEP .... Dipeptidase (DMAA)
DPER .... Donor Procurement Efficiency Rating [*Medicine*]
DPERPLA .... Delegacion del Parlamento Europeo para las Relaciones con los Paises de Latinoamerica [*Europe-Latin America Interparliamentary Assembly - ELAIA*] [*Luxembourg, Luxembourg*] (EAIO)
DPers .... Director of Personnel Services (SAUO)
DPersP .... Director of Personnel Planning (SAUO)
DPESE .... Densely Packaged Encased Standard Element (AAG)
dpe service... developing-printing-enlarging service (SAUS)
DPESO .... Department of Defense Product Engineering Services Office (MCD)
DPESO .... DoD Product Engineering Services Office (SAUS)
DPETD .... Department of the Premier, Economic and Trade Development [*Queensland*] [*Australia*]
DPEWS .... Designed-to-Price Electronic Warfare System (SAUS)
DPEWS .... Design-to-Price Electronics Warfare System [*Military*]
DPEWS .... Design-to-Price Electronic Warfare Suite (SAUS)
DPEX .... Distributed Processing Executive (SAUS)
DPEX .... Distributed Processing Executive Program
DPF .... Data Private Facility (SAUS)
DPF .... Data Processing Facility
DPF .... Data Processing Federation [*France*] (NITA)
DPF .... Data Processing Financial & General Corp. (SAUO)
DPF .... Deck Project Force (SAUS)
DPF .... Defatted Peanut Flour [*Food industry*]
DPF .... Defense Plasma Focus (SAUS)
DPF .... Deferred Pay Fund
DPF .... Denier per Filament [*Textile technology*]
DPF .... Dense Plasma Focus
DPF .... Dental Practioners Formulary (SAUS)
DPF .... Dental Practitioner's Formulary
DPF .... Deperming Facility (SAUS)
DPF .... Depression Position-Finder
DPF .... Diesel Particulate Filter [*Automotive emissions*]
DPF .... Differential Pressure Feedback (KSC)
DPF .... Differential Procedure Feedback [*Military*]
DPF .... Digital Parching Field (SAUS)
DPF .... Digital Parching Frame (SAUS)
DPF .... Disciples Peace Fellowship (EA)
DPF .... Discrete Packet Format (SAUS)
DPF .... Distance Precedence Function (SAUS)
DPF .... Diversified Processed Foods [*Vancouver Stock Exchange symbol*]
DPF .... Divorced Professional Female (ADWA)
DPF .... DPF, Inc. (SAUO)
DPF .... Drill Press Feed
DPF .... Driving Point Function [*Control system*] (IAA)
DPF .... Drug Policy Foundation (EA)
DPF .... Dual Polarized Frequency (SAUS)
DPF .... Dual Porosity Filter [*Automotive engineering*]
DPF .... Dual Program Feature
DPF .... Dynamic Pressure Feedback
DPFAG .... Data Processing, Financial and General (IAA)
DPF&G .... Data Processing Financial & General Corp. (SAUO)
DPFC .... Defense Program Field Council (SAUO)
dPFC .... Direct Plaque-Forming Cell [*Immunology*]
DPFC .... Dolly Parton Fan Club (EA)
DPFC .... Double Pole, Front Connected [*Switch*]
DPFD .... Deptford [*Region of London*]
DPFG .... Data Processing Functional Group (SAUO)
DPFLP .... Democratic Popular Front for the Liberation of Palestine (BJA)
DPFM .... Discrete Time Pulse Frequency Modulation (IAA)
DPFM .... Dual-Polarization Frequency Modulation (SAUS)
DPFN .... Directory Publishers' Forum-North America (NTPA)
DPFO .... Data Processing Field Office (MCD)
DPFP .... Double-Precision Floating Point [*Computer science*]
DPFR .... Diastolic Pressure-Flow Relationship [*Medicine*] (DMAA)
DPFT .... Desk, Double-Pedestal Flat-Top
DPFT .... Double Pedestal Flat Top (SAUS)
DPFZ .... Destor-Porcupine Fault Zone (SAUS)
DPG .... Dahlgren Proving Ground (SAUS)
DPG .... Damping (MSA)
DPG .... Danish Project Group (SAUO)
DPG .... Data of Permanent Grade (SAUS)
DPG .... Data Processing Group [*Army*] (AABC)
DPG .... Data Processor Group (SAUO)
DPG .... Date of Permanent Grade
DPG .... Debutanized Pyrolysis Gasoline

DPG Deck Plate Girder (SAUS)
DPG Dedicated Packet Group
DPG Defense Planning Guidance [*Formerly, Defense Guidance*] (DOMA)
DPG Defense Policy Guidance [*Military*]
DPG Defense Production Guarantees, Army
DPG Desulfurize Pyrolysis Gasoline [*Petroleum refining*]
DPG Detailed Planning Group (SAUO)
DPG Development Program Grant (MHDB)
DPG Diagnostic Programming Group (SAUO)
DPG Digital Pattern Generator
DPG Diphenylguanidine [*Organic chemistry*]
DPG Diphosphoglycerate [*Also, DPGA*] [*Biochemistry*]
dpg diphosphoglyceric acid (SAUS)
DPG Disodium Phosphoglycerate [*Organic chemistry*]
DPG Displacement Placentogram [*Medicine*] (MAE)
DPG Domestically Prohibited Goods (SAUS)
DPG Dripolene Pyrolysis Gasoline [*Lummus Crest, Inc. process*]
DPG Dugway Proving Ground [*Dugway, UT*] [*Army*] (AABC)
DPG Dugway/Tooele, UT [*Location identifier*] [*FAA*] (FAAL)
DPG Dumping
DPG Processing Group (SAUS)
DPGA Delaware Personnel and Guidance Association (SAUO)
DPGA Diphosphoglycerate [*Also, DPG*] [*Biochemistry*]
DPG Acid Diphosphoglyceric Acid (SAUS)
DPGE Dial Page, Inc. [*NASDAQ symbol*] (SAG)
DPGM Deputy Provincial Grand Master [*Freemasonry*] (ROG)
DPGM Diphosphoglyceromutase [*An enzyme*]
DPGN Diffuse Proliferative Glomerulonephritis [*Medicine*]
DPGp Data Processing Group [*Air Force*] (AFM)
DPGP Diphosphoglycerate Phosphatase [*An enzyme*] (DAVI)
DPGR Dugway Proving Ground [*Utah*] [*Army*]
DPGs Development Planning Groups (SAUO)
DPG-S Dugway Proving Ground Studies Branch [*Utah*] [*Army*]
DPG/TA Dugway Proving Ground Technical Analysis and Information Office [*Utah*] [*Army*]
DPH Delphi Automotive Systems [*NYSE symbol*] (SG)
DPH Department of Planning and Housing [*Victoria*] [*Australia*]
DPH Department of Public Health
DPH Department of Public Highways (SAUS)
DPH Depth of Hold
DPH Designated Pinch Hitter [*Later, DH*] [*Baseball*]
DPH Dew-Point Hygrometer (SAUS)
DPH Diamond Penetrator Hardness
DPH Diamond Point Hardness (SAUS)
DPH Diamond Pyramid Hardness (MSA)
dph Diamond-Pyramid Hardness (ABAC)
DPH Diaphragm (STED)
DPH Diphenhydramine [*Organic chemistry*] (DAVI)
DPH Diphenylhexatriene [*A fluorophore*] [*Organic chemistry*]
DPH Diphenylhydantoin [*Anticonvulsant*]
DPH Diploma in/of Public Health (SAUO)
DPH Diploma in Public Health [*British*]
DPH Disc Pack Handler (SAUS)
DPH Disintegrations per Hour
DPH Disk Pack Handler [*Computer science*] (IAA)
DPH Division for Physically Handicapped (EA)
D Ph Doctor of Philosophy
DPH Doctor of Public Health
DPH Doctor of Public Hygiene
DPH Domestic Packing House (SAUS)
DPH Double-Phase Hologram
DPHA Descripcion del Patrimonio Historico-Artistico Espanol [*Database*] [*Ministerio de Cultura*] [*Spanish*] [*Information service or system*] (CRD)
D Phar Doctor of Pharmacy
D Phar C Doctor of Pharmaceutical Chemistry
DPharm Doctor of Pharmacy (ADA)
D Ph C Doctor of Pharmaceutical Chemistry
D Phc Doctor of Pharmacology
DPHD Diploma in Public Health Dentistry (SAUS)
DPHD Division for Physical and Health Disabilities (EA)
DPHDent Diploma in Public Health Dentistry (ADA)
DPHE Doctor of Public Health Engineering
DPH Ed Doctor of Public Health Education
DPH Eng Doctor of Public Health Engineering
DPHGM Diaphragm (IAA)
D Phil Doctor of Philanthropy
D Phil Doctor of Philosophy
D Ph M Doctor of Philosophy in Metaphysics
DPHN Diamond Pyramid Hardness Number (SAUS)
DPHN Diploma in Public Health Nursing (ADA)
DPHN Doctor of Public Health Nursing
D Pho Doctor of Photography
DPhoto Directorate of Photography (SAUO)
DPHP Director, Post-Hostilities Plan (SAUO)
DPHQ Data Processing Headquarters (SAUS)
DPHRCSEng Diploma in Dental Public Health, Royal College of Surgeons of England [*British*] (DBQ)
D Ph S Doctor of Physical Science
D Ph Sc Doctor of Physical Science
DPHU Dispersed Phase Hold Up [*Chemical engineering*]
DPhy Doctor of Philosophy
D Phy Doctor of Physics
DPHy Doctor of Public Hygiene
DPHY UCD Physical (SAUS)
DPhys Diploma of Physiotherapy [*British*]
DPhysiol Diploma in Physiology
D Phys Med Diploma in Physical Medicine [*British*]
DPI Daily Permissible Intake [*Medicine*] (STED)
DPI Data Pathing, Incorporated (SAUO)
DPI Data Preparation Instruction (ACAE)
DPI Data Processing Industry (SAUS)
DPI Data Processing Installation
DPI Data Publishing International [*Netherlands*] [*Information service or system*] (IID)
DPI Days Post Inclubation [*Medicine*] (EDAA)
DPI Days Post Inoculation [*Medicine*] (DMAA)
DPI Deal Proneness Index [*Marketing*]
DPI Defense Plant Installation
DPI Delayed Procurement Item
DPI Departmental Personnel Instruction
DPI Department of Primary Industries (or Industry) (SAUO)
DPI Department of Production and Inspection (SAUO)
DPI Department of Public Information [*United Nations*]
DPI Department of Public Instruction (SAUS)
Dpi Dermatophagoides Pteronyssinus [*Medicine*] (EDAA)
DPI Design Publishing International (SAUS)
DPI Desired Point of Impact [*Military*]
DPI Detail Program Interrelationships (NASA)
DPI Detected Pulse Interference (CET)
DPI Deuterium Pellet Injector (SAUS)
DPI Device Programmer Interface [*Computer science*] (EECA)
DPI Dietary Protein Intake (STED)
dPI Difference Pressure Indicating [*Engineering*]
DPI Differential Pressure Indicator [*Automotive engineering*]
DPI Different Premises Information [*Telecommunications*] (TEL)
DPI Digital Printing and Imaging Association (NTPA)
DPI Digital Process Instrument [*Computer science*] (IEEE)
DPI Digital Pseudorandom Inspection (IEEE)
DPI (Dihydroxyphenylimino)imidazolidine [*Biochemistry*]
DPI Diphenylimide (SAUS)
DPI Diphosphoinositide [*Biochemistry*]
DPI Diploma of the Plastics Institute [*British*] (DI)
DPI Diptheria-Pertussis Immunization [*Medicine*] (EDAA)
DPI Director of Public Instruction
DPI Director of Public Instructions (SAUS)
DPI Disabled Peoples' International (EAIO)
DPI Disorderly Persons Investigation (SAUS)
DPI Disposable Personal Income
DPI Distillation Products Industries (SAUO)
DPI Distributed Program Interface (SAUS)
DPI Distributed Protocol Interface (SAUS)
DPI Division of Plant Industry (SAUO)
DPI Division of Project Implementation (SAUO)
DPI Domestic Product of Industry (MHDB)
DPI Doppler Perfusion Index [*Medicine*] (MELL)
DPI Dot Per Inch (SAUS)
DPI Dot Pitch Integer (SAUS)
DPI Dots Per Inch (WDMC)
dpi Dots-per-Inch [*Printing technology*]
DPI Dots Per Inch, dpi (SAUS)
DPI Double-Pendulum Interferometer (SAUS)
DPI Drug Prescribing Index (STED)
DPI Dry Powder Inhaler [*Pharmacy*]
DPI Dual Plug Inhibit (HAWK)
DPI Duoplasmation Ion
DPI Dynamic Personality Inventory [*Psychology*]
DPIA Diethylenetriamine Producers Importers Alliance (EA)
DPIA Disabled Peoples' International [*Australia*]
DPI-AISO Data Processing Installation-Automated Information Security Official (SAUS)
DPI-AISO Data Processing Installation-Automated Information System Office (SAUS)
DPIBF Diphenylisobenzofuran [*Organic chemistry*]
DPIC Death Penalty Information Center (EA)
DPIC Deputy Paymaster in Chief
DPIC Directorate of Photographic Interpretation Center (SAUO)
DPIC Drug and Poison Information Centre [*University of British Columbia*] [*Information service or system*] (IID)
DPICM Dual-Purpose Improved Conventional Munition (AABC)
DPICS Dyadic Parent-Child Interaction Coding System [*Psychology*]
DPI-CSO Data Processing Installation-Computer Security Official (SAUS)
DPIE Department of Primary Industries and Energy [*Australia*] (GEOI)
DPIEVETPLAN Department of Primary Industries & Energy Veterinary Emergency Plan (SAUO)
DPIF Department of Primary Industries and Fisheries (SAUO)
DPIF Destruct Package Installation Facility (SAA)
DPIF Driving-Point Impedance Function (SAUS)
DPIF Drug Product Information File [*American Society of Hospital Pharmacists*] [*Information service or system*] (IID)
DPIFE Department of Primary Industry, Fisheries, and Energy
DPIG Disaster Preparedness Improvement Grant (DEMM)
DPII Dairy Products Improvement Institute (EA)
DP-II Developmental Profile-II [*Alpern, Bell, and Shearer*] (TES)
DPIL Democracy and Peace (Iterim) League [*Myanmar*] [*Political party*]
DPIM Director of Programme Implementation Monitoring (SAUO)
DP-ING Data Processing (SAUS)
dp-ing durable pressing (SAUS)
DPI/O Data Processing Input/Output (SAUS)
DPIO District Public Information Office [*or Officer*] [*Navy*]

DPIP .... Dichlorophenolindophenol [*Also, DCIP, DCPI, DCPIP*] [*Analytical reagent*]
DPIP .... Dichlorophenol Indophenol Diphenyl Isophthalate (SAUS)
DPIP .... Diphenyl Isophthalate (EDCT)
DPIR .... Data Processing and Information Retrieval (DIT)
DPIR .... Detailed Photo Interpretation Report (DNAB)
DPI regulations... Australian Department of Primary Industry Regulations for the Carriage of Chille (SAUS)
DPIS .... Differential pressure indicator switch (SAUS)
DPIS .... Differential Pressure Isolation Switch (IEEE)
DPIS .... Duoplasmation Ion Source
DPIUSA........ Disabled Peoples' International USA (EA)
DP/IVCP........ Diastolic Pressure to Isovolumic Contraction Period (SAUS)
DPIWE .... Department of Primary Industries, Water and Environment [*Tasmania*] [*Atmosphere*] (ATR)
DPJ.............. Dementia Paralytica Juvenilis [*Medicine*] (DB)
DPJ.............. Democratic Party of Japan [*Political party*]
DPJ.............. Ohio Power Co. [*NYSE symbol*] (SAG)
DPJS............ Department of Prisons and Judicial Statistics (SAUO)
DPK .... Deer Park, NY [*Location identifier*] [*FAA*] (FAAL)
DPK .... Delta Psi Kappa [*Society*]
DPK .... Democratic Party of Kurdistan [*Iraq*] [*Political party*] (PPW)
DPK .... Diphenylketone (SAUS)
DPK .... Driscoll Play Kit [*Psychological testing*]
DPKC .... Diagnostic Problem-Knowledge Coupler
DPKC .... Domestic Poultry Keepers Council (SAUO)
DPKG .... Dolco Packaging Corp. [*NASDAQ symbol*] (SAG)
DPKO .... Department of Peace-keeping Operations (SAUO)
DPL.............. Dallas Public Library (SAUS)
DPL.............. Dataless Programming Language (SAUS)
DPL.............. Data Pathing Inc (SAUS)
DPL.............. Data Processing Language
DPL.............. Data Programming Language (GEOI)
DPL.............. Dayton Power and Light (SAUS)
DPL.............. Dayton Power and Light Co. (EFIS)
DPL.............. Dayton Public Library (SAUS)
dpl .... Death Place (GEAB)
DPL.............. Deferred Pastoral Lease (SAUS)
DPL.............. Deferred Payment License (SAUS)
DPL.............. Delhi Public Library (SAUS)
DPL.............. Delmarva Power & Light [*Federal Railroad Administration identification code*]
DPL.............. Denied Parties List (JAGO)
DPL.............. Denied Persons List
DPL.............. Denver Public Library, Denver, CO [*OCLC symbol*] (OCLC)
DPL.............. Deploy (AABC)
DPL.............. Descriptor Privilege Level [*Computer science*] (BYTE)
DPL.............. Design and Programming Language (IAA)
DPL.............. Detached Parts List (ACAE)
DPL.............. Detroit Public Library
DPL.............. Development Prototype Launcher
DPL.............. Diagnostic Peritoneal Lavage [*Medicine*] (STED)
DPL.............. Diagonal Proof Line [*Technical drawings*]
DPL.............. Diode-Pumped LASER (CIST)
DPL.............. Dipalmitoyl Lecithin [*Biochemistry*]
DPL.............. Diploma (ROG)
DPL.............. Diplomat (WGA)
DPL.............. diplomatic corps (SAUS)
DPL.............. Dipole (KSC)
DPL.............. Dipolog [*Philippines*] [*Airport symbol*] (OAG)
DPL.............. Director of Pioneers and Labour (SAUO)
DPL.............. Discrete Phase Loop (IAA)
DPL.............. Display and Panel (SAUS)
DPL.............. Distopulpolingual [*Dentistry*]
DPL.............. Distributed Program Link [*IBM Corp.*] (CIST)
DPL.............. Distribution Plot List
DPL.............. Divisional Programming List (SAUS)
DPL.............. Doctor of Patent Law
DPL.............. Document Processing Language (IAA)
DPL.............. Dome Petroleum Ltd. [*Canada*] [*ICAO designator*] (FAAC)
DPL.............. Double [*or Dual*] Propellant Loading (AFM)
DPL.............. DPL, Inc. [*Formerly, Dayton Power & Light Co.*] [*NYSE symbol*] (SPSG)
DPL.............. Drawing Parts List (ACAE)
DPL.............. Dual Propellant Loading
DPL.............. Dublin Public Libraries [*Ireland*] (TELE)
DPL.............. Due Process of Law [*Legal shorthand*] (LWAP)
DPL.............. Dunlop's Parochial Law [*A publication*] (DLA)
DPL.............. Duplex (IAA)
DPL.............. Durban Public Library (SAUS)
DPL.............. Dynex Petroleum Ltd. [*Toronto Stock Exchange symbol*]
DPL.............. Kenansville, NC [*Location identifier*] [*FAA*] (FAAL)
DPLa............ Distopulpolabial [*Dentistry*]
DPL&DMA ... Data Processing Librarians and Documentations Managers Association (SAUO)
DPLCS .... Digital Propellant Level Control System (KSC)
DPL/DMA..... Data Processing Librarians and Documentation Managers Association (SAUO)
DPLE............ Digital Principal Local Exchange
DPLF............ Data [*or Digital*] Phone Line Formatter
DPLF............ Digital Phone Line Formatter (SAUS)
DPLG .... Day Plane Guard [*Military*] (NVT)
DPLH .... Direct Productive Labor Hour (EEVL)
DPLIS .... Development Pilot Line Information System (SAUS)
DPLL............ Digital Phase-Locked Loop [*Space communication*]
DPLL............ Digital Phase Lock Loop (NITA)
DPLL............ Digital PLL (SAUS)
DPLLs.......... Digital Phase-Locked Loops (SAUS)
DPLM........... Domestic Public Land Mobile [*Telecommunications*] (TEL)
DPLM........... Dual Pulse LASER Microwelder
DPLMRS...... Domestic Public Land Mobile Radio Service (SAUS)
DPLN .... Deplane (SAUS)
DPLN .... Diffuse Proliferative Lupus Nephritis [*Medicine*]
DPLNMT ...... Deplanement (SAUS)
DPLO .... District Postal Liaison Officer [*Navy*]
DPLOA......... Draft Proposed Letter of Agreement
DPLR .... Department of Productivity and Labour Relations [*Western Australia*]
DPLR .... Doppler (MCD)
DPLS .... Data and Program Library Service of the Data and Computation (SAUS)
DPLS .... Deck Projector Landing Sight (ACAE)
DPLS .... Digital Private Line Service [*Telecommunications*] (CIST)
D-PIS........... Diplomate, American Board of Plastic Surgery (DHSM)
DPLS .... Division of Public Library Services (SAUO)
DPLU .... Department of Planning and Land Use (SAUS)
dplx .... Duplex (BARN)
DPLX .... Duplex (TRID)
DPLXR .... Diplexer (SAUS)
DPLXR .... Duplexer (MSA)
DPLY .... Deploy (KSC)
DPLY .... Display (SAUS)
Dpm .... Dampproof Membrane (DAC)
DPM............. Data Patch Module (SAUS)
DPM............. Data Plant Management [*Computer science*] (ELAL)
DPM............. Data Preparation and Maintenance (CAAL)
DPM............. Data Processing Machine (AAG)
DPM............. Data Processing Magazine (SAUS)
DPM............. Data Processing Manager
DPM............. Data Processing Model (SAUS)
DPM............. Data Processing Module (SAUS)
DPM............. Decays per Minute [*Radiochemistry*]
DPM............. Decimal Point Mechanism (SAUS)
DPM............. Decomposable Plant Material [*Soil science*]
DPM............. Defects per Million (VERA)
DPM............. Defense Prioritization Model (SAUO)
DPM............. Defense Products Marketing Inc. (SAUO)
DPM............. Defense Program Memorandum (AABC)
DPM............. Deferred Payment Mortgage (FOTI)
DPM............. Deflectable Photomultiplier
DPM............. Delhi Pacific Resources Ltd. [*Toronto Stock Exchange symbol*]
DPM............. Demand Planning Module
DPM............. Department Personnel Manual
DPM............. Depot Paymaster [*Military*] [*British*] (ROG)
DPM............. Deputy Prime Minister [*British*]
DPM............. Deputy Program Management [*DoD*]
DPM............. Deputy Program Manager (DOMA)
DPM............. Deputy Project Manager
DPM............. Deputy Provost Marshal [*British*]
DPM............. Designated for Prompt Mobilization
DPM............. Designated Project Manager
DPM............. Development Planning Memo (MCD)
DPM............. Development Program Manuals (AFIT)
DPM............. Development Proposal Manager (MCD)
DPM............. Diaminopimelic Acid [*Also, DAP, DAPA*] [*An amino acid*]
DPM............. Dichroic Parametric Mirror
DPM............. Diesel Particulate Matter [*Environmental chemistry*]
dpm .... Digital Panel Meter (IDOE)
DPM............. Digital Panel Meter [*Computer science*]
DPM............. Digital Plotter Map [*Military*] [*British*]
DPM............. Digital Power Meter (IAA)
DPM............. Diphenylmethane [*Organic chemistry*]
DPM............. Diphenylphosphinomethane (SAUS)
DPM............. Dipivaloylmethan (SAUS)
DPM............. Dipivaloylmethanate [*Organic chemistry*]
DPM............. Dipivaloylmethane (SAUS)
DPM............. Diploma in Psychological Medicine [*British*]
DPM............. Dipyridamole [*Medicine*] (EDAA)
DPM............. Directional Policty Matrix
DPM............. Director of Personnel Manning (SAUS)
DPM............. Directory of Paper Makers [*A publication*] (DGA)
DPM............. Direct Procurement Method [*Personal property*]
DPM............. Discontinue Previous Medication [*Pharmacology*]
dpm .... Disintegrations per Minute (IDOE)
DPM............. Disintegrations per Minute
DPM............. Disruptive Pattern Material [*British military*] (DMA)
DPM............. Distributed Plant Management (SAUS)
DPM............. Distributed Presentation Management (ELAL)
DPM............. Distributive Principle of Multiplication (SAUS)
DPM............. District Paymaster (SAUO)
DPM............. Divert Propulsion Module (ACAE)
DPM............. Division of Physician Manpower (SAUO)
DPM............. Divorced Professional Male (ADWA)
DPM............. Doctor of Pediatric Medicine (NADA)
DPM............. Doctor of Physical Medicine
DPM............. Doctor of Podiatric Medicine
DPM............. Doctor of Preventative Medicine
DPM............. Doctor of Psychiatric Medicine
DPM............. Documents per Minute [*Computer science*] (BUR)
dpm .... Documents per Minute (VLIE)
DPM............. Dopamine [*Medicine*] (MELL)

DPM............ Downtown People Mover
DPM............ Drafting Practice Manual
DPM............ Draft Presidential Memorandum [*DoD*]
DPM............ Dried Poultry Manure
DPM............ drill-pipe measurement (SAUS)
DPM............ Drop Physics Module (SAUS)
DPM............ Dual Point Memorandum
DPM............ Dual-Port Memory [*Computer science*] (MCD)
DPM............ dual port memory (SAUS)
DPM............ Dual Purpose Missile (KSC)
DPM............ Dynamic Pressure Measurements
DPM............ Dynamic Programming Method (SAUS)
DPMA.......... Dairy Pruducts Manufacturers Association (SAUO)
DPMA.......... Data Processing Management Association (EA)
DPMA.......... Data Processing Managers Association [*Communications term*] (DCT)
DPMA.......... Demand Priority Access Method (SAUS)
DPMA.......... Dictionary of Physics and Mathematics Abbreviations (SAUS)
DPMA.......... Dictionary of Physics and Mathematics Abbreviations, Signs, and Symbols [*A publication*]
DPMA.......... Distributive Principle of Multiplication over Addition [*Mathematics*]
DPMA.......... Drydocking Phased Maintenance Availability (SAUS)
DPMA.......... Dummy Part Master (MCD)
DPMA Quarterly... Data Processing Management Association Quarterly (journ.) (SAUS)
DPMAS........ Driver Performance Measurement and Analysis System (MCD)
DPMAWA..... Dairy Products Manufacturers' Association of Western Australia
DPMB.......... Defense Programs Management Board (SAUS)
DPMB-AF..... Directorate of Project Management B - Air Force
DPMC.......... Defense Procurement Management Course [*DoD*]
DPMC.......... Deli/Prepared Meats Committee (EA)
DPMC.......... Dental Practice Management Company (SAUO)
DPMC.......... Department of the Prime Minister and Cabinet [*Australia*]
DPMC.......... Director of Personnel, Marine Corps
DPMC.......... Dual-Port Memory Control [*Computer science*]
DPM/DPM.... Diploma in Psychological Medicine (SAUS)
DPMH.......... Direct Productive Man-Hours (AFIT)
DPMI........... DOS [*Disk Operating System*] Protected Mode Interface [*Computer science*] (PCM)
DPMI........... DuPont Photomasks [*NASDAQ symbol*] (SG)
DPMI........... DuPont Photomasks, Inc. [*NASDAQ symbol*] (SAG)
DPMIAC....... Defense Pest Management Information Analysis Center [*Database*] [*DoD*] [*Washington, DC*]
DPMIS......... Data Processing Management Information System (VLIE)
DPML........... Deputy Program Manager for Logistics (AFIT)
DPML........... Deputy Project Manager for Logistics (SAUO)
DPML........... Digital Portable Mathematics Library (SAUS)
DPMM.......... Dew Point Moisture Monitors [*Nuclear energy*] (NRCH)
DPMM.......... Division of Production and Materials Management [*Energy Research and Development Administration*]
DPMM.......... Dots per Millimeter (SAUS)
DPMO.......... Data Processing Machine Order (VLIE)
DPMO.......... Defense Prisoner of War/Missing Personnel Office
DPMO.......... Defense Productivity Measurement Office (ACAE)
DPMO.......... Defense Program Management Office [*DoD*]
DPMOAP...... [*Society of*] Data Processing Machine Operators and Programmers (NITA)
DPMOAP...... National Society of Electronic Data Processing Machine Operators and Programmers [*Inactive*]
DPMOAP...... Society of Data Processing (SAUS)
DPMOAP...... Society of Data Processing Machine Operators and Programmers (SAUO)
DPMP.......... Depot Plant Modernization Plan [*Army*]
DPMP.......... Digital Parcel Mapping Project (SAUO)
D-PMR......... Diplomate, American Board of Physical Medicine and Rehabilitation (DHSM)
DPMR.......... District Postmaster [*British*] (DCTA)
DPMR&F...... Data Processing Market Research and Forecasting (SAUS)
DPMS.......... Data Project Management System (IEEE)
DPMS.......... Departmental Property Management System
DPM/S......... Disintegrations per Minute/Second (DEN)
DPMS.......... Display Power Management Services (SAUS)
DPMS.......... Display Power Management Signaling [*Computer science*] (PCM)
DPMS.......... Display Power Management Standard [*Computer science*] (VERA)
DPMS.......... Display Power Management Support [*Computer science*] (PCM)
DPMS.......... Distributed Plant Management System (VLIE)
DPMS.......... DOS [*Disk Operating System*] Protected Mode Service (PCM)
DPMT........... Delayed Pony Motor Trip (SAUS)
DPMZ........... Dyno Polymers [*Federal Railroad Administration identification code*]
DPN............ Data Packet Network (GART)
DPN............ Data Processing Network [*Trademark of Northern Telecom Ltd.*] (IAA)
DPN............ Data Processing Node (SAUS)
DPN............ Deferred Purchase Note (EBF)
DPN............ Dermatosis Papulosa Nigra [*Medicine*] (EDAA)
DPN............ Diabetic Polyneuropathy [*Medicine*] (DMAA)
DPN............ Diabetic Proximal Neuropathy [*Medicine*] (MELL)
DPN............ Diamond Pyramid Hardness Number
dpn............. diamond pyramid number (SAUS)
DPN............ Diphosphonucleosidase (SAUS)
DPN............ Diphosphopyridine (WDAA)
DPN............ Diphosphopyridine Dinucleotide (EDCT)
DPN............ Diphosphopyridine Nucleotide [*Also, ARPPRN, NAD*] [*Biochemistry*]
DPN............ Diphosphoyridiniumnucleotid (SAUS)
Dpn............. Diplococcus Pneumoniae (SAUS)
D-PN........... Diplomate, American Board of Psychiatry and Neurology (DHSM)
DPN............ Dipropylnitrosamine [*Also, DPNA, NDPA*] [*Organic chemistry*]
DPN............ Disabling Pansclerotic Morphea [*Medicine*] (EDAA)
dpn............. Dispersion (SAUS)
DPN............ Dual Processing Node [*Computer science*] (VLIE)
DPN............ Dynamic Probabilistic Network (IDAI)
DPNA.......... Dipropylnitrosamine [*Also, DPN, NDPA*] [*Organic chemistry*]
DPNA.......... Dual-Port Network Adapter [*Telecommunications*] (PCM)
DPNase........ Diphosphopyridine Nucleotide Glycohydrolase [*Also, NaDase*] [*An enzyme*]
DPNC.......... Democratic Party of Nigeria and the Cameroons
DPNDA........ Diphenylnaphthalene Diamine (SAUS)
DPNDBL...... Dependable
DPNE.......... Division of Peaceful Nuclear Explosives [*AEC*]
DPNG.......... Deepening (FAAC)
DPNH.......... Dihydrodiphosphopyridine Nucleotide, Reduced Form (SAUS)
DPNH.......... Diphosphopyridine Nucleotide, Reduced Form [*Biochemistry*]
DPNH.......... Reduced Diphosphopyridine (SAUS)
DPNL........... Distribution Panel
DPN Number... Diamond Pyramid Hardness Number (SAUS)
DPNPH........ Data Packet Network-Packet Handler [*Computer science*] (VERA)
DP-NR......... Deproteinated Natural Rubber (SAUS)
DPNR.......... Deproteinized Natural Rubber
DPNR.......... Dignity Partners [*NASDAQ symbol*] (TTSB)
DPNR.......... Dignity Partners, Inc. [*NASDAQ symbol*] (SAG)
DPNS.......... Douglas Point Nuclear Station (GFGA)
DPNSS........ Digital Private Network Signalling System (NITA)
DPO............ Data Phase Optimization [*Computer science*] (VLIE)
DPO............ Data Processing Officer (TBD)
DPO............ Data Processing Operation
DPO............ Days Post-Ovulation [*Medicine*] (ADWA)
DPO............ Dayton Philharmonic Orchestra (SAUS)
DPO............ Defence Press Office (SAUS)
DPO............ Defense Program Operation (AAG)
DPO............ Delayed Pulse Oscillator
DPO............ Demokratische Partei Oesterreichs [*Democratic Party of Austria*] (PPE)
DPO............ Deployable Payloads Projects Office [*Kennedy Space Center*] [*NASA*] (NASA)
DPO............ Depot (MCD)
DPO............ Depot Property Officer
DPO............ Deputy Principal Officer [*Foreign Service*]
DPO............ Deputy Project Officer (SAUO)
DPO............ Development Planning Objective
DPO............ Development Planning Officer [*Military*]
DPO............ Development Project Officer (MCD)
DPO............ Devonport [*Tasmania*] [*Australia*] [*Airport symbol*] (OAG)
DPO............ Dial Pulse Orginating (SAUS)
DPO............ Dial Pulse Originating [*Telecommunications*] (TEL)
DPO............ Digital Processing Oscilloscope (MCD)
DPO............ Diphenylene Oxide (SAUS)
DPO............ Diphenyloxazole [*Organic chemistry*]
DPO............ Diphenyl Oxide [*Organic chemistry*]
DPO............ Director, Planning and Operations (MCD)
DPO............ Directory of Post Office (AFM)
DPO............ Direct Purchasing Organisation [*Commercial firm*] [*British*]
DPO............ Disabled Persons Organization [*Bahamas*] (EAIO)
DPO............ Disaster Preparedness Office (ACAE)
DPO............ Discontinued Post Office [*Deltiology*]
DPO............ Distributing Post Office
DPO............ District Pay Office (SAUO)
DPO............ District Personnel Office [*or Officer*] [*Navy*]
DPO............ District Plans Officer (SAUO)
DPO............ District Postal Office [*or Officer*] [*Navy*]
DPO............ District Post Office (SAUS)
DPO............ District Post Officer (SAUS)
dpo............. Dividend Payout Ratio [*Stock exchange term*]
DPO............ Divisional Pests Officer [*Ministry of Agriculture, Fisheries, and Food*] [*British*]
DPO............ Division of Production Operations (SAUO)
DPO............ Dormant Posting Order (SAUS)
DPO............ Double Pulse Operation
DPO............ Dripproof Open
DPO............ Drop Out (KSC)
DPO............ DSA [*Defense Supply Agency*] Planning Objective
DPO............ Duty Petty Officer [*Navy*] (DNAB)
DPO............ dynamic-positioning operator (SAUS)
DPO............ Placid Oil Co., Exploration Library, Dallas, TX [*OCLC symbol*] (OCLC)
DPO............ United States Postal Service, Washington, DC [*Library symbol*] [*Library of Congress*] (LCLS)
DPOA.......... Detroit Police Officers Association (SAUO)
DPOA.......... Dissatisfied Peugeot Owners of America (EA)
DPOA.......... Durable Power of Attorney (SAUS)
DPOAH........ Durable Power of Attorney for Health Care
DPOB.......... Date and Place of Birth
DPOC.......... Base de Documentos en Politica Criminal [*Criminal Law Documents Data Base*] [*United Nations Latin American Institute for Crime Prevention and Treatment of Offenders*] (IID)
DPOC.......... Delco Products Overseas Corporation (SAUO)
DPOC.......... Dynamic Processor Overload Control [*Telephone technology*]
DPOD.......... DSA [*Defense Supply Agency*] Objective Document
DPODP........ Double-Precision Orbit Determination Program [*NASA*]
DPOI........... Delay-On-Pull-In
DPOIR......... Dial Pulse Originating Incoming Register [*Telecommunications*]

DPOL .... Political Directorate [*Allied German Occupation Forces*]
DPolEco .... Doctor of Political Economy (NADA)
D Pol Sc ...... Doctor of Political Science
DPolSci .... Doctor of Political Science (NADA)
DPOM .... Data Processing Orders and Movements (VLIE)
DPopC .... Population Crisis Committee, Washington, DC [*Library symbol*] [*Library of Congress*] (LCLS)
DPopI .... Population Institute, Washington, DC [*Library symbol*] [*Library of Congress*] (LCLS)
DPopR .... Population Reference Bureau, Washington, DC [*Library symbol*] [*Library of Congress*] (LCLS)
DPOs .... Digital Processing Oscilloscopes (SAUS)
DPOS .... District Planning Officers Society [*British*]
DPO-SA .... Development Project Office for Selected Ammunition [*Army*] (RDA)
DPost .... Directorate of Armed Forces Postal Services (SAUO)
DPost .... Director of Postal Services (SAUO)
DPOST SW ... Doublke-Pole Single-Throw Switch (SAUS)
DpoTch .... DepoTech Corp. [*Associated Press*] (SAG)
DPOW .... Data Processing Order Worksheet (VLIE)
DPOW .... Directorate of Prisoners of War and Displaced Persons (SAUO)
DPOW .... Prisoners of War and Displaced Persons Directorate [*Allied German Occupation Forces*]
DPOWA .... Distributive, Processing, and Office Workers Union of America
DPP .... Dairy Produce Packers Ltd. [*British*]
DPP .... Damage Protection Plan (SAUS)
DPP .... Data Processing Policy (VLIE)
DPP .... Data Project Plan (AFIT)
DPP .... Date of Prescribed Period [*Social Security Administration*] (OICC)
DPP .... Days Postpollination [*Botany*]
DPP .... Decentralized Printing Program [*Army*]
DPP .... Decision Process Pattern (RDA)
DPP .... Deep Pseudopupil [*Optical effect*]
DPP .... Default Protection Plan [*Travel industry*] (TRID)
DPP .... Defence Planning and Policy (SAUS)
DPP .... Defense Procurement Program [*DoD*]
DPP .... Defense Program Planning (SAUS)
DPP .... Defense Program Projection (SAUS)
DPP .... Deferred Payment Plan [*Banking, finance*]
DPP .... Deferred Payment Program (SAUO)
DPP .... Delayed Procurement Program
DPP .... Delegate Production Policy (MCD)
DPP .... Demand Priority Protocol (SAUS)
DPP .... Democratic People's Party [*Taiwan*] [*Political party*] (ECON)
DPP .... Democratic Progressive Party [*Transkei*] [*Political party*] (PPW)
DPP .... Democratic Progressive Party [*Taiwan*] [*Political party*]
DPP .... Democratic Progressive Party South Africa (SAUO)
DPP .... Department of Procurement Policy (SAUS)
DPP .... Department of Public Prosecution (SAUS)
DPP .... Deployment Pointing Panels (NASA)
DPP .... Detailed Pass Plan (SAA)
DPP .... Detailed Project Plan
DPP .... Development Program Plan
DPP .... Dextran Phosphate Precipitate (SAUS)
DPP .... diastolic pulmonal pressure (SAUS)
DPP .... Diepdaume Mines [*Vancouver Stock Exchange symbol*]
DPP .... Differential Pulse Polarography [*Analytical chemistry*]
DPP .... differential puls polarography (SAUS)
DPP .... Digital Panel Printer (SAUS)
DPP .... Digital Parallel Processor
DPP .... Diketopyrrolopyrrole [*Organic chemistry*]
DPP .... Dimethoxyphenyl Penicillin [*Medicine*] (MAE)
DPP .... Dipeptidyl Peptidase [*An enzyme*]
DPP .... Diphenylimide Perylene (SAUS)
DPP .... Diphenylphosphinyl (SAUS)
DPP .... Diphenyl Phthalate [*Organic chemistry*]
DPP .... Diphloretin Phosphate [*Biochemistry*]
DPP .... Diphtheria Pertussis Prophylactic [*Medicine*]
DPP .... Diploma in Plant Pathology (ADA)
DPP .... Directorate of Publications and Printing (SAUO)
DPP .... Director of Personnel Planning [*Air Force*]
DPP .... Director of Procurement and Production [*Army*]
DPP .... Director of Public Prosecutions [*British*]
DPP .... Direct Participation Program (ODA)
DPP .... Direct Product Profitability [*Analysis*]
dpp .... dirty petroleum products (SAUS)
DPP .... Disabilities Prevention Program (SAUO)
DPP .... Disaster Preparedness Plan (DNAB)
DPP .... Disaster Prevention and Preparedness [*Marine science*] (OSRA)
DPP .... Discounted Payback Period (SAUS)
DPP .... Disease Prevention Program (SAUS)
DPP .... Display Processor Program (MCD)
DPP .... Disposable Plotter Pen [*Koh-I-Noor Rapidograph, Inc.*]
DPP .... Distributed Parallel Processing [*Computer science*]
DPP .... Distributed Phase Plate [*LASER technology*]
DPP .... Divisional Programming Practice (VLIE)
DPP .... Division of Personnel Preparation [*Department of Education*]
DPP .... Division of Polar Programs [*National Science Foundation*] [*Information service or system*] (IID)
DPP .... Drip Pan Pot [*of closed-loop ex-vessel machine*] [*Nuclear energy*] (NRCH)
DPP .... Dripproof Protected
DPP .... Driver Parallel Processor [*Computer science*] (TIMI)
DPP .... Dry Photo Process
DPP .... Dual Progress Plan [*Education*] (AEE)
DPP .... Dual-Purpose Packaging (DB)
DPP .... Duplicating Pattern Production (MCD)
DPP .... Dynamic Programming Procudure (SAUS)
DPP .... Political Party Democrats 66 [*Netherlands*] [*Political party*] (EAIO)
DPP .... Director of Public Prosecutions (ODA)
DPPA .... Dipalmitoyl Phosphatidyl Chloride (SAUS)
DPPA .... Diphenylphosphoryl Azide [*Organic chemistry*]
DPPA .... Double Pumped Parametric Amplifier
DPPB .... Defense Intelligence Information Systems Products Priorities Board (SAUO)
DPPB .... Disaster Preparedness Planning Board (AFM)
DPPC .... Data Processing Products Contract
DPPC .... Defense Planning and Programming Catalog (MCD)
DPPC .... Defense Planning Programming Category
DPPC .... Developmental Potential of Preschool Children [*Psychology*]
DPPC .... Development and Project Planning Centre [*University of Bradford*] [*British*] (IRC)
DPPC .... Dipalmitoyl Phosphatidylcholine [*Biochemistry*]
DPPC .... Diphenyl Phosphorochloridate [*or Diphenylphosphoric Acid Monochloride*] [*Organic chemistry*]
DPP-Cl .... Diphenylphosphinyl Chloride (SAUS)
DPPD .... Diphenylphenylenediamine [*Organic chemistry*]
DPPDB .... Digital Point Positioning Data Base (GEOI)
DPPE .... Data Processing Project Engineer
DPPE .... Dipalmitoyl Phosphatidylethanolamine [*Biochemistry*]
DPPG .... Data Processing Products Group (SAUO)
DPPG .... Defense Planning and Programming Guidance
DPPG .... Defense Policy Planning Guidance (NVT)
DPPG .... Department of Defense Policy Planning Guidance (SAUO)
DPPG .... DoD Policy Planning Guidance (SAUS)
DPPH .... Diphenylpicrylhydrazyl [*Analytical chemistry*]
DPPH .... Direct Product Person Hours (ACAE)
DPPIP .... Data Processor Program Interface Procedure (SAUS)
DPPM .... Differential Pulse Position Modulation (SAUS)
DPPM .... Dynamic Pulse Position Modulation [*LASER technology*]
DPPNGS ...... Douglas Point Project Nuclear Generating Station (NRCH)
DPPO .... Deepwater Ports Project Office [*Marine science*] (MSC)
DPPO .... Defense Productivity Program Office (ACAE)
DPPO .... Dental Preferred Provider Organization [*Insurance*] (WYGK)
DPPO .... Development Production Prove Out [*Army*] (RDA)
DPPO .... Direct Procurement Petty Officer
DPPO .... District Printing and Publications Office (SAUS)
DPPO .... District Publications and Printing Office
DPPO .... Division Police Petty Officer [*Navy*] (DNAB)
DPPP .... Deferred Premium Payment Plan [*Business term*] (IIA)
DPPROG ...... Data Processing Programming (SAUS)
DPPS .... Data Packets Per Second [*Communications term*] (DCT)
DPPS .... Department of Public Printing and Stationery (SAUS)
DPPS .... Digitally Programmable Power Supplies (SAUS)
DPPSO .... Data Processing Programming Support Office [*Military*]
DPPT .... Director of Personnel Procurement and Training [*Air Force*]
DPPWA .... Director of Public Prosecutions for Western Australia
DPPX .... Distributed Processing Programming Executive [*IBM*] (NITA)
DPPX .... Distributed Processing Programming Executive Base [*IBM Corp.*]
DPPX .... distributed processing programniing executive (SAUS)
DPPX/BASE ... Distributed Processing Programming Executive Base (SAUS)
DPPX/SP ...... Distributed Processing Programming Executive/ System Product (SAUS)
DPQ .... Data Processing Quality [*Computer science*] (VERA)
DPQ .... Defense Planning Questionnaire (MCD)
DPQ .... Defense Position Questionnaire (MCD)
DPQ .... Double-Precision Quantity
DPQCA .... Dairy Products Quality Checked Association (EA)
DPQMR .... Draft Proposal Qualitative Materiel Requirement
DPQS .... Draw-a-Person Quality Scale [*Psychology*]
DPR .... Daily Production Report
DPR .... Daily Pro Rata (SAUS)
D Pr .... Darling. Practice of the Scotch Court of Session [*A publication*] (DLA)
DPR .... Data Plotting Routine (SAUS)
DPR .... Data Processing Request
DPR .... Data Protection Register (NITA)
DPR .... Data Protection Registrar [*British*]
DPR .... Day Press Rate [*Telegraph rate*] (NTCM)
DPR .... Defect Prevention Reports
DPR .... Definition Phase Review (NASA)
DPR .... Degrees per Revolution
DPR .... Democratic Peoples Republic (SAUS)
DPR .... Demonstration Power Reactor (NRCH)
DPR .... Department of Pesticide Regulation [*California*] (SARE)
DPR .... Department of Physical Research [*British*]
DPR .... Department of Professional Regulation (SAUO)
DPR .... Department Performance Rating
DPR .... Deployment Position RADAR (MCD)
DPR .... Depolymerized Rubber
DPR .... Design and Partitioning for Restability (SAUS)
DPR .... Design Pressure Ratio (SAUS)
DPR .... Design Problem Report (ACAE)
DPR .... Development Planning Report (SAUS)
DPR .... Development Planning Reports (MCD)
DPR .... development planning review (SAUS)
DPR .... Dewan Perwakilan Rakyat (SAUS)
DPR .... Dial Pulse Receiver [*Telecommunications*] (PDAA)
DPR .... Dial Pulse Repeater [*Telecommunications*] (IAA)
DPR .... Diaminopropanoic Acid [*An amino acid*]
DPR .... diaminopropionic acid (SAUS)
DPR .... Diaper

DPR .... Diazo Print
DPR .... Differential Police Response (SAUS)
DPR .... Digital Pattern Recorder (SEWL)
DPR .... Digital Printer (SAUS)
DPR .... Digital Process Reporter (SAUS)
DPR .... Dihydropyridine [*Organic chemistry*]
DPR .... Directions and Program Review [*American Library Association*]
DPR .... Director of Public Relations
DPR .... Direct Particle Rolling (PDAA)
DPR .... Disabled Persons Railcard [*British*]
DPR .... Dispenser [*Technical drawings*]
DPR .... District Probate Registry
DPR .... Division of Physical Research [*Energy Research and Development Administration*]
DPR .... Domestic Policy Review
dpr .... double lapping of pure rubber (SAUS)
DPR .... Double Pulse Ranging (NG)
DPR .... Double Pure Rubber (IAA)
DPR .... Drogue Parachute Deployment
DPR .... Drug Price Review
DPR .... Dual Pen Recorder
DPR .... Dual-Port RAM (SAUS)
DPR .... Dual Precipitation Radar (SAUS)
DPR .... Dundee-Palliser Resources, Inc. [*Toronto Stock Exchange symbol*]
DPR .... Dunlop Precision Rubbers Division (SAUS)
DPR .... Dupree, SD [*Location identifier*] [*FAA*] (FAAL)
DPR .... Dye-to-Protein Ratio (SAUS)
DPR .... Dynamic Perception Resolution (DMAA)
dPR .... Electronic Purchase Requisition (SAUS)
DPR .... Puerto Rico Reports, Spanish Edition [*A publication*] (DLA)
D PR .... United States District Court for the District of Puerto Rico (DLA)
DPRA .... Development, Planning and Research Associates (SAUO)
DPRAM .... Dual-Port RAM (SAUS)
DPRB .... Defense Planning and Resources Board [*Formerly, Defense Resources Board*] (DOMA)
DPRC .... Data Processing Resources [*NASDAQ symbol*] (TTSB)
DPRC .... Data Processing Resources Corp. [*NASDAQ symbol*] (SAG)
DPRC .... Defence Policy and Requirements Committee [*British military*] (DMA)
DPRC .... Defense Program Review Committee [*Military*] (CAAL)
DPRDO .... Dawro Peoples Revolutionary Democratic Organization (SAUS)
DPREP .... Disk Preparation Processor [*Computer science*]
DPREP .... Disk Prepping (SAUS)
DPRF .... Drug Product Reference File [*US Public Health Service*] [*Information service or system*] (IID)
DPRF .... Dual Pulse Ranging Fuse
DPRK .... Democratic People's Republic of Korea [*Also known as North Korea*]
DPRL .... Digital Property Rights Language
DPRM .... Diploma of Physical and Rehabilitation Medicine (ADA)
D-PrM .... Diplomate, American Board of Preventive Medicine (DHSM)
DPR(N) .... Directorate of Public Relations (Naval) [*British*]
DPRO .... Defense Plant Representative Officer (RDA)
DPRO .... Defense Plant Representative Offices [*or Officers*] (RDA)
DPRO .... Defense Plant Representatives Office (DOMA)
DPRO .... Defense Procurement Resident Office (SAUO)
DPRO .... Digital Projection Readout (CAAL)
DPRO .... Disk Pack Reorganizer (SAUS)
DPRO .... District Public Relations Office [*or Officer*] [*Navy*]
DPROC .... Draft Proposed Required Operational Capability (MCD)
DProgC .... Directorate of Programme Control (SAUO)
DProGM .... Deputy Provincial Grand Master [*Freemasonry*]
DPRORM .... Drafting, Pay and Records Office, Royal Marines [*British*]
DPRO System ... Digital Position Read-Out System (SAUS)
D PROV GM ... Deputy Provincial Grand Master [*Freemasonry*] (ROG)
DPRP .... Disaster Prevention and Recovery Plan (SAUS)
DPRP .... Dripproof and Ratproof
DPRR .... Decommissioning Project Readiness Review (SAUS)
DPRR .... Department of Parks and Renewable Resources (SAUS)
DPRS .... Data Processing Requirements Summary
DPRS .... Derogatis Psychiatric Rating Scale [*Test*] (TMMY)
DPRS .... Directors' & Producers' Rights Society
DPRS .... Distributed Processing Reporting Service (SAUS)
DPRS .... Dynamic Preferential Runway System [*Aviation*]
DPRSD .... Depressed
DPRT .... Depart (AABC)
DPRT .... Drawing Parts Release Ticket (MCD)
DPRTF .... Drought Policy Review Task Force [*Australia*]
DPRX .... Deep Rock Refining [*Private rail car owner code*]
DPRX .... Direct Pharmaceutical Corp. [*NASDAQ symbol*] (COMM)
DPS .... Dales Pony Society [*British*] (BI)
DPS .... Database Publishing Software (SAUS)
DPS .... Data Package Set (CAAL)
DP(S) .... Data Packet (Subsystem) [*Telecommunications*] (TEL)
DPS .... Data Packet Switch (SAUS)
DPS .... Data Polling Signal (SAUS)
DPS .... Data Preparation Subsystem (SAUS)
DPS .... Data Presentation System (IAA)
DPS .... Data Present Signal
DPS .... Data Processing and Software (NASA)
DPS .... Data Processing Service (IAA)
DPS .... Data Processing Services Co. [*Information service or system*] (IID)
DPS .... Data Processing Software (SAUS)
DPS .... Data Processing Software System (NASA)
DPS .... Data Processing Standards [*NASA*] (KSC)
DPS .... Data Processing Station (SAUS)
DPS .... Data-Processing Station
DPS .... Data Processing System [*or Subsystem*]
DPS .... Data Processor Set (SAUS)
DPS .... Data Process Service (SAUS)
DPS .... Data Production Services (SAUS)
DPS .... Dead Poets' Society [*Film title*] (WDAA)
DPS .... Decimal Point Setting (SAUS)
DPS .... Decision Package Sets
DPS .... Decision Program Set
DPS .... Dedicated Printer Share [*AC DataLink*] [*Computer science*]
DPS .... Deep Passive Sensors (MCD)
DPS .... Defence Policy Staff [*British*]
DPS .... Defence Priorities System (SAUS)
DPS .... Defense Package Sets (TIMI)
DPS .... Defense Planning Staff [*Military*] (AABC)
DPS .... Defense Postgraduate School (SAUS)
DPS .... Defense Printing Service
DPS .... Defense Priorities System [*DoD*]
DPS .... Defense Protective Service (DOMA)
DPS .... Degrees per Second
DPS .... Delaware Pharmaceutical Society Inc. (SAUO)
DPS .... Delayed Primary Suture (SAUS)
DPS .... Delayed Printer Simulator
DPS .... Delegated Production System (SAUS)
DPS .... Delegate Production System (MCD)
DPS .... Demokratische Partei Saar [*Democratic Party of the Saar*] [*Germany*] [*Political party*] (PPE)
DPS .... Demokratska Partija Socijalista [*Democratic Party of Socialists*] [*Montenegro*] [*Political party*] (EY)
DPS .... DEM Production System (SAUO)
DPS .... Denison & Pacific Suburban Railway Co. [*AAR code*]
DPS .... Denpasar [*Indonesia*] [*Airport symbol*] (OAG)
DPS .... Departmental Processing System (SAUS)
DPS .... Department of Planetary Sciences (SAUS)
DPS .... Department of Polymer Science (SAUS)
DPS .... Department of Public Safety [*Arizona*]
DPS .... Department of the Permanent Secretary (SAUO)
DPS .... Descending Perineum Syndrome [*Medicine*] (MELL)
DPS .... Descent Power System [*NASA*]
DPS .... Descent Propulsion System
DPS .... Design and Procedure Standard [*NASA*]
DPS .... Design Problem Silver (SAUS)
DPS .... Design Problem Solver (SAUS)
DPS .... Destainer Power Supply [*Electrophoresis*]
DPS .... Detail Process Standard (MCD)
DPs .... Detention Pens (SAUS)
DPS .... Deterministic Pattern Search (SAUS)
DPS .... Detroit Public Schools [*Michigan*]
DPS .... Development and Proof Services [*Aberdeen Proving Ground, MD*] (MCD)
DPS .... Development Processing System (SAUS)
DPS .... Development, Production, Stockpiling (FOTI)
DPS .... Dewan Pengurus Sementara [*Provisional Management Board Section*] [*Indonesia*]
DPS .... Diagnostic Problem Solver [*Computer science*]
DPS .... Dialectic Problem Solver
DPS .... Dial Pulse Sender [*Telecommunications*] (PDAA)
DPS .... Differential Phase Shift (PDAA)
DPS .... Differential Phase Shifting (SAUS)
DPS .... Differential Power Switch
DPS .... Differential pressure switch (SAUS)
DPS .... Different Premises Subscriber [*Telecommunications*] (TEL)
DPS .... Digital Panel Meter [*Electronics*] (ECII)
DPS .... Digital Phase Shifter
DPS .... Digital Photogrammetry System (SAUS)
DPS .... Digital Plotter System
DPS .... Digital Positioning System (SAUS)
DPS .... Digital Power Supply
DPS .... Digital Print System (SAUS)
DPS .... Digital Processing System (SAUS)
DPS .... Digital Production System (GEOI)
DPS .... Digital Production System laboratory (SAUO)
DPS .... Digital Signal Processor (SAUS)
DPS .... Dimethylpolysiloxane [*Organic chemistry*] (MAE)
DPS .... Diode Phase Shifter
DPS .... Diphenylstilbene [*Organic chemistry*]
DPS .... Diphenyl Sulfone [*Organic chemistry*]
D Ps .... Diploma of Psychology (PGP)
DPS .... Director of Personal Services [*Navy*] [*British*]
DPS .... Director of Postal Services [*British*]
DPS .... Disc programming system (SAUS)
DPS .... Disintegrations per Second
DPS .... Disk Pack Storage (SAUS)
DPS .... Disk Processing System (IAA)
DPS .... Disk Programming System [*IBM Corp.*] (IEEE)
dPs .... displaced Palestinians (SAUS)
DPs .... Displaced Persons (SAUS)
DPS .... Display PostScript [*Computer science*] (VERA)
DPS .... Display Power Supply
DPS .... Display Processing System (SAUS)
DPS .... Display Process Status (AAEL)
DPS .... Distibuted Presentation Services (SAUS)
DPS .... Distributed Parameter System (SAUS)
DPS .... Distributed Presentation Services [*IBM Corp.*]
DPS .... Distributed Present Services [*IBM*] (NITA)
DPS .... Distributed Problem Solving (IDAI)

DPS .... Distributed Processing Support (SAUS)
DPS .... Distributed Processing System [*Honeywell, Inc.*]
DPS .... Distributed Programming System (IAA)
DPS .... Diversified Pharmaceutical Services (ECON)
DPS .... Dividend per Share [*Investment term*] (ADA)
DPS .... Divisional Programming Standard (SAUS)
DPS .... Division Primary Standards (AAG)
DPS .... Doctor of Political Science
DPS .... Doctor of Professional Studies (PGP)
D Ps .... Doctor of Psychology
DPS .... Doctor of Public Service
DPS .... Documentation and Programming System (SAUS)
DPS .... Document Processing System [*IBM Corp.*] [*Computer science*]
DPS .... Domestic Policy Staff (SAUS)
DPS .... Double-Page Spread (SAUS)
DPS .... Double Pole Snap (SAUS)
DPS .... Double-Pole, Snap Switch (IAA)
DPS .... Double-Pole Switch (SAUS)
DPS .... Draft Proposed Standard (SAUS)
DPS .... Dramatists Play Service [*Published new plays since 1936*]
DPS .... Dripproof Semienclosed
DPS .... Drogue Parachute System (SAA)
DPS .... Drought Preparedness [*US Army Corps of Engineers*]
DPS .... Dry Peridotite Solidus [*Geochemistry*]
DPS .... Dual Porosity Sinter
DPS .... Dynamic Path Selection (SAUS)
DPS .... Dynamic Philatelic Society
DPS .... Dynamic Processing System [*Mitsubishi*] (NITA)
DPS .... Dysesthetic Pain Syndrome [*Medicine*] (MELL)
DPS .... Movement for Rights and Freedoms (Bulgaria) [*Political party*] (PSAP)
DPS 6 .... trademark of Honeywell Corp. (SAUO)
DPSA .... Dartmoor Pony Society of America (EA)
DPSA .... Data Processing Sales Administration (SAUS)
DPSA .... Data Processing Suppliers Association (SAUO)
DPSA .... Data Processing Supplies Association [*Later, IOSA*] (MCD)
DPSA .... Deep Penetration Strike Aircraft
DPSA .... Diploma in Public and Social Administration (ADA)
DPSA .... Display Producers and Screen Printers Association (SAUO)
DPSA .... Distinguished Public Service Award (MUGU)
DPSA .... Doctor of Public School Art
DPSA .... Dual Polarized Sinuous Antenna (SEWL)
DPSA .... Seaman Apprentice, Data Processing Technician, Striker [*Navy rating*]
DPSB .... Defence Production Supply Board [*NATO*] (NATG)
DPSB .... Defense Program Strategy Board (SAUO)
DPSBad .... Distinguished Pistol Shot Badge [*Military decoration*] (AABC)
DPSC .... Data Processing Service Center
DPSC .... Defense Personnel Support Center (AFM)
DPSC .... Defense Petroleum Supply Center
DPSC .... Detainees Parents' Support Committee
DP Sc .... Doctor of Political Science
DPSc .... Doctor of Political, Social and Economic Sciences (CPGU)
DPSC .... Double Paper, Single Cotton [*Wire insulation*] (AAG)
DPSCA .... Darwin Pensioners and Senior Citizens' Association [*Australia*]
DPSCA .... Department of Political and Security Council Affairs [*UN*] [*Environment term*] [*International*] (EGA)
DPSCG .... Democratic Party of Socialists of Montenegro (Yugoslavia) [*Political party*] (PSAP)
DPSCPAC ..... Data Processing Service Center, Pacific (DNAB)
DPSCPAC ..... Data Processing Service Center Pacific Fleet (SAUO)
DPSCS .... Department of Public Safety and Correctional Services (SAUS)
DPSD .... Data Processing Systems Division (SAUO)
DPSD .... Dew Point Sensing Device
DPSD .... Dimensionless Power Spectral Density
DPSDR .... Douglas Process Standard Development Record [*DAC*]
DPS-EMS ..... Department of Public Safety - Emergency Medical Service (SAUS)
DPSH .... Direct Product Standard Hours (AFIT)
DPSI .... Dawson Production Services, Inc. [*NASDAQ symbol*] (SAG)
DPSI .... Dawson Production Svcs [*NASDAQ symbol*] (TTSB)
DPSK .... Department of the Private Secretary to the King (SAUO)
DPSK .... Differential Phased Shift Keying (SAUS)
DPSK .... Differential Phase Shift Keying [*Telecommunications*]
DPSK .... Digital Phase Shift Keying (SAUS)
DPSL .... Database Publishing Systems Limited
DPSM .... Diode Phase Shifter Module
DpSM .... Diploma in Surgery Medicine
DPSM .... Doctor of Public School Music
DPSM .... Dual-Purpose Submunitions [*Military*] (INF)
DPSMM .... Dynamically Partitioned Second Moment Model (SAUS)
DPSN .... Defence Packet Switched Network (SAUS)
DPSN .... Seaman, Data Processing Technician, Striker [*Navy rating*]
DPSO .... Data Processing Systems Office [*Picatinny Arsenal, NJ*]
DPSO .... Defense Projects Support Office [*NASA*]
DPSOR .... Digital Photogrammetric System-Orthophoto (SAUS)
DPSP .... Deferred Profit Sharing Plan (SAUS)
DPSP .... Diffuse Process Such as Pericarditis [*Cardiology*]
DPSPECIALIST... Data Processing Specialist (SAUS)
DPSPT .... Combat Consumption Support from D-Day to P-Day [*Military*] (AABC)
DPSR .... Daily Problem Status Report
DPSR .... Data Processing Service Request (NVT)
DPSR .... Data Processing System Requirements
DPSRAM ...... Dual-Port Static Random Access Memory (AAEL)
DPSS .... Data Processing and Services Subsystem (NOAA)
DPSS .... Data Processing Services Subsystem (SAUO)
DPSS .... Data Processing Subsystem
DPSS .... Data Processing Switching System [*Space Flight Operations Facility, NASA*]
DPSS .... Data Processing System Simulator (IEEE)
DPSS .... Deep Passive Sonobuoy System (MCD)
DPSS .... Department of Public Social Services
DPSS .... Director of Printing and Stationery Services [*Military*] [*British*]
DPSS .... Direct Program Search System (IAA)
DPSS .... Display Presentation Subsystem (IAA)
DPSS .... Domain Professional Support Service (SAUS)
DPSS .... Double-Pole, Snap Switch (IAA)
DPsSc .... Doctor of Psychological Science (ADA)
DPSSC .... Drugs and Poisons Schedule Standing Committee (SAUS)
DPSSL .... Diode-Pumped Solid State LASERS (AAEL)
DPSSO .... DSA [*Defense Supply Agency*] Performance Standards Support Office
DPS Switch... Double-Pole Snap Switch (SAUS)
DPST .... Deposit
DPST .... Disaster Preparedness Shelter Training (SAUO)
DPST .... Double Pole, Single Throw [*Switch*]
dpst .... Double-Pole, Single-Throw (IDOE)
DPST .... double-pole single-throw contact (SAUS)
DPST .... double-pole snap switch (SAUS)
DP-StE .... Democratic Party - Statia [*Netherlands Antilles*] [*Political party*] (EY)
D Ps Th .... Doctor of Psycho-Therapy
DPSTK .... Dipstick
DP-StM .... Democratic Party - St. Maarten [*Netherlands Antilles*] [*Political party*] (EY)
DPST-NC ..... Double-Pole Single-Throw - Normally Closed (SAUS)
DPSTNC ...... Double-Pole, Single-Throw, Normally Closed Switch (IAA)
DPST-NC ..... Double-Pole Single-Throw - Normally Open (SAUS)
DPST-NO ..... Double-Pole Single-Throw - Normally Open (SAUS)
DPSTNO ...... Double-Pole, Single-Throw, Normally Open Switch (IAA)
DPSTSW ...... Double-Pole, Single-Throw Switch
DPST Switch... Double-Pole Single-Throw Switch (SAUS)
DPSW .... Differential Pressure Seawater
DPSW .... Double-Pole Switch
DPSX .... Dipropyl(sulfophenyl)xanthine [*Organic chemistry*]
DPsy .... Diploma in Psychiatry (SAUS)
DPsy .... Diploma in Psychology (SAUS)
D Psych .... Diploma in Psychiatry [*British*]
D PSYCH ..... Doctor of Psychology (WDAA)
DPsychol ..... Doctor of Psychology
DPsyMedNeuro... Diploma in Psychiatric Medicine and Neurology
DPsySci .... Doctor of Psychological Science (NADA)
DPT .... Datapoint Corp. [*NYSE symbol*] (SPSG)
DPT .... Data Processing Technique (VLIE)
DPT .... Data Processing Theory (SAUS)
DPT .... Data Processing Time (SAUS)
DPT .... Data Punched Tape (SAUS)
DPT .... Days per Thousand
DPT .... Dedicated Planning Terminal (CAAL)
DPT .... Dedicated Programmable Timer (SAUS)
DPT .... Deep Pressure Touch
DPT .... Delayed Picture Transmission (SAUS)
DPT .... Demerol-Phenergan-Thorazine [*Drug regime*]
DPT .... Democratic Party of Tadzhikistan [*Political party*]
DPT .... Democratic Party of Turkmenistan [*Political party*] (PSAP)
DPT .... Dental Pantomogram (WDAA)
DPT .... Depart
Dpt .... Department (GEOI)
dpt .... Department (SHCU)
DPT .... Department
DPT .... Department of Petroleum Technology (SAUO)
DPT .... Department of Pharmacology and Toxicology (SAUS)
DPT .... Departure Control (MUGU)
DPT .... Depletion Perturbation Theory (PDAA)
dpt .... Deponent (ADWA)
DPT .... Deponent
DPT .... Deposit (ADA)
DPT .... Depot
DPT .... Depth
Dpt .... Dermatophagoides pteronyssinus [*House dust*]
DPT .... Descent Performance Test
DPT .... Description Price Transmittal (SAUS)
DPT .... Design Proof Test (SAUS)
DPT .... Design Proof Tests
DPT .... Development Project Team (MCD)
DPT .... Development Prototype (NG)
DPT .... Dew-Point Temperature [*Measure of humidity*]
DPT .... Dew Point Tester
DPT .... Diagnostic Prescriptive Teacher [*or Teaching*]
DPT .... Dial Pulse Terminating [*Telecommunications*] (TEL)
DPT .... Dichotic Pitch Discrimination Test [*Medicine*] (DMAA)
DPT .... Diesel Particulate Trap [*Automotive engineering*]
DPT .... Differential Polarization Telegraphy (SAUS)
DPT .... Differential Pressure Transducer
DPT .... Different Premises Telephone (SAUS)
DPT .... Different Premises Telephone Number [*Telecommunications*] (TEL)
DPT .... Digital Picture Terminal (NOAA)
DPT .... Digital Piezoelectric Translator [*Instrumentation*]
DPT .... Digital Pressure Transducer
DPT .... Dimethyltryptamine [*Hallucinogenic agent*] (DAVI)
DPT .... Dinitrosopentamethylenetetramine (SAUS)
DPT .... Dioptre (VLIE)

DPT............ Diphenyltrichloroethane [*Also, DPE*] [*Organic chemistry*]
DPT............ Diphosphothiamine [*Also, TDP, TPP*] [*Biochemistry*]
DPT............ Diphtheria, Pertusis, Typhoid (SAUS)
DPT............ Diphtheria, Pertussis, and Tetanus [*Also, DTP*] [*Immunology*]
DPT............ Diphtheritic Pseudotabes (DB)
DPT............ Diploma of Physio-Therapy [*British*]
DPT............ Dipropylphytamine (SAUS)
DPT............ Dipropyltryptamine [*Hallucinogenic agent*]
DPT............ Diptheria, Pertussia and Tetanus (SAUO)
DPT............ Director of Personnel and Training (SAUO)
DPT............ Director of Physical Therapy (SAUS)
DPT............ Director of Plans and Training [*Military*] (AABC)
DPT............ Director, Polaris Technical [*Missiles*]
DPT............ Dissatisfied Parents Together (EA)
DPT............ Distributed Processing Technology [*Computer science*]
DPT............ Distributed Profit Tax (SAUS)
DPT............ Doctor of Physical Therapy (PGP)
DPT............ Dripproof Totally Enclosed
DPT............ Drive Parameter Table [*Computer science*] (VERA)
DPT............ Drive Parameter Tracking [*Computer science*] (PCM)
DPT............ Dummy Part (MCD)
DPT............ Duplicating Pattern Tooling (MCD)
DPT............ Dye pentrant test (SAUS)
DPT............ Dynamic Packet Transport (SAUS)
DPT............ Dynamic Plume Test
DPTA............ Diaminopropanoltetraacetic Acid [*Also, DTA, DHPTA*] [*Organic chemistry*]
DPTA............ Diethylenetriamine Penta-Acetic Acid [*Organic chemistry*] (DAVI)
dpta............ diethylene triamine pentaacetic acid (SAUS)
dPTC............ Dispersed Human Parathyroid Cell [*Clinical chemistry*]
DPTC............ Dual Processor Terminal Controller (SAUS)
DPTDR............ Draft Proposed Training Device Requirement (MCD)
DPTE............ Data Processing Terminal Equipment (ACAE)
DPTE............ Deoxidized Phosphorus Copper, Tellurium Bearing (SAUS)
DPTH............ Depth (FAAC)
DPTH............ Dipentamethylenethiuram Hexasulfide [*Organic chemistry*]
DPTH............ Diphenylthiohydantoin [*Organic chemistry*]
DPTI............ Diastolic Pressure Time Index (AAMN)
DPTI............ diastolic pressure time index (SAUS)
DPTM............ Director of Plans, Training, and Mobilization [*DoD*]
DPTNAVSCI... Department of Naval Science (DNAB)
DPTO............ Director, Passenger Transportation Office (SAUO)
DPTO............ District Property Transportation Office [*or Officer*] [*Navy*]
DPTOE............ Draft Plan Table of Organization and Equipment (MCD)
DPtoTP............ Display Coordinates to Tablet Coordinates (SAUS)
DPtoTP............ Display Points to Tablet Points (VLIE)
DPTPM............ Diphtheria-Pertussis-Tetanus-Poliomyelitis-Measles [*Vaccine*] [*Medicine*] (DMAA)
DPTPrA............ Datapoint $1 cm Pfd [*NYSE symbol*] (TTSB)
DPTR............ Data Pointer [*Computer memory*] (BYTE)
DPTR............ Delta Petroleum [*NASDAQ symbol*] (SAG)
dptr............ Departure (TRID)
Dptr............ Diopter [*Medicine*] (EDAA)
DPTRAJ............ Double-Precision Trajectory Program [*NASA*]
DPTRAJ Program... Double-Precision Trajectory Program (SAUS)
Dp Trk............ Dump Truck (SAUS)
DPTRK............ Dumptruck (AABC)
DPTS............ Digital Programming Test Set (SAA)
DPTS............ Dimethylamino Pyridiniumtoluenesulfonic Acid [*Organic chemistry*]
DPTS............ Director of Physical Training and Sports [*Navy*] [*British*]
DPTSI............ Design Professions Technical Specialty Index [*National Society of Professional Engineers*] [*Information service or system*] (IID)
DPTT............ Double Pole, Triple Throw [*Switch*]
DPTTC............ Drilling and Production Technology Training Centre (SAUO)
DPTT SW............ Double-Pole, Triple-Throw Switch (SAUS)
DPT vaccine... Diptheria, Pertussis [*Whooping Cough*], and Tetanus Vaccine [*Also, called DTP vaccine*] (PAZ)
dpt vaccines... diphtheria pertussis, tetanus vaccines (SAUS)
DPTW............ Desk, Double-Pedestal Typewriter
DPTW............ Double-Pedestal Typewriter (SAUS)
DPTW Desk... Double-Pedestal Typewriter Desk (SAUS)
DPTX............ Distributed Processing Terminal Exchange [*Prime Computers*] (NITA)
DPTX............ Distributed Processing Terminal Executive (SAUS)
DPTX............ distributed processing terminal exehange (SAUS)
Dpty............ Deputy (TBD)
DPTY............ Deputy
dpty............ Diptych (VRA)
DPU............ Data Parallel Unit (SAUS)
DPU............ Data Path Unit [*Computer science*]
DPU............ Data Processing Unit
DPU............ Defects per Unit (ACAE)
dpu............ Defects per Unit (VLIE)
DPU............ Delayed Pressure Urticaria [*Dermatology*] (DAVI)
DPU............ Demand Processing Unit [*Military*]
DPU............ Democratic Party of Ukraine [*Political party*] (PSAP)
DPU............ Department of Public Utilities (SAUS)
DPU............ Depuy, Inc. [*NYSE symbol*] (SAG)
DPU............ Design Proof Unit (KSC)
DPU............ Differential Pressure Unit (DNAB)
DPU............ Digital Patch Unit
DPU............ Digital Processing Unit
DPU............ Digit Pick-Up (VLIE)
DPU............ Diphenylhydantoin [*Also, DPH*] [*Anticonvulsant*] (DAVI)
DPU............ Diphenylurea (SAUS)
DPU............ Dip Pick-Up (SAUS)
DPU............ Direct Pickup [*Telecommunications*] (OTD)
DPU............ Disabled Persons Unit [*United Nations*] (DUND)
DPU............ Disk Pack Unit [*Computer science*]
DPU............ Display Processor Unit (IAA)
DPU............ Dispositif de Protection Urbane [*Algeria*]
DPU............ Document Processing Unit [*Computer science*] (IAA)
DPU............ Driver Propulsion Unit
DPU............ Dual Processing Unit [*Computer science*] (WGA)
DPU............ Dual Processor Unit (SAUS)
DPU............ Dumpu [*New Guinea*] [*Airport symbol*] (AD)
DPU............ Duodenal Peptic Ulcer [*Medicine*] (EDAA)
DPU............ Dust Preparation Unit (SAUS)
DPU............ Dynamic Pulse Unit (SAUS)
DPU............ Organization of American States, Washington, DC [*Library symbol*] [*Library of Congress*] [*Obsolete*] (LCLS)
D Pub Adm... Doctor of Public Administration
DPUD............ Department of Planning and Urban Design (SAUO)
DPUD............ Department of Planning and Urban Development [*Western Australia*] [*Australia*]
DPUD............ Duodenal Peptic Ulcer Disease [*Medicine*] (MELL)
DP-UDC............ Democracia Popular - Union Democrata Cristiana [*People's Democracy - Christian Democratic Union*] [*Ecuador*] [*Political party*] (PPW)
DPUO............ Duty Directed Is Being Performed for Unit Issuing Order
DPUS............ Directory of Physicians in the United States [*A publication*] (MELL)
DPUSSA............ Department of the Permanent Under-Secretary of State for Air (SAUO)
DPUSSW............ Department of the Permanent Under-Secretary of State for War (SAUO)
DPV............ Design Point Vehicle
DPV............ Deutscher Verein zur Erforschung Palaestinas [*A publication*] (BJA)
DPV............ Differential Pulse Voltammetry [*Analytical chemistry*]
DPV............ Different Pulse Voltametry (DB)
DPV............ Diffuse and Perivascular [*Medicine*]
DPV............ Disabling Positional Vertigo [*Medicine*] (EDAA)
DPV............ Diver Propulsion Vehicle (DNAB)
DPV............ Dockside Proofing Vehicle
DPV............ Doppler Predict Voltage
DPV............ Dorsal Penis Vein [*Medicine*] (MELL)
DPV............ Dry Pipe Valve
DPV............ Duty Paid Value [*Business term*]
DPV............ Duty Paying Value (SAUS)
DPVM............ Demand-Page Virtual Memory [*Computer science*] (PDAA)
DPVM............ Discrete Process Variable Measurement [*Process control*]
DPVS............ Denver Peritoneovenous Shunt [*Medicine*] (DMAA)
DPVS............ Digitally-Programmed Voltage Source (IAA)
DPW............ Davis Polk & Wardwell, Library, New York, NY [*OCLC symbol*] (OCLC)
DPW............ Dealer Proceeds Withheld [*Automobile sales*]
DPW............ Department of Public Welfare
DPW............ Department of Public Works
DPW............ Die per Wafer (AAEL)
DPW............ Digital Power [*AMEX symbol*] (SG)
DPW............ Director of Prisoners of War [*British*] [*World War II*]
DPW............ Distal Phalangeal Width [*Medicine*] (DMAA)
dp/w............ drawbar pull/weight (SAUS)
DPWA............ Data Processing Work Assignment (SAUS)
DPWA............ Decorative Paving and Walling Association (SAUO)
DPWBR............ Deepwater Bridge, WV [*American Association of Railroads railroad junction routing code*]
DPWG............ Defence Planning Working Group [*of Defense Ministers*] [*NATO*] (NATG)
DPWG............ Development Plan Working Group (SAUO)
DPWG............ Drainage Program Working Group (SAUO)
DPWH............ Department of Parks, Wildlife, and Heritage [*Tasmania*] [*Australia*]
DPWM............ Double Pulsewidth Modulation (SAUS)
DPWM............ Double-Sided Pulse-Width Modulation [*Telecommunications*]
DPWO............ Devegadhi Public Welfare Organization (SAUS)
DPWO............ District Public Works Office
DPWP............ Director of Planning of War Production [*Air Ministry*] [*British*] [*World War II*]
DPWR............ Data Process Work Request (AAG)
DPWS............ Digital Photogrammetric Work Station (SAUS)
DPWS............ Dollars per Word Syndrome (SAUS)
DPWS............ Dual Purpose Weapon System
DPWTR............ Deep Water, WV [*American Association of Railroads railroad junction routing code*]
DPX............ Diethyl(phenyl)xanthine [*Organic chemistry*]
DPX............ Displaced Persons Executive [*Allied Military Government detachments, Red Cross teams, and UN Relief and Rehabilitation Administration Corps*] [*Post-World War II*]
DPX............ Duplex (ADA)
DPX............ Duplex Products, Inc. [*AMEX symbol*] (SPSG)
DPY............ Deploy (NASA)
dpy............ dipyridamole (SAUS)
DPZ............ Dale-Parizeau, Inc. [*Toronto Stock Exchange symbol*]
DPZ............ Deutsches Primatenzentrum GmbH Goettingen [*German Primate Center*] (GVA)
DQ............ Coastal Air Transport [*ICAO designator*] (AD)
DQ............ Dairy Queen [*Commercial firm*]
DQ............ Dash Quote (SAUS)
DQ............ Data Qualifier (SAUS)
DQ............ Decode Queue (SAUS)
DQ............ Deep Quest
DQ............ Definite Quantity (AFM)

DQ .... Deleted Quality Review Transaction [*IRS*]
DQ .... Design Qualification (MCD)
DQ .... Destination Queues [*Computer science*] (MDG)
DQ .... Detention Quarters [*British*]
DQ .... Deterioration Quotient [*Medicine*]
DQ .... Developmental Quotient (FOTI)
DQ .... Development Quotient
dQ .... differential of figure of merit (SAUS)
dQ .... differential of quantity (SAUS)
DQ .... Director of Quality (SAUS)
DQ .... Director of Quartering (SAUS)
DQ .... Directory enquiry (SAUS)
DQ .... Directory Enquiry Service [*Telecommunications*] (TEL)
DQ .... Direct Quenching (SAUS)
DQ .... Direct Question [*Legal testimony*]
DQ .... Disqualified
DQ .... Disqualify (ADWA)
dq .... Dominica [*MARC country of publication code*] [*Library of Congress*] (LCCP)
DQ .... Dormant Queue (VLIE)
DQ .... Dragon Quest (SAUS)
DQ .... Drawing Quality (DNAB)
D-Q .... Drocourt-Queant Line [*World War I*] [*Canada*]
dq .... dry quart (SAUS)
DQ .... Duquesne Capital [*NYSE symbol*] (SAG)
DQ .... Fiji [*Aircraft nationality and registration mark*] (FAAC)
DQ .... [*The*] Deccan Queen [*Indian Railway*] (TIR)
DQ .... Dispersion Quotient (ODA)
DQA .... Data Quality Assessment (ABAC)
DQA .... Defence Quality Assurance
DQA .... Design Quality Assurance [*Telecommunications*] (TEL)
DQA .... Division of Quality Assurance [*Department of Education*] (GFGA)
DQA .... D'Or Val Mines Ltd. [*Toronto Stock Exchange symbol*] [*Vancouver Stock Exchange symbol*]
DQA .... Drawing Quality Audit (MCD)
DQAA .... Department Quality Assurance Administrator (SAUO)
DQAB .... Defence Quality Assurance Board [*British*] (RDA)
DQABE .... Defence Quality Assurance Board Executive (SAUO)
DQABE .... Defense Quality Assurance Board Executive (SAUS)
DQADO .... DCAS [*Defense Contract Administration Services*] Quality Assurance Staff Development Office
DQAK .... Drawing Quality, Aluminum-Killed (SAUS)
DQC .... Data Quality Control
DQC .... Definite Quantity Control
DQC .... Delayed Quick Cure (MCD)
DQC .... Design qualification checklist (SAUS)
D-QC .... Drug-Quaternary Carrier [*Biochemistry*]
DQC .... Dynamic Quality Control
DQCB .... Disc Queue Control Block [*Computer science*] (ELAL)
DQCB .... Disk Queue Control Block [*Computer science*] (VLIE)
DQCB .... Distributed Queue Control Bus (SAUS)
DQCIR .... Directory Enquiry Computerized Information Retrieval System [*BT*] (NITA)
DQCM .... Data Quality Control Monitor
DQD .... Digital Quadrature Detection [*Instrumentation*]
dqd .... digitat quadrature detection (SAUS)
DQ-DAF .... Double-Quadrupole Dynamic Astigmatism and Focus [*Panasonic gun technology*]
DQDB .... Distributed Queue Dial Bus (SAUS)
DQDB .... Distributed Queue Double Bus (SAUS)
DQDB .... Distributed Queue Dual Bus [*Telecommunications*] (PCM)
DQDB .... Dual Queue Dual Bus (SAUS)
DQE .... Data Quality Engineering (SAUS)
DQE .... Data Quality Expert (SAUS)
DQE .... De Queen & Eastern Railroad Co. [*AAR code*]
DQE .... Descriptor Queue Element [*Computer science*] (IAA)
DQE .... Detective Quantum Efficiency [*Photon device*]
DQE .... DQE [*NYSE symbol*] (TTSB)
DQE .... DQE Co. [*Associated Press*] (SAG)
DQE .... DQE, Inc. [*NYSE symbol*] (SPSG)
DQENMR .... deuterium quadrupole echo NMR (SAUS)
DQF .... Division of Quality Enhancement (AIE)
DQF-COSY .... Double Quantum Filtered Correlation Spectroscopy (SAUS)
DQG .... Charlotte, NC [*Location identifier*] [*FAA*] (FAAL)
DQH .... Douglas, GA [*Location identifier*] [*FAA*] (FAAL)
DQI .... Cimber Air, Sonderjyllands Flyveselskab [*Denmark*] [*ICAO designator*] (FAAC)
DQI .... Data Quality Indicators
DQI .... Distributor Quality rating Index [*Chemical engineering*]
DQL .... Database Query Language [*Computer science*] (VERA)
DQL .... DataEase Query Language [*Search method*] [*Computer science*] (PCM)
DQL .... Dielectric Quilted Liner (UWER)
DQM .... Data Quality Management (BCP)
DQM .... Data Quality Monitors (MDG)
DQM .... Depot Quartermaster [*Marine Corps*]
DQM .... Digital Q Meter (SAUS)
DQM .... Digital Quadrature Modulation (UWER)
DQM .... Digital Quality Monitor
DQM .... Digital Queue Meter (SAUS)
DQM .... Divisional Quartermaster (SAUO)
DQM .... Division Quartermaster
DQM .... Dormant Queue Manager [*Computer science*] (VLIE)
DQMC .... Diffusion Quantum Monte Carlo Method (MEC)
DQMG .... Deputy Quartermaster General
DQMGO .... Deputy Quartermaster General of Ordnance (SAUS)
DQMGO .... Deputy Quartermaster-General of Ordnance (SAUO)
DQMS .... Data Quality Management System (SAUS)
DQMS .... Deputy Quartermaster-Sergeant [*British*]
DQMS .... Development Qualification and Monitoring System (SAUS)
DQN .... Depot Quartermaster, Norfolk, Virginia [*Marine Corps*]
DQN .... Diazonaphthoquinone-Sensitized Novolac [*Photoresist resin system*]
DQN .... Diazoquinone Novolac (EDCT)
DQO .... Data Quality Objective
DQO .... Wilmington, DE [*Location identifier*] [*FAA*] (FAAL)
DQO/OA .... Data Quality Objectives/Observational Approach (SAUS)
DQOP .... Directorate of Quartering Operations and Planning (SAUO)
DQOPP .... Data Quality Objectives Planning Process (SAUS)
DQP .... Depot Quartermaster, Philadelphia, Pennsylvania [*Marine Corps*]
DQP .... Designated Qualified Person [*Department of Agriculture*]
DQP .... Diode Qualification Program
DQ PACKET .... Data Qualifier Packet [*Communications term*] (DCT)
DQPH .... Depot Quartermaster, Pearl Harbor, Hawaii [*Marine Corps*]
DQ/PL .... Definite-Quantity Price List [*Type of contract*] (AAGC)
DQPrA .... Duqesne Cap L.P.8.375%'MIPS' [*NYSE symbol*] (TTSB)
DQPSK .... Differentially encoded quadriphase shift keying (SAUS)
DQPSK .... Differential Quadrature Phase-Shift Keying (AEBE)
DQPSK .... Differential Quadri-Phrase Shift Keying (CCCA)
DQPSK .... Digital Quadrature Phase Shift Keying (SAUS)
DQQ .... Depot Quartermaster, Quantico, Virginia [*Marine Corps*]
DQQ .... Digital Quarter Quadrangle (SAUS)
DQR .... Data Quality Report (SAUS)
DQR .... Depot Quartermaster, Richmond (SAUO)
DQR .... Depot Quartermaster, Richmond, Virginia [*Marine Corps*]
DQR .... Design Qualification Requirement
DQR .... Design, Quality, Reliabilty
DQR .... Dihydroquercetin Reductase [*An enzyme*]
DQR&S .... Design quality, reliability, and safety (SAUS)
DQRS .... Distributed Query and Retrieval System [*Telecommunications*] (PS)
DQRS .... Drawing Quality Rimmed Steel (SAUS)
DQrtg .... Directorate of Quartering (SAUO)
DQS .... Digital Quartz Servo [*Thomson video control system*] (NITA)
DQS .... distributed queuing system (SAUS)
DQS .... Dominant Quasi-Simple (SAUS)
DQS .... Drawing Quality Steel
DQS .... Index-Digest Quarterly System
DQSF .... Depot Quartermaster, San Francisco, California [*Marine Corps*]
DQSK .... Drawing Quality, Special-Killed [*Metallurgy*]
DQT .... Design Qualification Test (CTAS)
DQT .... Diode Qualification Test
DQT .... Division Quality Team (DOMA)
DQTP .... Design Qualification Test Plan (MCD)
DQTP .... Design Qualification Test Program (SAUS)
DQTP .... Diode Qualification Test Program
DQU .... Deganawidah-Quetzalcoatl University [*Initials preferred to spelled-out name*] [*California*]
DQU .... Dequincy, LA [*Location identifier*] [*FAA*] (FAAL)
DQU .... Duquesne Light Co. [*Later, DQE*] [*NYSE symbol*] (SPSG)
DQUEN .... De Queen, AR [*American Association of Railroads railroad junction routing code*]
DQUIN .... De Quincy, LA [*American Association of Railroads railroad junction routing code*]
DQUPrA .... Dunquesne Lt cm$2.10 Pfd [*NYSE symbol*] (TTSB)
DQUPrB .... Duquesne Lt 3.75% Pfd [*NYSE symbol*] (TTSB)
DQUPrC .... Duquesne Lt 4% Pfd [*NYSE symbol*] (TTSB)
DQUPrD .... Duquesne Lt4.10% Pfd [*NYSE symbol*] (TTSB)
DQUPrE .... Duquesne Lt 4.15% Pfd [*NYSE symbol*] (TTSB)
DQUPrG .... Duquesne Lt 4.20% Pfd [*NYSE symbol*] (TTSB)
DQV .... Deckerville, MI [*Location identifier*] [*FAA*] (FAAL)
DQV-K .... Penicillin V-Potassium Salt [*Medicine*] (EDAA)
DQW .... Double Quantum Well [*Physics*]
DQZ .... Duquesne Light 7.375% Bonds [*NYSE symbol*] (SG)
DR .... Advance Airlines [*ICAO designator*] (AD)
DR .... Coastal Healthcare Group, Inc. [*NYSE symbol*] (SAG)
DR .... Coastal Physican Grp [*NYSE symbol*] (TTSB)
DR .... Dacca Reports [*India*] [*A publication*] (DLA)
DR .... Dahlgren Rifle
DR .... Daily Record [*Penny newspaper in "He Knew He Was Right" by Anthony Trollope*]
DR .... Daily Relay (SAUS)
DR .... Daily Report
DR .... Daily Review
DR .... Dalhousie Review [*A publication*] (ANEX)
DR .... Damping Ratio (IAA)
D-R .... Damp Rag [*Decontamination method*] [*Nuclear energy*] (NRCH)
DR .... Danish Reactor (NRCH)
DR .... Danmarks Retsforbund [*Justice Party of Denmark*] (PPE)
DR .... Dardanelle & Russellville Railroad Co. [*AAR code*]
DR .... Dark Red [*Philately*]
DR .... Dark Resistance (SAUS)
DR .... Darkroom [*Photography*]
D/R .... Database Reference [*A publication*]
DR .... Data Rate [*Telecommunications*] (TEL)
DR .... Data Reader (SAUS)
DR .... Data Ready (SAUS)
DR .... Data Receiver [*or Recorder*]
DR .... Data Record [*Computer science*] (VLIE)
DR .... Data Recorder (MCD)
DR .... Data Recording (SAUS)
DR .... Data Recovery [*Computer science*] (ECII)

DR Data Reduction (KSC)
DR Data Register
DR Data Reorganizer (IAA)
DR Data Report
DR Data Request
DR Data Requirements [*NASA*]
DR Data Research (SAUS)
DR Date of Rank [*Air Force*]
DR Date Rape (MELL)
DR Daughter (ROG)
DR Daughters of the Revolution
DR Daunorubicin [*Antineoplastic drug*] (DAVI)
DR Dead Reckoning [*Navigation*]
DR Dead Rise (DS)
DR Deadroom (SAUS)
DR Dealer [*Automotive sales*]
DR Dear (ROG)
DR Death Rate
DR Death Row
Dr Debit (EBF)
DR Debit
DR Debit Record (FOTI)
DR Debit Request
dr Debtor (ADWA)
DR Debtor
Dr Debtor (EBF)
DR Debugging Routine (SAUS)
DR Decanus Ruralis [*Rural Dean*]
DR Decay Ratio (SAUS)
DR Decisions and Reports of the European Commission of Human Rights (SAFN)
DR Decorator Remodeling [*A publication*]
DR Deduced Reckoning [*Navigation*] (OA)
DR Defence Regulation (DAS)
DR Defense [*or Disaster*] Readiness (OICC)
DR Defense Research (SAUS)
DR Defensive Response [*Psychology*]
DR Deficiency Report [*Air Force*] (AFM)
DR Defined Readout [*Telecommunications*] (OA)
DR Degeneration Reaction
Dr Degree (SAUS)
dr Degree of Resilience (SAUS)
DR Degrees Rankine (KSC)
DR Dejerine-Roussy [*Syndrome*] [*Medicine*] (DB)
DR Delayed Release [*Tablet*] [*Medicine*] (EDAA)
DR Deliquency Report [*Military*] (VNW)
DR Delivery Rate [*DoD*]
DR Delivery Room [*Medicine*]
DR Delta Ray (SAUS)
DR Demodulation/Remodulation (IAA)
DR Demolition Rocket (NATG)
DR Denmarks Radio (SAUS)
DR Density Report [*Army*]
DR Dental Record (SAUS)
DR Dental Recruit
DR Deoxyribose (MELL)
DR Depart Dose [*Medicine*] (EDAA)
DR Departmental Report (SAUS)
DR Dependents Rate [*Air Force*] (AFM)
DR Deposition Rate [*Electrochemistry*]
DR Deposit Receipt [*Banking*]
DR Deputy Remembrancer [*A publication*] (DLA)
DR De-Rating and Rating Appeals [*England and Scotland*] [*A publication*] (DLA)
DR Derby Aviation, Ltd. (SAUO)
DR Derrick (DS)
DR Designator Register [*Computer science*]
DR Design report (SAUS)
DR Design Requirement
DR Design Review (AAG)
DR Despatch Rider [*Military*] [*British*]
DR Destination Release (SAUS)
DR Destroyer (SAUS)
DR Destroyer Flag [*Navy*] [*British*]
DR Destructive Reading (SAUS)
DR Detached Retina (MELL)
DR Detailed Report
DR Detection RADAR
DR Detector Response [*Medicine*] (EDAA)
DR Detergent- Resistant (SAUS)
DR Deuteronomy Rabba (BJA)
DR Deutsche Reichsbahn [*German Democratic Republic Railway*] (DCTA)
DR Deutsche Reichspartei [*German National Party*] [*Political party*] (PPE)
DR Deutsches Recht [*German Law*] (ILCA)
DR Deutsches Reich [*German Empire*]
DR Developer Release (SAUS)
DR Developmental Review (SAUO)
DR Development Report
DR Development-Right (MCD)
DR Deviation Range
DR Deviation Ratio
DR Deviation Report
DR Devin Register [*An association*] (EA)
DR Dextrorotatory (SAUS)
DR Diabetes-Resistant [*Medicine*]
DR Diabetic Retinopathy [*Medicine*]
DR Diagnostic Radiology [*Medicine*]
DR Diagnostic Routine (SAUS)
DR Diaper Rash (MELL)
dr Diastereomer Ratio (MEC)
DR Dielectric Reader (SAUS)
DR Dielectric Reading (SAUS)
DR Diesel Radial [*Aircraft engine*]
DR Dietary Restriction [*Medicine*]
dR differential of resistance (SAUS)
DR Differential Rate
DR Differential Reflectometry (AAEL)
DR Differential Relay
DR Differential Resistivity (UWER)
DR Diffused Resistor (UWER)
DR Diffuse Reflectance (SAUS)
DR Diffuse Reflection (UWER)
DR diferential rate (SAUS)
DR Digital Radio (SAUS)
DR Digital Radiography
DR Digital Radioscopy (SAUS)
DR Digital Recording (SAUS)
DR Digital Rectal [*Proctoscopy*]
DR Digital Representation (SAUS)
DR Digital Research (SAUO)
DR Digital Resolver
DR Digit Reading (SAUS)
DR Digit Receiver
DR Dihydrotestosterone Receptor [*Endocrinology*]
D/R Dining Room [*Therapy term*] (CTAA)
dr Dining Room (NTIO)
DR Dining Room
DR Diocesan Registry (GEAB)
DR Diode Rectifier (SAUS)
DR Diploma in Radiology [*British*]
D-R Diplomate, American Board of Radiology (DHSM)
D/R Directional Radio
DR Directive Antenna with Reflector
DR Directives
DR Director (ADA)
DR Director of Railways (SAUO)
DR Direct or Reserve (SAUS)
D/R Direct or Reverse (SAUS)
DR Direct Ratio (SAUS)
DR Direct Reading [*Spectroscopy*]
DR Direct Recording (IAA)
DR Direct Reduction [*Ironmaking process*]
DR Direct Repeat [*Genetics*]
D/R Direct/Reverse
DR Direct Route
DR Disaster Recovery (DA)
DR Disaster Representative [*Red Cross*]
DR Discharging Resistor
DR Discipline report (SAUS)
DR Disconnect Request (SAUS)
DR Discount Rate [*Banking*]
DR Disc reader (SAUS)
DR Discrepancy Record [*or Report*] (KSC)
DR Discrete Register (MCD)
DR Discrete Regulator (SAUS)
DR Disc Ridge Splitting [*Agriculture*]
DR Discrimination RADAR
DR Discrimination Reversal [*Neurophysiology*]
DR Disk Recorder (DEN)
DR Dispatch Reliability (NASA)
D/R Dispatch Rider [*Marine Corps*]
DR Dispersion Relation (SAUS)
DR displacement corrector (SAUS)
DR Display Racks [*Freight*]
DR Display Register (ACAE)
DR Display Result
DR Disposal Rate [*Of hormone metabolism*]
DR Disposition Record (NASA)
DR Dissociative Recombination [*Chemistry*]
D/R Distance to Cell Radius Ratio (CGWS)
DR Distant Range
DR Distant Reading (IAA)
DR Distant Reception (IAA)
DR Distinctive Ringing [*Communications term*] (DCT)
DR Distribution Regulation [*Office of Price Stabilization*] (DLA)
DR Distribution Request
DR Distributor
DR District Railway [*London*]
DR District Registry
DR Diurnal Rhythm [*Medicine*] (MEDA)
DR Divided Ringing (IAA)
DR Dividend Refund (FOTI)
DR Divide Registers (SAUS)
DR Division of Research [*Navy*]
DR Division Register (IAA)
DR Divisor [*Mathematics*]
DR DMR Group, Inc. [*Toronto Stock Exchange symbol*]
DR Dock Receipt

DR .... Doctor (EY)
Dr .... Doctor (WDAA)
DR .... Doctor of Radiology (SAUS)
DR .... Doctor of Religion
DR .... Document Reader (SAUS)
DR .... Document Register (MCD)
DR .... Document Report
DR .... Document Retrieval (SAUS)
DR .... Dogger [*Ship's rigging*] (ROG)
DR .... Dollar [*Monetary unit*] (ROG)
dr .... Dominican Republic [*IYRU nationality code*] [*MARC country of publication code*] [*Library of Congress*] (LCCP)
dr .... Door (VRA)
Dr .... Door
DR .... Door
DR .... Dorsal Raphe [*Brain anatomy*]
DR .... Dorsal Root [*of spinal nerve*] [*Anatomy*]
DR .... Dose Rate (SAUS)
DR .... Dose Ratio [*Medicine*]
DR .... Double Reading (SAUS)
DR .... Double Reduced [*Tinplate*]
DR .... Double Reduction (SAUS)
Dr .... Double Reduction Gearing (DS)
DR .... Double-Reduction gearing (SAUS)
d-r .... Double-Riveted (SAUS)
DR .... Double Royal [*Paper*] (ADA)
D/R .... Downrange
DR .... Down Repeated [*Football*]
DR .... Down Right [*The front right portion of a stage*] [*A stage direction*]
dr .... Drachm [*Unit of weight*] [*German*]
DR .... Drachma [*Monetary unit*] [*Greece*] (EY)
DR .... Draft
DR .... Drafting Request (MSA)
DR .... Draft Recommendation [*International Standards Organization*]
DR .... Draft Release (MCD)
DR .... Dragoon (ROG)
DR .... Drag Reduction (SAUS)
DR .... Drain (MSA)
dr .... Dram (IDOE)
DR .... Dram
DR .... Drama (ADA)
DR .... Draped [*Numismatics*]
DR .... Draw (WDAA)
Dr .... Drawer (EBF)
DR .... Drawer
Dr .... Drawing (SAUS)
DR .... Drawn (AABC)
DR .... Draw Ratio [*Plastics technology*]
Dr .... Dredger (SAUS)
DR .... D-Related [*Antigen*] [*Immunology*]
DR .... Dressed [*Fish processing*]
DR .... Dresser
DR .... Dressing [*Medicine*]
DR .... Dressing Room (DAC)
DR .... Dressing Station (SAUO)
DR .... Dress Rehearsal (MUGU)
Dr .... Drewry's English Vice Chancellors' Reports [*A publication*] (DLA)
Dr .... Dries [*Maps and charts*] [*British*]
DR .... Drifting (WEAT)
DR .... Drift Rate
DR .... Drill (MSA)
DR .... Drilling Regulation (SAUS)
DR .... Drill Kod (SAUS)
DR .... Drill Regulations
DR .... Drill Rig (UWER)
DR .... Drill Road (SAUS)
DR .... Drill Rod
DR .... Drive [*or Driver*] (AFM)
Dr .... Drive (TBD)
Dr .... Driver (MIST)
DR .... Driver (SAUS)
D/R .... Driver Records [*Motor vehicle violation code used in state of Maryland*] (MVRD)
DR .... Driver Responsibility [*Motor vehicle term used in state of Washington*] (MVRD)
DR .... Driver's Report (UWER)
DR .... Driving [*Motor vehicle violation code used in state of Maryland*] (MVRD)
DR .... Driving Record
DR .... Drug Receptor (MELL)
DR .... Drug Rehabilitation
DR .... Drug Residue (MELL)
DR .... Drug Resistance (MELL)
DR .... Drug-Resistant (UWER)
DR .... Drum (MUGU)
DR .... Drummer (WDAA)
Dr .... Drury's Irish Chancery Reports Tempore Napier [*1858-59*] [*A publication*] (DLA)
Dr .... Drury's Irish Chancery Reports Tempore Sugden [*A publication*] (DLA)
DR .... Dual Relationship
DR .... Ducted Rocket (MCD)
DR .... Ductus Reuniens (MELL)
DR .... Dummy Record (SAUS)
DR .... Dump Revenues [*Solid waste management*]
DR .... Duplicating Requisition (MCD)
DR .... Dutch Reformed Church (IIA)
DR .... Dynamic Radius [*Tires*]
DR .... Dynamic Range
DR .... Dynamic Reconfiguration (SAUS)
DR .... Dynamic Relaxation (ODA)
DR .... Dynamic Reprocessing (NITA)
DR .... Dynamic Routing (SAUS)
DR .... European Right [*European Parliament*] (ECED)
DR .... Increment of Response [*Psychology*]
Dr .... La Sainte Bible (1884) (Drioux) [*A publication*] (BJA)
DR .... National Distillers and Chemical Corp. (SAUO)
DR .... Reaction of Degeneration [*Physiology*]
DR .... Robin Avions [*Pierre Robin*] [*France*] [*ICAO aircraft manufacturer identifier*] (ICAO)
dr .... Drizzle and Rain (ODA)
DR .... Dry Riser (ODA)
DRA .... Dancers Responding to AIDS [*An association*]
DRA .... Data Reformatter Assembly
DRA .... Data Reproducing Apparatus (SAUS)
DRA .... Data Research Associates, Inc. [*Information service or system*] (IID)
DRA .... Data Resource Administrator
DRA .... Dead Reckoning Analyser (or Analyzer) (SAUS)
DRA .... Dead Reckoning Analyzer
DRA .... Decision Risk Analysis [*Army*]
DRA .... Defence Research Agency [*British*]
DRA .... Defense Reauthorization Act (BCP)
DRA .... Defense [*or Disaster*] Relief Act (OICC)
DRA .... Defense Reorganization Act
DRA .... Defense Research & Applications (SAUS)
DRA .... Deficit Reduction Act (ADWA)
Dra .... Deinococcus Radiophilus (SAUS)
DRA .... Delco Remy America
DRA .... Democratic Republic of Afghanistan
DRA .... Dependent Relative Allowance (DLA)
DRA .... Deputy Regional Administrator
DRA .... De-Rating Appeals [*England*] [*A publication*] (DLA)
DRA .... Designated Responsible Activity (MCD)
DRA .... Design Requirements Agreement (SPST)
DRA .... Design Review Agreement (MCD)
DRA .... Despite Resuscitation Attempts [*Medicine*] (MEDA)
DRA .... Detection, Recognition, and Acquisition (ACAE)
DRA .... Dextran-Reactive Antibody [*Medicine*] (DMAA)
DRA .... Diagnosis-Rework Action (AAG)
DRA .... Dielectric Rod Aerial (SAUS)
DRA .... Dielectric Rod Antenna
DRA .... Diffuse Reflection Attachment [*Spectroscopy*]
DRA .... Digital Read-In Assembly [*Computer science*]
DRA .... Digital Record Analyzer (SAUS)
DRA .... Digital Recorder Analyzer [*Computer science*]
DRA .... Directed Reading Activity [*Education*]
DRA .... Director of Royal Artillery [*British*]
DRA .... Direct Reckoning Analyzer (MUGU)
DRA .... Disaster Relief Act (COE)
DRA .... Discontinuous Reinforced Aluminum programme (SAUS)
DRA .... Discrete Recovery Area (KSC)
DRA .... Discretionary Routed Array (SAUS)
DRA .... Division of Ratepayer Advocates (SAUS)
DRA .... Divorce Registration Area [*Department of Health and Human Services*] (GFGA)
DRA .... Djibouti Relief Association
DRA .... DMR Group, Inc. Class A SV [*Toronto Stock Exchange symbol*]
DRA .... Document Release Authorization (KSC)
DRA .... Doppler RADAR
DRA .... Double Register Arithmetic (SAUS)
Dra .... Draco [*Constellation*]
DRA .... Drag Reducing Agent [*Petroleum pipeline transport*]
Dra .... Draper's Upper Canada King's Bench Reports [*A publication*] (DLA)
dra .... Dravidian [*MARC language code*] [*Library of Congress*] (LCCP)
DRA .... Dravidian Air Services Ltd. [*British*] [*ICAO designator*] (FAAC)
DRA .... Drawing Release Authorization
DRA .... Draw International Resources Corp. [*Formerly, Draw Resources Corp.*] [*Vancouver Stock Exchange symbol*]
DRA .... Drug-Related Admission (MELL)
DRA .... drum read amalifier (SAUS)
DRA .... Drum-Read Amplifier [*Computer science*] (CET)
DRA .... Dual Recovery Anonymous [*An association*] (SEAT)
DRA .... Dude Ranchers' Association (EA)
DRA .... Dynamic Range Adjustment (SAUS)
DRA .... dynamic resonance absorber (SAUS)
DRA .... Mercury, NV [*Location identifier*] [*FAA*] (FAAL)
DRA .... Sandoz AG [*Germany*] [*Research code symbol*]
DRAA .... Data Reduction and Analysis (SAUS)
DRAAG .... Design Review and Acceptance Group [*Reviews nuclear weapon designs for DoD*]
DRAB .... Downriver Residents Against Bowling (SAUO)
DRA (BB & S) .... Decisions in Review and Appeal Cases (Basutoland, Bechuanaland, and Swaziland) [*A publication*] (ILCA)
DRAC .... Defense Research Advisory Committee (NATG)
DRAC .... Dell Remote Assitant Card
DRAC .... Delta Region Aviation Command [*Military*] (VNW)
DRAC .... Director of the Royal Armoured Corps [*British*]
DRAC .... Director, Royal Armoured Corps (SAUO)
DRAC .... Distributed Read Address Counter
DrAc .... Doctor of Acupuncture [*British*] (DBQ)

Drac .... Draco [*Constellation*]
DRACAS .... Data Reporting, Analysis & Corrective Action System (SAUS)
DRACO .... Dead Reckoning Automatic Computer [*Obsolete*]
DRACO .... Driver and Accident Coordinated Observer (SAUO)
DRACO .... Legislative Drafting Committee (SAUO)
DRACOG .... Diploma of Royal Australian College of Obstetricians and Gynaecologists (BABM)
DRACON .... Drug Abuse Communications Network (SAUS)
DRACR .... Diploma of Royal Australasian [*Medicine*] (DMAA)
DRACR .... Diploma of Royal Australasian College of Radiologists [*Medical degree*] (CMD)
DRACS .... Direct Reactor Auxiliary Cooling System (SAUS)
DRACULA .... Data Repository for Addressing Combat Unified Logistics Analysis
DRACULA .... Dynamic Route Assignment Combining User Learning and Microsimulation [*Traffic management*]
DRAD .... Digital Remote Antenna Driver [*Telecommunications*] (ACRL)
DRAD .... Drill Adapter
dr ad .... drill adaptor (SAUS)
DRADA .... Depression and Related Affective Disorders Association (EA)
DRadEng .... Director of Radio Engineering (SAUO)
D/RADEX .... Digitized RADAR Experiment
Dra Dow .... Draper on Dower [*A publication*] (DLA)
DRADS .... Degradation of RADAR Defense System
DRAE .... Defence Research Analysis Establishment [*Canada*]
Dr Ae .... Doctor of Aviation
D Ra E .... Doctor of Radio Engineering
D Ra Eng .... Doctor of Radio Engineering
DRAERD .... Division of Reproductive, Abdominal, ENT[*Ear, Nose, and Throat*], & Radiological Devices [*Center for Devices and Radiological Devices*]
Dr Ae S .... Doctor of Aeronautical Science
Dr Ae Sc .... Doctor of Aeronautical Science
DRAFI .... Document Read and Format Translator (SAUS)
DRAFT .... Display Retrieval and Formatting Technique (MCD)
DRAFT .... Document Read and Format Translator
DRAFT .... Dynamic Reconfigurability Assisting Fault-Tolerance (SAUS)
Drager Bev .... Drager Review (journ.) (SAUS)
Dragns .... Dragoons [*Military unit*] [*British*] (DMA)
DRAGONAIR .... Hong Kong Dragon Airlines (FEA)
Dr Agr .... Doctor of Agriculture
DRAI .... Data Research Associates [*NASDAQ symbol*] (TTSB)
DRAI .... Data Research Associates, Inc. [*NASDAQ symbol*] (SAG)
DRAI .... Dead Reckoning Analog [*or Analyzer*] Indicator
Drain .... Drainage (SAUS)
DRA/INED .... Development Research Associates, Inc., Institute for New Enterprise Development
Drake Att .... Drake on Attachment [*A publication*] (DLA)
Drake Attachm .... Drake on Attachment [*A publication*] (DLA)
Drake U .... Drake University (GAGS)
DRAM .... Dataram
DRAM .... Department Risk Assessment Manager (SAUO)
DRAM .... Detection RADAR Automatic Monitoring (CET)
DRAM .... Digital Recorded Announcement Module (SAUS)
DRAM .... Display Random Access Memory [*Computer science*] (IAA)
DRAM .... Drama (ADA)
dram .... Dramatic (SHCU)
DRAM .... Dramatic
dram .... Dramatist (ADWA)
DRAM .... Dramatist (WDAA)
DRAM .... Dynamic Memory [*Computer science*]
DRAM .... Dynamic RAM [*Random Access Memory*] (NITA)
DRAM .... Dynamic Random Access Mechanization
DRAM .... Dynamic Random Access Memory [*Computer science*] (ACRL)
d-RAM .... Dynamic Random Access Memory [*Computer science*]
DRAM .... Dynamic Reliability, Availability, and Maintainability
DRAM .... Dynamic Response of Articulate Machinery [*MDI*] (NITA)
DRAMA .... Digital Radio and Multiplex Acquisition (SAUS)
DRAMA .... Digital Radio and Multiplexer Acquisition (MCD)
DRAMD .... Demand Return Disposal Average Monthly Demand
DRAMEDY .... Drama and Comedy [*Slice-of-life television show*]
DRA Memory .... Dynamic Random Access Memory (SAUS)
DRAMI .... Digital Range Measuring Instrument (SAUS)
DRAM PERS .... Dramatis Personae [*Characters of the Play*] [*Latin*]
DRAMS .... Data Reduction and Management System (SAUS)
DRAMS .... Digital Recording and Measuring System
DRAMs .... Dynamic Random Access Memories (SAUS)
DR & A .... Data Reduction and Analysis
DR & A .... Data Reporting and Accounting (AFM)
DR & A .... Data Requirements and Analysis (MCD)
DR & E .... Defense Research and Engineering [*DoD*]
Dr & Nap .... Drury's Irish Chancery Reports Tempore Napier [*1858-59*] [*A publication*] (DLA)
DR and O .... Depot Repair and Overhaul (SAUS)
Dr & S .... Doctor and Student [*A publication*] (DSA)
Dr & Sm .... Drewry and Smale's English Vice Chancellors' Reports [*1860-65*] [*A publication*] (DLA)
Dr & Sug .... Drury's Irish Chancery Reports Tempore Sugden [*A publication*] (DLA)
Dr & Wal .... Drury and Walsh's Irish Chancery Reports [*1837-40*] [*A publication*] (DLA)
Dr & War .... Drury and Warren's Irish Chancery Reports [*1841-43*] [*A publication*] (DLA)
DR&WG .... Data Reduction and Computing Work Group (SAUO)
DRANO .... Downriver Associated Narcotics Organization (SAUO)
DRANS .... Data Reduction and Analysis Subsystem (SAUS)
DRANS .... Data Reduction and Analysis System
DRAO .... Defense Reconstruction Assistance Office (SAUS)
DRAO .... Dominion Radio Astrophysical Observatory [*Herzberg Institute of Astrophysics, National Research Council of Canada*] [*Research center*] (RCD)
DRAP .... Deployment Readiness Assistance Program [*Military*]
DRAP .... Direct Reading Azimuth Protractor [*Bureau of Mines*]
dr ap .... Drachm, Apothecaries (SAUS)
dr ap .... Drachm Apothecaries' Weight [*Pharmacology*] (DAVI)
dr ap .... Dram, Apothecaries (SAUS)
DRAP .... Dram, Apothecary
DRAP .... Drapery
DRAPAC .... Design Rule and Process Architecture Council (AAEL)
DRAPE .... Data Recording and Processing Equipment
DRAPE .... Data Reduction and Processing Equipment (SAUS)
DRAPE .... Digital Recording and Playback Equipment (MCD)
Draper .... Draper's Upper Canada King's Bench Reports [*A publication*] (DLA)
Draper (Can) .... Draper's Upper Canada King's Bench Reports [*A publication*] (DLA)
Draper (Ont) .... Draper's Upper Canada King's Bench Reports [*A publication*] (DLA)
drapes .... draperies (SAUS)
DRAPF .... Data Reduction and Processing Facility (IAA)
DRAS .... Data Requirements Authorization Sheet (ACAE)
DRAS .... Defense Retiree and Annuitant Pay System [*DoD*]
DRAS .... Descending Reticular Activating System (DIPS)
DRAs .... Discretionary Routed Arrays (SAUS)
DRAS .... Django Reinhardt Appreciation Society [*Inactive*] (EA)
DRAs .... Drum Read Amplifiers (SAUS)
DRASER .... Doppler RADAR and Storm Electricity Research Group [*Norman, OK*] [*Department of Commerce*] (GRD)
DRASTIC .... Depth to Water, Recharge, Aquifer Media, Soil Media, Topography, Impact of the Vadose Zone, Conductivity (SAUS)
DRAT .... Data Reduction Analysis Tape
DRAT .... Data Reduction and Analysis Tape (SAUS)
DRAT .... Demonstration Reliability Acceptance Test
DRAT .... Differential Rheumatoid Agglutination Test [*Medicine*] (DMAA)
DRAT .... Digital Range and Angle Tracker (ACAE)
DRATE .... Difference of Rate
Dr Att .... Drake on Attachment [*A publication*] (DLA)
DR Av .... Doctor of Aviation (SAUS)
DRAV .... Dram, Avoirdupois
Drav .... Dravidian [*Family of languages from southern India and Sri Lanka*] (BARN)
dr avdp .... Drachm Avoirdupois (SAUS)
dr avdp .... Dram Avoirdupois (SAUS)
Dravo .... Dravo Corp. [*Associated Press*] (SAG)
DRAW .... Digital Read After Write disc (SAUS)
DRAW .... Direct Read after Write [*Computer science*]
DRAW .... Direct Read After Write Animation System (SAUS)
DRAW .... Drag Racing Association of Women
DRAW .... Drawing (SAUS)
DRAW Disk .... Direct Read After Write Disk (SAUS)
DRAX .... Drake Tank Car [*Private rail car owner code*]
DRAX .... Draxis Health, Inc. [*NASDAQ symbol*] (SAG)
DRAXF .... Draxis Health [*NASDAQ symbol*] (TTSB)
Draxis .... Draxis Health, Inc. [*Associated Press*] (SAG)
DRB .... Dartmouth College, Hanover, NH [*OCLC symbol*] (OCLC)
DRB .... Data Review Board [*Military*] (AFIT)
DRB .... Daunorubicin [*Daunomycin*] [*Also, D, DNR, R*] [*Antineoplastic drug*]
DRB .... DCS Retractable Bit System (SAUS)
DRB .... Decade Resolver Bridge
DRB .... Decimal Register Binary
DRB .... Defence (or Defense) Research Board (SAUO)
DRB .... Defence Research Board [*Canada*]
DRB .... Defense Resources Board
DRB .... Defense Review Board [*Aerospace*]
DRB .... Deficiency Review Board (AFIT)
DRB .... Demonstrated Reserve Base
DRB .... Departmental Records Branch [*Military*]
DRB .... Derby [*Australia*] [*Airport symbol*] (OAG)
DRB .... Design Requirements Baseline (NASA)
DRB .... Design Review Board
DRB .... Deutsche Reichsbahn [*German State Railways*] [*Pre-1945*]
DRB .... Diagnostic Readout Box (HAWK)
DRB .... Dichlororibofuranosylbenzimidazole [*Biochemistry*]
DRB .... Digital Radio Broadcasters (SAUO)
DRB .... Digital Readout Box [*Computer science*]
DRB .... Dimensional Review Board (SAUO)
DRB .... Disability Retirement Branch [*BUPERS*]
DRB .... Discarding Rotating Band [*Military*] (CAAL)
DRB .... Discharge Review Board (SAUS)
DRB .... Division Ready Brigade (SAUS)
DRB .... Double-Ring Break [*Ampoules*] (DB)
DRB .... Drainboard [*Technical drawings*]
DRB .... Drum Brakes
Drb .... Durban (SAUS)
DRB .... Dursunbey [*Turkey*] [*Seismograph station code, US Geological Survey*] [*Closed*] (SEIS)
DRBA .... Dharma Realm Buddhist Association (EA)
DRBC .... Delaware River Basin Commission [*Successor to INCODEL*]
DRBC .... Donkey Red Blood Cell (DB)
DRBCL .... Defence Research Board Chemical Laboratories (SAUO)
DRBG .... Drill Bushing
DRBH .... Defence Research Board Headquarters (SAUO)
Dr Bi Ch .... Doctor of Biological Chemistry

DrBiChem.... Doctor of Biological Chemistry (NADA)
Dr Bi Phy..... Doctor of Biophysics
DrBl............ Dark Blend [*Philately*]
DRBL.......... Design Requirements Baseline
DRBn.......... divisional reconnaissance battalion (SAUO)
DRBOND...... Dial-up Router Bandwidth On Demand (SAUS)
DRBOND...... Dial-up Router Bandwith On Demand (SAUS)
DRBU.......... Dharma Realm Buddhist University (SAUO)
DrBusAdm... Doctor of Business Administration (NADA)
DrBusAdmin... Doctor of Business Administration
DRC............ Dada Research Center (or Centre) (SAUO)
DRC............ Dain Rauscher [*NYSE symbol*] (SG)
DRC............ Damage Received in Collision [*Insurance*] (MARI)
DRC............ Damage Risk Contours
DRC............ Damage-Risk Criteria [*Tolerable limits for noise exposure*]
DRC............ Data access control system Return Code (SAUS)
DRC............ Data Range Changer (SAUS)
DRC............ Data Rate Changer
DRC............ Data Recording Camera
DRC............ Data Recording Code (SAUS)
DRC............ Data Recording Control (NITA)
DRC............ Data Recording Controller [*Computer science*] (BUR)
DRC............ Data Recovery Center (SAUS)
DRC............ Data Reduction Center [*or Complex*]
DRC............ Data Reduction Compiler [*or Computer*] (MCD)
DRC............ Data Reduction Computer (SAUS)
DRC............ Data Regeneration Code (SAUS)
DRC............ Data Resource Center [*Bureau of the Census*] (GFGA)
DRC............ Data Return Capsule [*or Container*]
DRC............ Data Return Code (SAUS)
DRC............ Daunorubicin (LDT)
DRC............ Daylight Rapid Contacting (DGA)
DRC............ Defence Requirements Committee [*British military*] (DMA)
DRC............ Defence Research Committee [*British*]
DRC............ Defence Review Committee [*NATO*] (NATG)
DRC............ Defense Research Corporation (ACAE)
DRC............ Defense Review Committee (SAUS)
DRC............ Deficit Reduction Coalition [*Defunct*] (EA)
DRC............ Delaware Railroad [*Federal Railroad Administration identification code*]
DRC............ Democratiaid Rhyddfrydol Cymru [*Welsh Liberal Democrats*] [*Political party*] [*Wales*] (EAIO)
DRC............ Democratic Republic of China (CINC)
DRC............ Democratic Republic of the Congo [*Later, Zaire*]
DRC............ Demographic Research Co., Inc. [*Information service or system*] (IID)
DRC............ Denver Railway Car Co. (SAUO)
DRC............ Denver Research Center (SAUS)
DRC............ Department of Rehabilitation and Correction (SAUS)
DRC............ Deployment Readiness Condition [*Army*] (AABC)
DRC............ Depot Repair Cycle (MCD)
DRC............ Deputy Regional Commander
DRC............ Deputy Regional Counsel (GFGA)
DRC............ Design Research Center [*Carnegie-Mellon University*] [*Research center*] (RCD)
DRC............ Design review comments (SAUS)
DRC............ Design Rule Check (AAEL)
DRC............ Design Rule Checker [*For integrated circuitry*]
DRC............ Design Rule Checks (SAUS)
DRC............ Design Rules Checking (SAUS)
DRC............ Device Release Command (SAUS)
DRC............ Dictionary Research Centre [*University of Exeter*] [*British*] (IRC)
DRC............ Dictionary Research Centre [*Macquarie University*] [*Australia*]
DRC............ Dielectric Relaxation Current (PDAA)
DRC............ Digital Radar Code (SAUS)
DRC............ Diminished Radix Complement (SAUS)
DRC............ Diminished Radix Complementation (DICI)
DRC............ Diploma of the Royal College of Science and Technology, Glasgow [*British*]
DRC............ Director of Reserve Components (SAUO)
DRC............ Direct-Reaction Calculation
DRC............ Direct Robotic Control (SAUS)
DRC............ Disability Review Council [*Military*] (AABC)
DRC............ Disability Rights Center (EA)
DRC............ Disappearing RADAR Contact (MCD)
DRC............ Disarmament Resource Center [*Defunct*] (EA)
DRC............ Disaster Recovery Center (DEMM)
DRC............ Disaster Research Center [*Ohio*] (AEBS)
DRC............ Discontinuous Reinforced Composite (SAUS)
DRC............ Discoverer Recovery Capsule [*NASA*]
DRC............ Discrete Rate Command (MCD)
DRC............ Disposal Release Confirmation (ACAE)
DRC............ Dispute Resolution Committee (SAUS)
DRC............ Distant Reading Compass
DRC............ District Recruiting Command [*Army*] (AABC)
DRC............ Division of Rehabilitation Counseling [*of the APGA*]
DRC............ Document Record Card
DRC............ Document Retrieval System (SAUS)
DRC............ Documents Review Committee [*American Occupational Therapy Association*]
DRC............ Dolphin Research Center (EA)
DRC............ Domaine de la Romanee-Conti [*French vintner*]
DRC............ Domain Relational Calculus (SAUS)
DRC............ Domestic Resource Cost (SAUS)
DRC............ Domestic Revenue Cost Coefficient [*Economics*]
DRC............ Donkey Red Cell [*s*]
DRC............ Dose Response Curve [*Medicine*]
DRC............ Double Rayon Covered (SAUS)
drc............ down right center (SAUS)
DRC............ Down Right Centre (SAUS)
DRC............ Downward Reflected Component (SAUS)
DRC............ Drawing Record Card (MCD)
DRC............ DRCA Medical Corp. [*AMEX symbol*] (SPSG)
DRC............ DRC Resources Corp. [*Vancouver Stock Exchange symbol*]
DRC............ Driver Re-education Course (SAUS)
DRC............ Driver Rehabilitation Clinic [*Motor vehicle violation code used in state of Maryland*] (MVRD)
DRC............ Dropped Rod Control [*Nuclear energy*] (NRCH)
DRC............ Drug Referral Center (SAUS)
DRC............ Drug Rehabilitation Center (SAUS)
DRC............ Dry Rubber Content
DRC............ Dual Receive Capability (SAUS)
DRC............ Dutch Reformed Church
DRC............ dynamic range compression (SAUS)
DRC............ Dynamic Research Console
DRC............ Dynamics Research Corp.
DRC............ Dynamics Research Corporation (SAUO)
DRC............ Triton Airlines, Inc. [*Canada*] [*ICAO designator*] (FAAC)
DRCA.......... Data Retrieval Corporation of America (SAUO)
DRCA.......... DRCA Medical Corp. [*Associated Press*] (SAG)
Dr Can L....... Doctor of Canon Law
DRCC.......... Data Referencing and Conditioning Centre (SAUO)
DRCC.......... Division Remote Computer Center (SAUO)
DRCC.......... Document Records Control Committee (SAUS)
DRCCA........ Division of Resources, Centers, and Community Activities [*National Cancer Institute*]
DRCCC........ Defense Regional Communications Control Center
DRCCC-FE.... Defense Regional Communications Control Center, Far East (CINC)
DRCCC-SEA... Defense Regional Communications Control Center, Southeast Asia (CINC)
DRCd.......... Defence (or Defense) Review Committee (SAUO)
DRCD.......... Drive Code [*Automotive emissions*]
DRCDE........ Development and Engineering Directorate [*Army*] (RDA)
DRCDG........ Data Recording (MSA)
DRCE.......... Drag Race Competition Engine [*Automotive engineering*]
Dr C Ec........ Droit Civil Ecclesiastique [*A publication*] (DLA)
DR-CG......... Data Reduction and Computing Group [*Range Commanders Council*] [*NASA*]
DRCG.......... Discrimination RADAR Control Group (AAG)
DR CHEM...... Doctor of Chemistry (WDAA)
DrchHu........ Dorchester Hugoton Ltd. [*Associated Press*] (SAG)
DRCIRD....... DARCOM International Relations Directorate (SAUO)
dr ck........... drill chuck (SAUS)
DRCL.......... Defence Research Chemical Laboratories [*Canada*]
DRCL.......... Distributed Robot Control Language (SAUS)
DRCM.......... Deletion Retention Contour Machine (SAUS)
DRCM.......... Department Records Control Manager (SAUO)
DRCM.......... Differential Reinforced Clostridial Medium (PDAA)
DRCM.......... Dutch Reformed Church Mission (SAUO)
DRCO.......... Dynamics Research [*NASDAQ symbol*] (TTSB)
DRCO.......... Dynamics Research Corp. [*NASDAQ symbol*] (NQ)
DRCOG........ Diploma of the Royal College of Obstetricians and Gynaecologists [*Australia*]
DRCOG........ Diploma of the Royal College of Obstetrics and Gynaecology [*British*]
Dr Com........ Doctor of Commerce
Dr Com........ Droit Commercial [*Commercial Law*] [*French*] (DLA)
DrComSc..... Doctor of Commercial Science
DRCP.......... Dual Range Channel Processor (SAUS)
DRCP.......... Dummy Rip Cord Pulls (DICI)
DRC Path..... Diploma of the Royal College of Pathologists [*British*]
DRCPM-NUC... Development Readiness Command Program Manager - Nuclear [*Army*]
DRCPR........ Differential Reactive Current Project Relay
DR/CR......... Data Requirements/Change Request (MCD)
DRCR.......... Design review completion report (SAUS)
Dr Cr Jus..... Doctor of Criminal Jurisprudence
DRCS.......... Directorate of Reserve Component Support [*DoD*]
DRCS.......... Distress Radio Call System [*Telecommunications*] (TEL)
Dr CS.......... Doctor of Commercial Science
DRCS.......... Dynamically Redefinable Character Set [*Computer science*]
DRCSA........ Distance Runners Club of South Australia
DRCT.......... Depot Repair Cycle Time
DRCT.......... Direct (AFM)
DRCT.......... Dry Rod Consolidation Technology (GAAI)
DRCT.......... Dynamic Recipe Control Table
DRCTN........ Direction (FAAC)
DRCTY........ Directly (MSA)
DRCTY........ Directory (AFM)
DRCU.......... DEW Line Record Communications Upgrade (SAUS)
dr/cu in....... Dram per Cubic Inch (SAUS)
Dr Cul S...... Doctor of Cultural Science
Dr Cul Sc..... Doctor of Cultural Science
DRCV.......... Distributor Retard Control Valve [*Automotive engineering*]
DRCVX........ Comstock Partners Capital Value Cl.A [*Mutual fund ticker symbol*] (SG)
DR-CWG...... Data Reduction and Computing Working Group [*Range Commanders Council*] [*NASA*]
DRCX.......... Denver Railway Car [*Federal Railroad Administration identification code*]
DRCZ.......... Don Russ [*Federal Railroad Administration identification code*]

DRD .... Data Reading Device [*Computer science*] (VERA)
DRD .... Data Recording Device [*Computer science*] (BUR)
DRD .... Data Reduction Division (SAUS)
DRD .... Data Requirement Description [*NASA*] (MCD)
DRD .... Data Requirements Document [*NASA*] (NASA)
DRD .... Data Resources Directory (ACAE)
DRD .... Data Resources Directory Publications Subsystem [*Department of Energy*] [*Database*]
DRD .... Defence Research Directors [*NATO*] (NATG)
DRD .... Defense Reactor Division (SAUS)
DRD .... Demand Return Disposal
DRD .... Department of Research Development (SAUO)
DRD .... Depressed Reticle Dive [*Military*]
DRD .... Design Requirement Drawing (MCD)
DRD .... Design Research Division (SAUO)
DRD .... Detailed Requirements Document (MCD)
DRD .... Device Reliability Data (ACAE)
DRD .... Diesel Reduction Drive
DRD .... Differenced-Range Doppler
DRD .... Differential Range De-Ramp (SAUS)
D Rd .... Dird Road (SAUS)
DRD .... Director [*or Directorate*] of Research and Development [*Air Force*]
DRD .... Direct-Reading Dosimeter (SAUS)
D Rd .... Dirt Road (SAUS)
DRD .... Disaster Response Division [*Office of U.S. Foreign Disaster Assistance*]
DRD .... Diver Restraint Device (SAUS)
DRD .... Dividend Received Deduction [*Finance*]
DRD .... Division of Reactor Development [*AEC*]
Dr D .... Doctor of Divinity
DRD .... Documentary Research Division [*Air Force*]
DRD .... Document Requirement Description (KSC)
DRD .... Doparesponsive Dystonia [*Medicine*]
DRD .... Dorsal Root Damage (MELL)
DRD .... Dorunda Station [*Australia*] [*Airport symbol*] [*Obsolete*] (OAG)
DRD .... Draw and Re-Draw [*Tin can manufacturing*]
DRD .... Draw Die [*Tool*] (MCD)
DRD .... Draw-Redraw (SAUS)
DRD .... Drill Rig Duty (SAUS)
DRD .... Drug-Related Dementia (MELL)
DRD .... Drum-Read Driver [*Computer science*]
DRD .... Dual Readout Devices (MCD)
DRD .... Duane Reade [*NYSE symbol*] (SG)
DRD1 .... Dopamine Receptor D1 (SAUS)
DRDA .... Director, Research and Development, Air [*Military*] [*Canada*]
DRDA .... Distributed Relational Data Architecture (SAUS)
DRDA .... Distributed Relational Database Access [*Computer science*] (TNIG)
DRDA .... Distributed Relational Database Algorithm (SAUS)
DRDA .... Distributed Relational Database Architecture [*IBM Corp.*] [*Computer protocol*] [*Computer science*] (PCM)
DRDA .... Distributed Remote Database Access (SAUS)
DRDA .... Division of Research Development and Administration [*University of Michigan*] [*Information service or system*] (IID)
DRDAAS .... Distributed Relational Database Architecture Application Server [*IBM Corp*] (VERA)
DRDBMS .... Distributed Relational DBMS [*Database Management System*] (CDE)
DRDC .... Dairy Research and Development Corp. [*Australia*]
DRDC .... Dairy Research and Development Corporation (SAUO)
DRDC .... Defence Research and Development Council (SAUO)
DRDC .... Drilling Resource Development Corporation (SAUO)
DRDCN .... Data Reduction (MSA)
DRD Corp .... Dairy Research & Development Corp. (SAUS)
DRD Corp .... Dairy Research & Development Corporation (SAUO)
DRDCS .... Director, Research and Development, Communications and Space [*Military*] [*Canada*]
DRDE .... Data Record Description Entry (SAUS)
DRDE .... Differential Read Data Enhancement [*Computer science*]
Dr DES .... Doctor of Design (PGP)
DRDF .... Densified Refuse-Derived Fuel (RDA)
DRDF .... difference RDF (SAUS)
DRD-FD .... Differential Range De-Ramp - Frequency Domain (SAUS)
DRDG RGE .... Dredging Range [*Nautical charts*]
DRDHP .... Director, Research and Development, Human Performance [*Military*] [*Canada*]
DRDL .... Data Requirements and Distribution List [*Navy*]
DRDL .... Defence Research & Development Laboratories (SAUS)
DRDL .... Defense Research and Development Laboratory [*India*]
DRDL .... Director, Research and Development, Land [*Military*] [*Canada*]
DRDM .... Director, Research and Development, Maritime [*Military*] [*Canada*]
DRDO .... Defence (or Defense) Research and Development Organization (SAUO)
DRDO .... Defence Research Development Organization [*India*]
DRDO .... Indian Defense Department (SAUO)
DRDOS .... Digital Research Disk Operating System [*Computer science*] (VERA)
DR-DOS .... Digital Research-Disk Operating System (SAUS)
DRDP .... Detection RADAR Data Processing (CET)
DRDP .... Digital Range Data Processor (MCD)
DRDP .... Director of Radar Data Processing (SAUO)
DRDP .... Director, Research and Development, Program Control [*Military*] [*Canada*]
DRDR .... Reparations, Deliveries and Restitution Directorate (SAUO)
DRDRCSEd .... Diploma in Restorative Dentistry, Royal College of Surgeons of Edinburgh [*British*] (DBQ)
DRDRM .... Director, Research and Development, Resource Management [*Military*] [*Canada*]
DRDS .... Degradation of RADAR Defense System
DRDS .... Dynamic Reconfiguration Data Set [*Computer science*] (VLIE)
DRDSS .... Division of Research and Demonstrations Systems Support [*Department of Health and Human Services*] (GFGA)
DRDT .... Daily Record of Dysfunctional Thoughts (SAUS)
DRDT .... Differential Range Delay Time
DRDT .... Division of Reactor Development and Technology [*AEC*]
DRDT & E .... Director, Research, Development, Test, and Evaluation [*Military*] (DNAB)
DRDTO .... Detection RADAR Data Takeoff [*Air Force*]
DRDW .... Direct Read During Write (VLIE)
DRDW Technique ... Direct Read During Write Technique (SAUS)
DRE .... Data Record Extension (SAUS)
DRE .... Data Recording Equipment (OA)
DRE .... Data Reduction Equipment
DRE .... Dead Reckoning Equipment (MSA)
DRE .... Defence Research Establishment [*Atlantic Canada*] [*UTLAS symbol*]
DRE .... Defense Research Engineering (UWER)
DRE .... Defense Research Establishment [*Israel*]
DRE .... Department of Real Estate (SAUS)
DRE .... Department of Rural Education [*of NEA*] [*Later, REA*] (EA)
DRE .... Destruction and Removal Efficiency [*Of waste incinerators*]
DRE .... Destruction Removal Efficiency (AAEL)
DRE .... Digital Radar Extractor (SAUS)
DRE .... Digital Rebalance Electronics (SAUS)
DRE .... Digital Rectal Exam [*Medicine*]
DRE .... Digital Rectal Examination [*Medicine*]
DRE .... Diploma in Remedial Electrolysis, Institute of Electrolysis [*British*] (DBQ)
DRE .... Directional Reservation Equipment [*Telecommunications*] (TEL)
DRE .... Directorate of Research and Engineering (SAUO)
DRE .... Directorate of Royal Engineers (SAUO)
DRE .... Director of Radio Equipment [*Navy*] [*British*]
DRE .... Director of Religious Education
DRE .... Director [*or Directorate*] of Research and Engineering [*Military*]
DRE .... Direct Reading Encoder
DRE .... Direct-Recording Electronic [*Technology*]
DRE .... Disassembly Reassembly Equipment (SAUS)
D/RE .... Disassembly/Reassembly Equipment [*Nuclear energy*] (NRCH)
DRE .... Display Remoting Enhancement (CCCA)
DRE .... Display Remoting Equipment (SAUS)
DRE .... District Reserve Equipment [*Army*] (AABC)
DRE .... Diversity Reception Equipment
DRE .... Divisional Road Engineer (SAUO)
DRE .... Doctor of Recreation Education (GAGS)
D Re .... Doctor of Religion
DRE .... Doctor of Religious Education
DRE .... Dokumentationsring Elektrotechnik [*Database*]
DRE .... Doppler RADAR Equipment
DRE .... Downrange Error [*NASA*]
DRE .... Drachma [*Monetary unit in Greece*] (EY)
DRE .... Drewrys Ltd. USA, Inc. (SAUO)
DRE .... Duke Realty Investments, Inc. [*NYSE symbol*] (SPSG)
DRE .... Duke-Weeks Realty [*NYSE symbol*] (SG)
DRE .... Michigan Airways, Inc. [*ICAO designator*] (FAAC)
DREA .... Defence Research Establishment, Atlantic [*Canada*]
DREA .... Dreco Energy Services Ltd. [*NASDAQ symbol*] (SAG)
DREAC .... Drum Experimental Automatic Computer (IAA)
DREAF .... Dreco Energy Svcs 'A' [*NASDAQ symbol*] (TTSB)
DREAM .... Data Requirements, Evaluation, and Management (ABAC)
DREAM .... Data Retrieval, Entry, and Management
DREAM .... Design Realization, Evaluation, and Modelling (MHDI)
DREAM .... Development Rehabilitation of the Environment through Arts and Media [*Philippines Earth Savers movement*]
DREAM .... Digital Recording and Measurement [*Computer science*] (MHDI)
DREAM .... Distributed Real-Time Ever Available Microcomputing Laboratory [*University of California, Irvine*] [*Research center*] (RCD)
DREAMS .... Data Retrieval, Entry, and Management Systems (DGA)
drec .... Descant Recorder
DREC .... Detection RADAR Electronic Component
DRec .... Directorate of Records (SAUO)
Dr Ec .... Doctor of Economics
DRECAM .... Dresdner Bank - Cash- Management-System (SAUS)
DrecoE .... Dreco Energy Services Ltd. [*Associated Press*] (SAG)
DRECP .... Design Release Engineering Change Proposal (MCD)
DREC Process ... Device Recognition Process (SAUS)
DRECT .... Conservation Technologies (SAUS)
DRECT .... Demonstration of Resource and Energy (SAUS)
DRECT .... Development of Resource and Energy Consetvation Technologies (SAUS)
DRED .... Daily Readiness [*Testing*] (MCD)
DRED .... Data Routing and Error Detecting (or Detector) (SAUS)
DRED .... Deferred Requisitioning of Engineering Drawings (SAUS)
DRED .... Detection RADAR Environmental Display [*Air Force*]
DRED .... Directed Rocket Engine Demonstrator
DR Ed .... Doctor of Religious Education
DRED .... Dredger (SAUS)
DRED .... Dredging (SAUS)
DRED .... Ducted Rocket Engine Development (MCD)
DREDF .... Disability Rights Education and Defense Fund (EA)
DREE .... Department of Regional Economic Expansion [*Canada*]
DREE .... Director of Royal Engineer Equipment (SAUO)
D Re E .... Doctor of Refrigeration Engineering
D Re Eng .... Doctor of Refrigeration Engineering

D-REF .... Data Reference [*Environment Canada*] [*Information service or system*] [*Information service or system*] (CRD)
DREF .... Distribution Research and Education Foundation (EA)
DREF .... Dose Rate Effectiveness Factor [*Toxicology of radiation*]
DREF System... Data Reference System (SAUS)
DREG .... Data Regulations (KSC)
DREG .... Dressing (MSA)
DREGE .... Diabetes Retrieval Element Generator and Executor
DREK .... Dead Reckoning (SAUS)
DrElectEngin... Doctor of Electrical Engineering (SAUS)
DRelEd .... Doctor of Religious Education
DREM .... Department of Rangeland Ecology and Management (SAUO)
DREM .... Department of Resources and Management (SAUO)
DREME .... Division of Research and Evaluation in Medical Education [*Ohio State University*] [*Research center*] (RCD)
DREN .... Defense Research and Engineering Network [*DoD*]
Dr En .... Doctor of English
Dr Eng .... Doctor of Engineering
DrEngin .... Doctor of Engineering (SAUS)
Dr Ent .... Doctor of Entomology
DREO .... Defence Research Establishment, Ottawa [*Canada*]
DREO .... Defense Research and Engineering Office [*DoD*]
DREO .... Design Revision Engineering Order (SAUS)
DREP .... Defence Research Establishment, Pacific [*Canada*]
DRep .... Ohio Decisions Reprint [*A publication*] (DLA)
D Repata ..... Director of Repatriation (SAUO)
DREPO .... District Reserve Electronics Program Officer
DRepr .... Ohio Decisions Reprint [*A publication*] (DLA)
DRES .... DARCOM [*Development and Readiness Command, Army*] Readiness Evaluation System (MCD)
DRES .... Defence Research Establishment, Suffield [*Canada*] (MCD)
DRES .... Dietary Risk Evaluation System [*Environmental Protection Agency*] (EPAT)
DRES .... Direct Reading Emission Spectrograph (NRCH)
D/RES .... Disassembly/resassembly equipment station (SAUS)
DRES .... Dresden [*City in East Germany*] (ROG)
DresB .... Dress Barn, Inc. [*Associated Press*] (SAG)
Dres Int Rev... Dresse on Internal Revenue Laws [*A publication*] (DLA)
DRESS .... Dendenkosha Real-time Sales and Inventory Management System (SAUS)
DRESS .... Depth Resolved Surface Coil Spectroscopy
Dressr .... Dresser Industries, Inc. [*Associated Press*] (SAG)
DRESTC .... Defence Research Establishment, Suffield, Test Centre [*British*] (NATG)
DRET .... Defence Research Establishment, Toronto [*Canada*]
DRET .... Defense Research Establishment, Toronto (SAUS)
DRET .... Direct Re-Entry Telecommunications (SAUS)
DRET .... Direct Reentry Telemetry [*Air Force*] (MCD)
DRET .... Dissociative Return Electron Transfer
DRETS .... Direct Reentry Telemetry System [*Air Force*]
DREV .... Defence Research Establishment in Valcarier (SAUS)
DREV .... Defence Research Establishment, Valcartier [*Canada*]
DREVX .... Dreyfus Fund [*Mutual fund ticker symbol*] (SG)
Drew .... Charles E. Drew Postgraduate Medical School (SAUS)
Drew .... Drewry's English Vice Chancellors' Reports [*A publication*] (DLA)
Drew .... Drew's Reports [*13 Florida*] [*A publication*] (DLA)
Drew & S..... Drewry and Smale's English Chancery Reports [*A publication*] (DLA)
Drew & S (Eng)... Drewry and Smale's English Chancery Reports [*A publication*] (DLA)
Drew & Sm... Drewry and Smale's English Chancery Reports [*A publication*] (DLA)
Drew Ch F... Drewry's Chancery Forms [*1876*] [*A publication*] (DLA)
Drew (Eng)... Drewry's English Chancery Reports [*A publication*] (DLA)
Drew Eq Pl... Drewry's Equity Pleading [*A publication*] (DLA)
DrewInd ...... Drew Industries, Inc. [*Associated Press*] (SAG)
Drew Inj ...... Drewry on Injunctions [*1841*] [*A publication*] (DLA)
Drew Pat ..... Drewry's Patent Law Amendment Act [*1838*] [*A publication*] (DLA)
drews .... direct readout equatorial satellite (SAUS)
DREWS .... Direct Readout Equatorial Weather Satellite
Drew Tr M... Drewry's Trade Marks [*1878*] [*A publication*] (DLA)
Drew U .... Drew University (GAGS)
Drexel Libr Q... Drexel Library Quarterly (journ.) (SAUS)
Drexel U ...... Drexel University (GAGS)
Drexlr .... Drexler Technology Corp. [*Associated Press*] (SAG)
DreyerG ...... Dreyer's Grand Ice Cream, Inc. [*Associated Press*] (SAG)
DREZ .... Dorsal Root Entry Zone [*Medicine*]
DRF .... Daily Replacement Factor [*Of lymphocytes*] [*Medicine*]
DRF .... Dairy Remembrance Fund (EA)
DRF .... Dance Research Foundation (EA)
DRF .... Dan River 'A' [*NYSE symbol*] (SG)
DRF .... Data Recovery Field [*Computer science*] (MWOL)
DRF .... Data Reporting Form
DRF .... Data Request Form [*NASA*] (NASA)
DRF .... Data Requirement Form (KSC)
DRF .... Deafness Relief Foundation (SAUO)
DRF .... Deafness Research Foundation (EA)
DRF .... Deliberate Reinforcement Force (SAUO)
DRF .... Depot Recovery Factor (MCD)
DRF .... Depreciation Reserve Fund [*Indian Railway*] (TIR)
DRF .... Depression Range Finder [*British military*] (DMA)
DRF .... Destiny Research Foundation (EA)
DRF .... Diamond Radiation Facility
DRF .... Differential Reinforcement [*Psychometrics*]
DRF .... Differentiation Retarding Factor [*Cytology*]
DRF .... Digital, Radio Frequency (MCD)
DRF .... Digital Raster File (SAUS)
DRF .... Direct Radiative Forcing [*Atmospheric science*]
DRF .... Direct Relief Foundation [*Later, DRI*]
DRF .... Dirty Rotten Form [*Slang*] (ADA)
D/RF .... Disassembly/reassembly fixture (SAUS)
DRF .... Disaster Relief Fund (SAUO)
DRF .... Disaster Response Force [*Military*]
DRF .... Discharge Ringing Frequency
DRF .... Discrepancy Report Form (SAUS)
DRF .... Distortion-Rate Function (SAUS)
DRF .... Division Ready Force [*Army*] (MCD)
DRF .... Doctorate Records File [*National Research Council*] [*Information service or system*] (CRD)
Dr F .... Doctor of Forestry
DRF .... Documentation Request Form (MCD)
DRF .... Documentation Requisition Form (SAUS)
DRF .... Dose Range Finding [*Medicine*] (DB)
DRF .... Dose Reduction Factor (DEN)
drf .... Draft (SAUS)
DRF .... Driver Related Factor [*National Highway Traffic Safety Administration Fatal Accident Recording System code*]
DRF .... Dry Rectifier
DRF .... Dual Role Fighter (MCD)
DRF .... Duke Realty Inv [*NYSE symbol*] (TTSB)
DRF .... Kenai, AK [*Location identifier*] [*FAA*] (FAAL)
DRF .... SAR Data Reception Facility (SAUS)
DRFB .... Doubly Refractile Fat Bodies [*Biochemistry*] (DAVI)
DRFC .... David Rappaport Fan Club (EA)
DRFC .... Del Reeves Fan Club (EA)
Dr Fi .... Doctor of Finance
DRFL .... Drainage Fluid [*Medicine*] (DAVI)
dr fl .... dram, fluid (SAUS)
DRflmnBad... Distinguished Rifleman Badge [*Military decoration*] (AABC)
DRFM .... Digital Radio Frequency Memory (ADWA)
DRFN .... Driefontein Consolidated [*NASDAQ symbol*] (NQ)
DRFNY .... Dviefontein Consol ADR [*NASDAQ symbol*] (TTSB)
DRFO .... Danube River Field Organization [*Allied German Occupation Forces*]
DRFP .... Design-Rated Full Power (DNAB)
DRFP .... Division of Retail Food Protection [*Food and Drug Administration*]
DRFP .... Draft Request for Proposal (MCD)
DRFR .... Division of Research Facilities and Resources [*National Institutes of Health*]
DRFS .... Defense Reactor Fuel Supply (SAUS)
DRFS .... destination rail freight station (SAUS)
DRFS .... Destination Rail Station [*MARAD*] (TAG)
drft .... draft (SAUS)
dr/ft .... Dram per Foot (SAUS)
DRFT .... Drift [*NWS*] (FAAC)
DR/FTIR ...... Diffuse Reflectance/Fourier Transform Infrared Spectroscopy (SAUS)
drftm .... draftsman (SAUS)
drftmn .... Draftsman (SAUS)
DRFTNG ...... Drafting
Drftsmn ...... Draftsman (SAUS)
DRFX .... Drill Fixture
DRG .... Data Reporting Guideline [*Environmental Protection Agency*]
DRG .... Data Resource Group (TIMI)
DRG .... Davey Resource Group (SAUO)
DRG .... Deering [*Alaska*] [*Airport symbol*] (OAG)
DRG .... Defense Research Group [*NATO*]
DRG .... Democratic Republic of Germany (SAUS)
DR-G .... Deputy Registrar-General [*British*]
DRG .... Detroit Rubber Group (SAUO)
DRG .... Development and Research Group (SAUO)
DRG .... Diagnosis Related Group (SAUO)
DRG .... Diagnosis-Related Group [*Insurance*] (WYGK)
DRG .... Diagnostic Related Group [*Medicine*]
DRG .... Dickinson Robinson Group Ltd. [*British*]
DRG .... Digital Ranging Generator [*Apollo*] [*NASA*]
DRG .... Digital Raster Graphic (SAUS)
DRG .... Directional Receiver Group (SAUO)
drg .... Dirigible (SAUS)
DRG .... Disaster Research Group [*National Academy of Sciences*]
DRG .... Division of Research Grants [*National Institutes of Health*]
DRG .... Dorsal Respiratory Group [*Medicine*]
DRG .... Dorsal Root Ganglia (SAUS)
DRG .... Dorsal Root Ganglion [*Neuroanatomy*]
DRG .... Double Reduction Gear (SAUS)
DRG .... Drag
drg .... Drainage (MELL)
DRG .... Drawing
Drg .... Dredger (SAUS)
DRG .... DRG, Inc. [*Toronto Stock Exchange symbol*]
DRG .... Drilling (SAUS)
DRG .... Drogue (KSC)
DRG .... During
Dr Ge .... Doctor of Geology
DRGE .... Drainage (MELL)
Dr Geo .... Doctor of Geography
DRGM .... Director-General of Repair and Maintenance (SAUO)
DRGMX .... Dreyfus GNMA [*Mutual fund ticker symbol*] (SG)
DRGN .... Distributed Real-Time Groove Network [*Computer science*]
DRGN .... Dragon
DRGP .... Digital Representation of Graphic Products (SAUS)
Dr GP .... Doctor of Geopolitics
DRGR .... Dredger (MSA)
DRGs .... Diagnosis-Related Groups (SAUO)

DRGS.......... Direct Readout Ground Station
DRGS.......... Direct Readout Ground System (ACAE)
DRGW.......... [*The*] Denver & Rio Grande Western Railroad Co. [*AAR code*]
DR/GW.......... Directorate of Ranges, Guided Weapons (SAUO)
DRGWR.......... Denver and Rio Grande Western Railroad (SAUS)
DRH.......... CDC Division of Reproductive Health (SAUS)
DRH.......... Data Reading Head (SAUS)
drh.......... Differential Reinforcement of High Rate [*B.F. Skinner*] (DIPS)
DRH.......... Digital Readout Head [*Computer science*]
DRH.......... Division of Radiological Health (SAUS)
DRH.......... Division of Reproductive Health (SAUO)
DRH.......... DriverHarris [*AMEX symbol*] (TTSB)
DRH.......... Driver-Harris Co. [*AMEX symbol*] (SPSG)
Drhc.......... Doctor Honoris Causa [*Honorary Doctor*] [*Latin*] (BARN)
DRHD.......... Drill Head
DRHI.......... Horton [*D.R.*], Inc. [*NASDAQ symbol*] (SAG)
Dr HL.......... Doctor of Humanities of Learning
DRHLA.......... Double-Conductor, Radio, High-Tension, Lead-Armored [*Cable*] (IAA)
DRHLA Cable... Double-conductor, Radio, High-Tension, Lead-Armoured Cable (SAUS)
DRHM.......... Durham [*City and county in England*]
DRHO.......... Divisional Road Haulage Officer (SAUO)
Dr Hor.......... Doctor of Horticulture
DR Hort.......... DR Horton, Inc. [*Associated Press*] (SAG)
DR Horton... DR Horton, Inc. [*Associated Press*] (SAG)
DRHP.......... Diagnosis and Remediation of Handwriting Problems [*Educational test*]
Dr HS.......... Doctor of Humanitarian Service
Dr Hy.......... Doctor of Hygiene
DRHY.......... Durham Transport [*Federal Railroad Administration identification code*]
DrHyg.......... Doctor of Hygiene (DAVI)
DRI.......... Darden Restaurants [*NYSE symbol*] (TTSB)
DRI.......... Darden Restaurants, Inc. [*NYSE symbol*] (SAG)
DRI.......... Data Rate Indicator (NASA)
DRI.......... Data Recording Instrument (IAA)
DRI.......... Data Recording Instrument Co. Ltd. (SAUO)
DRI.......... Data Recording Instruments Ltd. (SAUS)
DRI.......... Data Recording Interface (MCD)
DRI.......... Data Reduction Interpreter
DRI.......... Data Resources, Inc. [*Database originator and operator*] [*Information service or system*] (IID)
DRI.......... Data Routing Indicator
DRI.......... Davenport, Rock Island & North Western Railway Co. [*AAR code*]
DRI.......... Dead Reckoning Indicator (MSA)
DRI.......... Decision Relevant Information (SAUS)
DRI.......... Declarative Referential Integrity (SAUS)
DRI.......... Deductible Requirement Rider [*Health insurance*] (GHCT)
DRI.......... Defense Research Institute [*Later, DRI - Defense Research and Trial Lawyers Association*] (EA)
DRI.......... Defense Research Internet [*DoD*] (CIST)
DRI.......... Dental Research Institute [*University of California, Los Angeles*] [*Research center*] (RCD)
DRI.......... Denver Research Institute [*University of Denver*] [*Research center*]
DRI.......... Department of Resource Industries [*Queensland*] [*Australia*]
DRI.......... De Ridder, LA [*Location identifier*] [*FAA*] (FAAL)
DRI.......... Descent Rate Indicator [*Aviation*]
DRI.......... Desert Research Institute [*University of Nevada*] [*Research center*]
DRI.......... Development of Regional Impact [*Land use*]
DRI.......... Diabetes Research Institute [*University of Miami*] [*Research center*] (RCD)
DRI.......... Dietary Reference Intakes
DRI.......... Differential Refractive Index Detector (MCD)
DRI.......... Digital Reflective Imaging [*Pioneer*]
DRI.......... Digital Research, Inc.
DRI.......... Digit Record Identification (SAUS)
DRI.......... Directorate of Research and Information (SAUO)
DRI.......... Direct reading instruments (SAUS)
DRI.......... Direct Read-Out Infrared (PDAA)
dri.......... direct reduced iron (SAUS)
DRI.......... Direct Reduction Iron [*Ironmaking process*]
DRI.......... Direct Relief International (EA)
DRI.......... Direct Rooming In [*Medicine*] (DAVI)
DRI.......... Disaster Recovery Institute International (NTPA)
DRI.......... Disaster Research Institute (EAIO)
DRI.......... Discharge Readiness Inventory (MAE)
DRI.......... Document Retrieval Index
DRI.......... Document revision instruction receipt (SAUS)
DRI.......... Dose Rate Instrumentation
DRI.......... Drive
DRI.......... Dual Roll Idler
DRI.......... Duct removal/installation (SAUS)
DRI.......... Dynamic Response Index
DRI.......... Dynamic Rotation Isomeric (UWER)
D RI.......... United States District Court for the District of Rhode Island (DLA)
DRIB.......... Deoxyribose (SAUS)
dRib.......... Deoxyribose [*Genetics*] and Laboratory (DAVI)
DRI-BAS.......... DRI [*Data Resources, Inc.*] Bank Analysis Service [*Information service or system*] (CRD)
DRIC.......... Defence Research Information Centre [*Research center*] [*British*]
DRIC.......... Dental Research Information Center (DIT)
DRIC.......... Dispute Resolution Information Center (SAUS)
DRI-CEI.......... DRI [*Data Resources, Inc.*] Current Economic Indicators Data Bank [*Information service or system*] (CRD)
DRICO.......... Data Recording Instrument Company (SAUO)
DRICOM.......... DRI [*Data Resources, Inc.*] Commodities [*Information service or system*] (CRD)
DRID.......... Deflection Refractive Index Detector
drid.......... direct-readout image disector (SAUS)
DRID.......... Direct Readout Image Dissector [*Camera system*]
DRID.......... Double Radial Immunodiffusion [*Medicine*] (DMAA)
DRID.......... Double Radioisotope Derivative [*Medicine*] (EDAA)
DRIDAC.......... Drum Input to Digital Automatic Computer
DRIDR.......... De Ridder, LA [*American Association of Railroads railroad junction routing code*]
DRIE.......... Deep Reactive Ion Etching
DRIE.......... Department of Regional Industrial Expansion [*Canada*]
DriefC.......... Driefontein Consolidated Ltd. [*Associated Press*] (SAG)
DRIF.......... Defense Freight Railway Interchange Fleet [*Army*] (DNAB)
DRIF.......... Diabetes Research Institute Fund
DRIF.......... Disposal Regional Inventory File [*Military*] (AFIT)
DRI-FACS.......... DRI [*Data Resources, Inc.*] Financial and Credit Statistics [*Information service or system*] (CRD)
DRIFT.......... Diagnostic Retrievable Information for Teachers (SAUS)
DRIFT.......... Diffuse effectance infrared Fourier transform spectroscopy (SAUS)
DRIFT.......... Diffuse Reflectance Infrared Fourier Transform [*Spectrometry*]
DRIFT.......... Diversity Receiving Instrumentation for Telemetry
DRIFT.......... Dynamic Reliability Instantaneous Forecasting Technique
DRIFTEX.......... Drift-card Experiment in the Mediterranean Sea (SAUS)
DRIFTS.......... Diffuse Reflectance Infrared Fourier Transform Spectroscopy
DRIG.......... Digital Rate-Integrating Gyro (MCD)
DRIL.......... Detect, Recognize, Identify, and Locate [*Military*]
DRIL.......... Directorio Revolucionario Iberico de Liberta [*Revolutionary Directorate for Iberian Liberation*]
DRILL.......... Delaware Rapid Interlibrary Loan and Reference Service (SAUO)
DRILL.......... Delaware Rapid Interlibrary Loan Project [*Library network*]
DRILL.......... Direct Routing Investigation of Line Layouts (VLIE)
DRILL.......... Drilling
DRILRON.......... Drilling Squadron (SAUO)
DRILS.......... Defense Retail Interservice Logistic Support [*Military*]
DRIMS.......... Diagnostic Rifle Marksmanship Simulator (MCD)
dr/in.......... Dram per Inch (SAUS)
DRINC.......... Dairy Research, Inc. (EA)
Dr Ind.......... Doctor of Industry
D-ring.......... Capital-D-shaped ring (SAUS)
Dr Ing.......... Doctor Ingeniariae [*Doctor of Engineering*]
Drink.......... Drinking (MIST)
Drink.......... Drinkwater's English Common Pleas Reports [*1840-41*] [*A publication*] (DLA)
Drinkw.......... Drinkwater's English Common Pleas Reports [*1840-41*] [*A publication*] (DLA)
Drinkwater... Drinkwater's English Common Pleas Reports [*1840-41*] [*A publication*] (DLA)
Drinkw (Eng)... Drinkwater's English Common Pleas Reports [*1840-41*] [*A publication*] (DLA)
DRIP.......... Data Reduction Input Program [*Computer science*]
DRIP.......... Data Rich, Information Poor [*Medicine*] (AMHC)
DRIP.......... Dead Reckoning Information Processor (SAUS)
DRIP.......... Digital Ray and Intensity Projector
DRIP.......... Dividend Reinvestment Plan [*Also, DRP*]
DRIP.......... Downspout Rechargement Infusion Program [*Energy development program*]
DRIPP.......... Drip Proof (SAUS)
DRIPS.......... Dynamic Real-Time Information Processing System (MCD)
DRIR.......... Denver Rock Island Railroad [*Federal Railroad Administration identification code*]
DRIR.......... Direct Read-out Infra-Red (SAUS)
DRIR.......... Direct Readout Infrared Radiometer
DRIRC.......... Defence Research and Intramural Resources Committee (SAUS)
DRIRU.......... Dry Rotor Inertial Reference Unit [*NASA*] (NASA)
DRIS.......... Debt Reconstruction Interest Subsidy (SAUS)
DRIS.......... Defense Retail Interservice Support [*Military*] (MCD)
DRIS.......... Department of Defense Retail Interservice Support Program (SAUS)
DRIS.......... Diagnosis and Recommended Integrated System [*Plant pathology*]
DRIS.......... Diagnostic Radiology Information System (SAUS)
DRIS.......... Diffuse Reflectance Infrared Spectroscopy [*Physics*]
DRIS.......... Digital Read-In System [*Computer science*] (DNAB)
DRI-SEC.......... DRI [*Data Resources, Inc.*] US Equity and Debt Securities [*Information service or system*] (CRD)
DRISS.......... Digital Read-In Subsystem [*Computer science*]
DRIT.......... Diagnostic Retrievable Information for Teachers (SAUS)
DRIT.......... DTIC Retrieval and Indexing Terminology [*DoD*]
DRIU.......... Damage Repair Instruction Unit (SAUS)
DRI-UP.......... Decent Respectable Individuals-United for Progress (SAUS)
Dr Iur.......... Doctor of Laws
DRIV.......... Digital River, Inc. [*NASDAQ symbol*] (NASQ)
DRIV.......... Drive [*Automotive engineering*]
DRIVE.......... Dedicated Road Infrastructure for Vehicle safety in Europe [*Automotive navigation systems*]
DRIVE.......... Dedicated Road Infrastructure of Vehicle Safety [*European Community*] (MHDB)
DRIVE.......... Democratic Republican Independent Voter Education Committee [*Political Action Committee*]
DRIVE.......... Developing Resources for Instructors of Vocational Education (SAUS)
DRIVE.......... Digital Raster Imaging, Viewing, and Editing system (SAUS)
DRIVE.......... Document Read, Information Verify, and Edit
DRIVE.......... Document Review into Video Entry (SAUS)
DRIVE.......... Drive [*Commonly used*] (OPSA)
DRIVE.......... Driving

DRIVER .... Division of Research and Improvement, Vocational Education, and Rehabilitation [*Department of Education*]
DRIVES .... Drives [*Commonly used*] (OPSA)
DrivHar .... Driver-Harris Co. [*Associated Press*] (SAG)
DRIZ .... Drackett [*Federal Railroad Administration identification code*]
DRJ .... Data Requirements Justification [*Military*]
DRJ .... Discipline Rules for Judges (SAUO)
DrJ .... Doctor Juris [*Doctor of Law*]
DRJG .... Drill Jig
DRJI .... Drill Jig (AAG)
Dr JS .... Doctor of Judicial Science
Dr J Sc .... Doctor of Judicial Science
DrJU .... Doctor Juris Utriusque [*Doctor of Both Laws*]
Dr Jur .... Doctor Juris [*Doctor of Law*] (EY)
Dr Jur Can ... Doctor Juris Canonici [*Doctor of Canon Law*] [*Latin*]
Dr Jur et Rer Pol ... Doctor of Laws and Political Science
DRK .... Dark
DRK .... Data Record Key (SAUS)
DRK .... Data Request Keyboard
DRK .... Democratic People's Republic of Korea
DRK .... Derrick (MSA)
DRK .... Display Request Keyboard (KSC)
DRK .... Druk Air [*Bhutan*] [*ICAO designator*] (FAAC)
DRK .... Drunk [*FBI standardized term*]
DRKL .... Defence Research Kingston Laboratory [*Canada*] (MCD)
DRKN .... Durakon Industries [*NASDAQ symbol*] (TTSB)
DRKN .... Durakon Industries, Inc. [*NASDAQ symbol*] (NQ)
DRL .... Data Record Language (SAUS)
DRI .... Data Reduction Interpreter (SAUS)
DRL .... Data Reduction Laboratory
DRL .... Data Requirement List (KSC)
DRL .... Data Requirements Language
DRL .... Data Requirements List (SAUS)
DRL .... Data Retrieval Language [*National Institute of Standards and Technology*]
DRL .... Date Required to Load (AABC)
DRL .... Daytime Running Lights [*Automotive engineering*]
DRL .... Defense Research Laboratories (or Laboratory) (SAUO)
DRL .... Defense Research Laboratory
DRL .... Deliverables Requirement List (SAUS)
DRL .... Department of Romance Languages (SAUO)
DRL .... Derlan Industries Ltd. [*Toronto Stock Exchange symbol*]
DRL .... Design Report Letter (SAUS)
DRL .... Design Review List (MCD)
DRL .... Device Research Laboratory [*University of California, Los Angeles*] (UWER)
DRL .... Diamond Research Laboratory (SAUS)
drl .... Differential Reinforcement of Low Rate [*B.F. Skinner*] (DIPS)
DRL .... Differential Reinforcement of Low Rate [*Psychometrics*]
DRL .... differential reinforcement of low response rates (SAUS)
DRL .... Digital Readout Light [*Computer science*]
DRL .... DI Industries [*Formerly, Drillers, Inc.*] [*AMEX symbol*] (SPSG)
DRL .... Diode Resistor Logic (IAA)
DRL .... Directional Reference Locator
DRL .... Direct Retrieval Language (NITA)
DRL .... Dirty Region Logging (SAUS)
DRL .... Divisional Records List (VLIE)
DRL .... Division of Reactor Licensing [*AEC*]
DRL .... Document Requirement List (KSC)
DRL .... Dorsal Root Lumbar [*Medicine*] (EDAA)
DRL .... Double Rail Logic (VLIE)
DRL .... Drilling Research Laboratory (SAUS)
DRL .... Drug-Related Lupus [*Medicine*] (DMAA)
DRL .... Dynamically Reconfigurable Logic (SAUS)
Drlct .... derelict (SAUS)
Dr Lett .... Doctor of Letters (SAUS)
DRLG .... Danish Royal Life Guards (SAUS)
Drlg .... Drilling (SAUS)
DRLI .... Data Requirements List Item (SSD)
DRLI .... Drug Literature (SAUS)
Dr Lit .... Doctor of Literature
Dr Litt .... Doctor of Letters
Dr LL .... Doctor of Laws
DRLL .... Drill
DRLM .... Depolarized Reflected Light Microscopy
DRLM .... Digital Radar Land Mass (SAUS)
DRLMS .... Digital Radar Landmass Simulation System (SAUS)
DRLMS .... Digital RADAR Landmass Simulator
DRLR .... Dehri Rohtas Light Railway [*Indian Railway*] (TIR)
DRL/S .... Data Requirements List/Schedule
DRLS .... Del Rio Language Screening [*Speech and language therapy*] (DAVI)
DRLS .... Despatch Rider Letter Service (SAUO)
DRLS .... Despatch-Rider Letter-Service [*Military*] [*British*]
DRLS .... Dispatch Rider Letter Service (SAUS)
Dr LS .... Doctor of Library Science
DRLS .... Dragon Remote Launch System [*Military*] (MCD)
DRL/UT .... Defense Research Laboratory/University of Texas (MUGU)
DRlys .... Director of Railways (SAUO)
DRM .... Damaged Rim [*Tire maintenance*]
DRM .... Data Recording Medium (SAUS)
DRM .... Data Records Management (MCD)
DRM .... Data Resource Management (NITA)
DRM .... Data Retrieval Mode
DRM .... Dead Reckoning Module
DRM .... Decay Rate Meter
DRM .... Decay Repair Technician (SAUS)
DRM .... Decimal Rate Multiplier (IAA)
DRM .... Defense Research Member (AAGC)
DRM .... Defense Resource Management (AAGC)
DRM .... Defense Resources Model [*Congressional Budget Office*] (GFGA)
DRM .... Dental Repair Technician [*Navy*]
DRM .... Department of Resources and Management (SAUO)
DRM .... Depositional Remanent Magnetization (IAA)
DRM .... Design Reference Mission [*NASA*]
DRM .... Design Reference Model (KSC)
DRM .... Destination Release Mechanism (VERA)
DRM .... Destructive Readout Memory (DNAB)
DRM .... Detrital Remanent Magnetization [*Geophysics*]
DRM .... Development Rate Monitor (SAUS)
DRM .... Development Reactor Mock-Up
DRM .... Diagnostic Record Matching (VLIE)
DRM .... Diamond Shamrock [*NYSE symbol*] (TTSB)
DRM .... Diamond Shamrock Co. [*NYSE symbol*] (SPSG)
DRM .... Digital Radiometer
DRM .... Digital Radio Mondiale (SAUS)
DRM .... Digital Range Machine
DRM .... Digital Range Meter (SAUS)
DRM .... Digital Relief Mapping (SAUO)
DRM .... Digital Relief Maps (SAUO)
DRM .... Digital Rights Management
DRM .... Digital Road Map [*Digital Equipment Corp.*] (PCM)
DRM .... Diploma in Resource Management (ADA)
DRM .... Direction of Relative Movement [*Navigation*]
DRM .... Directorate for Resource Management [*CIA*]
DRM .... Direct Reduction Mortgage [*Banking*]
DRM .... Disaster Recovery Manager (DEMM)
DRM .... Disaster Resource Manager (SAUS)
DRM .... Display Refresh Memory (SAUS)
DRM .... Distributed Real time Multiprocessor (SAUS)
DRM .... Distributed Resource Management (SAUS)
DRM .... Distribution Requirements Module
DRM .... Divisional Railway Manager [*Indian Railway*] (TIR)
DRM .... DOD Reference Model (SAUS)
DRM .... Donor-Recipient Matching [*Medicine*] (MELL)
DRM .... Drafting [*or Drawing*] Room Manual
DRM .... Drama [*Greece*] [*Airport symbol*] (AD)
DRM .... Drawing Requirements Manual [*NASA*] (NASA)
DRM .... Dream
DRM .... Drum [*Shipping*]
DRM .... Drummond Island, MI [*Location identifier*] [*FAA*] (FAAL)
DRM .... Ducted Rocket Motor
DRM .... Dunraine Mines Ltd. [*Toronto Stock Exchange symbol*]
DRM .... Dynamic Recoil Mixing (SAUS)
DRM .... Dynamic Resources Management (VLIE)
DRMA .... Drama
DRMAJ .... Drum Major [*Marine Corps*]
DRMC .... Defense Resources Management Course (SAUO)
DRMD .... Duramed Pharmaceutical [*NASDAQ symbol*] (TTSB)
DRMD .... Duramed Pharmaceuticals, Inc. [*NASDAQ symbol*] (SAG)
DRME .... Division of Research in Medical Education (DMAA)
Dr Med .... Doctor of Medicine
DrMedUniv ... Doctor Medicinae Universae [*Latin*]
Dr Med Vet ... Doctor Medicinae Veterinariae [*Doctor of Veterinary Medicine*] [*Latin*]
DRMF .... Damon Runyon Memorial Fund for Cancer Research [*Later, DRWWCF*] (EA)
DRMFCR .... Damon Runyon Memorial Fund for Cancer Research, Inc [*Medicine*] (EDAA)
DRMI .... Dual Radio Magnetic Indicator (MCD)
DRML .... Defence Research Medical Laboratory [*Canada*]
DRMND .... Drummond, IL [*American Association of Railroads railroad junction routing code*]
DRMO .... Defense Reutilization and Marketing Office [*DoD*]
DRMO .... Defense Reutilization and Materials Organization (DOMA)
DRMO .... District Records Management Office [*or Officer*]
Dr Mont .... Doctor Rerum Montanarum [*Latin*]
DRMP .... Design Reference Mission Profile [*DoD*]
DRMP .... Division of Regional Medical Programs (SAUO)
DRMR .... Defense Re-utilization & Marketing Region (SAUS)
DRMS .... Data Record Management System (SAUS)
DRMS .... Data Resources Management System
DRMS .... Defense Reutilization and Marketing Service [*DoD*]
DRMS .... Deficiency Report Management System (ACAE)
DRMS .... Department of Defense Resource Management System (NG)
DRMS .... Design Rock-Mass Strength [*Mining technology*]
DRMS .... Digital Radiation Monitoring System (VLIE)
DRMS .... Distance Root Mean Square (FAAC)
DRMs .... drought relief measures (SAUS)
DRMS .... Drug Reaction Monitoring System [*Medicine*] (DMAA)
Dr MT .... Doctor of Mechanotherapy
DRMU .... Digital Remote Measurement Unit [*Computer science*] (VERA)
Dr Mus .... Doctor of Music
DRMV .... Digital Rights Management for Video (VLIE)
DRMX .... Danbury Railway Museum [*Private rail car owner code*]
DRMZ .... Drummond [*Federal Railroad Administration identification code*]
DRN .... Daily Reports Notice [*Air Force*] (AFM)
Drn .... Dairen (SAUS)
DRN .... Data Record Name (SAUS)
DRN .... Data Record Number (MCD)
DRN .... Data Reference Number

DRN .... Data Release Notice (DNAB)
DRN .... Data Routing Network (VLIE)
DRN .... Detroit River Navigation (SAUS)
drn .... Direction (SAUS)
DRN .... Directorate of Radio Navigation (SAUO)
DRN .... Dirranbandi [*Australia*] [*Airport symbol*] [*Obsolete*] (OAG)
DRN .... Disaster Research Newsletter (SAUO)
DRN .... Documentation Revision Notice (SAUS)
DRN .... Document Reference Number (SAUS)
DRN .... Document Release Notice [*Jet Propulsion Laboratory, NASA*]
DRN .... Document Revision Notice (MCD)
DRN .... Dorsal Raphe Nucleus [*Brain anatomy*]
DRN .... Dorsal Root Neurons [*Neuroanatomy*]
DRN .... Double-Round Nose
drn .... Drain (MIST)
DRN .... Drain (NASA)
DRN .... Drawn [*Cricket*] (ROG)
DRN .... Indonesian National Research Council (SAUO)
DRNA .... Desoxyribose Nucleic Acid (SAUS)
dRNA .... DNA[*Deoxyribonucleic Acid*]-like RNA[*Ribonucleic Acid*] [*Genetics*] (DOG)
dRNA .... Ribonucleic Acid, Diverse [*Biochemistry, genetics*]
DrNatSc .... Doctor of Natural Science
DrNatSci .... Doctor of Natural Science (NADA)
DrNatTechn ... Doctor Rerum Naturalium Technicarum [*Latin*]
DRNDP .... Diribonucleoside-3', 5'-Diphosphate (DB)
drng .... Drainage [*Medicine*] (DAVI)
DRNG .... Drainage
DRNK .... Cable Car Beverage [*NASDAQ symbol*] (TTSB)
DRNK .... Cable Car Beverage Corp. [*NASDAQ symbol*] (NQ)
DRNL .... Defence Research Northern Laboratory [*Canada*]
Dr No .... Drawing Number (SAUS)
Dr N Ph .... Doctor of Natural Philosophy
Dr N Sc .... Doctor of Natural Sciences
Dr N Sc .... Doctor of the Natural Sciences (SAUS)
DRnt .... Diagnostic Roentgenology [*Radiology*] (DAVI)
DRO .... Daily Receipt of Obligation [*Military*]
DRO .... Daily Report of Obligation [*Navy*] (NG)
DRO .... Daily Routine Order
DRO .... Dancing Room Only
DRO .... Danish Association of Medical Imaging (SAUO)
DRO .... Data Readout [*Navy*] (NVT)
DRO .... Day Room Orderly [*Army*]
DRO .... Delivery Release Order (SAUS)
DRO .... Demobilisation and Re-integration Office (SAUO)
DRO .... Desert Rose Resources [*Vancouver Stock Exchange symbol*]
DRO .... Design Requirements Overview (SAUS)
DRO .... Destructive Read-Only (SAUS)
DRO .... Destructive Read Operation (SAUS)
DRO .... Destructive Readout
DRO .... Destructive Read Out, Data Request Output (SAUO)
DRO .... Development Release Order
DRO .... Dielectric Resonator Oscillator (ACAE)
DRO .... Differential Reinforcement of Other Behavior [*Psychometrics*]
DRO .... Digital Readout [*Computer science*]
DRO .... Digital Readout Oscilloscope [*Computer science*]
DRO .... Digital Recording Oscilloscope (CIST)
DRO .... Digital Revision Overlay (SAUS)
dro .... Dinheiro [*Monetary unit*] [*Portugal*]
DRO .... Dining Room Orderly [*Military*] (VNW)
DRO .... Director of Recruiting and Organization [*Military*] [*British*]
DRO .... Directory of Religious Organizations [*A publication*]
DRO .... Direct Readout [*Computer science*]
DRO .... Direct Recording Oscillograph
DRO .... Disablement Resettlement Office [*or Officer*] [*British*]
DRO .... Disaster Recovery Operations (DEMM)
DRO .... Disposal Release Order [*DoD*]
DRO .... Divisional Records Office [*British military*] (DMA)
DRO .... Divisional Recruiting Officer (SAUO)
DRO .... Divisional Routine Order
DRO .... Division of Regional Operations (AAGC)
DRO .... Document Release Order (NASA)
DRO .... Domestic Route Order
DRO .... double resonant optical parametric oscillator (SAUS)
dro .... double-room occupancy (SAUS)
DRO .... Doubly Resonant Oscillator (IEEE)
DRO .... Drawing Requirement Outline
DRO .... Durango [*Colorado*] [*Airport symbol*] (OAG)
DRO .... Dynamic Runout [*Automotive engineering*]
DRO .... House Democratic Research Organization (EA)
DROC .... Democratic Republic of Congo (MILB)
DROD .... Delayed Readout Detector [*Satellite instrument*]
DROD .... digital read-out device (SAUS)
Dr of Eng ..... Doctor of Engineering
Dr of PE .... Doctor of Physical Education
Dr of Rec ..... Doctor of Recreation
Drof Sci in Engr ... Doctor of Science in Engineering (SAUS)
DROG .... Drogue
Droit CC .... Droit Civil Canadien [*A publication*] (DLA)
DROL .... Defense RDT & E [*Research, Development, Test, and Evaluation*] Online System [*DTIC*] (MCD)
DRO-LA .... Defense Research Office, Latin America [*Army*] (AABC)
DRO-LA .... Defense Research Office-Latin America (SAUS)
DRO-LA .... United States Army Element, Defense Research Office, Latin America (SAUO)
DROLLS .... Defense RDT&E On-Line System (AAGC)
DROLS .... Defense RDT & E [*Research, Development, Test, and Evaluation*] Online System [*DTIC*]
DROM .... Decoder Read-Only Memory
DROM .... Dromore [*District in Northern Ireland*] (ROG)
DROMDI ..... Direct Readout Miss Distance Indicator
DRON .... Data Reduction (MCD)
Drone Cop ... Drone on Copyrights [*A publication*] (DLA)
DROO .... Digital Readout Oscilloscope [*Computer science*]
DROO .... Durban Roodepoort Deep Ltd. [*NASDAQ symbol*] (SAG)
DROP .... Data Printout Program
DROP .... Distribution Register of Organic Pollutants [*In Water*] [*Environmental Protection Agency*]
DROP .... Distribution Register of Pollutants (SAUS)
DROP .... Dynamics of Rotating and Oscillating Free Drops (SAUS)
drop res .... Dropping Resistor (SAUS)
DROPS .... Demountable, Rack, Off-Loading, and Pick-Up System [*British Army*]
DRORM .... Draft & Records Officer, Royal Marines (SAUS)
DRORM .... Drafting and Records Office, Royal Marines [*British military*] (DMA)
DROS .... Data Returned from Overseas (SAUS)
DROS .... Date of Return from Overseas [*Army*]
DROS .... Date Returned from Overseas [*Military*]
DROS .... Dead Reckoning Own Ship
DROS .... Direct Readout Satellite
DROS .... disc resident operating system (SAUS)
DROS .... Disk Remote Operating System (SAUS)
DROS .... Disk Resident Operating System [*Computer science*] (IEEE)
Dr O Sc .... Doctor of the Science of Oratory
DROT .... Delayed Range on Target [*Air Force*]
DROT .... Direct Read Out Terminal (SAUS)
Dr OT .... Doctor of Occupational Therapy (PGP)
droupie .... Data groupie [*Person who likes to spend time in the company of programmers and data processing professionals.*] (CDE)
DROV .... Drovers Bancshares Corp. [*NASDAQ symbol*] (NASQ)
DROWS .... Direct Readout Weather Satellite
DRP .... Data Rapid Printer (SAUS)
DRP .... Data Reception Process [*Telecommunications*] (TEL)
DRP .... Data Record/Playback (CTAS)
DRP .... Data Reduction Procedure [*or Program*]
DRP .... Data Retrieval Program (CAAL)
DRP .... Dead Reckoning Plotter
DRP .... DECs Routing Protocol (SAUS)
DRP .... Defense Reactor Programs (SAUS)
DRP .... Degree of Reading Power [*Test*]
DRP .... Delayed Reenlistment Program [*Air Force*]
DRP .... Democratic Reform Party [*South Africa*] [*Political party*] (EY)
DRP .... Democratic Republican Party [*South Korea*] [*Political party*] (PPW)
DRP .... Demonstration Reprocessing Plant [*Nuclear energy*] (NUCP)
DRP .... Densest Random Packing [*Solid state physics*]
DRP .... Dental Radiography and Photography [*Journal*] [*Medicine*] (EDAA)
DRP .... Designated Repair [*or Rework*] Point [*Military*] (CAAL)
DRP .... Design Review Presentation (SAUS)
DRP .... Detailed refueling procedure (SAUS)
DRP .... Detected Radiant Power
DRP .... Deutsche Rechtspartei [*German Party of the Right*] [*Political party*] (PPE)
DRP .... Deutsches Reichspatent [*German State Patent*]
DRP .... Development Resources Panel [*United Nations Development Program*]
DRP .... Digital Recording Process
DRP .... Digoxin Reduction Products [*Clinical chemistry*]
DRP .... Directional Radiated Power [*Telecommunications*] (TEL)
DRP .... Directorate of Radio Production (SAUO)
DRP .... Directorate of Requirements and Programmes (SAUO)
DRP .... Director of Radio Production [*Air Ministry*] [*British*] [*World War II*]
DRP .... Direct Repair Program [*Automotive collision repairs*]
DRP .... Direct Requisitioning Procedure (DNAB)
DRP .... Disaster Recovery Plan [*Computer systems*]
DRP .... Discontinuously Reinforced Plastic
DRP .... Discoverer Research Program [*NASA*] (IAA)
DRP .... Dissolved Reactive Phosphorus [*Environmental science*]
DRP .... Distribution and Replication Protocol (SAUS)
DRP .... Distribution Reinvestment Program [*Stock exchange term*]
DRP .... Distribution Requirements Planning (GART)
DRP .... Distribution Resource Planning
DRP .... Dividend Reinvestment Plan [*Also, DRIP*]
DRP .... Divisional Records Practice (SAUS)
DRP .... Doctor of Regional Planning
DRP .... Documentation Research Project [*American Institute of Physics*]
DRP .... Dorsal Root Potential [*Anatomy*]
DRP .... Draft Requirements Package (MCD)
DRP .... Drawing Release Point (ACAE)
DRP .... Dredging Research Program [*U.S. Army Corps of Engineers*]
DRP .... Drill Plate [*Tool*] (MCD)
DRP .... Drone Recovery Platform (NVT)
DRP .... Drug-Related Problem (MELL)
DRP .... During Reporting Period
DRP .... Dynamic Rear Proportioning [*Automotive brake systems*]
DRP .... Dystrophin-Related Protein [*Biochemistry*]
DRPA .... Defense Research Projects Agency (SAUS)
DRPA .... Delaware River Port Authority
DRPA .... Distributed Relational Database Architecture (SAUS)
Dr Pa .... Doctor of Painting
Dr PA .... Doctor of Public Administration
DRPC .... Defence Research Policy Committee [*British*]

DRPC.......... Direct Reading Pocket Chamber
DRPC.......... Division Reliability Policy Committee (AAG)
Drpd.......... Dropped [*Army*]
DRPE.......... Dark-Rumped Petrel [*North American bird banding code*] (BIBA)
DRPE.......... Drill Plate [*Tool*] (AAG)
DRPG.......... Detroit Rubber and Plastics Group (SAUO)
DrPH.......... Doctor of Public Health (GAGS)
Dr PH.......... Doctor of Public Hygiene
Dr Pharm..... Doctor Pharmaciae [*Latin*]
Dr PH Hy..... Doctor of Public Health and Hygiene
Dr Phi.......... Doctor of Philanthropy
Dr Phil.......... Doctor of Philosophy (SAUS)
Dr Phil.......... Doctor Philosophiae [*Doctor of Philosophy*]
Dr Phil Fac Theol... Doctor Philosophiae Facultatis Theologicae [*Latin*]
Dr Phil Nat... Doctor of Natural Philosophy
Dr Philos..... Doctor of Philosophy
Dr Pho.......... Doctor of Photography
DRPHS.......... Dense Random Packing of Hard Spheres (MCD)
Dr Phy.......... Doctor of Physics
DRPI.......... Digital Rod Position Indication [*Nuclear energy*] (NRCH)
DRPL.......... Del Rio Public Library (SAUS)
DRPL.......... Drill Plate [*Tool*]
DRPLA.......... Dentatorubral Pallidoluysian Atrophy [*Medicine*]
DR Plot.......... Dead Reckoning Plot [*Navy*] (POLM)
DRPM.......... Direct Reporting Program Manager [*Navy*] (DOMA)
DRPO.......... Defense Resources Planning Operation (AAG)
DrPolSc.......... Doctor of Political Science (NADA)
Dr Pol Sci.... Doctor of Political Science
DRPP.......... Data Routing Patch Panel (MCD)
DRPP.......... Directorate of Research Programmes and Planning (SAUO)
DRPR.......... Drawing Practice (NG)
Dr Pr M.......... Doctor of Preventative Medicine
DRPS.......... Defence Radiological Protection Service (SAUS)
drps.......... digital random program selector (SAUS)
DRPS.......... disc real-time and programming system (SAUS)
DRPS.......... Disk Real-Time and Programming System [*Computer science*]
DRPS.......... Display Rapid Prototype System (ACAE)
drps.......... drapes (SAUS)
DRPS.......... Dry Reed Pushbutton Switch
DRPS.......... Dynamic Memory Relocation and Protection System (NITA)
Dr P Sc.......... Doctor of Physical Science
D RPT.......... Dead Reprint (DGA)
DRPTV.......... Ducted Rocket Propulsion Test Vehicle (MCD)
DRPZ.......... Drake Power [*Federal Railroad Administration identification code*]
DRQ.......... Data Ready Queue [*IBM Corp.*] (IBMDP)
DRQ.......... Data Request
DRQ.......... Diagnostic Radiographic Quality (MELL)
DRQ.......... Discomfort Relief Quotient [*Medicine*] (AAMN)
drq.......... Discomfort-Relief Quotient (DIPS)
DRQ.......... DMA Request (SAUS)
DRQ.......... Dril-Quip, Inc. [*NYSE symbol*] (SG)
DRR.......... Daily Regulatory Reporter
DRR.......... Data Read Register (SAUS)
DRR.......... Data Ready Reset (SAUS)
DRR.......... Data Recorder/Reproducer (MCD)
DRR.......... Data Redundancy Reduction [*or Removal*] (KSC)
DRR.......... Data Review Record [*Environmental Protection Agency*] (EPAT)
DRR.......... Department of Renewable Resources (SAUS)
DRR.......... Department of Rice Research (SAUO)
DRR.......... Deployment Readiness Review [*Aviation*] (FAAC)
DRR.......... Descent Rate RADAR
DRR.......... Design Release [*or Request*] Review
DRR.......... Design Requirements Review [*NASA*] (NASA)
DRR.......... Development Revision Record (KSC)
DRR.......... Digitally Reconstructed Radiography [*Medicine*] (DMAA)
DRR.......... Digital RADAR Relay
DRR.......... Directorate of Rice Research (SAUO)
DRR.......... Direct Reading Ratio (SAUS)
DRR.......... Direct Reading Receiver
DRR.......... Discounted Rate of Return [*Marketing*] (PDAA)
DRR.......... Disparity Reduction Rate [*Measures progress a country has made toward reconciling its current Physical Quality of Life Index with its optimum projected PQLI for the year 2000*] [*Overseas Development Council*]
DRR.......... Diversity Reception Receiver
DRR.......... Division of Research Resources [*Bethesda, MD*] [*National Institutes of Health*]
DRR.......... Document Release Record (NRCH)
DRR.......... Dorado Resources Ltd. [*Vancouver Stock Exchange symbol*]
DRR.......... Dorsal Root Reflex [*Medicine*] (EDAA)
DRR.......... Dough Rate of Reaction [*Food science*]
DRR.......... Drawing Release Record (SAUS)
DRR.......... Drawing revision record (SAUS)
DRR.......... Drug Research Reports (SAUO)
DRR.......... Durrie [*Australia*] [*Airport symbol*] [*Obsolete*] (OAG)
DRRA.......... Direct Reading Range Assessor (DNAB)
DRRA.......... Dura Automotive Sys'A' [*NASDAQ symbol*] (SG)
DRRA.......... Tessaoua [*Niger*] [*ICAO location identifier*] (ICLI)
Dr Ra E.......... Doctor of Radio Engineering (SAUS)
DrRaEng.......... Doctor of Radio Engineering (NADA)
DRRB.......... Data Requirements Review Board [*DoD*]
DRRC.......... Dogondoutchi [*Niger*] [*ICAO location identifier*] (ICLI)
Dr RCA.......... Doctor of the Royal College of Art
DRRD.......... Division of Reactor Research and Development [*Energy Research and Development Administration*]
DRRD.......... Dosso [*Niger*] [*ICAO location identifier*] (ICLI)
DRRE.......... Tera [*Niger*] [*ICAO location identifier*] (ICLI)
DrRec.......... Doctor of Recreation (NADA)
DrReEng...... Doctor of Refrigeration Engineering (NADA)
Dr Rer Comm... Doctor Rerum Commercialium [*Latin*]
Dr Rer Nat... Doctor Rerum Naturalium [*Doctor of Natural Science*] [*Latin*]
Dr Rer Pol... Doctor Rerum Politicarum [*Doctor of Political Science*] [*Latin*]
Dr Rer Soc Oec... Doctor Rerum Socialium Oeconomicarumque [*Latin*]
Dr Rer Tech... Doctor of Technical Science
DRRF.......... Division Rapid Reaction Force [*Army*] (AABC)
DRRG.......... Gaya [*Niger*] [*ICAO location identifier*] (ICLI)
DRRI.......... Bilma [*Niger*] [*ICAO location identifier*] (ICLI)
DRRI.......... Defense Race Relations Institute [*Air Force*]
DRRL.......... Digital RADAR Relay Link
DRRL.......... Tilabery [*Niger*] [*ICAO location identifier*] (ICLI)
DRRM.......... Maradi [*Niger*] [*ICAO location identifier*] (ICLI)
DRRN.......... Niamey Airport [*Niger*] [*ICAO location identifier*] (ICLI)
DRRP.......... La Tapoa [*Niger*] [*ICAO location identifier*] (ICLI)
DRRR.......... Niamey [*Niger*] [*ICAO location identifier*] (ICLI)
DRRS.......... Direct Reading Ratio Set (SAUS)
DRRT.......... Data Reception, Recording, and Transmission (MCD)
DRRT.......... Tahoua [*Niger*] [*ICAO location identifier*] (ICLI)
Dr R T Nap... Drury's Irish Chancery Reports Tempore Napier [*1858-59*] [*A publication*] (DLA)
Dr R T Sug... Drury's Irish Chancery Reports Tempore Sugden [*A publication*] (DLA)
DRRU.......... Ouallam [*Niger*] [*ICAO location identifier*] (ICLI)
DRRV.......... Niamey [*Niger*] [*ICAO location identifier*] (ICLI)
DRRX.......... Durect Corp. [*NASDAQ symbol*]
DRRZ.......... Dri-Rite [*Federal Railroad Administration identification code*]
DRS.......... Clarepine Industries, Inc. [*Toronto Stock Exchange symbol*]
DRS.......... Daily Receipt Sheet (SAUS)
DRS.......... Daily Release Sheet (SAUS)
DRS.......... Daily River Stages (NOAA)
DRS.......... Dairy Research Station (SAUS)
DRS.......... Dar Es Salaam [*Tanzania*] [*Geomagnetic observatory code*]
DRS.......... Data Rate Selector
DRS.......... Data Reaction System (AAG)
DRS.......... Data Receiving Station (KSC)
DRS.......... Data Receiving System (SAUS)
DRS.......... Data Recording Set
DRS.......... Data Recording System (MUGU)
DRS.......... Data Record Skip (SAUS)
DRS.......... Data Recovery System (SAUS)
DRS.......... Data Reduction Situation (SAUS)
DRS.......... Data Reduction Software (IAA)
DRS.......... Data Reduction System [*Computer science*]
DRS.......... Data Relay Satellite [*NASA*]
DRS.......... Data Relay Station (NASA)
DRS.......... Data Relay System (CAAL)
DRS.......... Data Requirements Specification (KSC)
DRS.......... Data Retrieval and Storage
DRS.......... Data Retrieval System [*Computer science*] (BUR)
DRS.......... Debtor Reporting System [*World Bank*]
DRS.......... Defense Research Sciences
DRS.......... Deficiency Reporting System [*Military*]
drs.......... degrees (SAUS)
DRS.......... Delayed Release Signal (SAUS)
DRS.......... Dementia Rating Scale [*Psychometric testing*]
DRS.......... Dendron Resource Surveys (SAUO)
DRS.......... Depolarized Rayleigh Scattering (UWER)
DRS.......... Descending Rectal Septum [*Medicine*] (EDAA)
DRS.......... Designator Ranging Subsystem (ACAE)
DRS.......... Design Recovery System (ACAE)
DRS.......... Design Requirement Sheet [*Military*]
DRS.......... Design Requirements Specifications (SAUS)
DRS.......... Detection and Ranging Set (CAAL)
DRS.......... Detection Ranging System (SAUS)
DRS.......... Development Reference Service [*Society for International Development*] (IID)
DRS.......... Development Requirements Specification [*Nuclear energy*] (NRCH)
DRs.......... Development Rights (SAUS)
DRS.......... Device Resource (SAUS)
DRS.......... Devon Record Society (SAUO)
DRS.......... Dexterous Robotics System [*NASA*] (SPST)
DRS.......... Diabetic Retinopathic Study [*National Eye Institute*]
DRS.......... Diagnostic Reading Scales [*Education*]
DRS.......... Diagnostic Research System (SAUS)
DRS.......... Diagnostic/Retrieval Sys [*AMEX symbol*] (TTSB)
DRS.......... Diagnostic/Retrieval Systems, Inc. [*AMEX symbol*] (SPSG)
DRS.......... Diagnostic Rework Sheets (AAG)
DRS.......... Diffuse Reflectance Spectroscopy (SAUS)
DRS.......... Diffuse Reflection Spectroscopy
DRS.......... Digital RADAR Simulator
DRS.......... Digital RADAR System
DRS.......... Digital Radio System (CCCA)
DRS.......... Digital Range Safety (NASA)
DRS.......... Digital Readout System [*Computer science*]
DRS.......... Digital Receiver Station [*Computer science*]
DRS.......... Digital Recording System
DRS.......... Digital Reference Sequence (SAUS)
D-R/S.......... Digital-to-Resolver/Synchro (SAUS)
DRS.......... Dipping-Reflector Sequence [*Geology*]
DRS.......... Director of Repair and Service [*British military*] (DMA)
DRS.......... Direct Receiving Station (ADWA)

DRS .... Direct Reception System (SAUS)
DRS .... Direct Recoil Spectroscopy (UWER)
DRS .... Direct Reference System (TRID)
DRS .... Direct relay satellite (SAUS)
DRS .... Direct Release System (SAUS)
DRS .... Disability Rating Scale (MELL)
DRS .... Disassembly Reassembly Station (SAUS)
D/RS .... Disassembly/Reassembly Station [*Nuclear energy*] (NRCH)
DRS .... Disc real-time system (SAUS)
DRS .... Discrepancy Reporting System [*NASA*]
DRs .... Discrepancy Reports (SAUS)
DRS .... Discrepancy Report Squawk [*NASA*] (SAA)
DRS .... Disc Resident System (SAUS)
DRS .... Disk Realtime System (SAUS)
DRS .... Disk Resident System [*Computer science*] (IAA)
DRS .... Dissolved Reactive Silica [*Environmental science*]
DRS .... Distributed Resource System (IAA)
DRS .... Divisional Records Standard (SAUS)
DRS .... Division of Reactor Safeguards (SAUO)
DRS .... Division of Reclamation Support (SAUO)
DRS .... Division of Research Services [*Bethesda, MD*] [*National Institutes of Health*]
DRS .... Division Reference Standards (AAG)
DRS .... Division Restructuring Study [*TRADOC*] [*Army*] (INF)
DRS .... Division Reverence Standard (SAUS)
DRS .... Django Reinhardt Society (EA)
DRS .... Doctors Reform Society of Australia (SAUO)
DRS .... Document Registration System (SAUO)
DRS .... Document Retrieval Services [*Information service or system*] (IID)
DRS .... Document Retrieval System
DRS .... DOE records schedule (SAUS)
DRS .... Dominion Research Station (SAUS)
DRS .... Domino Runtime Services (SAUS)
drs .... Doors (REAL)
DRS .... Doppler RADAR Set (DNAB)
DRS .... Dorset Record Society (SAUO)
DRS .... Double Radio Source (SAUS)
DRS .... Double Right Shift
DRS .... Downrange Ship (SAA)
drs .... drawers (SAUS)
DRS .... Drawing Record Summary (ACAE)
DRS .... Drenair [*Spain*] [*ICAO designator*] (FAAC)
DRS .... Dresden [*Germany*] [*Airport symbol*] (OAG)
DRS .... Dress
DRS .... Dressed [*Lumber*]
DRS .... Dressing (SAUS)
DRS .... Drive Recorder System
DRS .... Driver Resource (SAUS)
DRS .... Drives [*Postal Service standard*] (OPSA)
DRS .... Drowsiness (KSC)
DRS .... DRS Technologies [*AMEX symbol*] [*Formerly, Diagnostics/Retrieval Systems*] (SG)
DRS .... Dry Reed Switch
DRS .... Duane's Retraction Syndrome [*Medicine*] (MELL)
DRS .... Dynamic Reflectance Spectroscopy
DRS .... Dynamic Renal Scintigraphy [*Medicine*] (EDAA)
DRS .... Dynamic Report System [*Computer science*] (HODG)
DRSA .... Data Recording System Analyst (MUGU)
DRSA .... Dominican Republic Settlement Association (SAUO)
DRSAM .... Diploma of the Royal Scottish Academy of Music (SAUS)
DRSAM .... Diploma of the Royal Scottish Academy of Music and Drama
DRSAMD .... Diploma of the Royal Scottish Academy of Music and Dance (BARN)
DRSC .... Defence Required Strategic Capability
DRSC .... Development Studies and Research Centre (SAUO)
DRSC .... Direct RADAR Scope Camera
DRSC .... Direct Reading Scope Camera
Dr Sc .... Doctor of Science
DRSC .... Duplicate, replicate, split, or composite (SAUS)
Dr Sci .... Doctor of Science
Dr Sci Nat ... Doctor of Natural Sciences
Dr Sc Jur ..... Doctor of the Science of Jurisprudence
DRSCMOS ... Dual-Rail Static CMOS (SAUS)
DRSCPO ..... District Reserve Supply Corps Program Officer (DNAB)
Dr Sc Pol ..... Doctor of Political Sciences (EY)
DRSCR .... Digital Range Safety Command Receiver [*NASA*] (KSC)
DRSCS .... Digital Range Safety Command System [*NASA*] (MCD)
Dr Sc Techn ... Doctor of Technical Science
DRSE .... Drug-Related Side Effects [*Medicine*] (ODA)
DRSEM .... Deployable Receive Segment Engineering Model (MCD)
DRSF .... Disaster Response Support Facilities (SAUO)
DRSG .... Digital Recorder Signal Generator [*Computer science*]
DRSG .... Division Restructuring Study Group [*TRADOC*] [*Army*] (RDA)
DRSG .... Dominican Republic Study Group [*Defunct*] (EA)
drsg .... Dressing (ADWA)
DRSG .... Dressing [*Medicine*]
DRSGO .... Division Restructuring Study Group Office (SAUO)
DRSH .... Drill Shell
DRSHC .... Deletion Reason/Supply History Code
drsmkr .... Dressmaker (SAUS)
DRSN .... Defense Red Switch Network (SAUO)
DRSN .... Downrange Station [*Space launch term*] (ISAK)
DRSN .... Drifting Snow [*Meteorology*]
DRSNSW .... Doctors' Reform Society of New South Wales [*Australia*]
DRSO .... Danish Radio Symphony Orchestra (SAUS)
Dr So .... Doctor of Sociology
Dr So Sc ...... Doctor of Social Science
DRSP .... Death Row Support Project (EA)
DRSP .... Defense Reconnaissance Support Program
DRSP .... Digital RADAR Signal Processor (MCD)
dr/sq in .... Dram per Square Inch (SAUS)
DRSR .... Direct RADAR Scope Recorder (MCD)
DRSR .... Dresser (MSA)
DRSS .... Data Relay Satellite System [*NASA*]
DRSS .... Discrepancy Report Squawk Sheet [*NASA*] (NASA)
DRSS .... Division of Retirement and Survivors Studies [*Social Security Administration*] (GRD)
DRSs .... Document Retrieval Systems (SAUS)
DRSS .... Downrange Support Ship
DRSW .... Documentary Relations of the South West [*Arizona State Museum*] [*Tucson*] [*Information service or system*] (IID)
DRSX .... DOT Rail Service [*Private rail car owner code*]
DRT .... Darta [*France*] [*ICAO designator*] (FAAC)
Drt .... Dartmouth (BARN)
DRT .... Data Reckoning Tracer (MSA)
DRT .... Data Recording Terminal (SAUS)
DRT .... Data Recovery Tester [*Computer science*] (HGAA)
DRT .... Data Relay Terminal (ACAE)
DRT .... Data Relay Transponder (SAUS)
DRT .... Data Remote Transfer (SAUS)
DRT .... Data Review Technician
DRT .... Data Review Technique (SAUS)
DRT .... Daughters of the Republic of Texas (EA)
DRT .... Dead Reckoning Tracer [*RADAR*]
DRT .... Dead Reckoning Trainer
DRT .... Dead Right There (SAUS)
DRT .... Decade Ratio Transformer
DRT .... Decision Response Time
DRT .... Defect Review Tool (AAEL)
DRT .... Defense Research Technologies Inc. (SAUO)
DRT .... Del Rio [*Texas*] [*Airport symbol*] [*Obsolete*] (OAG)
DRT .... Department of Roads and Transport [*Tasmania*] [*Australia*]
DRT .... Department of Road Transport [*South Australia*] [*Australia*]
DRT .... Dermal Regeneration Template [*Medicine*] (MELL)
DRT .... Design Reference Timeline (MCD)
DRT .... Design Review Team (SAUO)
DRT .... Detroit River Tunnel [*Federal Railroad Administration identification code*]
DRT .... Deviation for Replacement Time
DRT .... Device Reference Table
DRT .... Device Rise Time [*Photomultipliers for scintillation counting*] (IEEE)
DRT .... Diagnostic Rhyme Test
DRT .... Digital Readout Timer [*Computer science*]
DRT .... Digital Rotary Transducer
DRT .... Diode Recovery Tester
drt .... Director [*MARC relator code*] [*Library of Congress*] (LCCP)
DRT .... Director of Railway Transport [*British military*] (DMA)
DRT .... Direct Reading Telemeter (IAA)
DRT .... Direct Reading Telemetering (SAUS)
DRT .... Direct Reading Totalizer
DRT .... Disaster Recovery Training (DNAB)
DRT .... Discrimination RADAR Transmitter (IAA)
DRT .... Dismounted Reconnaissance Team [*Army*] (INF)
DRT .... Distal Renal Tubular Acidosis [*Medicine*] (MELL)
DRT .... Distant Remote Transceiver (IAA)
DRT .... Distribution Requirement Table (MCD)
DRT .... Division Reconnaissance Team [*Warsaw Pact forces*]
DRT .... Dog Rescue Team (SAUS)
DRT .... Domain-Referenced Test [*Education*] (AEE)
DRT .... Dome Removal Tool
DRT .... Dorsal Root, Thoracic [*Medicine*] (DMAA)
dr t .... dram troy (SAUS)
DRT .... Drawing Release Ticket (MCD)
DRT .... Drill Template (MCD)
DRT .... Driver Reaction Time
DRTA .... Darwin Region Tourism Association [*Australia*]
DR-TA .... Directed Reading-Thinking Activity (EDAC)
DRTA .... Direct Reading Thinking Activity [*Education*] (AEE)
DRTA .... Driptank
DRTC .... Deputy Regional Transport Commissioner (SAUO)
DRTC .... Diabetes Research and Training Center [*Yeshiva University*] [*Research center*] (RCD)
DRTC .... Diabetes Research and Training Center [*University of Chicago*] [*Research center*] (RCD)
DRTC .... Diabetes Research and Training Center [*Washington University*] [*Research center*] (RCD)
DRTC .... Diploma of the Royal Technical College [*British*]
DRTC .... Documentation (SAUS)
DRTC .... Documentation Research and Training Centre
DRTD .... Disaster Recovery Training Department (SAUO)
DRTE .... Defence Research Telecommunication Establishment [*Canada*]
DRTE .... Dendrite International [*NASDAQ symbol*] (TTSB)
DRTE .... Dendrite International, Inc. [*NASDAQ symbol*] (SAG)
DRTE .... Doctor of Radio and Television Engineering
Dr Tech .... Doctor of Technology
Dr Techn .... Doctor of Technology
DRT Eng .... Doctor of Radio and Television Engineering
DRTE Report ... Defence Research Telecommunications Establishment, Report (SAUS)
Dr Theol .... Doctor of Theology
DRTI .... Dual Roll Trough Idler

DRTK .... GTS Duratek [*NASDAQ symbol*] (TTSB)
DRTK .... GTS Duratek Corp. [*NASDAQ symbol*] (NQ)
DRTL .... Diode Resistor Transistor Logic (MSA)
DRTM .... Disk Real-Time Monitor [*Computer science*]
Dr T Med ..... Doctor of Tropical Medicine
Dr T Nap ...... Drury's Irish Chancery Reports Tempore Napier [*1858-59*] [*A publication*] (DLA)
DRTO .... Directorate of Transport and Reconnaissance Operations (SAUO)
DRTP .... Drill Template
DRTP .... Dynatech Real Time Products (SAUS)
DRTR .... Dead Reckoning Trainer
Dr Trav .... Droit du Travail: Revue Mensuelle [*French*] [*A publication*] (DLA)
DRTRS .... District Report of Transported Resident Students
DRTS .... Data Relay and Tracking Satellite (SAUS)
DRTS .... Data Relay Test Satellite [*Sponsored by Japan Space Agency*]
DRTS .... Data Relay Tracking Satellite (SAUO)
DRTS .... Detecting, Ranging, and Tracking System (MCD)
DRTS .... Digital Recording Technique Study (ACAE)
DRTS .... Dose Record and Treatment Emergent Symptom [*Scale*] [*Medicine*] (DB)
DRTSA .... Defense Reconnaissance Tactical Support Activity (MCD)
Dr T Sug ...... Drury's Irish Chancery Reports Tempore Sugden [*A publication*] (DLA)
DRTV .... Direct Response Television (SAUS)
DRU .... Data Receiver Unit (SAUS)
DRU .... Data Recording Unit (SAUS)
DRU .... Data Recovery Unit (ADWA)
DRU .... Data Reference Unit
DRU .... Data Reorganization Utility [*Computer science*]
DRU .... Data Retrival Unit (GAVI)
DRU .... Demolition Research Unit
DRU .... Design Research Unit (SAUO)
DRU .... Digital Range Unit
DRU .... Digital Register Unit
DRU .... Digital Remote Unit [*Computer science*] (MCD)
DRU .... Direct Reporting Unit
DRU .... Disaccharide Repeating Unit [*Biochemistry*]
DRU .... Document Reproduction Unit
DRU .... Document Retention Unit [*IRS*]
DRU .... Drew University, Madison, NJ [*OCLC symbol*] (OCLC)
DRU .... Drive Unit
DRU .... Drummond, MT [*Location identifier*] [*FAA*] (FAAL)
DRU .... Drummond Petroleum Ltd. [*Toronto Stock Exchange symbol*]
Dru .... Drury's Irish Chancery Reports Tempore Sugden [*A publication*] (DLA)
Dru .... Drusila (SAUS)
DRU .... Dynamic Reference Unit (SAUS)
DRUA .... Data Recognition Users Association (SAUO)
Dru & Nap ... Drury's Irish Chancery Reports Tempore Napier [*1858-59*] [*A publication*] (DLA)
Dru & Sug ... Drury's Irish Chancery Reports Tempore Sugden [*A publication*] (DLA)
Dru & Wal ... Drury and Walsh's Irish Chancery Reports [*1837-40*] [*A publication*] (DLA)
Dru & War ... Drury and Warren's Irish Chancery Reports [*1841-43*] [*A publication*] (DLA)
DRUB .... Digital Remote Unit Buffer [*Computer science*] (MCD)
DRUC .... Disposition Record Unsatisfactory Condition (MCD)
DRUCC .... Divisional Rail Users Consultative Committee [*Indian Railway*] (TIR)
D Ru E .... Doctor of Rural Engineering
D Ru Eng ..... Doctor of Rural Engineering
Drug Abuse... Drug Abuse Council (SAUO)
Drug Abuse LR... Drug Abuse Law Review [*A publication*] (DLA)
Drug Abuse L Rev... Drug Abuse Law Review [*A publication*] (DLA)
Drug Cosmet Ind... Drug and Cosmetic Industry (journ.) (SAUS)
Drug Dev Ind Pharm... Drug Development and Industrial Pharmacy (journ.) (SAUS)
DRUGDOC .... Comprehensive Drug Literature Computer Tape Service (SAUS)
DrugE .... Drug Emporium, Inc. [*Associated Press*] (SAG)
DRUGINFO ... Drug Information (SAUS)
Drug Intel .... Drug Intelligence (journ.) (SAUS)
Drug Metabol Drug Interact... Drug Metabolism and Drug Interactions (SAUS)
Drug Metab Rev... Drug Metabolism Review (MEC)
DRUGR .... Drug Registry (SAUS)
Drug Rehab... Drug Rehabilitation Program (SAUS)
Drugs Aging... Drugs and Aging (SAUS)
Drugs Exp Clin Res... Drugs Under Experimental and Clinical Research (SAUS)
DRUID .... Digital Readout Unit and Interactive Displays (MCD)
DRUIDS .... Diffuse Reflectance Using Infrared Dispersive Spectrophotometry
DRUJ .... Distal Radioulnar Joint [*Anatomy*]
DRUL .... Downrange Up Link [*Apollo*] [*NASA*]
DRUM .... Deep Reflections from the Upper Mantle [*Geology*]
DRUM .... Dodge Revolutionary Union Movement
DRUMH .... Drumheller, AB [*American Association of Railroads railroad junction routing code*]
DRUMS .... Defensible Reasoning and Uncertainty Management Systems (EURO)
Dr UniPar .... Doctor of the University of Paris (SAUO)
DR UNIV PAR... Doctor of the University of Paris (ROG)
DRurSc .... Doctor of Rural Science (ADA)
DRurSci .... Doctor of Rural Science (NADA)
Drury .... Drury's Irish Chancery Reports [*A publication*] (DLA)
Drury & Wal... Drury and Walsh's Irish Chancery Reports [*1837-40*] [*A publication*] (DLA)
Drury & Wal (Ir)... Drury and Walsh's Irish Chancery Reports [*1837-40*] [*A publication*] (DLA)
Drury & War... Drury and Warren's Irish Chancery Reports [*1841-43*] [*A publication*] (DLA)
Drury & War (Ir)... Drury and Warren's Irish Chancery Reports [*1841-43*] [*A publication*] (DLA)
Drury C .... Drury College (GAGS)
Drury (Ir) ..... Drury's Irish Chancery Reports [*A publication*] (DLA)
Drury T Nap... Drury's Irish Chancery Reports Tempore Napier [*1858-59*] [*A publication*] (DLA)
Drury T Sug... Drury's Irish Chancery Reports Tempore Sugden [*A publication*] (DLA)
DRUs .... Directing Reporting Units (SAUS)
Dru T Nap.... Drury's Irish Chancery Reports Tempore Napier [*1858-59*] [*A publication*] (DLA)
Dru T Sug.... Drury's Irish Chancery Reports Tempore Sugden [*A publication*] (DLA)
Dru T Sugden... Drury's Irish Chancery Reports Tempore Sugden [*A publication*] (DLA)
DRUV .... Diffuse-Reflectance Ultraviolet-Visible [*Spectra*]
DRV .... Data Recovery Vehicle
DRV .... Deep-Diving Research Vehicle (SAUS)
DRV .... Deep-Diving Research Vehicles (KSC)
DRV .... Deep Research Vehicle [*or Vessel*] [*NOO*]
DRV .... Deep Research Vessel (SAUS)
DRV .... Deep-Sea Research Vehicle (FOTI)
DRV .... Democratic Republic of Vietnam [*North Vietnam*]
DRV .... Development Reentry Vehicle [*Aerospace*] (IAA)
DRV .... Device Driver (SAUS)
DRV .... Dravo Corp. [*NYSE symbol*] (SPSG)
DRV .... Drive [*Commonly used*] (OPSA)
DRV .... Dumont D'Urville [*Pointe Geologie, Adelie*] [*Antarctica*] [*Seismograph station code, US Geological Survey*] (SEIS)
DRVID .... Differenced-Range Versus Integrated Doppler [*Charged particle measurement*]
DRVID .... Difference Range Versus Integrated Doppler (SAUS)
DRVID .... Differential Range Versus Integrated Doppler (SAUS)
DRVN .... Democratic Republic of Vietnam [*North Vietnam*]
DRVN .... Driven [*Automotive engineering*]
DRVO .... Deputy Regional Veterinary Officer (SAUS)
DRVP .... Design requirements verification procedure (SAUS)
DRVR .... Driver (MSA)
DRVRPRES... Driver Presence [*National Highway Traffic Safety Administration Fatal Accident Recording System code*]
DRVS .... Diabetic Retinopathy Vitrectomy Study [*National Eye Institute*]
DRVS .... Doppler RADAR Velocity Sensor
DRVS .... Drill Vise
DRW .... Darwin [*Australia*] [*Airport symbol*] (OAG)
DRW .... Data Return Word (SAUS)
DRW .... Defence Radio Warfare (SAUS)
DRW .... Defensive Radio Warfare (NATG)
DRW .... Dennis R. Williams [*Designer's mark on US bicentennial dollar*]
DRW .... Directorate of Radio Warfare (SAUO)
DRW .... Dirty RADWASTE [*Nuclear energy*] (NRCH)
DRW .... Draw (SAUS)
drw .... Drawing (SAUS)
DRW .... Draw Format [*Computing*] (ODA)
DRWAW .... Distillery, Rectifying and Wine Workers International Union of America (SAUO)
DRWAW .... Distillery, Rectifying, Wine, and Allied Workers International Union of America [*Later, DWAW*] (EA)
DRWG .... Data Reduction Working Group (SAA)
DRWG .... Drawing (NATG)
DRWI .... Drew Industries, Inc. (MHDW)
DR WIND ..... Door or Window [*Freight*]
Drwl .... Dry Wall (DAC)
drwl .... Drywall (MIST)
DRWP .... Doppler Radar Wind Profiler (SAUS)
DRWS .... Dirty Radwaste System (SAUS)
DRWW .... Distillery, Rectifying and Wine Workers International Union of America (SAUO)
DRWW .... Distillery, Rectifying, Wine Workers (SAUS)
DRWWCF ..... Damon Runyon-Walter Winchell Cancer Fund (EA)
DRWY .... Denver Railway [*Federal Railroad Administration identification code*]
DRX .... Distributed Resource Executive (SAUS)
DRX .... Drachma [*Monetary unit*] [*Greece*]
DRX .... Drexel University, School of Library and Information Science, Philadelphia, PA [*OCLC symbol*] (OCLC)
DRX .... Drucox Petroleum [*Vancouver Stock Exchange symbol*]
DRX .... Dynamic Recrystallization (SAUS)
DRXR .... Drexler Technology [*NASDAQ symbol*] (TTSB)
DRXR .... Drexler Technology Corp. [*NASDAQ symbol*] (NQ)
DRY .... Dairy
DRY .... Democratic Party of Yemen [*Political party*] (PSAP)
DRY .... Deraya Air Taxi PT [*Indonesia*] [*ICAO designator*] (FAAC)
DRY .... destination rail yard (SAUS)
DRy .... Director of Railways (SAUO)
DRY .... Dreyfus Corp. (SAUO)
DRY .... Dryden Resources Corp. [*Vancouver Stock Exchange symbol*]
dry .... Drying (SAUS)
DRY .... Manchester, NH [*Location identifier*] [*FAA*] (FAAL)
DryCal .... Dreyfus California Municipal Income Fund [*Associated Press*] (SAG)
DryfMu .... Dreyfus Municipal Income Fund [*Associated Press*] (SAG)
DryfNY .... Dreyfus New York Municipal Income Fund [*Associated Press*] (SAG)
Drying Technol... Drying Technology (journ.) (SAUS)
dryp .... Drypoint (VRA)
Drypers .... Drypers Corp. [*Associated Press*] (SAG)

dry pt .... Dry Pint (SAUS)
dry qt .... Dry Quart (SAUS)
DRYR .... Dreyer's Grand Ice Cream, Inc. [*NASDAQ symbol*] (NQ)
DRYR .... Dreyer's Gr Ice Cr [*NASDAQ symbol*] (TTSB)
DrySM .... Dreyfus Strategic Municipal Bond Fund, Inc. [*Associated Press*] (SAG)
DryStG .... Dreyfus Strategic Government Income Fund [*Associated Press*] (SAG)
DryStrt .... Dreyfus Strategic Municipals [*Associated Press*] (SAG)
Drysys .... Drysys Equipment Ltd. (SAUO)
DRYWL .... Drywall
DRZ .... Deep Reconnaissance Zone [*Army*] (AABC)
DRZ .... Disturbed-Rock Zone [*Geology*]
Dr Z .... Doctor Zhivago (SAUS)
DRZA .... Agades-Sud [*Niger*] [*ICAO location identifier*] (ICLI)
DRZD .... Dirkou [*Niger*] [*ICAO location identifier*] (ICLI)
DRZG .... Goure [*Niger*] [*ICAO location identifier*] (ICLI)
DRZI .... Iferouane [*Niger*] [*ICAO location identifier*] (ICLI)
DRZL .... Arlit [*Niger*] [*ICAO location identifier*] (ICLI)
DRZL .... drizzle (SAUS)
DRZL .... drizzling rain (SAUS)
DRZM .... Maine-Soroa [*Niger*] [*ICAO location identifier*] (ICLI)
DRZN .... N'Guigmi [*Niger*] [*ICAO location identifier*] (ICLI)
DRZR .... Zinder [*Niger*] [*ICAO location identifier*] (ICLI)
DRZT .... Tanout [*Niger*] [*ICAO location identifier*] (ICLI)
DS .... Air Senegal [*ICAO designator*] (AD)
DS .... Code of Safety for Diving Systems (SAUS)
DS .... Compagnie Senegalaise de Transports Aeriens [*Senegal*] [*ICAO designator*] (ICDA)
D-S .... Dada-Surrealism
DS .... Dairy Shrine (EA)
DS .... Dajnavna Sigurnost [*Bulgarian Secret Police affiliated with the KGB*]
DS .... Dallas Semiconductor [*NYSE symbol*] (TTSB)
DS .... Dallas Semiconductor Corporation (SAUO)
DS .... Dallas Support Office (SAUO)
DS .... Dal Segno [*Repeat from the Sign*] [*Music*]
DS .... Dalton on Sheriffs [*A publication*] (DLA)
DS .... Dance Tuition Schools [*Public-performance tariff class*] [*British*]
DS .... Danish Standard (SAUS)
DS .... Danmarks Statistik [*Denmark*]
DS .... Dansk Samling [*Danish Union*] (PPE)
DS .... Dantrolene Sodium [*Muscle relaxant*]
DS .... Daoist Sanctuary (EA)
DS .... Dark Shadows [*Television program*]
ds .... Da Segno [*From the Sign*] [*Italian*] [*Music*] (WDAA)
DS .... Data Sample (SAUS)
DS .... Data Scanning (BUR)
DS .... Data Security (IAA)
DS .... Data Segment
DS .... Data Send, Double Sided (SAUO)
DS .... Data Sequence (SAUS)
DS .... Data Series (IAA)
DS .... Data Series (journ.) (SAUS)
DS .... Data Set [*Computer science*]
DS .... Data Sheet (NATG)
DS .... Data Signal (SAUS)
DS .... Data Sorter (SAUS)
DS .... Data Station [*Spectroscopy*]
DS .... Data Storage [*Computer science*] (NASA)
DS .... Data Strobe (TIMI)
DS .... Data Structure (SAUS)
DS .... Data Symbol (SAUS)
DS .... Data Synchronization (DEN)
DS .... Data System
DS .... Data Systems Technician [*Navy rating*]
DS .... Date of Service [*Military*]
DS .... Daughters of Scotia (EA)
D/S .... Day of Surgery (DAVI)
d/s .... Days after Sight (EBF)
DS .... Days after Sight [*Business term*]
D/S .... Days Sight (EBF)
DS .... Dead Air Space [*Physiology*]
D-S .... Dead Slow (SAUS)
DS .... Debenture Stock [*Investment term*] (ADA)
DS .... Debre-Semelaigne [*Syndrome*] [*Medicine*] (DB)
DS .... Debugging System
DS .... Decade Scaler (MSA)
DS .... Decanning Scuttle
DS .... Decimal Selector (SAUS)
DS .... Decimal Subtract
DS .... Decision and Switching
DS .... Decision Sheet (NATG)
DS .... Decision Support (GART)
DS .... Decision Symbol (SAUS)
DS .... Decistere [*Unit of measure*] (ROG)
DS .... Decoder Simulator (IAA)
DS .... Decommissioning Support (SAUS)
DS .... Decomposition Sintering (RDA)
DS .... Decompression Sickness (MELL)
DS .... Decontamination Shop [*Nuclear energy*] (NRCH)
DS .... Deep Screw (SAUS)
DS .... Deep Sedative (MELL)
DS .... Deep Sleep (MELL)
DS .... Deep Space (SEWL)
DS .... Deepstar [*A manned, self-propelled submersible vehicle built by Western Electric Corp.*]
DS .... Deep Structure (SAUS)
DS .... Default Segment [*Computer science*] (UWER)
DS .... Defect Scattering [*Physics*] (UWER)
DS .... Defence Secretariat [*Ministry of Defence*] [*British*]
DS .... Defense Secretary (SAUO)
DS .... Defense Support (CINC)
DS .... Defense Suppression
DS .... Deficiency System (SAUS)
DS .... Defined Substrate [*Medicine*] (MAE)
DS .... Define Storage
DS .... Define Symbol
DS .... Definition of a Storage Area (SAUS)
DS .... Definition of Symbol (SAUS)
DS .... Deflection Spectrometer (UWER)
DS .... Degree of Substitution
DS .... Dehydroepiandrosterone Sulfate [*Biochemistry*] (AAMN)
DS .... Dejerine-Sottas [*Sydnrome*] [*Medicine*] (DB)
DS .... Dekastere [*Unit of measure*] (ROG)
DS .... Dektra System (UWER)
DS .... Delayed Sensitivity [*Medicine*] (DMAA)
DS .... Delete String (SAUS)
DS .... Delimiter Statement (SAUS)
DS .... Delius Society (EA)
DS .... Delivery Schedule
DS .... Delivery Segment (SAUS)
DS .... Delivery System (UWER)
DS .... Delphian Society
DS .... Delphinium Society (EA)
DS .... Delta Society (EA)
DS .... Demand Scanner (VLIE)
DS .... Democracia Socialista [*Spain*] [*Political party*] (EY)
DS .... Demokraticheska Sgovor [*Democratic Alliance*] [*Bulgaria*] [*Political party*] (PPE)
DS .... Demokraticka Strana [*Democratic Party*] [*Former Czechoslovakia*] [*Political party*] (PPE)
DS .... Demokratikos Sinaspismos [*Democratic Coalition*] [*Greece*] [*Political party*] (PPE)
DS .... Demokratikos Synagermos [*Democratic Rally*] [*Greek Cyprus*] [*Political party*] (PPE)
DS .... Demolition Site (SAUS)
DS .... Demolition Squad (SAUO)
DS .... Denotational Semantics (SAUS)
DS .... Density Standard [*Medicine*] (MAE)
DS .... Dental Surgeon (SAUS)
DS .... Dental Surgery [*or Surgeon*] [*Medical Officer designation*] [*British*]
DS .... Departed Station (SAA)
DS .... Department of Sanitation (SAUS)
DS .... Department of State
DS .... Dependents School (SAUO)
DS .... Depenture Stock (SAUS)
DS .... Depolarization Shift [*Electrophysiology*]
DS .... Depot Ship (SAUS)
DS .... Depression Subtle [*Psychology*]
DS .... Deprivation Syndrome [*Medicine*] (DB)
DS .... Depth Sounder
DS .... Depth Sounding (SAUS)
DS .... Deputy Secretary (SAUS)
DS .... Deputy-Secretary [*British*]
DS .... Deputy Sheriff (DLA)
DS .... Dermatan Sulfate [*Biochemistry*]
DS .... Descent Stage [*NASA*] (KSC)
D/S .... Descent State [*NASA*] (KSC)
DS .... Descent System
DS .... Descriptive Statement (SAUS)
DS .... Desifrator (SAUS)
DS .... Designated Subcontractor (ACAE)
DS .... Designer Software [*Computer science*]
DS .... Design Selection (UWER)
DS .... Design Sheet
DS .... Design Specification (MCD)
DS .... Design Standards
DS .... Design System (UWER)
DS .... Desk Stand (IAA)
DS .... Destination Store (UWER)
DS .... Destroyer Squadron (SAUO)
DS .... Destroyer Surface-Effect Ship (MCD)
DS .... Desynchronized Sleep [*Medicine*] (MEDA)
DS .... Detached Service [*Army*]
DS .... Detailed Routings (VLIE)
DS .... Detail Specification (MCD)
DS .... Detection Sensitivity (ACAE)
DS .... Detection Systems (SAUS)
DS .... Detective Sergeant [*Scotland Yard*]
DS .... Detergent Sensitive (SAUS)
DS .... Deterministic System (SAUS)
DS .... Deuterated Solvent (SAUS)
DS .... Development System
DS .... Device Selector
DS .... Dextran Sulphate (DB)
D/S .... Dextrose and Saline [*Medicine*]
D/S .... Dextrose and Sodium Chloride [*Injection*] [*Pharmacology*] (DAVI)
d/s .... dextrose in saline (SAUS)
D/S .... dextrose/saline (SAUS)

DS Dextrose Stick (DAVI)
d/s Dhrystone per Second (VLIE)
DS Diagnostic Sensitivity (SAUS)
DS Dial System
DS diamond saw (SAUS)
DS Diamond-Star [*Society of Automotive Engineers auto manufacturer code for service information interchange*]
DS Diastolic Murmur [*Medicine*] (DB)
D/S Diastolic/Systolic [*Ratio*] [*Cardiology*]
DS Dibasic Salt (SAUS)
DS Dichotomous Sampler (COE)
DS Dickens Society (EA)
DS Dictionary of Spirituality (SAUS)
DS Dictionnaire de Spiritualite Ascetique et Mystique, Doctrine et Histoire [*Paris*] [*A publication*] (BJA)
DS Dielectric Spectroscopy
DS Diesel Severe [*Service*] [*Automotive engineering*]
DS Diesel Ship (SAUS)
DS Diesel Specialist (SAUS)
DS Diethyl Sulfate (SAUS)
DS Difference Sensation [*Psychology*]
DS Difference Spectrophotometry (SAUS)
DS Difference Spectroscopy
DS Difference, Starboard [*Navigation*]
DS Differential Spacing [*Typography*]
DS Differential Stimulus (SAUS)
DS Differentiated Service (SAUS)
DS Differentiated Staffing [*Education*] (AEE)
DS Diffuse Scleroderma [*Medicine*] (MELL)
DS Diffuse Surface (SAUS)
DS Digital Carrier Span (VLIE)
ds Digital Science [*Kodak*] [*Computer science*]
DS Digital Section (SAUS)
DS Digital Select (VLIE)
DS Digital Selection (SAUS)
DS Digital Service [*Computer science*] (DCDG)
DS Digital Services (SAUS)
DS Digital Signal
DS Digital Storage (SAUS)
DS Digital Store (SAUS)
DS digital subset (SAUS)
DS Digital Subsystem (SAUS)
DS Digital Switching [*Telecommunications*] (IAA)
DS Digital System
D-S Digital to Synchro (SAUS)
DS Digit Select (BUR)
DS Digit Selection (SAUS)
DS Digit Selector (SAUS)
DS Digit Sorting (SAUS)
DS Digit Switch (SAUS)
DS Digit Symbol [*Psychometrics*]
DS Dilated Space (SAUS)
DS Dilute Strength [*Chemistry*]
DS Dimension Statement (SAUS)
DS Dimethylaminostilben (SAUS)
DS Dinosaur Society (EA)
DS Diode Store (SAUS)
DS Diode Switch
DS Dioptric Strength
DS Diploma in Surgery [*Medical degree*] (CMD)
D-S Diplomate, American Board of Surgery (DHSM)
DS Diplomatic Security [*U.S. Department of State*] (BARN)
DS Diplomatic Service [*or Servant*] [*British*]
ds dip-slide (SAUS)
DS Dip Soldering
DS Directing Staff
DS Directing Station (IAA)
DS Directionally Solidified [*Metallurgy*]
DS Directional Solidification (SAUS)
DS Direction Sports (EA)
DS Director of Services [*Air Force*]
DS Director of Signals [*British military*] (DMA)
DS Directory Service (VERA)
DS Directory Synchronization (ACRL)
DS Directory System (SAUS)
DS Direct Sequence [*Telecommunications*] (TEL)
D/S Direct Ship (MCD)
DS Direct Signal (VLIE)
DS Direct Steamer
DS Direct Support [*Army*]
DS Disabled Spouse [*Title XVI*] [*Social Security Administration*] (OICC)
DS Disaster Services [*Red Cross*]
DS Discarding Sabot [*Navy*]
DS Discharge Summary [*Medicine*] (MELL)
DS Disclosure Statement (AAGC)
DS Disconnect Switch (MSA)
DS Discontinue (BUR)
DS Discrete System (SAUS)
DS Discriminating Stimulus [*Psychology*] (AEE)
DS disc storage (SAUS)
DS Disc system (SAUS)
D/S Disintegrations per Second
DS Disjunctive Syllogism [*Rule of inference*] [*Logic*]
DS Disk Station (SAUS)
DS Disk Storage [*Computer science*] (NASA)
DS Disk Store (SAUS)
DS Disk System
DS Disorganized Schizophrenia [*Medicine*] (MELL)
DS Dispersion Staining [*Analytical chemistry*]
DS Dispersion Strengthened [*Metallurgy*]
DS Dispersion Strengthening (SAUS)
DS Display and Storage (SAUS)
DS Display Screen
DS Display Section
DS Display Started (IAA)
DS Display Statement (SAUS)
DS Display Station (IAA)
DS Display Subsystem (MCD)
DS Disseminated Sclerosis [*Medicine*]
Ds Dissimulation [*Psychology*]
ds dissociation (SAUS)
DS Dissociator [*Genetics*]
DS Dissolved Solids
ds Distance (SAUS)
DS Distant (IAA)
DS Distant Surveillance
DS Distinguishing Sequence (SAUS)
DS Distributed Services (SAUS)
DS Distributed Single Layer (VLIE)
D/S Distributed/Stand-Alone [*Pricing*]
DS Distributed Synchronization (SAUS)
DS Distributed System
DS Distributed Systems (SAUS)
DS Distribution Services (VERA)
DS Distribution Space
DS Distributor Specialist (TIMI)
DS District Secretary [*British*]
D-S Ditlev-Simonsen Lines (SAUS)
D-S Ditley-Simonsen, Halfdan & Co. [*Steamship*] (MHDB)
DS Diver, Salvage [*Navy rating*]
DS Diverter station (SAUS)
DS Divide Statement (SAUS)
DS Diving Saucer
DS Divisional Superintendent [*British police*]
DS Division of Soils (SAUO)
DS Division of Systems and Licensing (SAUO)
DS Division/Station Code [*Searchable field*] [*Dialog*] (NITA)
DS Divorce Support [*An association*] (EA)
DS Docking Survey
DS Docking System
DS Dock Service
DS Doctor of Science
DS Doctor of Surgery
DS Doctrine Sponsor (COE)
DS Documented Sample (KSC)
DS Document Signed
DS Document Spacing (SAUS)
DS Documents Signed (SAUS)
DS Document Storage (VLIE)
D-S Doerfler-Stewart [*Test*] [*Medicine*] (MEDA)
DS Dokumentation Schweisstechnik [*Welding Documentation*] [*Federal Institute for Materials Testing*] [*Information service or system*] (IID)
DS Doll Show
DS Dolly Shot [*Cinematography*] (NTCM)
DS Dolphin Society (EA)
DS Domesday Survey [*Census-like record of the lands of England, 1085-86*]
DS Domestic Service [*Equipment specification*]
DS Dominion Securities Ltd. [*Toronto Stock Exchange symbol*] [*Vancouver Stock Exchange symbol*]
DS Dominus [*The Lord*] [*Latin*]
DS Donor's Serum [*Medicine*]
DS Door Switch (SAUS)
DS Doppler Science (ACAE)
DS Doppler Shift [*Physics*]
DS Doppler SONAR (IAA)
DS Double Sandwich
ds Double Screened (SAUS)
D/S Double-Screened [*Coal*]
DS Double Sided (SAUS)
DS Double-Sided [*Disks*] [*Computer science*]
DS Double Silk [*Wire insulation*] (AAG)
DS Double Slave [*LORAN stations*]
DS DoubleSlave (SAUS)
DS Double Space (SAUS)
DS Double Stitch [*Bookbinding*]
ds Double Stitched (SAUS)
DS Double Storage (SAUS)
DS Double Stout [*Brewing*] (ROG)
DS Double Stranded (OA)
ds Double-Stranded (DB)
DS Double Strength [*Medicine*]
DS Double Subdominance [*Ethology*]
DS Double Sunk (SAUS)
DS downsection (SAUS)
DS downslope (SAUS)
DS Downspout (AAG)
DS Down's Syndrome [*Medicine*]
DS Downstage [*Toward audience*] [*A stage direction*]

DS .... Downstream (AAG)
Ds .... Down syndrome (SAUS)
DS .... Downtime between Sorties [*Military*] (AFIT)
DS .... Dracula Society (EA)
DS .... Drafting Site [*NFPA pre-fire planning symbol*] (NFPA)
DS .... Draft Standard (VLIE)
DS .... Draft Stop [*Technical drawings*]
DS .... Drawing Society (EA)
DS .... Drawing Summary (AAG)
DS .... Dressed Sides [*of lumber*] (BARN)
DS .... Dressing Station (SAUO)
DS .... Dressler's Syndrome [*Medicine*] (MELL)
DS .... drilling superintendent (SAUS)
DS .... Drill Sergeant [*Army*]
DS .... Drill Ship (SAUS)
DS .... drill site (SAUS)
DS .... Drill Stem (SAUS)
DS .... drill string (SAUS)
DS .... Driver Services [*Motor vehicle term used in state of Washington*] (MVRD)
DS .... Drive Scanner (SAUS)
DS .... Drive Select (SAUS)
DS .... Drive Surface (SAUS)
DS .... Drive System
DS .... Driving Signal (SAUS)
DS .... Drone Squadron
D/S .... Dropped Shipped (DNAB)
DS .... Drop Siding
DS .... dropstones (SAUS)
DS .... Drug Screening (MELL)
DS .... Drug Store (SAUS)
DS .... Drugstore [*US maps*]
DS .... Drum Storage [*Computer science*] (IEEE)
DS .... Drum Store (SAUS)
DS .... Drum Switch
DS .... Dry Scrubber (EEVL)
DS .... Dry Season (SAUO)
DS .... Dry Socket [*Medicine*] (MELL)
DS .... Dry Spinning (SAUS)
DS .... Dry Sunk (ROG)
DS .... Dry Swallow [*Medicine*]
DS .... Dual Speed (SAUS)
DS .... Dual Spin (ACAE)
DS .... Dudley Herbarium of Stanford University [*San Francisco, CA*]
DS .... Dugdale Society (SAUO)
DS .... Dummy Section (SAUS)
DS .... Dummy Statement (SAUS)
D/S .... Duration of Status (SAUS)
DS .... Duration of Systole (MAE)
ds .... duration series (SAUS)
DS .... Durham & Southern Railway Co. [*AAR code*]
DS .... Dust Storm [*Astronomy*]
DS .... Duty Section [*Air Force*] (AFM)
DS .... Duty Status [*Air Force*] (AFM)
DS .... Dwarf Shoot [*Botany*]
DS .... Dwell Sounding (ACAE)
DS .... Dyestuffs
DS .... Dynamic Speaker (SAUS)
D/S .... Dynamic/Static Analysis (SAUS)
DS .... Dynamic Store (SAUS)
DS .... Dynamic Subroutine (SAUS)
DS .... Dynamic System (SAUS)
D/S .... Dynamic to Static
Ds .... dysprosium (SAUS)
DS .... Systolic Diameter (SAUS)
DS .... United States Department of State Library [*Division of Library and Reference Services*], Washington, DC [*Library symbol*] [*Library of Congress*] (LCLS)
ds .... Daylight Saving (ODA)
DS0 .... Digital Service Zero [*Telecommunications*] (DINT)
DS-0 .... Digital Signal Level 0 (SAUS)
DS1 .... Data Systems Technician, First Class [*Navy rating*]
DS1 .... Digital Signal 1 [*Telecommunications*]
DS-1 .... Digital Signal 1 format (SAUS)
DS-1 .... Digital Signal Level 1 (SAUS)
DS1 .... Digital Signal Level One (SAUS)
DS-1C .... Digital Signal level 1C (SAUS)
DS1/E1 .... Digital Signal Level 1/European Wide-area digital transmission scheme-level 1 (SAUS)
DS2 .... Data Systems Technician, Second Class [*Navy rating*]
DS2 .... Decision Support Display System (SAUS)
DS-2 .... Decontaminating Solution Number Two [*Chemical defense*] [*Army*] (RDA)
DS-2 .... Digital Signal 2 format (SAUS)
DS-2 .... Digital Signal 2. Physical interface for digital transmission at the rate of 6.312 Mbps (SAUS)
DS-2 .... Digital Signal Level 2 (SAUS)
DS2 .... Digital Signal Level Two (SAUS)
DS2T .... Deployment and Sustainment Support Tool
DS3 .... Data Systems Technician, Third Class [*Navy rating*]
DS3 .... Deep Space Surveillance System (SAUS)
DS3 .... Digital Signal 3 format (SAUS)
DS-3 .... Digital Signal Level 3 (SAUS)
DS3 .... Digital Signal Level Three (SAUS)
DS4 .... Direct Support Unit Standard Supply System [*Army*] (AABC)
DSA .... Dairy Science Abstracts [*Database*] [*Commonwealth Bureau of Dairy Science and Technology*] [*Information service or system*] (CRD)
DSA .... Dairy Science Association (SAUO)
DSA .... Dalcroze Society of America (EA)
DSA .... Danbury Airways, Inc. [*ICAO designator*] (FAAC)
DSA .... Danish Sisterhood of America (SAUO)
DSA .... Dante Society of America (EA)
DSA .... Dataroute Serving Area [*TransCanada Telephone System/Computer Communications Group*]
DSA .... Data Service Adapter [*Computer science*] (VERA)
DSA .... Data Set Adapter [*Computer science*]
DSA .... Data Set Adapter (or Adaptor) (SAUS)
DSA .... Data Signature Algorithm (SAUS)
DSA .... Data Signature Architecture (SAUS)
DSA .... Data Standard Algorithm (SAUS)
DSA .... Data Standard Architecture (SAUS)
DSA .... Data Standards and Administration (SAUS)
DSA .... Data Storage Algorithm (SAUS)
DSA .... Data Storage Architecture (SAUS)
DSA .... Data Systems Administration (NVT)
DSA .... Data Systems Analysts, Incorporated (SAUO)
DSA .... Data Systems Architecture (SSD)
DSA .... Date Society of America (SAUO)
DSA .... Day Sailer Association (EA)
DSA .... Deadly Serious Party of Australia [*Political party*]
DSA .... Deep Space Aerial (or Antenna) (SAUS)
DSA .... Deep Space Antenna [*Aerospace*] (IAA)
DSA .... Defence (or Defense) Shipping Authority (SAUO)
DSA .... Defence Services Asia (SAUS)
DSA .... Defence Supply Agency (SAUS)
DSA .... Defence Support Agency (SAUS)
DSA .... Defense Shipping Authority
DSA .... Defense Special Assessment [*Defense Intelligence Agency*] (DOMA)
DSA .... Defense Supply Advisor (DOMA)
DSA .... Defense Supply Agency [*Later, Defense Logistics Agency*] [*Alexandria, VA*]
DSA .... Defense Supply Association [*Later, ALA*] (EA)
DSA .... Defense Support Agency
DSA .... Defense Systems Analysis [*DoD*]
DSA .... Define Symbol Address [*Computer science*] (IAA)
DSA .... Delay Study Analysis
DSA .... Dell SCSI Array [*Computer science*]
DSA .... Demand Statement Analysis (SAUS)
DSA .... Democratic Socialists of America [*Political party*] (EA)
DSA .... Dense Sintered Alumina (SAUS)
DSA .... Dental Surgery Assistant [*British*]
DSA .... Deoxystreptamine (SAUS)
DSA .... Department of Substance Abuse (SAUS)
DSA .... Deployable Solar Array
DSA .... Depth & Simultaneous Attack (SAUS)
DSA .... Deputies for System Acquisition [*Army*]
DSA .... Deputy Scientific Adviser [*British*]
DSA .... Deputy Secretary to the Admiralty (SAUO)
DSA .... Deputy-Secretary to the Admiralty [*British*]
DSA .... Deputy Sector Advisor
DSA .... Deputy Senior Advisor
DSA .... Designated Security Agency (NATG)
DSA .... Designated Smoking Area (ACAE)
DSA .... Design Schedule Analysis
DSA .... Design Services Allocation (DNAB)
DSA .... Desired Start Address (SAUS)
DSA .... Destination Sub-Area (SAUS)
DSA .... Detense Supply Agency (SAUS)
DSA .... Developmental Sentence Analysis [*Education*]
DSA .... Development Service of America (SAUO)
DSA .... Development Signature Approval
DSA .... Device Specific Adapter (SAUS)
DSA .... Dial Service Analysis [*Telecommunications*] (TEL)
DSA .... Dial Service Assistance [*Telecommunications*] (CET)
DSA .... Dial Service Auxiliary [*Telecommunications*] (IAA)
DSA .... Dial System Assistance (SAUS)
DSA .... Dial System A-switchboard (SAUS)
DSA .... Dielectric Stimulated Arcing (PDAA)
DSA .... Diffusion Self-Aligned (SAUS)
DSA .... Diffusion Self-Aligning (SAUS)
DSA .... Diffusion Self-Alignment
DSA .... Digital Service Area [*Communications term*] (DCT)
DSA .... Digital Serving Area [*Telecommunications*] (TEL)
DSA .... Digital Signal Analyzer (IEEE)
DSA .... Digital Signature Algorithm [*Telecommunications*]
DSA .... Digital Signature Architecture (SAUS)
DSA .... Digital Signature Standard (SAUS)
DSA .... Digital Spectrum Analyzer (NVT)
DSA .... Digital Standard Algorithm (SAUS)
DSA .... Digital Standard Architecture (SAUS)
DSA .... Digital Storage Algorithm (SAUS)
DSA .... Digital Storage Architecture
DSA .... Digital Subtraction Angiography [*or Angiogram*] [*Medicine*]
DSA .... Digital Surface Analyzer (SAUS)
DSA .... Digital System Arrays (AGLO)
DSA .... Dimensionally Stabilized Anode
DSA .... Dimensionally Stable Anode (SAUS)
DSA .... Diploma in Social Administration
DSA .... Diplome en Sciences Administratives (DD)
DSA .... Directory Server/System Agent (SAUS)

DSA .... Directory Service Agent (OSI)
DSA .... Directory System Agent (DINT)
DSA .... Direct Selling Association (EA)
DSA .... Direct Service Activities (MCD)
DSA .... Direct Storage Access
DSA .... Direct Support Aircraft (ACAE)
DSA .... Disaster Support Area (GNE)
DSA .... Discrete Sample Analyzer
DSA .... Disc-Space-Accounting (SAUS)
DSA .... Dispersal Anchorage [*Navy*] (NVT)
DSA .... Display System Activity (AAEL)
DSA .... Distributed Sparse Array (ACAE)
DSA .... Distributed Systems Architecture [*Computer science*] (HGAA)
DSA .... District Senior Adviser (SAUS)
DSA .... District Senior Advisory (MCD)
DSA .... Divisional Service Area (SAUS)
DSA .... Division Senior Advisor [*US advisor to the Army of the Republic of Vietnam*] (VNW)
DSA .... Division Service Area [*Army*]
DSA .... Division Support Area (AABC)
DSA .... Docteur es Sciences Agricole [*Doctor of Agricultural Sciences*] (DD)
DSA .... Doctor of Agricultural Sciences (DD)
DSA .... Documentation Staging Area [*Military*]
DSA .... Dodecylsuccinic Anhydride [*Organic chemistry*]
DSA .... Donkey Society of Australia
DSA .... Doppler Shift Attenuation (SAUS)
DSA .... Doppler Spectrum Analyzer
DSA .... Double Strength A Grade [*Construction term*] (MIST)
DSA .... Double-Submerged Arc (PDAA)
DSA .... Down Sensor Assembly (PDAA)
DSA .... Down's Syndrome Association [*British*]
DSA .... Dozenal Society of America (EA)
DSA .... Dragonfly Society of America (EA)
DSA .... Drilling and Sawing Association [*British*] (DBA)
DSA .... Drillsite Supervisors Association (EA)
DSA .... Drillsite Supevisor Association (SAUS)
DSA .... Driving Standards' Agency [*British*] (WDAA)
DSA .... Drum Seiners Association [*Defunct*] (EA)
DSA .... Drum Store Adapter (SAUS)
DSA .... Duluth, South Shore & Atlantic Railroad [*AAR code*] [*Obsolete*]
DSA .... Duodecimal Society of America (AEBS)
DSA .... Dynamic Safety (SAUS)
DSA .... Dynamic Safety Suspension [*Automotive engineering*]
DSA .... Dynamic Scalable Architecture [*Computer science*] (VERA)
DSA .... Dynamic Screening Anomaly (SAUS)
DSA .... Dynamic Server Architecture (GART)
DSA .... Dynamic Shear Adhesion (PDAA)
DSA .... Dynamic Signal Analyzer
DSA .... Dynamic Spring Analysis
DSA .... Dynamic Storage Area (CMD)
DSA .... Sidley & Austin, Washington, DC [*Library symbol*] [*Library of Congress*] (LCLS)
DSA .... Spectro-Angular Density Method of Forecasting Ocean Waves [*Marine science*] (MSC)
DSA .... Supreme Lodge of the Danish Sisterhood of America (EA)
DSAA .... Dairy Shorthorn Association of Australia
DSAA .... Defense Security Assistance Agency
DSAA .... Direct Selling Association of Australia
DSAA .... Driving School Association of America (EA)
DSAA .... Driving School Association ofAmerica (SAUS)
DSA/AAO ..... Development Signature Approval - Advanced Assembly Outline
DSAB .... Dictionary of South African Biography [*A publication*]
DSAB .... Distributed Systems Architecture Board (SAUO)
DSABL .... Depth and Simultaneous Attack Battle Lab [*Army*] (SEWL)
dsabl .... disability (SAUS)
DSABL .... Disable (AABC)
DSABLSEVP... Disability Severance Pay
DSABS .... Defence Science Advisory Board (SAUS)
DSAC .... Data Set Authory Credential (SAUS)
DSAC .... Deceleration Spark Advance Control [*Automotive engineering*]
DSAC .... Defense Security Assistance Council (SAUO)
DSAC .... Defense Systems Affordability Council
DSAC .... Deputy Supreme Allied Commander (AABC)
DSAC .... Diaper Service Accreditation Council (EA)
DSAC .... Dixon Springs Agricultural Center [*University of Illinois*] [*Research center*] (RCD)
DSAC .... DLA Systems Automation Center (SAUO)
DSACAS .... Defense Supply Agency Contract Administration Services [*DoD*]
DSACEL .... Defense Supply Agency Contractor Experience List [*DoD*]
DSACEUR .... Deputy Supreme Allied Commander, Europe (NATG)
DSACS .... Defense Standard Ammunition Computer System [*DoD*] (GFGA)
DSACS .... Direct Support Armored Cannon System (SAUS)
DSACT .... Direct Sinoatrial Conduction Time [*Medicine*] (DMAA)
DSAD .... Data System Authorization Directory (SAUO)
DSAD .... Data Systems and Analysis Directorate (MCD)
DSAD .... Data Systems Application Division [*Agricultural Research Service*]
DSAD .... Data Systems Authorization Directory (AFIT)
DSAD .... Destruct Safe Arm Device
DSAD .... Director, Systems Analysis Division (SAUO)
DSADAP ...... Digital Synthetic Array Data Processor (ACAE)
DSAF .... Destination Subarea Address Field (SAUS)
DSAF .... Destination Subarea Field [*IBM Corp.*] (CIST)
D-SAFE .... Depot System Support Activity Far East [*US Army Materiel Command*]
DSA/FO .... Development Signature Approval - Fabrication Order
DSAFSM ...... Deputy Safeguard [*Missile defense*] System Manager (AABC)
DSAFSM ...... Deputy System Manager [*Army*] (AABC)
DSAG .... Dallas Audit Group (SAUO)
DSAG .... Defence Systems Analysis Group [*Canada*]
DSAH .... Defense Supply Agency Handbook [*DoD*]
DSAH .... Defense Supply Agency Headquarters (SAUO)
DSAHBK ...... Defense Supply Agency Handbook [*DoD*]
DSAI .... Digital Solar Aspect Indicator (IIA)
DSAI .... Drug Store Applicant Inventory [*Test*] [*London House, Inc.*] (TES)
DSAIER .... Defense Supply Agency Industrial Equipment Reserve [*DoD*]
DS-AIK .... Demokratiske Sosialister - Arbeidernes Informasjon Kommitte [*Democratic Socialists - Workers' Information Committee*] [*Norway*] [*Political party*] (PPE)
DSAirP .... Defence Supply Aircraft Panel (SAUO)
DSALD Code... Discount Allowed Code (SAUS)
DSAM .... Defense Supply Agency Manual [*DoD*]
DSAM .... Defense Systems Acquisition Management [*DoD*]
DSAM .... Direct Sequential Access Method (SAUS)
DSAM .... Doppler Shift Attenuation Method (SAUS)
DSAM .... Dual-Surface Attenuation Module (MCD)
DSAmnP ...... Defence Supply Ammunition Panel (SAUO)
DSA-MOS .... diffused self aligned MOS (SAUS)
DSAMOS ...... Diffusion Self-Aligned Metal-Oxide Semiconductor (BUR)
DSA-MOS .... diffusion self aligned MOS (SAUS)
DSA MOSFET... diffused self aligned MOS (SAUS)
DSAMOSFET... Diffusion Self-Aligned Metal-Oxide Semiconductor Field Effect Transistor [*Electronics*] (IAA)
DSA MOSFET... diffusion self aligned MOS (SAUS)
DSAMOST .... Diffusion Self-Aligned Metal-Oxide Semiconductor Transistor [*Electronics*] (IAA)
DSA MOST... Diffusion Self Aligned MOS Transistor (SAUS)
DSAMT .... Down Syndrome Association of Metropolitan Toronto
DSAN .... Debug Syntax Analysis [*Telecommunications*] (TEL)
DS & DH .... Data Switching and Data Handling (AFM)
DS & P .... Duell, Sloan & Pearce (SAUS)
DS & R .... Data Storage and Retrieval (MSA)
DS&RS .... Document Storage and Retrieval System (SAUO)
DS & S .... Data Systems and Statistics (AFM)
DS & SO ...... Data Systems and Statistics Officer [*Air Force*]
DS & T .... Directorate of Science and Technology (SAUS)
DSANSW ...... Down Syndrome Association of New South Wales [*Australia*]
DSANZ .... Direct Selling Association of New Zealand (SAUO)
DSAO .... Data Systems Automation Office [*Columbus, Ohio*] [*Military*]
DSAO .... Diplomatic Service Administration Office [*British*]
DSAP .... Data Self-Auditing Program [*Environmental Protection Agency*] (EPA)
DSAP .... Data Systems Automatic Program (SAUS)
DSAP .... Data Systems Automation Program
DSAP .... Dee Scofield Awareness Program [*Defunct*] (EA)
DSAP .... Defense Security Assistance Program (NVT)
DSAP .... Defense Supply Agency Poster [*DoD*] (MCD)
DSAP .... Defense Systems Application Program [*DoD*]
DSAP .... Designated Security-Assessed Position
DSAP .... Destination Link Service Access Point [*Computer science*] (VERA)
DSAP .... Destination Service Access Point
DSAP .... Directory Scope Analysis Program [*Bell System*]
DSAP .... Disseminated Superficial Actinic Porokeratosis [*Medicine*] (MAE)
DSAP .... DOE Special Analysis Project (SAUS)
DSAQ .... [*The*] Down Syndrome Association of Queensland
DSAR .... Daily Subsistance Allowance Rates [*Business travel*] (BARN)
DSAR .... Data-Sampling Automatic Receiver (MCD)
DSAR .... Defense Supply Agency Regulation [*DoD*]
DSARC .... Defense Systems Acquisition Review Council [*Pentagon board*] (MCD)
DSARMNT.... Disarmament
DSArmP .... Defence Supply Armament Panel (SAUO)
DSAS .... Data Set Analysis System [*Computer science*] (HGAA)
DSAS .... Data Sharing Architecture System (SAUS)
DSAS .... Del Shannon Appreciation Society (EAIO)
DSAS .... Dial Service Assistance Switchboard [*Telecommunications*] (CET)
dsas .... dial-service-assistance switchboard (SAUS)
DSAs .... Dimensionally Stable Anodes (SAUS)
DSAS .... Direct Support Aviation Section [*Army*]
DSAS .... Discrete Subaortic Stenosis [*Medicine*]
DSASBL .... Disassemble (IAA)
DSASC .... Defense Supply Agency Administrative Support Center [*DoD*]
D Sa Sc .... Doctor of Sacred Sciences
DSASO .... Deputy Senior Air Staff Officer [*British military*] (DMA)
DSASS .... Design Services Administrative Support System (SAUS)
DSA Switchboard... Dial Service Auxiliary Switchboard (SAUS)
DSAT .... Defensive Satellite (MCD)
DSAT .... Disk Storage Allocation Table (MCD)
DSAT .... Distributed System Administration Team (SAUS)
DSATC .... Descent so as to Cross (SAUS)
DSATR .... Descend So as to Reach [*Aviation*] (FAAC)
DSA Transistor... Diffusion Self-Aligned Transistor (SAUS)
DSATS .... DLA Standard Automation Transportation System (SAUS)
DS/ATSS ...... Direct Support/-Automatic est Support System (SAUS)
DSATX .... Descend So as to Cross [*Aviation*] (FAAC)
DSAV .... Dr Solomon's Anti-Virus [*Software*]
DSAW .... Directorate of Surface and Air Warfare (SAUO)
DSAW .... Dispersive Surface Acoustic Wave (MCD)
DSA-WRAO... Defense Supply Agency - Western Regional Audit Office [*DoD*]
DSA-YS .... Democratic Socialists of America - Youth Section (EA)
DSB .... Air Senegal, Societe Nationale de Transport Aerien [*ICAO designator*] (FAAC)

DSB .... Dahlgren Smoothbore
DSB .... Danish State Railways (SAUS)
DSB .... Danske Statsbaner [*Danish State Railways*]
DSB .... Data Set Block
DSB .... Debit sans Brene [*Charge without Abatement*] [*French*] [*Business term*]
DSB .... Debit sans Brevet [*Debt without Writ*] [*French*] [*Legal term*] (DLA)
DSB .... Debitum Sine Brevi [*Debt without Writ*] [*Latin*] [*Legal term*] (DLA)
DSB .... Decade Synchro Bridge (SAUS)
DSB .... Decade Synchronic Bridge
DSB .... Defence Signal Board [*British*]
DSB .... Defense Science Board [*DoD*]
DSB .... Defense Signals Board (SAUO)
DSB .... Demand Scheduled Bus (OA)
DSB .... Department of Small Business [*Australia*]
DSB .... Department of State. Bulletin [*A publication*]
DSB .... Department of Statutory Bodies (SAUS)
DSB .... De Sola Brothers (SAUS)
DSB .... Device Status Byte [*Computer science*] (BUR)
DSB .... Diagnostic Skills Battery [*Educational test*]
DSB .... Dial System B-position (SAUS)
DSB .... Dial System B-switchboard (SAUS)
DSB .... Dictionary of Scientific Biography [*A publication*]
DSB .... Digital Storage Buffer (IAA)
DSB .... digital switch board (SAUS)
DSB .... Digit Select Block (SAUS)
DSB .... Diplomatic Services Bureau
DSB .... direct satellite broadcasting (SAUS)
DSB .... Direct Sound Broadcast
DSB .... Direct Sounder Broadcast (ACAE)
DSB .... Direct Sounding Broadcast (EOSA)
DSB .... Direct Support Battery [*Army*] (ADDR)
DSB .... Disbursement
DSB .... Dispersion-Strengthened Brass (SAUS)
DSB .... Dispersion-Strengthened Bronze (SAUS)
DSB .... Distribution Switchboard
DSB .... Divine Science Bachelor
DSB .... Documentation Standards Committee (ECII)
DSB .... Document Status Bulletin (MCD)
DSB .... Double Sideband
DSB .... Double SideBand transmission (SAUS)
DSB .... Double Strand Break [*Genetics*]
DSB .... Double Strength B Grade [*Construction term*] (MIST)
DSB .... Drill Spacer Block (MCD)
DSB .... Drug Supervisory Body
DSB .... Dry Support Bridge (SAUS)
DSB .... Duracell Special Batteries (SAUS)
DSB .... Duty Steam Boat [*British military*] (DMA)
DSBA .... Delaware School Boards Association (SAUO)
DSBAM .... Double-Sideband Amplitude Modulation [*Telecommunications*] (TEL)
DSBAM .... Double SideBand Amplitude Module (SAUS)
DSBAMRC .... Double-Sideband Amplitude Modulation Reduced Carrier [*Telecommunications*] (IEEE)
DSBB .... Double Sheath Bronchial Brushing [*Medicine*] (DAVI)
DSBC .... DS Bancor [*NASDAQ symbol*] (TTSB)
DSBC .... DS Bancor, Inc. [*NASDAQ symbol*] (NQ)
DSBCO .... Defense Surplus Bidders Control Office
DSBDC .... Double Sideband, Decreased Carrier (SAUS)
DSBDC .... Double Sideband, Diminished Carrier (SAUS)
DSBDC .... Double Sideband, Discrete Carrier (SAUS)
DSBE .... Di-secondary-butyl Ether [*Organic chemistry*]
DSBEC .... Double-Sideband Emitted Carrier [*Telecommunications*] (TEL)
DSBG .... Disbursing (AFM)
DSBK .... Data Set by Key [*Computer science*] (IAA)
DSBL .... Disable (MSA)
DSBLD .... Disabled (SAUS)
DSBLTY .... Disability
DSBM .... Double Sideband Modulation (SAUS)
DSB Modulation ... Double Sideband Modulation (SAUS)
dsbn .... disband (SAUS)
DS Bnc .... DS Bancor, Inc. [*Associated Press*] (SAG)
DSBR .... Double-Strand Break Repair [*Genetics*]
DSBRC .... Double-Sideband Reduced Carrier [*Telecommunications*] (TEL)
DSBS .... Defense Science Board Subcommittee [*DoD*]
DSBs .... Digital Storage Buffers (SAUS)
DSBS .... Direct Sound Broadcasting by Satellite (SAUS)
DSBS .... Droughtmaster Stud Breeders' Society [*Australia*]
DSBSC .... Defense Science Board Subcommittee (SAUO)
DSBSC .... Double-Sideband Suppressed Carrier [*Modulation*]
DSB-SC .... double sideband suppressed carrier (SAUS)
DSB/SC .... Double Sideband with Suppressed Carrier (SAUS)
DSBSCAM .... Double Sideband, Suppressed Carrier Amplitude Modulation (SAUS)
DSBSCAM w/QM ... DSBSCAM with Quadrature Multiplexing (SAUS)
DSBSCASK ... Double Sideband, Suppressed Carrier Amplitude Shift Keyed (SAUS)
DSBT .... Deletable Soft Return (SAUS)
DSBT .... Donor-Specific Blood Transfusion [*Medicine*] (DMAA)
DSBTC .... Double-Sideband Transmitted Carrier [*Telecommunications*]
DSB (UN) .... Drug Supervisory Body of the United Nations
DSBV .... Double-Sealed Ball Valve
DSBWC .... Double Sideband with Carrier [*Modulation*] (IAA)
DSC .... Code of Safety for Dynamically Supported Craft (SAUS)
DSC .... Dangerous goods, Solid Cargoes and containers (SAUS)
DSC .... Data Selection Circuit (SAUS)
DSC .... Data Separator Card (MCD)
DSC .... Data Services Center [*International City Management Association*] [*Information service or system*] (IID)
DSC .... Data Services Company (SAUO)
DSC .... Data Set Controller
DSC .... Data Statistics Comparison Software [*Computer science*]
DSC .... Data Stream Compatability (IAA)
DSC .... Data Streaming Channel (VLIE)
DSC .... Data Sub-Central (SAUS)
DSC .... Data Synchronizer Channel
DSC .... Data Synchronizing Channel (VLIE)
DSC .... Data System Console (CAAL)
DSC .... Data Systems Controller (MCD)
DSC .... Data Systems Technician, Chief [*Navy rating*]
DSC .... Dealer Service Center [*Automotive industry*]
DSC .... Debye-Sears Cell [*Physics*]
DSC .... [*A*] Decade of Study of the Constitution [*Defunct*] (EA)
DSC .... Decent Suit of Civvies [*British slang military decoration*] [*World War I*]
DSC .... Decimal Classification System (SAUS)
DSC .... Decision Sciences Corp. (IID)
DSC .... Decommutator Synchronization Code (ACAE)
DSC .... Decussation of the Superior Cerebellar pedoncles (SAUS)
DSC .... Dedicated Signal Conditioner (MCD)
DSC .... Deep Submergence Computer (ACAE)
DSC .... Defence and Security Committee (SAUS)
DSC .... Defence (or Defense) Shipping Council (SAUO)
DSC .... Defence Security Command (SAUS)
DSC .... Defence Situation Centre (SAUS)
DSC .... Defense Shipping Council [*NATO*]
DSC .... Defense Space Council (SAUO)
DSC .... Defense Supplies Corporation (SAUO)
DSC .... Defense Supply Center (AABC)
DSC .... Defense Supply Corp. [*World War II*]
DSC .... Defensiveness Scale for Children [*Psychology*]
DSC .... Delaware State College [*Dover*]
DSC .... Delivered System Capability
DSC .... Dental Study Club (SAUS)
DSC .... Depot Supply Center
DSC .... Depot Support Concept (SAUS)
DSC .... Deputy Sheriff Clerk (ROG)
DSC .... Deputy Squadron Commander (SAUS)
DSC .... De Sanctis-Cacchione [*Syndrome*] [*Medicine*] (EDAA)
DSC .... Design Safety Criteria [*Nuclear energy*] (NRCH)
DSC .... Design Stability Code (VLIE)
DSC .... Detroit Stock Exchange (MHDB)
DSC .... Development Studies Center (SAUO)
DSC .... Difference Signal Control (SAUS)
DSC .... Differential Scanning Calorimeter [*or Calorimetry*] [*Instrumentation*]
DSC .... Differential Scanning Calorimetry (SAUS)
DSC .... differential scanning colorimetry (SAUS)
DSC .... Differential Signal Control
DSC .... Digital Scan Converter (MCD)
DSC .... digital selective call (SAUS)
DSC .... Digital Selective Calling
DSC .... Digital Set Point Control (IAA)
DSC .... digital set-point control (SAUS)
DSC .... Digital Signal Channel (SAUS)
DSC .... Digital Signal Conditioner (MCD)
DSC .... digital signal converter (SAUS)
DSC .... Digital Sound Corp. [*Telecommunications service*] (TSSD)
DSC .... Digital Source Collector
DSC .... Digital Spectrum Compatible (PS)
DSC .... Digital Stabilization Console
DSC .... Digital Subscriber Controller [*Telecommunications*]
DSC .... Digital Synchro Converter (ACAE)
DSC .... Digit Select Character [*Computer science*] (VLIE)
DSC .... Digit Selector Common [*Computer science*] (VLIE)
DSC .... Diploma of the Sydney Conservatorium of Music [*Australia*]
DSC .... Directed Scattering Coefficients (ARMP)
DSC .... Directional Solidification Crystal (SSD)
DSC .... Direct Satellite Communications
DSC .... Direct Self-Control (SAUS)
DSC .... Direct Semiconductor (SAUS)
DSC .... Direct Side-force Control (SAUS)
DSC .... Direct Strip Casting (SAUS)
DSC .... Direct Support Command (SAUS)
DSC .... Direct Synchronized Control (SAUS)
DSC .... Disappearance of Single Cell [*Assay*] [*Cytology*]
DSC .... Discone Antenna
DSC .... Disconnect (SAUS)
DSC .... Discount (SAUS)
DSC .... Discovery Channel (ADWA)
DSC .... Discrete System Concept
DSC .... Discrete Timesystems, Inc. [*Toronto Stock Exchange symbol*]
DSC .... Disc Storage Controller (SAUS)
DSC .... Disk Storage Controller [*Computer science*] (CMD)
DSC .... Disk Store Control (SAUS)
DSC .... Disodium Cromoglycate [*Pharmacology*]
DSC .... Displacement Shift Complete (SAUS)
DSC .... Dissolved Scrubbing Capacity (SAUS)
DSC .... Distant Station Connected [*Computer science*] (BUR)
DSC .... Distinct Switching Centre (SAUS)
DSC .... Distinguished Service Cross [*US and British*] [*Military decoration*]
DSC .... Distributed Service Coordinator (VLIE)
DSC .... Distribution of Stockage Code (AABC)

DSC .... District Switching Center [*Telecommunications*]
DSC .... District Switching Centre [*Telecommunications network*] (NITA)
DSC .... Disuccinimidyl Carbonate (SAUS)
DSC .... DIVAD Systems Controller (MCD)
DSC .... Divided Spouses Coalition [*Defunct*] (EA)
DSC .... Divisional Supply Column (SAUO)
DSC .... Doctor of Christian Science
DSC .... Doctor of Commercial Science
DSC .... Doctor of Science (ACAE)
DSc .... Doctor of Science (GAGS)
DSC .... Doctor of Surgical Chiropody
D Sc............ Doctor Scientiae [*Doctor of Science*] [*Latin*]
DSC .... Documentation Standards Committee [*British*] (DIT)
DSC .... Document Service Center
DSC .... document structuring conventions (SAUS)
DSC .... Document Supply Centre (SAUS)
DSC .... Document Support Centre (SAUO)
DSC .... Domestic Satellite Carrier [*Computer science*] (TNIG)
DSC .... Dominant-Subordinate Conflict [*Biology*]
DSC .... Donner Scientific Company (SAUO)
DSC .... Doppler Shift Compensation [*Physics*]
dsc............ Double Silk Covered (IDOE)
DSC .... Double Silk Covered [*Wire insulation*]
dsc............ Double-Silk Covering (SAUS)
DSC .... Down's Syndrome Congress [*Later, NDSC*] (EA)
DSC .... Downstage Center [*Toward audience*] [*A stage direction*]
DSC .... Drain Saturation Current
DSC .... Dry Sterile Dressing (SAUS)
DSC .... DSC Communications Corp. [*Associated Press*] (SAG)
DSC .... Duns Scotus College [*Detroit, MI*]
DSC .... Durable Sprayed Cladding (SAUS)
DSC .... Dynamically Self-Checked (SAUS)
DSC .... Dynamic Science Corporation (SAUO)
DSC .... Dynamic Sequential Control (AAG)
DSC .... Dynamic Slide Compensator
DSC .... Dynamic Stability Control [*Automotive*]
DSC .... Dynamic Standby Computer (KSC)
DSC .... International Die Sinkers' Conference
DSC .... Scottish Rite of Freemasonry, Southern Jurisdiction USA, Supreme Council Library, Washington, DC [*Library symbol*] [*Library of Congress*] (LCLS)
DSC .... South Carolina State Library, Columbia, SC [*OCLC symbol*] (OCLC)
DSC .... Sub-Committee on Dangerous Goods, Solid Cargoes and Containers (SAUO)
D SC .... United States District Court for the District of South Carolina (DLA)
DSCA .... Data Systems Coordinating Activity [*DoD*] (DNAB)
DSCA .... Default System Control Area [*Computer science*] (VLIE)
DSCA .... Department of State Correspondents Association (EA)
DScA............ Doctor of Science in Agriculture
DSCA .... Douglas Social Credit Association (SAUO)
DSCAB .... Department of State Contract Appeals Board (AAGC)
DScAdm............ Doctor in Administrative Sciences
DScAdmin............ Doctor in Administrative Science (SAUS)
DSCAEF .... Deputy Supreme Commander, Allied Expeditionary Force
DScAg............ Doctor of Science in Agriculture (ADA)
D Sc Agr............ Doctor of Science in Agriculture
DSc(Agric)... Doctor of Science in Agriculture (ADA)
D Scale............ Convective Scale (SAUS)
DSCAPRS .... Dental Suction Apparatus
DSCAT .... Data Set Catalog [*Computer science*] (IAA)
DSCB .... Data Set Control Block [*Computer science*]
DSCC .... Data Set Control and Correction (SAUS)
DSCC .... Datasouth Computer Corp. [*NASDAQ symbol*] (COMM)
DSCC .... Deep Space Communications Complex (MCD)
DSCC .... Deferred Specification Compliance Change (MCD)
DSCC .... Democratic Senatorial Campaign Committee [*Commercial firm*] (EA)
dscc............ Democratic Senatorial Campaign Committee
DSCC .... Desiccant [*Chemistry*]
DSCC .... Division Support Control Center [*Army*]
DScC............ Doctor of Commercial Science (SAUS)
DSCC .... Double Silk, Cotton Covered [*Wire insulation*] (IAA)
DSCC .... Double-Silk Cotton Covering (SAUS)
DSCCD .... Discount Code (SAUS)
DScCom............ Doctor of Commercial Science (SAUS)
D Sc Com.... Doctor of Science in Commerce
DSCD .... Directorate of Stores and Clothing Development [*British*]
DScD............ Doctor of Science and Didactics (ADA)
DScD............ Doctor of Science in Dentistry (WGA)
DS-CDMA ..... Direct Sequence CDMA (SAUS)
DS/CDMA..... Direct Sequence - Code Division Multiple Access (SAUS)
DSCDP .... Delaware State Central Data Processing (SAUS)
DSCE .... Dental Simulated Clinical Exercise (SAUO)
DScE............ Doctor of Science in Engineering
D Sc Ec............ Doctor of Science in Economics (SAUS)
DScEco............ Doctor of Science in Economics (NADA)
D Sc Econ.... Doctor of Science in Economics
DSCEMS .... Depth-Selective Conversion Electron Mossbauer Spectroscopy
DScEng............ Doctor of Science and Engineering (SAUS)
D Sc (Eng)... Doctor of Science (Engineering) (EY)
DScEng............ Doctor of Science in Engineering (SAUS)
DSCF .... Digital Switched Capacitor Filter (SAUS)
DSCF .... Doppler-Shifted Constant Frequency [*Biosonar research*]
dscf............ Dry Standard Cubic Feet (COE)
DSCF .... Dry Standard Cubic Feet (GFGA)
DScFin............ Doctor of Financial Science
DScFor............ Doctor of Science in Forestry (ADA)
DSCG .... Digital Scan Converter Group (TIMI)
DSCG .... Digital Sine/Cosine Generator (IAA)
DSCG .... Directional Solidification Crystal Growth (SSD)
DSCG .... Disodium Cromoglycate [*Pharmacology*]
DscGph............ Disc Graphics, Inc. [*Associated Press*] (SAG)
DSCH .... Dark Skies for Comet Halley [*Defunct*] (EA)
DSCH .... Dual Service Channel (SAUS)
DSC-HDTV... Digital Spectrum Compatible HDTV (SAUS)
D Sch Mus... Doctor of School Music
D Sc Hyg ..... Doctor of Science in Hygiene
DSCI .... Derma Sciences [*NASDAQ symbol*] (TTSB)
DSCI .... Derma Sciences, Inc. [*NASDAQ symbol*] (SAG)
D Sci .... Doctor of Science
DScI............ Doctor of Science in Industry (NADA)
D Sci H............ Doctor of Science and Hygiene
DSCIL .... Defense Supply Center Indication List (DNAB)
DSCIM .... Display Select Computer Input Multiplexer (MCD)
DSCIM .... Display System Computer Input Multiplexer [*NASA*] (NASA)
D Sc in VM... Doctor of Science in Veterinary Medicine
DSCIZ .... Dayton Signal Corps Inspection Zone (SAUS)
DScJur............ Doctor of Science of Jurisprudence (NADA)
DScJur............ Doctor of the Science of Jurisprudence (SAUS)
DSCL .... Displacement Shift Complete Lattice (SAUS)
D Sc L .... Doctor of the Science of Law
DSCl .... Durable Sprayed Cladding (PDAA)
DSCLO .... Disclosure-Online [*Information service or system*]
DSCM .... Data Systems Technician, Master Chief [*Navy rating*]
DSCM .... Diploma of the Sydney Conservatorium of Music (SAUS)
DSCM .... drugstore.com, Inc. [*NASDAQ symbol*] (SG)
dscm............ Dry Standard Cubic Meter (COE)
DSCM .... Dry Standard Cubic Meter (EG)
DSCMD .... Dallas Contract Management District (SAUS)
DScMil............ Doctor of Military Science (ADA)
DSCMO .... Decennial Systems and Contracts Management Office (SAUS)
DSCN .... Discontinue (SAUS)
DSCN .... Discontinued (VLIE)
DSCN .... Dispersion-Strengthened Cupro Nickel (SAUS)
D Scn............ Doctor of Scientology
DScNat .... Doctor of Natural Science [*Canada*] (ASC)
DScNat .... Doctor of Natural Sciences (SAUS)
DSCNT .... Descent [*Aviation*] (FAAC)
DSCO .... Deputy State Coordinating Officer [*Department of Emergency Management*] (DEMM)
D Sc O .... Doctor of the Science of Oratory
DSCONT .... Discontinue (MSA)
D Sc Os ...... Doctor of the Science of Osteopathy
DS Covered... Double-Silk Covered (SAUS)
DSCP .... Datascope Corp. [*NASDAQ symbol*] (NQ)
DSCP .... Data Service Command Processor (SAUS)
DSCP .... Data Services Command Processor [*Computer science*] (VLIE)
DSCP .... Defence Supply Construction Panel (SAUO)
DSCP .... Defense Satellite Communications Program (MCD)
DSCP .... Defense Suppression Concept Plan (MCD)
DSCP .... Detailed Site Characterization Plan (SAUS)
DSCP .... Diabetes Self-Care Program (SAUO)
DSCP .... Differentiated Services Code Point (SAUS)
DSCP .... Disk System Control Processor [*Computer science*] (VLIE)
DSCP .... Disk System Control Programming (SAUS)
DSCP .... Division Supply Control Point
DScP............ Doctor of Political Science
DScPol............ Doctor of Political Science (NADA)
DSCR .... Descrambler (SAUS)
DSCR .... description (SAUS)
DSCR .... Detailed Site Characterization Report (SAUS)
DSCR .... Discriminator (SAUS)
DSCR .... District Sub-Chief Ranger [*Ancient Order of Foresters*]
DSCR .... Doppler-Shifted Cyclotron Resonance (SAUS)
DSCRM .... Discriminator (MSA)
DSCRP .... Descriptor [*Computer science*]
DSCS .... Dallas Southern Clinical Society (SAUO)
DSCS .... Danube Sea Container Service (SAUS)
DSCS .... Data Systems Technician, Senior Chief [*Navy rating*]
DSCS .... Defense Satellite Communications System [*DoD*]
DSCS .... Defense Service Communications Satellite (ACAE)
DSCS .... Defense Space Communications Squadron
DSCS .... Defe Satellite Communications System (SAUS)
DSCS .... Desk Side Computer System [*General Electric Co.*]
DSCS .... digital selective calling system (SAUS)
DSCS .... Digital Simulator Computer System
dscs............ direct-set cheese starter (SAUS)
DSCs............ District Switching Centres (SAUS)
DScS............ Doctor of Social Science
DSCS .... Doorstop sample carrier system (SAUS)
DSCS NCF ... Defense Satellite Communications System Network Control Facility (MCD)
DSCSOC............ Defense Satellite Communications Systems Operations Center (DOMA)
DScSoc............ Doctor of Social Science
DSCSOC............ DSCS Operations Center (SAUO)
DSCS OCE .... Defense Satellite Communications System Operations Control Element (MCD)
DSc(Social Sciences)... Doctor of Science in the Social Sciences, University of Southampton [*British*] (DBQ)
DSCS PO ..... Defense Satellite Communications System Program Office (MCD)

DSCS-TD ...... Defense Satellite Communications Support Training Device
DSCS-TD ...... DSCS Training Device (SAUS)
DSCT ...... Defective Sectors Table (SAUS)
dsct ...... Descendant (GEAB)
DSCT ...... Dorsal Spinocerebellar Tract [*Medicine*] (EDAA)
DSCT ...... Double Secondary Current Transformer (MSA)
DScTech ...... Doctor of Science and Technology (SAUS)
D Sc Tech .... Doctor of Technical Science
DSC/TGA ...... differential scanning calorimeter/thermogravimetric analyzer (SAUS)
DSCTP ...... Defence Supply Clothing and Textile Panel (SAUO)
DSCU ...... Disk Store Control Unit (SAUS)
DScVM ...... Doctor of Science in Veterinary Medicine (GAGS)
DSCW ...... Directorate of Service Conditions and Welfare (SAUO)
DSD ...... Daily Staff Digest (SAA)
DSD ...... Data Scanner Distributor (SAUS)
DSD ...... Data-Scanner Distributor
DSD ...... Data Security Device (ACAE)
DSD ...... Data Set Definition [*Computer science*] (IBMDP)
DSD ...... Data Set Deletion (SAUS)
DSD ...... Data Status Display
DSD ...... Data Storage Device
DSD ...... Data Stream Direct [*Computer science*]
DSD ...... Data Structure Diagram
DSD ...... Data System Designator (SAUS)
DSD ...... Data Systems Designator (AFM)
DSD ...... Data Systems Division (SAUS)
DSD ...... Dayton Superior'A' [*NYSE symbol*] (SG)
DSD ...... Dead Sea Scrolls: Manual of Discipline (BJA)
DSD ...... DECHEMA [*Deutsche Gesellschaft fuer Chemisches Appartewesen, Chemische Technik, und Biotechnologie eV*] Stoffdaten Dienst [*DECHEMA Physical Property Data Service*] [*Information service or system*] (IID)
DSD ...... Deep Submergence Device (NVT)
DSD ...... Deep Suspended DIFAR [*Military*] (CAAL)
DSD ...... Defence Signals Directorate of Australia (CARL)
DSD ...... Defense Support Division (SAUO)
DSD ...... Defense Systems Division (ACAE)
DSD ...... Defense Systems Division, General Motors Corp. (SAUO)
DSD ...... Delta Sigma Delta [*An association*] (NTPA)
DSD ...... Demographic Surveys Division [*Census*] (OICC)
DSD ...... Departmental Science Development [*National Science Foundation*]
DSD ...... Department Science Development [*Medicine*] (EDAA)
DSD ...... Depression Sine Depression [*Psychology*]
DSD ...... Depressive Spectrum Disease (SAUS)
DSD ...... Depressive Spectrum Disorder (SAUS)
DSD ...... Deputy Secretary of Defense
DSD ...... Detailed System Design [*Computer science*]
dsd ...... Diamond-Square-Diamond [*Lipscomb polyhedral rearrangement in borane anion and carborane series*]
DSD ...... Digital Sailing Directions (SAUS)
DSD ...... Digital Sharing Device (SAUS)
DSD ...... Digital Standard Dump (SAUS)
DSD ...... Digital System Design (IEEE)
DSD ...... Digital System Diagram
DSD ...... Digital Systems Department (SAUO)
DSD ...... Diode Semiconductor Device
DSD ...... Director of Signal Department [*Obsolete*] [*Navy*] [*British*]
DSD ...... Director of Signal Division (SAUO)
DSD ...... Director of Staff Duties [*Military*] [*British*]
DSD ...... Direct-Search Discretized [*Computer science*]
DSD ...... Direct Service Dialing (SAUS)
DSD ...... Direct Service Dialling (SAUS)
DSD ...... Direct Stream Digital (ADWA)
DSD ...... Discharge Summary Dictated [*Medicine*] (DMAA)
DSD ...... Disk Storage Device [*Computer science*]
DSD ...... Disk Store Drive (SAUS)
DSD ...... Disposal Division (SAUS)
DSD ...... Divine Science Doctor
DSD ...... Doctrine and Systems Directorate [*Army*] (RDA)
DSD ...... Documentary Sight Draft (MARI)
DSD ...... Double-Single-Dummy [*in game of bridge*]
DSD ...... Double Switching Demodulator (SAUS)
DSD ...... Drop Size Distribution (ARMP)
DSD ...... Dry Sterile Dressing [*Medicine*]
DSD ...... Dry Surgical Dressing (SAUS)
DSD ...... DSIF [*Deep Space Instrumentation Facility*] Supply Depot [*NASA*]
DSD ...... Duales System Deutschland [*German recycling organization*]
DSD ...... Dual-Speed Drive
DSD ...... Dual-Stage Deployment [*Automotive safety systems*]
DSD ...... Dynamic System Display (SAUS)
DSD ...... La Desirade [*Guadeloupe*] [*Airport symbol*] (OAG)
D SD ...... United States District Court for the District of South Dakota (DLA)
DSD ...... United States Superintendent of Documents, Washington, DC [*Library symbol*] [*Library of Congress*] (LCLS)
DSDA ...... Dedicated and Switched Digital Access [*Tylink Corp.*]
DSDA ...... Dual-Stage Driver Airbag [*Automotive safety systems*]
DSDAR ...... Deputy and Scientific Director of Army Research
DSDBTL ...... Direct-current Switching Diffused Base Transistor Logic (SAUS)
DSDC ...... Data Segment Descriptor Cashe [*Computer science*] (VERA)
DSDC ...... Data Systems Design Center [*Air Force*]
DSDC ...... Direct Service Dial Capability (SAUS)
DSDC ...... Direct Services Dialing Capability [*Telecommunications*] (OSI)
DSDCS ...... Dynamic Sensor Display and Control Simulator (ACAE)
DSDD ...... Defense Subsystem Development and Demonstration (MCD)
DSDD ...... Double Sided Double Density [*Magnetic disc format*] (NITA)
DSDD ...... Double-Sided, Double-Density Disk [*Computer science*]
DSDDT ...... Double Sampling Dye Dilution Technique [*Medicine*] (EDAA)
DSDE ...... Directorate of Seaward Defence Equipment (SAUO)
DSDG ...... Department of the Superintendent of Demagnetization (SAUO)
DSD-HLB .... Disposal Division-High-Level Waste Branch (SAUS)
DSDI ...... Descendants of the Signers of the Declaration of Independence (EA)
DS Di ...... Doctor of Scientific Didactics
DSDIO ...... Director, Strategic Defense Initiative Organization [*Military*] (SDI)
DSDL ...... Data Storage Definition Language (SAUS)
DSDL ...... Data Storage Description Language
DSDL ...... Distributed System Definition Language (SAUS)
DSDLHP ...... Distributed Spatial Data Library Home Page (SAUO)
DSD-LLB ...... Disposal Division-Low-Level Waste Branch (SAUS)
DSDM ...... Dynamic Systems Development Method [*Computer science*] (ITCA)
dsDNA ...... Deoxyribonucleic Acid, Double-Stranded [*Genetics*] [*Biochemistry*]
dsDNA ...... Double-Stranded DNA (SAUS)
DSDO ...... Data System Design Office (SAUO)
DSDP ...... Data System Development Plan
DSDP ...... Deep Sea Diving Project (SAUS)
DSDP ...... Deep-Sea Drilling Project [*Later, IPOD*] [*National Science Foundation*]
DSDP ...... Double Source Differential Photocapacitance (AAEL)
DSDR ...... Design Section Drawing Record (MCD)
DSDRG ...... Data System Design and Research Group (SAUO)
DSDRS ...... DoD [*Department of Defense*] Standard Data Repository System
DSDS ...... Dataphone Switched Digital Service [*AT & T*]
DSDS ...... Data Storage and Distribution System (ADWA)
DSDS ...... Decision Support Display System (SAUS)
DSDS ...... Deep Sea Diving School (SAUO)
DSDS ...... Digital Synchro Data Source
DSDS ...... Document Survey Data Sheet (KSC)
DSDS ...... Dual-Source Dynamic Synchronous (DNAB)
DSDS ...... Dynamic Synchro Data Service [*or Source*] (MCD)
DSDS ...... Naval School Deep Sea Divers
DSDT ...... Data-Set Definition Table [*Computer science*]
DSDT ...... Deformographic Storage Display Tube [*IBM Corp.*]
DSDT ...... Discrete Space and Discrete Time
DSDT ...... Discrete-Space Discrete-Time (SAUS)
DSDTR ...... Delinquent Supplier Data Transmittal (MCD)
DSDU ...... Data Storage Distribution Unit (MCD)
DSDVOR ...... Double-Sideband Doppler Very-High-Frequency Omnidirectional Range [*FAA*]
DSDX ...... Dairy Shippers Dispatch [*Private rail car owner code*]
DSE ...... Dacca Stock Exchange [*Bangladesh*]
DSE ...... Dartmouth Society of Engineers (SAUO)
DSE ...... Data Set Extension [*IBM Corp.*] [*Computer science*] (BUR)
DSE ...... Data Set Extent (SAUS)
DSE ...... Data Storage Equipment
DSE ...... Data Structure Editor (SAUS)
DSE ...... Data Support Element (MCD)
DSE ...... Data Switching Equipment [*Computer science*] (ACRL)
DSE ...... Data Switching Exchange [*Telecommunications*]
DSE ...... Data Systems Engineering
DSE ...... Debye-Sears Effect [*Physics*]
DSE ...... Deep Sky Exploration
DSE ...... Department of School Education [*New South Wales, Victoria*] [*Australia*]
DSE ...... Department of State Expenditure (SAUS)
DSE ...... Depot Support Equipment (ACAE)
DSE ...... Derby Society of Engineers (SAUO)
DSE ...... Designated Spouse Equivalent
DSE ...... Dessie [*Ethiopia*] [*Airport symbol*] (OAG)
DSE ...... Detector, Selector, and Effector [*Social science*]
DSE ...... Detroit Stock Exchange (SAUO)
DSE ...... Developmental Supportability Engineering (SAUS)
DSE ...... Development Software Engineer (MWOL)
DSE ...... Development Student Engineer (MCD)
DSE ...... Development Supportability Engineering (ACAE)
DSE ...... Development Support Equipment
DSE ...... Diffuse Spasm of Esophagus [*Medicine*] (MELL)
DS/E ...... Digital Scrambler/Encoder (NITA)
DSE ...... Digital Select Emitter (IAA)
DSE ...... Digital Service Europe [*Communications term*] (DCT)
DSE ...... Digital Shaft Encoder
DSE ...... Digital Subtraction Echocardiogram [*Cardiology*] (DAVI)
DSE ...... Digit Selector Emitter (SAUS)
DSE ...... Dimensionally Stabilized Electrode [*Electrochemistry*]
DSE ...... Dimokratikos Stratos Ellados [*Greece*]
DSE ...... Directionally Solidified Eutectic (SAUS)
DSE ...... Directorate of Systems Engineering (AAG)
DSE ...... Director of Systems Evaluation (SAUO)
DSE ...... Direct Sequence Encoding [*Telecommunications*]
DSE ...... Direct Support Element [*Military*] (NVT)
DSE ...... Direct Switching Equipment (NITA)
DSE ...... Direct Switching Exchange [*Telecommunications*] (NITA)
DSE ...... Dispatch Service Emergency (SAUS)
DSE ...... Display Screen Equipment (HEAS)
DSE ...... Distal Sequence Element [*Genetics*]
DSE ...... Distal Stimulating Electrode (DB)
DSE ...... Distributed Systems Engineering (TIMI)
DSE ...... Distributed Systems Environment [*Honeywell, Inc.*] (BUR)
DSE ...... Dobutamine Stress Echoradiography [*Medicine*] (DMAA)
DSE ...... Doctor of Sanitary Engineering
DSE ...... Doctor of Science in Economics
DSE ...... Document Spacing Error (SAUS)

DSE .... Domain Software Environment (SAUS)
DSE .... Domestic Sewage Exclusion
DSE .... Draft Safety Evaluation (NRCH)
DSE .... Driver Screening Evaluator
DSE .... Dry Sheep Equivalent (SAUS)
DSE .... Dry Skin Eczema (MELL)
DSE .... Dual System Estimator [*Demography*]
DSE .... Dyad Symmetry Element [*Genetics*]
DSE .... Dynamic System Electronics
DSEA .... Data Station Emulation Adapter [*IBM Corp*] (VERA)
DSEA .... Data Storage Electronics Assembly [*Apollo*] [*NASA*]
DSEA .... Davis Submerged Escape Apparatus [*British military*] (DMA)
DSEA .... Deep Sea Exploration Association (SAUO)
DSEA .... Defense Security Assistance Agency (SAUO)
DSEA .... Delaware State Education Association (SAUO)
DSEA .... Directorate of Seamanship (SAUO)
DSEA .... Display Station Emulation Adapter (SAUS)
D Se A .... Doctor of Secretarial Arts
DSEB .... Defense Shipping Executive Board [*NATO*]
DSEB .... Discharged Servicemen's Employment Board [*Victoria*] [*Australia*]
DSEC .... Director of Security (AABC)
DSEC/DEF .... Deputy Secretary of Defense (SAUO)
DSECT .... Data Control Section (SAUS)
DSECT .... Data Section (SAUS)
DSECT .... Dummy Control Section [*Computer science*]
DSECT .... Dummy Section [*Computer science*] (ITCA)
DSED .... Defense Suppression Expendable Drone (MCD)
DSEDM .... Departure Sequencing Engineering Development Model [*FAA*] (TAG)
DSEE .... Designated Special Emphasis Engineering (KSC)
DSEE .... Distributed Software Engineering Environment (SAUS)
DSEE .... Domain Software Engineering Environment
DSEF .... Direct Selling Education Foundation (EA)
DSE/FAD .... Data Systems Environment Functions and Application Design [*Course*] [*Computer science*]
DSEG .... Data Systems Engineering Group (MCD)
DSEG .... Defense Systems Evaluation Group [*Air Force*]
DSEG .... Design Studies Evaluation Group [*NATO*]
DSEI .... Daily Summary of Enemy Intelligence [*World War II*]
DSEI .... Disabled Soldiers Embroidery Industry (SAUO)
DSEL .... Data Systems, Designators Exchange List (SAUS)
DSEL .... Deselect (SAUS)
DSEL .... Doctor of Science and English Literature
DSELCY .... Deselect Cycle (SAUS)
DSEM .... Danish Society for Engineering Metrology (SAUO)
DSEMIT .... Digit Selector Emitter (SAUS)
DS Eng .... Doctor of Sanitary Engineering
DSENGA .... Disengaging
DSENGR .... Data Systems Engineer
DSENQ .... Data Set Enqueue (SAUS)
DSENQ Table ... Data Set Enqueue Table (SAUS)
DSEO .... Data Systems Evaluation Office (SAUS)
DSEP .... Data Services Educational Profile
DSEP .... Defense Science and Engineering Program (MCD)
DSEP .... Distribution System Expansion Program (SAUS)
DSES .... Defense Systems Evaluation Squadron [*Air Force*] (AFM)
D Se Sc .... Doctor of Secretarial Science
DSESq .... Defense System Evaluation Squadron [*Air Force*]
D Se St .... Doctor of Secretarial Studies
DSESTS .... Direct Support Electrical System Test Sets (ACAE)
DSET .... Desert Sunshine Exposure Testing, Inc. (SAUS)
DSET .... DSET Corp. [*NASDAQ symbol*] (NASQ)
DSF .... Dainippon Silk Foundation (SAUO)
DSF .... Dairy Suppliers Foundation [*Defunct*] (EA)
DSF .... Danish Simulation Facility (ACAE)
DSF .... Data Scanning and Formatting
DSF .... Data Secured File (SAUS)
DSF .... Data Set Functions (SAUS)
DSF .... Daughters of St. Francis of Assisi [*Roman Catholic religious order*]
DSF .... David See Flying Services [*British*] [*FAA designator*] (FAAC)
DSF .... Day-Second-Foot [*Measurement*]
DSF .... Dead Space Free (AAEL)
DSF .... Defatted Soy Flour (OA)
DSF .... Defense Stock Fund [*DoD*]
DSF .... Delancey Street Foundation (EA)
DSF .... Delivery Sequence File (SAUS)
DSF .... Departmental Square Feet (MCD)
DSF .... Design Safety Factor
DSF .... Deutsch-Sowjetische-Freundschaft [*German-Soviet Friendship*] [*Common street name in East Germany*]
DSF .... Development Stimulating Factor [*Biochemistry*]
DSF .... Device support facility (SAUS)
DSF .... Diffuse Sound Field (MELL)
DSF .... Digital Simulation Facility (SAUS)
DSF .... Directional Solidification Furnace
DSF .... disc storage facility (SAUS)
DSF .... Disk Storage Facility [*Computer science*]
DSF .... Dispersion-strengthened ferritic (SAUS)
DSF .... Disulfiram [*Organic chemistry*]
DSF .... Division of Sea Fisheries (SAUS)
DSF .... Doctor of the Science of Forestry
DSF .... Drum Store Function (SAUS)
Dsf .... Dusseldorf (SAUS)
DSFA .... Defense Solid Fuels Administration [*Terminated, 1954*]
DSFAAS .... Domestic Solid Fuel Appliances Approval Scheme (PDAA)
DSFB .... David Syme Faculty of Business [*Chisholm Institute of Technology*] [*Australia*]
DSFC .... Dark Shadows Fan Club (EA)
DSFC .... Dinah Shore Fan Club (EA)
DSFC .... Direct Side Force Control [*Aviation*]
DSFC .... Dogman and the Shepherds Fan Club (EA)
DSFC .... Doppler Sonar Fish Counting (SAUS)
DSFF .... Downflow Stationary Fixed-Film [*Chemical engineering*]
DSFG .... Diamond Setters Fraternal Guild [*Defunct*] (EA)
DSFI .... Derogatis Sexual Functioning Inventory [*Psychology*]
DSFI .... Divine Science Federation International (EA)
DSFL .... Danish Society for Photogrammetry and Surveying (SAUO)
DSFLP .... Defense Supply Fuels and Lubricants Panel (SAUO)
DSFM .... Division of the State Fire Marshall (COE)
DSFR .... Detailed System Functional Requirements
DSFS .... Doppler Shift Frequency Spectrum
DSFSA .... District School Food Service Association (SAUO)
DSFT .... Detection Scheme with Fixed Thresholds [*Communication signal*]
DSFT .... Discrete Sliding Fourier Transform (PDAA)
DSFU .... Danish Sailors' and Firemen's Union (EA)
DSG .... Danzig Study Group [*German Philatelic Society*] (EA)
DSG .... Dataset Generator (SAA)
DSG .... Data Set Group (SAUO)
DSG .... Data Standards Group (SAUO)
DSG .... Data Systems Group [*Computer science*] (ACRL)
DSG .... Decision Support Graphics [*Hewlett-Packard Co.*]
DSG .... Deep Submergence Group
DSG .... Defense Steering Group [*Military*]
DSG .... Defense Suppression Group [*DoD*] (MCD)
DSG .... Defense Systems Group
DSG .... Democratic Study Group (EA)
DSG .... Deoxyspergualin [*Antineoplastic drug*]
DSG .... Deputy Secretary General (NATG)
DSG .... Deputy Surgeon-General (SAUO)
DSG .... Desaguadero [*Bolivia*] [*Seismograph station code, US Geological Survey*] [*Closed*] (SEIS)
DSG .... Designate (AABC)
dsg .... Designation (SAUS)
DSG .... Designatronics, Inc. [*AMEX symbol*] (COMM)
DSG .... Designer Shoe Guild (EA)
DSG .... Design Systems Group (HGAA)
DSG .... Desktop Systems Group [*Novell, Inc.*] (PCM)
DSG .... Development Studies Group (SAUO)
DSG .... Digital Signal Generation (SAUS)
DSG .... Digital Signal Generator
DSG .... Digital Symbology Generator (MCD)
DSG .... Directed Semantic Graph (SAUS)
DSG .... Directed Studies Group [*Air Force*] (AFM)
DSG .... Direct Support Group [*Army*] (AABC)
DSG .... Disuccinimidyl Glutarate [*Organic chemistry*]
DSG .... Divisional Support Group (SAUS)
DSG .... Double Strength Glass (SAUS)
Dsg .... Dressing [*Medicine*] (AMHC)
DSG .... Dressing [*Medicine*] (IDYL)
dsg .... Dressing [*Medicine*]
DSG .... Dry Sterile Gauze (MELL)
DSGA .... Double Conductor, Shipboard General Use, Armor [*Cable*] (IAA)
DSGB .... Duodecimal Society of Great Britain (SAUO)
DSGI .... DSG International Ltd. [*NASDAQ symbol*] (SAG)
DSGIF .... DSG International Ltd [*NASDAQ symbol*] (TTSB)
DSG Int .... DSG International Ltd. [*Associated Press*] (SAG)
DSGM .... Director Standing Group Memorandum [*NATO*] (NATG)
DSGMM .... Detailed Sensor Geometric Math Model (ACAE)
DSGN .... Design (AFM)
DSGN .... Designate (AFM)
dsgn .... designed (SAUS)
DSGN .... Designer (WDAA)
DSGND .... Designated (FAAC)
dsgnd .... Designed (SAUS)
DSGNG .... Designing
dsgnr .... Designator
DSGNR .... Designer
DSGp .... Directed Studies Group [*Air Force*] (AFM)
DSGR .... Disc Graphics [*NASDAQ symbol*] (TTSB)
DSGR .... Disc Graphics, Inc. [*NASDAQ symbol*] (SAG)
DSGRW .... Disc Graphics Wrrt [*NASDAQ symbol*] (TTSB)
DSGs .... Data Set Groups (SAUO)
DSGS .... Densely Spaced Geodetic Systems (ACAE)
DS/GS .... Direct Support/General Support (MCD)
DSGS(CAR) .... Deputy Secretary of the General Staff (Coordination and Reports) [*Army*] (AABC)
DSGSP .... Defence Supply General Stores Panel (SAUO)
D/Sgt .... Drill Sergeant [*British military*] (DMA)
DSGX .... Descartes Systems Group, Inc. [*NASDAQ symbol*] (NASQ)
DSH .... Data Store Handler (SAUS)
DSH .... Deactivated Shutdown Hours [*Electronics*] (IEEE)
DSH .... Deafness, Speech, & Hearing Publications, Inc. (AEBS)
DSH .... Deliberate Self Harm (SAUS)
DSH .... Deliberate Self-Harm Syndrome
DSH .... Designer Finance Trust [*NYSE symbol*] (SAG)
DSH .... Designer Holdings [*NYSE symbol*] (TTSB)
DSH .... Designer Holdings Ltd. [*NYSE symbol*] (SAG)
DSH .... Desparately Seeking Help (SAUS)
DSH .... Desperately Seeking Help [*Slang*] (VERA)
DSH .... Disproportionate Share Hospital (MHCS)

DSH .... Disproportionate Share Payments
dsh .... domestic short hair (SAUS)
DSH .... Drive Sample Hole (SAUS)
DSH .... Dushanbe [*Stalinabad*] [*Former USSR*] [*Seismograph station code, US Geological Survey*] (SEIS)
DSH .... Northeast Management, Inc. [*ICAO designator*] (FAAC)
Dsh .... Single-Breath Diffusion [*Medicine*] (EDAA)
DSH Abstracts ... Deafness Speach and Hearing Abstracts (SAUS)
DSHC .... Defence Service Homes Corporation (SAUO)
DSHD .... Double Sided and High Density (SAUS)
DS/HD .... Double Sided High-Density Disk [*Computer software*] (PCM)
DSHE .... Downstream Heat Exchanger (AAG)
DSHEA .... Dietary Supplement Health and Education Act [*1194*]
DSHEA .... Dietary Supplement Health and Education Act of 1994
D/SHLD .... Dust Shield [*Automotive engineering*]
DSHMRA ...... Deep Seabed Hard Mineral Resources Act
DSHP .... Disodium Hydrophosphate [*Inorganic chemistry*] [*Also, DSP*]
DSHR .... Delayed Skin Hypersensitivity Reaction [*Medicine*] (DMAA)
DSHR .... Dish-Rinsing
DSHS .... Deliberate Self-Harm Syndrome [*Medicine*] (MELL)
DSHS .... Department of Social and Health Services
DSI .... Daily Sum Insured [*Insurance*] (MARI)
DSI .... Dairy Society International [*Australia*]
DSI .... Dalcroze Society Incorporated (SAUO)
DSI .... Data Set Identifier
DSI .... Data Stream Interface (SAUS)
DSI .... Data Submitted Information (KSC)
DSI .... Data System Integration [*NASA*]
DSI .... Data Systems, Incorporated (SAUO)
DSI .... Data Systems Inquiry (AABC)
DSI .... Dead Sea Isaiah Scroll (BJA)
DSI .... Decision Sciences Institute (EA)
DSI .... Declassified Satellite Images (SAUO)
DSI .... Deep Shock Insulin [*Endocrinology*] (DAVI)
DSI .... Defense Security Installation (SAUS)
DSI .... Defense Simulation Internet [*Army*] (RDA)
DSI .... Defense Systems Incorporated (SAUO)
DSI .... Delivered Source Instructions
DSI .... Delivery to Surgery Interval [*Gynecology*]
DSI .... Depression Status Inventory [*Psychology*] (DB)
DSI .... Deputy Superintending Inspector (HEAS)
DSI .... DeSales Secular Institute (EA)
DSI .... Design Science Institute
DSI .... Desktalk Systems, Inc.
DSI .... Detailed Spectrum Investigation (SAUS)
DSI .... Dial Services Interface (SAUS)
DSI .... Digitally Sensed Image (DGA)
DSI .... Digital Satellite Images (SAUO)
DSI .... Digital Signal Interpolation (SAUS)
DSI .... Digital Signal Processor [*Computer science*]
DSI .... Digital Speech Interpolation [*Telephone channels*]
DSI .... Digital Speech Interpretation
DSI .... Digital Speech Interruption (ACAE)
DSI .... Digital Strain Indicator
DSI .... Digital Subtraction Imaging [*Cardiology*] (DAVI)
DSI .... Directorate of Scientific Information Service (SAUS)
DSI .... Directorate of Scientific Intelligence (SAA)
DSI .... Direct Sample Insertion (SAUS)
DSI .... Direct Support Item [*Army*]
DSI .... Disease Severity Index (SAUO)
DSI .... Dislocation-Solute Interaction (SAUS)
DSI .... Dissociative Surface Ionization [*Organic chemistry*]
DSI .... Distilled Spirits Institute [*Later, DISCUS*] (EA)
DSI .... Distilled Spirits Institute Inc. (SAUO)
DSI .... Distribution Sciences, Inc. [*Information service or system*] (IID)
DSI .... Divisional Safety Inspector [*Ministry of Agriculture, Fisheries, and Food*] [*British*]
DSI .... Division of Science Information [*National Science Foundation*] (IID)
DSI .... Dominion-Scottish Investments Ltd. [*Toronto Stock Exchange symbol*]
DSI .... Domini Social Index [*Stock exchange term*]
DSI .... Dont Say It (Write It) (SAUS)
DSI .... Double Sandwich Indirect
DSI .... Downey Financial [*NYSE symbol*] (TTSB)
DSI .... Down's Syndrome International (EA)
DSI .... Dreyfus Strategic Government [*NYSE symbol*] (SPSG)
DSI .... Dreyfus Strategic Gvts [*NYSE symbol*] (TTSB)
DSI .... Drinking Straw Institute [*Defunct*] (EA)
DSI .... Drug-Seeking Index (MEDA)
DSI .... Dual-Stage Inflation [*Automotive safety systems*]
DSI .... Dwelling Sculpture Institute [*Defunct*] (EA)
DSI .... Dynamic Side Impact [*Automotive safety*]
DSI .... Dynamic Skeleton Interface [*Computer science*] (VERA)
DSI .... Dynamic System Interchange (SAUS)
DSI .... Smithsonian Institution, Washington, DC [*Library symbol*] [*Library of Congress*] (LCLS)
DSIA .... Defense Suppression Integration Analysis (MCD)
DSIA .... Diaper Service Industry Association [*Later, NADS*] (EA)
DSIA .... Diaper Service Institute of America (SAUS)
DSI-AAA ...... Smithsonian Institution, Archives of American Art, Washington, DC [*Library symbol*] [*Library of Congress*] (LCLS)
DSIATP .... Defense Sensor Interpretation and Application Training Program (AFM)
DSI Bulletin ... Dairy Society International Bulletin (SAUO)
DSIC .... Demand Statement Index and Control (SAUS)
DSIC .... Documentation and Scientific Information Center (SAUS)
DSIC .... Dowty & Smiths Industries Controls (SAUS)
DSIC .... DSI Industries [*NASDAQ symbol*] (SAG)
DSICA .... Distilled Spirits Industry Council of Australia
DSID .... Data Set Identification [*Computer science*] (IBMDP)
DSID .... Destination Signaling Identifier (SAUS)
DSID .... Direct Sample Insertion Device (SAUS)
DSID .... Disposable Seismic Intrusion Detector (MCD)
DSID .... Divergence Source-Image Distortion [*Crystal*]
DSIDA .... Disodium Iminodiacetate [*Organic chemistry*]
DSIDBAD ...... Drill Sergeant Identification Badge [*Military decoration*] (GFGA)
DSIdentBad ... Drill Sergeant Identification Badge [*Military decoration*] (AABC)
DSIE .... Deutsche Stiftung fur Internationale Entwicklung [*German Foundation for International Development*] (EAIO)
DSIF .... Deep Space Instrumentation Facility
DSig .... Digital Signature Initiative [*Computer science*]
DSig .... Digital Signatures (SAUS)
DSig .... Digital Signatures Initiative (SAUS)
D Sig Co ...... Divisional Signal Company (SAUO)
DSigs .... Director of Signals (SAUS)
DSI-HMS ...... Smithsonian Institution, Hirshhorn Museum and Sculpture Garden, Washington, DC [*Library symbol*] [*Library of Congress*] (LCLS)
DSII .... Decom Systems, Inc. [*NASDAQ symbol*] (COMM)
DSI Ind .... DSI Industries [*Associated Press*] (SAG)
DSIIR .... Direct Support Imagery Interpretation Report (MCD)
DSIL .... Digital Simulation Language (SAUS)
DSIM .... Diagnostic Fault Simulation (VLIE)
DSIM .... Doctor of Science in Industrial Medicine
DSI-MAA ...... Smithsonian Institution, Museum of African Art, Washington, DC [*Library symbol*] [*Library of Congress*] (LCLS)
DSI-MHT ...... Smithsonian Institution, National Museum of History and Technology, Washington, DC [*Library symbol*] [*Library of Congress*] (LCLS)
D-SIMM .... Dual RAS SIMM (SAUS)
DSIMS .... dynamical SIMS (SAUS)
DSI-Mus ...... Smithsonian Institution, Museum Reference Center, Washington, DC [*Library symbol*] [*Library of Congress*] (LCLS)
DSIN .... Digital Software Information Network [*Computer science*] (CIST)
DSI-NAS ...... Smithsonian Institution, National Space and Air Museum, Washington, DC [*Library symbol*] [*Library of Congress*] (LCLS)
DS in BA ...... Doctor of Science in Business Administration
DSI-NCF ...... Smithsonian Institution, National Collection of Fine Arts, Washington, DC [*Library symbol*] [*Library of Congress*] (LCLS)
DS in Ge Engr ... Doctor of Science in Geological Engineering
DS in Gp Engr ... Doctor of Science in Geophysical Engineering
DS in Met Engr ... Doctor of Science in Metallurgical Engineering
DS in PE ...... Doctor of Science in Petroleum Engineering
DSI-NPG ...... Smithsonian Institution, National Portrait Gallery, Washington, DC [*Library symbol*] [*Library of Congress*] (LCLS)
DS in PRE ... Doctor of Science in Petroleum Refining Engineering
DSIP .... Delta-Sleep-Inducing Peptide
DSIP .... Development, Support and Integration Program (SAUO)
DSIP .... Domestic Science Information Program (SAUO)
DSIPS .... Digital Satellite Image Processing System (MCD)
DSIPT .... Dissipate [*NWS*] (FAAC)
DSIR .... Department of Scientific and Industrial Research [*of the Privy Council for Scientific and Industrial Research*] [*Later, SRC*] [*British*]
DSIR .... Department of Scientific and Industrial Research, Institute of Nuclear Sciences (SAUS)
DSIR .... Department of Scientific and Industrial Research, Wellington (SAUS)
DSIR .... Department of Scientific Industrial Research (SAUS)
DSIR .... Driver-Side Inflatable Restraint [*Automotive safety systems*]
DSIRnet ...... Government Network in New Zealand [*Communications term*] (DCT)
DSIS .... Defence Scientific Information Service [*Canada*] [*Information service or system*] (IID)
DSIS .... Defense Communications System SCF [*Satellite Control Facility*] Interface System (MCD)
DSIS .... Defense Satellite Interface System (ACAE)
DSIS .... Defense Scientific Information Services (SAUS)
DSIS .... Defense System Interaction Study (ACAE)
DSIS .... Department of Scientific Information Services (SAUS)
DSIS .... Development Support Information Service (SAUO)
DSIS .... Digital Software Integration Station (SAUS)
DSIS .... Digital Software Integration System (ACAE)
DSIs .... Directorate of Service Intelligence members or operatives (SAUS)
DSIS .... Director [*or Directorate*] of Scientific Information Service [*Canada*]
DSIS .... Distributed Statistical Information Services (EURO)
DSIS .... Distributed Support Information Standard (PCM)
DSISD .... Data Set Integrity for Shared Data (SAUS)
DSISI .... Double-Sided Inter-Symbol Interference (PDAA)
DSI-SOA ...... Smithsonian Institution, National Museum of Natural History, Office of Anthropology, Washington, DC [*Library symbol*] [*Library of Congress*] (LCLS)
DSISR .... Delinquent Supply Item Status Report (ACAE)
DSISS .... AMC Standard Installation Supply System (SAUS)
DSIT .... Data and Science Integration Team (SAUO)
D-site .... Decoy Site (SAUS)
DSITMS .... Direct Sampling Ion Trap Mass Spectrometry (ABAC)
DSIU .... Discrete Signal Interface Unit (DWSG)
DSIZ .... Diamond Shamrock Industries [*Federal Railroad Administration identification code*]
dsj .... differential space justifier (SAUS)
DSJ .... Differential Spacing Justifying [*Typography*] (SAA)
DSJ .... Discrete Sonic Jet
DSJ .... Doctor of the Science of Jurisprudence
DSJG .... Deputy Secretary John Garamendi (SAUO)

DSK .... Aero Algarve Lda. [*Portugal*] [*FAA designator*] (FAAC)
D Sk .... Daily Sketch (SAUS)
DSK .... Delay Shift Keying (IAA)
DSK .... Demokratikon Sosialistikon Komma [*Democratic Socialist Party*] [*Greece*] [*Political party*] (PPE)
DSK .... Demokratski Savez Kosovo [*Democratic Alliance of Kosovo*] [*Serbia*] [*Political party*] (EY)
DSK .... Deputy Seal Keeper [*British*] (ROG)
DSK .... Dera Ismail Khan [*Pakistan*] [*Airport symbol*] (OAG)
DSK .... Disk [*Computer science*]
DSK .... Disk Island [*Alaska*] [*Seismograph station code, US Geological Survey*] (SEIS)
DSK .... Disulfide Knot (SAUS)
DSK .... Down Stream Keyer (VLIE)
DSK .... Dvorak Simplified Keyboard [*Typewriter keyboard developed by August Dvorak in the 1920's*]
DskDt .... Desktop Data, Inc. [*Associated Press*] (SAG)
DSKY .... Display and Keyboard [*Computer science*]
DSKY .... Display System Keyboard (SAUS)
DSL .... Damage Severity Limit (SAUS)
DSL .... Dampier Salt Ltd (SAUS)
DSL .... Daru [*Sierra Leone*] [*Airport symbol*] (AD)
DSL .... Data Services Laboratory (SAUS)
DSL .... Data Set Label [*Computer science*]
DSL .... Data Simulation Language
DSL .... Data Specification Library (VLIE)
DSL .... Data Specifications Library (SAUS)
DSL .... Data Structures Language [*Computer science*] (BUR)
DSL .... Data Sublanguage (SAUS)
DSL .... Datura Stramonium Lectin (SAUS)
DSL .... Decalogue Society of Lawyers (EA)
DSL .... Deep Scattering Layer [*Undersea populations*]
DSL .... Deep South League (PSS)
DSL .... Defence Standards Laboratories [*British*]
DSL .... Defence Standards Laboratories (or Laboratory) (SAUO)
DSL .... Delivered Source Lines [*of Code*]
DSL .... Denver & Salt Lake Railroad [*AAR code*]
DSL .... Department of Surveys and Lands (SAUS)
DSL .... Depot Stockage List [*Army*]
DSL .... Depot Supply Level (ACAE)
DSL .... Depressed Sight Line (MCD)
DSL .... Design Language (VLIE)
DSL .... Design Simulation Language (SAUS)
DSL .... Detachable Side Locks [*Gunnery*]
DSL .... Detailed Ship Loading
DSL .... Detroit Signal Laboratory [*Army*]
DSL .... Development Support Library (IAA)
DSL .... Development System Library (SAUS)
DSL .... Dialogue Scripting Language [*Computer science*] (VERA)
DSL .... Diamond Sakha Airlines [*Former USSR*] [*FAA designator*] (FAAC)
DSL .... Dickinson School of Law [*Pennsylvania*]
DSL .... Diesel (MSA)
DSL .... Digital Simulation Language [*Computer science*] (CSR)
DSL .... Digital Subscriber Line [*Telecommunications*] (PCM)
DSL .... Digital Subscriber Loop (SAUS)
DSL .... Digital System Specification Language [*Computer science*] (VERA)
DSL .... Directory of Special Libraries (SAUS)
DSL .... Directory of Special Libraries and Information Centers [*A publication*]
DSL .... Direct Static Logic (SAA)
DSL .... Direct Swift Link (SAUS)
DSL .... Distal Sensory Latency [*Medicine*] (DMAA)
DSL .... Distributed Service Logic [*Computer science*] (VERA)
DSL .... Distributed Software Libraries (SAUS)
DSL .... Divisional Systems List (SAUS)
DSL .... Division of Systems and Licensing (SAUO)
DSL .... Doctor of Sacred Letters (CPGU)
DSL .... Doctor of Sacred Literature
DSL .... Document Style Language (ADWA)
DSL .... Document Summary List
DSL .... Domain-Specific Language (RALS)
DSL .... Domestic Substances List [*Canada*]
DSL .... Dominican Steamship Line (SAUS)
dsl .... doppler speed log (SAUS)
DSL .... Downey Financial [*NYSE symbol*] (SG)
DSL .... Downey Financial Corp. [*NYSE symbol*] (SAG)
DSL .... Downey S&L Assn. [*NYSE symbol*] (COMM)
DSL .... Downstage Left [*Toward audience*] [*A stage direction*]
DSL .... Downstream Load [*Communications term*] (DCT)
DSL .... Downwind Safety Limit
DSL .... Drawing and Specification Listing (NRCH)
DSL .... Drawing Status List (ACAE)
DSL .... Dual Shift Left (SAA)
DSL .... dynamic self locking (SAUS)
DSL .... Dynamic Simulation Language [*Computer science*]
DSL .... Dynamic Super Loudness (SAUS)
DSLA .... Directory of Special Libraries in Australia [*A publication*]
DSLAM .... Digital Subscriber Line Access Multiplexer (MLOA)
DSLB .... Digital Subscriber Line Board (SAUS)
DSLC .... Data Subscriber Line Carrier [*Computer science*] (HGAA)
DSLC .... Data Subscriber Loop Carrier (SAUS)
DSLC .... Digital Synchronizing Load Sensing Control [*Electronic controls*] [*Diesel engines*]
DSLCP .... Dynamically Switched Link Control Protocol [*Computer science*] (VERA)
DSLD .... Digital Seismic Listing Device (DWSG)
DSLE .... Directorate of Security and Law Enforcement [*Military*] (DNAB)
D-sleep .... desynchronized sleep (SAUS)
dsl elec .... diesel electric (SAUS)
DSLG .... Discreet Logic, Inc. [*NASDAQ symbol*] (SAG)
DSLGF .... Discreet Logic [*NASDAQ symbol*] (TTSB)
DSLI .... Department of Survey and Land Information (SAUO)
DSLIC .... Digital Subscriber Line Interface Circuit. (SAUS)
DSLIM .... Double-Sided Linear Induction Motor (PDAA)
DSLO .... Disaster Services Liaison Officer
DSLO .... Distributed Systems Licensing Option [*IBM Corp.*]
DSLP .... Danish Social-Liberal Party [*Political party*] (EAIO)
DSLP .... Diary of Social Legislation and Policy [*Australia*] [*A publication*]
DSLT .... Deck Surface Light (AAG)
DSLT .... Detection Scheme with Learning of Thresholds [*Communication signal*]
dsltd .... dry-salted (SAUS)
DSLTR .... Desalter (MSA)
DSLV .... Dissolved (NVT)
DSLX .... Degussa [*Private rail car owner code*]
DSM .... Danziger Statistische Mitteilungen [*Danzig*] [*A publication*]
DSM .... Data Service Manager (SAUS)
DSM .... Data Services Manager (VLIE)
DSM .... Data Set Manager (MCD)
DSM .... Data Specification Methodology (VLIE)
DSM .... Data Status Messages (KSC)
DSM .... Data Storage Memory
DSM .... Data Structure Manipulator (SAUS)
DSM .... Data Submodel (TIMI)
DSM .... Data Systems Manager (SAUS)
DSM .... Data Systems Modernization
DSM .... Dedicated Server Module (SAUS)
DSM .... Deep Space Measurement (KSC)
DSM .... Deep Sub-Micron (VLIE)
DSM .... Defence Studies Methodology [*British*]
DSM .... Defense Standardization Manual [*DoD*]
DSM .... Defense Subcontract Model (AAGC)
DSM .... Defense Suppression Missile
DSM .... Delta Sigma Modulator (IAA)
DSM .... Demand-Side Management
DSM .... Demand Statement Manipulation (SAUS)
DSM .... Demonstration Support Model (SAUS)
DSM .... Dense-Staining Material [*Cytology*]
DSM .... Department of Standards Malaysia (SAUS)
DSM .... Department of Survey and Mapping (SAUO)
DSM .... Deputy Stage Manager (WDAA)
DSM .... Design Specification Model (VLIE)
DSM .... Design Standards Manual (AAG)
DSM .... Design Station Manager (VLIE)
DSM .... Des Moines [*Iowa*] [*Airport symbol*] (OAG)
DSM .... Deterministic State Machine (SAUS)
DSM .... Detonation Sensing Module [*Automotive electronics*]
DSM .... Deutsche Sammlung von Mikroorganismen (DB)
DSM .... Development of Substitute Materials
DSM .... Development of Substitute Materials Digital Simulation Model (SAUS)
DSM .... Development Shop Memorandum (SAUS)
DSM .... Device Strategy Module (IAA)
DSM .... Dextrose Solution Mixture [*Medicine*] (MAE)
DSM .... Diagnostic and Statistical Manual (SAUS)
DSM .... Diagnostic and Statistical Manual of Mental Disorders [*A publication*]
DSM .... Diagnostic Statistical Manual
DSM .... Diamond-Shaped Murmur [*Medicine*] (MELL)
DSM .... Digital Scanning Electron Microscope
DSM .... Digital Select Matrix
DSM .... Digital Select Module (KSC)
DSM .... Digital Signal Microprocessor (SAUS)
DSM .... Digital Simulation Model (KSC)
DSM .... Digital Storage Media [*Computer science*]
DSM .... Digital Subscriber Modem [*Telecommunications*] (NITA)
DSM .... Digital System Model (SEWL)
DSM .... Dimethylsulfide (SAUS)
DSM .... Diploma in Social Medicine [*British*]
DSM .... Diploma in State Medicine (ROG)
DSM .... Direction of Systems Management
DSM .... Directorate of Servicing and Maintenance (SAUO)
DSM .... Directorate of Surveys and Mapping (SAUS)
DSM .... Director of Supply and Maintenance [*Army*]
DSM .... Direct Signal Monitoring [*Telecommunications*] (TEL)
DSM .... Direct Stiffness Method (SAUS)
DSM .... Direct Support Maintenance [*Army*]
DSM .... Discovery Mines Ltd. [*Toronto Stock Exchange symbol*]
DSM .... Discrete Source with Memory [*Computer science*] (HGAA)
DSM .... disc space management (SAUS)
DSM .... Disease State Management
DSM .... Disease-State Management (MHCS)
DSM .... Disk Sort/Merge [*Computer science*] (VLIE)
DSM .... Disk Space Management [*Computer science*]
DSM .... Disk Space Manager (SAUS)
DSM .... Display System, Multipurpose (ACAE)
DSM .... Disposable Surgical Mask (MELL)
DSM .... Distinguished Service Medal [*US and British*] [*Military decoration*]
DSM .... Distributed Shared Memory [*Computer science*]
DSM .... Distributed Systems Management [*Computer science*]
DSM .... District Sales Manager
DSM .... District Scout Master [*Scouting*]
DSM .... Dive Strategy Module (SAUS)

DSM .... Divisional Sergeant-Major [*British military*] (DMA)
DSM .... Division safety monitor (SAUS)
DSM .... Doctor of Sacred Music
DSM .... Don't Shoot Me [*Training term*] (LPT)
DSM .... Double Short Meter [*Music*]
DSM .... Dreyfus Strategic.Muni Bd Fd [*NYSE symbol*] (TTSB)
DSM .... Dreyfus Strategic Municipals, Inc. [*NYSE symbol*] (SPSG)
DSM .... Dried Skimmed Milk (SAUS)
DSM .... Dried Skim Milk
DSM .... Drink Skim Milk [*Dietetics*] (DAVI)
DSM .... Dry Skim Milk (SAUS)
DSM .... Dutch State Mines
DSM .... Dynamic Scattering Mode (IEEE)
DSM .... Dynamic Stiffness Modulus (PDAA)
DSM .... Dynamic Storage Mechanism (SAUS)
DSM .... United States Department of the Interior, Office of Surface Mining, Washington, DC [*Library symbol*] [*Library of Congress*] (LCLS)
DSMA .... Defense Supply Management Agency
DSMA .... Digital Sense Multiple Access [*Telecommunications*] (ACRL)
DSMA .... Direct Support Maintenance Activity [*Army*] (MCD)
DSMA .... Disodium Methyl Arsonate [*Herbicide*]
DSMA .... Disodium Monomethanearsonate (LDT)
DSMA .... Distributed Scheduling Mulitiple Access [*Telecommunications*] (OSI)
DSMA .... Divine Science Ministers Organization (EA)
DSMA .... Division of Small Manufacturers Assistance [*FDA*]
DSMA .... Doll Supply Manufacturers Association (EA)
DSMA .... Door and Shutter Manufacturers' Association [*British*]
DSMAC .... Digital Scene Matching Area Correlation (SAUS)
DSMAC .... Digital Scene Matching Area Correlator [*Navy*]
DSMB .... Data Safety Monitoring Board [*Generic term*]
DSMC .... Data Systems Management Course (SAUS)
DSMC .... Dealers Safety and Mobility Council (EA)
DSMC .... Defense Specification Management Course [*Army*]
DSMC .... Defense Systems Management College [*Fort Belvoir, VA*] [*Army*] (RDA)
DSMC .... Defense Systems Management Course [*Air Force*]
DSMC .... Direct Simulation Monte Carlo (SAUS)
D/SMC .... Dough/Sheet Molding Compound (SAUS)
DSM-CC .... Digital Storage Media - Command and Control (SAUS)
DSMC-PMC ... Defense Systems Management College - Program Management Course [*DoD*]
DSMD .... Demographic Statistical Methods Division (SAUS)
DSMD .... Discount Schedule and Marketing Data
dsmd .... Dismissed (MHDB)
DSMD .... Draft Ships Manpower Document [*Navy*] (CAAL)
DSMDPS .... Deployable Strategic Mission Data Preparation System (SAUS)
DSMetEng .... Doctor of Science in Metallurgical Engineering (NADA)
DSMG .... Designated Systems Management Group [*Military*]
DSMG .... Designed Systems Management Group (SAUO)
DSMGI .... Directorate of Strategic Military Geographic Information (SAUO)
DSMGP .... Designated Systems Management Group [*Military*]
DSMI .... Danish Society for Medical Informatics (SAUO)
DSM-III .... Diagnostic and Statistical Manual of Mental Disorders-third edition (SAUS)
DSM-III .... Diagnostic and Statistical Manual of the American Psychiatric Association (QSUL)
DSMIII-R ...... Diagnostic and Statistical Manual, 3rd Edition, Revised [*A publication*]
DSM-III-R .... Diagnostic and Statistical Manual of Mental Disorders [*A publication*]
DSMIT .... Distributed SMIT (SAUS)
DSMIV .... Diagnostic and Statistical Manual, 4th Edition [*A publication*]
DSM-IV .... Diagnostic and Statistical Manual of Mental Disorders 4th edition (SAUS)
DSM-IV-PC ... DSM-IV Primary Care Version (SAUS)
DSM-IV-TR ... DSM-IV Text Revision (SAUO)
DSML .... Directory Services Markup Language (GART)
DSMO .... Data Site Management Officer [*AT&T*] (CIST)
DSMO .... Dimethyl Sulfoxide [*Topical anti-inflammatory*] [*Medicine*] (DAVI)
DSMOA .... Defense and State Memorandum of Agreement (BCP)
DSMP .... Daughters of St. Mary of Providence [*Roman Catholic religious order*]
DSMP .... Defense Satellite Meteorological Program (LAIN)
DSM Project ... Development of Substitute Materials (SAUS)
DSMPU .... Digital Signal-Processing Microprocessor (GART)
DSMPW .... Director, Submarine Policy and Warfare [*Military*]
DSMR .... digital-subtracted magnetic resonance (SAUS)
DSMS .... Data Systems and Mathematics Staff [*Bureau of Radiological Health*] (IID)
DSMS .... Defense Systems Management School [*Fort Belvoir, VA*] (AABC)
DSMS .... depth selective MS (SAUS)
DSMs .... Deterministic State Machines (SAUS)
DSMS .... Document Service Management System (NITA)
DSMS .... Drawing Submittal Monitoring System [*MAC*]
DSMSB .... Die Set Manufacturers Service Bureau (EA)
dsmt .... Disarmament (SAUS)
DSMT .... Dual-Speed Magnetic Transducer
DSMTD .... Dismounted
DSMTI .... Discrete Signal Moving Target Indicator
DSMTP .... Defence Supply Mechanical Transport Panel (SAUO)
DSN .... Dance Services Network
DSN .... Data Set Name
DSN .... Data Set Number (SAUS)
DSN .... Data Smoothing Network [*Telecommunications*]
DSN .... Data Source Name [*Computer science*]
DSN .... Data Source Number (SAUS)
DSN .... Data Systems News (journ.) (SAUS)
DSN .... Deep Space Network [*NASA*]
DSN .... Defence Stock Number
DSN .... Defense Secure Network [*Military*]
DSN .... Defense Switched [*or Switchboard*] Network
DSN .... Delivery Service Notification (SAUS)
DSN .... Delivery Status Notification (SAUS)
DSN .... Dennison Manufacturing Co. (SAUO)
DSN .... Department of School Nurses (SAUS)
DSN .... Derived Services Network [*Telecommunications*] (NITA)
DSN .... Descriptive Supplement Number (SAUS)
dsn .... design (SAUS)
DSN .... Detroit Suburban Network [*Radio*]
DSN .... Developer Support News (SAUS)
DSN .... Digital Services Network (SAUO)
DSN .... Digital Signal Network (SEWL)
DSN .... Digital Switching Network [*Telecommunications*]
DSN .... Distributed Network System (SAUS)
DSN .... Distributed Sensor Network (MCD)
DSN .... Distributed Systems Network [*Hewlett-Packard Co.*]
DSN .... Doctor of Science in Nursing (PGP)
DSN .... Document Serial Number (ACAE)
DSN .... Dusing [*New York*] [*Seismograph station code, US Geological Survey*] [*Closed*] (SEIS)
DSN .... Marquette, MI [*Location identifier*] [*FAA*] (FAAL)
DSNA .... Dictionary Society of North America (EA)
DSNADNS .... Dihydroxy(hydroxydisulfonaphthylazo)naphthalenedisulfonic Acid [*An indicator*] [*Chemistry*]
DSND .... Descend [*Aviation*] (FAAC)
DSNDI .... Descend Immediately [*Aviation*] (FAAC)
DSN/DS .... DSN/Distributed Systems (SAUS)
DSNE .... Dispatch Service Non-Emergency (SAUS)
DSNET .... Defense Secure Network [*Computer science*] (RDA)
DSNG .... Durango & Silverton Narrow Gauge Railroad [*Federal Railroad Administration identification code*]
DSNI .... Deep Space Neck Infection [*Medicine*] (DMAA)
DSNI .... [*The*] DocketSearch Network, Inc. [*Information service or system*] (IID)
DSNL .... Direct Swift Network Link (SAUS)
DSN/IMF ...... DSN/Interactive Mainframe Facility (SAUS)
DSN/INP ...... DSN/Intelligent Network Processor (SAUS)
DSN/MRJE .... DSN/Multi-leavin Remote Job Entry (SAUS)
DSN/MTS .... DSN/Multipoint Terminal Software (SAUS)
DSNP .... Dassault-Sercel NP (SAUS)
DSNR .... Display Signal-to-Noise Ratio (SAUS)
DSN/RJE ...... DSN/Remote Job Entry (SAUS)
dsnrv .... double-swivel-nose reentry vehicle (SAUS)
DSNS .... Division of Space Nuclear Systems [*Energy Research and Development Administration*]
DSNS .... Doppler Sonar Navigation System (SAUS)
DSNSPEC .... Design Specification (TIMI)
DSNSW .... Deaf Society of New South Wales [*Australia*]
DSNT .... Data Set Name Table (SAUS)
DSNT .... Descent (KSC)
DSNT .... Distant (WEAT)
DSNTZ .... Desensitize (MSA)
DSNX .... Distributed System Node Executive (SAUS)
DSO .... Companion of the Distinguished Service Order [*Canada*] (DD)
DSO .... Dallas Support Office (SAUO)
DSO .... Dallas Symphony Orchestra (BARN)
DSO .... Data Security Officer (HGAA)
DSO .... Data Services Operations [*Informatics, Inc.*] (IID)
DSO .... Data Set Optimiser (or Optimizer) (SAUS)
DSO .... Data Set Optimizer [*Boole & Babbage, Inc.*]
DSO .... Data Store Organization (SAUS)
DSO .... Data Systems Office
DSO .... Days Sales Outstanding [*Business term*] (MHDB)
DSO .... Deck Stowage Only [*Shipping*]
DSO .... Deep Sky [*or Space*] Object [*Astronomy term*]
DSO .... Defence Sales Organisation [*Ministry of Defence*] [*British*]
DSO .... Defense Sciences Office [*Arlington, VA*] [*DoD*] (GRD)
DSO .... Defense Security Officer [*Military*]
DSO .... Defense Subsistence Office [*DoD*]
DSO .... Defense Systems Operations (SAUS)
DSO .... Defense Systems Operator (SAUS)
DSO .... Delayed Service Order (SAUS)
DSO .... Denver Symphony Orchestra (SAUS)
DSO .... Dependents Schooling Office [*Military*]
DSO .... Deputy Safety Officer (SAUS)
DSO .... Designate Senior Official (AAGC)
DSO .... Design Stop Order
DSO .... De Soto, Inc. (SAUO)
DSO .... DeSoto, Inc. [*NYSE symbol*] (SAG)
DSO .... Detailed Secondary Objective (MCD)
DSO .... Detailed Supplementary Objective (MCD)
DSO .... Detroit Symphony Orchestra (SAUO)
DSO .... Dielectrically-Stabilized Oscillator (SEWL)
DSO .... Digital Sampling Oscilloscope (SAUS)
DSO .... Digital Service Level Zero [*Telecommunications*] (ITD)
DSO .... Digital Storage Oscilloscope [*Gould, Inc.*]
DSO .... Directorate of Supply Operations (AFIT)
DSO .... Director of Site Operations [*Nuclear energy*] (NRCH)
DSO .... Direct Shipment Order (AAG)
dso .... direct shipping ore (SAUS)
DSO .... Direct System Output [*Computer science*] (MCD)

DSO .... Disaster Safety Officer (SAUO)
DSO .... Display Switching Oscilloscope
DSO .... Distal Subungual Onychomyosis
DSO .... Distinguished Service Order [*British*]
DSO .... District Sales Office
DSO .... District Security Office [*or Officer*] [*Navy*]
DSO .... District Service Office [*or Officer*] [*Navy*]
DSO .... District Signal Officer [*Navy*] (IAA)
DSO .... District Sorting Office [*British*] (ROG)
DSO .... District Staff Officer [*British*] (ROG)
DSO .... District Supply Office [*or Officer*] [*Navy*]
DSO .... Division Signal Officer [*Army*]
DSO .... Division Supply Officer [*Army*]
D So .... Doctor of Sociology
DSO .... Doctor of the Science of Oratory
DSO .... Document Services Office (SAUS)
DSO .... Donora Southern Railroad (SAUO)
DSO .... Donora Southern R. R. [*AAR code*]
DSO .... Drawing Sign Out (MCD)
DSO .... Duluth Symphony Orchestra (SAUS)
DSO .... Duty Signal Officer (SAUO)
DSO .... Dynamic Shared Object (SAUS)
DSO .... Evansville, IN [*Location identifier*] [*FAA*] (FAAL)
DSOAG......... Deputy Senior Officer, Assault Group [*British military*] (DMA)
DSOAU......... Deputy Senior Officer, Assault Unit (SAUO)
DSOB .... Dirksen Senate Office Building [*Washington, DC*] (DLA)
DSOC .... Defense Space Operations Committee (SAUO)
DSOC .... Democratic Socialist Organizing Committee [*Later, DSA*] (EA)
DSOC .... Division Support Operations Center (MCD)
DSOC .... Drug Suppression Operations Center (SAUO)
DSOC .... Dynamic Simulated Optimized Contact
DSoC .... Society of the Cincinnati, Washington, DC [*Library symbol*] [*Library of Congress*] (LCLS)
DSocS......... Doctor of Social Science
D Soc Sc ..... Doctor of Social Science
DSocSci....... Doctor of Social Science
DSODS......... Drug Specific Oral Delivery System [*Pharmacy*]
DSOFC .... Dark Shadows Official Fan Club (EA)
DSOFC .... David Selby Official Fan Club (EA)
DS of D........ Deputy Secretary of Defense (SAUO)
DSOM.......... Digital Systems Operations Panel (MCD)
DSOM.......... Distributed System Object Model [*Computer science*] (PCM)
DSOP.......... Digital Systems Operations Panel (SAUO)
DSOP.......... Draft Statement of Principles (SAUO)
DSOPS......... Direct Support Operations (NVT)
DSORDRS.... Disorders
DSORG .... Data Sequence Organisation (SAUS)
DSORG .... Data Set Organization (IAA)
DSOS........... Data Switch Operating System
D So Sc....... Doctor of Social Science
D So Se....... Doctor of Social Service
DSOT........... Daily Systems Operability Test [*for surface-to-air missiles*]
DSOTS......... Demonstration Site Operational Test Series
DSOW.......... Denmark Strait Overflow Water [*Oceanography*]
DSP .... Data Service Partition (SAUS)
DSP .... Dataset Printer (SAA)
DSP .... Data Source Panel (MCD)
DSP .... Data Standardization Project [*DoD*]
DSP .... Daughters of St. Paul, Missionary Sisters of the Catholic Editions [*Roman Catholic religious order*]
DSP .... Days since Planting [*Botany*]
DSP .... Decessit sine Prole [*Died without Issue*] [*Latin*]
DSP .... Decreased Sensory Perception (MELL)
DSP .... Deep-Sea Particles
DSP .... Deep South Petroleum [*Vancouver Stock Exchange symbol*]
DSP .... Deep Space Probe
DSP .... Deep Submergence Program (MCD)
DSP .... Defence Support Program (SAUS)
DSP .... Defense Development Sharing Program [*US and Canada*] (RDA)
DSP .... Defense Satellite Platform [*Strategic Defense Initiative*]
DSP .... Defense Satellite Program (MCD)
DSP .... Defense Science Program
DSP .... Defense Services Program (SAUS)
DSP .... Defense Standardization Program [*DoD*]
DSP .... Defense Support Program
DSP .... Delayed Sleep Phase (MELL)
DSP .... Delta Sigma Phi (SAUS)
DSP .... Delta Sigma Pi [*An association*] (NTPA)
DSP .... Demisit-Sene-Prole [*Died without issue*] [*Latin*]
DSP .... Democratic Socialist Party [*India*] [*Political party*] (PPW)
DSP .... Democratic Socialist Party [*Ireland*] [*Political party*] (PPW)
DSP .... Democratic Socialist Party [*South Korea*] [*Political party*] (PPW)
DSP .... Democratic Socialist Party [*Australia*] [*Political party*]
DSP .... Democratic Socialist Party [*Japan*] [*Political party*] (PPW)
DSP .... Dense Star Polymer (DB)
DSP .... Dentsply International, Inc. (SAUO)
DSP .... Department of State Planning (SAUO)
DSP .... Departure Sequencing Program [*FAA*] (TAG)
DSP .... Deployable Solar Panel
DSP .... Derogatis Stress Profile [*Personality development test*] [*Psychology*]
DSP .... Designated Stock Point
DSP .... Desilication Product (SAUS)
Dsp .... Dessertspoon (ADA)
DSP .... Detachment Support Package (MCD)
DSP .... Detroit Steel Products (SAUS)
DSP .... Deutsche Sex Partei [*German*] [*Political party*]
DSP .... Device Stop (SAUS)
DSP .... Device Support Processor [*Computer science*] (ITCA)
DSP .... Dextran Sulphate Precipitable (OA)
DSP .... Diarrhetic Shellfish Poisoning [*Medicine*]
DSP .... Dibasic Sodium Phosphate (SAUS)
DSP .... Differential Signal Processing (AAEL)
DSP .... Digital Signal Processing [*Telecommunications*] (ACRL)
DSP .... Digital Signal Processing Chip [*Computer science*] (MHDB)
DSP .... Digital Signal Processing Techniques (ACAE)
DSP .... Digital Signal Processor [*Computer science*]
DSP .... Digital Sound Processing (SAUS)
DSP .... Digital Speckle-Pattern Interferometry (ACAE)
DSP .... Digital Strip Printer
DSP .... Digital Subtraction Phlebography [*Medicine*] (DMAA)
DSP .... Dimensionally-Stable Polyester [*Tire manufacturing*]
DSP .... Directorate of Special Projects (SAUO)
DSP .... Director for Security Plans and Programs (ACAE)
DSP .... Director of Selection and Personnel [*British*]
DSP .... Director of Selection of Personnel (SAUO)
DSP .... Director Selector Panel
DSP .... Directory Service Protocol [*Telecommunications*] (OSI)
DSP .... Directory Synchronization Protocol (SAUS)
DSP .... Directory System Protocol [*Computer science*] (TELE)
DSP .... Direct Supply Platoon (SAUO)
DSP .... Direct Support Plan (MCD)
DSP .... Direct Support Platoon
DSP .... Direct System Platemaker
DSP .... Disassemble Sequence Parameter (IAA)
DSP .... Disodium Phosphate [*or Dibasic Sodium Phosphate*] [*Also, DSHP*] [*Inorganic chemistry*]
DSP .... Dispensary (DNAB)
DSP .... Display (SAUS)
DSP .... Display Simulation Program
DSP .... Display System Protocol [*Telecommunications*] (ACRL)
DSP .... Disposition [*Motor vehicle term used in state of Washington*] (MVRD)
DSP .... Distilled Spirits Plant
DSP .... Distributed System Program [*Computer science*]
DSP .... Distribution Point
DSP .... Dithiobis(succinimidylpropionate) [*Organic chemistry*]
DSP .... Division Standard Practice (AAG)
D Sp .... Doctor of Speech
DSP .... Doctor of Surgical Podiatry (WGA)
DSP .... Documentation Standards Package (SAUS)
DSP .... Document Search Pattern (SAUS)
DSP .... Document Services for Printing [*Xerox Co.*] (PCM)
DSP .... Domain Specific Part [*Telecommunications*] (OSI)
DSP .... Domain Specific System (SAUS)
DSP .... Doppler Spectrum Processor
DSP .... Double Silver Plate
DSP .... Double Silver Plated (SAUS)
DSP .... Downstream Processing (SAUS)
DSP .... Drain Source Protected (IAA)
DSP .... Drive Sample Pulse (SAUS)
DSP .... Dryland Salinity Program (SAUO)
DSP .... DSP Communications [*NYSE symbol*] (SG)
DSP .... DSP Technology, Inc. [*Associated Press*] (SAG)
DSP .... Dual Speed
dsp............ Duell, Sloan & Pearce, Inc. (SAUO)
DSP .... Dynamic Sequence Parameters (SAA)
DSP .... Dynamic Shift Pattern [*Automotive transmissions*]
DSP .... Dynamic Speaker
DSP .... Dynamic Subscription Promotion
DSP .... Dynamic Support Program [*Computer science*]
DSPA .... Data Systems Participating Agency (DNAB)
DSPA .... Deep-Submersible Pilots Association (SAUO)
DSPA .... Desert Sportsman Pilots Association (SAUO)
DSPA .... Dual-Stage Passenger Airbag [*Automotive safety systems*]
DSPAR......... Distributed System Partition (VLIE)
DSPAUG ...... Defense Support Program Augmentation (ACAE)
DSPB .... Digital Signal Processing Board (SAUS)
DSPC .... Defense Petroleum Supply Center (SAUO)
DSPC .... Defense Small Purchase Course [*DoD*] (RDA)
DSPC .... Direct Shell Production Casting [*Metallurgy*]
DSPC .... Direct Strip Production Complex [*Steel manufacturing*]
DSPC .... Disaturated Phosphatidylcholine [*Biochemistry*]
DSPC .... Distearoyl Phosphatidylcholine [*Biochemistry*]
DSPC .... DSP Communications [*NASDAQ symbol*] (SAG)
dspcb.......... dispatch (SAUS)
dspcb.......... dispatcher (SAUS)
DSPCH......... Dispatch (AABC)
dspch.......... Dispatcher (SAUS)
DSPChip ...... Digital Signal Processing Chip (VLIE)
DSPCm .... DSP Communications [*Associated Press*] (SAG)
DSPD .... Delayed Sleep-Phase Disorder (MELL)
DSPD .... Disalicylidenepropanediamine [*Organic chemistry*]
DSPD .... Double Stage Phase Diversity (SAUS)
DSPE .... Data Set Pointer Entry (SAUS)
DSP-E .... Defense Satellite Platform-East [*Strategic Defense Initiative*]
DSPE .... Division of Scientific Personnel and Education [*National Science Foundation*]
DSPE .... UCD Special (SAUS)
DSPEC .... Design Specification
D SPEC .... Process Specification (AAGC)
DSPECT .... Dynamic Single Photon Emission Computer Tomography (SAUS)

DSPF .... Data Services Planning Form
DSPG .... Defense Special Projects Group (MCD)
DSPG .... Defense Systems Planning Group (SAUO)
DSPG .... Distributed Single-Point Ground (SAUS)
DSPG .... Drill Service in Paygrade [*Military*] (DNAB)
DSPG .... DSP Group [*NASDAQ symbol*] (TTSB)
DSPG .... DSP Group, Inc. [*NASDAQ symbol*] (SAG)
DSP Gp .... DSP Group, Inc. [*Associated Press*] (SAG)
DSPH .... Diopter Spherical
DSPI .... Digital Speckle-Pattern Interferometry (SAUS)
DSPI .... Display Indicator (SAUS)
DSPL .... Decessit sine Prole Legitima [*Died without Legitimate Issue*] [*Latin*]
DSPL .... Definitized Spare Parts List (AAG)
DSPL .... Disciplinary
DSPL .... Displacement [*Nautical term*] (NTA)
DSPL .... Display
DSPL .... Display System Programming Language (COE)
DSPL .... Disposal
DSPL .... Douglas Space Physics Laboratory (MUGU)
DSPLC .... Displace (FAAC)
DSPLC .... display controller (SAUS)
DSPLCD .... Displaced
dspln .... disciplinary (SAUS)
DSPLN .... Discipline (AFM)
DSPLY .... Display (IAA)
DSPM .... Decessit sine Prole Mascula [*Died without Male Issue*] [*Latin*]
DSPM .... Designated Subsystems Project Manager [*NASA*] (NASA)
DSPM .... Digital Signal Processing Multiprocessor (SAUS)
DSPM .... Displacement (SAUS)
DSPM .... Double Strokes per Minute (MSA)
DSPMI .... Displacement (SAUS)
DSPMO .... Defense SAAMS [*Special Airlift Assignment Missions*] Program Management Office [*DoD*]
DSPMS .... Decessit sine Prole Mascula Superstita [*Died without Surviving Male Issue*] [*Latin*]
DSPMT .... Displacement (VLIE)
DSPN .... Deterministic Stochastic Petri Net (VLIE)
DSPN .... Direct Sequence Pseudo Noise (SEWL)
DSPN .... Dispensary
DSPN .... Disposition (AFM)
DSPN .... Distal Symmetric Polyneuropathy [*Medicine*] (TAD)
DSPNAME .... Dynamic Support Program Name (SAUS)
DSPNSG .... Dispensing
DSPO .... Defense Support Project Office (SAUO)
dspo .... disposal (SAUS)
DSPO .... Dispose (AABC)
dspo .... disposition (SAUS)
DSPO .... Duty Security Petty Officer [*Navy*] (DNAB)
DSPP .... Disodium Phenylphosphate (SAUS)
DSPR .... Defense Supply Procurement Regulation [*Military*]
DSPRL .... Dispersal (FAAC)
DSPRM .... Digital Signal Processor Resource Manager [*Computer science*]
DS-Prothese .... drum-to-stapes prothesis (SAUS)
dsprsl .... Dispersal (SAUS)
DSPS .... Decessit sine Prole Superstita [*Died without Surviving Issue*] [*Latin*]
DSPS .... Deep Sea Production System (SAUO)
DSPS .... Delayed Sleep Phase Syndrome
DSPS .... Digital Signal Processing System
DSPS .... Digital Signal Processors [*Computer science*]
DSPS .... Disabled Students' Programs and Services
DSPS .... Dynamic Ship Positioning System (SAUS)
DSPSL .... Disposal
DSPSWS .... Defence Support Program Satellite Warning System (SAUS)
DSP-Syndrom .... Diarrhetic Shellfish Poisoning-Syndrom (SAUS)
DSPT .... Decision Support Problem Technique (VLIE)
DSPT .... Diagnostic Spelling Potential Test [*Educational test*]
DSPT .... Display Station Pass-Thru (SAUS)
DSPT .... Dominican School of Philosophy and Theology (SAUS)
DSPT .... DSP Technology, Inc. [*NASDAQ symbol*] (NQ)
DSPU .... Downstream Physical Unit [*Computer science*]
DSPV .... Decessit sine Prole Virile [*Died without Male Issue*] [*Latin*] (ADA)
DSPView .... Digital Signal Processor View (SAUS)
DSP-W .... Defense Satellite Platform-West [*Strategic Defense Initiative*]
DSPY .... Display (GAVI)
DSQ .... Deaf Society, Queensland [*Australia*]
DSQ .... Digital Squelch (SAUS)
DSQ .... Director of Supplies and Quartering [*British military*] (DMA)
DSQ .... Discharged to Sick Quarters
DSQ .... Disqualified [*Racing*] (IYR)
DSQ .... downstream quartz (SAUS)
DSQD .... Double-Sided Quad-Density [*Disk drive*] [*Scottsdale Systems*] [*Computer science*]
D-squad .... Death squad (SAUS)
DSR .... Daily Service Report
DSR .... Daily Shipping Report (SAUS)
DSR .... Daily Status Report (AAG)
DSR .... Dairo Air Services Ltd. [*Uganda*] [*ICAO designator*] (FAAC)
DSR .... Damage Survey Report [*Department of Emergency Management*] (DEMM)
DSR .... Danmarks Radio (EY)
DSR .... Dasher Resources [*Vancouver Stock Exchange symbol*]
DSR .... Data and Software Resources (SAUO)
DSR .... Data Scanning and Routing
DSR .... Data Service Request (SAUS)
DSR .... Data Set Ready [*Model signal*]
DSR .... Data Set Register (SAUS)
DSR .... Data Signalling/Set Rate (VLIE)
DSR .... Data Specification Request
DSR .... Data Storage and Retrieval (MCD)
DSR .... Data Survey Report (AAG)
DSR .... Date Set Ready (SAUS)
DSR .... Daughters of St. Rita of the Immaculate Heart [*Roman Catholic religious order*]
DSR .... Debt Service Ratio (ODBW)
DSR .... Defense Source Register (MCD)
DSR .... Defense Subsistence Region [*DoD*]
DSR .... Defense Suppression Rocket
DSR .... Delayed Sound Reinforcement
DSR .... Delivery Status Report (NUMA)
DSR .... Dental Service Report (SAUS)
DSR .... Departmental Staff Records (AIE)
DSR .... Depolymerized Scrap Rubber [*Waste recycling*]
DSR .... De Ridder, LA [*Location identifier*] [*FAA*] (FAAL)
DSR .... Desire (FAAC)
DSR .... desired fuel load (SAUS)
DSR .... Detroit Street Railways (SAUS)
DSR .... Device Service Routine (VLIE)
DSR .... Device State Register (NITA)
DSR .... Device Status Register (SAUS)
DSR .... Device Status Report [*Computer science*] (VERA)
DSR .... Diagnostic Shift Register (SAUS)
DSR .... Differentiation with Symmetrical Reinforcement
DSR .... Digital Satellite Radio (PS)
DSR .... Digital Shift Register
DSR .... Digital Standard Runoff (VLIE)
DSR .... Digital Stepping Recorder
DSR .... Digit Storage Relay
DSR .... Director of Scientific Research [*British*]
DSR .... Director of Surveillance and Reconnaissance [*Army*]
DSR .... Direct Scope Radar (ACAE)
DSR .... Direct Seeded Rice (SAUO)
DSR .... Direct Ship Release (MCD)
DSR .... Direct Ship Requirements (MCD)
DSR .... Direct Solar Radiation (ARMP)
DSR .... Direct Space Refinement
DSR .... Direct Stage Recorder (MCD)
DSR .... Direct Storage Recorder
DSR .... Discrete Speech Recognition
DSR .... Discriminating Selector Repeater (DEN)
DSR .... Discrimination Selector Repeater (SAUS)
DSR .... Display System Replacement [*FAA*] (TAG)
DSR .... Distributed State Response
DSR .... District Sales Representative (SAUS)
DSR .... Division of Solar Research [*Energy Research and Development Administration*]
DSR .... Division of Sponsored Research [*Massachusetts Institute of Technology*] (MCD)
DSR .... Division of Sponsored Research [*University of South Florida*] [*Research center*] (RCD)
DSR .... Document Search and Research [*Xerox Corp.*]
DSR .... Document Search and Retrieval (SAUS)
DSR .... Document Status Report [*Military*]
DSR .... Downstage Right [*Toward audience*] [*A stage direction*]
DSR .... Drangdhara State Railway [*Indian Railway*] (TIR)
DSR .... Dry scrap recycle (SAUS)
DSR .... Dry Sterile Dressing [*Medicine*] (MELL)
DSR .... Dual Shift Right (IAA)
DSR .... Dummy Stowage Receptacle
DSR .... Dynamic Segment Relocation (VLIE)
DSR .... Dynamic Service Register (SAUS)
DSR .... Dynamic Shift Register
DSR .... Dynamic Sideband Regulator
DSR .... Dynamic Spatial Reconstructor [*X-ray scanning machine*]
DSR .... Dynamic Status Recording (SAUS)
DSR .... Dynamic Storage Relocation (SAUS)
DSR .... Dynamic Storage Report (SAUS)
DSR .... Digital Subtraction Radiography (ODA)
DSRA .... Directorate of Supplementary Radio Activities (SAUO)
DSRA .... Dockyard Ship Riggers' Association [*A union*] [*British*]
DSRB .... Data Services Request Block [*IBM Corp.*] (CIST)
DSRC .... Dakota Southern Railway [*Federal Railroad Administration identification code*]
DSRC .... Data Systems Requirements Committee (ACAE)
DSRC .... David Sarnoff Research Center [*RCA*] (MCD)
DSRC .... Dedicated Short Range Communications
DSRC .... Distant Space Radio Center (IAA)
DSRC .... Double Sideband Reduced Carrier [*Telecommunications*] (IAA)
DSRCT .... Desmoplastic Small Round-Cell Tumor [*Medicine*] (MELL)
DSRD .... Data Systems Research and Development [*Oak Ridge National Laboratory*]
DSRD .... Depot Support Requirement Document (ACAE)
DSRD .... Directorate of Signals Research and Development (SAUO)
DSRE .... Defense Subsistence Region - Europe (AABC)
DSREDS .... Digital Storage and Retrieval of Engineering Data System [*Army*] (MCD)
DSRF .... Debt Service Reserve Fund [*Information service or system*] (HCT)
DSRG .... Data System Review Group (SAUO)
DSRG .... Director of Sport and Inspector of Recreational Grounds (SAUO)
DSRG .... Director of Sport of Recreational Grounds (SAUS)
DSRGD .... Disregard (FAAC)

DSRI .... Danish Science Research Institute (SAUO)
DSRI .... Danish Space Research Institute
DSRI .... Data Set to Record Interface (SAUS)
DSRI .... Destination Station Routing Indicator (SAUS)
DSRI .... Digital Standard Relational Interface [*Computer science*] (VERA)
DSRI .... Dynamic Selection of Runtime Location (GART)
DSRK .... Deutsche Schiffs Revision und Klassifikation [*German ship classification society*] (DS)
DSR/LOC ...... Debt Service Reserve/Letter of Credit Program [*Investment term*]
DSRN .... Data Set Reference Number (SAUS)
DSRN .... Defense Switched Red Network [*Military*] (SEWL)
dsRNA .... Double-Stranded Ribonucleic Acid [*Biochemistry, genetics*]
dsRNase ...... Double-Stranded Ribonuclease
DSRO .... Danish-Swedish Refugee Organisation (SAUO)
DSRO .... Designated Self-Regulatory Organization (MHDB)
DS-RP .... Deafness Sensorineural, Recessive Profound [*Medicine*] (MELL)
DSRP .... Democratic and Social Republican Party [*Mauritania*] [*Political party*] (EY)
DSRPAC ...... Defense Subsistence Region, Pacific [*DoD*] (DNAB)
DS/RPIE ...... Direct Support Real Property Installed Equipment (AFIT)
DSRR .... Delta Southern Railroad [*Federal Railroad Administration identification code*]
DSRR .... Digital Short Range Radio (SAUS)
DSRS .... Data Signalling Rate Select (IAA)
DSRS .... Data Storage and Retrieval System (COE)
DSRS .... Deep Submergence Rescue System [*Navy*] (NVT)
DSRS .... Defense Software Repository System (SAUO)
DSRS .... Direct Scope Recording System (MCD)
DSRS .... Distal Splenorenal Shunt [*Medicine*]
DSRS .... Drug Services Research Survey (ADWA)
DSRT .... Deep Sea Reversing Thermometer (SAUS)
DSRT .... Desert [*Board on Geographic Names*]
DSR-TKA ...... Delta Sigma Rho-Tau Kappa Alpha (EA)
DSRV .... Deep Sea Recovery Vehicle (SEWL)
DSRV .... Deep Submergence Rescue Vehicle [*Navy*]
DSRV .... Deep Submergence Research Vessel
DSRW .... Dry-Sand, Rubber-Wheel (SAUS)
DSS .... Data Sampling System (SAUS)
DSS .... Data Selection System (SAUS)
DSS .... Data Server System
DS/S .... Data Services Segment (SAUS)
DSS .... Data Set Security (SAUS)
DSS .... Data Source Status (SAUS)
DSS .... Data Specification System (SAUS)
DSS .... Data Station Selector (SAUS)
DSS .... Data Storage Segment (SAUS)
DSS .... Data Storage Set (MCD)
DSS .... Data Storage System
DSS .... Data Summary Sheets (MCD)
DSS .... Data Support Section (ARMP)
DSS .... Data Switching System
DSS .... Data Systems Services (SAUS)
DSS .... Data Systems Specification
DSS .... Data Systems Staff (COE)
DSS .... Data Systems Supervisor (MCD)
Dss .... Deaconess (SAUS)
DSS .... Dead Sea Scrolls (BJA)
DSS .... Deaf Supportive Services (SAUS)
DSS .... Decision and Simulation System [*Computer science*]
DSS .... Decision Support Software (NITA)
DSS .... Decision Support System
DSS .... Decompression Staging System (SAUS)
DSS .... Decorstone Industry [*Vancouver Stock Exchange symbol*]
DSS .... Deep Sea Sediments (SAUS)
DSS .... Deep Seismic Sounder (or Sounding) (SAUS)
DSS .... Deep Seismic Sounding [*Geophysics*]
DSS .... Deep Seismic Sounding Program [*Former USSR*]
DSS .... Deep Space Station [*NASA*]
DSS .... Deep Space Surveillance (SEWL)
DSS .... Deep Submergence Systems [*Navy*]
DSS .... Defence Signals Staff (SAUO)
DSS .... Defense Satellite System (ACAE)
DSS .... Defense Security Service
DSS .... Defense Signals Staff (NATG)
DSS .... Defense Supply Service [*DoD*]
DSS .... Defense Switched Services (SAUO)
DSS .... Dejerine-Sottas Syndrome [*Medicine*]
DSS .... Dengue Shock Syndrome [*Medicine*]
DSS .... Department of Social Security [*British*]
DSS .... Department of Social Services [*in various governmental agencies*]
DSS .... Department of Special Services
DSS .... Department of State Services [*Western Australia*] [*Australia*]
DSS .... Department of Supply and Service [*Canada*] (IMH)
DSS .... Department Store System (SAUS)
DSS .... Department Summary Schedule [*NASA*] (NASA)
DSS .... Depot Status Schedule (SAUS)
DSS .... Depot Supply System [*Army*]
DSS .... Deputy of Space Systems [*Air Force*]
DSS .... Design Specification
DSS .... Desktop Security Suite [*McAfee Associates, Inc.*] [*Computer science*]
DSS .... Developmentally Stable Strategy (SAUS)
DSS .... Developmental Sentence Scoring [*for the hearing-impaired*]
DSS .... Development Support System (SAUS)
DSS .... Device, Simulator, and Simulation [*Army*] (RDA)
DSS .... Diagnostic Simulation System
DSS .... DIALOG Statistical Service (SAUS)
DSS .... Digital Satellite System
DSS .... Digital Scene Simulation [*Computer graphics used in cinematography*] (WDMC)
DSS .... Digital Signal Standard [*Telecommunications*] (ACRL)
DSS .... Digital Signal Synchronizer
DSS .... Digital Signature Standard [*National Institute of Standards and Technology*]
DSS .... Digital Simulator System
DSS .... Digital Storage Subsystem (SAUS)
DSS .... Digital Storage System
DSS .... Digital Subscriber Signaling System [*Telecommunications*] (ACRL)
DSS .... Digital Subset [*or Subsystem*]
DSS .... Digital Switched Services [*Telecommunications*] (ACRL)
DSS .... Digital Switching Subsystem (SAUS)
DSS .... Digital Switching System [*Telecommunications*] (TEL)
DSS .... Dimethylsilapentane Sulfonate [*Organic chemistry*]
DSS .... Dioctyl Sodium Sulfosuccinate [*Organic chemistry*]
DSS .... Diploma in Sanitary Science (ROG)
DSS .... Diploma of Specialized Studies (SAUS)
DSS .... Directed Stationing System [*DoD*]
DSS .... Directorate of Scientific Services (SAUO)
DSS .... Director of Social Services (WDAA)
DSS .... Director [*or Directorate*] of Statistical Services [*Air Force*]
DSS .... Directory and Security Services [*IBM Corp*] (VERA)
DSS .... Direct Satellite Service (DCDG)
DSS .... Direct Satellite System
DSS .... Direct State Services
DSS .... Direct Station Selection [*Telecommunications*]
DSS .... Direct Station Selector (SAUS)
DSS .... Direct Subsystem (MCD)
DSS .... Direct Supply Support [*Military*]
DSS .... Direct Support System [*Army*]
DSS .... Disabled Student Services
DSS .... Discrete Sync System (SAUS)
DSS .... Disc Storage Subsystem (SAUS)
DSS .... Disc Storage System (SAUS)
DSS .... Disc Subsystem (SAUS)
DSS .... Disc Support System (NITA)
DSS .... Disk Storage Subsystem (SAUS)
DSS .... Disk Storage System [*or Subsystem*] [*Computer science*] (IAA)
DSS .... Disk Subsystem (SAUS)
DSS .... Disk Support System (SAUS)
DSS .... Display Stocker Status (AAEL)
DSS .... Display Subsystem (SAUS)
DSS .... Distributed Satellite Software (SAUS)
DSS .... Distributed Secure System (SAUS)
DSS .... Distributed Security Service [*Computer science*] (VERA)
DSS .... Distributed System Satellite (IAA)
DSS .... Distributed System Simulator
DSS .... Distribution and Switching System (MCD)
DSS .... Distribution System Simulator (SAUS)
DSS .... Disuccinimydyl Suberate [*Organic chemistry*]
DSS .... Division of Safeguards and Security [*Energy Research and Development Administration*]
DSS .... Division of Safety Studies (SAUS)
DSS .... Doctor of Sacred Scripture (SAUS)
DSS .... Doctor of Sanitary Science
DSS .... Doctor of Science in Surgery
DSS .... Doctor of Secretarial Science
DSS .... Doctor of Social Science (SAUS)
DSS .... Doctor of Social Service
DSS .... Doctor Sacrae Scripturae [*Doctor of Holy Scripture*]
DSS .... Documentation Support Services (NASA)
DSS .... Document Search System (SAUS)
DSS .... Documents Signed
DSS .... Document Storage System (NITA)
DSS .... Docusate Sodium (SAUS)
DSS .... Domain SAP Service (SAUS)
DSS .... Domestic Sewage Study [*Environmental science*] (COE)
DSS .... Dosage-Sensitive Sex [*Reversal*] [*Genetics*] [*Medicine*]
DSS .... Double Security System (SAUS)
DSS .... Double-Shell Slurry (ABAC)
DSS .... Double-Sided Scrubber (SAUS)
DSS .... Double-Simultaneous Stimulation (DIPS)
DSS .... Double Spot System
DSS .... Double-Spot System (SAUS)
DSS .... Downshift Solenoid [*Automotive term*] (HAWK)
DSS .... Draughting Software System [*Gould Electronics Ltd. Computer Systems*] [*Software package*] (NCC)
DSS .... Drill Sergeant School [*Army*] (AABC)
DSS .... Drum Storage System
DSS .... Drum Store System (SAUS)
dss .... dry surface storage (SAUS)
DSS .... Duchess (ROG)
DSS .... Dynamic Simulation System (MCD)
DSS .... Dynamic Steady State
DSS .... Dynamic Support System (MCD)
DSS .... Dynamic Systems Simulator (ACAE)
DSS .... Dynamic Systems Synthesizer (SAUS)
DSS .... Dynamic System Synthesizer
DSS .... Dyslexia Screening Survey [*Psychology*]
DSS .... Society of Slovene Composers (SAUO)
DSS .... Duplex Stainless Steel (ODA)
DSS1 .... Digital Subscriber Signaling One [*Telecommunications*] (OSI)

DSSA .... Defence Subsistence Supply Agency (SAUO)
DSSA .... Development Society of Southern Africa (EAIO)
DSSA .... Direct Supply Support Activity [*Army*] (AABC)
Dssa .... Dottoressa [*Female Doctor*] [*Italian*]
DSS & A .... Duluth, South Shore & Atlantic Railroad [*Nickname: Damned Slow Service and Abuse*] [*Obsolete*]
DSS & R .... Document Storage Search and Retrieval [*Air Force*]
DSSAT .... Decision Support System for Agrotechnology Transfer (SAUO)
DSSB .... Data Selection and Storage Buffer (IAA)
DSSB .... Double Single-Sideband (MSA)
DSSC .... Deep Space Station Complex (SAUO)
DSSC .... Defense Subsistence Supply Center [*Later, Defense Personnel Support Center*]
DSSC .... Department of the Secretary of State of Canada (SAUS)
DSSC .... Derived Services Switching Centre (NITA)
dSSc .... Diffuse Systemic Sclerosis
DSSc .... Diploma in Sanitary Science [*British*]
DS Sc .... Doctor of Sanitary Science (SAUS)
DSSc .... Doctor of Social Science (GAGS)
DSSC .... Double-Sideband Suppressed Carrier [*Modulation*] (IEEE)
DSSC .... Double Silk, Single Cotton [*Wire insulation*] (IAA)
DSSCP .... Defence Supply Statistical Clearing Panel (SAUO)
DSSCS .... Defense Special Security Communications System [*Pronounced "discus"*]
DssCSA .... Deaconess Community of St. Andrew [*Anglican religious community*]
DSSD .... Data Structure and System Development (SSD)
DSSD .... Decennial Statistical Studies Division (SAUS)
DSSD .... Direct Supply Support Depot [*Military*] (AFM)
DSSD .... Direct Support Supply Depot (SAUO)
DSSD .... Double-Sided Single-Density Disk [*Computer science*]
DSSD .... Double-Stroke Solid-Die (SAUS)
DSSD .... drop and salt size distribution (SAUS)
DSSD .... Dry Surface Storage Demonstration (SAUS)
DSSE .... Daily Summary Spare Engines (SAUS)
DSSE .... Design Selection Specification Engineer
DSSE .... Developmental Software Support Environment [*Army*]
DSSE .... Directory System Service Element [*Telecommunications*] (OSI)
DSSEAT .... Deep-Sea System for Evaluating Acoustic Transducers (SAUS)
DSSEP .... Dermatomal Somatosensory Evoked Potential [*Medicine*] (DMAA)
DSSEP .... Developmental Software Support Environment Plan [*Army*]
DSSF .... Double-Shell Slurry Feed (ABAC)
DSSFK .... Defense Subsistence Storage Facility (SAUO)
DSSG .... Defense & Space Systems Group (CCCA)
DSSG .... Defense Science Study Group (SAUO)
DSSG .... Defense Suppression Analysis Evaluation Steering Group (SAUO)
DSSH .... Department of Social Services and Housing (SAUS)
DSSI .... Data Systems & Software, Inc. [*NASDAQ symbol*] (SAG)
DSSI .... Digital Standard Systems Interconnect (SAUS)
DSSI .... Digital Storage System Interconnect [*Computer science*] (VLIE)
DSSI .... Digital Storage Systems Interconnect
DSSI .... Duke Social Support Index (DMAA)
DSSII .... Displaced System Support Item Identification
DSSJ .... Deceptive Self-Screening Jammer (MCD)
DSSM .... Dedicated Solar Sortie Mission [*Aerospace*] (MCD)
DSSM .... Defense Superior Service Medal [*Military decoration*]
DSSM .... Digital Signal Sinusoidal Modulation (PDAA)
DSSM .... Digital Single Sideband Modulator (SEWL)
DSSM .... Division of State Systems Management [*Social and Rehabilitation Service, HEW*]
DSSM .... Drawing Stimulus Strategy Measure
DSSM .... Dynamic Sequencing and Segmentation Model (SAUS)
DSSM .... Dynamic Sequencing and Segregation Model [*Computer science*] (OA)
DSSN .... Data Set Serial Number (SAUS)
DSSN .... Disbursing Station Symbol Number [*Military*] (AFM)
DSSN .... Seaman, Data Systems Technician, Striker [*Navy rating*]
DSSNY .... Dental Society of the State of New York (SAUO)
DSSO .... Data System Support Organization (COE)
DSSO .... Defense Supply Sales Office (SAUO)
DSSO .... Defense Surplus Sales Office
DSSO .... Defense Systems Support Organization (SAUS)
DSSO .... Defense System Support Office (SAUO)
DSSO .... District Ships Service Office [*or Officer*] [*Navy*]
DSSO .... Division Signal Supply Office (SAUO)
DSSO .... Duty Space Surveillance Officer [*Air Force*] (AFM)
DSSP .... Deep Sea Submergence Project (SAUS)
DSSP .... Deep Submergence System Program (ACAE)
DSSP .... Deep Submergence Systems Project Office [*Arlington, VA*] [*Navy*]
DSSP .... Deep Submergency Systems Project (SAUS)
DSSP .... Deep Submerge Systems Project (SAUS)
DSSP .... Defense Standardization and Specification Program [*DoD*] (RDA)
DSSP .... Deflection Single Shot Probability (SAUS)
DSSP .... Depot Support Supply Plan (AFIT)
DSSP .... Direct Supply Support Point [*Military*]
DSSP .... Direct Support Supply Point (SAUO)
DSSP .... Division Support Slice Program (MCD)
DSSPO .... Deep Submergence Systems Project Office [*Navy*]
DSSP/SSD ... Department Supply Storage Point/Stock Storage Depot [*DoD*]
DSSPTO .... Deep Submergence Systems Project Technical Office [*San Diego, CA*] [*Navy*]
DSSR .... Deep Space Surveillance RADAR (MCD)
DSSRG .... Deep Submergence Systems Research Group (SAUO)
DSSRG .... Deep Submergence Systems Review Group [*Navy*]
DSSS .... Deep Space Surveillance Satellite [*Military*]
DSSS .... Deep Space Surveillance System (ACAE)
DSSS .... Defense Special Security System (MCD)
DSSS .... Direct Sequence Spread Spectrum [*Telecommunications*] (IAA)
DSSS .... Division of Special Schools and Services (OICC)
DSSS .... Division of Supplemental Security Studies [*Department of Health and Human Services*] (GRD)
DS-SSDA ..... Direct Sequence-Spread Spectrum Multiple Access (SAUS)
DSSSL .... Document Style Semantics and Specification Language [*ISO/IEC*] [*Computer science*]
DSSSP .... Division of Student Support and Special Programs [*Office of Education*]
DSST .... Digit Symbol Substitution Task (DMAA)
DSST .... Digit Symbol Substitution Test [*Medicine*] (EDAA)
DSST .... Director of Supply and Secretariat Training [*British military*] (DMA)
DSST .... Driver Stage Silicon Transistor
DSST .... Dunlop Self-Supporting Tire
DS Storage... Delayed-Staging Storage (SAUS)
DSSTP .... Development Site System Training Program (SAA)
DS Structure... Diffusion Substrate Structure (SAUS)
DS-Struktur... Diffusion Substrate Structure (SAUS)
DSSU .... Dismounted Soldier System Unit [*Military*] (SEWL)
DSSV .... Deep Submergence Search Vehicle [*Research submarine*] [*Navy*]
DSSW .... Defense Supply Services, Washington (ACAE)
DSS-W .... Defense Supply Service - Washington [*DoD*]
DST .... Danstar Resources Ltd. [*Vancouver Stock Exchange symbol*]
DST .... Data Segment Table (IAA)
DST .... Data Service Task (SAUS)
DST .... Data Source Terminal (MCD)
DST .... Data Station Terminal (SAUS)
DST .... Data Storage Terminal
DST .... Data Summary Tape (OA)
DST .... Data Systems Test [*Formerly, DAT*]
DST .... Daylight Saving Time
DST .... Decision Support Template [*Military*] (INF)
DST .... Decoding Skills Test [*Richardson and DiBenedetto*] (TES)
DST .... Dedicated Search Team (WDAA)
DST .... Dedicated Service Tools (VLIE)
DST .... Deep Sleep Therapy
DST .... Defence & Space Talks (SAUS)
DST .... Defense Suppression Threat (ACAE)
DST .... Dermatology and Syphilology Technician [*Navy*]
DST .... Desensitization Test [*Allergy*]
DST .... Desensitization Time (SAUS)
DST .... Design Basis Tornadoes [*Environmental science*] (COE)
DST .... Design-Specified Transformer (IAA)
DST .... Design Support Test (MCD)
DST .... Destination (VLIE)
DST .... Destructor [*Military*]
DST .... Detailed System Test
DST .... Development Sentence Types [*Medicine*] (EDAA)
DST .... Development Suitability Test (MCD)
DST .... Device Service Task (VLIE)
DST .... Device Start (SAUS)
DST .... Dexamethasone Suppression Test [*Clinical chemistry*]
DST .... Diagnostic sensitivity test (SAUS)
DST .... Dielectric Strength Test
DST .... Differential Skin Surface Temperature
DST .... Differential Survey Treatment (NTCM)
DST .... Digital Subscriber Terminal
DST .... Digit-Symbol Substitution Test [*Psychiatry*]
DST .... Dihydrostreptomycin [*Also, DHS, DHSM*] [*Antimicrobial agent*]
DST .... Dimensional Special Tooling (NASA)
DST .... Diploma, Sante du Travail [*Medical degree*] (CMD)
DST .... Direction de la Surveillance du Territoire [*Directorate of Territorial Surveillance*] [*France*]
DST .... Directorate of Science and Technology (HEAS)
DST .... Director of Sea Transport [*British military*] (DMA)
DST .... Director of Supplies and Transport [*British*]
DST .... Direct Satellite Terminal (SAUS)
DST .... Direct Screw Transfer
DST .... Direct Sounding Transmission [*Meteorology*]
DST .... Direct Support Team (SAUO)
DST .... Direct-Viewing Storage Tube
DS-T .... Discarding Sabot Tracer (SAUS)
DS/T .... Discarding Sabot/Training [*British military*] (DMA)
DST .... Discrete Sine Transform (PDAA)
DST .... Discrete Slant Transform (SAUS)
DST .... Disc Storage Terminal (NITA)
DST .... Display Storage Tube (CET)
DST .... Disproportionate Septal Thickening [*Medicine*] (EDAA)
DST .... Disston, Inc. (SAUO)
DST .... Distort (FAAC)
DST .... Distributed Systems Terminal (SAUS)
dst .... Distributor [*MARC relator code*] [*Library of Congress*] (LCCP)
DST .... District
DST .... Disuccinimidyl Tartrate [*Organic chemistry*]
DST .... Doctor of Sacred Theology
D St .... Doctor of Statistics
DST .... Dodecanoylsarcosyltaurine [*Crustacean detergent*]
DST .... Donor Specific Transfusion
DST .... Door Stop (AAG)
DST .... Dot Sequential Transmission (IAA)
DST .... Double Set Triggers [*Gunnery*]
DST .... double-shell tank (SAUS)
DST .... Double Spot Tuning

DST............ Double Summer Time [*Daylight Saving Time two hours ahead of Standard Time*] [*British*]
DST............ Douglas Sleeper Transport [*Aviation*]
DST............ Downhole Systems Team (SAUS)
DST............ Downsized Tester (SAUS)
DST............ Drill Stem Test (ADA)
DST............ Driver Skill Trainer (SAUS)
DST............ Drop Survival Time
DST............ DST Systems, Inc. [*NYSE symbol*] (SAG)
DST............ Dursunbey [*Turkey*] [*Seismograph station code, US Geological Survey*] (SEIS)
DST............ Dust [*Tea trade*] (ROG)
DST............ Dynamic Stability Test (NASA)
DST............ Missoula, MT [*Location identifier*] [*FAA*] (FAAL)
DSTA........... Diagnostic Screening Test: Achievement [*Educational test*]
DSTA........... Distribution Assembly [*Ground Communications Facility, NASA*]
d stab......... Direction Stability (SAUS)
DST & DD.... Developing Systems Training and Devices Directorate [*Army*]
DStAP.......... Saint Anselm's Abbey, Washington, DC [*Library symbol*] [*Library of Congress*] (LCLS)
DStatC......... Directorate of Statistics and Costing (SAUO)
DSTB........... Danmarks Statistiks TidsseriedataBank [*Denmark*] [*Information service or system*] (CRD)
DSTC........... Daylight Saving Time Coalition [*Inactive*] (EA)
DSTC........... Distance (FAAC)
DSTC........... Distributed Systems Technology Centre [*Australia*] (DDC)
DSTC........... Double-Sideband Transmitted Carrier [*Telecommunications*] (IAA)
DSTC........... Due Submit to Correction (SAUS)
DSTCD......... District Code (SAUS)
DSTD........... Design service training database (SAUS)
DSTD........... Double-Sided, Triple-Deposit
DSTDI.......... Division of Scientific and Technological Documentation and Information (SAUS)
DSTDP......... Distearyl Thiodipropionate [*Organic chemistry*]
d-std vehicle... driver-seated vehicle (SAUS)
DSTE........... Data Subcarrier Terminal Equipment (SAUS)
DSTE........... Data Subscriber Terminal Equipment [*Telecommunications*] (IAA)
DSTE........... Defense System Terminal Equipment (MCD)
DSTE........... Digital Subscriber Terminal Equipment (AFM)
D St E.......... Doctor of Structural Engineering
D St Eng....... Doctor of Structural Engineering
DSTF........... Delta Spin Test Facility (MCD)
DSTF........... Double-shell tank farm (SAUS)
DstFear........ Destron Fearing Corp. [*Associated Press*] (SAG)
DSTFSG....... Deep-Sea Test Facilities Study Group (SAA)
d-stg vehicle... driver-standing vehicle (SAUS)
DSTI............ Directorate of Scientific and Technical Intelligence [*British*]
DSTI............ Division of Scientific and Technical Information [*International Atomic Energy Agency*] (DIT)
D St J.......... Dame of Justice/Grace of the Order of St. John of Jerusalem [*British*]
DStJ............ Saint Joseph Seminary, Washington, DC [*Library symbol*] [*Library of Congress*] (LCLS)
DSTL............ Diagnostic Screening Test: Language [*Educational test*]
DSTL............ Digital Studio-to-Transmitter Link (SAUS)
DSTL............ Digital Summation Threshold Logic (SAUS)
DSTL............ Distill
DSTL............ Division System Training Leader (SAA)
DSTLD......... Distilled
DSTLN......... Distillation (SAUS)
DSTLT......... Distillate
DSTM........... Datastream Systems [*NASDAQ symbol*] (TTSB)
DSTM........... Datastream Systems, Inc. [*NASDAQ symbol*] (SAG)
DSTM........... Diagnostic Screening Test: Math [*Educational test*]
DSTMM........ Detailed Sensor Thermal Math Model (ACAE)
DSTN........... Destination (KSC)
DSTN........... Double Supertwisted Nematic [*Video technology*] (PCM)
D Stn........... Dressing Station (SAUS)
DSTN........... Dual-Scan Twisted Nematic [*Communications term*] (DCT)
DSTND......... Destined (FAAC)
DSTO........... Datastrobe (SAUS)
DSTO........... Defence Sciences and Technology Organization (SAUS)
DSTO........... Defense Sciences and Technology Organization (SAUS)
DSTO........... Deputy Sea Transport Officer (SAUO)
DSTO........... District Sea Transport Officer (SAUO)
DSTO........... District Supply and Transport Officer [*British military*] (DMA)
DSTO........... Divisional Sea Transport Officer (SAUO)
DSTOSR....... Double-shell tanks operational safety requirement (SAUS)
DSTP........... Data Self-Test Program
DSTP........... Data System Technology Program (SAUS)
DSTP........... Delaware State Testing Program
DSTP........... Director of Strategic Target Planning [*Military*]
DSTP........... Draft Site Treatment Plan [*Department of Energy*]
DStPC.......... Saint Paul's College, Washington, DC [*Library symbol*] [*Library of Congress*] (LCLS)
dstpn........... dessert spoon (SAUS)
DSTPS......... Director of Strategic Target Planning Staff [*Offutt AFB*] [*Military*] (CINC)
DSTR........... Deserter [*Military*] (AABC)
DSTR........... Destructor [*Military*]
DSTR........... Diagnostic Screening Test: Reading [*Educational test*]
DSTR........... Distort (VLIE)
DSTR........... Distribution (MCD)
DSTR........... Distributor (SAUS)
DSTR........... Dorsal Striatum [*Neuroanatomy*]
DSTR........... Down-Stream (SAUS)
DSTR........... Dual Stage Target Recognizer (ACAE)
DSTR........... DualStar Technologies Corp. [*NASDAQ symbol*] (SAG)
DSTR........... Dynamic Systems Test Rig [*Helicopters*] [*Army*] (RDA)
DST-REF...... Destination Reference (SAUS)
DSTRU......... DualStar Technologies Unit [*NASDAQ symbol*] (TTSB)
DSTRW........ DualStar Technologies Wrrt'A' [*NASDAQ symbol*] (TTSB)
DSTS........... Defensive System Technology Study (CCCA)
DSTS........... Desk Side Time Shared [*General Electric Co.*] [*Computer science*]
DSTS........... Destruct System Test Set
DSTS........... Diagnostic Screening Test: Spelling [*Educational test*]
DSTS........... Dockside Training Simulator
DSTS........... Dynamic Sound Test System
DSTSA......... Double-shell tank sampling analysis (SAUS)
DSTSPN....... Dessertspoon (WGA)
DST Sys....... DST Systems, Inc. [*Associated Press*] (SAG)
DSTT........... Dictionary of Scientific and Technical Terms (SAUS)
DSTU........... Digital Signal Transfer Unit (DWSG)
DSTU........... Draft Standards for Trial Use (SAUS)
DSTUMS....... Digital Signal Transfer Unit and Multi Sensor (ACAE)
DSTWCD...... Double-shell tank waste characterization database (SAUS)
DSU............ Data Selector Unit (OA)
DSU............ Data Sequentializer Unit [*Computer science*] (VLIE)
DSU............ Data Service Unit [*Telecommunications*]
DSU............ Data Servicing Unit (CTAS)
DSU............ Data Storage Unit
DSU............ Data Switching Unit (ACAE)
DSU............ Data Synchronization [*or Synchronizer*] Unit
DSU............ Daughters and Sons United [*An association*] (EA)
DSU............ Day Surgery Unit (MELL)
DSU............ Decoder Switching Unit
DSU............ Democratic and Social Union [*Mauritania*] [*Political party*] (EY)
DSU............ Deployment Sensor Unit (ACAE)
DSU............ Deskewing Synchronizer Unit (SAUS)
DSU............ Deutsche Soziale Union [*German Social Union*] (PPW)
DSU............ Device Selection Unit (SAUS)
DSU............ Device Switching Unit (SAUS)
DSU............ Device-Switching Unit
DSU............ Dictionary of Scientific Units (SAUS)
DSU............ Digital Service Unit [*Signal converting device*] [*Telecommunications*] (TSSD)
DSU............ Digital Standard Update (SAUS)
DSU............ Digital Storage Unit (DIT)
DSU............ Digital Synchronization Unit (HGAA)
DSU............ Direct Supply Unit [*Army*] (VNW)
DSU............ Direct Support Unit [*Army*]
DSU............ Disc Storage Unit (ACAE)
DSU............ Disk Storage Unit [*Computer science*] (MSA)
DSU............ Disk Subsystem Unit [*Computer science*] (VLIE)
DSU............ Disk Synchronizer Unit (SAUS)
DSU............ Display Support Unit (MCD)
DSU............ Dispute Settlement Understanding
dsu............. dissemination services unit (SAUS)
DSU............ Distribution Service Unit [*IBM Corp.*] (VERA)
DSU............ Drum Storage Unit
DSUA.......... Dynamic Special-Use Airspace [*FAA*] (TAG)
DSUCR........ Doppler-Shifted Ultrasonic Cyclotron Resonance (PDAA)
DSU/CSU..... Data Servicing Unit / Channel Servicing Unit (HGAA)
DSU/CSU..... Digital Service Unit/Channel Service Unit [*Communications term*] (DCT)
DSUE.......... [*A*] Dictionary of Slang and Unconventional English [*A publication*]
DSUE.......... Doubly Stochastic User Equilibrium [*Traffic management*]
DSU/GSU..... Direct Support Unit/General Support Unit [*Computer system*]
DSU-GSU..... Direct Support Units-General Support Units (SAUO)
DSUH.......... Direct Suggestion under Hypnosis
DSUM......... Data Summary (ADWA)
DSUP.......... Defensive System Upgrade Program [*Military*] (SEWL)
DSUPHTR.... Desuperheater
D-SUPT....... Detective Superintendent
DSUR.......... Data Storage Unit Receptacle (MCD)
D Sur.......... Doctor of Surgery
DSurg......... Dental Surgeon (SAUS)
D Surg........ Dental Surgery (SAUS)
DS/USA....... Disabled Sports USA [*An association*] [*Established in 1967 by disabled Vietnam veterans*] (NRGU)
DSUWG....... Data Systems Users Working Group (ACAE)
DSV............ Damping Structural Vibrations
DSV............ Dansville, NY [*Location identifier*] [*FAA*] (FAAL)
DSV............ Deep Submarine Vehicle (SAUS)
DSV............ Deep Submergence Vehicle [*Navy symbol*]
DSV............ Defence Suppression Vehicle (SAUS)
DSV............ Design, Specification and Verification (SAUS)
DSV............ Detected Safety Violation
DSV............ Digital Sum Variation [*Telecommunications*]
DSV............ Digitaria Striate Virus [*Plant pathology*]
DSV............ Dilute Solution Viscosity (SAUS)
DSV............ Director of Special Visits (SAUO)
DSV............ Diving Support Vessel (DS)
DSV............ Double Silk Varnish [*Wire insulation*] (AAG)
DSV............ Douglas Space Vehicle
DSV............ Drum Safety Valve (DS)
DSV............ Dynamic Self-Verification (IAA)
DSV............ Dynamic Signature Verification (SEWL)
DSVD.......... Digital Simultaneous Voice and Data (CDE)
DS/VD......... Director of Salvage Department [*Navy*] [*British*]
DSVL.......... Doppler SONAR Velocity Log (MCD)

DSVOPS....... Duty as an Operator or Crewmember of an Operational Self-Propelled Submersible Including Underseas Exploration and Research Vehicles [*Military*] (DNAB)
DSVP.......... Director of Small Vessels Pool [*Admiralty*] [*British*]
DSVP.......... Downstream Venous Pressure [*Physiology*] (MAH)
DSVR.......... Design Specification Validation Report (SEWL)
DS/VSE....... Decision Support/VSE (SAUS)
DSVT.......... Digital Secure Voice Telephone [*Telecommunications*] (TEL)
DSVT.......... Digital Secure Voice Terminal (CCCA)
DSVT.......... Digital Subscriber Voice Terminal (MCD)
DSVY.......... Director of Survey [*British military*] (DMA)
DSW........... Data Status Word
DSW........... Deep-Sea Winch
DSW........... Defense Suppression Weapon (ACAE)
DSW........... Delivered with Standard Wiring
DSW........... Department of Social Welfare [*New Zealand*] (WDAA)
DSW........... Designator Storage Word (SAUS)
DSW........... Device Status Word (CMD)
DSW........... Diesel Sea Water (DNAB)
DSW........... Differential Shunt Winding [*Wiring*] (DNAB)
D/SW.......... Dimmer Switch [*Automotive engineering*]
DSW........... Director of Special Weapons [*Army*]
DSW........... Direct-Step-on-the-Wafer [*Microelectronics*]
DSW........... Discovery West Corp. [*Toronto Stock Exchange symbol*]
DSW........... Doctor of Social Welfare
DSW........... Doctor of Social Work
DSW........... Door Switch
DSW........... Drum Switch
DSWA.......... Defense Special Weapons Agency (SAUS)
DSWA.......... Dry Stone Walling Association [*British*] (DBA)
DSWC.......... Disposable solid waste cask (SAUS)
DSW exposure... direct-step-on-wafer exposure (SAUS)
DSWI.......... Deep Surgical Wound Infection [*Medicine*] (DMAA)
DSWL.......... Deswell Industries, Inc. [*NASDAQ symbol*] (SAG)
DSWLF......... Deswell Industries [*NASDAQ symbol*] (TTSB)
DSW-machine... direct-step-on-wafer machine (SAUS)
DSWP.......... Director of Surface Weapons Projects [*Navy*] [*British*]
DSWR.......... Deep Space Warning Radar (SAUS)
DSWR.......... Digital Short-Wave Radio (SAUS)
DSWS.......... Deep Submergence Weapon System [*Also, DEXTOR*] (MCD)
DSWS.......... Direct Support Weapon System (MCD)
DSWS.......... Disorders of Sleep-Wake Schedule (MELL)
DSWS.......... Division Support Weapon System (MCD)
DSW system... direct-step-on-wafer system (SAUS)
DSWV.......... Director of Special Weapons and Vehicles [*Military*] [*British*]
DSWW.......... Deswell Industries, Inc. [*NASDAQ symbol*] (SAG)
DSWWF......... Deswell Inds Wrrt [*NASDAQ symbol*] (TTSB)
DSX........... Data Systems Executive (SAUS)
DSX........... Digital Service Cross-Connect (MLOA)
DSX........... Digital Signal Cross-Connect [*Telecommunications*]
DSX........... Digital signal cross connection equipment (SAUS)
DSx........... Digital Signal, Level X [*Computer science*] (VLIE)
DSX........... Digital System Cross-Connect [*Telecommunications*] (ACRL)
DSX........... Distributed Systems Executive [*IBM Corp.*]
dsx........... Doublesex
DSX-1......... Digital Cross Connect, Level 1 [*Communications term*] (DCT)
DSX-1......... Digital Signal Cross-Connect Level 1 (CDE)
DSX1/3........ Digital Signal Cross-Connect between Levels 1 and 3 (VLIE)
DSXBT......... Deep Shipboard Expendable Bathythermograph [*Oceanography*]
DSXBT......... Digitized Shipboard Expandable Bathythermograph (SAUS)
DSY........... Diesel Supply [*Federal Railroad Administration identification code*]
DSy........... Digit Symbol [*Psychology*] [*Medicine*] (EDAA)
DSY........... Dorsey Corp. (SAUO)
DSYG.......... Deputy Secretary General (NATG)
DSYS.......... Data Sys Network Corp. [*NASDAQ symbol*] (TTSB)
DSYS.......... Data Systems Network Corp. [*NASDAQ symbol*] (SAG)
DSYSW......... Data Sys Network Wrrt [*NASDAQ symbol*] (TTSB)
DSYT.......... Dorsey Trailers [*NASDAQ symbol*] (TTSB)
DSYT.......... Dorsey Trailers, Inc. [*NASDAQ symbol*] (SAG)
D Sy Th....... Doctor of Systematic Theology
DSZ........... Decrement and Skip on Zero (SAUS)
DSZ........... Madison, WI [*Location identifier*] [*FAA*] (FAAL)
DT............ Daily Telegraph [*A publication*]
DT............ Dakota Territory (ROG)
DT............ Dark Trace
DT............ Data (VLIE)
DT............ Data Table [*Computer science*] (ELAL)
DT............ Data Tablet (TIMI)
DT............ Data Tabulation (OICC)
DT............ Data Tape (SAUS)
DT............ Data Technique (SAUS)
DT............ Data Telecommunication (SAUS)
DT............ Data Terminal
DT............ Data Text [*Computer science*] (VLIE)
DT............ Data Transcriber
DT............ Data Transducer (SAUS)
DT............ Data Transfer (SAUS)
DT............ Data Translator (IEEE)
DT............ Data Transmission
DT............ Date (AFM)
dt............ Date (WDMC)
DT............ Date and Time (SAUS)
DT............ Date of Treatment (SAUS)
DT............ Daughter
DT............ Daylight Time
DT............ Days after Transplanting [*Botany*]
DT............ Day Tracer (SAUS)
DT............ Dead Time
DT............ Dealer Team (SAUS)
D/T........... Deaths Total Ratio [*Measurement*] [*Medicine*] (DAVI)
DT............ Debits Tax (ADA)
DT............ Decatur Junction Railway [*Federal Railroad Administration identification code*]
DT............ Decay Time (MSA)
DT............ Deccan Trap [*Geology*]
DT............ Decision Table [*Computer science*]
DT............ Decision Technology (UWER)
DT............ Decision Time (SAUS)
DT............ Decision Tree [*Medicine*] (EDAA)
dt............ Decitonne
DT............ Declaration of Taking (SAUS)
DT............ Dedicated Terminal (SAUS)
DT............ Deduction Theorem [*Logic*]
DT............ Deep Tank (MSA)
DT............ Deep Thought (SAUS)
DT............ Defensive Tackle [*Football*]
DT............ Defensive Target [*Military*]
DT............ Deferred Telegram
DT............ Defibrillation Threshold [*Medicine*] (EDAA)
DT............ Definition Term (SAUS)
DT............ Deflection Temperature (SAUS)
DT............ Deformation Twin (SAUS)
DT............ Dejerine-Thomas [*Syndrome*] [*Medicine*] (DB)
DT............ Delayed Time (KSC)
DT............ Delay Time (UWER)
DT............ Delirium Tremens [*Also, DT's*] [*Hallucinatory condition of advanced alcoholism*]
DT............ Delivery Time
DT............ Delta Technique (SAUS)
DT............ Deltorphin [*Biochemistry*]
DT............ Dental Technician [*Navy rating*]
dT............ Deoxythymidine (DB)
DT............ Deoxythymidine [*Organic chemistry*]
DT............ Department of Tactics (SAUO)
DT............ Department of Tourism (SAUS)
DT............ Department of Trade [*British*] (DS)
DT............ Department of Transportation (SAUO)
DT............ Department Training
DT............ Depletion Transistor (SAUS)
DT............ Deployment Transaction (SAUS)
DT............ Depressed Temperature (UWER)
DT............ Depression of Transmission (SAUS)
DT............ Descriptor Table (SAUS)
DT............ Design and Technology (DET)
DT............ Design Temperature (UWER)
DT............ Design Test (UWER)
DT............ Desk Top
DT............ Desmoid Tumor [*Medicine*] (MELL)
DT............ Desoxynucleotidyl-Terminal-transferase (SAUS)
DT............ Desoxyribonylthymin (SAUS)
DT............ Destructive Testing (SAUS)
DT............ Detecting Heads [*JETDS nomenclature*] [*Military*] (CET)
DT............ Detection and Tracking (SEWL)
DT............ Detection Theory (SAUS)
DT............ Detection Threshold (CAAL)
D/T........... Detection/Tracker (NVT)
dt............ detective (SAUS)
DT............ Detention Time (COE)
DT............ Detoxification [*Medicine*] (DHP)
DT............ Detroit Terminal Railroad Co. [*AAR code*]
DT............ Deuterium-Tritium (UWER)
DT............ Deuterium-Tritium Ratio (SAUS)
D-T........... Deuterium-Tritium Reaction [*Fusion program*]
Dt............ Deuteronomy [*Old Testament book*]
DT............ deuteron-triton (SAUS)
DT............ Deutsche Telekom AG [*NYSE symbol*] (SAG)
DT............ Deutsche Theologie [*A publication*] (BJA)
DT............ Developed Template (MCD)
DT............ Developmental Testing (SAUS)
DT............ Development Test [*or Testing*] (MCD)
DT............ Development Type (AABC)
DT............ Diagnostic Technique (SAUS)
DT............ Diagnostic Time [*Computer science*] (DNAB)
DT............ Dial Tone [*Telecommunications*] (TEL)
DT............ Diastolic Time [*Cardiology*]
dt............ Dickite (SAUS)
d/t........... dictaphone typist (SAUS)
DT............ Diesel tester (SAUS)
DT............ Diesel Trawler (SAUS)
DT............ Die Template (MSA)
DT............ Dietetic Technician (HCT)
DT............ Diet Therapy (MELL)
DT............ Difference Threshold [*Psychology*] (IAA)
dt............ Differential of Time (IDOE)
DT............ Differential Time (IEEE)
DT............ Differentiating Transformer (SAUS)
DT............ Diffraction Theory (SAUS)
DT............ Digital Technique
DT............ Digital Telemetering (IAA)
DT............ Digital Test Measurement System (NASA)

DT .... Digital Tracker
DT .... Digital Translator (SAUS)
DT .... Digital Transmission (SAUS)
DT .... Digital Transmission and Routing System (SAUS)
DT .... Digital Transmitter (SAUS)
DT .... Digitoxin (DB)
DT .... Digit Track (SAUS)
DT .... Digit Tube (IEEE)
DT .... Digroup Terminal [*Telecommunications*] (TEL)
D/T .... Dilutions to Threshold [*Olfactory*]
dt .... dinette (SAUS)
D-T .... Dinner Theater
DT .... Diode Transistor (IAA)
dT .... Diphtheria (ADWA)
dt .... Diphtheria and Tetanus Toxoid [*or Toxin*] [*Immunology*] (DAVI)
DT .... Diphtheria, Tetanus [*Medicine*]
DT .... Diphtheria Toxin [*Biochemistry*]
DT .... Dip Test (UWER)
DT .... Dip Tube
DT .... Directorate of Tests (SAUS)
DT .... Director of Transport [*British military*] (DMA)
DT .... Direct Tension (UWER)
DT .... Discharge Tomorrow [*Medicine*] (EDAA)
DT .... Discharge Tube (IAA)
DT .... Disconnector Trap
DT .... Discrepancy Tag
DT .... Discrete Time (SAUS)
DT .... Disc tape (SAUS)
DT .... Disc Turntable [*A record player*] (WDMC)
D/T .... Disk Tape [*Computer science*] (IEEE)
DT .... Disk Technician [*Computer science*]
DT .... Disk to Tape (SAUS)
DT .... Dispensing Tablet [*Medicine*] (DMAA)
DT .... Dispersion Time (NATG)
DT .... Displacement ton (BARN)
DT .... Displacement Transducer (KSC)
DT .... Display Terminal (IAA)
DT .... Display Test (ACAE)
DT .... Display Translator (MCD)
DT .... Distance Test
DT .... Distant Terminal [*Communications term*] (DCT)
DT .... Distant Transmission (IAA)
DT .... Distillation Test (UWER)
DT .... Distillation Tower (UWER)
DT .... Distributed Transaction (SAUS)
DT .... Distributive Trades [*Department of Employment*] [*British*]
DT .... District Trust Co. [*Toronto Stock Exchange symbol*]
DT .... Diuretic Therapy [*Medicine*] (MELL)
DT .... Diver, Second Class [*Navy rating*]
DT .... Diversional Therapy [*Psychiatry*] (DAVI)
DT .... Divisional Train (SAUO)
DT .... Docklands Taskforce [*Victoria*] [*Australia*]
DT .... Doctor of Technology
DT .... Doctor of Theology
DT .... Documentation Terminology (SAUS)
DT .... Document Terminator (SAUS)
DT .... Document Title [*European Space Agency-Information Retrieval System*] [*Searchable fields*] (NITA)
dt .... Document Type (MEC)
DT .... Document Type [*Online database field identifier*]
DT .... Dog Tick (MELL)
DT .... Doit [*Debit*] [*French*]
DT .... Domain Theory (SAUS)
DT .... Dominant Trait (MELL)
DT .... Double Tachycardia [*Cardiology*]
DT .... Double Threat (SAUS)
DT .... Double Throw [*Switch*]
DT .... Double Time
DT .... Double Torsion (SAUS)
DT .... Double Track [*Engineering acoustics*] (IAA)
DT .... Double Tube
DT .... Doubling Time (SAUS)
DT .... Down Through [*Clairvoyance experiment*]
DT .... Downtime [*Computer science*] [*Telecommunications*] (AAG)
DT .... Dow Theory [*Stock market analysis*]
Dt .... Draft (SAUS)
DT .... Drain Tile [*Technical drawings*]
DT .... Drama Tree (EA)
DT .... Draught
DT .... Dravon Tube (SAUS)
DT .... Dressed or Tanned [*Freight*]
DT .... Dressing Table [*Classified advertising*] (ADA)
DT .... Drift Tube (SAUS)
DT .... Drilling Technician (SAUS)
DT .... Drilling Technology (SAUS)
DT .... Drilling Template (SAUS)
DT .... Drive Tube
DT .... Driving Trace [*Automotive emissions*]
DT .... Drop Tank (KSC)
DT .... Drop Test Report
DT .... Drop Top (OA)
DT .... Drop Tower (SAUS)
DT .... Drop Tube (SAUS)
DT .... Drug Therapy (MELL)
DT .... Drug Toxicity (MELL)
DT .... Drum Transfer (CET)
DT .... Drum Trap (DAC)
DT .... Dry Ton (SAUS)
DT .... Dry Toned [*Copier*] [*Reprography*]
DT .... Dry Traction [*Tire design*]
DT .... Dual Tandem [*Aviation*] (DA)
DT .... Dual Terminal (SAUS)
DT .... Dual Tires
DT .... Due to (SAUS)
DT .... Dumb Terminal [*Computer science*] (GART)
DT .... Dummy Target (OA)
DT .... Dump tank (SAUS)
DT .... Dump Telemetry
DT .... Duration of Tetany [*Medicine*]
Dt .... duration tetanus (SAUS)
Dt .... Duration Tetany (SAUS)
DT .... Dust-Tight (MSA)
DT .... Dust Turn (OA)
DT .... Duty Technician (SAUS)
DT .... Dwell Time (AAG)
DT .... Dye Testing
DT .... Dylan Thomas (SAUS)
DT .... Dynamic Tear (OA)
DT .... Dynamic Test (AAEL)
DT .... Dynamic Tester
DT .... TAAG-Angola Airlines [*ICAO designator*] (AD)
DT .... TAAG Linhas Aereas de Angola [*Angola*] [*ICAO designator*] (ICDA)
DT .... Telefunken (Pressed by Decca) [*Record label*] [*Great Britain*]
dT .... Tetanus booster with diptheria booster (SAUS)
DT .... Tornado Damper (SAUS)
DT .... United States Department of the Treasury, Washington, DC [*Library symbol*] [*Library of Congress*] (LCLS)
DT .... [*USA*] Department of Treasury (ODA)
DT .... Damage Tolerant (ODA)
DT .... Dead from Tumour [*Medicine*] (ODA)
dT .... Thymidine [*Biochemistry*] (ODA)
DT1 .... Data Form 1 (SAUS)
DT1 .... Dental Technician, First Class [*Navy rating*]
DT2 .... Data Form 2 (SAUS)
DT2 .... Dental Technician, Second Class [*Navy rating*]
DT3 .... Dental Technician, Third Class [*Navy rating*]
DTA .... Daily Travel Allowance [*Business term*] (WDAA)
DTA .... Daisy Testability Analyser (NITA)
DTA .... Dakka Tourist Agency [*Israel*]
DTA .... Dance Teachers' Association (AIE)
DTA .... Data File [*Computer science*]
DTA .... Data Transfer Area [*Computer science*]
DTa .... Deep Tank Aft (DS)
DTA .... Deep Transverse Arrest [*Obstetrics*]
DTA .... Default Transfer Area [*Computer science*] (PCM)
DTA .... Defense Transport Administration [*Terminated, functions transferred to Interstate Commerce Commission*]
DTA .... Defense Transportation Administration (SAUS)
DTA .... Delta, UT [*Location identifier*] [*FAA*] (FAAL)
DTA .... Democratic Turnhalle Alliance [*Namibia*] [*Political party*] (EY)
DTA .... Dental Therapy Assistant (RDA)
DTA .... Dentonia Resources Ltd. [*Vancouver Stock Exchange symbol*]
DTA .... Department of Transitional Assistance (SAUO)
DTA .... Design and Test Alliance [*Technology research group*]
DTA .... Desktop Administrator [*Computer science*] (GART)
DTA .... Detailed Traffic Analysis [*Telecommunications*] (TEL)
DTA .... Detroit Edison 7.625% 'QUIDS' [*NYSE symbol*] (TTSB)
DTA .... Detroit Edison Co. [*NYSE symbol*] (SAG)
DTA .... Detroit Teachers Association (SAUO)
DTA .... Detroit Tooling Association (EA)
DTA .... Development Test Article
DTA .... Diaminopropanoltetraacetic Acid [*Also, DPTA, DHPTA*] [*Organic chemistry*]
DTA .... Diethylenetriamine [*Also, DETA*] [*Organic chemistry*]
DTA .... Differential Thermal [*or Thermogravimetric*] Analysis [*or Analyzer*]
DTA .... Differential Thermal Analyzer (SAUS)
DTA .... Differential Thermal Arrest (SAUS)
DTA .... differential thermoanalysis (SAUS)
DTA .... differential thermoanalyzer (SAUS)
DTA .... Differential Turn Angle (SAUS)
DTA .... Digital Throttle Actuator [*Automotive engineering*]
DTA .... Dimethyl-Triazeno-Acetanilide (DICI)
DTA .... Diphtheria Toxin, A Strain [*Immunology*]
DTA .... Diploma in Tropical Agriculture (ADA)
DTA .... Direct Tape Access [*Computer science*]
DTA .... Direct Transit Area (SAUS)
DTA .... Disk Transfer Address (ADWA)
DTA .... Disk Transfer Area [*Computer science*] (BYTE)
DTA .... Disk Turbine Assembly
DTA .... Dispersion-Toughened Alumina (SAUS)
DTA .... Distributing Terminal Assembly [*Electronics*]
DTA .... Distributive Trades' Alliance [*British*] (BI)
DTA .... District Traffic Agent
DTA .... Divisao de Exploracao dos Transportes Aereos [*Angolan airline*]
DTA .... Division Tactical Area [*Army*]
DTA .... Document Tracking and Accountability system (SAUS)
DTA .... Dominion Traffic Association [*Canada*]
DTA .... Double Tape Armored [*Heavy-duty telephone buried cable*]
dta .... double tape armored cable (SAUS)
DTA .... Dovetail Anchor [*Technical drawings*]

DTA.......... Dual Trace Amplifier
DTA.......... Due to Arrive
DTA.......... Dynamic Test Article (SAUS)
DTA.......... Dynamic Traffic Assignment [*Traffic management*]
DTA.......... TAAG, Linhas Aereas de Angola [*ICAO designator*] (FAAC)
DTAA.......... Diamond Trade and Precious Stone Association of America (NTPA)
DTAA.......... Diamond Trade Association of America [*Later, DTPSAA*] (EA)
DTAA.......... Di-Tryptophan Aminal Acetaldehyde [*Biochemistry*]
DTAA.......... Diversional Therapy Association of Australia
DTAARA.......... Data Area (SAUS)
DTAB.......... Demountable Tape Automated Bonding (SAUS)
DTAB.......... Dodecyltrimethylammonium Bromide [*Organic chemistry*]
DTABL.......... Decision Table Processor [*IBM Corp.*]
DTAC.......... Department of Tactics (SAUO)
DTAC.......... Dodecyltrimethylammonium Chloride [*Organic chemistry*]
DTACC.......... Deployable Tactical Air Control Center (SAUO)
DTACC.......... Deployed Tanker/Airlift Control Center (SAUO)
DTACCS.......... Director/Telecommunications and Command and Control System (MCD)
DTACCS.......... Director, Telecommunications and Command and Control Systems (SAUO)
DTACK.......... Data Transfer Acknowledge [*Computer memory management*]
DTAD.......... Digital Telephone Answering Device (SAUS)
DtaDimn.......... Data Dimensions, Inc. [*Associated Press*] (SAG)
DtaDoc.......... Data Documents, Inc. [*Associated Press*] (SAG)
DTAE.......... Department of Technical and Adult Education (SAUO)
DTAE.......... Depot Test and Acceptance Equipment (ACAE)
DTAF.......... (Dichlorotriazinyl)aminofluorescein [*Also, DCTAF*] [*Analytical biochemistry*]
DTAF.......... Document Translation Assistance Facility (SAUS)
DTAF.......... Dynamic Tactical Area File [*Military*] (CAAL)
DTAFE.......... Department of Technical and Further Education [*Australia*]
DTAG.......... Defense Trade Advisory Group (AAGC)
DTAG.......... Destination Tag [*Communications term*] (DCT)
DTAG.......... Digitale Telekable AG [*NASDAQ symbol*] (SAG)
Dta IO.......... Data I-O Corp. [*Associated Press*] (SAG)
DTAL.......... David Taylor Aerodynamics Laboratory (SAUO)
DTAM.......... Daily Traffic Assignment Model [*Aviation*]
DTAM.......... Descend to and Maintain [*Aviation*] (FAAC)
DTAM.......... Distributor Total Available Market (TIMI)
DTAM.......... Document Transfer, Access and Manipulation [*Computer science*] (VERA)
DTAM.......... Document Transfer and Manipulation (SAUS)
DTAM.......... Data Transfer, Access, and Manipulation (ODA)
DtaMea.......... Data Measurement Corp. [*Associated Press*] (SAG)
DTAMS.......... Data Transmission and Message System (SAUS)
DT&C.......... Department of Transport and Communications (SAUO)
DT&E.......... Demonstration, Testing and Evaluation (SAUS)
DT&E.......... Design, Testing, and Evaluation (ABAC)
DT&E.......... Developmental Test and Evaluation (SAUS)
DT & E.......... Development, Test, and Evaluation (AFM)
DT & E.......... Development, Test, and Experimentation
DT & FE.......... Department of Technical and Further Education (SAUS)
DT & G.......... Double Tongue and Groove (DAC)
DT & I.......... Detroit, Toledo & Ironton Railroad Co. [*Nickname: Damned Tough and Independent*]
DTAO.......... During the Temporary Absence Of [*Military*]
DTAP.......... Defense Technology Area Plan [*Defense Technical Information Center*]
DTaP.......... Diphtheria, Tetanus, and Acellular Pertussis (ADWA)
DTaP.......... Diptheria and Tetanus Toxoids Combined with Acellular Pertussis Vaccine [*Medicine*] (MELL)
DTAP.......... Direct Transfer Application Part [*Computer science*] (VERA)
DtaProc.......... Data Processing Resurces Corp. [*Associated Press*] (SAG)
DTAR.......... Decision Theoretic Adaptive Radar (ACAE)
DTARS.......... Digital Transmitting and Routing System (IEEE)
DtaRsh.......... Data Research Associates, Inc. [*Associated Press*] (SAG)
DTAS.......... Data Transmission and Switching
DTAS.......... Diagnostic Test of Arithmetic Strategies
DTAS.......... Diffuse Thalamic Activating System (SAUS)
DTAS.......... Digital Test Access System (SAUS)
DTAS.......... Digital Time Assignment Speech Interpolation (SAUS)
DTAS.......... Digital Transmission And Switching (SAUS)
DTAS.......... Digital Transmission and Switching System (ACAE)
DTAS.......... Digitas, Inc. [*NASDAQ symbol*] (SG)
DTASI.......... Digital Time Assignment Speech Interpolation (PDAA)
DTAS System... Digital Transmission and Switching System (SAUS)
DTASW.......... Department of Torpedo and Anti-Submarine Warfare (SAUS)
DTASW.......... Director, Torpedo, Anti-Submarine, and Mine Warfare [*British military*] (DMA)
DTAT.......... Depot Turn-Around Time (MCD)
DtaTrn.......... Data Translation Corp. [*Associated Press*] (SAG)
DTAU.......... Digital Test Access Unit (SAUS)
DtaWks.......... DataWorks Corp. [*Associated Press*] (SAG)
Dtawtc.......... Datawatch Corp. [*Associated Press*] (SAG)
Dtawtch.......... Datawatch Corp. [*Associated Press*] (SAG)
DTAX.......... Descend to and Cross [*Aviation*] (FAAC)
D Tax.......... Dominion Tax Cases [*CCH Canadian Ltd.*] [*Information service or system*] [*A publication*] (DLA)
DTAZ.......... Dominion Terminal Association [*Federal Railroad Administration identification code*]
DTB.......... Danish Tourist Board (EAIO)
DTB.......... Danmarks (SAUS)
DTB.......... Danmarks Tekniske Bibliotek [*National Technological Library of Denmark*] [*Information service or system*] (IID)
DTB.......... Data Transfer Bus (SAUS)
DTB.......... Decimal to Binary [*Computer science*] (BUR)
DTB.......... Delayed Time Base (IAA)
DTB.......... Desktop Broadcasting [*Computer science*] (GART)
DTB.......... Destroyer Tactical Bulletin [*Navy*]
DTB.......... Detroit Edison 7.54% 'QUIDS' [*NYSE symbol*] (SG)
DTB.......... Deutsche Terminboerse [*Derivatives market*] [*Germany*]
DTB.......... Deviation Test Bridge
DTB.......... Ditaurobilirubin [*Biochemistry*]
DTB.......... Dithiobiuret [*Organic chemistry*]
DTB.......... Dominica Tourist Board (EAIO)
DtB.......... Down The Back (SAUS)
DTB.......... Dynamic Transaction Backout [*IBM Corp.*] (CIST)
DTB.......... Dynamic Translation Buffer
DTBA.......... Date to Be Advised (MARI)
dtba.......... Date to Be Agreed (AIA)
DTBA.......... (Dimethyltriazenol)benzoic Acid [*Antineoplastic drug*]
DTBB.......... Di-Tertiary-Butylbiphenyl [*Organic chemistry*]
DTBC.......... Digital Time Base Corrector (PDAA)
dtbc.......... disturbance (SAUS)
DTBC.......... Di-tert-butylcatechol [*Organic chemistry*]
DTBC.......... Di-tert-butylcresol [*Organic chemistry*]
DTBC.......... D-Tubocurarine [*Pharmacology*] (DAVI)
DTBC.......... Lower Canada Reports (Decisions des Tribunaux du Bas-Canada) [*1850-67*] [*A publication*] (DLA)
DtBdcst.......... Data Broadcasting Corp. [*Associated Press*] (SAG)
DTBE.......... Defense Telecommunications Research Establishment (SAUS)
DTBHQ.......... Di-tert-butylhydroquinone [*Organic chemistry*]
DT BIOL.......... Deutsche Biologische Literatur [*German Biological Literature*] [*Also, DBL*] [*Database*] [*Forschungsinstitut Senckenberg*] [*Information service or system*]
DTBN.......... Di-T-butyl Nitroxide [*Organic chemistry*]
DTBN.......... Di-tert-butylnaphthalene [*Organic chemistry*]
DTBP.......... Dedicated Total Buried Plant [*Telecommunications*] (TEL)
DTBP.......... Di-tert-butyl Peroxide [*Organic chemistry*]
DTBP.......... Di-Tert-Butylphenol [*Biochemistry*]
DTC.......... Darwin Turf Club [*Australia*]
DTC.......... Data communications and Terminal Controller (SAUS)
DTC.......... Data Technical Control
DTC.......... Data Technology Corp.
DTC.......... Data Terminals & Communications, Inc.
DTC.......... Data Test Center [*Telecommunications*] (TEL)
DTC.......... Data Transfer Cartridge (SAUS)
DTC.......... Data Transfer Complete (SAUS)
DTC.......... Data Transmission Center (KSC)
DTC.......... Data Transmission Channel (CMD)
DTC.......... Data Transport Computer
DTC.......... Day Training Center (SAUS)
DTC.......... Day Treatment Center [*Medicine*] (DAVI)
DTC.......... Dead Time Correction
DTC.......... Decision Threshold Computer
DTC.......... Deep Tow Camera (SAUS)
DTC.......... Defense Technical Center
DTC.......... Defense Trade Controls (POLM)
DTC.......... Dental Technician, Chief [*Navy rating*]
DTC.......... Department of Technical Cooperation [*British*]
DTC.......... Department of Trade and Commerce (SAUS)
DTC.......... Deposition Thickness Controller (IAA)
DTC.......... Depository Transfer Check [*Banking*]
DTC.......... Depository Trust Co.
dtc.......... depository trust company (SAUO)
DTC.......... Deposit-Taking Company [*Generic term that originated in Hong Kong*]
DTC.......... Depot Training Center
DTC.......... Deputy Town Clerk (SAUS)
DTC.......... Desert Test Center [*Fort Douglas, UT*] [*Army*] (AABC)
DTC.......... Desert Tortoise Council (EA)
DTC.......... Desert Training Center [*Army*]
DTC.......... Design/Test Contractor (KSC)
DTC.......... Design-Time Component
DTC.......... Design to Cost (MCD)
DTC.......... Design to Cut (MHDB)
DTC.......... Desktop Communication (SAUS)
DTC.......... Desk Top Computer
DTC.......... DeskTop Conferencing [*Fujitsu Networks Industry, Inc.*] [*Computer science*] (PCM)
DTC.......... Desktop Tactical Computer (ACAE)
DTC.......... Detection Threshold Computer [*Telecommunications*] (TEL)
DTC.......... Developmental Test Command [*Army*]
DTC.......... Developmental Training Center [*Indiana University*] [*Research center*] (RCD)
DTC.......... Dextro-Tubocurarine [*Organic chemistry*]
DTC.......... Diagnostic Trouble Code [*Automotive engineering*]
DTC.......... Diamond Trading Company (SAUO)
DTC.......... Dictionnaire de Theologie Catholique [*A publication*] (ODCC)
DTC.......... Diethyldithiocarbamate (SAUS)
DTC.......... Differential temperature controller (SAUS)
DTC.......... Differential Thermal Coating (SAUS)
DTC.......... Differential Throttle Control
DTC.......... Digital Tape Conversion
DTC.......... Digital Television Camera
DTC.......... Digital to Tone Converter
DTC.......... Digital Transmit Command (SAUS)
DTC.......... Digital Trunk Controller (SAUS)
DTC.......... Di group Terminal Controller (SAUO)

DTC............ Diode Transistor Compound (SAUS)
DTC............ Diploma in Textile Chemistry (ADA)
DTC............ Direct Thermocouple Control [*Electronics*] (AAEL)
DTC............ Direct-to-Consumer [*Sales*]
DTC............ Direct Torque Control [*Electric motors*]
DTC............ Disciplinary Training Center
DTC............ Discrete-Time Control (SAUS)
DTC............ Display Test Chamber
DTC............ Display Timing Control
DTC............ Distal Transverse Crease (MELL)
DTC............ Distance Traveled Count (SAUS)
DTC............ Distributed Transaction Coordinator [*Computer science*] (VERA)
DTC............ Distribution Traffic Control (VLIE)
DTC............ Dithiocarbamate [*Organic chemistry*]
DTC............ Dithiocarb Sodium (LDT)
DTC............ Division training coordinator (SAUS)
DTC............ Doctor of Textile Chemistry
DTC............ Document de Transport Combine [*Combined Transport Document*] [*French*] [*Business term*]
DTC............ Documento de Transporte Combinado [*Combined Transport Document*] [*Spanish*] [*Business term*]
DTC............ Documento di Trasporto Combinato [*Combined Transport Document*] [*Italian*] [*Business term*]
DTC............ Document Transformation Component (IAA)
DTC............ Dominion Tax Cases [*CCH Canadian Ltd.*] [*Information service or system*] [*A publication*] (DLA)
DTC............ Domtar, Inc. [*NYSE symbol*] [*Toronto Stock Exchange symbol*] [*Vancouver Stock Exchange symbol*] (SPSG)
DTC............ Doppler Translation Channel
DTC............ Downtime Code [*Military*] (AFIT)
DTC............ Draft Technical Corrigendum [*Correction*] [*Telecommunications*] (OSI)
DTC............ Driveability Test Chamber [*Automotive engineering*]
DTC............ Driving Trailer Car [*Indian Railway*] (TIR)
DTC............ DSIF [*Deep Space Instrumentation Facility*] Telemetry and Command Subsystem [*NASA*]
dTC............ d-Tubocurarine [*Muscle relaxant*]
DTC............ Dynamic Tape Tension Control (VLIE)
DTC............ Dynamic Test Chamber (ACAE)
DTC............ Dynatech Tactical Communications (SAUS)
DTC............ International Trade Commission, Washington, DC [*Library symbol*] [*Library of Congress*] (LCLS)
DTC............ United States International Trade Commission, Washington, DC [*OCLC symbol*] (OCLC)
DTC............ Docklands Transportation Consortium (ODA)
DTCCS......... Defense Telecommunications Command and Control System (MCD)
DTCD.......... Department of Technical Cooperation for Development [*UN*] [*Internationl*] [*Environment term*] (EGA)
DTCD.......... Diploma in Tuberculosis and Chest Diseases [*British*]
DTCD.......... Department of Technical Cooperation for Development (ODA)
DTCH.......... Detached
DTCH.......... Diploma in Tropical Child Health [*British*]
DT Ch.......... Doctor of Textile Chemistry
DTCH.......... Dutch
DTChem....... Doctor of Technical Chemistry (NADA)
DTC/LCC...... Design to Cost / Life Cycle Cost (SSD)
DTCM.......... Dental Technician, Master Chief [*Navy rating*]
DTCN.......... Direction Technique des Constructions Navales [*French naval design bureau*] (DOMA)
DTCP.......... Development Training Communication Programme (SAUS)
DTCP.......... Diode Transistor Compound Pair [*Electronics*] (OA)
DTCP.......... Division of Tropical Crops and Pastures, Commonwealth Scientific and Investigation Research Organisation (SAUS)
DTCP.......... Dual Tape Carrier Package (SAUS)
DTCR.......... Data Transfer and Certification Record (KSC)
DTCS.......... Data Transmission and Control System (AAG)
DTCS.......... Data Trend Channel Set (SAUS)
DTCS.......... Dental Technician, Senior Chief [*Navy rating*]
DTCS.......... Digital Tank Control System (SAUS)
DTCS.......... Digital Test Command System
DTCS.......... Discrete-Time Control System (SAUS)
DTCS.......... Drone Target Control System [*Military*] (MCD)
DTCS.......... Drone Tracking and Control System [*Military*] (MCD)
DTCS.......... DynCorp Tri-Cities Services Inc. (SAUO)
DTCU.......... Data Transmission Control Unit [*Burroughs Corp.*]
DTCW.......... Data Transfer Command Word (NASA)
DTCXO........ Digital Temperature Compensated Quarz Oscillator (SAUS)
DTD............ Damage-Tolerance Design (SAUS)
DTD............ Data Terminal Display
DTD............ Data Transfer Device (SEWL)
DTD............ Data Transfer Done
DTD............ Data Transport Device (SAUS)
DTD............ Data Type Definition [*Computer science*] (TELE)
DTD............ Dated (AFM)
dtd............ Datur Talis Dosis [*Give Of Such A Dose*] [*Pharmacology*] (DAVI)
DTD............ Dekoratie voor Trouwe Dienst [*Decoration for Devoted Service*] [*South Africa*]
DTD............ Dentur Tales Doses [*Give in Such Doses*] [*Pharmacy*]
DTD............ Department of Tank Design [*British*] (MCD)
dtd............ Detached (SAUS)
DTD............ Detailed Test Description (MCD)
DTD............ Detailed Troop Decontamination [*Military*] (INF)
DTD............ Detroit Edison 8.50% 'QUIDS' [*NYSE symbol*] (TTSB)
DTD............ Detroit Edison Co. [*NYSE symbol*] (SAG)
DTD............ Dial Tone Delay (SAUS)
DTD............ Diastrophic Dysplasia [*Medicine*]
DTD............ Difficult to Deliver [*US Postal Service*]
DTD............ Digital Television Display (ELAL)
DTD............ Digital Terrain Data [*Army*]
DTD............ Digital Topographic Data (MCD)
DTD............ Dimethyl Tin Difluoride (SAUS)
DTD............ Diploma in Tuberculous Diseases [*British*]
DTD............ Directorate of Technical Development (MCD)
DTD............ Directorate of Training Developments [*Army*]
DTD............ Director of Trade Divisional (SAUO)
DTD............ Direct-to-Disc [*Recording system*] (WDAA)
dtd............ direct to disc (SAUS)
DTD............ Disk to Disk [*Computer science*] (VLIE)
DTD............ Dismounted Training Day [*Military*] (INF)
DTD............ Doctor of Textile Dyeing
DTD............ Document Type Definition [*Computer science*] (PCM)
DTD............ Droplet Technology Demonstration (SAUS)
DTD............ Dual-Threshold Deployment [*Automotive safety systems*]
DTD............ Dual Trace Display
DTD............ Washington, DC [*Location identifier*] [*FAA*] (FAAL)
DTD............ Director of Technical Development (ODA)
DTDC.......... Desolventizer-Toaster-Dryer-Cooler [*Oil technology*]
DT Des........ Doctor of Textile Design
DTDGA........ Dithiodiglycolic Acid (SAUS)
DTDM.......... Deterministic Time Division Multiplexing [*FAA*] (TAG)
DTDM.......... Dithio Dimorpholine (SAUS)
DTDMA........ Distributed Time Division Multiple Access [*System*] [*DoD*]
DTDMAC...... Ditallowdimethylammonium Chloride (SAUS)
dTDP........... Deoxyribosylthymine Diphosphate [*Biochemistry*]
DTDP.......... Deoxythymidine Diphosphate [*Biochemistry*]
DTDP.......... Diisotridecyl Phthalate
DTDP.......... Ditridecyl Phthalate [*Organic chemistry*]
DTDR.......... Draft Training Device Requirement (MCD)
DTDRS........ Direct-to-Disc Recording System (SAUS)
DTDS.......... Digital Television Display System
DTDS.......... Disaster Tolerant Disk System (SAUS)
DTDSP........ Directorate of Technical Data and Standardization Policy (SAUO)
DTDT.......... David Taylor Dance Theatre
DT/DT......... Drop Tube/Drop Tower [*Facility*]
DTDU.......... Dichloro-bis(trifluoromethyl)diphenylurea [*Insectproofing agent for wool*]
DT/DV......... Deposit Ticket/Debit Voucher [*Computer science*]
DTE............ Data Ten to Eleven (PDAA)
DTE............ Data Terminal Emulator (SAUS)
DTE............ Data Terminal Equipment [*Computer science*]
DTE............ Data Terminating Equipment (SAUS)
DTE............ Datatracker International [*Vancouver Stock Exchange symbol*]
DTE............ Data Transfer Equipment (SAUS)
DTE............ Data Transmission Equipment [*Computer science*] (UWER)
DTE............ Data Transmission Exchange (SAUS)
DTE............ Datentransfereinrichtung (SAUS)
DTE............ Dayton, TN [*Location identifier*] [*FAA*] (FAAL)
DTE............ Deaminotyrosyl-Tyrosine Ethyl Ester (UWER)
dte............ Dedicatee [*MARC relator code*] [*Library of Congress*] (LCCP)
DTE............ Deep Texture Editor (VLIE)
DTE............ Defence Technology Enterprises Ltd. [*British*] (IRUK)
DTE............ Dental Training Establishment (SAUO)
DTE............ Departed Transshipment Export (SAUS)
DTE............ Depot Tooling Equipment
DTE............ Destructive Testing Equipment (SAUS)
DTE............ Detroit Edison Co. [*NYSE symbol*] (SPSG)
dte............ development (SAUS)
DTE............ Development, Test, and Evaluation (ACAE)
DTE............ Development Test Equipment (SAUS)
DTE............ Diagnostic Test Equipment (WDAA)
DTE............ Dial Telephone Exchange (DNAB)
DTE............ Diamond Tool Engineering Co.
DTE............ Dibromotetrafluoroethane
DTE............ Differential Thermal Expansion (SAUS)
DTE............ Digital Target Extractor (SAUS)
DTE............ Digital Television Encoder
DTE............ Digital Television Equipment (KSC)
DTE............ Digital Test Executive (SAUS)
DTE............ Digital Transmission Equipment (IAA)
DTE............ Digital Tune Enable (IAA)
DTE............ Diplomacy Test of Empathy [*Psychology*]
dte............ diploma test of empathy (SAUS)
DTE............ Display Tester Element (VLIE)
DTE............ Distance to Empty [*Automotive driver information display*]
DTE............ Dithioerythritol [*Organic chemistry*]
DTE............ Doctor of Textile Engineering
DTE............ Domain and Type Enforcement (SAUS)
DTE............ Dresser Transportation Equipment Division [*Federal Railroad Administration identification code*]
DTE............ Drop Tube Facility (SAUS)
DTE............ DTE Energy [*NYSE symbol*] [*Formerly, Detroit Edison*] (SG)
DTE............ Dual Track Etcher
DTE............ Dumb Terminal Emulator [*Computer science*] (VLIE)
DTE............ Dynamic Tear Energy (PDAA)
DTE............ Tamas Darida Enterprise [*Hungary*] [*ICAO designator*] (FAAC)
DTEA.......... Data Telemetry Exploitation Aid (MCD)
DTEA.......... Developmental Training Effectiveness Analysis [*Military*]
DTeaching... Diploma in Teaching
DTEAS........ Detection Track Evaluation and Assignment Systems [*Navy*] (NG)
DTE-C......... A Character Mode DTE [*Communications term*] (DCT)

D-TEC .... Durable-Technic [*Automobile engines*]
D Tech .... Doctor of Technology
D Tech Chem... Doctor of Technical Chemistry (EY)
DTechnol ..... Doctor of Technology
DTED .... Department of Trade and Economic Development (SAUO)
DTED .... Digital Terrain Elevation Data [*Military*]
DTED .... Digital Terrain Elevation Data Information System (SAUS)
DTE/DCE ...... Data Terminal Equipment/Data Communications Equipment (SAUS)
DTEE .... Division of Technology and Environmental Education [*Office of Education*]
DTEFLA .... Diploma in the Teaching of English as a Foreign Language to Adults
DTEK .... Display Technologies [*Formerly, La-Man Corp.*] [*NASDAQ symbol*]
DTEM .... Deep Transient Electromagnetic System (SAUS)
DT Eng .... Doctor of Textile Engineering
DTENT .... Date of Entry (SAUS)
DTEO .... Defence Test and Evaluation Organisation (SAUO)
DTE-P .... A Packet Mode DTE [*Communications term*] (DCT)
DTEP .... Democratic Tradition Education Project [*Australia*]
DTEP .... Desktop Electronic Publishing
DTEP .... Digital Transmission Evaluation Project (SAUO)
DTEPrF .... Detroit Edison 7.74% Dep Pfd [*NYSE symbol*] (TTSB)
DTEPrI .... Detroit Edison 7.75% Dep Pfd [*NYSE symbol*] (TTSB)
DTER .... Dither
DTEV .... Deutsche Telecom eV [*Germany*] [*Telecommunications*]
DTF .... Daily Transaction File
DTF .... Dairy Trade Federation [*British*] (ECON)
DTF .... Data Test Facility (SAUS)
DTF .... Data to Follow (SAUS)
DTF .... Data Transfer Facility [*Computer science*] (CIST)
DTF .... Data Transmission Factor
DTF .... Data Transmission Feature
DTF .... Data Transmission Function
DTF .... Data Transmittal Form (MCD)
DTF .... Date to Follow [*Telecommunications*] (TEL)
DTF .... Debre-De Toni-Fanconi [*Syndrome*] [*Medicine*] (DB)
DTF .... Dedicated Terminal Facility [*Telecommunications*] (TSSD)
DTf .... Deep Tank Forward [*Shipping*] (DS)
DTF .... Default-the-File (SAUS)
DTF .... Define the File [*Computer science*] (BUR)
DTF .... Definite Tape File [*Computer science*] (OA)
DTF .... Definite Type File [*Computer science*] (VLIE)
DTF .... Dental Traders Federation (SAUS)
DTF .... Dental Treatment Facility
DTF .... Department of Treasury and Finance [*Australia*]
DTF .... Desk Top Facsimile (SAUS)
DTF .... Detector Transfer Function (MAE)
DTF .... Deterministic Transfer Function (SAUS)
DTF .... Detritiation Factor
DTF .... Development Test Facility (SSD)
DTF .... Development Test Flight (SAUS)
DTF .... Diagnostic Turbulent Flux [*Marine science*] (OSRA)
DTF .... Dial Tone First [*Telecommunications*] (TEL)
DTF .... Diamond Thin-Film [*Coating technology*]
DTF .... Dicyanomethylenetrinitrofluorene [*Organic chemistry*]
DTF .... Digital Tape Format (SAUS)
dtf .... dilutent-free formulation (SAUS)
DTF .... Direct to Film [*Printing technology*]
DTF .... Direct Transfer Filter (SAUS)
DTF .... Disabilities Task Force [*Australia*]
DTF .... Distance to Fault (SEWL)
DTF .... Distributed Test Facility (VLIE)
DTF .... Diving Test Facility (SAUS)
DTF .... Division of Training and Facilities [*Office of Education*]
DTF .... Document Transmission Facility [*Computer science*] (VLIE)
DTF .... Domestic Textiles Federation [*British*] (BI)
DTF .... Domestic Traffic Federation (SAUO)
DTF .... Dow Chemical Co., Texas Division, Freeport, TX [*OCLC symbol*] (OCLC)
DtF .... Down The Front (SAUS)
DTF .... Dried Tree Fruit
DTF .... Drone Target Facility [*Military*]
DTF .... Drone Test Facility [*Military*]
DTF .... Drop Tower Facility (SAUS)
DTF .... Dry Tortugas Island, FL [*Location identifier*] [*FAA*] (FAAL)
DTF .... Duff/Phelps Utilities Tax-Free Income [*NYSE symbol*] (SPSG)
DTF .... Dynamic Test Fixture [*Military*] (MCD)
DTF .... Dynamic Track Follower (SAUS)
DTF .... Dynamic Track Following [*Electronics*]
DTF .... Dynamic Tracking Filter (SAUS)
DTFA .... Digital Transfer Function Analyzer (IAA)
dtfc .... differential temperature-flow controller (SAUS)
DTFCD .... Define the File for a Card Device (SAUS)
DTFCD .... Define The File for Card Device (SAUS)
DTFCN .... Define the File for Console (SAUS)
DTFD .... Diagnostic Test Flow Diagram (MCD)
DTFDA .... Define the File for Direct Access (SAUS)
DTFDI .... Define the File Device Independent (SAUS)
DTFDI .... Define the File for Device Independence (SAUS)
DTFDI .... Define The File for Device Independent (SAUS)
DTFDR .... Define the File Data Recorder (SAUS)
DTFDW .... Deciduous Tree Fruit Disease Workers [*An association*] (EA)
DTFIS .... Define the File for Indexed Sequential (SAUS)
DTFMR .... Define the File for Magnetic Reader (SAUS)
DTFMT .... Define the File for Magnetic Tape (SAUS)
DTFOR .... Define the File for Optical Reader (SAUS)
DTFPH .... Define the File for Physical input-output multiplexer (SAUS)
DTFPR .... Define the File for Printer (SAUS)
DTFPT .... Define the File for Paper Tape (SAUS)
DTFSR .... Define the File for Serial Device File (SAUS)
DTFT .... depletion-mode thin-film transistor (SAUS)
DTFT .... Discrete Time Fourier Transform (SAUS)
DTFT .... Discrete-Time Fourier Transform (VLIE)
DTG .... Data Time Group (SAUS)
DTG .... Data Transmission Generator (MCD)
DTG .... Defence Technology Group (SAUO)
DTG .... Dental Technician (General) [*U.S. Navy enlisted rating*] (AUER)
DTG .... Derivative Thermogravimetry
DTG .... Development Training Group
DTG .... Differential ThermoGravimetry (DICI)
DTG .... Diffuse Toxic Goiter [*Medicine*] (MELL)
DTG .... Digital Tape Generation (SAUS)
DTG .... Digital Transmission Group (SAUS)
DTG .... Direct Trunk Group (SAUO)
DTG .... Display Transmission Generator
DTG .... Distance to Go (SAUS)
DTG .... Dollar Thrifty Auto Grp [*NYSE symbol*] (SG)
DTG .... Dry Tuned Gyro (ACAE)
DTG .... Dual Track Geneva
DTG .... Dwight, IL [*Location identifier*] [*FAA*] (FAAL)
DTG .... Dynamically Tuned Gyro [*Inertial sensor*] (IEEE)
DTG .... Dynamically Tuned Gyroscope (SAUS)
D-TGA .... Dextrotransposition of the Great Arteries [*Cardiology*] (DAVI)
DTGA .... Differential Thermogravimetric Analysis (SAUS)
d-TGA .... D-transposition of the great arteries (SAUS)
DTGS .... Deuterated Triglycine Sulfate [*Organic chemistry*]
DTGW .... Director of Guided Weapons Trials [*British military*] (DMA)
DTH .... Dance Theater Harlem (SAUO)
DTH .... Dance Theater of Harlem
DTH .... Death Valley [*California*] [*Airport symbol*] (OAG)
DTH .... Delayed-Type Hypersensitivity [*Immunology*]
DTH .... Detroit Edison 7.375% 'QUIDS' [*NYSE symbol*] (SG)
DTH .... Dimensional testing head (SAUS)
DTH .... Diploma in Tropical Health
DTH .... Diploma in Tropical Hygiene [*British*]
DTH .... Direct to Home [*Satellite broadcast mode*] [*Canada*]
DTh .... Doctor of Theology [*Canada*] (ASC)
D Th .... Doctor of Theology
DTh .... Double Throat (SAUS)
DTH .... Down-The-Hill radios (SAUS)
DTH .... Technical University of Denmark (SAUO)
D Theol .... Diploma in Theology [*British*]
D Theol .... Doctor of Theology
DTheolC .... Sulpician Seminary Theological College, Washington, DC [*Library symbol*] [*Library of Congress*] (LCLS)
DTHK .... Digital Think, Inc. [*NASDAQ symbol*] (SG)
DThom .... Divus Thomas [*Piacenza*] (BJA)
DThomP .... Divus Thomas [*Piacenza*] (BJA)
D ThPT .... Diploma in Theory and Practice of Teaching (SAUS)
DThPT .... Diploma in Theory and Practice of Teaching (Durham University) [*British*]
DTHS .... Director of Treatment and Hospital Services (SAUO)
DTHy .... Sandoz [*Italy*] [*Research code symbol*]
DTI .... Data Phase Systems (SAUS)
DTI .... Data-Tech Institute [*Clifton, NJ*] (TSSD)
DTI .... Data Transfer Interface (SAUS)
DTI .... Defense Technical Information Center, Alexandria, VA [*OCLC symbol*] (OCLC)
DTI .... Departed Transshipment Import (SAUS)
DTI .... Department of the Treasury, Internal Revenue Service, Washington, DC [*Library symbol*] [*Library of Congress*] (LCLS)
DTI .... Department of Trade and Industry [*British*]
DTI .... Deposit-Taking Institution (ADA)
DTI .... Design Technical Information [*or Instruction*] (KSC)
DTI .... Detroit, Toledo & Ironton Railroad Co. [*AAR code*]
DTI .... Development Test Instrumentation (NASA)
DTI .... Development through Industry
DTI .... De.V.ry Technical Institute (SAUO)
DTI .... Dial Test Indicator
DTI .... Digital Technology Inc. (SAUS)
DTI .... Digital Test Indicator (IAA)
DTI .... Director of Tactical Investigation [*Military*] [*British*]
DTI .... Director Train Indicator
DTI .... Direct Trader Input [*Customs term*] (DCTA)
DTI .... Display Technologies, Inc. (PCM)
DTI .... Display Terminal Interchange
DTI .... Dissolved Transport Index [*Geochemistry*]
DTI .... Distortion Transmission Impairment [*Telecommunications*] (TEL)
DTI .... Division of Technical Information [*AEC*]
DTI .... Domestic Technology Institute (EA)
DTI .... Doppler Time Intensity (SEWL)
DTI .... Double Thickness of Insulation (SAUS)
DTI .... Drug and Therapeutic Information [*Later, Medical Letter*] (EA)
DTI .... Durham Technical Institute [*Durham, NC*]
DTIA .... Dive Travel Industry Association (TRID)
DTIB .... Decision Table Information Bulletin (HGAA)
DTIB .... Defense Technology and Industrial Base
DTIC .... Deconvoluted Total Ion Current [*Spectrometry*]
DTIC .... Defense Technical Information Center [*Formerly, DDC*] [*Alexandria, VA*] [*DoD*] [*Information service or system*]

DTIC .... (Dimethyltriazenyl)imidazolecarboxamide [*Dacarbazine*] [*Also, DIC*] [*Antineoplastic drug*]
DTIC-ACT-D ... DTIC [*Dacarbazine*], Actinomycin D [*Dactinomycin*] [*Antineoplastic drug regimen*]
DTICC .... Defense Technological and Industrial Cooperation Committee (SAUS)
DTICC .... Korea Defense Technological and Industrial Cooperation Committee (SAUO)
DTICH .... Delayed Traumatic Intracerebral Hematoma [*Medicine*] (MELL)
DTID .... Defense Turn-In Document (SAUO)
DTID .... Disposal Turn-In Document [*Military*]
DTIDC .... Division of Technical Information and Document Control (SAUS)
DTIE .... Division of Technical Information Extension [*Later, Technical Information Center*] [*AEC*]
DTIF .... Digital Table Interchange Format (GART)
DTIF .... Digital Transmission Interface Frame (SAUS)
DTII .... D T Industries [*NASDAQ symbol*] (TTSB)
DTII .... DT Industries, Inc. [*NASDAQ symbol*] (SAG)
d-time .... dream time (SAUS)
DT Inds .... DT Industries, Inc. [*Associated Press*] (SAG)
DTIP .... Detoxification Inpatient [*Medicine*] (DHP)
DTIP .... Digital Tune in Progress (IAA)
DTIR .... Defense Technical Intelligence Report (MCD)
DTIS .... Defense Technical Information Service (SAUO)
DTIS .... Defense Technical Integration Services (SAUS)
DtIs .... Deutero-Isaiah (BJA)
DTIS .... Drill Time in Service [*Military*] (DNAB)
DTIW .... Defense Technical Information Web [*Military*]
DTIZ .... Determan Industries [*Federal Railroad Administration identification code*]
DTK .... Datatech Systems Ltd. [*Toronto Stock Exchange symbol*]
DTK .... Dietrich, AK [*Location identifier*] [*FAA*] (FAAL)
DTKR .... Developmental Tasks for Kindergarten Readiness [*Child development test*]
DTL .... Dal-Tile Intl. [*NYSE symbol*] (SG)
DTL .... Data Training Ltd. [*British*] (NITA)
DTL .... Data Transistor Logic (SAUS)
DTL .... Datel Industries Ltd. [*Toronto Stock Exchange symbol*] [*Vancouver Stock Exchange symbol*]
DTL .... Dead Time Log
DTL .... Deep Trench Latrine [*British military*] (DMA)
DTL .... Definite Time Limit (SAUS)
DTL .... Degree of Total Leverage [*Finance*]
DTL .... Delta Teen-Lift (EA)
DTI .... Department of Trade and Industry (SAUS)
DTL .... Depolarization Transmission Loss (SAUS)
DTL .... Designated Transit List (MLOA)
DTL .... Desk Top Library (SAUS)
DTL .... Detail (AABC)
DTL .... Detailed Time Line (SPST)
DTL .... Detroit Lakes [*Minnesota*] [*Airport symbol*] [*Obsolete*] (OAG)
DTL .... Detroit Testing Laboratory (SAUS)
DTL .... Dialog Tag Language (SAUS)
DTL .... Dictogrraph Telephone Limited (SAUO)
DTL .... Diode Transfer Logic (SAUS)
DTL .... Diode-Transistor Logic
dtl .... diode transistor logic (SAUS)
DTL .... Direct to Licensee
DTL .... Direct-to-Line (SAUS)
DTL .... Disburse To Location (SAUS)
DTL .... Double Transistor Logic (SAUS)
DTL .... Down the Line (SAUS)
DTL .... Duct Transmission Loss [*Facility*] (MCD)
DTL .... United States Department of the Treasury, Washington, DC [*OCLC symbol*] (OCLC)
DTL .... Drift-Tube Linac (ODA)
DTLA .... Detroit Tests of Learning Aptitude [*Education*]
DTLA .... Dynamic Transmit Level Adjustment (SAUS)
DTLA-2 .... Detroit Tests of Learning Aptitude-2 [*Hammill*] (TES)
DTLA-P .... Detroit Tests of Learning Aptitude-Primary [*Hammill and Bryant*] (TES)
DTLB .... Dual Translation Lookaside Buffer [*Computer science*] (VERA)
DTLC .... Two-Dimensional Thin Layer Chromatography (UWER)
DTLCC .... Design to Life-Cycle Cost
Dtl-Dtl .... Detail to Detail (SAUS)
Dtl-Hdg .... Detail to Heading (SAUS)
DTL IE .... Designated Transit List Information Ethernet (MLOA)
DTLN .... Data Transmission Network Corp. [*NASDAQ symbol*] (NQ)
DTLN .... Data Transmission Ntwk [*NASDAQ symbol*] (TTSB)
DT Logic .... Diode-Transistor Logic (SAUS)
DTLOM .... Doctrine, Training, Leader Development, Organization, and Materiel [*Army*] (INF)
DTLOMS .... Doctrine, Training, Leader Development, Organization, Materiel and Soldier (SAUS)
DTLOMS .... Doctrine, Training, Leader Development, Organization, Materiel, and the Soldier [*Army education program*] (INF)
DTLOMS .... Doctrine, Training, Leadership, Operations, Materiel and Soldiers (SAUS)
DTLOMS-P ... Doctrine, Training, Leader Development, Organization, Materiel and Soldiers-Policy [*Army*]
DTLS .... Descriptive Tests of Language Skills (EDAC)
DTLS .... Descriptive Top Level Specification (ACAE)
DTLS .... Digital Television Lightware System (SAUS)
DTLS .... Digital Television Lightwave System (SAUS)
DTLS-A .... Diagnostic Test of Library Skills-Advanced Edition (TMMY)
DTL/TTL .... Diode-Transistor Logic/Transistor-Transistor Logic (SAUS)
DTL/TyL .... Diode Transistor Logic/Transistor Transistor Logic (SAUS)
DTLU .... Digital Terminal Line Unit [*Telecommunications*] (ACRL)
DTLU .... Digital Trunk and Line Unit [*Communications term*] (DCT)
DTLZ .... Diode-Transistor Logic with Zener Diode [*Electronics*] (IAA)
DTLZD .... Diode Transistor Logic with Zener Diodes (SAUS)
DTM .... Carnegie Institution of Washington [*District of Columbia*] [*Seismograph station code, US Geological Survey*] [*Closed*] (SEIS)
DTM .... Dataram Corp. [*AMEX symbol*] (SPSG)
DTM .... Data Transfer Module (ACAE)
DTM .... Data Transmission Medium (SAUS)
DTM .... Date Time Module (GART)
DTM .... Deceleration Throttle Modulator [*Automotive engineering*]
DTm .... Deep Tank Midship [*Shipping*] (DS)
DTM .... Defect Test Monitor [*Electronics*] (AAEL)
DTM .... Delay Timer Multiplier (IEEE)
DTM .... Demonstration Test Motor (MCD)
DTM .... Dermatophyte Test Medium (AAMN)
DTM .... Descriptive training manual (SAUS)
DTM .... Descriptive training material (SAUS)
dtm .... designed to meet (SAUS)
DTM .... Design Test Model
DTM .... Design to Market (SAUS)
DTM .... Desktop Manufacturing
DTM .... Deterministic Turing Machine (SAUS)
DTM .... Detroit, Toledo & Milwaukee Railroad [*Federal Railroad Administration identification code*]
DTM .... Deutsche Tourenwagen Meisterschaft [*German Touring Car Championship*]
DTM .... Developmental Telemetry (ACAE)
DTM .... Developmental Test Model
DTM .... Development Telemetry Equipment (MCD)
DTM .... Device Test Module
DTM .... Diagnostic Test Mode [*Automotive engineering*]
DTM .... Difficult to Monitor (ACII)
DTM .... Digital Talk-Out Module
DTM .... Digital Television Monitor
DTM .... digital terrain map (SAUS)
DTM .... Digital Terrain Model (MCD)
DTM .... Digital Terrain Modelling (SAUS)
DTM .... Digital Topographic Model (ACAE)
DTM .... Digital Transient Model (SAUS)
DTM .... Digital Transportation Marketplace
DTM .... Digital Troposcatter MODEM (MCD)
DTM .... Digital Trunk Module [*Telecommunications*]
DTM .... Diocesan Travelling Mission [*Roman Catholic*]
DTM .... Diploma in Tropical Medicine [*British*]
DTM .... Director of Telecommunications Management [*Abolished, 1970*] [*Air Force*]
DTM .... Director of Torpedos and Mining Department (SAUO)
DTM .... Director of Transport and Movements [*British military*] (DMA)
DTM .... Directory of Texas Manufacturers [*University of Texas at Austin*] [*Information service or system*] (CRD)
DTM .... Display Technology and Manufacturing (SAUS)
DTM .... Display Time (SAUS)
DTM .... Doctor of Tropical Medicine
DTM .... Dortmund [*Germany*] [*Airport symbol*] (OAG)
DTM .... Draft Technical Manual
Dtm .... draught moulded (SAUS)
DTM .... Drift-Type Mines (SAUO)
DTM .... Driver transfer machine (SAUS)
DTM .... Dual Thruster Module (ACAE)
DTM .... Dual Tone Multifrequency (SAUS)
DTM .... Dual Transport Module (NOAA)
DTM .... Duration Time Modulation (IAA)
DTM .... Dynamic Tensile Modulus [*Materials testing*]
DTM .... Dynamic Test Model [*Spacecraft*]
DTM .... Dynamic Transient Master control block (SAUS)
DTma .... Deep Tank Midship Aft [*Shipping*] (DS)
DTMA .... Desoxycorticosterone Trimethylacetate [*Pharmacology*] (DAVI)
DTM & H .... Diploma in Tropical Medicine and Hygiene [*British*]
DTMB .... David W. Taylor Model Basin [*Also, DATMOBAS,TMB*] [*Later, DTNSRDC, NSRDC*] [*Washington, DC*]
DTMB .... Defense Traffic Management Branch (DNAB)
DTMB .... Monastir/Habib Bourgiba [*Tunisia*] [*ICAO location identifier*] (ICLI)
DTMC .... Di(p-chlorophenyl)trichloromethylcarbinol [*Miticide*]
DTMC .... DTM Corp. [*NASDAQ symbol*] (NASQ)
DTMD .... Dento-Med Industries, Inc. [*NASDAQ symbol*] (COMM)
DTMD .... Determined (NVT)
DTMD .... Differential Temperature Measuring Device
DTME .... Design-To-Manufacture Environment (SAUS)
DTMF .... Data Tone Multiple Frequency (SAUS)
DTmf .... Deep Tank Midship Forward [*Shipping*] (DS)
DTMF .... Desktop Management Task Force (SAUS)
DTMF .... Dial Tone Multiple Frequency [*Telecommunications*] (MLOA)
dtmf .... dual-tome multifrequency (SAUS)
DTMF .... Dual Tone Modulated Frequency [*Telecommunications*]
DTMF .... Dual-Tone Modulated Multi-Frequency [*Telecommunications*] (AGLO)
DTMF .... Dual Tone Multifrequency [*Telecommunications*]
DTMF .... Dual Tone Multifrequency Signalling (NITA)
DTMH .... Diploma in Tropical Medicine and Hygiene
DTMH .... Diplomate of Tropical Medicine and Hygiene (SAUS)
DTMI .... Dairy Training and Merchandising Institute [*Later, MTI*] (EA)
DTML .... Diode-Transistor Micrologic (IAA)
dt mld .... draft moulded (SAUS)

DTMLD .... Draught Moulded [*British*] (IAA)
DTMN .... Datamation (journ.) (SAUS)
DTMO .... Design [*or Development*], Test, and Mission Operations [*NASA*]
DTMO .... Digital Test Measurement System (SAUS)
DTMO .... District Traffic Management Office (SAUO)
DTMO .... District Transport & Movements Officer (SAUO)
DTMO .... District Transportation Management Office (SAUO)
DTMOC .... District Transport & Movements Operation Centre (SAUS)
DTMP .... DCPS Management Panel (SAUS)
dTMP .... De Novo Thymidylate [*Synthesis*] [*Biochemistry*] (DAVI)
dTMP .... Deoxyribosylthymine Monophosphate [*Biochemistry*]
DTMP .... Deoxythymidine Monophosphate [*Biochemistry*]
DTMP .... Deoxythymidylic Acid (SAUS)
DTMPH .... Diploma in Tropical Medicine and Public Health
DTMPN .... Defect Test Monitor Phase Number [*Electronics*] (AAEL)
DTMR .... Defense Traffic Management Regulation (COE)
DTMR .... Defense Traffic Management Regulations (AAGC)
DTMR .... Denver Terminal Railroad [*Federal Railroad Administration identification code*]
DTMRS .... Data Transmission and Message Routing System (SAUS)
DTMS .... Data Base and Transaction Management System [*IBM Corp.*]
DTMS .... Database and Transaction Management System (SAUS)
DTMS .... Data Transmission and Multiplexing System (ACAE)
DTMS .... Dedicated Transmission Measurement System (SAUS)
DTMS .... Defense Traffic Management Service
DTMS .... Delivery and Transport Management System [*Software package*] [*British*]
DTMS .... Descriptive Test of Mathematics Skills (EDAC)
DTMS .... Desktop Marketing System [*CD-ROM*] [*Computer science*]
DTMS .... Development, Test, and Mission Support (MCD)
DTMS .... Digital Test Measurement [*or Monitor*] System
DTMS .... Disaster Transportation Management System (SAUO)
DTMS .... Document Transfer and Manipulation Services [*Computer science*] (VERA)
DTMT .... Dual-Tone Multifrequency [*Telephone*] (WDMC)
DTMV$_{max}$ ..... Diastolic Transmembrane Voltage, Maximum [*Cardiology*] (DAVI)
DTN .... [*The*] Daily Times of Nigeria [*A publication*]
DTN .... Dalmatian Resources Ltd. [*Vancouver Stock Exchange symbol*]
DTN .... Data Transfer Network (SAUS)
DTN .... Data Transmission Network (SAUO)
DTN .... Data Transporting Network
DTN .... Defence Telecommunications Network [*British military*] (DMA)
DTN .... Defence Teleprinter Network (SAUS)
DTN .... Defense Telecommunications Network (SAUS)
DTN .... Defense Telephone Network (SAUS)
DTN .... Defense Teleprinter Network (NATG)
DTN .... Detain (AABC)
DTN .... Detection (IAA)
dtn .... Detonation (SAUS)
DTN .... Digital Equipment Corp., Spit Brook, Nashua, NH [*OCLC symbol*] (OCLC)
DTN .... Digital Television Network
DTN .... Diphtheria Toxin Normal [*Medicine*]
DTN .... Diploma of Teaching (Nursing)
D Tn .... Director of Transportation (SAUO)
DTN .... Drug Trade News [*A publication*]
DTN .... DuMont Television Network [*1946-55*]
DTN .... SAR Data Transfer Network within the CDHS (SAUS)
DTN .... Shreveport, LA [*Location identifier*] [*FAA*] (FAAL)
DTNB .... Dithiobis(nitrobenzoic acid) [*Analytical biochemistry*]
DTNB .... Dithionitrobenzoic Acid [*Organic chemistry*]
DTNC .... North Carolina Department of Transportation [*Federal Railroad Administration identification code*]
dtng .... Detuning (SAUS)
DTNHEB .... Dithiobis(nitrohydroxyethylbenzamide) [*Biochemistry*]
DTNM .... Date-Time-Next Meeting (DI)
DTNS .... Digital Test Measurement System (SAUS)
DTNS .... Dragon Terminal Night Sight [*Military*] (MCD)
DTNSRDC .... David W. Taylor Naval Ship Research and Development Center [*Later, DTRC*] [*Bethesda, MD*]
DTNSRDC/ASED ... David W. Taylor Naval Ship Research and Development Center Aviation and Surface Effects Department [*Bethesda, MD*]
DTNSRDC/CID ... David W. Taylor Naval Ship Research and Development Center Central Instrumentation Department [*Bethesda, MD*]
DTNSRDC/CMLD ... David W. Taylor Naval Ship Research and Development Center Computation Mathematics/Logistics Department [*Bethesda, MD*]
DTNSRDCDET ... David W. Taylor Naval Ship Research and Development Center Detachment (DNAB)
DTNSRDC/FMD ... David W. Taylor Naval Ship Research and Development Center Financial Management Department [*Bethesda, MD*]
DTNSRDC/MAT ... David W. Taylor Naval Ship Research and Development Center Materials Department [*Annapolis, MD*]
DTNSRDC-NLHP ... David W. Taylor Naval Ship Research and Development Center Naval Laboratories History Program [*Bethesda, MD*]
DTNSRDC/PAS ... David W. Taylor Naval Ship Research and Development Center Propulsion and Auxiliary Systems Department [*Annapolis, MD*]
DTNSRDC-PASD ... David W. Taylor Naval Ship Research and Development Center Propulsion and Auxiliary Systems Department [*Annapolis, MD*]
DTNSRDC/SAD ... David W. Taylor Naval Ship Research and Development Center Ship Acoustics Department [*Bethesda, MD*]
DTNSRDC/SDD ... David W. Taylor Naval Ship Research and Development Center Systems Development Department [*Bethesda, MD*]
DTNSRDC/SHD ... David W. Taylor Naval Ship Research and Development Center Ship Hydromechanics Department [*Bethesda, MD*]
DTNSRDC/SME ... David W. Taylor Naval Ship Research and Development Center Ship Materials Engineering Department [*Annapolis, MD*]
DTNSRDC/SPD ... David W. Taylor Naval Ship Research and Development Center Ship Performance Department [*Bethesda, MD*]
DTNSRDC/SSID ... David W. Taylor Naval Ship Research and Development Center Ship Systems Integration Department [*Bethesda, MD*]
DTNTN .... Detention of Pay (DNAB)
DTO .... Daily Tasking Order (SAUS)
DTO .... Data Takeoff [*Air Force*]
DTO .... Data Terminal Operator [*Computer science*]
DTO .... Date Take-Off (SAUS)
DTO .... Dealer Tags Only [*Motor vehicle violation code used in state of Maryland*] (MVRD)
DTO .... Decentralized Toll Office [*Telecommunications*] (TEL)
dto .... Dedicator [*MARC relator code*] [*Library of Congress*] (LCCP)
DTO .... Defense Technology Objective [*Military*]
DTO .... Defense Transportation Order [*Department of Commerce*]
DTO .... Delayed Test Objective (ACAE)
DTO .... Dental Therapists of Ontario (SAUS)
DTO .... Denton, TX [*Location identifier*] [*FAA*] (FAAL)
DTO .... Deodorized Tincture of Opium [*Pharmacy*]
DTO .... Detailed Test Objective [*NASA*]
DTO .... Deuterium-Tritium Oxide (SAUS)
DTO .... Development Test Objective (ACAE)
DTO .... Digitally Tuned Oscillator (SEWL)
DTO .... Digital Testing Oscilloscope (IEEE)
DTO .... Director of Training and Operations (SAUO)
DTO .... Direct Termination Overflow [*MCI Communications Corp.*] [*Telecommunications*]
DTO .... Direct Turn-Over (NG)
DTO .... Disburse-to-Order (SAUS)
DTO .... District Training Office [*or Officer*] [*Navy*]
DTO .... District Transportation Officer
DTO .... District Transport Officer (SAUO)
DTO .... Division Transportation Office [*or Officer*]
DTO .... Dollar Tradeoff
dto .... dollar trade off (SAUS)
D-to-A .... Digital-to-Analog [*Converter*] [*Computer science*]
DTOA .... due time of arrival (SAUS)
DTOC .... Division Tactical Operations Center
DTOCSE .... Division Tactical Operations Center Support Element (SAUO)
D to D .... Dawn to Dusk (SAUS)
D-to-D .... Digital-to-Digital
D to D .... Dusk to Dawn (SAUS)
DTOD .... Director of Trade and Operations Division (ODA)
DTOE .... Draft Table of Organization and Equipment [*Military*] (INF)
DTOL .... Digital Test-Oriented Language [*Computer science*] (PDAA)
DTOM .... De Tomaso Industries, Inc. [*NASDAQ symbol*] (SAG)
DTomaso ..... De Tomaso Industries, Inc. [*Associated Press*] (SAG)
DTOP .... Daily Turn On Procedures [*Computer science*] (MCD)
DTOP .... Desktop Data, Inc. [*NASDAQ symbol*] (SAG)
DTOP .... Detoxification Outpatient [*Medicine*] (DHP)
DTOP .... Digital Topographic Data (SAUS)
DTOSC .... Design to Operations and Support Cost
DTOT .... Development Test, Operational Test (SAUS)
DT/OT .... Development Test/Operational Test
DTP .... Dairy Termination Program [*Department of Agriculture*]
DTP .... Dance Touring Program [*National Endowment for the Arts*]
DTP .... Datagram Transport Protocol (SAUS)
DTP .... Data Tape Punch (IAA)
DTP .... Data Transfer Process (SAUS)
DTP .... Data Transfer Protocol [*Telecommunications*] (OSI)
DTP .... Data Translation Project (SAUS)
DTP .... Data Transmission Process (SAUS)
DTP .... Data Type Punch (SAUS)
DTP .... Deer and Turkey Permits (SAUO)
DTP .... Defense Trade Policy [*Office of*] (DOMA)
DTP .... Delta Theta Phi [*An association*] (NTPA)
DTP .... Dental Technician (Prosthetic) [*U.S. Navy enlisted rating*] (AUER)
DTp .... Department of Transport [*British*] (DS)
DTP .... Depth Telemetering Pinger
DTP .... Design & Technical Planning (SAUS)
DTP .... Design to Price (NVT)
DTP .... Desktop Publishing [*Computer science*]
DTP .... Detailed Planning (SAUS)
DTP .... Detailed Test Plan [*or Procedure*]
DTP .... Detailed Test Procedure (SAUS)
DTP .... Developmental Therapeutics Program [*National Cancer Institute*]
DTP .... Development Test Plan (ACAE)
DTP .... Development Threat Package
DTP .... Diagnostic-Therapeutic Pair (SAUS)
DTP .... Diameter True Position (AAEL)
dtp .... Diethyldithiophosphate [*Organic chemistry*]
DTP .... Differential Twisted Pair (ACAE)
DTP .... Diode Test Program
DTP .... Diphtheria, Tetanus, Pertussis [*Also, DPT*] [*Immunology*]
DTP .... Diphtheria, Tetanus, Poliovirus [*Vaccine*] [*Medicine*]
DTP .... Directory Tape Processor
DTP .... Direct Tape Processor [*Computer science*] (ECII)
DTP .... Discrete Transient Protection (SAUS)
DTP .... Display Translator Program (MCD)
DTP .... Distal Tingling on Percussion [*Medicine*]
DTP .... Distal Tingling on Pressure [*Medicine*] (MELL)
DTP .... Distributed Transaction Processing (HGAA)
DTP .... Dithiophosphate (SAUS)

DTP .... Document Transfer Profile [*Computer science*] (VERA)
DTP .... Dolph-Tchebyscheff Pattern
DTP .... Doppler Techniques Proposal
DTP .... Double Test Position
DTP .... Driver Training Platoon [*British military*] (DMA)
DTP .... Drum Timing Pulse
DTP .... Dynamic Testing Program (AAG)
DTP .... Dynamic Test Panel
DTP .... U.S. Department of Transportation-Pueblo Test Center [*Federal Railroad Administration identification code*]
DTPA .... Diethylenetriaminepentaacetate (SAUS)
DTPA .... Diethylenetriaminepentaacetic Acid [*Also, DETP, DETPA*] [*Chelating agent*]
dtpa .... diethylenetriamine pentaacetic acid (SAUS)
DTPA .... Dynamic Transient Pool Area [*Computer science*] (ELAL)
DTPA Acid ... Diethylenetriamine Penta-Acetic Acid (SAUS)
dtpb .... divider time pulse distributor (SAUS)
DTPB .... Divider Time Pulse Distributor Board (MCD)
DTPC .... Defense Transportation Policy Council [*MTMC*] (TAG)
DTPC .... Desert Tortoise Preserve Committee (EA)
DTPD .... Divider Time Pulse Distributor (SAUS)
DTPEW .... Design-to-Price Electronic Warfare [*Military*] (CAAL)
DTPEWS ...... Design-to-Price Electronic Warfare Suite [*Navy*] (MCD)
DTPEWS ...... Design-to-Price Electronic Warfare System (SAUS)
DTPGS .... Digital Test Program Generation System (MCD)
DTPH .... Department of Tropical Public Health [*Medicine*] (EDAA)
DTPH .... Diploma in Tropical Public Health [*British*]
DTPI .... Diamond Technology Partners, Inc. [*NASDAQ symbol*] (NASQ)
DTPL .... Domain Tip Propagation Logic (MCD)
DTPM .... Distributed Transaction Processing Middleware (RALS)
DTPM .... Dynamic Transient Pool Management [*Computer science*] (ELAL)
DTPMT .... Date of Payment (SAUS)
DTPP .... Demonstration Tokamak Power Plant (SAUS)
DTPR .... Detailed Test Procedures (NASA)
DTPS .... Day-Timer Pen Scheduler
DTPS .... Dialer Token Pairs (SAUS)
DTPS .... Diffuse Thalamic Projection System (DIPS)
DTPS .... Diffusion Transfer Processing System [*Reprography*]
DTPS .... Director of Transport (SAUS)
DTPS .... Dublin Typographical Provident Society (SAUO)
DTPSAA .... Diamond Trade and Precious Stone Association of America (EA)
DTPT .... Dedicated Theater Planning Terminal [*Military*] (MCD)
DTPT .... DeltaPoint, Inc. [*NASDAQ symbol*] (SAG)
D Tpt .... Director of Transport (SAUO)
DTPT .... Transport Directorate (SAUO)
DTP vaccine ... Diptheria, Tetanus, and Pertussis [*Whooping Cough*] Vaccine [*Also, called the DPT vaccine*] (PAZ)
DTQP .... Desk-Top Quality Publishing (VLIE)
DTR .... Daily Transaction Registering [*or Reporting*] [*Computer science*]
DTR .... Danish Air Transport [*ICAO designator*] (FAAC)
DTR .... Data Tape Reader (SAUS)
DTR .... Data Tape Recorder (IAA)
DTR .... Data Tecnology Research, Inc. (EFIS)
DTR .... Data Telemetering Register
DTR .... Data Telemetry Register (SAUS)
DTR .... Data Terminal Reader
DTR .... Data Terminal Ready [*Computer science*] [*Telecommunications*]
DTR .... Data Transfer Rate
DTR .... Data Transfer Register
DTR .... Data Translator (MCD)
dtr .... Daughter (GEAB)
DTR .... Dedicated Token Ring (SAUS)
DTR .... Deep Tendon Reflex [*Physiology*]
DTR .... Defense Test Range (MCD)
DTR .... Definite-Time Relay (MSA)
DTR .... Delivery Truck Ramp (UWER)
DTR .... Demand Totalizing Relay (KSC)
DTR .... Dental Technician (Repair) [*U.S. Navy enlisted rating*] (AUER)
DTR .... Dental Treatment Room (MHCS)
DTR .... Department of Trade [*British*] (ADA)
DTR .... Desktop Replacement [*Computer science*]
DTR .... Desk Top Reproduction [*Computer science*] (VERA)
Dtr .... Deuteronomy Rabba (BJA)
DTR .... Development and Test Resource (SAUS)
DTR .... Development test report (SAUS)
DTR .... Development Trouble Report
DTR .... Diamond T Register (EA)
DTR .... Diatec Resources Ltd. [*Vancouver Stock Exchange symbol*]
DTR .... Dielectric Tape Reading (SAUS)
DTR .... Dietetic Technician Registered (NUJO)
DTR .... Diffusion Transfer [*Reprography*]
DTR .... Diffusion Transfer Reversal [*Reprography*]
DTR .... Digital Tape Recorder
DTR .... Digital Telemetering Register
DTR .... Digital Test Report (ACAE)
DTR .... Digital Trunk (SAUS)
DTR .... Diploma in Therapeutic Radiology [*British*]
DTR .... Directorate of Technical Research [*Navy*] [*Canada*]
DTR .... Discharge-Tube Recifier (SAUS)
DTR .... Disposable Tape Reel [*Computer science*]
DTR .... Distribution Tape Reel [*Computer science*]
DTR .... Diurnal Temperature Range [*Climatology*]
DTR .... Division of Tax Research
DTR .... Document Filing and Retrieval (SAUS)
d/tr .... documents against trust receipt (SAUS)
DTR .... Document Transmittal Record (NRCH)
DTR .... Double-Taxation Relief (ODBW)
DTR .... Downtime Radio (SAUS)
DTR .... Downtime Ratio [*Computer science*] [*Telecommunications*] (TEL)
DTR .... Draft Technical Report [*Telecommunications*] (OSI)
DTR .... DTE Ready (SAUS)
DTR .... Duty Type Rating (SAUS)
DTr .... Trinity College, Washington, DC [*Library symbol*] [*Library of Congress*] (LCLS)
DTRA .... Defense Technical Review Activity [*or Agency*] [*Military*] (AABC)
DTRA .... Defense Threat Reduction Agency
DTRA .... Development Test Requirements Assessment [*Military*]
DTRACS .... Defense Transportation Reporting and Control System
DTRC .... David W. Taylor Research Center [*Bethesda, MD*] [*United States Space and Naval Warfare Systems Command*] (GRD)
DTRC/CMLD... David W. Taylor Research Center Computation Mathematics/ Logistics Department [*Bethesda, MD*]
DTRC/PAS.... David W. Taylor Research Center Propulsion and Auxiliary Systems Department [*Bethesda, MD*]
DTRC/SHD ... David W. Taylor Research Center Ship Hydromechanics Department [*Bethesda, MD*]
DTRC/SME .. David W. Taylor Research Center Ship Materials Engineering Department [*Bethesda, MD*]
DTRC/SSID... David W. Taylor Research Center Ship Systems Integration Department [*Bethesda, MD*]
DTRCT .... Date of Receipt (SAUS)
DTRD .... Development Test Requirements Document [*NASA*] (NASA)
DTR/DSR ..... Data Terminal Reader/Data Storage and Retrieval (SAUS)
DTRE .... Defence (or Defense) Telecommunications Research Establishment (SAUO)
DTRE .... Defence Telecommunications Research Establishment [*British*]
DTRE .... Diploma in Therapeutic Radiology and Electrology
DTREM .... Dust, Thermal, and Radiation Engineering Measurements Package [*NASA*]
DTREM Package... Dust, Thermal, and Radiation Engineering Measurements Package (SAUS)
DTRF .... Daily Transaction Register File [*Computer science*]
DTRF .... Darlington Tritium Removal Facility (SAUS)
DTRF .... Data Transmittal and Routing Form (NRCH)
DTRG .... Dry Tuned Rate Gyro (ACAE)
DTRIX .... Delaware: Limited-Term Govt. Cl.A [*Mutual fund ticker symbol*] (SG)
DTRL .... digital trunk logic (SAUS)
DTRM .... Determine (FAAC)
DTRM .... Dual Thrust Rocket Motor
DTRO .... Director of Transport and Reconnaissance Operations (SAUO)
DTRP .... Diploma in Town and Regional Planning (ADA)
DTRR .... Danbury Terminal Railroad [*Federal Railroad Administration identification code*]
DTRS .... Data Transmission and Routing System (SAUS)
DTRS .... Development Test Requirement Specification (NRCH)
DTRS .... Distress (MSA)
DT/RSS .... Data Transmission/Recording Subsystem
DTRT .... Deteriorate
Dtrt .... Detroit (SAUS)
DTRT .... Do the Right Thing [*Also, DWIM*] [*In data processing context, translates as "Guess at the meaning of poorly worded instructions"*]
DTRTT .... Digital Temperature Recovery Time Test [*Medicine*] (EDAA)
DTRX .... Detrex Corp. [*NASDAQ symbol*] (NQ)
DTRX .... Detrex Corporation [*NASDAQ symbol*] (TTSB)
DTRY .... Dietary
DTS .... Dallas Transit System (SAUO)
DTS .... Dartmouth Training Squadron (SAUO)
DTS .... Data Tape Service (SAUS)
DTS .... Data Telecom Service (SAUO)
DTS .... Data Terminal Screen (SAUS)
DTS .... Data Terminal Set (NVT)
DTS .... Data Terminal System (IAA)
DTS .... Data Terminal Systems, Inc. (SAUO)
DTS .... Data Test Station
DTS .... Data Transfer Sequence (IAA)
DTS .... Data Transfer System [*Army*] (AABC)
DTS .... Data Transformation Services [*Computer science*] (VLIE)
DTS .... Data Transmission Service (IAA)
DTS .... Data Transmission Subsystem (CCCA)
DTS .... Data Transmission System [*Air Force*]
DTS .... Data Transport System (SAUS)
DTS .... Date-Time Stamp (AGLO)
DTS .... Defect Tracking System (VLIE)
DTS .... Defense Telephone Service [*DoD*]
DTS .... Defense Transportation System [*DoD*]
DTS .... Defensive Technology Study [*Military*] (SDI)
DTS .... Delaware Technical and Community College, Southern Campus, Georgetown, DE [*OCLC symbol*] (OCLC)
dts .... Delirium Tremens (DIPS)
DT's .... Delirium Tremens [*Also, DT*] [*Hallucinatory condition of advanced alcoholism*]
DTS .... Delta Transfer Stage (SAUS)
DTS .... Dense Tar Surface (or Surfacing) (SAUS)
DTS .... Dense Tar Surfacing
DTS .... Dense Tubular System
DTS .... Department of Technology and Society (EA)
DTS .... Desk Top Server (CDE)
DTS .... Detailed Test Specification
DTS .... Detailed Type Specification (MCD)

DTS.......... Detecting Transition Sequence (SAUS)
DTS.......... Detector Test System
DTS.......... Detector Tracker Switch
DTS.......... [*The*] Detroit & Toledo Shore Line Railroad Co. [*AAR code*]
DTS.......... Developer Technical Support (CDE)
DTS.......... Development and Test Support
DTS.......... Development Test Satellite
DTS.......... Diagnostic and Test System (SAUS)
DTS.......... Diagnostic Test Sequence (SAUS)
DTS.......... Diagnostic Test Set (IAA)
DTS.......... Dialog Terminal System (IAA)
DTS.......... Diametral Tensile Strength [*Material science*]
DTS.......... Dielectric Tape Scanning (SAUS)
DTS.......... Differential Temperature Switch (NRCH)
DTS.......... Differential Transmission Spectrum
DTS.......... Diffusion Total System (SAUS)
DTS.......... Digital Tandem Switch
DTS.......... Digital Telemetry System
DTS.......... Digital Telephone System
DTS.......... Digital Television System (MCD)
DTS.......... Digital Termination Service [*Data transmission*]
DTS.......... Digital Termination System [*Telecommunications*]
DTS.......... Digital Terrain System (SAUS)
DTS.......... Digital Test System (MCD)
DTS.......... Digital Theater Systems [*Surround-sound technology*] (PS)
DTS.......... Digital Titration System
DTS.......... Digital Tracking System [*or Subsystem*]
DTS.......... Digital Transmission Systems [*Telecommunications*] (ACRL)
DTS.......... Digital Tuning System (AAEL)
DTS.......... Diphtheria Toxin Sensitivity [*Medicine*] (EDAA)
DTS.......... Diploma in Theological Studies
D-TS.......... Diplomate, American Board of Thoracic Surgery (DHSM)
DTS.......... Diplomatic Telecommunications Service (FAAC)
DTS.......... Diplomatic Telecommunication System (SAUS)
DTS.......... Direct To SOM (SAUS)
DTS.......... Discrete Time Sample [*Medicine*] (MEDA)
DTS.......... Discrete-Time Series (SAUS)
DTS.......... Discrete-Time Signal (SAUS)
DTS.......... Discrete-Time System (SAUS)
DTS.......... Distributed Time Server [*Computer science*] (VERA)
DTS.......... Distributed Time Service [*Computer science*] (VERA)
DTS.......... District Traffic Superintendent [*British railroad term*]
DTS.......... Dix Tracking Station (SAUS)
DTS.......... Docket tracking system (SAUS)
DTS.......... Doctor of Textile Science
DTS.......... Domestic Transmission System [*ITT*] [*Telecommunications*] (TEL)
DTS.......... Domestic Transmission Systems, Inc. (SAUO)
DTS.......... Donor Specific Transfusion [*Hematology*] (DAVI)
DTS.......... Doppler Tracking Station
DTS.......... Double Thermostat and Safety [*Nuclear energy*] (OA)
DTS.......... Double Throw Switch
DTS.......... Double-Throw Switch (SAUS)
DTS.......... Dovetail Anchor Slot [*Technical drawings*]
DTS.......... DSIF [*Deep Space Instrumentation Facility*] Tracking and Monitor-Control Subsystem [*NASA*]
DTS.......... Dual Tracer Scintigraphy [*Medicine*] (ODA)
DTS.......... Dynamic Test Station (SAUS)
DTS.......... Dynamic Test System
DTS.......... Dynamic Transient Segment (VLIE)
DTS.......... Dynamic Transient Segment register save (SAUS)
DTS.......... Deep-Sleep Therapy (ODA)
DTSA.......... Defense Technology Security Administration
DTSA.......... Discrete Time Series Analysis (SAUS)
DTSC.......... DARCOM [*Development and Readiness Command, Army*] Technical Steering Committee (MCD)
DTSC.......... Data Transmission Subcommittee (SAUO)
DTSC.......... Defense Telecommunication System Center (LAIN)
DTSC.......... Denver Technical Support Center (SAUS)
DTSC.......... Department of Toxic Substances Control (DOGT)
DTSC.......... Digital Transit Switching Centre [*Computer science*] (VLIE)
DTSC.......... Drum Test Self Check (VLIE)
DTSC Routine... Drum Test Self Check Routine (SAUS)
DTSD.......... Development Test Supportability Demonstration [*Army*]
DTSD.......... Directorate of Tactics and Staff Duties (SAUO)
DTSD.......... Director of Tactical and Staff Duties Division [*British military*] (DMA)
DTSD.......... Director of Training and Staff Duties Division [*Navy*] [*British*]
DTSE&E....... Director, Test, Systems Engineering, and Evaluation (SAUS)
DTSG.......... Data Transmission Study Group [*Military*]
DTSI.......... Datron Systems [*NASDAQ symbol*] (TTSB)
DTSI.......... Datron Systems, Inc. [*NASDAQ symbol*] (NQ)
DTSM.......... Data Base and Transaction Management (SAUS)
DTSP.......... Down through Sealed Packs [*Clairvoyance experiment*]
DTSR.......... Datakit Terminal Send/Receive [*Computer science*] (VLIE)
DTSR.......... Department of Tourism, Sport, and Racing [*Queensland*] [*Australia*]
DTSR.......... Department of Tourism, Sport, and Recreation [*Tasmania*] [*Australia*]
DTSRS.......... Dynamic Transient Segment Register Save [*Computer science*] (ELAL)
DTSS.......... Dartmouth Time-Sharing System [*Computer science*]
DTSS.......... Data Transmission Simulation System (SAUS)
DTSS.......... Digital Time Synchronization Protocol (SAUS)
DTSS.......... Digital Topographic Support System [*Army*] (RDA)
DTSS.......... Digitized Terrain Support System (SAUS)
DTSS.......... Dynamic Tracking Suspension System [*Automotive engineering*]
DTS System... Disk Time-Sharing System (SAUS)
DTST.......... Defense Technology Study Team
DTST.......... Defensive Technologies Study Team (ACAE)
DTSTP.......... Derivative Truncated Sequential Test Program (ACAE)
DTS-W.......... Defense Telephone Service - Washington [*DoD*]
DTSX.......... Data Transport Station for X.25 (VLIE)
DTSX.......... Digital Transmission Systems, Inc. [*NASDAQ symbol*] (SAG)
DTSXU.......... Digital Transmission Sys Unit [*NASDAQ symbol*] (TTSB)
DTSY.......... Digital Transmission System
DTT.......... Data Transfer Timing
DTT.......... Data Transition Tracking
DTT.......... Data Transmission Technique (SAUS)
DTT.......... Data Transmission Terminal (NITA)
DTT.......... Decommissioning Technology Tracking (SAUS)
DTT.......... Defective Tracks Table (SAUS)
DTT.......... Design Thermal Transient [*Nuclear energy*] (NRCH)
DTT.......... Design Transition Temperature (NRCH)
DTT.......... Desk Top Trainer (SAUS)
DTT.......... Detent [*Mechanical engineering*]
DTT.......... Detroit [*Michigan*] [*Airport symbol*] (OAG)
DTT.......... Developmental Technician Team (MCD)
DTT.......... Diagnostic and Therapeutic Team [*Medicine*] (EDAA)
DTT.......... Dictionary of Technical Terms (SAUS)
DTT.......... Difficult to Test [*Audiology*]
DTT.......... Digital Terrestrial Television (WDAA)
dtt.......... diphtheria tetanus toxin (SAUS)
DTT.......... Diphtheria-Tetanus Toxoid [*Medicine*]
DTT.......... Director of Technical Training [*British military*] (DMA)
DTT.......... Direct Transverse Traction [*Orthopedics*] (DAVI)
DTT.......... Disk to Tape [*Computer science*] (VLIE)
DTT.......... Dithiothreitol [*Organic chemistry*]
DTT.......... Doctor of Textile Technology
DTT.......... Doctrinal and Tactical Training [*Army*] (INF)
DTT.......... Domain Tip Technology (IAA)
DTT.......... Double Twin Tube [*Fluorescent lighting*]
DTT.......... Drag Disk-Turbine Transducer [*Nuclear energy*] (NRCH)
DTT.......... Driver Training Tank (SAUS)
DTT.......... Duplicate Title Transferred [*Library science*]
DTT.......... Dynamic Test Target [*Military*] (CAAL)
DTTA.......... Tunis/Carthage [*Tunisia*] [*ICAO location identifier*] (ICLI)
DTTAC.......... Distributive Trades Technology Advisory Centre [*University of Stirling*] [*British*] (CB)
DTTB.......... Bizerte/Sidi Ahmed [*Tunisia*] [*ICAO location identifier*] (ICLI)
DTTB.......... Digital Terrestrial TV Broadcasting (SAUO)
DTTC.......... Diethylthiatricarbocyanine [*Organic chemistry*]
DTTC.......... Director of Translation and Terminology Coordination (SAUO)
DTTC.......... Tunis [*Tunisia*] [*ICAO location identifier*] (ICLI)
DTTD.......... Dedicated Test Training Detachment (MCD)
DTTD.......... Remada [*Tunisia*] [*ICAO location identifier*] (ICLI)
DTTF.......... Deviation in Time to Failure (SAUS)
DTTF.......... Digital Tape and Tape Facility (SAUS)
DTTF.......... Gafsa [*Tunisia*] [*ICAO location identifier*] (ICLI)
DTTG.......... Gabes [*Tunisia*] [*ICAO location identifier*] (ICLI)
DTTI.......... Bordj El Amri [*Tunisia*] [*ICAO location identifier*] (ICLI)
DTTJ.......... Jerba/Zarzis [*Tunisia*] [*ICAO location identifier*] (ICLI)
DTTK.......... Kairouan [*Tunisia*] [*ICAO location identifier*] (ICLI)
DTTL.......... Data Transition Tracking Loop
DTTL.......... Kelibia [*Tunisia*] [*ICAO location identifier*] (ICLI)
DT/TM.......... Delayed Time/Telemetry (KSC)
DTTN.......... Distributed Tactical Test Network (ACAE)
DTTN.......... Jendouba [*Tunisia*] [*ICAO location identifier*] (ICLI)
DTTP.......... Deoxyribonucleoside Triphosphate (SAUS)
dTTP.......... Deoxyribosylthymine Triphosphate [*Biochemistry*]
DTTP.......... Deoxythymidine Triphosphate [*Biochemistry*]
DTTP.......... Documents to the People [*Government Documents Round Table*] [*American Library Association*]
DTTR.......... El Borma [*Tunisia*] [*ICAO location identifier*] (ICLI)
DtTrns.......... Data Translation II, Inc. [*Associated Press*] (SAG)
DtTrNw.......... Data Transmission Network Corp. [*Associated Press*] (SAG)
DTTS.......... Day Television Tracking System [*Military*]
DTTS.......... Defense Transportation Tracking System (SAUS)
DTTS.......... Dynamic Track-Tensioning System [*Army*] (RDA)
DTTT.......... Dynamic Time-Temperature Transformation (SAUS)
DTTU.......... Data Transmission Terminal Unit [*Burroughs Corp.*]
DTTV.......... Digital Terrestrial Television (AAEL)
DTTV.......... Tunis [*Tunisia*] [*ICAO location identifier*] (ICLI)
DTTW.......... Doctors to the World [*An association*] (EA)
DTTX.......... Sfax/El Maou [*Tunisia*] [*ICAO location identifier*] (ICLI)
DTTY.......... Digital-to-Teletype
DTTZ.......... Tozeur/Nefta [*Tunisia*] [*ICAO location identifier*] (ICLI)
DTU.......... Data Telecommunication Unit (SAUS)
DTU.......... Data Terminal Unit [*Telecommunications*]
DTU.......... Data Terminating Unit (TEL)
DTU.......... Data Transfer Unit
DTU.......... Data Transformation Unit (SAUS)
DTU.......... Data Transmission Unit
DTU.......... Delft Technical University (SAUO)
DTU.......... Demand Transmission Unit [*Computer science*] (VERA)
DTU.......... Department for Timber Utilisation (SAUO)
DTU.......... Dial Terminal Unit (CAAL)
DTU.......... Digital Tape Unit (IEEE)
DTU.......... Digital Telemetry Unit
DTU.......... Digital Test Unit (ACAE)
DTU.......... Digital Time Unit (SAUS)
DTU.......... Digital Transmission Unit (IEEE)
DTU.......... Digital Tuning Unit (IAA)
DTU.......... Di group Terminal Unit (SAUO)

DTU .... Display Terminal Unit (CMD)
DTU .... Distance Transmitter Unit (SAUS)
DTU .... Dominican Trade Union (SAUO)
DTU .... Dorozhno-Transportnyy Upravleniye [*Road and Transportation Directorate*] [*Former USSR*] (LAIN)
DTU .... Dual Toplogical Unitarization (SAUS)
DTUC .... Data Transfer Unit Cartridge (SAUS)
DTUC .... David Thompson University Centre [*Nelson, BC*] [*Pronounced "dee-tuck"*] [*Canada*]
DTUL .... Deflection Temperature under Load [*Plastics technology*]
DTUN .... Detroit & Canada Tunnel Corp. [*NASDAQ symbol*] (NQ)
DTUN .... Detroit & Cda Tunl [*NASDAQ symbol*] (TTSB)
Dt Univ .... Detroit University (SAUO)
DTUOC .... Digital Tire Uniformity Optimizer Computer (PDAA)
DTUPC .... Design to Unit Production Cost [*Army*]
dtur .... departure (SAUS)
DTUS .... Diathermy, Traction, and Ultrasound [*Medicine*] (EDAA)
DTUTF .... Digital Tape Unit Test Facility [*NASA*]
DTUTL .... Digital Tape Unit Tape Facility (SAUS)
DTUX .... Dallas Terminal Railway & Union [*Federal Railroad Administration identification code*]
DTV .... Centre Airlines, Inc. [*ICAO designator*] (FAAC)
DTV .... Data Translation and Verification (SAUS)
DTV .... Day Television [*Sensing equipment*]
DTV .... Design Test Vehicle (ACAE)
DTV .... Desktop Video [*Telecommunications*] (PCM)
DTV .... Deutscher Taschenbuch Verlag [*Publisher*]
DTV .... Development Test Vehicle (SAUS)
DTV .... Digital Television (MSA)
DTV .... Digital to Television (NITA)
DTV .... Diploma in Tropical Veterinary Health
DTV .... Disc Thickness Variation [*Automotive brakes*]
DTV .... Disney Television [*Animated music video program*] [*Cable-television*]
DTV .... Diver Transport Vehicle (PDAA)
DTV .... Drivers Terminal Viewer (TIMI)
DTV .... Driver's Thermal Viewer [*Tank technology*] [*Army*]
DTV .... Drop Test Vehicle (IAA)
DTV .... Due to Void (MAE)
DTV .... Dynamic Test Vehicle
DT/VAC .... Diphtheria-Tetanus Vaccine [*Medicine*]
DTVC .... Desktop Video Conferencing (SAUO)
DTVC .... Desktop Videoconferencing
DTVC .... Digital Transmission and Verification Converter (KSC)
DTVE .... Digital Television Element (CCCA)
DTVECCU .... Digital Television Equipment Cluster Control Unit [*Military*]
DTVM .... Differential Thermocouple Voltmeter
DTVM .... Diploma in Tropical Veterinary Medicine [*British*]
DTVMI .... Developmental Test of Visual Motor Integration [*Medicine*] (EDAA)
DTVP .... Developmental Test of Visual Perception [*Frostig*]
DTVS .... Data Type Verification System (SAUS)
DTVS .... Distributor Thermo-Vacuum Switch [*Automotive engineering*]
DTW .... Dance Theater Workshop (EA)
DTW .... Dealer Tankwagon [*Gasoline*]
DTW .... Department of Transport and Works [*Northern Territory*] [*Australia*]
DTW .... Detroit [*Michigan*] [*Airport symbol*]
DTW .... Digital Equipment Corp., Tewkesbury, Tewkesbury, MA [*OCLC symbol*] (OCLC)
DTW .... Director, Torpedoes & Weapons (SAUS)
DTW .... Dry Tank Weight
DTW .... Dual Tandem Wheels [*Aviation*]
DTW .... Duty to Warn (MELL)
DTW .... Dynamic Time Warping
DTWA .... Dual Trailing Wire Antenna (SAUS)
DTWP .... Defense Transuranic Waste Program (SAUS)
DTWP .... Director of Tactical and Weapons Policy (SAUS)
DTWP .... Director of Tactical and Weapons Policy Division (SAUO)
DTWS .... Dial Teletypewriter Service (IAA)
DTWX .... Dial Teletypewriter Exchange
DTWX .... Dial Teletypewriter Exchange Service (SAUS)
DTWX Service ... Dial Teletypewriter Exchange Service (SAUS)
DTx .... Dallas Texans [*National Football League*] [*1960-62*] (NFLA)
DTX .... Dedicated Terminal Facility [*Telecommunications*] (TSSD)
DTX .... Deltex [*Slovakia*] [*ICAO designator*] (FAAC)
DTX .... Dendrotoxin [*Biochemistry*]
DTX .... Detoxification (AAMN)
DTX .... Discontinuous Transmission (SAUS)
DTX .... Dominion Textile [*NASDAQ symbol*] (TTSB)
DTX .... Dominion Textile, Inc. [*Toronto Stock Exchange symbol*]
D T Y .... Dirty (SAUS)
DTY .... Draw Texturized Yarn (SAUS)
Dty .... Duty (MIST)
DTYCSA .... Discount to Yield Compounded Semi-Annually [*Finance*]
DTY CY .... Duty Cycle (SAUS)
DTYD .... Development Trust for the Young Disabled [*British*] (IRUK)
DTYO .... Duty Officer [*Military*]
DTYP .... Daguerreotype (VRA)
DTZ .... Diatrizoate (MAE)
DTZ .... Division Tactical Zone [*Army*] (AABC)
DU .... Dalhousie University (SAUO)
DU .... Dayton Union Railway [*Federal Railroad Administration identification code*]
DU .... Decision Unit [*Management*] (RDA)
DU .... Decubitus Ulcer [*Dermatology*] (DAVI)
DU .... Defense Unit [*Military*]
D/U .... Delay Unit [*Telecommunications*] (TEL)
DU .... Deleted Unpostable [*IRS*]
DU .... Delivery Unit (SAUS)
DU .... Demarcation Unit (MCD)
DU .... Denatured Uranium [*Nuclear reactor technology*]
DU .... Denison University (SAUO)
DU .... Density Unknown [*Medicine*] (MAE)
DU .... Deoxyuridine [*Medicine*] (EDAA)
dU .... Deoxyuridine [*Biochemistry*] (MAE)
DU .... De Paul University (SAUO)
DU .... Depleted Uranium
DU .... Deregulation Unit (HEAS)
D/U .... Desired-to-Undesired (SAUS)
DU .... Detector Unit (SAUS)
DU .... Device Upgrade
DU .... Dextrinizing Unit (SAUS)
DU .... Diabetic Urine [*Endocrinology*] (DAVI)
DU .... Diagnosis Undetermined [*or Unknown*] [*Medicine*]
du .... Dial Unit (MAE)
DU .... Diazouracil [*Pharmacology*]
DU .... Diazyme Unit [*Of hydrolytic enzyme activity*]
DU .... [*A*] Dictionary of the Underworld [*A publication*]
DU .... Died Unmarried (WDAA)
DU .... Digital Unit
DU .... Dillard University (SAUO)
DU .... Dimensioning Unit [*Telecommunications*] (TEL)
D-U .... Diplomate, American Board of Urology (DHSM)
DU .... Diploma, Urology [*Medical degree*] (CMD)
DU .... Disk Unit (IAA)
DU .... Disk Usage (SAUS)
DU .... Disk Used (SAUS)
DU .... Display Unit (NASA)
DU .... Display, Upper
DU .... Disposal Unit (DAC)
DU .... Dissemination and Utilization (SAUS)
DU .... Distant Unit (SAUS)
DU .... Distribution Uniformity (ADWA)
DU .... Distribution Unit (KSC)
DU .... Diversity University [*On-line education*] [*Information retrieval*]
Du .... D-Load Ultimate (SAUS)
DU .... Dobson Unit [*Measure of ozone*]
DU .... Dockers' Union [*British*]
DU .... Docteur d'Universite [*Doctor of the University*] [*Canada*] (DD)
DU .... Doctor of the University
DU .... Doctor of the University of Essex [*British*] (DI)
DU .... Documentation Unit
DU .... Dog Unit [*Veterinary medicine*]
DU+ .... Dog Unit Positive [*Biochemistry*] (DAVI)
DU .... Doshisha University (SAUO)
DU .... Double Uptake [*Boilers*]
DU .... Drake University (SAUO)
DU .... Drew University (SAUO)
DU .... Drexel University (SAUO)
DU .... Driver Unit (ACAE)
du .... drug use (SAUS)
Du .... Dual (BJA)
DU .... Dual-Use
DU .... Du Bois Chemicals, Inc. (SAUO)
Du .... Ducal (SAUS)
Du .... Duchy (NTIO)
DU .... Duchy
DU .... Ducks Unlimited (EA)
DU .... Ducks Unlimited New Zealand Inc. (SAUO)
DU .... Due
Du .... Duke (WDAA)
DU .... Duke University (SAUO)
DU .... Dump (SAUS)
DU .... Dundee University (SAUO)
DU .... Dunlop [*Tire casing code*]
DU .... Duodenal Ulcer [*Medicine*]
DU .... Duplex [*Radio*] (NATG)
DU .... Duquesne University (SAUO)
DU .... Durham University (SAUO)
DU .... Duripan [*Soil biology*] (QSUL)
DU .... Duroxide Uptake [*Radiology*] (DAVI)
DU .... Dust [*ICAO*] (FAAC)
DU .... Dust in Suspension in the Air (WEAT)
Du .... Dutch (ADWA)
DU .... Dutch
DU .... Duty Cycle [*Military*]
DU .... Dwelling Unit [*Household census*]
DU .... Philips-Duphar NV [*Netherlands*] [*Research code symbol*]
DU .... Roland Air [*ICAO designator*] (AD)
D/U .... Up/Down Input (UWER)
Du .... Urea Dialysance [*Medicine*] (MAE)
DUA .... Death Under Anaesthesia
DUA .... Deer Unlimited of America (EA)
DUA .... Device Unit Address (SAUS)
DUA .... Digital Uplink Assembly
DUA .... Digitronics Users Association [*Later, IUA*] (EA)
DUA .... Directory User Agent [*Computer science*] (TNIG)
DUA .... Disaster Unemployment Assistance [*Disaster Relief Act*]
DUA .... Distance Vector Algorithms (SAUS)
DUA .... Dorsal Uterine Artery [*Medicine*] (MELL)
dua .... Duala [*MARC language code*] [*Library of Congress*] (LCCP)
DUA .... Dual Resources Ltd. [*Vancouver Stock Exchange symbol*]

DUA............ Durant, OK [*Location identifier*] [*FAA*] (FAAL)
DUAC.......... Derry Unemployed Action Committee (SAUO)
DUADS........ Duluth Air Defense Sector (SAUS)
DUAH........... Department of Urban Affairs and Housing (SAUS)
DUAL........... Distributed Update Algorithm (ACRL)
DUAL........... Dual Drilling [*NASDAQ symbol*] (TTSB)
DUAL........... Dual Drilling Co. [*NASDAQ symbol*] (SAG)
DUAL........... Dynamic Universal Assembly Language [*Computer science*]
DUALABS..... Data Use Access Laboratories Inc. (NITA)
DUA Labs..... Date Use and Access Laboratories (SAUS)
dual ADF..... dual automatic direction-finder (SAUS)
DUAL-COMM... Data Use and Access Laboratories - Communications, Inc. [*Information service or system*] (IID)
DualDrl........ Dual Drilling Co. [*Associated Press*] (SAG)
DUALEXTAC... Dual Salvo Attack Tactic [*Navy*] (NVT)
DualStar...... DualStar Technologies Corp. [*Associated Press*] (SAG)
DualStr........ DualStar Technologies Corp. [*Associated Press*] (SAG)
Duane Nat... Duane on the Law of Nations [*A publication*] (DLA)
Duane Road L... Duane's Road Laws of Pennsylvania [*A publication*] (DLA)
DUAP........... Dante University of America Press (SAUO)
DUAP........... Dual-Use Applications Program
DUART......... Dual Universal Asynchronous Receiver/Transmitter [*Motorola, Inc.*]
DUAS........... Uralic and Altaic Studies Department [*Indiana University*] [*Research center*] (RCD)
DUAT........... Direct User Access Terminal (DA)
DUAT........... Direct User Access Terminal System (PIPO)
DUAT........... Dual User Access Terminal [*Computer science*] (CIST)
DUATS......... Direct User Access Terminal System [*Aviation*] (FAAC)
DUB............. Deep Underground Basing (ACAE)
dub.............. diameter underback (SAUS)
DUB............. Distinguished Unit Badge (SAUS)
dub.............. double (SAUS)
DUB............. Dubai Airwing [*United Arab Emirates*] [*ICAO designator*] (FAAC)
dub.............. dubber (SAUS)
dub.............. dubbing (SAUS)
DUB............. Dubious (ADA)
DUB............. Dubitans [*or Dubius*] [*Doubting or Dubious*] [*Latin*]
DUB............. Dubitatur [*It Is Doubted*] [*Legal term*] (DLA)
Dub.............. Dublin (ADWA)
DUB............. Dublin [*Ireland*] [*Airport symbol*] (OAG)
DUB............. Dublin [*City and county in Ireland*]
DUB............. Dublin Rathfarnham Castle [*Ireland*] [*Seismograph station code, US Geological Survey*] [*Closed*] (SEIS)
DUB............. Dubowitz [*Score*] [*Obstetrics*] (DAVI)
DUB............. Dubuque [*Diocesan abbreviation*] [*Iowa*] (TOCD)
DUB............. Dysfunctional Uterine Bleeding [*Medicine*]
Dub.............. Trinity College of Dublin (SAUO)
DUBAL......... Dubai Aluminium Co. (SAUO)
DUBAL......... Dubai Aluminium Company (SAUS)
DUBC........... Dublin University Boat Club (SAUO)
DUBD........... Director of Unexploded Bombs Department (SAUO)
DUBD........... Director of Unexploded Bombs Disposal Department (SAUS)
DUBDD......... Director of Unexploded Bomb Disposal Department [*Navy*] [*British*]
DUBDD......... Director of Unexploded Bombs Disposal Department (SAUO)
DUBL........... Double
Dubl............ Dublin (ADWA)
DUBL........... Dublin [*City and county in Ireland*]
Dubl............ Dubliner (SAUS)
DUBLI.......... Dublin, GA [*American Association of Railroads railroad junction routing code*]
DUBLIN........ Dublin, TX [*American Association of Railroads railroad junction routing code*]
Dublin Committee... International Trade Union Committee for Peace and Disarmament (SAUO)
Dubner CBG... Character Background Generator [*Television*] (WDMC)
DUBS........... Durham University Business School
DUBU........... Dubuque, IA [*American Association of Railroads railroad junction routing code*]
DUC............. Data Utilization Center [*Navy*] (NVT)
DUC............. Data Utilization Console
DUC............. Decision Unit Coordinator [*Environmental science*] (COE)
DUC............. Defined User Command (IAA)
DUC............. Demonstration Unity Capsule (SAUS)
DUC............. Dense Upper Cloud [*ICAO*] (FAAC)
DUC............. Digital Uplink Command (MCD)
DUC............. Distinguished Unit Citation [*Military decoration*]
DUC............. Distributable Union Catalog [*Harvard University*] [*Microfiche*] (NITA)
DUC............. Division of Unemployment Compensation [*A publication*] (DLA)
DUC............. Doctor of the University of Calgary
DUC............. Document Usage Card (ACAE)
DUC............. Dragon under Cover (MCD)
DUC............. Dual-Access Utility Circuit (SAUS)
DUC............. Dual Capable (SAUS)
DUC............. Duarte [*California*] [*Seismograph station code, US Geological Survey*] (SEIS)
DUC............. Duchess
DUC............. Duff & Phelps Utilities & Corporate Bond Trust [*NYSE symbol*] (SPSG)
DUC............. Duff/Phelps Util & Cp Bd Tr [*NYSE symbol*] (TTSB)
DUC............. Duncan [*Oklahoma*] [*Airport symbol*] [*Obsolete*] (OAG)
DUC............. Durban University College (SAUO)
DUC............. University Club, Washington, DC [*Library symbol*] [*Library of Congress*] (LCLS)
DUCA........... United States Court of Appeals for the District of Columbia, Washington, DC [*Library symbol*] [*Library of Congress*] (LCLS)
DU Canada... Ducks Unlimited of Canada (FOTI)
Du Cange..... Du Cange's Glossarium [*A publication*] (DLA)
DUCC........... Deep Underground Command Center (MCD)
DUCC........... Dual Universal Serial Communicator Controller [*Signetics Corp.*] (NITA)
DUCCS......... Duke University Clinical Cardiology Study [*Cardiology study*]
DUCE........... Denied Usage Channel Evaluator [*Telecommunications*] (TEL)
DUCE........... Distinguished Unit Citation Emblem [*Military decoration*]
Duc Gl......... Ducange's Glossarium [*A publication*] (DLA)
DUCH........... Duchess (ROG)
DUCK........... Duckwall-Alco Stores [*NASDAQ symbol*] (TTSB)
DUCK........... Duckwall-Alco Stores, Inc. [*NASDAQ symbol*] (SAG)
DUCKEX....... Duck, N.C. Experiment (SAUS)
Duck Mountain... Duck Mountain Provincial Park in western Manitoba and adjacent Saskatchewan (SAUS)
Duckwall...... Duckwall-Alco Stores, Inc. [*Associated Press*] (SAG)
DUCO........... Department of Unified and Combined Operations (SAUO)
DUCO........... Duplex Controller (IAA)
DUCO........... Dupont Colors Paints (SAUO)
Ducom......... Ducommun, Inc. [*Associated Press*] (SAG)
DUCON......... Duty Connection
DUCOSY...... Duplex Control System (SAUS)
DUCR........... Duracraft Corp. [*NASDAQ symbol*] (SAG)
DUCS........... Deep Underground Communications System (AFM)
DUCS........... Defense Unit Classification System
DUCS........... Department of University Computer Systems [*University of Connecticut*] [*Research center*] (RCD)
DUCS........... Display Unit Control System (IAA)
DUCSOOP.... Drexel University Computer Simulator of Operations with an Online Program (SAUO)
DUCT........... Diverse Use of Communication Technology
duct............ Ductile (SAUS)
DUCTS......... Ductwork Services [*Focus Software Consultants*] [*Software package*] (NCC)
DUCY........... Duty Cycle (IAA)
dud.............. dependably undependable (SAUS)
DUD............. Design under Design
DUD............. Duchenne Muscular Dystrophy [*Medicine*] (DB)
Dud.............. Dudley (SAUS)
Dud.............. Dudley's Georgia Reports [*A publication*] (DLA)
DUD............. Dunedin [*New Zealand*] [*Airport symbol*] (OAG)
DUD............. Duodenal Ulcer Diet [*Medicine*] (MELL)
DUD............. duodenal ulcer disease (SAUS)
DUDAT......... Due Date
DUDC........... University of the District of Columbia, Washington, DC [*Library symbol*] [*Library of Congress*] (LCLS)
DUDFCD....... Denver Urban Drainage and Flood Control District (SAUS)
Dud (GA)..... Dudley's Georgia Reports [*A publication*] (DLA)
Dud (Geo).... Dudley's Georgia Reports [*A publication*] (DLA)
Dudl............ Dudley's Georgia Reports [*A publication*] (DLA)
Dudley (GA)... Dudley's Georgia Reports [*A publication*] (DLA)
dUDP........... Deoxyuridine Diphosphate [*Biochemistry*]
Dud R.......... Dudley's Georgia Reports [*A publication*] (DLA)
DUDST & K'S BART... Dudstone and King's Barton [*England*]
DUDT........... Duluth, Union Depot & Transfer [*Federal Railroad Administration identification code*]
DUE............. Date Use Identifier (SAUS)
DUE............. Detection of Unauthorized Equipment [*Bell Laboratories*]
due.............. distal upper extremity (SAUS)
DUE............. Distinguished Unit Emblem [*Military decoration*]
DUE............. DNA [*Deoxyribonucleic Acid*] Unwinding Element [*Genetics*]
DUE............. Drug Use Evaluation
DUE............. Dundo [*Angola*] [*Airport symbol*] (OAG)
DUEG........... Development Unit Executive Group [*Scotland*] (AIE)
DUEGG......... Dual Energy Gamma Group [*Nuclear energy*] (NRCH)
DUEL........... Data Update Edit Language [*Computer science*]
DUER........... Design Unit Engineering Report (SAUS)
DUER........... Digital UHF [*Ultra-High Frequency*] ECCM Radio [*Electronic Counter-Countermeasures*] [*Army*]
Duer............ Duer's New York Superior Court Reports [*A publication*] (DLA)
Duer Const Jur... Duer's Constitutional Jurisprudence [*A publication*] (DLA)
Duer Ins...... Duer on Insurance [*A publication*] (DLA)
Duer Mar Ins... Duer on Marine Insurance [*A publication*] (DLA)
Duer (NY)..... Duer's New York Superior Court Reports [*A publication*] (DLA)
Duer Rep..... Duer on Representation [*A publication*] (DLA)
DUET........... Distance University Education via Television [*Mount Saint Vincent University*] [*Halifax, NS*] [*Telecommunications service*] (TSSD)
DUET........... Drug Use Education Tips (DB)
DUET........... Dual Emitter Transistor [*Electronics*]
DUETS......... Duo-Mode Electric Transport System, Inc.
DUF............. Chavis, KY [*Location identifier*] [*FAA*] (FAAL)
DUF............. Database Update File (SAUS)
DUF............. Diffusion Under Field (SAUS)
DUF............. Diffusion under [*Epitaxial*] Film (IEEE)
DUF............. downward utilization factor (SAUS)
DUF............. Drug Use Forecasting (SAUS)
DUF............. Duff & Phelps Corp. [*NYSE symbol*] (SPSG)
DUF............. Phoenix Duff & Phelps [*NASDAQ symbol*] (TTSB)
DUF............. Phoenix Duff & Phelps Corp. [*NYSE symbol*] (SAG)
Duff............. Duffield (SAUS)
Duff............. Duffle (SAUS)
Duff............. Duff's Feudal Conveyancing [*Scotland*] [*A publication*] (DLA)
Duff Conv..... Duff's Feudal Conveyancing [*Scotland*] [*A publication*] (DLA)
DUFFEL........ Dutch Far East Lines (SAUS)

DUFJC .... Duffs Junction, PA [*American Association of Railroads railroad junction routing code*]
DUFL .... Dusky Flycatcher [*North American bird banding code*] (BIBA)
Du Fl .... Dutch Flemish (SAUS)
DUFLE .... Digital Universal Fault Locating Equipment (SAUS)
DUFLY .... Duty Involving Flying [*Military*]
DUFLYTECH... Duty Involving Flying as a Technical Observer [*Military*]
DUFONT .... El du Pont de Nemours & Co. (SAUO)
DUFONT .... El du Pont de Nemours & Company (SAUS)
DufPCr .... Duff & Phelps Credit Rating Co. [*Associated Press*] (SAG)
DufPhCr .... Duff & Phelps Credit Rating Co. [*Associated Press*] (SAG)
DUFPr .... Phoenix Duff/Phelphs $1.50 Cv Pfd [*NYSE symbol*] (TTSB)
DufPTF .... Duff & Phelps Utilities Tax Free Income [*Associated Press*] (SAG)
DufPUC .... Duff & Phelps Utility & Corporate Bond Trust [*Associated Press*] (SAG)
DufPUtil .... Duff & Phelps Utilities & Income, Inc. [*Associated Press*] (SAG)
Dufresne .... Dufresne's Glossary [*A publication*] (DLA)
DUG .... Datapac User Group (SAUO)
DUG .... Douglas [*Arizona*] [*Airport symbol*] (OAG)
DUG .... Dugway [*Utah*] [*Seismograph station code, US Geological Survey*] (SEIS)
Dug Mon .... Dugdale's Monasticon [*A publication*] (DLA)
Dug Sum .... Dugdale on Summons [*A publication*] (DLA)
DUH .... Data Upper Half Byte (IAA)
DUH .... Duke University Hospital (SAUO)
DUI .... Data Use Identifier (AFM)
DUI .... Distinctive Unit Insignia [*Military*] (INF)
DUI .... Diving Unlimited International Inc. (SAUO)
DUI .... Driving under the Influence (DHSM)
DUI .... Drug Use Index [*Psychology*]
DUI .... Duisburg [*Germany*] [*Airport symbol*] (AD)
DUIB .... Diureido isobutane (SAUS)
DUIB .... Document User Information Block (SAUS)
DUID .... Driving Under the Influence of Drugs (MELL)
DUIL .... Driving under the Influence of Liquor
DUINS .... Duty under Instruction
DUINS/TEMDUINS STU... Duty under Instruction or Temporary Duty under Instruction as a Student [*Military*] (DNAB)
DUJ .... Digital Urology Journal (SAUS)
DUJ .... Du Bois [*Pennsylvania*] [*Airport symbol*] (OAG)
DUJ .... E. I. Du Pont de Nemours & Co., Jackson Laboratory, Wilmington, DE [*OCLC symbol*] (OCLC)
DUJ .... Juris Utriusque Doctor [*Doctor of Both Laws; i.e., Canon and Civil Law*]
DUK .... Dead Upon Keyboard (SAUS)
DUK .... Duke Energy [*NYSE symbol*] [*Formerly, Duke Power*] (SG)
DUK .... Duke, Nat, New York NY [*STAC*]
DUK .... Duke Power [*NYSE symbol*] (TTSB)
DUK .... Duke Power Co. [*NYSE symbol*] (SPSG)
Duke .... Duke Power Co. [*Associated Press*] (SAG)
Duke .... Duke's Law of Charitable Uses [*A publication*] (DLA)
Duke BAJ .... Duke Bar Association. Journal [*A publication*] (DLA)
Duke BA Jo... Duke University Bar Association. Journal [*A publication*] (DLA)
Duke B Ass'n J... Duke Bar Association. Journal [*A publication*] (DLA)
Duke Ch Us... Duke on Charitable Uses [*1676*] [*A publication*] (DLA)
Duke Math J... Duke Mathematical Journal (SAUS)
DukeP .... Duke Power Co. [*Associated Press*] (SAG)
DukeR .... Duke Realty Investments Capital Shares [*Associated Press*] (SAG)
DukeRlty .... Duke Realty Investments Capital Shares [*Associated Press*] (SAG)
Duke U .... Duke University (GAGS)
DUKPrA .... Duke Pwr 6.375%'A'Pfd [*NYSE symbol*] (TTSB)
DUKPrS .... Duke Pwr 7.72%'A'Pfd [*NYSE symbol*] (TTSB)
DUKW .... Amphibious Truck, 2 1/2-ton Cargo
DUKWS .... Detroit United Kaiser Works (SAUO)
DUL .... Data Unit Length (SAUS)
DUL .... Design Ultimate Load (SAUS)
DUL .... Devon Union List (SAUO)
DUL .... Diffuse Undifferentiated Lymphoma [*Oncology*]
DUL .... Duke University Library (SAUO)
DUL .... Duluth [*Minnesota*] [*Seismograph station code, US Geological Survey*] [*Closed*] (SEIS)
DUL .... Duluth, MN [*American Association of Railroads railroad junction routing code*]
DUL .... Durham University Library (SAUO)
DULC .... Democratic Unionist Loyalist Coalition (SAUO)
DULC .... Dulcis [*Sweet*] [*Pharmacy*]
Dulck .... Dulcken's Eastern District Reports [*Cape Colony, South Africa*] [*A publication*] (DLA)
DULN .... Duke University Library Notes (journ.) (SAUS)
DULZ .... Dupont Lead [*Federal Railroad Administration identification code*]
DUM .... Deep Underwater Missile (SAUS)
DUM .... Died Unmarried [*Genealogy*]
DUM .... Disc User Multi-Access Unit (NITA)
DUM .... Dorsal Unpaired Median (PDAA)
DUM .... Dublin University Mission
DUM .... Dumb UTP Mini-hub (SAUS)
DUM .... Dumb UTP Multiport repeater (SAUS)
DUM .... Dummy (MSA)
DUM .... Dumont D'Urville [*France*] [*Geomagnetic observatory code*]
dum .... Dutch, Middle [*MARC language code*] [*Library of Congress*] (LCCP)
DUMA .... Dubai Marine Areas (BJA)
DUMAND .... Deep Underwater Muon and Neutrino Detection [*Astrophysics*]
DUMAND .... Deep Underwater Muon and Neutrino Detection (or Detector) (SAUS)
DUMB .... Deep Underground Missile Basing
DUMB .... Defensive Umbrella (SAUS)
Dumb .... Dumbarton (SAUS)
DUMBER .... Dull, Unrealistic, Mediocre, Boring, Evaporating, Rote (see SMARTER) [*Training term*] (LPT)
DUMBO .... Down Under the Manhattan Bridge Overpass [*New York*]
DUMBO .... Duke University Medical Board (SAUO)
DUMC .... Duke University Medical Center (SAUO)
DUMC .... Dutch Union Map Catalogue (TELE)
DUMD .... Deep Underwater Measuring Device
DUMETI .... Dorsal Unpaired Median Extensor-Tibiae (PDAA)
Dumf .... Dumfries (SAUS)
DUMF .... Dumfriesshire [*County in Scotland*]
Dumf & Gall... Dumfries and Galloway (SAUS)
Dumf Gal .... Dumfries and Galloway [*Region of Southern Scotland, established in 1975*] (WGA)
DUML .... Diabetic Ulcer Meal [*Airline notation*]
dUMP .... Deoxyuridine Monophosphate [*Biochemistry*]
dUMP .... Deoxyuridylate [*Biochemistry*] (DAVI)
DUMPGEN ... Dump Generation (SAUS)
DUMPS .... Deficiency of UMP synthase (SAUS)
DUMR .... Display Unit Mounting Rack (ACAE)
DUMR .... Dust and Moisture
DUMS .... Deep Unmanned Submersibles
DUMU .... Disk User Multi-Access Unit (SAUS)
DUM Unit .... Disk User Multi-access Unit (SAUS)
DUMV .... Dulcamara Mottle Virus [*Plant pathology*]
DUN .... Data Users' Note [*NASA*] (MCD)
DUN .... Death of Ur-Nammu (BJA)
DUN .... Depth Under Notch (PDAA)
DUN .... Dial-Up Networking [*Computer science*]
DUN .... Dispatch Unit Number (SAUS)
DUN .... Douglas United Nuclear, Inc. (KSC)
DUN .... Down unloaded normal (SAUS)
Dun .... Dunbar (SAUS)
Dun .... Duncan (SAUS)
Dun .... Dundalk (SAUS)
Dun .... Dundas (SAUS)
Dun .... Dundee (SAUS)
DUN .... Dundo [*Angola*] [*Seismograph station code, US Geological Survey*] (SEIS)
Dun .... Dundrennan (SAUS)
DUN .... Dunedin [*New Zealand*] (ROG)
Dun .... Dunellen (SAUS)
Dun .... Dunelm (SAUS)
Dun .... Dunfermline (SAUS)
DUN .... Dunford BAE [*British*] [*ICAO designator*] (FAAC)
Dun .... Dungarvan (SAUS)
Dun .... Dungeness (SAUS)
Dun .... Dunglas (SAUS)
Dun .... Dunglison (SAUS)
Dun .... Dun Laoghaire (SAUS)
Dun .... Dunlap (SAUS)
Dun .... Dunlop (SAUS)
Dun .... Dunmore (SAUS)
Dun .... Dunn (SAUS)
Dun .... Dunnachie (SAUS)
DUN .... Dunnage
Dun .... Dunning (SAUS)
Dun .... Dunnsville (SAUS)
Dun .... Dunoon (SAUS)
Dun .... Dunscore (SAUS)
DUN .... Dunsfold BAE [*British*] [*FAA designator*] (FAAC)
Dun .... Dunsmuir (SAUS)
Dun .... Dunstable (SAUS)
Dun .... Dunstan (SAUS)
Dun .... Dunvegan (SAUS)
Dun .... Dunwood (SAUS)
Dun .... Dunwoody (SAUS)
Dun & Cum... Dunphy and Cummins' Remarkable Trials [*A publication*] (DLA)
Dunb .... Dunbarton (SAUS)
DUNB .... Dunbartonshire [*County in Scotland*]
DUNBL .... Dunblane (ROG)
DunBrd .... Dun & Bradstreet [*Associated Press*] (SAG)
DUNC .... Deep Underwater Nuclear Counting
Dunc .... Duncan (SAUS)
DUNC Device... Deep Underwater Nuclear Counting Device (SAUS)
DUNCE .... Dial Up Network Connection Enhancement (SAUS)
Dunc Eccl L... Duncan's Scotch Parochial Ecclesiastical Law [*A publication*] (DLA)
Dunc Ent Cas... Duncan's Scotch Entail Cases [*A publication*] (DLA)
Dunc Ev .... Duncombe on the Law of Evidence [*A publication*] (DLA)
Dunc Man .... Duncan's Manual of Summary Procedure [*A publication*] (DLA)
Dunc Mer Cas... Duncan's Mercantile Cases [*1885-86*] [*Scotland*] [*A publication*] (DLA)
Dunc Merc Cas... Duncan's Mercantile Cases [*1885-86*] [*Scotland*] [*A publication*] (DLA)
Dunc NP .... Duncombe's Nisi Prius [*A publication*] (DLA)
DUNDA .... Dundas, OH [*American Association of Railroads railroad junction routing code*]
DUNDEE .... Down Under Doppler and Electricity Experiment (SAUS)
DUNDIS .... Direction of United Nations Databases and Information Systems (SAUO)
DUNDIS .... Directory of United Nations Datahouses and Information Systems (SAUS)
Dund LC .... Dundee Law Chronicle [*1853-58*] [*A publication*] (DLA)
DUNELM .... Bishop of Durham [*British*]

DUNELM ...... Dunelmensis [*Of Durham*] [*Signature of Bishops of Durham*] [*Latin*] (ROG)
DUNES .... Detecting Ulcers caused by NSAIDS [*Nonsteroidal Anti-Inflammatory Drugs*] Early with Sucrose
DUNF .... Democratic United National Front [*Sri Lanka*] [*Political party*] (ECON)
DUNG .... Dog Unit Negative (DAVI)
Dungl Med Dict ... Dunglison. Dictionary of Medical Science and Literature [*A publication*] (DLA)
DUNGN .... Dunagan, TX [*American Association of Railroads railroad junction routing code*]
DUNIS .... Directory of United Nations Information Systems [*Database*] [*Inter-Organisation Board of the United Nations*] [*Information service or system*] (CRD)
DUniv .... Doctor of the University
DUNK .... Dunkeld (ROG)
DUNK .... Dunkeswell [*England*]
DUNL .... Dunlin [*North American bird banding code*] (BIBA)
Dunl .... Dunlop, Bell, and Murray's Scotch Court of Session Cases, Second Series [*1838-62*] [*A publication*] (DLA)
Dunl Abr ...... Dunlap's Abridgment of Coke's Reports [*A publication*] (DLA)
Dunl Adm Pr ... Dunlop's Admiralty Practice [*A publication*] (DLA)
Dun L & T ... Dun's Landlord and Tenant in Ireland [*A publication*] (DLA)
Dunl B & M ... Dunlop, Bell, and Murray's Scotch Court of Session Cases, Second Series [*1838-62*] [*A publication*] (DLA)
Dunl (Ct of Sess) ... Dunlop, Bell, and Murray's Scotch Court of Session Cases, Second Series [*1838-62*] [*A publication*] (ILCA)
Dunl F .... Dunlap's Forms [*A publication*] (DLA)
Dunl L PA .... Dunlop's Laws of Pennsylvania [*A publication*] (DLA)
Dunl L US .... Dunlop's Laws of the United States [*A publication*] (DLA)
Dunlop .... Dunlop, Bell, and Murray's Scotch Court of Session Cases, Second Series [*1838-62*] [*A publication*] (DLA)
Dunlop PR ... Dunlop Precision Rubbers Division (SAUS)
Dunl Paley Ag ... Dunlap's Paley on Agency [*A publication*] (DLA)
Dunl Par ...... Dunlop on Parochial Law [*Scotland*] [*A publication*] (DLA)
Dunl Pr .... Dunlop's Admiralty Practice [*A publication*] (DLA)
DUNMIRE .... Dundee University Numerical Method Information Retrieval Experiment [*British*] (NITA)
DUNMIRE .... Retrieval System (SAUS)
Dunn .... Dunning's English King's Bench Reports [*1753-54*] [*A publication*] (DLA)
Dunning .... Dunning's English King's Bench Reports [*1753-54*] [*A publication*] (DLA)
DUNRK .... Dunkirk, NY [*American Association of Railroads railroad junction routing code*]
DUNS .... Data Universal Numbering System [*Dun's number*] [*Business term*]
DUNS .... Deep Underground Support Center [*Air Force*] (DNAB)
DUNS .... Dun & Bradstreet (AAGC)
DUNST .... Dunstable [*Municipal borough in England*]
DUO .... Datatron Users' Organization
DUO .... Disk Unseen Object
DUO .... DOS [*Disk Operating System*] under OS [*Operating System*]
DUO .... Duetto [*Duet*] [*Music*] (ROG)
DUO .... Duodecimo [*Book up to 20 centimeters in height*]
DUOD .... Duodenum [*Anatomy*]
duodec .... duodecimo (SAUS)
duol .... duologue (SAUS)
DUOW .... Distributed Unit of Work [*Computer science*] (VERA)
DUP .... Data User Part [*Integrated Services Digital Network*] [*Telecommunications*] (OSI)
DUP .... Data User Port (SAUS)
DUP .... Data User Program [*Computer science*] (UWER)
DUP .... Dedicated User Port [*Telecommunications*] (ACRL)
DUP .... Defense Unit Platform
DUP .... Delft University Press [*Netherlands*] (UWER)
DUP .... Democratic Unification Party [*South Korea*] [*Political party*] (PPW)
DUP .... Democratic Unionist Party [*Sudan*] [*Political party*] (PD)
DUP .... Democratic Unionist Party [*Northern Ireland*] [*Political party*]
DUP .... Diploma of the University of Paris
DUP .... Diplomate of the University of Paris (SAUS)
DUP .... Disk Utility Program [*IBM Corp.*] [*Computer science*]
DUP .... Distinguished University Professor
DUP .... Diundecyl Phthalate [*Organic chemistry*]
DUP .... Docteur de l'Universite de Paris [*Doctor of the University of Paris*] [*French*] (BARN)
DUP .... Dump Utility Program (SAUS)
DUP .... Duplan Corp. (SAUO)
DUP .... Duplex [*Watchmaking*] (ROG)
DUP .... Duplicate (AFM)
dup .... Duplicate (VRA)
dup .... duplicating (SAUS)
DUP .... Duplication
DUP .... Du Pont Canada, Inc. [*Toronto Stock Exchange symbol*]
DUP .... Duquesne University Press (SAUO)
DUP .... E. I. DuPont de Nemours & Co., Lavoisier Library, Wilmington, DE [*OCLC symbol*] (OCLC)
DUP .... National Society, Daughters of Utah Pioneers (EA)
DUP .... Ulster Democratic Unionist Party [*Northern Ireland*] [*Political party*] (PPW)
DUPA .... Drug Users Parent Aid (SAUS)
du pa .... duplicating pattern (SAUS)
DUPAC .... Duke University Preventive Approach to Cardiovascular Disease
DUPAR .... Dewhurst and Partner Ltd. (SAUO)
DUPART .... Data Up-Date Procedure at a Remote Terminal (SAUS)
DUPC .... Delayed Under Program Control (ACAE)
DUPC .... Displayed under Program Control
Dup Const .... Duponceau on the Constitution [*A publication*] (DLA)
DUPE .... Duplicate (AABC)
dupe .... duplicate copy (SAUS)
dupe neg ..... duplicate negative (SAUS)
dupes .... duplicate copies (SAUS)
dupes .... duplicates (SAUS)
DUP-FIL .... Duplicate Filing [*IRS*]
DUPI .... Defense Unit Platform Interceptor [*Strategic Defense Initiative*]
Dup Jur .... Duponceau on Jurisdiction of United States Courts [*A publication*] (DLA)
dupl .... Duplicate (BJA)
DUPL .... Duplication (SAUS)
Duplex .... Duplex Products, Inc. [*Associated Press*] (SAG)
dupli .... duplicate (SAUS)
dupli .... duplicated (SAUS)
dupli .... duplication (SAUS)
DUPLICS ...... Dublin Public Libraries Computerised System (SAUS)
DUPLX .... Duplex (NASA)
DUPLXR .... Duplexer (NASA)
DUPNG .... Duplicating
DuPnt .... DuPont [*E. I.*] de Nemours [*Associated Press*] (SAG)
DUPNT .... Dupont-Wilkes Barre Branch, PA [*American Association of Railroads railroad junction routing code*]
DUPO .... Dupo, IL [*American Association of Railroads railroad junction routing code*]
Duponceau US Cts ... Duponceau on Jurisdiction of United States Courts [*A publication*] (DLA)
DuPont .... DuPont [*E. I.*] de Nemours [*Associated Press*] (SAG)
Du Pont Inf Serv ... Du Pont Information Service (journ.) (SAUS)
Du Pont Mag ... Du Pont Magazine (journ.) (SAUS)
Du Pont Mag Eur Ed ... Du Pont Magazine, European Edition (journ.) (SAUS)
DuPontP .... DuPont Photomasks, Inc. [*Associated Press*] (SAG)
DUPPA .... Dual Path Protection Arrangement [*AT & T*]
DUPS .... Defense Unit Platform Subsystem [*Strategic Defense Initiative*]
DUPS .... Duplicates (SAUS)
DUPX .... El Dupont de Nemours [*Federal Railroad Administration identification code*]
DUPX .... El Dupont de Nemours [*Private rail car owner code*]
DUPZ .... Duke Power [*Federal Railroad Administration identification code*]
DUQ .... Duncan/Quamichan Lake [*Canada*] [*Airport symbol*] [*Obsolete*] (OAG)
Duq .... Duquesne Light Co. [*Associated Press*] (SAG)
DUQ .... Duquesne University Library, Pittsburgh, PA [*OCLC symbol*] (OCLC)
DuqCap .... Duquesne Capital [*Associated Press*] (SAG)
Duquesne U ... Duquesne University (GAGS)
DUR .... Down unloaded restricted (SAUS)
DUR .... Driving under Revocation (SARE)
DUR .... Drug Usage Review (MEDA)
DUR .... Drug Utilization Review [*Medicine*]
DUR .... Duracell International [*NYSE symbol*] (SPSG)
DUR .... Duracell Intl. [*NYSE symbol*] (TTSB)
Dur .... Durango (SAUS)
Dur .... Duration [*Medicine*] (AMHC)
DUR .... Duration
DUR .... Durban [*South Africa*] [*Airport symbol*] (OAG)
Dur .... Durham (ADWA)
DUR .... Durham [*England*] [*Seismograph station code, US Geological Survey*] (SEIS)
DUR .... Durham [*City and county in England*]
DUR .... Durham Resources, Inc. [*Toronto Stock Exchange symbol*]
DUR .... During
dur .... duris (SAUS)
Dur .... Durium [*Record label*] [*Italy*]
DUR .... Duro-Test Corp. (SAUO)
DUR .... Durus [*Hard*] [*Pharmacy*]
DURA .... Durability (MCD)
DURA .... Dura Pharmaceuticals [*NASDAQ symbol*] (TTSB)
DURA .... Dura Pharmaceuticals, Inc. [*NASDAQ symbol*] (SAG)
DURA .... Duration (SAUS)
Duracel .... Duracell International [*Associated Press*] (SAG)
Duracrft ...... Duracraft Co. [*Associated Press*] (SAG)
Dural .... Duraluminum (SAUS)
duralumin .... durable aluminum-copper-magnesium-manganese alloy (SAUS)
Duramed ...... Duramed Pharmaceuticals, Inc. [*Associated Press*] (SAG)
DURAN .... Durant, OK [*American Association of Railroads railroad junction routing code*]
DuraPh .... Dura Pharmaceuticals, Inc. [*Associated Press*] (SAG)
Durb ADR .... Durban Roodepoort Deep Ltd. [*Associated Press*] (SAG)
DURC .... Dublin University Rowing Club (SAUO)
DURC .... Durden [*Federal Railroad Administration identification code*]
DURC .... During Climb [*Aviation*] (FAAC)
DURD .... Department of Urban and Regional Development (SAUS)
DURD .... During Descent [*Aviation*] (FAAC)
DUR DOL ..... Durante Dolore [*While Pain Lasts*] [*Pharmacy*]
DUR DOLOR ... Durante Dolore [*While Pain Lasts*] [*Pharmacy*]
Dur Dr Fr ..... Duranton's Droit Francais [*A publication*] (DLA)
DURELAS ..... Duty as His Relief [*Military*] (DNAB)
Durf .... Durfee's Reports [*2 Rhode Island*] [*A publication*] (DLA)
Durfee .... Durfee's Reports [*2 Rhode Island*] [*A publication*] (DLA)
DURG .... During (FAAC)
durgc .... during climb (SAUS)
durgd .... during descent (SAUS)
DURH .... Durham [*City and county in England*]
DURH LI ...... Durham Light Infantry [*Military unit*] [*British*] (ROG)

DURHM .... Durham, NC [*American Association of Railroads railroad junction routing code*]
DURI .... Duriron Co. [*NASDAQ symbol*] (SAG)
DUrI .... Urban Institute, Washington, DC [*Library symbol*] [*Library of Congress*] (LCLS)
Durie .... Durie's Scotch Court of Session Decisions [*1621-42*] [*A publication*] (DLA)
DURIP .... Defense University Research Instrumentation Program (SAUO)
Duriron .... Duriron Co. [*Associated Press*] (SAG)
Durkn .... Durakon Industries, Inc. [*Associated Press*] (SAG)
Dur Mus ...... Durban Museum (SAUS)
DURN .... Duration (FAAC)
Durn & E ..... Durnford and East's (Term) Reports [*1785-1800*] [*England*] [*A publication*] (DLA)
DURND .... Durand, MI [*American Association of Railroads railroad junction routing code*]
DURR .... Delaware & Ulster Rail Ride [*Federal Railroad Administration identification code*]
DURS .... Dockside Underway Replenishment Simulator [*Navy*] (DNAB)
DURS .... Dursley [*England*]
DUS .... Data Utilization Station
DUS .... Data Utilization System (ACAE)
DUS .... Democratic Union of Slovakia [*Political party*] (PSAP)
DUS .... Denver Union Stockyard [*Federal Railroad Administration identification code*]
DUS .... Department of Urban Services (SAUO)
DUS .... Deputy Under Secretary of State (SAUS)
DUS .... Design Unit Specification (SAUS)
DUS .... Diagnostic Utility System
DUS .... Diploma of the University of Southampton [*British*]
DUS .... Disk Utility System [*Computer science*] (VLIE)
DUS .... Distinctness, Uniformity and Stability (SAUS)
DUS .... Division of Undergraduate Studies (SAUS)
DUS .... Dockside Underway Replenishment Simulator [*Navy*] (NVT)
DUS .... Dollar Unit Sampling (ADA)
DUS .... Doppler Ultrasound Stethoscope (MEDA)
DUS .... Driver Units Speaker
DUS .... Driving under Suspension (SARE)
DUS .... Dusheti [*Former USSR*] [*Seismograph station code, US Geological Survey*] (SEIS)
DUS .... Dusseldorf [*Germany*] [*Airport symbol*] (OAG)
DUS .... Dusty Mac Mines Ltd. [*Vancouver Stock Exchange symbol*]
DUS .... Marshfield, WI [*Location identifier*] [*FAA*] (FAAL)
DUSA .... Deputy Under Secretary of the Army (AABC)
DUSA .... Dispensatory of the United States of America (SAUS)
DUSA .... DUSA Pharmaceuticals [*NASDAQ symbol*] (TTSB)
DUSA .... DUSA Pharmaceuticals, Inc. [*Associated Press*] (SAG)
DUSAA .... Davison United States Army Airfield (AABC)
DUSAM .... Dummy Surface-to-Air Missile
DUSB .... United States Brewers Association, Washington, DC [*Library symbol*] [*Library of Congress*] (LCLS)
DUSC .... Deep Underground Support Center [*Air Force*]
DUSC .... Defense Underground Support Center (SAUO)
DUSC .... Drug Utilisation Sub-Committee [*Australia*]
DUSC .... United States Supreme Court, Washington, DC [*Library symbol*] [*Library of Congress*] (LCLS)
DUSCOOP .... Drexel University Computer Simulator of Operations with an Online Program (SAUO)
DUSD .... Data Services Division [*Census*] (OICC)
DUSD .... Data User Services Division (SAUS)
DUSD .... Data Users Services Division [*Computer science*] (VLIE)
DUSD .... Deputy Under Secretary of Defense (RDA)
DUSD .... Dongola Unit School District (SAUO)
DUSD (A) ..... Deputy Under Secretary of Defense (Acquisitions) (AAGC)
DUSD(AP) .... Deputy Under-Secretary of Defense (Acquisition Policy) (DNAB)
DUSD(AT) .... Deputy Under Secretary of Defense (for Advanced Technology) (RDA)
DUSD(C$_3$I) .... Deputy Under-Secretary of Defense (Communications, Command, Control, and Intelligence) (DNAB)
DUSD C3I .... Deputy Undersecretary of Defense for Communications, Command, Control and Intelligence (SAUO)
DUSD(ES) .... Deputy Under Secretary of Defense (Environmental Security) (BCP)
DUSDP .... Deputy Under Secretary of Defense for Policy
DUSD (P) ..... Deputy Under Secretary of Defense-Policy (AAGC)
DUSD(PR) .... Deputy Under-Secretary of Defense (Policy Review) (DNAB)
DUSDRE ...... Deputy Under Secretary of Defense for Research and Engineering (SAUO)
DUSDRE(C^{3}I) ... Deputy Under Secretary of Defense for Research and Engineering (Communications, Command, Control, and Intelligence) [*Military*]
DUSDRE (T & E) ... Deputy Under Secretary of Defense for Research and Engineering (Test and Evaluation) [*Military*]
DUSD (T&E) ... Deputy Under Secretary of Defense-Test and Evaluation (AAGC)
DUSFC .... Deputy Undersecretary for Field Coordination [*HUD*]
DUSIGN ...... To Duty Assigned By [*Military*]
DUSN .... Deputy Under-Secretary of the Navy (DNAB)
DUSN .... Diffuse Unilateral Subacute Neuroretinitis [*Ophthalmology*]
DUSNWS ..... Director, United States Naval Weather Service
DUSO .... Dar es Salaam University Student Organization (SAUO)
DUSO .... Data User Service Office (SAUS)
DUSO .... Developing Understanding of Self and Others [*Educational tool*]
DUSODA ...... For Duty or Such Other Duty as [*Command or Activity Indicated*] May Assign [*Military*]
DUSOI .... Duke Severity of Illness [*Checklist*]
DUSS .... Deep Underground Sanguine System [*Navy*] (MCD)
DUSS .... Deep Underground Support System (SAUS)
DUST .... Deferred User Service Tasks (SAUS)
DUST .... Dual-Use Science and Technology [*Army*] (SEWL)
DUSTA .... Duty Station [*Navy*]
DUSTER ...... Dual Stage Target Recognition (ACAE)
dus/testing ... distinctness,uniformity, and stability testing (SAUS)
DUSTSONDE ... Balloon-Borne Particle Counter (SAUS)
DUSTWUN ... duty status-whereabouts unknown (SAUS)
DustyM .... Dusty Mac Oil & Gas Ltd. [*Associated Press*] (SAG)
DUSW .... Director of Undersea Warfare, Ministry of Defence, London (NATG)
DUT .... Dalian University of Technology (SAUO)
DUT .... Darmstadt University of Technology (SAUO)
DUT .... Delft University of Technology (SAUO)
DUT .... Denver Union Terminal Railway [*Federal Railroad Administration identification code*]
DUT .... Depot Unit Tester (ACAE)
DUT .... Deutsche Umsiedlungstreuhandgesellschaft [*A publication*] (BJA)
DUT .... Device under Test
DUT .... Diode Under Test (IAA)
DUT .... Drainage Unions and Trusts [*Australia*]
DUT .... Duke Energy [*NYSE symbol*]
DUT .... Duke Energy 6.60% Sr Notes'C' [*NYSE symbol*] (SG)
dut .... dunnage untreated (SAUS)
DUT .... Duplication Technician, Photolithography [*Navy rating*]
Dut .... Dutch (DIAR)
dut .... Dutch [*MARC language code*] [*Library of Congress*] (LCCP)
DUT .... Dutch
DUT .... Dutch Harbor [*Alaska*] [*Airport symbol*] (OAG)
DUTA .... Display Unit Test Assembly (MCD)
D Utah .... United States District Court for the District of Utah (DLA)
Dut & Cowd Rev ... Dutton and Cowdrey's Revision of Swift's Digest of Connecticut Laws [*A publication*] (DLA)
DUTC .... Dallas Union Terminal [*AAR code*]
Dutch .... Dutcher's Law Reports [*25-29 New Jersey*] [*A publication*] (DLA)
DUTE .... Digital Universal Test Equipment (MCD)
DUTH .... Dusky Thrush [*North American bird banding code*] (BIBA)
DUTN .... Duotone (VRA)
dUTP .... Deoxyuridine Triphosphate [*Biochemistry*]
DUTPase .... Deoxyiauridine Triphosphatase [*An enzyme*]
DUT pin .... device under test pin (SAUS)
DUTS .... Decision Unit Tracking System [*Nuclear energy*] (NRCH)
DUTSCAT ..... Delft University of Technology Scatterometer (SAUO)
Dutton .... EP Dutton & Co (SAUS)
DutyF .... Duty Free International, Inc. [*Associated Press*] (SAG)
DUV .... Damaging Ultraviolet (DB)
DUV .... Dangerous Ultraviolet (DB)
DUV .... Data Under Voice [*Bell System*]
DUV .... Daughters of Union Veterans of the Civil War, 1861-1865 (EA)
DUV .... Deep Ultraviolet [*Lithography*]
DUV .... Dispersive Ultraviolet [*Automotive engineering*]
Duv .... Duvall's Canada Supreme Court Reports [*A publication*] (DLA)
Duv .... Duvall's Reports [*62, 63 Kentucky*] [*A publication*] (DLA)
Duval .... Duvall's Canada Supreme Court Reports [*A publication*] (DLA)
Duvall .... Duvall's Canada Supreme Court Reports [*A publication*] (DLA)
DUVAS .... Derivative Ultraviolet Absorption Spectrometer [*Instrumentation*]
Duv (Can) .... Duvall's Canada Supreme Court Reports [*A publication*] (DLA)
DUVCW .... Daughters of Union Veterans of the Civil War (SAUO)
DUVD .... Direct Ultrasonic Visualization of Defects (PDAA)
DUVT .... Duval Transportation of the Carolinas [*Federal Railroad Administration identification code*]
DUW .... Director of Underwater Weapons [*British*]
DUWA .... Dusky Warbler [*North American bird banding code*] (BIBA)
DUWCAL ...... Duluth Weapons Calibration System
DUWIR .... Dual Wavelength Infrared (SAUS)
DUWM .... Director of Underwater Weapon Material Department (SAUO)
DUWP .... Director of Underwater Weapons Projects [*Navy*] [*British*]
DUX .... Data Utility Complex (IAA)
DUX .... Dumas, TX [*Location identifier*] [*FAA*] (FAAL)
Dux .... Duxbury's High Court Reports [*South African Republic*] [*1895*] [*A publication*] (DLA)
DUXX .... Donner-Hanna Coke [*Private rail car owner code*]
DV .... Daily Value [*Nutrition*]
DV .... Damage and Vulnerability (MCD)
DV .... Damped Vibration (UWER)
d/v .... Danube View
DV .... Data Vetting
DV .... Data Volume (SAUS)
DV .... Day Visitor (SAUO)
DV .... Death Valley Resources [*Vancouver Stock Exchange symbol*]
DV .... Decimal Value (SAUS)
D/V .... Declared Value (WDAA)
DV .... Decomposition Voltage (UWER)
DV .... Defective Vision (ADA)
DV .... Dei Verbum [*Dogmatic Constitution on Divine Revelation*] [*Vatican II document*]
DV .... Delaware Valley Railroad [*Federal Railroad Administration identification code*]
DV .... Delta Velocity (KSC)
DV .... Demand Valve
DV .... Demonstration and Validation (MCD)
D/V .... Demonstration/Validation (SAUS)
D/V .... Demonstration/Validation Phase (SAUS)
DV .... Denver Support Office (SAUO)
DV .... Deo Volente [*God Willing*] [*Latin*]
DV .... Depended Variable (IAA)
DV .... Dependent Variable (AAMN)

DV Dependent Vehicle
DV Designated Verification (SAUS)
DV Designee for Verification [*NASA*] (NASA)
DV Design Verification (AAEL)
DV Desired Value (UWER)
dv Desk View (VLIE)
DV DESQview Script (SAUS)
DV Development and Verification (SAUS)
DV Device
DV DeVry, Inc. [*NYSE symbol*] (SAG)
DV diagnosis undetermined (SAUS)
DV Diana Vreeland [*Fashion editor, 1903-1989*]
DV Dianhydrogalactitol and VP-16 [*Antineoplastic drug regimen*] (DAVI)
DV Diesel Vessel (SAUS)
DV Difference in Volume [*Medicine*] (EDAA)
dv Differential of Velocity (IDOE)
dV differential of voltage (SAUS)
DV Differential Velocity (KSC)
DV Differential Voltage (IEEE)
DV Differential Voltmeter (SAUS)
DV Different Version
D/V Diffusion per Unit Volume [*Measurement*] (DAVI)
DV Digital Vibration [*Medicine*] (EDAA)
DV Digital Video
DV Digital Voice (MCD)
DV Dilute Volume [*Chemistry*]
DV Diploma in Venereology (ADA)
DV Diploma, Venereology [*British*] [*Medical degree*] (CMD)
DV Directed Verdict [*Legal term*]
DV Direct View (ACAE)
DV Direct Vision [*Aviation*]
DV DirectVision [*Home-information service of KPIX-TV*]
DV Direct Voice (NTCM)
DV Direct Voltage (IAA)
DV Disbursement Voucher (AFM)
DV Discontinuous Vulcanization (SAUS)
DV Discovery Vessel (SAUS)
DV Disease Variable [*Medicine*]
DV dispatch ship (SAUS)
DV Dispersal Vessel (SAUS)
DV Distance Vector (SAUS)
DV Distemper Virus
DV Distinguished Visitor
DV Distressed Vehicle (KSC)
dv Dive (SAUS)
DV Diversity Visa (SAUS)
DV Diverter Valve (KSC)
DV Divide
DV Divinitas (BJA)
DV Division [*Mathematics*] (ROG)
DV Division Flag [*Navy*] [*British*]
DV Division of Validation [*Social Security Administration*]
DV Division Piece [*Rotary piston meter*]
DV Divisionsverfuegung [*or Divisionsverordnung*] [*Divisional Order*] [*German military - World War II*]
DV Divisor [*Mathematics*] (IAA)
DV Divorce [*Facetious translation of DV, Deo Volente (God Willing)*] (DSUE)
DV Divorced
DV Doctor of Veterinary Science (CPGU)
DV Domestic Violence (WDAA)
DV Domiciliary Visit [*Medicine*]
DV Dorsal-ventral (SAUS)
dv dorsiventral (SAUS)
DV Dorsoventral [*Anatomy*]
DV Dorso-Ventralis (SAUS)
dv dorsovolar (SAUS)
DV Douay Version [*Bible*]
DV Double Valve [*Stutz car model designation*]
DV Double Vibrations [*Cycles*]
DV Double Vision
DV Doubtful-Very [*Theatrical term*] [*Facetious translation of DV, Deo Volente (God Willing)*] (DSUE)
DV Drift Voltage
D/V Dual Valuation [*Insurance*] (MARI)
DV Dual Valve
DV Dummy Variable (SAUS)
DV Dump Valve (IEEE)
DV Durchgangsvermittlung [*Long-distance telephone exchange*] [*German military - World War II*]
DV Dutch RCA [*Victor*] [*Record label*]
DV Nantucket Airlines [*ICAO designator*] (AD)
DV Volumetric Diffusivity (SAUS)
DV District Valuer (ODA)
DVA Adams County School District No. 12, Northglenn, CO [*OCLC symbol*] (OCLC)
DVA Data Valid (SAUS)
DVA Department of Veterans Affairs [*Canada*]
DVA Department of Veterans Affairs [*Formerly, Veterans Administration*]
DVA Designed, Verified, and Assigned Date [*Telecommunications*] (TEL)
DVA Design Verification Article (SAUS)
DVA Deutsche Verlags-Anstalt [*Publishing company*]
DVA Developmental Venous Anomaly [*Medicine*] (EDAA)
DVA Differential Voltage Amplifier
D/V_A Diffusion per Unit of Alveolar Volume [*Medicine*] (DAVI)
DVA Digital Voice Announcer (SAUS)
DVA Diminished Visual Acuity
DVA Diploma in Veterinary Anaesthesia [*British*]
DVA Directory of Visual Arts Organizations [*Arts Midwest*] [*Information service or system*] (CRD)
DVA Discovery Airways [*ICAO designator*] (FAAC)
DVA Discovery Value Accounting (ADA)
DVA Disco Vision Associates [*Videodisc manufacturer*] (NITA)
DVA Distal Visual Acuity [*Eye Examination*] [*Medicine*] (EDAA)
DVA Distance Vector Algorithm (SAUS)
DVA Distance Visual Acuity [*Ophthalmology*]
DVA Distributed Voting Algorithm (RALS)
DVA Diverse Vector Area [*FAA*] (TAG)
DVA Divinylacetylene [*Organic chemistry*]
DVA Doctor of Visual Aids (NADA)
DVA Document Validation Audit [*NASA*] (MCD)
DVA Dunkirk Veterans Association [*Leeds, England*] (EAIO)
DVA Duration of Voluntary Apnea [*Physiology*]
DVA Dynamic Visual Acuity (IEEE)
DVA United States Veterans Administration, Washington, DC [*Library symbol*] [*Library of Congress*] (LCLS)
DVA Digital Video Angiography [*Medicine*] (ODA)
DVAB Defense Vocational Aptitude Battery [*Military*] (NVT)
DVAC Distributor Vacuum Advance Control [*Automotive engineering*]
DVACS Data Verification, Access and Control System [*Computer science*] (VLIE)
DVAD Dollar Value of Annual Demands (AFIT)
DVA Date Designed, Verified and Assigned Date (SAUS)
DVAL Data Link Vulnerability Analysis [*DoD*] (RDA)
DVAL Data Link Vulnerability Joint Task Force (SAUO)
DVAL Demonstration and Validation (MCD)
D-value Death value (SAUS)
DV & D Diploma in Venereology and Dermatology (ADA)
DV&RS Director of Veterinary and Remounts Services (SAUO)
DVAR Data Value-Added Reseller
DVARS Doppler Velocity Altimeter RADAR Set [*Military*] (CAAL)
dva test Duration of Voluntary Apnea Test (SAUS)
DVAV Dorsoventral Abdominal Vibration [*Entomology*]
DVB Department of Veterans Benefits [*Veterans Administration*]
DVB Device Base Control Block [*Computer science*] (IBMDP)
DVB Device Vector Base (VLIE)
DVB Diamminedichloroplatinum [*Cisplatin*], Vindesine, Bleomycin [*Antineoplastic drug regimen*]
DVB Digital Video Bandwidth
DVB Digital Video Broadcast (SAUS)
DVB Digital Video Broadcasting (TELE)
DVB Digital Video Broadcasting Group (SAUO)
DVB Disability Veiling Brightness [*Optics*] (IAA)
DVB Divinylbenzene [*Organic chemistry*]
DVB Volta Bureau for the Deaf, Washington, DC [*Library symbol*] [*Library of Congress*] (LCLS)
DVBD Diesel V-Belt Drive
DVB/DAVIC Digital Video Broadcasting/Digital Audio-Visual Council (VLIE)
DVBID Division of Vector-Borne Infectious Diseases (SAUS)
DVBIRD Digital Video Broadcasting Integrated Receiver Decoder [*Communications term*] (DCT)
DVBST Direct View Bistable Storage Tube (SAUS)
DVC Community College of Denver, North Campus, Westminster, CO [*OCLC symbol*] (OCLC)
DVC Damodar Valley Corporation (SAUO)
DVC Delaware Valley Conference (SAUS)
DVC Deputy Vice-Chancellor (SAUS)
DVC Desktop Video Conferencing (SAUO)
DVC Device (MSA)
DVC Diablo Valley College (SAUS)
DVC Digital/Desktop Video Conferencing (VLIE)
DVC Digital Valve Controller (ACII)
DVC Digital Video Camera (SAUS)
DVC Digital Video Cassette (DOM)
DVC Digital Video Communication [*Military*] (CAAL)
DVC Digital Video Compression
DVC Digital Video Conference (SAUS)
DVC Digital Voice Card [*Computer science*] (VLIE)
DVC Digital Voice Communication (SAUS)
DVC Digital Voice Communications
DVC Digital Voice Computer (COE)
DVC Digital Voice Controller (MCD)
DVC Direct Variable Cost
DVC Direct View Console (MCD)
DVC Direct View Cueing (SAUS)
DVC Direct Visualization of Vocal Cords (MELL)
DVC Divanillylidenecyclohexanone [*or Divanillalcyclohexanone*] [*Pharmacology*]
DVC Dove Creek, CO [*Location identifier*] [*FAA*] (FAAL)
DVC Dynamic Visual Camouflage [*Army*] (INF)
DVC Direct Viable Count [*Microbiology*] (ODA)
D/VCAS Deputy Vice Chief of the Air Staff (SAUO)
DVCC Disease Vector Control Center (SAUO)
DVCCS Differential Voltage-Controlled Current Source (IEEE)
DVCDN Device Down (VLIE)
DVCHC Delaware Valley Collegiate Hockey Conference (PSS)
DVCMF Doxorubicin [*Adriamycin*], Vincristine, Cyclophosphamide, Methotrexate, Fluorouracil [*Antineoplastic drug regimen*]
DVCND Device down Command (SAUS)
DVCO DavCo Restaurants [*NASDAQ symbol*] (TTSB)

DVCO .... Davco Restaurants, Inc. [*NASDAQ symbol*] (SAG)
DVCO .... Digital Voltage Controlled Oscillator (SEWL)
DVCO .... Dual Voltage Controlled Oscillator (SAUS)
DVCP .... Direct View Control Panel (ACAE)
DVCR .... Digital Videocassette Recorder (CDE)
DVCR .... Digital Video Cassette Recording (SAUS)
DVCS .... Data/Voice Communications System (SSD)
DVCS .... Devices
DVCS .... Digital Voice Communications System (MCD)
DVCS .... Domestic Violence Crisis Service [*Australian Capital Territory*] [*Australia*]
DVCSA .... Delaware Valley College of Science and Agriculture (SAUS)
DVCSB .... Delaware Valley Consumer Sounding Board (SAUO)
DVCUP .... Device up (SAUS)
DVCZ .... Davco Coal [*Federal Railroad Administration identification code*]
D/VD .... Data/Voice Data (MCD)
DVD .... Delta Velocity Display
DVD .... Design Verification Demonstration
DVD .... Detail Velocity Display (IEEE)
DVD .... Deutsche Vereinigung fuer Datenschutz [*German Data Protection Organization*]
DVD .... Developmental Verbal Dyspraxia
DVD .... Digital Versatile Disc [*Computer science*]
DVD .... Digital Versatile Disk (PCM)
DVD .... Digital Video Disc (SAUS)
DVD .... Digital Video Disk
DVD .... Diploma in Venereology and Dermatology
DVD .... Directorate of Vehicle Development (SAUO)
DVD .... Direct Vendor Delivery [*DoD*]
DVD .... Direct-View Device [*Night vision*]
DVD .... Dissociated Vertical Deviation [*Ophthalmology*]
DVD .... Dissociated Vertical Divergence [*Ophthalmology*] (DAVI)
DVD .... Divide [*Commonly used*] (OPSA)
DVD .... Double Vessel Disease [*Medicine*] (DB)
DVD .... Dover Downs Entertainment [*NYSE symbol*] (SG)
DVD .... Dover Downs Entertainment, Inc. [*NYSE symbol*] (SAG)
DVD .... Thurmont, MD [*Location identifier*] [*FAA*] (FAAL)
DVDA .... Dollar Volume Discount Agreement (SAUS)
DVDALV .... Double Vessel Disease with an Abnormal Left Ventricle [*Cardiology*]
DVDC .... Divisional Vendor Data Coordinator (MCD)
DVDCCA .... DVD Copy Control Association (SAUO)
DVDM .... Data Voice Digital Multiplexer (CCCA)
DVDP .... Dry Valley Drilling Project [*National Science Foundation*]
DVD-R .... Digital Versatile Disk-Recordable (ADWA)
DVD-R .... Digital Video Disc-Recordable
DVDR .... Direct-View Diagnostic Region
DVD-RAM .... Digital Versatile Disk-Random Access Memory (ADWA)
DVD-ROM .... Digital Versatile Disk-Read Only Memory (ADWA)
DVD-RW .... Digital Versatile Disk-Read-Write (ADWA)
DVD-R/W .... Digital Video Disc-Rewritable
DVDS .... Digital Video Display System
DVDV .... Differential Vacuum Delay Valve [*Automotive engineering*]
DVDY .... Diving Duty [*Military*]
DVE .... Community College of Denver, North AEC Project, Westminster, CO [*OCLC symbol*] (OCLC)
DVE .... Data Value Element (SAUS)
DVE .... Device End (SAUS)
DVE .... Devnic Energy, Inc. [*Toronto Stock Exchange symbol*]
DVE .... Differential Vector Equation
DVE .... Digital Video Effect [*Video technology*] (PCM)
DVE .... Diploma of Vocational Education [*British*] (DET)
DVE .... Distributed Virtual Environment (SEWL)
DVE .... Division of Vocational Education [*Department of Education*] (GFGA)
Dve .... Drive
DVE .... Driver's Vision Enhancer [*Military*]
DVE .... Duck Virus Enteritis
DVECC .... Disease Vector Ecology and Control Center [*Military*] (NVT)
DV Ed .... Doctor of Vocational Education
DVEG .... Derwent Valley Environment Group [*Australia*]
DVEO .... Defense Value Engineering Services Officer
DVER .... Design Rule Verification (AAEL)
DVES .... Defense Value Engineering Services (SAUS)
DVESO .... DoD [*Department of Defense*] Value Engineering Services Office (IEEE)
DVET .... Data Vetting program (SAUS)
DVET .... Department of Vocational Education and Training (SAUS)
D Vet Med .... Doctor of Veterinary Medicine
DVetSc .... Doctor of Veterinary Science (ADA)
DVF .... Diane Von Furstenberg [*Couturiere*]
DVF .... Digital Variable Frequency (SAUS)
DVF .... Dried Vine Fruit
DVF .... Dualbowl Vibratory Feeder
DVF .... Society of the Descendants of Washington's Army at Valley Forge (EA)
DVFC .... Danny Vann Fan Club (EA)
DVFD .... Direct View Filament Display (MCD)
DVFE .... Director, Vehicle and Field Engineering [*Canada*] [*Military*]
DVFO .... Digital Variable Frequency Oscillator (SAUS)
DVFO .... Digital Variable-Frequency Oscillator (IEEE)
DVFR .... Day Visual Flight Rules [*FAA*] (TAG)
DVFR .... Defence Visual Flight Rules (SAUS)
DVFR .... Defense Visual Flight Rules
DVG .... Deutsche Veterinaermedizinische Gesellschaft [*German Veterinary Association*] (GVA)
DVG .... Digital Video Generator [*Computer science*]
DVG .... Dunvagen [*Publisher*]
DVH .... Dark, Hard & Vitreous (SAUO)
DVH .... Dental, Visual, and Hearing Insurance
DVH .... Diploma in Veterinary Hygiene [*British*]
DVH .... Divide or Halt (IAA)
DVH .... Division for the Visually Handicapped (EA)
DVH .... Driver's Vision Enhancer (SEWL)
D-VHS .... Data-VHS (CDE)
D-VHS .... Digital VHS (SAUS)
DVHSP .... Digital Video High-Speed Processor [*Computer science*] (CIST)
DVI .... Deep Venous Incompetence [*Medicine*] (EDAA)
DVI .... Deuel Vocational Institution (SAUS)
DVI .... Device Independent (SAUS)
DVI .... Device-Independent Format [*Computer science*]
DVI .... Difference Vegetation Index (SAUS)
DVI .... Digital Vascular Imaging [*Roentgenology*]
DVI .... Digital Versatile Interactive (RALS)
DVI .... Digital Video Imaging (CPH)
DVI .... Digital Video Interactive [*CD-ROM technology*] [*General Electric Co.*]
DVI .... Digital Video Interface (SAUS)
DVI .... Direct Voice Input (DA)
DVI .... Doppler Systolic Velocity Integral (DB)
DVI .... Dover Industries Ltd. [*Toronto Stock Exchange symbol*]
DVI .... Driver Vehicle Interface (SEWL)
DVI .... Dust Veil Index [*of atmosphere*]
DVI .... DVI Corp. [*NYSE symbol*] (SPSG)
DVI .... DVI, Inc. [*Associated Press*] (SAG)
DVI .... dynamic viscosity index (SAUS)
DVI .... Information Management Specialists, Denver, CO [*OCLC symbol*] (OCLC)
D VI .... United States District Court for the District of the Virgin Islands (DLA)
DVIA .... Dual Video Adapter (SAUS)
DVIC .... DVI, Inc. [*NASDAQ symbol*] (SAG)
DVID .... Digital Video Systems [*NASDAQ symbol*] (TTSB)
DVID .... Digital Video Systems, Inc. [*NASDAQ symbol*] (SAG)
DVIDU .... Digital Video Sys Unit [*NASDAQ symbol*] (TTSB)
DVIDW .... Digital Video Sys Wrrt'A' [*NASDAQ symbol*] (TTSB)
DVIDZ .... Digital Video Sys Wrrt'B' [*NASDAQ symbol*] (TTSB)
DVI Inc .... DVI, Inc. [*Associated Press*] (SAG)
DVIIS .... Direct View Image Intensifier System (ACAE)
DVILL .... Danville, KY [*American Association of Railroads railroad junction routing code*]
dvin .... deviation (SAUS)
DVIP .... Digital Video Integrator and Processor (MCD)
DVIR .... Driver Vehicle Inspection Report [*FHWA*] (TAG)
DVIS .... Datavision, Inc. [*NASDAQ symbol*] (COMM)
DVIS .... Digital Vascular Imaging System [*Roentgenology*] (MCD)
DVITS .... Digital Video Imagery Transfer System (SAUS)
DVITS .... Digital Video Imagery Transmission System (DOMA)
DVIU .... Direct Vision Internal Urethrotomy [*Medicine*] (MAE)
DVJ .... Colorado Supreme Court Library, Denver, CO [*OCLC symbol*] (OCLC)
DVJB .... Danish Veterinary and Agricultural Library (SAUS)
DVJB .... Danmarks Veterinaer- og Jordbrugsbase [*Danish Veterinary and Agricultural Library Catalogue*] [*Information service or system*]
DVK .... Danville, KY [*Location identifier*] [*FAA*] (FAAL)
DVK .... Davis-Keays Mining [*Vancouver Stock Exchange symbol*]
DVL .... Data/Voice Logger (SAUS)
DVL .... Deep Vastus Lateralis [*Medicine*] (EDAA)
DVL .... Delta Velocity Launch
DVL .... Del-Val Financial Corp. [*NYSE symbol*] (COMM)
DVL .... Develop (MSA)
DVL .... Devils Lake [*North Dakota*] [*Airport symbol*] (OAG)
DVL .... Digital Video Link (VERA)
DVL .... Direct Voice Line (CET)
DVL .... Distance Velocity Laboratory
DVL .... Dorsal Velar Lobe
DVLA .... Driver and Vehicle Licensing Agency [*Formerly, Driver and Vehicle Licensing Centre*] [*British*] (ECON)
DVLBI .... Differential Very Long Baseline Interferometry (MCD)
DVLC .... Driver and Vehicle Licensing Center (SAUS)
DVLC .... Driver and Vehicle Licensing Centre [*British*] (DCTA)
DVLG .... DeVlieg Bullard, Inc. [*NASDAQ symbol*] (SAG)
DVLP .... Daunomycin, Vincristine, L-Asparaginase, Prednisone [*Antineoplastic drug regimen*] (DAVI)
DVLP .... Develop (SAUS)
DVLP .... Development
DVLPD .... developed (SAUS)
Dvlpmt .... Development
DVLPR .... Developer
DVLPT .... development (SAUS)
DVLR .... Derwent Valley Light Railway (SAUO)
DVLX .... Freeport-McMoran Sulphur [*Private rail car owner code*]
DVM .... Data over Voice Multiplexer [*Telecommunications*] (ACRL)
DVM .... Decessit Vita Matris [*Died during the Lifetime of the Mother*] [*Latin*]
DVM .... Design Verification Model (ACAE)
DVM .... Diel Vertical Migration [*Zooplankton*]
DVM .... Digital Velocity Meter
DVM .... Digital Video Memory (SAUS)
DVM .... Digital Voltage Meter (SAUS)
dvm .... Digital Voltmeter (IDOE)
DVM .... Digital Voltmeter
DVM .... Directional Variable Microphone
DVM .... Discontinuous Variational Method
DVM .... Discrete Variational Method (SAUS)

DVM............ Discrete Variation Method
DVM............ Displaced Virtual Machine
DVM............ Displayed Virtual Machine (SAUS)
DVM............ Distributed Virtual Memory [*Computer science*]
DVM............ Divisional Veterinary Manager (SAUS)
DVM............ Doctor of Veterinary Medecine (SAUS)
DVM............ Doctor of Veterinary Medicine
DVM............ Double Vacuum Melting (PDAA)
DVM............ Doxurubicin [*Adriamycin*], Vincristine, Methotrexate [*Antineoplastic drug regimen*]
DVMA.......... Direct Virtual Memory Access [*Computer science*]
DVM and S... Doctor of Veterinary Medicine and Surgery (SAUS)
DVMD.......... Digital Voltmeter Display (SAUS)
DVMD.......... Digital Volt-Ohmmeter Display (IAA)
DVME.......... Director of Vehicle and Marine Engineering (SAUO)
DVME.......... Dulbecco-Vogt Modified Eagle's [*Medium for cell growth*]
DVMR.......... Division of Veterinary Medical Research [*Department of Health and Human Services*] (GRD)
DVMRP........ Distance Vector Multicast Routing Protocol [*Computer science*] (VERA)
DVMS.......... Digital Voice Messaging System [*Computer science*] (ELAL)
DVMS.......... Doctor of Veterinary Medicine and Science (NADA)
DVMS.......... Doctor of Veterinary Medicine and Surgery
DVMT.......... Daily Vehilce-Miles of Travel [*FHWA*] (TAG)
DVN............ Community College of Denver, North Campus, Westminster, CO [*OCLC symbol*] (OCLC)
DVN............ Davenport, IA [*Location identifier*] [*FAA*] (FAAL)
DVN............ Daytime Versus Nighttime (SAUS)
DVN............ Devisavit Vel Non [*Issue of fact as to whether a will in question was made by the testator*] [*Latin*] [*Legal term*] (DLA)
DVN............ Devon (SAUS)
DVN............ Devon Energy [*AMEX symbol*] (TTSB)
DVN............ Devon Energy Corp. [*AMEX symbol*] (CTT)
DVN............ Devonion Resources [*Vancouver Stock Exchange symbol*]
DVN............ Devonshire Regiment (SAUO)
dvn............. division (SAUO)
DVN............ Dorsal Vagal Nucleus (DB)
DVN............ Dorsal Ventricular Nerve (SAUS)
DvN............ D. Van Nostrand (SAUS)
DVNA.......... Direct View Navigation Aid (SAUS)
DVNA.......... Direct-View Navigation Aid
DVNG.......... Diving
DVNG DY..... Diving Duty [*Military*] (DNAB)
DVNIGMI...... Far East Hydrometeorological Institute, State Committee on Hydrometeorology (SAUO)
DVNIGMI...... Far East Hydrometeorological Institute, State Committee on Hydrometeorology, Vladivostok (SAUS)
DVNM.......... Death Valley National Monument (SAUS)
Dvnport........ Devonport (SAUS)
DVNT.......... Diversinet Corp. [*NASDAQ symbol*] (SG)
DVNV.......... Dendrobium Vein Necrosis Virus [*Plant pathology*]
DVO............ Davao [*Philippines*] [*Airport symbol*] (OAG)
DVO............ Davenport Industries Ltd. [*Vancouver Stock Exchange symbol*]
DVO............ Decimal Voltage Output
DVO............ Deep Venus Obstruction [*Medicine*] (EDAA)
DVO............ Delta Velocity On/Off
DVO............ Diffuse Viewing Only (SARE)
DVO............ Direct View Optics
DVO............ Divisional Veterinary Officer [*Ministry of Agriculture, Fisheries, and Food*] [*British*]
DVO............ Durchfuehrungsverordnung [*Executive Decree*] [*German*] (ILCA)
DVO............ District Veterinary Officer (ODA)
DVOC.......... Delaware Valley Ornithological Club (SAUO)
D-VOF.......... Defense Mapping Agency Vertical Obstruction File (DNAB)
DVOM.......... Digital Video Optic MODEM [*Modulate/Demodulate*] (DWSG)
DVOM.......... Digital Volt-Ohmmeter
DVOM.......... Digital Volt Ohm Milliammeter (IDOE)
dvom........... Digital Volt Ohm Milliammeter (IDOE)
DVOP.......... Disabled Veterans Outreach Program [*Department of Labor*]
DVOPS........ Disabled Veterans Outreach Program Specialist [*Veterans Administration*]
DVOR.......... Doppler Vertical Omni-Range (SAUS)
DVOR.......... Doppler Very High Frequency Omnidirectional Range [*FAA*] (TAG)
DVOR.......... Doppler very high frequency omni-range (SAUS)
DVOR.......... Doppler VHF [*Very High Frequency*] Omnirange
DVOSI......... Divinyloxydimethylsilane [*Organic chemistry*]
DVOT.......... Delayed Velocity on Target (ACAE)
DVOT.......... Delayed Voltage on Target (SAUS)
DVOT.......... Dog Vomit on Toast [*Creamed beef or tuna on toast*] [*Military slang*]
DVP............ Damodar Valley Project (SAUO)
DVP............ Data Validation Program [*NASA*]
DVP............ Daunorubicin, Vincristine, Prednisone [*Antineoplastic drug*] (CDI)
DVP............ Davenport Downs [*Queensland*] [*Airport symbol*] (AD)
DVP............ Decessit Vita Patris [*Died during the Lifetime of the Father*] [*Latin*]
DVP............ Delivery Versus Payment
DVP............ Delta Velocity Planet
DVP............ Demokratische Volkspartei [*Democratic People's Party*] [*Germany*] (PPE)
DVP............ Dense Vortex Plasma
DVP............ Design Verification Period (MCD)
DVP............ Design Verification Program [*or Plan*] (MCD)
DVP............ Desktop Video Publishing (AGLO)
DVP............ Deutsche Volkspartei [*German People's Party (1919-1933)*] (PPE)
DVP............ Devran Petroleum Ltd. [*Vancouver Stock Exchange symbol*]
DVP............ Differential Value Profile [*Psychology*]
DVP............ Digital Video Plotter (SAUS)
DVP............ Digital Video Producer [*Asymetrix Co.*] (PCM)
DVP............ Digital Voice Privacy [*Telecommunications*]
dvp............. direct vision panel (SAUS)
DVP............ Discounted Present Value (SAUS)
DVP............ Distance Visual Point (SAUS)
DVP............ Distinguished Visitor Program [*Army*]
DVP............ Divide or Proceed (IAA)
DVP............ Domestic Violence Project (EA)
DVP............ University of Denver, Denver, CO [*OCLC symbol*] (OCLC)
DVPDF......... Dry Vacuum Pump Discharge Filter
DVPF........... Dry Vacuum Pump Filter
DVPH.......... Diploma in Veterinary Public Health (ADA)
DVPL-ASP.... Daunorubicin, Vincristine, Prednisone, L-Asparaginase [*Antineoplastic drug regimen*]
DVPMP........ Deutsche Vereinigung gegen Politischen Missbrauch der Psychiatrie [*Germany*]
DVPPI.......... Daylight View Plan Position Indicator (CET)
DVPPI.......... Daylight-View Plan-Position Indicator (SAUS)
DVPR.......... Design Verification Plan and Report
DVQ............ Distinguished Visitor Quarters [*Military*] (DOMA)
DVR............ Community College of Denver, Red Rocks Campus, Golden, CO [*OCLC symbol*] (OCLC)
DVR............ Department [*or Division*] of Vocational Rehabilitation [*Later, DTVE*] [*Department of Education*] (OICC)
DVR............ Derotational Varus Osteotomy [*Orthopedics*] (DAVI)
DVR............ Design and Verification Routine [*Sperry Univac*] (NITA)
DVR............ Design Validation Report (SEWL)
DVR............ Design Verification Rig (MCD)
DVR............ Devco Railway [*Cape Breton Development Corp. - Coal Div.*] [*AAR code*]
DVR............ Device Driver (SAUS)
DVR............ Device Register (SAUS)
DVR............ Digital Vascular Reactivity (DB)
DVR............ Digital Video Recording (NTCM)
DVR............ Diver (MSA)
DVR............ Division of Vocational Rehabilitation (SAUO)
DVR............ Doctor in Veterinary Radiology
DVR............ Doctor of Veterinary Radiology (SAUS)
DVR............ Document Validation Report
DVR............ Double Valve Replacement [*Medicine*]
DVR............ Driver (AABC)
DVR............ Lebanon, NH [*Location identifier*] [*FAA*] (FAAL)
DVR............ Van Riebeeck Decoration [*British military*] (DMA)
DVRABAD.... Driver Badge, Amphibious Vehicles [*Military decoration*]
DVRG.......... Deja Vu Research Group (EAIO)
DVRG.......... Diverge (FAAC)
DVRI........... Direct View RADAR Indicator [*Military*] (CAAL)
DVRMBAD... Driver Badge, Motorcycles [*Military decoration*]
DvrMechBadA... Driver and Mechanic Badge, Amphibious Vehicles [*Military decoration*] (AABC)
DvrMechBadM... Driver and Mechanic Badge, Motorcycles [*Military decoration*] (AABC)
DvrMechBadMech... Driver and Mechanic Badge, Mechanic [*Military decoration*] (AABC)
DvrMechBadOp... Driver and Mechanic Badge, Operator [*Military decoration*] (AABC)
DvrMechBadT... Driver and Mechanic Badge, Tracked Vehicles [*Military decoration*] (AABC)
DvrMechBadW... Driver and Mechanic Badge, Wheeled Vehicles [*Military decoration*] (AABC)
DVRO.......... Digital Video Receive Only (SAUS)
DVRP.......... Divisional Vehicle Recovery Point (SAUO)
DVRP.......... Domestic Violence Recovery Program (SAUS)
DVRRE........ Digital Video Record-Reproduce Equipment (ACAE)
DVRS.......... Diversco, Inc. [*NASDAQ symbol*] (COMM)
DVRSN........ Diversion (FAAC)
DVRT.......... Differential Variable Rotary Transducer [*Electronics*]
DVRTBAD.... Driver Badge, Tracked Vehicles [*Military decoration*]
DVRWBAD... Driver Badge, Wheeled Vehicles [*Military decoration*]
DVS............ Data Value Standard (SAUS)
DVS............ Data Visualization Sites (SAUO)
DVS............ Davis [*Australia*] [*Geomagnetic observatory code*]
DVS............ Delta Valley & Southern Railway Co. [*AAR code*]
DVS............ Denver Special Librarians, Denver, CO [*OCLC symbol*] (OCLC)
DVS............ Descriptive Video Services [*for the sight-impaired*] [*Public Broadcasting Service*]
DVS............ Design Verification Specification (NASA)
DVS............ devise [*Legal shorthand*] (LWAP)
DVS............ Digital Video System (SAUS)
DVS............ Digital Video Systems (SAUO)
DVS............ Digital Voice System (MCD)
DVS............ Digital Voltage Source
DVS............ Director of Veterinary Services [*Military*] [*British*]
DVS............ Display Vehicle Status (AAEL)
DVS............ Division of Veterinary Services (SAUS)
DVS............ Division of Vital Statistics [*Department of Health and Human Services*] (DAVI)
DVS............ Doctor of Veterinary Science
DVS............ Doctor of Veterinary Surgery
DVS............ Doppler Velocity Sensor
DVS............ Dynamic Vacuum Seal
DVS............ Dynamic Vertical Sensor (IAA)
DVSA.......... Dierkundige Vereniging van Suidelike Afrika [*Zoological Society of Southern Africa - ZSSA*] (EAIO)

DVSA .... Diversa Corp. [*NASDAQ symbol*] (SG)
DVSAI .... Division of Veterinary Services and Animal Industry (SAUS)
DVSc .... Doctor of Veterinary Science [*Canada*] (ASC)
DVSC .... Doctor of Veterinary Surgery
DV Sci .... Doctor of Veterinary Science
DVSFD .... Diversified
DVSG .... Diabetic Vitrectomy Study Group (SAUS)
DVSI .... Digital Vibration Survey Instrument
DVSINIT .... Device Session Initialization (SAUS)
DVSL .... District Venture Scout Leader (SAUS)
DVSM .... Diploma in Veterinary State Medicine
DVSM .... Diploma of Veterinary State Medicine (SAUS)
DVSO .... Denver Support Office (SAUS)
DVSP .... digital video subtraction phlebography (SAUS)
DVST .... Daylight Viewing Storage Tube (SAUS)
DVST .... Daylight-Viewing Storage Tube (SAUS)
DVST .... Direct View Bistable Storage (SAUS)
DVST .... Direct View bistable Storage Tube (SAUS)
DVST .... Direct View Storage Tube (SAUS)
DVST .... Direct-View Storage Tube [*Princeton Electronic Products*]
DVSWS .... UROHEALTH Sys Wrrt [*AMEX symbol*] (TTSB)
DVT .... Davic Enterprise, Inc. [*Vancouver Stock Exchange symbol*]
DVT .... Deep Vein Thrombosis (SAUS)
DVT .... Deep Venous [*or Vein*] Thrombosis [*Medicine*]
DVT .... Delta Voice Terminal (SAUS)
DVT .... Design, verification and testing (SAUS)
DVT .... Design Verification Test
DVT .... Development Verification Testing (RDA)
DVT .... Device Vector Table [*Computer science*] (ELAL)
DVT .... Digital Video Terminal [*Telecommunications*] (ACRL)
DVT .... Digital Voice Terminal (SAUS)
DVT .... Dynamic Velocity Taper (PDAA)
DVT .... Phoenix, AZ [*Location identifier*] [*FAA*] (FAAL)
D VT .... United States District Court for the District of Vermont (DLA)
DVTA .... Delaware Valley Translators Association (SAUO)
DVTE .... Division of Vocational and Technical Education [*Formerly, DVR*] [*Office of Education*]
DVTF .... Domestic Violence Task Force (SAUS)
DVTL .... Dovetail (MSA)
DVTMDS .... (Divinyl)tetramethyldisilazane [*Organic chemistry*]
dvtp .... development (SAUS)
DVTP .... Divide Time Pulse (IAA)
DVTR .... Digital Video Tape Recorder (NITA)
DVTVM .... Digital Vacuum Tube Voltmeter (SAUS)
DVTVM .... Digital Vacuum-Tube Voltmeter (IAA)
DVTW .... Delay Valve Two-Way [*Automotive engineering*]
DVU .... Delta Velocity Ullage
DVU .... Design Verification Unit (SAUS)
DVU .... Deutsche Volksunion [*German People's Union*] [*Political party*] (PD)
DVU .... Orbi [*Former USSR*] [*ICAO designator*] (FAAC)
DVV .... Downward Vertical Velocity [*NWS*] (FAAC)
DVVI .... Data, Voice, Video Integration (DINT)
DVVV .... Distributor Vacuum Vent Valve [*Automotive engineering*]
DVW .... Davenport [*Washington*] [*Seismograph station code, US Geological Survey*] (SEIS)
DVWP .... Deo Volente, Weather Permitting (SAUS)
DVX .... Daphne Virus X [*Plant pathology*]
DVX .... Data Voice Exchange (MCD)
DVX .... Denver Area Project, Denver, CO [*OCLC symbol*] (OCLC)
DVX .... Digital Voice Exchange [*Telecommunications*] (TEL)
DVXI .... Direct Vision Times One [*Medicine*] (DAVI)
DVZ .... Arapahoe Community College, Littleton, CO [*OCLC symbol*] (OCLC)
DVZ .... Mocksville, NC [*Location identifier*] [*FAA*] (FAAL)
DW .... Association of Drinkwatchers International [*Defunct*] (EA)
DW .... Commonwealth Workshop on Building and Planning in the Third World (SAUO)
DW .... Daily Wear Contact Lenses
DW .... Daisy Wheel [*Printer*]
DW .... Damage Waiver [*Insurance*]
DW .... Dangerous Weapon
DW .... Danville & Western Railway [*Federal Railroad Administration identification code*]
DW .... Darling Wife (ADWA)
DW .... Darrell Waltrip [*Race car driver*]
DW .... Data Warehouse (or Warehousing) (SAUS)
DW .... Data Word (NASA)
DW .... Data Word Buffer [*Computer science*] (MDG)
DW .... Daughters of Wisdom [*Montfort Sisters*] [*Roman Catholic religious order*]
D/W .... Dead Weight (EBF)
D/w .... Deadweight (MARI)
DW .... Deadweight
DW .... Dean Witter Organization (SAUO)
DW .... Decentralized Warehouse (AFIT)
DW .... Deck Watch [*A small chronometer*] [*Navy*]
DW .... Deep Water [*Nautical charts*]
DW .... Defensive Weapons (ACAE)
DW .... Define Word (PCM)
DW .... Deionized Water [*Pharmacology*] (DAVI)
DW .... Delayed Weather
DW .... Delivered Weight [*Business term*] (ADA)
DW .... Demineralized Water (NRCH)
DW .... Density Wave (SAUS)
DW .... Department of Waters (SAUS)
DW .... Detonation Wave (SAUS)
DW .... Detroit & Western [*AAR code*]
DW .... Deutsche Welle [*Radio network*] [*Germany*]
DW .... Developed Width (AAG)
DW .... Development Workbench (GART)
DW .... Development Workshop on Building and Planning in the Third World (SAUO)
DW .... Device Wait (SAUS)
DW .... Deworming (MELL)
D/W .... Dextrose in Water [*Medicine*]
dw .... diameter width (SAUS)
DW .... Die Welding (SAUS)
DW .... Director of Works [*Air Ministry*] [*British*]
D/W .... Direct Writing (MUGU)
DW .... Disabled Widow [*or Widower*] [*Social Security Administration*] (OICC)
D/W .... Discussed With [*Medicine*]
DW .... Disc Width [*Pisciculture*]
DW .... Dishwasher [*Classified advertising*]
DW .... Dislocated Worker [*Job Training and Partnership Act*] (OICC)
DW .... Display Write [*Software*]
DW .... Distilled Water
DW .... Dividend Warrant (ROG)
DW .... DLT Deutsche Regional [*ICAO designator*] (AD)
DW .... DLT Luftverkehrsgesellschaft mbH [*Germany*] [*ICAO designator*] (ICDA)
DW .... Dock Warehouse [*Shipping*] (ROG)
D/W .... Dock Warrant (EBF)
DW .... Does not Want (SAUS)
DW .... Doing Well (MELL)
DW .... Domestic Water (AAG)
DW .... Do not Want (SAUS)
DW .... Don't Want [*Telecommunications*] (TEL)
DW .... Double Wall
DW .... Double Warp (SAUS)
DW .... Double Weight
DW .... Double Wire [*Indian Railway*] (TIR)
DW .... Double Word [*Computer science*]
DW .... Downy Woodpecker [*Ornithology*]
DW .... drawworks (SAUS)
DW .... Drew Industries [*AMEX symbol*] (TTSB)
DW .... Drew Industries, Inc. [*AMEX symbol*] (SAG)
DW .... Dried Weight (SAUS)
DW .... Drinking Water (AAG)
DW .... Drop and Block Wire [*Telecommunications*] (TEL)
DW .... Drop Weight (SAUS)
DW .... Drop-Weight
DW .... Drop Wire
DW .... Drum Write [*Computer science*]
DW .... Dry Weight
DW .... Drywell (NRCH)
dw .... dry wine (SAUS)
DW .... Dual Wheel (SAUS)
DW .... Dual Wheels [*Aviation*]
DW .... Duke of Wellington's West Riding Regiment [*Military unit*] [*British*]
DW .... Dumbwaiter (MSA)
DW .... Durbin-Watson [*Procedure*] [*Statistics*]
dw .... Dust Wrapper [*Also, Dust Jacket*] (WDMC)
DW .... Dust Wrapper [*Paper cover for a hardbound book*]
DW .... Dwarfishness (SAUS)
dw .... Dwarf Mouse [*Medicine*] (DMAA)
D/W .... Dying with Dignity (ADWA)
DW .... Dynamic Wave (SAUS)
DW .... Sandoz AG [*Switzerland*] [*Research code symbol*]
DW .... Track for Deep Draft Vessels [*Nautical term*] (NTA)
DW3 .... Duke World Wide Web
DWA .... Daily Weighted Average [*Data sampling*]
DWA .... Damaging Winds Algorithm [*Marine science*] (OSRA)
DWA .... Deadly Weapon Act
DWA .... Delaware Division of Libraries, Dover, DE [*OCLC symbol*] (OCLC)
DWA .... Died of Wounds Resulting from Action with Enemy [*Military*]
DWA .... Digital Watch Association (EA)
DWA .... Director of War Archives [*British*]
DWA .... Dirty Writers of America [*Satirical*]
DWA .... Distributive Workers of America (SAUS)
DWA .... Diwan [*France*] [*FAA designator*] (FAAC)
DWA .... Double-Wire Armor
DWA .... Double Wire Armoured (SAUS)
DWA .... Double Word Address (SAUS)
DWA .... Drug Wholesalers Association [*Later, NWDA*] (EA)
DWA .... Dutch Warmblood Association (EA)
DWA .... Driving Without Awareness (ODA)
DWAA .... Dog Writers' Association of America (EA)
DWAAF .... Director of Women's Auxiliary Air Force [*British*]
DWAC .... Director, Women's Army Corps (AABC)
DWAC .... Distributed Write Address Counter
DWAF .... Department of Water Affairs and Forestry (SAUS)
DW & P .... Duluth, Winnipeg & Pacific Railway
DW&WR .... Dublin, Wicklow, and Wexford Railway (SAUO)
DWANGO .... Dialup Wide-Area Network Game Organization Corp. (SAUO)
Dwango .... Dial-Up Wide Area Network Gaming Operation [*Computer science*]
DWAPS .... Defense Warehousing Automated Processing System (SAUS)
Dwar .... Dwarris on Statutes [*A publication*] (DLA)
DWARF .... Deception Waveform Receiver Facility (SAUS)
DWARN .... Dakota Women of All Red Nations (EA)
Dwar St .... Dwarris on Statutes [*A publication*] (DLA)
DWASP .... Defense Warehousing and Shipping Program [*Military*]

DWASP........ DLA Standard Warehousing and Shipping Automated System (SAUS)
DWASUCY... Data Word a Setup Cycle (SAUS)
DWAT......... Deadweight All Told [*Shipping*]
DWAV......... Dual Wide Avionics Van (DWSG)
DWAW......... Distillery, Wine, and Allied Workers International Union (EA)
DWAZX........ Mgn. Stanley D. Witter MSMS Arizona [*Mutual fund ticker symbol*] (SG)
DWB........... Daily Wireless Bulletin (IAA)
DWB........... Designers' Workbench (TEL)
DWB........... Development Workbook (SAUS)
DWB........... Direct Wafer Bonding (CIST)
DWB........... Disabled Widow [*or Widower*] Benefits [*Social Security Administration*] (OICC)
DWB........... Dismissed for Want of Bond [*Legal term*] (DLA)
DWB........... Documenter's Workbench [*AT & T*] [*Computer science*]
DWB........... Double with Bath [*Hotel room*]
DWB........... Dual Walking Beam
DWB........... Library, US Weather Bureau (SAUS)
DWB........... Soalala [*Madagascar*] [*Airport symbol*] (OAG)
DWBA......... Direct Wire Burglar Alarm
DWBA......... Direct-Wire Burglar Alarm (SAUS)
DWBA......... Distored Wave Born Approximation (SAUS)
DWBA......... Distorted-Wave Born Approximation (SAUS)
DWBA......... Distorted Wave-Borne Approximation
DWBC......... Deep Western Boundary Current [*Oceanography*]
DWBL......... Dismounted Warfighting Battle Laboratory (INF)
DWBM......... Office of Defense Waste Byproducts Management (SAUO)
DWBO......... District War Bond Office [*or Officer*] [*Navy*]
DW Buffer.... Data Word Buffer (SAUS)
DWC........... Damaged Weapons Control (DNAB)
DWC........... Data Word Cycle [*Computer science*] (VLIE)
DWC........... Dead Weight Capacity (SAUS)
DWC........... Deadweight Capacity
DWC........... Democratic Workers' Congress [*Ceylon*]
DWC........... Detroit, MI [*Location identifier*] [*FAA*] (FAAL)
DWC........... Digital Wireless Communications (SAUS)
DWC........... Discolored Wood Columns [*Plant pathology*]
DWC........... Dislocated Worker Center [*Job Training and Partnership Act*] (OICC)
DWC........... Display and Weapon Control (DNAB)
DWC........... Dissolved Water Color [*Environmental chemistry*]
DWC........... Douglas World Cruiser (ACAE)
DWC........... dry water content (SAUS)
DWC........... Morgan Stanley Group, Inc. [*AMEX symbol*] (SAG)
DWC4......... Deployable WWMCCS Command, Control and Communications Capability (SAUO)
DWCA......... Decorative Window Coverings Association (NTPA)
DWCAX........ Mgn. Stanley D. Witter MSMS California [*Mutual fund ticker symbol*] (SG)
DWCC......... Deadweight Cargo Capacity [*Shipping*]
DWCC......... Differential White Cell Count [*Medicine*] (MELL)
DWCD......... Drinking Water Criteria Document [*Environmental Protection Agency*] (AEPA)
DWCH......... Datawatch Corp. [*NASDAQ symbol*] (SAG)
DWCM......... Dried Weight of Cell Mass (OA)
DWCOORD(N)... Director of Weapons Coordination (Naval) [*British*]
DWCP......... Detroit-Wayne County Port (SAUS)
DWCR......... Double Whole-Cell Recording [*Neurophysiology*]
DWCS......... Defueling Water Cleanup System (GAAI)
DWCT......... Deadweight Cargo Tons (SAUS)
DWCX......... David Witherspoon [*Private rail car owner code*]
DWD........... Daily Wafer Demand (TIMI)
DWD........... Data Word (SAUS)
DWD........... Dead Wind (SAUS)
DWD........... Dean Witter, Discover & Co. [*NYSE symbol*] (SPSG)
DWD........... Deepest Working Depth
DWD........... Deep Water Dump
dwd............ died while drinking (SAUS)
DWD........... Died with Disease [*Medicine*]
DWD........... Directorate of Weapons Development (SAUO)
DWD........... Director of Wreck Dispersal Department (SAUO)
DWD........... Director of Wreck Disposal
DWD........... Driving While Drugged
DWD........... Driving While Drunk [*Police term*]
DWD........... Drum Write Drive (SAUS)
DWD........... Drum Write Driver [*Computer science*]
DWD........... Dumbwaiter Door
DWD........... Dying With Dignity (SAUO)
DWD........... Dynamic Weather Display
DWDCTR...... Drum Word Counter (SAUS)
DWDI.......... Draw Die [*Tool*] (AAG)
DWDisc........ Dean Witter Discover & Co. [*Associated Press*] (SAG)
DWDL......... Diffuse Well-Differentiated Lymphocytic [*Oncology*]
DWDL......... Diffuse, Well-Differentiated, Lymphoma [*Oncology*] (DAVI)
DWDL......... Donald W. Douglas Laboratory [*McDonnell Douglas Corp.*]
DWDLL........ Diffuse, Well-Differentiated, Lymphocytic Lymphoma [*Oncology*] (DAVI)
DWDM......... Dense Wave Division Multiplexing [*Lucent*]
DWDM......... Dense Wavelength Division Multiplexer
DWDM......... Dense Wavelength Division Multiplexer (or Multiplexing) (SAUS)
DWDS......... Defense Waste Disposal Safety (SAUS)
DWDsc......... Dean Witter Discover & Co. [*Associated Press*] (SAG)
DWE........... Decreased Wage Earner [*Social Security Administration*] (DHP)
DWE........... Delivery with Equipment (MCD)
DWE........... distance measuring equipment (SAUS)
DWE........... Divco-Wayne Electronics (SAUO)
DWE........... Division of Wildlife and Ecology (SAUO)
DWE........... Doppler Wind Experiment (ACAE)
DWE........... Tulsa, OK [*Location identifier*] [*FAA*] (FAAL)
DWEC......... District War Executive Committee (SAUO)
DWED......... Department of Western Economic Diversification (SAUS)
DWED......... Dry Well Equipment Drain (SAUS)
DWED......... Drywell Equipment Drain (IEEE)
DWEDS....... Drywell Equipment Drain Sump (NRCH)
DWEL......... Discrete Wire Equivalence List (VLIE)
DWEL......... Drinking Water Equivalent Level [*Environmental Protection Agency*]
DWEL......... Dwelling (MSA)
Dwell.......... Dwelling (DIAR)
DWEM......... Dead White European Males [*Derogatory appellation for Western culture*]
DWEP......... Domestic Workers and Employers Project (SAUO)
DWER......... Directorate of Weapons and Engineering Research [*Canada*]
DWES......... Director of Weapons Equipment, Surface [*British military*] (DMA)
DWEST....... Deep Water Environmental Survival Training [*Navy*]
DWET......... Directorate of Weapons Effect Tests (MCD)
DWEU......... Director of Weapons Equipment, Underwater [*British military*] (DMA)
DWF........... Daily Water Flow (IAA)
DWF........... Data Word Format (SAUS)
DWF........... Deep Water Fording Kit [*Army*]
DWF........... Delta Waterfowl Foundation (NTPA)
DWF........... Directional Warhead Fuze
DWF........... Disk Work File (SAUS)
DWF........... Divorced White Female [*Classified advertising*]
DWF........... Dollywood Foundation (EA)
DWF........... Drawing Web Format [*Computer science*] (PCM)
DWF........... Dry Weather Flow (IAA)
DWF........... Duty Weather Forecaster (SAA)
Dwf............ Dwarf [*Horticulture*]
DWFD......... Dry Well Floor Drain (SAUS)
DWFD......... Drywell Floor Drain (IEEE)
DWFDS....... Drywell Floor Drain Sump (NRCH)
DWFG......... Digital Waveform Generator (SEWL)
DWFK......... Deep Water Fording Kit (SAUS)
DWFLX........ Mgn. Stanley D. Witter MSMS Florida [*Mutual fund ticker symbol*] (SG)
DWFM......... Draw Form [*Tool*] (AAG)
DWG........... Deadweight Gauge
DWG........... Democracy Working Group (SAUO)
DWG........... Designated Work Group
DWG........... Diamond Walnut Growers (EA)
DWG........... Digital Waveform Generator (MCD)
DWG........... Discipline Working Group (SAUS)
DWG........... Domain Work Group (AAEL)
DWG........... Drawing (AFM)
dwg............ Drawing (VRA)
DWG........... Dwelling (ADA)
DWG........... DWG Cigar Corp. (SAUO)
dwg-ho........ dwelling house (SAUS)
DWGI.......... Dean Witter Government Income Trust [*Associated Press*] (SAG)
DWGNRA..... Delaware Water Gap National Recreation Area (COE)
DWH........... Data Ware Housing (SAUS)
DWH........... Diploma in Women's Health
DWH........... DISA Western Hemisphere (SAUS)
DWh........... Driving Wheel (SAUS)
DWH........... Houston, TX [*Location identifier*] [*FAA*] (FAAL)
DWH........... Washington Hall Junior College, Washington, DC [*Library symbol*] [*Library of Congress*] (LCLS)
DWHBP....... Displaced Workers Health Benefits Program (SAUS)
DWHC......... Washington Hospital Center, Medical Library, Washington, DC [*Library symbol*] [*Library of Congress*] (LCLS)
DWHO......... Washington Hospital Center, Medical Library, Washington, DC [*Library symbol*] [*Library of Congress*] (LCLS)
DWHS......... De Witt Clinton High School (SAUO)
DWI........... Danish West Indies
DWI........... Data Word In (MCD)
DWI........... Descriptive Word Index (SAUS)
DWI........... Descriptor Word Index
DWI........... Died without Issue (DLA)
DWI........... Differential Wave Impedance (DEN)
DWI........... Directional Wireless Installation [*British military*] (DMA)
DWI........... Director of Office and War Information (SAUO)
DWI........... Disaster Welfare Information (SAUO)
DWI........... Disaster Welfare Inquiry (SAUO)
DWI........... Divco-Wayne Industries (SAUO)
DWI........... Drawn and Wall Ironed [*Metal printing*] (DGA)
DWI........... Driving While Impaired (SAUS)
DWI........... Driving While Intoxicated [*Legal term*]
DWI........... Drop Weight Index (SAUS)
DWI........... Durable Woods Institute (EA)
DWI........... Durham Wheat Institute (SAUS)
DWI........... Durum Wheat Institute [*Later, MNF*] (EA)
DWI........... Dutch West Indies
DWI........... Washington International College, Washington, DC [*Library symbol*] [*Library of Congress*] (LCLS)
DWIA......... Distorted Wave Impulse Approximation
DWIC......... Disaster Welfare Inquiry Center [*Federal disaster planning*]
DWIC......... DWI Corp. [*NASDAQ symbol*] (COMM)
DWICA........ Deep Water Isotopic Current Analyzer [*TVA*] (MSC)
Dwig........... Dwiggins (SAUS)
DWIGH........ Dwight, IL [*American Association of Railroads railroad junction routing code*]

Dwight .... Dwight's Charity Cases [*England*] [*A publication*] (DLA)
DWIM .... Division for Women in Medicine [*Defunct*] (EA)
DWIM .... Do What I Mean [*Also, DTRT*] [*In data processing context, translates as "Guess at the meaning of poorly worded instructions"*]
DWIM Analyzer... Do-What-I-Mean Analyzer (SAUS)
DWIM Anmalyzer... Do-What-I-Mean Analyzer (SAUS)
DWIMC .... Do What I Mean, Correctly [*Computer hacker terminology*] (NHD)
DWIMNWIS... Do What I Mean, Not What I Say (SAUS)
DWIMNWIS... Do What I Meant, Not What I Said
DWIMS .... Defense Waste Information Management System (SAUS)
DWIN .... Doctor Who Information Network [*Canada*] (EAIO)
DWIND .... Do What I Need Done [*Also, DWIM*] [*In data processing context, translates as "Guess at the meaning of poorly worded instructions"*] (PCM)
D-WIP .... Defense-Wide Intelligence Plan [*DoD*]
DWIPS .... Digital Weather Processing System (SAUS)
DWIS .... Do What I Say [*Computer science*]
DWISNWID... Do what I say not what I do (SAUS)
DWK .... German Company for Republic Reprocessing Nuclear Fuel Materials (SAUS)
D Wks .... Director of Works (SAUS)
DWL .... Data Word Length (SAUS)
DWL .... Depressed Water Leg [*Nuclear energy*] (NRCH)
dwl .... derived working level (SAUS)
DWL .... Derived Working Limit (NUCP)
DWL .... Designed Water Line [*Technical drawings*]
DWL .... Designed Waterline Length [*Boating*]
D W L .... design water line (SAUS)
DWL .... Desired Work Load
DWL .... Detergent Worker's Lung [*Medicine*] (MELL)
DWL .... DeWolfe Cos. [*AMEX symbol*] (TTSB)
DWL .... [*The*] DeWolfe Cos., Inc. [*AMEX symbol*] (SAG)
DWL .... Displacement Water Line
DWL .... displacement waterline (SAUS)
DWL .... Distillers and Winegrowers Limited (SAUO)
DWL .... Dominant Wavelength
DWL .... Doppler Wind LIDAR (SAUS)
DWL .... Dowel
DWL .... Downwind Localizer (SAUS)
DWL .... Drywell (NRCH)
dwl .... Dwelling (VRA)
DWLC .... Deadweight Loading Capacity (SAUS)
DWLFBD .... Double-Wall Fiberboard
DWLG .... Dwelling (AABC)
DWLLNG .... Dwelling
DWLTX .... Mgn.Stanley D. Witter Limited Municipal [*Mutual fund ticker symbol*] (SG)
DWM .... Dangerous Waste Material (SAUS)
DWM .... Dead White Male
DWM .... Degrees of Word Meaning [*Test*] (TMMY)
DWM .... Deputy Worshipful Master [*Freemasonry*] (ROG)
DWM .... Destination Warning Marker
DWM .... Destination Word Marker (CMD)
DWM .... Deutsche Waffen- und Munitionsfabriken [*German Weapons and Munitions Factory*] [*World War II*]
DWM .... Directory of Women's Media [*A publication*]
DWM .... Diskless Workstation Management [*Computer science*] (VERA)
DWM .... Divine Word Missionaries [*See also SVD*] [*Italy*] (EAIO)
DWM .... Divorced White Male [*Classified advertising*]
DWM .... Dogwood [*Missouri*] [*Seismograph station code, US Geological Survey*] (SEIS)
DWMC .... Dedicated Wooden Money Collectors (EA)
DWMD .... Defense Waste Management Division (SAUS)
DWMI .... Diamond Wheel Manufacturers Institute (EA)
Dw Mil .... Dwyer on the Militia Laws [*A publication*] (DLA)
DWML .... Due West Motor Line [*AAR code*]
DWMP .... Defense Waste Management Plan (GAAI)
DWMS .... Demineralized Water Makeup System [*Nuclear energy*] (NRCH)
DWMSTD .... Defense Work Measurement Standard Time Date (SAUO)
DWMSTDP... Defense Work Measurement Standard Time Data Program [*Air Force*] (AFM)
DWMT .... Discrete Wavelet Multi Tone (SAUS)
DWMT .... Discrete Wavelet Multi-Tone (VLIE)
DWMT .... Division of Waste Management and Transportation [*Energy Research and Development Administration*]
DWN .... County Down (SAUS)
DWN .... Darwin, MN [*Location identifier*] [*FAA*] (FAAL)
DWN .... Dawn Air, Inc. [*ICAO designator*] (FAAC)
DWN .... Down (KSC)
DWN .... Downdraft (DA)
DWN .... Drawn (MSA)
DWNAV(N)... Director of Weapons Navigation (Naval) [*British*]
DWNC .... Disabled Women's Network of Canada (FOTI)
DWNDFTS... Downdrafts [*NWS*] (FAAC)
DWNJX .... Mgn. Stanley D. Witter MSMS New Jersey [*Mutual fund ticker symbol*] (SG)
dwnstrs .... Downstairs (ADWA)
DWNTN .... Downtown
DWO .... Delta Wing Orbiter (KSC)
DWO .... Department Work Order (MCD)
DWO .... Development Work Order
DWO .... Directorate of War Organization [*RAF*] [*British*]
DWO .... Direct Writing Oscillograph
DWOHX .... Mgn. Stanley D. Witter MSMS Ohio [*Mutual fund ticker symbol*] (SG)
DWOP .... Dismissed without Prejudice [*Legal shorthand*] (LWAP)
DWord .... Double Word
DWP .... Daisy Wheel Printer (VLIE)
DWP .... Dalbandin [*Pakistan*] [*Airport symbol*] (AD)
DWP .... Decommissioning Work Plan (SAUS)
DWP .... Deep Water Port [*Marine science*] (MSC)
DWP .... Deepwater Port (SAUS)
DWP .... Defence White Paper (SAUS)
DWP .... Defense Waste Programs (SAUS)
DWP .... Democratic Workers Party (SAUO)
DWP .... Department of Water and Power (COE)
DWP .... Design with a Purpose [*Nonprofit corporation*]
DWP .... Digital Waveform Pattern (SAUS)
DWP .... Director of Weapons Production [*British military*] (DMA)
DWP .... Dismissed for Want of Prosecution [*Legal term*] (DLA)
DWP .... Dismissed with Prejudice [*Legal shorthand*] (LWAP)
DWP .... Displaced Worker Program (OICC)
DWP .... District of Columbia Public Library, Washington, DC [*OCLC symbol*] (OCLC)
DWP .... Division of Water Planning (SAUO)
DWP .... Duluth, Winnipeg & Pacific Railway [*AAR code*]
dwp .... dyna whirlpool (SAUS)
DWP .... Dyna Whirlpool Process (SAUS)
DWP .... Public Library of the District of Columbia, Martin Luther King Memorial Library,Washington, DC [*Library symbol*] [*Library of Congress*] (LCLS)
DWP .... Webb [*Del E.*] Properties Corp. (MHDW)
DWPA .... Deep Water Ports Act [*1974*] (MSC)
DWPAX .... Mgn. Stanley D. Witter MSMS Pennsylvania [*Mutual fund ticker symbol*] (SG)
DWPC .... Division of Water Pollution Control (SAUS)
DWPF .... Defense Waste Processing Facility [*Department of Energy*]
DWPH .... Dual wall percussion hammer (SAUS)
DWPL .... Drinking Water Priority List [*1988*] (LDOE)
DWP(N) .... Director of Weapons Production (Naval) [*British*]
DWPNT .... Dew Point [*NWS*] (FAAC)
dwpnt .... dewpoint (SAUS)
DWPO .... District War Plans Officer
DW Point ..... Double Wire Point (SAUS)
DWPROD(N)... Director of Weapons Production (Naval) [*British*]
DWPS .... Deployable War Planning System (SAUO)
Dw Pt .... Dew Point (SAUS)
DWQGV .... Drinking Water Quality Guideline Value [*World Health Organization*]
DWQRC .... Drinking Water Quality Research Center [*Florida International University*]
DWR .... Data Word Register (SAUS)
DWR .... Data Write Register (SAUS)
DWR .... Development Work Request
DWR .... Digital Wired Recorder
DWR .... Dirty Word Remover [*Graffiti-removing chemical*]
DWR .... Display Writer (VLIE)
DWR .... Divided Winding Rotor (SAUS)
DWR .... Divided Winding-Rotor
DWR .... Divisional Work Request (AAG)
DWR .... Division of Water Resources (SAUO)
DWR .... Division of Wildlife Resources (SAUO)
DWR .... Doppler Weather Radar (ADWA)
DWR .... Drawer (MSA)
DWR .... Dry Weight Rank Method (SAUS)
DWR .... Dual Wavelength Ratio (ARMP)
DWR .... Duke of Wellington's Regiment [*Military unit*] [*British*]
DWR .... Du-Well Resources Ltd. [*Vancouver Stock Exchange symbol*]
DWR .... United States Walter Reed Army Medical Center, Post/Patient Library, Washington,DC [*Library symbol*] [*Library of Congress*] (LCLS)
DWRA .... Defense Western Regional Audit Office [*DoD*]
DWRA .... Dry Wrinkle Recovery Angle [*Textile technology*]
DWRAF .... Director of the Women's Royal Air Force [*British military*] (DMA)
DWRC .... Denver Wildlife Research Center [*Colorado*] [*Department of Agriculture*] (GRD)
DWRC .... Descend Well to Right of Course [*Aviation*] (FAAC)
DWRC .... Descent Well to Right Course (SAUS)
DWRDS .... Director, Weapons Research and Development, Surface [*British military*] (DMA)
DWRDU .... Director, Weapons Research and Development, Underwater [*British military*] (DMA)
DWRGLU ..... Dock, Wharf, Riverside, and General Labourers' Union [*British*]
DWR-I .... United States Walter Reed Army Medical Center, Research Institute, Washington, DC [*Library symbol*] [*Library of Congress*] (LCLS)
DWRI .... Walter Reed Army Institute of Research, Washington, DC [*Library symbol*] [*Library of Congress*] (LCLS)
DWRIA .... died of wounds received in action (SAUS)
DWRM .... Division of Water Resources (SAUO)
DWR-M .... United States Walter Reed Army Medical Center, Medical Library, Washington, DC [*Library symbol*] [*Library of Congress*] (LCLS)
DWRNS .... Department of the Director, Women's Royal Naval Service [*British*]
DWRP .... Dee Weather Radar Project (SAUS)
DWRP .... Director of Weapons Resources and Programmes [*British military*] (DMA)
DWR-P .... Walter Reed Army Medical Biomechanical Research Center, Forest Glen, MD [*Library symbol*] [*Library of Congress*] (LCLS)
DWRTO .... Defense Western Regional Telecommunications Office [*DoD*]
DWRX .... DataWorks Corp. [*NASDAQ symbol*] (SAG)
DWS .... Damped Working Set (SAUS)
DWS .... Dandy-Walker Syndrome [*Medicine*] (MELL)
DWS .... Deck Working Space

DWS .... Deep Water Sediments (SAUS)
DWS .... Defense Weapons System
DWS .... Demineralized Water System (SAUS)
DWS .... Department of Water Supply (SAUS)
DWS .... Depot Working Standards
DWS .... Design Wind Speed (SAUS)
DWS .... Design Work Study
DWS .... Detailed Work Statement (MCD)
DWS .... Detroit Waldhorn Society (EA)
DWS .... Development Work Statement (NRCH)
DWS .... Diffusing Wave Spectroscopy
DWS .... Direct Wet Seedbed (SAUO)
DWS .... Disaster Warning Satellite [*NASA*] (NASA)
DWS .... Disaster Warning System [*National Weather Service*]
DWS .... Dispenser Weapon System (SAUS)
DWS .... Display Writer System (VLIE)
DWS .... Distributed Wargaming System [*Military*] (SEWL)
DWS .... Doppler Wind Sensor (EOSA)
DWS .... Doppler Wind Sounder (SAUS)
DWS .... Dorcas Welfare Society [*Later, Community Services*] (EA)
DWS .... Double Whammy Syndrome [*Medicine*] (MELL)
DWS .... Double White Silk (SAUS)
DWS .... Double White Silk Covered [*Wire insulation*]
DWS .... Double Wound Silk (SAUS)
DWS .... Drinking Water Standard
DWS .... Drop Wood Siding [*Technical drawings*]
DWS .... Dry Workshop [*NASA*] (KSC)
DWS .... Dynamic Work Storage (SAUS)
DWS .... Orlando, FL [*Location identifier*] [*FAA*] (FAAL)
DWS .... Washington Star, Washington, DC [*Library symbol*] [*Library of Congress*] (LCLS)
DWSA .... Deterministic Writing Stack Acceptor (SAUS)
DWSA .... Director of Weapon Systems Analysis [*Army*] (AABC)
DWSBX .... Mgn. Stanley D. Witter Short Term Bond Fund [*Mutual fund ticker symbol*] (SG)
DWSC .... Director of Welfare and Service Conditions [*British military*] (DMA)
DWSEE .... DOE/Westinghouse School for Environmental Excellence (SAUS)
DWSF .... Dry Well Storage Facility (ABAC)
DWSGAE .... Department of Water Supply, Gas and Electricity (SAUS)
DWSHX .... Mgn. Stanley D. Witter Short-Term U.S. Treas. [*Mutual fund ticker symbol*] (SG)
DWSMC .... Defense Weapons System Management Center
DWSN .... Dandy-Walker Syndrome Network (ADWA)
DWSN .... Dawson Geophysical [*NASDAQ symbol*] (TTSB)
DWSN .... Dawson Geophysical Co. [*NASDAQ symbol*] (NQ)
DWSO .... Drainage and Water Supply Officer [*Ministry of Agriculture, Fisheries, and Food*] [*British*]
DWSO .... Drainange and Water Supply Officer (SAUO)
DWSP(N) .... Director of Weapons Surface Projects (Naval) [*British*]
DWSR .... Direct Wet Seeded Rice (SAUO)
DWSR .... Dodge Wayfarer Sportabout Registry [*Defunct*] (EA)
DWSRF .... Drinking Water State Revolving Fund (SAUS)
DWSS .... Data Highway Service System (SAUS)
DWSS .... Double Wiper Slide Switch (SAUS)
DWSS .... Double Wipe Slide Switch
DWST .... Demineralized Water Storage Tank [*Nuclear energy*] (NRCH)
Dw Stat .... Dwarris on Statutes [*A publication*] (DLA)
DW Statistic .... Durbin-Watson Statistic (SAUS)
DWStK .... Deutsche Waffen Stillstandkommission [*German Armistice Commission, in France*] [*World War II*]
DWSUCy .... Data Word Set-Up Cycle (SAUS)
DWT .... Dahl-Wade-Till Valve [*Medicine*]
DWT .... Deadweight
DWT .... Deadweight Tester
DWT .... Deadweight Tonnage (ADWA)
Dwt .... Deadweight tonnes (SAUS)
dwt .... Deadweight Tons [*Industrial hygiene term*] (OHS)
DWT .... Deadweight Tons [*Shipping*]
DWT .... Deck Watch Time [*Navigation*]
DWT .... Demineralized Water Tank (SAUS)
DWT .... Denarius Weight [*Pennyweight*] [*Latin*]
DWT .... Dichotic Word Test (DB)
DWT .... Directory Watch (SAUS)
DWT .... Discrete Walsh Transform (SAUS)
DWT .... Discrete Wavelet Transformation (DOM)
DWT .... Division Wing Team [*Air Force*] (MUSM)
DWT .... Dog Wags Tail [*Airspace effects*]
DWT .... Double-Weight [*Paper*]
dwt .... double weight (SAUS)
DWT .... Drop-Weight Test [*Nuclear energy*] (NRCH)
DWT .... Duck Waddle Test (MELL)
dwt .... Pennyweight [*Measurement*] (DAVI)
DWT .... Wesley Theological Seminary, Washington, DC [*Library symbol*] [*Library of Congress*] [*OCLC symbol*] (LCLS)
DWTC .... Cargo Deadweight (SAUS)
DWTC .... Federale Diensten voor Wetenschappelijke, Technische en Culturele aangelegenheden (SAUO)
DWTF .... Daily and Weekly till Forbidden [*Advertising*]
DWTF .... Decontamination and Waste Treatment Facility
DWTI .... Dataware Technologies [*NASDAQ symbol*] (TTSB)
DWTI .... Dataware Technologies, Inc. [*NASDAQ symbol*] (SAG)
dw tk .... drinking water tank (SAUS)
DWTM .... Defense Waste Transportation Management (SAUS)
DWTM .... Office of Defense Waste and Transportation Management [*Washington, DC*] [*Department of Energy*] (GRD)
DWTMC .... Domestic Water Tank Manufacturers Council [*Defunct*]
DWTP .... Domestic Wastewater Treatment Plant (BCP)
DWTR .... Descend Well to Right [*Aviation*] (FAAC)
DWTR .... Descent Well to Right (SAUS)
DWTrfCy .... Data Word Transfer Cycle (SAUS)
DWTS .... Dangerous Waste Tracking System (SAUS)
DWTS .... Digital Wideband Transmission System (MCD)
DWTT .... Decontamination Waste Treatment Tank (SAUS)
DWTT .... Drop-Weight Tear Test
DWU .... Dakota Wesleyan University [*South Dakota*]
DWU .... Distillery, Wine, and Allied Workers Union (BARN)
DWUC .... Democratic Women's Union of Canada
DWUI .... Driving While under the Influence (OICC)
dwuld .... dewooled (SAUS)
DWUWA .... Disabled Workers' Union of Western Australia
DWV .... Data With Voice (SAUS)
DWV .... Dielectric Withstand Voltage (MCD)
DWV .... Drain, Waste, and Vent [*System*]
DWV .... Drain, Waste and Ventilation System (SAUS)
DWV .... Drain, Waste and Vent Pipe (SAUS)
DWVP-A .... Directorate of Weapons and Vehicle Procurement - Army
DWVP-A-VEH .... Directorate of Weapons and Vehicle Procurement - Army - Vehicles
DWV Pipe .... Drain, Waste, and Vent Pipe (SAUS)
DWW .... Davis Water & Waste [*NYSE symbol*] (TTSB)
DWW .... Davis Water & Waste Industries, Inc. [*NYSE symbol*] (SPSG)
DWW .... Direct Write-on-Wafer (SAUS)
DWW .... Distillery, Wine, and Allied Workers International Union
dww .... downward (SAUS)
DWW .... Wilmington Institute Free Library and the New Castle County Free Library, Wilmington, DE [*OGLC symbol*] (OCLC)
DWW .... Woodrow Wilson International Center for Scholars, Washington, DC [*Library symbol*] [*Library of Congress*] (LCLS)
DWW .... Wright International Express, Inc. [*ICAO designator*] (FAAC)
DWWBFC .... Don Winters and the Winters Brothers Fan Club [*Defunct*] (EA)
DWWSSN .... Digital World-Wide Standardised Seismograph Network [*Australia*]
DWY .... Gadsden, AL [*Location identifier*] [*FAA*] (FAAL)
DwyerGp .... Dwyer Group, Inc. [*Associated Press*] (SAG)
D Wyo .... United States District Court for the District of Wyoming (DLA)
DWYR .... Dwyer Group [*NASDAQ symbol*] (TTSB)
DWYR .... Dwyer Group, Inc. [*NASDAQ symbol*] (SAG)
DWYSYWD .... Do What You Say You Will Do
DX .... Aerotaxi (SAUS)
DX .... Danair [*ICAO designator*] (AD)
DX .... Data Exchange (VLIE)
DX .... Data Extraction (CAAL)
DX .... Data Transfer [*Computer science*]
DX .... Deep Donor in III-V Compounds (AAEL)
DX .... Defect Unknown Complex (SAUS)
dx .... Defense Exhibit (SAUS)
DX .... De Luxe (SAUS)
DX .... Deluxe White (MIST)
DX .... Destroyer Experimental (MCD)
DX .... Dextran (MAE)
dx .... Diagnosis (ADWA)
DX .... Diagnosis
Dx .... Diagnosis
DX .... Diagnosis Code
DX .... Differential Crosstalk (SAUS)
dx .... differential of reactance (SAUS)
dx .... differential of x (SAUS)
Dx .... Diffusing Capacity of the Lung Expressed as Volume [*Medicine*] (DAVI)
DX .... Digital Index [*Photography*]
DX .... Direct Current (VLIE)
DX .... Direct Current Switching (SAUS)
DX .... Direct Exchange [*Army*] (AABC)
DX .... Direct Expansion
DX .... Direct Expansion Coil (SAUS)
DX .... Directory exchange (SAUS)
DX .... direct transmission (SAUS)
DX .... Distance [*Radio term*] (EA)
DX .... Distance long (SAUS)
DX .... distance radio reception or transmission (SAUS)
DX .... Distance Reception (SAUS)
dx .... Distant (SAUS)
DX .... Distant Radio Reception (AEBE)
DX .... Distant Reception (SAUS)
DX .... Distant Transmission (SAUS)
DX .... Document Transfer (SAUS)
DX .... Document Transmission (SAUS)
DX .... Double Cash Ruled [*Stationery*]
DX .... Double Exposure [*Photography*] (GOBB)
DX .... Duplex [*Signaling*] [*Telecommunications*] (MSA)
DX .... Duplex Repeater (SAUS)
DX .... Duplex Signaling [*Communications term*] (DCT)
DX .... Duplex signalling (SAUS)
DX .... Dynex Capital [*NYSE symbol*] (SG)
DX .... Long Distance [*Amateur radio shorthand*] (WDAA)
DX .... Daylight Exposure [*Photography*] (ODA)
DXA .... Deferred Cancellation Area [*Travel industry*] (TVEL)
DXA .... Direct Exchange Activity (AABC)
DXA .... Directory Exchange Agent [*Computer science*] (VERA)
DXA .... Document Exchange Architecture [*Data General*] (NITA)

DXA .... Dual Energy X-Ray Absorptiometry [*Painless bone mass test*] [*Medicine*]
DXAK .... Atakpame/Akpaka [*Togo*] [*ICAO location identifier*] (ICLI)
DXAM .... Distributed Indexed Access Method [*IBM Corp*] (CIST)
DXB .... Drawing Exchange Binary (SAUS)
dxb............ Drawing Interchange Binary [*Computer science*] (VLIE)
DXB .... Dubai [*Trucial Oman*] [*Airport symbol*] (AD)
DXB .... Dubai [*United Arab Emirates*] [*Airport symbol*] (OAG)
DXBS .... Bassari [*Togo*] [*ICAO location identifier*] (ICLI)
DXC .... Data Exchange Control
DXC .... Digital Cross-Connect (SAUS)
DXC .... Digital Cross-Connect System (SAUS)
DXC .... Digital/Direct Cross-Connect (VLIE)
DXC .... Penn-Dixie Cement (SAUS)
DXC .... Penn-Dixie Cement Corp. (SAUO)
DXCC .... DX Century Club (SAUO)
DX Coil........ Direct Expansion Coil (SAUS)
DXCP .... Dynex Capital, Inc. [*NASDAQ symbol*] (NASQ)
Dxd .... Discontinued [*Medicine*] (DAVI)
DXD .... Discontinued [*Medicine*] (EDAA)
dxd............ Discontinued [*Medicine*] (EDAA)
DXD .... Dixie [*Australia*] [*Airport symbol*] [*Obsolete*] (OAG)
DXD .... Drexore Developments, Inc. [*Vancouver Stock Exchange symbol*]
dxda-mc ...... ductile metals experimental diamond abrasive-metal clad (SAUS)
DXDP .... Dapango [*Togo*] [*ICAO location identifier*] (ICLI)
dXDP .... Deoxyxanthosine Diphosphate [*Biochemistry*]
DX/DXG........ ASW [*Antisubmarine Warfare*], Gun, and Missile Escort Ship [*Navy symbol*]
DXE............ Data Transmitting Equipment (MSA)
DXE............ Dexter, MO [*Location identifier*] [*FAA*] (FAAL)
DXE............ Dixylylethane [*Organic chemistry*]
DXF............ Autocads Digital Exchange Format (SAUS)
DXF............ Data/Drawing Exchange Format (SAUS)
DXF............ Data Exchange File [*Computer science*]
DXF............ Data Exchange Format (AAEL)
DXF............ Data Transfer Facility (SAUS)
DXF............ Digital Exchange Format (SAUS)
DXF............ Drawing Exchange File [*Computer science*] (PCM)
DXF............ Drawing Exchange Format (SAUS)
DXF............ Drawing Interchange File (ADWA)
DXF............ Drawing Interchange Format
DXF file .... Document Exchange Format File (CDE)
DXG .... Dyonix Greentree Technologies, Inc. [*Vancouver Stock Exchange symbol*]
DXG .... Guided Missile Destroyer [*Navy symbol*]
DXGN............ Guided Missile Destroyer, Nuclear-Propulsion [*Navy symbol*]
DXH .... Dexleigh Corp. [*Toronto Stock Exchange symbol*]
DXHO............ Hahotoe [*Togo*] [*ICAO location identifier*] (ICLI)
DXI............ Data Exchange Interface [*Computer science*]
DXI............ Direct Exchange Item [*Army*] (AABC)
DXKP .... Anie/Kolokope [*Togo*] [*ICAO location identifier*] (ICLI)
DXL............ Dorset Exploration Ltd. [*Toronto Stock Exchange symbol*]
DXM............ Dexamethasone [*Also, D, DEX*] [*Antineoplastic drug*]
dxm .... dexanmethasone (SAUS)
DXM............ Dextromethorphan (SAUS)
DXMG .... Sansanne-Mango [*Togo*] [*ICAO location identifier*] (ICLI)
dXMP............ Deoxyxanthosine Monophosphate [*Biochemistry*]
DXMZ............ DX Marketing & Refining [*Federal Railroad Administration identification code*]
DXNG............ Niamtougou [*Togo*] [*ICAO location identifier*] (ICLI)
DXO .... Disco S.A. ADS [*NYSE symbol*] (TTSB)
DXP .... Dallas Express Airlines, Inc. [*FAA designator*] (FAAC)
DXP .... Detroit, MI [*Location identifier*] [*FAA*] (FAAL)
DXP .... Dynamic Extended Pathing (SAUS)
DXPE .... DXP Enterprises, Inc. [*NASDAQ symbol*] (NASQ)
DXR .... Danbury [*Connecticut*] [*Airport symbol*] [*Obsolete*] (OAG)
DXR .... Daxor Corp. [*AMEX symbol*] (SPSG)
DXR .... Deep X-Ray
DXR .... Deex Resources Corp. [*Vancouver Stock Exchange symbol*]
DXR .... Doxorubicin [*Also, D, DOX*] [*Formerly, ADR, Adriamycin*] [*Antineoplastic drug*]
DXRA .... DXplorers Radio Association (SAUO)
DXRD .... Dynamic X-Ray Diffraction [*Physics*]
DXRL .... Deep X-Ray Lithography (SAUS)
DX/RSTS...... Document Transmission/Resources Time-Sharing (SAUS)
DX/RSTS...... Document Transmission/Resource Time Sharing (SAUS)
DXRT .... Deep X-Ray Therapy [*Medicine*] (EDAA)
DXS .... Data Exchange System [*Texas Instruments, Inc.*]
DXS .... Dextran Sulfate [*Organic chemistry*]
DXS .... Directory Exchange Server [*Computer science*] (VERA)
DXSK .... Sokode [*Togo*] [*ICAO location identifier*] (ICLI)
DXS/OS........ Data Exchange System/Operating System (NITA)
DXS/OS........ DXS Operating System (SAUS)
DXSST .... Data Exchange System Statement Translator [*Texas Instruments, Inc.*]
DXS-ST .... Data Exchange System-Statement Translator (SAUS)
DXS/ST .... DXS Statement Translator (SAUS)
DXS/TL .... Data Exchange System/Transaction Language (NITA)
DXS/TL .... DXS Transaction Language (SAUS)
DXT............ Dalton, MA [*Location identifier*] [*FAA*] (FAAL)
DXT............ Data Extract (SAUS)
DXT............ Data Extract Facility (SAUS)
DXT............ Deep X-Ray Therapy
DXT............ Dextrose [*Pharmacology*]
DXT............ Dhoxaton [*Greece*] [*Airport symbol*] (AD)
DXT............ Dixon Ticonderoga [*AMEX symbol*] (TTSB)
DXT............ Dixon Ticonderoga Co. [*AMEX symbol*] (SPSG)
DXTA .... Tabligbo [*Togo*] [*ICAO location identifier*] (ICLI)
dXTP............ Deoxyxanthosine Triphosphate [*Biochemistry*]
DXTZ............ Display Crosstell Zone (SAA)
DXU .... Drexel University, Philadelphia, PA [*OCLC symbol*] (OCLC)
DX-W .... Direct Exchange - Wholesale (MCD)
DXX .... Madison, MN [*Location identifier*] [*FAA*] (FAAL)
DXXX .... Lome/Tokoin [*Togo*] [*ICAO location identifier*] (ICLI)
DXY .... Derby [*England*] [*Airport symbol*] (AD)
D-XYL .... D-Xylose [*In urine*] [*Gastroenterology*] (DAVI)
DXYN .... Dixie Group [*NASDAQ symbol*]
DXYN .... Dixie Group, Inc. [*NASDAQ symbol*] (NASQ)
DXYN .... Dixie Yams [*NASDAQ symbol*] (TTSB)
DXYN .... Dixie Yarns, Inc. [*NASDAQ symbol*] (NQ)
DXZE............ Dixie River Railroad [*Federal Railroad Administration identification code*]
DY............ Alyemda Democratic Yemen [*ICAO designator*] (AD)
Dy............ Catholic Douay Version [*of the Bible*] [*1609*] (BJA)
DY............ Daf Yomi (BJA)
DY............ Dahomey (SAUO)
DY............ Daily (ROG)
DY............ Dairy Yield (OA)
DY............ Dandy [*Ship's rigging*] (ROG)
DY............ Day (MSA)
DY............ Deflection Yoke
DY............ Delinquent Year [*IRS*]
dy .... Delivery (ODBW)
DY............ Delivery
Dy............ Delivery (WDAA)
DY............ Democratic Yemen Airlines (ALYEMDA) [*People's Democratic Republic of Yemen*] [*ICAO designator*] (ICDA)
DY............ Demy [*Half*] [*Size of paper*] (ROG)
DY............ Dense Parenchyma [*Medicine*] (DMAA)
DY............ Density
Dy............ Dependency [*Psychology*]
DY............ Deputy
DY............ Deputy Director [*KSC Directorate*] (MCD)
DY............ Derbyshire Yeomanry [*British military*] (DMA)
DY............ Design Year [*DoD*]
DY............ De Young Memorial Museum (SAUO)
dy .... Died Young (GEAB)
dY .... differential of admittance (SAUS)
dy .... differential of y (SAUS)
DY............ Dockyard
dy .... dock yard (SAUS)
DY............ Dorset Yeomanry (SAUO)
Dy............ Douay Bible (SAUS)
DY............ Double Y [*Hepateiportico-Jejunostomy*] [*Medicine*] (EDAA)
DY............ Duty (AFM)
DY............ Dycom Industries [*NYSE symbol*] (TTSB)
DY............ Dycom Industries, Inc. [*NYSE symbol*] (SPSG)
Dy............ Dyer's English King's Bench Reports [*73 English Reprint*] [*A publication*] (DLA)
DY............ Dyke-Young [*Syndrome*] [*Medicine*] (DB)
DY............ Dylan (SAUS)
dy .... Dynamic (SAUS)
DY............ Dynamotor (SAUS)
DY............ Dynamotors [*JETDS nomenclature*] [*Military*] (CET)
dy .... Dyne (SHCU)
Dy............ Dyne [*Unit of force*] [*Also, D, dyn*] [*Preferred unit is N, Newton*]
DY............ Dynode (IAA)
dy .... dysplasia (SAUS)
Dy............ Dysprosium [*Chemical element*]
dy .... Dystrophia Muscularis [*Mouse*] [*Medicine*] (EDAA)
DY1............ Dyersburg [*Tennessee*] [*Seismograph station code, US Geological Survey*] [*Closed*] (SEIS)
DY2............ Lassiter [*Tennessee*] [*Seismograph station code, US Geological Survey*] [*Closed*] (SEIS)
DY3............ Tiptonville [*Tennessee*] [*Seismograph station code, US Geological Survey*] [*Closed*] (SEIS)
DY4............ Samburg [*Tennessee*] [*Seismograph station code, US Geological Survey*] [*Closed*] (SEIS)
DY5............ Lassiter Corners [*Tennessee*] [*Seismograph station code, US Geological Survey*] [*Closed*] (SEIS)
DYA .... Alyemda-Democratic Yemen Airlines [*ICAO designator*] (FAAC)
DYA .... Deflection Yoke Amplifier
DYA .... Department of Youth Authority (SAUS)
DYA .... Dependent Youth Activities (SAUO)
DYA .... Dynamics Corp. Amer [*NYSE symbol*] (TTSB)
DYA .... Dynamics Corp. of America [*NYSE symbol*] (SPSG)
DYA .... Dysart [*Australia*] [*Airport symbol*] (OAG)
DYAN .... Dyansen Corp. [*NASDAQ symbol*] (COMM)
DYANA............ Dynamic Analyzer
DYANA............ Dynamic Analyzer-programmer (SAUS)
DYANA............ Dynamic Interpretation of Natural Language (EURO)
DYANA............ Dynamics analyser programmer Computing (SAUS)
dyana............ dynamics analyzer (SAUS)
DYANA............ Dynamics Analyzer Programmer [*Computer program*] (NITA)
DYANA............ dynamics analyzer-programmer (SAUS)
dyb............ do your best (SAUS)
DYB .... Dynamic Braking
DYB .... Dynamic Breaking (SAUS)
DYC .... Dalmys (Canada) Ltd. [*Toronto Stock Exchange symbol*]
DYC .... Detroit Yacht Club (SAUS)

DYC .... Direct Yaw Control [*Automotive engineering*]
DYC .... Dominion Yeast Company (SAUO)
DYC .... Dycam, Inc. [*AMEX symbol*] (SAG)
Dycam .... Dycam, Inc. [*Associated Press*] (SAG)
Dyche & P Dict... Dyche and Pardon's Dictionary [*A publication*] (DLA)
DYCMOS .... Dynamic CMOS (SAUS)
DYCMOS .... Dynamic Complementary Metal Oxide Semiconductor (IAA)
DYCO .... Dycom Industries, Inc. [*NASDAQ symbol*] (COMM)
Dycom .... Dycom Industries, Inc. [*Associated Press*] (SAG)
DYCOMS .... Dynamics and Chemistry of Marine Stratocumulus (SAUS)
DYCON .... Dynamic Control
DYCONTR .... Duty Controller [*Air Force*]
DYCOP .... Dynamic Console for Operations Planners
DYCS .... Department of Children and Youth Services (SAUO)
DYD .... Dock Yard (SAUS)
DYD .... Dockyard
DYDAT .... Dynamic Data Allocator (DNAB)
DYDE .... Dynamic Debugger
dydff .... dyed and fully finished (SAUS)
DYE .... Dyeing (SAUS)
DYE .... Dynamic Air [*Netherlands*] [*ICAO designator*] (FAAC)
DYER .... Dyer, IN [*American Association of Railroads railroad junction routing code*]
Dyer .... Dyer's English King's Bench Reports [*73 English Reprint*] [*A publication*] (DLA)
Dyer (Eng) ... Dyer's English King's Bench Reports [*73 English Reprint*] [*A publication*] (DLA)
Dyer's .... Short for Dyer's Compendium [*3 volume listing of civil war regiments*] [*Civil War term*]
Dyersbg .... Dyersburg Corp. [*Associated Press*] (SAG)
DYF .... Damned Young Fools [*Officers under the age of thirty*] [*British naval slang*]
DYF .... Democratic Youth Front (SAUS)
DYF .... Drag Your Feet (DAVI)
DYFAMED .... Atmospheric Dynamics and Fluxes in the Mediterranean Sea (SAUS)
DYFS .... Division of Youth and Family Services (SAUS)
DYFUS .... Dynamic Fuze Simulator [*RADAR*]
DYG .... Discovery Gold Explorations Ltd. [*Vancouver Stock Exchange symbol*]
DYG .... Drying
DYG .... Dyeing (SAUS)
DYG .... Dying
DYGN .... Dynagen, Inc. [*NASDAQ symbol*] (SAG)
DYGNW .... DynaGen Inc. Wrrt [*NASDAQ symbol*] (TTSB)
DYH .... Double Yellow Headed Amazon [*Bird*]
DYHBIFC .... Don Youngblood and the Hoosier Bears International Fan Club [*Defunct*] (EA)
DYHM .... Dynamic Homes [*NASDAQ symbol*] (TTSB)
DYHM .... Dynamic Homes, Inc. [*NASDAQ symbol*] (SAG)
DYHR .... Dehydrator (MSA)
DYII .... Dynacq International, Inc. [*NASDAQ symbol*] (SAG)
DYIL .... Dynacq Intl. [*NASDAQ symbol*] (TTSB)
DYJHIW .... Dont you just hate it when (SAUS)
dykes .... diagonal wire cutters (SAUS)
DYL .... Doylestown, PA [*Location identifier*] [*FAA*] (FAAL)
DYLEX .... Damn Your Lame Excuses [*Facetious translation for the name of a Toronto-based specialty store chain*]
DYLG .... Democratic Youth League of Ghana (SAUS)
DYM .... Diamantina Lakes [*Queensland*] [*Airport symbol*] (AD)
DYMAC .... Dynamic material control (SAUS)
dymaxion .... dynamic maximum (SAUS)
Dym Death Dut... Dymond's Death Duties [*15th ed.*] [*1973*] [*A publication*] (DLA)
DYMM .... De Young Memorial Museum (SAUS)
DYMO .... Dynamotion/ATI [*NASDAQ symbol*] (TTSB)
DYMO .... Dynamotion ATI Corp. [*NASDAQ symbol*] (SAG)
DYMO .... Dynamotion/ATT [*NASDAQ symbol*] [*Formerly, Cybernetics Products*] (SG)
DYMOZ .... Dynamotion/ATI Wrrt'A' [*NASDAQ symbol*] (TTSB)
DYMP .... Dynamotion ATI Corp. [*NASDAQ symbol*] (SAG)
DYMTF .... DynaMotive Technologies [*NASDAQ symbol*] (TTSB)
DYMV .... Desmodium Yellow Mottle Virus [*Plant pathology*]
DYMX .... Dynamex, Inc. [*NASDAQ symbol*] (SAG)
DYMZ .... Dynamotion ATI Corp. [*NASDAQ symbol*] (SAG)
DYN .... Detectability of Yes-No
DYN .... Diarios y Noticias [*News agency*] [*Argentina*] (EY)
DYN .... Drives You Nuts [*Coined by Erma Bombeck*]
dyn .... Dynamic [*Medicine*] (EDAA)
DYN .... Dynamic
DYN .... Dynamic Systems Project (SAUO)
DYN .... Dynamic Ventures, Inc. [*ICAO designator*] (FAAC)
DYN .... Dynamiting [*FBI standardized term*]
DYN .... Dynamo (MSA)
DYN .... Dynamometer [*Engineering*] (DEN)
DYN .... Dynamotor (IAA)
Dyn .... Dynasty (BJA)
DYN .... Dynasty Resources, Inc. [*Vancouver Stock Exchange symbol*]
DYN .... DynCorp Tri-Cities Services, Inc. (SAUO)
dyn .... Dyne [*Unit of force*] [*Also, D*] [*Preferred unit is N, Newton*] (DEN)
DYN .... Dynegy, Inc. [*NYSE symbol*] [*Formerly, NGC Corp.*]
DYNA .... Dynaflow [*Automotive engineering*]
DYNA .... Dynamic Analyzer (MCD)
DYNA .... Dynamic Analyzer-programmer (SAUS)
DYNA .... Dynamics Analyzer programmer (SAUS)
dyna .... dynamite (SAUS)
Dyna .... Dynamotion ATI Corp. [*Associated Press*] (SAG)
Dynacq .... Dynacq International, Inc. [*Associated Press*] (SAG)
Dynag .... Dynagen, Inc. [*Associated Press*] (SAG)
Dynagn .... Dynagen, Inc. [*Associated Press*] (SAG)
DynaGp .... Dyna Group International, Inc. [*Associated Press*] (SAG)
DYNAL .... Dynamic Analysis (NRCH)
DYNAM .... Dynamic (WGA)
DynAm .... Dynamics Corp. of America [*Associated Press*] (SAG)
dynam .... dynamite (SAUS)
Dynam .... Dynamotion ATI Corp. [*Associated Press*] (SAG)
DYNA-METRIC... Dynamic Multi-Echelon Technique for Repairable Item Control (SAUS)
DYNAMETRICS... Combat Capabilities Assessment Tool (SAUS)
DYNAMIT .... Dynamic Allocation of Manufacturing Inventory and Time (MHDB)
DYNAMO .... Dynamic Action Management Operation (SAUS)
DYNAMO .... Dynamic Action Management Operations [*BSD*]
DYNAMO .... Dynamic Allocation Model (SAUS)
DYNAMO .... Dynamic Automatic Monitoring (CET)
DYNAMO .... Dynamic Magneto-Optical Correlator [*Instrumentation*]
DYNAMO .... Dynamic Model (SAUS)
DYNAMO .... Dynamic Model Continuous Time Simulation (BUR)
DYNAMO .... Dynamic Modeller (SAUS)
DYNAMO .... Dynamic Modelling (SAUS)
Dynamo .... Dynamotion ATI Corp. [*Associated Press*] (SAG)
DYNAMO-S... Dynamic Modeller- Simulator (SAUS)
DYNAMOWS... Dynamic Manned Orbital Weapon System (IAA)
Dynamx .... Dynamex, Inc. [*Associated Press*] (SAG)
DYNANA .... Dynamic Analyzer (HGAA)
DYNARM .... Dynamic Arm Programmer [*Computer science*]
DYNASAR .... Dynamic Systems Analyzer [*General Electric Co.*] (IEEE)
DYNA-SOAR... Dynamic Soaring [*Space flight*]
DYNAT .... Dynamic Accuracy Tester [*General Electric Co.*]
dynatac .... dynamic adaptive total area coverage (SAUS)
Dyn Atmos Oceans... Dynamics of Atmospheres and Oceans [*A publication*] (PABS)
DYNAVIS .... Dynamic Video Display System (SAUS)
DYNC .... Dynamic Classics Ltd. [*NASDAQ symbol*] (COMM)
dyncm .... dyne centimeter (SAUS)
DYN/CM .... Dynes per Centimeter
DYN/CM² .... Dynes per Square Centimeter
DYNDADIS .... Dynamic Data Display System (SAUS)
DYNFET .... Dynamic Four Phase Non-overlapping Clock Field Effect Transistor (SAUS)
DYNG .... Dyeing
Dyng .... Dynagen, Inc. [*Associated Press*] (SAG)
DynHlth .... Dynamic Healthcare Technologies, Inc. [*Associated Press*] (SAG)
DynHm .... Dynamic Homes, Inc. [*Associated Press*] (SAG)
DynHom .... Dynamic Homes, Inc. [*Associated Press*] (SAG)
DYNIMAN .... Dynamic Information Management Systems (SAUS)
DYNM .... Dynamotor
DynMatl .... Dynamic Materials Corp. [*Associated Press*] (SAG)
DYNMC .... Dynamic
DYNMT .... Dynamite (MSA)
DYNMT .... Dynamometer [*Engineering*]
DYNMX .... Dynamic Mixing Model [*Marine science*] (OSRA)
dyno .... dynamite, undiluted drugs (SAUS)
DYNO .... Dynamometer [*Engineering*] (KSC)
DynOil .... Dynamic Oil Ltd. [*Associated Press*] (SAG)
DYNPOS .... Dynamic Positioning (RIMS)
Dyn Res .... Dynamic Resistance (SAUS)
DynRsh .... Dynamics Research Corp. [*Associated Press*] (SAG)
Dyn Suppr ... Dynamic Suppression (SAUS)
DYNSYS .... Dynamics Systems Simulator (SAUS)
DYNT .... Dynatronics Corp. [*NASDAQ symbol*] (TTSB)
DYNT .... Dynatronics Laser Corp. [*NASDAQ symbol*] (NQ)
DYNTACS .... Dynamical Tactical Simulator
DYNTACS-X... Dynamic Tactical Simulator - Enhanced
Dyntcl .... Dynatec International, Inc. [*Associated Press*] (SAG)
DYNTOX .... Dynamic Toxic Model (EEVL)
DYNTOX .... Dynamic Toxics Model (SAUS)
DyntrCp .... Dynatronics Corp. [*Associated Press*] (SAG)
DYNX .... Dynatec International, Inc. [*NASDAQ symbol*] (NQ)
DYNX .... Dynatec Intl. [*NASDAQ symbol*] (TTSB)
DYO .... Diocesan Youth Officer [*Church of England*]
DYO .... Duke of York's Own [*British military*] (DMA)
DYO .... Rutland, VT [*Location identifier*] [*FAA*] (FAAL)
DYOH .... Do Your Own Homework (ADWA)
DYOL .... Dynamic Oil Ltd. [*NASDAQ symbol*] (NQ)
DYOLF .... Dynamic Oil Ltd. [*NASDAQ symbol*] (TTSB)
DYP .... Directory Yellow Pages [*Telecommunications*] (TEL)
DYP .... Dogru Yol Partisi [*Correct Way Party*] [*Turkey*] [*Political party*] (EY)
DYPOL .... Dynamic Planning Of Liquidity (SAUS)
Dypol .... Dynamic Programming of Liquidity (SAUS)
DYPR .... Drypers Corp. [*NASDAQ symbol*] (SAG)
DYPS .... Dynamic Programming System [*Computer science*] (IAA)
DYPSP .... Disabled Young People's Services Program [*Australia*]
DYPT .... Dependent Youth Part-Time (SAUO)
DYQ .... Greeneville, TN [*Location identifier*] [*FAA*] (FAAL)
D/Yr .... Days per Year (SAUS)
DYR .... Dyersburg, TN [*Location identifier*] [*FAA*] (FAAL)
dy r .... dynamic response (SAUS)
DYR .... Dynamo Resources [*Vancouver Stock Exchange symbol*]
DYRAD .... Dynamic Resolver Angle Digitizer
DYRQRPRCHT... Duties Require Parachuting [*Army*] (AABC)
DYS .... Abilene, TX [*Location identifier*] [*FAA*] (FAAL)
DYS .... Department of Youth Services (SAUS)

DYS .... Derbyshire (SAUS)
DYS .... Distribucion y Servico ADS [*NYSE symbol*] (SG)
DYS .... Division of Youth Services (SAUS)
DYS .... Duke of York's Royal Military School [*British military*] (DMA)
DYS .... Dysgerminoma [*Oncology*]
Dys .... Dysphagia [*Therapy term*] (CTAA)
DYSAC .... Digitally Simulated Analog Computer (SAUS)
DYSAC .... Digital Simulated Analog Computer (MCD)
DYSAC .... Dynamic Storage Analog Computer (IEEE)
DYSEAC .... Digital High-Speed Standard Eastern Automatic Computer
dysen .... dysentery (SAUS)
DYSIM .... Dynamic Simulator (CTAS)
DySIS .... Dynamic Software and Integrated Solutions, Inc. (SAUS)
dyslex .... dyslexia (SAUS)
dyslex .... dyslexic (SAUS)
DYSM .... Dysmenorrhea [*Medicine*]
dysp .... dyspepsia (SAUS)
DYSTAC .... Dynamic Storage Allocation Language (SAUS)
DYSTAC .... Dynamic Storage Analog Computer
DYSTAL .... Dynamic Storage Allocation [*Computer science*] (CIST)
DYSTAL .... Dynamic Storage Allocation Language [*in FORTRAN*] [*Computer science*]
Dy Sum Proc... Dyett's Summary Proceedings [*A publication*] (DLA)
DYSYS .... Digital Dynamic System Simulator (SAUS)
DYSYS .... Dynamic System Simulator (SAUS)
DYT .... Dynatronics Laser Corp. [*Vancouver Stock Exchange symbol*]
DYTAPS .... Dynamic Tongue and Palatometric Shapes [*System to help the deaf speak*]
DYTC .... Dynatech Corp. [*NASDAQ symbol*] (NQ)
DytchC .... Dynatech Corp. [*Associated Press*] (SAG)
DYTON .... Dayton, WA [*American Association of Railroads railroad junction routing code*]
DYTR .... Dyatron Corp. [*NASDAQ symbol*] (COMM)
DYTRPT .... Dye Transfer Print (VRA)
dyu .... do your utmost (SAUS)
DYU .... Dushanbe [*Former USSR*] [*Airport symbol*] (OAG)
DYUU .... Delta Luminance Color Difference
DYV .... Dolly Varden Minerals [*Vancouver Stock Exchange symbol*]
DYW .... Daly Waters [*Northern Territory, Australia*] [*Airport symbol*] (AD)
DYW .... Detached Youth Worker (AIE)
DYW .... Dynamic Youth Workers (SAUS)
D-YWHF .... Dozen-Year White House Foul-Up Cycle [*Reference to the 1949 "mess in Washington," 1961 Bay of Pigs disaster, 1973 Watergate scandal, and 1985 Iran-CONTRA affair*] [*Term coined by William Safire*]
DYX .... DiaSys Corp. [*AMEX symbol*]
DYZO .... Dror Young Zionist Organization [*Later, YKM*] (EA)
DZ .... Algeria [*ANSI two-letter standard code*] (CNC)
DZ .... Danger Zone [*Nautical term*] (HRNC)
DZ .... Dead Zone (SAUS)
DZ .... Decimal Zoned (SAUS)
DZ .... Definitive Zone
DZ .... Deformed Zone (UWER)
DZ .... Department of Zoology (SAUO)
DZ .... Depleted Zone (SAUS)
DZ .... Detection Zone (SAUS)
DZ .... Diazepam [*Also, D, DAP*] [*A sedative*]
DZ .... Dictionary of Zoology (SAUS)
dZ .... differential of impedance (SAUS)
DZ .... Disease (DAVI)
dz .... Disease [*Medicine*] (EDAA)
DZ .... Disruption Zone [*Military*] (INF)
DZ .... Dissociated Zircon (PDAA)
DZ .... Distillation Zone (UWER)
DZ .... dizygot (SAUS)
DZ .... Dizygotic [*Genetics*]
DZ .... Dizziness (KSC)
dz .... dizzy (SAUS)
DZ .... Doctor of Zoology
DZ .... Double Zeta (MEC)
DZ .... Double Zeta Basis (UWER)
DZ .... Douglas Airways [*ICAO designator*] (AD)
DZ .... Dozen
dz .... Dozen
dz .... dozens (SAUS)
DZ .... Drizzle [*Meteorology*]
DZ .... Dropping Zone (PIAV)
DZ .... Drop Zone [*For parachute troops and gliders*] [*Military*]
DZ .... Druckzuender [*Pressure Igniter*] [*German military - World War II*]
DZ .... Durand-Zunin [*Syndrome*] [*Medicine*] (DB)
DZA .... Algeria [*ANSI three-letter standard code*] (CNC)
DZA .... dizygotic twins raised apart (SAUS)
DZA .... Dizygotic Twins Reared Apart [*Genetics*]
DZA .... Doppler Zeeman Analyser [*British*]
DZA .... Doppler Zeeman Analyzer (SAUS)
DZA .... Drop Zone Area [*Military*]
DZA .... Dzaoudzi [*Comoro Islands*] [*Airport symbol*] (OAG)
DZAAS .... Drop Zone Assembly Aid System [*Military*] (INF)
DZaE .... Embassy of Zaire, Washington, DC [*Library symbol*] [*Library of Congress*] (LCLS)
DZAPO .... Cytosine Arabinoside, Azacytidine, Prednisone, Vincristine, Daunomycin [*Antineoplastic drug regimen*] (DAVI)
DZC .... Dispersed Zirconia Ceramics (UWER)
DZCO .... Drop Zone Control Officer [*Military*] (AFM)
DZF .... Dokumentationszentrale Feinwerktechnik [*Precision Technology Documentation Center*] [*Originator, operator, and database*] [*Germany*] [*Information service or system*] (IID)
DZFC .... Dread Zeppelin Fan Club (EA)
dzg .... dizygotic (SAUS)
DZH .... Dzhafr [*Former USSR*] [*Seismograph station code, US Geological Survey*] [*Closed*] (SEIS)
DZIP .... Driver Zipcode [*National Highway Traffic Safety Administration Fatal Accident Recording System code*]
DZJ .... Pensions for Secure Living (Czech Rep.) [*Political party*] (PSAP)
DZM .... Miami-Dade Public Library System, Miami, FL [*OCLC symbol*] (OCLC)
DZNE .... Douzaine [*Dozen*] [*French*]
DZool .... Doctor of Zoology (ADA)
DZP .... Diazepam [*Also, D, DAP, DZ*] [*Antiepileptic drug*]
DZ PR .... Dozen Pairs (SAUS)
DZR .... Double Zigzag Rectifier
DZS .... Drop Zone Study [*Military*] (MCD)
DZSO .... Drop Zone Safety Officer [*Military*] (AABC)
DZST .... Drop Zone Support Team [*Army*] (INF)
DZT .... Digit Zero Trigger (IAA)
DZT .... Dizygotic (MELL)
DZT .... Dizygotic Twins (SAUS)
DZT .... Dzhergetal [*Former USSR*] [*Seismograph station code, US Geological Survey*] [*Closed*] (SEIS)
DZTK .... Daisytek International Corp. [*NASDAQ symbol*] (SAG)
DZTK .... Daisytek Intl. [*NASDAQ symbol*] (TTSB)
DZTL .... diode-coupled Z-diodes transistor logic (SAUS)
DZTL .... Diode Zener Diode Transistor Logic [*Electronics*] (IAA)
DZTL .... diode Zener-diode transistor logic (SAUS)
Dzun .... Dzungaria (SAUS)

E
By Acronym

E .... Activation Energy (SAUS)
E .... Air Dose [*Also called air exposure, referring to radiation exposure*] (DAVI)
E .... Air Force Training Category [*Inactive duty training periods and 30 days active duty training per year*]
E .... American Export-Isbrandtsen Lines (SAUS)
E .... Amphibian [*Russian aircraft symbol*]
E .... Anchor Examined (SAUS)
e .... Angle of Downwash (SAUS)
E .... Applied Voltage (UWER)
e .... Base of Natural Logarithms [*Mathematics*] (DAVI)
E .... Cases in the Eastern District's Local Division of the Supreme Court [*1910-46*] [*South Africa*] [*A publication*] (DLA)
e .... charge of electron (SAUS)
e .... charge of positron (SAUS)
E .... Church of England School [*British*]
e .... Coefficient of Impact (SAUS)
e .... Coefficient of Resilience (SAUS)
e .... Coefficient of Restitution (SAUS)
E .... Cold Polar Climate (UWER)
E .... Color Excess [*Astronomy*]
E .... Constant Electric Field (SAUS)
E .... Constant Energy (SAUS)
E .... Cutoff Voltage (SAUS)
E .... Declared or Paid in the Preceding 12 Months [*Investment term*] (DFIT)
E .... Eagle A corps/division level analytical model used primarily for DIS research (SAUS)
E .... Eagle Airways (SAUS)
e .... ear (SAUS)
E .... Earl
E .... Early [*Genetics*]
E .... Early Warning (SAUS)
E .... Earnings [*Finance*]
E .... Ear, Nose, and Throat [*Medical Officer designation*] [*British*]
E .... Earth [*Wind triangle problems and relative movement problems*]
E .... Easily
e .... East (WDMC)
E .... East [*or Eastern*]
E .... Easter
E .... Easterly (WDAA)
E .... eastern longitude (SAUS)
E .... Eastern Standard Time
E .... East's English King's Bench Term Reports [*A publication*] (DLA)
E .... Easy [*Phonetic alphabet*] [*World War II*] (DSUE)
E .... Easy to Move [*Horticulture*]
e .... eccentric (SAUS)
e .... Eccentricity [*of application of load*] [*Aerospace*] (AAG)
E .... eccentricity of a curve (SAUS)
E .... Ecclesiastical (DLA)
E .... Ecclesiastical District [*Maps*] (ROG)
E: .... ECCS (SAUS)
E .... Echelon (SAUS)
E .... Echinococcus [*Genus of tapeworms*] (UWER)
E .... Echo [*Phonetic alphabet*] [*International*] (DSUE)
E .... Echo-code for letter E (SAUS)
E .... Eclairage [*Illumination*] [*French*]
E .... Economic Community (SAUS)
E .... Economics (ADA)
E .... Ecstacy [*Synthetic stimulant*]
E .... Ectopia [*Dislocation, displacement or malposition*] [*Medicine*] (EDAA)
E .... Edema [*Medicine*]
E .... Edge [*Lumber*]
E .... Edinburgh [*City in Scotland*] (ROG)
E .... Edison (SAUS)
E .... Edison cap (SAUS)
E .... Edition
E .... Edrophonium [*A cholinergic*] [*Anesthesiology*]
E .... Educated
E .... Education (SAUS)
E .... Edward [*Phonetic alphabet*] [*Royal Navy*] [*World War I*] (DSUE)
E .... effciency (SAUS)
E .... Effect (WDMC)
e .... effective (SAUS)
E .... Effectiveness (CAAL)
E .... Effectivity (SAUS)
E .... Effector [*Biology*]
E .... Effects (WDMC)
E .... Efficiency [*or Efficient*]
e .... Efficient (SAUS)
E .... Effort (CDAI)
E .... Egg (UWER)
E .... Egyptian
E .... Eigenvalue (UWER)
E .... Eighteen "Great" Choral Preludes [*Bach*]
E .... Einspritz [*Fuel-injection*] [*As in 280 E, the model number of a Mercedes-Benz automobile*]
E .... Einsteinium [*Also see Es*] [*Chemical element*]
E .... Einstein unit of energy (SAUS)
E .... ejection click (SAUS)
E .... Ejection Release [*Communications term*] (DCT)
E .... Ekuele [*Currency of Equatorial Guinea*] (UWER)
E .... Elaborate [*Used in correcting manuscripts, etc.*]
E .... Elastance (MAE)
e .... elastic (SAUS)
E .... Elasticity (SAUS)
E .... Elastic Modulus (UWER)
E .... Elbow (DAC)
E .... Eldest
E .... Eldisine [*Also, VDS*] [*Antineoplastic drug*]
E .... electic field strength (SAUS)
E .... Electric (ADA)
e .... Electric
E .... electric affinity (SAUS)
e .... Electric Charge [*Electricity*] (DAVI)
E .... Electric Charge [*Medicine*] (EDAA)
E .... electric field (SAUS)
E .... Electric Field Strength [*Symbol*]
E .... Electric Field Vector
E .... electric force (SAUS)
E .... electric gradient (SAUS)
e .... Electric Intensity (SAUS)
E .... Electricity (NTCM)
E .... electric potential (SAUS)
E .... electric potential difference (SAUS)
E .... Electric Shutoff [*NFPA pre-fire planning symbol*] (NFPA)
E .... electric voltage (SAUS)
E .... Electrochemical Equivalent (UWER)
E .... Electrode (SAUS)
E .... Electrode Potential
e .... electromagnetic (SAUS)
E .... Electromagnetic Force [*Physics*] (DAVI)
E .... Electromotive (SAUS)
E .... Electromotive Force [*Symbol*] [*See also EMF, V*] [*Electrochemistry*]
E .... Electron (STED)
e .... Electron [*A nuclear particle*]
e .... Electron Charge (IDOE)
E .... Electronic [*Automotive engineering*]
E .... Electronic Capability [*Designation for all US military aircraft*]
e .... electronic charge (SAUS)
E .... Electronic Countermeasures [*Military*]
E .... Electronics Program [*Association of Independent Colleges and Schools specialization code*]
E .... Electrophoretic Analysis [*Botany*]
E .... Element (IAA)
e .... Elementarladung (SAUS)
e .... Elementary Charge [*of a proton*] [*Symbol*] [*IUPAC*]
e .... eletric field vector (SAUS)
E .... Elevation Angle (NASA)
E .... Elevator [*Technical drawings*] (NFPA)
E .... Elimination Reaction (ODA)
E .... Elizabeth (SAFN)
E .... Ell
E .... Ellipse (SAUS)
E .... Elliptical (for galaxies) (SAUS)
E .... Elocution
E .... Elohist (SAUS)
E .... Elohist Source [*Biblical scholarship*]
E .... Eluviate (UWER)
E .... Elysium Mons [*A filamentary mark on Mars*]
E .... Emalangeni [*Monetary unit*] [*Swaziland*] (BARN)
E .... Eman (SAUS)

E .... Embassy
E .... EMBRAER [*Empresa Brasileira Aeronautica SA*] [*Brazil*] [*ICAO aircraft manufacturer identifier*] (ICAO)
E .... Embroidery [*Quilting*]
E .... Embryo [*Botany*]
E .... embryon (SAUS)
E .... Embryonic
E .... Emerald (UWER)
E .... Emergency [*Symbol placed in neighborhood windows to indicate that resident will aid passing schoolchildren in the event of an emergency*]
E .... Eminence (DLA)
E .... Eminent [*Freemasonry*]
E .... Emissive Power (SAUS)
e .... Emitter (IDOE)
E .... Emitter (MSA)
E .... Emma [*Novel by Jane Austen*]
E .... Emmetropia [*Also, EM*] [*Ophthalmology*]
E .... Emperor (ROG)
E .... Empfindichkeit [*Susceptibility to Stimulation*] [*Psychology*]
e .... Emphatic [*Linguistics*]
E .... Employee [*Legal shorthand*] (LWAP)
E .... Empty
e .... emulsifer (SAUS)
E .... Emulsifier (SAUS)
e .... emulsion (SAUS)
E .... Enable (SAUS)
E .... Enamel (AAG)
E .... Enamelled (SAUS)
E .... Enantiomeric Ratio
E .... Encephalitis [*Medicine*] (STED)
E .... Enclosure (UWER)
E .... Encounter [*Time*]
E .... End [*Football*]
E .... Endamoeba [*Biology*] (UWER)
E .... Endangered Animal [*Medicine*] (DMAA)
E .... Endocrinology
E .... Endogenous (MELL)
E .... Endometriosis [*Medicine*] (UWER)
E .... Endoplasmic [*Freeze etching in microscopy*]
E .... Endospore [*Biology*] (UWER)
E .... Endotoxin [*Microbiology*]
e .... Endurance (SAUS)
E .... Enema [*Medicine*]
E .... Enemy (ADA)
E .... Energy [*Symbol*] [*IUPAC*]
E .... energy density (SAUS)
e .... energy of gas (SAUS)
E .... Enflurane [*Also, ENF*] [*An anesthetic*]
E .... Engine
e .... Engineer (ADWA)
E .... Engineer [*or Engineering*]
E .... engineering (SAUS)
E .... England (ROG)
E .... English
E .... English Shilling (WDAA)
E .... Engorged [*Medicine*] (EDAA)
E .... ENI S.p.A.ADS [*NYSE symbol*] (TTSB)
E .... Enlisted [*Often in combination with numbers to denote serviceman's grade*]
E .... Entamoeba [*Microbiology*] (MAE)
E .... Entering [*FBI standardized term*]
E .... Enterococcus [*Medicine*] (EDAA)
E .... Entertainment [*Wire service code*] (NTCM)
E! .... Entertainment Television [*Also, E! Entertainment*] [*A cable network*] [*Los Angeles, California*] (WDMC)
(E) .... Entgegen [*Opposed*] [*Chemistry*] [*German*]
E .... Entrainment (SAUS)
E .... Entrance
E .... Entry [*Horse racing*]
E .... Entscheidung [*Decision, Judgment*] [*German*] (ILCA)
E .... Entwurf [*Draft*] [*German*] (ILCA)
E .... E-Number (ODA)
E .... Environment [*Psychology*]
E .... Envoy Extraordinary and Minister Plenipotentiary (SAUS)
E .... Enzyme (AAMN)
E .... Enzyme, Free [*Enzyme kinetics*]
e .... Eodem [*In the Same Place, Title Explained*] [*Latin*] (ILCA)
E .... Eosinophil [*Hematology*]
E .... Eotvos (SAUS)
E .... Ephelis (MELL)
E .... Epicondyle [*Medicine*] (EDAA)
E .... Epidermis
E .... Epidermophyton [*Genus of ringworms*] (UWER)
E .... Epiglottis [*Anatomy*] (UWER)
E .... Epinephrine [*Endocrinology*]
E .... Episode (UWER)
E .... Epistle
E .... Epithelium [*Anatomy*]
E .... Epsilon (NUCP)
-E .... Equal (SAUS)
E .... Equation of Time (ROG)
E .... Equator (WDAA)
E .... Equatorial [*Air mass*]
E .... Equipment (NFPA)
E .... Equity (DLA)
E .... Equivalent
e .... equivalent quantities (SAUS)
E .... Erase Protected (SAUS)
E .... Erbium [*Chemical element*] [*Symbol is ER*] (ROG)
E .... Erepsin [*Biochemistry*] (UWER)
E .... Erg [*Unit of work*] (GPO)
e .... Erg (IDOE)
E .... Ericksen Number [*Physics*] (UWER)
E .... Erie [*Diocesan abbreviation*] [*Pennsylvania*] (TOCD)
E .... Eriodictyol [*Organic chemistry*]
E .... Erlang [*Unit*] [*Statistics*] [*Telecommunications*]
E .... Erogenic
E .... Erroneous (SAUS)
e .... Error (ADWA)
E .... Error [*Computer science*] (BUR)
E .... Errors [*Baseball*]
E .... Error Score
E .... Erythrocyte [*Hematology*]
E .... Erythroid [*Medicine*] (EDAA)
E .... Erythromycin [*Also, ERY, ERYC, ETM*] [*Antibacterial compound*]
E .... Escape (ROG)
E .... Escherichia [*Bacterial strain*]
E .... Escudo [*Monetary unit*] [*Chile, Portugal*]
E .... Esophagus [*Anatomy*]
E .... Esophoria (STED)
E .... Esophoria for Distance [*Ophthalmology*]
E .... Espana [*Spain*]
E .... Especial [*Designation on brandy labels*]
E .... Espionage (SAUS)
E .... essential (SAUS)
E .... Estate Agency [*London Stock Exchange*]
E .... Ester [*Organic chemistry*] (MAE)
E .... Estimate
e .... estimated (SAUS)
E .... Estimated Commercial Readability (UWER)
E .... estimated weight (SAUS)
E .... Estradiol [*Medicine*] (DAVI)
E .... Estrogen [*Biochemistry*] (UWER)
E .... Eta (NUCP)
E .... Ethanol
E .... Ethmoid Sinus [*Medicine*] (DAVI)
e .... Ethyl [*As substituent on nucleoside*] [*Biochemistry*]
E .... Ethylene (UWER)
E .... Etiology [*Medicine*] (DAVI)
E .... Euler Number [*Fluid mechanics*]
E .... Eurocard [*Credit card*] [*British*]
e---- .... Europe [*MARC geographic area code*] [*Library of Congress*] (LCCP)
E .... European [*British military*] (DMA)
E .... Euston Railway Station [*British*] (ROG)
E .... Eutectic (UWER)
E .... Evangelist [*Church calendars*]
E .... Evaporation
E .... Evaporativity (SAUS)
E .... Evening
E .... Evensong
E .... Event (UWER)
E .... Evidence [*Law*]
E .... Evolution (SAUS)
e .... Ex [*From*] [*Latin*] (MAE)
E .... Exa [*A prefix meaning multiplied by 10^{18}*] [*SI symbol*]
E .... Excellence (UWER)
E .... "Excellence in Production" [*Army-Navy "E" awarded manufacturers*] [*World War II*]
E .... Excellency
E .... Excellent
E .... Excellent Skiing Conditions
e .... Exchange (QSUL)
E .... Exchequer [*British*] (DLA)
E .... Excitation (UWER)
E .... Excitatory Tendency [*Psychology*]
E .... Exciton [*Solid-state physics*] (UWER)
E .... Exclusion
E .... Execute (SAUS)
E .... Execution (MHDB)
E .... Executive (SAUS)
E .... Exempt [*from traceability*] [*NASA*] (NASA)
E .... exhaust (SAUS)
E .... Exkursion (SAUS)
E .... Exoplasmic [*Freeze etching in microscopy*]
E .... Exotoxin [*Microbiology*] (UWER)
E .... Expectation
E .... Expected Value
E .... Expended (SAUS)
E .... Expenditure [*Economics*]
E .... Expenses
E .... Experience
E .... experiment (SAUS)
E .... Experimental [*When preceding vessel classification*] [*Navy symbol*]
E .... Experimental Group (DIPS)
E .... Experiment Compartment
E .... Experimenter [*Psychology*]
E .... Expert Slope [*Skiing*]
E .... Expire [*Medicine*] (DAVI)
E .... Expired [*Gas*] [*Medicine*]

E ..... Expired Air [*Medicine*] (DMAA)
E ..... expired gas (SAUS)
E ..... Explained [*Statement of import of decision in cited case, not merely a restatement of the facts*] [*Legal term*] (DLA)
E ..... Explicit
e ..... Exponent (VLIE)
E ..... Exponent
E ..... Exponential [*Mathematics*]
e ..... exponential number (SAUS)
E ..... Export
E ..... Export Service [*Queen's award*] [*British*]
E ..... Exposure
E ..... Exposure Level (SAUS)
E ..... Expression (MHDI)
E ..... extended word (SAUS)
E ..... Extension (SAUS)
e ..... external (SAUS)
E ..... Extinction [*Neurophysiology*]
E ..... Extra (ADWA)
E ..... Extraction Fraction (MAE)
E ..... Extralymphatic [*Medicine*]
E ..... Extraordinary (SAUS)
E ..... Extraordinary Ray [*Direction of*]
e ..... extrapolated value of a length (SAUS)
E ..... Extra Wide [*Women's shoe width*] [*More than one "E" indicates increasing wideness, up to EEE*]
E ..... Extrinsic (SAUS)
E ..... Eye
E ..... Eye Infection [*Classification system used by doctors on Ellis Island to detain, re-examine, and possibly deny entry to certain immigrants*]
E ..... Farbenfabriken Bayer [*Germany*] [*Research code symbol*]
E ..... filament supply voltage (SAUS)
E ..... Fraunhofer line caused by iron (SAUS)
E ..... Glutamic Acid [*One-letter symbol; see Glu*] [*An amino acid*]
E ..... Glutamyl (SAUS)
E ..... Green Strain (UWER)
E ..... Hotels and Restaurants [*Public-performance tariff class*] [*British*]
E ..... Illuminance [*Symbol*]
E ..... Index of Forecasting Efficiency (DIPS)
E ..... Internal Energy (DAVI)
E ..... Irradiance [*Symbol*] [*IUPAC*]
E ..... Kinetic Energy (MELL)
E ..... License Class [*Motor vehicle violation code used in state of Maryland*] (MVRD)
E ..... Lilangeni [*Currency of Swaziland*] (UWER)
E ..... Mathematical Expectation [*Statistics*] (DAVI)
E ..... Medium Wide [*Men's shoe width*] [*More than one "E" indicates increasing wideness, up to EEEE*]
E ..... Modulus of Elasticity [*Mechanics*]
E ..... Musical Note [*or Key*] (ODA)
e ..... Naperian [*or Natural*] Logarithm Base [*2.7182818*]
E ..... Nupac [*Communications term*] (DCT)
E ..... Oxidation Reduction Potential (UWER)
e ..... Partial Water Vapor Pressure [*Meteorology*] (BARN)
e ..... Permittivity [*Physics*] (BARN)
E ..... Pitch Diameter (UWER)
E ..... Polar Climates (UWER)
E^+ ..... Positron [*Also called positive electron*] [*Symbol*] [*Physics*] (DAVI)
E ..... Potential (DIPS)
E ..... Potential Difference (UWER)
E ..... pulse amplitude (SAUS)
E ..... Redox Potential [*Organic chemistry*] (DAVI)
E ..... Richmond [*Branch in the Federal Reserve Regional banking system*] (BARN)
E ..... Second-Class Merchant Ship (ODA)
E ..... Shoe Width Grater than D (BARN)
E ..... Sleet [*Meteorology*]
E ..... Spain [*IYRU nationality code*] (IYR)
E ..... Spanish [*Language in tables*] (BARN)
E ..... Special Electronic Missile [*Department of Defense*] (UWER)
E ..... Standard Potential [*Symbol*] [*Physics*] (DAVI)
e ..... [*The*] Fifth Vertical Row of Squares from the Left on a Chessboard (ODA)
E ..... Torpedo Boat [*German symbol*]
e ..... Transcendental Number 2.718.212 (ODA)
E ..... Unreliable Source of Intelligence [*Military*]
E ..... Voltage (CET)
E ..... Water Vapor Pressure
e ..... Wet Air Without Rain [*Meteorology*] (BARN)
e ..... Elder (ODA)
E ..... Electromeric Effect (ODA)
e ..... Equatorial Conformation [*Chemistry*] (ODA)
e0 ..... effective (SAUS)
E1 ..... Basic Airman [*Air Force*]
E1 ..... Electrical Repairs [*Nautical term*] (NTA)
E_1 ..... Estrone [*Endocrinology*]
E-1 ..... European Digital Signal 1. European standard for digital physical interface at 2.048 Mbps. (SAUS)
E1 ..... European Standard Transmission Speed of 2048 Mb/s (VLIE)
E1 ..... Private [*Marine Corps*]
E1 ..... Recruit [*Army*]
E1 ..... Seaman Recruit [*Navy*]
E2 ..... Airman [*Air Force*]
E2 ..... Estradiol [*Also, E-diol, ES*] [*Endocrinology*]
E2 ..... Private 2 [*Army*]
E2 ..... Private First Class [*Marine Corps*]
E2 ..... Seaman Apprentice [*Navy*]
E-2C ..... Hawkeye Grumman [*Carrier-based airborne early warning*] [*Navy*] (POLM)
E2CL ..... emitter emitter-coupled logic (SAUS)
E^2DIS ..... Environmental Effects for Distributed Interactive Simulation [*Army*]
E2DIS ..... Environmental Effects for Distribution Interactive Simulation (SAUO)
E2EG ..... Ear to Ear Grin (SAUS)
E2EG ..... Ear To Ear Grin (Slang) (SAUS)
E^2I ..... Endoatmospheric/Exoatmospheric Interceptor [*Army*] (DOMA)
E2IC ..... elevated electrode integrated circuit (SAUS)
E2L ..... emitter emitter-coupled logic (SAUS)
E2L ..... emitter-to-emitter coupled logic (SAUS)
E2PROM ..... Electrically Erasable Programmable Read Only Memory (AEBE)
E3 ..... Airman, First Class
E-3 ..... Airman Second Class [*Air Force*] (UWER)
E^3 ..... Education and Experience in Engineering [*Illinois Institute of Technology program*]
E^3 ..... Electromagnetic Environmental Effect (CAAL)
E3 ..... Electromagnetic Environmental Effects
E^3 ..... Electromagnetic Environment Effects
E3 ..... Electronic Entertainment Expo (ADWA)
E^3 ..... Emerging Ethnic Engineers [*An association*]
E3 ..... End-to-End Encryption (SAUS)
E_3 ..... Estriol [*Endocrinology*]
E-3 ..... European Digital Signal 3. European standard for digital physical interface at 34.368 Mbps (SAUS)
E3 ..... Lance Corporal [*Marine Corps*]
E3 ..... Private First Class [*Army*]
E3 ..... Seaman [*Navy*]
E4 ..... Corporal [*Army, Marine Corps*]
E_4 ..... Estetrol [*Endocrinology*] (DAVI)
E-4 ..... European Digital Signal 4. European standard for digital physical interface at 139.264 Mbps. (SAUS)
E4 ..... Petty Officer, Third Class [*Navy*]
E4 ..... Sergeant [*Air Force*]
E4 ..... Specialist 4 [*Army*]
E-4B ..... National Airborne Operations Center (SAUO)
E4E ..... Enterprise for the Environment
E4OD ..... Electronic 4-Speed Overdrive [*Automotive term*] (HAWK)
E5 ..... Petty Officer, Second Class [*Navy*]
E5 ..... Sergeant [*Army, Marine Corps*]
E5 ..... Specialist 5 [*Obsolete*] [*Army*]
E5 ..... Staff Sergeant [*Air Force*]
E6 ..... Petty Officer, First Class [*Navy*]
E6 ..... Specialist 6 [*Obsolete*] [*Army*]
E6 ..... Staff Sergeant [*Army, Marine Corps*]
E6 ..... Technical Sergeant [*Air Force*]
E7 ..... Chief Petty Officer [*Navy*]
E7 ..... Gunnery Sergeant [*Marine Corps*]
E7 ..... Master Sergeant [*Air Force*]
E7 ..... Platoon Sergeant
E7 ..... Specialist 7 [*Obsolete*] [*Army*]
E8 ..... First Sergeant [*Army, Marine Corps*]
E8 ..... Master Sergeant [*Army, Marine Corps*]
E8 ..... Senior Chief Petty Officer [*Navy*]
E8 ..... Senior Master Sergeant [*Air Force*]
E8 ..... Specialist 8 [*Obsolete*] [*Army*]
E9 ..... Chief Master Sergeant [*Air Force*]
E9 ..... Command Sergeant Major [*Army*]
E9 ..... Master Chief Petty Officer [*Navy*]
E9 ..... Master Chief Petty Officer of the Coast Guard
E9 ..... Master Gunnery Sergeant [*Marine Corps*]
E9 ..... Sergeant Major [*Marine Corps*]
E9 ..... Sergeant Major of the Army
E9 ..... Specialist 9 [*Obsolete*] [*Army*]
E9 ..... Staff Sergeant Major [*Army*]
e12 ..... elongation in 2 inches (SAUS)
E-28 ..... Form EOIR-28, Notice of Entry of Appearance (SAUS)
E_3-3GI ..... Estriol-3-Glucosiduronate [*Pharmacology*] (DAVI)
E85 ..... Motor Fuel Containing 15 Percent Gasoline and 85 Percent Ethyl Alcohol [*Industrial hygiene term*] (OHS)
E911 ..... Enhanced 911 (SAUS)
EA ..... Address Field Extension (SAUS)
EA ..... Airbus Industrie [*France*] [*ICAO aircraft manufacturer identifier*] (ICAO)
ea--- ..... Alps Region [*MARC geographic area code*] [*Library of Congress*] (LCCP)
EA ..... Army Industrial Engineering Activity (AAGC)
EA ..... Basque Solidarity (Spain) [*Political party*] (PSAP)
ea ..... Each (NTIO)
EA ..... Each
EA ..... EA Industries [*NYSE symbol*] (TTSB)
EA ..... Early (ROG)
ea ..... Early (VRA)
EA ..... Early American
EA ..... Early Amniocentesis [*Medicine*] (MELL)
EA ..... Early Antigen [*Immunochemistry*]
EA ..... early antigens (SAUS)
EA ..... Earnings Asset (EBF)
EA ..... Earphone Amplifier
EA ..... Earth (IAA)
EA ..... Earth Acquisition (ACAE)
EA ..... East Africa

EA .... East African Airways Corp. (SAUO)
EA .... East Anglia [*England*] (ROG)
EA .... Easterline Angus (SAA)
EA .... Eastern Africa Law Reports [*A publication*] (DLA)
EA .... Eastern Air Lines, Inc. [*ICAO designator*]
EA .... Eastern Area
EA .... Eastern Measurements Office (SAUO)
Ea .... East's English King's Bench Term Reports [*A publication*] (DLA)
Ea .... East's Notes of Cases [*1785-1821*] [*Bengal, India*] [*A publication*] (DLA)
EA .... Easy Axis (SAUS)
EA .... Ebstein's Anomaly [*Cardiology*]
Ea .... Eccelerating Voltage (SAUS)
E/A .... Ecology Action (SAUS)
EA .... Economic Adviser
EA .... Economic Analysis
EA .... Economic Area (OTD)
EA .... Edetic Acid (MELL)
EA .... Edge Act [*Banking*]
EA .... Edgewood Arsenal [*Aberdeen Proving Ground, MD*] [*Army*]
EA .... Editorial Alteration [*Publishing*] (WDMC)
EA .... Editorial Assistant [*Publishing*]
EA .... Education Act (SAUO)
EA .... Educational Advisor
EA .... Educational Age
EA .... Educational Alliance (EA)
EA .... Educational Art
EA .... Educational Management [*Educational Resources Information Center (ERIC) Clearinghouse*] [*University of Oregon*] (PAZ)
EA .... Education Alternatives
EA .... Education Association (AIE)
EA .... Education des Adultes (SAUO)
EA .... Educators to Africa [*Later, ETAA*] (EA)
EA .... Effective Address [*Computer science*] (MDG)
EA .... Effective Area
EA .... Efficient Algorithm (SAUS)
EA .... Egg Albumin
EA .... Egyptian Army
EA .... Eighth Army (MCD)
EA .... El-Amarna (BJA)
EA .... Elastic Anisotropy (UWER)
EA .... Elder Abuse (MELL)
EA .... Eleanor Association (EA)
EA .... Electric Actuator (SAUS)
EA .... Electric Affinity [*Physics*] (DAVI)
EA .... Electrical Actuator (SEWL)
EA .... Electrical Artificer [*Navy*] [*British*]
EA .... Electrical Association (SAUO)
EA .... Electrically-Alterable (SAUS)
EA .... Electric Antenna [*Automobile accessory*]
E(A) .... Electrician (Aviation) [*U.S. Navy enlisted rating*] (AUER)
EA .... Electrics Association (SAUO)
EA .... Electroabsorption (SAUS)
EA .... Electroacoustics (SAUS)
EA .... Electro Actuators (SAUS)
EA .... Electroanalysis (SAUS)
EA .... Electroanesthesia [*Medicine*] (AAMN)
EA .... Electrocardiographic Amplifier
EA .... Electron Acceptor (UWER)
EA .... Electron Affinity (ABAC)
EA .... Electronic Accelerator [*Automotive engineering*]
EA .... Electronic Addition (SAUS)
EA .... Electronic Array (IAA)
EA .... Electronic arrays (SAUS)
EA .... Electronic Artificer (SAUS)
EA .... Electronic Arts
EA .... Electronic Arts, Inc.
EA .... Electronic Assembly
EA .... Electronic Associates (SAUS)
EA .... Electronic Associates, Inc. [*NYSE symbol*] (SPSG)
EA .... Electronic Attack (COE)
EA .... Electrophilic Addition (UWER)
EA .... Electrophysiologic Abnormality [*Medicine*] (DB)
EA .... Electrostatic Analyzer (IAA)
EA .... Element Activity (ELAL)
EA .... Elemental Analysis (SAUS)
EA .... Elementary Assignment (IAA)
EA .... Elettronica Aster SpA (SAUS)
E-A .... Elimination-Addition (UWER)
EA .... Ellagic Acid
EA .... Elliptical Aperture (SAUS)
EA .... Embryonic Antibody [*Medicine*] (MELL)
EA .... Embryonic Antigen (DB)
EA .... Emergency Acquisition [*Nautical term*] (NTA)
EA .... Emergency Action (MCD)
EA .... Emergency Addressee [*Aeromedical evacuation*]
EA .... Emergency Area (AFM)
EA .... Emergency Assessment [*Environmental science*] (COE)
EA .... Emergency Assistance (TAD)
EA .... Emirates Airlines [*United Arab Emirates*] (MENA)
EA .... Emotions Anonymous (EA)
EA .... Employers' Association [*British*] (DCTA)
EA .... Employment Act (OICC)
EA .... Enabling Objective [*Military training*]
EA .... Enamelled Asbestos Covered [*Electric wire*] (UWER)
EA .... Encyclopedia of Associations [*Information service or system*] [*A publication*]
EA .... End Address (SAUS)
EA .... Endangerment Assessment (GNE)
EA .... End Article (DNAB)
EA .... End of Answer (SAUS)
EA .... Endometrial Ablation [*Medicine*] (MELL)
EA .... Endometriosis Association (EA)
EA .... Ends Annealed (SAUS)
EA .... Enemy Action (SAUS)
EA .... Enemy Aircraft
EA .... Enemy Area (IAA)
EA .... Energy Absorbing
EA .... Energy Absorption (AAG)
EA .... Energy Analysis (ELAL)
EA .... Energy Association (SAUO)
E/a .... Energy per Atom (UWER)
EA .... Enforcement Action [*Nuclear energy*] (NRCH)
EA .... Enforcement Agreement [*Environmental Protection Agency*] (GFGA)
EA .... Engagement Area [*Military*] (INF)
EA .... Engelbert's Aquarians (EA)
EA .... Engine Assembly
EA .... Engineer Admiral (SAUO)
EA .... Engineer Agency (SAUO)
E/A .... Engineer/Architect (DAC)
EA .... Engineering Adhesive (UWER)
EA .... Engineering Aid [*Navy rating*]
EA .... Engineering Aide [*Military*] (POLM)
EA .... Engineering Analysis (ACAE)
EA .... Engineering Assignment
EA .... Engineering Authority (SAUS)
EA .... Engineer Rear-Admiral [*Navy*] [*British*]
EA .... English Actors [*A publication*]
EA .... English Association [*British*] (EAIO)
EA .... English-Pressed Allegro [*Record label*]
EA .... Enlisted Allowance (SAUS)
EA .... Enlistment Allowance [*Military*]
EA .... Enquiry Agency [*British*]
EA .... Enrolled Agent [*IRS*]
EA .... Entered Apprentice [*Freemasonry*]
EA .... Enterprise Agency (WDAA)
EA .... Enterprise Agreement (GART)
EA .... Enterprise Allowance (ODBW)
EA .... Enterprise America (EA)
EA .... Enterprise Analysis (SAUS)
EA .... Enterprise of the Americas (SAUO)
EA .... Entertaining Allowance [*British military*] (DMA)
EA .... Enthalpimetric Analysis [*Analytical chemistry*]
EA .... Entwicklungsalter [*Developmental Age*] [*Psychology*]
EA .... Enumeration Area [*Statistics*]
EA .... Environment Abstracts (UWER)
EA .... Environment Agency (HEAS)
EA .... Environmental Action (EA)
EA .... Environmental Agency (ACAE)
EA .... Environmental Assessment (MCD)
EA .... Environmental Assessment team (SAUO)
EA .... Environmental Audit [*Environmental Protection Agency*] (GFGA)
EA .... Environmental Auditing (SAUS)
EA .... Environment Analysis [*Computer science*] (ELAL)
EA .... Environment Assessment (SAUS)
EA .... Environment Australia (SAUO)
EA .... Epidural Abscess [*Medicine*] (MELL)
EA .... Epidural Anesthesia [*Medicine*]
EA .... Epilepsy Abstracts (SAUS)
EA .... Equal Angle (ACAE)
EA .... Equalizing Line Amplifier (IAA)
EA .... Equipment Alignment
EA .... Erythrocyte Amboceptor [*Immunology*]
EA .... Erythrocyte-Antibody [*Complex*] [*Immunochemistry*]
EA .... Erythrocyte Antiserum [*Medicine*] (MELL)
EA .... Erythromycin Acistrate [*Antibacterial*]
EA .... Erythromycylamine [*Antibacterial*]
EA .... Escort Aircraft (CINC)
EA .... Escrowed Authenticator (SAUS)
EA .... Escrowed Authenticator Cryptography (VERA)
EA .... Esperanto Association (SAUO)
EA .... Espionage Acid (SAUS)
EA .... Esters of Acrylic Acid (SAUS)
EA .... Estivoautumnal [*Malaria*]
Ea .... Estonia (MILB)
EA .... Estonian Aid (EA)
EA .... Ethacrynic Acid [*A diuretic*] [*Pharmacology*] (DAVI)
Ea .... Ethanamine (UWER)
EA .... Ethanolamine [*Also, Etn, OLAMINE*] [*Organic chemistry*]
EA .... Ethnic Anonymous (EA)
EA .... Ethoxyacetylene (UWER)
EA .... Ethyl Acrylate [*Organic chemistry*]
EA .... ethyl alcohol (SAUS)
EA .... Ethylene-Diamine Dinitrate/Ammonium Nitrate Explosive
EA .... European Army (SAUO)
EA .... European co-operation for Accreditation (SAUS)
EA .... Europe Assistance (SAUO)
EA .... Eusko Alkartasuna [*Basque Solidarity*] [*Spain*] [*Political party*]
EA .... Evaluation Agree [*Canada*] (DD)
EA .... Evangelical Alliance [*British*] (BI)

EA .... Even Address (SAUS)
EA .... Event Action (VLIE)
EA .... Event Analysis (SAUS)
EA .... Evolutionary Acquisition (AAGC)
EA .... Evolutionary Acquisition Strategy [*Army*]
EA .... Evolutionary Algorithm (IDAI)
EA .... Examining for Aphasia [*Psychology*]
EA .... Excess Air (UWER)
EA .... Excise Act [*Canada*]
EA .... Executive Agency (SAUS)
EA .... Executive Agent (SAUS)
EA .... Executive Assistant
EA .... Exhaust Air (OA)
EA .... Expectancy Age [*Education*]
EA .... expedited acknowledgment (SAUS)
EA .... Experimental Agent (ACAE)
e/a .... experimental aircraft (SAUS)
EA .... Experiment Assembly (KSC)
EA .... Explicit Atom (UWER)
EA .... Export Administration
EA .... Exportakademie (SAUS)
EA .... Export Annual Data [*Department of Commerce*] (GFGA)
EA .... Extended Abstract (SAUS)
EA .... Extended Accumulator (IAA)
EA .... Extended Address (SAUS)
EA .... Extended-Address [*Computer science*]
EA .... Extended Address/Attribute (SAUS)
EA .... Extended Aeration Process [*Sludge treatment*]
EA .... Extended Attribute [*Computer science*]
EA .... Extender Amplifier (SAUS)
EA .... external access (SAUS)
EA .... External Affairs (SAUS)
EA .... External Affairs Department [*Canada*]
E/A .... Extra Time Allowed [*Indian Railway*] (TIR)
EA .... Extrinsic Alveolitis (PDAA)
EA .... Parke, Davis & Co. [*Research code symbol*]
EA1 .... Engineering Aid, First Class [*Navy rating*]
EA2 .... Engineering Aid, Second Class [*Navy rating*]
EA3 .... Engineering Aid, Third Class [*Navy rating*]
EA-6B .... Prowler Grumman [*Tactical electronic jamming aircraft*] [*Navy*] (POLM)
EA75 .... Explosives Act 1875 (HEAS)
e-aa- .... Albania [*MARC geographic area code*] [*Library of Congress*] (LCCP)
EAA .... Eagle [*Alaska*] [*Airport symbol*] (OAG)
EAA .... Earth Attitude Angle (ADWA)
EAA .... East Africa Association (EA)
EAA .... East African Airways Corp. [*African airline*]
EAA .... East African Airways, Nairobi (SAUO)
EAA .... East African Artillery [*British military*] (DMA)
EAA .... Eastern Arts Association (AEBS)
EAA .... Ecclesiastical Archivists Association [*Italy*] (EAIO)
EAA .... Economic Accounts for Agriculture (EURO)
EAA .... Economic Activity Analysis
EAA .... Ecuadorean American Association (EA)
EAA .... Edinburgh Architectural Association (SAUO)
EAA .... EDP [*Electronic Data Processing*] Auditors' Association
EAA .... Educational Audiology Association (SAUS)
EAA .... Education Amendment Act (SAUS)
EAA .... Elastic Active Aerodynamics [*Mitsubishi*] [*Automotive engineering*]
EAA .... Electrical Aerosol Analyzer [*Instrumentation*]
EA(A) .... Electrical Artificer, Air [*British military*] (DMA)
EAA .... Electric Auto Association (EA)
EAA .... Electro-Acoustic Subassembly (SAUS)
EAA .... Electroacupuncture Analgesia [*Medicine*] (STED)
EAA .... Electronic Accounting Automaton (SAUS)
EAA .... Electronics Association of Australia (SAUO)
EAA .... Electrothermal Atomic Absorption [*Physics*] (DAVI)
EAA .... Emergency Assistance to Adults [*Medicine*] (EDAA)
EAA .... Empire Athletic Association (PSS)
EAA .... Employment Agents Association (SAUO)
EAA .... Encyclopedia of American Associations [*Later, EA*] [*A publication*]
EAA .... Encyclopedia of Astronomy and Astrophysics [*A publication*]
EAA .... End-Article Application Code [*Military*]
EAA .... Engineer and Architecture Association (SAUO)
EAA .... Engineer in Aeronautics and Astronautics
EAA .... Engineering Alumni Association (SAUO)
EAA .... Engineering and Architects Association
EAA .... Engineers and Architects Association (SAUO)
EAA .... Entertainment Agents Association [*British*]
EAA .... Environemental Assessment Association (NTPA)
EAA .... Environmental Assessment Act (SAUS)
EAA .... Environment of Evolutionary Adaptedness
EAA .... Epilepsy Association of America [*Later, EFA*]
EAA .... Equipment Approval Authority (AFM)
EAA .... Equity Access Account [*Revolving mortgage-credit account*] [*Merrill Lynch & Co.*]
EAA .... Essential Amino Acid [*Nutrition*]
EAA .... Ethyl Acetoacetate [*Organic chemistry*]
EAA .... Ethylanthranilic Acid [*Organic chemistry*]
EAA .... Ethylene Acrylic Acid [*Organic chemistry*]
EAA .... Ethylene-Acrylic Acid Copolymer (EDCT)
EAA .... Euro-American Alliance (EA)
EAA .... European Academy of Anaesthesiology (EA)
EAA .... European Accounting Association [*Brussels, Belgium*] (EAIO)
EAA .... European Air Agency (SAUO)
EAA .... European Aluminium Association [*Germany*] (EA)
EAA .... European Athletic Association [*Paris, France*]
EAA .... Europeans Against Apartheid (SAUO)
EAA .... Everglades Agricultural Area
EAA .... Evrytanian Association of America (EA)
EAA .... Excitatory Amino Acid [*Neurophysiology*]
EAA .... Excretory Amino Acid
EAA .... Experimental Aircraft Association (EA)
EAA .... Experimental Aviation Association (SAUO)
EAA .... Export Administration Act [*1979*]
EAA .... Export Advertising Association (DGA)
EAA .... External Access Applique (SAUS)
EAA .... Extrinsic Allergic Alveolitis [*Medicine*]
EAA .... Transporte Aereo Andino SA [*Venezuela*] [*ICAO designator*] (FAAC)
EAAA .... European Association of Advertising Agencies
EAAACD .... EAA [*Experimental Aircraft Association*] Antique/Classic Division (EA)
EAAAF .... EAA [*Experimental Aircraft Association*] Aviation Foundation (EA)
EA(A)APP .... Electrical Artificer (Air), Apprentice [*British military*] (DMA)
EAABSH .... English Association of American Bond and Share Holders [*Commercial firm*] (EA)
EAAC .... East African Academy (SAUO)
EAAC .... East African Airways Corp. [*African airline*]
EAAC .... East African Armoured Corps [*British military*] (DMA)
EAAC .... European Academy of Allergology and Clinical Immunology (SAUO)
EAAC .... European Agricultural Aircraft Centre (SAUS)
EAAC .... European Agricultural Aviation Centre [*Later, International Agricultural Aviation Centre*]
EAAC .... European Association of Audiophonological Centres (EA)
EAAC .... Experimental Aircraft Association of Canada (SAUO)
EA ACC .... Each Accident [*Insurance*]
EAACI .... European Academy of Allergology and Clinical Immunology (EAIO)
EAACP .... European-African Airlift Command Post (SAUO)
EAADS .... Enhanced Area Air Defense System
EAAE .... European Association of Agricultural Economists (EA)
EAAEC .... East African Army Educational Corps [*British military*] (DMA)
EAAES .... East African Agricultural Economics Society (SAUO)
EAAFR .... European Academic Association for Financial Research (EAIO)
EAAFRO .... East African Agriculture and Forestry Research Organization
EAAFRO .... European African Agricultural and Forestry Research Organization (SAUS)
EAAH .... Essential Amino Acids plus Histidine [*Nutrition*]
EAAI .... Essential Amino Acid Index (SAUS)
EAAI .... Export Advertising Association, Incorporated (SAUO)
EAAJ .... East African Agricultural and Forestry Journal [*A publication*]
EAAL .... European and American Airways, Limited (SAUO)
EAAM .... European Association for Aquatic Mammals (EA)
EAAM .... European Association of Automobile Manufacturers [*Belgium*] (EAIO)
EAAMC .... East African Army Medical Corps [*British military*] (DMA)
EAandina .... Embotelladora Andina SA [*Associated Press*] (SAG)
EA & OC .... Engineering Administration and Operations Control [*Military*]
EA & P .... East Asian and Pacific [*Series*] [*A publication*]
EAA neuron .... Excitatory Amino Acid neuron (SAUS)
EAAOC .... East African Army Ordnance Corps [*British military*] (DMA)
EA-AP .... Encyclopedia of Associations: Association Periodicals [*A publication*]
EAAP .... European Association for Animal Production [*ICSU*] [*Italian*] (SLS)
EAAPD .... Eastern Air Procurement District (SAUS)
EAAR .... Economists Allied for Arms Reduction (SAUS)
EAARM .... European Academy for Advanced Research in Marketing (SAUO)
EAARS .... Exercise After Action Reporting System (SAUS)
EAAS .... East Asian Art Society
EAAS .... Environmental Analysis and Assessment Section (SAUS)
EAAS .... European Association for American Studies [*Italy*] (EAIO)
EAASC .... East African Army Service Corps (SAUO)
EAASCS .... East Asian Art Society Chinese School
EAASH .... European Academy of Arts, Sciences, and Humanities (EAIO)
EAASN .... European Association for American Studies Newsletter (SAUO)
EAASN .... European Association for American Studies Newsletter (journ.) (SAUS)
EAASY .... Educator's Automated Authoring System (VLIE)
EAAT .... Electronic Aircraft Air Temperature (ACAE)
EAAT .... Excitatory Amino-Acid Transporter [*Neurochemistry*]
EAATS .... Eastern ARNG Aviation Training Site (SAUS)
EAAUA .... EAA [*Experimental Aircraft Association*] Ultralight Association [*Defunct*] (EA)
EAAZ .... East Alcoa Aluminum [*Federal Railroad Administration identification code*]
EAB .... Abbse [*Yemen Arab Republic*] [*Airport symbol*] (OAG)
EAB .... Aberfoyle [*Scotland*] [*Seismograph station code, US Geological Survey*] (SEIS)
EAB .... Eagle Air Ltd. [*Switzerland*] [*ICAO designator*] (FAAC)
EAB .... Economic Advisory Board [*Department of Commerce*] [*Washington, DC*] (EGAO)
EAB .... Economic Affairs Bureau (EA)
EAB .... Economic Analysis Bureau (SAUS)
EAB .... Educational Activities Board (SAUO)
EAB .... Educational Advisory Board [*British*]
EAB .... Education Appeal Board [*Department of Education*] (GFGA)
EAB .... Effective Address Buffer [*Computer science*] (VLIE)
EAB .... Elective Abortion [*Obstetrics*] (DAVI)
EAB .... Electrical Approvals Board (Victoria)
EAB .... Elongation-at-Break [*Textile technology*]
EAB .... Emergency Actions Book
EAB .... Emergency Air Breathing (SAUS)
EAB .... Emergency Air Breathing System (DNAB)
EAB .... Enemy Activities Branch [*British military*] (DMA)

EAB............ Energy Absorption
EAB............ Energy Advisory Board (SAUS)
EAB............ Engineer Aviation Battalion (SAUO)
EAB............ Engineering Action Board (SAUO)
EAB............ Engineering Activity Board (SAUO)
EAB............ Enterprise Access Builder (SAUS)
EAB............ Environmental Appeal Board (SAUO)
EAB............ Esperanto-Asocio de Britujo [*British*]
EAB............ Ethics Advisory Board [*HEW*]
EAB............ Ethnic Affairs Bureau (SAUS)
EAB............ European American Bank (NITA)
EAB............ European Arab Bank (SAUS)
EAB............ European Asian Bank (SAUS)
EAB............ European Associations Bureau (SAUO)
EAB............ Exclusion Area Boundary [*Nuclear energy*] (NRCH)
EAB............ Executive Advisory Board [*Army*] (RDA)
EAB............ Extended Attribute Byte (SAUS)
EAB............ External Access Box (SAUS)
EAB............ Extra-Anatomic Bypass [*Medicine*] (MEDA)
EABC............ Edison Animal Biotechnology Center [*Ohio University*] [*Research center*] (RCD)
EABC............ European Amateur Baseball Confederation (EA)
EABC............ European/ASEAN [*Association of Southeast Asian Nations*] Business Council (DS)
EABF............ effective renal blood flow (SAUS)
EABF............ Entertainment Artists' Benevolent Fund (WDAA)
EABI............ Engineering Agency for Resources Inventories (SAUS)
EABL............ Eastern Bluebird [*North American bird banding code*] (BIBA)
EABM............ Electroactive Biologic Material (DB)
EABM............ Electronically Addressable Bulk Memory [*Computer science*] (VLIE)
EABN............ Engineer Aviation Battalion [*Military*]
EABP............ Encyclopedia of Afterlife Beliefs and Phenomena [*A publication*]
EABR............ East Asia Blocking Ridge [*Meteorology*]
EABRD............ Electrically Activated Bank Release Device (IEEE)
EABRD............ Electrically Actuated Band Release Device (SAUS)
EABRNet............ East Asia Biosphere Reserve Network (SAUO)
EABS............ Erotic Art Book Society [*Commercial firm*] (EA)
EABS............ Euro-Abstracts [*Commission of the European Communities*] [*Information service or system*]
EABT............ European Association for Behavior Therapy (EA)
EABV............ Effective Arterial Blood Volume
EAC............ Early American Coppers (EA)
EAC............ Early Analysis Capabilities (ACAE)
EAC............ East Africa Conference (SAUS)
EAC............ East African Community [*Formed in 1967*] [*Formerly, EACSO*] (AF)
EAC............ East African Countries (UWER)
EAC............ East Asiatic Company Limited (SAUO)
EAC............ East Australian Current [*Oceanography*]
EAC............ Eastern Air Command [*CBI Theater*] [*World War II*]
EAC............ Eastern Arizona College [*Formerly, EAJC*] [*Thatcher*]
EAC............ Echelon Above Corps [*Military*] (RDA)
EAC............ Economic Adjustment Committee (MCD)
EAC............ Economic Advisory Council (SAUO)
EAC............ Economic and Agriculture Census (SAUS)
EAC............ Education Advisory Committee (SAUO)
EAC............ Education Affairs Committee (SAUS)
EAC............ Educational Advisory Committee [*AIAA*]
EAC............ Educational Assessment Center [*University of Washington*] [*Research center*] (RCD)
EAC............ Effective Acoustic Center
EAC............ Effective Atomic Charge
EAC............ Effective Attenuation Coefficient (PDAA)
EAC............ Ehrlich Ascites Carcinoma [*Cells*] [*Oncology*]
EAC............ Eire Air Corps (SAUO)
EAC............ Eire Army Corps
EAC............ Electrical Apparatus Company (SAUO)
EAC............ Electroacupuncture [*Medicine*] (STED)
EAC............ Electroanalytical Chemistry (UWER)
EAC............ Electronic Air Cleaner
EAC............ Electronic Air Control [*Automotive engineering*]
EAC............ Electronic Analog Computer (UWER)
EAC............ Electronic Assistance Corporation (SAUO)
EAC............ Electronic Autocollimator [*Optics*] (IAA)
EAC............ Electronics Association of California (SAUO)
EAC............ Electro-Optical Area Correlator [*Missile guidance system*]
EAC............ Embraer Aircraft Corporation (SAUO)
EAC............ Emerald Agricultural College
EAC............ Emergency Action Cell (SAUS)
EAC............ Emergency Action Center (SAUO)
EAC............ Emergency Action Communications (MCD)
EAC............ Emergency Action Console [*Navy*] (CINC)
EAC............ Emergency Action Coordinator (SAUO)
EAC............ Employee Account Code (SAUS)
EAC............ Employee Activities Committee (SAUS)
EAC............ Empowerment Assistance Council (SAUO)
EAC............ Encyclopedia of Analytical Chemistry (SAUO)
EAC............ End-Around Carry
EAC............ Energy Absorbing Capacity (NASA)
EAC............ Energy Absorption Characteristics (AAG)
EAC............ Engineer Amphibian Command [*World War II*]
EAC............ Engineering Accreditation Commission of ABET (SAUS)
EAC............ Engineering Advisory Committee (SAUO)
EAC............ Engineering Advisory Council (SAUO)
EAC............ Engineering Affairs Council (SAUO)
EAC............ Engineering Aid, Chief [*Navy rating*]
EAC............ Engineering Applications Centre [*University of Strathclyde*] [*British*] (CB)
EAC............ Engineering Automation and Control (PCM)
EAC............ Environmental Action Coalition (EA)
EAC............ Environmental Action Committee (SAUO)
EAC............ Environmental Advisory Committee (SAUS)
EAC............ Environmental Affairs Committee (SAUO)
EAC............ Environmental Assesment Center (SAUO)
eac............ Environmental Assessment Council, Inc. (SAUO)
EAC............ Environmentally Assisted Crack [*Metallurgy*]
EAC............ Epiphany Apostolic College [*New York*]
EAC............ Equipment Availability Constant (MCD)
EAC............ Equity Appreciation Certificate [*Investment term*]
EAC............ Equivalent Annual Cost
EAC............ Erlich Ascites Carcinoma [*Medicine*] (EDAA)
EAC............ Error Alert Control (OA)
EAC............ Erthrocyte, Antibody, Complement [*Medicine*] (STED)
EAC............ Erythema Action [*Medicine*] (STED)
EAC............ Erythema Annualre Centrifugum [*Medicine*] (STED)
EAC............ Erythrocyte Amboceptor Complement [*Immunology*]
EAC............ Erythrocyte-Antibody Complement [*Immunochemistry*]
eac............ erythrocyte antibody complement (SAUS)
EAC............ Estate Agents Cooperative (SAUS)
EAC............ Estate Agents' Council [*British*] (BI)
EAC............ Estimate at Completion (NASA)
EAC............ Estimated Acquisition Cost [*of drug products*] [*HEW*]
EAC............ Estimated Arrival Carrier (MCD)
EAC............ Estimated Cost at Completion (SAUS)
EAC............ Ethnic American Coalition (of Eastern Europeans) (EA)
EAC............ Ethyl Acetamidocinnamate [*Organic chemistry*]
EAC............ Eudismic Affinity Correlation (DB)
EAC............ Euro-Asia Capital Ltd. [*Vancouver Stock Exchange symbol*]
EAC............ Euro-Asia Centre (SAUO)
EAC............ European Accident Code (SAUO)
EAC............ European Accreditation of Certification (SAUS)
EAC............ European Activities Committee (SAUO)
EAC............ European Advisory Commission (SAUO)
EAC............ European Advisory Committee [*Allied German Occupation Forces*]
EAC............ European Advisory Council (EAIO)
EAC............ European Air Charter (SAUO)
EAC............ European Association for Co-Operation
EAC............ European Association of Conservatories (EA)
EAC............ European Astronaut Centre [*Astronomy term*]
EAC............ European Astronautic Center (SAUS)
EAC............ European Atomic Commission (NATG)
EAC............ Evaluation Analysis Center [*Army*]
EAC............ Evangelical Association of the Caribbean (EAIO)
EAC............ Evaporative Air Cooler
EAC............ Except Approach Clearance [*Aviation*] (OA)
EAC............ Executive Air Charter [*ICAO designator*] (FAAC)
EAC............ Exhaust Air Control [*Automotive engineering*]
EAC............ Exhibitors Advisory Council
EAC............ Expect Approach Clearance (SAUS)
EAC............ Expectations about Counseling Questionnaire (EDAC)
EAC............ Expected Approach Clearance [*Aviation*] (AFM)
EAC............ Expedition Advisory Centre [*Royal Geographical Society*] [*British*] (CB)
EAC............ Experiment Apparatus Container
EAC............ Extended Arithmetic Chip
EAC............ Exterior Auditory Canal [*Medicine*] (EDAA)
EAC............ External Auditory Canal [*Anatomy*]
EACA............ Constructionman Apprentice, Engineering Aid, Striker [*Navy rating*]
EACA............ East Africa Court of Appeal Reports (SAUO)
EACA............ Epsilon-Aminocaproic Acid [*Pharmacology*]
EACA............ Eta-Amino-N-Caproic Acid (SAUS)
EACA............ European Association of Charter Airlines (EAIO)
EACA............ European Athletics Coaches Association (EAIO)
EACA............ Law Reports, Court of Appeals of Eastern Africa [*A publication*] (DLA)
EAC/ABET............ Engineering Accreditation Commission of the Accreditation Board for Engineering Technology
EACACT............ Eastern African Centre for Agricultural Credit Training (SAUS)
EAC-AIA............ EEC Advisory Council of the Asbestos International Association (EAIO)
EACBP............ European-American Committee on Reactor Physics (SAUS)
EACC............ East Asia Christian Conference [*Later, Christian Conference of Asia - CCA*]
EACC............ Ecuadorean-American Chamber of Commerce (SAUO)
EACC............ Egyptian American Chamber of Commerce [*Defunct*] (EA)
EACC............ Electronic Asset Control Center (AFM)
EACC............ Emergency Action Control Console (SAUS)
EACC............ Emergency Alternate Command Center (CINC)
EACC............ Environmental Assessment Command Center [*Nuclear energy*] (NRCH)
EACC............ Error Adaptive Control Computer (IEEE)
EACC............ European-American Chamber of Commerce (NTPA)
EACC............ European Association of Audiophonological Centres (SAUO)
EAC COMM............ Echelon Above Corps Communications [*Army*] (DOMA)
EACC-PDH............ Employee Assistance Certification Commission-Professional Development Hours (SAUS)
EACC-USA............ European-American Chamber of Commerce in the United States
EACD............ Eczematous Allergic Contact Dermatitis [*Dermatology*]
EACE............ Euro American Cultural Exchange (EA)
EACE............ European Association of Cognitive Ergonomics (EAIO)

EACEM........ European Association of Consumer Electronic Manufacturers [*EEC*] (PDAA)
EACF........ Employer Identification Number Assignment Control Card File [*IRS*]
EACF........ Extension and Acceleration of Financial Confidence (EURO)
EA/CG........ Ecology Action/Common Ground [*An association*]
EACG........ European Association of Exploration Geophysicis (SAUO)
EACH........ East Camden & Highland Railroad Co. [*AAR code*]
EACH........ Essential Access Community Hospital
EACH........ European Alzheimer Clearing House (SAUS)
EACHG........ East Chicago, IN [*American Association of Railroads railroad junction routing code*]
EACHS........ East African Cargo Handling Services (PDAA)
EACHS........ East African Cargo Handling Services Ltd. (SAUO)
EACI........ Ecology Action Educational Institute (UWER)
EACIC........ Echelons Above Corps Intelligence Center (SAUO)
EACL........ Energie Atomique du Canada, Limitee [*Atomic Energy of Canada Ltd.*]
EACL........ European Association for Chinese Law (EAIO)
EACL........ European Chapter of the Association for Computational Linguistics (VLIE)
EACLALS...... European Branch Association for Commonwealth Literature and Language Studies (SAUO)
EACLN........ Expect Approach Clearance [*Aviation*] (FAAC)
EACM........ Engineering Aid, Master Chief [*Navy rating*]
EACMFS...... European Association for Cranio-Maxillo-Facial Surgery (EAIO)
EACMR........ European Advisory Committee for Medical Research (SAUO)
EACN........ Constructionman, Engineering Aid, Striker [*Navy rating*]
EACN........ Equivalent Alkane Carbon Number [*of crude oil*]
EACN........ European Air Chemistry Network
EACNG........ Emergency Advisory Committee for Natural Gas [*Terminated, 1977*] [*Department of the Interior*] (EGAO)
EACNL........ Expect Approach Clearance Not Later Than [*Aviation*] (FAAC)
EACNSW...... Ethnic Affairs Commission of New South Wales
EACO........ EA Engineering Systems [*NASDAQ symbol*] (NQ)
EACO........ EA Engr Science/Tech [*NASDAQ symbol*] (TTSB)
EACO........ Engineers and Architects Council of Oregon (SAUO)
EACOA........ Endometrioid Endocarcinoma of Ovary [*Medicine*] (MELL)
EA Com........ East African Command (SAUO)
EACON service... Euro-Asia Container Service (SAUS)
ea content... effective-agent content (SAUS)
EACOS........ European Air Combat Operations Staff [*Military*]
EACP........ European Area Communications Plan [*Military*] (AABC)
EACPD........ Emergency Advisory Committee for Political Defense
EACPI........ European Association of Country Planning Institutions (EAIO)
EACR........ Engineering Analysis Closing Report [*Automotive safety*]
EACR........ European Association for Cancer Research (EAIO)
EACRO........ European Association of Contract Research Organisations (or Organizations) (SAUS)
EACRONATAL... Eastern African Centre for Research on Oral Traditions and African National Languages (SAUO)
EACROTANAL... East African Centre for Research in/on Oral Traditions and African National Languages (SAUO)
EACRP........ European-American Committee on Reactor Physics
EACRP........ Extrapolated Alternating Direction Implicit (PDAA)
EACS........ Electronic Automatic Chart System (OA)
EACS........ Engineering Aid, Senior Chief [*Navy rating*]
EACS........ EP/EO [*Employee Plans/Exempt Organization*] Application Control System [*IRS*]
EACS........ European Allied Contacts Section [*Supreme Headquarters, Allied Expeditionary Force*] [*World War II*]
EACS........ European Association for Chinese Studies (SAUO)
EACS........ European Association of Chinese Studies (EA)
EACS........ European Association of Classification Societies (SAUO)
EACSO........ East African Common Services Organization [*Later, EAC*]
EACT........ Emergency Action Coordination Team [*Department of Energy*]
EACTA........ European Association of Cardiothoracic Anaesthesiologists [*Cambridge, England*] (EAIO)
EACV........ Electronic Air Control Valve [*Automotive emissions*]
EACVD........ Electron-Assisted Chemical Vapor Deposition [*Coating technology*]
EAD........ Eadem [*The Same*] [*Pharmacy*]
EAD........ Earliest Arrival Date (AABC)
EAD........ Early After-Depolarization [*Medicine*] (MELL)
EAD........ East Australian Daylight (SAUS)
EAD........ Easy Axis Dispersion [*Solid-state physics*] (UWER)
EAD........ Echelon Above Division [*Military*] (MCD)
EAD........ Economic Analysis Division [*Federal Emergency Management Agency*] [*Information service or system*] (IID)
EAD........ Effective Air Distance
EAD........ Electrically Alterable Device (NASA)
EAD........ Electroacoustic Dewatering (SAUS)
EAD........ Empire Air Day (SAUS)
EAD........ Employer Association of Detroit (SAUO)
EAD........ Employment Authorization Document (SAUS)
EAD........ Enable Application Developer [*Computer science*] (PCM)
EAD........ Encoded Archival Description (TELE)
EAD........ Encoded Archival Description Project (SAUS)
EAD........ Encoding Archival Description (SAUS)
EAD........ Endo-Atmospheric Decoy
EAD........ Energy and Air Division [*Office of Research and Development*] [*Environmental Protection Agency*] (EPA)
EAD........ Engineering Aid, Draftsman [*Navy rating*] [*Obsolete*]
EAD........ Enlisted Assignment Document [*Military*] (DNAB)
E-AD........ Enterprise Applications Development (GART)
EAD........ Entry Acceptance Data (DS)
EAD........ Entry on Active Duty [*Army*]
EAD........ environmental assessment determination (SAUS)
EAD........ Equilibrium Air Distillation (AAG)
EAD........ Equipment Allocation Document (MCD)
EAD........ Equipment Allowance Document (ELAL)
EAD........ Equipment Availability Date (MCD)
EAD........ Equivalent Air Depth [*Deep-sea diving*]
EAD........ Error Adjusted (WDAA)
EAD........ Escort Air Defence mission (SAUS)
EAD........ Estimated Availability Date [*Military*] (AFM)
EAD........ Ethyl Azodicarboxylate [*Organic chemistry*]
EAD........ European Area Differential (SAUS)
EAD........ European Association of Decaffeinators [*France*] (EAIO)
EAD........ Evaluation and Analysis Division [*Environmental science*] (COE)
EAD........ Evaluation and Development (IAA)
EAD........ Exchequer and Audit Department (SAUO)
EAD........ Excitation Absorbed Dose (UWER)
EAD........ Exogenous Antigen Disease [*Medicine*] (MELL)
EAD........ Expected Achievement Date [*Therapy term*] (CTAA)
EAD........ Expected Availability Date (MCD)
EAD........ Expendable Acoustic Device [*Military*] (CAAL)
EAD........ Extended Active Duty
EAD........ Extended Air Defense [*NATO*]
EAD........ Extended Air-Defense Testbed (SAUS)
EAD........ External Aerodynamic Diffusion
EAD........ External Affairs Department (SAUO)
EAD........ Extracranial Arterial Disease [*Medicine*] (STED)
EAD........ Nevada, MO [*Location identifier*] [*FAA*] (FAAL)
EADA........ East African Diploma in Agriculture (SAUS)
EADA........ Eighth Armored Division Association (EA)
EADAS........ Eastern Association of College Deans and Advisers of Students (AEBS)
EADAS........ Engineering and Administrative Data Acquisition System [*Bell System*]
EADASNM.... EADAS/Network Management (SAUS)
EADASNM.... Engineering and Administrative Data Acquisition System/Network Management (VLIE)
EADASS........ Engineering and Administrative Data Acquisition System (SAUS)
EADB........ East African Development Bank [*Uganda*] (AF)
EADB........ Emergency Authorities Database [*Department of Defense*] (DEMM)
EADB........ Experimental Arctic Data Buoy (MSC)
EADC........ Eastern Air Defense Command (SAA)
EADC........ Energy Analysis and Diagnostic Center [*Department of Energy*]
EADC........ Ethylaluminum Dichloride [*Organic chemistry*]
EAD C2........ Extended Air Defense Command and Control [*Army*] (RDA)
EADCC........ Eastern Air Defense Control Center (SAA)
EADCS........ Extended Activity Duty in a Commissioned Status (SAUS)
EADCU........ Enemy Ammunition Disposal and Collection Unit [*Military*] [*British*]
EADD........ East African Development Division (SAUO)
E-ADD........ Epileptic Attentional Deficit Disorder [*Medicine*] (DMAA)
EAD/EAC...... Echelon Above Division / Echelon Above Corps (SAUS)
EADF........ Eastern Air Defense Force
EADF........ Elliptical Aperture with Dynamic Focus (VERA)
EaDI........ Easy Access Data Interchange [*Unisys Corp.*] (IT)
EADI........ Electronic Altitude Director Indicator (SAUS)
EADI........ Electronic Attitude and Direction Indicator
EADI........ Electronic Attitude Directional Indicator (SAUS)
EADI........ Electronic Attitude Direction Indicator (SAUS)
EADI........ Electronic Attitude Director Indicator
EADI........ European Association of Development Research and Training Institutes (EAIO)
EADI........ Extrapolated Alternating Direction Implicit (SAUS)
EADIZ........ Entering Air Defense Identification Zone [*Aviation*] (FAAC)
EADP........ European Association of Directory Publishers (EA)
EADPTA........ Exotic Animal Disease Preparedness Trust Account
EADRI........ European Association of Development Research and Training Institutes
EADS........ Early Amnion Deficit Spectrum [*Medicine*] (EDAA)
EADS........ Echelons Above Division Study [*Military*] (AABC)
EADS........ Emergency Assistance Dispatch System
EADS........ Engineering Administrative Data Systems (MCD)
EADS........ Engineering Analysis and Design Synthesis (SAUS)
EADS........ Engineering Analysis Data System
EADS........ Environmental Assessment Data Systems [*Discontinued*] [*Environmental Protection Agency*] [*Information service or system*] (IID)
EADS........ European Aeronautic Defence & Space Co.
EADSC........ Enhanced Apple Digital Sound Chip [*Computer science*]
EADSIM........ Extended Air Defense Simulation [*Army*] (RDA)
EADTB........ Extended Air Defense Test Bed [*Army*] (RDA)
EAdV........ Equine Adenovirus (SAUS)
EADX........ Echelons Above Division - Expanded [*Military*] (MCD)
EAE........ Aerosevicios Ecuatorianos CA [*Ecuador*] [*ICAO designator*] (FAAC)
EAE........ East African English (SAUS)
EAE........ Ecology Action East [*An association*] (EA)
EAE........ Edetic Acid Eugenics [*Medicine*] (MELL)
EAE........ Elastic After Effect (UWER)
EAE........ Emae [*Vanuatu*] [*Airport symbol*] (OAG)
EAE........ Emergency Action Element (SAUS)
EAE........ Energy and the Environment [*A publication*]
EAE........ Environmentally Assisted Embrittlement (UWER)
EAE........ Ethylaminoethanol [*Organic chemistry*]
EAE........ European Academy of Endodontists (SAUO)
EAE........ European Economic Area (SAUO)
eae........ experimental allergic encephalitis (SAUS)
EAE........ Experimental Allergic Encephalomyelitis [*Medicine*] (AAMN)

EAE .... Experimental Autoimmune Encephalomyelitis [*Medicine*]
EAE .... Extended Arithmetic Element
EAEB .... East Anglian Examinations Board (AIE)
EAEBP .... European Association of Editors of Biological Periodicals (DIT)
EAEC .... East African Economic Community
EAEC .... East African Engineering Consultants (SAUO)
EAEC .... East Asian Economic Caucus
EAEC .... Enteroadherent Escherichia Coli [*Medicine*] (EDAA)
EAEC .... European Airlines Electronic Committee
EAEC .... European Atomic Energy [*Medicine*] (EDAA)
EAEC .... European Atomic Energy Commission (SAUS)
EAEC .... European Atomic Energy Community [*Also, EURATOM*] (DCTA)
EAEC .... European Automotive Engineers Cooperation
EAEE .... European Association for Earthquake Engineering (PDAA)
EAEE .... Evangelische Arbeitsgemeinschaft fuer Erwachsenenbildung in Europa [*Protestant Association for Adult Education in Europe*] (EAIO)
EAEF .... Energy Action Educational Foundation [*Later, EAEP*] (EA)
EAEG .... East Asian Economic Group [*Australia*]
EAEG .... European Association of Exploration Geophysicists (EAIO)
EAEI .... Ecology Action Educational Institute (EA)
EA/EIS .... Environmental Assessment/Environmental Impact Statement [*Army*] (RDA)
EAEM .... European Airlines Electronics Meeting (PDAA)
EAEME .... East African Electrical and Mechanical Engineers [*British military*] (DMA)
EAENF .... Engineering and Allied Employers National Federation (SAUO)
EA Eng .... EA Engineering Systems [*Associated Press*] (SAG)
EAEO .... Equal Access End Office (CCCA)
EAEP .... Energy Action Educational Project of C/LEC [*Defunct*] (EA)
EAEP .... European Association for Earthquake Prediction (SAUO)
EAER .... East African Economic Review (journ.) (SAUS)
EAERE .... European Association of Environmental and Resource Economists (EERA)
EAES .... electron excited AES (SAUS)
EAES .... Environment Atmospheric Environment Service (SAUS)
EAES .... European Atomic Energy Society
EAESP .... European Association of Experimental Social Psychology (EA)
EAET .... East African External Telecommunications Co. (PDAA)
EAET .... East African External Telecommunications Company (SAUO)
EAETB .... Efficienoy and Alternative Energy Technology Branch (SAUS)
EAETLFEM ... European Association for the Exchange of Technical Literature in the Field of Ferrous Metallurgy (SAUO)
EAETLFFM ... European Association for the Exchange of Technical Literature in the Field of Ferrous Metallurgy [*Luxembourg*] (EA)
EAEVE .... European Association of Establishments for Veterinary Education (GVA)
EAEWA .... Engineering and Allied Employers West of England Association (SAUO)
EAF .... Earth Awareness Fair (SAUO)
EAF .... Earth Awareness Foundation (EA)
EAF .... Earth's Armed Forces (SAA)
EAF .... East Africa (SAUS)
EAF .... Economic Accounts for Forestry (EURO)
EAF .... Educational Accountability Function (OICC)
EAF .... Education and Research Foundation (SAUO)
EAF .... EECONET Action Fund (SAUS)
EAF .... Effort Adjustment Factor
EAF .... Egyptian Air Force
EAF .... Electric Arc Furnace [*Steelmaking*]
EAF .... Electric Arc Furnaces (SAUS)
EAF .... Electron Arc Furnace (IAA)
EAF .... Emergency Action File [*Air Force*] (AFM)
EAF .... Emergency Assistance to Families [*Medicine*] (EDAA)
EAF .... Emery Air Freight Corp. (SAUO)
EAF .... Employment Agents' Federation of Great Britain (BI)
EAF .... Engineering Analysis Facility (SSD)
EAF .... Environmental Action Foundation (EA)
EAF .... Eosinophil-Activating Factor [*Immunology*]
EAF .... Equivalent Availability Factor (IEEE)
EAF .... European Aviation Air Charter Ltd. [*British*] [*FAA designator*] (FAAC)
EAF .... Exhaust Air Filter
EAF .... Expeditionary Airfield (MCD)
EAF .... Experiment Analysis Form (KSC)
EAF .... Experimenter's Analysis Facility (ADWA)
EAF .... Extra-Articular Fracture [*Medicine*] (MELL)
EAF .... Fairbanks, AK [*Location identifier*] [*FAA*] (FAAL)
EAFB .... Edwards Air Force Base [*California*]
EAFB .... Eglin Air Force Base [*Florida*]
EAFB .... Elison Air Force Base [*Alaska*] (KSC)
EAFB .... Ellington Air Force Base [*Texas*] (KSC)
EAFB .... Ellsworth Air Force Base [*South Dakota*] (SAA)
EAFC .... Eastern Area Frequency Coordinator
EAFC .... Eastern Association of Fire Chiefs (SAUO)
EAFDEV .... Effort Adjustment Factor, Development [*Military*]
EAFE .... Europe, Australia, and Far East
EAFFRO .... East African Freshwater Fisheries Research Organization
EAFHS .... Eighth Air Force Historical Society (EA)
EAFL .... East Africa Feeder Line (SAUS)
EAFMAIN ..... Effort Adjustment Factor, Maintenance [*Military*]
EAFORD .... International Organisation for the Elimination of All Forms of Racial Discrimin ation [*Geneva, Switzerland*] (EAIO)
EAFPEB .... European Armed Forces Professional Entertainment Branch (SAUO)
EAFPED .... European Armed Forces Professional Entertainment Division (SAUO)
E Afr .... East Africa
E African LJ ... East African Law Journal [*A publication*] (DLA)
E Afr LR .... East Africa Law Reports [*A publication*] (DLA)
E Afr L Rev ... Eastern Africa Law Review [*A publication*] (DLA)
EAFRO .... East Africa Fisheries Research Organization (SAUO)
EAFRO .... East African Fishery Research Organization (SAUS)
EAFS .... Effective Aerial Film Speed (SAUS)
EAFS .... European Academy of Facial Surgery (EAIO)
EAG .... Eagle Flying Services Ltd. [*British*] [*ICAO designator*] (FAAC)
EAG .... Eaglet Mines Ltd. [*Toronto Stock Exchange symbol*] [*Vancouver Stock Exchange symbol*]
EAG .... Eagle Wireless Intl. [*AMEX symbol*] (SG)
EAG .... Economic Analysis Group [*General Accounting Office*] [*Washington, DC*] (GRD)
EAG .... Edmonton Art Gallery (SAUS)
EAG .... Electroantennogram [*Entomology*]
EAG .... Electroarteriography [*Medicine*] (MELL)
EAG .... Electrotechnical Association of Greece (SAUO)
EAG .... ELINT [*Electronic Intelligence*] Advisory Group (AABC)
EAG .... Empty (or Express) [*Anal glands*] (SPVS)
EAG .... End of Area Group (SAUO)
EAG .... Environmental Analysis Group [*Army*]
EAG .... Environmental Assessments Group (SAUS)
EAG .... Equipment Advisory Group
E-AG .... European Atlantic Group [*British*] (DBA)
EAG .... Evaluation and Analysis Group [*Bureau of Ordnance*] [*Washington, DC*] [*Navy*] (MCD)
EAG .... Experimental Miscellaneous Auxiliary [*Navy symbol*]
EAG .... Exposure Assessment Group [*Environmental Protection Agency*] (GFGA)
EAG .... Extended Active Gate (ACAE)
EAG .... External Advisory Group (EURO)
EAG .... Ministry of External Affairs, Government Documents [*UTLAS symbol*]
EAG .... Economists Advisory Group (ODA)
EAGA .... East Asian Growth Area [*International Trade*]
EAGA .... Episcopal Actor's Guild of America (EA)
Eag & Y .... Eagle and Younge's English Tithe Cases [*A publication*] (DLA)
Eag & Yo .... Eagle and Younge's English Tithe Cases [*A publication*] (DLA)
EAGB .... Executives Association of Great Britain [*England*] (EAIO)
EAGB .... Eyewear Association of Great Britain (SAUO)
EAGBR .... Eagle Bridge, NY [*American Association of Railroads railroad junction routing code*]
EAGE .... Electrical Aerospace Ground Equipment (TEL)
EAGER .... Electronic Audit Gauger
EAGF .... Electrically Augmented Gravity Filter [*Chemical engineering*]
EAGGF .... European Agricultural Guidance and Guarantee Fund [*Also known as FEOGA*]
EAGL .... Eagle Financial Corp. (MHDW)
EAGL .... Eagle Hardware & Garden [*NASDAQ symbol*] (TTSB)
EAGL .... Eagle Hardware & Garden, Inc. [*NASDAQ symbol*] (SAG)
EAGL .... East Atlantic Gymnastics League (PSS)
EAGLA .... Eagle Lake, TX [*American Association of Railroads railroad junction routing code*]
EAGLE .... Educational Assessment Guidelines Leading [*Toward*] Excellence
EAGLE .... Elevation Angle Guidance Landing Equipment
EAGLE .... Energy Absorbing Gas Lithium Ejector (MCD)
EAGLE .... Environmental Assessment of Great Lakes Ecosystems [*United States Fish and Wildlife Service*] (ASF)
EAGLE .... EOS Atmospheric Global LIDAR Experiment (SAUS)
EAGLE .... European Association for Grey Literature Exploitation [*Database producer*] (EAIO)
EAGLE .... Exchange on Ageing, the Law and Ethics (SAUO)
EAGLE .... Expense Analysis of Gross Laboratory Effort (SAUS)
EAGLE .... Experiment and Guidance Loop Evaluator
EAGLE .... Extended Application of Ground LASER Equipment (MCD)
EagleBcp .... Eagle Bancorp, Inc. [*Associated Press*] (SAG)
Eagle Bull .... Eagle Bulletin [*A publication*] (UWER)
EaglFnce .... Eagle Finance Corp. [*Associated Press*] (SAG)
EaglFncl .... Eagle Financial [*Associated Press*] (SAG)
EaglPac .... Eagle Pacific Industries, Inc. [*Associated Press*] (SAG)
Eag Mag Com ... Eagle's Magistrate's Pocket Companion [*A publication*] (DLA)
EAGMI .... Eagle Mills, AR [*American Association of Railroads railroad junction routing code*]
EAGO .... European Association for/of Gynaecologists and Obstetricians (SAUO)
EAGO .... European Association of Gynaecologists and Obstetrician (SAUS)
EAGPA .... Eagle Pass, TX [*American Association of Railroads railroad junction routing code*]
EagPnt .... Eagle Point Software Corp. [*Associated Press*] (SAG)
EAGR .... Eared Grebe [*North American bird banding code*] (BIBA)
EAGR .... East African Geographical Review [*A publication*]
EAGS .... English and Germanic Studies [*A publication*]
EAGS .... European Association of Exploration Geophysics [*International Council of Scientific Unions*]
Eag T .... Eagle's Law of Tithes [*2nd ed.*] [*1836*] [*A publication*] (DLA)
EAH .... Eastern Air Transport, Inc. [*FAA designator*] (FAAC)
EAH .... Effective Antenna Height (OTD)
EAH .... El Arish [*Egypt*] [*Airport symbol*] (AD)
EAH .... Engineering Association of Hawaii (SAUO)
EAH .... Epochs of Ancient History [*A publication*]
EAH .... European Academy of History (EA)
EAH .... Express Attention Handling (SAUS)
EAHA .... European Association of Hospital Administrators (EA)
EAHC .... East Africa High Commission (SAUO)
EAHC .... East Asia Hydrographic Commission [*Marine science*] (OSRA)
EAHC .... Essex Archaeological and Historical Congress (SAUO)

EAHCA .... Education for All Handicapped Children [*1975*] (DIPS)
EAHCA .... Education of All Handicapped Children Act
EAHCCL .... Educators' Ad Hoc Committee on Copyright Law (EA)
eahf .... eczema, asthma, and hay fever (SAUS)
EAHF .... Eczema, Asthma, Hay Fever [*Medicine*]
EAHHFC .... Engel's Angels in Humperdinck Heaven Fan Club (EA)
EAHIL .... European Association of Health Information and Libraries [*Stockholm, Sweden*] (EAIO)
EAHILC .... Erie Area Health Information Library Cooperative [*Library network*]
EAHLG .... Equine Antihuman Lymphoblast Globulin [*Immunochemistry*] (MAE)
EAHLS .... Equine Antihuman Lymphoblast Serum [*Immunochemistry*] (MAE)
EAHM .... European Association of Hospital Managers [*France*] (EAIO)
EAHP .... European Association of Haematopathology (SAUO)
EAHP .... European Association of Hospital Pharmacists (EAIO)
EAHQ .... Ethylanthrahydroquinone [*Organic chemistry*]
EAHTMA ...... Engineers' and Allied Hand Tool Makers' Association [*British*] (BI)
EAHY .... European Architectural Heritage Year [*1975*]
EAI .... East Asian Institute (SAUS)
EAI .... Economic Abstracts International [*Database*] (NITA)
EAI .... Education Audit Institute [*Washington, DC*]
EAI .... Electronic-Aided Instruction (IAA)
EAI .... Electronic Arts Intermix
EAI .... Electronic Associates, Inc.
EAI .... Emphysema Anonymous, Inc. (EA)
EAI .... Emulsifying Activity Index [*Food analysis*]
EAI .... Encyclopedia of American Industries [*A publication*]
EAI .... Engineering Advance Information (SAUS)
EAI .... Engineers and Architects Institute [*Defunct*]
EAI .... Entergy Arkansas, Inc. Capital I [*NYSE symbol*] (SAG)
EAI .... Enterprise Application Integration (RALS)
EAI .... Enterprise for the Americas Initiative [*Bush administration*]
EAI .... Equal-Appearing Intervals (EDAC)
EAI .... Equip and Install (IAA)
EAI .... Ethyl Acetimidate [*Biochemistry*]
EAI .... European Airbus Industry (SAUO)
EAI .... Expanded Academic Index (UWER)
EAI .... External Authoring Interface (SAUS)
EAIA .... Early American Industries Association (EA)
EAIB .... European Association of International Booksellers (SAUO)
EAIC .... East African Industrial Council (SAUO)
EAIC .... East Asian Insurance Corporation (SAUO)
EAIC .... Electronic Air Inlet Controller (MCD)
EAID .... Electronic Anti-Intrusion Device (DNAB)
EAID .... Engine Air Intake Duct [*Hovercraft*]
EAID .... Equipment Authorization Inventory Data [*Air Force*] (AFM)
EAID .... Equipment Authorizations Inventory Document (SAUS)
EAID .... ESRO [*European Space Research Organization*] Advanced Imaging Detector [*Satellite*]
EAIDL .... Equipment Authorization Inventory Data Listing [*Air Force*] (AFM)
EAIDS .... Equipment Authorization Inventory Data System [*Air Force*] (AFIT)
EAIHILC .... Erie Area Health Information Library Cooperative (SAUS)
EAII .... Engineering Animation [*NASDAQ symbol*] (TTSB)
EAIM .... End Article Item Manager (AFIT)
EAIM .... European Alliance for Information Management (SAUS)
EAIMB .... East Africa Industries Management Board (SAUO)
EAIN .... Education Alternative, Inc. [*NASDAQ symbol*] (SAG)
EAIN .... Education Alternatives [*NASDAQ symbol*] (TTSB)
EA-IO .... Encyclopedia of Associations: International Organizations [*A publication*]
EAIR .... End Article Identity Record
EAIR .... Enterprise Analysis integration Review (SAUS)
EAIR .... European Higher Education Society (SAUO)
EAIR .... Extended Area Instrumentation RADAR (MCD)
EAIRO .... East African Industrial Research Organization (SAUO)
EAIS .... East Antarctic Ice Sheet
EAIS .... Extended Area Instrumentation System (MCD)
EAISR .... East Africa Institute of Social Research (SAUO)
EAITC .... External Affairs and International Trade Canada [*Government agency*]
EAJ .... Editor, Army Journal (SAUS)
EAJA .... Equal Access to Justice Act [*1980*]
EAJC .... Eastern Arizona Junior College [*Later, EAC*]
EAJCC .... European Association of Jewish Community Centres (EAIO)
EAJ Criminol... East African Journal of Criminology [*A publication*] (DLA)
EAJP .... East Asia Journalism Program (EA)
EAK .... East Kootenay Community College Library [*UTLAS symbol*]
EAK .... Einleitung in die Assyrischen Koenigsinschriften [*A publication*] (BJA)
EAK .... Electronic Acupuncture Kit [*Medicine*] (EDAA)
EAK .... Ethyl Amyl Ketone [*Organic chemistry*]
EAK .... Kenya [*International vehicle registration*] (ODBW)
EAKI .... Eastern Kingbird [*North American bird banding code*] (BIBA)
EAL .... Eagle Industry [*Vancouver Stock Exchange symbol*]
EAL .... Early American Life Insurance Association (EA)
EAL .... Early American Literature [*A publication*] (ANEX)
EAL .... East Asian Library (SAUS)
EAL .... East Asiatic Line (SAUS)
EAL .... Eastern Airlines Inc. (SAUO)
EAL .... Economic Alert List (CARL)
EAL .... Educational Assistance Ltd. (PCM)
EAL .... Ehrenfest Adiabatic Law [*Physics*]
EAL .... Electromagnetic Amplifying Lens
EAL .... Electronic Associates Limited (NITA)
EAL .... Electronics Appointments, Limited (SAUO)
EAL .... Emergency Action Level [*Nuclear energy*] (NRCH)
EAL .... Engineer Acquisition Letter (AAGC)
Eal .... English as an additional language (SAUS)
EAL .... Environmental Acoustics Laboratory [*Pennsylvania State University*] [*Research center*] (RCD)
EAL .... Environmental Awareness Lubricant
EAL .... Equalized Assessed Valuation
EAL .... Equipment Air Lock [*Nuclear energy*] (NRCH)
EAL .... Equipment Applications List (MCD)
EAL .... Equivalent Age Load (IAA)
EAL .... Estimated [*or Expected*] Average Life
EAL .... Ethanolamine Ammonia Lyase [*An enzyme*]
EAL .... Ethiopia Air Lines
EAL .... Ethiopian Airlines (SAUO)
EAL .... Ethiopian Airlines Share Company (SAUO)
EAL .... European cooperation for Accreditation of Laboratories (SAUS)
EAL .... Executive Appointments Limited (SAUO)
EAL .... Expected Average Life [*Physics*] (IAA)
EAL .... Extended Average Level (UWER)
EAL .... Philippine Eagle Airlines [*FAA designator*] (FAAC)
EALA Bull .... East African Library Association Bulletin (SAUO)
EALB .... East African Literature Bureau
EALCAE .... Ecumenical Association of Laity Centres and Academies in Europe [*See also OVATE*] [*Germany*] (EAIO)
EALCC .... East Anglian Librarians (SAUS)
EALCR .... East African Leprosy Research Centre (SAUO)
EALIS .... Egyptian Association of Archives, Librarianship and Information Science (SAUO)
EALJ .... East African Law Journal [*A publication*] (DLA)
EALJS .... Egyptian Association of Archives, Librarianship and Information Science (SAUO)
EALM .... Electron-Beam Addressed Light Modulator (PDAA)
EALM .... Electronic Address Light Modulator
EALM .... Electronically Addressed Light Modulator (SAUS)
EALM .... European Association of Livestock Markets [*See also AEMB*] [*Belgium*] (EAIO)
EALP .... East African Light and Power (SAUS)
EALR .... East Africa Law Reports [*A publication*] (DLA)
EALRGA .... East Asian Library Resources Group of Australia
EALS .... English & American Literature Section [*Association of College and Research Libraries*] [*American Library Association*]
EALT .... earliest anticipated launch time (SAUS)
E-ALT .... ERS-1 Altimeter (SAUS)
EAM .... Eastern Atlantic and Mediterranean (SAUS)
EAM .... Economic and Applied Microbiology (SAUS)
EAM .... electric accounting machine (SAUS)
EAM .... Electric Adding Machine (SAUS)
EAM .... Electric Addition Mechanism (SAUS)
EAM .... Electrical Accounting Machine (NITA)
EAM .... Electrical and Mechanical (SAUS)
EAM .... Electrically Alterable Memory [*Computer science*]
EAM .... Electrically Memory (SAUS)
EAM .... Electro-Absorption Modulator (AAEL)
EAM .... Electromechanic Accounting Machine (SAUS)
EAM .... Electronic Accounting Machine [*Computer science*]
EAM .... Electronic Accounting Machinery (SAUS)
eam .... electronic accounting methods (SAUS)
EAM .... Electronic Automatic Machinery
EAM .... Elementary Access Method (IAA)
EAM .... Embedded-Atom Method [*Model of interatomic interaction*]
EAM .... Emergency Action Message [*Navy*] (NVT)
EAM .... Encapsidated Adenovirus Minichromosome
EAM .... Endo-N-Acetylmuramidase (DB)
EAM .... Entered Apprentice Mason [*Freemasonry*] (ROG)
EAM .... Enterprise Asset Management (GART)
EAM .... Environmental ALARA Memorandum (SAUS)
EAM .... Environmental Aspects of Mining (SAUO)
EAM .... Equipment Acquisition Manual (DNAB)
EAM .... Equipment Asset Management (GART)
EAM .... Ergonomic Accident Model [*Engineering*]
EAM .... Ethnikon Apelephtherotikon Metopon [*National Liberation Front*] [*Greek*] (PPE)
EAM .... Ethylene-Acrylate Copolymer (SAUS)
EAM .... Evanescent Access Method [*Sperry UNIVAC*]
EAM .... [*The*] Evangelical Alliance Mission [*An association*] (NTCM)
EAM .... Ewald Ernst Air-Service [*Germany*] [*FAA designator*] (FAAC)
EAM .... exercise and monitoring (SAUS)
EAM .... Extended Answer Message (SAUS)
EAM .... Extended Answer Message indication (SAUS)
EAM .... External Auditory Meatus [*Anatomy*]
EAM .... Nejran [*Saudi Arabia*] [*Airport symbol*] (OAG)
EAMA .... Etats Africains et Malgache Associes [*Associated African and Malagasy States*]
EAM/AIF .... Expense Appropriation Management/Army Industrial Fund
EAMAS .... Emergency Action Message Authentication System [*Military*]
EAMC .... Eastern Atlantic and Mediterranean Command [*Military*]
EAMC .... European Airlines Montparnasse Committee (SAUO)
EAMC .... European Air Materiel Command (SAUO)
EAMCBP .... European Association of Makers of Corrugated Base Papers (EAIO)
EAM Co .... Engineer Aviation Maintenance Company (SAUO)
EAMD .... Engineered Average Monthly Demand [*Military*]
EAMD .... Equivalent Aerodynamic Median Diameter [*of atmospheric particulates*]
EAMDA .... European Alliance of Muscular Dystrophy Associations (SAUO)
EAME .... Europe-Africa-Middle East (TIMI)
EAME .... European, African, Middle Eastern (SAUS)

EAME AACS ... Europe, Africa and Middle East Airways and Communication Service (SAUO)
EAMECM ... European-African-Middle Eastern Campaign Medal [*Military decoration*]
EAMEDPM ... Electric Accounting Machine and Electronic Data Processing Machine
EAMF ... European Association of Music Festivals (EA)
EAMFRO ... East African Marine Fisheries Research Organization (USDC)
EAMFS ... European Association for Maxillo-Facial Surgery (EA)
EAMG ... Electric Arc Metallizing Gun
EAMG ... Experimental Autoimmune Myasthenia Gravis [*Medicine*]
EAMHD ... Engineering Aspects of Magnetohydrodynamics [*A publication*] (MCD)
EAMHMS ... European Association of Museums of the History of Medical Sciences [*See also AEMHSM*] (EAIO)
EAMI ... Expansion Anchor Manufacturers Institute (EA)
EAM Indication ... Extended-Answer-Message Indication (SAUS)
EAM-Institute ... European Advanced Materials Institute (SAUO)
EAMJ ... East African Management Journal [*A publication*]
EAMLS ... East Africa Military Labour Service (SAUO)
EAMLS ... East African Military Labour Service [*British military*] (DMA)
EAMM ... Early Alert Motivation Mail-out Flyer (SAUS)
EAMM ... Electronic Access to Medieval Manuscripts
EAMP ... Engine Analytical Maintenance Program [*Navy*] (NVT)
EAMP ... Envoy Extraordinaire and Minister Plenipotentiary (SAUS)
EAMR ... Engineering Advance Material Release (KSC)
EAMREA ... Environmental Impact Assessment of Mineral Resource Exploitation and Exploration in Antarctica (SAUS)
EAMRX ... Evergreen Amer. Retire. Cl.Y [*Mutual fund ticker symbol*] (SG)
EAMS ... Educational Assistance Management System (TIMI)
EAMS ... Empire Air Mail Scheme (SAUS)
EAMS ... Euro-Arab Management School [*Granada, Spain*] (ECON)
EAM/SELREL ... Emergency Action Message/Selected Release (MCD)
EAMSP ... East African Marine Science Programme (SAUS)
EAmst ... Elsevier Amsterdam (SAUS)
EAMT ... Expanded Alternative Minimum Tax
EAMTC ... European Association of Management Training Centres
EAMTM ... European Association of Machine Tool Merchants [*British*] (EAIO)
EAMTMC ... Eastern Area Military Traffic Management Command (AFIT)
EAMTMTS ... Eastern Area, Military Traffic Management and Terminal Service (AABC)
EAMU ... East Africa Malaria Unit, Amani (SAUO)
EAMU ... Electric Accounting Machine Unit
EAMVBD ... East African Institute of Malaria and Vector-Borne Disease [*Tanzania*] (PDAA)
e-an- ... Andorra [*MARC geographic area code*] [*Library of Congress*] (LCCP)
EAN ... Association Internationale de Numerotation des Articles [*International Article Numbering Association*] (EAIO)
EAN ... Eastern Mines Ltd. [*Vancouver Stock Exchange symbol*]
EAN ... Effective Atomic Number
EAN ... Emergency Action Notification [*Civil Defense*]
EAN ... Engineering Association of Nashville (SAUO)
EAN ... Enriched Air Nitrox (SAUS)
EAN ... Equivalent Atomic Number
EAN ... European Academic Network (SAUO)
EAN ... European Advanced Networking (Protocol) (SAUS)
EAN ... European Article Number [*Equivalent of Universal Product Code*]
EAN ... European Article Number, Extragalactic Area Network, (SAUS)
EAN ... European Article Numbering Association (SAUO)
EAN ... Expenditure Account Number
EAN ... Experimental Allergic Neuritis [*Medicine*]
EAN ... Experimental Autoimmune Neuritis [*Medicine*]
EAN ... Express Airways Nigeria Ltd. [*ICAO designator*] (FAAC)
EAN ... External Access Network (SAUS)
EAN ... Extragalactic Area Network (SAUO)
EAN ... International Article Numbering Association (SAUO)
EAN ... Wheatland, WY [*Location identifier*] [*FAA*] (FAAL)
EANA ... Esperanto Association of North America [*Defunct*] (EA)
EANA ... European Alliance of News Agencies
EANAC ... European Association of Nurses in AIDS Care (SAUS)
EANC ... Elastically Active Network Chain (UWER)
EANC ... Estonian American National Council (EA)
EANCO ... Emergency Actions Noncommissioned Officer [*Army*] (AABC)
E & A ... Ecclesiastical and Admiralty Reports [*1853-55*] [*A publication*] (DLA)
E & A ... Engineering and Acquisition
E & A ... Errata and Addenda (NRCH)
E & A ... Error and Appeal [*Legal term*] (DLA)
E&A ... Euthanasia and Aftercare (SPVS)
E & A ... Evaluate and Advise [*Medicine*] (MELL)
E&A ... Evaluation and Assistance Visits (SAUS)
E and A ... Exchequer and Audit Department [*British government*]
E & A ... Spinks' English Ecclesiastical and Admiralty Reports [*A publication*] (DLA)
E & A ... Upper Canada Error and Appeal Reports [*A publication*] (DLA)
E & A Co ... Eastern and Australian Steamship Company (SAUO)
E & AD ... Exchequer and Audit Department [*British government*] (RDA)
E & AR ... Error and Appeal Reports [*Canada*] [*A publication*] (DLA)
E & AUC ... Grant's Error and Appeal Reports [*A publication*] (DLA)
E & B ... Ellerman & Bucknall Steamship Co. (MHDW)
E & B ... Ellis and Blackburn's English Queen's Bench Reports [*118-120 English Reprint*] [*A publication*] (DLA)
EANDC ... Edgewood Arsenal Nuclear Defense Center [*Maryland*] [*Army*]
E&C ... Electronics and Control (ACAE)
E & C ... Engineering and Construction
EANDC ... European-American Nuclear Data Committee [*OECD*]
E & CB1S ... Edge and Center Bead on One Side [*Technical drawings*]
E & CB1S ... Edge and Centre Bead One Side (SAUS)
E & CB2S ... Edge and Centre Bead on Two Side (SAUS)
E & CB2S ... Edge and Center Bead on Two Sides [*Technical drawings*]
E & CB2S ... Edge and Centre Bead Two Sides (SAUS)
E&CC ... Education and Communication Center (TIMI)
E&CF ... Events and Causal Factors [*Environmental science*] (COE)
E & CN ... Engine and Crew Navigation (SAUS)
E&CV1S ... Edge & Center V One Side (SAUS)
e & cV 1 s ... edge and center-V one side (SAUS)
E & CV1S ... Edge and Center V on One Side [*Technical drawings*]
E & CV2S ... Edge and Center V on Two Sides [*Technical drawings*]
E&CV2S ... Edge & Center V Two Sides (SAUS)
e & cV 2 s ... edge and center-V two sides (SAUS)
E & D ... Education and Development
E&D ... Eldery & Disabled (SAUO)
E & D ... Engineering and Development Directorate [*Johnson Space Center*] [*NASA*] (NASA)
E & D ... Experimental and Demonstration Projects
e & d ... exploration and development (SAUS)
E&DCP ... Evaluation and Data Collection Plan [*Environmental science*] (COE)
E & DO ... Experimental and Development Operations (MCD)
E&E ... Ecology & Environment, Inc. (EFIS)
E & E ... Ellis and Ellis' English Queen's Bench Reports [*A publication*] (DLA)
E & E ... Escape and Evasion
E & E ... Evacuation and Evasion
E&E ... Evasion and Escape [*Military*] (POLM)
E and E ... Evasion and Escape (SAUS)
E & E ... Eye and Ear (MELL)
e & e ... Each and Every (ODA)
E & EA ... Each and Every Accident [*Insurance*] (AIA)
e&ea ... Each and Every Accident (MARI)
E & ED ... English and Empire Digest [*A publication*] (DLA)
E & E Dig ... English and Empire Digest [*A publication*] (DLA)
E & EL ... Each and Every Loss [*Insurance*] (AIA)
e&el ... Each and Every Loss (MARI)
E & EO ... Each and Every Occurrence [*Insurance*] (AIA)
e&eo ... Each and Every Occurrence (MARI)
E&EO ... Errors and Omissions Excepted (SAUS)
E&ERFTS ... Elementary & Reserve Training School (SAUO)
E&ERFTS ... Elementary & Reserve Training School, at Sywell before WWII. (SAUS)
E & ES ... Environmental and Energy Systems
E&ET ... Energy and Environmental Technologies (SAUS)
e&f ... ebb and flood (SAUS)
E & F ... Economic and Financial [*Plans*] [*British*]
E & F ... Elder and Fyfes Ltd. [*Shipping*] (ROG)
E & FC ... Examined and Found Correct (ADA)
E&G ... Educational and General [*Expenditure*]
E & Ger St ... English and German Studies (journ.) (SAUS)
E & GVR ... Ellesmere & Glyn Valley Railway [*Later, GVR*] [*Wales*]
E&H ... Elderly and Handicapped [*TRB*] (TAG)
E&H ... Environment and Health (COE)
E & H ... Environment and Heredity
E & H ... Euchromatin and Heterochromatin [*Medicine*] (MELL)
E & HC ... Emory and Henry College (SAUS)
E&HCD ... Environmental and Health Compliance Division (SAUS)
E&HPD ... Environmental and Health Protection Division (SAUS)
E&I ... Electrical and Instrumentation (SAUS)
E & I ... Endocrine and Infertility [*Endocrinology and obstetrics*] (DAVI)
E&I ... Engineering and Installation (CCCA)
E & I ... English and Irish Appeals, House of Lords [*A publication*] (DLA)
E & I ... Equip and Install (MSA)
E & I ... Examination and Inventory (AFIT)
E & I App ... Law Reports, House of Lords, English and Irish Appeals [*1866-75*] [*A publication*] (DLA)
E & ID ... Education and Information Dissemination
E&IR ... Education and International Relations Committee (SAUS)
E & L ... Elrick & Lavidge, Inc. (WDMC)
E & L ... Engineering and Laboratory (KSC)
E & L ... Equity & Law [*Brokerage group*] [*British*]
E&M ... Ear & Mouth [*Communications term*] (DCT)
E&M ... Earth & Magnet (MLOA)
E & M ... Effectiveness and Maintainability (MCD)
E & M ... Electrical and Mechanical (KSC)
E & M ... Endocrine and Metabolism [*Medicine*] (DAVI)
E and M ... Endocrine and Metabolism (SAUS)
E&M ... Engineering and Maintenance Division (SAUS)
E and M ... Erection and Maintenance (SAUS)
E & M ... Erection and Maintenance
E & MC ... Electrical and Mechanical Compatibility [*Military*]
E & MCC ... Electrical and Mechanical Capability Committee
E & MCWG ... Electrical and Mechanical Capability Working Group
E & MIWG ... Electrical and Mechanical Interface Working Group [*Strategic Defense Initiative*]
E and MJ ... Engineering and Mining Journal (SAUS)
E & MJ Eng Min J ... E & MJ Engineering and Mining Journal (journ.) (SAUS)
E & ML ... Environmental and Morale Leave [*Military*]
E&M leads ... Ear and Mouth Lead [*A headpiece unit used by telephone operators and broadcasters*] (WDMC)
E & MR ... Energy & Mineral Resources [*Business Publishers, Inc.*] [*No longer available online*] [*Information service or system*] (CRD)
E&MT ... Engineering and Manufacturing Technologies (SAUS)
E & NR ... Esquimalt and Nanaimo Railway (SAUS)
E&O ... Errors & Omissions (EBF)
E&O ... Erros & Omissions (TDOB)

E and OE ..... Errors and Omissions Excepted [*Insurance*]
E&OSD .... Environmental and Occupational Safety Division (SAUS)
E & OT .... Enemy and Occupied Territories Department [*Ministry of Economic Warfare*] [*British*] [*World War II*]
E & P .... Earnings and Profit (ADA)
e&p .... earnings and profits (SAUS)
E&P .... Editor & Publisher (WDMC)
E and P .... Editor and Publisher (SAUS)
E & P .... Electronics & Power (journ.) (SAUS)
E & P .... Equipment and Parts (SAUS)
E & P .... Exercise and Plans (CINC)
E & P .... Exploration and Production [*In organization name Oil Industry International Exploration & Production Forum*]
E & P .... Extraordinary and Plenipotentiary
E & P .... Oil Industry International Exploration and Production Forum (EAIO)
E&P Forum ... Exploration and Production Forum (SAUS)
E & P Forum ... Oil Industry International Exploration and Production Forum (EA)
E & PL .... Entry and Postlanding [*NASA*] (KSC)
E&R .... Education and Research (SAUS)
E & R .... Ends and Rings [*Architecture*] (ROG)
E & R .... Engineering and Repair [*Department*] [*Navy*]
E & R .... engineering and research (SAUS)
E & R .... Equal and reactive [*Ophthalmology*] (DAVI)
E & R .... Equal and Regular [*Ophthalmology*] (DAVI)
E&R .... Evasion and Recovery (SEWL)
E & RFTS ..... Elementary and Reserve Flying Training School [*British military*] (DMA)
EANDRO ...... Electrically-Alterable Non-Destructive Read Out [*Computer science*] (IAA)
E & S .... Erosion and Sediment
E&S .... Error and Sensitivity (COE)
E & S .... Evans & Sutherland Computer Corp.
E & S .... Excess and Surplus Business [*Insurance*]
E&SA .... environmental and safety activity (SAUS)
E & SA .... Europe and South Africa container line (SAUS)
E & S NC ..... Engineers and Scientists Non-Construction [*Army*] (RDA)
e & sp .... equipment and spare (SAUS)
E and SP ...... Equipment and Spare Parts (SAUS)
E & SP .... Equipment and Spare Parts
E & ST .... Employment and Suitability Test [*Aerospace*] (AAG)
E & T .... Education and Training [*Navy*]
E & T .... Employment and Training
E & U .... Erosion and Ulcer [*Medicine*] (MELL)
E&V .... Endangered and Vulnerable (EERA)
E&V .... Evaluation and Validation (SAUS)
E & W .... England and Wales
E & WIDC .... East and West India Dock Co. [*Shipping*] (ROG)
E & WLR ..... East and West London Railway [*British*] (ROG)
E & WR ...... Elmira and Williamsport Railway [*British*] (ROG)
E&WS .... Electrical and Wireless School (SAUS)
E & Y .... Eagle and Younge's English Tithe Cases [*A publication*] (DLA)
E&Y .... Ernst & Young (SAUO)
EANG .... Epidemic Acute Nonbacterial Gastroenteritis [*Medicine*] (MEDA)
EANGUS ...... Enlisted Association of the National Guard of the United States
EANHS .... East African Natural History Society (EAIO)
EANPC .... European Association for National Productivity Centers [*See also AECNP*] (EAIO)
EANRRC ...... East African Natural Resources Research Council [*Kenya*] (PDAA)
EANS .... Emergency Action Notification System [*White House Teletype network*] [*Civil Defense*]
EANS .... Empire Air Navigation School (SAUO)
EANS .... European Article Numbering System (PDAA)
EANS .... European Association of Neurosurgical Societies (EAIO)
EANSL .... Eastern Africa National Shipping Line Ltd (SAUS)
EANSW .... Electricity Authority of New South Wales (SAUS)
EANTC .... European Advanced Networking Test Center (VERA)
EANYS .... Energy Association of New York State (SRA)
EAO .... Economy Act Order
EAO .... Education Assistance Office (SAUS)
EAO .... Egyptian Antiquities Organization (EA)
EAO .... Electrical Assembly Order (MCD)
EAO .... Emergency Actions Officer [*Army*] (AABC)
EAO .... Enterprise Application Outsourcing (GART)
EAO .... Environmental Assessment Office (SAUS)
EAO .... European Association of Orthodontists (SAUO)
EAO .... Expense Accounts Officer (SAUO)
EAOA .... Eastern Authorities Orchestral Association [*British*]
eaoe .... Errors and Omissions Excepted (SAUS)
EAOG .... European Association of Organic Geochemists (EAIO)
EAON .... Except as Otherwise Noted
EAOS .... Easy Access Ordering System [*Automated book ordering system, Blackwells North America*] (NITA)
EAOS .... End of Active Obligated Service [*Navy*] (POLM)
EAOS .... Enhanced Artillery Observer Subsystem (SAUS)
EAOS .... Environment Australia On-line Service (SAUS)
EAOS .... European Association of Oral Surgeons (SAUO)
EAOS .... Expiration of Active Obligated Service [*Military*]
EAOSY .... Emergency Action Officer System (SAUO)
EAOT .... End of Arm Tooling [*Robotics*]
EAOUG .... East Anglia Online User Group (SAUO)
EAP .... East Africa Protectorate [*Later, Kenya*]
EAP .... Easton Area Public Library, Easton, PA [*OCLC symbol*] (OCLC)
EAP .... Ecological Agriculture Projects [*See also PAE*] [*Sainte Anne De Bellevue, PQ*] (EAIO)
EAP .... economically active population (SAUS)
EAP .... Ectopic Abdominal Pregnancy (MELL)
EAP .... Edgar Allan Poe [*Initials used as pseudonym*]
EAP .... Edgil Access Processor (SAUS)
EAP .... Education Abroad Program (SAUS)
EAP .... Educational Activities (ACII)
EAP .... Educational Assistance Program (SAUS)
EAP .... Educational Awareness Project (EA)
EAP .... Effective Air Path
EAP .... Electro-Absorption Avalanche Photodiode [*Instrumentation*]
EAP .... Electroacupuncture
EAP .... Electronic Access Project
EAP .... Electronic Assembly Plant (SAUS)
EAP .... Electronics and Power (SAUS)
EAP .... Electronics Assembly Plant [*College Station, TX*] [*Westinghouse Electric Corp.*]
EAP .... Elvis Aaron Presley (ADWA)
EAP .... Embedded Avionic Processor (ACAE)
EAP .... Emergency Action Plan (SARE)
EAP .... Emergency Action Procedure [*Military*] (NVT)
EAP .... Emergency Assembly Point
EAP .... Employee Assistance Personnel [*Psychology*] (DAVI)
EAP .... Employee Assistance Program [*Health care*] (HCT)
EAP .... Employee Assistance Programs (SAUS)
EAP .... Emulator Application Program (MHDB)
eap .... engines, armament, and pyrotechnics (SAUS)
EAP .... English for Academic Purposes
EAP .... Entered Apprentice [*Freemasonry*] (ROG)
EAP .... Environment Actions Plan [*Commonwealth*] (EERA)
EAP .... Environmental Action Plan [*Environmental Protection Agency*] (ERG)
EAP .... Environmental Action Programme for Central and Eastern Europe (SAUS)
EAP .... Environmental Affairs Program (SAUS)
EAP .... Environmental Analysis and Planning (PDAA)
EAP .... Environmental Assistance Procedure
EAP .... Environment Assistance Program (EERA)
EAP .... Epiallopregnanolone [*Endocrinology*]
EAP .... Equipment Alignment Procedure (MCD)
EAP .... Equipment and Parts (SAUS)
EAP .... Equity Adjustment Program (ACAE)
EAP .... Equivalent Air Pressure
EAP .... Erythrocyte Acid Phosphatase [*Hematology*]
EAP .... Esophageal Atrial Pacing [*Medicine*]
EAP .... Ethanolamineperchlorate (MCD)
EAP .... Europaeische Arbeiterpartei [*European Workers' Party*] [*Germany*] [*Political party*] (PPE)
EAP .... Evoked Action Potential [*Neurophysiology*]
EAP .... Expedited Appeals Process [*Social Security Administation*] (DHP)
EAP .... Expenditure Analysis Plan (TEL)
EAP .... Experimental Activity Proposal [*Nuclear energy*] (NRCH)
EAP .... Experimental Aircraft Programme [*British*]
EAP .... Experimental Aircraft Project (SAUS)
EAP .... Extended Active Duty [*Military*] (MUSM)
EAP .... Extended Arithmetic Processor (MHDB)
EAP .... Extensible Authentication Protocol [*Computer science*]
EAP .... Eye Artifact Potential
EAP .... Office of Environmental Assurance, Permits and Policy (SAUS)
EAPA .... Embedded-Alumina-Particle Aluminide [*Chemical coating*]
EAPA .... Employee Assistance Professionals Association (EA)
EAPA .... Employee Assistance Program Association
EAPA .... Employment Aptitude Placement Association (SAUO)
EAPA .... Energy Abstracts for Policy Analysis [*National Science Foundation*] [*A publication*] (MCD)
EAPA .... European Asphalt Pavement Association (EA)
EAPA .... European Association of Psychological Assessment (SAUS)
EAP&T .... East African Post and Telecommunications (SAUO)
EAPAUS ...... Employment Agencies Protective Association of the United States [*Later, National Employment Association*]
EAPC .... East African Pioneer Corps [*British military*] (DMA)
EAPC .... European Aero-Philately Club (SAUO)
EAPC .... European American Phytomedicines Coalition (SAUS)
EAPCC .... European Association of Poison Control Centers (EAIO)
EAPCCCT .... European Association of Poisons Control Centers and Clinical Toxicologists [*Sweden*] (EAIO)
EAP-CJCS .... Emergency Action Procedures of the Chairman of the Joint Chiefs of Staff (COE)
EAPCO .... East African Pesticides Control Organization (PDAA)
EAPD .... Eastern Air Procurement District
EAPD .... Electroabsorption Photodiode [*Electronics*] (EECA)
EAPE .... Eddy Available Potential Energy (SAUS)
EAPE .... Evangelical Association for the Promotion of Education (EA)
EA PER .... Each Person [*Insurance*]
EAPF .... Electrically Augmented Pressure Filter [*Chemical engineering*]
EAPFBO ...... European Association of Professional Fire Brigade Officers (EA)
EAPFP .... European Association of Passive Fire Protection (SAUS)
EAPFS .... Electron Appearance Potential Fine Structure (DB)
EAPFS .... Extended Appearance Potential Fine Structure (PDAA)
EAPFSS ...... Electron Appearance Potential Fine Structure Spectroscopy (UWER)
EAPFSS ...... Extended Appearance Potential Fine Structure Spectroscopy (UWER)
EAPG .... Eastern Atlantic Planning Guidance [*NATO*] (NATG)
EAPG .... European Association of Petroleum Geologists (QUAC)
EAPG .... European Association of Petroleum Geoscientists (SAUO)
EAPGE .... European Association of Petroleum Geoscientists and Engineers (SAUO)
EAPH .... East African Publishing House [*Kenya*]

EAPHSS ...... European Association of Programmes in Health Services Studies (EAIO)
EAPI ...... East-West Environment and Policy Institute [*East-West Center*] [*Research center*] (RCD)
EAP-JCS ...... Emergency Action Procedures of the Joint Chiefs of Staff (SAUO)
EAPL ...... East Australian Pipeline Ltd. [*Commercial firm*]
EAPL ...... Engineering Assembly Parts List
EAPLR ...... East Africa Protectorate Law Reports [*A publication*] (DLA)
EAPM ...... European Association for Personnel Management (SAUS)
EAPM ...... European Association of Perinatal Medicine (EAIO)
EAPM ...... European Association of Personnel Management [*Paris, France*] (EA)
EAPM ...... European South Pacific and Magellan Conference (SAUS)
EAPO ...... Electrical Armaments Program Office [*Army*]
EAPP ...... Engineered Australia Plan Party [*Political party*]
EAPP ...... European Association for the Promotion of Poetry (EA)
EAPP ...... European Association of Personality Psychology (SAUS)
EAPPCFC ...... Electronically Adjustable Proportionally Pressure Compensated Flow Control
EAPPM ...... European Association for Product and Process Modelling in the Building Industry (SAUS)
EAPR ...... Europaische Gesellschaft fur Kartoffelforschung [*Netherlands*] (EAIO)
EAPR ...... European Association for Potato Research (EAIO)
EAPROM ...... Electrically Alterable Programmable Read-Only Memory [*Computer science*]
EAPROM ...... Electronically Alterable Programmable Read-Only Memory (SAUS)
EA Prot LR ... East Africa Protectorate Law Reports [*A publication*] (DLA)
EAPS ...... Electronic Air Particle Separator
EAPS ...... Engine Air Particle Separator
EAPS ...... European Association for Population Studies (EA)
EAPS ...... European Association of Professional Secretaries [*Paris, France*] (EAIO)
EAPSB ...... Edgar Allan Poe Society of Baltimore (EA)
EAPSS ...... Electronic Intelligence Analysis Processing Subsystem (MCD)
EAPT ...... East African Post and Telecommunications (SAUS)
EAPU ...... Electrical Auxiliary Power Unit (DNAB)
EAPU ...... External Auxiliary Power Unit
EAPV ...... Eastern Arctic Patrol Vessels (SAUS)
EAQ ...... Ethylanthraquinone [*Organic chemistry*]
EAQ ...... Eudismic Affinity Quotient (DB)
EAR ...... early asthmatic reaction (SAUS)
EAR ...... Earnings Allowance Rate
EAR ...... Earnings-at-Risk [*Incentive pay plan*]
EAR ...... East African Railways Corp. (SAUO)
EAR ...... Eastern American Realm (SAUO)
EAR ...... Edwin Arlington Robinson (SAUS)
EAR ...... Effective Address Register [*Computer science*] (IAA)
EAR ...... Electric Alignment Reticle (ACAE)
EAR ...... Electroencephalographic Audiometry [*Medicine*] (DB)
EAR ...... Electromagnetic Activity Receiver (DNAB)
EAR ...... Electron Affinity Rule (SAUS)
EAR ...... Electronically Agile RADAR
EAR ...... Electronic Analog Resolver (WDAA)
EAR ...... Electronic and Aerospace Report (IAA)
EAR ...... Electronic & Aerospace Report (journ.) (SAUS)
EAR ...... Electronic Array Radar (SAUS)
EAR ...... Electronic Audio Recognition
EAR ...... Electronic Aural Responder (IAA)
EAR ...... Elliniki Aristera [*Greek Left Party*] [*Political party*] (EY)
EAR ...... Emergency Action Report [*Military*]
EAR ...... Emergency Action Room (CCCA)
EAR ...... Employee Appraisal Record
EAR ...... Employee Attitude Research (IEEE)
EAR ...... Encyclopedia of American Religions [*A publication*]
EAR ...... Energy-Absorbing Resin (PDAA)
EAR ...... Energy Audit Report [*Navy*]
EAR ...... Engineering Abstract Report [*Defense Supply Agency*]
EAR ...... Engineering All Risks (MARI)
EAR ...... Engineering Analysis Report (KSC)
EAR ...... Engineering Analysis Request (ACAE)
EAR ...... Engineering and Research (IAA)
EaR ...... Entartungs-Reaktion [*Reaction of Degeneration*] [*German*]
EAR ...... Enterprise Analysis Review (SAUS)
EAR ...... environmental ALARA review (SAUS)
EAR ...... Environmental Auditing Roundtable [*Environmental Protection Agency*] (EPA)
EAR ...... Eroded Area Rate (SAUS)
EAR ...... Error Analysis Routine (SAUS)
EAR ...... Escape and Rescue
ear ...... estimate after release (SAUS)
EAR ...... Estimated Additional Resources
EAR ...... Estimated Assumed Resources [*Minerals*]
EAR ...... European Association of Radiology (EA)
EAR ...... European Autocat Recycling (SAUO)
EAR ...... Experimental Alcoholic Rhabdomyolysis [*Medicine*]
EAR ...... Experimental & Recent [*Music*] (WDAA)
EAR ...... Experimental Array RADAR [*Army*]
EAR ...... Expired Air Resuscitation (ADA)
EAR ...... Export Administration Regulation [*Department of Commerce*]
EAR ...... Extended Address Register [*Computer science*] (ELAL)
EAR ...... External Access Register (SAUS)
EAR ...... External Address Register (SAUS)
EAR ...... Extravehicular Aerospace Routing
EAR ...... Hearx Ltd. [*AMEX symbol*] (SAG)
EAR ...... Kearney [*Nebraska*] [*Airport symbol*] (OAG)
EARA ...... Educational Assistance Reimbursement Application (SAUS)
EARA ...... Environmental Auditors Registration Association (COBU)
EARA ...... Equipment Authorization Review Activity (MCD)
EARAC ...... East Anglian Regional Advisory Council for Further Education (AIE)
EAR & H ...... East African Railways and Harbours (SAUS)
EAR & H Magazine ... East African Railways and Harbours Magazine (journ.) (SAUS)
EARB ...... Electronics and Avionics Requirements Board (ACII)
EARB ...... Engineering Associates Registration Board (SAUS)
EARB ...... European Airlines Research Bureau
EARB ...... Export Administration Review Board
EARBA ...... Enhanced Adaptive Rate Based Algorithm (SAUS)
EARBICA ...... East African Regional Branch of the International Council on Archives (SAUO)
EARC ...... East African Reconnaissance Corps [*British military*] (DMA)
EARC ...... East African Research Centre (SAUO)
EARC ...... Eastern Aerospace Rescue and Recovery Center [*Air Force*]
EARC ...... Eastern Air Rescue Center (SAUS)
EARC ...... Eastern Association of Rowing Colleges (EA)
EARC ...... Educational Administration Resource Centre [*Information service or system*] (IID)
EARC ...... Elemental Analysis Research Center [*Department of Health and Human Services*] (GRD)
EARC ...... Elimination of Ambiguity in Radiotelephony Call Signs (SAUS)
EARC ...... Extraordinary Administrative Radio Conference [*ITU*]
EARCCUS ...... East African Regional Committee for Conservation and Utilisation of Soil
EARCOM ...... East Africa Regional Remote Sensing Management Committee (SAUO)
EARCOM ...... East Asia Regional Council of Overseas Schools (SAUO)
EARCOS ...... East Asia Regional Council of Overseas Schools (EA)
EARCUS ...... East African Regional Committee for Utilization of Soils (SAUO)
EARDC ...... Edwards Aquifer Research and Data Center (SAUO)
EAREC ...... Essential Airborne Radio Equipment Characteristic (SAUS)
EARFLAP ...... Emergency Action Reporting for Logistics Action Programming [*Military*] (AFM)
EARFRO ...... East African Agriculture Forestry Research Organization (SAUS)
EARG ...... Environmental Adaptation Research Group (SAUO)
Ear Hear ...... EAR AND HEARING (BALTIMORE MD) (SAUS)
EARI ...... Engineer Agency for Resources Inventories [*Army Corps of Engineers*]
EARI ...... Equipment Acceptance Requirements and Inspections (AAG)
EARIC ...... East African Research Information Center (SAUS)
EARIS ...... Egyptian-American Rural Improvement Service (SAUO)
EARISS ...... Energy and Angle-Resolved-Ion Scattering Spectrometer (UWER)
EARL ...... Easy Access Report Language [*Computer science*] (MHDB)
EARL ...... Electronic Access to Resources in Libraries [*British*] (TELE)
EARL ...... Electronically Accessible Russian Lexicon
EARL ...... Environmental ALARA Review Letter (SAUS)
EARL ...... Environmental Awareness Reading List [*Department of the Interior*]
EARL ...... Esso Australia Resources Ltd. [*Commercial firm*]
EARL ...... Extended Algorithmic "R" Language
EARLI ...... European Association for/on Research on Learning and Instruction (SAUS)
EARLI ...... European association for research on learning and instruction (SAUS)
EARLI ...... European Association on Research on Learning and Instruction (SAUS)
EARLO ...... Enhanced Airlift Reporting for Logistics and Operations (SAUS)
EARLPRADATE ... Earliest Practicable Date
eArmyU ...... Army University Access Online
Earn ...... Earnshaw's Gold Coast Judgments [*1909-10*] [*Ghana*] [*A publication*] (DLA)
EARN ...... Engineering Alumni Recruiting Network
EARN ...... Environmental Access Research Network [*Founded in 1986*] (NRGU)
EARN ...... European Academic Research Network [*A computer network*]
Ear Nose Throat J ... EAR, NOSE, AND THROAT JOURNAL (CLEVELAND OH) (SAUS)
Earnshaw ...... Gold Coast Judgments, by Earnshaw [*1909-10*] [*Ghana*] [*A publication*] (DLA)
EARO ...... Eastern African Regional Office (SAUS)
EAROM ...... Electrically Alterable Read-Only Memory [*Computer science*]
EAROM ...... Electronically Alterable Read Only Memory (SAUS)
EAROPH ...... East Asia Regional Organization for Planning and Housing
EAROPH ...... Eastern Regional Organization for Planning and Housing (SAUO)
EAROS ...... Electrically Alterable Read-Only Store [*Computer science*]
ear ox ...... Ear oximetry (STED)
EARP ...... Environmental Assessment and Review Process (SAUO)
EARP ...... Environmental Assessment and Review Program (SAUS)
EARP ...... Environmental Assessment Review Panel (SAUS)
EARP ...... Equipment Antiriot Projector [*British*] (MCD)
EARPC ...... East African Royal Pioneer Corps (SAUO)
EARR ...... Extended Aortic Root Replacement [*Medicine*] (EDAA)
EARRS ...... Engineering Automated Release and Record System (MCD)
EARRVI ...... Exchange in Array Rows Row Values according to Indices (SAUS)
EARS ...... East African Reconnaissance Squadron [*British military*] (DMA)
EARS ...... Electro-Acoustic Rating System (PDAA)
EARS ...... Electromagnetic Aircraft Recovery System [*Military*] (SEWL)
EARS ...... Electronic Access to Reference Services (SAUS)
EARS ...... Electronic Airborne Reaction System (SAUS)
EARS ...... Electronically Agile Radar System (SAUS)
EARS ...... Electronic Approval and Routing Systems (SAUS)
EARs ...... Electronic Aural Responders (SAUS)
EARS ...... Electronic Authoring and Routing System (SAUS)
EARS ...... Electronic Authorization and Routing System (SAUS)
EARS ...... Elliot Automation RADAR System (IAA)

EARS .... Emergency Airborne Reaction System (MCD)
EARS .... Emergency AUTODIN Release System (SAUS)
EARS .... Emergency Automated Response Subsystem [*National Oceanic and Atmospheric Administration*]
EARS .... Enhanced Accident Response System [*Automotive engineering*]
EARS .... En Route Analysis and Reporting System [*FAA*] (TAG)
EARS .... Entry to Anesthesia Record by Speech
EARS .... Environmental Activities Reporting System (SAUS)
EARS .... Environmental Analog Recording System
EARS .... Environmental Analysis and Remote Sensing (SAUS)
EARS .... Epilepsy Abstracts Retrieval Service (NITA)
EARS .... Epilepsy Abstracts Retrieval System (PDAA)
EARS .... Ethernet Alto Research Generator Scanning Laser Output Terminal [*Laser printer*] (NITA)
EARS .... Executive Audial Rehabilitation Society
EARS .... Explicit Archive and Retrieval System (SAUS)
EARS .... External Audio Receptor System (SAUS)
EARSC .... European Association of Remote Sensing Companies (SAUO)
EARSC .... European Assoc. of Remote Sensing Companies (SAUO)
EARSEC .... European Airborne Remote Sensing Capabilities (SAUS)
EARSEL .... European Association of Remote Sensing Laboratories (EA)
EAR Set .... Electronically Agile Radar Set (SAUS)
EARSF .... European Airborne Remote Sensing Facility (SAUO)
EA-RSL .... Encyclopedia of Associations: Regional, State, and Local Organizations [*A publication*]
earssn .... early season (SAUS)
EART .... Earth Sciences and Map Library (SAUS)
Earth G .... Earth Garden [*A publication*]
Earthgr .... Earthgrains Co. [*Associated Press*] (SAG)
EarthKAM .... Knowledge Acquired by Middle Schools [*Program*]
Earth Obs Remote Sens... Earth Observation and Remote Sensing [*A publication*] (PABS)
Earthq Eng Struct Dyn... Earthquake Engineering and Structural Dynamics (journ.) (SAUS)
Earthsat .... Earth Satellite Corp. (SAUS)
EARTHSAT .... Earth Satellite Corporation (SAUS)
EarthSc .... Earth Sciences, Inc. [*Associated Press*] (SAG)
Earth Sci Rev... Earth Science Reviews [*A publication*] (UWER)
Earth-Sci Rev... Earth-Science Reviews [*A publication*] (PABS)
Earth Station... trademark of Earth Computer Technologies (SAUS)
Earth Surf Process Landf... Earth Surface Processes and Landforms (journ.) (SAUS)
Earth Syst Monit... Earth System Monitor [*A publication*] (PABS)
EarthT .... Earth Technology Corp. [*Associated Press*] (SAG)
EARTS .... En Route Automated Radar Tracking System [*FAA*] (TAG)
EARV .... Emergency Ambulance Response Vehicle (SAUO)
Earw .... Earwalker's Manchester Court-Leet Records [*England*] [*A publication*] (DLA)
EARY .... Eastern Alabama Railway [*Federal Railroad Administration identification code*]
EAS .... Early American Society (EA)
EAS .... Earth and Atmospheric Sciences (SAUO)
EAS .... Earth Aspect Sensor
EAs .... East African Shilling [*Monetary unit*]
EAS .... East Asian Seas (SAUS)
EAS .... East Australian Standard (SAUS)
EAS .... Eastern Analytical Symposium
EAS .... Eastern Apicultural Society of North America (EA)
EAS .... Eastern College, St. Davids, PA [*OCLC symbol*] (OCLC)
EAS .... Econometric Analysis System (SAUO)
EAS .... Economic Analysis Staff [*Department of Agriculture*] (GFGA)
EAS .... Education Administration Specialist (PGP)
EAS .... Educational Analog Simulator
EAS .... Egyptian Academy of Sciences (SAUS)
EAS .... Electron Accelerator System (IAA)
EAS .... Electronic Accounting System (SAUS)
EAS .... Electronic Activation System [*Automotive brakes*]
EAS .... Electronic Actuation System
EAS .... Electronic Air Suspension [*Automotive engineering*]
EAS .... Electronic Air Switching [*Automotive engineering*]
EAS .... Electronic Altitude Sensor (DNAB)
EAS .... Electronic Animation System (SAUS)
EAS .... Electronic Article Surveillance
EAS .... Electronic Article System (SAUS)
EAS .... Electronic Automatic Switch (IAA)
EAS .... Electronique Aerospatiale [*France*]
EAS .... Electrophilic Aromatic Substitution (UWER)
EAS .... Elemental Analysis System [*Medicine*] (EDAA)
EAS .... E-Mail Application Server [*Computer science*] (HODG)
EAS .... Emergency Action System (SAUS)
EAS .... Emergency Alert System [*Telecommunications*] (OTD)
EAS .... Employee Aptitude Survey [*Psychology*] (AEBS)
EAS .... Employee Auxiliary Services (MCD)
EAS .... End-Around Shift
EAS .... Energy Absorbing Steering
EAS .... Engineering Administration System (SAUS)
EAS .... Engineering Aid, Surveyor [*Navy rating*] [*Obsolete*]
EAS .... Engineering Analysis Services [*Auto industry supplier*]
EAS .... Engineering Assistance Section [*Environmental science*] (COE)
EAS .... Engineering Automated Systems (MCD)
EAS .... Enlisted Assignment System
EAS .... Enterprise Access System [*Dynatech*] (VERA)
EAS .... Enterprise Agreement for Software (GART)
EAS .... Enterprise Allowance Scheme [*for the self-employed*] [*British*]
EAS .... Environmental Activities Staff [*Automotive industry*]
EAS .... Environmental Analysis Section (SAUS)
EAs .... Environmental Assessments (SAUO)
EAS .... Environmental Assessment Scale [*Occupational therapy*]
EAS .... Enzyme Alarm System (SAUS)
EAS .... Equal Access Signaling [*Communications term*] (DCT)
EAS .... Equipment Acquisition Strategy (ADA)
EAS .... Equivalent Air Speed
EAS .... Error Analysis Study
EAS .... Essential Air Servicer [*Department of Transportation*]
EAS .... Essential Auxiliary Support [*Nuclear energy*] (NRCH)
EAS .... Essex Archaeological Society (SAUO)
EAS .... Essex Archaeological Society (SAUO)
EAS .... Essex Society for Archaeology and History (SAUO)
EAS .... Estimated Air Speed (MCD)
EAS .... Estonian Academy of Sciences (SAUS)
EAS .... Estonian Association of Scientists
EAS .... Europe Aero Service
EAS .... European Accident Statement
EAS .... European Agriculture Society (SAUO)
EAS .... European Aquaculture Society (EA)
EAS .... European Association for Supervision (SAUO)
EAS .... European Astronomical Society
EAS .... European Atherosclerosis Society (EA)
EAS .... European Atomic Society (SAUO)
EAS .... Evaluation and Advisory Service [*Educational testing service*] (AEBS)
EAS .... Evaluation and Analysis Staff [*Bureau of Ordnance*] [*Washington, DC*] [*Navy*] (MCD)
EAS .... Excutive Aerospace (Pty) Ltd. [*South Africa*] [*ICAO designator*] (FAAC)
EAS .... Executive Aerospace Ltd. [*FAA designator*] [*South Africa*] (FAAC)
EAS .... Executive Agreement Series [*A publication*] (DLA)
EAS .... Executive Air Services Proprietary Ltd. [*Australia*] (ADA)
EAS .... Executive Assignment Service [*Civil Service Commission*]
EAS .... Exercise Angioscintigraphy [*Medicine*]
EAS .... Expense Assignment System (SAUS)
EAS .... Experimental Antenna System (ACAE)
EAS .... Experimental Army Satellite (SAUS)
EAS .... Experiment Analysis System (UWER)
EAS .... Experiment Assurance System [*Nuclear energy*] (NRCH)
EAS .... Experimenter-Administered Stimulation [*Psychology*]
EAS .... Expert Agent Selection (DINT)
EAS .... Expiration of Active Service [*Marine Corps*]
EAS .... Extended Address Set (CCCA)
EAS .... Extended Announcement System (SAUS)
EAS .... Extended Area Service [*Communications term*] (DCT)
EAS .... Extensive Air Shower [*Cosmic ray physics*]
EAS .... External Agency Simulator (MCD)
EAS .... External Anal Sphincter [*Medicine*] (EDAA)
EAS .... External Archival Storage [*Computer science*] (BARN)
EAS .... San Sebastian [*Spain*] [*Airport symbol*] (OAG)
EAS .... Endotoxin-Activated Serum (ODA)
EASA .... East African School of Aviation [*Kenya*] (PDAA)
EASA .... Electrical Apparatus Service Association (EA)
EASA .... Electrical Apparatus Service Association, Inc.
EASA .... Electronics Association of South Australia
EASA .... Emergency Air Staff Actions (AFM)
EASA .... Engineer Automation Support Activity [*Army Corps of Engineers*]
EASA .... Engineering Association of South Africa (SAUO)
EASA .... Engineers Association of South Africa (SAUO)
EASA .... Entertainment Arts Socialist Association (SAUO)
EASA .... European Academic Software Award (SAUO)
EASA .... European Aviation Safety Authority (SAUS)
EASA .... External Architectural Students Association [*British*] (BI)
EASAA .... European Association of South Asian Archaeologists [*British*] (EAIO)
EASAL .... Easy Application Language [*Computer science*] (MHDB)
EASAMS .... Elliott Automation Space and Advanced Military Systems (MCD)
EASAP .... East Asian Seas Action Programme (SAUS)
EASB .... Electronic Area Support Base [*Air Force*]
EASC .... East African Service Corps [*British military*] (DMA)
EASC .... East Asian Studies Center [*Indiana University*] [*Research center*] (RCD)
EASC .... Eastern Administrative Support Center [*Marine science*] (OSRA)
EASC .... Elmira Area Soaring Corporation (SAUO)
EASC .... Emergency Avoidance Solidification Campaign (SAUS)
EASC .... Employers Association of South Carolina (SRA)
EASC .... Ethylaluminum Sesquichloride [*Organic chemistry*]
EASC .... Exploration of Alternative Concepts (MCD)
Easco .... Easco, Inc. [*Associated Press*] (SAG)
EASCO .... East African Common Services Organization (WDAA)
EASCO .... European Association of Schools and Colleges of Optometry (EA)
EASCOM .... Eastern Command [*World War II*]
EASCOMINT... Extended Air Surveillance Communications Intercept [*Air Force*]
EASCON .... Electronic and Aerospace Systems Conference (SAUS)
EASCON .... Electronics and Aerospace Systems Convention (MCD)
EASCON .... Electronics and Aerospace Systems Convention and Exposition (SAUS)
EASD .... Empowerment for African Sustainable Development (SAUO)
EASD .... Equal Access Service Date (SAUS)
EASD .... European Association for the Study of Diabetes [*See also AEED*] (EAIO)
EASDAQ .... European Association of Securities Dealers Automated Quotation [*System*]
EASE .... Easement [*Legal term*] (DLA)
EASE .... Easy Access System Europe (VERA)
EASE .... Econolite Automatic Sensing Equipment

EASE........... Editing, Arranging, and Sequencing Environment [*Computer science*] (BYTE)
EASE........... Educational and Scientific Establishment (IIA)
EASE........... Elastic Analysis for Structural Engineering (NRCH)
EASE........... Electrical Automatic Support Equipment
EASE........... Electronic Airborne Systems Evaluator (SAUS)
EASE........... Electronic Analog and Simulation Equipment (SAUS)
EASE........... Electronic Analog Simulating Equipment [*Computer science*]
EASE........... Electronic Assisted Solicitation Exchange (AAGC)
EASe........... Electronic Auditory Stimulation Effect
EASE........... Elementary Adult Sex Education (EDAC)
EASE........... Elicited Articulatory System Evaluation (TES)
EASE........... Embedded Advance Sampling Environment [*Hewlett-Packard Co.*]
EASE........... Emigrant's Assured Savings Estate [*Banking program*]
EASE........... Encoder for Algorithmic Syntactic English (SAUS)
EASE........... Engineering Analysis Software Environment
EAS-E........... Engineering and Survey-Exchange (SAUO)
EASE........... Engineering Applications for Support Engineers [*British*]
EASE........... Engineering Automatic System for Solving Equations
EASE........... Environmental Associated Services & Engineering (EFIS)
EASE........... Equal Area SSMI [*Special Sensor Microwave Imager*] Earth Grid [*Marine science*] (OSRA)
EASE........... Equipment and Software Emulator (AAEL)
EASE........... Escape and Survival Equipment (PDAA)
EASE........... Estimation and Assessment of Substance Exposure (HEAS)
EASE........... European Association for Special Education
EASE........... European Association of Science Editors [*European Association of Earth Sc ience Editors and European Life Sciences Editors*] [*Formed by a merger of*] (EAIO)
EASE........... Experimental Assembly of Structures in Extravehicular Activity [*Space technology*]
EASEC........... East Asian Stock Exchange Conference (SAUO)
EASE Grid.... Equal Area SSMI [*Special Sensor Microwave Imager*] Earth Grid [*Marine science*] (OSRA)
EASel........... Engineers Adhesive Selector Program
EASEMT........ Easement [*British*] [*Legal term*] (ROG)
EASEP........... Early Apollo Scientific Experiments Package [*or Payload*] [*NASA*]
EASEy........... Encoder for Algorithmic Syntactic English, Easy Version (SAUS)
EA sh........... East African shilling (SAUS)
EASH........... Shilling [*Monetary unit in Tanzania*]
EASHP........... European Association of Senior Hospital Physicians (PDAA)
EASHW........ European Agency for Safety and Health at Work (EURO)
EASI........... East Asia Strategy Initiative [*Military*]
EASI........... Electrical Accounting for the Security Industry [*IBM Corp.*] (IEEE)
EASI........... Electronic Acquisition Systems Instrumentation [*Vehicle testing*] [*Automotive engineering*]
EASI........... Engineered Air Systems Inc. (SAUS)
EASI........... Engineered Support Systems, Inc. [*NASDAQ symbol*] (NQ)
EASI........... Enhanced Asynchronous SCSI Interface (VLIE)
EASI........... Environmental Alliance for Senior Involvement (SAUO)
EASI........... Epioptics Applied to Semiconductor Interfaces (VLIE)
EASI........... Equal Access to Softward and Information
EASI........... Estimate of Adversary Sequence Interruption [*Nuclear energy*] (NRCH)
EASI........... European Academic Supercomputer Initiative (VLIE)
EASI........... European Academic Supercomputing Initiative (SAUO)
EASI........... European Association for Shipping Informatics (SAUO)
EASI........... European Association for Shipping Informatics (SAUS)
EASI........... European Association of Shipping Informatics [*Brussels, Belgium*] (EAIO)
EASI........... Expanded Additional Skill Identifier [*Military*] (AABC)
EASI........... Expected Amount of Sample Information [*Statistics*]
EASIAC........ Easy Instruction Automatic Computer (IAA)
EASIAP........ Engineering and Applied Sciences Industrial Affiliates Program (SAUS)
EASIC........... Evaluating Acquired Skills in Communication [*Language ability test*]
EASIE........... EJS/ECP Automated Status Information and Exception System (MCD)
EASI/IMP...... Expert Analysis System Interface / Interface Management Package (SAUS)
EASI-ISAE.... Educating Authors for Simulated Interaction: Intercommunication Software for Appreciating Educators (EURO)
EASILY........ Experimental Avionics Simulation and Integration Laboratory
EASINet...... European Academic Supercomputer Initiative Network (VLIE)
EASINET...... European Area Sales and Information Network (SAUS)
EASI/PACE... Expert Analysis System Interface / Picture Analysis, Correction and Enhancement (SAUS)
EASIT........... European Association for Software Access and Infomation Transfer (PDAA)
EASIZ........... Ecology of the Antarctic Sea Ice Zone (SAUO)
EASL........... Ealing Association of Student Librarians (SAUO)
EASL........... Easel Corp. [*NASDAQ symbol*] (SAG)
EASL........... Electroacoustic Systems Laboratory
EASL........... Engineering Analysis and Simulation Language [*Computer science*]
EASL........... Engineering Approved Source List
EASL........... Experimental Assembly and Sterilization Laboratory [*NASA*]
EASLS........... East African Scientific Literature Service (SAUS)
EASLY........... Easley, SC [*American Association of Railroads railroad junction routing code*]
EASM/RSF... External Armament Stores Management/Remote Set Fuze (MCD)
EASMT........... Easement [*British*] [*Legal term*] (ROG)
EASNA........... Employee Assistance Society of North America (EA)
EASO........... EASX Railroad [*Federal Railroad Administration identification code*]
EASOE........... European Arctic Stratosphere (or Stratospheric) Ozone Experiment (SAUO)
EASP........... Edgewood Arsenal Special Publication [*Army*]
EASP........... Educational Advice Service Project (AIE)
EASP........... Educational Advisory Sewices Project (SAUS)
EASP........... Electric Arc Spraying (SAUS)
EASP........... Employee Auxiliary Service Personnel (MCD)
EASP........... European Association for Signal Processing [*Lausanne, Switzerland*] (MCD)
EASP........... European Atlantic Seaboard Project (SAUO)
EASS........... Engine Automatic Stop and Start System (PDAA)
EASSG........ European Accountancy Students Study Group (PDAA)
EASSS........ European Access to Seafloor Survey Systems [*Southampton Oceanography Centre*] [*British*]
EASS System... Engine Automatic Stop and Start System (SAUS)
EAST........... East Asia Studies Library (SAUS)
EAST........... East Australian Standard Time
east........... easterly (SAUS)
EAST........... Eastern (WDAA)
EAST........... Eastern Academy of Sexual Therapy [*Later, SSTAR*] (EA)
EAST........... Eastern Association for the Surgery of Trauma (SAUS)
EAST........... Eastern Australian Standard Time (SAUS)
East........... Eastern Reporter [*A publication*] (ILCA)
East........... east of the Mississippi, eastern states of the U.S. (SAUS)
EAST........... Eastover Corp. [*NASDAQ symbol*] (NQ)
East........... East's English King's Bench Term Reports [*A publication*] (DLA)
East........... East's Notes of Cases in Morley's East Indian Digest [*A publication*] (DLA)
EAST........... Electric Arc Shock Tunnel [*NASA*]
EAST........... Elevated-Arm Stress Test [*Medicine*] (EDAA)
EAST........... Emory Angioplasty vs. Surgical Trial [*Medicine*] (EDAA)
EAST........... Enhanced Adult Sensory Threshold
EAST........... Euro-Arab Sea Trailer-Line (SAUS)
EAST........... European Academy of Science and Technology
EAST........... European Assistance for Science and Technology (SAUO)
EAST........... Evaluation and Subsystem Training (SAA)
EAST........... Experimental Army Satellite Tactical
EAST........... External Rotation, Abduction Stress Test [*Medicine*]
East........... Far East (SAUS)
East Af........ East Africa Court of Appeals Reports [*A publication*] (DLA)
EASTAF........ Eastern Transport Air Force
East Afr J Criminol... East African Journal of Criminology [*A publication*] (DLA)
East Afr LJ... East African Law Journal [*A publication*] (DLA)
East Afr L Rep... East Africa Law Reports [*A publication*] (DLA)
East Afr L Rep... Eastern Africa Law Reports [*Durban*] [*A publication*] (DLA)
East Afr Med J... EAST AFRICAN MEDICAL JOURNAL (NAIROBI) (SAUS)
EASTASAC... East African Society of African Culture
Eastbay........ Eastbay, Inc. [*Associated Press*] (SAG)
East Bloc..... Albania, Bulgaria, Czechoslovakia, East Germany, Hungary, Poland, Romania, Yugoslavia (SAUS)
East Car U... East Carolina University (GAGS)
East Cent Okla St U... East Central Oklahoma State University (GAGS)
EastChm...... Eastman Chemical Co. [*Associated Press*] (SAG)
EASTCO....... East Coast
Eastco.......... Eastco Industrial Safety Corp. [*Associated Press*] (SAG)
EASTCOBASE... East Coast Base
EASTCOMMRGN... Eastern Communications Region [*Military*] (AFM)
EASTCON..... Eastern Sea Frontier Control Local of Shipping in Gulf of Maine
EASTCON..... Eastern States International Construction Expo and Conference [*Associated General Contractors of America - Carolinas Branch*] (TSPED)
EASTCON..... Electronic Aerospace Systems Convention
East Conn St U... East Connecticut State University (GAGS)
EASTCONRADREG... Eastern Continental Air Defense Region (DNAB)
East DC......... Eastern District Court Reports [*South Africa*] [*A publication*] (DLA)
East DL......... Eastern Districts, Local Division, South African Law Reports [*A publication*] (DLA)
EASTEC........ Eastern States Exposition Center (SAUS)
EASTEC........ Eastern Testing Exposition/Conference (SAUS)
EastEn.......... Eastern Enterprises [*Associated Press*] (SAG)
East (Eng).... East's English King's Bench Term Reports [*A publication*] (DLA)
Eastern Econ J... Eastern Economic Journal [*A publication*] (JLIT)
Eastern Europ Econ... Eastern European Economics [*A publication*] (JLIT)
Eastern J Int L... Eastern Journal of International Law [*A publication*] (ILCA)
Eastern J In'tl L... Eastern Journal of International Law [*A publication*] (DLA)
Eastern J of Internat L... Eastern Journal of International Law [*A publication*] (DLA)
eastern S-P-F... Eastern Spruce Pine or Fir [*Softwood*] (MIST)
East Europe... International Market Letter: East Europe [*A publication*] (DLA)
EASTH........ Easthamstead [*England*]
East Ill U...... Eastern Illinois University (GAGS)
EASTINDIACON... Australia/East India Outward Shipping Conference (SAUS)
East J Int L... Eastern Journal of International Law [*A publication*] (DLA)
East Ky U...... Eastern Kentucky University (GAGS)
East L........... East London (SAUS)
East L........... East Lothian (SAUS)
EastLant...... Eastern Atlantic (SAUS)
EASTLANT.... Eastern Atlantic Area [*NATO*]
EASTLANTMEDCOM... Eastern Atlantic and Mediterranean Command [*Military*]
East Librn..... Eastern Librarian (journ.) (SAUS)
East Los....... East Los Angeles, California (SAUS)
East LR......... Eastern Law Reporter [*Canada*] [*A publication*] (DLA)
East LR (Can)... Eastern Law Reporter [*Canada*] [*A publication*] (DLA)
EASTLS........ East African Scientific and Technical Literature Service (SAUS)
EASTM......... European Association for Marine Sciences and Techniques [*Marine science*] (OSRA)
East Mich U... Eastern Michigan University (GAGS)
East Mont C... Eastern Montana College (GAGS)

EASTN .... Eastern
East N Mex U... Eastern New Mexico University (GAGS)
East N of C... East's Notes of Cases in Morley's East Indian Digest [*A publication*] (DLA)
EASTOMP.... East-Ocean Meeting Point
East Ore C... Eastern Oregon College (GAGS)
EASTPAC..... Eastern Pacific (ACAE)
EASTPAC..... Eastern Pacific Area (MUGU)
EASTPAC..... Eastern Pacific Command [*Navy*]
East PC........ East's Pleas of the Crown [*A publication*] (DLA)
East PC (Eng)... East's Pleas of the Crown (England) [*A publication*] (DLA)
East Phil...... Eastern Philharmonic (SAUS)
East Phil...... Eastman Philharmonia (SAUS)
East Pl Cr.... East's Pleas of the Crown [*A publication*] (DLA)
East Punjab... All India Reporter, East Punjab [*1948-50*] [*A publication*] (DLA)
East Rep...... Eastern Reporter [*A publication*] (DLA)
EASTROLANT... Eastern Tropical Atlantic (SAUS)
EASTROPAC... Eastern Tropical Pacific [*Oceanographic expedition*]
EASTROPIC... Cooperative Survey of the Eastern Tropical Pacific (MSC)
EASTSEAFRON... Eastern Sea Frontier
East Stroudsburg U... East Stroudsburg University of Pennsylvania (GAGS)
EASTT.......... Experimental Army Satellite Tactical Terminals
East Tenn St U... East Tennessee State University (GAGS)
East Tex St U... East Texas State University (GAGS)
East US Bus L Rev... Eastern United States Business Law Review [*A publication*] (DLA)
EastUtl......... Eastern Utilities Association [*Associated Press*] (SAG)
East Va Med Sch... Eastern Virginia Medicine School (GAGS)
East Wash U... Eastern Washington University (GAGS)
East-West Committee... Committee of the ICC and the Chambers of Commerce of Socialist Countries for the Development of East-West Trade and Economic Cooperation (SAUO)
East-West Ser Econ Bus Environ... East-West Series in Economics, Business, and the Environment [*A publication*] (JLIT)
EASV............ Engine Angular Speed Variation [*Automotive engineering*]
E/A SVC....... E/A Supervisor Call (SAUS)
EASVO......... European Association of State Veterinary Officers (GVA)
EASY............ Automated Economic Analysis System (SAUO)
EASY............ Early Acquisition System [*Army*] (AABC)
EASY............ Efficient Assembly System [*Honeywell, Inc.*] [*Assembler language*]
EASY............ Emergency Action System (SAUO)
EASY............ Engine Analyzer Systems [*Air Force*] (MCD)
EASY............ Engineering Analysis System (SAUS)
EASY............ Evasive Aircraft System (MCD)
EASY............ Exception Analysis System (IAA)
EASY............ Exchange Assembly System (SAUS)
easy............. expense-account spending money (SAUS)
EAT.............. Aerliest Arriving Time (SAUS)
EAT.............. Air Transport Ltd. [*Slovakia*] [*ICAO designator*] (FAAC)
EAT.............. Brinker International [*Formerly, Chili's, Inc.*] [*NYSE symbol*] (SPSG)
EAT.............. Earliest Arrival Time
EAT.............. Earnings after Taxes (ADWA)
EAT.............. East African Time
EAT.............. East Africa Tanzania (SAUS)
EAT.............. Eastern Air Transport
EAT.............. Eating Attitude Test (EDAC)
EAT.............. Ectopic Atrial Tachycardia [*Cardiology*] (DAVI)
EAT.............. Edinburgh Articulation Test (STED)
EAT.............. Education Apperception Test (STED)
EAT.............. Ehrlich Ascites Tumor [*Oncology*]
EAT.............. elective replacement time (SAUS)
EAT.............. Electroacoustic Testing (SAUS)
EAT.............. Electroacoustic Transducer (UWER)
EAT.............. Electroaerosol Therapy [*Medicine*]
EAT.............. Electronic Angle Tracking (PDAA)
E/AT............. Electrons per Atom
EAT.............. Emergency Action Termination [*Telecommunications*] (OTD)
EAT.............. Employment Appeal Tribunal [*British*]
EAT.............. Encoder Address Translator
EAT.............. End-Around Test
EAT.............. Engineering Analysis Team [*NASA*]
EAT.............. Entity Alignment Time (VLIE)
EAT.............. Environmental Acceptance Test (NASA)
EAT.............. Equipment Acceptance Test (MCD)
EAT.............. Estimated Approach Time [*Aviation*] (PIAV)
EAT.............. Estimated Arrival Time (WDAA)
EAT.............. European Advanced Technologies (SAUS)
EAT.............. European Advertising Tripartite [*Brussels, Belgium*] (EA)
EAT.............. European Association of Teachers [*See also AEDE*] (EAIO)
EAT.............. Expected Approach Time (PIPO)
EAT.............. Experimental Autoimmune Thymitis [*Medicine*]
EAT.............. Experimental Autoimmune Thymitis/Thyroiditis [*Medicine*] (STED)
EAT.............. Experiments in Art and Technology (EA)
EAT.............. External Air Transportability (MCD)
EAT.............. PNR Food Industries Ltd. [*Toronto Stock Exchange symbol*]
EAT.............. Tanzania [*International vehicle registration*] (ODBW)
EAT.............. Wenatchee [*Washington*] [*Airport symbol*] (OAG)
EATA............ East Asia Travel Association (EAIO)
EATA............ Enhanced AT Attachment [*Computer science*]
EATA............ Enhanced AT Bus Attachment (SAUS)
EATA............ European Association for/of Transactional Analysis (SAUO)
EATB............ East Anglia Tourist Board [*British*] (DCTA)
EATC............ Ecology and Analysis of Trace Contaminants [*Program*] [*Oak Ridge National Laboratory*] (IID)
EATC............ Ehrlich Ascites Tumor Cell [*Oncology*]
EATC............ Electric Armor Test Carrier [*Military*] (SEWL)
EATC............ Electronic Automatic Temperature Control [*Automotive engineering*]
EATC............ European Aviation Training Center (SAUS)
EATCHIP...... European Air Traffic Control Harmonization and Integration Program [*Eurocontrol*]
EATCHIP...... European Air Traffic Control Harmonization Implementation Project (SAUS)
Eat Cont....... Eaton's Supplement to Chipman on Contracts [*A publication*] (DLA)
EATCQ......... Expressed Attitude Toward Confrontation Questionnaire (EDAC)
EATCS.......... European Association for Theoretical Computer Science (EAIO)
EATD............ European Association of Technical Divers (SAUS)
EATD............ Expanded Advanced Terminal Defense Study
EATDS.......... Expanded Advanced Terminal Defense Study (MCD)
EATE............ Electronic Automatic Test Equipment (GART)
Eaterie......... Eateries, Inc. [*Associated Press*] (SAG)
EATF............ Externally Applied Thermal Field [*Physics*] (ODA)
EATI............. Entities, Actions, Tasks, and Interactions (SAUS)
EATI............. Equipment and Tool Institute [*Glenview, IL*]
EATI............. European Addiction Training Institute (EURO)
EATIC........... East African Tuberculosis Investigation Centre [*Kenya*] (PDAA)
EATJP........... European Association for the Trade in Jute Products (EA)
EATM............ Edgewood Arsenal Technical Memorandum [*Army*]
EATMS.......... Electroacoustic Transmission Measuring System [*Telecommunications*] (TEL)
EATMS.......... European Air Traffic Management System (SAUS)
EATN............ Bank of East Tennessee [*NASDAQ symbol*] (COMM)
EATN............ European AIDS Treatment News (SAUS)
EatnVan....... Eaton Vance Corp. [*Associated Press*] (SAG)
EATO............ Euro-Asia Trade Organisation
EATO............ Euro-Asia Trade Organization, Taipei, Taiwan (SAUO)
EATON......... Eaton, CO [*American Association of Railroads railroad junction routing code*]
Eaton........... Eaton Corp. [*Associated Press*] (SAG)
EATP............ European Association for Textile Polyolefins (EAIO)
EATPHHSA... European Association of Training Programmes in Hospital and Health Services Administration (SAUO)
EATR............ Edgewood Arsenal Technical Report [*Army*]
EATR............ Enroute Air Traffic Regulation (MCD)
EATR............ Environment Assessment Technical Report (SAUS)
EATR............ Equilibrium Air Total Radiation
EATRO......... East African Trypanosomiasis Research Organization (SAUO)
EATS............ Eateries, Inc. [*NASDAQ symbol*] (NQ)
EATS............ Efficiency of Assistive Technology and Services (EURO)
EATS............ Empire Air Training Scheme [*British military*] (DMA)
EATS............ Enforcement Activities Tracking System (FOTI)
EATS............ Engine Acceleration Temperature Schedule
EATS............ Equipment Accuracy Test Station
EATS............ European Air Transport Service
EATS............ Extended Area Test System [*Navy*]
EATS............ Extended Area Tracking System (SAUS)
EATT............ Evaluation and Technology Transfer (SAUS)
EATTA.......... East African Tea Trade Association (EA)
EATU............ East African Telecommunications Union (SAUS)
EATU............ Eastern African Telecommunications Union (SAUS)
EATWG........ Executive Agency Transfer Working Group (SAUO)
EATWOT...... Ecumenical Association of Third World Theologies [*India*]
EATX............ Electronic Automatic Transaxle [*Automotive engineering*]
EAU.............. American University, Washington, DC [*OCLC symbol*] (OCLC)
EAU.............. Auchinoon [*Scotland*] [*Seismograph station code, US Geological Survey*] (SEIS)
e-au-........... Austria [*MARC geographic area code*] [*Library of Congress*] (LCCP)
EAU.............. Eagle European Airways [*British*] [*FAA designator*] (FAAC)
EAU.............. Early Assistance Unit
EAU.............. East Africa Uganda (SAUS)
EAU.............. Eau Claire [*Wisconsin*] [*Airport symbol*] (OAG)
EAU.............. Emergency Accommodation Unit (ADA)
EAU.............. Emergency Action Unit (SAUS)
EAU.............. Emergency Assistance Unit (SAUS)
EAU.............. Enabled Artists United [*An association*] (EA)
EAU.............. Energy Absorber Unit (SAUS)
EAU.............. Energy Absorbing Unit [*Automotive engineering*]
EAU.............. Engine Analyzer Unit (DWSG)
EAU.............. Engineer Aviation Unit (SAUS)
EAU.............. Equivalent Average Unit (SAUS)
EAU.............. Erase All Unprotected (VLIE)
EAU.............. European Association of Urology
EAU.............. Experimental Allergic Uveitis [*Ophthalmology*]
EAU.............. Experimental Autoimmune Uveitis [*Medicine*] (STED)
EAU.............. Experimental Autoimmune Uveoretinitis [*Immunology*]
EAU.............. Extended Arithmetic Unit (IAA)
EAU.............. Uganda [*International vehicle registration*] (ODBW)
EAUCL......... Eau Claire, WI [*American Association of Railroads railroad junction routing code*]
EAUG............ European Atex Users Group [*Deventer, Netherlands*] (EAIO)
EA-UPDS...... Encyclopedia of Associations: Updating Service [*A publication*]
EAUS............ Enterprise Association of the United States (EA)
EAUs............ Extended Arithmetic Units (SAUS)
EAUTC.......... Engineer Aviation Unit Training Center [*Military*]
EAUXCP....... East Auxiliary Airborne Command Post (MCD)
EAV.............. Bettles, AK [*Location identifier*] [*FAA*] (FAAL)
EAV.............. Eagle Aviation Luftfahrt Ges.MbH [*Austria*] [*FAA designator*] (FAAC)
EAV.............. Effective Angular Velocity
EAV.............. Engine Assembly Vehicle
EAV.............. Enteric Adenovirus [*Medicine*] (EDAA)
EAV.............. Equine Abortion Virus [*Medicine*] (DMAA)

EAV .... Explosive-Actuated Valve
EAV .... Extended Application Verification [*Computer science*] (VLIE)
EAV .... Viner [*E. A.*] Holdings [*Toronto Stock Exchange symbol*]
EAVA .... European Association of Veterinary Anatomists (EA)
EAVA .... European Association of Video Associations (SAUO)
EAVC .... Edinburgh Artillery Volunteer Corps [*British military*] (DMA)
EAVC .... Enhanced Atrioventricular Conduction [*Medicine*] (EDAA)
EAVE .... European Audiovisual Entrepeneurs [*EC*] (ECED)
EAVE .... Experimental Autonomous Vehicle [*Underwater robot*]
EAVE-EAST ... Experimental Autonomous Vehicle - East (SAUS)
EA VEH .... Each Vehicle [*Insurance*]
EAVES .... Eavesdropping (DLA)
EAVF .... Electrically Augmented Vacuum Filter [*Chemical engineering*]
Eavg .... Average Voltage (SAUS)
EAVK .... E.A. Viner Holdings Ltd. [*NASDAQ symbol*] (COMM)
EAVM .... Extramedullary Arteriovenous Malformation [*Medicine*] (STED)
EAVN .... Eaton Vance [*NASDAQ symbol*] (TTSB)
EAVN .... Eaton Vance Corp. [*NASDAQ symbol*] (NQ)
EAVPO .... East African Veterinary Research Organization (SAUS)
EAVRO .... East African Veterinary Research Organization (SAUO)
EAVS .... Emergency Action Voice System (SAUS)
EAVSoM .... European Association for the Visual Studies of Man (SAUO)
EAW .... Easy Washer [*Laboratory science*]
eaw .... Electrical Association for Women (SAUO)
EAW .... Electrical Association for Women [*British*]
EAW .... Electric Arc Weld
EAW .... Employment at Will
EAW .... environmental assessment worksheet (SAUS)
EAW .... Equivalent Average Word [*Mathematics*] (IAA)
EAW .... Ethnic Aged Worker
EAW .... European Airways Ltd. [*British*] [*FAA designator*] (FAAC)
EAWA .... East Africa Wins Again [*Used by US Diplomatic Corps in Nairobi, Kenya, to express dispair at bureaucratic obstacles*]
EAWC .... Exploring Ancient World Cultures
EAWEP .... East Asia and Western Pacific (CARB)
EAWLS .... East African Wild Life Society (GNE)
EAWOP .... European Association for Work and Organizational Psychology (SAUO)
EAWP .... Eastern Atlantic War Plan [*NATO*] (NATG)
EAWP .... Ethnic Aged Working Party [*Australia*] [*Political party*]
EAWR .... Employment at Will Reporter [*A publication*] (DLA)
EAWRC .... East and West Radio Club (SAUS)
EAWS .... Enlisted Aviation Warfare Specialist
EAWUSA .... Electrical and Allied Workers Union of South Africa (SAUO)
EAX .... Eastern Air Executive Ltd. [*British*] [*ICAO designator*] (FAAC)
EAX .... Electronic Automated Exchange (SAUS)
EAX .... Electronic Automatic Exchange [*See also ESS*] [*General Telephone & Electronics*] [*Telecommunications*]
EAX .... Electronic Automatic Switch (ECII)
EAX .... Environmental Audio Extensions [*Computer science*]
EAY .... elastic Auger yield (SAUS)
EAY .... European Alliance of YMCAs (SAUO)
EAZ .... East African pound (SAUS)
EAZ .... Empfindlicher Aufschlagzuender [*Superquick impact fuze*] [*German military - World War II*]
EAZO .... Energetically-Active Zones of the Ocean (SAUO)
EAZO .... Energy Active Zones of the Ocean (CARB)
EAZWVS .... European Association of Zoo and Wildlife Veterinary Surgeons (GVA)
EB .... Avitour Airlines (SAUS)
eb--- .... Baltic States [*MARC geographic area code*] [*Library of Congress*] (LCCP)
EB .... Bureau of Economic and Business Affairs (SAUO)
EB .... Die Heilige Schrift in Deutscher Uebersetzung. Echter-Bibel [*Wuerzburg*] [*A publication*] (BJA)
EB .... Early Bargain [*Stock exchange term*] [*British*] (DCTA)
EB .... Early Bird (SAUS)
EB .... Early Bronze [*Age*]
EB .... Early Burst [*Premature explosion of a warhead*]
EB .... EarthBank Association of North America (EA)
EB .... Eastbound
EB .... Easter Bunny (SAUS)
Eb .... Ebba (SAUS)
Eb .... Ebed (SAUS)
EB .... Ebony (SAUS)
EB .... Economic and Business affairs (SAUS)
EB .... ectopic beat (SAUS)
EB .... Edge Brightness (SAUS)
E/B .... Edges Bevelled [*Printing*] (DGA)
EB .... Education Board (SAUO)
EB .... Edwards Brothers [*Printer*]
EB .... Ehrlich Bober Financial Corp. [*AMEX symbol*] (COMM)
eb .... Electric Bass
EB .... Electric Boat (MCD)
EB .... Electric Braking (SAUS)
EB .... Electricity Board [*British*]
E/B .... Electrode per Bit (EECA)
EB .... Electron Beam
EB .... Electron Bombardment (SAUS)
E-B .... Electron-Bombardment (SAA)
EB .... Electronic Banking (VERA)
EB .... Electronic Beam [*Electronics*]
EB .... Electronic Book (TELE)
EB .... Electronic Bourse (ECON)
EB .... Electronic Broadcasting (SAUS)
EB .... Elementary Block (VLIE)
EB .... Elementary Body [*Hematology*]
EB .... Emeraldine Base (UWER)
EB .... Emergency Box (MCD)
EB .... Emergency Brake (WDAA)
EB .... Emissions Balancing [*Environmental Protection Agency*] (GFGA)
EB .... Emitter Base (IAA)
EB .... Emphysematous Bullae [*Pulmonary medicine*]
EB .... enclose building (SAUS)
EB .... Enclosure Building (SAUS)
EB .... Encoder Buffer (IAA)
EB .... Encyclopaedia Biblica [*A publication*]
EB .... Encyclopaedia Britannica [*A publication*] (WDAA)
EB .... Encyclopaedia Britannica, Inc.
EB .... End Bracket [*Computer science*] (VLIE)
EB .... End Bracket Erase Bit (SAUS)
EB .... Ending Balance (TIMI)
EB .... End of Block [*Computer science*] (VLIE)
EB .... End-of Block (SAUS)
EB .... Endometrial Biopsy [*Medicine*]
EB .... Energy Balance (SAUS)
EB .... Energy Bond (UWER)
EB .... Engine Bulletin (MCD)
EB .... Engine Burn [*NASA*]
EB .... Engineer Battalion [*Military*]
EB .... Engineering Biophysics (SAUS)
EB .... Engineering Bulletin (MCD)
EB .... English Baron (ROG)
EB .... English Bias (ACAE)
EB .... English Bible
EB .... English Breakfast (TRID)
EB .... Enlistment Bonus [*Military*] (AABC)
EB .... Environmental Buoy [*Marine science*] (MSC)
EB .... Environment and Behavior (journ.) (SAUS)
EB .... Epidermolysis Bullosa [*Dermatology*]
EB .... Epstein-Barr [*Virus*]
EB .... Equal Brake (OA)
EB .... Equipment Bay (KSC)
EB .... Equipment Bay, Equipment Building (SAUS)
EB .... Equipment Branch [*Air Force*] [*British*]
EB .... Equipment Building (AAG)
EB .... Erase Band (UWER)
EB .... Erase Bit (SAUS)
EB .... Erasing Bit (SAUS)
EB .... Erbium [*Symbol is Er*] [*Chemical element*] (ROG)
EB .... Error Bell (SAUS)
EB .... Escape Beat [*Medicine*] (MELL)
e-b .... estate-bottled (SAUS)
E-B .... Estate-Bottling [*Wine*]
EB .... Estradiol Benzoate [*Endocrinology*]
E-B .... Etch-Bleach [*Photography*] (DGA)
EB .... Ethidium Bromide [*Trypanocide*] [*Also, ETB, Etd Br*] [*Biochemical analysis*]
EB .... Ethiopian Birr [*Monetary Unit*] (BARN)
EB .... Ethylbenzene [*Organic chemistry*]
EB .... Ethylbenzoate (UWER)
EB .... Ethylene Bromide [*Same as DBE, EDB*] [*Organic chemistry*]
EB .... Ethylene-Butene (SAUS)
EB .... Ettore Bugatti [*Auto engineer*] [*French*]
EB .... Evaluation Branch [*BUPERS*]
EB .... Evan's Blue [*Fluorescent dye*]
EB .... Event Block [*Computer science*] (IAA)
EB .... Evolutionary Biology (SAUS)
EB .... ExaByte (SAUS)
EB .... Excisional Biopsy [*Medicine*] (MELL)
EB .... Executive Board
EB .... Executive Bulletin
EB .... Exercise Book (SAUS)
EB .... Expansion Bolt [*Technical drawings*]
EB .... Experimental Breeder (SAUS)
EB .... Experimental Buoy [*Marine science*] (MSC)
EB .... Exponential Born (SAUS)
EB .... [*The*] Expositor's Bible [*A publication*]
EB .... Exposure Back (SAUS)
EB .... Extended Benefits [*Unemployment insurance*]
EB .... Extended Born [*Solid-state physics*] (UWER)
EB .... Extension Bulletin (SAUS)
EB .... External Burning (RDA)
EB .... Eye Bolt (SAUS)
EB .... Eyepiece Box
EB .... L'Equilibre Biologique [*France*] [*Research code symbol*]
EB .... Pennsylvania Commuter Airlines [*Airline code*]
EB1S .... Edge Bead One Side [*Lumber*] (DAC)
e-B2B .... electronic Business-to-Business (SAUO)
eb 2 s .... edge bead two sides (SAUS)
EBA .... Early Birds of Aviation [*Defunct*] (EA)
EBA .... Ecole des Beaux Arts [*Paris, France*]
EBA .... Ecu Banking Association (SAUO)
EBA .... Edison Birthplace Association (EA)
EBA .... Education Boards Association (SAUO)
EBA .... Elba Island [*Italy*] [*Airport symbol*] [*Obsolete*] (OAG)
EBA .... Electric Boat Association [*British*] (DBA)
EBA .... Electron Beam Accelerator
EBA .... Emergency Breathing Apparatus
EBA .... Endemic Bird Area
EBA .... Energy Business Association (SAUO)

EBA............ Engineer Battlefield Assessment [*Military*] (INF)
EBA............ English Bowling Association
EBA............ Enriched Brucella Blood Agar [*Culture media*]
EBA............ Enterprise Bargaining Agreement (SAUO)
EBA............ Enterprise-Based Agreement
EBA............ Environmental Ballistics Associates (SAUS)
EBA............ Environmental Bankers Association
EBA............ Epidermolysis Bullosa Acquisita (DB)
EBA............ Epizootic Bovine Abortion
EBA............ Erythrocyte Binding Antigen [*Immunology*]
EBA............ Ethoxybenzoic Acid [*Dental cement*]
EBA............ Ethyl(benzyl)aniline [*Organic chemistry*]
EBA............ Ethyl Bromoacetate [*Organic chemistry*]
EBA............ Ethyl(butyl)amine [*Organic chemistry*]
EBA............ Ethylene Butyl Acrylate [*Organic chemistry*]
EBA............ Euro Banking Association
EBA............ Eurobelgian Airlines, NV [*Belgium*] [*FAA designator*] (FAAC)
EBA............ European Broadcasting Area (SAUS)
EBA............ European Business Associates [*Information systems marketing organization*] (NITA)
EBA............ European Business Associates On-line (SAUO)
EBA............ European Heating Boilers Association (SAUO)
EBA............ evaluation basis accident (SAUS)
EBA............ evaluation basis audit (SAUS)
EBA............ Experimental Ballistics Associates [*Defunct*] (EA)
EBA............ Experimental Behavioral Analyzer
EBA............ Extended Batch Language (SAUS)
EBA............ O-Ethoxybenzoic Acid (SAUS)
EBAA.......... Electric Boat Association of the Americas (EA)
EBAA.......... European Business Aircraft Association (PIAV)
EBAA.......... European Business Aviation Association (EAIO)
EBAA.......... Eye Bank Association of America (EA)
EBAC.......... European Bank Advisory Committee (SAUS)
EBAD.......... exfoliative broncho-alveolar disease (SAUS)
EBAE.......... European Bureau of Adult Education (EAIO)
EBAF.......... Equipment Blockage and Failure (SAUS)
EBAILL........ European Bureau for the Allocation of International Long Lines (NATG)
EBAL.......... Aalst [*Belgium*] [*ICAO location identifier*] (ICLI)
EBAM.......... Amougies [*Belgium*] [*ICAO location identifier*] (ICLI)
EBAM.......... Electron Beam Accessed Memory [*Computer science*] (ELAL)
EBAM.......... Electron-Beam-Accessible Memory (SAUS)
EBAM.......... Electron Beam Access Method (PDAA)
EBAM.......... Electron-Beam-Addressed Memory [*Air Force*]
EBAM.......... electron beamed access memory (SAUS)
EBAM.......... Electronic Beam-Addressable Memory (SAUS)
EB & BB...... Eastbound Basing and Billing Book
EB & E........ Ellis, Blackburn, and Ellis' English Queen's Bench Reports [*1858*] [*A publication*] (DLA)
EB&F.......... Equipment Blockage and Failure (SAUS)
EB & F........ Equipment Blockages and Failures [*Telecommunications*] (TEL)
EB&RA........ Engineer Buyers and Representatives Association (SAUO)
EB & S........ Ellis, Best, and Smith's English Queen's Bench Reports [*A publication*] (DLA)
EB & SR...... Engineer Boat and Shore Regiment [*Army*]
EBAP.......... Eldisine [*Vindesine*], BCNU , Adriamycin, Prednisone [*Carmustine*] [*Antineoplastic drug regimen*]
EBAP.......... External Burning-Assisted Projectile [*Military*] (DNAB)
EB-APGA...... European Branch of the American Personnel Guidance Association (SAUO)
EBAPS........ Engine Bleed Air Precooler System
EBAR.......... Edited Beyond All Recognition (SAUS)
EBAS.......... Electron Beam Activated Switch (PDAA)
EBAS.......... Electronic Beam Activated Switch (IAA)
EBASA........ Ethyl(benzyl)anilinesulfonic Acid [*Organic chemistry*]
EB ASB........ Ebony Asbestos (SAUS)
EBAW.......... Antwerp-Anvers [*Belgium*] [*ICAO location identifier*] (ICLI)
EBAY.......... Eastbay, Inc. [*NASDAQ symbol*] (SAG)
EBAY.......... eBay, Inc. [*NASDAQ symbol*] (SG)
EBB............ Economic Bulletin Board [*Information service or system*] (IID)
EBB............ Electronic Bulletin Board [*Department of Commerce*] [*Washington, DC*] [*Information service or system*] (IID)
EBB............ Elias Baseball Bureau (SAUS)
EBB............ Elizabeth Barrett Browning (SAUS)
EBB............ Entebbe/Kampala [*Uganda*] [*Airport symbol*] (OAG)
EBB............ Equivalent Block Body (SAUS)
EBB............ European Brazilian Bank [*London, England*]
EBB............ Extra Best Best [*Steel wire*]
EBBA.......... Eastern Bird Banding Association (EA)
EBBA.......... English Basket Ball Association
EBBA.......... Estuarine and Brackish-Water Biological Association (SAUO)
EBBA.......... (Ethoxybenylidene)butylaniline [*Organic chemistry*]
EBBA News... Eastern Bird Banding Association News (journ.) (SAUS)
EBBB.......... Brussels [*Belgium*] [*ICAO location identifier*] (ICLI)
EBBD.......... Central Data Bank, EUROCONTROL [*Belgium*] [*ICAO location identifier*] (ICLI)
EBBE.......... Beauvechain [*Belgium*] [*ICAO location identifier*] (ICLI)
EBBF.......... Equitable Benefit-Based Financing
EBBL.......... Klein Brogel [*Belgium*] [*ICAO location identifier*] (ICLI)
EBBR.......... Brussels/National [*Belgium*] [*ICAO location identifier*] (ICLI)
EBBR.......... Energy-Balance Bowen Ratio (CARB)
EBBS.......... Brussels [*Belgium*] [*ICAO location identifier*] (ICLI)
EBBS.......... Engineering Bulletin Board System
EBBS.......... European Brain and Behaviour Society (PDAA)
EBBT.......... Brasschaat [*Belgium*] [*ICAO location identifier*] (ICLI)
EBBU.......... Brussels [*Belgium*] [*ICAO location identifier*] (ICLI)
EBBV.......... Brussels [*Belgium*] [*ICAO location identifier*] (ICLI)
EBB Wire..... Extra Best Best Wire (SAUS)
EBBX.......... Bertrix [*Belgium*] [*ICAO location identifier*] (ICLI)
EBC............ Aero Ejecutivo de Baja California SA de CV [*Mexico*] [*ICAO designator*] (FAAC)
EBC............ Bay Area Library and Information System [*Library network*]
EBC............ Beam Electron-Beam Coating (SAUS)
EBC............ Brevard Community College, Cocoa, FL [*OCLC symbol*] (OCLC)
EBC............ Eastern Baptist College (SAUO)
EBC............ Eastern Boundary Current (SAUS)
EBC............ Echelons Below Corps [*Army*] (DOMA)
EBC............ EdperBrascan Corp.'A' [*AMEX symbol*] (SG)
EBC............ Educational Broadcasting Corp. (EA)
EBC............ Educational Broadcasting Corporation (SAUO)
EBC............ EISA Bus Controller (SAUS)
EBC............ Electoral Boundaries Commission [*Victoria, Australia*]
EBC............ Electron Beam Channeling (UWER)
EBC............ Electron Beam Coating
EBC............ Electron Beam Control
EBC............ Electron Beam Curing [*Chemical technology*]
EBC............ Electron Beam Cutting [*Engraving*] [*Welding*]
EBC............ Electronic Batch Control
EBC............ Electronic Business Communications (SAUS)
EBC............ Emergency Beacon Corporation (SAUO)
EBC............ Employee Bay Out (SAUS)
EBC............ Employee Benefits Cases (DLA)
EBC............ Emulated Buffer Computer (MCD)
EBC............ Enamel Bonded Single Cotton [*Wire insulation*] (AAG)
EBC............ End Breguet Cruise [*SST*]
EBC............ Energy Band Calculations [*Solid-state physics*] (UWER)
EBC............ English Benedictine Congregation (SAUO)
EBC............ English Butter Conference (SAUO)
EBC............ Enterprise-Based Committee [*Australia*]
EBC............ Environmental Business Council
EBC............ Epoxy Bond Coating
EBC............ Equivalent Boron Content (SAUS)
EBC............ Eugene Ballet Company [*Eugene, OR*]
EBC............ Euro-board computer (SAUS)
EBC............ European Banking Company Ltd. (SAUO)
EBC............ European Bibliographical Center
EBC............ European Billiards Confederation
EBC............ European Brewery Convention
EBC............ Existing Building Center (SAUS)
EBC............ Expositor's Bible Commentary [*A publication*]
EBC............ External Baggage Container (DNAB)
EBCA.......... Department of Energy Board of Contract Appeals (AAGC)
EBCA.......... (Ethoxybenzylidene)cyanoaniline [*Also, PEBAB*] [*Organic chemistry*]
EBCA.......... External Branch Condition Address [*Telecommunications*] (TEL)
EB Car........ Electric Baggage Car (SAUS)
EBCB.......... European Bank of Computer programs in Biotechnology (SAUS)
EBCB.......... European Business Coalition for Brussels (SAUO)
EBCCD........ Electron-Bombarded Charge Coupled Device (SEWL)
EBC-CLIO..... European Bibliographical Center CLIO Press (SAUS)
EBCD.......... Extended Binary-Coded Decimal [*Computer science*]
EBCD.......... Extended Binary Coded Decimals (SAUS)
EBCD Code... Extended Binary Coded Decimal Code (SAUS)
EBCDI.......... Extended Binary-Coded Decimal Interchange [*Computer science*] (IAA)
EBCDIC........ Expanded Binary Coded Decimal Interchange Code (SAUS)
EBCDIC........ Extended Binary Coded Data Interchange Code (SAUS)
EBCDIC........ Extended Binary-Coded Decimal Interchange Code [*Computer science*]
EBCDI code... extended binary-coded decimal interchange code (SAUS)
EBCDIC........ extended binary coded decimal interchange code (SAUS)
EBCDS........ Extended Binary Coded Decimals (SAUS)
EBCE.......... Electron Beam Control Electronics
EBCE.......... Experience-Based Career Education
EBCE-MD..... Experience-Based Career Education for Mentally Disabled Students (OICC)
ebcf............ early-B-cell-factor (SAUS)
EBCG.......... European Biotechnology Coordinating (or Coordination) Group (SAUO)
EBCG.......... Experimental Buried Collector Gauge
EBCHR........ Electron Beam Cold-Hearth Refining (SAUS)
EBCI.......... Charleroi/Gosselies [*Belgium*] [*ICAO location identifier*] (ICLI)
EBCI.......... Eagle Bancorp, Inc. [*NASDAQ symbol*] (NQ)
EBCI.......... European Biological Control Laboratory (ECON)
EBCI.......... External Branch Condition Input [*Telecommunications*] (TEL)
EBC-IVH...... Electronic Braking Control - Four Wheel Hybrid [*Automotive engineering*]
EBCM.......... Electronic Brake Control Module [*Automotive engineering*]
EBCM.......... Extended Boundary Condition Method
EBCP.......... Eastern Bancorp, Inc. [*NASDAQ symbol*] (SAG)
EBCP.......... Evidence-Based Clinical Practice (SAUO)
EBCS.......... Electronic Business Communications System
EBCS.......... European Barge Carrier System (PDAA)
EBCSM........ East Bay Council on Surveying and Mapping (SAUO)
EBCT.......... Electron Beam Computed Tomography
EBCT.......... Empresa Brasileira de Correios e Telegrafos [*State enterprise*] [*Brazil*] (EY)
EBCT.......... Empty Bed Contact Time [*Environmental Protection Agency*]
EBCT.......... Extended Battlefield Contact Team (MCD)
EBCV.......... Chievres [*Belgium*] [*ICAO location identifier*] (ICLI)
ebd............ Ebenda (BJA)

EBD .... Economic Batch Determination
ebd .... education by discussion (SAUS)
EBD .... Effective Billing Date (TEL)
EBD .... Effective Biological Dose (SAUS)
EBD .... Electron-Beam Deflection (UWER)
EBD .... Electronic Brake-Force Distribution [*Anti-lock brake systems*] [*Automotive engineering*]
EBD .... El Obeid [*Sudan*] [*Airport symbol*] (OAG)
EBD .... Emergency Boot Disk (SAUS)
EBD .... Emotional and Behavioural Difficulties (AIE)
EBD .... Emotional/Behavioral Disorder
EBD .... Epidermolysis Bullosa Dystrophia [*Dermatology*]
EBD .... Equivalent Binary Digit
EBD .... Eucaloric Balanced Diet
EBD .... Extrinsic Boundary Dislocation (SAUS)
EBD .... Eye Ball Down (MCD)
EBDC .... Enamel Bonded Double Cotton [*Wire insulation*]
EBDC .... Ethylenebis(dithiocarbamate) [*Organic chemistry*]
EBDCs .... ethylenebisdithiocarbamates (SAUS)
EBDD .... Epidermolysis Bullosa Dystrophic Dominant [*Dermatology*]
EBDE .... Electronic Business Data Exchange (SAUS)
EBDI .... Electronic Business Data Interchange (SAUS)
EBDI .... Electronic Business Document Interchange
EBDI .... External Breathing Direct Injection [*Chrysler Corp.*] [*Automotive engineering*]
EBDIK .... EBDIC for Kana characters (SAUS)
EBDJ .... Evidence- based dentistry-BDJ (SAUS)
EBDO .... European Developmental Biology Organization (SAUS)
EBDP .... Enamel Bonded Double Paper [*Wire insulation*]
EBDR .... Epidermolysis Bullosa Dystrophic Recessive [*Dermatology*]
EBDS .... Emotional or Behavior Disorder Scale [*Test*] (TMMY)
EBDS .... Enamel Bonded Double Silk [*Wire insulation*]
EBDV .... Exhaust Blow-Down Volume
EBDW .... Beam Electron-Beam Direct-Write (SAUS)
e-be- .... Belgium [*MARC geographic area code*] [*Library of Congress*] (LCCP)
EBE .... Electron Beam Evaporator
EBE .... Electron Binding Energy
EBE .... evaluation basis earthquake (SAUS)
EBE .... Experimental Bridging Establishment [*British*]
EBE .... Extraterrestrial Biological Entity
E-BEAM .... Electron Beam (AAEL)
e-beam .... Electron Beam
EBEB .... EB, Inc. [*NASDAQ symbol*] (SAG)
EBEC .... Encyclopaedia Britannica Educational Corp.
EBEC .... Encyclopedia Britannica Educational Corporation (SAUS)
EBEE .... Electron Beam Evaporation Equipment
EBEM .... Electron Beam Evaporation Module
EBEP .... Electron-Beam-Excited Plasma (UWER)
EBER .... Equivalent Binary Error Rate (SAUS)
EBERAS .... Event-by-Event Recording and Sorting [*Electronics*]
Ebersole .... Ebersole's Reports [*59-80 Iowa*] [*A publication*] (DLA)
Ebersole (IA)... Ebersole's Reports [*59-80 Iowa*] [*A publication*] (DLA)
EbertRV .... Reallexikon der Vorgeschichte [*M. Ebert*] [*A publication*] (BJA)
EBES .... Electric Beam Exposure System [*Integrated circuit*] [*Bell Laboratories*]
EBES .... Electron Beam Engraving System (NITA)
EBES .... Electron Beam Exposure System (SAUS)
EBES .... Electronic Banking Economics Society (NTPA)
EBF .... Early B-cell Factor [*Biochemistry*]
EBF .... Economic and Business Foundation
EBF .... Electric Bomb Fuze (NG)
EBF .... Electron-Beam Focusing (SAUS)
EBF .... Electron-Bombardment Furnace
EBF .... Electronic Book Format (TELE)
EBF .... Encyclopaedia Britannica Film (IIA)
EBF .... English Bowling Federation (DBA)
EBF .... Ennis Business Forms, Inc. [*NYSE symbol*] (SPSG)
EBF .... Erythroblastosis Fetalis [*Hematology*]
EBF .... estimated blood flow (SAUS)
EBF .... Europaeische Baptistische Foderation [*European Baptist Federation - EBF*] (EAIO)
EBF .... Europaeische Baptistische Frauenunion [*European Baptist Women's Union - EBWU*] (EAIO)
EBF .... Externally Blown Flap [*Aviation*]
EBFA .... Electron Beam Fusion Accelerator
ebfa .... electron-beam fusion accelerator (SAUS)
EBFBRG .... European Bank of Frozen Blood of Rare Groups [*Amsterdam, Netherlands*] (EAIO)
EBFC .... Ed Bruce Fan Club [*Defunct*] (EA)
EBFC .... Elvis Brothers Fan Club (EA)
EBFC .... Eric Braeden Fan Club (EA)
EBFG .... East Bay Fan Guild (EA)
EBFN .... Koksijde [*Belgium*] [*ICAO location identifier*] (ICLI)
EBFP .... Enhanced Blue Fluorescent Protein
EBFR .... Enclosure Building Filtration Region (SAUS)
EBFS .... Enclosure Building Filtration System (IEEE)
EBFS .... Florennes [*Belgium*] [*ICAO location identifier*] (ICLI)
EBF-STOL .... Externally Blown Flap - Short Takeoff and Landing (SAUS)
EB Function... Emitter Base Function (SAUS)
EBFYC .... European Baptist Federation Youth Committee (EAIO)
EBG .... Ecobank Ghana (EY)
EBG .... Economic Bulletin of Ghana [*A publication*]
EBG .... El Bagre [*Colombia*] [*Airport symbol*] (OAG)
EBG .... Electroblepharogram (DB)
EBG .... electron-beam engraving (SAUS)
EBG .... Electron Beam Generator
EBG .... Electron Beam Gun
EBG .... Electronics Buyers' Guide [*A publication*] (NITA)
ebg .... Elsewhere Below Ground (SAUS)
EBGB .... Brussels/Grimbergen [*Belgium*] [*ICAO location identifier*] (ICLI)
EBGL .... Glons [*Belgium*] [*ICAO location identifier*] (ICLI)
EBGS .... Extracorporeal Blood Gas System [*Medicine*] (DB)
EBGT .... Gent/St. Denijs Westrem [*Belgium*] [*ICAO location identifier*] (ICLI)
EBH .... Black Hill [*Scotland*] [*Seismograph station code, US Geological Survey*] (SEIS)
EBH .... Engine Block Heater [*Automotive engineering*]
EBH .... Epibromohydrin [*Organic chemistry*]
EBH .... Epidermolysis Bullosa Hereditaria [*Dermatology*]
EBH .... Ergonomic Book Holder
EBHC .... equated busy hour call (SAUS)
EBHC .... Evidence-Based Health Care (SAUS)
EBHN .... Hoevenen [*Belgium*] [*ICAO location identifier*] (ICLI)
EBHP .... Ethylbenzene Hydroperoxide [*Organic chemistry*]
EBHSS .... Electron Beam High Speed Scan (SAUS)
EBHT .... Electron Beam High Throughput Lithography
EBI .... Earnings Before Interest
EBI .... Echo Bay Finance Corp. [*AMEX symbol*] (SPSG)
EBI .... Economics and Business Information Group (SAUO)
EBI .... [*The*] Educational Broadcasting Institute [*National Association of Educational Broadcasters*] (NTCM)
EBI .... Effective Buying Income [*Portion of gross income after subtracting taxes, food, clothing, and housing expenditures*]
EBI .... Electromagnetic Bone Stimulator [*Orthopedics*] (DAVI)
EBI .... Electron Beam Induced (SAUS)
EBI .... Electron Beam Instrumentation (MELL)
EBI .... Electron-Beam Interference (UWER)
EB-I .... electron beam separator (SAUS)
EBI .... Elsevier Business Information
EBI .... Emerson Books, Inc. (DGA)
EBI .... Emerson Books, Incorporated (SAUO)
EBI .... Emetine Bismuth Iodide [*Pharmacology*]
EBI .... Encyclopaedia Biblica [*A publication*] (BJA)
EBI .... Equality Bancorp [*AMEX symbol*] (SG)
EBI .... Equivalent Background Input
EBI .... Equivalent Background Investigation (SAUS)
EBI .... Equivalent/Extended Background Input/Investigation (SAUS)
EBI .... Ergosterol Biosynthesis Inhibitor [*Biochemistry*]
EBI .... Estradiol Binding Index [*Biochemistry*] (DMAA)
EBI .... European Bioinformatics Institute
EBI .... Everly Brothers International [*Defunct*] (EA)
EBI .... Expanded Background Investigation (AFM)
EBI .... Experience and Background Inventory [*Management and supervision test*]
EBI .... Exploding Bridgewire Initiator (ACAE)
EBI .... Extended Background Input (SAUS)
EBI .... Extended Background Investigation (SAUS)
EBI .... Extended BIOS Interface (SAUS)
EBI .... Extensive Background Investigations (SAUS)
EBI .... Eye Ball In
EBIAT .... Earnings Before Interest and After Taxes [*Accounting*] (PDAA)
EBIB .... Energy Bibliography (SAUS)
EBIB .... Energy Bibliography and Index [*Center for Energy and Mineral Resources - Texas A & M University*] [*College Station, TX*] [*Bibliographic database*]
EB-IBCCA .... Editorial Board for the International Bathymetric Chart of the Caribbean Sea and the Gulf of Mexico (SAUS)
EB-IBCEA .... Editorial Board for the International Bathymetric Chart of the Central Eastern Atlantic (SAUS)
EB-IBCM .... Editorial Board for the International Bathymetric Chart of the Mediterranean and its Geological/Geophysical Series (SAUS)
EB-IBCWIO... Editorial Board for the International Bathymetric Chart of the Western Indian Ocean (SAUS)
EB-IBCWP.... Editorial Board for the International Bathymetric Chart of the Western Pacific (SAUS)
EBIC .... EFTA [*European Free Trade Association*] Brewing Industry Council (EAIO)
EBIC .... Electron Beam Induced Conduction (SAUS)
EBIC .... Electron Beam Induced Conductivity (SAUS)
EBIC .... Electron-Beam-Induced Current [*Photovoltaic energy systems*]
EBIC .... Electron-Bombardment-Induced Conductivity
EBIC .... European Banks International Corporation (SAUO)
EBIC .... European Banks International Company (SAUS)
EBIC .... European Business Information Centre (EURO)
EBIC method... electron-beam induced current method (SAUS)
EBICON .... Electron-Bombardment-Induced Conductivity
EBID .... Electron-Bombardment Induced Desorption (UWER)
EBIF .... European Button Industries Federation [*British*] (EAIO)
EBIFC .... Elmer Bird International Fan Club (EA)
EBIG .... Electron Beam Inert Gas (PDAA)
EBIL .... Electron Beam Injector Laboratory (SAUS)
e-bill .... Electronic Bill (GART)
EBIM .... Elections Before Independence Movement (SAUO)
EBIM .... Ethernet Bridge Interface Module (SAUS)
EBIO .... European Beet Industries Organization (SAUO)
EBIOC .... Electron Beam-Induced Oxide Charging
EBIP .... European Biotechnology Information Project [*British Library*] [*Information service or system*] (IID)
EBIR .... Electron Beam Image Recorder (SAUS)
EBIR .... Electron-Bombardment-Induced Response
EBIRD .... Electron Beam Ionization of Semiconductor Devices (PDAA)

EBIS............ East Bay Information Service [*Library network*]
EBIS............ Economic Business Information Service (SAUS)
EBIS............ Economic Information Systems (SAUS)
EBIS............ Electron Beam Ion Source (IEEE)
EBIS............ Employee Benefits Infosource [*International Foundation of Employee Benefit Plans*] [*Information service or system*] (CRD)
EBIS............ Employment Barrier Identification Scale [*Employment test*]
EBIS............ Encyclopedia of Business Information Sources [*A publication*]
EBIS............ ESCAP [*Economic and Social Commission for Asia and the Pacific*] Bibliographic Information System [*Thailand*] [*United Nations*] [*Information service or system*] (IID)
EBIS............ ESCAP Bibliographic Information Systems (SAUO)
EBIS............ Ethylenebisisothiocyanate Sulfide [*Organic chemistry*]
EBIS............ Exothermic Bimetallic Ignition System (MCD)
EBISD......... Electron Beam Ionization of Semiconductor Devices (SAUS)
EBIS/IRD...... EBIS Integrated Rural Development (SAUS)
EBIST.......... Expert Bradley Infantry Squad Training Test [*Army*] (INF)
EBIT............ Earnings before Interest and Taxes [*Accounting*]
Ebit............ Earnings before interests and Taxes (SAUS)
EBIT............ Electron Beam Injected Transistor (SAUS)
EBIT............ Electron Beam Injection Transistor (SAUS)
EBIT............ Electron Beam Ion Trap [*Developed at Lawrence Livermore and Lawrence Berkeley National Laboratories*] [*Atomic physics*]
ebit............ electron-beam ion trap (SAUS)
E-bit............ Error bit (SAUS)
EBIT............ European Broadband Interconnect Trial (SAUS)
EBITA.......... Earnings before Interest, Taxes, Depreciation, and Amortization [*Investment term*] (DFIT)
EBITD.......... Earnings before Interest Taxes and Depreciation
EBITDA........ Earnings before Interest, Taxes, Depreciation, and Amortization [*Business term*]
EBITS.......... Estimated Earnings before Interest and Taxes
EBIV............ Electron-Beam-Induced Voltage [*Photovoltaic energy systems*]
EBIV............ Electron Beam Induce Voltage (SAUS)
EBIV............ Electron Bombardment Induced Voltage (SAUS)
EBJ............ Emitter-Base Junction (SAUS)
EBJ............ Esbjerg [*Denmark*] [*Airport symbol*] (OAG)
EBJ............ European Biophysics Journal (SAUO)
EBJ............ European Business Journal [*A publication*]
E-B junction... emitter base junction (SAUS)
EBK............ Eastern Bakeries Ltd. [*Toronto Stock Exchange symbol*]
EBK............ Easy Bleaching Kraft [*Pulp and paper technology*]
EBK............ Embryonic Bovine Kidney
EBKH.......... Balen/Keiheuvel [*Belgium*] [*ICAO location identifier*] (ICLI)
EBKT.......... Kortrijk-Wevelgem [*Belgium*] [*ICAO location identifier*] (ICLI)
EBL............ Austin, TX [*Location identifier*] [*FAA*] (FAAL)
EBL............ Broadlaw [*Scotland*] [*Seismograph station code, US Geological Survey*] (SEIS)
EBL............ East Branch & Lincoln [*Federal Railroad Administration identification code*]
EBL............ Eastern Basketball League
EBL............ Electric Heated Back Light [*Automotive engineering*]
EBL............ Electron-Beam Laser (UWER)
EBL............ Electron Beam Lithography (IAA)
EBL............ Electron Beam-pumped semiconductor Laser (SAUS)
EBL............ Electronic Bearing Line [*RADAR technology*]
EBL............ Encyclopaedia Biblica [*A publication*] (ROG)
EBL............ Endemic Burkitt's Lymphoma [*Medicine*]
EBL............ Endoscopic Band Ligation (MELL)
EBL............ Energy Budget Level
EBL............ Enzootic Bovine Leukemia
EBL............ Enzootic Bovine Leukosis (SAUS)
EBL............ Estimated Blood Loss [*Medicine*]
EBL............ European Bridge League (EAIO)
EBL............ Event-Based Language [*1979*] [*Computer science*] (CSR)
EBL............ Extended Batch Language (CDE)
EBL............ Exterior Ballistics Laboratory (SAUS)
EBL............ External Blood Loss (ADWA)
EBL............ Eye Ball Left (MCD)
EBLAN.......... Eblanencis [*Signature of the Bishops of Dublin*] (ROG)
EBLB.......... Elsenborn [*Belgium*] [*ICAO location identifier*] (ICLI)
EBLF.......... Electron Beam Lithography Facility [*British*]
EBLG.......... Liege/Bierset [*Belgium*] [*ICAO location identifier*] (ICLI)
EBLH.......... Liege/Bierset [*Belgium*] [*ICAO location identifier*] (ICLI)
EBLI............ Electronics Business Leading Indicator (SAUS)
EBLIDA........ European Bureau of Library Information and Documentation Associations (AIE)
EBLUL.......... European Bureau for Lesser Used Languages (EA)
EBLV.......... Elderberry Latent Virus [*Plant pathology*]
EBM............ Early-Break-Make [*Computer science*]
EBM............ Echo Bay Mines (SAUO)
EBM............ Ecosystem-Based Management (SAUO)
EBM............ Electric Backing Memory (SAUS)
EBM............ Electric Billing Machine (SAUS)
EBM............ Electric Buffer Memory (SAUS)
EBM............ Electromagnetic Billetmaker (SAUS)
EBM............ Electron Beam Machining [*Manufacturing term*]
EBM............ Electron Beam Melted (SAUS)
EBM............ Electron Beam Melting (IAA)
EBM............ Electron Beam Method
EBM............ Electron Beam Microanalysis
EBM............ Electron Beam Multiplier (IAA)
EBM............ Electronic Battle Management (SAUS)
EBM............ Electronic Bearing Marker [*Navigation*] (OA)
EBM............ Empresa Bacaladera Mexicana (SAUS)
EBM............ Energy Balance Model [*Climatology*]
EBM............ Energy Balance Models (SAUO)
EBM............ Engagement Battle Manager (ACAE)
EBM............ English Beet Molasses (SAUS)
EBM............ Enterprise Business Model [*Australia*]
EBM............ Esen Bulak [*Mongolia*] [*Seismograph station code, US Geological Survey*] [*Closed*] (SEIS)
EBM............ Estimation-before-Modeling (MCD)
EBM............ Europaeische Baptistische Mission [*European Baptist Mission*] [*Germany*] (EAIO)
EBM............ European Baptist Mission (EAIO)
EBM............ Evidence-Based Medicine
EBM............ Expressed Breast Milk [*Medicine*]
EBM............ Extended Branch Mode
EBMA.......... E & B Marine, Inc. [*NASDAQ symbol*] (SAG)
EBMA.......... Elastic Braid Manufacturers Association [*Later, EFMC or EFMCNTA*] (EA)
EBMA.......... Electron Beam Microprobe Analysis (SAUS)
EBMA.......... Engine, Booster Maintenance Area
EBMA.......... European Butylated Hydroxytoluene-BHT-Manufacturers Association (SAUO)
EBMB.......... Melsbroek [*Belgium*] [*ICAO location identifier*] (ICLI)
EBMD.......... Electron Beam Mode Discharge
EBMDA........ Eastern Building Material Dealers Association (SRA)
EBME.......... Eagle's Basal Medium with Earle's Salts [*Culture medium*]
EBMF.......... Electron Beam Microfabricating System (SAUS)
EBMF.......... Electron Beam Microfabricator (IAA)
EBMI............ Brussels [*Belgium*] [*ICAO location identifier*] (ICLI)
EBMI............ E&B Marine, Inc. [*NASDAQ symbol*] (COMM)
EBMLM........ Electron Beam Membrane Light Modulator [*Army*] (MCD)
EBMO.......... Moorsele [*Belgium*] [*ICAO location identifier*] (ICLI)
EBMR.......... Evidence Based Medicine Reviews (SAUS)
EBMS.......... Energy Balance Models (EERA)
EBMSC........ Enduring Battle Management Support Center (SAUO)
EBMT.......... European Bone Marrow Transplantation
EBMT.......... European Cooperative Group for Bone Marrow Transplantation (SAUS)
EBMT.......... Munte [*Belgium*] [*ICAO location identifier*] (ICLI)
EBMUD........ East Bay Municipal Utility District (SAUS)
EbN............ East by North
ebn............ Ebonized (VRA)
ebn............ Ebony (VRA)
EBN............ Endosperm Balance Number [*Genetics*]
EBN............ Eurobird-Net info (SAUS)
EBN............ European Broadcast News (SAUS)
EBN............ European Business innovation centre Network (SAUO)
EBN............ Evidence-Based Nursing (SAUS)
EBNA.......... EBV [*Epstein-Barr Virus*] Nuclear Antigen [*Immunochemistry*]
EBNA.......... Epstein-Barr Nuclear Antigen [*Virus*] [*Immunology*]
EBND.......... Eastbound (FAAC)
EBNF.......... Extended Backus-Naur Form
EBNI............ Electricity Board for Northern Ireland (BI)
EBNIC.......... European Biotechnology Node for Interaction with China (EURO)
EBNM.......... Namur-Suarlee [*Belgium*] [*ICAO location identifier*] (ICLI)
EB/NO.......... Energy per Bit to Noise (CCCA)
Eb/No.......... Signal Bit Energy/Noise Level (SAUS)
EBNY.......... Edition Bookbinders of New York (EA)
EBO............ Employee Benefits Officer (TBD)
EBO............ European Banking Operation (SAUS)
EBO............ European Community Baroque Orchestra (EURO)
EBO............ Evaluation by Objective (ACAE)
EBO............ Experimental Biology Online (SAUS)
EBO............ Extrahepatic Biliary Obstruction [*Medicine*]
EBO............ Eye Ball Out
E-boat.......... enemy boat (SAUS)
E-boat.......... Enemy Torpedo Boat (WDAA)
E/BOD.......... Electrolytic Biological Oxygen Demand
EBONE.......... European Backbone (SAUO)
EBONE.......... European IP backBONE (SAUS)
EBONTA........ (Ethylenebis(oxyethylenenitrilo))tetraacetic Acid [*Also, EGTA*] [*Organic chemistry*]
EBOR.......... Eboracensis [*Signature of the Bishop of York*] (ROG)
EBOR.......... Eboracum [*York*] [*County in England*] [*Latin*] (ROG)
EBOR.......... Experimental Beryllium Oxide Reactor [*Later, BORE*]
EBOR-CX...... Experiment Beryllium Oxide Reactor - Critical Assembly (SAA)
EBOS.......... Oostende [*Belgium*] [*ICAO location identifier*] (ICLI)
E-box.......... Electronic Box
EBOZ.......... Ebola Virus, Zaire Strain (ADWA)
EBP............ Eisenbindendes Protein (SAUS)
EBP............ Electric Bilge Pump
EBP............ Electron Beam Pumping (AAEL)
EBP............ Electronic Bill Presentment (GART)
EBP............ Electronic Book Player (TELE)
EBP............ Enamel-Bonded Single Paper [*Wire insulation*] (IAA)
ebp............ enamel single paper bonded (SAUS)
EBP............ End Boiling Point (SAUS)
EBP............ Environmental Biology Program (SAUO)
EBP............ Environmentaly Benign Processing [*Engineering*]
EBP............ Epidural Blood Patch [*Medicine*]
EBP............ Estradiol-Binding Protein [*Biochemistry*]
EBP............ Etch Back Process (IAA)
EBP............ European Books in Print (TELE)
EBP............ European Business Program (EURO)
EBP............ Exhaust Back Pressure
EBP............ Explanation of Benefit Payment [*Insurance*]

EBP .... Extended Basal Period
EBPA .... Electron Beam Parametric Amplifier
EBPA .... Ethylbenzene Producers Association (EA)
EBPAD .... Ethoxylated Bisphenol A Dimethacrylate [*Organic chemistry*]
EBPE .... European Biotech Partnering Event
EBPG .... Electron Beam Pattern Generator
EBPI .... Environmental Business Publishing, Inc. (IID)
EBPN .... Early Babylonian Personal Names [*A publication*] (BJA)
EBPP .... Electronic Bill Presentment and Payment
E-BPR .... Enhanced Bottom Pressure Recorder [*Marine science*] (OSRA)
EbpS .... EBSCO Publishing & EBSCO Subscription Service Service, Birmingham, AL [*Library symbol*] [*Library of Congress*] (LCLS)
EBPS .... European Baptist Press Service [*of the European Baptist Federation*] (EAIO)
EBPSUSA .... El Bireh Palestine Society of the USA (EA)
EB-PVD .... Electron Beam - Physical Vapor Deposition (SAUS)
EBQ .... Economic Batch Quantity (SAUS)
EBQ .... Empire Brass Quintet (SAUS)
EBQ .... Experience and Background Questionnaire [*Test*]
Ebr .... De Ebrietate [*Philo*] (BJA)
EBR .... East Bengal State Railway [*Indian Railway*] (TIR)
EBR .... Ebro Roquetas [*Spain*] [*Seismograph station code, US Geological Survey*] (SEIS)
EBR .... Edge Bead Removal (AAEL)
EBR .... Electron Beam Readout
EBR .... Electron Beam Recorder [*or Recording*]
EBR .... Electron Beam Recording (SAUS)
EBR .... Electron Beam Regulator
EBR .... Electron Beam Remelting (IAA)
EBR .... Electron Beam Reproducer (SAUS)
EBR .... Electronic Batch Record
EBR .... Electronic Beam Recording Method (SAUS)
EBR .... Emergency Bomb Release (CINC)
EBR .... Emu Bay Railway (SAUS)
EBR .... Emulsion Butadiene Rubber
E-BR .... emulsion butadiene ruber (SAUS)
E BR .... Encyclopaedia Britannica [*A publication*] (ROG)
EBR .... Engine Braking Regulation [*Automotive engineering*]
EBR .... Engineering Business Report (SAUS)
EBR .... Enterprise Backup and Restore [*Computer science*] (VERA)
EBR .... Environmental Bill of Rights (SAUO)
EBR .... Epoxy Bridge Rectifier
EBR .... Excessive Burst Rate (SAUS)
EBR .... Experimental Beryllium Oxide Reactor (SAUS)
EBR .... Experimental Breeder Reactor
EBR .... Extended-Partition Root Record (SAUS)
EBR .... External Beam Radiation
EBR .... Eye Ball Right (MCD)
EBRA .... Emergency Banking Relief Act
EBRA .... Engineer Buyers' and Representatives' Association [*British*]
EBRA .... European Biomedical Research Association (GVA)
EBRC .... Economic and Budget Review Committee [*Victoria, Australia*]
EBRD .... Electron Beam Rotating Disk (SAUS)
EBRD .... European Bank for Reconstruction and Development [*Economic assistance for Eastern Europe*] [*Proposed*]
EBRD .... Export Business Division (SAUS)
EBRD .... Export Business Relations Division [*Department of Commerce*]
EBRG .... Earth-Based Radio Guidance
EBRI .... Employee Benefit Research Institute (EA)
EBRII .... Experimental Breeder Reactor II [*Environmental Protection Agency*]
EBRJC .... East Bridge Junction, LA [*American Association of Railroads railroad junction routing code*]
EBRNT .... East Braintree, MA [*American Association of Railroads railroad junction routing code*]
EBROM .... Electronic Book-Read Only Memory (SAUS)
EBROM .... Extended BIT [*Binary Digit*] Read Only Memory [*Computer science*] (IAA)
EBRPD .... East Bay Regional Park District (SAUS)
EBRS .... European Businessmen Readership Study [*Database*] [*Research Services Ltd.*] [*Information service or system*] (CRD)
EBRSC .... Electronic Bulletin of the Rough Set Community (VLIE)
EBRT .... External-Beam Radiation Therapy (ADWA)
EBS .... CANEBSCO Subscription Service Ltd. [*ACCORD*] [*UTLAS symbol*]
EBS .... Derma: Epidermolysis Bullosa Simplex (SAUS)
EBS .... Eagle Butte [*South Dakota*] [*Seismograph station code, US Geological Survey*] (SEIS)
EbS .... East by South
EBS .... Eastern Baptist Theological Seminary, Philadelphia, PA [*OCLC symbol*] (OCLC)
EBS .... Eastern Base Section [*Mediterranean and England*] [*Army*] [*World War II*]
EBS .... Eastern Bering Sea
EBS .... EBI Capital Trust I [*AMEX symbol*] (NASQ)
EBS .... Ebone Boundary System (SAUS)
EBS .... Ecological Basis of Sustainable Forestry (FOTI)
EBS .... Edinburgh Biblical Society (SAUO)
EBS .... Edison Brothers Stores, Inc. [*NYSE symbol*] (SPSG)
EBS .... Educational Broadcast Satellite (MCD)
EBS .... Elastic Back Strap (MELL)
EBS .... Electrical Brain Stimulation (DIPS)
EBS .... Electric Backing Store (SAUS)
EBS .... Electric Bond and Share (IAA)
EBS .... Electric Brain Stimulator
EBS .... Electron Beam Scanlaser (VLIE)
EBS .... Electron Beam Semiconductor
EBS .... Electron Beam System
EBS .... Electron-Bombarded Semiconductor
EBS .... Electron Bombarded Silicon (SAUS)
EBS .... Electron-Bombardment Silicon (KSC)
EBS .... Electronic Band Spectra
EBS .... Electronic Band Spectrum (SAUS)
EBS .... Electronic Beam Squint-Tracking System (SAUS)
EBS .... Electronic Bombarded Silicon
EBS .... Electronic Braking System
EBS .... Electronic Business Solutions [*Computer science*]
EBS .... Eli-Fly SpA [*Italy*] [*ICAO designator*] (FAAC)
EBS .... Elmo bumpy square (SAUS)
EBS .... Emergency Bed Service [*Medicine*]
EBS .... Emergency Borating System (IEEE)
EBS .... Emergency Breathing Subsystem (MCD)
EBS .... Emergency Breathing System
EBS .... Emergency Broadcast Station (SAUS)
EBS .... Emergency Broadcast System [*Formerly, CONELRAD*]
EBS .... Emergency Bypass Surgery (MELL)
EBS .... Enamel Bonded Single Silk [*Wire insulation*] (AAG)
ebs .... enamel single cotton (SAUS)
EBS .... Energy Band Structure (IAA)
EBS .... Engine Breather Separator
EBS .... Engineered Barrier System [*Waste disposal*]
EBS .... English Bookplate Society (BARN)
EBS .... Enrichment Business Services (SAUS)
EBS .... Environmental Baseline Survey (BCP)
EBS .... Epidermolysis Bullosa Simplex [*Dermatology*]
EBS .... Equal Breath Sounds (MELL)
EBS .... Equivalent Barrier Speed [*Automotive safety testing*]
EBS .... Eridania-Beghin Say [*France*] (ECON)
EBS .... Ernest Bloch Society (EA)
EBS .... Ethiopian Broadcasting Service (SAUS)
EBS .... Ethylene Bistearamide [*Organic chemistry*]
EBS .... Euroabstracts (SAUS)
EBS .... European Business Satellite (SAUS)
EBS .... European Business Studies (SAUO)
EBS .... European Bussiness School (SAUS)
EBS .... Excess Burst Size (SAUS)
EBS .... Experimental Building Station
EBS .... Extended Boolean Search
EBS .... External Bulk Store (SAUS)
EBS .... Extruded Bar Solder
EBS .... Webster City, IA [*Location identifier*] [*FAA*] (FAAL)
EBSA .... Estuarine and Brackish-Water Sciences Association (EAIO)
EBSA .... Ethylbenzenesulfonic Acid [*Organic chemistry*]
EBSA .... European Bio-Safety Association (SAUO)
EBSC .... Elder-Beerman Stores Corp. [*NASDAQ symbol*] (NASQ)
EBSC .... European Bird Strike Committee (PDAA)
EBSD .... Electron Backscatter Diffraction (SAUS)
EBSD .... European Business Services Directory [*A publication*]
EBSF .... National Black Survival Fund [*Emergency Black Survival Fund*] [*Acronym is based on former name,*] (EA)
EBSH .... Saint-Hubert [*Belgium*] [*ICAO location identifier*] (ICLI)
EBSI .... Eagle Bancshares, Inc. [*NASDAQ symbol*] (NQ)
EBSI .... electron-bombarded silicon interface (SAUS)
EBSICON .... Electron Bombarded Silicon-target (SAUS)
Ebs Inf .... Ebsworth on the Law of Infants [*A publication*] (DLA)
EBSK .... Epidermolysis Bullosa Simplex-Koebner [*Dermatology*]
EBSL .... Zutendaal [*Belgium*] [*ICAO location identifier*] (ICLI)
EBSLG .... European Business School Librarians Group [*London Business School*] [*Information service or system*] (IID)
e BSNO .... Brake Specific Nitric Oxide (SAUS)
EBSP .... Electron Backscattered Spectroscopy (UWER)
EBSP .... Electron Backscattering Pattern (MCD)
EBSP .... Spa/La Sauveniere [*Belgium*] [*ICAO location identifier*] (ICLI)
EBSR .... Engineer Boat and Shore Regiment [*Army*]
EBSR .... Eye-Bank for Sight Restoration (EA)
EBSRVR .... East Bengal State Railway Volunteer Rifles [*British military*] (DMA)
EBSS .... Earles Balanced Salt Solution [*Media for cell culture*]
EBSS .... Education and Behavioral Sciences Section [*Association of College and Research Libraries*]
EBST .... Educational Broadcasting Services Trust (AIE)
EBST .... Sint-Truiden [*Belgium*] [*ICAO location identifier*] (ICLI)
EBSU .... Saint-Hubert [*Belgium*] [*ICAO location identifier*] (ICLI)
EBSV .... Exchange-Biased Spin Valve (UWER)
EBSWC .... Epidermolysis Bullosa Simplex - Weber Cockayne [*Dermatology*]
EBSZ .... Semmerzake [*Belgium*] [*ICAO location identifier*] (ICLI)
EBT .... Early Bedtime (DAVI)
EBT .... earnings before taxes (SAUS)
EBT .... Earth-Based Tug [*NASA*]
EBT .... East Broadtop Railroad & Coal [*Federal Railroad Administration identification code*]
EBT .... Eccentric Bottom Tapping (SAUS)
EBT .... Echelons Below Theater [*Military*] (MCD)
EBT .... Effective Blocking Technique (SAUS)
EBT .... Electroless Bath Treatment (SAUS)
EBT .... Electron Beam [*Fluorescence*] Technique
EBT .... Electron Beam Tomography [*Imaging science*]
EBT .... Electron Beam Transmission
EBT .... Electron Deam Technique (SAUS)
ebt .... electronically blown flap (SAUS)
EBT .... Electronic Benefits Transfer [*Department of Agriculture*] (GFGA)
EBT .... Electronic Book Technologies, Inc. (PCM)
EBT .... Elmer Bumpy Torus (EDCT)

EBT .... Elmo Bumpy Torus [*Nuclear energy*]
EBT .... Engine Block Test (SAUS)
EBT .... Engine Braking Torque [*Automotive engineering*]
EBT .... English Bull Terrier (SPVS)
EBT .... Enid Board of Trade (EA)
EBT .... Epicardial Breakthrough [*Cardiology*]
EBT .... ERIN Biodiversity Team (SAUS)
ebt .... erythroblastosis foetalis (SAUS)
EBT .... Ethylidenebis(tryptophan) [*Biochemistry*]
EBT .... European Business Trends (EURO)
EBT .... Examination Before Trial (DHSM)
EBT .... Executive Business Transport [*Aircraft*]
ebt .... externally blown flap (SAUS)
EBT-1 .... Elmo Bumpy Torus-One (MCD)
EB/TCC .... Executive Bureau of the Temporary Committee of the Council (SAUO)
EBTCM .... Electronic Brake and Traction Control Module (HAWK)
EBTF .... ECC [*Emergency Control Center*] Bypass Test Facility [*Nuclear energy*] (NRCH)
EBTG .... Everything But the Girl [*British band*]
EBTI .... European Binding Tariff Information (SAUO)
EBTN .... Goetsenhove [*Belgium*] [*ICAO location identifier*] (ICLI)
EBTP .... Elmo Bumpy Torus Proof of Principle (SAUS)
EBT-P .... Elmo Bumpy Torus-Proof of Principle (MCD)
EBTR .... Electronic Bearing-Time Recorder
EBT-R .... Elmo Bumpy Torus Reactor [*Conceptual design study*] [*Nuclear energy*]
EBTS .... ECC Bypass Test Facility (SAUS)
EBTS .... Electron Beam Test System (ACAE)
EBT-S .... Elmo Bumpy Torus-Scale (MCD)
EBTs .... equivalent blackbody temperatures (SAUS)
EBTTC .... European Baptist Theological Teachers' Conference [*Germany*] (EAIO)
EBTX .... Theux-Verviers [*Belgium*] [*ICAO location identifier*] (ICLI)
EBTY .... Tournai/Maubray [*Belgium*] [*ICAO location identifier*] (ICLI)
e-bu- .... Bulgaria [*MARC geographic area code*] [*Library of Congress*] (LCCP)
EBU .... Engine Build-Up [*Automotive engineering*]
EBU .... English Bridge Union (BI)
EBU .... European Badminton Union (EA)
EBU .... European Blind Union (EA)
EBU .... European Board of Urology (SAUS)
EBU .... European Boxing Union
EBU .... European Broadcasting Union [*Switzerland*]
EBU .... Eye Ball Up (MCD)
EBU .... St. Etienne [*France*] [*Airport symbol*] (OAG)
EBUC .... Etch Back Uniformity Calculation (IAA)
EBUFF .... East Buffalo, NY [*American Association of Railroads railroad junction routing code*]
EBUL .... Ebullition (SAUS)
EBUL .... Ursel [*Belgium*] [*ICAO location identifier*] (ICLI)
EBUM .... Brussels [*Belgium*] [*ICAO location identifier*] (ICLI)
EBUR .... Brussels [*Belgium*] [*ICAO location identifier*] (ICLI)
EBU Review... European Broadcasting Union Review (journ.) (SAUS)
EBURN .... Eburneus [*Made of Ivory*] [*Pharmacy*] (ROG)
e-business... Electronic Business (ADWA)
EBUSW .... Executive Board of United Steel Workers (SAUO)
EBV .... Effective Blood Volume [*Medicine*] (DB)
EBV .... Efferent Branchial Vein [*Anatomy*]
EBV .... Electron-Bombardment Vehicle
EBv .... Epstein-Barr Virus (MELL)
EBV .... Epstein-Barr Virus
EBV .... Estimated Blood Volume [*Hematology*]
EBV .... Estimated Breeding Value [*Agricultural science*]
EBV .... Every Block is a Village [*Chicago community development program*]
EBV .... Extended Binary Vectors (VLIE)
EBV .... Electron-Beam Vaporization [*Physics*] (ODA)
EBV-1 .... Epstein-Barr Virus Type 1 (MELL)
EBV-2 .... Epstein-Barr Virus Type 2 (MELL)
EBVA .... Brussels [*Belgium*] [*ICAO location identifier*] (ICLI)
EB-VCA .... Epstein-Barr Viral Capsid Antigen [*Medicine*] (STED)
EBVCA .... Eptein-Barr Virus Capsid Antigen [*Medicine*] (PDAA)
EBVD .... Electron-Beam Vapor Deposition (SAUS)
EBVDNA .... Epstein-Barr Virus-Determinated Nuclear Antigen [*Medicine*] (STED)
EBVDNA .... Epstein-Barr Virus-Determined Nuclear Antigen [*Medicine*] (DB)
EBVEA .... Epstein-Barr Virus Early Antigen [*Medicine*] (STED)
EBVNA .... Epstein-Barr Virus Nuclear Antigen [*Medicine*] (STED)
EBVP .... Epidoxorubicin, Bleomycin, Vinblastine, Prednisone [*Antineoplastic drug regimen*]
EBVS .... European Board of Veterinary Specialisation (GVA)
EBVT .... Exterior Ballistic Verification Projectile (MCD)
EBW .... Ebolowa [*Cameroon*] [*Airport symbol*] (AD)
EBW .... E B Wilson [*Indian Railway*] (TIR)
EBW .... Effective Bandwidth
EBW .... Electron Beam Welding (MUGU)
EBW .... Elwyn Brooks White (SAUS)
EBW .... Empty Body Weight (OA)
EBW .... Exploding Bridge-Wire
ebw .... exploding bridge wire (SAUS)
EBWE .... Weelde [*Belgium*] [*ICAO location identifier*] (ICLI)
EBW-HV .... Electron Beam Welding - High Vacuum
EBWM .... Brussels [*Belgium*] [*ICAO location identifier*] (ICLI)
EBW-MV .... Electron Beam Welding - Medium Vacuum
EBW-NV .... Electron Beam Welding - Nonvacuum
EBWR .... Experimental Boiling Water Reactor
EBWs .... Exploding Bridgewires (SAUS)
EBWS .... Exploding Bridge-Wire System (KSC)
EBWU .... European Baptist Women's Union (EAIO)
EBX .... Electronic Book Exchange (SAUS)
EBX .... Electronic Branch Exchange (VLIE)
EBY .... Elsag Bailey Process Auto NV [*NYSE symbol*] (SPSG)
EBY .... European Blue Cross Youth Association (EAIO)
EBY .... Neah Bay, WA [*Location identifier*] [*FAA*] (FAAL)
EBYC .... European Bureau for Youth and Childhood
e by i .... execution by injection (SAUS)
E by N .... east by north (SAUS)
E by R .... English by Radio (SAUS)
E by S .... east by south (SAUS)
EBZ .... Effective Beaten Zone (SAUS)
EBZ .... Epidermal Basement Zone (STED)
EBZ .... Estradiol 3-Benzoate (SAUS)
EBZ .... Exercise Benefit Zone [*Aerobic dance*]
EBZH .... Hasselt [*Belgium*] [*ICAO location identifier*] (ICLI)
EBZR .... Zoersel [*Belgium*] [*ICAO location identifier*] (ICLI)
EBZW .... Genk/Zwartberg [*Belgium*] [*ICAO location identifier*] (ICLI)
EC .... Air Ecosse [*ICAO designator*] (AD)
EC .... Arm Experiment Center (SAUS)
EC .... Commission of the European Communities (SAUO)
EC .... Disabilities and Gifted Education [*Educational Resources Information Center (ERIC) Clearinghouse*] [*Council for Exceptional Children*] (PAZ)
EC .... Ear Clamp [*Medicine*]
EC .... Earlham College (SAUO)
EC .... Early Childhood (ADA)
EC .... Early China
EC .... Early Closing [*Nautical term*] (NTA)
EC .... Early-Closing Day [*British*]
EC .... Earth Closet [*British*] (ROG)
EC .... Earth Comet (SAUS)
EC .... Earth Council [*Costa Rica*] (EERA)
EC .... Earth Coverage (CCCA)
EC .... Earth Coverage antenna (SAUS)
EC .... Earth Coverage East Center (SAUS)
EC .... Earth Current (SAUS)
EC .... East African Airways (SAUS)
EC .... East Caribbean
EC .... East Carolina (SAUO)
EC .... East Carolina Railway [*AAR code*]
EC .... East Center (SAUS)
EC .... East Central [*Refers especially to London postal district*]
EC .... East Centre (SAUS)
EC .... East Coast
EC .... Eastern Cedar [*Utility pole*] [*Telecommunications*] (TEL)
EC .... Eastern Central
EC .... Eastern College (SAUO)
EC .... Eastern Command [*British*]
EC .... Eaton Corporation (SAUO)
Ec .... Ecclesiastes [*Old Testament book*] (BJA)
Ec .... Ecclesiastic (SAUS)
EC .... Ecclesiastical Commissioner [*British*] (DAS)
EC .... Echo-Cancellation [*Data transmission*] (BYTE)
EC .... Echo Check (VLIE)
EC .... Echo Controller [*Telecommunications*] (TEL)
EC .... Eclipse
EC .... Eco Corp. [*Toronto Stock Exchange symbol*]
EC .... Ecology Center (EA)
ec .... economic (SAUS)
ec .... economical (SAUS)
EC .... Economic Analysis [*Program*] [*Department of State*]
ec .... Economics (ELAL)
EC .... Economics
EC .... Economics Council (SAUO)
EC .... Economy Cartridge (SAUS)
EC .... Economy Class (UWER)
Ec .... Ecossais [*Scottish*] [*Freemasonry*] [*French*]
Ec .... Ectoconchion [*Medicine*] (EDAA)
Ec .... Ectoparasitic [*Biology*]
EC .... Ectopia Cordis [*Medicine*] (MELL)
EC .... Ecuador [*ANSI two-letter standard code*] (CNC)
ec .... Ecuador [*IYRU nationality code*] [*MARC country of publication code*] [*Library of Congress*] (LCCP)
Ec .... Ecuador (MILB)
EC .... Ecumenical Celebrations (EA)
EC .... eddy correlation (SAUS)
EC .... Eddy Current [*Electromagnetism*] (NRCH)
EC .... Edge Clamp (SAUS)
EC .... Edge Connector
E/C .... Edges Cut [*Printing*] (DGA)
EC .... Edgewood College (SAUO)
EC .... Edgeworth Cramer [*Chromatography*] (UWER)
EC .... Editing Character (SAUS)
EC .... Editor Compiler (SAUS)
EC .... Educational Centre (SAUO)
EC .... Educational Committee (SAUO)
EC .... Educational Communications [*An association*] (EA)
EC .... Educational Computer (SAUS)
EC .... Education Center (SAUO)
EC .... Education Code (OICC)
EC .... Effect Concentration (EEVL)
EC .... effective clearance (SAUS)
EC .... Effective Concentration [*Instrumentation*]

EC .... Effective Conductivity
EC .... Ego Control [*Psychology*]
EC .... Ejection Click [*Cardiology*]
EC .... Elastic Center [*Mechanics*] (UWER)
EC .... Elastic Collision [*Mechanics*] (UWER)
EC .... Elastic Constant (UWER)
EC .... Elder Craftsmen (EA)
EC .... Election Cases [*A publication*] (DLA)
EC .... Election Commission (SAUS)
EC .... Electrical Coding (WDAA)
EC .... Electrical Combat, Electric Commerce (SAUS)
EC .... Electrical Communication (SAUS)
EC .... Electrical Conductivity
EC .... Electrical Conductor (SAUS)
EC .... Electrically Coated (SAUS)
EC .... Electric Calculator (SAUS)
EC .... Electric Cipher [*or Coding*] Machine Repairman [*Navy rating*]
EC .... Electric Circuit (SAUS)
EC .... Electric Coding (SAUS)
EC .... electric conductivity (SAUS)
EC .... Electric Control (SAUS)
EC .... Electric Controller (SAUS)
EC .... Electric Current
EC .... Electricity Commission [*British*] (DAS)
EC .... Electricity Council [*British*]
EC .... [*The*] Electrification Council
EC .... Electrocapillary (SAUS)
EC .... Electrocautery [*Medicine*] (MELL)
EC .... Electrochemical [*or Electrochemistry*]
EC .... Electrochemical Detection (DB)
EC .... Electrochromic [*Optics*]
EC .... Electrocoating
EC .... Electrocondensation (UWER)
EC .... Electroconductivity
EC .... Electrode Catheter [*Medicine*] (MELL)
EC .... Electrode Current (SAUS)
EC .... Electrolysis Cell (SSD)
EC .... Electrolytic Capacitor (SAUS)
EC .... Electrolytic Cell (UWER)
EC .... Electrolytic Corrosion (SAUS)
EC .... Electromagnetic Communications (ELAL)
EC .... Electromagnetic Compatibility (ELAL)
EC .... Electromechanical Computer (SAUS)
EC .... Electron Capture [*Radioactivity*]
EC .... Electron Cloud (SAUS)
EC .... Electron Coupled (DEN)
EC .... Electron Coupling (SAUS)
EC .... Electron Cyclotron (SAUS)
EC .... Electronically Commutated [*Motor*] [*Electrical engineering*]
EC .... Electronically Coupled (VLIE)
EC .... Electronic Calculator [*or Computer*] (BUR)
EC .... Electronic Calibration
EC .... Electronic Cash/Commerce (SAUS)
EC .... Electronic Ceramic (SAUS)
EC .... Electronic Charge (ELAL)
EC .... Electronic Cinematography (WDMC)
EC .... Electronic Circuit (SAUS)
EC .... Electronic Coding
EC .... Electronic Combat
EC .... Electronic Commerce [*Computer science*] (RDA)
EC .... Electronic Communicator (journ.) (SAUS)
EC .... Electronic Comparator
EC .... Electronic Components (journ.) (SAUS)
EC .... Electronic Computer (MCD)
EC .... Electronic Conductivity
EC .... Electronic Contact (ELAL)
EC .... Electronic Counter
EC .... Electronic-Coupled (SAUS)
EC .... Electronics and Control
EC .... Electronics Card (ACAE)
EC .... Electronics Chassis
EC .... Elemental Carbon (CARB)
EC .... Element Contractor (NASA)
EC .... Element Count [*Searchable field*] [*Dialog*] [*Information service or system*] (NITA)
EC .... Elevation Center (ACAE)
EC .... Elevation Console
EC .... Elevation Control (ACAE)
EC .... Elevation Correction (SAUS)
EC .... Elifrits Constant (SAUS)
EC .... Elizabeth City [*North Carolina*] (UWER)
EC .... Elizabethtown College (SAUO)
EC .... Ellerman Container Line (SAUS)
EC .... Ellis-Van Creveld [*Syndrome*] [*Medicine*] (DB)
EC .... Elmhurst College (SAUO)
EC .... Elmira College (SAUO)
EC .... Elon College (SAUO)
EC .... Elvis in Canada [*An association*] (EAIO)
EC .... Embarkation Commandant [*Military*] [*British*]
EC .... Embedded Computer (SAUS)
EC .... Embryonal Carcinoma [*Medicine*]
EC .... Emergency Call (IAA)
EC .... Emergency Capability
EC .... Emergency Cargo [*Vessel*] (IIA)
EC .... Emergency Chaplain [*Army*] [*British*]
E/C .... Emergency Charges
EC .... Emergency Commission [*British*]
EC .... Emergency Contraceptive
EC .... Emergency Coordinator (CET)
ec .... Emerging Company (ADWA)
EC .... Emerson College (SAUO)
EC .... Eminent Chaplain [*Freemasonry*] (ROG)
EC .... Eminent Commander [*Freemasonry*] (ROG)
EC .... Eminent Conductor [*Freemasonry*] (ROG)
EC .... Emission Control (SAUS)
EC .... Emmanuel College (SAUO)
EC .... employee convenience (SAUS)
EC .... Employment Code [*IRS*]
EC .... Employment Counseling (OICC)
EC .... Emulator Control (IAA)
EC .... Emulsible Concentrate
ec .... emulsifiable concentrate (SAUS)
EC .... Emulsifying Capacity [*Food technology*]
EC .... Enamel Coated (SAUS)
EC .... Enamel Covered
ec .... Enamel-Covered (IDOE)
EC .... Enamel Covering (SAUS)
EC .... Enameled Copper [*Wire insulation*] (IAA)
ec .... Enamelled Copper (SAUS)
EC .... Enamel Single Cotton [*Wire insulation*] (AAG)
EC .... Enciclopedia Cattolica [*Vatican City*] [*A publication*] (BJA)
EC .... Encode (SAUS)
E/C .... Encoder Coupler (NASA)
EC .... En Cuenta [*On Account*] [*Spanish*] [*Business term*]
EC .... Encyclopedia Canadiana [*A publication*]
EC .... End Carry (SAUS)
EC .... End Cell (SAUS)
EC .... End Chain (SAUS)
EC .... End Chain, Exchange Carrier, European Community (SAUS)
EC .... Ending Character (SAUS)
E/C .... Endoscopy/Cystoscopy [*Medicine*] (MAE)
EC .... Endothelial Cell [*Medicine*]
EC .... Endotracheal Catheter [*Medicine*] (MELL)
EC .... Enemy Capabilities (MCD)
EC .... Energy Charge
EC .... Energy Commission (SAUS)
EC .... Energy Concepts Company (SAUS)
EC .... energy constant (SAUS)
EC .... Energy Cost (SAUS)
E/C .... energy-to-cost ratio (SAUS)
EC .... Engagement Controller [*Navy*] (NVT)
EC .... Engelhard Corp. [*Formerly, ENG*] [*NYSE symbol*] (SPSG)
EC .... Engine Change (MCD)
EC .... Engine Control (MCD)
EC .... Engine Cutoff [*Aerospace*] (MCD)
EC .... Engineer Captain [*Navy*] [*British*]
EC .... Engineer Circular [*Army Corps of Engineers*]
EC .... Engineering Center (SAUS)
EC .... Engineering Ceramics (SAUS)
EC .... Engineering Change (MCD)
EC .... Engineering change, equipment controller (SAUS)
EC .... Engineering Cognizant Authority (MCD)
EC .... Engineering Construction
EC .... Engineering Corps
EC .... Engineering Council (ACII)
EC .... Engineering Critical (MCD)
EC .... Engineers Club (SAUS)
EC .... English Chancery (DLA)
EC .... English Chancery Reports [*American Reprint*] [*A publication*] (DLA)
Ec .... English Conditions [*Insurance*] (EBF)
EC .... English Conditions [*Insurance*]
EC .... English Constitution (ADA)
EC .... Enriched Condition (SAUS)
EC .... Entente Council [*See also CE*] (EAIO)
EC .... Enteric Coated [*Pharmacy*]
EC .... Entering Complaint [*Medicine*]
EC .... Enterochromaffin Cells [*Medicine*]
EC .... Enterprise Characterization (VLIE)
EC .... Enterprise Community (PA)
EC .... Entorhinal Cortex [*Brain anatomy*]
EC .... Entrance Complaint [*Medicine*] (MEDA)
EC .... Entries Closed (ROG)
EC .... Entry Code [*Computer science*]
EC .... Entry Controller
EC .... Entry Corridor (UWER)
EC .... Environmental Capacity (EERA)
EC .... Environmental Chamber (KSC)
EC .... Environmental Chemistry (SAUS)
EC .... Environmental Complexity
EC .... environmental compliance (SAUS)
EC .... Environmental Control (KSC)
EC .... Environmental Coordinator (SAUO)
EC .... Environmental Corrosion (UWER)
EC .... Environmental Cracking (UWER)
EC .... Environmentally Correct (PS)
EC .... Environment Canada
EC .... Environment Centre (SAUO)
EC .... Environment Condition (CAAL)
EC .... Enzyme Code (DB)
EC .... Enzyme Commission [*of the International Union of Biochemistry*]

EC .... Enzyme Commission Code (EDCT)
EC .... Enzyme Commission (-System) (SAUS)
EC .... EPCOT [*Experimental Prototype Community of Tomorrow*] Center [*Walt Disney World*]
EC .... Epidermal Cell
EC .... Epilepsy Concern Service Group (EA)
EC .... Episcopal Church
EC .... Episcopal Communicators (EA)
EC .... Equalization-Cancellation [*Medicine*] (EDAA)
EC .... Equation Cruncher [*Computer science*]
EC .... Equipment Check (VLIE)
EC .... Equipment Controller (CET)
E/C .... Equipment or Component
EC .... Equivalency Class [*Statistical algorithm*]
EC .... Erase Character (VLIE)
EC .... Erb-Charcot [*Syndrome*] [*Medicine*] (DB)
EC .... Erection Computer
EC .... Ergocryptine [*Organic chemistry*]
EC .... Erosion Control [*Type of water project*]
EC .... Erosion-Corrosion (UWER)
EC .... Error Code [*Computer science*]
EC .... Error Control (SAUS)
EC .... Error Control Active [*Modem status information light*] [*Computer science*] (IGQR)
E/C .... Error Correcting [*or Correction*] [*Computer science*]
EC .... Error Correction (SAUS)
EC .... Error Counter (OA)
EC .... Erskine College (SAUO)
EC .... Erythrocyte [*Anatomy*] (UWER)
EC .... Erythrocyte Creatine [*Clinical chemistry*]
EC .... Escherichia Coli [*Microorganism*]
EC .... Escort Convoy (CINC)
EC .... Esophageal Chalasia [*Medicine*] (MELL)
EC .... Essentiality Code (NASA)
EC .... Essex College (SAUO)
EC .... Established Church
EC .... Esterified Cholesterol (OA)
EC .... Estimated Concentration (SAUS)
E/C .... Estriol [*or Estrogen*]/Creatinine [*Ratio*] [*Clinical chemistry*] (AAMN)
EC .... Estrogen Conjugate [*Endocrinology*]
E/C .... estrogen-creatinine ratio (SAUS)
e/c .... estrogen-to-creatinine (SAUS)
E-C .... Ether-Chloroform [*Mixture*]
e-c .... ether chloroform (SAUS)
EC .... Ethiopian Calendar (SAUS)
EC .... Ethiopian Commentator [*A publication*]
EC .... Ethyl Cellulose
EC .... Ethyl Centralite (OA)
EC .... Ethyl Corp. (KSC)
EC .... Etling Clearinghouse (EA)
EC .... Eton College [*British*] (ROG)
EC .... Euler Cauchy [*Method*] (UWER)
EC .... EURAIL [*European Railway*] Community (EAIO)
EC .... Eureka College (SAUS)
EC .... Eurocard [*Credit card*] [*British*] (ADA)
EC .... Eurocheque [*Credit card*] [*British*]
EC .... Euro-Children (EAIO)
EC .... EuroCity [*Railroad*]
EC .... European Cellars [*Commercial firm*] [*British*]
EC .... European Chapter (SAUS)
EC .... European Command (SAUO)
EC .... European Commission
EC .... European Communities or Commission of the European Communities (SAUS)
EC .... European Communities (or Community) (SAUO)
EC .... European Community [*Collective name given to the consolidation of the European Coal and Steel Community, the Common Market, and the European Atomic Energy Community*]
EC .... European Companions (EAIO)
ec--- .... Europe, Central [*MARC geographic area code*] [*Library of Congress*] (LCCP)
EC .... Evaluation Center (NATG)
EC .... Evangel College (SAUS)
EC .... Evangelical College (SAUO)
EC .... Evangelicals Concerned (EA)
EC .... Evansville College (SAUO)
EC .... Evaporative Cooling (SAUS)
EC .... Event Code [*Searchable field*] [*Dialog*] [*Information service or system*] (NITA)
EC .... Event Condition (VLIE)
EC .... Event Count (NITA)
EC .... Event Counter (NITA)
EC .... Events Controller (MCD)
EC .... Events Coupler (MCD)
EC .... Evolutionary Computing (SEWL)
EC .... Examining Circulars
EC .... Excellent Companion [*Freemasonry*] (ROG)
EC .... Excellent Condition [*Doll collecting*]
EC .... Exceptional Children Abstracts [*A publication*] (IID)
EC .... Exchange Capacity [*Geology*] (UWER)
EC .... Exchange Carrier (SAUS)
EC .... Exchange Centre (SAUS)
EC .... Exchange Chromatography
EC .... exchange clause (SAUS)
EC .... Excitation-Contraction [*Medicine*] (MELL)
E-C .... Excitation-Contraction [*Physiology*]
EC .... Excitatory Center [*Neurology*] (DAVI)
EC .... Exclusion Chromatography (EDCT)
EC .... Ex Commission [*Upon Order*]
EC .... Ex-Coupon [*Investment term*]
EC .... Excretory Cell
EC .... Executable Code (SAUS)
EC .... Execution Cycle [*Computer science*] (IAA)
EC .... Executive Clock (ACAE)
EC .... Executive Committee (NATG)
EC .... Executive Control (SAUS)
EC .... Executive Council (ADA)
EC .... Exempli Causa [*For the Sake of Example*] [*Latin*]
EC .... Exercise Command (ACAE)
EC .... Exercise Commander [*NATO*] (NATG)
EC .... Exercise Countermeasure (SPST)
EC .... Exeter College (SAUS)
EC .... Exhaust Close (SAUS)
EC .... Exhaust Closes [*Valve position*]
EC .... Exhaust Coefficient (SAUS)
EC .... Expander Cell (IAA)
EC .... Expansion Coefficient (UWER)
EC .... Expansive Classification
EC .... Expansive Concrete (SAUS)
EC .... Experimental Chemist (SAUS)
EC .... Experimental Chemistry (SAUS)
EC .... Experimental Control (MAE)
EC .... Experimentation Command [*Army*] (MCD)
EC .... Experiment Canister (MCD)
EC .... Experiment Center (ARMP)
EC .... Experiment Computer (MCD)
EC .... Expert Committee (SAUO)
EC .... Expiratory Center [*Physiology*]
EC .... Explorers Club (EA)
EC .... Express Consent [*Motor vehicle violation code used in state of Maryland*] (MVRD)
EC .... Extended Control [*Mode*] [*Computer science*]
EC .... Extended Coverage [*Insurance*]
EC .... Extension and Conversion [*Public buildings*]
EC .... Extension Course
EC .... Exterior Closet (ADA)
EC .... External Combustion
EC .... Extracapsular (CPH)
EC .... Extracellular [*Hematology*]
ec .... extra choice (SAUS)
EC .... Extra Control [*Wire*] [*Telecommunications*] (TEL)
EC .... Extra Coordination
EC .... Extracorporeal Circulation (UWER)
EC .... Extracranial [*Medicine*]
EC .... Eye Care (EA)
EC .... Eye Chair (SAUS)
EC .... Eyes Closed [*Ataxia*]
EC .... IOC Executive Council (SAUS)
EC .... Ontario Election Cases [*1884-1900*] [*Canada*] [*A publication*] (DLA)
EC .... Worthington Biochemical Corp. [*Research code symbol*]
EC .... Ethylene [*or Ethene*] Carbonate [*Chemistry*] (ODA)
EC-1 .... Emission Control 1 Gasoline [*ARCO*]
EC3SE .... Enhanced C3 Survivability and Endurance (SAUO)
EC50 .... Effective Concentration 50 (SAUS)
EC-50 .... effective concentration at which 50% of worms will leave sediment (SAUS)
EC_{50} .... Effective Concentration at which Light Emission Is Reduced by 50% [*Instrumentation*]
EC50 .... effective concentration for a specific response in 50% of a given population (SAUS)
EC_50 .... Effective Concentration, Median Value
EC-130 .... Hercules and Compass Call [*Air Force*] (POLM)
EC-130V .... Hercules Surveillance Aircraft [*Coast Guard*] (POLM)
EC-135 .... Stratolifter [*Air Force*] (POLM)
ECA .... Bureau of Educational and Cultural Affairs (SAUO)
ECA .... Department of Economic Affairs of the United Nations
ECA .... Early Closing Association [*British*]
ECA .... Early Comparability Analysis (RDA)
ECA .... Earth Central Angle
ECA .... Earth Coverage Antenna (SAUS)
ECA .... Earth-Crossing Asteroid [*Astronomy*]
ECA .... Earthmovers and Contractors Association (SAUO)
ECA .... Earth-orbit-Crossing Asteroid
ECA .... East Coast Africa (SAUS)
ECA .... Eastern Central Motor Carriers Association, Agent, Akron OH [*STAC*]
ECA .... Echinococcus Antibody [*Medicine*] (MELL)
ECA .... Echo suppression Allowed (SAUS)
ECA .... Economic Adjustment Committee (SAUO)
EcA .... Economic Adviser (SAUS)
ECA .... Economic Commission Administration (SAUO)
ECA .... Economic Commission for Africa [*Addis Ababa, Ethiopia*] [*See also CEA*] [*United Nations*] (EAIO)
ECA .... Economic Commission for Agriculture (SAUO)
ECA .... Economic Commission for Latin America (SAUO)
ECA .... Economic Commission of Africa (SAUS)
ECA .... Economic Community for Africa (EPAT)
ECA .... Economic Control Agency [*Allied German Occupation Forces*]
ECA .... Economic Cooperation Act [*of 1948*]
ECA .... Economic Cooperation Administration [*Administered aid under Marshall Plan; abolished, 1951*]

ECA............. Economic Cooperation Agreement (EERA)
ECA............. Economische Commissie voor Africa [*Economic Commission for Africa*] [*United Nations*]
ECA............. Ecumenical Clergy Association [*Later, AGEI*] (EA)
ECA............. Educational and Cultural Affairs (SAUS)
ECA............. Educational Centres Association [*British*]
ECA............. Educational Communication Association (EA)
ECA............. [*The*] Educational Corp. of America (ECON)
ECA............. Eigenvalue Change Analysis
ECA............. El Cajon [*California*] [*Seismograph station code, US Geological Survey*] [*Closed*] (SEIS)
ECA............. El Camino Resources, Inc. [*Vancouver Stock Exchange symbol*]
ECA............. Electrical Contact Analyzer (IAA)
ECA............. Electrical Contractors' Association [*British*] (BI)
ECA............. Electrical Control Activity (MCD)
ECA............. Electrocardioanalyzer [*Medicine*] (AAMN)
ECA............. Electrochemical Affinity (UWER)
ECA............. electrochemical analysis (SAUS)
ECA............. Electrochemical Anode (UWER)
ECA............. Electrode Catheter Ablation [*Medicine*] (MELL)
ECA............. Electromagnetic Compatibility (ACAE)
ECA............. Electronic Commerce Acquisition (AAGC)
ECA............. Electronic Commerce Association (SAUO)
ECA............. Electronic Confusion Area
ECA............. Electronic Control Amplifier (MCD)
ECA............. Electronic Control Assembly [*Ford Motor Co.*]
ECA............. Electronic Controller Assembly (SAUS)
ECA............. Electronics & Computer Assembly (SAUS)
eca............. electronics control assembly (SAUS)
ECA............. Electronics Corporation of America (SAUO)
ECA............. Elsa Clubs of America [*Defunct*] (EA)
ECA............. Embroidery Council of America (EA)
ECA............. Emergency Call Announcer [*Hearing technology*]
ECA............. emergency changeover acknowledgement signal (SAUS)
ECA............. Emergency Controlling Authority (DA)
ECA............. Employment Conditions Abroad [*British*] [*An association*] (DBA)
ECA............. Encal Energy [*NYSE symbol*] (SG)
ECA............. Endocervical Aspiration [*Medicine*] (MELL)
ECA............. Endocervical Aspirator [*Medicine*] (MELL)
ECA............. Endothelial Cytotoxic Activity [*Medicine*] (EDAA)
ECA............. energy conversion area (SAUS)
ECA............. Engine Computer Assembly [*Automotive engineering*]
ECA............. Engine Cycle Analysis
ECA............. Engineer Cognizant Authority
ECA............. Engineering and Computer Science Association (SAUO)
ECA............. Engineering Change Analysis
ECA............. Engineering Change Announcement
ECA............. Engineering Change Authorization
ECA............. Engineering Contractors Association (EA)
ECA............. Engineering Cost Analysis (SAUS)
ECA............. Engineering Critical Assessment (SAUS)
ECA............. English Curling Association
ECA............. Enhanced Credit Authority (SAUO)
ECA............. Ensign Class Association [*Defunct*] (EA)
ECA............. Enter Control Area [*Aviation*]
ECA............. Enteric Coated Aspirin (MELL)
ECA............. Enterobacterial Common Antigen [*Immunology*]
ECA............. Environmental Change in Africa (SAUO)
ECA............. Environmental Choice Australia
ECA............. Environmental Contaminants Authority (EERA)
ECA............. Environmental Control Administration [*Later, EPA*]
ECA............. Environmental Control Assembly (SAUS)
ECA............. Environment Canada Atlantic (SAUO)
ECA............. Environment Conservation Authority (SAUS)
ECA............. Environment Council of Alberta (SAUO)
ECA............. eosinophil chemotactic activity (SAUS)
ECA............. Epidemiologic Catchment Area [*Department of Health and Human Services*] (GFGA)
ECA............. Epoxy Curing Agent
ECA............. Equipment Condition Analysis (MSA)
ECA............. Ericson Class Association (EA)
ECA............. Erythrina Cristagalli Agglutinin (SAUS)
ECA............. Etched Card Assembly (IAA)
ECA............. Ethacrynic Acid [*Diuretic*] [*Medicine*] (EDAA)
ECA............. Ethacrynic Acid [*Biochemistry*]
ECA............. Ethylcarboxylate Adenosine [*Biochemistry*]
ECA............. Eurocypria Airlines Ltd. [*Cyprus*] [*ICAO designator*] (FAAC)
ECA............. European Catering Association [*Germany*] (EAIO)
ECA............. European Choral Association (EA)
ECA............. European Civil Affairs
ECA............. European Collaborative Action (SAUS)
ECA............. European Combat Aircraft (PDAA)
ECA............. European Commission on Agriculture [*FAO*] [*United Nations*]
ECA............. European Communications Area [*Military*]
ECA............. European Confederation of Agriculture
ECA............. European Court of Auditors (EURO)
ECA............. Europe China Association (EA)
ECA............. Evangelical Church Alliance (EA)
ECA............. Event, Condition, Action (SAUS)
ECA............. Exceptional Circumstances Allowance [*Legal term*] (DLA)
ECA............. Excess Charge Adjudication [*Health insurance*] (GHCT)
ECA............. Exchange Carrier Association (EA)
ECA............. Exchange Control Act (SAUS)
ECA............. Executive Chef Association [*Defunct*] (EA)
ECA............. Experimental Combat Aircraft (SAUS)
ECA............. Explosives Corp. of America (MCD)
ECA............. Explosives Corporation of America (SAUO)
ECA............. Export Control Act (MCD)
ECA............. Export Credit Agency (FOTI)
ECA............. Express Carriers Association (NTPA)
ECA............. Extended Central Area (DOAD)
ECA............. Extended Coverage Altitude (SAA)
ECA............. External Carotid Artery [*Medicine*] (MELL)
eCAADe....... Education in Computer Aided Architectural Design in Europe (SAUO)
ECAAR........ Economists Allied for Arms Reduction [*An association*] (EA)
ECAART....... European Conference on Accelerators in Applied Research and Technology (SAUS)
ECAB........... Department of Energy Contract Adjustment Board (AAGC)
ECAB........... Early Case Assessment Bureau (SAUO)
ECAB........... Economic (SAUS)
ECAB........... Economic Abstracts (journ.) (SAUS)
ECAB........... Elder Citizens Advisory Board (SAUS)
ECAB........... Employees' Compensation Appeals Board [*Department of Labor*]
ECAB........... Engineering Committee for the American Bicentennial
ECAB........... Executive Committee of the Army Board [*British*]
E-CABG....... Endarterectomy and Coronary Atery Bypass Graft [*Medicine*] (EDAA)
ECAC........... Eastern College Athletic Conference (EA)
ECAC........... Electromagnetic Compatibility Analysis Center [*Illinois Institute of Technology*] [*Annapolis, MD*]
ECAC........... Electronic Compatibility Analysis Center (SAUO)
ECAC........... Engineering College Administrative Council
ECAC........... Enhanced Counter Air Capability [*Military*]
ECAC........... European Civil Aviation Commission (SAUO)
ECAC........... European Civil Aviation Conference [*See also CEAC*] (EAIO)
ECAC........... Extra-Curricular Activities Center (SAUS)
ECACC......... European Collection of Animal Cell Cultures [*Cell bank*] (ECON)
ECACC......... European Collection of Cell Cultures (SAUS)
ECACC......... European Council of American Chambers of Commerce (EA)
ECAC/US-CRS... European Civil Aviation Conference/United States Working Group on Computer Reservation Systems (SAUO)
ECAD........... Commonwealth NGO Consortium for Agricultural Development Programmes (SAUO)
ECAD........... electrical characterization and diagnostics (SAUS)
ECAD........... Electronical Computer Aided Design (SAUS)
ECAD........... Electronic Computer-Aided Design [*Computer science*] (BYTE)
ECAD........... Engineer Control and Advisory Detachment [*Air Force*]
ECAD........... Engineering Computer-Aided Design
ECAD........... Error Check Analysis Diagram (IAA)
ECAD........... European Cities Against Drugs (SAUS)
ECAD........... European Civil Affairs Division [*US Military Government, Germany*]
ECAD........... European NGO Consortium for Agricultural Development (SAUS)
ECAD........... European NGO Consortium for Agricultural Development Programme (SAUO)
ECAD........... Existing Chemical Assessment Division [*Environmental Protection Agency*]
ECADR......... Nordic Council for Alcohol and Drug Research (EA)
ECAE........... Educational Center for Applied Ekistics (EA)
ECAE........... Electronic Computer-Aided Engineering (AAEL)
ECAE........... Engineering Change Analysis Evaluation (ACAE)
ECAE........... European Community of Atomic Energy (SAUS)
ECAETC....... East Central AIDS Education and Training Center (SAUO)
ECAF........... Excess Cost Adjudication Function [*Army*]
ECAFE......... Economic Commission for Africa and the Far East (SAUO)
ECAFE......... Economic Commission for Asia and the Far East [*Later, ESCAP*] [*United Nations*]
ECAG........... Equipment Change Analysis Group (SAA)
ECAHTI....... European Committee for Agricultural and Horticultural Tools and Implements (EA)
ECAI........... Electronic Cultural Atlas Initiative (SAUO)
ECAI........... European Conference on Artificial Intelligence (VERA)
ECAL........... Electronic Calibration (ADWA)
ECAL........... Enjoy Computing And Learn (SAUS)
ECAL........... Equipment Calibration [*Military*] (NVT)
ECAM........... Electric Control and Manufacturing (IAA)
ECAM........... Electric Controller and Manufacturing (SAUS)
ECAM........... Electronically Computer Aided Manufacturing (ACAE)
E-cam........... electronic camera (SAUS)
ECAM........... Electronic Centralized Aircraft Monitor (SAUS)
ECAM........... Electronic Centralized Aircraft Monitoring System
ECAM........... Energy Conservation and Management (MCD)
ECAM........... ERTS Command Auxiliary Memory (MCD)
ECAM........... Extended Communications Access Method (WDAA)
ECAM........... Extended Content Addressable (SAUS)
ECAM........... Extended Content-Addressable Memory [*Computer science*] (MHDB)
ECAMA......... European Citric Acid Manufacturers Association [*of the European Council of Chemical Manufacturers' Federations*] (EAIO)
ECAMP......... Environmental Compliance Assessment and Management Program [*Air Force*] (DOMA)
ECAMS......... Enhanced Comprehensive Asset Management System (MCD)
ECAMS......... Enhanced Computer Automated Maintenance System (SAUS)
ECAMWP..... European Committee of Associations of Manufacturers of Welding Products (EA)
ECAN........... Electronic Calibration and Normalization (KSC)
ECAN........... Electronic Consumer Advertising Network [*Data Corp. of America*]
ECAN........... Excitation, Calibration, and Normalization (SAUS)
ECAN........... Exitation, Calibration, and Normalization (SAUS)
EC&A........... Engineering Coordination and Analysis Section (SAUS)
EC & D......... Electromagnetic Cover and Deception (MCD)
EC & D......... Electronic Cover and Deception (PDAA)
EC & DB....... Encourage Coughing and Deep Breathing [*Medicine*]

EC & M........ Environmental Control and Mechanism (SAA)
Ec & Mar..... Notes of Cases, English Ecclesiastical and Maritime Courts [*1844-50*] [*A publication*] (DLA)
ECANSW...... Electrical Contractors' Association of New South Wales [*Australia*]
ECAO........... Electrical Contractors Association of Ontario [*Canada*]
ECAO........... Enteric Cytopathogenic Avian Orphan [*Medicine*] (EDAA)
ECAO........... Environmental Criteria and Assessment Office [*Environmental Protection Agency*] (GRD)
ECAO/CIN..... Environmental Criteria and Assessment Office, Cincinnati [*Ohio*] [*Environmental Protection Agency*] (GRD)
ECAO/RTP.... Environmental Criteria and Assessment Office, Research Triangle Park [*North Carolina*] [*Environmental Protection Agency*] (GRD)
ECAO Virus... Enteric Cytopathogenic Avian Orphan Virus (SAUS)
ECAP........... Electrical [*or Electronic*] Circuit Analysis Program
ECAP........... Electric Circuit Analysis Program (NITA)
ECAP........... Electric Companies' Advertising Program
E-Cap.......... Electrolytic Capacitor (SAUS)
ECAP........... Electronic Circuit Analysis Program (ECII)
ECAP........... Electronic Combat Action Plan (SAUS)
ECAP........... Electronic Control Analyzer and Programmer [*Automotive engineering*]
ECAP........... Electronic Control Assembly - Pitch (IAA)
ECAP........... Electronic Control Assembly-Roll (SAUS)
ECAP........... Electronic Current Analysis Program (IAA)
ECAP........... Electronic Customer Access Program (SAUS)
ECAP........... Employee Counseling and Assistance Program [*Environmental Protection Agency*] (EPA)
ECAP........... Energy-Compensated Atom Probe (SAUS)
ECAP........... Energy Crisis Assistance Program [*Federal government*]
ECAP........... Enhanced Cobra Armament Program [*Military*]
ECAP........... Environmental Compatibility Assurance Program [*Navy*]
ECAP........... Environmental Cooperation with Asia Program (EERA)
ECAP........... Error Check Analysis Program (IAA)
ECAP........... European Conflict Analysis Project [*NATO*]
ECaP........... Exceptional Cancer Patients [*Therapy program*]
ECAPA......... European Citric Acid Planufactures Association (SAUO)
ECAPB......... Engineering Unit Capability (SAUS)
ECAPE......... Exploratory Committee on Assessing the Progress of Education [*Later, NAEP*]
ECA-PMO..... Electronic Commerce Acquisition-Program Management Office (AAGC)
ECAPS......... Emergency Capability System (SAA)
ECAPT......... European Congress of American Parents and Teachers (SAUO)
ECAR........... East Central Area Reliability Coordination Agreement [*Regional power council*]
ECAR........... Economy Car (TRID)
ECAR........... Electronic Control Assembly - Roll (KSC)
ECAR........... Electronic Control Assembly Roll (SAUS)
ECAR........... Engineering Concern Action Report [*Industrial engineering*]
ECAR........... European Civil Affairs Regiment
ECAR........... European College for Animal Reproduction (GVA)
ECARBICA.... East and Central African Regional Branch of the International Council on Archives (SAUO)
ECARBS....... Economic Census Advertising and Response Behavior Study [*Bureau of the Census*] (GFGA)
ECAREG....... Eastern Canada Traffic Regulation Office (SAUS)
ECARL......... Expendable Cluster Aircraft Rocket Launcher
ECARP......... Environmental Conservation Acreage Reserve Program [*Department of Agriculture*]
ECARS......... Electronic Coordinatograph and Readout System
E-CARS........ Enhanced Airline Communications and Reporting System (DA)
ECART......... European Conference on Advances in Rehabilitation Technology (SAUO)
ECAS........... Earth-Crossing Asteroid
ECAS........... Economic Community of Central African States (SAUO)
ECAS........... Electrical Contractors' Association of Scotland (EAIO)
ECAS........... Electronically Controlled Air Suspension
ECAS........... Electronic Chemical Agent Alarm System (SAUS)
ECAS........... Electronics Cleaning Advisory Service (SAUS)
ECAS........... Energy Conversion Alternatives Study [*NASA*]
ECAS........... Engineering Change Automated System (SAUS)
ECAS........... Engineering Change Automation System
ECAS........... Enhanced Cobra/TOW [*Tube-Launched, Optically-Tracked, Wire-Guided*] Armament System [*Military*] (MCD)
ECAS........... Enter Controlled Airspace [*Air Traffic Control*] (FAAC)
ECAS........... Environmental Compliance Assessment System (BCP)
ECAS........... Euro-Citizen Action Service (EURO)
ECAS........... European Council of/on African Studies (SAUO)
ECAS........... Exchange Card Architecture Specification (SAUS)
ECAS........... Experiment Computer Application Software (MCD)
ECASAAMA... European Campaign Against South African Aggression on Mozambique and Angola (SAUO)
ECASC......... EPIC Center for Adhesives, Sealants, and Coatings [*Research center*] (RCD)
E-CASE........ Enterprise Computer-Aided Software Engineering (GART)
e-cash......... Electronic Cash (ADWA)
E-cash......... Electronic Cash (ITCA)
ECASIA........ European Conference on Applications of Surface and Interface Analysis (SAUS)
ECA Signal... Emergency Changeover Acknowledgement Signal (SAUS)
ECASS......... Electronically Controlled Automatic-Switching System (DEN)
ECASS......... Experimental Computer-Aided Shop Scheduling (IAA)
ECASS......... Export Control Automated Support System [*Department of Commerce*]
ECASTAR..... Energy Conservation Assessment of Systems, Technologies, and Requirements
EC-AT.......... Electronically Controlled Automatic Transmission [*Mazda*] [*Automotive engineering*]
ECAT........... Electronic Card Assembly and Test (SAUS)
ECAT........... [*Federal*] Electronic Commerce Acquisition Team (AAGC)
ECAT........... Emergency Committee for American Trade (EA)
ECAT........... Emission Computerized Axial Tomography
ECAT........... Environmental Centres for Administration and Technology (EURO)
ECAT........... Equipment Category
ECAT........... Error Correction and Translation (SAUS)
ECAT........... European Centre for Automatic Translation [*Luxembourg*] (NITA)
ECATA......... European Consortium in Advanced Training for Aeronautics (EURO)
ECATR......... Early Comparability Analysis Time Requirement [*Army*]
ECATRA....... European Car and Truck Rental Association (EA)
E-CATS........ Electronic Catalog System [*Environment term*] (EGA)
ECATS......... Electronic Combat Airborne Training System (SAUS)
ECATS......... Expandable Computerized Automatic Test System (MCD)
ECATS......... Expendable Computerized Automatic Test System (SAUS)
EcATT.......... Economic Awareness Teacher Training (AIE)
ECATV......... Educational Cable Television (NTCM)
ECAW........... European Council for Animal Welfare (EA)
ECAY........... Electronic Control Assembly - Yaw (IAA)
ECAY........... Electronic Control Assembly Yaw (SAUS)
ECB............. Echelons Corps and Below [*Army*]
ECB............. Echelons Corps Level and Below [*Military*]
ECB............. Economic Cruising Boost (SAUS)
ECB............. Eddy Current Brake [*Mechanical engineering*]
ECB............. Edit Control Block (SAUS)
ECB............. Efferent Cochlear Bundle (PDAA)
ECB............. Electrically Controlled Birefringe (SAUS)
ECB............. Electrically Controlled Birefringence [*Telecommunications*] (TEL)
ECB............. Electronic Claims Billing (HGAA)
ECB............. Electronic Codebook
ECB............. Electronic Codebook Event Control Block (SAUS)
ECB............. Encyclopedia of College Basketball [*A publication*]
ECB............. Encyclopedia of Consumer Brands [*A publication*]
ECB............. Energy Conservation Board (SAUS)
ECB............. Engineer Construction Battalion (CINC)
ECB............. Engineering Change Board (SAUS)
ECB............. Engineering Control Board (AAG)
ECB............. Enhanced Cordless Base (CGWS)
ECB............. Enhanced Cubic Grain [*Photography*]
ECB............. Environmental and Conservation Bureau [*Australian Capital Territory*]
ECB............. Environmental Chemistry and Biology [*Marine science*] (OSRA)
ECB............. Environmental Conservation Board (SAUS)
ECB............. Environment Coordination Board [*United Nations*]
ECB............. Equipment Control Board (KSC)
ECB............. Etched Circuit Board
ECB............. Ethylene Copolymer Blends with Bitumen (EDCT)
ECB............. European Central Bank
ECB............. European Chemicals Bureau (SAUS)
ECB............. European Conference on Biomaterials (SAUS)
ECB............. European Congress of Biotechnology
ECB............. European Coordination Bureau for International Youth Organizations G2 [*See also BEC*] (EAIO)
ECB............. European Corn Borer [*Agronomy*]
ECB............. Europe card bus (SAUS)
ECB............. Event Control Block [*Computer science*] (BUR)
ECB............. Events Control Buffer [*NASA*] (NASA)
ECB............. Export Control Bulletin [*Department of Commerce*]
ECB............. Newcombe, KY [*Location identifier*] [*FAA*] (FAAL)
ECB............. Electronic Components Board (ODA)
ECB9........... Ninth European Congress on Biotechnology (SAUO)
ECBA........... Eastern Coast Breweriana Association (EA)
ECBA........... Eastern College Basketball Association (EA)
ECBA........... European Citizens Band Association (SAUO)
ECBA........... European Communities Biologists Association [*Belgium*] (EAIO)
ECBA........... European Communities Biologists Organization [*University of Bremen*] (EAIO)
ECBA........... European Community Biologists Association (SAUS)
ECBC........... Eastern Collegiate Bowling Conference (PSS)
ECBC........... Edgewood Chemical Biological Center
ECBC........... Empress Chinchilla Breeders Cooperative (EA)
ECBC........... External Call Barring Circuit (IAA)
ECBD........... Exploration of Common Bile Duct [*Medicine*] (DMAA)
ECBF........... E. C. Brown Foundation (EA)
ECBF........... Episcopal Church Building Fund (EA)
ECBF........... European Community Banking Federation [*Belgium*] (EAIO)
ECBI............ Eyberg Child Behavior Inventory (EDAC)
ECBM........... English Continental Book Market (SAUS)
ECBM........... Episcopal Commission for Black Ministries (EA)
ECBMD......... Emergency Committee to Boycott Mother's Day
echo............ enteric cytopathogenic bovine orphan (SAUS)
ECBO........... Enterocytopathogenic Bovine Virus
ECBO........... European Cell Biology Organization (EAIO)
ECBO Virus... Enteric Cytopathogenic Bovine Orphan Virus (SAUS)
ECB-P.......... Excellence-in-Competition Badge (Pistol) [*Military decoration*]
ECBR........... East Cooper & Berkeley Railroad [*Federal Railroad Administration identification code*]
ECB-R.......... Excellence-in-Competition Badge (Rifle) [*Military decoration*]
ECBS........... Early Childhood Behavior Scale [*Test*] (TMMY)
ECBS........... Electronically Controlled Braking System [*Automotive engineering*]
ECBS........... Engineer Combat Battalions (CINC)
ECBS........... European Committee for Banking Standards (EURO)

ECBS .... Engineering of Computer-Based Systems (ODA)
ECBTE .... European Committee for Building Technical Equipment [*See also CEETB*] (EAIO)
ECBV .... Effective Circulating Blood Volume [*Physiology*]
ECC .... Early Childhood Consultant (SAUO)
ECC .... Earth Conservation Corps
ECC .... Earth Continuity Conductor [*Electronics*] (BARN)
ECC .... East Carolina College [*Later, ECU*] [*North Carolina*]
ECC .... East Coast Canada (SAUS)
ECC .... East Coast Carriers Conference, New York NY [*STAC*]
ECC .... East Coast Conference (PSS)
ECC .... Eastern Claims Conference (EA)
ECC .... Eastman Chemical Company (SAUO)
ECC .... Eccentric (AAG)
ECC .... ECC International Ltd. [*Formerly, Educational Computer Corp.*] [*NYSE symbol*] (SPSG)
Ecc .... Ecclesiastes [*Old Testament book*] (BJA)
Ec C .... Ecclesiastical Council (SAUO)
ECC .... Ecclesiastical Courts Commission (SAUO)
ECC .... Economic Council of Canada
ECC .... Eddy Current Clutch [*Mechanical engineering*]
ECC .... Edema, Clubbing, and Cyanosis [*Medicine*] (DAVI)
ECC .... Educational Computer Corporation (SAUO)
ECC .... Educational Cultural Complex (SAUO)
ECC .... Effective Creep Compliance
ECC .... Effects Control Center [*Army*]
ECC .... Eighty Column Card (SAUS)
ECC .... El Camino College [*Torrance, CA*]
ECC .... El Centro [*California*] [*Seismograph station code, US Geological Survey*] [*Closed*] (SEIS)
ECC .... E-Learning Courseware Certification Vanguard Circle
ECC .... Electrical Commuter Car
ECC .... Electrical Connectivity Check (VERA)
ECC .... Electrical Continuous Cloth (IAA)
ecc .... electrically-continuous cloth (SAUS)
ECC .... Electric Construction Company (SAUO)
ECC .... Electric Coordinating Council (SAUO)
ECC .... Electricity Consumers' Council [*British*]
ECC .... Electrocardiocorder [*Medicine*]
ECC .... Electrochemical Cathodes (MCD)
ECC .... Electrochemical Concentration Cell (MCD)
ECC .... Electrochemichromic [*Optoelectronics*]
ECC .... Electrocorticogram [*Neurology*] (DAVI)
ecc .... electron capture (SAUS)
ECC .... Electron Channeling Contrast (SAUS)
ECC .... Electron-Coupled Control (IAA)
ECC .... Electron Coupling Control (SAUS)
ECC .... Electronically controllable coupler (SAUS)
ECC .... Electronic Calibration Center [*National Institute of Standards and Technology*]
ECC .... Electronic Carburetor Control [*Automotive engineering*]
ECC .... Electronic Card Chips (SAUS)
ECC .... Electronic Climate Control [*Automotive engineering*]
ECC .... Electronic Commerce Canada (DDC)
ECC .... Electronic Common Control [*Telecommunications*] (TEL)
ECC .... Electronic Components Code (NATG)
ECC .... Electronic Components Conference
ECC .... Electronic Computer Center (SAUS)
ECC .... Electronic Computer Concepts (HGAA)
ECC .... Electronic Counter Control Measure
ECC .... Electronic Counting Circuit (SAUS)
ECC .... Electronic-Courier Circuit (DNAB)
ECC .... Electronics Capital Corporation (SAUO)
ECC .... Electronics Control Corporation (SAUO)
ECC .... Electronized Chemicals Corporation (SAUO)
ECC .... Elgin Community College [*Illinois*]
ECC .... Elliptic Curve Crypto (SAUS)
ECC .... Elliptic Curve Cryptography [*Computer science*] (IGQR)
ECC .... Elliptic Curve Cryptosystem (VERA)
ECC .... Ellsworth Community College [*Iowa*] [*Formerly, EJC*]
ECC .... Embedded Control Channel (SAUS)
ECC .... Embryonal Cell Carcinoma [*Medicine*] [*Medicine*] (DMAA)
ECC .... Emergency Cardiac Care
ECC .... Emergency Combat Capability
ECC .... Emergency Conservation Committee [*Defunct*]
ECC .... Emergency Control Center (CINC)
ECC .... Emergency Core Cooling [*or Coolant*] [*Nuclear energy*]
ECC .... Emitter-Coupled Circuit [*Electronics*] (HGAA)
ECC .... Empire Coke [*Federal Railroad Administration identification code*]
ECC .... Employees' Compensation Commission
ECC .... Endocervical Cone [*or Conization*] [*Gynecology*] (DAVI)
ECC .... Endocervical Curettage [*or Curretings*] [*Gynecology*] (DAVI)
ECC .... Energy Conservation Caucus [*Defunct*] (EA)
ECC .... Energy Conservation Coalition (EA)
ECC .... Energy Conservation Committee (SAUS)
ECC .... Energy Conservation Council
ECC .... Energy Content Curve (NOAA)
ECC .... Energy Control Center (SAUS)
ECC .... Engagement Control Center [*Army*]
ECC .... Engineering Casualty Control [*Military*] (NVT)
ECC .... Engineering Change Center (ACAE)
ECC .... Engineering Change Committee (SAUO)
ECC .... Engineering Change Control
ECC .... Engineering Change Coordination (MCD)
ECC .... Engineering Change Correction (SAUS)
ECC .... Engineering Control Center (ACAE)
ECC .... Engineering Control Code (SAUS)
ECC .... Engineering Critical Component (KSC)
ECC .... English Ceramic Circle [*An Association*] [*British*] (EAIO)
ECC .... English Chamber Choir
ECC .... English China Clay (SAUS)
ECC .... English China Clays Ltd. (ECON)
ECC .... English Conservation Center (SAUS)
ECC .... Enhanced Control Cellular [*Telecommunications*]
ECC .... Enlisted Classification Code
ECC .... Enlisted Correspondence Course
ECC .... Enter Cable Change (VLIE)
ECC .... Enteric Coated Capsule (SAUS)
ECC .... enteric coated capsule, extracorporeal circulation (SAUS)
ECC .... Enterprise Cooperation Community (GART)
ECC .... Environmental Control Canister
ECC .... Environmental Control Council (SAUO)
ECC .... Environment Concept Car [*Volvo Motor Co.*]
ECC .... Equatorial Communications Co. [*Mountain View, CA*] [*Telecommunications*] (TSSD)
ECC .... Equatorial Countercurrent [*Oceanography*]
ECC .... Equipment Category Code [*Military*] (AABC)
ecc .... equipment classification control (SAUS)
ECC .... Equipment Configuration Control (AAG)
ecc .... equipment control classification (SAUS)
ECC .... Eras of the Christian Church [*A publication*]
ECC .... Erie Community College (SAUS)
ECC .... Error Check and Control (SAUS)
ECC .... Error Check Circuit (SAUS)
ECC .... Error Check Code (SAUS)
ECC .... Error Check Correction (SAUS)
ECC .... Error Checking and Correcting (SAUS)
ECC .... Error Checking and Correction [*Computer science*]
ECC .... Error Checking Circuitry (SAUS)
ECC .... Error Checking Code (NITA)
ECC .... Error Control and Correction (SAUS)
ECC .... Error Control Circuitry [*Algorithm to verify data*] [*Computer science*] (PCM)
ECC .... Error Controlled Code (SAUS)
ECC .... Error Correcting Circuitry (SAUS)
ECC .... Error-Correcting Circuitry [*Computer science*] (IAA)
ECC .... Error Correcting Code (SAUS)
ECC .... Error Correction and Control
ECC .... Error Correction Capability [*Computer software quality*]
ECC .... Error Correction Circuit (VERA)
ECC .... Error Correction Circuitry (SAUS)
ECC .... Error Correction Code
ECC .... Error Correction Control (SAUS)
ECC .... Ertl Collectors Club [*Commercial firm*] (EA)
ECC .... Escherichia Coli [*Microorganism*]
ECC .... Essex Community College, James A. Newpher Library, Baltimore, MD [*OCLC symbol*] (OCLC)
ECC .... Estimated Correction Cost (MCD)
ECC .... Estimated Creatinine Clearance [*Medicine*] (EDAA)
ECC .... Ethiopian Collectors Club (EA)
ECC .... Ethnic Communities Council (SAUO)
ECC .... Ethyl Chlorocarbonate (SAUS)
ECC .... Eton College Chronicle [*A publication*] [*British*]
ECC .... Eurasian Communist Countries (MCD)
ECC .... European Commercial Cases (SAFN)
ECC .... European Communist Countries (MCD)
ECC .... European Communities Commission (SAUS)
ECC .... European Community Commission (MCD)
ECC .... European Competence Center (SAUS)
ECC .... European Consensus Conference (SAUS)
ECC .... European Consultative Commission (SAUO)
ECC .... European Coordinating Committee
ECC .... European Coordinating Council (SAUO)
ECC .... European Coordination Committee (SAUS)
ECC .... European Crystallographic Committee [*International Council of Scientific Unions*]
ECC .... European Cultural Centre [*Geneva, Switzerland*]
ECC .... European Cultural Commission (SAUS)
ECC .... European Cultural Cooperation (SAUO)
ECC .... European Economic Community (TDOB)
ECC .... Europe Container Care (SAUS)
ECC .... Evacuation Coordination Center (DOMA)
ECC .... Everett Community College [*Formerly, EJC*] [*Washington*]
ECC .... Exceptional Child Center [*Utah State University*] [*Research center*] (RCD)
ECC .... Exchange Control Copy [*Business term*] (DS)
ECC .... Excitement, Choreiform Movements, and Circling [*Characterizations of a medical syndrome*]
ECC .... Ex-Communist Country
ECC .... Execute Control Cycle (IAA)
ECC .... Executive and Congressional Communications [*Environmental Protection Agency*] (COE)
ECC .... Executive Chair Car [*Indian Railway*] (TIR)
ECC .... Executive Committee of the Comintern (SAUO)
ECC .... Executive Communications and Control (DOMA)
ECC .... Executive Computer Concepts (SAUS)
ECC .... Executive Computer Course (VLIE)
ECC .... Executive Coordinating Committee (SAUS)
ECC .... Exercise Control Centre [*Australia*]
ECC .... Expanded Community Calling [*Telecommunications*] (TEL)

ECC............ Experimental Computer Complex
ECC............ Export Consultants Corporation (SAUO)
ECC............ Exposition and Conference Council (EA)
ECC............ Extended Core Configuration (SAUS)
ECC............ External Cardiac Compression
ECC............ External Chest Compression [*Medicine*]
ECC............ Extracorporeal Circulation [*Medicine*]
ECC............ Energy-Conscious Construction (ODA)
ECCA........... East Caribbean Currency Authority (SAUO)
ECCA........... Electronic Component Checkout Area (AAG)
ECCA........... European Coil Coating Association
ECCAA......... Executive Chefs de Cuisine Association of America [*Later, Chefs de Cuisine Association of America*] (EA)
ECCAI.......... European Coordinating Committee for Artificial Intelligence (VERA)
Ecc & Ad...... Spinks' English Ecclesiastical and Admiralty Reports [*1853-55*] [*A publication*] (DLA)
ECCANE....... East Coast Conference on Aerospace and Navigational Electronics (MCD)
EC Car......... Electric Combined Car (SAUS)
ECCAS......... Economic Community of Central African States [*See also CEEAC*] [*Bangui, Central African Republic*] (EAIO)
ECCAS......... Engineer Command and Control Automation System [*Army*] (RDA)
ECCB........... Eastern Caribbean Central Bank [*Formerly, East Caribbean Currency Authority*] [*Basseterre, St. Christopher*] (GEA)
ECCB........... Eighteenth Century: A Current Bibliography (SAUS)
ECCB........... Electronic Components Certification Board (EA)
ECCB........... Engineering Change Control Board (NASA)
ECCB........... Equipment to Computer Converter Buffer (DNAB)
ECCB........... European Coca-Cola Collectors (SAUO)
ECCC........... Ecology Center Communications Council [*Defunct*] (EA)
ECCC........... Electronically Controlled Converter Clutch [*Automotive engineering*]
ECCC........... Engineering Change Classification Concurrence (ACAE)
ECCC........... English Country Cheese Council (BI)
ECCC........... European Command Coordinating (or Coordination) Committee (SAUO)
ECCC........... European Command Coordination Committee [*Military*] (AABC)
ECCC........... European Communications Coordinating Committee (SAUO)
ECCC........... European Communities Chemistry Committee (EA)
ECCC........... European Community Computer Club (SAUO)
ECCCA......... Education Committee of County Councils Association (SAUO)
ECCCAC....... East Carolina Community College Athletic Conference (PSS)
ECC circuit... error-checking and correcting circuit (SAUS)
ECCCM......... Electronic Countermeasures [*Military*] (IAA)
ECCCO......... European Culture Collections Curators Organisation (SAUO)
ECCCO......... European Culture Collections Curators Organization (SAUS)
ECC Code..... Error Check and Correction Code (SAUS)
ECCCS......... Electronic Command, Communication, and Control System (ACAE)
ECCCS......... Emergency Command Control Communications System
ECCCS......... European Command and Control Communications System (SAUO)
ECCCS......... European Command and Control Console System [*DoD*]
ECCCS......... European Society for the Study of Cognitive Systems (SAUO)
ECCD........... Electric Cockpit Control Device (SAUS)
ECCD........... Electronic Cockpit Control Device (SAUS)
ECCDA......... Eastern Connecticut Clam Diggers Association [*Defunct*] (EA)
ECCE........... European Council of Civil Engineers (SAUS)
ECCE........... Exchange and Cooperation between Culture and Enterprise (SAUO)
ECCE........... Extra Capsular Cataract Extraction (SAUS)
ECCE........... Extracapular Cataract Extraction [*Ophthalmology*]
ECCEN......... Eccentric (IAA)
ECCET......... Engineering Casualty Control Evaluation Team [*Navy*] (ANA)
ECCFD......... European Commission for the Control of Foot-and-Mouth Disease
ECCFPP....... European Conference on Controlled Fusion and Plasma Physics (SAUS)
ECCHO......... Electronic Check Clearing House Organization
ECC HOM..... Ecce Homo [*Behold the Man*] [*Latin*] (ROG)
ECCI........... Eastern Canada Cat Institute (ROAS)
ECCI........... Emergency Core Cooling Injection [*Environmental science*] (COE)
ECCI........... Evening College Characteristics Index (EDAC)
ECCI........... Executive Committee Communist International (SAUO)
ECCI........... Executive Council of the Communist International (SAUO)
ECCI........... Experimental Consultative Conference of Industrialists (NATG)
ECC Int....... ECC International Ltd. [*Formerly, Educational Computer Corp.*] [*Associated Press*] (SAG)
ECCJ........... European Communities Court of Justice (DLA)
Eccl............ Ecclesiastes [*Old Testament book*]
eccl............ ecclesiastic (WDAA)
eccl............ Ecclesiastical (SHCU)
ECCL........... Ecclesiastical
Eccl............ Ecclesiazusae [*of Aristophanes*] [*Classical studies*] (OCD)
ECCL........... Equipment and Component Configuration Listing (DNAB)
ECCL........... Erie City and County Library (SAUS)
ECCL........... Error Checking and Correction Logic [*Computer science*] (IAA)
ECCL........... Essex County Cooperating Libraries [*Library network*]
ECCL........... Scriptores Ecclesiastici [*Ecclesiastical Authors*] [*Latin*] (ROG)
ECCLA......... European Committee for Co-operation with Latin-America (SAUS)
Eccl & Ad.... Ecclesiastical and Admiralty [*Legal term*] (DLA)
Eccl & Ad.... Spinks' English Ecclesiastical and Admiralty Reports [*A publication*] (DLA)
Eccl & Adm... Spinks' Ecclesiastical and Admiralty [*Upper Canada*] [*A publication*] (DLA)
Eccles......... Ecclesiastes [*Old Testament book*]
eccles......... ecclesiastic (SAUS)
eccles......... Ecclesiastical (VRA)
ECCLES....... Ecclesiastical
EcclesR....... Ecclesiastes Rabbah (BJA)
Eccl Gk........ Ecclesiastical Greek (ADWA)
Eccl R.......... English Ecclesiastical Reports [*A publication*] (DLA)
Eccl Rep...... Ecclesiastical Reports [*England*] [*A publication*] (DLA)
ECCLS.......... European Committee for Clinical Laboratory Standards [*Kent, England*]
Eccl Stat...... Ecclesiastical Statutes [*A publication*] (DLA)
Ecclus.......... Ecclesiasticus [*Old Testament book*] [*Apocrypha*]
ECCM........... East Caribbean Common Market (DS)
ECCM........... Eastern Caribbean Common Market (SAUS)
ECCM........... Electronic Counter Counter Measure (SAUS)
ECCM........... Electronic Counter-Countermeasures [*Military*]
ECC memory... Error-Correcting Code Memory [*Computer science*]
ECCMF......... European Council of Chemical Manufacturers Federations (SAUO)
ECCMO......... Electronic Counter-Countermeasures Operator [*Military*] (CET)
ECCN........... Eccentricity (SAUS)
ECCN........... European Child Care Network (EURO)
ECCN........... Export Control Classification Number (SAUS)
ECCN........... Export Control Commodity Number (AAGC)
ECCNE......... Electric Coordinating Council of New England (SAUO)
ECCNP......... European Conference on Computer Network Protocols (VLIE)
ECCNR......... European Committee for the Conservation of Nature and Natural Resources (SAUS)
ECCNSW...... Ethnic Communities Council of New South Wales [*Australia*]
ECCO........... Educational Computer Consortium of Ohio (SRA)
ECCO........... Emergency Committee of the Christian Organizations (SAUO)
ECCO........... Engineering Command Control and Operation (SAUS)
ECCO........... Engineers Coordinating Council of Oregon (SAUO)
ECCO........... Environmental Council of Concrete Organizations
ECCO........... Error Checking and Correcting Coder (VLIE)
ECCO........... Ethyl Cellulose and Caster Oil (SAA)
ECCO........... European Cardiology Congress Organization (SAUS)
ECCO........... European Conference of Conscripts Organisations (EAIO)
ECCO........... European Conference of Conscripts Organization (SAUS)
ECCO........... European Conference on Clinical Oncology (SAUO)
ECCO........... European Culture Collections' Organization (EAIO)
ECC-OCC...... Enlisted/Officer Combined Correspondence Course [*Military*] (DNAB)
ECCOFEX..... European Commission Coordinating Committee of Options and Future Exchanges (EURO)
ECCOIL........ Eastern Construction Co. in Laos (CINC)
ECCO Virus... Enteric Cytopathogenic Cat Orphan Virus (SAUS)
ECCP........... East Coast Coal Port [*Shipping*] [*British*]
ECCP........... Eielson Consolidated Command Post (SAUO)
ECCP........... Engineering Concepts Curriculum Project
ECCP........... Equivalent Cost Contract Price (SAUS)
ECCP........... European Committee on Crime Problems
ECCP........... Examination of Clinical Counseling (SEAT)
ECCP........... Executive Committee on Commercial Policy [*Abolished, 1944*]
ECCR........... Electronic Cash and Credit Register (HGAA)
ECCR........... Engineering Calibration Cycle Request (SAUS)
ECCR........... European Centre for Credit Ratings (SAUO)
ECCR........... experimental gas-cooled reactor (SAUS)
ECCRA......... Eastern Canada - Caribbean Rate Association (SAUS)
ECCRA......... Eastern Canada-Caribbean Rate Association (SAUO)
ECC RAM..... Error Checking and Correcting Random-Access Memory
ECCRAM...... Error Checking and Correction Random Access Memory (SAUS)
ECCRDSS..... European Coordination Centre for Research and Documentation in Social Science (SAUS)
ECCREDI...... European Council for Construction, Research, Development and Innovation (SAUS)
ECCS........... ECCS, Inc. [*NASDAQ symbol*] (SAG)
ECCS........... Economic Cent Call Seconds (SAUS)
ECCS........... Economic Hundred Call Seconds [*Telecommunications*] (TEL)
ECCS........... Electrolytic Chromium-Coated Steel (SAUS)
ECCS........... Electronically Changeable Control Store (SAUS)
ECCS........... Electronically Changeable Control Stores (VLIE)
ECCS........... Electronic Case Control System (SAUS)
ECCS........... Electronic Concentrated Control System [*Computerized car fuel system*]
ECCS........... Electronic Concentrated Engine Control System (SAUO)
ECCS........... Electronic Cycling Clutch Switch [*Automotive engineering*]
ECCS........... Emergency Command and Control System (DEMM)
ECCS........... Emergency Core-Cooling System [*Nuclear energy*]
ECCs........... Emitter Coupled Circuits (SAUS)
ECCS........... Employee Charity and Community Services
ECCS........... Engine and Component Control System (SAUS)
ECCS........... Engineer Command and Control System [*Software*]
ECCS........... Engineering of Complex Computer Systems
ECCS........... European Committee for Consultant Services (EA)
ECCS........... European Convention for Construction Steelwork (SAUS)
ECCSA......... Ethnic Communities Council of South Australia
ECCSEC....... Ecumenical Commission for Church and Society in European Community (SAUO)
ECCSL......... Emitter-Coupled Current-Steered Logic [*Electronics*] (MSA)
ECCSL......... Emitter Coupled Current Steering Logic (SAUS)
ECCT........... Enhanced Computer Controlled Teletext (SAUS)
ECCT........... Error Correction Console Technician (IAA)
ECC technique... error-checking and correcting technique (SAUS)
ECCTIS........ Educational Counselling and Credit Transfer Information Service [*Information service or system*] (IID)
ECCTO......... Association of European Chemical Coastal Tanker Owners (SAUO)
ECCTO......... European Chemical Coastal Tanker Owners
ECCTO......... European Committee for Cocoa Trade Organisations (EERA)
ECCTO......... European Community Cocoa Trade Organization (EAIO)
ECCTT......... Engineering Casualty Control Training Team [*Navy*]
ECCTYC....... English Council of California Two-Year Colleges (EDAC)

ECCU English Cross Country Union (BI)
ECCW Electoral College of the Church of Wales (SAUO)
ECD detection (SAUS)
ECD Early-Closing Day [*British*]
ecd early closing day (SAUS)
ECd East Caribbean dollar (SAUS)
ECD East Central District (SAUS)
ECD East Coast Division (SAUS)
ECD Ecosystem Conservation Directorate (SAUO)
ECD Educational and Cultural Development Program
ECD Effective Cutoff Diameter [*Particulate measurement*]
ECD Efficiency of Conversion of Digested Material [*Physiology*]
ECD Electric Chart Drive (SAUS)
ECD Electric Control Drive
ECD Electrochemical Debarring (SAUS)
ECD Electrochemical Deburring
ECD Electro-Chemical Degradation
ECD Electrochemical Deposition [*Metallurgy*]
ECD Electrochemical Detector (DB)
ECD Electrochromeric Display (SAUS)
ECD Electrochromic Display [*Instrumentation*]
ECD Electron Capture Decay (SAUS)
ECD Electron-Capture Detection [*Instrumentation*]
ECD electron capture detection (SAUS)
ECD Electron Capture Detector (LDOE)
ECD Electron Catch Detector (SAUS)
ECD Electron Current Detector (SAUS)
ECD Electronic Calculator Device (SAUS)
ECD Electronic Cash Disbursements (SAUS)
ECD Electronic Command Division (SAUO)
ECD Electronic Communications Division [*Air Force*] (AFM)
ECD Electronic Components Division (SAUS)
ECD Electronic Control Drive (SAUS)
ECD Electronic Controlled Deceleration
ECD Electrostatic Charge Decay [*Electronics*] (ODA)
ECD Elk Chute Ditch [*Missouri*] [*Seismograph station code, US Geological Survey*] (SEIS)
ECD Emergency Category Designation
ECD Emission Control Device [*Automotive engineering*]
ECD Endocardial Cushion Defect
ECD Endothelial Cell Density [*Anatomy*]
ECD energy control device (SAUS)
ECD Energy Conversion Devices, Inc.
ECD Engineering Change Directive (ACAE)
ECD Engineering Control Drawing (MCD)
ECD Engineers Club of Dayton (SAUS)
ECD Enhanced Casing Design [*Tire engineering*]
ECD Enhanced Color Display [*Computer monitor*]
ECD Enhanced Compact Disk (PCM)
ECD Enhanced Console Driver [*Computer science*]
ECD Entry Corridor Display (KSC)
ECD Environmental Chemistry Division (SAUO)
ECD Environmental Conditions Determination (AAG)
ECD Episcopal Conference of the Deaf (EA)
ECD Epithelial Corneal Dystrophy [*Medicine*] (MELL)
ECD Equal Charge Displacement [*Fission*]
ECD Equipment Configuration Data (SAUS)
ECD Equivalent Carbon Dioxide [*Climatology*]
ECD Equivalent Circulating Density [*Well drilling*]
ECD Equivalent Current Dipole [*Magnetism*]
ECD Error Control Device (TEL)
ECD error correction (SAUS)
ECD Error Correction Decoder (VLIE)
ECD Escherichia Coli Database [*Genetics*]
ECD Estimated Completion Date
ECD Ethoxycoumarin Deethylase [*An enzyme*]
ECD European Communications Division [*Military*]
ECD European Consultants Directory [*A publication*]
ECD Except Change Departure to Read [*Aviation*] (FAAC)
ECD Exploratory Career Development (DNAB)
Ecd Extensible Compound Document [*Programming language*] [*Computer science*] (PCM)
ECD Prospect, AK [*Location identifier*] [*FAA*] (FAAL)
ECD Ethyl Cysteinate Dimer [*Chemistry*] (ODA)
ECDA Engine Control Development Area (KSC)
ECDB Electrochemical Deburring (IAA)
ECDB Electronic Components Data Bank (SAUS)
ECDB Emissions Certification Data Base (SAUS)
ECDB Engineering Change Data Base (VLIE)
ECDC Early Childhood Direction Center
ECDC Economic Cooperation among Developing Countries [*United Nations*]
ECDC Electro-Chemical Diffused Collector (SAUS)
ECDC Electrochemical Diffused-Collector Transistor
ecdc electrochemical diffused collector transistor (SAUS)
ECDC Electronically Commutated Direct Current (SAUS)
ECDC Electronic Commerce in Developing Countries (SAUO)
ECDC Electronic Components Development Committee (SAUO)
ECDC Energy Capital Development Corporation (SAUO)
ECDC Engineering Configuration Data Control (AAG)
ECDC Ethiopian Community Development Council (EA)
ECDC External Countdown Clock
ECDCC Early Childhood Day Care Center [*University of Alabama*] [*Research center*] (RCD)
ECDC transistor electrochemical-diffused-collector transistor (SAUS)
ECDD Environment Canada Data Dictionary (SAUO)
ECDD Exceeded (VLIE)
ECDDS East Coast District Dental Society (SAUS)
ECDES EC Digital Evaluation System (MCD)
ECDES Electronic Combat Digital Evaluation System (SAUS)
ECDEU Early Clinical Drug Evaluation Unit [*Medicine*] (DB)
ECDF Equipment Characteristics Data File (SAUS)
ECDFTT Employment-Corrected Double Factorial Terms of Trade [*Economics*]
ECDG Electrochemical Discharge Grinding [*Manufacturing term*]
ECDGF Embryonal Carcinoma Derived Growth Factor [*Biochemistry*]
ECDGF Endothelial Cell-Derived Growth Factor [*Biochemistry*]
ECDI Early Childhood Diagnostic Instrument [*Mason and Stewart*] (TES)
ECDI Editorial Code and Data, Inc. (IID)
ecdi electronic course deviation indicator (SAUS)
ECDIN Environmental Chemicals Data and Information Network [*Commission of the European Communities*] [*Chemical databank*] (IID)
ECDIN European Chemical Data and Infomation Network [*EURATOM*] (PDAA)
ECDIS Electronic Chart Display and Information System [*Computer science*]
ECDIS Electronic Chart Display Informations System (SAUS)
ECDIS Electronic Chart Display System (SAUS)
ECDL Emergency Carbon Dioxide Limit (SAA)
ECDL European Computer Driving Licence (VLIE)
ECDL European Computer Driving License (SAUO)
ECDL External Cavity Diode Laser (ARMP)
ECDM Electrical Discharge Machining (SAUS)
ECDM Electrochemical and Electrical Discharge Machining (PDAA)
ECDM Electrochemical Discharge Machining [*Manufacturing term*] (IAA)
ECDMMRL European Committee for the Development of the Meuse and Meuse/Rhine Links (EAIO)
ecdn electrical cables down (SAUS)
ECDO Electronic Combat Duty Officer (SAUS)
ECDO Electronic Community Deal Office [*Telecommunications*] (TEL)
ECDO Electronic Community Dial Office (VLIE)
ECDO Enterocytopathogenic Dog Orphan Virus
ECDO European Cell Death Organization
ECDOC European Communities Commission Documentation (SAUS)
ECDO Virus Enteric Cytopathogenic Dog Orphan Virus (SAUS)
ECDP Estimating Controlled Data Package (SAUS)
ECDPM European Centre for Development Policy (EURO)
ECD Program Educational and Cultural Development Program (SAUS)
ECDR Encoder (SAUS)
ECDR Engineering Control Distribution Report (MCD)
ECDR Electrostatic Corona Discharge (ODA)
ECDs Effective Cutoff Diameters (SAUS)
ECDSA Elliptic Curve Digital Signature Algorithm (DINT)
ECDT Electrochemical Diffused-Transistor (IAA)
ECDU Electrical Coupling Display Unit (KSC)
ECDU Enhanced Control & Display Unit (SAUS)
ECDU European Christian Democratic Union [*Brussels, Belgium*] Political party] (EAIO)
ECDW Electronic Cooling Distilled Water (DNAB)
ECE Clearinghouse on Early Childhood Education (SAUS)
ECE Early Childhood Education
ECE East Central Europe (ECON)
ECE Echo Control Equipment [*Telecommunications*] (TEL)
ECE Economic Commission for Europe [*United Nations*] (IRC)
ECE Economic Commission for Europe of the UN (SAUS)
ECE Economic Commission of Europe (SAUS)
ECE Economic Committee of Europe (SAUO)
ECE Economic Coverage Endorsement
ECE E. Coyote Enterprises (SAUS)
ECE Eddy Current Energy
ECE Effective Conversion Efficiency
ECE El Campo, TX [*Location identifier*] [*FAA*] (FAAL)
ECE Electrical and Computer Engineering (ACAE)
ECE Electrical Checkout Equipment (KSC)
ECE Electrical Conversion Electronics (ACAE)
ECE Electric Control Equipment (SAUS)
ECE Electrochemical, Chemical, Electrochemical [*Chemical mechanism*]
ECE Electrochemical Electrode (SAUS)
ECE Electro-Chemical Engine
ECE Electrochemical Equivalent (IAA)
ECE electron-cyclotron emission (SAUS)
ECE Electronic Commerce Europe Association (SAUS)
ECE Electronic Communications Engineer (SAUS)
ECE Electronic Control Enable (ACAE)
ECE Element Characteristics Equation
ECE Eligible Capital Expenditure (FOTI)
ece eligible capital expenditure (SAUS)
ECE Endocervical Ecchymosis [*Gynecology*] (DAVI)
ECE Endothelin-Converting Enzyme [*Biochemistry*]
ECE Engineering Capacity Exchange (IEEE)
ECE Environmental Consulting Engineering (SAUS)
ECE Environmental Contaminant Evaluation [*Fish and Wildlife Service program*]
ECE Environmental Control Equipment
ECE Episcopal Center for Evangelism (EA)
ECE European Commodities Exchange [*of the European Economic Community*] (EA)
ECE Evangelical Church of Eritrea
ECE Executive Committee of Economics (SAUO)
ECE Executive Communications Exchange (MHDI)
ECE Exemption for Coal Extraction (SAUO)
ECE Experiment Checkout Equipment (MCD)
ECE Export Council for Europe (ILCA)

ECE .... Extended Coverage Endorsement [*Insurance*]
ECE .... External Combustion Engine [*Steam bus*]
ECE .... Extrachromosomal Element [*Genetics*]
ECEA .... Ethyl(chloroethyl)aniline [*Organic chemistry*]
ECEA .... Exceptional Child Education Abstracts (SAUS)
ECE & R Center... Eaton Corp., Engineering & Research Center (SAUO)
ECEAP .... Early Childhood Education Assistance Program
ECEB .... East Coast Editorial Board (SAUO)
ECEBA .... Energy Conservation in Existing Buildings Act of 1976
ECEC .... East Carolina Engineers Club (SAUS)
ECEC .... Effective Cation and Exchange Capacity [*Soil science*]
ECEC .... European Centre for Environmental Communication (SAUS)
EC/EDI .... Electronic Commerce / Electronic Data Interchange [*DoD*]
ECEF .... Earth-Centered, Earth-Fixed
ECEF .... Electronic Commerce Executive Forum (AG)
ECEFP .... Executive Committee on Economic Foreign Policy [*Terminated*] (EGAO)
ECEFT .... Early Childhood Embedded Figures Test (EDAC)
ECE/HBP ...... Economic Commission for Europe-Committee on Housing, Building and Planning (SAUO)
ECEJ .... Early Childhood Education Journal [*A publication*] (BRI)
ECEJAETA .... European Chamber of Extra-Judicial Adjudicators and Expert Technical Advisers [*See also CEASPECT*] (EA)
ECEL .... Epithermal Critical Experiment Laboratory [*Nuclear energy*]
ECEL .... European Council for Environmental Law (PDAA)
ECELL .... Electrochemical Cell (MCD)
ECELR .... Epithermal Critical Experiment Laboratory Reactor (SAUS)
ECEMG .... Evoked Compound Electromyography [*Neurology*] (DAVI)
ECEMP .... Electron Caused Electromagnetic Pulse (ACAE)
ECEO .... Economic Crime Enforcement Office (SAUO)
ECEO .... Enteric-Cytopathogenic-Equine-Orphan (SAUS)
ECEO Virus... Enteric Cytopathogenic Equine Orphan Virus (SAUS)
ECEP .... Equivalent CEP
ECEP .... Experiment Checkout Equipment Processor (NASA)
ECEPE .... European Corporate Electronic Publishing Exhibition (SAUS)
ECEPS .... Electronic Converter Electric Power Supply (PDAA)
ECER .... Exceptional Child Education Resources [*Formerly, ECEA*] [*Council for Exceptional Children*] [*Bibliographic database*] [*A publication*]
ECER .... Exceptional child information resources (SAUS)
ECERM .... Environment Code of Ethics for Rangeland Managers (EERA)
ECES .... Educational and Career Exploration System (SAUS)
ECES .... Education and Career Exploration System (SAUS)
ECES .... European Consumer Electronics Show (SAUO)
ECES .... Evaluation Contractors Estimating System
ECESDB .... European Commodities Exchange Statistical Database [*United Nations*] (DUND)
ECESP .... European Committee for Economic and Social Progress (SAUO)
ECET .... Ecological Centre of Study and Protection of the East-European Tundra (SAUO)
ECET .... Electrical and Computer Engineering Technology (ACAE)
ECET .... Electronic Control Assembly - Engine Thrust (KSC)
ECET .... Electronic Control Engine Thrust (SAUS)
ECETOC .... European Chemical Industry Ecology and Toxicology Centre [*Belgium*] (PDAA)
ECE-UN .... Economic Commission of Europe of the United Nations (SAUO)
ECF .... Earth Center Finding (ACAE)
ECF .... Earth Crust Formation
ECF .... East Cavalry Field (SAUO)
ECF .... East Coast Fever [*Veterinary medicine*]
ECF .... Eastern Counties Farmers Ltd. (SAUO)
ECF .... Echo Control Factor [*Telecommunications*] (TEL)
ECF .... Echo Frame (SAUS)
ECF .... Edgar Cayce Foundation (SAUO)
ECF .... Effective Capillary Flow [*Medicine*] (MAE)
ECF .... Effective Cutoff Frequency
ECF .... Elecrical Council of Florida (SRA)
ECF .... Electrical Contractors Federation (SAUO)
ECF .... Electrically Conductive Film (MCD)
ECF .... Electric Crystal Field (UWER)
ECF .... Electrochemical Fluorination [*Chemical synthesis*]
ECF .... Electrochemical Forming [*Manufacturing term*] (IAA)
ECF .... Electro-Conductive Film (SAUS)
ECF .... Electronic Commerce Finland (SAUS)
ECF .... Elemental Chlorine-Free [*Pulp and paper processing*]
ECF .... Element Change Factor (MCD)
ECF .... Element Charge Factor (SAUS)
ECF .... Element Circuit Function (SAUS)
ECF .... Eleventh Commandment Fellowship (EA)
ECF .... Ellsworth Convertible Growth & Income Fund, Inc. [*AMEX symbol*] (SPSG)
ECF .... Emergency Cooling Function [*Nuclear energy*] (NRCH)
ECF .... Emergency Cooling Functionality (SAUS)
ECF .... Emission Contribution Fraction (OA)
ECF .... Employees' Compensation Fund (NG)
ECF .... Energy of Crush Factor [*Automotive safety*]
ECF .... Engineering Central Files
ECF .... Enhanced Connectivity Facilities (CDE)
ECF .... Enhanced Cytotoxicity Factor [*Biochemistry*]
ECF .... Eosinophil Chemotactic Factor [*Hematology*]
ECF .... Episcopal Charismatic Fellowship (SAUS)
ECF .... Equivalency Capability File (MCD)
ECF .... Error Correction Feature (SAUS)
ECF .... Erythroid Colony Formation [*Hematology*] (DMAA)
ECF .... Ethyl Chloroformate (LDT)
ECF .... Eurocopter [*France*] [*ICAO designator*] (FAAC)
ECF .... European Caravan Federation (EA)
ECF .... European Coffee Federation (EAIO)
ECF .... European Commission on Forestry and Forestry Products (SAUS)
ECF .... European Composites Forum (SAUS)
ECF .... European Conference on Fracture (SAUS)
ECF .... European Cultural Foundation (EAIO)
ECF .... European Cyclist Federation (EURO)
ECF .... "Evangelize China" Fellowship (EA)
ECF .... Excess Chiasma Frequency [*Genetics*]
ECF .... Ex-Communist Forces (SAUS)
ECF .... Expanded Code File (SAUS)
ECF .... Expended Core Facility [*Nuclear energy*]
ECF .... Experimental Cartographic Facility [*Air Force*]
ECF .... Export Cargo Form [*Shipping*]
ECF .... Extended Care Facility (WYGK)
ECF .... Externally Caused Failure
ECF .... Extracapsular Fracture [*Medicine*] (MELL)
ECF .... Extracellular Fluid [*Physiology*]
ECF .... extracellular fluid, extended care facility (SAUS)
ECF .... Eye Contolled Focus [*Camera technology*]
ECFA .... Eastern College Football Association (PSS)
ECFA .... Emergency Community Facilities Act of 1970
ECF-A .... Eosinophil Chemotactic Factor of Anaphylaxis [*Immunochemistry*]
ECFA .... European Committee for Future Accelarators (SAUS)
ECFA .... European Committee for Future Activities (PDAA)
ECFA .... European Committee on Future Accelerators [*Nuclear energy*]
ECFA .... Evangelical Council for Financial Accountability (EA)
ECFB .... Ethyl Cellulose Perfluorobutyrate
ECF Black .... Extra Conducted Furnace Black (SAUS)
ECFC .... Eastern Collegiate Football Conference (PSS)
ECFC .... Employers Council on Flexible Compensation (EA)
ECFCI .... European Center of Federations of the Chemical Industry (SAUS)
ECFCI .... European Centre (or Center) of Federations of the Chemical Industry (SAUO)
ECFD .... Executive Council on Foreign Diplomacy (EA)
ECFD .... Executive Council on Foreign Diplomats (EA)
ECFI .... Eastern Caribbean Farm Institute (SAUO)
ECFI .... Electronic Company Filing Index [*Disclosure Information Group*] [*Information service or system*] (IID)
ECFI .... European Court of First Instance (EURO)
ECF-IUF .... European Committee of Food, Catering, and Allied Workers' Unions within the IUF [*International Union of Food and Allied Workers' Associations*] (EAIO)
ECF/IUF .... European Committee of Food, Catering and Allied Workers Unions within the IUF/INT (SAUS)
ECFL .... Emergency Crop and Feed Loans [*New Deal*]
ECFM .... Eddy Current Flow Meter [*Nuclear energy*] (NRCH)
ECFM .... European Committee of the Manufacturers of Foundry Machines (SAUO)
ECFMG .... Educational Commission for Foreign Medical Graduates (EA)
ECFMS .... Educational Council for Foreign Medical Students (DAVI)
ECFO .... Electronic Control Functions Objective (TIMI)
ECFP .... East Coast Forestry Project (SAUS)
ECFR .... Executive Communication Region (SAUS)
ECFRC .... Electronic Component Reliability Center (SAUS)
ECFRPC .... East Central Florida Regional Planning Council (SAUO)
ECFS .... East Coast Flying Service (SAA)
ECFS .... Eastern Caribbean Fibre-Optic System (SAUO)
ECFS .... Empire Central Flying School (SAUO)
ECFS .... Export Credit Facilitation Scheme [*Australia*]
ECFSA .... Episcopal Churchpeople for a Free Southern Africa (EA)
ECFSOV .... Episcopal Council for Foreign Students and Other Visitors [*Defunct*] (EA)
ECFT .... Extraluminal Contractile Force Transducer (SAUS)
ECFTU .... European Confederation of Free Trade Unions [*Later, ETUC*]
ECFTUE .... International Centre of Free Trade Unionists in Exile (SAUO)
ECFV .... Extracellular Fluid Volume [*Physiology*]
ECG .... Eccentric Gear (SAUS)
ECG .... Echocardiogram [*Cardiology*] (DAVI)
ECG .... Economic Control Group (SAUO)
ECG .... Ecosystem Conservation Group [*Marine science*] (MSC)
ECG .... Ecosystems Conservation Group (EERA)
ECG .... Effective Center of Gravity (SAUS)
ECG .... Electrocapiogram [*Medicine*]
ECG .... Electrocardiogram [*Also, EK, EKG*] [*Medicine*]
ECG .... Electrocardiograph [*Also, EKG*] (MSA)
ECG .... Electrocardiography [*Medicine*] (MELL)
ECG .... Electrochemical Grinding (IEEE)
ECG .... Electro-Epitaxial Crystal Growth [*Materials processing*]
ECG .... Electrolytic Chloride Generator (DWSG)
ECG .... Electronic Character Generation [*Electronography*] (DGA)
ECG .... Electronic Character Generator [*Television*] (WDMC)
ECG .... Electronic Component Group
ECG .... Elizabeth City, NC [*Location identifier*] [*FAA*] (FAAL)
ECG .... Emergency Coordination Group [*Military*]
ECG .... Endocrine Gland [*Medicine*] (MELL)
ECG .... Energy Coordinating Group [*Twelve-nation coalition*]
ECG .... Engineering Consulting Group (SAUO)
ECG .... Engineering Craftsmen's Guild [*A union*] [*British*]
ECG .... Environmental Compliance Group (SAUO)
ECG .... Environmental Control Group (CAAL)
ECG .... Environmental Coordinating Group (SAUO)
ECG .... Envirosystems Consulting Group, Inc. (EFIS)
ECG .... Epicathechin Gallate [*Biochemistry*]
ECG .... Equine Chorionic Gonadotropin [*Endocrinology*]

ECG European Contact Group on Urban Industrial Mission (EAIO)
ECG Evaporative Cooling Garment [*Spacesuit*] [*NASA*]
ECG Exercise Control Group [*Army*]
ECG Explicitly Correlated Gaussian (MEC)
ECG Export Credit Guarantee (DLA)
ECGAI Education Council of the Graphic Arts Industry [*Later, GATF*] (EA)
EC Games European Economic Community Games (SAUO)
ECGB East Coast of Great Britain [*Shipping*]
EC-GC Electron Capture-Gas Chromatograph (ADWA)
ECGC Electron-Capture Gas Chromatography
ECGC Empire Cotton Growing Corp. [*British*] (BI)
ECGC Essex County Gas Co. [*NASDAQ symbol*] (NQ)
ECGC Export Credit and Guarantee Corporation (SAUO)
ECGD Export Credits Guarantee Department [*British*]
ECGF Endothelial Cell Growth Factor [*Cytochemistry*]
ECGF European Container Glass Federation (EA)
ECGI Electronically Controlled Gasoline Injection [*Automotive fuel systems*]
ECGL Economic Comrnunity of the Great Lakes Countries (SAUS)
ECGLC Economic Community of the Great Lakes Countries [*See also* CEPGL] [*Gisenye, Rwanda*] (EAIO)
ECGLC Electron Capture Gas-Liquid Chromatography
ECGM Electrocardiagraphic Monitoring [*Medicine*] (MELL)
ECGM Episcopal Council for Global Mission (EA)
ECGO Amer Eco [*NASDAQ symbol*] (SG)
ECGO American Eco Corp. [*NASDAQ symbol*] (SAG)
ECGOF Amer Eco Corp. [*NASDAQ symbol*] (TTSB)
ECG Press Eccentric Gear Press (SAUS)
ECGS Endothelial Cell Growth Supplement [*Cytochemistry*]
ECGS Evaporative Cooling Garment System [*NASA*]
ECGX EC Gaston Railroad [*Federal Railroad Administration identification code*]
ECH Early Childhood Health
ECH Earth Coverage Horizon Measurement (SAUS)
ECH Earth Coverage Horn [*Satellite communications*]
ECH Echelon
ECH Echery [*France*] [*Seismograph station code, US Geological Survey*] (SEIS)
ECH Echlin, Inc. [*NYSE symbol*] (SPSG)
ECH Echlin Manufacturing Co. (SAUO)
ECH Echo Cancellation Hybrid [*Telecommunications*] (NITA)
ECH Eddy-Current Heating (EECA)
ECH Electrochemical Honing [*Manufacturing term*]
ECH Electron Cyclotron Harmonic [*Planetary Physics*]
ECH Electron Cyclotron Heating [*Nuclear energy*]
ECH Empire Clearing House for Raw Materials (SAUO)
ECH Employment Clearing House (SAUO)
ECH Endocardial Hemorrhage [*Medicine*] (MELL)
ECH Engine Compartment Heater (AAG)
ECh English Channel (SAUS)
ECH Enhanced Call Handling [*Telecommunications*] (ITD)
ECH Epicardial Hemorrhage [*Medicine*] (MELL)
ECH Epichlorohydrin [*Organic chemistry*]
ECH Episodic Cluster Headache (MELL)
ECH Epochs of Church History [*A publication*]
ECH Erase Character (SAUS)
ECH Ethylcyclohexane (SAUS)
ECH Ethylene Chlorhydrin (DB)
ECH European Country Hotels (SAUS)
ECH Extended Care Hospital (DAVI)
ECH Ketchikan, AK [*Location identifier*] [*FAA*] (FAAL)
ECH Movement Echelon [*MTMC*] (TAG)
ECHA Eastern College Hockey Association (EA)
ECHA Executive Committee for Humanitarian Affairs [*United Nations*]
ECHAM European Centre/Hamburg Model (SAUO)
ECHB East Coast/Hawkes Bay Conservancy (SAUS)
EchBF Echo Bay Finance Corp. [*Associated Press*] (SAG)
ECHC European Colloquium on Heterocyclic Chemistry
ECHD Ann Arbor ECTD HD System (SAUS)
echd Echeloned (SAUS)
ECHE Ealing College of Higher Education [*England*]
E-Check Electronic Check (ITCA)
E-Check Emergency Check (SAUS)
Echelon Echelon International Corp. [*Associated Press*] (SAG)
ECHH Electro-Catalytic Hyper-Heaters (GNE)
ECHIN Echinococcus [*Microorganism*] (DAVI)
ECHIVAL European Climate and Hydrological Project on Interactions between Vegetation, Atmosphere and Land (SAUS)
ECHIVAL European International Project on Climate and Hydrological Interactions between Vegetation, Atmosphere and Land surfaces (SAUS)
ECHIVAL European International Project on Climate and Hydrological Interactions between Vegetation, the Atmosphere and the Land-Surface (SAUS)
ECHIVAL European International Project on Climatic and Hydrological Interactions between Vegetation, Atmosphere and Land Surface (SAUS)
Echlin Echlin, Inc. [*Associated Press*] (SAG)
ECHM Earth Coverage Horizon Measurement (PDAA)
ECHO Each Community Helps Others [*Environmental Protection Agency*]
ECHO East Coast Hang Out [*Computer network*]
ECHO East Coast Hazards Observation [*Sampling program*]
echo Echocardiogram [*Therapy term*] (CTAA)
ECHO Echocardiogram [*Cardiology*]
ECHO Echocardiography (QSUL)
ECHO Echoencephalogram [*Neurology*]
echo Echogram [*Radiology*] (DAVI)
echo Echoplex [*Telecommunications protocol*] (CDE)
ECHO EC Host Organisation (SAUS)
ECHO Echo, TX [*American Association of Railroads railroad junction routing code*]
ECHO Educational Concern for Hunger Organization (EA)
ECHO Efficient Car-Handling Operations (SAUS)
ECHO Elder Cottage Housing Opportunity
ECHO [*The*] Electonic Clearing House, Inc. [*NASDAQ symbol*] (NQ)
ECHO Electronic Case-Handling in Offices (SAUO)
ECHO Electronic Clearing House [*NASDAQ symbol*] (TTSB)
ECHO Electronic Communications for the Home and Office [*Marina Del Ray, CA*] [*Telecommunications service*] (TSSD)
ECHO Electronic Compating Hospital-Oriented (SAUS)
ECHO Electronic Components Harmonization Organization (SAUO)
ECHO Electronic Computing Health Organization (SAUS)
ECHO Electronic Computing Health-Oriented Organization (SAUO)
ECHO Electronic Computing, Hospital-Oriented (IEEE)
ECHO Electronic Computing Hospital-Oriented Group (SAUO)
ECHO Electronic Controlled High Output (SAUS)
ECHO Enterocytopathogenic Human Orphan Virus
ECHO Environmental Conservation Hotlinks (SAUO)
ECHO Environment, Conservation, and Hunting Outreach [*An association*]
ECHO Equipment for Charity Hospitals Overseas [*British*] (DI)
ECHO Etoposide, Cyclophosphamide, Hydroxydaunomycin [*Adriamycin*], Oncovin [*Vincristine*] [*Antineoplastic drug regimen*]
ECHO European Commission Host Organization [*Commission of the European Communities*] [*Host system*] [*Luxembourg*] [*Information service or system*] (IID)
ECHO European Communities (or Community) Host Organisation (SAUO)
ECHO European Community Host Organisation (SAUS)
ECHO European Community Humanitarian Office
ECHO Evidence for Community Health Organization (SAUO)
ECHO Evolution of Competing Hierarchical Organizations
ECHO Exchange Clearing House (NUMA)
ECHO Exchange Clearing House Organization [*European bank coalition*] (ECON)
ECHO Expanded Characteristics Option [*Metallurgy*]
ECHO Experimental Contract Highlight Operation [*NASA*]
ECHO Expo Collectors - Historians Organization (EA)
ECHO Hungarian Economic Information Service (IID)
EchoBay Echo Bay Mines Ltd. [*Associated Press*] (SAG)
EchoC EchoCath, Inc. [*Associated Press*] (SAG)
EchoCG Echocardiography [*Medicine*] (EDAA)
EchoCth EchoCath, Inc. [*Associated Press*] (SAG)
Echo-Eg Echoencephalography [*Medicine*] (EDAA)
Echo-RNV Echoradionuclide Ventriculography [*Medicine*] (EDAA)
EchoStar EchoStar Communications Corp. [*Associated Press*] (SAG)
EchoStr EchoStar Communications Corp. [*Associated Press*] (SAG)
ECHO Virus Enteric Cytopathogenic Human Orphan Virus (SAUS)
Echo-VM Echoventriculometry [*Medicine*] (EDAA)
ECHP European Community Household Panel (EURO)
ECHR Emergency Coalition for Haitian Refugees (EA)
ECHR European Commission of Human Rights (EA)
ECHR European Convention on Human Rights (SAFN)
ECHR European Court of Human Rights (SAUO)
ECHR50 European Convention for the Protection of Human Rights and Fundamental Freedoms of 4 November 1950 (SAFN)
ECHS Evander Childs High School (SAUS)
ECHSA Elderly Citizens Homes of South Australia
ECHSCP Exeter Community Health Services Computer Project [*Medicine*] (EDAA)
ECHT EchoCath, Inc. [*NASDAQ symbol*] (SAG)
ECHT European Conference on Hypermedia Technology (VERA)
ECHTA EchoCath Inc.'A' [*NASDAQ symbol*] (TTSB)
ECHTU EchoCath Inc. Unit [*NASDAQ symbol*] (TTSB)
ECHTW EchoCath Inc. Wrrt [*NASDAQ symbol*] (TTSB)
ECHTZ EchoCath Inc. Wrrt'B' [*NASDAQ symbol*] (TTSB)
ECI Cast Iron Electrode (SAUS)
ECI Earth Centered Inertia (Inertials) (SAUS)
ECI Earth-Centered Inertial [*System*]
ECI Earth Central Inertial (SAUS)
ECI Earth Consultants, Inc. (EFIS)
ECI East Coast of Ireland [*Shipping*]
ECI Eastern Carolina Aviation, Inc. [*ICAO designator*] (FAAC)
ECI Eddy Current Inspection (SAUS)
ECI Edgell Communications, Inc. [*Database producer*] (IID)
ECI effective conductivity index (SAUS)
ECI Efficiency of Conversion of Ingested Material [*Physiology*]
ECI Efficient Channel Integration (VERA)
ECI Election Commission of India (SAUO)
ECI Electrical Circuit Interrupter (KSC)
ECI Electric Classifieds Incorporated (SAUO)
ECI Electrocerebral Inactivity (MAE)
ECI Electrochemical Interface (SAUS)
ECI electronically controlled injection (SAUS)
ECI Electronic Cascade Impactor [*For aerosol analysis*]
ECI Electronic Communications, Inc.
ECI Electronic Communications Incorporated (SAUO)
ECI Electronic Communications Index
ECI Electronic Communications Instrument (ACAE)
ECI Electronic Computer Ignition [*Automotive engineering*]
ECI Electronic Control Instrumentation
ECI Electronic Controlled Injection [*Automotive engineering*]
ECI Electronic Counters, Incorporated (SAUO)

ECI .... Emergency Coolant Injection [*Nuclear energy*] (NRCH)
ECI .... Employee Cost Index
ECI .... Employment Consultants Institute (COBU)
ECI .... Employment Cost Index (OICC)
ECI .... Encor Energy Corp. Inc. [*Toronto Stock Exchange symbol*] [*Vancouver Stock Exchange symbol*]
ECI .... Enemy Countries Intelligence [*Ministry of Economic Warfare*] [*British*] [*World War II*]
ECI .... Engine Component Improvement (SAUS)
ECI .... Engineering Change Incorporation (AAG)
ECI .... Engineering Change Information
ECI .... Engineering Change Instruction
ECI .... Environmental Carcinogen Information [*Department of Energy*] [*Information service or system*] (IID)
ECI .... Environmental Clearinghouse, Inc. [*An association*] (EA)
ECI .... Eosinophilic Cytoplasmic Inclusion [*Medicine*] (STED)
ECI .... Equipment and Component Index (DNAB)
ECI .... Equipment Change Information
ECI .... Equipment Configuration Item (SAUS)
ECI .... Equity Capital for Industry [*British*]
ECI .... Equity Capital Investment (SAUS)
ECI .... Error Cause Identification [*Military*] (AFM)
ECI .... Essential Controls and Instrumentation [*Nuclear energy*] (NRCH)
ECI .... EURATOM [*European Atomic Energy Community*] Classified Information
ECI .... Euro Capital Invest (SAUO)
ECI .... European Confederation of Independents [*Germany*] (EAIO)
ECI .... European Construction Institute (SAUS)
ECI .... European Cooperation for Informatics (SAUO)
ECI .... European Co-operation in Informatics (SAUS)
ECI .... European Federation of Trade Unions for Energy, Chemical, and Miscellaneous Industries (EA)
ECI .... Evangelism Center International (EA)
ECI .... Evaporative Cooling Institute (EA)
ECI .... Excel Communications, Inc. [*NYSE symbol*] (SAG)
ECI .... Executives Consultants, Inc. [*An association*] (EA)
ECI .... Executives Consultants Incorporated (SAUO)
ECI .... Experimental Cities, Inc. (EA)
ECI .... Export Consignment Identifer (SAUS)
ECI .... Export Consignment Identifying Number (DS)
ECI .... Extended Compressor at Idle [*Automotive term*] (HAWK)
ECI .... Extension Course Institute [*Air Force*]
ECI .... External Call Interface (SAUS)
ECI .... External Charge Injector (UWER)
ECI .... Extracorporeal Irradiation [*Medicine*]
ECIA .... Education Consolidation and Improvement Act [*1981*]
ECIAB .... Executive Council of the Imperial Agricultural Bureau (SAUO)
ECIAB .... Executive Council of the Imperial Agricultural Bureaux (SAUO)
ECIAF .... Eastern Caribbean Institute for Agricultural (or Agriculture) and Forestry (SAUO)
ECIAF .... Eastern Caribbean Institute for Agriculture and Forestry (SAUS)
ECIB .... Extracorporeal Irradiation of Blood [*Medicine*]
ECIC .... Electric Consumers Information Committee (EA)
ECIC .... Electronic Components Information Center [*Battelle Memorial Institute*]
ECIC .... Environmental Carcinogen Information Center (SAUS)
ECIC .... European Centre for International Co-opera tion (SAUS)
ECIC .... Export Credits Insurance Corp. [*Canada*]
ECIC .... Extracranial-Intracranial [*Medicine*]
ECICS .... European Customs Inventory of Chemical Substances (EURO)
ECICS .... Export Credit Insurance Corporation of Singapore (SAUO)
ECID .... electron capture induced decomposition (SAUS)
ECID .... Emission Circular Intensity Differential [*Spectroscopy*]
ECID .... En Route Computer Identification (KSC)
ECIE .... Executive Council on Integrity and Efficiency (AAGC)
ECIEL .... Estudios Conjuntos sobre Integracion Economica Latinoamericana [*Program*]
ECIEL .... Programa de Estudios Conjuntos sobre la Integracion Economica Latinoamericana [*Program of Joint Studies for Latin American Economic Integration*] (EAIO)
ECI Env .... ECI Environmental, Inc. [*Associated Press*]
ECIF .... Electronic Components Industry Federation [*British*]
EC-IGBP .... Executive Committee IGBP (SAUO)
ECII .... Energy Conserving - Second Generation [*Automotive engineering*]
ECII .... Equity Corp. Intl. [*NASDAQ symbol*] (TTSB)
ECII .... Equity Corporation International [*NASDAQ symbol*] (SAG)
ECIIB .... Enemy Civilian Internee Information Bureau [*Military*] (AABC)
ECIIB(Br) .... Enemy Civilian Internee Information Bureau (Branch) [*Military*] (AABC)
ECIICS .... European Conference on Integrated Interactive Computing Systems (SAUS)
EC-IIP .... European Communities-International Investment Partners (SAUO)
ECIL .... ECI Telecom Ltd. [*NASDAQ symbol*] (NQ)
ECIL .... Electronics Corporation of India Limited (SAUO)
ECIL .... Emission Control Information Label [*Automotive engineering*]
ECIL .... emitter coupled injection logic (SAUS)
ECIL .... Expected Confidence Interval Length [*Statistics*]
ECIL .... Extracorporeal Irradiation of Lymph (MAE)
ECILF .... ECI Telecom Ltd. (MHDW)
ECILs .... Emitter Coupled Injection Logics (SAUS)
ECIM .... European Commission for Industrial Marketing (SAUS)
ECIMOT .... European Central Inland Movements of Transport
ECIN .... Electronics Missiles & Communications, Inc. [*NASDAQ symbol*] (COMM)
ECIN .... EMCEE Broadcast Products [*NASDAQ symbol*] (TTSB)
ECIN .... EMCEE Broadcast Products, Inc. [*NASDAQ symbol*] (SAG)
ECI Number ... Export Consignment Identifying Number (SAUS)
ECIO .... European Conference on Integrated Optics (SAUS)
ECIO .... Experiment Computer Input/Output (NASA)
EC-IOA .... European Committee of the International Ozone Association [*See also CEAIO*] (EA)
ECIP .... Energy Conservation Investment Program [*DoD*] (MCD)
ECIP .... European CAD Integration Project (NITA)
ECIP .... European Computer Program Information Centre (SAUS)
ECIP .... European Cooperation in Information Processing (PDAA)
ECIPL .... Engineering Change Identity Parts List [*McDonnell Douglas Aircraft Corp.*]
ECIPS .... Electronic Combat Integrated Pylon System [*Military*] (SEWL)
ECIR .... European Centre for Industrial Relations (EURO)
ECIRC .... European Computer Industry Research Centre (PDAA)
ECIS .... Earth-Centered Inertial System (SAA)
ECIS .... Electrical Cell-Substrate Impedance Sensing [*for cell-culture study*]
ECIS .... Emory Center for International Studies [*Emory University*] [*Research center*] (RCD)
ECIS .... Engineering Careers Information Service (AIE)
ECIS .... Engineering Careers Information System
ECIS .... Environmental Concern Interaction Score
ECIS .... Equipment Control Information System [*Medicine*] (EDAA)
ECIS .... Error Correction Information System [*NASA*]
ECIS .... European Colloid and Interface Society
ECIS .... European Community Information Service (EA)
ECIS .... European Council of International Schools (EA)
ECIS .... Extension and Change of Immigration Status (ADA)
ECISAP .... Electronic Combat International Security Assistance Program [*Military*] (SEWL)
ECISS .... European Committee for Iron and Steel Standards (SAUO)
ECITC .... European Committee for Informations Technology, Testing and Certification (SAUS)
ECITC .... European Committee for IT [*Information Technology*] Testing and Certification (OSI)
ECI Tel .... ECI Telecom Ltd. [*Associated Press*] (SAG)
ECITER .... Electron Cyclotron International Thermonuclear Experimental Reactor (SAUS)
ECITO .... European Central Inland Transport Organization
ECIUSAF .... Extension Course Institute, United States Air Force (SAUS)
ECIWA .... European Committee of Importers and Wholesalers Associations (SAUS)
ECIX .... Electronic Component Information Exchange [*Computer science*] (AGLO)
ECIX .... Electronic Component Interchange (SEWL)
ECIX .... Erman [*Private rail car owner code*]
ECIY .... Earl of Chester's Imperial Yeomanry [*British military*] (DMA)
ECIZ .... Erie County Industrial Development Agency [*Federal Railroad Administration identification code*]
ECJ .... Berlin European [*ICAO designator*] (FAAC)
ECJ .... Court of Justice of the European Communities (DLA)
ECJ .... Erie County Jail (SAUS)
ECJ .... Etudes Publies par des Peres de la Compagnie de Jesus [*A publication*] (BJA)
ECJ .... European Court of Justice (JAGO)
ECJA .... Eastern Collegiate Judo Association (SAUO)
ECJC .... East Central Junior College [*Decatur, MS*]
ECJCC .... European Council of Junior Chambers of Commerce (SAUO)
ECJCS .... European Council of Jewish Community Services (EA)
ECJF .... Emergency Council of Jewish Families (EA)
ECJS .... East Coast Joint Service, Stock [*Railroad*] [*British*] (ROG)
ECK .... Brooklyn Eckfords (SAUS)
ECK .... East Coast Airlines Ltd. [*Kenya*] [*ICAO designator*] (FAAC)
ECK .... Eckankar [*Medicine*] (EDAA)
ECK .... Eckerd Corp. [*NYSE symbol*] (SPSG)
ECK .... Ecology Center Kiel (SAUS)
ECK .... Embryonic Chicken Kidney
ECK .... Emergency Communications Key
ECK .... Engine Change Kit
ECK .... Epidermal Cytokeratin [*Cytology*]
ECK .... Equipment Check (VLIE)
ECK .... Extracellular kalium [*Potassium*] (STED)
ECK .... Peck, MI [*Location identifier*] [*FAA*] (FAAL)
ECKC .... Engineers Club of Kansas City (SAUS)
ECKD .... Extended Count-Key Data (SAUS)
Eckerd .... Eckerd Corp. [*Associated Press*] (SAG)
ECKL .... Eckler Industries [*NASDAQ symbol*] (TTSB)
ECKL .... Eckler Industries, Inc. [*NASDAQ symbol*] (SAG)
Eckler .... Eckler Industries, Inc. [*Associated Press*] (SAG)
ECKLU .... Eckler Industries Unit [*NASDAQ symbol*] (TTSB)
ECKLW .... Eckler Industries Wrrt [*NASDAQ symbol*] (TTSB)
ECKO .... Eddy-Current Killed Oscillator [*Engineering instrumentation*]
ECL .... East Coast Laboratory [*Environmental Science Services Administration*]
ECl .... East Coast India (SAUS)
ECl .... East Coast Ireland (SAUS)
ECL .... Eclectic (WGA)
ECL .... Eclectic Language (SAUS)
ECL .... Eclipse (WDAA)
ECL .... Eclipse Mining [*Vancouver Stock Exchange symbol*]
Ecl .... Eclogues [*of Vergil*] [*Classical studies*] (OCD)
ECL .... Ecolab, Inc. [*NYSE symbol*] (SPSG)
ECL .... Eddy Current Loss [*Electromagnetism*]
ECL .... Edinburgh City Libraries (SAUS)
ECL .... Effluent Charge Law [*1976*]

ECL .... Egyptian Confederation of Labor
ECL .... Electrical (IAA)
ECL .... Electrical Communication Laboratory (SAUS)
ECL .... Electrocardiograph Log (SAUS)
ECL .... Electrochemiluminescence
ECL .... Electrogenerated Chemiluminescence (STED)
ECL .... Electronic Components Laboratory
ecl .... electronic crash locator (SAUS)
ECL .... Ellerman City Liners (SAUS)
ECL .... Emerson College, Boston, MA [*OCLC symbol*] (OCLC)
ECL .... Emitter Control Logic (SEWL)
ECL .... Emitter-Coupled Logic [*Electronics*]
ECL .... emitter-coupled transistor logic (SAUS)
ECL .... Encyclopedia of Comparative Letterforms (SAUS)
ECL .... End Communication Layer (VLIE)
ECL .... Endicott Computation Laboratory (SAUS)
ECL .... Energy Conversion Laboratory [*MIT*] (MCD)
ECL .... Energy Conversion, Limited (SAUS)
ECL .... Engine Coolant Level [*Automotive engineering*]
ECL .... Engineering Change List (MCD)
ECL .... Engineering Computer Laboratory [*University of Southern California*] [*Research center*] (RCD)
ECL .... Engineering Computing Laboratory (SAUO)
ECL .... Engineering Configuration List (MCD)
ECL .... English China Clays International Ltd. [*British*] (IRUK)
ECL .... English Church Leaders [*A publication*]
ECL .... English Comprehension Level [*Army*] (AABC)
ECL .... Enhanced Chemiluminescence [*Analytical chemistry*]
ECL .... Enterochromaffin-Like [*Biochemistry*]
ECL .... Enterprise Container (SAUS)
ECL .... Entertainment Corporation Limited (SAUO)
ECL .... Entry Closed Loop (NASA)
ECL .... Environmental Chemical Laboratory (SAUO)
ECL .... Environmental Chemistry Laboratory [*Environmental Protection Agency*] (GFGA)
ECL .... Environmental Conservation Law [*New York, NY*] [*A publication*]
ECL .... Equipment Component List [*Army*] (AABC)
ECL .... Equipment Configuration List (ACAE)
ECL .... Equipment Control List (ACAE)
ECL .... Equivalent Chain Length [*of fatty acids*] [*Biochemistry*]
ECL .... Equivalent Chlorine [*Analytical Chemistry*]
ECL .... Error Correction Logic (VLIE)
ECL .... Establishment Communications Link (VLIE)
ECL .... Euglobulin Clot Lysis [*Hematology*]
ecl .... Eurocheque International (SAUO)
ECL .... European Calibration Line
ECL .... Europe-Canada Line (SAUS)
ECL .... Eurotec Consultants Ltd. [*Information service or system*] (IID)
ECL .... Evets Communications Ltd. [*Telecommunications service*] (TSSD)
ECL .... Exchange Control Logic (KSC)
ECL .... Execution Control Language (SAUS)
ECL .... Execution Control List (SAUS)
ECL .... Executive Control Language [*Computer science*]
ECL .... Exposure Control Limit [*Environmental science*]
ECL .... Extended Center Line (WDAA)
ECL .... Extended Control Language (SAUS)
ECL .... Extend of Cerebral Lesion [*Neurology*] (DAVI)
ECL .... Extracapillary Lesion [*Cardiology*] (DAVI)
ECL .... Emergency Cooling Limit [*Physics*] (ODA)
ECLA .... Economic Commission for Latin America [*Database originator*] [*Later, ECLAC*] [*United Nations*]
ECLA .... Economic Commission for Latin America and the Caribean (SAUS)
ECLA .... European Clothing Association [*Belgium*] (EAIO)
ECLA .... European Community Library Association (SAUO)
ECLA .... European Company Lawyers' Association (EURO)
ECLA .... Evangelical Church Library Association (EA)
ECLAC .... Economic Commission for Latin America and the Caribbean [*See also CEPAL*] [*Santiago, Chile*] [*United Nations*] (EAIO)
ECLAIR .... Encouraging Agro-Industrial Research -European Collaborative Linkage of Agriculture and Industry trough Research (SAUS)
ECLAIR .... European Collaborative Linkage of Agriculture and Industry through Research [*EC*] (ECED)
ECLAIR .... Extensible Class Library for Information Retrieval (SAUS)
ECLAS .... European Commission Library Automated System [*Database*] [*EC*] (ECED)
ECLAT .... European Computer Leasing and Trading Association (SAUO)
ECLAT .... European Computer Lessors and Trading Association (PDAA)
ECLAT .... European Conference on Laser Treatment (SAUS)
ECLAT Association... European Computer Leasing and Trading Association (SAUO)
ECLATEL .... Empresa Commercial Latinoamericana de Telecommunicaciones [*Latin America Commercial Telecommunications Enterprise*] (PDAA)
ECLC .... Eastern Collegiate Conference (PSS)
ECLC .... Emergency Civil Liberties Committee [*Later, NECLC*] (EA)
ECLE .... European Centre for Leisure and Education (EA)
ECLEC .... Eclectic (ROG)
eclec .... Eclectic (STED)
eclec .... eclecticism (SAUS)
ECLG .... Edit-Compile-Link-and- Go-Zyklus (SAUS)
ECLG .... European Consumer Law Group (EA)
ecli .... Eclipse (BARN)
ecli .... ecliptic (SAUS)
ECLIM .... European Conference on LASER Interaction with Matter and LASER Thermonuclear Fusion (PDAA)
ECLIPS .... European Convention of Library and Information Products and Services (SAUS)
ECLIPS .... Expanded Calculator Link Processing System [*Computer science*]
ECLIPS .... Experimental Cloud Lidar Polot Study (EERA)
ECLIPSE .... Electronic Clipping Service (HGAA)
ECLIS .... Economics and Cultural Landscape Information System (SAUS)
ECLL .... Europe Canada Lakes Line (SAUS)
ECLM .... Economic Community for Livestock and Meat [*See also CEBV*] (EAIO)
ECLM .... Electronic Compass Logic Module [*Automotive navigation systems*]
ECLM .... European Corporation for Laboratory Medicine (SAUO)
ECLO .... Emergency Centre for Locust Operations (EERA)
ECLO .... Emitter-Coupled Logic Operator [*Electronics*]
ECLOF .... Ecumenical Church Loan Fund
ECLP .... Eclipsys Corp. [*NASDAQ symbol*] (NASQ)
ECLP .... Executive Committee of the Labour Party (SAUO)
ECLPS .... Eclipse (ABBR)
ECLPSD .... Eclipsed (ABBR)
ECLPSG .... Eclipsing (ABBR)
EclpSurg .... Eclipse Surgical Technologies, Inc. [*Associated Press*] (SAG)
ECLR .... European Competition Law Review [*A publication*] (DLA)
ECLS .... Environmental Control and Life Support [*NASA*] (NASA)
ECLS .... Export Contact List Services (JAGO)
ECLSS .... Environmental Control and Life Support (SAUO)
ECLSS .... Environmental Control and Life Support Subsystem [*NASA*] (MCD)
ECLSS .... Environmental Control and Life Support System (SAUO)
ECLSS .... Extended Campus Library Services Section [*Association of College and Research Libraries*]
ECLSTCL .... Ecclesiastical (ABBR)
ECLT .... English Comprehensive Level Test [*DoD*]
ECLT .... Euglobulin Clot Lysis Time [*Clinical chemistry*]
ECLTA .... European Computer Lessors and Trading Association (SAUO)
ECL-Technologie... Emitter Coupled Logic (SAUS)
ECLTM .... Eclecticism (ABBR)
ECL-TTL .... Emitter-Coupled Logic/Transistor-Transistor Logic (SAUS)
ECLX .... ELM-Central Rail Leasing [*Private rail car owner code*]
ECM .... ECM Paytel [*Vancouver Stock Exchange symbol*]
ECM .... Ectomycorrhyzae (SAUS)
ECM .... Effective Calls Meter [*Telecommunications*] (NITA)
ECM .... Effective Complex Modulus
ECM .... Electrical Conductivity Measurement
ECM .... Electrically-Commutated Motor [*General Electric Co.*] (PS)
ECM .... Electric Calculating Machine (SAUS)
ECM .... Electric [*or Electronic*] Cipher Machine [*or Coding*]
ECM .... Electric Coding Machine (VLIE)
ECM .... electric control equipment (SAUS)
ECM .... Electric Controller and Manufacturing (IAA)
ECM .... Electric Controller & Manufacturing Company (SAUO)
ECM .... Electric Counter Measure (CCCA)
ECM .... Electrochemical Machining
ECM .... Electrochemical Metallizing (SAUS)
ECM .... Electrochemical Milling (SAUS)
ECM .... electronically commutated motor (SAUS)
ECM .... Electronic Combat Measures [*Military*] (LAIN)
ECM .... electronic control equipment (SAUS)
ECM .... Electronic Control Module [*Instrumentation*]
ECM .... Electronic Countermeasure [*Military*]
ECM .... electronic counter-measurement (SAUS)
ECM .... Elementary Circulation Mechanism
ECM .... Ellipsoid Collector Mirror
ECM .... embedded cluster method (SAUS)
ECM .... Embryonic Chicken Muscle
ECM .... emergency changeover message (SAUS)
ECM .... Emergency Conservation Measures
ECM .... Emerging Company Marketplace (DFIT)
ECM .... Emission Characteristics Monitor
ECM .... Enchondromatosis [*Medicine*] (MELL)
ECM .... Ends Center Matched (SAUO)
ecm .... ends matched, center (SAUS)
ECM .... Energy Center Netherlands (SAUS)
ECM .... Energy Conservation Measure (AAGC)
ECM .... Engine Condition Monitoring
ECM .... Engine Control Module [*General Motors' computer system*]
ECM .... Engineering Change Management (SAUS)
ECM .... Engineering Change Memo (KSC)
ECM .... Engineering Coordination Memorandum [*Military*]
ECM .... Engineers Club of Minnestoa (SAUS)
ECM .... Enhanced Coprocessor Mount, Entity Coordination Management (SAUS)
ECM .... Enterprise Client Migration (GART)
ECM .... Enterprise Commerce Management (VLIE)
ECM .... Enterprise Compliance Management (GART)
ECM .... Enterprise Configuration Manager (VLIE)
ECM .... Enterprise Content Management
ECM .... Entity Connection Management (SAUS)
ECM .... Entity Coordination Management (VERA)
ECM .... Environmental Coal Mining (SAUO)
ECM .... Environmentally Conscious Manufacturing (SAUS)
ECM .... Equipment Condition Monitoring
ECM .... Equivalence Class Mask
ECM .... Equivalent Current Method (SAUS)
ECM .... Error Correcting/Correction Mode (SAUS)
ECM .... Error Correcting Memory (VLIE)
ECM .... Error Correcting Mode (SAUS)
ECM .... Error Correction Mode [*Computer science*]

ECM .... Erythema Chronicum Migrans [*Dermatology*]
ECM .... Esophagocardiomyotomy [*Medicine*] (MELL)
ECM .... Eton College Mission (SAUO)
ECM .... Etude en Commun de la Mediterranee [*Cooperative Investigations in the Mediterranean - CIM*] [*French*] (MSC)
ECM .... European Christian Mission
ECM .... European Christian Movement (SAUO)
ECM .... European Common Market
ECM .... European Conference on Mixing (SAUO)
ECM .... Evangelical and Catholic Mission (EA)
ECM .... Evasive Combat Maneuver (MCD)
ECM .... Event Control Module [*Chromatography*]
ECM .... Exco Capital Markets [*Money brokers*] [*British*]
ECM .... Extended Capacity Memory [*Computer science*] (IAA)
ECM .... Extended Control Mode (VLIE)
ECM .... Extended Conventional Memory [*Computer science*]
ECM .... Extended Core Memory [*Computer science*] (MCD)
ECM .... Extended Core Module [*Computer science*] (IAA)
ECM .... External Cardiac Massage [*Medicine*] (ADA)
ECM .... External Chemical Messenger (DIPS)
ECM .... External Configuration Model (MLOA)
ECM .... External Core Memory (SAUS)
ECM .... External Crystalline Massif [*Geology*]
ECM .... Externally Controlled Machine (VLIE)
ECM .... Extracellular Mass [*Medicine*] (MELL)
ECM .... Extracellular Material [*Physiology*]
ECM .... Extracellular Matrix [*Cytology*]
E/CM3 .... Electrons per Cubic Centimeter
ECMA .... East Coast Magnetic Anomaly [*Geophysics*]
ECMA .... Eastern Cosmetic Manufacturers Association
ECMA .... Electronic Computer Manufacturers Association
ECMA .... Embalming Chemical Manufacturers Association [*Westport, CT*] (EA)
ECMA .... Engineering College Magazines Associated (EA)
ECMA .... Ethylcholine Mustard Aziridinium [*Picrate*] [*Biochemistry*]
ECMA .... European Association for Standardising Information and Communication Systems (SAUO)
ECMA .... European Carton Makers Association (PDAA)
ECMA .... European Catalysts Manufacturers Association [*of the European Council of Chemical Manufacturers' Federation*] (EAIO)
ECMA .... European Collectors and Modellers Association (EAIO)
ECMA .... European Community Marketing Authorisation Number (ECON)
ECMA .... European Computer Manufacturer Association (SAUS)
ECMA .... European Computer Manufacturers (SAUS)
ECMA .... European Computer Manufacturers Address (SAUS)
ECMA .... European Computer Manufacturers Association [*Switzerland*]
ECMAA .... Ethiopian Community Mutual Assistance Association (EA)
ECMALGOL... European Computer Manufacturer Association Algorithmic Language (SAUO)
ECMALGOL... European Computer Manufacturers Association Algorithmic Language
ECM & MR... European College of Marketing and Marketing Research (SAUS)
ECMA PCTE... European Computer Manufacturer's Association Portable Common Tools Environment (HODG)
ECMAST .... European Conference on Multimedia Applications, Services, and Techniques (EURO)
ECMB .... European Committee for Mini-Basketball [*See also CEMB*] [*Germany*] (EAIO)
ECMB .... European Conference on Molecular Biology
ECM/BFT ...... Error Correction Mode/Binary File Transfer [*Computer science*] (PCM)
ECMBR .... European Committee on Milk-Butter-Fat Recording
ECM/BRV ..... Electronic Countermeasures Ballistic Reentry Vehicle [*Military*]
ECMC .... Electric Cable Makers' Confederation [*British*] (BI)
ECMC .... Electronic Circuit Making Equipment (SAUS)
ECMC .... Electronic Countermeasures Environment (SAUS)
ECMC .... Emergency Crisis Management Center (SAUO)
ECMC .... Enhanced Crisis Management Capability (SAUS)
ECMC .... Episcopal Church Missionary Community (EA)
ECMC .... Erie County Medical Center (SAUS)
ECMC .... European Container Manufacturers Committee (EA)
ECMCA .... Eastern Central Motor Carriers Association
EC-MCA .... External Carotid - Middle Cerebral Artery [*Anatomy*]
ECMCS .... European Conference on Mixing and Centrifugal Separation
ecmd .... electronic countermeasures display (SAUS)
ECM-D .... Engineering Change Management-Development
ECME .... Economic Commission for the Middle East [*United Nations*] (DS)
ECME .... Electronic Checkout Maintenance Equipment (IAA)
ECME .... Electronic Circuit-Making Equipment [*Computer science*]
ECME .... Electronic Countermeasures (SAUS)
ECME .... Electronic Countermeasures Environment [*Military*]
ECME .... Electronic Counter Measures Equipment (SAUS)
ECMEA .... European Conference of Meteorological Experts for Aeronautics
ECMED .... Electro-Chemical Moving Electrode Deburring (SAUS)
ECMELINT... Electronic Countermeasures Electronic Intelligence [*Military*] (IAA)
ECMEN .... European Coastal and Marine Ecological Network (SAUS)
ECMEP .... European Committee of Manufacturers of Electrical machines and Power electronics (SAUS)
ECMES .... Electronic Combat Modeling and Evaluation [*Military*] (SEWL)
ECMEX .... Electronic Countermeasures Exercise [*Military*] (NVT)
ECMF .... Electronic Combat Mission Folder (SAUS)
ECMF .... European Community Mortgage Federation [*Brussels, Belgium*] (EA)
ECMHP .... East Coast Migrant Health Project (EA)
e-c mix .... ether-chloroform mixture (SAUS)
ECMJ .... Electronic Counter Measures Jammer (ACAE)
ECML .... Electronic Commerce Modeling Language
ECMM .... European Community Monitoring Mission (EURO)
ECMO .... Electronic Countermeasures Officer [*Navy*] (NVT)
ecmo .... enteric cytopathogenic monkey organ (SAUS)
ECMO .... Enterocytopathogenic Monkey Orphan Virus
ECMO .... Extra-Corporal Membrane Oxynegation (ACAE)
ECMO .... Extracorporeal Membrane Oxidation [*Medicine*] (MELL)
ecmo .... extracorporeal membrane oxygenation (SAUS)
ECMO .... Extracorporeal Membrane Oxygenator [*Respirator*]
ECMob .... Electronic Countermeasures Observer [*Military*]
EC Mode ...... Extended Control Mode (SAUS)
ECMO Virus... Enteric Cytopathogenic Monkey Orphan Virus (SAUS)
ECMP .... Electro-Chemical Machining Process (SAUS)
ECMP .... Electronic Counter Measures Plan (SAUS)
ECMP .... Electronic Countermeasures Program [*Military*]
ECMP .... Enteric-Coated Microspheres of Pancrelipase
ECMP&R ...... EC Master Plan and Roadmap (SAUS)
ECM Process... Electro-Chemical Machining Process (SAUS)
ECMR .... Eastern Contract Management Region [*Air Force*]
ECMR .... Effective Common Mode Rejection [*Electronics*] (IAA)
ECMR .... Electrochemical Metal Removal (SAUS)
ECMR .... Electronic Control of the Mixture Ratio
ECMR .... Equipment Calibration Maintenance Record (MCD)
ECMRA .... European Association for Business Research, Planning, and Development in the Chemical Industry [*Formerly, European Chemical Market Research Association*] [*British*]
ECMRA .... European Chemical Market Research Association (EDCT)
ECMRON ...... Electronic Countermeasures Squadron [*Military*] (IAA)
ECMRWF ..... European Centre for Medium-Range Weather Forecasts (PDAA)
ECMS .... Electronic Copyright Management System (TELE)
ECMS .... Employee Concerns Management System (SAUS)
ECMS .... Engine Condition Monitoring System (SAUS)
ECMS .... Engine Configuration Management System
ECMSA .... Electronics Command Meteorological Support Agency [*Army*] (MCD)
ECM-SIG ...... Environmentally Conscious Manufacturing Strategic Initiative Group (SAUO)
ECMSN .... Electronic Countermeasures Mission [*Military*]
ECMST .... European Centre for Marine Science and Technology (SAUO)
ECMT .... Ecomat, Inc. [*NASDAQ symbol*] (SAG)
ECMT .... Electronic Combat Maintenance Training (SAUS)
ECMT .... European Conference of Ministers of Transport (EAIO)
ECMTNG ...... Electronic Countermeasures Training [*Military*] (NVT)
ECMU .... Electronic Countermeasures Upgrade (SAUS)
ECMU .... Extended Core Memory Unit [*Computer science*] (NVT)
ECM Unit ..... Electronic Controlled Military Unit (SAUS)
ECMWF .... European Center for Medium-Range Weather Forecasting
ECMWF .... European Center (or Centre) for Medium-range Weather Forecasting (or Forecasts) (SAUO)
ECN .... Effective Carbon Number [*Chemistry*]
ECN .... El Condor Resources [*Vancouver Stock Exchange symbol*]
ECN .... Electronic Change Notice (HGAA)
ECN .... Electronic Commerce Network (GART)
ECN .... Electronics Communications Network (GART)
ECN .... Emergency Communication Network [*Highway*] [*Telecommunications*] (TEL)
ECn .... End Connector (SAUS)
ECN .... Energy Research Foundation, Netherlands (SAUS)
ECN .... Engineering Change Notice
ECN .... Engineering Computer Network (SAUS)
ECN .... Environmental Change Network
ECN .... Environmental Communications Network [*Proposed environmental information exchange network*]
ECN .... Epoxy Creosol Novolac [*Resin*]
ECN .... Equipage Category Number (MSA)
ECN .... Equipment Category Number (SAUO)
ECN .... Equivalent Carbon Number (SAUS)
ECN .... Ercan [*Cyprus*] [*Airport symbol*] (OAG)
ECN .... Essential Emergency Communications Network, Minimum (COE)
ECN .... European Chemical News [*Reed Business Publishing Ltd.*] [*Information service or system*] (CRD)
ECN .... European Consulting Network (TELE)
ECN .... European Counter Network (VERA)
ECN .... Explicit Congestion Notification [*Telecommunications*] (ACRL)
ECN .... Export Clearance Number
ECN .... Extended Care Nursery [*Neonatology*] (DAVI)
ECNA .... East Cape News Agency (SAUS)
ECNA .... East Coast of North America (SAUS)
ECNAIS .... European Council of National Associations of Independent Schools [*Denmark*] (EAIO)
ECNAMP ...... East Caribbean Natural Area Management Program (EAIO)
ECNAP .... Eastern Caribbean Natural Area Management Program (EERA)
ECN-APL ...... Equippage Category Numbered Allowance Parts List (DNAB)
EC/NBC .... Environmental Control / Nuclear, Biological & Chemical (SAUS)
ECNC .... Economic Committee of the Nordic Council (SAUO)
ECNC .... El Condor Resources Ltd. [*NASDAQ symbol*] (SAG)
ECNC .... European Centre for Nature Conservation (EERA)
EC-NC/AC.... Earth Coverage to Narrow Coverage / Area Coverage (SAUS)
EC-NCI .... Electron-Capture Negative Chemical Ionization [*Spectrometry*]
ECNDT .... European Council for Nondestructive Testing (EA)
ECNE .... Electric Council of New England (SAUO)
ECNE .... Enterprise Certified NetWare Engineer (SAUS)
ECNE .... Enterprise Certified Novell Engineer (SAUS)
ECNF .... European Central NOTAM [*Notice to Airmen*] Facility [*Military*]
ECNG .... East Central Nuclear Group
ECNL .... Equivalent-Continuous Noise Level (PDAA)
ECNM .... Engineers Club of Northern Minnesota (SAUS)

ECNMC........ Economic
ECNO.......... Engineering Change Notice One (SAUS)
ECNOS......... Eastern Atlantic, Channel and North Sea Orders for Ships [*NATO*] (NATG)
ECNOS......... Engineering Change Notice System (SAUS)
ECNP.......... Environmental Coalition on Nuclear Power (EA)
ECNP.......... European College Of Neuropsychopharmacology (SAUS)
ECNR.......... European Council for Nuclear Research (DCTA)
ECNR.......... Executive Council for National Recovery [*New Deal*]
ECNRT......... Emitter-Controlled Negative Resistance Triode
ECNS.......... Electronic Communication Networks
ECNS.......... Electronic Trading Systems [*Finance*]
ECNSW........ Electricity Commission of New South Wales (SAUO)
ECNSW........ Environment Centre, New South Wales [*Australia*]
ECNT.......... Environment Centre, Northern Territory [*Australia*]
ECNT.......... Environment Centre of the Northern Territory [*State*] (EERA)
EC-number... Enzyme Classification Number
ECO............ Aero Sierra Eco, SA de CV [*Mexico*] [*FAA designator*] (FAAC)
ECO............ Cabinet Economic Committee (SAUO)
ECO............ Complex Relation Object (SAUS)
ECO............ Earth Communications Office (EERA)
ECO............ Earth-Crossing Orbit (SEWL)
ECO............ East Central Oklahoma State University, Ada, OK [*OCLC symbol*] (OCLC)
ECO............ East Coast Airlines [*Australia*] [*ICAO designator*] (FAAC)
ECO............ East Coast Overseas (SAUS)
ECO............ Eastern Counties Omnibus Co. Ltd. [*British*]
ECO............ Echo Bay Mines Ltd. [*AMEX symbol*] (SPSG)
eco............ ecologist (SAUS)
ECO............ Ecology (WDAA)
ECO............ Economic (ABBR)
ECO............ Economic Cooperation Organization
eco............ economics (SAUS)
eco............ economist (SAUS)
ECO............ economizer (SAUS)
ECO............ Ecorail [*Federal Railroad Administration identification code*]
ECO............ Ecumenical Committee on the Andes [*Defunct*] (EA)
ECO............ Effective Citizens Organization [*Later, PAC*] (EA)
ECO............ Electric Cooperative of Oklahoma
eco............ Electron-Coupled Oscillator (IDOE)
ECO............ Electron-Coupled Oscillator
ECO............ Electron Coupled Oscillator, Electronic Commerce Forum (SAUS)
ECO............ Electronic Central Office [*Within network*] [*Telecommunications*] (TEL)
ECO............ Electronic Checkout
ECO............ Electronic Combat Officer (SAUS)
ECO............ Electronic Commerce Forum (SAUO)
ECO............ Electronic-Commerce Outsourcing (GART)
ECO............ Electronic Contact Operate
ECO............ Electronic Contact Operator (SAUS)
ECO............ ELINT Collection Outstation (SAUS)
ECO............ emergency changeover order signal (SAUS)
ECO............ Emergency Commissioned Officer [*British military*] (DMA)
ECO............ Emergency Control Officer (IAA)
ECO............ Emergency Coordinating Officer [*Department of Emergency Management*] (DEMM)
ECO............ Encyclopaedia of Chess Openings
ECO............ Energy Conservation Opportunities [*Federal Energy Administration*]
ECO............ energy conservation opportunity (SAUS)
ECO............ Engine Check-Out (SAUS)
ECO............ Engine Checkout System [*Aerospace*] (AAG)
ECO............ Engine Combustion (NASA)
ECO............ Engine Cutoff [*Aerospace*] (MCD)
ECO............ Engineering Central Office (SAUS)
ECO............ Engineering Change Order
ECO............ Engineering Checkout (ACAE)
ECO............ Engineering Cognizant Office (ACAE)
ECO............ Engineering Control Office [*Telecommunications*] (TEL)
ECO............ Engineers Club of Omaha (SAUS)
ECO............ English Chamber Orchestra
ECO............ Entry Clearance Officer [*Immigration*] (DLA)
ECO............ Environmental Careers Organization (AEPA)
ECO............ Environmental Commission of Ontario [*Canada*] (FOTI)
ECO............ Environmental Communicators Organisation [*British*] (DBA)
ECO............ Environmental Conservation Organization
ECO............ Environmental Control Organization [*Proposed in 1970 by Walter J. Hickel, Secretary of the Interior*]
ECO............ Environmental Crisis Operation [*University of British Columbia*]
ECO............ Environmentally Conscious Oil [*A trademark*] [*Automotive lubricant*]
ECO............ Environment and Conservation Organizations (SAUS)
ECO............ Epichlorohydrin Copolymer [*Organic chemistry*]
ECO............ Epichlorohydrin Ethylene Oxide [*Organic chemistry*] (RDA)
ECO............ Equipment Control Officer [*Air Force*] (AFM)
Eco............ Escherichia Coli [*Microorganism*]
ECO............ Esperantista Centra Oficejo (SAUO)
E/CO.......... Ethylene/Carbon Monoxide (SAUS)
ECO............ European Coal Organization
ECO............ European Consultants Organisation
ECO............ European Consumers Organization [*Belgium*] (EAIO)
ECO............ Ex Caelis Oblatus
ECO............ Exempted by Commanding Officer
ECO............ Experience Critique Orgel [*Nuclear reactor*] [*Italy*]
ECO............ Exploring Career Options [*Test*] (TES)
ECO............ Extra-Contractual Obligations (MARI)
ECO2.......... ECO2, Inc. [*Associated Press*] (SAG)
ECO157........ Escherichia Coli 0157 [*Virulent strain of the bacterium E. coli*] [*Medicine*] (MELL)
ECOA.......... Economic Co-operation Act of 1948 (SAUO)
ECOA.......... Equal Credit Opportunity Act [*1974, 1976*]
ECOA.......... Equal Employment Opportunity Act (TDOB)
ECOA.......... Equipment Company of America (SAUO)
ECOAA......... European Congress on Obstetrical Anaesthesia and Analgesia (SAUS)
Eco & Soc... Economic and Social (SAUS)
ECOC.......... Eastern Counties Omnibus Co. Ltd. [*British*] (DCTA)
ECOC.......... Engineering Club of Oklahoma City (SAUS)
ECOC.......... European Conference on Optical Communications (VERA)
ECOC.......... European Congress on Optical Communication (SAUS)
ECOCAB....... Economic Cabinet [*British*]
ECOCAS....... Economic Community of Central African States (SAUS)
ECOCEN....... Economic Cooperation Center (SAUS)
ECOCEN....... Economic Co-operation Centre for the Asian and Pacific Region (SAUS)
ECOCEN....... Economic Co-ordination Centre for the Asian and Pacific Regions (SAUO)
ECOCO......... Ecological Consortium (EERA)
ECO/COM..... Economic/Commercial Section [*Foreign service*]
ECOCOM...... Economic Commission for Europe [*United Nations*] (DS)
Ecod........... Encoder (SAUS)
ECOD.......... Error Classification, Omission, or Deficiency (MCD)
ECOD.......... Estimated Cost of Damage (MCD)
ECOD.......... Ethoxycoumarin O-Deethylase [*An enzyme*]
ECOD.......... European Consortium for Ocean Drilling (SAUS)
ECOD.......... European Science Foundation Consortium for the Ocean Drilling Program (SAUS)
ECOD.......... Export Control Operations Division (SAUS)
ECODU......... European Control Data Users Association (SAUO)
ECODU......... European Control Data User's Organization (EA)
ECODU......... European Control of Data Users Group (SAUS)
ECODU Association... European Control Data Users Association (SAUO)
ECODUG....... European Control Data Users Group (SAUO)
ECO-ED........ World Congress on Education and Communication on Environment and Development (SAUO)
ECOF.......... Engineering Change Order Factor (MCD)
ECOFIN........ Economic and Financial Council of Ministers [*EC*] (ECED)
ecofuel........ ecology fuel (SAUS)
ECOG.......... Eastern Cooperative Oncology Group [*Research center*] (RCD)
ECoG.......... Electrocorticogram (DIPS)
ECOG.......... Electrocorticogram [*or Electrocorticographic*]
ECoG.......... Electrocorticography (DB)
ECOG.......... Electronics Coordinating Group [*Army*] (RDA)
ECoG.......... Electrocochlegraphy [*Medicine*] (ODA)
ECOGAS....... European Council of General Aviation Support (PIAV)
Ecogen......... Ecogen, Inc. [*Associated Press*] (SAG)
ECOGEO....... Ecogeographer (ABBR)
ecogeo......... ecogeography (SAUS)
ECOGEOC..... Ecogeographic (ABBR)
ECOGEOR..... Ecogeographer (ABBR)
Ecogn.......... Ecogen, Inc. [*Associated Press*] (SAG)
Ecography.... Ecography (SAUS)
ECOIN......... European Core Inventory of Chemicals (SAUO)
ECOIN......... European Core Inventory of Existing Substances [*Chemicals which are exempt from new product regulations*]
ECOL........... American Ecology Corp. [*NASDAQ symbol*] (SAG)
ECOL........... Ecological (SAUS)
ECOL........... Ecologist (SAUS)
ecol............ Ecology (BEE)
ECOL........... Ecology
ECOL........... Environmental Conservation Library of Minnesota (SAUS)
ECOL........... Environmental Council of Lenawee (SAUO)
ECOLA......... Extending Concepts through Language Activities [*Education*] (AEE)
Ecolab......... Ecolab, Inc. [*Associated Press*] (SAG)
Ecol Appl...... Ecological Applications [*A publication*] (PABS)
Ecol Bull...... Ecological Bulletin (MEC)
ECOLC......... Ecologic (ABBR)
ECOLCL........ Ecological (ABBR)
ECOLCLY...... Ecologically (ABBR)
ecolcrit........ ecological criticism (SAUS)
ecolcrit........ ecology critic (SAUS)
ECOLE......... Amer Ecology [*NASDAQ symbol*] (TTSB)
ECOLE......... European Collaboration in Oncology Literature Evaluation (SAUS)
ECOLE......... Evaluation by Computer of the Learning Environment (PDAA)
Ecol Econ..... Ecological Economics [*A publication*] (PABS)
EcolEn......... Ecology & Environment [*Associated Press*] (SAG)
Ecol Eng...... Ecological Engineering [*A publication*] (PABS)
Ecol Freshwat Fish... Ecology of Freshwater Fish [*A publication*] (PABS)
E coli.......... Escherichia Coli (DOG)
Ecol Ind Regions... Ecology of Industrial Regions [*A publication*] (PABS)
Ecol Law Q... Ecology Law Quarterly [*A publication*] (PABS)
Ecol Lett....... Ecology Letters [*A publication*] (PABS)
Ecol Manage Restor... Ecological Management & Restoration [*A publication*] (PABS)
Ecol Mediterr... Ecologia Mediterranea (SAUS)
Ecol Model... Ecological Modelling [*A publication*] (PABS)
Ecol Monogr... Ecological Monographs (SAUS)
Ecol Monogr... Ecological Monographs (journ.) (SAUS)
Ecolo.......... Parti Ecologiste [*Ecologist Party*] [*Belgium*] (PPW)
ECOLO......... Party of Ecologists (SAUO)
Ecolog Econ... Ecological Economics [*A publication*] (JLIT)
ECOLOS....... Ecological Coalition on the Law of the Sea (FOTI)

Ecol Restor... Ecological Restoration [*A publication*] (PABS)
Ecol Soc Am... Ecological Society of America (BARN)
ECOLST........ Ecologist (ABBR)
ECOM........... Army Electronics Command (SAUO)
ECOM........... Electric Computer-Oriented Mail (SAUS)
E-com.......... Electronic Commerce (ITCA)
ECom........... Electronic Commerce Promotion Council of Japan (SAUO)
ECOM........... Electronic Computer-Originated Mail (TIMI)
E-Com.......... Electronic Computer-Originated Mail Services [*Postal Service*] [*United States*] [*Defunct*] (WDMC)
ECOM........... Electronic Computer Originated Mail System (SAUS)
E-COM......... Electronic Mail (SAUS)
ECOM........... Electronics Command [*Fort Monmouth, NJ*] [*Army*]
ECOM........... Especialidades Consumidas por la Seguridad Social [*Ministerio de Sanidad y Consumo*] [*Spain*] [*Information service or system*] (CRD)
ECOM........... Extended Communications Module (SAUS)
ECOM........... United States Army Electronic Command (SAUO)
ECOMA........ European Computer Measurement Association
Eco-Manage Auditing... Eco-Management and Auditing [*A publication*] (PABS)
ECOMARGE... ecology of the continental margins (SAUS)
ECOM Association... European Computer Measurement Association (SAUO)
Ecomat........ Ecomat, Inc. [*Associated Press*] (SAG)
ECOMCON.... Emergency Communications Control [*Fictitious military unit in film "Seven Days in May"*]
ECOMED...... Ecological Mediterranean [*An association*] [*Turkey*] (EAIO)
ECOMINE...... Economics Minerals (NITA)
ECOM LABS... Electronics Command R & D [*Research and Development*] Laboratories [*Army*] (MCD)
ECOMM......... early communications (SAUS)
e-commerce... Electronic Commerce (ADWA)
ECOMMRGN... Eastern Communications Region [*Air Force*]
ECOMOG...... Economic Community Monitoring Group [*West Africa*]
ECOMOG...... Economic Community of West African States Monitoring Group (SAUS)
ECOMOG...... ECOWAS Cease-Fire Monitoring Group (SAUS)
ECOMONOC... Ecological Monitoring of the Oceans Programme (SAUO)
E COMP....... Excellent Companion [*Freemasonry*]
ECOMP........ Federal Coordinator for Ocean Mapping and Prediction [*Marine science*] (OSRA)
ECOMS........ Early Capability Orbital Manned Station
ECOM System... Electronic Computer-Originated Mail System (SAUS)
Econ............ Economic (WDAA)
econ............ Economics (BEE)
Econ............ Economics (DD)
ECON........... Economics (EY)
Econ............ Economies (DIAR)
econ............ economiser (SAUS)
econ............ Economist (ADWA)
Econ............ Economist [*A publication*] (BRI)
ECON........... Economize (SAUS)
ECON........... Economizer (SAUS)
Econ............ Economy (MIST)
ECON........... Economy
ECON........... Electromagnetic Emission Control (IEEE)
ECON........... Electronic Conference (TIMI)
ECON........... Extended Console System (MHDB)
Econ Act...... Economic Activity [*A publication*]
Econ Activ... Economic Activity [*A publication*]
ECONADS..... Economic Advisers
Econ Aff....... Economic Affairs [*A publication*] (JLIT)
Econ Anal Workers' Manage... Economic Analysis and Workers' Management [*A publication*] (JLIT)
Econ Bot...... Economic Botany [*A publication*] (PABS)
Econ Bus Bull... Economic and Business Bulletin [*A publication*] (JLIT)
Econ Bus Educ... Economics and Business Education [*A publication*] (JLIT)
ECONC........ Economic (ABBR)
ECONCL...... Economical (ABBR)
ECONCLY.... Economically (ABBR)
Econ Comput Econ Cybern St... Economic Computation and Economic Cybernetics Studies and Research (SAUS)
Econ Design... Economic Design [*A publication*] (JLIT)
Econ Devel Cult Change... Economic Development and Cultural Change [*A publication*] (JLIT)
Econ Devel Quart... Economic Development Quarterly [*A publication*] (JLIT)
Econ Educ Rev... Economics of Education Review [*A publication*] (JLIT)
ECONET....... Environmental Communications Network
ECONFIG...... Ethernet Configuration [*Computer science*] (AGLO)
Econ Finan Modelling... Economic Financial Modelling [*A publication*] (JLIT)
Econ Finan Rev... Economic and Financial Review [*A publication*] (JLIT)
Econ Forum... Economic Forum [*A publication*] (JLIT)
Econ Geog... Economic Geography (journ.) (SAUS)
Econ Geogr... Economic Geographer (UWER)
Econ Geol.... Economic Geologist (UWER)
Econ Geol.... Economic Geology [*A publication*] (UWER)
Econ Geol.... Economic Geology and the Bulletin of the Society of Economic Geologists (SAUO)
Econ Geol.... Economy Geology and the Bulletin of the Society of Economic Geologists (SAUS)
Econ Hist R... Economic History Review (journ.) (SAUS)
Econ HR...... Economic History Review (journ.) (SAUS)
Econ Ind Democracy... Economic and Industrial Democracy [*A publication*] (JLIT)
Econ Innovation New Tech... Economics of Innovation and New Technology [*A publication*] (JLIT)
Econ Inquiry... Economic Inquiry [*A publication*] (JLIT)
Econ Intell Umt Spec Rep... Economist Intelligence Unit Special Report (journ.) (SAUS)
ECONIS........ Economics Information System (SAUS)
Econ Issues... Economic Issues [*A publication*] (JLIT)
Econ J......... Economic Journal [*A publication*] (BRI)
Econ J......... Economic Journal (journ.) (SAUS)
Econ J Econ Assoc... Economics: The Journal of the Economics Association [*A publication*] (JLIT)
Econ Jour.... Economic Journal (journ.) (SAUS)
Econ Jrnl..... Economic Journal (SAUS)
ECONL......... Economical (ABBR)
Econ Lab Relat Rev... Economic and Labour Relations Review [*A publication*] (JLIT)
Econ Letters... Economics Letters [*A publication*] (JLIT)
EconMin...... Economics Minister
Econ Modelling... Economic Modelling [*A publication*] (JLIT)
Econ Monog... Economic Monographs [*A publication*]
Econ Monogr Econ Soc Aust NZ... Economic Society of Australia and New Zealand. Economic Monograph [*A publication*]
ECONMST.... Economist
Econ N......... Economic News [*A publication*]
Econ Notes... Economic Notes [*A publication*] (JLIT)
ECONOMAN... Effective Control of Manpower (AFM)
Econom Anc Gr... [*The*] Economics of Ancient Greece [*A publication*] (OCD)
ECONOMET... Econometric (ABBR)
economet.... econometrician (SAUS)
economet.... econometrics (SAUS)
economet.... econometrist (SAUS)
Econometric Rev... Econometric Reviews [*A publication*] (JLIT)
Economy Hist... Economy and History [*A publication*] (JLIT)
Economy Soc... Economy and Society [*A publication*] (JLIT)
Econ O/P Tr... Economy Output Transformer (SAUS)
Econ Paps... Economic Papers [*A publication*]
Econ Perspect... Economic Perspectives [*A publication*] (JLIT)
Econ Philos... Economics and Philosophy [*A publication*] (JLIT)
Econ Plann... Economic Planning (Montreal) [*A publication*] (PABS)
Econ Planning... Economics of Planning [*A publication*] (JLIT)
Econ Politics... Economics and Politics [*A publication*] (JLIT)
Econ Pol Rev... Economic Policy Review [*A publication*] (JLIT)
Econ R......... Economic Review (journ.) (SAUS)
Econ Rec..... Economic Record [*A publication*] (JLIT)
Econ Soc Rev... Economic and Social Review [*A publication*] (JLIT)
ECONST....... Economist (ABBR)
Econ Stand (CCH)... Economic Standards (Commerce Clearing House) [*A publication*] (DLA)
Econ Stud.... Economic Studies (journ.) (SAUS)
Econ Stud Quart... Economic Studies Quarterly [*A publication*] (JLIT)
Econ Survey... Economic Survey of Ancient Rome [*A publication*] (OCD)
ECON System... Extended Console System (SAUS)
Econ Systems... Economic Systems [*A publication*] (JLIT)
Econ Systems Res... Economic Systems Research [*A publication*] (JLIT)
Econ Theory... Economic Theory [*A publication*] (JLIT)
Econ Tr........ Economy Transformer (SAUS)
Econ Transition... Economics of Transition [*A publication*] (JLIT)
ECONY......... Economy (ABBR)
ECONZ......... Economize (ABBR)
ECONZD....... Economized (ABBR)
ECONZG....... Economizing (ABBR)
ECONZR....... Economizer (ABBR)
ECOO........... Educational Computing Organization of Ontario (EDAC)
ECOOP......... European Conference on Object Orientated Programming (VERA)
ECOP........... Electronic Co-Pilot (SAUS)
ECOP........... Energy Conservation Opportunity Program (SAUS)
ECOP........... Extension Committee on Organization and Policy [*Department of Agriculture*] (EA)
ECO/PAHO/WHO... Pan American Center for Human Ecology and Health (SAUO)
ECO/PAHWHO... Pan American Center for Human Ecology and Health (SAUO)
ECOPC......... Experimental Changes of Practice Committees [*British Post Office*] (PDAA)
ECOPHYS..... Ecophysiologic (ABBR)
ecophys....... ecophysiologist (SAUS)
ecophys....... ecophysiology (SAUS)
Ecoplan International... Centre for Economic Research and Industrial Planning (SAUO)
ECOPS......... European Committee on Ocean and Polar Science
Eco Pty........ Ecology Party (SAUO)
ECOR........... Economic Order (SAUS)
ECOR........... eddy correlation (SAUS)
ECOR........... Engineer Change Order Request (AAG)
ECOR........... Engineering Commission on Ocean Resources (SAUS)
ECOR........... Engineering Committee on Oceanic Research (USDC)
ECOR........... Engineering Committee on Oceanic Resources [*Later, SUT*] [*United Nations*]
ECOR........... Error Control Register [*Computer science*] (IAA)
EcoR........... Escherichia Coli RY (SAUS)
ECOR........... estimate of cost and obligation requirements (SAUS)
ECorA.......... Erythrina Corallodendron Agglutinin (SAUS)
ECORC......... Eastern Cereal and Oilseed Research Centre [*Ottawa, Canada*]
Ecorep......... European Confederation of Real Estate Professions (SAUO)
EcoR I.......... Escherichia Coli 1 RY-13 I [*Microbiology*] (UWER)
ECORIB........ Ecologically-Fueled Rigid Inflatable Boat
EcoR II......... Escherichia Coli II R-245 [*Microbiology*] (UWER)
EcoRISK....... Ecological Research Information System Kiel (SAUS)
ECORQ......... Economic Order Quantity (SAUS)
ECORS......... Eastern Counties Operational Research Society (PDAA)

EcoR V......... Escherichia Coli V [*Microbiology*] (UWER)
ECOS.......... Education and Career Opportunities System
ECOS.......... Electrical Check-Out System
ECOS.......... EMSP Common Operating System (SAUS)
ECOS.......... Energy Conservation and Substitution (SAUS)
ECOs.......... Engineering Change Orders (SAUS)
ECOS.......... Environmental Compliance Online System (SAUS)
ECOS.......... Environmental Council of the States (EPAT)
ECOS.......... Evans Environmental [*NASDAQ symbol*] (TTSB)
ECOS.......... Experiment Computer Operating System (MCD)
ECOS.......... Experiment Computer Operational Software (SAUS)
ECOS.......... Extended Communications Operating System (HGAA)
ECOS.......... Extracardiac Obstructive Shock [*Medicine*] (MELL)
ECOSA......... Economic Community of South Africa (SAUS)
ECOSA......... European Conference on Optical Systems and Applications (PDAA)
ECOSA......... European Consumer Safety Association (EURO)
ECOSAL....... Equipo de Conferencias Sindicales de America Latina [*Committee for Latin American Trade Union Conferences*]
ECOSAT....... Ecosystems Science and Technology (SAUS)
EcoSci......... EcoScience Corp. [*Associated Press*] (SAG)
ECOSEC....... European Cooperation Space Environment Committee
ECO Signal... Electronic Contact Operate Signal (SAUS)
ECO Signal... Emergency Changeover Order Signal (SAUS)
ECOSOC....... Committee of Experts on the Transport of Dangerous Goods of the United Nations Economic and Social Council [*RSPA*] (TAG)
ECOSOC....... Economic and Social Committee [*EC*] (ECED)
ECOSOC....... Economic and Social Council [*ICSU*] [*United Nations*]
EcoSoil........ Eco Soil Systems, Inc. [*Associated Press*] (SAG)
ECOSOL....... European Centre of Studies on Linear Alkylbenzene [*Belgium*] (EAIO)
Ecosph......... Ecosphere (UWER)
ECOSS......... European Conference on Surface Science
EcoSSP........ Escherichia Coli Single-Stranded Protein
ECOST......... European Cooperation on Science and Technology [*British*]
ECOSY......... Exclusive Correlation Spectroscopy (SAUS)
ECOSYS....... Ecosystem (ABBR)
eco system... ecological system economic system (SAUS)
ECO System... Engine Chek-Out System (SAUS)
ECOTAGE..... Ecological Sabotage [*Tactic used by radical environmentalists*]
ECOTEC....... Economy Compact Technology [*Automotive engines*]
Eco-Tech...... Economic-Technology (SAUS)
ECOTOX....... Ecotoxicological Database Retrieval System (AEPA)
Ecotoxicol Environ Saf... Ecotoxicology and Environmental Safety (journ.) (SAUS)
EcoTyre........ EcoTyre Technologies, Inc. [*Associated Press*] (SAG)
ecou............ electric clip-on unit (SAUS)
ecou............ electronic clip-on unit (SAUS)
ECOWAF...... Economic Community of West African States (SAUO)
ECOWARM... European Committee for Water Resources Management (SAUO)
ECOWAS...... Economic Commission of West African States (EERA)
ECOWAS...... Economic Community of West African States [*Treaty signed May 28, 1975*]
ECOX........... Eagle Cotton Oil [*Private rail car owner code*]
ECOX........... Educational Communications on Exhibit [*Commercial firm*]
ECOX........... Engineered Carbons [*Private rail car owner code*]
ECOZ........... Ecolab [*Federal Railroad Administration identification code*]
ECP............. Central Newspapers, Inc. Class A [*NYSE symbol*] (SPSG)
ECP............. Congolese Progressive Students [*Zaire*] (PD)
EC/P............ Early Childhood/Primary
ECP............. Early Childhood Programs (SAUO)
ECP............. Early Churches in Palestine [*A publication*] (BJA)
ECP............. East Cleveland Public Library, East Cleveland, OH [*OCLC symbol*] (OCLC)
ECP............. Eastman Chemical Products, Inc. (SAUO)
ECP............. Eclipse Capital Corp. [*Toronto Stock Exchange symbol*]
ECP............. Edinburgh County Police [*British*] (ROG)
ECP............. Education Center Publications (MCD)
ECP............. Effective Cable Pair (SAUS)
ECP............. Effective Core Potential
ECP............. Effector Cell Precursor [*Medicine*] (DMAA)
ECP............. Efficient Component Pricing [*Business term*] (ECON)
ECP............. Egyptian Communist Party [*Political party*] (PD)
ECP............. Electrical Contact Plate
ECP............. Electrical Control Package
ECP............. Electrically Compensated Pyrometer
ECP............. Electrically-Conducting Polymer
ECP............. Electric Current Perturbation [*Method*] [*Southwest Research Institute*]
ECP............. Electric Power Converter (ACAE)
ECP............. Electrochemical Processing (SAUS)
ECP............. Electro-Conductive Plastic
ECP............. Electromagnetic Capability Program (SAUS)
ECP............. Electromagnetic Compatibility Program [*Air Force*]
ECP............. Electromagnetic Containerless Processing [*Materials processing*]
ECP............. Electron Channeling Pattern (MCD)
ECP............. Electronic Calculating Punch
ECP............. Electronic Channelling Pattern (SAUS)
ECP............. Electronic Check Presentment [*Finance*]
ECP............. Electronic Circuit Protector
ECP............. Electronic Coding Pad (SAUS)
ECP............. Electronic Color Prepress (DGA)
ECP............. Electronic Combat Pilot (SAUS)
ECP............. Electronic Commerce Platform (FOTI)
ECP............. Electronic Control Products (MUGU)
ECP............. Electronics and Computing for Peace (SAUO)
ECP............. Electronmagnetic Compatibility Program (SAUS)
ECP............. Electrostatic Card Printer (SAUS)
ECP............. Eligible Capital Property (FOTI)
ECP............. Elliptical Cavity Pump
ECP............. Emergency Change Package (SAUS)
ECP............. Emergency Command Precedence (DNAB)
ECP............. Emergency Communications Plan (NUCP)
ECP............. Emergency Conservation Program [*Department of Agriculture*] (EGAO)
ECP............. Emitter-Coupled Pair [*Electronics*] (IAA)
ECP............. Emitter Current Programmer (MELL)
ECP............. Employee Communications Program (SAUS)
ECP............. Employee Concerns Program (SAUS)
ECP............. Emulator Control Program (IAA)
ECP............. Encryption Control Protocol (SAUS)
ECP............. Endocardial Potential (DB)
ECP............. Endogenous Circadian Phase [*Physiology*]
ECP............. Energy Charge Potential
ECP............. Energy Conversion Program (SAUS)
ECP............. Engagement Control Panel (MCD)
ECP............. Engineered Coated Products, Inc. (SAUO)
ECP............. Engineering Change Package (SAUS)
ECP............. Engineering Change Program
ECP............. Engineering Change Proposal
ECP............. Engineering Change Proposed (SAUS)
ECP............. Engineering Control Proposal
ECP............. English Centre of PEN (EAIO)
ECP............. English Collective of Prostitutes (DI)
ECP............. Enhanced Call Processing [*Telecommunications*] (ITD)
ECP............. Enhanced Capabilities Port [*Computer science*]
ECP............. Enhanced Capability Port (SAUS)
ECP............. Enhanced Communication Port [*Microsoft Corp.*]
ECP............. Enhanced Communication Protocol (SAUS)
ECP............. Enhanced/Extended Capabilities Port (SAUS)
ECP............. Enkephalin-Containing Polypeptide [*Physiological chemistry*]
ECP............. Enlisted Commissioning Program [*Military*] (DNAB)
ECP............. Enteric Cytopathogenic Swine Orphan Virus (DB)
ECP............. Entry Control Point (MCD)
ECP............. Environmental Compliance Program (SAUS)
ECP............. Eosinophil Cationic Protein [*Immunology*]
ECP............. Equipment Collecting Point [*Military*] [*British*]
ECP............. Equipment Conversion Package [*Telecommunications*] (TEL)
ECP............. Erosion Control Plan [*Environmental science*] (COE)
ECP............. Erythrocyte Coproporphyrin [*Hematology*] (MAE)
ECP............. Escherichia Coli Polypeptides
ECP............. Estimated Critical Position [*Nuclear energy*] (NRCH)
ECP............. Estonian Communist Party (SAUO)
ECP............. Estradiol Cyclopentanepropionate [*Endocrinology*]
ECP............. Estradiol cypionate (SAUS)
ECP............. Ethiopian Communist Party [*Political party*] (PD)
ECP............. Euro-Commercial Paper [*Finance*]
ECP............. European Cancer Prevention Organization (SAUO)
ECP............. European Committee of Crop Protection
ECP............. European Organization for Cancer Prevention Studies
ECP............. European Organization for Cooperation in Cancer Prevention Studies (SAUO)
ECP............. Evangeli Christi Proedicatur [*Preacher of the Gospel of Christ*] [*Latin*] (ROG)
ECP............. Evaporative Cooling Processor
ECP............. Examiner of Commercial Practices (SAUS)
ECP............. Excessive Cross-Posting (SAUS)
ECP............. Exchange Core Polarization (SAUS)
ECP............. Executive Control Program [*Computer science*]
ECP............. Exemplary Course Project
ECP............. Exessive CrossPosting (SAUS)
ECP............. Expandable Communications Processor (SAUS)
ECP............. Explicitly Coded Program (MCD)
ECP............. Extended Capabilities Port (SAUS)
ECP............. Extended Capability Port [*Telecommunications*] (PCM)
ECP............. Extended Coherent Processing (SEWL)
ECP............. External Cardiac Pressure [*Medicine*] (DMAA)
ECP............. External Casing Packer (SAUS)
ECP............. External Communications Processor (SAUS)
ECP............. External Compliance Programs [*Environmental Protection Agency*] (GFGA)
ECP............. External Control Panel
ECP............. External Counterpulsation [*Medicine*]
ECP............. Extracellular Products
ECP............. Free Cytoprophyrin in Erythrocytes [*Hematology*] (DAVI)
ECPA........... Early Childhood Program Aid
ECPA........... Effective Cell Pair Area [*Electrochemistry*]
ECPA........... Electric Consumer Protection Act of 1986
ECPA........... Electronic Communications Piracy Act of 1986
ECPA........... Energy Conservation and Production Act [*1976*] (MCD)
ECPA........... Energy Consumers and Producers Association (EA)
ECPA........... Evangelical Christian Publishers Association (EA)
ECPA........... Expert Committee on Post Adjustments [*United Nations*]
ECPAC......... East County Performing Arts Center (SAUS)
ECPAT......... End Child Prostitution and Trafficking [*An association*]
ECPAT......... End Child Prostitution in Asian Tourism [*An association*]
ECPC........... Economic Classification Policy Committee [*BTS*] (TAG)
ECPC........... Edge Connector Programmable Cartridge
ECPC........... Enlarged Committee for Program and Coordination [*United Nations Development Program*]
ECPC........... Ethnic Cultural Preservation Council [*Also known as Association of North American Museums, Libraries, Archives, Cultural Centers, and Fraternal Organizations*] (EA)

ECPC........... European Civil Peace Corps (EURO)
ECPC........... European Communist Party Conference
ECPC........... Experimental Climate Prediction Center
ECPCDP....... Euro-Commercial Paper and Certificates of Deposit Programme [*Finance*]
ECPCM......... East Coast passive continental margin (SAUS)
ECPCR......... Expression Cassette Polymerase Chain Reaction [*Genetics*]
ECPD........... Engineers Council for Professional Development [*Later, ABET*] (EA)
ECPD........... Export Cargo Packing Declaration (DS)
ECPD........... External Counterpressure Device [*Medicine*] (MELL)
ECPE........... European Centre of Public Enterprise (EAIO)
ECPE........... External Combustion Piston Engine (PDAA)
ECPECC........ Ecuadorian Committee of the Pacific Economic Cooperation Council
ECP/EPP...... Enhanced Capabilities Port/Enhanced Parallel Port (SAUS)
ECPG........... electrochemical potential gradient (SAUS)
ECPGB......... Entrance Cable Protector Ground Bar (SAUS)
ECPGR......... Expert Committee on Plant Gene Resources [*Canadian Agricultural Services Coordinating Committee*]
ECPH........... [*The*] Electronic Communications Privacy Act
ECPH........... European Committee of Private Hospitals [*Belgium*] (EAIO)
ECPHIN........ European Community Pharmaceutical Information Network (SAUO)
ECPI........... Electronic Computer Programming (SAUS)
ECPI........... Electronic Computer Programming Institute [*Ceased operation, 1976*]
ECPI........... European Consumer Price Index (EURO)
ECPIP.......... Electric Companies' Public Information Program
ECPIU.......... Electronic Circuit Plug-In Unit
ECPM........... Environmental Control and Processing Module (SAUS)
ECPMAOA...... Executive Committee's Panel on Meteorological Aspects of Ocean Affairs [*WMO*] (MSC)
ECPNL......... Equivalent Continuous Perceived Noise Level (PDAA)
ecpnl........... equivalent continuous preceived noise level (SAUS)
ECPO........... Eastern College Personnel Officers
ECPO........... Engineering Computer Processing Operation (ACAE)
ecpo............ enteric cytopathogenic porcine orphan (SAUS)
ECPO........... Enteric Cytopathogenic Porcine Orphan Virus
ECPO........... Environmental Characterization Projects Office (SAUS)
ECPOG......... Electrochemical Potential Gradient
EC Pole........ Eastern Cedar Pole (SAUS)
ECPO Virus... Enteric Cytopathogenic Porcine Orphan Virus (SAUS)
ECPP........... Enterprise Collaborative Processing Portals (VLIE)
EC-PPC........ Epoxy Chopped Pre-Preg Compounds (SAUS)
ECPR........... Electrically Calibrated Pyroelectric Radiometer
ECPR........... European Confederation of Public Relations [*France*] (EAIO)
ECPR........... European Conference on Psychosomatic Research (SAUO)
ECPR........... European Consortium for Political Research [*Colchester, Essex, England*] (EAIO)
ECPR........... External Cardiopulmonary Resuscitation [*Medicine*] (MELL)
ECPRD......... European Centre for Parliamentary Research and Documentation [*See also CERDP*] [*Luxembourg, Luxembourg*] (EAIO)
ECPR Filter... Electrically Calibrated Pyroelectric Filter (SAUS)
ECPS........... Eastern Counties Poultry Society (SAUO)
ECPS........... Effective Candlepower Second [*Photography*] (WDMC)
ECPS........... Electronic Compendium of Pharmaceuticals and Specialties (SAUS)
ECP-S.......... Engineering Change Proposal-Software
ECPS........... Engineering Change Proposal System (DNAB)
ECPS........... English Connemara Pony Society (DBA)
ECPS........... Enhanced Chemical Protection Suit (ACAE)
ECPS........... Environment and Consumer Protection Service [*EEC*] (DS)
ECPS........... European Centre for Population Studies (EA)
ECPS........... European Council for Payments Systems
ECPS........... Expanded Control Program Store (SAUS)
ECPs........... Extended Capabilities Ports [*Computer science*]
ECPS........... Extended Control Program Support [*IBM Corp.*]
ECPS........... Extracellular Polysaccharide (SAUS)
ECPSA......... European Consumer Product Safety Association [*EC*] (ECED)
ECP System... Electronic Control and Power System (SAUS)
ecpt............ egress cockpit procedure trainer (SAUS)
ECPT........... Electronic Coin Public Telephone (VLIE)
ECPT........... Ethylcamptothecin [*Antineoplastic drug*]
ECPT........... European Committee for the Prevention of Torture
ECPT........... European Confederation for Physical Therapy (EAIO)
ECPT........... European Conference of Postal and Telecommunications Administrations (SAUO)
ECPTA......... European Conference of Postal and Telecommunication Administrations (SAUS)
ECPTT......... Electronic Combat Part Task Trainer (ACAE)
ECPWS......... Engineering Change Proposal Work Statement (AAG)
ECPY........... Electronic Control Assembly - Pitch and Yaw (KSC)
ECQAC......... Electronic Components Quality Assurance Committee (BARN)
ECQAC......... Electronics Component Quality Assessment Committee (SAUS)
ECQB........... Electrochemical Quartz Crystal Balance (AAEL)
ECR............. Air Charter Express AS [*Norway*] [*ICAO designator*] (FAAC)
ECR............. Canada Law Reports, Exchequer Court [*A publication*] (DLA)
ECR............. Earth Centered Rotating (SAUS)
ECR............. Earth Centered Rotational (ACAE)
ECR............. East Coast Railway [*Indian Railway*] (TIR)
ECR............. East Coast Repository at LDEO (SAUO)
ECR............. Eastern Counties Railway [*British*] (ROG)
ECR............. Economic Cleanup Responsibility Act (SAUS)
ECR............. Economy Cylinder Rating [*Engine technology*]
ECR............. Edit, Count, Recode (IAA)
ECR............. Edit, Count, Record (SAUS)
ECR............. Effective Cleaning Radius (ABAC)
ECR............. Efficient Consumer Response [*Marketing incentive*] (ECON)
ECR............. Electrical Chart Recorder (TIMI)
ECR............. Electrical Contact Resistance (PDAA)
ECR............. Electrochemical Reaction
ECR............. Electro-Chemical Resistant [*Automotive cooling systems*]
ECR............. Electro-Conductive Resin (SAUS)
ECR............. Electron Cyclotron Resolution (SAUS)
ECR............. Electron Cyclotron Resonance (IEEE)
ECR............. Electron Cyclotron Response (SAUS)
ECR............. Electronic Cash Register
ECR............. Electronic Character Recognition (VLIE)
ECR............. Electronic Classroom [*Training term*] (LPT)
ECR............. Electronic Combat and Reconnaissance (SAUS)
ECR............. Electronic Control Receiver (SAUS)
ECR............. Electronic Control Relay (IEEE)
ECR............. Electronic Countermeasures and Reconnaissance
ECR............. Electronics Combat Reconnaissance
ECR............. Embedded Computer Resources (MCD)
ECR............. Embossed Character Reader [*Banking*]
ECR............. Emergency Chemical Restraint (DAVI)
ECR............. Emergency Combat Readiness (AAG)
ECR............. Emergency Conference Room (SAUS)
ECR............. Emergency Coolant Recirculation [*Nuclear energy*] (NRCH)
ECR............. Emergency Cooling Recirculation (SAUS)
ECR............. Emitted Coherent Radiation
ECR............. Employee Concerns Reporting (SAUS)
ECR............. Endogenous Circadian Rhythm (PDAA)
ECR............. Enemy Contact Report [*NATO*] (NATG)
ECR............. Energy Consumption Rate
ECR............. Energy Control Report [*Navy*]
ECR............. Enforcement Case Review (EEVL)
ECR............. engine-control room (SAUS)
E CR............ Engineer Commander [*Navy*] [*British*] (ROG)
ECR............. Engineering Change Report (KSC)
ECR............. Engineering Change [*or Correction*] Request [*or Requirement*]
ECR............. Engineering Change Requirement (SAUS)
ECR............. Engineering Change Review (SAUS)
ECR............. Engineering Concept Review
ECR............. Enterprise Customer Resource (VLIE)
ECR............. Entry Control Roster (MCD)
ECR............. Environmental Characterization Report (SAUS)
ECR............. Environmental Control Report [*A publication*] (EAAP)
ECR............. Environmental Criteria Report (ACAE)
ECR............. Equipment Control Record (MCD)
ECR............. Error Cause Removal [*Quality control*]
ECR............. Error Control Receiver (IEEE)
ECR............. Error Correcting Routine (SAUS)
ECR............. Estimate Change Request (NRCH)
ECR............. European Chemical Reports (SAUS)
ECR............. European Collaborative Radar (SAUS)
ECR............. European Commercial Register [*EC*] (ECED)
ECR............. European Court Reports [*European Communities*] [*A publication*] (DLA)
ECR............. Except Change Route to Read [*Aviation*] (FAAC)
ECR............. Excess Carrier Ratio (IAA)
ECR............. Exchequer Court Reports [*Canada Department of Justice*] [*Information service or system*] (CRD)
ECR............. Execute Command Request (KSC)
ECR............. Executive Communication Region (SAUS)
ECR............. Executive Control Routines
ECR............. Executive Council Resolution (SAFN)
ECR............. Experimental Coherent RADAR (MCD)
ECR............. Export Control Regulations [*Department of Commerce*]
ecr.............. extended chromosome region (SAUS)
ECR............. Extended Coverage Range [*Insurance*] (IAA)
ECR............. External Channels Ratio
ECR............. External Control Register (OA)
ECR............. Extraordinary Contractual Relief (AAGC)
ECR............. Extraordinary Contractual Relief Reporter [*A publication*] (AAGC)
ECRA........... East Coast Racing Association (SAUO)
ECRA........... Economic Cleanup Responsibility Act (COE)
ECRA........... Electric Car Racing Association
ECR/A.......... Engineering Change Request/Authorization (AFM)
ECRA........... Environmental Cleanup and Responsibility Act [*1983*] (ERG)
ECRA........... European Car Rental Association (SAUO)
ECRA........... Excess and Casualty Reinsurance Association (EA)
ECRB........... Engineering Change Review Board (ACAE)
ECRB........... Export Control Review Board
ECRB........... Extensor Carpi Radialis Brevis [*Anatomy*]
ECRC........... Early Childhood Resource Center
ECRC........... Earth Colonization Research Center (SAUS)
ECRC........... Eastern Canada Response Corporation (FOTI)
ECRC........... Elderly Care Research Center [*Case Western Reserve University*] [*Research center*] (RCD)
ECRC........... Electricity Council Research Center [*British*] (MCD)
ECRC........... Electronic Commerce Resource Center (VLIE)
ECRC........... Electronic Component Reliability Center [*Battelle Memorial Institute*] (MCD)
ECRC........... Electronic Components Research Center
ECRC........... Engineering College Research Council (EA)
ECRC........... Engineering Contracts Requirement Committee (SAUO)
ECRC........... Environmental and Contaminants Research Center [*U.S. Geological Survey*]
ECRC........... Equipment Category Rollup Code [*Army*]
ECRC........... European Community Research Council
ECRC........... European Computer Industry Research Centre
ECRC........... European Computer Research Centre (SAUS)

ECR-CVD...... Electron-Cyclotron Resonance - Chemical Vapor Deposition (SAUS)
ECRD.......... Eddy Current Resonance Digitizing (SAUS)
ECRDC........ Electronic Component Research and Development Center (SAUS)
ECRDC........ Electronic Component Research and Development Centre (SAUO)
ECRDC........ Electronic Cornponent Research and Development Center (SAUS)
ECRDG........ Electronic Component Research and Development Grant [*Canada*]
ECRE........... Edinburgh Centre of Rural Economy [*British*] (CB)
ECRE........... European Consultation on Refugees and Exiles
ECRE........... European Council on Refugees and Exiles
ECREA......... European Conference of Radiotelegraphy Experts for Aeronautics
Ec Rec......... Economic Record [*A publication*]
ECREEA....... European Conference of Radio and Electronic Equipment Association (CIST)
ECRF........... Edited Collections Report File [*IRS*]
ECRF........... Electron Cyclotron Resonance Frequency (SAUS)
ECRF........... Essential Commodities Reserve Fund (SAUO)
ECRF........... Externally Coupled Resonator Filter (MCD)
ECRH........... Electron Cyclotron Resonance Heating (MCD)
ECRI............ East Central Reservoir Investigation [*Department of the Interior*] (GRD)
ECRI............ Economic Cycle Research Institute
ECRI............ Emergency Care Research Institute (EA)
ECRI............ Exemplary Center for Reading Instruction [*Maine*] (EDAC)
ECRIB.......... European Commissary Resale Item Board (SAUO)
ECRIE.......... European Center for Research and Information Exchange [*Belgium*] (EAIO)
ECRIM......... Engineering Construction and Related Industries Manpower [*British*]
ECRL........... East Central Regional Library System [*Library network*]
ECRL........... Eastern Caribean Regional Library (SAUO)
ECRL........... European Council for Rural Law (SAUO)
ECRL........... Extensor Carpi Radialis Longus [*Muscle or tendon*] [*Anatomy*] (DAVI)
ECRM.......... ECRM, Inc. [*NASDAQ symbol*] (SAG)
eCRM.......... e-Customer Relationship Management
ECRM.......... Electronic Character Recognition Machine (DGA)
ECRM.......... Euronorm Certified Reference Material
ECRO........... Erection Counter Readout
ECRO........... European Chemoreception Research Organization [*Research center*] [*Switzerland*] (IRC)
ECROC......... Engineering Council Regional Organisation Committee (ACII)
ECRO Virus... Enteric Cytopathogenic Rodent Orphan Virus (SAUS)
ECRP........... Earcap Reference Point (SAUS)
ECRP........... Employee Concerns/Response Program (SAUS)
ECRP........... Energy Coal and Recycling Page (SAUO)
ECRR........... Engineering Change Request and Record (MCD)
ECRR........... European Conference on Radio Relay Systems (SAUO)
ECRS........... Earthwork/Center for Rural Studies (EA)
ECRS........... East Chapman Research Station (SAUO)
ECRS........... East Coast Radar System (SAUS)
ECRS........... Economic and Contingency Reserve Stock [*Military*]
ECRs........... edited cloud reports (SAUS)
ECRS........... Embedded Computer Resource Standards (SAUS)
ECRS........... Empty Car Routing System (SAUS)
ECRs........... Enemy Contact Reports (SAUS)
ECRS........... Equipment Control Record System [*Army*]
ECRS........... Event Classification and Reporting System (SAUS)
ECRT........... Emergency Crisis Response Team (CARL)
ECRT........... European Confederation of Retail Tobacconists [*Luxembourg*] (EA)
ECRU........... Eastern Counties Rugby Union (SAUO)
ECRU........... Emergency Communications Research Unit [*Carleton University*] [*Canada*] [*Research center*] (RCD)
ECRV........... Extended Curve (VLIE)
ECRWP........ East Chestnut Ridge Waste Pile (SAUS)
ECRX........... Econo-Rail [*Private rail car owner code*]
e-cs-........... Czechoslovakia [*MARC geographic area code*] [*Library of Congress*] (LCCP)
ECS............. Early Childhood Services (ADA)
ECS............. Eccentric Shaft (SAUS)
ECS............. Echo Control Subsystem [*Telecommunications*] (TEL)
ECS............. Ecological Classification System (SAUO)
ECS............. Economic Census Staff [*Census*] (OICC)
ECS............. Economic Committe for Scotland (SAUO)
ECS............. Economics (ABBR)
ECS............. Economy Class Syndrome [*Thromboembolism resulting from cramped seating*]
ECS............. Ecos Resources [*Vancouver Stock Exchange symbol*]
ECS............. Editorial Consulting Services (SAUS)
ECS............. Editorial Coordination Services (SAUS)
ECS............. Educational Career Service [*Later, EHCS*] [*An association*] (EA)
ECS............. Educational Counselling Service [*British Council*] (AIE)
ECS............. Education Commission of the States (EA)
ECS............. Elective Cosmetic Surgery
ECS............. Electrical Connector Subassembly
ECS............. Electrical Control System (SAUS)
ECS............. Electrocardiogram Simulator (SAUS)
ECS............. Electrocardioscanner
ECS............. Electrocerebral Silence [*Medicine*] (CPH)
ECS............. Electrochemical Science (SAUS)
ECS............. Electrochemical Series (SAUS)
ECS............. Electrochemical Society (EA)
ECS............. Electrochemical Society, Inc. (SAUO)
ECS............. Electro Convulsive Shock (SAUS)
ECS............. Electroconvulsive Shock
ECS............. Electromagnetic Compatibility Society (SAUO)
ECS............. Electronically Controlled Suspension [*Mitsubishi*] [*Automotive engineering*]
ECS............. Electronic Chart System
ECS............. Electronic Circulating Store (SAUS)
ECS............. Electronic Claims Submission (MEDA)
ECS............. Electronic Combat Squadron
ECS............. Electronic Communication Society (VLIE)
ECS............. Electronic Communication System (SAUS)
ECS............. Electronic Composing System
ECS............. Electronic Control and Surveillance (SAUS)
ECS............. Electronic Control Sensor (MCD)
ECS............. Electronic Control Switch (IEEE)
ECS............. Electronic Control System (SAUS)
ECS............. Electronic Cooling System (SAUS)
ECS............. Electronic Countermeasures Squadron [*Military*] (MUSM)
ECS............. Electronic Countermeasures System [*Military*]
ECS............. Electronic Counter Services
ECS............. Electronic Courier Systems [*Eatontown, NJ*] (TSSD)
ECS............. Electronic Crosconnect System (SAUS)
ECS............. Electronic Cross-Connect System (VLIE)
ECS............. Electronics Control System
ECS............. Elitegroup Computer Systems [*Taiwan*] (VERA)
ECS............. Embedded Computer Systems
ECS............. Embedded Computing System (SAUS)
ECS............. Embedded Control Software (VLIE)
ECS............. Embedded Control System (RALS)
ECS............. Emergency Call System [*AT & T*]
ECS............. Emergency Communications Staff (SAUO)
ECS............. Emergency Control Station [*Nuclear energy*] (NRCH)
ECS............. Emergency Coolant System (MSA)
ECS............. Emergency Core Cooling System [*Environmental science*] (COE)
ECS............. Emission Control System (MCD)
ECS............. Emperor's Clothes Syndrome
ECS............. Employee Communication Survey (SAUS)
ECS............. Employment Counseling Service (SAUS)
ECS............. Empty Coaching Stock [*Railway term*] (DCTA)
ECS............. Enable Control System
ECS............. Encryption Control Signal (SAUS)
ECS............. Encyclopedia of Cognitive Science [*A publication*]
ECS............. End Cell Switch (IAA)
ecs............. ends cut square (SAUS)
ECS............. Energy Communication Services (SAUS)
ECS............. Energy Conservation Service (SAUS)
ECS............. Energy Conversion Subsystem (SSD)
ECS............. Energy Conversion System (PDAA)
ECS............. Engagement Controller Set
ECS............. Engagement Control Station (ACAE)
ECS............. Engagement Control System [*Navy*] (MCD)
ECS............. Engine Control System [*Facetious translation: Expect Catastrophe Soon*]
ECS............. Engineering Change Schedule (AAG)
ECS............. Engineering Change Sheet (NATG)
ECS............. Engineering Change Summary
ECS............. Engineering Contract Services (ACAE)
ECS............. Engineering Control System
ECS............. English Citizen Series [*A publication*]
ECS............. Enhanced Chip Set (SAUS)
ECS............. Enterprise Communications System (SAUS)
ECS............. Environmental Chamber Shroud (SAUS)
ECS............. Environmental Chiefs of Staff (FOTI)
ECS............. Environmental Compliance Section (SAUS)
ECS............. Environmental Conditioning System (SAUS)
ECS............. Environmental Conservation Service [*Canada*]
ECS............. Environmental Control Shroud [*Nuclear energy*] (NRCH)
ECS............. Environmental Control Subsystem (SAUO)
ECS............. Environmental Control System [*NASA*]
ECS............. Environmental Control System (Subsystem) (SAUS)
ECS............. environment control system (SAUS)
ECS............. EOSDIS Core System (SAUO)
ECS............. Episcopal Church of Sudan (SAUO)
ECS............. Episcopal Community Services (SAUS)
ECS............. Equatorial Coordinate System (SAUS)
ECS............. Equatorial Currents System [*Oceanography*]
ECS............. Equipment Compiler System (IAA)
ECS............. Equipment Concentration Sites [*Military*] (AABC)
ECS............. Equipment Configuration Study (SAUS)
ECS............. Equipment Construction Site (MCD)
ECS............. Equipment Control System (SAUS)
ECS............. Erosion Control Standard [*Environmental science*] (COE)
ECS............. Error Correction Serve (SAUS)
ECS............. Error Correction Servo [*or Signals*] (AAG)
ecs............. error correction servomechanism (SAUS)
ECS............. Error Correction Signal (SAUS)
ecs............. error correction signals (SAUS)
ECS............. Established Church of Scotland (ROG)
ECS............. Etched Circuit Society [*Defunct*] (EA)
ECS............. Etched Circuits Society (SAUS)
ECS............. Ethical Culture Schools (SAUO)
ECS............. Ethiopian Catholic Secretariat
ECS............. Ethnic Children's Service [*Australia*]
ECS............. European Ceramic Society (SAUO)
ECS............. European Chemical Society
ECS............. European Committee for Coordination of Standards (SAUO)
ECS............. European Committee for Standardization (SAUS)
ECS............. European Common Standard (VLIE)
ECS............. European Common Standard, Embedded Computing System (SAUS)
ECS............. European Communication Satellite

ECS European Communications Satellite System (SAUS)
ECS European Communication System (SAUS)
ECS European Components Service (SAUO)
ECS European Confederation of Scouts (EAIO)
ECS Europe Computer Systems [*Computer leasing company*] (NITA)
ECS Evaporation Control System [*Automobile antipollution device*]
ECS Exact Cubic Search [*Mathematics*]
ECS Exchangeable Cation State (SAUS)
ECS Executive Compensation Service
ECS Executive Control System [*Computer science*]
ECS Executive Counselling Service [*Australia*]
ECS Exhaust Collection System [*Automotive emissions*]
ECS Exhaust Control System
ECS Exospheric Composition Studies (MUGU)
ECS Expanded Character Set [*Computer science*] (ELAL)
ECS Expanded Control Store (SAUS)
ECS Experienced Control Scales (EDAC)
ECS Experimental Communications Satellite [*NASA*]
ECS Exploder Control Sensor (MCD)
ECS Extended Character Set [*Computer science*] (PCM)
ECS Extended Control Store (SAUS)
ECS Extended Core Storage [*Computer science*]
ECS Exterior Communications System [*Military*] (CAAL)
ECS External Calling Sequence [*Computer science*]
ECS External Communication System (SAUS)
ECS Extracapillary Space
ECS Extracellular-Like, Calcium-Free Solution [*Medicine*]
ECS IEEE Electromagnetic Compatability Society (EA)
ECS Newcastle, WY [*Location identifier*] [*FAA*] (FAAL)
ECS2 Executive Control Subordinate System (SAUO)
ECSA Eastern, Central, and Southern Africa (SAUO)
ECSA Eastern College Soccer Association (EA)
ECSA EEC [*European Economic Community*] Ship Owners Association [*Belgium*] (EAIO)
ECSA Embedded COMSEC Software Algorithm (SAUS)
ECSA Episcopal Churchmen for South Africa (EA)
ECSA Episcopal Church People for a Free Southern Africa (SAUO)
ECSA Estuarine and Coastal Sciences Association [*Scotland*] (EAIO)
ECSA European Chips and Snacks Association [*British*] (EAIO)
ECSA European Chlorinated Solvent Association (EAIO)
ECSA European Communication Security Agency
ECSA European Community Shipowners' Associations [*Belgium*] (EAIO)
ECSA European Computing Services Association
ECSA Exceptional Civilian Service Award (RDA)
ECSA Exchange Carriers Standards Association (EA)
ECSA Expanded Clay and Shale Association [*Later, LAPA*] (EA)
ECSA Extended Common Storage Area [*IBM Corp.*] (CIST)
ECSAMR Emergency Committee to Save America's Marine Resources (EA)
ECS/API Enhanced Character Set/All Purpose Interface [*Xerox Corp.*]
ECSAS Electronic Counter measures Signal Analysis System (SAUS)
ECSC East Central State College [*Later, East Central Oklahoma State University*]
ECSC Eastern Collegiate Skiing Conference (PSS)
ECSC EcoScience Corp. [*NASDAQ symbol*] (SAG)
ECS-C Electronic Communication System for Commerce (SAUS)
ECSC Electronic Countermeasure Sub-Committee (SAUO)
ECSC Enamelled Single Cotton Covered (SAUS)
ECSC Energy Conservation and Solar Centre [*British*] (CB)
ECSC European Coal and Steel Community [*France, West Germany, Italy, BENELUX*]
ECSC European Community for Steel and Coal (SAUS)
ECSC European Conference on Satellite Communications (MCD)
ECSC European Continental Shrine Club (SAUO)
ECSC European Customer Support Centre (SAUS)
ECSC Exchange Carriers Standards Commission [*Communications term*] (DCT)
ECSCA English Cocker Spaniel Club of America (EA)
ECSCF Eastern Connecticut State College Foundation (SAUO)
ECSCK entry control systems card key (SAUS)
ECS-CM Extended Core Storage-Central Memory (SAUS)
ECS/CMS Embedded Computer System/Configuration (SAUS)
ECSCW European Conference on Computer Supported Cooperative Work
ECSE Advisory Committee for Electrical, Computer, and Systems Engineering [*Terminated, 1985*] (EGAO)
ECSE Early Childhood Special Education
ECSEC European Center for Scientific/Engineering Computing (SAUS)
ECSEDA Eastern Caribbean States Export Development Agency [*Dominica*] (EY)
ECSEL Engineering Coalition of Schools for Excellence in Education and Leadership (SAUS)
ECSF Electronic Combat Support Flight [*Military*] (SEWL)
ECSF European Civil Service Federation (EAIO)
ECSG ECsoft Group Plc [*NASDAQ symbol*] (NASQ)
ECSG Electronic Connector Study Group (EA)
ECSG Eurocom Crypto Sub Group (SAUO)
ECSG European Cooperative Study Group (SAUO)
ECSGY Ecsoft Group [*NASDAQ symbol*] (SAG)
ECSGY ECsoft Group ADR [*NASDAQ symbol*] (SG)
ECSH Edgewood College of the Sacred Heart [*Wisconsin*]
ECS/HCS Educational Career Service/Health Career Service [*Later, EHCS*] [*An association*] (EA)
ECSI Emergency Committee to Suspend Immigration (EA)
ECSI Endocardial Solutions, Inc. [*NASDAQ symbol*] (NASQ)
ECSI European CAD [*Computer-Aided Design*] Standardization Initiative [*Computer science*]
ECSI European Customer Satisfaction Index (EURO)
ECSI European Custom Systems Integration (SAUO)
ECSI Export Cargo Shipping Instruction (DS)
ECSIL Experimental Cross Section Information Library [*University of California, Livermore*]
ECSIM European Centre for Study and Information on Multinational Corporations (SAUO)
ECSIM European Centre for Study and Information on Multinational Corporations (SAUS)
ECSIR European Consortium for Software Access and Information Transfer in Research and Teaching (SAUO)
ECSJ Electro-Chemical Society of Japan (SAUS)
ECSL Enforcement Compliance Schedule Letter [*Environmental Protection Agency*] (EG)
ECSL European Centre for Space Law (CARB)
ECSL Extended Control and Simulation Language [*Computer science*] (PDAA)
ECSLA East-Central State School Libraries Association (SAUO)
ECSLA European Centre of Studies on Linear Alkylbenzene (EAIO)
ECSM Event Capture Storage Mode
ECSM Exeter Camborne School of Mines (SAUO)
ECSMA European Copper Sulphate Manufacturers' Association (EAIO)
ECSN European Climate Support Network (SAUS)
ECSN European Concrete Societies Network (SAUO)
ECSO Effective Concentration of Substance for 50% Survival of Organism
ECSO Electronic Component Sales Operation (SAUS)
ECSO Enterocytopathogenic Swine Orphan Virus
ECSO European Communications Satellite Organization (SAUS)
ECSOB Eastern College Soccer Officials Bureau [*Later, ECSA*]
ECSOC Electronic Conference on Synthetic Organic Chemistry (SAUO)
ECSOCO Economic and Social Council (SAUO)
Ecsoft Ecsoft Group [*Associated Press*] (SAG)
ECSO Virus Enteric Cytopathogenic Swine Orphan Virus (SAUS)
ECSP Electronic Command Signal Processor (SAUS)
ECSP Electronic Command Signal Programmer (MCD)
ECSP Electronics Control Signal Processor [*HELLFIRE*]
ECSP Electronic Specialist
ECSP Employee Counseling Services Program (COE)
ECSP Enhanced Consumer Spending Patterns [*National Planning Data Corp.*] [*Information service or system*] (CRD)
ECSP Extended Corresponding States Principle [*Physical chemistry*]
ECS Press Eccentric Shaft Press (SAUS)
ECSR Economic Computation & Economic Cybernetics Studies and Research (SAUO)
ECSR Economic Computation & Economic Cybernetics Studies and Research (journ.) (SAUS)
ECSS Electrical Command and Stability System (PDAA)
ECSS Equipment Concentration Site System [*Army*]
ECSS European Committee for the Study of Salt (EA)
ECSS European Communication Satellite System
ECSS European Conference on Surface Science (SAUS)
ECSS Extendable Computer System Simulator [*Programming language*] [*1973*]
ECSS Extended Computer System Simulator (SAUS)
ECSSA European Centre for Studies of Sulfuric Acid (EAIO)
ECSSID Environmental Defense Fund (SAUO)
ECSSID European Conference in Social Science Information and Documentation (SAUS)
ECSSID European Cooperation in Social Science Information and Documentation
ECSSID European Development Fund (SAUO)
ECSSS Eighteenth Century Scottish Studies Society (EA)
ECST Ecstasy (ABBR)
ECST Electronic Control of Spark Timing (PDAA)
ECST Emergency Condensate Storage Tank [*Nuclear energy*] (NRCH)
ECSTASY Economical Storage and Access System [*Computer science*]
ECSTASY Electronic Control for Switching and Telemetering Automobile Systems [*Automotive engineering*]
ECSTC Ecstatic (ABBR)
ECSTC Eighteenth-Century Short Title Catalogue [*A publication*]
ECSTC Elizabeth City State Teachers College (SAUS)
ECSTCY Ecstatically (ABBR)
ECSU Educational Cooperative Service Unit (SAUS)
ECSU Electrical Certification Support Unit (HEAS)
EC SW End Cell Switch (SAUS)
ECSW Engagement Controller Software
ECSW Extended Channel Status Word [*Computer science*] (MHDB)
ECSWTR European Centre for Social Welfare Training and Research [*See also CEFRAS*] [*United Nations*] (EAIO)
ECSYT Ecosystem (ABBR)
ECSZ Eastern California Shear Zone [*Geology*]
ECSZ Elgin Crop Service [*Federal Railroad Administration identification code*]
ECT Earliest Completion Time (SAUS)
ECT Earth-Centered True
ECT Echo Cancellation Technique (SAUS)
ECT Eddy Current Test [*Nuclear energy*] (NRCH)
ECT Eddy Current Testing (SAUS)
ECT Edge Crush Test [*Packaging*]
ECT Edit Control Table (SAUS)
ECT [*The*] Egyptian Coffin Texts [*A publication*] (BJA)
ECT Electric Checking Tabulator (SAUS)
ECT Electrochemical Turning [*Manufacturing term*]
ECT Electroconvulsive Therapy [*or Treatment*] [*Medicine*]
ECT electroconvulsive therapy, enteric coated tablet (SAUS)

ECT............ Electroconvulsive Treatment (SAUS)
ECT............ Electronically Controlled Transmission [*Automotive engineering*]
ECT............ Electronic and Control Technology (NITA)
ECT............ Electronic Controlled Transmission (SAUS)
ECT............ Electronic Control Technology (SAUS)
ECT............ Electronic Coolant Temperature
ECT............ Ellsworth [*Connecticut*] [*Seismograph station code, US Geological Survey*] (SEIS)
ECT............ Emergency Cooling Tower [*Nuclear energy*] (NRCH)
ECT............ Emission Computed Tomography
ECT............ Emission-Controlled Tomography (SAUS)
ECT............ Emissionscomputertomographie (SAUS)
ECT............ Encyclopedia of Chemical Technology [*A publication*]
ECT............ Engine Coolant Temperature [*Automotive engineering*]
ect............ engine cut off time (SAUS)
ECT............ Engine Cutoff Timer [*Aerospace*] (KSC)
ECT............ English Composition Test [*Education*] (AEBS)
ECT............ Enhanced Computer Tomography [*Radiology*] (DAVI)
ECT............ Enteric Coated Tablet [*Pharmacology*]
ECT............ Environmental Concept Truck [*Automotive engineering*]
ECT............ Environmental Control Table
ECT............ Environmental Control Technology (SAUS)
ECT............ Environment Control Table (SAUS)
ECT............ Equicohesive Temperature (SAUS)
ECT............ Equivalence Conversion Training (SAUS)
ECT............ Error Control Translator
ECT............ Error Control Transmitter
ECT............ Estimated Cloud Time [*Drinking slang*]
ECT............ Estimated Completion Time [*Business term*]
ECT............ Euglobulin Clot Test [*Clinical chemistry*] (MAE)
ECT............ European Compression Technique [*Bone screw and internal fixation*] [*Orthopedics*] (DAVI)
ECT............ European Container Terminus (SAUS)
ECT............ Europe Combined Terminal (SAUS)
ECT............ Europe Container Terminus (SAUS)
ECT............ Evans Clear Tunnel (OA)
ECT............ Evaporative Cooling Techniques
ECT............ Evaporator Condensate Tank [*Environmental science*] (COE)
ECT............ Executive Career Trac [*A publication*]
ECT............ Experiment Control Team (ACAE)
ECT............ Explicit Call Transfer [*Telecommunications*] (DOM)
ECT............ Explosive Cutting Tape
ECT............ Exposure Control Technique
ECT............ Extortionate Credit Transactions [*FBI standardized term*]
ECTA........... Early Childhood Teachers' Association [*Australia*]
ECTA........... Eastern Caribbean Tourist Association (SAUO)
ECTA........... Economics and Commercial Teachers Association (SAUO)
ECTA........... Electrical Contractors Trading Association (SAUS)
ECTA........... Electronics Component Test Area (AAG)
ECTA........... Error-Correcting Tree Automation [*Computer science*]
ECTA........... European Communities Trade Mark Association (EURO)
ECTA........... European Competitive Telecommunications Association (SAUO)
ECTA........... European Cutting Tools Association (EA)
ECTA........... Everyman's Contingency Table Analyzer (PDAA)
ECTAA.......... Group of National Travel Agents' Associations within the EEC (EAIO)
ECTAR.......... Electronic Countermeasures Tactical Action Report (SAUS)
ECTAR.......... Electronic Tactical Action Report (AFM)
ECTC........... East Carolina Teachers College (SAUO)
ECTC........... East Coast Telecommunications Center [*Defense Communications System*] (RDA)
ECTC........... Eastern Coal Transportation Conference (EA)
ECTC........... Engineer Corps Training Center (SAUO)
ECTCT.......... Eccentricity (ABBR)
ECTD........... Electronics Command Technical Description (ACAE)
ECTD........... Emission Control Technology Division [*Environmental Protection Agency*] (GFGA)
ECTED.......... Electronic Combat Threat Environment Description (SAUS)
ECTEL.......... European Telecommunications and Professional Electronics Industry [*Europe an Conference of Associations of Telecommunications Industries and European Conference of Radio and Electronic Equipment Associations*] [*Formed by a merger of*] (EAIO)
ECTEOLA........ Epichlorohydrin Triethanolamine [*Organic chemistry*]
ECTEOLA-C...... Epichlorohydrin Triethanolamine Cellulose (SAUS)
ECTF........... East Coast Test Facility (ACAE)
ECTF........... Edinburgh Centre for Tropical Forests (SAUO)
ECTF........... Engineering Change Tracking File (SAUS)
ECTF........... Enhanced Computer Telephony Forum (GART)
ECTF........... Enterprise Computer Telephony Forum (SAUO)
ECTFE.......... Ethylene-Chlorotrifluoroethylene [*Organic chemistry*]
ECTFE.......... Ethylene-Chlorotrifluoroethylene Copolymer (EDCT)
E-CTFE......... Polyethylene-Cochlorotrifluoroethylene [*Plastics*]
ECTG........... European Channel Tunnel Group [*Planning a proposed tunnel between England and France under the English Channel*]
ECTH........... Electro-Catheter [*NASDAQ symbol*] (TTSB)
ECTH........... Electro Catheter Corp. [*NASDAQ symbol*] (SAG)
ECTI........... Eddy Current Testing Instrument
ECTI........... Erie County Technical Institute [*New York*]
ECTL........... Elcotel, Inc. [*NASDAQ symbol*] (NQ)
ECTL........... Electronic Communal Temporal Lobe (SAUS)
ECTL........... Emitter-Coupled Transistor Logic [*Electronics*]
ECTMAC......... East Coast Trawl Management Advisory Committee (EERA)
ECTMM.......... European Committee of Textile Machine Manufacturers (SAUO)
ECTMPCHD....... European Collaborative Trial of Multifactorial Prevention of Coronary Heart Diseases (SAUS)
ECTN........... Eastern Canada Telemetered Network (SAUS)
ECTN........... European Children's Television (EURO)
Ecto........... Ectoparasitic [*Biology*]
ECTOC.......... Electronic Conference on Trends in Organic Chemistry
ectohorm....... ectohormonal (SAUS)
ECTOHORM....... Ectohormone (ABBR)
ECTP........... Enhanced Communication Transport Protocol (SAUS)
ECTPWF......... European Confederation for Trade in Paint, Wall- and Floorcoverings (EAIO)
ECTR........... Endoscopic Carpal Tunnel Release [*Medicine*] (MELL)
ectr........... endoscopic carpal-tunnel release (SAUS)
ECTR........... Extended Connection Table Representation (NITA)
ECTS........... Electrical Cable Test Set
ECTS........... Electric Circuit Test Set
ECTS........... Electronic Combat Training Seminar (SAUS)
ECTS........... Electronic Combat Training System [*Military*] (SEWL)
ECTS........... Electronic Custom Telephone Set [*or System*] (NRCH)
ECTS........... Engine Coolant Temperature Sensor [*Automotive engineering*]
ECTS........... European Calcified Tissue Society (EA)
ECTS........... European Computer Trade Show [*London*] (VERA)
ECTS........... European Conference on Telecommunications by Satellite
ECTS........... European Credit Transfer System (SAUS)
ECTS........... Executive Correspondence Tracking System (SAUS)
ECTU........... Electrochemical Technology Unit (SAUS)
ECTUA.......... European Counsil for Telecommunications Users Association (SAUS)
ECTUEA......... European Committee of Trade Unions in Entertainment and Arts (SAUO)
ECTUNAMAC...... East Coast Tuna Management Advisory Committee (EERA)
ECTV........... Electronically-Controlled Throttle Valve [*Automotive engineering*]
ECTWT.......... Ecumenical Coalition on Third World Tourism (EA)
ECU............ East Carolina University [*Formerly, ECC*] [*Greenville, NC*]
ECU............ Echo suppression Denied (SAUS)
ECU............ Economic Crime Unit (SAUS)
ECU............ Ecuador [*ANSI three-letter standard code*] (CNC)
Ecu............ Ecuador (VRA)
Ecu............ Ecuadorean (SAUS)
ECU............ Ecumania (ABBR)
ECU............ Ecumenism (WDAA)
ECU............ EISA Configuration Utility (SAUS)
ECU............ Electrical Conversion Unit
ECU............ Electrocautery Unit [*Medicine*] (MELL)
ECU............ Electrochemical Unit
ECU............ Electronic Cabling Unit
ECU............ Electronic Computing Unit (IAA)
ECU............ Electronic Control Unit
ECU............ Electronic Conversion Unit (IEEE)
ECU............ Electronic Coupling Unit (MCD)
ECU............ Emergency Care Unit (ADWA)
ECU............ Emission Control Unit (SAUS)
ECU............ Emitter Classification Unit (SEWL)
ECU............ Energy Conservation and Utilization (SAUS)
ECU............ Energy Conservation Update [*A publication*]
ECU............ Engine Calibration Unit [*Automotive engineering*]
ECU............ Engine Change Unit (MCD)
ecu............ engine compatability unit (SAUS)
ECU............ Engine Control Unit
ECU............ English Church Union
ECU............ Entry Computer
ECU............ Environmental Control Unit
ECU............ Environmental Crimes Unit [*Environmental Protection Agency*] (GFGA)
ECU............ Environment Conditioning Unit (MCD)
ECU............ environment control unit (SAUS)
ECU............ Equipment Control Unit (AFIT)
ECU............ Euclid Public Library, Euclid, OH [*OCLC symbol*] (OCLC)
ECU............ European Chiropractors' Union (EAIO)
ECU............ European Clearing Union (SAUO)
ECU............ European Currency Unit [*European monetary system*] (AF)
Ecu............ European Currency Unit (SAFN)
ecu............ European Currency Unit (SHCU)
ECU............ European Customs Union (SAUO)
ECU............ Evidence Control Unit (GOBB)
ECU............ Exabyte Control Unit (SAUS)
ECU............ Exercise Control Unit (SAUS)
ECU............ Extended Care Unit [*Medicine*] (DHSM)
ECU............ Extensor Carpi Ulnaris [*Muscle or tendon*] [*Anatomy*] (DAVI)
ecu............ extra closeup (SAUS)
ECU............ Extreme Close-Up [*Television*]
ECUA........... Ecuador
Ecua........... Republic of Ecuador (SAUS)
Ecuad.......... Ecuadorean (DIAR)
ECUBE.......... Energy Conservation Using Better Engineering (PDAA)
E-Cubed........ Energy, Environment and Economics (SAUS)
ECUC........... Education Credit Union Council (EA)
Ecu Con........ Ecumenical Conference (SAUS)
Ecu Con........ Ecumenical Council (SAUO)
ecufuel........ eucalyptus-tree fuel (SAUS)
ECUI........... Extreme Close-Up Indeed [*Photography*] [*British*] (NTCM)
ECUK........... East Coast of the United Kingdom [*Shipping*]
E-CUK.......... East Coast of United Kingdom (SAUS)
ECUK........... East Coast United Kingdom (SAUO)
ECUM........... Ecumenic (ABBR)
Ecum........... Ecumenical (SAUS)
ECUMEN......... Ecumenical (ABBR)
ecumen......... ecumenicist (SAUS)
ecumen......... ecumenicity (SAUS)

ecumen........ ecumenics (SAUS)
ecumen........ ecumenism (SAUS)
ECUML........ Ecumenical (ABBR)
ECUMLSM... Ecumenicalism (ABBR)
ECUMLY...... Ecumenically (ABBR)
ECUMN....... Ecumenic (ABBR)
ECUMNL...... Ecumenical (ABBR)
ECUMNLY.... Ecumenically (ABBR)
ECUMNM..... Ecumenism (ABBR)
ECUP.......... European Copyright User Platform (TELE)
ECURIE........ European Community Urgent Radiological Information Exchange (SAUS)
ECURIE........ European system for notification in case of radiological emergencies (SAUO)
ECUs............ European Currency Units (SAUS)
ECUSA......... Episcopal Church of the U.S.A. (SAUS)
ecusat.......... ecumenical satellite (SAUS)
ECUSAT....... Ecumenical Satellite Commission
ECUSATCOM... Ecumenical Satellite Commission (SAUS)
ECUT............ Energy Conservation and Utilization Technology Program (SAUS)
ECUT............ Energy Conversion and Utilization Technologies Program [*Department of Energy*]
ECV............. Earned Community Visit (WDAA)
ECV............. Elderberry Carlavirus [*Plant pathology*]
ECV............. Electric Cargo Vehicle (SAUS)
ECV............. Electric Clock Valve
ECV............. Electronic Combat Vehicle (ACAE)
ECV............. Enamel Single Cotton Varnish [*Wire insulation*] (AAG)
ECV............. Energy Conservation Vehicle [*British Leyland*]
ECV............. Enteric Coronavirus [*Medicine*] (EDAA)
ECV............. Epithelial Cell Vacuolization [*Medicine*] (MELL)
ECV............. Esperantist Club of Veterans [*See also VEK*] [*Wolfhagen, Federal Republic of Germany*] (EAIO)
ecv.............. estimated cash value (SAUS)
ECV............. Extended Content Verification (VLIE)
ECV............. External Cephalic Version [*Gynecology*]
ECV............. Extracellular Volume [*Hematology*]
ECV............. Extracorporeal Volume [*Medicine*] (MAE)
ECVA........... European College of Veterinary Anaesthesia (GVA)
ECVAC......... Endorsers Conference for Veterans Affairs Chaplaincy (EA)
ECVAM......... European Center for the Validation of Alternative Methods [*To animals for biological testing, Italy*]
ECVCN......... European College of Veterinary and Comparative Nutrition (GVA)
ECVD........... Extracellular Volume of Distribution [*Medicine*] (EDAA)
ECVE........... Extracellular Volume Expansion [*Hematology*] (CPH)
ECVFI.......... European Committee for the Valves and Fittings Industry [*Germany*] (EAIO)
ECVFP.......... Expanded Charted Visual Flight Procedures [*FAA*] (TAG)
ECVIM-CA.... European College of Veterinary Internal Medicine-Companion Animals (GVA)
ECVO........... European College of Veterinary Ophthalmologists (GVA)
ECVP........... European College of Veterinary Pathologists (GVA)
ECVP........... European Community Visitors Program
ECVPH-PM-FS... European College for Veterinary Public Health, Population Medicine, and Food Scince (GVA)
ECVS........... European College of Veterinary Surgeons (GVA)
ECVT........... Electro-Continuously Variable Transmission [*Subaru*] [*Automotive engineering*]
ECVT........... Electronically Controlled Continuously Variable Transmission
ECW............ Eastern Coach Works [*British*] (DCTA)
ECW............ Effluent Cooling Water [*Environmental science*] (COE)
ECW............ Electronic Combat Wing [*Military*]
ECW............ Electronic Cooling Water (DNAB)
ECW............ Emergency Conservation Work [*Succeeded by CCC, 1937, now obsolete*]
ECW............ Emergency Cooling Water [*Nuclear energy*] (NRCH)
ECW............ Engineering Construction World (journ.) (SAUS)
ECW............ Envipco Canada [*Vancouver Stock Exchange symbol*]
ECW............ Episcopal Church Women
ECW............ Essays on Canadian Writing [*A publication*] (ANEX)
ECW............ essential cooling water (SAUS)
ECW............ European Council of Women [*Belgium*] (EAIO)
ECW............ Extracellular Water [*Physiology*]
ECWA.......... East Coast Wrestling Association (PSS)
ECWA.......... Economic Commission for Western Africa (SAUS)
ECWA.......... Economic Commission for Western Asia [*Later, ESCWA*] [*United Nations*]
ECWA.......... Economic Community of West Africa (SAUO)
ECWA.......... Environment Centre of Western Australia [*Australia*]
ECWAG........ Emergency Community Water Assistance Grants (SAUO)
ECWAS........ Economic Community of West African States [*Treaty signed May 28, 1975*]
ECWC.......... Empire Collegiate Wrestling Conference (PSS)
ECWC.......... Employers' Council on Workers' Compensation [*Canada*]
ECWC.......... Extended Cold/Wet Clothing Systems [*Military*] (INF)
ECWCS........ Extended Cold Weather Clothing System [*Army*] (INF)
ECWD.......... Effluent Cooling Water Drainage [*Environmental science*] (COE)
ECWD.......... Error Channel Word (VLIE)
ECWG.......... Emergency Communications Working Group [*DoD*]
ECWG.......... Environmental Characterization Working Group
ECWG.......... Evaluation Coordination Working Group [*Navy*]
ECWIM......... European Committee of Weighing Instrument Manufacturers (EAIO)
EC Wire....... Enamel-Covered Wire (SAUS)
EC WIRE..... Extra Control Wire (MSA)
ECWP.......... Egyptian Communist Workers' Party [*Political party*] (PD)
ECWP.......... Emergency Cooling Water Pond [*Nuclear energy*] (NRCH)
ECWP.......... Eurocom Crypto Working Party (SAUO)
ECWPH........ Emergency Cooling Water Pumphouse [*Nuclear energy*] (NRCH)
ECWS.......... Eastern Chemical Waste Systems (EFIS)
ECWS.......... Element Control Workstation [*NASA*] (SPST)
ECWS.......... English Civil War Society [*British*] (DBA)
ECWS.......... Environment Control Workstation (SAUS)
ECWS.......... essential cooling water system (SAUS)
ECWS.......... European Centre for Work and Society (EA)
ECWSS........ Extreme Cold Weather Sleep System [*Army*]
EC-WTA....... Executive Committee - Western Traffic Association (SAA)
ECWU.......... Energy and Chemical Workers Union [*See also STEC*]
ECX............ Electronically Controlled Telephone Exchange (DEN)
ecx............ Electronic Catalogs
EC-X........... Emission Control Experimental
ECx............ Experimental Concentration-Percent (FFDE)
ECY............ Economy Inns, Inc. [*Vancouver Stock Exchange symbol*]
ECY............ European Conservation Year (SAUS)
ECY 70........ European Conservation Year (SAUS)
ECY 70........ European Conservation Year 1970 (SAUO)
ECYC.......... Earl of Chester's Yeomanry Cavalry [*British military*] (DMA)
ECYC.......... European Confederation of Youth Clubs (EA)
E-cycle........ Execution Cycle [*Computer science*] (NITA)
ECYE........... Federation of National Committees in the International Christian Youth Exchange (SAUO)
ECYEB......... European Community Youth Exchange Bureau (AIE)
ECYFC......... European Committee for Young Farmers and 4H Clubs (EA)
ECYFC4HC... European Committee for Young Farmers and 4H Clubs [*Germany*] (EAIO)
ECYO........... European Community Youth Orchestra [*British*] (EAIO)
ECYU........... Elizabethan Club of Yale University (EA)
ECZ............ Church of Christ in Zaire (D. Rep. Congo) [*Political party*] (PSAP)
ECZ............ East Cape [*New Zealand*] [*Seismograph station code, US Geological Survey*] (SEIS)
ECZ............ Ethycarbazole [*Organic chemistry*]
ECZM.......... Eczema (ABBR)
ED.............. Canadian Efficiency Decoration [*Military*] (DD)
ED.............. Consolidated Edison Co. of New York, Inc. [*NYSE symbol*] (SPSG)
Ed.............. Department of Education [*Cabinet department*]
E_d.............. Depth Dose [*Radiation therapy*] (DAVI)
ED.............. Doctor of Engineering
ED.............. Early Deceleration (SAUS)
ED.............. Early Difference [*Medicine*] (EDAA)
ED.............. Earth-Dawn (SAUO)
ED.............. Earth Detector (SAUS)
ED.............. Eastern District [*ATSC*]
ED.............. Eastern District Court Reports [*South Africa*] [*A publication*] (DLA)
E/D+........... Eating and Drinking [*Normally*] (SPVS)
ED.............. Eating Disorder (MELL)
ED.............. Economically Deprived [*Medicine*] (EDAA)
ED.............. Economically Disadvantaged (OICC)
ED.............. Economic Development [*A publication*]
ED.............. Economics Division [*US Military Government, Germany*]
ED.............. Ectodermal Dysplasia [*Medicine*]
ED.............. Ectopic Depolarization [*Medicine*] (DMAA)
ED.............. Edema (SAUS)
ED.............. Edema, Emergency department (SAUS)
Ed.............. Eden's English Chancery Reports Tempore Northington [*28 English Reprint*] [*1757-66*] [*A publication*] (DLA)
Ed.............. Edgar's Decisions, Scotch Court of Session [*1724-25*] [*A publication*] (DLA)
ED.............. Edge (VLIE)
ED.............. Edge Device (SAUS)
ED.............. Edge Distance
Ed.............. Edible
ed.............. edidif (SAUS)
ED.............. Edinburgh [*City in Scotland*]
ED.............. Edit [*or Edited*]
ed.............. Edited By (WDMC)
ed.............. Edition (WDAA)
ED.............. Edition
ed.............. editit (SAUS)
Ed.............. Editor (AL)
ed.............. Editor (WDAA)
ED.............. Editor (EY)
Ed.............. Editorial (AL)
ED.............. Editorial Division (SAUO)
Ed.............. Edmond (SAUS)
Ed.............. Edson (SAUS)
ed.............. educate (SAUS)
ed.............. Education (BEE)
ED.............. Education
Ed.............. Education (DD)
ED.............. Educational [*FCC*] (NTCM)
ED.............. Educational Drama
ED.............. Educational Institution Program (NTCM)
ED.............. Education Department [*British military*] (DMA)
ED.............. Educator (SAUS)
ED.............. Edulcorata [*Sweetened*] [*Pharmacy*] (ROG)
'Ed............. 'Eduyyoth (BJA)
ED.............. Effective Date Unit Enters Federal Active Duty (SAUO)
ED.............. Effective Diameter [*TII*] (TAG)
ED.............. Effective Dose
ED.............. Effective Dosis (SAUS)
ED.............. Efficiency Decoration [*Military*] [*British*]

ED.............. Egg Diameter [*Pisciculture*]
ED.............. Ehlers-Danlos Syndrome [*Medicine*] (MAE)
ED.............. Ejaculatory Dysfunction [*Medicine*] (MELL)
ED.............. Elasticity of Demand [*Economics*] (DCTA)
E/D.............. Elbow Disarticulation [*Orthopedics*]
ED.............. Elbow Dislocation (MELL)
ED.............. Elder Dempster Line (SAUS)
ED.............. Election District
ED.............. Electrical Damage (ADWA)
ED.............. Electrical Department [*Navy*] [*British*]
ED.............. Electrical Differential
ED.............. electrical discharge (SAUS)
ED.............. Electrical Drawing (IAA)
ED.............. Electric-Diesel
ED.............. Electric Dipole (SAUS)
ED.............. Electric Dynamic [*Motors*]
ED.............. Electrochemical Detector [*Instrumentation*]
ED.............. Electrochemical Diffused (IAA)
ED.............. Electrodecantation (SAUS)
ED.............. Electrodeposited (AAEL)
ED.............. Electrodeposition (SAUS)
ED.............. Electrodermal (SAUS)
ED.............. Electrodiagnosis (SAUS)
ED.............. Electrodialysis [*Medicine*]
ED.............. Electrodynamic (DEN)
E-D.............. Electro-Dynamics (SAUS)
ED.............. Electron Density (SAUS)
ED.............. Electron Device (MCD)
ED.............. Electron Diffraction
ED.............. Electronic Design (SAUS)
ED.............. electronic desorption (SAUS)
ED.............. Electronic Detection (LAIN)
ED.............. Electronic Development (MCD)
ED.............. Electronic Device (VLIE)
ED.............. Electronic Differential [*Analyzer*]
ED.............. Electronic Digital [*Analyzer*]
ED.............. Electronic Digital analyzer (SAUS)
ED.............. Electronic Display
ed.............. electronic displays (SAUS)
ED.............. Electronic Document
ED.............. Electronic Dummy [*Engineering acoustics*] (IAA)
ED.............. Electrostatic Discharge (IAA)
ED.............. Electrostatic Storage Deflection (IAA)
ED.............. Elevation Data (SAUS)
E-D.............. Elsevier-Dutton (SAUS)
E/D.............. Embarkation/Disembarkation
ED.............. Embryonic Day
ED.............. Embryonic Death [*Medicine*] (EDAA)
ED.............. Emergency Delivery (SAUS)
ED.............. Emergency Department [*of a hospital*]
ED.............. Emergency Destruction (MCD)
ED.............. Emergency Distance [*Aviation*] (DA)
ED.............. Emotional Disorder [*Medicine*] (EDAA)
ED.............. Emotional Disturbance
ED.............. Emotionally Deprived
ED.............. Emotionally Disabled (OICC)
ED.............. Emotionally Disturbed (WDAA)
ED.............. [*The*] Emphatic Diaglott [*1942*] [*A publication*] (BJA)
ED.............. Employability Development (OICC)
ED.............. Employment Department (HEAS)
ED.............. Encoded Data (SAUS)
E/D.............. Encode/Decode (VLIE)
E/D.............. encoder-to-digital (SAUS)
ED.............. Encryption Device (VLIE)
ED.............. End Delimiter (TNIG)
ED.............. End-Diastole [*Cardiology*]
ED.............. End Door
ED.............. Ending Delimiter [*Telecommunications*] (ACRL)
ED.............. End of Data [*Computer science*] (IAA)
ED.............. End of Date (SAUS)
E/D.............. End-of-Descent (GAVI)
ED.............. Endogenous Depression [*Medicine*] (EDAA)
ED.............. Enemy Dead
ED.............. Energy Dispersive (EDCT)
ED.............. Energy Division (CARB)
ED.............. Enforcement Division [*Environmental Protection Agency*] (GFGA)
ED.............. Engine Designer (DS)
ED.............. Engine Drive (MSA)
ED.............. Engineering Data
ED.............. Engineering Demonstration (SAUS)
ED.............. Engineering Department [*Navy*] [*British*]
ED.............. Engineering Depot
ED.............. Engineering Design
ED.............. Engineering Designer (SAUS)
ED.............. Engineering Development
ED.............. Engineering Directive (NASA)
ED.............. Engineering Directorate (SAUS)
ED.............. Engineering Division
ED.............. Engineering Document
ED.............. Engineering Draftsman
ED.............. Engineering Drawing (SAUS)
ED.............. Engineering Duty [*Navy*]
ED.............. Engineering Dynamics Ltd. (SAUS)
ED.............. English Duke (ROG)
ED.............. Enhanced Density (VERA)
ED.............. Enhancement Depletion (IAA)
E-D.............. Enhancement-Depletion Logic (NITA)
ED.............. Entering Diagnosis [*Medicine*] (MELL)
ED.............. Entertainment Duty (DLA)
ED.............. Entner-Doudoroff [*Hexose metabolic pathway*]
ED.............. Entry Date [*British Library Automated Information Service and National Library of Medicine*] [*Searchable field*] [*Information service or system*] (NITA)
ED.............. Enumeration District [*Census*]
ED.............. Envelope Drawing (MSA)
ED.............. Environmental Damage (EERA)
E/D.............. Environmental Devices, Inc., Sacramento, California (SAUS)
ED.............. Environmental Disruption
ED.............. Enzephalitis disseminata (MS) (SAUS)
ED.............. Enzymatic Deficiencies
ED.............. Epidural [*Brain anatomy*]
ED.............. Epileptiform Discharge (DB)
ED.............. Epithelial Defect (SAUS)
ED.............. Equilibrium Dialysis [*Analytical chemistry*]
ED.............. Equipment Delay (CAAL)
ED.............. Equipment Depot (SAUS)
ED.............. Equipment Description
ED.............. Equipment Development (journ.) (SAUS)
ED.............. Equivalent Dose (QUAC)
ED.............. Erase Digital [*Signal*]
ED.............. Erase Display (VLIE)
ED.............. Erb Disease [*Medicine*] (MELL)
ED.............. Erectile Dysfunction [*Medicine*] (MELL)
ED.............. ERIC [*Educational Resources Information Center*] Document
ED.............. Errata Data [*Dialog*] [*Searchable field*] [*Information service or system*] (NITA)
ED.............. Error Detecting [*or Detection*] [*Computer science*]
ED.............. Error Detection (SAUS)
ED.............. Erythema Disease [*Medicine*] (LDT)
ED.............. Erythema Dose [*Medicine*]
ED.............. Erythrocyte Density (DB)
ED.............. Esaki Diode [*Electronics*]
ED.............. Esophageal Diverticulum [*Medicine*] (MELL)
ED.............. Esquerra Democratica [*Democratic Left*] [*Spain*] [*Political party*] (PPE)
ED.............. Establishment Date [*IRS*]
ED.............. Estate Duty (DLA)
ED.............. Estimated Date (AAG)
ED.............. Estimated Dose (SAUS)
ED.............. Ethyldichloroarsine [*Medicine*] (ADDR)
ED.............. Ethynodiol [*Pharmacology*]
ED.............. Euclidean Distance Matrix [*Statistics*]
ED.............. EUCOM Directive (SAUS)
ED.............. Eurodefence
ED.............. European Democratic Group [*European Parliament*] (ECED)
ed--- .... Europe, Southeastern [*MARC geographic area code*] [*Library of Congress*] (LCCP)
ED.............. Evaluation and Development (IAA)
ED.............. Evaluation Directive [*Environmental science*] (COE)
ED.............. Evening Duties (WDAA)
ED.............. Event Dispatcher (SAUS)
ED.............. Every Day
ED.............. Evidence of Disease (DAVI)
ED.............. Evolutionary Distance
ED.............. Exception Data (VLIE)
ED.............. Excess Distribution (ADA)
ED.............. Exchequer Division, English Law Reports [*A publication*] (DLA)
ED.............. Excused from Duty
ED.............. Ex-Dividend [*Without the right to dividend*] [*Finance*]
ED.............. Executive Director
ED.............. Exertional Dyspnea [*Medicine*] (DAVI)
ED.............. Exhaust Dampers [*Nuclear energy*] (NRCH)
ED.............. Existence Doubtful [*Navigation charts*]
ED.............. Expanded Display
E-D.............. Expansion Deflection (AAG)
ED.............. Expansion Drum (SAUS)
ED.............. Expedited Data (VLIE)
ED.............. Experimental Design
ED.............. Experimental Duty (SAUS)
ED.............. experiment design (SAUS)
ED.............. Exploratory Development [*Military*]
ED.............. Explosive Device
ED.............. Export Declaration (SAUS)
ED.............. Exports Directorate [*British*]
ED.............. Exposure Draft [*Business term*]
ED.............. Extended Definition Television [*in ED Beta*] [*Sony Corp.*]
ED.............. Extended Duration (OICC)
ED.............. Extension Shaft Disconnect [*Nuclear energy*] (IAA)
ED.............. Extensive Disease [*Medicine*]
ED.............. Extensor Digitorum [*Muscle or tendon*] [*Orthopedics*] (DAVI)
ED.............. External Declaration (SAUS)
ED.............. External Deflector (SAUS)
ED.............. External Delay [*Computer science*] (IAA)
ED.............. External Device [*Computer science*]
ED.............. External Diameter [*Measurement*] (DAVI)
ED.............. Extraction Dialysis [*For separation of mixtures*]
ED.............. Extractive Distillation (SAUS)
ED.............. Extra Dividend [*Banking*] (ADA)
ED.............. Extra Divident (SAUS)
ED.............. Extra Duty (ACAE)

ED............... Extra-High-Density [*Floppy disk technology*] (PCM)
ED............... Extra-Low Dispersion [*Instrumentation*]
ED............... Extra-Low Dispersion Glass (SAUS)
ED............... Extrusion Die (MCD)
ED............... Sunbird [*ICAO designator*] (AD)
ED............... U.S. Department of Education
ED............... Economic Dispatch (ODA)
ED.IT............ Education and Information Technology [*Educational viewdata service*] (NITA)
ED3A............. ethylenediaminetriacetic acid (SAUS)
ED10............. Ten Percent Effective Dose (SAUS)
ED50............. Effective Dose 50 (SAUS)
ED_{50}............. Effective Dose, Median
ED50............. Median Effective Dose
EdA.............. Advanced Degree in Education (GAGS)
EDA.............. Aerolinas Nacionales del Ecuador SA [*ICAO designator*] (FAAC)
EDA.............. Early Departure Allowance (FOTI)
EDA.............. Early Departure Authorized
EDA.............. Eating Disorders Association (EAIO)
EDA.............. Economic Development Administration [*Formerly, Office of Appalachian Assistance*] [*Terminated*] [*Department of Commerce*]
EDA.............. Economic Development Agency (SAUO)
EDA.............. Economic Development Agreement (SAUS)
EDA.............. Economic Development Association (SAUO)
EDA.............. Ecosystem Dynamics and the Atmosphere (SAUS)
EDA.............. Educational Drama Association [*Defunct*] (EAIO)
EDA.............. Education Development Associates [*Information service or system*]
EDA.............. Effective Doubleword Address [*Computer science*] (IAA)
EDA.............. Electrical Development Advisory Division (SAUO)
EDA.............. Electrical Development Association
EDA.............. Electric Development Association (SAUO)
EDA.............. Electrodermal Audiometry [*Otolaryngology*]
EDA.............. Electron Donor-Acceptor
EDA.............. Electronic Data Acquisition (SAUS)
EDA.............. Electronic Defense Association (SAUO)
EDA.............. Electronic Dental Anesthesia
EDA.............. Electronic Design Automation [*Computer science*]
EDA.............. Electronic Development Associates Inc. (SAUS)
EDA.............. Electronic Differential Analyzer
EDA.............. Electronic Digital Analyzer (MCD)
EDA.............. Electronic Display Assembly (NASA)
EDA.............. Electronic Document Authorization (CDE)
EDA.............. Elevation Difference Accuracy (CARB)
EDA.............. Elevation Drive Assembly (MCD)
EDA.............. Embedded Direct Analysis (SAUS)
EDA.............. Embedded Document Architecture [*PenPoint*] [*Computer science*]
EDA.............. Emergency Declaration Area [*Environmental Protection Agency*]
EDA.............. Emergency Distance Available [*Aviation*] (AIA)
EDA.............. Employment Development Act (SAUS)
EDA.............. Enacie Demokratiki Aristera [*United Democratic Left Party*] [*Greek*] (BARN)
EDA.............. Encoder/Decoder Assembly (MCD)
EDA.............. End-Diastolic Area [*Cardiology*]
EDA.............. Energy-Dispersive Analysis (SAUS)
EDA.............. Engineering Design Activities (SAUS)
EDA.............. Engineering Design Agreement
EDA.............. English Draughts Association (DBA)
EDA.............. Enterprise Data Access [*Computer science*] (HODG)
EDA.............. Environmental Damage and its Assessment (SAUS)
EDA.............. Environmental Development Administration (COE)
EDA.............. Environmental Development Agency (SAUS)
EDA.............. Epidermal Abscess [*Medicine*] (MELL)
EDA.............. Epidural Anesthesia [*Medicine*] (MELL)
EDA.............. Equal Diffusivities Approximation (SAUS)
EDA.............. Equipment Design Agent
EDA.............. Equipment Disposition Authorization
eda.............. equivalent design axles (SAUS)
EDA.............. Erbium-Doped fiber Amplifiers (SAUS)
EDA.............. Erection Digital Assembly
EDA.............. Error and Dispersion Analysis (MCD)
EDA.............. Error Detector Assembly
EDA.............. Estimated Date of Arrival (NG)
EDA.............. Estimated Date of Availability (AAG)
EDA.............. Ethiopian Democratic Alliance (SAUS)
EDA.............. Ethyl Diazoacetate [*Organic chemistry*]
EDA.............. Ethylene Diacrylate [*Organic chemistry*]
EDA.............. Ethylenediamenetetraacetic Acid
EDA.............. Ethylenediamine [*Organic chemistry*]
EDA.............. European Dairy Association (EURO)
EDA.............. European Democratic Alliance [*Political movement*] (ECON)
EDA.............. European Demolition Association (EA)
EDA.............. European Desalination Association [*Glasgow, Scotland*] (EAIO)
EDA.............. European Dichromate Producers Association (SAUS)
EDA.............. European Disposables Association [*Belgium*] (PDAA)
EDA.............. European Dyslexia Association (SAUS)
EDA.............. Evolutionary Defense Acquisition (AAGC)
EDA.............. Excess Defense Article (AFIT)
EDA.............. Execution Damage Assessment (SAA)
EDA.............. Exhaust Deflection Angle
EDA.............. Explorative Datenanalyse (SAUS)
EDA.............. Exploratory Data Analysis [*Statistics*]
EDA.............. Explosive Distributors Association [*Defunct*] (EA)
EDA.............. Extensive-Dilatancy Anisotropy [*Geology*]
EDA.............. External Data Accepted (SAUS)
EDA.............. External Data Aiding [*Computer science*] (PDAA)
EDA.............. Extreme Disablement Adjustment
Ed A2.......... Advanced Degree in Education
EDAA........... Frankfurt Am Main, USAFE [*United States Air Force in Europe*] [*Germany*] [*ICAO location identifier*] (ICLI)
EDAAL.......... Eastern Division (SAUS)
EDAAS.......... Expert Disclosure Analysis and Avoidance System [*Environmental protection agency*] (NITA)
EDAB........... Bitburg [*Germany*] [*ICAO location identifier*] (ICLI)
EDAB........... Early Deploying Armored Bridge (MCD)
EDAC........... Early Defibrillation/Advanced Care [*Medicine*] (MELL)
EDAC........... Earth Data Analysis Center (SAUO)
EDAC........... Economic Defense Advisory Committee (SAUO)
EDAC........... Edac Technologies [*NASDAQ symbol*] (TTSB)
Edac........... Edac Technologies Corp. [*Associated Press*] (SAG)
EDAC........... Electromechanical Digital Adapter Circuit (VERA)
EDAC........... Electron Donor Acceptor Complex
EDAC........... Electronic Design Automation Companies (SAUO)
EDAC........... Electronic Dive Angle Control
EDAC........... Electronics Development Analysis Center (SAUS)
EDAC........... Engineering Decision Analysis Company (SAUO)
EDAC........... Engineering Decision Analysis Corporation, Inc. (SAUO)
EDAC........... Engineering Design Advisory Committee (SAUO)
EDAC........... Equipment Distribution and Condition [*Statistical reporting system*] [*Military*] (AFM)
EDAC........... Error Detecting and Correcting (SAUS)
EDAC........... Error Detection and Correction
EDAC........... Error Detection & Correction Unit (SAUS)
EDAC........... Ethyl(dimethylaminopropyl)carbodiimide [*Also, EDC, EDCI*] [*Organic chemistry*]
EDAC........... European Conference on Design Automation (SAUS)
EDAC........... Evaluation, Dissemination, and Assessment Center for Bilingual Education (EDAC)
EDAC........... Exhibit and Display Association of Canada
EDAC........... Kindsbach [*Germany*] [*ICAO location identifier*] (ICLI)
EDA Complex... Electron Donar Acceptor Complex (SAUS)
EDACS.......... Enhanced Digital Access Communications System (CGWS)
EDACS.......... Environmental Data Access and Control System (HGAA)
EDACT.......... Engineering Drawings to Automatic Control Tapes (PDAA)
EDAD........... Spangdahlem [*Germany*] [*ICAO location identifier*] (ICLI)
EDAF........... Rhein-Main Air Base [*Germany*] [*ICAO location identifier*] (ICLI)
EDAG........... Ethiopian Democratic Action Group
EDAH........... Hahn [*Germany*] [*ICAO location identifier*] (ICLI)
EDAI........... Engineering Design Advance Information (DNAB)
EDAK........... Kindsbach [*Germany*] [*ICAO location identifier*] (ICLI)
EDAL........... Engineering Design and Analysis Laboratory [*University of New Hampshire*] [*Research center*] (RCD)
EDAL........... Sollingen [*Germany*] [*ICAO location identifier*] (ICLI)
EDALHAB....... Engineering Design and Analysis Laboratory Habitat
EDAM........... Edatrexate [*Antineoplastic drug*] (CDI)
EDAM........... Educational Distributors of Manitoba (SAUS)
EDAM........... Electron-Dense Amorphous Material [*Medicine*] (DMAA)
EDAM........... Electronic Design and Manufacture (IAA)
EDAM........... Experiments, Drill, and Maintenance
EDAM........... Zweibrucken [*Germany*] [*ICAO location identifier*] (ICLI)
EDAMS.......... Electronic Data and Management System
EDAN........... Lahr [*Germany*] [*ICAO location identifier*] (ICLI)
EDANA.......... European Disposables and Nonwovens Association
ED & C......... Electrodesiccation and Curettage [*Medicine*] (AAMN)
ED&C........... European Coal and Steel Community (EBF)
ED&D........... Expert Dungeons & Dragons (SAUS)
ED & I......... Engineering, Design, and Inspection
ED&M........... Electronic Desing and Manufacture (SAUS)
ED & T......... Equipment Development and Test Report [*Forest Service*]
ED & T Report... Equipment Development and Test Report (SAUS)
EDANS.......... Ethylenediaminenaphthalenesulfonic Acid (SAUS)
EDANSW......... Electrical Development Association of New South Wales [*Australia*]
EDAO........... Gates [*Germany*] [*ICAO location identifier*] (ICLI)
EDA - OER...... Economic Develapment Administration, Office of Economic Research (SAUS)
EDAP........... Eating Disorders Awareness and Prevention (SAUO)
EDAP........... EDAP TMS S.A. [*NASDAQ symbol*] (NASQ)
EDAP........... Employee Development and Assistance Programme (AIE)
EDAP........... Engagement Decision Analysis Process [*DoD*]
EDAP........... Environmental Design Alignment Process
EDAP........... Extraordinary Data Availability and Protection (SAUS)
EDAP........... May [*Germany*] [*ICAO location identifier*] (ICLI)
EDAPS.......... Electronic Data Processing System
EDAPS.......... Embedded Diagnostics and Prognostics Synchronization
EDAPS.......... Energy Data and Projection System (SAUS)
EDAQ........... Electrical Development Association of Queensland [*Australia*]
EDAQ........... Rotz [*Germany*] [*ICAO location identifier*] (ICLI)
EDAR........... Education Department Acquisition Regulation (AAGC)
EDAR........... Ramstein [*Germany*] [*ICAO location identifier*] (ICLI)
EDARC.......... Electronic Design Automation Research Center [*University of California*]
ED Ark......... United States District Court for the Eastern and Western Districts of Arkansas (DLA)
EDARR.......... Engineering Drawing and Assembly Release Record (AAG)
EDAS........... Ecosystem Dynamics and the Atmosphere Section (SAUS)
EDAS........... Engineering Design and Simulation System [*Graphic Data Ltd.*] [*Software package*] (NCC)
EDAS........... Enhanced Data-Acquisition System [*Computer science*] (ODBW)
EDAS........... Enlisted Distribution and Assignment System [*DoD*]

EDAS .... ERIC [*Educational Resources Information Center*] Data Access System [*Search system*]
EDAS .... Eta Data Assimilation System (SAUS)
EDAS .... Sembach [*Germany*] [*ICAO location identifier*] (ICLI)
Ed Asia Oceania... Education in Asia and Oceania [*A publication*]
Ed Asia Pacif... Education in Asia and the Pacific [*A publication*]
EDA/SQL ...... Enterprise Data Access/SQL [*Structured Query Language*] (CDE)
EDASRE .... Engineering Drawing Automated Storage and Retrieval Equipment (SAUS)
Ed Ass .... Eddis. Administration of Assets [*1880*] [*A publication*] (DLA)
EDASS .... EMSL-Cinci Equivalency Statistical System (SAUS)
EDASS .... Environmental Data Acquisition Sub-System (SAUS)
EDAT .... Electronic Data Technologies [*NASDAQ symbol*] (COMM)
EDATE .... Effective Date (SAUS)
EDATS .... Executive Data System (DNAB)
EDATS .... Extra-Deep Armed Team Sweep [*Military*]
EDAV .... Electrical Development Association of Victoria [*Australia*]
EDAV .... Siegenberg [*Germany*] [*ICAO location identifier*] (ICLI)
EDAVR .... Enlisted Distribution and Verification Report
EDAW .... Wiesbaden [*Germany*] [*ICAO location identifier*] (ICLI)
EDAWA .... Electrical Development Association of Western Australia [*Australia*]
EDAX .... energy disperse analysis x-ray (SAUS)
EDAX .... energy disperse analyzer X-ray (SAUS)
EDAX .... Energy Dispersion Analyzer X-ray (SAUS)
EDAX .... Energy Dispersive Analysis by X-Ray [*Photovoltaic energy systems*]
EDAX .... energy dispersive analysis of X-rays (SAUS)
EDAX .... Ramstein [*Germany*] [*ICAO location identifier*] (ICLI)
Edax Ed .... Edax Editor (journ.) (SAUS)
EdB .... Bachelor of Education (SAUS)
Ed B .... Bachelor of Education
EDB .... Broward Community College, Fort Lauderdale, FL [*OCLC symbol*] (OCLC)
EDB .... Early Dry Breakfast [*Medicine*]
EDB .... Earned Depletion Base (SAUS)
EDB .... Economic Defense Board [*Later, Board of Economic Warfare*] [*World War II*]
EDB .... Economic Development Board [*Singapore*]
EDB .... Economics Defense Board (SAUO)
EDB .... Edible (ABBR)
Edb .... Edinburgh (SAUS)
EDB .... Educational Data Bank (IEEE)
EDB .... Eerdmans Dictionary of the Bible [*A publication*]
EDB .... El Debba [*Sudan*] [*Airport symbol*] [*Obsolete*] (OAG)
EDB .... Electrodynamic Balance [*Physical chemistry*]
EDB .... Electronic Data Bank (SAUS)
EDB .... Elongated Die Bushing
EDB .... Embedded Database (SAUS)
EDB .... Emergency Dispersal Bases (NATG)
EDB .... End of Data Block [*Computer science*] (CET)
EDB .... Energy Database [*Department of Energy*] [*Information service or system*]
EDB .... Energy Development Board (COE)
EDB .... Engineering Data Bank [*GIDEP*]
EDB .... Engineering Data Base (SAUS)
EDB .... Environmental Data Book (NASA)
EDB .... Environmental Data Buoy (SAUS)
edb .... ethene dibromide (SAUS)
EDB .... Ethylene Dibromide [*Same as DBE, EB*] [*Organic chemistry*]
EDB .... Event Database
EDB .... Excise Duty Bulletins [*Revenue Canada - Customs and Excise*] [*Information service or system*] (CRD)
EDB .... Experience Data Base (SAUS)
EDB .... Export Data Branch (SAUO)
edb .... extended double base (SAUS)
EDB .... Extensional Database (RALS)
EDB .... Extensor Digitorum Brevis [*Anatomy*]
EDB .... Extradimensional Being
EDB .... Extruded Double Base (SAUS)
EDBA .... Berlin [*Germany*] [*ICAO location identifier*] (ICLI)
EDBAR .... Edith and Dana Bennett Agricultural Roundtable (EA)
EDBB .... Berlin/Tempelhof [*Germany*] [*ICAO location identifier*] (ICLI)
EDBC .... extra-dense barium crown (SAUS)
EDBD .... Environmental Data Base Directory [*National Oceanographic Data Center*] [*Database*] (MSC)
EDBG .... Berlin/Gatow [*Germany*] [*ICAO location identifier*] (ICLI)
EDBHPA ...... Ethylenediaminebis(hydroxyphenylacetic acid) [*Also, EDDHA, EDHPA*] [*Organic chemistry*]
EDBI .... Electronic Distributors Research Institute (SAUS)
Ed Bills .... Eddis on Bills of Exchange [*A publication*] (DLA)
EDBISS .... European Directory of Business Information Sources (SAUS)
edbiz .... educational business (SAUS)
Ed BL .... Eden's Bankrupt Law [*A publication*] (DLA)
EDBL .... Edible
EDBMS .... Engineering Data Base Management System (SAUS)
EDBP .... Epidemiology, Demography, and Biometry Program [*National Institute on Aging*] [*Department of Health and Human Services*]
Ed Bro .... Eden's Edition of Brown's English Chancery Reports [*1757-66*] [*A publication*] (DLA)
EDBS .... Educational Data Base Management System [*Computer science*] (MHDB)
EDBS .... Educational Database System [*Computer System Research Group*] [*University of Toronto*] (NITA)
EDBS .... Engineering Data Bank System (MCD)
EDBS .... Expert Database System [*Computer science*] (ODBW)
EDBSA .... Engine Drivers' Board of South Australia
EDBT .... Berlin/Tegel [*Germany*] [*ICAO location identifier*] (ICLI)
EDC .... Earth Day Canada (FOTI)
EDC .... Earth Resources Observation Systems Data Center (SAUO)
EDC .... Eastern Defense Command [*Army*]
EDC .... Eastern Defense Community (SAUO)
EDC .... Eastern District Court Reports [*South Africa*] [*A publication*] (DLA)
EDC .... Eastman Dental Center [*University of Rochester*] [*Research center*] (RCD)
EDC .... Economic Development Committee [*Nickname: "Little Neddie"*] [*British*]
EDC .... Economic Development Corporation (SAUS)
EdC .... EDCO, Springfield, MO [*Library symbol*] [*Library of Congress*] (LCLS)
EDC .... Edincik [*Turkey*] [*Seismograph station code, US Geological Survey*] (SEIS)
EDC .... Educational Development Center (SAUS)
EDC .... Educational Development Corporation (SAUO)
EDC .... Educational Development Council (SAUO)
EDC .... Education Development Center [*Defunct*] (EA)
EDC .... Effective Date of Change (MCD)
EDC .... Effective Date of Contract (SAUS)
EDC .... Effective Dielectric Constant (SAUS)
EDC .... Effective Dynamic Compliance (MEDA)
EDC .... Electrical Discharge (ACAE)
EDC .... Electrical Distribution Center [*Army*]
EDC .... Electrode Dark Current
EDC .... Electro Development Corporation (SAUO)
EDC .... Electronic Damping Control [*Automotive engineering*]
EDC .... Electronic Data Collection (SAUS)
EDC .... Electronic Data Communications
EDC .... Electronic Demand Charger
EDC .... Electronic Desk Calculator (IEEE)
EDC .... Electronic Diesel Control [*Automotive engineering*]
EDC .... Electronic Digital Computer
EDC .... Electronic Discharge LASER (MCD)
EDC .... Electronic Displacement Control [*Hydraulics*]
EDC .... Electronic Document Collection
EDC .... Electronics Design Center [*Case Western Reserve University*] [*Research center*] (RCD)
EDC .... Electronics Development Corporation (SAUO)
EDC .... electrooptic directional coupler (SAUS)
EDC .... Electrostatic Discharge Control (SAUS)
EDC .... Electrotechnical Divisional Council (SAUO)
EDC .... Emergency Decontamination Center [*Nuclear energy*] (NRCH)
EDC .... Emergency Digital Computer
EDC .... Enamel Double Cotton [*Wire insulation*] (AAG)
EDC .... Encyclopedie des Citations [*A publication*]
EDC .... End-Detonating Cartridge [*Explosive*]
EDC .... End-Diastolic Count [*Cardiology*]
EDC .... Energy Discharge Capacitor (IAA)
EDC .... Energy Distribution Curve [*Electron*]
EDC .... Engagement Direction Center (SAA)
EDC .... Engine-Drive Compressor (DNAB)
EDC .... Engineering Data Consultants (SAUS)
EDC .... Engineering Data Control
EDC .... Engineering Design Center (SAUS)
EDC .... Engineering Design Change
EDC .... Engineering Design Consultants (SAUS)
EDC .... Engineering Distributed Computing (TIMI)
EDC .... Engineering Documentation Center [*NASA*] (KSC)
EDC .... Engineering Document Control (ACAE)
EDC .... Engineering Drawing Change (SAUS)
EDC .... Enhanced Data Correction (SAUS)
EDC .... Enterprise Database Connectivity (SAUS)
EDC .... Environmental Data Center (SAUS)
EDC .... Environmental Discrimination Circuit (SAUS)
EDC .... EROS [*Earth Resources Observation Systems*] Data Center [*Marine science*] (MSC)
EDC .... Error Detecting Code
EDC .... Error Detection and Correction (NATG)
EDC .... Error-Detection Code (SAUS)
EDC .... Escalation during Construction (MCD)
EDC .... Estimated Date of Completion
EDC .... Estimated Date of Completion of Loading (SAUS)
EDC .... Estimated Date of Conception [*Obstetrics*] (DAVI)
EDC .... Estimated [*or Expected*] Date of Confinement [*Obstetrics*]
EDC .... estimated or expected date of confinement (SAUS)
EDC .... Ethiopian Democratic Coalition (SAUS)
EDC .... Ethiopian Democratic Organization Coalition
EDC .... Ethylcarbodiimide Chloride (SAUS)
EDC .... Ethyl(dimethylaminopropyl)carbodiimide [*Also, EDAC, EDCI*] [*Organic chemistry*]
EDC .... Ethylene Dichloride [*Organic chemistry*]
EDC .... European Danube Commission (SAUS)
EDC .... European Defense Communications System (ACAE)
EDC .... European Defense Community [*NATO*]
EDC .... European Disarmament Conference
EDC .... European Documentation Centre [*University of Dundee*] [*Dundee, Scotland*] (DLA)
EDC .... European Documentation Centre - Lecce (SAUS)
EDC .... Evaluation Documentation Center [*Department of Health and Human Services*] [*Information service or system*] (IID)
EDC .... Event Driven Component
EDC .... Excessive Duty Cycle [*Military*]
EDC .... Expect Departure Clearance (SAUS)

EDC.......... Expect Departure Clearance At [*Aviation*] (FAAC)
EDC.......... Expected Date of Confinement [*Medicine*] (DHSM)
E/DC.......... Expected/Dual-Command Travel Time
EDC.......... Experimental Display Concept [*Space shuttle*] [*NASA*]
EDC.......... Experiment Development Center [*NASA*] (KSC)
EDC.......... Exploder Dynamo Condenser (SAUS)
EDC.......... Explosive Disposal Control
EDC.......... Export Development Corp. [*Canada*]
EDC.......... Extended Device Control (MHDB)
EDC.......... Extensor Digitorum Communis [*Muscle or tendon*] [*Anatomy*] (DAVI)
EDC.......... External Data Carrier (SAUS)
EDC.......... External-Device Code [*Computer science*] (MDG)
EDC.......... External Disk Channel (SAUS)
EDC.......... External Disk/Drum Channel
EDC.......... Extractive Distillation Column [*Chemical engineering*]
EDC.......... Extra Dark Color (ADA)
EDC.......... Electron-Distribution Curve [*Physics*] (ODA)
EDC-16.......... Error Detection Correction 16-Bit (SAUS)
EDCA.......... Educate (ABBR)
EDCA.......... Employment Department Clerks' Association [*A union*] [*British*]
EDCA.......... Executive Director for Conventional Ammunition
EDCA.......... Gluecksburg [*Germany*] [*ICAO location identifier*] (ICLI)
EDCAB.......... Educable (ABBR)
EDCAD.......... Educated (ABBR)
EDCAG.......... Educating (ABBR)
ED Cal.......... United States District Court for the Eastern District of California (DLA)
EdcAlt.......... Education Alternative, Inc. [*Associated Press*] (SAG)
EDCAN.......... Education (ABBR)
EDCANL.......... Educational (ABBR)
EDCARS.......... Engineering Data Computer-Assisted Retrieval System [*Air Force*] (GFGA)
EDCARS.......... Engineering Data Computer Automated Retrieval System (SAUS)
EDCATR.......... Educator (ABBR)
EDCAV.......... Educative (ABBR)
EDCB.......... Bueckeburg [*Germany*] [*ICAO location identifier*] (ICLI)
EDCBL.......... Educable (ABBR)
EDCC.......... Electronic Data Council of Canada (SAUO)
EDCC.......... Emergency Defence Communications Centre (SAUS)
EDCC.......... Error Detection and Correction Controller (SAUS)
EDCC.......... Goch [*Germany*] [*ICAO location identifier*] (ICLI)
EDCCI.......... Economic Development Committee for the Clothing Industry (SAUO)
EDCD.......... EDIFACT Composite Elements Directory (AG)
EDCD.......... Engineering Data Control Department (ACAE)
EDCE.......... Electric-Drive Control Electronics (SEWL)
EDCE.......... Rheine-Bentlage [*Germany*] [*ICAO location identifier*] (ICLI)
EDCEN.......... Education Center [*Army*] (AABC)
EDC Equipment... Error Detection and Correction Equipment (SAUS)
EDCF.......... Endothelial-Derived Contraction Factor (DB)
EDCF.......... endothelium-derived constricting factor (SAUS)
EDCF.......... European Defence Community Forces (SAUO)
EDCG.......... Educating (ABBR)
EDCG.......... Eggebek [*Germany*] [*ICAO location identifier*] (ICLI)
EDCG.......... Error Detection Code Generator
EDCGC.......... Elliott District Community Government Council [*Australia*]
Ed Ch.......... Edwards' New York Chancery Reports [*A publication*] (DLA)
EDCH.......... Hurth [*Germany*] [*ICAO location identifier*] (ICLI)
Ed Ch R.......... Edwards' New York Chancery Reports [*A publication*] (DLA)
EDCI.......... Energetic Dynamic Cardiac Insufficiency [*Cardiology*] (DMAA)
EDCI.......... Ethyl(dimethylaminopropyl)carbodiimide [*Also, EDAC, EDC*] [*Organic chemistry*]
EDCI.......... Itzehoe Hungriger Wolf [*Germany*] [*ICAO location identifier*] (ICLI)
ed cit.......... Editio Citata [*Edition Cited*] [*Latin*]
EDCK.......... Kiel-Holtenau [*Germany*] [*ICAO location identifier*] (ICLI)
EDCL.......... Celle [*Germany*] [*ICAO location identifier*] (ICLI)
EDCL.......... EDIFACT Codes List Directory (AG)
edcl.......... electric discharge coaxial laser (SAUS)
EDCL.......... Electric-Discharge Convection LASER [*Navy*]
EDCI.......... Ethylcarbodiimide Chloride (SAUS)
EDC-L.......... European Documentation Centre-Lecce (SAUS)
EDCLMDA.... Eastern Dry Cleaning and Laundry Machinery Distributors Association [*Defunct*] (EA)
EDCM.......... Aachen/Merzbruck [*Germany*] [*ICAO location identifier*] (ICLI)
EDC (M).......... Electrochemical Depolarization CO^2[*Carbon Dioxide*] (Module)
EDC(M).......... Electrochemical Depolarized Carbon Dioxide (Module) [*NASA*] (NASA)
EDC(M).......... Electrochemical Depolarized (Module) (SAUS)
EDCM.......... Extracted, Dialyzed Crab Meat (SAUS)
EdcMge.......... Education Management Corp. [*Associated Press*] (SAG)
EDCMR.......... Effective Date of Change of Morning Report [*Military*]
EDCN.......... Education (ADA)
EDCN.......... Engineering Drawing Change Notice [*Nuclear energy*] (NRCH)
EDCN.......... Equipment Design Change Notice (SAUS)
EDCN.......... Experimental Data Communications Network (MCD)
EDCN.......... Nordholz [*Germany*] [*ICAO location identifier*] (ICLI)
EDCO.......... Economic Developers Council of Ontario [*Canada*] (FOTI)
EDCO.......... Edison Control Corp. [*NASDAQ symbol*] (NQ)
EDCO.......... Editing Committee (SAUS)
EDCo.......... Educational Development Corp. [*Defunct*] (EA)
EDCO.......... Educational Development Corporation (SAUO)
EDCOM.......... Editor and Compiler
edcom.......... editor-compiler (SAUS)
EDCOM.......... Educational Computing Network (SAUS)
EDCOMER.... European Documentation Centre and Observatory on Migration and Ethnic Relations (EURO)
Ed Comment... Editorial Comment (DLA)
EDCOM Network... Educational Computing Network (SAUS)
Ed Comp Con... Educational Computing Conference (SAUS)
EDCOR.......... Economic Development Corps [*Philippines*]
EDCP.......... Engineering Design Change Proposal
E/DCP.......... Equipment/Document Change Proposal (NATG)
EDCP.......... Ethyl Dichlorophosphate [*Organic chemistry*]
EDCP.......... External Data Channel Processor (NOAA)
EDCPF.......... Environmental Data Collection and Processing Facility [*Tucson, AZ*] [*Army*] (AABC)
Ed CR.......... Edwards' New York Chancery Reports [*A publication*] (DLA)
EDCR.......... Engineering Design Change Request (MCD)
EDCR.......... Rotenburg/Wumme [*Germany*] [*ICAO location identifier*] (ICLI)
EDCs.......... Economic Development Committees (SAUS)
EDCS.......... Ecumenical Development Cooperative Society (EAIO)
EDCS.......... End-Diastolic Chamber Stiffness [*Medicine*] (DMAA)
EDCS.......... End-Diastolic Circumferential Stress [*Medicine*] (DMAA)
EDCS.......... Engineering Data Control System (SAUS)
EDCS.......... Engineering Design Change Schedule
EDCS.......... Engineering Document Control System (HGAA)
EDCs.......... European Documentation Centres (SAUO)
EDCS.......... Extended Defense Communication System (CINC)
EDCS.......... Schleswig [*Germany*] [*ICAO location identifier*] (ICLI)
EDCSA.......... Effective Date of Change of Strength Accountability [*Military*]
EDCT.......... Estimated Departure Clearance Time [*FAA*] (TAG)
EDCT.......... Expected Departure Clearance Time (PIPO)
EDCTU.......... Electronic Development and Compatibility Test Unit
EDCU.......... Butzweilerhof [*Germany*] [*ICAO location identifier*] (ICLI)
EDCU.......... Eight Digit Calculator Unit (SAUS)
EDCU.......... Error Detection and Correction Units (SAUS)
EDCV.......... Enamel Double Cotton Varnish [*Wire insulation*]
EDCW.......... External-Device Control Word [*Computer science*]
EDCW.......... Werl [*Germany*] [*ICAO location identifier*] (ICLI)
EDCX.......... Ethyl-Dow Chemical [*Private rail car owner code*]
Ed D.......... Doctor of Education (SAUS)
EDD.......... Earliest Delivery Date [*Navy*] (DOMA)
EDD.......... Earliest Departure Date (SAUS)
EDD.......... Earliest Due Date
EDD.......... Early Differentiation (DB)
EDD.......... Eastern Development Division [*Air Force*]
EDD.......... Eastman Dental Dispensary (SAUS)
EDD.......... Economic Development District [*EDA*]
EDD.......... Economic Development Division (SAUS)
EDD.......... Eddied (ABBR)
Edd.......... Edited by (SAUS)
EDD.......... Editions (ROG)
EDD.......... Editors (ROG)
EDD.......... Effective Drug Duration [*Medicine*] (MAE)
EDD.......... Electric Displacement Density
EDD.......... Electrodermal Diagnosis [*Controversial medical technique*]
EDD.......... Electronic Data Display
EDD.......... Electronic Dehydration Dryer
EDD.......... Electronic Document Delivery [*Software*]
EDD.......... Electronic Document Distribution [*Computer science*] (ELAL)
EDD.......... Employment Development Department (SAUS)
EDD.......... End Delivery Date (AAG)
EDD.......... End-Diastolic Diameter [*Cardiology*]
EdD.......... End-Diastolic Dimension [*Cardiology*]
EDD.......... Energy Distribution Difference (SAUS)
EDD.......... Enforcement Decision Document [*Environmental Protection Agency*] (ERG)
EDD.......... Engagement Data Display (MCD)
EDD.......... Engineering and Development Directorate [*Johnson Space Center*] [*NASA*]
EDD.......... Engineering Data Depository (MSA)
EDD.......... Engineering Design Data (AAG)
EDD.......... Engineering Development and Design (SAUS)
EDD.......... Engineering Development Department (SAUS)
EDD.......... Engineering Development Division [*Pacific Marine Environmental Laboratory*] (USDC)
EDD.......... English Dialect Dictionary [*A publication*]
EDD.......... Enterprise Data Distribution [*Computer science*] (VERA)
EDD.......... Envelope Delay Distortion
EDD.......... Environmental Data Directory [*Database*] (EERA)
EDD.......... Enzyme-Digested Delta Endotoxin [*of Bacillus thuringiensis*] [*Biological control*]
EDD.......... Equipment Data Display
EDD.......... Equipment Density Data
EDD.......... Equipment Development Division [*Britain's national phone-tapping center*]
EDD.......... Essential Data Duplicator [*Utilico Microware*]
EDD.......... Estimated Date of Departure [*or Detachment*] [*Military*] (DNAB)
EDD.......... Estimated Delivery Date
EDD.......... Estimated Departure Date (SAUS)
EDD.......... Event Data Distributor (MCD)
EDD.......... Exchange of Digital Data (SAUS)
EDD.......... Expected Date of Delivery [*Obstetrics*]
EDD.......... Experimental Destroyer (SAUS)
EDD.......... Expert Database Designer [*Computer science*]
EDD.......... Explosives Detection Devices [*FAA*] (TAG)
EDD.......... Extra Deep Drawing [*Metal industry*]
EDD.......... Exactly Delayed Detonator (ODA)
EDDA.......... Bonn, Frankfurt Am Main [*Germany*] [*ICAO location identifier*] (ICLI)
EDDA.......... Electronic Demand Deposit Accounting (VLIE)
EDDA.......... Electronic Digital Data Acquisition (SAUS)

EDDA .... Electronic Directory of German Databases [*Information service or system*] (IID)
EDDA .... Ethylenediaminediacetic Acid [*Organic chemistry*]
EDDC .... East Coast Documents Distribution Center
EDDC .... Extended Distance Data Cable (VLIE)
EDDD .... Error Detection and Decision Feedback (SAUS)
EDDD .... Expanded Direct Distance Dialing [*Telecommunications*]
EDDD .... Frankfurt Am Main [*Germany*] [*ICAO location identifier*] (ICLI)
EDDF .... Error Detection and Decision Feedback
EDDF .... Frankfurt Am Main [*Germany*] [*ICAO location identifier*] (ICLI)
EDDFEC .... Estimated Date of Departure Far East Command [*Military*]
EDDH .... Hamburg [*Germany*] [*ICAO location identifier*] (ICLI)
EDDHA .... Ethylenediaminedi-O-Hydroxyphenylacetate [*or -hydroxyphenylacetic Acid*] [*Also, EDBHPA, EDHPA*] [*Organic chemistry*]
EDDI .... Ethylenediamine Dihydriodide [*Organic chemistry*]
EDDIC .... Experimental Development, Demonstration, and Integration Center [*Army*]
EDDIE .... Environmental Distribution of Dynamic Item Entries (SAA)
EDDIS .... Electronic Document Delivery: Integrated Solutions [*Project*] (AIE)
EDDK .... Koeln-Bonn [*Germany*] [*ICAO location identifier*] (ICLI)
EDDL .... Duesseldorf [*Germany*] [*ICAO location identifier*] (ICLI)
EDDM .... Muenchen [*Germany*] [*ICAO location identifier*] (ICLI)
EDDN .... Nuernberg [*Germany*] [*ICAO location identifier*] (ICLI)
EDDNTC .... Endodontic
EDDP .... Electron Dipole-Dipole Polarization
EDDP .... Engineering Design Data Package (AAG)
EDDP .... Engineering Design Documentation Procedures (MCD)
EDDQ .... Extra-Deep-Drawing-Quality [*Steel*]
EDDR .... Electron Dipole-Dipole Reservoir (NASA)
EDDRA .... Exchange on Drug Demand Reduction Action (SAUS)
EDDS .... Early Docking Demonstration System (IAA)
EDDS .... Electron Devices Data Service [*National Institute of Standards and Technology*]
EDDS .... Electronic Document Delivery Service (TELE)
E-D DS .... Elsevier-Dutton Distribution Services (SAUS)
EDDS .... Emergency Detection and Decision System
EDDS .... Enhanced Defense Logistics Agency Distribution System (AAGC)
EDDS .... Ethylenediaminedisuccinic [*Organic chemistry*]
EDDS .... European Data Distribution System (SAUS)
EDDS .... Executive Data Display System (HGAA)
EDDS .... Stuttgart [*Germany*] [*ICAO location identifier*] (ICLI)
EDDS Acid ... Ethylene Diamine-disuccinic Acid (SAUS)
EDDU .... Rhein [*Germany*] [*ICAO location identifier*] (ICLI)
EDDUS .... Electronic Data Display and Update System (SAUS)
EDDV .... Hannover [*Germany*] [*ICAO location identifier*] (ICLI)
EDDW .... Bremen [*Germany*] [*ICAO location identifier*] (ICLI)
EDDY .... Maastricht [*Germany*] [*ICAO location identifier*] (ICLI)
EDDZ .... Frankfurt Am Main [*Germany*] [*ICAO location identifier*] (ICLI)
EDE .... Economic Development Foundation (SAUO)
EDE .... Edenton, NC [*Location identifier*] [*FAA*] (FAAL)
EDE .... Effective Dose Equivalent (COE)
EDE .... Electrical Design Engineering
EDE .... Electronic Data Exchange [*DoD*]
EDE .... Electronic Defense Evaluator
EDE .... Electronic Design Engineering (SAUS)
EDE .... Elevator Design Engineering (SAUS)
EDE .... Elliptic [*or Exact*] Differential Equation
EDE .... Emergency Decelerating [*Relay*] (IEEE)
EDE .... Emerging Mkts Income Fund II [*NYSE symbol*] (TTSB)
EDE .... Emitter Dip Effect (IEEE)
EDE .... Empire District Electric Co. [*NYSE symbol*] (SPSG)
EDE .... Encrypt-Decrypt-Encrypt (SAUS)
EDE .... Engineering Design Establishment (SAUS)
EDE .... Engineering Development Establishment [*Australia*]
EDE .... Environmental Data and Ecological Parameters Data Base [*International Societyof Ecological Modelling*] [*Information service or system*] (IID)
EDE .... Esquerda Democratica Estudantil [*Democratic Student Left*] [*Portugal*] [*Political party*] (PPE)
EDE .... Experimental Demolition Establishment [*British*]
EDE .... Experimental Escort Ship (SAUS)
EDE .... External Document Exchange (HGAA)
EDEA .... Amberg [*Germany*] [*ICAO location identifier*] (ICLI)
EDEAC .... EPRI [*Electric Power Research Institute*] Database for Environmentally Assisted Cracking [*Battelle Memorial Institute*] [*Information service or system*] (IID)
EDEB .... Ansbach [*Germany*] [*ICAO location identifier*] (ICLI)
EDEC .... Aschaffenburg [*Germany*] [*ICAO location identifier*] (ICLI)
EDECN .... European Development Education Curriculum Network
EDECN .... European Development Education Network (SAUO)
EDECWS ...... Emergency Diesel Engine Cooling Water System [*Nuclear energy*] (NRCH)
EDED .... EDIFACT Data Elements Directory (AG)
EDED .... Error Detection Encoder-Decoder [*Ground Communications Facility, NASA*]
EDED .... Kaiserlautern [*Germany*] [*ICAO location identifier*] (ICLI)
EDEE .... Heidelberg, United States Army [*Germany*] [*ICAO location identifier*] (ICLI)
EDEEN .... Engineering Division Electrical Engineering Newsletter (SAUO)
EDEF .... Babenhausen [*Germany*] [*ICAO location identifier*] (ICLI)
EDEG .... Bad Kissingen [*Germany*] [*ICAO location identifier*] (ICLI)
EDEH .... Bad Kreuznach [*Germany*] [*ICAO location identifier*] (ICLI)
EDEI .... Miesau-West [*Germany*] [*ICAO location identifier*] (ICLI)
EDEJ .... Bamberg [*Germany*] [*ICAO location identifier*] (ICLI)
EDEK .... Baumholder [*Germany*] [*ICAO location identifier*] (ICLI)
EDEK .... Unified Democratic Union of the Center (Cyprus) [*Political party*] (PSAP)
EDEL .... Bayreuth [*Germany*] [*ICAO location identifier*] (ICLI)
EDEL .... Edelbrock Corp. [*NASDAQ symbol*] (SAG)
Edelbrck ...... Edelbrock Corp. [*Associated Press*] (SAG)
EDELS .... Emergency Diesel Engine Lubrication System [*Nuclear energy*] (NRCH)
EDEM .... European Defence Equipment Market (SAUS)
EDEM .... Muenchen, Hospital, Perlacher Forst [*Germany*] [*ICAO location identifier*] (ICLI)
EDEN .... Eden Bio Science [*NASDAQ symbol*]
Eden .... Eden's English Chancery Reports [*28 English Reprint*] [*A publication*] (DLA)
EDEN .... Emma Dorothy Eliza Nevitte Southworth [*American novelist, 1818-99*] [*Acronym used as pseudonym*]
EDEN .... Engineering Design Network (ACAE)
EDEN .... European Dermato-Epidemiology Network (SAUO)
EDEN .... Evaluated Disposition toward the Environment [*Student attitude test*]
EDEN .... Maurice Rose [*Germany*] [*ICAO location identifier*] (ICLI)
Eden Bankr... Eden's Bankrupt Law [*A publication*] (DLA)
EDENDOR .... Electrically Detected Electron Nuclear Double Resonance (AAEL)
Eden (Eng)... Eden's English Chancery Reports [*28 English Reprint*] [*A publication*] (DLA)
Eden Pen Law... Eden's Principles of Penal Law [*A publication*] (DLA)
Eden's Prin PL... Eden's Principles of Penal Law [*A publication*] (DLA)
EDENT .... Edentate (ABBR)
edent .... Edentulous [*Toothless*] [*Dentistry*] (DAVI)
EDEO .... Bremerhaven [*Germany*] [*ICAO location identifier*] (ICLI)
EDEO .... Episcopal Division Ecumenical Officers (SAUS)
EDEP .... Budingen [*Germany*] [*ICAO location identifier*] (ICLI)
EDEP .... Electrodeposition (SAUS)
EDEPR .... Electrically Detected Electron Paramagnetic Resonance (AAEL)
EDEPrA .... Empire Dist El,4 3/4% Pfd [*NYSE symbol*] (TTSB)
EDEPrB .... Empire Dist El,5% Pfd [*NYSE symbol*] (TTSB)
EDER .... Crailsheim [*Germany*] [*ICAO location identifier*] (ICLI)
EDE Relay ... Emergency Decelerating Relay (SAUS)
EDES .... Darmstadt [*Germany*] [*ICAO location identifier*] (ICLI)
EDES .... Ethnikos Demokratikos Ellinikos Stratos [*National Democratic Greek Army*] (PPE)
EDESA .... Economic Development of Equatorial and Southern Africa
EDESS .... Emergency Diesel Engine Starting System [*Nuclear energy*] (NRCH)
EDET .... Elevation Data Edit Terminals (RDA)
EDET .... Engine Detector (MCD)
EDET .... Erlangen [*Germany*] [*ICAO location identifier*] (ICLI)
EDETATE ...... Ethylenediaminetetraacetate [*Also, EDTA, enta*] [*USAN*] [*Organic chemistry*]
Ed et Ord ..... Edits et Ordonnances [*Lower Canada*] [*A publication*] (DLA)
EDEU .... Giebelstadt [*Germany*] [*ICAO location identifier*] (ICLI)
EDEUCHEM... European Association of Editors of Periodicals in Chemistry and Physics (SAUO)
EDEV .... Friedberg [*Germany*] [*ICAO location identifier*] (ICLI)
EDEW .... Enhanced Distant Early Warning
EDEW .... Fuerth [*Germany*] [*ICAO location identifier*] (ICLI)
EDEX .... Fulda [*Germany*] [*ICAO location identifier*] (ICLI)
EDEXIM .... European Data base on Export-Import of certain dangerous chemicals (SAUS)
edexs .... education of exceptional students (SAUS)
EDEY .... Zweibrucken [*Germany*] [*ICAO location identifier*] (ICLI)
EDEZ .... Germersheim [*Germany*] [*ICAO location identifier*] (ICLI)
EDF .... Anchorage, AK [*Location identifier*] [*FAA*] (FAAL)
EDF .... Earliest Deadline First (RALS)
EDF .... Earthquake Data File [*Marine science*] (MSC)
EDF .... East Daggafontein [*Vancouver Stock Exchange symbol*]
EDF .... Economics of Distribution Foundation (EA)
EDF .... Edited Detail File (SAUS)
Ed F .... Educational Forum [*A publication*] (BRI)
EDF .... Electrical Discharge Forming [*Manufacturing term*] (IAA)
EDF .... Electric Depth Finder
EDF .... Electric-Drive Fan [*Automotive engineering*]
EDF .... Electricite de France
EDF .... Electricity Development Fund [*Australia*]
EDF .... Electrophoresis Duplicating Film [*For analytical chemistry*]
EDF .... Elmendorf AFB (SAUS)
EDF .... Elongatable Dow Fiber [*Dow Chemical Co.*]
EDF .... Elongation, Derotation, and Lateral Flexion [*Medicine*]
EDF .... Emergency Decontamination Facility [*Energy Research and Development Administration*]
EDF .... Emerging Markets Income Fund [*NYSE symbol*] (SPSG)
EDF .... Empirical Distribution Function [*Statistics*]
EDF .... Engineering and Development Facility (SAUS)
EDF .... Engineering Data File
EDF .... Engineering Data Form (SAUS)
EDF .... Engineering Demonstration Facility (SAUS)
EDF .... Engineering Design Format (ACAE)
EDF .... Enlisted Dining Facility [*Military*]
EdF .... Enroles de Force [*Forced Conscripts*] [*Luxembourg*] (PPE)
EDF .... Environmental Defense Fund (EA)
EDF .... Environmental Defense Fund, Inc. (SAUO)
EDF .... Epidermal Cell Derived Factor [*Biochemistry*]
EDF .... Erythroid Differentiation Factor [*Endocrinology*]
EDF .... Estimated Date of Flight (SAUS)
EDF .... Estimated Duration of Flight (SAUS)
EDF .... European Defense Force (NATG)
EDF .... European Development Fund (EY)
EDF .... European Disability Forum (EURO)

EDF........ Everyman Defense Fund (SAUS)
EDF........ Execution Diagnostic Facility (HGAA)
EDF........ Experiment Data Facility [*NASA*] (KSC)
EDF........ Experiment Data Frame (SAUS)
EDF........ Exploratory Development Facility (SAUS)
EDF........ External Delay Factor [*Computer science*]
EDF........ Extra Dense Flint (SAUS)
EDFA........ Electronic Differential Analyzer (MSA)
EDFA........ Employer Dentists Federation of Australia
EDFA........ Erbium-Doped Fiber Amplifier [*Materials science*]
EDFB........ Eastern Deciduous Forest Biome [*Ecological biogeographic study*]
EDFB........ Reichelsheim [*Germany*] [*ICAO location identifier*] (ICLI)
EDFC........ Aschaffenburg-Grossostheim [*Germany*] [*ICAO location identifier*] (ICLI)
EDFC........ Edifice (ABBR)
EDFCN........ Edification (ABBR)
EDFD........ Edified (ABBR)
EDF-DOC........ EDF- documentations (SAUS)
EDF-DOC........ Electricite de France [*Bibliographic database*] [*French*]
EDFE........ Egelsbach [*Germany*] [*ICAO location identifier*] (ICLI)
EDFE........ Engineer District, Far East (CINC)
EDFF........ Frankfurt [*Germany*] [*ICAO location identifier*] (ICLI)
EDFG........ Edge Device Functional Group
EDFG........ Edifying (ABBR)
EDFG........ Extended Data Flow Graph
EDFG........ Gelnhausen [*Germany*] [*ICAO location identifier*] (ICLI)
EDFI........ Electronic Direct Fuel Injection [*Automotive fuel systems*]
EDF-III........ Engineering Development Facility (SAUS)
EDFK........ Bad Kissingen [*Germany*] [*ICAO location identifier*] (ICLI)
Ed-Flex........ Education Flexibility Partnership Act of 1999
EDFM........ Educational FM Station (NTCM)
EDFM........ Electronic Design for Manufacture
EDFM........ Extended Disk File Management System [*Computer science*] (VLIE)
EDFM........ Mannheim-Neuostheim [*Germany*] [*ICAO location identifier*] (ICLI)
EDFMIS........ Department of Education Financial Management Information System (GFGA)
EDFM System... Extended Disk File Management System (SAUS)
EDFN........ Marburg-Schoenstadt [*Germany*] [*ICAO location identifier*] (ICLI)
EDFO........ Economic Development Financing Organization [*Greece*]
EDFO........ Michelstadt [*Germany*] [*ICAO location identifier*] (ICLI)
EDFORUM........ Educators Forum [*Columbus, OH*] [*Information service or system*] (IID)
EDFP........ Engine Driven Fire Pump (IEEE)
EDFQ........ Allendorf/Eder [*Germany*] [*ICAO location identifier*] (ICLI)
EDFR........ Effective Date of Federal Recognition [*Military*]
EDFR........ Rothenburg [*Germany*] [*ICAO location identifier*] (ICLI)
EDFRL........ Erbium-Doped Fiber Ring LASER [*Physics*]
EDFS........ Schweinfurt-Sud [*Germany*] [*ICAO location identifier*] (ICLI)
ED-FTGA........ Eastern Dark-Fired Tobacco Growers Association (EA)
EDFU........ Mainbullau [*Germany*] [*ICAO location identifier*] (ICLI)
EDFV........ Worms [*Germany*] [*ICAO location identifier*] (ICLI)
EDFW........ Wuerzburg-Schenkenturm [*Germany*] [*ICAO location identifier*] (ICLI)
EDFX........ Fuldatal [*Germany*] [*ICAO location identifier*] (ICLI)
EDFY........ Edify Corp. [*NASDAQ symbol*] (TTSB)
EDFYD........ Edified (ABBR)
EDFYG........ Edifying (ABBR)
Edg........ Edgar (SAUS)
Edg........ Edgar's Reports, Scotch Court of Session [*1724-25*] [*A publication*] (DLA)
EDG........ Edge (SAUS)
EDG........ Edgewood Arsenal, MD [*Location identifier*] [*FAA*] (FAAL)
EDG........ Edinburgh Department of Geology (SAUO)
EDG........ Electrical Discharge Grinding [*Manufacturing term*]
EDG........ Electrodermatogram (SAUS)
EDG........ Electrodischarge Grinding (SAUS)
EDG........ Electrodynamic Gradient (SAUS)
EDG........ Electrodynamic Gradient Freeze [*Crystal growing technique*]
EDG........ Electrodynogram [*For evaluation of walking gait*]
EDG........ Electronic Development Group [*Military*] (AFIT)
EDG........ Electronic Dot Generation (DGA)
EDG........ Emergency Diesel Generator (NRCH)
EDG........ Employment Department Group (HEAS)
EDG........ Environmental Database Gateway (SAUO)
EDG........ Equivalent Dielectric Guide (SAUS)
EDG........ European Democratic Group (SAUO)
EDG........ Executive Development Group (SAUO)
EDG........ Exploratory Development Goal [*Military*]
EDGA........ European Graphic Dealers Association (SAUO)
Edgar........ Edgar's Reports, Scotch Court of Session [*1724-25*] [*A publication*] (DLA)
EDGAR........ Education Department General Administrative Regulations [*Department of Education*] (GFGA)
EDGAR........ Electronic Data Gathering, Analysis, and Retrieval [*Securities and Exchange Commission pilot project*] (IID)
EDGAR........ Electronic Gathering, Analysis and Retrieval System (SAUS)
EDGAR........ Experimental Data Gathering and Reduction (MCD)
EDGAR System... Electronic Document Gathering, Analysis and Retrieval System (SAUS)
EDGB........ Breitscheid/Dillkreis [*Germany*] [*ICAO location identifier*] (ICLI)
EDGB........ Export Development Grants Board (SAUS)
Edg C........ Canons Enacted under King Edgar [*A publication*] (DLA)
EDGCAIES........ Emergency Diesel Generator Combustion Air Intake and Exhaust System [*Nuclear energy*] (NRCH)
EDGD........ Edged (ABBR)
EDGE........ Electronic Data Gathering Equipment
EDGE........ Electronic Document Gathering Environment [*A.B. Dick*] [*Updatable fiche system*] (NITA)
EDGE........ Energy Data Geographical Explorer (SAUS)
EDGE........ Engineering data gathering equipment (SAUS)
EDGe........ Engineering, Design and Geosciences Group (SAUO)
EDGE........ Enhanced Data Rate for Global Evolution
EDGE........ Enhanced Data rate for GSM Evolution (SAUS)
EDGE........ Enhanced Digital Geodetic Environment (SEWL)
EDGE........ Ergonomic Digitally Generated Environments [*Chrysler Corp.*]
EDGE........ Evolution through Dynamic Group Experience
EDGE........ Experimental Display Generator
EDGE........ Extensible Display Geometry Engine (SAUS)
EDGE........ Visual Edge Systems, Inc. [*NASDAQ symbol*] (SAG)
EDGECON........ Edge Connector (SAUS)
EDGEP........ European Democratic Group in the European Parliament [*Brussels, Belgium*] [*Political party*] (EAIO)
EDGF........ Electrodynamic Gradient Freeze (SAUS)
EDGF........ Endothelial-Derived Growth Factor [*Biochemistry*]
EDGF........ Eye-Derived Growth Factor [*Biochemistry*]
EDGG........ Edging (ABBR)
EDGK........ Korbach [*Germany*] [*ICAO location identifier*] (ICLI)
EDGL........ Ludwigshafen-Unfallklinik [*Germany*] [*ICAO location identifier*] (ICLI)
Edg Leas........ Edges' Forms of Leases [*A publication*] (DLA)
EDGM........ Mosbach-Lohrbach [*Germany*] [*ICAO location identifier*] (ICLI)
EDGN........ Nordenbeck [*Germany*] [*ICAO location identifier*] (ICLI)
EDGNS........ Edginess (ABBR)
EDGNSW........ Export Development Group of New South Wales [*Australia*]
EDGO........ Oedheim [*Germany*] [*ICAO location identifier*] (ICLI)
EDGR........ Edgier (ABBR)
EDGS........ Electronic Data Gathering System [*Computer science*] (ECII)
EDGST........ Edgiest (ABBR)
EDGT........ Elevation Data Editing Terminal (SAUS)
EDGW........ Edgewise (MSA)
EDGW........ Wolfhagen/Granerberg [*Germany*] [*ICAO location identifier*] (ICLI)
EDGWD........ Edgewood, IL [*American Association of Railroads railroad junction routing code*]
EDGWS........ Edgewise (ABBR)
EDGYR........ Edgier (ABBR)
EDGYST........ Edgiest (ABBR)
EDH........ Efficient Deck Hand (NATG)
EDH........ Efficient Deck Hand certificate (SAUS)
EDH........ Ego-Distonic Homosexuality (SAUS)
EDH........ Engineering Design Handbook (MCD)
EDH........ Ethylenedihydrazine (MCD)
EDH........ Execution Data Handler (SAUS)
EDH........ Sturgeon Bay, WI [*Location identifier*] [*FAA*] (FAAL)
EDHA........ Hamburg [*Germany*] [*ICAO location identifier*] (ICLI)
EDHAG........ EDH Advisory Group (SAUO)
EDHASA........ Editora y Distribuidora Hispano-Americana Sociedad Anonima [*Publisher's imprint*] [*Spain*]
EDHB........ Grube [*Germany*] [*ICAO location identifier*] (ICLI)
EDHC........ Luchow/Rehbeck [*Germany*] [*ICAO location identifier*] (ICLI)
EDH Certificate... Efficient Deck Hand Certificate (SAUS)
EDHE........ Experimental Data Handling Equipment
EDHE........ External Data Handling Equipment (SAUS)
EDHE........ Uetersen [*Germany*] [*ICAO location identifier*] (ICLI)
EDHF........ Endothelium-Derived Hyperpolarizing Factor [*Physiology*]
EDHG........ Luneburg [*Germany*] [*ICAO location identifier*] (ICLI)
EDHI........ Hamburg/Finkenwerder [*Germany*] [*ICAO location identifier*] (ICLI)
EDHK........ Enose Demokratikou Hellinikou Kentrou [*Union of the Greek Democratic Center*] (PPE)
EDHL........ Luebeck/Blankensee [*Germany*] [*ICAO location identifier*] (ICLI)
EDHM........ Hartenholm [*Germany*] [*ICAO location identifier*] (ICLI)
EDHN........ Neumuenster [*Germany*] [*ICAO location identifier*] (ICLI)
EDHP........ Engine Driven Hydraulic Pump (MCD)
EDHPA........ Ethylenediaminedi-O-Hydroxyphenylacetic Acid [*Also, EDBHPA, EDDHA*] [*Organic chemistry*]
EDHS........ ECS Data Handling System (SAUS)
EDHS........ ECS Document Handling System (SAUS)
EDHS........ Engineering Design Handbook Series (MCD)
EDHSC........ EDH Steering Committee (SAUO)
EDHX........ Bad Bramstedt [*Germany*] [*ICAO location identifier*] (ICLI)
Edi........ Diaphragmatic Electrical Activity
EDI........ Eating Disorder Inventory [*Psychology*]
EDI........ Echo Doppler Indicator [*Telecommunications*] (IAA)
EDI........ Economically Disadvantaged Income (ADA)
EDI........ Economic-Damage Index [*Environmental technology*]
EDI........ Economic Development Institute [*of the International Bank for Reconstruction and Development*]
EDI........ Edinburgh [*Scotland*] [*Airport symbol*] (OAG)
EDI........ Edinburgh [*Scotland*] [*Seismograph station code, US Geological Survey*] (SEIS)
EDI........ Edingtonite [*A zeolite*]
EDI........ Editek, Inc. [*AMEX symbol*] (SPSG)
EDI........ Editor [*Computer science*]
EDI........ Educational Data Information Ltd. [*Information service or system*] (IID)
EdI........ Education Index
EDI........ Electrical Deflection Indicator
EDI........ Electromagnetic Discharge Imaging (SAUS)
EDI........ Electron Diffraction Instrument
EDI........ Electron Drift Instability (SAUS)
EDI........ Electron Drift Instrument
EDI........ Electronical Data Interchange (SAUS)
EDI........ Electronic Data/Document Interchange (SAUS)

EDI Electronic Data Exchange (EBF)
EDI electronic data input (SAUS)
EDI Electronic Data Intelligence (DOMA)
EDI Electronic Data Interchange (MHCS)
EDI Electronic Data Interchange Council of Canada (FOTI)
EDI Electronic Design, Inc.
EDI Electronic Devices, Incorporated (SAUO)
EDI Electronic Dissemination of Information (GFGA)
EDI Electronic Document Interchange
EDI Endosseous Dental Implant (MELL)
EDI End System Identifier (SAUS)
EDI Engineering Data Identifier (ACAE)
EDI Engineering Data Interchange (ACAE)
EDI Engineering Demonstrated Inspection (AAG)
EDI Engineering Department Instruction (SAUS)
EDI Engineering Depreciation Index (TIMI)
EDI Engineering Disposal Instruction [*Air Force*] (SEWL)
EDI Enhanced Data Set Integrity [*Computer science*] (HODG)
EDI Ensured Data Integrity
EDI Environmental Diagnostics, Inc.
EDI eosinophile derived inhibitor (SAUS)
EDI Epitaxy Diffusion Insulation (SAUS)
EDI Epitaxy Diffusion Isolation (SAUS)
EDI Eponyms Dictionaries Index [*A publication*]
EDI Equivalent-Damage Index (CARB)
EDI Error Detection Instrument (IAA)
EDI Estimated Daily Intake [*Toxicology*]
EDI European Defense Initiative (SAUO)
EDI European Drug Index (SAUO)
EDIA Electronic Data Interchange Association (EA)
EDIA Engineering Department Instruction Amendment (SAUS)
EDIA European Dry Ice Association (SAUO)
EDIA Giessen [*Germany*] [*ICAO location identifier*] (ICLI)
EDIAC Electronic Display of Indexing Association and Content (PDAA)
EDIAC Engineering Decision Integrator and Communicator
EDIAP Energy Division Information Analysis Program (SAUS)
EDIB Ethyl Diiodobrassidate (SAUS)
EDIB Goeppingen [*Germany*] [*ICAO location identifier*] (ICLI)
EDIBANX EDI Bank Alliance Network Exchange (SAUS)
EDIBUILD Pan European User Group for the Construction Industry within the EDI area (SAUO)
EDIC Economic Documentation and Information Centre Ltd. [*British*] [*Database producer*] (IID)
edic electric diesel injection control (SAUS)
EDIC Engineering Data Identification and Control (SAUS)
EDIC Equipment Dictionary [*Navy*] (MCD)
EDIC Exploration Drilling Incentive Program (SAUS)
EDIC Grafenwoehr [*Germany*] [*ICAO location identifier*] (ICLI)
EDICA EDI Coalition of Associations (AG)
EDICC Electronic Data Interchanges Council of Canada (EAIO)
EDICESA Ecumenical Documentation and Informatin Centre for Eastern and Southern Africa (SAUO)
EDICO Educational Information Conference (SAUS)
EDICON EDI Community for the Construction Industry (SAUS)
EDICS European Dealer Information and Communication System (SAUS)
Edict Edicts of Justinian [*A publication*] (DLA)
EDICT Engineering Departmental Interface Control Technique (SAUS)
EDICT Engineering Department Interface Control Task [*or Technique*]
EDICT Engineering Document [*or Drawing*] Information Collection Task [*or Technique*]
EDICUSA EDI Council of the U.S.A. (SAUO)
EDID Extended Display Identification Data [*Computer science*] (VERA)
EDID Hanau [*Germany*] [*ICAO location identifier*] (ICLI)
Edie Edith (SAUS)
EDIE European Direct Investment in Europe (EURO)
EDIE Heidelberg [*Germany*] [*ICAO location identifier*] (ICLI)
EDI/EC Electronic Data Interchange/Electronic Commerce [*Computer science*] [*Army*] (RDA)
EDI/EDA Electronic Data Interchange and Electronic Data Access
EDIES EDC Digital Image Enhancement System (SAUS)
EDIES EROS Digital Image Enhancement Systems (SAUS)
EDIF Edificio
EDIF Electronic Data Interchange Format (SAUS)
EDIF Electronic Design Interchange Format [*Computer science*]
EDIF Heilbronn [*Germany*] [*ICAO location identifier*] (ICLI)
EDIFACT Electronic Data Interchange for Administration, Commerce, and Transport [*Economic Commission for Europe*]
EDIFACT Electronics Data Interchange For Administration, Commerce, and Trade [*Telecommunications*] (ACRL)
EDIFC Ethel Delaney International Fan Club (EA)
EDIFICE EDIFACT-Subset Elektroindustrie (SAUS)
EDIFICE Pan-European EDI group of the electronics industry (AG)
EDIG European Defence Industrial (or Industry) Group (SAUO)
EDIG Feucht [*Germany*] [*ICAO location identifier*] (ICLI)
EDIH Hohenfels [*Germany*] [*ICAO location identifier*] (ICLI)
EDII Augsburg Hospital [*Germany*] [*ICAO location identifier*] (ICLI)
EDII Environmental Dynamics Incorporated (SAUO)
EDIJ Bohmer [*Germany*] [*ICAO location identifier*] (ICLI)
EDIK Enossi Dimokratikou Kentrou [*Union of Democratic Centre Party*] [*Greece*] [*Political party*] (EY)
EDIK Illesheim [*Germany*] [*ICAO location identifier*] (ICLI)
EDIL Electronic Document Interchange between Libraries (TELE)
EDIL Karlsruhe [*Germany*] [*ICAO location identifier*] (ICLI)
EDILAN Editora Internacional de Libros Antiguos (SAUS)
EDILIB Editeurs, Libraires & diffuseurs francophones (SAUO)
EDILIBE Electronic Data Interchange for Libraries and Booksellers in Europe (TELE)
ED III United States District Court for the Eastern District of Illinois (DLA)
EDIM Electronic Data Interchange Message (SAUS)
EDIM Epidemic [*or Epizootic*] Diarrhea of Infant Mice
EDIM Epizootic Diarrhea of Infant Mice (DB)
EDIM Equipment Design Information Memo
EDIM Kirchgons [*Germany*] [*ICAO location identifier*] (ICLI)
EDIMB Edimbourg [*Edinburgh*] (ROG)
EDIMS EDI Messaging System (SAUS)
EDIMS Environmental Data and Information Management Systems [*Marine science*] (OSRA)
EDIN Economic Development Information Network [*Indiana University*] [*Information service or system*] (IID)
EDIN Edinburgh [*City in Scotland*]
EDIN Educational Insights, Inc. [*NASDAQ symbol*] (SAG)
EDIN Electronic Data Interchange Network (SAUS)
EDIN Engineering Design Integration System [*NASA*] (MCD)
EDIN Kitzingen [*Germany*] [*ICAO location identifier*] (ICLI)
Edinb LJ Edinburgh Law Journal [*A publication*] (DLA)
Edinboro U Edinboro University of Pennsylvania (GAGS)
EDINBURG Edinburgensis [*Signature of Bishops of Edinburgh*] (ROG)
ED IN CH Editor-in-Chief (WDAA)
EDINET Education Instruction Network (WDAA)
EDI-NET Electronic Data Interchange Network (TSSD)
Ed Inj Eden on Injunctions [*1821*] [*A publication*] (DLA)
Edin N Phil J Edinburgh Journal of Natural Philosophy (MEC)
E-D Inverter Enhancement-Depletion Inverter (SAUS)
EDIO Butzbach (Schloss) [*Germany*] [*ICAO location identifier*] (ICLI)
EDIO Energy Disaggregated Input-Output Model [*Department of Energy*] (GFGA)
E-Diol Estradiol [*Also, E2, ES*] [*Endocrinology*]
EDIP Error Detection and Indication Package (SAUS)
EDIP European Defense Improvement Program [*NATO*] (MCD)
EDIP Landstuhl [*Germany*] [*ICAO location identifier*] (ICLI)
EDIPS EROS Digital Image Processing System (SAUS)
EDIQ Herzo Base [*Germany*] [*ICAO location identifier*] (ICLI)
EDIR Ecartometrie Differentielle Infra-Rouge (SAUS)
EDIR Ludwigsburg [*Germany*] [*ICAO location identifier*] (ICLI)
EDIS Edison National Historic Site
EDIS Educational Documentation and Information System (SAUS)
EDIS Electrical Distribution Information System (SAUO)
EDIS Electronic Distributorless Ignition System [*Automotive engineering*]
EDIS Electronic Document Information System (SAUS)
EDIS Elektronisches Dokumentations und Informations System [*Information retrieval system*] [*France*] (NITA)
EDIS Emergency Digital Information Service (INF)
EDIS Engineering Data Information System (IEEE)
EDIS Engineering Design Information System (SAUS)
EDIS Environmental Data and Information Service [*Later, NESDIS*]
EDIS European Defence Industry Study (SAUS)
EDIS Executive Directorate Industrial Security (MCD)
EDIS Exploratory Drill Incentives System (SAUS)
EDIS Nellingen [*Germany*] [*ICAO location identifier*] (ICLI)
EdisBr Edison Brothers Stores [*Associated Press*] (SAG)
EdisCtr Edison Control Corp. [*Associated Press*] (SAG)
e-disk Emulated-Disk (CDE)
Edisto Edisto Resources Corp. [*Associated Press*] (SAG)
EDIT Edited (ROG)
EDIT Editing (SAUS)
EDIT Editing File Concerning On-going Projects (SAUS)
EDIT Edition
edit Editor (ADWA)
EDIT Editor (ROG)
EDIT Editorial (WDAA)
EDIT Editor Instruction (SAUS)
EDIT Editor Program (SAUS)
EDIT Electronic Diagnostic and Technical Information Tools [*Army*]
EDIT Electronic Dissemination of Information Technology (SAUS)
EDIT Emulsion Direct Imaging Technology [*Computer science*]
EDIT Engineering Design Intelligent Terminal (SAUS)
EDIT Engineering Development Integration Test
EDIT Engineering Document Image Transmission (SAUS)
EDIT Error Deletion by Iterative Transmission
EDIT Error Detection by Iterative Transmission (SAUS)
EDIT Estate Duties Investment Trust (DLA)
EDIT Examining, Diagnosis, Identification, and Training (PDAA)
EDIT Eye-Slaved Display Integration and Test
EDIT Nuernberg, Hospital [*Germany*] [*ICAO location identifier*] (ICLI)
EDIT RGB Computer & Video [*NASDAQ symbol*] (TTSB)
EDITAR Electronic Digital Tracking and Ranging
editar electronic digital tracking and ranging unit (SAUS)
EDITEAST Association of Editors in the South East Asian Region (SAUO)
EDITEAST South-East Asia Association of Science Editors (PDAA)
Editek Editek, Inc. [*Associated Press*] (SAG)
EDITH Emergency Drill in the Home [*Fire Department drill exercise*]
EDITH Estate Duties Investment Taxes [*British*]
EDITH Exit Drills in the Home (SAUS)
EDITOR Electronic Data Input Through Optical Recognition (SAUS)
EDITOR ERTS Data Interpretation and Tenex Operations Recorder (SAUS)
EDITP Engineering Development Integration Test Program (IAA)
EDITS Educational and Industrial Testing Service
EDITS Educators Information Technology System (SAUS)
EDITS Electronic Data Information Technical Service (DIT)
EDITS Electronic [*Warfare*] Data Integration Test System (MCD)

EDITS.......... Experimental Digital Television System
EDITSPEC.... Editing Specifications (MCD)
EDIU........... Heidelberg [*Germany*] [*ICAO location identifier*] (ICLI)
EDIUP......... Existing Documents Improvement and Updating (MCD)
EDIV........... Pirmasens [*Germany*] [*ICAO location identifier*] (ICLI)
EDIW.......... Wuerzburg, Hospital [*Germany*] [*ICAO location identifier*] (ICLI)
EDIX........... Electronic Designs [*NASDAQ symbol*] (TTSB)
EDIX........... Electronic Designs, Inc. [*NASDAQ symbol*] (SAG)
EDIX........... Schwaebisch Gmuend [*Germany*] [*ICAO location identifier*] (ICLI)
EDIXW........ Electronic Designs Wrrt [*NASDAQ symbol*] (TTSB)
EDIZ........... Schwabach [*Germany*] [*ICAO location identifier*] (ICLI)
EDJ............. End Of Job (SAUS)
EDJT........... Economic Development Job Training (SAUS)
e-dk-.......... Denmark [*MARC geographic area code*] [*Library of Congress*] (LCCP)
EDK............. Enose Demokratikou Kentrou [*Union of the Democratic Center*] [*Greek*] (PPW)
EDK............. Schweizerische Konferenz der kantonalen Erziehungsdirektoren (SAUS)
EDKB.......... Bonn/Hangelar [*Germany*] [*ICAO location identifier*] (ICLI)
EDKD.......... Altena/Hegenscheid [*Germany*] [*ICAO location identifier*] (ICLI)
EDKE........... Dierdorf/Wienau [*Germany*] [*ICAO location identifier*] (ICLI)
EDKF........... Bergneustadt/Auf Dem Dumpel [*Germany*] [*ICAO location identifier*] (ICLI)
EDKI............ Betzdorf/Kirchen [*Germany*] [*ICAO location identifier*] (ICLI)
EDKL........... Leverkusen [*Germany*] [*ICAO location identifier*] (ICLI)
EDKM.......... Meschede/Schuren [*Germany*] [*ICAO location identifier*] (ICLI)
EDKN.......... Wipperfurth/Neye [*Germany*] [*ICAO location identifier*] (ICLI)
EDKS........... Siegerland [*Germany*] [*ICAO location identifier*] (ICLI)
EDKV........... Dahlemer Binz [*Germany*] [*ICAO location identifier*] (ICLI)
EDKW.......... Werdohl/Kuntrop [*Germany*] [*ICAO location identifier*] (ICLI)
ED KY.......... United States District Court for the Eastern District of Kentucky (DLA)
EDKZ........... Meinerzhagen [*Germany*] [*ICAO location identifier*] (ICLI)
EDL............. Consolidated Ed 7.75%'QUICS' [*NYSE symbol*] (TTSB)
EDL............. Economic Dislocation Loans [*Small Business Administration*]
EDL............. Edit Decision List
EDL............. Edition Deluxe
edl.............. edition de luxe (SAUS)
EDL............. Editor-Linking (SAUS)
EDL............. Educational Developmental Laboratories [*of McGraw Hill, Inc.*]
EDL............. Elder Dempster Lines (SAUS)
EDL............. Eldoret [*Kenya*] [*Airport symbol*] [*Obsolete*] (OAG)
EDL............. Electrical Discharge Lamp (SAUS)
EDL............. Electrical Discharge LASER (MCD)
EDL............. Electrical Double Layer [*Chemistry*] (ODA)
EDL............. Electric Delay Line
EDL............. Electric Discharge Laser (SAUS)
EDL............. Electric Double Layer
EDL............. Electrodeless Discharge Lamp
EDL............. Electro-Dynamic Laser (ACAE)
EDL............. Electrodynamic Levitation (PDAA)
EDL............. Electromagnetic Delay Line [*Computer science*] (ELAL)
EDL............. Electron Devices Laboratory
EDL............. Electron Discharge Laser (SAUS)
EDL............. Electronic Defense Laboratory
EDL............. Electrostatic Deflecting Lens (PDAA)
EDL............. Embedded Design Language [*Computer science*] (PDAA)
EDL............. Emulation Design Language [*Computer science*] (MHDB)
EDL............. Encapsulator Definition Language (SAUS)
EDL............. Encapsulator Description Language (SAUS)
EDL............. Encapsulator/Enterprise Definition/Description Language (SAUS)
EDL............. End-Diastolic Length [*Cardiology*]
EDL............. End-Diastolic Load [*Medicine*] (MELL)
EDL............. Engineering Data Library (SAUS)
EDL............. Engineering Development Laboratory
EDL............. Engineering Drawing List
EDL............. Enterprise Definition Language (SAUS)
EDL............. Enterprise Description Language (SAUS)
EDL............. Entry, Descent, and Landing [*Planetary science*]
EDL............. Equipment Development Laboratory (SAUS)
EDL............. Essential Drug List [*Medicine*] (DB)
EDL............. Estimated Date of Labor [*Obstetrics*] (DMAA)
EDL............. Ethernet Data Link (ADWA)
EDL............. Euro Disneyland [*France*]
EDL............. Everglades Digital Library [*Database*]
EDL............. Every-Day Life [*Psychological testing*]
EDL............. Executive Data Link [*IBM Corp.*]
EDL............. Exotic Disease Laboratory (SAUO)
EDL............. Extensor Digitorum Longus [*Anatomy*]
EDL............. South African Law Reports, Eastern Districts Local Division [*South Africa*] [*A publication*] (DLA)
EDL............. Economic Discard Limits (ODA)
EDLA........... Arnsberg [*Germany*] [*ICAO location identifier*] (ICLI)
EDLA........... Exotic Dancers League of America (EA)
ED LA.......... United States District Court for the Eastern District of Louisiana (DLA)
EDLB........... Borkenberge [*Germany*] [*ICAO location identifier*] (ICLI)
EDLC........... Edwardian Drama and Literature Circle (EA)
EDLC........... Ethernet Data Link Control [*Computer science*] (VERA)
EDLC........... Kamp/Lintfort [*Germany*] [*ICAO location identifier*] (ICLI)
EDLCC......... Electronic Data Local Communications Central [*or Complex*]
EDLCC......... Electronic Data Local Communications Complex (SAUS)
EDLCC......... Electronic Data Local Control Center (SAUO)
EDICT.......... Engineering Document Information Collection Technique (SAUS)
EDLD........... Dinslaken/Schwarze Heide [*Germany*] [*ICAO location identifier*] (ICLI)
ED/LD......... Emotionally Disturbed/Learning Disabled
EDLD........... Employee Daily Labor Distribution (AAG)
EDLE........... Essen/Muelheim [*Germany*] [*ICAO location identifier*] (ICLI)
EDLF........... Endogenous Digitalis-Like Factor [*Biochemistry*]
EDLF........... Grefrath/Niershorst [*Germany*] [*ICAO location identifier*] (ICLI)
EDLG........... Muenster/Osnabruck [*Germany*] [*ICAO location identifier*] (ICLI)
EDLH........... Hamm/Lippewiesen [*Germany*] [*ICAO location identifier*] (ICLI)
EDLI............ Bielefeld/Windelsbleiche [*Germany*] [*ICAO location identifier*] (ICLI)
EDLIN.......... Editor (SAUS)
EdLiNC........ Education and Library Networks Coalition
Ed LJ........... Edinburgh Law Journal [*A publication*] (DLA)
EDLK........... Krefeld/Egelsberg [*Germany*] [*ICAO location identifier*] (ICLI)
EDLL........... Duesseldorf [*Germany*] [*ICAO location identifier*] (ICLI)
EDLM.......... Eritrean Democratic Liberation Movement
EDLM.......... Marl/Loemuhle [*Germany*] [*ICAO location identifier*] (ICLI)
EDLN........... Engineering Development Logic Network (NASA)
EDLN........... Moenchengladbach [*Germany*] [*ICAO location identifier*] (ICLI)
EDLNA......... Exotique Dancers League of North America (SAUS)
E/D-Inverter... enhancement/depletion inverter (SAUS)
EDLO........... Oerlinghausen [*Germany*] [*ICAO location identifier*] (ICLI)
EDLP........... Engineering Development Laboratory Program (KSC)
EDLP........... Every Day Low Pricing [*Business term*]
EDLP........... Paderborn/Lippstadt [*Germany*] [*ICAO location identifier*] (ICLI)
EDLQ........... Essen [*Germany*] [*ICAO location identifier*] (ICLI)
EDLR........... Ecosystem Dynamics and Living Resources (SAUS)
EDLS........... Ethernet Data Link Service (SAUS)
EDLS........... Stadtlohn/Wenningfeld [*Germany*] [*ICAO location identifier*] (ICLI)
EDIT............ education and information technology (SAUS)
EDLT........... Muenster/Telgte [*Germany*] [*ICAO location identifier*] (ICLI)
EDLW.......... Dortmund/Wickede [*Germany*] [*ICAO location identifier*] (ICLI)
EDLX........... Wesel/Romerwardt [*Germany*] [*ICAO location identifier*] (ICLI)
edm............. Early Day Motion [*British*] (BARN)
EDM............ Early Diastolic Murmur [*Medicine*]
EDM............ Edgar Dale Media Center, Columbus, OH [*OCLC symbol*] (OCLC)
EDM............ Edmonston [*Strain*] [*Medicine*] (DB)
EDM............ Edmonton [*Alberta*] [*Seismograph station code, US Geological Survey*] (SEIS)
EDM............ Electrical Discharge [*or Electrodischarge*] Machine [*or Machining*]
EDM............ Electrical Disintegration Machining [*Nuclear energy*] (NRCH)
EDM............ Electric Dipole Moment [*Physics*]
EDM............ Electric Discharge Machine (SAUS)
EDM............ Electric Drive Mechanism (KSC)
EDM............ Electro-Discharge Machine (SAUS)
EDM............ Electro-Discharge Machining (SAUS)
edm............. electromagnetic discharge measuring (SAUS)
EDM............ Electromagnetic Distance Measurement [*Geology*]
EDM............ Electromagnetic Distance Measuring (SAUS)
EDM............ Electron Density Map [*Crystallography*]
EDM............ Electron Discharge Machining (SAUS)
EDM............ Electronic Data Memory (SAUS)
EDM............ Electronic Design and Manufacture (IAA)
EDM............ Electronic Design Machining (AAEL)
EDM............ Electronic Design Management system (SAUS)
EDM............ Electronic Distance Measurement (NITA)
EDM............ Electronic Distance Measurer (SAUS)
EDM............ Electronic Distance Measuring
EDM............ electronic distance-measuring instrument (SAUS)
EDM............ Electronic Distance Meter
EDM............ Electronic Distribution Measurement
EDM............ Electronic Distributor Modulator [*Automotive engineering*]
EDM............ Electronic Document Management (SAUS)
EDM............ Electronic Drafting Machine
edm............. electrostatic discharge machining (SAUS)
EDM............ Emergency Defense Message (ACAE)
EDM............ Employability Development Model (OICC)
EDM............ Encyclopedic Dictionary of Mathematics [*A publication*]
EDM............ End of Month (EBF)
EDM............ Enforced Dipole Moment
EDM............ Engine Data Multiplexer (SAUS)
EDM............ Engineering Data Management
EDM............ Engineering Design Machine
EDM............ Engineering Design Memorandum
EDM............ Engineering Development Machine (SAUS)
EDM............ Engineering Development Mode (SAUS)
EDM............ Engineering Development Model
EDM............ Engineering Disposition Management [*Air Force*] (SEWL)
EDM............ Engineering Drafting Machine
EDM............ Engineering Drafting Manual [*Air Force*]
EDM............ Engineering Drawing Microfilm (MCD)
EDM............ Enterprise Data Model (GART)
EDM............ Enterprise Desktop Manager (SAUS)
EDM............ Entity Data Model (SAUS)
EDM............ Environmental Data Manager (SAUO)
EDM............ Environmental Observation Mission (ACAE)
EDM............ Equine Degenerative Myeloencephalopathy [*Equine term*] (TED)
EDM............ Equipment Code Department Master (MCD)
EDM............ Equipment Deadlined for Maintenance [*Army*] (AABC)
EDM............ Eritrean Democratic Movement
EDM............ Error Detection Mechanism (SAUS)
EDM............ Error Diagnostic Message (SAUS)
EDM............ Event Driven Monitor (VLIE)
EDM............ Evolutionary Design Methodology (VLIE)
EDM............ Executive Doctorate in Management

EDM............ Exploratory Development Model [*Military*]
EDM............ Extended Data Message [*Computer science*] (VERA)
EDM............ Extramucosal Duodenal Myotomy [*Medicine*] (EDAA)
Ed M............ Master of Education
EDM .... Energy-Density Model [*Physics*] (ODA)
EDMA............ Augsburg/Muehlhausen [*Germany*] [*ICAO location identifier*] (ICLI)
EDMA............ Ethylene Dimethacrylate [*Organic chemistry*]
EDMA............ Ethylene Glycol Dimethacrylate [*Organic chemistry*]
EDMA............ European Diagnostics Manufacturer Association (SAUS)
EDMA............ European Direct Marketing Association [*Jona/SG, Switzerland*] (EAIO)
EDMA............ Extended Direct Memory Access [*Computer science*]
EDMAG............ European Defence Manufacturers Group (SAUS)
EDMALC...... European Direct Marketing Association List Council [*Jona/SG, Switzerland*] [*Inactive*] (EA)
Edmark........ Edmark Corp. [*Associated Press*] (SAG)
EDMARS...... Educational Document Management and Retrieval System [*Database*] [*Japan*]
EDMAX........ Educational Management Exchange (SAUS)
EDMB............ Biberach Aerodrome Riss [*Germany*] [*ICAO location identifier*] (ICLI)
EDMC............ Education Management [*NASDAQ symbol*] (SG)
EDMC............ Education Management Corp. [*NASDAQ symbol*] (SAG)
EDMC............ El Dorado Motor Corp. [*NASDAQ symbol*] (COMM)
EDMC............ Energy Data and Modeling Center [*Institute of Energy Economics*] [*Japan*] [*Database producer*] (IID)
EDMCC........ European Distributed Memory Computing Conference (VERA)
EDMD............ Electronic Document Message Directory (VLIE)
EDMD............ Emery-Dreifuss Muscular Dystrophy [*Medicine*] (EDAA)
EDME............ Eggenfelden, Nieder Bayern [*Germany*] [*ICAO location identifier*] (ICLI)
EDME............ Electronic Distance Measuring Equipment (MCD)
EDMED........ European Directory of Marine Environmental Data [*Marine science*] (OSRA)
EDMEN........ Engineering Division Mechanical Engineering Newsletter (SAUO)
EDMERP...... European Directory of Marine Environmental Research Projects (SAUO)
Edm Exch Pr... Edmund's Exchequer Practice [*A publication*] (DLA)
EDMF............ Euclid-IS Data Management Facilities (SAUS)
EDMF............ Extended Data Management Facility
EDMF............ Fuerstenzell Bei Passau [*Germany*] [*ICAO location identifier*] (ICLI)
EDMG............ Ethiopian Democratic Movement Group (SAUO)
EDMG............ Gunzburg/Donauried [*Germany*] [*ICAO location identifier*] (ICLI)
EDMH............ Gunzenhausen [*Germany*] [*ICAO location identifier*] (ICLI)
EDMI............ Electron-Dense Mitochondrial Inclusions [*Oncology*]
EDMI............ Electronic Distance-Measuring Instrument
EDMI............ Employees of Diplomatic Missions [*A publication*]
EDMI............ European Dun's Market Identifiers [*Information service or system*] (IID)
EDMI............ Illertissen [*Germany*] [*ICAO location identifier*] (ICLI)
ED Mich....... United States District Court for the Eastern District of Michigan (DLA)
EDMICS....... Engineering Data Management Information Control System [*DoD*]
Ed M in BT Ed... Master of Education in Business Teacher Education
Ed M in Phy Ed... Master of Education in Physical Education
E/D MISFET... enhancement/depletion MISFET (SAUS)
EDMIX........ Engineering Data Management Information Control System (ACAE)
EDMJ............ Jesenwang [*Germany*] [*ICAO location identifier*] (ICLI)
EDMK............ Edit and Mark (VLIE)
EDMK............ Edmark Corp. [*NASDAQ symbol*] (SAG)
EDMK............ Kempten/Durach [*Germany*] [*ICAO location identifier*] (ICLI)
EDML............ Electric Discharge Mixing LASER (PDAA)
EDML............ Landshut [*Germany*] [*ICAO location identifier*] (ICLI)
EDMM............ Muenchen [*Germany*] [*ICAO location identifier*] (ICLI)
EDMMA........ European Dessert Mixes Manufacturers' Association [*EC*] (ECED)
EDMN............ Edmonton [*Canada*] (ABBR)
EDMO............ Electron Devices for Microwave and Opto-electronic applications (SAUS)
EDMO............ Oberpfaffenhofen [*Germany*] [*ICAO location identifier*] (ICLI)
ED MO........ United States District Court for the Eastern District of Missouri (DLA)
Edmonds' St at Large... Edmonds' New York Statutes at Large [*A publication*] (DLA)
ED-MOS....... enhancement/depletion-load MOS technology (SAUS)
E/D-MOS....... Enhancement/Depletion - Metal Oxide Semiconductor (SAUS)
ED-MOS....... enhancement/depletion MOSFET (SAUS)
E/D MOSFET... enhancement/depletion-load MOS technology (SAUS)
EDMOSFET... Enhancement Depletion Metal-Oxide Semiconductor Field-Effect Transistor (IAA)
E/D-MOSFET... enhancement/depletion metal-oxide semi conductor field-effect transistor (SAUS)
E/D MOSFET... enhancement/depletion MOSFET (SAUS)
EDMP............ Engineering Data Management Plan (SAUS)
EDMP............ Ethyl (Diisopropylamino)ethylmethyl-phosphonite [*Nerve gas intermediate*] [*Organic chemistry*]
EDMP............ Vilsbiburg [*Germany*] [*ICAO location identifier*] (ICLI)
EDMQ............ Donauworth/Genderkingen [*Germany*] [*ICAO location identifier*] (ICLI)
EDMR............ Ottobrunn [*Germany*] [*ICAO location identifier*] (ICLI)
EDMS............ Electra Data Management System
EDMs............ Electric Dipole Moments (SAUS)
EDMS............ Electronic Design Management System (SAUS)
EDMS............ Electronic Device and Materials Symposium (SAUS)
EDMS............ Electronic Document Management System
EDMS............ Engineering Database Modelling System (VLIE)
EDMS............ Engineering Data Management Service (SAUS)
EDMS............ Engineering Data Management System [*Jet Propulsion Laboratory, NASA*]
EDMS............ Engineering Data Microreproduction System [*DoD*]
EDMS............ Engineering Document Management System [*Computer science*]
EDMS............ Enterprise Data Management System [*Computer science*] (HODG)
EDMS............ Enterprise Desktop Mangement Services (SAUS)
EDMS............ Enterprise Document Management Systems (VLIE)
EDMS............ Evolutionary Data Management System (IAA)
EDMS............ Extended Data Management System [*Xerox Corp.*]
EDMS............ Extended Diagnostic & Maintenance System (SAUS)
EDMS............ Straubing/Wallmuehle [*Germany*] [*ICAO location identifier*] (ICLI)
Edm Sel Ca... Edmonds' New York Select Cases [*A publication*] (DLA)
Edm Sel Cas... Edmonds' New York Select Cases [*A publication*] (DLA)
Edm Stat...... Edmonds' New York Statutes at Large [*A publication*] (DLA)
EDMT............ Tanheim [*Germany*] [*ICAO location identifier*] (ICLI)
EDMU............ Muenchen [*Germany*] [*ICAO location identifier*] (ICLI)
EDMUND...... Sir Edmund Hillary Foundation (SAUO)
Edmundites... Society of St. Edmund (SAUO)
EDMV............ Vilshofen [*Germany*] [*ICAO location identifier*] (ICLI)
EDMW............ Deggendorf/Steinkirchen [*Germany*] [*ICAO location identifier*] (ICLI)
EDMX............ Oberschleissheim [*Germany*] [*ICAO location identifier*] (ICLI)
EDMY............ Muehldorf [*Germany*] [*ICAO location identifier*] (ICLI)
edn............ Edition (WDAA)
EDN............ Edition
edn............ Education (WDAA)
EDN............ Education
EDN............ Electrical Design News (journ.) (SAUS)
EDN............ Electrodesiccation [*Medicine*]
EDN............ Emergency Data Network (SAUO)
EDN............ Engine Deflector Nozzle
EDN............ Engineering Department Notice (AAG)
EDN............ Engineering Discrepancy Notice [*Nuclear energy*] (NRCH)
EDN............ Enterprise, AL [*Location identifier*] [*FAA*] (FAAL)
EDN............ Environmental Data Network (SAUO)
EDN............ Eosinophil Derived Neurotoxin [*Immunology*]
EDN............ Expedited Data Negotiation (VLIE)
EDN............ Experimental Data Network (SAUS)
EDN............ Exploratory Data Network (SAUS)
EDNA............ Ahlhorn [*Germany*] [*ICAO location identifier*] (ICLI)
EdNA............ Education Network Australia (SAUS)
EDNA............ Emergency Department Nurses Association [*Later, ENA*] (EA)
EDNA............ Environmental Designation for Noise Abatement (EEVL)
EDNB............ Koeln-Wahn [*Germany*] [*ICAO location identifier*] (ICLI)
Ednbgh........ Edinburgh (SAUS)
EDNC............ United States District Court for the Eastern District of North Carolina (DLA)
EDND............ Diepholz [*Germany*] [*ICAO location identifier*] (ICLI)
EDNEED....... Empirical Determination of Nationally Essential Educational Data (SAUS)
EDNET........ Edinburgh Network [*Edinburgh Regional Computer Centre*] [*British*] (NITA)
Ed News Philos J... Edingurgh New Philosophical Journal (journ.) (SAUS)
EDNF............ Ehlers-Danlos National Foundation (EA)
EDNF............ Endogenous Digitalis-Like Natriuretic [*Medicine*] (EDAA)
EDNF............ Extradural Neurofibroma [*Medicine*] (EDAA)
EDNF............ Fassberg [*Germany*] [*ICAO location identifier*] (ICLI)
EDNG............ Geilenkirchen [*Germany*] [*ICAO location identifier*] (ICLI)
EDNH............ Egg Development Neurosecretory Hormone (SAUS)
EDNH............ Husum [*Germany*] [*ICAO location identifier*] (ICLI)
EDNJ............ Jever [*Germany*] [*ICAO location identifier*] (ICLI)
EDNK............ Koeln-Bonn [*Germany*] [*ICAO location identifier*] (ICLI)
ednl............ Educational (WDAA)
EDNL............ Educational (WGA)
EDNL............ Leck [*Germany*] [*ICAO location identifier*] (ICLI)
EDNM............ Muenster [*Germany*] [*ICAO location identifier*] (ICLI)
EDNN............ Norvenich [*Germany*] [*ICAO location identifier*] (ICLI)
EDNO............ Oldenburg [*Germany*] [*ICAO location identifier*] (ICLI)
EDNP............ Ethyl Dinitropentanoate [*An explosive*]
EDNP............ Hopsten [*Germany*] [*ICAO location identifier*] (ICLI)
EDNQ............ Hohn [*Germany*] [*ICAO location identifier*] (ICLI)
Edns............ Editions [*A publication*]
EDNS............ Enhanced Domain Name Service (SAUS)
EDNS............ Expected Demand not Supplied (ODBW)
EDNT............ Edunetics Ltd. [*NASDAQ symbol*] (SAG)
EDNT............ Wittmundhafen [*Germany*] [*ICAO location identifier*] (ICLI)
EDNV............ Kalkar [*Germany*] [*ICAO location identifier*] (ICLI)
EDNW............ Wunstorf [*Germany*] [*ICAO location identifier*] (ICLI)
EDNX............ Goch [*Germany*] [*ICAO location identifier*] (ICLI)
EDNY............ Eastern District, New York (SAUS)
EDNY............ United States District Court for the Eastern District of New York (DLA)
EDO............ Economic Development Office (SAUS)
EDO............ Economic Development Officer (FOTI)
EDO............ Economic Development Operations
EDO............ Edgewood, NM [*Location identifier*] [*FAA*] (FAAL)
EDO............ EDO Corp. [*NYSE symbol*] (SPSG)
EDO............ EDO-Western, manufacturer of reentry sonar system and seismic recorders (SAUS)
EDO............ Effective Diameter of Objective [*Optics*]
EDO............ Electric Data Output (SAUS)
EDO............ Employee Development Officer
EDO............ Engineering Duties Only (SAUS)
EDO............ Engineering Duty Officer [*Military*]
EDO............ Engineering Duty Only [*Aerospace*]
EDO............ Enhanced/Extended Data Output (SAUS)
EDO............ Equipment Design Objectives (SAUS)
EDO............ Error Demodulator [*or Determination*] Output (MCD)
EDO............ Error Detector Output (SAUS)

EDO .... Error Determination Output (SAUS)
EDO .... Estate Duty Office [*British*]
EDO .... European Distributing Operation (SAUO)
EDO .... Executive Director of Operations (IAA)
EDO .... Experimental Development Operations (SAUS)
EDO .... Exploratory Development Objective [*Military*]
EDO .... Export Development Office [*Department of Commerce*] (IMH)
EDO .... Extended Data Out [*Computer science*]
EDO .... Extended Data Out/Extra Data Output (SAUS)
EDO .... Extended Data Output
EDO .... Extended Data Output Memory [*Computer science*]
EDO .... Extended Duration Orbiter [*NASA*]
EDO .... Office of Executive Director for Operations [*Nuclear energy*] (NRCH)
EDOA .... European Database on AIDS (SAUS)
EDOA .... Schweinfurt [*Germany*] [*ICAO location identifier*] (ICLI)
EDOB .... Garlstedt/Clay Kaserne [*Germany*] [*ICAO location identifier*] (ICLI)
EDOC .... Echterdingen [*Germany*] [*ICAO location identifier*] (ICLI)
EDOC .... Economic Development Opportunity Committee [*Department of Labor*]
EDOC .... Effective Date of Change (AFM)
EDOC .... Electrical Description of Operation Chart (IAA)
EDOC .... Estimated Date of Confinement [*Medicine*] (EDAA)
EDOC .... Expected Date of Confinement
EDOCC .... Enhanced Deep Operations Coordination Center (SEWL)
EDO DRAM... Enhanced Data Output Dynamic Access Random [*Computer science*]
EDODRAM ... Extended Data Out Dynamic Random Access Memory (SAUS)
EDOE .... Ulm [*Germany*] [*ICAO location identifier*] (ICLI)
EDOF .... Wertheim [*Germany*] [*ICAO location identifier*] (ICLI)
EDOG .... Bad Cannstatt Hospital [*Germany*] [*ICAO location identifier*] (ICLI)
EDOH .... Emery [*Germany*] [*ICAO location identifier*] (ICLI)
EDOI .... Vilseck [*Germany*] [*ICAO location identifier*] (ICLI)
EDOJ .... Bonn (Bad Godesberg-Plittersdorf) [*Germany*] [*ICAO location identifier*] (ICLI)
EDOK .... Frankfurt-North [*Germany*] [*ICAO location identifier*] (ICLI)
ED Okla .... United States District Court for the Eastern District of Oklahoma (DLA)
EDOL .... Frankfurt City [*Germany*] [*ICAO location identifier*] (ICLI)
EDOM .... Worms [*Germany*] [*ICAO location identifier*] (ICLI)
EDOMP .... EDO Medical Project (SAUS)
EDOMP .... Educational Development of Military Personnel
EDON .... Kaiserslautern [*Germany*] [*ICAO location identifier*] (ICLI)
EDONM .... Eddie-Dampened Quasi-Normal Markovian [*Equation*] [*Marine science*] (OSRA)
EDONSW...... Environmental Defender's Office, New South Wales [*Australia*]
Ed Op........... Edmonton Opera Association (SAUO)
EDOP .... Elimination of Discharge of Pollutants (DICI)
EDOP .... ER-2 Doppler Radar (SAUS)
EDOP .... Schwaebisch Hall/Hessental [*Germany*] [*ICAO location identifier*] (ICLI)
EDOPAC....... Enlisted Personnel Distribution Office Pacifiic Fleet (SAUS)
EDOQ .... Heidelberg, United States Army [*Germany*] [*ICAO location identifier*] (ICLI)
EDOR .... Coleman [*Germany*] [*ICAO location identifier*] (ICLI)
EDOR .... File Editor (SAUS)
EDORAM..... Enhanced Data Output Random Access Memory (VLIE)
EDO RAM..... Extended Data Out RAM [*Radom Access Memory*] (CDE)
EDORAM..... Extended Data Out Random Access Memory (SAUS)
EDORM .... Ethiopian Democratic Officers Revolutionary Movement (SAUO)
EDOS .... Effective Date of Supply
EDOS .... Electronic Distribution of Software [*Consumer market*] (NITA)
EDOS .... Enhanced DOS for Windows (SAUS)
EDOS .... EOS Data and Operations System (SAUO)
EDOS .... Estimated Delivery Dates of Supply [*Army*] (INF)
EDOS .... Extended Disk Operating System [*Computer science*] (BUR)
EDOS .... Kaiserslautern (Kapaun) [*Germany*] [*ICAO location identifier*] (ICLI)
EDOSCOL.... Engineering Duty Officer School [*Military*] (DNAB)
EDOS-MSO.... Extend Disk Operating System - Multistage Operations (SAUS)
EDOS-MSO... Extended Disc Operating System-Multistage Operations [*Fujitsu*] [*Japan*] (NITA)
EDOS/MSO... Extended Disk Operating System/Multi-Stage Operation (SAUS)
EDOS/RJE.... Extended Disc Operating System with Remote Job Entry (PDAA)
EDOS/RJE.... Extended Disk Operating System with Remote Job Entry facilities (SAUS)
EDOT .... Effective Date of Training (SAUS)
EDOT .... Finthen [*Germany*] [*ICAO location identifier*] (ICLI)
EDOU .... Wiesbaden [*Germany*] [*ICAO location identifier*] (ICLI)
EDOV .... Bad Tolz [*Germany*] [*ICAO location identifier*] (ICLI)
EDOW .... Wildflecken [*Germany*] [*ICAO location identifier*] (ICLI)
EDOX .... Augsburg/Gablingen [*Germany*] [*ICAO location identifier*] (ICLI)
EDOY .... Leighton Barracks [*Germany*] [*ICAO location identifier*] (ICLI)
EDOZ .... Bad Hersfeld [*Germany*] [*ICAO location identifier*] (ICLI)
EDP.............. Early Decision Plan [*Medical school entrance program*]
EDP.............. Early Detection Program [*Medicine*] (EDAA)
EDP.............. Early Development Planning
EDP.............. Earth Dynamics Program [*Smithsonian Astrophysical Observatory*]
EDP.............. eco-domestic product (SAUS)
EDP.............. Economical Data Processing (SAUS)
EDP.............. Economic Development Program
EDP.............. Edema disease principle (SAUS)
EDP.............. EDP-Electricidade Portugal ADS [*NYSE symbol*] (SG)
EDP.............. Educational Data Processing (NITA)
EDP.............. Education des perceptions (SAUS)
ED-P .... Education-Psychology Library (SAUS)
EDP.............. Effective Depth of Penetration (SAUS)
EDP.............. Effective Directives and Plans (MUGU)
EDP.............. Electric Data Printing (SAUS)
EDP.............. Electric Dot Printer (SAUS)
EDP.............. Electrodeposition (EG)
EDP.............. Electron Decay Profile
EDP.............. Electron Dense Particles [*Chemistry*] (DAVI)
EDP.............. Electron Density Profile (ACAE)
EDP.............. Electron Diffraction Pattern
EDP.............. electronic data point (SAUS)
EDP,............. Electronic Data Processing (MHCS)
EDP.............. Electronic Data Processor (ACAE)
EDP.............. Electronic Digital Pipette [*Instrumentation*]
EDP.............. Electronic Display Panel
EDP.............. Electronic Document Processing (SAUS)
EDP.............. Electrophoresis Duplicating Paper [*For analytical chemistry*]
EDP.............. Electrophoretic Display (SAUS)
EDP.............. Embedded Data Processor (SSD)
EDP.............. Emergency Defense Plan [*Later, GDP*] (NATG)
EDP.............. Emergency Department Physician (NUJO)
EDP.............. Emergency Deployment Plans (SAUO)
EDP.............. Emergency Distribution Plan [*DoD*] (AFIT)
EDP.............. Emotionally Disturbed Person (LAIN)
EDP.............. Employment Development Plan [*Job Training and Partnership Act*] (OICC)
EDP.............. End-Diastolic Pressure [*Cardiology*]
EDP.............. Engagement Decision Point [*Military*] (SEWL)
EDP.............. Engineering Data Package [*Air Force*] (AFIT)
edp .... engineering data processing (SAUS)
EDP.............. Engineering Design Plan
EDP.............. Engineering Design Proposal (AAG)
EDP.............. Engineering Development Phase (OAG)
EDP.............. engineering development plan (SAUS)
EDP.............. Engineering Drawing Procedure (ACAE)
EDP.............. Enhanced Dot Pitch (SAUS)
EDP.............. Enterprise Development Programme [*University of Glasgow*] (AIE)
EDP.............. Environmental Development Plan (SAUO)
EDP.............. Environmental Protection Division (EERA)
EDP.............. Environment Determination Program (SAA)
EDP.............. Epatite Degenerative-Proliferativa [*A strain of mouse hepatitis virus*]
EDP.............. Equipment Data Package (MCD)
EDP.............. Equipment Deadlined for Parts [*Army*]
EDP.............. Equipment Distribution Plan (MCD)
EDP.............. Estimated Date of Publication (AAG)
EDP.............. Ethylene Diamine Pyrocatechol
EDP.............. European Defence Plan (SAUS)
EDP.............. European Defence Products (SAUO)
EDP.............. European Depository Receipt (EBF)
EDP.............. European Development Pole (EURO)
EDP.............. European Digitization Program (SAUS)
EDP.............. Event Display Process (SAUS)
EDP.............. Expedite Departure Path [*FAA*] (TAG)
EDP.............. Expeditious Discharge Program [*Army*]
EDP.............. Experimental Data Processor (SAUS)
EDP.............. Experimental Development
EDP.............. Experimental Development Program (SAUS)
EDP.............. Experimental Dynamic Processor (MUGU)
EDP.............. Extended Data Tape (SAUS)
EDP.............. Extended Delivery Point (SAUS)
EDP.............. Extended Density Platform (CIST)
EDP.............. External Data Processing (SAUS)
EDP.............. External Diploma Program
EDPA .... Environmental Data Planning Associates, Inc. (SAUO)
EDPA .... Erhardt Development Prehension Assessment
EDPA .... Exhibit Designers and Producers Association (EA)
EDPA .... Exhibition Designers and Producers Association (SAUS)
ED PA .... United States District Court for the Eastern District of Pennsylvania (DLA)
EDPAA .... EDP [*Electronic Data Processing*] Auditors Association (EA)
EDPAA .... International EDP Auditors Association (SAUS)
edpac........... electronic data processing air conditioning (SAUS)
EDPAC .... Estimated Departure from Pacific (CINC)
EDPACS .... Electronic Data Processing Audit, Control and Security (SAUS)
EDP Address... Electronic Data Processing Address (SAUS)
EDPAF .... EDP Auditors Foundation (SAUS)
EDPAF .... Electronic Data Processing Auditors Foundation (SAUS)
EDP Analyzer... Electronic Data Processing Analyzer (SAUS)
EDPAP .... enddiastolic pulmonary artery pressure (SAUS)
ED pathway... Entner-Doudoroff pathway (SAUS)
EDPC .... Electronic Data Processing Center
edp crimes... electronic data-processing crimes (SAUS)
EDPD .... Electronic Data Processing Device (IAA)
EDPD .... Electronic Data Processing Devison (SAUS)
EDPD .... Electronic Data Processing Equipment (SAUS)
EDPD .... Energy-Dependent Photoelectron Diffraction (PDAA)
EDPE............ Electronic Data Processing Equipment
ed-ped-psych-soc... education-pedagogy-psychology-sociology (SAUS)
EDPEO .... Electronic Data Processing Equipment Office (IAA)
EDPEP .... Electronic Data Processing Education Program (MHDI)
EDP/ER .... Electronic Data Processing/Europe Report (SAUS)
EDPF............ Experimental Distributed Processing Facility (ACAE)
EDPF............ Fritzlar [*Germany*] [*ICAO location identifier*] (ICLI)
EDPH .... Neuhausen Ob Eck [*Germany*] [*ICAO location identifier*] (ICLI)
Ed Philos J... Edinburgh Philosophical Journal (journ.) (SAUS)
EDPI............. Electronic Data Processing Institute (HGAA)
EDP In-Depth Rep... EDP In-Depth Reports (journ.) (SAUS)

EDP/IR .... Electronic Data Processing/Industry Report
EDP-IR .... Electronic Data Processing - Information Retrieval
EDPIS .... Electronic Data Processing and Information System (SAUS)
EDPITAF ...... Educational Development Projects Implementing Task Force (SAUO)
EDP/JR .... Electronic Data Processing/Japan Report (SAUS)
EDPL .... Altenstadt [*Germany*] [*ICAO location identifier*] (ICLI)
Ed PL .... Eden's Principles of Penal Law [*A publication*] (DLA)
EDPL .... Eminent Domain Procedure Law [*New York, NY*] [*A publication*]
EDPLA .... European Polymer Dispersion and Latex Association (SAUS)
EDPLOT .... Engineering Data Plotting [*Computer science*]
EDPM .... Electronic Data Processing Machine [*Also translated by some users of such equipment as "Every Damn Problem Multiplied"*]
EDPM .... Electronic Data Processing Magnetic [*Tape*]
EDPM .... Laupheim [*Germany*] [*ICAO location identifier*] (ICLI)
EDP Machine... Electronic Data Processing Machine (SAUS)
EDPN .... Mendig [*Germany*] [*ICAO location identifier*] (ICLI)
EDPO .... Electronic Data Processing Operation (SAUS)
EDPO .... Electronic Data Processing Organization (SAUS)
EDPOR .... Electronic Data Processing Operations Research (IAA)
EDP-OR .... Electronic Data Processing-Operations Research (SAUS)
EDP/PR .... Electronic Data Processing/Performance Review (SAUS)
EDPPrB .... Consol Ed NY,6% Cv B Pref [*NYSE symbol*] (TTSB)
EDPR .... Department of Education Procurement Regulations [*A publication*] (AAGC)
EDPR .... Electronic Data Performance Review (SAUS)
EDPR .... Electronic Data Processing Review (SAUS)
EDPR .... Engineering Development Part Release (KSC)
EDPR .... Roth [*Germany*] [*ICAO location identifier*] (ICLI)
EDPrA .... Consol Ed NY,$5 Pfd [*NYSE symbol*] (TTSB)
EDPrC .... Consol Ed NY,4.65% C Pfd [*NYSE symbol*] (TTSB)
EDP-RC .... Expeditious Discharge Program for the Reserve Components [*Army*] (MCD)
EDPRESS ..... Educational Press Association of America (EA)
EDPRICE ...... Energy Detente International Price/Tax Series [*Lundberg Survey, Inc.*] [*No longer available online*] [*Information service or system*] (CRD)
EDPS .... Electronic Data Processing System
EDPS .... Electronic Dew Point Sensor
EDPS .... Electronic Distributor Parts Show (SAUS)
EDPS .... Enhanced DPS (SAUS)
EDPS .... Equipment Distribution Planning Studies [*Army*] (AABC)
EDPS .... European Data Protection Supervisor (EURO)
EDPS .... Exploratory Development Program Summary [*Military*]
EDPS .... Straubing/Mitterharthausen [*Germany*] [*ICAO location identifier*] (ICLI)
EDPSG .... European Diabetes Pregnancy Study Group [*of the European Association for the Study of Diabetes*] (EAIO)
EDP System... Electronic Data Processing System (SAUS)
EDPT .... Electronic Data Processing Test (AFM)
EDPT .... Enhanced Drive Parameter Table [*Computer science*]
EDPT .... Niederstetten/Bad Mergentheim [*Germany*] [*ICAO location identifier*] (ICLI)
EDPW .... Ethylenediamine-Pyrocatechol-Water [*Mixture for etching silicon sensors*]
EDPW .... European Drug Prevention Weeks (EURO)
EDQ .... Economic Distribution Quantity (AFIT)
EDQ .... Extensor Digiti Quinti [*Muscle*] [*Anatomy*] (DAVI)
EDQA .... Electronic Devices Quality Assurance
EDQC .... Coburg/Brandensteinsebene [*Germany*] [*ICAO location identifier*] (ICLI)
EDQD .... Bayreuth [*Germany*] [*ICAO location identifier*] (ICLI)
EDQE .... Burg Feuerstein [*Germany*] [*ICAO location identifier*] (ICLI)
EDQF .... Ansbach/Petersdorf [*Germany*] [*ICAO location identifier*] (ICLI)
EDQH .... Herzogenaurach [*Germany*] [*ICAO location identifier*] (ICLI)
EDQK .... Kulmbach [*Germany*] [*ICAO location identifier*] (ICLI)
EDQL .... Lichtenfels [*Germany*] [*ICAO location identifier*] (ICLI)
EDQM .... Hof [*Germany*] [*ICAO location identifier*] (ICLI)
EDQN .... Neumarkt, Oberpfalz [*Germany*] [*ICAO location identifier*] (ICLI)
EDQNM .... Eddie-Dampened Quasi-Normal Markovian [*Equation*] (USDC)
ED/QP .... Engine Development / Qualification Plan (SAUS)
EDQP .... Rosenthal-Field Plossen [*Germany*] [*ICAO location identifier*] (ICLI)
EDQT .... Hassfurt/Mainwiesen [*Germany*] [*ICAO location identifier*] (ICLI)
EDQW .... Weiden, Oberpfalz [*Germany*] [*ICAO location identifier*] (ICLI)
EDQY .... Coburg/Steinrucken [*Germany*] [*ICAO location identifier*] (ICLI)
EDR .... Earliest Date of Release (WDAA)
EDR .... Early Departure Release At (SAA)
EDR .... Early Device Release (SAUS)
EDR .... Early Diastolic Relaxation [*Medicine*] (MELL)
EDR .... Edgemont Resources [*Vancouver Stock Exchange symbol*]
EDR .... Edrophonium [*Medicine*] (MELL)
EDR .... Educator's Desk Reference [*A publication*]
EDR .... Edward River [*Australia*] [*Airport symbol*] (OAG)
EDR .... Effective Direct Radiation
EDR .... Electrical Distance Recorder [*British military*] (DMA)
EDR .... Electric Digital Reading (SAUS)
EDR .... electric dispersion reactor (SAUS)
EDR .... Electrodermal Reaction (SAUS)
EDR .... Electrodermal Response
EDR .... Electrodialysis Reversal (ADWA)
EDR .... Electrodialysis Reversing
EDR .... Electromagnetic Dent Removal [*Aviation*]
EDR .... Electron Decay Rate
EDR .... Electron-Dense Region [*in Microorganisms*]
EDR .... Electronic Data Reader (SAUS)
EDR .... Electronic Data Reading (SAUS)
EDR .... Electronic Data Recorder (SAUS)
EDR .... Electronic Data Recording (SAUS)
EDR .... Electronic Decoy Rocket
EDR .... Electronic Dictionary Research (IDAI)
EDR .... Electronic Diesel Regulation [*Automotive engineering*]
EDR .... Electronic Digit Reading (SAUS)
EDR .... Electronic Document Reader (SAUS)
EDR .... Emergency Distance Required [*Aviation*] (AIA)
EDR .... Employee Data Record
EDR .... Encyclopedic Dictionary of Religion
EDR .... Engineering Data Representative (SAUS)
EDR .... Engineering Data Requirements (AAG)
EDR .... Engineering Department [*or Division*] Report
EDR .... Engineering Design Review (NASA)
EDR .... Engineering Disposition Request [*Air Force*] (SEWL)
EDR .... Engineering Division Report (SAUS)
EDR .... Engineering Drawing Release
EDR .... Environmental Data Records
EDR .... Environmental Data Resources, Inc. (IID)
EDR .... Environmental Deterioration Rating (PDAA)
EDR .... Enzyme-Dependent Reaction [*Medicine*] (MELL)
EDR .... Equipment Damage Report (SAUS)
EDR .... Equipment Decontamination Room [*Nuclear energy*] (NUCP)
EDR .... Equipment Design Review (SAUS)
EDR .... Equivalent Direct Radiation
EDR .... Error Detection Routine (SAUS)
EDR .... Estimated Date of Resumption (AAG)
EDR .... Ethanol-Disulfiram Reaction [*Pharmacology*]
EDR .... European Depositary Receipt [*Investment term*]
EDR .... European Depository Receipt (SAUS)
EDR .... Event Data Recorder
EDR .... [*The*] Executive Desk Register [*Information service or system*] (IID)
EDR .... Exo Defense Regime (ACAE)
EDR .... Expect Departure Release (SAUS)
EDR .... Expect Departure Release At [*Aviation*] (FAAC)
EDR .... Experience Data Report (AAGC)
EDR .... Experimental Development Requirements (CINC)
EDR .... Experiment Data Record
EDR .... Exploratory Development Request [*Military*]
EDR .... Exploratory Development Requirement [*Military*]
EDR .... External Data Ready (SAUS)
EDR .... External Developer Release (SAUS)
EDR .... Lineas Aereas Eldorado Ltd. [*Colombia*] [*ICAO designator*] (FAAC)
EDR .... Roscoe's Eastern District Reports [*Cape Of Good Hope*] [*A publication*] (DLA)
EDR .... Except During Rain (ODA)
EDRA .... Engineering Drawing Release Authorization
EDRA .... Environmental Design Research Association (EA)
EDRA .... European Digital Road-mapping Association
EDRAM .... Enhanced Dynamic Random Access Memory [*Computer science*]
EDRAM .... Extended Dynamic Random Access Memory (SAUS)
EDRAS .... Economic Data Retrieval and Application System (BUR)
EDRAW .... Erasable Direct Read After Write [*Computer science*] (IAA)
EDRB .... Engineering Design Review Board (SAA)
EDRC .... Economic and Development Review Committee (SAUO)
EDRC .... Engineering Design Research Center [*Pittsburgh, PA*] [*National Science Foundation*] (GRD)
EDRCC .... Electronic Data Remote Communications Complex
Ed RD .... Doctor of Religious Education
EDRE .... Emergency Deployment Readiness Exercise [*Army*] (INF)
EdReAn .... Educational Research Analysts (EA)
Ed Res Perspectives... Education Research and Perspectives [*A publication*]
E-dress .... Electronic Address (ADWA)
EDRF .... Bad Duerkheim [*Germany*] [*ICAO location identifier*] (ICLI)
EDRF .... Endothelial-Derived Relaxing Factor [*Biochemistry*]
EDRF .... Endothelium-Derived Vascular Relaxant Factor [*Biochemistry*]
EDRF .... Epithelium-Derived Relaxation Factor [*Animal physiology*] (QSUL)
EDRF .... Experience Demand Replacement Factor [*Navy*]
EDRI .... Electronic Distributors' Research Institute
EDRI .... Environmental Data Research Institute (SAUO)
EDRIS .... Engineering Data Requisition and Index System (SAUS)
EDRJ .... Saarlouis/Dueren [*Germany*] [*ICAO location identifier*] (ICLI)
EDRK .... Koblenz/Winningen [*Germany*] [*ICAO location identifier*] (ICLI)
EDRL .... Effective Damage Risk Level
EDRL .... Engineering Data Records and Lists (ACAE)
EDRL .... Lachen/Speyerdorf [*Germany*] [*ICAO location identifier*] (ICLI)
EDRLS .... Engineering Data Records and Lists System (ACAE)
EDRO .... Office of Executive Director of Regional Operations [*Nuclear energy*] (NRCH)
EDRP .... European Demonstrtion Reprocessing Plant [*Nuclear energy*] (NUCP)
EDR-RC .... Expeditious Discharge Program for the Reserve Components [*Military*]
EDRS .... Education Document Reproduction Service
EDRS .... Education Document Reproductive Service (SAUS)
EDRS .... Enforcement Document Retrieval System [*Environmental Protection Agency*] (EPA)
EDRS .... Engineering Data Release System (ACAE)
EDRS .... Engineering Data Retrieval System [*Military*]
EDRS .... ERIC [*Educational Resources Information Center*] Document Reproduction Service [*Department of Education*] [*Alexandria, VA*]
EDRS .... European Data Relay Satellite
EDRs .... European Depository Receipts (SAUS)
EDRS .... Expanded Data Reporting System (PDAA)
EDRS .... Saarbruecken [*Germany*] [*ICAO location identifier*] (ICLI)
EDRT .... Effective Date of Release from Training

EDRT .... Trier/Foehren [*Germany*] [*ICAO location identifier*] (ICLI)
EDRY .... Speyer [*Germany*] [*ICAO location identifier*] (ICLI)
EDRZ .... Pirmasens/Zweibruecken [*Germany*] [*ICAO location identifier*] (ICLI)
EDS .... Early Deployment System (ABAC)
EDS .... earth data systems (SAUS)
EDS .... Echo Depth Sounder
EDS .... Economic Development Service (SAUO)
EDS .... Edema Disease of Swine [*Medicine*] (DMAA)
EDS .... Edisto Resources Corp. [*AMEX symbol*] (SPSG)
Eds .... Editions (WDMC)
eds .... Editions
EDS .... Editorial Data Systems
eds .... Editors (DIAR)
EDS .... Editors (SAUS)
Eds .... Editors (WDMC)
EDS .... Educational Data System (IAA)
EDS .... Educational Delivery System (OICC)
Ed S .... Educational Specialist
EDS .... Education Specialist (SAUO)
EDS .... Egg Drop Syndrome [*Medicine*] (DMAA)
EDS .... Ehlers-Danlos Syndrome [*Medicine*]
EDS .... El Dorado Systems Canada [*Vancouver Stock Exchange symbol*]
EDS .... Electrical Discharge Sawing (SAUS)
EDS .... Electrical Discharge Slice (SAUS)
EDS .... Electrical Distribution System (MCD)
EDS .... Electric Data Scanning (SAUS)
EDS .... Electric Data Storage (SAUS)
EDS .... Electric-Discharge Sintering (SAUS)
EDS .... Electric Drive System (SAUS)
EDS .... Electrodynamic Suspension [*Railway technology*] (PS)
EDS .... Electromagnetic Data Storage (SAUS)
EDS .... Electron Devices Society (EA)
EDS .... electron dispersive x-ray (SAUS)
EDS .... Electronic Data Service (SAUS)
EDS .... Electronic Data Station (SAUS)
EDS .... Electronic Data Storage (IAA)
EDS .... Electronic Data Submission (HGEN)
EDS .... Electronic Data Switching (ELAL)
EDS .... Electronic Data Switching System [*Computer science*] (TEL)
EDS .... Electronic Data System (IEEE)
EDS .... Electronic Data Systems [*NYSE symbol*] (SG)
EDS .... Electronic Data Systems Corporation (SAUS)
EDS .... Electronic Data Systems Federal Corp.
EDS .... Electronic Data Systems Ltd. [*Information service or system*] (IID)
EDS .... Electronic Design Section (SAA)
EDS .... Electronic Devices Society (SAUO)
EDS .... Electronic Diesel System [*Automotive engineering*]
EDS .... Electronic Differential Lock System [*Automotive engineering*]
EDS .... Electronic DIP Switch (SAUS)
EDS .... Electronic Directory Service [*Communications term*] (DCT)
EDS .... Electronic Distribution Show (ITD)
EDS .... Electronic Distribution System (MCD)
EDS .... Electronic Document Service
EDS .... Electronic Document Storage (SAUS)
EDS .... Electronic Document Storage Systems (NITA)
EDS .... Electronic Switching System (SAUS)
EDS .... Emamel Double-Silk (SAUS)
EDS .... Emergency Deorbit System [*NASA*] (KSC)
EDS .... Emergency Detection System
EDS .... Emergency Disablement System
EDS .... Emergency Distribution System (MCD)
EDS .... Emery-Dreifuss Syndrome [*Medicine*] (EDAA)
EDS .... Employability Development Services [*US Employment Service*] [*Department of Labor*]
EDS .... Enamel Double Silk [*Wire insulation*] (AAG)
EDS .... Energy Data System [*Databank*] [*Environmental Protection Agency*] (IID)
EDS .... Energy Depot Systems
EDS .... Energy-Dispersive (SAUS)
EDS .... Energy Dispersive Spectrometer (SAUS)
EDS .... Energy-Dispersive Spectrometry (SAUS)
EDS .... Energy Dispersive Spectroscopy
EDS .... Energy Dispersive System [*Microscopy*]
EDS .... Energy-Dispersive X-Ray Spectroscopy (EDCT)
EDs .... Engagement Direction Station (SAA)
EDS .... Engine Diagnostic System
EDS .... Engine Dynamometer Schedule [*Automotive emissions testing*]
EDS .... Engineering Data Sales (SAUS)
EDS .... Engineering Data Service (SAUS)
EDS .... Engineering Data Sheet
EDS .... Engineering Data Software
EDS .... Engineering Data System (SAUS)
EDS .... Engineering Data Systems [*DoD*]
EDS .... Engineering Design Simulator
EDS .... Engineering Design System (ELAL)
EDS .... Engineering Development Section (SAUS)
EDS .... Engineering Drafting Software [*Calcomp Ltd.*] [*Software package*] (NCC)
EDS .... English Dialect Society
EDS .... Enter Day Stop [*Investment term*] (NUMA)
EDS .... Enter Day Stop Order (ADWA)
EDS .... Entreprise Diffusion SystSme (SAUS)
EDS .... Entry Data Subsystem
EDS .... Environmental Data Service [*Later, NESDIS*] [*Washington, DC*] [*National Oceanic and Atmospheric Administration*] (EA)
EDS .... Epigastric Distress Syndrome [*Medicine*] (EDAA)
EDS .... Episcopal Divinity School (SAUS)
EDS .... Equatorial Dynamics Study [*Marine science*] (MSC)
EDS .... Equipment Decontamination Station [*Military*]
EDS .... equipment disposition system (SAUS)
EDS .... Error Detection System (KSC)
EDS .... Error Diagnostic Signal (SAUS)
EDS .... Estimated Date of Separation
EDS .... Estimated Daughter Superiority [*Genetics*] (OA)
EDS .... European Declarative System (EURO)
EDS .... European Demonstration Scheme (SAUS)
EDS .... European Distribution System [*DoD*]
EDS .... Evolution Development System (SAUS)
EDS .... Excess Disposition System (MCD)
EDS .... Excessive Daytime Sleepiness
EDS .... Excessive Daytime Somnolence [*Medicine*]
EDS .... Exchangeable Disc Stores (NITA)
EDS .... Exchangeable Disk Storage [*Computer science*]
EDS .... Executive Display Subsystem (SAUS)
EDS .... Experimental Distributed System (SAUS)
EDS .... Experiment Data System
EDS .... Expert Debugging System (SAUS)
EDS .... Explosive Detection Systems [*FAA*] (TAG)
EDS .... Explosive Device System (KSC)
EDs .... Explosive Disposal specialists (SAUS)
EDS .... Express Delivery Service
EDS .... Extended Data Stream [*Medicine*] (MEDA)
EDS .... External Drum Store (SAUS)
EDS .... Extradimensional Shift [*Psychometrics*]
EDS .... Exxon Donor Solvent Process [*Coal liquefaction*]
EDS .... IEEE Electron Devices Society (EA)
EDS .... Orangeburg, SC [*Location identifier*] [*FAA*] (FAAL)
EdS .... Specialist in Education (GAGS)
EDSA .... Eating Disorders Shared Awareness (ADWA)
EDSA .... Effective Date of Change in Station Assignment [*Military*]
EDSA .... Electronic Data Storage Automatic computer (SAUS)
EDSA .... Electronic Document Systems Association (NTPA)
EDSA .... Epifanio de los Santos [*Avenue where Philippine President Marcos' government tanks were stopped by unarmed citizens*] [*In the EDSA Revolution of February, 1986*]
EDSA .... European Distribution System Aircraft [*DoD*]
EDSA .... Expert Dataflow and Static Analysis Tool (SAUS)
EDSA .... Expert Debugging System for Ada (SAUS)
EDSA .... Landsberg [*Germany*] [*ICAO location identifier*] (ICLI)
EDSAC .... Electronic Data Storage Automatic Computer (IAA)
edsac .... electronic delayed-storage automatic computer (SAUS)
EDSAC .... Electronic Delay Storage Automatic Calculator [*or Computer*] [*1949*]
EDSAC .... Electronic Discrete Sequential Automatic Computer [*University of Manchester, 1949*] [*British*] (IEEE)
EDSA Computer ... Electronic Data Storage Automatic Computer (SAUS)
EDSAI .... Educational Dealers and Suppliers Association International (EA)
EDSA-IL .... Electric Service Dealers Association of Illinois (SRA)
EDSA Int'l .... Educational Dealers and Suppliers Association International (NTPA)
EDS & R ...... Engineering Data Storage and Retrieval [*Military*]
EDS and R ..... Engineering Data Store and Retrieval (SAUS)
EDSAR .... Engineering Drawing Status and Release (DNAB)
EDSAT .... Center for Educational Diffusion and Social Application of Satellite Telecommunications (SAUS)
EDSAT .... Educational Satellite (SAUS)
edsat .... educational television satellite (SAUS)
EDSB .... Buchel [*Germany*] [*ICAO location identifier*] (ICLI)
EDSC .... Enamel Double-Silk Covered (SAUS)
EDSC .... Engineering Data Service Center [*Air Force*]
EDSC .... Engineering Data Support Center [*Air Force*] (CET)
EDSC .... European Deaf Swimming Championships [*British*]
EDSC .... Exotic-Diseases Sub-Committee of Animal Health Committee (SAUO)
EDS Center ... Electronic Data Switching Center (SAUS)
ED-Schneiden ... electrical discharge slice (SAUS)
EDS Corp ..... Electronic Data Systems Corporation (SAUO)
EDSD .... EDIFACT Segments Directory (AG)
EDSD .... Electronic Defense Systems Division (SAUO)
EDSD .... Engineering and Development Services Department [*Naval Air Development Center*]
EDSD .... Leipheim [*Germany*] [*ICAO location identifier*] (ICLI)
EDSDM .... Electronic Document Storage Datamanagement (SAUS)
EDSE .... Edison Sault Electric Co. (MHDW)
EDSE .... Equixated Dendritic Solidification Experiment (SAUS)
EDSE .... Erding [*Germany*] [*ICAO location identifier*] (ICLI)
EDSE .... ESELCO, Inc. [*NASDAQ symbol*] (SPSG)
EDS/EELS ...... Energy-Dispersive Spectroscopy/Electron Energy Loss Spectroscopy (SAUS)
EDSF .... Fuerstenfeldbruck [*Germany*] [*ICAO location identifier*] (ICLI)
EDSFC .... Electronic Data Systems Federal Corp.
EDS-FS .... European Distribution System Forward Stockage (SAUO)
EDSG .... Bremgarten [*Germany*] [*ICAO location identifier*] (ICLI)
EDSG .... Electrooptical Data Systems Group (SAUO)
EDSG .... Energy Demand Steering Group (SAUO)
EDSI .... Educational Data Systems, Incorporated (SAUO)
EDSI .... Enhanced Small Device Interface (SAUS)
EDSI .... Equivalent Delivered Source Instructions
EDSI .... equivalent number of delivered source instructions (SAUS)
EDSI .... Ingoldstadt [*Germany*] [*ICAO location identifier*] (ICLI)
EDSIL .... Engineering Development Systems Integration Laboratory
EDSIM .... Editor + Simulator (SAUS)
EDSIM .... Event-Based Discrete Simulation (PDAA)

ED SK .... Engineering Department Sketch (MSA)
EDSK .... Kaufbeuren [Germany] [ICAO location identifier] (ICLI)
EDSL .... End-Diastolic Segment Length [Cardiology]
EDSL .... Enhanced Digital Subscriber Line [AT&T] (CIST)
EDSL .... Extended Digital Subscriber Line (SAUS)
EDSL .... Lechfeld [Germany] [ICAO location identifier] (ICLI)
EDSM .... Electro-Optical Data Systems Manufacturing (ACAE)
EDSM .... Memmingen [Germany] [ICAO location identifier] (ICLI)
EDSN .... Ejercito Defensor de la Soberania Nacional [Defending Army of the National Sovereignty of Nicaragua]
EDSN .... Neubiberg [Germany] [ICAO location identifier] (ICLI)
EDS-NWT ..... Eskimo Dog Society of the Northwest Territories [Defunct] (EA)
EDSO .... European Deaf Sports Organization (SAUO)
Ed Sp .... Education Specialist
EDSP .... Electronic Discrimination Signal Processor (ACAE)
EDSP .... Engineering Design Support to Production (MCD)
EDSP .... Exchange Delivery Settlement Price (NUMA)
EDSP .... Pferdsfeld [Germany] [ICAO location identifier] (ICLI)
Ed Spec ...... Educational Specialist (SAUS)
Ed Spec ...... Education Specialist
EDSR .... Electronic Digital Slide Rule (IAA)
EDSR .... Electronic Document Storage and Retrieval (SAUS)
EDS/R .... Engineering Data Storage and Retrieval Project [Picatinny Arsenal] [Dover, NJ] [Military]
EDSR .... Exploratory Development Summary Report [Military]
EDSRA .... Earth Data System Reference Application (VERA)
EDSS .... Electronic Data Switching System (SAUS)
EDSS .... Engineering and Development Support Services (KSC)
EDSS .... Environmental Data Support System (MCD)
EDSS .... Environment Decision-Making Support System [Computer science] (EERA)
EDSS .... Equipment Deployment and Storage System [MTMC] (TAG)
EDSS .... European Digital Subscriber System (SAUO)
EDSS .... Expanded Disability Status Scale [Clinical medicine]
EDSS .... Expanded Kurtzke Disability Status Scale [Medicine]
EDSS .... Expert Decision-Support System [Computer science] (ODBW)
EDSS .... Explosives Detection Security System (SAUS)
EDSS .... Extended Disability Status Scale [Medicine]
EDSS1 .... European Digital Subscriber Signalling System No. 1 (SAUS)
EDS System... Electronic Data Switching System (SAUS)
EDST .... Eastern Daylight Saving Time
EDST .... Elastic Diaphragm Switch Technology [IBM Corp.] (MCD)
EDST .... Electric Diaphragm Switch Technique (SAUS)
EDSTAC ...... Endocrine Disruptor Screening and Testing Advisory Committee
ED STAFF .... Editorial Staff (DGA)
EDSTAT ...... Educational Statistics [Search system]
EDSTAT ...... Educational Statistics Information Access Service [Databank] (NITA)
EDSTM .... Environmental Data Service Technical Memoranda [National Oceanic and Atmospheric Administration] (NOAA)
EDSTN .... Edmundston, NB [American Association of Railroads railroad junction routing code]
EDSTO .... Eddystone, PA [American Association of Railroads railroad junction routing code]
EDSU .... Neuburg [Germany] [ICAO location identifier] (ICLI)
EDSV .... Enamel Double Silk Varnish [Wire insulation]
EDSV .... Mebstetten [Germany] [ICAO location identifier] (ICLI)
EDSWS .... Edisto Resources Wrrt [AMEX symbol] (TTSB)
EDSX .... Electronic Digital Signal Cross-Connect [Telecommunications] (CIST)
EdSys .... Editorial System
EDT .... Early Decay Time (SAUS)
EDT .... Eastern Daylight Saving Time (SAUS)
EDT .... Eastern Daylight Time
EDT .... Edict (ABBR)
EDT .... Edisto Resources Corp. [AMEX symbol] (SAG)
EDT .... Edit (ABBR)
EDT .... Edit Data Transmission (COE)
EDT .... Editor
EDT .... Educom (SAUS)
EDT .... Effective Date of Training
EDT .... Effective Diagenetic Temperature [Geology]
EDT .... Electrical Discharge Tube (MSA)
EDT .... Electric Data Transmission (SAUS)
EDT .... Electric Discharge Tube (SAUS)
EDT .... Electrodeless Discharge Tube
EDT .... Electronic Data Transmission (AAG)
EDT .... Electronic Design Transfer (SAUS)
EDT .... Employability Development Team (OICC)
EDT .... End Data Transmission (SAUS)
EDT .... End-Diastolic Thickness [Medicine] (MELL)
EDT .... End of Data Transfer (SAUS)
EDT .... Energy Dissipation Tests (NRCH)
EDT .... Engineer Design Test (SAUS)
EDT .... Engineering Defense Training (SAUO)
EDT .... Engineering Description Tape (IAA)
EDT .... Engineering Design Test
EDT .... Engineering Development Test
EDT .... Engineering Drawing Tree
EDT .... Enumerated Data Type (ACAE)
EDT .... Equipment Downtime
EDT .... Equipment Drain Tank [Nuclear energy] (NRCH)
EDT .... Erb, Dill, and Toombs (SAUS)
EDT .... Estimated Delivery Times
EDT .... Estimated Departure Time
EDT .... Estimated Discharge Time
EDT .... Ethylenediamine Tartrate [Organic chemistry]
EDT .... European Deaf Telephone (MWOL)
EDT .... Exchange Data Terminal (SAUS)
EDT .... Executive Display Terminal (SAUS)
EDT .... Expected Downtime (SAUS)
EDT .... explosive detonation trench (SAUS)
EDT .... Extended Data Tape (SAUS)
EDT .... Energy Design Technique (ODA)
EDTA .... Aalen-Heidenheim/Elchingen [Germany] [ICAO location identifier] (ICLI)
EDTA .... Edathamil (MAE)
EDTA .... Edetate Calcium Disodium [Medicine] (MTAA)
EDTA .... Edetic Acid [Organic chemistry] (AAMN)
EDTA .... Ethylendiamin-tetra-acetat (SAUS)
EDTA .... Ethylenediaminetetraacetate [Also, EDETATE, enta] [Organic chemistry]
edta .... ethylene diamine tetra-acetic (SAUS)
EDTA .... Ethylenediaminetetra-Acetic Acid [Also called edathamil and edetic acid] [Organic chemistry] (DAVI)
EDTA .... Ethylene Diaminetetracetic Acid (DOG)
EDTA .... Ethylenedinitrilo Tetraacetic Acid [Organic chemistry] (NRCH)
EDTA/ERA .... European Dialysis and Transplant Association-European Renal Association (SAUO)
EDTAN .... Ethylenediaminetetraacetonitrile [Also, EDTN] [Organic chemistry]
EDTB .... Baden-Baden [Germany] [ICAO location identifier] (ICLI)
EDTC .... Electronic Desk Top Computer (SAUS)
EDTC .... Electronic Desktop Computer (VLIE)
EDTC .... Engine Drag Torque Control [Automotive engineering]
EDTC .... Engineering Design Test, Contractor (MCD)
EDTC .... Engineering Development and Test Center [Mack Trucks, Inc.] [Allentown, PA]
EDTC .... Ethyldipropylthiocarbamate (SAUS)
EDTCC .... Electronic Data Traffic Control Center [or Complex]
EDTCC .... Electronic Data Traffic Control Complex (SAUS)
EDTCC .... Electronic Data Transmission Communications Center (SAUO)
EDTCC .... Electronic Data Transmission Communications Central
EDTCC .... Electronic Data Transmission Control Center (SAUO)
EDTCS .... Engine Dynamometer Test Control System [Automotive engineering]
EDTD .... Donaueschingen/Villingen [Germany] [ICAO location identifier] (ICLI)
EDTD .... Edit Description (SAUS)
EDTD .... Edited (ABBR)
EDTE .... Effective Date [Military] (AFIT)
EDTE .... Schwenningen Am Nickar [Germany] [ICAO location identifier] (ICLI)
ED Tenn ...... United States District Court for the Eastern District of Tennessee (DLA)
EDTEP .... Engineering Design Test and Evaluation Program
ED Tex .... United States District Court for the Eastern District of Texas (DLA)
EDTF .... Freiburg/Breisgau [Germany] [ICAO location identifier] (ICLI)
EDTG .... Editing (ABBR)
EDTG .... Engineering Design Test, Government (MCD)
EDTH .... Heubach, Wurttemberg [Germany] [ICAO location identifier] (ICLI)
Ed Theory .... Educational Theory [A publication] (BRI)
EDTI .... Explosive Demolition Technical Instructions (SAUS)
EDTK .... Karlsruhe/Forchheim [Germany] [ICAO location identifier] (ICLI)
EDTL .... Editorial (ABBR)
EDTL .... Electronic Technology & Devices Laboratory [Army] (RDA)
EDTLZ .... Editorialize (ABBR)
EDTLZD ...... Editorialized (ABBR)
EDTLZG ...... Editorializing (ABBR)
EDTM .... Mengen [Germany] [ICAO location identifier] (ICLI)
EDTN .... Edition (ABBR)
EDTN .... Ethylenediaminetetraacetonitrile [Also, EDTAN] [Organic chemistry]
EDTN .... Nabern/Teck [Germany] [ICAO location identifier] (ICLI)
EDTNA .... European Dialysis and Transplant Nurses Association (SAUO)
EDTNA/ERCA... European Dialysis and Transplant Nurses Association / European Renal Care Association (SAUS)
EDTNA/ERCA... European Dialysis and Transplant Nurses Association/European Renal Care Association [Formerly, European Dialysis and Transplant Nurses Associaton] (EA)
EDTO .... Offenburg/Baden [Germany] [ICAO location identifier] (ICLI)
EDTP .... Engineer Design Test Plan (ACAE)
EDTPDU .... Expedited Data Transport Protocol Data Unit (SAUS)
EDTPDUEGP... exterior gateway protocol (SAUS)
EDTPO .... Ethylenediaminetetra(methylenephosphonic Acid) [Organic chemistry]
EDTR .... Editor (ABBR)
EDTR .... Experimental, Developmental, Test, and Research
EDTRASUPPDET... Education and Training Support Detachment [Military] (DNAB)
EDTRASUPPTRADEV FEO... Education and Training Support Training Device Field Engineering Office [Military] (DNAB)
EDTRSP .... Editorship (ABBR)
EDTS .... Ann Arbor Evaluation and Development Test System (SAUS)
EDTS .... Electrodepositer Technology Society (SAUO)
EDTS .... Equipment Drain Treatment System [Nuclear energy] (NRCH)
EDTS .... Evaluation and Development Test System (SAUO)
EDTS .... Expanded Data Transfer System (SEWL)
EDTSP .... Editorship (ABBR)
EDTSR .... Electronic Dial Tone Speed Register [Bell System]
EDTV .... Enhanced [or Extended] Definition Television (PCM)
EDTV .... Extended-Definition Television [in ED Beta] [Sony Corp.] (PS)
EDTX .... Schwaebisch Hall/Weckrieden [Germany] [ICAO location identifier] (ICLI)
EDTY .... Friedrichshafen-Lowental [Germany] [ICAO location identifier] (ICLI)
EDTZ .... Konstanz [Germany] [ICAO location identifier] (ICLI)
EDU .... Dundee [Scotland] [Seismograph station code, US Geological Survey] (SEIS)
EDU .... Early Deploying Unit (MCD)

EDU .... Eating Disorder Unit [*Medicine*] (DAVI)
EDU .... Edit Display Unit (VLIE)
EDU .... Education (ADA)
edu .... Education (BEE)
Edu .... Education (AL)
Edu .... Educational (AL)
EDU .... Educational Institutions (SAUS)
EDU .... Educational Institutions (Domain Name) (SAUS)
edu .... educational, Internet-Domain (SAUS)
edu .... Educational Organization [*Internet address domain name*] (CDE)
EDU .... EDUcation institution (SAUS)
Edu .... Educo [*Record label*]
EDU .... Electrical Distribution Unit
EDU .... Electronic Display Unit
EDU .... Electronic Distributor Unit [*Automotive engineering*]
EDU .... Encoder-Decoder Unit (ACAE)
EDU .... Endue (ABBR)
EDU .... Engine Diagnostic Unit (SAUS)
EDU .... Engineering Development Unit [*NASA*] (NASA)
EDU .... Enterprise and Deregulation Unit (AIE)
EDU .... Environmental Diving Unit [*Marine science*] (MSC)
EDU .... Equipment Dependent Uptime (AAEL)
EDU .... Error Detection Unit (CCCA)
EDU .... Ethiopian Democratic Union [*Political party*] (PD)
EDU .... Europaeische Demokratische Union [*European Democratic Union*] [*Austria*] (EAIO)
EDU .... Experimental Development Unit (SAUS)
EDU .... Experimental Diving Unit [*Research center*] [*British*]
EDU .... Exponential Decay Unit [*Physics*] (IAA)
EDU .... Form Description Utility [*Computer science*] (ELAL)
EDU .... Ministry of Education, Information Centre [*Ontario*] [*UTLAS symbol*]
EDUBU .... East Dubuque, IL [*American Association of Railroads railroad junction routing code*]
EDUC .... Educated [*or Education*] (AFM)
educ .... Educated (WDAA)
Educ .... Education (DIAR)
educ .... Education (VRA)
EDUC .... Education
educ .... Educational (ADWA)
EDUC .... Educational Development Corp. [*NASDAQ symbol*] (NQ)
educasting ... Educational Broadcasting (SAUS)
EDUCATE ..... End-user Courses in Information Access through Communication Technology (SAUS)
Educational Film ... Educational Film Library Association (SAUO)
EDUCATSS ... Education Cataloguing Support System [*UTLAS symbol*]
EDUCB .... Educable (ABBR)
Educ Chem ... Education in Chemistry (MEC)
Educ Comput ... Educational Computing (journ.) (SAUS)
EDUCD .... Educated (ABBR)
Educ Digest ... Educational Digest (SAUS)
Educ Econ .... Education and Economics [*A publication*] (JLIT)
EDUCG .... Educating (ABBR)
EducIns .... Educational Insights, Inc. [*Associated Press*] (SAG)
EDUC International ... Association of Advisers on Education in International Religious Congregations (SAUO)
EDUCL .... Educational
Educ Libr Bull ... Education Libraries Bulletin (journ.) (SAUS)
EDUCN .... Education
Educnl .... Educational
EDUCNLST ... Educationalist (ABBR)
EDUCOM ...... Educational Communications/ Interuniversity Communications Council (SAUO)
EDUCOM ...... Educational Use of Computers
EDUCOM ...... Interuniversity Communications Council (EA)
EDUCOM Bull ... EDUCOM Bulletin (journ.) (SAUS)
EDUCOM Rev ... EDUCOM Review (journ.) (SAUS)
Educ Pr .... Educational Press (SAUS)
Educ Pr .... Educational Press Association of America (SAUO)
Educ Pub ..... Educational Publications Services (SAUS)
Educ Pub ..... Educational Publishers (SAUS)
Educ R .... Educational Review (journ.) (SAUS)
EDUCR .... Educator (ABBR)
educrat .... educational bureaucrat (SAUS)
Educ Rec ..... Educational Record (journ.) (SAUS)
Educ Tecbnol ... Educational Technology (journ.) (SAUS)
Educ Theatre J ... Educational Theatre Journal (journ.) (SAUS)
EDUCTL .... Educational (SAUS)
Educ + Train ... Education + Training (journ.) (SAUS)
Educ Train Technol Int ... Educational and Training Technology International (journ.) (SAUS)
EDUCV .... Educative (ABBR)
EDUD .... Detmold [*Germany*] [*ICAO location identifier*] (ICLI)
EDUD .... Eating, Drinking, Urinating and Defaecating (SPVS)
EduDv .... Educational Development Corp. [*Associated Press*] (SAG)
EDUG .... European Datamanager Users Group [*London, England*] (CSR)
EDUH .... Hildesheim [*Germany*] [*ICAO location identifier*] (ICLI)
EDUI/O .... Error Detection Unit Input/Output
EDUK .... Rheindahlen [*Germany*] [*ICAO location identifier*] (ICLI)
EduKan .... Western Kansas Community College Virtual Education Consortium
EDUL .... Laarbruch [*Germany*] [*ICAO location identifier*] (ICLI)
EDUM .... Educational Media (journ.) (SAUS)
EduMOO ...... Educational Multi-User Object Oriented [*Computer science*]
EDUN .... Nordhorn Range [*Germany*] [*ICAO location identifier*] (ICLI)
EDUNET .... Education Network [*EDUCOM*]
Edunetic ...... Edunetics Ltd. [*Associated Press*] (SAG)
EDUO .... Guetersloh [*Germany*] [*ICAO location identifier*] (ICLI)
EDUP .... Ethiopian Democratic Unionist Party
EDUP .... Ethiopian Democratic Unity Party [*Political party*] (EY)
EDUR .... Bruggen [*Germany*] [*ICAO location identifier*] (ICLI)
EDUR .... Engineering Drawing Usage Record [*DAC*]
EDUS .... Edusoft Ltd. [*NASDAQ symbol*] (SAG)
EDUS .... Soest [*Germany*] [*ICAO location identifier*] (ICLI)
EDUSAT .... Educational Satellite (KSC)
EDUSAT System ... Education-Television Satellite System (SAUS)
EDUSE .... Edusoft Ltd [*NASDAQ symbol*] (TTSB)
Edusoft .... Edusoft Ltd. [*Associated Press*] (SAG)
EDUT .... EduTrek International, Inc. [*NASDAQ symbol*] (NASQ)
EDUT .... EduTrek Intl.'A' [*NASDAQ symbol*] (SG)
edutainment ... educational entertainment (SAUS)
edutele .... educational television (SAUS)
edutherap .... educational therapist (SAUS)
edutherap .... educational therapy (SAUS)
EDUW .... Wildenrath [*Germany*] [*ICAO location identifier*] (ICLI)
'Eduy .... 'Eduyyoth (BJA)
EDV .... Eastern Diverging Volcanism [*Geology*]
EDV .... Electro-Dynamic Venturi (PDAA)
EDV .... Electronic Depressurizing Valve (MCD)
EDV .... Elektronische Datenverarbeitung [*Electronic Data Processing - EDP*] [*German*]
EDV .... Emission Data Vehicle [*Exhaust emissions testing*] [*Automotive engineering*]
EDV .... End-Diastole Volume (SAUS)
EDV .... End-Diastolic Volume [*Cardiology*]
EDV .... Epidermodysplasia Verruciformis [*Medicine*]
EDV .... Equivalent Daylight Visibility (PDAA)
EDVA .... Bad Gandersheim [*Germany*] [*ICAO location identifier*] (ICLI)
EDVA .... Erbium doped Fiber Amplifier (SAUS)
ED VA .... United States District Court for the Eastern District of Virginia (DLA)
EDVAC .... Electron Discrete Variable Automatic Compiler (SAUS)
EDVAC .... Electronic Digital Variable Automatic Computer (SAUS)
EDVAC .... Electronic Digital-Vernier Analog Computer (SAA)
EDVAC .... Electronic Discrete Variable Automatic Calculator [*or Computer*] (MCD)
EDVAC .... Electronic Discrete Variable Automatic Computer (SAUS)
EDVAC .... Electronic Discrete Variable Computer (SAUS)
EDVAP .... Electronic Digital-Vernier Analog Plotter (MUGU)
EDVB .... Braunschweig [*Germany*] [*ICAO location identifier*] (ICLI)
EDVC .... Celle/Arloh [*Germany*] [*ICAO location identifier*] (ICLI)
EDVE .... Braunschweig [*Germany*] [*ICAO location identifier*] (ICLI)
EdVENT .... Educational Events [*Timeplace, Inc.*] [*Waltham, MA*] [*Information service or system*] (IID)
EDVH .... Hodenhagen [*Germany*] [*ICAO location identifier*] (ICLI)
EDVI .... End-Diastolic Volume Index [*Cardiology*] (DAVI)
EDVI .... Hoxter/Holzminden [*Germany*] [*ICAO location identifier*] (ICLI)
EDVK .... Kassel/Calden [*Germany*] [*ICAO location identifier*] (ICLI)
EDVL .... Holleberg [*Germany*] [*ICAO location identifier*] (ICLI)
EDVM .... Kassel-Mittelfeld [*Germany*] [*ICAO location identifier*] (ICLI)
EDVN .... Northeim [*Germany*] [*ICAO location identifier*] (ICLI)
EDVP .... Peine/Eddesse [*Germany*] [*ICAO location identifier*] (ICLI)
EDVR .... Enlisted Distribution and Verification Report
EDVR .... Rinteln [*Germany*] [*ICAO location identifier*] (ICLI)
EDVS .... Salzgitter/Drutte [*Germany*] [*ICAO location identifier*] (ICLI)
EDVU .... Uelzen [*Germany*] [*ICAO location identifier*] (ICLI)
EDVV .... Hannover [*Germany*] [*ICAO location identifier*] (ICLI)
EDVX .... Gifhorn [*Germany*] [*ICAO location identifier*] (ICLI)
EDVY .... Porta Westfalica [*Germany*] [*ICAO location identifier*] (ICLI)
EDW .... Earth Departure Window [*Aerospace*]
Edw .... Edward (SAFN)
EDW .... Edwards [*California*] [*Airport symbol*] [*Obsolete*] (OAG)
EDW .... Edwards Air Force Base [*California*] [*TACAN station*] (NASA)
Edw .... Edwards' Chester Palatine Courts [*England*] [*A publication*] (DLA)
Edw .... Edwards' English Admiralty Reports [*A publication*] (DLA)
Edw .... Edwards' New York Chancery Reports [*A publication*] (DLA)
Edw .... Edwards' Reports [*2, 3 Missouri*] [*A publication*] (DLA)
EDW .... El Dorado & Wesson Railway Co. [*AAR code*]
EDW .... Electron Density Wave (SAUS)
EDW .... Elementary Data Word (SAUS)
edw .... energy dump window (SAUS)
EDW .... Enterprise Data Warehouse (VLIE)
EDW .... Estimated Dry Weight [*Nephrology*] (DAVI)
EDWA .... Enterprise Data Warehouse Architecture (VLIE)
EDWA .... Evaluation, Decision and Weapon Assignment [*Army*]
EDWA .... Norden-Hage [*Germany*] [*ICAO location identifier*] (ICLI)
EDWAA .... Economic Dislocation and Worker Adjustment Assistance [*Department of Labor*]
EDWAAA ...... Economic Dislocation and Worker Adjustment Assistance Act of 1988 (WYGK)
Edw Abr .... Edwards' Abridgment of Prerogative Court Cases [*A publication*] (DLA)
Edw Abr .... Edwards' Abridgment, Privy Council [*A publication*] (DLA)
Edw Adm ...... Edwards' English Admiralty Reports [*A publication*] (DLA)
Edw Adm (Eng) ... Edwards' English Admiralty Reports [*A publication*] (DLA)
Edw Adm Jur ... Edwards' Admiralty Jurisdiction [*1847*] [*A publication*] (DLA)
Edwards .... Edwards [*A. G.*] & Sons, Inc. [*Associated Press*] (SAG)
Edwards' Chr R ... Edwards' New York Chancery Reports [*A publication*] (DLA)
Edwards' Rep ... Edwards' New York Chancery Reports [*A publication*] (DLA)
ED Wash ...... United States District Court for the Eastern District of Washington (DLA)
EDWB .... Bremerhaven/Am Luneort [*Germany*] [*ICAO location identifier*] (ICLI)
Edw Bail ...... Edwards on the Law of Bailments [*A publication*] (DLA)

Edw Bailm ... Edwards on the Law of Bailments [*A publication*] (DLA)
Edw Bills ..... Edwards on Bills and Notes [*A publication*] (DLA)
Edw Bills & N... Edwards on Bills and Notes [*A publication*] (DLA)
Edw Brok & F... Edwards on Factors and Brokers [*A publication*] (DLA)
EDWC .... Damme [*Germany*] [*ICAO location identifier*] (ICLI)
EDWC .... Electrical Discharge Wire Cutting [*Manufacturing term*]
Edw Ch .... Edwards' New York Chancery Reports [*A publication*] (DLA)
Edw Chan .... Edwards' New York Chancery Reports [*A publication*] (DLA)
Edw Ch (NY)... Edwards' New York Chancery Reports [*A publication*] (DLA)
Edw Conf ..... Edward the Confessor (King of England) (DLA)
EDWD .... Lemwerder [*Germany*] [*ICAO location identifier*] (ICLI)
EDWE .... Emden [*Germany*] [*ICAO location identifier*] (ICLI)
Edw Eccl Jur... Edwards on Ecclesiastical Jurisdiction [*A publication*] (DLA)
EDWF .... Leer-Nuttermoor [*Germany*] [*ICAO location identifier*] (ICLI)
Edw Fac ...... Edwards on Factors and Brokers [*A publication*] (DLA)
EDWG .... Wangerooge [*Germany*] [*ICAO location identifier*] (ICLI)
Edw Gam ..... Edwards' Law of Gaming [*A publication*] (DLA)
EDWH .... Oldenburg/Hatten [*Germany*] [*ICAO location identifier*] (ICLI)
EDWI .... Wilhelmshaven/Mariensiel [*Germany*] [*ICAO location identifier*] (ICLI)
EDWIN .... Editorial Word Processing International Network (DGA)
ED Wis .... United States District Court for the Eastern District of Wisconsin (DLA)
EDWJ .... Juist [*Germany*] [*ICAO location identifier*] (ICLI)
Edw Jur ...... Edwards' Juryman's Guide [*A publication*] (DLA)
EDWL .... Langeoog [*Germany*] [*ICAO location identifier*] (ICLI)
Edw Lead Dec... Edwards' Leading Decisions in Admiralty [*Edwards' Admiralty Reports*] [*A publication*] (DLA)
EDWM .... Electrodynamic Wattmeter (SAUS)
EDWM .... Weser-Wumme [*Germany*] [*ICAO location identifier*] (ICLI)
Edw MO .... Edwards' Reports [*2, 3 Missouri*] [*A publication*] (DLA)
EDWN .... Nordhorn/Klausheide [*Germany*] [*ICAO location identifier*] (ICLI)
EDWNT .... Endowment (ABBR)
Edw (NY) ..... Edwards' New York Chancery Reports [*A publication*] (DLA)
EDWO .... Osnabruck/Atterheide [*Germany*] [*ICAO location identifier*] (ICLI)
Edw Part ...... Edwards on Parties in Chancery [*A publication*] (DLA)
Edw PC .... Edwards' English Prize Cases [*A publication*] (DLA)
Edw Pleas ... Edwards' Pleasantries of the Courts of New York [*A publication*] (DLA)
Edw Pr Cas... Edwards' English Prize Cases [*A publication*] (DLA)
Edw Pr Ct Cas... Edwards' Abridgment of Prerogative Court Cases [*A publication*] (DLA)
EDWQ .... Ganderkesee-Atlas Aerodrome [*Germany*] [*ICAO location identifier*] (ICLI)
EDWR .... Borkum [*Germany*] [*ICAO location identifier*] (ICLI)
ED/WR .... Edge Wear [*Deltiology*]
Edw Rec ...... Edwards on Receivers in Equity [*A publication*] (DLA)
Edw Ref ...... Edwards on the Law of Referees [*A publication*] (DLA)
Edw Rep ...... Edwards' New York Chancery Reports [*A publication*] (DLA)
EDWS .... Norden/Norddeich [*Germany*] [*ICAO location identifier*] (ICLI)
Edw St Act... Edwards on the Stamp Act [*A publication*] (DLA)
EDWT .... Nordenham-Einswarden [*Germany*] [*ICAO location identifier*] (ICLI)
EDWTH .... End-Diastolic Wall Thickness [*Cardiology*]
Edw (Tho).... Edwards' English Admiralty Reports [*A publication*] (DLA)
EDWU .... Varrelbusch [*Germany*] [*ICAO location identifier*] (ICLI)
EDWV .... Verden/Scharnhorst [*Germany*] [*ICAO location identifier*] (ICLI)
EDWVL .... Edwardsville, IL [*American Association of Railroads railroad junction routing code*]
EDWW .... Bremen [*Germany*] [*ICAO location identifier*] (ICLI)
EDWY .... Norderney [*Germany*] [*ICAO location identifier*] (ICLI)
EDX .... Denergy-Dispersive X-Ray Analysis (AAEL)
EDX .... Edna, TX [*Location identifier*] [*FAA*] (FAAL)
EDX .... Electrical Industry Data Exchange [*Computer science*]
EDX .... Electrodiagnosis [*Medicine*]
EDX .... Electronic Data Exchange (EEVL)
EDX .... Energy Dispersive X-Ray
EDX .... Energy-Dispersive X-Ray Analysis Event Driven Executive (SAUS)
EDX .... energy dispersive X-ray analyzer (SAUS)
EDX .... energy-dispersive x-ray fluorescence (SAUS)
EDX .... Event Driven Executive [*IBM Corp.*]
EDXA .... Energy Dispersive X-Ray Analysis [*or Analyzer*] [*Also, EDXRA*]
EDX Analysis... Energy Dispersive X-ray Analysis (SAUS)
EDXB .... Heide/Busum [*Germany*] [*ICAO location identifier*] (ICLI)
EDXC .... European DX Council [*Huntingdon, Cambridgeshire, England*] (EAIO)
EDXD .... Energy Dispersive X-Ray Diffraction [*Atomic structure determination*]
EDXE .... Rheine/Eschendorf [*Germany*] [*ICAO location identifier*] (ICLI)
EDXF .... Energy Dispersive X-Ray Fluorescence [*Spectrometry*]
EDXF .... Flensburg/Schaferhaus [*Germany*] [*ICAO location identifier*] (ICLI)
EDXH .... Helgoland/Dune [*Germany*] [*ICAO location identifier*] (ICLI)
EDXM .... St. Michaelisdonn [*Germany*] [*ICAO location identifier*] (ICLI)
EDXO .... St. Peter/Ording [*Germany*] [*ICAO location identifier*] (ICLI)
EDXR .... Rendsburg/Schachtholm [*Germany*] [*ICAO location identifier*] (ICLI)
EDXRA .... Energy Dispersive X-Ray Analysis [*or Analyzer*] [*Also, EDXA*]
EDXRD .... Energy-Dispersive X-Ray Diffraction (SAUS)
EDXRF .... electron diffraction X-ray fluorescence (SAUS)
EDXRF .... Energy Dispersive X-Ray Fluorescence [*Spectrometry*]
EDXRF .... Excitation Dispersive X-Ray Fluorescence [*Chemical analysis*]
EDXRS .... Energy Dispersive X-Ray Spectrometry
EDXS .... Energy Dispersive X-Ray Spectrum
EDXW .... Westerland/Sylt [*Germany*] [*ICAO location identifier*] (ICLI)
EDX/WDX..... Energy-Dispersive X-Ray Analysis/Wavelength Dispersive X-Ray Analysis (UWER)
EDXY .... Wyk Auf Fohr [*Germany*] [*ICAO location identifier*] (ICLI)
EDY .... Educationally Disadvantaged Youth (EDAC)
EDYA .... Ampfing/Waldkraiburg [*Germany*] [*ICAO location identifier*] (ICLI)
EDYB .... Arnbruck [*Germany*] [*ICAO location identifier*] (ICLI)
EDYG .... Beilingries [*Germany*] [*ICAO location identifier*] (ICLI)
EDYG .... Eddying (ABBR)
EDYL .... Leutkirch/Unterzeil [*Germany*] [*ICAO location identifier*] (ICLI)
EDYN .... Envirodyne Inds [*NASDAQ symbol*] (TTSB)
EDYN .... Envirodyne Industries, Inc. [*NASDAQ symbol*] (SAG)
EDYN .... Nittenau/Bruck [*Germany*] [*ICAO location identifier*] (ICLI)
EDYNMT ...... Electric Dynamometer [*Engineering*]
EDYR .... Regensburg-Oberhub [*Germany*] [*ICAO location identifier*] (ICLI)
EDYV .... Vogtareuth [*Germany*] [*ICAO location identifier*] (ICLI)
EDZ .... Emission Density Zoning [*Environmental Protection Agency*] (GFGA)
EDZA .... Mittenwald-Luttensee [*Germany*] [*ICAO location identifier*] (ICLI)
EDZB .... Bergen-Hohne [*Germany*] [*ICAO location identifier*] (ICLI)
EDZD .... Ulm [*Germany*] [*ICAO location identifier*] (ICLI)
EDZE .... Sengwarden [*Germany*] [*ICAO location identifier*] (ICLI)
EDZF .... Fuerstenfeldbruck [*Germany*] [*ICAO location identifier*] (ICLI)
EDZG .... Oldenburg [*Germany*] [*ICAO location identifier*] (ICLI)
EDZH .... Garmersdorf [*Germany*] [*ICAO location identifier*] (ICLI)
EDZI .... Trier [*Germany*] [*ICAO location identifier*] (ICLI)
EDZJ .... Idar-Oberstein [*Germany*] [*ICAO location identifier*] (ICLI)
EDZK .... Karlsruhe [*Germany*] [*ICAO location identifier*] (ICLI)
EDZL .... Flensburg [*Germany*] [*ICAO location identifier*] (ICLI)
EDZM .... Muenster-Gievenbeck [*Germany*] [*ICAO location identifier*] (ICLI)
EDZN .... Koblenz [*Germany*] [*ICAO location identifier*] (ICLI)
EDZO .... Motne-Centre, Offenbach [*Germany*] [*ICAO location identifier*] (ICLI)
EDZQ .... Quickborn [*Germany*] [*ICAO location identifier*] (ICLI)
EDZR .... Aurich [*Germany*] [*ICAO location identifier*] (ICLI)
EDZS .... Bredstedt [*Germany*] [*ICAO location identifier*] (ICLI)
EDZT .... Altenstadt [*Germany*] [*ICAO location identifier*] (ICLI)
EDZU .... Appenweiler [*Germany*] [*ICAO location identifier*] (ICLI)
EDZW .... Offenbach [*Germany*] [*ICAO location identifier*] (ICLI)
EDZX .... Traben-Trarbach [*Germany*] [*ICAO location identifier*] (ICLI)
EDZY .... Weiden [*Germany*] [*ICAO location identifier*] (ICLI)
EE .... Aeronautical Engineering (SAUS)
EE .... Basque Left (Spain) [*Political party*] (PSAP)
EE .... Eagle Commuter Airlines [*ICAO designator*] (AD)
EE .... Early English [*Language, etc.*]
EE .... Earthquake Engineer (SAUS)
EE .... Earthquake Engineering (SAUS)
EE .... Eased Edge (DAC)
EE .... Eastern Establishment [*Politics*]
EE .... Eastern European (MWOL)
EE .... Echo Equalizer (IAA)
EE .... Ecological Efficiency (FOTI)
EE .... Economic Efficiency (SAUS)
EE .... Ecosystem Evaluation (GNE)
EE .... Edge Effect (UWER)
EE .... Edison Effect (UWER)
EE .... Edit Error [*Military*] (AFIT)
EE .... Educational Establishment (SAUS)
EE .... Edward Elgar [*Publisher*] [*British*]
EE .... El Paso Electric [*AMEX symbol*] (TTSB)
EE .... Eject Enable (ACAE)
E/E .... Electrical/Electronic
EE .... Electrical Engineer [*or Engineering*]
EE .... Electrical Equipment (SAUS)
EE .... Electrically-Erasable (SAUS)
EE .... Electrical or Electronics Engineer (SAUS)
EE .... Electric Electric (SAUS)
ee .... electric eye (SAUS)
EE .... Electrodynamic Explorer [*NASA*]
EE .... Electronic Editing [*Telecommunications*]
EE .... Electronic Editions [*Cowles Publishing Co.*] [*Information service or system*] (IID)
EE .... Electronic Engineering
EE .... Electronics Engineer (SAUS)
EE .... Electronics Engineering Division [*Coast Guard*]
EE .... Electronics to Electronics
E-E .... Electronic-to-Electronic (AGLO)
EE .... Elementary English (journ.) (SAUS)
EE .... Elements of Expense [*Army*] (AABC)
EE .... Elevator Equipment Room [*NFPA pre-fire planning symbol*] (NFPA)
EE .... Ellis & Eastern [*Federal Railroad Administration identification code*]
EE .... El Paso Electric Co. [*AMEX symbol*] (SAG)
EE .... Elrington Engineering (SAUS)
EE .... Embassador Extraordinary [*Diplomacy*] [*British*] (ROG)
EE .... Embryo Extract
EE .... Emergency Establishment [*Military*] (NATG)
EE .... Emerson Electric Co. (MCD)
EE .... Emotion Engine (SAUS)
EE .... Employee (OICC)
ee .... Enantiomeric Excess (MEC)
EE .... Enantiomeric Excess [*Organic chemistry*]
EE .... End Effector (MCD)
EE .... Endocardial Endothelium (SAUS)
E-E .... End to End [*Technical drawings*] (NASA)
EE .... End-to-End [*Anastomosis*] [*Medicine*] (DAVI)
EE .... Enentarzid (BJA)
EE .... Energy Efficiency [*Electrochemistry*]
EE .... Energy Efficiency and Renewable Energy, Office of (SAUS)
EE .... Energy Engineer (SAUS)
EE .... Energy Engineering (SAUS)
EE .... Energy Enterprises [*Information service or system*] (IID)
EE .... Energy Expenditure
EE .... Engagement Effectiveness [*Army*] (AABC)
EE .... Enge's Entourage (EA)

EE .... Engineering Economics
EE .... Engineering Estimate
EE .... engineering evaluation (SAUS)
EE .... English Earl (ROG)
EE .... English Electric [*Commercial firm*] [*British*]
EE .... English Ell [*Unit of measure*] (ROG)
EE .... English Estates [*British*] (GEA)
EE .... English Exchequer Reports [*A publication*] (DLA)
EE .... Enki and Eridu (BJA)
EE .... Enolether (SAUS)
EE .... Enter Exponent [*Computer science*]
EE .... Environmental Economics
EE .... Environmental Education
EE .... Environmental Encyclopedia [*A publication*]
EE .... Environmental Engineer (SAUS)
EE .... Environmental Engineering (SAUS)
EE .... Environmental Equipments Ltd., Wokingham (SAUS)
EE .... Envoy Extraordinary [*Department of State*]
EE .... Equation Error (VLIE)
EE .... Equine Encephalitis
EE .... Equine Encephalomyelitis (SAUS)
EE .... Equipment Engaged (SAUS)
EE .... Equipment Engaged Tone [*Telecommunications*] (IAA)
EE .... Equity Earnings [*Accounting*]
EE .... Equity Exchequer [*Legal term*] (DLA)
EE .... Error Expected (IAA)
EE .... Errors Accepted (ELAL)
EE .... Errors Excepted [*Business term*]
E-E .... Erythematous-Edematous [*Reaction*] [*Medicine*]
EE .... Essential Elements (SAUS)
EE .... Esterified Estrogen [*Medicine*] (MELL)
EE .... Estonia [*Internet country code*]
EE .... Etch Epitaxial Refill (VLIE)
EE .... Ethniki Enosis [*National Unity Party*] [*Greek*] (PPE)
EE .... Ethynyl Estradiol [*Endocrinology*]
EE .... Euer Ehrwuerden [*Your Reverence*] [*German*]
EE .... Eurocity Express [*Airline*] [*British*]
ee-- .... Europe, Eastern [*MARC geographic area code*] [*Library of Congress*] (LCCP)
EE .... Euzkadiko Ezkerra [*Basque Left*] [*Spain*] [*Political party*] (PPE)
EE .... Evolutionary Ecology (SAUS)
EE .... Evreiskaia Entsiklopediia [*A publication*] (BJA)
EE .... Executair Ltd. [*Nigeria*] [*ICAO designator*] (ICDA)
EE .... Execution Element (VLIE)
EE .... Executive Engineer [*British*] (DCTA)
EE .... Exoelectron (PDAA)
EE .... Exoelectron Emission (PDAA)
EE .... Exoerythrocyte (SAUS)
EE .... Exoerythrocytic [*Medicine*]
EE .... Expenditure and Employment (OICC)
EE .... Experimental Establishment [*RAF*] [*British*]
EE .... Expiration of Enlistment
EE .... Explosives Engineer (SAUS)
EE .... Explosives Engineering (SAUS)
EE .... Exponential Equation
EE .... Export Enforcement
ee .... expressed emotion (SAUS)
EE .... Extended Edition [*IBM Corp.*] (BYTE)
EE .... External Ear (MELL)
EE .... External Entity
EE .... External Environment
ee .... extra effciency (SAUS)
EE .... Eye and Ear
EE .... Office of Energy Efficiency and Renewable Energy (SAUS)
EE3ME .... Ethinyloestradiol-3-Methyl Ether [*or Mestranol*] [*Pharmacology*] (DAVI)
EEA .... Adrian College, Adrian, MI [*OCLC symbol*] (OCLC)
EEA .... Eastern Economic Association
EEA .... Economic Espionage Act [*1996*]
EEA .... Ecurie Ecosse Association Ltd. [*British*] (BI)
EEA .... Educational Exhibitors' Association [*British*] (BI)
EEA .... Egyptian Electricity Authority (SAUO)
EEA .... Electrical and Electronic Abstracts (SAUS)
EEA .... Electrical Engineering Abstracts (journ.) (SAUS)
EEA .... Electric Energy Association [*Later, EEI*] (EA)
EEA .... Electroencephalic Audiometry [*Medicine*] (MAE)
EEA .... Electromagnetic Energy Association (NTPA)
EEA .... Electromagnetic Environment Analysis
EEA .... Electronic Engineering Association [*British*]
EEA .... Electrostatic Energy Analyzer [*Instrumentation*]
EEA .... Emergency Employment Act [*1971*]
EEA .... Empresa Ecuatoriana de Aviacion [*Ecuador*] [*ICAO designator*] (FAAC)
EEA .... End-to-End Anastomosis [*Medicine*]
EEA .... End zu End Anastomosierung (SAUS)
EEA .... Energy and Environmental Analysis [*Environmental Protection Agency*] (GFGA)
EEA .... Energy and Environmental Applications (SAUS)
EEA .... Energy and Environmental Assessment (SAUO)
EEA .... Engineering Evaluation Article (AAG)
EEA .... Environmental Education Act (SAUS)
EEA .... Equal Employment Act
EEA .... Error Exit hddress (SAUS)
EEA .... Essential Elements of Analysis
EEA .... Estimated Expenditure of Ammunition (AABC)
EEA .... Ethical Education Association (SAUO)
EEA .... Ethylene-Ethyl Acetate [*Organic chemistry*]
EEA .... Ethylene Ethyl Acrylate (SAUS)
EEA .... Ethylene-Ethyl Acrylate [*Copolymer*] [*Organic chemistry*]
EEA .... Ethylene Ethylacrylate Copolymer (EDCT)
EEA .... Euonymus Europaeus Acetone Powder (SAUS)
EEA .... Euonymus Europaeus Agglutinin (SAUS)
EEA .... Europaeische Evangelische Allianz [*European Evangelical Alliance - EEA*] (EAIO)
EEA .... European Economic Agreement [*Political party*] (PSAP)
EEA .... European Economic Area (ECON)
EEA .... European Environment Agency
EEA .... European Environmental Agency (SAUS)
EEA .... Evaluation Elements of Analysis (MCD)
EEA .... Excellence in Education Act (GFGA)
EEA .... exhaust-emission analyzer (SAUS)
EEA .... Explosive Embedment Anchor (PDAA)
EEAA .... Employee Educational Assistance Act of 1978 (WYGK)
EEAA .... Environmental Education Advisers Association [*British*] (DBA)
EEAC .... Energy and Education Action Center (SAUS)
EEAC .... Equal Employment Advisory Council (EA)
EEAF .... Environmental Enterprises Assistance Fund (SAUO)
EEAIE .... Electrical, Electronic and Allied Industries, Europe (SAUO)
EEAIE .... Electrical, Electronic, and Allied Industries of Europe (SAUS)
EE & H .... Electricity, Electronics, and Hydraulics School (DNAB)
EE & MP .... Envoy Extraordinary and Minister Plenipotentiary [*Department of State*]
ee & o .... excuses, errors, and omissions (SAUS)
EE & RM .... Elementary Electrical and Radio Material [*Training School*] [*Navy*]
EE&RM .... Elementary Electrical and Radio Material Training School (SAUS)
EE & W .... Emperor of the East and West [*Freemasonry*] (ROG)
EEAP .... Emergency Egress Air Pack [*NASA*] (KSC)
EEAP .... Enlisted Education Advancement Program [*Military*] (DNAB)
EEAP .... Environmental Effects Assessment Panel
EEAPROM .... Electrically Erasable and Programmable Read-Only Memory (VLIE)
EEARM .... Elementary Electrical and Radio Material (SAUS)
EEAS .... Energy and Economic Analysis Section (SAUS)
EEAS .... Externally Excited Adaptive System (SAUS)
EEASA .... Engineering Employers' Association, South Australia
EEAT .... Emergency Expected Approach Time (DNAB)
EEAT .... Emotional-Ethical Attitudes Test [*Psychometrics*]
EEAT .... End, Evening Astronomical Twilight (MCD)
EEATCS .... Early External Active Thermal Control System [*NASA*] (SPST)
EEAW .... Environmental Education Association of Washington
EEB .... Bendix Engineering Development Center, Southfield, MI [*OCLC symbol*] (OCLC)
EEB .... Eastern Electricity Board [*British*]
EEB .... Ecology and Evolutionary Biology [*A discipline division*]
EEB .... Economic Engineering Branch [*Army Tank Automotive Command*] [*Warren, MI*]
EEB .... Educational Employees Board (SAUS)
EEB .... Effective External Boundary [*Forestry*]
EEB .... Euroberlin [*France*] [*ICAO designator*] (FAAC)
EEB .... European Environmental Bureau [*Belgium*]
EEB .... European Environment Bureau (EERA)
EEB .... European Export Bank (SAUS)
EEB .... Exports to Europe Branch [*British Overseas Trade Board*] (DS)
EEBA .... Energy Efficient Building Association (EA)
EEBC .... Ether Ester Block Copolymer
EEBCS .... Electrical Equipment Bay Cooling System
EEBD .... Emergency Escape Breathing Device [*Navy*] (CAAL)
EE-BE .... Ending Event - Beginning Event (SAA)
eEBES .... Varian Corporations EBES (SAUO)
EEBIC .... Eastern Europe Business Information Center [*Department of Commerce*]
EEBIC .... Emergent and Evolutionary Behaviour, Intelligence, Computation (VLIE)
EEBM .... Eastern Europe Bible Mission (EA)
EEBO .... Early English Books Online
EEC .... Clearinghouse on Elementary and Early Childhood Education (SAUS)
EEC .... East Erie Commercial Railroad [*AAR code*]
EEC .... Economic Education for Clergy (EA)
EEC .... Ectrodactylia, Ectodermal Dysplasia, Cleft Lip and Palate
EEC .... Ectrodactyly, Ectodermal Dysplasia Elefting [*Syndrome*] [*Medicine*] (DAVI)
EEC .... Educational Equity Concepts [*An association*] (EA)
EEC .... Education Equipment Centre (SAUS)
EEC .... Education Exploration Center
EEC .... EECO, Inc. [*NASDAQ symbol*] (COMM)
EEC .... Electoral Education Centre [*Australia*]
EEC .... Electrical and Electronics Commission
EEC .... Electrical Export Corp. [*Defunct*]
EEC .... Electrochemical Equipment Committee [*Military*]
EEC .... Electron Energy Corporation (ACAE)
EEC .... Electronic Engine Control
EEC .... Electronic Engine Controls (ACAE)
EEC .... Electronic Equipment Committee [*NASA*] (KSC)
EEC .... Electronic Experimental Centre (SAUO)
EEC .... Electronics Explosive-Emission Cathode (ODA)
EEC .... Emergency Essential Civilians (SAUS)
EEC .... Emerson Electric Co.
EEC .... Emerson Electric Company (SAUO)
EEC .... Encased Elastic Cylinder
EEC .... End of Equilibrium Cycle [*Nuclear energy*] (NRCH)
EEC .... Enemy Exports Committee [*British*] [*World War II*]

EEC .... Engine Electronic Control (MCD)
EEC .... Engineered Electronics Company (SAUO)
EEC .... English Electric Company (SAUO)
EEC .... English Electric Computers [*British*] (NITA)
EEC .... English Electronic Computers (SAUS)
EEC .... Enlisted Evaluation Center [*Army*]
EEC .... Enough Is Enough Club [*Defunct*] (EA)
EEC .... Enteropathogenic Escherichia Coli [*Also, EPEC*] [*Medicine*]
EEC .... Environmental Elements Corp. [*NYSE symbol*] (SPSG)
EEC .... Environmental Elements Corp., Baltimore, Md. (SAUS)
EEC .... Environmental Engineering Committee (COE)
EEC .... Environmental Engineering Consultants, Inc. (EFIS)
EEC .... Equal Employment Council (SAUO)
EEC .... Equilibrium Equivalent Concentration [*Nuclear energy*] (NUCP)
EEC .... Estimated Environmental Concentration (EES)
EEC .... Estimated Exposure Concentration [*Toxicology*]
EEC .... EUROCONTROL Experimental Center (SAUS)
EEC .... Europa Esperanto-Centro [*European Esperanto Centre - EEC*] (EAIO)
EEC .... European Ecological Centre (SAUO)
EEC .... European Economic Commission (SAUO)
EEC .... European Economic Communities (SAUS)
EEC .... European Economic Community [*Common Market*]
EEC .... European Economic Cooperation (SAUO)
EEC .... European Economic Council (SAUO)
EEC .... EUROPEAN UNION (SAUS)
EEC .... Evaporation [*or Evaporative*] Emission Control [*Automobile antipollution device*]
EEC .... Evaporative Emission Control (SAUS)
EEC .... EXAMETNET [*Experimental Inter-American Meteorological Rocket Network*] Executive Committee [*NASA*]
EEC .... Exhaust Emmission Control [*Automotive engineering*]
EEC .... Expected Environmental Concentration [*Environmental science*]
EEC .... Extendable Exit Cone (MCD)
EEC .... Extended Error Correction (SAUS)
EEC .... Extended Exit Cone (SAUS)
EEC .... Extendible Exit Cone (SAUS)
EEC .... High explosive, general-purpose (SAUS)
EEC .... St. Clair Community College, Port Huron, MI [*OCLC symbol*] (OCLC)
EEC .... Energy-Energy Correlation (ODA)
EECA .... Emergency Energy Conservation Act [*1979*]
EECA .... Engineering Economic Cost Analysis (MCD)
EE/CA .... Engineering Evaluation and Cost Analysis (BCP)
EE/CA .... Engineering Evaluation/Cost Analysis (DOGT)
EECA .... European Electronic Component Manufacturers Association (EAIO)
EEC-AAMS ... Association of the European Economic Community and the Associated African and Malagasy States (SAUO)
EEC-ACP .... EEC-African, Caribbean and Pacific countries (SAUS)
EEC Bulletin... European Economic Community Bulletin (journ.) (SAUS)
EECC .... Electronic Engineering Co. (EFIS)
EECC .... Environmental Epidemiology and Cancer Centre [*British*] (IRUK)
EECCS .... European Ecumenical Commission for Church and Society [*Formerly, Ecumenical Commission for Church and Society*] (EA)
EECD .... Endothelial-Epithelial Corneal Dystrophy [*Medicine*] (DMAA)
EECE .... Emergency Economic Committee for Europe [*A "Western Nation" organization*] [*Post-World War II*]
EEC/EC .... European Economic Community (EBF)
EEC/EURAM... European Economic Community/European Research on Advanced Materials (SAUS)
EECF .... Earthnet ERS-1 Central Facility (SAUS)
EECG .... Electroencephalography (DB)
EECGDR .... Entente Europeenne du Commerce en Gros des Deux-Roues (EA)
EECGS .... Emergency Evaporative Coolant Garment System (PDAA)
EECIS .... Electrical, Environmental Control, and Instrumentation Systems Specialist [*NASA*]
EECL .... Effective Equivalent Chlorine [*Analytical chemistry*]
EECL .... Emitter-Emitter Coupled Logic [*Electronics*] (IEEE)
EECL .... Encyclopedia of European Community Law [*A publication*] (DLA)
EECL .... Equivalent Electrical Cable Length (SAUS)
EEC-LCM .... European Economic Community - Liaison Committee of Midwives (EAIO)
EECM .... East European Chemical Monitor [*Business International*] [*Vienna, Austria*] [*Information service or system*] (IID)
EECM .... Electronic Engine Control Module
EECM .... End-to-End Call Manager [*Telecommunications*] (DINT)
EECMA .... European Electronic Component Manufacturers Association (CIST)
EECMB .... Electrical Equipment Certification Management Board (HEAS)
EECMOS .... Electrically Erasable Complementary MOS (SAUS)
EECMWF .... European Centre for Medium Range Weather Forecasting (SAUS)
EECMY .... Ethiopian Evangelical Church Mekane Yesus
EECN .... Ecogen, Inc. [*NASDAQ symbol*] (SPSG)
EECNW .... Ecogen Inc. Wrrt [*NASDAQ symbol*] (TTSB)
EECo .... Eastern Edison Company (SAUO)
EECO .... Electronic Engineering Company (SAUO)
EECo .... Engineered Electronics Company (SAUO)
EECO .... European Economic Cooperation Organization (SAUO)
EECO .... European Endoscopy Congress (SAUS)
EECOD .... European Ecumenical Organization for Development [*Brussels, Belgium*] (EAIO)
EECOM .... [*The*] Canadian Network for Environmental Education & Communication [*Reseau Canadien d'Education et de Communication Relatives a l'Environnement*] (AC)
EECOM .... CSM [*Command and Service Module*] Environmental and Electrical Systems Engineer [*NASA*]
EECOM .... Electrical, Environmental, and Communications
EECOM .... Electrical, Environmental, Consumables, and Mechanical Systems (MCD)
e-economy... Electronic Economy (FOTI)
EECP .... Emergency Energy Conservation Program (OICC)
E ECP .... Expedited Engineering Change Proposal
EECS .... Electrical Engineering and Computer Service (SAUS)
EECS .... Electronic Engine Control System [*OC Johnson & Associates, Inc.*] [*Automotive engineering*]
EECS .... Equal Employment Compliance Section [*Employment and Training Administration*] (OICC)
EECs .... Estimated Environmental Concentrations (SAUS)
EECS .... Evaporative Emission Control System [*Automotive engineering*]
EECS .... Electrical-Energy Conversion System (ODA)
EEC-SLC .... European Economic Community - Shipbuilders' Linking Committee [*Brussels, Belgium*] (EAIO)
EEC-Syndrom... ectrodactyly-ectodermal dysplasia-clefting-Syndrom (SAUS)
EECT .... Early Entry Contracting Team [*Army*]
EECT .... End, Evening Civil Twilight [*Navigation*]
EECT .... End to End Call Trace (SAUS)
EEC-V .... Electronic Engine Control - 5th Generation [*Automotive engineering*]
EECW .... Emergency Exchanger Cooling Water (IEEE)
EED .... Elastic Energy Density (WDAA)
EED .... Electrical and Electronics Division (SAUS)
EED .... Electrical Engineering Department (SAUS)
eed .... electrical explosive device (SAUS)
EED .... Electro (Electrical) Explosive Device (SAUS)
EED .... Electroexplosive Device
EED .... Electromagnetic Explosive Device (SAUS)
EED .... Electron Energy Distribution (SAUS)
EED .... Electronic Engineering Division [*Coast Guard*]
EED .... Electronic Evidence Discovery [*Company*]
EED .... Electronic Explosive Device (NVT)
EED .... Emergency Escape Device
EED .... Emitter Edge Dislocations (SAUS)
EED .... Energy and Environment Division (SAUO)
EED .... Energy Efficient Design
EED .... Energy, Environment and Development (SAUS)
EED .... Environmental Equipment Division (SAUS)
EED .... Environment and Energy Directory (SAUO)
EED .... Epizootic Epitheliotropic Disease [*Ichthyology*]
EED .... Equipment Engineering Department (COE)
EED .... Erase to End of Display (SAUS)
EED .... Essential Elements Of Data (SAUS)
EED .... Estimated Exposure Dose [*Toxicology*]
EED .... European Enterprises Development Co. [*Luxembourg*]
EED .... European Enterprises Development Company S.A. (SAUO)
EED .... European Environmental Database (SAUO)
EED .... Exo-Earth Discoverer (SAUS)
EED .... Exposure Evaluation Division [*Environmental Protection Agency*] (GFGA)
EED .... Externally Mounted Electrical Device
EED .... Needles, CA [*Location identifier*] [*FAA*] (FAAL)
EED .... Wayne State University, Division of Library Science, Detroit, MI [*OCLC symbol*] (OCLC)
EED .... Effective Equivalent Dose (of Radiation) [*Physics*] (ODA)
EEDA .... Edmonton Economic Development Authority (SAUS)
EEDB .... Energy and Economics Data Bank [*IAEA*] [*United Nations*] (DUND)
EEDB .... Energy and Environment Data Base [*Oak Ridge National Laboratory*] [*Database*]
EEDB .... ERDA [*Energy Research and Development Agency*] Energy Database [*Database*] (NITA)
EEDF .... Electron Energy Distribution Function (AAEL)
EEDM .... External Event Detection Module [*Computer science*] (MDG)
EEDO .... Economic and Employment Development Officer
EEDP .... European Association of Directory Publishers (SAUO)
EEDP .... Evaluation, Experimental and Development Projects (OICC)
EEDP .... Expanded Electronic tandem switching Dialing Plan (SAUS)
EEDQ .... Ethoxycarbonylethoxydihydroquinone [*Pharmacology*]
EEDQ .... Ethyl 1,2-Dihydro-2-Ethoxy-1-Quinolinecarboxylate (SAUS)
EEDS .... Early English Dialect Society (SAUO)
EEDS .... Electric-Electronic Distribution System [*Automotive engineering*]
EEDS .... Electro-Explosive Decices (SAUS)
eeds .... Electro-Explosive Devices (SAUS)
EEDS .... European Electrostatic Discharge Association [*British*] (EAIO)
EEDSKs .... Early Entry Deployment Support Kids
EEE .... Brainerd, MN [*Location identifier*] [*FAA*] (FAAL)
EEE .... Canadian 88 Energy [*AMEX symbol*] (SG)
EEE .... Detroit Edison Co., Information Services, Detroit, MI [*OCLC symbol*] (OCLC)
EEE .... Eastern Equine Encephalitis [*Virus*] (DAVI)
EEE .... Eastern Equine Encephalomyelitis [*Virus*]
EEE .... Ecology Ethology and Evolution (SAUO)
EEE .... Edema, Erythema, and Exudate [*Medicine*] (MELL)
EEE .... Electrical and Electronics Engineer (journ.) (SAUS)
EEE .... Electrical, Electronic, and Electromechanical
EEE .... Electrical Engineering Exposition
EEE .... Electromagnetic Environmental Effect (ACAE)
EEE .... Electromagnetic Environment Experiment [*NASA*] (MCD)
EEE .... Electronic, Electrical, Electromechanical (SAUS)
EEE .... Electronic Entertainment Expo, Los Angeles (SAUS)
EEE .... Electronic Equipment Engineering [*A publication*]
EEE .... Energy Economics and Environment (SAUO)
EEE .... Energy Efficient Engine
EEE .... Energy Efficient Environments (SAUO)
EEE .... Engine and Electrical Engineering [*Automotive engineering*]

EEE .... engineering, education, enforcement (SAUS)
EEE .... Enterprise Extended Edition (SAUS)
EEE .... Environmental-Ecological Education [*Office of Education program*]
EEE .... Equal, Effective, Elected [*Canada's Triple E Senate movement*]
EEE .... Error [*International telex abbreviation*] (WDMC)
EEE .... Essential Elements of Evaluation (SAUS)
EEE .... European Economics Editor (SAUO)
EEE .... Exoelectron Emission (PDAA)
EEE .... Experimental Enterococcal Endocarditis (DB)
EEE .... Expert en Evaluation d'Entreprises [*French*] (ASC)
EEE .... External Ear Effect [*Audiology*]
EE/EB .... Eastern European EDIFACT Board (AG)
EEEC .... Electromagnetic Energy Environment Criteria [*Army*] (AABC)
EEEC .... Energy and Environmental Engineering Center (SAUO)
E/EEC .... Extendable and Expandable Exit Cone [*Space launch term*] (ISAK)
EEEC .... Extraepithelial Enterochromaffin Cells [*Cytology*]
EEED .... Electronic & Electrical Engineering Division (SAUS)
EEEE .... eMachines, Inc. [*NASDAQ symbol*] (SG)
EEEEE .... Erase [*British naval signaling*]
EEEI .... Energy, Economics and Environment Institute [*Defunct*] (EA)
EEEP .... End-Expiratory Esophageal Pressure [*Medicine*] (MAE)
EEEP .... Entry Employment Experience Program (SAUS)
EEES .... Electronic Equipment Environment Survey (AFM)
EEES .... End-Effector Exchange System (ABAC)
EEET .... Electronic Excitation Energy Transfer (SAUS)
EEEU .... End Effector Electronics Unit (MCD)
EEEV .... Eastern Equine Encephalomyelitis Virus [*Medicine*] (DMAA)
EEE-Virus ..... Eastern-Enquine-Encephalitis-Virus (SAUS)
EEF .... Earth Ecology Foundation (EA)
EEF .... Effective Enemy Fire (SAUS)
EEF .... Egypt Exploration Fund [*A publication*] (ABAR)
EEF .... Egyptian Expeditionary Force [*Military*] [*British*]
EEF .... Eisenhower Exchange Fellowships (EA)
EEF .... Electrical Enhancement Factor
EEF .... Encircled Energy Function (PDAA)
EEF .... Engineering Employers' Federation [*British*] (DCTA)
EEF .... Erickson Educational Foundation [*Later, J2CP Information Services*]
EEF .... Estimate of Enemy Force (SAUS)
EEF .... European Ecological Federation (SAUS)
EEF .... Exoerythrocytic Form [*Phase of malaria parasite*]
EEF .... Export Expansion Facility [*Export-Import Bank of the US*]
EEF .... Export Expansion Fund (SAUS)
EEF .... Exxon Education Foundation
EEF .... Ford Motor Co., Engineering and Research Library, Dearborn, MI [*OCLC symbol*] (OCLC)
EEF .... Sisters Island, AK [*Location identifier*] [*FAA*] (FAAL)
EEFAMOS .... Electrically-Erasable Floating Gate Avalanche-Injection Metal-Oxide Semiconductor [*Computer science*] (IAA)
EEFC .... Economic Education Foundation for Clergy [*Later, EEC*] (EA)
EEFF .... Electrostatically Enhanced Fabric Filtration
EEFHA .... East European Family History Association (EA)
EEFI .... Essential Elements of Friendly Information [*Army*] (AABC)
EEFIS .... Evasion and Escape Fingerprint Identification System
EEFM .... Egyptian Exploration Fund. Memoirs [*A publication*] (ROG)
EEFSU .... Eastern Europe and Former Soviet Union (SAUO)
EEFT .... Electronic Environmental Test Facility (SAUS)
EEG .... Echo-Encephalography [*Medicine*] (MELL)
EEG .... Electroencephalogram [*or Electroencephalography*] [*Medicine*]
EEG .... Electro Encephalograph (SAUS)
EEG .... Electroencephalograph (DIPS)
EEG .... Electroencephalographic (DIPS)
EEG .... Electroencephalography (QSUL)
EEG .... Electromagnetic Environment Generator (ACAE)
EEG .... Electronics Engineering Group [*Military*]
EEG .... Employee Exposure Guidelines [*General Motors Corp.*]
EEG .... Employment and Enterprise Group (AIE)
EEG .... Environmental Education Group [*Defunct*] (EA)
EEG .... Environmental Effects Group [*Army*] (RDA)
EEG .... Environmental Engineers Group (SAUO)
EEG .... Environmental Evaluation Group (SAUO)
EEG .... Essence Export Group [*British*] (BI)
EEG .... European Expedition Guild (EA)
EEG .... Europese Economische Gemeenschap [*European Economic Community*]
EEG .... Evaporative Emissions Generator [*Gasoline testing*] [*Organic chemistry*]
EEG .... Great Lakes Bible College, Lansing, MI [*OCLC symbol*] (OCLC)
EEGA .... Electroencephalographic Audiometry (DB)
EEG Journal ... Electroencephalography Journal (SAUS)
EEGL .... Emergency Exposure Guidance Level [*Environmental science*] (COE)
EEGS .... Environmental and Engineering Geophysical Society (NTPA)
EEG Society ... Electroencephalographic Society (SAUO)
EEG T .... Electroencephalographic Technologist [*Neurology*] (DAVI)
EEGT .... Electroencephalograph Technician [*Medicine*] (EDAA)
EEH .... EMU [*Extra-Vehicular Mobility Unit*] Electrical Harness
EEH .... Exploration in Economic History (SAUS)
EEH .... Siena Heights College, Adrian, MI [*OCLC symbol*] (OCLC)
ee/ha .... ewe equivalents per hectare (SAUS)
EEHLLAPI .... Entry Emulator High Level Language Application Programming Interface (SAUS)
EEHLLAPI .... OS/2 Extended Edition High Level Language Application Programming Interface (SAUS)
EEHO .... Either End Hop Off (SAUS)
EEHOC .... Empty Equipment Handdover Charge (SAUS)
EEHP .... Ecology and Evolution Home Page (SAUO)
EEI .... EBSCO Electronic Information [*EBSCO Industries, Inc.*] [*Information service or system*] (IID)
EEI .... Ecology & Environment [*AMEX symbol*] (SPSG)
EEI .... Edison Electric Institute (EA)
EEI .... Educational Expeditions International [*Later, Earthwatch*]
EEI .... Electrical and Electromagnetic Interference (KSC)
EEI .... Electrical Energy, Incorporated (SAUO)
EEI .... Electronic Emission Intelligence [*Military*]
EEI .... Ellis Enterprises, Inc. (IID)
EEI .... Energy and Environment Information (SAUS)
EEI .... Environmental Enterprises, Inc. (EFIS)
EEI .... Environmental Equipment Institute [*Defunct*] (EA)
EEI .... Equipment to Equipment Interface [*Computer science*] (VERA)
EEI .... Essential Elements of Information [*Military*]
EEI .... Evans Economics, Inc. [*Database producer*] [*Information service or system*] (IID)
EEI .... Excel Energy, Inc. [*Toronto Stock Exchange symbol*]
EEI .... Exo-Earth Imager (SAUS)
EEI .... External Environment Interface [*Computer science*]
EEI .... Hillsdale College, Mossey Learning Center, Hillsdale, MI [*OCLC symbol*] (OCLC)
EEIA .... Electrical and Electronic Insulation Association [*British*] (DBA)
EEIB .... Enemy Equipment Intelligence Branch [*World War II*]
EEIB .... Environmental Engineering Intersociety Board
EEIBA .... Electrical and Electronic Industries Benevolent Association (SAUO)
EEI Bulletin ... Edison Electric Institute Bulletin (journ.) (SAUS)
EEIC .... Electrical/Electronics Insulation Conference (EA)
EEIC .... Element of Expense/Investment Code (AFM)
EEIC .... Elevated Electrode Integrated Circuit (MHDI)
EEIC .... Environmental Education and Information Committee (EERA)
EEIC .... European Electronic Intelligence Center (MCD)
EEIG .... European Economic Interest Grouping
EEII .... Eby Elementary Identification Instrument [*Educational test*]
E/E Inverter ... Enhancement/Enhancement Inverter (SAUS)
EE-IS .... Basque Left - Left for Socialism (PPW)
EEIS .... Encyclopedia of Environmental Information Sources [*A publication*]
EEIS .... End-to-End Information System (NASA)
EEIS .... Enemy Equipment Identification Service [*World War II*]
EEIS .... European Environmental Information System (SAUO)
EEIS .... Evanston Early Identification Scale [*Psychology*]
EEIST .... Enemy Equipment Intelligence Service Team [*World War II*]
EEJ .... Capital Library Cooperative, Mason, MI [*OCLC symbol*] (OCLC)
EEJ .... Equatorial Electrojet
EEK .... Eek [*Alaska*] [*Airport symbol*] (OAG)
EEK .... Epoxy Experimental Kit
EEK .... Kellogg Community College, Battle Creek, MI [*OCLC symbol*] (OCLC)
EEL .... Ecology and Epidemiology Laboratory (SAUO)
EEL .... Economic Education League (SAUO)
EEL .... Edge-Emitting LASER (CIST)
EEL .... Electrical Equipment List (MCD)
EEL .... Electromagnetic Effects Laboratory [*Army*] (RDA)
EEL .... Electron Energy Loss (SAUS)
EEL .... Emergency Exposure Limits (AFM)
EEL .... Emitter-Emitter Coupled Logic [*Electronics*] (IAA)
EEL .... Emitter-to-Emitter coupled Logic (SAUS)
EEL .... Engineering Electronics Laboratory
EEL .... English Electric Limited (SAUO)
EEL .... Entomology Environmental Laboratory (SAUS)
EEL .... Environmental Education Link (SAUO)
EEL .... Environmental Effects Laboratory [*Army*]
EEL .... Environmental Exposure Level [*Toxicology*]
EEL .... Epsilon Extension Language (SAUS)
EEL .... Erase to End of Line (SAUS)
EEL .... Eurasian Express Line (SAUS)
EEL .... Evans Electroselenium Limited [*as in EEL analyzer, used in biochemical analysis*] [*British*]
EEL .... Exclusive Exchange Line [*Telecommunications*]
EEL .... Experimental & Electronic Laboratories (SAUS)
EEL .... Lansing Community College, Lansing, MI [*OCLC symbol*] (OCLC)
EELC .... Electronic Equipment Liquid Cooler (ACAE)
EELC .... Ethnic Employees of the Library of Congress (EA)
EEIChil .... Empresa Nacional de Electridad de Chile [*Associated Press*] (SAG)
EELFS .... Electron Energy Loss Fine Structure
EELFS .... electron energy loss Fourier spectroscopy (SAUS)
EELL .... Equivalent Electrical Lobe Length (SAUS)
EELM .... electron energy loss microscopy (SAUS)
EELM .... English Electric Leo Marconi (SAUS)
EELM .... English Electronic-Leo-Marconi Computers Ltd (SAUS)
EELN .... E-Loan, Inc. [*NASDAQ symbol*] (SG)
E/E-Inverter ... enhancement/enhancement inverter (SAUS)
EELR .... Extended Emission Line Region [*Spectrometry*]
EELS .... Early Entry Lethality and Survivability [*Military*] (INF)
EELS .... Elecricity Emitter Location System (SAUS)
EELS .... electron energy loss spectral (SAUS)
EELS .... Electron Energy Loss Spectroscopy [*Also, ELS*]
EELS .... Electron Energy Loss Spectrum (SAUS)
EELS .... Electronic and Editing Layout System [*Telecommunications*] (DGA)
EELS .... Electronic Emitter Location System (MCD)
EELS .... Electronic Emitter Locator System (SAUS)
EELS .... Engineering Electronic Library, Sweden (SAUS)
EELS-EDX ..... Electron Energy Loss Spectroscopy/Energy-Dispersive X-Ray Analysis (SAUS)
EELUT .... Eastern Energy and Land Use Team [*Kearneysville, WV*] [*Department of the Interior*] (GRD)

EELV .... End-Expiratory Lung Volume [*Medicine*] (MELL)
EELV .... Evolved Expendable Launch Vehicle [*NASA*] (ECON)
EELX .... Evans Equipment Leasing [*Private rail car owner code*]
EEM .... Earth Entry Module [*NASA*] (KSC)
EEM .... Earth Exchange Museum [*Sydney, New South Wales, Australia*]
EEM .... Eastern European Mission [*Later, SGA*]
EEM .... Ebauches Electronic Marin
EEM .... Ectodermal Dysplasia, Ectrodactyly, Macular Dystrophy Syndrome [*Medicine*] (DMAA)
EEM .... Effective Elastic Modulus
EEM .... Effective Engineering Management
EEM .... Effective Exposure Method (KSC)
EEM .... Eigenmode Expansion Method (PDAA)
EEM .... Electron Emission Mass Spectroscopy (ACAE)
EEM .... Electronic Engineers Master (MUGU)
EEM .... Electronic Engine Management (SAUS)
EEM .... Electronic Equipment Modification
EEM .... Electronic Equipment Monitoring (IEEE)
EEM .... Electrostatic Electron Microscope
EEM .... Emission Electron Microscope (IAA)
EEM .... Emission Electron Miscroscope (PDAA)
EEM .... Energy Efficient Mortgage (SAUO)
EEM .... Engineer Electrical and Mechanical (SAUS)
EEM .... Engineering Evaluation Model (KSC)
EEM .... Engineering Experimental Memo
EEM .... Ensemble for Early Music
EEM .... Environmental Effects Monitoring (FOTI)
EEM .... Erythema exsudativum multiforme (SAUS)
EEM .... Essential Equipment Monitor [*Environmental science*] (COE)
EEM .... Excess Exchange Material (AFIT)
EEM .... Excessive Eye Movement [*Medicine*] (EDAA)
EEM .... Excitation-Emission Matrix [*Fluorometry*]
EEM .... exercise evaluation methodology (SAUS)
EEM .... Expendable Electronic Markers (NVT)
EEM .... Experienced Export Manager [*American Society of International Executives*] [*Designation awarded by*]
EEM .... Exponential Ensemble Mutagenesis [*Technique for studying genetic sequences*]
EEM .... Extended Memory Management (SAUS)
EEM .... External Expansion Module [*Sun*] (VERA)
EEM .... Extrapolated End-Point Method [*Nuclear energy*] (NRCH)
EEM .... Michigan State University, East Lansing, MI [*OCLC symbol*] (OCLC)
EEM .... Morgan Stanley Finance Markets Ltd. Capital Units [*NYSE symbol*] (SAG)
EEMA .... Electrical and Electronic Manufacturers Association (SAUO)
EEMA .... European Electronic Messaging Association (DDC)
EEMA .... European Environmental Management Association (SAUS)
EEMAC .... Electrical and Electronic Manufacturers Association of Canada (EAIO)
EEMD .... Electronic Equipment Maintainability Datebook (MCD)
EEMDA .... Electrical-Electronics Materials Distributors Association [*Later, LEMDA*] (EA)
EEME .... Endocardial Elastomyofibrosis [*Medicine*] (EDAA)
EEME .... Ethinylestradiol Methyl Ether (MAE)
EEMG .... Evoked Electromyogram (DB)
EEMIS .... Energy Emergency Management Information System (PDAA)
EEMJEB .... Electrical and Electronic Manufacturers Joint Education Board
EEMK .... Electronic Equipment Maintenance Kit
EEMM .... [*The*] Egyptian Expedition. Metropolitan Museum of Art [*New York*] [*A publication*] (BJA)
EEMRL .... Equivalent Electrical Main Ring Length (SAUS)
EEMS .... Electronic Engine Management System
EEMS .... Emissions Elements Needs Survey (SAUS)
EEMS .... Energy Emergency Management System [*Environmental science*] (COE)
EEMS .... Enhanced Expanded Memory Specifications [*AST, Quadram*]
EEMS .... Enhanced Expanded Memory Support (SAUS)
EEMS .... Enhanced Expanded Memory System (ADWA)
EEMS .... European Environmental Mutagen Society [*Leiden, Netherlands*] (EAIO)
EEMS .... European Environment Monitoring Satellite (SAUS)
EEMT .... Electronic Equipment Maintenance Trainer (MCD)
EEMT .... Energy Emergency Management Team [*Environmental science*] (COE)
EEMT .... Environmental Engineering Management Team
EEMTIC .... Electrical and Electronic Measurement and Test Instrumentation Conference (MCD)
EEMTR .... Enhanced Enlisted Master Tape Record (AABC)
EEMUA .... Engineering Equipment and Materials User's Association [*British*]
EEN .... Brattleboro, Vermont-Keene, New Hampshire [*Airport symbol*] (AD)
EEN .... Eastern Educational Television Network [*Boston, MA*] [*Telecommunications service*] (TSSD)
EEN .... Eden Resources Ltd. [*Vancouver Stock Exchange symbol*]
EEN .... Education for Enterprise Network (AIE)
EEN .... Emergency Engineering Notice (MCD)
EEN .... Environmental Education Network (SAUO)
EEN .... Equipment Engineering Notice (SAUS)
EEN .... Estonian Educational and Research Network (SAUO)
EEN .... Evangelical Environmental Network (SAUO)
EEN .... Even-Even Nucleus
E'EN .... Evening (ROG)
een .... exceptional educational needs (SAUS)
EEN .... Keene [*New Hampshire*] [*Airport symbol*] (OAG)
EENC .... European Experimental Nuclear Magnetic Resonance Conference (SAUO)
EENET .... Emergency Education Network [*Federal Emergency Management Agency*] (GFGA)
EENET .... Estonian Educational and Research Network (SAUO)
EENG .... Early English [*Language*] (DGA)
EEng .... Electrical Engineering (DD)
EENGR .... Electrical Engineer (FAAC)
EENR .... Economic Evaluation of Natural Resources (EERA)
EENT .... Early Evening Nautical Twilight [*Navigation*] (MCD)
EENT .... End, Evening Nautical Twilight [*Navigation*]
EENT .... End of Evening Nautical Twilight (SAUS)
EENT .... Eyes, Ears, Nose, and Throat [*Medicine*]
EENWR .... Exe Estuary National Wildlife Refuge (SAUS)
EENX .... Equipment Enterprise [*Private rail car owner code*]
EEO .... Ealing Electro-Optics [*British*]
EEO .... Effective Equal Opportunity
EEO .... Electroendosmosis [*Analytical biochemistry*]
EEO .... Electronic Editorial Office (SAUS)
EEO .... Elliptical Earth Orbit
EEO .... Energy Efficiency Office (SAUS)
EEO .... Environmental Emergencies Officer (FOTI)
EEO .... Equal Employment Office (SAUS)
EEO .... Equal Employment Officer
EEO .... Equal employment opportunities (SAUS)
EEO .... Equal Employment Opportunity
EEO .... Equal Employment Opportunity Office (SAUS)
EEO .... European Electro-Optics Conference and Exhibition
EEO .... Executive Engineering Order (SAUS)
EEO .... Expedite Engineering Order (MCD)
EEO .... Extremely Elliptical Orbit [*Telecommunications*] (ACRL)
EEOA .... Equal Employment Opportunity Act (OICC)
EEOA .... Equal Employment Opportunity Agency
EEOAA .... Equal Employment Opportunity Action Agency (ACAE)
EEO/AA .... Equal Employment Opportunity/Affirmative Action (SAUS)
EEOAC .... Equal Employment Opportunity Advisory Council (DNAB)
EEOB .... Enemy Electronic Order Of Battle (SAUS)
EEOC .... Economic Employment Opportunity Committee (SAUO)
EEOC .... Equal Employment Opportunity Commission
EEOC Compl Man... Equal Employment Opportunity Commission Compliance Manual [*Commerce Clearing House*] (DLA)
EEODIRSYS... Equal Employment Opportunity Directives System (DNAB)
EEOED .... Emergency Earth Orbital Escape Device (KSC)
EEOO .... Equal Employment Opportunity Officer [*DoD*]
EEOOA .... Equal Employment Opportunity Officer Activity
EEOP .... Equal Educational Opportunities Program [*HEW*]
EEOP .... Equal Employment Opportunity Program (MCD)
EEOS .... Equality of Educational Opportunity Survey [*1965*]
EEOS .... European Earth Observation System (SAUS)
EEOS Technique... Effective Equation-of-State Technique (SAUS)
EEOW .... Engineering Officer of the Watch [*Navy*]
EEP .... Early Experience Program (VERA)
EEP .... Earth Equatorial Plane
EEP .... Eastern Equatorial Pacific
EEP .... East European Program (EERA)
EEP .... Economic Education Project [*Public Media Center*] (EA)
EEP .... Educational Extension Page (SAUO)
EEP .... Education Excellence Partnership
EEP .... Einstein Equivalence Principle [*Gravity*]
EEP .... Electrode Electrostatic Precipitator
EEP .... Electroencephalophony [*Medical electronics*] (IEEE)
EEP .... Electromagnetic Emission Policy (VLIE)
EEP .... Electronic Emission Policy (SAUS)
EEP .... Electronic Evaluation and Procurement (MHDB)
EEP .... Electronic Event Programmer (MHDB)
EEP .... Electronics Equipment Package (SAUS)
EEP .... Elliptical Error Probability (CAAL)
EEP .... Emergency Essential Personnel (AFM)
EEP .... Employee Evaluation Program (SAUO)
EEP .... End Exercise Point (FAAC)
EEP .... End Expiratory Pressure (AAMN)
EEP .... endexpiratory pressure (SAUS)
EEP .... End to End Protocol (IAA)
EEP .... Energy Engineering Program [*Navy*]
EEP .... Engine Environment Protection (SAUS)
EEP .... Engineering Experimental Phase [*National Data Buoy Project*]
EEP .... Engineering Experimental Phase Buoy (SAUS)
EEP .... Enormously Entertaining Prodigy
EEP .... Entry Exit Procedure [*Computer science*] (VERA)
EEP .... Entry Point (SAUS)
EEP .... Environmental Easement Program [*Department of Agriculture*]
EEP .... Environmental Enhancement Program
EEP .... Environmental Experiments Program [*National Science Foundation*]
EEP .... Epsilon Eta Phi [*Later, Phi Chi Theta*]
EEP .... Equivalent Effective Photon (DB)
EEP .... Esperanza Explorations Ltd. [*Vancouver Stock Exchange symbol*]
EEP .... Ethyl Ethoxypropionate [*Organic chemistry*]
EEP .... European Educational Project (EURO)
EEP .... European Endangered species Programmes (SAUS)
EEP .... European Exchange Program (EURO)
EEP .... Exit Point (SAUS)
EEP .... Experimental Education Program
EEP .... Experiment Electronic Package (SAUS)
EEP .... Explorations in Eastern Palestine [*A publication*] (BJA)
EEP .... Export Enhancement Program [*Department of Agriculture*]
EEP .... External Economic Policy [*British*]
EEP .... Lansing Public Library, Lansing, MI [*OCLC symbol*] (OCLC)

EEPA........... Electromagnetic Energy Policy Alliance (EA)
EEPA........... Environmental Expenditure on Protection and Abatement (EERA)
EEPA........... European Food Phosphates Producers Association (SAUO)
EEPA........... European Food Service and Packaging Association (SAUO)
EEPAC......... Eastern Electronics Packaging Conference (SAUS)
EEPAL......... electrical erasable programmable array logic (SAUS)
EEPAL......... Electrically Erasable Programmable Array Logic (SAUS)
EEP Buoy..... Engineering Experimental Phase Buoy (SAUS)
EEPC........... Eastern Export Promotion Council (SAUO)
EEPC........... Energy and Environmental Policy Center [*Harvard University*] [*Research center*] (RCD)
EEPC........... India Engineering Export Promotion Council (EA)
EEPCD......... Early Education for Children with Disabilities Program Project [*Established under the Individuals with Disabilities Education Act (IDEA)*] (PAZ)
EEPD........... Energy Production and Delivery (IAA)
EEPES......... Greek Seed Trade Association (SAUO)
EEPI........... Extraretinal Eye Position Information [*Ophthalmology*]
EEPLA......... electrical erasable programmable logic array (SAUS)
EEPLA......... Electrically Erasable Programmable Logic Array (SAUS)
EEPLD......... Electrically Erasable Programmable Logic Device (AAEL)
EEPLD......... Electrically Erasable Programmable Read-Only Memory (SAUS)
EEPLO Device... Electrically Erasable Programmable Logic Device (SAUS)
EEPM........... Electrical and Electronic Properties of Materials
EEPNL......... Estimated Effective Perceived Noise Level
EEPOL......... Electrically-Erasable Programmable Logic Device [*Computer science*] (IAA)
EEPROM...... Electrically Erasable, Programmable, Read-Only Memory [*Computer science*]
EEPROM...... Electronical Erasable Programmable Read Only Memory (SAUS)
EEPROM...... Electronically Erasable and Programmable Read Only Memory (SAUS)
EEPROM...... Electronic Erasable Programmable Read-Only Memory (SAUS)
EEPROMs.... Electronically Erasable and Programmable Read Only Memories (SAUS)
EEPS........... Eastern European Politics and Societies (SAUS)
EEPS........... Emergency Electrical Power System (MCD)
EEPSEA....... Economy and Environment Program for Southeast Asia
EEPVS......... Electrical Equipment Protection Room Ventilation System [*Nuclear energy*] (NRCH)
EER............. Early Emissions Reduction [*Environmental science*]
EER............. Eerie (ABBR)
EER............. EER Systems, Inc. [*FAA designator*] (FAAC)
EER............. Electroencephalic Response [*Medicine*] (MAE)
EER............. Electroencephalographic Response [*Medicine*] (STED)
EER............. Electrolyte Electroreflectance (SAUS)
EER............. Electronic/Electrical Equipment Rack (ACAE)
EER............. Electronic Equipment Representative (MCD)
EER............. Elevated Electric Railway [*South London Railway*] (ROG)
EER............. Emergency English for Refugees [*Pennsylvania*] (EDAC)
EER............. Encounter Energy Resources Ltd. [*Toronto Stock Exchange symbol*]
EER............. Energy and Environment Research (SAUO)
EER............. Energy Efficiency Ratio [*Home appliance electric output*]
EER............. English Ecclesiastical Reports [*A publication*] (DLA)
EER............. Enlisted Evaluation Report [*DoD*] (GFGA)
EER............. Entered Employment Rate [*Job Training and Partnership Act*] (OICC)
EER............. Envelope Elimination and Restoration
EER............. Environmental Effects Report [*Military*]
EER............. Equipment Evaluation Report (NG)
EER............. Etch Epitaxial Refill (SAUS)
EER............. European Exhibit Reactor (SAUS)
E'ER............ Ever (ROG)
EER............. Excess Emission Report [*Environmental Protection Agency*] (ERG)
EER............. Expendable-Expendable-Reusable
EER............. Experimental Ecological Reserves [*Project*] [*National Science Foundation*]
EER............. Explosive Echo Ranging
EER............. Extended Endocardial Resection [*Medicine*]
EER............. Extended Entity-Relationship Model (VLIE)
EER............. external engineering review (SAUS)
EER............. University of Michigan, School of Library Science, Ann Arbor, MI [*OCLC symbol*] (OCLC)
EER............. Equilibrium Equivalent Radon [*Physics*] (ODA)
EERA........... Education Evaluation and Remedial Assistance Program [*Connecticut*] (EDAC)
EERA........... Electrical and Electronic Retailers Association (SAUO)
EERA........... Electrical Equipment Representatives Association (EA)
EERA........... Explosive Excavation Research Agency [*Formerly, NCG*] [*Army*] (RDA)
EERC........... Earth Environment and Resources Conference (SAUS)
EERC........... Earthquake Engineering Research Center [*University of California, Berkeley*] (IID)
EERC........... Energy and Environmental Research Center [*University of North Dakota*]
EERC........... Explosive Echo Ranging Charge (NG)
EERD........... Electronic Equipment Reliability Databook (MCD)
EERF........... Eastern Environmental Radiation Facility [*Environmental Protection Agency*] (IID)
EERF........... Sample Data Base (SAUS)
EERI........... Earthquake Engineering Research Institute (EA)
EERI........... Environmental and Ecological Reserach Institute (SAUO)
EERI........... Experience, Education, and Research Institute (SAUS)
EERJ........... External Expansion Ramjet (PDAA)
EERL........... Earthquake Engineering Research Laboratory (SAUS)
EERL........... Eastern Environmental Radiation Laboratory [*Environmental Protection Agency*]
EERL........... Electrical Engineering Research Laboratory (KSC)
EERL........... Explosive Excavation Research Laboratory [*Army Engineer Waterways Experiment Station*] [*Livermore, CA*]
EERNS......... Eeriness (ABBR)
EERO........... European Environmental Research Organization
EERO........... Explosive Excavation Research Office [*Livermore, CA*] [*Army*]
EEROC......... Expedited Essential Required Operational Capability
EEROM......... Electrically Erasable Read-Only Memory [*Computer science*] (MDG)
EERP........... Extended Endocardial Resection Procedure [*Medicine*] (STED)
EERR........... Eerier (ABBR)
EERRHV....... Emergency Escape Ramp for Runaway Heavy Vehicle (PDAA)
EERS........... Earthquake Early Reporting System [*Marine science*] (MSC)
EERS........... elevated environmental risk summary (SAUS)
EERS........... Expeditionary Equipment Report System
EERST......... Eeriest (ABBR)
EERU........... Environmental Emergency Response Unit (COE)
EERWA......... Enlisted Efficiency Report Weighted Average [*Army*]
EERX........... Eccles & Eastern Railroad [*Federal Railroad Administration identification code*]
EERY........... Eerily (ABBR)
EES............. Early Docking Demonstration System (SAA)
EES............. Earth and Environmental Sciences (SAUO)
EES............. Eco-Energy System
EES............. Ecotoxicology and Environmental Safety (SAUS)
EES............. Educational Employment Service
EES............. Education and Enrichment Section of the National Council on Family Relations (EA)
EES............. Effectiveness Evaluation System
EES............. Egypt Exploration Society (EA)
EES............. Ejection Escape Suit (NASA)
EES............. Electrical Equipment Shelter
EES............. Electric Energy Systems (SAUS)
EES............. Electro Explosive Subsystem (ACAE)
EES............. Electromagnetic Environment Simulator
EES............. Electronic Emission Security (NATG)
EEs............. Electronic Engineers (SAUS)
EES............. Electronic Environment Simulator
EES............. Electronics Engineering Squadron [*Military*]
EES............. Emergency Ejection Suits (MCD)
EES............. Emergency Environmental Services, Inc. (EFIS)
EES............. Emergency Establishment Supplements (NATG)
EES............. Emergency Evacuation Study [*Military*] (MCD)
EES............. Emergency Evaluation Study [*Military*]
EES............. Emergency Exhaust System (GOBB)
EES............. Encyclopedia of Endangered Species [*A publication*]
EES............. Encyclopedia of Environmental Science (SAUS)
EES............. Endoscopic Esophageal Sclerotherapy [*Medicine*]
EES............. End to End System
EES............. Energy and Environmental Studies (SAUO)
EES............. Energy Extension Service [*Department of Energy*]
EES............. Engineering Equation Solver [*Macintosh*] [*Computer science*]
EES............. Engineering Experiment Station [*University of Missouri, Columbia*] [*Research center*] (RCD)
EES............. Enlisted Evaluation System [*Army*]
EES............. Environmental Education Server (SAUO)
EES............. Environmental Effects Statement [*Australia*]
EES............. Environmental Engineering Section
EES............. Environment Effects Statement (EERA)
EES............. Erythromycin Ethylsuccinate [*Antimicrobial compound*]
EES............. Escrowed Encryption Standard (VERA)
EES............. E-Section Escape Suit [*Military*]
EES............. Ethyl Enthanesulfate [*Organic chemistry*] (MAE)
EES............. European Economic Space
EES............. European Employment Strategy (EURO)
EES............. European Exchange Service (SAUO)
EES............. European Exchange System
EES............. Evangelical Education Society of the Protestant Episcopal Church (EA)
EES............. Evaporative Emission System [*Automotive engineering*]
EES............. Examining and Entrance Station [*Air Force*]
EES............. Expedient Excavation of Soils (SAUS)
EES............. External Environment Simulator (ACAE)
EES............. Spring Arbor College, Spring Arbor, MI [*OCLC symbol*] (OCLC)
EES............. Electron-Energy Spectroscopy [*Physics*] (ODA)
EESA........... Education for Economic Security Act [*1988*]
EESA........... Electrical and Engineering Staff Association [*British*]
EESB........... Earth and Environmental Science Building (SAUS)
EESB........... Electrical and Electronics Standards Board [*American National Standards Institute*] [*Telecommunications*]
EESC........... Earth and Environmental Sciences Center (SAUO)
EESC........... Eastern Europe Solidarity Campaign (EAIO)
EESC........... East European Solidarity Committee [*Defunct*] (EAIO)
EESC........... Energy and Environment Study Conference (SAUS)
EESC........... Environmental and Energy Study Conference (EA)
EESC........... Erie Engineering Societies Council (SAUO)
EESC........... European EDIF Steering Committee (SAUO)
EESCM......... Enhanced Engine Starting Control and Monitor
EESD........... Electromechanical and Environmental Systems Division (SAUS)
EESD........... European Electronic Security Division [*Military*]
EESE........... Electric Energy Systems Engineering (SAUS)
EESE........... Energy Efficient Services and Equipment
EESG........... Evoked Electrospinogram [*Medicine*] (AAMN)
EESI........... Earth Environment Satellite Initiative (SAUS)

EESI .... Earth Environment Space Initiatives (SAUS)
EESI .... Eastern Environmental Services, Inc. [*NASDAQ symbol*] (NQ)
EESI .... Environment and Energy Study Institute (GNE)
EESL .... Environmental Ecological and Support Laboratory [*Environmental Protection Agency*] (GFGA)
EESLC .... Electronic Equipment Shop Liquid Cooler (ACAE)
EESMB .... Electrical and Electronics Standards Management Board
EES/NCFR .... Education and Enrichment Section of the National Council on Family Relations (EA)
EESP .... Enterprise Extended Services Portals (VLIE)
EESRT .... Entrance Examinations Schools of Health Related Technologies [*Psychological Corp.*] (TES)
EESS .... Earth Exploration Satellite Service (SAUS)
EESS .... Encyclopedia of Engineering Signs and Symbols (SAUS)
EESS .... Environmental Effects on Space Systems
EESS .... Evaporative Emission SHED [*Sealed Housing for Evaporative Determinations*] System [*Automotive engineering*]
EESTEC .... Electrical Engineering Students European Association (SAUO)
EEST/PD ...... Emergency Establishment Supplement Table of Personnel Distribution [*NATO*] (NATG)
EESV .... End to End Service Validation (SAUS)
EESWS .... Emergency Equipment Service Water System [*Nuclear energy*] (NRCH)
EET .... Eames Eye Test (SAUS)
EET .... Eastern European Time (DCTA)
EET .... Edge Enhancement Technology [*Tandy*]
EET .... Education Equivalency Test
EET .... Effective Elastic Thickness [*Mechanics*]
EET .... Electrical Engineering Technologist (SAUS)
EET .... Electrical Engineering Technology (VLIE)
EET .... Electrical Equipment Trailer
EET .... Electronic Educational Toys (TIMI)
EET .... Electronic EGR [*Exhaust Gas Recirculation*] Transducer [*Automotive engineering*]
EET .... Electronic Excitation Transfer (SAUS)
EET .... Electronic Exhaust Transducer (SAUS)
EET .... Electronic Exposure Timer (KSC)
EET .... Electronics Engineering Technician (SAUS)
EET .... Electronics Engineering Technologist (SAUS)
EET .... Electronics Engineering Technology (SAUS)
EET .... Elevated Electron Temperature (UWER)
EET .... Emergency Evacuation Trainer (SAUS)
EET .... End to End Test (SAUS)
EET .... Energy Efficient Transport (MCD)
EET .... Engage Enemy Target
EET .... Engineering Evaluation Test (NG)
EET .... Enhanced Environment Technology (MWOL)
EET .... Entry Elapsed Time (MCD)
EET .... Environmental Engineering Technologist (SAUS)
EET .... Environmental Engineering Technology (SAUS)
EET .... Epoxyeicosatrienoic Acid (UWER)
EET .... Epoxy-Encapsulated Transistor
EET .... Equator Earth Terminal
EET .... Equipment Engaged Tone [*Telecommunications*] (TEL)
EET .... Equivalent Exposure Time (KSC)
EET .... Erythrozyten-Eisenturnover (SAUS)
EET .... Estimated Elapsed Time [*ICAO*] (FAAC)
EET .... Etruscan Enterprises Ltd. [*Vancouver Stock Exchange symbol*]
EET .... Event Elapsed Time (MCD)
EET .... Excitation Energy Transfer
EET .... Explosive-to-Electric Transducer
EETB .... Electronic Electrical Termination Building [*NASA*] (NASA)
EETC .... Electronic Equipment Technical Committee [*NASA*] (KSC)
EETCB .... Eternally Elvis TCB [*Taking Care of Business*] (EA)
EETD .... Environmental Emergencies Technology Division (SAUS)
EETDN .... End-to-End Transit Delay Negotiation (VLIE)
EETEP .... Extended Eligibility Temporary Entry Permit
EETF .... Electromagnetic Environmental Test Facility (SAUS)
EETF .... Electronic Environmental Test Facility (MUGU)
EETFC .... Environmental Effects, Transport, and Fate Committee (COE)
EET-i .... EE Times - interactive (SAUS)
EETIN .... Environmental Education, Training and Information Network (SAUO)
EETLA .... Expanded Extended Three-Letter Acronym (UWER)
EETO .... Emergencies Engineering Technologies Office (FOTI)
EETP .... Engineering Evaluation Test Program (SAUS)
EETP .... Executive Employment Transition Policy (FOTI)
EETPU .... Electrical, Electronic, Telecommunication, and Plumbing Union [*British*] (DCTA)
EETS .... Early English Text Society [*Oxford, England*]
EETs .... Emission estimating techniques (SAUS)
EETS .... Engineering Evaluation Test Station (ACAE)
EETU .... Electrical Electronic Telecommunication Union (SAUO)
EETV .... Electrophoresis Equipment Test Verification [*Military*]
EEU .... Engineering Evaluation Use (TIMI)
EEU .... Environmental Evaluation Unit (SAUS)
EEU .... Eurofly [*Italy*] [*ICAO designator*] (FAAC)
EEU .... European Economic Unit (SAUS)
EEU .... European Esperanto Union (EA)
EEU .... Extravehicular Excursion Unit (SSD)
EEU .... University Microfilms International, Ann Arbor, MI [*OCLC symbol*] (OCLC)
EEUA .... Electrical Equipment Users Association (OSI)
EEUA .... End-to-End Ureteral Anastomosis [*Medicine*] (MELL)
EEUA .... Engineering Equipment Users' Association [*British*] (BI)
EEUR .... Earth Environment University Roundtable [*of America*]
EEV .... Eastern Equine Virus (MELL)
EEV .... Effective Exhaust Velocity (UWER)
EEV .... Encircling Endocardial Ventriculotomy [*Cardiology*]
EEV .... English Electric Valve [*Electronics company*]
EEV .... Extracellular Enveloped Virus
EEVeTec ...... Equipment, Environment, Velocity, Technique, Conditioning [*Sports medicine*]
EEVF .... East Eifel Volcanic Field [*Geology*] [*Germany*]
EEVIP .... Early Extended Validation Integration Program (SAUS)
EEVIR .... Evaporator Equalized Values in Receiver (HAWK)
EEVL .... Edinburgh Engineering Virtual Library [*Project*] (TELE)
EEVT .... Electrophoresis Equipment Verification Test
EEW .... Epoxy per Equivalent Weight (SAUS)
EEW .... Extraordinary Electromagnetic Wave
EEW .... Neenah, WI [*Location identifier*] [*FAA*] (FAAL)
EEW .... Willard Library, Battle Creek, MI [*OCLC symbol*] (OCLC)
EEWC .... Evangelical and Ecumenical Women's Caucus (EA)
EEWD .... Enhanced Exchange Wide Dial (SAUS)
EEWT .... Elementary Exercises Without Troops (SAUS)
EEX .... EEX Corp. [*NYSE symbol*] [*Formerly, Enserch Exploration*] (SG)
EEX .... Electronic Egg Exchange [*Computer program*]
EEX .... emergency exit (SAUS)
EEX .... Enserch Exploration, Inc. [*NYSE symbol*] (SAG)
EEX .... Essex Petroleum [*Vancouver Stock Exchange symbol*]
EEX .... Excess Exception Code [*Air Force*] (AFIT)
EEX .... Michigan State Library Services, Lansing, MI [*OCLC symbol*] (OCLC)
EEXCEL .... Educational Excellence for Children with Environmental Limitations (SAUS)
EEY .... Winchester, VA [*Location identifier*] [*FAA*] (FAAL)
eez .... eastern economic zone (SAUS)
EEZ .... Economic Exclusion Zone (SEWL)
EEZ .... Electronic Exclusion Zone (SAUS)
EEZ .... Eurofly SPA [*Italy*] [*ICAO designator*] (FAAC)
EEZ .... Exclusive Economic Zone [*Offshore sovereignty*] [*ICSU*]
EF .... Each Face [*Technical drawings*]
EF .... Eagle Forum (EA)
EF .... Ear Foundation (EA)
EF .... Early Finish
EF .... Earth First (EA)
EF .... East Florida [*Obsolete*] (ROG)
EF .... Economic Forecasting (FOTI)
EF .... Ectopic Focus [*Cardiology*]
EF .... Eddy Flow (UWER)
EF .... Edema Factor [*Medicine*]
EF .... Edge Filter (SAUS)
EF .... Edge Finishing (DNAB)
EF .... Educational Foundation (SAUO)
EF .... Effective (ABBR)
EF .... Effective Fire (SAUS)
EF .... Effective Force (SAUS)
EF .... Efficiency (ADWA)
EF .... Eglin Field [*Florida*] [*Air Force*] (MCD)
EF .... Ehrmann Foundation (SAUO)
EF .... Ejection Factor [*Cardiology*] (DAVI)
EF .... Ejection Fraction [*Cardiology*]
EF .... Elastic Fibril [*Medicine*] (DMAA)
EF .... Elastic Force (UWER)
EF .... Elect of Fifteen [*Freemasonry*] (ROG)
EF .... Electric Field (DB)
EF .... electric fog horn (SAUS)
EF .... Electric Furnace (SAUS)
EF .... Electrofining (SAUS)
EF .... Electrofinishing (UWER)
EF .... Electroflotation (PDAA)
ef .... electrofocus (SAUS)
EF .... Electroforming (SAUS)
EF .... Electron Focusing (UWER)
EF .... Electronic Filing (NITA)
EF .... Electroviscous Fluid (UWER)
EF .... Eleftherofronon [*Free Opinion Party*] [*Greek*] (PPE)
EF .... Elevation Finder [*Military*]
EF .... Elliptic Filter (SAUS)
EF .... Elongation Factor [*Biochemistry, genetics*]
EF .... Embedded Figures [*Psychometrics*]
EF .... Embryo-Fetal [*Neonatology and obstetrics*] (DAVI)
EF .... Embryo Fibroblast [*Medicine*] (DMAA)
EF .... Emergency Facilities (AAG)
EF .... Emergency Facility (SAUS)
EF .... Emergency Fix
EF .... Emergency Fleet (SAUS)
EF .... Emerson Foundation (SAUO)
EF .... Emission Factor [*Environmental Protection Agency*] (GFGA)
EF .... Emitter Follower [*Electronics*] (MCD)
EF .... Emotional Factor [*Psychology*] (DAVI)
EF .... Empirical Formula (UWER)
EF .... Employed Full Time [*Chiropody*] [*British*]
EF .... Encephalitogenic Factor (MAE)
EF .... Endeavour Forum [*Australia*]
EF .... Endeavour Foundation [*Australia*]
EF .... End Fetch (SAUS)
EF .... Endfile (SAUS)
EF .... End Fitting (COE)
EF .... Ending Flag Value for Data Input [*Computer science*]
EF .... Endoplasmic Fracture [*Freeze etching in microscopy*]
EF .... Endothoracic Fascia [*Medicine*] (STED)

EF .... Endurance Factor [*Cardiology*] (DAVI)
E/F .... Enemy/Friendly (MCD)
EF .... En Foco [*An association*] (EA)
EF .... Engineering Foundation (EA)
EF .... English Finish [*Paper*]
EF .... Enrichment Factor (SAUS)
EF .... Entered From (SAA)
EF .... Enteric Fistula [*Medicine*] (MELL)
EF .... Enterprise Foundation (EA)
EF .... Entire Function (SAUS)
EF .... Entry Fee
EF .... Envelope Follower (SAUS)
EF .... Environmental Factor
EF .... Environment Funds (SAUS)
EF .... Eosinophilic Fasciitis [*Medicine*]
EF .... Epicondylar Fracture [*Medicine*] (MELL)
EF .... Epithelial Focus (DB)
EF .... Epithelial Force (Assay) [*Oncology*]
EF .... Equalization Fund (SAUS)
EF .... Equilibrium Field (MCD)
EF .... Equipment Factor (CAAL)
EF .... Equivalent Focal Length [*Optics*]
EF .... Equivalent Focus [*Medicine*] (DAVI)
EF .... Erlenmeyer Flask (UWER)
EF .... Error Factor (IEEE)
EF .... Error-Free (SAUS)
EF .... error free region (SAUS)
ef .... error function (SAUS)
EF .... Erythroblastosis Fetalis (DB)
EF .... Erythrocytic Fragmentation (AAMN)
EF .... Ethos Foundation (EA)
EF .... Etruscan Foundation (EA)
EF .... Eurodata Foundation (EAIO)
EF .... European Foundation (DS)
EF .... European Fund (SAUO)
EF .... [*The*] Europe Fund [*NYSE symbol*] (SPSG)
EF .... Eurotransplant Foundation (EA)
EF .... Evaluation Finder (SAUS)
EF .... Evangelische Freiheit [*A publication*] (BJA)
EF .... Evergreen Foundation (EA)
EF .... Everyman's Fiction [*Series published by J. M. Dent & Sons*] [*British*]
EF .... Execution Function [*Computer science*] (ELAL)
EF .... Executive Forum (EA)
EF .... Executive Function (SAUS)
EF .... Exhaust Fan (AAG)
EF .... Exoplasmic Fracture [*Freeze etching in microscopy*]
EF .... Expectant Father (ODA)
EF .... Expedited Forwarding [*Computer science*] (SEWL)
EF .... Expeditionary Force
EF .... Experimental Flight
EF .... Exposed Facility (SSD)
ef .... exposure factor (SAUS)
EF .... Exposure Frequency (EEVL)
EF .... Expressional Fluency [*Research test*] [*Psychology*]
EF .... Extended Facility [*IBM Corp.*]
EF .... Extended Field [*Radiation therapy*] (DAVI)
E/F .... Extension/Flexion [*Medicine*]
EF .... External Flag [*Computer science*] (ELAL)
EF .... External Flaps (AAG)
EF .... Extractable Fluorescence
EF .... Extra Fine [*Threads*]
EF .... Extremely Fine [*Condition*] [*Antiquarian book trade and numismatics*]
EF .... Extrinsic Factor [*Vitamin B_{12}*] [*Also, APA, APAF, LLD*]
EF .... Eye Focus
EF .... Far Eastern Air Transport [*ICAO designator*] (AD)
EF .... Edge-to-Face (ODA)
EF-111 .... Raven Tactical Electronic Jamming Aircraft [*Air Force*] (POLM)
EFA .... Category E Flying Accident [*British military*] (DMA)
EFA .... Eastern Finance Association (EA)
EFA .... Economic and Financial Adviser (SAUS)
EFA .... Eddy Family Association (EA)
EFA .... Editorial Freelancers Association (EA)
EFA .... Edmondson Family Association (EA)
EFA .... Educational Foundation of America (SAUO)
EFA .... Education for All (SAUO)
EFA .... Education for All Forum
EFA .... Effective Filtration Area
EFA .... EFTA-Finnland Association (SAUO)
EFA .... Ego Function Assessment [*Test*] (TMMY)
EFA .... Electrical Floor Warming Association [*British*] (BI)
EFA .... Electrinium Foundation of America (EA)
EFA .... Electronics Field Activity
EFA .... Elliot Flight Automation (SAUS)
EFA .... En Famille Agency (WDAA)
EFA .... Engineering Field Activity (MCD)
EFA .... Engine Fault Analysis (ODA)
EFA .... Enginemen and Firemen's Association [*A union*] [*British*]
EFA .... Enhancing Factor of Allergy [*Medicine*] (MELL)
EFA .... Enterprise Flexibility Agreement [*Australia*]
EFA .... Entire Field Available (FAAC)
EFA .... Environmental Financing Authority [*Expired, 1975*] [*Environmental Protection Agency*]
EFA .... Epilepsy Foundation of America (EA)
EFA .... Equilibrium Float Altitude [*Balloon flight*]
EFA .... Erbium-Doped Fiber Amplifier (SAUS)
EFA .... Eskridge Family Association (EA)
EFA .... Essential Fatty Acid [*Biochemistry*]
EFA .... Esterified Fatty Acid (SAUS)
EFA .... Eton Fives Association (SAUO)
EFA .... European Fairytale Association [*See also EMG*] [*Rheine, Federal Republic of Germany*] (EAIO)
EFA .... European Federation of Agricultural Workers Trade Unions (SAUS)
EFA .... European Federation of Agricultural Workers' Unions [*EC*] (ECED)
EFA .... European Federation of Agricultural Workers Unions within the Community (SAUO)
EFA .... European Federation of Asthma and Allergy Associations (SAUS)
EFA .... European Fighter Aircraft
EFA .... European Film Alliance (SAUO)
EFA .... European Finance Association (EAIO)
EFA .... European Free Alliance [*See also ALE*] [*Brussels, Belgium*] Political party] (EAIO)
EFA .... European Free Associations (SAUO)
EFA .... Evangelical Friends Alliance [*Later, EFI*] (EA)
EFA .... Everglades Forever Act
EFA .... Evolutionary Factor Analysis [*Statistics*]
EFA .... Examining for Aphasia [*J. Eisenson*] (DIPS)
EFA .... Examining for Aphasia, Third Edition [*Test*] (TMMY)
EFA .... Excess Fare Allowance
EFA .... Experimental Flight Approval (SAUS)
EFA .... Experiment Flight Applications (NASA)
EFA .... Extended File Attribute [*Software feature*] [*Computer science*] (PCM)
EFA .... Exteneded Finite Automation [*Computer science*] (CIST)
EFA .... External Function Acknowledgement (SAUS)
EFA .... Extrafamily Adoptee (MAE)
EFA .... Eyepiece Focusing Adjustment [*Optics*] (ROG)
EFA .... International Franchise Association (JAGO)
EFAA .... Aavahelukka [*Finland*] [*ICAO location identifier*] (ICLI)
EFAA .... Expedited Funds Availability Act (EBF)
EFAAD .... European Federation for the Advancement of Anaesthesia in Dentistry [*Italy*] (EAIO)
EFAB .... Electrochemical Fabrication
EFAB .... Environmental Financial Advisory Board [*Environmental Protection Agency*] (EGAO)
EFAC .... European Field Archery Championship (SAUO)
EFAC .... Extended File Access Control (SAUS)
EFACB .... Effaceable (ABBR)
EFACD .... Effaced (ABBR)
EFACF .... European Folk Art and Craft Federation [*Zurich, Switzerland*] (EAIO)
EFACG .... Effacing (ABBR)
EFACR .... Effacer (ABBR)
EFACT .... Effacement (ABBR)
EFACW .... Export Finance Assistance Center of Washington (SAUO)
EFAD .... Essential Fatty Acid Deficiency [*Medicine*]
EFAD .... European Federation of the Associations of Dietitians (EAIO)
EFAG .... Economic and Financial Aspect Group (SAUO)
EFAG .... Emergency Field Arresting Gear (MCD)
EFAH .... European Forum for the Arts and Heritage (EURO)
EFAI .... Educational Foundation for the Apparel Industry [*Later, EFFI*] (EA)
EFAL .... Alavus [*Finland*] [*ICAO location identifier*] (ICLI)
EFAL .... Electronic Flash Approach Light (IAA)
EFAMS .... Enhanced Fuel and Armament Management System (SAUS)
EF&I .... Engineer Furnish and Install [*Telecommunications*] (ITD)
EF & I .... Engineer, Furnish and Install (SAUS)
EF & LTC .... Enemy Fuels and Lubricants Technical Committee
EF&P .... End Fitting Delta Pressure (COE)
EFANSW .... Electoral Funding Authority of New South Wales [*Australia*]
EFAP .... Elastic Frame Analysis Program [*Structures & Computers Ltd.*] [*Software package*] (NCC)
EFAP .... Environmentally Friendly Accreditation Program [*Australia*]
EFAPIT .... Euromarket Federation of Animal Protein Importers and Traders (EAIO)
EFAPP .... Enrico Fermi Atomic Power Plant [*Decommissioned*] (NRCH)
EFAR .... Economic Feeder Administration and Relief (TEL)
EFAR .... Error Factor Analysis and Reduction (ADA)
EFAR .... European Federation for AIDS Research
EFARS .... Engineer Federal Acquisition Regulation Supplement [*A publication*] (AAGC)
EFAS .... Electronic flash approach light system (SAUS)
EFAS .... Electronic Flash Approach System
EFAS .... Embryo-Fetal Alcohol Syndrome (MELL)
EFAS .... Emergency Feedwater Actuation Signal [*Nuclear energy*] (NRCH)
EFAS .... Engine Failure Assist System (ACAE)
EFAS .... Enhance Fault Alarm System (SAUS)
EFAS .... En Route Flight Advisory Services [*FAA*]
EFAS .... European Foot & Ankle Societies (SAUS)
EFAS .... European Foot and Ankle Society (SAUS)
EFAS .... Evanescent-Field Absorbance Sensor (SAUS)
EFAT .... Essential Field Artillery Task [*Army*]
EFATCA .... European Federation of Air Traffic Controllers Associates (SAUS)
EFATCA .... European Federation of Air Traffic Controllers Association
EFATO .... Engine Failure At or After Take-Off [*Aviation*] (PIAV)
EFAVA .... Educational Foundation for Audio-Visual Aids (SAUO)
EFAX .... eFax.com, Inc. [*AMEX symbol*] (SG)
EFB .... Eight Fathom Bight [*Alaska*] [*Airport symbol*] (OAG)
EFB .... Electric Feedback
EFB .... Electric Flash Butt Welding (SAUS)
EFB .... Electrode Film Barrier
EFB .... Electrofluidized Bed [*Chemical engineering*]
EFB .... Electronic Feedback (SAUS)
EFB .... Elemental Function Block (SAUS)

EFB .... Emerging Flux Regions (SAUS)
EFB .... Engineering Field Bulletin (MCD)
EFB .... Engineering Foundation Board (SAUO)
EFB .... Eppley Foundation for Research (SAUO)
EFB .... Error Free Block (SAUS)
EFB .... Error-Free Region (SAUS)
EFB .... Europaeische Foderation Biotechnologie [*European Federation of Biotechnology*] (EAIO)
EFB .... Evening School for Foreign Born
EFB .... Experimental Fighting Biplane [*British military*] (DMA)
EFBC .... Empire Federal Bancorp, Inc. [*NASDAQ symbol*] (NASQ)
EFBD .... Emergency Feed Baron Detector (IEEE)
EFBI .... Enterprise Federal Bancorp [*NASDAQ symbol*] (TTSB)
EFBI .... Enterprise Federal Bancorp, Inc. [*NASDAQ symbol*] (SAG)
EFBPBI .... European Federation of the Brush and Paint Brush Industries (EA)
EFBS .... E. F. Benson Society (EAIO)
EFBS .... European Federation of Building Societies (EAIO)
EFBTE .... Eastern Federation of Building Trades' Employers [*British*] (BI)
EFBWW .... European Federation of Building and Woodwork (SAUS)
EFBWW .... European Federation of Building and Woodworkers (EA)
EFC .... Earth-Fixed Coordinate (MCD)
efc .... earth fixed coordinate (SAUS)
EFC .... Eastern Football Conference
EFC .... Economic and Finance Committee (SAUO)
EFC .... Educational Facilities Center (SAUS)
EFC .... EFC Bancorp [*AMEX symbol*] (SG)
EFC .... Efface (ABBR)
EFC .... Effective Full-Charge [*Weaponry*] (RDA)
EFC .... Elastin Fragment Concentration [*Medicine*] (EDAA)
EFC .... Electrical Field Current
EFC .... Electrical Frequency Control (MCD)
EFC .... Electric Fuel Control [*Automotive engineering*]
EFC .... Electrochemical Fuel Cell
EFC .... Electrofluid Converter
EFC .... Electromechanical Fuel Cell (SAUS)
EFC .... Electronic Fabrication Center (SAUS)
EFC .... Electronic Flow Compensation [*Automotive emissions*]
EFC .... Electronic Flow Control
EFC .... Electronic Frequency Control
EFC .... Elfquest Fan Club (EA)
EFC .... Elvira Fan Club (EA)
EFC .... Emergency Fleet Corp. [*Defunct, 1936*]
EFC .... Emergency Foster Care (ADA)
EFC .... Emitter Follower Cascade (SAUS)
EFC .... Empire Financial Corporation (SAUO)
EFC .... Employment Focus Course (WDAA)
EFC .... Encampment for Citizenship [*An association*] (EA)
EFC .... Endogenous Fecal Calcium [*Medicine*] (MAE)
efc .... engineered for color (SAUS)
EFC .... Engineering Field Change (MSA)
EFC .... Enterprise Fabric Connectivity (VLIE)
EFC .... Ephemeral Fever of Cattle [*Veterinary science*] (DB)
EFC .... Equipment Functional Check (KSC)
EFC .... Equivalent Full Charge
EFC .... Ernest Fan Club [*Defunct*] (EA)
EFC .... Escort Force Commander [*NATO*] (NATG)
EFC .... Estimated Final Cost
EFC .... Etched Flexible Circuitry
EFC .... European Federal Constitution (SAUO)
EFC .... European Federation of Corrosion (EA)
EFC .... European Forestry Commission
EFC .... Eurythmics Fan Club (EA)
EFC .... Evangelical Fellowship of Canada (FOTI)
efc .... Evergreen Fir Corporation (SAUO)
EFC .... Exile Fan Club (EA)
EFC .... Expected Family Contribution [*Department of Education*] (GFGA)
EFC .... Expected Fraction of Casualties (MCD)
EFC .... Expected Further Clearance (GAVI)
EFC .... Expect Further Clearance [*FAA*] (TAG)
EFC .... Expect Further Clearance At [*Aviation*] (FAAC)
EFC .... Expeditionary Force Canteens [*Official supply organization*] [*World War I*] [*British*]
EFC .... Experimental Forecast Center (SAUS)
EFC .... Extended Freeman Code (SAUS)
EFC .... External Fission Counter [*Environmental science*] (COE)
EFCA .... Equity Funding Corporation of America (SAUO)
EFCA .... European Federation of Engineering Consultancy Associations (SAUS)
EFCA .... Evangelical Free Church of Australia
EFCAT .... European Football Commentators Association Television (EA)
EFCATS .... European Federation of Catalysis Societies
EFCB .... Emergency Financial Control Board [*Later, FCB*]
EFCC .... European Federation of Conference Cities (SAUO)
EFCC .... Externally Fired Combined Cycle (SAUS)
EFCCCI .... Early Four Cylinder Chevrolet Club, International [*Defunct*] (EA)
EFCD .... Effaced (ABBR)
EFCE .... European Federation of Chemical Engineering [*See also EFCIW*] (EAIO)
EFCE .... European Federation of Chemical Engineers (SAUO)
EFCEM .... European Federation of Catering Equipment Manufacturers (EA)
EFCG .... Effacing (ABBR)
EFCGU .... European Federation of Chemical and General Workers Union (SAUS)
EFCGU .... European Federation of Chemical and General Workers Unions (EAIO)
EFChE .... European Federation of Chemical Engineering
EFCI .... Explicit Forward Congestion Identification (SAUS)
EFCI .... Explicit Forward Congestion Indication [*Telecommunications*] (MLOA)
EFCI .... Explicit Forward Congestion Indicator [*Telecommunications*] (ACRL)
EFCIW .... Europaeische Foderation fuer Chemie-Ingenieur-Wesen [*European Federation of Chemical Engineering - EFCE*] (EAIO)
EFCL .... Error-Free Communication Link (IAA)
EFCN .... Explicit Forward Congestion Notification [*Telecommunications*] (MLOA)
EFCNT .... Effacement (ABBR)
EFCO .... English French Cultural Organization (SAUO)
EFCOG .... Energy Facilities Contractors Group (AAGC)
EFCOM .... Electricity Flow Computer (SAUS)
EF Condition .... Extremely Fine Condition (SAUS)
EFCOR .... Effect Corona (IAA)
EFCR .... Effacer (ABBR)
EFCR .... Equivalent Full Charge Rounds (SAUS)
EFCR .... Experimental Fast Ceramic Reactor
EFCS .... Earth-Fixed Coordinate System (MCD)
EFCS .... Electrical Flight Control System (SAUS)
EFCS .... Electronic Filmless Camera System (SEWL)
EFCS .... Electronic Flight Control System
EFCS .... Electronic Fuel Control System
EFCS .... Emitter Follower Current Switch [*Electronics*] (IAA)
EFCS .... Engineer Fuel Control System (ACAE)
EFCS .... Enhanced Fire Control System (SAUS)
EFCS .... European Federation for Company Sports (EAIO)
EFCS .... European Federation of Cytological Societies (SAUO)
EFCS .... European Federation of Cytology Societies (EAIO)
EFCSM .... European Federation of Ceramic Sanitaryware Manufacturers (EA)
EFCT .... Effect (ABBR)
EFCT .... Einstein Family Correspondence Trust (WDAA)
EFCT .... European Federation of Congress Towns (SAUO)
EFCTA .... Effectuate (ABBR)
EFCTAD .... Effectuated (ABBR)
EFCTAG .... Effectuating (ABBR)
EFCTB .... Effectible (ABBR)
EFCTC .... European Federation of Connective Tissue Clubs (SAUO)
EFCTD .... Effected (ABBR)
EFCTEC .... European Fluorocarbon Technical Committee [*Belgium*] (EAIO)
EFCTG .... Effecting (ABBR)
EFC Time .... Expected Further Clearance Time (SAUS)
EFCTL .... Effectual (ABBR)
EFCTLNS .... Effectualness (ABBR)
EFCTLT .... Effectuality (ABBR)
EFCTLY .... Effectually (ABBR)
EFCTR .... Effector (ABBR)
EFCTV .... Effective (ABBR)
EFCTVNS .... Effectiveness (ABBR)
EFCTVY .... Effectively (ABBR)
EFCUA .... Extreme Fuel - Critical, Unspecified Area [*NASA*]
EFCV .... Excess Flow Check Valve [*Nuclear energy*] (NRCH)
EFCW .... Eagle Finance [*NASDAQ symbol*] (TTSB)
EFCW .... Eagle Finance Corp. [*NASDAQ symbol*] (SAG)
EFCX .... Electrical Fuel Corp. [*NASDAQ symbol*] (SAG)
EFCX .... Electric Fuel [*NASDAQ symbol*] (TTSB)
EFCX .... Evergreen Freight Car Express (SAUS)
EFD .... Earliest Finish Date
EFD .... Early Failure Detection
EFD .... Economic Flat transformer Design (SAUS)
EFD .... Electric Flux Density
EFD .... Electrofluid Dynamic [*Process*] (MCD)
efd .... electro fluid dynamics (SAUS)
EFD .... Electronic Forms Designer [*Microsoft Corp.*] (PCM)
EFD .... Ellington Field, Houston (SAUS)
EFD .... End of Form Description (SAUS)
EFD .... Enemy Forward Disposition [*Military*]
EFD .... Energy Flux Density
EFD .... Enfield Resources [*Vancouver Stock Exchange symbol*]
EFD .... Engineered Fasteners Division [*Townsend Co.*]
EFD .... Engineering Facilities Depot
EFD .... Engineering Field Divisions [*Military*]
EFD .... Engineering Flow Diagram (NRCH)
EFD .... Episode Free Day [*Medicine*] (MELL)
EFD .... Equivalent Full Discharge (SAUS)
EFD .... Erlenmeyer Flask Deformity [*Medicine*] (MELL)
EFD .... European Faculty Directory [*A publication*]
EFD .... European Force Design (SAUO)
EFD .... Event Forwarding Discriminator (VLIE)
EFD .... Excused from Duty
EFD .... Executive Flight Detachment (AAG)
EFD .... Experimental Facilities Department (SAUO)
EFD .... Extended Functional Dependency (SAUS)
EFD .... Houston, TX [*Location identifier*] [*FAA*] (FAAL)
EFDA .... Epoxyfarnesyl Diazoacetate [*Organic chemistry*]
EFDA .... European Federation of Data processing Associations (SAUS)
EFDA .... European Formula Drivers Association (EAIO)
EFDA .... European Funeral Directors' Association (EAIO)
EFDA .... Expanded Function Dental Auxiliary [*HEW program*]
EFDARS .... Electronic Flight Data and Recording System (MCD)
EFDARS .... Expandable Flight Data Acquisition and Recording System (SAUS)
EFDAS .... Electronic Flight Data Accumulation Service
EFDAS .... Epsilon Flight Data Acquisition System (IAA)
EFDB .... Environmental Fate Data Bases (SAUO)
EFDEX .... Electronic Food and Beverage Exchange

EFD-Generator... electro fluid dynamic generator (SAUS)
EFDO .... European Film Development Office (SAUS)
EFDP .... European Federation of Data Processing (SAUO)
EFDPA .... European Federation of Data Processing Associations (SAUO)
EFDPMA ...... Education Foundation of the Data Processing Management Association (SAUO)
EFDPR .... European Federation of Diary Retailers (SAUS)
EFDS .... eFunds Corp. [*NASDAQ symbol*]
EFDS .... Equipment and Floor Drainage System [*Nuclear energy*] (NRCH)
EFDS .... Error Free Deciseconds (SAUS)
EFDSA .... English Folk Dance & Song Association (WDAA)
EFDSS .... English Folk Dance and Song Society [*British*]
EFDSS .... Environmental Flows Decision Support System (SAUS)
EFE .... Early Fuel Evaporation [*Automotive technology*]
EFE .... Early Fuel Evaporative System (SAUS)
EFE .... Emitter Feature Extractor (SAUS)
EFE .... Endocardial Fibroelastosis [*Medicine*]
efe .... endoctrinal fibro-elastosic (SAUS)
EFE .... Ermolino Flying Test Research Enterprise [*Former USSR*] [*FAA designator*] (FAAC)
efe .... expected field emergence (SAUS)
EFE .... External Field Emission
EFEA .... European Free Exchange Area (NATG)
EFEC .... Efforts From Ex-Convicts (SAUS)
EFECS .... Engine Fuel Economy Control System [*Automotive engineering*]
EFEDA .... ECHIVAL Field Experiment in a Desertification Threatened Area (SAUS)
EFEDA .... Echival Field Experiment in Desertification-Threatened Area (SAUS)
EFEDA .... European Field Experiment in Desertification-Threatened Area (SAUS)
EFEDA .... European Field Experiment in Desertification-Threatened Areas (SAUS)
EFEDA .... European International Project on Climate and Hydrological Interactions (SAUS)
EFEDA .... European International Project on Climate and Hydrological Interactions between Vegetation, Atmosphere and Landsurfaces (SAUS)
EFEDTA .... European Field Experiment in Decertification Threatened Area (SAUO)
EFEHV .... Educational Fund to End Handgun Violence (EA)
EFEI .... Equivalent Fuel Efficiency Improvement
EFEI .... European Federation of Electronic Industries (SAUO)
EFEM .... Effeminate (ABBR)
EFEM .... Energy Filtering Electron Microscope
EFEM .... Energy Filtering Electron Microscopy (SAUS)
EFEMA .... Association des Fabricants Europeens d'Emulsifants Alimentaires [*Association of European Manufacturers of Food Emulsifiers*] (EAIO)
EFEMA .... Emergency Fund for European Mountain Areas (SAUO)
EFEMA .... European Food Emulsifiers Manufacturers Association (SAUO)
EFEMAY .... Effeminately (ABBR)
EFEMC .... Effeminacy (ABBR)
EFEMNS .... Effeminateness (ABBR)
EFEMY .... Effeminately (ABBR)
EFEO .... Ecole Francaise d'Extreme Orient [*French School of the Far East*]
EFERVS .... Effervesce (ABBR)
EFERVSD .... Effervesced (ABBR)
EFERVSG .... Effervescing (ABBR)
EFERVSNC .... Effervescence (ABBR)
EFERVST .... Effervescent (ABBR)
E-FES .... Enhanced-Force Entry Switch [*Military*]
EFES .... Tampere [*Finland*] [*ICAO location identifier*] (ICLI)
E-FET .... enhancement FET (SAUS)
EFET .... Enhancement Mode Field Effect Transistor (IAA)
EFET .... Enontekio [*Finland*] [*ICAO location identifier*] (ICLI)
EFET .... Epoxy Field Effect Transistor
EFEU .... Eura [*Finland*] [*ICAO location identifier*] (ICLI)
EFEx .... Ejection Fraction (during) Exercise [*Medicine*] (EDAA)
EFF .... Eastern Fishermen's Federation [*See also FPE*] [*Canada*]
EFF .... Educational Freedom Foundation (EA)
Eff .... Effacement [*Obstetrics*] (DAVI)
eff .... effciency (SAUS)
EFF .... Effect (AFM)
Eff .... Effective [*Legal term*] (DLA)
EFF .... Effective [*Motor vehicle violation code used in state of Maryland*] (MVRD)
eff .... Effective (TRID)
EFF .... Effectiveness (SAUS)
EFF .... Efferent [*Anatomy*]
EFF .... Effervescent [*Pharmacy*] (ROG)
eff .... Efficiency (ADWA)
EFF .... Efficiency
eff .... efficient (SAUS)
EFF .... Effigy (ROG)
EFF .... Effluent
EFF .... Electric Flow Field
EFF .... Electronic Font Foundry (SAUO)
EFF .... Electronic Freedom Foundation [*Telecommunications*]
EFF .... Electronic Frontier Foundation (EA)
EFF .... Empirical Force Field [*Physical chemistry*]
EFF .... Engine Fuel Flow (SAUS)
EFF .... English for Foreigners
EFF .... Enterprise, Family, and Freedom [*Australia*] [*Political party*]
EFF .... Equipped for the Future [*National Institute for Literacy project*]
EFF .... European Franchise Federation [*France*] (EAIO)
EFF .... European Franchising Federation (SAUO)
EFF .... European Furniture Federation
EFF .... Expandable File Family [*Computer science*] (MHDB)
EFF .... Experimenal Forecast Facility [*Marine science*] (OSRA)
EFF .... Experimental Forecast Facility [*National Weather Service*] (USDC)
EFF .... Explosively Formed Fragment (SAUS)
EFF .... Extended Fringe Field (SAUS)
EFF .... Extended Fund Facility [*International Monetary Fund*]
EFF .... Westair Aviation Ltd. [*Ireland*] [*ICAO designator*] (FAAC)
EFFA .... Eastern Frosted Foods Association (SAUO)
EFFA .... European Federation of Flight Engineers (SAUO)
EFFA .... European Flavour and Fragrance Association [*Belgium*] (EAIO)
EFFAS .... European Federation of Financial Analysts' Societies (EA)
EFFAS .... European Federation of Foot and Ankle Societies (SAUS)
EFFBR .... Enrico Fermi Fast Breeder Power Reactor
EFFBR .... Enrico Fermi Fast Breeder Reactor (SAUS)
EFFCTS .... Effects [*Automotive advertising*]
effcy .... effciency (SAUS)
EFFCY .... Efficiency (AABC)
EFF DIODE... Efficiency Diode (SAUS)
EFFE .... Environmentalists for Full Employment [*Defunct*] (EA)
EFFE .... European Federation of Flight Engineers
EFFE .... Experiment in Free-Form Education (AEBS)
EFFECT .... Effective (ABBR)
EFFECT .... Effectivity (ABBR)
EFFECT .... Environmental Forecasting for the Effective Control of Traffic [*Traffic management*]
EFFER .... Efferent (ABBR)
EFFF .... Electrical Field-Flow Fractionation [*Electrochemical separation method*]
EFFFL .... Efficiency Full Load (IAA)
EFFG .... Effectuating (ROG)
EFFGRO .... Efficient Growth [*Computer program*] (NASA)
EFFI .... Educational Foundation for the Fashion Industries (EA)
EFFI .... Electronic Fiber Fineness Indicator
EFFI .... Electronic Forum for Industry [*British*]
EFFI Bulletin... Electronic Forum for Industry Bulletin (journ.) (SAUS)
effic .... Efficiency (ADWA)
EFFIC .... Efficiency (ROG)
Effie .... Award for Effective Advertising (SAUS)
Effie .... Euphemia (SAUS)
EFFIG .... Effigies (ROG)
Effigy Mounds... Effigy Mounds National Monument on the Mississippi in northeastern Iowa (SAUS)
EFFL .... Efflorescence (SAUS)
EFFL .... Efflorescent (ABBR)
efflor .... Efflorescent (SAUS)
Effluent Water Treat J... Effluent and Water Treatment Journal (SAUS)
Effl Water Treat J... Effluent and Water Treatment Journal (journ.) (SAUS)
EFFM .... Eastern Federation of Feed Merchants (SRA)
EFFM .... European Federation of Fiber Cement Manufacturers [*EC*] (ECED)
EffMgt .... Effective Management Systems [*Associated Press*] (SAG)
EFFNCY .... Efficiency (ADWA)
EFFO .... Forssa [*Finland*] [*ICAO location identifier*] (ICLI)
EFFORPA .... Elliptic Function First-Order Ripple Phase Approximation
EFFOST .... European Federation for/of Food Science and Technology (SAUO)
EFFoST .... European Federation of Food Science and Technology (EA)
EF Foundation... Educational Foundation for Foreign Study (EA)
EFFT .... Effete (ABBR)
Efft .... Effort (SAUS)
EFFU .... Epithelial Focus-Forming Unit [*Oncology*]
EFFUNDAT .... Effundatur [*Let It Be Poured Out*] [*Pharmacy*] (ROG)
Effy .... Efficiency (SAUS)
EFG .... Earthquake Finger Gateway (SAUO)
EFG .... Economic Forestry Group [*British*]
EFG .... Edge-Defined Film-Fed Growth [*Photovoltaics*]
EFG .... Edward FitzGerald (SAUS)
efg .... Effigy (VRA)
EFG .... Efogi [*Papua New Guinea*] [*Airport symbol*] (OAG)
EFG .... Electric Field Gradient [*of crystals*]
EFG .... Elemental and Functional Group (SAUO)
EFG .... engineering flow diagram (SAUS)
EFG .... Environmental Fund for Georgia (SAUO)
EFGS .... Easterling Family Genealogical Society (EA)
EFGS .... Edge Following as Graph Searching (SAUS)
EFGTF .... Entrained-Flow Gasification Test Facility
EFGY .... Effigy (ABBR)
EFH .... Earth Far Horizon [*NASA*] (KSC)
EFH .... Echo-Free Hole [*Meterology*]
EFH .... Eileen F Hodges (SAUS)
EFH .... Enge's Flaming Hearts (EA)
EFH .... Engine Flight Hours
EFH .... Explosive Follicular Hyperplasia [*Medicine*] (EDAA)
EFHA .... Esperanto Family History Association [*Later, EEFHA*] (EA)
EFHA .... Halli [*Finland*] [*ICAO location identifier*] (ICLI)
EFHAM .... Effingham, IL [*American Association of Railroads railroad junction routing code*]
EFHBM .... Eosinophilic Fibrohistiocytic Bone Marrow [*Medicine*] (EDAA)
EFHC .... Emanuel Foundation for Hungarian Culture (EA)
EFHF .... Helsinki/Helsinki-Malmi [*Finland*] [*ICAO location identifier*] (ICLI)
EFHK .... Helsinki/Vantaa [*Finland*] [*ICAO location identifier*] (ICLI)
EFHL .... Hailuoto [*Finland*] [*ICAO location identifier*] (ICLI)
EFHM .... Hameenkyro [*Finland*] [*ICAO location identifier*] (ICLI)
EFHN .... Hanko [*Finland*] [*ICAO location identifier*] (ICLI)
EF Horn .... Electrical Fog Horn (SAUS)

EFHP........ Haapavesi [*Finland*] [*ICAO location identifier*] (ICLI)
EFHT........ Ahtari [*Finland*] [*ICAO location identifier*] (ICLI)
EFHV........ Hyvinkaa [*Finland*] [*ICAO location identifier*] (ICLI)
EFI........ Educational Forces Inventory (SAUS)
EFI........ Educational Futures, Inc. (EA)
efi........ Efik [*MARC language code*] [*Library of Congress*] (LCCP)
EFI........ Electromechanical Frequency Interference (SAUS)
EFI........ Electronic Facility Instruction (SAA)
EFI........ Electronic Flash Illuminator
EFI........ Electronic Flight Instruments (WDAA)
EFI........ Electronic Fluid Injection (SAUS)
EFI........ Electronic Fuel Injection (EAGT)
EFI........ Electronic Funds Transfer (SAUS)
EFI........ Electronics For Imaging, Inc (SAUS)
EFI........ Embedded Figures Test (SAUS)
EFI........ Emissary Foundation International (EA)
EFI........ Engineered, Furnished and Installed (SAUS)
EFI........ Engineering Flight Test (SAUS)
EFI........ Enrico Fermi Institute [*University of Chicago*]
EFI........ Environic Foundation International (EA)
EFI........ Equestrian Federation of Ireland (EAIO)
EFI........ Error Free Interval (NITA)
EFI........ Error Function Integral (SAUS)
EFI........ European Flight Information (SAUS)
EFI........ European Forest Institute
EFI........ Evangelical Friends International (EA)
EFI........ Expedited Flow Indicator [*Telecommunications*] (ACRL)
EFI........ Expeditionary Force Institutions [*Military*] [*British*]
EFI........ Exploding Foil Initiator (ACAE)
EFI........ Export Financing Institution (FOTI)
EFi........ extended field irradiation (SAUS)
e-fi-........ Finland [*MARC geographic area code*] [*Library of Congress*] (LCCP)
EFIA........ European Fertiliser (or Fertilizer) Import Association (SAUO)
EFIA........ European Fertilizer Importers' Associations (EAIO)
EFIB........ Eastern Freight Inspection Bureau
EFIB........ European Freight Inspection Bureau (SAUS)
EFIBCA........ European Flexible Intermediate Bulk Container Association (PDAA)
EFIC........ Efficacy (ABBR)
EFIC........ EFI Electronics Corp. [*NASDAQ symbol*] (SAG)
EFIC........ Export Finance and Insurance Corporation (SAUO)
EFICNC........ Efficiency (ABBR)
EFICNT........ Efficient (ABBR)
EFICNTY........ Efficiently (ABBR)
EFICNY........ Efficiency (ABBR)
EFICO........ Electrical Fitting Inventory Control Branch
EFICON........ Electronic Financial Control
EFICP........ Electronic Flight Instrument Control Panel (MCD)
EFICU........ Efficacious (ABBR)
EFICY........ Efficiently (ABBR)
EFID........ Electric-Field In-Process Dressing (SAUS)
EFID........ Electronic Flight Instrument Display (SAUS)
EFIE........ Electric Field Integral Equation (PDAA)
EFIEA........ European Forum on Integrated Environmental Assessment (EURO)
EFIEI........ EFI Electronics Corp. [*Associated Press*] (SAG)
E-field........ electric field (SAUS)
EFIF........ Export Finance and Insurance Fund
EFIFC........ European Federation of Investment Funds and Companies (ECON)
EFIG........ Emission Factor and Inventory Group [*Environmental Protection Agency*] (AEPA)
EFII........ Electronics for Imaging [*NASDAQ symbol*] (SAG)
EFII........ Electronics for Imaging, Inc. [*Associated Press*] (SAG)
EFII........ I Salmi [*Finland*] [*ICAO location identifier*] (ICLI)
EFIK........ Kiikala [*Finland*] [*ICAO location identifier*] (ICLI)
EFIL........ European Federation for Intercultural Learning (EAIO)
EFIL........ Ilmajoki [*Finland*] [*ICAO location identifier*] (ICLI)
EFILA........ European Forum for Implementors of Library Applications (TELE)
EFILC........ Engineers Foreign Language Circle (SAUS)
EFILWC........ European Foundation for the Improvement of Living and Working Conditions (EURO)
EFI (M)........ Electronic Fuel Injection (Metering) [*Automotive engineering*]
EFIM........ Immola [*Finland*] [*ICAO location identifier*] (ICLI)
EFIN........ Environmental Financing Information Network [*Environmental Protection Agency*] (AEPA)
EFINS........ Enrico Fermi Institute for Nuclear Studies [*University of Chicago*]
EFIP........ European Federation of Interconnection and Packaging (SAUS)
EFIR........ Educational Fund for Individual Rights [*Defunct*] (EA)
EFIR........ European Flight Information Region (SAUS)
EFIRA........ Electric-Field-Induced Infrared Absorption (PDAA)
EFIRA Spectroscopy... Electric Field-induced Infrared Absorption Spectroscopy (SAUS)
Efird........ Efird's Reports [*45-56 South Carolina*] [*A publication*] (DLA)
EFIS........ Electronic Flight Information Systems [*FAA*] (TAG)
EFIS........ Electronic Flight Instrumentation System (SAUS)
EFIS........ Electronic Flight Instrument System
EFISC........ Enhanced Fast Instruction Set Computer (SAUS)
EFISGA........ England, France, Ireland, Scotland, Germany, and Aborigines [*See also TUPONA*] [*Suggested early name for Canada*]
EFISH........ Electric Field-Induced Second Harmonic Generation [*Physics*]
EFISHG........ Electric-Field-Induced Second-Harmonic Generation
EFISM........ Enhanced Footprint Improved Sensing Munition (ACAE)
EFISP........ Enrico Fermi International School of Physics (SAUS)
EFISS........ Empirical Foundations of Information and Software Sciences (SAUO)
EFIT........ Electronic Facial Identification Technique
EFIV........ Ivalo [*Finland*] [*ICAO location identifier*] (ICLI)
EFJC........ Europaische Foderation Junger Chore [*European Federation of Young Choirs*] (EAIO)
EFJG........ Educational Foundation for Jewish Girls [*Later, Jewish Foundation for Educationof Women*] (EA)
EFJM........ Jamijarvi [*Finland*] [*ICAO location identifier*] (ICLI)
EFJO........ Joensuu [*Finland*] [*ICAO location identifier*] (ICLI)
EFJP........ Jakalapaa [*Finland*] [*ICAO location identifier*] (ICLI)
EFJY........ Jyvaskyla [*Finland*] [*ICAO location identifier*] (ICLI)
EFK........ Newport [*Vermont*] [*Airport symbol*] (AD)
EFK........ Newport, VT [*Location identifier*] [*FAA*] (FAAL)
EFKA........ Kauhava [*Finland*] [*ICAO location identifier*] (ICLI)
EFKE........ Kemi [*Finland*] [*ICAO location identifier*] (ICLI)
EFKG........ Kumlinge [*Finland*] [*ICAO location identifier*] (ICLI)
EFKH........ Kuhmo [*Finland*] [*ICAO location identifier*] (ICLI)
EFKI........ Kajaani [*Finland*] [*ICAO location identifier*] (ICLI)
EFKJ........ Kauhajoki [*Finland*] [*ICAO location identifier*] (ICLI)
EFKK........ Kruunupyy [*Finland*] [*ICAO location identifier*] (ICLI)
EFKL........ Helsinki [*Finland*] [*ICAO location identifier*] (ICLI)
EFKM........ Kemijarvi [*Finland*] [*ICAO location identifier*] (ICLI)
EFKR........ Karsamaki [*Finland*] [*ICAO location identifier*] (ICLI)
EFKS........ Kuusamo [*Finland*] [*ICAO location identifier*] (ICLI)
EFKT........ Kittila [*Finland*] [*ICAO location identifier*] (ICLI)
EFKU........ Kuopio [*Finland*] [*ICAO location identifier*] (ICLI)
EFKV........ Kivijarvi [*Finland*] [*ICAO location identifier*] (ICLI)
EFKY........ Kymi [*Finland*] [*ICAO location identifier*] (ICLI)
EFL........ Argostolion [*Greece*] [*Airport symbol*] (OAG)
EFL........ Educational Facilities Laboratories [*Defunct*] (EA)
EFL........ Educational Facilities Laboratory (SAUS)
EFL........ Effective Focal Length [*Optics*]
EFL........ Effluent (MSA)
EFL........ Egptian Federation of Labour (SAUS)
E FL........ Ell, Flemish [*Unit of measure*] (ROG)
EFL........ Emerging Markets Floating Rate Fund [*NYSE symbol*] (SAG)
EFL........ Emitter Follower Logic [*Electronics*]
EFL........ Emitter-Function Logic (MED)
EFL........ Ending File Label (SAUS)
EFL........ Engineering Field Laboratory (SAUS)
EFL........ English as a First Language (SAUS)
EFL........ English as a Foreign Language
EFL........ Equivalent Focal Length [*Optics*]
EFL........ Error Frequency Limit [*Computer science*] (IAA)
EFL........ Explosion and Flame Laboratory [*British*] (IRUK)
EFL........ External Finance Limit
EFL........ Folkways (Ethnic Folkways Library) [*Record label*]
EFLA........ Educational Film Library Association (EA)
EFLA........ Education Film Library Association (SAUS)
EFLA........ Education for Librarianship - Australia [*A publication*]
EFLA........ European Foundation for Landscape Architecture [*EC*] (ECED)
EFLA........ Extended Four Letter Acronym (SAUS)
EFLA........ Vesivehmaa [*Finland*] [*ICAO location identifier*] (ICLI)
EFLA Bulletin... Educational Film Library Association Bulletin (journ.) (SAUS)
EFLAI........ Educational Film Library Association, Incorporated (SAUO)
EFLC........ Engineers Foreign Language Circle (PDAA)
EFLC........ European Foundation for Library Cooperation (TELE)
EF Length.... Equivalent Focal Length (SAUS)
EFLIC........ Educational Film Library Lending Committee (SAUS)
EFLIC........ Effective Legislation Committee (SAUS)
EFLIC........ Equity Funding Life Insurance Company (SAUO)
E Flip-Flop... Exclusive Flip-Flop (SAUS)
EFLM........ Extended Flight Line Maintenance (ACAE)
EFLO........ European Food Law Association (SAUO)
EFLOR........ Effloresce (ABBR)
EFLORD........ Effloresced (ABBR)
EFLORG........ Efflorescing (ABBR)
EFLORNC........ Efflorescence (ABBR)
EFLORT........ Efflorescent (ABBR)
EFLP........ Lappeenranta [*Finland*] [*ICAO location identifier*] (ICLI)
EFL Process... Emitter-Function-Logic Process (SAUS)
EFLU........ Effluent (ABBR)
EFL-UAR........ Egyptian Federation of Labor - United Arab Republic [*Obsolete*]
EFLUNC........ Effluence (ABBR)
EFLUVA........ Effluvia (ABBR)
EFLUVL........ Effluvial (ABBR)
EFLUVM........ Effluvium (ABBR)
EFLWC........ European Food Law Association (SAUO)
EFM........ Eight-Fourteen Modulation (SAUS)
EFM........ Eight to Fourteen Modulation (IAA)
EFM........ Electric Field Meter
EFM........ electronical fetal monitoring (SAUS)
EFM........ Electronic Fetal Monitor (ADWA)
EFM........ Electronic Fetal Monitoring [*Medicine*]
efm........ electronic fuel management (SAUS)
EFM........ Electronic Fuel Metering [*Automotive engineering*]
EFM........ Electronics for Medicine
EFM........ Engineer Field Manual (SAUS)
EFM........ Engineering Feasibility Model (MCD)
EFM........ Enhanced Fighter Maneuverability (MCD)
EFM........ Epifluorescence Microscopy
EFM........ European Federalist Movement
EFM........ Evangelistic Faith Missions (EA)
EFM........ Expeditionary Force Message [*Low-rate cable or radio message selected from a list of standard wordings*]
EFM........ Explosives Factory Maribyrnong (SAUS)
EFM........ Extended Flygare Method (SAUS)
EFM........ Extensive Field Maintenance [*Military*] (NG)

EFM .... External Fetal Monitoring [*Obstetrics*] (DAVI)
EFM .... Palm Beach Junior College, Lake Worth, FL [*OCLC symbol*] (OCLC)
EFMA .... Emergency Farm Mortgage Act of 1933
EFMA .... European Fertilizer Manufacturers Association (EAIO)
EFMA .... European Financial Management and Marketing Association (EAIO)
EFMA .... European Fittings Manufacturers Association (EAIO)
EFMA .... Evangelical Fellowship of Mission Agencies (EA)
EFMA .... Evangelical Foreign Missions Association (EA)
EFMA .... Mariehamn [*Finland*] [*ICAO location identifier*] (ICLI)
EFMB .... Expert Field Medical Badge [*Military decoration*] (AABC)
EFMC .... Educators Fund Management Corporation (SAUO)
EFMC .... E for M Corp. [*NASDAQ symbol*] (SAG)
EFMC .... Elastic Fabric Manufacturers Council of the Northern Textile Association
EFMC .... European Federation for Medicinal Chemistry (SAUS)
EFMC .... European Federation for/of Medical Chemistry (SAUO)
EFMC .... European Federation of Medical Chemistry (SAUS)
EFMC .... European Federation of Medicinal Chemistry (EAIO)
EFMC-ISMC ... EFMC International Symposium on Medicinal Chemistry (SAUO)
EFMCNTA .... Elastic Fabric Manufacturers Council of the Northern Textile Association (EA)
EFMD .... European Foundation for Management Development (EAIO)
EFME .... Menkijarvi [*Finland*] [*ICAO location identifier*] (ICLI)
EFMF .... Environmental Fluid Mechanics Foundation [*Monash University*] [*Australia*]
EFMG .... Electric Fuse Manufacturers Guild [*Defunct*] (EA)
EFMI .... Elastic Fabric Manufacturers Institute [*Later, EFMC or EFMCNTA*] (EA)
EFMI .... European Federation for Medical Informatics (EAIO)
EFMI .... European Federation for/of Medical Information (SAUO)
EFMI .... Mikkeli [*Finland*] [*ICAO location identifier*] (ICLI)
EFMK .... European Federation of Masseurs-Kinesitherapeutes (SAUO)
EFMLS .... Eastern Federation of Mineralogical and Lapidary Societies (SAUO)
EFMM .... Education for Mission and Ministry (SAUS)
EFMO .... Effigy Mounds National Monument
EFMO .... European Foundation for Management Development (SAUO)
EFMP .... Emergency Food and Medical Program
EFMP .... Exceptional Family Member Program [*Army*] (INF)
EFMP .... Extended File Management Package (ACAE)
EFMS .... Eucharistic Franciscan Missionary Sisters (TOCD)
EFMS .... Experimental Flight Management System [*Aviation*] (DA)
EFMV .... estimated fair market value (SAUS)
EFN .... Euro-American Financial [*Vancouver Stock Exchange symbol*]
EFN .... European Federation of Naturopaths (SAUO)
EFN .... Extrafloral Nectary [*Botany*]
EFN .... Palm Beach Junior College, North Campus Library, Lake Worth, FL [*OCLC symbol*] (OCLC)
EFNCP .... European Forum on Nature Conservation and Pastoralism (SAUS)
EFNEA .... European Federation of National Engieering Associations (SAUO)
EFNEP .... Expanded Food and Nutrition Education Program [*Department of Agriculture*]
EF-Net .... Eris Free Net (SAUS)
EFNIR .... Exhibition/Festival for New Instrumental Resources (SAUS)
EFNMS .... European Federation of National Maintenance Societies [*Sweden*]
EFNRA .... Educational Foundation of the National Restaurant Association (EA)
EFNS .... Educational Foundation for Nuclear Science (EA)
EFNSW .... Esperanto Federation of New South Wales [*Australia*]
EFNT .... Efficient Networks [*NASDAQ symbol*] (SG)
EFNU .... Nummela [*Finland*] [*ICAO location identifier*] (ICLI)
EFO .... East Fork, AK [*Location identifier*] [*FAA*] (FAAL)
EFO .... EIFEL Follow-On (SAUS)
EFO .... Electronic Flame-Off (AAEL)
EFO .... Electronic Functions Objective (TIMI)
EFO .... Engineers Foundation of Ohio (SAUO)
EFO .... Equivalent Field Office [*Environmental Protection Agency*] (EPAT)
EFO .... Error, Freak, Oddity
EFOA .... European Fuel Oxygenates Association (EAIO)
EFOCC .... Errors, Freaks and Oddities Collector's Club (EA)
EFOC/LAN .... European Fiber Optic Communications and Local Area Network Exposition [*Information Gatekeepers, Inc.*]
EFOCS .... Evanescent Fiber Optic Chemical Sensor (AAEL)
EFOGM .... Enhanced Fiber-Optic-Guided Missiles [*DoD*]
EFOMP .... European Federation of Organizations for Medical Physics [*EC*] (ECED)
EFONX .... Evergreen Foundation Cl.Y [*Mutual fund ticker symbol*] (SG)
EFOP .... Economic Feasibility of Projects (SAUS)
EFOP .... Economic Feasibility of Projects and Investments
EFOP .... Expanded Function Operator Panel (MHDB)
EFOP .... Oripaa [*Finland*] [*ICAO location identifier*] (ICLI)
EFOR .... Equivalent Forced Outage Rate (IEEE)
EFOR .... experimental fast oxide reactor (SAUS)
EFOR .... Oritkari [*Finland*] [*ICAO location identifier*] (ICLI)
E-FORM .... Electronic Form (SAUS)
e-forms .... Electronic-Forms (CDE)
EFOs .... errors, freaks, and oddities (SAUS)
EFOSS .... Engineer Family of Systems Study (MCD)
EFOU .... Oulu [*Finland*] [*ICAO location identifier*] (ICLI)
EFOV .... Effective Field of View (SAUS)
EFP .... Economical File Processing (SAUS)
EFP .... Effective Filtration Pressure [*Physiology*]
EFP .... Electric Fire Pump [*Nuclear energy*] (NRCH)
EFP .... Electric Fuel Propulsion (SAUS)
EFP .... Electrofluid Dynamic Process (SAUS)
EFP .... Electronic Field Production (IEEE)
EFP .... Emergency Firing Panel
EFP .... End Forming Press
efp .... end of flight plan (SAUS)
EFP .... Endoneurial Fluid Pressure (PDAA)
EFP .... Enhanced Flux Pinning (SAUS)
EFP .... Enrico Fermi Power Plant (SAUS)
EFP .... Error-Free Performance
EFP .... ESA [*European Space Agency*] Furnished Property
EFP .... Escaped Federal Prisoner
EFP .... Europaeische Foederalistische Partei [*European Federalist Party*] [*Austria*] (PPE)
EFP .... European Federation of Parasitologists (EAIO)
EFP .... European Federation of Periodontology (SAUS)
EFP .... European Federation of Purchasing (PDAA)
EFP .... Exchange for Physicals [*Commodities exchange*]
EFP .... Expanded Function operator Panel (SAUS)
EFP .... Explosively-Formed Penetrator [*Army*] (RDA)
EFP .... Explosively Formed Plate
EFP .... Explosively Formed Projectile [*Military*] (MUSM)
EFP .... Einstein-Fokker-Planck [*Mathematics*] (ODA)
EFPA .... Educational Film Producers Association (SAUO)
EFPA .... European Federation for the Protection of Waters (SAUO)
EFPA .... European Food Phosphates Producers' Association (EAIO)
EFPA .... European Food Service and Packaging Association [*British*] (EAIO)
EFPB .... Employers Federation of Papermakers and Boardmakers (SAUO)
EFPC .... East Fork Poplar Creek (SAUS)
EFPD .... Effective Full Power Day (KSC)
EFPD .... Equivalent Full Power Day (SAUS)
EFPE .... Pello [*Finland*] [*ICAO location identifier*] (ICLI)
EFPH .... Equivalent Full Power Hour [*FCC*]
EFPH .... Evaluating Fallout Protection in Homes [*Later, HFPS*] [*Civil Defense*]
EFPI .... Council of Educational Facility Planners International (SAUO)
EFPI .... Essential Fuzzy Prime Implicant (SAUS)
EFPI .... European Federation of the Plywood Industry (EA)
EFPI .... Piikajarvi [*Finland*] [*ICAO location identifier*] (ICLI)
EFPIA .... European Federation of Pharmaceutical Industries' Associations (EA)
EFPK .... Pieksamaki [*Finland*] [*ICAO location identifier*] (ICLI)
EFPL .... English and Foreign Philosophical Library [*A publication*]
EFPM .... Effective Full Power Month (NRCH)
EFPM .... Employers' Federation of Paper Makers (DGA)
EFPO .... Pori [*Finland*] [*ICAO location identifier*] (ICLI)
EFPPA .... European Federation of Professional Psychologists Associations (EA)
EFPROUT ..... Effecting Promotion, Procedure Outlined [*Military*] (DNAB)
EFPS .... European Federation of Productivity Services [*Stockholm, Sweden*] (EA)
EFPS .... Rovaniemi [*Finland*] [*ICAO location identifier*] (ICLI)
EFPU .... Pudasjarvi [*Finland*] [*ICAO location identifier*] (ICLI)
EFPV .... Eisenhower Foundation for the Prevention of Violence [*Later, Milton S. Eisenhower Federation*] (EA)
EFPW .... European Federation for the Protection of Waters
EFPWCM ...... European Federation of Pallet and Wooden Crate Manufacturers (EA)
EFPY .... Effective Full-Power Years (NRCH)
EFPY .... Pyhasalmi [*Finland*] [*ICAO location identifier*] (ICLI)
EFPZ .... Export Free Processing Zone
EFQ .... Estimated fuel quantity consumed (SAUS)
EFQFFM .... European Federation of Quick Frozen Food Manufacturers [*Belgium*] (EAIO)
EFQM .... European Foundation for Quality Management (EURO)
EFR .... Echo Free Room
EFR .... Effective Filtration Rate [*Physiology*]
EFR .... Efficient Food Service Response (GART)
EFR .... Electro-Flux Remelting [*Metal industry*]
EFR .... Electronic Failure Report
EFR .... electronic film recording (SAUS)
EFR .... Elf Air Ltd. [*Russian Federation*] [*ICAO designator*] (FAAC)
E FR .... Ell, French [*Unit of measure*] (ROG)
EFR .... Elliott Forbes-Robinson [*Race car driver*]
EFR .... Emergency Fund Request
EFR .... Emerging Flux Region (OA)
EFR .... Engine Firing Rate (NVT)
EFR .... Engine Flat Rate
EFR .... Enhanced Full Rate (SAUS)
EFR .... Entrained-Flow Reactor [*Chemical engineering*]
EFR .... Environmental Flow Requirements of Australia's Waterways (EERA)
EFR .... Equipment Failure Rate
EFR .... Equipment Failure Reporting (TIMI)
EFR .... European Fast Reactor [*Physics*]
EFR .... Exact Finite Range
EFR .... Expect Further Routing [*Aviation*] (FAAC)
EFR .... Extended-Field Radiotherapy [*Radiology*]
EFR .... External Function Request (SAUS)
EFRA .... Electronic Forms Routing and Approval (SAUS)
EFRA .... Electronic forms, routing, and authorization (SAUS)
EFRA .... Rautavaara [*Finland*] [*ICAO location identifier*] (ICLI)
EFRAG .... Red Blood Cell Fragility [*Test*] [*Hematoloy*] (DAVI)
EFRAP .... Electronic Feeder Route Analysis Program (SAUS)
EFRAP .... Exchange Feeder Route Analysis Program [*Bell System*]
EFRAPS .... Extracted Feature Rectification and Processing System (SAUS)
EFRC .... Education Funding Research Council (EA)
EFRC .... Edwards Flight Research Center [*NASA*]
EFRH .... Pattijoki [*Finland*] [*ICAO location identifier*] (ICLI)
EFris .... East Frisian (ADWA)
EFRIS .... External Finished Reports Information Subsystem [*Computer science*]
EFRN .... Rantasalmi [*Finland*] [*ICAO location identifier*] (ICLI)

EFRNT .... Effrontery (ABBR)
EFRO .... Electronic Failure Report Only
EFRO .... Rovaniemi Airport [*Finland*] [*ICAO location identifier*] (ICLI)
EFRP........... European Federation for Retirement Provision (ECON)
EFRR .... Effingham Railroad [*Federal Railroad Administration identification code*]
EFRT........... Effort (ABBR)
EFRT........... European Federation of Retail Traders [*Belgium*] (EAIO)
EFRT........... External Floating Roof Tank [*Engineering*]
EFRTLS........ Effortless (ABBR)
EFRTLSNS ... Effortlessness (ABBR)
EFRTLSY...... Effortlessly (ABBR)
EFRV........... Kiuruvesi [*Finland*] [*ICAO location identifier*] (ICLI)
EFRVS .... Effervesce (ABBR)
EFRVSD ...... Effervesced (ABBR)
EFRVSG ...... Effervescing (ABBR)
EFRVSNC..... Effervescence (ABBR)
EFRVST....... Effervescent (ABBR)
EFRY........... Rayskala [*Finland*] [*ICAO location identifier*] (ICLI)
EFS .... Earth-Fixed System
efs .... economic farm surplus (SAUS)
EFS .... Edinburgh Festival Society (SAUO)
EFS .... Effective Field Stimulation [*Medicine*] (EDAA)
EFS .... Effective Fighting Strength (SAUS)
EFS .... Electric Field-Induced Spectra
EFS .... Electric Field Strength
EFS .... Electric Front Seats [*Automotive classified advertising*]
EFS .... Electronic Filing System (SAUS)
EFS .... Electronic Financial Services (GART)
EFS .... Electronic Firing Switch (SAUS)
EFS .... Electronic Firing Switches [*Military*] (NG)
EFS .... Electronic Frequency Selection (IEEE)
EFS .... Electronic Frontier Society (SAUO)
EFS .... Electronic Funds Services (GOBB)
EFS .... Emergency Feeding Service [*Civil Defense*]
EFS .... Emergency Feedwater System [*Nuclear energy*] (NRCH)
EFS .... Encrypted/Enterprise File System (SAUS)
EFS .... Encrypted File System (SAUS)
EFS .... Encrypted (or Encrypting) File System (SAUS)
EFS .... Encrypting File System [*Computer science*]
EFS .... End File Statement (SAUS)
EFS .... End of Frame Sequence [*Telecommunications*] (ACRL)
EFS .... Enhanced Flight Screener (SAUS)
EFS .... Enhanced Flight Screening (DOMA)
EFS .... Enhance Financial Services Group [*NYSE symbol*] (SAG)
EFS .... Enterprise File System (SAUS)
efs .... equivalent standard fillet (SAUS)
EFS .... Error Free Seconds (TEL)
EFS .... Europe Falcon Service [*France*] [*ICAO designator*] (FAAC)
EFS .... Event Free Survival [*Medicine*]
EFS .... Exchange of Futures for Swap [*Investment term*] (NUMA)
EFS .... Experimental Firing Ship
EFS .... Export Facilitation Scheme [*Motor vehicles*] [*Australia*]
EFS .... Extended Feature Supplements (SAUS)
EFS .... External File System (BYTE)
EFS .... External Function Store [*Computer science*] (ELAL)
EFS .... Extrafield Sensitivity [*Photonics*]
EFSA........... England Football Supporters Association (DBA)
EFSA........... European Federation of Sea Anglers (EAIO)
EFSA........... Savonlinna [*Finland*] [*ICAO location identifier*] (ICLI)
EFSE .... Engineering Factory Support Equipment (SAA)
EFSE .... Selanpaa [*Finland*] [*ICAO location identifier*] (ICLI)
EFSEC......... Energy Facility Site Evaluation Council (SAUO)
EFSG........... European Federation of Serials Groups (SAUO)
EFSG........... European Fire and Security Group, Loss Prevention Certification Board (SAUS)
EFSH........... Equine Follicle Stimulating Hormone [*Endocrinology*]
EFSIM......... Explosive Foam Shock Initiation Model (SAUS)
EFSJ............ Sonkajarvi-Jyrkka [*Finland*] [*ICAO location identifier*] (ICLI)
EFSM .... Extended Finite-State Machine (SAUS)
EFSO........... Sodankyla [*Finland*] [*ICAO location identifier*] (ICLI)
EFSORPA..... Elliptic Function Second-Order Ripple Phase Approximation
EFSP........... Electrolytic Fused-Salt Process
EFSP........... Electronic Family Security Program [*of Sun Life Assurance Co. of Canada*]
EFSP........... Emergency Food and Shelter Program [*FEMA*]
EFSR........... Electronic Field Seaman Recruit [*Military*] (IAA)
EFSS........... E. F. Schumacher Society (EA)
EFSS........... Emergency Food Supply Scheme [*World Food Program*]
EFSS........... Experimental Flight Systems Section [*Langley*]
EFSSS......... Engine Failure Sensing and Shutdown System [*NASA*] (KSC)
EFST .... Essential Fire Support Task [*Army*]
EFSU........... Suomussalmi [*Finland*] [*ICAO location identifier*] (ICLI)
EFSUMB ..... European Federation for the Study of Ultrasound in Medicine and Biology (SAUO)
EFSUMB ..... European Federation of Societies of Ultrasound in Medicine and Biology (EAIO)
EFT .... Earliest Finish Time (SAUS)
EFT .... Early Finish Time
EFT .... Effect (MSA)
EFT .... Efficient File Treatment (SAUS)
EFT .... Electrical Fast Transient (SAUS)
EFT .... Electronic Funds Transfer [*Banking*]
EFT .... Electronic Fund Tape [*Banking*]
EFT .... Electrostatically Focused Tube
EFT .... Embedded Figures Test [*Psychology*]
EFT .... Emergency Flight Termination (AFM)
EFT .... Engineering Feasibility Test (CAAL)
EFT .... Engineering Field Test (SAUS)
EFT .... Engineering Flight Test
EFT .... Enhanced File Transfer (SAUS)
EFT .... Enhanced Forecaster Tools [*Forecast Systems Laboratory*] [*Branch*] (USDC)
EFT .... Eno Foundation for Transportation (EA)
EFT .... Erythrocyte Fragility Test [*Medicine*] (MELL)
EFT .... Essential-Familial Tremor [*Medicine*] (MELL)
EFT .... Etchingham Family Tree (EA)
EFT .... Euro File Transfer (SAUS)
EFT .... European File Transfer (SAUS)
EFT .... Experimental Flight Test
EFT .... External Function Translator
EFT .... Oklahoma Executive Jet Charter, Inc. [*FAA designator*] (FAAC)
EFTA........... Economic Recovery Tax Act of 1981 (EBF)
EFTA........... Effectuate (ABBR)
EFTA........... Electronic Funds Transfer Association [*Washington, DC*] (EA)
EFTA........... Electronic Fund Transfer Act [*1978*]
EFTA........... Enrolled Federal Tax Accountant [*EFTA Institute*] [*Designation awarded by*]
EFTA........... ERADCOM [*Electronics Research and Development Command*] Flight Test Activity
EFTA........... European Fair Trade Association [*Netherlands*] (EAIO)
EFTA........... European Flexographic Technical Association (PDAA)
EFTA........... European Foreign Trade Association
EFTA........... European Free Trade Agreement (SAUO)
EFTA........... European Free Trade Area (DS)
EFTA........... European Free Trade Association (EERA)
EFTAD......... Effectuated (ABBR)
EFTAG......... Effecting (ABBR)
EFTAM......... Electronic File Transfer Access Method (VLIE)
EFTAPA....... European Free Trade Association-Plastics Association (SAUS)
EFTA-TUC.... Trade Union Committe for the European Free Trade Area (SAUO)
EFTC........... Edwards Flight Test Center [*NASA*]
EFTC........... EFTC Corp. [*NASDAQ symbol*] (NASQ)
EFTC........... Electrical Fair Trading Council (SAUO)
EFTC........... Electronic Fab Technology [*NASDAQ symbol*] (SAG)
EFTC........... Elementary Flying Training College [*British*]
EFTC........... European Fluorocarbon Technical Committee [*of the European Council of Chemical Manufacturers' Federations*] [*Belgium*] (EAIO)
EFTC........... European Freight Timetable Conference (EAIO)
EFTCBFC..... Elvis Forever TCB [*Taking Care of Business*] Fan Club (EA)
EFTD........... Economic, Financial and Transit Department (SAUO)
E/FTE.......... Eject/Fail to Eject (ACAE)
EFTE........... Tervola [*Finland*] [*ICAO location identifier*] (ICLI)
EFTEC......... European Fluorocarbon Technical Committee [*of the European Council of Chemical Manufacturers' Federations*] (EAIO)
EFTEM......... Energy-Filtering Transmission Electron Microscopy (SAUS)
EF Thread.... Extra Fine Thread (SAUS)
EFTI............ Engineering Flight Test Inspector
EFTI............ Engineering Flight Test Instrumentation (AAG)
EFTIR.......... Emission Fourier Transform Infrared Spectroscopy (AAEL)
EFTL............ Effectual (ABBR)
EFTMI.......... European Federation for Medical Informatics (SAUO)
EFTO........... Encrypted for Transmission Only
EFTO........... Encrypted for Transmission Overseas (MCD)
EFTO........... Encrypt for Transmission Only [*Military*]
EFTP........... Easy File Transfer Protocol (SAUS)
EFTP........... Error File Teaching Package (NITA)
EFTP........... Ethernet File Transfer Protocol (SAUS)
EFTP........... Tampere-Pirkkala [*Finland*] [*ICAO location identifier*] (ICLI)
EFTPOB....... Electronic Funds Transfer at Point of Banking
EFTPOS....... Electronic Funds Transfer at Point of Sale
EFTPoS....... Electronic Funds Transfer at Point of Sales (EERA)
EFT POS...... Electronic Funds Transfer initiated at Point of Sale (SAUS)
EFTPS......... Electronic Federal Tax Payment System (VLIE)
EFTR........... Engineering Flight Test Report
EFTR........... Ethernet Frequency Translator (SAUS)
EFTRO......... European Federation of Tobacco Retail Organizations (EAIO)
EFTS........... Electronic Funds Transfer Service (SAUS)
EFTS........... Electronic Funds Transfer System [*or Service*] [*Banking*] [*National Science Foundation*]
EFTS........... Elementary Flying Training School [*British*]
EFT's.......... Expanded Field [*Prism*] Telescopes [*Instrumentation*]
EFTS........... Teisko [*Finland*] [*ICAO location identifier*] (ICLI)
EFTSU......... Equivalent Full-Time Student Unit
EFTTA......... European Fishing Tackle Trade Association (EAIO)
EFTU........... Engineering & Fastener Trade Union (WDAA)
EFTU........... Turku [*Finland*] [*ICAO location identifier*] (ICLI)
EFTUNMW... European Federation of Trade Unions of Non-Manual Workers [*Belgium*] (EY)
EFTV........... Effectivity
EFTVNS....... Effectiveness (ABBR)
EFTVY......... Effectively (ABBR)
EFU............ Eastern Enterprises [*NYSE symbol*] (SPSG)
EFU............ Eastern Gas & Fuel Associates (SAUO)
EFU............ Edit Follow-up (SAUS)
efu............. environmental force unit (SAUS)
EFU............ Equivalent Fatality Unit [*National Highway Traffic Safety Administration*]
EFU............ Europaische Frauen Union [*Austria*] (EAIO)

EFU .... European Film Union (SAUO)
EFU .... European Forecast Unit (SAUS)
EFU .... Evaluation and Follow-Up [*Medicine*] (MELL)
EFULG .... Effulgent (ABBR)
EFULGNC ..... Effulgence (ABBR)
EFUS .... Effuse (ABBR)
EFUSD .... Effused (ABBR)
EFUSG .... Effusing (ABBR)
EFUSN .... Effusion (ABBR)
EFUSV .... Effusive (ABBR)
EFUSVNS ..... Effusiveness (ABBR)
EFUSVY ...... Effusively (ABBR)
EFUT .... Utti [*Finland*] [*ICAO location identifier*] (ICLI)
EFUV .... Extreme And Far Ultraviolet (SAUS)
EFV .... Electric Field Vector
EFV .... Epilepsy Foundation of Victoria [*Australia*]
EFV .... Equestrian Federation of Victoria [*Australia*]
EFV .... Equilibrium Flash Vaporization (PDAA)
EFV .... Excess Flow Valve
EFV .... Extracellular Fluid Volume [*Physiology*]
EFVA .... Educational Foundation for Visual Aids (SAUS)
EFVA .... Educational Foundation for Visual Arts [*British*]
EFVA .... European Federation of Vending Associations (EA)
EFVA .... European Foundation for Visual Aids (SAUO)
EFVA .... Vaasa [*Finland*] [*ICAO location identifier*] (ICLI)
EFV-Analyse... equilibrium flash vaporisation analysis (SAUS)
EFVC .... Expiratory Flow-Volume Curve [*Medicine*]
EFVI .... Viitasaari [*Finland*] [*ICAO location identifier*] (ICLI)
EFVL .... Vaala [*Finland*] [*ICAO location identifier*] (ICLI)
EFVP .... El Salvador Film and Video Projects [*Later, El Salvadore Media Projects*] (EA)
EFVR .... Varkaus [*Finland*] [*ICAO location identifier*] (ICLI)
EFVS .... Electronic Fighting Vehicle System [*Army*]
EFVU .... Vuotso [*Finland*] [*ICAO location identifier*] (ICLI)
EFW .... Effective Fall-out Wind (SAUS)
EFW .... effective line width (SAUS)
EFW .... Electric Field and Waves
EFW .... Emergency Feedwater [*System*] [*Nuclear energy*] (NRCH)
EFW .... Energy from Waste Program (SAUS)
EFW .... Estimated Fetal Weight [*Obstetrics*] (DAVI)
EFW .... Executive Financial Woman [*National Association of Bank Women*] [*A publication*]
EFW .... Jefferson, IA [*Location identifier*] [*FAA*] (FAAL)
EFW .... Electric Front Windows (ODA)
EFWA .... Eastern Farmworkers Association (SAUO)
EFWB .... Wredeby [*Finland*] [*ICAO location identifier*] (ICLI)
EF/WM .... Ejection Fraction/Wall Motion [*Medicine*] (EDAA)
EFWRC .... Engineering Foundation Welding Research Council (SAUO)
EFWS .... Emergency Feedwater System [*Nuclear energy*] (NRCH)
EFWS .... Evaluation of Foreign Weapons Systems (MCD)
EFWST .... Emergency Feedwater Storage Tank [*Nuclear energy*] (NRCH)
EFW/TS .... Energy from Waste Transfer Station (SAUS)
EFX .... Equifax, Inc. [*Formerly, Retail Credit Co.*] [*NYSE symbol*] (SPSG)
EFX .... Special Effects (NTCM)
EFY .... End of Fiscal Year (AFM)
EFYC .... European Federation of Young Choirs [*See also EFJC*] (EA)
EFYL .... Ylivieska-Raudaskyla [*Finland*] [*ICAO location identifier*] (ICLI)
EFZ .... Electronic Final Zero
EFZ .... Exclusive Fishing Zone
EFZ .... Extended Fisheries Zone (SAUS)
EG .... Early Gate (ACAE)
EG .... Earth Gate (ACAE)
EG .... Eaves Gutter (SAUS)
EG .... Ecological Genetics (SAUS)
EG .... Economic Geography [*A publication*] (BRI)
EG .... Economic Growth (SAUO)
EG .... Economics and Government [*Office of Management and Budget*]
EG .... Edge Grain
eg .... Edges Gilt [*Bookbinding*] (BARN)
Eg .... Egidius de Fuscarariis [*Deceased, 1289*] [*Authority cited in pre-1607 legal work*] (DSA)
Eg .... Egwene (SAUS)
EG .... Egypt [*ANSI two-letter standard code*] (CNC)
Eg .... Egypt (SHCU)
Eg .... Egyptian (ADWA)
EG .... Egyptian (ROG)
EG .... Ejusdem Generis [*Of the Same Kind*] [*Latin*]
EG .... Electric Generator (SAUS)
E(G) .... Electrician (General) [*U.S. Navy enlisted rating*] (AUER)
eg .... electrogalvanized (SAUS)
EG .... Electrogalvanizing [*Automotive engineering*]
EG .... Electrographic (SAUS)
EG .... Electron Gas (SAUS)
EG .... Electron Gun (OA)
EG .... Electronic Guidance (AAG)
EG .... Else Good [*In good condition except for defects mentioned*] [*Antiquarian book trade*]
EG .... Emergency Generator (NRCH)
EG .... Emergency Generator Room [*NFPA pre-fire planning symbol*] (NFPA)
EG .... Emergency Grade [*Automotive engineering*] [*Polymer Steel Corp.*]
EG .... Employment Guide (CAAL)
EG .... Enamel Glass (SAUS)
EG .... Enamel Single Glass [*Wire insulation*] (IAA)
EG .... End Group (VLIE)
EG .... Endoglucanases [*An enzyme*]
EG .... Engelbert's "Goils" [*An association*] (EA)
EG .... Engineering Geologist
EG .... Engineering Geology (SAUS)
EG .... Engineers Guild (SAUS)
EG .... Engine Generator (SAUS)
E/G .... Engine-Generator
EG .... enhanced gold (SAUS)
EG .... Enteric Ganglion [*Neurology*]
EG .... Enteroglucagon (DB)
EG .... Entry Guidance [*NASA*] (NASA)
EG .... Envelope Generator (SAUS)
EG .... Environment Generator [*Computer software*]
EG .... Enziklopedyah Shel Galuyot (BJA)
EG .... Eosinophilic Granuloma [*Medicine*]
eg .... Equatorial Guinea [*MARC country of publication code*] [*Library of Congress*] (LCCP)
EG .... Equatorial Guinea (MILB)
EG .... Equipment Ground (SAUS)
EG .... Erb-Goldflam [*Disease*] [*Medicine*] (DB)
eg .... erythrocyte ghost (SAUS)
EG .... Escort Group
EG .... Esophagogastrectomy [*Medicine*]
EG .... Esquerra Gallega [*Galician Left*] [*Political party*] (PPW)
EG .... Estate Gazette [*A publication*] (DLA)
EG .... Estrogen Gel [*Medicine*] (MELL)
EG .... Estrone Glucuronide [*Endocrinology*]
EG .... Ethylene Glycol [*Organic chemistry*]
EG .... European Greens [*Brussels, Belgium*] Political party] (EAIO)
EG .... Evil Grin [*Slang*] (VERA)
EG .... Execution Guidance (SAUS)
EG .... Executive Generator
EG .... Exempli Gratia [*For Example*] [*Latin*]
EG .... Exfoliation Glaucoma [*Medicine*] (MELL)
EG .... Ex Grege [*Among the Rest*] [*Latin*]
EG .... Existential Generalization [*Rule of quantification*] [*Logic*]
EG .... Expenditure Greater Than [*Dialog*] [*Searchable field*] [*Information service or system*] (NITA)
EG .... Experimental Assistant, Gunnery [*British military*] (DMA)
EG .... Experimental Glider
EG .... Experimental Group
EG .... Expert Gunner [*Army*]
EG .... Experts Group (VLIE)
EG .... Exploration Geochemist (SAUS)
EG .... Exploration Geochemistry (SAUS)
EG .... Exploration Geophysicist (SAUS)
EG .... Exploration Geophysics (SAUS)
EG .... Exploratory Group (NATG)
EG .... External Declaration (SAUS)
EG .... External Genitalia [*Medicine*] (DAVI)
eg .... For Example [*Exempli Gratia*] [*Latin*] (WDMC)
eg .... for instance (SAUS)
EG .... Grid Voltage (SAUS)
EG .... Roederer Aviation [*ICAO designator*] (AD)
EGA .... Agnes Scott College, Decatur, GA [*OCLC symbol*] (OCLC)
EGA .... Die Entwicklung der Glyptik Waehrend der Akkad-Zeit [*A publication*] (BJA)
EGA .... East German Army (CINC)
EGA .... Ecuato Guineana de Aviacion [*Equatorial Guinea*] [*ICAO designator*] (FAAC)
EGA .... Edge Gradient Analysis
EGA .... Efferent Glomerular Arteriole [*Medicine*] (MELL)
EGA .... Effluent [*or Evolved*] Gas Analysis
EGA .... Electric Generation Association (NTPA)
EGA .... Elizabeth Garrett Anderson Hospital [*British*] (DI)
EGA .... Embroiderers' Guild of America (EA)
EGA .... Eminent Grand Almoner [*Freemasonry*] (ROG)
EGA .... End Game Analysis
EGA .... Engineering and Grant Administration (SAUO)
EGA .... Engineering Assistant
EGA .... enhanced graphics (SAUS)
EGA .... Enhanced Graphics Adapter [*Computer technology*]
EGA .... Enhanced Graphics Array (ADWA)
EGA .... Environmental Governance in Asia (SAUO)
EGA .... Environment Generation & Analysis (SAUS)
EGA .... Equato-Guinean de Aviacion [*Airline*] [*Equatorial Guinea*]
EGA .... Estimated Gestational Age
EGA .... Ethics in Government Act (SAUS)
EGA .... Ethylglycolacetate (SAUS)
EGA .... Evolved Gas Analysis [*Chemistry*]
EGA .... Exhaust Gas Analyzer (MCD)
EGA .... Export Guarantees Act
EGA .... Extended Graphics Adapter (SAUS)
EGA .... Extended Graphics Array [*Computer science*] (EERA)
EGA .... Extragalactic Astronomy (SAUS)
EGA .... European Golf Association (ODA)
EGAA .... Belfast/Aldergrove [*British*] [*ICAO location identifier*] (ICLI)
EGAA .... Emergency General Account of Advances
EGAA .... Enhanced Graphics Acquisition and Analysis [*Computer science*]
EGAAE .... European Group of Artists of the Ardennes and the Eifel (EAIO)
EGAB .... Enniskillen/St. Angelo [*British*] [*ICAO location identifier*] (ICLI)
EGAC .... Belfast Harbour [*British*] [*ICAO location identifier*] (ICLI)
EGAC .... Egyptian Accreditation Council (SAUS)
EGA/CGA ..... Enhanced Graphics Adapter/Color Graphics Adapter (SAUS)
EGACT .... Embroiderers' Guild of the Australian Capital Territory
EGAD .... Electric Power Generation and Distribution (MCD)

EGAD .... Electromagnetic Gas Detector (SAUS)
EGAD .... Electronegative Gas Detector
EGAD .... Electronic Ground Automatic Destruct [*Air Force*]
EGAD .... Newtownards [*British*] [*ICAO location identifier*] (ICLI)
EGADS .... Electronic Ground Automatic Destruct Sequencer [*Air Force*]
EGAE .... Londonderry/Eglinton [*British*] [*ICAO location identifier*] (ICLI)
EGAF .... East German Air Force (SAUO)
EGAL .... Egalitarian
EGAL .... Elevation Guidance for Approach and Landing [*Aviation*]
EGAL .... Langford Lodge [*British*] [*ICAO location identifier*] (ICLI)
EGALSM .... Egalitarianism (ABBR)
EGALTR .... Egalitarian (ABBR)
EGALTRM .... Egalitarianism (ABBR)
EGA/MDA .... Enhanced Graphics Adapter/Monochrome Display Adapter (SAUS)
EGAMS .... Evolved Gas Analysis Mass Spectrometry (MCD)
Egan Bills .... Egan. Bills of Sale [*4th ed.*] [*1882*] [*A publication*] (DLA)
EG & G .... Edgerton, Germeshausen & Grier (SAUS)
EG&G .... Edgerton, Germeshausen and Grier Corp. (SAUO)
EG&G .... Edgerton, Germeshauser, and Greer (SAUS)
EG&G .... EG&G Idaho, Inc. (SAUO)
EG&G/ID .... EG&G Idaho, Inc. (GAAI)
EG&GRF .... EG&G Rocky Flats, Inc. (SAUO)
EG&G-STL .... EG&G-Special Technology Laboratory (SAUO)
EGAO .... Encyclopedia of Governmental Advisory Organizations [*A publication*]
EGAP .... End Game Analysis Program (MCD)
EGARD .... Environmental Gammaray and Radon Detector (ODA)
EGAS .... Eastern Gas (SAUS)
EGAS .... Educational Grants Advisory Service (AIE)
EGAS .... Energas Co. (MHDW)
EGAS .... Energy Search [*NASDAQ symbol*] (SG)
EGAS .... European Group for Atomic Spectroscopy (EAIO)
EGASCAC .... Educational Guidance Associates School and College Advisory Center [*Formerly, SCAC*] (EA)
EGAT .... Educational Goal Attainment Tests (STED)
EGATS .... EUROCONTROL Guild of Air Traffic Controllers (SAUS)
EGATS .... Eurocontrol Guild of Air Traffic Services (SAUO)
EGB .... Eastern Gas Board (SAUS)
Egb .... Egbert (SAUS)
EGB .... Episcopal Guild for the Blind (EA)
EGB .... Expected Gentlemanly Behavior (DSUE)
EGBAR .... Everything's Going to Be All Right
EGBB .... Birmingham [*British*] [*ICAO location identifier*] (ICLI)
EGBD .... Extrinsic Grain Boundary Dislocation (SAUS)
EGBDF .... Every Good Boy Deserves Favour [*Title of play by Tom Stoppard*]
EGBDF .... Every Good Boy Does Fine [*or Deserves Favor*] [*Mnemonic guide to notes on the treble clef*]
EGBE .... Coventry [*British*] [*ICAO location identifier*] (ICLI)
EGBE .... Ethylene Glycol Butyl Ether (SAUS)
EGBG .... Leicester [*British*] [*ICAO location identifier*] (ICLI)
EGBJ .... Gloucester and Cheltenham/Staverton [*British*] [*ICAO location identifier*] (ICLI)
EGBK .... Northampton/Sywell [*British*] [*ICAO location identifier*] (ICLI)
EGBM .... Tatenhill [*British*] [*ICAO location identifier*] (ICLI)
EGBN .... Nottingham [*British*] [*ICAO location identifier*] (ICLI)
EGBO .... Halfpenny Green [*British*] [*ICAO location identifier*] (ICLI)
EGBOK .... Everythings going to be ok (SAUS)
EGBP .... Pailton [*British*] [*ICAO location identifier*] (ICLI)
EGBPS .... Equilibrium-Gated Blood Pool Study [*Medicine*] (STED)
EGBPS .... Equilibrium-Grated Blood Pool Study [*Hematology*] (DAVI)
EGBS .... Shobdon [*British*] [*ICAO location identifier*] (ICLI)
EGBUS .... External Genitalia, Bartholin, Urethral, Skene's Glands [*Medicine*] (DMAA)
EGBW .... Wellesbourne Mountford [*British*] [*ICAO location identifier*] (ICLI)
EGC .... Bergerac [*France*] [*Airport symbol*] [*Obsolete*] (OAG)
EGC .... Eagle [*Colorado*] [*Seismograph station code, US Geological Survey*] [*Closed*] (SEIS)
EGC .... Early Gastric Cancer [*Medicine*] (STED)
EGC .... Early Gastric Carcinoma [*Medicine*] (MELL)
EGC .... Early Glottic Carcinoma [*Medicine*] (MELL)
EGC .... East Gippsland Coalition (EERA)
EGC .... East Greenland Current (SAUS)
EGC .... Ebony Gold Corp. [*Vancouver Stock Exchange symbol*]
EGC .... Economic Growth Center [*Yale University*] (PDAA)
EGC .... Educational Guidance Center for the Mentally Retarded [*Defunct*] (EA)
EGC .... Effective Government Committee (EA)
egc .... electrogalvanized coated (SAUS)
EGC .... Electronic Governor Control [*Automotive engineering*]
EGC .... Electronic Gyro Compass
EGC .... Elution Gas Chromatography [*Medicine*] (EDAA)
EGC .... Eminent Grand Commander [*Freemasonry*] (ROG)
EGC .... Empire Gas Corporation (SAUO)
EGC .... Engineer Group, Construction [*Military*]
EGC .... Enhanced Group Call (SAUS)
EGC .... Enhanced Group Calling (SAUO)
EGC .... Enhanced Group Call System (SAUS)
EGC .... Environmental Geochemistry (SAUS)
EGC .... Epigallocathechin [*Biochemistry*]
EGC .... Epiglottic Cartilage [*Medicine*] (MELL)
EGC .... Epithelioid A Globoid Cell [*Medicine*] (AAMN)
EGC .... Epithelioid-Globoid Cell [*Medicine*] (STED)
EGC .... equipment grounding conductor (SAUS)
EGC .... Euro Glass Club (SAUO)
EGC .... Excess Gate Current (SAUS)
EGC .... Executive Group of Companies [*Engineering Council*] (ACII)
EGC .... Experiments Ground Computer [*NASA*] (NASA)
EGC .... Exploration Geochemistry (SAUS)
EGC .... Exposure Growth Curve
EGC .... Extremenly Gruntled Customer (SAUS)
EGC .... World Government Corporation (SAUO)
EGCA .... Coal Aston [*British*] [*ICAO location identifier*] (ICLI)
EGCA .... Engineering and Grading Contractors Association (SAUO)
EG-CAE .... Experts Group for Command Application Environment (VLIE)
EGCAS .... Energy and Global Change Analysis Section (SAUS)
EGCB .... Manchester/Barton [*British*] [*ICAO location identifier*] (ICLI)
EGCC .... Manchester International [*British*] [*ICAO location identifier*] (ICLI)
EGCCT .... Intergovernmental Commission for Cooperation of Socialist Countries in the Field of Computer Technology (SAUO)
EGCD .... Woodford [*British*] [*ICAO location identifier*] (ICLI)
EGCE .... Wrexham/Borras [*British*] [*ICAO location identifier*] (ICLI)
EGCF .... Sandtoft [*British*] [*ICAO location identifier*] (ICLI)
EGCG .... Epigallocatechin Gallate [*Biochemistry*]
EGCG .... Strubby [*British*] [*ICAO location identifier*] (ICLI)
EGCH .... Holyhead [*British*] [*ICAO location identifier*] (ICLI)
EGCI .... Doncaster [*British*] [*ICAO location identifier*] (ICLI)
EGCI .... Export Group for the Construction Industries [*British*]
EGCJ .... Sherburn-In-Elmet [*British*] [*ICAO location identifier*] (ICLI)
EGCL .... Electro-Generated Chemiluminescene (PDAA)
EGCL .... Fenland [*British*] [*ICAO location identifier*] (ICLI)
EGCM .... Eddy-resolving General Circulation Model (SAUS)
EGCM .... Endgame Countermeasures (SAUS)
EGCM .... European Group for Cooperation in Management (PDAA)
EGCM .... European Group of Cellulose Manufacturers [*Defunct*] (EA)
EGCMA .... European Gas Control Manufacturers Association (SAUO)
EGCMC .... European Glass Container Manufacturers' Committee [*British*] (EAIO)
EGCN .... Northern Area Maintenance Unit [*British*] [*ICAO location identifier*] (ICLI)
EGCPM .... European Group of Corrugated Paper Makers (EAIO)
EGCR .... Experimental Gas-Cooled Reactor
E/GCR .... Extended Group Coded Recording [*Computer science*] (IBMDP)
EGCR .... Extragalactic Cosmic Ray
EGCRNR .... Eilat Gulf Coral Reef Nature Reserve (SAUS)
EGCS .... Engine Governing Control System [*Diesel engines*]
EGCS .... English Guernsey Cattle Society [*British*]
EGCS .... Environmental Generation Control System (ACAE)
EGCS .... Extended Graphic Character Set (VLIE)
EGCS .... Sturgate [*British*] [*ICAO location identifier*] (ICLI)
EG-CT .... Experts Group for Conformance Testing (VLIE)
EGCV .... Exhaust Gas Check Valve [*Automotive engineering*]
EGCZ .... Economy Gas [*Federal Railroad Administration identification code*]
EGD .... Effluent Gas Detection (BARN)
EGD .... Effluent Guidelines Division [*Environmental Protection Agency*]
EGD .... Electrogasdynamic [*Generator*]
EGD .... Environmental Graphic Designer (SAUS)
EGD .... Esophagogastroduodenoscopy [*Medicine*]
EGD .... Estates Gazette Digest of Cases [*A publication*] (DLA)
EGD .... Evolved Gas Detection [*Chemistry*]
EGD .... Epithermal Gold Deposit (ODA)
EGDA .... Brawdy [*British*] [*ICAO location identifier*] (ICLI)
EGDA .... Ethylene Glycol Diacetate [*Organic chemistry*]
EGDB .... Plymouth (Mount Wise) [*British*] [*ICAO location identifier*] (ICLI)
EGDC .... Chivenor [*British*] [*ICAO location identifier*] (ICLI)
EGDC .... Estates Gazette Digest of Cases [*A publication*] (DLA)
EGDD .... Royal Air Force Supervisory Centre Communications [*British*] [*ICAO location identifier*] (ICLI)
EGDE .... Ethylene Glycol Dimethyl Ether [*Also, DME, GLYME*] [*Organic chemistry*]
EGDF .... Embryonic Growth and Development Factor [*Biochemistry*]
egdg .... electrogasdynamic generator (SAUS)
EGDG .... St. Mawgan [*British*] [*ICAO location identifier*] (ICLI)
EGDH .... Royal Air Force 1 Group [*British*] [*ICAO location identifier*] (ICLI)
EG-DIR .... Experts Group on Directory (VLIE)
EGDJ .... Upavon [*British*] [*ICAO location identifier*] (ICLI)
EGDK .... Kemble [*British*] [*ICAO location identifier*] (ICLI)
EGDL .... Lyneham [*British*] [*ICAO location identifier*] (ICLI)
EGDM .... Boscombe Down [*British*] [*ICAO location identifier*] (ICLI)
EGDMA .... Ethylene Glycol Dimethacrylate [*Organic chemistry*]
EGDN .... Ethylene Glycol Dinitrate [*Organic chemistry*]
EGDN .... Netheravon [*British*] [*ICAO location identifier*] (ICLI)
EGDO .... Ethiopia Gabooye Democratic Organization (SAUS)
EGDP .... Portland [*British*] [*ICAO location identifier*] (ICLI)
EGDR .... Culdrose [*British*] [*ICAO location identifier*] (ICLI)
EGDS .... Bulford/Salisbury Plain [*British*] [*ICAO location identifier*] (ICLI)
EGDS .... Equipment Group Design Specifications (NATG)
EGDS .... Extragalactic Distance Scale (SAUS)
EGDT .... Wroughton [*British*] [*ICAO location identifier*] (ICLI)
EGDV .... Hullavington [*British*] [*ICAO location identifier*] (ICLI)
EGDX .... St. Athan [*British*] [*ICAO location identifier*] (ICLI)
EGDY .... Yeovilton [*British*] [*ICAO location identifier*] (ICLI)
EGE .... Eagle, CO [*Location identifier*] [*FAA*] (FAAL)
EGE .... Electricity-Generated Emissions (SAUS)
EGE .... Elevated Glandular Epidermis
EGE .... Emergency Ground Egress (MCD)
EGE .... Engelbert's Golden Eagles (EA)
EGE .... Enhanced Greenhouse Effect (EERA)
EGE .... Eosinophilic Gastroenteropathy [*Medicine*]
EGE .... Equine Granulocytic Ehrlichiosis [*Equine term*] (TED)
EGE .... Ethylene Glycol Ether (AAEL)
ege .... expected grade equivalent (SAUS)

e-ge-........... Germany, East [*MARC geographic area code*] [*Library of Congress*] (LCCP)
EGEAS .... Electric Generating Expansion Analysis System (ODA)
EGECON....... Electronic Geographic Coordinate Navigation (MCD)
EGECON System... Electronic Geographic Coordinate Navigation System (SAUS)
EGEO .... Eagle Geophysical, Inc. [*NASDAQ symbol*] (NASQ)
E GER .... East Germany
Eg Ext .... Egan on Extradition [*1846*] [*A publication*] (DLA)
EGF............. AMR American Eagle, Inc. [*ICAO designator*] (FAAC)
EGF............. Electrical Grapple Fixture (MCD)
EGF............. Electrodynamic Gradient Freeze (SAUS)
EGF............. Energy Guideline Factors
EGF............. Englefield Resources [*Vancouver Stock Exchange symbol*]
EGF............. Epicorum Graecorum Fragmenta [*A publication*] (OCD)
EGF............. Epidermal Growth Factor [*Endocrinology*]
egf.............. epidermal growth factors (SAUS)
EGF............. Europaeische Go Foderation [*European Go Federation - EGF*] [*Austria*] (EAIO)
EGF............. European Go Federation (SAUO)
EGF............. European Grassland Federation (EA)
EGFC........... Cardiff/Tremorfa [*British*] [*ICAO location identifier*] (ICLI)
EGFC........... Eagle Financial [*NASDAQ symbol*] (SAG)
EGFE........... Haverfordwest [*British*] [*ICAO location identifier*] (ICLI)
EGFF........... Cardiff [*British*] [*ICAO location identifier*] (ICLI)
EGFH .... Swansea [*British*] [*ICAO location identifier*] (ICLI)
EGFI............ Weston-Super-Mare [*British*] [*ICAO location identifier*] (ICLI)
EGFR .... Epidermal Growth Factor Receptor [*Biochemistry*]
EGFRK .... Epidermal Growth Factor Receptor Kinase [*An enzyme*]
EG-FT........... Experts Group on File Transfer (VLIE)
EGF-URO ..... Epidermal Growth Factor - Urogastrone [*Endocrinology*]
EGG .... Edinburgh Geology and Geophysics (SAUO)
EGG .... Educational Growth Group (DICI)
EGG .... EG & G, Inc. [*NYSE symbol*] (SPSG)
EGG .... Eggerton [*England*]
EGG .... Electric Glue Gun
EGG .... Electrogastrogram [*Medicine*]
EGG .... Electrogastrograph (SAUS)
EGG .... Electrogastrography [*Medicine*] (STED)
EGG .... Electrogoniogram (LDOE)
EGG .... Electrogoniography (LDOE)
eGG .... Electronic Gourmet Guide [*America Online Greenhouse program*]
EGG .... Engineering Geology Group (SAUO)
EGG .... Environmental Geology Group (SAUO)
EGG .... Equine Gamma Globulin [*Medicine*] (EDAA)
EGG .... Evaporating Gaseous Globules (SAUO)
EGGA .... European General Galvanizers Association (EA)
EGGA .... London [*British*] [*ICAO location identifier*] (ICLI)
EGGB .... London [*British*] [*ICAO location identifier*] (ICLI)
EGGC .... London [*British*] [*ICAO location identifier*] (ICLI)
EGGD .... Bristol/Lulsgate [*British*] [*ICAO location identifier*] (ICLI)
Egg Dam...... Eggleston on Damages [*A publication*] (DLA)
EGGE .... Bletchley [*British*] [*ICAO location identifier*] (ICLI)
EGGF .... Uxbridge [*British*] [*ICAO location identifier*] (ICLI)
Egghead ...... Egghead, Inc. [*Associated Press*] (SAG)
EGGN .... United Kingdom International NOTAM Office [*ICAO location identifier*] (ICLI)
EGGO .... London [*British*] [*ICAO location identifier*] (ICLI)
EGGP........... Liverpool [*British*] [*ICAO location identifier*] (ICLI)
EGGQ........... Liverpool [*British*] [*ICAO location identifier*] (ICLI)
EGGR .... Redhill [*British*] [*ICAO location identifier*] (ICLI)
EGGS........... Egghead.com, Inc. [*NASDAQ symbol*] (SG)
EGGS........... Egghead, Inc. [*NASDAQ symbol*] (NQ)
EGGS........... Environmental and GeoGraphical Science (SAUO)
eggsan......... egg sandwich (SAUS)
EGGW........... Luton [*British*] [*ICAO location identifier*] (ICLI)
eggwich....... egg sandwich (SAUS)
EGGX .... Shanwick [*British*] [*ICAO location identifier*] (ICLI)
EGGY .... United Kingdom MOTNE Centre [*ICAO location identifier*] (ICLI)
EGH .... Epidermal Growth Hormone [*Medicine*] (EDAA)
EGH .... Equine Growth Hormone (DB)
EGH .... Europaische Gesellschaft fuer Herbologie [*European Weed Research Society*] (EAIO)
EGH .... Everton's Genealogical Helper [*A publication*]
EGHA .... Compton Abbas [*British*] [*ICAO location identifier*] (ICLI)
EGHC .... Land's End/St. Just [*British*] [*ICAO location identifier*] (ICLI)
EGHD .... Plymouth/Roborough [*British*] [*ICAO location identifier*] (ICLI)
EGHE .... Scilly Isles/St. Mary's [*British*] [*ICAO location identifier*] (ICLI)
EGHG .... Yeovil [*British*] [*ICAO location identifier*] (ICLI)
EGHH .... Bournemouth/Hurn [*British*] [*ICAO location identifier*] (ICLI)
EGHI .... Southampton [*British*] [*ICAO location identifier*] (ICLI)
EGHJ............ Bembridge [*British*] [*ICAO location identifier*] (ICLI)
EGHK .... Penzance/Eastern Green [*British*] [*ICAO location identifier*] (ICLI)
EGHL .... Lasham [*British*] [*ICAO location identifier*] (ICLI)
EGHM .... Hamble [*British*] [*ICAO location identifier*] (ICLI)
EGHN .... Sandown (Isle Of Wight) [*British*] [*ICAO location identifier*] (ICLI)
EGHO .... Thruxton [*British*] [*ICAO location identifier*] (ICLI)
EGHP .... Employer Group Health Plan [*Department of Health and Human Services*] (GFGA)
EGHR .... Chichester/Goodwood [*British*] [*ICAO location identifier*] (ICLI)
EGHS .... Henstridge [*British*] [*ICAO location identifier*] (ICLI)
EGHT .... EightXEight, Inc. [*NASDAQ symbol*] (SAG)
EGHTFD .... Eightfold (ABBR)
EGHTH .... Eightieth (ABBR)
Egi .... Egidius de Losano [*Authority cited in pre-1607 legal work*] (DSA)
EGI.............. Egilsstadir [*Iceland*] [*Seismograph station code, US Geological Survey*] (SEIS)
EGI.............. Electronic Gasoline Injection [*Automotive engineering*]
EGI.............. Embedded GPS/INU programme (SAUS)
EGI.............. End of Group Indicator (SAUO)
EGI.............. Exhaust Gas Ignition [*Automotive emissions*]
EGI.............. Explosive Gas Indicator
e-gi-............ Gibraltar [*MARC geographic area code*] [*Library of Congress*] (LCCP)
EGI.............. Valparaiso, FL [*Location identifier*] [*FAA*] (FAAL)
Egid .... Egidius de Fuscarariis [*Deceased, 1289*] [*Authority cited in pre-1607 legal work*] (DSA)
Egid Bellam... Egidius Bellamera [*Deceased, 1407*] [*Authority cited in pre-1607 legal work*] (DSA)
EGIF............ Equipment Group Interface
EGIFO .... Edward Grey Institute of Field Ornithology (BARN)
EGIG .... International Glaciological Expedition to Greenland (SAUO)
EGIL............ Electrical, General Instrumentation, and Lighting Engineer (MCD)
EGIL............ Environmental, General Instrumentation, Life Support [*NASA*] (KSC)
EGIS............ East German Intelligence Service (SAUO)
EGIS............ Encyclopedia of Geographic Information Sources [*A publication*]
EGIS............ European Geographical Information Systems Symposia (EERA)
EGIS............ European GIS (SAUS)
EGIS............ Executive Guide to Information Sources [*Later, EBIS*] [*A publication*]
EGIS............ Exhaust Gas Ionization Sensor [*Automotive engineering*]
EGIU .... Error Generator Injection Unit (VLIE)
EGIZ............ Essex Group [*Federal Railroad Administration identification code*]
EGJ .... Eagle Jet Charter, Inc. [*FAA designator*] (FAAC)
EGJ .... Esophagogastric Junction [*Anatomy*] (DAVI)
EGJA........... Alderney, Channel Islands [*British*] [*ICAO location identifier*] (ICLI)
EGJB........... Guernsey, Channel Islands [*British*] [*ICAO location identifier*] (ICLI)
EGJC........... Eagle Grove Junior College [*Iowa*]
EGJ/IFJ .... European Group of Journalists/International Federation of Journalists [*EC*] (ECED)
EGJJ .... Jersey, Channel Islands [*British*] [*ICAO location identifier*] (ICLI)
EGK............. Dayton, OH [*Location identifier*] [*FAA*] (FAAL)
EGK............. Ein Grosser Komponist [*A Great Composer*] or Ein Genialer Komponist [*A Great Genius of a Composer*] [*Suggested interpretations for the adopted surname of German composer Werner Egk. Egk maintained that he chose the name in honor of his wife*]
EGKA .... Shoreham [*British*] [*ICAO location identifier*] (ICLI)
EGKB .... Biggin Hill [*British*] [*ICAO location identifier*] (ICLI)
EGKC .... Bognor Regis [*British*] [*ICAO location identifier*] (ICLI)
EGKE........... Challock [*British*] [*ICAO location identifier*] (ICLI)
EGKH .... Lashenden/Headcorn [*British*] [*ICAO location identifier*] (ICLI)
EGKK .... London/Gatwick [*British*] [*ICAO location identifier*] (ICLI)
EGKM........... West Malling [*British*] [*ICAO location identifier*] (ICLI)
EGKR .... Redhill [*British*] [*ICAO location identifier*] (ICLI)
EGKS .... Europaeische Gemeinschaft fuer Kohle und Stahl [*European Coal and Steel Community*] [*German*] (DCTA)
EGKT........... Early Grand Knight Templar [*Freemasonry*] (ROG)
EGL............. Capital Trading Aviation Ltd. [*British*] [*ICAO designator*] (FAAC)
EGL............. Eagle
EGL............. Eagle Global Logistics
EGL............. Eagle Precision Technologies, Inc. [*Toronto Stock Exchange symbol*]
EGL............. Eclectic Grand Lodge [*Freemasonry*] (ROG)
EGL............. Eglin Air Force Base [*Florida*] (SAA)
EGL............. Encyclopedia of Georgia Law [*A publication*] (DLA)
EGL............. Eosinophilic Granuloma of the Lung [*Medicine*]
EGL............. Equipment Group Laboratories (MCD)
EGL............. Equipment Guide List (NVT)
EGL............. European Group of Lymphology [*Belgium*] (EAIO)
EGL............. Expected Grade Level [*Education*]
EGL............. External Germinal Layer [*Cytology*]
EGL............. External Granular Layer (PDAA)
EGL............. Extragalactic Light
EGL............. Gala Law [*Scotland*] [*Seismograph station code, US Geological Survey*] (SEIS)
EGL............. Neghelli [*Ethiopia*] [*Airport symbol*] (AD)
EGLA........... Bodmin [*British*] [*ICAO location identifier*] (ICLI)
EGLB........... Brooklands [*British*] [*ICAO location identifier*] (ICLI)
EGLB........... Eagle BancGroup, Inc. [*NASDAQ symbol*] (SAG)
EglBGp......... Eagle BancGroup, Inc. [*Associated Press*] (SAG)
EglBsh .... Eagle Bancshares [*Associated Press*] (SAG)
EGLD .... Denham [*British*] [*ICAO location identifier*] (ICLI)
EGLE........... Eagle Food Centers [*NASDAQ symbol*] (SAG)
Egle .... Every Ghanaian Living Everywhere (SAUS)
EgleRiv....... Eagle River Interactive, Inc. [*Associated Press*] (SAG)
EgleUSA ...... Eagle USA Airfreight, Inc. [*Associated Press*] (SAG)
EglFd.......... Eagle Food Centers, Inc. [*Associated Press*] (SAG)
EGLG .... Panshanger [*British*] [*ICAO location identifier*] (ICLI)
EglHrd .... Eagle Hardware & Garden, Inc. [*Associated Press*] (SAG)
EGLI............ Esperantista Go-Ligo Internacia [*International Esperantist League for Go - IELG*] (EAIO)
EGLI............ Essay and General Literature Index
EGLISI .... Service de Presse de l'Eglise du Silence [*Belgium*]
EGLJ .... Chalgrove [*British*] [*ICAO location identifier*] (ICLI)
EGLK........... Blackbushe [*British*] [*ICAO location identifier*] (ICLI)
EGLL............ London City [*British*] [*ICAO location identifier*] (ICLI)
EGLM........... Exchangeable General Linear Model [*Statistics*]
EGLM........... White Waltham [*British*] [*ICAO location identifier*] (ICLI)
EGLMSFCMS... Elves', Gnomes', and Little Men's Science Fiction, Chowder, and Marching Society (EA)
EGLMT......... Ejector-Launcher, Guided Missile, Transporter

EGLN .... London/Heathrow [*British*] [*ICAO location identifier*] (ICLI)
EGLO .... eGlobe, Inc. [*NASDAQ symbol*] (SG)
EGLO .... Executive TeleCard, Ltd. [*NASDAQ symbol*] (NASQ)
EGLS .... Electroglas, Inc. [*NASDAQ symbol*] (SAG)
EGLS .... Old Sarum [*British*] [*ICAO location identifier*] (ICLI)
EGLT .... Euglobin Lysis Time [*Medicine*] (EDAA)
EGLW .... London [*British*] [*ICAO location identifier*] (ICLI)
EGM .... East Greenland Margin (SAUS)
EGM .... Electrogel Machining (SAUS)
EGM .... Electrogram (MAE)
EGM .... Electronic Governor Module (IEEE)
EGM .... El Golfo De Santa Clara [*Mexico*] [*Seismograph station code, US Geological Survey*] (SEIS)
EGM .... Emergency General Meeting (SAUO)
EGM .... Empire Gallantry Medal [*British*]
EGM .... Enhanced Graphics Module (SAUS)
EGM .... Enhanced Graphics Monitor [*Computer technology*]
EGM .... Epitaxial Growth by Melting (SAUS)
EGM .... European Glass Container Manufacturers (SAUS)
EGM .... European Glass Container Manufacturers' Committee [*British*]
EGM .... Excellent Grand Master [*Freemasonry*] (ROG)
EGM .... Extraordinary General Meeting [*British*] (ADA)
EGM .... Sege [*Solomon Islands*] [*Airport symbol*] (OAG)
EGMBE .... Ethylene Glycol Monobutyl Ether (SAUS)
eGmbH .... Eingetragene Gesellschaft mit Beschraenkter Haftung [*Registered Company with Limited Liability*] [*German*] (ILCA)
EGmc .... East Germanic (ADWA)
EGMC .... Equipment Group Management Committee (TIMI)
EGMC .... Southend [*British*] [*ICAO location identifier*] (ICLI)
EGMD .... Lydd [*British*] [*ICAO location identifier*] (ICLI)
EGME .... Elevation Gimbal Mounted Electronics (ACAE)
EGME .... Ethylene Glycol Methyl Ether (PIPO)
EGME .... Ethylene Glycol Monomethyl Ether [*A poison*] [*Organic chemistry*]
EGMEX .... Eastern Gulf of Mexico
EGMF .... Edvard Grieg Memorial Foundation (EA)
EGMH .... Manston [*British*] [*ICAO location identifier*] (ICLI)
EGMIA .... Educational Group of the Musical Instrument Association (SAUO)
EGMIA .... Educational Group of the Music Industries Association [*British*] (BI)
EGMIS .... East German Military Intelligence Services (SAUO)
EGM of C .... Excellent Grand Master of Ceremonies [*Freemasonry*] (ROG)
Egmonts .... Egmont Islands in the Chagos Archipelago northwest of Diego Garcia (SAUS)
EGMR .... East Griqualand Mounted Rifles [*British military*] (DMA)
EGMRSA .... Edible Gelatin Manufacturers Research Society of America (SAUO)
EGMS .... Education of Girls in Mathematics and Science
EGMT .... Elapsed Greenwich Mean Time (KSC)
EGMTR .... Eglin Gulf Missile Test Range [*Florida*] [*Air Force*]
EGN .... Eagle's Nest [*New York*] [*Seismograph station code, US Geological Survey*] (SEIS)
EGN .... El Geneina [*Sudan*] [*Airport symbol*] (OAG)
EGN .... Energen Corp. [*NYSE symbol*] (SPSG)
EGN .... Environmental Geology Notes (SAUO)
EGN .... Experimental Glomerulonephritis [*Medicine*]
EGN .... Express Group Newspapers [*British*]
EGNA .... Eucharistic Guard for Nocturnal Adoration [*Defunct*] (EA)
EGNA .... Hucknall [*British*] [*ICAO location identifier*] (ICLI)
EGNB .... Brough [*British*] [*ICAO location identifier*] (ICLI)
EGNB .... Enteric Gram Negative Bacteria [*Medicine*] (MELL)
EGNC .... Carlisle [*British*] [*ICAO location identifier*] (ICLI)
EGND .... Huddersfield/Crosland Moor [*British*] [*ICAO location identifier*] (ICLI)
EGNE .... Repton/Gamston [*British*] [*ICAO location identifier*] (ICLI)
EGNF .... Nether Thorpe [*British*] [*ICAO location identifier*] (ICLI)
EGNG .... Preston and Blackburn/Samlesbury [*British*] [*ICAO location identifier*] (ICLI)
EGNH .... Blackpool [*British*] [*ICAO location identifier*] (ICLI)
EGNI .... Skegness/Ingoldmells [*British*] [*ICAO location identifier*] (ICLI)
EGNJ .... Humberside [*British*] [*ICAO location identifier*] (ICLI)
EGNL .... Barrow/Walney Island [*British*] [*ICAO location identifier*] (ICLI)
EGNM .... Leeds and Bradford [*British*] [*ICAO location identifier*] (ICLI)
EGNO .... Warton [*British*] [*ICAO location identifier*] (ICLI)
EGNOS .... European Geostationary Navigation Overlay Service (SAUS)
EGNOS .... European Geostationary Navigation Overlay System
E/GNP .... Energy/Gross National Product [*Fuel use ratio*]
EGNR .... Ein Gedi Nature Reserve (SAUS)
EGNR .... Hawarden [*British*] [*ICAO location identifier*] (ICLI)
EGNS .... Isle Of Man/Ronaldsway [*British*] [*ICAO location identifier*] (ICLI)
EGNSW .... Embroiderers' Guild of New South Wales [*Australia*]
EGNT .... Expositer's Greek New Testament [*A publication*]
EGNT .... Newcastle [*British*] [*ICAO location identifier*] (ICLI)
EGNV .... Tees-Side [*British*] [*ICAO location identifier*] (ICLI)
EGNW .... Wickenby [*British*] [*ICAO location identifier*] (ICLI)
EGNX .... East Midlands [*British*] [*ICAO location identifier*] (ICLI)
EGO .... Eccentric Geophysical Observatory [*Also, EOGO*] [*NASA*]
EGO .... Eccentric Orbiting Geophysical Observatory (ACAE)
EGO .... Economie/gouvernements/organisations (SAUS)
EGO .... Educational Growth Opportunities (SAUS)
EGO .... Ego Resources Ltd. [*Toronto Stock Exchange symbol*]
EGO .... Electronic Grading Operator
EGO .... Excellent Grand Orator [*Freemasonry*] (ROG)
EGO .... Exhaust Gas Oxygen [*Automotive engineering*]
EGO .... Experimental Geophysical Orbiting [*Vehicle*]
EGO .... Exposed Gate Oxide (TIMI)
EGOB .... Burtonwood [*British*] [*ICAO location identifier*] (ICLI)
EGOBOO .... Ego Boost
EGOC .... Bishops Court [*British*] [*ICAO location identifier*] (ICLI)
EGOCO .... European Group of Oil Companies (SAUO)
EGOD .... Llanbedr [*British*] [*ICAO location identifier*] (ICLI)
EGOE .... Ternhill [*British*] [*ICAO location identifier*] (ICLI)
EGOMAC .... Effect of Gravity on Methane-Air Combustion
EGOQ .... Mona [*British*] [*ICAO location identifier*] (ICLI)
EGOR .... Exhaust Gas Oxygen Sensor Return [*Automotive engineering*]
EGOS .... European Group for Organizational Studies [*British*] (SLS)
EGOS .... Exhaust Gas Oxygen Sensor [*Automotive engineering*]
EGOS .... Shawbury [*British*] [*ICAO location identifier*] (ICLI)
EGOT .... Erythrocyte Glutamic Oxaloacetic Transaminase (AAMN)
egot .... erythrocyte glutamic oxaloacetic transminase (SAUS)
EGOTH .... Egyptian Government Organization for Tourism and Hotels
EGOV .... Valley [*British*] [*ICAO location identifier*] (ICLI)
EGOW .... Woodvale [*British*] [*ICAO location identifier*] (ICLI)
EGOY .... West Freugh [*British*] [*ICAO location identifier*] (ICLI)
EGP .... Eagle Pass [*Texas*] [*Airport symbol*] [*Obsolete*] (OAG)
EGP .... Eagle Pass Resources [*Vancouver Stock Exchange symbol*]
EGP .... Eagle-Picher Co. (SAUO)
EGP .... Early Greek Philosophy [*1930*] [*A publication*] (OCD)
EGP .... Eastern Group of Painters, Montreal [*1938*] [*Canada*] (NGC)
EGP .... EastGroup Properties, Inc. [*NYSE symbol*] [*Formerly, EastGroup Properties SBI*] (SG)
EGP .... Egypt (ROG)
EGP .... Ejercito Guerrillero de los Pobres [*Guerrilla Army of the Poor*] [*Guatemala*]
EGP .... Electron Gun Problem (SAUS)
EGP .... Electronic Graphics Processing (SAUS)
EGP .... Elliptical Gear Planetary
EGP .... Embezzlement of Government Property
EGP .... Eminentra Granularis Posterior [*Anatomy*]
EGP .... Environmental Genome Project [*National Institute of Environmental Health Sciences*]
EGP .... Environmental Geology Page (SAUO)
EGP .... Ethno-, Geo-, Polycentric (SAUS)
EGP .... European Glaciological Programme (SAUS)
EGP .... Evolved Gas Profile [*Chemistry*]
EGP .... Exhaust Gas Pressure
EGP .... Experimental Geodetic Payload [*Japan*]
EGP .... Experimental GOES [*Goestationary Operational Environmental Satellite*] Platform [*Marine science*] (MSC)
EGP .... Exploration Geophysics (SAUS)
EGP .... Extended Guide Projectile [*Navy*] (MCD)
EGP .... Extensive Gateway Protocol (SAUS)
EGP .... Exterior Gateway Protocol [*Computer science*]
EGP .... External Gateway Protocol (RALS)
EGP .... Extra-Solar Giant Planet
EGP .... Thai Aerospace Services Co. Ltd. [*FAA designator*] (FAAC)
EGPA .... Egyptian General Petroleum Authority (SAUS)
EGPA .... Erlangen General Purpose Array (SAUS)
EGPA .... European Group of Public Administration [*See also GEAP*] [*Brussels, Belgium*] (EAIO)
EGPA .... Export Grape and Plum Act [*1960*]
EGPA .... Kirkwall [*British*] [*ICAO location identifier*] (ICLI)
EGPACOM .... Environmental Group, Pacific Command (CINC)
EGPAS .... European General Product Acceptance Specifications (SAUO)
EGPB .... Sumburgh [*British*] [*ICAO location identifier*] (ICLI)
EGPC .... Egyptian General Petroleum Company (SAUO)
EGPC .... Egyptian General Petroleum Corp.
EGPC .... Wick [*British*] [*ICAO location identifier*] (ICLI)
EGPD .... Aberdeen/Dyce [*British*] [*ICAO location identifier*] (ICLI)
EGPE .... Extended Generalized Programming Environment (SAUS)
EGPE .... Inverness/Dalcross [*British*] [*ICAO location identifier*] (ICLI)
EGPF .... East Greenland Polar Front [*Oceanography*]
EGPF .... Glasgow [*British*] [*ICAO location identifier*] (ICLI)
EGPH .... Edinburgh [*British*] [*ICAO location identifier*] (ICLI)
EGPH .... Electro-Galvanized and Phosphated [*Metallurgy*]
EGPI .... Islay/Port Ellen [*British*] [*ICAO location identifier*] (ICLI)
EGPJ .... Fife/Glenrothes [*British*] [*ICAO location identifier*] (ICLI)
EGPK .... Prestwick [*British*] [*ICAO location identifier*] (ICLI)
EGPL .... Benbecula [*British*] [*ICAO location identifier*] (ICLI)
EGPM .... Scatsta [*British*] [*ICAO location identifier*] (ICLI)
EGPMF .... Error Gap Probability Mass Function
EGPN .... Dundee (Riverside Park) [*British*] [*ICAO location identifier*] (ICLI)
EGPO .... Stornoway [*British*] [*ICAO location identifier*] (ICLI)
EGPQ .... Edinburgh [*British*] [*ICAO location identifier*] (ICLI)
EGPR .... Barra [*British*] [*ICAO location identifier*] (ICLI)
EGPS .... Electric Ground Power System [*Aerospace*] (AAG)
EGPS .... Extended General Purpose Simulator [*National Electronics Conference*] (IEEE)
EGPS .... Peterhead/Longside [*British*] [*ICAO location identifier*] (ICLI)
EGPT .... Eagle Point Software [*NASDAQ symbol*] (TTSB)
EGPT .... Eagle Point Software Corp. [*NASDAQ symbol*] (SAG)
EGPT .... Perth/Scone [*British*] [*ICAO location identifier*] (ICLI)
EGPU .... Tiree [*British*] [*ICAO location identifier*] (ICLI)
EGPW .... Unst (Shetland Isles) [*British*] [*ICAO location identifier*] (ICLI)
EGPWS .... Enhanced Ground Proximity Warning System [*Aviation*]
EGPX .... Scottish Air Traffic Control Centre [*British*] [*ICAO location identifier*] (ICLI)
EGPY .... Dounreay/Thurso [*British*] [*ICAO location identifier*] (ICLI)
EGQ .... Embroiderers' Guild of Queensland [*Australia*]
EGQ .... Emmetsburg, IA [*Location identifier*] [*FAA*] (FAAL)
EGQB .... Ballykelly [*British*] [*ICAO location identifier*] (ICLI)
EGQJ .... Machrihanish [*British*] [*ICAO location identifier*] (ICLI)
EGQK .... Kinloss [*British*] [*ICAO location identifier*] (ICLI)
EGQL .... Leuchars [*British*] [*ICAO location identifier*] (ICLI)

EGQM .... Boulmer [*British*] [*ICAO location identifier*] (ICLI)
EGQN .... Buchan [*British*] [*ICAO location identifier*] (ICLI)
EGQP .... Edinburgh [*British*] [*ICAO location identifier*] (ICLI)
EGQQ .... Prestwick [*British*] [*ICAO location identifier*] (ICLI)
EGQR .... Saxa Vord [*British*] [*ICAO location identifier*] (ICLI)
EGQS .... Lossiemouth [*British*] [*ICAO location identifier*] (ICLI)
EGQT .... Edinburgh [*British*] [*ICAO location identifier*] (ICLI)
EGR .... Eagle River Mines [*Vancouver Stock Exchange symbol*]
EGR .... Early Growth Response [*Biochemistry*]
EGR .... Earned Growth Rate [*Finance*] (ODBW)
EGR .... Earthgrains Co. [*NYSE symbol*] (TTSB)
egr .... egress (SAUS)
EGR .... Electrographic Recorder (CAAL)
EGR .... Electronic Governor Regulator (IEEE)
EGR .... Embossed Groove Recording
EGR .... Emission Gas Recirculation (SAUS)
EGR .... Empire Grade Road [*California*] [*Seismograph station code, US Geological Survey*] (SEIS)
egr .... Engraver [*MARC relator code*] [*Library of Congress*] (LCCP)
EGR .... Enhanced Guardrail (MCD)
egr .... erythrocyte glutathione reductase (SAUS)
EGR .... Erythrocyte Glutatione Reductase [*An enzyme*]
EGR .... Excellent Grand Recorder [*Freemasonry*] (ROG)
EGR .... Exhaust Gas Recirculation [*Engines*]
EGR .... Exhaust Gas Recycle (SAUS)
e-gr- .... Greece [*MARC geographic area code*] [*Library of Congress*] (LCCP)
EGRA .... Equilibrium-Gated Radionuclide Angiography [*Medicine*] (DMAA)
EGRA .... Glasgow [*British*] [*ICAO location identifier*] (ICLI)
EGRATT .... European Research Group for Alternatives in Toxicity Testing
EGRB .... London [*British*] [*ICAO location identifier*] (ICLI)
EGRC .... Exhaust Gas Recirculation Control [*Valve*] [*Automotive engineering*]
EGRC .... Manchester [*British*] [*ICAO location identifier*] (ICLI)
EGRCV .... Exhaust Gas Recirculation Control Valve [*Automotive engineering*]
EGRD .... Bristol [*British*] [*ICAO location identifier*] (ICLI)
EGRD .... Eye Guard
EGRE .... Malvern [*British*] [*ICAO location identifier*] (ICLI)
EGR Engine... Exhaust Gas Recirculation Engine (SAUS)
EGREP .... Extended Fixed Global Regular Expression Print (SAUO)
EGREP .... Extended Global Regular Expression Print [*Unix*] (VERA)
EGRESS .... Emergency Global Rescue, Escape, and Survival System [*NASA*]
EGRESS .... Evaluation of Glide Reentry Structural Systems
EGRET .... Energetic Gamma Ray Experiment Telescope [*NASA*]
EGRET .... Energetic Gamma-Ray Explorer Telescope (SAUS)
EGRET .... Epidemiological, Graphics, Estimation, and Testing [*Program*]
EGRET .... Explorer Gamma-Ray-Experiment Telescope (SAUS)
EGRG .... Cardiff City [*British*] [*ICAO location identifier*] (ICLI)
EGRH .... High Wycombe [*British*] [*ICAO location identifier*] (ICLI)
Egr High ...... Egremont on the Law of Highways [*A publication*] (DLA)
EGRI .... Southampton [*British*] [*ICAO location identifier*] (ICLI)
EGRJ .... Upavon [*British*] [*ICAO location identifier*] (ICLI)
EGRK .... Ocean Station Vessel Romeo [*British*] [*ICAO location identifier*] (ICLI)
EGRL .... Ocean Station Vessel Lima [*British*] [*ICAO location identifier*] (ICLI)
EGRM .... Ocean Station Vessel Mike [*British*] [*ICAO location identifier*] (ICLI)
EGRN .... Norwich [*British*] [*ICAO location identifier*] (ICLI)
EGROM .... Erasable Graphics Read Only Memory (TIMI)
EGRP .... E Trade Group [*NASDAQ symbol*] (SG)
EGRP .... Plymouth [*British*] [*ICAO location identifier*] (ICLI)
EGRR .... Bracknell [*British*] [*ICAO location identifier*] (ICLI)
EGRS .... Egress (KSC)
EGRS .... Electronic and Geodetic Ranging Satellite (IAA)
EGRS .... Exhaust Gas Recirculation Sensor [*Automotive engineering*]
EGRS .... Extragalactic Radio Source
EGRS .... Sullom Voe [*British*] [*ICAO location identifier*] (ICLI)
EGRT .... Exhaust Gas Recirculation Temperature [*Automotive term*] (HAWK)
EGRT .... Newcastle [*British*] [*ICAO location identifier*] (ICLI)
EGRU .... Ocean Station Vessel Charlie [*British*] [*ICAO location identifier*] (ICLI)
EGRV .... Exhaust Gas Recirculation Valve [*Automotive engineering*]
EGRV .... Exhaust Gas Recirculation Vent [*Automotive engineering*]
EGRVA .... Exhaust Gas Recirculation Valve Actuator [*Automotive engineering*]
EGRVP .... Exhaust Gas Recirculation Vacuum Port [*Automotive engineering*]
EGRW .... Nottingham [*British*] [*ICAO location identifier*] (ICLI)
EGRY .... Leeds [*British*] [*ICAO location identifier*] (ICLI)
EGS .... East Greenland Shelf (SAUS)
EGS .... Economic General Staff [*British*]
EGS .... Economic geology series (SAUS)
EGS .... Edge Guide System
EGS .... Egilsstadir [*Iceland*] [*Airport symbol*] (OAG)
EGS .... Electrical Galvanic Stimulation [*Physiology*]
EGS .... Electric Geospace Shuttle (SAUS)
EGS .... Electrogalvanized Steel
EGS .... Electrographic Seizure [*Neurophysiology*]
EGS .... Electronic Gear Selection [*Heavy-duty vehicles*]
EGS .... Electronic-Glide Slope (NG)
EGS .... Electronic Governor System [*Heavy-duty automotive engines*]
EGS .... Electronic Grade Silicon (SAUS)
EGS .... Electronic Guidance Section (SAUS)
EGS .... Electronics-Grade Silicon (SAUS)
EGS .... Electronics Guidance Section (SAUS)
EGS .... Electronics Guidance Station (SAUS)
EGS .... Elementary Gliding School [*British military*] (DMA)
EGS .... Emergency Generator System (ACAE)
EGS .... Emil Gilels Society (EA)
EGS .... Employment Guarantee Scheme (SAUS)
EGS .... Endovascular Grafting System (SAUS)
EGS .... Engineering Graphics System (SAUS)
EGS .... English and German Studies (journ.) (SAUS)
EGS .... English Goethe Society [*British*]
EGS .... Enhanced Graphics System [*Commodore*] (VERA)
EGS .... Environmental and Geographical Science (SAUO)
EGS .... Ethylene Glycol Succinate [*Organic chemistry*]
EGS .... Europaeische Gesellschaft fuer Schriftpsychologie und Schriftexpertise [*European Society of Handwriting Psychology - ESHP*] (EAIO)
EGS .... European Geophysical Society (EAIO)
EGS .... Excellent Grand Secretary [*Freemasonry*] (ROG)
EGS .... Excluded Goods Schedule
EGS .... Exhaust Gas System
EGS .... Experimental Geodetic Satellite (SAUS)
EGS .... Extended Generalized Shuffle (SAUS)
EGS .... Extended Graphic Subsystem (SAUS)
EGS .... Extension of the Gastric Shield
EGS .... External Guide Sequence [*Genetics*]
EGSA .... Electrical Generating Systems Association (EA)
EGSA .... Embroiderers' Guild of South Australia
EGSA .... Shipdham [*British*] [*ICAO location identifier*] (ICLI)
EGSB .... Bedford/Castle Mill [*British*] [*ICAO location identifier*] (ICLI)
EGSC .... Cambridge [*British*] [*ICAO location identifier*] (ICLI)
EGSCCP .... European Graduate Summer Course on Computational Physics (SAUS)
EGSD .... Great Yarmouth/North Denes [*British*] [*ICAO location identifier*] (ICLI)
EGSE .... Electrical [*or Electronic*] Ground-Support Equipment
EGSE .... Electronic Ground Support Equipment (SAUS)
EGSE .... Ipswich [*British*] [*ICAO location identifier*] (ICLI)
EG-SEA-AI.... European Group for Structural Engineering Applications of Artificial Intelligence (SAUS)
EGSF .... Peterborough (Conington) [*British*] [*ICAO location identifier*] (ICLI)
EGSG .... Stapleford [*British*] [*ICAO location identifier*] (ICLI)
EGSH .... Norwich [*British*] [*ICAO location identifier*] (ICLI)
EGSIPS .... Electronic Guides for Standardizing Items of Procurement and Supply (MCD)
EGSJ .... Polstead [*British*] [*ICAO location identifier*] (ICLI)
EGSK .... Hethel [*British*] [*ICAO location identifier*] (ICLI)
EGSL .... Andrewsfield [*British*] [*ICAO location identifier*] (ICLI)
EGSM .... Beccles [*British*] [*ICAO location identifier*] (ICLI)
E-GSM .... Extended Global System for Mobile Communication (CGWS)
EGSMA .... Electrical Generating Systems Marketing Association [*Later, EGSA*] (EA)
EGSMA .... Geological Survey and Mining Authority (SAUS)
EGSN .... Bourn (Cambs) [*British*] [*ICAO location identifier*] (ICLI)
EGSP .... Electronic Glossary and Symbol Panel (IAA)
EGSP .... Electronics Glossary and Symbol Panel (SAUO)
EGSP .... Peterborough/Sibson [*British*] [*ICAO location identifier*] (ICLI)
EGSR .... Earls Colne [*British*] [*ICAO location identifier*] (ICLI)
EGSS .... Ethnic and Genealogical Sourcebook Series [*A publication*]
EGSS .... London/Stansted [*British*] [*ICAO location identifier*] (ICLI)
EGST .... Elmsett [*British*] [*ICAO location identifier*] (ICLI)
EGSW .... Weeley [*British*] [*ICAO location identifier*] (ICLI)
EGSWG .... European Geophysical Society Working Group on Tsunami [*Marine science*] (OSRA)
EGT .... Eagle Airways Ltd. [*British*] [*ICAO designator*] (FAAC)
EGT .... Ecdysteroid Glucosyl Transferase [*An enzyme*]
EGT .... Egypt
EGT .... Elapsed Ground Time (MCD)
EGT .... Embroiderers' Guild of Tasmania [*Australia*]
EGT .... Eminent Grand Treasurer [*Freemasonry*] (ROG)
EGT .... Entreprise de Gestion Touristique [*Algeria*] (EY)
EGT .... Equipment Group Tester (SAUO)
EGT .... Equivalent Gear Train
EGT .... Estimated Ground Time (MCD)
EGT .... European Geotraverse [*A collaborative lithosphere study*]
EGT .... Excellent Grand Tabernacle [*Freemasonry*] (ROG)
EGT .... Exhaust Gas Temperature
EGT .... [*The*] Expositor's Greek Testament [*A publication*] (BJA)
EGT .... Extended Glaciological Timescale [*Climatology*]
EGT .... Wellington, KS [*Location identifier*] [*FAA*] (FAAL)
EGT .... Einstein-Invariant Gauge Theory (of Gravitation) [*Physics*] (ODA)
EGTA .... Aylesbury/Thame [*British*] [*ICAO location identifier*] (ICLI)
EGTA .... Esophageal Gastric Tube Airway [*Medicine*]
EGTA .... Ethylene Glycol Bis(aminoethyl ether)tetraacetic Acid [*Also, EBONTA*] [*Organic chemistry*]
EGTA .... Ethylene Glycol Tetra-Acetic Acid [*Organic chemistry*] (DAVI)
EGTA .... European Group of Television Advertising (EA)
EGTB .... Wycombe Air Park/Booker [*British*] [*ICAO location identifier*] (ICLI)
EGTC .... Cranfield [*British*] [*ICAO location identifier*] (ICLI)
EGTD .... Dunsfold [*British*] [*ICAO location identifier*] (ICLI)
EGTD .... Electric Gun & Turret Drive (SAUS)
EGTE .... Exeter [*British*] [*ICAO location identifier*] (ICLI)
EGTF .... Electron Gun Test Facility (SAUS)
EGTF .... Fairoaks [*British*] [*ICAO location identifier*] (ICLI)
EGTG .... Bristol/Filton [*British*] [*ICAO location identifier*] (ICLI)
EGTH .... Hatfield [*British*] [*ICAO location identifier*] (ICLI)
EGTI .... Exhaust Gas Temperature Indicator
EGTI .... Leavesden [*British*] [*ICAO location identifier*] (ICLI)
EGTK .... Oxford/Kidlington [*British*] [*ICAO location identifier*] (ICLI)
EGTO .... Egyptian General Trade Organization (SAUO)
EGTO .... Rochester [*British*] [*ICAO location identifier*] (ICLI)
EGTR .... Eglin Gulf Test Range [*Florida*] [*Air Force*]
egtr .... Electric Guitar
EGTR .... Elstree [*British*] [*ICAO location identifier*] (ICLI)
EGTRRA .... Economic Growth and Tax Relief Reconciliation Act [*2001*]

EGTS........... Emergency Gas Treatment System [*Nuclear energy*] (NRCH)
EGTS........... Exhaust Gas Temperature Switch [*Automotive term*] (HAWK)
EGTT........... London Air Traffic Control Center [*British*] [*ICAO location identifier*] (ICLI)
EGTYF.......... European Good Templar Youth Federation [*Norway*] (EAIO)
EGU........... English Golf Union (BI)
EGUA........... Upper Heyford [*British*] [*ICAO location identifier*] (ICLI)
EGUB........... Benson [*British*] [*ICAO location identifier*] (ICLI)
EGUC........... Aberporth [*British*] [*ICAO location identifier*] (ICLI)
EGUD........... Abingdon [*British*] [*ICAO location identifier*] (ICLI)
EGUF........... Farnborough [*British*] [*ICAO location identifier*] (ICLI)
EGUH........... High Wycombe [*British*] [*ICAO location identifier*] (ICLI)
EGUHM.......... Extra Gentleman Usher to His Majesty [*British*]
Eguin Baro... Eguinarius Baro [*Deceased, 1550*] [*Authority cited in pre-1607 legal work*] (DSA)
EGUK........... Waterbeach [*British*] [*ICAO location identifier*] (ICLI)
EGUL........... Lakenheath [*British*] [*ICAO location identifier*] (ICLI)
EGUM........... Manston [*British*] [*ICAO location identifier*] (ICLI)
EGUN........... Fast Pulse Electron Gun [*NASA*] (NASA)
EGUN........... Mildenhall [*British*] [*ICAO location identifier*] (ICLI)
EGUO........... Oakington [*British*] [*ICAO location identifier*] (ICLI)
EGUP........... Sculthorpe [*British*] [*ICAO location identifier*] (ICLI)
EGUS........... Lee-On-Solent [*British*] [*ICAO location identifier*] (ICLI)
EGUU........... Uxbridge [*British*] [*ICAO location identifier*] (ICLI)
EGUW........... Wattisham [*British*] [*ICAO location identifier*] (ICLI)
EGUY........... Wyton [*British*] [*ICAO location identifier*] (ICLI)
EGV........... Eagle River, WI [*Location identifier*] [*FAA*] (FAAL)
EGV........... Embroiderers' Guild of Victoria [*Australia*]
EGV........... Exit Guide Vane
EGVA........... Fairford [*British*] [*ICAO location identifier*] (ICLI)
EGVB........... Bawdsey [*British*] [*ICAO location identifier*] (ICLI)
EGVC........... Northolt [*British*] [*ICAO location identifier*] (ICLI)
EGVG........... Woodbridge [*British*] [*ICAO location identifier*] (ICLI)
EGVI........... Greenham Common [*British*] [*ICAO location identifier*] (ICLI)
EGVJ........... Bentwaters [*British*] [*ICAO location identifier*] (ICLI)
EGVN........... Brize Norton [*British*] [*ICAO location identifier*] (ICLI)
EGVO........... Odiham [*British*] [*ICAO location identifier*] (ICLI)
EGVP........... Middle Wallop [*British*] [*ICAO location identifier*] (ICLI)
EGVT........... Wethersfield [*British*] [*ICAO location identifier*] (ICLI)
EGVW........... Bedford [*British*] [*ICAO location identifier*] (ICLI)
EGW........... Edge Gateway (SAUS)
EGW........... Edgewater Resources Ltd. [*Vancouver Stock Exchange symbol*]
EGW........... Electrogas Welding
EGW........... Enamel Guild: West (EA)
EGW........... Engineering Writer
EGW........... Equipment Ground Wire
e-gw-........... Germany, West [*MARC geographic area code*] [*Library of Congress*] (LCCP)
EGWA........... Embroiderers' Guild of Western Australia
EGWB........... Ministry of Defence, United Kingdom [*ICAO location identifier*] (ICLI)
EGWC........... Cosford [*British*] [*ICAO location identifier*] (ICLI)
EGWD........... West Drayton [*British*] [*ICAO location identifier*] (ICLI)
EGWE........... Henlow [*British*] [*ICAO location identifier*] (ICLI)
EGWI........... London [*British*] [*ICAO location identifier*] (ICLI)
EGWL........... North Luffenham [*British*] [*ICAO location identifier*] (ICLI)
EGWN........... Halton [*British*] [*ICAO location identifier*] (ICLI)
EGWS........... Enhanced General War System (SAUS)
EGWS........... Stanmore Park [*British*] [*ICAO location identifier*] (ICLI)
EGWU........... Northolt [*British*] [*ICAO location identifier*] (ICLI)
EGWX........... CINCFLEETWOC [*British*] [*ICAO location identifier*] (ICLI)
EGWZ........... Alconbury [*British*] [*ICAO location identifier*] (ICLI)
EGX........... Egegik [*Alaska*] [*Airport symbol*] (OAG)
EGX........... Energex Minerals Ltd. [*Toronto Stock Exchange symbol*] [*Vancouver Stock Exchange symbol*]
EGX........... Engex, Inc. [*AMEX symbol*] (SPSG)
e-gx-........... Germany [*MARC geographic area code*] [*Library of Congress*] (LCCP)
EGXB........... Binbrook [*British*] [*ICAO location identifier*] (ICLI)
EGXC........... Coningsby [*British*] [*ICAO location identifier*] (ICLI)
EGXE........... Leeming [*British*] [*ICAO location identifier*] (ICLI)
EGXG........... Church Fenton [*British*] [*ICAO location identifier*] (ICLI)
EGXH........... Honington [*British*] [*ICAO location identifier*] (ICLI)
EGXI........... Finningley [*British*] [*ICAO location identifier*] (ICLI)
EGXJ........... Cottesmore [*British*] [*ICAO location identifier*] (ICLI)
EGXN........... Newton [*British*] [*ICAO location identifier*] (ICLI)
EGXP........... Scampton [*British*] [*ICAO location identifier*] (ICLI)
EGXS........... Swinderby [*British*] [*ICAO location identifier*] (ICLI)
EGXT........... Wittering [*British*] [*ICAO location identifier*] (ICLI)
EGXU........... Linton-On-Ouse [*British*] [*ICAO location identifier*] (ICLI)
EGXV........... Leconfield [*British*] [*ICAO location identifier*] (ICLI)
EGXW........... Waddington [*British*] [*ICAO location identifier*] (ICLI)
EGXZ........... Topcliffe [*British*] [*ICAO location identifier*] (ICLI)
EGY........... Columbus Energy [*AMEX symbol*] (TTSB)
EGY........... Columbus Energy Corp. [*AMEX symbol*] (SPSG)
EGY........... Egypt [*ANSI three-letter standard code*] (CNC)
Egy........... Egypt (VRA)
egy........... Egyptian [*MARC language code*] [*Library of Congress*] (LCCP)
EGY........... Egyptian (ROG)
EGY........... Egyptian Air Force [*FAA designator*] (FAAC)
EGY........... Egyptology
EGY........... English Bay, AK [*Location identifier*] [*FAA*] (FAAL)
EGY........... Triton Energy Corp. [*Toronto Stock Exchange symbol*]
EGYB........... Brampton [*British*] [*ICAO location identifier*] (ICLI)
EGYC........... Coltishall [*British*] [*ICAO location identifier*] (ICLI)
EgyCny........ Energy Conversion Devices, Inc. [*Associated Press*] (SAG)
EGYD........... Cranwell [*British*] [*ICAO location identifier*] (ICLI)
EGYE........... Barkston Heath [*British*] [*ICAO location identifier*] (ICLI)
EGYH........... Holbeach [*British*] [*ICAO location identifier*] (ICLI)
EGYK........... Elvington [*British*] [*ICAO location identifier*] (ICLI)
EGYM........... Marham [*British*] [*ICAO location identifier*] (ICLI)
Egyp........... Egypt (SAUS)
Egyp........... Egyptian (DIAR)
EGYP........... Egyptian (ROG)
Egyp........... egyptology (SAUS)
EGYP........... Mount Pleasant [*British*] [*ICAO location identifier*] (ICLI)
Egypt........... Arab Republic of Egypt (SAUS)
EGYPT........... Eager to Grab Your Pretty Top [*Correspondence*] [*Bowdlerized version*] (DSUE)
Egypt........... Egyptian (BEE)
EGYPT........... Egyptian (ROG)
Egypt Comput J... Egyptian Computer Journal (journ.) (SAUS)
Egyptol........ Egyptologist (SAUS)
egyptol........ Egyptology (ADWA)
EGYPTOL..... Egyptology (ROG)
EGYR........... Watton [*British*] [*ICAO location identifier*] (ICLI)
EGZ........... Estimated Ground Zero (SAUS)
EH........... Assistant Secretary for Environment, Safety, and Health (SAUS)
EH........... Derma: Epidermolysis Hyperkeratosis (SAUS)
EH........... Early Hebrew (BJA)
EH........... Easily Hydrolyzable (SAUS)
EH........... Eclosion Hormone [*Entomology*]
EH........... Economie et Humanism [*Economy and Humanism*] [*An association*] (EAIO)
EH........... Educationally Handicapped
EH........... Effective Height (SAUS)
EH........... Eggs in Hatching [*Parcel Post*]
EH........... Electra House (SAUS)
EH........... Electrical Hydraulics
EH........... Electric Heater (AAG)
EH........... Electric Hoist (IAA)
EH........... Electrohydraulic [*Nuclear energy*] (NRCH)
EH........... Electrohydrodynamic Ionization
EH........... Electron Hole (SAUS)
EH........... Eminent Herald [*Freemasonry*] (ROG)
EH........... Emotionally Handicapped [*Psychology*]
EH........... Encyclopaedia Hebraica [*Jerusalem*] [*A publication*] (BJA)
EH........... Endometrial Hyperplasia [*Medicine*] (MELL)
EH........... Engineering Hardware (SAUS)
EH........... Engineering Hydrology (SAUS)
EH........... Engine Heater [*Automotive accessory*]
EH........... Engine Hoods
EH........... English Heritage (WDAA)
EH........... English Horn
EH........... English Hymnal [*Episcopalian*]
EH........... Enlarged Heart [*Medicine*]
EH........... Enlil Hymn (BJA)
EH........... environmental and health protection (SAUS)
EH........... environmental and health site safety representative (SAUS)
EH........... Environment, Safety and Health, Office of (SAUS)
EH........... Epidermolysis Hyperkeratosis (SAUS)
EH........... Epidermolytic Hyperkeratosis [*Dermatology*]
EH........... Epidural Hematoma [*Medicine*] (MELL)
EH........... Epochs of History [*A publication*]
EH........... Epoxide Hydrolase [*An enzyme*]
EH........... Equilibrium Humidity (WDAA)
EH........... Equitable Handicap [*Sailing*]
EH........... Equivalent Hertz (SSD)
EH........... Equivalent Hour (ACAE)
EH........... Erase Head (SAUS)
EH........... Erasing Head (SAUS)
EH........... Eridu Hymn (BJA)
EH........... Ernest Hemingway (SAUS)
EH........... Escort Helicopter (CINC)
EH........... Essential Hypertension [*Medicine*]
EH........... Ethiopian Herald [*A publication*]
EH........... Ets Haim Seminary [*Amsterdam*] (BJA)
EH........... Euskal Herritarrok [*Spain*] [*Political party*]
EH........... Evacuation Hospital (SAUS)
EH........... Even ha-'Ezer, Shulhan 'Arukh (BJA)
EH........... Everlasting Heritage [*A variety of sweet corn*]
EH........... Exegetisches Handbuch zum Alten Testament [*Muenster*] [*A publication*] (BJA)
EH........... Exercise Head
EH........... Experimental Herbicide (SAUS)
EH........... Extended Hueckel [*Molecular orbit*] [*Atomic physics*]
EH........... Extra Hazardous (AAG)
EH........... Extra [*or Extremely*] High
EH........... Extramedullary Hematopoiesis [*Hematology*] (DAVI)
EH........... Extrude Hone (SAUS)
Eh........... Heater Voltage (SAUS)
EH........... Office of Environment, Safety and Health (SAUS)
eH........... Oxidation-Reduction Potential [*Symbol*] (MAE)
E_h........... Redox Potential [*Symbol*] [*Organic chemistry*] (DAVI)
EH........... Western Sahara [*ANSI two-letter standard code*] (CNC)
EH-1........... Equine Herpesvirus, type 1 (SAUS)
EHA........... Early Hemi Association (EA)
EHA........... Early History of Assyria [*A publication*] (BJA)
EHA........... East Hampton Aire [*ICAO designator*] (FAAC)
EHA........... Economic History Association (EA)
EHA........... Educational Handwork Association (SAUO)

EHA............ Education for All Handicapped Children Act (AIE)
EHA............ Education of the Handicapped Act [*1968*]
EHA............ Edward Hamilton Aitken [*Author*] [*Initials used as pseudonym*]
EHA............ Effective Halfword Address (SAUS)
EHA............ Electrical Harness Assembly (KSC)
EHA............ Electric Heating Association (EA)
EHA............ Electric-Hydraulic Actuator (SAUS)
EHA............ Electrohydraulic Actuator
EHA............ Electro-Hydrostatic Actuator (SAUS)
EHA............ Elkhart, KS [*Location identifier*] [*FAA*] (FAAL)
EHA............ Emergency and Humanitarian Action (SAUO)
EHA............ Emergency and Humanitarian Assistance
EHA............ Emotional Health Anonymous (EA)
EHA............ Enkephalin-Hydrolyzing Activity
EHA............ En Route High Altitude
eha............ enroute high altitude (SAUS)
EHA............ Environmental Health Association (WDAA)
EHA............ Environmental Hygiene Agency [*Army*] (MCD)
EHA............ Environmental Protection Agency, Region I Library, Boston, MA [*OCLC symbol*] (OCLC)
EHA............ Enziklopedyah la-Hafirot ha-Arkheologiyot be-Erez Yisrael [*A publication*] (BJA)
EHA............ Equipment Handover Agreement [*Shipping*] (DS)
EHA............ Ethyl Hexyl Acetate (SAUS)
EHA............ Ethylhexyl Acrylate [*Organic chemistry*]
EHA............ Ethyl Hexyl Alcohol (SAUS)
EHA............ European Helicopter Association (PDAA)
EHA............ Expect Higher Altitude (FAAC)
EHAA............ Amsterdam [*Netherlands*] [*ICAO location identifier*] (ICLI)
EHAA............ Epidemic Hepatitis-Associated Antigen [*Immunochemistry*]
EHAA............ Epidermic Hepatitis-Associated Antigen [*Immunology*] (DAVI)
EHAA............ Every Hand an Adventure [*Bridge bidding method*]
EHAC............ Early Heart Attack Care
EHAC............ Enroute High Altitude Chart [*Aviation*] (PIPO)
EHAC............ National Environmental Health Science and Protection Accreditation Council (EA)
EHAG............ Emergency Housing Assistance Grant (SAUO)
EHAG............ Employee Health Assurance Group [*Medicine*]
EHAL............ Ameland [*Netherlands*] [*ICAO location identifier*] (ICLI)
EHAM............ Amsterdam/Schiphol [*Netherlands*] [*ICAO location identifier*] (ICLI)
EHAM............ Electronic Home Arrest Monitor (SEWL)
EHAMP............ Easthampton, MA [*American Association of Railroads railroad junction routing code*]
EHA-MR............ Equitable Handicap Associated-Measured Rating [*Boating*]
EH&AMPS............ Environment, Health, and Safety (SAUS)
EH&S............ Environmental Health and Safety (ACAE)
EH & S............ Environmental, Health, and Safety
EHAP............ Employee Health Assistance Program (SAUS)
EHAP............ Experimental Housing Allowance Program [*Department of Housing and Urban Development*] (GFGA)
EHAP............ Extremely Hazardous Air Pollutant [*Environmental science*]
EHAS............ East Hertshire Archaeological Society [*British*]
EHAT............ Equipment Historical Availability Trend [*Military*]
EHAT............ Exegetisches Handbuch zum Alten Testament [*Muenster*] [*A publication*] (BJA)
EHATS............ Electro Hydraulic Actuator Test Set (ACAE)
EHB............ Electro-Hydraulic Brake [*Automotive engineering*]
EHB............ Elevate Head of Bed [*Medicine*] (DAVI)
EHB............ Environmental Hearing Board (SAUS)
EHB............ Environmental Protection Agency, Environmental Research Laboratory, Narragansett, RI [*OCLC symbol*] (OCLC)
EHB............ Extra Hard Black [*Pencil leads*] (ROG)
EHBA............ Extrahepatic Biliary Atresia [*Medicine*]
EHBD............ Weert/Budel [*Netherlands*] [*ICAO location identifier*] (ICLI)
EHBF............ Essential High Blood Pressure [*Cardiology*] (DAVI)
EHBF............ Estimated Hepatic Blood Flow [*Medicine*]
EHBF............ Exercise Hyperemia Blood Flow [*Medicine*] (MAE)
EHBF............ Extrahepatic Blood Flow [*Medicine*]
EHBK............ Maastricht/Zuid-Limburg [*Netherlands*] [*ICAO location identifier*] (ICLI)
EHBP............ Essential High Blood Pressure (MELL)
EHC............ Education for all Handicapped Children act [*1975 federal law*] (PAZ)
EHC............ Elastic Hysteresis Constant
EHC............ Electrical Heating Control (MCD)
EHC............ Electrical Height Calculator (IAA)
EHC............ Electrically Heated Catalyst
EHC............ Electrochemical Hydrogen Cracking (SAUS)
EHC............ Electrohydraulic Control (NRCH)
EHC............ Electrohydrodynamic Convection [*Physics*]
EHC............ Electronically Heated Catalysts [*Automotive engineering*]
EHC............ Electronic Hardware Corporation (SAUO)
EHC............ Emergency Housing Consortium
EHC............ Emergency Housing Corp.
EHC............ Emergency Housing Corporation (SAUO)
EHC............ Emory and Henry College [*Virginia*]
EHC............ Enterohepatic Circulation [*Medicine*]
EHC............ Enterohepatic Clearance [*Biochemistry*] (DAVI)
EHC............ Environmental Hazard Communication
EHC............ Environmental Health Center (AEPA)
EHC............ Environmental Health Committee [*Environmental Protection Agency*] (GFGA)
EHC............ Environmental Health Conferences (SAUO)
EHC............ Environmental Health Criteria (SAUS)
EHC............ Environmentally Hazardous Chemical
EHC............ Error Handling Chip (SAUS)
EHC............ Essential Hypercholesterolemia [*Medicine*] (MAE)
EHC............ Ethylenic Hydrocarbon (SAUS)
EHC............ Ethylhydrocuprein (DB)
EHC............ European Helicopter Cooperation (SAUO)
EHC............ European Holographic Connection (SAUO)
EHC............ European Hotel Corporation (SAUO)
EHC............ Extended Health Care [*Insurance*]
EHC............ Extended Hospital Care [*Veterans Administration*] (GFGA)
ehc............ external heart compression (SAUS)
EHC............ Extra-Heavy Crude [*Petroleum technology*]
EHC............ Extrahepatic Cholestasis [*Medicine*]
EHC............ Extra High Conversion (SAUS)
EHC............ Effective Heat Capacity (ODA)
EHCA............ Education for All Handicapped Children Act
EHCAC............ Egyptian High Commission of Automatic Control (SAUS)
EHCC............ European Hop Culture Committee (SAUO)
EHCD............ Environment, Housing, and Community Development (SAUS)
EH-CF............ Entamoeba Histolytica-Complement Fixation [*Immunochemistry*] (DAVI)
EHCI............ Emergency and Hazardous Chemical Inventory [*Environmental science*] (COE)
EHCLS............ Encapsulated Harpoon Command and Launch System (MCD)
EHCM............ Editor "Hebrew Christians' Magazine" [*Pseudonym used by Nathan Davis*]
EHCN............ Experimental Hybrid Computer Network (MHDB)
EHCS............ Educational and Health Career Services (EA)
EHCS............ Electro-Hydraulic Control System
EHD............ E.H. Darby Aviation [*FAA designator*] (FAAC)
EHD............ Elastohydrodynamic
EHD............ Electrohemodynamics
EHD............ Electrohydrodimerization [*Organic chemistry*]
EHD............ Electron-Hole Drop [*Semiconductor physics*]
EHD............ Employee Health Department
EHD............ Engineer Historical Division [*Army*]
EHD............ Entity Hierarchy Diagram (TIMI)
EHD............ Environmental Health Directorate (SAUO)
EHD............ Environmental Hypersensitivity Disease [*Medicine*] (MELL)
EHD............ Epizootic Hemorrhagic Disease [*Veterinary medicine*]
EHD............ Experimental Husbandry Farm (SAUS)
EHD............ Extended-Height-to-Diameter [*Aviation*]
EHD............ Extra High Duty (SAUS)
EHDA............ Electrical Housewares Distributors Association [*Defunct*] (EA)
EHDA............ Electrohydrodynamic Atomization (SAUS)
EHDA............ Ethylhexadecyldimethylammonium Bromide [*Blood count diluent*]
EHDA............ Etidronate Sodium [*Pharmacology*] (DAVI)
EHDB............ De Bilt [*Netherlands*] [*ICAO location identifier*] (ICLI)
EHDC............ EMP Hardened Dispersal Communications (SAUS)
EHDHP............ Electrohydrodynamic Heat Pipe [*NASA*]
EHDI............ Electronic Horizontal Director Indicator [*Aviation*] (PDAA)
EHDL............ Deelen [*Netherlands*] [*ICAO location identifier*] (ICLI)
EHDM............ Enhanced Hierarchical Development Methodology (SAUS)
EHDP............ Ethanehydroxydiphosphonate [*or -diphosphonic Acid*] [*Also, HEDP*] [*Organic chemistry*]
EHDP............ Ethylenehydroxydiphosphonate [*Organic chemistry*]
EHDP............ Venraij/De Peel [*Netherlands*] [*ICAO location identifier*] (ICLI)
EHDPP............ Ethylhexyl Diphenyl Phosphate [*Organic chemistry*]
EHDR............ Drachten [*Netherlands*] [*ICAO location identifier*] (ICLI)
EHDR............ Erection, Holddown, and Release [*Aerospace*] (AAG)
EHDTV............ Enhanced High Definition Television (SAUS)
EHDV............ Epizootic Hemorrhagic Disease Virus [*Veterinary medicine*] (DMAA)
EHE............ Embassy Home Entertainment [*Video distributor*]
EHE............ Enterprise in Higher Education (SAUS)
EHE............ Epithelioid Hemangioendothelioma [*Medicine*] (STED)
EHE............ External Heat Exchanger (SAUS)
eHEAL............ Electronic Health Economics Analysis Letters (ADWA)
EHEC............ Enterohemorrhagic Escherichia Coli
EHEC............ Ethyl(hydroxyethyl)cellulose [*Organic chemistry*]
EHECA............ Emergency Highway Energy Conservation Act [*1974*]
EheG............ Ehegesetz [*Marriage Law*] [*German*] (ILCA)
EHEH............ Eindhoven [*Netherlands*] [*ICAO location identifier*] (ICLI)
eHEL............ Electronic Health Economics Letters (ADWA)
E-HEMT............ Enhancement-Mode High-Electron-Mobility Transistor (SAUS)
EHEP............ Experimental High-Energy Physics (SAUS)
EHES............ Environmental Health Engineering Services [*Army*] (AABC)
EHF............ Electrical Historical Foundation [*Defunct*] (EA)
EHF............ Electrohydraulic Forming
EHF............ electrohydraulic Fragmentation [*Medicine*] (DAVI)
EHF............ Elevated HF antenna (SAUS)
EHF............ Encoding Header Field [*Computer science*] (VERA)
EHF............ End Half
EHF............ Engineers Hall of Fame (SAUS)
EHF............ Environmental Health Forum (SAUO)
EHF............ Epidemic Hemolytic Fever [*Medicine*] (EDAA)
EHF............ Epidemic Hemorrhagic Fever [*Disease encountered by American troops during the Korean War*]
EHF............ European Habitats Forum (SAUS)
EHF............ European Hockey Federation (SAUO)
EHF............ Exophthalmos-Hyperthyroid Factor [*Endocrinology*] (AAMN)
EHF............ Experimental Husbandry Farm [*British*]
EHF............ Exponential Hazard Function
EHF............ Extra High Frequency (SAUS)
ehf............ extreme high-frequency (SAUS)
EHF............ Extremely High Factor (STED)
EHF............ Extremely High Frequencies (SAUS)
EHF............ Extremely High Frequency [*Electronics, radio wave*]

EHF Frequencies above 30GHz (SAUS)

EHFA Electric Home and Farm Authority [*Terminated, 1947*]

EHFB Electrical Historical Foundation Board (SAUO)

EHFC Emmylou Harris Fan Club (EA)

EHF SATCOM Extra-High-Frequency Satellite Communication

EHF SATCOM Extremely High Frequency Satellite Communication (SAUS)

EHG Edinburgh Home Guard [*British military*] (DMA)

EHG Edvard Hagerup Grieg (SAUS)

EHG Electro-Hydrodynamic Power Generation (SAUS)

EHG energy heat gain (SAUS)

EHG Executive Health Group [*Medicine*] (EDAA)

ehg extra high grade (SAUS)

EHG Electro-Hydraulic Governor (ODA)

EHGG Groningen/Eelde [*Netherlands*] [*ICAO location identifier*] (ICLI)

EHGR Gilze-Rijen [*Netherlands*] [*ICAO location identifier*] (ICLI)

EHGV 'S Gravenhage [*Netherlands*] [*ICAO location identifier*] (ICLI)

EHH Esophageal Hiatal Hernia [*Medicine*] (MEDA)

EHH Ever Heard of Him [*Facetious criterion for determining insignificance of Supreme Court Justices*] [*Proposed by University of Chicago professor David P. Currie*]

EHHE Environmental Hazards and Health Effects (ADWA)

EHHO Hoogeveen [*Netherlands*] [*ICAO location identifier*] (ICLI)

EHHS Erasmus Hall High School (SAUS)

EHHV Hilversum [*Netherlands*] [*ICAO location identifier*] (ICLI)

EHI EH Industries Ltd. (SAUS)

EHI Electronic Height Indicator (MCD)

EHI Emergency Homes, Inc.

EHI Emergency Homes, Incorporated (SAUO)

EHI Employee Health Insurance

EHI Environmental Health Institute [*Pittsfield, MA*]

EHI Expanded Helicopter Industries [*Military*]

EHI Experimental Homes, Incorporated (SAUO)

EHIA Environmental Health Impact Assessment (FOTI)

EHIA European Herbal Infusions Association (EA)

EHIC Emergency Hurricane Information Center [*Marine science*] (MSC)

EHIC Energetic Heavy Ion Composition Experiment [*NASA*]

EHICS Employer Health Insurance Cost Survey [*Department of Health and Human Services*] (GFGA)

EH-IHA Complement Histolytica-Indirect Hemagglutination [*Hematology*] (DAVI)

EHIP Employee Health Insurance Plan (DHSM)

EHIP European HAWK Improvement Program (SAUS)

EHIS Emission History Information System [*Environmental Information Agency*]

EHIS Encyclopedia of Health Information Sources [*A publication*]

EHIS Environmental Health Information Services (ADWA)

EHJ Emanuel Haldeman-Julius (SAUS)

EHK Electrode Heater Kit

EHK Epidermolytic Hyperkeratosis [*Dermatology*]

EHKD De Kooy (Den Helder) [*Netherlands*] [*ICAO location identifier*] (ICLI)

EHL Eastern Hockey League

EHL Effective Halflife [*Nuclear science*]

ehl effective half life (SAUS)

EHL Elastohydrodynamic Lubrication

EHL El Bolson [*Argentina*] [*Airport symbol*] (OAG)

EHL Electrohydraulic Lithotripsy [*Medicine*] (HCT)

EHL Electrohydraulic Lithotriptor [*Nephrology and urology*] (DAVI)

EHL Electron-Hole Liquid Model [*Physics*]

EHL Endogenous Hyperlipidemia [*Medicine*] (MAE)

Ehl English as a home language (SAUS)

EHL Environmental Health Laboratory [*Air Force*]

EHL Essential Hyperlipidemia [*Medicine*] (STED)

EHL Evaporative Heat Loss (SAUS)

EHL Extensor Hallucis Longus [*Anatomy*]

EHLE Lelystad [*Netherlands*] [*ICAO location identifier*] (ICLI)

EHL(K) Environmental Health Laboratory, Kelly Air Force Base

EHLLAPI Emulator High-Level Language Application Programming Interface [*Computer science*] (PCM)

EHLLAPI Extended High-Level Language Application Program Interface [*Computer science*]

EHL-M Environmental Health Laboratory, McClellan Air Force Base

EHLS Division of Environmental Health Laboratory Sciences (SAUO)

EHLS Environmental Health Laboratory Sciences Division [*Atlanta, GA*] [*Department of Health and Human Services*] (GRD)

EHLW Leeuwarden [*Netherlands*] [*ICAO location identifier*] (ICLI)

EHM Advisory Committee for Earthquake Hazard Mitigation [*Washington, DC*] [*National Science Foundation*] (EGAO)

EHM Cape Newenham [*Alaska*] [*Airport symbol*] (OAG)

EHM Earthquake Hazard Maps (SAUO)

E/H/M Eggs per Hen per Month (SAUS)

EHM Electrohydraulic Motor

EHM Encyclopedia of Holistic Medicine [*A publication*]

EHM Engine Health Monitoring (MCD)

EHM engine heavy maintenance (SAUS)

EHM Environmental Hazards Management (SAUO)

EHM Environmental Hazards Management Institute [*University of New Hampshire*] [*Research center*] (RCD)

EHM Environmental Health Forum (SAUO)

EHM Extended Hueckel Method (SAUS)

EH/M Extension Hose/Mouthpiece (MCD)

EHM Eye-Hand-Muscle (SAA)

EHMA Electric Hoist Manufacturers Association (SAUO)

EHMA European Healthcare Management Association (EAIO)

EHMA European Hotel Managers Association (EA)

EHMA Evangelism and Home Missions Association (EA)

EHMC Nieuw Milligen [*Netherlands*] [*ICAO location identifier*] (ICLI)

EHME Employee Health Maintenance Examination

EHMI Environmental Hazards Management Institute (GNE)

EHML Nieuw Milligen [*Netherlands*] [*ICAO location identifier*] (ICLI)

EHMO Extended Hueckel Molecular Orbit [*Atomic physics*]

EHMS Electrohydrodynamic Ionization Mass Spectrometry

EHMS Engine Health Monitoring System

EHMZ Middelburg/Midden Zeeland [*Netherlands*] [*ICAO location identifier*] (ICLI)

EHN End Hunger Network (EA)

EHN Environmental Health Network [*Defunct*] (EA)

EHN Environmental Health News [*Database*] [*Occupational Health Services, Inc.*] [*Information service or system*] (CRD)

EHN European Host Network [*Computer science*]

EHN Exploring Human Nature [*National Science Foundation project*]

EHNA Erythro(hydroxynonyl)adenine [*Biochemistry*]

EHNP Edwin I. Hatch Nuclear Plant (NRCH)

EHNP Emmeloord/Noord-Oostpolder [*Netherlands*] [*ICAO location identifier*] (ICLI)

EHO Early Hebrew Orthography [*A publication*] (BJA)

EHO Environmental Health Office (SAUS)

EHO Environmental Health Officer [*British*] (DCTA)

EHO Estimated Hourly Output [*Electronics*] (AAEL)

EHO Extrahepatic Obstruction [*Medicine*]

EHO extra high output (SAUS)

EHO Shelby, NC [*Location identifier*] [*FAA*] (FAAL)

EHOG Association of the European Host Operators Group (SAUO)

EHOG European Host Operators Group [*EURONET*] [*Luxembourg*]

EHOM Electronics Hardover Monitor (SAA)

EHOP Employee Home Ownership Plan [*Human resources*] (WYGK)

EHOP Equal Housing Opportunity Plan (SAUO)

EHosp Evacuation Hospital (SAUS)

EHOT External Hydrogen/Oxygen Tank (NASA)

EHP Di-(2-Ethylhexyl) Hydrogen Phosphate [*Organic chemistry*] (DAVI)

EHP Effective Horsepower

EHP Electrical Hull Penetration

EHP Electric Horsepower

EHP Electron Hole Pair (SAUS)

EHP Electron-Hole Pairs (ACRL)

EHP Electron-Hole Plasma (AAEL)

EHP Electron-Hole Potential Method [*Physics*]

EHP Environmental Health Perspective (SAUO)

EHP Environmental Health Program (SAUS)

Ehp Equivalent Horse Power (SAUS)

ehp Equivalent Horsepower (DOMA)

EHP Error Handling Package (SAUS)

EHP Estimated Horsepower

EHP Excessive Heat Production (MAE)

EHP Extra-High Potency

EHP Extra-High Pressure (ROG)

EHP Extrinsic Hyperpolarizing Potential

EHP Office of Environmental and Health Protection (SAUS)

EHPA Ethylhexyl Phosphoric Acid (SAUS)

EHPA Ethylhexyl Phosphoric Hour (SAUS)

EHPAC Emergency Health Preparedness Advisory Committee [*Terminated, 1973*] (EA)

EHPC Electro-Hydraulic Proportional Control [*Automotive engineering*]

EHPC Environmental Health Policy Committee [*World Health Organization*]

EHPC Extended High Priority Command (ADWA)

EHPF European Health Policy Forum (EAIO)

EHPG Ethylenebis(hydroxyphenylglycine) [*Organic chemistry*]

EHPH Electric Horsepower Hour (IAA)

EHPH Extrahepatic Portal Hypertension [*Medicine*] (MAE)

EHPL Estimated Half-Power Life (SAUS)

EHPM Electrohydraulic Pulse Motor

EHPM European Federation of Associations of Health Product Manufacturers (EAIO)

EHPRG European High Pressure Research Group (EA)

EHPRN European Health Policy Research Network [*British*] (ECON)

EHPT Eddy Hot Plate Test [*Clinical chemistry*] (AAMN)

EHR Earned Hour Ratio (NASA)

EHR Economic History Review (journ.) (SAUS)

EHR Education and Human Resources (SAUS)

EHR Emergency Heat Removal [*Nuclear energy*] (NRCH)

EHR English Historical Review [*A publication*] (BRI)

ehr enhanced reflector (SAUS)

EHR Environmental Health Review (ADWA)

EHR Error Handling Routine (SAUS)

EHR European Human Rights (EAIO)

EHR Euthanize for Humane Reasons [*ASPCE terminology*]

EHR Events History Recorder (MCD)

EHR evoked heart rate response (SAUS)

EHR Explosive Hazard Reduction (SAUS)

EHR Extra-High Reliability

EHRA Endurance Horse Registry of America (EA)

EHRC European Humanities Research Centre [*University of Warwick*] [*British*] (CB)

EHRD Rotterdam [*Netherlands*] [*ICAO location identifier*] (ICLI)

EHRF Equine Health Research Fund [*Equine term*] (TED)

EHRR European Human Rights Reports [*A publication*] (SAFN)

EHRS Environmental Health Research Staff (SAUO)

EHRS European Histamine Research Society (EAIO)

EHS Earth Horizon Scanner

EHS Earth-Lunar Horizon Sensor

EHS Ecclesiastical History Society (EAIO)

EHS............ Ectopic-Hypercalcemia Syndrome [*Medicine*] (MELL)
EHS............ Electrical Horology Society (EA)
EHS............ Electric Heated Seats [*Automotive classified advertising*]
EHS............ Elitos SpA [*Italy*] [*ICAO designator*] (FAAC)
EHS............ Elongating Hypocotyl Section [*Botany*]
EHS............ Emergency Health Service [*HEW*]
EHS............ Emergency Hospital Scheme
EHS............ Employee Health Service (MELL)
EHS............ Englebreth-Holm-Swarm Sarcoma Cells [*Cell biology*] (QSUL)
EHS............ Environmental Health Sciences (SAUO)
EHS............ Environmental Health Service [*US Government*]
EHS............ Environmental Health Specialist
EHS............ Environmental Health Standards (EERA)
EHS............ Environmental Health System (SAUO)
EHS............ Environmental Hydro Systems (SAUO)
EHS............ Estonian Educational Society (EA)
EHS............ European Home System (SAUO)
EHS............ Experimental Horticulture Station [*British*]
EHS............ Experiment Horticulture Station (SAUS)
EHS............ Exploding Head Syndrom [*Common and totally benign condition in which patients are alarmed by a sudden loud noise in the twilight stage of sleep*] [*Medicine*] (EDAA)
EHS............ Extra-High Strength [*Steel*] [*Telecommunications*] (TEL)
EHS............ Extraordinarily Hazardous Substance [*Industrial hygiene term*] (OHS)
EHS............ Extreme High Shot [*Photography*]
EHS............ Extremely hazardous materials (SAUS)
EHS............ Extremely Hazardous Substances
EHSA............ Enhanced High System Availability (DINT)
EHSB............ Soesterberg [*Netherlands*] [*ICAO location identifier*] (ICLI)
EHSC............ United States Army Engineering and Housing Support Center (AAGC)
EHSD............ Electronic Horizontal Situation Display [*Aviation*] (PDAA)
EHSD............ Environment, Health and Safety Division (SAUO)
EHSDS............ Experimental Health Services Delivery Systems [*HEW*]
EHSE............ Hoeven/Seppe [*Netherlands*] [*ICAO location identifier*] (ICLI)
EHSI............ Electronic Horizontal Situation Indicator
EHSP............ Environment Health Safety Program (SAUS)
EHST............ Electronic Hair Styling [*NASDAQ symbol*] (TTSB)
EHST............ Electronic Hair Styling, Inc. [*NASDAQ symbol*] (SAG)
EHST............ Engellireth-Holm Swarm Tumor [*Medicine*]
EHST............ Stadskanaal [*Netherlands*] [*ICAO location identifier*] (ICLI)
EHSV............ Electrohydraulic Servo Valve (MCD)
EHSX............ Essex Hybrid Seed [*Private rail car owner code*]
EHT............ East Hartford, CT [*Location identifier*] [*FAA*] (FAAL)
EHT............ Effective Hydration Temperature [*Archeology, geology*]
EHT............ Electric Heat Tracing (ACII)
EHT............ Electrothermal Heat Thruster (SAUS)
EHT............ Electrothermal Hydrazine Thruster
EHT............ Electrothermally Heated Thrusters (ACAE)
EHT............ Emitter Homing Technology (ACAE)
EHT............ Employer Health Tax (FOTI)
EHT............ Essential Hypertension (MELL)
EHT............ Extended Huckel Theory [*Atomic physics*]
EHT............ Extra-High Tension
EHT............ Extremely High Tension (SAUS)
EHT............ Eye Head Tracker (ACAE)
EHTB............ Extended Hueckel Tight-Binding [*Quantum mechanics*]
EHTD............ Equivalent Heat Transfer Dimensionality [*Process engineering*]
EHTE............ Deventer/Teuge [*Netherlands*] [*ICAO location identifier*] (ICLI)
EHTO............ European Health Telematics Observatory (SAUO)
EHTP............ East Harlem Tutorial Program [*New York*]
EHTPS............ Extra-High-Tension Power Supply (EECA)
EHTR............ Emergency Highway Traffic Regulation [*Federal disaster planning*]
EHTR............ Enhanced Heat Transfer Reformer [*Engineering*]
EHTRC............ Emergency Highway Traffic Regulation Center [*Federal disaster planning*] (AABC)
EHTS............ Emergent Hydrophyte Treatment System
EHTW............ Enschede/Twenthe [*Netherlands*] [*ICAO location identifier*] (ICLI)
EHTX............ Texel [*Netherlands*] [*ICAO location identifier*] (ICLI)
EHU............ Electric Heating Unit
e-hu-............ Hungary [*MARC geographic area code*] [*Library of Congress*] (LCCP)
EHV............ Electric and Hybrid Vehicles
EHV............ Electric Heart Vector [*Cardiology*]
EHV............ Electric Heat Vector [*Physics*] (DAVI)
EHV............ electric hybrid vehicle (SAUS)
EHV............ Electrohydraulic Valve (MCD)
EHV............ El Hato [*Venezuela*] [*Seismograph station code, US Geological Survey*] (SEIS)
EHV............ Equine Herpes Virus
EHV............ Europaischer Holzhandelsverband [*European Timber Association*] [*EC*] (ECED)
EHV............ Extra-High Voltage [*FPC*]
EHV............ Extremely High Voltage (SAUS)
EHV1............ Equine Herpesvirus 1 [*Equine term*] (TED)
EHV4............ Equine Herpesvirus 4 [*Equine term*] (TED)
EHVA............ Electrohydraulic Valve Actuator (IAA)
EHVB............ Valkenburg [*Netherlands*] [*ICAO location identifier*] (ICLI)
EHVIST............ Ethical and Human Value Implications of Science and Technology (SAUS)
EHVK............ Volkel [*Netherlands*] [*ICAO location identifier*] (ICLI)
EHW............ Environmental Health Watch (SAUS)
EHW............ Equivalent Hours Worked (SAUS)
EHW............ Ethnic Health Worker [*Australia*]
EHW............ European Heathland Workshop (SAUS)
EHW............ Evolvable HardWare (SAUS)
EHW............ Extreme High Water
EHW............ extremely hazardous waste (SAUS)
EHWO............ Woensdrecht [*Netherlands*] [*ICAO location identifier*] (ICLI)
EHWS............ Electric Hot Water Service [*Classified advertising*] (ADA)
ehws............ extreme-high-water-level spring tides (SAUS)
EHX............ emergency heat exchanger (SAUS)
EHX............ Experiment Dedicated Heat Exchanger (MCD)
EHY............ Engage High Yield
EHYB............ Ypenburg [*Netherlands*] [*ICAO location identifier*] (ICLI)
e/h/yr............ eggs per hen per year (SAUS)
EHz............ Exahertz (ADWA)
EI............ Airline Carrier code (SAUS)
EI............ Air Lingus [*ICAO designator*] (AD)
EI............ Early Intervention
EI............ Early Iron Age [*Archeology*] (BJA)
EI............ Earned Income
E/I............ Earned Premium to Incurred Loss Ratio [*Insurance*]
EI............ Earth Inductor (SAUS)
EI............ East India (ROG)
EI............ East Indies
EI............ Eat-In [*Kitchen*] [*Classified advertising*]
EI............ Echo Intensity [*Marine science*] (OSRA)
EI............ Ecoforestry Institute - United States (EA)
EI............ Ectopic Implantation [*Medicine*] (MELL)
EI............ Ecumenical Institute [*World Council of Churches*] (EA)
EI............ Educational Insights
EI............ Educational Intervention (SAUS)
EI............ Educationally Impaired
EI............ Education International (SAUS)
EI............ Effectiveness Index (MCD)
EI............ Eire (SAUS)
EI............ Eisenhower Institute (EA)
EI............ Eisenhower World Affairs Institute (EA)
EI............ Elderhostel, Inc. (EA)
EI............ Electrical Industries (SAUS)
EI............ Electrical Instrument (SAUS)
EI............ Electrical Insulation (MCD)
EI............ Electric Iron (SAUS)
EI............ Electrogist International (SAUS)
EI............ Electro Industries (SAUS)
EI............ Electro Institute (SAUS)
EI............ Electro Instruments (SAUS)
EI............ Electrolyte Imbalance [*Physiology*]
EI............ Electromagnetic Interference
EI............ Electronic Ignition [*Automotive engineering*]
EI............ electronic imaging (SAUS)
EI............ Electronic Imaging Conference and Exposition (ITD)
EI............ electronic injection (SAUS)
EI............ Electronic Installation
EI............ Electronic Instruction (MCD)
EI............ Electronic Intelligence (ACAE)
EI............ Electronic Interface (MCD)
EI............ Electronic Interference
EI............ Electron Impact [*Mass spectrometry*]
EI............ Electron-Impact Ionization (EDCT)
EI............ Electron Ionization [*Spectrometry*]
EI............ Eligible Individual [*Social Security Administration*]
EI............ Elmwood Institute (EA)
EI............ Emaus Internacional [*Emmaus International*] (EA)
EI............ Embrittlement Index (PDAA)
EI............ Emergency Injection [*Nuclear energy*] (NRCH)
EI............ Emergency International (EA)
EI............ Emery Industries, Incorporated (SAUO)
EI............ Emigrant Institute [*Sweden*]
EI............ Emission Index
EI............ Emissions Inventory [*Environmental Protection Agency*] (GFGA)
EI............ Emmission Index (SAUS)
EI............ Emotional Intelligence (MELL)
EI............ Emotionally Impaired
EI............ Empathy Inventory [*Teacher evaluation test*]
EI............ Employee Involvement [*Human resources*] (WYGK)
EI............ Employer Identification (SAUS)
EI............ Employment Insurance (FOTI)
EI............ Employment Inventory [*George Paajanen*] (TES)
EI............ Empowerment Inventory [*Test*] (TMMY)
EI............ Emulsion In [*Photography*] (WDMC)
EI............ Enable Interrupt (MHDB)
EI............ Enamelled Iron (SAUS)
EI............ Endevco, Inc. (EFIS)
EI............ End Injection (IEEE)
EI............ End Item
EI............ Endocrinology Index [*Publication*] [*Medicine*] (EDAA)
E/I............ Endorsement Irregular [*Banking*]
EI............ Enemy Intelligence
EI............ energy index (SAUS)
EI............ Energy Information Administration (SAUO)
EI............ Energy Intake (ODA)
EI............ Energy North, Inc. [*NYSE symbol*] (SAG)
EI............ Engineering Index (ECII)
EI............ Engineering Index, Incorporated (SAUO)
Ei............ Engineering Information [*An association*] [*Also, an information service or system*] (EA)
Ei............ Engineering Information, Inc. (SAUO)
EI............ Engineering Information, Incorporated (SAUS)
E-I............ Engineering-Installation (AFM)

EI .... Engineering Instruction
EI .... Engineering Investigation (MCD)
EI .... Engineering Item (MCD)
EI .... English Institute (EA)
EI .... Entayant Institute (EA)
EI .... Enterprise Integration (SAUS)
EI .... Entrepreneurial Institute [*Australia*]
EI .... Entry Interface (NASA)
EI .... Entsiklopedyah 'Ivrit [*or Enziklopedyah 'Ivrit*] (BJA)
EI .... Environmental Illness (SAUO)
EI .... Environmental Impact (NASA)
EI .... Environmentally Ill [*Medicine*]
EI .... Environment Institute (SAUS)
EI .... Enzyme Inhibitor [*Biochemistry*]
EI .... Eosinophilic Index [*Medicine*] (MAE)
EI .... Epilepsy International (EAIO)
EI .... Epitheliogenesis [*Equine term*] (TED)
EI .... Epitheliogenesis Imperfecta [*Equine term*] (TED)
EI .... Equilibrium Index (SAUS)
EI .... Equipment Integration [*Electronics*] (AAEL)
EI .... Equipment Item (MCD)
EI .... Error Increments (SAUS)
EI .... Error Indicator [*Computer science*]
EI .... Erythema Infectiosum [*Medicine*] (MELL)
EI .... Esalen Institute (EA)
EI .... Essential Information [*An association*] (EA)
EI .... Essex Institute (SAUS)
EI .... Establishment Inspection [*Federal government*]
ei .... estrogen index (SAUS)
EI .... Ethyleneimine [*Organic chemistry*]
EI .... Eugene Ionesco (SAUS)
EI .... Eunice Institute (SAUS)
EI .... European Initiative (SAUO)
EI .... Evaluation Indication (SAUS)
EI .... Evaluation Instrumentation (AAG)
EI .... Exact Interest [*Banking*]
EI .... Exaltation of Inanna [*A publication*] (BJA)
EI .... Excessively Included [*Colored gemstone grade*]
EI .... Excretory Index [*Medicine*] (EDAA)
EI .... Execution Interrupt (SAUS)
EI .... Executive Instruments [*Ghana*] [*A publication*] (DLA)
EI .... Ex-Interest [*Without the right to interest*] [*Finance*]
EI .... Existential Instantiation [*Rule of quantification*] [*Logic*]
EI .... Exit Instruction (SAUS)
EI .... Expander Input (SAUS)
EI .... Expansion Interface [*Electronics*] (ACRL)
E/I .... Expiration-Inspiration [*Ratio*] [*Physiology*]
EI .... Explosives Inspectorate (HEAS)
EI .... Exponential Integral
Ei .... exponential integral function (SAUS)
EI .... Exposure Index [*Photography*]
EI .... Extensions for Independence [*An association*] (EA)
EI .... External Interconnect (SAUS)
EI .... External Interrupt (SAUS)
EI .... External Irradiation (ODA)
EI .... Extra-Illustrated
E-I .... Extraversion-Introversion [*Psychology*]
EI .... Eye Balls In (SAA)
ei--- .... Iberian Peninsula [*MARC geographic area code*] [*Library of Congress*] (LCCP)
EI .... Irina Dunn Environment Independents [*Political party*] [*Australia*]
EI .... Earth Interface (ODA)
EIA .... Early Infantile Autism [*Medicine*] (MELL)
EIA .... Early Iron Age [*Archeology*]
EIA .... East Indian Association (SAUO)
EIA .... Economic Impact Area (SAUS)
EIA .... Economic Impact Assessment
EIA .... Education Improvement Act of 1984
EIA .... Education Industries Association [*Later, NSSEA*] (EA)
EIA .... Electrical Industries Association
EIA .... Electric Industries Associaton (SAUS)
EIA .... Electric Industries of America (SAUS)
EIA .... Electroimmunoassay [*Clinical medicine*]
EIA .... Electronic Industries Association [*Formerly, RETMA*] (EA)
EIA .... Electronic Industries Association of Canada (SAUO)
EIA .... Electronic Industry Association (SAUS)
EIA .... Electronic Interference Absorption (SAUS)
EIA .... Electronic Invoicing Automaton (SAUS)
EIA .... Electronics Industries Association (SAUS)
EIA .... Electronics Industry Association (SAUS)
EIA .... Electronics Institute of America (SAUO)
EIA .... Elevator Industries Association (EA)
EIA .... Empire Industries Association (SAUO)
EIA .... Employee Involvement Association
EIA .... End Item Application (MCD)
EIA .... Endotoxin Inactivating Agent (OA)
EIA .... Energetic Ion Analysis [*Surface analysis*]
EIA .... Energy Independence Authority
EIA .... Energy Information Administration [*Department of Energy*] (IID)
EIA .... Energy Information Agency
EIA .... Engineering Industries Association [*British*] (EAIO)
EIA .... Engineering Inspectors' Association [*A union*] [*British*]
EiA .... English in Action (EA)
EIA .... enterprise information architecture (SAUS)
EIA .... Enterprise Integration of Applications (VLIE)
EIA .... Envelope Institute of America
EIA .... Environmental Impact Analysis (SAUO)
EIA .... Environmental Impact Appraisal [*Nuclear Regulatory Commission*] (GFGA)
EIA .... Environmental Impact Assessment [*Environmental Protection Agency*] (MCD)
EIA .... Environmental Industry Associations (NTPA)
EIA .... Environmental Information Abstracts (SAUS)
EIA .... Environmental Information Association (NTPA)
EIA .... Environmental Initiative for the Americas (SAUO)
EIA .... Environmental Investigation Agency (BARN)
EIA .... Environmental Protection Agency, Region II Library, New York, NY [*OCLC symbol*] (OCLC)
EIA .... Environment Impact Assessment (SAUS)
EIA .... Environment Institute of Australia (EERA)
EIA .... Enzyme Immunoassay [*Analytical biochemistry*]
EIA .... Enzyme-Linked Immunosorbent Assay [*Clinical chemistry*]
EIA .... Enzymoimmunoassay (DB)
EIA .... Equine Infectious Anemia
EIA .... Equipment Interchange Association [*Defunct*] (EA)
EIA .... Eucalyptus Improvement Association (EA)
EIA .... European Information Association [*EC*] (ECED)
EIA .... Euskal Iraultzako Alderdia [*Basque Revolutionary Party*] (PPW)
EIA .... Evergreen International Airlines [*ICAO designator*] (FAAC)
EIA .... Exercise-Induced Anaphylaxis [*Medicine*]
EIA .... Exercise-Induced Asthma [*Medicine*]
EIA .... Experiment Integration Analysis (ACAE)
EIA .... Extended Interaction Amplifier
EIA .... International Association for the Evaluation of Educational Archievement (SAUO)
EIA .... International Ergonomics Association (SAUO)
EIAA .... Electronic Industry Association of Alberta (SAUO)
EI/AA .... Environmental Investigation and Alternatives Analysis (BCP)
EIAA .... Shannon/Ballygirreen [*Ireland*] [*ICAO location identifier*] (ICLI)
EIAB .... Extra-Intracranial Arterial Bypass [*Cardiology*] (DMAA)
EIAC .... Eastern Intercollegiate Athletic Conference (PSS)
EIAC .... Ecological Information and Analysis Center
EIAC .... Electronic Industries Association of Canada
EIAC .... Energy Information Administration Clearinghouse
EIAC .... Environmental Information Analysis Center [*Battelle Memorial Institute*] (IID)
EIAC .... Ergonomics Information Analysis Centre [*University of Birmingham*] [*British*] (CB)
EIA/CEG .... EIAs Consumer Electronics Group (SAUO)
EIA Code .... Electronic Industries Association Code (SAUO)
EIAD .... End Item Allocation Document (AAG)
EIA/EIS .... Environmental Impact Assessment/Environmental Impact Statement
EIA/EPUB .... Energy Information Administration Electronic Publication System [*Database*] [*Department of Energy*] [*Information service or system*] (CRD)
EIAG .... Exeter Industrial Archaeology Group [*British*] (DBA)
EIAJ .... Electric Industries Association of Japan (SAUO)
EIA-J .... Electronic Industries Association - Japan
EIA-J .... Electronic Industries (or Industry) Association of Japan (SAUO)
EIAJ .... Electronics Industries Association of Japan (SAUS)
EIA - J .... Electronics Industry Association of Japan (SAUS)
EIAK .... Electronics Industries Association of Korea (SAUS)
EIALC .... Environmental Impact Assessment for Life Cycle [*Army*]
EIAMUG .... European Intelligent Actuation and Measurement User Group (ACII)
EI & T .... Emplacement, Installation, and Test (CET)
EIAP .... Employer Information Access Project (SAUS)
EIAP .... environmental impact analysis process (SAUS)
EIAP .... Environmental Impact Analysis Program [*or Project*] [*Department of the Interior*] (GRD)
EIAP .... Environmental Impact Assessment Project (SAUS)
EIAR .... Environmental Impact Analysis Report (SAUS)
EIARD .... European Initiative for Agricultural Research for Development (EURO)
EIA RS .... Earlier designation of EIA Recommended Standards documents (SAUS)
EIAS .... Electoral Institute of South Africa
EIAS .... Electron Image Animation System [*Computer science*]
EIASA .... Energia e Industrias Aragonesas Sociedad Anonima [*Spain*]
EIASA .... Extractive Industries Association of South Australia
EIASM .... European Institute for Advanced Studies in Management [*Information service or system*] (IID)
EIASN .... End Item Assembly Sequence Number (NASA)
EIA/TIA .... Electronic Industries Association/ Telecommunications Industry Association (SAUO)
EIA/TIA .... Electronics Industry Association and the Telecommunications Industry Association (PCM)
EIAV .... Equine Infectious Anemia Virus
EIB .... Economic Impact Budget
EIB .... Edinboro State College, Edinboro, PA [*OCLC symbol*] (OCLC)
EIB .... Egyptian International Bank (IMH)
EIB .... Electrical Interface Building [*NASA*] (KSC)
EIB .... Electronic Information Bulletin [*Navy*]
EIB .... Electronics Information Branch [*Navy*] (MCD)
EIB .... Electronics Installation Bulletin
EIB .... Electrophoretic Immunoblotting [*Medicine*] (MELL)
EIB .... Elsevier International Bulletins (SAUS)
EIB .... Emissions Inventory Branch (SAUS)
EIB .... Engineering Information Bureau (SAUS)
EIB .... Engineering Instruction Bulletin (KSC)
EIB .... Enterprise Information Base (VLIE)
EIB .... Environmental Improvement Board (SAUS)

EIB.............. Environment Information Bureau (SAUO)
EIB.............. Error Information Block (VLIE)
EIB.............. Error Interrupt Buffer (VLIE)
EIB.............. European Installation Bus (SAUO)
EIB.............. European Investment Bank (AF)
EIB.............. Europese Investeringsbank [*European Investment Bank*]
EIB.............. Execute Interface Block [*IBM Corp.*] (CIST)
EIB.............. Execution Interface Block (VLIE)
EIB.............. Exercise-Induced Bronchiospasm [*Medicine*]
EIB.............. exercise-induced bronchoconstriction (SAUS)
EIB.............. Expert Infantryman Badge [*Military decoration*]
EIB.............. Export Import Bank (SAUO)
E-IB.............. Export-Import Bank
EIB.............. Export-Import Bank of Washington (SAUO)
EIB.............. External Intelligence Bureau (MCD)
EIB.............. Extractive Industries Board [*Victoria, Australia*]
EIBA.............. Electrical Industries Benevolent Association [*British*] (BI)
EIBA.............. English Indoor Bowling Association [*British*] (DBA)
EIBA.............. Ethylene-(Isobutyl Acrylate) [*Organic chemistry*]
EIBA.............. European International Business Association [*Brussels, Belgium*] (EA)
EIBAD.............. Expert Infantryman Badge [*Military decoration*]
EIBIEM.............. Enhanced Interactive Business Integrating Environment Manager (SAUS)
EIBIS.............. Engineering In Britain Information Services (SAUS)
EIBL.............. Eastern Intercollegiate Baseball League (PSS)
EIBs.............. Elsevier International Bulletins (SAUS)
EIBUS.............. Export-Import Bank of the United States [*Formerly, EIB(W)*]
EIB(W).............. Export-Import Bank (of Washington) [*Later, EIBUS*]
EIC.............. Early Installation Centre (SAUO)
EIC.............. Earned Income Credit
EIC.............. Earth Images Catalog (SAUO)
EIC.............. Earth Inductor Compass
EIC.............. Earth-Ionosphere Cavity
EIC.............. Earthquake Information Center (SAUO)
EIC.............. Easter Island [*Seismograph station code, US Geological Survey*] (SEIS)
EIC.............. Easter Island Committee (EA)
EIC.............. East India Co. [*1600-1858*] [*British*]
EIC.............. East Indian Company (SAUO)
EIC.............. Ecology International Corporation (SAUO)
EIC.............. Economic Intelligence Committee [*Military*]
EIC.............. Educational Information Center [*Office of Education*]
EIC.............. Education Information Center [*Georgia State Department of Education*] [*Information service or system*] (IID)
EIC.............. Education Interchange Council, Inc. (SAUO)
EIC.............. Effective Inlet Valve Closing [*Automotive engineering*]
EIC.............. Elastase Inhibitory Capacity [*Physiology*]
EIC.............. electret ionization chamber (SAUS)
EIC.............. Electrical Industry Committee (SAUO)
EIC.............. Electrical Insulation Committee [*Military*]
EIC.............. Electrical Insulation Conference [*Later, EEIC*] (MCD)
EIC.............. Electrically Insulated Coating
EIC.............. Electromagnetic Interference Control (IAA)
EIC.............. Electronic Industry Council (SAUO)
EIC.............. Electronic Institute of Canada (HGAA)
EIC.............. Electronic Instrument Cluster (VLIE)
EIC.............. Electron-Induced Conduction (IAA)
EIC.............. Electron Ionization Cross Section
EIC.............. Electrostatic Ion Cyclotron [*Seismology*]
EIC.............. Elevator Code (NFPA)
EIC.............. Embar Information Consultants [*Information service or system*] (IID)
EIC.............. Emotional Inertia Concept (SAUS)
EIC.............. Emplaced Instrument Complex [*Aerospace*]
EIC.............. Employer Identification Code (AABC)
EIC.............. Employment and Immigration Canada (SAUS)
EIC.............. Employment and Immigration Canada Library [*UTLAS symbol*]
EIC.............. Enamel Insulating Compound
EIC.............. End Item Code
EIC.............. End Item Contract
EIC.............. Energy Industries Council [*British*] (DS)
EIC.............. Energy Information Center [*Battelle Memorial Institute*] (IID)
EIC.............. Energy Information Centre [*Australia*]
EIC.............. Engineer In Charge (SAUS)
E-I-C.............. Engineer-In-Charge [*Television*] (WDMC)
EIC.............. Engineer In Chief (SAUO)
EIC.............. Engineering and Integration Contractor (SAUS)
EIC.............. Engineering Information Center
EIC.............. Engineering Installation Center [*Military*]
EIC.............. Engineering Institute of Canada
EI/C.............. Engineer Inspector-in-Chief (SAUS)
EIC.............. Entertainment Industries Council (EA)
EIC.............. Environmental Industries (or Industry) Council (SAUO)
EIC.............. Environmental Industry Council (EA)
EIC.............. Environmental Information Center (SAUS)
EIC.............. Environmental Protection Agency, Region II Field Office, Edison, NJ [*OCLC symbol*] (OCLC)
EIC.............. Environment Information Center, Inc. [*Database producer*]
EIC.............. Enzyme Immunochromatography
EIC.............. Enzyme Inhibitor Complex (DB)
EIC.............. Epilepsy Information Center [*Medicine*] (EDAA)
EIC.............. Equipment Identification Code
EIC.............. Equipment Installation and Checkout (MUGU)
EIC.............. Equipment Interstage Container
EIC.............. Equitable of Iowa [*NYSE symbol*] (TTSB)
EIC.............. Equivalent IC (SAUS)
EIC.............. Essays in Criticism [*A publication*] (ANEX)
EIC.............. European Independents Confederation (EAIO)
EIC.............. European Information Centre (AIE)
EIC.............. European Insurance Committee [*Paris, France*] (EA)
EIC.............. European International Contractors (SAUS)
EIC.............. European Investment Center (SAUS)
EIC.............. Examiner in Charge (EBF)
EIC.............. Exciton Impurity Complex (SAUS)
EIC.............. Exercise Intelligence Center [*Military*] (CINC)
EIC.............. Exhibitors in Cable [*An association*] (EA)
EIC.............. Experimental Intercom (NASA)
EIC.............. Experiment Integration Center (MCD)
e-ic-.............. Iceland [*MARC geographic area code*] [*Library of Congress*] (LCCP)
EICA.............. Electronics Corporation of America (SAUO)
EICA.............. Experimental Integrated Conformed Array
EICAM.............. Electronic Installation Change and Maintenance (DNAB)
EICAS.............. Engine Indication and Crew Advisory System
EICAS.............. Engine Indication and Crew Alerting System (MCD)
EICAVR.............. European Institute for Computer Anti-Virus Research (VERA)
EICB.............. Extra-Intracranial Bypass [*Medicine*] (PDAA)
EICBL.............. Eastern Independent Collegiate Basketball League
EICC.............. Emergency Information and Coordination Center [*Federal Emergency Management Agency*]
EICC.............. Emergency Information Control Center (SAUS)
EICD.............. Electrical Interface Control Document (MCD)
EICDP.............. Environmental Impacts and Criteria Development Project (SAUO)
EICDT.............. Ego-Ideal and Conscience Development Test [*Personality development test*] [*Psychology*]
EI Cen.............. El Centro (SAUS)
EICF.............. European Investment Casters Federation [*Netherlands*] (PDAA)
EIC-FET.............. European Information Centre of Charles University for/of Further Education of Teachers (SAUO)
EICG.............. Electromagnetic Interference Control Group (AAG)
EICG.............. Electronic/Infrared Crystal Growth (SAUS)
e-i children... emotionally-impaired children (SAUS)
EI-CI Changeover... Electron Ionization - Chemical Ionization Changeover (SAUS)
EICK.............. Cork [*Ireland*] [*ICAO location identifier*] (ICLI)
EIC-LDA.............. Equipment Indentification Code - Lowest Designated Assembly (SAUO)
EICM.............. Employer's Inventory of Critical Manpower
EICMC.............. Enterprise Integration Corporate Management Council (SAUO)
EICMS.............. Engine In-Flight Condition Monitoring System (MCD)
EIC-NE.............. Educational Improvement Center - Northeast [*Information service or system*]
EI CO.............. East India Co. [*1600-1858*] [*British*] (ROG)
EICo.............. East India Company (SAUO)
EICO.............. Electronic Instrument Corporation (SAUO)
EICON.............. Electronic Index Console (SAUS)
EICP.............. European Index of Consumer Prices (EURO)
EICR.............. Eastern Interior Coal Region (SAUS)
EICR.............. Eppley Institute for Cancer Research (SAUS)
EICS.............. East India Civil Service [*British*] (ROG)
EICS.............. East India Company's Service [*British*]
EICS.............. Electromagnetic Intelligence Collection System
EICS.............. Environmental Impact Computer System [*Database*] [*Army Corps of Engineers*]
EICS.............. Equipment Identification Coded System (DNAB)
EICSB.............. Electrical, Instrumentation and Control System Branch (SAUO)
EICT.............. External Isovolumic Contraction Time [*Laboratory*] (DAVI)
EICV.............. Engine Idling Control Valve (SAUS)
EICW.............. Electrostatic Ion Cyclotron Waves [*Seismology*]
EICX.............. Edlow International [*Private rail car owner code*]
EID.............. East India Dock
EID.............. Egg-Infective Dose [*Clinical chemistry*]
EID.............. Eider Resources Minieres, Inc. [*Toronto Stock Exchange symbol*]
EID.............. Electrical Inspection Directorate (IAA)
EID.............. Electric Inertial Dynamometer [*Automotive emissions*]
EID.............. Electroimmunodiffusion [*Clinical medicine*] (MAE)
EID.............. Electromagnetic Impulse Deicing [*System under development by NASA*]
EID.............. Electronic Identification Device (SEWL)
EID.............. Electronic Induction Desorption (DB)
EID.............. Electronic Information Display (SAUS)
EID.............. Electronic Infusion Device [*Pharmacology*] (DAVI)
EID.............. Electronic Installation Design [*Navy*]
EID.............. Electronic Instrument Digest (journ.) (SAUS)
EID.............. Electronic Intrusion Detection
EID.............. Electronic Intrusion Detector (SAUS)
EID.............. Electronics Intelligence Digest (SAUS)
EID.............. Electron Impact [*or Induced*] Desorption
EID.............. electron impact dissoziation (SAUS)
EID.............. electron induced desorption (SAUS)
EID.............. Electron-induced Ion Desorption (SAUS)
EID.............. Electron-Stimulated Ion Desorption (SAUS)
EID.............. Embryo Infective Dose
EID.............. Emergency Infusion Device [*Medicine*]
EID.............. Emergency Isolation Device (HEAS)
EID.............. Emerging Infectious Diseases (SAUS)
EID.............. Emitter Identification (MCD)
EID.............. Emitting Identifier (SAUS)
EID.............. Empresa de Investigacao e Desenvolvimento de Electronica SA (SAUS)
EID.............. End Item Delivery (AAG)
EID.............. End Item Description (AAG)

EID.............. End Item Designators
EID.............. End Item Documentation (MCD)
E-ID.............. Energy-Information Database [*International Research and Evaluation*] [*Information service or system*] (CRD)
EID.............. Engineering Information Department (SAUO)
EID.............. Engineering Installation Division [*Military*]
EID.............. Engineering Item Description (AAG)
EID.............. Environmental Impacts Division (SAUS)
EID.............. Environmental Information Directory [*Later, Gale Environmental Sourcebook*] [*A publication*]
EID.............. Environmental Information Division [*Air Force Air Training Command*] (IID)
EID.............. Equi-Illuminating Dimming (SAUS)
EID.............. Equipment Interface Development
EID.............. Equipment Interface Document (CAAL)
EID.............. Espace d'Interpellation Democratique [*Forum for Democratic Consultation*] [*Mali*]
EID.............. Eugenic Insemination by Donor
EID.............. European Investment Bank (GNE)
EID.............. Export Insurance Division [*of the Ministry of International Trade and Industry*] [*Japan*]
EID.............. Exposure Intensity Distribution (IAA)
EID.............. Research Laboratory for Equine Infectious Diseases [*Cornell University*] [*Research center*] (RCD)
EIDA.............. Engineering Industries Development Agency (SAUS)
EIDAP.............. Emitter Isolated Difference Amplifier Paralleling [*Bell System*]
EIDB.............. Dublin [*Ireland*] [*ICAO location identifier*] (ICLI)
EIDC.............. Eastern Investment and Development Corporation (SAUO)
EIDC.............. East Indian Defence Committee
EIDC.............. East Indian Defense Commission (SAUS)
EIDC.............. Experimental International Data Centre [*Australia*]
EIDC.............. Extreme Intervertebral Disk Collapse [*Medicine*] (MELL)
EIDCT.............. Educational Institute of Design, Craft, and Technology [*British*]
EIDD.............. Epileptic Intentional Deficit Disorder (MELL)
EIDD.............. Experiment Interface Definition Document (MCD)
EIDE.............. Enhanced Integrated Device Electronics (MWOL)
EIDE.............. Extended Integrated Drive Electronics [*Computer science*]
EIDEBOEWABEW... Economic Intelligence Division of the Enemy Branch of the Office of Economic Warfare Analysis of the Board of Economic Warfare (SAUS)
EIDED.............. Escuela Interamericana de Educacion Democratica
eid it.............. emergency identification light (SAUS)
EIDL.............. Economic Injury Disaster Loan [*Small Business Administration*]
EIDLT.............. Emergency Identification Light [*Aerospace*] (AAG)
EIDM.............. Ethiopian Islamic Democratic Movement (SAUO)
EIDOS.............. Electronic Information Delivery Online System [*Information retrieval*]
EIDOSTAS.... European Infrastructure for Document Supply in Technology and Applied Sciences (TELE)
EIDP.............. Early Intervention Developmental Profile [*Speech and language therapy*] (DAVI)
EIDP.............. Early Intervention Developmental Program [*Therapy term*] (CTAA)
EIDP.............. End Item Data Package (NASA)
EIDs.............. East India Docks (SAUS)
EIDS.............. Eidos plc [*NASDAQ symbol*] (NASQ)
EIDS.............. Electronic Information Delivery System [*Individual learning center equipped with head sets and video monitors*]
EIDS.............. Electronic Information Display System
EIDS.............. Equipment Integration Design Section
EIDS-ASSIST... Electronic Information Delivery System - Authoring Software System for Instructive Simulation and Training
EIDSO.............. Engineer Information and Data Systems Office [*Army*] (AABC)
EIDSO.............. Engineering Information and Data Systems Office (SAUS)
EIDSY.............. Eidos PLC ADR [*NASDAQ symbol*] (SG)
EIDW.............. Dublin [*Ireland*] [*ICAO location identifier*] (ICLI)
EIDX.............. Electronics Industry Data Exchange association (SAUO)
EIE.............. Easily-Ionized Element (SAUS)
EIE.............. Electronic Industrial Engineering (SAUO)
EIE.............. Electronic Information Exchange [*National Message Center, Inc.*] [*Overland Park, KS*] [*Telecommunications service*] (TSSD)
EIE.............. Electronics Industry Exhibition (SAUS)
EIE.............. End Item Equipment
eie.............. end-item equipment (SAUS)
EIE.............. English Institute Essays (journ.) (SAUS)
EIE.............. Error Interrupt (SAUS)
e-ie-.............. Ireland [*MARC geographic area code*] [*Library of Congress*] (LCCP)
EIE.............. Equilibrium Isotope Effect [*Chemistry*] (ODA)
EIEA.............. Emergency Immigrant Education Act [*1984*] (GFGA)
EIEA.............. Entertainment Industry Employers' Association [*Australia*]
EIE-AF.............. Experienced International Executive - Air Forwarding [*American Society of International Executives, Inc.*] [*Designation awarded by*]
EIEB.............. Experienced International Executive - Banking [*American Society of Intern ational Executives, Inc.*] [*Designation awarded by*]
EIEC.............. Emergency Incident of Environmental Contamination [*Environmental Protection Agency*]
EIEC.............. English Industrial Estates Corp.
EIEC.............. Enteroinvasive E. coli [*Medicine*] (MELL)
EIEC.............. European Institute of Ecology and Cancer [*Formerly, European Institute of Cancerology*] (EA)
EIE-C.............. Experienced International Executive - Credit [*American Society of Interna tional Executives, Inc.*] [*Designation awarded by*]
EIED.............. Electrically Initiated Explosive Device
EIEE.............. Early Infantile Epileptic Encephalopathy [*Medicine*] (STED)
EIE-EM.............. Experienced International Executive - Export Management [*American Society of International Executives, Inc.*] [*Designation awarded by*]
EIE-F.............. Experienced International Executive - Forwarding [*American Society of Int ernational Executives, Inc.*] [*Designation awarded by*]
EIEIO.............. Earthwide Internet Education and Information Organization (SAUS)
EIEIO.............. Easily-Ionized-Element Interface Observation (SAUS)
EIEIO.............. Empowering Individuals with Disabilities Through Education, Information, and Opportunity [*Farmer outreach program*] [*Montana State University*]
EIEIO.............. Engineering Industries Export Intelligence Officer [*British*] (DI)
EIEIT.............. Enterprise Interoperability and Emerging Information Technologies (SEWL)
EIEM.............. Electrical Installation Equipment Manufacturers Association (SAUO)
EIEM.............. Environmental Interference Effects Model (MCD)
EIE-M.............. Experienced International Executive - Marketing [*American Society of Inte rnational Executives, Inc.*] [*Designation awarded by*]
EIEMA.............. Electrical Installation Equipment Manufacturers Association [*British*] (DBA)
EIEN.............. Endometrial Intraepithelial Neoplasia [*Medicine*] (MELL)
EI-EO.............. Eye Balls In - Eye Balls Out (SAA)
EIEP.............. Emergency Immigrant Education Program (SAUO)
EIES.............. Electronic Information Exchange System [*Pronounced "eyes"*] [*New Jersey Institute of Technology*] [*Computer network*] [*Telecommunications*]
EIES.............. Electronic Information Interchange system (SAUS)
EIES.............. Electron Impact Emission Spectroscopy [*Photovoltaic energy systems*]
EIES.............. Esprit Information Exchange System (SAUO)
EIES.............. European Information Exchange Service for the Communication between Harbour Areas (SAUO)
EIESP.............. European Institute of Education and Social Policy (AIE)
EIE System... Electronic Information Exchange System (SAUS)
EIE-TM.............. Experienced International Executive - Traffic Management [*American Societ y of International Executives, Inc.*] [*Designation awarded by*]
EIF.............. Dukaryotic Initiation Factor (STED)
EIF.............. ECCM Improvement Factor (SAUS)
EIF.............. Elderly Invalids Fund (SAUO)
EIF.............. Electrochemical Industries (Frutarom) Ltd. [*AMEX symbol*] (SPSG)
EIF.............. Electronic Industries Foundation (EA)
EIF.............. End Item Failure
EIF.............. Enterprise Integration Framework (VLIE)
EIF.............. Erythema-Inducing Factor [*Hematology*]
eIF.............. Erythrocyte Initiation Factor [*Medicine*] (EDAA)
EIF.............. Erythrocyte Initiation Factor
eIF.............. Eukaryotic Initiation Factors [*Biochemistry*]
EIF.............. European Internet Forum (EURO)
EIF.............. European Internet Foundation (SAUO)
EIF.............. Executive Inventory File [*Civil Service Commission*]
EIF.............. Exercise in Futility (SAUS)
EIF.............. Exhibition Industry Federation [*British*] (DBA)
EIF.............. External Information Flow (SAUS)
EIF.............. Pittsfield, MA [*Location identifier*] [*FAA*] (FAAL)
EIFA.............. Eastern Intercollegiate Football Association (SAUO)
EIFA.............. Element Interface Functional Analysis (NASA)
EIFAC.............. European Inland Fisheries Administration Commission (SAUS)
EIFAC.............. European Inland Fisheries Advisory Commission [*Food and Agriculture Organization*] [*United Nations*] (ASF)
EIFAC.............. European Inland Fisheries Advisory Committee (SAUS)
EIFDC.............. Eterna International Foundation for Disabled Children (EA)
EIFEL.............. Electronic Information C2 System For The Luftwaffe (SAUS)
EIFF.............. Enemy Identification Friend or Foe
eiff.............. Enemy Identification-Friend or Foe (SAUS)
EIFI.............. Electrical Industries Federation of Ireland (BI)
EIFI.............. European Industrial Fasteners Institute [*EC*] (ECED)
Eif Jud Act... Eiffe on the Irish Judicature Act [*A publication*] (DLA)
EIFL Direct... Electronic Information for Libraries Direct
EIFOV.............. Effective Instantaneous Field of View
EIFS.............. Economic Impact Forecast System [*Army*] (RDA)
EIFS.............. Extended Inter Frame Space (SAUS)
EIFS.............. Exterior Insulation and Finish System [*Sto Industries*]
EIFS.............. Exterior Insulation Finishing Systems
EIG.............. Electronic Image Generator
EIG.............. Electronics Installations Group [*Military*]
EIG.............. Elephant Interest Group (EA)
EIG.............. Emitter Identification Guide (NG)
EIG.............. Energy Information Guide [*A publication*]
EIG.............. Engineering Installation Group [*Military*]
EIG.............. Exchange Information Group (NATG)
EIG.............. Voltage Inner Gimbal
EIGA.............. Ethics in Government Act
EIGA.............. European Industrial Gases Association (SAUS)
EIGFET.............. Equivalent Insulated Gate Field Effect Transistor (IAA)
E-IGFET.............. Equivalent Insulated-Gate Field Effect Transistor (SAUS)
Eight-C St.... Eighteenth-Century Studies [*A publication*] (BRI)
Eight Great... Eight Great Inslands of Japan (SAUS)
EIGL.............. Eastern Intercollegiate Gymnastic League (EA)
EIGM.............. Gormanston County Meath [*Ireland*] [*ICAO location identifier*] (ICLI)
EIGRP.............. Enhanced Interior Gateway Routing Protocol [*Telecommunications*] (ACRL)
EIGS.............. Ethiopian Institute of Geological Survey (SAUS)
EIH.............. East India House (ROG)
EIH.............. Economic Indicator's Handbook [*A publication*]
EIH.............. Error Interrupt Handler (SAUS)

EIHR .... Eisenhower Institute for Historical Research [*Smithsonian Institution*]
EIHSW .... European Institute of Hunting and Sporting Weapons (EAIO)
EII .... Earth Island Institute (EA)
EII .... Electronically Invisible Interconnect [*Computer science*]
EII .... Encoded Item Identifier (CAAL)
EII .... Engineering Item Identification
EII .... Environmental Information Index (SAUO)
EII .... Ethnic Identification Index (BJA)
EIIA .... Electro Instrument Industry Association (SAUS)
EIIA .... European Information Industry Association [*Database producer*] (IID)
EIIC .... Emerald Isle Immigration Center (EA)
EIIC .... Entertainment Industry Interim Council [*Australia*]
EIIC .... European Intracular Implantiens Council (SAUO)
EIIF .... Electronics and Information Industries Forum (SAUS)
EIIG .... Earned Income Initiatives Group (SAUS)
EIII .... Association of the European Independent Informatics Industry (PDAA)
EIII .... Association of the European Independent Informatics (or Information) Industry (SAUS)
eiii .... Electrical Industry Information Institute (SAUS)
EIII .... European Independent Informatics Industry (SAUO)
EIII .... European Independent Information Industry (SAUS)
EIIP .... Engineering Industries Internalisation Program [*Australia*]
EIIS .... Ecological Incident Information Systems [*Environmental Protection Agency*] (AEPA)
EIIS .... Energy Industry Information System (IEEE)
EIIV .... Electronics Interface Integrated Validation (KSC)
EIJ .... Egyptian Islamic Jihad [*Government term*] (GA)
EIK .... Eat-In Kitchen [*Classified advertising*]
EIK .... Extended Interaction Klystron [*Electronics*] (IAA)
EIKN .... Connaught Regional Airport [*Ireland*] [*ICAO location identifier*] (ICLI)
EIKON .... Gesellschaft der Freunde der Ikonenkunst (EAIO)
EIL .... Egyptian International Line (DS)
EIL .... Eilat [*Israel*] [*Seismograph station code, US Geological Survey*] (SEIS)
Eil .... Eileen (SAUS)
EIL .... Electrical Insulating Liquid (PDAA)
EIL .... Electro Chemical Inds. (Frutarom) Ltd. [*AMEX symbol*] (SAG)
EIL .... Electronic Instruments Laboratory (SAUS)
EIL .... Electronic Instruments Limited [*as in EIL electrode, used in biochemistry*] [*British*]
EIL .... Electron Injection LASER
EIL .... Emergency Identification Light (SAUS)
EIL .... Engineers India Limited (SAUO)
Eil .... English as an international language (SAUS)
EIL .... Environmental Impairment Liability
EIL .... Environmental Impairment Liability Insurance (SARE)
EIL .... Equipment Identification List (DNAB)
EIL .... Esprit International Limited (SAUO)
EIL .... Essays on International Law [*A publication*] (ILCA)
EIL .... Event Index Log [*NASA*] (KSC)
EIL .... Experiment in International Living/School for International Training (EA)
EIL .... Explosive Investigative Laboratory [*Navy*]
EIL .... Fairbanks, AK [*Location identifier*] [*FAA*] (FAAL)
EILC .... Egg Industry Licensing Committee [*Victoria, Australia*]
EILI .... E.I.L. Instruments, Inc. [*NASDAQ symbol*] (COMM)
EILIS .... Electronic Integrated Library and Information Service (SAUS)
EILL .... Elegant Illusions, Inc. [*NASDAQ symbol*] (SAG)
EILNET .... Eastern Idaho Library Net Consortium
Eil Wom .... Eiloart's Laws Relating to Women [*1878*] [*A publication*] (DLA)
EIM .... Effective Index Method (PDAA)
EIM .... Elastomeric Insulation Material
EIM .... Electrical Instrument Makers (SAUO)
EIM .... Electronic Image Management [*Computer science*] (AGLO)
EIM .... Electronic Imaging in Medicine [*Computer graphics*]
EIM .... Elite Insurance Management Ltd. [*Toronto Stock Exchange symbol*] [*Vancouver Stock Exchange symbol*]
EIM .... End Item Manager (AFIT)
EIM .... End of Information Marker [*Computer science*] (IAA)
EIM .... Engine Inventory Manager [*Air Force*] (AFIT)
EIM .... Enterprise Information Management [*Seagate*]
EIM .... Enterprise Integration Modelling (VLIE)
EIM .... Environmental Industries Marketplace [*A publication*]
EIM .... Environmental Information Management (SAUS)
EIM .... E-Sim Ltd. [*AMEX symbol*] (SG)
EIM .... European Institute for the Media (EA)
EIM .... European Interactive Media [*Joint venture of Philips International and PolyGram BV International*]
EIM .... European Interprofessional Market (ECON)
EIM .... Excitability-Inducing Material [*Biochemistry*]
EIM .... Explosive Inventory Manager [*Military*]
EIM .... Explosive Investigation Manager
EIM .... Explosives Investigation Memorandum [*Navy*] (MCD)
EIM .... Express Instant Manager (VLIE)
EIM .... Eyelet-Installing Machine
EIMA .... Electrical Insulating Materials Association (SAUO)
EIMA .... Exterior Insulation Manufacturers Association (EA)
Eimac .... Eitel-McCullough (SAUS)
EIMAM .... Environmental Instrumentation Measurement and Monitoring (IAA)
EIM&M .... Environmental Instrumentation Measurement and Monitoring (SAUS)
EIMB .... Electronics Installation and Maintenance Book (SAUO)
EIMB .... Electronics Installation and Maintenance Bulletin
EIMC .... East India Military College (SAUO)
EIMC .... Electronic Image Motion Compensation (ACAE)
EIMC .... English Institute Materials Center
EIME .... Electronic Instrument Manufacturers Exhibit (MUGU)
EIME .... Mhic Easmuinn Baldonnel, County Dublin [*Ireland*] [*ICAO location identifier*] (ICLI)
EIMECH .... Electro Mechanical
EIMET .... Engineering Information Meetings (NITA)
EIMF .... End Item Maintenance Form
EIM F .... End Item Maintenance Form (SAUS)
EIMI .... Exercise-Induced Myocardial Ischemia [*Medicine*] (MELL)
EIMM .... East India Metal Merchants Association (SAUO)
EIMO .... Electronic Interface Management Office (SAUO)
EIMO .... Electronic Interference Management Office (SAUS)
EIMO .... Engineering Interface Management Office (SAUO)
EIMR .... Equipment Item Material Requirements
EIMS .... Electronic Image Motion Stabilization (ACAE)
EIMS .... Electronic Ink and Moisture System [*Printing*] (DGA)
EIMS .... Electronic Institutional [*or Integrated*] Media System
EIMS .... Electron Impact Mass Spectrometry
EIMS .... Electron Ionization Mass Spectrometry
EIMS .... Electron Ionization Mass Spectroscopy (ACAE)
EIMS .... End Item Maintenance Sheets (MCD)
EIMS .... Engineering and Implementation Methods System (SAUO)
EIMS .... Engineering Installation Management System [*Air Force*] (CET)
EIMS .... Environmental Information Management System
EIMS .... European Innovation Monitoring System (SAUO)
EIMTS .... End Item Maintenance Transmittal Sheet
EIMU .... Environmental Information Management Unit (EERA)
EIMWT .... Echo Integration-Mid Water Trawl [*Marine science*] (OSRA)
EIN .... Aer Lingus Teoranta [*Ireland*] [*ICAO designator*] (FAAC)
EIN .... Echelon International Corp. [*NYSE symbol*] (SAG)
EIN .... Educational Information Network [*Princeton, NJ*]
EIN .... Education Information Network (SAUS)
EIN .... Eindhoven [*Netherlands*] [*Airport symbol*] (OAG)
EIN .... Electronic Information Network (SAUS)
EIN .... Employer Identification Number [*IRS*]
EIN .... Endometrial Intraepithelial Neoplasia [*Medicine*] (MELL)
EIN .... Engineer Intelligence Note
EIN .... Engineer Intelligence Notice (SAUS)
EIN .... Engine Identification Number [*Automotive engineering*]
EIN .... Environmental Information Networks Inc. [*Database producer*] (IID)
EIN .... Environment Information Network (SAUS)
EIN .... Equipment Installation Notice (AAG)
EIN .... Erase Input (SAUS)
EIN .... Eulerian Iterative Nonsteady [*Method*] [*Mathematics*]
EIN .... European Informatics Network (NITA)
EIN .... European Information Network [*Telecommunications*] (TEL)
EIN .... Excitatory Interneuron [*Neurophysiology*]
EIN .... Experimental Integrated Network
EIN .... External Interlace
EINA .... Exodus International - North America (EA)
E in C .... Engineer-in-Charge [*Army*]
E in C .... Engineer-in-Chief
E-in-CD .... Engineer-in-Chief's Department [*British military*] (DMA)
E Ind .... East Indian (SAUS)
E Ind .... East Indies
EINDES .... Employer ID No. Data Entry System on the PDP 11/70s (SAUS)
EINE .... EINE Is Not Emacs (SAUS)
EINECS .... European Inventory of Existing Chemical Substances (SAUS)
EINECS .... European Inventory of Existing Commercial Chemical Substances [*Which will be exempt from new product regulations*]
EINECS .... European Inventory of Existing Commercial Substances (SAUS)
E in EE .... Engineer in Electrical Engineering
EINET .... Enterprise Integration Network [*Information service or system*] (IID)
EINI .... Electron Irradiation and Neutron Irradiation (IAA)
EINIS .... European Integrated Network of Image and Services (EAIO)
e-ink .... Electronic Ink (ADWA)
E in ME .... Engineer in Mechanical Engineering
EIN Method ... Eulerian Iterative Nonsteady Method (SAUS)
EINN .... Shannon [*Ireland*] [*ICAO location identifier*] (ICLI)
EINP .... Elk Island National Park (SAUS)
EINS .... Electronic Information Network System (SAUS)
E INS .... Engineer Inspector [*Navy*] [*British*] (ROG)
EINS .... European Information Network Services (SAUS)
Einspr .... Einspruch [*Objection, Opposition, Caveat*] [*German*] (ILCA)
EinstnN .... Einstein Noah Bagel Corp. [*Associated Press*] (SAG)
E Int .... Equal Interval [*Isophase navigation light*]
EINZ .... Export Institute of New Zealand (SAUS)
EIO .... Electric Induction Oven
EIO .... Electronics and Industrial Operations (SAUS)
EIO .... Emergency Information Officer [*Civil Defense*]
EIO .... Execute Input-Output (IAA)
EIO .... Extended Interactive Oscillator (PDAA)
EIOBL .... Equipment Item Out of Balance (AFIT)
EIOC .... Early Initial Operational Capability (MCD)
EIOC .... Equivalent Input Offset Current
EIOD .... Equivalent Instruction or Duty
EIOHC .... European International Oil Hydraulic Commission (SAUO)
EIOI .... Expedition Internationale de l'Ocean Indien [*International Indian Ocean Expedition - IIOE*] [*French*] (MSC)
EIO-IMS .... Early Initial Operational-Information Management System (MCD)
EIOL .... European Infrastructure for Open Learning (SAUO)
EIONET .... European Environment Information and Observation NETwork (SAUS)
EIOP .... End of the Initial Operating Period [*Department of Housing and Urban Development*] (GFGA)

EIOP.......... European Integration On-Line Papers (EURO)
EIOP.......... External Input-Output Processor (IAA)
EIOS.......... Execute Input/Output System (SAUS)
EIOS.......... Extended Input-Output System (IAA)
EIO System... Execute Input/Output System (SAUS)
EIOV.......... Equivalent Input Offset Voltage
EIP.......... Association Mondiale pour l'Ecole Instrument de Paix [*World Association for the School as an Instrument of Peace*] [*Geneva, Switzerland*] (EAIO)
EIP.......... Early Imprints Project (SAUS)
EIP.......... Early Intervention Program
EIP.......... Economic Incentive Program (EEVL)
EIP.......... Economic Inventory Policy
EIP.......... Economic Inventory Procedures [*Army*] (AABC)
EIP.......... Educational Improvement Process [*Indiana*] (EDAC)
EIP.......... Educational Incentive Plan [*Red Cross*]
EIP.......... Educational Investing and Planning Programme (SAUO)
EIP.......... EIP Microwave, Inc. [*Associated Press*] (SAG)
EIP.......... Elective Interruption of Pregnancy [*Obstetrics*] (STED)
EIP.......... Electronic Implementation Procedure (SAUS)
EIP.......... Electronic Incentive Program (SAUS)
EIP.......... Electronic Installation Plan (NG)
EIP.......... Electronics for Peace (PDAA)
EIP.......... electron image projection (SAUS)
EIP.......... Elementary Information Process (RALS)
EIP.......... Emergency Implementation Procedure (NRCH)
EIP.......... Emitter Identification Program [*RADAR*] (MCD)
EIP.......... Emulator Interface Program (IAA)
EIP.......... End-Inspiratory Pause [*Respiration*]
EIP.......... End Item Parameter
EIP.......... Engineering and Installation Plan (SAUS)
EIP.......... Engineering Installation Plan (CET)
EIP.......... Engine Inspection Party (SAUO)
EIP.......... Enterprise Information Portal [*Computer science*]
EIP.......... Enterprise Integration Program (TIMI)
EIP.......... Environmental Impact Assessment (SAUO)
EIP.......... Environmental Impact Planning (SAUO)
EIP.......... Environmental Improvement Program (SAUO)
EIP.......... Environmental Innovation Program (SAUS)
EIP.......... Environmental Interface Processor (SAUS)
EIP.......... Equipment Improvement Program [*Electronics*] (AAEL)
EIP.......... Equipment Improvement Project
EIP.......... Equipment in Place (MCD)
EIP.......... Equipment Installation Procedure [*Telecommunications*] (TEL)
EIP.......... ERA [*Equal Rights Amendment*] Impact Project [*Defunct*] (EA)
EIP.......... Ethical Investments Policy (WDAA)
EIP.......... Ethylene Interpolymer Alloy
EIP.......... Evolutionary Implementation Plan (SAUS)
EIP.......... EXEC Interchange Program (SAUS)
EIP.......... Execute Interface Program (SAUS)
EIP.......... Executive Interface Program [*Computer science*] (HGAA)
EIP.......... Exoatmospheric Interceptor Propulsion (MCD)
EIP.......... Experiment Implementation Plan [*NASA*]
EIP.......... Export Industrial Park (SAUS)
EIP.......... Extended Internet Protocol (VERA)
EIP.......... Extended IP (Internet) (SAUS)
EIP.......... Extensor Indicis Proprius [*Anatomy*]
EIP.......... External Input (ACAE)
EIPA.......... Ethyl(isopropyl)amiloride [*Organic chemistry*]
EIPA.......... Ethylisopropylaniline [*Organic chemistry*]
EIPA.......... European Institute of Public Administration (EA)
EIPAS.......... Educational Innovation Programme for Development in the Arab States (SAUO)
E-IPB.......... Electronic version of IGOSS Products Bulletin (SAUS)
EIPBN.......... Electron, Ion, and Photon Beam Technology and Nanofabrication (SAUS)
EIPC.......... European Institute of Printed Circuits (EA)
EIPC.......... Extended Interprocess Communication (SAUS)
EIPDAS.......... Educational Innovation Programme for Development in Arab States (SAUO)
EIPG.......... Energy Investment Promotion Group (EURO)
EIPG.......... European Industrial Planning Group [*NATO*]
EIPH.......... Exercise-Induced Pulmonary Hemorrhage [*Veterinary medicine*]
EIPM.......... EIP Microwave [*NASDAQ symbol*] (TTSB)
EIPM.......... EIP Microwave, Inc. [*NASDAQ symbol*] (NQ)
EIPO.......... European IGAC Project Office (SAUS)
EIPO.......... European IGAC Project Office Steering Committee (SAUO)
EIPPA.......... European Isopropanol Producers Association (SAUO)
EIPR.......... European Intellectual Property Review (SAFN)
EIPS.......... Endogenous Inhibitor of Prostaglandin Synthase [*Biochemistry*]
EIPSL.......... Entry Age Normal with Frozen Initial Past Service Liability [*Business term*]
EIPT.......... Electronic Industry Production and Test Equipment (IMH)
EIPU.......... Education and Inmate Programs Unit (AGLO)
EIQ.......... Emission Inventory Questionnaire [*Environmental science*] (FFDE)
eir.......... earned income relief (SAUS)
EIR.......... Earthquake Information Requests (SAUO)
EIR.......... East Indian Railway
EIR.......... economic impact region (SAUS)
EIR.......... Either (ROG)
EIR.......... electric input ratio (SAUS)
EIR.......... Electron-Ion Recombination
EIR.......... Electrostatic Image Reproducer (ACAE)
EIR.......... Emerald Isle Resources, Inc. [*Vancouver Stock Exchange symbol*]
EIR.......... Emergency Information Readiness [*Civil Defense*]
EIR.......... Employee Incident Report (MCD)
EIR.......... employee invention report (SAUS)
EIR.......... Endangerment Information Report [*Environmental Protection Agency*] (ERG)
EIR.......... End Item Requirement (AAG)
EIR.......... Energy Information Resource (MCD)
EIR.......... Engineering Information Report [*Telecommunications*] (TEL)
EIR.......... Engineering Information Request [*Nuclear energy*] (NRCH)
EIR.......... Engineering Investigation Request
EIR.......... Environmental Impact Rep (SAUS)
EIR.......... Environmental Impact Report [*Environmental Protection Agency*]
EIR.......... Environmental Impact Review
EIR.......... Equipment Identification Center (SAUO)
EIR.......... Equipment Identification Register
EIR.......... Equipment Identity Register (SAUS)
EIR.......... Equipment Improvement Recommendations [*Military*]
EIR.......... Equipment Improvement Report [*DoD*]
EIR.......... Equipment Inoperable Record [*Nuclear energy*] (NRCH)
EIR.......... Equipment Installation Record (MCD)
EIR.......... Equipment Interchange Receipt (SAUS)
EIR.......... Error Interrupt Request (SAUS)
EIR.......... Establishment Inspection Report [*Federal government*]
EIR.......... Excess Information Rate [*Telecommunications*] (ACRL)
EIR.......... Expanded Infrared (DNAB)
EIR.......... Explosive Incident Report (ACAE)
EIR.......... Exposure Information Report [*Environmental science*] (COE)
Eir.......... Lambard's Eirenarcha [*A publication*] (DLA)
EIR.......... Error-Indicating Recording (ODA)
EIRAC.......... Entertainment Industry Referral and Assistance Center (EA)
EIRB.......... European Investment Research Bureau [*Information service or system*] (NITA)
EIRC.......... Eastern Illinois Railroad [*Federal Railroad Administration identification code*]
EIRD.......... Economics Information Resources Directory [*A publication*]
EIRD.......... Engineering Information Report Date [*Telecommunications*] (TEL)
EIRD.......... Engineering Instrumentation Requirements Document
EIRD.......... Equipment Integration Requirements Document (SAUO)
EIRD.......... Experiment Integration Requirements Document [*NASA*]
EIRD.......... Experiment Interface Requirements Document (SAUS)
EIRE.......... Emerald Isle Bancorp, Inc. [*NASDAQ symbol*] (SAG)
EIRENE.......... European Information Researchers Network (IID)
EIRI.......... Early Intervention Research Institute [*Utah State University*] [*Research center*] (RCD)
EIRI.......... Energy Information Resources Inventory [*Database*] [*Department of Energy*] [*Information service or system*] (CRD)
EIRIS.......... Ethical Investment Research Service [*British*] [*Information service or system*]
EIRMA.......... European (SAUS)
EIRMA.......... European Industrial Research Management Association [*France*]
EIRnv.......... Extra-Incidence Rate in Nonvaccinated [*medicine*] (STED)
EIRNV.......... Extra Incidence Rate in Non-Vaccinated Groups [*Medicine*] (BABM)
eiro.......... evaluation of infra-red-optics (SAUS)
EIRP.......... Effective/Equivalent Isotropically Radiated Power (SAUS)
EIRP.......... Effective Instantaneous [*or Isotropic*] Radiated Power [*Telecommunications*]
EIRP.......... Effective Irradiated Power (SAUS)
EIRP.......... Effective Isotopic Radiated Power (SAUS)
EIRP.......... Effective Isotropically Radiated Power (SAUS)
EIRP.......... Effective Isotropic Radiated Power [*Telecommunications*] (WDMC)
EIRP.......... Environmental Impact Research Program [*Army*] (RDA)
EIRP.......... Equivalent Isotropically Radiated Power [*Microwave transmission*]
EIRR.......... Eastern Idaho Railroad [*Federal Railroad Administration identification code*]
EIRR.......... European Industrial Relations Review (SAFN)
EIRS.......... Education Information Resources Service (SAUS)
EIRS.......... Engineering and Industrial Research Station [*Mississippi State University*] [*Research center*] (RCD)
EIRs.......... Environmental Impact Reports (SAUS)
EIRS.......... Ethical Investment Research Service [*London, England*] [*Information service or system*] (IID)
EIRT.......... Equivalent Isotropic Radiated Power [*Telecommunications service*] (BARN)
EIRT.......... Executive Independent Review Team (MCD)
EIRV.......... Error Interrupt Request Vector [*Computer science*] (ELAL)
EIRv.......... Extra Incidence Rate in Vaccinated Groups [*Biochemistry*] (DAVI)
EIRv.......... Extra Incidence Rate of Vaccinated Groups [*Medicine*] (DMAA)
EIRWL.......... Exploring Internet Resources at Washington and Lee (SAUO)
EIS.......... Beef Island [*British Virgin Islands*] [*Airport symbol*] (AD)
EIS.......... Digests of Environmental Impact Statements (SAUS)
EIS.......... Early Implementation System (SAUS)
EIS.......... Earth Landing System (SAUS)
EIS.......... Earthnet Info Server (SAUO)
EIS.......... East India Service (SAUO)
EIS.......... Economic Impact Studies (SAUS)
EIS.......... Economic Information Service (SAUS)
EIS.......... Economic Information System [*International Monetary Fund*] [*Information service or system*] (IID)
EIS.......... Economic Information Systems Inc. (SAUO)
EIS.......... Economic Lot Size (SAUS)
EIS.......... Ecosystem Information System (SAUO)
EIS.......... Educational Institute of Scotland
EIS.......... Education Information Services (SAUS)
EIS.......... Education in Science (AIE)
EIS.......... Effluent Inventory System [*Nuclear energy*] (NRCH)
EIS.......... Electrical and Instrument Shop (NRCH)

EIS.............. Electrical Induction Steel (SAUS)
EIS.............. Electrical Integration System (NASA)
eis.............. electrical intersection splice (SAUS)
EIS.............. Electric Induction Steel (IAA)
EIS.............. Electric Inertia Simulation [*Automotive emissions*]
EIS.............. Electric Information Storage (SAUS)
EIS.............. Electrochemical Impedance Spectroscopy (AAEL)
EIS.............. Electroluminescence Screen (SAUS)
EIS.............. Electrolyte Insulator Semiconductor (IAA)
EIS.............. Electromagnetic Intelligence System
EIS.............. Electron Energy Loss Spectroscopy (SAUS)
EIS.............. Electronet Information Systems, Inc. [*Information service or system*] (IID)
EIS.............. Electronic Ignition System [*Automotive engineering*]
EIS.............. Electronic Image Stabilizer [*Photography*]
EIS.............. Electronic Imaging Section (SAUS)
EIS.............. Electronic Imaging System [*Computer graphics*]
EIS.............. Electronic Information Series [*Information service or system*] (IID)
EIS.............. Electronic Information Services [*Industry*] (IT)
EIS.............. Electronic Information Standards (ADWA)
EIS.............. Electronic Inquiry System (PDAA)
EIS.............. Electronic Instrument System (SAUS)
EIS.............. Electronics Installations Squadron [*Military*]
EIS.............. Electron Impact Spectrometry (SAUS)
eis.............. electron impact spectroscopy (SAUS)
EIS.............. Element Symbol (SAUS)
EIS.............. Emergency Information System [*Software package*] [*Research Alternatives, Inc.*]
EIS.............. Emergency Injection System [*Nuclear energy*] (NRCH)
EIS.............. Emissions Impact Statement [*Environmental Protection Agency*] (GFGA)
EIS.............. Emissions Inventory System [*Environmental Protection Agency*] (GFGA)
EIS.............. Emitter Location System (SAUS)
EIS.............. Employee Information System (MCD)
EIS.............. Employment Incentive Scheme
EIS.............. End Interruption Sequence [*Computer science*]
EIS.............. End Item Specification (AAG)
EIS.............. End Item Subdivision (MCD)
EIS.............. Endoscopic Injection Scleropathy [*Medicine*] (STED)
EIS.............. Energy and Industry Subgroup (EERA)
EIS.............. Energy Information Systems [*UNIDO*] [*United Nations*] (DUND)
EIS.............. Energy-Loss Spectroscopy (SAUS)
EIS.............. Engineering Index Service (SAUS)
EIS.............. Engineering Information Series (SAUS)
EIS.............. Engineering Information Service (SAUS)
EIS.............. Engineering Information System (MCD)
EIS.............. Engineering Installation Squadron (SAUO)
EIS.............. Engineering Integrity Society (COBU)
EIS.............. Entered in Service [*Military*]
EIS.............. Enterprise/Executive Information System (SAUS)
EIS.............. Enterprise Information Systems
EIS.............. Enterprise Investment Scheme [*British*] (ECON)
EIS.............. Entry Into Service (SAUS)
EIS.............. Environmental Imaging Spectrometer (SAUS)
EIS.............. Environmental Impact Service (USDC)
EIS.............. Environmental Impact Statement [*Environmental Protection Agency*]
EIS.............. Environmental Impact Statements [*Heiner and Co.*] (NITA)
EIS.............. Environmental Impact Study
EIS.............. Environmental Industry Sector (FOTI)
EIS.............. Environmental Information Services
EIS.............. Environmental Information System [*National Science Foundation*]
EIS.............. Environmental Inventory System (GNE)
EIS.............. Environmental Law Society (SAUO)
EIS.............. Environment Information System (SAUS)
EIS.............. Epidemic Intelligence Service [*of the Centers for Disease Control*]
EIS.............. Epidemiological Investigation Service (SAUO)
EIS.............. Epidemiology Information System [*Database*] [*Oak Ridge National Laboratory*] [*Information service or system*] (CRD)
EIS.............. Epson Informations System (SAUS)
EIS.............. Equal Load Sharing (SAUS)
EIS.............. Equipment Information Series (SAUS)
EIS.............. Equipment Information System (SAUS)
EIS.............. equipment interface system (SAUS)
EIS.............. Ericsson Information Systems (SAUS)
EIS.............. Error Likely Situation (SAUS)
EIS.............. Erwin Identity Scale [*Psychology*] (DHP)
EIS.............. Eurasian Ice Sheet [*Climatology*]
EIS.............. European Information System (SAUO)
EIS.............. European Invertebrate Survey (SAUS)
EIS.............. Evaluation Information System (SAUS)
EIS.............. Excelsior Income Shares, Inc. [*NYSE symbol*] (SAG)
EIS.............. Executive Information Service [*or Software or System*]
EIS.............. Executive Information Systems (SAUS)
EIS.............. Expanded Inband Signaling [*Telecommunications*] (TEL)
EIS.............. Expendable Instrument System
EIS.............. Experiment Information System
EIS.............. Experiment Initiator System (SAUS)
EIS.............. Export Intelligence Service (DS)
EIS.............. Extended Instruction Set [*Honeywell, Inc.*]
EIS.............. Exxon Information System (SAUS)
EIS.............. Eyes in the Sky
EIS.............. Tortola [*British Virgin Islands*] [*Airport symbol*] (OAG)
EIS7.............. Region 7 EIS 404 Program (SAUS)
EISA.............. Eastern Intercollegiate Skiing Association (PSS)
EISA.............. EEG Aperiodic-Interval Spectrum Analysis [*Neurology*]
EISA.............. EEG interval spectrum analysis (SAUS)
EISA.............. Electroencephalogram Interval Spectrum Analysis [*Medicine*] (STED)
EISA.............. Electronics Industry Standards Association
EISA.............. Enhanced/Extended Industry Standard Architecture (SAUS)
EISA.............. Enhanced Industry Standard Architecture [*Computer hardware*] (PCM)
EISA.............. European Imaging and Sound Association (VERA)
EISA.............. European Independent Steelworks Association (EAIO)
EISA.............. Extended Industrial Systems Architecture (SAUS)
EISA.............. Extended Industry Standard Adapter (SAUS)
EISA.............. Extended Industry Standard Architecture [*Computer science*]
EISA.............. extended industry standards association (SAUS)
EISA.............. Extended International Standard Architecture (RALS)
EISAC.............. European Imaging Spectroscopy Aircraft Campaign (SAUS)
EISA/ISA.............. Extended Industry Standard Architecture/Industry Standard Architecture (SAUS)
EISA/MCA.............. Extended Industry Standard Architecture/ Microchannel Architecture (SAUS)
EIS/AS.............. Emissions Inventory System/Area Source [*Environmental Protection Agency*] (GFGA)
EISB.............. Electrical Industry Study Board (EA)
EISB.............. Electronic Imaging Standards Board (VERA)
EISC.............. Eastern Illinois State College [*Later, EIU*]
EISC.............. Electronic Industry Show Corp. [*Defunct*] (EA)
EISC.............. Entertainment Industry Support Committee [*Defunct*] (EA)
EISC.............. Environmental Information Service Center [*Environmental Protection Agency*] (AEPA)
EISC.............. EUCOM Intelligence Summary Cable (SAUS)
EISCAT.............. European Incoherent Scatter (SAUS)
EISCAT.............. European Incoherent Scatter Facility (SAUS)
EISCAT.............. European Incoherent Scattering (SAUS)
EISCAT.............. European Incoherent Scattering Scientific Association
EISCAT.............. European Incoherent Scatter Organisation (SAUS)
EISCAT.............. European Incoherent Scatter Radar Facility/Scientific Association (SAUO)
EISCAT.............. European Incoherent Scatter Radar System (SAUS)
EISD.............. Engineering and Industrial Software Directory [*Engineering Information, Inc.*] [*Information service or system*] (CRD)
EISD.............. European Information Systems Division (SAUO)
EISD.............. Explosives Ingredients Sources Database [*Chemical Propulsion Information Agency*]
EISE.............. Extendable Integration Support Environment [*Air Force*]
EISEP.............. Expanded In-Home Services for the Elderly Program (BARN)
EISF.............. Elastic Incoherent Structure Factor [*of spectra*]
EISG.............. Energy Information Systems Group [*Department of Energy*] [*Also, an information service or system*] (IID)
EISI.............. EIS International [*NASDAQ symbol*] (TTSB)
EISI.............. Electronic Information Systems, Inc. [*NASDAQ symbol*] (SAG)
EISIM.............. Electron Impact Selected Ion Monitoring [*Instrumentation*]
EIS Intl.............. EIS International [*Associated Press*] (SAG)
EISL.............. Eastern Intercollegiate Swimming League (PSS)
EISL.............. Shannon [*Ireland*] [*ICAO location identifier*] (ICLI)
EISMINT.............. European Ice-Sheet Modelling Initiative (SAUS)
EISN.............. Environmental Information and Support Network (EERA)
EISN.............. Experimental Integrated Switched Network
EISO.............. Educational Information System for Ontario (SAUS)
EISO.............. Engineering and Integrated Support Office (SAUO)
EISO.............. Engineering and Integration Supply Office (ACAE)
EISO.............. Environmental Information Society of Ontario (SAUO)
EISO.............. Environmental Information System Office [*National Science Foundation*]
EISP.............. Engineering and Installation Support Plan (SAUS)
EISP.............. Equivalent Industrial Standard Process (MCD)
EISPACK.............. eigensystem package subroutine computing facility (SAUS)
EIS Plants.............. Economic Information Systems plants (SAUS)
EIS Plants.............. Economic Information Systems-Plants [*Information service or system*] (NITA)
EIS/PS.............. Emissions Inventory System/Point Source [*Environmental Protection Agency*] (GFGA)
EIS/PS&AS.............. Emissions Inventory Subsystem/Point Source and Area Source (EAGT)
EISS.............. Economic Impact Study System (SAUS)
EISS.............. Encyclopedia of Information Systems and Services [*Later, IID*] [*A publication*]
EISs.............. Environmental Impact Statements (SAUS)
EISS.............. European Intelligence Support System (SAUS)
EISS.............. European Intelligence System Support (SAUS)
EISSWA.............. Experimental Information Service in Two Social Welfare Agencies (PDAA)
EISU.............. Eastern Illinois State University (SAUO)
EISU.............. Shannon [*Ireland*] [*ICAO location identifier*] (ICLI)
EISV.............. Extrinsic Irradiated Silicon Vidicon
EISYS.............. Earth Information System [*Commercial firm*]
EIT.............. Economies in Transition (ACII)
EIT.............. Eilat [*Israel*] [*Airport symbol*] (AD)
EIT.............. Electrical Impedance Tomography [*Medicine*] (BARN)
EIT.............. Electrical Information Test
EIT.............. Electrical Installation Test [*or Technician*]
EIT.............. Electrical Insulation Tape
EIT.............. Electrical Intersystems Test
EIT.............. Electric Information Technique (SAUS)
EIT.............. Electromagnetically Induced Transparency [*Optics*]
EIT.............. Electromagnetic Interference Testing
EIT.............. Electron-Bombardment Ion Thrustor

EIT .... Electronic Information Technology (FOTI)
EIT .... Electronic Information Technology [*Hardware manufacturer*]
EIT .... Electronic Installation Technician
EIT .... Encoded Information Type (SAUS)
EIT .... Encoding Information Type (SAUS)
EIT .... Engineering Index Thesaurus [*A publication*]
EIT .... Engineer-in-Training
eit .... engineer in training (SAUS)
EIT .... Enterprise Integration Technologies [*Commercial firm*]
EIT .... Enterprise Investments Trust [*Australia*]
EIT .... Entry Interface Time (MCD)
EIT .... Environmental Interaction Theory of Personality (PDAA)
EIT .... Environmental Issues Test (EDAC)
EIT .... Erythrocyte Iron Turnover (SAUS)
EIT .... (Erythrofuranosyl)imidazolinethione [*Antineoplastic drug*]
EIT .... Erythroid Iron Turnover [*Hematology*]
EIT .... European Institute for Trans-National Studies in Group and Organizational Development (EA)
EIT .... European Institute of Technology [*International Consortium of Industrial Firms*]
EIT .... Europe Industry and Technology Division [*Department of Trade*] [*British*]
EIT .... Extreme-Ultraviolet Imaging Telescope [*Instrumentation*]
e-it- .... Italy [*MARC geographic area code*] [*Library of Congress*] (LCCP)
EITA .... Eastern Intercollegiate Tennis Association (PSS)
EITA .... Electric Industrial Truck Association (SAUO)
EITB .... Engineering Industry Training Board [*British*]
EITB .... Enzyme-Linked Immunoelectrotransfer Blot (Technique) [*Clinical chemistry*]
EITC .... Earned Income Tax Credit
EITCA .... United States-Soviet Union Agreement to Facilitate Economic, Industrial and Technical Cooperation (SAUO)
EITD .... Electronic Industry Telephone Directory (SAUO)
EITE .... European Institute of Transuranium Elements (SAUS)
EITF .... Emerging Issues Task Force (EBF)
EITF .... Environmental Institute Task Force (SAUS)
EITI .... European Interconnect Technology Initiative (SAUO)
EITO .... European Information Technology Observatory (SAUO)
EITP .... End Item Test Plan (MCD)
eitp .... environmental interaction theory of personality (SAUS)
EITS .... East Integrated Test Stand (KSC)
EITS .... Educational and Industrial Testing Service
EITS .... Encoded Information Types (SAUS)
EITS .... Express International Telex Service (MHDB)
EITT .... Employee Involvement Task Team (ACAE)
EITT .... Export/Import Transit Time (VLIE)
EITZ .... English Inshore Traffic Zone (DS)
EIU .... Eastern Illinois University [*Formerly, EISC*] [*Charleston*]
EIU .... Economic and Industrial Understanding [*British*] (DET)
EIU .... Economist Intelligence Unit [*British*]
EIU .... Electronic Interconnect Unit (TIMI)
EIU .... Electronic Interface Unit
EIU .... Engine Interface Unit (NASA)
EIU .... Enid, OK [*Location identifier*] [*FAA*] (FAAL)
EIU .... Equipment Inventory Update [*Telecommunications*] (TEL)
EIU .... European Ichthyological Union (SAUO)
EIU .... Even If Used (RIMS)
EIU .... Executive Independent Utilities (SAUS)
EIU .... Experimental Information Unit (SAUS)
EIUF .... European ISDN User Forum (SAUO)
EIV .... Effective Initial Value
EIV .... Engine Installation Vehicle
EIV .... Entsiklopedyah 'Ivrit [*or Enziklopedyah 'Ivrit*] (BJA)
EIV .... External Iliac Vein (MELL)
EIVA .... Eastern Intercollegiate Volleyball Association (PSS)
EIVR .... Engineering Information Visit Request (SAUS)
EIVR .... Exchange of Information, Visits, and Reports
EIVT .... Electrical and Instrumentation Verification Tests [*NASA*] (NASA)
EIVT .... Electrical Interface Verification Test [*NASA*] (NASA)
EIVT .... Electronic Installation Verification Test [*NASA*] (NASA)
EIW .... Economic Information Warfare (SEWL)
EIW .... Enamel Insulated Wire
EIW .... European Institute for Water (EAIO)
EIW .... New Madrid, MO [*Location identifier*] [*FAA*] (FAAL)
EIWA .... Eastern Intercollegiate Wrestling Association (PSS)
EIWA .... EASTERN IOWA BASINS (SAUS)
EIWA .... Escala Inteligencia Wechsler Para Adultes [*Weschler Adult Intelligence Scale*] [*Psychology*] (DAVI)
EIWG .... EM International Working Group (SAUO)
EIWH .... European Institute of Womens Health (SAUS)
EIWLS .... Extended Iterative Weighted Least Squares [*Statistics*] (PDAA)
EI/WS .... End Item/Weapon System [*Army*]
EIWS .... Engineering Installation Workload Schedule (CET)
EIX .... Edison International [*NYSE symbol*] [*Formerly, SCEcorp*] (SG)
EIX .... Elders IXL Canada, Inc. [*Toronto Stock Exchange symbol*]
EIX .... electrochemical ion exchange (SAUS)
EIX .... Enterprise Information Exchange (VLIE)
EIY .... Ein Yahav [*Israel*] [*Airport symbol*] [*Obsolete*] (OAG)
EIZ .... Emery Industries [*Federal Railroad Administration identification code*]
EJ .... Die Entstehung des Judentums [*A publication*] (BJA)
EJ .... Eccles-Jordan circuit (SAUS)
EJ .... Economic Journal (journ.) (SAUS)
EJ .... Eject (KSC)
EJ .... Ejus [*Of Him, or Of Her*] [*Latin*]
EJ .... Elbow Jerk [*Medicine*] (EDAA)
Ej .... Elbow Jerk [*Medicine*] (EDAA)
EJ .... Electrojet (IAA)
EJ .... Electronic Jamming
EJ .... Electronic Journalism
EJ .... Electronic Junction (SAUS)
EJ .... Elizabeth Jones [*Designer's mark, when appearing on US coins*]
EJ .... Encyclopaedia Judaica [*A publication*]
E-J .... Endicott-Johnson (SAUS)
EJ .... End of Job (VLIE)
EJ .... English Journal [*A publication*] (BRI)
EJ .... ERIC Journal (SAUS)
EJ .... Everest & Jennings International [*AMEX symbol*] (SPSG)
EJ .... exajoule (SAUS)
EJ .... Expansion Joint
EJ .... Expendable Jammer (LAIN)
EJ .... New England Airlines [*ICAO designator*] (AD)
EJA .... Barrancabermeja [*Colombia*] [*Airport symbol*] (OAG)
EJA .... Engineering Job Analysis (KSC)
EJA .... Environmental Protection Agency, Region III Library, Philadelphia, PA [*OCLC symbol*] (OCLC)
EJA .... Equal Justice for All (FOTI)
EJA .... Esperanta Jura Asocio [*Esperanto Law Association*] [*See also ELA*] [*British*] [*England*] (EAIO)
EJA .... Ethiopian Journalists Association (SAUS)
EJA .... European Journal of Archaeology [*A publication*] (ABAR)
EJA .... Executive Jet Aviation, Inc. [*ICAO designator*] (FAAC)
EJ & E R Y... Elgin, Joliet & Eastern Railway (SAUS)
EJASA .... Electronic Journal of the Astronomical Society of the Atlantic [*A publication*]
Ejava .... Embedded Java (VLIE)
EJB .... Ectopic Junctional Beat [*Cardiology*]
EJB .... Enterprise Java Beans (VLIE)
EJB .... Environmental Protection Agency, Headquarters Library, Washington, DC [*OCLC symbol*] (OCLC)
EJB .... European Journal of Biochemistry (SAUS)
EJC .... Eccles-Jordan Circuit [*Electronics*]
EJC .... Edison Junior College (SAUS)
EJC .... Electrical Joint Compound (IAA)
EJC .... Electronic Journal Collection
EJC .... Electronic Journal of Communication (SAUO)
EJC .... Ellsworth Junior College [*Iowa*] [*Later, ECC*]
EJC .... Ely Junior College [*Minnesota*] [*Later, Vermilion Community College*]
EJC .... Enciclopedia Judaica Castellana [*A publication*] (BJA)
EJC .... Endicott Junior College [*Beverly, MA*]
EJC .... Engineers Joint Council [*Superseded by AAES*] (EA)
EJC .... Engineers Junior College (SAUS)
EJC .... Environmental Protection Agency, Law Library, Washington, DC [*OCLC symbol*] (OCLC)
EJC .... Espoir de la Jeunesse Camerounaise [*Hope of the Cameroonese Youth*]
EJC .... Estherville Junior College [*Iowa*]
EJC .... European Journalism Centre (EURO)
EJC .... Eveleth Junior College [*Later, Mesabi Community College*] [*Minnesota*]
EJC .... Everett Junior College [*Later, ECC*] [*Washington*]
EJC .... Grupo de Aviacion Ejecutiva, SA de CV [*Mexico*] [*FAA designator*] (FAAC)
EJCC .... Eastern Joint Computer Conference
EJCC .... Eastern Joint Computer Council (SAUO)
EJCDC .... Engineers Joint Contract Documents Committee (AAGC)
EJCNC .... Engineers Joint Council Nuclear Congress (IEEE)
EJCSC .... European Joint Committee of Scientific Cooperation [*Council of Europe*] (PDAA)
EJCT .... Eject
EJCT .... Engineering Joint Council Thesaurus (NITA)
EJC/TEST .... Engineering Joint Council, Thesaurus of Engineering and Scientific Terms (SAUO)
EJCTR .... Ejector
EJD .... DeBartolo Realty [*NYSE symbol*] (TTSB)
EJD .... DeBartolo Realty Co. [*NYSE symbol*] (SAG)
EJD .... Environmental Protection Agency, Region III Field Office, Annapolis, MD [*OCLC symbol*] (OCLC)
EJE .... Chicago Outer Belt R. R. [*AAR code*]
EJE .... Electric Junction Equation
EJE .... Elgin, Joliet & Eastern Railway Co. [*AAR code*]
EJE .... Environmental Protection Agency, OTS [*Office of Toxic Substances*] Technical Information Center, Washington, DC [*OCLC symbol*] (OCLC)
EJE .... Executive Jet Aviation SA [*Switzerland*] [*FAA designator*] (FAAC)
EJEA .... Empire Journal of Experimental Agriculture [*A publication*]
EJEC .... Eject (SAUS)
EJEC .... Ejection (SAUS)
Eject .... Ejector (SAUS)
EJF .... Equal Justice Foundation (EA)
EJF .... Estimated Junction Frequency [*Telecommunications*] (TEL)
E-JFET .... Enhancement-Mode Junction Field-Effect Transistor [*Electronics*]
EJGAAF .... Earl J. Goldberg Aplastic Anemia Foundation [*Founded in 1979*] (NRGU)
EJGS .... Eminent Junior Grand Steward [*Freemasonry*] (ROG)
EJGX .... Ernest and Julio Gallo Winery [*Private rail car owner code*]
EJH .... Wedjh [*Saudi Arabia*] [*Airport symbol*] (OAG)
EJHC .... East Jayhawk Conference (PSS)
EJI .... European Journal of Immunology [*Medicine*] (EDAA)
EJI .... Expansion Joint Institute
EJIC .... Education and Job Information Center (SAUS)

EJIL .... European Journal of International Law [*A publication*] (SAFN)
EJ Korvette... , Corvettes [*Zwillenberg*] [*Department store chain name derived from the owner's name, a business parter, and a Canadian warship*]
EJM .... American Air Services, Inc. [*ICAO designator*] (FAAC)
EJM .... Etudes sur le Judaisme Medieval [*A publication*] (BJA)
EJM .... European Journal of Mineralogy [*A publication*] (STAH)
EJMA .... Educational Jewelry Manufacturers Association [*Defunct*] (EA)
EJMA .... Expansion Joint Manufacturers Association (EA)
EJN .... Ejection
EJN .... Endicott Johnson Corp. (SAUO)
EJN .... External Jugular Vein (MELL)
EJN ST .... Ejection Seat (MSA)
EJO .... Earp, Joseph O., Seattle WA [*STAC*]
EJO .... Electronic Journal of Oncology (SAUS)
EJO .... Electronic Journals Online (SAUS)
EJO .... Engineering Job Order (MCD)
EJO .... Nejo [*Ethiopia*] [*Airport symbol*] (AD)
EJOB .... European Joint Optical Bistability Programme [*To develop an optical computer*]
EJOB Project... European Joint Optical Biostability Project (SAUS)
EJOGR .... European Journal of Obstetrics and Gynecology and Reproductive Biology (SAUS)
EJOTF .... Earth-Jupiter Orbiter Transfer Flight (PDAA)
E-Journal ..... Electronic Journal (TNIG)
EJP .... European Journal of Physics [*A publication*]
EJP .... Exchange Jump
EJP .... Excitatory Junctional Potential [*Neurophysiology*]
EJPC .... European Justice and Peace Commissions (EAIO)
EJPEA .... Emergency Jobs Programs Extension Act of 1976
EJR .... Detroit, MI [*Location identifier*] [*FAA*] (FAAL)
EJR .... East Jersey Railroad & Terminal Co. [*AAR code*]
EJRMG .... Edmond James Rothschild Memorial Group [*Foundation*]
EJRS .... Emergency Joint Reporting Structure (SAUS)
EJS .... East Jordan & Southern R. R. [*AAR code*]
EJS .... Electronic Journal of Surgery and Specialistic Medicine (SAUS)
EJS .... Engineering Job Sheet (MCD)
EJS .... Enhanced JTIDS [*Joint Tactical Information Distribution System*] System [*Air Force*]
EJS .... Ethical Judgement Scale (EDAC)
EJT .... Aero Ejecutiva SA [*Mexico*] [*ICAO designator*] (FAAC)
EJT .... Eccles-Jordan Trigger [*Electronics*]
EJT .... Eject (VLIE)
EJT .... Engineering Job Ticket
EJT .... Extended Joint Test (MCD)
EJTA .... Emergency Jobs Training Act (SAUS)
EJTF .... Electronic Journals Task Force (SAUS)
EJU .... European Journal of Ultrasound (SAUS)
EJU .... European Judo Union (EAIO)
EJU .... Exports to Japan Unit [*British Overseas Trade Board*] (DS)
EJUA .... Emergency Jobs and Unemployment Assistance Act (SAUS)
EJUAA .... Emergency Jobs and Unemployment Assistance Act
EJud .... Encyclopaedia Judaica: Das Judentum in Geschichte und Gegenwart [*Berlin*] [*A publication*] (BJA)
EJUSB .... European Joint Utilities Services Board (SAUO)
EJUSD .... Ejusdem [*Of the Same*] [*Latin*]
EJV .... Equity Joint Venture [*Business term*]
EJV .... External Jugular Vein [*Anatomy*]
EJWG .... Eco-Justice Working Group [*Joint Strategy and Action Committee and National Council of the Churches of Christ in the USA*] (EA)
EJX .... Eject X (VLIE)
Ek .... Cathode Voltage (SAUS)
EK .... Eastern Knight [*Freemasonry*] (ROG)
EK .... Eastman Kodak Co. [*NYSE symbol*] (SPSG)
EK .... Einschluss-Korper [*Inclusion body*] [*Medicine*]
EK .... Einzelkommentar [*A publication*] (BJA)
EK .... Eklutna Project Office (SAUO)
EK .... Electrocardiogram [*Also, ECG, EKG*] [*Medicine*]
EK .... Electrokinetic
EK .... Electrokinetics (SAUS)
EK .... Enkephalin [*Brain peptide, subclass of endorphin*]
EK .... Erase Key (SAUS)
EK .... Erythrokinase [*Biochemistry*] (DAVI)
EK .... Esperantski Klub (SAUO)
ek .... even keel (SAUS)
EK .... Masling Commuter Services [*ICAO designator*] (AD)
EKA .... Enterprise Knowledge Architecture (GART)
EKA .... Environmental Protection Agency, Region IV Library, Atlanta, GA [*OCLC symbol*] (OCLC)
EKA .... Eskdalemuir Array [*Scotland*] [*Seismograph station code, US Geological Survey*] (SEIS)
EKA .... Eureka/Arcata [*California*] Murray Field [*Airport symbol*] [*Obsolete*] (OAG)
EKABX .... Evergreen Small Co. Growth Cl.B [*Mutual fund ticker symbol*] (SG)
EKAE .... Aero [*Denmark*] [*ICAO location identifier*] (ICLI)
EKAH .... Tirstrup [*Denmark*] [*ICAO location identifier*] (ICLI)
EkahR .... Ekah Rabbah (BJA)
EKAT .... Anholt [*Denmark*] [*ICAO location identifier*] (ICLI)
EKAV .... Avno [*Denmark*] [*ICAO location identifier*] (ICLI)
EKB .... Edgeworth-Kuiper Belt [*Panetary science*]
EKB .... Electronic Keyboard
EKB .... Electronic Knowledge Bank
EKB .... Environmental Protection Agency, Library Services, Research Triangle Park, NC [*OCLC symbol*] (OCLC)
EKB .... Extended Kalman- Bucy (SAUS)
EKBBX .... Evergreen Balanced Cl.B [*Mutual fund ticker symbol*] (SG)
EKBI .... Billund [*Denmark*] [*ICAO location identifier*] (ICLI)
EKBS .... Electronic Keyboard System
EKC .... East Kansas City Aviation, Inc. [*ICAO designator*] (FAAC)
EKC .... Eastman Kodak Co.
EKC .... Eastman Kodak Company (SAUO)
EKC .... Ek Chor Ching Motorcycle [*NYSE symbol*] (SPSG)
EKC .... Electrokinetic Chromatography
EKC .... Environmental Protection Agency, Environmental Research Laboratory, Gulf Breeze,FL [*OCLC symbol*] (OCLC)
EKC .... Epidemic Keratoconjunctivitis [*Ophthalmology*]
EKC .... Ethylketocyclazocine [*Biochemistry*]
EKCA .... Kobenhavn [*Denmark*] [*ICAO location identifier*] (ICLI)
EKCH .... Kobenhavn/Kastrup [*Denmark*] [*ICAO location identifier*] (ICLI)
EK Chor .... Ek Chor China Motorcycle [*Associated Press*] (SAG)
EKCI .... Esperantista Kolektanta Centra Informejo (SAUO)
EKCO .... Ekco Group [*Associated Press*] (SAG)
EKCO .... E K Cole Ltd. (WDAA)
EKCZ .... East Kentucky Coal Docks [*Federal Railroad Administration identification code*]
EKD .... Electronic Key Distribution (SAUS)
EKD .... Environmental Protection Agency, Environmental Research Laboratory, Athens, GA [*OCLC symbol*] (OCLC)
EKD .... Epic Data, Inc. [*Toronto Stock Exchange symbol*] [*Vancouver Stock Exchange symbol*]
EKD .... Eucaloric Ketogenic Diet
EKD .... Evangelische Kirche Deutschlands
EKDK .... Kobenhavn [*Denmark*] [*ICAO location identifier*] (ICLI)
EKDMX .... Evergreen Diversified Bond Cl.B [*Mutual fund ticker symbols*] (SG)
EKE .... Biloxi, MS [*Location identifier*] [*FAA*] (FAAL)
EKE .... Eddy Kinetic Energy (SAUS)
EKE .... Ekereku [*Guyana*] [*Airport symbol*] (OAG)
EKE .... Environmental Protection Agency, Library, Research Triangle Park, NC [*OCLC symbol*] (OCLC)
EKE .... Equatorial Kerr Effect [*Physics*] (ODA)
EKEB .... Esbjerg [*Denmark*] [*ICAO location identifier*] (ICLI)
EKEBX .... Evergreen Tax Free Cl.B [*Mutual fund ticker symbol*] (SG)
E KENT R ..... East Kent Regiment [*Military unit*] [*British*] (ROG)
EKF .... Environmental Protection Agency, ESRL [*Environmental Sciences Research Laboratory*], Meteorology Laboratory, Research Triangle Park, NC [*OCLC symbol*] (OCLC)
EKF .... Extended Kalman Filter (AAEL)
EKFC .... Elvis Is King Fan Club (EAIO)
EKG .... Carlsbad, CA [*Location identifier*] [*FAA*] (FAAL)
EKG .... Effective Kilogram (NRCH)
EKG .... Electrocardiogram [*Also, ECG, EK*] [*Medicine*]
EKG .... Electrocardiograph [*Also, ECG*] (NASA)
EKG .... Electrocardiography [*Medicine*] (MELL)
ekg .... electrokardiogram (SAUS)
EKG .... Electrokymogram (SAUS)
EKG .... Electrokymography (SAUS)
EKG .... Epidemic Keratoconjunctivitis [*Ophthalmology*] (DAVI)
EKGAX .... Evergreen Global Opport. Cl.A [*Mutual fund ticker symbol*] (SG)
EKGF .... Gormfelt [*Denmark*] [*ICAO location identifier*] (ICLI)
EKGH .... Gronholt [*Denmark*] [*ICAO location identifier*] (ICLI)
EKH .... Elkhorn Ranch [*California*] [*Seismograph station code, US Geological Survey*] (SEIS)
EKHBX .... Evergreen High Yield Cl.B [*Mutual fund ticker symbol*] (SG)
EKHG .... Herning/Skinderholm [*Denmark*] [*ICAO location identifier*] (ICLI)
EKHO .... Lindtorp [*Denmark*] [*ICAO location identifier*] (ICLI)
EKHS .... Hadsund [*Denmark*] [*ICAO location identifier*] (ICLI)
EKHSIN .... Eastern Kentucky Health Science Information Network (SAUS)
EKHV .... Haderslev [*Denmark*] [*ICAO location identifier*] (ICLI)
EKI .... Corpus Christi, TX [*Location identifier*] [*FAA*] (FAAL)
EKI .... Ekaton Industries, Inc. [*Toronto Stock Exchange symbol*]
EKI .... E. Khashoggi Industries
EKI .... Electronic Keyboarding, Inc. [*Information service or system*] (IID)
EKI .... Elkhart [*Indiana*] [*Airport symbol*] (OAG)
EKI .... Esperanto en Komerco Kaj Industrio [*Institute for Esperanto in Commerce and Industry*] (EA)
EKIAP .... East Kimberley Impact Assessment Program (EERA)
EKIAX .... Evergreen Intermed. Term Bond Cl.A [*Mutual fund ticker symbol*] (SG)
EKIF .... Employer Identification Number Key Index File [*IRS*]
EKIP .... Eastman Kodak Inst. Print Film (VRA)
EKJBX .... Evergreen Strategic Growth Cl.B [*Mutual fund ticker symbol*] (SG)
EKK .... Evangelisch-Katholischer Kommentar zum Neuen Testament [*A publication*] (BJA)
EKKA .... Karup [*Denmark*] [*ICAO location identifier*] (ICLI)
EKKE .... Epanastatiko Kommunistiko Komma Ellados [*Revolutionary Communist Party of Greece*] (PPW)
EKKL .... Kalundborg [*Denmark*] [*ICAO location identifier*] (ICLI)
EKKM .... Arhus/Kirstinesminde [*Denmark*] [*ICAO location identifier*] (ICLI)
EKL .... Evangelisches Kirchenlexikon. Kirchlich-Theologisches Handwoerterbuch [*A publication*] (BJA)
EKLAX .... Evergreen Latin America Cl.A [*Mutual fund ticker symbol*] (SG)
EKLF .... Erythroid Kruppel-Like Factor [*Medicine*]
EKLS .... Laeso [*Denmark*] [*ICAO location identifier*] (ICLI)
EKLV .... Lemvig [*Denmark*] [*ICAO location identifier*] (ICLI)
EKM .... Edwald-Kornfeld Method
EKM .... Elkhart, IN [*Location identifier*] [*FAA*] (FAAL)
EKM .... Enterprise Knowledge Management (HODG)
EKMA .... Empirical Kinetic Modeling Approach [*Air pollution research*]
EKMB .... Maribo [*Denmark*] [*ICAO location identifier*] (ICLI)
EKMC .... Karup [*Denmark*] [*ICAO location identifier*] (ICLI)

EKMI .... Danish Meteorological Institute [*Denmark*] [*ICAO location identifier*] (ICLI)
EKMK .... Karup [*Denmark*] [*ICAO location identifier*] (ICLI)
EKMN .... Koster Vig [*Denmark*] [*ICAO location identifier*] (ICLI)
EKMS .... Electronic Key Management System (SEWL)
EKN .... Ecology of Knowledge Network (EA)
EKN .... Elkins [*West Virginia*] [*Airport symbol*] (OAG)
EKN .... Eta Kappa Nu [*Fraternity*]
EKNA .... Eureka Springs & North Arkansas Railroad [*Federal Railroad Administration identification code*]
EKNE .... Department of Elementary, Kindergarten, and Nursery Education [*of NEA*] [*Later, American Association of Elementary, Kindergarten, Nursery Educators*]
EKNF .... Elementary Key Normal Form (SAUS)
EKNM .... Morso [*Denmark*] [*ICAO location identifier*] (ICLI)
EK/NOD .... Eastman Kodak/Navy Ordnance District (AAG)
EKNS .... Nakskov [*Denmark*] [*ICAO location identifier*] (ICLI)
EKO .... Edgeworth Kuiper Belt Object [*Planetary science*]
EKO .... Ekco Group [*NYSE symbol*] (SPSG)
Eko .... Eko [*Record label*] [*France*]
EKO .... Elko [*Nevada*] [*Airport symbol*] (OAG)
EKO .... Elko [*Nevada*] [*Seismograph station code, US Geological Survey*] [*Closed*] (SEIS)
EKO .... Internacia Ekologia-Ekonomia Akademio [*International Ecological-Economic Academy*] [*Bulgaria*] (EAIO)
EKOAX .... Evergreen Omega Fund Cl.A [*Mutual fund ticker symbol*] (SG)
EKOD .... Odense/Beldringe [*Denmark*] [*ICAO location identifier*] (ICLI)
EKodak .... Eastman Kodak Co. [*Associated Press*] (SAG)
EK of N .... Election Knight of Nine [*Freemasonry*] (ROG)
EKOL .... European Kompass Online [*Reed Information Services Ltd.*] [*Information service or system*]
EKOPO .... Evreiskii Komitet Pomoshchi [*Shanghai*] (BJA)
EKP .... A/S Eksportfinans [*Export Finance*] [*NYSE symbol*] (SPSG)
EKP .... Eestimaa Kommunistlik Partei
EKP .... Eksportfinans Capital Securities [*NYSE symbol*] (SAG)
EKP .... Enterprise Knowledge Portal [*Computer science*]
EKP .... Epikeraprosthesis [*Ophthalmology*]
EKP .... Evreiskaia Kommunisticheskaia Partiia [*Political party*] (BJA)
EKP .... Wisconsin Rapids, WI [*Location identifier*] [*FAA*] (FAAL)
EKPB .... Krusa-Padborg [*Denmark*] [*ICAO location identifier*] (ICLI)
EKPBX .... Evergreen Cap. Preserv. & Income Cl.B [*Mutual fund ticker symbol*] (SG)
EKPPr .... A/S Eksportcinans 8.70% Pfd [*NYSE symbol*] (TTSB)
EKQ .... Monticello, KY [*Location identifier*] [*FAA*] (FAAL)
EKR .... East Kent Regiment [*Military unit*] [*British*]
EKR .... EQK Realty Investors I SBI [*NYSE symbol*] (SPSG)
EKR .... EQK Realty Inv I SBI [*NYSE symbol*] (TTSB)
EKR .... Meeker, CO [*Location identifier*] [*FAA*] (FAAL)
EKRC .... Elisabeth Kubler-Ross Center (EA)
EKRD .... Randers [*Denmark*] [*ICAO location identifier*] (ICLI)
EKRECC .... East Kentucky Rural Electric Cooperative Corporation (SAUO)
EKRK .... Kobenhavn/Roskilde [*Denmark*] [*ICAO location identifier*] (ICLI)
EKRN .... Ronne [*Denmark*] [*ICAO location identifier*] (ICLI)
EKRR .... Ro [*Denmark*] [*ICAO location identifier*] (ICLI)
EKRS .... Ringsted [*Denmark*] [*ICAO location identifier*] (ICLI)
EKS .... Electrocardiogram Simulator
EKS .... Electronic Keyboard System
EKS .... Electronic Key System [*Telecommunications*] (NITA)
EKS .... Elks, Inc. [*Toronto Stock Exchange symbol*]
EKS .... Energetic Komprimierendes System [*Nuclear science*] (OA)
EKS .... Engpasskonzentrierte Strategie [*Bottleneck-focused strategy*] [*German*] [*Business term*]
EKS .... Epidemic Kaposi's Sarcoma [*Medicine*] (MELL)
EKS .... Excessive Key Strokes [*Computer science*] (PCM)
EKSAX .... Evergreen Strategic Income Cl.A [*Mutual fund ticker symbol*] (SG)
EKSB .... Sonderborg [*Denmark*] [*ICAO location identifier*] (ICLI)
EKSC .... Eastern Kentucky State College [*Later, EKU*]
EKSD .... Esperanto Klubo San Diego (SAUS)
EKSD .... Spjald [*Denmark*] [*ICAO location identifier*] (ICLI)
EKSM .... Evreiskii Kommunisticheskii Soiuz Molodezhi (BJA)
EKSN .... Sindal [*Denmark*] [*ICAO location identifier*] (ICLI)
EKSP .... Skrydstrup [*Denmark*] [*ICAO location identifier*] (ICLI)
Eksprt .... A/S Eksportfinans [*Export Finance*] Capital Securities [*Associated Press*] (SAG)
Eksprt .... Eksportfinans Capital Securities [*Associated Press*] (SAG)
EKSS .... End of Key Stage Statements [*British*] (DET)
EKSS .... Samso [*Denmark*] [*ICAO location identifier*] (ICLI)
EKST .... Sydfyn/Tasinge [*Denmark*] [*ICAO location identifier*] (ICLI)
EKSTC .... East Kentucky State Teachers College (SAUO)
EKSU .... Electronic Key Service Unit (SAUS)
EKSV .... Skive [*Denmark*] [*ICAO location identifier*] (ICLI)
EKT .... Ektachrome (VRA)
EKT .... Electrokinetic Transducer (SAUS)
EKT .... Eskilstuna [*Sweden*] [*Airport symbol*]
EKT .... Grupo Elektra SA de CV [*NYSE symbol*] (SAG)
EKTD .... Tonder [*Denmark*] [*ICAO location identifier*] (ICLI)
EKTS .... Electronic Key Telephone Sets (SAUS)
EKTS .... Electronic Key Telephone System
EKTS .... Thisted [*Denmark*] [*ICAO location identifier*] (ICLI)
EKTX .... E. Kahn's Sons [*Private rail car owner code*]
eku .... earliest known usage (SAUS)
EKU .... Eastern Kentucky University [*Formerly, EKSC*] [*Richmond*]
EKU .... European Karate Union (SAUO)
EKV .... Electromagnetic Kill Vehicle (ACAE)
eKv .... Electron Kilovolt (EY)
EKV .... Erythrokeratodermia Variabilis [*Medicine*] (EDAA)
EKV .... Exoatmospheric Kill Vehicle [*Military*]
EKV .... Weeksville, NC [*Location identifier*] [*FAA*] (FAAL)
EKVA .... Vandel [*Denmark*] [*ICAO location identifier*] (ICLI)
EKVB .... Viborg [*Denmark*] [*ICAO location identifier*] (ICLI)
EKVD .... Vamdrup [*Denmark*] [*ICAO location identifier*] (ICLI)
EKVF .... East Kent Volunteer Fencibles [*British military*] (DMA)
EKVG .... Vagar, Faroe Islands [*Denmark*] [*ICAO location identifier*] (ICLI)
EKVH .... Vesthimmerland [*Denmark*] [*ICAO location identifier*] (ICLI)
EKVJ .... Stauning [*Denmark*] [*ICAO location identifier*] (ICLI)
EKVL .... Vaerlose [*Denmark*] [*ICAO location identifier*] (ICLI)
EKW .... Eisenbahnkesselwagen [*Railway tank car*] [*German military - World War II*]
EKW .... Electrical Kilowatts
ekW .... Equivalent Kilowatt (SAUS)
EKW .... Worcester, MA [*Location identifier*] [*FAA*] (FAAL)
EKWBX .... Evergreen Precious Metals Cl.B [*Mutual fund ticker symbol*] (SG)
EKY .... Electrokymogram
EKY .... Electrokymography (SAUS)
EKYT .... Alborg [*Denmark*] [*ICAO location identifier*] (ICLI)
EKZBX .... Evergreen Intl. Growth Cl.B [*Mutual fund ticker symbol*] (SG)
el--- .... Benelux Countries [*MARC geographic area code*] [*Library of Congress*] (LCCP)
EL .... Each Layer [*Technical drawings*]
el .... each layer, educational level (SAUS)
EL .... Early Latent [*Medicine*]
EL .... Eastern League [*Baseball*]
EL .... Eastern Lines
EL .... East Longitude (ROG)
E-L .... Eaton-Lambert Syndrome [*Medicine*] (MEDA)
EL .... Economic League [*British*]
EL .... Economics Laboratory, Inc.
EL .... Ectopia Lentis [*Medicine*] (MELL)
EL .... Educational Leadership [*A publication*] (BRI)
EL .... Educational Level (SAUS)
EL .... Education Level
EL .... Education Library [*A publication*]
EL .... Egg Length
EL .... Einfache Lafette [*Single-barreled mount*] [*German military - World War II*]
El .... Elamite (BJA)
EL .... Elasticity (SAUS)
EL .... Elastic Level (SAUS)
EL .... Elastic Limit
El .... Elayne (SAUS)
El .... Elberfelder Bibel [*1905*] (BJA)
El .... Elbert (SAUS)
EL .... Elbow (SAUS)
El .... Elchies' Dictionary of Decisions, Scotch Court of Session [*A publication*] (DLA)
EL .... Eldest (ROG)
EL .... Elect [*or Election*]
EL .... Election Laws
El .... Electra [*of Euripides*] [*Classical studies*] (OCD)
EL .... Electric
EL .... Electrical Laboratory (SAUS)
EL .... Electrical Latching (IAA)
EL .... Electrician [*British military*] (DMA)
EL .... Electric LASER (MCD)
EL .... Electric Life (SAUS)
EL .... Electric Light
EL .... Electric Line (SAUS)
EL .... Electrohome Ltd. [*Toronto Stock Exchange symbol*]
EL .... Electroluminescence
EL .... Electroluminescent (IDOE)
EL .... electroluminescent displays (SAUS)
EL .... Electroluminescent Lamp (SAUS)
EL .... Electronic Library Inc. (IID)
EL .... Electronics Command [*Army*] (MCD)
EL .... Electronics Laboratory
EL .... Electron Lens (SAUS)
EL .... Electrotechnical Laboratory (SAUS)
EL .... Electrum [*Numismatics*]
EL .... Element
EL .... Elementary
el .... elements (SAUS)
EL .... Elevate (SAUS)
el .... Elevated (SHCU)
EL .... Elevated [*Railway*] [*Also, L*]
el .... Elevated Railroad (ADWA)
el .... Elevated Train (SHCU)
EL .... Elevation (AAG)
el .... Elevation (SHCU)
EL .... Elevation Angle (SAUS)
EL .... Elevator (MIST)
El .... Elevator (SAUS)
EL .... Eligible Layout
EL .... Eligible Liability [*British*]
EL .... Eli Lilly & Co. [*Research code symbol*]
El .... Eline
el .... Elixir [*Pharmacology*] (MAE)
EL .... Elongation (WDAA)
EL .... elopement status (SAUS)
EL .... Emergency Laparotomy [*Medicine*] (MELL)
EL .... Emergency Legislation

EL .... emergency lighting (SAUS)
EL .... Emergency Locator Beacon (SAUS)
EL .... EMILY's List (EA)
EL .... Emitter Locator (SAUS)
EL .... Employment Law (SAFN)
EL .... End Line (SAUS)
EL .... End of Line [*Computer science*] (ELAL)
EL .... End of the Line (VLIE)
EL .... Endurance Limit [*Mechanical engineering*]
EL .... Energy Loss (IAA)
EL .... Engineering Laboratories [*Army*] (MCD)
EL .... Engineering Letter [*Telecommunications*] (TEL)
EL .... Engineer Lieutenant [*Navy*] [*British*]
EL .... English Leicester (SAUS)
EL .... Entrance Left [*A stage direction*] [*Theater*] (WDMC)
EL .... Entry local (SAUS)
E/L .... Entry/Landing (NASA)
EL .... Entry Level (SAUS)
EL .... Entry Lock [*Diving apparatus*]
EL .... Environmental Laboratory
EL .... Ephemerides Liturgicae [*A publication*] (ODCC)
EL .... Ephemerides Lovanienses (BJA)
EL .... Epidemic Listeriosis [*Medicine*] (MELL)
EL .... Epidemiological Laboratory [*Air Force*]
EL .... Epitaxial Layer (ODA)
EL .... Epworth League (SAUS)
EL .... Equal (SAUS)
EL .... Equal Length (SAUS)
EL .... Equipment List (SAUS)
EL .... Equivalent Length [*Engineering*]
EL .... Erase Line (VLIE)
EL .... Erie-Lackawanna Railway Co. [*Absorbed into Consolidated Rail Corp.*] [*AAR code*]
EL .... Erythroleukemia [*Medicine*] (MAE)
EL .... Estee Lauder Companies, Inc. [*NYSE symbol*] (SAG)
EL .... Etched Lead (IAA)
EL .... Euroleft Coalition (Bulgaria) [*Political party*] (PSAP)
EL .... Evangelical Lutheran (ROG)
EL .... Even Lot [*Investment term*]
EL .... Everyman's Library (ODA)
EL .... Excess Limit
EL .... Exchange Line [*Telecommunications*] (TEL)
EL .... Excimer Laser [*Medicine*] (MELL)
EL .... Executive Level (SAUS)
EL .... Exercise Limit [*Medicine*]
EL .... Expected Loss
EL .... Expenditure Less Than [*Dialog*] [*Searchable field*] [*Information service or system*] (NITA)
EL .... Experience Level (AAEL)
EL .... Explicit Language (SAUS)
EL .... Exploration Lease (ADA)
EL .... Exploration License (FOTI)
EL .... Exploratory Laparotomy [*Medicine*] (MELL)
EL .... Explosion Limit (SAUS)
EL .... Exposure Level (GNE)
EL .... Exterior Lighting [*Automotive engineering*]
EL .... External Labium (SAUS)
EL .... External Lamina (OA)
E-L .... External Lid [*Ophthalmology*] (DAVI)
EL .... External Link (MHDB)
EL .... External Logic (SAUS)
EL .... Extracorporeal Lithotripsy [*Medicine*] (ODA)
EL .... extra light fuel oil (SAUS)
el .... extra line (SAUS)
EL .... Extra Low (SAUS)
EL .... Eye Lens (MSA)
EL .... Eymard League (EA)
EL .... Lauder (Estee) Co. [*NYSE symbol*] (TTSB)
EL .... Nihon Kinkyori Airways [*ICAO designator*] (AD)
EL .... Electron Lattice (ODA)
EL1 .... Extensible Language one (SAUS)
EL2 .... Elongation in Two Inches
ELA .... Eagle Lake, TX [*Location identifier*] [*FAA*] (FAAL)
ELA .... Eastland Air [*Australia*] [*ICAO designator*] (FAAC)
ELA .... Edmonton Library Association (SAUO)
ELA .... Education Law Association (NTPA)
ELA .... Egyptian Library Association (SAUO)
ELA .... Eighth Lively Art [*Advertising award*]
ELA .... Elastomer Lubricating Agent (SAUS)
ELA .... Elazig [*Turkey*] [*Seismograph station code, US Geological Survey*] [*Closed*] (SEIS)
ELA .... Electric League of Arizona (SRA)
EIA .... electronic industries association (SAUO)
ELA .... Electronic Library Association [*Defunct*] (EA)
ELA .... Electron Linear Accelerator
ELA .... Eligible Legalized Alien (GFGA)
ELA .... Endometrial LASER Ablation [*Medicine*]
ELA .... Endotoxin-Like Activity (DB)
ELA .... English Language Amendment [*Proposed*]
ELA .... Enmekar and the Lord of Aratta (BJA)
ELA .... En Route Low Altitude
ELA .... Enterprise License Agreement (SAUS)
ELA .... Environmental Law Alliance (SAUO)
ELA .... Environmental Protection Agency, Region V Library, Chicago, IL [*OCLC symbol*] (OCLC)
ELA .... Equilibrium-Line Altitude [*Glaciation*]
ela .... Equilibrium-Line Altitude [*Level on a glacier at which accumulation and ablation are in balance*] (SAUS)
ELA .... Equine Lymphocyte Alloantigen [*Genetics, immunochemistry*]
ELA .... Equipment Leasing Association [*British*] (DBA)
ELA .... Ernest K. Lehmann & Associates, Inc. [*Also, an information service or system*] (IID)
ELA .... Esperanto Law Association [*British*] [*England*] (EAIO)
ELA .... Establishment License Application [*Food & Drug Administration*]
ELA .... Ethical Library [*A publication*]
ELA .... Ethiopian Library Association (SAUO)
ELA .... European Laser Association (EA)
ELA .... Experimental Lakes Area [*A collection of 48 small lakes near the Ontario-Manitoba border*] [*Canada*]
ELA .... Exploration Licence Application [*Australia*]
ELA .... Expressive Language Age [*of the hearing-impaired*]
ELA .... Extended Line Adapter (MHDB)
ELA .... Extender Lens Assembly (SAUS)
ELA .... Extra Large Apertures [*Optics*] (ROG)
ELA .... Revolutionary People's Struggle [*Government term*] (GA)
ELA .... Electronic Learning Aid (ODA)
elab .... elaborately (SAUS)
elab .... elaborating (SAUS)
elab .... elaboration (SAUS)
elab .... elaborative (SAUS)
ELAB .... Environmental Laboratory Advisory Board [*Environmental Protection Agency*]
ELAB .... External Loop Airlift Bioreactor [*Chemical engineering*]
ELAC .... East Los Angeles College (SAUS)
el-ac .... Electro-Acoustic (GROV)
ELAC .... Electroacoustic (IAA)
ELAC .... Elevator & Aileron Computer (SAUS)
ELAC .... Enroute Low Altitude Chart [*Aviation*] (PIPO)
ELAC .... European LIDAR Airborne Campaign (SAUS)
ELACS .... Extended Life Attitude Control System [*NASA*]
E LACT .... E Lacte [*With Milk*] [*Pharmacy*]
ELAD .... Extracorporeal Liver-Assist Device [*Medicine*] (ECON)
ELADEX .... Electronic Adapter for Telex (SAUS)
ELADI .... Electronic Atlas of Agenda 21 (SAUS)
ELADIS .... European Local Administrative Data Integration Study (EURO)
ELADO .... El Dorado, KS [*American Association of Railroads railroad junction routing code*]
ELADS .... Early Launch Air Defense System (MCD)
ELADS .... Early Launch Display System (SAUS)
ELAF .... Electron Linear Acceleration Facility (SAUS)
ELAFB .... Ellsworth Air Force Base [*South Dakota*] (KSC)
ELAFB .... Ellworth Air Force Base (SAUS)
ELAG .... European Library Automation Group (PDAA)
ELAIA .... European Parliament Delegations for Latin America [*Luxembourg*] (EAIO)
ELAIA .... Europe-Latin America Interparliamentary Assembly [*See also DPERPLA*] [*Luxembourg, Luxembourg*] (EAIO)
ELAIN .... Export License Application and Information Network (JAGO)
ELAIN .... Export License Application Information Network (SAUS)
EL AL .... El Al Israel Airlines (SAUS)
EL AL .... Every Landing, Always Late [*Humorous interpretation of El Al Airlines*]
ELALR .... External Loop Air Lift Reactor [*Chemical engineering*]
ELAM .... Elamex S.A. de C.V. [*NASDAQ symbol*] (NASQ)
ELAM .... Endothelial Leukocyte Adhesion Molecule [*Cytology*]
ELAM .... Escuela Latinoamericana de Matematica (SAUO)
Elamex .... Elamex SA de CV [*Associated Press*] (SAG)
ELAMF .... Elamex S.A.de C.V. Cl I [*NASDAQ symbol*] (TTSB)
ELaMod .... Empresas La Moderna SA [*Associated Press*] (SAG)
ELAMP .... Elamex SA de CV [*NASDAQ symbol*] (SAG)
ELAMS .... Electronic Laboratory Animal Monitoring System
ELAN .... Educational/Elementary Language (SAUS)
ELAN .... Educational Language (SAUS)
ELAN .... Education LANguage (SAUS)
Elan .... Elan Corp. [*Associated Press*] (SAG)
ELAN .... Electrologic Language (IAA)
ELAN .... Elementary Language [*Programming language*] (NITA)
ELAN .... Emulated Local Area Network (SAUS)
ELAN .... Environment in Latin-America Network (EERA)
ELAN .... Error Logging and Analysis [*Computer science*] (CIST)
ELAN .... European LAN (SAUS)
ELAN .... Extended Local Area Network [*Defunct*] (TSSD)
ELANC .... Enhanced LAN Controller (SAUS)
ELANC .... Enhanced Local Area Network Controller (SAUS)
E LANC R .... East Lancashire Regiment [*Military unit*] [*British*] (ROG)
El & B .... Ellis and Blackburn's English Queen's Bench Reports [*118-120 English Reprint*] [*A publication*] (DLA)
El & Bl .... Ellis and Blackburn's English Queen's Bench Reports [*118-120 English Reprint*] [*A publication*] (DLA)
El & Bl (Eng) .... Ellis and Blackburn's English Queen's Bench Reports [*118-120 English Reprint*] [*A publication*] (DLA)
El & El .... Ellis and Ellis' English Queen's Bench Reports [*A publication*] (DLA)
El & El (Eng) .... Ellis and Ellis' English Queen's Bench Reports [*A publication*] (DLA)
EL & Eq .... English Law and Equity Reports [*American Reprint*] [*A publication*] (DLA)
EL & P .... Electric Light & Power (journ.) (SAUS)
EL & P .... Elliptical (SAUS)
EL & P .... Emulsified Liquid Propellant (SAUS)
EL & P .... English Language Programs (SAUS)

EL & P .... Extended Long-Play (SAUS)
EL & P .... Extra Low Pressure (SAUS)
EL & S .... Electronic Laboratories and Services
ELANE .... Electronics Association for the North East (SAUO)
E Lan R .... East Lancashire Regiment [*Military unit*] [*British*] (DAS)
ELANs .... Emulated LANs (SAUS)
ELANT .... East Atlantic [*Satellite*] (DOMA)
Elantec .... Elantec Semiconductor, Inc. [*Associated Press*] (SAG)
ELANY .... Elan Corp. PLC (MHDW)
ELAP .... Emergency Legal Assistance Project
ELAP .... Ethernet Link Access Protocol [*Computer science*] (VERA)
ELAP .... EtherTalk Link Access Protocol [*Computer science*] (ACRL)
ELAR .... Enemy Launch Acceptability Region [*Military*] (SEWL)
ELARC .... Electronic Light Arc
ELAS .... Earth Laboratory Applications Software
ELAS .... Earth Resources Laboratory Application Software
ELAS .... Education Law Advisers Service (AIE)
ELAS .... Elastic (MSA)
ELAS .... Elasticity (SAUS)
ELAS .... Elastic Networks [*NASDAQ symbol*]
ELAS .... Ellenikos Laikos Apeleutherotikos Stratos [*Hellenic People's Army of Liberation*] [*Military arm of EAM*] [*Greek*]
ELAS .... Emergency Logistical Air Support (SAUS)
ELAS .... Emitter Location and Analysis System (MCD)
ELAS .... Equilibrium Problems of Linear Structures
ELAS .... Extended Lymphadenopathy Syndrome [*Medicine*]
Elasm .... Elasmobranchia (SAUS)
elasmobranchs... elasmobranch fishes (SAUS)
elast .... elasticity (SAUS)
Elast Noteb... Elastomers Notebook (journ.) (SAUS)
ELAT .... Elaterium [*To Stimulate or Incite*] [*Pharmacy*] (ROG)
ELAT .... English Language Aptitude Test (DNAB)
ELAT .... Enzyme-Linked Antiglobulin Test [*Immunology*] (DAVI)
ELAT .... Estimated Latitude (FAAC)
ELATE .... Engineers' Language for Automatic Test Equipment
ELATS .... Expanded Litton Automatic Test Station (MCD)
ELB .... Bachelor of English Literature
ELB .... Early-Labeled Bilirubin [*Medicine*] (MELL)
ELB .... Early Light Breakfast [*Medicine*]
Elb .... Egyptian pound (SAUS)
ELB .... El Banco [*Colombia*] [*Airport symbol*] (OAG)
elb .... Elbow (IDYL)
ELB .... Elbow (MSA)
ELB .... Eldorado Bancorp [*AMEX symbol*] (SPSG)
ELB .... Electric Battery (IAA)
ELB .... Electronically Limited Braking
ElB .... electronic brake (SAUS)
ELB .... Electronic Lean Burn (ADA)
ELB .... Emergency Location Beacon (SAUS)
ELB .... Emergency Locator Beacon
ELB .... English Language Battery (SAUS)
ELB .... Environmental Protection Agency, Library, Environmental Research Center, Cincin nati, OH [*OCLC symbol*] (OCLC)
ELB .... Environment Liaison Board [*British*] (DI)
ELB .... Export Licensing Branch [*British Overseas Trade Board*] (DS)
ELB .... Exposed Location Buoy [*Nautical term*] (NTA)
ELB .... Extended Littoral Battlespace [*Military*] (SEWL)
ELB .... Florida P&L 7.05% CABCO Tr Debs [*NYSE symbol*] (SG)
ELBA .... Electronics and Biotechnology Advanced (SAUS)
ELBA .... Emergency Location Beacon (COE)
ELB-A .... Emergency Location Beacon - Aircraft (PDAA)
elba .... emergency location beacon aircraft (SAUS)
ELBA .... English Language Books Abroad [*A publication*]
El B & E ...... Ellis, Blackburn, and Ellis' English Queen's Bench Reports [*A publication*] (DLA)
El B & El ..... Ellis, Blackburn, and Ellis' English Queen's Bench Reports [*A publication*] (DLA)
El B & S ...... Ellis, Best, and Smith's English Queen's Bench Reports [*A publication*] (DLA)
El B & S (Eng)... Ellis, Best, and Smith's English Queen's Bench Reports [*A publication*] (DLA)
ELBAS .... English Language Books Abroad (SAUS)
Elbasa .... Electronica Basica SA (SAUS)
ELBI .... Eldorado Bancshares, Inc. [*NASDAQ symbol*] (NASQ)
Elbit .... Elbit Ltd. [*Associated Press*] (SAG)
ElbitLtd .... Elbit Ltd. [*Associated Press*] (SAG)
ElbitMd .... Elbit Medical Imaging Ltd. [*Associated Press*] (SAG)
ElbitSys .... Elbit Systems Ltd. [*Associated Press*] (SAG)
ElbitVis .... Elbit Vision Systems Ltd. [*Associated Press*] (SAG)
El Bl & El .... Ellis, Blackburn, and Ellis' English Queen's Bench Reports [*A publication*] (DLA)
El Bl & El (Eng)... Ellis, Blackburn, and Ellis' English Queen's Bench Reports [*A publication*] (DLA)
ELBO .... Electronics Boutique Hldgs [*NASDAQ symbol*] (SG)
ELBO .... Hellenic Vehicle Industry SA (SAUS)
ELBOWS .... No Erasures, No Leaves Torn Out, No Blank Spaces, No Overturning, No Writing between Lines, Statements to Be in Exact Words [*Directions for written reports*] [*Scotland Yard*]
ELBS .... electronic brake system (SAUS)
ELBS .... English Language Book Society [*British*]
ELBT .... Elbit Ltd. [*NASDAQ symbol*] (NQ)
ELBT .... English Language Books by Title [*A publication*]
ELBTF .... Elbit Ltd. [*NASDAQ symbol*] (TTSB)
ELBTN .... Elberton, GA [*American Association of Railroads railroad junction routing code*]
ELBUG .... Electronic Key [*Amateur radio shorthand*] (WDAA)
ELBW .... Extremely Low Birth Weight [*Obstetrics*] (ADA)
ELC .... Early Landed Cognac [*British*]
El C .... El Centro (SAUS)
ELC .... Elcho Island [*Australia*] [*Airport symbol*] (OAG)
ELC .... Elco [*Illinois*] [*Seismograph station code, US Geological Survey*] (SEIS)
ELC .... El Coco Explorations Ltd. [*Vancouver Stock Exchange symbol*]
ELC .... Electric Cable (IAA)
ELC .... Electric City [*AMEX symbol*]
ELC .... electrocoagulation (SAUS)
ELC .... Electronic Level Control [*General Motors Corp.*] [*Automotive engineering*]
ELC .... Electronic Library Computer
ELC .... Electronic Light Control (SAUS)
ELC .... Electronic Load Controller
ELC .... Electronic Location Center (SAUS)
ELC .... Element Count (SAUS)
ElC .... Elevator Code
ELC .... Embedded Linking and Control (SAUS)
ELC .... Emission-Limited Current (SAUS)
ELC .... Employee Learning Centre (SAUO)
ELC .... End Launch Connector (TIMI)
ELC .... End of Line Code (SAUS)
ELC .... Entrepreneurial Leadership Center (EA)
ELC .... Environmental Law Centre (EERA)
ELC .... Environmental Liaison Center (SAUS)
ELC .... Environmental Protection Agency, Motor Vehicle Emission Laboratory, Ann Arbor, MI [*OCLC symbol*] (OCLC)
ELC .... Environment Leisure Centre (SAUO)
ELC .... Environment Liaison Centre [*Later, ELCI*] (EAIO)
ELC .... Errett Lobban Cord [*Auto industrialist*]
ElC .... espace intercostal (SAUS)
ELC .... Essential Light Chain
ELC .... Euro City Line, Stuttgart [*Federal Republic of Germany*] [*FAA designator*] (FAAC)
ELC .... European Industral Food Additives and Food Enzymes Liaison Committee (SAUO)
ELC .... European Industrial Food Additives Liaison Committee and Food Enzymes (SAUS)
ELC .... European Labour Committee (SAUO)
ELC .... European Language Council (EURO)
ELC .... European Liaison Committee for Management Development (SAUO)
ELC .... European Liaison Committee Management Education Training (SAUO)
ELC .... Europe's Largest Companies [*ELC International*] [*Information service or system*] (CRD)
ELC .... Evangelical Lutheran Church [*Later, ELCA*]
ELC .... Excellent Low Cost (SAUS)
ELC .... Exchange Line Capacity (SAUS)
ELC .... Expression-Linked Copy (MELL)
ELC .... Expression-Linked Extra Copy [*Genetics*]
ELC .... External Locus of Control [*Psychology*]
ELC .... Extra-Low Carbon
ELC .... Extra-Low Carbon Steel (SAUS)
ELC .... Extra Low Cost (SAUS)
ELCA .... Earth Landing Control Area (SAUS)
ELCA .... Earth Landing Control Assembly [*NASA*] (KSC)
ELCA .... Education Landscape Contractors Association (SAUO)
ELCA .... Electronic Linear Circuit Analysis (PDAA)
ELCA .... Electronic Linear Circuit Analysis programme (SAUS)
ELCA .... Enzyme-Linked Coagulation Assay [*Clinical chemistry*]
ELCA .... European Landscape Contractors Association (EAIO)
ELCA .... Evangelical Lutheran Church in America [*Formed by merger of ALC, ELC, and LCA*]
ELC Acts ...... Expiring Law Continuance Acts (DLA)
ELCAF .... Extended-Life Cabin Air Filter
ELCAG .... ELINT [*Electronic Intercept*] Collection/Analysis Guide [*Air Force*]
El Caj .... El Cajon (SAUS)
El Cajohn ..... El Cajon, California (SAUS)
El Cap .... El Capitan Dam (SAUS)
El Cap .... El Capitan Reservoir (SAUS)
ELCAP .... End-Use Load and Conservation Assessment Program (SAUS)
ELCAP .... End-Use Load and Consumer Assessment Program (SAUS)
ELCA Program... Electronic Linear Circuit Analysis Program (SAUS)
elcar .... electric car (SAUS)
ELCAR .... [*The*] Elkhart Carriage & Motor Car Co. [*Automobile manufacturer (1909-1915), later, Elcar Motor Co. (1916-1931)*] [*Acronym also used as car name*]
ElcArt .... Electronic Arts, Inc. [*Associated Press*] (SAG)
El Cas .... Election Cases [*A publication*] (DLA)
ELCAS .... Elevated Causeway System (CAAL)
El Cas .... New York Election Cases (Armstrong's) [*A publication*] (DLA)
ElCash .... ELectronic Cash (SAUS)
El Cas (NY)... New York Election Cases (Armstrong's) [*A publication*] (DLA)
ElCath .... Electro Catheter Corp. [*Associated Press*] (SAG)
ELCB .... Earth Leakage Circuit Breaker
ELCB .... Earth-Leakage Circuit-Breaker or Earth-Leakage Contact-Breaker (SAUS)
ELCC .... Electronics Communications [*NASDAQ symbol*] (TTSB)
ELCC .... Electronics Communications Corp. [*NASDAQ symbol*] (SAG)
ElcChm .... Electro Chemical Industries (Frutarom) Ltd. [*Associated Press*] (SAG)
ElcCm .... Electronics Communications Corp. [*Associated Press*] (SAG)
ELCCW .... Electronics Communications Wrrt'A' [*NASDAQ symbol*] (TTSB)
ELCD .... Electrolytic Conductivity Detector

ELCD............ Evaporative Loss Control Device [*Automobile antipollution device*]
ELCEN......... El Centro, CA [*American Association of Railroads railroad junction routing code*]
ElcFuel........ Electric Fuel Corp. [*Associated Press*] (SAG)
ElcGas......... Electric & Gas Technology, Inc. [*Associated Press*] (SAG)
ELCH........... El Chico Restaurants [*NASDAQ symbol*] (TTSB)
ELCH........... El Chico Restaurants, Inc. [*NASDAQ symbol*] (SPSG)
Elch............ Elchies. Court of Session Cases [*Scotland*] [*A publication*] (DLA)
ELCH........... Evangelical Lutheran Church in America (BARN)
ElChico........ El Chico Restaurants, Inc. [*Associated Press*] (SAG)
Elchies......... Elchies. Court of Session Cases [*Scotland*] [*A publication*] (DLA)
Elchies' Dict... Elchies' Dictionary of Decisions, Scotch Court of Session [*A publication*] (DLA)
ELCI............ Employers' Liability Compulsory Insurance (HEAS)
ELCI............ Environmental Liaison Center/International (SAUS)
ELCI............ Environment Liaison Centre International (EAIO)
ELCIC.......... Evangelical Lutheran Church in Canada (FOTI)
ELCID.......... Electronics Command & Information Display Concept (SAUO)
ELCID.......... Enforcement of Law Through Court Intervention and Diversion (SAUS)
ELCINA........ Electronic Component Industries Association
ElcIntl.......... Electocon International, Inc. [*Associated Press*] (SAG)
ELCl............ Extra-Low Chloride (SAUS)
ElClear......... Electronic Clearing House, Inc. [*Associated Press*] (SAG)
ELCM........... Electronic Load Control Module [*Indian Railway*] (TIR)
ELCMED....... Electromedical
ELCMTLG..... Electrometallurgical
ELCN........... Elco Industries, Inc. [*NASDAQ symbol*] (NQ)
ELCN........... European Laboratories Communications Network (SAUS)
ELCN........... European Laboratory Computer Network (SAUS)
ELCO........... Elcom International [*NASDAQ symbol*] (SAG)
ELCO........... Electrolytic Capacitor (DEN)
elco............ Electrolytic Condenser (SAUS)
ELCO........... Electrostatic Coaxial (SAUS)
ELCO........... Eli Lilly and Co. (EFIS)
ELCO........... Eliminate and Count [*Coding*] [*Computer science*]
ELCO........... European Liaison Committee for Osteopaths (EA)
Elcom.......... Elcom International [*Associated Press*] (SAG)
ELCOM......... Electronics and Communications (SAUS)
ELCOM......... Electronics and Computers [*Cambridge Scientific Abstracts*] [*Bethesda, MD*] [*Bibliographic database*]
ELCOMA...... Electronic Components and Materials (SAUS)
ELCOMA...... Electronic Components and Materials Division (SAUS)
ELCON......... Electricity Consumers Resource Council (EA)
ELCON......... Equipment Loss Consolidator
ElCondor...... El Condor Resources Ltd. [*Associated Press*] (SAG)
Elcor........... Elcor Corp. [*Associated Press*] (SAG)
Elcotel......... Elcotel, Inc. [*Associated Press*] (SAG)
ELCP........... European Lake Coring Project (QUAC)
ELCPLTG...... Electroplating
ELCR........... Engineer Lieutenant-Commander [*Navy*] [*British*]
ELCRA......... Elliott-Larsen Civil Rights Act [*Michigan*]
ElcRetl......... Electronic Retailing Systems International [*Associated Press*] (SAG)
ElcRnt.......... Electro Rent Corp. [*Associated Press*] (SAG)
ELCS........... Earth leakage circuit breaker (SAUS)
ELCS........... Electronic Control Systems, Inc. [*NASDAQ symbol*] (COMM)
ELCS........... Experimental Labor Control System (IAA)
ElcSci.......... Electro Scientific Industries, Inc. [*Associated Press*] (SAG)
ElcSen......... Electro Sensors [*Associated Press*] (SAG)
ELCSMI........ European Liaison Committee for the Sewing Machine Industries [*Defunct*] (EA)
ELCT........... Electricity (SAUS)
ELCT........... Electronic (AABC)
ELCTC......... Electric Contact
ELCTCBR..... Electric Contact Brush
ELCTD......... Elected
ELCTD......... Electrode (MSA)
ELCTEX........ Enforcement Liaison Certification for Transport of Explosives (HEAS)
ELCTLT........ Electrolyte
ELCTLT........ Electrolytic (SAUS)
Elctmg......... Electromagnetic Sciences, Inc. [*Associated Press*] (SAG)
Elctph.......... Electropharmacology, Inc. [*Associated Press*] (SAG)
Elctphr......... Electropharmacology, Inc. [*Associated Press*] (SAG)
elctr............ Electronic (VRA)
ELCTRG....... Electric Contact Ring
Elctrgls........ Electroglas Inc. [*Associated Press*] (SAG)
ELCTRLGST... Electrologist
ELCTRM...... Electronic Room (IAA)
elct rm......... electronics room (SAUS)
ELCTRMCHNCL... Electromechanical
ELCTRN....... Electron
elctrpl......... Electroplate (VRA)
ELCTRYLS... Electrolysis
Elctsrc......... Electrosource, Inc. [*Associated Press*] (SAG)
ELCU........... Electrical Control Unit (PDAA)
ELD............. Earth Launch Date [*Aerospace*]
ELD............. East Longitude Date
ELD............. Economic Load Dispatching (BUR)
ELD............. Economic Lot Size (SAUS)
ELD............. Edge-Lighted Display
ELD............. edge lit display (SAUS)
ELD............. Egg Lethal Dose
ELD............. Ehrlich-Lettre Hyperdiploid [*Mouse ascites tumor*]
eld.............. Elder (VRA)
ELD............. Elder Tech Ltd. [*Vancouver Stock Exchange symbol*]
ELD............. Eldest
ELD............. Eldon Industries, Inc. [*NYSE symbol*] (COMM)
ELD............. El Dorado [*Arkansas*] [*Airport symbol*] (OAG)
ELD............. Electrical System (SAUS)
eld.............. electric load dispatcher (SAUS)
ELD............. Electroless Deposition (SAUS)
ELD............. Electroluminescent Diode
ELD............. Electro luminescent display (SAUS)
ELD............. Electroluminescent Display [*Computer science*]
ELD............. Electrolytic Display (PDAA)
ELD............. Electrolytic Liquid Display (SAUS)
ELD............. Electronic Lie Detector
ELD............. Electronic Liquor Dispenser (TRID)
ELD............. Electron Landau Damping (SAUS)
ELD............. Electrostatic Defelection (SAUS)
ELD............. Embryo Lethal Dose (OA)
ELD............. Emergency Laparotomy Drain [*Medicine*] (MELL)
ELD............. Encapsulated Light Diffusion (IAA)
ELD............. Endolymphatic Duct [*Medicine*] (MELL)
ELD............. Energy Level Diagram
ELD............. Engineering Logic Diagram
ELD............. Environmental Protection Agency, Library, Environmental Research Laboratory, Du luth, MN [*OCLC symbol*] (OCLC)
ELD............. Error Logging Device
ELD............. European Law Digest [*A publication*] (SAFN)
ELD............. Expendable LASER Decoy (SEWL)
ELD............. Export Licence Department (SAUO)
ELD............. Extra-Long Distance
ELD............. Federation of Liberal and Democratic Parties of the European Community [*Brussels, Belgium*] Political party] (EAIO)
ELD............. Office of the Executive Legal Director [*Nuclear energy*] (NRCH)
ELDATRAWP... Electronic Data Transmission Working Party [*Army*] (AABC)
ELDC........... Economic Load Dispatching Computer (SAUS)
ELDC........... Equivalent Load Duration Curve
ELDC........... European Lead Development Committee [*EC*] (EA)
ELDEC......... European Lead Development Committee [*EC*] (ECED)
ELDEMA....... Electronic Detection Machine (PDAA)
ElDes.......... Electronic Designs, Inc. [*Associated Press*] (SAG)
ELDG........... Electrical, Defective, Government [*Government-furnished equipment*] (DNAB)
El Dict......... Elchies' Dictionary of Decisions, Scotch Court of Session [*A publication*] (DLA)
EL DIEFF...... Lew David Feldman [*New York bookseller; phonetic spelling of his initials forms name of company*]
El Dig.......... Eller's Minnesota Digest [*A publication*] (DLA)
ELDISC........ Electrical Disconnect (MCD)
el-dl............ electric locomotive-diesel locomotive (SAUS)
ELDMK........ Earth Landmark [*NASA*]
ELDO........... Eldorado [*Cadillac automobile*]
ELDO........... European Launcher Development Organization [*Superseded by European Space Agency*]
ELDO........... European Organization for the Development and Construction of Space Vehicle Launchers (SAUS)
ELDO........... European Space Launcher Development Organization (SAUS)
ELDO........... European Space Vehicle Launcher Development Organization (SAUS)
ELDOC......... Documentation by Electronic Means Program (SAUS)
ELDOME...... Electra Radome (SAUS)
ELDOR......... El Dorado, AR [*American Association of Railroads railroad junction routing code*]
ELDOR......... Electron Double Resonance (SAUS)
ELDOR......... Electron Electron Double Resonance [*Physics*]
ELDORA....... Electra Doppler Radar (SAUS)
Eldorad........ Eldorado Bancorp [*Associated Press*] (SAG)
ELDP........... European Lake Drilling Program (QUAC)
ELDP........... European Lake Drilling Project (SAUS)
ELDP........... Executive Leadership Development Program (ACAE)
ELDR........... Elder
ELDR........... European Federation of Liberal, Democratic, and Reform Parties (EAIO)
ELDR........... Federation of Liberal, Democratic and Reform Parties of the European Community (SAUO)
ELDRED....... European Lakes, Dams, and Reservoirs Database (EURO)
ELDRLY....... Elderly
ELDRO......... Eldorado, IL [*American Association of Railroads railroad junction routing code*]
ELDS........... Editorial Layout Display System
ELDV........... Electrically Operated Depressurization Valve (MCD)
ELE............. Earth Leading Edge (ACAE)
ELE............. El Adem [*Libya*] [*Airport symbol*] (AD)
ELE............. Electronic Launching Equipment
Ele.............. Eledoisin [*Biochemistry*]
ELE............. Elementary Flying Training School [*British*] (MCD)
ELE............. El Paso Energy Corp. [*Vancouver Stock Exchange symbol*]
ELE............. El Real [*Panama*] [*Airport symbol*] (OAG)
ELE............. Emergency Lighting Equipment
ELE............. Empresa Nacional de Electricidad SA ADS [*NYSE symbol*] (SPSG)
ELE............. Empresa Nacionale de Espana SA [*NYSE symbol*] (SAG)
ELE............. Endesa SA ADS [*NYSE symbol*] [*Formerly, Empresa Nac'l. Elec. ADS*] (SG)
ELE............. Engine Life Expectancy (NG)
ELE............. Equine leukoencephalomalacia (SAUS)
ELE............. Equivalent Logic Element
ELE............. Estimated Life Expectancy (MCD)
ELE............. SW Electricity Board [*British*] [*ICAO designator*] (FAAC)

ELEA........ Evangelical Lutheran Education Association (EA)
e-learning.... Electronic Learning (FOTI)
ELEC.......... Elect
ELEC.......... Election (ROG)
ELEC.......... Election Law Enforcement Commission (SAUS)
ELEC.......... Elector [*or Electoral*] (WDAA)
ELEC.......... Electorate (ROG)
Elec.......... Elector, Electorate (SAUS)
Elec.......... Electra (SAUS)
Elec.......... Electric (AAGC)
ELEC.......... Electric (AFM)
elec.......... Electric (REAL)
elec.......... Electrical (MIST)
elec.......... Electrician (MIST)
ELEC.......... Electrician (SAUS)
elec.......... Electricity (SHCU)
ELEC.......... Electricity (WDAA)
Elec.......... Electro [*Record label*] [*Finland*]
elec.......... electroelectuary (SAUS)
ELEC.......... Electron (WDAA)
elec.......... Electronic (GROV)
ELEC.......... Electronic (NASA)
Elec.......... Electronic (TBD)
ELEC.......... Electronics
ELEC.......... Electronics (journ.) (SAUS)
ELEC.......... Electuarium [*Electuary*] [*Pharmacy*] (ROG)
ELEC.......... European League for Economic Cooperation
ElecAs........ Electronic Associates, Inc. [*Associated Press*] (SAG)
Elec C......... Elections Code [*A publication*] (DLA)
ElecCm........ Electronics Communications Corp. [*Associated Press*] (SAG)
ELECD......... Electrode (SAUS)
ELECD......... Element Code (MCD)
ElecDes....... Electronic Designs, Inc. [*Associated Press*] (SAG)
elecdis........ Electronic Distributor (SAUS)
ELEC/DR....... Electric Residential Service (SAUS)
Elec Engr..... Electronic Engineer (SAUS)
ELECENGRSCOL... Electrical Engineering School (SAUS)
Elec Engr Scol... Electrical Engineer School (SAUS)
ElecFab....... Electronic Fab Technology [*Associated Press*] (SAG)
Elec Gr........ Electronic Grade (SAUS)
ElecHair....... Electronic Hair Styling, Inc. [*Associated Press*] (SAG)
Elec LR........ Election Law Reports [*India*] [*A publication*] (DLA)
ELECMECH... Electrical Mechanical (IAA)
ELECN......... Electrician (AFM)
ELECN......... Electronic (SAUS)
Elecnc Des... Electronic Design (journ.) (SAUS)
Elecnc Engg... Electronic Engineering (journ.) (SAUS)
ELECO......... Engineering and Lighting Equipment Company (SAUO)
ELECOM........ Electronic Computer (SAUS)
ELECOM........ Electronic Computing
ELECOMPS..... Electronic Components (NITA)
ELECOMPs..... Electronics Components Data Bank (SAUS)
ELECPROC... Electrostatic Process (IAA)
elecpub........ electronic publishing (SAUS)
ELECPWRPLNTENGR... Electric Power Plant Engineer (IAA)
ELECSS........ Electronic Combat Satellite System (ACAE)
Elec stim..... Electrical Stimulation (AMHC)
ELECSYS...... Integrated Electronic Engineering System (SAUS)
ELECSYSCOM... Electronic Systems Command [*Also, NESC*] [*Navy*]
ELECT.......... Election (AABC)
Elect.......... Elector (SAUS)
elect.......... electoral (SAUS)
ELECT.......... Electric (SAUS)
elect.......... Electrical (BEE)
ELECT.......... Electrical
elect.......... Electrician (SAUS)
ELECT.......... Electricity (SAUS)
ELECT.......... Electrolyte (KSC)
elect.......... Electrolytic (SAUS)
elect.......... Electronic (ADWA)
ELECT.......... Electronic (MCD)
ELECT.......... Electronics (SAUS)
ELECT.......... Electuarium [*Electuary*] [*Pharmacy*]
ELECTC........ Electronic Control
Elect Cas..... Election Cases [*A publication*] (DLA)
Elect Cas NY... New York Election Cases (Armstrong's) [*A publication*] (DLA)
ELECTCIRDESGNR... Electronic Circuit Designer (IAA)
elec tech..... electrical technician (SAUS)
ELECTECH.... Electronics Technician (DNAB)
elec tech..... electronic technician (SAUS)
ElecTel........ Electronic Telcommunications, Inc. [*Associated Press*] (SAG)
ELECTENGR... Electronic Engineer (IAA)
Elect Engr.... Electronics Engineer (SAUS)
ELECTHYDR... Electrohydraulic (KSC)
elect in........ electricity installed (SAUS)
ELECTL........ Electrical
ELECTL........ Electrolytic
Electl Wkly... Electrical Weekly [*A publication*]
ELECTLY....... Electrically
ELECTMAINTCO... Electronic Maintenance Co. [*Military*] (DNAB)
ELECTMECH... Electromechanical (KSC)
ELECTMG...... Electromagnetic
Electn.......... Electrician (SAUS)
elect pd....... electricity planned (SAUS)
ELECTPKGENGR... Electronic Packaging Engineer (IAA)
ELECTR........ Electric
ELECTR........ Electrician (SAUS)
electr.......... Electricity (BEE)
ELECTR........ Electronics (NASA)
Electra........ Electrical, Electronics, and Communication Trades Association (ODA)
electraac..... electronic auto analysis clinic (SAUS)
Electr China... Electricity for China (journ.) (SAUS)
ELECTRCL.... Electrical
ELECTRCN... Electrician
Electr Commun... Electrical Communication (journ.) (SAUS)
Electr Constr Maint... Electrical Construction and Maintenance (journ.) (SAUS)
Electr Contract... Electrical Contractor (journ.) (SAUS)
ELECTRCTY... Electricity
ELECTRE...... French books in print catalogue (SAUS)
Electr Eng.... Electrical Engineer (SAUS)
Electr Eng Jap... Electrical Engineering in Japan (journ.) (SAUS)
Electr Eng Jpn... Electrical Engineering in Japan (journ.) (SAUS)
Elect Rep..... Election Reports [*Ontario*] [*A publication*] (DLA)
Electr: Equip... Electrical Equipment (journ.) (SAUS)
ELECTREX.... International Electrotechnical Exhibition [*British Electrical and Allied Manufacturers Association*]
electr h p.... Electrical Horse-Power (SAUS)
electr h p hr... Electrical Horse Power Hour (SAUS)
electr h p hrs... Electrical Horse Power Hours (SAUS)
ELECTRL...... Electrical
ELECTRL...... Electrolyte (IAA)
electrl......... Electrolytic (SAUS)
Electr Mach Power Syst... Electric Machines and Power Systems (journ.) (SAUS)
Electr Manuf... Electrical Manufacturing (journ.) (SAUS)
ELECTRN..... Electrician (IAA)
electro......... electrocute (SAUS)
electro......... electrocution (SAUS)
ELECTRO..... Electronics (KSC)
ELECTRO..... Electrotype (ROG)
ELECTROCHEM... Electrochemistry
Electro-Chem Engr... Electrochemical Engineer (SAUS)
Electrochem Technol... Electrochemical Technology (journ.) (SAUS)
Electrocomponent Sci Technol... Electrocomponent Science and Technology (journ.) (SAUS)
Electroencephalogr Clin Neurophysiol... Electroencephalography and Clinical Neurophysiology (Limerick) (SAUS)
electrogen... electrogenesis (SAUS)
ELECTROL... Electrolysis (IAA)
electrolev.... electronically levitated (SAUS)
electrolev.... electronic levitation (SAUS)
Electro-Mech Engr... Electro-Mechanical Engineer (SAUS)
electromusic... electronic music (SAUS)
ELECTRON... Electronic (SAUS)
Electron Bus... Electronic Business (journ.) (SAUS)
Electron Commun Eng J... Electronics & Communication Engineering Journal [*A publication*] (CABS)
Electron Commun Jap... Electronics and Communications in Japan (journ.) (SAUS)
Electron Components... Electronic Components (journ.) (SAUS)
Electron Des... Electron Design (journ.) (SAUS)
Electron Des... Electronic Design (journ.) (SAUS)
Electron Des Autom... Electronic Design Automation (journ.) (SAUS)
Electron Educ... Electronic Education (journ.) (SAUS)
Electron Eng... Electronic Engineering (journ.) (SAUS)
ELECTRONENGR... Electronics Engineer
Electron Equip News... Electronic Equipment News (journ.) (SAUS)
Electron Green J... Electonic Green Journal [*A publication*] (PABS)
Electron Imaging... Electronic Imaging (journ.) (SAUS)
Electron Ind... Electronics Industry (journ.) (SAUS)
Electron Inf Plan... Electronics Information and Planning (journ.) (SAUS)
Electron Learn... Electronic Learning (journ.) (SAUS)
Electron Lett... Electronics Letters (journ.) (SAUS)
Electron Libr... Electronic Library (journ.) (SAUS)
Electron Manuf Test... Electronics Manufacture and Test (journ.) (SAUS)
Electron Microsc... Electron Microscopy (SAUS)
Electron Microsc Rev... Electron Microscopy Review (journ.) (SAUS)
Electron Opt Beport... Electron Optics Reporter (journ.) (SAUS)
Electron Opt Publ Rev... Electronic and Optical Publishing Review (journ.) (SAUS)
Electron Packag Prod... Electronic Packaging and Production (journ.) (SAUS)
Electron Prod... Electronic Production (journ.) (SAUS)
Electron Prod... Electronic Products (journ.) (SAUS)
Electron Prod Des... Electronic Product Design (journ.) (SAUS)
Electron Prog... Electronic Progress (journ.) (SAUS)
Electron Publ Bus... Electronic Publishing Business (journ.) (SAUS)
Electron Purch... Electronics Purchasing (journ.) (SAUS)
ElectronTest... Electronics Test (journ.) (SAUS)
Electron Times... Electronic Times (journ.) (SAUS)
Electron Today... Electronics Today (journ.) (SAUS)
Electron Today Int... Electronics Today International (journ.) (SAUS)
Electron Wirel World... Electronics and Wireless World (journ.) (SAUS)
Electron Wkly... Electronics Weekly (journ.) (SAUS)
Electron World Wirel World... Electronics World + Wireless World (journ.) (SAUS)
electro-ocu... electro-oculogram (SAUS)
Electro-Opt... Electro-Optics (journ.) (SAUS)
ELECTRO-OPTINT... Electrooptical Intelligence [*DoD*]
electrophonics... electrophonic instruments (SAUS)
ELECTROPHYS... Electrophysical (SAUS)
ELECTROPHYS... Electrophysics (IAA)
Electro - RAM... Electro-mechanical Redundant Actuator Mechanism (SAUS)
electrosen... electrosensitive (SAUS)
electrosen... electrosensitivity (SAUS)

electrostat... electrostatic copy (SAUS)
electrostat... electrostatic printing (SAUS)
Electrotech News... Electrotechnical News (journ.) (SAUS)
ELECTROTECHNOL... Electrotechnology (SAUS)
Electro-Technol... Electro-Technology (journ.) (SAUS)
Electrovette... electric-batterypowered Chevette (SAUS)
Electr Power Syst Res... Electric Power Systems Research (journ.) (SAUS)
ELECTRPROG... Electronic Progress (SAUS)
ElectrProg.... Electronic Progress (journ.) (SAUS)
Electr Rev.... Electrical Review (journ.) (SAUS)
Electr Times... Electrical Times (journ.) (SAUS)
Electr Veh Dev... Electric Vehicle Developments (journ.) (SAUS)
ELECTRWARFARE... Electronic Warfare (SAUS)
ElectrWarfare... Electronic Warfare (journ.) (SAUS)
Electr World... Electrical World (journ.) (SAUS)
ELECTY........ Electricity
ELED........... Edge-Emitting Light Emitting Diode (SAUS)
ELED........... Edge Light Emitting Diode (IAA)
ELED........... Entry-Level Employee Development (SAUS)
ELEED......... Elastic Low-Energy Electron Diffraction (PDAA)
EleglII......... Elegant Illusions, Inc. [*Associated Press*] (SAG)
ELEICH......... European Local Environmental Information Clearing House (SAUO)
ELEK........... Electronic (MSA)
ELEK........... Elek Tek, Inc. [*NASDAQ symbol*] (SAG)
Elek........... Elektra [*Record label*]
ElekTek........ Elek Tek, Inc. [*Associated Press*] (SAG)
ELEM........... Element (MSA)
elem........... Element (VRA)
Elem........... Elementary (AL)
ELEM........... Elementary (MSA)
elem........... Elementary (NTIO)
ELEM........... Equine Leukoencephalomalacia [*Medicine*] (EDAA)
ELEMCH......... Elementary Charge [*of a Proton*] (IAA)
ElEng........... Electronic Engineering (DD)
ELEOP......... Electro Optics Division (ACII)
ELEP........... Electronic Converter Electric Power (SAUS)
ELEP........... Electronic converter of Electric Power (SAUS)
ELEP........... European Federation of Anti-Leprosy Associations (SAUO)
elepb fol........ Elephant Folio-Books [*About 23 inches high*] (SAUS)
ElepCstl........ Elephant & Castle Group, Inc. [*Associated Press*] (SAG)
elephantocade... elephant parade (SAUS)
ELEPLTG....... Electroplating (SAUS)
ELES........... Energy-Loss Electron Spectroscopy
ELES........... Expanded Liquid Engine Simulation (MCD)
ELES........... Expanded Liquid Engine System (ACAE)
ELES........... Extended Linear Expenditure System
e-less.......... e-less novel written by British author Ernest Vincent Wright in 1933 with more than 50,000 words without the letter e (SAUS)
ELET........... Ellett Brothers [*NASDAQ symbol*] (TTSB)
ELET........... Ellett Brothers, Inc. [*NASDAQ symbol*] (SAG)
ELETREX....... International Electrical Engineers Exhibition (SAUS)
elev........... Elevate (DAVI)
elev........... Elevation (ADWA)
ELEV........... Elevation (AFM)
Elev........... Elevator (MIST)
ELEV........... Elevator
elev........... elevatorion (SAUS)
ELEV........... Elevon [*Aviation*] (NASA)
ELEV........... Extremely Low-Emitting Vehicle [*Automotive engineering*]
ELEVAR......... Elevated Acquisition RADAR (PDAA)
ElevenYBB...... Eleven Years of Bible Bibliography [*A publication*] (BJA)
ELEX........... Electronics (MSA)
ELEX........... Electronics Exercise [*Military*] (NVT)
ELEX........... Elexsys International, Inc. [*NASDAQ symbol*] (SAG)
Elexsys......... Elexsys International, Inc. [*Associated Press*] (SAG)
ELF............. Early Lunar Flare
ELF............. Earth Liberation Front
ELF............. Eclectic Literary Forum (SAUS)
ELF............. Education Liberation Front
ELF............. Ejected Lunar Flare (SAUS)
ELF............. Elected Lunar Flare (ACAE)
ELF............. Elective Low Forceps [*Delivery*] [*Obstetrics*] (DAVI)
elf.............. electric-light fitting (SAUS)
ELF............. Electroluminescent Ferroelectric
ELF............. Electroluminescent Ferroelectricity (SAUS)
ELF............. Electromagnetic Field
ELF............. Electromotive Force [*Electrochemistry*] (IAA)
ELF............. Electronic Commerce Forum (SAUS)
ELF............. Electronic Location Finder
ELF............. Electronic Logging Facility (SAUS)
ELF............. Electron LASER Facility [*Physics*]
ELF............. Electrostatic Levitator Facility (SSD)
ELF............. Element Lifting Fixture (ACAE)
ELF............. Elevator Load Feel (MCD)
ELF............. Elf Aquitaine ADS [*NYSE symbol*] (TTSB)
ELF............. El Fasher [*Sudan*] [*Airport symbol*] (OAG)
El F............. El Ferrol (SAUS)
ELF............. E-L Financial Corp. Ltd. [*Toronto Stock Exchange symbol*]
ELF............. Elginfield [*Ontario*] [*Seismograph station code, US Geological Survey*] (SEIS)
ELF............. Eliminate Legal-Size Files [*An association*]
ELF............. Ellipsometry, Low Field [*Microscopy*]
ELF............. Elvish Linguistic Fellowship (EA)
ELF............. Emergency Land Fund [*Later, FSC/LAF*] (EA)
ELF............. Engine Lube Filter
ELF............. Eritrean Liberation Front [*Ethiopia*] (PD)
ELF............. Esperanto-Ligo Filatelista [*Philatelic Esperanto League - PEL*] (EAIO)
ELF............. European Landworkers Federation
ELF............. Everybody Loves Fudge [*in Keebler Co. brand of cookies "E. L. Fudge"*]
ELF............. Executable and Linkable Format [*Unix*] (VERA)
ELF............. Executable and Linking Format (SAUS)
ELF............. Expeditionary Logistics Facility (MCD)
ELF............. Explosive-Actuated Light Filter (NG)
ELF............. Explosive Lens Flashbinder
ELF............. Extensible Language Facility [*Computer science*] (IEEE)
ELF............. Extensible Linking Format (SAUS)
ELF............. Extension Language Facility [*Computer science*] (AGLO)
ELF............. External Labor Force [*Medicine*] (EDAA)
ELF............. Extra Light Fast [*Ink*] (DGA)
ELF............. Extra-Light Flint (SAUS)
ELF............. Extra Low Frequency (SAUS)
elf.............. extra low frequncy (SAUS)
ELF............. Extremely Low Frequency [*Electronics, radio wave*]
ELF............. Extremely Low Frequency [*New LINUX binary format*] (SAUS)
ELFA........... Electric Light Fittings Association [*British*] (BI)
ELFA........... Enzyme-Linked Fluorescence Assay
ElfAquit........ Elf Aquitaine [*Associated Press*] (SAG)
ElfAquit........ Societe National ELF Aquitaine [*National ELF Aquitaine Co.*] [*Associated Press*] (SAG)
ELFC........... Electroluminescent Ferroelectric Cell
ELFC........... Elvis Lives On Fan Club (EA)
ELFE........... Extremely Low Frequency Effect (SAUS)
ELF EM field... Extremely Low Frequency Electromagnetic Field (LDOE)
ELF-ERAP...... Essences et Lubrifiants de France - Entreprise de Recherches et d'Activites Petrolieres [*French oil company*]
ELFEXT......... Equal Level Far End Crosstalk (SAUS)
ELFH........... Early Labeled-Fragment Hybridization [*Analytical biochemistry*]
ELF-HELP...... Educators, Librarians, and Families-Helping Loving Prescholars (SAUS)
ELFIA........... Enzyme-Linked Fluorescence Immunoassay [*Immunology*] (QSUL)
ELFIS........... Ernaehrungs-, Land-, und Forstwissenschaftliches Informations-System [*German Information System on Food, Agriculture, and Forestry*] [*Zentralstelle fuer Agrardokumentation und -Information*] [*Information service or system*]
El Fo........... Elephant Folio (WGA)
ElfOv........... Elf Overseas Ltd. [*Associated Press*] (SAG)
ELF/PLF....... Eritrean Liberation Front/Peoples Liberation Forces (SAUS)
ELF-PLF....... Eritrean Liberation Front - Popular Liberation Forces [*Ethiopia*] (PD)
ELF-PLF-REVCOM... ELF-PLF-Revolutionary Committee (SAUS)
ELFR........... Extremely Low Frequency Radiation
ELF-RC......... Eritrean Liberation Front - Revolutionary Command [*Ethiopia*] (PD)
ELF-UO......... ELF-United Organization (SAUS)
ELG............. Alpi Eagles SpA [*Italy*] [*ICAO designator*] (FAAC)
ELG............. Education Librarians Group (SAUO)
ELG............. El Cap Gold Mines [*Vancouver Stock Exchange symbol*]
ELG............. Electrolytic Grinding (IEEE)
Elg............. Elgar (SAUS)
Elg............. Elgin (SAUS)
ELG............. El Golea [*Algeria*] [*Airport symbol*] (AD)
El G............. El Paso Natural Gas Co. (SAUO)
El G............. El Paso Natural Gas Company (SAUS)
ELG............. Emergency Landing Ground
ELG............. Emergency Lifting Gear (WDAA)
ELG............. Equal Life Group [*Depreciation class*]
ELG............. European Liaison Group [*Army*] (AABC)
ELG............. European Library Group (SAUO)
ELG............. European Lymphology Group [*See also GEL*] [*Brussels, Belgium*] (EAIO)
ELG............. Emission-Line Galaxy [*Astronomy*] (ODA)
ELGA........... (French) Study of African Squall Lines (SAUS)
ELGAS......... Electricity and Gas (SAUS)
ELGB........... Emergency Loan Guarantee Board
ELGBA......... European Low Gravity Research Association (SAUO)
E-IGFET........ Ehanchement Insulated Gate Field-Effect Transistor (SAUS)
E-IGFET........ Equivalent Insulated Gate Field-Effect Transistor (SAUS)
ELGI........... European Lubricating Grease Institute [*An association*]
EL-GIEU........ Erector-Launcher Ground Interface Electronics Unit (MCD)
ELGIN.......... Elgin, IL [*American Association of Railroads railroad junction routing code*]
ELGMT......... Erector-Launcher, Guided Missile, Transportable
ELGNC......... Elegance
ELGNT......... Elegant
ELGO........... European Launcher for Geostationary Orbit (SAUO)
ELGRA......... European Low Gravity Research Association (SAUS)
ELGSS......... Ev. [*Evangelical*] Lutheran Good Samaritan Society (EA)
ELG System... Equal Life Group System (SAUO)
ELGT........... Electric & Gas Technology [*NASDAQ symbol*] (TTSB)
ELGT........... Electric & Gas Technology, Inc. [*NASDAQ symbol*] (NQ)
ELGX........... Elgrae Tank Car Line [*Private rail car owner code*]
ELH............. Early Life History [*Marine science*] (OSRA)
ELH............. Egg-Laying Hormone [*Endocrinology*]
ELH............. Endolymphatic Hydrops [*Medicine*] (DAVI)
ELH............. English Literary History (journ.) (SAUS)
ELH............. Enol-Lactone Hydrolase (SAUS)
ELH............. Entity Life History (SAUS)
ELH............. Equine Luteinizing Hormone [*Endocrinology*]
e-lh-........... Liechtenstein [*MARC geographic area code*] [*Library of Congress*] (LCCP)
ELH............. North Eleuthera [*Bahamas*] [*Airport symbol*] (OAG)

ELHCY .... Elkhorn City, KY [*American Association of Railroads railroad junction routing code*]
ELHI .... Elementary and High School [*Acronym refers to books published for this market*]
el-hi .... Elementary and High School Levels [*Textbook publishing*] (WDMC)
ElHi .... Elementary/High School (WDAA)
ELHILL .... Lister Hill System [*Search system*]
ELHS .... Earth-Lunar Horizon Sensor (SAUS)
ELHWS .... Electric Hot Water Service [*Classified advertising*] (ADA)
ELHYD .... Electrohydraulic
ELI .... Early Latent Infection [*Medicine*]
ELI .... Economic Literature Index [*American Economic Association*] [*Information service or system*] (IID)
ELI .... Educational Leadership Institute (EA)
eli .... electricity installed (SAUS)
ELI .... Electric League of Indiana (SRA)
ELI .... Electronic Line Indicator [*Tennis*]
ELI .... ELE Energy, Inc. [*Vancouver Stock Exchange symbol*]
Eli .... Elijah (ODA)
ELI .... Elim [*Alaska*] [*Airport symbol*] (OAG)
Eli .... Elite [*Record label*] [*Europe*]
ELI .... Elite Pharmaceuticals [*AMEX symbol*] (SG)
ELI .... elixir (SAUS)
ELI .... Elizabethville [*Zaire*] [*Later, KVA*] [*Geomagnetic observatory code*]
ELI .... Embedded LISP Interpreter (SAUS)
ELI .... Emitter Location and Identification
ELI .... Endomorphin-Like Immunoreactivity
ELI .... Energy Law Institute (EA)
ELI .... Energy Loss Image (SAUS)
ELI .... English Language Institute [*University of Michigan*] [*Research center*] (RCD)
ELI .... English language Interface (SAUS)
ELI .... English Language Interpreter (NITA)
ELI .... Entry Level Item [*Bureau of Labor Statistics*] (GFGA)
ELI .... Environmental Language Inventory [*Speech and language therapy*] (DAVI)
ELI .... Environmental Law Institute (EA)
ELI .... Environment Liaison International (SAUS)
ELI .... Equitable Life Interpreter [*Computer*]
ELI .... European Light Infantry [*British military*] (DMA)
ELI .... exercise lability index (SAUS)
ELI .... Expression-Library Immunization [*To develop a vaccine*]
ELI .... Extended Lubrication Interval [*Automotive engineering*]
ELI .... Extensible Language I [*Computer science*]
ELI .... Extra-Low Impurity [*Metals*]
ELI .... Extra-Low Interstitial [*Alloy*]
ELI .... Heliarcos [*Spain*] [*FAA designator*] (FAAC)
Eli .... nickname for a student or aluminus of Yale University (SAUO)
Eli .... Elias (ODA)
ELIA .... Elementary Imprint Assistance [*Writing system for the blind*]
ELIA .... English Language Institute of America (WDAA)
ELIA .... Enhanced Luminescent Immunoassay [*Analytical biochemistry*]
ELIA .... Enzyme-Labelled Immunoassay (DB)
ELIA .... Enzyme-Linked Immunoassay (MELL)
ELIA .... European League of Institutes of the Arts [*British*]
ELIA .... Expert System for Landsat Image Analysis (SAUS)
ELIAS .... Earth Limb Infrared Atmospheric Structure (SAUS)
ELIAS .... Earth Limb Infrared Atomic Structure (ACAE)
ELIAS .... Entry Level Interactive Applications Systems [*Computer science*]
ELIAS .... Environment Libraries Automated System [*Environment Canada*] [*Database*] [*Information service or system*] (IID)
ELIAS .... Environment Library Integrated Automated System (SAUO)
ELIAS .... Expandable Level Interactive Application System (HGAA)
ELIAS-I .... Entry Level Interactive Application System-One (SAUS)
eLib .... Electronic Libraries Programme (SAUS)
ELIB .... Environmental Legal Information Base (SAUO)
ELIC .... Electric Lamp Industry Council [*British*] (BI)
ELICIANT ..... Eliciantur [*Let Be Drawn*] [*Pharmacy*] (ROG)
ELICOS .... English Language Intensive Courses for Overseas Students (SAUO)
ELICT .... Enzyme-Linked Immunocytochemical Technique [*Clinical chemistry*] (DMAA)
ELID .... Electrolytic-in-Process-Dressing [*Optics manufacturing*] (RDA)
ELID .... Electrostatic Latent Image Development (IAA)
E-LIDAR .... Experimental Lidar (EOSA)
ELIEDA .... Enzyme-Linked Immunoelectric Diffusion Assay [*Clinical chemistry*]
ELIFE .... Enhancement of Life Support, Europe (MCD)
elig .... Eligible (ADWA)
ELIG .... Eligible (AFM)
ELIGATA ...... Eastern Languages International Group of ATA (SAUO)
ELIG RET ..... Eligible for Retirement (DNAB)
ELIM .... Eliminate (AFM)
elim .... eliminated (SAUS)
ELIM .... Eliminator [*Automotive engineering*]
ELIM .... Enlisted Loss Inventory Model (MCD)
ELIM .... Evangelical Lutherans in Mission [*Group opposing the Missouri Synod of the Lutheran Church*]
ELIMS .... Enhanced Logistics Information Management System
ELIN .... Estacado Library Information Network
ELIN .... Exhibit Line Item Number (MCD)
ELINCS .... European List of Notified Chemical Substances (SAUS)
e-line .... Expo Line [*Expository line*] [*Photograph caption*] (WDMC)
ELINT .... Electromagnetic Information (SAUS)
ELINT .... Electromagnetic Intelligence
ELINT .... Electromagnetic Intercept (SAUS)
ELINT .... Electronic Intelligence [*or Intercept*] [*Meaning of ELINT determined by reference to before (Intercept) and after (Intelligence) analysis of reconnaissance mission results*]
ELINT .... Electronic Intelligence Satellite (NITA)
ELINT .... electronics intelligence. (SAUS)
elints .... Electronic Intelligence Gathering Vessels (SAUS)
ELINTS .... Electronic Intelligence Ship (SAUS)
ELINT TGU ... Electronic Intelligence Technical Guidance Unit (MCD)
ELIP .... Electrostatic Latent Image Photography (IEEE)
ELIP .... Elliptical (FAAC)
ELIPA .... Experienced Librarians and Information Personnel in the Developing Countries of Asia and Oceania [*Korea Advanced Institute of Science and Technology*] [*Seoul*] [*Information service or system*] (IID)
ELIPA .... Experienced Library and Information Personnel in Asia and Oceania (SAUS)
ELIPS .... Electron Image Projection System (SAUS)
ELIPS .... Electron Image Projetion System (SAUS)
elipt .... Elipitically (ADWA)
ELIRT .... Environmental Laboratories Information Retrieval Technique (PDAA)
ELIS .... Editing System of Logic Information (SAUS)
ELIS .... Electrical Installation System (EURO)
ELIS .... Electronic Legislative Information System (SAUS)
ELIS .... Electronic Library Information Service (SAUS)
ELIS .... Electronic Library Information System [*Library network*] (IT)
ELIS .... Encyclopaedia of Library and Information Science (SAUS)
ELIS .... Encyclopedia of Legal Information Sources [*A publication*]
ELIS .... Encyclopedia of Library and Information Science (SAUS)
ELIS .... Environmental Law Information System (SAUO)
ELISA .... An Electronic Messaging System Operated by Helsinki Telephone Company in Finland [*Communications term*] (DCT)
ELISA .... Electronic Intelligence Search and Analysis (ACAE)
ELISA .... Electronic Library Information Service at the Australian National University
ELISA .... Enzyme-Linked [*or Labeled*] Immunoadsorbent Assay [*Immunochemistry*]
ELISA .... Enzyme-Linked Immunosorbant Assay (EDCT)
ELISE .... Electronic Library Image Server for Europe project (SAUS)
ELISE .... Electronic Library Image Service for Europe (TELE)
ELISE .... European Network for the Exchange of Information on Local Employment Initiatives [*EC*] (ECED)
ELIST .... Enhanced Logistics Intratheater Support Tool [*DoD*]
ELIT .... Electronics Information Test
ELITE .... Electric Insertion Transfer Experiment (SAUS)
ELITE .... Electronic Library and Teleservices (TELE)
ELITE .... Electronic Library Information Transfer Experimentation (SAUS)
ELITE .... Electronic Library Teleservices (SAUS)
ELITE .... Enhanced Level I Technician Education [*Automotive service industry*]
ELITE .... Enterprise Learning through Information Technology [*University of Durham*] (AIE)
ELITE .... Executive Level Interactive Terminal Environment (RDA)
ELITE .... Extended Long-Range Integrated Technology Evaluation
ELITF .... Executive Level Interactive Terminal (ACAE)
ELIX .... Electric Lightwave'A' [*NASDAQ symbol*] (SG)
ELIX .... Electric Lightwave, Inc. [*NASDAQ symbol*] (NASQ)
Elix .... Elixer (AMHC)
elix .... Elixir (IDYL)
ELIX .... Elixir [*Pharmacology*]
Eliz .... Elizabethan (ADWA)
ELIZ .... Elizabethan (ROG)
ELIZ .... Ellsworth Industries [*Federal Railroad Administration identification code*]
Eliz .... Queen Elizabeth (DLA)
ELIZA .... Artificial Intelligence System [*Runs on IBM systems*] (HODG)
ELIZA .... Elizabeth, MS [*American Association of Railroads railroad junction routing code*]
Elizabeths .... Elizabeth Islands (SAUS)
ELJ .... Eljer Industries [*NASDAQ symbol*] (TTSB)
ELJ .... Eljer Industries, Inc. [*NYSE symbol*] (SPSG)
ELJ .... El Recreo [*Colombia*] [*Airport symbol*] (OAG)
ELJ .... Executive-Legislative-Judicial
ELJ .... Expendable LASER Jammer (MCD)
Eljer .... Eljer Industries, Inc. [*Associated Press*] (SAG)
ELK .... Eesti Lennukompani [*Estonia*] [*ICAO designator*] (FAAC)
ELK .... Elcor Corp. [*NYSE symbol*] (SPSG)
ELK .... Elk City, OK [*Location identifier*] [*FAA*] (FAAL)
ELK .... Elko [*Nevada*] [*Seismograph station code, US Geological Survey*] (SEIS)
ELK .... Emerald Lake Resources, Inc. [*Toronto Stock Exchange symbol*]
ELK .... Enosis Laikou Kommatos [*Union of Populist Parties*] [*Greek*] (PPE)
ELK .... Esperantista Lingva Komitato (SAUO)
ELK .... Ethniko Laiko Komma [*National Populist Party*] [*Greek*] (PPE)
ELK .... Extension Language Kit [*Computer science*] (VERA)
ELK .... External Link (SAUS)
ELKE .... Elevated Kinetic Energy Weapon
Elk Island .... Elk Island National Park east of Edmonton, Alberta (SAUS)
ELKO .... Elko, NV [*American Association of Railroads railroad junction routing code*]
ELKR .... Elk River Railroad [*Federal Railroad Administration identification code*]
ELKRAFT ...... Danish Electric Utility (SAUS)
ELKX .... Elkem Metal [*Federal Railroad Administration identification code*]
ELL .... Eccentric Leveling Lugs (SAUS)
ell .... elbow (SAUS)
El L .... Electrical Lieutenant (SAUS)

ELL .... Electrosensory Lateral Line-Lobe [*Biology*]
ELL .... Ellipsometry [*Surface analysis*]
ELL .... Elmali [*Turkey*] [*Seismograph station code, US Geological Survey*] (SEIS)
ELL .... Empire Lacrosse League (PSS)
ELL .... English Language and Literature [*Publication*] (SAUS)
ELL .... English Language Laboratory
Ell .... English language learning (SAUS)
ELL .... Environmental Law Library (SAUO)
ELL .... Equivalent Loudness Level
ELL .... Estonian Air [*ICAO designator*] (FAAC)
ELL .... Excimer LASER Lithography
ELL .... Extremely Low Luminosity [*Astronomy*]
ELL .... Huntsville, AL [*Location identifier*] [*FAA*] (FAAL)
ELLA .... Eastern Lamp and Lighting Association (EA)
ELLA .... European Long Lines Agency [*NATO*]
Ell & Bl .... Ellis and Blackburn's English Queen's Bench Reports [*118-120 English Reprint*] [*A publication*] (DLA)
Ell & Ell .... Ellis and Ellis' English Queen's Bench Reports [*A publication*] (DLA)
Ell Ann .... Ellison. Law of Annuities [*A publication*] (DLA)
Ell B & Ell ... Ellis, Blackburn, and Ellis' English Queen's Bench Reports [*A publication*] (ILCA)
Ell B & S ..... Ellis, Best, and Smith's English Queen's Bench Reports [*A publication*] (DLA)
Ell Bl & Ell ... Ellis, Blackburn, and Ellis' English Queen's Bench Reports [*A publication*] (DLA)
ELLC .... Enhanced Logical Link Control (SAUS)
El L Cr .... Electrical Lieutenant Commander (SAUS)
ELLC Tyre .... Extra Low Load Capacity Tyre (SAUS)
Ell D & Cr .... Ellis. Debtor and Creditor [*1822*] [*A publication*] (DLA)
ELLDE .... Ellendale, DE [*American Association of Railroads railroad junction routing code*]
Ell Deb .... Elliot's Debates on the Federal Constitution [*A publication*] (DLA)
Ell Dig .... Eller's Minnesota Digest [*A publication*] (ILCA)
Ell Dip Code ... Elliot's American Diplomatic Code [*A publication*] (DLA)
ELLE .... Elle Looks Like Emacs (SAUS)
ELLECTRA .... Electrical, Electronics, and Communications Trades Association (SAUO)
ELLECTRA .... trademark of the London Electricity Board (SAUS)
Ellerman ...... Ellerman Lines Ltd (SAUS)
Ellesm Post N ... Ellesmere's Post Nati [*A publication*] (DLA)
EllettBr .... Ellett Brothers, Inc. [*Associated Press*] (SAG)
ELLI .... European Lifelong Learning Initiative (SAUO)
ELLIAS .... Expandable Level Interactive Application System (SAUS)
Ellices .... Ellice Islands now called Tuvalu (SAUS)
Ell Ins .... Ellis on Fire and Life Insurance and Annuities [*A publication*] (DLA)
Elliot Deb Fed Const ... Elliot's Debates on the Federal Constitution [*A publication*] (DLA)
Elliott App Proc ... Elliott's Appellate Procedure [*A publication*] (DLA)
Elliott Roads & S ... Elliott on Roads and Streets [*A publication*] (DLA)
Elliott Supp ... Elliott's Supplement to the Indiana Revised Statutes [*A publication*] (DLA)
ellip .... elliptic (SAUS)
ellip .... elliptically (SAUS)
ELLIP .... Elliptocytosis [*Medicine*] (EDAA)
ELLIPT .... Elliptical
ELLIPT .... Ellipticity (SAUS)
ELLIS .... Ellis Air Lines (SAUS)
Ellis .... Ellis Island Immigration Examination Station, New York (SAUS)
Ellis .... Ellis on Insurance [*A publication*] (DLA)
ELLIS .... English Language Learning and Improvement Service [*State Library of South Australia*]
ELLIS .... English Language Learning Instruction System
ELLIS .... Eulisp Linda System (SAUS)
ELLIS .... European Legal Literature Information Service [*London, England*]
Ellis & Bl ..... Ellis and Blackburn's English Queen's Bench Reports [*118-120 English Reprint*] [*A publication*] (DLA)
Ellis Dr & Cr ... Ellis. Debtor and Creditor [*1822*] [*A publication*] (DLA)
ELLL .... Electrosensory Lateral Line [*Invertebrate zoology*]
ELLP .... Elliptocytes [*Biochemistry*] (DAVI)
ELLPAT .... Environmental Lead Laboratory Proficiency Analytical Testing (SARE)
ELLSA .... Enzyme-Linked Ligand Sorbent Assay [*Analytical biochemistry*]
Ells Cop Man ... Ellsworth's Copyright Manual [*A publication*] (DLA)
ELLT .... Electric Light (IAA)
el lt .... electric lighting (SAUS)
ELLTAB .... ERL/NASA Look-Up-Table Classification System (SAUS)
Ell Trade ...... Ellet on the Laws of Trade [*A publication*] (DLA)
ELLX .... Luxembourg/Luxembourg [*ICAO location identifier*] (ICLI)
ELM .... Corning-Elmira [*New York*] [*Airport symbol*] (AD)
ELM .... Department of Environment and Land Management (SAUS)
ELM .... Early Language Milestone Scale (MEDA)
ELM .... Eastern Atlantic and Mediterranean [*Military*]
ELM .... Easy-to-Learn Mail program (SAUS)
ELM .... Edgar Lee Masters (SAUS)
ELM .... Elaboration-Likelihood Model [*R.E Petty & J. T. Cacioppo*] (DIPS)
ELM .... Elasticity buffer and Link Manager (SAUS)
ELM .... Electrical Length Measurement (IAA)
ELM .... ELectronic Mail (SAUS)
ELM .... ELectronic Mailer (SAUS)
ELM .... Electronics Module (ADWA)
ELM .... Element (AABC)
elm .... Element (MILB)
ELM .... Elementary Loop Model (SAUS)
ELM .... Element Load Model
ELM .... Element Load Module (SAUS)
ELM .... Elma [*New York*] [*Seismograph station code, US Geological Survey*] [*Closed*] (SEIS)
ELM .... Elmira [*New York*] [*Airport symbol*] (OAG)
ELM .... Emitter Location Method
ELM .... Empresas La Moderna SA [*NYSE symbol*] (SAG)
ELM .... Empresas La Moderna SAADS [*NYSE symbol*] (TTSB)
ELM .... Emulsion Liquid Membrane [*Chemical separation technology*]
ELM .... Endings [*of nerves*] to Lip Muscle
elm .... energy-loss meter (SAUS)
ELM .... Environmental Library of Minnesota (SAUS)
ELM .... Epiluminescence Microscopy
ELM .... Eritrea Liberation Movement (SAUO)
ELM .... Error Latency Model (SAUS)
ELM .... Error Log Manager [*Computer science*] (ELAL)
ELM .... Expendable Light Markers (NVT)
ELM .... Experimental Logistics Module (SSD)
ELM .... Extended Length Measure (SAUS)
ELM .... Extended Length Message (DA)
ELM .... Extended Length Methods (MCD)
ELM .... Extended Lunar Mission [*NASA*] (KSC)
ELM .... Extended Lunar Module (SAUS)
ELM .... External Limiting Membrane
ELM .... Extra Low Mass (SAUS)
ELM .... La-Rouche-Sur-Yon [*France*] [*Airport symbol*]
ELM .... Edge-Localized Mode (ODA)
ELMA .... Electric Lamp Manufacturers Association (SAUO)
ELMA .... Electric Lamp Manufacturers' Association of Great Britain Ltd. (BI)
ELMA .... Electro-Mechanical Aid (SAUS)
ELMA .... Emergency Lighting Manufacturers Association [*Defunct*] (EA)
ELMAP .... Exchange Line Multiplexing Analysis Program (TEL)
Elm Arch Jur ... Elmes on Architectural Jurisprudence [*A publication*] (DLA)
ELMAS .... ELectrochemical MicroAnalytical System (SAUS)
ELMC .... Electrical Load Management Center (ADWA)
ELMCH .... Electromechanical
ELMD .... Electromotive Division [*Federal Railroad Administration identification code*]
Elm Dig .... Elmer's New Jersey Digest of Laws [*A publication*] (DLA)
Elm Dilap .... Elmes on Ecclesiastical Civil Dilapidation [*A publication*] (DLA)
ELME .... Emitter Location Method
ELMECH .... Electromechanical (NASA)
EL MECH ..... Electromechanical (SAUS)
ELMER .... Electromechanical Robot (SAUS)
Elmer Lun .... Elmer's Practice in Lunacy [*A publication*] (DLA)
Elmer R Rice ... Elmer Reizenstein (SAUS)
Elmers .... Elmers Restaurants, Inc. [*Associated Press*] (SAG)
Elm Exec Dep ... Elmes' Executive Departments of the United States [*A publication*] (DLA)
ELMF .... European Large Magnetic Field Facility
ELMG .... Electromagnetic Sci [*NASDAQ symbol*] (TTSB)
ELMG .... Electromagnetic Sciences, Inc. [*NASDAQ symbol*] (NQ)
ELMG .... EMS Technologies [*NASDAQ symbol*] (SG)
ELMG .... Engine Life Management Group [*Navy*]
Elmi .... electron microscopy (SAUS)
ELMI .... Enhanced Local Management Interface (DINT)
ELMIG .... Electronic Library Membership Initiative Group [*ALA*] (NITA)
ELMINT .... Electromagnetic Intelligence
Elmira C ...... Elmira College (GAGS)
ELMIRD .... Electromagnetic Liquid Metal Inclusion Removal Device (SAUS)
Elm Lun .... Elmer's Practice in Lunacy [*A publication*] (DLA)
ELMN(A) ..... Electrical Mechanician (Air) [*Navy rating*] [*British*]
ELMN(AW) ... Electrical Mechanician (Air Weapon) [*British military*] (DMA)
Elm NJ Laws ... Elmer's New Jersey Digest of Laws [*A publication*] (DLA)
ELMNT .... Element
ELMO .... Electronic Map Ordering (SAUS)
ELMO .... El Morro National Monument
ELMO .... Engineering and Logistics Management Office [*MERDC*] [*Army*]
ELMO .... Engineering Lunar Model Obstacle [*NASA*] (PDAA)
ELMO .... European Laundry and Dry Cleaning Machinery Manufacturers Organization (EA)
elmobile ...... electric automobile (SAUS)
ELMR .... Estuarine Living Marine Resources Program [*National Oceanic and Atmospheric Administration*]
ElmrSv .... Elmira Savings Bank FSB [*Associated Press*] (SAG)
ELMS .... Earth Limb Measurement Satellite [*NASA/Air Force*]
ELMS .... Earth Limb Measurement System [*NASA*] (SSD)
ELMS .... Earth Limit Measurement Satellite (ACAE)
ELMS .... Educators of Library Media Specialists Section [*American Association of School Librarians*]
ELMS .... Elastic Loop Mobility System [*NASA*]
ELMS .... Elements
ELMS .... Elmer's Restaurants, Inc. [*NASDAQ symbol*] (NQ)
ELMS .... Engineering Lunar Model Surface
ELMS .... Environment and Land Management Sector (SAUS)
ELMS .... Equipment Library Management System (SAUS)
ELMS .... Experimental Library Management System
ELMSIM .... Engine Life Management Simulation Model (PDAA)
ELMSS .... Educators of Library Media Specialists Section [*American Association of School Librarians*] [*American Library Association*]
ELMT .... Electronic Mechanic Technician
ELMT .... Elements [*on Urinalysis*] [*Biochemistry*] (DAVI)
ELMTNO ...... Element Numbers [*On urinalysis*] [*Biochemistry*] (DAVI)
ELMU .... Environment Law and Machinery Unit (EERA)
El Mus .... East London Museum (SAUS)
elmwd .... Elmwood (VRA)
E Ln .... East London (SAUS)

ELN .... Ejercito de Liberacion Nacional [*National Liberation Army*] [*Peru*] (PD)
ELN .... Ejercito de Liberacion Nacional [*National Liberation Army*] [*Bolivia*] (PD)
ELN .... Elan Corp. [*NYSE symbol*] (SAG)
ELN .... Elan Corp. ADS [*NYSE symbol*] (TTSB)
ELN .... Electronic Laboratory Notebook
ELN .... Ellensburg, WA [*Location identifier*] [*FAA*] (FAAL)
ELN .... Encapsulated Lymph Node [*Medicine*] (MELL)
ELN .... English Language Notes [*A publication*] (ANEX)
ELN .... English Language Notes (journ.) (SAUS)
ELN .... EnviroLink Network (SAUO)
ELN .... Environmental Librarian's Network (ADWA)
ELN .... National Liberation Army [*Government term*] (GA)
ELN .... Nordic East International Aircraft, AB [*Sweden*] [*ICAO designator*] (FAAC)
ELN.WS A.... Elan Corp. ADS Wrrt'98 [*NYSE symbol*] (TTSB)
ELNA .... Esperanto League for North America (EA)
ELNA .... Esperanto-Ligo de Nord-Ameriko (SAUO)
ELND .... Elective Node Dissection [*Medicine*]
ELNEO .... Elastase-Neomycin Gene [*Genetics*]
ELNES .... Electron Loss Near Edge Structure [*Electron microscopy*]
ELNES .... Energy-Loss Near Edge Structure (AAEL)
eLNet .... Educators' Learning Network
ELNET .... European Library Networks meeting (SAUS)
ELNET .... European Library Netwroks meeting (SAUS)
ELNG .... Elongate (MSA)
elngn .... elongation (SAUS)
ELNGT .... Elongate (FAAC)
ELNI .... Ethernet Local Network Interconnect (SAUS)
ELNK .... Earthlink Network [*NASDAQ symbol*] (SG)
ELNK .... Earthlink Network, Inc. [*NASDAQ symbol*] (SAG)
El/NI .... Electron Irradiation and Neutron Irradiation (SAUS)
ELNM .... Edison Laboratory National Monument (SAUS)
ELNM .... Edison Laboratory National Monument, West Orange, New Jersey (SAUS)
ELNS .... European League for a New Society [*See also LIENS*] [*Paris, France*] (EAIO)
ELNT .... Elantec Semiconductor [*NASDAQ symbol*] (TTSB)
ELNT .... Elantec Semiconductor, Inc. [*NASDAQ symbol*] (SAG)
ELO .... Eldorado Minerals & Petroleum [*Vancouver Stock Exchange symbol*]
ELO .... Electric Light Orchestra [*Rock music group*]
elo .... elocution (SAUS)
Elo .... Eloheimo (SAUS)
elo .... eloquence (SAUS)
ELO .... Ely, MN [*Location identifier*] [*FAA*] (FAAL)
ELO .... Enabling Learning Objective [*Training term*] (LPT)
ELO .... epitaxiales laterales Aufwachsen (SAUS)
ELO .... epitaxial lateral overgrowth (SAUS)
ELO .... Epitaxial Lift-Off (SAUS)
ELO .... Epoxidized Linseed Oil [*Organic chemistry*]
ELO .... European Leisure Organization (SAUO)
ELO .... Evangelical Literature Overseas (EA)
ELO .... Eye Lens Obsolescence [*Ophthalmology*]
ELO .... Logiealmond [*Scotland*] [*Seismograph station code, US Geological Survey*] (SEIS)
ELOA .... Educational Leave of Absence (ABAC)
ELOC .... Eastern Line of Communication [*World War II*]
ELOC .... Elastomeric-Oriented Copolyester (PDAA)
Eloc .... Elocution
ELOCARS ..... Electro-Optical Collection and Analysis Reporting System (MCD)
ELO-CATS .... Electro-Optical Collection and Analysis Targeting System
ELOD .... Electronic Design (journ.) (SAUS)
ELOD .... Erasable LASER Optical Disk [*Computer science*] (IAA)
ELOG .... Epitaxially Laterally Overgrown Gallium (AAEL)
ELOG .... European Landowning Organization Group (EAIO)
ELOI .... Emergency Letter of Instructions
ELOISE .... European Land-Ocean Interaction Studies (SAUO)
Eloise .... European large-orbiting instrumentation for solar experimentation (SAUS)
ELOISE .... European Large Orbiting Instrumentation for Solar Experiments
ELOK .... Evangelical-Lutheran Ovambo-Kavango (SAUS)
E Lon .... East Longitude
ELON .... Echelon Corp. [*NASDAQ symbol*] (NASQ)
E Long .... East Longitude (HGAA)
ELONG .... Elongate (VLIE)
ELONG .... Elongation (MSA)
E Longs .... East Longitudes (SAUS)
EL-OP .... Electro-Optics Industries Ltd.
ELOP .... Estimated Length of Program [*Medicine*] (DAVI)
ELOP .... Extended Logic Plan (SAUS)
ELOQ .... Eloquence [*or Eloquent*] (ROG)
ELOQ .... Eloquent, Inc. [*NASDAQ symbol*] (SG)
ELOR .... Extended Lunar Orbital Rendezvous [*NASA*] (KSC)
ELORM .... Extended Lunar Orbital Rendezvous Mission [*NASA*] (KSC)
ELOS .... Electronic Line-of-Sight [*Military*]
ELOS .... Estimated Length of Stay [*Medicine*] (DAVI)
ELOS .... Experimental Land Observing System (ACAE)
ELOS .... Extended Line-of-Sight (CAAL)
ELOS .... Extralymphatic Organ Site [*Oncology*] (DAVI)
ELOT .... Executone Info Sys [*NASDAQ symbol*] (SG)
ELOT .... Hellenic Organization for Standardization [*Greece*] (DDC)
ELOTARLOCS... Electro-Optical Target Locating System (MCD)
E Loth .... East Lothian (SAUS)
ELOX .... Elcon [*Private rail car owner code*]
ELOX .... Electrical Spark Erosion
ELOY .... eLoyalty Corp. [*NASDAQ symbol*] (SG)
ELP .... Aerolineas Ejecutivas de San Luis Potosi SA de CV [*Mexico*] [*ICAO designator*] (FAAC)
ELP .... Comp Paranaense Energia'B' ADS [*NYSE symbol*] (SG)
ELP .... Edge-Lit Panel (DNAB)
elp .... electricity planned (SAUS)
ELP .... Electric Light Pole
ELP .... Electrolytic Polishing (MCD)
ELP .... Electronic Label Printing [*Diagraph Corp.*]
ELP .... Electronic Line Printer
ELP .... Electronic Printer (MCD)
ELP .... Electrophoresis [*Laboratory*] (DAVI)
ELP .... Electropolishing (SAUS)
ELP .... Element Processor (NITA)
ELP .... Elliptical (MSA)
ELP .... El Pangue [*Chile*] [*Seismograph station code, US Geological Survey*] (SEIS)
ELP .... El Paso [*Texas*] [*Airport symbol*] (OAG)
ELP .... El Paso, TX [*Location identifier*] [*FAA*] (FAAL)
ELP .... Emergency Loading Procedure
ELP .... Emerson, Lake & Palmer [*Rock music group*]
ELP .... Emission Line Polarimeter (SAUS)
ELP .... Emulsified Liquid Propellant
ELP .... Endogenous Limbic Potentials [*Neurophysiology*]
ELP .... Energy Loss Peak [*Physics*]
ELP .... Engine Lube and Purge [*System*]
ELP .... English Language Program (MCD)
ELP .... English Level Program (ACAE)
ELP .... Environmental Leadership Program (LDOE)
ELP .... Equipment Loan Program (SAUS)
ELP .... Error Localization Program (SAUS)
ELP .... Estimated Learning Potential
ELP .... European Labour Party (SAUO)
ELP .... European Library and Publishers (SAUS)
ELP .... European Library Publishers (TELE)
ELP .... Excess Leave Program (SAUO)
ELP .... Extreme Limb Photometer [*Instrumentation*]
ELP .... Equivalent Local Potential (ODA)
ELPA .... El Paso Electric Co. [*NASDAQ symbol*] (NQ)
ELPA .... Eyring Low-Profile Antenna (SAUS)
ELPAS .... El Paso, TX [*American Association of Railroads railroad junction routing code*]
ElPasNG ...... El Paso Natural Gas Co. [*Associated Press*] (SAG)
ElPasoE .... El Paso Electric Co. [*Associated Press*] (SAG)
El Paso Trial Law Rev... El Paso Trial Lawyers Review [*A publication*] (DLA)
ElPasT .... El Paso Tennessee Pipeline [*Associated Press*] (SAG)
ELPAT .... Environmental Lead Proficiency Analytical Testing Program
ELPAVG .... Equity Linked Life Insurance Policy with an Asset Value Guarantee (DICI)
ELPB .... Engine Logistics Planning Board [*Air Force*] (AFIT)
elpc .... electroluminescence photo conductor (SAUS)
ELPC .... Electroluminescent - Photoconductive (SAUS)
EL-PC .... Electroluminescent-Photoconductive (MCD)
ELPC .... Electroluminescent Photoconductor (SAUS)
ELPC .... Even Longitudinal Parity Check (VLIE)
ELPE .... Electroluminescent-Photoelectric
ELPEX .... Electronic Production Equipment Exhibition (SAUS)
ELPEX .... International Electronic Production Equipment Exhibition (SAUO)
ELPFA .... Ester-Linked Phospholipid Membrane Analysis [*Analytical biochemistry*]
ELPG .... Electric Light and Power Group
ELPGA .... European Liquefied Petroleum Gas Association (EA)
ELPH .... Elliptical Head (IEEE)
Elph .... Elphinstone, Norton, and Clark. Interpretation of Deeds [*1885*] [*A publication*] (DLA)
Elph Conv .... Elphinstone's Introduction to Conveyancing [*A publication*] (DLA)
ELPHEV .... Electrically Modulated Control Clutch
Elph Interp Deeds... Elphinstone's Rules for Interpretation of Deeds [*A publication*] (DLA)
ELPHR .... Experimental Low-Temperature Process Heat Reactor
ELPHR Concept... Experimental Low Temperature Process Heat Reactor Concept (SAUS)
ELPN .... Electric League of the Pacific Northwest (SRA)
ELPNEU .... Electropneumatic
ELPO .... Electrodeposition (SAUS)
ELPO .... Electronic Products (journ.) (SAUS)
ELPO .... Electro-Phosphate Coating [*Metallurgical engineering*]
ELPO .... Electrostatic Primer [*Automotive manufacturing*]
ELPR .... Electroluminescent-Photoresponsive (IAA)
ELPS .... English Language Proficiency Survey [*Department of Education*] (GFGA)
ELPSO .... El Paso, IL [*American Association of Railroads railroad junction routing code*]
ELP Tire .... Extra Low Pressure Tire (SAUS)
ELQ .... El Quisco [*Chile*] [*Seismograph station code, US Geological Survey*] [*Closed*] (SEIS)
ELQ .... Gassim [*Saudi Arabia*] [*Airport symbol*] (OAG)
ELQC .... Electroluminescent Quantum Counter
ELR .... Earned Loss Ratio [*Insurance*]
ELR .... Eastern Law Reporter [*Canada*] [*A publication*] (DLA)
ELR .... East London Railway (ROG)
ELR .... Eldon Resources Ltd. [*Vancouver Stock Exchange symbol*]
ELR .... Election Law Reports [*India*] [*A publication*] (DLA)
ELR .... Electronic Label Reader (SAUS)

ELR............ Electronic Line Replacement [*Cinematography*] (WDMC)
Elr............ Elevator (SAUS)
ELR............ Elrom Aviation & Investments [*Israel*] [*ICAO designator*] (FAAC)
ELR............ Emergency Locking Retractor (SAUO)
ELR............ Engineering Laboratory Report
ELR............ Engineering Liaison Request (KSC)
ELR............ Environmental Law Reporter [*A publication*] (COE)
ELR............ Environmental Report (SAUS)
ELR............ Environment Lapse Rate (DA)
ELR............ Equal Listener Response [*Scale*]
ELR............ Equal Listener Response Scale (SAUS)
ELR............ Error Logging Register (MHDB)
ELR............ European Law Review [*A publication*] (SAFN)
ELR............ Exchange Line Relay [*Telecommunications*] (IAA)
ELR............ Execution Local/Remote (VLIE)
ELR............ Existing Lapse Rate (DA)
ELR............ Expanded Low-voltage Range (SAUS)
ELR............ Expected Loss Ratio [*Insurance*]
ELR............ Experimental Launching Round (SAA)
ELR............ Export Licensing Regulations (ODBW)
ELR............ Extra Long Range [*ICAO designator*] (FAAC)
ELR............ Rapid City, SD [*Location identifier*] [*FAA*] (FAAL)
ELRA............ Electronic RADAR
ELRA............ European Language Resources Association (EURO)
elra............ European Leisure and Recreation Association (EAIO)
ELRA............ European Logistics and Relief Association (SAUO)
ELRAC........ Electronic Reconnaissance Accessory
ELRAC........ Electronic Reconnaissance Accessory Set (SAUS)
ELRAC........ Electronic Reconnaissance Accessory system (SAUS)
ELRACS........ Electronic Reconnaissance Accessory System (SAUS)
ELRAC System... Electronic Reconnaissance Accessory System (SAUS)
ELRAFT........ Efficient Logic Reduction Analysis of Fault Trees (PDAA)
ELRAT........ Electrical Ram Air Turbine (PDAA)
ELRC............ Electro Rent [*NASDAQ symbol*] (TTSB)
ELRC............ Electro Rent Corp. [*NASDAQ symbol*] (NQ)
ELRDL........ Electronics Research and Development Laboratory (SAUO)
ELREN........ El Reno, OK [*American Association of Railroads railroad junction routing code*]
El Reno........ Federal Reformatory, El Reno, Oklahoma (SAUS)
EL Rev........ European Law Review [*A publication*] (SAFN)
ELRF............ Eyesafe LASER Rangefinder (RDA)
ELRFTD........ Eye-Safe LASER Range Finder Training Device (MCD)
ELRIC........ Employers Labor Relations Information Committee (EA)
ELRN............ Elron Electronic Industries Ltd. [*NASDAQ symbol*] (NQ)
ELRNF........ Elron Electrn Ind Ord [*NASDAQ symbol*] (TTSB)
ELRNF........ Elron Electronic Industries Ltd. (MHDW)
ElRnv........ extra incidence rate in nonvaccinated groups (SAUS)
ELRO............ Electronics Logistics Research Office
Elron............ Elron Electronic Industries [*Associated Press*] (SAG)
ElronEl........ Elron Electronic Industries, Ltd. [*Associated Press*] (SAG)
ELR Scale.... Equal Listener Response Scale (SAUS)
ELRTS........ Elevated Light Rail Transit System [*Indian Railway*] (TIR)
ELRUM........ Eldon Avenue Revolutionary Union Movement
ElRv............ extra incidence rate in vaccinated groups (SAUS)
ELRW............ Elron Elektronic Industries [*NASDAQ symbol*] (SAG)
ELRWF........ Elron Electric Ind Wrrt [*NASDAQ symbol*] (TTSB)
ELS............ Early Lunar Shelter [*NASA*] (KSC)
ELS............ Earnings and Leave Statements (SAUO)
ELS............ Earth Landing System [*or Subsystem*] [*NASA*]
ELS............ Earth Limb Sensor (ACAE)
ELS............ Eastern Lake Survey (SAUO)
ELS............ Eastern Launch Site (MCD)
ELS............ East London [*South Africa*] [*Airport symbol*] (OAG)
ELS............ Eath Landing System (SAUS)
ELS............ Eaton-Lambert Syndrome [*Medicine*] (DMAA)
ELS............ Ecolabelling Schemes (SAUS)
ELS............ Economic Lot Size (MHDW)
ELS............ Education Learning Services (AIE)
ELS............ Elector-Optic Level Sensor
ELS............ Electrical Laser System (SAUS)
ELS............ Electrical System
ELS............ Electric Limit Switch
ELS............ Electro-magnetic Launcher System (SAUS)
ELS............ Electron Energy Loss Spectroscopy [*Also, EELS*]
ELS............ Electronic Levelling Suspension (SAUS)
ELS............ Electronic Library System [*Aviation*]
ELS............ Electronic Speciality (IAA)
ELS............ Electronic Specialty Co. (SAUO)
ELS............ Electron Loss Spectroscopy (DB)
ELS............ Electrophoretic Light Scattering [*Analytical chemistry*]
ELS............ Electrostatic Loudspeaker (DEN)
ELs............ elevated railways (SAUS)
ELS............ Elevon Load System [*Aviation*] (MCD)
ELS............ Elizabethan Literary Society (SAUO)
ELS............ Elizabeth Linington Society (EA)
ELS............ Elm Leaf Scorch [*Plant pathology*]
ELS............ El Sal Air [*El Salvador*] [*ICAO designator*] (FAAC)
EIS............ El Salvador (MILB)
ELS............ Elsevier [*Published by the Elsevier family*] (ROG)
ELS............ Elsinore Corp. [*AMEX symbol*] (SPSG)
ELS............ Emergency Landing Site (SSD)
ELS............ Emergency Landing Strip (SAUS)
ELS............ Emergency Lighting Supply (DNAB)
ELS............ Emergency Lighting System (DNAB)
ELS............ Emitter Location System [*Air Force*]
ELS............ Emitter Locator System (SAUS)
ELS............ Enchiridion Locorum Sanctorum [*A publication*] (BJA)
ELS............ Encyclopedia of Life Science [*A publication*]
ELS............ Encyclopedia of Life Sciences [*A publication*]
ELS............ Endolymphatic Sac [*Medicine*] (MELL)
ELS............ Energy Loss Spectroscope (SAUS)
ELS............ Energy-Loss Spectroscopy
ELS............ Enterprise Library Service (GART)
ELS............ Entry Level System [*Computer science*]
ELS............ Environmental Labelling Schemes (EERA)
ELS............ Environmental Law Service (SAUS)
ELS............ Environmental Law Society (SAUO)
ELS............ Eosinophilic Lymphfolliculosis of the Skin [*Kimura disease*] [*Dermatology*]
ELS............ Equidistant Letter Sequences [*Computer analysis of texts*]
ELS............ Error Likely Situation (IEEE)
ELS............ Escanaba & Lake Superior Railroad Co. [*AAR code*]
ELS............ Evangelical Lutheran Synod
ELS............ Exchange Line Selector [*Telecommunications*] (IAA)
ELS............ External Lamina Substance (OA)
ELS............ Extra-Long Staple [*Cotton*]
ELS............ Extreme Long Shot [*Photography*] (WDMC)
ELS............ Harvard Environmental Law Society (EA)
ELS............ Electronic Lodgement Service (ODA)
ELSA............ Electronic Library SGML Applications (SAUS)
ELSA............ Electronic Lobe Switching Antenna (PDAA)
ELSA............ Electronic Selective Archives [*Swiss News Agency*] [*Information service or system*] (IID)
ELSA............ Emergency Life Support Apparatus (PDAA)
ELSA............ Energy Loss Spectral Analysis (SAUS)
ELSA............ English Language Skills Assessment in a Reading Context [*Educational test*]
ELSA............ Environmental Life-Support Assembly [*NASA*] (KSC)
ELSA............ Estonian Learned Society of America (EA)
ELSA............ European Lead Stabilizers Association (SAUS)
ELSA............ European League of Stuttering Associations (SAUS)
ELSA............ Evaluation and Learning Systems Approach (FOTI)
ELSA............ Experimental System for Simulation and Animation (SAUS)
ELSAC........ Ealing Library School Students Action Committee (SAUS)
ElsagB........ Elsag Bailey Process Automation [*Associated Press*] (SAG)
El Sal........ El Salvador (SAUS)
El Salv........ El Salvador
ELSASSER... Elsaess-Lothringen Partei [*Alsace-Lorraine Party*] [*German*] (PPE)
ELSB............ Edge-Lighted Status Board [*Navy*]
ELSBM........ Exposed Location Single-Buoy Mooring (DNAB)
ELSC............ Earth Landing Sequence Controller [*NASA*] (NASA)
EL-SC........ Elastic Scattering (SAUS)
ELSC............ Electronic Library System Cabinet
El School J... Elementary School Journal (SAUS)
El School T... Elementary School Teacher (journ.) (SAUS)
Elscint........ Elscint Ltd. [*Associated Press*] (SAG)
ELS Cotton... Extra-Long Stable Cotton (SAUS)
ELSD............ Evaporative Light Scattering Detector [*Chemistry*]
ELSDN........ Elsdon, IL [*American Association of Railroads railroad junction routing code*]
ELSE............ Earth and Life Sciences Editors (SAUS)
ELSE............ Economic Learning and Social Evolution
ELSE............ Electrical Launch Support Equipment [*NASA*] (KSC)
ELSE............ Electro-Sensors, Inc. [*NASDAQ symbol*] (NQ)
ELSE............ European Association of Editors of Biological Periodicals (SAUS)
ELSE............ European Life Sciences Editors (SAUS)
ELSE............ Executive Luxury Special Edition [*Concept car*]
elsec............ electronic security (SAUS)
ELSEC........ Electronic Security [*Air Force*]
ELSECOM.... Electrotechnical Sectorial Committee for Testing and Certification (SAUO)
ELSEGIS...... Elementary and Secondary Education General Information Survey [*Department of Education*] (GFGA)
El Sel DO Tp Rd... Electronic Selector Dropout Tape Read (SAUS)
ELSET........ Element Set (ACAE)
elsets........ elements sets (SAUS)
Elsev App Sci... Elsevier Applied Science (SAUS)
Elsevier........ Elsevier NV [*Associated Press*] (SAG)
Elsevier Sci... Elsevier Scientific Publishing Co (SAUS)
Elsev NH...... Elsevier North Holland (SAUS)
Elsev Sci...... Elsevier Science Publishing Co. (SAUO)
Elsev Sci...... Elsevier Science Publishing Company (SAUS)
Elsev Seq...... Elsevier Sequoia (SAUS)
ELSEWH...... Elsewhere [*Manuscripts*] (ROG)
ELSG............ Executive Level Steering Group (SAUO)
El Sgndo...... El Segundo (SAUS)
ELSH............ Extended Length Super HIPPO [*High Internal Pressure Producing Orifice*] (MCD)
ELSI............ Ecological Life Systems Institute [*San Diego, CA*] (CROSS)
ELSI............ Electronic Licensing & Security Initiative (ITCA)
ELSI............ Electrosource, Inc. [*NASDAQ symbol*] (NQ)
ELSI............ Ethical, Legal and Social Implications [*Genetic research*]
ELSI............ Ethical, Legal, and Social Issues (HGEN)
ELSI............ Extra Large Scale Integrated (SAUS)
ELSI............ Extra-Large-Scale Integration [*Computer science*] (TEL)
ELSI............ Extremely Large Scale Integration (VLIE)
ELSIE............ Edmond's Learning Style Identification Exercise (EDAC)
ELSIE............ Electronic Letter Sorting and Indicating Equipment (SAUS)
ELSIE............ Electronic Letter Sorting and Indicator Equipment
elsie............ electronic letter-sorting and indicator equipment (SAUS)

ELSIE .... Electronic Location and Status Indicating Equipment (IAA)
ELSIE .... Electronic Signaling and Indicating Equipment (IEEE)
elsie .... electronic signalling and indicating equipment (SAUS)
ELSIE .... Electronic Speech Information Equipment [*System developed by Britain's Department of Transport to facilitate bus transit*]
ELSIE .... Emergency Life-Saving Instant Exit [*Aircraft*] [*Air Force*]
Elsinor .... Elsinore Corp. [*Associated Press*] (SAG)
ELSJC .... Elsmere Junction, DE [*American Association of Railroads railroad junction routing code*]
El S L .... Electrical Sub-Lieutenant (SAUS)
ELSO .... El Nino-Southern Oscillation [*Experiment*]
ELSO .... Extracorporeal Life Support Organization (SAUS)
ELSOR .... Education Libraries Sharing of Resources [*Network*]
ELSOR .... Education Libraries Sharing of Resources Network (SAUS)
ELSP .... Economic Lot Scheduling Problem
ELSPA .... European Leisure Software Publishers' Association (WDAA)
ELSPECS .... Electronic Components Specification Database (SAUS)
ELSPECS .... Electronic Specifications [*Databank of specifications issued by national agencies*] (NITA)
EL-SPT .... Electrolytes on Urine Spot [*Test*] [*Biochemistry*] (DAVI)
ELSS .... Electronic Legislative Information System (SAUS)
ELSS .... Electronic Legislative Search System [*Commerce Clearing House, Inc.*] [*Information service or system*]
ELSS .... Electronic Legislative System (SAUS)
ELSS .... Emergency Life Support System
ELSS .... Emplaced Lunar Scientific Station [*Aerospace*]
ELSS .... Emplaced Search Lunar Scientific Station (SAUS)
EISs .... Environmental impact statements (SAUS)
ELSS .... Environmental, Life, and Social Sciences (SAUS)
ELSS .... Environmental Life-Support System (MCD)
ELSS .... EVA [*Extravehicular Activity*] Life-Support System [*NASA*]
ELSS .... Extravehicular Life Support System (ACAE)
EL-SSC .... Electronic Switching System Control [*Telecommunications*] (TEL)
ELSSE .... Electronic Sky Screen Equipment [*Air Force*]
ELSSOC .... EL Salvador Solidarity Campaign [*British*]
ELSSS .... Electronic Society for Social Scientists
ELST .... Endolymphatic Sac Tumors [*Oncology*]
ELST .... Extra-Long Staple (SAUS)
ELSTPT .... Electrostatic Print (VRA)
ELSUR .... Electronic Surveillance Index [*FBI file of persons overheard on wiretaps*]
ELSW .... Elsewhere (FAAC)
Els W Bl .... Elsley's Edition of William Blackstone's English King's Bench Reports [*A publication*] (DLA)
ELSWITCH .... Electronic Switching (SAUS)
Elswth .... Elsworth Convertible Growth & Income Fund, Inc. [*Associated Press*] (SAG)
Elsyn Parl .... Elsynge on Parliaments [*A publication*] (DLA)
ELT .... Each Less Than
ELT .... Eagle's Law of Tithes [*2nd ed.*] [*1836*] [*A publication*] (ILCA)
ELT .... East London Telecommunications [*Commercial firm*] [*British*]
ELT .... Electrocardiography and Basal Metabolism Technician [*Navy*]
ELT .... Electrometer (DEN)
ELT .... Electronic Level Transducer (SAUS)
ELT .... Electronic Light Table (SAUS)
ELT .... Electronic Locator Transmitter (VLIE)
ELT .... Electronic Technician
elt .... Element (ELAL)
ELT .... Element
ELT .... Elliott Aviation, Inc. [*FAA designator*] (FAAC)
ELT .... Elliott Beechcraft of Omaha, Inc. [*ICAO designator*] (FAAC)
ELT .... Elscint Ltd. [*NYSE symbol*] (SPSG)
ELT .... Eltsovka [*Former USSR*] [*Seismograph station code, US Geological Survey*] (SEIS)
ELT .... Emergency Location Transmitter (SAUS)
ELT .... Emergency Locator Transmitter
ELT .... Emission Limitations (OTD)
ELT .... Endoscopic LASER Therapy [*Medicine*]
ELT .... Enforcement of Laws and Treaties [*Program*] [*Coast Guard*]
ELT .... Engineering Laboratory Technician
E Lt .... Engineer Lieutenant (SAUS)
ELT .... English Language Teaching
ELT .... English Literature in Transition 1880-1920 [*A publication*] (BRI)
ELT .... Entry Level Training
ELT .... Environmental Team Leader [*Nuclear energy*] (NRCH)
ELT .... Euglobulin Lysis Test [*Medicine*] (MELL)
ELT .... Euglobulin Lysis Time [*Clinical chemistry*]
ELT .... European Letter Telegram
ELT .... Extended Lapped Transform [*Telecommunications*]
ELT .... Extended Long Tank (MCD)
ELT .... Extremely Large Telescope (SAUS)
ELTA .... EHF Lightweight Transportable Antenna (SAUS)
ELTA .... English Lawn Tennis Association (SAUO)
ELTA .... European Learning Technology Association (AIE)
ELTAD .... Emergency Locator Transmitter Automatic Deployable [*Navigation*] (OA)
ELTAF .... Emergency Location Transmitter, Automatic Fixed (SAUS)
ELTAP .... Emergency Locator Transmitter Automatic Portable [*Navigation*] (OA)
ELTC .... Electric (SAUS)
ELTC .... Enlisted Loss to Commissioned Status [*Military*]
ELTC .... European Lubricant Testing Committee
E Lt-Cdr .... Engineer Lieutenant-Commander (SAUS)
Elt Com .... Elton on Commons and Waste Lands [*A publication*] (DLA)
Elt Copyh .... Elton on Copyholds [*A publication*] (DLA)
ELTD .... Engineering Level Test Document (ACAE)
ELTD .... English Language Test Design (ACAE)
ELTD .... Eurobike Limited (EA)
ELTDA .... English Language Teaching Development Aid (SAUS)
ELTE .... Elegant Tern [*North American bird banding code*] (BIBA)
eltec .... electrical technician (SAUS)
ELTEC .... Electronics Technician (NOAA)
eltec .... electronic technician (SAUS)
Eltec .... Electronic Technology [*Automotive engineering*]
ELTEC .... ELINT [*Electronic Intelligence*], Technical (MCD)
ELTEX .... Electronic Telex Exchange (SAUS)
ELTEX .... Electronic Time-Division Telex Exchange (SAUS)
ELTG .... European Logistics Task Group (MCD)
ELTHE .... Evaluation of Learning Technology in Higher Education (SAUS)
ELTI .... Elapsed-Time Indicator (MCD)
ELTI .... English Language Teaching Institute (SAUS)
ELTIC .... English Language Teaching In Cameroon (SAUS)
ELTIS .... European Local Transport Information (EURO)
ELTLV .... English League for the Taxation of Land Values (SAUO)
ELTN .... Eltron International, Inc. [*NASDAQ symbol*] (SAG)
ELTN .... Eltron Intl. [*NASDAQ symbol*] (TTSB)
Elton Com .... Elton on Commons and Waste Lands [*A publication*] (DLA)
Elton Copyh .... Elton on Copyholds [*A publication*] (DLA)
ELTOS .... English Language Teaching Orientation Seminar (SAUO)
ELTP .... English Language Test Program (ACAE)
ELTP .... English Language Training Program (SAUO)
ELTR .... Elegant Trogon [*North American bird banding code*] (BIBA)
ELTR .... Emergency Locator Transmitter Receiver
Eltrax .... Eltrax System, Inc. [*Associated Press*] (SAG)
ELTRC .... Electric (IAA)
ELTRN .... Electron [*A nuclear particle*]
ELTRNC .... Electronic
Eltron .... Eltron International, Inc. [*Associated Press*] (SAG)
ELTS .... Emergency Locator Transmitters (SAUS)
ELTSA .... End Loans to Southern Africa [*An association*] (EAIO)
ELT Signal .... Emergency-Load-Transfer Signal (SAUS)
Elt Ten of Kent .... Elton's Tenures of Kent [*A publication*] (DLA)
ELTV .... Ejection Launch Test Vehicle (NG)
ELTW .... Enlisted Loss to Warrant Status [*Military*]
ELTX .... Eltrax Sys [*NASDAQ symbol*] (TTSB)
ELTX .... Eltrax Systems, Inc. [*NASDAQ symbol*] (SAG)
ELTX .... Solvay Polymers [*Federal Railroad Administration identification code*]
ELU .... El Oued [*Algeria*] [*Airport symbol*] (OAG)
ELU .... English Lacrosse Union (BI)
ELU .... Environmental Load Unit [*Recycling, emissions*] [*Automotive engineering*]
ELU .... Existing Carrier Line-Up (SAUS)
ELU .... Extension Lay Volunteers (SAUO)
e-lu- .... Luxembourg [*MARC geographic area code*] [*Library of Congress*] (LCCP)
elut .... Elutriation (SAUS)
El Util .... Electric Utilities (SAUS)
ELUX .... Electrolux AB [*NASDAQ symbol*] (NQ)
EluxAB .... Electrolux AB [*Associated Press*] (SAG)
ELUXY .... Electrolux AB Cl'B'ADR [*NASDAQ symbol*] (TTSB)
ELV .... Earth Launch Vehicle [*NASA*]
ELV .... Edit-Level Video (NTCM)
ELV .... Efferent Lymphatic Vessel [*Medicine*] (MELL)
ELV .... Electrically Operated Valve
elv .... Elevation (VRA)
ELV .... Elfin Cove [*Alaska*] [*Airport symbol*] (OAG)
ELV .... Elfin Cove, AK [*Location identifier*] [*FAA*] (FAAL)
ELV .... Enclosed-Frame Low Voltage (IEEE)
ELV .... Erythroid Leukemia-Inducing Virus [*Medicine*] (DB)
ELV .... Expandable Launch Vehicle (SAUS)
ELV .... Expendable Launch Vehicle [*NASA*] (KSC)
ELV .... Experimental Launch Vehicle (SAUS)
ELV .... Extension Lay Volunteers (EA)
ELV .... Extra-Low Voltage
ELVA .... Elle Va [*She Goes*] [*Racing car*] [*French*]
ELVA .... Emergency Low Visibility Approach (COE)
ELVAC .... Electric Furnace Melting, Ladle Refining, Vacuum Degassing and Continuous Casting (SAUS)
el vent .... Electrically Ventilated (SAUS)
ELVES .... Emissions of Light and Very Low Frequency Perturbations Due to Electromagnetic Pulse Sources
ELVIL .... European Legislative Virtual Library (TELE)
ELVIRA .... Electronic Library and Visual Information Research project (SAUS)
ELVIS .... Electroluminescent Vertical Indication System
ELVIS .... Electromagnetic Very weak Instabilities Saturated (SAUS)
ELVIS .... Electrovisual System (MUGU)
ELVIS .... Esco-laser-Vision und Videotex-Informations- System (SAUS)
ELVIS .... Expanding Linear Visualization Information Structure (VLIE)
ELVIS .... Export Licensing Voice Information System (SAUS)
ElvisNet EPFC .... Elvisnet Elvis Presley Fan Club (EA)
ELVN .... Eleven (NASA)
ELW .... Anderson, SC [*Location identifier*] [*FAA*] (FAAL)
ELW .... Earth Launch Window [*Aerospace*] (AAG)
ELW .... Electric Weld (IAA)
ELW .... Electronic Warfare (CAAL)
ELW .... Enhanced Land Warrior [*Military*] (RDA)
ELW .... Extended Linked Well (SAUS)
ELW .... Extreme Low Water
ELW .... Webster College, Eden Theological Seminary, Webster Groves, MO [*OCLC symbol*] (OCLC)
ELWAR .... Electronic Warfare

ELWCR .... Erodible Land and Wetland Conservation and Reserve Program (COE)
ELWCY .... Ellwood City, PA [*American Association of Railroads railroad junction routing code*]
ELWD .... Extra-Long Working Distance [*Microscopy*]
elwh .... elsewhere (SAUS)
ELWIU .... Essays in Literature [*A publication*] (ANEX)
ELWK .... Equivalent Live Weight Killed (EEVL)
El Wld .... Electrical World (SAUS)
Elw Mal .... Elwell on Malpractice and Medical Jurisprudence [*A publication*] (DLA)
Elw Med Jur... Elwell on Malpractice and Medical Jurisprudence [*A publication*] (DLA)
elws .... extreme-low-water-level spring tides (SAUS)
ELWS .... Extreme Low Water of Spring Tide
ELWTH .... Ellsworth, KS [*American Association of Railroads railroad junction routing code*]
ELWW .... European Laboratory without Walls (EURO)
elx .... Elamite [*MARC language code*] [*Library of Congress*] (LCCP)
ELX .... Exol Industries Ltd. [*Vancouver Stock Exchange symbol*]
ELX .... Keeler, MI [*Location identifier*] [*FAA*] (FAAL)
elxr .... elixir (SAUS)
ELXS .... ELXSI Corp. [*NASDAQ symbol*] (NQ)
ELXSI .... ELXSI Corp. [*Associated Press*] (SAG)
ELXT .... Elbow Extension [*Sports medicine*]
ELY .... Callaway Golf Co. [*NYSE symbol*] (SAG)
ELY .... Easterly
ELY .... El Al-Israel Airlines Ltd. [*ICAO designator*] (FAAC)
ELY .... Ely [*Nevada*] [*Airport symbol*] (OAG)
ELY .... Ely [*Nevada*] [*Seismograph station code, US Geological Survey*] [*Closed*] (SEIS)
ELY .... Ely, NV [*Location identifier*] [*FAA*] (FAAL)
ELYC .... East Lothian Yeomanry Cavalry [*British military*] (DMA)
ELYRA .... Elyria, OH [*American Association of Railroads railroad junction routing code*]
ELZ .... Elazig [*Turkey*] [*Seismograph station code, US Geological Survey*] (SEIS)
ELZ .... Elizabethtown College, Elizabethtown, PA [*OCLC symbol*] (OCLC)
ELZ .... Elzevir [*Elsevier*] [*Published by the Elsevier family*] (ROG)
ELZ .... Environmental Living Zone (SAUS)
ELZ .... Extensive Landuse Zone [*Australia*] (EERA)
ELZ .... Wellsville, NY [*Location identifier*] [*FAA*] (FAAL)
ELZC .... Emergency Lead-Zinc Committee [*Later, Lead-Zinc Producers Committee*] (EA)
ELZTN .... Elizabethtown, KY [*American Association of Railroads railroad junction routing code*]
EM .... Die Evangelischen Missionen (BJA)
EM .... DOE Office of the Assistant Secretary for Environmental Management (SAUS)
EM .... Earl Marshal [*British*]
EM .... Early Melanoma [*Medicine*] (MELL)
EM .... Early Memory [*Medicine*] (EDAA)
EM .... Early Midcourse (ACAE)
EM .... Early Minoan [*Archeology*] (BJA)
EM .... Earth Mass
EM .... Eastern Mediterranean (SAUS)
EM .... Eastern Megalopolis [*Proposed name for possible "super-city" formed by growth and mergers of other cities*]
EM .... East Mark [*Monetary unit*] [*Germany*]
EM .... East Midlands [*England*]
EM .... Easton Minerals [*Vancouver Stock Exchange symbol*]
EM .... Ebony Man [*Johnson Publishing Co., Inc.*] [*A publication*]
EM .... Economical Methods [*A line of Varian spectrometers*]
EM .... Edge Medium [*Automotive engineering*]
EM .... Edgmoor & Manetta Railway [*AAR code*]
EM .... Educational Marketer [*A publication*]
EM .... Education Manual [*Military*]
EM .... Edward Medal [*British*]
em .... effciency modulation (SAUS)
EM .... Effective Mass (ODA)
EM .... Effective Modulus (SAUS)
EM .... Efficience Medal (SAUS)
EM .... Efficiency Medal
EM .... Efficiency Modulation
EM .... Egyptian Mysteries [*Freemasonry*] (ROG)
EM .... Ejection Murmur [*Cardiology*]
EM .... Elastic Membrane [*Medicine*] (EDAA)
EM .... Elastic Modulus (SAUS)
EM .... Elective Masonry [*Freemasonry*] (ROG)
EM .... Electrical and Mechanical (ODA)
EM .... Electrical Mechanic (SAUS)
e/m .... Electric Charge to Mass (IEEE)
EM .... Electrician's Mate [*Navy rating*]
EM .... Electric Machinery (SAUS)
EM .... Electric Memory (SAUS)
EM .... Electric Mirrors [*Automotive classified advertising*]
EM .... Electric Motors (MCD)
EM .... Electrodeposition Memo
EM .... Electrolytic Meter (SAUS)
EM .... Electromagnetic (TIMI)
EM .... Electromagnetic Conductivity (SAUS)
EM .... Electromagnetic Memory (SAUS)
EM .... Electromagnetic Radiation (SAUS)
EM .... Electromagnetism (SAUS)
EM .... Electromechanical
EM .... Electromechanic Memory (SAUS)
EM .... Electromechanics (SAUS)
EM .... Electrometallurgist (SAUS)
EM .... Electrometallurgy (SAUS)
EM .... Electrometer (SAUS)
EM .... Electrometric (SAUS)
EM .... Electromicroscopic [*or Electromicroscopy*]
EM .... Electromigration
EM .... Electromotive (VLIE)
EM .... Electro-Motive Corporation (SAUO)
EM .... Electromotor (SAUS)
e/m .... electron charge/electron mass ratio (SAUS)
EM .... Electronic Countermeasures Malfunction [*Military*] (IAA)
EM .... Electronic Magnetic Slip Couplings (DS)
EM .... Electronic Mail [*Telecommunications*]
E/M .... Electronic Measurements (SAUS)
EM .... Electronic Measurement (IAA)
EM .... Electronic Memory (SAUS)
EM .... Electronic Multiplier (SAUS)
EM .... Electronics Manufacturing Group (SAUO)
EM .... Electron Micrograph (DB)
EM .... Electron Microprobe
EM .... Electron Microscope
EM .... Electron Microscopy [*Medicine*] (MELL)
EM .... Electron Multiplier (SAUS)
EM .... Electrophoretic Mobility [*Analytical biochemistry*]
EM .... Electrostatic Memory (SAUS)
EM .... Elemental Metal (UWER)
EM .... Elevation Model (NRCH)
EM .... Elicotteri Meridionali SpA (SAUS)
EM .... Emanation (ADA)
EM .... Embargo (ADA)
E-M .... Embden-Meyerhof [*Glycolytic pathway*] [*Biochemistry*]
em .... emendavit (SAUS)
EM .... E. Merck [*Laboratories*]
Em .... Emergence [*Biology*]
EM .... Emergency (NASA)
EM .... Emergency Maintenance (BUR)
EM .... Emergency Management
EM .... Emergency Manning [*Nautical term*] (NTA)
EM .... Emergency Medicine [*Medical specialty*] (DHSM)
EM .... Emergency Message (CINC)
em .... emergency mobilizalion (SAUS)
EM .... Emergency Mobilization (SAUS)
em .... Emeritus [*Obtain by Service*] [*Latin*]
EM .... Eminence
EM .... Eminent (ROG)
em .... Emirates (BEE)
EM .... Emission
EM .... Emission Measure (ODA)
EM .... Emission Monochromator [*Spectroscopy*]
EM .... Emission Pump (SAUS)
EM .... Emitter (MSA)
Em .... Emmetropia [*Eye Examination*] [*Medicine*] (EDAA)
EM .... Emmetropia [*Also, E*] [*Ophthalmology*]
EM .... Emotionally Disturbed
EM .... Emphasized (VLIE)
EM .... Empire Airlines [*ICAO designator*] (AD)
EM .... Empirical Mathematics (ECON)
EM .... Emulated Machine (VLIE)
Em .... Emulsion (SAUS)
EM .... Encoder Matrix (SAUS)
EM .... End Matched
EM .... end-member (SAUS)
EM .... End of Media (SAUS)
EM .... End of Medium [*Computer science*]
em .... end of medium character (SAUS)
EM .... End of Message [*Computer science*] (IAA)
EM .... Endosteal Marrow [*Hematology*]
EM .... Endothelial Medium [*Anatomy*] (UWER)
EM .... Energy Management
EM .... Energy Maneuverability (MCD)
EM .... Energy Meter (UWER)
EM .... Energy Method (UWER)
EM .... Energy Module (SPST)
EM .... Engineered Magnetics Inc. (SAUS)
EM .... Engineering Management (MCD)
EM .... Engineering Manual (IEEE)
EM .... Engineering Manufacture (UWER)
EM .... Engineering Material (SAUS)
EM .... Engineering Mathematics (UWER)
EM .... Engineering Mechanician
EM .... engineering mechanics (SAUS)
EM .... Engineering Memorandum
EM .... Engineering Metrology (UWER)
EM .... Engineering Model
EM .... Engineering Module (NASA)
EM .... Engineering of Mines (SAUS)
EM .... Engineer Manager
EM .... Engineer Manual [*Army Corps of Engineers*]
EM .... Engineer of Mines [*or Mining*]
EM .... Engineer of Mining (SAUS)
EM .... Engine Maintenance
EM .... Engine Modification [*Automotive engineering*]
EM .... English Market

EM English Marquess (ROG)
E/M English/Metric
EM Engraving Master (MCD)
EM Enhanced Monitoring [*Environmental Protection Agency*]
EM Enhanced Mutagenesis [*Genetics*] (ODA)
EM Enlisted Man [*or Men*]
EM Enlisted Member (AABC)
EM Enlisted Men (SAUS)
EM Enriched Mantle [*Geology*]
EM Enterprise Model (AAEL)
EM Entertainment Marketing (EFIS)
EM Entity Module [*Computer science*]
EM Entsiqlopedia Miqra'it-Encyclopaedia Biblica [*Jerusalem*] [*A publication*] (BJA)
EM Environmental Management (NRCH)
EM Environmental Measurements Laboratory (SAUO)
EM Environmental Modelling (ODA)
EM Environmental Monitoring
EM Environmental Restoration and Waste Management (EGAO)
EM Environment Management (SAUS)
EM Environment Matters [*A publication*]
EM Enzyme Mechanism (SAUS)
EM Ephemerides Mariologicae (BJA)
EM Epigraphical Museum [*Epigraphic notation*]
EM Episcopus et Martyr [*Bishop and Martyr*] [*Latin*]
EM Epitaxial Mesa
EM Equimomental (SAUS)
EM Equine Morbillivirus [*Veternary medicine*]
EM Equipment Maintenance and Performance Reporting System (SAUS)
EM Equipment Management (MCD)
EM Equitum Magister [*Master of the Horse*] [*British*]
EM Erasable Memory [*Computer science*] (KSC)
EM Ergonovine Maleate [*Medicine*] (EDAA)
EM Error Message (SAUS)
EM Error Multiplier
EM Erthrocyte Mass [*Hematology*] (CPH)
EM Erythema Migrans [*Medicine*] (MELL)
EM Erythema Multiforme [*Hematology*] (CPH)
EM Erythrocyte Mass [*Hematology*] (MAE)
EM Erythromycin (DB)
EM Escape Motor
EM Esophageal Manometry/Motility [*Medicine*] (EDAA)
EM espaces morts (SAUS)
EM Estimated Man Hours (DNAB)
EM Estramustine (DB)
E-M Etat-Major [*Headquarters*] [*French military*]
EM Ethoxylated Monoglyceride (OA)
EM Etna & Montrose R. R. [*AAR code*]
EM Euromissile (ACAE)
EM European Movement
EM Evaluation Missile (ACAE)
EM Evaluation Model (NRCH)
EM Evangelist and Martyr [*Church calendars*]
EM Evans Medical Ltd. [*Great Britain*] [*Research code symbol*]
EM Event Management (SAUS)
EM event manager (SAUS)
EM Evergreen Marine Corp. [*Taiwan*]
EM Exact Match (IAA)
Em exameter (SAUS)
EM Excellent Masons [*Freemasonry*] (ROG)
EM Exception Monitor (NASA)
EM Excerpta Medica Foundation [*Database producer*]
EM Executive Memorandum
EM Exerpta Medica (SAUO)
EM Expanded Memory (SAUS)
EM Expanded Memory Manager (BYTE)
EM Expanded Metal
EM Expectation Maximization [*Statistics*]
EM Experimental Memo
EM Experimental Model (SAUS)
EM Explanatory Memorandum
EM explicit microphysics (SAUS)
EM Export Monthly Data [*Department of Commerce*] (GFGA)
EM Exposure Meter (IAA)
EM Extended Memory [*Computer science*] (ELAL)
EM Extensible Machine (PDAA)
EM Extensions Manager [*Apple*] (VERA)
EM Extensive Metabolizer (DB)
EM External Memorandum
EM External Memory (SAUS)
EM External Monitor [*Obstetrics*] (DAVI)
EM External Monitoring (SAUS)
EM Extracellular Matrix [*Medicine*] (MELL)
EM Extractive Metallurgist (SAUS)
EM Extractive Metallurgy (SAUS)
EM Extra Milers [*Later, EMC*] (EA)
EM Extra-Mural (AIE)
EM Extraordinary Maintenance (SAUO)
EM Eye Movement (SAUS)
EM Hammond's Air Service [*ICAO designator*] (AD)
EM Heli-Air-Monaco [*Monaco*] [*ICAO designator*] (ICDA)
E_m Maximum Junction Field (IDOE)
E_m Maximum Voltage (IDOE)
EM Mining Engineer (PGP)
EM Office of Environmental Management (SAUS)
EM Office of Environmental Restoration and Waste Management (SAUO)
e/m Ratio of Charge to Mass [*Physics*] (DAVI)
EM1 Electrician's Mate, First Class [*Navy rating*]
Em2 Brasilia [*Airplane code*]
EM2 Electrician's Mate, Second Class [*Navy rating*]
EM3 Electrician's Mate, Third Class [*Navy rating*]
EM-4 Office of Policy and Program Information within EM (SAUO)
EM-10 Office of Planning and Resource Management witnin EM (SAUO)
EM-40 Office of Environmental Restoration within EM (SAUO)
EM-50 Office of Technology Development within EM (SAUO)
EM-60 Office of Facility Transition and Management (SAUO)
EMA East Midlands [*England*] [*Airport symbol*] (OAG)
EMA East Midlands Airport [*England*]
EMA Easy Magnetization Axis (AAEL)
EMA Educational Maintenance Allowances (SAUS)
EMA Effective Mass Approximation
EMA Effective Mechanical Advantage [*Bone-muscle physiology*]
EMA Effective Medium Approximation (SAUS)
EMA Egyptian Aviation Co. [*ICAO designator*] (FAAC)
EMA Egyptian Moslem Association [*Australia*]
EM(A) Electrical Mechanic (Air) [*British military*] (DMA)
EMA Electrodynamics of the Middle Atmosphere (SAUS)
EMA Electromagnetic Accelerometer [*Navigation*]
EMA Electromagnetic-Acoustic Transducer (SAUS)
EMA Electromagnetic Analysis (NASA)
EMA Electromagnetic Armour (SAUS)
EMA Electromantle
EMA Electro-Mechanical Actuator (SAUS)
EMA Electronic Mail Association (EA)
EMA Electronic Maintenance Assembly
EMA Electronic-Making Apparatus (IAA)
EMA Electronic Manufacturers Association (SAUS)
EMA Electronic Mathematic Automation (IAA)
EMA Electronic Measuring Apparatus (IAA)
EMA Electronic Messaging Association (VERA)
EMA Electronic Microanalyzer (DB)
EMA Electronic Missile Acquisition
EMA Electronics Manufacturers Association [*Defunct*] (EA)
EMA Electronics Materiel Agency [*Army*]
EMA Electron Microprobe Analyzer [*Also, EMPA*]
EMA Elephant Managers Association (GVA)
EMA Elm [*Alabama*] [*Seismograph station code, US Geological Survey*] (SEIS)
EMA eMagin Corp. [*AMEX symbol*] (SG)
EMA Emergency Assistance [*Medicine*] (DAVI)
EMA Emergency Assistant [*Medicine*] (DAVI)
EMA Emergency Management Agency
EMA Emergency Management Assistance [*Federal Emergency Management Agency*] (GFGA)
EMA Emergency Management Australia (SAUO)
EMA Emergency Medicine Assembly (ADWA)
EMA Emergency Minerals Administration [*Department of the Interior*]
EMA Emergency Movements Atomic [*Military*] (AABC)
EMA Employment Management Association (EA)
EMA Employment Medical Adviser (HEAS)
EMA Energy Managers' Association [*Australia*]
EMA Engineered Materials Abstracts [*Materials Information*] [*Information service or system*] [*A publication*]
EMA Engineering Methods Analysis (MCD)
EMA Engineers' and Managers' Association [*A union*] [*British*] (DCTA)
EMA Engine Maintenance Area (AAG)
EMA Engine Manufacturers Association (EA)
EMA Engine Manufacturing Association (SAUO)
EMA English Men of Action [*A publication*]
EMA Enrollment Management and Administration (SAUS)
EMA Entering Markets Abroad (SAUS)
EMA Enterprise Management Architecture [*Computer science*] (TNIG)
EMA Enterprise Marketing Automation (HODG)
EMA Entertainment Managers Association of Great Britain and Ireland (SAUO)
EMA Envelope Manufacturers Association [*Later, EMAA*] (EA)
EMA Environmental Management Agency (SAUS)
EMA Environmental Management Association (EA)
EMA Environmental Media Association (SAUO)
EMA Environmental Mediation Association (SAUO)
EMA Environmental Protection Agency, Region VI Library, Dallas, TX [*OCLC symbol*] (OCLC)
EMA Epithelial Membrane Antigen [*Immunology*]
EMA Equal Mental Age [*Psychometrics*]
EMA Equipment Maintenance Agreement
EMA Equipment Market Abstracts [*Predicast Inc.*] [*Database*] (NITA)
EMA Equity Market Analysis [*MMS International*] [*Information service or system*] (CRD)
EMA Essential Maintenance Action (MCD)
EMA Ethopian Mapping Authority (SAUS)
EMA Ethylene-Maleic Anhydride [*Copolymer*] [*Organic chemistry*]
EMA Ethylene-Methacrylate Copolymer (EDCT)
EMA Ethylene Methyl Acetate [*Plastic technology*]
EMA Ethylene Methyl Acrylate [*Photovoltaic energy systems*]
EMA Ethyl Methacrylate [*Organic chemistry*]
EMA European Maritime Area (SAUS)
EMA European Marketing Association [*Brixham, Devonshire, England*] (EA)
EMA European Monetary Agreement
EMA European Motorcycle Association [*Defunct*] (EA)

EMA............ Evangelical Missionary Alliance [*British*]
EMA............ Evaporated Milk Association (EA)
EMA............ Excellence in Mining Award (SAUO)
EMA............ Exchequer Master's Associate [*British*] (ROG)
EMA............ Expediting Management Association (EA)
EMA............ Exposition Management Association (EA)
EMA............ Extended Memory Addressing (SAUS)
EMA............ extended memory area (SAUS)
EMA............ Extended Mercury Autocode (SAUS)
EMA............ Extended Mercury Autocoder (IEEE)
EMA............ Extended Mission Apollo [*NASA*]
EMA............ Externally Mounted Assembly
EMA............ External Mounting Assembly (SAUS)
EMA............ Extra Memory Adapter (SAUS)
EMA............ Extra Mileage Allowance [*Travel industry*] (TRID)
EMA............ Extramural Absorption [*Fiber optics*]
EMA............ Society for Human Resource Management/Employment Management Association (NTPA)
EMAA.......... Engineering Materials Achievement Award (SAUS)
EMAA.......... Envelope Manufacturers Association of America (EA)
EMAA.......... Ethylene Methacrylic Acid [*Organic chemistry*]
EMAA.......... European Mastic Asphalt Association (EA)
EMABC........ Electronics Manufacturers Association of British Columbia (SAUO)
EMABIC....... Emission/Absorption Inversion Codes (MCD)
EMAC.......... Ecole Afrioaine de la Meterologie et de d'Aviation Civile [*East African School of Meteorology and Civil Aviation*] [*Republic of Niger*] (PDAA)
EMAC.......... Educational Media Association of Canada
EMAC.......... Electromechanical Averaging Circuit
EMAC.......... Electronics Manufacturers Association of Canada (SAUO)
EMAC.......... Emergency Management Advisory Committee [*Environmental science*] (COE)
EMAC.......... Environmental Restoration and Waste Management Advisory Committee [*Department of Energy*] (EGAO)
EMAC.......... Equipment Maintenance and Control [*Online database*]
EMAC.......... Ethylene-Methyl Acrylate Copolymer (SAUS)
EMAC.......... European and Mediterranean Association of Coloproctology (EAIO)
EMAC.......... European Market Awareness and Education Committee (SAUO)
EMAC.......... European Marketing Academy (EAIO)
EMAC.......... European Music and Audiovisual Center (SAUO)
EMAC.......... Examination for Master Addictions Counselors (SAUS)
EMAC.......... Exercise-Associated Muscle Cramping
EMAC-94/95... European Multisensor Airborne Campaign-94/95 (SAUS)
EMACC........ Energy Materials Coordinating Committee (SAUO)
E MacD........ Edward MacDowell (SAUS)
EMA-CE........ Etoposide, Methotrexate, Actinomycin D (Dactinomycin), and Citrovorum Factor [*Medicine*] (EDAA)
EMA Coating... Extramural Absorption Coating (SAUS)
EMACS......... Editing Macros [*Computer science*] (NHD)
EMACS......... Editor MACroS (SAUS)
EMACS......... Eight Megabytes And Constantly Swapping (SAUS)
EMACS......... Engine Monitoring and Control System
E-MAD......... Engineer-Maintenance Assembly-Disassembly [*NERVA program*]
EMAD.......... Engine Maintenance Assembly and Disassembly (GAAI)
EMAD.......... Engine Maintenance Assembly and Disassembly Facility (SAUS)
EMAD.......... Engine Modification and Disassembly (SAUS)
EMAD.......... Equatorial Middle Atmosphere Dynamics (SAUS)
EMAD.......... European Marketing and Advertising Agencies (SAUO)
EMAE.......... Electrical and Mechanical Assistant Engineer [*British military*] (DMA)
EMag.......... Electricity and Magnetism (SAUS)
EMAG.......... Electron Microscopy and Analysis Group (SAUO)
E Mag.......... E Magazine [*A publication*] (BRI)
EMAG.......... Ethnic Minorities Action Group [*Australia*]
EMAI........... Elizabeth Macarthur Agricultural Institute [*Australia*]
EMAIG......... East Midlands Agricultural Information Group (SAUO)
E-MAIL......... Electronic Mail (EEVL)
e-mail.......... Electronic Mail [*Computer science*]
email........... Electronic Mail [*Internet language*] [*Computer science*]
E-MAIL......... Electronic-Mail (AGLO)
E-mail.......... Electronic mail [*Computer science*] (EERA)
EMAIL.......... Electronic Mail (TNIG)
E-MAIL......... EPAs Electronic Mail System (SAUS)
EMAK.......... Equity Marketing [*NASDAQ symbol*] (TTSB)
EMAK.......... Equity Marketing, Inc. [*NASDAQ symbol*] (SAG)
EMAL.......... Electron Microbeam Analysis Laboratory (SAUS)
EMALS......... Electro-Magnetic Aircraft Launch System (SAUS)
EMALS......... Electromagnetic Air Launch System
EM/AM......... Emergency Message - Alert Message (CINC)
EMAN.......... Ecological Monitoring and Assessment Network [*Canada*] (QUAC)
EMAN.......... Economy Car, Manual Transmission (TVEL)
EMAN.......... Economy Car with Manual Transmission (TRID)
Eman.......... Emanation [*Medicine*] (EDAA)
EM & C........ Engelhard Minerals & Chemicals Corp. [*Later, Engelhard Corp.*]
EM&CD........ Environmental Monitoring and Compliance Department (SAUS)
EM&M......... Electronics Memories and Magnetics Corp. (SAUO)
EM&MM....... Encyclopedia of Millennialism and Millenial Movements [*A publication*]
EM & R........ Equipment Maintenance and Readiness (SAUS)
EM & S........ Equipment Maintenance and Support (MHDB)
EMANI......... Electronic Mathematics Archiving Network Initiative [*Springer-Verlag*]
EMANJ......... Educational Media Association of New Jersey
EMAnj......... Educational Media Association of New Jersey
EMAP.......... East Midlands Allied Press [*British*] (DI)
EMAP.......... Electromagnetic Array Profiling (SAUS)
EMAP.......... Encyclopedia of Minorities in American Politics [*A publication*]
EMAP.......... Environmental Mapping and Assessment Program (SAUO)
EMAP.......... Environmental Monitoring and Analysis Program (SAUS)
EMAP.......... Environmental Monitoring and Assessment Program [*Environmental Protection Agency*]
EMAP.......... Evoked Muscle Action Potential [*Neurophysiology*]
EMAP.......... Export Marketing Assistance Program [*Australia*]
Em App........ Emergency Court of Appeals [*United States*] (DLA)
EMAR.......... Experimental Memory - Address Register
EMARL......... Edit Master and Activity Review List (MCD)
EMARS......... Energy Mineral Activity Recommendation System (SAUO)
EMAS.......... Eco-Management Audit Scheme (ACII)
EMAS.......... Edinburgh Modular Arm System
EMAS.......... Edinburgh Multiaccess System (HGAA)
EMAS.......... Electro-Acoustic Music Association of Great Britain (EAIO)
EMAS.......... Electromagnetic Acoustic System (SAUS)
EMAS.......... Electro-Magnetic Armament System (SAUS)
EMAS.......... Emergency Medical Advisory Service (SAUO)
EMAS.......... Emergency Message Action System (SAUS)
EMAS.......... Emergency Message Authentication System [*USEUCOM*] (AABC)
EMAS.......... Employment Medical Advisory Service [*Department of Employment*] [*British*]
EMAS.......... Enforcement Management and Accountability System [*Environmental Protection Agency*] (GFGA)
EMAS.......... Engine Management and Analysis System [*Automotive engineering*]
EMAS.......... Environmental Management Audit Scheme (SAUS)
EMAS.......... Equipment Marking Accounting System (SAUS)
EMAS.......... Exercise Message Analysis System (SAUS)
EMASA......... Electrical Manufacturers' Association of South Australia
EMASAR....... Ecological Management of Arid and Semi Arid Rangelands (EERA)
EMASAR....... Ecological Management of Semi-Arid Rangelands in Africa, the Near East and Middle East (SAUO)
EMASHE....... Establishing Multimedia Authoring Skills in Higher Education (AIE)
EMAST......... European Marketing Advisory System for Transfer and/of Technology (SAUO)
EMAT.......... Electromagnetic Acoustic Transducer [*Engineering*]
EMAT.......... Electromagnetic Acoustic Transducer Testing (PDAA)
EMAT.......... Electro-Mechanical Automatic Transmission
EMAT.......... Expendable Mobile Acoustic Target (MCD)
EMATS......... Emergency Message Automatic Transmission System [*Military*]
EMATS......... Emergency Mission Automatic Transmission Service (SAUO)
EMATS......... Emergency Mission Automatic Transmission System (SAUS)
EMATS......... Experimental Message Automatic Transmission System (SAUS)
EMATS......... Experiment Manipulation And Transportation System (SAUS)
EMATS-AF... Emergency Message Automatic Transmission System - Air Force
EMATS-JCS... Emergency Message Automatic Transmission System - Joint Chiefs of Staff
EMATT......... Expendable Mobile ASW [*Antisubmarine Warfare*] Tracking Target [*Navy*] (CAAL)
EMATT......... Expendable Mobile ASW [*Air-to-Surface Weapon*] Training Target [*Navy*] (DWSG)
EMA-UK....... European Marketing Association United Kingdom (SAUO)
EMAV.......... Electromagnetic Relief Valve [*Engineering instrumentation*] (IAA)
EM(AW)....... Electrical Mechanic (Air Weapon) [*British military*] (DMA)
EMAX.......... Electronic Multiplex Automatic Exchange (SAUO)
Emb............ Bandeirante [*Airplane code*]
EMB............ Early-Make-Break [*Computer science*]
EMB............ East Midlands Branch (SAUS)
EMB............ Egg Marketing Board (SAUS)
EMB............ Electrical Modernization Bureau (SAUS)
EMB............ Electromagnetic Brakes (HAWK)
EMB............ Electromagnetic Braking (SAUS)
EMB............ Electro-Mechanical Battery
EMB............ Electro-Mechanical Brake [*Automotive engineering*]
EMB............ Electron Beam Microanalysis
EMB............ Electron-Beam Microprobe (UWER)
EMB............ Electronic Maintenance Book (IAA)
EMB............ Electronic Material Bulletin [*Army*] (MCD)
Emb............ Emballage (SAUS)
EMB............ Embankment
EMB............ Embargo (ADA)
EMB............ Embark (AABC)
EMB............ Embassy (AFM)
Emb............ Embasy
EMB............ Embolism [*Medicine*] (EDAA)
emb............ Embolism [*Medicine*] (EDAA)
EMB............ Emboss (MSA)
EMB............ Embossed (SAUS)
EMB............ Embossing (SAUS)
EMB............ Embroidered
EMB............ Embroidery
emb............ Embryo (MELL)
EMB............ Embryology (ROG)
EMB............ Empire Marketing Board [*For motion pictures in England*]
EMB............ Empresa Brasileira de Aeronautica SA [*Brazil*] [*ICAO designator*] (FAAC)
EMB............ Emulator Board (SAUS)
EMB............ Endometrial Biopsy [*Gynecology*] (DAVI)
EMB............ Endomyocardial Biopsy [*Medicine*]
EMB............ Energy Mobilization Board
EMB............ Engineering in Medicine and Biology (MCD)
EMB............ Engineering Metalbond (SAUS)
EMB............ English Beet Molasses (PDAA)
EMB............ Enhanced Master Burst [*Computer science*] (VERA)
EMB............ Environmental Management Bureau (SAUS)
EMB............ Environmental Medicine Branch [*NASA*] (KSC)

EMB.......... Environmental Protection Agency, R. S. Kerr Environmental Research Laboratory, Ada, OK [*OCLC symbol*] (OCLC)
EMB.......... Eosin-Methylene Blue [*Dye combination*]
EMB.......... Ethambutol [*An antituberculosis drug*]
EMB.......... Ethambutol Hydrochloride [*Pharmacology*]
EMB.......... Ethambutol-Myambutol [*Tuberculous therapy*] [*Medicine*] (EDAA)
EMB.......... European Molecular Biology Conference
EMB.......... Experimental Model Basin [*Navy*]
EMB.......... Explosive Mental Behavior (BABM)
EMB.......... Explosive Motor Behavior [*Neurochemistry*]
EMB.......... Extended Memory Block [*Computer science*] (PCM)
EMB.......... Extractive Membrane Bioreactor [*Chemical engineering*]
EMBA.......... Emba Mink Breeders Association (EA)
EMBA.......... European Marine Biological Association (SAUS)
EMBA.......... European Methylbromide Association (SAUS)
EMBA.......... Executive Master of Business Administration (GAGS)
EMBARC.......... Electronic Mail Broadcast to a Roaming Computer [*Telecommunications*] (PCM)
EMBARC.......... Embarc [*Electronic Mail Broadcast to a Roaming Computer*] Communications Service [*Boyton Beach, FL*] (CDE)
EMBARCO.......... Embarkation Control (SAUS)
EMBARK.......... Embarkation (DSUE)
EMBASE.......... Excerpta Mediça Database [*Trademark*] [*Elsevier*] [*Bibliographic database*]
EMBB.......... Electronic Mail Building Block (SAUS)
EMBBS.......... Emergency Medicine Bulletin Board System (ADWA)
EMBD.......... Embedded (WEAT)
embd.......... Embroidered (SAUS)
EMBDU.......... Ethnic Minority Business Development Unit [*British*]
EMBERS.......... Emergency Bed Request System [*Computer science*]
EMBET.......... Error Model Best Estimate of Trajectory (PDAA)
EMBEZ.......... Embezzlement (DLA)
EMBGN.......... Engineering in Medicine and Biology Group Newsletter [*Medicine*] (EDAA)
embgo.......... embargo (SAUS)
EMBH.......... Etched Mesa Buried Heterostructure (SAUS)
EMBI.......... European Molecular Biology Laboratory
embk.......... embark (SAUS)
EMBKMT.......... Embankment
embkn.......... embarkation (SAUS)
Embkn Pt.......... Embarkation Point (SAUS)
EMBL.......... Eniwetok Marine Biological Laboratory [*Marine science*] (MSC)
EMBL.......... European Molecular Biology Laboratory [*Research center*] [*Germany*] (IRC)
EMBL.......... European Mology Biology Laboratory (SAUS)
EMBLA.......... East Midland Branch of Library Association (SAUO)
EMBL Data Library... European Molecular Biology Laboratory Data Library (DOG)
EMBM.......... Environment-Mapped Bump Mapping [*Computer science*]
EMBnet.......... European Molecular Biology Data Network (SAUS)
EMBO.......... Embarkation Officer [*Marine Corps*]
EMBO.......... Embarkation Order [*Marine Corps*]
EMBO.......... EMBO Journal (SAUS)
embo.......... embossing (SAUS)
EMBO.......... Eta-Maleimidocaproyloxysuccinimide (SAUS)
EMBO.......... European Molecular Biology Organisation (or Organization) (SAUO)
EMBO.......... European Molecular Biology Organization [*ICSU*] [*Germany*]
EMBOFF.......... Embassy Officer
EmbOff.......... Embasy Office
EMB of GP... Elected Members Board of General Purposes [*Freemasonry*] (ROG)
EMBO J.......... EMBO Journal (SAUS)
EMB Press... Embossing Press (SAUS)
embr.......... Embroidered (SAUS)
embr.......... Embroidery (VRA)
EMBR.......... Embroidery
EMBR.......... Embryo
EMBR.......... Embryo Development Corp. [*NASDAQ symbol*] (SAG)
EMBR.......... Epoxy-Modified Bisphenol Resin [*Plastics*]
EMBR.......... Equipment Management Balance Register (AFIT)
EMBRAC.......... Embracery [*Legal term*] (DLA)
EMBRAPA.......... Agricultural and Livestock Research Center for the Semi-Arid Tropic (SAUO)
EMBRATEL... Empresa Brasileira de Telecomunicacoes [*Brazilian Telecommunications Enterprises*]
Embrex.......... Embrex, Inc. [*Associated Press*] (SAG)
embrs.......... Embrasure (VRA)
Embrx.......... Embrex, Inc. [*Associated Press*] (SAG)
EMBRY.......... Embryology
Embryo.......... Embryo Development Corp. [*Associated Press*] (SAG)
EMBRYOL.......... Embryology
EMBS.......... Committee for European Marine Biological Symposia (SAUO)
embs.......... Embossed (VRA)
EMBS.......... Embossed [*Deltiology*]
EMBS.......... Energy Management Bumper System [*Automobile safety*]
EMBS.......... Engineering in Medicine and Biology Society [*Institute of Electrical and Electronic Engineers, Inc.*]
EMBS.......... IEEE Engineering in Medicine and Biology Society (EA)
EMBSSY.......... Embassy
embsy.......... embassy (SAUS)
EMBT.......... Emergency Ballast Tank (DNAB)
EMBTEL.......... Embassy Telegram (NATG)
EMBWA.......... Egg Marketing Board of Western Australia
EMBX.......... Embrex, Inc. [*NASDAQ symbol*] (SPSG)
EMBXW.......... Embrex Inc. Wrrt [*NASDAQ symbol*] (TTSB)
EMC.......... Canada Centre for Remote Sensing Library [*UTLAS symbol*]
EMC.......... Early Midcourse (ACAE)
EMC.......... Eastern Mapping Center (SAUS)
EMC.......... Eastern Mennonite College [*Virginia*]
EMC.......... Eastern Minerals and Chemicals (SAUO)
EMC.......... Ecuadorian Minerals Corporation (SAUO)
EMC.......... Educational Media and Technology Center
EMC.......... Educational Media Council [*Defunct*] (EA)
EMC.......... Educational Modulation Center
EMC.......... Education Media Council (SAUS)
EMC.......... Effective Minimum Complement (WDAA)
EMC.......... Eighty Meter Community (SAUS)
EMC.......... Einstein Medical Center (ODA)
EMC.......... Elastomeric-Molding Compound (SAUS)
EMC.......... Elastomeric Molding Tooling Compound (MCD)
EMC.......... Electrical Metallic Conduit (DAC)
EMC.......... Electrician's Mate, Chief [*Navy rating*]
EMC.......... Electromagnetic Capability
EMC.......... Electromagnetic Casting (SAUS)
EMC.......... Electromagnetic Coil (SAUS)
EMC.......... Electromagnetic Compatibility (TIMI)
EMC.......... Electro-Magnetic Compliance
EMC.......... Electromagnetic Control
EMC.......... Electromagnetic Coupling (SAUS)
EMC.......... Electromagnetic Cyclotron
EMC.......... Electromechanochemical
EMC.......... Electronic Mail Courier
EMC.......... Electronic Manifold Card [*Clippard Instrument Laboratory, Inc.*] [*Cincinnati, OH*]
EMC.......... Electronic Material Change
EMC.......... Electronic Materials Conference (SAUS)
EMC.......... Electronic Media Center (VLIE)
EMC.......... Electronic Media Claims [*Department of Health and Human Services*] (GFGA)
EMC.......... Electronic Mode Control (IAA)
EMC.......... Electronic Modules Corporation (SAUO)
EMC.......... Electronic Money Council (SAUO)
EMC.......... Electronic Music Consortium (EA)
EMC.......... Electronics Maintenance Center (SAUO)
EMC.......... Electronics Management Center (SAUS)
EMC.......... Electronics/Management Center (SAUO)
EMC.......... Electronics Marketing Corporation (SAUO)
EMC.......... Electron Microscopy (MAE)
EMC.......... Electron Microscopy Center for Materials Research [*Argonne, IL*] [*Argonne National Laboratory*] [*Department of Energy*] (GRD)
EMC.......... Elektronik Mekanik Cihaziar Ticaret Ltd. (SAUO)
EMC.......... E-Mail Connection (VLIE)
EMC.......... EMC Corp. [*NYSE symbol*] (SPSG)
EMC.......... Emergency Management Coordinator [*Nuclear energy*] (NRCH)
EMC.......... Emergency Medical Care (DAVI)
EMC.......... Emergency Medical Center
EMC.......... Emergency Message Changes (MCD)
EMC.......... Emerging and other Communicable Diseases Surveillance and Control (SAUO)
EMC.......... Emitter Coupled Logic (VLIE)
EMC.......... Emmanuel College, Boston, MA [*OCLC symbol*] (OCLC)
EMC.......... Employee-Management Cooperation
EMC.......... Encephalomyocarditis [*Virus*]
EMC.......... End Center Matched [*of lumber*] (BARN)
EMC.......... End Mollycoddling in America (SAUS)
EMC.......... End of Major Cycle [*Military*]
EMC.......... End of Medium Character [*Computer science*] (ELAL)
EMC.......... Endometrial Cancer [*Medicine*] (MELL)
EMC.......... Endometrial Carcinoma [*Medicine*] (MELL)
EMC.......... Endometrial Curettage [*Medicine*] (MELL)
EMC.......... Energy Management Center
EMC.......... Energy Management Corp. (EFIS)
EMC.......... Engineered Military Circuit [*Leased long lines established in continental US*] [*Military*]
EMC.......... Engineering Maintenance Center (SAUS)
EMC.......... Engineering Manpower Commission (EA)
EMC.......... Engineering Military Circuits (SAUS)
EMC.......... Engineering Mock-Up Critical Experiment [*Nuclear energy*] (NRCH)
EMC.......... Engineer Maintenance Center
EMC.......... Engineer Maintenance Control [*Army*]
EMC.......... Engine Maintenance Center (AAG)
EMC.......... Engine Manufacturers' Committee (EAIO)
EMC.......... Engine Modification Committee (SAUO)
EMC.......... Engine Monitor Computer
EMC.......... Enhanced Memory Chip (SAUS)
EMC.......... Enterprise Storage Co.
EMC.......... Environmental Management Committee (EERA)
EMC.......... Environmental Medical Centre [*Australia*]
EMC.......... Environmental Modeling Center (SAUO)
EMC.......... environmental monitoring and compliance (SAUS)
EMC.......... Environmental Monitoring Center (SAUS)
EMC.......... Environment Management Committee [*Australia*]
EMC.......... Enzepalomyocarditis (SAUS)
EMC.......... Enzyme-Modified Cheese
EMC.......... Equality Mining Company (SAUO)
emc.......... equilibrium moisture contend (SAUS)
EMC.......... Equilibrium Moisture Content
EMC.......... Equipment Maintenance Council [*Defunct*] (EA)
EMC.......... Equipment Management Code [*Air Force*] (AFIT)
EMC.......... Equivalent Mission Cycle
EMC.......... Essential Mixed Cryoglobulinemia [*Medicine*] (MELL)
EMC.......... Etched Metal Circuit

EMC........ Ethylmercuric Chloride (SAUS)
EMC........ European Mathematical Council (EA)
EMC........ European Mechanics Colloquium (SAUS)
EMC........ European Mechanics Committee (EAIO)
EMC........ European Metals Conference (SAUS)
EMC........ European Microwave Conference (SAUS)
EMC........ European Military Communication (IEEE)
EMC........ European Monetary Committee (SAUO)
EMC........ European Muon Collaboration [*Nuclear physics*]
EMC........ Evergreen Marine Corporation, Taipei (SAUO)
EMC........ Every Member Canvas [*Fundraising term*] (NFD)
EMC........ Excess Minority Carrier [*Electronics*] (OA)
EMC........ Excess Minority Carriers (SAUS)
EMC........ Executive Management Committee (SAUS)
EMC........ Executive Management Course (DOMA)
EMC........ Exercise Monitoring and Control (MCD)
EMC........ Experiment Management and Control (SAUS)
EMC........ Experiment Mock-Up Converters (KSC)
EMC........ Explicit Multiplexing Capability (SAUS)
EMC........ Export Management Companies (SAUO)
EMC........ Export Management Company
EMC........ Extended Mass Change
EMC........ Extended Math Coprocessor [*Computer science*]
EMC........ Extended Model Checker [*Computer science*]
EMC........ Extended Multiplexer Channel (NITA)
EMC........ External Multiplexer Channel (MHDB)
EMC........ Extra Miler Club (EA)
EMC........ Eye-Motion Camera
EMC........ Eye-Movement Camera (VLIE)
e-mc-........ Monaco [*MARC geographic area code*] [*Library of Congress*] (LCCP)
EMC........ Winnemucca, NV [*Location identifier*] [*FAA*] (FAAL)
Emc²........ Electronic Mail Communication Center [*Naples, FL*] [*Telecommunications service*] (TSSD)
EMCA........ Electronic Motion Control Association [*Defunct*] (EA)
EMCA........ Ethnic Minority Council of America (SAUO)
EMCAB........ Electromagnetic Compatibility Advisory Board (MCD)
EMC & R........ Emergency Medical Care and Rescue
EM Car........ Electric Mail Car (SAUS)
EmCare........ EmCare Holdings, Inc. [*Associated Press*] (SAG)
EMCASS........ Expert Motor Carrier Selection System (SAUS)
EMCB........ Earth-Mounded Concrete Bunker (ODA)
EMCB........ Electrician's Mate, Construction Battalion [*Navy rating*] [*Obsolete*]
EMCB........ Endomyocardial Biopsy [*Medicine*] (MELL)
EMCBC........ Electrician's Mate, Construction Battalion, Communications [*Navy rating*] [*Obsolete*]
EMCBD........ Electrician's Mate, Construction Battalion, Draftsman [*Navy rating*] [*Obsolete*]
EMCBG........ Electrician's Mate, Construction Battalion, General [*Navy rating*] [*Obsolete*]
EMCBL........ Electrician's Mate, Construction Battalion, Line and Station [*Navy rating*] [*Obsolete*]
EMCC........ Easy Magic Cookery Council [*Defunct*] (EA)
EMCC........ Eckert-Mauchly Computer Company (SAUS)
EMCC........ Electromagnetic Control Compatibility
EMCC........ Emergency Medicine and Crisis Care [*Database*]
EMCC........ Emergency Mission Control Center [*NASA*]
EMCC........ Essential Motor Control Center (AAG)
EMCC........ European Military Communications Coordinating Committee (SAUO)
EMCC........ European Municipal Credit Community
EMCCC........ European Military Communications Co-Ordinating Committee [*NATO*]
EMCCS........ Emergency Medical Command and Communications System
EMCD........ Electro-Magnetically Controlled Differential [*Powertrain*] [*Automotive engineering*]
EMCD........ Electromechanical Control Diagram (MCD)
EMCDAS........ Electro-Magnetic Compatibility Data Acquisition System [*Telecommunications*] (PDAA)
EMCDAS........ Electro-Magnetic Compatibility Data Requisition System (SAUS)
EMCDB........ Elastomer-Modified Cast Double-Base (MCD)
EMCE........ Eastern Montana College of Education (SAUO)
EMCEE........ EMCEE Broadcast Products, Inc. [*Associated Press*] (SAG)
EMCEE........ Master of Ceremonies
EMCF........ Edna McConnel Clark Foundation (SAUO)
EMCF........ Employer Master Control File [*State Employee Security Agency*] (OICC)
EMCF........ European Monetary Co-Operation Fund [*Bank for International Settlements*] (EY)
EMCFA........ Electromagnetic Compatibility Frequency Analysis (SSD)
EMCFOM........ Electromagnetic Compatibility Figure of Merit [*Telecommunications*] (TEL)
EMCG........ EMCORE Group [*NASDAQ symbol*] (TTSB)
EMCG........ Emcor Group
EMCGS........ Electromagnetic Centimeter Gram Second (IAA)
EMCI........ EMC Insurance Group, Inc. [*NASDAQ symbol*] (NQ)
EMCI........ Engineering Model Configuration Inspection (MCD)
EMC In........ EMC Insurance Group, Inc. [*Associated Press*] (SAG)
EMCIS........ Experimental Military Command Information System (MCD)
EMCLASS........ Excerpta Medica Classifcation System (SAUS)
EMCM........ Electrician's Mate, Master Chief [*Navy rating*]
EMCMF........ Embarked Mine Countermeasures Force
EMCML........ Electromagnetic Countermeasures Launcher (SAUS)
EMCO........ Ecological Monitoring Coordinating Office (SAUO)
EMCO........ Electro-Mechanics Company (SAUO)
EMCO........ EMCO Ltd. [*Associated Press*] (SAG)
EMCO........ Engineering Measurements Co. [*NASDAQ symbol*] (NQ)
EMCO........ ESF Management Committee for the ODP (SAUO)
EMCO........ International Board of Cooperation for the Developing Countries (SAUO)
EMCOF........ European Monetary Co-Operation Fund
EMCOM........ Educational Media Catalogs on Microfiche (SAUS)
EMCOM........ Environmental Management Career Opportunities for Minorities (SAUS)
EM COMP........ Electromagnetic Compatibility (SAUS)
EMCON........ Electromagnetic Contamination (MCD)
EMCON........ Electromagnetic-emission Control (SAUS)
EMCON........ Electro-magnetic Radiation Control (SAUO)
EMCON........ Electronic Emission Control (SAUO)
EMCON........ Electron Microscopy Congress
EMCON........ EMCON, Corp. [*Associated Press*] (SAG)
EMCON........ Emergency Control (SAUS)
EMCON........ Emery Control (IAA)
EMCON........ Emission Control (CAAL)
EMCOPS........ Electromagnetic Compatibility Operational System (PDAA)
EMCP........ Electromagnetic Compatibility Program [*Air Force*] (AFM)
EMCP........ Electromagnetic Containerless Processing (SAUS)
EMCP........ Electronic Modular Control Panel [*Motor-generator set design*]
EMCP........ Emergency Military Construction Program
EMCR........ EmCare Holdings [*NASDAQ symbol*] (TTSB)
EMCR........ EmCare Holdings, Inc. [*NASDAQ symbol*] (SAG)
EMCR........ Equipment Maintenance Change Record (MCD)
EMCRF........ Engineering Materials Characterization Research Facility [*Louisiana State University*] [*Research center*] (RCD)
EMCRF........ European and Mediterranean Cereal Rusts Foundation (EAIO)
EMCRO........ Experimental Medical Care Review Organization [*Program of the National Center for Health Services Research and Development*]
EMCS........ Electrician's Mate, Senior Chief [*Navy rating*]
EMCS........ Electromagnetic Compatibility Society (SAUO)
EMCS........ Electromagnetic Compatibility Standardization [*Program*] [*Telecommunications*] (IEEE)
EMCS........ Energy Management and Controls Society (EA)
EMCS........ Energy Management and Control System
EMCS........ energy management control system (SAUS)
EMCS........ Energy Monitoring and Control System (SAUS)
EMCS........ Environmental Management and Control System (AAGC)
EMCS........ Eta-Maleimidocaproyloxysuccinimide (SAUS)
EMCS........ Excerpta Medica Computer System (SAUS)
EMCSR........ European Meeting on Cybernetics and Systems Research (SAUO)
Em Ct App........ Emergency Court of Appeals [*United States*] (DLA)
EMCTCU........ European-Middle-east Channel and Traffic Control Unit (SAUS)
EMCTP........ Electromagnetic Compatibility Test Plan (IEEE)
EMCU........ Evergreen Maritime Container Unit (SAUS)
EMC USA........ Estonian Music Center, USA (EA)
EMCV........ Eggplant Mottled Crinkle Virus [*Plant pathology*]
EMCV........ Encephalomyocarditis Virus
EMC Virus........ Encephalomyocarditis Virus (SAUS)
EMCWA........ Electrical Manufacturing and Coil Winding Association (NTPA)
EMCWP........ European Mediterranean Commission on Water Planning (EA)
EMCYX........ Evergreen Micro Cap Fund Cl.Y [*Mutual fund ticker symbol*] (SG)
EMD........ Each Military Department (LAIN)
EMD........ Effective Miss Distance (ACAE)
EMD........ Electrical Mechanical Disassociation [*Medicine*]
EMD........ Electric Motor Driven
EMD........ Electrolytic Manganese Dioxide [*For use in batteries*]
EMD........ Electromagnetic Damping (SAUS)
EMD........ Electromagnetic Defense (CAAL)
EMD........ Electromagnetic Motion Detector (PDAA)
EMD........ Electromechanical Dissociation
EMD........ electromotive diesel (SAUS)
EMD........ Electro-Motive Division [*General Motors Corp.*]
EMD........ Electromotive Driven (SAUS)
EMD........ Electro Motor Driven (SAUS)
EMD........ Electromyocardial Dissociation [*Medicine*] (MELL)
EMD........ Electronic Map Display
EMD........ Electronic Marcel Dassault [*France*]
EMD........ Electronic Measurement and Display (ACAE)
EMD........ Element Merge and Distribution (VLIE)
EMD........ EM diffraction (SAUS)
EMD........ Emerald [*Australia*] [*Airport symbol*] (OAG)
EMD........ Emergency Medical Division (DoT) [*Medicine*] (EDAA)
EMD........ Emergency Medical Doctor (IDYL)
EMD........ Emerging Markets Income Fund [*NYSE symbol*] (SPSG)
EMD........ Emory University School of Dentistry, Atlanta, GA [*OCLC symbol*] (OCLC)
EMD........ Employment Medical Division (HEAS)
EMD........ EMSP Maintenance Device (SAUS)
EMD........ Energy and Minerals Division [*GAO*] (AAGC)
EMD........ Energy Management Display (SAUS)
EMD........ Engineering and Manufacturing Development [*Military*]
EMD........ Engineering and Manufacturing Development Phase (SAUS)
EMD........ Engineering Magnetics Division (SAUS)
EMD........ Engineering Manufacturing Development (SEWL)
EMD........ Engineering Master Drawing (MCD)
EMD........ Engineering Mechanics Division [*American Society of Civil Engineers*] (MCD)
EMD........ Engine Management Display (MCD)
EMD........ Engine Model Derivative (ACAE)
EMD........ Engine Monitor Display (MCD)
EMD........ Enhanced Microbial Degradation [*Biochemistry*]
EMD........ Entry Monitor Display (KSC)
EMD........ Environmental Management Division (SAUS)
EMD........ Equilibrium Mode Distribution (SAUS)

EMD .... Equipment Maintenance Directive (ACAE)
EMD .... Equipment Manufacturers Design
EMD .... Equivalent Martin Day (PDAA)
EMD .... Erythema Multiforme [*Medicine*] (MELL)
EMD .... Esophageal Motility Disorder [*Medicine*]
EMD .... Esophageal Myotonia Dystrophica [*Medicine*] (MELL)
EMD .... European Market Development
EMD .... Exploration and Mining Division (SAUO)
EMD .... Exploration Map Data (RDA)
EMD .... Export Market Development [*Grants*]
EMD .... Extractive Metallurgy Division (SAUS)
EMD .... Eye Movement Density (SAUS)
EMD .... Eye Movement Desensitization [*Medicine*]
EMD .... Eye-Movement Device
EMD .... Marshalltown, IA [*Location identifier*] [*FAA*] (FAAL)
EMDA .... Emergency Distance Available [*Aviation*]
EMDAAL .... East Midlands Division of the Association of Assistant Librarians (SAUO)
EMDAS .... Expanded MINUTEMAN Data Analysis System (SAUS)
EMDB .... Engineering Master Data Base (VLIE)
EMDB .... Equipment Maintenance Data Base (SAUS)
EMDEF .... Electronic Map Display Experimental Facility (ACAE)
EMDG .... Euromissile Dynamics Group (PDAA)
EMDGA .... Export Market Development Grants Act [*Australia*]
EMDI .... Energy Management Display Indicator
EMDI .... Engineering Manufacturing Division Instruction (SAUS)
EMDI .... Estimated Maximum Daily Intake [*Toxicology*]
EMDI .... Extended Mission Duration Items (SAUS)
EMDIF .... Elementary Messages of Discrete Frequency (SAUS)
EMDIR .... Electronic Mail Directory (VLIE)
EMDL .... East Midlands [*England*]
EMDOC .... European Management Documentation Group (SAUO)
EM DOM ...... Eminent Domain [*Legal term*] (DLA)
EMDP .... Electromotive Difference of Potential
EMDP .... Energy Management Development Program (SAUS)
EMDP .... Engine Model Derivative Program [*Air Force*] (DOMA)
EMDP .... Executive and Management Development Program [*Defense Mapping Agency*] (DNAB)
EMDP .... Export Market Development Programme (SAUS)
EMDR .... Emulated Machine Description Record (VLIE)
EMDR .... Eye-Movement Desensitization and Reprocessing [*Psychotherapy*]
EMDRIA .... EMDR International Association (SAUS)
EMDS .... Electro-Magnetic Design System [*Computer simulation*]
EMDS .... Electronic Material Data Service (MUGU)
EMDS .... Electronic Music Delivery System (SEWL)
EMDS .... Emergency Management Decision Support system (SAUS)
EMDS .... European Meteorological Data System (SAUS)
EMDU .... Electronic Media Development Unit (SAUO)
EMDU .... Enhanced Main Display Unit (DWSG)
EMDUP .... European MOS-1 Data Utilization Programme (SAUS)
EMDV .... Eggplant Mottled Dwarf Virus [*Plant pathology*]
EME .... CEMR [*Canada Energy Mines and Resources*] Headquarters Library [*UTLAS symbol*]
EME .... Earth-Mars-Earth
EME .... Earth-Moon-Earth [*Extraterrestrial communications*]
EME .... Earth - Moon - Earth (Connection) (SAUS)
EME .... East Midlands Electricity [*British*] (WDAA)
EME .... Ecgonine Methyl Ester [*Organic chemistry*]
EME .... Electrical and Mechanical Engineering [*or Engineers*]
EME .... Electrical & Mechanical Engineers (SAUS)
EME .... Electric Multipole Expansion (SAUS)
EME .... Electromagnetically Equivalent (SAUS)
EME .... Electromagnetic Effect
EME .... Electromagnetic Effectiveness (SAUS)
EME .... electromagnetic emission (SAUS)
EME .... Electromagnetic Emissions (OTD)
EME .... Electromagnetic Energy (IEEE)
EME .... Electromagnetic Environment (MCD)
EME .... Electromantle Extraction
EME .... Electromechanical Energy (SAUS)
EME .... Electromedical Equipment (SAUS)
EME .... Electronics Materials Engineering
EME .... EMCOR Group [*NYSE symbol*]
EME .... Emden [*Germany*] [*Airport symbol*] (OAG)
EME .... Emergency Power Engineering (HGAA)
eme .... Emerging Market Economics Ltd. [*England*]
EME .... Emerging Market Economy (ECON)
EME .... Emetic [*Pharmacy*] (ROG)
EME .... Emetine [*Antiamebic compound*]
EME .... Encapsulated Mediastinal Effusion [*Medicine*] (EDAA)
EME .... Energy and Man's Environment [*Utility-funded curriculum program*]
EME .... Environmental Measurements Experiment
EME .... Environmental Mine Engineering (SAUS)
EME .... Epidemic Myalgic Encephalomyelitis [*Medicine*] (EDAA)
EME .... Established Market Economy
EME .... European Machine Tool Exhibition (SAUO)
EME .... Extension Memory (SAUS)
EME .... Extraordinary Minister of the Eucharist (SAUS)
EME .... Foreign & Colonial Emerging Middle East Fund, Inc. [*NYSE symbol*] (SAG)
EME .... Metro Express, Inc. [*ICAO designator*] (FAAC)
EMEA .... Electronic Maintenance Engineering Association
EMEA .... Employment and Earnings (journ.) (SAUS)
EMEA .... European Medicines Evaluation Agency [*London*]
EMEA .... Europe, Middle East and Africa
EMEB .... East Midlands Electricity Board (SAUO)
EMEC .... Electrical and Mechanical Engineering Committee [*British*]
EMEC .... Electrical Maintenance Engineering Center (SAUO)
EMEC .... Electromagnetic Effects Capability (NASA)
EMEC .... Electromagnetic Effects Compatibility [*NASA*] (NASA)
EMEC .... Electronic Maintenance Engineering Center [*Military*] (IEEE)
EMEC .... Engineers Manual for Emergency Construction [*Army Corps of Engineers*]
EMECA .... European Major Exhibition Centers Association (SAUO)
EMECS .... Environmental Management of Enclosed Coastal Seas (EERA)
EMED .... Entrepreneur Management and Executive Development (SAUO)
EMED .... EuroMed Inc. [*NYSE symbol*] (TTSB)
EMEDCA ...... Electro-Medical Agreement Group (SAUS)
EMEDS .... Electro-Mechanical Expulsive De-Icing System
EMEF .... Environmental Management and Enrichment Facilities (SAUS)
EMEFS .... Eulerian Model Evaluation Field Study (SAUS)
EMEG .... Electromagnetic Environment Generator
EMEG .... Environmental Media Evaluation Guide (SAUS)
EM/EH .... Environmental Management/Environmental Health (SAUS)
EMEI .... Equipment Management Exception Indicator (AFIT)
EMELEC .... trademark of East Midlands Electricity Board (SAUS)
EMEM .... Eagle's Minimum Essential Medium [*Culture medium*]
EMEMS .... Elastomeric Micro Electro Mechanical System (AAEL)
emend .... emendating (SAUS)
EMEND .... Emendatio [*Emendation*] [*Latin*]
emend .... emendatory (SAUS)
EMEP .... Co-operative Programme for Monitoring and Evaluation of the Long-Range Transboundary of Air Pollutants in Europe (SAUO)
EMEP .... European Model and Evaluation Program (SAUS)
EMEP .... European Monitoring and Evaluation Programme [*Environmental research*]
EMEP .... Evaluation Monitoring European Pollution (SAUS)
EMEP-CCC ... EMEP-Chemical Coordination Centre (SAUS)
EMEPS .... Electronic Message Privacy System (SAUS)
EM equipment... earthmoving equipment (SAUS)
EMER .... Electromagnetic Environment Recorder (MCD)
EMER .... Electromagnetic Molecular Electronic Resistance [*Medicine*] (EDAA)
EMER .... Electromagnetic Molecular Electronic Resonance (PDAA)
emer .... Emegency (SAUS)
emer .... Emerald [*Philately*]
emer .... Emergency (ADWA)
EMER .... Emergency (KSC)
EMER .... Emergency Travel (TRID)
EMER .... Emergent Group, Inc. [*NASDAQ symbol*] (SAG)
Emer .... Emerita (AL)
Emer .... Emeritus (CMD)
EMER .... Emeritus
EMER .... Emerson, MB [*American Association of Railroads railroad junction routing code*]
EMer .... Mercury [*Record label*] [*Great Britain*]
EMERCOM ... Federation State Committee of Emergencies (SAUO)
EMERCOM ... Russian Federation State Committee of Emergencies (SAUO)
EMERCOM ... Russian Ministry for Civil Defense, Emergencies and the Elimination of Consequences of Natural Disasters (SAUO)
Emer Ct App... Emergency Court of Appeals [*United States*] (DLA)
EMERG .... Emergency (AABC)
EMERGCON... Emergency Condition [*Navy*] (ANA)
EMERGCONS... Emergency Conditions (SAUS)
Emergency Med... Emergency Medicine [*A publication*] (PABS)
Emerg Lib.... Emergency Librarian [*A publication*] (BRI)
Emerg Med Clin North Am... Emergency Medicine Clinics of North America [*Philadelphia, PA*] (SAUS)
Emergnt .... Emergent Group, Inc. [*Associated Press*] (SAG)
Emerig Ins... Emerigon on Insurance [*A publication*] (DLA)
Emerig Mar Loans... Emerigon on Maritime Loans [*A publication*] (DLA)
Emer Ins ...... Emerigon on Insurance [*A publication*] (DLA)
Emerit .... Emeritus Corp. [*Associated Press*] (SAG)
Emeritus ...... Emeritus Corp. [*Associated Press*] (SAG)
Emer Mar Lo... Emerigon on Maritime Loans [*A publication*] (DLA)
EmerR .... Emerson Radio Corp. [*Associated Press*] (SAG)
Emerson & Haber Pol & Civ Rits... Emerson and Haber's Political and Civil Rights in the United States [*A publication*] (DLA)
Emerson C... Emerson College (GAGS)
EMES .... Earth Monitoring Educational System (SAUS)
EMES .... Electrical, Mechanical, and Environmental Systems (MCD)
EM/ES .... Emergence and Establishment [*Agriculture*]
E-MESFET.... Enhancement-Metal Semiconductor Field Effect Transistor (HGAA)
E Met .... Engineer of Metallurgy
E-Meter .... electrical-resistance galvanometer (SAUS)
E (Meter) ..... Electropsychometer [*Device for measuring emotional response through electrical conductivity of subject's skin*]
EMETF .... Electromagnetic Environmental Test Facility [*Fort Huachuca, AZ*] [*Army*] (AABC)
EMETS .... Emmetsburg, IA [*American Association of Railroads railroad junction routing code*]
EMEU .... East Midlands Education Union [*British*] (AIE)
EMEX .... Equatorial Mesoscale Experiment [*National Oceanic and Atmospheric Administration*]
EMEX .... Equatorial Monsoon Experiment (SAUS)
EMEX .... International Machinery and Equipment Exhibition (SAUS)
EMF .... Effective Mass Filter (SAUS)
EMF .... Elastomyofibrosis [*Medicine*] (MELL)
EMF .... Electric and Magnetic Field
EMF .... Electro-Machine Fixture (MCD)
EMF .... Electromagnetic Field [*Industrial hygiene term*] (OHS)

EMF........ Electromagnetic Field/Force (SAUS)
EMF........ Electromagnetic Flow [*or Florometer*] [*Cardiology*]
EMF........ Electromagnetic Flowmeter (MAE)
EMF........ Electromagnetic Force (NASA)
EMF........ electromagnetic forming (SAUS)
EMF........ Electromagnetic Frequency
EMF........ Electromnagnetic Forming (SAUS)
emf........ Electromotive Force (IDOE)
EMF........ Electromotive Force [*See also E, V*] [*Electrochemistry*]
EMF........ Electronic Fetal Monitoring [*Medicine*] (MELL)
EMF........ Electronic Mail Facility [*Postal Service*]
EMF........ Electronic Manufacturing Facility (IAA)
EMF........ Electronics Metal Finishing Corporation (SAUS)
EMF........ Electron Microscope Facility (SAUS)
emf........ Eletromotive Force (SAUS)
EMF........ Emergency Medicine Foundation (EA)
EMF........ Endomyocardial Fibrosis [*Cardiology*]
EMF........ Energy Modelling Forum (SAUS)
EMF........ Engineering Master File (SAUS)
EMF........ Enhanced Metafile [*Computer science*]
EMF........ Enhanced Metafile Format [*Microsoft Corp.*] (PCM)
EMF........ Enlisted Master File [*Army*] (INF)
EMF........ Enterprise Middleware Framework (GART)
EMF........ Environmental Management Framework (SAUO)
EMF........ Equipment Maintenance Facility [*Deep Space Instrumentation Facility, NASA*]
EMF........ Erythrocyte Maturation Factor [*Hematology*]
emf........ erythrocyte maturing factor (SAUS)
EMF........ Europaeische Motel Foderation [*European Motel Federation*] (EA)
EMF........ European Management Forum (SAUS)
EMF........ European Market France (SAUO)
EMF........ European Metalworkers' Federation in the Community [*EC*] (ECED)
EMF........ European Missionary Fellowship
EMF........ European Monetary Fund [*Proposed*]
EMF........ European Mountain Forum (SAUS)
EMF........ European Multimedia Forum (DDC)
EMF........ Evaluate Memory Fit (SAUS)
EMF........ Evaporated Milk Formula [*Dietetics*] (DAVI)
EMF........ Event Marketing Funds [*Business term*]
EMF........ Everitt-Metzger-Flanders [*Early automobile*] [*Facetious translation: Every Mechanical Failure*]
EMF........ Every Minute Fix-It (IIA)
emf........ every morning fix (SAUS)
EMF........ Every Morning Fixum [*An old car*] [*Slang*]
EMF........ Evolving Magnetic Feature (OA)
EMF........ Excerpta Medica Foundation [*Database producer*] (EA)
EMF........ Explosive Metal Forming
EMF........ Templeton Emerging Markets Fund, Inc. [*NYSE symbol*] (SPSG)
EMFA........ Electrician's Mate, Fireman Apprentice [*Navy rating*]
EMFA........ Excerpta Medica Foundation of Amsterdam [*Netherlands*] [*Medicine*] (EDAA)
Emfac........ Emery Industries, Inc. [*Research code symbol*]
EMFBI........ Excuse Me For Butting In (SAUS)
EMFCS........ Enhanced Mortar Fire Control System [*Military*] (INF)
EMF/ELF........ Electromagnetic Field/Extra-Low Frequency (GOBB)
EMFF........ Edward Mulhare's Foundation of Friends (EA)
EMFF........ Edward Mulhare's Foundations (EA)
EMFF........ Electromagnetic Form Factor
EMFGA........ Eastern Metropolitan Fruit Growers' Association [*Australia*]
EMFI........ [*USA*]Energy and Minerals Field Institute (ODA)
EMFJ........ European Musical Festival for Youth (SAUO)
EMFJ........ Europees Muziekfestival voor de Jeugd [*European Music Festival for the Youth*] (EAIO)
EMFM........ Electromagnetic Flowmeter
EMFN........ Electrician's Mate, Fireman [*Navy rating*]
EMFP........ Electromagnetic Flow Probe [*Analytical biochemistry*]
EMFP........ Ethnic/Racial Minority Fellowship Programs (ADWA)
EMFR........ Electromotive Force Recorder (SAUS)
EMF RAPID... Electric and Magnetic Fields Research and Public Information Dissemination Program (SAUO)
EMFT........ Early-Morning Fuzzy Thinking
EMFT........ Extended Multiprogramming with a Fixed number of Tasks (SAUS)
EMFU........ Ethoxymethylfluorouracil [*Antineoplastic drug*]
EMG........ Eastern Management Group (HGAA)
EMG........ Eastmaque Gold Mines Ltd. [*Toronto Stock Exchange symbol*] [*Vancouver Stock Exchange symbol*]
EMG........ Educational Management Group (SAUO)
EMG........ Electromagnetic Generator (SAUS)
EMG........ Electromagnetic Gravity Data (SAUS)
EMG........ Electro-Magnetic Gun (SAUS)
EMG........ Electromagnetic Gyro
EMG........ Electrometrogram [*Recording of changes in electric potential of the uterine muscle*] [*Medicine*] (EDAA)
EMG........ Electromigration (AAEL)
EMG........ Electromyelogram [*Medicine*] (MELL)
EMG........ Electromyelography [*or Electromyelogram*] [*Neurology*] (DAVI)
EMG........ Electromyogram [*or Electromyographic, Electromyography*]
EMG........ Electromyograph (DIPS)
EMG........ Electromyographic
EMG........ Electromyography (QSUL)
EMG........ Electron Micrograph [*Medicine*] (EDAA)
EMG........ Electronmyogram (SAUS)
Emg........ Emergency [*Medicine*] (EDAA)
emg........ Emergency (SAUS)
EMG........ Emergency Management Guide [*Environmental science*] (COE)
EMG........ [*The*] Emerging Markets Infrastructure Fund [*NYSE symbol*] (SPSG)
EMG........ Emerging Mkts Infrastructure [*NYSE symbol*] (TTSB)
EMG........ Encyclopedia of the Mouse Genome (HGEN)
EMG........ Energy Managers' Group [*Australia*]
EMG........ Engine Monitoring Group (SAUO)
EMG........ Equipment Management Group
EMG........ Essential Monoclonal Gammopathy [*Medicine*] (MELL)
E-MG........ Etat-Major General [*General Headquarters*] [*French military*]
EMG........ Eurocom Main Group (SAUO)
EMG........ Europaeische Maerchengesellschaft [*European Fairytale Association - EFA*] [*Germany*] (EAIO)
EMG........ Executive Mansion and Grounds [*i.e., the White House and its grounds*] [*Executive Office of the President*]
EMG........ Exomphalos, Macroglossia, and Giantism [*Syndrome*] [*Medicine*]
EMG........ Exophthalmos-Macroglossia-Gigantism [*Medicine*] (EDAA)
EMG........ Exploration and Mining Geology (SAUO)
EMG........ Exponentially Modified Gaussian [*Mathematical function*]
EMG........ Extension Module Group (ACRL)
EMG........ Externally Mounted Gun (SAUS)
EMG........ Eye-Movement Gauge
EMG........ Shreveport, LA [*Location identifier*] [*FAA*] (FAAL)
EMG Analysis... Electromyographic Analysis (SAUS)
EMGB........ East Midlands Gas Board (SAUO)
EMGB........ Engine-Mounted Gear Box (MCD)
EMGBL........ Ethyl(methyl)-Gamma-Butyrolactone [*Biochemistry*]
EMGCU........ East Mengo Growers Cooperative Union (SAUO)
Emgcy........ Emergency (SAUS)
EMGE........ Electronic Maintenance Ground Equipment (KSC)
EmgGer........ Emerging Germany Fund [*Associated Press*] (SAG)
EMG Investigation... Electromyographic Investigation (SAUS)
EmgMkt........ [*The*] Emerging Markets Infrastructure Fund [*Associated Press*] (SAG)
EMGN........ Extramembranous Glomerulonephritis [*Medicine*] (AAMN)
EMGO........ Emperor Goose [*North American bird banding code*] (BIBA)
EMGORS........ Electromyogram Sensors [*For control of artificial limbs*]
EMGSX........ Midas Fund [*Mutual fund ticker symbol*] (SG)
EmgTgr........ Emerging Tigers Fund [*Associated Press*] (SAG)
EMGTN........ Equivalent Megatonnage [*Military weapon index*] (MCD)
EMGWS........ Electromagnetic Gun Weapon System
EMGY........ Emergency (ADWA)
EMH........ Educable Mentally Handicapped
EMH........ Efficient Market Hypothesis (ADA)
emh........ electrical, mechanical, and hydraulic (SAUS)
EMH........ Electronic Mail Handling
EMH........ Emhart Corp. (SAUO)
EMH........ Epochs of Modern History [*A publication*]
EMH........ Estimated Man-Hours (AFIT)
EMH........ Expedited Message Handling [*Computer science*] (ELAL)
EMH........ External Message Handler (SAUS)
EMHA........ Electronically-Monitored Home Arrest (SAUS)
EMHC........ Experimental Mine Hunter, Coastal (SAUS)
EMHI........ Estonian Meteorological and Hydrological Institute (SAUO)
EMHR........ East Mahaney & Hazelton Railroad [*Federal Railroad Administration identification code*]
EMHR........ Estimated Maximum Heart Rate [*Aerobic dance*]
EMHS........ Electronic Message Handling System (SAUS)
EMHS........ Electronic Message Handling Systems (SAUS)
EMHT........ Early to Mid-Holocene Transition
EMI........ Early Manufacturing Involvement (TIMI)
EMI........ Eastern Microwave, Inc. [*Telecommunications service*] (TSSD)
EMI........ Eaton Vance Michigan Municipal Income Trust [*AMEX symbol*] (NASQ)
EMI........ Ecology for Mineral Industries (SAUO)
EMI........ Educable Mentally Impaired (ADWA)
EMI........ Educationally Mentally Impaired
EMI........ Egg Marketing Inspectorate (GVA)
EMI........ Elderly and Mentally Infirmed (MELL)
EMI........ electomagnetic interference (SAUS)
EMI........ Electrical & Musical Industries Ltd. [*British*]
EMI........ Electrical Measuring Instrument (IAA)
EMI........ Electric & Musical Industrie (SAUS)
EMI........ Electric, and Musical Industries (SAUS)
EMI........ Electric Music Instrument (SAA)
EMI........ Electro Magnetic Immunity (SAUS)
EMI........ Electromagnetic Impulse (IAA)
EMI........ Electromagnetic Induction (SAUS)
EMI........ Electro Magnetic Influence (SAUS)
EMI........ Electromagnetic Interface
EMI........ Electromagnetic Interference (HAWK)
EMI........ electromagnetic radiation interference (SAUS)
EMI........ Electronic and Musical Industries Ltd [*Medicine*] (EDAA)
EMI........ Electronic Maintenance Inspector
EMI........ Electronic Memories, Incorporated (SAUO)
EMI........ Electronics and Medical Instrumentation [*Medicine*] (EDAA)
EMI........ Electron Magnetic Interference (SEWL)
EMI........ Electrostatic Multipole Interaction (SAUS)
EMI........ Emergency Management Institute
EMI........ Emergency Medical Identification (MELL)
EMI........ Emergency Medical Information
EMI........ EMI Music Publishing
EMI........ Emirau [*Papua New Guinea*] [*Airport symbol*] (OAG)
EMI........ EMI [*formerly, Electric & Musical Industries Ltd.*] Special Issues [*Record label*] [*Great Britain*]
EMI........ Employers Mutual Indemnity Ltd.
EMI........ Enable Manual Input (SAUS)

EMI .... Encore Marketing International [*AMEX symbol*] (SAG)
EMI .... End of Message Indicator (SAUS)
EMI .... Energy and Minerals Institute (SAUO)
EMI .... Engineering and Manufacturing Instructions (NRCH)
EMI .... Environmental Management, Incorporated (SAUO)
EMI .... Environmental Measurements, Incorporated (SAUO)
EMI .... Environmental Mediation International [*Defunct*] (EA)
EMI .... Environmental Mutagen Information [*Department of Energy*] [*Information service or system*] (IID)
EMI .... Environment Management Industries (EERA)
EMI .... Environment Management Industry
EMI .... Enzyme and Microbore Immobilization [*Biochemistry*]
EMI .... Equipment Manufacturers Institute (NTPA)
EMI .... Equipment Manufacturing Incorporated (SAUO)
EMI .... European Monetary Institute (ECON)
EMI .... Evangelical Ministries, Inc. (EA)
EMI .... Excavation Engineering and Earth Mechanics Institute [*Colorado School of Mines*] [*Research center*] (RCD)
EMI .... Exchange of Medical Information [*Program*] [*Veterans Administration*]
EMI .... Experiences in Mathematical Ideas (EDAC)
EMI .... Experiments in Musical Intelligence
EMI .... Expressible Moisture Index
EMI .... External Machine Interface (SAUS)
EMI .... External Memory Interface (SAUS)
EMI .... External Muon Identifier [*Atomic physics*]
EMI .... Extractive Metallurgy Institute (EA)
EMI .... Extra Military Instruction
EMI .... Premium Air Shuttle, Ltd. [*Nigeria*] [*FAA designator*] (FAAC)
EMI .... Westminster, MD [*Location identifier*] [*FAA*] (FAAL)
EMI .... Earth Mechanics Institute (ODA)
EMIA .... Employers' Mutual Indemnity Association Ltd. [*Australia*] [*Commercial firm*]
EMIA .... Enzyme Membrane Immunoassay [*Biochemistry*]
EMIAA .... Environment Management Industry Association of Australia (EERA)
EMIAC .... Electric & Musical Industries [*later, EMI Ltd.*] Analogue Computer (DEN)
EMI-AC .... Electro Magnetic Influence AC (SAUS)
Emiat .... Empresa Importadora y Exportadora de Suministros Tecnicos [*Import-export board*] [*Cuba*] (EY)
EMIAZ .... Export Meat Industry Advisory Committee (SAUO)
EMIB .... European Master's in International Business
EMIBS .... Executive Master of International Business Studies (PGP)
EMIC .... Electromagnetic Impulse Capability
EMIC .... Electromagnetic Interference and Compatibility
EMIC .... Electromagnetic Interference Control (SAUS)
EMIC .... Electronic Materials Information Center (SAUS)
EMIC .... Emergency Maternity and Infant Care
EMIC .... Engineering Management Inquiry Console (SAUS)
EMIC .... Environmental Mutagen Information Center [*Environmental Information System Office*]
EMIC BACK ... Environmental Mutagen Information Center Backfile [*Medicine*] (EDAA)
EMICE .... Electromagnetic Interference Control Engineer (IEEE)
E-MICR .... Electron Microscopy [*Organic chemistry*] (DAVI)
EMID .... Electromagnetic Intrusion Detector (NVT)
EMID .... Emergency Medical Information Devices
Emid .... Environmentally-Mediated Intellectual Decline (SAUO)
EMID .... Export Market Development Incentive (SAUS)
EMIDEC .... Electrical & Musical Industries Data Electronic Computer (SAUS)
EMIDEC .... EMI [*formerly, Electric & Musical Industries Ltd.*] Data Electronic Computer [*British*]
E Midl .... East Midland (SAUS)
EMIDS .... Experiment for the Management of Information Data System (SAUS)
EMIE .... Educational Media Institute Evaluation Project (SAUS)
EMIE .... Educational Media Institutes Evaluation [*Project*]
EMIE .... Education Management Information Exchange (SAUS)
EMIE .... Ethnic Materials Information Exchange
EMIEL .... EMI Electronics, Limited (ACAE)
EMIERT .... Ethnic Materials and Information Exchange Round Table [*American Library Association*] (EA)
EMIETF .... Ethnic Materials Information Exchange Task Force [*Later, EMIERT*] (EA)
emig .... emigrant (SAUS)
emig .... emigration (SAUS)
EMIG .... EM International working Group (SAUO)
EMILAS .... Energy Management in Lighting Award Scheme [*British*]
EMILM .... Electro-Absorbtive Modulated Isolated LASER Module (AAEL)
EMILY .... Early Money Is Like Yeast [*Political fund raising campaign for female Democrats running for the US Senate*]
EMIM .... Executive Master of International Management
EMIM .... External Mixer Interface Module (NITA)
EMIMA .... Electrical and Mechanical Instrument Makers' Association [*A union*] [*British*]
Emin .... Eminence (SAUS)
EMIN .... Eminent (ROG)
EMInco .... [*The*] Emerging Markets Income Fund [*Associated Press*] (SAG)
EMInco2 .... Emerging Markets Income Fund II, Inc. [*Associated Press*] (SAG)
EMIND .... European Modular Interactive Network Designer (CIST)
EM in Geol ... Mining Engineer in Geology
EMInS .... Emergency Management Information System (SAUS)
EMINT .... Electromagnetic Intelligence (MSA)
EMINT .... Electronic Intelligence (FOTI)
EMINWA .... Environmentally Sound Management of Inland Water [*United Nations*]
EMINWAR .... Environmentally Sound Management of Inland Waters (EERA)
EMIP .... Equivalent Means Investment Period
EMIP .... European Market for Infrastructural Projects (SAUS)
EMIP .... Experimental Manned Interceptor Program (IAA)
EMIP .... Extended Management Improvement Program [*Military*]
EMIPr .... Encore Mkt Intl Cv Partic Pfd [*ECM Symbol*] (TTSB)
EMiqr .... Entsiqlopedia Miqra'it-Encyclopaedia Biblica [*Jerusalem*] [*A publication*] (BJA)
EMIR .... EDP [*Electronic Data Processing*]-Microfilm-Integrated-Retrieval [*German Patent Office*]
EMIR .... Electromagnetic Interference Resolution (SAUS)
EMIRA .... Ezegodnik Muzeja Istorii i Ateizma [*Moscow*] (BJA)
EMIRE .... Early Manned Planetary Interplanetary RoundTrip Experiment (SAUS)
EMI/RFI .... Electromagnetic Interference/Radio Frequency Interference (SAUS)
EMIRS .... Electrochemically Modulated Infrared Reflectance Spectroscopy
EMIRS .... Electrochemically-Modulated Infrared Reflectance Spectroscopy (SAUS)
EMIRS .... Electrochemically Modulated Infrared Spectroscopy (EDCT)
EMIRTEL .... Emirates Telecommunications Corp. Ltd. (TEL)
EMIS .... Ecosystem of Machines Information System
EMIS .... EDIS Management and Information System (SAUS)
EMIS .... Educational Management Information System
EMIS .... Effluent Management Information System [*Computer science*] (PDAA)
EMIS .... Electromagnetic Intelligence System
EMIS .... Electromagnetic Isotope Separation [*Uranium enrichment*]
EMIS .... Electronic Mail Integration Services (ACAE)
EMIS .... Electronic Markets and Information Systems, Inc. [*Information service or system*]
EMIS .... Electronic Materials and Information System (SAUS)
EMIS .... Electronic Materials Information Service [*Institution of Electrical Engineers*] [*Database*] (IID)
EMIS .... Emergency Medical Indentification Symbol (MELL)
EMIS .... Emisphere Technologies, Inc. [*NASDAQ symbol*] (SAG)
EMIS .... Emission (KSC)
EMIS .... Employee Management Information System (SAUS)
EMIS .... Energy Management Information System (SAUS)
EMIS .... Engineering Maintenance Information System (SAUO)
EMIS .... Engineering Management Information System [*Defense Supply Agency*]
EMIS .... English Monumental Inscription Society (SAUS)
EMIS .... Enrichment Marketing Information System (SAUS)
EMIS .... European Metallurgy Information System (SAUS)
EMIS .... Evangelical Missions Information Service (EA)
EMIS .... Executive Equipment Management Information System (ACAE)
EMIS .... Exercise Message Intercept System (SAUS)
EMIS .... Extension Management Information System [*Department of Agriculture*]
EMISARI ...... Emergency Management Information System and Reference Index (SAUS)
EMISEC .... Emission Security (AFM)
EMISM .... Electromagnetic Interference Safety Margin (ACAE)
EMISMS .... Electromagnetic Interference Safety Margins (SAUS)
EMISS .... Electromolecular Instrument Space Simulator
EMISS .... Emission (SAUS)
EmisTch .... Emisphere Technologies, Inc. [*Associated Press*] (SAG)
EMIT .... Elbit Medical Imaging Ltd. [*NASDAQ symbol*] (SAG)
EMIT .... Electromagnetic Induction Tweeter
EMIT .... Electromagnetic Interference (SAA)
EMIT .... Electromagnetic Interference Testing
EMIT .... Embedded Micro-Interface Technoloy [*Telecommunications*]
EMIT .... Emergency Message Initiation Terminal (MCD)
EMIT .... Emzyme Mutiplication Immunoassay Technique [*Medicine*] (EDAA)
EMIT .... Engineering Management Information Technique
emit .... enzyme-multiplied immunoassay (SAUS)
EMIT .... Enzyme Multiplied Immunoassay Technique [*Clinical chemistry*] [*Syva Co. trade mark*]
EMIT .... Enzyme Multiplied Immunoassay Test [*Clinical chemistry*] [*Generic*]
EMIT .... Enzyme-multiplied-immuno-technique (SAUS)
EMI-tran ...... Electro Magnetic Influence - Transient (SAUS)
EMITS .... Electromagnetic Instrument Test System (MCD)
EMITS .... Electromagnetic Interference Test System [*Navy*] (MCD)
EMITT .... Emittatur [*Let It Be Discharged*] [*Pharmacy*] (ROG)
EMJC .... East Mississippi Junior College [*Scooba, MS*]
EMJH .... Ellinghausen, McCullough, Johnson, Harris [*Medium*] [*Microbiology*]
Emjo .... Emmanuel Jobe (SAUS)
EMJR .... electronic maintenance job request (SAUS)
EMK .... Edward Moore Kennedy [*American politician*]
EMK .... Electrical Meter Kit
EMK .... Electro-Motorische Kraft [*Electromotive Force*] [*German*]
EMK .... Emergency Medical Kit (MCD)
EMK .... Emmonak [*Alaska*] [*Airport symbol*] (OAG)
EMKO .... Ethyl Michler's Ketone Oxime (PDAA)
EMKR .... EMCORE Corp. [*NASDAQ symbol*] (NASQ)
EML .... Earthquake Mechanisms Laboratary (SAUS)
EML .... Eastern Co. [*AMEX symbol*] (SPSG)
EML .... Economic Models Ltd. [*British*] (NITA)
EML .... Educational Materials Laboratory
EML .... Electrical Metrology Laboratory (MCD)
EML .... Electromagnetic Laboratory [*NASA*] (GFGA)
EML .... Electromagnetic Launcher [*Military*] (SDI)
EML .... Electromagnetic Levitation (ACAE)
EML .... Electromagnetic Levitator
EML .... Electromechanical Laboratories (MUGU)
EML .... Electronic Mail (file name extension) (SAUS)
EML .... Electronic Media Literacy (SAUS)

E-ML .... Electronic-Media Literacy [*or Literate*]
EML .... Electronic Media Literate (SAUS)
EML .... Electronic Microsystems Ltd (SAUS)
EML .... Electron Microscopy Laboratory (SAUS)
EML .... Elementary Math Library [*IBM Corp.*]
EML .... Element Management Layer [*Computer science*] (VERA)
Eml .... Emanliter (SAUS)
EML .... Emco Ltd. [*Toronto Stock Exchange symbol*]
EML .... Emergency Manning Level (CET)
EML .... Emission Measurement Laboratory (SAUO)
EML .... Emory University Division of Librarianship, Atlanta, GA [*OCLC symbol*] (OCLC)
EML .... Empire Lines, Inc.
EML .... Emulator (IAA)
EML .... Emulator Machine Language [*Computer science*] (MHDB)
eml .... Emulsion (VRA)
EMl .... End of Medium (SAUS)
EML .... Engineering Materials List [*Nuclear energy*]
EML .... Engineering Mechanics Laboratory [*National Institute of Standards and Technology*] (IEEE)
EML .... English Men of Letters [*A publication*]
EML .... Environmental and Morale Leave [*Military*] (POLM)
EML .... Environmental Measurements Laboratory [*Department of Energy*] (GRD)
EML .... Environmental Measuring Laboratory (SAUS)
EML .... Equal Matrix Languages [*Computer science*] (PDAA)
EML .... Equatorial Magnetosphere Laboratory (MCD)
EML .... Equipment Maintenance Log [*Army*] (AABC)
EML .... Equipment Modification List (MCD)
EML .... Error Management Logic (SAUS)
EML .... Erythema Nodosum Leprosum [*Medicine*] (EDAA)
EML .... Established Measured Loss (CIST)
EML .... Estimated Maximum Loss (MARI)
EML .... Estimated Month of Loss
EML .... European Media Lab, Heidelberg (SAUS)
EML .... European Media Laboratory (SAUO)
EML .... Expanded Metal Lath
EML .... Expected Measured Loss [*Telecommunications*] (TEL)
EML .... Experimental Meteorology Laboratory
EML .... Extended Media List [*British*]
EML .... Exterior Metal Loss (SAUS)
EMLA .... Electromechanical Linear Actuator
EMLA .... European Medical Laser Association (SAUS)
EMLA .... Eutectic Mixture of Local Anesthetics [*Topical anesthetic cream*]
EMLAT .... Modern Language Aptitude Test-Elementary [*Education*] (AEE)
EMLB .... Erythromycin Lactobionate [*Medicine*] (EDAA)
EMLC .... Experimental Manpower Laboratory for Corrections (OICC)
EMLD .... Emerald (ROG)
EMLD .... Emerald Financial Corp. [*NASDAQ symbol*] (NASQ)
EMLEC .... Encore Marketing Intl. [*ECM Symbol*] (TTSB)
EMLF .... Eastern Mineral Law Foundation (EA)
EMLI .... Environmental Measurements Laboratory Impactor [*Sampling instrument*]
EMLIS .... Exploratory Modelling of Library and Information Systems (SAUS)
EMLIS Project ... Exploratory Modelling of Library and Information Systems Project (SAUS)
EMLNG .... External Mammary Lymph Node Group [*Medicine*] (MELL)
em log .... electromagnetic log (SAUS)
EMLR .... Engineering Manufacturing Liaison Release (KSC)
EMI/RFI .... Electromagnetic Interference and Radio Frequency Interference (SAUS)
EMLT .... EMCO, Ltd. [*NASDAQ symbol*] (NASQ)
EMLTF .... EMCO Ltd. [*NASDAQ symbol*] (SAG)
EMLTS .... Electromagnetic Levitation Transportation System (SAUS)
EMLX .... Emulex Corp. [*NASDAQ symbol*] (NQ)
EMM .... CANMET [*Canada Centre for Mineral and Energy Technology*] Library [*Canada Energy, Mines, and Resources*] [*UTLAS symbol*]
EMM .... Eagle's Minimal Medium [*Animal physiology*] (QSUL)
EMM .... Earth, Moon, and Mars [*Astronomy*]
EMM .... East Machias [*Maine*] [*Seismograph station code, US Geological Survey*] (SEIS)
EMM .... Ebers-MOLL [*Metallo-Organic Liquid LASER*] Model [*Electronics*] (OA)
EMM .... Electrical and Mechanical Maintenance (IAA)
EMM .... Electricity Market Model [*Department of Energy*] (GFGA)
EMM .... Electric Matrix Memory (SAUS)
EMM .... Electromagnetic Measurement (IEEE)
EMM .... Electromagnetic Moment (SAUS)
EMM .... Electromanometric (SAUS)
EMM .... Electromechanical Machining [*Manufacturing term*]
EMM .... electromechanical manipulator (SAUS)
EMM .... Electromechanical Mockup (KSC)
EMM .... Electronic Magnetic Memory (SAUS)
EMM .... Electronic Manufacturing Manual (IAA)
EMM .... Electronic Memories & Magnetics (SAUS)
EMM .... Electronic Memories and Magnetics Corp. (SAUS)
EMM .... Electronic Memory and Magnetics (IAA)
EMM .... Electron Mirror Microscope (IAA)
EMM .... Emma-Nik Aviation Services Ltd. [*Nigeria*] [*FAA designator*] (FAAC)
EMM .... Emmanuel College [*Boston, MA*] (ROG)
Emm .... Emmanuel College, Cambridge (SAUS)
EMM .... Emmenagogue [*Promoting Menstruation*] [*Pharmacy*] (ROG)
EMM .... Emory University, A. W. Calhoun Medical Library, Atlanta, GA [*OCLC symbol*] (OCLC)
EMM .... Engineering Management Manual
EMM .... Entente Medicale Mediterraneenne [*Mediterranean Medical Entente*] (EAIO)
EMM .... Enterprise Mail Manager (SAUS)
EMM .... Entity Motion and Modeling (SAUS)
EMM .... Environment Mining Model (SAUO)
EMM .... Episcopal Migration Ministries (SAUO)
EMM .... Error Matrix Method (SAUS)
EMM .... Erythema Multiforme Major [*Medicine*] (EDAA)
EMM .... Expanded Memory Manager
EMM .... Experiences in Marketing Management (MCD)
EMM .... Extended Memory Manager (SAUS)
EMM .... Extended Memory Module (SAUS)
EMM .... Extended Midcourse Mode [*Navy*] (CAAL)
EMM .... Kemmerer, WY [*Location identifier*] [*FAA*] (FAAL)
e-mm- .... Malta [*MARC geographic area code*] [*Library of Congress*] (LCCP)
EMMA .... Electronic Mask-Making Apparatus (IAA)
EMMA .... Electronic Mathematic Model-Analog (PDAA)
EMMA .... Electron Manual Metal Arc (OA)
EMMA .... Electron Microscope Microanalyzer (SAUS)
EMMA .... Electron Microscope-Microprobe Analyser (SAUS)
EMMA .... electron microscop microprobe analysis (SAUS)
EMMA .... Electron Microscopy and Microanalysis (IEEE)
EMMA .... Emergency Medicine Management Association [*Defunct*] (EA)
EMMA .... Engineering Maintenance Mockup Aid (ACAE)
EMMA .... Engineering Mock-Up and Manufacturing Aid (MCD)
EMMA .... Environmental Monitoring in Metropolitan Areas [*Air quality management*]
EMMA .... Equalized Maintenance, Maximum Availability (PDAA)
EMMA .... Equitorial Mount with Mirrors for Acceleration (SAUS)
EMMA .... Ethylene Methyl Methacrylate [*Organic chemistry*]
EMMA .... European Marine Motorways (EURO)
EMMA .... European Mouse Mutant Archive
EMMA .... European MultiMedia Award (VERA)
EMMA .... Exceptional Merit Media Awards [*National Women's Political Caucus*]
EMMA .... Expanded Metal Manufacturers Association [*Defunct*] (EA)
EMMA .... Expeditious Monitor and Maintenance Analyst [*Computer*] [*NASA*]
EMMA .... Expert Missile Maintenance Aid (ACAE)
EMMA .... Explosives Munitions Manufacturing Area (BCP)
EMMA .... Extra MARC [*Machine-Readable Catalog*] Material (NITA)
EMMA .... Eye-Movement Measuring Apparatus [*Ophthalmology*] (DAVI)
EMMADS .... Electronic Master Monitor and Display System (ACAE)
EMMAQUA ... Equitorial Mount with Mirrors for Acceleration with Water Spray (SAUS)
EMMC .... Corps of Engineers Manual for Military Construction [*Army*]
EMMC .... Engineers Manual for Military Construction [*Army Corps of Engineers*] [*A publication*] (AAGC)
EMMCC .... Erection Mechanism Motor Control Center
Emm Coll ..... Emmanuel College-Cambridge (SAUS)
EMME .... Ethernet Management Module [*Telecommunications*]
EmMex .... Emerging Mexico Fund [*Associated Press*] (SAG)
EMMGB .... Eaton's Motor Machine Gun Battery [*British military*] (DMA)
EMMI .... environmental method monitoring index (SAUS)
EMMI .... Environmental Monitoring Methods Index [*Environmental Protection Agency*] (AEPA)
EMMI .... ESO Multi Mode Instrument (SAUS)
EMMI .... Euregional Multimedia Information (EURO)
EMM Investigation ... Electromanometric Investigation (SAUS)
EMMIS .... Electronics Maintenance Management Information System (SAUO)
EMMIS .... Electronics Manufacturing Management Information System (SAUS)
EMMIS .... Environmental Monitoring Management Information System (SAUS)
EmmisBd ..... Emmis Broadcasting Corp. [*Associated Press*] (SAG)
EmMkFlt ...... Emerging Markets Floating Rate Fund [*Associated Press*] (SAG)
EMML .... Electromechanical Machine Laboratory (SAUS)
EMMP .... Environmental Monitoring and Mitigation Plan (ABAC)
EMMP .... Equipment Maintenance Management Program [*Air Force*]
EMMPS .... Emergency Military Manpower Procurement System (MCD)
EMMPS .... Enhanced MEECN [*Minimum Essential Emergency Communications Network*] Message Processing System
EMMR .... Eastern Museum of Motor Racing (EA)
EMMRIT .... Electronic Warfare Signal Intelligence Material Management Realignment Implementation Task Group
EMMS .... Edinburgh Medical Missionary Society (SAUO)
EMMS .... Electronic Mail and Message Systems
EMMS .... Emmis Broadcasting'A' [*NASDAQ symbol*] (TTSB)
EMMS .... Emmis Broadcasting Corp. [*NASDAQ symbol*] (SAG)
EMMS .... Emmis Communications "A" [*NASDAQ symbol*] [*Formerly, Emmis Broadcasting*]
EMMS .... Emmis Communications Corp. [*NASDAQ symbol*] (NASQ)
EMMSA .... Envelope Makers' and Manufacturing Stationers' Association (DGA)
EMMSE .... Educational Modules for Materials Science and Engineering (SAUS)
EMMTAC .... Executive Manpower Management Technical Assistance Center [*Civil Service Commission*]
EMMTAP .... Executive Manpower Management Technical Assistance Plan [*Civil Service Commission*]
EMMU .... Extended Memory Management Unit (SAUS)
EMMV .... Extended Mandatory Minute Ventilation [*Medicine*] (EDAA)
EMN .... , and Nancy [*Dickerman*] [*Cook*] [*Democratic Party activists*]
EMN .... Eastmain Resources, Inc. [*Toronto Stock Exchange symbol*]
EMN .... Eastman Chemical [*NYSE symbol*] (TTSB)
EMN .... Eastman Chemical Co., Inc. [*NYSE symbol*] (SPSG)
EMN .... Electromagnetic Moving Coil and Neutralized Winding (IAA)
EMN .... Engineering Management Network (NASA)
EMN .... Equivalent Manufacturers Number (SAUS)
EMN .... Escuadron de la Muerte Nuevo [*New Death Squad*] [*El Salvador*] (PD)

EMN Nema [*Mauritania*] [*Airport symbol*] (OAG)
EMND Equine Motor Neuron Disease [*Equine term*] (TED)
EMNE Early Modern English [*Language, etc.*]
EMNM El Morro National Monument (SAUS)
EMO Earth Physics Library [*Canada Energy Mines and Resources*] [*UTLAS symbol*]
EMO Electric Motor-Operated (NRCH)
EMO Electromagnetic Oscillograph (SAUS)
EMO Electromechanical Optical (AAG)
EMO Electromechanical Oscillator (SAUS)
EMO Electronic Maintenance Officer (SEWL)
EMO Electronics Material Officer
EMO Elk Mountain Observatory (SAUS)
EMO Embarkation Medical Official [*Military*] [*British*]
EMO Emergency Management Office (SAUS)
EMO Emergency Management Organization [*Environmental science*] (COE)
EMO Emergency Measurement Organization (SAUO)
EMO Emergency Measures Organization [*Canada*]
EMO Emergency Off (SAA)
EMO Emergency Services Organization (SAUS)
EMO Emo [*Papua New Guinea*] [*Airport symbol*] (OAG)
EMO Emollient (ROG)
EMO Emosson [*Switzerland*] [*Seismograph station code, US Geological Survey*] (SEIS)
EMO Engage Missile Orders [*Military*] (CAAL)
EMO Engineering Maintainability Organization (SAUS)
EMO Engineering Maintenance Officer (DNAB)
EMO Environmental Management Office (DOMA)
EMO Environmental Medicine Officer [*Military*]
EMO Epstein and Macintosh, Oxford [*Ether inhaler and Oxford bellows*] [*Anesthesiology*] (DAVI)
EMO Equipment Management Office [*Air Force*] (AFIT)
EMO Equipment Move Order (AAG)
EMO European Manufacturing Operation (SAUO)
EMO Examining Medical Officer (SAUS)
EMO Export Meat Order
EMO TCW/DW Emerging Markets Opportunities Trust [*NYSE symbol*] (SAG)
EMO TCW/DW Emerg Mkt Opp Tr [*NYSE symbol*] (TTSB)
EMOA Encyclopedia of Medical Organizations and Agencies [*A publication*]
EMOC EOSDIS Mission Operations Center (SAUO)
EMOC EOS Missions Operations Center (SAUS)
EMOD Erasable Magneto-Optical Disk [*Computer science*] (IAA)
EMOD Erasable Memory Octal Dump [*Computer science*]
E Mod E Early Modern English (BARN)
EMO Dig Emergency Measurement Organization Digest (SAUO)
EMO Dig Emergency Measurement Organization Digest (journ.) (SAUS)
EMOFICO Committee for Environmental Monitoring of Forest Insect Control Operations
EMOG Enstatite, Magnesite, Olivine, Graphite [*Geology*]
EMOL Excerpta Medica On Line (SAUS)
EMOL Excerpta Medica Online [*Information service or system*] (NITA)
EMOLI East Moline, IL [*American Association of Railroads railroad junction routing code*]
EMOLL Emolliens [*Mollifying, Healing*] [*Pharmacy*] (ROG)
EMON Emons Transportation Group [*NASDAQ symbol*] (TTSB)
EMON Environmental Monitoring & Testing Corp. [*NASDAQ symbol*] (NQ)
EMON Exception Monitoring (MCD)
e-money Electronic Money (ADWA)
Emons Emons Holding, Inc. [*Associated Press*] (SAG)
EMORG East Midland Operational Research Group (SAUS)
EMORS East Morris, IL [*American Association of Railroads railroad junction routing code*]
Emory U Emory University (GAGS)
EMOS Earth Mean Orbital Speed
EMOS Eastern Mediterranean Optical System [*Communications term*] (DCT)
EMOS ECMWF Meteorological Operational System (SAUS)
EMOS Enhanced Military Operation System (SAUS)
EMOS Enhancement Metal-Oxide Semiconductor (BUR)
EMOS Entry Military Occupational Specialty (AABC)
EMOS European Meteorological Satellite (SAUS)
emot emotion (SAUS)
EMOT Emotional
EMOT Estimated Minimum Operating Temperature [*Engineering*]
EMOTA European Mail Order Traders' Association [*EC*] (ECED)
emoticon Emotional Icon [*Expression of emotion typed into a message using standard keyboard characters*] (CDE)
EMOV Electromagnetically Operated Valve (NRCH)
EMOV Elm Mottle Virus [*Plant pathology*]
EMP Association of students of the European Management Programme (SAUO)
EMP Elastomer Modified Plastomer (SAUS)
EMP Electrician's Mate (Power and Light) [*U.S. Navy enlisted rating*] (AUER)
EMP Electric Membrane Property [*Medicine*] (EDAA)
EMP Electromagnetic (SAUS)
EMP Electromagnetic Power [*or Pulse*]
EMP Electromagnetic Propagation
EMP Electromagnetic Prospecting (SAUS)
EMP Electro-Magnetic Pulse
emp electromagnetic pulses (SAUS)
EMP Electromechanical Power [*or Pulse*]
EMP Electromolecular Propulsion [*Electrochemistry*]
EMP Electronic Manuscript Project [*Association of American Publishers*] [*Information service or system*] (IID)
EMP Electronic Materials Programme (ODA)
EMP Electronic Multiplying Punches (DEN)
EMP Electron Microprobe
EMP Embden-Meyerhof-Parnas [*Hexose metabolic pathway*] [*Biochemistry*]
EMP Embden-Meyerhof Pathway (DB)
EMP Emergency Medical Personnel (MCD)
EMP Emission Pattern (SAUS)
EMP Empennage [*Aerospace engineering*]
emp Emperor (VRA)
EMP Emperor [*or Empress*]
emp Empire (ADWA)
EMP Empire
EMP Empire Air Service, Inc. [*ICAO designator*] (FAAC)
EMP Empire Co. Ltd. [*Toronto Stock Exchange symbol*]
Emp Empire District Electric Co. [*Associated Press*] (SAG)
EMP Empire of Carolina, Inc. [*AMEX symbol*] (SPSG)
Emp Empirical (DIAR)
EMP Emplastrum [*Plaster*] [*Pharmacy*]
EMP Employables (OICC)
EMP Employee [*or Employer*] (DCTA)
EMP Employment [*Motor vehicle violation code used in state of Maryland*] (MVRD)
emp Employment (SAUS)
EMP Emporia, KS [*Location identifier*] [*FAA*] (FAAL)
emp Empress (ADWA)
EMP End of Month Payment [*Business term*]
EMP Energy Management Plan (MCD)
EMP Engineering, Mathematics, and Physical Sciences [*Military*]
EMP Engineering Mine Plough (SAUS)
EMP Engineering Modification Proposal (NG)
EMP Environmental Management Plan
EMP Environmental Management Programs (SAUS)
EMP Environmental Measurement Payload (SAUS)
EMP Environmental Measure Package (ACAE)
EMP Environmental Monitoring and Prediction [*Subcommittee*] [*Marine science*] (OSRA)
EMP Environmental Monitoring Plan (SAUS)
EMP Environmental Monitoring Program
EMP Environment Management Program (EERA)
EMP Ephemerides of the Minor Planets (DICI)
EMP Epidermal Melanin Pigmentation [*Dermatology*]
EMP EPO [*Erythroprotein*] Mimetic Peptide [*Biochemistry*]
EMP Equipment Mounting Plate (NASA)
EMP Equivalent Monthly Payment
EMP Erasable Memory Program [*Computer science*]
EMP Erythrocyte Membrane Protein [*Biochemistry*]
EMP Estuary Management Plan
EMP Ethyl Mercury Phosphate (BARN)
EMP Evaluated Maintenance Programming
EMP Excessive Multiple Posting [*Computer science*] (VERA)
EMP Excessive Multi-Posting (SAUS)
EMP Exciton-Magnetic Polaron [*Physics*] (ODA)
EMP Executive Management Program (DD)
EMP Ex Modo Praescripto [*In the Manner Prescribed*] [*Pharmacy*]
EMP Experimental and Molecular Pathology [*Medicine*] (EDAA)
EMP Exponentially Mapped Past (SAUS)
EMP Export Marketing Plan (JAGO)
EMP External Membrane Potential/Protein [*Medicine*] (EDAA)
EMP External Power Monitor
EMP Extramedullary Plasmacytoma [*Medicine*] (EDAA)
EMP Extraocular Muscle Palsy [*Medicine*] (MELL)
EMP Ecological Monitoring Programme (ODA)
EMPA Electron Microprobe Analysis [*Also, EMA*]
EM/PA Engine Maintenance through Progressive Analysis (SAUS)
EMPA Equipment Maintenance through Progressive Analysis [*Automotive service and lubricants*]
EMPA European Military Press Association (SAUO)
EMPA Executive Master of Public Affairs (PGP)
EMPAC Engineering Management Planning and Control (SAUS)
EMPAC Enterprise Maintenance Planning and Control (GART)
EMPAC Ethnic Millions Political Action Committee (EA)
EMP AGCY Employment Agency (WDAA)
EMPAR European Multifunction Phased Array Radar (SAUS)
EMPAR European Multifunction Phased-Array RADAR (MCD)
EMPASS Electromagnetic Performance of Air and Ship Systems
EMPASS Electromagnetic Performance of Aircraft and Ships System (SAUS)
EMPATF Emergency Management Preparedness and Assistance Trust Fund (DEMM)
empath empathetic (SAUS)
empath empathy (SAUS)
EM Pathway Embden-Meyerhof Pathway (SAUS)
EMPB Effervescent Magnetic Peroxoborate
EMPB Embroidery Manufacturers Promotion Board [*Later, SEMPB*] (EA)
EMPB Emergency Mobilization Preparedness Board [*DoD*]
EMPB Ethyl(methyl)(piperidyl)barbituric Acid [*Biochemistry*]
EMPC Educational Media Producers Council [*of the National Audio-Visual Association*] [*Later, NAVA Materials Council*]
EMPC Equipment Modification Procurement Costs (MCD)
EMPC European Manpower Committee (SAUO)
EMPC Electrostatic Molecular Potential Contour [*Chemistry*] (ODA)
EmpCar Empire of Carolina, Inc. [*Associated Press*] (SAG)
EMPD Electromotive Potential Difference (SAUS)

empd .... employed (SAUS)
EMPD .... Engineering Physics and Mathematics Division (SAUS)
EMPD .... Ethoxy-meta-phenylenediamine [*Organic chemistry*]
EMPDA .... Educational Media Producers and Distributors Association (SAUO)
EMPDAC ...... Educational Media Producers and Distributors Association of Canada
EmpDist .... Empire District Electric Co. [*Associated Press*] (SAG)
EMPE .... Emperor Penguin [*North American bird banding code*] (BIBA)
EMPE-AERIS... Electronic Mobile Positioning Equipment-Aerial Electronic Range Instrumentation (SAUS)
EMPE-AERIS... Electronic Mobile Positioning Equipment-Aerial Electronic Range Instrumentation System (SAUO)
EMPEP .... Erythrocyte Membrane Protein Electrophoretic Pattern [*Clinical chemistry*] (AAMN)
EMPF .... Electronics Manufacturing Productivity Facility (MCD)
EMPG .... Electrical/Mechanical Power Generation Subsystem
EMPG .... Excerpta Medica/EMBASE Publishing Group (IID)
EMPGS .... Electrical/Mechanical Power Generation Subsystem (MCD)
emph .... emphasis (SAUS)
EMPH .... Emphysema [*Medicine*]
EMPHAS ...... Emphysema plus Asthma [*Medicine*]
EMPHASIS ... Evaluation Management Using Past History Analysis for Scientific Inventory Simulation
emphy .... emphysema (SAUS)
emphy .... emphysematous (SAUS)
emphy .... emphyteusis (SAUS)
emphy .... emphyteuta (SAUS)
emphy .... emphyteutic (SAUS)
EMPI .... EMPI, Inc. [*NASDAQ symbol*] (NQ)
EMPI .... Engineering Manual Preparation Instruction [*Army Materiel Command*]
EMPI .... Enterprise Master Person Index (GART)
EMPI .... European Motor Products, Inc. [*Auto industry supplier*]
EmpIca .... Empresas Ica Sociedad Controladora [*Associated Press*] (SAG)
EMPIN .... Emporia, IN [*American Association of Railroads railroad junction routing code*]
EMPIRE .... Early Manned Planetary-Interplanetary Round-Trip Expedition (SAUS)
EMPIRE .... Early Manned Planetary-Interplanetary Round Trip Experiment
EMPIRE .... Early Manned Planetary Interruptionless Reconnaissance Expedition (SAUO)
EMPIRE .... Early Manned Planetary Interruptionless Round-Trip Expedition (SAUS)
EMPIRE .... Electromagnetic Performance Information Research (PDAA)
EMPIRE .... Electromagnetic Phenomena Interference Repository (PDAA)
EMPIRE .... Electronic Multipurpose Intelligence Retaliatory Equipment (IAA)
EMPIRES ..... Excerpta Medica Physicians Information Retrieval and Education Service [*Elsevier Science Publishers*] [*Information service or system*]
Empirical Econ... Empirical Economics [*A publication*] (JLIT)
EMPIS .... Engineering Materials and Processes Information Service (SAUS)
EMPIS .... Engineering Materials and Process Information Service (SAUS)
EMPIS .... Environmental Management and Planning Information System (SAUS)
EMPKG .... Electromechanical Packaging (SAUS)
empl .... Emplace (SAUS)
EMPL .... Emplacement (AABC)
EMPL .... Emplane [*British*]
EMPL .... Emplastrum [*Plaster*] [*Pharmacy*] (ROG)
EMPL .... Employ [*or Employee*] (AABC)
EMPL .... Employed
Empl .... Employee (TBD)
EMPL .... Employer (ROG)
empl .... Employment (PROS)
EMPL .... Engineering Master Parts List (KSC)
EMPL .... Estimated Maximum Probable Loss (MARI)
EMPL .... Extensible Microprogramming Language [*Computer science*] (MHDB)
EMPLAST..... Emplastrum [*Plaster*] [*Pharmacy*] (ROG)
Empl Comp App Bd... Decisions of the Employees' Compensation Appeals Board [*Department of Labor*] (DLA)
empld .... employed (SAUS)
EMPLEE .... Employee
EMPLMNT.... Employment
Emplmt .... Employment (TBD)
Employee Rel L Rev... Employee Relations Law Review [*A publication*] (AAGC)
Employers' Rev... Employers' Review [*A publication*]
Empl Prac Dec... Employment Practices Decisions [*Commerce Clearing House*] [*A publication*] (DLA)
Empl Prac Guide... Employment Practices Guide [*Commerce Clearing House*] [*A publication*] (DLA)
EMPLR .... Employer
Empl R .... Employers' Review [*A publication*]
Empl'rs Liab... Employers' Liability (DLA)
Empl Saf'y & Health Guide... Employment Safety and Health Guide [*A publication*] (DLA)
EMPLT .... Employment (SAUS)
EmplySl .... Employee Solutions, Inc. [*Associated Press*] (SAG)
EMPMC .... Effective Medical Practice and Managed Care (SAUO)
EMPMD .... Electronic, Magnetic and Photonic Materials Division (SAUS)
EMPNO .... Employee Number (MCD)
EMPOR .... Emporia, VA [*American Association of Railroads railroad junction routing code*]
EMPOR .... Emporium
Emporia St U... Emporia State University (GAGS)
EMPP .... Electromagnetic Pulse Protection (SAUS)
EMP pathway... Embden-Meyerhof-Parnas pathway (SAUS)
EMPPO .... European and Mediterranean Plant Protection Organization (SAUS)
EMPR .... Electromagnetic Pulse Radiation (SAUS)
EMPR .... Electromagnetic Pulse Response (SAUS)
EMPR .... Ethernet Multiport Repeater (SAUS)
EMPRA .... Emergency Mulitple Person Rescue Apparatus (PDAA)
EMPRESS .... Electromagnetic Pulse Radiation Environment Simulator for Ships [*Navy*] (MCD)
EMPRESS .... EnvironMental Pulse Radiation Environment Simulator for Ships (SAUS)
EMPRESS .... Expert Mission Planning and Replanning Scheduling System (ACAE)
EMPRO .... Emergency Proposal (NATG)
EMPRS .... Enroute Mission Planning and Rehearsal System (SEWL)
EMPRU .... Rural Employment (SAUS)
EMPS .... Electromagnetic Pulse Simulator (MCD)
EMPS .... Electronic Maintenance Publication System (MCD)
EMPS .... Electronic Message Privacy System (SAUS)
EMPS .... Elevation Matrix Processing System (SAUS)
EMPS .... Emergency Power Supply (MSA)
EMPS .... Ethernet Multiport Station (SAUS)
EMPS .... Exertional Muscle Pain Syndrome [*Medicine*] (MELL)
EMPSA .... Electro-resistance Multichannel Particle-Size Analyzer (SAUS)
EMPSKD ...... Employment Schedule [*Navy*] (ANA)
EMPSKED .... Employment Schedule (NVT)
EMPST .... Energy, Matter, Personality, Space, Time (SAUS)
empsz .... emphasize (SAUS)
EMPT .... Early College Mathematics Placement Testing Program
EMPT .... Electronic Maintenance Proficiency Test
EMPTA .... Ethyl Methylphosphonothioic Acid
emp vesic.... Blistering Plaster [*Latin for emplastrum vesicatorium*] [*Medicine*] (EDAA)
Emp Vesic ... Emplastrum Vesicatorum [*A Blister*] [*Medicine*]
EMQ .... Economic Manufacturing Quality
EMQ .... Electromagnetic Quiet
EMQ .... Ethoxyquin [*Antioxidant*] [*Organic chemistry*]
EMR .... Augusta, GA [*Location identifier*] [*FAA*] (FAAL)
EMR .... Department of Energy, Mines and Resources Canada (SAUO)
EMR .... Earthquake Maps and Reports (SAUO)
EMR .... Eastern & Midlands Railway [*British*] (ROG)
EMR .... Eastern Mediterranean Region (SAUS)
EMR .... Eastern Missile Range (ACAE)
EMR .... Echo Mountain Resources Ltd. [*Vancouver Stock Exchange symbol*]
EMR .... Eddy-Making Resistance (SAUS)
EMR .... Educable Mentally Retardate [*or Retarded*]
EMR .... Effective Management Responsibility
EMR .... electomagnetic radiation (SAUS)
EMR .... Electrolytic Metal Recovery (SAUS)
EMR .... Electromagnetic Radiation (AFM)
EMR .... Electromagnetic Relay (SAUS)
EMR .... Electromagnetic Resonance (WDAA)
EMR .... Electromagnetic Response (SAUO)
EMR .... Electromagnetic Riveting (PDAA)
EMR .... Electromechanical Relay [*Power switchgear*] (IEEE)
EMR .... Electromechanical Research (IEEE)
EMR .... Electromechanical Research, Incorporated (SAUS)
EMR .... Electronic-Combat Multi-Function RADAR [*Military*] (SEWL)
EMR .... Electronic Mail Registration (SAUS)
EMR .... Electronic Management Reporting (SAUS)
EMR .... Electronic Medical Record (SAUS)
EMR .... Electronic Metering Rack [*Diesel engines*]
EMR .... Electronic Module Retard [*Automotive engineering*]
EMR .... Electronic Moisture Recorder
EMR .... Electronic Motor Regulation
EMR .... Electron Magnetic Resonance (SAUO)
EMR .... Eletromagnetic Radiation (SAUS)
EMR .... Emergency Mechanical Restraint [*Medicine*] (DAVI)
EMR .... Emergency Medical Responders
EMR .... Emergency Medical Response (SAUO)
EMR .... Emerson Electric Co. [*NYSE symbol*] (SPSG)
EMR .... Emgold Mining [*Vancouver Stock Exchange symbol*] [*Formerly, Emperor Gold*] (SG)
EMR .... Emission Maintenance Reminder [*Automotive engineering*]
EMR .... Emotionally Mentally Retarded [*Psychology*]
EMR .... Emperor Gold [*VS Symbol*] (TTSB)
EMR .... Empty, Measure, and Record [*Nursing*] (DAVI)
EMR .... EMR Schlumberger Co [*Medicine*] (EDAA)
EMR .... Endoscopic Mucosal Resection [*Medicine*] (MELL)
EMR .... Energy, Mines, and Resources [*Canadian government department*]
EMR .... Engineering Malfunction Report (MCD)
EMR .... Engineering Master Report (SAUS)
EMR .... Engineering Model Report (SAUS)
EMR .... Engineering Modification Requirements (MCD)
EMR .... Engine Maintenance Reminder [*Automotive engineering*]
EMR .... Engine Mature Ratio (SAUS)
EMR .... Engine Mission Ratio (SAUS)
EMR .... Engine Mixture Ratio
EMR .... Enhanced Metafile Record (SAUS)
EMR .... Enhanced Monitoring Rule [*For industrial plant emissions*]
EMR .... Enlisted Manning Report [*Air Force*]
EMR .... Enter Move Request (AAEL)
EMR .... Environmental Management Report [*Environmental Protection Agency*] (GFGA)
EMR .... Equipment Maintenance Record [*Army*] (AABC)
EMR .... Equipment Maintenance Report (SAUS)
EMR .... Error Monitor Register (KSC)
EMR .... Essential Metabolism Ratio [*Medicine*] (DMAA)
EMR .... Essential Minimum Repairs (SAUS)

EMR........ Exclusive Marketing Rights [*Business term*]
EMR........ Executive Management Responsibility (MCD)
EMR........ Executive Management Review (NG)
EMR........ Explosive Mishap Report (ACAE)
EMR........ External Mold Release [*Plastic fabrications*]
EMR........ Extra-Mural Rotations (GVA)
EMR........ Eye Movement Record [*Medicine*] (EDAA)
EMR........ Geological Survey of Canada Library [*Canada Energy Mines and Resources*] [*UTLAS symbol*]
EMRA........ Electrical Manufacturers Representive Association (SAUS)
EMRA........ Electronics Materiel Readiness Activity [*Army*]
EMRA........ Emergency Medical Response Agency (ADWA)
EMRA........ Emergency Medicine Residents' Association (EA)
EMRA........ Executive Master of Rehabilitation Administration (PGP)
EMRAAT........ Extended Medium Range Air to Air Technology (ACAE)
EMRACSE........ East Midland Regional Advisory Committee on Special Education [*British*] (AIE)
EMRAT........ Emergency Ram-Air Turbo-alternator (SAUS)
EMRB........ European Marketing Research Board [*British*]
EMRB........ European Market Research Bureau (SAUO)
EMRC........ Electronic Media Rating Council (EA)
EMRC........ Energy Mines Resources Canada (SAUO)
EMRC........ European Medical Research Councils [*ESF*] (PDAA)
EMRE........ Electromagnetic Radiation Effect [*Military*]
EMREL........ Emission Release (NVT)
em-related... emission-related (SAUS)
EMRF........ European Monetary Reserve Fund [*Common Market*]
EMRG........ Electromagnetic Radiation Generator
EMRG........ Electro Magnetic Rail Gun [*Military*] (ACAE)
EMRG........ eMerge Interactive 'A' [*NASDAQ symbol*] (SG)
EMRG........ Energy and Mineral Resources Group (SAUO)
EMRH........ Electromagnetic Radiation Hazard (MCD)
EMRH........ Emergency Manual Release Handle (MCD)
EMRIC........ Educational Media Research Information Center
emrl........ Emerald (VRA)
EMRL........ Emerald Capital Holdings, Inc. [*NASDAQ symbol*] (SAG)
EMRL........ Engineering (SAUS)
EMRL........ Engineering Materials Research Laboratory [*Brown University*] (PDAA)
EMRL........ Engineering Mechanics Research Laboratory [*Texas University*] (MCD)
EMRL........ Equipment Maintenance Requirements List (MCD)
EMRLB........ East Midland Regional Library Bureau (SAUS)
EMRLD........ Excimer Mid-Range Laser Device & Kill Assessment (SAUS)
EMRLD........ Excimer, Mid-Range [*or Moderate-Power*], Raman-Shifted LASER Device
EMRLD........ Excimer Moderate-Power Raman-Shifted Laser Device (SAUS)
EmrldCH........ Emerald Capital Holdings, Inc. [*Associated Press*] (SAG)
EmrldIsle........ Emerald Isle Bancorp, Inc. [*Associated Press*] (SAG)
EMRLS........ Eastern Massachusetts Regional Library System [*Information service or system*] (IID)
EMRLS........ Eastern Metropolitan Regional Library Service (SAUS)
EMRLS........ East Midlands Regional Library Service (SAUO)
EMRLS........ East Midlands Regional Library System (SAUS)
EMRO........ Eastern Mediterranean Regional Office [*World Health Organization*] [*Information service or system*] (IID)
EMRO........ Electromagnetic Radiation Operational
EMRO........ Emergency Management & Response Office (SAUS)
EMRO........ European Media Research Organizations (SAUO)
EMRODA........ Electronic Maintenance Repair Operation Distributors Association (SAUO)
EMRODA........ Electronic MRO [*Maintenance Repair Operation*] Distributors Association (EA)
EMRP........ Effective Monopole-Radiated Power (TEL)
EMRP........ Effective Monopulse Radiated Power (SAUS)
EMRPO........ Electromagnetic Radiation Project Office [*Naval Medical Research and Development Command*] [*Bethesda, MD*]
EM-RPSTL... Electronic Media Publications (Repair Parts Special Tools Lists) (SAUS)
EMRRI........ Energy and Mineral Resources Research Institute [*Iowa State University*] [*Research center*] (RCD)
EMRS........ East Malling Research Station [*British*] (ARC)
EMRS........ Electromagnetic Radiation System (MCD)
EMRS........ Electronic Medical Record System (ADWA)
EMRS........ Emergency Management Requirements Study (SAUO)
EMRS........ Emergency Medicine Research Society [*Manchester, England*] (EAIO)
EMRS........ Engineering Management Requirements Special [*McAir*]
E-MRS........ European-Materials Research Society (EAIO)
EMRSA........ Eastern Mediterranean Region Staff Association (SAUO)
EMRSC........ Experimental Medical Research Support Center (SAA)
EmrsEl........ Emerson Electric Co. [*Associated Press*] (SAG)
EMRT........ Electronic Market-Research Terminal
EMRT........ Emergency Medical Response Team (SAUO)
EMRU........ Electro-Magnetic Release Unit (PDAA)
EMRU........ Employment Market Research Unit (AIE)
EMRY........ Eastern Maine Railroad [*Federal Railroad Administration identification code*]
EMS........ Earl Marshal's Secretary [*Pseudonym used by James Dalloway*]
EMS........ Early Morning Specimen [*Medicine*]
EMS........ Early Morning Stiffness (MELL)
EMS........ Early Mortality Syndrome
EMS........ early myelosclerosis (SAUS)
EMS........ Earnings per Manshift (SAUS)
EMS........ Earth and Mineral Sciences (SAUO)
EMS........ Earth-Moon System (SEWL)
EMS........ Earthquake Monitoring System (NRCH)
EMS........ Economics Management Staff [*Department of Agriculture*] (GFGA)
EMS........ Edinburgh Mathematical Society (SAUO)
EMS........ Editorial Management System (DGA)
EMS........ Education Management System [*Military*]
EMS........ Eire Marine Service (SAUO)
EMS........ Elaine Music Shop [*Record label*]
EMS........ Electrical Muscle Stimulation [*Physiology*]
EMS........ Electrician's Mate (Shop) [*U.S. Navy enlisted rating*] (AUER)
EMS........ Electric Matrix Store (SAUS)
EMS........ Electro-Magnetic pulse Shielding (SAUS)
EMS........ Electromagnetic Separation (SAUS)
EMS........ Electromagnetic Sounding (ACAE)
EMS........ Electromagnetic Spectrum (NITA)
EMS........ Electromagnetic Stirring (SAUS)
EMS........ Electromagnetic Submarine [*Navy*]
EMS........ Electromagnetic Surveillance [*Air Force*]
EMS........ Electromagnetic Susceptibility (IEEE)
EMS........ Electromagnetic Suspension [*Railway technology*] (PS)
EMS........ Electromechanical System (SAUS)
EMS........ Electro Mechanical Systems Ltd (SAUS)
EMS........ Electromechanical Systole (DB)
EMS........ Electromotive Series (SAUS)
EMS........ Electromotive Surface [*Electrochemistry*] (IAA)
EMS........ Electromyosignal [*Computer science*]
EMS........ Electromyostimulation [*Medicine*] (DAVI)
EMS........ Electronic Magnetic Store (SAUS)
EMS........ Electronic Mail Service [*Telecommunications*]
EMS........ Electronic Mail System [*Postal Service*]
EMS........ Electronic Management System
EMS........ Electronic Measurement System (SAUS)
EMS........ Electronic Medical System [*or Service*]
EMS........ Electronic Meeting Services [*Clinton, MD*] [*Telecommunications*] (TSSD)
EMS........ Electronic Meeting System (RALS)
EMS........ Electronic Message Service [*Computer science*] (ELAL)
EMS........ Electronic Message System
EMS........ electronic messaging system (SAUS)
EMS........ Electronic Microsystem (IAA)
EMS........ Electronic Monitoring System (SAUS)
EMS........ electronic multishot instrument (SAUS)
ems........ electronic muscle stimulation (SAUS)
EMS........ Electronic Muscle Stimulator [*Medicine*] (CPH)
EMS........ Electronic Music Studio (SAUO)
EMS........ Electronic Music Synthesizer (SAUO)
EMs........ Electron Micrographs (SAUS)
EMS........ Electron Microscope [*Medicine*] (EDAA)
EMS........ Electron Microscopy Society (SAUO)
EMS........ electron modulation spectroscopy (SAUS)
EMS........ Electron-Momentum Spectrometer
EMS........ Electron Momentum Spectroscopy (SAUS)
EMS........ Electron Multiplex Switch
EMS........ Element Management System [*Computer science*] (TNIG)
EMS........ Elephant Memory System [*Computer science*]
EMS........ Elvis Presley Memorial Society of Syracuse, New York (EA)
EMS........ E-Mail Shorthand (SAUS)
EMS........ Embessa [*Papua New Guinea*] [*Airport symbol*] (OAG)
EMS........ Emergency Management System [*Environmental science*] (COE)
EMS........ Emergency Medical Service
EMS........ Emergency Mission Support [*Air Force*]
EMS........ Emergency Procedures for Ships Carrying Dangerous Goods (SAUO)
EMS........ Emergency Services (SAUO)
EMS........ Emergency Signal (BUR)
EMS........ Emission Spectrograph
EMS........ EMS Systems Ltd. [*Vancouver Stock Exchange symbol*]
EMS........ Emulator Machine Support (VLIE)
EMS........ Emulator Monitor System (IAA)
EMS........ Endometriosis [*Medicine*] (EDAA)
EMS........ Endoscopic Mucosectomy (MELL)
EMS........ Energy Emergency System [*Environmental science*] (COE)
EMS........ Energy Management System
EMS........ Enforcement Management Subsystem [*Environmental Protection Agency*]
EMS........ Enforcement Management System (GNE)
E/MS........ Engineering and Mining Journal (SAUS)
EMS........ Engineering Management Selection AG (SAUO)
EMS........ Engineering Management Society (SAUO)
EMS........ Engineering Master Schedule
EMS........ Engineering Material Specification (SAUS)
EMS........ Engineering Modeling System (SAUS)
EMS........ Engine Management System [*Army*]
EMS........ Engine Monitoring System
EMS........ English Madrigal School (SAUO)
EMS........ English Market Selection [*Cigars*]
EMS........ English Men of Science [*A publication*]
EMS........ Enhanced Memory Services (SAUS)
EMS........ Enhanced Memory Specifications [*Computer science*]
EMS........ Enhanced Mobility System [*LTV Aerospace and Defense Co.*]
EMS........ Enterprise Management System (FOTI)
EMS........ Enterprise Messaging Server (CDE)
EMS........ Enterprise Modeling Server (PCM)
EMS........ Enterprise Modelling System (VLIE)
EMS........ Enterprisewide Marketing System (GART)
EMS........ Entry Monitoring System (SAUS)

EMS............ Entry Monitor Subsystem (SAUS)
EMS............ Entry Monitor System [*or Subsystem*] [*NASA*]
EMS............ Environmental Management Service (SAUS)
EMS............ Environmental Management Subsystem [*Environmental Protection Agency*] (GFGA)
EMS............ Environmental Management System [*Mitsubishi Electric*]
EMS............ Environmental Monitoring Satellite (SAUS)
EMS............ Environmental Monitoring Stations (SAUS)
EMS............ Environmental Monitoring System (SAUS)
EMS............ Environmental Mutagen Society (EA)
EMS............ Eosinophilia Myalgia Syndrome [*Medicine*]
EMS............ Equilibrated Metal Surface [*Catalyst science*]
EMS............ Equilibrium Mode Simulator (TEL)
EMS............ Equipment Maintenance Squadron [*POMO*] (MCD)
EMS............ Equipment Management System (SAUS)
EMS............ Ericsson Manufacturing Systems [*Commercial firm*] [*British*]
EMS............ Error Mean Square
EMS............ Erythropoietic Marrow Scanning [*Medicine*] (EDAA)
EMS............ Essential Multiplexing System (SAUS)
EMS............ Ethyl Methanesulfonate [*or Ethyl Methanesulfonic Acid*] [*Experimental mutagen*]
EMS............ Eucharistic Missionary Society (TOCD)
EMS............ Europa Mining Strikes (SAUO)
EMS............ European Management Services (SAUO)
EMS............ European Mapping Standards (SAUO)
EMS............ European Mariculture Society (EAIO)
EMS............ European Marketing Systems (SAUO)
EMS............ European Mathematical Society (VERA)
EMS............ European Media Studies (SAUO)
EMS............ European Mobile Satellite (SAUS)
EMS............ European Monetary System (AF)
EMS............ Evangelical Missiological Society (EA)
EMS............ Event Management System (SAUS)
EMS............ Exception Management System
EMS............ Excess Mileage Surcharge [*Travel industry*] (TRID)
EMS............ Expanded Memory Services (SAUS)
EMS............ Expanded Memory Specification [*Computer science*]
EMS............ Expanded Memory Support (SAUS)
EMS............ Expanded Memory System [*Computer science*]
EMS............ Expected Mean Squares (SAUS)
EMS............ Expenditure Management System (FOTI)
EMS............ Experimental Monitoring Satellite (MCD)
EMS............ Experiment Management System (ACAE)
EMS............ Experiment Mounting Structure (SAUS)
EMS............ Export Marketing Service [*Department of Agriculture*]
EMS............ Exposure Modeling System [*Office of Pesticides and Toxic Substances*] (COE)
EMS............ Express Mail Service [*Generic term*]
EMS............ Extended Main Storage (VLIE)
EMS............ Extended Main Store (SAUS)
EMS............ Extended Maintenance Service (IAA)
EMS............ Extended Memory Specification (SAUS)
EMS............ Extended Memory Store [*Computer science*] (ECII)
EMS............ Extended Memory Support (SAUS)
EMS............ Extended Messaging Services [*Computer science*] (PCM)
EMS............ Extended Monitor System (VLIE)
EMS............ Extra-Mural Studies (GVA)
EMS............ IEEE Engineering Management Society (EA)
EMS............ Preferred Flights, Inc. [*Canada*] [*ICAO designator*] (FAAC)
EMS............ Society for Macedonian Studies (SAUO)
EMS............ Surveys and Mapping Library [*Canada Energy Mines and Resources*] [*UTLAS symbol*]
EMSA.......... Eastern Marathon Swimming Association (EA)
EMSA.......... Electrician's Mate, Seaman Apprentice [*Navy rating*]
EMSA.......... Electronics Material Support Agency (SAUS)
EMSA.......... Electronics Materiel Support Agency [*Army*]
EMSA.......... Electron Microscope Society of America (SAUO)
EMSA.......... Electron Microscope Surface Area (PDAA)
EMSA.......... Electron Microscopy Society of America (EA)
EMSA.......... Electrophoretic Mobility Shift Assay [*Analytical biochemistry*]
EMSA.......... Eugene Meylan, SA
EMSA.......... European Marine Step Association (SAUS)
EMSAP......... Early Medical School Acceptance Program (GAGS)
EMSATIME... EMS Arrival Time [*National Highway Traffic Safety Administration Fatal Accident Recording System code*]
EMSAW......... En Route Minimum Safe Altitude Warning [*FAA*] (TAG)
E-MSAW...... Enroute Minimum Safe Altitude Warning [*Aviation*] (PIPO)
EMSC.......... Educational Media Selection Center [*National Book Committee*]
EMSC.......... Eisenhower Mathematics/Science Consortium (SAUS)
EMSC.......... Electrical Manufacturers Standards Council (BARN)
EMSC.......... Electromechanical Stop Clock
EMSC.......... Electronic Mail Standards Committee (SAUO)
EMSC.......... Electronic Message Service Center (IAA)
EMSC.......... Emergency Medical Services for Children (ADWA)
EMSC.......... Engine Monitoring System Computer (VLIE)
EMSC.......... Equipment Maintenance Service Center (SAUO)
EMSC.......... European-Mediterranean Seismological Centre (SAUO)
EMSC.......... European-Mediterranean Siesmology Center
EMSC.......... Experimental Mine Sweeper, Coastal (SAUS)
EMSCOM...... Emergency Medical Services Communications (SAUS)
EMSCOM System... Emergency Medical Services Communications System (SAUS)
E/MSCS......... Enhanced Manual SHORAD [*Short Range Air Defense*] Control System [*Army*]
EMSD.......... Electrical Measurements and Standards Division [*National Institute of Standards and Technology*] (GRD)
EMSD.......... Environmental Monitoring Systems Division [*Environmental Protection Agency*] (GFGA)
EMSD.......... Equipment Major Subdivision
EMSEC......... Electro-Magnetic Security (SAUS)
EMSEC......... Emanations Security (AABC)
EMSEC......... Emission Security
EMSG.......... European Maintenance System Guide (SAUO)
EMSHOSP.... EMS Hospital [*National Highway Traffic Safety Administration Fatal Accident Recording System code*]
EMSI............ Effective Management Systems [*NASDAQ symbol*] (SAG)
EMSI............ Electromagnetic Sensing and Interpretation (SAUS)
EMSI............ Electronic Mail Standard Identification (SAUS)
EMSI............ Electron Microscopy Society of India (SAUO)
EMSI............ Ellipsomicroscopy
EMSI............ Ellipsomicroscopy for Surface Imaging
EMSI............ Emergency Medical Services Instructor (SAUO)
EMS-I.......... Environmental Modeling Systems, Inc. [*Computer science*]
EMSI............ European Myeloma Study Group for Interferon (SAUO)
EMSIB.......... Eastern Mediterranean Special Service Intelligence Bureau [*World War I*] [*British*]
EMSIDE........ Electromagnetic Signature Identification and Data Evaluation (SAUO)
EMSILR........ Executive Master of Science in Industrial and Labor Relations (PGP)
EM/SIM........ Emulator/Simulator (MCD)
EMSIS.......... Emergency Shipping Information System [*MARAD*] (TAG)
EMSIW......... Effective Mgmt Sys Wrrt [*NASDAQ symbol*] (TTSB)
EMSKED...... Employment Schedule
EMSL........... Electronic Material Sciences Laboratory
EMSL........... Electron Microscopy Service Laboratory (EFIS)
EMSL........... Environmental and Molecular Science Laboratory (DOMA)
EMSL........... Environmental Moleculer Sciences Laboratory (SAUO)
EMSL........... Environmental Monitoring and Support Laboratory (SAUS)
EMSL........... Environmental Monitoring and Surveillance Laboratory (SAUO)
EMSL........... Environmental Monitoring Support Laboratory (COE)
EMSL........... Environmental Monitoring Support Systems Laboratory (SAUS)
EMSL........... Environmental Monitoring Systems Laboratory [*Environmental Protection Agency*] (CARB)
EMSL........... European Microwave Signature Laboratory [*Italy*]
EMSL/CIN.... Environmental Monitoring and Support Laboratory, Cincinnati [*Ohio*] [*Environmental Protection Agency*] (GRD)
EMSL-LV...... Environmental Monitoring Systems Laboratory at Las Vegas (SAUO)
EMSL-LV...... Environmental Monitoring Systems Laboratory - Las Vegas (SAUS)
EMSL/LV...... Environmental Monitoring Systems Laboratory, Las Vegas [*Nevada*] [*Environmental Protection Agency*] (GRD)
EMSL/RTP... Environmental Monitoring Systems Laboratory, Research Triangle Park [*North Carolina*] [*Environmental Protection Agency*] (GRD)
EM/SME....... Electronics Manufacturing Group of the Society of Manufacturing Engineers (SAUO)
EMSN.......... Electrician's Mate, Seaman [*Navy rating*]
EMSN.......... Emission (MSA)
EMSN.......... External-Mix Spray Nut
EMSNTIME... EMS Notification Time [*National Highway Traffic Safety Administration Fatal Accident Recording System code*]
EMSO........... Education Society [*Later, Psychology Society - PS*] (EA)
EMSO........... Electronic Memory Systems Organization [*Burroughs Corp.*]
EMSO........... European Mobility Service Office [*Army*] (AABC)
EMSP........... Electromagnetic Pulse Survivability Military Standardization Program (SAUO)
EMSP........... Enhanced Modular Signal Processor (MCD)
EMSq........... Equipment Maintenance Squadron [*Air Force*]
EMSR........... Electrician's Mate, Ship Repair [*Navy rating*] [*Obsolete*]
EMSR........... Electronic Material Shipment Request [*Navy*]
EMSR........... Employment Service Review [*A publication*]
EMSRG......... Electrician's Mate, Ship Repair, General Electrician [*Navy rating*] [*Obsolete*]
EMSRS......... Electrician's Mate, Ship Repair, Shop Electrician [*Navy rating*] [*Obsolete*]
EMSRT......... Electrician's Mate, Ship Repair, I.C. Repairman [*Navy rating*] [*Obsolete*]
EMSS........... Einstein Extended Medium Sensitive Survey [*Cosmology*]
EMSS........... Electromagnetic Servoactuator System (NASA)
EMSS........... Electromechanical Subsystem (SAUS)
EMSS........... Electro-Mechanical System Simulator [*Computer-aided engineering*]
EMSS........... Electronic Message Service System [*Telecommunications*] (TEL)
EMSS........... Elsevier Materials Science Series (SAUS)
EMSS........... Emergency Manual Switching System [*Telecommunications*] (NITA)
EMSS........... Emergency Medical Service System
EMSS........... Emergency Mission Support System [*Air Force*]
EMSS........... E. Mitchell Scientific Society (SAUO)
EMSS........... Emulated Multispectral Scanner (SAUS)
EMSS........... Enviromod Software Server (SAUO)
EMSS........... Environmental Management Support Services (FOTI)
EMSS........... Experimental Manned Space Station [*Air Force*]
EMSS........... Experimental Man Space Station (SAUS)
EMSS........... Experimental Mobile Satellite System (DA)
EMSS Act..... Emergency Medical Services Systems Act (SAUS)
EM-SSC....... Electromechanical Switching System Control (SAUO)
EMST........... enhanced multichannel tracking (SAUS)
EMST........... Executive Master of Science in Taxation (PGP)
EMSTB......... Elevated Multi Sensor Test Bed (ACAE)
EM STOP..... Emergency Stop (SAUS)
EMSTRP...... Equipment Management System Training Requirements Program [*Navy*] (NG)
EMSU........... Early Morning Specimen of Urine (MELL)
EMSU........... Educational Media Services Unit (SAUO)
EMSU........... Electromagnetic Simulation Unit (MCD)

EMSU.......... Environmental Meteorological Support Unit [*National Weather Service*]
EMSU.......... environmental monitoring systems upgrade (SAUS)
EMSU.......... Epidemiology and Medical Statistics Unit (HEAS)
EMSU.......... Europaeiche Mittelstands-Union [*European Medium and Small Business Union*] [*EC*] (ECED)
EMSU.......... European Medium and Small Business Union (PDAA)
EMSUBS...... Equipment Management Subsystem (DNAB)
EMT.......... American Medical Response [*NYSE symbol*] (SPSG)
EMT.......... Each More Than
EMT.......... Early Memory Test (SAUS)
EMT.......... Early Missile Test
EMT.......... Eastern Mediterranean (SAUS)
EMT.......... Edited Machine Translation (SAUO)
EMT.......... Effective Mass Theory (AAEL)
EMT.......... Elapsed Maintenance Time
EMT.......... Elapsed Method of Training (MCD)
EMT.......... Electrical Mate Test (KSC)
EMT.......... Electrical Mechanical Tubing
EMT.......... Electrical Metallic Tubing
EMT.......... Electrical Metal Tubing (SAUS)
EMT.......... Electrician's Mate, Telephone [*Coast Guard rating*] [*Obsolete*]
EMT.......... electromagnetic technology (SAUS)
EMT.......... Electromagnetic Theory (SAUS)
EMT.......... Electromagnetic Thrust [*Propulsion for ship or submarine*]
EMT.......... Electromagnetic Tubing (SAUS)
EMT.......... Electromechanical Team
EMT.......... Electromechanical Technology
EMT.......... Electromechanical Test (NASA)
EMT.......... electromechanical transmission (SAUS)
EMT.......... Electronic Maintenance Technician [*FAA*]
EMT.......... Electronic Mind Tester
EMT.......... Electron Microscope Tomography
EMT.......... Electron Microscopy Technician [*Medicine*] (EDAA)
EMT.......... Electrostatic Memory Tube (SAUS)
EMT.......... Elemental Method of Training
EMT.......... El Monte, CA [*Location identifier*] [*FAA*] (FAAL)
EMT.......... Embalmer [*Navy rating*]
EMT.......... Embedded Management Tool (SAUS)
EMT.......... Embratel Participacoes ADS [*NYSE symbol*] (SG)
EMT.......... Emergency Management Team [*Nuclear energy*] (GFGA)
EMT.......... Emergency Medical Tag
EMT.......... Emergency Medical Team (MELL)
EMT.......... Emergency Medical Technician
emt.......... emergency medical technique (SAUS)
EMT.......... Emergency Medical Technologist (SAUS)
EMT.......... Emergency Medical Treatment [*Military*] (AABC)
EMT.......... Emmet [*California*] [*Seismograph station code, US Geological Survey*] (SEIS)
EMT.......... Emory University, Pitts Theological Library, Atlanta, GA [*OCLC symbol*] (OCLC)
EMT.......... Empire Resources [*Vancouver Stock Exchange symbol*]
Em T.......... Employment Taxes, Social Security Act Rulings [*Internal Revenue Service*] [*A publication*] (DLA)
EMT.......... Empty
EMT.......... Emulator Trap (MHDB)
EMT.......... End of Magnetic Tape [*Computer science*] (MDG)
EMT.......... energy management technology (SAUS)
EMT.......... Engineering Model Transport
EMT.......... Enzyme-Multiplied Immunoassay Technique [*Biophysics*] (QSUL)
EMT.......... Equivalent Megaton (SAUS)
EMT.......... Equivalent Megatonnage [*Military weapon index*]
EMT.......... Equivalent Megatons (SAUS)
EMT.......... Ergonovine Maleate Test [*Medicine*] (MELL)
EMT.......... Erythrocyte Mobility Test [*Medicine*] (EDAA)
EMT.......... European Mean Time (SAUO)
EMT.......... European Mediterranean Tropo (SAUS)
EMT.......... European Mediterranean Troposphere (IEEE)
EMT.......... Evaluation Modality Test [*Psychology*]
EMT.......... Evaluation Monitoring Team (MCD)
EMT.......... Exact Manning Table (SAA)
EMT.......... Executive Management Team (NRCH)
EMT.......... Expanded Mobility Truck (MCD)
EMT.......... Express Master Tape (VLIE)
EMT.......... Extended Mobility Tire [*Automotive technology*] (PS)
emt.......... Extreme Margin Trip (SAUS)
EMT.......... Energy-Momentum Tensor (ODA)
EMTA.......... Electro-Mechanical Trade Association (SAUO)
EMTA.......... Electro-Medical Trade Association [*British*] (BI)
EMT-A.......... Emergency Medical Technician, Ambulance (DHSM)
EMTA.......... Emerging Markets Traders Association (EA)
EMTA.......... Endomethylenetetrahydrophthalic Acid [*Organic chemistry*]
EMTAC......... Emergency Machine Tool Armament Corps [*British*] [*World War II*]
EMTAD......... Empress Message to All Districts (WDAA)
EMTAGS...... Excerpta Medica Broader Tags (SAUS)
EMTALA...... Emergency Medical Treatment and Active Labor Act
EMT-ALS...... Emergency Medical Technician-Advanced Life Support [*Medicine*] (MTAA)
EMTB.......... Electro Mechanical Test Building (ACAE)
EMTC.......... Electronic Module Test Console (ACAE)
EMTC.......... Emergency Management Training Center (DEMM)
EMTC.......... External Mass Transfer Control (SAUS)
EMTD.......... Estimated Maximum Tolerated Dose [*Toxiclolgy*] (LDT)
EMTDB......... ESCAP [*Economic and Social Commission for Asia and the Pacific*] Maritime Transport Database [*United Nations*] (DUND)
EMTDP......... Environmental Mutagen Test Development Program [*National Institute of Environmental Health Sciences*]
EMTE.......... Electromagnetic Test Environment
EMTE.......... Electromagnetic Threat Environment [*Military*] (SEWL)
EMTE.......... European Machine Tool Exhibition (PDAA)
EMTEC......... Edison Materials Technology Center [*Military*]
EMTEC......... European Marine Trade Exhibition and Congress (SAUO)
EMTECH........ Electromagnetic Technology
EMTED......... Electromagnetic Test and Evaluation Data (IAA)
EMTED......... Electromagnetic Test and Evaluation Data System (SAUS)
EMTEDS....... Electromagnetic Test Environment Data System (MCD)
EMTED System... Electromagnetic Test and Evaluation Data System (SAUS)
EMTel.......... Emerging Markets Telecommunications Fund [*Associated Press*] (SAG)
EMTF.......... Electronic Mail Task Force [*Communications term*] (DCT)
EMTF.......... Equivalent Mean Time to Failure (SAUS)
EMTF.......... Estimated Mean Time to Failure
EMTG.......... Electron Microscope Techniques Group (SAUO)
EM Therapy... Electromagnetic Therapy (SAUS)
EMTI.......... Edge-Mounted Threaded Inserts
EMT-I.......... Emergency Medical Technician, Intermediate [*Also, IEMT*] (DHSM)
EMTI.......... Enhanced Moving Target Indicator [*Air Force*] (DOMA)
EMT Instruction... Emulator Trap Instruction (SAUS)
EMT-IV......... Emergency Medical Technician-Intravenous [*Medicine*] (MTAA)
EMTM.......... Electron Microscope Technique Meeting (PDAA)
EMTM.......... Executive Master's in Technology Management
EMT-MAST... Emergency Medical Technician-Military Antishock Trousers [*Medicine*] (EDAA)
EMTN.......... European Meteorological Telecommunications Network (PDAA)
EMTP.......... electromagnetic transience program (SAUS)
EMTP.......... Electro-Magnetic Transient Program (SAUS)
EMTP.......... Electromagnetic Transients Program (SAUS)
EMT-P.......... Emergency Medical Technician, Paramedic (DHSM)
EMTR.......... Effective Marginal Tax Rate
EMTR.......... Emitter (MSA)
EMTR.......... Enlisted Master Tape Record [*Army*] (AABC)
EMTS.......... Electronic Money Transfer System
EMTs.......... Emergency Medical Technicians (SAUS)
EMTS.......... Environmental Methods Testing Site [*Environmental Protection Agency*] (GFGA)
EMTS.......... Environmental Monitoring Testing Site (EEVL)
EMTS.......... Ethylmercurithiosalicylate [*Organic chemistry*]
EMTS.......... Ethylmercury-P-Toluenesulfonamide [*Organic chemistry*]
EMTS.......... Ethylmercury-P-Toluenesulfonanilide (SAUS)
EMTS.......... Exposure Monitoring Test Site [*Environmental Protection Agency*] (ERG)
EMTT.......... Expanded Mobility Tactical Truck (MCD)
EMTTF......... Equivalent Mean Time to Failure
EMTTF......... Estimated Mean Time to Failure (SAUS)
EMTU.......... Enhanced Master Terminal Unit
EMTUG........ European Manufacturing Technology Users Group (SAUS)
EMU.......... Early Morning Urine (MELL)
EMU.......... Eastern Michigan University [*Ypsilanti*]
EMU.......... Eccentric Mailbox User [*Electronic mail systems*] (NITA)
EMU.......... Economic and Monetary Union
EMU.......... Economic and Monetary Union of the European Community (EBF)
EMU.......... Education for Mutual Understanding (SAUO)
EMU.......... Electrical Multiple Unit (SAUS)
EMU.......... Electric Multiple Unit [*Passenger trains*] (DCTA)
emu.......... Electromagnetic Unit (ADWA)
EMU.......... Electromagnetic Unit
emu.......... Electromagnetic Units (ABAC)
EMU.......... Electromotive Unit (SAUS)
EMU.......... Electronic Materials Unit (SAUO)
EMU.......... Electronic Message Unit (SAUS)
EMU.......... Electronic Messaging Utility (GART)
EMU.......... Electronic Mock-Up [*Computer-aided design*]
EMU.......... Elevation Measuring Unit (SAUS)
EMU.......... Emory University, Atlanta, GA [*OCLC symbol*] (OCLC)
EMU.......... Emulator (MSA)
EMU.......... Emultek, Ltd. [*AMEX symbol*] (NASQ)
EMU.......... EMU of capacitance (SAUS)
EMU.......... EMU of current (SAUS)
EMU.......... EMU of electric potential (SAUS)
EMU.......... EMU of inductance (SAUS)
EMU.......... EMU of resistance (SAUS)
EMU.......... Energy Management and Utilization Division (SAUS)
EMU.......... Energy Management Unit (PCM)
EMU.......... Engineering Mock-Up
EMU.......... Engineering Model Unit [*NASA*] (NASA)
EMU.......... Engine Maintenance Unit (SAUS)
EMU.......... Engine Monitoring Unit [*Automotive electronics*]
EMU.......... Engine Multiplexing Unit (MCD)
EMU.......... Enterprise Messaging Utility (GART)
EMU.......... Environmental Measurement Unit (MCD)
EMU.......... Environmental Monitoring Unit (SAUS)
EMU.......... Epilepsy Monitoring Unit [*Medicine*] (MELL)
EMU.......... Europaeische Musikschul-Union [*European Music School Union*] [*Linz, Austria*] (SLS)
EMU.......... Europaische Musikschul-Union [*European Union of Music Schools*] (EAIO)
EMU.......... European Mineworkers' Union [*Zambia*]
EMU.......... European Monetary Union
EMU.......... European Monetary Unit [*Proposed*]
EMU.......... Expanded Memory Unit (SAUS)

EMU .... Extended Memory Unit (NASA)
EMU .... Extravehicular Maneuvering Unit (SAUS)
EMU .... Extravehicular Mobility Unit [*NASA*] (KSC)
EMUA .... European Monetary Unit of Account
EMUDS .... Extravehicular Maneuvering Unit Decontamination System (SSD)
EMUG .... European MAP [*Manufacturing Automation Protocol*] Users Group [*Automotive engineering*]
emui .... emulsion (SAUS)
EMUL .... Emulate (VLIE)
Emul .... Emulation (DIAR)
EMUL .... Emulsion (MSA)
Emulex .... Emulex Corp. [*Associated Press*] (SAG)
EMULS .... Emulsum [*Emulsion*] [*Medicine*] (ROG)
EMUNX .... Evergreen Short-Intermed. Munic. Cl.Y [*Mutual fund ticker symbol*] (SG)
EMUO .... Early Morning Urine Osmolality [*Medicine*]
EMUO .... Ethiopian Muslim Unity Organization (SAUS)
EMUS .... Early Morning Urine Specimen (MELL)
EMUS .... Electronic Multiplexing System (SAUS)
emut .... electric multiple-unit train (SAUS)
EMUT .... Enhanced Manpack UHF [*Ultra High Frequency*] Terminal
EMU-TV .... Extravehicular Mobility Unit-Television
EMUX .... Electrical Multiplex
EMUX .... Electrical Multiplexer Unit (SAUS)
EMUX .... Electronic Multiple Bus (ACAE)
emux .... electronic multiplexer (SAUS)
EMUX .... Electronic Multiplexing (SAUS)
EMV .... Eggplant Mosaic Virus [*Plant pathology*]
EMV .... Egress Maintenance Vehicle
EMV .... Electromagnetic Velocity (KSC)
EMV .... Electromagnetic Voltage (CAAL)
EMV .... Electromagnetic Volume (IAA)
EMV .... Electromagnetic Vulnerability
eMv .... Electron Megavolt (EY)
EMV .... Electron Multiplier Voltage (ABAC)
EMV .... Emporia, VA [*Location identifier*] [*FAA*] (FAAL)
EMV .... Equine Morbillivirus
EMV .... Every Member Visit [*Fundraising term*] (NFD)
EMV .... Expected Monetary Value
EMV .... Expected Monetary Values (SAUS)
EMV .... Eyes, Motor, Voice [*Glasgow Coma Scale*] [*Medicine*]
EMVC .... Early Mitral Valve Closure [*Medicine*] (EDAA)
EMVEC .... Eastern Massachusetts-Vermont Energy Control (SAUO)
EMVER .... Experimento Meteoologico del Verano [*Marine science*] (OSRA)
EMVER .... Experimento Meteorologico del Verano (USDC)
EMVER .... Experimento Meteorologico de Verano (SAUS)
EMVJ .... Etched Multiple Vertical Junction [*Photovoltaic energy systems*]
EMVP .... Electro-Magnetic Velocity Profiler [*Oceanography*] (MSC)
EMVW .... Electromagnetic Wave (SAUS)
EMW .... Electrical Megawatt
EMW .... Electromagnetic Warfare (MCD)
EMW .... Electromagnetic Wave
EMW .... Electromagnetic Window
EMW .... Engineering and Mine Warfare [*Army*]
EMW .... Engineering Maintenance Workers (SAUO)
EMW .... Equipment Manufacturers Workmanship
EMW .... Equivalent Mud Weight [*Well drilling technology*]
EMW .... Evangelical Movement of Wales
EMWAC .... European Microsoft Windows NT Academic Centre (SAUO)
EM Wave .... Electromagnetic Wave (SAUS)
EMWDS .... Expanded Missile Warning Display System (SAUS)
EMWeek .... Electrical Merchandising Week (SAUS)
EM Week .... Electrical Merchandizing Week (journ.) (SAUS)
EMWF .... Electromagnetic Wave Form
EMWG .... Electronic Module Working Group (ACAE)
EMWO .... Engineering Mock-Up Work Order
EMWP .... Esperantist Movement for World Peace [*See also MEM*] [*Tours, France*] (EAIO)
EMWS .... Ethnic Minorities and Women in Science [*National Science Foundation*]
EMX .... Electronic Message Exchange (SAUS)
EMX .... Electronic Mobile Exchange (VLIE)
EMX .... Electronic Support Measures (ACAE)
EMX .... Electron Microprobe X-Ray Analyzer
EMX .... El Maiten [*Argentina*] [*Airport symbol*] (OAG)
EMX .... Enterprise Mail Exchange [*Soft-Switch, Inc.*]
EMXA .... Electron Microprobe X-Ray Analyzer
EMXRF .... Electron Microprobe X-Ray Fluorescence
Emy .... Emergency (DS)
EMY .... Emergency List [*Navy*] [*British*]
EN .... Air Caravane [*ICAO designator*] (AD)
EN .... E & N Railway [*Federal Railroad Administration identification code*]
EN .... Early Negative
EN .... Earthcare Network (EA)
EN .... Earth Vote Network (EA)
EN .... Eastern Airways [*British*] [*ICAO designator*] (ICDA)
EN .... echinoid (SAUS)
EN .... Edge Number [*Film stock identification number*] (NTCM)
En .... Edinburgh, National Library of Scotland (SAUO)
EN .... efferentes Neuron (SAUS)
EN .... Efferent Nerve [*Medicine*] (MELL)
EN .... Egress Node (ACRL)
EN .... Electroless Nickel
EN .... Electronarcosis [*Medicine*] (EDAA)
EN .... Electronegative (SAUS)
EN .... Electronegativity (MEC)
EN .... Electronic News (journ.) (SAUS)
EN .... Element Number [*Computer science*]
EN .... Elevation Nonridge (SAUS)
EN .... Emergency Number (SAUS)
EN .... End (SAUS)
en .... endemic (SAUS)
EN .... Endemic Nephropathy (PDAA)
EN .... End Node (ACRL)
EN .... Endocardium (ADWA)
EN .... Endo Laboratories, Inc. [*Research code symbol*]
EN .... Endoscopy [*Medicine*] (MELL)
En .... Endosperm [*Botany*]
EN .... Endothelial Nucleus [*Medicine*] (EDAA)
En .... Enema [*Medicine*] (EDAA)
en .... Enema [*Medicine*] (EDAA)
EN .... Enema [*Medicine*]
EN .... Enemy (AABC)
EN .... Enforcement Notification (NRCH)
EN .... Engineering Note [*or Notice*]
EN .... Engineman [*Navy rating*]
EN .... Englisch (SAUS)
En .... English (SAUS)
EN .... Enki and Ninhursag (BJA)
En .... Enoch (BJA)
EN .... Enrolled Nurse
en .... Enstatite [*CIPW classification*] [*Geology*]
EN .... Entanglement Network (EA)
EN .... Enteral Nutrition [*Medicine*]
EN .... Enteric [*Medicine*] (EDAA)
EN .... Enteritis Necroticans [*Medicine*] (MELL)
EN .... Entrapment Neuropathy [*Medicine*] (MELL)
EN .... Entry Name (SAUS)
EN .... Envelope [*Unit of issue*] [*Military*] (DNAB)
EN .... Epidemic Nephritis [*Medicine*] (EDAA)
EN .... Equipment Number (NITA)
EN .... Equivalent Noise Voltage (SAUS)
EN .... Eras of Nonconformity [*A publication*]
EN .... Erythema Nodosum [*Medicine*]
EN .... Esquimalt & Nanaimo Railway Co. [*AAR code*]
EN .... Essentially Negative (MELL)
EN .... Estrada Nacional [*National Highway*] [*Spanish*] (BARN)
EN .... Ethiopia News [*A publication*]
EN .... Ethylenediamine [*Organic chemistry*]
en .... ethylene diamine (SAUS)
E/N .... Euro/NATO
EN .... Euro-Nevada Mining [*Toronto Stock Exchange symbol*] (SG)
EN .... Euro-Nevada Mining Corp. Ltd. [*Toronto Stock Exchange symbol*]
EN .... Europa Norm (SAUO)
EN .... Europa Nostra [*Historic preservation organization*] (EA)
EN .... European Norm (SAUO)
EN .... European Norms (SARE)
EN .... European Standard (SAUO)
EN .... Europeene Norme [*European Standard*]
en--- .... Europe, Northern [*MARC geographic area code*] [*Library of Congress*] (LCCP)
EN .... Evening News (SAUS)
EN .... Event Name [*Dialog*] [*Searchable field*] [*Information service or system*] (NITA)
EN .... Exception Noted
en .... exceptions noted (SAUS)
EN .... Excess Noise (SAUS)
EN .... Explosive Neutralization (SEWL)
EN .... Export Network [*British*] [*Information service or system*] (CRD)
EN .... External Name (SAUS)
EN .... Ezrat Nashim [*Defunct*] (EA)
En .... Engineer (ODA)
EN1 .... Engineman, First Class [*Navy rating*]
En1C .... Engineer First Class (SAUS)
En 1 c .... Engineman first class (SAUS)
EN2 .... Engineman, Second Class [*Navy rating*]
EN3 .... Engineman, Third Class [*Navy rating*]
ENA .... Eastern News Agency [*Bangladesh*] (FEA)
ENA .... Eastern North America (SAUS)
ENA .... Ecole Nationale d'Administration [*France*] (ECON)
ENA .... Electronic Networking Association [*Defunct*] (IID)
ENA .... Elkan N. Adler Collection [*Jewish Theological Seminary of America, New York*] (BJA)
ENA .... Emergency Nurses Association (EA)
ENA .... Employment Nursing Adviser (HEAS)
ENA .... Enable (NASA)
ENA .... Energetic Neutral Atom [*Imaging*]
ENA .... Engineering Next Assembly (MCD)
EN(A) .... Engineman (Aviation) [*U.S. Navy enlisted rating*] (AUER)
ENA .... English Newspaper Association
ENA .... Enova Corp. [*NYSE symbol*] [*Formerly, San Diego Gas & Electric*] (SG)
ENA .... Enrolled Nursing Aide (ADA)
ENA .... Enterprise Networking Association (SAUS)
ENA .... Environmental Protection Agency, Region VII Library, Kansas City, MO [*OCLC symbol*] (OCLC)
ENA .... Espana, Direccion General de Aviacion Civil [*Spain*] [*ICAO designator*] (FAAC)
ENA .... Ethiopian News Agency
ENA .... Ethylnitrolic Acid [*Organic chemistry*]

ENA .... Europe and North Africa (SAUO)
ENA .... European Networking Associates (VERA)
ENA .... European Neuroscience Association (EAIO)
ENA .... European Neurosciences Association [Bussum, Netherlands] (SLS)
ENA .... European Nitrators Association (SAUS)
ENA .... Evening News Association
ENA .... Experimental Negotiating Agreement [Steelworkers contract]
ENA .... Extended Network Addressing [IBM Corp.] (VERA)
ENA .... Extractable Nuclear Antibody [Immunology] (DAVI)
ENA .... Extractable Nuclear Antigen [Immunology]
ENA .... Extractable Nuclear Antigens (SAUS)
ENA .... extrathyroidal neck radioactivity (SAUS)
ENA .... Kenai [Alaska] [Airport symbol] (OAG)
ENA .... Kenai, AK [Location identifier] [FAA] (FAAL)
ENAA .... Epithermal Neutron Activation Analysis [Analytical chemistry]
ENAB .... Evening Newspaper Advertising Bureau [Business term]
ENAB .... Evening Newspaper Advertising Bureau Ltd. (SAUO)
ENAB .... Exports to North America Branch [British Overseas Trade Board] (DS)
ENABL .... Enable (VLIE)
ENABLD .... Enabled (SAUS)
ENABLE .... Education and Neighborhood Action for Better Living Environment
ENABOL .... Empresa Naviera Boliviana [Shipping company] [Bolivia] (EY)
ENAC .... Electronic Numerical Integrator and Calculator [Early computer, 1946] (DCTA)
en ac .... Enemy Activity (SAUS)
ENAC .... Energetic Neutral Atom Camera (SAUS)
ENAC .... Expanded National Agency Check [DoD]
ENACEOS .... ENAC for (SAUS)
ENACEOS .... ENAC for EOS (SAUS)
ENACEOS .... Energetic Neutral Atom Camera for EOS (SAUS)
ENACT .... Effective National Action to Control Tobacco
ENACT .... Engineering Application of Computer Technology
ENACT .... Environmental Action for Survival [Defunct] (EA)
ENADS .... Enhanced Network Administration System [Telecommunications] (TEL)
ENAF .... Employer Identification Number Name and Address File [IRS]
ENAFOOD .... European NGOs Network on Agriculture, Food and Development (SAUO)
ENAL .... Alesund/Vigra [Norway] [ICAO location identifier] (ICLI)
ENALIM .... Evolving Natural Language Information Model [Computer science] (MHDI)
ENAM .... Enamel (KSC)
enam .... Enameled (MIST)
ENAM .... European North Atlantic Margin (QUAC)
ENAM BD .... Enamelled Board (DGA)
ENAM BLR .... Enamelled Blotter (DGA)
ENAMD .... Enameled (ROG)
enamd .... enamelled (SAUS)
ENAN .... Andoya [Norway] [ICAO location identifier] (ICLI)
ENAN .... Education Native American Network (AEPA)
ENANB .... Enteric [or Epidemic] NANB Hepatitis [Non-A, Non-B] [Medicine]
EN and T .... Ear, Nose, and Throat (SAUS)
EN & T .... Ears, Nose, and Throat
ENAO .... Employment and National Arbitration Order (SAUO)
ENAPN .... Eastern North America Phenological Network
ENAR .... Biometric Society, Eastern North American Region (SAUO)
ENAR .... Eastern North American Region (SAUS)
ENAS .... Ny Alesund (Svalbard) [Norway] [ICAO location identifier] (ICLI)
ENASA .... Empresa Nacional de Autocamiones SA [National Truck Manufacturing Company] [Spain]
ENAT .... Alta [Norway] [ICAO location identifier] (ICLI)
ENAT .... En Route Air Traffic Control [A publication]
ENATD .... Explosive Neutralization Advanced Technology Demonstration (SEWL)
ENB .... Earth Negotiations Bulletin (SAUS)
ENB .... East New Britain (SAUS)
ENB .... Eneabba [Australia] [Airport symbol] (OAG)
ENB .... English National Ballet (SAUO)
ENB .... English National Board (SAUS)
ENB .... English National Board Careers Advisory Centre [British] (CB)
ENB .... English National Board for Nursing, Midwifery and Health Visiting (SAUS)
ENB .... Ethylidenenorborene [Organic chemistry]
ENB .... Explosives Notified Body (HEAS)
ENBA .... Economics News Broadcasters Association (EA)
EnBA .... Ethylene normal Butyl Acrylate (SAUS)
ENBC .... Energy BioSystems [NASDAQ symbol] (TTSB)
ENBC .... Energy Biosystems Corp. [NASDAQ symbol] (SAG)
ENBD .... Bodo [Norway] [ICAO location identifier] (ICLI)
ENBJ .... Bjornoya [Norway] [ICAO location identifier] (ICLI)
enbl .... Enable (ELAL)
ENBL .... Enable (MSA)
ENBL .... Forde/Bringeland [Norway] [ICAO location identifier] (ICLI)
ENBLD .... Enabled (SAUS)
ENBL Signal ... Enable Signal (SAUS)
ENBM .... Bomoen [Norway] [ICAO location identifier] (ICLI)
ENBN .... Bronnoysund/Bronnoy [Norway] [ICAO location identifier] (ICLI)
ENBO .... Bodo [Norway] [ICAO location identifier] (ICLI)
ENBR .... Bergen/Flesland [Norway] [ICAO location identifier] (ICLI)
ENBR .... Enbridge, Inc. [NASDAQ symbol] (NASQ)
ENBR .... Engineering Branch (SAUO)
ENBRI .... European Network of Building Research Institutes. (SAUS)
ENBS .... Batsfjord [Norway] [ICAO location identifier] (ICLI)
ENBS .... Early Neurobehavioral Score (MELL)
ENBS .... English National Ballet School
ENBV .... Berlevag [Norway] [ICAO location identifier] (ICLI)
ENBX .... Einstein/Noah Bagel [NASDAQ symbol] (SG)
ENBX .... Einstein Noah Bagel Corp. [NASDAQ symbol] (SAG)
ENC .... Eastern Nazarene College, Wollaston, MA [OCLC symbol] (OCLC)
ENC .... ECC Group ADR [Formerly, English China Clays ADR] [NYSE symbol] (SPSG)
Enc .... Edinburgh, New College (SAUO)
ENC .... Eisenhower National Clearinghouse
ENC .... Electroencephalography Technician [Navy]
ENC .... electronic navigation chart (SAUS)
ENC .... Electron-Nuclear Coupling (IAA)
ENC .... Emergency National Council Against US Intervention in Central America/The Caribbean (EA)
ENC .... Emergency News Center (DEMM)
enc .... Encaustic (VRA)
enc .... Encipher (SAUS)
ENC .... Enclose [Technical drawings]
enc .... Enclosed (WDMC)
enc .... Enclosure (WDMC)
ENC .... Enclosure
enc .... enclosure(s) (SAUS)
ENC .... Encode (NASA)
ENC .... Encoded (file name extension) (SAUS)
ENC .... Encoder (SAUS)
ENC .... Encore (ADWA)
enc .... Encourage (DAVI)
Enc .... Encourage [Medicine] (EDAA)
Enc .... Encyclopaedia (SAUS)
Enc .... Encyclopedia (DIAR)
ENC .... Encyclopedia
ENC .... Enesco Group [NYSE symbol] (SG)
ENC .... Engineering Command (AAG)
ENC .... Engineman, Chief [Navy rating]
ENC .... English China Clays ADR [NYSE symbol] (TTSB)
ENC .... Enlisted Cancelled (SAUS)
ENC .... Enlistment Canceled [Military]
ENC .... Entanglement Network Coalition (SAUS)
ENC .... Enteral Nutrition Council (EA)
ENC .... Environmental Control [Medicine] (EDAA)
ENC .... Equivalent Noise Charge
ENC .... equivalent noise current (SAUS)
ENC .... Euromin Canada Ltd. [Vancouver Stock Exchange symbol]
ENC .... Euronational Certificate (SAUS)
ENC .... European Networking Center (HGAA)
ENC .... Exhaust Nozzle Control
ENC .... Exon Nuclear Company Inc. (SAUO)
ENC .... Exxon Nuclear Corporation (SAUO)
ENC .... Nancy [France] [Airport symbol] (OAG)
EnCa .... Endometrial Carcinoma [Oncology]
ENCA .... European Naval Communications Agency [NATO]
ENCA .... Oslo Caa [Norway] [ICAO location identifier] (ICLI)
ENCAC .... Eastern College Athletic Conference (PSS)
Encad .... Encad, Inc. [Associated Press] (SAG)
ENCAP .... Encapsulation (MSA)
ENCAR .... Enclosed Cryocondenser for Air Recovery
ENCAR .... Enclosed Cryopump for Air Sample Recovery (SAUS)
Enc Arch .... Gwilt's Encyclopedia of Architecture [A publication] (DLA)
EN-CAS .... Environmental Concerns and Safety (SAUS)
ENCATT .... Engineer CATT (SAUS)
ENCATT .... Engineering CATT [Army] (RDA)
EncBibl .... Encyclopaedia Biblica [Jerusalem] [A publication] (BJA)
Enc Brit .... Encyclopaedia Britannica [A publication] (WDAA)
ENCC .... Emergency Network Control Center (MCD)
ENCC .... Encore Computer [NASDAQ symbol] (TTSB)
ENCC .... Encore Computer Corp. [NASDAQ symbol] (SAG)
ENCC .... Environment(al) Noise Control Committee (SAUS)
ENCC .... Environment Noise Control Committee (EERA)
Enc Can .... Encyclopaedia Canadiana (SAUS)
Enc Can .... Encyclopedia Canadiana (SAUS)
ENCD .... Eighteen-Nation Committee on Disarmament (SAUO)
ENCD .... Encad, Inc. [NASDAQ symbol] (SAG)
encd .... Enclosed (SAUS)
ENCD .... Encode (MSA)
Enc Dict .... Encyclopedia Dictionary, Edited by Robert Hunter [1879-88] [A publication] (DLA)
ENCDR .... Encoder (MSA)
ENCE .... Enemy Situation and Correlation Element [Military] (SEWL)
ENCE .... Enemy Situation Correlation Element (SAUS)
ENCE .... Extendable Nozzle Cone
ENCEL .... Engineer Cellular Teams (SAUO)
ENCFOM .... Electromagnetic Compatibility Figure of Merit (SAUS)
Enc Forms ... Encyclopedia of Forms [A publication] (DLA)
Enc Ins US ... Insurance Year-Book [A publication] (DLA)
EncJud .... Encyclopaedia Judaica [Jerusalem] [A publication] (BJA)
Enc Jud .... Encyclopedia Judaica (SAUS)
ENCL .... Enclose (KSC)
Encl .... Enclosed (EBF)
encl .... Enclosed (WDMC)
Encl .... Enclosure (EBF)
ENCL .... Enclosure (ROG)
encl .... Enclosure (WDMC)
Enc Law .... American and English Encyclopedia of Law [A publication] (DLA)
ENCLD .... Enclosed (ROG)
enclg .... enclosing (SAUS)

enclit .... enclitic (SAUS)
ENCLO .... Enclosure
ENCLOD .... Enclosed (ROG)
ENCLOSG .... Enclosing (ROG)
ENCM .... Engineman, Master Chief [*Navy rating*]
ENCMM .... Ethernet Network Control + Management Modeul (SAUS)
ENCMM .... Ethernet Network Control + Management Module (SAUS)
ENCMP .... Economists' National Committee on Monetary Policy (EA)
ENCN .... Kristiansand/Kjevik [*Norway*] [*ICAO location identifier*] (ICLI)
ENCO .... Energy Company [*Slogan and brand name used by Humble Oil & Refining Co.*] [*Later, Exxon*]
ENCOE .... British National Committee on Ocean Engineering (SAUO)
ENCOM .... Engineer Command [*Army*] (DOMA)
ENCOM .... Engineer Construction Command [*Army*]
Encon .... Encon Systems [*Commercial firm*] [*Associated Press*] (SAG)
ENCON .... Energy Conservation (SAUS)
ENCON .... Environmental Conservation (SAUS)
ENCON .... Environmental Conservation Program (SAUS)
ENCON Program... Energy Conservation Program (SAUO)
ENCOR .... Energy Corporation Ltd. (SAUO)
ENCORD .... Interdepartmental Committee on Energy Development and Research (SAUO)
Encore .... Encore Computer Corp. [*Associated Press*] (SAG)
Encore .... Encore Marketing International [*Associated Press*] (SAG)
ENCORE .... Encouragement, Normalcy, Counseling, Opportunity, Reaching out, Energies revived (SAUS)
ENCORE .... Enlarged Compact by Response (IAA)
ENCORE .... Enlisted Navy Career Options for Reenlistment (DOMA)
ENCORE .... Enrichment of Nutrients on Coral Reefs Experiment [*Australia*]
ENCORE .... Environment and Coastal Resource Project (SAUO)
ENCORE .... European Network of Catchments organized for Research on Eurosystems (SAUO)
Encore Aust... Encore Australia [*A publication*]
EncoreW .... Encore Wire Corp. [*Associated Press*] (SAG)
Encour .... Encouragement (DIAR)
ENCP .... Encercorp Inc. [*NASDAQ symbol*] (TTSB)
ENCP .... European Naval Communications Plan [*NATO*] (NATG)
Enc Pl & Pr... Encyclopedia of Pleading and Practice [*A publication*] (DLA)
ENCR .... Encoder (SAUS)
Encr .... Encore Marketing International [*Associated Press*] (SAG)
ENCR .... Encrypted (MCD)
ENCR .... Enscor, Inc. [*NASDAQ symbol*] (NQ)
ENCR .... European Council for Nuclear Research (SAUO)
ENCR .... European Network of Cancer Registries (SAUO)
ENCRF .... Enscor Inc. [*NASDAQ symbol*] (TTSB)
ENCS .... Engineman, Senior Chief [*Navy rating*]
ENCSD .... Encased (MSA)
enct .... encounter (SAUS)
ENCTR .... Encounter (FAAC)
ENCU .... Environmental Control Unit (MCD)
Enc US Sup Ct Rep... Encyclopedia of United States Supreme Court Reports [*A publication*] (DLA)
ency .... Encyclopedia (ADWA)
ENCY .... Encyclopedia
EncyBibl .... Encyclopaedia Biblica (SAUO)
EncyBrit .... Encyclopaedia Britannica (SAUO)
encyc .... Encyclopedia (ELAL)
ENCYC .... Encyclopedia
Encyc .... Encyclopedia of the Laws of England [*2 eds.*] [*1897-1919*] [*A publication*] (DLA)
EncycBrit .... Encyclopaedia Britannica (SAUO)
Encyc Brit .... Encyclopedia Britannica [*A publication*]
encycl .... Encyclopedia
Ency L & P... American and English Encyclopedia of Law and Practice [*A publication*] (DLA)
Ency Law .... American and English Encyclopedia of Law [*A publication*] (DLA)
Ency of Ev... Encyclopedia of Evidence [*A publication*] (DLA)
Ency of Forms... Encyclopedia of Forms and Precedents [*A publication*] (DLA)
Ency of L & Pr... Encyclopedia of Law and Practice [*A publication*] (DLA)
Ency of Pl & Pr... Encyclopedia of Pleading and Practice [*A publication*] (DLA)
Ency P & P... Encyclopedia of Pleading and Practice [*A publication*] (DLA)
Ency US Sup Ct... Encyclopedia of United States Supreme Court Reports [*A publication*] (DLA)
Ency US Sup Ct Rep... Encyclopedia of Pleading and Practice. Supplement [*A publication*] (DLA)
END .... Early Neonatal Death (MELL)
END .... Earth Net Dial
END .... Electronic Null Detector
END .... Eliminate the National Debt (EA)
END .... Endicott (SAUS)
END .... End Notch Discrimination (EA)
END .... Endocrinology [*Medical specialty*] (DHSM)
END .... End of Data [*Computer science*] (SAA)
end .... Endoreduplication (MAE)
END .... Endorphin [*Medicine*] (EDAA)
End .... Endorsed (EBF)
END .... Endorsed [*or Endorsement*] [*Business term*]
End .... Endorsement (EBF)
END .... Endowed (ROG)
END .... endrin (SAUS)
END .... Endurance (IAA)
END .... Endurance Minerals [*Vancouver Stock Exchange symbol*]
END .... Engineman (Diesel) [*U.S. Navy enlisted rating*] (AUER)
END .... Enhancement Newcastle Disease (SAUS)
END .... Enid, OK [*Location identifier*] [*FAA*] (FAAL)
END .... Entente Nationale Democratique [*National Democratic Entente*] [*Monaco*] [*Political party*] (PPE)
END .... Environment Near Death (SAUS)
END .... Environment News Digest [*A publication*] (EAAP)
END .... Equipes Notre-Dame [*Teams of Our Lady - TOOL*] [*Paris, France*] (EAIO)
END .... Equivalent Narcotic Depth (SAUS)
END .... Equivalent Neutral Density (DGA)
END .... European Nuclear Disarmament [*British*]
END .... Exaltation Newcastle Disease
END .... External Negative Differential (PDAA)
ENDA .... ENDA [*Enviroment and Development*] Caribe [*An association*] (EAIO)
ENDA .... Environmental Training Program (SAUO)
ENDA .... Environment and National Development in Africa (SAUO)
ENDADR .... End Address [*of Main Memorix Section*] [*Computer science*] (IAA)
ENDAR .... Endoatmospheric Non-Nuclear Defense Application Review
End Ard Car... End Around Carry (SAUS)
ENDA-TM .... Environnement et Developpement du Tiers Monde [*Environment and Development of the Third World*] (EAIO)
ENDA TW .... Environment and Development in the Third World (SAUS)
End Bdg Ass... Endlich on Building Associations [*A publication*] (DLA)
ENDC .... Eighteen-Nation Disarmament Committee [*or Conference*] [*Later, CCD*] [*Convened March 14, 1962; actually attended by 17 nations, with France absent*]
ENDC .... Eighteen-Nation Disarmament Conference (SAUO)
ENDC .... Eighteen-Nations Disarmament Commission (SAUO)
ENDC .... European Network Design Center (SAUO)
End Cd .... End of Card (SAUS)
ENDCE .... Endurance (FAAC)
ENDCRNLGST... Endocrinologist
Endeavour ... ENDEAVOUR (OXFORD) (SAUS)
endec .... Encoder-Decoder (AEBE)
ENDECJA .... Stronnictwo Narodowej Demokracji [*Nationalist Democratic Party*] [*Poland*] (PPE)
ENDEE .... Endorsee [*Legal shorthand*] (LWAP)
ENDEF .... European Non-Destructive Evaluation (EURO)
END EFF .... End Effector
ENDER .... Endoatmospheric Non-Nuclear Definition and Requirements Study [*Military*]
ENDER .... Endorser [*Legal shorthand*] (LWAP)
Endesa .... Empresa Nacionale de Espana SA [*Associated Press*] (SAG)
ENDEX .... End Date of an Exercise (MCD)
ENDEX .... End of Discussion [*Training term*] (LPT)
ENDEX .... Enviromental Index (USDC)
ENDEX .... Environmental Data Index [*National Oceanic and Atmospheric Administration*] (MCD)
ENDEX .... Environmental Index [*Marine science*] (OSRA)
ENDEX .... exvironmental index (SAUS)
End Exe .... End Execute (SAUS)
ENDF .... Evaluated Nuclear Data File [*National Nuclear Data Center*] [*Information service or system*]
ENDFL .... Evaluated Nuclear Data File, Livermoore (SAUO)
ENDG .... Ending (FAAC)
ENDG .... Endogen, Inc. [*NASDAQ symbol*] (SAG)
End Guar .... Endorsement Guaranteed (MHDW)
ENDI .... Dagali [*Norway*] [*ICAO location identifier*] (ICLI)
ENDI .... End Item (TVEL)
ENDIF .... Enterprise Network Data Interconnectivity Family [*Telecommunications*]
End Interp St... Endlich's Commentaries on the Interpretation of Statutes [*A publication*] (DLA)
End Interp Stat... Endlich's Commentaries on the Interpretation of Statutes [*A publication*] (ILCA)
ENDIPS .... End Users Image Processing System (SAUS)
EnDIVE .... Enhanced DIVE (SAUS)
ENDIX .... Environmental Data Index (SAUS)
ENDL .... Evaluated Nuclear Data Library
Endl Bldg Ass'ns... Endlich on Building Associations [*A publication*] (DLA)
ENDLF .... Eelam National Democratic Liberation Front [*Sri Lanka*] [*Political party*] (EY)
End Ln .... End of Line (SAUS)
Endl Vac .... Endless Vacation [*A publication*]
ENDMT .... Endorsement [*Legal shorthand*] (LWAP)
end mth .... end of month (SAUS)
ENDO .... Endoatmospheric (ACAE)
endo .... Endocrine (ADWA)
ENDO .... Endocrine [*or Endocrinology*] (WDAA)
Endo .... Endocrinology (SAUS)
Endo .... Endodontics [*Dentistry*] (DAVI)
ENDO .... Endometriosis (ADWA)
ENDO .... Endoscopy [*or Endoscope*] [*Medicine*] (DAVI)
ENDO .... Endotracheal [*Medicine*] (DAVI)
Endo .... Endotracheal [*Medicine*] (EDAA)
ENDO .... Ethiopian National Democratic Organization (SAUS)
ENDOB .... Electron-Nuclear Double Resonance (SAUS)
Endoc .... Endocrinology
ENDOC .... Environmental (SAUS)
ENDOC .... Environmental Information and Documentation Centres Database [*Commission of the European Communities*] [*Information service or system*] (CRD)
ENDOC .... Environmental Information and Documentation Centres On-line Directory (SAUO)
endocrin .... endocrinological (SAUS)
endocrin .... endocrinologist (SAUS)

ENDOCRIN... Endocrinology
endocrino.... endocrinologist (SAUS)
endocrino.... endocrinology (SAUS)
endocrino.... endocrinopathy (SAUS)
endocrino.... endocrinosis (SAUS)
endocrino.... endocrinotherapy (SAUS)
endocrino.... endocrinous (SAUS)
ENDOCRINOL... Endocrinology
Endocrinol Metab Clin North Am... Endocrinology and Metabolism Clinics of North America [*Philadelphia, PA*] (SAUS)
Endocr J...... Endocrine Journal [*Tokoyo*] (SAUS)
Endocr Res... Endocrine Research [*New York, NY*] (SAUS)
Endocr Rev... Endocrine Reviews [*Baltimore, MD*] (SAUS)
EndocSoc..... Endocrine Society (SAUO)
Endogen...... Endogen, Inc. [*Associated Press*] (SAG)
endo-H......... Endoglucosaminidase-H [*An enzyme*]
ENDOMET.... Endometrium [*Anatomy*]
Endo Metab Clinics N Am... Enodcrine and Metabolism Clinics of North America (MEC)
ENDO-PAC.... Endo-Atmospheric Penetration Aids Concept
End Op Sup... End Operation Suppress (SAUS)
ENDOR......... Electron-Nuclear Double Resonance
ENDORPHIN... Endogenous Morphine [*or Endomorphin*] [*Also, ENM*] [*Brain peptide*]
ENDORPHINE... Endogenous Morphine (ACAE)
ENDORST.... Endorsement (ROG)
Endoscopy... ENDOSCOPY (STUTTGART) (SAUS)
Endovas....... Endovascular Technologies, Inc. [*Associated Press*] (SAG)
ENDOW........ Endowment (ROG)
ENDOW........ Environmental Design of Waterways [*U.S. Army Corps of Engineers*]
ENDP........... Endpaper (ADA)
ENDP........... Ethiopian National Democratic Party
ENDP........... Exception to National Disclosure Policy
ENDPLAN.... Endurability Plan (SAUS)
ENDPRM..... Endpaper Map [*Publishing*]
ENDR........... Endorsement [*Motor vehicle term used in state of Washington*] (MVRD)
ends............ endpapers (SAUS)
ENDS........... Ends Segment (SAUS)
ENDS........... Environmental Data Services [*Publisher*] [*British*]
ENDS........... Environmental Data Services Limited (SAUS)
ENDS........... European Nuclear Documentation System [*Information service or system*]
END SIM..... Endgame Simulation (SAUS)
Endsonc....... Endosonics Corp. [*Associated Press*] (SAG)
ENDSR......... End Subroutine (SAUS)
ENDT........... Electroneurodiagnostic Technologist (HCT)
ENDT........... Endorsement
ENDU........... Bardufoss [*Norway*] [*ICAO location identifier*] (ICLI)
ENDU........... Ethiopian National Democratic Union (SAUO)
ENDVR......... Endeavor
endvrg......... endeavoring (SAUS)
end wk......... end of week (SAUS)
end yr.......... end of year (SAUS)
ENE............. East-Northeast
E/NE........... Effective/Non-Effective (SAUS)
ENE............. Ende [*Indonesia*] [*Airport symbol*] (OAG)
ENE............. Energize (IAA)
ENE............. Enron Capital Trust I TOPRS [*NYSE symbol*] (SAG)
ENE............. Enron Corp. [*NYSE symbol*] [*Toronto Stock Exchange symbol*] (SPSG)
ENE............. Enterprise Network Event (SAUS)
ENE............. Enterprise Networking Event [*Telecommunications*] (OSI)
ENE............. Environment Encyclopedia [*A publication*]
ENE............. Estimated Net Energy (OA)
ENE............. Ethylnorepinephrine [*Also, ENS*] [*Pharmacology*]
ENE............. Kennebunk, ME [*Location identifier*] [*FAA*] (FAAL)
e-ne-........... Netherlands [*MARC geographic area code*] [*Library of Congress*] (LCCP)
ENEA........... European Neuro-Endocrinological Association (SAUO)
ENEA........... European Nuclear Energy Agency (DS)
ENEA........... European Nuclear Energy Agreement (SAUS)
ENEA........... European Nuclear Energy Association (SAUO)
ENEA........... Italian National Agency for New technology, Energy and the Environment (SAUS)
ENEA........... National Agency for New Technology, Energy and the Environment (SAUO)
ENEC........... Energy and Economics Data Bank [*IAEA*] [*Information service or system*]
ENEC........... European Nuclear Energy Community (SAUS)
ENEC........... Extendable Nozzle Exit Cone (MCD)
ENEC........... Extended Nozzle Exit Cones (SAUS)
ENECS......... European Inventory of Existing Chemical Substances (SAUO)
ENED........... EcoNet Environmental Directory (SAUO)
ENED........... Education Network for Environment and Development (AIE)
ENEF........... English New Education Fellowship (BI)
ENeG........... Electroneurography [*Medicine*] (EDAA)
ENEK........... Ekofisk [*Norway*] [*ICAO location identifier*] (ICLI)
EnEl............ Enuma Elis (BJA)
ENEM........... Enema [*Medicine*] (ROG)
enent........... Eventuality (SAUS)
ENEO........... Ebrei nell'Europa Orientale (BJA)
ENEP........... Expanded Nutrition Education Program (SAUO)
ENEPrA....... Enron Cap Res 9% 'A' Pfd [*NYSE symbol*] (TTSB)
ENEPrC....... Enron Capital LLC'MIPS' [*NYSE symbol*] (TTSB)
ENEPrJ........ ENRON $10.50 Cv 2nd Pfd [*NYSE symbol*] (TTSB)
ENER........... Energize (AAG)
ENER........... Energy Conv Devices [*NASDAQ symbol*] (TTSB)
ENER........... Energy Conversion Devices, Inc. [*NASDAQ symbol*] (SAG)
ENERDEMO... Conservation and Renewable Energy Demonstration Program (SAUS)
ENERG......... Energicamente [*With Energy*] [*Music*]
ENERGE....... Energicamente [*With Energy*] [*Music*] (ROG)
Energy Autom... Energy and Automation (journ.) (SAUS)
Energy Build... Energy and Buildings (journ.) (SAUS)
Energy Cont (P-H)... Energy Controls (Prentice-Hall, Inc.) [*A publication*] (DLA)
Energy Convers... Energy Conversion (journ.) (SAUS)
Energy Convers Manage... Energy Conversion and Management (journ.) (SAUS)
Energy Dev... Energy Developments (journ.) (SAUS)
Energy Econ... Energy Economics [*A publication*] (JLIT)
Energy Environ... Energy & Environment [*A publication*] (PABS)
Energy Explor Exploit... Energy Exploration & Exploitation [*A publication*] (PABS)
Energy Fuels... Energy and Fuels (journ.) (SAUS)
Energy J...... Energy Journal (journ.) (SAUS)
ENERGYLINE... Energy On-Line (SAUS)
Energy L Serv... Energy Law Service [*A publication*] (DLA)
Energy Manage... Energy Management (journ.) (SAUS)
Energy Mgmt (CCH)... Energy Management (Commerce Clearing House) [*A publication*] (DLA)
Energy Prog... Energy Progress (journ.) (SAUS)
Energy Res... Energy Research [*A publication*] (PABS)
Energy Res Rep... Energy Research Report (journ.) (SAUS)
Energy Stud Rev... Energy Studies Review [*A publication*] (JLIT)
Energy Systems... Lockheed Martin Energy Systems, Inc. (SAUO)
Energy Syst Policy... Energy Systems and Policy (journ.) (SAUS)
Energy Users Rep (BNA)... Energy Users Reports (Bureau of National Affairs) [*A publication*] (DLA)
ENERN......... East-Northeastern (FAAC)
Enersis......... Enersis Co. [*Associated Press*] (SAG)
ENES........... European and Near East Section [*Friends World Committee for Consultation*] [*Luxembourg*]
ENET........... Engineering Network (SAUS)
ENET........... EqualNet Holding [*NASDAQ symbol*] (TTSB)
ENET........... EqualNet Holding Corp. [*NASDAQ symbol*] (SAG)
Enet............ Ethernet (ITD)
ENET........... European Nuclear Energy Tribunal (SAUO)
ENET........... Evaluation Network [*An association*] (EA)
ENEV........... Evenes [*Norway*] [*ICAO location identifier*] (ICLI)
ENEWD......... European Network for East-West Dialogue (EA)
ENEWS......... Effectiveness of Navy Electronic Warfare Systems
ENEX........... ENEX Resources [*NASDAQ symbol*] (TTSB)
ENEX........... Enex Resources Corp. [*NASDAQ symbol*] (NQ)
ENEX-ASIA... International Electrical and Electronic Engineering Exhibition [*Interfama Pte. Ltd.*]
EnexRs......... Enex Resources Corp. [*Associated Press*] (SAG)
ENF............. Employment of Naval Forces [*Course*] (DNAB)
ENF............. End-Notched Flexure (SAUS)
ENF............. Enfamil [*Medicine*] (EDAA)
ENF............. Enfield Corp. Ltd. [*Toronto Stock Exchange symbol*]
ENF............. Enflurane [*Also, E*] [*An anesthetic*]
ENF............. Enforcement (DCTA)
ENF............. Equipment Not Operationally Ready to Fire [*Military*] (MCD)
ENF............. Equivalent Normal Form (SAUS)
ENF............. European Nuclear Force (SAUO)
ENF............. Extradural Neurofibroma [*Medicine*] (EDAA)
ENF............. Omaha, NE [*Location identifier*] [*FAA*] (FAAL)
ENFA........... Fireman Apprentice, Engineman, Striker [*Navy rating*]
ENFB........... Oslo/Fornebu [*Norway*] [*ICAO location identifier*] (ICLI)
ENFC........... Elvis Now Fan Club (EA)
ENFCMNT.... Enforcement
ENFD........... Enfield [*Borough of London*]
Enf'd........... Enforced [*Legal term*] (DLA)
ENFD........... Forde [*Norway*] [*ICAO location identifier*] (ICLI)
ENFE........... Experimental Intercomputer Network Front End (SAUS)
ENFE........... Experimental Network Front End (SAUS)
ENFET......... enhancement mode field-effect transistor (SAUS)
ENFET......... Enzyme-Based Field-Effect Transistor (SAUS)
ENFET......... Enzyme Field Effect Transistor [*Electrochemistry*]
ENFET......... enzyme-sensitive field-effect transistor (SAUS)
ENFG........... Fagernes/Leirin [*Norway*] [*ICAO location identifier*] (ICLI)
ENFIA......... Exchange Network Facilities for Interstate Access [*Computer science*] (TNIG)
ENFIA......... Exchange Network Facilities Interconnecting Arrangement [*Tariffs*] [*Telecommunications*]
ENFL........... Floro [*Norway*] [*ICAO location identifier*] (ICLI)
ENFLD......... Enfield, IL [*American Association of Railroads railroad junction routing code*]
ENFM........... Engine Family [*Automotive emissions*]
ENFN........... Fireman, Engineman, Striker [*Navy rating*]
ENFO........... Forus [*Norway*] [*ICAO location identifier*] (ICLI)
ENFOMAIN... Enforcement Main Computer (COE)
ENFOR......... Energy from the Forest Program [*Canada*]
ENFORM...... Engineering Numeric Corporation Information Management System (SAUO)
ENFP........... Extrovert, Intuitive, Feeling, Perceptive [*Meyers-Briggs Type Indicator*]
ENFR........... Frigg [*Norway*] [*ICAO location identifier*] (ICLI)
enft............. enforcement (SAUS)
ENFUEM...... Energy & Fuels [*A publication*]
ENFY........... Fyresdal [*Norway*] [*ICAO location identifier*] (ICLI)

ENFZ.......... Fritzoe [*Norway*] [*ICAO location identifier*] (ICLI)
ENG.......... Army Corps of Engineers (AAGC)
ENG.......... Destec Energy [*NYSE symbol*] (SPSG)
ENG.......... Electronic News Gathering [*Television news coverage*]
ENG.......... Electronystagmogram [*or Electrostagmography*] [*Neurology*] (DAVI)
ENG.......... Electronystagmograph (SAUS)
ENG.......... Electronystagmography [*Medicine*]
ENG.......... Electronystagnogram (SAUS)
ENG.......... Empty Net Goals [*Hockey*]
ENG.......... Engagement (ADA)
ENG.......... Engelhard Minerals and Chemical Corp. (SAUO)
ENG.......... Engine (AFM)
Eng.......... Engine (MIST)
eng.......... engine (SAUS)
ENG.......... Engineer [*or Engineering*] (EY)
Eng.......... Engineer (GAGS)
eng.......... Engineer (NTIO)
ENG.......... Engineer Hill [*Alaska*] [*Seismograph station code, US Geological Survey*] (SEIS)
eng.......... Engineering (DD)
ENG.......... Engineering Order (SAUS)
ENG.......... Engineer Officer [*Navy*] [*British*]
ENG.......... Engineman (Gasoline) [*U.S. Navy enlisted rating*] (AUER)
Eng.......... England (VRA)
ENG.......... England [*or English*]
eng.......... English [*MARC language code*] [*Library of Congress*] (LCCP)
Eng.......... English Reports (N. C. Moak) [*A publication*] (DLA)
Eng.......... English's Reports [*6-13 Arkansas*] [*A publication*] (DLA)
Eng.......... Engorged [*Medicine*] (EDAA)
ENG.......... Engrave
ENG.......... Engraver (ROG)
ENG.......... Engraving (SAUS)
EN(G).......... Enrolled Nurse (General) [*British*] (DBQ)
ENG.......... Enzootic nasal granuloma of cattle (SAUS)
ENGA.......... Emergency Natural Gas Act of 1977
ENGA.......... Engage (MSA)
ENGA.......... Engage Technologies [*NASDAQ symbol*] (SG)
ENGA.......... Engaging (SAUS)
Eng Adm...... English Admiralty Reports [*A publication*] (DLA)
Eng Adm R... English Admiralty Reports [*A publication*] (DLA)
ENGAGMT..... Engagement (ROG)
Eng Anal...... Engineering Analysis (journ.) (SAUS)
Eng&Bus...... Engineering & Business (DD)
Eng and Germ Stud... English and German Studies (journ.) (SAUS)
Eng & Ir App... Law Reports, English and Irish Appeal Cases [*A publication*] (DLA)
Eng Appl Artif Intell... Engineering Applications of Artificial Intelligence (journ.) (SAUS)
ENG-AUDIT... GICS Engineer Audit Tracking System (SAUS)
Eng Avn Bn... Engineer Aviation Battalion (SAUO)
ENGBAT...... Engineer Battalion [*Military*]
ENGBCA...... Corps of Engineers Board of Contract Appeals [*Army*]
ENGBCA...... Engineers Board of Contract Appeals (SAUS)
EngBiosy...... Energy Biosystems Corp. [*Associated Press*] (SAG)
ENG C&A..... Army Corps of Engineers Claims and Appeals Board (AAGC)
Eng-Capt...... Engineer-Captain (SAUO)
Eng C Bn..... Engineer Combat Battalion (SAUO)
Eng C Bn..... Engineer Construction Battalion (SAUO)
Eng CC........ English Crown Cases [*American Reprint*] [*A publication*] (DLA)
Eng Ch........ English Chancery [*Legal term*] (DLA)
Eng Ch........ English Chancery Reports [*American Reprint*] [*A publication*] (DLA)
EngChin....... English China Clays Ltd. [*Associated Press*] (SAG)
Eng CL........ English Common Law Reports [*A publication*] (DLA)
ENGCOM...... Engineer Command (SAUO)
ENGCOM...... Engineering Command (MCD)
ENGCOMDC... Engineer Commissioner, District of Columbia [*Military*] (AABC)
Eng Com LR... English Common Law Reports [*A publication*] (DLA)
Eng Comput... Engineering Computers (journ.) (SAUS)
Eng Comput... Engineering with Computers [*Publication*] (SAUS)
Eng: Cornell Q... Engineering: Cornell Quarterly (journ.) (SAUS)
Eng Cr Cas... English Crown Cases [*American Reprint*] [*A publication*] (DLA)
Eng Cybern... Engineering Cybernetics (journ.) (SAUS)
Eng D.......... Doctor of Engineering
ENGD.......... Engrossed (ROG)
Eng Department... Department of Engineers (SAUS)
Eng Department... Engineering Department (SAUS)
Eng Des....... Engineering Design (journ.) (SAUS)
Eng Dig....... Engineering Digest (journ.) (SAUS)
Eng Div....... Engineering Division (SAUS)
eng dvr....... engine driver (SAUS)
EngE.......... English in England (SAUS)
Eng Eccl...... English Ecclesiastical Reports [*A publication*] (DLA)
Eng Ecc R.... English Ecclesiastical Reports [*A publication*] (DLA)
Eng Econ...... Engineering Economist [*A publication*] (CABS)
eng/efp camera... electronic news-gathering/electronic field-production camera (SAUS)
Engelhard Ind Tech Bull... Engelhard Industries, Inc.; Technical Bulletin (SAUO)
Engelhard Ind Tech Bull... Engelhard Industries, Inc., Technical Bulletin (journ.) (SAUS)
ENG ERR..... Engineering Error (WDAA)
Engex.......... Engex, Inc. [*Associated Press*] (SAG)
Eng Exch...... English Exchequer Reports [*A publication*] (DLA)
eng fnd....... engine foundation (SAUO)
Eng Fract Mech... Engineering Fracture Mechanics (journ.) (SAUS)
engg.......... Engineering (ADWA)
Eng'g.......... Engineering [*A publication*] (DLA)
ENGG.......... Engineering (WGA)
Eng Geol...... Engineering Geology [*A publication*] (CABS)
enggmt........ engagement (SAUS)
Eng Hist R... Engineering Historical Review (journ.) (SAUS)
eng hn........ English Horn (BARN)
Eng hrn....... English horn (SAUS)
Eng Hse....... Engine House (SAUS)
ENGI.......... Engineering Library (SAUS)
ENGID......... Engineer Identification Report (SAUO)
ENGID......... Engine Identification Report [*Air Force*]
Engin.......... Engineer (DIAR)
Engin.......... Engineering (BEE)
engin.......... Engineering (NTIO)
ENGIN......... Engineering
Eng Ind....... Engineering Industries (journ.) (SAUS)
ENGING....... Engineering
Engin M....... Engineering Magazine (journ.) (SAUS)
ENG INT...... Engage Intercept (CAAL)
Eng Ir App... Law Reports, English and Irish Appeal Cases [*A publication*] (DLA)
engitist....... engineer + scientist (SAUS)
Eng J.......... Engineering Journal (journ.) (SAUS)
Eng Judg..... Scotch Court of Session Cases Decided by the English Judges [*1655-61*] [*A publication*] (DLA)
ENGL.......... England
ENGL.......... Engle Homes [*NASDAQ symbol*] (SPSG)
Engl.......... English (DD)
ENGL.......... English (ROG)
Eng L & Eq... English Law and Equity Reports [*American Reprint*] [*A publication*] (DLA)
Eng L & Eq R... English Law and Equity Reports [*American Reprint*] [*A publication*] (DLA)
Eng Lasers... Engineering Lasers (journ.) (SAUS)
Eng Law & Eq... English Law and Equity Reports [*American Reprint*] [*A publication*] (DLA)
ENGLD......... England
EnglhCp....... Engelhard Corp. [*Associated Press*] (SAG)
Engl Hist Rev... English Historical Review (journ.) (SAUS)
EnglHm........ Engle Homes, Inc. [*Associated Press*] (SAG)
English........ English's Reports [*6-13 Arkansas*] [*A publication*] (DLA)
English Lit.... English literature (SAUS)
ENG LIT....... English Literature (WDAA)
Engl Stud..... English Studies (journ.) (SAUS)
ENG-LT........ Engineer Lieutenant [*Navy*] [*British*] (ROG)
ENG(M)........ Enrolled Nurse, General (Mental Nursing) [*British*] (DI)
ENGM.......... Oslo/Gardermoen [*Norway*] [*ICAO location identifier*] (ICLI)
Eng Mater Des... Engineering Materials and Design (journ.) (SAUS)
EngMea........ Engineering Measurements Co. [*Associated Press*] (SAG)
Eng Med....... Engineering in Medicine (journ.) (SAUS)
ENG(MS)....... Enrolled Nurse, General (Mental Sub-Normal Nursing) [*British*] (DI)
engmt.......... Engagement (SAUS)
ENGN.......... Engineering
ENGN.......... Grimsmoen [*Norway*] [*ICAO location identifier*] (ICLI)
EngND......... Engineers for Nuclear Disarmament (SAUO)
Eng News..... Engineering News (journ.) (SAUS)
Eng News-Rec... Engineering News-Record (journ.) (SAUS)
ENGNG......... Engineering
ENG-NMCS... Engine Not Mission Capable - Supply (AFIT)
ENGNR......... Engineer
EngnSu......... Engineered Support Systems, Inc. [*Associated Press*] (SAG)
ENGO.......... Environmental Non-Governmental Organization (SAUO)
ENGO.......... Environment Non-Governmental Organizations (SAUS)
Eng Opt....... Engineering Optics [*A publication*] (CABS)
ENGORC...... Engineer Officers Reserve Corps
Eng Outlook... Engineering Outlook (journ.) (SAUS)
Eng Pews..... English on Church Pews [*A publication*] (DLA)
Eng Pl......... English Pleader [*A publication*] (DLA)
Eng Pr Cas... Roscoe's English Prize Cases [*A publication*] (DLA)
Engr.......... Engineer (PGP)
engr.......... Engineer (PROS)
ENGR.......... Engineer
Engr.......... Engineering (AL)
engr.......... Engraved (WDMC)
ENGR.......... Engraved
ENGR.......... Engraver (ROG)
engr.......... Engraver (WDMC)
Engr.......... Engraving (DIAR)
engr.......... Engraving (WDMC)
ENGR.......... Engravings (ROG)
Engr Amph Regt... Engineer Amphibian Regiment (SAUO)
Eng R & C Cas... English Railway and Canal Cases [*A publication*] (DLA)
Engr Avn Bn... Engineer Aviation Battalion (SAUO)
Engr Avn Cam Bn... Engineer Aviation Camouflage Battalion (SAUO)
Engr Avn Rgt... Engineer Aviation Regiment (SAUO)
Engr Bn........ Engineer Battalion (SAUS)
ENGRBN....... Engineer Battalion [*Military*]
ENGRCEN..... Engineering Center
Engr D......... Doctor of Engineering
ENGRD......... Engineered
ENGRE......... Engineer Element
Eng Re........ English Reports, Full Reprint [*A publication*] (DLA)
Eng Rep....... English Reports, Full Reprint [*A publication*] (DLA)
Eng Rep....... English Reports (N. C. Moak) [*American Reprint*] [*A publication*] (DLA)
Eng Rep....... English's Reports [*6-13 Arkansas*] [*A publication*] (DLA)
Eng Rep Anno... English Reports, Annotated [*A publication*] (DLA)

Eng Rep R... English Reports, Full Reprint [*A publication*] (DLA)
Eng Rep Re... English Reports, Full Reprint [*A publication*] (DLA)
Engr Equip... Engineer Equipment (SAUS)
ENGREQUIPMAINTRPRPLT... Engineer Equipment Maintenance Repair Platoon (DNAB)
ENGRFAC..... Engineering Facility
Engr FM....... Engineer Field Manual (SAUS)
ENGRG......... Engineering
ENGRING..... Engineering
ENG RM....... Engine Room (WDAA)
ENGRMAINTCO... Engineer Maintenance Co. [*Military*] (DNAB)
ENGRPLT..... Engineer Platoon (DNAB)
Eng RR Ca... English Railway and Canal Cases [*A publication*] (DLA)
Engr Regt.... Engineer Regiment (SAUO)
Engr-Res...... Engineer Reserve Corps (SAUO)
Engrs Aust... Engineers Australia [*A publication*]
ENGRSPTBN... Engineer Support Battalion (DNAB)
Engr Topo Co... Engineer Topographical Company (SAUO)
Eng Ru Ca... English Ruling Cases [*A publication*] (DLA)
Eng Rul Cas... English Ruling Cases [*A publication*] (DLA)
ENGRV......... Engrave
engrv.......... engraver (SAUS)
ENGRV......... Engraving
ENGRVR...... Engraver
ENGRY......... Energy
Eng Ry & C Cas... English Railway and Canal Cases [*A publication*] (DLA)
ENGS........... Engines (SAUS)
ENGS........... Engross (ROG)
EngSc.......... Engineering Science (DD)
Eng Sc D...... Doctor of Engineering Science
Eng Sc Ecc... English and Scotch Ecclesiastical Reports [*A publication*] (DLA)
ENGSOC....... Engineering Society (SAUO)
ENGSS......... Engineering Schoolship [*Navy*] (NVT)
ENGSTAT..... Engine Status (SAUS)
ENGSTAT..... Engine Status Report [*Air Force*]
Eng Struct.... Engineering Structures (journ.) (SAUS)
Eng Stud...... English Studies (journ.) (SAUS)
ENGSY......... Energis PLC ADS [*NASDAQ symbol*] (SG)
ENGT........... Engrossment (ROG)
EngTech....... Engineering Technician (ACII)
Eng Tech...... Engineering Technician (journ.) (SAUS)
EngTech....... Engineering Technology (DD)
Eng Technol... Engineering Technologist (journ.) (SAUS)
ENGV........... Engine V-Belt
EngWst......... Energy West, Inc. [*Associated Press*] (SAG)
ENGX........... Englehard [*Private rail car owner code*]
ENGY........... Energy (MSA)
Engynth........ Energy North, Inc. [*Associated Press*] (SAG)
EngyRsh....... Energy Research Corp. [*Associated Press*] (SAG)
EngyVen....... Energy Ventures [*Associated Press*] (SAG)
ENH............. Earth Near Horizon [*NASA*] (KSC)
ENH............. Educable Neurologically Handicapped
EN-H........... Elsevier North-Holland (SAUS)
ENH............. Enshi [*China*] [*Airport symbol*] (OAG)
Enh.............. Hymnal Prayer of Enheduanna (BJA)
ENHA........... Hamar/Stafsberg [*Norway*] [*ICAO location identifier*] (ICLI)
Enhance........ Enhance Financial Services Group [*Associated Press*] (SAG)
ENHB........... Heggebakken [*Norway*] [*ICAO location identifier*] (ICLI)
ENHD........... Haugesund/Karmoy [*Norway*] [*ICAO location identifier*] (ICLI)
ENHE........... Encounter in Health Education
ENHF........... Hammerfest [*Norway*] [*ICAO location identifier*] (ICLI)
ENHK........... Hasvik [*Norway*] [*ICAO location identifier*] (ICLI)
ENHN........... Harnmoen [*Norway*] [*ICAO location identifier*] (ICLI)
ENHNCD...... Enhanced [*ICAO designator*] (FAAC)
ENHNCMNT... Enhancement [*ICAO designator*] (FAAC)
ENHO........... Hopen [*Norway*] [*ICAO location identifier*] (ICLI)
ENHR........... essential national health research (SAUS)
ENHR........... Essential National Health Research - African Network (SAUS)
ENHS........... European Natural Hygiene Society (EAIO)
ENHS........... Hokksund [*Norway*] [*ICAO location identifier*] (ICLI)
ENHV........... Honningsvag/Valan [*Norway*] [*ICAO location identifier*] (ICLI)
ENI............. Effective Networks, Inc. [*Telecommunications service*] (TSSD)
ENI............. Elan Industries, Inc. [*Vancouver Stock Exchange symbol*]
ENI............. Elective Neck Irradiation [*Medicine*] (EDAA)
ENI............. Electro Nucleonics, Inc. (SAUO)
ENI............. Enemy Initiated Incident [*Vietnam*]
ENI............. Energy equivalent of the Network Input (SAUS)
ENI............. Energy Networks, Inc. (EFIS)
ENI............. Enersis SA [*NYSE symbol*] (SPSG)
ENI............. Enersis S.A. ADS [*NYSE symbol*] (TTSB)
ENI............. Equivalent Noise Input (DEN)
ENI............. Europe and New Independent States (SAUO)
ENI............. Excepted Net Income
ENIAC.......... Electronic Numerical Integrater and Computer (AEBE)
ENIAC.......... Electronic Numerical Integrator Analyzer and Computer (SAUS)
ENIAC.......... Electronic Numerical Integrator and Automatic Calculator (SAUS)
ENIAC.......... Electronic Numerical Integrator and Automatic Computer (SAUO)
ENIAC.......... Electronic Numerical Integrator and Calculator [*Early computer, 1946*]
ENIAC.......... Electronic Numerical Integrator and Computer (IDOE)
ENIAC.......... Electronic Numeric Integrator And Calculator (SAUS)
ENIAK.......... Electronic Numerical Integrator and Computer (SAUS)
ENIC............ Enid Central Railroad [*Federal Railroad Administration identification code*]
ENIC............ European National Information Centres on Academic Recognition and Mobility (SAUO)
ENIC............ European Network for Information on Children (SAUS)
ENIC............ Voltage Negative-Impedance Converter [*Electronics*] (ECII)
ENICO.......... Exxon Nuclear Idaho Company (SAUO)
ENID............ Endnote ID (SAUS)
ENID............ Enid, OK [*American Association of Railroads railroad junction routing code*]
ENID............ Environmental Industries Directory [*A publication*]
ENIDS.......... Ethnic Name Identification System (SAUS)
ENIG............ Electronic Nuclear Instrumentation Group (MCD)
ENIG............ Enrolled Nurse Interest Group [*Australia*]
ENIG............ Environment Information Group (EURO)
ENIMS......... European Nuclear Medicine Society (SAUO)
ENIP............ Estonian National Independence Party [*Political party*]
ENIRF.......... Enemy Initiated Incident Responded to by Friendly Forces [*Vietnam*]
ENIS............ Eastern Nigeria Information Service Corporation (SAUO)
ENIS............ European Nuclear Information Service (SAUS)
EnisBu......... Ennis Business Forms, Inc. [*Associated Press*] (SAG)
ENIT............ Ente Nazionale Italiano per il Turismo [*Italian National Tourist Board*]
ENITH.......... European Network for Information Technology in Human Services (SAUO)
ENJ............. Enjoin [*Legal shorthand*] (LWAP)
ENJ............. Nort Jet [*Spain*] [*ICAO designator*] (FAAC)
ENJA........... European New Jazz (SAUO)
ENJA........... Jan Mayen [*Norway*] [*ICAO location identifier*] (ICLI)
ENJB........... Jarlsberg [*Norway*] [*ICAO location identifier*] (ICLI)
ENJJPT........ Euro-NATO Joint Jet Pilot Training
En Jnl.......... Energy Journal [*A publication*] (BRI)
ENJOYT........ Enjoyment (ROG)
ENJPT.......... European-NATO Joint Jet Pilot Training (SAUS)
EnJu............ Encyclopaedia Judaica [*Jerusalem*] [*A publication*] (BJA)
ENK............. Endo-atmospheric Non-nuclear Kill (SAUS)
ENK............. Enerteck Energy Technologies Corp. [*Vancouver Stock Exchange symbol*]
enk.............. England [*MARC country of publication code*] [*Library of Congress*] (LCCP)
ENK............. Enkephalin [*Brain peptide, subclass of Endorphin*]
ENK............. Enniskillen [*Northern Ireland*] [*Airport symbol*] (AD)
ENK............. Enter Key [*Computer science*] (IAA)
ENK............. Expected Number of Kills [*Military*] (MCD)
ENKA........... Kautokeino [*Norway*] [*ICAO location identifier*] (ICLI)
ENKB........... Kristiansund/Kvernberget [*Norway*] [*ICAO location identifier*] (ICLI)
ENKJ........... Kjeller [*Norway*] [*ICAO location identifier*] (ICLI)
ENKR........... Kirkenes/Hoybuktmoen [*Norway*] [*ICAO location identifier*] (ICLI)
ENL............. Centralia, IL [*Location identifier*] [*FAA*] (FAAL)
ENL............. Ejercito Nacional de Liberacion [*National Liberation Army*] [*Nicaragua*] (PD)
ENL............. Eldorado Nuclear Limited (SAUO)
ENL............. Elsevier NV [*NYSE symbol*] (SAG)
ENL............. Elsevier NV ADS [*NYSE symbol*] (TTSB)
enl.............. Enamel (VRA)
ENL............. Enamel
En L............ Engineer Lieutenant [*Navy*] [*British*] (DMA)
E n l............ English as a national language (SAUS)
ENL............. Enlarge [*or Enlargement*]
enl.............. Enlarged (WDMC)
ENL............. Enlargement (SAUS)
enl.............. Enlisted (ADWA)
ENL............. Enlistment (AFM)
ENL............. Equivalent Noise Level
ENL............. Erythema Nodosum Leproticum [*Medicine*]
ENL............. European Network Laboratories (SAUO)
ENL............. Eye Notochord Length [*Fish anatomy*]
En L Cr........ Engineer Lieutenant Commander (SAUS)
En L Cr........ Engineer Lieutenant-Commander [*Navy*] [*British*] (DMA)
ENLDEVDISTSYS... Enlisted Development and Distribution Support System [*Military*] (DNAB)
ENLF........... Eelam National Liberation Front [*Sri Lanka*]
ENLG........... Enable Level Group (MHDB)
ENLG........... Enlarge (MSA)
ENLGD......... Enlarged
EnlghtS........ Enlighten Software Solutions [*Associated Press*] (SAG)
enlgmnt....... Enlargement (VRA)
ENLI............ Lista [*Norway*] [*ICAO location identifier*] (ICLI)
ENLIST........ Engineering Library Indexing and Searching Technique (SAUS)
ENLK........... Leknes [*Norway*] [*ICAO location identifier*] (ICLI)
ENLMAUSTSYS... Enlisted Master File Automated System (SAUO)
ENLN........... Eastern Nigeria Legal Notice [*A publication*] (DLA)
ENLPERMGTCEN... Enlisted Personnel Management Center [*Navy*] (DNAB)
Enl Pers....... Enlisted Personnel (SAUS)
ENLR........... Eastern Nigeria Law Reports [*1956-60*] [*A publication*] (DLA)
ENLRG......... Enlarge
ENM............. Emmonak, AK [*Location identifier*] [*FAA*] (FAAL)
ENM............. Endogenous Morphine [*or Endomorphin*] [*Also, ENDORPHIN*] [*Brain peptide*]
enm............. English, Middle [*MARC language code*] [*Library of Congress*] (LCCP)
ENM............. English Numbering Machines (SAUS)
ENM............. English Numbering Machines Ltd. (SAUO)
EN(M)......... Enrolled Nurse (Mental) [*British*] (DBQ)
ENM............. Environmental Noise Model (EEVL)
ENMAN........ Engine Management (SAUS)
ENMC........... Encore Medical Corp. [*NASDAQ symbol*] (NASQ)
ENMC........... European Neuromuscular Centre for the Coordination of Medical and Scientific Affairs (SAUO)
ENMCC......... Expanded National Military Command Center (MCD)
ENMCC......... Extended National Military Command Center (SAUS)

ENMD......... EntreMed, Inc. [*NASDAQ symbol*] (SAG)
ENMES......... Engines Not Mission Capable Supply (SAUS)
En Met......... Environmental Metrology [*Medicine*] (EDAA)
ENMG......... Electroneuromyographic (PDAA)
EN(MH)......... Enrolled Nurse (Mental Handicap) [*British*] (DBQ)
ENMH......... Mehamn [*Norway*] [*ICAO location identifier*] (ICLI)
ENMI......... Olso [*Norway*] [*ICAO location identifier*] (ICLI)
ENML......... Enamelon, Inc. [*NASDAQ symbol*] (NASQ)
ENML......... End Mill
ENML......... Molde/Aro [*Norway*] [*ICAO location identifier*] (ICLI)
ENMLD......... Enameled
ENMLNG......... Enameling
ENMOD......... Convention on the Prohibition of Military or any other Hostile use of Environmental Modification Techniques (SAUO)
ENMOD......... ENMOD Convention: Convention on the Prohibition of Military or Any Other Hostile Use of Environmental Modification Techniques (SAUS)
ENMOD......... Entity Module (SAUS)
Enmod......... Environmental Modifcation (SAUS)
ENMOD......... Environmental Modification
ENMOD......... Environment Modification Convention (EERA)
ENMR......... Executive for National Military Representatives [*Supreme Headquarters Allied Powers Europe*] (NATG)
ENMS......... European Nuclear Medical Society (EAIO)
ENMS......... Mosjoen/Kjaerstad [*Norway*] [*ICAO location identifier*] (ICLI)
ENMU......... Eastern New Mexico University
ENN......... Emergency Notification Network (SAUS)
Enn......... Enneades [*of Plotinus*] [*Classical studies*] (OCD)
ENN......... Ennisteel Corp. [*Toronto Stock Exchange symbol*]
ENN......... Environmental News Network (SAUO)
ENN......... Equity Inns [*NYSE symbol*] (SG)
ENN......... European Neurological Network (SAUS)
ENN......... Expand Nonstop Network (MHDB)
ENN......... Nenana, AK [*Location identifier*] [*FAA*] (FAAL)
ENNA......... Banak [*Norway*] [*ICAO location identifier*] (ICLI)
ENNG......... Ethyl-nitronitrosoguanidine [*Organic chemistry*]
ENNI......... EnergyNorth, Inc. [*NASDAQ symbol*] (NQ)
ENNK......... Endo-Atmospheric Non-Nuclear Kill (MCD)
ENNK......... Narvik/Framnes [*Norway*] [*ICAO location identifier*] (ICLI)
ENNKAS......... Endoatmospheric Non-Nuclear Kill Applications Study [*DoD*]
ENNKCIS......... Endoatmospheric Non-Nuclear Kill Controls Implementation Study [*DoD*]
ENNM......... Namsos [*Norway*] [*ICAO location identifier*] (ICLI)
ENNO......... Notodden [*Norway*] [*ICAO location identifier*] (ICLI)
ENNS......... Early Neonatal Neurobehavior Scale (MEDA)
ENNS......... Equity Inns [*NASDAQ symbol*] (SAG)
ENNWR......... Eastern Neck National Wildlife Refuge (SAUS)
ENO......... Emerging Healthcare Organization (ADWA)
ENO......... English National Opera
ENO......... Enoch & Cie [*Publisher*]
Eno......... Enolase (DB)
ENO......... Enolase [*An enzyme*]
eno......... Enough (GEAB)
ENO......... Enough
ENO......... Extraordinary Nuclear Occurrence (NRCH)
ENO......... Kenton, DE [*Location identifier*] [*FAA*] (FAAL)
e-no--......... Norway [*MARC geographic area code*] [*Library of Congress*] (LCCP)
ENOA......... Ellington Navigators/Observers Association (EA)
ENOA......... Extended Non-Owned Automobile Coverage [*Insurance*]
ENOB......... Bodo Oceanic [*Norway*] [*ICAO location identifier*] (ICLI)
ENOB......... Effective Number Of Bit (SAUS)
ENOC......... Association of the European National Olympic Committees [*See also ACNOE*] [*Brussels, Belgium*] (EAIO)
ENOC......... European National Olympic Committee (SAUO)
ENOCC......... Emergency Network Operations Control Center (MCD)
Enoch Pratt... Enoch Pratt Free Library (SAUS)
ENOD......... Employee Not on Duty [*FRA*] (TAG)
ENOG......... Electroneurography [*Medicine*] (EDAA)
ENOH......... Endoatmospheric Non-Nuclear Optical Homing (ACAE)
ENOL......... Enology
ENOL......... Orland [*Norway*] [*ICAO location identifier*] (ICLI)
ENORS......... Engine Non-Operational Requires Spares (SAUS)
ENORS......... Engine Not Operationally Ready - Supply [*Air Force*]
ENORW......... East Norwood, OH [*American Association of Railroads railroad junction routing code*]
Enos......... Book of Enos (SAUS)
eNOS......... Endothelial Nitric Oxide Synthase [*An enzyme*]
ENOS......... European Network of Ocean Stations (SAUO)
ENOS......... Oslo [*Norway*] [*ICAO location identifier*] (ICLI)
ENOV......... Orsta-Volda/Hovden [*Norway*] [*ICAO location identifier*] (ICLI)
ENOW......... European Network of Women (EURO)
ENOWD......... Europaeisches Netzwerk fuer den Ost-West-Dialog [*European Network for East-West Dialogue - ENEWD*] (EAIO)
ENP......... Egmont National Park (SAUS)
ENP......... Elderly Nutrition Programs (SAUO)
ENP......... Electrodeless Nickel Plating (SAUS)
ENP......... Electroless Nickel Plating
ENP......... Embedded NPrinter (SAUS)
ENP......... Emergency Nurse Practitioner (WDAA)
ENP......... Enable Presentation (SAUS)
ENP......... Endotoxin Neutralizing Protein [*Biochemistry*]
ENP......... Energy Programs [*Database*] [*Energy, Mines, and Resources, Canada*] [*Information service or system*] (CRD)
ENP......... Enerplus Resources Corp. [*Toronto Stock Exchange symbol*]
ENP......... Enron Liquids Pipeline L.P. [*NYSE symbol*] (TTSB)
ENP......... Enron Liquids Pipiline Ltd. [*NYSE symbol*] (SPSG)
ENP......... EntrePort Corp. [*AMEX symbol*]
ENP......... Estimated [*Time At or Over*] Next Position (BARN)
ENP......... Ethernet Node Processor (SAUS)
ENP......... Ethyl-P-Nitrophenylthiobenzene Phosphate [*Organic chemistry*] (DAVI)
ENP......... Etosha National Park (SAUS)
ENP......... European Neuroscience Programme [*Defunct*] [*France*] (EAIO)
ENP......... Everglades National Park
ENP......... Exceptional Needs Payment [*Legal term*] (DLA)
ENP......... Extractable Nucleoprotein [*Biochemistry*]
ENP/A......... Eastern North Pacific/Atlantic (SAUS)
EnPA......... Environmental Performance Agreement (EPAT)
ENPC......... Ecole Nationale des Ponts et Chaussees [*Graduate School of International Business*] [*France*]
ENPC......... Emergency Nursing Pediatric Course (SAUS)
ENPCAF......... Ethyl N-Phenylcarbamoylazoformate [*Organic chemistry*]
ENPEP......... Energy and Power Evaluation Program [*Computer science*]
ENPMA......... Eastern National Park and Monument Association (SAUO)
ENPMA......... enquire (SAUS)
ENPMA......... enquiry (SAUS)
ENPOCON......... Environmental Pollution Control (PDAA)
ENPOCON......... Environmental Pollution Control Exhibition (SAUO)
ENPP......... Electronics New Product Preview (SAUS)
En Psn......... Enemy Position (SAUS)
ENPT......... En Pointe Tech [*NASDAQ symbol*] (TTSB)
ENPV......... Expected Net Present Value (SAUS)
ENQ......... American Media, Inc. [*Formerly, Enquirer/Star Group*] [*NYSE symbol*] (SAG)
ENQ......... Amer Media Cl'A' [*NYSE symbol*] (TTSB)
ENQ?......... Are You There? [*Computer science*] (DOM)
ENQ......... Enqueue (SAUS)
ENQ......... Enquiry [*Transmission control character*]
ENQ......... Enquiry character (SAUS)
ENQ Character... Enquiry Character (SAUS)
ENQWS......... Amer Media Wrrt [*NYSE symbol*] (TTSB)
ENR......... Effort Net Return [*Motivation model*] [*Business term*]
ENR......... Emissora Nacional de Radiodifusao [*Radio network*] [*Portugal*]
ENR......... Energizer Holdings [*NYSE symbol*] (SG)
ENR......... Energy and Natural Resources (DLA)
ENR......... Enertec Corp. [*Toronto Stock Exchange symbol*]
ENR......... Engineering Narrative Report [*Defense Supply Agency*]
ENR......... Engineering News-Record (journ.) (SAUS)
ENR......... Enoyl Reductase [*An enzyme*]
ENR......... Enrollment (ROG)
ENR......... En Route (NVT)
ENR......... Ensor Air [*Czechoslovakia*] [*ICAO designator*] (FAAC)
ENR......... Enterprise Network Roundtable (SAUS)
ENR......... Environment and Natural Resources (SAUO)
ENR......... Eosinophilic Nonallergic Rhinitis [*Medicine*]
ENR......... Epoxidized Natural Rubber
ENR......... Equivalent Noise Ratio [*or Resistance*] [*Electronics*] (IEEE)
ENR......... Equivalent Noise Resistance (SAUS)
ENR......... Excess Noise Ratio
E/NR......... Exercised/Not Repositioned [*Sports medicine*]
ENR......... External Number Repetition (VLIE)
ENR......... Extrathyroidal Neck Radioactivity [*Radiology*]
ENRA......... Mo I Rana/Rossvoll [*Norway*] [*ICAO location identifier*] (ICLI)
ENRAT......... En Route, Arrival at _____ [*Military*] (NVT)
ENRC......... European Nuclear Research Centre (NUCP)
ENRC......... European Nuclear Research Committee (SAUS)
EnrCR......... Enron Capital Resources Ltd. [*Associated Press*] (SAG)
ENREP......... Directory of Environmental Research Projects in the European Communities [*EURONET*] [*Information service or system*]
ENREP......... Environmental Research Projects in the European Communities (SAUS)
ENREP......... Permanent Inventory of Environmental Research (SAUO)
ENRESA......... Nuclear Waste Management Authority (SAUO)
ENRFOSCOMD... En Route This Station from Oversea Command
Enrgn......... Energen Corp. [*Associated Press*] (SAG)
EnrGP......... Enron Global Power & Pipeline [*Associated Press*] (SAG)
ENRGZ......... Energize (MSA)
ENRI......... Electronic Navigation Research Institute (SAUO)
EnRI......... Environmental Retraining and Internship (SAUS)
ENRIC......... Environment and Natural Resources Information Center (SAUO)
ENRICH......... European Network for Global Change Research (SAUS)
ENRICH......... European Network for Research in Global Change (SAUS)
ENRICH......... European Network for Research on Global Change (CARB)
ENRIN......... Environmental and Natural Resources Information Network (SAUS)
ENRIN......... Environment and Natural Resource Information Networks (SAUS)
ENRIN......... Environment and Natural Resources Information Networking (SAUS)
Enriron Prot Eng... Environmental Protection Engineering (journ.) (SAUS)
ENRL......... Enrollment (AABC)
EnrLLC......... Enron Capital Corp. LLC [*Associated Press*] (SAG)
ENRM......... Environmental and Natural Resource Management (SAUS)
ENRM......... Environment and Natural Resource Management (SAUS)
ENRM......... Rorvik/Ryum [*Norway*] [*ICAO location identifier*] (ICLI)
Enrn......... Enron Corp. [*Associated Press*] (SAG)
ENRO......... Roros [*Norway*] [*ICAO location identifier*] (ICLI)
Enron......... Enron Corp. [*Associated Press*] (SAG)
Enron98......... Enron Corp. [*Associated Press*] (SAG)
EnronLq......... Enron Liquids Pipeline [*Associated Press*] (SAG)
ENRPAE......... En Route to/from Public Affairs Event [*Military*] (NVT)
ENRS......... Eastern Neuroradiological Society (SAUS)
ENRS......... Eastern Nursing Research Society (SAUO)

ENRS .... Electronic News Release Service (SAUO)
ENRS .... Rost [*Norway*] [*ICAO location identifier*] (ICLI)
ENRSVC .... En Route and Provide Service to Units Indicated [*Military*] (NVT)
ENRT .... En Route
EN RX .... enable receive (SAUS)
ENRX .... United States Enrichment [*Federal Railroad Administration identification code*]
ENRY .... Rygge [*Norway*] [*ICAO location identifier*] (ICLI)
ENRZ .... Enhanced Non-Return to Zero (IAA)
ENRZ .... Enhanced NRZ (SAUS)
ENS .... Electron News Service [*Evans Economics, Inc.*] [*Information service or system*] (CRD)
ENS .... Electrostatic Nonmetallic Separator (SAUS)
ENS .... El Nino, Pacific SST (SAUS)
ENS .... Emergency Notification System
ENS .... Empresa Naviera Sanra (SAUS)
ENS .... Energy Nova Scotia [*Database*] [*Nova Scotia Research Foundation Corp.*] [*Information service or system*] (CRD)
ENS .... Enschede [*Netherlands*] [*Airport symbol*] (OAG)
ens .... Ensemble [*Group*] [*French*]
ENS .... ENSERCH Corp. [*NYSE symbol*] (TTSB)
ENS .... Enserch Exploration [*NYSE symbol*] [*Toronto Stock Exchange symbol*]
ENS .... Ensign (AABC)
ens .... Ensign (GEAB)
Ens .... Ensign (SHCU)
ENS .... Enteral Nutritional Support [*Medicine*] (EDAA)
ENS .... Entergy Services, Inc. [*ICAO designator*] (FAAC)
ENS .... Enteric Nervous System [*Neurobiology*]
ENS .... Enterprise Naming Service [*Banyan Systems, Inc.*] [*Telecommunications*] (PCM)
ENS .... Enterprise Network Services [*Banyan*] [*Computer science*]
ENS .... Enterprise Network Switch (SAUS)
ENS .... Enterprise Network System (SAUO)
ENS .... Epidermal Nevus Syndrome [*Medicine*]
ENS .... Ethnic, Nationalist, and Separatist [*Conflicts or wars*]
ENS .... Ethylnorsuprarenin [*Also, ENE*] [*Pharmacology*]
ENS .... Europaeische Kernenergie-Gesellschaft [*European Nuclear Society - ENS*] (EAIO)
ENS .... European Nervous System
ENS .... European Network for Science [*Marine science*] (OSRA)
ENS .... European Neurological Society [*Switzerland*]
ENS .... European News Service (SAUO)
ENS .... European Nuclear Society (NUCP)
ENS .... Exhibition for National Security (SAUO)
ENS .... Experimental Navigation Ship
ENS .... Explosive Neutralization System (SEWL)
ENS .... Extended Network Services (MHDB)
ENS .... Extended Nylon Shaft
ENS .... Empty Nest Syndrome (ODA)
ENSA .... Enterprise Network Storage Architecture (VLIE)
ENSA .... Entertainments National Service Association [*Facetiously translated as "Every Night Something Awful"*] [*Military*] [*British*]
ENSA .... Environmental Services of America, Inc. [*NASDAQ symbol*] (SAG)
ensb .... Ensemble (VRA)
ENSB .... Equivalent Noise Sideband
ENSB .... Svalbard/Longyear [*Norway*] [*ICAO location identifier*] (ICLI)
Ensc .... Enserch Corp. [*Associated Press*] (SAG)
ENSCA .... European Natural Sausage Casings Association (EA)
ENSCE .... Enemy Situation Correlation Element [*DoD*]
ENSCO .... Energy Service Co. [*Associated Press*] (SAG)
ENSCO .... Environmental Services Corp. (EFIS)
ENSCO .... Environmental Systems Co. (EFIS)
Enscor .... Enscor, Inc. [*Associated Press*] (SAG)
ENSD .... Sandane/Anda [*Norway*] [*ICAO location identifier*] (ICLI)
ENSDF .... Evaluated Nuclear Structure Data File [*National Nuclear Data Center*] [*Information service or system*]
ENSDHE .... European Network for Staff Development in Higher Education (SAUO)
ENSDU .... Expedited Network Service Data Unit (VLIE)
ENSEARCH ... Environmental Management Association of Malaysia (SAUO)
ENSEC .... Electronics for National Security (SAUO)
ENSEC .... European Nuclear Steelmaking Club [*British*] (NUCP)
Ensen .... Ensenada (SAUS)
EnsExp .... Enserch Exploration, Inc. [*Associated Press*] (SAG)
ENSF .... Statfjord-A [*Norway*] [*ICAO location identifier*] (ICLI)
ENSG .... Ensuing (ROG)
ENSG .... Sogndal/Haukasen [*Norway*] [*ICAO location identifier*] (ICLI)
ENSH .... Svolvaer/Helle [*Norway*] [*ICAO location identifier*] (ICLI)
ENSI .... Environment and School Initiatives Project (EERA)
ENSI .... Equivalent Noise Sideband Input (MCD)
ENSIC .... Environmental Sanitation Information Center [*Asian Institute of Technology*] [*Thailand*] [*Information service or system*] (IID)
ENSIM .... Environmental Simulator (IAA)
ENSIP .... Engine Structural Integrity Program (ACAE)
ENSIP .... ENSO Intercomparison Project (SAUS)
ENSIP .... Turbine Engine Structural Integrity Program (SAUO)
ENSIQ .... ENS - Information Query (SAUS)
ENSIT .... Enemy Situation (MCD)
ENSITN .... Enemy Situation (SAUS)
ENSK .... Stokmarknes/Skagen [*Norway*] [*ICAO location identifier*] (ICLI)
En SL .... Engineer Sub-Lieutenant [*Navy*] [*British*] (DMA)
ENSLA .... Eastern Nigeria School Libraries Association (SAUO)
ENSLY .... Ensley, AL [*American Association of Railroads railroad junction routing code*]
ENSMT .... ENS - Management Tool (SAUS)
ENSN .... Skien/Geiteryggen [*Norway*] [*ICAO location identifier*] (ICLI)
ENSO .... El Nino and Southern Oscillation [*Coupled oceanic-atmospheric change*]
ENSO .... Envirosource, Inc. [*NASDAQ symbol*] (SAG)
ENSO .... Stord [*Norway*] [*ICAO location identifier*] (ICLI)
ENSP .... Engineering Specification [*Air Force*]
ENSPrE .... ENSERCH Dep Adj cm E Pfd [*NYSE symbol*] (TTSB)
ENSPrF .... ENSERCH Dep Adj cm F Pfd [*NYSE symbol*] (TTSB)
ENSR .... Sorkjosen [*Norway*] [*ICAO location identifier*] (ICLI)
Ensrch .... Enserch Corp. [*Associated Press*] (SAG)
ENSS .... European Navigation Satellite System
ENSS .... Exterior Nodal Switching Subsystem [*Computer science*] (ACRL)
ENSS .... Svartnes [*Norway*] [*ICAO location identifier*] (ICLI)
ENST .... Sandnessjoen/Stokka [*Norway*] [*ICAO location identifier*] (ICLI)
ENSTINET .... Egyptian National Scientific and Technical Information Network
ensu .... Ensuing (GEAB)
ENSURE .... Emergency Non-Standard Urgent Requirements (ACAE)
ENSURE .... Engineering Surveillance Report (MCD)
ENSURE .... Expedited Non-Standard Urgent Requirements for Equipment [*Army*] (AABC)
ENSV .... Stavanger [*Norway*] [*ICAO location identifier*] (ICLI)
ENSVTA .... Eesti Noukogude Sotsialistliku Vabariigi Teaduste Akadeemia (SAUO)
ENSY .... EnSys Environmental Products [*NASDAQ symbol*] (TTSB)
ENSY .... EnSys Environmental Products, Inc. [*NASDAQ symbol*] (SAG)
ENSYN .... Electromagnetic Environment Synthesizer (NVT)
ENSYN .... Environmental Synthesizer [*Navy*]
ENSYS .... Electromagnetic Environment Synthesizer (DNAB)
EnSys .... EnSys Environmental Products, Inc. [*Associated Press*] (SAG)
ENT .... Aerolineas Argentinas (SAUS)
Ent .... Coke's Book of Entries [*1614*] [*England*] [*A publication*] (DLA)
ENT .... Department of Entomology (SAUS)
ENT .... Ear, Nose, and Throat [*Medicine*] (EDAA)
ENT .... Ear, Nose, Throat (SAUS)
ENT .... Ears, Nose, and Throat
ENT .... Effective Noise Temperature (SAUS)
ENT .... Electrical Nonmetallic Tubing
ENT .... Emergency Negative Thrust
ENT .... Eniwetok [*Marshall Islands*] [*Airport symbol*] (OAG)
ENT .... Entebbe [*Uganda*] [*Seismograph station code, US Geological Survey*] [*Closed*] (SEIS)
ENT .... Enter (MUGU)
Ent .... Entered (SAUS)
ENT .... Entering [*FBI standardized term*]
ent .... Enterotoxin [*Medicine*] (EDAA)
ENT .... Enterprise [*United States Postal Service last word addressing abbreviation*]
Ent .... Enterprise
ENT .... Entertainment
Ent .... Entire [*Philately*]
ENT .... Entity
Ent .... Entomologie (SAUS)
ENT .... Entomology
ENT .... Entrada
ENT .... Entrance (ROG)
ent .... Entrance [*A stage direction*] (WDMC)
ENT .... Entry (NASA)
ENT .... Entry equivalent Noise Temperature (SAUS)
ENT .... Environmental Test (MCD)
ENT .... Enzootic Nasal Tumor [*Medicine*] (EDAA)
ENT .... EQUANT N.V. ADS [*NYSE symbol*] (SG)
ENT .... Equivalent Noise Temperature [*Electronics*]
ENT .... EuroNATO Training (SAUS)
ENT .... Event Number Translator
ENT .... Exhaust Nozzle Temperature (KSC)
ENT .... Extranodular Tissue (DB)
ENT .... Holmstrom Flyg AB [*Sweden*] [*ICAO designator*] (FAAC)
ENT .... Otorhinolaryngology [*Medicine*] (DAVI)
Ent .... Rastell's Entries [*A publication*] (DLA)
ENTA .... Environmental Test Area (SAUS)
enta .... Ethylenediaminetetraacetate [*Also, EDETATE, EDTA*] [*Organic chemistry*]
ENTAB .... Entry Table (VLIE)
ENTAC .... Engine-Teleguide Anti-Char (SAUS)
ENTAC .... Engin Teleguide Anti-Char [*Antitank Missile*] [*French*]
ENTAC .... Entrance National Agency Check [*Military*] (AABC)
Ent & Sports Law ... Entertainment and Sports Lawyer [*A publication*] (DLA)
EntArk .... Entergy Arkansas, Inc. Capital I [*Associated Press*] (SAG)
entbl .... Entablature (VRA)
ENTC .... Eastern Nuclear Training Center (SAUS)
ENTC .... Engine Negative Torque Control (MSA)
ENTC .... Entronics Corp. [*NASDAQ symbol*] (COMM)
ENTC .... Tromso/Langnes [*Norway*] [*ICAO location identifier*] (ICLI)
ENTCE .... Entrance (ROG)
ENTD .... Entered
ENTEC .... Enterotoxigenic Escherichia coli (SAUS)
ENTELEC .... Energy Telecommunications and Electrical Association (EA)
Entente .... Council of the Entente
ENTER .... Enterprise (DLA)
Entergy .... Entergy Corp. [*Associated Press*] (SAG)
enterobact ... enterobacteriologist (SAUS)
enterobact ... enterobacterium (SAUS)
enterov .... enterovioform (SAUS)
ENTERPRISE ... Evaluating New Technologies for Roads Program Initiatives in Safety and Efficiency [*FHWA*] (TAG)

Enters......... Enterprises (AAGC)
Entertainment LJ... Entertainment Law Journal [*A publication*] (DLA)
ENTEX......... European Technical Exporters (SAUO)
EntFedB........ Enterprise Federal Bancorp, Inc. [*Associated Press*] (SAG)
ENTG.......... Entering (ROG)
ENTG.......... Euro-NATO Training Group [*An association*] (EAIO)
ENTG.......... European NATO Training Group (SAUO)
EntGlf.......... Entergy Gulf States [*Associated Press*] (SAG)
ENTH.......... Ear-Nose-Throat Hospital (SAUS)
ent hall....... entrance hall (SAUS)
ENTIS.......... Engine Teleguide Anti-Char Automatic Data System for the Army in the Field (SAUO)
ENTJ.......... Extrovert, Intuition, Thinking, Judging (SAUS)
ENTJ.......... Extrovert, Intuitive, a Thinker, and Judger [*Keirsey Temperament Test Result*] [*Psychology*]
ENTL.......... Entitle (AABC)
EntLA.......... Entergy Louisiana, Inc. [*Associated Press*] (SAG)
EntLA.......... Entergy Louisiana, Inc. Capital I [*Associated Press*] (SAG)
Ent LR.......... Entertainment Law Review [*A publication*] (SAFN)
entn.......... entertain (SAUS)
ENTNAC....... Entrance National Agency Check [*Military*] (NVT)
ENTO.......... CSIRO Division of Entomology (SAUO)
ENTO.......... Entomology (AABC)
ENTO.......... Torp [*Norway*] [*ICAO location identifier*] (ICLI)
EntOil.......... Enterprise Oil Co. [*Associated Press*] (SAG)
entom.......... Entomology (ADWA)
ENTOM........ Entomology
ENTOMA...... Entomological Society of America (SAUO)
ENTOMOL.... Entomologic
ENTOMOL.... Entomological (SAUS)
ENTOMOL.... Entomologist (SAUS)
Entomol....... Entomology (BEE)
Entomol Rev... Entomological Review (journ.) (SAUS)
ENTP.......... Enter Packed (SAUS)
ENTP.......... European Network of Training Partnerships (EURO)
ENTPROL..... (Ethylenedinitrilo)tetrakis(propanol) [*Organic chemistry*]
ENTPS......... Expanded Near-Term Prepositioning Ships
ENTR.......... Eneteractive, Inc. [*NASDAQ symbol*] (SAG)
ENTR.......... Enter (SAUS)
ENTR.......... Entire
ENTR.......... Entrance [*Maps and charts*] (MSA)
entr.......... Entrance (VRA)
ENTR.......... Trondheim [*Norway*] [*ICAO location identifier*] (ICLI)
ENTRACE..... Entrance (ROG)
Entract......... Eneteractive, Inc. [*Associated Press*] (SAG)
Entractv....... Eneteractive, Inc. [*Associated Press*] (SAG)
EntreMd....... EntreMed, Inc. [*Associated Press*] (SAG)
ENTRI.......... Environmental Treaties and Resource Indicators [*Internet resource*]
Entries Antient... Rastell's Old Entries [*So cited in Rolle Abridgment*] [*A publication*] (DLA)
ENTROP....... Entropy (SAUS)
ENTRPRNR... Entrepreneur
ENTRPRS..... Enterprise
ENTRPT....... Entrepot
EntrSys....... Enterprise Systems, Inc. [*Associated Press*] (SAG)
ENTRTN....... Entertainment
ENTRW........ Enteractive Inc. Wrrt [*NASDAQ symbol*] (TTSB)
ENTS.......... Physicians' Specialty Corp. [*NASDAQ symbol*] (NASQ)
ENT/SAT...... Entertainment Satellite [*Proposed*] (MCD)
Entsch.......... Entscheidung [*Decision, Judgment*] [*German*] (ILCA)
ENTSOC....... Entomological Society of Canada (FOTI)
ENTSPR....... Entsprechend [*Corresponding*] [*German*]
Ent Sta Hall... Entered at Stationers' Hall [*British*] (BARN)
ENT Surgery... Ear, Nose, Throat Surgery (SAUS)
ENTU.......... Entrust Technologies [*NASDAQ symbol*] (SG)
EnTUSA........ Environmental Tech USA, Inc. [*Associated Press*] (SAG)
Ent W.......... Entertainment Weekly [*A publication*] (BRI)
ENTW.......... Entwistle Co. [*NASDAQ symbol*] (COMM)
Entw.......... Entwurf [*Draft*] [*German*] (ILCA)
EN TX.......... Enable Transmit [*Status activation code*] (NITA)
ENU.......... Enugu [*Nigeria*] [*Airport symbol*] (OAG)
ENU.......... Essential/Nonessential/Update [*Telecommunications*] (TEL)
ENU.......... Ethylnitrosourea [*Organic chemistry*]
Enuc.......... Enucleation [*Medicine*] (EDAA)
ENUF.......... Enough [*Amateur radio shorthand*] (WDAA)
ENUF.......... Everybody Now Undo Foul-ups (SAUS)
ENUM.......... Enumeration (MSA)
ENUM.......... Enumerator (SAUS)
ENUN.......... Enunciation (ROG)
ENUP.......... Ethiopian National Unity Party (SAUO)
enur.......... enuresis (SAUS)
enus.......... end user (SAUS)
En Users Rep... Energy Users Report [*Commerce Clearing House*] [*A publication*] (DLA)
enutech........ enuresis technology (SAUS)
ENUWAR...... Environmental Consequences of Nuclear War [*International Council of Scientific Unions*]
ENUWAR...... Environmental Effects of Nuclear War, Nuclear Winter Ecology Group (SAUO)
ENV.......... CET Environmental Services [*AMEX symbol*] (SAG)
env.......... Envelope [*Refers to the envelope that surrounds cells*] [*Biochemistry*] (DAVI)
ENV.......... Envelope
ENV.......... Environ [*About*] [*French*]
ENV.......... Environment (ACAE)
Env.......... Environment [*A publication*] (BRI)
ENV.......... Environmental Pollution Monitoring and Research Programme (SAUS)
ENV.......... Environmental Safety Systems, Inc. [*Toronto Stock Exchange symbol*]
ENV.......... Environs (SAUS)
ENV.......... Enviropact, Inc. [*AMEX symbol*] (COMM)
ENV.......... Envoy (ROG)
Env.......... Envoy Extraordinary (SAUS)
ENV.......... Equivalent Noise Voltage
ENV.......... Erdbeernekrosevirus
ENV.......... Europeene Norme Vorausgabe [*European Prestandard*] (OSI)
ENV.......... Wendover, UT [*Location identifier*] [*FAA*] (FAAL)
ENVA.......... Trondheim/Vaernes [*Norway*] [*ICAO location identifier*] (ICLI)
ENVANAL..... Environmental Analysis [*Program*]
ENVD.......... Vadso [*Norway*] [*ICAO location identifier*] (ICLI)
EnvE.......... Environmental Engineer (SAUS)
ENVEC........ Environmental Economics (EERA)
ENVEIS........ Environmental Engineering Information System (BCP)
EnvEle........ Environmental Elements Corp. [*Associated Press*] (SAG)
ENVEX......... Environmental Extremists
Env-Ext........ Envoy-Extraordinary (SAUS)
Env Extr........ Envoy Extraordinary (DLA)
Env-Extr........ Envoy-Extraordinary (SAUS)
ENVG.......... Efferent Vein from Nephridial Gland [*Anatomy*]
ENVG.......... Envirogen, Inc. [*NASDAQ symbol*] (SAG)
ENVGEN....... Environment Generator [*Computer software*]
ENVGW........ Envirogen Inc. Wrrt [*NASDAQ symbol*] (TTSB)
ENVI.......... Environmental Design Library (SAUS)
ENVI.......... Envirosafe Services, Inc. [*NASDAQ symbol*] (COMM)
ENVI.......... Envirosphere Company (SAUS)
ENVI.......... Envirotest Systems'A' [*NASDAQ symbol*] (TTSB)
ENVI.......... Envirotest Systems, Inc. [*NASDAQ symbol*] (SAG)
ENVICAN...... Ministry of Environment (SAUO)
ENVIR.......... Environment (MSA)
envir.......... Environment (VRA)
ENVIR.......... Environmental Information and Retrieval System (SAUS)
ENVIREX...... Environmental Engineering Exhibition (SAUS)
Envirln.......... Envirodyne Industries, Inc. [*Associated Press*] (SAG)
envirl.......... Environmental (DD)
ENVIRN........ Environment
Envir News... Environment News [*A publication*]
ENVIROBIB... Environmental Periodicals Bibliography [*Environmental Studies Institute*] [*Information service or system*]
ENVIROFATE... Environmental Fate [*Environmental Protection Agency*] [*Information service or system*] (CRD)
ENVIROLINE... Environmental Science Index On Line (SAUS)
ENVIROLINE... Environment Information On-Line [*Database*] [*Environment Information Center, Inc.*] [*New York, NY*]
environ........ Environment (ADWA)
ENVIRON..... Environmental
ENVIRON..... Environmental Information Retrieval On-Line [*Environmental Protection Agency*]
environ........ environmentalism (SAUS)
environ........ environmentalist (SAUS)
Environ Behav... Environment and Behavior [*A publication*] (PABS)
Environ Can Environ Update... Environment Canada, Environment Update (journ.) (SAUS)
Environ Can Notice Publ... Environment Canada, Notice of Publications (journ.) (SAUS)
Environ Claims J... Environmental Claims Journal [*A publication*] (PABS)
Environ Conserv... Environmental Conservation [*A publication*] (CABS)
Environ Devel Econ... Environment and Development Economics [*A publication*] (JLIT)
Environ Econ Pol Stud... Environmental Economics and Policy Studies [*A publication*] (JLIT)
Environ Eng... Environmental Engineering (journ.) (SAUS)
Environ Eng Policy... Environmental Engineering and Policy [*A publication*] (PABS)
Environ Eng Sci... Environmental Engineering Science [*A publication*] (PABS)
Environ Eng World... Environmental Engineering World [*A publication*] (PABS)
ENVIROnet... Space Environment information service (SAUO)
Environ Ethics... Environmental Ethics [*A publication*] (PABS)
Environ Exp Bot... Environmental and Experimental Botany (SAUS)
Environ Exp Bot... Environmental and Experimental Botany (journ.) (SAUS)
Environ Fluid Mech... Environmental Fluid Mechanics [*A publication*] (PABS)
Environ Geochem Health... Environmental Geochemistry and Health [*A publication*] (PABS)
Environ Geol... Environmental Geology [*A publication*] (PABS)
Environ Health Perspect... Environmental Health Perspectives [*Research Triangle Park, NC*] (SAUS)
Environ Hist... Environmental History [*A publication*] (PABS)
Environ Hist Rev... Environmental History Review [*A publication*] (PABS)
Environ Int... Environment International (journ.) (SAUS)
Environ Liability... Environmental Liability [*A publication*] (PABS)
Environ Manage... Environmental Management [*A publication*] (PABS)
Environ Manager... Environmental Manager [*A publication*] (PABS)
Environ Mol Mutag... Environmental and Molecular Mutagenesis [*A publication*] (PABS)
Environ Monit Assess... Environmental Monitoring and Assessment (MEC)
Environ Mutagenesis... Environmental Mutagenesis (journ.) (SAUS)
Environ Pollut... Environmental Pollution (MEC)
Environ Pollut... Environmental Pollution (journ.) (SAUS)
Environ Prof... Environmental Professional [*A publication*] (PABS)
Environ Prog... Environmental Progress [*A publication*] (PABS)
Environ Prot... Environmental Protection [*A publication*] (PABS)

Environ Prot Eng... Environment Protection Engineering [*A publication*] (PABS)
Environ Qual Manage... Environmental Quality Management [*A publication*] (PABS)
Environ Quart... Environmental Quarterly (journ.) (SAUS)
Environ Res... Environmental Research (journ.) (SAUS)
Environ Res... Environmental Research [*New York, NY*] (SAUS)
Environ Resource Econ... Environmental and Resource Economics [*A publication*] (JLIT)
Environ Resour Econ... Environmental & Resource Economics [*A publication*] (PABS)
Environ Rev... Environmental Review (SAUS)
Environ Rev... Environmental Review (journ.) (SAUS)
Environ Sci Technol... Environmental Science and Technology (journ.) (SAUS)
Environ Sci Technol A... Environmental Seience and Technology A (journ.) (SAUS)
Environ Softw... Environmental Software (journ.) (SAUS)
Environ Software... Environmental Software [*A publication*] (CABS)
Environ Solutions... Environmental Solutions [*A publication*] (PABS)
Environ Space Sci... Environmental Space Sciences (journ.) (SAUS)
Environ Technol... Environmental Technology [*A publication*] (PABS)
Environ Technol Lett... Environmental Technology Letters (journ.) (SAUS)
Environ Toxicol... Environmental Toxicology [*A publication*] (PABS)
Environ Toxicol Chem... Environmental Toxicology and Chemistry [*A publication*] (PABS)
Environ Toxicol Pharmacol... Environmental Toxicology and Pharmacology [*A publication*] (PABS)
Environ Toxicol Water Qual... Environmental Toxicology and Water Quality [*A publication*] (PABS)
Environ Urban... Environment and Urbanization [*A publication*] (PABS)
Environ Values... Environmental Values [*A publication*] (JLIT)
Environ Views... Environment Views [*A publication*] (PABS)
Environ Waste Manage... Environmental & Waste Management [*A publication*] (PABS)
Enviro-TRADE... Environmental Technologies for Remedial Action Data Exchange [*Environment term*] (EGA)
Envirotst...... Envirotest Systems, Inc. [*Associated Press*] (SAG)
Envir Poll Contr... Environmental Pollution Control (SAUS)
Envir Rep..... Environment Reporter [*Bureau of National Affairs*] [*A publication*] (DLA)
ENVISA........ European Space Agency Environmental Satellite (SAUS)
ENVISAT...... environmental satellite (SAUS)
ENVISAT...... Environmental Satellite Mission (SAUO)
ENVISAT...... ESA Earth observation satellite (SAUS)
ENVISAT...... European Space Agency Environmental Satellite (SAUO)
Envitec.......... Environmental Technics (SAUS)
Envitec.......... Environmental Technology (SAUS)
Env LM......... Environmental Law Monthly [*A publication*]
Env LR.......... Environmental Law Reports [*A publication*]
ENVM........... Environment Model
Envmt.......... Envirometrics Inc. [*Associated Press*] (SAG)
ENVMT.......... Environment (AFM)
Envmt........... Environment (DIAR)
ENVMTL......... Environmental
Envmtrc....... Envirometrics, Inc. [*Associated Press*] (SAG)
ENVN........... Tromso [*Norway*] [*ICAO location identifier*] (ICLI)
Envoy........... Envoy Corp. [*Associated Press*] (SAG)
ENVPD.......... Environmental Protection Division (SAUS)
EnvperB......... Environmental Periodicals Biography
ENVPREDRSCHF... Environmental Prediction Research Facility [*Monterey, CA*] [*Navy*]
ENVPREDRSCHFAC... Naval Environmental Prediction Research Facility [*Marine science*] (MSC)
Envpsych..... Environmental Psychology [*City University of New York*] [*Defunct*] [*Information service or system*] (CRD)
EnvPwr........ Environmental Power Corp. [*Associated Press*] (SAG)
ENVR........... Envirocare Facility [*Clive, UT*] (GAAI)
ENVR........... Envirodyne Industries, Inc. [*NASDAQ symbol*] (COMM)
ENVR........... Environmental (KSC)
ENVR........... Environmental Tech USA [*NASDAQ symbol*] (TTSB)
ENVR........... Environmental Tech USA Inc. [*NASDAQ symbol*] (SAG)
Envrg........... Envirogen, Inc. [*Associated Press*] (SAG)
Envrgen........ Envirogen, Inc. [*Associated Press*] (SAG)
ENVRNMTL... Environmental
EnvrOne....... Environment One Corp. [*Associated Press*] (SAG)
EnvrTc......... Environmental Tectonics Corp. [*Associated Press*] (SAG)
EnvrTch........ Environmental Technology Corp. [*Associated Press*] (SAG)
ENVRW........ Environmental Tech USA Wrrt [*NASDAQ symbol*] (TTSB)
Envs............ Environmentalists (SAUS)
ENVS............ Envirosure Management Corp. [*NASDAQ symbol*] (COMM)
Envsrc.......... Envirosource, Inc. [*Associated Press*] (SAG)
EnvSvc......... Environmental Services of America, Inc. [*Associated Press*] (SAG)
ENV-SYS...... Environmental System (MCD)
ENVT............ Environmental
EnvT............. Environmental Tech USA, Inc. [*Associated Press*] (SAG)
ENVT............ Environmental Tectonics Corp. (MHDW)
EnvTcCp....... Environmental Technology Corp. [*Associated Press*] (SAG)
Envtl Affairs... Environmental Affairs [*A publication*] (DLA)
Envtl F......... Environmental Forum [*A publication*] (DLA)
Envtl L Rev... Environmental Law Review [*A publication*] (DLA)
Envtl L Rptr... Environmental Law Reporter [*A publication*] (DLA)
Envtl Pol'y & L... Environmental Policy and Law [*A publication*] (DLA)
Env't Reg Handbook... Environment Regulation Handbook [*A publication*] (DLA)
Env't Rep (BNA)... Environment Reporter (Bureau of National Affairs) [*A publication*] (DLA)
ENVV........... Bergen [*Norway*] [*ICAO location identifier*] (ICLI)
EnvWste...... Enviropur Waste Refining & Technology, Inc. [*Associated Press*] (SAG)
ENVY........... Envoy Corp. [*NASDAQ symbol*] (SPSG)
ENVY........... Vaeroy [*Norway*] [*ICAO location identifier*] (ICLI)
ENW............ Effects of Nuclear Weapons [*AEC-DoD book*]
ENW............ Elgin National Industries, Inc. (SAUO)
ENW............ Elgin National Watch Co. (SAUO)
ENW............ El Nino, Pacific SST (SAUS)
ENW............ Emergency Nursing World (SAUO)
ENW............ English the New Way [*Education*] (AEBS)
ENW............ Ethnic NewsWatch [*Softline Information Co.*]
ENW............ Kenosha, WI [*Location identifier*] [*FAA*] (FAAL)
ENWGS........ Enhanced Naval Warfare Gaming System (GFGA)
ENWGS........ Enhanced Navy War Gaming System (SAUS)
ENWR.......... Erie National Wildlife Refuge (SAUS)
ENWR.......... Eufaula National Wildlife Refuge (SAUS)
ENWV.......... Endwave Corp. [*NASDAQ symbol*]
ENX............. Eaton Manufacturing Company (SAUO)
ENX............. Enexco International Ltd. [*Vancouver Stock Exchange symbol*]
ENY............. Ashland, WI [*Location identifier*] [*FAA*] (FAAL)
ENY............. Elsevier New York (SAUS)
ENY............. European Original New York Seltzer Ltd. [*Vancouver Stock Exchange symbol*]
ENY............. Yanan [*China*] [*Airport symbol*] (OAG)
ENZ............. Enscor, Inc. [*Toronto Stock Exchange symbol*]
ENZ............. Enzo Biochem [*AMEX symbol*] (TTSB)
ENZ............. Enzo Biochem, Inc. [*AMEX symbol*] (SPSG)
enz.............. Enzymatic [*or Enzyme*] (MAE)
Enz.............. Enzyme
ENZ............. Enzymes (SAUS)
ENZ............. New Zealand Air Services Ltd. [*ICAO designator*] (FAAC)
ENZ............. Nogales, AZ [*Location identifier*] [*FAA*] (FAAL)
enza............ influenza (SAUS)
ENZN.......... Enzon, Inc. [*NASDAQ symbol*] (NQ)
ENZO.......... Ethernet Needing Zero Overhead
EnzoBi......... Enzo Biochem, Inc. [*Associated Press*] (SAG)
Enzon........... Enzon, Inc. [*Associated Press*] (SAG)
ENZV........... Stavanger/Sola [*Norway*] [*ICAO location identifier*] (ICLI)
ENZY........... Enzymatics, Inc. [*NASDAQ symbol*] (SAG)
Enzymat....... Enzymatics, Inc. [*Associated Press*] (SAG)
Enzyme Protein... Enzyme and Protein (SAUS)
Enzyme Protein... Enzyme and Protein [*Basel*] (SAUS)
EO............... Aeroamerica [*ICAO designator*] (AD)
EO............... Aero America, Inc. [*ICAO designator*] (ICDA)
EO............... Air Nordic Sweden [*ICAO designator*] (AD)
eo---........... Danube River and Basin [*MARC geographic area code*] [*Library of Congress*] (LCCP)
EO............... Earth Observation
EO............... Earth Orbit [*NASA*] (KSC)
EO............... Eastern Orthodox
EO............... Easter Offerings [*to a church*]
E/O............. East Of [*In outdoor advertising*] (WDMC)
EO............... Echos d'Orient [*A publication*] (ODCC)
E/O............. Edges Opened [*Publishing*] (DGA)
EO............... Editorial Operations (SAUS)
EO............... Education Officer [*Military*]
EO............... Education Otherwise [*British*] [*An association*] (DBA)
EO............... Ego Overcontrol [*Psychology*]
EO............... Eight Ones (SAUS)
EO............... Elbow Orthosis [*Medicine*]
EO............... Electoral Office [*Australia*]
E_0............... Electric Affinity [*Symbol*] [*Physics*] (DAVI)
E/O............. Electrical-to-Optical (ACRL)
EO............... Electrolytic Oxidation
EO............... Electronic Office (SAUS)
EO............... Electronics Lock Overhead [*NASA*] (SPST)
EO............... Electron Optics (SAUS)
EO............... Electro-Optic (SAUS)
EO............... Electro-Optical
EO............... Electro-Optically (SAUS)
EO............... Electrosmosis (SAUS)
EO............... Elementary Operation (IAA)
EO............... Elliptical Orbit [*Aerospace*] (AAG)
EO............... Emergency Officer [*Nuclear energy*] (NRCH)
EO............... Emergency Operation (ADWA)
EO............... Emergency Order (VLIE)
EO............... Employers Organization (DCTA)
EO............... Employment Officer
EO............... Emulsion Out [*Photography*] (WDMC)
EO............... Enable Output [*Davey Air Services*] [*Computer science*] (MHDB)
EO............... End Office [*Telecommunications*] (TEL)
EO............... End of Operation [*Computer science*] (IAA)
EO............... End-On (SAUS)
EO............... End Order (SAUS)
EO............... Enemy Occupied (SAUS)
E/O............. Engineering/Operations [*NASA*] (NASA)
EO............... Engineering Order
EO............... Engineer Officer [*Navy*] [*British*]
EO............... Engine Oil
EO............... Engine Out (NASA)
EO............... English [*Communion*] Office [*Episcopalian*]
EO............... Entertainments Officer [*Military*] [*British*]
EO............... environmental officer (SAUS)
E/O............. Eocene/Oligocene [*Geological boundary zone*]
eo................ Eosinophil [*Hematology*]
EO............... Eosinophil(s) [*Medicine*] (EDAA)
Eo............... Eotvos Number [*Fluid mechanics*]

EO .... Equal Opportunity
EO .... Equal Opportunity Program Office [*Kennedy Space Center Directorate*] [*NASA*] (NASA)
EO .... Equilibrium Orbit (SAUS)
EO .... Equipment Operator [*Navy rating*]
EO .... Equivalent Orifice (IAA)
EO .... Erasable Optical (VLIE)
EO .... Erasable Optical Disk (ITCA)
EO .... Errors and Omissions [*Insurance*]
EO .... Ethylene Oxide [*Organic chemistry*]
EO .... Europe Online (VERA)
EO .... Even-Odd
EO .... Examining Officer (ROG)
EO .... Excise Officer (ROG)
EO .... Exclusive Or [*Gates*] [*Computer science*]
EO .... Executive Office [*or Officer*]
EO .... Executive Order [*Rule or regulation having the force of law, issued by the President with congressional authorization*]
EO .... Executive Organ (SAUS)
EO .... Executive Outcomes (SAUS)
EO .... Exempt Organization [*IRS*]
EO .... Exhaust Opens [*Valve position*]
EO .... Ex Officio [*By Virtue of Office*] [*Latin*]
EO .... Expander Output (SAUS)
EO .... Expected [*Patient*] Outcome [*Medicine*] (DAVI)
EO .... Expected Output
EO .... Experimental Officer [*Also, ExO, XO*] [*Ministry of Agriculture, Fisheries, and Food*] [*British*]
EO .... Explosive Ordnance [*Military*] (AFM)
EO .... Exponent Overflow (SAUS)
EO .... Export Office (ROG)
EO .... Extend and Offset (VLIE)
EO .... Extended Operations
EO .... Eye Balls Out (SAA)
EO .... Eyes Open [*Ataxia*]
EO .... Ethoxylated Sulphonates [*Chemistry*] (ODA)
EO-1 .... Earth Observing One [*NASA*]
EO1 .... Edge Oya [*Norway*] [*Seismograph station code, US Geological Survey*] (SEIS)
EO1 .... Equipment Operator, First Class [*Navy rating*]
EO2 .... Equipment Operator, Second Class [*Navy rating*]
EO3 .... Equipment Operator, Third Class [*Navy rating*]
EOA .... Early Operational Assessment [*Military*]
EOA .... Eastern Orthopaedic Association (SAUS)
EOA .... Economic Oil Association (SAUO)
EOA .... Economic Opportunity Act [*1964*] [*Repealed, 1974*]
EOA .... Education Officers Association (SAUO)
EOA .... Effective On or About [*Business term*]
EOA .... Effective Orifice Area [*Medicine*] (EDAA)
EOA .... Egyptian Orthopedic Association (SAUS)
EOA .... Electro-Optical Assembly (MCD)
EOA .... Electro-Optics Augmentation
EOA .... End of Activity (ADWA)
EOA .... End of Address [*Computer science*]
EOA .... Energy Office [*Department of Agriculture*] (OICC)
EOA .... English Orienteering Association (BI)
EOA .... Enterprise Object Architecture (HODG)
EOA .... Environmental Protection Agency, Region VIII Library, Denver, CO [*OCLC symbol*] (OCLC)
EOA .... Epithelioma [*Medicine*]
EOA .... Equal Opportunity Advisor [*DoD*]
EOA .... Equal Opportunity Assistants (SAUO)
EOA .... Erosive Osteoarthritis [*Medicine*]
EOA .... Esophageal Obturator Airway [*Medicine*] (DMAA)
EOA .... Essential Oil Association (SAUO)
EOA .... Essential Oil Association of the United States (EA)
EOA .... Ethics Officer Association
EOA .... Examination, Opinion, and Advice [*Medicine*]
EOA .... Exercise Operating Area (NVT)
EOA .... External Oblique Aponeurosis [*Medicine*] (MELL)
EOA .... External Ostomy Appliance [*Medicine*] (MELL)
EOAA .... Eastern Ontario Archivists Association (SAUO)
EO/AA .... Equal Opportunity/Affirmative Action (SAUS)
EOAAD .... European Organization for Aid to Animals in Distress (SAUO)
EOAB .... European Office of Aerospace Research (SAUS)
EOAC .... Earth Observation Advisory Committee (SAUS)
EOAD .... Educational Organizations and Agencies Directory [*A publication*]
EOAE .... Earth-Orientated Applications Experiment (MCD)
EOAM .... End of the Accounting Month (ACAE)
EO & SP ...... Economic Order and Stockage Policy (AFIT)
EOAP .... Earth Observations Aircraft Program [*NASA*]
EOAP .... Equipment Oil Analysis Program [*Air Force*] (MCD)
EOAQ .... End of the Accounting Quarter (ACAE)
EOAR .... European Office of Aerospace Research
EOAR .... European Office of the Office of Aerospace Research (SAUO)
EOARD .... European Office of Aerospace Research and Development
EOARDC .... European Office of the Air Research and Development Command (SAUS)
EOATC .... European Organization for Research on Treatment of Cancer (SAUS)
EOAU .... Electro-Optical Alignment Unit (AAG)
EOB .... Eastern Orchestral Board [*British*] [*An association*] (DBA)
EOB .... Educational Opportunity Bank
EOB .... Electronic Order of Battle (MSA)
EOB .... Electro-Optical Bench [*Army*]
EOB .... Emergency Observation Bed [*Medicine*]
EOB .... Encyclopedia of Business [*A publication*]
EOB .... End of Battle [*Time*] (MCD)
EOB .... End of Block [*Computer science*]
EoB .... End of Blowdown (SAUS)
EOB .... End of Bombardment
EOB .... End of Boost (ACAE)
EOB .... End of Buffer (MCD)
EOB .... End of Burn (MCD)
EOB .... End of Bus (ACRL)
EOB .... End Of Business (SAUS)
EOB .... Enemy Order of Battle (AFM)
EOB .... Engineering and Operations Building [*NASA*]
EOB .... Environmental Protection Agency, NEIC Library, Denver, CO [*OCLC symbol*] (OCLC)
EOB .... Eocene/Oligocene Boundary [*Palaeontology*]
EOB .... Equal Opportunity Board [*Victoria, Australia*]
EOB .... Estimated on Berth
EOB .... Executive Office Building [*Washington, DC*]
EOB .... Expense Operating Budget (AFM)
EOB .... Explanation of Benefits
EOB .... Exstrophy of Bladder [*Medicine*] (MELL)
EOBC .... Early-Onset Breast Cancer (MELL)
EOBC .... Edmonton Oilers Booster Club [*Defunct*] (EA)
EOBCC .... Electronic Order of Battle Control Center
EOBCC .... End of Battle Control Center (MCD)
EOBM .... End of Block Mark (SAUS)
EOB Mark .... End of Block Mark (SAUS)
EOBP .... Explanation of Benefit Payment [*Insurance*]
EOBS .... Enrichment Operations and Business Services (SAUS)
EOBs .... Explanation of Benefits (SAUS)
EOBT .... Estimated Off-Block Time [*ICAO designator*] (FAAC)
EOC .... Early Operational Capability (ACAE)
EOC .... Early Ovarian Cancer (MELL)
EOC .... Earth Observation Center (CARB)
EOC .... Eastern Oregon College
EOC .... Economic Opportunity Commission (SAUS)
EOC .... Edge of Coverage (SAUS)
EOC .... Edge of Cutter (MSA)
EOC .... Edsel Owner's Club (EA)
EOC .... Educational Opportunity Center [*Higher Education Act*]
EOC .... Elastic Optic Coefficient (AAEL)
eoc .... electric overhead crane (SAUS)
EOC .... Electronic Operations Center [*Military*]
EOC .... Electro-Optic Countermeasure (TIMI)
EOC .... Elementary Operated Control (PDAA)
EOC .... Elementary Operation Control (SAUS)
EOC .... Elva Owners Club [*Worthing, West Sussex, England*] (EAIO)
EOC .... Embedded Operations Channel [*Telecommunications*] (ACRL)
EOC .... Emergency Operating Center [*Civil Defense*]
EOC .... Emergency Operational Capability (AAG)
EOC .... Emergency Operation Centre (SAUS)
EOC .... Emergency Operations Center [*Military*]
EOC .... Emissions Opportunity Cost
eoc .... emotional-organic combination (SAUS)
EOC .... Empresa Nacional de Electridad de Chile [*NYSE symbol*] (SAG)
EOC .... Empresa Nac'l De El Chile, ADS [*NYSE symbol*] (SG)
EOC .... Empresa Nac'l De Electric ADS [*NYSE symbol*] (TTSB)
EOC .... End of Card [*Computer science*] (CMD)
EOC .... End of Chain (ELAL)
EOC .... End Of Character (SAUS)
EOC .... End of Charge [*Physics*] (ODA)
EOC .... End of Cluster (SAUS)
EOC .... End of Communication (SAUS)
EOC .... End of Construction (NG)
EOC .... End of Contents (SAUS)
EOC .... End of Contract (AAG)
EOC .... End of Conversation (ECII)
EOC .... End of Conversion
EOC .... End of Convert (SAUS)
EOC .... End of Count (ACAE)
EOC .... End of Course (AFM)
EOC .... End of Cycle (NRCH)
EOC .... End of Cylinder (SAUS)
EOC .... Enema of Choice [*Medicine*] (MELL)
EOC .... Enemy Oil Committee [*US*]
EOC .... Engineered Operating Cycle
EOC .... Engineering Operations Control (MCD)
EOC .... Engine Order Capability (NASA)
EOC .... Engine Out Capability (MCD)
EOC .... Enterprise Operations Center (GART)
EOC .... Environment One Corporation (SAUO)
Eoc .... Eocene [*Second epoch of the Cenozoic Era*] (BARN)
EOC .... EOS Operations Center (SAUO)
EOC .... Epiphyseal Ossification Center [*Medicine*] (MELL)
EOC .... Epithelial Ovarian Cancer (MELL)
EOC .... Equal Opportunities Commission [*British*]
EOC .... Equal Opportunity Cases [*Australia*] [*A publication*]
EOC .... Equal Opportunity Commission [*Western Australia*]
EOC .... Equal Opportunity Compliance (SSD)
EOC .... Equipment Operational Control
EOC .... Equivalent Operational Capability (ACAE)
EOC .... Erbium Oxide Crystal
EOC .... Ercoupe Owners Club (EA)
EOC .... Error of Closure
EOC .... Ethoxycaffeine (SAUS)

EOC .... Ethylene Oxide Cycle (SAUS)
EOC .... Even-Odd Check (SAUS)
EOC .... Executive Officers Council (SAUO)
EOC .... Executive Officers Council of the National Association of Real Estate Boards (EA)
EOC .... Experimental Operations Center
EOC .... Experimentation Operations Center (SAUS)
EOC .... Explosive Ordnance Components [*Military*] (MCD)
EOC .... Extended Operating Cycles (SAUS)
EOC .... Extended Overhaul Cycle (NVT)
EOC .... Electron-Optical Camera (ODA)
EOCA .... Constructionman Apprentice, Equipment Operator, Striker [*Navy rating*]
EOCA .... Early Onset Cerebellar Ataxia [*Medicine*]
EOCA .... Electronic Office Centers of America, Inc. [*Schaumburg, IL*] [*Telecommunications*] (TSSD)
EOC and WPA... Editors Organizing Committee and Writers' and Publishers' Alliance for Disarmament (EA)
EOCAP .... Earth Observation Commercialization Application Program (SAUO)
EOCAP .... Earth Observations Commercial Applications Program (SAUS)
EOCAP .... Earth Observations Commercialization Applications Program (SAUS)
EOCAP .... Earth Observing Commercialization and Applications Program (SAUS)
EOCC .... Emergency Operations Control Center [*Environmental Protection Agency*]
EOCC .... Engineering Operational Casualty Control (NVT)
EOCC .... European Options Clearing Corporation (SAUO)
EOCC .... Experiment and Operations Control Center (ACAE)
EOCCD .... European Organisation for the Control of Circulatory Diseases (PDAA)
EOCCM .... Electro-Optical Counter-Countermeasures (MCD)
EOCCT .... End-of-Course Comprehensive Testing
EOCD .... Economic Organization for Cooperation and Development (SAUO)
EOCD .... Error, Omission, Clarification, or Deficiency (MCD)
EOCD .... Executive Office of Communities and Development (SAUO)
EOCI .... Electric Overhead Crane Institute [*Later, Crane Manufacturers Association of America*] (EA)
EOCM .... Electro-Optical Countermeasures (MCD)
EOCM .... Equipment Operator, Master Chief [*Navy rating*]
E-OCMS .... Electro-Optical Countermeasures System (ACAE)
EOCN .... Constructionman, Equipment Operator, Striker [*Navy rating*]
EOCN .... Emergency Operations Communications Network (SAUS)
EOCNO .... Emergency Operations Center Notification Officer [*Environmental science*] (COE)
EOCOM .... Electro-Optic Countermeasure (TIMI)
EOCP .... Emergency Out of Commission for Parts
EOCP .... Engine Out of Commission for Parts
EOCR .... Experimental Organic Cooled Reactor
EOCS .... Equipment Operator, Senior Chief [*Navy rating*]
EOCT .... End-of-Cycle Test [*Army training*] (INF)
EO CT .... Eosinophil Count [*Hematology*] (DAVI)
EOCTS .... Electro Optical Contact Test Set (ACAE)
EOCV .... End-of-Charge Voltage [*Automotive engineering*]
EOCY .... End of Calendar Year
EOD .... Date of Entering Office
EOD .... Earth Observations Division [*Johnson Space Center*] [*NASA*]
EOD .... Economic Objectives Department [*Ministry of Economic Warfare*] [*British*] [*World War II*]
EOD .... Education Outcomes Division [*Washington, DC*] [*Department of Education*] (GRD)
EOD .... Electric Organ Discharge [*Electrophysiology*]
EOD .... electronic overcurrent detector (SAUS)
EOD .... Electro Optical Division (ACAE)
EOD .... Electro Optic Developments Ltd. (SAUO)
EOD .... Electro-Optic Device (SAUS)
EOD .... Electro-Optic Display
EOD .... Electro-Optics Division (TIMI)
EOD .... Elements of Data (MSA)
EOD .... Emergency Ordnance Disposal
EOD .... Employee on Duty [*FRA*] (TAG)
EOD .... End of Data [*Computer science*]
EOD .... End of Date (SAUS)
EOD .... End of Day (AFM)
EOD .... End of Deck (SAUS)
EOD .... End of Dialing [*Telecommunications*] (TEL)
EOD .... End of Discussion [*Computer hacker terminology*]
EOD .... End of Document (SAUS)
EOD .... End-Organ Dysfunction [*Medicine*] (MELL)
EOD .... Engineering Operating Directives (MCD)
EOD .... Engineering Operations Division [*Environmental Protection Agency*] (GFGA)
EOD .... Engine Object Damage (SAUS)
EOD .... Entered on Duty (SAA)
EOD .... Entering Office Date (DNAB)
EOD .... Entrance on Demand (COE)
EOD .... Entrance on Duty (EEVL)
EOD .... Entry on Duty (MUGU)
EOD .... Environmental Observation Division (SAUS)
EOD .... Environmental Operations Division (SAUS)
EOD .... Eraseble Optical Disc (SAUS)
EOD .... Established Onset of Disability (OICC)
EOD .... Estimated on Dock (KSC)
EOD .... Estimated Operational Date (CINC)
EOD .... Ethylene Oxide Decontamination (SAUS)
eod .... Every Other Day (MELL)
EOD .... Every Other Day
EOD .... Expected Occupancy Date
EOD .... Explosive Ordinance Disposal [*Military*] (VNW)
EOD .... Explosive, Ordnance, Demolition (SAUS)
EOD .... Explosive Ordnance Detachment [*Army*] (RDA)
EOD .... Explosive Ordnance Device [*Military*] (MCD)
EOD .... Explosive Ordnance Disposal [*Military*]
EOD .... Explosives Ordnance Depot (SAUS)
EOD .... Extent of Disease (MELL)
EODA .... Electronic Organ Distributors Association (SAUO)
EODAD .... End of Data Address [*Computer science*] (HGAA)
eodad .... end-of-data-set address (SAUS)
EODAP .... Earth and Ocean Dynamic Applications Program [*NASA*] (PDAA)
EODARS .... Electro-Optical Direction and Ranging System (IAA)
EODB .... End of Data Block [*Computer science*] (MCD)
EODB .... Explosive Ordnance Disposal Bulletin [*Military*]
EODBAD .... Explosive Ordnance Disposal Badge [*Military decoration*] (GFGA)
EODC .... Earth Observation Data Centre (EERA)
EODC .... Earth Observing Data Centre (SAUS)
EODC .... Eastern Ontario Development Corporation (SAUO)
EODC .... End Of Data Carrier (SAUS)
EODC .... Explosive Ordnance Disposal Center [*DoD*]
EODC .... Explosive Ordnance Disposal Control [*Military*] (AABC)
EODCC .... EOD Control Center
EODD .... Electro-Optical Digital Deflector (SAUS)
EODD .... Electro-Optic Digital Deflector (IEEE)
EODE .... Explosive Ordnance Disposal Evaluator
EODF .... Explosive Ordnance Disposal Flight [*Military*]
EODG .... Explosive Ordnance Disposal Group [*Military*] (NVT)
EODGRU .... Explosive Ordnance Disposal Group [*Military*]
EODGRUDET... Explosive Ordnance Disposal Group Detachment [*Military*] (DNAB)
EODGRULANT... Explosive Ordnance Disposal Group, Atlantic [*Military*]
EODGRUPAC... Explosive Ordnance Disposal Group, Pacific [*Military*]
EODMS .... Earth Observation Data Management Systems (SAUS)
EODMS .... Earth Observations Data Management Systems (SAUS)
EODMU .... Explosive Ordnance Disposal Mobile Unit [*Military*] (DNAB)
EODN .... Explosive Ordnance Disposal, Nuclear [*Military*] (NVT)
EODP .... Earth and Ocean Dynamics Program (SAUO)
EODP .... Engineering Order Delayed for Parts
EODPP .... Epidemiology and Oral Disease Prevention Program [*Bethesda, MD*] [*National Institute of Dental Research*] [*Department of Health and Human Services*] (GRD)
EODR .... Electro-Optic Digital Reflector (SAUS)
EODS .... Electro-Optic Direction Sensor
EODS .... European Occupational Diseases Statistics (EURO)
EODS .... Explosive Ordnance Disposal School [*Indian Head, MD*] [*Military*]
EODS .... Explosive Ordnance Disposal Squadron [*Military*]
EODSBad .... Explosive Ordnance Disposal Specialist Badge [*Military decoration*] (AABC)
EODSupvBad... Explosive Ordnance Disposal Supervisor Badge [*Military decoration*] (AABC)
EODT .... explosive ordnance disposal technology (SAUS)
EODT & T.... Explosive Ordnance Disposal Technology and Training Center [*Military*]
EODTC .... Electro-Optic Display Test Chamber
EODTECHCEN... Explosive Ordnance Disposal Technical Center [*Military*] (DNAB)
EODTECHCTR... Explosive Ordnance Disposal Technical Center [*Military*] (POLM)
EODTEU .... Explosive Ordnance Disposal Training and Evaluation Unit [*Military*] (DNAB)
EODTIC .... Explosive Ordnance Disposal Technical Information Center [*Military*] (DNAB)
EODU .... Explosive Ordnance Disposal Unit [*Military*] (NVT)
EODWP .... Explosive Ordnance Disposal Interservice Working Party (SAUO)
EOE .... Early Operational Evaluation [*Army*]
EOE .... Earth Orbit Ejection [*Aerospace*] (MCD)
EOE .... Earth Orbit Equipment [*Aerospace*]
EOE .... Edge of Earth (IAA)
EOE .... Electronic-Optic-Electronic (IAA)
EOE .... Electronic Order Exchange (SAUS)
EOE .... Element of Expense
EOE .... End of Extent [*Computer science*] (IBMDP)
EOE .... Enemy Occupied Europe [*World War II*]
EOE .... Equal Opportunity Employer
EOE .... Errors and Omissions Excepted [*Insurance*]
EOE .... Errors and Omissions Expected (SAUS)
EOE .... Ethiodized Oil Emulsion [*Clinical chemistry*]
EOE .... Ethyloxaergoline [*Biochemistry*]
EOE .... European Options Exchange [*Netherlands*]
EOE .... Newberry, SC [*Location identifier*] [*FAA*] (FAAL)
EOEC .... Early-Onset Endocarditis [*Medicine*] (MELL)
EOEC .... End of Equilibrium Cycle [*Nuclear energy*] (NRCH)
EOED .... Earth Orbit Escape Device [*Aerospace*]
EOEL .... End of Equilibrium Life [*Nuclear energy*] (NUCP)
EOEM .... Electronic Original Equipment Manufacturer (SAUS)
EOEM .... Electronic Original Equipment Market
EOE M/F .... Equal Opportunity Employer, Male/Female (OICC)
EOE M-F-H... Equal Opportunity Employer, Male-Female-Handicapped
EOEMS .... European Organisation for the Exploitation of Meteorological Satellites (SAUO)
EOEPR .... European Organization for Experimental Photogrammetric Research (SAUO)
EO/EW .... Electro Optical / Electronic Warfare [*DoD*]
EOF .... Earth Orbital Flight [*Aerospace*] (AAG)
EOF .... Editorials on File (SAUS)
EOF .... Electro-Optic Force

EOF............ Electroosmotic Flow [*Physical chemistry*]
EOF............ Emergency Operating Facility [*Civil Defense*]
EOF............ Emergency Operations Facility [*Nuclear energy*] (NRCH)
EOF............ Empirical Orthogonal Function [*Statistics*]
EOF............ empirical orthogonal function(s), an alternative terminology for PCA (SAUS)
EOF............ End of Field (TIMI)
EOF............ End of File [*Computer science*]
EOF............ End Of File/Flame (SAUS)
EOF............ End Of Flame (SAUS)
eof............ end of flight (SAUS)
EOF............ End of Form [*Computer science*] (IAA)
EOF............ end of frame (SAUS)
EOF............ End of Frequencies (SAUS)
EOF............ Energy Optimizing Furnace (SAUS)
EOF............ Enterprise Objects Framework [*Computer science*] (VERA)
EOF............ Essential Operating Facilities (SAUS)
EOF............ Eurodollar Overseas Fund SA, Luxembourg (SAUO)
EOF............ Expected Operations Forecast [*NWS*] (FAAC)
EOFB............ End of Facsimile Block (SAUS)
EOFC............ Electro-Optical Fire Control [*Military*] (PDAA)
E of Cov....... Trial of the Earl of Coventry [*A publication*] (DLA)
EOFCS............ Electro-Optical Fire Control Subsystem (SAUS)
EOFCS............ Electro-Optical Fire Control System [*Military*] (CAAL)
E of E............ Expiration of Enlistment
EOFEA............ Equal Opportunity and Full Employment Act (OICC)
EOFL............ End of File Label (SAUS)
E of M............ Error of Measurement (WDAA)
E of M............ Error of Metabolism [*Medicine*] (EDAA)
EOF mark..... End-of-File Mark [*Computer science*]
EOFO............ End Of File Option (SAUS)
EOFR............ End of File Record (SAUS)
EOFRt............ End Of File Record (SAUS)
EOFS............ End Of File Statement (SAUS)
E of S............ Expiration of Service
EOFT............ Engine Oil Filterability Test
EOFY............ End of Fiscal Year
EOG............ Educational Opportunity Grant
EOG............ Effect on Guarantees
EOG............ Electroculogram (SAUS)
EOG............ Electrograph (KSC)
EOG............ Electrolytic Oxygen Generator (DNAB)
EOG............ Electrooculogram [*or Electrooculography*] [*Medicine*]
EOG............ Electrooculograph (DIPS)
EOG............ Electro-Oculography (ADWA)
EOG............ Electroolfactogram [*Medicine*]
EOG............ End-On Generator [*Car*] [*Indian Railway*] (TIR)
EOG............ English Opera Group (SAUO)
EOG............ Enron Oil & Gas [*NYSE symbol*] (SPSG)
EOG............ Ethrane, Oxygen, and Gas [*Nitrous oxide*] [*Anesthesiology*] (DAVI)
EOG............ Executive Office of the Governor (DEMM)
EOG............ Voltage Outer Gimbal
EOGB............ Electro-Optical Glide Bomb (MCD)
EOGB............ Electro-Optical Guided Bomb (VNW)
EOGB............ Electro-Optically Guided Bomb (SAUS)
EOGBS............ Early Onset Group B Streptococcal [*Infection*] [*Medicine*] (EDAA)
EOGO............ Eccentric Orbital Geophysical Observatory [*Also, EGO*] [*NASA*] (MUGU)
EOGO............ Elliptical Orbiting Geological Observatory (SAUS)
EOGs............ Educational Opportunity Grants (SAUS)
EOGS............ Electrooptical Guidance Section (SAUS)
EO/GW............ Electro-Optical Guided Weapons
EOH............ Emergency Operation Headquarters [*Army*] (AABC)
EOH............ Encyclopedia of Hoaxes [*A publication*]
EOH............ End of Heading (SAUS)
EOH............ End of Overhaul
EOH............ Engine Overhaul (SAUS)
EOH............ Equipment on Hand (AABC)
EOH............ Equipment Operator, Hauling [*Navy rating*]
EOH............ Experiment Operations Handbook (KSC)
eohp............ Except as Otherwise Herein Provided (MARI)
EOHP............ Except as Otherwise Herein Provided
eohp............ except otherwise herein provided (SAUS)
EOHPC............ European Oil Hydraulic and Pneumatic Committee [*Italy*] (EAIO)
EOHR............ Egyptian Organisation of Human Rights
EOHT............ External Oxygen and Hydrogen Tanks (NASA)
EOHY............ End of the Half Year (ACAE)
EOI............ Earth Observation Images (SAUO)
EOI............ Earth Observation Initiative
EOI............ Earth Orbit Insertion [*NASA*] (KSC)
EOI............ Eday [*Orkney Islands*] [*Airport symbol*] (OAG)
EOI............ Electronic Operating Instructions (DNAB)
EOI............ Electro-Optical Imaging (PDAA)
EOI............ Electro Optical Instrumentation (ACAE)
EOI............ End of Identify (SAUS)
EOI............ End of Identity [*Computer science*] (IAA)
EOI............ End Of Idle (SAUS)
EOI............ End of Information (NITA)
EOI............ End of Injection [*Automotive engineering*]
EOI............ End of Input [*Computer science*]
EOI............ End of Inquiry [*Computer science*]
EOI............ End of Interpreter (SAUS)
EOI............ End of Interrupt [*Computer science*] (VERA)
EOI............ End of Interrupts (SAUS)
EOI............ End of Irradiation (ABAC)
EOI............ End of Item (ELAL)
EOI............ end or identify (SAUS)
EOI............ Equipment Operating Instructions
EOI............ European Organ Index (EURO)
EOI............ Evidence of Insurability
EOI............ Expression of Interest
EOI............ International Labour Welfare Organization (SAUO)
EOIATS............ Electro Optical Identification and Tracking System (ACAE)
EOIC............ Ethylene Oxide Industry Council (EA)
EO-ICL............ European Organization of the International Confederation of Labour (SAUO)
EO-ICWG...... Earth Observation Int. Coordination Working Group (SAUS)
EO-ICWG...... Earth Observations International Coordination Working Group (EOSA)
EOID............ Electro-Optical Ion Detection [*Spectroscopy*]
EOIEC............ Effects of Initial Entry Conditions (SAA)
EOIG............ Enemy Oil Intelligence Group [*Ministry of Economic Warfare*] [*British*] [*World War II*]
EOIM............ Environmental Oxygen Interaction with Materials (SAUO)
EOIM............ Evaluation of Oxygen Interaction with Materials (MCD)
EOI Monitor... Earth Orbit Insertion Monitor (SAUS)
E/O-IMS....... Engineering/Operations - Information Management System (NASA)
EOIR............ Electro-Optical Infrared
EO/IR............ Electro-Optic/Infrared (RDA)
EOIR............ Executive Office for Immigration Review [*Department of Justice*] (GFGA)
EOIS............ Electro-Optical Imaging System (IEEE)
EOI Signal... End-of-Identity Signal (SAUS)
EOISS............ Equal Opportunity Information and Support System (DNAB)
EOITS............ Electro-Optical Identification and Tracking System (MCD)
EOIU............ End Of Interaction Unit (SAUS)
EOJ............ Egyptian Orthodontic Journal (SAUS)
EOJ............ End of Job [*Computer science*]
EOJ............ Extrahepatic Obstructive Jaundice [*Medicine*] (MELL)
EOJS............ End Of Job Statement (SAUS)
EOK............ Keokuk, IA [*Location identifier*] [*FAA*] (FAAL)
EOKA............ Ethnike Organosis Kypriakou Agonos [*National Organization of Cypriot Fighters*] [*Greece*]
EOKA............ Ethniki Organosis Kyprion Agoniston [*Cypress*]
EOL............ Earth Observations Laboratory (SAUO)
EOL............ Earth Observatory Laboratory (SAUS)
EOL............ Earth Orbit Launch [*NASA*] (KSC)
EOL............ Economic Opportunity Act Loan
eol............ effective operational length (SAUS)
EOL............ electromagnetic unit (SAUS)
EOL............ Electro Optical Laboratory (ACAE)
EOL............ Electro-Optics and Laser International Exhibition and Conference [*British*] (ITD)
EOL............ Elf Overseas Ltd. [*NYSE symbol*] (SPSG)
EOL............ Emir Oils Ltd. [*Vancouver Stock Exchange symbol*]
EOI............ End Of Item (SAUS)
EOL............ End of Lecture [*Online dialog*]
EOL............ end-of-letter (SAUS)
EOL............ End of Life
EOL............ End of Line (CDE)
EOL............ End Of Line/List (SAUS)
EOL............ End of Line Termination (MIST)
EOL............ End of List [*Computer science*] (IAA)
EOL............ Engine-Off Landing (SAUS)
Eol............ Eolic (SAUS)
EOL............ Europe Online (SAUS)
EOL............ Executive Office of Labor (SAUO)
EOL............ Ex Oriente Lux [*A publication*] (BJA)
EOL............ Expected Operating Life (ACAE)
EOL............ Expression-Oriented Language [*Computer science*]
EOL............ Neola, IA [*Location identifier*] [*FAA*] (FAAL)
EOLA............ Eola, IL [*American Association of Railroads railroad junction routing code*]
EOLAB............ Electro-Optics Laboratory [*University of Michigan*] [*Research center*] (RCD)
EOLAS............ [*The*] Irish Science and Technology Agency [*Information service or system*] (IID)
EOLAS - ISTA... EOLAS - the Irish Science and Technology Agency (EAIO)
EOLB............ End of Line Block [*Computer science*] (CET)
eolb............ end-of-line block (SAUS)
EOLC............ Earth Orbital Launch Configuration [*NASA*] (KSC)
EOLC............ End-of-Life Care (MELL)
EOLC............ End of Line Code (ACAE)
EOLCS............ Engine Oil Licensing and Certification System [*American Petroleum Institute*]
EOLE............ Earth Orbiting Lab Equipment (ACAE)
EOLLL............ Ernest Orland Lawrence Livermore Laboratory [*University of California*] (KSC)
EOLM............ Electron-Optical Light Modulator (SAUS)
EOLM............ Electro-Optical Light Modulator
EOLM............ End of Line Marker [*Computer science*]
EOLMA............ Ernest Orlando Lawrence Memorial Award (SAUS)
EOLN............ End of Line [*Computer science*]
EO-LOROPS... Electro-Optical - Long Range Oblique Panamoric Camera (SAUS)
EOLORPS............ Electro-Optical Long-Range Protection System [*Military*] (DWSG)
EOLPrA............ Elf Overseas Ltd 8.50% Pfd'A' [*NYSE symbol*] (TTSB)
EOLPrB............ Elf Overseas Ltd 7.625% Pfd'B' [*NYSE symbol*] (TTSB)
EOLR............ Electrical Objective Loudness Rating (IEEE)
EOLS............ Eastern Ontario Library System (SAUS)
EOLT............ End of Logical Tape [*Computer science*]
EOLT............ End Of Logic Tape (SAUS)

EOLV .... Electro-Optic Light Valve
EOM .... Earth Observation Magazine (SAUO)
EOM .... Earth Observation Mission [*NASA*]
EOM .... Earth Orbital Mission [*NASA*]
EOM .... Ease of Maintenance [*Quality management*]
EOM .... Eastern Ocean Margin (SAUS)
EOM .... Egyptian Order of Merit
EOM .... Electron Optic Method (SAUS)
EOM .... Electro-Optical Modulator
EOM .... Electrooptic- Light Modulator (SAUS)
EOM .... Electro-Optic Modulator (SAUS)
EOM .... Emergency Operational Message (SAUS)
EOM .... Employment Office Manager (ADA)
EOM .... End Of Meckerei (SAUS)
EOM .... End of Medium [*Computer science*] (BUR)
EOM .... End of Message [*Computer science*]
EOM .... End Of Message/Meckerei (SAUS)
EOM .... end of message signal (SAUS)
EOM .... End of Mission
eom .... End Of Month [*Billing*] (WDMC)
EOM .... End of Month [*Business term*]
EOM .... end of months following (SAUS)
EOM .... Energize Output M [*Symbol language*]
EOM .... Energize Output Medium [*Medicine*] (EDAA)
EOM .... Engineering Operations Manual [*NASA*] (NASA)
EO-M .... Engine Oil-Mack
EOM .... Enjoyment of Music Series, EMI [*Record label*] [*Great Britain*]
EOM .... Equal Ocular Movement [*Medicine*] (DMAA)
EOM .... Equation of Motion (NASA)
EOM .... Erasable Optical Memory (SAUS)
EOM .... Erim Ocean Model (SAUS)
EOM .... Ethoxymethyl [*Organic chemistry*]
EOM .... European Options Market (DCTA)
EOM .... Every Other Month (ADA)
EOM .... Executives on the Move [*A publication*]
EOM .... Exercise Object Model [*Training term*] (LPT)
EOM .... Expendable Ordnance Management [*Navy*] (DOMA)
EOM .... External Ocular Movement [*Medicine*]
EOM .... external ocular muscles (SAUS)
EOM .... External Otitis Media [*Medicine*] (EDAA)
EOM .... Extractable Organic Matter [*Environmental chemistry*]
EOM .... Extraction of Other Minerals (SAUO)
EOM .... Extraocular Motion (ADWA)
EOM .... Extra- Ocular Movement (SAUO)
EOM .... Extraocular Movement [*or Motion*] [*Ophthalmology*]
eom .... extra-ocular movements (SAUO)
EOM .... Extra Ocular Muscles (SAUS)
EOM .... Extraocular Muscles [*Ophthalmology*]
EOMA .... Emergency Oxygen Mask Assembly (KSC)
EOMB .... Explanation of Medicare [*or Medical*] Benefits
EOMC .... Engineering Order Map Correction (MCD)
EOMC .... Engineering Order Material Revision Data Collection (MCD)
EOMET .... Electro-Optics Meteorology (SAUS)
EOMF .... End of Minor Frame (MCD)
EOMF .... Exempt Organization Master File [*IRS*]
EOMF .... Extraocular Motion Full (ADWA)
EOMG .... End of Message Group (SAUO)
EOMI .... End of Message Incomplete [*Computer science*] (IAA)
EOMI .... Extraocular Motion [*or Movement*] Intact [*Ophthalmology*] (DAVI)
EOMI .... Extraocular Muscles Intact [*Ophthalmology*]
EOMIA .... Ecclesiae Occidentalis Monumenta Iuris Antiquissima [*A publication*] (ODCC)
EOM NI .... Extraocular Eye Movements Normal [*Medicine*] (EDAA)
EOMR .... Engineering Order List of Material Revision (MCD)
EOMRU .... End of Message Recovery Unit (SAUS)
EOMS .... Earth Orbital Military Satellite [*NASA*] (IAA)
EOMS .... End of Message Sequence [*Computer science*] (CET)
eoms .... end-of-message sequence (SAUS)
EOMS .... End of Message Signal [*Communications term*] (DCT)
EOMSF .... Earth Orbital Military Space Force (MCD)
EOMTC .... Eugene O'Neill Memorial Theater Center (EA)
EOMV .... End-of-Mix Viscosity (MCD)
EON .... Advanced Other Network (SAUS)
EON .... Edge of Network (VLIE)
EON .... End of Number [*Computer science*] (IAA)
EON .... End of Number Control Character (SAUS)
EON .... Enhanced Information Concerning Other Networks (SAUO)
EON .... Enhanced Other Networks (SAUS)
EON .... Equipment Operator, Construction Equipment [*Navy rating*]
EON .... Ethylene Oxide Number [*Surfactant technology*]
EON .... Everything or Nothing Film Production (WDAA)
EON .... Peotone, IL [*Location identifier*] [*FAA*] (FAAL)
EONC .... eOn Communications [*NASDAQ symbol*] (SG)
EONE .... Environment-One [*NASDAQ symbol*] (TTSB)
EONE .... Environment One Corp. [*NASDAQ symbol*] (SAG)
EON Information... Enhanced Other Networks Information (SAUS)
EONR .... European Organization for Nuclear Reserch (NUCP)
EONZ .... Outdoor Education Association of New Zealand (SAUO)
EOO .... Electro-Optics Organization (SAUS)
EOO .... End of Output (SAUS)
EOO .... Equal Opportunity Office (SAUS)
EOO .... Extensible Object Orientation
EOOC .... Exchange-Oriented Operator Control (IAA)
EOOE .... Erreur ou Omission Exceptee [*Error or Omission Excepted*] [*French*]
eooe .... error or omission excepted (SAUS)
EOOE .... Errors and Omissions Excepted (SAUS)
eooe .... errors or omissions excepted (SAUS)
EOOF .... European Olive Oil Federation [*Italy*] (EAIO)
EOOFC .... Electro-Magnetic On-Off Fan Clutch [*Automotive engineering, cooling systems*]
EOOW .... Engineering Officer of the Watch [*Navy*] (NVT)
EOP .... Earth and Ocean Physics [*NASA*] (NASA)
EOP .... Earth Observations Programs [*NASA*]
EOP .... Earth Orbit Plane [*Aerospace*] (AAG)
EOP .... Educational Opportunity Programs (SAUS)
EOP .... Efficiency of Plating [*Microbiology*]
EOP .... Electrical-Optical (VLIE)
EOP .... Electronic Overload Protection
EOP .... Electro-Optic Projector
EOP .... Emergency Observation Post (SAUS)
EOP .... Emergency Off-take Point (SAUS)
EOP .... Emergency Operating Procedure [*Nuclear energy*] (NRCH)
EOP .... Emergency Operating Program (OICC)
EOP .... Emergency Operations Plan [*Civil Defense*]
EOP .... Emergency Outpatient [*Medicine*] (HGAA)
EOP .... Emergency Oxygen Pack [*NASA*] (KSC)
EOP .... Emission Offset Policy (SAUS)
EOP .... Employee Ownership Plan (WGA)
EOP .... Encyclopedia of Occultism and Parapsychology [*A publication*]
EOP .... End of Page (VLIE)
EOP .... End of Paragraph
EOP .... End of Part (MCD)
eop .... end of passage (SAUS)
EOP .... End of Period
EOP .... End of Pipe (EEVL)
EOP .... End of Procedure [*Computer science*]
EOP .... End of Program [*Computer science*]
EOP .... End of Project (ACAE)
EOP .... End of Push [*Spectroscopy*]
EOP .... Endogenous Opioid Peptides [*Medicine*] (MEDA)
EOP .... End Operation (VLIE)
EOP .... End Output [*Computer science*] (IEEE)
EOP .... Engineering Operating Procedure (MCD)
EOP .... Engineering Operational Procedure (SAUS)
EOP .... Engine Oil Pressure (SAUS)
EOP .... English for Occupational Purposes (AIE)
EOP .... Equal Employment Opportunity (SAUS)
EOP .... Equal Opportunity Policy (OICC)
EOP .... Equal Opportunity Programs (MCD)
EOP .... Equational Prover
EOP .... Equipment Operating [*or Operational*] Procedure (AAG)
EOP .... Equipment Operations Procedure: Executive Office of the President (SAUS)
EOP .... Equity Office Properties Trust [*NYSE symbol*] [*Formerly, Beacon Properties*] (SG)
EOP .... Even-Odd Predominance (SAUS)
EOP .... Exchange Offering Prospectus (SAUS)
EOP .... Executive Office of the President
EOP .... Executive Office of the President of the United States (SAUS)
EOP .... Executive Office of the President, Washington, DC [*OCLC symbol*] (OCLC)
EOP .... Experimental Operating Procedure (SAA)
EOP .... Experiment of Opportunity Payload (ACAE)
EOP .... Experiment of Opportunity Program (SAUS)
EOP .... experiment operation plan (SAUS)
EOP .... Experiment Operations Panel
EOP .... Experiments of Opportunity (NASA)
EOP .... External Occipital Protuberance [*Medicine*] (MELL)
EOP .... External Output (ACAE)
EOP .... Extraoptic Photoreceptors
EOPAG .... ERS-1 Operation Plan Advisory Group (SAUO)
EOPAP .... Earth and Ocean Physics Applications Program [*NASA*]
EOPC .... Electro-Optical Phase Change (SAUS)
EOPC .... Electro-Optic Phase Change (IEEE)
EOPF .... End of Powered Flight
EOPM .... Electro-Optic Phase Modulated (SAUS)
EOPM .... Electro-Optic Phase Modulation (CARB)
EOPM .... Electro-Optic Phase Modulator (SAUS)
EOPO .... Ethylene Oxide Propylene Oxide Copolymer (EDCT)
EOPP .... Earth Observation Preparatory Program (ACAE)
EOPP .... Employment Opportunities Pilot Program [*Department of Labor*]
EOPR .... Engineering Order Purchase Request (SAA)
EOPS .... Electronic Oil Pressure Sensor [*Automotive engineering*]
EOPS .... Equal Opportunity Programs and Services (SAUS)
EOPS .... Equal Opportunity Program Specialist [*Navy*] (NVT)
EOPS .... Extended Opportunity Program and Services (SAUS)
EOPs .... Extended Opportunity Programs (SAUS)
EOPTO .... Electro-Optical Technology Program Office [*Navy*] (GRD)
EOPTS .... emergency operating procedure tracking system (SAUS)
eoq .... economical ordering quantity (SAUS)
EOQ .... Economic Ordering Quantity (SAUS)
EOQ .... Economic Order Quantity
EOQ .... Educational Orientation Questionnaire (EDAC)
EOQ .... End of Quarter (AFM)
EOQ .... End of Query (VLIE)
EOQ .... End of the Quarter (ACAE)
EOQ .... European Organization for Quality [*Switzerland*] (EAIO)
EOQC .... European Organisation for Quality Control (SAUS)
EOQC .... European Organisation on Quality Control (SAUS)
EOQI .... Equal Opportunity Quality Indicator [*Navy*] (NVT)

EOQL .... End of Qualified Life (ODA)
EOQS .... European Organisation for Quality Control (SAUS)
EOQT .... Economic Order Quality Techniques [*Course*] [*Military*] (DNAB)
EOR .... Earth Observing Radar (SAUS)
eor .... earth orbital rendezvous (SAUS)
EOR .... Earth Orbit Rendezvous [*NASA*]
EOR .... El Dorado [*Venezuela*] [*Airport symbol*] (AD)
EOR .... Electro-Optical Reconnaissance (VLIE)
EOR .... Electro-Optical Rectifier (MCD)
EOR .... Electro-Optical Research
EOR .... Emergency Operations Center (SAUS)
EOR .... End-of-Range (UWER)
EOR .... End of Record [*Computer science*]
EOR .... End of Reel
EOR .... End of Report (ELAL)
EOR .... End of Run [*Telecommunications*] (TEL)
EOR .... End of Runway (SAUS)
EOR .... Engine Order
EOR .... Enhanced Oil Recovery [*Petroleum engineering*]
EOR .... Equaled Olympic Record (SAUS)
EOR .... Equal Opportunities Review [*A publication*]
EOR .... Equipment Operationally Ready (AABC)
EOR .... Error Of Reading (SAUS)
EOR .... Estimates of Recuperability (SAUS)
EOR .... Exchange Option Rental
EOR .... Exclusive Operating Room [*Medicine*] (DAVI)
EOR .... Exclusive Or [*Gates*] [*Computer science*]
EOR .... Exclusive Or (auch: XOR) (SAUS)
EOR .... Exclusive or. Computing (SAUS)
EOR .... Exclusive Or Logical (SAUS)
EOR .... Explosive Ordnance Reconnaissance [*Military*]
EORA .... Elderly Onset Rheumatoid Arthritis [*Medicine*] (DAVI)
EORA .... Explosive Ordnance Reconnaissance (SAUS)
EORA .... Explosive Ordnance Reconnaissance Agent [*Military*] (AABC)
EORBS .... Earth Orbiting Recoverable Biological Satellite
EORC .... Earth Observation Research Center [*Japan*]
EORC .... Emergency Operations Research Center
EORC .... End Of Record Character (SAUS)
EORC .... Engineering Officers Reserve Corps
EORCU .... European Ozone Research Coordinating Unit (SAUO)
EORDC .... Essential Oils Research and Development Committee [*Tasmania, Australia*]
EOR Dig .... Equal Opportunities Review Discrimination Law Case Digest [*A publication*]
EORF .... Electron Optical Recording Facility
EORI .... [*USA*] Economic Opportunity (ODA)
EORL .... Emergency Officers' Retired List [*Army*]
EORLS .... Eastern Ontario Regional Library System (SAUS)
EORM .... Environmental and Occupational Risk (AAEL)
EORQ .... Engineering Order Request for Quotation (SAA)
EO/RR .... Equal Opportunity/Race Relations [*Navy*] (NVT)
EORS .... Emergency Oil Spill Response System (SAUS)
EORS .... End of Routing Signal [*Communications term*] (DCT)
EORSA .... Episcopalians and Others for Responsible Social Action (EA)
EORSAT .... Electronic Ocean Reconnaissance Satellite (SAUS)
EORSAT .... ELINT Ocean RECCE Satellite (SAUS)
EORSAT .... ELINT [*Electronic Intelligence*] - Ocean Reconnaissance Satellite (MCD)
EORT .... Equipment Operational Readiness Trends [*Report*] (MCD)
EORTC .... European Organization for Research and Treatment of Cancer (SAUS)
EORTC .... European Organization for Research on the Treatment of Cancer [*Research center*] [*Switzerland*] (IRC)
E Orth .... Eastern Orthodox
EOS .... Early Operational Signal (SAUS)
EOS .... Earth Observation Satellite [*NASA*] (OSRA)
EOS .... Earth Observation System (SAUO)
EOS .... Earth Observatory Satellite [*NASA*]
EOS .... Earth Observatory Spacecraft (SAUS)
EOS .... earth observing (SAUS)
EOS .... Earth Observing Satellite (SAUO)
EOS .... Earth Observing System [*NASA*]
EOS .... Earth Observing System - Proposed U.S. Satellite (SAUS)
EOS .... Earth Orbital Shuttle [*NASA*] (KSC)
EOS .... Earth Orbit Shuttle (SAUS)
EOS .... Earth Orbit Station
EOS .... Earth Orientation Service (SAUO)
EOS .... Earth to Orbit Shuttle (SAUS)
EOS .... Economic Order Splitting (SAUS)
EOS .... Educational Online Sources (SAUO)
EOS .... Effect on System
EOS .... Efficiency of Survival [*Genetics*]
EOS .... Egyptian Organization for Standardization (SAUO)
EOS .... Egyptian Orthodontic Society (SAUS)
EOS .... Electrical Optical Systems GmbH (SAUS)
EOS .... Electrical Output Spaces (SAUS)
EOS .... Electrical Overstress (AAEL)
EOS .... Electronic Office Service (SAUS)
EOS .... Electronic Office System (VLIE)
EOS .... Electronic Optical System (SAUS)
EOS .... Electronic Output Strategy (GART)
EOS .... electron optical system (SAUS)
EOS .... Electro-Optical System [*Electronics*] (ECII)
EOS .... Electro-Optical Systems, Inc. [*Subsidiary of Xerox Corp.*]
EOS .... Electrophenesis Operations in Space
EOS .... Electrophoresis Operations in Space (SAUS)
EOS .... Electrophoretic Operations in Space [*Without gravity*]
EOS .... Element of Service (VLIE)
EOS .... Eligibility On-Site (MEDA)
EOS .... Eligible for Overseas (SAUS)
EOS .... Eligible for Overseas Service
EOS .... Elipse of Skin [*Medicine*] (DAVI)
EOS .... Elsevier Oceanographic Series (SAUS)
EOS .... Emergency Operating Center (SAUO)
EOS .... Emergency Operations Simulation [*Civil Defense*]
EOS .... Emergency Operations Staff (MCD)
EOS .... Emergency Operations System
EOS .... Emergency Oxygen Supply [*or System*]
EOS .... Emergency Oxygen System (SAUS)
EOS .... Employed Operational State (SAUS)
EOS .... Enclosed Operating Station [*Military*] (CAAL)
EOS .... End of Scan (TIMI)
EOS .... End of Screen (SAUS)
EOS .... End-of-Screen [*Computer science*] (MHDB)
EOS .... End of Season [*Business term*]
EOS .... End of Segment [*Computer science*] (IAA)
EOS .... End of Select (SAUS)
EOS .... End of Selection (SAUS)
EOS .... End Of Selection signal (SAUS)
EOS .... End of Sequence (SAUS)
EOS .... End-of-Sequence [*Computer science*] (MHDB)
EOS .... End of Service (MCD)
EOS .... End Of Session (SAUS)
EOS .... End of Step (SAUS)
EOS .... End-of-Step [*Computer science*] (MHDB)
EOS .... End of String [*Computer science*] (IAA)
EOS .... End of Study [*Medicine*] (EDAA)
EOS .... End Operation Suppress (VLIE)
EOS .... Energy of State
EOS .... Engineering Operating Station [*Military*] (CAAL)
EOS .... Engineering Operating System
EOS .... Engine Overhaul Shop (SAUS)
EOS .... Enhanced Operating System [*Computer science*] (PDAA)
EOS .... Enterprise Optimization System (VLIE)
EOS .... Enter Stop Order (SAUS)
Eos .... Eosinophile (SAUS)
EOS .... Eosinophilen (SAUS)
EOS .... Eosinophilene (SAUS)
EOS .... Eosinophils [*Hematology*]
EOS .... Equal Opportunity Specialist (AAGC)
EOS .... Equate Operand Spaces (SAUS)
EOS .... Equation of State
EOS .... Equipment and Ordnance Stores (SAUS)
EOS .... ERIN On-line Service [*Commonwealth*] (EERA)
EOS .... Etasable Optical Storage [*Computer science*] (ODBW)
EOS .... Ethylene Oxide Sterilizer (MCD)
EOS .... Eugene O'Neill Society (EA)
EOS .... European Optical Society
EOS .... European Orthodontic Society (PDAA)
EOS .... European Overnight Service (SAUO)
EOS .... Exhaust Oxygen Sensor [*Automotive engineering*]
EOS .... Exodus Online Services [*Computer science*]
EOS .... Expiration of Obligated Service [*Military*]
EOS .... Extended Operating System [*DoD*]
EOS .... Extraordinary Occasion Service [*Associated Press*] (IIA)
EOS .... Greek National Mountaineering Association (SAUO)
EOS .... Institute for the Study of Earth Oceans and Space (SAUS)
EOS .... Neosho, MO [*Location identifier*] [*FAA*] (FAAL)
Eos .... Weekly publication of American Geophysical Union (SAUO)
EOSA .... Electro-Optic Sensor Assembly
EOSA .... Explosive Ordnance Safety Approval [*Military*] (MUGU)
EOSA .... Explosive Ordnance Safety Arming (ACAE)
EOS-A .... first NPOP (SAUS)
E-O SAEL .... Electro-Optical Sensors Atmospheric Effects Library (RDA)
EOS-AERO ... Earth Observing System-Aerosols (SAUS)
EOS-AERO ... EOS Aerosol Mission (SAUS)
EOS-ALT .... EOS-Altimetry (SAUS)
EOS-ALT .... EOS Altimetry Mission (SAUS)
EOS-AM1 .... Earth Observing System-Morning (SAUS)
EOSAT .... Earth Observation Satellite (SAUS)
EOSAT .... Earth Observation Satellite Co. [*Joint venture of RCA Corp. and Hughes Aircraft Co.*]
EOSAT .... Earth Observation Satellite Corporation (SAUS)
EOSC .... Earth Observations Science Committee (SAUO)
EOSC .... Eastern Oregon State College
EOSC .... Egyptian Organisation for Standardisation & Quality Control (SAUS)
EOSC .... Extended Operating System Card [*Computer science*] (IAA)
EOSCC .... Equine ocular squamous-cell carcinoma (SAUS)
EOS-Chem .... Earth Observing Satellite-Chemistry [*NASA*]
EOS-CHEM ... Earth Observing System-Chemistry (SAUS)
EOS-CHEM ... EOS Chemistry Mission (SAUO)
EOS-COLOR ... Earth Observing System-Color (SAUS)
EOSCOR .... Extended Observation of Solar and Cosmic Radiation [*National Center for Atmospheric Research*]
EOSD .... Emergency Operations Systems Development [*Civil Defense*]
EOSD .... Equipment on Station Date [*Army*] (AABC)
EOSDIS .... Earth Observing Satellite Data and Information System (SAUO)
EOSDIS .... Earth Observing System comprehensive Data and Information System (SAUS)
EOSDIS .... Earth Observing System Data and Information System

EOSDIS .... Earth Observing System Data and Information System of NASA (SAUS)
EOSDIS .... Earth Observing System Data Information System (SAUS)
EOSDIS .... EOS Data and Information System (SAUS)
EOSDIS .... EOS Data Information System (SAUS)
EOSDIS .... EOS Data Information System for information on Distributed Data Centers (SAUS)
EOSEQ .... End Order Sequence (SAUS)
EOS/ESD ...... Electrical Overstress/Electrostatic Discharge Association (EA)
EOS/ESD Association... Electrical Overstress and Electrostatic Discharge Association (SAUO)
EOSF .... Electro-Optical Simulation Facility (SAUS)
EOSH .... Earth Observing System Handbook (SAUO)
EOSI .... Earth Observation Science Initiative
EOSi .... EOS International
Eosin .... Eosinophil [*Hematology*] (WGA)
eosin B .... Dibromodinitrofluorescein [*A dye*] [*Biochemistry*] (DAVI)
eosins .... eosinophils (SAUS)
Eosm .... Effective Osmolarity [*Medicine*] (EDAA)
EOSM .... Electro-Optical Support Measures (SEWL)
EOSMD .... Extended Operating System Magnetic Drum [*Computer science*] (IAA)
EOSMOR ...... European Society for Market and Opinion Research
EOS/MT .... Extended Operating System for Magnetic Tapes (DNAB)
EOSO .... Escort Oilers Supervising Officer [*Navy*]
EOSP .... Earth Observation Satellites Program (SAUO)
EOSP .... Earth Observing Scanner Polarimeter
EOSP .... Earth Observing Scanning Polarimeter (CARB)
EOSP .... Economic Order and Stockage Procedure
eosp .... economic order and stocking procedure (SAUS)
EOSPC .... Electro-Optical Signal Processing Computer
EOS-PM .... Earth Observing System-Afternoon (SAUS)
EOS PM .... Earth Observing System (afternoon pass) (SAUS)
EOSR Signal... End of Status Request Signal (SAUS)
EOSRU .... End Of Session Recovery Unit (SAUS)
EOSS .... Earth Orbital Space Station [*NASA*] (MCD)
EOSS .... Electro-Optical Sensor System [*Navy*] (MCD)
EOSS .... Electro-Optical Simulation [*or Sighting*] System [*for missiles*] [*Army*] (MCD)
EOSS .... Electro-Optic Sensor System (SAUS)
EOSS .... Emergency Operational Sequencing System (MCD)
EOSS .... Engineering Operational Sequence System (DNAB)
EOSS .... Engineering Operational Sequencing System (SAUS)
EOS SAR ...... Earth Observing System Satellite Synthetic Aperture Radar (SAUS)
EOST .... Electrical Output Storage Tube (SAUS)
EOST .... Emergency Operations Simulation Techniques [*Civil Defense*]
EOSTAG .... Earth Observation Scientific and Technical Advisory Group (SAUS)
EOS Trans Am Geophys Union... EOS Transactions of the American Geophysical Union (journ.) (SAUS)
EOSX .... East Ohio Stone [*Private rail car owner code*]
EOT .... Eagle Ocean Transport (SAUS)
EOT .... Earth-Observed Time [*NASA*]
EOT .... Effective Oxygen Transport (MAE)
EOT .... Electric Overhead Travelling
EOT .... Electrooptical Technology (SAUS)
EOT .... Emergency Operations Team [*Environmental Protection Agency*] (GFGA)
EOT .... End Of Table (SAUS)
EOT .... End of Tape [*Computer science*]
EOT .... End of Task [*Computer science*]
EOT .... End of Terrace (ODA)
EOT .... End of Test [*Computer science*]
EOT .... End of Text [*Computer science*]
EOT .... End of Thread (ADWA)
EOT .... End of Tour [*Air Force*] (AFM)
EOT .... End of Track
EOT .... End of Transaction (SAUS)
EOT .... End of Transfer (AAEL)
EOT .... End of Transmission [*Computer science*]
EOT .... End of Type (SAUS)
EOT .... Enemy-Occupied Territory
EOT .... Energy Optimized Technology [*German-manufactured car tire*] [*Continental Gummi-Werke AG*]
EOT .... Engineering and Operations Training [*Navy*]
EOT .... Engine Oil Temperature [*Automotive engineering*]
EOT .... Engine Order Telegraph (DNAB)
EOT .... Eott Energy Partners [*NYSE symbol*] (SAG)
EOT .... EOTT Energy Partners L.P. [*NYSE symbol*] (TTSB)
EOT .... Equal Opportunity and Treatment [*Army program*]
EOT .... Equation of Time (ACAE)
EOT .... Exhaust Outlet Temperature [*Automotive engineering*]
EOT .... End of Tape [*Computing*] (ODA)
EOTA .... Eastern Ontario Trails Alliance [*Canada*]
EO(T)A .... Engineering Officers' (Telecommunications) Association [*British*]
EOTA .... European Organisation for Technical Approvals (SAUS)
EOTADS .... Electro-Optical Target Acquisition and Designation System [*Military*]
EOTADS .... Electro-Optical Target Acquisition / Designation System (SAUS)
EOTC .... Education Outside the Classroom (SAUO)
EOTC .... Electro-Optic Test Chamber
EOTC .... European Organization for Testing and Certification (SAUO)
EOTD .... Electro-Optical Tracking Device
EOTD .... Engine Outlet Temperature Differential [*Automotive engineering*]
EOTD .... Enhanced Observed Time Difference (GART)
EOTDA .... Electro-Optical Tactical Decision Aids (SEWL)
EOTF .... Electro-Optics Test Facility
EOTI .... Ecology on the Internet (SAUO)
EOTL .... End of Tape Label (SAUS)
EOT Label.... End of Tape Label (SAUS)
EOT Mark..... End of Tape Mark (SAUS)
EOTP .... End Of Tape Pulse (SAUS)
EOTP .... European Organization for Trade Promotion (SAUS)
EOT Pulse.... End of Tape Pulse (SAUS)
EOTR .... Eastern Ozone Transport Region [*Environmental science*] (COE)
EOTR .... End Of Transmission Record (SAUS)
EOTS .... Earth Orbiting Teleoperator System [*Spacecraft*] [*NASA*]
EOTS .... Electron Optic Tracking System (MUGU)
EOTS .... Electro Optical Threat Sensor (ACAE)
EOTS .... Electro-Optical Threat Sensor (SAUS)
EOTS .... Electro-Optical Tracking System (IDOE)
EOTS .... Electro-Optic Tracking System (SAUS)
EOTS .... End of Transmission Signal [*Communications term*] (DCT)
EOTS .... Engineer Officers Training School (SAUS)
EOTT .... End Office Toll Trunking (SAUS)
EottEn .... Eott Energy Partners [*Associated Press*] (SAG)
EOTV .... Electric Orbital Transfer Vehicle (SEWL)
EOTV .... Expendable Orbital Transfer Vehicle (ACAE)
EOU .... Electro-Optical Unit
EOU .... End of User [*Computer hacker terminology*] (NHD)
EOU .... Enemy Objective Unit [*of US*] [*in London*]
EOU .... Epidemic Observation Unit [*Medicine*]
EOU .... Export Orientated Units (EURO)
EOUG .... European Oracle User Group (VERA)
EOUSA .... Executive Office for United States Attorneys [*Department of Justice*]
EOUST .... Executive Office for United States Trustees [*Department of Justice*] (BARN)
EOV .... Columbia, SC [*Location identifier*] [*FAA*] (FAAL)
EOV .... Economic Order Van (AABC)
EOV .... Electrically Operated Valve
EOV .... End Of Visibility (SAUS)
EOV .... End of Volume [*Computer science*]
EOVAC .... Elecro Optical Vulnerability Assessment Code (ACAE)
EOVM .... End of Valid Message [*Computer science*] (IAA)
EOVR .... Electro Optical Viewing and Ranging (ACAE)
EOVS .... Electro-Optical Viewing System (MCD)
EOVs .... Explanation of Votes (EERA)
eow .... Early Open Water (SAUS)
EOW .... Electro-Optional Warfare (SAUS)
EOW .... Empty Operational Weight (SAUS)
EOW .... End of Watch [*Military*] (GOBB)
EOW .... End of Week (ACAE)
EOW .... End of Word [*Computer science*]
EOW .... Energy over Weight (MCD)
EOW .... Engineering Order Wire (SAUS)
EOW .... Engineering Order Wire circuits (SAUS)
EOW .... Engineering Order Worksheet
EOW .... Engineer of the Watch [*Military*] (MUSM)
EOW .... Engineer's Order Wire
EOW .... Engine Out Warning
EOW .... Engine over the Wing
EOW .... Equal Opportunities for Women (SAUS)
EOW .... Every Other Week
EOWA .... English Olympic Wrestling Association
EO-WCL .... European Organization of the World Confederation of Labour (SAUO)
E-OWDS .... Electro-Optical Weapon Delivery System (ACAE)
EOWG .... Earth Observation Working Group (SAUO)
EOWPVT ...... Expressive One-Word Picture Vocabulary Test [*Intelligence test*]
EOWPVT:UE... Expressive One-Word Picture Vocabulary Test: Upper Extension [*Intelligence test*]
EOWS .... Electro-Optical Weapons System
EOWTF .... Every Other Week Til Forbid [*Advertising*] (DOAD)
EOWTF .... Every Other Week Till Forbid (NTCM)
EOx .... Elsevier Oxford (SAUS)
EOX .... End of Exklusive (SAUS)
EOX .... Extractable Organic Chlorine (SAUS)
EOX .... extractable organic halide (SAUS)
EOX .... Extractable Organic Halogen [*Environmental chemistry*] (FFDE)
EOY .... End of Year
EOYFS .... End of Year Financial Statement
EOZ .... Elorza [*Venezuela*] [*Airport symbol*] (OAG)
EP .... Eagle-Picher (SAUS)
EP .... Early Philosophies [*A publication*]
EP .... Early Positive
EP .... Earned Premium [*Insurance*]
EP .... Earning Power [*Business term*]
E/P .... Earning/Price Ratio (EBF)
EP .... Earnings Price [*Investment term*]
EP .... Earth Penetrating (SAUS)
EP .... Earth Penetrator [*Weapon*]
EP .... Earth Plate (SAUS)
EP .... Earth Probe (SAUS)
EP .... Earth Protectors (GNE)
EP .... Eastward Position
EP .... Easy Projection (PDAA)
EP .... EBSCO Publishing
EP .... Ebury Press [*Publisher*] [*British*]
EP .... Ecclesiastical Parish
EP .... Echo Prospecting (SAUS)
EP .... Economic Planning (MCD)
EP .... Economic Planning. Journal for Agriculture and Related Industries [*A publication*]

EP .... Economic Policy [*British*]
EP .... Ectopic Pacemaker (MELL)
EP .... Ectopic Pregnancy [*Obstetrics*]
EP .... Edematous Pancreatitis [*Medicine*] (MELL)
EP .... Edible Portion [*of a food*]
EP .... Edito Princeps [*First edition*] [*Latin*] (WDAA)
EP .... Educational Psychologist (ODA)
EP .... Educational Publication [*NASA*]
EP .... Effective Par [*Investment term*]
EP .... Effective Pressure (SAUS)
EP .... Effective Production
EP .... Egyptian Pattern [*British military*] (DMA)
EP .... Egyseg Partja [*Party of Unity*] [*Hungary*] (PPE)
EP .... Elastic Peak (SAUS)
EP .... Elbow Pitch (MCD)
EP .... Electrically Conducting Polymer [*Electronics*] (ODA)
EP .... Electrically Polarized [*Relay*]
EP .... Electrical Panel (NG)
EP .... Electrical Polarization (SAUS)
EP .... Electrical Power (SAUS)
EP .... Electrical Properties (SAUS)
EP .... Electrical Propulsion (AAG)
EP .... Electrical Prototype
E/P .... Electrical-to-Pneumatic [*Converter*] (NRCH)
EP .... Electric Power (NRCH)
EP .... Electric Primer
EP .... Electrode Plasma [*Energy source*]
EP .... Electrode Potential (SAUS)
EP .... Electrolytic Polishing (SAUS)
EP .... Electrolytic Printing (SAUS)
EP .... Electronic and Desktop Publishing
EP .... Electronic Package
EP .... Electronic Packaging (SAUS)
EP .... Electronic Post [*British Post Office*] [*Defunct*] (TSSD)
EP .... Electronic Printer
EP .... Electronic Printing (SAUS)
EP .... Electronic Processing (IAA)
EP .... Electronic Protect (SAUS)
EP .... Electronic Protection (SEWL)
EP .... electronic publisher (SAUS)
EP .... Electronic Publishing (TELE)
EP .... Electronics Panel
EP .... Electron Pair (MEC)
EP .... Electron Paramagnetic
EP .... Electron Photon
EP .... Electron Probe (SAUS)
E/P .... Electron/Proton (MCD)
EP .... Electrophony (SAUS)
EP .... Electrophoresis
EP .... Electrophotographic (COE)
EP .... Electrophotographic Engine (SAUS)
EP .... Electrophotography (SAUS)
EP .... Electrophysiologic (SAUS)
EP .... Electrophysiology
ep .... electrophysiology procedure (SAUS)
EP .... Electroplate
EP .... Electroplating (SAUS)
EP .... Electro Pneumatic (SAUS)
EP .... Electropneumatic
EP .... Electropolish (AAEL)
EP .... Electropolishing (SAUS)
EP .... Electropositive (SAUS)
EP .... Electroprecipitin (DB)
EP .... Electropulse (SAUS)
EP .... Electrostatic Powder
EP .... Electrostatic Precipitator [*Also, ESP*]
EP .... Elementary Particles (SAUS)
EP .... Element Processor (SAUS)
EP .... Elephantine Papyri (BJA)
EP .... Eligible Participant (OICC)
EP .... Elongated Punch
EP .... Elopement Precaution [*Medicine*] (EDAA)
EP .... Emancipation Proclamation (SAUO)
EP .... Emergence Planning (SAUS)
EP .... Emergency Physician (MELL)
EP .... Emergency Planning (NATG)
EP .... Emergency Preparedness [*Nuclear energy*] (NRCH)
EP .... Emergency Procedures (MCD)
EP .... Emission Policy (NATG)
EP .... Employee Participation (ADA)
EP .... Employee Plan [*IRS*]
EP .... Employment Program (SAUS)
EP .... Employment Protection [*Act*] [*British*]
EP .... Empowerment Project (EA)
EP .... Emulation Processing (SAUS)
EP .... Emulation Program [*IBM Corp.*] (BUR)
EP .... Emulation System (SAUS)
EP .... Emulator Program [*Computer science*] (ELAL)
EP .... Emulsion Polymer (SAUS)
EP .... Ending Period (AABC)
EP .... End of Program [*Computer science*]
EP .... Endogenous Pyrogen [*Immunology*]
EP .... Endoperoxide [*Medicine*] (EDAA)
EP .... Endorphin [*Biochemistry*]
EP .... Endorser Potential [*Advertising term*]
EP .... Endothia parasitica [*Plant pathology*]
EP .... End Paper (SAUS)
E/P .... End-Paper [*Bibliography*]
ep .... End Papers [*Publishing*] (WDAA)
ep .... End Paragraph [*Typesetting command*] (WDMC)
EP .... End Point [*Distilling*]
EP .... End Printing (SAUS)
EP .... End-Use Product [*Environmental Protection Agency*]
EP .... Enemy Position
EP .... Energy Policy (SAUS)
EP .... Engagement Planning (ACAE)
EP .... Engineering Paper
EP .... Engineering Personnel [*Coast Guard*]
EP .... Engineering Phase (MCD)
EP .... Engineering Plastics (SAUS)
EP .... Engineering Practice (NG)
EP .... Engineering Print (KSC)
EP .... Engineering Procedure
EP .... Engineering Project
EP .... Engineering Proposal
EP .... Engineering Prototype (ACAE)
EP .... Engineer Pamphlet [*Army Corps of Engineers*]
EP .... Engineer Personnel [*Marine Corps*]
ep .... English Partnership
EP .... English Patent (IAA)
EP .... Enlisted Personnel (AABC)
EP .... En Passant [*In Passing*] [*Chess*]
EP .... En Route Penetration [*Aviation*] (FAAC)
EP .... Enteropeptidase [*Medicine*] (EDAA)
EP .... Enterprise Portal (GART)
EP .... Entrainment Pressure
EP .... Entrucking Point [*Military*]
EP .... Entry Point (BUR)
EP .... Entry Protected (ACAE)
ep .... Envelope (WDMC)
EP .... Environmental Park [*Australia*]
EP .... Environmental Physiology (SAUS)
EP .... Environmental Planner (COE)
EP .... Environmental Pollution [*A publication*] (NOAA)
EP .... Environmental Profile [*Environmental Protection Agency*] (GFGA)
EP .... environmental project (SAUS)
EP .... environmental protection (SAUS)
EP .... Environmental Protective Plan (MCD)
EP .... Enzootic pneumonia (SAUS)
EP .... Enzyme Presoak [*for laundry*]
EP .... Enzyme-Product [*Biochemistry*] (DAVI)
EP .... Enzyme-Product Complex [*Enzyme kinetics*]
EP .... Eosinophilic Pneumonitis [*Medicine*] (DB)
EP .... Eparchy (ROG)
Ep .... Ephesians [*New Testament book*] (BJA)
EP .... Epicardial Electrogram [*Cardiology*] (DMAA)
EP .... Epicardium (SAUS)
ep .... Epidote (SAUS)
EP .... Epileptic (AIE)
EP .... Epiotic [*Ear anatomy*]
EP .... Episcopalian
EP .... Episcopus [*Bishop*] [*Latin*]
EP .... Epistle
EP .... Epistola [*Epistle, Letter*] [*Latin*] (ROG)
Ep .... Epistulae [*of St. Jerome*] [*Classical studies*] (OCD)
Ep .... Epistulae [*of Augustine*] [*Classical studies*] (OCD)
Ep .... Epistulae [*of Epicurus*] [*Classical studies*] (OCD)
EP .... Epitaxial Planar [*Electronics*]
EP .... Epithelial [*or Epithelioid*] [*Histology*] (DAVI)
EP .... Epithelial Proliferation [*Histology*]
EP .... Epoxide [*Medicine*] (EDAA)
EP .... Epoxide Plastic
EP .... Epoxy (EDCT)
EP .... Epping [*Urban district in England*]
EP .... Equilibrium Partitioning (EEVL)
EP .... Equilibrium Point (FOTI)
EP .... Equine Piroplasmosis (PDAA)
EP .... Equipment Piece (NRCH)
EP .... Equipment Practice [*Telecommunications*] (TEL)
EP .... Equipment Publication (AABC)
EP .... Equipotential (SAUS)
EP .... Equivalence Principle [*Physics*]
EP .... Equivalent Part (ACAE)
EP .... equivalent personnel (SAUS)
EP .... Erasmus Press, Lexington, KY [*Library symbol*] [*Library of Congress*] (LCLS)
EP .... Erb Paralysis [*Medicine*] (MELL)
EP .... Ergot Poisoning (MELL)
EP .... Error Print (VLIE)
EP .... Error Probable (ACAE)
EP .... Error Program (SAUS)
EP .... Erythrocyte Protoporphyrin [*Hematology*]
EP .... Erythrophagocytosis [*Hematology*]
EP .... Erythropoietic Porphyria [*A genetic disorder*]
Ep .... Erythropoietin [*Also, EPO*] [*Hematology*]
EP .... Erythrose Phosphate [*Biochemistry*] (BARN)
EP .... Essential Power (COE)
EP .... Estimated Position [*Navigation*]
EP .... Estrogen Patch (MELL)
EP .... Etched Plate

EP .... Ethylene Propylene (SAUS)
EP .... Ethylene-Propylene (SAUS)
EP .... Ethylene-Propylene Copolymer (EDCT)
EP .... Eurographic Press (SAUS)
EP .... European Parliament
EP .... European Plan [*Hotel room rate*]
EP .... Europrime Capital [*Vancouver Stock Exchange symbol*]
EP .... Evaluation Plan
EP .... Evaluation Program (SAUS)
E/P .... Evaporation and Percolation (BCP)
EP .... Evening Prayer
EP .... Evoked Potential [*Neurophysiology*]
EP .... Evolutionary Programming (IDAI)
EP .... exceptions passed (SAUS)
EP .... Excess Profits
EP .... Execution Planning [*Environmental science*] (COE)
EP .... Executive Pension [*British*]
EP .... Executive Program (MCD)
EP .... Exeption Passed (SAUS)
EP .... Exercise Practice (SAUS)
EP .... Existing Prison (WDAA)
ep .... exit pupil (SAUS)
EP .... Expanded Polystyrene (ADA)
EP .... Expectancy Phenomenon
EP .... Expected Pay-Off
EP .... Experienced Playgoer [*Theatrical*]
EP .... Experience Points (VLIE)
EP .... Experimental Physicist (SAUS)
EP .... Experimental Physics (SAUS)
EP .... Experimental Product (EEVL)
EP .... Exploration Permit [*Australia*]
EP .... Explorer Platform [*NASA*]
EP .... Explosion-Proof
EP .... Export Propensity
EP .... EXPRESS Pallet (SAUS)
EP .... Exprisoner
EP .... Extended Performance (SAUS)
ep .... Extended Play (IDOE)
EP .... Extended Play
EP .... Extended Playing (SAUS)
EP .... Extended Port (SAUS)
EP .... Extended Processor (SAUS)
EP .... Extended Programmability (SAUS)
EP .... Extension Pay [*British military*] (DMA)
EP .... Externally Powered [*Gun*] (MCD)
EP .... External Phloem [*Botany*]
EP .... External Pressure
EP .... External Production
EP .... External Programs [*Environmental science*] (COE)
EP .... External Publication
EP .... Extraction Procedure [*Chemical engineering*]
EP .... Extraordinary and Plenipotentiary (ODA)
EP .... Extra Player [*Baseball term*] (NDBD)
EP .... Extra Point [*Football*]
EP .... Extra Protection (SAUS)
EP .... Extra Pulse (SAUS)
EP .... Extreme Power (VLIE)
EP .... Extreme Pressure (MSA)
ep .... Eyepiece (SAUS)
EP .... Office of Domestic and International Energy Policy (SAUS)
E_p .... Peak Voltage (IDOE)
E_p .... Plate Voltage (IDOE)
EP .... Presbyterian, Church of England [*Military*] (ROG)
ep--- .... Pyrenees Region [*MARC geographic area code*] [*Library of Congress*] (LCCP)
EP .... Tropic Air Services [*ICAO designator*] (AD)
EP .... Early Picture (ODA)
EP2DS .... Electronic Properties of Two-Dimensional Systems (SAUS)
EP3 .... Extensible PERL PreProcessor (SAUS)
EPA .... Earth's Polar Axis (KSC)
EPA .... Eastern Provincial Airways [*Labrador*]
EPA .... Eastern Psychological Association
EPA .... Ecological Planning and Assessment (SAUO)
EPA .... Economic Price Adjustment
EPA .... Edge Path Adapter (CDE)
EPA .... Educational Paperback Association (EA)
EPA .... Educational Press Association of America (SAUO)
EPA .... Educational Priority Area (WDAA)
EPA .... Educational Publishers Association
EPA .... Educational Puppetry Association [*British*] (BI)
EPA .... Eicosapentaenoic Acid [*Biochemistry*]
epa .... eicosapentanoic acid (SAUS)
EPA .... Eire Philatelic Association (EA)
EPA .... Electrical Power Association (SAUO)
EPA .... Electronic Publishing Abstracts [*Information service or system*] (NITA)
EPA .... Electron Probe Analyzer
EPA .... Emergency Powers Act [*British*] [*World War II*]
EPA .... Emergency Provisions Act (SAUO)
EPA .... Emission Parameter Analyzer (SAUS)
EPA .... Empire Parliamentary Association [*Later, CPA*] [*Australia*]
EPA .... Empire Press Agency (DGA)
EPA .... Employee Plan Administrators
EPA .... Employer-Paid Advertising
EPA .... Employment Protection Act [*1975*] [*British*] (DCTA)
EPA .... Enduring Power of Attorney [*Legal term*] (WDAA)
EPA .... Energetic Particles Analyzer [*Astrophysics*]
EPA .... Energy-Performance Assessment (USA) (ODA)
EPA .... Energy Policy Act (SAUS)
EPA .... Engineering Practice Amendment (AAG)
EPA .... Engineering Product Assumptions
EPA .... English Pool Association [*British*] (DBA)
EPA .... Enhanced Performance Architecture [*Computer science*] (TNIG)
EPA .... Entertainments Protection Association (SAUO)
EPA .... Entry Point Address (SAUS)
EPA .... Environmental Pesticide Act (SAUO)
EPA .... Environmental Planning Authority (SAUS)
EPA .... Environmental Protection Act (SAUS)
EPA .... Environmental Protection Agency [*Government agency formed in 1970*]
EPA .... Environmental Protection Agency on Global Warming (SAUO)
EPA .... Environmental Protection Agency, Washington (SAUS)
EPA .... Environment Planning Authority (EERA)
EPA .... Environment Pollutions Agency [*British*]
EPA .... Environment Protection Agency [*Australia*] (EERA)
EPA .... Environment Protection Authority [*Western Australia*] [*State*] (EERA)
EPA .... Epidermolysis Bullosa Acquisita [*Dermatology*]
EPA .... Equal Pay Act [*US*] (OICC)
EPA .... Equatorial Pitch Angle [*Geophysics*]
EPA .... Equity Principle Auditions (BARN)
EPA .... Erect Posterior-Anterior [*Radiology*]
EPA .... Erythroid Potentiating Activity [*Hematology*]
EPA .... Essential Pharmacy Allowance
EPA .... Estimated Position Arc [*Navy*] (NVT)
EPA .... Estimated Profile Analysis (VLIE)
EPA .... Ether-Isopentane-Ethanol [*Solvent system*]
EPA .... Ethylbenzene Producers Association (EA)
EPA .... Europaeisches Patentamt [*European Patent Office - EPO*] (EAIO)
EPA .... European Parent Association (AIE)
EPA .... European Photochemistry Association (EAIO)
EPA .... European Production Agency (EBF)
EPA .... European Productivity Agency
EPA .... European Productivity Association (SAUO)
EPA .... Evangelical Press Association (EA)
EPA .... Evasive Plan of Action (SAUS)
EPA .... Executive Protective Agency (SAUS)
EPA .... Exoatmospheric Penetration Aid
EPA .... Exophthalmus Producing Activity (SAUS)
EPA .... Expanded Polystyrene Association (SAUO)
EPA .... Exparc [*Russian Federation*] [*ICAO designator*] (FAAC)
EPA .... Ex Patriates Association [*British*] (DBA)
EPA .... Export Pound Account [*Special type of currency*] [*United Arab Republic*]
EPA .... Extended Performance Analysis (VLIE)
EPA .... Extended Performance Architecture (SAUS)
EPA .... Extended Planning Annex
EPA .... Extended Power Aging (ACAE)
EPA .... External Page Address (VLIE)
EPA .... Extrinsic Plasminogen Activator [*Hematology*]
EPA .... L'Economie des Pays Arabes [*A publication*] (BJA)
EPA .... Electron-Positron Annihilation [*Physics*] (ODA)
EPAA .... Educational Press Association of America [*Later, EDPRESS*] (EA)
EPAA .... Emergency Petroleum Allocation Act
EPAA .... Employing Printers Association of America [*Defunct*] (EA)
EPAA .... Environmental Programs Assistance Act (GFGA)
EPAA .... Epithermal Neutron Activation Analysis (SAUS)
EPAA .... European Primary Aluminum Association [*Later, European Aluminium Association - EAA*] (IID)
EPAA .... Exciter Power Amplifier Assembly [*Electricity*] (DWSG)
EPAAR .... Environmental Protection Agency Acquisition Regulations (GFGA)
EPAAR .... EPA Acquisition Regulations (SAUO)
EPA/ARB .... Environmental Protection Agency/Air Resources Board
EPA/AWMA .... Environmental Protection Agency/Air and Waste Management Association (SAUO)
EPABX .... Electronic Private Automatic Branch Exchange [*Telecommunications*] (MCD)
EPABX .... Electronic Private Automatic Business Exchange (SAUS)
EPAC .... Eastern Pacific (CCCA)
EPAC .... East Pacific (SAUO)
EPAC .... Economic Planning Advisory Council (EERA)
EPAC .... Electronic Production Aids Catalogue (SAUO)
EPAC .... Emergency Preparedness Advisory Committee (SAUO)
EPAC .... Energetic Particle Composition Instrument [*Astrophysics*]
EPAC .... Enhanced Perceptual Audio Coder [*Computer science*]
EPAC .... Entraineurs en Patinage Artistique du Canada [*Figure Skating Coaches of Canada - FSCC*]
EPAC .... Expanded Polystyrene Association of Canada (SAUO)
EPAC .... External Program Advisory Committee (SAUS)
EPACA .... Evaluate, Plan, Action, Check, Amend (BB)
EPACASR .... Environmental Protection Agency Chemical Activities Status Report [*Databa se*] [*Environmental Protection Agency*]
EPACASR .... EPA Chemical Activities Status Report (SAUO)
EPACCI .... Economic Planning and Advisory Council for the Construction Industries (SAUO)
EPACML .... Environmental Protection Agency Composite Model for Landfills [*Formerly, EPASMOD*]
EPAct .... Energy Policy Act (ADWA)
EPACT .... Energy Policy Act of 1992 [*BTS*] (TAG)
EPACT .... Environmental Policy Act (SAUO)
EPACT .... Environmental Protection Agency's Control Techniques (COE)

EPACT......... National Energy Policy Act [*Legislation passed in 1992*] [*Department of Energy*] (PS)
EPAD.......... Electrically Powered Actuation Device (ADWA)
EPAD.......... Electrical Power and Distribution (SAUS)
EPAD.......... Enlisted Personnel Assignment Document [*Navy*] (NVT)
EPAD.......... Error Protecting Packet Assembler/Disassembler [*Telecommunications*] (OSI)
EPADC........ East Pakistan Agricultural Development Corporation (SAUO)
EPA-DC........ Environmental Protection Agency - District of Columbia (SAUO)
EP-Add........ Extreme Pressure Additive (SAUS)
EP Additive... Extra Pressure Additive (SAUS)
EPADOC....... Document Control System (SAUS)
Ep ad Tryph... Epistula ad Tryphonem [*of Quintilian*] [*Classical studies*] (OCD)
EPAG.......... Ecological Planning and Assessment Group (SAUO)
EPAGM........ Environmental Protection Agency Grants Administration Manual
EPAI.......... Exchange of Publicity Available Information (VLIE)
EPAIRS........ Environmental Protection Agency Information Retrieval System (SAUS)
EPAIS.......... Encyclopedia of Public Affairs Information Sources [*A publication*]
EPA J.......... EPA Journal (journ.) (SAUS)
EPAL.......... Electrical Programmable Array Logic (SAUS)
EPALIT......... ERL-Gulf Breeze Text Data Management (SAUS)
EPALL.......... Emergency Preparedness at Local Level (EERA)
EPAM.......... Elementary Perceiver and Memorizer [*University of California*] [*Learning theory*] [*Computer device*]
EPAM.......... Emergency Priorities and Allocations Manual [*DoD*]
Epam.......... Epaminondas [*of Nepos*] [*Classical studies*] (OCD)
EPAMS........ Experimental Prototype Automatic Meteorological System (MCD)
EPAN.......... Electronic Purchasing Agent Network [*Service of Data Corp. of America*]
EP & A........ Exercise Plans and Analysis Division (MCD)
EP&BC........ Environment Protection and Biodiversity Conservation Bill (SAUS)
EP & D........ Electrical Power and Distribution (CET)
ep & d........ electric power and distribution (SAUS)
EP&M.......... Engineering Physics and Mathematics (SAUS)
EPANTS........ NTIS/EPA Report System (SAUS)
EPANY........ Export Packers Association of New York [*Defunct*] (EA)
EPAP.......... Expiratory Positive Airway Pressure [*Medicine*]
EPA-PRD..... Environmental Protection Agency - Pesticide Regional Division
epaq.......... electronic parts of assessed quality (SAUS)
EPAQ.......... Extended Personality Attributes Questionnaire (EDAC)
E-PAR.......... Electronic Warfare/Radioelectronic Parity Study
EPARCS....... Enhanced Perimeter Acquisition Radar Attack Characterization System (SAUS)
EPARCS....... Enhanced Perimeter Acquisition RADAR Characterization System (PDAA)
EPARCS....... Enhanced Perimeter Acquisition Raid (SAUS)
Ep Arist........ Epistle of Aristeas [*Biblical*] (RION)
EP (ARR)..... Act Environment Protection [*Alligator Rivers Region*] [*Act 1978*] [*Commonwealth*] (EERA)
EP(ARR)...... Environment Protection (Alligator Rivers Region) Act (SAUS)
EPAS.......... Electric Power-Assisted Steering
EPAS.......... Energetic Particle Anisotropy Spectrometer
EPAS.......... Exercise Production and Analysis System (SAUS)
EPAS.......... Experimental Project Apollo-Soyuz [*Acronym used as name of a cologne created to commemorate the first joint US/Russian manned space flight*]
EPASA........ Electron Probe Analysis Society of America [*Later, MAS*] (EA)
EPASMOD.... Environmental Protection Agency Subsurface Fate and Transport Model [*Later, EPACML*]
EPASYS....... European Patents Administration System [*Information service or system*] (NITA)
EPAT.......... Earliest Possible Arrival Time (MCD)
EPAT.......... Earliest Probable Arrival Time (SAUS)
EPAT.......... Early Psychosis Assessment Team (ADWA)
EPAT.......... Every Pupil Achievement Test (EDAC)
EPATH........ Ejection Path [*National Highway Traffic Safety Administration Fatal Accident Recording System code*]
EPA/TSCA.... Environmental Protection Agency/Toxic Substance Control Act (SAUS)
EPA-V.......... Environmental Protection Agency, Region V (SAUS)
EPAW.......... Enhanced Post Attack WWMCCS (SAUS)
EPAX.......... Paxon Polymer [*Private rail car owner code*]
EPAYS.......... Environmental Protection Agency Payroll System (GFGA)
EPAYS.......... EPA Payroll System (SAUS)
EPB............ Early Premature Beat (SAUS)
EPB............ Earth Pressure Balance [*Civil engineering*]
EPB............ Eastern Pacific Aviation Ltd. [*Canada*] [*ICAO designator*] (FAAC)
EPB............ East Pacific Barrier [*Oceanography*]
EPB............ Economic Policy Board [*Department of the Treasury*]
EPB............ Editorial Production Branch [*BUPERS*]
EPB............ Effective Physiological Base (SAUS)
EPB............ Ejercito Popular Boricua [*Puerto Rican Popular Army*] (PD)
EPB............ Electrode per Bit (SAUS)
EPB............ Electronically Proportioned Braking
EPB............ Electronic Planning Board (SAUS)
EPB............ Electronic Publishing Business [*Electronic Publishing Ventures, Inc.*] [*Information service or system*] (IID)
EPB............ Electro-Proportional Valve [*Hydraulics*]
EPB............ Energy Pulse Bonding [*Electronics*]
EPB............ Engineering Process Bulletin
EPB............ Enlisted Performance Branch (SAUO)
EPB............ Enlisted Programs Branch [*BUPERS*]
EPB............ Environmental Periodicals Bibliography [*Environmental Studies Institute*] [*Information service or system*]
EPB............ Environmental Pre-Language Battery [*Speech and language therapy*] (DAVI)
EPB............ Environmental Protection Board [*British*] (BARN)
EPB............ Equipment Parts Bin
EPB............ Equivalent Passband (MCD)
EPB............ Equivalent Pension Benefit [*British*]
EPB............ Ethylpyridinium Bromide [*Organic chemistry*]
EPB............ Eucrite Parent Body [*Meteorite geology*]
EPB............ Export Promotion Bureau [*Pakistan*]
EPB............ Extensor Pollicis Brevis [*Anatomy*]
EPB............ External Proton Beam
EPBA.......... European Portable Battery Association
EpBarn........ Epistle of Barnabas (BJA)
EPBC Act..... Environmental Protection and Biodiversity Conservation Act [*1999*] (AUSE)
EPBI............ Epoxy-Beta-Ionone [*Biochemistry*]
EP-BL.......... Ethylene Propylene Block Copolymer (SAUS)
EPBLFC........ Elvis Presley Burning Love Fan Club (EA)
EPBM.......... Earth Pressure Balance Machine [*Excavation*]
epbm.......... electroplated base metal (SAUS)
EPBM.......... Electroplated Britannia Metal (IIA)
EPBM.......... Enhanced Probability-Based Matching (SAUS)
EPBN.......... European Plant Biotechnology Network (EURO)
EPBS.......... Earth-Pressure Balanced Shield (SAUS)
EPBX.......... Electronic Private Branch Exchange [*Telecommunications*]
EPC............ Conti-Flug Koln/Bonn [*Germany*] [*ICAO designator*] (FAAC)
EPC............ Earth Potential Compensation [*Telecommunications*] (TEL)
EPC............ Earth Prelaunch Calibration [*NASA*] (KSC)
EPC............ Eastern Pilgrim College [*Later, United Weslayan College*] [*Pennsylvania*]
EPC............ East's Pleas of the Crown [*A publication*] (DLA)
EPC............ Easy Processing Carbon (SAUS)
EPC............ Easy Processing Channel
EPC............ Economic Policy Commission (SAUS)
EPC............ Economic Policy Committee [*OECD*]
EPC............ Economic Policy Council [*UNA-USA*]
EPC............ Ectoplacental Cone [*Embryology*]
EPC............ Edge Perforated Card (SAUS)
EPC............ Edge Punched Card (IAA)
EPC............ Editoral Processing Center (SAUS)
EPC............ Editorial Policy Committee (SAUS)
EPC............ Editorial Processing Center
EPC............ Editor's Presentation Copy
EPC............ Educational Policies Commission [*Defunct*] (EA)
EPC............ Educational Publishers Council [*British*]
EPC............ Education Products Center (SAUS)
EPC............ Effective Production Coefficient
EPC............ Egg Phosphatidylcholine [*Biochemistry*]
EPC............ Ejercito del Pueblo Costarricense [*Costa Rica*] [*Political party*] (EY)
EPC............ Ejercito Popular Catalan [*Catalan Popular Army*] [*Spain*] (PD)
EPC............ Elastic Performance Coefficient [*Textile testing*]
EPC............ Elder Flowers, Peppermint, and Composition Essense [*Patent medicine ingredients*] [*British*]
EPC............ Electrically-Pulsed Chamber (PDAA)
EPC............ Electrical Parameter Check (SAUS)
EPC............ Electric Power Club (SAUO)
EPC............ Electric Power Corporation (SAUO)
EPC............ Electric Propulsion Conference (SAUS)
EPC............ Electrolytic Photocell (SAUS)
EPC............ Electronic Page Composition (DGA)
EPC............ Electronic Pain Control [*Apparatus*] [*Neurology*] (DAVI)
EPC............ Electronic Parts Committee of Aerospace Industries Association (SAUO)
EPC............ Electronic Plane Conversion (SAUS)
EPC............ Electronic Power Conditioner
EPC............ Electronic Power Control [*Off-highway equipment*] [*Hydraulics*]
EPC............ Electronic Pressure Control (HAWK)
EPC............ Electronic Program Control
EPC............ Electronic Publishing Committee [*Association of American Publishers*] [*Information service or system*] (IID)
EPC............ Electron Photon Cascade
EPC............ Electroplate on Copper (SAUS)
EPC............ Electropowder Coating (UWER)
EPC............ Electro Prismatic Collimator (SAUS)
EPC............ Elementary Processing Centers
EPC............ Elevated Plasma Cholesterol (MELL)
EPC............ Elsevier Publishing Companies Amsterdam (SAUO)
EPC............ Elsevier Publishing Company (SAUO)
EPC............ Embedded Print Command [*Computer science*] (HGAA)
EPC............ Emergency Planning Canada
EPC............ Emergency Planning Commission (SAUS)
EPC............ Emergency Preparedness Coordinator (SAUO)
EPC............ Emergency Propaganda Committee [*London*] [*World War II*]
EPC............ Emulsion Polymers Council (NTPA)
EPC............ Endoscopic Pancreatocholangiography [*Medicine*] (MELL)
EPC............ End Plate Current
EPC............ End Products Committee [*of WPB*] [*World War II*]
EPC............ Engagement Planning Control (ACAE)
EPC............ Engineering Part Card
EPC............ Engineering Parts Counter (SAUS)
EPC............ Engineering Process Specification (SAUS)
EPC............ Engineering, Procurement, and Construction
EPC............ Engine Performance Computer (PDAA)
EPC............ Engin Principal de Combat (SAUS)
EPC............ English Prize Cases [*Legal*]

EPC .... Environmental Forecast Center (SAUS)
EPC .... Environmental Policy Center (EA)
EPC .... Environmental Pollution Control
EPC .... Environmental Protection Committee (SAUO)
EPC .... Environmental Protection Control (SAUS)
EPC .... Environmental Protection Council [*Tasmania, Australia*]
EPC .... Environment Protection Council (SAUO)
EPC .... Epilepsy Partialis Continua [*Medicine*]
EpC .... Epithelial Cell [*Cytology*]
EPC .... Equipotential Cathode
EPC .... Error-Position Code (UWER)
EPC .... Error Protection Code (NASA)
Epc .... Erythrocyte Particle Counter [*Hematology*]
EPC .... Erythroid Progenitor Cells [*Hematology*]
EPC .... Esperanto Publishing Company Ltd. (SAUO)
EPC .... Esso Petroleum Company (SAUO)
EPC .... Ethiopian Petroleum Corporation (SAUO)
EPC .... Ethyl Phenylcarbamate [*Plant regulator*] [*Organic chemistry*]
EPC .... European Confederation of Plastics Convertors [*EC*] (ECED)
EPC .... European Palaeoclimate and Man Project (SAUO)
EPC .... European Paleoclimate (SAUS)
EPC .... European Paleoclimate and Man (SAUS)
EPC .... European Parliamentary Constituency (WDAA)
EPC .... European Patent Convention
EPC .... European Pension Committee [*France*] (EAIO)
EPC .... European Planning Council (SAUO)
EPC .... European Policy Committee (HEAS)
EPC .... European Political Community (NATG)
EPC .... European Political Cooperation
EPC .... European Popular Circle (EAIO)
EPC .... Evaluation and Planning Centre for Health Care [*London School of Hygiene and Tropical Medicine*] [*British*] (CB)
EPC .... Evaporative Pattern Casting [*Automotive engineering*]
EPC .... Even Parity Check (VLIE)
EPC .... Event-Driven Process Chain (GART)
epc .... every poor cluck (SAUS)
EPC .... Evidence-Based Practice Centers (ADWA)
EPC .... Excess Profits Tax Council Ruling or Memorandum [*Internal Revenue Bureau*] [*A publication*] (DLA)
EPC .... Executive Policy Committee [*Western Australia*] [*State*] (EERA)
EPC .... Exercise Planning Committee (SAUO)
EPC .... Exhaust Port Combustion
EPC .... Expendable Pattern Casting [*Metallurgy*] (UWER)
EPC .... Expended Processing Capacity (SAUS)
EPC .... Experimental Patrol Craft (SAUS)
EPC .... Experiment Package Console (ACAE)
EPC .... Experiment Point Control [*NASA*]
EPC .... Experiment Pointing and Control (SAUS)
EPC .... Experiment Pointing Control (SAUO)
EPC .... Extended Parity Checking (SAUS)
EPC .... Extended Performance Compound [*Automobile tires*]
EPC .... Extended Plotter Code (VLIE)
EPC .... Extended Plotter Commands (SAUS)
EPC .... External Pneumatic Compression [*Medicine*]
EPC .... External Power Contractor (NASA)
EPC .... Extra-Pair Copulation [*Biology*]
EPC .... Honolulu, HI [*Location identifier*] [*FAA*] (FAAL)
EPC .... Roscoe's English Prize Cases [*A publication*] (DLA)
EPCA .... Electronic Pest Control Association (EA)
EPCA .... Emergency Price Control Act of 1942
EPCA .... Employment Protection Consolidation Act [*1978*] [*British*] (DLA)
EPCA .... Energy Policy and Conservation Act [*1975*]
EPCA .... European Petrochemical Association [*Database producer*]
EPCA .... Extended Principle Components Analysis (SAUS)
EPCA .... External Pressure Circulatory Assist [*Cardiac treatment*]
epca .... external-pressure circulatory assist (SAUS)
EPCA .... International Study Group for the Detection and Prevention of Cancer (SAUO)
EPCA .... Energy Production and Consumption Account (ODA)
EPCAC .... Ecumenical Program on Central America and the Caribbean (EA)
EPCAD .... Electronics Packaging Computer-Aided Design (CIST)
EPCAF .... El Paso Coalition Against the Fence (SAUS)
EP Car .... Electric Passenger Car (SAUS)
EPCB .... Electric Plant Control Benchboard (SAUO)
EPC Black .... Easy Processing Carbol Black (SAUS)
EPC Black .... Easy Processing Channel Black (SAUS)
EPCC .... Environment Policy Coordinating Committee [*Commonwealth*] (EERA)
EPCC .... European Power Capacitors Corporation (SAUO)
EPCCC .... Eastern Pennsylvania Community College Conference (PSS)
EPCCFC .... Elvis Presley Circle City Fan Club (EA)
EPCCS .... Emergency Positive Control Communications System
EPCCT .... Emergency Planning Committee for Civil Transportation [*US and Canada*]
EPCDC .... Electrical Power Conditioning, Distribution, and Control (MCD)
EPCE .... Electrical Power Consuming Equipment (SPST)
Ep cell .... Epithelial Cell [*Medicine*] (AMHC)
ep cells .... epithelial cells (SAUS)
EPCER .... Experimental Patrol Craft, Escort and Rescue
epcg .... endoscopic pancreaticholangiography (SAUS)
EPCG .... Endoscopic Pancreatocholangiography [*Medicine*] (AAMN)
EPCG .... Environment Priorities and Coordination Group (SAUS)
EPCGS .... Export Promotion Capital Goods Scheme (EURO)
EPCI .... Enhanced Peripheral Communication Interface [*Motorola, Inc.*]
EPCI .... Enhanced Programmable Circuit Interface (SAUS)
EPCI .... Enhanced Programmable Communication Interface (SAUS)
EPCI .... Enhanced Proliferation Control Initiative (SAUS)
EPCI .... Entry Point Control Item (MHDB)
EPCI .... European Photographic Chemical Industry (SAUS)
EPCIA .... Expanded Polystyrene Cavity Insulation Association [*British*] (DBA)
EPCM .... Electropulse Chemical Machining (SAUS)
EPCM .... Engineering, Procurement and Construction Management (SAUS)
EPCM .... Essential Procedures for Clinical Microbiology (SAUO)
EPCMA .... Export Packing-Case Manufacturers Association (SAUO)
EPCO .... Emergency Power Cutoff [*NASA*] (KSC)
EPCO .... Engineer Procurement Office [*Army*]
EPCO .... Engine Parts Coordinating Office [*Navy*]
EPCO .... Enrichment Project Coordination Office (SAUS)
E-P Converter ... Electro-Pneumatic Converter (SAUS)
EPCOT .... Experimental Polyester Costumes Of Tomorrow (SAUS)
EPCOT .... Experimental Prototype Community of Tomorrow [*Disney World*] [*Facetious translation: "Every Person Comes Out Tired"*]
EPCOT .... Extremely Profitable Corporation Of Today (SAUO)
EPCOT Center ... Experimental Prototype Community Of Tomorrow (SAUS)
EPCP .... Electric Plant Control Panel
EPCP .... Electric Propulsion Control Panel (SAUO)
EPCP .... Equivalent Public-Cost Contract Price (SAUS)
EPCR .... Emergency Planning and Community Right to Know Act, 1986 (EERA)
EPCRA .... Emergency Planning and Community Right-to-Know Act [*1986*]
EPCRA .... Emergency Planning and Community Right-to-Know Agency (SAUS)
EPCRA .... Emergency Preparedness and Community Right to Know Act (EEVL)
epcrbs .... emergency-position communication radio beacons (SAUS)
EPC Reader ... Edge Punched Card Reader (SAUS)
EPCRTK .... Emergency Planning and Community Right-to-Know Act [*1986*]
EPCRTKA .... Emergency Planning and Community Right-to-Know Act (COE)
EPCS .... Earnings and Profits Calculation System
EPCs .... Editorial Processing Centers (SAUS)
EPCS .... Electronic Plane Conversion System (SAUS)
ePCS .... Electronic Publishing Clearing Services
EPCS .... Engineer Functional Components System (AABC)
EPCS .... English Playing-Card Society (DBA)
EPCS .... Equitable Pioneers Cooperative Society (SAUO)
EPCS .... Experiment Point Control Subsystem (SAUO)
EPCS .... Experiment Point Control System [*or Subsystem*] [*NASA*] (KSC)
EPCU .... Electrical Power Control Unit (MCD)
EPCU .... ensemble de preparation charges utiles (SAUS)
EPCX .... Enterprise Products [*Private rail car owner code*]
EPD .... Earliest Parole Date (WDAA)
EPD .... Earliest Possible Date
EPD .... Earliest Practicable Date (AFIT)
EPD .... Early Packet Discard (DINT)
EPD .... Early Packet Disguard [*Communications term*] (DCT)
EPD .... Earth Potential Difference (IAA)
EPD .... Eastern Procurement Division [*Navy*]
EPD .... Eastern Production District [*Navy*]
EPD .... Educational Planning District (SAUO)
EPD .... Electrical Power Distribution (SAUS)
EPD .... Electric Potential Difference
EPD .... Electric Power Database [*Electric Power Research Institute*] [*Information service or system*] (IID)
EPD .... Electric Power Distribution
EPD .... Electric Power Distributor (SAUS)
EPD .... Electronic Product Definition [*Engineering design*]
EPD .... Electronic Products Department (SAUO)
EPD .... Electronic Programming Device (SAUS)
EPD .... Electronic Proximity Detecting (SAUS)
EPD .... Electronic Proximity Detector (MCD)
EPD .... Electrophotographic Display (DGA)
EPD .... Emergency Planning District [*Environmental science*] (EPAT)
EPD .... Emergency Preparedness Department (SAUS)
EPD .... Emergency Preparedness Division (SAUS)
EPD .... Emergency Procedures Document (MCD)
EPD .... Energetic Particles Detector [*Geophysics*]
EPD .... Energy Programs Division (SAUS)
EPD .... Engineering Planning Document
EPD .... Engineering Procedure Directive
EPD .... Enlisted Personnel Directorate [*Army*]
EPD .... Enlisted Personnel Division [*Navy*]
EPD .... Enterprise Products Partners [*NYSE symbol*] (SG)
EPD .... Entry Products Division (SAUO)
EPD .... Environmental Policy Database (SAUO)
EPD .... Environmental Protection Devices (MCD)
EPD .... Environmental Protection Division
EPD .... Eplett Dairies Ltd. [*Toronto Stock Exchange symbol*]
EPD .... Equilibrium Peritoneal Dialysis [*Medicine*] (BARN)
EPD .... Etch Pitch Density (PDAA)
EPD .... Etch-Pit Density (ODA)
EPD .... etch pit density (SAUS)
EPD .... European Pollen Database (QUAC)
EPD .... European Programming Document (SAUO)
EPD .... European Progressive Democrats (PPE)
EPD .... Excellent Policy Duty (SAUS)
EPD .... Excess Profits Duty
epd .... excess profts duty (SAUS)
EPD .... Exchange Parameter Definitions [*Telecommunications*] (TEL)
EPD .... Expected Progeny Difference [*Agricultural science*]
EPD .... Experimental Physics Department (SAUS)
EPD .... Exponential Power Distribution [*Statistics*]
EPD .... Extraction and Processing Division (SAUS)

EPD .... Extra Police Duty [*Extra cleaning chores*] [*Military*]
EPDA .... Educational Professional Development Assistance [*Office of Education*]
EPDA .... Education Professions Development Act [*1965*]
EPDA .... Education Professions Development Administration (SAUS)
EPDA .... Emergency Powers Defence Act [*British*] [*World War II*]
EPDA .... Environmental Protection Data Base (SAUS)
EPDA .... Ethiopian Peoples' Democratic Alliance
EPDA .... Exhibit Producers and Designers Association (SAUO)
EPDAN .... Elastic-Plastic Deformation Analysis (SAUS)
EPDB .... Electrical Power Data Base (SAUS)
EPDB .... Electrical Power Distribution Board (SAUS)
EPDB .... Electrical Power Distribution Box (MCD)
EPDB .... Environmental Protection Data Base [*Environmental Protection Agency*]
EPDB .... Experiment Power Distribution Box (NASA)
EPDC .... Economic Power Dispatch Computer
EPDC .... Electrical Power Distribution and Control (NASA)
EPDC .... Electric Power Development Center (SAUS)
EPDC .... Electric Power Development Corporation (SAUS)
EPDC .... Electronic Park Distance Control
EPDC .... Energy Policy Development and Conservation (SAUS)
EPDCC .... Elementary Potential Digital Computing Component
EPDCC .... European Pressure Die Casting Committee (EA)
EPDCE .... Elementary Potential Digital Computing Element (IAA)
EPDCS .... Electrical Power Distribution and Control System (KSC)
EPDE .... Electronic Product Data Exchange (SAUS)
EPDF .... Electronic Publishing Demonstration Facility (SAUS)
EPDF .... Embedded Portable Document Format [*Computer science*] (VERA)
EPDF .... Engineer Performance Description Form [*Test*]
EPDG .... Execution Plan Data Generation (SAUO)
EPDGP .... Eyre Penninsula Division of General Practice (SAUS)
ep disc .... extended-play disc (SAUS)
EPDL .... Emergency Powers Defence Law (SAUO)
EPDM .... Enterprise Performance Data Manager [*Computer science*] (HODG)
EPDM .... Epidemiological (SAUS)
epdm .... epidemiologist (SAUS)
EPDM .... Epidemiology (SAUS)
EPDM .... Ethiopian People's Democratic Movement [*Political party*]
EPDM .... Ethylene Propylene Diene Modified (SAUS)
EPDM .... Ethylene-Propylene-Diene Monomer [*Rubber, ASTM nomenclature*]
epdm .... ethylene propylene diene monomer (SAUS)
EPDM .... Ethylene-Propylene-Dimonomer (SAUS)
EPDM .... Ethylene-Propylene Terpolymer (SARE)
EPDM .... ethylene-propylene terpolymer rubber (SAUS)
EPD/McGraw-Hill... Educators' Professional Development/McGraw-Hill
EPDML .... Epidemiology [*or Epidemiological*]
EPDMLGY .... Epidemiology
EPDM rubber... ethylene-propylene diene monomer rubber (SAUS)
EPDO .... Enlisted Personnel Distribution Office [*Navy*]
EPDOCONUS... Enlisted Personnel Distribution Office, Continental United States [*Navy*]
EPDOLANT... Enlisted Personnel Distribution Office, Atlantic Fleet [*Navy*]
EPDOPAC.... Enlisted Personnel Distribution Office, Pacific Fleet [*Navy*] (MUGU)
EPDP .... Eelam People's Democratic Party [*Sri Lanka*] [*Political party*] (EY)
EPDP .... Engineering Program Definition Plan (MCD)
EPDP .... Experiment Power Distribution Box (SAUS)
EPD/RDIS .... Electric Power Database/Research and Development Information System [*Electric Power Research Institute*] [*Information service or system*] (IID)
EpDRF .... Epithelial-Derived Relaxant Factor (DB)
EPDS .... Edinburgh Postnatal Depression Scale
EPDS .... Electrical Power and Distribution Subsystem (SAUS)
EPDS .... Electrical Power Distribution System [*or Subsystem*] (KSC)
EPDS .... Electric Power Distribution System (SAUS)
EPDS .... Electronic Parts Distributors' Show
EPDS .... Electronic Processing and Dissemination System [*Computer science*] (DOMA)
EPDS .... ELINT Processing and Dissemination System (SAUS)
EPDS .... Environmental Planning Database System (SAUS)
EPDS .... European Data Relay Satellite (SAUO)
EPDS .... Experiment Power and Data System (SAUS)
EPDT .... Estimated Project Duration Time
EPDU .... Electrical Power Distribution Unit (SAUS)
EPDU .... Ethiopian People's Democratic Union (EA)
EPDWO .... Engineering and Product Development Work Order
EPDX .... Forest Products Chemical [*Private rail car owner code*]
EPE .... Earth-Pointing Error (MCD)
EPE .... Economic Policy towards Eire [*British*]
EPE .... Editorial Project for Education (SAUS)
EPE .... Editorial Projects for Education Inc. (SAUO)
EPE .... Editorial Projects in Education (EA)
epe .... electrical parts and equipment (SAUS)
EPE .... Electrical Power Engineering (SAUS)
EPE .... Electrical Power Engineering Co. (SAUO)
EPE .... Electronic Packaging Engineering (SAUS)
EPE .... Electronic Parts and Equipment (NATG)
EPE .... Electron-Plastic Effect (SAUS)
EPE .... Electrophoresis Experiment [*NASA*] (MCD)
EPE .... Electrostatic Probe Experiment
EPE .... Elvis Presley Enterprises (WDAA)
EPE .... Emergency Passenger Exit
EPE .... Emergency Preparedness Evaluation [*Nuclear energy*] (NRCH)
EPE .... Energetic Particles Explorer [*Satellite*] [*NASA*]
EPE .... Engineering Progress Exposition (SAUS)
EPE .... Enhanced Performance Engine (MCD)
EPE .... Environmental Performance Evaluation (SAUS)
EPE .... Environmental Programme for Europe (SAUS)
EPE .... Environmental Protection Expenditure (EURO)
EPE .... Erythropoietin-Producing Enzyme [*Hematology*] (MAE)
EPE .... Ethniki Politiki Enosis [*National Political Union*] [*Greek*] (PPE)
EPE .... European Conference on Power Electronics and Applications (SAUS)
EPE .... European Partners for the Environment (SAUS)
EPE .... European Party (SAUO)
EPE .... Experimental and Proving Establishment [*Canada*] (MCD)
EPE .... Explosion-Proof Enclosure
EPE .... Extended Period of Eligibility [*Social Security Administration*] (GFGA)
EPE .... Pellston, MI [*Location identifier*] [*FAA*] (FAAL)
EPEA .... Electrical Power Engineers' Association [*A union*] [*British*]
EPEA .... Environmental Protection Encouragement Agency (SAUS)
EPEA .... Experiment Pointing Electronic Assembly [*NASA*]
EPEA .... Exploratory Project for Economic Alternatives (EA)
EPEAA .... Employing Photo-Engravers Association of America [*Defunct*] (EA)
EPEB .... Ecosystem Processes and Effects Branch [*Army*]
EPEC .... Electric Programmer, Evaluator, Controller (SAA)
EPEC .... Emerson Programmer, Evaluator and Controller (SAUS)
EPEC .... Emerson Programmer-Evaluator-Controller [*Computer science*]
EPEC .... Enteropathogenic Escherichia coli [*Also, EEC*] [*Medicine*]
EPED .... Environmental Processes and Effects Division [*Army*]
Epedemiol ... Epedemiologist (SAUS)
epedemiol ... epedemiology (SAUS)
EPEDS .... Energy Price and Expenditure Data System (SAUS)
EPEEA .... Enlisted Personnel Enlistment Eligibility Activity [*Army*]
EPEM .... Association of Electronic Parts and Equipment Manufacturers (SAUO)
EPEM .... Electric Parts and Equipment Manufacturers (SAUS)
EPEN .... Greek National Political Society (PPW)
epenth .... epenthesis (SAUS)
epenth .... epenthetic (SAUS)
EP/EO .... Employee Plans/Exempt Organization [*IRS*]
EPER .... Emergency Project for Equal Rights (EA)
EPERA .... Extractor Parachute Emergency Release Assembly (PDAA)
E-PERM ...... Electret-Passive Environmental Radon Monitor [*Rad-Elec, Inc.*]
E-PERS ...... Enlisted Personnel (DNAB)
E Persnl ...... Employed Personnel (SAUS)
EPES .... elastic peak electron spectroscopy (SAUS)
EPES .... Emergency Procedures Expert System (ACAE)
EPESD .... Elsevier Publishing Earth Sciences Department (SAUO)
EPESE .... Established Populations for Epidemiologic Studies of the Elderly [*Department of Health and Human Services*] (GFGA)
EPET .... European Production Efficienca Factor (SAUS)
EPEX .... Edge Petroleum Corp. [*NASDAQ symbol*] (NASQ)
EPEX .... Epoxy Resin Extender (SAUS)
EPF .... Early Pregnancy Factor [*Medicine*] (DMAA)
EPF .... Earth Preservation Fund (GNE)
EPF .... Easy Processing Furnace (SAUS)
EPF .... Easy Programming Facility (SAUS)
EPF .... Education Projects Fund [*British Council/Overseas Development Administration*] (DS)
EPF .... Electronic Power Feed (NITA)
EPF .... Emergency Plant Facilities
EPF .... Employment Policy Foundation (EA)
EPF .... Endocarditis Parietalis Fibroplastica (DB)
EPF .... End of Programmed Flight (MCD)
EPF .... Endothelial Proliferating Factor [*Biochemistry*]
EPF .... Engine and Propeller Factor [*IOR*] [*Yacht racing*]
EPF .... Environmental Protection Facility (SAUS)
EPF .... Eosinophil-Producing Factor (DB)
EPF .... Epidemiological Flight [*Military*]
EPF .... Epidermal Proliferation Factor [*Animal physiology*] (QSUL)
EPF .... Episcopal Peace Fellowship (EA)
EPF .... Equilibrium Porous Flow [*Chemistry*]
EPF .... Erase Preceding Field (SAUS)
EPF .... Esparros [*France*] [*Seismograph station code, US Geological Survey*] (SEIS)
EPF .... Established Program Financing
EPF .... Esthonian Popular Front (CARL)
EPF .... European Packaging Federation [*Denmark*] (SLS)
EPF .... European Polar Forum (SAUS)
EPF .... European Psycho-Analytical Federation (EA)
EPF .... Exophthalmos-Producing Factor [*Endocrinology*]
epf .... exopthalmos-producing factor (SAUS)
EPF .... Expected Provident Fund
EPF .... Exploitation Products File (MCD)
EPF .... Extended Payload Fairing [*Space launch term*] (ISAK)
EPF .... Extra-Pair Fertilization [*Biology*]
EPF .... Eye Protection Factor
EPFA .... Established Program Financing Act (SAUS)
EPFA .... European Plasma Fractionation Association
EPFB .... Easy Processing Furnace Black (SAUS)
EPF Black .... Easy Processing Furnace Black (SAUS)
EPFC .... Euro-Pacific Finance Corporation (SAUO)
EPFCL .... Elvis Presley Fan Club of Luxembourg (EAIO)
EPFCL .... Esso Pakistan Fertilizer Co. Ltd (SAUO)
EPFIF .... European Pet Foods Industry Federation (SAUO)
EPFL .... East Pakistan Federation of Labour (SAUO)
EPFL .... Ecole Polytechnique Federale de Lausanne [*Swiss Federal Institute of Technology, Lausanne*] (ECON)
EPFL .... Enoch Pratt Free Library (SAUS)
EPFM .... Elastic-Plastic Fracture Mechanics (SAUS)
EPF-Rua ...... easy processing furnace black (SAUS)

EPFS .... Equipment Pool for Field Spectroscopy (SAUS)
EPFSU .... Earth's Physical Features Study Unit (EA)
EPFT .... Elastic-Plastic Fracture Toughness (SAUS)
EPFTR .... Expert Panel on the Facilitation of Tuna Research [*Marine science*] (MSC)
EPFV .... Exhaust Pseudo-Flow Velocity
EPG .... Ecole Polytechnique, Publications Officielles [*UTLAS symbol*]
EPG .... Economic Policy Group
EPG .... Economic Pressure on Germany Committee [*War Cabinet*] [*British*] [*World War II*]
EPG .... Edit Program Generator
EPG .... Eggs per Gram [*Parasitology*]
EPG .... Egle Party of Ghana (SAUO)
EPG .... Electrical Power Generator (NASA)
EPG .... Electrolytic Plunge Grinder
EPG .... Electronic Program Guide [*Cable-television system*]
EPG .... Electronic Proving Ground [*Army*] (MCD)
EPG .... Electronics Proving Ground (SAUS)
EPG .... Electropneumogram [*Medicine*]
EPG .... Electrostatic Particle Guide (OA)
EPG .... Electrostatic Power Generator
EPG .... Eletronic Program-Guide (SAUS)
EPG .... El Paso Energy [*Formerly, El Paso Natural Gas*] [*NYSE symbol*]
EPG .... El Paso Natural Gas [*NYSE symbol*] (TTSB)
EPG .... El Paso Natural Gas Co. [*NYSE symbol*] (SPSG)
EPG .... El Paso Tennessee Pipeline [*NYSE symbol*] (SAG)
EPG .... Emergency Power Generator
EPG .... Emergency Procedure Guidelines (IAA)
EPG .... Eminent Persons Group [*Group of elder statesmen from Commonwealth countries*]
EPG .... Empire Gold Resources Ltd. [*Vancouver Stock Exchange symbol*]
EPG .... Employee Participation Group
EPG .... Engineering Policy Group (SAUO)
EPG .... Eniwetok Proving Ground [*AEC*]
EPG .... Environmental Protection Group (SAUO)
EpG .... EP Group of Companies, Microform Division, Wakefield, Yorkshire, United Kingdom [*Library symbol*] [*Library of Congress*] (LCLS)
EPG .... Esterified Propoxylated Glycerol [*Organic chemistry*]
EPG .... European Participating Governments [*In the F-16 fighter program*]
EPG .... European Press Group
EPG .... European Programme Group [*NATO*]
EPG .... Exercise Planning Group [*Environmental science*] (COE)
EPG .... Exercise Planning Guidance (SAUS)
EPG .... Exhaust Pressure Governor [*Diesel engines*]
EPG .... Experimental Proving Ground (SAUS)
EPG .... Extended Planning Guidance (MCD)
EPG .... Externally Powered Machine Gun (SAUS)
EPG .... Weeping Water, NE [*Location identifier*] [*FAA*] (FAAL)
EPG .... Electropalatogram [*or Electropalatology*] [*Medicine*] (ODA)
EPGA .... effective peak ground acceleration (SAUS)
EPGA .... Emergency Petroleum and Gas Administration [*Department of the Interior*]
EPGA .... Emergency Petroleum and Gas Administration, Department of Transportation (SAUO)
EPGCR .... Experimental Prototype Gas-Cooled Reactor
EPGD .... Gdansk/Rebiechowo [*Poland*] [*ICAO location identifier*] (ICLI)
EPGR .... Electrical Potential Gradient Radiosonde [*Meteorology*]
EPGRS .... Employment Policy Grievance Review Staff [*OSA*]
EPGS .... Electric Power Generation System
EPGS .... El Paso Geological Sciences (SAUO)
EPGS .... EOS Polar Ground Stations (SAUS)
EPGS .... Export Programme Grants Scheme (SAUS)
EPH .... Edema, Proteinuria, and Hypertension [*Medicine*] (MELL)
EPH .... Electric Process Heating (MCD)
EPH .... Electrochemical Plating and Honing [*Manufacturing term*] (IAA)
EPH .... Electronic Package Housing
EPH .... Electronic Payment Handling (SAUS)
EPH .... Electronic Print Head (TIMI)
EPH .... Employ the Physically Handicapped
EPH .... ephedrine hydrochloride (SAUS)
EPH .... Ephemeris and Attitude (SAUS)
Eph .... Ephesians [*New Testament book*]
EPH .... Ephraim
EPH .... Ephrata, WA [*Location identifier*] [*FAA*] (FAAL)
EPH .... Epibromohydrin (GNE)
EPH .... Episodic Paroxysmal Hemicrania [*Medicine*] (MELL)
EPH .... Epoch Capital Corp. [*Vancouver Stock Exchange symbol*]
EPH .... Expected Period of Hospitalisation
EPH .... Explosion-Proof Housing
EPH .... Extensor Proprius Hallucis [*Medicine*] (MELL)
EPH .... Extrapyramidal Hypertonia [*Medicine*] (MELL)
EPHC .... Eastern Pacific Hurricane Center [*San Francisco*] [*National Weather Service*] (NOAA)
EPHDP .... Electronic Public Health Development Project (ADWA)
Eph Epigr .... Ephemeris Epigraphica [*A publication*] (OCD)
Ephes .... Ephesians [*New Testament book*] (ROG)
EPHGEN .... Ephemeris Generator Program (SAUS)
EPHI .... Electropharmacology, Inc. [*NASDAQ symbol*] (SAG)
EPhi .... English Philips [*Record label*]
EPHIN .... Electron Proton Helium Instrument (ADWA)
EPHIW .... Electropharmacology Inc. Wrrt [*NASDAQ symbol*] (TTSB)
EPHL .... Eastern Professional Hockey League
ephmer .... ephemeral (SAUS)
ephmer .... ephemerides (SAUS)
EPhMRA .... European Pharmaceutical Marketing Research Association (EAIO)
EPHO .... Ephemeris - Orbit
EPHOS .... European Procurement Handbook for Open Systems (SAUS)
EPHR .... Ephemeris - Reentry
Ephr .... Ephraim (BJA)
EPHS .... Electrically Powered Hydraulic Steering
EPHSOC .... Ephemera Society [*British*]
EPHSOC .... Ephemera Society of America (EA)
EPI .... Consolidated Ed 7.35%'PINES' [*NYSE symbol*] (SG)
EPI .... Eagle-Picher Industries, Inc. (SAUO)
EPI .... Earth Path Indicator
EPI .... Echo-Planar Imaging [*Physics*]
EPI .... Economic Performance Indicator [*New York Stock Exchange*]
EPI .... Economic Policy Institute (EA)
EPI .... Economic Procurement Item (NATG)
EPI .... Educational Planning Institute (EA)
EPI .... Educational Priority Indices (AIE)
EPI .... Edwards Personality Inventory [*Psychology*]
EPI .... Ehrenreich Photo-Optical Industries, Inc.
EPI .... Electrical Patents Index (SAUS)
EPI .... Electrical Pulse Interference [*Communications term*] (DCT)
EPI .... Electric Power Institute (SAUS)
EPI .... Electronic Position Indicator
EPI .... Electronic Process, Incorporated (SAUO)
EPI .... Electronic Processors Inc. (NITA)
EPI .... Electronic Products Inc. (SAUS)
EPI .... Electronic Products Incorporated (SAUO)
EPI .... Electron Photon Interaction
EPI .... Electron Probe Instrument (SAUS)
EPI .... Electro-Pyrolysis, Incorporated (SAUO)
EPI .... Elevation Position Indicator [*Aviation*]
EPI .... Emergency Position Indicator (SAUS)
EPI .... Emergency Public Information [*Civil Defense*]
epi .... emotional-physiologic illness (SAUS)
EPI .... Emulsion Polymers Institute (EA)
EPI .... Engineering Physics Institute (SAUS)
EPI .... Engineering Projects India, Limited (SAUS)
EPI .... Engine Performance Indicator (NG)
EPI .... Entraide aux Peuples Isoles (SAUO)
EPI .... Environmental Policy Institute (EA)
EPI .... Environmental Preference Inventory
EPI .... Environmental Priorities Initiative
EPI .... environmental productivity index (SAUS)
EPI .... Environmental Protection Initiative (SAUS)
EPI .... Epichlorohydrin (SAUS)
EPI .... Epidote [*Petrology*]
epi .... Epidural [*Medicine*] (DAVI)
Epi .... epikeratophakia (SAUS)
EPI .... Epilogue (ROG)
Epi .... Epinephrine [*Medicine*] (AMHC)
EPI .... Epinephrine [*Endocrinology*]
EPI .... Epistilbite [*A zeolite*]
EPI .... Epitaxial (IAA)
epi .... Epitaxially grown material (SAUS)
EPI .... Epithelial [*or Epithelium*] [*History*] (DAVI)
Epi .... Epithelial [*Animal physiology*] (QSUL)
epi .... epithelium (SAUS)
EPI .... ESOC Precipitation Index (SAUS)
EPI .... Estes Park Institute
EPI .... European Paper Institute [*Research center*]
EPI .... European Participating Industry
EPI .... European Product Index (SAUS)
EPI .... Evaluation Position Indicator (SAUS)
EPI .... Evoked Potential Index [*Neurophysiology*]
EPI .... Exocrine pancreatic insufficiency (SAUS)
EPI .... Expanded Plan Indicator
EPI .... Expanded Position Indicator
EPI .... Expanded Programme on Immunization [*World Health Organization*]
EPI .... Expanded Program of Immunization (SAUS)
EPI .... Expanded Program on Immunization (SAUS)
EPI .... Expanded Program on Immunization. Pan American Health Organization (SAUS)
EPI .... Expected Point of Impact (SAUS)
EPI .... Export Polygraph International (SAUS)
EPI .... Extension Producing Interneuron [*Neurology*]
EPI .... External Presentation Interface (SAUS)
EPI .... Extrapyramidal Involvement (DIPS)
EPI .... Eysenck Personality Inventory [*Psychology*]
EPI .... Institute of Professional Representatives before the European Patent Office (SAUO)
EPI .... Effective-Pair Interaction (ODA)
EPIA .... Electric Power Industry Abstracts [*Utility Data Institute*] [*Information service or system*]
EPIA .... End Poverty in America Society (EA)
EPIAI .... EP [*Elvis Presley*] Impersonators Association International (EA)
EPIB .... Emergency Position-Indicating Beacon (SAUS)
EPIB .... Environmental Protection Information Bulletin (SAUS)
EPIC .... Early Purchase Individual Contract (SAUS)
EPIC .... Earth-Pointing Instrument Carrier [*A satellite*]
EPIC .... East Central Pennsylvania Council on Interlibrary Cooperation (SAUO)
EPIC .... Ecumenical Partnership for International Concerns (SAUO)
EPIC .... Educational Products Information Exchange (HGAA)
EPIC .... Education Professional for Indian Children (SAUS)
EPIC .... Electranically Processed Inter-unit Cabling (SAUS)
EPIC .... Electrical Properties Information Center (SAUS)

EPIC............ Electric Properties Information Center (SAUO)
EPIC............ Electromagnetic Principle Investigators Council [*An association*]
EPIC............ Electronically-Processed Inter-Unit Cabling (PDAA)
EPIC............ Electronically Programmed Injection Control [*Automotive engineering*]
EPIC............ Electronic Page Image Composer (DGA)
Epic............ Electronic Payroll Information Collection (SAUS)
EPIC............ Electronic Photochromic Integrating Cathode-Ray [*Tube*]
EPIC............ Electronic Portable Information Center [*Computer science*]
EPIC............ Electronic Precision Industries Cooperative (SAUO)
EPIC............ Electronic Price Information Computer
EPIC............ Electronic Printer Image Construction (DGA)
EPIC............ Electronic Privacy Information Center
EPIC............ Electronic Product Information Center [*Buick's computerized information network and database*]
EPIC............ Electronic Production and Inventory Control (IAA)
EPIC............ Electronic Products Information Center (SAUS)
EPIC............ Electronic Properties Information Center [*DoD*]
EPIC............ Electronic Publishing Initiative at Columbia
EPIC............ Electronic Publishing Initiative at Columbia University
EPIC............ Electron Position Proton Intersecting Complex (SAUS)
EPIC............ Electron-Positron Intersecting Complex (PDAA)
EPIC............ Electron Proton Interaction Complex (SAUS)
EPIC............ El Paso [*Texas*] Intelligence Center [*Drug Enforcement Administration; Border Patrol; US Customs Service; Bureau of Alcohol, Tobacco, and Firearms; FAA; US Coast Guard*]
EPIC............ Elyria Project for Innovative Curriculum (EDAC)
EPIC............ Embedded Post-Beamformer Interference Canceler (CAAL)
EPIC............ Emergency Programs Information Center [*Database*]
EPIC............ Employment of Personnel in Computing (PDAA)
EPIC............ End Poverty in California [*Slogan used by Upton Sinclair during campaign as Democratic candidate for governor of California, 1934*]
EPIC............ Energy Conservation Program Guide for Industry and Commerce [*Department of Commerce*]
EPIC............ Energy Policy Information Center [*Defunct*] (EA)
EPIC............ Engineering and Production Information Control (SAUO)
EPIC............ Engineering Performance Information Center (SAUS)
EPIC............ Engineering Physics Information Center (SAUS)
EPIC............ Engineering Planning Information Coordination (SAUS)
EPIC............ Engineering Projects Information Center (SAUS)
EPIC............ Engineers Public Information Council (SAUO)
EPIC............ Engine Program Information Center (SAUO)
EPIC............ Enhanced Performance Implanted CMOS [*Texas Instruments, Inc.*]
EPIC............ Entry Point Interface Control
EPIC............ Environmental Management Program Integrating Contractor (SAUS)
EPIC............ Environmental Photographic Interpretation Center [*Environmental Protection Agency*]
EPIC............ Environmental Process Improvement Center (BCP)
EPIC............ Epic Design Technology [*NASDAQ symbol*] (TTSB)
EPIC............ Epic Design Technology, Inc. [*NASDAQ symbol*] (SAG)
EPIC............ Epic Health Group, Inc. [*NASDAQ symbol*] (COMM)
EPIC............ Epicor Software [*NASDAQ symbol*] (SG)
EPIC............ Epitactic Integrated Circuit (SAUS)
EPIC............ Epitaxial Passivated Integrated Circuits (MCD)
EPIC............ Equatorial Pacific Information Collection [*Marine science*] (OSRA)
EPIC............ Equatorial Pacific Interocean Circulation (SAUS)
EPIC............ Equitrac's Professional Internet Client [*Computer science*]
EPIC............ Erosion Productivity Impact Calculator (GNE)
EPIC............ Estates Property Investment Co. [*British*]
EPIC............ Estimate of Properties for Industrial Chemistry [*Universite de Liege*] [*Database*]
EPIC............ etched and polycrystalline-carried integrated circuit (SAUS)
EPIC............ European Photon Imaging Camera (SAUS)
EPIC............ European Product Information Cooperation (SAUS)
EPIC............ European Proliferation Information Centre [*British*] (CB)
EPIC............ European Public sector Information systems Conference (SAUS)
EPIC............ Evaluating Prolonged Intensive Combat (SAUO)
EPIC............ Evaluator Programmer Integrated Circuit [*NASA*]
EPIC............ Evidence Photographers International Council (EA)
EPIC............ Exchange Price Indicators [*Database*] [*British*]
EPIC............ Exchange price indicators datebase (SAUS)
EPIC............ Exchange Price Information Computer (MHDB)
EPIC............ Executive Planning Information and Communication system (SAUS)
EPIC............ Exhaust Plume Interference Characterization [*NASA*] (KSC)
EPIC............ Explicitly Parallel Instruction (SAUS)
EPIC............ Explicitly Parallel Instruction Computing [*Computer science*]
EPIC............ Explicit Parallelism Instruction Computing
EPIC............ Export Processing Industry Coalition
EPIC............ Exports Payments Insurance Corporation (SAUS)
EPIC............ Extended Performance and Increased Capability
EPIC............ Extended Program for Individual Compensation (SAUS)
EPIC............ External Pneumatic Intermittent Compression
EPIC............ Extraterrestrial Photographic Information Center [*NASA*]
EPIC............ Working group for European Product Information Co-operation (SAUO)
EPICA........... Ecumenical Program for Inter American Communication and Action [*Later, EPCAC*] (EA)
EPICA........... Ecumenical Program on Central America and the Caribbean (EA)
EPICA........... European Polar Ice Coring in Antarctica (SAUS)
EPICA........... European Program for Ice Coring in Antarctica [*Proposed start up date, 1997*]
EPICA........... European Programme on Sea Ice Coring in Antarctica (SAUS)
EPICC........... Equity in Prescription Insurance and Contraceptive Coverage Act
EpicDes....... Epic Design Technology, Inc. [*Associated Press*] (SAG)
epicen......... epicenter (SAUS)
EPICS........... Energetic Pion Channel and Spectrometer (PDAA)
EPICS........... Engine Production and Information Control System (PDAA)
EPICS........... Enlisted Personnel Individualized Career System [*Military*] (MCD)
EPICs........... Etched and Polycrystalline-carried Integrated Circuits (SAUS)
EPICS........... European Petrochemical Industry Computerized System [*Parpinelli Tecnon*] [*Italy*] [*Information service or system*] (IID)
EPICS........... Experimental Physics & Industrial Control System (SAUS)
EPICS........... Extended Power in Composition Systems (DGA)
EPICS........... Extended Purpose Inline Console System (SAUS)
EPIC System... Engineering Planning Information Coordination System (SAUS)
Epict............ Epictetus (SAUS)
Epict Diss.... Epicteti Dissertationes [*of Arrian*] [*Classical studies*] (OCD)
EPIC Technique... Epitactic-Integrated Circuit Technique (SAUS)
EPIC-Verfahren... epitatic-integrated circuit technique (SAUS)
EPID............ Electrophoretic Image Display [*Analytical chemistry*] (IAA)
EPID............ Epidemic
EPID............ Epidemiological Studies (SAUO)
EPIDC.......... East Pakistan Industrial Development Corporation (SAUO)
EPIDC.......... East Pakistan Industrial Development Council (SAUO)
EPIDEM........ Epidemiological (ADA)
Epidemiol Bull... Epidemiological Bulletin [*Wahington, DC*] (SAUS)
Epidemiol Infect... Epidedmiology and Infection [*Cambridge, England*] (SAUS)
Epidemiol Mikrobiol Imunol... Epidemiologie, Mikrobiologie, Imunologie (SAUS)
Epidemiology... Epidemiology [*Baltimore, MD*] (SAUS)
Epidemiol Prev... Epidemiologia E Prevenzione (SAUS)
Epidemiol Rev... Epidemiologic Reviews [*Baltimore, MD*] (SAUS)
EPIDermIS... Erlanger Patient Informations of the Dermatology Internet Service (SAUO)
EPIDs........... Electrophoretic Image Devices (SAUS)
EPIDS........... Enlisted Personnel Information Delivery System (SAUS)
EPIDSP......... Electronic Publishing and Internet Data Servers Project (SAUS)
EPIE............ Educational Products Information Exchange
EPIE............ Educational Progress through Information and Evaluation (SAUO)
EPIE............ Eskimo Pie [*NASDAQ symbol*] (TTSB)
EPIE............ Eskimo Pie Corp. [*NASDAQ symbol*] (SAG)
EPIE/CU....... Educational Products Information Exchange/Consumers Union (SAUO)
EPIEI........... Educational Products Information Exchange Institute [*Later, EPIE Institute*] (EA)
epig............ epigastric (SAUS)
epig............ epigeal (SAUS)
epig............ epigenesis (SAUS)
epig............ epigenetic (SAUS)
epig............ epigenic (SAUS)
epig............ epigeous (SAUS)
epig............ epiglottal (SAUS)
epig............ epiglottic (SAUS)
epig............ epiglottis (SAUS)
epig............ epigone (SAUS)
epig............ epigonic (SAUS)
epig............ epigonus (SAUS)
EPIG............ Epigram (WDAA)
epig............ epigrammatism (SAUS)
epig............ epigrammatize (SAUS)
epig............ epigrammatized (SAUS)
epig............ epigrammatizing (SAUS)
Epig............ Epigraphy (DIAR)
epig............ epigynous (SAUS)
epig............ epigyny (SAUS)
EPIGAS........ Epigastrium [*The part above the stomach*] [*Pharmacy*] (ROG)
Epigr........... Epigrammata [*Classical studies*] (OCD)
Epigr........... Epigrammata Super Exilio [*of Seneca the Younger*] [*Classical studies*] (OCD)
Epigr Gr....... Epigrammata Graeca ex Lapidibus Conlecta [*A publication*] (OCD)
EPII............ Eagle Pacific Indus [*NASDAQ symbol*] (TTSB)
EPII............ Eagle Pacific Industries, Inc. [*NASDAQ symbol*] (SAG)
EPIL............ Encyclopedia of Public International Law [*A publication*] (SAFN)
EPIL............ Engineering Projects India Limited (SAUO)
EPIL............ Epilepsy
EPIL............ Epilogue
EPIL............ European Partnership for Insurance Co-operation [*Proposed*] (ECON)
Epilepsia..... Epilepsia [*New York, NY*] (SAUS)
EPILEPSYLINE... Epilepsy on-Line Institutes of Health, National Institute of Neurological and Communicative Disorders and Stroke (SAUS)
Epilepsy Res... Epilepsy Research [*Amsterdam*] (SAUS)
Epilepsy Res Suppl... Epilepsy Research. Supplement [*Amsterdam*] (SAUS)
EPIM............ Ethernet Port Interface Module [*Computer science*] (VERA)
EPIN............ Electronic Personnel Information Network [*Data Corp. of America*]
EPIN............ Electronic Public Information Network (SAUS)
Epin............ Epinomis [*of Plato*] [*Classical studies*] (OCD)
epineph....... Epinephrine [*Endocrinology*] (DAVI)
epingrad..... equal participation in the great American dream (SAUS)
EPINT.......... Executive Program Initialize
EPIO............ Employment Prospects by Industry and Occupation [*A publication*] (ADA)
EPIP............ Electrons Per Incident Photon (SAUS)
EPIP............ Emergency Plan Implementing Procedure [*Nuclear energy*] (NRCH)
EPIP............ Environmental Protection Implementation Plan (SAUS)
EP (IP)........ Environment Protection (Impact of Proposals) [*Act 1974*] [*Commonwealth Act*] (EERA)
Epiph........... Epiphania (SAUS)
EPIPH.......... Epiphany
EPIQ............ Electronic Processing, Inc. [*NASDAQ symbol*] (NASQ)
EPIRB.......... Emergency Position-Indicating Radio Beacon (MCD)
EPIRBs........ Emergency Position Indicating Radio Beacons (AAGC)

EPIRBS .... Emergency Position-Indicating Radio Beacon System (SAUS)
EPIREPT ...... Epidemiological Report
EPIS .... Electronic Program Identification System (SAUS)
Epis .... Episcopal (SHCU)
EPIS .... Episcopal
EPIS .... Episiotomy [*Obstetrics*]
Epis .... Epistle (ADWA)
EPIS .... Epistle
EPIS .... Europe Presse Information Service (SAUS)
EPIS .... Exchange Price Information Service [*Finance*] [*British*]
EPIS .... Extramural Programs Information System (SAUS)
Episc .... Episcopal (DIAR)
EPISC .... Episcopal [*or Episcopalian*] (WDAA)
Episc .... Episcopalian (ADWA)
Episc .... Episcopus [*Bishop*] [*Latin*]
EPISCPL ...... Episcopal
Epist .... Epistle (ADWA)
Epist .... Epistulae [*Classical studies*] (OCD)
EPISTLE .... European Process Industries STEP Technical Liaison Executive (SAUO)
EPISTLE .... Evaluation,Preparation and Interpretation System for Text and Language Entities (SAUS)
Epistolog Graec... Epistolographi Graeci [*A publication*] (OCD)
EPISTOM ..... Epistomium [*A Stopper*] [*Pharmacy*]
EPI System... Electronic Position Indicator System (SAUS)
EPIT .... Epitaph
Epit .... Epitomae [*of Livy*] [*Classical studies*] (OCD)
Epit .... Epitome [*Classical studies*] (OCD)
EPIT .... Epitome
EPIT .... Equipment Procurement and Installation Team (PDAA)
epith .... epithelial (SAUS)
EPITH .... Epithelium [*Medicine*]
EPITH .... Epithet (ROG)
epithal .... epithalamic (SAUS)
epithal .... epithalamion (SAUS)
Epithelial Cell Biol... Epithelial Cell Biology [*London*] (SAUS)
Epitope .... Epitope, Inc. [*Associated Press*] (SAG)
Epit Oxyrh.... Epitome Oxyrhynchica [*of Livy*] [*Classical studies*] (OCD)
EPITS .... Essential Program Information, Technologies or Systems [*DoD*] (RDA)
epivag .... epivaginitis (SAUS)
Ep Jer .... Epistle of Jeremiah [*Biblical*] (RION)
EPK .... Early Prenatal Karyotype [*Medicine*] (DAVI)
EPK .... Electronic Press Kit
EPK .... Embryonic Porcine Kidney (SAUS)
EPK .... Epitek International, Inc. [*Toronto Stock Exchange symbol*]
EPK .... Equipotential Kathode
EPK .... Ethnikon Phileleftheron Komma [*National Liberal Party*] [*Greek*] (PPE)
EPK .... Ethyl Propyl Ketone (SAUS)
EPK .... Partido Comunista de Euzkadi/Euzkadiko Partidu Komunista [*Basque Communist Party*] (PPW)
E_{pk} .... Peak Voltage (IDOE)
EPKK .... Krakow/Balice [*Poland*] [*ICAO location identifier*] (ICLI)
EPKL .... European Pan-Keltic League (EA)
E_{pk-pk} .... Peak-to-Peak Voltage (IDOE)
EPL .... Early Programming Language [*Computer science*]
EPL .... Economic Policy and Licensing (SAUO)
EPL .... Economic Programming Language (SAUS)
EPL .... Edmonton Public Library [*UTLAS symbol*]
EPL .... Education for Public Library (SAUS)
EPL .... Effective Path Length (SAUS)
EPL .... Effective Patient Life (STED)
EPL .... Effective Privilege Level [*Computer science*]
EPL .... Ejercito Popular de Liberacion [*Popular Liberation Army*] [*El Salvador*] (PD)
EPL .... electrical parts list (SAUS)
EPL .... Electrical Power Level (MCD)
EPL .... Electric Power Line (SAUS)
EPL .... Electronic, Electrical, and Electromechanical Parts List (NASA)
EPL .... Electronic Intelligence Parameter Limits
EPL .... Electronic Intelligence Parameter Limits List (SAUS)
EPL .... Electronic Parameter List (SAUS)
EPL .... Electronic Parties List [*On-line version of List of Parties Excluded from Federal Procurement and Non-Procurement Programs*] (AAGC)
EPL .... Electronic Products Laboratory (IAA)
EPL .... Electronic switching system Program Language (SAUS)
EPL .... Electronic Switching Systems Programming Language [*Computer science*] (MHDB)
EPL .... Electron Projection Lithography (AAEL)
EPL .... Electron Prototype Laboratory (SAUS)
EPL .... Electroplate (MSA)
EPL .... Elliptically Polarized Light
EPL .... Embryonic Porcine Lung (SAUS)
EPL .... Emergency Power Level (KSC)
EPL .... Emitter Parameter List (SEWL)
EPL .... Emitter Position Location
EPL .... Emitter Program Library (CAAL)
EPL .... Emitter Programs Listing (CARL)
EPL .... Encoder Programming Language [*Computer science*]
EPL .... Energy Partners [*NYSE symbol*]
EPL .... Engineering Parts List (KSC)
EPL .... enhanced photoluminescence (SAUS)
EPL .... Environmental Planning Lobby [*New York*] [*Medicine*] (EDAA)
EPL .... Environmental Pollution Licensing (SAUO)
EPL .... Environmental Protection Limit (NRCH)
EPL .... Equal Protection of the Law [*Legal shorthand*] (LWAP)
EPL .... Equipment Performance Log
EPL .... Erie County Library, Erie, PA [*OCLC symbol*] (OCLC)
EPL .... Erie Public Library (SAUS)
EPL .... Essential Phospholipid [*Medicine*] (EDAA)
EPL .... European Program Library (ELAL)
EPL .... Evaluated Products List (SAUS)
EPL .... Evansville Public Library (SAUS)
EPL .... Excess Profits Levy [*British*]
EPL .... Exciter Power Logic (SAUS)
EPL .... Exclusive Prospecting License (SAUS)
EPL .... Executive Professional Leadership (AEBS)
EPL .... Express Programming Language (SAUS)
EPL .... Extensible Programming Language (SAUS)
EPL .... Extensor Pollicis Longus [*Anatomy*]
EPL .... External Plexiform Layer (STED)
epl .... extreme pressure lubricant (SAUS)
e-pl- .... Poland [*MARC geographic area code*] [*Library of Congress*] (LCCP)
EPL .... Exact Power Law (ODA)
EPLA .... Electronics Precedence List Agency
EPLA .... Eritrean People's Liberation Army [*Ethiopia*] [*Political party*] (EY)
EPLAB .... Eppley Laboratory, Inc. (SAUS)
EPLAF .... European Planning Federation [*British*] (EA)
EPLAN .... Econometric Planning Language (SAUS)
EPLAN .... Elastic Plastic Analysis (SAUS)
EPLAN .... Emergency Plan [*Environmental science*] (COE)
EPLAN .... Exonometric Planning Language (SAUS)
EPLANS .... Engineering, Planning, and Analysis Systems [*Telecommunications*] (TEL)
EPLB .... Environmental Pre-Language Battery [*Speech and language therapy*] (DAVI)
EPLD .... Electrically Programmable Logic Device [*Computer science*]
EPLD .... Enhanced Programmable Logic Device (SAUS)
EPLD .... Erasable Programmable Logic Device (NITA)
EPL/DRL ...... Engineering Parts List/Drawing Release List (KSC)
EPLF .... Eritrean People's Liberation Front [*Ethiopia*] (PD)
EPLI .... Employment Practices Liability Insurance
EPLIB .... Environment Programme Library [*Database*] [*UNEP*] [*United Nations*] (DUND)
EPLJ .... Environmental and Planning Law Journal [*Australia*] [*A publication*]
EPLO .... Electronic Plotting (SAUS)
EPLO .... Emergency Preparedness Liaison Officer (DEMM)
EPLOT .... Enhanced Performance Lasers for Optical Transmission (SAUO)
EPLP .... European Parliamentary Labor Party [*European Community*] [*Political party*]
EPLRS .... Enhanced Position Location Reporting System [*Army*] (INF)
EPLS .... Eastern Peninsula Library System [*Library network*]
EPLT .... Electocon International, Inc. [*NASDAQ symbol*] (SAG)
EPLT .... Electrocon International, Inc. [*NASDAQ symbol*] (NQ)
EPLTF .... Electrocon Intl. [*NASDAQ symbol*] (TTSB)
EPM .... Earth-Probe-Mars [*Angle*]
EPM .... Ecole Polytechnique, Bibliotheque [*Montreal*] [*UTLAS symbol*]
EPM .... Economic Performance Monitoring (OA)
EPM .... Economic Planning Machine [*British*]
EPM .... Education for Public Management [*Program*] [*Civil Service Commission*] (RDA)
EPM .... Educator's Purchasing Master [*A publication*]
EPM .... Eight Phases Modulation (VLIE)
EPM .... Elastic Plastic Membrane
EPM .... Elderfield Pyrimidine Mustard (DB)
epm .... electric pedestrian mover (SAUS)
EPM .... Electric Power Monthly [*A publication*] (GFGA)
EPM .... Electric Printing Machine (SAUS)
EPM .... Electric Printing Mechanism (SAUS)
EPM .... electric pulse motor (SAUS)
EPM .... Electronic Pacemaker [*Cardiology*] (DAVI)
EPM .... Electronic Parts Manual
EPM .... Electronic Permanent Memory (SAUS)
EPM .... Electronic Photocomposing Machine (DGA)
EPM .... Electronic Postmark (SEWL)
EPM .... Electronic Protective Measures (SAUS)
EPM .... Electron Parts Manual (SAUS)
EPM .... Electron Probe Microanalysis [*Also, EPMA*]
EPM .... Electrophoretic Mobility (STED)
EPM .... Electro Print Marking (SAUS)
EPM .... Emigration Portfolio Manager [*Investment term*]
EPM .... Empirical Pseudopotential Method [*Physics*]
EPM .... Encyclopedia of Protest Movements [*A publication*]
EPM .... Energy-Protein Malnutrition
EPM .... Engineering Procedure Memorandum [*Nuclear Regulatory Commission*] (GFGA)
EPM .... Engineering Procedures Manual
EPM .... Engineering Prototype Model (SAUS)
EPM .... Engine Peak Meter [*Automotive engineering*]
EPM .... Engine Powertrain Management [*Automotive engineering*]
EPM .... Enhanced Editor for Presentation Manager (VLIE)
EPM .... Enhanced Pulse Modulation (SAUS)
EPM .... Enterprise Performance Management (VLIE)
EPM .... Enterprise Process Management (VLIE)
EPM .... Enterprise Production Management (GART)
EPM .... Environmental Planning and Management (EERA)
EPM .... Environmental Program Manager (SAUS)
EPM .... Environmental Programme for the Mediterranean (SAUO)

EPM .... Environmental Project Manager (COE)
EPM .... Environmental Protection Management (COE)
EPM .... Environmental Protection Manual (SAUS)
EPM .... Equine protozoal myeloencephalitis (SAUS)
EPM .... Equivalent per Million (IAA)
EPM .... Equivalents per Million (DNAB)
EPM .... Ethylene-Propylene Monomer (SAUS)
EPM .... Ethylene-Propylene rubber (SAUS)
EPM .... Evolutionary Project Management (VLIE)
EPM .... Evolution Protest Movement (SAUO)
EPM .... Execute Processor Monitor (SAUS)
epm .... explosions per minute (SAUS)
EPM .... External Polarization Modulation (IEEE)
EPM .... External Protection Material (MCD)
EPM .... Extract of Particulate Matter (QDA)
EPMA .... Electronic Parts Manufacturers Association (SAUO)
EPMA .... Electronic Printing Machine (SAUS)
EPMA .... Electron Probe Microanalysis [*Also, EPM*]
EPMA .... Electron Probe Microanalyzer (SAUS)
EPMA .... Electron-Probe X-Ray Microanalysis [*Biophysics*] (QSUL)
EPMAC .... Enlisted Personnel Management Center [*Navy*] (NVT)
EPMARKUP... European Publishers' Markup User Group
EPMaRV ...... Earth Penetrating Maneuverable Reentry Vehicle [*Military*]
EPMAU .... Expected Present Multiattribute Utility (IEEE)
EPMCC .... Enesco Precious Moments Collectors' Club (EA)
EPMD .... Engineering Physics and Mathematics Division (SAUS)
EPMD .... Enlisted Personnel Management Directorate
EPMD .... Eric and Parrish Making Dollars [*Rap recording group*]
EPMF .... Employees' Plan Master File [*IRS*]
EPMFC .... Earth Potential for Manned Flight Computation (SAUS)
EPMI .... European Printer Manufactorers and Importers (SAUS)
EPMIS .... Emergency Preparedness Management Information System (SAUS)
EPMMA .... European Proprietary Medicines Manufacturers Association [*Belgium*] (EAIO)
EPMP .... Emergency Preparedness Management Plan [*Environmental science*] (COE)
EPMP .... Ethyl(para-Nitrophenyl)methylphosphonate [*Biochemistry*]
EPMR .... Embarked Personnel Material Report [*Navy*] (ANA)
EPMS .... Electronic Publishing Management System
EPMS .... Engineering Performance Management System (NASA)
EPMS .... Engineering Performance Measurement System (MCD)
EPMS .... Engineering Project Management System (MCD)
EPMS .... Engine Performance Monitoring System (MCD)
EPMS .... Enlisted Personnel Management System [*Army*] (AABC)
EPMU .... Environmental and Preventive Medicine Unit (SAUO)
EPN .... Early Public Notification (FOTI)
EPN .... Effective Perceived Noise [*Aviation*]
EPN .... Electronic-highway Platform Netherlands (SAUS)
EPN .... Engineering Part Number [*Automotive engineering*]
EPN .... Engineering Program Notice (AFIT)
EPN .... Epena [*Congo*] [*Airport symbol*] (OAG)
EPN .... Epoxidized Phenol Novolac (SAUS)
EPN .... Epoxy Phenol Novolac (SAUS)
epn .... ethyl paranitrophenyl (SAUS)
EPN .... Ethyl-Para-Nitrophenyl Phenylphosphonothioate [*An insecticide*]
EPN .... Ethyl-P-Nitrophenyl Phenylphosphorothioate (SAUS)
EPN .... Excitatory Premotor Neuron [*Neurology*]
EPN .... Extended Parliamentary Network
EPN .... external point name (SAUS)
EPN .... External Priority Number [*Computer science*] (OA)
epnd .... effective-perceived noise decibels (SAUS)
epndB .... Effective Perceived Noise Decibel [*Electronics*] (MED)
EPNdB .... Effective-Perceived-Noise Decibel Level [*Aviation*]
EPNdB .... Effective Perceived Noise level dB (SAUS)
EPNDB .... Effective Perceived Noise-level Decibels (SAUS)
EPNdB .... Effective Perceived Noise Level in Decibels (SAUS)
EPNdB .... Equivalent Perceived Noise Level in Decibels (SAUS)
EPNDbL .... Effective Perceived Noise Decibel Level (SAUS)
EPNG .... El Paso Natural Gas (SAUS)
EPNI .... effective perceived noise level (SAUS)
EPNL .... Effective-Perceived-Noise Level [*Aviation*]
EPNL .... Equivalent Perceived Noise Level (SAUS)
EPNLDB .... Effective Perceived Noise-Level Decibel [*Aviation*] (IIA)
EPN Level.... Effective Perceived Noise Level (SAUS)
EPNP .... Epoxy(nitrophenoxy)propane [*Organic chemistry*]
EPNS .... Electroplated Nickel Silver
EPNS .... English Place-Name Society
EPO .... Centers for Disease Control and Prevention. Epidemiology Program Office (SAUO)
EPO .... Earth Parking Orbit [*Apollo*] [*NASA*]
EPO .... Ekco Products Co. (SAUO)
EPO .... Elected Public Official
EPO .... Electron Plasma Oscillation [*Astrophysics*]
EPO .... Electrostatic Plasma Oscillator
EPO .... Element Project Office [*NASA*] (NASA)
EPO .... Emergency Planning Office [*Environmental science*] (COE)
EPO .... Emergency Planning Officer [*Army*]
EPO .... Emergency Power Off
EPO .... Energy Policy Office [*Formerly, National Energy Office*] [*Executive Office of the President*] [*Abolished, 1974*]
EPO .... Energy Program Office (SAUO)
EPO .... Engine Project Office [*NASA*] (KSC)
EPO .... Engine Propeller Order (MSA)
EPO .... Enlisted Programs Officer (DNAB)
EPO .... Enterprise Profit Optimization
EPO .... Environmental, Population, and Organismic Biology
EPO .... environmental protection officer (SAUS)
EPO .... Eosinophil Peroxidase [*An enzyme*]
EPO .... EOS Project Office (SAUO)
EPO .... Epichlorohydrin Ethylene Oxide [*Organic chemistry*]
EPO .... Epidemiology Program Office [*Department of Health and Human Services*] (GRD)
EPO .... Erythropoietin [*Also, Ep*] [*Hematology*]
EPO .... Estuarine Programs Office [*National Oceanic and Atmospheric Administration*]
EPO .... European Patent Office [*Germany*] (PDAA)
EPO .... European Patent Organisation (HEAS)
EPO .... European Policy Office of WWF (SAUO)
EPO .... European Political Organization (SAUO)
EPO .... Evershed Power Optics (SAUS)
EPO .... Examination Procedure Outline [*Weighing equipment*]
EPO .... Exclusive Provider Organization [*Medicine*]
EPO .... Experimental Processing Operation (SAUS)
EPO .... Experiment Performance Option
EPO .... Expiratory Port Occlusion (STED)
EPO .... Expo Oil [*Vancouver Stock Exchange symbol*]
e-po- .... Portugal [*MARC geographic area code*] [*Library of Congress*] (LCCP)
EPOA .... Eastcoast Petroleum Operators' Association [*Canada*]
EPOA .... Exercise Plan of Analysis (MCD)
EPOA .... External Plant Operators' Association of South Australia
EPOC .... Early Parts on Change (SAUS)
EPOC .... Earthquake Prediction Observation Centre (SAUO)
EPOC .... Eastern Pacific Oceanic Conference
EPOC .... Eastern Pacific Oceanographic Conference (SAUO)
EPOC .... Employers' Perceptions of Colleges (AIE)
EPOC .... Employment Policy and Organization Committee [*British*] (DCTA)
EPOC .... Engineering Parts on Change (SAUS)
EPOC .... Engineers Procurement Office (SAUO)
EPOC .... Environment Protection Policy (EERA)
EPOC .... Equity Policy Center (EA)
EPOC .... Erythropoietic Protoporphyria (SAUS)
EPOC .... ESCAP [*Economic and Social Commission for Asia and the Pacific*] Pacific Operations Center [*Vanuatu*]
EPOC .... ESCAP Pacific Operations Centre (SAUS)
EPOC .... Evening Primrose Oil Capsules [*Trade name*] [*British*]
EPOC .... External Payload Operations Center
EPOCA .... Environmental Project on Central America [*Defunct*] (EA)
EPOCH .... Early Parts On Change Hold (SAUS)
EPOCH .... Educational Programming of Cultural Heritage (AEBS)
EPOCH .... European Programme for Climatology and Natural Hazards (SAUO)
EPOCH .... European Programme on Climate and Hazards (SAUS)
EPOCH .... European Programme on Climate and Natural Hazards (SAUS)
EPOCH .... European Programme on Climatology and natural Hazards (SAUO)
EPOCS .... Easten Pacific Ocean Climate Study (SAUO)
EPOCS .... Equatorial Pacific Ocean Climate Studies [*National Oceanic and Atmospheric Administration*]
Epod .... Epodi [*of Horace*] [*Classical studies*] (OCD)
EPOE .... End Piece of Equipment
EPOI .... Ehrenreich Photo-Optical Industries, Inc.
EPOL .... Elementary Procedure Oriented Language (VLIE)
EPOL .... Entirely Pulled-Out Length (VLIE)
EPOMA .... Explosive and Pyrotechnic Ordnance Manufacturing Association (SAUO)
EPOP .... Each Pays Own Postage
EPOP .... ESA Polar Orbiting Platform (SAUS)
EPOP .... European Polar-Orbiting Platform (EOSA)
EPOQUE .... European Parliament On-Line Query System (SAUO)
EPOR .... Electronics Performance and Operational Report (DNAB)
EPOR .... Erythropoietin Receptor [*Hematology*]
EPORT .... Eastport, ID [*American Association of Railroads railroad junction routing code*]
EPOS .... Earthquake Phenomena Observation System [*Japan*] (USDC)
EPOS .... Electronic Point-of-Sale [*Computer science*]
EPOS .... Engineered Plastics on Screen (SAUS)
EPOS .... Engineering and Project-Management Oriented Support (VLIE)
EPOS .... Engineering and Project management Oriented Support system (SAUS)
EPOS .... Epson Praxis-Orientiertes Text-System (SAUS)
EPOS .... European Pediatric Orthopaedic Society (SAUS)
EPOS .... European Polarstern Study (SAUS)
EPOS .... European Pool of/on Studies and Analysis (SAUO)
EPOS .... European PTT Open Learning System (SAUO)
EPOSS .... Environmental Protection Oil Sands Systems (PDAA)
EPOW .... Emergency Power Off Warning (SAUS)
EPOW .... Enemy Prisoners of War (SAUO)
EPOW .... Extraction Procedure for Oily Wastes [*Environmental science*] (COE)
EPP .... Concord, NH [*Location identifier*] [*FAA*] (FAAL)
EPP .... Earth Physics Program
EPP .... Editions Phonographiques Parisiennes - Allegro Label [*Record label*] [*France*]
EPP .... Educable sur le plan pratique (SAUS)
EPP .... Education Purchase Plan (SAUS)
EPP .... Effective Program Projections
EPP .... Electrical Power Panel (MCD)
EPP .... Electric Power Plant (MCD)
EPP .... Electromagnetic Wave Propagation Panel (SAUS)
EPP .... Electronic Packaging and Production (SAUS)
EPP .... Electronic Postproduction (NTCM)
EPP .... Electronic Publishers Partners (SAUS)
EPP .... Electron Pair Production (VLIE)

EPP .... Electrostatic Plotter/Printer (SAUS)
EPP .... Emergency Power Package (NG)
EPP .... Emergency Preparedness Plan (SAUS)
EPP .... Employee Protection Program (SAUS)
EPP .... End Plate Potential
EPP .... End Point Prediction
EPP .... Energy Policy and Planning (SAUS)
EPP .... Energy Policy Project (SAUO)
EPP .... Engineered Polypropylene [*Plastics*] [*Automotive engineering*]
EPP .... Engineering and Public Policy [*Graduate program, Carnegie-Mellon University*]
EPP .... Enhanced Parallel Port (PCM)
EPP .... Enhanced Parallel Protocol (SAUS)
EPP .... Enron Global Power & Pipeline Co. [*NYSE symbol*] (SAG)
EPP .... Enron Global Pwr/Pipeln LLC [*NYSE symbol*] (TTSB)
EPP .... Environmental Professional Page (SAUO)
EPP .... Environmental Protection Authority [*Atmosphere*] (ATR)
EPP .... Environmental Protection Program (CAAL)
EPP .... Environment Protection Program (EERA)
EPP .... Epiphyseal Plate [*Medicine*] (MELL)
EPP .... Epistolae [*Epistles, Letters*] [*Latin*] (ROG)
EPP .... Equal Payment Plan
EPP .... Equal Pressure Point (MAE)
EPP .... Equipment Procurement Program (SAUO)
EPP .... Erythropoietic Protoporphyria [*A genetic disorder*]
EPP .... Estimating Price Policy
EPP .... Ethernet Packet Processor (CDE)
EPP .... European Pallet Pool (PDAA)
EPP .... European People's Party - Federation of Christian Democratic Parties of the European Community [*Brussels, Belgium*]
EPP .... European Producer Price
EPP .... Evangelical People's Party (Netherlands) [*Political party*] (PSAP)
EPP .... Excess Personal Property
EPP .... Exchangeable-Potassium-Percentage
EPP .... Executive Peachpack (SAUS)
EPP .... Executive Pension Plan (ODBW)
EPP .... Executive Plan Program (ACAE)
EPP .... Extra-Pair Paternity [*Biology*]
EPP .... Eysenck Personality Profiler [*Psychology*]
E_{p-p} .... Peak-to-Peak Voltage (IDOE)
EPPA .... Emissions Prediction and Policy Analysis
EPPA .... Employee Polygraph Protection Act of 1988
EPPA .... Established Pattern of Psychodynamic Adaptation
EPPA .... Established Pattern of Psychodynamic Adaption (SAUS)
EPPAA .... European Pure Phosphoric Acid Producers' Association [*Belgium*] (EAIO)
EPPAPA .... European Pure Phosphoric Acid Producers' Association [*Belgium*] (EAIO)
EPPASF .... Elvis Presley Performing Arts Scholarship Foundation (EA)
EPPASFV .... Elvis Presley Performing Arts Scholarship Foundation of Virginia [*Later, EPPASF*] (EA)
EP/PB .... Electroplated / Pressure Bonded (SAUS)
EPPB .... End Positive-Pressure Breathing (MELL)
EPPB .... Export Promotion Programme Budget [*British*]
EPPC .... Edge Physics and Particle Control (SAUS)
EPPC .... Ethics and Public Policy Center (EA)
EPPC .... European Palaeobotanical and Palynological Conference (SAUO)
EPPCMM .... European Printing and Paper Converting Machinery Manufacturers (SAUS)
EPPCO .... Environmental Pollution Processors Corporation (SAUO)
EPPCO .... Environmental Pollution Processors Corporation, Hudson, Ohio (SAUS)
EPPD .... Energy Planning and Policy Development (SAUS)
EPPD .... Entomology and Plant Pathology Division (SAUO)
EPPD .... Estate Planning for Persons with Disabilities [*An association*] (PAZ)
EPPD .... Externally Powered Prosthetic Device (SAUS)
EPPHI .... Educators of Professional Personnel for the Hearing Impaired
EPPI .... Eastern Pennsylvania Psychiatric Institute
EPPI .... Electronic Plan Position Indicator (IAA)
EPPI .... Electronic Programmed Procurement Information (NG)
EPPI .... Enhanced Programmable Peripheral Interface (SAUS)
EPPI .... Expanded Plan-Position Indicator (MED)
EPPIA .... Ecumenical Peace Program in Asia (SAUO)
EPPIC .... Early Psychosis Prevention and Intervention Centre [*Australia*]
EPPIC .... Educate People - Protect Innocent Children [*Defunct*] (EA)
EPPIP .... Environmental Protection Program Implementation Plan (SAUS)
EPPK .... Derma: Epidermolysis Palmoplantar Keratoderma (SAUS)
EPPK .... Epidermolytic Palmoplantar Keratoderma [*Medicine*]
EPPL .... Electronic Preferred Parts List [*Jet Propulsion Laboratory, NASA*]
EPPL .... El Paso Public Library (SAUS)
EPPL .... Emergency Production Planning List [*Army*]
EPPL .... Environmental Planning And Programming Language (SAUS)
EPPL .... Epithelial Possibly Precancerous Lesion
EPPL .... Excess Personal Property List
EPPMA .... Expanded Polystyrene Product Manufacturers' Association [*British*] (BI)
EPPO .... Earth Physics and Physical Oceanography Program [*NASA*]
EPPO .... Emergency Planning Office of Ontario (SAUS)
EPPO .... European and Mediterranean Plant Protection Organization [*See also OEPP*] (EAIO)
EPPO .... European Plant Protection Organization (SAUS)
EPPO .... Poznan/Lawica [*Poland*] [*ICAO location identifier*] (ICLI)
EPPO Program... Earth Physics and Physical Oceanography Program (SAUS)
EPPP .... Electronic Publications Pilot Project [*National Library of Canada*]
EPPP .... Emergency Production Planning Program [*Navy*] (NG)
EPPP .... Employee Profit Participation Plan (SAUS)
EPPP .... Examination for Professional Psychology Programs (DIPS)
EPPPI .... Expanded Partial Plan Position Indicator (IAA)
EPPR .... Emergency Prevention, Preparedness and Response (SAUS)
EPPR .... Engineering Procurement Proposal Request (SAUS)
EPPR .... Environmental Protection Agency Procurement Regulations [*A publication*] (AAGC)
EPPRP .... Emergency Planning, Preparedness, and Response Program [*Environmental science*] (COE)
EPPS .... Edwards Personality Preference Schedule (SAUS)
EPPS .... Edwards Personal Preference Scale [*or Schedule*] [*Psychology*]
EPPS .... Edwards Personal Preference Schedule (SAUS)
EPPS .... Electrical Power/Pyro Sequential System (MCD)
EPPS .... Electronic Page Printing System (SAUS)
EPPS .... Electronic Pipe Proving System (SAUO)
EPPS .... Electronic Pre Press Systems (SAUS)
EPPS .... Electronic Publishing and Prepress Systems (DGA)
EPPs .... End-Plate Potentials [*Medicine*] (EDAA)
EPPS .... Engineering Procurement Planning Sheet (SAUS)
EPPs .... Enhanced Parallel Ports [*Computer science*]
EPPS .... Ethylpiperazinepropanesulfonic Acid (SAUS)
EPPS .... Expedited Passenger Processing System (FOTI)
EPPT .... Electrical Power Production Technician (IAA)
EPPT .... European Printer Performance Test (ODBW)
EPPTS .... Electrical Power Production Technician Specialist (SAUS)
EPPT/S .... Electrical Power Production Technician/Specialist (AAG)
EPPVS .... Emergency Propulsive Propellant Venting System
EPQ .... Economic Production Quantity (AAGC)
EPQ .... Economic Purchasing Quantity (SAUS)
EPQ .... Educational Process Questionnaire [*Institute for Behavioral Research in Creativity*] (TES)
EPQ .... Embarrassing Personal Question [*National Security Agency screening procedure*]
EPQ .... Engineering Qualification Trials (DOMA)
EPQ .... European Parliamentary Question (EURO)
EPQ .... Eysenck Personality Questionnaire [*Personality development test*] [*Psychology*]
EPQM .... European Foundation for Quality Management (SAUO)
EPR .... Early Progressive Resistance [*Medicine*] (EDAA)
EPR .... Earnings Price Ratio
epr .... earnings-to-price ratio (SAUS)
EPR .... Eastern Pakistan Rifles [*British military*] (DMA)
EPR .... Eastern Public Radio Network (SAUS)
EPR .... Eastern Punjab Railway [*Indian Railway*] (TIR)
EPR .... East Pacific Rise [*Geology*]
EPR .... Economic Production Rate (MCD)
EPR .... Education in Personal Relationships (AIE)
EPR .... Effective Production Rate (SAUS)
EPR .... Effector-Cell Protease Receptor [*Biochemistry*]
EPR .... Einstein-Podolsky-Rosen [*Quantum mechanics*]
EPR .... Einstein-Podolsky-Rosen experiment (SAUS)
EPR .... electon paragmagnetic resonance (SAUS)
EPR .... Electrical Pressure Regulator (IEEE)
epr .... electric propulsion rocket (SAUS)
EPR .... Electrochemical Potentiokinetic Reactivation [*Metallurgical test*]
EPR .... Electromechanical Potentiokinetic Reactivation Test [*Nuclear energy*] (NRCH)
epr .... electronic paramagnetic resonance (SAUS)
EPR .... Electronic Parts Reliability
EPR .... Electronic Planning and Research (SAUS)
EPR .... Electronic Procurement Regulation [*Defense Supply Agency*]
EPR .... Electron Paramagnetic Resonance [*Also, ESR*] [*Physics*]
EPR .... Electro-Phonetic Resistor (SAUS)
EPR .... Electrophrenic Respiration [*Medicine*]
EPR .... Elimination of Purchase Requirement [*Department of Agriculture*]
EPR .... El Paraiso Resources Ltd. [*Vancouver Stock Exchange symbol*]
EPR .... Emergency Parts Requisition (KSC)
EPR .... Emergency Personnel Record (SAUS)
EPR .... Emergency Physical Restraint [*Medicine*] (DAVI)
EPR .... EMI Prevention Rule (SAUS)
EPR .... Engineering Parts Release (KSC)
EPR .... Engineering Planning Report
EPR .... Engineering Power Reactor
EPR .... Engineering Purchase Request (SAUS)
EPR .... Engineer Photographic and Reproduction [*Marine Corps*]
EPR .... Engine Power [*or Pressure*] Ratio
EPR .... Engine Pressure Ratio (GAVI)
EPR .... Enlisted Performance Report (SAUS)
EPR .... Enriched Pulverised Refuse (PDAA)
EPR .... Entertainment Properties Tr [*NYSE symbol*] (SG)
EPR .... Entry Point Register (SAUS)
EPR .... Environmental Policy Research (SAUO)
EPR .... equal pressure point (SAUS)
EPR .... Equipment Performance Report
EPR .... Equipment Performance Requirement (SAUS)
EPR .... Equipotential Region
EPR .... Equivalent Parallel Resistance (DEN)
EPR .... Equivalent Parallel Resistor (SAUS)
EPR .... Error Pattern Register
EPR .... Error-Prone Repair (GNE)
EPR .... Esperance [*Australia*] [*Airport symbol*] (OAG)
EPR .... Essential Performance Requirements (NATG)
EPR .... Estimated Price Request (MCD)
EPR .... Estradiol Production Rate [*Endocrinology*] (MAE)
EPR .... Ethylene-propylene Resin (SAUS)

EPR............. Ethylene Propylene Rubber [*Organic chemistry*]
EPR............. European Pressurized Watercooled Reactor (SAUS)
EPR............. Evaluation Project Report [*Air Force*]
EPR............. Evaporator Pressure Regulator (DNAB)
EPR............. Excess Parts Request (SAUS)
EPR............. Exhaust Pressure Ratio
EPR............. Exhaust Pressure Regulator [*Automotive engineering*]
EPR............. Experimental Power Reactor (MCD)
EPR............. Explosion-Proof Relay
EPR............. Expreso Aereo [*Peru*] [*ICAO designator*] (FAAC)
EPR............. External Power Relay (MCD)
EPR............. Extreme Pressure Ratio [*Military*]
EPR............. Eye Point of Regard [*NASA*]
EPR............. WHO Panafrican Centre for Emergency Preparednees and Response (SAUO)
EPRA............ Early Planning for Retirement (SAUS)
EPRA............ Eastern Psychiatric Research Association (EA)
EPRA............ Economic Policy Resource Center (SAUO)
EPRA............ Electronic Production Resources Agency [*Military*]
EPRA............ European Phenolic Resins Association (SAUS)
ePRAI........... Escherichia Coli Phosphoribosyl Anthranilate Isomerase
EPRC............ Educational Policy Research Center (SAUS)
EPRC............ European Policies Research Centre [*University of Strathclyde*] [*Glasgow, Scotland*] [*Database producer*] (IID)
EPRCA........... Enhanced Proportional Rate Control Algorithm
EPRD............ Electrical Power Requirements Data
EPRD............ Emergency Plans and Readiness Division [*of OEP*] [*Terminated*]
EPRDC........... Electric Power Research and Development Center (SAUO)
EPRDCC.......... Electric Power Resources Development Coordination Council (SAUO)
EPRDF........... Ethiopian People's Revolutionary Democratic Front [*Political party*] (ECON)
EPR-DPG......... East Pacific Rise Detailed Planning Group (SAUO)
EP Record....... Extended Playing Record (SAUS)
EPRF............ Energy Probe Research Foundation [*Canada*] (IRC)
EPRF............ Environmental Prediction Research Facility [*Monterey, CA*] [*Navy*]
EPRF............ Exhausted Publications Reference File (MCD)
EPRG............ Emergency Planning Review Guideline [*Nuclear energy*] (NRCH)
EPR/G........... End-Paper Rubbed, Else Good [*Condition*] [*Antiquarian book trade*]
EPRI............ Electric Power Research Institute [*Palo Alto, CA*] (ECON)
EPRI............ Electronic Power Research Institute (SAUS)
EPRI............ Engine Pressure Ratio Indicator
EPRI............ Environmental Protection Research Institute
EPRICS.......... Emergency Power Ride through Capability System [*Nuclear energy*] (NUCP)
EPRI-HVTRC...... Electric Power Research Institute, High Voltage Transmission Research Center [*Research center*] (RCD)
E-print......... Electronic Print (ADWA)
EPRI RDS........ Electric Power Research Institute - Research and Development Information System (SAUS)
EPRI RDS........ EPRI Research and Development Information System (NITA)
EPRI RDS........ EPRI research and development information system (SAUS)
EPRL............ Electric Power Research Laboratory [*Arizona State University*] [*Research center*] (RCD)
EPRL............ Warszawa [*Poland*] [*ICAO location identifier*] (ICLI)
EPRLF........... Eelam People's Revolutionary Liberation Front [*Sri Lanka*] [*Political party*]
EPRM............ Equipment Performance Report Management System (MCD)
EPRN............ Eastern Public Radio Network (NTCM)
EPRN............ Emergency Program Release Notice [*NASA*] (NASA)
EPRO............ Eastern Professional River Outfitters Association (EA)
EPRO............ Etudes Preliminaires aux Religions Orientales dans l'Empire Romain [*A publication*] (BJA)
EPROI........... Expected Project Return on Investment [*Finance*] (PDAA)
EPROM........... Electrically Programmable Read-Only Memory [*Computer science*] (MCD)
EPROM........... Electronically Programmable Read Only Memory (SAUS)
EPROM........... erasable and programmable read only memory (SAUS)
EPROM........... Erasable Programmable Read-Only Memory [*Computer science*] (MCD)
EPROM........... Erasable Programmable ROM (SAUS)
E-PROM.......... Erasable PROM (SAUS)
EPRP............ Employee Problem Resolution Procedure (ACAE)
EPRP............ Ethiopian People's Revolutionary Party [*Political party*] (PD)
EPRS............ Effective Projected Radiant Surface (SAUS)
EPRS............ Egyptian Periodontal Restorative Society (SAUS)
EPRS............ Electron Paramagnetic Resonance Spectroscopy
EPRS............ Electron Pulse Radiolysis System [*Medicine*] (MELL)
EPRS............ Engineering Proposal Requirement Specification (SAUS)
EPRS............ Eprise Corp. [*NASDAQ symbol*] (SG)
EPRT............ Engine Pressure Ratio Transmitter (HLLA)
EPRTCS.......... Emergency Power Ride-Through Capability System [*Nuclear energy*] (NRCH)
EPR Technique... Equi-Potential Ring Technique (SAUS)
ePrv............ Enolpyruvate [*Biochemistry*]
EPRY............ East Penn Railways [*Federal Railroad Administration identification code*]
EPRZ............ Rzeszow/Jasionka [*Poland*] [*ICAO location identifier*] (ICLI)
EPS............. Acute Extrapyramidal Syndrome [*Medicine*]
EPS............. Early Production System (SAUS)
EPS............. Early Prolific Straightneck Summer Squash
EPS............. Earnings per Share [*Finance*]
EPS............. Earth and Planetary Sciences (SAUO)
EPS............. Earth-Probe-Sun [*Angle*]
EPS............. Econometric Programme System (SAUO)
EPS............. Economic Programming System (SAUS)
EPS............. Editor Press Service (SAUO)
EPS............. Educational Policy Studies (SAUO)
EPS............. Educational Products Strategy (TIMI)
EPS............. Elastosis Perforans Serpiginosa [*Medicine*]
EPS............. Electrical Power Storage (ROG)
EPS............. Electrical Power Supply
EPS............. Electrical Power System [*or Subsystem*]
EPS............. Electrical Power System (Subsystem) (SAUS)
EPS............. Electrical Programmed Stimulation [*Medicine*] (CPH)
EPS............. Electric Pencil System (SAUS)
EPS............. Electric Power Source (MCD)
EPS............. Electric Power Steering System [*Automotive engineering*]
EPS............. Electric Power Storage (SAUS)
EPS............. Electric Power Subsystem (SAUS)
EPS............. Electric Power Supply (SAUS)
EPS............. Electric Power System [*or Subsystem*] (NRCH)
EPS............. Electric Propulsion System
EPS............. Electric Protection Services (EFIS)
EPS............. Electrochemical Photocapacitance Spectroscopy
EPS............. Electromagnetic Position Sensor
EPS............. Electronic Payments System
EPS............. Electronic Performance Support [*Training term*] (LPT)
EPS............. Electronic Permanent Store (SAUS)
EPS............. Electronic Plate Scanner (DGA)
EPS............. Electronic Power Shift (SAUS)
EPS............. Electronic Power Steering [*Mitsubishi*] [*Automotive engineering*]
EPS............. Electronic Prepress System (DGA)
EPS............. Electronic Programmable Speedometer
EPS............. Electronic Protection System (IIA)
EPS............. Electronic Publishing System (BYTE)
EPS............. Electron-Proton Spectrometer
EPS............. Electrophoresis Power Supply (SAUS)
EPS............. Electrophysiologic Study
EPS............. Electropneumatic Gear Shift [*System*]
EPS............. electro-pneumatic shift control (SAUS)
EPS............. Electrostatic Powder Spraying (SAUS)
EPS............. El Paso Southern Railway Co. [*AAR code*]
EPS............. Email Postal Software [*Computer science*]
EPS............. Embedded and Personal Systems
EPS............. Embedded PServer (SAUS)
EPS............. Embossing Press Station
EPS............. Emergency Pest Suppression (WPI)
EPS............. Emergency Power Subsystem (SAUS)
EPS............. Emergency Power Supply
EPS............. Emergency Power System
EPS............. Emergency Preparedness Staff [*Office of Solid Waste and Emergency Response*] (COE)
EPS............. Emergency Pressurization System
EPS............. Emergency Pressurizing System (SAUS)
EPS............. Emergency Procurement Service [*Later, Defense Materials Service*]
EPS............. Emotional Problems Scales [*Test*] (TMMY)
EPS............. Encapsulated Post-Script [*Computer science*]
EPS............. Encapsulated PostScript File [*Computer science*] (EERA)
EPS............. Encapsulated PostScript (file name extension) (SAUS)
EPS............. Encapsulated Postscript Image Format (AAEL)
EPS............. Encoder Power Supply
EPS............. Endoscopic Paravariceal Sclerotherapy [*Medicine*]
EPS............. Energetic Particle Sensor (ACAE)
EPS............. Energetic Particles Satellite [*NASA*] (MUGU)
EPS............. Engineered Performance Standards (SAUS)
EPS............. Engineering & Professional Services Inc. (SAUS)
EPS............. Engineering Performance Standards
EPS............. Engineering Planning Skeleton (MCD)
EPS............. Engineering Print System [*Xerox*]
EPS............. Engineering Procedures Services (MCD)
EPS............. Engineering Process Specification (SAUS)
EPS............. Engineering Product Description (SAUS)
EPS............. Engineering Purchase Specification
EPS............. English Philological Studies (journ.) (SAUS)
EPS............. Enterprise Parallel Server (SAUS)
EPS............. Entertainment Production Services [*British*]
EPS............. Entry Processing Station (SAUS)
EPS............. Environmental Priorities Strategies [*Volvo*] [*Automotive engineering*]
EPS............. Environmental Protection Service, West Vancouver [*Environment Canada*] [*Research center*] (RCD)
EPS............. Environmental Protection Shelter (MCD)
EPS............. Environmental Protection Specialist (SAUO)
EPS............. Environmental Protection System (AAG)
EPS............. Environmental Purification Systems, Inc.
EPS............. Enzyme Pancreatic Secretion [*Medicine*] (MELL)
EPS............. Epps Air Service, Inc. [*ICAO designator*] (FAAC)
EPS............. Equilibrium Problem Solver (IEEE)
EPS............. Equipment Policy Statement [*Army*] (AABC)
EPS............. Equipotential Surface
EPS............. Equivalent Point Source (SAUS)
EPS............. Equivalent Prior Sample [*Information*] [*Statistics*]
EPS............. Escape Propulsion System (SAUS)
EPS............. Essay-Proof Society (EA)
EPS............. Ethiopian Philatelic Society (EA)
EPS............. Ethiopian Postal Service (SAUS)
EPS............. Eumetsat Polar System (SAUS)
EPS............. European Passenger Services [*British*] (ECON)
EPS............. European Physical Society (EAIO)
EPS............. European Polar Satellite
EPS............. European Polar Segment (SAUS)

EPS............ European Polar System (SAUS)
EPS............ Evaluation Planning System (SAUS)
EPS............ Even Parity Select
EPS............ Event Processing System
EPS............ Excitation Power Supply (MCD)
EPS............ Executive Picture Show (SAUS)
EPS............ Executive Planning Section [*British military*] (DMA)
EPS............ Executive Profile Survey [*Management and supervision test*]
EPS............ Executive Protection Service [*Soviet*] (CARL)
EPS............ Executive Protective Service [*Formerly, White House Police; later, USSS/UD*]
EPS............ Exercise Planning Staff [*NATO*] (NATG)
EPS............ Exercise Production System (SAUS)
EPS............ Exocellular Polysaccharide [*Biochemistry*]
EPS............ Exophthalmos-Producing Substance [*Endocrinology*]
EPS............ Exotic Pathology Society [*Paris, France*] (EAIO)
EPS............ Expandable [*or Expanded*] Polystyrene [*Plastics Technology*]
eps............ expanded polystyrene (SAUS)
EPS............ Experimental Power Supply (NASA)
EPS............ Experimental Procurement Service
EPS............ Experimental Prototype Silo (SAA)
EPS............ Experimental Psychology Society [*British*]
EPS............ Experimental Publications System [*Defunct*]
EPS............ Experiment Pointing System [*NASA*]
EPS............ experiment protection subsystem (SAUS)
EPS............ Exploration Procedure Systems (SAUO)
EPS............ Export Promotion Services (JAGO)
EPS............ Expressed Prostatic Secretion [*Physiology*]
EPS............ Extended Polar Satellite (SAUS)
EPS............ Extensible Programming System [*Computer science*] (CSR)
EPS............ External Page Storage [*Computer science*] (BUR)
EPS............ Extracellular Polysaccharide [*Medicine*] (EDAA)
EPS............ extrapyramidalmotorisches System (SAUS)
EPS............ Extrapyramidal Side-Effect [*Syndrome*] [*Medicine*] (DB)
EPS............ Extrapyramidal Symptoms [*Medicine*]
EPS............ Extrapyramidal Syndrome [*Neurology and psychiatry*] (DAVI)
EPS............ Extruded Polystyrene (SAUS)
EPS............ Eye Protection Shutter
EPS............ Ezra Pound Society (EA)
EPS............ Primary Earnings per Share (SAUS)
EPS............ Sandinista Popular Army (Nicaragua) [*Political party*] (PSAP)
EPSA............ Early Page Space Allocation [*Computer science*] (VERA)
EPSA............ Educational Program in Systems Analysis (RDA)
EPSA............ Electrostatic Particle Size Analyzer
EPSA............ Elevated Prostate-Specific Antigen [*Medicine*] (MELL)
EPSA............ Energy Products and Services Administration (SAUS)
EPSA............ Energy Products and Services Association (NTPA)
EPSA............ European Pharmaceutical Students Association (SAUO)
EPSAL............ Elevated Prostate-Specific Antigen Level [*Medicine*] (MELL)
EPS Angle... Earth-Probe-Sun Angle (SAUS)
EPSAT............ Estimation of Precipitation from Satellite (SAUS)
EPSAT............ Evaluation des Pluies par Satellite (SAUO)
EPSC............ Emergency Petroleum Supply Committee [*Terminated, 1976*] (EA)
EPSC............ EPSCO, Inc. [*NASDAQ symbol*] (COMM)
EPSC............ Ethiopian Peace and Solidarity Committee (SAUS)
EPSC............ Excitatory Postsynaptic Current [*Neurophysiology*]
EPSCG............ European Parliamentary and Scientific Contact Group (SAUO)
EPSCG............ Groupe de Contact Parlementaire et Scientifique [*European Parliamentary and Scientific Contact Group*] (EA)
EPSCoR............ Experimental Program to Stimulate Competitive Research [*National Science Foundation*]
EPSCS............ Enhanced Private Shared Communications Service (GART)
EPSCS............ Enhanced Private Switched Communications Service [*Pronounced "ep-sis"*] [*AT & T*]
EPSD............ Electronics and Power Sources Directorate [*Army*] (RDA)
EPSD............ E-Point to Septal Distance (DB)
EPSDT............ Early and Periodic Screening, Diagnosis, and Treatment
EPSDT............ Early Periodic Screening Diagnosis Treatment (SAUO)
EPSDU............ Experimental Process System Development Unit [*Photovoltaic energy systems*]
EPSE............ Encapsulated Postscript Format [*Computer science*] (AGLO)
EPSE............ extrapyramidal side-effects (SAUS)
EPSEIS............ Encyclopedia of Physical Sciences and Engineering Information Sources [*A publication*]
EPSEP............ Environmental Protection, Safety and Emergency Planning (SAUS)
EPSF............ Early Postsurgical Fitting [*Medicine*]
EPSF............ Employee Profile Security File [*IRS*]
EPSF............ Encapsulated Post-Script Draw Format [*Computer science*]
EPSF............ Encapsulated PostScript File [*Computer science*] (CIST)
EPSF............ Encapsulated Postscript File Format (SAUS)
EPSF............ Encapsulated PostScript Format (SAUS)
EPSF............ Expenditure Per Sortie Factor (SAUS)
EPSFC............ Ethiopian Peace, Solidarity and Friendship Committee (SAUS)
EPSG............ Electronic Publishing Specialist Group (NITA)
EPSG............ Epiphytic Plant Study Group [*British*] (DBA)
EPSG............ European Pineal Study Group (EAIO)
EPSI............ Device Independent Encapsulated PostScript (SAUS)
EPSI............ Earnings per Share Issued [*Finance*]
EPSI............ Encapsulated PostScript Interchange [*Computer science*] (VERA)
EPSI............ Encapsulated Postscript Interchange Format (SAUS)
EPSI............ Energy and Process Systems Inc. (SAUO)
EPSI............ Erikson Psychosocial Stage Inventory [*Psychology*]
EPSIA............ Eastern Professional Ski Instructors Association [*Formerly, EPSTI*] (EA)
EPSIG............ Electronic Publishing Special Interest Group [*Association of American Publishers*]
EPSILON...... Evaluation of Printed Subject Indexes by Laboratory Investigation (SAUS)
EPSIS............ Educational Programs and Studies Information Service (SAUS)
EPSIS............ Education Program and Studies Information Services (SAUS)
EPSL............ Eastern Primary Standards Laboratory
EPSL............ Emergency Power Switching Logic (NRCH)
EPSLN............ Epsilon
EPS Logic.... Execute Processor Start Logic (SAUS)
EPsM............ Educational and Psychological Measurement (journ.) (SAUS)
EPSMA............ European Power Supply Manufacturers Association (SAUO)
EPS MOD Germany... Exercise Planning Staff MOD Germany (SAUO)
EPSOC............ Earth-Physics Satellite Observation [*or Observing*] Campaign [*Smithsonian Astrophysical Observatory*]
EPSOC............ Ephemera Society of America (EA)
EPSP............ Employees Profit Sharing Plan (FOTI)
EPSP............ Enolpyruvylshikimic Acid Phosphate [*Organic chemistry*]
EPSP............ European Peer Support Project (EURO)
EPSP............ Excitatory Postsynaptic Potential [*Neurophysiology*]
EPSP............ Experiment Power Switching Panel (MCD)
EPSP............ Extra Prime Skills Program (DICI)
EPSPS............ Enolpyruvylshikimatephosphate Synthase [*An enzyme*]
EPSRC............ Engineering and Physical Sciences Research Council [*British*]
EPSRG............ Exhibit Planning and Study Review Group (SAUO)
EPSS............ Electrical Power Subsystem (ADWA)
EPSS............ Electronic Performance Support System (CDE)
EPSS............ Enhanced Packet Switching Service (SAUS)
EPSS............ E-Point Septal Separation (DB)
EPSS............ Experimental Packet Switched Service (SAUS)
EPSS............ Experimental Packet-Switched System (SAUS)
EPSS............ Experimental Packet Switching Service (SAUS)
EPSS............ Experimental Packet Switching System [*Telecommunications*]
EPSSC............ Ecological and Physical Sciences Study Center (SAUS)
EPST............ Electric Power Statistics (journ.) (SAUS)
EPST............ Encyclopedia of Polymer Science and Technology [*A publication*]
EPST............ Extended Partition Specification Table [*Computer science*] (ELAL)
EPSTF............ Electrical Power System Test Facility [*NASA*] (KSC)
EPSTI............ Eastern Professional Ski Touring Instructors [*Later, EPSIA*] (EA)
Eps Vle............ Epsom Vale (SAUS)
EPT............ Early Pregnancy Test
EPT............ Economic Power Transmission
EPT............ Edge Point Threshold (SAUS)
ept............ egress procedures trainer (SAUS)
EPT............ Electric Power Transmission (ADA)
EPT............ Electricstatic Printing Tube (SAUS)
EPT............ Electromagnetic Propagation Tool (SAUS)
EPT............ Electronic Perspective Transformation System (SAUO)
EPT............ Electron Polar Zone (SAUS)
EPT............ Electrostatic Printing Tube
EPT............ El Paso [*Texas*] [*Seismograph station code, US Geological Survey*] (SEIS)
EPT............ Emergency Procedure Trainer [*NASA*] (NASA)
EPT............ Empire of the Petal Throne (SAUS)
EPT............ Endoscopic Papillotomy [*Medicine*]
EPT............ End-Point Temperature [*Food science*]
EPT............ Engineering Programming and Technology (VLIE)
EPT............ English Placement Test [*Education*]
EPT............ Environmental Proof Test (IAA)
EPT............ Environment Policy and Technology Project (SAUS)
EPT............ Epitope, Inc. [*AMEX symbol*] (SPSG)
EPT............ Epsilon Pi Tau (EA)
EPT............ Equipment Performance Tracking (AAEL)
EPT............ Ethylene-Propylene-Diene Terpolymer (EDCT)
EPT............ Ethylene Propylene Terpolymer [*Organic chemistry*]
EPT............ Euro Petroleum Corp. [*Toronto Stock Exchange symbol*] [*Vancouver Stock Exchange symbol*]
EPT............ Evoked Potential Technique [*Neurophysiology*]
EPT............ Examination Division Planning Tape [*IRS*]
EPT............ Excess Profits Tax
EPT............ Executive Process Table (VLIE)
EPT............ Experimental Prototype Test (MCD)
EPT............ External Page Table (VLIE)
EPT............ External Pipe Thread [*Technical drawings*]
EPT............ External Protocol Termination (SAUS)
EPT............ Extraction Procedure Toxicity
EPTA............ Electric Propulsion Trajectory Analysis
EPTA............ Electrophysiological Technologists' Association (EAIO)
EPTA............ European Parliamentary Technology (EURO)
EPTA............ European Piano Teachers Association (EAIO)
EPTA............ European Power Tool Association (EAIO)
EPTA............ European Pultrusion Technology Association [*Plastics*]
EPTA............ Expanded Program for Technical Assistance (SAUS)
EPTA............ Expanded Program of Technical Assistance [*United Nations*]
EPTAQ............ Executive Program Task Assignment Queue Manager (MCD)
EPTC............ East Portland Traction [*Federal Railroad Administration identification code*]
EPTC............ Electronic Programmable Transmission Control [*Off-highway vehicles*]
EPTC............ Ethyl Dipropylthiocarbamate [*Organic chemistry*]
EPTC............ Ethylpropylthiocarbamate (SAUS)
EPTC............ European Passenger Timetable Conference (SAUO)
EPTC............ European Petroleum Technical Corporation (SAUO)
EPTC............ Extraction Procedure Toxicity Characteristic [*Environmental Protection Agency*]

EPTD........... Ethylphosphonothioicdichloride [*Organic chemistry*]
EPTE........... Existed Prior to Enlistment [*Especially, dependency or physical defect*] [*Military*]
EPTE........... Existed Prior to Entry [*Military*]
EP Tech....... EP Technologies, Inc. [*Associated Press*] (SAG)
EPTFC......... Elvis Presley Tribute Fan Club [*Defunct*] (EA)
EPTFE......... Expanded Polytetrafluoroethylene [*Organic chemistry*]
EPTG........... Electronic Publication Technology Group [*Defunct*] (EA)
EPTI........... Existed Prior to Induction [*Especially, dependency or physical defect*] [*Military*]
EPTI........... Export Performance Taxation Incentive (SAUS)
EPTK........... EP Technologies, Inc. [*NASDAQ symbol*] (SAG)
EPTL........... Estates, Powers, and Trusts Law [*A publication*]
EPTLD......... East Portland, OR [*American Association of Railroads railroad junction routing code*]
EPTO........... Engineer Packaging Technical Office [*Merged with General Equipment Command*]
EPTO........... Epitope, Inc. [*NASDAQ symbol*] (COMM)
EP TOX....... Extraction Procedure for Toxicity Characteristics [*Environmental science*] (COE)
EP tox......... Extraction Procedure Toxicity (EEVL)
EPTox......... Extraction Procedure Toxicity
EP TOX....... Extraction Procedure Toxicity Test (SARE)
EPTR........... Ethylene Propylene Terpolymer Rubber (SAUS)
EPTRS......... Export Promotion Techniques Research (SAUO)
EPTS........... Electronic Problem Tracking System (VLIE)
EPTS........... Engine Power Trim System
EPTS........... Existed Prior to Entry Service [*Military*]
EPTS........... Existed Prior to Service (SAUS)
EPT System... Electronic Perspective Transformation System (SAUS)
EPTT........... Comite Europeen de l'Internationale du Personnel des Postes, Telegraphes et Telephones [*European Committee of the Postal, Telegraph and Telephone International*] [*EC*] (ECED)
EPTT........... Extraction Procedure Toxicity Test (SAUS)
EPTTC......... European Passenger Train Timetable Conference (EA)
EPTU........... Events per Time Unit (NASA)
EPTW........... Educational Programs that Work [*Department of Education*] [*Information service or system*] (IID)
EPU............. East Promontory [*Utah*] [*Seismograph station code, US Geological Survey*] (SEIS)
EPU............. Economic Planning Unit [*Generic term*] (DS)
EPU............. Electrical Power Unit
EPU............. Electronic Power Unit (IDOE)
EPU............. Electronic Purchasing by Units (SAUS)
EPU............. elliptically polarizing undulator (SAUS)
EPU............. Emergency Power Unit (IDOE)
EPU............. Empire Press Union (DGA)
EPU............. Entry Processing Unit [*Computer science*] (DCTA)
EPU............. Environmental Physiology Unit [*Simon Fraser University*] [*Canada*] [*Research center*] (RCD)
EPU............. Environmental Policy Unit (SAUO)
EPU............. Epidermal Proliferative Unit (PDAA)
EPU............. Essential Power Unit (SAUS)
EPU............. European Payments Union
EPU............. European Political Union (SAUO)
EPU............. European Press Photo Agencies Union (SAUO)
EPU............. European Pressphoto Union (SAUO)
EPU............. Events per Unit Time (TIMI)
EPU............. Execution Processing Unit (SAUS)
EPU............. Executive Processing Unit
EPU............. Expandable Processor Unit (SAUS)
EPU............. Extended Processing Unit (VLIE)
EPU............. External Programmer Unit (VLIE)
EPUB........... Electronic Publication (VLIE)
EPUB........... Electronic Publishing System [*ITT Dialcom*] [*Database*]
EPUB........... Entertainment Publications, Inc. [*NASDAQ symbol*] (COMM)
e-publishing... Electronic Publishing (ADWA)
EPUBS......... Electronic Publishing Abstracts [*The Research Association for the Paper and Board, Printing and Packaging Industries*] [*Database*]
EPUNIT....... European Payments Unit (SAUO)
EPUP........... El Paso Union Passenger Terminal [*Federal Railroad Administration identification code*]
EPUR........... Envirogen Waste Refining & Technology, Inc. [*NASDAQ symbol*] (SAG)
EPUR........... Envirogen Waste Refining/Tech [*NASDAQ symbol*] (TTSB)
EPURE......... Etude de la Protection des Usagers de la Route et de l'Environement [*St udy of Road User Safety and Environmental Protection*] [*French*] [*Automotive engineering*]
e-purse........ Electronic Purse (ADWA)
EPUS........... Episcopus [*Bishop*] [*Latin*]
EPUT........... Events per Unit Time
EPUTS......... Emergency Power Unit Test Set
EPUU........... Enhanced PLRS [*Position Location Reporting System*] User Unit [*Air Force*]
EPUU........... Enhanced PLRS User Unit. Communications (SAUS)
EPUU/MLS... EPLRS [*Enhanced Position Location Reporting System*] User Unit/ Microwave Landing System (MCD)
EPUY........... Education Program for Unemployed Youth (SAUS)
EPV............. Earth Probe near Limb of Venus [*Angle*]
EPV............. Electric Polarization Vector
EPV............. Electric Powered Vehicle
EPV............. Electropneumatic Valve
EPV............. Emergency Pressurization Valve (MCD)
EPV............. Entomopox Virus [*Medicine*] (EDAA)
EPV............. Evangelische Progressieve Volkspartij [*Evangelical Progressive People's Party*] [*Netherlands*] (PPW)
EPV............. Extended Precision Vector (ADWA)
EPV............. External Pressure Vessel
EPV............. External Pudendal Vein [*Medicine*] (MELL)
EPVA........... Eastern Paralyzed Veterans Association (SAUO)
EPVS........... Emergency Propellant Venting System
EPVT........... English Picture Vocabulary Test [*Educational test*] (EDAC)
EPVTS......... English Picture Vocabulary Tests [*Educational test*]
EPW............. Earth-Penetrating Warhead (RDA)
EPW............. Earth Penetrating Weapon (ACAE)
EPW............. Earth Penetrator Warhead (SAUS)
EPW............. Earth Penetrator Weapon (MCD)
EPW............. Electric Pressure Wave
EPW............. electron plasma wave (SAUS)
EPW............. Elektra Power, Inc. [*Vancouver Stock Exchange symbol*]
EPW............. Elliptically Polarized Wave
EPW............. end-point weighing (SAUS)
EPW............. end-point weight (SAUS)
EPW............. Enemy Prisoner of War [*Army*] (AABC)
EPW............. Ephrata [*Washington*] [*Seismograph station code, US Geological Survey*] (SEIS)
EPW............. Ethyl-acetate Pyridine-Water (SAUS)
EPW............. Expected Probability of Winning (FOTI)
EPWA........... Warszawa/Okecie [*Poland*] [*ICAO location identifier*] (ICLI)
EPWG........... Electromagnetic Propagation Working Group [*Army*]
EPWG........... Energy Production Working Group [*Australia*]
EPWG........... Environmental Projects Working Group [*NASA*] (NASA)
EPWIB......... Enemy Prisoner of War Information Bureau [*Army*] (AABC)
EPWIB(Br)... Enemy Prisoner of War Information Bureau (Branch) [*Army*] (AABC)
epwm........... electroplated white metal (SAUS)
EPWM......... Electroplate on White Metal (SAUS)
EPWM......... Electroplate White Metal (IAA)
EPWR........... Emergency Power
EPWS........... Emergency Production Weapons Schedule [*Navy*] (NG)
EP-X........... Efficient Personal-Experimental [*Concept vehicle*]
EPX............. Electronic Patrol, Experimental (MCD)
EPX............. Electronic Payments Exchange, Inc. (TBD)
EPX............. Eurotech Packet Exchange (SAUS)
EPXMA......... Electron Probe X-Ray Microanalyzer
EPY............. Expanded Planning Yard (SAUS)
EPY............. Extra-Pair Young [*Biology*]
EPZ............. Electron Polar Zone
EPZ............. Emergency Planning Zone [*Nuclear emergency planning*]
EPZ............. Export Processing Zone (ECON)
EPZA........... Export Processing Zone Administration (SAUS)
EPZA........... Export Processing Zone Authority
EPZGA......... effective peak zero ground acceleration (SAUS)
EQ............... Earthquake (SAUO)
EQ............... Economic Questionnaire (SAUO)
EQ............... Economic Quotient
EQ............... Educational Quotient [*Psychology*]
EQ............... Elders Quorum (SAUS)
EQ............... Emergency Quota [*Indian Railway*] (TIR)
EQ............... Emo Questionnaire [*Psychology*]
EQ............... Emotional Quotient (ADWA)
EQ............... Employment Questionnaire (ACAE)
EQ............... Encephalization Quotient
EQ............... End-Quench (SAUS)
EQ............... Energy Quotient
EQ............... Engineering Quality
EQ............... Enquiries [*Telecommunications*] (TEL)
EQ............... Enquiry (SAUS)
EQ............... Enthusiasm Quotient (SAUS)
EQ............... Environmental Qualification (COE)
EQ............... Environmental Quality
eq............... Equal (COE)
EQ............... Equal
EQ............... Equality (ROG)
EQ............... Equalization [*Electronics*]
eq............... equalization quotient (SAUS)
EQ............... Equalizer
EQ............... Equal To (VLIE)
EQ............... Equate (SAUS)
EQ............... Equation (KSC)
Eq............... Equation (MIST)
eq............... Equation (SHCU)
eq............... Equations (ADWA)
EQ............... Equator (WDAA)
EQ............... Equatorial
EQ............... Equerry
EQ............... Eques [*Knight*] [*Latin*] (ROG)
EQ............... Equestrian (ROG)
EQ............... Equilibrium (SAUS)
Eq............... Equipe (SAUS)
EQ............... Equipment (BUR)
EQ............... Equipmentman [*Military*] (DNAB)
EQ............... Equipment Qualification (NRCH)
Eq............... Equitable [*Legal term*] (DLA)
EQ............... Equitable Co. [*NYSE symbol*] (SPSG)
EQ............... Equitable Cos. [*NYSE symbol*] (TTSB)
Eq............... Equites [*Knights*] [*of Aristophanes*] [*Classical studies*] (OCD)
Eq............... Equity (SAFN)
EQ............... Equity
Eq............... Equity Court [*or Division*] [*Legal term*] (DLA)

Eq .... Equity Reports [*A publication*] (DLA)
EQ .... Equivalency (SAUS)
Eq .... Equivalent (AMHC)
EQ .... Equivalent
eq .... equivalent (ABAC)
eq .... equivalent weight (SAUS)
EQ .... Erythroplasia of Queyrat (SAUS)
EQ .... Ethnic Quotient
EQ .... Ethoxyquin (SAUS)
EQ .... Example Query (SAUS)
EQ .... Experiment Inquiries (SAUS)
EQA .... Educational Quality Assessment Program [*Pennsylvania*] (EDAC)
EQA .... El Dorado, KS [*Location identifier*] [*FAA*] (FAAL)
EQA .... Environmental Quality Abstracts (journ.) (SAUS)
EQA .... Environmental Quality Administration (SAUS)
EQA .... Equipment Quality Analysis
EQA .... European Quality Alliance [*Proposed merger between four European airlines*] (ECON)
EQA .... OCLC [*Online Computer Library Center*] Europe, Birmingham, England [*OCLC symbol*] (OCLC)
EQAA .... Environmental Quality Advisory Agency (SAUS)
Eq Ab .... Abridgment of Cases in Equity [*1667-1744*] [*A publication*] (DLA)
EQAB .... Environmental Quality Advisory Board (SAUS)
EQAD .... Electrical Quality Assurance Directorate (SAUS)
eq & wd .... earthquake and war damage (SAUS)
EQAS .... Energy Quick Advice Service (SAUO)
EQ AUR .... Eques Auratus [*Knight Bachelor*] [*Latin*] (ROG)
EQB .... Chambersburg, PA [*Location identifier*] [*FAA*] (FAAL)
EQB .... Environmental Quality Board (COE)
EQBLE .... Equitable [*Legal term*] (ROG)
EQBM .... Engineering/Qualification Back-Up Model (ACAE)
EQC .... Environmental Quality Control
EQC .... Environmental Quality Council [*Terminated, 1970*] (MCD)
EQC .... Equipment Check (SAUS)
EQC .... Equipment Quality Analysis (SAUS)
EQC .... Equipment Quantities Committee (SAUO)
EQC .... European Question Committee (HEAS)
EQC .... Externally Quenched Counter
EQC .... External Quality Control (ODA)
Eq Ca Ab .... Equity Cases Abridged [*A publication*]
Eq Ca Abr .... Abridgment of Cases in Equity [*1667-1744*] [*A publication*] (DLA)
Eq Cas .... Equity Cases [*A publication*] (DLA)
Eq Cas .... Gilbert's English Equity Cases [*A publication*] (DLA)
Eq Cas Abr .... Equity Cases Abridged [*2 vols.*] [*21, 22 English Reprint*] [*A publication*] (DLA)
Eq Cas Abr (Eng) .... Equity Cases Abridged [*2 vols.*] [*21, 22 English Reprint*] [*A publication*] (DLA)
Eq Cas Mod .... Equity Cases [*A publication*] (DLA)
EQCC .... Entry Query Control Console [*Computer science*]
EQCC .... Environmental Quality Control Committee
EQCM .... Electrochemical Quartz-Crystal Microbalance [*Biochemistry*]
EQCM .... Master Chief Equipmentman [*Navy rating*]
EQCO .... European Quality Control Organization (SAUS)
Eq Concn .... Equilibrium Concentration (SAUS)
EQ CONV .... Equitable Conversion (DLA)
EQCRT .... Equipment Certified (FAAC)
EQD .... Electrical Quality Assurance Directorate [*British Ministry of Defense*] [*Research center*]
EQD .... Established Quarter of Disability [*Social Security Administration*] (OICC)
EQDB .... Equipment Qualification Data Bank [*Information service or system*] (IID)
EQDD .... Equipment Density Data (AABC)
Eq Draft .... Equity Draftsman (Van Heythuysen's, Edited by Hughes) [*A publication*] (DLA)
EQE .... English Qualifying Exam [*Western Michigan University*] (TES)
EQE .... Equivalent Quantum Efficiency (MCD)
EQE .... Esquisure, Inc. [*AMEX symbol*] (SAG)
EQE .... Event Queue Element [*Computer science*] (MCD)
EQEEB .... Equivalent Queue Extended Erlang B (VLIE)
EQF .... Elswick Quick-Firing Gun
EQF .... Eolian Quartz Flux (SAUS)
EQF .... Equity Funding Corporation of America (SAUO)
EQG .... Equalizing (VLIE)
EQ gate .... Electronics Equivalence Gate (ODA)
EqGth1 .... Equipment Growth Fund 1 (PLM) [*Associated Press*] (SAG)
EqGth2 .... Equipment Growth Fund 2 (PLM) [*Associated Press*] (SAG)
EQGth3 .... Equipment Growth Fund III (PLM) [*Associated Press*] (SAG)
Eq Guin .... Equatorial Guinea (SAUS)
Eqhv .... Equipment Operator, Heavy [*Construction term*] (MIST)
EQI .... Electric Quadrupole Interaction (SAUS)
EQI .... electronic control module (SAUS)
EQ-i .... Emotional Quotient Inventory
EQI .... Environmental Quality Index (PDAA)
EqI .... Equity Income [*Finance*]
EQIA .... Environmental Quality Improvement Act of 1970
EqIowa .... Equitable of Iowa Companies [*Associated Press*] (SAG)
EQIP .... Environmental Quality Incentives Program (SAUO)
EQIP .... Environmental Quality Information Panel (SAUS)
EQIS .... Environmental Quality Information Services Program [*Navy*]
eqiv .... equivalent (SAUS)
Eq Judg .... Equity Judgments, by A'Beckett [*New South Wales*] [*A publication*] (DLA)
EQK Rt .... EQK Realty Investors [*Associated Press*] (SAG)
EQL .... Earthquake Light
EQL .... Earthquake Locator (SAUO)
EQL .... English Query Language (CIST)
EQL .... Environmental Quality Laboratory [*California Institute of Technology*]
eql .... Equal (ELAL)
EQL .... Equal (MSA)
EQL .... Equalizer (SAUS)
EQL .... Equally (SAUS)
EQL .... Equatorial Airlines of Sao Tome and Principe [*ICAO designator*] (FAAC)
EQL .... Equilization (MLOA)
EQL .... Estimated Quantitation Limit (ABAC)
EQL .... Expected Quality Level
EQLIPSE .... Evaluation and Quality in Library Performance Systems (TELE)
EQL SP .... Equally Spaced (SAUS)
Eqlt .... Equipment Operator, Light [*Construction term*] (MIST)
EQLY .... Equally [*Legal term*] (ROG)
EQM .... Environmental Quality Magazine (journ.) (SAUS)
eqm .... equal-flow manifold (SAUS)
EQM .... Equitable Real Estate Shopping [*Later, Midwest Real Estate Shopping Center Ltd.*] [*NYSE symbol*] (SPSG)
EQM .... Midwest Real Estate Shopping Centers Ltd. [*NYSE symbol*] (SAG)
EQMal .... European Quaternary Malacologists (SAUO)
EQMD .... EquiMed [*NASDAQ symbol*] (SAG)
EQMD .... EquiMed Inc. [*NASDAQ symbol*] (TTSB)
Eqmd .... Equipment Operator, Medium [*Construction term*] (MIST)
EQMD .... European Quatermaster Depot (SAUO)
Eqmm .... Equipment Operator, Master Mechanic [*Construction term*] (MIST)
EQMT .... Equipment (SAUS)
EQN .... Equation
EQN .... Equine
EQN .... Equine Resources Ltd. [*Vancouver Stock Exchange symbol*]
eqn prdx .... equine paradox (SAUS)
EQNX .... Equinox Systems [*NASDAQ symbol*] (TTSB)
EQNX .... Equinox Systems, Inc. [*NASDAQ symbol*] (SAG)
EQO .... Environmental Quality Objective [*British*] (DCTA)
EQO .... Environmental Quality Office [*HUD*] (OICC)
EQO .... Environment Quality Objective (SAUO)
Eqol .... Equipment Operator, Oilers [*Construction term*] (MIST)
EQOPPINFOSYS .... Equal Opportunity Information and Support System (DNAB)
EQP .... Elders quorum president (SAUS)
EQP .... Employer Quality Partnership
EQP .... Englehard, NC [*Location identifier*] [*FAA*] (FAAL)
EQP .... Equip (SAUS)
EQP .... Equipment (CINC)
EQP .... Equity Preservation Corp. [*Toronto Stock Exchange symbol*] [*Vancouver Stock Exchange symbol*]
Eq PA .... Equal Pay Act [*1970*] [*British*] (DCTA)
EqPac .... Equatorial Pacific [*Project*] [*Marine science*] (OSRA)
EQPAC .... Equatorial Pacific (USDC)
EQPCE .... Earthquake Preparedness Center of Expertise (SAUO)
EQPCHK .... Equipment Check (SAUS)
EQPFOR .... Equipment Foreman
EQPMT .... Equipment (MDG)
eqpt .... Equipment (MILB)
EQPT .... Equipment
eqq .... electric quadripole-quadripole (SAUS)
EQQ .... Electric Quadrupole-Quadrupole
Eq R .... Common Law and Equity Reports [*1853-55*] [*A publication*] (DLA)
EQR .... Electronic Industries Quality Registry (SAUS)
EQR .... Equity Reserve Corp. [*Toronto Stock Exchange symbol*]
EQR .... Equity Residential Property Trust [*NYSE symbol*] (SPSG)
Eq R .... Gilbert's English Equity Reports [*1705-27*] [*A publication*] (DLA)
Eq R .... Harper's South Carolina Equity Reports [*A publication*] (DLA)
EQRD .... Equipment Ready Date (SAUS)
Eq R (Eng) .... Equity Reports [*England*] [*A publication*] (DLA)
EQREP .... Equipment Report (MCD)
Eq Rep .... Equity Reports [*A publication*] (DLA)
Eq Rep .... Equity Reports, Published by Spottiswoode [*A publication*] (DLA)
Eq Rep .... Gilbert's English Equity Reports [*1705-27*] [*A publication*] (DLA)
Eq Rep .... Harper's South Carolina Equity Reports [*A publication*] (DLA)
EQRPrA .... Equity Res Prop Tr 9.375% Pfd [*NYSE symbol*] (TTSB)
EQRPrB .... Equity Res Prop Tr 9.125%Pfd [*NYSE symbol*] (TTSB)
EQS .... Environmental Quality Staff [*Tennessee Valley Authority*] [*Knoxville, TN*] (GRD)
EQS .... Environmental Quality Standard [*British*] (DCTA)
EQS .... Equality Search (ACAE)
eqs .... equations (SAUS)
EQS .... Equatorial Scatter
eqs .... equivalents (SAUS)
EQS .... Equivalent to Sheathed Explosive (IAA)
EQS .... Equus II, Inc. [*AMEX symbol*] (SPSG)
EQS .... Esquel [*Argentina*] [*Airport symbol*] (OAG)
EQS .... European Committee for Quality System Assessment and Certification (SAUS)
EQS .... Exact Quadratic Search [*Mathematics*]
EQSA .... Environmental Quality Standard Agency (SAUS)
EQSA .... Extended Quasi-Static Approximation [*Materials research*]
EQSB .... Equitable Federal Savings Bank [*NASDAQ symbol*] (SAG)
EQSB .... Equitable Fed Svgs Bank [*NASDAQ symbol*] (TTSB)
EQSC .... Environmental Quality Study Council (SAUO)
eq sp .... equally spaced (SAUS)
EQSTTRN .... Equestrian
EQT .... Engineering Qualification Test
EQT .... Environmental Qualification Test
EQT .... Environmental Quality Technology

EQT Equation of Time [*Navigation*]
Eqt Equipment (SAUS)
EQT Equitable Resources, Inc. [*Formerly, Equitable Gas Co.*] [*NYSE symbol*] (SPSG)
EQT Equivalent Training (AFM)
EQTBL Equitable
EqtCos Equitable Companies, Inc. [*Associated Press*] (SAG)
EqtFedl Equitable Federal Savings Bank [*Associated Press*] (SAG)
EqtOil Equity Oil Co. [*Associated Press*] (SAG)
Eq Tr Equipment Trust (EBF)
EqtR Equity Residential Property Trust [*Associated Press*] (SAG)
EqtResc Equitable Resources, Inc. [*Formerly, Equitable Gas Co.*] [*Associated Press*] (SAG)
EQTV Extended Quality Television (ACRL)
EQTX Equitex, Inc. [*NASDAQ symbol*] (NQ)
EQTY Equity
EQTY Equity Oil [*NASDAQ symbol*] (TTSB)
EQTY Equity Oil Co. [*NASDAQ symbol*] (NQ)
EqtyInn Equity Inns [*Associated Press*] (SAG)
EqtyMkt Equity Marketing, Inc. [*Associated Press*] (SAG)
EqtyRsd Equity Residential Property Trust [*Associated Press*] (SAG)
EQU Equal (SAUS)
EQU Equate (MDG)
equ equation (SAUS)
Equ Equerry (SAUS)
Equ Equity [*Business term*]
Equ Equuleus [*Constellation*]
EQU Equus Petroleum [*Vancouver Stock Exchange symbol*]
Equa Equator (SAUS)
Equa Equatorial (SAUS)
EQUAATE Electronic Quality Assurance Automatic Test Equipment (SAUS)
Equa C Cur Equatorial Counter-current (SAUS)
EQUAL Equalizer (SAUS)
EQUALANT Equatorial Atlantic (MSC)
EQUALANT Equatorial Atlantic Survey [*Marine science*] (OSRA)
EqualN EqualNet Holding Corp. [*Associated Press*] (SAG)
Equal Opp Equal Opportunity [*A publication*]
EQUAP Engineering Qualification Approval Program (SAUS)
EQUAPAC Cooperative Survey of the Pacific Equatorial Zone (SAUS)
EQUAPAC Equatorial Pacific
EQUARIDGE International Study of the Equatorial Segment of the Mid-Atlantic Ridge (SAUS)
equat equator (SAUS)
EQUAT Equatorial (ROG)
EQUATE Electronic Quality Assurance Test Equipment [*System*] [*Army*] (RDA)
EQUAT GUI Equatorial Guinea (WDAA)
Equatorials Equatorial Islands in the central and South Pacifc Ocean, also called the Line Islands (SAUS)
EQUEL Embedded QUEL (SAUS)
EQUEL Embedded Query Language (SAUS)
EQUEL/C Embedded Query Language written in C (SAUS)
EQUI Equivest Finance, Inc. [*NASDAQ symbol*] (SAG)
Equifx Equifax, Inc. [*Formerly, Retail Credit Co.*] [*Associated Press*] (SAG)
EQUIL Equilibrium (MSA)
equilib Equilibrium (AAMN)
EquiMed EquiMed [*Associated Press*] (SAG)
equimol Equimolecular (SAUS)
equin Equinoctial (SAUS)
equin equinox (SAUS)
Equine Vet J Equine Veterinary Journal [*London*] (SAUS)
equinl Equinoctial (SAUS)
equinol equinologist (SAUS)
equinol equinology (SAUS)
Equinox Equinox Resources Ltd. [*Associated Press*] (SAG)
EQUIP Engineering Quality Improvement
EQUIP Enterprise Quality Improvement Program [*Australia*]
EQUIP Equation Input Processor (SAUS)
Equip Equipment (AAGC)
equip Equipment (DD)
EQUIP Equipment
EQUIP Equipment Usage Information Programme (SAUO)
EQUIP ERIC/QUERY Interface Program (SAUS)
EQuIP Evaluation and Quality Improvement Program (SAUS)
EQUIP C/I Equipment Control and Integration [*Electronics*] (AAEL)
EQUIP RTC Equipment Real-Time Control [*Electronics*] (AAEL)
EQUIPT Equipment (WGA)
Equisure Equisure, Inc. [*Associated Press*] (SAG)
Equitex Equitex, Inc. [*Associated Press*] (SAG)
Equitrc Equitrac Corp. [*Associated Press*] (SAG)
EquityCp Equity Corporation International [*Associated Press*] (SAG)
Equity Rep Common Law and Equity Reports [*1853-55*] [*A publication*] (DLA)
Equity Rep Equity Reports (Gilbert) [*England*] [*A publication*] (DLA)
Equity Rep Harper's South Carolina Equity Reports [*A publication*] (DLA)
equiv Equiavlent (SHCU)
equiv Equivalence (ADWA)
EQUIV Equivalent (AFM)
Equiv Equivalent (IDOE)
equiv Equivalent (NTIO)
Equiv Amt Equivalent Amount (SAUS)
Equiv Conc Equivalent Concentration (SAUS)
Equivsn Equivision, Inc. [*Associated Press*] (SAG)
Equivst Equivest Finance, Inc. [*Associated Press*] (SAG)
equiv wt Equivalent Weight [*Chemistry*]
Equl Equuleus (SAUS)
E QUOL VEH E Quolibet Vehiculo [*In Any Vehicle*] [*Pharmacy*]
E QUOV LIQ E Quovis Liquido [*In Any Liquid*] [*Pharmacy*]
EQUUS Equus Gaming Co. Ltd. [*NASDAQ symbol*] (SAG)
EQUUS Equus Gaming LP [*NASDAQ symbol*] (TTSB)
EquusG Equus Gaming Co., Ltd. [*Associated Press*] (SAG)
EquusII Equus II, Inc. [*Associated Press*] (SAG)
EQUX Equistar Chemicals [*Private rail car owner code*]
EQV Equivalence (IAA)
EQV Equivalent (SAUS)
EQV Equivest International Financial Corp. [*Vancouver Stock Exchange symbol*]
EQW Emitter Quantum Well (SAUS)
Eqwa Eccentric Quadrant Walking Aid (SAUS)
EQWin EQuIS for Windows [*Computer science*]
EQX Equator Crossing
EQX Equinox Resources Ltd. [*Toronto Stock Exchange symbol*] [*Vancouver Stock Exchange symbol*]
EQY Equity One [*NYSE symbol*] (SG)
EQY Monroe, NC [*Location identifier*] [*FAA*] (FAAL)
EQZ Seymour, IN [*Location identifier*] [*FAA*] (FAAL)
ER [*The*] Earlham Review [*A publication*]
ER Early Release (MCD)
ER Early Reticulocyte (STED)
E/R Early Run
ER Earned Run [*Baseball*]
ER Earnings Record (SAUS)
ER Earnings Report [*Business term*]
ER Earth Radii
ER Earth Radius (SAUS)
ER Earth Rate
ER Earth Resources (MCD)
ER Earth Return (SAUS)
ER Eastern Railway [*Indian Railway*] (TIR)
ER Eastern Range (SAUO)
ER Eastern Region (SAUS)
ER Eastern Rite News Service
ER East Riding (SAUS)
ER East Riding of Yorkshire [*Administrative county in England*]
ER East River [*New York*]
ER East's English King's Bench Term Reports [*A publication*] (DLA)
ER Easy to Reach [*Telecommunications*] (TEL)
ER Echo Ranging
ER Economic Region (SAUS)
ER Economic Regulations [*Civil Aeronautics Board*]
ER Ecosystem Restoration [*Environmental Protection Agency*] (EPAT)
ER Ecumenical Review [*A publication*] (BRI)
E/R Edges Red [*Publishing*] (DGA)
e/r editing/reviewing (SAUS)
ER Editor Routine (SAUS)
ER Educational Radio (SAUS)
ER Educational Ratio
ER Educational Resources [*Auckland, NZ*]
ER Educational Review (journ.) (SAUS)
ER Edwardus Rex [*King Edward*] [*Latin*]
ER Effectiveness Ratio (MCD)
ER Effectiveness Report [*Military*]
ER Effective Resistance (SAUS)
ER Efficacy Ratio (STED)
ER Efficiency Review [*DoD*]
ER Ego Resiliency [*Psychology*]
ER Egress Router (ACRL)
ER Egyptian Railways (DCTA)
ER Ejection Rate [*Medicine*]
ER Elastic Recoil (SAUS)
ER Elastoresistance (SAUS)
ER Elder
ER Eleanor Roosevelt [*1884-1962*]
ER Election Reports [*Ontario*] [*A publication*] (DLA)
ER Electrical Resistance (MSA)
ER Electrical Resistivity (EEVL)
E(R) Electrician (Radio) [*U.S. Navy enlisted rating*] (AUER)
ER Electric Reader (SAUS)
ER Electrolytic Rectifier (SAUS)
ER Electrolytic Reduction (SAUS)
ER Electrolytic Refining (SAUS)
ER Electronic Ram (SAUS)
ER Electronic Reader (SAUS)
ER Electronic Reconnaissance
ER Electronic Recording
ER Electronic Review (journ.) (SAUS)
ER Electron Recording (SAUS)
ER Electro-Refined (SAUS)
ER Electro-Refining [*Environmental science*] (COE)
ER Electroreflectance (EDCT)
ER Electroresection (STED)
ER Electro-Rheological
ER Electrorheology [*Physics*]
ER Eley-Rideal Mechanism [*Chemistry*]
ER Elizabetha Regina [*Queen Elizabeth*] [*Latin*]
ER Elizabeth Regina [*Queen Elizabeth*] (DLA)
ER Embryo Replacement [*Gynecology*]
ER Emergency Receiver (SAUS)
ER Emergency Recovery (SAUS)
ER Emergency Relief
ER Emergency Request
ER Emergency Rescue

ER.............. Emergency Reserve
ER.............. Emergency Response [*Nuclear energy*] (NRCH)
ER.............. Emergency Room [*Medicine*]
er.............. employee relations (SAUS)
ER.............. Employer (OICC)
er.............. Enantiomer Ratio (MEC)
ER.............. End of Run (IAA)
er.............. Endoplasmic Reticulum (DOG)
ER.............. Endoplasmic Reticulum [*Cytology*]
ER.............. End Routine (SAUS)
ER.............. Energy Related Health Research Laboratory (SAUO)
ER.............. Energy-Related Health Research Laboratory (SAUS)
ER.............. energy research (SAUS)
ER.............. Energy Research, Office of (SAUS)
ER.............. Energy Resources (SAUS)
ER.............. Energy Review (journ.) (SAUS)
ER.............. Engineering Record
ER.............. Engineering Regulations [*A publication*]
ER.............. Engineering Release (MCD)
ER.............. Engineering Report
ER.............. Engineering Request (ACAE)
ER.............. Engineering Route [*Telecommunications*] (TEL)
ER.............. Engineer Relations [*ACE*] (AAGC)
ER.............. Engine Relay (SAUS)
ER.............. Engine Room [*Force*]
ER.............. English Reports [*Legal*]
ER.............. English Reports, Full Reprint [*A publication*] (DLA)
ER.............. English Revised Version [*of the Bible*] [*A publication*] (BJA)
ER.............. Enhanced Radiation (SAUS)
ER.............. Enhanced Radiation Weapon
ER.............. Enhanced Reactivation [*Medicine*] (DMAA)
er.............. enhanced recovery (SAUS)
ER.............. Enhancement Ratio
ER.............. Enhancement request (SAUS)
ER.............. Enlisted Reservist (SAUO)
ER.............. Enoyl Reductase [*An enzyme*]
E/R.............. En Route
ER.............. Entity Relationship [*Computer science*] (PCM)
E-R.............. Entity-Relationship (SAUS)
ER.............. Entrance Right [*A stage direction*] [*Theater*] (WDMC)
ER.............. Entry Remote (SAUS)
ER.............. enviromental resistance (SAUS)
ER.............. Environmental Report (NRCH)
ER.............. Environmental Requirement
ER.............. Environmental Resistance
ER.............. Environmental Resource (SAUS)
ER.............. Environmental Restoration [*Metallurgy*]
ER.............. Environment Reporter (journ.) (SAUS)
ER.............. Epidemiologic Research (COE)
ER.............. Epigastric Region (STED)
ER.............. Equine Rhinopneumonia [*Medicine*] (DMAA)
ER.............. Equipment Readiness [*DoD*]
ER.............. Equipment Record
ER.............. Equipment Regulations (SAUS)
ER.............. Equipment Related (DNAB)
ER.............. Equipment Repair (SAUS)
ER.............. Equipment Repairer [*British military*] (DMA)
ER.............. Equipment Requirement
ER.............. equivalent radius (SAUS)
ER.............. Equivalent Roentgen
ER.............. Equivalent Round (MCD)
Er.............. Erbium [*Chemical element*]
ER.............. Ergonomics
Er.............. Eritrea (MILB)
ER.............. Eritrea [*Internet country code*]
ER.............. Errata
ER.............. Erroneous
ER.............. Error [*Baseball*]
ER.............. Error Rate [*Statistics*]
ER.............. Error Recorder
ER.............. Error Recovery (BUR)
ER.............. Error Register (SAUS)
ER.............. Error Relay
ER.............. Error Retrieval [*Computer science*] (ECII)
ER.............. Erskine Register (EA)
'Er.............. 'Erubin [*or 'Eruvin*] (BJA)
ER.............. Erythrocyte [*Hematology*]
ER.............. Erythrocyte Receptor [*Medicine*] (MELL)
ER.............. Erythrocyte Rosette [*Hematology*]
ER.............. Escape Rhythm [*Medicine*] (MELL)
ER.............. Esophageal Reflux [*Medicine*] (MELL)
ER.............. Esophageal Rupture (STED)
ER.............. Essex Regiment (SAUO)
ER.............. Established Reliability (MCD)
ER.............. Establishment Reliability (SAUS)
ER.............. Estimated Rental (ROG)
ER.............. Estimating Relationship (AFIT)
ER.............. Estradiol Receptor [*Endocrinology*]
ER.............. Estrogen Receptor [*Endocrinology*]
ER.............. Ethiopian Review [*A publication*]
ER.............. European Right [*Political movement*] (ECON)
E/R.............. Evacuation/Replacement [*Jar technique*] [*Microbiology*]
ER.............. Evaluation Record [*LIMRA*]
ER.............. Evaluation Report
ER.............. Evaluation Routine (SAUS)
ER.............. Evaporation Rate (SAUS)
ER.............. Evaporation Residue (ODA)
ER.............. Event Rule (SAUS)
ER.............. Evidence Rules (SAUO)
ER.............. Evoked Response [*Neurophysiology*]
ER.............. Exception Report (SAUS)
ER.............. Exception Reporting (MCD)
ER.............. Excess Reserves (MHDB)
ER.............. Exchange Ratio (MCD)
ER.............. Exchange Register (SAUS)
ER.............. Exchange Rolls
ER.............. Executive Request [*Computer science*]
ER.............. Executive Reserve
ER.............. Executive Risk, Inc. [*NYSE symbol*] (SAG)
ER.............. Executive Routine (SAUS)
E/R.............. Exercised/Repositioned [*Sports medicine*]
ER.............. Exeter Railway (SAUO)
ER.............. Exfiltration Rocket (SEWL)
ER.............. Exodus Rabbah (BJA)
ER.............. Expected Result (IAA)
ER.............. Expedite Requirement (KSC)
ER.............. Expeditious Repair (ACAE)
ER.............. Expense Report (AAG)
ER.............. Expert Rifleman
ER.............. Expiratory Reserve (STED)
ER.............. Explanation Report [*NASA*] (NASA)
ER.............. Explicit Rate (MLOA)
ER.............. Explicit Route (ELAL)
ER.............. Exploratory Research (ABAC)
ER.............. Explosives Report
ER.............. Exponent Register (SAUS)
ER.............. Exposure Range (SAUS)
ER.............. Express Route (SAUS)
ER.............. Ex-Rights [*Without Rights*] [*Investment term*]
ER.............. Extended Range
ER.............. Extended Release [*Pharmacy*]
ER.............. External Ratio (ABAC)
ER.............. External Reduction (STED)
ER.............. External Reflection (SAUS)
ER.............. External Register (SAUS)
ER.............. External Relations (WDAA)
ER.............. External Report
ER.............. External Resistance [*Physics*]
ER.............. External Rotation [*Myology*]
ER.............. Extraction Ratio (STED)
ER.............. Extraordinary Contractual Relief Reporter [*A publication*] (AAGC)
ER.............. Extrarespiratory
ER.............. Extra Restricted (ADA)
ER.............. Extremely Reinforcing (SAUS)
er.............. extremely rough (SAUS)
ER.............. Eye Research [*Defunct*] (EA)
ER.............. Here [*Amateur radio shorthand*] (WDAA)
ER.............. Office of Energy Research (SAUO)
ER.............. Office of Environmental Restoration (SAUS)
er---.............. Rhine River and Basin [*MARC geographic area code*] [*Library of Congress*] (LCCP)
ER-2.............. Earth Resources-2 (SAUS)
ER-2.............. Earth Resources-2 (aircraft) (SAUS)
ER2.............. Earth Resources-2 (satellite) (SAUS)
ER-2.............. Extended Range U-2 (SAUS)
ERA.............. Early Retirement Adjustment (EERA)
ERA.............. Earned Run Average [*Baseball*]
ERA.............. Earthquake Risk Analysis (PDAA)
ERA.............. Eastern Railroad Association [*Defunct*] (EA)
ERA.............. Ecological Risk Assessment (ABAC)
ERA.............. Economic Regulatory Administration (MCD)
ERA.............. Economic Regulatory Agency (COE)
ERA.............. Ecosophical Research Association (SAUO)
ERA.............. Educational Rankings Annual [*A publication*]
ERA.............. Educational Recording Agency
ERA.............. Education and Religious Affairs [*US Military Government, Germany*]
ERA.............. Education Reform Act [*1988*] (AIE)
ERA.............. Education Research Assistant (ADA)
ERA.............. Education Review Association [*Australia*]
ERA.............. Effective Range Approximation (SAUS)
ERA.............. Effective Rate of Assistance [*International trade*]
ERA.............. Egyptian Research Account [*London*] [*A publication*] (BJA)
ERA.............. Egyptians Relief Association (EA)
ERA.............. Electrical and Allied Industries Research Association (SAUO)
ERA.............. Electrically Reconfigurable Array (CDE)
ERA.............. Electrical [*or Electronic*] Replaceable Assembly
ERA.............. Electrical Representatives Association
ERA.............. Electrical Research Association [*British*]
ERA.............. Electrical Response Activity
ERA.............. electrical response audiometry (SAUS)
ERA.............. Electric Railroaders Association (EA)
ERA.............. Electric Research Association (SAUS)
ERA.............. Electric Response Audiometry (AAMN)
ERA.............. Electroencephalic Evoked Response Audiometry (DB)
ERA.............. Electronic Reading Automation [*Information retrieval*]
ERA.............. Electronic Realty Associates (SAUS)
ERA.............. Electronic Remittance Advice
ERA.............. Electronic Rentals Association [*British*] (BI)
ERA.............. Electronic Replaceable Assemby (SAUS)
ERA.............. Electronic Representatives Association (EA)

ERA............ electronic research administration (SAUS)
ERA............ Electronic Research Association [*British*]
ERA............ Electronic Retailing Association [*Trade group*]
ERA............ Electronic Revision and Approval [*Computer science*]
ERA............ Electronic Routing and Approval (TIMI)
ERA............ Electronics Representatives Association (SAUS)
ERA............ Electron Ring Accelerator
ERA............ Electroshock Research Association [*Later, International Psychiatric Library Service*]
ERA............ Elliniki Radiophonia [*Greek radio*] (EY)
ERA............ Ellison, R. A., Cincinnati OH [*STAC*]
ERA............ Emergency Relief Administration
ERA............ Employment Rights Act [*1996*] (WDAA)
ERA............ Energy Reduction Analysis (SAUS)
ERA............ Energy Reorganization Act [*1974*]
ERA............ Energy Resources of Australia (EERA)
ERA............ Engineering Records Automation (SAUS)
ERA............ Engineering Release Authorization
ERA............ Engineering Rental Agreement
ERA............ Engineering Request Authorization (AAG)
ERA............ Engineering Research Associates (MCD)
ERA............ Engineering Research Associates Inc. (SAUO)
ERA............ Engineering Research Association (SAUS)
ERA............ Engineer Rear-Admiral [*Navy*] [*British*]
ERA............ Engine-Room Artificer [*Obsolete*] [*Navy*] [*British*]
ERA............ English Racing Automobiles Ltd. [*British*]
ERA............ English Reports, Annotated [*A publication*] (DLA)
ERA............ Entity Relationship Attribute (SAUS)
ERA............ Environmental Protection Agency, Region IX Library, San Francisco, CA [*OCLC symbol*] (OCLC)
ERA............ Environmental Resources Analysis (SAUS)
ERA............ Environmental Resources of Australia [*Commercial*] (EERA)
ERA............ Environmental Risk Assessment (SARE)
ERA............ Enzyme Rate Analyzer
ERA............ Enzymic Radiochemical Assay [*Clinical chemistry*]
ERA............ Equal Rights Advocates (EA)
ERA............ Equal Rights Amendment [*Proposed constitutional amendment which supports equal rights regardless of sex*]
ERA............ Equipment Rental Agreement
ERA............ Equitable Reserve Association [*Neenah, WI*] (EA)
ERA............ ERA Technology (SAUO)
Era............ Erato [*Record label*] [*France*]
ERA............ Erigavo [*Somalia*] [*Airport symbol*] (AD)
ERA............ Eritrean Relief Agency (SAUS)
ERA............ Eritrean Relief Organization (SAUS)
ERA............ Estradiol Receptor Assay [*Medicine*] (MELL)
ERA............ Estrogen Receptor Assay [*Clinical chemistry*]
ERA............ Eurocommander SA [*Spain*] [*ICAO designator*] (FAAC)
ERA............ European Ramblers' Association (EAIO)
ERA............ European Regional Airlines (PDAA)
ERA............ European Regional Airlines Association [*British*] (EAIO)
ERA............ European Research Associates
ERA............ European Research Workers Association (SAUO)
ERA............ European Rotogravure Association [*Germany*] (PDAA)
ERA............ European Rum Association (EAIO)
ERA............ Evangelical Radio Alliance [*British*] (BI)
ERA............ Evaporative Rate Analysis [*Surface technology*]
ERA............ Evoked Response Audiometry [*Neurophysiology*]
ERA............ Exabiology and Radiation Assembly (SAUS)
ERA............ Excess Rent Allowance [*British*]
ERA............ Exchange Rate Agreement [*Banking*] [*British*]
ERA............ Executive Recruitment Association (COBU)
ERA............ Executive Resource Associates (AAGC)
ERA............ Exercise-Related Anaphylaxis [*Medicine*] (MELL)
ERA............ Exobiology and Radiation Assembly (SSD)
ERA............ Expedited Removal Action [*Environmental science*] (FFDE)
ERA............ Expedited Response Action (ABAC)
ERA............ Expense for Return of Absentee [*Military*]
ERA............ Explosive Reactive Armor [*Tank design*]
ERA............ Extended Range Ammunition (MCD)
ERA............ Extended-Range ASROC [*Antisubmarine Rocket*] [*Navy*] (NVT)
ERA............ Extended Registry Attributes (SAUS)
ERA............ External Release Agent
ERA............ Extra-Regimental Assignment [*Army*] (INF)
ERAA............ emergency readiness assurance appraisal (SAUS)
ERAA............ Equipment Review and Authorization Activity [*Military*] (AFM)
ERAAM............ Extended-Range Air-to-Air Missile (MCD)
ERAB............ Energy Research Advisory Board [*Department of Energy*]
ERAC............ Electromagnetic Radiation Advisory Council
ERAC............ Electronic Random Action Control
ERAC............ Environmental Research Assessment Committee [*National Research Council*]
ERAC............ Handicap International [*France*] (EAIO)
ERACE............ electrical remediation at contaminated environments (SAUS)
ERACOM............ Era Computer Corporation (SAUO)
ERAD............ Economic and Regulatory Analysis Division [*Environmental Protection Agency*] (GFGA)
ERAD............ Eliminate Records Administration and Duplication (SAUO)
ERAD............ Energy Research and Development (DNAB)
ERAD............ Enroute RADAR [*Aviation*] (FAAC)
ERAD............ En Route Radial (SAUS)
erad............ erased (SAUS)
ERAD............ Erie Army Depot
ERADCOM............ Electronics Research and Development Command [*Later, LABCOM*] [*Adelphi, MD*] [*Army*]
ERADCOM/ASL... Electronics Research and Development Command Atmospheric Sciences Laboratory [*Army*]
ERA-EDTA.... European Renal Association - European Dialysis and Transplant Association (SAUS)
ERAF............ Earth Resources Aircraft Facility [*NASA*]
ERAFSSO..... Emergency Reaction Air Force Special Security Office (SAUS)
ERAI............ Embry-Riddle Aeronautical Institute (SAUS)
ERAI............ Emby-Riddle Aeronautical Institute (SAUS)
ERAJFS........ Emergent Reading Ability Judgements for Favorite Storybooks Scale (EDAC)
ERAM............ Earth Resources Applications Mission [*NASA*] (KSC)
eRAM............ Embedded Random Access Memory [*Computer science*]
ERAM............ Equipment Reliability, Availability, and Maintainability (AAEL)
ERAM............ Extended Range Anti Armor Mine (ACAE)
ERAM............ Extended Range Antiarmor Munition
ERAM............ Extended Range Antitank Mine (MCD)
ERAM............ Extended Range Aviation Munition (ACAE)
ERAM............ Extended Range Mine (ACAE)
ERAMS............ Environmental Radiation Ambient Monitoring System [*Environmental Protection Agency*]
ERAN............ Examine and Repair as Necessary
ER&D............ Educational Research and Dissemination [*Program*]
ER & D............ Energy Research and Development
ER & S............ Electrolytic Refinery and Smelting (SAUS)
ER&S............ Exploratory Research and Study (SAUS)
ER&SD............ Employee Relations and Services Division (SAUO)
ER&WM............ environmental restoration and waste management (SAUS)
ERANOS............ ERANOS Foundation (SAUO)
ERANS............ Engineering Research Association for Nuclear Steelmaking (SAUO)
ERAP............ Earth Resources Aircraft Program [*NASA*]
ERAP............ Earth Resources Aircraft Project (SAUS)
ERAP............ Economic Research Action Project [*Students for a Democratic Society*] [*Defunct*]
ERAP............ Economic Research and Action Project (SAUS)
ERAP............ Emergency Readiness Assurance Plan [*Environmental science*] (COE)
ERAP............ Environmental Remedial Action Project (SAUS)
ERAP............ Error Recording Analysis Procedure (SAUS)
ERAP............ Error Recording and Analysis Procedure (ACAE)
ERAP............ Exchange Feeder Route Analysis Programme (SAUO)
ERAPS............ Enhanced Range Acoustic Path Sonobuoy (SAUS)
ERAPS............ Expendable Reliable Acoustic Path Sensor [*or Sonar or Sonobuoy*] (MCD)
ERAPS............ Expendable Reliable Acoustic Path Sonobuoy (SAUS)
ERAPT............ Electronic Reverse Auctioning Project Team
ERAR............ Error Return Address Register (SAUS)
ERAR............ Experience Retention Action Request (SAA)
ERAS............ East Riding Archaeological Society (SAUO)
ERAS............ Educational Resources Allocation Systems
ERAS............ EIN [*Employer Identification Number*] Research and Assignment System [*IRS*]
ERAS............ Electronic Reconnaissance Access Set
ERAS............ Electronic Residency Application Service (SAUS)
ERAS............ Electronic Routing and Approval System (SAUS)
ERAS............ Endogenous Reninangiotensin System [*Medicine*] (MELL)
ERAS............ En Route Advisory Service [*Aeromedical evacuation*]
ERAS............ Erase (SAUS)
Eras............ Erasmus (SAUS)
ERASE............ Eat Right and Slim Easily [*Weight Watchers, Inc., competition*]
ERASE............ Electromagnetic Radiation Source Elimination (NVT)
ERASE............ Electronic Radiation Source Eliminator (ACAE)
ERASE............ Emitted Radiation from Special Engines (MCD)
eraser............ elevated radiation seeker rocket (SAUS)
ERASER............ Elevated Radiation Seeking Rocket
ERASER............ Elevation Radiation Seeker Rocket (SAUS)
ERASER............ Enhanced Recognition and Sensing Radar (ADWA)
Erasmus............ Evaluation and Ranking of Alternative Sites for Major Users of Seaports (SAUS)
ERASP............ Education Resource Allocation in Schools Project [*Australia*]
ER ASROC... Extended-Range Antisubmarine Rocket [*Navy*] (SAA)
ERAST............ Environmental Research Aircraft and Sensor Technology
ERAST............ Environmental Research Aircraft Sensor Technology (SAUS)
ERATO............ Exploratory Research for Advanced Technology [*Japan*]
ERATO............ Extended Range Automatic Targeting of Otomat missile (SAUS)
Eratosth............ Eratosthenes [*275-194BC*] [*Classical studies*] (OCD)
E-RAU............ Embry-Riddle Aeronautical University [*Formerly, ERSA*] [*Daytona Beach, FL*]
Er Av............ Earned Average [*Baseball*]
ERB............ Earth's Radiation Budget [*Meteorology*]
ERB............ Ecclesiastical Relations Branch [*BUPERS*]
ERB............ Economic Requirement Batching
ERB............ Economic Resources Board (SAUO)
ERB............ Edgar Rice Burroughs [*1875-1950*] [*Author of Tarzan books*]
ERB............ Editorial Review Board (SAUO)
ERB............ Educational Records Bureau (EA)
ERB............ Educational Research Bulletin (journ.) (SAUS)
ERB............ Educational Rewards Bureau
ERB............ Education Research Branch (AIE)
ERB............ Edwards Rocket Base (MUGU)
ERB............ Electricians Registration Board (SAUS)
erb............ electron beam recording (SAUS)
ERB............ Electronic Recording Beam (MDG)
ERB............ Emergency Radio Beacon
ERB............ Emergency Relief Bureau (SAUO)
ERB............ Employee Recognition Bonus (TIMI)

ERB .... Employment Relations Board [*Usually preceded by abbreviation of state name*]
ERB .... Engineering Reference Branch [*Department of the Interior*]
ERB .... Engineering Review Board [*NASA*] (NASA)
ERB .... Engineers Registration Board [*Council of Engineering Institutions*] [*British*]
ERB .... Engine Relay Box (MCD)
ERB .... Enlisted Record Brief [*Army*] (AABC)
ERB .... Environmental Protection Agency, Environmental Monitoring and Support Laboratory, Las Vegas, NV [*OCLC symbol*] (OCLC)
ERB .... Environmental Response Branch (SAUO)
ERB .... Environmental Review Board (COE)
ERB .... Epic Resources (BC) Ltd. [*Vancouver Stock Exchange symbol*]
erb .... epigram record bureau (SAUS)
ERB .... Equipment Review Board (SAUS)
ERB .... Execution Request Block (SAUS)
ERB .... Executive Resources Board [*NASA*] (RDA)
ERB .... Executive Review Board (ACAE)
ERB .... Experiment Review Board [*Nuclear Regulatory Commission*] (NRCH)
ERBB2 .... Avian erythroblastic leukemia viral oncogene (SAUS)
ERBC .... Equine Red Blood Cells (SAUS)
ERB-Dom ..... Edgar Rice Burroughs Domain [*as in organization, Friends of ERB-Dom*]
ERBE .... Earth Radiation Budget (SAUS)
ERBE .... Earth Radiation Budget Experiment [*NASA*]
ERBE .... Earth Radiometer Backscatter Experiment (SAUS)
ERBE .... ERB experiment (SAUS)
ERBE-NS ...... Earth Radiation Budget Experiment Non-Scanner (SAUS)
ERBE-S .... Earth Radiation Budget Experiment Scanner (SAUS)
ERBES .... Earth Radiation Budget Explorer Satellite (CARB)
ERBE-S .... ERBE Scanner (SAUS)
ERBF .... Effective Renal Blood Flow [*Medicine*]
er bh .... engine room bulkhead (SAUS)
ERBI .... Earth Radiation Budget Instrument
ERBM .... Electronic Range/Bearing Marker (SAUS)
ERBM .... Extended-Range Ballistic Missile
ERBOS .... Earth Radiation Budget Observation Satellite (PDAA)
ERBP .... Equilibrium Reflux Boiling Point [*Brake fluid*]
ERB-PACK .... Earth Radiation Budget Package (SAUS)
ERBS .... Earth Radiation Budget Satellite [*NASA*] (MCD)
ERBS .... Earth Resources Budget Satellite
ERBS .... Emergency Radio Broadcast System (GOBB)
ERBS .... Expanded Range Bench Stock
ERBSS .... Earth Radiation Budget Satellite System [*NASA*] (MCD)
ErbStG .... Erbschaftsteuer- und Schenkungssteuergesetz (SAUS)
ERBUT .... Engine Requisition and Build-Up Time (MCD)
ERC .... Eagle Readiness Center (SAUS)
erc .... earnings-related compensation (SAUS)
ERC .... Earth Rate Compensation
ERC .... Earth Resources Consultants (SAUS)
ERC .... Earth Resources Corporation (SAUO)
ERC .... Easily Recognizable Code (DINT)
ERC .... Ebenezer Rail Car [*Federal Railroad Administration identification code*]
ERC .... Echo-Rhino-Coryza [*Virus*] [*Usage obsolete*]
ERC .... Economic Reform Club (SAUO)
ERC .... Economic Research Committee (SAUO)
ERC .... Economic Research Council [*Research center*] [*British*] (IRC)
ERC .... Economic Resources Corp. [*OEO-Department of Labor project*] (EA)
ERC .... Ecosystems Research Center [*Cornell University, EPA*] [*Research center*] (RCD)
ERC .... Ecumenical Resource Consultants (EA)
ERC .... Edge Reading Controller
ERC .... Educational Reference Center [*National Institute of Education*]
ERC .... Educational Research Center [*New Mexico State University*] [*Research center*] (RCD)
ERC .... Educational Research Centre [*Australia*]
ERC .... Educational Research Committee (SAUO)
ERC .... Educational Research Council of America (AEBS)
ERC .... Educational Resources Center (AEBS)
ERC .... Education and Resource Centre [*South Australia*]
ERC .... Education Relations Commission (SAUS)
ERC .... Eject Rocket Container
ERC .... Elections Research Center (EA)
ERC .... Electonic Remote Control [*Automotive electronic systems*]
ERC .... Electrical Research Committee (SAUO)
ERC .... Electrical Rule Checker [*For integrated circuitry*]
ERC .... Electric Regulation Co.
ERC .... Electric Regulation Company (SAUO)
ERC .... Electric Research Council (SAUO)
ERC .... electronic repair center (SAUS)
ERC .... Electronic Ride Control [*Automotive engineering*]
ERC .... Electronic Rule Check (SAUS)
ERC .... Electronics Research Center [*NASA*]
ERC .... Electronics Research Council (SAUO)
ERC .... Electron Reflection Coefficient
ERC .... Eligibility Review Committee [*Social security*] [*Australia*]
ERC .... El Reno College [*Oklahoma*]
ERC .... Emergency Relocation Center (NRCH)
ERC .... Emergency Rescue Committee (SAUO)
ERC .... Emergency Response Center (SAUS)
ERC .... Emergency Response Commission (GNE)
ERC .... Emergency Response Coordinator (SAUO)
ERC .... Emission Reduction Credit [*Environmental Protection Agency*] (GFGA)
ERC .... Empire Rheumatism Council (SAUO)
E-R-C .... Employee Relocation Council (EA)
ERC .... Employment Rehabilitation Center (SAUS)
ERC .... Endometriosis Research Center (ADWA)
ERC .... Endoscopic Retrograde Cholangiography [*Medicine*]
ERC .... Energy Research [*AMEX symbol*] (SG)
ERC .... Energy Research Centre (EERA)
ERC .... Energy Resources Center [*University of Illinois at Chicago*] [*Research center*] (RCD)
ERC .... Energy Resources Council [*Terminated, 1977*]
ERC .... Engineering and Research Center (SAUS)
ERC .... Engineering Readiness Center (SAUO)
ERC .... Engineering Research Center [*New Mexico State University*] (RCD)
ERC .... Engineering Research Center program (SAUO)
ERC .... Engineering Research Council (NRCH)
ERC .... Engineering Rule Check (SAUS)
ERC .... Engineer Reserve Corps (SAUO)
ERC .... English Red Cross (SAUO)
ERC .... English Resource Centre (SAUO)
ERC .... English Ruling Cases [*A publication*] (DLA)
ERC .... Enlisted Reserve Corps [*Later, Army Reserve*]
ERC .... En Route Chart [*Aviation*]
erc .... en-route chart (SAUS)
ERC .... Enteric Cytopathic Human Orphan-Rhino-Coryza Virus (DMAA)
ERC .... Environmental Reporter Cases [*Bureau of National Affairs*] [*A publication*] (DLA)
ERC .... Environmental Research Center [*Environmental Protection Agency*]
ERC .... Environmental Research Consortium
ERC .... Environmental Resources Center
ERC .... Environmental Response Center [*Department of Energy*] (IID)
ERC .... Environmental Science Research consortia (SAUS)
ERC .... Epic Record Co. [*Record label*] [*New York*]
ERC .... Epilepsy Research Center [*Baylor College of Medicine*] [*Research center*] (RCD)
ERC .... Epping Realty Corp. [*Vancouver Stock Exchange symbol*]
ERC .... Equal Rights Congress (EA)
ERC .... Equatorial Ring Current (IEEE)
ERC .... Equipage Repair Part Consumable (AFIT)
ERC .... Equipment Readiness Codes [*or Criteria*] (MCD)
ERC .... Equipment Record Card (AAG)
ERC .... Equivalent Release Concentration (AAEL)
ERC .... Eritrean Relief Committee (EA)
ERC .... Error Retry Count [*Computer science*] (IAA)
ERC .... Erythropoietin-Responsive Cell [*Hematology*]
ERC .... Erzincan [*Turkey*] [*Airport symbol*] (AD)
ERC .... Esquerra Republicana de Catalunya [*Catalan Republican Left*] [*Spain*] [*Political party*] (PPE)
ERC .... Essentials Review Committee [*American Occupational Therapy Association*]
ERC .... ESSO [*Standard Oil*] Resources Canada Ltd. [*UTLAS symbol*]
ERC .... Esso Rosources Canada Ltd. [*ICAO designator*] (FAAC)
ERC .... Estonian Relief Committee (EA)
ERC .... Estrogen Receptor, Cytosolic [*Endocrinology*]
ERC .... Ethics Resource Center (EA)
ERC .... Euro Info Centre (SAUS)
ERC .... European Radiocommunication Committee (SAUO)
ERC .... European Registry of Commerce (DS)
ERC .... European Rheumatology Congress [*Medicine*] (EDAA)
ERC .... Evaluation Research Center [*University of Virginia*] [*Research center*] (RCD)
ERC .... Evaluation Research Corporation (SAUO)
ERC .... Evaluation Review Committee (EERA)
ERC .... Event Recorder (NASA)
ERC .... Events Recorder Console (MCD)
ERC .... Excessive Requirements Cost (EERA)
ERC .... Exemplary Rehabilitation Certificate [*Department of Labor*]
ERC .... Expatriate Resources Co. [*British*]
ERC .... Expendability Repair Classification (AAG)
ERC .... expiratory reserve capacity (SAUS)
ERC .... Explicit Route Control (SAUS)
ERC .... Explosives Research Center [*Bruceton, PA*] [*Bureau of Mines*]
ERC .... Extended Range Cap [*Navy*] (ANA)
ERC .... Extended Research Checkout (SAUO)
ERC .... Externally Received Component
ERC .... External Reflected Component (SAUS)
ERC .... External Relations Committee (SAUS)
ERCA .... Educational Research Council of America [*Defunct*] (EA)
ERCA .... Ejercito Rojo Catalan de Liberacion [*Spain*] [*Political party*] (EY)
ERCA .... Electrochemically Regenerable Absorber (SAUS)
ERCA .... Electrochemically Regenerable Carbon Dioxide Absorber (NASA)
ERCA .... Emergency Relief and Construction Act
ERCA .... Emergency Response and Community Awareness (SAUS)
ErCam .... Camaldolese Hermits of the Congregation of Monte Corona (TOCD)
ercam .... Camaldolese Hermits of the Congregation of Monte Corona (TOCD)
ER CAM .... Eremitarum Camaldulensium [*Monk Hermits of Camaldoli*] [*Roman Catholic religious order*]
ERCB .... Energy Resources Conservation Board (SAUO)
ERCB .... Exploitation de Renseignements Contenus dans les Brevets [*Patent Information Exploitation - PIE*] [*Canadian Patent Office*]
ERCC .... Edinburgh Regional Computing Center [*British*]
ERCC .... Energy Research Corp. [*NASDAQ symbol*] (SAG)
ERCC .... Engine Requirement Coordinating Committee (SAUS)
ERCC .... Enroute Control Center [*Aviation*] (DA)
ERCC .... Erecting (SAUS)
ERCC .... Error Checking and Correcting (SAUS)

ERCC .... Error Checking and Correction [*Computer science*]
ERCC .... Error Checking and Correction Code (SAUS)
ERCC .... Expendability, Recoverability Cost Code (AAG)
ERCCC .... Error Checking and Correcting Code (SAUS)
ERCC Code... Error Checking and Correcting Code (SAUS)
ERCDC .... Energy Resources Conservation and Development Commission (SAUS)
ERCEM .... European Regional Conference on Electron Microscopy (SAUS)
ERCF .... Eglin RADAR Control Facility [*Florida*] [*Air Force*] (MCD)
ERCG .... Emergency Response Coordination Group (SAUO)
ERCG .... Erecting
ERCHCW .... European Regional Clearing House for Community Work (EAIO)
ERCI .... ERC Industries [*NASDAQ symbol*] (SAG)
ERCIA .... Egg Research and Consumer Information Act [*1974*]
ERCIM .... European Consortium on Informatics and Mathematics (SAUS)
ERCIM .... European Research Consortium for Informatics and Applied Mathematics (SAUO)
ERCIM .... European Research Consortium for Informatics and Mathematics (DDC)
ERCIM .... European Research Consortium for Information and Mathematics (VERA)
ERC Ind .... ERC Industries, Inc. [*Associated Press*] (SAG)
Erck .... Erck's Ecclesiastical Register [*1608-1825*] [*England*] [*A publication*] (DLA)
ERCL .... Environmental Research Chemistry Laboratory (SAUO)
ERCMAP .... Entity Relationship to Codasyl Mapping (SAUS)
ERCMIS .... Environmental Requirements/Capabilities Management Information System (MCD)
ERCMS .... ELINT [*Electronic Intelligence*] Requirements and Capabilities Management System (MCD)
ERCN .... Employee Record Change Notice
ERCO .... Electric Reduction Company (SAUO)
ERCO .... Energy Resources Co., Inc. (EFIS)
ERCO .... Engineering and Research Corporation (SAUO)
ERCO .... Engineering Representation & Consultants Co. (SAUO)
ERCO .... European Chemoreception Research Organization (SAUO)
ERCOCFA .... Eleanor Roosevelt's Centennial Observance Committee of Friends and Admirers (EA)
ERCOFTAC ... European Research Community on Flow, Turbulence and Combustion (SAUO)
ERCOS .... Embedded, Real-Time, Compliant Operating System
ERCOT .... Electric Reliability Council of Texas [*Regional power council*]
ERCP .... Emergency Response Concept Plan (SAUS)
ERCP .... Endoscopic Retrograde Cannulation of Pancreatic Duct [*Medicine*] (DAVI)
ERCP .... endoscopic retrograde cannulation of the papilla (SAUS)
ERCP .... Endoscopic Retrograde Cholangiopancreatographic [*Exam*] [*Medicine*]
ERCP .... Endoscopic Retrograde Cholangiopancreatography (QSUL)
ercp .... endoscopic retrograde cholangio-pancreatography (SAUS)
ERCR .... Electronic Retina Computing Reader
ERCR .... Engineering Release Change Record
ERCR .... Erector
ERCR .... Error Cause Register [*Computer science*] (IAA)
ERCS .... ECM Resistant Communications System (SAUS)
ERCS .... Elective Repeat Cesarean Section [*Obstetrics*]
ERCS .... Emergency Response Cleanup Services (GNE)
ERCS .... Emergency Response Contract Services [*Environmental science*] (COE)
ERCS .... Emergency Rocket Command System (SAUS)
ERCS .... Emergency Rocket Communications System
ERCSS .... European Regional Communications Satellite System (SAUS)
ERCT .... Erecting
ERCTR .... Erector
ERCU .... Edinburgh Royal Choral Union (SAUO)
ERCW .... Emergency [*or Essential*] Raw Cooling Water [*Nuclear energy*] (NRCH)
ERCWS .... Emergency Raw Cooling Water System [*Environmental science*] (COE)
ERCX .... Excel Railcar [*Private rail car owner code*]
ERD .... Early Retirement for Disability (MELL)
ERD .... Earth Resources Data (SAUS)
ERD .... Eastern Recruiting Division
ERD .... Ecological Research Division (SAUO)
ERD .... Ecosystems Research Division [*Athens Library*],[*Environmental Protection Agency*] (AEPA)
E/RD .... Edges Rounded [*Publishing*] (DGA)
ERD .... Elastic Recoil Detection
ERD .... Electronic Reading Device (SAUS)
ERD .... Electronic Recording Device (SAUS)
ERD .... Electronic Reference Document
ERD .... Electronic Research Directorate [*Air Force*]
ERD .... Electrostatic Recording Device (SAUS)
ERD .... Eligible Rollover Distribution [*Business term*]
ERD .... Emergency Recovery Display [*Bell System*]
ERD .... Emergency Relief Desk [*Eritrea*]
ERD .... Emergency Repair Disc (SAUS)
ERD .... Emergency Repair Disk [*Computer science*] (AGLO)
ERD .... Emergency Reserve Decoration [*British*]
ERD .... Emergency Response Division [*Environmental Protection Agency*] (GFGA)
ERD .... Emergency Return Device [*Aerospace*]
ERD .... End Routing Domain [*Computer science*] (TNIG)
ERD .... Energy Research and Development Inventory [*Information service or system*] (NITA)
ERD .... Entity-Relation Diagram (SAUS)
ERD .... Entity-Relationships Diagram [*Computer science*]
ERD .... Environmental Restoration Division (SAUS)
ERD .... Equipment Readiness Data
ERD .... Equipment Readiness Date [*Army*] (AABC)
ERD .... Equipment Readiness Drawing (MCD)
ERD .... Equipment Requirements Data [*Army*]
ERD .... Equivalent Residual Dose
ERD .... Erdek [*Turkey*] [*Seismograph station code, US Geological Survey*] (SEIS)
ERD .... ERD Waste Corp. [*Associated Press*] (SAG)
ERD .... Error Recording Device
ERD .... Estimated Receival Date (KSC)
ERD .... Estimated Release Date (AAG)
ERD .... Estuarine Research Data (SAUO)
ERD .... Evoked Response Detector [*Neurophysiology*] (MCD)
ERD .... Expense for Return of Deserter [*Military*]
ERD .... Experiment Requirements Document (KSC)
ERD .... Exponentially Retrograded Diode
ERD .... Expressed Reading Difficulty (EDAC)
ERD .... External Relations Division (SAUS)
ERD .... Extrapolated Response Dose (ODA)
ERD .... exudative RD (SAUS)
ERD .... Exudative Research & Development (SAUS)
ERD .... Environmental Radiation Data (ODA)
ERDA .... Economic Regional Development Agreements (SAUS)
ERDA .... Elastic Recoil Detection Analysis [*Physics*]
ERDA .... Electronic Resources Development Agency
ERDA .... Electronics Research and Development Activity [*Army*]
ERDA .... Electronics Research and Development Agency (SAUS)
ERDA .... Energy Research and Development Administration [*Superseded by Department of Energy, 1977*]
ERDA .... Energy Research and Development Agency [*Information service or system*] (NITA)
ERDA .... Energy System Acquisition Advisory Board (SAUO)
ERDA .... Engineering Research and Development in Agriculture (SAUS)
ERDA .... European Refrigeration Development Association (SAUO)
ERDAA .... Electronics Research and Development Activity Analysis [*Army*] (MCD)
ERDABCA .... Energy Research and Development Administration Board of Contract Appeals (AAGC)
ERDAC .... Energy Research and Development Advisory Council
ERDAF .... Energy Research and Development in Agriculture and Food (SAUS)
ERDAM .... Energy Research and Development Administration Manual [*A publication*] (IEEE)
ERD&DAA .... Environmental Research, Development, and Demonstration Authorization Act (EEVL)
ERDA-RDD... Energy Research and Development Administration, Division of Reactor Development and Demonstration (PDAA)
ERDA-RECON... ERDA Remote Console (SAUS)
ERDAS .... Earth Resource Data Analysis
ERDAS .... Earth Resources Digital Analysis System Software [*Computer science*] (EERA)
ERDB .... Environmental Radiofrequency Data Base (SAUS)
ERDC .... Earth Resources Data Center [*NASA*]
ERDC .... Eastern Region Development Corporation (SAUO)
ERDC .... East Region Development Corp.
ERDC .... East Region Development Corporation (SAUO)
ERDC .... Electronic Research and Development Command [*Army*]
ERDC .... Energy Research and Development Corporation (SAUO)
ERDC .... Engineering Research and Development Center [*University of Nevada, Reno*] [*Research center*] (RCD)
ERDC .... Engineering Research and Development Council (SAUO)
erdc .... equine respiratory disease complex (SAUS)
ERDC .... Exploratory Research and Development Center (SAUS)
ERDD .... European Research and Development Database
ERDDA .... Extended Resolution Digital Differential Analyzer (SAUS)
ERDDAA .... Environmental Research Development and Demonstration Authorization Act (GFGA)
ERDDAA .... Environmental Research Development and Demonstration Authorization Act of 1978 (COE)
ERDE .... Engineering Research and Development Establishment (SAUO)
ERDE .... Explosive Research and Development Establishment [*British*]
ERDEC .... Edgewood Research, Development and Engineering Center [*Army*] (RDA)
ERDET .... Error Detection (PDAA)
ERDF .... European Regional Development Fund [*See also FEDER*] [*Brussels, Belgium*] (EAIO)
ERDI .... Energy and Resource Development Institute [*Clemson University*] [*Research center*] (RCD)
ERDI .... Energy Research and Development Inventory [*Marine science*] (MSC)
ERDI .... ERD Waste Corp. [*NASDAQ symbol*] (SAG)
ERDIC .... Energy Research, Development, and Information Centre (ODA)
ERDIP .... Experimental Research and Development Incentives Program [*National Science Foundation*]
ERDL .... Electronic Research and Development Laboratory [*Army*] (MCD)
ERDL .... Engineer Research and Development Laboratories (SAUS)
ERDL .... Experimental Reactor Development Laboratory (SAUS)
ERDL .... Explosives Research and Development Laboratorie (SAUS)
ERDL .... Extended Range Data Link [*Bomb*] (MCD)
ERDL .... Exxon Research and Development Laboratories [*Formerly, Esso Research Laboratory*]
ERDM .... Employment Rehabilitation Divisional Manager (AIE)
ERDMC .... Environmental Restoration Document Management Center (SAUS)

ERDP .... Environmental Review and Documentation Program (SAUS)
ERDR .... Earth Rate Directional Reference
ERDR .... STAT Healthcare [*NASDAQ symbol*] (TTSB)
ERDR .... Stat Healthcare, Inc. [*NASDAQ symbol*] (SAG)
ERDRW .... Stat Healthcare Wrrt'A' [*NASDAQ symbol*] (TTSB)
ERDS .... Earth Resource Data System (SAUS)
ERDS .... Educational Research Document Delivery System (SAUS)
ERDS .... Emergency Response Data System (ODBW)
ERDS .... Environmental Radiation Data System [*Environmental Protection Agency*] (GFGA)
ERDS .... Environmental Recording Data Set (SAUS)
ERDS .... Environmental Review and Documentation System (SAUS)
ERDS .... Equipment Recall Data System (MCD)
ERDS .... Error Recording Data Set (SAUS)
ERDS .... European Reliability Data System (SAUO)
ERDSAT .... Earth Observation Satellite And Modular Platform (SAUS)
ERDT .... Electronic Research and Development Technician (IAA)
ERE .... East Carolina University, Greenville, NC [*OCLC symbol*] (OCLC)
ERE .... Echo Range Equipment
ERE .... Echo Return Error (VLIE)
ERE .... Ecumenical Research Exchange Center, Rotterdam (SAUO)
ERE .... Edison Responsive Environment [*Automated learning system*]
ERE .... Elite Resources Corp. [*Vancouver Stock Exchange symbol*]
ERE .... Emergency Rescue Equipment
ERE .... Employee Related Expense (SAUS)
ERE .... Encyclopedia of Religion and Ethics (SAUS)
ERE .... Energy Requirement for Energy (SAUS)
ERE .... Entity Relationship Editor (VLIE)
ERE .... Erave [*Papua New Guinea*] [*Airport symbol*] (OAG)
ERE .... Erevan [*Former USSR*] [*Seismograph station code, US Geological Survey*] (SEIS)
ERE .... Ericsson Radar Electronics (SAUS)
ERE .... Erie Airways, Inc. [*ICAO designator*] (FAAC)
ERE .... Estrogen-Responsive Element [*Endocrinology*]
ERE .... Ethylene-Responsive Element [*Biochemistry*]
ERE .... Event Recorder Evaluator (VLIE)
ERE .... Extended Red Emission [*Spectroscopy*]
ERE .... Extensional Rheology Experiment (SAUS)
ERE .... External Rotation in Extension [*Orthopedics*] (DAVI)
ERE .... Extra Regimental Employment (SAUS)
ERE .... Extra-Regimentally Employed [*List*] [*Military*] [*British*]
EREAC .... Environmental Radiation Exposure Advisory Committee (SAUO)
EREC .... Electronic Reconnaissance (MCD)
EREC .... Energy Efficiency and Renewable Energy Clearinghouse
EREC .... Enlisted Records and Evaluation Center [*Fort Benjamin Harrison, IN*] [*Army*]
EREC .... Enlisted Records Evaluation Center (SAUO)
erec .... Erection (MIST)
EREC .... Erection (ROG)
EREC .... Exxon Research and Engineering Co. [*Information service or system*] (IID)
ERECO .... European Economic Research and Advisory Consortium [*Belgium*] (EAIO)
ERECT .... Erection
ERECTN .... Erection (ROG)
EREF .... Energy Research and Education Foundation
ER-EIA .... estrogen receptor enzyme immunoassay (SAUS)
EREP .... Earth Resources Experimental Program (SAUO)
EREP .... Earth Resources Experiment Package [*Skylab*] [*NASA*]
EREP .... Earth Resources Package [*NASA*] (NASA)
EREP .... End Results Evaluation Program [*Later, SEER*] [*National Cancer Institute*]
EREP .... Environmental Record Editing and Printing program (SAUS)
EREP .... Environmental Recording Editing and Printing (SAUO)
EREP .... Environmental Recording, Editing, and Printing Program (BUR)
EREP .... Environment Record Edit and Print (SAUS)
EREP .... Equipment Replacement and Enhancement Program [*Computer science*]
EREP .... Error Recording, Edit, and Print (VLIE)
EREP .... Error recording editing and printing (SAUS)
EREP .... Error Recovery Executive Program (VLIE)
EREPP .... Earth Resources Experiment Package Program [*Skylab*] [*NASA*]
ERES .... Electronic Reflected Energy System [*Acoustics*]
ERES .... Electronic Resucitation Evaluation System (SAUS)
ERES .... Environmental Record Editing and Statistics [*Fujitsu*] [*Japan*] (NITA)
ERES .... Erie Western Railway Co. [*AAR code*]
ERES .... Erlanger Rechner-Entwurfs-Sprache [*Programming language*] [*1974*]
ERESC .... European Register of Stolen Computers (SAUO)
ER et I .... Edwardus Rex et Imperator [*Edward King and Emperor*] [*Latin*]
ERETS .... Edwards Rocket Engine Test Station [*NASA*] (IAA)
E-RETS .... Enhanced Remote Target System [*Military*] (INF)
ERETS .... Experimental Rocket Engine Test Station (SAA)
EREW .... Exclusive Read, Exclusive Write [*Computer science*]
ERF .... Early Renal Failure [*Medicine*]
ERF .... Education and Research Foundation (SAUO)
ERF .... Edward R.Fodon (SAUS)
ERF .... Eesti Rahvusfond (SAUO)
ERF .... Egg-Release Pheromone [*Biology*]
ERF .... Electronic counter-countermeasures Remote Fill (SAUS)
ERF .... Electronic Repair Facility [*Military*]
ERF .... Electro-Rheological Fluids [*American Cyanamid Co.*]
ERF .... Ellipsoidal Reflector Floodlight (WDMC)
ERF .... Emergency Recovery Force
ERF .... Emergency Response Facility (MCD)
ERF .... Emergency Response Fund (SAUO)
ERF .... Employer's Return File [*IRS*]
ERF .... Energy Rejection Filter
ERF .... Enerplus Resources Fund Series 'B' Trust Units [*Toronto Stock Exchange symbol*]
ERF .... Engineering Research Facility (ADWA)
ERF .... Entrainment Release Factor [*Nuclear energy*] (NRCH)
ERF .... Epoxy Resins Formulators Division (SAUS)
ERF .... Erfurt [*Germany*] [*Airport symbol*] (OAG)
ERF .... Error Function
ERF .... Established Risk Factor (PDAA)
ERF .... Estuarine Research Federation (EA)
ERF .... European Redistribution Facility
ERF .... European Regional File (SAUO)
ERF .... Event Report Function (VLIE)
ERF .... Exchange Reference File (ADA)
ERF .... Excitatory Receptive Field [*Physiology*]
ERF .... Expected Response File
ERF .... Explosion Release Factor [*Nuclear energy*] (NRCH)
ERF .... Exponential Reliability Function
ERF .... External Rotation in Flexion [*Orthopedics*] (DAVI)
ERF .... Eye Research Foundation (DAVI)
ERFA .... European Radio Frequency Administration (SAUS)
ERFA .... European Radio Frequency Agency [*Later, ARFA*] [*NATO*]
ERFAA .... European Radio Frequency Allocation Agency (SAUO)
ERFAA .... European Radio-Frequency Allocation Agency (SAUS)
ERFB .... Extended-Range Full Bore (PDAA)
ERFC .... Eddie Rabbitt Fan Club (EA)
ERFC .... Error Function Complement (SAUS)
ERFC .... Error Function Complementary
ERFC .... Erythrocyte Rosette-Forming Cells [*Hematology*]
ERFC .... Evaluation Rapide des Fonctions Cognitives [*Rapid evaluation of cognitive functions in psychiatric illnesses*] [*Medicine*] (EDAA)
ERFCS .... emergency response facility computer system (SAUS)
ERFD .... Airborne Particulate and Precipitation Data (SAUS)
ERFDADS ..... emergency response facility data acquisition and display system (SAUS)
ERFDP .... Earth Resources Flight Data Processor [*NASA*]
ERFEN .... Regional Study of the El Nino Phenomenon [*Peru-Chile-Columbia-Ecuador*] [*Marine science*] (OSRA)
ERFI .... Error Function, Integral (SAUS)
ERFI .... Error Function, Inverse
ERFIS .... emergency response facility indication system (SAUS)
ERFIS .... Emergency Response Facility Information System [*Nuclear energy*] (NRCH)
ERFPI .... Extended Range Floating Point Instruction (VLIE)
ERFPI .... Extended Range Floating Point Interpretive System (SAUS)
ERFPI .... Extended-Range Floating Point Interpretive System
ERFPIS .... Extended-Range Floating Point Interpretive System (IAA)
ERFPI System ... Extended Range Floating Point Interpretive System (SAUS)
ERFS .... Electrophysiological Ring Finger Splinting [*Medicine*] (EDAA)
ERFS .... Extended-Range Fuel System (DOMA)
ERF-SA .... Edward R.Foden South Africs (SAUS)
ERFU .... Environmental Restoration and Facilities Update (SAUS)
ERFU .... Environmental Restoration and Facilities Upgrade (SAUS)
ERFU .... Environmental Restoration and Facilities Upgrade Program (SAUO)
ERG .... Earth-Oriented Research Working Group (SAUO)
ERG .... Education Reference Group (SAUO)
erg .... electrical resistance gage (SAUS)
ERG .... Electrolyte Replacement with Glucose [*Medicine*] (MEDA)
ERG .... Electromagnetic Radiation Generator
ERG .... electro-magnetic rail gun (SAUS)
ERG .... Electronic Rentals Group [*Commercial firm*] [*British*]
ERG .... Electron Radiograph (SAUS)
ERG .... Electron Radiography (IAA)
ERG .... Electroretinogram [*Medicine*]
ERG .... Electroretinograph (SAUS)
ERG .... Electroretinography (LDOE)
ERG .... Emergency Recovery Group
ERG .... Emergency Response Guide [*RSPA*] (TAG)
ERG .... Emergency Response Guidebook (SAUO)
ERG .... Emergency Response Guidelines [*Nuclear energy*] (NRCH)
ERG .... Empirical Research Group (HGAA)
ERG .... Employment Resources Group [*British*]
ERG .... Endocrine Research Group [*University of Calgary*] [*Research center*] (RCD)
ERG .... Endoplasmic Reticulum of Golgi [*Cytology*]
ERG .... Energy-Related General [*National Science Foundation research office*]
ERG .... Energy-Related Graduate [*National Science Foundation trainee program*]
ERG .... Energy Research for the Governors
ERG .... Energy Research Group (SAUO)
ERG .... Engineering Release Group (AAG)
ERG .... Engineer Reactors Group [*Army*]
ERG .... Enhancement and Review Group (AAEL)
ERG .... Enriching and Reprocessing Group (SAUO)
ERG .... Environmental Research Group
ERG .... Environmental Research Group, Inc. (SAUO)
ERG .... Environmental Restoration Group (SAUO)
ERG .... Erase Gap [*Computer science*]
Erg .... Ergaenzung [*Amendment, Supplement*] [*German*] (DLA)
ERG .... Ergometer (MCD)
ERG .... ERG Resources, Inc. [*Formerly, Energy & Resources (CAM) Ltd.*] [*Toronto Stock Exchange symbol*]
ERG .... Eromanga [*New Hebrides*] [*Airport symbol*] (AD)

ERG .... Executive Review Group
ERG .... Existence, Relatedness, and Growth [*Basic human needs suggested by Clayton P. Alderfer*]
ERG .... External Review Group (SAUO)
ERGATT .... European Research Group for Alternatives in Toxicity Testing (GVA)
ERG/(CM² S)... Ergs per Square Centimeter Second [*Unit of work*]
ERGI .... Enjoin for Responsible Government [*An association*] (EA)
ERGLIA .... Environmental Research Geographic Location Information Act (COE)
ERGM .... Extended-Range Gun Munition [*Military*] (SEWL)
ERGO .... Energy Rich Glucose Optimized Drink [*Military*] (INF)
ERGO .... Environmental Review Guide for Operations [*US Army Corps of Engineers*]
ergo .... ergonomics (SAUS)
ERGO .... Ergo Science [*NASDAQ symbol*] (TTSB)
ERGO .... Euthanasia Research and Guidance Organization (EA)
ERGODATA... Banque de Donnees Internationales de Biometrie Humaine et d'Ergonomie [*International Database of Human Biometrics and Ergonomics*] [*Universite Rene Descartes*] [*France*] [*Information service or system*] (CRD)
ERGODATA... Ergonomy Data [*Information service or system*] [*France*] (NITA)
ERGOM .... European Research Group on Management (SAUO)
ergon .... ergonomic (SAUS)
ergon .... ergonomical (SAUS)
ERGON......... Ergonomics (ADA)
ergp .... emergency removal gate pass (SAUS)
ERGP .... Extended Range Guided Projectiles (MCD)
ERGS .... Earth Geodetic Satellite [*Air Force*] (SAUS)
ERGS .... Electronic Route Guidance System (OA)
ERGS .... En Route Guidance System (IEEE)
ERG/S .... Ergs per Second [*Unit of work*]
ERGS .... Experimental Route Guidance System (IAA)
ERH .... Eastern Region Headquarters, Bohemia (SAUS)
ERH .... Egg-Laying Release Hormone [*Endocrinology*]
ERH .... Elastomeric Rotary-Wing Head [*Military*] (CAAL)
ERH .... Electric Reading Head (SAUS)
ERH .... Equilibrium Relative Humidity (SAUS)
ERH .... ERA Helicopters, Inc. [*ICAO designator*] (FAAC)
Erh .... Erhard (SAUS)
ERH .... Erith Herbarium [*Borough Museum*] [*British*]
ERH .... Ethiopian Refugee Help-Line (EAIO)
ERHD .... Exposure-Related Hypothermic Death (MELL)
ERHPA .... Efficient Reliable High-Power Amplifier (MCD)
ERHS .... Evangelical and Reformed Historical Society
ERHSA-UCC... Evangelical and Reformed Historical Society and Archives, United Church of Christ (EA)
ERHS-UCC ... Evangelical and Reformed Historical Society, United Church of Christ [*Later, ERHSA-UCC*] (EA)
ERI.............. Ear Research Institute [*Later, HEI*] (EA)
ERI.............. Earthquake Research Institute
ERI.............. Ecological Research and Investigations (SAUO)
ERI.............. Economic Research Institute [*Utah State University*] [*Research center*] (RCD)
ERI.............. Educational Research Information
ERI.............. Education and Research Institute [*Washington, DC*] (EA)
ERI.............. EGFR [*Epidermal Growth Factor Receptor*] Related Inhibitor [*Biochemistry*]
ERI.............. Ekwal Reading Inventory (EDAC)
ERI.............. Eleanor Roosevelt Institute (EA)
ERI.............. Electronic Resources, Incorporated (SAUO)
ERI.............. Electronics Research Laboratory [*Montana State University*] [*Research center*] (RCD)
ERI.............. Ellef Ringnes Island [*Canada*]
ERI.............. Elm Research Institute (EA)
ERI.............. Emergency Response Indictor
ERI.............. Employee Relations Index
ERI.............. End of Recorded Information [*Computer science*]
ERI.............. Energy Research Institute (EA)
ERI.............. Energy Resources Incorporated (SAUO)
ERI.............. Energy Resources Institute [*University of Oklahoma*] [*Research center*] (RCD)
ERI.............. Engineering Research Institute [*Iowa State University*] [*Research center*] (AAG)
ERI.............. Engineer Restructuring Initiative [*Army*]
ERI.............. Enterprise Resources [*Vancouver Stock Exchange symbol*]
ERI.............. Entomological Research Institute
ERI.............. Environmental Research Institute (EA)
ERI.............. Environmental Resource Institute (SAUO)
ERI.............. Environmental Response Inventory [*Research test*] [*Psychology*]
ERI.............. Equitable Resources, Inc. (EFIS)
ERI.............. Equivalent Reference Illuminance (SAUS)
Eri.............. Eridamus [*Constellation*]
Eri.............. Eridanus (SAUS)
ERI.............. Erie [*Pennsylvania*] [*Airport symbol*] (OAG)
ERI.............. Erie, PA [*Location identifier*] [*FAA*] (FAAL)
ERI.............. Erindale Campus Library, University of Toronto [*UTLAS symbol*]
ERI.............. Erionite [*A zeolite*]
ERI.............. Essig Research Incorporated (SAUO)
ERI.............. Ethical Reasoning Inventory (EDAC)
ERI.............. Eureka Ridge [*Idaho*] [*Seismograph station code, US Geological Survey*] [*Closed*] (SEIS)
ERI.............. Executive Resources International [*British*]
ERI.............. Expressive-Regressive Index
ERI.............. Extended Range Interceptor (ACAE)
ERI.............. Extravehicular Reference Information [*NASA space program*]
ERI.............. Eyes Right (EA)
ERIA............ Electroradioimmunoassay [*Clinical chemistry*]
ERIC............ Educational Research and Information Center (SAUS)
ERIC............ Educational Resources [*formerly, Research*] Information Center [*Department of Education*] [*Bibliographic database*] [*Washington, DC*]
ERIC............ Education Resources Information Center (SAUS)
ERIC............ Effective Rate of Interest and Charges
ERIC............ Electronic Remote and Independent Control
ERIC............ Electronic Retailing Investment Corp. [*Acronym is also the name of an electronic vending kiosk*]
ERIC............ Emergency Response Intervention Card (HEAS)
ERIC............ Energy Rate Input Controller (IEEE)
ERIC............ Enterobacterial Repetitive Intergenic Consensus [*Genetics*]
ERIC............ Environmental Research and Information Centre [*Commercial*] (EERA)
ERIC............ Environmental Research Information Center (SAUO)
ERIC............ Ericsson [*L. M.*] Telephone Co. [*NASDAQ symbol*] (NQ)
ERIC............ ERISA [*Employee Retirement Income Security Act*] Industry Committee (EA)
ERIC............ European Road Information Centre (SAUO)
ERICA .... Effective Reading in Content Areas (EDAC)
ERICA .... European Research into Consumer Affairs [*England*] [*Research center*] (IRC)
ERICA .... Experiment on Rapidly Intensifying Cyclones and Anticyclones (SAUS)
ERICA .... Experiment on Rapidly Intensifying Cyclones in the Atlantic (SAUS)
ERICA .... Experiment on Rapidly Intensifying Cyclones over the Atlantic [*National Oceanic and Atmospheric Administration*]
ERICA .... Eye-Gaze Response Interface Computer Aid [*Computer designed for the physically handicapped that responds to user's eye movements*] [*Designed by Thomas Hutchinson*]
ERIC/ACVE... Educational Resources Information Center/Clearinghouse on Adult, Career, and Vocational Education [*Department of Education*] (IID)
ERIC-AE .... Educational Resources Information Center - Adult Education (SAUS)
ERIC/AE .... Educational Resources Information Center/Adult Education [*Department of Education*] (AEBS)
ERIC/AE .... ERIC Clearinghouse on Adult Education (SAUS)
ERIC/C .... Central ERIC (SAUS)
ERICCA........ Equal Rights in Clubs Campaign for Action [*British*] (DI)
ERIC/CAPS... Educational Resources Information Center/ Clearinghouse on Counseling and Personnel Services (SAUS)
ERIC/CAPS... Educational Resources Information Center/Clearinghouse on Counseling and Personnel Services [*Department of Education*] [*University of Michigan*] [*Research center*] (IID)
ERIC/CAPS... ERIC Clearinghouse on Counceling and Personnel Services (SAUS)
ERIC/CCE..... ERIC Clearinghouse on Career Education (SAUS)
ERIC/CE ...... Educational Resources Information Center/Clearinghouse in Career Education [*Ohio State University*] (IID)
ERIC/CE ...... ERIC Clearinghouse on Adult Career and Vocational Education (SAUS)
ERIC/CEA..... Educational Resources Information Center/ Clearinghouse on Educational Administration (SAUS)
ERIC/CEA..... Educational Resources Information Center/Clearinghouse on Educational Administration [*University of Oregon*] [*Department of Education*] (AEBS)
ERIC-CEA..... ERIC - Clearinghouse on Educational Administration (SAUS)
ERIC/CEC..... Educational Resources Information Center/ Clearinghouse for Educational Change (SAUS)
ERIC/CEC..... ERIC Clearinghouse on Exceptional Children (SAUS)
ERIC/CEF..... ERIC Clearinghouse on Education Facilities (SAUS)
ERIC/CEM.... Educational Resources Information Center/ Clearinghouse on Educational Management (SAUS)
ERIC/CEM.... Educational Resources Information Center/Clearinghouse on Educational Management [*Department of Education*] [*University of Oregon*] [*Eugene*] [*Research center*]
ERIC/CEM.... ERIC Clearinghouse on Educational Management (SAUS)
ERIC/CHE..... Educational Resources Information Center/Clearinghouse on Higher Education (IID)
ERIC/CHE..... ERIC Clearinghouse on Higher Education (SAUS)
ERIC/CHESS... Educational Resources Information Center/Clearinghouse for Social Studies/SocialScience Education [*Department of Education*] [*Information service or system*] (IID)
ERIC/CHESS... ERIC Clearinghouse for Social Science Education (SAUS)
ERIC / CHESS... ERIC Clearinghouse for Social Studies (SAUS)
ERIC/CIR...... Educational Resources Information Center/ Clearinghouse on Information Resources (SAUS)
ERIC/CIR...... Educational Resources Information Center/Clearinghouse on Information Resources (SAUO)
ERIC-CIR...... ERIC -- Clearinghouse on Information Resources (SAUS)
ERIC/CIR...... ERIC/Clearinghouse on Information Resources (SAUS)
ERIC/CLIS.... Educational Resources Information Center/Clearinghouse for Library Information Sciences
ERIC/CLIS.... ERIC Clearinghouse for Library and Information Sciences (SAUS)
ERIC-CLIS.... ERIC -- Clearinghouse on Library and Information Sciences (SAUS)
ERIC / CLIS... ERIC Clearinghouse on Library and Information Sciences (SAUS)
ERIC/CLL ..... Educational Resources Information Center/ Clearinghouse on Languages and Linguistics (SAUS)
ERIC/CLL ..... Educational Resources Information Center/Clearinghouse on Languages and Linguistics [*Department of Education*] [*Center for Applied Liguistics*] (IID)
ERIC/CLL ..... ERIC Clearinghouse on Languages and Linguistics (SAUS)
ERIC-CLIS.... ERIC - Clearinghouse on Library and Information Sciences (SAUS)
ERIC-CIR...... ERIC - Clearinghouse on Information Resources (SAUS)

ERIC/CLS ..... Educational Resources Information Center/ Clearinghouse for Library and Information Sciences (SAUS)
ERIC/CRCS... Educational Resources Information Center/Clearinghouse on Reading and Communication Skills (SAUO)
ERIC/CRESS... Educational Resources Information Center/ Clearinghouse on Rural Education and Small Schools (SAUS)
ERIC/CRESS... Educational Resources Information Center/Clearinghouse on Rural Education and Small Schools [*Department of Education*] [*New Mexico State University*] [*Research center*] (IID)
ERIC / CRESS... ERIC Clearinghouse on Rural Education and Small Schools (SAUS)
ERIC/CRIER... Educational Resources Information Center/ Clearinghouse on Retrieval Information and Evaluation on Reading (SAUS)
ERIC/CRIER... Educational Resources Information Center/Clearinghouse on Retrieval of Information and Evaluation on Reading [*Indiana University*] [*Department of Education*] (AEBS)
ERIC-CRIER... ERIC -- Clearinghouse on Retrieval Information and Evaluation on Reading (SAUS)
ERIC/CRIER... ERIC Clearinghouse on Retrieval of Information and Evaluation on Reading (SAUS)
ERIC/CUE ..... Educational Resources Information Center/Clearinghouse on Urban Education [*Department of Education*] [*Columbia University*] (IID)
ERIC/CUE ..... ERIC Clearinghouse on Urban Education (SAUS)
ERIC/EC .... Educational Resources Information Center/Clearinghouse on Handicapped and GiftedChildren [*Department of Education*] [*Information service or system*] (IID)
ERIC/ECE ..... Educational Resources Information Center/ Clearinghouse on Early Childhood Education (SAUS)
ERIC/ECE ..... ERIC Clearinghouse on Early Childhood Education (SAUS)
ERIC/EEC ..... ERIC Clearinghouse on Elementary and Early Childhood Education (SAUS)
ERIC/EECE ... Educational Resources Information Center/Clearinghouse on Elementary and Early Childhood Education [*Department of Education*] [*University of Illinois*] (IID)
ERIC/EM ...... ERIC Clearinghouse on Educational Media (SAUS)
ERIC/EM ...... ERIC Clearinghouse on Educational Media and Technology (SAUS)
ERIC-EM .... ERIC - on Educational Media (SAUS)
ERIC/EMT .... ERIC Clearinghouse on Educational Media and Technology (SAUS)
ERIC/HE .... Educational Resources Information Center/Clearinghouse on Higher Education [*George Washington University*] [*Research center*] (EA)
ERIC/HE .... ERIC Clearinghouse on Higher Education (SAUS)
ERIC/IR .... Educational Resources Information Center/Clearinghouse for Information Resources [*Department of Education*] [*Syracuse University*] [*Research center*] (IID)
ERIC/IR .... ERIC Clearinghouse on Information Resources (SAUS)
ERIC-IR .... ERIC - on Information Resources (SAUS)
ERIC/IRCD ... Educational Resources Information Center/Information Retrieval Center on the Disadvantaged [*Horace Mann-Lincoln Institute Teachers College*] [*Columbia University*] [*Department of Education*] (AEBS)
ERIC-IRCD ... ERIC - Information Retrieval Center on the Disadvantaged (SAUS)
ERIC/IRCD ... ERIC Information Retrieval Center on the Disadvantaged (SAUS)
ERIC/JC........ ERIC Clearinghouse for Junior Colleges (SAUS)
ERIC-IR .... ERIC - Information Resources (SAUS)
ERIC-IRCD ... ERIC - Information Retrieval Center on the Disadvantaged (SAUS)
Ericofon .... Ericsson telephone (SAUS)
ERIC-PRF..... ERIC Processing and Reference Facility (SAUS)
ERICR .... Eleanor Roosevelt Institute for Cancer Research
ERIC/RCS..... Educational Resources Information Center/Clearinghouse on Reading and Communication Skills [*Department of Education*] [*Urbana, IL*]
ERIC/RCS..... ERIC Clearinghouse on Reading and Communication Skills (SAUS)
ERICS .... Emergency Rocket Communications Subsystem (ACAE)
ERIC/SMAC... ERIC Clearinghouse for Science and Mathematics Education (SAUS)
ERIC/SMEAC... Educational Resources Information Center/Clearinghouse for Science, Mathematics,and Environmental Education [*Department of Education*] [*Information service or system*] (IID)
ERIC/SMEAC... ERIC Science, Mathematics and Environmental Education Analysis Center (SAUS)
ERIC/SP .... Educational Resources Information Center/School Personnel [*Department of Education*] [*Washington, DC*]
ERIC/SP .... ERIC Clearinghouse on School Personnel (SAUS)
EricT............ Ericsson [*L.M.*] Telephone Co. [*Associated Press*] (SAG)
ERIC/TE........ Educational Resources Information Center/Clearinghouse on Teacher Education
ERIC/TE........ ERIC Clearinghouse on Teacher Education (SAUS)
EricTel .... Ericsson Telephone [*Associated Press*] (SAG)
ERIC/TM .... Educational Resources Information Center/Clearinghouse on Tests, Measurement, and Evaluation [*Department of Education*] [*Educational Testing Service*] (IID)
ERIC/TM ...... ERIC Clearinghouse on Tests, Measurements and Evaluation (SAUS)
ERIC/TME .... Educational Resources Information Center/ Clearinghouse on Tests, Measurement, and Evaluation (SAUS)
ERICY .... Ericsson(LM) Tel'B'ADR [*NASDAQ symbol*] (TTSB)
ERICY .... Ericsson, L.M., Tel'B'ADS [*NASDAQ symbol*] (SG)
ERICZ........... Ericsson L M Tel [*NASDAQ symbol*] (TTSB)
ERICZC .... Educational Reptiles in Captivity Zoological Compound (EA)
ERID .... Emerging and Reemerging Infectious Diseases [*Medicine*]
Erid.............. Eridamus [*Constellation*]
ERIE............. Eastern Regional Institute for Education
ERIE............. Environmental Resistance Inherent in Equipment
Erie.............. Erie County Legal Journal [*Pennsylvania*] [*A publication*] (DLA)
ERIE............. Erie Indemnity 'A' [*NASDAQ symbol*] (TTSB)
ERIE............. Erie Indemnity Co. [*NASDAQ symbol*] (SAG)
ERIE............. Erie Mining [*Federal Railroad Administration identification code*]
ERIE............. Erie, PA [*American Association of Railroads railroad junction routing code*]
Erie Co Leg J... Erie County Legal Journal [*Pennsylvania*] [*A publication*] (DLA)
Erie Co L J (PA)... Erie County Law Journal (Pennsylvania) [*A publication*] (DLA)
ERI/EDI .... Early Retirement Incentive/Early Departure Incentive (FOTI)
ERiEI............ Eastern Regional Institute for Education (SAUS)
ErieInd......... Erie Indemnity Co. [*Associated Press*] (SAG)
Erie LJ......... Erie County Legal Journal [*Pennsylvania*] [*A publication*] (DLA)
Erie Phil ...... Erie Philharmonic (SAUS)
ERIG .... Ecological Research and Investigations Group (SAUO)
ERILCO .... Exchange of Ready for Issue in Lieu of Concurrent Overhaul
erild............ earth rotation in lunar distances (SAUS)
ERIM............ Environmental Research Institute of Michigan [*Research center*] (RCD)
ERIN .... Earth Resources Information Network (SAUS)
ERIN .... Environmental Resources Information Network [*Australia*]
ERINT .... Extended Range Interceptor [*Air Force*]
ERINT .... Extended Range Interceptor Technology (SAUS)
ERINT .... Extended-Range Intercept Technology Missile [*Army*]
ERIP............. Early Retirement Incentive Program [*Generic term*]
ERIP............. Energy-Related Inventions Program [*Department of Energy and National Bureau of Standards*]
ERIP............. ENERLINKS: Australian Energy Research, Development and Demonstration Projects (SAUO)
ERIP............. Engineering Research Initiation Program [*National Science Foundation*]
ERIP............. Experiment Requirement and Implementation Plan (SAUS)
ERIPS .... Earth Resources Image [*or Interactive*] Processing System
ERIPS .... Earth Resources Interactive Processing System (SAUS)
ERIR .... Extended-Range Instrumentation RADAR (PDAA)
ERIS............. Earth-Reflecting Ionospheric Sounder [*Air Force*] (MCD)
ERIS............. Earth Resources Information System (SAUS)
ERIS............. Earth Resources Inventory System (SAUS)
ERIS............. Economic Resource Impact Statement
ERIS............. Electrostatic Reflex Ion Source (SAUS)
ERIS............. Emergency Resources Identification Equipment (IAA)
ERIS............. Emergency Resources Identification System (SAUS)
ERIS............. Emergency Response Information System [*Nuclear Regulatory Commission*] (GFGA)
ERIS............. Energy Research Information System (SAUS)
ERIS............. Enforcement Case Support Expert Resources Inventory System (SAUS)
ERIS............. Engineering Resins Information System [*General Electric Co.*]
ERIS............. Environmental Resource Information Services [*Australia*]
ERIS............. Environmental Resources Information System [*Computer science*] (EERA)
ERIS............. Equal Rank-Intervals Set (VLIE)
ERIS............. Equipe de Recherche Interdisciplinaire en Sante [*Universite de Montreal, Quebec*] [*Canada*]
ERIS............. European Research Information Service (SAUS)
ERIS............. Exoatmospheric Reentry Interceptor System (SAUS)
ERIS............. Exoatmospheric Re-entry vehicle Interception System (SAUS)
ERIS............. Exoatmospheric Reentry Vehicle Interceptor Subsystem [*Army*] (RDA)
ERISA .... Early Retirement Income Security Act (SAUS)
ERISA .... Employee Retirement Income Security Act [*of 1994*] (AAGC)
ERISA .... Employee Retirement Income Security Act of 1974 [*Also facetiously translated as Every Ridiculous Idea Since Adam*]
ERISA .... Employee Retirment Income Security Act (EBF)
ERISA .... Employment Retirement Income Security Act (SAUO)
ERIS ML ...... European Research Information Service on Modern Languages (SAUS)
ERISS .... Employment Research and Information Supply (SAUO)
ERISTAR ...... Earth Resources Information Storage, Transformation, Analysis, and Retrieval
Erit.............. Eritrea
ERIV............. Eagle River Interactive [*NASDAQ symbol*] (TTSB)
ERIV............. Eagle River Interactive, Inc. [*NASDAQ symbol*] (SAG)
ERIW .... European Research Institute for Welding (PDAA)
ERJ .... Alexandria, LA [*Location identifier*] [*FAA*] (FAAL)
ERJ .... Eurojet Italia [*Italy*] [*ICAO designator*] (FAAC)
ERJ .... Extended-Range Juno [*Survey meter for radiation*]
ERJ .... External Ramjet
ERJA............ E R Johnson Association (SAUO)
ERJE .... Extended Remote Job Entry
erk .... enroute kit (SAUS)
ERK.............. Ethniko Rizospastiko Komma [*National Radical Party*] [*Greek*] (PPE)
ERK.............. Experimental Research Kit
ERK.............. Extracellular-Signal-Regulated Kinase [*An enzyme*]
ERKE............ Excess Rotational Kinetic Energy (SAUS)
ERKO .... Estrogen Receptor Knockout [*Mouse strain*]
ERL.............. Earth Resources Laboratory [*Later, NSTL*] [*NASA*] (KSC)
ERL.............. Echo Return Loss [*Telecommunications*]
ERL.............. Economic Retention Level (AFIT)
ERL.............. Effective Refractory Length [*Ophthalmology*] (DAVI)
E(RL) .... Electrician (Radio Land Wire Operator) [*U.S. Navy enlisted rating*] (AUER)
ERL.............. Electromagnetic Radiation Laboratory (SAUS)
ERL.............. Electronic Reference Library (VLIE)
ERL.............. Electronics Research Laboratory [*University of California, Berkeley*] [*Research center*] (RCD)
ERL.............. Electronics Research Laboratory [*Massachusetts Institute of Technology*] [*Research center*] (MCD)
ERL.............. Emergency Reference Level [*Nuclear energy*] (NRCH)
ERL.............. emergency response level (SAUS)

ERL............ Ending Reel Label (SAUS)
ERL............ Energy Research Laboratories (EERA)
ERL............ Enteric Reference Laboratory [*London*] [*Medicine*] (EDAA)
ERL............ Environmental Research Laboratories [*Boulder, CO*] [*National Oceanic and Atmospheric Administration*]
ERL............ Environmental Resources Library (SAUS)
ERL............ Environmental Resources Limited (SAUO)
ERL............ Environmental Resources Ltd. [*British*]
ERL............ Equine Research Laboratory [*University of California, Davis*]
ERL............ Equipment Requirement List (MCD)
ERL............ Equipment Revision Level (IAA)
Erl............ Erl (SAUS)
Erl............ Erlass [*Decree, Edict, Order*] [*German*] (ILCA)
Erl............ Erload (SAUS)
ERL............ Error Line (AGLO)
ERL............ Error Location (SAUS)
ERL............ ESSA [*Environmental Science Services Administration*] Research Laboratories
ERL............ Euralair [*France*] [*ICAO designator*] (FAAC)
ERL............ European Requirements List [*Military*] (AABC)
ERL............ Event Record Log
ERL............ Explosives Research Laboratory (SAUS)
ERL............ Extended-Range Lance [*Missile*] (MCD)
ERL............ Extended Relational Language (SAUS)
ERL............ Extraneous Residue Limit [*Toxicology*]
ERL............ Eye Research Laboratories [*University of Chicago*] [*Research center*] (RCD)
ERLAP........ European Reference Laboratory for Air Pollution (SAUS)
ERLAS........ Earth Resources Laboratory Application Software (SAUO)
ERL/ATH...... Athens Environmental Research Laboratory [*Athens, GA*] [*Environmental Protection Agency*] (GRD)
ERL-C......... Environmental Research Laboratory Narragansett [*Environment term*] (EGA)
ERLC........... Exponential Run Length Code (SAUS)
ER-ICA........ estrogen receptor immunocytochemical assay (SAUS)
ERL/COR...... Corvallis Environmental Research Laboratory [*Corvallis, OR*] [*Environmental Protection Agency*] (GRD)
E/RLD......... Edges Rolled [*Publishing*] (DGA)
ERL/DUL...... Duluth Environmental Research Laboratory [*Minnesota*] [*Environmental Protection Agency*] (GRD)
ERLE........... Echo Return Loss Enhancement
ERLE........... Energy-Related Laboratory Equipment [*Defunct*]
ERLE........... excess research laboratory equipment (SAUS)
Erle Tr Un.... Erle on the Law of Trade-Unions [*A publication*] (DLA)
ERL/GB........ Gulf Breeze Environmental Research Laboratory [*Gulf Breeze, FL*] [*Environmental Protection Agency*] (GRD)
ERLink......... Emergency Response Link (SEWL)
ERLL........... Enhanced Run Length Limited [*Computer science*] (BYTE)
ERL-N......... Environmental Research Laboratory, Narragansett [*Environmental Protection Agency*]
ERL/NARR... Narragansett Environmental Research Laboratory [*Narragansett, RI*] [*Environmental Protection Agency*] (GRD)
ERLR........... Eastern Region of Nigeria Law Reports [*A publication*] (DLA)
ERLS........... Economic Release Lot-Size
ER-LSS........ Environmental Research Literature Search and Storage (SAUS)
ERLTM......... Environmental Research Laboratories Technical Memorandum (SAUO)
ERLTM......... ESSA [*Environmental Science Services Administration*] Research Laboratories. Technical Memorandum [*A publication*]
ERLUA......... Environmental Research Laboratory, University of Arizona
ERL-UCB...... University of California, Berkeley Electronics Research Laboratory [*Research center*] (RCD)
ERLV........... Erysimum Latent Virus [*Plant pathology*]
ERLY........... Early
ERLY........... ERLY Indus [*NASDAQ symbol*] (TTSB)
ERLY........... ERLY Industries, Inc. [*NASDAQ symbol*] (SAG)
ERM............ Earth Re-Entry Module (MCD)
ERM............ Earth Resistivity Meter
ERM............ Earth Resource Mapping (SAUS)
ERM............ Earth Resource Monitoring (SEWL)
ERM............ Earth Return Module [*NASA*] (KSC)
ERM............ Edge Reading Meter
ERM............ Eesti Rahva Muuseum (SAUO)
ERM............ Effective Relaxation Modulus
ERM............ Ejection Restraint Mechanism (ACAE)
ERM............ Elastic Reservoir Molding (DICI)
erm............ elastic reservoir moulding (SAUS)
ERM............ Electrical Research Memorandum
ERM............ Electric Research and Management (SAUS)
ERM............ Electrochemical Relaxation Methods
ERM............ Electronic Recording Machine (SAUS)
ERM............ Electronic Records Management
ERM............ Electronics Right Management (VLIE)
ERM............ EMC and Radio Matters (SAUS)
ERM............ Emergency Radiation Monitor
ERM............ Energy Research Management (MCD)
ERM............ Engine Room
ERM............ En Route Metering [*FAA*] (TAG)
ERM............ Enterprise Reference Model (AAEL)
ERM............ Enterprise Relationship Management
ERM............ Enterprise Risk Management
ERM............ Entity-Relationships Model (HGAA)
ERM............ environmental and radiological monitoring (SAUS)
ERM............ Environmental Resources Management
ERM............ Environmental Resources Management, Inc. [*Database producer*] (IID)
ERM............ Epiretinal Membrane [*Ophthalmology*]
ERM............ Erimo [*Japan*] [*Seismograph station code, US Geological Survey*] (SEIS)
ERM............ Ermine [*Heraldry*]
ERM............ Error Recovery Manager (SAUS)
ERM............ Error Recovery Module (SAUS)
ERM............ European Rate Mechanism (SAUS)
ERM............ European Red Mite [*Insect*]
ERM............ Evaporate Rate Monitor (IAA)
ERM............ Evaporation Rate Monitor (AAEL)
ERM............ Evaporation Rate Monitoring (SAUS)
ERM............ Exact Repeat Mission [*of GEOSAT*] [*Navy*] (GFGA)
ERM............ Exchange-Rate Mechanism [*European Economic Union*] (ECON)
ERM............ Explosives Research Memorandum
ERM............ Exposure Radical Mastectomy (MELL)
ERM............ Extended Radical Mastectomy [*Medicine*] (STED)
ERM............ Ezrin-Radixin-Moesin [*Cytology*]
e-rm-.......... Romania [*MARC geographic area code*] [*Library of Congress*] (LCCP)
ERMA.......... Electrical Reproduction Method of Accounting (SAUS)
ERMA.......... Electronic Reading Method of Accounting (SAUS)
ERMA.......... Electronic Recording Machine (SAUS)
ERMA.......... Electronic Recording Machine Accounting
ERMA.......... Electronic Recording Method of Accounting (SAUS)
ERMA.......... Emergency Refugee and Migration Assistance [*Department of State*]
ERMA.......... Engineering Reprographic Management Association [*Later, ERS*]
ERMA.......... Engineering Reprographics Management Association (SAUS)
ERMA.......... Environmental Restoration Monitoring and Assessment Program (SAUS)
ERMA.......... Environmental Risk Management Authority (SAUS)
ERMA.......... Environment Resources Management Association (SAUO)
ERMA.......... Ernest Read Music Association [*British*] (DBA)
ERMA.......... Expansion Rate Measuring Apparatus
ERMA.......... Extended Red Multialkali [*Cathode*]
ERMAC........ Echo-Ranging Masked Acoustic Communications
ERMAC........ Electromagnetic Radiation Management Advisory Council [*US Government*]
ERMA Cathode... Extended Red Multi-Alcali Cathode (SAUS)
ERMA Cathode... Extended Red Multi-Alkali Cathode (SAUS)
ERMA-Katode... extended red multialkali cathode (SAUS)
ERMAN........ Earth Resources Management (SAUS)
ERMAN........ Earth Resources Management System (SAUS)
ERMAN System... Earth Resources Management System (SAUS)
ERMBE......... Energy-Related Minority-Owned Business Enterprise
ERMC.......... Environmental Restoration Management Contractor (SAUO)
ERMC.......... Europe Regional Monitoring Center (SAUO)
ERMCA........ Energy and Resources Management Conservation Authority (SAUS)
ERMCO........ European Ready Mixed Concrete Organization (EAIO)
ERMD.......... Environment and Resource Management Division [*World Wildlife Fund-United States*]
Ermes.......... European Messaging System (SAUO)
ERMES......... European Radio Message (or Messaging) System (SAUO)
ERMES......... European Radio Message Service (SAUO)
ERMES......... European Radio Messaging System
ERMG.......... Enroute Metering [*Aviation*] (FAAC)
ERMI........... Electronic Radio Manufacturing Industry (SAUO)
ERMING....... Ermington [*England*]
ERMISS....... Explosion-Resistant Multi-Influence Sweep System (NATG)
ER-MLRS..... Extended Range, Multiple Launch Rocket System [*Army*]
ER model..... Entity Relationship Model [*Computer science*]
ERMP.......... Energy Research Management Project [*Federal interagency group*]
ERMP.......... Environment Management and Review Program (EERA)
ERMP.......... Ethnic Records Microform Project (SAUS)
ermpl.......... employee (SAUS)
ER/MRT....... Equipment Removal/Material Review Tag [*Military*] (MCD)
ERMS.......... Educational Resource Management System (SAUS)
ERMS.......... Electrical Resistivity Measuring System (SAUO)
ERMS.......... Electroluminescent Runway Marking System [*Aviation*]
Erms........... electron root mean square (SAUS)
ERMS.......... E-Mail Response Management System (GART)
ERMS.......... Emergency Radiation Monitoring System (GNE)
ERMS.......... Environmental Resources Mapping System [*Computer science*] (EERA)
ERMS.......... European Register of Marine Species (SAUO)
ERMS.......... Exacerbating-Remitting Multiple Scelrosis (MELL)
ERMU.......... Experimental Remote Maneuvering Unit
ERMV.......... Cherry European Rusty Mottle Virus (SAUS)
ERMV.......... European Rusty Mottle Virus (SAUS)
ERN............ Eastern
ERN............ Ecological Research Network (SAUO)
ERN............ Educational Radio Network
ERN............ Effective Radiation Node (SAUS)
ERN............ Effectivity Revision Notice (ACAE)
ERN............ Electronic RADAR Navigation (DNAB)
ERN............ Engineering Reference Number
ERN............ Engineering Release Notice (MSA)
ERN............ Environmental Research News (SAUO)
Ern............ Ernest (SAUS)
ERN............ Ernestine [*Alaska*] [*Seismograph station code, US Geological Survey*] [*Closed*] (SEIS)
ERN............ Error-Related Negativity [*Neurophysiology*]
ERN............ Explicit Route Number (SAUS)
ERN............ Explosives Research Note

ERN .... External Recurrent Neural Network (AAEL)
ERNA .... Engineer, Royal Naval Artillery [*Navy*] [*British*] (ROG)
ERNA .... Equilibrium Radionuclide Angiography [*Cardiology*] (CPH)
ERNAS .... European Review of Native American Studies [*A publication*]
ERNET .... Education and Research Network [*India*] [*Computer science*] (TNIG)
ERNets .... Energy Research Networks (SAUO)
ERNIC .... Earnings-Related National Insurance Contribution [*British*] (DCTA)
ERNIE .... Electronic Random Number and Indicating Equipment [*Used for selecting winning premium bond numbers*] [*British*]
ERNIE .... Electronic random number indicator equipment (SAUS)
Ernie .... Ernest (SAUS)
ERNK .... Enlya Ruzgariya Netwa Kurdistan [*National Front for the Liberation of Kurdistan*] [*Turkey*] [*Political party*]
ERNLR .... Eastern Region of Nigeria Law Reports [*A publication*] (DLA)
ERNO .... Entwicklungsring Nord Organisation [*Space Division of European Consortium*]
ERNO .... European Research National Organization (MCD)
ERNS .... Emergency Response Notification System [*Environmental Protection Agency*] (EPA)
ERNS .... Ernst Home Center [*NASDAQ symbol*] (TTSB)
ERNS .... Ernst Home Center, Inc. [*NASDAQ symbol*] (SAG)
ErnstHm .... Ernst Home Center, Inc. [*Associated Press*] (SAG)
ERO .... Early Retirement Opportunity [*Business term*]
ERO .... Early Return Option (SAUS)
ERO .... Eastman-Rochester Orchestra (SAUS)
ERO .... Eldred Rock, AK [*Location identifier*] [*FAA*] (FAAL)
E(RO) .... Electrician (Radio Operator) [*U.S. Navy enlisted rating*] (AUER)
ERO .... Electronic Repair Order [*Automobile service*]
ERO .... Elementary Relaxation Oscillator [*Instrumentation*]
ERO .... Emergency Repair Overseer [*Navy*]
ERO .... Emergency Response Officer [*Environmental science*] (COE)
ERO .... Emergency Response Organization [*Environmental science*] (COE)
ERO .... Employer Relations Officer
ERO .... Energy Research Office [*Department of Energy*] (OICC)
ERO .... Engineering Regional Organisation (ACII)
ERO .... Engineering Release Operations (NASA)
ERO .... Engineering Release Order [*Formerly, ROD*]
ERO .... Engine Running Offload (SAUS)
ERO .... Engine Running On (SAUS)
ERO .... Engine Running On Load (SAUS)
ERO .... Enterprise Resource Optimization (GART)
ERO .... Environmental Response Organization (SAUS)
ERO .... Environmental Restoration Organization (SAUS)
ERO .... Equipment Repair Order (DNAB)
ERO .... ERO, Inc. [*Associated Press*] (SAG)
Ero .... Erosion (SAUS)
ERO .... European Radiocommunications Office (DDC)
ERO .... European Regional Office (SAUS)
ERO .... European Regional Organization (SAUS)
ERO .... European Regional Organization of the ICFTU
ERO .... European Regional Organization of the International Dental Federation (EAIO)
ERO .... European Research Office [*British*]
ERO .... evoked response olfactometry (SAUS)
ERO .... Exclusive Retailers Organization (SAUO)
ERO .... Extended Range Ordnance (SAUS)
ERO .... Sundor International Air Services Ltd. [*Israel*] [*ICAO designator*] (FAAC)
EROAT .... Echo Ranging Operated Acoustic Torpedo [*Military*] (IAA)
EROC .... Ecological Rates of Change (SAUO)
EROC .... Ecological Response to Change (SAUS)
EROC .... En-Route Obstacle Clearance Criteria (SAUS)
EROC .... Environmental Restoration Opportunities Conference
EROCP .... Extended Remote Operator Control Panel (SAUS)
EROD .... Ethoxyresorufin O-Deethylase [*An enzyme*]
EROI .... Energy Return on Investment
EROI .... Engineering Return on Investment (TIMI)
EROI .... ERO, Inc. [*NASDAQ symbol*] (SAG)
EROICA .... Estimation and retrieval of organic properties (SAUS)
EROM .... electronically alterable read-only memory (SAUS)
EROM .... Electron Readout Measurement (MCD)
EROM .... Erasable Read-Only Memory [*Computer science*]
EROM .... Erasable ROM [*Computer science*] (ECII)
EROMDA .... Eastern Regional Office Machine Dealers Association Convention (TSPED)
EROMM .... European Register of Microform Masters (TELE)
E-room .... engine room (SAUS)
EROOS .... Entity-Relationship Object-Oriented Specifications (ITCA)
EROP .... Executive Review of Overseas Programs [*Army*] (AABC)
EROP .... Extensions and Restrictions of Operators (IEEE)
EROPA .... Eastern Regional Organization for Public Administration GG2 [*Manila, Philippines*] [*See also OROAP*]
EROPS .... Extended Range Operations (PIAV)
EROS .... Earth Resources Observation Satellite (SAUO)
EROS .... Earth Resources Observation System [*United States of America*] [*Military*] (EERA)
EROS .... Earth Resources Observation Systems [*US Geological Survey*]
EROS .... Earth Resources Observing Satellite (USDC)
EROS .... Earth Resources Observing System (SAUO)
EROS .... Eelam Revolutionary Organization [*Sri Lanka*] [*Political party*]
EROS .... Electric Resonance Optothermal Spectrometer
EROS .... Electric Resonance Optothermal Spectroscopy
EROS .... Eliminate Range Zero System (SAUS)
EROS .... Elimination of Range Zero System [*Aviation*]
EROS .... Engineering Records Organisation System [*Applied Research of Cambridge Ltd.*] [*Software package*] (NCC)
EROS .... Engine Repair and Overhaul Squadron [*British Royal Air Force*]
EROS .... Environment and RADAR Operations Simulator
EROS .... Equipment Required on Site (MCD)
EROS .... Estimate Range Zero System (SAA)
EROS .... European River Ocean System (CARB)
EROS .... European Rivers Outflow Studies (SAUS)
EROS .... Event-Related Optical Signal [*Imaging science*]
EROS .... Experience de Recherche d'Objets Sombres [*Astronomy*]
EROS .... Experience de Recherches d'Objets Sombres [*Experiment on Investigations int o Dark Objects*]
EROS .... Experimental Reflector Orbital Shot [*NASA project*]
EROS .... Experimental Reflector Orbit Shot (SAUS)
EROS .... Extendable Realtime Operating System (SAUS)
EROS .... USGS Earth Resources Observing System (SAUS)
EROS-2000 ...... European River Ocean System (SAUS)
EROS-2000 ...... European River-Ocean Systems Programme (SAUS)
EROSAT .... ELINT [*Extended-Range Interceptor Technology*] Ocean Reconnaissance Satellite (DOMA)
EROSP .... Earth Resources Observation Systems Program (SAUS)
EROW .... Executive Right of Way [*Telecommunications*] (TEL)
EROWS .... Expandable Remote-Operated Weather Station (SAUO)
EROWS .... Expendable Remote Operating Weather Station [*Air Force*]
EROX .... Erox Corp. [*NASDAQ symbol*] (SAG)
EroxCp .... Erox Corp. [*Associated Press*] (SAG)
ERP .... Early Receptor Potential [*of the eye*]
ERP .... early refractory period (SAUS)
ERP .... Early Release of Prisoners (WDAA)
ERP .... Earthquake Reporting and Prediction (NOAA)
ERP .... Earth Reference Point (SAUS)
ERP .... Earth Reference Pulse (IAA)
ERP .... Earth Resources Program (SAUS)
ERP .... Easy Revolving Plan (SAUS)
ERP .... ECM Resistant Communications System (SAUS)
ERP .... Ecological Research Project (SAUO)
ERP .... Econometric Research Program [*Princeton University*] [*Research center*] (RCD)
ERP .... Economic Recovery Program (SAUO)
ERP .... Economic Review Period
ERP .... Economic Rights Program [*Later, WERP*] (EA)
ERP .... Educational Reimbursement Program (SAA)
ERP .... Effected Radiative Power (SAUS)
ERP .... Effected Radioactive Power
ERP .... Effective Radiated Power [*Radio transmitting*]
ERP .... Effective Radiation Power (SAUS)
ERP .... Effective Rating Point (WDMC)
ERP .... Effective Refractory Period
ERP .... Ejercito Revolucionario del Pueblo [*People's Revolutionary Army*] [*El Salvador*] (PD)
ERP .... Ejercito Revolucionario del Pueblo [*People's Revolutionary Army*] [*Argentina*] (PD)
ERP .... Electronic Radiated Power (PDAA)
ERP .... Electronic Reliability Panel of Electronic Parts Committee of Aerospace Industries Association of America, Inc. (SAUO)
ERP .... Electronic Requirement Plan [*Navy*]
ERP .... Electronic Road Pricing (PDAA)
ERP .... Electronics Research Paper (SAUS)
erp .... electro rustproofing (SAUS)
ERP .... Electrostatic Reversal Printing
ERP .... Elevated Release Point [*Nuclear energy*] (NRCH)
ERP .... Eligibility Review and Reemployment Assistance Program [*Employment Service*] [*Department of Labor*]
ERP .... Elodoisin-Related Peptide [*Medicine*] (DMAA)
ERP .... Emergency Recorder Plot (IAA)
ERP .... Emergency Relocation Point (DOMA)
ERP .... Emergency Requirements Plan (SAUS)
ERP .... Emergency Response Plan (SARE)
ERP .... Emergency Response Program [*Environmental science*] (COE)
ERP .... Emergency-Room Physician (MEDA)
ERP .... Emergency Rubber Project [*National Research Council*]
ERP .... Emerson Radio and Phonograph (SAUS)
ERP .... Emissive Radio Power (SAUS)
ERP .... Emitted Radio Power (IAA)
ERP .... Emitter Radiated Power (SAUS)
ERP .... Endocardial Resection Procedure [*Cardiology*]
ERP .... Endoscopic Retrograde Pancreatography [*Medicine*]
ERP .... End Reporting Period
ERP .... End Response (IAA)
ERP .... Enforcement Response Policy [*Environmental Protection Agency*] (GFGA)
ERP .... Engineered Restoration Procedure
ERP .... Engineering Release Package
ERP .... Engineering Requirements Plan [*for Military Assistance Programs*]
ERP .... Enroute Reporting Point [*MTMC*] (TAG)
ERP .... Enterprise Resource Planning (ACII)
ERP .... Environmental Research Papers (MCD)
ERP .... Environmental Research Parks (SAUO)
ERP .... Environmental Research Program (SAUO)
ERP .... Environmental Research Project (SAUS)
ERP .... Environmental Response Policy
ERP .... Environmental Responsibility Program [*An association*] (EA)
ERP .... Environmental Restoration Program (SAUS)
ERP .... Enzyme-Releasing Peptide (MELL)
ERP .... Equine Rhinopneumonitis [*Medicine*] (MAE)

ERP............. Equipment Repair Parts
ERP............. Equipment Replacement Program [*Computer science*]
ERP............. Equipment Requirement Program (MCD)
ERP............. Equipment Requirements Plan (SAUO)
ERP............. Equivalent Radiated Power
ERP............. equivalent radiation power (SAUS)
ERP............. Equivalent Reduction Potential (SAUS)
ERP............. Erase, Record, and Playback (NTCM)
ERP............. Error-Recovery Package [*Computer science*] (MDG)
ERP............. Error-Recovery Procedure [*Computer science*]
ERP............. Erythropoietin (SAUS)
ERP............. Establishment Reporting Plan [*Social Security Administration*] (GFGA)
ERP............. Estimated Reseller Price
ERP............. Estimated Resident Population [*Demographics*] [*Australia*]
ERP............. Estrogen Receptor Protein [*Endocrinology*]
ERP............. Euler-Rodrigues Parameter [*Physics*]
ERP............. European Reconstruction Program (SAUO)
ERP............. European Recovery Program
ERP............. Event-Related Potential [*Neurophysiology*]
ERP............. Evoked Response Potential (SAUS)
ERP............. Expanded Relations Program [*Army*] (DOMA)
ERP............. Exploratory Research Program (TIMI)
ERP............. Extended Range Projectile (SAUS)
ERP............. Extended-Range Projectile
ERP............. Extended Range Proximity (SAUS)
ERP............. Extended Range Pyrometer (AAEL)
ERP............. exterior router protocol (SAUS)
ERP............. External Ramjet Program (SAUS)
ERP............. External Research Program (SAUS)
ERP............. Eye Reference Point [*NASA*] (KSC)
ERPA........... Electronic Production Resources Agency (SAUO)
ERPA........... Emergency Response Planning Area [*Environmental science*] (COE)
ERPA........... European Rotogravure Packaging Association (SAUO)
ERPA........... Evader Replica Penetration Aids (ACAE)
ERPA........... Office of Exploratory Research and Problem Assessment [*National Science Foundation*]
ERP Adm..... European Recovery Program Administration (SAUO)
ERPAL.......... Electronic Repair Parts Allowance List [*Navy*]
ERP-AVN...... effective refractory period of the AV-node (SAUS)
ERPC........... Eastern Railroad Presidents Conference [*Later, ERA*] (EA)
ERPC........... Eglin Refugee Processing Center [*Florida*] [*Air Force*] (MCD)
ERPC........... Emerson Radio & Phonograph Corp. [*Later, Emerson Radio Corp.*]
ERPD........... Electronic Reconnaissance Procurement Division
ERPD........... Experimental RADAR Prediction Device (MCD)
ERPF........... Effective Renal Plasma Flow [*Medicine*]
ERPF........... Estimated Renal Plasma Flow [*Medicine*] (MELL)
ERPFI.......... Extended-Range Floating-Point Interpretive System (SAUS)
ERPG........... Emergency Response Planning Guideline [*Environmental science*]
ERPG-2........ Emergency Response Guidelines-2 (SAUS)
ERPL........... Equipment Repair Parts List
ERPLD......... Extended-Range Phase-Locked Demodulator (IEEE)
ERPLS......... Eastern Regional Public Library System (SAUS)
ERPLV......... Effective Refractory Period of Left Ventricle [*Medicine*] (EDAA)
ERPM.......... East Rand Proprietary Mines Ltd., South Africa (SAUS)
ERPM.......... Engineering Requirements and Procedures Manual (MCD)
ERPN........... Eastern Region Public Notice [*Nigeria*] [*A publication*] (DLA)
ERPN........... European
ERPO........... Earth Resources Project Office (MCD)
ERPPO......... Engineer Repair Parts Packaging Office [*Merged with General Equipment Command*]
ER-PR.......... Effectiveness Report - Performance Report [*Air Force*] (AFM)
ERPR........... Exponentially Restored, Poisson-Released
ERPS........... Electrolytic Reactants Production System (IAA)
ERPS........... Environmental Radiation Protection Standard (NUCP)
ERPS........... Environmental Restoration Program Support (SAUS)
ERPS........... Equipment Release Priority System [*DoD*]
ERPS........... Equipment Requisitioning Priority System [*Military*]
ERPSL......... Essential Repair Part Stockage List [*Military*] (AABC)
ERPSL......... Essential Repair Stock List (SAUS)
ERPTUAC..... European Recovery Program Trade Unions Advisory Committee (SAUO)
ERPTUAC..... European Recovery Program Trade Unions Advisory Program (SAUO)
ERQ............ Economic Reorder Quantity (ADA)
ERQ............ Economic Repair Quantity
ERQ............ Endorsement Request (TVEL)
ERQ............ End Request (IAA)
ERQC.......... Engineering Reliability and Quality Control (AAG)
Err............... [*The*] Comedy of Errors [*Shakespearean work*]
ERR............ Eagle Ridge Resources Ltd. [*Vancouver Stock Exchange symbol*]
ERR............ Eastern Resources Research (SAUO)
ERR............ Economic Rate of Return
ERR............ Economic Retention Requirement (AFIT)
ERR............ Edaville Railroad [*Federal Railroad Administration identification code*]
ERR............ Efficiency and Renewables Research Section (SAUS)
E(RR).......... Electrician (Radio Repair) [*U.S. Navy enlisted rating*] (AUER)
ERR............ Electronic Requirements Report (DNAB)
ERR............ Elk River Reactor
ERR............ Employer Relations Representative
ERR............ Engineering Release Record (AAG)
ERR............ Engineering Reliability Review (MCD)
ERR............ Engineering Research Report
ERR............ Engine Removal Report
ERR............ Erie Railroad
ERR............ Errata [*Error*] [*Latin*] (NVT)
ERR............ Errol, NH [*Location identifier*] [*FAA*] (FAAL)
ERR............ Erroneous (SAUS)
ERR............ Error (MCD)
ERR............ Error description (SAUS)
err............... Estonian Soviet Socialist Republic [*MARC country of publication code*] [*Library of Congress*] (LCCP)
ERR............ Estrogen Receptor-Related
ERR............ Explosive Echo Ranging (SAUS)
ERR............ Extended Range Rocket [*Aerospace*]
ERR............ Energy Release Rate (ODA)
ERRA.......... Eritrean Relief and Rehabilitation Association
ERRAIS....... Environmental Restoration and Remedial Action Information System (SAUS)
ERRAN........ Error Analysis (SAUS)
Err & App.... Error and Appeal Reports [*Canada*] [*A publication*] (DLA)
err & app..... error and appeals (SAUS)
ERRAP........ Environmental Resources Research and Assistance Program [*US Army Corps of Eng ineers*]
ER/RB......... Enhanced Radiation/Reduced Blast
ERRC.......... Eastern Regional Research Center [*Department of Agriculture*] [*Philadelphia, PA*] (GRD)
ERRC.......... Employment Relations Resource Centre [*British*] (AIE)
ERRC.......... Error Character (SAUS)
ERRC.......... Error Correction
errc.............. expandability, recoverability, repairability cost (SAUS)
ERRC.......... Expendability, Recoverability, Repairability Code (SAUS)
ERRC.......... Expendability, Recoverability, Repairability Cost (NASA)
ERRC.......... Expendability/Recoverability/Repair Capability (NASA)
ER/RC......... Extended Result/Response Code (SAUO)
ERRCC........ Expendability, Recoverability, Repairability Cost Category
ERR CNTR... Error Counter
ERRD.......... Emergency and Remedial Response Division [*Environmental Protection Agency*] (GFGA)
ERRDEP...... Error Variance Dependent on Level [*Statistical test*]
ERRDF........ Earth Resources Research Data Facilities (SAUS)
ERRDF........ Earth Resources Research Data Facility
ERREAC...... Employee Relocation Real Estate Advisory Council [*Later, E-R-C*] (EA)
ERRET........ Error Return Point (MCD)
ERRI........... Environmental Resources Research Institute [*Pennsylvania State University*] [*Information service or system*] (IID)
ERRIS......... Emergency and Remedial Response Information System [*Environmental science*] (COE)
ERRN.......... Expedite Release Request Notice (MCD)
ERRON........ Erroneous
erron........... Erroneously (ADWA)
ERRP.......... EGF [*Epidermal Growth Factor*] Receptor-Related Protein [*Biochemistry*]
ERRS.......... Efficiency and Renewables Research Section (SAUS)
ERRS.......... Environmental Response and Referral Service [*Oak Ridge National Laboratory*] (IID)
ERRSAC....... Eastern Regional Remote Sensing Applications Center (SAUO)
ERRSAC....... Eastern Region Remote Sensing Application Center (SAUS)
ERRSYS....... Errata System (SAUS)
ERRT.......... Economic Research Round Table (EA)
ERS............ Early Reporting System (SAUS)
ERS............ Earnings-Related Supplement [*British*]
ERS............ Earth Recources Survey (SAUS)
ERS............ Earth Recovery Subsystem [*NASA*] (KSC)
ERS............ Earth Reference System (ACAE)
ERS............ Earth Regeneration Society (EA)
ERS............ Earth Remote-Sensing (SAUO)
ERS............ Earth Remote Sensing Satellite (EERA)
ERS............ Earth Research From Space (SAUS)
ERS............ Earth Resources Satellite [*NASA*]
ERS............ Earth Resources Survey [*NASA*]
ERS............ Eastern Radiological Society (SAUO)
ERS............ Eastern Railway Supply [*Federal Railroad Administration identification code*]
ERS............ Eastern Range Ships
ERS............ Economic Research Service [*Department of Agriculture*] [*Washington, DC*]
ERS............ Economic Retention Stock
ERS............ Educational Research Service (EA)
ERS............ Edwards Rocket Site (SAUS)
ERS............ Electoral Reform Society [*British*]
ERS............ Electrical Resistance Strain (OA)
ERS............ Electric Railway Society (EAIO)
ERS............ Electric Reconnaissance Set (SAUS)
ERS............ Electric Resistant Strain (SAUS)
ERS............ Electrolytic Refining and Smelting Company [*Australia*] [*Commercial firm*]
ERS............ Electronic Rear Steering [*Automotive engineering*]
ERS............ Electronic Reconnaissance Set
ERS............ Electronic Reconnaissance System
ERS............ Electronic Register-Sender [*Telecommunications*] (TEL)
ERS............ Electronic Remote Switching (MCD)
ERS............ Electronic Repair Station
ERS............ Electronic Rig Stats [*Pennwell Publishing Co.*] [*Information service or system*] (IID)
ERS............ Element Requirements Specification (SAUS)
ERS............ Elevated Radio System
ERS............ Elizabethan Railway Society [*British*] (BI)
ERS............ Emergency Radio System (SAUS)

ERS .... Emergency Recovery Section
ERS .... Emergency Release System (SAUS)
ERS .... Emergency Relocation Site [*Military*]
ERS .... Emergency Reporting System [*Telecommunications*] (TEL)
ERS .... Emergency Response Service (SAUS)
ERS .... Emergency Response System (MELL)
ERS .... Emergency Road Service [*American Automobile Association*]
ERS .... Employee Relocation Service (SAUS)
ERS .... Employees Retirement System (SAUO)
ERS .... End-Around Shift (SAUS)
ERS .... Endoscopic Retrograde Sphincterotomy [*Medicine*]
ERS .... Energy Research Section (SAUS)
ERS .... Energy Return System [*In ERS 2000, brand name of Reebok International Ltd.*]
ERS .... Engineering Release System
ERS .... Engineering Reprographic Society (EA)
ERS .... Engineering Research Station [*British*]
ERS .... Engineers Register Study (SAUS)
ERS .... Engine Room Supervisor (DNAB)
ERS .... Enterprise Resource Sharing (SAUS)
ERS .... Entry and Recovery Simulation (MCD)
ERS .... Environmental Research Satellite [*NASA*]
ERS .... Environmental Resources Services (SAUO)
ERS .... Environmental Resource Studies (SAUS)
ERS .... Equilibrium Radiation Spectra
ERS .... Equipment Record System (KSC)
ERS .... Equipment Requirement Specification
ERS .... Erased (MSA)
ERS .... Ergonomics Research Society [*British*] (BI)
ERS .... Eros Resources [*Vancouver Stock Exchange symbol*]
ERS .... Error Report Suppression [*Computer science*] (VERA)
ERS .... ESA [*European Space Agency*] Remote Sensing Satellite
ERS .... Estimated Release Schedule (AAG)
ERS .... Ethylene Response Sensor [*Botanical genetics*]
ERS .... European Radar Satellite (SAUS)
ERS .... European Radio Satellite (SAUS)
ERS .... European Recreation Society (SAUO)
ERS .... European Remote Sensing (SAUO)
ERS .... European Remote Sensing Satellite (SAUS)
ERS .... European Research Satellites (SAUO)
ERS .... European Rhinologic Society (EA)
ERS .... European (Space Agency) Remote Sensing Satellite System (EERA)
ERS .... Evaluated Receipts Settlement (SAUS)
ERS .... Evaluation Record Sheet (MCD)
ERS .... Event Reporting Standard (AAEL)
ERS .... Exception Reporting System (SAUS)
ERS .... Expanded RADAR Service (AFM)
ERS .... Experience Rating System [*Health insurance*] (GHCT)
ERS .... Experimental RADAR System
ERS .... Experimental Research Society [*Defunct*] (EA)
ERS .... Experimental Retrieval System (SAUS)
ERs .... Export Restraints (SAUO)
ERS .... Export Return Scheme [*Australia*]
ERS .... Expression-Regulating Sequence (DB)
ERS .... External Random Storage (SAUS)
ERS .... External Reflection Spectroscopy
ERS .... External Regulation System (IEEE)
ERS .... Extremal Regulation System (PDAA)
ERS .... Windhoek-Eros [*Namibia*] [*Airport symbol*] (OAG)
ERS .... Engine Repair Section (ODA)
ERS-1 .... Earth Remote Sensing Satellite-1 (MCD)
ERS-1 .... Earth Resources Satellite 1 (SAUS)
ERS-1 .... ESA Remote Sensing Satellite (SAUS)
ERS-1 .... European Radio Satellite (SAUS)
ERS-1 .... European Remote Sensing Satellite-1 (EERA)
ERS-1 .... European Research Satellite - 1 (SAUS)
ERS-1 .... European Space Agency Remote Sensing Satellite (SAUO)
ERS-1/ERS-2... European Remote Sensing Satellite (SAUS)
ERS-1/ERS-2... European Remote-sensing Satellite-1/-2 (SAUS)
ERS-2 .... European Remote Sensing Satellite-2 [*Marine science*] (OSRA)
ERS-11 .... European Research Satellite (SAUS)
ERSA .... Economic Research and Statistics Service (SAUS)
ERSA .... Electronic Research Supply Agency
ERSA .... Embry-Riddle School of Aviation [*Later, E-RAU*] [*Florida*]
ERSA .... Emergency Relocation Site Afloat (MCD)
ERSA .... Extended-Range Strike Aircraft [*for low-level missions*] [*Air Force*]
ERSAC .... Environmental Remote Sensing Applications Consultants Ltd. (SAUO)
ERSAF .... Environment Remote Sensing Analysis Facility (SAUS)
ERSAF .... European Remote Sensing Aircraft Facility (SAUS)
ERSAL .... Environmental Remote Sensing Applications Laboratory [*Oregon State University*] [*Research center*] (RCD)
ERSAR .... Earth Resources Synthetic Aperture Radar (SAUS)
ERSATS .... Earth Resource Survey Satellite (PDAA)
ERSB .... Expendable Radio Sonobuoy (IAA)
ERSC .... Egyptian Remote Sensing Center (SAUS)
ERSC .... Environmental Remote Sensing Center (SAUS)
ERSC .... Extended Range and Space Communication (SAUO)
ERSC .... Extended-Range and Space Communication (MCD)
ERSC .... Extended Range Sub-Calibre (SAUS)
ERSCP .... End Refueling and Start Climb Point (SAA)
ERSCRE .... Engineer and Railway Staff Corps, R.E. (SAUO)
ERSD .... Electronic Range Scoring Device (MCD)
ERSD .... Engineering Research Services Division [*North Carolina State University*] [*Research center*] (RCD)
ERSDAC .... Earth Resources Satellite Data Analysis Center [*Japan*] (EERA)
ERS-DC .... ERS Data Centre (SAUS)
ERSDIS .... Earth Resources Satellite Data And Information System (SAUS)
ERSE .... Electrical Automatic Support Equipment (SAUS)
ERSE .... Electronic Airborne Systems Evaluator (SAUS)
ERSER .... Expanded Reactance Series Resonator
ERSFF .... Eastern Region SEATO [*Southeast Asia Treaty Organization*] Field Forces (CINC)
ERSFP .... Earth Resources Survey Flights Program [*NASA*]
ERSI .... Elastomeric Reusable Surface Insulation (NASA)
ERSI .... Electric Remote Speed Indicator (IAA)
ERSI .... Electronic Retailing Systems International [*NASDAQ symbol*] (SAG)
ERSI .... Environmental Research Systems Institute (SAUS)
ERSIR .... Earth Resources Shuttle Imaging RADAR
ersir .... earth-resources shuttle-imaging radar (SAUS)
ERSIS .... Earth Resources Spectral Information System (SAUS)
Ersk .... Erskine's Institutes of the Law of Scotland [*A publication*] (DLA)
Ersk .... Erskine's Principles of the Law of Scotland [*A publication*] (DLA)
Ersk Dec ...... Erskine's United States Circuit Court, Etc., Decisions [*35 Georgia*] [*A publication*] (DLA)
Erskine I ...... Erskine's Institutes of the Law of Scotland [*8 eds.*] [*1773-1871*] [*A publication*] (DLA)
Erskine Inst... Erskine's Institutes of the Law of Scotland [*8 eds.*] [*1773-1871*] [*A publication*] (DLA)
Ersk Inst ...... Erskine's Institutes of the Law of Scotland [*8 eds.*] [*1773-1871*] [*A publication*] (DLA)
ERSKN .... Erskine, MN [*American Association of Railroads railroad junction routing code*]
Ersk Prin...... Erskine's Principles of the Law of Scotland [*A publication*] (DLA)
Ersk Speech... Erskine's Speeches [*A publication*] (DLA)
Ersk Speeches... Erskine's Speeches [*A publication*] (DLA)
ERSNA .... Efferent Renal Sympathetic Nerve Activity [*Physiology*]
E-R S O .... Eastman-Rochester Symphony Orchestra (SAUS)
ERSO .... Electronic Research and Support Organization [*Taiwan*] (NITA)
ERSOS .... Earth Resources Survey Operational Satellite (SAUO)
ERSOS .... Earth Resource Survey Operational Satellite (SAUS)
ERSOS .... Earth Resource Survey Operational System (TEL)
ERSP .... Earth Resources Spaceflight Program (SAUO)
ERSP .... Earth Resources Survey Program [*NASA*]
ERSP .... Eesti Rahvusliku Soltumatuse Partei [*Estonian National Independence Party*] [*Political party*] (EAIO)
ERSP .... Electronic Reservations Service Provider [*Travel industry*] (TRID)
ERSP .... Encapsulated Ring-Shell Projector (SAUS)
ERSP .... Enroute Spacing Program [*Aviation*] (FAAC)
ERSP .... Epipolar Rectified Stereo Pair (SAUS)
ERSP .... European Remote Sensing Program (SAUS)
ERSP .... Event-Related Slow-Brain Potential [*Neurophysiology*]
ERSP .... Event-Related Slow Potential [*Medicine*] (EDAA)
ERSP .... Expendable Recoverable Sound Projector [*Navy*] (CAAL)
ERSPRC .... Earth Resources Survey Program Review Committee [*NASA*] (NOAA)
ERSR .... Equipment Reliability Status Report
ERSS .... Earth Remote-Sensing Satellite (SAUO)
ERSS .... Earth Resources Satellite Survey (SAUO)
ERSS .... Earth Resources Satellite System (IEEE)
ERSS .... Earth Resources Survey Satellite [*NASA*] (IAA)
ERSS .... Earth Resources Survey Satellites (SAUS)
ERSS .... Establishment Registration Support System (SAUO)
ERSS .... European Remote Sensing Satellite (SAUO)
ERSS .... Extended Range Surveillance System (ACAE)
ERSSP .... European Remote Sensing Satellite Programme (SAUS)
ER/STA .... Energy Research/Science and Technology Advisor (SAUS)
ERSTC .... Ergonomics Research Society Training Committee (SAUO)
ERSU .... Energy Research Support Unit (SAUO)
ERT .... Earth Received Time [*Astronomy*]
ert .... Earth Relative Time (ADWA)
ERT .... Earth Resources Technology (SAUO)
ERT .... Educational Requirements Test
ERT .... Effective Reference Time
ERT .... Egyptian Religious Texts and Representations [*New York*] [*A publication*] (BJA)
ERT .... Electrical Resistance Temperature
ERT .... Electrical Resistance Thermometer (SAUS)
ERT .... Electrical Resistance Tomography (SAUS)
ERT .... Electric and Radio Trading (journ.) (SAUS)
ERT .... Electron Ray Tube (SAUS)
ERT .... Elementary Renewal Theorem
ERT .... Emergency Repair Team [*Nuclear energy*] (GFGA)
ERT .... Emergency Response Team (NRCH)
ERT .... Emergency Response Time (AAEL)
ERT .... Emergency Response Training
ERT .... Emergency Room Technician (SAUS)
ERT .... Emergency Room Triage (MELL)
ERT .... Encoder-Receiver-Transmitter [*Telecommunications*]
ERT .... Energy Resources Technology (SAUS)
ERT .... Enershare Technology Corp. [*Vancouver Stock Exchange symbol*]
ERT .... Engineering Release Ticket
ERT .... Engine Rotor Tester
ERT .... Enhanced Readiness Test (ABAC)
ERT .... Ente de Radiodiffusion y Television [*Radio and television network*] [*Argentina*]
ERT .... Environmental Research & Technology (SAUS)
ERT .... Environmental Research and Technology, Inc. [*Concord, MA*] (MCD)
ERT .... Environmental Research and Technology, Information Center, Concord, MA [*OCLC symbol*] (OCLC)
ERT .... Environmental Response Team [*Environmental Protection Agency*]

ERT............. Environment Round Table (EERA)
ERT............. Enzyme Replacement Therapy [*Medicine*] (MELL)
ERT............. Equipment Removal Tag (MCD)
ERT............. Equipment Repair Time
ERT............. Estimated Removal Time (SAUS)
ERT............. Estimated Repair Time [*Telecommunications*] (TEL)
ERT............. Estrogen Replacement Therapy [*Medicine*]
ERT............. European Round Table (EAIO)
ERT............. European Roundtable of Industrialists, Bruxelles (SAUS)
ERT............. Execute Reference Time (MCD)
ERT............. Execution Reference Time (CCCA)
ERT............. Executive Reference Time
ERT............. Exhibits Round Table [*American Library Association*]
ERT............. Expected Run-Time
ERT............. Extended-Range TOW [*Tube-Launched, Optically Tracked Wire-Guided (Weapon)*] (MCD)
ERT............. Extended-Release Tablets [*Medicine*] (MELL)
ERT............. Extended Research Telescope
ERT............. External Radiation Therapy [*Medicine*]
ERT............. Excess Retention Tax (ODA)
ERT-A......... Advance Element of the Emergency Response Team (SAUO)
ERTA........... Economic Recovery Tax Act [*1981*]
ERTA........... Emergency Railroad Transportation Act, 1933
ERT-A......... Emergency Response Team-Advance Element (SAUO)
ERTA........... Energy Research and Technology Administration (COE)
ERTA........... European Road Transport Agreement (ILCA)
ERTA Bulletin... European Free Trade Association Bulletin (journ.) (SAUS)
ERTAQ......... Environmental Response Team Air Quality Model [*Environmental Protection Agency*] (GFGA)
ERTAQ......... ERT air quality (SAUS)
ERTAQ......... ERT Air Quality Model (SAUO)
ERTBP......... Emergency Restart Transaction Backout Program (SAUS)
ERTC........... Emergency Rescue Team Chief [*Air Force*]
ERTC........... Engineer Replacement Training Center
ERTC........... European Regional Test Center (NATG)
ERTC........... European Regional Travel Commission (SAUO)
ERTCS......... Emergency Recirculation and Tritium Cleanup System (SAUS)
ERTE........... Edinburgh Remote Terminal Emulator (SAUS)
ERTE........... Exact Radiative Transfer Equation (SAUS)
ERTEC......... Eastern Region Teacher Education Consortium (AIE)
ERTG........... Economic [*or Economical*] Radioisotope Thermoelectric Generator
ERTH........... Earth [*Freight*]
ERTH........... EarthShell Corp. [*NASDAQ symbol*] (SG)
ERTH........... Environmental Resources Technology [*Information service or system*] (IID)
Erthlink........ Earthlink Network, Inc. [*Associated Press*] (SAG)
erthwk......... Earthwork (VRA)
erthwr.......... Earthenware (VRA)
ERTI............ Electron-Ray Tuning Indicator (DEN)
ERTN........... Exhaust [*Oxygen Sensor*] Return [*Automotive engineering*]
ERT-N......... National Emergency Response Team (SAUO)
ERTOR......... Effective Radiational Temperature of the Ozone-Layer Region (SAUS)
ERTP........... Earth Reference Pulse (SAUS)
ERTS........... Earth Resources Technology Satellite [*Later, LANDSAT*] [*NASA*]
ERTS........... Earth Resources Technology Satellite Program (SAUS)
ERTS........... Edwards Rocket Test Site (KSC)
ERTS........... Electronic Arts [*NASDAQ symbol*] (TTSB)
ERTS........... Electronic Arts, Inc. [*NASDAQ symbol*] (SAG)
ERTS........... ELINT [*Electronic Intelligence*] Receiver Test System (MCD)
ERTS........... Emergency Remote Tracking Station [*Navy*] (ANA)
ERTS........... Environmental Radiological Technical Specifications [*Nuclear energy*] (NRCH)
ERTS........... Environmental Resources Technology Satellite (NRCH)
ERTS........... Error Rate Test Set (TEL)
ERTS-1........ Earth Resources Technology Satellite-1 (EOSA)
ERTTO......... Ecologically Responsive Tractor Transmission Oil [*Lubricants*]
ERTU........... Egyptian Radio and Television Union [*Political party*] (PSAP)
E-R Tube..... Electron Recording Tube (SAUS)
ERU............. Earth Rate Unit [*NASA*] (KSC)
ERU............. Eastern Rugby Union of America (EA)
ERU............. Education Review Unit [*South Australia*]
ERU............. Ejector Release Unit (MCD)
ERU............. Electronic Reconnaissance Unit (MCD)
ERU............. Emergency Reaction Unit (SAUS)
ERU............. Emergency Recovery Unit
ERU............. Emergency Recovery Utility (SAUS)
ERU............. Emergency Response Unit (SAUO)
ERU............. Emission Reduction Unit (SAUS)
ERU............. Endorectal Ultrasound [*Medicine*] (EDAA)
ERU............. English Rugby Union
ERU............. Equipment Replaceable Unit (ACAE)
ERU............. Error Return address Update (SAUS)
ERU............. Erume [*Papua New Guinea*] [*Airport symbol*] (OAG)
ERU............. External Relations Unit (SAUO)
ERU............. External Run Unit (MHDB)
'Erub........... 'Erubin (BJA)
ERUCA......... East Rand Urban Councils Association (SAUO)
ERUHG......... External Representation of the Ukrainian Helsinki Group (EA)
ERUN........... Education Research Unit News [*Australian Union of Students*] [*A publication*] (ADA)
ER Unit........ Equivalent Roentgen Unit (SAUS)
ERUPT......... Elementary Reliability Unit Parameter Technique (PDAA)
ERV............. Earth Return Vehicle (ACAE)
ERV............. ECM [*Electronic Countermeasures*] - Resistant Voice
ERV............. Efferent Renal Vein [*Anatomy*]
ERV............. Electromagnetic Relief Valve [*Engineering instrumentation*]
ERV............. Electronic Repair Vehicle (PDAA)
ERV............. Emergency Relief Valve [*Environmental science*] (COE)
ERV............. Emergency Rendezvous (SAUS)
ERV............. Emergency Rescue Vehicle (SAUS)
ERV............. Endogenous Retrovirus
ERV............. Energy Recovery Ventilators
ERV............. English Revised Version [*of the Bible*] [*A publication*] (BJA)
ERV............. Entry Research Vehicle
ERV............. Equine Rhinopneumonitis Virus [*Veterinary science*] (DB)
ERV............. Equine rhinovirus (SAUS)
ERV............. Europese Rum Vereniging [*European Rum Association*] [*EC*] (ECED)
ERV............. Expiratory Reserve Volume [*Physiology*]
ERV............. Extract Release Volume [*Food technology*]
ERV............. Kerrville, TX [*Location identifier*] [*FAA*] (FAAL)
ERVAD......... Engineering Release for Vendor Article Data [*Later, PRVD*] (AAG)
ERVIN......... Energy Research Video Network [*Video conferencing*]
ERVm........... English Revised Version [*of the Bible*], Margin
ERVSC......... Engineer and Railway Volunteer Staff Corps [*Army*] [*British*]
ERW............. Elastic Resist Weld (DNAB)
ERW............. Electrical Resistance Weld
ERW............. Electric Rear Window [*Automotive classified advertising*]
ERW............. Electric Resistance Welded (SAUS)
ERW............. Electric Resistance Welding (SAUS)
ERW............. Electronic Resistance Welding (SAUS)
erw.............. electro-resistance welding (SAUS)
ERW............. Enhanced Radiation Weapon
ERW............. Environmentally-Responsive Workstation
ERW............. Explosive Radial Warhead (ACAE)
ERWE........... Enhanced Radar Warning Equipment (SAUS)
Erwin........... Entity Relationship for Windows (CDE)
ERWM......... Environment Restoration and Wate Management (COE)
ERWMP....... Environmental Restoration and Waste Management Programs (SAUS)
ERWMTD..... Environmental Restoration and Waste Management Technology Development (SAUS)
ERWP........... European Railway Wagon Pool (EA)
ER(WR)........ Earnings Record (Wage Record) [*Social Security Administration*] (OICC)
ERWRE......... Earthenware [*Freight*]
ERWS........... Engineering Release Work Sheet (AAG)
ERWTS......... Enhanced Return Wave Tracker System (ACAE)
ERX............. Electronic Remote Switching (IAA)
Erx............... Empty Spiracles-Related Retinal-Homeobox
ERY............. Early (FAAC)
ERY............. East Riding of Yorkshire [*Administrative county in England*] (ROG)
ERY............. East Riding Yeomanry [*Military unit*] [*British*]
ERY............. Erysipelas [*Medicine*]
Ery............... Erysipelothrix [*A bacteria*] (DAVI)
ery............... erysipelothrixia (SAUS)
Ery............... erythrocyte (SAUS)
ERY............. Erythromycin [*Also, E, ERYC, ETM*] [*Antibacterial compound*]
ERY............. Newberry, MI [*Location identifier*] [*FAA*] (FAAL)
ERYC........... Erythromycin [*Also, E, ERY, ETM*] [*Antibacterial compound*]
ERYIY......... East Riding of Yorkshire Imperial Yeomanry [*British military*] (DMA)
ER Yorks...... East Riding, Yorkshire (SAUS)
ERYTHR....... Erythromycin [*Also, E, ERY, ETM, ERYC*] [*An antibacterial compound*] (DAVI)
erythro......... Erythrocyte [*Hematology*] (DAVI)
ERZ............. Eastern Rift Zone [*Geology*]
ERZ............. Erzurum [*Turkey*] [*Airport symbol*] (OAG)
ERZ............. Erzurum [*Turkey*] [*Seismograph station code, US Geological Survey*] (SEIS)
ERZ............. Extended Reconnaissance Zone [*Army*] (AABC)
ES............... Abbott Laboratories Ltd. [*Great Britain*] [*Research code symbol*]
ES............... Air Atlantique [*ICAO designator*] (AD)
ES............... Eagle Squadron [*British military*] (DMA)
ES............... Early Shock [*Medicine*]
e/s............... early shorn (SAUS)
ES............... Early Successional [*Botany*]
ES............... Earned Surplus
ES............... Earth Save [*An association*] (EA)
ES............... Earth Sciences Division [*Army Natick Laboratories*]
ES............... Earth Spring (OA)
ES............... Earth Station
ES............... Earth Switch (IAA)
ES............... Earth to Space (IAA)
ES............... EASCO Corporation (SAUO)
ES............... Eastern Stainless Steel Corp. (SAUO)
ES............... Eastern States (ADA)
E/S.............. East Side [*In outdoor advertising*] (WDMC)
ES............... East Sussex (SAUS)
ES............... Ebenezer Society (EA)
ES............... Echo Sounder (SAUS)
ES............... Echo Sounding
ES............... Echo Suppressor [*Telecommunications*] (TEL)
ES............... Econometric Society (EA)
ES............... Economic and Social Department (SAUS)
ES............... Economic Studies [*Bureau of the Census*]
ES............... Edge Salicornia Zone [*Ecology*]
ES............... Edinaya Systema [*Unified System*] [*Russian*] [*Computer science*]
ES............... Edison Screw
ES............... Editing Symbol (SAUS)
es................ Edmund Scientific Consumer Science Division

ES .... Educational Services [*Publisher*]
ES .... Educational Specialist
ES .... Educational Studies [*A publication*] (BRI)
ES .... Education Society (SAUO)
ES .... Effect Size
ES .... Efros and Schlovskii (SAUS)
Es .... Ego Strength [*Psychology*]
ES .... Ego Stress [*Test*] [*Psychology*] (DAVI)
ES .... Egypt Suez [*Crude oil*]
ES .... Einheitliche Systematik [*Library science*]
Es .... Einsteinium [*Preferred form, but also see E*] [*Chemical element*]
ES .... Ejection Sound [*Cardiology*]
ES .... Elasticities of Substitution [*Statistics*]
ES .... Elasticity of Supply [*Economics*] (DCTA)
ES .... Elastic Scattering (SAUS)
ES .... Elastic Stockings (MELL)
ES .... Elastic Suspensor
ES .... Elder Statesman
ES .... Eldest Son
ES .... Electrical Schematic (SAUS)
ES .... Electrical Section (IAA)
ES .... Electrical Shutter (UWER)
ES .... Electrical Sounding (PDAA)
es .... Electrical Stimulation (IDYL)
ES .... Electrical stimulation (SAUS)
ES .... Electrical Stimulus
ES .... Electrical System (SAUS)
ES .... Electric Scanner (SAUS)
ES .... Electric Seats [*Automotive accessory*]
ES .... Electric Starting (ADA)
ES .... Electric Storage (SAUS)
ES .... Electric Store (SAUS)
ES .... Electrochemical Society
E/S .... Electrode Signalling [*British military*] (DMA)
ES .... Electrolytic Storage (SAUS)
ES .... Electrolytic Store (SAUS)
ES .... Electromagnetic Storage
ES .... Electromagnetic Store (SAUS)
ES .... Electromagnetic Switch (SAUS)
ES .... Electromagnetic Switching (IEEE)
ES .... Electromechanical Society (SAUO)
ES .... Electronic Science (UWER)
ES .... Electronic Section [*National Weather Service*]
ES .... Electronic Service
ES .... Electronic Shop Major [*Coast Guard*]
ES .... Electronic Shutter (SAUS)
ES .... Electronic Specialty (IAA)
ES .... Electronic Spectroscopy (SAUS)
ES .... Electronic Spectrum (UWER)
ES .... Electronic Standard
ES .... Electronic Storage (SAUS)
ES .... Electronic Store (SAUS)
ES .... Electronic Structure (UWER)
ES .... Electronic Support (SAUS)
ES .... electronic switch (SAUS)
ES .... Electronic Switching [*Telecommunications*]
ES .... Electronic Systems
ES .... Electron Shell (UWER)
ES .... Electron Spectroscopy (SAUS)
ES .... Electron Spectrum (UWER)
ES .... Electron Synchrotron [*Nuclear energy*]
ES .... Electrophoresis Society (NTPA)
ES .... Electroshock [*Psychology*]
ES .... Electroslag (UWER)
ES .... Electrospray [*Ionization*] [*Physics*]
ES .... Electrostatic
es .... Electrostatical (SAUS)
ES .... Electrostatic Separator (SAUS)
ES .... Electrostatic Spray
ES .... Electrostatic Spraying
ES .... Electrostatic Storage
ES .... Electrostatic Store (SAUS)
ES .... Electrostatis (SAUS)
ES .... Electrostimulation [*Medicine*] (EDAA)
ES .... Electrostriction (SAUS)
ES .... Electrosurgery [*Medicine*] (EDAA)
ES .... Element Signal [*Dialog*] [*Searchable field*] [*Information service or system*] (NITA)
ES .... Elenchus Suppletorius ad Elenchum Bibliographicum Biblicum [*A publication*] (BJA)
ES .... Eligible for Separation
ES .... Eligible Spouse [*Social Security Administration*]
ES .... Ellis Air Lines
ES .... Ells Scotch (ROG)
ES .... elopement status (SAUS)
es .... El Salvador [*MARC country of publication code*] [*Library of Congress*] (LCCP)
ES .... Embryonal Stem [*Cell line*]
ES .... Embryonic Shield
ES .... Embryonic Stem [*Medicine*] (MELL)
ES .... Embryonic System [*Medicine*]
ES .... Embryo Sac [*Botany*]
ES .... Embryo Stem Cell
ES .... Emergency Service
ES .... Emergency Standards (SAUS)
e(S) .... Emergent S Wave [*Earthquakes*]
ES .... emission spectrometry (SAUS)
ES .... Emission Spectrum [*Spectroscopy*]
ES .... Emotional Stress (MELL)
ES .... Employee Services Division (SAUS)
ES .... Employee Suggestion (AAG)
ES .... Employer Services [*State Employee Security Agency*] (OICC)
ES .... Employment Service [*US*] (KSC)
ES .... Emulsifying Salts [*Food technology*]
ES .... Enamelist Society (EA)
ES .... Enamel Single Silk [*Wire insulation*] (AAG)
ES .... Endocrine Society (EA)
ES .... End of Study
ES .... Endogenous Substance [*Biology*]
ES .... Endometritis-Salpingitis [*Medicine*] (DMAA)
ES .... Endoplasmic Surface [*Freeze etching in microscopy*]
ES .... Endoscopic Sclerosis [*Medicine*] (DAVI)
ES .... Endoscopic Sclerotherapy [*Medicine*]
ES .... Endoscopic Sphincterotomy [*Medicine*]
es .... End Scale (SAUS)
ES .... End Sheet [*Publishing*]
ES .... End Strength
ES .... End System [*Computer science*] (TNIG)
ES .... End-Systole [*Cardiology*]
ES .... End to Side [*Portacaval shunt*] [*Medicine*] (AAMN)
ES .... Enema Saponis [*Medicine*]
ES .... Enemy Status (MCD)
ES .... Energy Safer (SAUS)
ES .... Energy Sampling (SAUS)
ES .... energy saver (SAUS)
ES .... Energy Sector (FOTI)
ES .... Energy Spectrum (ODA)
ES .... Enforcement Stategy [*Environmental Protection Agency*] (GFGA)
ES .... Enforcement Strategy (SAUO)
ES .... Engagement Simulation [*Military*] (INF)
ES .... Engineered Safeguards [*Nuclear energy*] (NRCH)
ES .... Engineering and Society
ES .... Engineering Services
ES .... Engineering Specification
ES .... Engineering Staff (SAUO)
ES .... Engineering Standard
ES .... Engineering Standardization (SAUS)
ES .... Engineering Study
ES .... Engineering Support (SAUS)
E/S .... Engineer/Service [*Aerospace*] (AAG)
ES .... Engineer Stores (SAUS)
ES .... Engine-Sized [*Paper*]
ES .... engine sizing (SAUS)
ES .... Enginesmith [*British military*] (DMA)
es .... engine speed (SAUS)
ES .... English Studies: A Journal of English Language and Literature [*A publication*] (ANEX)
ES .... English Studies (journ.) (SAUS)
ES .... Enhanced Security (SAUS)
ES .... enhanced silver (SAUS)
ES .... Enhanced Surveillance (SAUS)
E-S .... En Route Supplement
E/S .... En Suite (ADA)
ES .... Enterprise Statistics [*A publication*]
ES .... Enter Statement (SAUS)
ES .... Entomological Society (ODA)
ES .... Entotic Sound [*Medicine*] (MELL)
ES .... Entrainment Separator (EEVL)
ES .... Environmental Safety (EA)
ES .... Environmental Services (EERA)
ES .... Environmental Studies (SAUS)
ES .... Environmental Survey
ES .... Enzyme Substrate (SAUS)
ES .... Enzyme-Substrate Complex [*Enzyme kinetics*]
ES .... Eosinophils (SAUS)
ES .... Ephphatha Services (EA)
ES .... Epigraphic Society (EA)
ES .... Epileptic Syndrome [*Medicine*] (DMAA)
ES .... Eprova Ltd. [*Switzerland*] [*Research code symbol*]
ES .... Equal Section [*Technical drawings*]
ES .... Equipment Section
ES .... Equipment Serviceability (MCD)
ES .... Equipment Shelf (SAUS)
ES .... Equipment Specialist [*Military*] (AFIT)
ES .... Equipment Specification
ES .... Equipment Status (MCD)
ES .... Equivalence Statement (SAUS)
ES .... Erasable Storage (SAUS)
ES .... Erasable Store (SAUS)
ES .... Ergonomics Society [*British*]
ES .... Erkennungssignal [*Recognition signal*] [*German military - World War II*]
ES .... Errata Sheet
ES .... Errored Second (SAUS)
ES .... Errored Seconds [*Computer science*] (VERA)
ES .... Error Satisfaction (SAUS)
ES .... Erysipelothrix-Selective (SAUS)
ES .... Escape System (MCD)
ES .... Escort Ship (CINC)
ES .... ESER-System (SAUS)

ES Esophageal Scintigraphy [*Medicine*] (DAVI)
ES Esophageal Spasm [*Medicine*] (MELL)
ES Esophagus [*Anatomy*] (DAVI)
ES Esophoria [*Ophthalmology*] (DAVI)
ES establishment data (SAUS)
ES Esterase (DB)
ES Esther [*Old Testament book*]
ES Estimate (ROG)
ES Estimated Standard [*Statistics*] (DAVI)
ES Estimated Tax [*IRS*]
ES Estradiol [*Also,* E_2, *E-diol*] [*Endocrinology*]
Es Estriol [*Endocrinology*] (AAMN)
ES Ethnological Society (COE)
ES Eugenics Society (SAUO)
ES Eureka Society (EA)
ES Eurodollar (SAUS)
ES European Space Agency (SAUO)
ES European Standard (SAUO)
es--- Europe, Southern [*MARC geographic area code*] [*Library of Congress*] (LCCP)
ES Eurosam (SAUS)
ES Euroscience [*An association*]
ES Eutectic Solidification (SAUS)
ES Evangelization Society (EA)
ES Eversley Series [*A publication*]
ES Evolutionary Stable Strategy (SAUS)
ES EW Support (SAUS)
ES Exchangeable Sodium (OA)
ES Excitation Spectrum (SAUS)
ES Exclusive of Sheeting
ES Exclusive Segment (SAUS)
ES Excretory-Secretory
ES Executable Statement (SAUS)
ES Execute Statement (SAUS)
ES Executive Schedule [*U.S. Civil Service*] (BARN)
ES Executive Secretariat (USDC)
ES Executive Secretary
ES Exempt Security
ES Exercise Scenario (SAUS)
ES Exercise Specialist (SAUO)
ES Existential Study [*Psychology*]
ES Exit Statement (SAUS)
ES Exoplasmic Surface [*Freeze etching in microscopy*]
ES Expanded Storage (SAUS)
ES Expansion Speaker (SAUS)
ES Expectation Score (MAE)
ES Expendable Second Stage (SAUS)
ES Experimental Station
ES Experimental Study [*Research*] (DAVI)
ES Experiment Segment (MCD)
ES Experiment Support System (SAUS)
ES Expert System [*Computer science*]
ES Explicit Storage (SAUS)
es exploratory shaft (SAUS)
ES Export Surpluses [*British*]
ES Exsmoker (DAVI)
ES Extended Segment (ACAE)
ES Extended Service [*Automotive engineering*]
ES Extended Sleeper [*In truck name Aero ES*] [*Volvo White Truck Corp.*] [*Automotive engineering*]
ES Extended Support (VLIE)
ES Extension Service [*Department of Agriculture*]
ES Extension Shaft [*Nuclear energy*] (NUCP)
ES Extension Station (IAA)
ES Exterior Surface
ES External Services [*British Broadcasting Corp.*]
ES External Shield (IAA)
ES External Statement (SAUS)
ES External Store
ES Extraction Steam [*System*] [*Nuclear energy*] (NRCH)
ES Extra Data Segment (SAUS)
ES Extradatensegment (SAUS)
ES Extra Segment [*Computer science*]
ES Extra Series
ES Extra Slow [*Photography*] (DGA)
es Extra Soft (SAUS)
ES Extra Stiff (SAUS)
ES Extrastriate [*Neurology*]
ES Extrasystole [*Cardiology*] (DAVI)
ES Extreme Spread (SAUS)
ES Extruded Shape (SAUS)
ES Eye Stalk
ES IEEE Education Society (EA)
E_s Screen Voltage (IDOE)
ES Spain [*ANSI two-letter standard code*] (CNC)
ES Electronic Structure (ODA)
ES1 EliteSwitch/1 (SAUS)
ES001 Estuarine Water Quality Model (SAUS)
ES2 European Silicon Structures (NITA)
E/S^3 Engineering and Scientific Support System [*IBM Corp.*]
ESA Airship Rigger [*U.S. Navy enlisted rating*] (AUER)
ESA Department of Economic and Social Affairs (SAUS)
ESA Earth Scanner Assembly (ACAE)
ESA Earth Sciences Associates (SAUS)
ESA Earth Sensor Assembly (ACAE)
ESA Earth Station - Arabia
ESA Eastern Ski Association [*Later, USSA*] (EA)
ESA Eastern Surfing Association (EA)
ESA Ecole Superieure des Affaires [*High Business School*] [*Information service or system*] (IID)
ESA Ecological Society of America (EA)
ESA Ecological Society of Australia (SAUO)
ESA Ecological Society of Equatorial South America (SAUO)
ESA Economic and Social Affairs (SAUS)
ESA Economic and Statistical Analysis (SAUS)
ESA Economics and Statistics Administration (USDC)
ESA Economic Society of Australia
ESA Economic Stabilization Act [*Wage-price controls*] [*Expired April 30, 1974*]
ESA Economic Stabilization Administration
ESA Economic Stabilization Agency [*Terminated, 1953*]
ESA Educational Settlements Association (SAUO)
ESA Educational Supplies Association (WDAA)
ESA Educational Supply Association (SAUO)
ESA Education Sector Analysis
ESA Egyptian Survey Authority (SAUS)
ESA Ejercito Salvadoreno Anticomunista [*Salvadoran Anti-Communist Army*] (PD)
ESA Ejercito Segredo Anti-Comunista [*Secret Anti-Communist Army*] [*Guatemala*] (PD)
ESA Electrically Supported [*or Suspended*] Accelerometer
ESA Electrically Suspended Accelerometer (SAUS)
ESA Electrical Stress Analysis
ESA Electrical Supply Authorities (SAUS)
ESA Electrical Surge Arrester (SAUS)
ESA Electric Seat Adjustment [*Automotive engineering*]
ESA Electric Spark Alloying (SAUS)
ESA Electric Supply Authority (SAUS)
ESA Electrokinetic Sonic Amplitude [*Determination of electrokinetic potential*]
ESA Electrolysis Society of America [*Later, SCME*] (EA)
ESA Electronically Scanned Array (ACAE)
ESA Electronically Scanning Antenna (SAUS)
ESA Electronically-Scanning Array (SAUS)
ESA Electronically Steerable Antenna (SAUS)
ESA Electronically Steerable Array (MCD)
ESA Electronic Security Alarm [*Automobile theft preventive*]
ESA Electronic Security Alaska [*Air Force*]
ESA Electronic Signature Authentication (SAUS)
ESA Electronics System Analyst (SAUS)
ESA Electronic-Static Amplifier (SAUS)
ESA Electronic Subsystems Analysis (MCD)
ESA Electronic Surge Arrester
ESA Electronic System Assembly Operation (TIMI)
ESA Electron Scan Antenna [*FAA*]
ESA electron stimulated adsorption (SAUS)
ESA Electrostatic Analyzer
ESA Electrosurgical Arthroscopy (DB)
ESA Emergency Safe Altitude (MCD)
ESA Employee Standards Administration
ESA Employment and Social Affairs (EURO)
ESA Employment Service Agency [*Department of Employment*] [*British*]
ESA Employment Standards Administration [*Department of Labor*]
ESA Endangered Species Act [*1973*]
ESA End of Storage Area (SAUS)
ESA End-of-Storage Area (VLIE)
ESA End-Systolic Areas [*Cardiology*]
ESA Energy Security Act [*1980*]
ESA Energy-Separating Agent [*Chemical engineering*]
ESA Engineering Service Agreements (VLIE)
ESA Engineering Study Authorization Division [*NASA*] (KSC)
ESA Engineering Supply Area (NASA)
ESA Engineering Support Activity [*Military*]
ESA Engineering Support Assembly (NASA)
ESA Engineers and Scientists of America [*Defunct*]
ESA Engineer Stores Assignment [*British*]
ESA Engineer Surveyors' Association [*A union*] [*British*]
ESA Engine Service Association (EA)
ESA English, Scottish & Australian Bank Ltd. (ADA)
ESA Enterprise Service Agreement (GART)
ESA Enterprise-Specific Agreement
ESA Enterprise Systems Architecture [*IBM Corp*] (VERA)
ESA Entomological Society of America (EA)
ESA Entomological Society of Australia
ESA Environmental and Safety Activities (SAUS)
ESA Environmentally Sensitive Area [*British*]
ESA Environmental Protection Agency, Region X Library, Seattle, WA [*OCLC symbol*] (OCLC)
ESA Environmental Sciences Association (NTPA)
ESA Environmental Services Agency (SAUO)
ESA Environmental Services Association (SAUO)
ESA Environmental Site Assessment (COE)
ESA Environmental Site Audit (COE)
ESA Environmental Study Area
ESA Epigraphic South Arabian (BJA)
ESA Epiphyllum Society of America (EA)
ESA Episcopal Synod of America (EA)
ESA Epyphyllum Society of America (SAUO)
ESA Equalized Sidelobe Aerial (SAUS)
ESA Equalized Sidelobe Antenna

ESA .... Equatorial South America (CARB)
ESA .... Equipment Service Association (EA)
ESA .... Equivalent Snowline Altitude
ESA .... Ergonomics Society of Australia
ESA .... Esa Ala [*Papua New Guinea*] [*Airport symbol*] (OAG)
ESA .... Esa Ala [*Papua New Guinea*] [*Seismograph station code, US Geological Survey*] (SEIS)
ESA .... Ethernet Station Adapter (SAUS)
ESA .... EURATOM Supply Agency (SAUS)
ESA .... European Satellite Agency [*Marine science*] (OSRA)
ESA .... European Satellite Agency/European Space Agency (USDC)
ESA .... European Schoolmagazine Association (SAUO)
ESA .... European Space Agency [*See also ASE*] (EAIO)
ESA .... European Space Association
ESA .... European Space Research Organisation (SAUS)
ESA .... European Spice Association [*EC*] (ECED)
ESA .... European Strabismological Association (EAIO)
ESA .... European Sulphuric Acid Association (SAUS)
ESA .... European Supply Agency (NATG)
ESA .... European Suzuki Association [*British*] (EAIO)
ESA .... European Switching Center (SAUO)
ESA .... European System of integrated economic Accounts (SAUO)
ESA .... Euthanasia Society of America [*Later, SRD*] (EA)
ESA .... Evangelicals for Social Action (EA)
ESA .... Exceptional Service Award (SAUS)
ESA .... Exchange of Services Agreement (FOTI)
ESA .... Excited-State Absorption
ESA .... Executive Storage Area (IAA)
ESA .... Executive Suite Association (NTPA)
ESA .... Exercise-Safety Association (EA)
ESA .... Exer-Safety Association (EA)
ESA .... Expanded Save Area (VLIE)
ESA .... Expiration of Service Agreement [*Military*] (AABC)
ESA .... Exploratory Shaft Facility (SAUS)
ESA .... Explosive Safe Area [*NASA*]
ESA .... Explosive Safety Approval (MUGU)
ESA .... Explosives Storage Area
ESA .... Export Screw Association (SAUO)
ESA .... Extended Service Agreement
ESA .... Extended Service Area (SAUS)
ESA .... Extended Stay Amer. [*NYSE symbol*] (SG)
ESA .... Externally Specified Address (CAAL)
ESA .... Extra Services Agreement [*Environmental science*] (COE)
ESA .... Extra Shift Authorization (SAUS)
ESA .... Seagreen Air Transport [*Antigua and Barbuda*] [*ICAO designator*] (FAAC)
ESA 370 .... Enterprises System Architecture [*Computer science*]
ESA 390 .... Enterprise System Architecture [*Computer science*]
ESAA .... Economic Stimulus Appropriations Act (OICC)
ESAA .... Electrical Supply Authorities Association (SAUO)
ESAA .... Electricity (SAUS)
ESAA .... Electricity Supply Association of Australia (EERA)
ESAA .... Emergency School Aid Act [*1972*]
ESAA .... Employment Security Administration Account
ESAA .... English Schools' Athletic Association (BI)
ESAA .... English Setter Association of America (EA)
ESAA .... European Special Activities Area [*Military*]
ESAAB .... Energy System Acquisition Advisory Board (SAUS)
ESAAB .... Energy System Aquisition Advisory Board (SAUO)
ESAAB .... Energy Systems Acquisition Advisory Board (SAUS)
ESAAB .... Energy Systems Advisory Acquisition Board (SAUS)
ESAB .... Energy Supplies Allocation Board
ESABR .... European Society for Animal Blood-Group Research (SAUO)
ESAC .... Economics and Social Affairs Committee (SAUO)
ESAC .... Education Service Advisory Committee (AIE)
ESAC .... Electrical Systems and Controls (ACII)
ESAC .... Electronic Shock Absorber Control
ESAC .... Electronic Surveillance Assistance Center (VLIE)
ESAC .... Electronic Systems Assistance Center [*Telecommunications*] (TEL)
ESAC .... Endangered Species Advisory Committee [*Commonwealth*] (EERA)
ESAC .... Environmental Studies Association of Canada (EERA)
ESAC .... Environmental Systems Applications Center [*NASA*]
ESAC .... Evangelical Social Action Commission (EA)
ESACCS .... Earth Stabilized Aircraft Center Coordinate System (ACAE)
ESACT .... Engineering and Systems Analysis for the Control of Toxics Technology Center [*University of California at Los Angeles*] [*Research center*] (RCD)
ESACT .... European Association for Animal Cell Technology (SAUS)
ESACT .... European Society for Animal Cell Technology (EA)
ESACT .... European Society of Animal Cell Technology (SAUS)
ESAD .... Earth Science and Applications Division [*NASA*] (EOSA)
ESAD .... Empirically Supported Algorithm Driven [*Computer science*]
ESADA .... Empire State Atomic Development Associates, Inc.
ESADS .... Earth Science and Applications Data System [*National Oceanic and Atmospheric Administration*]
ESAE .... European Society for Atomic Energy (SAUO)
ESAE .... European Society of Association Executives (EA)
ESAEINZ .... Electric Supply Authority Engineers Institute of New Zealand (SAUS)
ESAER .... European Space Agencys Earth Resources (SAUS)
ESAF .... East and Southern Africa Banking Supervisors Group (SAUO)
ESAF .... Electronic Safe Arming and Firing Device (DWSG)
ESAF .... Endothelial Cell Stimulating Angiogenesis Factor (DB)
ESAF .... Energy Systems Award Fee (SAUS)
ESAF .... Enhanced Structural Adjustment Facility [*IMF*] (ECON)
ESAF .... Extended Structural Adjustment Facility (SAUO)
ESAFA .... Employment Security Administrative Financing Act of 1954
ESAFT .... Electrically Steerable Antenna Feed Techniques (NG)
ESAG .... Expression Site-Associated Genes
ESAI .... Expanded Situational Awareness Insertion [*Air Force*] (SEWL)
ESAIDAM .... Eastern and Southern African Initiative in Debt and Reserves Management (SAUS)
ESAIDARM .... Eastern and Southern African Initiative in Debt and Reserves Management (ECON)
ESAIRA .... Electronically Scanning Airborne Intercept RADAR Antenna
ESA-IRS .... ESA Information Retrieval Service (SAUS)
ESA-IRS .... European Space Agency Information Retrieval Service [*Italy*]
ESA IRS .... European Space Agency - Information Retrieval System (SAUS)
ESAIT .... ERS-1 Science and Applications Team (SAUS)
ESAL .... Elan Systems Application Language (SAUS)
E Sal .... El Salvador (VRA)
ESAL .... Engine Start after Launch [*Navy*] (CAAL)
ESAL .... Equivalent Single Axle Load
ESALB .... East Alburgh, VT [*American Association of Railroads railroad junction routing code*]
ESA-IRS .... European Space Agency information retrieval service (SAUS)
ESAM .... Earth Sensor Assembly Module (SAUS)
E Sam .... Eastern Samoa (SAUS)
ESAM .... Evangelization Society of African Missions (SAUO)
ESAM .... Evolutionary Surface-to-Air Missile [*Military*]
ESAM .... Extendable Stiff Arm Manipulator [*NASA*]
ESAM .... Institute for Environmental Science and Management (SAUO)
ESAMRDC .... East and Southern Africa Mineral Resources Development Center (SAUS)
ESAMRDC .... Eastern and Southern African Mineral Resources Development Center
ESAMS .... Elliott Automation Space and Advanced Military Systems
ESAMS .... Energy Systems Action Management System (SAUS)
ESAMS .... Enhanced Surface to Air Missile Simulation (ACAE)
ESAMS .... Enhanced Surface-to-Air Missile Simulator (SEWL)
ES&A .... English, Scottish and Australian Bank Ltd. (SAUO)
ES&AMPH .... Environment, Safety, and Health (SAUS)
ES & H .... Environmental Safety and Health [*Environmental Protection Agency*] (EPA)
ES&H .... environment, safety and health (SAUS)
ES&H .... Environment, Safety, and Health Program (COE)
ES&H .... Office of Environment, Safety, and Health
ES&HC .... Environment, Safety and Health Compliance (SAUS)
ES & P .... Engineering Systems and Procedures (MCD)
ES&R .... Enviro-Systems & Research Inc. (SAUO)
ES & R .... Enviro-Systems & Research Incorporated, Roanoke, Va. (SAUS)
ES & S .... Engineering Services and Safety (NRCH)
ES&T .... Environmental Science and Technology (SAUO)
ES & T .... Environmental Science & Technology (journ.) (SAUS)
ES&T .... Environment, Science and Technology (SAUO)
ES & WQIAC ... Effluent Standards and Water Quality Information Advisory Committee (DICI)
ESANET .... ESA [*European Space Agency*] Network [*Information service or system*] (NITA)
ESANET .... European Space Agency Information Network (PDAA)
ESANET .... European Space Agency Network (SAUS)
ESANN .... European Symposium on Artificial Neural Networks (VERA)
ESANZ .... Economic Society of Australia and Nea Zealand (SAUS)
ESANZ .... Electrical Supply Authorities of New Zealand (SAUS)
ESAO .... Earth Sciences Assistance Office [*Department of the Interior*] (GRD)
ESAO .... European Society for Artificial Organs (EA)
ESAOA .... Eastern Ski Area Operators Association (EA)
ESAP .... Economics and Systems Analysis Program (SAUS)
ESAP .... Economic Structural Adjustment Program (SAUS)
ESAP .... Emergency School Assistance Program
ESAP .... Employment Security Automation (SAUS)
ESAP .... Employment Security Automation Project [*Department of Labor*]
ESAP .... Environmental Self-Assessment Program
ESAP .... Evoked Sensory Action Potential [*Neurophysiology*]
ESAPADIC .... English-Speaking Africa Patent Documentation and Information Centre (SAUS)
ESAPP .... Energy System Acquisition Project Plan (SAUS)
ESAPS .... Experimental Strain Analysis Processing System (SAUS)
ESAR .... Economic Synthetic Aperture Radar (ACAE)
ESAR .... Electromagnetic Spectrum Allocation Request [*Army*] (RDA)
ESAR .... Electronically Scanned Array RADAR (IEEE)
ESAR .... Electronically Steerable Array RADAR
esar .... electronically-steered array radar (SAUS)
ESAR .... Employment Service Automatic Reporting System (SAUS)
ESAR .... Energy Systems acquisition review (SAUS)
ESAR .... Extended Subsequent Application Review (AAGC)
ESARA .... Electronically Scanned Airborne Intercept Radar (SAUS)
ESARBICA .... Eastern and Southern African Regional Branch of the International Council on Archives [*Nairobi, Kenya*] (EAIO)
ESARCC .... Endangered Species Act Reauthorization Coordinating Committee (EA)
ESARG .... Energy Systems Administrative Reference Guide (SAUS)
Esarh .... Esarhaddon (BJA)
ESARIPO .... Industrial Property Organization for English-Speaking Africa [*Nairobi, Kenya*] (EAIO)
ESARS .... Earth Surveillance and Reconnaissance Simulator (SAUS)
ESARS .... Earth Surveillance and Rendezvous Simulator
ESARS .... Employment Service Automated [*or Automatic*] Reporting System [*Department of Labor*]
ESARS .... Expert System for Accessing Remotely Sensed Data (SAUS)
ESAR System ... Employment Service Automatic Reporting System (SAUS)

ESARTS .... En Route Stand-Alone Radar Training System [*FAA*] (TAG)
ESAs .... Eastern Socially Attractives (SAUS)
ESAS .... Education Student Assistance System
ESAS .... Electronically Steerable Antenna System [*Navy*] (CAAL)
ESAS .... Electronic Solar Array Simulator (ACAE)
ESAS .... Engineered Safeguards Actuation System [*Nuclear energy*] (NRCH)
ESAS .... Enhanced Situation Awareness System (SAUS)
ESAS .... Event Sensing and Analysis System (DNAB)
ESAS-2 .... Elastic Structural Analysis System - Two Dimensional [*Structures & Computers Ltd.*] [*Software package*] (NCC)
ESASA .... Ethnic Schools Association of South Australia
ESASC .... Elementary School Administrative Supervisory Certificate
ESA/SDS ..... ESA Space Documentation Service (SAUS)
ESASI .... European Society of Air Safety Investigators (PDAA)
ESA System... Easy, Speedy Accounting System (SAUS)
ESAT .... Electronic Shift Automatic Transmission [*Automotive engineering*]
ESAT .... Employee Satisfaction
ESAT .... Environmentally Sound and Appropriate Technology (PDAA)
ESAT .... Environmental Services Assistance Team (SAUO)
ESAT .... ERB Solar Analysis Tape (SAUS)
ESAT .... Esat Telecom Group ADS [*NASDAQ symbol*] (SG)
eSat .... except Saturday (SAUS)
ESAT .... Extrasystolic Atrial Tachycardia [*Medicine*] (MELL)
ESATA .... Executive Subroutines for Afterheat Temperature Analysis [*Computer program*] [*NASA*]
ESATC .... European Space Agency Technical Center (SAUS)
ESATCOM .... Emergency Satellite Communications System (DEMM)
ESATT .... European Science and Technology Transfer Network (SAUO)
ESAU .... Expert System AOB Update (SAUS)
ESA (UN) ..... Department of Economic and Social Affairs of the United Nations [*Later, Depart ment of Social Affairs*]
ESAURP .... Eastern and Southern African Universities Research Project (SAUO)
ESAUSA .... Estonian Student Association in the United States of America [*Defunct*] (EA)
ESAVD .... European Society Against Virus Diseases (SAUO)
ESAVS .... European School for Postgraduate Veterinary Training and Continuing Education (EURO)
ESAW .... European Statistics on Accidents at Work (EURO)
ESAWC .... Evaluation Staff, Air War College (SAUS)
ESAWC .... Evaluation Staff, War College [*Air Force*]
ESAWR .... Early Settlers Association of the Western Reserve (EA)
ESAX .... East Saxon [*Dialect of Old English*] [*Language, etc.*]
ESB .... Aerosaba SA de CV [*Mexico*] [*FAA designator*] (FAAC)
ESB .... Ankara-Esenboga [*Turkey*] [*Airport symbol*] (OAG)
ESB .... Earth Station - Brazil
ESB .... Economic Stabilization Board [*World War II*]
ESB .... Educational Service Branch [*BUPERS*]
ESB .... Education Support Centre [*Australia*]
ESB .... Effective Sample Base [*Advertising*] (DOAD)
ESB .... Effective School Battery [*Educational test*]
ESB .... Electrical Simulation of Brain (SAUS)
ESB .... Electrical Standards Board (SAUO)
ESB .... Electrical Stimulation of the Brain
ESB .... Electrical Supply Board (SAUO)
ESB .... Electrical Systems Branch [*NASA*] (KSC)
ESB .... Electricity Supply Board (ACII)
ESB .... Electric Storage Battery
ESB .... Electric Storage Battery Co. (EFIS)
ESB .... Electronic Stimulation of the Brain (SAUS)
ESB .... Electrostimulation of the Brain (DIPS)
ESB .... Elektromotroischer Systembaukasten
ESB .... Emergency Services Bureau [*Queensland, Australia*]
ESB .... Emerging Small Business (AAGC)
ESB .... Empennage Support Beam [*Aerospace engineering*] (MCD)
ESB .... Empire State Building (SAUS)
ESB .... Engineering Services Building (SAUS)
ESB .... Engineering Societies Building (SAUS)
ESB .... Engineering Society of Baltimore (SAUO)
ESB .... Engineering Society of Buffalo (SAUO)
ESB .... Engineering Support Building (SAUS)
ESB .... Engineer Special Brigade [*Military*]
ESB .... English-Speaking Background (ADA)
ESB .... English-Speaking Board (SAUO)
ESB .... English-Speaking Board (International) [*British*]
ESB .... Environmental Protection Agency, ERC [*Environmental Research Center*] Library, Corvallis, OR [*OCLC symbol*] (OCLC)
ESB .... Environmental Specimen Banking (SAUS)
ESB .... Environmental Studies Board [*National Academy of Sciences*]
ESB .... Esa Ala [*D'Entrecasteaux Islands*] [*Seismograph station code, US Geological Survey*] (SEIS)
ESB .... Espirito Santo Overseas [*NYSE symbol*] (SPSG)
ESB .... Essential Switching Box (MCD)
ESB .... Eugenics Society Bulletin [*Medicine*] (EDAA)
ESB .... European Schoolbooks Ltd. [*British*]
ESB .... European Society for Biomechanics (SAUO)
ESB .... European Society of Biomechanics (EA)
ESB .... European Soil Bureau (EURO)
ESB .... European Standardisation Board (SAUO)
ESB .... Executive for Small Business
ESB .... Executive Safety Board (SAUS)
ESB .... Executive Support Board [*Army*] (RDA)
ESB .... Executive Support Branch (HEAS)
ESB .... Experiments Systems Branch [*NASA*] (KSC)
ESB .... Explosive Safety Board [*Military*]
ESB .... Export Services Branch (SAUO)
ESB .... Extra Strong Bitter [*Beer*] [*British*]
ESBA .... Eastern Sovereign Base Area [*British military*] (DMA)
ESBA .... Eastern States Bankcard Association (SAUO)
ESBA .... Ethyl-sec-butylamiline [*Organic chemistry*]
ESBAR .... Epitaxial Schottky Barrier (VLIE)
ESBC .... Electronics Small Business Council
ESBCY .... European Society for Blue Cross Youth (EA)
ESBFCOA ..... Eastern States Blast Furnace and Coke Oven Association (EA)
ESBFS .... East of Scotland Brass Founders' Society [*A union*]
ESBG .... European Savings Bank Group [*EC*] (ECED)
ESBK .... [*The*] Elmira Savings Bank [*NASDAQ symbol*] (NQ)
ESBK .... Elmira Svgs Bk FSB NY [*NASDAQ symbol*] (TTSB)
ESBL .... Engine Start before Launch [*Navy*] (CAAL)
ESBM .... Equipment Section Boost Motor [*Space launch term*] (ISAK)
ESBO .... Electronic Selection and Bar Operating (IAA)
ESBO .... Environmental and Safety Business Opportunities [*Bureau of National Affairs*]
ESBOA .... Electricity Supply Board Officiers Association (SAUO)
ESBO Circuit... Electronic Selection and Bar-Operating Circuit (SAUS)
ESBP .... European Society for Biochemical Pharmacology (SAUS)
ESBP .... European Society for/of Biochemical Pharmacology (SAUO)
ESBPrA .... Espirito Santo Oversecs 8.50% Pref [*NYSE symbol*] (TTSB)
ESBR .... Electronic Stacked Beam Radar (SAUS)
E-SBR .... Emulsion Styrene Butadiene Rubber (SAUS)
ESBRA .... Emerging Small Business Reserve Amount (AAGC)
ESBRS .... Elementary School Behavior Rating Scale [*Devereaux*] [*Psychology*]
ESBT .... Expert System Building Tool [*Computer science*]
ESBTC .... [*USA*] European Space Battery Test Center (ODA)
ESBVM .... Ecumenical Society of the Blessed Virgin Mary (EA)
ESC .... Earthspirit Community (EA)
ESC .... Earth Station - Congo
ESC .... Eastern Simulation Council
ESC .... Echo Suppressor Control [*Telecommunications*] (TEL)
ESC .... Ecological Science Centre (SAUS)
ESC .... Ecological Science Co-operative (SAUS)
ESC .... Ecological Study Center [*Oak Ridge National Laboratory*]
ESC .... Economic and Social Committee [*EC*] (ECED)
ESC .... Economic and Social Council [*United Nations*]
ESC .... Economic Sciences Corp. [*Information service or system*] (IID)
ESC .... Economist, Food Information Group (SAUO)
ESC .... Edison Screw Cap [*Electronics*] (EECA)
ESC .... Educational Scientific Computer (VLIE)
ESC .... Educational Systems Corp. [*Defunct*] (EA)
ESC .... Educational Systems Corporation (SAUO)
ESC .... Education Service Center (SAUS)
ESC .... Education Systems Incorporated (SAUO)
ESC .... EISA System Component (SAUS)
ESC .... EISA System Component Escape (SAUS)
ESC .... Electrical Safety Committee (SAUS)
ESC .... Electrical Skin Conductivity (SAUS)
ESC .... Electric Steering Column Adjustment [*Automotive engineering*]
ESC .... Electric Surface Current
ESC .... Electromechanical Slope Computer (MAE)
ESC .... Electromechanical Stop Clock
ESC .... Electronic Scan Converter
ESC .... Electronic Security Command (MCD)
esc .... electronic service change (SAUS)
ESC .... Electronic Shop Computer
ESC .... Electronic Spark Control [*Automotive*]
ESC .... Electronic Specialty Company (SAUO)
ESC .... Electronic Speed Control (SAUS)
ESC .... Electronics Systems Center (SAUS)
ESC .... Electronic Still Camera
ESC .... Electronic Structural Correlator (SAUS)
ESC .... Electronic Supervisory Control (MCD)
ESC .... Electronic Support Centre (SAUS)
ESC .... Electronic Switching Center (CET)
ESC .... Electronic Systems Center [*Air Force*]
ESC .... Electronic Systems Command [*Also, NESC*] [*Navy*]
ESC .... Electron Shop Computer (SAUS)
ESC .... Electroskin Conductance [*Medicine*] (EDAA)
ESC .... Electroslag Casting (SAUS)
ESC .... Electrostatic Chuck (AAEL)
ESC .... Electrostatic Collector
ESC .... Electrostatic Compatibility (IEEE)
ESC .... Electrostatic Space Cleaner (SAUS)
ESC .... Elementary School Center [*An association*] (EA)
ESC .... Elongation-Sensitive Cell (PDAA)
ESC .... El Salvador [*Chile*] [*Seismograph station code, US Geological Survey*] [*Closed*] (SEIS)
ESC .... Embryonic Stem Cell [*Cytology*]
ESC .... Emeritus Corp. [*AMEX symbol*] (SAG)
ESC .... Employment Security Commission of North Carolina (SAUO)
ESC .... Employment Studies Centre [*University of Newcastle, Australia*]
ESC .... Employment Support Center (EA)
ESC .... Emulation Sub-Channel (SAUS)
ESC .... Enamel Single-Covered [*Wire insulation*] (DEN)
ESC .... Endangered Species Committee [*Environmental Protection Agency*] (EPA)
ESC .... End-Systolic Count [*Cardiology*]
ESC .... Energy Security Corporation (SAUO)
ESC .... Energy Systems Center [*University of Nevada*] [*Research center*] (RCD)
ESC .... Engineering and Scientific Computing (SAUS)
ESC .... Engineering Sequential Camera (KSC)

ESC Engineering Service Circuit
ESC Engineering Society of Cincinnati (SAUO)
ESC Engineering Standards Committee (SAUO)
ESC Engineering Support Center (SAUS)
ESC Engineers and Scientists of Cincinnati (SAUS)
ESC Engineer Studies Center (MCD)
ESC Engine Start Command (KSC)
ESC Engine Supervisory Control (SAUS)
ESC England Steel Castings Corporations Ltd. (SAUO)
ESC English Shakespeare Co. (ECON)
ESC English Shepherd Club (EA)
ESC English Ski Council [*British*] (DBA)
ESC English-Speaking Country
ESC English Stage Company (SAUO)
ESC English Steel Corporation (SAUO)
ESC Enhanced Satellite Capability (SEWL)
ESC Enrichment Survey Committee (SAUO)
ESC Entomological Society of Canada (BARN)
ESC Environmental Sciences Catalog (SAUO)
ESC Environmental Stress Crack [*or Cracking*] [*Plastics*]
ESC Environmental Studies Center [*State University of New York at Buffalo*] [*Research center*] (RCD)
ESC Environmental Study Conference [*House of Representatives*]
ESC Environmental Supercomputer Center (SAUO)
ESC Environment Sensitive Cracking (SAUS)
ESC Epoxy Spray Coater
ESC Equipment Section Container
ESC Equipment Serviceability Criteria [*Military*]
ESC Equipment Storage Container (KSC)
ESC Error Status Code (SAUS)
ESC Erythropoietin-Sensitive Stem Cell [*Hematology*]
Esc Escadrille [*Military*] (BARN)
ESC Escalator [*Technical drawings*]
ESC Escanaba [*Michigan*] [*Airport symbol*] (OAG)
ESC Escanaba, MI [*Location identifier*] [*FAA*] (FAAL)
ESC Escape (NASA)
Esc Escape (SHCU)
ESC Escape Character [*Keyboard*] (KSC)
ESC Escaped (SAUS)
esc Escapement (SAUS)
ESC Escobilla [*Little Broom*] [*Flamenco dance term*] [*Spanish*]
ESC Escompte [*Discount, Rebate*] [*French*]
ESC Escort (AABC)
Esc Escort [*Record label*]
Esc Escrow [*Legal term*] (DLA)
ESC Escudo [*Monetary unit*] [*Chile, Portugal*]
ESC Escutcheon
ESC Esplanade Centre Holdings [*Vancouver Stock Exchange symbol*]
ESC Estonian Shipping Company (SAUO)
ESC European National Shippers Councils (SAUS)
ESC European Security Community (SAUS)
ESC European Security Conference [*Soviet-sponsored*]
ESC European Seismological Commission (EAIO)
ESC European Serials Conference (SAUS)
ESC European Shippers' Councils [*Netherlands*] (DS)
ESC European Social and Economic Committee (SAUO)
ESC European Social Charter (SAUO)
ESC European Society of Cardiology (MCD)
ESC European Society of Climatotherapy [*See also FEC*] [*Briancon, France*] (EAIO)
ESC European Society of Culture [*See also SEC*] (EAIO)
ESC European Software Contractors (SAUS)
ESC European Space Conference
ESC European Sport Shooting Confederation (EAIO)
ESC European Standardisation Council (SAUO)
ESC European Statistics Center (SAUO)
ESC European Steering Committee (SAUS)
ESC European Support Center (Novell) (SAUS)
esc evanescent (SAUS)
ESC Evanescent Space Charge (PDAA)
ESC Even Small Caps [*Publishing*] (WDMC)
ESC Evoked Synaptic Currents [*Neurophysiology*]
ESC Exchange Servicing Center [*Telecommunications*] (TEL)
ESC Executive Search Council [*Defunct*] (EA)
ESC Executive Seminar Center [*Civil Service Commission*]
ESC Executive Service Corps (SAUS)
ESC Executive Steering Committee (DOMA)
ESC Executive Support Center [*Army*]
ESC Executive Systems Corp. [*An association*] [*Defunct*] (EA)
ESC Expandable Shelter Containers (MCD)
E/SC Expected/Single-Command Travel Time
ESC Expedited Site Characterization [*Argonne National Laboratory*] [*Environmental science*]
ESC Expedited Site Characterization project (SAUS)
ESC Experimental Safety Car (SAUS)
ESC Export Supply Center (SAUS)
ESC Ex Senatus Consulto [*By Decree of the Senate*] [*Latin*]
esc extended core storage (SAUS)
ESC Extended Service Coverage [*Automotive engineering*]
ESCA Electron Spectroscopic Chemical Analysis (SAUS)
ESCA Electron Spectroscopy for Chemical Analysis
ESCA Endangered Species Conservation Act of 1969
ESCA Engineer Supply Control Agency (SAUO)
ESCA English Schools Cricket Association (BI)
ESCA English Schools Cycling Association (SAUO)
ESCA Escalade, Inc. [*NASDAQ symbol*] (NQ)
ESCA European Computer Service Association (SAUO)
EScA Executive and Scientific Appointments, Ltd. [*Commercial firm*] [*British*]
ESCA Executive Stewards' and Caterers' Association [*Later, IFSEA*]
ESCA Exposition Service Contractors Association (EA)
ESCA Extended Source Calibration Area [*Nuclear energy*] (NRCH)
ESCAD Energy Soft Computer-Aided Design [*Energy Soft Computer Systems Ltd.*] [*Software package*] (NCC)
Escalde Escalade, Inc. [*Associated Press*] (SAG)
Escalon Escalon Medical Corp. [*Associated Press*] (SAG)
ESCAM Enhanced SORTS Capability Assessment Module (SAUS)
ESCAN Electronics & Space Corporation of Canada Ltd. (SAUS)
ESCAN Escanaba, MI [*American Association of Railroads railroad junction routing code*]
E Scan E Scanner (SAUS)
ESCAP Economic and Social Commission for Asia and the Pacific [*UN division*] (NITA)
ESCAP Economic Social Commission for Asia and the Pacific (SAUS)
ESCAP Economic Soil Commission - Asia Pacific (SAUS)
E S Cap Edison Scraw Cap (SAUS)
escap escapologist (SAUS)
escap escapology (SAUS)
ESCAP European Society of Child and Adolescent Psychiatry (EA)
ESCAP United Nations Economic and Social Commission for Asia and the Pacific [*Bangkok, Thailand*] (EAIO)
ESCAPAC Escape PAC (MCD)
ESCAPE European Symposium on Computer Aided Process Engineering
ESCAPE Evaluation of Strategies to Address Climate Change by Adapting to and Preventing Emissions (SAUS)
ESCAPE Expansion Symbolic Compiling Assembly Program for Engineers
ESCAPE Expeditious Sales, Catalog, and Property Evaluation [*Defense Logistics Services Center project*] [*DoD*]
ESCAPER Emergency System of Control Allowing Pilot Escape and Recovery (MCD)
ESCAP/PCHIS United Nations Economic and Social Commission for Asia and the Pacific, Clearinghouse and Information Section (SAUS)
ESCAP/TIAI ESCAP Network for Technological Information on Agro- Industries (SAUS)
ESCAP/TIAI ESCAP Network for Technology Information on Agro-Industries (SAUO)
ESCAP/TIS ESCAP Trade Information Service (SAUO)
ESCAP/TPC ESCAP Trade Promotion Centre (SAUO)
ESCAR Experimental Superconducting Accelerating Ring [*Atomic physics*]
ESCARFOR Escort Carrier Force
Escarp Escarpment (SAUS)
ESCAT Emergency Security Control Air Traffic (SAUO)
ESCAT Emergency Security Control of Air Traffic (AFM)
ESCAWT European Steering Committee for APr Workshop Technology (SAUO)
ESCB European System of Central Banks (WDAA)
ESCBA Escape Self-Contained Breathing Apparatus (SARE)
ESCC Electrical Standards Coordinating Committee (SAUO)
ESCC electrolyte-steroid-cardiopathy by calcification (SAUS)
ESCC Enamelled Single Cotton Covered (SAUS)
ESCC Enamel Single, Cotton Covered [*Wire insulation*] (IAA)
ESCC Engineering Sequential Camera Coverage (KSC)
ESCC Enhanced Serial Communications Controller (SAUS)
ESCC Epidural Spinal Cord Compression [*Medicine*] (MELL)
ESCC Evans & Sutherland Computer Corp. [*NASDAQ symbol*] (NQ)
ESCC Evans&Sutherl'd Computer [*NASDAQ symbol*] (TTSB)
ESCC External Stress Corrosion Cracking (SAUS)
ESCC Stockholm [*Sweden*] [*ICAO location identifier*] (ICLI)
ESCCD Electrical Short-Circuit Current Decay (ODA)
ESCCP Engineering and Scientific Career Continuation Pay [*Air Force*]
ESCD end stage cardiac disease (SAUS)
ESCD Engineering Specification Control Document (AAG)
ESCD Extended Setup Configuration Data (SAUS)
ESCD Extended System Configuration Data [*Computer science*] (AGLO)
ESCD Extended System Contents Directory (SAUS)
ESCE Enemy Situation Correlation Element [*Air Force*]
ESCERC European Semiconductor Device Research Conference
ESCES Experimental Satellite Communications Earth Station (SAUO)
ESCES Experimental Space Communication Earth Station [*Telecommunications*] (TEL)
ESCF Electronic Systems Compatibility Facility [*NASA*]
ESCF European Seed Capital Funds (EURO)
ESCF Linkoping/Malmen [*Sweden*] [*ICAO location identifier*] (ICLI)
ESCG Earth Science Catalogue Gopher (SAUO)
ESCGS Electrostatic Centimeter Gram Second (IAA)
escgs Electrostatic Centimetre-Gram-Second (SAUS)
ESCH Earth Station - Chile
ESCH Electrolyte-Steroid-Cardiopathy by Hyalinization (SAUS)
ESCH Escherichia [*Bacterial strain*]
ESCHAT Eschatological (ADA)
E School L Rev Eastern School Law Review [*A publication*] (DLA)
ESCHR El Salvador Committee for Human Rights (EAIO)
ESCI Earth Sciences [*NASDAQ symbol*] (TTSB)
ESCI Earth Sciences, Inc. [*NASDAQ symbol*] (NQ)
ESCI Electric Space Conditioning Institute (SAUO)
ESCI Environmental Science Citation Index (SAUS)
ESC/I Epson Standard Code for Image Readers (SAUS)
ESCI European Society for Clinical Investigation (EAIO)
ESCIM European Centre for Study and Information on Multinational Corporations (SAUO)

ESCIM.......... European Centre for Study and Information on Multinational Corporations (SAUS)
ESCIP.......... Employee Suggestion Cost Improvement Proposal (SAUS)
ESCIS.......... Encyclopedia of Senior Citizens Information Sources [*A publication*]
ESCK.......... Norrkoping/Bravalla [*Sweden*] [*ICAO location identifier*] (ICLI)
ESCL.......... Electronic Systems Compatibility Laboratory [*NASA*]
ESCL.......... Elias Sourasky Central Library (SAUS)
ESCL.......... Escalator (MSA)
ESCL.......... Evans Signal Corps Laboratory (SAUS)
ESCL.......... Soderhamn [*Sweden*] [*ICAO location identifier*] (ICLI)
EscIn.......... Escalon Medical Corp. [*Associated Press*] (SAG)
ESCM.......... Engine Systems Control Module [*Automotive engineering*]
ESCM.......... Equipment Support Center, Mannheim [*Germany*]
ESCM.......... Erosion and Sedimentation Control Measures [*Environmental science*] (COE)
ESCM.......... ESC Medical Systems Ltd. [*NASDAQ symbol*] (SAG)
ESCM.......... Extended Services Communications Manager [*IBM Corp.*]
ESCM.......... Uppsala [*Sweden*] [*ICAO location identifier*] (ICLI)
ESCMed.......... ESC Medical Systems Ltd. [*Associated Press*] (SAG)
ESCMF.......... ESC Medical Systems [*NASDAQ symbol*] (TTSB)
ESCMIA.......... Education, Scientific and Cultural Material Import Act (SAUO)
ESCMT.......... Engineering Societies Committee for Manpower Training (SAUS)
ESCN.......... Electrolyte and Steroid-Produced Cardiopathy Characterized by Necrosis [*Medicine*]
escn.......... electrolyte-and-steroid-produced cardiopathy characterized by necrosis (SAUS)
ESCN.......... Electrolyte-Steroid-Cardiopathy by Necrosis (SAUS)
ESCN.......... Stockholm/Tullinge [*Sweden*] [*ICAO location identifier*] (ICLI)
ESCO.......... Earth Station - Colombia
ESCO.......... Easco, Inc. [*NASDAQ symbol*] (SAG)
ESCO.......... Educational, Scientific, and Cultural Organization (BARN)
ESCO.......... Electrical Steel Company (SAUO)
ESCO.......... Energy Service Co.
ESCO.......... Energy Service Company (SAUO)
ESCO.......... Energy Systems Conference Office (SAUS)
ESCO.......... Engineered Systems Co. (SAUO)
ESCO.......... Engineers Supply Control Office [*Army*]
ESCO.......... Engineer Supply Control Office (SAUO)
ESCO.......... Equipment Survey Control Office (SAUO)
Esco.......... ESCO Electronics [*Associated Press*] (SAG)
ESCO.......... ESF Scientific Committee for ODP (SAUO)
ESCo.......... Estonian Shipping Company (SAUO)
ESCO.......... European Satellite Communications Organization (SAUS)
ESCO.......... European Satellite Consulting Organization [*France*] [*Telecommunications*]
ESCO.......... European Sterility Congress Organization (SAUO)
ESCO2.......... Energy Specific Carbon Dioxide [*Automotive emissions*]
ESCOE.......... Engineering Societies Commission on Energy [*Defunct*] (EA)
ESCOFAR.......... Eastern Counties Farmers Ltd. (SAUO)
Escom.......... Electrical Supply Commission (SAUS)
ESCOMO.......... Escort Cost Model
ESCON.......... Enterprise Systems Connect (SAUS)
ESCON.......... Enterprise Systems Connection [*IBM Corp.*]
ESCON.......... Enterprise Systems Connection architecture (SAUS)
ESCON.......... Estimated Consumption [*of gasoline*] [*Computer model*]
ESCOP.......... Experimental Stations Committee on Organization and Policy [*National Association of State Universities and Land-Grant Colleges*]
ESCOR.......... Economic and Social Committee for Overseas Research (SAUO)
ESCOR.......... Economic and Social Council Official Records (SAUO)
ESCORON.... Escort-Scouting Squadron
ESCORP.......... Examination Services Corporation (SAUS)
ESCORT.......... Electronic System for Control of Receipt Transactions (MCD)
ESCORTDIV... Escort Division
ESCORTFIGHTRON... Escort Fighter Squadron
ESCOS.......... Electronic Security Combat Operations Staff [*Military*]
ESCOs.......... Energy Service Companies (SAUO)
ESCP.......... Earth Science Curriculum Project [*Education*]
ESCP.......... Employee Counseling Services Program (SAUS)
ESC/P.......... Epson Printer Language (SAUS)
ESC/P.......... Epson Standard Code for Printers (SAUS)
ESCP.......... European Society of Clinical Pharmacy (SAUS)
ESCP.......... Expendable Surface Current Probe [*Coast Guard*]
escp.......... expendable surface-current probe (SAUS)
ESCP2.......... Epson Specific Code / Protocol 2 (SAUS)
ESCPB.......... European Society of Comparative Physiology and Biochemistry (EAIO)
ESCP Newsletter... Earth Science Curriculum Project Newsletter (journ.) (SAUS)
ESCR.......... Economic and Social Research Council (SAUO)
ESCR.......... Environmental Stress-Cracking Resistance (SAUS)
ESCR.......... Environmental Stress-Crack Resistance [*Plastics*]
escr.......... escrow (SAUS)
ESCR.......... External Standard Channel Ratio (ODA)
ESCRG.......... Escort Guard
Escriche Dict... Escriche's Dictionary of Jurisprudence [*A publication*] (DLA)
ESCRTC.......... Eastern Signal Corps Replacement Training Center
ESCRU.......... Episcopal Society for Cultural and Racial Unity [*Defunct*] (EA)
ESCS.......... Eccentrically Stiffened Cylindrical Shell
ESCs.......... Ecological Science Centres (SAUO)
ESCs.......... Ecological Science Co-operatives, formerly Ecological Science Centres (SAUS)
ESCS.......... Economics, Statistics, and Cooperatives Service [*Later, ERS, SRS*] [*Department of Agriculture*]
ESCS.......... Electrical Spinal Cord Stimulation [*Medicine*] (EDAA)
ESCS.......... Electronic Spacecraft Simulator (IAA)
ESCS.......... Emergency Satellite Communications (SAUS)
ESCS.......... Emergency Satellite Communications System
ESCS.......... Enlisted Signal Corps School
Esc Sh.......... Escort Ship (SAUS)
ESCSI.......... Expanded Shale, Clay, and Slate Institute (EA)
ESCSP.......... European Society of Corporate and Strategic Planners [*Belgium*] (PDAA)
ESCT.......... Elapsed Spacecraft Time
ESCTC.......... Eastern Signal Corps Training Center (SAUS)
ESCTS.......... Explosive Set Circuit Test System (DWSG)
ESCU.......... Extended Service and Cooling Umbilical (NASA)
ESCVS.......... European Society for Cardiovascular Surgery (EAIO)
ESCVS.......... European Society of Cardiovascular Surgery (SAUS)
ESCWA.......... Economic and Social Commission for Asia and the Pacific (SAUS)
ESCWA.......... Economic and Social Commission for Western Art (SAUO)
ESCWA.......... Economic and Social Commission for Western Asia [*Iraq*] [*United Nations*] [*Research center*] (IRC)
ESCWS.......... Essential Service Cooling Water System [*Nuclear energy*] (NRCH)
ESCX.......... First Security Bank [*Private rail car owner code*]
ESD.......... Earliest Start Date
ESD.......... Earth Sciences Division [*Army Natick Laboratories*] (NOAA)
ESD.......... East San Diego (SAUS)
ESD.......... Eastsound [*Washington*] [*Airport symbol*] (OAG)
ESD.......... Echo Sounding Device [*Navigation*]
ESD.......... Ecologically-Sustainable Development
ESD.......... Ecological Sciences Division [*Oak Ridge National Laboratory*]
ESD.......... Economic Surveys Division [*Census*] (OICC)
ESD.......... Educational Service and Demonstration Centers [*Washington*] (EDAC)
ESD.......... Education Service District (SAUS)
ESD.......... Effective Standard Deviation [*of chemical standardized solutions*]
ESD.......... Electrical Overstress/Electrostatic Discharge Association, Inc.
ESD.......... Electric Spike Defence (SAUS)
ESD.......... Electronic Semiconductor Device (SAUS)
ESD.......... Electronic Service Delivery (FOTI)
esd.......... electronic smoke detector (SAUS)
ESD.......... Electronic Software Distribution
ESD.......... Electronics Systems Division [*Air Force*] (DOMA)
ESD.......... Electronic Summation Device (MAE)
ESD.......... Electronic System Design (SAUS)
ESD.......... Electronic Systems Division [*Hanscom Air Force Base, MA*]
ESD.......... Electronique Serge Dassault [*French manufacturer*] (NITA)
ESD.......... Electron Spectrographic Diffraction
ESD.......... Electron-Stimulated Desorption [*Spectroscopy*]
ESD.......... Electroocular Symbol Display
ESD.......... Electro Sound Group, Inc. [*AMEX symbol*] (COMM)
ESD.......... Electrostatic Discharge (MCD)
ESD.......... Electrostatic Dissipation
ESD.......... Electrostatic Dissipative (SARE)
ESD.......... Electrostatic Sensitive Device (PDAA)
ESD.......... Electrostatic Storage Deflection
ESD.......... Element Status Display (SAUS)
ESD.......... Elongated Single Domain
ESD.......... Emergency Service Division (SAUS)
ESD.......... Emergency Services Department (SAUO)
ESD.......... Emergency Shutdown (MCD)
ESD.......... Emergency Shutdown Device [*Environmental science*] (COE)
ESD.......... emission spectrometric detector (SAUS)
ESD.......... Emission Spectrometric Device [*Medicine*] (EDAA)
ESD.......... Emission Standards Division (AUEG)
ESD.......... Employment Security Department (SAUS)
ESD.......... Ending Sequence Done
ESD.......... End of Screening Date [*DoD*]
ESD.......... end sequence done (SAUS)
ESD.......... End System Designator (GART)
ESD.......... End-Systolic Diameter [*or Dimension*] [*Cardiology*]
ESD.......... energy spectral density (SAUS)
ESD.......... Energy Storage Device (IAA)
ESD.......... Energy Systems Division (ACAE)
ESD.......... Engineered Systems & Development Corp. (EFIS)
ESD.......... Engineering Service Division (SAUO)
ESD.......... Engineering Services Department (SAUS)
ESD.......... Engineering Society of Detroit (EA)
ESD.......... Engineering Standardization Directives
ESD.......... Engineering Support Documentation
ESD.......... English as a Secondary Dialect
Esd.......... English as a second dialect (SAUS)
ESD.......... Enhanced Small Device Interface (SAUS)
ESD.......... Entry Systems Division [*IBM division*] (CDE)
ESD.......... Environmental Satellite Data [*National Oceanic and Atmospheric Administration*] (GFGA)
ESD.......... Environmental Sciences Division [*Oak Ridge National Laboratory*]
ESD.......... Environmental Sensing Device (IAA)
ESD.......... Environmental Services Department (SAUO)
ESD.......... Environmental Services Division [*Environmental Protection Agency*] (GFGA)
ESD.......... Environmental Sex Determination [*Biology*]
ESD.......... Environmental Systems Division [*Army*]
ESD.......... Environment Strategies Division [*Commonwealth*] (EERA)
ESD.......... EPAs Emissions Standards Division (SAUS)
ESD.......... Epidemiological Information Service (SAUO)
ESD.......... Equipment Statistical Data
ESD.......... Equipment Supply Depot [*British military*] (DMA)
ESD.......... Equivalent Sphere Diameter (SAUS)
ESD.......... Equivalent Spherical Diameter [*of a particle*]

ESD .... Equivalent Stylized Day [*Of wartime combat*]
Esd .... Esdras [*Apocrypha*] (BJA)
ESD .... Esophagus, Stomach, and Duodenum [*Gastroenterology*] (DAVI)
ESD .... Esterase D [*An enzyme*]
ESD .... Estimated Shipping Date
ESD .... Estimated Standard Deviation [*Mathematics*]
ESD .... Euratom Safeguards Directorate (ODA)
ESD .... European System Design (SAUS)
ESD .... Exoskeletal Device [*Medicine*] (EDAA)
ESD .... Experiment Systems Division (MCD)
ESD .... Explanation of Significant Differences (BCP)
ESD .... Exploitation Support Data (SEWL)
ESD .... Exponential-Slope Difference [*Statistics*]
ESD .... Export Services Division (SAUO)
ESD .... Export Supply Directorate (SAUS)
ESD .... Ex-Stock Dividend [*Investment term*]
esd .... extended school day (SAUS)
ESD .... Extension Shaft Disconnect [*Nuclear energy*] (NRCH)
ESD .... External Symbol Dictionary [*A publication*]
ESD .... Extra Soil Defense [*Fabric treatment*]
ESD .... Electromagnetic Shower Detector (ODA)
ESDA .... Earth-Science Data Acquisition (SAUS)
ESDA .... Earth Sciences Data Standards (SAUS)
ESDA .... Earth Sciences Data Standards Council (SAUO)
ESDA .... Electronic System Design Automation (SAUS)
ESDA .... Electrostatically Deployed Antenna (ACAE)
ESDA .... European Society for Dermatological Research (SAUO)
ESDA .... Ljungbyhed [*Sweden*] [*ICAO location identifier*] (ICLI)
ESDAC .... European Space Data Analysis Centre (SAUS)
ESDAC .... European Space Data Center (MCD)
ESDAC .... European Space Data Center (Darmstadt, Germany) (SAUS)
ESDAG .... Earth-Science Data Acquisition Guidelines (SAUS)
ESDB .... Angelholm [*Sweden*] [*ICAO location identifier*] (ICLI)
ESDB .... Earth Station Database (SAUS)
ESDB .... Endangered Species Database ReachScan Link (AEPA)
ESDC .... Environmental Sciences Division Complex (SAUS)
ESDC .... Equipment Sliding Drawer Cabinet
ESDC .... Equipment Statistical Data Card
ESDC .... Extended Salvage Depth Capability (MCD)
ESDC .... Extra Segment Descriptor Cache [*Computer science*] (VERA)
ESDCD .... Earth and Space Data Computing Division (SAUS)
ESDD .... Earth Science Data Directory (EERA)
ESDD .... Earth Systems Science Committee [*Intrenational*] [*Environment term*] (EGA)
ESDD .... Regional Military Command Subcenter South [*Sweden*] [*ICAO location identifier*] (ICLI)
ESDE .... Electrostatic Discharge Effects (MCD)
ESDE .... Engineer Stores Development Establishment (SAUS)
ESDE .... Expert System Development Environment (VLIE)
ESDERC .... European Semiconductor Device Research Conference (PDAA)
ESD/EW .... Electronic Systems Division Eastwing [*Hanscom Air Force Base, MA*]
ESDF .... Ronneby [*Sweden*] [*ICAO location identifier*] (ICLI)
ESD-Generator... Electrostatic Discharge Generator (SAUS)
ESDI .... Enhanced Small Device [*or Disk*] Interface [*Computer science*]
ESDI .... Enhanced Small Disk Interface (SAUS)
ESDI .... Enhanced Small/System Device Interface (SAUS)
ESDI .... Enhanced Small Systems Interface (SAUS)
ESDI .... Enhanced Standard Device Interface [*Computer science*] (VERA)
ESDI .... Enhanced Storage Device Interface (SAUS)
ESDI .... Enhanced System Device Interface [*Computer science*] (DDC)
ES:DI .... Extra Segment:Destination Index [*Computer science*]
ESDIAD .... Electron-Stimulated Desorption Ion Angular Distribution [*For study of surfaces*]
ESDIAD .... ESD ion angular distribution (SAUS)
ESDIIR .... Ecologically Sustainable Development Intersectoral Issues Report (EERA)
ESDIM .... Earth System Data and Information Management [*National Oceanic and Atmospheric Administration*] (USDC)
ESDIM .... Environmental Science Data Integration and Management (SAUS)
ESD/IPC .... Environmental Satellite Distribution/Interactive Processing Center (SAUO)
ESDIS .... Earth Science Data and Information System (CARB)
ESDL .... Electronic Software Distribution and Licensing (CDE)
ESDL .... Electro Technical Laboratory System Description Language (SAUS)
ESDL .... Ethiopian Somali Democratic League
ESDM .... Ethiopian Somali Democratic Movement
ESDM .... Expert System Development Methodology (VLIE)
ESDM .... Extended Services Database Manager [*Computer science*] (AGLO)
ESDN .... electron stimulated desorption of neutrals (SAUS)
ESDN .... Extended Software Defined Network [*Computer science*] (HGAA)
ESDP .... Engineering and Science Development Program (TIMI)
ESDP .... Evolutionary System for Data Processing (IAA)
esdp .... external stores data package (SAUS)
ESD plastic... ElectroStatic Dissipative plastic (SAUS)
ESDR .... Electrical System Design Report
Esdr .... Esdras [*Biblical*] (RION)
ESDR .... External System Design Report (VLIE)
ESDRP .... Evreiskaia Sotsialdemokraticheskaia Rabochaia Partiia (BJA)
ESDS .... Economic and Social Data System [*Agency for International Development*] [*Database*]
ESDS .... Electronic Software Delivery System (GART)
ESDS .... Electrostatic Discharge Simulator
ESDS .... Elemental Standard Data System (NG)
ESDS .... Enclosed Space Detector System (SAUS)
ESDS .... Entry Sequence Data Set (HGAA)
ESDS .... Entry-Sequenced Data System (SAUS)
ESDS .... Environmental Satellite Data System (SAUS)
ESDSC .... Ecologically Sustainable Development Steering Committee [*Commonwealth*] (EERA)
ES-DSMA..... Ephphatha Services - Division for Service and Mission in America (EA)
ESD System... Emergency Shut-Down System (SAUS)
ESDT .... Electrostatic Storage Display Tube (IAA)
ESD TDR...... Electronic Systems Division, Technical Documentary Reports [*AFSC*]
ESDTR .... Electronic Selector Dropout Tape Read (VLIE)
ESDU .... Engineering Sciences Data Unit
ESDU .... Event Storage and Distribution Unit
ESDV .... Emergency Shutdown Valve (TIMI)
ESDX .... Environmental Services Data Exchange (AG)
ESDX .... Environment and Safety Data Exchange (VLIE)
ESE .... Avesen SA de CV [*Mexico*] [*ICAO designator*] (FAAC)
ESE .... Earth Sensor Electronics (ACAE)
ESE .... East-Southeast
ESE .... Editorial System Engineering, Inc. (SAUO)
ESE .... Electrical Support Equipment
ESE .... Electric Sequence Equipment (SAUS)
ESE .... Electronic Security Environment (SAUS)
ESE .... Electronic Security Europe (SAUO)
ESE .... Electronic Stock Evaluator Corp.
ESE .... Electronic Storage Element [*Computer science*] (CIST)
ESE .... Electronic Support Equipment (MCD)
ESE .... Electronic System Evaluator
ESE .... Electron Spin Echo [*Physics*]
ESE .... Electrostatische Einheit [*Electrostatic unit*] [*Physics*] (DAVI)
ESE .... Emergency Strike Effort [*Military*]
ESE .... Energy Systems Evaluation (SAUS)
ESE .... Engineering Associate of the Society of Engineers, Inc. [*British*] (DBQ)
ESE .... Engineering Support Equipment (KSC)
ESE .... Engineers Stores Establishment (SAUS)
Ese .... Ensenada (SAUS)
ESE .... Environmental Science & Engineering, Inc. (EFIS)
ESE .... Environmental Science Education (AIE)
ESE .... Environmental Simulation Equipment (SAUS)
ESE .... Environment, Safety and Economics (SAUS)
ESE .... Ephemeris fuer Semitische Epigraphik [*A publication*] (BJA)
ESE .... ESCO Electronics [*NYSE symbol*] (SPSG)
ESE .... Estec Systems [*Vancouver Stock Exchange symbol*]
ESE .... Ethernet Switching Engine (SAUS)
ESE .... European Stock Exchange
ESE .... EVA [*Extravehicular Activity*] Support Equipment [*NASA*] (NASA)
ESE .... Experimental Simulation Equipment (SAUS)
ESE .... Experiment Support Equipment
ESE .... Expert System Environment [*IBM Corp.*] (CIST)
ESE .... Extended Selling Enterprise (GART)
ESE .... Extravehicular Support Equipment (SSD)
ESEA .... Electrical Supply Engineers Association (SAUO)
ESEA .... Elementary and Secondary Education Act [*1965*]
ESEA .... EPA/State Enforcement Agreement (SAUO)
ESEAFE .... Environmental Safety and Economic Aspects of Fusion Energy (SAUS)
ESEC .... Earth Science Education Conference (SAUO)
ESEC .... Earth Station - Ecuador
ESEC .... European Software Engineering Conference (VERA)
ESEC .... European Symposium on Engineering Ceramics (SAUS)
ESECA .... Energy Supply and Environmental Coordination Act of 1974
ESECOM .... Environmental Safety and Economic (SAUO)
ESECRP .... Energy Systems Employee Concerns/Response Program (SAUS)
ESECS .... European Security Studies (SAUS)
ESED .... Electronic Systems Engineering Department [*Naval Weapons Support Center*] [*Crane, IN*]
ESED .... Emission Standards and Engineering Division [*Environmental Protection Agency*] (GFGA)
ESED .... Environmental System and Effects Division [*NASA*]
ESEE .... European Society for Engineering Education
ESEE .... European Society of Engineering Education (SAUO)
ESEEM .... Electron Spin Echo Envelope Modulation [*Physics*]
ESEEM .... ESE envelope modulation (SAUS)
ESEERCO ..... Empire State Electric Energy Research Corporation (SAUO)
ESEF .... Electrotyping and Stereotyping Employers Federation (SAUO)
ESEF .... European Science and Environment Forum [*An association*]
ESEG .... Earth Station - Egypt
ESEG .... Electronic Systems Engineering Group (SAA)
ESEGP .... Energy Systems External Gopher Project (SAUS)
ESELCO .... ESELCO, Inc. [*Associated Press*] (SAG)
ESEM .... Electron Spin Echo Modulation [*Physics*]
ESEM .... Electron Spin Envelope Modulation (SAUS)
ESEM .... Environmental Scanning Electron Microscope
ESEM .... Eski Sark Eserleri Muezesi [*Istahbul*] (BJA)
ESEM .... European Seminar on Ethno-Musicology (SAUS)
ESEM .... European Society for Engineering and Medicine
ESEN .... Escuela Superior de Economia y Negocios [*El Salvador*]
ESEO .... Energy Systems Engineering Organization (SAUS)
ESEP .... Centre for European Social and Economic Policy (SAUO)
ESEP .... Extreme Somatosensory Evoked Potential [*Medicine*] (MELL)
ESERN .... East-Southeastern (FAAC)
ESES .... Earth-Moon Space Exploration Study
ESES .... Electrical Status Epilepticus during Sleep [*Medicine*] (MELL)
ES-ES .... End System to End System (VLIE)

ESES .... Existing Stationary Emission Source [*Environmental Protection Agency*]
ESESD .... Elementary and Secondary Education Statistics Division [*Department of Education*] (GFGA)
ESE/VM .... Expert System Environment/Virtual Machine [*Computer science*]
ESEWD .... East-Southeastward (FAAC)
ESEX .... Electronic Propulsion Space Experiment (SEWL)
ESEX .... Essex Corp. [*NASDAQ symbol*] (NQ)
ESF .... Alexandria [*Louisiana*] [*Airport symbol*] (OAG)
ESF .... Alexandria, LA [*Location identifier*] [*FAA*] (FAAL)
ESF .... Earth Society Foundation (EA)
ESF .... Eastern Sea Frontier
ESF .... Ecoles Sans Frontieres [*Education Without Frontiers*] [*An association*] (EAIO)
ESF .... Economic Support Fund [*Agency for International Development*]
ESF .... Edge Spread Function (SAUS)
ESF .... Electronic Support Fund (ACAE)
ESF .... Electrostatic Air Filter (PDAA)
ESF .... Electrostatic Focusing [*Electronics*]
ESF .... Electrostrictive Force (SAUS)
ESF .... Elementary Symmetric Function (MCD)
ESF .... Emergency Support Function [*Department of Emergency Management*] (DEMM)
ESF .... engineered safeguards feature (SAUS)
ESF .... Engineered Safety Feature [*Nuclear energy*] (NRCH)
ESF .... Engineering-Scale Facility (SAUS)
ESF .... Engineering Specification Files
ESF .... Engineering Structural Foam
ESF .... Engineering Systems Flight [*Military*]
ESF .... Environmental Safety Facility [*Stanford University*]
ESF .... Environmental Support Facility (SAUS)
ESF .... Equivalent Standard Fillet (SAUS)
ESF .... Erythropoietic Stimulating [*or Erythropoietin Switching*] Factor [*Hematology*]
ESF .... Esperantic Studies Foundation (EA)
ESF .... Espirito Santo Financial [*NYSE symbol*] (SPSG)
ESF .... Espirito Santo Finl ADS [*NYSE symbol*] (TTSB)
ESF .... Ethynylphenoxysulfone (SAUS)
ESF .... Eureka Software Factory (SAUO)
ESF .... European Schools Federation (EA)
ESF .... European Science Foundation (EAIO)
ESF .... European Security Forum
ESF .... European Simmental Federation (EAIO)
ESF .... European Social Fund
ESF .... European Surfing Federation (EAIO)
ESF .... Even Side Flat
ESF .... Exchange Stabilization Fund (ECON)
ESF .... Expanded Sample Frame (NTCM)
ESF .... Explosive-Safe Facility
ESF .... Export Success Fund (SAUS)
ESF .... Extended Spooling Facility (IAA)
ESF .... Extended Super Frame [*Telecommunications*]
ESF .... Extended Superframe Format [*Telecommunications*] (ACRL)
ESF .... External Source Format (CDE)
ESFA .... Emergency Solid Fuels Administration
ESFA .... Engineered Safety Feature Actuation [*Nuclear energy*] (NRCH)
ESFAC .... engineered safety feature actuation cabinet (SAUS)
ESFAC .... Esso Standard Fertilizer and Agricultural Chemical Company (SAUO)
ESFAES .... Estimates Safety Factors Against Embarkment Sliding [*Military*]
ESFAS .... Engineered Safety Features Actuation System [*Nuclear energy*] (NRCH)
ESFAS .... European Society of Foot and Ankle Surgeons (SAUS)
ESFC .... Energy Systems Finance College (SAUS)
ESFC .... Equivalent Specific Fuel Consumption (NG)
ESFC .... Extended Specific Fuel Consumption (WDAA)
ESFE .... Errored Second, Far End (VLIE)
ESFEDS .... European Taxonomic, Floristic and Biosystematic Documentation System (SAUS)
ESF/EPC ...... ESF/European Palaeoclimate and Man Project (SAUO)
ESFH .... Hasslosa [*Sweden*] [*ICAO location identifier*] (ICLI)
ESFI .... Epitaxial Silicon Film on Isolators (SAUS)
ESFI .... Epitaxial Silicon Films on Insulators (MCD)
ESFI .... Epitaxial Silicon-on-Insulator (SAUS)
ESFI .... Knislinge [*Sweden*] [*ICAO location identifier*] (ICLI)
ESFJ .... Extroversion Sensing Feeling Judging (ADWA)
ESFJ .... Sjobo [*Sweden*] [*ICAO location identifier*] (ICLI)
ESFK .... Electrostatically-Focused Kylstron (IAA)
ESFKA .... Electrostatically Focused Klystron Amplifier (SAUS)
ESFL .... End Systolic Force-Length Relationship [*Medicine*] (DB)
ESFLG .... Emergency Support Function Leaders Group (SAUO)
ESFM .... Ecologically Sustainable Forest Management (SAUS)
ESFM .... European Society of Feline Medicine (GVA)
ESFM .... Moholm [*Sweden*] [*ICAO location identifier*] (ICLI)
ESFMU .... Extended Superframe Monitoring Unit [*Computer science*] (CIST)
ESFO .... Engineering Support Field Office [*Federal disaster planning*]
ESFP .... Environment-Sensitive Fracture Processes (PDAA)
ESFP .... Extroversion Sensing Feeling Perception (ADWA)
ESFPA .... Empire State Forest Products Association (SRA)
ESFPS .... Earth Stabilized Fixed Point System (ACAE)
ESFQ .... Kosta [*Sweden*] [*ICAO location identifier*] (ICLI)
ESFR .... Early Suppression Fast Response [*Sprinkler program for fire protection*]
ESFR .... Rada [*Sweden*] [*ICAO location identifier*] (ICLI)
ESFS .... engineered safeguards feature system (SAUS)
ESFS .... Engineered Safety Features System [*Nuclear energy*] (NRCH)
ESFSM .... Energy Systems facility safety manager (SAUS)
ESFSWR ...... Extra-Special Flexible Steel Wire Rope [*British*]
ESFT .... exponential sum fitting of transmission (SAUS)
ESFU .... Enhanced Standard Format Unit (SAUS)
ESFU .... Vaxjo/Urasa [*Sweden*] [*ICAO location identifier*] (ICLI)
ESFVS .... Engineered Safety Feature Ventilation System [*Nuclear energy*] (NRCH)
ESFY .... Byholma [*Sweden*] [*ICAO location identifier*] (ICLI)
ESG .... Earth Station - Greece
ESG .... Edith Stein Guild (EA)
ESG .... Editorial Support Group
ESG .... Edit Sync Guide (NTCM)
ESG .... Education Service Group [*Bibliographic Retrieval Services*] [*Information service or system*] (IID)
ESG .... Education Support Grant [*British*] (DET)
ESG .... Electrically [*or Electrostatically*] Suspended Gyro (MSA)
ESG .... Electronic Scene Generator (ACAE)
ESG .... Electronic Security Group [*Military*]
ESG .... Electronic Sports Gathering [*Television*] (WDMC)
ESG .... Electronic Sweep Generator
ESG .... Electrospinogram [*Medicine*] (MEDA)
ESG .... Electrosplanchnography (SAUS)
ESG .... Electrostatic Gyroscope (IEEE)
ESG .... Emergency Shelter Grants Program [*Department of Housing and Urban Development*] (GFGA)
ESG .... Empirical Study Group (SAUS)
ESG .... Empiric Studies Group (SAA)
ESG .... Engineering Service [*or Support*] Group (AAG)
ESG .... Engineering Support Gated (ACAE)
ESG .... Engineering Support Group (SAUO)
ESG .... Engineer Studies Group [*Office of the Chief of Engineers*]
ESG .... Engineer Support Group (SAUS)
ESG .... Engine Speed Governor
ESG .... English Standard Gauge
ESG .... Environmental Sampling Group (SAUO)
ESG .... Environmental Sciences Group [*Boulder, CO*] [*Department of Commerce*] (GRD)
ESG .... Environmental Support Group (SAUO)
ESG .... Equivalent Signal Generator (SAUS)
ESG .... Estrogen [*Endocrinology*] (AAMN)
ESG .... Ethnobotany Specialist Group (EA)
ESG .... Exchange Software Generator (TEL)
ESG .... Expanded Sweep Generator (CET)
esg .... extended-sweep generator (SAUS)
ESG .... UN/EDIFACT Steering Group (AG)
ESGA .... Backamo [*Sweden*] [*ICAO location identifier*] (ICLI)
ESGA .... Electrically Supported [*or Suspended*] Gyro Accelerometer
ESGA .... Electrically Suspended Gyro Accelerometer (SAUS)
ESGC .... Alleberg [*Sweden*] [*ICAO location identifier*] (ICLI)
ESGEO .... ESRO Geostationary Earth Orbiting Satellite (SAUS)
ESGEP .... European Study Group for Electronic Patents (SAUO)
ESGG .... Goteborg/Landvetter [*Sweden*] [*ICAO location identifier*] (ICLI)
ESGH .... Herrljunga [*Sweden*] [*ICAO location identifier*] (ICLI)
ESGI .... Alingsas [*Sweden*] [*ICAO location identifier*] (ICLI)
ESGJ .... Jonkoping [*Sweden*] [*ICAO location identifier*] (ICLI)
ESGK .... Falkoping [*Sweden*] [*ICAO location identifier*] (ICLI)
ESGL .... Lidkoping [*Sweden*] [*ICAO location identifier*] (ICLI)
ESGLD .... European Study Group on Lysosomal Diseases (EAIO)
ESGLNLA ..... European Support Groups for Liberation and Nonviolence in Latin America (EAIO)
ESGM .... Electrostatically Supported Gyro Monitor [*Navy*]
ESGM .... European Society of Gastrointestinal Motility [*Louvain, Belgium*] (EAIO)
ESGM/SINS ... Electrostatically Supported Gyro Monitor/Ships Inertial Naviation System [*Navy*]
ESGN .... Electrically Suspended Gyro Navigation
ESGN .... Electronically Suspended Gyro Navigator (SAUS)
ESGO .... Vargarda [*Sweden*] [*ICAO location identifier*] (ICLI)
ESGP .... Earth Science Geostationary Platform (ACAE)
ESGP .... Emergency Shelter Grant Program [*HUD*]
ESGP .... Goteborg/Save [*Sweden*] [*ICAO location identifier*] (ICLI)
ESGQ .... Skovde [*Sweden*] [*ICAO location identifier*] (ICLI)
ESGR .... Employer Support of the Guard and Reserve
ESGS .... Stromstad/Nasinge [*Sweden*] [*ICAO location identifier*] (ICLI)
ESGSSFDB ... Empiric Studies Group Simulated SAC [*Strategic Air Command*] Force Data Base (SAA)
ESGT .... Trollhattan/Vanersborg [*Sweden*] [*ICAO location identifier*] (ICLI)
ESGU .... Experimental Sheet Growth Unit [*Photovoltaic energy systems*]
ESGV .... Varberg [*Sweden*] [*ICAO location identifier*] (ICLI)
ESGX .... Boras-Viared [*Sweden*] [*ICAO location identifier*] (ICLI)
ESGY .... Saffle [*Sweden*] [*ICAO location identifier*] (ICLI)
ESH .... Earl Scheib, Inc. [*AMEX symbol*] (COMM)
ESH .... Earth System History (QUAC)
ESH .... Electric Strip Heater (OA)
ESH .... Electric Surface Heating (HEAS)
ESH .... Electronically Swept Head (SAUS)
ESH .... End System Hello [*Computer science*] (TNIG)
ESH .... End System Hello PDU (SAUS)
ESH .... Environmental Safety and Health (COE)
ESH .... Environment, Safety, and Health [*ESH*] (AAEL)
ESH .... Equivalent Solar Hour [*NASA*]
ESH .... Equivalent Standard Hours (MCD)
ESH .... European Society of Haematology (ODA)
ESH .... Harbor Defense SONARman [*Navy*]

ESH............ Human Resources, Institutions, and Agrarian Reform Division [*FAO*] [*United Nations*] [*Italy*] [*Information service or system*] (IID)
ESH............ Scheib (Earl) [*AMEX symbol*] (TTSB)
ESH............ Scheib [*Earl*], Inc. [*AMEX symbol*] (SPSG)
ESH............ Shoreham-By-Sea [*England*] [*Airport symbol*] (OAG)
ESH............ Western Sahara [*ANSI three-letter standard code*] (CNC)
ESHA.......... Abisko [*Sweden*] [*ICAO location identifier*] (ICLI)
ESHAC........ Electric Space Heating and Air Conditioning (MCD)
ESHAC........ Electric Space Heating and Air Conditioning Committee (SAUS)
ESH&QA...... environmental, safety, health and quality assurance (SAUS)
E-SHAP........ Etopside, Cisplatin, Arabinosylcytosine, Methylprednisolone [*Antineoplastic drug*] (CDI)
ESHB........... Electrical Stimulation - Hot Boning [*Meat processing*]
ESHB........... Goteborg/Eastern Hospital [*Sweden*] [*ICAO location identifier*] (ICLI)
ESHC........... Environmental, Safety and Health Compliance Directorate (SAUS)
ESHC........... Stockholm/Southern Hospital [*Sweden*] [*ICAO location identifier*] (ICLI)
ESHCH......... Environmental, Safety and Health Concerns Hotline (SAUS)
ESHD........... End Stage Heart Disease [*Medicine*] (CPH)
ESHD........... Environment, Safety and Health Division (SAUO)
ESHE........... Landskrona [*Sweden*] [*ICAO location identifier*] (ICLI)
ESHECRS..... Employee Safety, Health and Environmental Concerns Response System (SAUS)
EshedR........ Eshed Robotec 1982 Ltd. [*Associated Press*] (SAG)
ESHG........... Electric-field-induced Second Harmonic Generation (SAUS)
ESHG........... European Society of Human Genetics (SAUS)
ESHG........... Stockholm/Gamla Stan [*Sweden*] [*ICAO location identifier*] (ICLI)
ESHH........... Enthronement of the Sacred Heart in the Home (EA)
ESHH........... Helsingborg/Harbour [*Sweden*] [*ICAO location identifier*] (ICLI)
ESHI............ Ingmarso [*Sweden*] [*ICAO location identifier*] (ICLI)
ESHK........... Earth Station - Hong Kong
ESHL............ Eastern Seaboard Herpetological League (SAUS)
ESHL............ Stockholm/Huddinge Hospital [*Sweden*] [*ICAO location identifier*] (ICLI)
ESHM........... Malmo/Harbour [*Sweden*] [*ICAO location identifier*] (ICLI)
ESHN........... Nacka [*Sweden*] [*ICAO location identifier*] (ICLI)
ESHO........... Skovde/Hospital [*Sweden*] [*ICAO location identifier*] (ICLI)
ESHP........... Electrical Servo-Hydraulic Pump
ESHP........... Empire State Historical Publications [*Series*]
ESHP........... Equivalent Shaft Horsepower [*Air Force*]
eshp............ established standard horsepower (SAUS)
ESHP........... European Society of Handwriting Psychology (EAIO)
ESHPH......... European Society for the History of Photography (EA)
ESHQC......... Environment, Safety, Health and Quality Committee (SAUS)
ESHR........... Akersberga [*Sweden*] [*ICAO location identifier*] (ICLI)
ESHR........... Eastern Shore Railroad Incorporated [*Federal Railroad Administration identification code*]
ESHR........... Energy Systems Human Resources (SAUS)
ESHS........... Egyptian Society of Historical Studies (SAUO)
ESHs........... Equivalent Standard Hours (SAUS)
ESHS........... Sandhamn [*Sweden*] [*ICAO location identifier*] (ICLI)
ESHT........... Electroslag Hot Topping (SAUS)
ESHU........... Emergency Ship Handling Unit [*Navy*]
ESHU........... environmental, safety and health upgrade (SAUS)
ESHU........... Uppsala/Akademiska [*Sweden*] [*ICAO location identifier*] (ICLI)
ESHV........... Vaxholm [*Sweden*] [*ICAO location identifier*] (ICLI)
ESHW........... Vastervik Hospital [*Sweden*] [*ICAO location identifier*] (ICLI)
ESI.............. EagleScan Incorporated (SAUO)
ESI.............. Early School Inventory [*Test*] (TMMY)
ESI.............. Early Screening Inventory [*Child development test*]
ESI.............. Early Supplier Involvement (AAGC)
ESI.............. Earned Self-Image [*Psychology*]
ESI.............. Earth Science Index (SAUO)
ESI.............. Earth Sciences Information (SAUS)
ESI.............. Earth Station Interface (ACAE)
ESI.............. Earth Station - Iran
ESI.............. Earth Systems Institute (SAUS)
ESI.............. Economic Strategy Institute (RDA)
ESI.............. Educational Services, Inc. [*Later, EDC*]
ESI.............. Educational Services, International (EA)
ESI.............. Educational Sport Institute (EA)
ESI.............. Educreative Systems, Inc.
ESI.............. Electrical Specialties, Incorporated (ACAE)
ESI.............. Electrical System Integration (MCD)
ESI.............. Electricity Supply Industry (SAUS)
ESI.............. Electromagnetic Sciences, Incorporated (SAUO)
ESI.............. Electronic System Integration (KSC)
ESI.............. Electron Spectroscopic Imaging
esi.............. Electro Scientific Industries (SAUO)
ESI.............. Electrospray Ionization [*Physics*]
ESI.............. Electrostatic Induction (SAUS)
ESI.............. Electro-Static Interference (VLIE)
ESI.............. Elementary and Secondary School Index [*Research test*] [*Psychology*]
ESI.............. Emergency Stop Indicator [*Aerospace*] (AAG)
ESI.............. Employee Safety Inventory [*London House, Inc.*] (TES)
Esi.............. Empresa de Suministros Industriales [*Import-export board*] [*Cuba*] (EY)
ESI.............. Emulsion Stability Index [*Food analysis*]
ESI.............. End of Segment Indicator (SAUS)
ESI.............. End System Identifier [*Telecommunications*] (ACRL)
ESI.............. Energy Systems, Inc., El Cajon, Calif. (SAUS)
ESI.............. Engineering and Scientific Interpreter (IEEE)
ESI.............. Engineering Services, Inc. (EFIS)
ESI.............. Enhanced Serial Interface [*Communication protocol*] [*Computer science*] (PCM)
ESI.............. Enhanced Serial Interface (specification) (SAUS)
ESI.............. Entertainment Systems International [*Database producer*] (IID)
ESI.............. Environmental Science Index [*Environmental Information Center Inc.*] [*Database*] (NITA)
ESI.............. Environmental Severity Index
ESI.............. Environmental Studies Institute (SAUS)
ESI.............. Environmental Sustainability Initiative
ESI.............. Epidural Steroid Injection [*Medicine*] (MELL)
ESI.............. Equivalent Spherical Illumination (PDAA)
ESI.............. Equivalent Step Index (SAUS)
ESI.............. ESI International [*Washington, D.C.*] (AAGC)
ESI.............. Espinosa [*Brazil*] [*Airport symbol*] (OAG)
ESI.............. Essential Sustainment Items (DOMA)
ESI.............. Essex International [*Microprocessor manufacturer*] (NITA)
ESI.............. ethernet serial interface (SAUS)
ESI.............. Ethiopian Standards Institution
ESI.............. Ethylene-Styrene copolymers (SAUS)
ESI.............. Executive Security International [*Institute for training bodyguards*] [*Aspen, CO*]
ESI.............. Executives' Secretaries, Inc. [*Later, EWI*] (EA)
ESI.............. Expanded Site Inspection (BCP)
ESI.............. Experiment Information System (VLIE)
ESI.............. Extended Service Interval [*Automotive engineering*]
ESI.............. externally specified (SAUS)
ESI.............. Externally Specified Index
ESI.............. Extremely Sensitive Information [*Army*] (AABC)
ESI.............. ITT Educational Services, Inc. [*NYSE symbol*] (SAG)
ESIA............ Externally-Specified Index Address (IAA)
ESIA............ Karlsborg [*Sweden*] [*ICAO location identifier*] (ICLI)
ESIAC.......... Electronic Satellite Image Analysis Console [*NASA*]
ESIAC.......... Electronic Satellite Imaging Analysis Console (SAUS)
ESIB............ European Students Information Buro (SAUO)
ESIB............ Satenas [*Sweden*] [*ICAO location identifier*] (ICLI)
ESIBEEP...... Electricity Supply Industry Building Energy Estimating Program [*Electricity Council*] [*British*]
ESIC............ Earth Science Information Center (SAUS)
ESIC............ Earth Station - Ivory Coast
ESIC............ Ecological Sciences Information Center [*Oak Ridge National Laboratory*]
ESIC............ Ecological Sciences Information System (SAUS)
ESIC............ Environmental Science and Information Center (SAUS)
ESIC............ Environmental Science Information Center [*National Oceanic and Atmospheric Administration*]
ESIC............ Europees Studie en Informatie Centrum [*Later, European Center for Research and Information*] [*Belgium*] (EAIO)
ESICCS........ Earth Stabilized Interceptor Centered Coordinate System (ACAE)
ESID............ electron stimulated ion desorption (SAUS)
ESID............ European Information System Division (SAUO)
ESID............ External Symbol Identification (SAUS)
ESIDOG........ European Society for Infectious Diseases in Obstetrics and Gynecology (SAUO)
ESIE............ electron stimulated ion emission (SAUS)
ESIE............ Expert System Inference Engine [*Artificial intelligence system*] (HODG)
ESIF............ Energy Systems Inventors Forum (SAUS)
ESIF............ European Service Industries Forum (EURO)
ESIG............ Electronic Simulated Image Generation
ESIG............ Environmental and Societal Impacts Group [*National Center for Atmospheric Research*]
ESIG............ Eugenics Special Interest Group [*Defunct*] (EA)
ESIG............ European SMDS Interest Group (SAUO)
ESIG............ Exemplary Service in Government
ESIG............ Exemplary Systems in Government award (SAUS)
ESII............ Regional Military Command Subcenter West [*Sweden*] [*ICAO location identifier*] (ICLI)
ESIIO.......... European Symposium of Independent Inspecting Organizations (EA)
ESIL............ Egyptian Society of International Law, Kairo (SAUO)
ESIL............ Essential Support Items List
ESIL............ European Standard Inventory List (NATG)
ESIM............ Earth Science Information Manager (SAUS)
ESI-MS........ Electrospray Ionization Mass Spectrometry
ESIMS.......... Engineering Svcs Information Management System (SAUS)
ESIMV.......... expiration synchronized intermittend mandatory ventilation (SAUS)
ESIN............ Earth Science Information Network (SAUS)
ESIN............ Elisabeth Sladen Information Network [*Actress featured in TV series "Dr. Who"*] [*British*] (EA)
ESIND.......... Electricity Supply Item Name Directory [*A publication*]
ESIO............ Earth Science Information Office (SAUS)
ESIO............ Electro Scientific Ind [*NASDAQ symbol*] (TTSB)
ESIO............ Electro Scientific Industries, Inc. [*NASDAQ symbol*] (NQ)
ESIOA.......... Extended Serial Input/ Output Adapter (SAUS)
ESIOA.......... External Serial Input/Output Adapter (SAUS)
ESI-P........... Early School Inventory-Preliteracy [*Nurss and McGauvran*] (TES)
ESIP............ Embedded Computer Resource Support (SAUS)
ESIP............ Employee Savings Investment Plan (SAUS)
ESIP............ Employment Service Improvement Program [*Department of Labor*]
ESIPP.......... Earth Science Image Processing Package (SAUS)
ESIR............ Electronically Stimulated Incarnation Recall
ESIR............ European Society for Impotence Research (SAUS)
ESIS............ Earth Science Information System (SAUS)
ESIS............ Earth Station - Israel
ESIS............ Electronic Store Information System (IAA)
ESIS............ Element Structure Information Set [*Computer science*] (VERA)

ES-IS .... End System-Intermediate System [*Computer science*] (TNIG)
ES-IS .... End System to Intermediate System Protocol (SAUS)
ESIS .... Environmentally Sensitive Investment System (SAUS)
ESIS .... ESA Space Information Systems (SAUS)
ESIS .... European Shielding Information Service [*EURATOM*] [*Databank*] (IID)
ESIS .... European Space Information System
ESIS .... Executive Selection Inventory System
ESISS .... Experimental Submarine Integrated Sonar System (SAUS)
ESI Standard ... Electricity Supply Industry Standard (SAUS)
ESIT .... Egyptian Society for Information Technology (NITA)
ESIT .... Electrical System-Integrated Test (SSD)
ESITB .... Electricity Supply Industry Training Board (SAUO)
ESITC .... Electrical Supply Industry Training Committee (AIE)
e-site .... Electronic Site (ADWA)
ESIX .... Enterprises Systems, Inc. [*NASDAQ symbol*] (SAG)
ESIX .... Enterprise Systems [*NASDAQ symbol*] (TTSB)
ESIX .... Enterprise Systems, Inc. [*NASDAQ symbol*] (SAG)
ESJ .... Earth Station - Jordan
ESJ .... Epithelial Stromal Junction [*Anatomy*]
ESJ .... Escort Screening Jammer [*Military*]
ESJCP .... Engineers and Scientists Joint Committee on Pensions (SAUS)
ESJO .... Earth Science Journals Online (SAUO)
ESJWG .... Earth Science Joint Working Group (SAUS)
ESJWG .... Earth Sciences Joint Working Group (SAUS)
ESK .... Earth Station - Kenya
ESK .... Electrostatic Klystron
ESK .... Engineering Sketch
ESK .... Environmental Sensor Kit (MCD)
ESK .... Eskdalemuir [*Scotland*] [*Seismograph station code, US Geological Survey*] (SEIS)
Esk .... Eskimo (ADWA)
esk .... Eskimo [*MARC language code*] [*Library of Congress*] (LCCP)
ESK .... Eskimo [*Language, etc.*]
ESK .... Eurosky Airlines [*Austria*] [*FAA designator*] (FAAC)
ESK .... Telecommunications Censorship Technician [*Navy*]
ESKA .... Ekranolytny Spassatyelny Kater Amphibiya [*Screen-Effect Amphibious Lifeboat*] [*Former USSR*]
ESKA .... Gimo [*Sweden*] [*ICAO location identifier*] (ICLI)
ESKB .... Stockholm/Barkarby [*Sweden*] [*ICAO location identifier*] (ICLI)
ESKC .... European Student Korfball Committee (SAUO)
ESKC .... Sundbro [*Sweden*] [*ICAO location identifier*] (ICLI)
ESKC .... Telecommunications Censorship Technician, Chief [*Navy*]
ESKCM .... Telecommunications Censorship Technician, Master Chief [*Navy*]
ESKCS .... Telecommunications Censorship Technician, Senior Chief [*Navy*]
ESKD .... Dala-Jarna [*Sweden*] [*ICAO location identifier*] (ICLI)
ESKD .... End-Stage Kidney Disease (MELL)
ESKE .... Enhanced Station-Keeping Equipment [*Air Force*] (DOMA)
ESKH .... Eksharad [*Sweden*] [*ICAO location identifier*] (ICLI)
ESKI .... Stockholm [*Sweden*] [*ICAO location identifier*] (ICLI)
Eskimo .... Eskimo Pie Corp. [*Associated Press*] (SAG)
ESKIMO .... Explosive Safety Knowledge Improvement Operation (MCD)
ESKK .... Karlskoga [*Sweden*] [*ICAO location identifier*] (ICLI)
ESKL .... Norrkoping [*Sweden*] [*ICAO location identifier*] (ICLI)
ESKM .... Mora/Siljan [*Sweden*] [*ICAO location identifier*] (ICLI)
ESKN .... Nykoping/Oxelosund [*Sweden*] [*ICAO location identifier*] (ICLI)
ESKO .... Munkfors [*Sweden*] [*ICAO location identifier*] (ICLI)
ESKOM .... Electricity Supply Commission (SAUS)
ESKR .... Stockholm Radio [*Sweden*] [*ICAO location identifier*] (ICLI)
ESKRM .... Evreiskii Soiuz Kommunisticheskoi Rabochei Molodezhi (BJA)
ESKS .... Strangnas [*Sweden*] [*ICAO location identifier*] (ICLI)
ESKT .... Tierp [*Sweden*] [*ICAO location identifier*] (ICLI)
ESKU .... Sunne [*Poland*] [*ICAO location identifier*] (ICLI)
ESKV .... Arvika [*Sweden*] [*ICAO location identifier*] (ICLI)
ESKW .... Gavle/Avan [*Sweden*] [*ICAO location identifier*] (ICLI)
ESKX .... Bjorkvik [*Sweden*] [*ICAO location identifier*] (ICLI)
Esky .... Esquire [*A publication*] [*New York, NY*] (WDMC)
ESL .... Eagle Shipping Ltd (SAUS)
ESL .... Earth Science Links (SAUO)
ESL .... Earth Sciences Laboratory [*Boulder, CO*] [*National Oceanic and Atmospheric Administration*]
ESL .... Earth Station - Libya
ESL .... Eastern Steamship Lines (SAUO)
ESL .... Effective Series Inductance (SAUS)
ESL .... Egg Stalk Length
ESL .... Elbit Symbolic Language (SAUS)
ESL .... Electrical Services League (SAUS)
ESL .... Electromagnetic Systems Laboratories, Inc.
ESL .... Electron Beam Switched Latch (SAUS)
ESL .... electronic sailing list (SAUS)
ESL .... Electronic Software Licensing [*Software*] (CDE)
ESL .... Electronics Sciences Laboratory (SAUO)
ESL .... Electronic Support Laboratory
ESL .... Electronic Systems Laboratory (MCD)
ESL .... Electro-Science Laboratories Inc. (SAUO)
ESL .... Electroscience Laboratory [*Ohio State University*] [*Research center*] (RCD)
ESL .... Emergency Stand Alone (SAUS)
ESL .... Encoded Synthetic Libraries [*Chemistry*]
ESL .... Endangered Species List (SAUS)
ESL .... End-Systolic Length [*Cardiology*]
ESL .... Engineering and Services Laboratory [*Tyndall Air Force Base, FL*] [*Air Force*] (GRD)
ESL .... Engineering Services Laboratory (SAUO)
ESL .... Engineering Societies Library (MCD)
ESL .... Engineer Sub-Lieutenant [*Navy*] [*British*] (ROG)
ESL .... English as a Second Language
ESL .... Environmental Sustainment Laboratory (RDA)
ESL .... Environmental Systems Laboratory [*Virginia Polytechnic Institute and State University*] [*Research center*] (RCD)
ESL .... Equipment Status List (ACAE)
ESL .... Equipment Status Log (DNAB)
ESL .... Equivalent Series Inductance (SAUS)
ESL .... Essential Service Line [*Telecommunications*] (TEL)
ESL .... Esterline Technologies [*NYSE symbol*] (TTSB)
ESL .... Etac Sales Ltd. [*Toronto Stock Exchange symbol*]
ESL .... European Systems Language (IAA)
ESL .... Evans Signal Laboratory [*Army*]
ESL .... Exceeding Speed Limit
ESL .... Expected Significance Level
ESL .... Extended Service Life [*Military*] (CAAL)
ESL .... External Set Loop [*Electronics*] (ECII)
ESL .... Eye Standard Length [*Fish anatomy*]
ESL .... Kessel, WV [*Location identifier*] [*FAA*] (FAAL)
ESLA .... English as a Second Language Allowance [*Australia*]
ESLAB .... European Space Laboratory
ESLAFA .... Latin American School of Applied Physics (SAUO)
ESLAR .... European Space Research Laboratory (SAUS)
ESLAT .... English as a Second Language (EDAC)
E-SLATS .... Executive Strike Leader Attack Training School (DOMA)
ESLC .... Elementary School Library Collection
ESLD .... End-Stage Liver Disease [*Medicine*]
ESLD .... Engineering School Libraries Association (SAUO)
ESLE .... Electronic Survivor Location Equipment (SAUS)
esle .... engineering special laboratory equipment (SAUS)
ESLE .... Equivalent Station Location Error
ES/LES .... Equipment Section/Loaded Equipment Section
ESLF .... End-Stage Liver Failure (MELL)
ESLH .... Electrical Stimulation of the Lateral Hypothalamus [*Medicine*]
ESLH .... Estimated Standard Labor Hours (AAGC)
ESLI .... Elementary Science Leadership Institute (SAUS)
ESLI .... End-of-Service-Live Indicator [*Industrial hygiene term*] (OHS)
ESLI .... Esperantista Sak-Ligo Internacia [*International Esperantist Chess League - IECL*] (EAIO)
ESLI .... Esperanto Sak-Ligo Internacia (SAUO)
ESLIMS .... Energy Systems Laboratory Information Management System (SAUS)
ESLJ .... East St. Louis Junction Railroad (SAUO)
ESLJ .... [*The*] East St. Louis Junction R. R. [*AAR code*]
E-SLM .... Electrically addressed Spatial Light Modulator (SAUS)
ESLO .... Ethnic Schools Liaison Officer [*Australia*]
ESLO .... European Satellite Launching Organization (MCD)
ESLO .... European Society of Limnology and Oceanography (SAUO)
ESLO .... European Space Launcher Organization
ESLOA .... English as a Second Language Oral Assessment
ESLP .... Electric Shocklike Pain (MELL)
ESLR .... Events Select Logic and Rates (MCD)
ESLS .... Elementary and Secondary Education Longitudinal Studies [*Department of Education*] (GFGA)
ESLS .... English School of Lutanist Songwriters (SAUO)
ESLs .... Expected Significance Levels (SAUS)
ESLT .... Elbit Systems Ltd. [*NASDAQ symbol*] (SAG)
ESLT .... Equipment Section Leakage Test
ESLX .... Essroc Logansport [*Federal Railroad Administration identification code*]
ESM .... Earth Station - Mexico
ESM .... Earth Systems Model [*Climatology*]
ESM .... Eastman School of Music (SAUS)
ESM .... East Surrey Militia [*British military*] (DMA)
ESM .... Edible Structural Material (SAUS)
ESM .... Edible Structure Material
ESM .... Edmund Sixtus Muskie [*American politician*]
ESM .... Education Simulation Model (SAUS)
ESM .... Effectiveness Simulation Model
ESM .... Ejection Systolic Murmur [*Cardiology*]
ESM .... Elastomeric Shield Material [*Plastic technology*]
ESM .... Elastomeric Solid Material
ESM .... Electrical Stimulation of the Midbrain
ESM .... Electromagnetic Support Measures (ACAE)
ESM .... Electromatic Speed Meter (IAA)
ESM .... Electronically controlled System with Magnetic Field coupling (SAUS)
ESM .... Electronic Sequencing Module
ESM .... Electronic Service Manual (AAEL)
ESM .... Electronic Shop Minor [*Coast Guard*]
ESM .... Electronic Signal Monitoring (PDAA)
ESM .... Electronic Stores Measures (SAUS)
ESM .... Electronic Support Measures [*Instrumentation*] (IEEE)
ESM .... Electronic Surveillance Measures
ESM .... Electronic Switch Module
ESM .... Electronic Warfare Support Measures [*Formerly, EWSM*] (AABC)
Es M .... Electrostatic Memory (SAUS)
ESM .... Emerald Star Mining [*Vancouver Stock Exchange symbol*]
ESM .... Emergency Shipment Memorandum
ESM .... Employment Security Manual (OICC)
ESM .... Endometrial Stromal Meiosis [*Medicine*] (MELL)
ESM .... Ends Standard Matched (SAUS)
ESM .... Enemy Situation Map (SAUS)
ESM .... Energy Storage Modulator
ESM .... Engineering Material Specification
ESM .... Engineering Scab Melter (ABAC)
ESM .... Engineering Schedule Memo (SAUS)

ESM .... Engineering Schedule Memorandum
ESM .... Engineering Service Memo (SAUS)
ESM .... Engineering Service Memorandum (MCD)
ESM .... Engineering Shop Memo (SAUS)
ESM .... Engineering Society of Milwaukee (SAUO)
ESM .... Engineers and Scientists of Milwaukee (SAUS)
ESM .... Enterprise Storage Manager [*Computer science*] (HODG)
ESM .... Environmental System Module (MCD)
ESM .... Environmental Systems Monitor (IAA)
ESM .... Equipment Support Module (ACAE)
ESM .... Equivalent Standard Minute (SAUS)
ESM .... Erector Spinae Muscle [*Medicine*] (MELL)
ESM .... Error Satisfaction Method (SAUS)
ESM .... Escort Mission
ESM .... Esmeraldas [*Ecuador*] [*Airport symbol*] (OAG)
ESM .... Ethernet Switching Module (SAUS)
ESM .... Ethosuximide [*Medicine*] (DMAA)
ESM .... European Society for Microcirculation (EA)
ESM .... European Society for Mycobacteriology (EA)
ESM .... EW Support Measures (SAUS)
ESM .... Excellence in Surface Mining (SAUO)
ESM .... Experimental Safety Motorcycle (SAUS)
ESM .... Experiment Service Module (SAUS)
ESM .... Experiments Systems Monitor [*NASA*] (KSC)
ESM .... Experiment Support Module (ACAE)
ESM .... Extended State Machine
ESM .... External Storage Module [*Sun*] (VERA)
e-sm- .... San Marino [*MARC geographic area code*] [*Library of Congress*] (LCCP)
ESM .... Underwater Mechanic [*Obsolete*] [*Navy*]
ESM .... Winston-Salem State University, Winston-Salem, NC [*OCLC symbol*] (OCLC)
ESMA .... Electrical Sign Manufacturers Association
ESMA .... Electric Sign Manufacturers Association (SAUO)
ESMA .... Electronic Sales-Marketing Association [*Defunct*] (EA)
ESMA .... Emmaboda [*Sweden*] [*ICAO location identifier*] (ICLI)
ESMA .... Engraved Stationery Manufacturers Association (EA)
ESMA .... Episcopal Society for Ministry on Aging (EA)
ESMA .... Essential Manning
ESMA .... Expert System Maintenance Aid (ACAE)
ESMB .... Borglanda [*Sweden*] [*ICAO location identifier*] (ICLI)
ESMB .... Explosive Stand-Off Minefield Breacher [*Military*] (SEWL)
ESMC .... Eastern Space and Missile Center [*Patrick Air Force Base, FL*] [*Also, ETR*] [*Air Force*]
ESMC .... Eastern Space and Missile Center, Cape Canaveral, Florida (SAUS)
ESMC .... Eastern Space and Missile Command (ACAE)
ESMC .... Electronic Structure of Materials Centre [*Flinders University, Australia*]
ESMC .... Engineering Societies Monograph Committee (SAUS)
ESMC .... Environmental System Management Controller (MCD)
E-SMC .... Epoxy-Matrix Sheet Molding Compound (SAUS)
ESMC .... Escalon Medical Corp. [*NASDAQ symbol*] (SAG)
ESMC .... Karlshamn [*Sweden*] [*ICAO location identifier*] (ICLI)
ESMCL .... Escalon Med Corp. Wrrt'B' [*NASDAQ symbol*] (TTSB)
ESMCW .... Escalon Med Corp. Wrrt'A' [*NASDAQ symbol*] (TTSB)
ESMD .... Embedded Storage Module Disk [*Computer science*] (VERA)
ESMD .... Enhanced Storage Module Device [*Computer science*] (VERA)
ESMD .... Extended Storage Module Drives [*Computer science*] (AGLO)
ESMDC .... Expandable Shielded Mild Detonating Cord [*Space launch term*] (ISAK)
ESMDIS .... Earth System Model Information System (SAUS)
ESME .... Eastern Space and Missile Center (SAUS)
ESME .... Eslov [*Sweden*] [*ICAO location identifier*] (ICLI)
ESME .... Excited State Mass Energy
ESM/ECM .... Electronic Support Measures/Electronic Countermeasures (SAUS)
ESMF .... Efficient Separable Median Filter (SAUS)
ESMF .... Eleanor Steber Music Foundation [*Defunct*] (EA)
ESMF .... Fagerhult [*Sweden*] [*ICAO location identifier*] (ICLI)
ESMG .... Ljungby/Feringe [*Sweden*] [*ICAO location identifier*] (ICLI)
ESMH .... Hoganas [*Sweden*] [*ICAO location identifier*] (ICLI)
ESMI .... Energy Studies Measurement Instrument (SAUS)
ESMI .... Sovdeborg [*Sweden*] [*ICAO location identifier*] (ICLI)
ESMJ .... Kagerod [*Sweden*] [*ICAO location identifier*] (ICLI)
ESMK .... Kristianstad/Everod [*Sweden*] [*ICAO location identifier*] (ICLI)
ESML .... Expendable/durable Supplies and Materials List (SAUS)
ESML .... Expendable Supplies and Materials List (MCD)
ESML .... Landskrona/Viarp [*Sweden*] [*ICAO location identifier*] (ICLI)
ESMM .... Equivalent Square Miles of Mapping (NOAA)
ESMM .... Malmo [*Sweden*] [*ICAO location identifier*] (ICLI)
ESMMC .... Enhanced SMMC [*FAA*] (TAG)
ESMN .... Lund [*Sweden*] [*ICAO location identifier*] (ICLI)
ESM/NCTR .... Electronic Support Measure / Non-Cooperative Target Recognition
ESMO .... Earth Station - Morocco
ESMO .... Electronics System Measures Operator (MCD)
ESMO .... European Society for Medical Oncology (EA)
ESMO .... European Society for/of Medical Oncology (SAUO)
ESMO .... Explosive Standoff Mine Clearer [*Military*] (SEWL)
ESMO .... Oskarshamn [*Sweden*] [*ICAO location identifier*] (ICLI)
ESMOA .... Electrotypers' and Stereotypers' Managers and Overseers Association [*British*] (BI)
Esmor .... Esmor Correctional Services [*Commercial firm*] [*Associated Press*] (SAG)
ESMP .... Anderstorp [*Sweden*] [*ICAO location identifier*] (ICLI)
ESMP .... El Salvador Media Projects (EA)
ESMP .... Energy Systems Mentor Program (SAUS)
ESMQ .... Kalmar [*Sweden*] [*ICAO location identifier*] (ICLI)
ESMR .... Electrically Scanned Microwave Radiometer [*NASA*]
ESMR .... Electrical Scanning Microwave Radiometer (SAUS)
ESMR .... Electronically Scanning Microwave Radiometer (SAUS)
ESMR .... Electronic Scanning Microwave Radiometer [*Marine science*] (OSRA)
ESMR .... Enhanced Specialized Mobile Radio (DCDG)
ESMR .... Esmor Correctional Services [*NASDAQ symbol*] (SAG)
ESMR .... Trelleborg [*Sweden*] [*ICAO location identifier*] (ICLI)
ESMRI .... Engraved Stationery Manufacturers Research Institute (EA)
ESMRW .... Esmor Correct'l Svcs Wrrt [*NASDAQ symbol*] (TTSB)
ESMS .... East Sullivan Monzonitic Stock (SAUS)
ES-MS .... Electrospray Ionization Mass Spectrometry
ESMS .... Emission Standards for Moving Sources [*Environmental science*] (COE)
ESMS .... Enterprise System Managed Storage (GART)
ESMS .... Environment and Special Measurement System (MCD)
ESMS .... European Satellite Multimedia Services (SAUS)
ESMS .... European Society for/of Medical Sociology (SAUO)
ESMS .... European Society of Medical Sociology (SAUS)
ESMS .... Malmo/Sturup [*Sweden*] [*ICAO location identifier*] (ICLI)
ESMSA .... 18 Square Meter Sailing Association (EA)
ESMST .... European Society of Membrane Science and Technology (EA)
ESMT .... Electronic Shop Minor Telephone and Teletype [*Coast Guard*]
ESMT .... Halmstad [*Sweden*] [*ICAO location identifier*] (ICLI)
ESMTP .... Extended Simple Mail Transfer Protocol (RALS)
ESMTP .... Extended Simple Message Transport Protocol [*Computer science*] (VERA)
ESMTP .... Extended SMTP (Internet) (SAUS)
ESMU .... Electronic Systems Mockup (KSC)
ESMV .... Hagshult [*Sweden*] [*ICAO location identifier*] (ICLI)
ESMWT .... Engineering, Science, and Management War Training
ESMWTP .... Engineering, Science, and Management War Training Program (HGAA)
ESMX .... Vaxjo/Kronoberg [*Sweden*] [*ICAO location identifier*] (ICLI)
ESMY .... Smalandsstenar [*Sweden*] [*ICAO location identifier*] (ICLI)
ESMZ .... Olanda [*Sweden*] [*ICAO location identifier*] (ICLI)
ESN .... Earth Science Network (ACAE)
ESN .... Earth-Sun Coordinate System
ESN .... Easton [*Maryland*] [*Airport symbol*] (AD)
ESN .... Easton, MD [*Location identifier*] [*FAA*] (FAAL)
ESN .... ECS Science Network (SAUS)
ESN .... Educationally Subnormal
ESN .... Effective Segment Number (IAA)
ESN .... Elastic Stop Nut [*Hardware*]
ESN .... Electrical Sensitivity Network (EA)
ESN .... Electronic Security Number [*Cellular telephones*] (WDMC)
ESN .... Electronic Serial Number
ESN .... Electronic Switched Network [*Computer science*] (VERA)
ESN .... Encyclopaedia Sefardica Neerlandica [*A publication*] (BJA)
ESN .... Energy Systems News (SAUS)
ESN .... Engineering Shipping Notice (AAG)
ESN .... Engineers Society of Norway
ESN .... English-Speaking Nations [*of NATO*]
ESN .... Equipment Serial Number (ACRL)
ESN .... Error Sequence Number [*Computer science*]
ESN .... Essence Biotech [*Vancouver Stock Exchange symbol*]
ESN .... Essential (AABC)
ESN .... Estrogen-Stimulated Neurophysin [*Endocrinology*]
ESN .... European Scientific Notes [*Office of Naval Research, London*] (PDAA)
ESN .... European Society for Nematologists (SAUS)
ESN .... European Society for Neurochemistry (EA)
ESN .... European Society of Nematologists (EAIO)
ESN .... European Society of Neuroradiology (EA)
ESN .... Executive Suite Network [*An association*] (EA)
ESN .... Extended Systems Networking (SAUS)
ESN .... External Segment Name (MHDB)
ESNA .... Economic Security Employees' National Association [*Canada*]
ESNA .... Elastic Stop Nut Corp. of America
ESNA .... Elastic Stop Nut Corporation of America (SAUO)
ESNA .... Electrical Survey-Net Adjuster
esna .... electrical survey net adjuster (SAUS)
ESNA .... Empire State Numismatic Association (SAUO)
ESNA .... Hallviken [*Sweden*] [*ICAO location identifier*] (ICLI)
ESNB .... Solleftea [*Sweden*] [*ICAO location identifier*] (ICLI)
ESNC .... Educational Statistics, National Center (OICC)
ESNC .... Hede/Hedlanda [*Sweden*] [*ICAO location identifier*] (ICLI)
ESNCD .... European Society for Noninvasive Cardiovascular Dynamics (EA)
ESND .... Sveg [*Sweden*] [*ICAO location identifier*] (ICLI)
ESNET .... Energy Sciences Network [*DOE-funded network*] (AAGC)
ESnet .... Energy Sciences Network [*Department of Energy*]
Esnet .... Energy Systems Network (SAUS)
ESNet .... Food Safety Network
ESNETT .... Engineering and Science Network on Thinking (EA)
ESNF .... Farila [*Sweden*] [*ICAO location identifier*] (ICLI)
ESNG .... Engineering Subworking Group (SAUO)
ESNG .... Gallivare [*Sweden*] [*ICAO location identifier*] (ICLI)
ESN-H .... Elsevier North-Holland (SAUS)
ESNH .... Hudiksvall [*Sweden*] [*ICAO location identifier*] (ICLI)
ESNI .... Kubbe [*Sweden*] [*ICAO location identifier*] (ICLI)
ESNICVD .... European Society for Noninvasive Cardiovascular Dynamics (EAIO)
ESNJ .... Jokkmokk [*Sweden*] [*ICAO location identifier*] (ICLI)
ESNK .... Kramfors [*Sweden*] [*ICAO location identifier*] (ICLI)
ESNL .... Lycksele [*Sweden*] [*ICAO location identifier*] (ICLI)
ESN(M) .... Educationally Subnormal-Moderate [*Medicine*] (DMAA)

ESNM Optand [*Sweden*] [*ICAO location identifier*] (ICLI)
ESNN Sundsvall-Harnosand [*Sweden*] [*ICAO location identifier*] (ICLI)
ESNO Ornskoldsvik [*Sweden*] [*ICAO location identifier*] (ICLI)
ESNP Pitea [*Sweden*] [*ICAO location identifier*] (ICLI)
ESNQ Kiruna [*Sweden*] [*ICAO location identifier*] (ICLI)
ESNR European Society of Neuroradiology (SAUS)
ESNR Orsa [*Sweden*] [*ICAO location identifier*] (ICLI)
ESNS Coexistence (Slovakia) [*Political party*] (PSAP)
ESNS Skelleftea [*Sweden*] [*ICAO location identifier*] (ICLI)
ESNS Educationally Subnormal, Serious (ODA)
ESNSW Entomological Society of New South Wales (EERA)
ESNT Sattna [*Sweden*] [*ICAO location identifier*] (ICLI)
ESNTL Essential
ESNU Umea [*Sweden*] [*ICAO location identifier*] (ICLI)
ESNV Vilhelmina [*Sweden*] [*ICAO location identifier*] (ICLI)
ESNZ Entomological Society of New Zealand (ODA)
ESO Avitat [*British*] [*ICAO designator*] (FAAC)
ESO Echo Suppressor, Originating End [*Telecommunications*] (TEL)
ESO Economic Stabilization Office (OICC)
ESO Ectrospinal Orthosis [*Medicine*] (EDAA)
ESO Educational Services Office [*or Officer*] [*Navy*]
ESO Education Services Officer (AAGC)
ESO Electrical Spinal Orthosis
ESO Electronics Supply Office [*or Officer*]
ESO Electronic Standards Office [*Navy*]
ESO Electronic Support Measure (SAUS)
ESO Embarkation Staff Officer [*Military*] [*British*]
ESO Emergency Security Operations (AFM)
ESO Emergency Security Option (SAUS)
ESO Emergency Senior Official (SAUO)
ESO Emergency Services Organization (SAUO)
ESO Emergency Support Organization (NRCH)
ESO Enforcement Specialist Office [*National Enforcement Investigations Center*] (COE)
ESO Engineering Science Order (SAUO)
ESO Engineering Service Order (AAG)
ESO Engineering Sign-Off
ESO Engineering Stop Order (AAG)
ESO Entomological Society of Queensland (EERA)
ESO Entry Server Offering (SAUS)
ESO Eosophagoscopy [*Medicine*] (EDAA)
ESO Epoxidized Soybean Oil [*Organic chemistry*]
eso Esophagoscopy [*Medicine*] (DAVI)
ESO Esophagus [*Anatomy*] (DAVI)
eso Esophagus [*Medicine*] (EDAA)
Eso Esoteric [*Record label*]
ESO European School of Oncology (SAUS)
ESO European School of Osteopathy (SAUO)
ESO European Southern Observatory [*ICSU*] [*Research center*] [*Germany*] (IRC)
ESO European Standardisation Organisation (SAUO)
ESO Event Sequence Override
ESO Energy Services Operator (ODA)
ESOA Employee Stock Ownership Association (SAUO)
ESOA Epiphyllum Society of America
ESOA European Society of Osteoarthrology [*Former Czechoslovakia*] (SLS)
ESOAA Eight Sheet Outdoor Advertising Association [*Independence, MO*] (EA)
ESOB Eastern Soccer Officials Bureau [*Later, ECSA*] (EA)
ESOC Emergency Supply Operations Center [*Defense Supply Agency*] (MCD)
ESOC Environmentally Safe Oil Change [*Automobile service*]
ESOC European Space Operations Center
ESoCE European Society of Concurrent Engineering (SAUS)
ESOD Erythrocyte Superoxide Dismutase [*An enzyme*]
ESOE Orebro [*Sweden*] [*ICAO location identifier*] (ICLI)
ESOFC Erika Slezak Official Fan Club (EA)
ESO-FHWA Emergency Standby Order - Federal Highway Administration [*Federal disaster planning*]
ESOH Environmental Safety and Occupational Health (BCP)
ESOH Equipment and Supplies on Hand (SAUS)
ESOH Hagfors [*Sweden*] [*ICAO location identifier*] (ICLI)
ESOL Employee Solutions, Inc. [*NASDAQ symbol*] (SAG)
ESOL English for Speakers of Other Languages (FOTI)
ESOL English to Speakers of Other Languages [*Program*]
ESOL Program English to Speakers of Other Languages Program (SAUS)
ESOMAR European Society for Opinion and Market Research [*Netherlands*]
ESOMAR European Society for Opinion Surveys and Market Research (SAUS)
ESON Endosonics Corp. [*NASDAQ symbol*] (SAG)
ESONE European Standard Organization of Nuclear Electronics (SAUS)
ESONE European Standards on Nuclear Electronics Committee [*Switzerland*]
ESONEC European Standards of Nuclear Electronics Committee (SAUS)
ESOP Employee Share Ownership Plan (SAUO)
ESOP Employee Share-Ownership Plans (SAFN)
ESOP Employee Stock Option [*or Ownership*] Plan [*Tax plan*]
ESOP Employee Stock Ownership Plan (AAGC)
ESOP Engineering Student Officer Program [*Air Force*]
ESOP European Space Operations Centre (SAUS)
ESOP European Subpolar Ocean Programme (SAUS)
ESOP evolutionary system for on-line processing (SAUS)
esoph esophageal (SAUS)
ESOPH Esophagus [*Anatomy*]
ESOPRS European Society of Ophthalmic Plastic and Reconstructive Surgery (EAIO)
ESOPS Employment Service Online Placement System [*Computer science*]
ESOR Electronically-Scanned Optical Receiver (PDAA)
ESOR Emergency Standoff Range (NVT)
ESOR Rescue Coordination Center [*Sweden*] [*ICAO location identifier*] (ICLI)
ESORCU European Stratigraphic Ozone Research Co-ordinating Unit (SAUS)
ESORICS European Symposium on Research in Computer Security (VERA)
ESOS Stockholm [*Sweden*] [*ICAO location identifier*] (ICLI)
ESOT Employee Stock Ownership Trust
ESOT Esoteric [*or Esoterica*] (WDAA)
esot esoterica (SAUS)
ESOW Engineering Statement of Work (NASA)
ESOW Vasteras/Hasslo [*Sweden*] [*ICAO location identifier*] (ICLI)
ESP Early Shipment Programm (SAUS)
ESP Early Support Program (HGAA)
ESP Early Systolic Paradox [*Cardiology*] (DAVI)
ESP Earth-Surface Potential
ESP Earth Systems Program (SAUO)
ESP Eastern Special Passenger [*Eastern Airlines*]
ESP Eastern State Penitentiary (SAUO)
ESP East Sepik Province (SAUS)
ESP East Stroudsburg, PA [*Location identifier*] [*FAA*] (FAAL)
esp easy solution possible (SAUS)
ESP Echeloned Series Processor (PDAA)
ESP Ecological Statistics Package (SAUS)
ESP E-Commerce Service Provider (VLIE)
ESP Economic Software Package (SAUS)
ESP Economic Stabilization Program [*Internal Revenue Service*]
ESP Economic Sufficiency Plan (OICC)
ESP Economic Support Funds (GNE)
ESP Economy Systems Plate
ESP Edge-Supported Pulling [*Photovoltaic energy systems*]
ESP Edit, Save and Plot Technology (SAUS)
ESP Educational Software Products [*Commercial firm*] (PCM)
ESP Educational Support Personnel
ESP effciency speed power rectifier (SAUS)
ESP Effective Sensory Projection [*Neurology*] (DAVI)
ESP Effective Systolic Pressure [*Cardiology*] (DAVI)
ESP efficiency speed-power rectifier (SAUS)
ESP Efficient Ship Project (SAUS)
ESP Eldorado String Processor (SAUS)
ESP Electrically Susceptible Patient [*Medicine*] (EDAA)
ESP Electrical Submersible Pump (SAUS)
ESP Electrical Systems Panel [*Apollo Spacecraft Program Office*] [*NASA*]
ESP Electric Service Priority (SAUO)
ESP Electric Service Provider (AGLO)
ESP Electric Shock Protector (MELL)
ESP Electromagnetic Subsurface Profiling (SAUS)
esp electro-magnetic surface profiler (SAUS)
ESP Electronic Security Profile [*of Equitable Life Assurance Society*]
ESP Electronic Seismic Photography
ESP Electronic Server Pad [*Restaurant computer device manufactured by Remanco Systems, Inc.*]
ESP Electronic Shock Protection (SAUS)
ESP Electronic Short Pathfinder (SAUS)
ESP Electronic Smart Power [*Automotive engineering*]
ESP Electronic Social Psychology
ESP Electronic Specification Package (BTTJ)
ESP Electronics System Plan (SAUS)
ESP Electronic Stability Program [*Automotive engineering*]
ESP Electronic Standard Procedure (MCD)
ESP Electronic Still Photography (CDE)
ESP Electronic Subsystem Project (ACAE)
ESP Electronic Supervisory Panel (MCD)
ESP Electronic Systems Planning (RDA)
ESP Electron Spin Polarization
ESP Electron Stream Potential (MSA)
esp electro-selective pattern (SAUS)
ESP Electroselective Pattern Metering [*Olympus cameras*]
ESP Electrosensitive Paper (MHDB)
ESP Electrosensitive Programming
ESP Electro Sensor Panel [*Toyota*]
esp electro-sensory panel (SAUS)
ESP Electroshock Protection (MCD)
ESP Electrosonic Profiler
ESP Electro-Static Precipitation (SAUS)
ESP Electrostatic Precipitator [*Also, EP*]
ESP Electro- Static Probe (SAUS)
ESP Electrostatic Probe (IAA)
ESP Elevated Stabilized Platform [*Aircraft*]
ESP Elevator / Escalators Power (SAUS)
ESP Elimination of Solvation Procedure [*Chemistry*]
ESP Elizabeth S. Priori [*Medicine*] (EDAA)
ESP Elsevier Science Publishers
ESP Elsevier Science Publishing (SAUS)
ESP [*The*] Emanu El Single Person (BJA)
ESP Emergency Stowage Plan (SAUS)
ESP Emerson Select Protection (SAUS)
ESP Employee Savings Program
ESP Employee Stock Purchase [*Software*]
ESP Employee Suggestion Program (SAUS)
ESP Employer School Program (OICC)
ESP Employment Service Potential [*Department of Labor*]
ESP Emulation Sensing Processor [*Quality Micro Systems*]
ESP Emulex SCSI [*Small Computer System Interface*] Processor (CDE)
ESP Encapsulating Security Payload [*Computer science*]

ESP .... Encapsulating Security Protocol (VLIE)
ESP .... Endangered Species Program [*Australia*]
ESP .... Endangered Species Protection Act (SAUS)
ESP .... End of Segment Pulse [*Military*]
ESP .... Endometritis, Salpingitis, and Peritonitis [*Medicine*] (MELL)
ESP .... End Systolic Pressure [*Cardiology*]
ESP .... endsystolic pressure (SAUS)
ESP .... Energetic Storm Particle
ESP .... Energy Services Planning
ESP .... Energy System Parameters (SAUO)
ESP .... Energy Systems Procedure (SAUS)
ESP .... Engineering Schedule Plan
ESP .... Engineering Service Project (MCD)
ESP .... Engineering Service Publications (AAG)
ESP .... Engineering Signal Processor
ESP .... Engineering Society of Pennsylvania (SAUO)
ESP .... Engineering Software Package
ESP .... Engine Sequence Panel (AAG)
ESP .... Engine Service Platform (KSC)
ESP .... Engine Start Panel
ESP .... English for Scientific Purposes [*Education*] [*British*]
ESP .... English for Specific Purposes [*Education*] (PDAA)
ESP .... Enhanced Serial Port (PCM)
ESP .... Enhanced Serial Processor [*Communication protocol*] [*Computer science*] (PCM)
ESP .... Enhanced Service Provider [*Online database service*]
ESP .... Enrichment Safeguards Program (SAUS)
ESP .... En Route Spacing Program [*FAA*] (TAG)
ESP .... Enterprise Server Platform (SAUS)
ESP .... Enterprise Storage Platform (GART)
ESP .... Entire Shape Plan (VLIE)
ESP .... Environmentally Sound Prevention [*Activity*] (COE)
ESP .... Environmentally Sound Products (SAUO)
ESP .... environmental sampling procedure (SAUS)
ESP .... Environmental Sketches in Perspective [*Computer program*]
ESP .... Environmental Studies Program (SAUO)
ESP .... Environmental Surveillance Procedure (SAUS)
ESP .... Eosinophil Stimulation Promoter [*Medicine*] (MAE)
ESP .... Epidermal Soluble Protein [*Biochemistry*] (DAVI)
ESP .... Epsilon Sigma Phi [*An association*] (NTPA)
ESP .... Equipment Status Panel (AAG)
ESP .... Equipment Support Plan (MCD)
ESP .... Equivalent Sum of Products (SAUS)
ESP .... Espeair [*Chechoslovakia*] [*FAA designator*] (FAAC)
Esp .... Especially (DIAR)
esp .... Especially (WDMC)
ESP .... Especially
esp .... Esperanto [*MARC language code*] [*Library of Congress*] (LCCP)
ESP .... Espey Manufacturing & Electronics, Inc. [*AMEX symbol*] (SPSG)
ESP .... Espey Mfg & Electr [*AMEX symbol*] (TTSB)
Esp .... Espinasse's English Nisi Prius Reports [*1793-1810*] [*A publication*] (DLA)
ESP .... Espionage [*FBI standardized term*]
Esp .... Esplanade (SAUS)
ESP .... Espressivo [*With Expression*] [*Music*]
ESP .... Essential Service Protection [*Communications term*] (DCT)
ESP .... Estimated Selling Price (SAUS)
ESP .... Estimated Street Price (FOTI)
ESP .... E-Tech Speedy Protocol (CDE)
ESP .... Ethernet Serial Port [*Computer science*] (VERA)
ESP .... Ethnic Schools Program [*Australia*]
ESP .... European Science Foundation (SAUS)
ESP .... European Society of Pathology (EAIO)
ESP .... European Specialist Publishers Dictionary [*A publication*]
ESP .... Evoked Synaptic Potential [*Neurophysiology*]
ESP .... Exceptional Sales Person (SAUS)
ESP .... Exchangeable-Sodium-Percentage
ESP .... Exchange Sale Property
ESP .... Exchange Stock Portfolio [*Investment term*] (MHDW)
ESP .... Execution Scheduling Processor (SAUS)
ESP .... Executive and Scheduling Program (SAUS)
ESP .... EX-OR Sum of Products (SAUS)
ESP .... Expandable Stored Program
ESP .... Expanded Spread Profile [*Seismology*]
ESP .... Expendable Signal Processor (SAUS)
ESP .... Expendables System Programmer (SAUS)
ESP .... Experimental Solids Proposal (SAUS)
ESP .... Experiment Sensing Platform (NASA)
ESP .... Expert Searching and Pricing
ESP .... Expert Systems for Producibility (TIMI)
ESP .... Exploratory Studies Program (SAUS)
ESP .... Extended Segment Processing (SAUS)
ESP .... Extended Self-Contained PROLOG [*Programming language*]
ESP .... Extended Service Plan [*Ford Motor Co.*]
ESP .... Extended Service Program
ESP .... Extended Services Processor (DINT)
ESP .... Extended Storage Platelet Pack [*Hematology*]
ESP .... Extended Streamflow Prediction (NOAA)
ESP .... Externally Stored Program (VLIE)
ESP .... Externally Supported Processor [*Mainframe computer*] (NITA)
ESP .... External Services Provider (GART)
ESP .... External Standard Pulse [*Instrumentation*]
ESP .... Extracellular Signaling Protein [*Biochemistry*]
ESP .... Extrasensory Perception
ESP .... Extravehicular Support Pack [*or Package*] [*NASA*]
ESP .... extravehicular support package (SAUS)
ESP .... Spain [*ANSI three-letter standard code*] (CNC)
ESP .... Emotional Selling Proposition [*Commerce*] (ODA)
ESP-1 .... Elizabeth S. Priori-1 [*Virus named after one of the scientists who isolated it*]
ESPA .... Electrical Stimulation Produced Analgesia (DB)
ESPA .... Electronically Steerable Phased Array [*SPADATS*] (MCD)
espa .... electronically steered phased array (SAUS)
ESPA .... Elementary and Secondary Principals Association (SAUO)
ESPA .... Elementary School Proficiency Assessment
ESPA .... Elementary School Proficiency Test
ESPA .... Elvis Special Photo Association (EA)
ESPA .... European Shipping Press Association (SAUO)
ESPA .... Evening Student Personnel Association [*Later, Evening Student Association*] (EA)
ESPA .... Exhaust Systems Professional Association [*Defunct*] (EA)
ESPA .... Lulea/Kallax [*Sweden*] [*ICAO location identifier*] (ICLI)
ESP Act .... Endangered Species Protection Act (SAUS)
ESP Act .... Endangered Species Protection Act 1992 [*Commonwealth*] (EERA)
Esp Act .... Espinasse. Actions on Statutes [*A publication*] (ILCA)
Espantuguese... Spanish-Portuguese (SAUS)
ESPAR .... Electronically Steerable Phased Array Radar (ACAE)
ESPAW .... Elementary School Principals' Association of Washington
ESPAWS .... Enhanced Self-Propelled Artillery Weapon System (MCD)
ESPAWSS ...... Enhanced Self-Propelled Artillery Weapon System Study (MCD)
ESPB .... European Society of Biochemical Pharmacology (SAUO)
Esp Bank ...... Espinasse's Law of Bankrupts [*1825*] [*A publication*] (DLA)
ESPC .... Education Systems & Publications Corporation (SAUO)
ESPC .... Elsevier Scientific Publishing Company (SAUO)
ESPC .... Emergency Status Precedence Code [*DoD*]
ESPC .... European Space Power Conference (SAUS)
ESPC .... Expendable Stored Project Contract (DNAB)
ESPC .... Ostersund/Froson [*Sweden*] [*ICAO location identifier*] (ICLI)
ESPD .... Endangered Species Protection Board (SAUO)
ESPD .... Export Services and Promotions Division [*British Overseas Trade Board*] (DS)
ESPD .... Export Services and Promotions Divisions (SAUS)
ESPD .... Gunnarn [*Sweden*] [*ICAO location identifier*] (ICLI)
Esp Dig .... Espinasse's Digest of the Law of Actions at Nisi Prius [*1812*] [*A publication*] (ILCA)
ESPE .... Earth Sensor Processing Electronics (ACAE)
ESPE .... Emergency Support Period Extension (ACAE)
ESPE .... European Society for Paediatric Endocrinology (SAUS)
ESPE .... European Society for Pediatric Endocrinology (EAIO)
ESPE .... United Socialist Alliance of Greece (PPW)
ESPE .... Vidsel [*Sweden*] [*ICAO location identifier*] (ICLI)
ESPEC .... Electrical Specification
E-Spec .... Equipment Specification [*Nuclear energy*] (NRCH)
ESPEC .... Especially
ESPEC .... Ethernet Specification [*Computer science*] (BTTJ)
E SPEC .... Material Specification (AAGC)
ESPEN .... Estimated Tax Penalty [*IRS*]
ESPEN .... European Society for Parenteral & Enteral Nutrition (WDAA)
ESPER .... Easy Simple Programming by Expert System (VLIE)
Esper .... Esperanto (SAUS)
ESPES .... Especialidades Farmaceuticas Espanolas Data Bank [*Spanish Pharmaceutical Specialities Data Bank*] [*Spanish Drug Information Center*] [*Information service or system*] (IID)
Esp Ev .... Espinasse on Penal Evidence [*A publication*] (DLA)
Espey .... Espey Manufacturing & Electronics, Inc. [*Associated Press*] (SAG)
ESPF .... Experimental SAR Processing Facility (SAUS)
ESPG .... Boden [*Sweden*] [*ICAO location identifier*] (ICLI)
ESPG .... Espionage (AABC)
ESP/GC & EE... Equipment Spare Package / Ground Communications and Electronic Equipment (SAUS)
ESP/GC & EE... Equipment Spare Package/Ground Communications and Electronic Equipment
ESPHI .... European Society for/of Paediatric Haematology and Immunology (SAUO)
ESPHI .... European Society for Paediatric Haematology and Immunology (EAIO)
ESPI .... Education Service of the Plastics Industry (AIE)
ESPI .... Electronic Space Products, Incorporated (ACAE)
ESPI .... Electronic Speckle-Pattern Interferometer (OA)
ESPI .... Electron Speckle Pattern Interferometry
ESPI .... Engineering Standard Practice Instruction (MCD)
ESPI .... e.spire Communications [*NASDAQ symbol*] [*Formerly, American Communications Services*]
ESPI .... Etched Sensitized Projected Image [*Circuit board manufacture*]
ESPICE .... Extended Simulation Program with an Integrated Circuit Emphasis (VLIE)
ESPIF .... Electro-Optical Sensor Performance Integration Facility (ACAE)
ESPIN .... Emergency Spare Parts Information Network (SAUO)
ESPIP .... Efficient Separations and Processing Integrated Program (SAUS)
ESPIP .... Efficient Separations/Processes Integrated Program (SAUS)
EspirSan ...... Espirito Santo Financial Holding [*Associated Press*] (SAG)
ESPJ .... Heden [*Sweden*] [*ICAO location identifier*] (ICLI)
ESPL .... Electronic Switching Programming Language
Espl .... Esplanade (DD)
ESPL .... Extensible Structure Processing Language [*1969-71*] [*Computer science*] (CSR)
ESPL 1 .... Electronic Switching Programming Language No. 1 (SAUS)
ESPLAF .... European Planning Federation (SAUO)
ESPLAF .... European Strategic Planning Federation [*British*] (EAIO)
Esplish .... Spanish-English (SAUS)

ESPM .... Energy Supply Planning Model [*National Science Foundation*]
ESPN .... Entertainment and Sports Programming Network [*Television*]
ESPN .... European Society for Pediatric Nephrology [*Switzerland*] (SLS)
ESPN .... European Society of Paediatric Nephrology (SAUS)
Esp NP .... Espinasse's English Nisi Prius Reports [*1793-1810*] [*A publication*] (DLA)
ESPNT .... East Point, GA [*American Association of Railroads railroad junction routing code*]
ESPO .... European Sea Ports Organisation (EURO)
ESPOA .... Electricity Supply Professional Officers Association (SAUO)
ESPOD .... Electronic System Precision Orbit Determination [*Air Force*] (MCD)
ESPOIR .... European Shoe Programme On Instant Response (SAUO)
ESPOIR .... European Symposium on Polar Platform Opportunities and Instrumentation for Remote Sensing (SAUS)
ESPOL .... Executive System Problem-Oriented Language [*Burroughs Corp.*] [*Computer science*] (BUR)
ESPOL .... Executive System Programming Oriented Language (SAUS)
ESPP .... Employee Stock Purchase Plan (AAGC)
ESPP .... Regional Military Command Subcenter North [*Sweden*] [*ICAO location identifier*] (ICLI)
Esp Pen Ev ... Espinasse on Penal Evidence [*A publication*] (DLA)
ESPPI .... Expanding and Specialty Paper Products Institute [*Defunct*] (EA)
Esp P St ...... Espinasse on Penal Statutes [*A publication*] (DLA)
ESPQ .... Early School Personality Questionnaire [*Psychology*]
ESPR .... English Society for Psychical Research (SAUO)
Espr .... Espressivo [*With Expression*] [*Music*]
ESPR .... European Society of Paediatric Radiology (EA)
ESPRA .... Empire State Paper Research Associates
ESPRAF .... ESP [*Extrasensory Perception*] Research Associates Foundation [*Defunct*] (EA)
ESP Rectifier ... Efficiency Speed Power Rectifier (SAUS)
Espres .... Espressivo [*With Expression*] [*Music*]
ESPRESS ..... Espressivo [*With Expression*] [*Music*]
ESPRI .... Education Service of the Plastics and Rubber Institute (SAUO)
ESPRI .... Empire State Paper Research Institute [*College of Environmental Science and Forestry at Syracuse*] [*Research center*] (RCD)
ESPRIT .... Electronic Still Photography at Rochester Institute of Technology [*A publication*]
ESPRIT .... Espatriate Turin [*Italy*] [*An association*]
ESPRIT .... Estimation of Signal Parameters by Rotational Invariance Techniques (SAUS)
ESPRIT .... European programme of research in information technology (SAUS)
ESPRIT .... European Specific Programme for Research and Technological Development in the field of Information Technology (SAUS)
ESPRIT .... European Starter Project for the Research in Information Technology (SAUS)
ESPRIT .... European Strategic Program for Research and Development in Information Technology (EDCT)
ESPRIT .... European Strategic Program for Research and Development in Information Technology and Telecommunications [*Research center*] [*Belgium*] (IRC)
ESPRIT .... European Strategic Programme of Research and Development in Information Technology (SAUS)
ESPRIT .... Eye-Slaved Projected Rafter Inset [*Simulator*]
ESPRP .... Energy Systems and Policy Research Program [*University of Wisconsin - Madison*] [*Research center*] (RCD)
EsprSan .... Espirito Santo Financial Holding [*Associated Press*] (SAG)
ESPS .... Education Systems Partition Supervisor (VLIE)
ESPS .... Entropic Signal Processing System (SAUS)
ESPS .... European Stroke Prevention Study
ESPS .... Experiment Segment and Pallet Simulator [*NASA*] (NASA)
ESPS .... Experiment Segment Pallet Simulator (SAUS)
EspSan .... Espirito Santo Overseas Ltd. [*Associated Press*] (SAG)
ESPT .... Executive Sequence Parameter Table (SAA)
ESPU .... European Society for Paediatric Urology (SAUS)
ESPVR .... endsystolic pressure-volume relationship (SAUS)
ESPWO .... Exigencies of the Service Having Been Such as to Preclude the Issuance of Competent Written Orders in Advance
ESQ .... Enlisted Separation Questionnaire [*Military*] (DNAB)
ESQ .... Environmental Symptoms Questionnaire (PDAA)
ESQ .... ESQ: A Journal of the American Renaissance [*A publication*] (ANEX)
ESQ .... Esquimalt & Nanaimo Railway [*Federal Railroad Administration identification code*]
esq .... Esquire (BEE)
ESQ .... Esquire
Esq .... Esquire [*Record label*] [*British*]
ESQ .... Extra-Special Quality [*Steel cable*] [*Ship's equipment*] (DS)
ESQA .... English Slate Quarries Association (SAUO)
ESQA .... Environment, Safety, Health and Quality Assurance (SAUO)
ESQA .... Extended System Queue Area (SAUS)
ESQC .... Elastic Scattering Quantum Chemistry
EsqCm .... Esquire Communications [*Commercial firm*] [*Associated Press*] (SAG)
EsqCom .... Esquire Communications [*Commercial firm*] [*Associated Press*] (SAG)
ESQD .... Explosives Safety Quality Distance (DNAB)
Esq Ins .... Esquirol on Insanity [*A publication*] (DLA)
ESQIS .... Energy Systems Quality Information System (SAUS)
ESQL .... Embedded Structured Query Language (SAUS)
ESQL/C .... Embedded Structured Query Language and Tools for C Language [*Computer science*] (HGAA)
ESQO .... Arboga [*Sweden*] [*ICAO location identifier*] (ICLI)
ESQP .... Berga [*Sweden*] [*ICAO location identifier*] (ICLI)
ESQR .... Esquire
ESQRE .... Esquire [*Gentleman*] (ROG)
Esqrr .... Esquire (SAUS)
ESQS .... Esquire Communications [*NASDAQ symbol*] (SAG)
ESQST .... Ego Strength Q-Sort Test [*Psychology*]
ESQSW .... Esquire Communications Wrrt [*NASDAQ symbol*] (TTSB)
ESQT .... Extended Sterilization Qualification Test
ESQV .... Visby [*Sweden*] [*ICAO location identifier*] (ICLI)
ESR .... Early Site Review [*Nuclear energy*] (NRCH)
ESR .... Early Storage Reserve
ESR .... Earthquake Seismology Research (SAUO)
ESR .... Earth Science Research (SSD)
ESR .... Earth Station Remote (SAUS)
ESR .... East Surrey Regiment [*Military unit*] [*British*]
ESR .... Economic Subregion [*Bureau of the Census*]
ESR .... Eco-Socialist Review (SAUS)
ESR .... Edge-Stabilized Ribbon [*Photovoltaic energy systems*]
ESR .... Editorial Status Report
ESR .... Educators for Social Responsibility (EA)
ESR .... Effective Search Radius (MCD)
ESR .... Effective Series Resistance [*Electronics*] (IAA)
ESR .... Effective Shunt Resistance [*Electronics*] (IAA)
ESR .... Effective Signal Radiated
ESR .... Effective SONAR Range [*Navy*] (NVT)
ESR .... Effective Sunrise
ESR .... Egyptian State Railway (ROG)
ESR .... Einstein Stoke Radius [*Medicine*] (DMAA)
ESR .... EISCAT [*European Incoherent Scatter Scientific Association*] Svalbard Radar
ESR .... Electrical Skin Resistance (LDOE)
esr .... electrical skin resistance (SAUS)
ESR .... Electrical Substitution Radiometer (SAUS)
ESR .... Electric Skin Resistance [*Neurology*] (DAVI)
ESR .... Electric Sliding Roof [*Automotive accessory*]
ESR .... Electric Store Register (SAUS)
ESR .... Electronically Scanned Radar (SAUS)
ESR .... Electronic Scanning RADAR
ESR .... Electronic Send/Receive
ESR .... Electronic Slide Rule (WDAA)
ESR .... Electronic Summary Report (SAUS)
ESR .... Electronic Surface Recorder (PDAA)
ESR .... Electronic Systems Reliability (MCD)
ESR .... Electron Spin Resonance [*Also, EPR*] [*Physics*]
ESR .... Electro-Slag Refined steel (SAUS)
ESR .... Electroslag Refining (SAUS)
ESR .... Electroslag Remelt (SAUS)
ESR .... Electroslag Remelting [*Steel alloy*]
ESR .... electroslag remelting furnace (SAUS)
esr .... electro-slag resmelting (SAUS)
ESR .... El Salvador [*Chile*] [*Airport symbol*] (OAG)
ESR .... Employment Service Representative
ESR .... Employment Status Recode [*Bureau of the Census*] (GFGA)
E-SR .... emulsion synthetic rubber (SAUS)
ESR .... Engineering Service Requests (MUGU)
ESR .... Engineering Societies Library (SAUO)
ESR .... Engineering Stop Release (SAUS)
ESR .... Engineering Summary Report
ESR .... Engineering Support Request (NASA)
ESR .... Engineering Surveys Reproduction Ltd. (SAUO)
ESR .... Environmental Resources Services (SAUO)
ESR .... Environmental Science Research [*Concept car*] [*Automotive engineering*]
ESR .... environmental surveillance report (SAUS)
ESR .... Environmental System Resources [*National Science Foundation*] (MCD)
ESR .... Equipment Status Report [*Air Force*]
ESR .... Equipment Status Reporting (SAUS)
ESR .... Equipment Supervisory Rack [*Telecommunications*] (TEL)
ESR .... Equivalent Series Resistance
ESR .... Equivalent Series Resistor (SAUS)
ESR .... Equivalent Service Rounds [*A standard for indicating gun erosion*]
ESR .... Error Search Routine (SAUS)
ESR .... Erythrocyte Sedimentation Rate [*Hematology*]
ESR .... Escape Road [*Hawaii*] [*Seismograph station code, US Geological Survey*] (SEIS)
ESR .... Essex Scottish Regiment of Canada [*Military unit*]
ESR .... Estimated Sedimentation Rate (SAUS)
ESR .... European Security Region [*Military*]
ESR .... European Staff Requirement (SAUS)
ESR .... Event Service Routine (AGLO)
ESR .... Event Storage Record (SAA)
ESR .... Excelsior Airlines Ltd. [*Ghana*] [*ICAO designator*] (FAAC)
ESR .... Exchangeable Sodium Ratio (SAUS)
ESR .... Executive Service Requests (MCD)
ESR .... Executive Summary Requirements (MCD)
ESR .... Expedite Shipping Request (MCD)
ESR .... Experimental Storage Ring
ESR .... Experimental Superheat Reactor
ESR .... Extended Self-contained Ring (SAUS)
ESR .... Extension Service Review (journ.) (SAUS)
ESR .... External Standard Ratio
ESR .... Extrahepatic Shunt Ratio [*Medicine*]
ESR .... Grouped Communication-Electronics and Meteorological Reporting System (SAUO)
ESR .... Electric Sunroof (ODA)
ESRO .... European Space Research Organization (SAUS)
ESRA .... Eastern Ski Representatives Association (EA)

ESRA .... Emergency Ship Repair Act of 1954
ESRA .... Employment Services Regulatory Authority [*Australia*]
ESRA .... Envelope Systems Research Apparatus (SAUS)
ESRA .... European Society of Regional Anaesthesia (EA)
ESRA .... Extended Slotted Ring Architecture (SAUS)
ESR Analysis... Electron Spin Resonance Analysis (SAUS)
ESRANGE..... European Sounding Rocket Range (SAUS)
ESRANGE..... European Space Range [*Sweden*] (MCD)
ESRANGE..... European Space Research (SAUS)
ESRANGE..... European Space Research Range (SAUS)
ESRB .... Entertainment Software Rating Board
ESRB .... European Society for Radiation Biology [*Formerly, Association of Radiobiologists from EURATOM Countries*] (EA)
ESRC .... Economic and Social Research Council [*British*]
esrc .... electronics recovery control (SAUS)
ESRC .... Engineering and Services Readiness Center (SAUO)
esrc .... engine surge recovery control (SAUS)
ESRC .... Environmental Science Research Center (SAUO)
ESRC .... European Science Research Council (NUCP)
ESRC .... Electricity Supply Research Council (ODA)
ESRD .... End Stage Renal Disease [*Medicine*]
ESRD .... Equipment Shipment Ready Date [*Army*] (AABC)
ESRD .... external-supertheater reheater D-type boiler (SAUS)
ESREF.......... ESG Re Ltd [*NASDAQ symbol*] (SG)
ESRF.......... Easter Seal Research Foundation of the National Easter Seal Society (EA)
ESRF.......... Electrical Systems Repair Facilities (MCD)
ESRF.......... End Stage Renal Failure [*Medicine*]
ESRF.......... Environmental Studies Research Fund (SAUO)
ESRF.......... Environmental Studies Revolving Funds (SAUS)
ESRF.......... Environmental Studies Revolving Funds report (SAUO)
ESRF.......... European Squash Rackets Federation (EA)
ESRF.......... European Student Relief Fund (SAUO)
ESRF.......... European Synchrotron Radiation Facility [*High-energy physics*] (ECON)
ESRG .... Earth Sciences Review Group (SAUO)
ESRI.......... Earth Sciences and Resources Institute [*University of South Carolina at Columbia*] [*Research center*] (RCD)
ESRI.......... Economic and Social Research Institute (ACII)
ESRI.......... Ekwall/Shanker Reading Inventory-Third Edition [*Test*] (TMMY)
ESRI.......... Engineering and Statistical Research Institute [*Canada*] (ARC)
ESRI.......... Environmental Systems Research Institute
ESRI.......... Environmental Systems Research Institute, Inc. (SAUS)
ESRI.......... Environmental Systems Research Institute Pty Ltd [*Commercial*] (EERA)
ESRI.......... European Space Research Institute (SAUO)
ESRI.......... Exploding Simon Research Institute (SAUO)
ESRIG .... European SR Implementors Group (SAUO)
ESRIN .... European Space Research Institute
ESRISAT ...... Earth Science and Related Information Selected Annotated Titles (SAUS)
ESRL.......... Earth Sciences and Research Laboratory (SAUO)
ESRL.......... Earth-to-Space Railgun Launcher (MCD)
ESRL.......... Eastern Shore Regional Library Resource Center [*Library network*]
ESRL.......... Environmental Sciences Research Laboratory [*Environmental Protection Agency*] (GRD)
ESRL/RTP.... Environmental Sciences Research Laboratory/Research Triangle Park [*Environmental Protection Agency*]
ESRM.......... Electroslag Remelting (PDAA)
ESRM.......... Energy Systems Records Manager (SAUS)
ESRO .... Engineering Stop and Release Order [*Aerospace*]
ESRO .... European Space Research Organization [*Superseded by ESA*]
ESRO .... European Space Research Organization Satellite (SAUS)
ESRO-SDS ... ESRO Space Documentation Service (SAUS)
ESRP .... Emergency Substitute in a Regular Position [*Education*]
ESRP .... Employee Software Royalty Program (TIMI)
ESRP .... Environmental Standard Review Plan (NRCH)
esrp .... Equivalent Semi-isotropic Radiated Power (SAUS)
ESRP .... European Society for Radiation Protection (SAUO)
ESRP .... European Supersonic Research Programme (SAUO)
ESRP .... Evreiskaia Sotsialisticheskaia Rabochaia Partiia (BJA)
ESR Process... Electroslag remelting Process (SAUS)
ESRR .... Early Site Review Report [*Nuclear energy*] (NRCH)
ESRS .... Early Sites Research Society (EA)
ESRS .... Electronic Scanning RADAR System (MCD)
ESRS .... European Society for Rural Sociology
ESRS .... European Synchroton Radiation Source (PDAA)
ESRS .... European Synchrotron Radiation Source [*High-energy physics*]
ESR Spectroscopy... Electron Spin Resonance Spectroscopy (SAUS)
ESRT.......... Electroslag Refining Technology [*Chemical engineering*] (IAA)
ESRU .... Electrical Stimulating and Recording Unit
ESRU .... English Schools' Rugby Union (BI)
ESRU .... Environmental Sciences Research Unit [*Cranfield Institute of Technology*]
ESRU .... European Society of Residents in Urology (SAUS)
ESRX .... Express Scripts 'A' [*NASDAQ symbol*] (TTSB)
ESRX .... Express Scripts, Inc. [*NASDAQ symbol*] (NASQ)
ESS.......... Earle's Salt Solution (OA)
ESS.......... Earth-Science Shelf (SAUO)
ESS.......... Earth-Sighting Simulator [*NASA*]
ESS.......... Earth Station - Sudan
ESS.......... Earth System Sciences (SAUS)
ESS.......... Eastern Sea Road Service (SAUS)
ESS.......... Eastern Sociological Society (AEBS)
ESS.......... Echo Suppression Subassembly (SAUS)
ESS.......... Echo Suppression Subsystem [*Telecommunications*] (TEL)
ESS.......... Echo Suppression System (SAUS)
ESS.......... Ecologically Sustainable Society (EERA)
ESS.......... Educational Services Section [*Navy*]
ESS.......... Educational Subscription Service, Inc.
ESS.......... Education Support Staff (AIE)
ESS.......... Effective Sunset
ESS.......... Efficient Sensing System (SAUS)
ESS.......... Electrical Spike Simulator
ESS.......... Electrical Standards Set
ESS.......... Electrical Standards System (SAUS)
ESS.......... Electrical Supervisory Subassembly (IAA)
ESS.......... Electroexplosive Device (SAUS)
ESS.......... Electronic Intelligence Support System (MCD)
ESS.......... Electronic Scanning Sensor (SAUS)
ESS.......... Electronic Scanning Spectrometer
ESS.......... Electronic Science Section (IAA)
ESS.......... Electronic Security Squadron [*Military*]
ESS.......... Electronic Security Strategic [*Military*]
ESS.......... Electronic Security Surveillance
ESS.......... Electronic Security System
ESS.......... Electronic Sequence Switching
ESS.......... Electronic Special Service GmbH (SAUO)
ESS.......... Electronic Speech Synthesis (IAA)
ESS.......... Electronic Speed Switch
ESS.......... Electronic Spreadsheet (CDE)
ESS.......... Electronics Systems Source (MCD)
ESS.......... Electronic Still Store [*Television*] (WDMC)
ESS.......... Electronic Surveillance System
ESS.......... Electronic Switching System [*See also EAX*] [*Telecommunications*]
ESS.......... Electronic Synchro-Shift
ESS.......... Electronic Systems Sector (AAGC)
ESS.......... Electron Spin Spectra [*Physics*] (IAA)
ESS.......... Electron Spin Spectrum (SAUS)
ESS.......... Electropneumatic Service System [*Truck engineering*]
ESS.......... Electroslag Surfacing (SAUS)
ESS.......... Electrostatic Spraying (SAUS)
ESS.......... Elementary School Science (SAUS)
ESS.......... Elementary Science Study [*National Science Foundation*]
ESS.......... ELINT [*Electronic Intelligence*] Support System (DWSG)
ESS.......... Emergency Ship Service [*Navy*] (MSA)
ESS.......... Emergency Short Stay [*in hospital*] [*British*]
ESS.......... Emergency Social Services [*Civil Defense*]
ESS.......... Emergency Survival System
ESS.......... Emplaced Scientific Station [*Aerospace*]
ESS.......... Employment Security System [*Department of Labor*]
ESS.......... Empty Sella Syndrome [*Medicine*]
ess.......... empty solution set (SAUS)
ESS.......... EMSP System Software (SAUS)
ESS.......... Encyclopedia of the Social Sciences [*A publication*]
ESS.......... Endoatmospheric Summer Study
ESS.......... Endostreptosin [*Medicine*] (EDAA)
ESS.......... Energy Storage Subsystem (SAUS)
ESS.......... Energy Storage System
ESS.......... Energy Systems Standard (SAUS)
ESS.......... Engagement Sensor Set
ESS.......... Engagement Simulation Systems [*Environmental science*] (COE)
ESS.......... Engineered Safety System (IEEE)
ESS.......... Engineering Equipment Surveillance System (SAUS)
ESS.......... Engineering Scheduling System (SAUS)
ESS.......... Engineering Source Selection
ESS.......... Engineering Standard Specification (MCD)
ESS.......... Engineering Surveillance System (SAUS)
ESS.......... Engineer Specialized Services
ESS.......... Engine Speed Synchronizer
ESS.......... Engine Start Signal
ESS.......... Engine Synchro-Shift [*Automotive transmissions*]
ESS.......... English Speaking Society (SAUO)
ESS.......... Enterprise Storage Server (SAUS)
ESS.......... Enterprise Support Service
ESS.......... Entry Survival System
ESS.......... Environmental Science and Society (SAUS)
ESS.......... Environmental Science and Society: An Economic and Institutional Analysis (SAUS)
ESS.......... Environmental Science Section (SAUO)
ESS.......... Environmental Science Services (SAUS)
ESS.......... Environmental Services Section (SAUO)
ESS.......... Environmental Stress Screen [*Durability testing*]
ESS.......... Environmental Stress Screening (MCD)
ESS.......... Environmental Stress Sensing [*Automotive engineering*]
ESS.......... Environmental Support Solutions (SAUO)
ESS.......... Environmental Support System (MCD)
ESS.......... Environmental Survey Satellite (ACAE)
ESS.......... Equipment Section Shell
ESS.......... Equipment Support Section (IGSL)
ESS.......... Equipment Surveillance System (SAUS)
ESS.......... Equivalent Sensor System (ACAE)
ESS.......... Equivalent State Subset (IAA)
ESS.......... Erection Subsystem
ESS.......... Erythrocyte-Sensitizing Substance [*Hematology*]
Ess.......... Essays (DIAR)
ESS.......... Essence
ESS.......... Essential
ess.......... essential expendable sound source (SAUS)
ESS.......... Essex [*County in England*]

ESS............ Essex Property Trust, Inc. [*NYSE symbol*] (SAG)
ESS............ Esstra Industries Corp. [*Vancouver Stock Exchange symbol*]
ESS............ Establishment Subsystem (SAUS)
ESS............ Estimating System Survey (AAGC)
ESS............ European Silicon Structures (NITA)
ESS............ European Spallation Source [*High-energy physics*] (ECON)
ESS............ European Special Situations Fund [*EEC*]
ESS............ European Symposium for Stereology (SAUS)
ESS............ Euthyroid Sick Syndrome [*Medicine*] (DMAA)
ESS............ Evaluation SAGE [*Semiautomatic Ground Environment*] Sector (IAA)
ESS............ Evaporation/Solidification System [*Nuclear energy*] (NRCH)
ESS............ Event Scheduling System
ESS............ Evolutionarily Stable Strategy
ESS............ Evolutionary Satellite Strategy (SAUO)
ESS............ Evolutionary Stable Strategy
eSS............ except Saturday and Sunday (SAUS)
ESS............ Excited Skin Syndrome [*Dermatology*]
ESS............ Executive's Shopping Service
ESS............ Executive Suites and Services [*Business term*]
ESS............ Executive Support Subsystem (SAUS)
ESS............ Executive Support System
ESS............ Executive Systems Software (SAUS)
ESS............ Exercise Support system (SAUS)
ESS............ Expendable Second Stage [*Space shuttle*] [*NASA*]
ESS............ Expendable Signal System (ACAE)
ESS............ Expendable Sound Source
ESS............ Experimental SAGE [*Semi-Automatic Ground Environment*] Sector
ESS............ Experiment Subsystem Simulator [*NASA*] (NASA)
ESS............ Experiment Support System (MCD)
ESS............ Expert Statistical System
ESS............ Explained Sum of Squares [*Data Analysis*]
ESS............ Exploitation Support Segment (SAUS)
ESS............ Explosive Safety Survey (NVT)
ESS............ Extended Security Services (FOTI)
ESS............ Extended System Software (HODG)
ESS............ External Serial Storage (SAUS)
ESS............ External Stores Support [*Military*] (POLM)
ESS............ External Suspension System (SAUS)
ESS............ Middleton Island, AK [*Location identifier*] [*FAA*] (FAAL)
ESS............ Northern Essex Community College, Haverhill, MA [*OCLC symbol*] (OCLC)
ESS............ TAES [*Tecnicas Aereas de Estudios y Servicios SA*] [*Spain*] [*ICAO designator*] (FAAC)
ESSA............ Earth Station - South Africa
ESSA............ Economists', Sociologists', and Statisticians' Association
ESSA............ Electronic Scanning and Stabilizing Aerial (SAUS)
ESSA............ Electronic Scanning and Stabilizing Antenna
ESSA............ Elliotdale Sheepbreeders' Society of Australia
ESSA............ Embassy Social Secretaries Association (EA)
ESSA............ Emergency Safeguards System Activation (IEEE)
ESSA............ Endangered Species Scientific Authority [*US Fish and Wildlife Service*] [*Terminated 1979, functions transferred to Department of the Interior*]
ESSA............ English Schools' Swimming Association (BI)
ESSA............ Enterprise Support Services for Africa [*Funded by CIDA - Canadian International Development Agency*]
ESSA............ Environmental and Social Systems Analyst (SAUS)
ESSA............ Environmental and Social Systems Analysts Ltd.
ESSA............ Environmental Science Services Admininistration Satellite (SAUS)
ESSA............ Environmental Science Services Administration [*Later, National Oceanic and Atmospheric Administration*]
ESSA............ Environmental Science Services Agency (SAUO)
ESSA............ Environmental Survey Satellite (TEL)
ESSA............ Environnmental Science Services Administration (SAUS)
ESSA............ European Single Service Association (EA)
ESSA............ European Supersonic Aviation Limited (SAUO)
ESSA............ Stockholm/Arlanda [*Sweden*] [*ICAO location identifier*] (ICLI)
ESS ADF...... Electronic Switching System Arranged with Data Features
Ess Ang Sax Law... Essays on Anglo-Saxon Law [*A publication*] (DLA)
ESSAR......... Early Site Safety Analysis Report [*Nuclear energy*] (NRCH)
ESSAR......... EBASCO Standard Safety Analysis Report [*Nuclear energy*] (NRCH)
ESSA Satellites... Environmental Science Services Administration Satellites (SAUS)
Essays CW... Essays on Canadian Writing [*A publication*] (BRI)
Essays Phys... Essays in Physics (journ.) (SAUS)
ESSB............ Electrical Self-Stimulation of the Brain (DIPS)
ESSB............ Electronic Supply Support Base [*Air Force*]
ESSB............ Stockholm/Bromma [*Sweden*] [*ICAO location identifier*] (ICLI)
ESSBR......... Electronically Scanned Stacked Beam RADAR [*Program*]
ESSC............ Earth Station - Scandinavia
ESSC............ Earth System Science Committee [*US governmental interagency group*]
ESSC............ Earth Systems Science Committee (EERA)
ESSC............ Electronic Standards Subcommittee (SAUS)
ESSC............ Emergency Support Schedule Changes (ACAE)
ESSC............ End Sweep Support Carrier [*Navy*] (DNAB)
ESSC............ Environmental Science Services Administration (SAUS)
ESSC............ Environmental Studies Service Center (ACAE)
ESSC............ Environmental Systems Science Centre
ESSC............ Eskilstuna/Ekeby [*Sweden*] [*ICAO location identifier*] (ICLI)
ESSC............ European Space Science Committee
ESSC............ European Sport Shooting Confederation (EAIO)
ESSCCA....... Easter Seal Society for Crippled Children and Adults (DHP)
ESSCIRC...... European Solid-State-Circuits Conference (PDAA)
ESSCO......... Electronic Space Structurers Corporation (SAUO)
ESSCO......... Electronic Space Systems Corporation (SAUS)
ESSCO......... Employee Support Services Company [*Military*]
ESSCO......... Environmental Science & Services Corporation (SAUO)
ESSD........... Borlange [*Sweden*] [*ICAO location identifier*] (ICLI)
ESSD........... Environmentally Sound and Sustainable Development (EERA)
ESSD........... Environment Supply Sensing Device (MCD)
ESSDERC...... European Solide State Research Conference (SAUS)
ESSDERC...... European Solid State Device Research Conference (PDAA)
ESSE........... Earth Station - Senegal
ESSE........... Earth System Science Education (SAUS)
ESSE........... EBASCO Services, Inc. Site Support Engineering [*Nuclear energy*] (NRCH)
ESSE........... Stockholm/Ska-Edeby [*Sweden*] [*ICAO location identifier*] (ICLI)
ESSEF......... ESSEF Corp. [*Associated Press*] (SAG)
ESSEN......... Essential
ESSENTIAL... European Systems Strategy for the Evolution of New Technology in Advanced Learning (SAUO)
Essequibos... Essequibo Islands (SAUS)
ESSERGY..... Essential Energy (MCD)
ESSEX......... Effects of Subsurface Explosions [*Project*] [*Army and DNA*] (RDA)
ESSEX......... Enhanced Satellite Survivability Experiment (ACAE)
Essex........... Essex Corp. [*Associated Press*] (SAG)
ESSEX......... Essex Technical and Commercial Library Service (SAUS)
ESSEX......... Experimental Solid-State Exchange [*Communication system*] (MCD)
ESSF........... Edmonton Space Sciences Foundation (SAUO)
ESSF........... ESSEF Corp. [*NASDAQ symbol*] (NQ)
ESSF........... Hultsfred [*Sweden*] [*ICAO location identifier*] (ICLI)
ESSFL......... Electron Steady-State Fermi Level
ESSFLO....... Electronic Switching System Flow Chart
ESSFLO Chart... Electronic Switching System Flow Chart (SAUS)
ESSFNR....... Exercise Simulation for Flexible Nuclear Response (SAUS)
ESSFNR....... Exercise Simulation System for Flexible Nuclear Response (MCD)
ESSFTA........ English Springer Spaniel Field Trial Association (EA)
ESSG........... Electrical Steel Standard Gauge (SAUS)
ESSG........... Engineer Strategic Studies Group [*Army*] (AABC)
ESSG........... Ludvika [*Sweden*] [*ICAO location identifier*] (ICLI)
ESSH........... Laxa [*Sweden*] [*ICAO location identifier*] (ICLI)
ESSI............ Earth Search Sciences Incorporated (SAUO)
ESSI............ Eco Soil Systems, Inc. [*NASDAQ symbol*] (SAG)
ESSI............ Electronic Support Systems Incorporated (SAUO)
ESSI............ Employment Security Systems Institute
ESSI............ Entrepreneurial Style and Success Indicator [*Test*] (TMMY)
ESSI............ European Software and Systems Initiative (VERA)
ESSI............ Visingso [*Sweden*] [*ICAO location identifier*] (ICLI)
ESSII........... Expert System For Satellite Image Interpretation (SAUS)
ESSIP........... Earth System Science Internet Project
ESSK............ Gavle-Sandviken [*Sweden*] [*ICAO location identifier*] (ICLI)
ESSL............ Eastern Secondary Standards Laboratory
ESSL............ Eco Soil Systems [*NASDAQ symbol*] (SG)
ESSL............ Linkoping/SAAB [*Sweden*] [*ICAO location identifier*] (ICLI)
ESSLR......... Eye-Safe Simulated LASER Range Finder (MCD)
ESSLR......... Eye-Soft System Laser Rangefinder (ACAE)
ESSM........... Brattforsheden [*Sweden*] [*ICAO location identifier*] (ICLI)
ESSM........... Electronic Shop, Shelter-Mounted [*Army*]
ESSM........... Emergency Ship Salvage Material [*Navy*] (NG)
ESSM........... Evolved Sea Sparrow Missile (DOMA)
ESSM/EWWS... Electronic Warfare Support Measures / Electronic Warfare Warning System [*Army*]
ESSMT......... Engine Start System Maintenance Trainer (DWSG)
ESSN........... European Senior Service Network (EURO)
ess neg........ Essentially Negative (MAE)
ESSNSS....... Electronic Supply Segment of the Navy Supply System
ESSNTL........ Essential
ESSO........... Elected Spanish Speaking Officials (EA)
ESSO........... Embarkation Supply and Stores Officer [*Military*] [*British*]
ESSO........... Esso Shipping (SAUS)
ESSO........... Esso Shipping Standard Oil (SAUS)
ESSO........... Standard Oil [*Trademark in foreign use only; superseded in US, 1973, by Exxon*]
Esso Mag..... Esso Magazine (journ.) (SAUS)
Esso Oilways Int... Esso Oilways International (journ.) (SAUS)
ESSOPE....... Expert System for Spacecraft Operation Planning and Execution (SAUS)
ESSOR......... Essai Orgel [*Orgel test reactor*] [*Italy*]
ESSP........... Earliest Scram Set Point [*Nuclear energy*] (NRCH)
ESSP........... Earth System Science Pathfinders (SAUO)
ESSP........... Eddy Statistics Scientific Panel (SAUO)
ESSP........... Elementary School Science Project
ESSP........... Elephant Species Survival Plan
ESSP........... Engineers Society of Saint Paul (SAUO)
ESSP........... Norrkoping/Kungsangen [*Sweden*] [*ICAO location identifier*] (ICLI)
ESSPO......... Electronic Supporting Systems Project Office [*Air Force*]
ESSPO......... Electronic Support Systems Project Office (SAUS)
ESSPO......... Electronic Systems Support Project Office (SAUS)
ess pos........ essentially positive (SAUS)
ESSQ........... Error Spectrum Shaping Quantizer (SAUS)
ESSQ........... Karlstad [*Sweden*] [*ICAO location identifier*] (ICLI)
ESSQs......... Error Spectrum Shaping Quantizers (SAUS)
ESSR........... European Society for Sleep Research (SAUO)
ESSR........... Expected Sample Size Ratio [*Statistics*]
ESSRA......... Economic and Social Science Research Association [*British*]
ESSS........... Electronic Security Surveillance System (SAUS)
ESSS........... Electronic Sensors and Systems Sector (SEWL)
ESSS........... Endangered Species Scientific Subcommittee [*Commonwealth*] (EERA)
ESSS........... Engineering/Scientific Support System (SAUS)

ESSS........... Environmental Science Services Administration (SAUS)
ESSS........... External Stores Support System [or Subsystem] (MCD)
ESSS........... Stockholm Aeronautical Fixed Telecommunication Network Center [Sweden] [ICAO location identifier] (ICLI)
ESSSSA...... Egyptian Society of Solid-State Science and Applications (SAUO)
ESST........... Eastern Equatorial Pacific Sea Surface Temperature [Oceanography]
ESST........... Eastern Standard Summer Time [Australia]
ESST........... ESS Technology, Inc. [NASDAQ symbol] (SAG)
ESST........... [The] European Interuniversity Association on Society, Science, and Technology [Lausanne, Switzerland] (ECON)
ESST........... European Master in Society, Science, and Technology [Swiss Federal Institute of Technology, Lausanne] (ECON)
ESST........... Torsby/Fryklanda [Sweden] [ICAO location identifier] (ICLI)
ESSTech...... ESS Technology, Inc. [Associated Press] (SAG)
ESSU........... Electronic Selective Switching Unit
ESSU........... Eskilstuna [Sweden] [ICAO location identifier] (ICLI)
ESSV........... Visby [Sweden] [ICAO location identifier] (ICLI)
ESSW........... Vastervik [Sweden] [ICAO location identifier] (ICLI)
ESSWACS...... Electronic Solid-State Wide-Angle Camera System (MCD)
ESSX........... Electronic Switching Systen eXchange (SAUS)
ESSX........... Vasteras/Johannisberg [Sweden] [ICAO location identifier] (ICLI)
EssxBc......... Essex Bancorp, Inc. [Associated Press] (SAG)
EssxPT......... Essex Property Trust, Inc. [Associated Press] (SAG)
ESSY........... Earth Station - Syria
ESSZ........... Vangso [Sweden] [ICAO location identifier] (ICLI)
EST............. Boundary Estimate Message [Aviation code]
EST............. Earliest Starting Time (SAUS)
EST............. Early Start Time
EST............. Earth Station - Turkey
EST............. Eastern Standard Time
EST............. Eastern Summer Time (IAA)
EST............. Echo Suppressor, Terminating End [Telecommunications] (TEL)
EST............. Effective Study Test [Study skills test]
EST............. Elastic Surface Transformation (IAA)
EST............. Electrical Surface Treatment [Polymer bonding]
EST............. Electric Shock Threshold [Medicine] (EDAA)
EST............. Electroconvulsive Shock Therapy (DIPS)
EST............. Electrolytic Sewage Treatment (IAA)
EST............. Electronic Security Tactical [Military]
EST............. Electronic Sequencer Timer
EST............. Electronic Shop Major Telephone and Teletype [Coast Guard]
EST............. Electronic Social Transformation
EST............. Electronic Spark Timing [Automotive engineering]
EST............. Electronics Sea Trials (MCD)
EST............. Electronic Support Training (SEWL)
EST............. Electroshock Therapy [Psychology]
EST............. Electroshock Threshold [Medicine] (DB)
EST............. Electroshock Treatment [Therapy term] (CTAA)
EST............. Electro-Sleep Therapy (DIPS)
EST............. Electrostatic Storage Tube (ACAE)
EST............. Electrostatic Store Tube (SAUS)
EST............. Elementary Scattering Theory (SAUS)
EST............. Element Simulation Technique (SAUS)
EST............. Elmo Snakey Torus (MCD)
EST............. Embedded Sensor Technique
EST............. Emergency/Salvage Tender (WDAA)
EST............. Emergency Service Team [Environmental science] (COE)
EST............. Emergency Support Team [National Guard] (DEMM)
EST............. Emerging Sciences and Technologies (SAUS)
EST............. Empire Social Telegram (IAA)
EST............. Endodermal Sinus Tumor [Oncology]
EST............. Endoscopic Sphincterotomy [Medicine]
EST............. Energy Saving Trust (AIE)
EST............. Energy Systems Toastmasters (SAUS)
EST............. Engineering Ellipsoidal Shell Tokamak [Nuclear] (ODA)
EST............. Engineering Sub Task (MCD)
EST............. Engineering Support Team (KSC)
EST............. Engineer/Service Test [Aerospace] (MCD)
EST............. Engineers Society of Tulsa (SAUO)
EST............. English in Science and Technology (SAUS)
EST............. Enlistment Screening Test [Military]
EST............. En Route Support Team [Military] (AFIT)
EST............. Enroute Support Teams (SAUO)
EST............. Entry Systems Technology [IBM] (PCM)
EST............. Environmental System Test (SAUS)
EST............. Environment Sport and Territories (SAUS)
EST............. Environment, Sport and Tourism (SAUO)
EST............. Eparchy of Saint Thomas the Apostle [Diocesan abbreviation] (TOCD)
EST............. Epidemiology and Sanitation Technician [Navy]
EST............. Equilibrium Surface Thermochemistry
EST............. Equipment Status Telemetry (ACAE)
EST............. Equity Silver Mines Ltd. [Toronto Stock Exchange symbol] [Vancouver Stock Exchange symbol]
est............. Erhard Seminars Training
EST............. Essential Subjects Test [Marine Corps] (DOMA)
Est............. Establish (EBF)
EST............. Established (EY)
est............. Established (VRA)
EST............. Establishment (WDAA)
EST............. Estancia [New Mexico] [Seismograph station code, US Geological Survey] (SEIS)
est............. Estate (GEAB)
EST............. Estate
Est............. Estates (SAUS)
EST............. Esteemed (ADA)
EST............. Esterase [An enzyme]
Est............. Esther [Old Testament book]
EST............. Estherville, IA [Location identifier] [FAA] (FAAL)
Est............. Estimate (EBF)
EST............. Estimate [or Estimation] (EY)
est............. Estimate (WDMC)
EST............. Estimated (MIST)
est............. Estimated (SHCU)
EST............. Estimation (SAUS)
est............. estimator (SAUS)
Est............. Estonia (SHCU)
EST............. Estonia
Est............. Estonian (ADWA)
est............. Estonian [MARC language code] [Library of Congress] (LCCP)
Est............. Estrogen [Biochemistry] (DAVI)
EST............. Estuary [Maps and charts]
EST............. European Satellite Team (SAUO)
EST............. European Society of Toxicology (EAIO)
EST............. European Staff Target (SAUO)
EST............. Excellent Satellite Tracker (SAUO)
EST............. Exercise Stress Testing
EST............. Exhaust System Terminal (KSC)
EST............. Expanded Service Test (SAUS)
EST............. Expanded Service Testing
EST............. Expressed Sequence Tag [Genetics]
EST............. Ex-Ship's Tackle (LDOE)
EST............. Extended Standard Theory [Linguistics]
est............. external static pressure (SAUS)
EST............. Flugfelag Austerlands Ltd. Egilsstadir [Iceland] [ICAO designator] (FAAC)
EST............. Portfolio of Environment Sport and Territories (SAUO)
EST............. University of New Hampshire, Jackson Estuarine Laboratory, Durham, NH [OCLC symbol] (OCLC)
ESTA........... Earth Sciences Technologies Association (SAUO)
ESTA........... Earth Science Teachers Association [British] (DBA)
ESTA........... Electronically-Synchronised Transmission Assembly (PDAA)
ESTA........... Electronic System Test Equipment (SAUS)
ESTA........... Electroshock Therapy Apparatus [Psychology]
ESTA........... Energy Systems Trade Association [British] (DBA)
ESTA........... Entertainment Services and Technology Association (NTPA)
ESTA........... Environmentally Sound Technology Assessment (GNE)
ESTA........... Escape System Test Article (MCD)
ESTA........... Ettlernet Station Adapter (SAUS)
ESTA........... European Science and Technology Assembly
ESTA........... European Security Transport Association (EA)
ESTAB.......... Establish [or Establishment] (KSC)
estab........... Established (ADWA)
ESTAB.......... Establishment
ESTABD....... Established (ROG)
estab est..... established estimate (SAUS)
establ.......... Establishment (GEAB)
Established Church... Established Church of England (SAUS)
ESTABLT...... Establishment (ROG)
estabt.......... Establishment (SAUS)
ESTAE.......... Extended Specify Task Abnormal Exit (VLIE)
e-stamp....... Electronic Stamp (ADWA)
Est & Trusts... Estates and Trusts [Legal term] (DLA)
EstANG........ Eastern American Natural Gas Trust [Associated Press] (SAG)
EstANG........ Estern American Natural Gas Trust [Associated Press] (SAG)
ESTAR.......... Electronically-Scanned Thin Array RADAR (SSD)
ESTAR.......... Electronically Scanned Thinned Array Radiometer (MCD)
ESTAR.......... Electronically Steered Thinned Array Radiometer (SAUS)
ESTAR.......... Estimated Arrival (SAUS)
ESTAR.......... Estimated Arrival Date
ESTATES...... Estates [Commonly used] (OPSA)
ESTB........... Establish [or Establishment] (AFM)
Estb............ Established (TBD)
ESTBD......... Established
estbl........... establishment (SAUS)
ESTBT......... Establishment (SAUS)
ESTC........... Eastern Tape Center (SAUS)
ESTC........... Eighteenth Century Short Title Catalogue [British Library] [Bibliographic database] [London, England]
ESTC........... Electrochemical Science and Technology Center (SAUS)
ESTC........... English Short Title Catalogue [Research Libraries Group]
ESTC........... European Space Technology Center [Netherlands] (KSC)
ESTC........... European Space Tribology Center (SAUS)
ESTC........... Explosives Safety Transport Committee (HEAS)
ESTC........... Explosives Storage & Transport Committee (SAUS)
ESTC........... Explosive Storage and Transportation Committee (SAUO)
ESTCA.......... Empire State Tattoo Club of America (EA)
ESTCA.......... Error-Sensitive Test Case Analysis (MCD)
Estco........... Eastco Industrial Safety [Associated Press] (SAG)
ESTCP.......... Environmental Security Technology Certification Program [Army] (RDA)
ESTD........... Electronic Standard (MSA)
ESTD........... Energy Systems Telecommunications Department (SAUS)
ESTD........... Energy Systems Training and Development (SAUS)
ESTD........... Established (ADA)
ESTD........... Establishment (SAUS)
estd............ Estimated (GEAB)
ESTD........... Estimated
ESTE........... Engineering Special Test Equipment (AAG)
ESTE........... Estate

ESTEAM....... Enrichment Science and Technology for Exceptionally Able and Motivated Pupils (AIE)
ESTEC.......... European Space Agency Technical Center (SAUS)
ESTEC.......... European Space Research and Space Technology Centre (EOSA)
ESTEC.......... European Space Research and Technology Centre (CARB)
ESTEC.......... European Space Research Technology Center (CCCA)
ESTEC.......... European Space Technology Center [*Netherlands*]
Estee.......... Estee's District Court of Hawaii [*A publication*] (DLA)
Estee (Hawaii)... Estee's District Court of Hawaii [*A publication*] (DLA)
EsteeL......... Estee Lauder Companies, Inc. [*Associated Press*] (SAG)
ESTEEM....... Empower Self through Education and Eating Management
ESTEER........ Electric Power Steering
ESTELLE...... extended state transition language (SAUS)
ESTF........... Electronic System Test Facility (IAA)
ESTF........... Environmental Systems Test Facility (KSC)
ESTF........... Exploratory Shaft Task Force (SAUS)
ESTF........... Exploratory Shaft Test Facility (SAUS)
EStG........... Einkommensteuergesetz [*Income Tax Law*] [*German*] (DLA)
ESTG........... Estimating (IAA)
Est Gifts & Tr J... Estates, Gifts, and Trusts Journal [*A publication*] (DLA)
Estgp.......... Eastgroup Properties [*Associated Press*] (SAG)
ESTH........... Economic Swiss Time Holding
Esth........... Esther [*Old Testament book*]
ESTH........... Esthetic
esth........... esthetics (SAUS)
Esth........... Esthonia (SAUS)
Esthr.......... Book of Esther (SAUS)
ESTHR......... Emergency Short Term Home Relief (SAUS)
EsthR.......... Esther Rabbah (BJA)
ESTI........... Eclipse Surgical Technologies, Inc. [*NASDAQ symbol*] (SAG)
EST-I........... Environmental System Test-Phase I (SAUS)
ESTI........... Estimation (VLIE)
ESTI........... European Solar Test Installation (EURO)
ESTIB.......... Environmental Science and Technology Internet Bowl
ESTIC.......... Ethiopian Science and Technology Information Centre (SAUS)
E/S TIEP...... Engineering/Service Test and Independent Evaluation Program [*Army*] (AABC)
EST-II.......... Environmental System Test-Phase II (SAUS)
ESTIMD........ Estimated (ROG)
ESTIV.......... European Society of Toxicology in Vitro (GVA)
ESTJ........... Extroversion Sensing Thinking Judging (ADWA)
ESTL........... East Saint Louis, IL [*American Association of Railroads railroad junction routing code*]
ESTL........... Electronic Systems Test Laboratory [*NASA*]
ESTL........... European Space Tribology Laboratory
estm........... estimate (SAUS)
Estm........... Estimated (DLA)
estmd.......... estimated (SAUS)
estmg.......... estimating (SAUS)
estmn.......... estimation (SAUS)
Estmr.......... Estimator (SAUS)
ESTMTN....... Estimation
ESTMTR....... Estimator
Estn........... Eastern (TBD)
ESTN........... Eastern
ESTN........... Endstone [*Horology*]
ESTN........... Estimation
EstnBc......... Eastern Bancorp, Inc. [*Associated Press*] (SAG)
EstnCo......... Eastern Co. [*Associated Press*] (SAG)
EstnEn......... Eastern Environmental Services [*Associated Press*] (SAG)
ESTO........... Eastco Industrial Safety Corp. [*NASDAQ symbol*] (NQ)
ESTO........... Electronic Systems Technology Office (VERA)
ESTO........... Engineer/Service Test Office [*Aerospace*]
Esto........... Estonia (VRA)
ESTO........... Estonian World Festival
ESTO........... Europaeische Studentenvereinigung in Osterreich
ESTO........... European Science and Technology Observatory (SAUS)
ESTO........... European Students Travel Organization (SAUO)
est of sitn.... Estimate of Situation (SAUS)
ESTOOOAHCF... Emergency Situations That Occur Outside of a Health Care Facility
ESTOP......... Estoppel [*Legal shorthand*] (LWAP)
ESTOP & W... Estoppel and Waiver [*Legal term*] (DLA)
e-store......... Electronic Store (ADWA)
ESTOW........ Eastco Indl Safety Wrrt [*NASDAQ symbol*] (TTSB)
ESTP........... Earth Science Technical Plan (SAUS)
ESTP........... Electronic Satellite Tracking Program (SAUS)
ESTP........... Electronic Systems Test Program [*NASA*]
ESTP........... Exploratory Shaft Test Plan (SAUS)
ESTP........... Extroversion Sensing Thinking Perception (ADWA)
ESTPER........ European Severe Trauma Perspective (EURO)
Est Plan Rev... Estate Planning Review [*A publication*] (DLA)
Est Powers & Trusts... Estates, Powers, and Trusts [*Legal term*] (DLA)
ESTPP.......... Earth Science Teacher Preparation Project (SAUS)
Est Prac....... Estee's Code Pleading, Practice, and Forms [*A publication*] (DLA)
Est Prac Pl... Estee's Code Pleading, Practice, and Forms [*A publication*] (DLA)
ESTR........... ElectroStar Inc. [*NASDAQ symbol*] (TTSB)
ESTR........... Environment, Science and Technology Resources (SAUS)
ESTR........... Environment, Science and Technology Resources statistical package (SAUO)
EstR........... Esther Rabbah (BJA)
ESTRA......... English-Speaking Tape Respondents Association [*British*] (BI)
ESTRA......... Estradiol [*Biochemistry*] (DAVI)
ESTRA......... Experimental STOL Transport Research
ESTRAC....... European Satellite Tracking, Telemetry and Telecommand Network (SAUS)
ESTRAC....... European Space Satellite Tracking and Telemetry Network (MCD)
ESTRACK..... European Satellite Tracking (SAUS)
ESTRACK..... European Space Satellite Tracking and Telemetry Network (BARN)
ESTRACK..... European Space Tracking (SAUS)
Estr B.......... Estero Bay (SAUS)
ESTRI.......... Electronic Standards for Transfer of Regulatory Information (SAUS)
ESTRIFF....... Encryptic Secure Tracking RADAR Identification Friend or Foe (NATG)
Estrlne......... Esterline Corp. [*Associated Press*] (SAG)
ESTRN......... Eastern
ESTRO......... European Society for Therapeutic Radiology and Oncology (EAIO)
ESTRO......... European Society of Therapeutic Radiation and Oncology (SAUO)
ESTS........... Echo Suppressor Testing System [*Telecommunications*] (TEL)
ESTS........... Electronic Systems Test Set (MCD)
ESTs........... Engineers, Scientists, and Technicians (SAUS)
ESTS........... Estates [*Postal Service standard*] (OPSA)
ESTS........... European Small Tanker Service (SAUS)
ESTSC......... Energy Science and Technology Software Center (CIST)
ESTSD......... Eastside
EstSSR......... Estonian Soviet Socialist Republic
est str......... Estimated Strength (SAUS)
Estt........... Establishment [*British military*] (DMA)
EstTX FS...... East Texas Financial Services, Inc. [*Associated Press*] (SAG)
ESTU........... Electronic System Test Unit
ESTU........... European Student Theatre Union (SAUO)
Estuarine Coastal Shelf Sci... Estuarine and Coastal Shelf Science (SAUS)
Estuarine Coastal Shelf Sci... Estuarine Coastal and Shelf Science (journ.) (SAUS)
ESTV........... Electronic Shelf Thermal Vacuum (ACAE)
ESTV........... Error Statistics by Tape Volume [*Computer science*] (IBMDP)
est w.......... Estimated Weight (SAUS)
Estwind........ Eastwind Group, Inc. (The) [*Associated Press*] (SAG)
Est Wt......... Estimated Weight [*Measurement*] (DAVI)
Esty........... Estuary (SAUS)
ESU............ East Stroudsburg University
ESU............ Electricity Supply Union [*British*]
ESU............ Electronic Sequencing Unit [*for helicopters*] [*Army*] (RDA)
ESU............ Electronic Services Unlimited [*New York, NY*] [*Telecommunications*] (TSSD)
ESU............ Electronic Setup (WDMC)
ESU............ Electronic Storage Unit (SAUS)
ESU............ Electronic Switching Unit [*Telecommunications*] (MCD)
esu............ Electrostatic Unit (IDOE)
ESU............ Electrostatic Unit
ESU............ Electrosurgical Unit [*Medicine*]
ESU............ Emergency Services Unit (LAIN)
ESU............ Employee Skills Upgrade
ESU............ Emporia State University (SAUO)
ESU............ Empty Signalling Unit (SAUS)
ESU............ Empty Signal Unit [*Telecommunications*] (TEL)
ESU............ Endangered Species Unit [*Commonwealth*] (EERA)
ESU............ Energy Studies Unit [*University of Strathclyde*] [*Scotland*] (IRC)
ESU............ Engineering Setup [*Television*] (WDMC)
ESU............ Engine Service Unit (AAG)
ESU............ English Speaking Union [*British*] (EAIO)
E-SU........... English-Speaking Union (SAUO)
ESU............ English-Speaking Union of the United States (EA)
ESU............ Enormous State University [*Fictitious school often featured in comic strip "Tank McNamara"*]
ESU............ Enterprise Support Unit
ESU............ Environmental Simulation Unit (PDAA)
ESU............ ESU of capacitance (SAUS)
ESU............ ESU of current (SAUS)
ESU............ ESU of electric potential (SAUS)
ESU............ ESU of inductance (SAUS)
ESU............ ESU of resistance (SAUS)
ESU............ Esutoru [*Uglegorsk*] [*Former USSR*] [*Seismograph station code, US Geological Survey*] [*Closed*] (SEIS)
ESU............ Europa Study Unit (EA)
ESU............ European Showmen's Union [*EC*] (ECED)
ESU............ European Size Unit (EURO)
ESU............ Exchange Signalling Unit (SAUS)
ESU............ Exercise Support Unit (SAUS)
ESU............ External Stabilisation Unit (SAUS)
ESU............ External Store Unit (SAUS)
ESUA........... Amsele [*Sweden*] [*ICAO location identifier*] (ICLI)
ESUAME....... Ethiopian Students Union in Africa and the Middle East (SAUO)
ESUB........... Arbra [*Sweden*] [*ICAO location identifier*] (ICLI)
E-Sub.......... Excitor Substance (DAVI)
ESUC........... English Speaking Union of the Commonwealth (EAIO)
ESUE........... Ethiopian Students Union in Europe (SAUO)
ESUE........... Idre [*Sweden*] [*ICAO location identifier*] (ICLI)
ESUF........... Fallfors [*Sweden*] [*ICAO location identifier*] (ICLI)
E Suffolk...... East Suffolk (SAUS)
ESUG........... Gargnas [*Sweden*] [*ICAO location identifier*] (ICLI)
ESUH........... Harnosand/Myran [*Sweden*] [*ICAO location identifier*] (ICLI)
ESUIC.......... English Speaking Union International Council (EAIO)
ESUK........... Kalixfors [*Sweden*] [*ICAO location identifier*] (ICLI)
ESUL........... Ljusdal [*Sweden*] [*ICAO location identifier*] (ICLI)
ESUM.......... Mohed [*Sweden*] [*ICAO location identifier*] (ICLI)
eSun........... except Sunday (SAUS)
ESUN.......... Sundsvall [*Sweden*] [*ICAO location identifier*] (ICLI)
ESUNA........ Ethiopian Students Union of North America
ESUPRA...... Empire State Utilities Power Resources Associates (SAUO)

ESUR .... Ramsele [*Sweden*] [*ICAO location identifier*] (ICLI)
E SURR R .... East Surrey Regiment [*Military unit*] [*British*] (ROG)
ESUS .... Asele [*Sweden*] [*ICAO location identifier*] (ICLI)
ESUS .... Electronically-Agile Solid-State Universal Surveillance (PDAA)
ESUSA .... Endangered Spiecies Distribution File (SAUS)
ESUSI .... Estates Staff Union of Society India (SAUO)
E Sussex .... East Sussex (SAUS)
ESUT .... Evaluation of Small Unit Training (MCD)
ESUT .... Hemavan [*Sweden*] [*ICAO location identifier*] (ICLI)
ESU/UFE .... European Showmen's Union/Union Foraine Europeenne (EA)
E-SUUS .... English-Speaking Union of the United States (SAUS)
ESUV .... Alvsbyn [*Sweden*] [*ICAO location identifier*] (ICLI)
ESUY .... Edsbyn [*Sweden*] [*ICAO location identifier*] (ICLI)
ESV .... Earth Satellite Vehicle [*Air Force*]
ESV .... Earth Station - Venezuela
ESV .... Ego Support Value [*Psychology*]
ESV .... Elastic Space Vehicle
ESV .... Electrostatic Voltmeter (DEN)
ESV .... Emergency Shutoff Valve (KSC)
ESV .... Emergency Stop Valve (SAUS)
ESV .... Emergy Support Vessel (SAUS)
ESV .... Enamel Single Silk Varnish [*Wire insulation*] (AAG)
esv .... enamel single varnish (SAUS)
ESV .... End-Systolic Volume [*Cardiology*]
ESV .... Energy Service Co. [*AMEX symbol*] (SPSG)
ESV .... Energy Systems Values (SAUS)
ESV .... ENSCO International [*AMEX symbol*] [*Formerly, Energy Service*] (SG)
ESV .... Enserv Corp. [*Toronto Stock Exchange symbol*]
ESV .... Entomological Society of Victoria [*Australia*]
ESV .... Error Statistics by Volume [*Computer science*] (BUR)
ESV .... Esophageal Valve [*Anatomy*]
ESV .... Essential Service Value [*Telecommunications*] (IEEE)
ESV .... Expanded Service Volume (SAUS)
ESV .... Experimental Safety Vehicle [*Later, Research Safety Vehicle*] [*Department of Transportation*]
ESV .... Extension Society Volunteers [*Defunct*]
ESV .... extrasystolies ventriculaires (SAUS)
ESVA .... Avesta [*Sweden*] [*ICAO location identifier*] (ICLI)
ESVEM .... Electrophysiological Study Versus Electrocardiographic Monitoring [*Medical study*]
ESVF .... Frolunda [*Sweden*] [*ICAO location identifier*] (ICLI)
ESVG .... Gagnef [*Sweden*] [*ICAO location identifier*] (ICLI)
ESVH .... Hallefors [*Sweden*] [*ICAO location identifier*] (ICLI)
ESVI .... End-Systolic Volume Index [*Cardiology*] (DMAA)
ESVID .... East Side Voice of Independent Detroit (SAUO)
ESVK .... Katrineholm [*Sweden*] [*ICAO location identifier*] (ICLI)
ESVM .... Electrostatic Voltmeter (SAUS)
ESVM .... Malung [*Sweden*] [*ICAO location identifier*] (ICLI)
ESVN .... Executive-Secure Voice Network
ESVOT .... European Society of Veterinary Orthopaedics and Traumatology (GVA)
ESVP .... European Society of Veterinary Pathology (EA)
ESVQ .... Koping [*Sweden*] [*ICAO location identifier*] (ICLI)
ESVR .... Examination Status Verification Report (NVT)
ESVS .... Escape Suit Ventilation System (MCD)
ESVS .... Escape System Ventilation System (NASA)
ESVS .... Siljansnas [*Sweden*] [*ICAO location identifier*] (ICLI)
ESW .... Economic and Sector Work
ESW .... Electroslag Welding
ESW .... Emergency Service Water [*Nuclear energy*] (NRCH)
ESW .... Engagement Software (ACAE)
ESW .... Engineering Specification Worksheet
ESW .... Engineering Statement of Work (MCD)
ESW .... Engine Status Word (MCD)
ESW .... Enhanced Sludge Washing (ABAC)
ESW .... Environmental Site of the Week (SAUO)
ESW .... Error Status Word [*Computer science*] (BUR)
ESW .... ESSA [*Environmental Science Services Administration*] World [*A publication*]
ESW .... Essential Service Water [*Nuclear energy*] (NRCH)
ESW .... Ethical Society of Washington (EA)
ESW .... Externally Sourced Worker (GART)
e-sw- .... Sweden [*MARC geographic area code*] [*Library of Congress*] (LCCP)
ESWA .... Engineering Shop Work Authorization (SAA)
ESWD .... Emergency Service Water Discharge [*Nuclear energy*] (NRCH)
ESWI .... Emergency Service Water Intake [*Nuclear energy*] (NRCH)
ESWI .... Norrkoping [*Sweden*] [*ICAO location identifier*] (ICLI)
ESWJS .... English and Scottish Wholesale Joint Societies (SAUO)
ESWL .... Electrohydraulic Shock Wave Lithotripsy (ADWA)
ESWL .... Electroshock Wave Lithotripsy [*Medicine*] (MELL)
ESWL .... Equivalent Single Wheel Load (MCD)
ESWL .... Estimated Surface Wheel Load (CINC)
ESWL .... Extracorporeal Shockwave Lithotripsy [*Medicine*]
ESWMO .... Energy Systems Waste Management Operations (SAUS)
ESWP .... Energy Systems Wellness Program (SAUS)
ESWP .... Engineers Society of Western Pennsylvania (SAUO)
ESWP .... Essential Sight Words Program (EDAC)
ESWR .... Escalante Western Railroad [*Federal Railroad Administration identification code*]
ESWS .... Earth Satellite Weapon Systems
ESWS .... Emergency Service Water Screening [*Nuclear energy*] (NRCH)
ESWS .... Emergency Service Water System [*Nuclear energy*] (IEEE)
ESWS .... Enlisted Surface Warfare Specialist (DNAB)
ESWS .... Essential Service Water System [*Nuclear energy*] (NRCH)
ESWSS .... Emergency Service Water Supply System [*Nuclear energy*] (NRCH)
ESWTR .... Enhanced Surface Water Treatment Rule (SAUO)
Esx .... Essex (SAUS)
ESX .... Essex Bancorp, Inc. [*AMEX symbol*] (SPSG)
ESX .... Essex County College, Newark, NJ [*OCLC symbol*] (OCLC)
ESX .... Extended Systems Executive (SAUS)
EsxCty .... Essex County Gas Co. [*Associated Press*] (SAG)
ESY .... Earth Station - Yugoslavia
ESY .... Engineering Society of York (SAUO)
ESY .... Episcopal Service for Youth (EA)
ESY .... E-Systems, Inc. [*NYSE symbol*] (COMM)
ESY .... Executive Aviation Services Ltd. [*Nigeria*] [*ICAO designator*] (FAAC)
ESY .... Extended School Year
ESY .... West Yellowstone, MT [*Location identifier*] [*FAA*] (FAAL)
ESYA .... Extended School Year Aid
ESYD .... Hellenic Accreditation Council (SAUO)
e-sz- .... Switzerland [*MARC geographic area code*] [*Library of Congress*] (LCCP)
ET .... Code of Professional Conduct (SAUS)
ET .... Committee FID Education and Training (SAUO)
ET .... Earliest Time [*Business term*]
ET .... Early Treatment (SAUS)
ET .... Earth Terminal (HGAA)
ET .... Earth Tide (SAUS)
ET .... Eastern Telegraph (IAA)
ET .... Eastern Telegraph Co. (SAUO)
ET .... Eastern Time (GPO)
ET .... Easter Term
ET .... East Texas (SAUS)
ET .... Eaton Trust Co. [*Toronto Stock Exchange symbol*]
ET .... Ebbinghaus Test [*Psychology*] (DAVI)
ET .... Eddy-Current Testing [*Electromagnetism*]
E/T .... Edges Trimmed [*Publishing*] (DGA)
ET .... Edge Thickness [*Technical drawings*]
ET .... Edge-Triggered (IEEE)
ET .... Educational Technician (SAUS)
ET .... Educational Technology (SAUS)
ET .... Educational Television [*FCC*] (NTCM)
ET .... Educational Test [*British military*] (DMA)
ET .... Educational Therapy
ET .... Educational Training
ET .... Effectiveness Teams (TIMI)
ET .... Effective Temperature
Et .... Egypt (MILB)
ET .... Egypt
ET .... Ejection Time
ET .... Elapsed Time
ET .... Electrical Technician (IAA)
ET .... Electrical Time
ET .... Electrical Transcription
ET .... Electrical/Transformer Room [*NFPA pre-fire planning symbol*] (NFPA)
ET .... Electrical Typewriter (CMD)
ET .... Electric Telegraph
ET .... Electric Truck
et .... electric typewriter (SAUS)
ET .... Electrode Track
ET .... Electrolytic Tank (SAUS)
ET .... Electronics Technician [*Navy rating*]
ET .... Electronics Technology (SAUS)
ET .... Electronic Technician
ET .... Electronic Teleprinter (SAUS)
ET .... Electronic Test
ET .... Electronic Time [*Fuze*] (MCD)
ET .... Electronic Timer (SAUS)
et .... electronic timing (SAUS)
ET .... Electronic Transcription [*Radio*] (WDMC)
ET .... Electronic Transformers (MCD)
ET .... Electronic Typewriter
ET .... Electron Transfer
ET .... Electron Transition (ODA)
ET .... Electron [*or Electronic*] Tube (MCD)
ET .... Electron Tunneling (SAUS)
ET .... Electrophoretic Type [*Medicine*] (MELL)
ET .... Electrothermal [*Gun classification*]
ET .... Elementary Training (SAUS)
ET .... Elevated Temperature (MCD)
ET .... Elongated Tokamak (ODA)
ET .... Embedded Trainer (SAUS)
ET .... Embedded Training [*Army*] (RDA)
ET .... Embryo Transfer
ET .... EMCLASS Terms [*Online database field identifier*]
ET .... Emergency Takeover
ET .... Emergency Tank [*Nuclear energy*] (NRCH)
ET .... Emergency Tender (WDAA)
ET .... Emergency Treatment [*Dentistry*]
ET .... Emerging Technology
ET .... Emissions Trading [*Environmental Protection Agency*]
ET .... Empathy Test [*Psychology*]
ET .... Employment and Training choices (SAUS)
ET .... Employment Training [*British*]
ET .... Emptying Time (ODA)
ET .... Ending Tape (SAUS)
ET .... Endocrine Therapy [*Medicine*] (MELL)
ET .... End of Tape [*Computer science*] (CET)
ET .... End of Text [*Computer science*]

ET End of Transaction (SAUS)
ET Endogenous Transcript [*Genetics*]
ET Endothelin [*Biochemistry*]
ET Endothermic (SAUS)
ET Endotoxin [*Microbiology*]
ET Endotracheal [*Medicine*] (AAMN)
ET Endotracheal Tube [*Medicine*]
ET Endotrachial (ADWA)
ET End Terminal (ACAE)
ET End-Tidal [*Physiology*]
ET End Transaction (TVEL)
ET Energy Technologist (SAUS)
ET Energy Technology (SAUS)
ET Energy Transfer (IAA)
ET Engaged Tone [*Telecommunications*] (TEL)
ET Engage Test [*Manual exchanges*] [*Telecommunications*] (NITA)
ET Engineering Technician (SAUS)
ET Engineering Technologist (SAUS)
ET Engineering Technology (MCD)
ET Engineering Test
E/T Engineering Testing (SAUS)
ET Engineering Thermoplastics (SAUS)
ET Engineer Training
ET Engine Turned [*Watchmaking*] (ROG)
ET English Text
ET English Title [*Online database field identifier*]
ET English Translation
ET Enhanced Telephone
ET Enhancement Technology (SAUS)
ET Enterically Transmitted [*Medicine*]
ET Enterostomal Therapist [*Gastroenterology*]
ET Enterotoxin (MELL)
ET Entertainment Tax (DLA)
ET Entertainment Television [*Also, E! Entertainment*] [*A cable network*] [*Los Angeles, California*] (WDMC)
ET Entertainment Tonight [*Television program*]
ET Entrenching Tool [*Shovel/pick combination*] [*Military*] (VNW)
ET Environmental Technician
ET Environmental Technologist (SAUS)
ET Environmental Technology (SAUS)
ET Environmental Test
ET Enziklopedyah [*or Entsiklopedyah*] Talmudit (BJA)
ET Ephemeris Time [*Astronomy*]
ET Epidemic Threshold (MELL)
ET Epileptic Transients (SAUS)
ET Equal Taper (OA)
ET Equation of Time [*Navigation*]
ET Equipment Test
ET Equipment Time
ET Equivalent Term (SAUS)
ET Equivalent Training (AABC)
ET Erection Torquer (SAA)
ET Erector Transporter (SAUS)
ET Ergotamine Tartrate (DICI)
e/t ergotin tartrate (SAUS)
E/T Escape Tower [*NASA*] (KSC)
ET Escort Trains (CINC)
ET Esophageal Trunk (SAUS)
ET Esotropia [*Ophthalmology*] (DAVI)
ET Esotropia for Distance [*Ophthalmology*]
ET Essential Thrombocythemia [*Hematology*]
ET Essential Tremor [*Neurophysiology*]
ET Estate and Gift Tax Ruling [*A publication*] (DLA)
ET Estate Tax
ET Estern Time (SAUS)
ET Estimated Time
ET Estimated Time of Arrival (DAVI)
ET Estimation Theory (SAUS)
ET Ethics and Transparency (Nicaragua) [*Political party*] (PSAP)
ET Ethionamide [*An antibacterial compound*] (DAVI)
ET Ethiopia [*ANSI two-letter standard code*] (CNC)
et Ethiopia [*MARC country of publication code*] [*Library of Congress*] (LCCP)
ET Ethiopian Airlines [*ICAO designator*] (AD)
ET Ethyl (MIST)
Et Ethyl [*Organic chemistry*]
ET Ethylenedithiotetrathiafulvalene (SAUS)
Et Ethyl Group [*Organic chemistry*] (DAVI)
ET Ethyltoluene [*Organic chemistry*]
Et Etienne (SAUS)
ET Etiocholanolone Test (DB)
et Etiology (AAMN)
ET European Theater
et--- Europe, East Central [*MARC geographic area code*] [*Library of Congress*] (LCCP)
ET Eustachian Tube [*Anatomy*]
ET Evaluation Team (SAUS)
ET Evaluation Test (IAA)
ET Evaluation Tool [*Training term*] (LPT)
ET Evapotranspiration [*Hydrology*]
ET Event Timer (NASA)
ET Event Trend (COE)
E/T Everhart-Thornley (SAUS)
ET Exchange Telegraph (SAUS)
ET Exchange Terminal (SAUS)
ET Exchange Termination [*Telecommunications*]
ET Exchange Transfusion [*Medicine*] (DMAA)
ET Excise Tax [*Canada*]
ET Excitation Transport (ODA)
ET Executive Team (NRCH)
ET Exercise Testing [*Medicine*]
ET Exercise Training (DB)
ET Exercise Treadmill (AAMN)
ET Exodus Trust (EA)
ET Exothermic (SAUS)
ET Expander Tube
ET Expenditure Targets [*Medical care proposal*]
ET Expiratory Time (MELL)
ET Explosive Technology
ET Express Transportation (SAUS)
ET Ex-Tapol [*Political Prisoner*] [*Indonesia*]
ET Extended Take [*Recording term*]
ET Extended Technology (ITCA)
ET Extended Test (SAUS)
ET Extended Threat (SAUS)
ET External Tank [*NASA*]
ET External Training (HEAS)
ET Extraterrestrial [*Also used in film title "ET - The Extra-Terrestrial"*]
et extra terrestrial (SAUS)
ET Extrathoracic
ET Extruded Tube (SAUS)
ET Eye Travel
ET Frame enclosed elevator with self-closing traps (SAUS)
E(T) Intermittent Esotropia [*Ophthalmology*] (DAVI)
et Engineering Time (ODA)
ET1 Electronics Technician, First Class [*Navy rating*]
ET2 Electronics Technician, Second Class [*Navy rating*]
ET3 Electronics Technician, Third Class [*Navy rating*]
ET-3 Erythrocyte Tri-Iodothyronine [*Hematology*] (DAVI)
ET$_4$R Effective T$_4$ Ratio [*Endocrinology*]
ETA A subsidiary of Control Data Corporation that manufactures supercomputers (SAUO)
ETA Basque Fatherland and Liberty [*Government term*] (GA)
ETA Basque Nation and Liberty (Spain) [*Political party*] (PSAP)
ETA Earth Tangential Angle (ACAE)
ETA Educational Telecommunications for Alaska (SAUS)
ETA Educational Television Association (EAIO)
ETA Educational Theater Association (EA)
ETA Education through Aviation
ETA Effectiveness Training Associates
ETA Effects Test Area [*Army*]
ETA Ejector Thrust Augmentation [*Air Force*]
ETA Electra North West [*Vancouver Stock Exchange symbol*]
ETA Electrical Thermal Analysis
ETA Electronics Technicians Association International (NTPA)
ETA Electron-Transfer Agent (DB)
ETA Electrothermal Analyzer (SAUS)
ETA Electrothermal Atomization [*For spectrometry*]
ETA Elemental Times in Agriculture (SAUS)
ETA Emanation Thermal Analysis
ETA Embroidery Trade Association (EA)
ETA Embryo Toxicity Assay (ADWA)
ETA Emery Trade Association (SAUO)
ETA Employment and Training Administration [*Formerly, Manpower Administration*] [*Department of Labor*]
ETA Employment Training Administration (SAUS)
ETA Endotracheal Airway [*Medicine*] (MELL)
ETA Endotracheal Anesthesia [*Medicine*] (MELL)
ETA Endotracheal Aspirates [*Medicine*] (MEDA)
ETA Energetic Transient Array (SAUS)
ETA Energy Tax Act [*1978*]
ETA Energy Technology Assessment Model (SAUO)
ETA engagement training aid (SAUS)
ETA Engineering Task Assignment
ETA English Teachers Association (SAUO)
ETA Entertainment Trades Alliance [*British*]
ETA Environmental Test Article (NASA)
ETA Environment Teachers' Association (EERA)
ETA Equipment Transfer Aisle (NRCH)
ETA Equipment Transfer Authorization (SAUS)
ETA Equivalent Target Area (MCD)
ETA Escorted Temporary Absence (FOTI)
ETA Esperanto Teachers Association [*British*]
ETA Estimated Target Assurance
ETA Estimated Time of Acquisition (KSC)
ETA Estimated [*or Expected*] Time of Arrival
eta Estimated Time of Arrival (EBF)
ETA Estimated Time to Acquisition (SAUS)
ETA Estrellas del Aire SA de CV [*Mexico*] [*ICAO designator*] (FAAC)
Eta Eterna [*Record label*] [*Germany*]
ETA Ethionamide [*Antibacterial*]
ETA Ethiopian Teachers Association (SAUO)
ETA Europaischer Holzhandelsverband [*European Timber Association*] [*EC*] (ECED)
ETA European Tallying-Association (SAUO)
ETA European Taxpayers Association (EA)
ETA European Teachers Association (BARN)
ETA European Tennis Association (EAIO)
ETA European Thermographic Association (SAUS)
ETA European Throwsters Association (EA)

ETA .... European Thyroid Association (EAIO)
ETA .... European Tropospheric-Scatter Army [*Communications system*]
ETA .... European Tube Association [*EC*] (ECED)
ETA .... European Tugowners Association (EAIO)
ETA .... Euzkadi ta Azkatasuna [*Basque Fatherland and Freedom*] [*Spain*] (PD)
ETA .... Evangelical Training Association (EA)
ETA .... Event Tree Analysis [*Engineering*]
ETA .... Exception Time Accounting
ETA .... Excise Tax Act [*Canada*]
ETA .... Expected Time of Arrival
ETA .... Expected to Arrive (SAUS)
ETA .... Expected Turnaround [*Computer science*]
ETA .... Expect to Arrive
ETA .... Experimental Test Accelerator [*Nuclear physics*]
ETA .... Explosive Transfer Assembly (MCD)
ETA .... Express Transport Association (SAUO)
ETA .... External Tank Attachment (MCD)
ETA .... Extraterrestrial Activity
ETA .... Extraterrestrial Actuality
eta .... Viscosity [*Symbol*] [*Organic chemistry*] (DAVI)
ETAA .... Eastern Townships Agricultural Association (SAUO)
ETAA .... Educators to Africa (EA)
ETAA .... Eelam Tamils Association of America (EA)
ETAA .... Electrothermal Atomic Absorption [*Analytical technique*]
ETAADS .... Engine Technical and Administrative Data System (PDAA)
ETAAS .... Electrothermal Atomic Absorption Spectrometry
ETAB .... Emerging Technologies Advisory Board
ETAb .... English Teaching Abstracts (journ.) (SAUS)
ETAB .... Environmental Testing Advisory Board [*Dow Chemical Co.*]
ETAB .... Executive Technical Advisory Board (AAEL)
ETAB .... Expanded Technical Assistance Board [*United Nations*]
ETAB .... Extrathoracic Assisted Breathing [*Medicine*] (DNAB)
ETABC .... Extrathoracic Assisted Breathing and Circulation [*Medicine*] (DNAB)
ETAC .... Electrically Tuned Aerial Coupler (SAUS)
ETAC .... Electrically Tuned Antenna Coupler
ETAC .... Electronics Technical Applications Center [*Air Force*]
ETAC .... Enlisted Tactical Air Controller [*Army*] (INF)
ETAC .... Enlisted Tactical Application (DOMA)
ETAC .... Enlisted Terminal Attack Controller (SAUS)
ETAC .... Enrichment Technology Applications Center (SAUS)
ETAC .... Environmental Technical Applications Center [*Air Force*]
ETAC .... Environment Technical Advisory Committee (EERA)
ETAC .... Equilibrium Transfer Alkylating Cross-Link (SAUS)
Et Ac .... Ethyl Acetate [*Medicine*] (EDAA)
ETAC .... European Trade Association for Composite Materials (SAUS)
ETACCS .... European Theater Air Command and Control Study [*DoD*]
ETAC-L .... Equilibrium Transfer Alkylating Cross-Link (SAUS)
ETACS .... Electronic Time and Alarm Control System [*Mitsubishi*] [*Automotive engineering*]
ETACS .... Extended Total Access Communications System (VLIE)
ETACS .... Extended Total Access Communication System (SAUO)
ETACSY .... Exclusive Tailored Correlation Spectroscopy (SAUS)
ETAD .... Ecological and Toxicological Association of the Dyes and Pigments Manufacturers (SAUS)
ETAD .... Ecological and Toxicological Association of the Dyestuffs Manufacturing Industry [*Basel, Switzerland*] (EAIO)
ETADM .... Embedded Trainer Advanced Development Mode (SAUS)
ETADS .... Enhanced Transportation Automated Data System [*Air Force*]
ETAE .... Ethyl Tertiary Amyl Ether [*Gasoline blending*]
ETAF .... epidermal thymocyte activating factor (SAUS)
ETAFF .... European Technical Association for Furniture Finishes [*Defunct*]
ETAG .... End TAG (SAUS)
ETAG .... European Tourism Action Group (SAUO)
ETA-I .... Electronics Technicians Association, International (EA)
e-tailing .... Electronic Retailing (ADWA)
ETAIRS .... Employment and Training Automated Information and Retrieval System [*Department of Labor*] [*Database*]
ET AL .... Et Alibi [*And Elsewhere*] [*Latin*]
et al .... Et Alii [*or Et Aliae or Et Alia*] [*And Others*] [*Latin*] (GPO)
Et Alc .... Ethyl Alcohol [*Organic chemistry*] (DAVI)
ET AL FREQ ... Et Alii Frequentis [*And in Many Other (Passages)*] [*Latin*] (ROG)
ETAM .... Anklam [*Germany*] [*ICAO location identifier*] (ICLI)
ETAM .... Entry Telecommunication Access Method
ETA-M .... Euzkadi ta Azkatasuna [*Basque Fatherland and Freedom*] Military Fr ont [*Spain*]
ETAM .... Everything to Attract Men (BB)
ETAM .... Experimental Transmitting Antenna Modular Model (MCD)
ETA/MDUSAS... Engineering Technology Analysts, Inc. Mobile Drilling Unit Structural Analysis System (SAUO)
ETA/MDUSAS... Engineering Technology Analysts / Mobile Drilling Unit Structural Analysis Syste (SAUS)
ETAMS .... Employment and Training Administration Management System [*Department of Labor*]
ETAN .... European Technology Assessment (SAUO)
ETA/NAME ... Engineering Technology Analysts / Naval Architecture Marine Engineering (SAUS)
ET&A .... Education, Training and Awareness (SEWL)
ET & E .... Engineering Test and Evaluation (MCD)
ET & E .... Environmental Technology and Economics [*A publication*]
ET&I .... Engineering, Test, and Inspection (SAUS)
ET & MO .... Education, Training, and Military Operations [*Army*] (RDA)
ET&W .... Energy Trade and Wholesale
ET & WNC .... East Tennessee & Western North Carolina Railroad Co. (IIA)
ETANN .... Electrically Trainable Analog Neural Network [*Intel Corp.*] [*Computer science*] (PCM)
ETANN .... Electrically Trainable Analog Neural Network (Intel) (SAUS)
ETANN .... Electrically Trainable Artificial Neural Network (SAUS)
ETAP .... Elevated Temperature Aluminum Program (ACAE)
ETAP .... Employee Tuition Assistance Plan
ETAP .... Expanded Technical Assistance Program [*United Nations*]
ETAP .... Extended Task Analysis Procedure [*Education*] (AIE)
ETAP .... Extended Technical Assistance Program (SAUS)
ETAPC .... European Technical Association for/of Protective Coatings (SAUO)
ETAPC .... European Technical Association for Protective Coatings [*Belgium*] (SLS)
ETAP/FAO .... Expanded Technical Assistance Program/FAO (SAUS)
ETA-PM .... Euzkadi ta Azkatasuna [*Basque Fatherland and Freedom*] Political-Military Front [*Spain*]
ETAQ .... English Teachers Association of Queensland (SAUO)
ETARO .... Employment and Training Administration Regional Office [*Department of Labor*]
ETARS .... Enroute Tracking Automatic RADAR Service [*Aviation*] (FAAC)
ETAS .... Effective True Airspeed (AFM)
ETAS .... Elevated Target Acquisition Sensor (ACAE)
ETAS .... Elevated Target Acquisition System
ETAS .... Emergency Technical Assistance (VLIE)
ETAS .... Escort Towed Array Sensor [*Later, TACTAS*] [*Navy*] (MCD)
ETAS .... Escort Towed Array Sonar (SAUS)
ETAS .... Escort Towed Array System (SAUS)
ETASS .... Escort Towed Array SONAR System [*Navy*] (PDAA)
ETASS .... European Tick-Borne Encephalitis [*Medicine*] (PDAA)
ETASS .... Evaluation of the Army Study System (MCD)
ETASS .... Experimental Towed Array Sonar System (SAUS)
ETAT .... Education and Training Advisory Team (CINC)
ETAW .... Evapotranspiration of Applied Water (ADWA)
ETAWA .... English Teachers' Association of Western Australia
ETAWG .... Engineering Test Area Working Group (SAA)
etb .... early to bed (SAUS)
ETB .... Elastic Top and Bottom [*Military-issue clothing*] [*British*] (DSUE)
ETB .... Electrical Time Base
ETB .... Electronic Test Block
ETB .... Elvis Teddy Bears (EA)
ETB .... End of Text Block [*Computer science*] (ACRL)
ETB .... End of Transmission Blank (SAUS)
ETB .... End of Transmission Block [*Computer science*]
etb .... end of transmission block character (SAUS)
ETB .... End of Transmitted Block (ACAE)
ETB .... Engineering Technical Bulletin (ACAE)
ETB .... Engineering Test Basis (KSC)
ETB .... English Tourist Board
ETB .... Enlisted Training Branch [*BUPERS*]
ETB .... Environmental Technology Building (ABAC)
ETB .... Equipment Transfer Bag [*NASA*]
ETB .... Estimated Time of Berthing [*Navigation*]
ETB .... Ethidium Bromide [*Trypanocide*] [*Also, EB, Etd Br*] [*Biochemical analysis*]
ETB .... Etobicoke Public Library [*UTLAS symbol*]
ETB .... Excise Tax Bulletins (SAUO)
ETB .... Expected Time of Berthing (SAUS)
ETB .... Experimental Test Bed (MCD)
ETB .... Extreme Terrain Bike [*Military*] (INF)
ETB .... West Bend, WI [*Location identifier*] [*FAA*] (FAAL)
ETBA .... Energy Trace and Barrier Analysis (LDOE)
ETBA .... Hellenike Trapeza Biomechanikes Anaptyxeos
ETBC .... East Texas Baptist College
ETB Character... End of Transmission Block Character (SAUS)
ETBE .... Ethyl Tertiary-Butyl Ether [*Fuel additive*]
ETBH .... Barth [*Germany*] [*ICAO location identifier*] (ICLI)
ETBN .... Berlin/Schonefeld [*Germany*] [*ICAO location identifier*] (ICLI)
ETBO .... Engineering Test Base Office (AAG)
ETBPR .... European Theater Bureau of Public Relations [*World War II*]
ETBS .... Berlin/Schonefeld [*Germany*] [*ICAO location identifier*] (ICLI)
ETBYLAW .... Bylaws of the American Institute of Certified Public Accountants (SAUO)
etc .... And So Forth [*Et cetera*] [*Latin*] (WDMC)
ETC .... Early Typewriter Collectors Association (EA)
ETC .... Earth Terminal Complex
ETC .... Earth Terrain Camera [*NASA*] (MCD)
ETC .... East Texas Central Railroad [*Federal Railroad Administration identification code*]
ETC .... Easycoder to COBOL (SAUS)
ETC .... Educational Technology Center [*Harvard University*] [*Department of Education*] [*Research center*] (RCD)
ETC .... Educational Travel Connection [*Oracle Corp.*] [*Information service or system*] (IID)
ETC .... Education & Training Command (SAUS)
ETC .... effective thermal conductivity (SAUS)
ETC .... Effluent Treatment Cell (PDAA)
ETC .... Elapsed Time Code
ETC .... El Centro [*Colombia*] [*Seismograph station code, US Geological Survey*] (SEIS)
ETC .... Electra Title Corp. [*Vancouver Stock Exchange symbol*]
ETC .... Electrical Technician Certificate (SAUS)
ETC .... Electrical Trade Council (EA)
ETC .... Electric Tube Corporation (SAUO)
ETC .... Electroacoustic Torpedo Countermeasure (MCD)
ETC .... electrochoc (SAUS)
ETC .... Electronics Technician Chief [*Military*] (SEWL)

ETC .... Electronic Table Calculator (SAUS)
ETC .... Electronic Technician Certificate (SAUS)
ETC .... electronic telephone circuit (SAUS)
ETC .... Electronic Temperature Control
ETC .... Electronic Text Corp. [*Information service or system*] (IID)
ETC .... Electronic Throttle Control [*Automotive engineering*]
ETC .... Electronic Time Card (SAUS)
ETC .... Electronic Time Clock (VLIE)
ETC .... Electronic Toll Center [*AT & T*]
ETC .... Electronic Toll Collection [*FHWA*] (TAG)
ETC .... Electronic Tool Company (NITA)
ETC .... Electronic Traction Control [*Automotive engineering*]
ETC .... Electronic Transaction Cycle (HGAA)
ETC .... Electronic Transmission Control [*Automotive engineering*]
etc .... electronic travel computer (SAUS)
ETC .... Electronic Tube Corporation (SAUO)
ETC .... Electronic Tuner Control (SAUS)
ETC .... Electronic Tuning Control (IAA)
ETC .... Electronic Typing Calculator (IAA)
ETC .... Electron Transport Chain [*Medicine*] (EDAA)
ETC .... Electro Tech Corporation (SAUO)
ETC .... Electrothermal-Chemical (RDA)
ETC .... Electrothermal Circuit (SAUS)
ETC .... Electro-Thermal-Circuits (SAUS)
ETC .... Eleven Thirty Conversion (SAUS)
ETC .... Emergency Training Centre [*British*]
etc .... employee timecard (SAUS)
ETC .... Employee Transportation Coordinator [*MOCD*] (TAG)
ETC .... Empresario de Transporte Combinado [*Combined Transport Operator*] [*Business term*] [*Spanish*]
ETC .... Enclosed Track Conveyor
ETC .... Energy Technology Center
ETC .... Energy Transfer Control [*Aviation*]
ETC .... Engineering and Training Center [*NASA*] (KSC)
ETC .... Engineering Test Capsule
ETC .... Engineering Test Center (MCD)
ETC .... Engineering Tooling Coordination
ETC .... Engineering Training Center (ACAE)
ETC .... engineering training course (SAUS)
ETC .... Engineer Training Centre (SAUO)
ETC .... Engine Technical Commission
ETC .... Engine Technical Committee (SAUO)
ETC .... Engine Test Chamber (MCD)
ETC .... English Translucent China (SAUS)
ETC .... Enhanced Throughput Cellular [*AT & T*] [*Telecommunications*] (PCM)
ETC .... Enhanced Throughput Cellular (modem protocol) (SAUS)
ETC .... Enthusiasm, Teamwork, Creativity (FOTI)
ETC .... Entrepreneur de Transport Combine [*Combined Transport Operator*] [*Business term*] [*French*]
ETC .... Environmental Technology Center (SAUS)
ETC .... Environmental Technology Council (NTPA)
ETC .... Environmental Tectonics [*AMEX symbol*] (TTSB)
ETC .... Environmental Tectonics Corp. [*AMEX symbol*] (SPSG)
ETC .... Environmental Tectonics Corporation (SAUO)
ETC .... Environmental Test Chamber
ETC .... Environmental Testing & Certification Corp. (EFIS)
ETC .... Environmental Testing Corporation (SAUO)
ETC .... Episcopal Travel Club (SAUS)
ETC .... Equal-Time Commutation
ETC .... Equal-Time Commutator (SAUS)
ETC .... Equipment Transit Centre (SAUO)
ETC .... Equipment Trust Certificate
ETC .... Estimated Time of Compilation (VLIE)
ETC .... Estimated Time of Completion
ETC .... Estimated Time of Conception [*Obstetrics*] (DAVI)
ETC .... Estimated Time of Correction
ETC .... Estimate Time to Complete (SAUS)
ETC .... Estimate to Complete [*Cost*] (AAGC)
ETC .... Estimate to Completion (SAUS)
ETC .... Et Cetera [*And So Forth*] [*Latin*]
ETC .... Ethiopian Tourism Commission (SAUO)
ETC .... Ethylene Carbonate (SAUS)
ETC .... European Tax Confederation (EAIO)
ETC .... European Taxi Confederation [*Belgium*] (EAIO)
ETC .... European Tea Committee (EA)
ETC .... European Technology Centre (SAUS)
ETC .... European Telecommunications Standards Institute (SAUO)
ETC .... European Test Conference (SAUS)
ETC .... European Tool Committee (EA)
ETC .... European Topic Centre (EURO)
ETC .... European Touring Car
ETC .... European Tourist Conference (SAUO)
ETC .... European Toy Confederation [*France*] (EAIO)
ETC .... European Trade Committee [*British Overseas Trade Board*] (DS)
ETC .... European Traffic Committee
ETC .... European Translations Centre [*Later, International Translations Centre*]
ETC .... European Transport Council (SAUO)
ETC .... European Travel Commission (EA)
ETC .... Euro Travellers Cheque [*Thomas Cook International*]
ETC .... Excess-Three Code (VLIE)
ETC .... Exchange Terminal Circuit (ACRL)
ETC .... Exempt Telecommunications Company (SAUO)
ETC .... Expected Time of Completion (RIMS)
ETC .... Expected to Complete (SAUS)
ETC .... Expected Total Cost
ETC .... Experimental Techniques Centre [*Brunel University*] [*British*] (CB)
ETC .... Explosion of the Total Contents [*Insurance*] (DS)
ETC .... Explosive Transient Camera [*Astronomy*]
ETC .... Export Trading Company [*Department of Commerce*]
ETC .... Extended Technicolor (SAUS)
ETC .... Extended Text Compositor [*Applied Data Research, Inc.*]
ETC .... Extendible Compiler (SAUS)
ETC .... Extraterrestrial Civilization
ETCA .... Edge Tool Cutters' Association [*A union*] [*British*]
ETCA .... Emergency Terrain Clearance Altitude
ETCA .... Ethiopian Transport Corporation Authority (SAUO)
ETCA .... ET Intertank Carrier Plate Assembly (SAUS)
ETCA .... Etudes Techniques et Constructions Aerospatiales [*Belgium*]
ETCA .... Export Trading Company Act of 1982
ETC-AQ .... European Topic Centre on Air Quality (SAUS)
ETCAWIS .... East Tennessee Chapter of the Association for Women in Science (SAUO)
ETCC .... Eastern Tank Carrier Conference
ETCC .... Electronic Touch Climate Control (HAWK)
ETCC .... Environmental Test Control Center (AAG)
ETCCC .... European Testing and Certification Coordination Council (JAGO)
ETC/CDS .... European Topic Centre on Catalogue of Data Sources (SAUS)
ETCD .... Estimated Task Completion Date (AAG)
ETCE .... Energy Sources Technology Conference and Exhibition (ITD)
Etcetera .... East-West Technical Cooperation in the Research & Development of Electronic Trading (SAUO)
ETCF .... European Technical Committee for Fluorine [*of the European Council of Chemical Manufacturers' Federations*] [*Belgium*] (EAIO)
ETCFC .... Earl Thomas Conley Fan Club (EA)
ETCG .... Elapsed-Time Code Generator
ET(CG)R .... Electric Target (Converted Gallery) Range (SAUS)
ETCH .... Etching (MSA)
etch .... Etching (VRA)
ETCHPS .... East Tennessee Chapter Health Physics Society (SAUO)
ETCI .... Electronic Tele-Communications, Inc. [*NASDAQ symbol*] (NQ)
ETCI .... [*The*] Electro-Technical Council of Ireland (ACII)
ETCI .... Engineering Technologist Certification Institute (EA)
ETCIA .... Electronic Tele Comm'A' [*NASDAQ symbol*] (TTSB)
ETCM .... Electronics Technician, Master Chief [*Navy rating*]
ETC/NC .... European Topic Centre on Nature Conservation (SAUS)
ETCO .... Cottbus [*Germany*] [*ICAO location identifier*] (ICLI)
ETCO .... [*The*] Earth Technology Corp. (USA) [*NASDAQ symbol*] (NQ)
ETCO .... Emergency Traffic Coordinating Officer [*Army*] (AABC)
ETCO .... Equipment Transfer/Change Order (SAUS)
ETCO .... Equipment Transfer or Change Order (NASA)
ETCO .... European Transplant Coordinators Organization (SAUS)
ETCO .... External Tanks Corporation (SAUO)
ETCOM .... European Testing and Certification for Office and Manufacturing Protocol (OSI)
ETCP .... Engineering Technical Change Package (MCD)
ETCR .... Equivalent Effective Temperature Corrected for Radiation (PDAA)
ETCR .... Estimated Time of Crew's Return
ETCRRM .... Electronic Teleprinter Cryptographic Regenerative Repeater Mixer (NATG)
ETCS .... Electronics Technician, Senior Chief [*Navy rating*]
ETCS .... Electronic Throttle Control System [*Automotive engineering*]
ETCS .... Engine Temperature Control System
ETCS .... European Train Control System [*Indian Railway*] (TIR)
ETCS .... External Threshold Clutter Select (ACAE)
ETCSi .... Electronic Throttle Control System with Intelligence [*Automotive engines*]
ETCTA .... Electrical Trades' Commercial Travellers' Association [*British*] (BI)
ETCX .... Tennessee Eastern Railroad [*Federal Railroad Administration identification code*]
ETCX .... Tennessee Eastman [*Private rail car owner code*]
ETD .... Economics and Technology Division [*Environmental Protection Agency*] (GFGA)
ETD .... Effective Transfer Date [*Military*] (AFM)
ETD .... Electrical Terminal Distributor (KSC)
ETD .... Electric Typewriter Division (SAUS)
ETD .... Electronic Tactical Display [*Military*]
ETD .... Electronic Theses and Dissertation [*Database*]
ETD .... Electronic Time Delay
ETD .... Electronic Transfer Device (SAUS)
ETD .... Embedded Temperature Detector (IAA)
ETD .... End of Train Device (SAUS)
ETD .... Energy Technologies Division (SAUO)
ETD .... Engineering Technology Division (SAUS)
ETD .... Engineering Test Directive
ETD .... English Teaching Division (SAUS)
ETD .... Ensemble Threshold Detector (ACAE)
ETD .... Environments and Threats Directorate [*Army*]
ETD .... Equipment Technical Director (MCD)
ETD .... Equivalent Transmission Density [*Photography*] (OA)
ETD .... Estimated [*or Expected*] Time of Departure
ETD .... Estimated Turnover Date (MCD)
ETD .... Etude
ETD .... Eustachian Tube Dysfunction [*Medicine*] (MELL)
ETD .... Event Time Digitizer
ETD .... Expected Time of Departure (RIMS)
etd .... Expected to Depart (SAUS)
ETD .... Experiment Test Document (ACAE)
ETD .... Exploratory Battery Technology Development and Testing (SAUS)
etd .... extension trunk dialing (SAUS)

ETD .... Extension Trunk Dialling (SAUS)
ETD .... External Tank Door (MCD)
ETDAIP .... Experimental Technology Development and Application Incentives Program (SAUS)
ETDAS .... Early Treatment Diabetic Retinopathy Study (SAUS)
ETDB .... Energy Technology Database (SAUS)
Etd Br .... Ethidium Bromide [*Trypanocide*] [*Also, EB, ETB*] [*Biochemical analysis*]
ETDC .... EADAS [*Engineering and Administrative Data Acquisition System*] Traffic Data Center [*Bell System*]
ETDC .... Electrotechnical Division Council (SAUO)
ETDCFRL .... European Training and Development Center for Farming and Rural Life (SAUS)
ETDCFRL .... European Training and Development Centre for Farming and Rural Life (EA)
ETDD .... Electrical Time Division Demultiplexer (SAUS)
ETDD .... Electrical Time Division Demultiplexer/Demultiplexing (SAUS)
ETDD .... Electrical Time Division Demultiplexing (SAUS)
ETDE .... Energy Technology Data Exchange [*Department of Energy*] (GFGA)
ETDE .... Experimental Target Designation Equipment
ETDI .... Electronic Trade Data Interchange (VLIE)
ETDI .... Eurasian Target Data Inventory [*File*] (MCD)
ETDL .... Electronics Technology and Devices Laboratory [*Fort Monmouth, NJ*] [*Army*] (RDA)
ETDM .... Electrical Time Division Multiplexer (SAUS)
ETDM .... Electrical Time Division Multiplexer/Multiplexing (SAUS)
ETDM .... Electrical Time Division Multiplexing (SAUS)
E-TDMA .... Enhanced Time Division Multiple Access (CGWS)
E-TDMA .... Extended Time Division Multiple Access [*Telecommunications*] (ACRL)
ETDN .... Dresden [*Germany*] [*ICAO location identifier*] (ICLI)
ETDN .... Electronic Ticket Delivery Network [*Travel industry*] (TRID)
ETDP .... Emergency Traffic Disposition Plan [*Military*]
ETDP .... Expert Tsunami Database for the Pacific [*Marine science*] (OSRA)
ETDRS .... Early Treatment Diabetic Retinopathy Study
ETDS .... Elapsed Time Distribution System (MCD)
ETDS .... Electronic Theft Detection System (SAUS)
ETDT .... Extrusion Trim and Drill Template
ETD-transistor... easy to drive transistor (SAUS)
ETE .... Earth-to-Earth (SEWL)
ETE .... Earth Trailing Edge (ACAE)
ETE .... Educational and Training Establishment [*Military*] [*British*]
ETE .... Effluent Thermal Effect (IAA)
ETE .... Electrical Technician Electrician (SAUS)
ET/E .... Electrical Technician/Electrician (AAG)
ETE .... Electromagnetic Test Environment (MCD)
ETE .... Electronic Test Equipment
ETE .... Electrothermal Engine
ETE .... Electrothermal Excitation (SAUS)
ETE .... electrothermical evaporation (SAUS)
ETE .... Emergency Transceiver Equipment
ETE .... End to End (NASA)
ETE .... Engineering Support Test Equipment [*Deep Space Instrumentation Facility, NASA*]
ETE .... Engineering Test Equipment (CAAL)
ETE .... Engineering Test Evaluation (AAG)
ETE .... Engineering Thermoplastic Elastomers (SAUS)
ETE .... Engineering Time Estimate
ETE .... Engineer Training Establishment (SAUO)
ETE .... Enhanced Tactical Fighter Engineering (MCD)
ETE .... Entry to Exit (SAUS)
ETE .... Estimated Time En Route
ETE .... Estimated Time of Ejection (SAUS)
Ete .... Eterna [*Record label*] [*Germany*]
ETE .... Evacuation-Time Estimated (ODA)
ETE .... Even Transversal Electric (SAUS)
ETE .... Expected Time Enroute (SAUS)
ETE .... Expendable Threat Emitter (DWSG)
ETE .... Expendable Turbine Engine
ETE .... Experimental Tunneling Establishment [*British*]
ETE .... External Telecommunications Executive (IAA)
ETE .... External Test Equipment (IAA)
ETE .... Metemma [*Ethiopia*] [*Airport symbol*] (OAG)
ETEC .... Effective Thermal Expansion Coefficient
ETEC .... Electronic Truck Engine Control System [*Automotive engineering*]
ETEC .... Electro-Technology (journ.) (SAUS)
ETEC .... Energy Technology (SAUS)
ETEC .... Energy Technology Engineering Center [*Canoga Park, CA*] [*Department of Energy*] (GRD)
ETEC .... Enteroinvasive Escherichia Coli (ADWA)
ETEC .... Enterotoxigenic Escherichia coli [*Water pollution indicator*]
ETEC .... Equal Tension Containment [*Tire design*]
ETEC .... Etec Systems, Inc. [*NASDAQ symbol*] (SAG)
ETEC .... European Timber Exporters Convention (SAUO)
ETEC .... European Timber Exportes Convention (SAUS)
ETEC .... Expendable Turbine Engine Concept (ACAE)
ETEC .... Extension Trunk Dialing [*Telecommunications*] (PDAA)
ETEC-E .... Electronics & Telecommunications Evaluation Center - Europe (SAUS)
ETECG .... Electronics Test Equipment Coordination Group [*Military*]
EtecSys .... Etec Systems, Inc. [*Associated Press*] (SAG)
ETEDES .... Electromagnetic Test Environment Data System (SAUS)
ETEDM .... End-to-End Data Management (SAUS)
ETEDS .... Electromagnetic Test Environment Data System
ETEE .... Educational Technologies for European Enterprises (SAUO)
ETEF .... Erfurt [*Germany*] [*ICAO location identifier*] (ICLI)
ETEK .... E-Tek Dynamics, Inc. [*NASDAQ symbol*] (NASQ)
ETEMA .... Education Technology and Equipment Manufacturing Association (AIE)
ETEMA .... Engineering Teaching Equipment Manufacturers Association (SAUS)
ETEMA .... European Terrestrial Ecosystem Modelling Activity (SAUS)
ETEN .... European Teacher Education Network (SAUO)
ETER .... East Troy Electric Railroad Museum [*Federal Railroad Administration identification code*]
ETER .... Epichlorohydrin-Ethylene Oxide-Allylglycidyl Ether Terpolymer (SAUS)
ETER .... Estimated Time en Route (ACAE)
eter .... estimated time enroute (SAUS)
ETES .... Early Training Estimation System (ACAE)
E-TES .... Earth-Orbiting Thermal Emission Spectrometer (SAUS)
ETES .... European Television Service (SAUS)
ETES .... Exotic Threat Emitter System (SAUS)
ET/EST .... Engineering Test / Expanded Service Test [*Military*]
Et Ex .... Etudes et Expansion (EA)
ETEX .... European Tracer Experiment (SAUS)
E-Text .... Electronic Text
ETF .... Earth Terminal Facility (CCCA)
ETF .... Eastern Task Force
ETF .... Eastfield Resources [*Vancouver Stock Exchange symbol*]
ETF .... Economic Transactions Framework
ETF .... Education Task Force [*Government Documents Round Table*] [*American Library Association*]
ETF .... Effluent Treatment Facility
ETF .... Eglin Test Facility [*Florida*] [*NASA*] (KSC)
ETF .... Electronically Tunable Filter
ETF .... Electronic Time Fuze (SAUS)
ETF .... Electronic Toll Fraud (SAUS)
ETF .... Electronic Transfer of Funds (SAUO)
ETF .... Electronic Tuning Fork
ETF .... Electron Transfer Flavins (SAUS)
ETF .... Electron-Transferring Flavoprotein [*Biochemistry*]
etf .... electron-transferring flavorprotein (SAUS)
ETF .... Electrothermal Filter
ETF .... Embryo Toxic Factor [*Medicine*]
ETF .... Emerging Markets Telecommunications Fund [*NYSE symbol*] (SAG)
ETF .... Engineering Test Facility (SAUS)
ETF .... Engine Test Facility [*Arnold Air Force Base, TN*] [*Air Force*] (MCD)
ETF .... Enhanced Tactical Fighter (MCD)
ETF .... Enhanced-Technology Fighter (MCD)
ETF .... Enriched Text Format (SAUS)
ETF .... Environmental Task Force (EA)
ETF .... Environmental Test Facility [*Fort Huachuca, AZ*] [*United States Army Electronic Proving Ground*] (GRD)
ETF .... Equipment Test Facility (SAUS)
ETF .... Error Threshold Firing (ACAE)
ETF .... Estimated Time of Flight
ETF .... European Technology Facility (EURO)
ETF .... European Training Foundation [*EC*] (ECED)
ETF .... European Transfer Format (SAUS)
ETF .... Eustachian Tube Function [*Medicine*]
ETF .... Evaluation Task Force [*Defunct*] (EA)
ETF .... Exchange-Traded Fund
ETF .... Explosives Testing Facility (SAA)
ETF .... Export Task Force (EA)
ETFA .... Engine Test Facility Addition (SAUS)
ETFA .... European Technological Forecasting Association (PDAA)
ETFC .... Ernest Tubb Fan Club (EA)
ETFD .... Electronic Toll Fraud Device (SAUS)
ETFE .... Ethylene-Tetrafluoroethylene [*Organic chemistry*]
ETFE .... Ethylene-Tetrafluoroethylene Copolymer (EDCT)
ETFE .... ethyl-tetrahydro-furfuryl ether (SAUS)
ETFIR .... Emergency Task Force for Indochinese Refugees [*Defunct*] (EA)
ETFL .... Each Thousand Foot Level (FAAC)
ETFL .... Friedland [*Germany*] [*ICAO location identifier*] (ICLI)
ETFO .... Electronics Technical Field Office [*FAA*]
ETFRN .... European Tropical Forest Research Network (EERA)
ETFRN Newsletter... ETFRN (European Tropical Forest Research Network) Newsletter (SAUS)
ETFS .... East Texas Financial Services, Inc. [*NASDAQ symbol*] (SAG)
ETFS .... Electronic Countermeasure Transmitter Frequency Set Up [*Military*] (IAA)
ETFS .... Exchange-Traded Funds
ETFT .... enhancement-mode thin-film transistor (SAUS)
ETG .... Eatonton [*Georgia*] [*Seismograph station code, US Geological Survey*] (SEIS)
ETG .... Eclipse Task Group (SAUS)
ETG .... Electrical Test Group (NRCH)
ETG .... Electrical Thermal Generators (KSC)
ETG .... Electronics Training Group (SAUS)
ETG .... Electronic Target Generator [*Military*] (DA)
ETG .... Electronic Thickness Gauge
ETG .... Electronic Training Group (SAUS)
ETG .... Electronic Truck Governor [*Cummins Engine*] [*Automotive engineering*]
ETG .... Electronic Turbine Governor
ETG .... Electrothermal Gun
ETG .... Emulation Test Generator (SAUS)
ETG .... Enhanced Target Generator (CTAS)
ETG .... Enterprise Transaction Gateway [*Computer science*] (VERA)
ETG .... Environmental Technologies Group
ETG .... European TrainingGroup (SAUO)

ETG............ EWOS Technical Guide (SAUS)
ETG............ External Thermal Garment
ETG............ Keating, PA [*Location identifier*] [*FAA*] (FAAL)
ETGCR........ Exogenous Triglyceride Clearance Rate [*Medicine*]
etgm........... estimate to get money (SAUS)
Etgom.......... European Teaching Group of Orthopaedic Medicine (SAUO)
ETGS........... East Tennessee Geological Society (SAUO)
ETGS........... Edge Tool Grinders' Society [*A union*] [*British*]
ETGT........... Equal To or Greater Than
ETGTS......... Electronic Text and Graphics Transfer System
ETH............ Elat [*Israel*] [*Airport symbol*] (OAG)
ETH............ Elixir Terpin Hydrate [*Pharmacy*]
ETH............ Error Trap Handling [*Military*]
ETH............ Ethan Allen Interiors, Inc. [*NYSE symbol*] (SPSG)
ETH............ Ethanol [*or ethyl alcohol*] [*Organic chemistry*] (DAVI)
eth............ Ether (AAMN)
Eth............ Ether [*Medicine*] (EDAA)
eth............ Ethic (SAUS)
eth............ ethical (SAUS)
ETH............ Ethics
ETH............ Ethionamide [*Medicine*] (EDAA)
ETH............ Ethiopia [*ANSI three-letter standard code*] (CNC)
Eth............ Ethiopia (VRA)
Eth............ Ethiopian (ADWA)
ETH............ Ethiopian Airlines Corp. [*ICAO designator*] (FAAC)
eth............ Ethiopic [*MARC language code*] [*Library of Congress*] (LCCP)
ETH............ Ethmoid [*Medicine*] (EDAA)
eth............ ethmoid (SAUS)
eth............ ethmoidal (SAUS)
eth............ ethnic (SAUS)
ETH............ Ethnology [*Medicine*] (EDAA)
ETH............ Ethrane [*Medicine*] (EDAA)
ETH............ Ethyl (SAUS)
Eth............ Ethylene (RIMS)
ETH............ Extraterrestrial Hypothesis
ETH............ Wheaton, MN [*Location identifier*] [*FAA*] (FAAL)
ETH ACET.... Ethyl Acetate (SAUS)
EthanAln...... Ethan Allen Interiors, Inc. [*Associated Press*] (SAG)
ethanol........ ethyl alcohol or grain alcohol (SAUS)
ETH/C.......... Elixir Terpin Hydrate with Codeine [*Pharmacy*]
ETHC........... Ethical Holdings Ltd. [*NASDAQ symbol*] (SAG)
ETHCY......... Ethical Holdings Ltd ADS [*NASDAQ symbol*] (TTSB)
ETHD........... Heringsdorf [*Germany*] [*ICAO location identifier*] (ICLI)
eth dat......... ethic dative (SAUS)
ETHEL.......... European Tritium Handling Experimental Laboratory (SAUS)
EthEnoch...... Ethiopic Book of Enoch [*A publication*] (BJA)
ether........... ethyl ether (SAUS)
Ethernet....... Xerox Local Area Network System (SAUO)
EtherTalk..... Adaptation der AppleTalk-Architektur (SAUS)
Eth Eud........ Ethica Eudemia [*of Aristotle*] [*Classical studies*] (OCD)
ETHIC.......... Electric Trace Heating Industry Council [*British*] (DBA)
EthicHld....... Ethical Holdings Ltd. [*Associated Press*] (SAG)
ETHICS........ Effective Technical and Human Implementation of Computer Systems [*Implementation methodology*] (NITA)
ETHICS........ ETH Library Information Control System (SAUS)
Ethiop......... Ethiopia (SAUS)
ETHIOP........ Ethiopic [*Language, etc.*] (ROG)
ETHN........... Ethnic Studies Library (SAUS)
Eth Nic......... Aristotle's Nicomachean Ethics [*A publication*] (DLA)
Eth Nic......... Ethica Nicomachea [*of Aristotle*] [*Classical studies*] (OCD)
ethno.......... ethnology (SAUS)
ethnoc......... ethnocide (SAUS)
Ethnog......... Ethnographer (SAUS)
ETHNOG....... Ethnography (ADA)
Ethnog......... Ethnography (DIAR)
ethnog......... ethnography (SAUS)
ethnograph... ethnography (SAUS)
ETHNOL....... Ethnological (SAUS)
ethnol.......... Ethnologist (ADWA)
Ethnol.......... Ethnology (DIAR)
ETHNOL....... Ethnology
ethnol.......... ethnology (SAUS)
ethnomus.... ethnomusicologist (SAUS)
ethnomus.... ethnomusicology (SAUS)
ethnomusi... ethnomusicologist (SAUS)
ethnomusi... ethnomusicology (SAUS)
ethnophaul... ethnophaulism (SAUS)
ethnosci....... ethnoscience (SAUS)
ETHO........... Ethylene Oxide [*Organic chemistry*] (KSC)
ethog........... ethogram (SAUS)
ethog........... ethographer (SAUS)
ethog........... ethographic (SAUS)
ethog........... ethography (SAUS)
ETHOL......... Ethanol (IDYL)
ethol........... Ethology
ETHOS......... European Telematics Horizontal Observatory Service (EURO)
ETHPA......... Epoxytetrahydrophthalmic Anhydride (SAUS)
ETHRC......... East Timor Human Rights Committee (EA)
ETHSX......... EV Worlwide Health Sciences Cl.A [*Mutual fund ticker symbol*] (SG)
Ethyl........... Ethyl Corp. [*Associated Press*] (SAG)
ETI.............. Economically-Targeted Investment
ETI.............. Economics & Technology, Inc. [*Telecommunications service*] (TSSD)
ETI.............. Economic Thickness of Insulation (SAUS)
ETI.............. Educational Travel Incorporated (SAUO)
ETI.............. Education and Training Institute (SAUS)
ETI.............. Education Technology Institute (SAUS)
ETI.............. Education Turnkey Institute (SAUS)
ETI.............. Effective Thyroxine Index (SAUS)
ETI.............. Ejection Time Index (MELL)
ETI.............. Elapsed-Time Indicator
ETI.............. Electric Test Installation
ETI.............. Electric Tool Institute [*Later, Power Tool Institute*] (EA)
ETI.............. Electrochemical Time Indicator [*Army*] (MCD)
ETI.............. Electronic Technical Institute (EA)
ETI.............. Emerging Technologies Initiative (SAUS)
ETI.............. Employment and Training Institute [*University of Wisconsin-Milwaukee*]
ETI.............. Encapsulated Toroidal Inductor
ETI.............. Endotracheal Intubation [*Medicine*] (MELL)
ETI.............. Engine Test Information
ETI.............. Environmental Technology Initiative [*Environmental Protection Agency*]
ETI.............. Environmental Teratology Information [*Department of Energy*] [*Information service or system*] (IID)
ETI.............. Environmental Transporters, Inc. (EFIS)
ETI.............. Equipment and Tool Institute (EA)
ETI.............. Estimated Information (FAAC)
ETI.............. Estimated Time of Interception
ETI.............. European Toy Institute (EAIO)
ETI.............. European Transuranium Institute [*Germany*]
ETI.............. Executive Tours International
ETI.............. Executor and Trustee Institute [*Australia*]
ETI.............. Exhaust Trail Indicator [*Military*] (NVT)
ETI.............. Expert Center for Taxonomic Identification [*The Netherlands*] (EERA)
ETI.............. Extended Terminal Interface (SAUS)
ETI.............. Extraction Tool Insert
ETI.............. Extraterrestrial Intelligence
ETIA............ European Tape Industry Associaton (PDAA)
ETIBS.......... Enhanced Tactical Information Broadcast System (SAUO)
ETIC............ English-Teaching Information Center [*British Council*] (PDAA)
ETIC............ Environmental Technical Information Center (SAUS)
ETIC............ Environmental technology information center (SAUS)
ETIC............ Environmental Teratology Information Center [*Department of Energy*] (IID)
ETIC............ Estimated Time for Completion (COE)
ETIC............ Estimated Time in Commission [*Army*] (AABC)
E ticket........ Electronic Ticket [*Travel industry*] (TRID)
ETICS.......... Ebara Technical Information Control System (SAUS)
ETICS.......... Embedded Tactical Information Control System (SEWL)
ETIF............ Employer Identification Number Taxpayer Information File [*IRS*]
ETIG............ Equine Tetanus Immune Globulin (MELL)
ETIH............ Error Terminate Interrupt Handler (MCD)
ETII............. External-to-Internal Interface (MCD)
ETIL............ East Tennessee Indian League (SAUS)
ETIM........... Elapsed Time [*Aviation*] (FAAC)
E-time......... Execution Time (CDE)
E-TIME........ Execution Time (VLIE)
ETIMR......... Electric Target Intermediate Marksmanship Range
ETIMS......... Electron Transfer Ionization Mass Spectroscopy (MCD)
ET INT AL.... Et Inter Alia [*And Among Others*] [*Latin*] (ROG)
etio............ etiocholandone (SAUS)
ETIO........... Etiocholanolone [*A pyrogen*] [*Medicine*] (MAE)
etio............ etiology (SAUS)
Etiol........... Etiology (AMHC)
etiol........... Etiology [*Therapy term*] (CTAA)
ETIOL......... Etiology
ETIP........... East Turkestan Islamic Party [*Government term*] (GA)
ETIP........... Experimental Technology Incentives Program [*National Institute of Standards and Technology*]
ETIP........... Experiment Technology Incentives Program (SAUS)
ETIPT......... Environmental Technology Integrated Process Team
ETIR........... Environmental Thermal Infrared
ETIS........... Elapsed Time Indicator System (SAUS)
ETIS........... Environmental Technical Information System [*Army*] [*Information service or system*] (IID)
ETIs........... Environmental Tolerance Indices (SAUS)
ETIS........... European Technical Information Service [*Information broker and database originator*] (NITA)
ETIS........... European Telecommunications Informatics Services (EURO)
ETIS........... Extruded Tunnel Lining System (SAUS)
ETISALAT..... Emirates Telecommunications Corp. Ltd. [*Telecommunications service*] (TSSD)
ETIS-MARFO... ETIS in machine readable (SAUS)
ETIS-MARFO... ETIS [*European Technical Information Service*] in Machine Readable For m (NITA)
ETIS-MARFO... ETTS in machine readable form (SAUS)
ETIS-MARFO... European and Technical Information Service in Machine-Readable Form (SAUS)
ETIS-MARFO... European Economic and Technical Information Service in Machine-Readable (SAUS)
ETIYRA........ El Toro International Yacht Racing Association (EA)
ETJ............. extraterritorial jurisdiction (SAUS)
ETJC........... Engineering Trades' Joint Council [*British*] (DCTA)
ETK............. Eicosanoyl(trifluoroacetyl)kanamycin [*Antiviral*]
ETK............. Electron Tube Klystron
ETK............. Embedded Toolkit for Windows [*Computer science*] (MWOL)
ETK............. Embryonic Turkey Kidney
ETK............. Entek Oil & Gas [*Vancouver Stock Exchange symbol*]
ETK............. Erythrocyte Transketolase (DB)
ETK............. Expected Time to Kill [*Military*] (ACAE)

ETK .... Explosive Testing Kit (MCD)
ETKM .... Every Test Known to Man [*or Mankind*] [*Medicine*] (CPH)
ETKZ .... Kyritz [*Germany*] [*ICAO location identifier*] (ICLI)
ETL .... Earliest Time to Launch [*Navy*] (CAAL)
ETL .... Eastern Lights Resources Ltd. [*Vancouver Stock Exchange symbol*]
ETL .... Eastern Trunk Line (IAA)
ETL .... Educational Technology Language [*University of Western Ontario*] [*Canada*] (NITA)
ETL .... Effective Testing Loss [*Telecommunications*] (TEL)
ETL .... Electrical Testing Laboratory [*Portsmouth Naval Shipyard, NH*]
ETL .... Electric Traction Line (SAUS)
ETL .... Electrolytic Tinning Line (PDAA)
ETL .... Electronic Technology Laboratory [*Air Force*] (MCD)
ETL .... Electronic Testing Laboratories (SAUO)
ETL .... Electrotechnical Laboratory (MCD)
ETL .... Emergency Time Limit
ETL .... Emergency Tolerance Limit (SAUS)
ETL .... Emitter Follower Transistor Logic [*Electronics*] (IAA)
ETL .... Ending Tape Label [*Computer science*] (BUR)
ETL .... Endorsed Tools List (SAUS)
ETL .... Energy Technology Programs (SAUS)
ETL .... Engineering Test Laboratory (AAG)
ETL .... Engineer Technical Letter [*Army Corps of Engineers*]
ETL .... Engineer Topographic Laboratories [*Fort Belvoir, VA*] [*Army*] (MCD)
ETL .... Engineer Topographic Laboratory (SAUS)
ETL .... Environmental Technology Laboratory [*Environmental Research Laboratories*] (USDC)
ETL .... Environmental Test Laboratory [*Jet Propulsion Laboratory, NASA*]
ETL .... Envrionmental Technology Laboratory (SAUS)
ETL .... Epitaxial Transistor Logic (SAUS)
ETL .... Equipment Test Laboratory (ACAE)
ETL .... Ericsson Telephones Limited, London (SAUO)
ETL .... [*The*] Essex Terminal Railway Co. [*AAR code*]
ETL .... Etching by Transmitted Light
ETL .... European Testing Laboratory (SAUS)
ETL .... Explosive Transfer Lines [*Military*]
ETL .... Extract, Transform, Load (SAUS)
ETL .... Patterson Aviation Co. [*ICAO designator*] (FAAC)
ETLA .... Extended Three Letter Acronym
ETLARS .... Electronics and Telecommunications Literature Analysis Retrieval System [*Computer science*] (IID)
ETLC .... Extraction Thin-Layer Chromatography (DB)
ETLG .... Enable This Level Group [*Computer science*] (MHDI)
ETLL .... Educational Technology and Language Learning (AIE)
ETLM .... Leipzig/Mockau [*Germany*] [*ICAO location identifier*] (ICLI)
ETLO .... Equipment Transfer or Loan Order
ETLOW .... External Tank Lift-Off Weight [*NASA*] (NASA)
ETLS .... Leipzig [*Germany*] [*ICAO location identifier*] (ICLI)
ETLT .... Equal To or Less Than
ETLX .... Export Tank Lines [*Private rail car owner code*]
ETM .... Educational Training Material (MCD)
ETM .... Elaborately-Transformed Manufacture
ETM .... Elapsed-Time Meter
ETM .... Electrically Transmitted Message
ETM .... Electrical Tactical Map
ETM .... Electrical Time Measurement
ETM .... Electronics Technician's Mate [*Navy rating*]
ETM .... Electronic Telephone Manager (SAUS)
ETM .... Electronic Test and Maintenance (IAA)
ETM .... Electronic Test and Measurement (MCD)
ETM .... Electro-Thermomigration (SAUS)
ETM .... Elemental Time Monitor (PDAA)
ETM .... Element Test and Maintenance (CIST)
ETM .... Embedded Training Material [*Military*]
ETM .... Emery Testing Machine [*Nineteenth-century hydraulic testing machine*] (RDA)
ETM .... Ending Tape Maker (SAUS)
ETM .... End of Tape Marker [*Computer science*] (IAA)
ETM .... Energy Transfer Module [*Aviation*] (MCD)
ETM .... Engineering Test Model (KSC)
ETM .... Engineering Test Motor (SAUS)
ETM .... Enhanced Thematic Mapper [*Geoscience*]
ETM+ .... Enhanced Thematic Mapper Plus (SAUS)
ETM .... Enhanced Timing Module (IEEE)
ETM .... Entercom Communications'A' [*NYSE symbol*] (SG)
ETM .... Enter Trapping Mode (SAA)
ETM .... Erythromycin [*Also, E, ERY, ERYC*] [*Antibacterial compound*]
ETM .... Escrowed to Maturity [*Finance*]
ETM .... Ethylenethiuram Monosulfide (SAUS)
ETM .... Even Transversal Magnetic (IAA)
ETM .... Exchange Telephone Manager (SAUS)
ETM .... Excise Tax Memoranda [*Revenue Canada - Customs and Excise*] [*Information service or system*] (CRD)
ETM .... Experimental Test Model (IAA)
ETM .... Extension Training Management [*Military*] (INF)
ETM .... Extension Training Materials [*Army*]
ETM .... Extension Training Memorandum [*Civil Defense*]
ETM .... External Technical Memorandum
ETM .... External Tympaniformic Membrane (SAUS)
ETM .... External Tympaniform Membrane [*Zoology*]
ETM .... Extraterrestrial Material
ETM .... Transportes Aereos Tamaulipas, SA de CV [*Mexico*] [*FAA designator*] (FAAC)
ETMA .... Educational Television for the Metropolitan Area
ETMA .... Elapsed Time/Maintenance Action (MCD)
ETMA .... Engineering Tooling Manufacturing Aid (ACAE)
ETMA .... English Timber Merchants' Association (BI)
ETMA .... European Television Magazines Association (SAUO)
ETMA-A .... Engineering Tooling and Manufacturing Aide (SAUS)
ETMB .... Electrical Techniques in Medicine and Biology (MCD)
ETMC .... European Telephone Marketing Council [*of the European Direct Marketing Organization*] [*Jona, Switzerland*] (EA)
ETMD .... Essential Technical Medical Data
ETMD .... Extendable Tubular Member Device [*Aerospace*]
ETMD .... Extended Thematic Mapper Derivative (SAUS)
ETME .... [*The*] European Turf Management Exhibition [*British*] (ITD)
ETMF .... Elapsed Terminal Measurement Facility (VLIE)
ETMF .... Elapsed Time Multiprogramming Factor
ETMF .... Execution Time Multiplication Factor (SAUS)
ETMF .... Extended Telecommunications Modules Feature (VLIE)
ETMG .... Electron Tube Management Group (SAA)
ETMG .... Magdeburg [*Germany*] [*ICAO location identifier*] (ICLI)
ETMO .... Education, Training, and Military Operations (SAUS)
ETMOD .... Environmental Tritium Model (SAUS)
ETMP .... Enhanced Terrain Masked Penetration (TIMI)
ETMPA .... East Tennessee Minority Professionals Association (SAUO)
ETMS .... Earth Terminal Measurement System (SAUS)
ETMS .... Enhanced Traffic Management System [*FAA*] (TAG)
ETMS .... Ernst Toller Memorial Society [*Later, ISSE*] (EA)
ETMSDG .... East Tennessee Mass Spectrometry Discussion Group (SAUO)
ETMSR .... Electronics Technician's Mate, Ship Repair [*Navy rating*]
ETMT .... Ethoxy(trichloromethyl)thiadiazole [*Fungicide*]
ETMWG .... Electronic Trajectory Measurements Working Group [*IRIG*] [*Range Commanders Council*] [*White Sands Missile Range, NM*]
ETMX .... Entertrainment Line [*Federal Railroad Administration identification code*]
ETN .... Eastern Technical Net [*Air Force*]
ETN .... Eastland, TX [*Location identifier*] [*FAA*] (FAAL)
ETN .... Eaton Corp. [*NYSE symbol*] (SPSG)
ETN .... Educational Telecommunications Network
ETN .... Educational Telephone Network [*University of North Dakota*] [*Grand Forks*] (TSSD)
ETN .... Education Teleconferencing Network (SAUS)
ETN .... Electrical Terminal Nut
ETN .... Electronics Technician, Communications [*Navy rating*]
ETN .... Electronic Tandem Network (ACRL)
ETN .... engineering test notice (SAUS)
ETN .... Equipment Table Nomenclature (AFM)
ETN .... Equivalent to New (VLIE)
ETN .... Erythrityl Tetranitrate [*Medicine*] (MELL)
Etn .... Ethanol (SAUS)
Etn .... Ethanolamine [*Also, EA, OLAMINE*] [*Organic chemistry*]
ETN .... Extension Teleconferencing Network [*Texas A & M University*] [*College Station, TX*] [*Telecommunications service*] (TSSD)
ETN1 .... Electronics Technician, Communications, First Class [*Navy rating*] (DNAB)
ETN2 .... Electronics Technician, Communications, Second Class [*Navy rating*] (DNAB)
ETN3 .... Electronics Technician, Communications, Third Class [*Navy rating*] (DNAB)
ETNA .... East Timor News Agency
ETNA .... Electrolevel-Theodolite Naval Alignment System (SAUS)
ETNA .... Electronic-Theodolite Naval Alignment
ETNAM .... European Theater Network Analysis Model (MCD)
ET-NANBH .... Enterically Transmitted Non-A, Non-B Hepatitis [*Medicine*]
ETNA System .... Electrolevel-Theodolite Naval Alignment System (SAUS)
ETNF .... Estimated Time to Next Failure (MCD)
ETNG .... East Tennessee Natural Gas (SAUS)
ETNP .... Eastern Tropical North Pacific Sea
ETNS .... Electronic Train Number System (PDAA)
ETNSA .... Electronics Technician, Communications Seaman Apprentice [*Navy rating*]
ETNSN .... Electronics Technician, Communications Seaman [*Navy rating*]
EtNu .... ethylnitrosourea (SAUS)
ETNVT .... Edinaia Tovarnaia Nomenklatura Vneshney Torgovli [*Commodity nomenclature system used in international trade*]
ETO .... Earth-to-Orbit (SEWL)
eto .... electric truck operator (SAUS)
ETO .... Electronics Technology Office (SAUS)
ETO .... Electronic Temperature Offset
ETO .... Electronic Temperature Offsetting (SAUS)
ETO .... Electronic Trading Opportunity (SAUS)
ETO .... Emergency Test Operation
ETo .... endotoxine (SAUS)
ETO .... Energy Technology Office [*Department of Energy*] (OICC)
ETO .... Engineer-to-Order (GART)
ETO .... Ephemeris-Tuned Oscillator
ETO .... Equalized Transmission Only [*Communications term*] (DCT)
ETO .... Equipment Transfer Order (SAUS)
ETO .... Essentials-Tools-Objects [*Apple*] (VERA)
ETO .... ESSO [*Standard Oil*] Turbo Oil
ETO .... Estimated Takeoff (KSC)
ETO .... Estimated Time Off
ETO .... Estimated Time of Operations [*NASA*] (KSC)
ETO .... estimated time of overfly (SAUS)
ETO .... Estimated Time of Ovulation [*Gynecology*]
ETO .... Estimated Time Over (SAUS)
ETO .... Estimated Time Over Significant Point (SAUS)
ETO .... Ethylene Oxide [*Organic chemistry*]
ETO .... European Telecommunications Office (DDC)

ETO .... European Theater of Operations [*World War II*]
ETO .... European Transportation Organization (SAUS)
ETO .... European Transport Organization [*ECE*]
ETO .... Eustachian Tube Obstruction [*Medicine*]
ETO .... Evadale, TX [*Location identifier*] [*FAA*] (FAAL)
ETO .... Exchange-Traded Option
ETO .... Expiration of Term of Obligation [*Military*]
ETO .... Explosive Test Operator (RDA)
ETO .... Express Transportation Order [*Army*] (AABC)
ETO .... extended time observations (SAUS)
ETO .... Extensive Time Observations (ACAE)
ETOA .... Estimated Time of Arrival (MELL)
E-to-B .... Emulsion to Base (VLIE)
ETOC .... Electronic Table of Contents Service (SAUS)
ETOC .... Emergency Technical Operations Center [*DoD*]
ETOC .... Estimated Time of Correction [*NASA*] (KSC)
ETOC .... Estimated Time Out of Commission
ETOC .... Expected Total Operating Cost (PDAA)
E-to-E .... Electronics-To-Electronics (WDMC)
E-to-E .... Emulsion to Emulsion (VLIE)
E to E .... End to End [*Telecommunications*]
ETOFY .... Elvis, This One's for You Fan Club (EA)
ETOG .... European Technical Operations Group
Et OH .... estimated turn around point (SAUS)
Et OH .... estimated turning point (SAUS)
ETOH .... Ethanol (SAUS)
ETOH .... Ethyl Alcohol [*or Ethanol*]
Et OH .... extra temporal perception (SAUS)
ETOL .... Evil Twin On Line (SAUS)
ETOM .... Electron Trapping Erasable Optical Memory (SAUS)
ETOM .... Electron Trapping Optical Memory [*Computer science*]
ETOMA .... Environmental Threshold of Measurement Accuracy
ETOMEP .... European Technical Office for Medicinal Products (SAUO)
ETON .... Eton, MO [*American Association of Railroads railroad junction routing code*]
ETOP .... Engineering Technical Operating Procedure
ETOP .... Environmental Threat and Opportunity Profile
ETOP .... Extended-Range Twin-Engine Operation [*Aviation*]
ETOPS .... Engines Turn Or Passengers Swim (SAUS)
ETOPS .... Extended Range Twinjet Operation [*Aviation*] (DA)
ETOPS .... Extended Range Twin Operations (SAUS)
ETOPS .... Extended Twin-engine Operations (SAUS)
ETOPS .... Extended Twin-Engine Over Water Operations [*OST*] (TAG)
ETOS .... Extended Tape Operating System (BUR)
ETO Signal ... Electronic Temperature-Offsetting Signal (SAUS)
ETOT .... Estimated Time Over Target
ETOUSA .... European Theater of Operations, United States Army [*Pronounced "ee-too-sah"*] [*World War II*]
ETOV .... Estimated Time Over [*Aviation*] (FAAC)
ETOW .... Eastern Theater of War (SAUS)
ETown .... E'Town Corp. [*Formerly, Elizabethtown Water*] [*Associated Press*] (SAG)
ETOX .... Ethylene Oxide [*Organic chemistry*] (MAE)
ETP .... Early Termination of Pregnancy (ADWA)
ETP .... Eastern Tennis Patrons (EA)
ETP .... Eastern Tropical Pacific [*Marine science*] (OSRA)
ETP .... Eastern Tropical Pacific Ocean
ETP .... East Timor Project [*Defunct*] (EA)
ETP .... Eccentricity, Tilt, Precession [*Oceanography*]
ETP .... Education and Training Program (SAUS)
ETP .... Effluent Treatment Plant (PDAA)
ETP .... Elastomeric Thermoplastic [*Organic chemistry*]
ETP .... Elastometric Thermoplastic
ETP .... Electrical Tough Pitch [*Copper*]
ETP .... Electrolytic Tough-Pitch [*Copper grade*]
ETP .... Electronic Tape Printer (IAA)
ETP .... Electronic Technical Publishing (IAA)
ETP .... Electronic Tough Pitch [*Copper*] (NITA)
ETP .... Electron Temperature Probe
ETP .... Electron Transfer [*or Transporting*] Particle
ETP .... Electron Transfer Process (SAUS)
ETP .... Electron Transport Particle (SAUS)
ETP .... Electron Tube Panel
ETP .... Elevated Training Platform
ETP .... Eligible Termination Payment (ADA)
ETP .... Eltopia [*Washington*] [*Seismograph station code, US Geological Survey*] (SEIS)
ETP .... Embedded Training Package (SAUS)
ETP .... Emergency Technology Program [*Oak Ridge National Laboratory*]
ETP .... Emergency Tour Plot (SAUS)
ETP .... Emissions Trading Policy [*Environmental Protection Agency*] (GFGA)
ETP .... Empire Test Pilots School [*British*] [*ICAO designator*] (FAAC)
ETP .... Engineering Test Plan (SAUS)
ETP .... Engineering Test Program [*NASA*] (KSC)
ETP .... Engineering Thermoplastic [*Plastics technology*]
ETP .... Engineered Technical Products (SAUS)
ETP .... Engine Test Panel [*Aerospace*] (AAG)
ETP .... Enterprise Oil [*NYSE symbol*] (SPSG)
ETP .... Enterprise Oil ADS [*NYSE symbol*] (TTSB)
ETP .... Entire Transaction Propagator (HODG)
ETP .... Entire Treatment Period [*Medicine*]
ETP .... Environmental Technology Programs (SAUS)
ETP .... Environmental Test Program (AAG)
ETP .... Environmental Training Project [*World Wildlife Fund-United States*]
ETP .... Ephedrine, Theophylline and Phenobarbital [*Medicine*] (MELL)
ETP .... Equal Time Point
ETP .... Equipment Test Plan (NASA)
ETP .... Equi-Time Point (SAUS)
ETP .... Equivalent Top Product
ETP .... Estimated Time of Penetration (SAUS)
ETP .... Estimated Turnaround Point
ETP .... Estimated Turning Point (SAUS)
ETP .... European Telecommunications Platform (SAUO)
ETP .... European Training Programme in Brain and Behavior Research [*of the European Science Foundation*] [*France*] (EA)
ETP .... European Training Programme in Brain and Behaviour Research (SAUO)
ETP .... European Trunking Plan (SAUS)
ETP .... Eustachian Tube Pressure [*Medicine*] (MAE)
ETP .... Evaluation Test Plan
ETP .... Executive Training Programme (WDAA)
ETP .... Experimental Test Procedure (MCD)
ETP .... Exportable Training Package [*Army*]
ETP .... Extended Tape Processing (IAA)
ETP .... Extended Term Plan (BUR)
ETP .... Extended Transaction Processing (SAUS)
ETP .... Exterior Thermoplastic
ETP .... External Tracking Processor (ACAE)
ETP .... Potential Evapotranspiration [*Hydrology*]
ETPA .... Electronically Tunable Parametric Amplifier
ETPA .... Emergency Technical Provisions Act of 1976
ETPAE .... Ethyl-Terminated Polyarylene Ether [*Organic chemistry*]
ETPB .... Ethyltrioxaphosphabicyclooctane (SAUS)
ETPBBR .... European Training Programme in Brain and Behavior Research [*of the European Science Foundation*] [*France*] (EAIO)
ETPC .... Electrolytic Tough-Pitch Copper (AAEL)
ETPCC .... European Technical Pneumatic Controls Commission (SAUO)
ETPCUG .... East Tennessee Personal Computer Users Group (SAUO)
ETPD .... Emerging Technology Program Database (SAUS)
ETPD .... Essential Tremor and Parkinson's Disease [*Neurophysiology*]
ETPD .... Estimated Time of Parachute Deployment (MUGU)
ETPE .... Elevated Temperature Polyethylene
ETPI .... Eastern Telecommunications Philippines, Inc. [*Manila*]
ETPL .... Endorsed Tempest Products List (SEWL)
ETPMI .... East Tennessee Project Management Institute (SAUS)
ET-PNL .... Engine Test Panel [*Aerospace*] (AAG)
ETPO .... Eastern Tropical Pacific Ocean (SAUS)
ETPO .... European Trade Promotion Organization (DS)
ETPPr .... Enterprise Oil Pref'A'ADS [*NYSE symbol*] (TTSB)
ETPPrB .... Enterprise Oil Pref 'B' ADS [*NYSE symbol*] (TTSB)
ETPR .... Engineering Test Part Release (SAA)
ETPR .... Execution Time Print Routing (SAUS)
ETPRO .... Employment Tax Problem Resolution Off (SAUS)
ETPS .... Educational Theorem Proving System (IDAI)
ETPS .... Empire Test Pilots' School [*British*]
ETPS .... Engineering Test Program Spares (SAA)
ETPS .... Enterprise (SAUS)
ETPS .... Experimental Test Pilot School (SAUS)
ETPY .... Electronic Control Assembly - Thrust Vector, Pitch and Yaw (IAA)
ETQ .... Education, Training and Qualifications Committee (ACII)
ETQAP .... Education and Training in Quality Assurance Practices [*American Society for Quality Control*] (NRCH)
ETQR .... External Total Quality and Reliability (AAEL)
ETR .... Early Token Release [*Computer science*]
ETR .... Eastern Test Range [*See also ESMC*] [*Air Force*]
ETR .... Easygrowth Treasury Receipts (SAUS)
ETR .... Easy-to-Reach (SAUS)
ETR .... Education, Training and Research Associates (EA)
ETR .... Effective Tax Rate
etr .... effective thyroid ratio (SAUS)
ETR .... Effective Thyroxinbinding Ratio (SAUS)
ETR .... Effective Thyroxine Ratio [*Medicine*]
ETR .... Effective Transmission Rate (SAUS)
ETR .... Elapsed Time Recorder (SAUS)
ETR .... Electric Target Range (SAUS)
ETR .... Electronically Tuned Receiver
ETR .... Electronics Technician, (RADAR) [*Navy rating*]
ETR .... Electronic Toll Route
ETR .... Electronic Trouble Report
ETR .... Electron Transfer Reaction (SAUS)
ETR .... Electron Transport Rate [*Physical chemistry*]
ETR .... Electron Tube Rectifier
ETR .... Element Test Review (SAUS)
ETR .... Embedded Training Requirement [*Military*]
ETR .... Emergency Tension Retractor [*Mercedes Benz*] [*Automotive engineering*]
ETR .... Emergency Treatment Record (MELL)
ETR .... Employer Trip Reduction [*Environmental Protection Agency*]
ETR .... Encrypted Traffic Report (CET)
ETR .... End of Track [*Electronics*] (ECII)
ETR .... End-of-Treatment Response [*Medicine*]
ETR .... Energy Test Reactor
ETR .... Engineered to Reliance (SAUS)
ETR .... Engineering Test Reactor
ETR .... Engineering Test Record (IAA)
ETR .... Engineering Test Request [*NASA*] (KSC)
ETR .... Engineer Technical Letter [*ACE*] (AAGC)
ETR .... Engine Transaction Report (NVT)
ETR .... Entergy Corp. [*NYSE symbol*] (SPSG)
ETR .... Environmental Test Report

ETR .... Epitympanic Recess [*Medicine*] (DAVI)
ETR .... Equal Transit Rate (ADWA)
ETR .... Equipment Temporarily Removed (MCD)
ETR .... Erient Resources, Inc. [*Vancouver Stock Exchange symbol*]
ETR .... Estates and Trusts Reports (SAFN)
ETR .... Estimated Time of Repair (NG)
ETR .... Estimated Time of Restoral (SAUS)
ETR .... Estimated Time of Restore (SAUS)
ETR .... Estimated Time of Return
ETR .... Estimated Time to Repair (SAUS)
etr .... Etcher [*MARC relator code*] [*Library of Congress*] (LCCP)
ETR .... Ethylthioribose [*Biochemistry*]
Etr .... Etruria (ADWA)
Etr .... Etruscan (SAUS)
ETR .... ETSI Technical Report (SAUO)
ETR .... Evansville Terminal [*Federal Railroad Administration identification code*]
ETR .... Execution Time Ratio (SAUS)
ETR .... Expected Time of Response
ETR .... Expected Time of Return (SAUS)
ETR .... Experimental Test Reactor [*Nuclear energy*] (OA)
ETR .... Experiment Tape Recorder (SAUS)
ETR .... Export Traffic Release
ETR .... Export Transport Release
ETR .... Extended Temperature Range (IAA)
ETR .... External Technical Report
ETR .... External Timing Register
ETR1 .... Electronics Technician, (RADAR), First Class [*Navy rating*] (DNAB)
ETR2 .... Electronics Technician, (RADAR), Second Class [*Navy rating*] (DNAB)
ETR3 .... Electronics Technician, (RADAR), Third Class [*Navy rating*] (DNAB)
ETRA .... Eastern Test Range [*Formerly, Atlantic Missile Range*] [*Air Force*]
ETRA .... East Tennessee Resource Agency (SAUS)
etra .... electronic radar (SAUS)
ETRA .... Estimated Time to Reach Altitude
ETRA .... Excise Tax Reduction Act
ETRAC .... Enhanced Tactical RADAR Correlator [*Military*]
e-trader .... Electronic Trader (ADWA)
ETRC .... Educational Television and Radio Center [*Later, EBC*]
ETRC .... Engineering Test Reactor Critical (SAUS)
ETRC .... Engineering Test Reactor Critical Facility
ETRC .... Entree Corp. [*NASDAQ symbol*] (COMM)
ETRC .... Equitrac Corp. [*NASDAQ symbol*] (SAG)
ETRC .... Expected Total Remnant Costs
ETRCF .... Engineering Test Reactor Critical Facility (SAUS)
Etr Cities .... [*The*] Etruscan Cities and Rome [*A publication*] (OCD)
ETR-CX .... Engineering Test Reactor Critical Assembly (SAUS)
ETRE .... Entre Computer Centers, Inc. [*NASDAQ symbol*] (COMM)
ETREC .... English Language Teaching Resource Centre (SAUS)
ETRI-PEC .... Electronics and Telecommunications Research Institute-Protocol Engineering Center (VLIE)
ETRIS .... Eastern Test Range Instrumentation Ship (DNAB)
ETRJC .... Etter Junction, TX [*American Association of Railroads railroad junction routing code*]
ETRL .... Environmental Toxicology Research Laboratory [*National Environmental Research Center*]
ETRM .... External Tank Rocket Motor
ETRO .... Estimated Time of Return to Operation [*Military*] (AFM)
ETRO .... Estimated Time to Return to Operational Status (SAUS)
ETROD .... Eastern Test Range Operations Directive [*Air Force*] (NASA)
ETRP .... Education and Training Programme (SAUO)
ETRP .... Engineering Test and Rework Plan (ACAE)
ETRP .... Exploratory Technology Research Program (SAUS)
ETRR .... Export Traffic Release Request [*MTMC*] (TAG)
ETRS .... Employee Time Reporting System (FOTI)
ETRs .... Encrypted Traffic Reports (SAUS)
ETRS .... European Tissue Repair Society
ETRs .... Execution Time Ratios (SAUS)
ETRSA .... Electronics Technician, (RADAR) Seaman Apprentice [*Navy rating*]
ETRSN .... Electronics Technician, (RADAR) Seaman [*Navy rating*]
ETRT .... Electronically Tuned Receiver Tuner
ETRTO .... European Technical Rim and Tyre Organisation (PDAA)
ETRTO .... European Tyre and Rim Technical Organisation [*Belgium*]
ETRU .... Emergency Target Relay Unit (MCD)
Etru .... Etruria (VRA)
Etrus .... Etruscan (DIAR)
ETRX .... Arkansas Power and Light [*Private rail car owner code*]
ETRY .... East Tennessee Railway [*Federal Railroad Administration identification code*]
ETRY .... Eatery
etry .... entirely (SAUS)
ETS .... Board of Education for the City of Etobicoke [*UTLAS symbol*]
ETS .... East Stroudsburg State College, East Stroudsburg, PA [*OCLC symbol*] (OCLC)
ETS .... Econometric Time-Series [*Computer program*] (PCM)
ETS .... Ecumenical Theological Seminary (EA)
ETS .... Educational Talent Search (EA)
ETS .... Educational Teleconference System [*University of Missouri - Columbia*] [*Telecommunications*] (TSSD)
ETS .... Educational Television Stations [*National Association of Educational Broadcasters*] (AEBS)
ETS .... Educational Testing Service (EA)
ETS .... Educational Time-sharing System (SAUS)
ETS .... Educational Training Service (SAUO)
ETS .... Educational TV Services [*Oklahoma State University*] [*Stillwater*] (TSSD)
ETS .... Edwards Test Station [*NASA*]
ETS .... Effective Time Slice (SAUS)
ETS .... Effective Tip Speed (SAUS)
ETS .... EIB Tool Software (SAUS)
ETS .... Electrical Test Set (SAUS)
ETS .... Electrical Test Setup [*NASA*] (KSC)
ETS .... Electrical Transcranial Stimulation (DIPS)
ETS .... Electro Depositors Technical Society (SAUO)
ETS .... Electrodepositors Technical Society (SAUO)
ETS .... Electronics Technician (Sonar) [*U.S. Navy enlisted rating*] (AUER)
ETS .... Electronic Tandem Switching [*Telecommunications*] (TEL)
ETS .... Electronic Teleaccounting System (SAUS)
ETS .... Electronic Telegraphic System (SAUS)
ETS .... Electronic Telegraph Service (SAUS)
ETS .... Electronic Telegraph System
ETS .... Electronic Test Set
ETS .... Electronic Test Stand
ETS .... Electronic Test Station
ETS .... Electronic Test Systems (SAUS)
ETS .... Electronic Timing Set
ETS .... Electronic Torque Split [*Automotive engineering*]
ETS .... Electronic Tracking System (TIMI)
ETS .... Electronic Traction System [*Automotive engineering*]
ETS .... Electronic Trading System (GART)
ETS .... Electronic Translation System (SAUS)
ETS .... Electronic Translator System [*Bell System*]
ETS .... Electronic Typing System (VLIE)
ETS .... Electron Transmission Spectroscopy
ETS .... Electron Transport System
ETS .... electron tunneling spectroscopy (SAUS)
ETS .... Elementary Transition System (VLIE)
ETS .... Elmwood Taco and Sub (SAUS)
ETS .... Elucidatio Terrae Sanctae (BJA)
ETS .... Embedded Tool Suite (SAUS)
ETS .... Emergency Telecommunications Service (SAUS)
ETS .... Emergency Telephone Service
ETS .... Emergency Temporary Standard [*OSHA*]
ETS .... Emergency Transponder System (SAUS)
ETS .... Emerging Technologies Services [*Telecommunications*] (OTD)
ETS .... Emissions Tracking System [*Environmental Protection Agency*] (EPAT)
ETS .... Empire Telecommunications [*British*] [*World War II*]
ETS .... Employment Transfer Scheme [*British*]
ETS .... Endless Tangent Screw
ETS .... Energy Transfer System (MCD)
ETS .... Energy Transmission System [*Automotive engineering*]
ETS .... Engagement Tracking Station (SAA)
ETS .... Engagement Training Simulator (SAUS)
ETS .... Engineered Time Standards (NG)
ETS .... Engineering and Technical Service (AFM)
ETS .... Engineering Tactical System
ETS .... Engineering Task Summary (SAUS)
ETS .... Engineering Test Satellite
ETS .... Engineering Time Standards [*Navy*] (NVT)
ETS .... Engineering Time Study (MCD)
ETS .... Engine Test Stand [*Nevada*] [*Seismograph station code, US Geological Survey*] [*Closed*] (SEIS)
ETS .... Engine Test Stands [*NERVA program*]
ETS .... English Text-to-Speech
ETS .... Enquiry Terminal System [*International Computers Ltd.*]
ETS .... Entry Terminal System (VLIE)
ETS .... Environmental Technical Specifications (NRCH)
ETS .... Environmental Technology Seminar (EA)
ETS .... Environmental Testing Section [*Social Security Administration*]
ETS .... Environmental Test Specification (IEEE)
ETS .... Environmental Tobacco Smoke [*Industrial hygiene term*] (OHS)
ETS .... Environmental Transfer Service, Inc. (EFIS)
ETS .... Environment Table Simulation (SAA)
ETS .... Episcopal Theological School
ETS .... Equal Time Spacing
ETS .... Equipment Training School (SAUO)
ETS .... Equivalent Target Size (SAA)
ETS .... Equivalent Time Sampling (SAUS)
ETS .... Estimated Time of Sailing [*Navigation*]
ETS .... Estimated Time of Separation [*Military*] [*Slang*]
ETS .... ETS International, Inc. [*Vancouver Stock Exchange symbol*]
et s .... Et Suivants [*And Following*] [*French*] (ILCA)
ETS .... European Telecommunications Standard (OSI)
ETS .... European Telecommunications Systems (SAUS)
ETS .... European Telefon System (SAUS)
ETS .... European Telephone Service (CCCA)
ETS .... European Telephone System [*DoD*]
ETS .... European Teratology Society (EA)
ETS .... European Treaty Series [*Council of Europe*] [*A publication*] (DLA)
ETS .... European Troop Strength (DOMA)
ETS .... European Trust Services (EURO)
ETS .... Evaluated Testbed System (SSD)
ETS .... Evaluation Test Specification
ETS .... Evaluation Trainers
ETS .... Evaluator Trainer System (ACAE)
ETS .... Evangelical Theological Society (EA)
ETS .... Evangelical Tract Society [*British*] (DBA)
ETS .... Event Time Simulator (SAUS)

ETS .... Excited Triplet State [*Electronics*] (AAEL)
ETS .... Executable Test Suite (SAUS)
ETS .... Exercise Thallium Scintigraphy [*Medicine*] (ODA)
ETS .... Exhaust-Gas Turbo-Supercharger
ETS .... Expected Time of Sailing (RIMS)
ets .... Expected to Sail (SAUS)
ETS .... Expeditionary Test Set (MCD)
ETS .... Experimental Technical Satellite (SAUS)
ETS .... Experimental Test Site (SAUS)
ETS .... Expiration of Term of Service [*Military*]
ets .... expiration of time of service (SAUS)
ETS .... Expiration Term of Service [*Army*]
ETS .... Expiration Time of Service (SAUS)
ETS .... External Tank System (MCD)
ETS .... External Time-Sharing (IAA)
ETS .... External Transcribed Spacer [*Genetics*]
ETS .... Extramural Tracking System (SAUS)
ETS .... Extra Telecoms Service [*British*]
ETS .... Earth Thermal Storage (ODA)
ETSA .... Educators'-Employers' Tests and Services Associate (AEBS)
ETSA .... Electricity Trust of South Australia [*State*] (EERA)
ETSA .... electron transport system activity (SAUS)
ETSA .... English Table Soccer Association (DBA)
ETSA .... Ethyl Trimethylsilylacetate [*Organic chemistry*]
ETSA .... European Textiles Services Association (EURO)
ETSA .... Seaman Apprentice, Electronics Technician, Striker [*Navy rating*]
ETSACI .... Electronic Tandem Switching Adminstration Channel Interface (SAUS)
ETSAL .... Electronic Terms for Space Age Language
ETSC .... East Tennessee State College [*Later, East Tennessee State University*]
ETSC .... East Texas State College [*Later, East Texas State University*]
ETSC .... Electrically-Excited Thermally-Stimulated Current
ETSC .... Electronic Technical Support Center [*DiagSoft*]
ETSC .... Emergency Technical Services Corporation (SAUO)
ETSC .... Employment and Training Service Center (EA)
ETSC .... Engineering Teratechnology Steering Committee (SAUO)
ETSC .... European Telecommunications Standardization Institute (SAUO)
ETSCA .... English Toy Spaniel Club of America (EA)
ETSCO .... Engineering and Technical Societies Council (SAUO)
ETSD .... Education and Training Support Detachment [*Military*] (DNAB)
ETSD .... Enhanced Thermionically Supported Discharge [*Materials technology*]
ETSE .... Echo Track & Significance Estimator (SAUS)
ETSE .... Engineering Test Support Equipment (SAA)
ETSEP .... External Tank Separation [*NASA*] (NASA)
et seq .... And The Following [*A notation*] (WDMC)
ET SEQ .... Et Sequens [*or Et Sequentes, Et Sequentia*] [*And the Following*] [*Latin*]
et seqq .... Et Sequentes [*And the Following*] [*Latin*] (BARN)
ETSF .... Educational Testing Service File (SAUS)
ETSF .... Educational Testing Service Test Collection File (EDAC)
ETSF .... Electronic Trading Standard Format (SAUS)
ETSG .... Elevated Temperature Strain Gauge
ETSI .... Energy Transportation Systems, Inc.
ETSI .... European Telecommunications (SAUS)
ETSI .... European Telecommunications Standards Institute
ETSI .... European Telecommunications Standards Institution (SAUS)
ETSI .... European Telecommunication Standardization Institute (SAUS)
ETSI .... Executive Telecom System, Inc. [*Database producer*] (IID)
ETSIC .... Educational Testing Service Test Collection (SAUS)
ETS Int .... ETS International, Inc. [*Associated Press*] (SAG)
ETSL .... Estimated Total Shelf Life (OA)
ETSMA .... European Tyre Stud Manufacturers Association (PDAA)
ETSN .... Seaman, Electronics Technician, Striker [*Navy rating*]
ETSO .... Extended Time-Sharing Option (SAUS)
ETSP .... Entitled to Severance Pay
ETSP .... Eurasian Tree Sparrow [*North American bird banding code*] (BIBA)
ETSP .... Evaluation of Testing in Schools Project (AIE)
ETSPL .... Equivalent Threshold Sound Pressure Level
ETSPL .... Extended Telephone System (SAUS)
ETSPL .... Extended Telephone Systems Programming Language [*Computer science*] (MHDB)
ETSQ .... Electrical Time, Superquick
ET SQQ .... Et Sequens [*or Et Sequentes, Et Sequentia*] [*And the Following*] [*Latin*]
ETSR .... Extraterrestrial Solar Spectral Irradiance (ADWA)
ETSREQ .... Engineering and Technical Services Request (ACAE)
ETSS .... Electronic Tandem Switching System (SAUS)
ETSS .... Electronic Telecommunication Switching System (MCD)
ETSS .... Engineering and Technical Services Specialist [*DoD*]
ETSS .... Engineering Time-Sharing System (SAUS)
ETSS .... Entry Time-Sharing System [*IBM Corp.*] [*Computer science*]
ETSS .... Evaluation of Total System Survivability (MCD)
ETSS .... Experimental Time-Sharing System (SAUS)
ETSS .... Extended Training Service Specialist [*Environmental science*] (COE)
ETSS .... External Tank Separation Subsystem [*NASA*] (NASA)
ETSSC .... ERADCOM [*Electronics Research and Development Command*] Tactical Software Support Center (MCD)
ETSSP .... ETS Status Panel (SAUS)
ETST .... Electronic Technical Suitability Test
ETST .... Engineering Test-Service Test (SAUS)
ET/ST .... Engineer Test/Service Test [*Aerospace*]
ETST .... English Test, Spelling Test (SAUS)
ETSTAC .... East Tennessee Special Technology Access Center (SAUS)
ETSTC .... East Texas State Teachers College (SAUO)
ETSTC .... Educational Testing Service Test Collection (IID)
ETSU .... East Tennessee State University [*Formerly, East Tennessee State College*]
ETSU .... East Texas State University [*Formerly, East Texas State College*]
ETSU .... Energy Technology Support Unit at Harwell [*British*]
ETSV .... Eastern Tennessee Seismic Zone [*Geology*]
ETS-VIII .... Engineering Test Satellite-VIII [*Developed to study geostationary satellite bus technologies*]
ETT .... Early Thrust Termination
ETT .... Easy to Test [*Audiology*]
ETT .... Efficiency Tracer Technique (SAUS)
ETT .... Elapsed Time Totalizer (ACAE)
ETT .... ElderTrust SBI [*NYSE symbol*] (SG)
ETT .... Electromagnetic Thickness Tool [*Gas well*]
ETT .... Electronically Tuned Tuner
ETT .... Electronic Tensile Tester
ETT .... Electron Tube, Triode
ETT .... Electrothermal Thrusters (SAUS)
ETT .... Elizabethan Theatre Trust (SAUS)
ETT .... End of Tape Test [*Computer science*]
ETT .... Endotracheal Tube [*Medicine*]
ETT .... Environmental Treatment & Technologies Corp. (MHDW)
ETT .... Epinephrine Tolerance Test [*Medicine*] (MELL)
ETT .... Equipment Task Time
ETT .... Estimated Time of Track
ETT .... Estimated Travel Time [*Army*] (AABC)
ETT .... Etaiyapuram [*India*] [*Geomagnetic observatory code*]
ETT .... Etana Tech Corp. [*Vancouver Stock Exchange symbol*]
ETT .... European Telecomunications and Technology (SAUO)
ETT .... Evasive Target Tank [*Army*] (RDA)
ETT .... Excess Travelling Time
ETT .... Exercise Tolerance Test [*Medicine*]
ETT .... Exercise Treadmill Test [*Cardiology*] (DAVI)
ETT .... Expected Test Time
ETT .... Explosion Tear Test [*Military*]
ETT .... Extended Time Tests
ETT .... Extraction/Transformation/Transport [*Computer science*] (GART)
ETT .... Extrathyroidal Thyroxine [*Endocrinology*] (MAE)
ETT .... Extrusion Trim Template
etta .... electronic temperature trip and alarm (SAUS)
ETTA .... English Table Tennis Association
ETTA .... Evangelical Teacher Training Association [*Later, ETA*] (EA)
Ett Ad .... Etting's American Admiralty Jurisdiction [*A publication*] (DLA)
ETTC .... Engine Test Technology Centre [*Worcester, England*]
ETTC .... Environmental Technology Technical Council
ETTC .... Environmental Technology Transfer Committee (BCP)
ETTC .... Estimated Total Target Cost
ETTDC .... Electronics Trade and Technology Development Corporation (SAUO)
ETTI .... Eastern Tufted Titmouse [*North American bird banding code*] (BIBA)
ETTI .... EcoTyre Technologies [*NASDAQ symbol*] (TTSB)
ETTI .... EcoTyre Technologies, Inc. [*NASDAQ symbol*] (SAG)
ETTI .... End Translation Time Indicator (IAA)
ETTI .... European Technology Transfer Initiative (EURO)
ETTIW .... EcoTyre Technologies Wrrt [*NASDAQ symbol*] (TTSB)
ETTM .... Electronic Toll and Traffic Management [*Highway engineering*]
ETTM .... Electronic Tolls and Traffic Management (PS)
ETTM .... Electronic Tool and Traffic Management
ETTM .... Expanded Tactical Telemetry (ACAE)
ETTN .... Etryol Trinitate (SAUS)
ETTN .... European Technology Transfer Network (EURO)
ETTO .... Extractor Tool
ETTP .... East Tennessee Technology Park (SAUS)
ETTP .... Etch Template [*Tool*] (AAG)
ETTR .... Estimated Time to Repair (SAUS)
ETTS .... Edge Tool Trade Society [*A union*] [*British*]
ETTU .... English Table Tennis Union (SAUO)
ETTU .... European Table Tennis Union (EA)
ETTUC .... European Teachers Trade Union Committee [*EC*] (ECED)
ETTX .... East Texas Transportation [*Federal Railroad Administration identification code*]
ETU .... East Traverse Mountains [*Utah*] [*Seismograph station code, US Geological Survey*] (SEIS)
ETU .... Electrical Trades Union [*British*]
ETU .... Electronic Text Unit (SAUS)
ETU .... Electronic Translator Unit [*Telecommunications*]
ETU .... Electronic Unit
etu .... electron tube (SAUS)
ETU .... Emergency and Trauma Unit
ETU .... Emergency Treatment Unit
ETU .... Employment and Training Unit [*Work Incentive Program*]
ETU .... Engineering Test Unit
ETU .... Enhanced Telephone Unit
ETU .... Erection Timing Unit
ETU .... Ethylene Thiourea [*Organic chemistry*]
Etu .... Etude [*Record label*]
ETU .... European Trade Union Institute (SAUO)
ETU .... European Triathlon Union (EA)
ETU .... Expected Total Utility
ETUC .... European Trade Union Confederation [*Formerly, ECFTU*]
ETUCF .... European Trade Union of Food and Allied Workers (SAUS)
ETUCO .... European Trade Union College (EURO)
ETUCTCL .... European Trade Union Committee for Textiles, Clothing, and Leather [*Belgium*] [*Belgium*] (EAIO)
ETUC Youth ... European Trade Union Confederation-Youth (SAUO)
ETUDE .... English Teachers in University Departments of Education (AIE)

ETUDE .... European Trade Union Distance Education (EURO)
ETUI .... European Trade Union Institute [Belgium]
ETUI .... European Trans-Uranium Institute [Karlsruhe, Germany]
ETUT .... Enhanced Tactical User Terminal (DOMA)
ET UX .... Et Uxor [And Wife] [Latin]
ETV .... E4L, Inc. [NYSE symbol] (SG)
ETV .... Educational Television
ETV .... Ejection Test Vehicle (NG)
ETV .... Electric Test Vehicle [Department of Energy]
ETV .... Electric Transfer Vehicle (SAUS)
ETV .... Electronic Training Village (EURO)
ETV .... Electronic Transfer Vehicle [MTMC] (TAG)
ETV .... Electrothermal Vaporization
ETV .... Elevating Transfer Vehicle (PDAA)
ETV .... Engineering Television Mode
ETV .... Engineering Test Vehicle (KSC)
ETV .... Engine Test Vehicle (SAUS)
ETV .... Environmental Technology Verification Program (EPAT)
ETV .... Epitaxial Tuning Varactor
ETV .... Epitaxial Tuning Vector (SAUS)
ETV .... Europaeischer Tabakwaren-Grosshandels-Verband [European Tobacco Wholesalers' Union] (EAIO)
ETVA .... External Tank Vent Arm (MCD)
ETVC .... Environmental Test Vacuum Center (SAA)
ETVCS .... Electronic Three-Vortex Control System
ETVG .... European Tumour Virus Group (EAIO)
Et Vir .... Et Viri [And Husband] [Latin]
ETVM .... Electrostatic Transistorized Voltmeter
ETVP .... Engineering Test Vehicle Program (SAUO)
ETVS .... Educational Television by Satellite (NTCM)
ETVS .... Enhanced Terminal Voice Switching [FAA] (TAG)
ETW .... Early Threat Warner (SAUS)
ETW .... Effectiveness Training for Women [A course of study]
etw .... empty tank weight (SAUS)
ETW .... End of Tape Warning [Computer science] (CET)
etw .... end-of tape warning (SAUS)
ETW .... Enemy Throw Weight (ACAE)
ETW .... Entertainment This Week [TV program]
ETW .... Equipment Trials Wing [Military] [British]
ETW .... Equivalent Test Weight [Automotive emissions]
ETW .... Error Time Word (KSC)
ETW .... E'town Corp. [Formerly, Elizabethtown Water] [NYSE symbol] (SPSG)
ETW .... European Transonic Wind-Tunnel
ETW .... European Trans-Sound Wind Tunnel (SAUS)
ETW .... Executive Television Workshop [New York, NY]
ETW .... New Town, ND [Location identifier] [FAA] (FAAL)
ETWA .... English Tiddlywinks Association (DBA)
ETWN .... East Tennessee & Western North Carolina Railroad Co. [AAR code]
ETWN .... Wriezen [Germany] [ICAO location identifier] (ICLI)
ETWTC .... European Tire and Wheel Technical Conference (SAUS)
ETX .... East Texas, PA [Location identifier] [FAA] (FAAL)
ETX .... Eburnetoxin [Biochemistry]
ETX .... End of Text [Computer science]
ETX .... End of Text Character [Communications term] (DCT)
etx .... end of text character (SAUS)
ETX .... End of Transmission (GAVI)
ETX .... End of Transmission Text (SAUS)
ETX .... European Air Taxi [British] [FAA designator] (FAAC)
ETX/ACK .... End-of-Text/Acknowledge [Computer science] (MHDB)
ETX Character... End of Text Character (SAUS)
ETXR .... End of Text Exit Routine (SAUS)
ETY .... Equivalent Taxable Yield (EBF)
ety .... Etymology [or Etymologist] (WGA)
ETY .... Finnish Energy Economy Association (SAUO)
ETYA .... Eicosatetraynoic Acid [Organic chemistry]
ETYM .... Etymological (SAUS)
Etym .... Etymology [Medicine] (EDAA)
etym .... Etymology (SHCU)
ETYM .... Etymology [or Etymologist]
Etym Magn... Etymologicum Magnum [Twelfth century AD] [Classical studies] (OCD)
Etymol .... Etymology
ETYP .... Engine Type [Automotive emissions]
E-type .... Jungian extrovert type (SAUS)
ETyre .... EcoTyre Technologies, Inc. [Associated Press] (SAG)
ETYS .... eToys, Inc. [NASDAQ symbol] (SG)
ETZ .... Eastern Time Zone (SAUS)
ETZ .... Electron Transparent Zone [Biochemistry]
ETZ .... Etz Lavud Ltd. [AMEX symbol] (SPSG)
ETZ .... Etz Lavud Ltd Ord [AMEX symbol] (TTSB)
ETZ .... Nantucket, MA [Location identifier] [FAA] (FAAL)
ETZA .... Etz Lavud Ltd 'A' [AMEX symbol] (TTSB)
EtzLav .... Etz Lavud Ltd. [Associated Press] (SAG)
EtzLv .... Etz Lavud Ltd. [Associated Press] (SAG)
EU .... Agri-residue Utilized for Energy supply (SAUS)
E/U .... Edges Untouched [Publishing] (DGA)
EU .... Edinburgh University (SAUO)
EU .... Ehime University (SAUO)
EU .... Ehrlich Unit [Laboratory] (DAVI)
EU .... Ehrlich Units [Clinical chemistry]
EU .... Ejector Unit (MCD)
EU .... Electronics Unit (SAUS)
EU .... Electronic Unit
EU .... Electron Unit
EU .... Elms Unlimited [Superseded by ERI]
EU .... Embarkation Unit (SAUS)
EU .... Emergency Unit (CPH)
EU .... Emission Unilateral (SAUS)
EU .... Emory University (SAUO)
EU .... Emotionally Unstable (MELL)
EU .... Empresa Ecuatoriana de Aviacion [Ecuador] [ICAO designator] (ICDA)
EU .... Emulator Program (IAA)
EU .... Endotoxin Unit [Clinical chemistry]
EU .... End-User [Computer science]
EU .... Energy Unit (IAA)
EU .... Engineering Unit (MCD)
EU .... Engineering Use
E/U .... Engineer/User [Aerospace] (AAG)
EU .... enriched uranium (SAUS)
eu .... Entropy Unit (ABAC)
EU .... Entropy Unit
EU .... Enzyme Unit [Analytical biochemistry]
EU .... Episcopalians United (EA)
EU .... Equatorial Undercurrent [Marine science]
eU .... Equivalent Uranium
EU .... Erection Unit
EU .... Error Unavoidable
EU .... Esterase Unit (DB)
E-U .... Etats-Unis [United States] [French]
EU .... Ethical Union (SAUO)
EU .... Ethnic United [An association] (EA)
EU .... Ethyleneurea [Organic chemistry]
EU .... Etiology Unknown [Medicine] (MELL)
Eu .... Euler Number [IUPAC] [Fluid mechanics]
Eu .... Euler unit (SAUS)
EU .... Europe
EU .... European Union [Formerly, European Community]
Eu .... Europium [Chemical element]
Eu .... Eustace (SAUS)
Eu .... Eustatia (SAUS)
EU .... Euthroid [Endocrinology] (DAVI)
EU .... Evacuation Unit [Army]
EU .... Evangelical Union [British]
EU .... Exchange Unit (SAUS)
EU .... Exchange, Unlimited (DNAB)
EU .... Excretory Urogram [Radiology] (DAVI)
EU .... Execution Unit [Computer science]
EU .... Expected Utility
EU .... Experience Unit
EU .... Experimental Unit (NASA)
EU .... Exponent Underflow (SAUS)
EU .... Exposed Uninfected [Medicine]
eu .... external upset (SAUS)
EU .... Extremadura Unida [Spain] [Political party] (EY)
Eu .... Norwich Pharmacal Co. [Research code symbol]
EUA .... Eastern Underwriters Association [Later, ISO]
EUA .... Eastern Utilities Associates [NYSE symbol] (SPSG)
EUA .... Electrical Utility Application (IAA)
EUA .... Erase Unprotected to Address (VLIE)
EUA .... Estados Unidos Americanos [United States of America] [Spanish]
EUA .... Eua Tonga Island [South Pacific] [Airport symbol] (OAG)
EUA .... Europe Air [France] [ICAO designator] (FAAC)
EUA .... European Area Headquarters [Red Cross]
EUA .... European Units of Account [Economics]
EUA .... European University of America (SAUO)
EUA .... Examination under Anesthesia [Medicine]
eua .... examination under anesthetic (SAUS)
EUA .... Examine Under Anesthesia (SAUS)
EUA .... exam under anesthesia (SAUS)
EUA .... Exchange Users Association (EA)
EUA .... Executive Unit of Account (WDAA)
EUA .... Extended User Area [Computer science]
EUA .... Extended User Authentication [Computer science]
EUA .... Faculty of Library Science, University of Alberta [EDUCATSS] [UTLAS symbol]
EUAC .... Equivalent Uniform Annual Cost
EUADC .... End User Application Development Center (VLIE)
EUAEM .... European Congress on Electron Microscopy (SAUS)
EUAIS .... European Union of Arab and Islamic Studies [See also UEAI] (EAIO)
EUB .... Alberta Energy and Utilities Board (SAUO)
EUB .... Emergency Utility Building (NRCH)
EUB .... Energy and Utilities Board (SAUS)
EUB .... Essential User Bypass. Communications (SAUS)
EUB .... Estados Unidos do Brasil [United States of Brazil] [Portuguese]
EUB .... Evangelical United Brethren [Church]
EUB .... School of Library Service, Dalhousie University [EDUCATSS] [UTLAS symbol]
EUBL .... Europa Unuigo de Blindaj Laboruloj (SAUO)
EUBS .... European Underseas Bio-Medical Society (EAIO)
EUBU .... Eurasian Bullfinch [North American bird banding code] (BIBA)
EUC .... Emergency Unemployment Compensation [Account]
EUC .... End Use Check
EUC .... End-User Certificate
EUC .... End User Computing [AT & T]
EUC .... Enhanced/Extended UNIX Code (SAUS)
EUC .... Equatorial Undercurrent [Marine science] (MSC)
EUC .... Equivalent Uranium Content (SAUS)
Euc .... Euclid [Second century BC] [Classical studies] (OCD)

EUC............. Euclidean [*Mathematics*]
EUC............. Euclid R. R. [*AAR code*]
EUC............. Eureka Canyon [*California*] [*Seismograph station code, US Geological Survey*] (SEIS)
EUC............. Eurocontrol [*Belgium*] [*ICAO designator*] (FAAC)
EUC............. European Union of Coachbuilders (EA)
EUC............. Extended Unit Cell (SAUS)
EUC............. Extended Unix Code (VLIE)
EUC............. Library Studies Program, Concordia University [*EDUCATSS*] [*UTLAS symbol*]
EUCA........... European Federation of Associations of Coffee Roasters (EA)
EUCA........... European Federation of Coffee Roasters Associations (SAUO)
EUCA........... Extended Unemployment Compensation Account
EUCAPA...... European Capsules Association [*EC*] (ECED)
EUCAR........ European Council for Automotive Research and development (SAUO)
EUCARPIA.... European Association for Research on Plant Breeding (EAIO)
EUCAS......... European Chemical Abstracts Search (SAUS)
EUCAS......... EUropean Conference on Applications of Superconductivity (SAUS)
EUCATEL...... European Conference of Associations of Telecommunications Industries (OSI)
EUCC........... Computing Center [*Emory University*] [*Research center*] (RCD)
EUCC........... Employers' Unemployment Compensation Council (EA)
EUCD........... Emotionally Unstable Character Disorder (MEDA)
EUCDW........ European Union for/of Christian Democratic Workers (SAUO)
EUCEMEC.... European Centre for Medical Demography and Health Economics (SAUO)
EUCEPA....... Europaeischer Verband fuer Zellstoff und Papiertechnik [*European Liaison Committee for Pulp and Paper*] (EAIO)
EUCEPA....... European Liason Committee for Cellulose and Paper (SAUS)
EUCF............ Enriched Uranium Conversion Facility (SAUS)
EUCF............ Equivalent Uniform Cash Flow
EUCFM......... Enriched Uranium Conversion Facility Modification (SAUS)
EUCG........... Electric Utility Cost Group (NTPA)
EUCH........... Eucharist (ROG)
EUCHEMAP... European Committee of Chemical Plant Manufacturers [*EC*] (ECED)
EU-CHIP....... Euro-Chinese Information Point (EURO)
EUCIB.......... European Collaborative Interspecies Backcross [*Genetic mapping resource*]
EUCIB.......... European Collaborative Interspecific Backcross (HGEN)
EUCIG.......... European CALS Industry Group (SAUS)
EUCL............ End User Common Line [*Telecommunications*] (OTD)
Eucl............. Euclid (SAUS)
EUCLEX........ European Cloud and Radiation Experiment (SAUO)
EUCLID........ Easily Used Computer Language for Illustration and Drawing [*European Community*] (MHDB)
EUCLID........ European Cooperative Longterm Initiative for Defense [*NATO*]
EUCLID........ Experimental Unpowered Climbing Dispenser (SAUS)
EUCLID........ Experimental Use Computer, London Integrated Display
EUCLIDE...... Easily Used Computer Language for Illustrations and Drawings (SAUS)
EUCLIDES.... European Standard for Clinical Laboratory Data Exchange between Independent Information Systems (SAUO)
EUCLIU........ Easily Used Computer Language for Illustrations and Drawings (SAUS)
EUCLI........... European Universal Communications Line Interface (SAUS)
EUCOFEL..... Union Europeenne du Commerce de Gros en Fruits et Legumes [*European Union of the Fruit and Vegetable Wholesale, Import, and Export Trade*] [*Brussels, Belgium*] (EAIO)
EUCOFF....... European Conference on Flammability and Fire Retardants
EUCOLAIT.... Union Europeenne du Commerce des Produits Laitiers et Derives [*European Union of Importers, Exporters, and Dealers in Dairy Products*] (EAIO)
EUCOM........ European Command [*Military*]
EUCOM AIDES... European Theater Air Command and Control System (SAUO)
EUCOMED.... European Confederation of Medical Suppliers Associations (EA)
EUCOMM-Z... [*US*] European [*Command*] Communications Zone (DOMA)
EUCON......... Energy Utilization and Conversation Exhibition and Conference (PDAA)
EUCONEC..... Europaische Konferenz der Industrie Elektrischer Kondensatoren [*European Conference of the Industry of Electrical Capacitors*] [*EC*] (ECED)
EUCONEC..... European Conference of the Industry of Electrical Capacitors (SAUO)
EUCONEC..... European Conference on Industrial Electrical Capacitors (SAUO)
EUCOR......... European Commissary Region (SAUO)
EUCORG...... European Cooperation Research Group [*European parliamentarians*]
EUCP........... Emergency Urgent Change Package [*Army*] (AABC)
EUCPS......... European University Centre for/of Peace Studies (SAUO)
EUCREX....... European Cirrus Research Experimetn (SAUS)
EUCREX....... European Cloud Radiation Experiment (SAUS)
EUCS........... Edinburgh University Computing Service (SAUO)
EUCUS......... Emergency Unitized Cargo Unloading System [*Navy*] (CAAL)
EUD............. Euro Direct Airlines UK Ltd. [*British*] [*FAA designator*] (FAAC)
EUD............. European Union of Dental Medicine Practitioners (SAUO)
EUD............. European Union of Dentists (PDAA)
EUD............. Extended Upper Deck
EUD............. Library Techniques, Sheridan College [*EDUCATSS*] [*UTLAS symbol*]
EUDA........... End-Users of Derivatives Association, Inc. (ECON)
EUDAC......... European Command Defense Analysis Center (SAUO)
EUDAC......... European Defense Analysis Center (MCD)
EUDAC......... European Distribution and Accounting Agency of the Military Committee, London [*US Army*] (AABC)
EUDAT......... End-User Data Access Tools (SAUS)
EUDAT......... European Association for the Development of Databases in Education and Training (EURO)
EUDC........... European Urban Driving Cycle [*Automotive emissions*]
EUDC........... Extra-Urban Driving Cycle [*Automotive emissions*]
EUDG........... European Datamanager User Group (SAUO)
EUDH........... European Union of Developers and House Builders [*Belgium*] (EAIO)
EUDIF.......... European Documentation and Information Network for Women (EURO)
EUDISED...... European Documentation and Information System for Education [*Council of Europe*] [*Database*] (IID)
EUDO........... Eurasian Dotterel [*North American bird banding code*] (BIBA)
EUDS........... Electronic Unit Design Section
EUE.............. Extended User Employment [*Military training*]
EUE.............. Universite de Montreal, Ecole de Bibliotheconomie [*EDUCATSS*] [*UTLAS symbol*]
EUE.............. University of Essex Library, Colchester, England [*OCLC symbol*] (OCLC)
EU/ECHO...... European Community Humanitarian Office (SAUO)
EUEP........... European Environmental Programme (SAUS)
Euer............. Euer. Doctrina Placitandi [*England*] [*A publication*] (DLA)
EUESS......... European Union of Export Service Suppliers (SAUO)
EUF.............. Electroultrafiltration
EUF.............. End User Facility
EUF.............. End-User Forum [*Computer science*] (AGLO)
EUF.............. Equivalent Unavailability Factor (IEEE)
EUF.............. Eufaula, AL [*Location identifier*] [*FAA*] (FAAL)
EUF.............. European Underwater Federation (SAUO)
EUF.............. European Union of Federalists
EUF.............. Library Technician Program, Fraser Valley College [*EDUCATSS*] [*UTLAS symbol*]
EUFA........... Eufaula BancCorp [*NASDAQ symbol*] (TTSB)
EUFA........... Eufaula BancCorp, Inc. [*NASDAQ symbol*] (SAG)
EUFA........... European Union Football Associations
Eufaula....... Eufaula BancCorp, Inc. [*Associated Press*] (SAG)
EUFMC........ Electric Utilities Fleet Managers Conference
EUFMD........ European Commission for the Control of Foot and Mouth Disease (SAUS)
EUFODA....... European Food Distributors Association (PDAA)
EUFODA....... European Foodstuffs Distributors Association (SAUS)
EUFOS......... European Federation of Societies for ORL, Head and Neck Surgery (SAUO)
EUFTG......... End User Facility Task Group (SAUO)
EUFTT.......... European Union of Film and Television Technicians (BARN)
EUG............. CEGEP [*College d'Enseignement General et Professionnel*], Trois-Rivieres, Bibliotheque [*EDUCATSS*] [*UTLAS symbol*]
EUG............. Eugene [*Oregon*] [*Airport symbol*] (OAG)
EUG............. Eugene, OR [*Location identifier*] [*FAA*] (FAAL)
EUG............. European Union of Geosciences [*Strasbourg, France*]
EUG............. Excretory Urography [*Medicine*] (MELL)
EUG............. Extrauterine Gestation [*Medicine*] (EDAA)
EUGBX......... Mgn. Stanley D. Witter European Growth Cl.B [*Mutual fund ticker symbol*] (SG)
EUGEN......... Eugene, OR [*American Association of Railroads railroad junction routing code*]
EUGEN......... Eugenics (ADA)
EUG LY........ Euglobulin Lysis [*Also, fibrinolysin and plasmin*] [*Biochemistry*] (DAVI)
Eugn............ eugenics (SAUS)
EUGO........... European Goldfinch [*North American bird banding code*] (BIBA)
EUGP........... Eurasian Golden-Plover [*North American bird banding code*] (BIBA)
EUGX........... Equity Union Grain [*Private rail car owner code*]
EUGX........... Farmar [*Federal Railroad Administration identification code*]
EUH............. Expected Utility Hypothesis
EUH............. Library Technician Program, Mohawk College [*EDUCATSS*] [*UTLAS symbol*]
EUI.............. Electronic Unit Injector [*or Injection*] [*Automotive Engineering*]
EUI.............. Enciclopedia Universal Illustrada, Espasa [*A publication*]
EUI.............. End-User Interface [*Computer science*] (AGLO)
EUI.............. Enemy Unit Identification [*Military*]
EUI.............. Energy Utilization Index (SAUS)
EUI.............. Euravia [*Spain*] [*ICAO designator*] (FAAC)
EUI.............. European University Institute [*Florence, Italy*] (AIE)
EUI.............. extended user interface (SAUS)
EUI.............. SAIT [*Southern Alberta Institute of Technology*] Library Technician Program [*UTLAS symbol*]
EUID........... Effective User IDentification (SAUS)
EuIG........... Europium Iron Garnet (PDAA)
E-UIOF........ European Region of the International Union of Family Organization (SAUO)
EUIPA......... Electric Utility Industrial Power Association (EA)
EUIT........... Educational Uses of Information Technology (CIST)
EUJ............. Georgian College [*EDUCATSS*] [*UTLAS symbol*]
EUJS........... European Union of Jewish Students (EA)
EUK............. Ecoropa UK [*An association*] (EAIO)
EUK............. Eureka Resources, Inc. [*Vancouver Stock Exchange symbol*]
EUK............. Library Technician Program, Kelsey Institute [*EDUCATSS*] [*UTLAS symbol*]
e-uk-........... United Kingdom [*MARC geographic area code*] [*Library of Congress*] (LCCP)
EUKA........... Eureka Southern Railroad [*Federal Railroad Administration identification code*]
EUKE........... Eurasian Kestrel [*North American bird banding code*] (BIBA)
e-uk-en....... England [*MARC geographic area code*] [*Library of Congress*] (LCCP)
e-uk-ni........ Northern Ireland [*MARC geographic area code*] [*Library of Congress*] (LCCP)
e-uk-st........ Scotland [*MARC geographic area code*] [*Library of Congress*] (LCCP)

e-uk-ui .... United Kingdom Miscellaneous Islands [*MARC geographic area code*] [*Library of Congress*] (LCCP)
e-uk-wl .... Wales [*MARC geographic area code*] [*Library of Congress*] (LCCP)
EUL .... Economic Useful Life (SAUS)
EUL .... Edinburgh University Library (SAUO)
EUL .... End User Layer Gateway (VLIE)
EUL .... Euralair International [*France*] [*ICAO designator*] (FAAC)
EUL .... Everyman s University Library (SAUO)
EUL .... Expected Upper Limit [*Clinical psychology*]
EUL .... Extensive User Library
EUL .... School of Library Technology, Lakehead University [*EDUCATSS*] [*UTLAS symbol*]
EULA .... End User License Agreement (IGQR)
EULA .... End-User Licensing Agreement (SAUS)
EULA .... Euro-Latin American Bank Ltd.
EULA .... European-Latinamerican Bank Ltd. (SAUO)
EULABANK ... Euro-Latin America Bank Ltd. [*British*] (EY)
EULAR .... European League Against Rheumatism (EAIO)
EULEP .... European Late Effects Project Group (PDAA)
EULER .... European Libraries and Electronic Resources in Mathematical Sciences (TELE)
EULOGIA ...... Edinburgh University Library Online for General Information Access (NITA)
EULTG .... End User Language Task Group (SAUO)
EUM .... Entraide Universitaire Mondiale [*World University Service - WUS*] (EAIO)
Eum .... Eumenides [*of Aeschylus*] [*Classical studies*] (OCD)
EUM .... Eureka Mesa [*New Mexico*] [*Seismograph station code, US Geological Survey*] (SEIS)
EUM .... European-Mediterranean [*Military*]
EUM .... External Urethral Meatus [*Medicine*] (EDAA)
EUM .... Graduate School of Library Science, McGill University [*EDUCATSS*] [*UTLAS symbol*]
EUMABOIS ... Comite Europeen des Constructeurs de Machines a Bois [*European Committee of Woodworking Machinery Manufacturers*] (EAIO)
EUMABOIS ... European Committee of Woodworking Machinery Manufacturers (SAUS)
EUM-AFTN ... European Mediterranean Aeronautical Fixed Telecommunications Network (PDAA)
EUMAPRINT ... European Committee of Associations of Printing and Paper Converting Machinery (EA)
EUMC .... Enameled Utensil Manufacturers Council (SAUO)
EUMC .... Entraide Universitaire Mondial du Canada [*World University Service of Canada - WUSC*]
EuMC .... European Microwave Conference (SAUO)
EUMC .... European Microwave Conference and Exhibition [*British*] (ITD)
EUMD .... Extended Unit Manning Document (SAUS)
EUMEAF .... Europe, Middle East and Africa (SAUO)
EUMELI .... Eutrophic, Mesotrophic and Oligotrophic (SAUS)
EUMELI .... eutrophic, mesotrophic, and oligotrophic sites (SAUS)
EUMESAT .... European Organisation for the Exploitation of Meteorological Satellites (SAUO)
EUMETSAT ... European Meteorological Satellite (MCD)
EUMETSAT ... European Organization for the Exploitation of Meteorological Satellites
EUMETSTAT ... European Meteorological Satellite (SAUS)
EUMOTIV ..... European Association for the Study of Economic, Commercial, and Industrial Motivation [*Belgium*] (PDAA)
EUMR .... Emergency Unsatisfactory Material Report (MCD)
EUMS .... European Union of Music Schools [*See also EMU*] (EA)
EUMT .... Europaeische Union Gegen den Missbrauch der Tiere [*European Union for the Prevention of Cruelty to Animals*] [*Switzerland*] (EAIO)
EUMV .... Euphorbia Mosaic Virus [*Plant pathology*]
EUN .... Egyptian University Network (SAUO)
EUN .... El Aaiun [*Morocco*] [*Airport symbol*] (AD)
EUN .... Electronic University Network [*TeleLearning Systems*] [*San Francisco, CA*] [*Computer science*]
EUN .... Enhanced Urban Network [*Traffic management*]
Eun .... Eunuchus [*of Terence*] [*Classical studies*] (OCD)
EUN .... Laayoune [*Morocco*] [*Airport symbol*] (OAG)
EUN .... Library Technician Program, Niagara College [*EDUCATSS*] [*UTLAS symbol*]
EUN .... University of Newcastle, Newcastle-Upon-Tyne, England [*OCLC symbol*] (OCLC)
Eun .... Wynne's Eunomus [*A publication*] (DLA)
EUNEASO ..... European Near-Earth Asteroids Search Observatories (SAUS)
EUNET .... EuropaNET (SAUS)
EUNET .... European Organisation for Packaging and the Environment (EURO)
EUNET .... European UNIX Network [*Computer science*] (ACRL)
EUnet .... Europe Network
Euni .... Eunice (SAUS)
EUNICEF ...... European Command Nuclear Interface Element Fastbreak (MCD)
EUNIE .... EUCOM Nuclear Interface Element (SAUS)
EUNIE-F .... EUCOM Nuclear Interface Element-Fastbreak (SAUS)
EUNIS .... European Nature Information System (SAUO)
EUNIT .... European Network of Intercultural Teacher Education (SAUO)
EUO .... Emergency Use Only (SAUS)
EUO .... English Usage Orientation [*Form*] [*Western Michigan University*] (TES)
EUO .... Enriched Uranium Operations (SAUS)
EUO .... Eurotech, Ltd. [*AMEX symbol*]
EUO .... Library Technician Program, Algonquin College [*EDUCATSS*] [*UTLAS symbol*]
EUORCOMP ... European Computing Congress and Exhibition (SAUS)
EU-OSHA ..... European Agency for Safety and Health at Work (EURO)
EUP .... Early Upper Paleolithic
EUP .... Eastern Upper Peninsula [*Michigan*]
EUP .... Edinburgh Paperback [*A publication*]
EUP .... Edinburgh University Press [*Publisher*] [*Scotland*]
EUP .... Electric Utility Pump
EUP .... Electronic Unit Pump [*Diesel engines*]
EUP .... End-Use Product (EEVL)
EUP .... English Universities Press
EUP .... Environmental Use Permit (HGAA)
EUP .... Equipment Upgrade Program [*Army*]
EUP .... Estimated Unit Price (MCD)
Eup .... Eupolis [*Fifth century BC*] [*Classical studies*] (OCD)
EUP .... Europa Petroleum [*Vancouver Stock Exchange symbol*]
EUP .... Experimental Use Permit [*Environmental Protection Agency*]
EUP .... Extrauterine Pregnancy (MELL)
EUPA .... European Union for the Protection of Animals (PDAA)
EUPC .... Electric Utility Planning Council (SAUO)
EuPC .... European Plastics Converters [*Belgium*] (EAIO)
EUPE .... European Union for Packaging and the Environment [*EEC*] (PDAA)
EUPEPTIC .... Evaluation of Unitary Programs for Effecting Plural Tasks in Index Construction (NITA)
euph .... euphemizing (SAUS)
EUPH .... Euphonium [*Musical instrument*]
euph .... Euphonium
EUPH .... Euphonix, Inc. [*NASDAQ symbol*] (SAG)
EU/PHARE .... European Union-Poland, Hungary, Albania, Romania, Estonia (SAUO)
EUPHEM ...... Euphemism (ROG)
euphem ...... Euphemistic (ADWA)
Euphie .... Euphemia (SAUS)
Euphnx .... Euphonix, Inc. [*Associated Press*] (SAG)
euphon .... euphonic (SAUS)
euphon .... euphonically (SAUS)
euphon .... euphony (SAUS)
EUPJ .... Experimental Underwater Pump Jet
EUPRAC .... European Public Relations Advisory Committee
EUPREN .... European Primate Resources Network
EUPRIO .... European Association of University Information and Public Relation Officers (SAUO)
EUPRISO ...... European Union of Public Relations - International Service Organization [*See also UERP*] (EAIO)
EUPSA .... European Union of Paediatric Surgical Associations (PDAA)
EUQ .... Emory University Quaterly (journ.) (SAUS)
EUQ .... John Abbott College Library [*EDUCATSS*] [*UTLAS symbol*]
EUR .... Bureau of European Affairs (SAUO)
EUR .... Electrically Transmitted Unsatisfactory Report
EUR .... Emergency Unsatisfactory Report [*Military*] (AFM)
EUR .... Engineering Unsatisfactory Report [*Military*] (AFIT)
EUR .... Equipment Unsatisfactory Report
EUR .... Eureka [*Nevada*] [*Seismograph station code, US Geological Survey*] (SEIS)
EUR .... Eureka, MT [*Location identifier*] [*FAA*] (FAAL)
Eur .... Euripides [*Fifth century BC*] [*Classical studies*] (OCD)
EUR .... Eurocan Ventures Ltd. [*Vancouver Stock Exchange symbol*]
Eur .... Eurochord [*Record label*] [*France*]
EUR .... Eurojet SA [*Spain*] [*ICAO designator*] (FAAC)
EUR .... Europe [*or European*] (AFM)
Eur .... Europe (VRA)
Eur .... European (AAGC)
EUR .... European Region [*USTTA*] (TAG)
EUR .... European Unit Routes (SAUS)
EUR .... European University Radio (SAUO)
EUR .... European Utility Requirements (SAUO)
EUR .... Executive Utility Routine (SAUS)
EUR .... Library Technician Program, Red River Community College [*EDUCATSS*] [*UTLAS symbol*]
e-ur- .... USSR [*Union of Soviet Socialist Republics*] [*MARC geographic area code*] [*Library of Congress*] (LCCP)
EURA .... Energy User Research Association (SAUO)
EURA .... European Renderers Association (EAIO)
EURABANK ... European-American Bank [*Databank on activities of non-US banks*] (NITA)
EURAC .... Europe Accessoires (SAUS)
EURAC .... European Requirements and Army Capabilities (AABC)
EurACS .... European Association of Classification Societies (EAIO)
EURACS .... European Radar Cross Section (SAUS)
EURADA .... European Association of Development Agencies (EURO)
EURADH .... European Adhesion Congress and Exhibition (SAUS)
Eur Adhes Seal ... European Adhesives and Sealants (journ.) (SAUS)
EURADIO ..... European Radio (SAUO)
EURADIS ...... European Agricultural Documentation and Information System (SAUS)
EURADIS ...... European Agriculture Documentation and Information System (SAUO)
EURADOS .... European Radiation Dosimetry Group
Eurafric .... Europe and Africa (SAUS)
EURAFRICA ... Europe and Africa
EURAG .... Federation Europeenne des Personnes Agees [*European Federation for the Welfare of the Elderly*] (EAIO)
EUR-AGRIS ... European Agricultural Information System (SAUS)
e-ur-ai .... Armenian Soviet Socialist Republic [*MARC geographic area code*] [*Library of Congress*] (LCCP)
Eurail .... European Railways (SAUS)
EURAILPASS ... European Railway Passenger [*Ticket*]
Eurailpass ... European tourist railroad pass (SAUS)

e-ur-aj .... Azerbaijan Soviet Socialist Republic [*MARC geographic area code*] [*Library of Congress*] (LCCP)
EURAL .... European Air Lines
EURALARM... Association des Constructeurs Europeens de Systemes d'Alarme Incendie et Vol [*Association of European Manufacturers of Fire and Intruder Alarm Systems*] (EAIO)
EURALARM... Association of European Manufacturers of Fire and Intruder Alarm Systems (SAUO)
EURALARM... European Association of Fire Alarm Systems Manufacturers (SAUO)
EURAM .... European Research and Advanced Materials Programme (SAUO)
EURAM .... European Research in Advanced Materials (SAUS)
EURAM .... European Research on Advanced Materials
EUR ANP ..... European Air Navigation Plan [*ICAO*] (DA)
Eur Appl Res Rep... European Applied Research Report (journ.) (SAUS)
Eur Appl Res Rep Nucl Tec... European Applied Research Reports, Nuclear Science Technology Section (journ.) (SAUS)
Eur Arb .... European Arbitration [*A publication*] (DLA)
EURAS .... Association Europeenne l'Anodisation [*European Anodisers' Association*] (EA)
EURAS .... European Advertising Service (SAUO)
EURAS .... European Anodisers Association (SAUS)
EURAS .... European Anodizers Association (SAUS)
EURASAFRICA... Europe, Asia, and Africa
EURASAP..... European Association for the Science of Air Pollution (EAIO)
EURASBANK... European Asian Bank (SAUS)
EURASEP..... European Association of Scientists for Experiments on Pollution (SAUO)
EURASEP..... European Assoc. of Satellite Experiments on Pollution (SAUS)
EURASHE..... European Association of Higher Education (SAUO)
Eurasia .... Europe and Asia (SAUS)
EURASIP...... European Association for Signal Processing (EAIO)
Eur Ass Arb... European Assurance Arbitration [*1872-75*] [*A publication*] (DLA)
EuRaTIN ...... European Research and Technology Information Network (EURO)
EURATN....... European Aeronautical Telecommunication Network (EURO)
Euratom ...... European Atomic Energy Commission (WA)
EURATOM.... European Atomic Energy Committee (SAUS)
EURATOM.... European Atomic Energy Community [*Also, EAEC*]
EURATOM SA... EURATOM Supply Agency (SAUO)
Eur Biophys J... European Biophysics Journal (journ.) (SAUS)
e-ur-bw........ Belorussian Soviet Socialist Republic [*MARC geographic area code*] [*Library of Congress*] (LCCP)
e-urc-.......... Central Black Soil Region, RSFSR [*MARC geographic area code*] [*Library of Congress*] (LCCP)
Eur Child Adolesc Psychiatry... European Child and Adolescent Psychiatry (SAUS)
EURCO........ European Composite Unit [*European Economic Community*]
EURCOM...... European Command [*Military*]
Eur Conslt Ass Deb... Council of Europe, Debates of the Consultative Assembly [*A publication*] (DLA)
EURCOR ...... European Commissary Region (SAUO)
Eur Ct H R ... European Court of Human Rights (SAUS)
EURDA......... Etudes d'Urbanisme de Developpement et d'Amenagement [*du Territoire*]
EURDEP....... European Union Radiological Data Exchange Platform (SAUO)
e-ure- .... East Siberian Region, RSFSR [*MARC geographic area code*] [*Library of Congress*] (LCCP)
EUREAU....... Union des Associations des Distributeurs d'Eau de Pays Membres des Communautes Europeennes [*Union of the Water Supply Associations from Countries of the European Communities*] (EAIO)
EURECA....... European Research Cooperation Agency (SAUS)
EURECA....... European Research Coordination Agency (SAUS)
EURECA....... European Retrievable Carrier [*Space shuttle experiment*]
EURECA....... European Retrieval Carrier (SAUS)
EURECOM.... Institut Eurecom (SAUO)
EURED .... European Unified Research on Educational Development (AIE)
EuReDatA .... European Reliability Data Association
EUREKA....... European Advanced Technology Programme [*British*]
EUREKA....... European Research and Cooperation Agency (SAUO)
EUREKA....... European Research and Co-ordination Agency (SAUS)
EUREKA....... European Research Cooperation Agency [*Non-defense research study group including eighteen European countries*]
EUREKA....... European Research Coordinating Agency (SAUO)
EUREKA....... European Research Coordination Agency (SAUS)
EUREKA....... Europe, Research, Co-operation, Action (SAUS)
EUREKA....... Evaluation of Uranium Resources and Economic Analysis [*Department of Energy*] (GFGA)
EUREL .... Association Europeenne des Reserves Naturelles Libres [*European Association for Free Nature Reserves*] [*Inactive*] (EAIO)
EUREL .... Convention of National Societies of Electrical Engineers of Western Europe (EAIO)
EUREL .... European Association for Free Nature Reserves (SAUO)
EURELFA ..... European Committee of Electric Light Fittings Association (SAUO)
EUREM .... European Conference on Electron Microscopy (SAUS)
EUREMAIL ... Conference Permanente de l'Industrie Europeenne de Produits Emailles
EURENCO .... European Information Center for Engineers and Consultants (SAUO)
e-ur-er......... Estonian Soviet Socialist Republic [*MARC geographic area code*] [*Library of Congress*] (LCCP)
EURES......... European Employment Services (SAUO)
EURESCO..... European Research Conferences (HGEN)
EUREX......... Enriched Uranium Extraction (PDAA)
EURF .... Experience Usage Replacement Factor [*Navy*]
e-urf-.......... Far Eastern Region, RSFSR [*MARC geographic area code*] [*Library of Congress*] (LCCP)
EUR FCB...... European Frequency Coordinating Body [*ICAO*] (DA)
EURGEEIA.... European Ground Electronics Engineering Installation Agency (SAUO)
e-ur-gs......... Georgian Soviet Socialist Republic [*MARC geographic area code*] [*Library of Congress*] (LCCP)
EURI .... Enriched Uranium Recovery Improvement (SAUS)
EURICAS..... European Research Institute for Civil Aviation Safety (SAUO)
EURIFI .... European Association of Research Institutes for Furniture (SAUS)
EURILIA .... European Initiative in Library and Information in Aerospace (TELE)
EURIM .... European Conference on Research into Information Management (SAUS)
EURIM .... European Conference on Research into Management of Information (NITA)
EURIM .... European Conference on Research into the Management of Information Systems and Libraries (PDAA)
EURIM .... European conference on Research of Information services and libraries Management (SAUS)
EURIMA .... European Insulation Manufacturers Association (PDAA)
EURING........ European Union for Bird Ringing [*Europe*] (EERA)
Eurip........... Euripides (SAUS)
EURIPA........ European Information Industry Association [*Formerly, European Information Providers Association*] [*Information retrieval*] (IID)
EURIPA........ European Information Providers Association (NITA)
EURIS .... Euromar Imaging Spectrometer (SAUS)
EURIS .... European Information Service [*Belgium*] (NITA)
EURISIS........ European Information System for Industrial Security (SAUS)
EURISOTOPE... EURATOM Radioisotope Information Bureau (SAUS)
EURISY........ European Assoc. for the Int. Space Year (SAUS)
EURISY........ European Association for the International Space Year (SAUO)
Eur J Biochem... European Journal of Biochemistry (SAUS)
Eur J Cancer... European Journal of Cancer (SAUS)
Eur J Cancer B Oral Oncol... European Journal of Cancer. Part B, Oral Oncology (SAUS)
Eur J Clin Invest... European Journal of Clinical Investigation (SAUS)
Eur J Eng Educ... European Journal of Engineering Education (journ.) (SAUS)
Eur J Mech Eng... European Journal of Mechanical Engineering (journ.) (SAUS)
Eur J Mineral... European Journal of Mineralogy (journ.) (SAUS)
Eur J Nucl Med... European Journal of Nuclear Medicine (journ.) (SAUS)
Eur J Sociol... European Journal of Sociology (SAUS)
e-urk-.......... Caucasus [*MARC geographic area code*] [*Library of Congress*] (LCCP)
e-ur-kg......... Kirghiz Soviet Socialist Republic [*MARC geographic area code*] [*Library of Congress*] (LCCP)
e-ur-kz .... Kazakh Soviet Socialist Republic [*MARC geographic area code*] [*Library of Congress*] (LCCP)
e-url- .... Central Region, RSFSR [*MARC geographic area code*] [*Library of Congress*] (LCCP)
Eur L Dig ..... European Law Digest [*A publication*] (DLA)
e-ur-li .... Lithuanian Soviet Socialist Republic [*MARC geographic area code*] [*Library of Congress*] (LCCP)
Eur L Newsl... European Law Newsletter [*A publication*] (DLA)
Eur L Rev .... European Law Review [*A publication*] (DLA)
e-ur-lv .... Latvian Soviet Socialist Republic [*MARC geographic area code*] [*Library of Congress*] (LCCP)
EURMEDS.... European Meteorological Data systems (SAUO)
e-ur-mv........ Moldavian Soviet Socialist Republic [*MARC geographic area code*] [*Library of Congress*] (LCCP)
e-urn- .... Northwestern Region, RSFSR [*MARC geographic area code*] [*Library of Congress*] (LCCP)
EURNAVFACENGCOM... European Division Naval Facilities Engineering Command
EURO .... Enriched Uranium Recovery Operations (SAUS)
EURO .... European Congress on Operational Research (SAUO)
EURO .... European Regional Office (SAUS)
EURO .... European Regional Office of FAO (SAUO)
e-uro- .... Soviet Central Asia [*MARC geographic area code*] [*Library of Congress*] (LCCP)
EURO-AIM ... European Organization for an Audiovisual Independent Market (SAUO)
EUROAVIA ... Association of European Aeronautical and Astronautical Students (PDAA)
EUROBA....... European Professional Fair for Industry and Handicraft of Bakery, Confectionery,Pastry, Biscuits, Chocolate, and Ice Cream Making
EUROBASE... European Database [*Databank on election results*] (NITA)
EUROBAT..... Association of European Battery Manufacturers (EA)
EUROBATS... Agreement on the Conservation of Bats in Europe (SAUO)
EUROBIT...... European Association of Manufacturers of Business Machines and Data Processing Equipment [*Frankfurt, Federal Republic of Germany*] (EAIO)
EUROBIT...... European Association of Manufacturers of Business Machines and Information Technology (SAUS)
EUROBITUMA... European Bitumen Association (SAUO)
EUROBITUME... European Bitumen Association (EA)
Eurobonds ... European bonds (SAUS)
EUROBRAZ... European Brazilian Bank
EUROBRAZ... European Brazilian Bank Ltd. (SAUO)
EUROBUILD... European Organization for the Production of New Techniques and Methods in Building (SAUS)
EUROBUILD... European Organization for the Promotion of New Techniques and Methods in Building (EA)
EUROC......... European Recovery Operations Center (SAUO)
EUROC......... European Recovery Operations Centre (SAUS)
EUROC......... European Rescue Operation Center (SAUO)
EUROCAE..... European Organization for Civil Aviation Electronics [*France*] (PDAA)
EUROCAEM... European Organization for Civil Aviation Electronics Manufacturers (SAUO)

EuroCAIRN... European Co-operation for Academic and Industrial Research Networking (SAUS)
EUROCARE... European Conservation and Restoration (SAUO)
EUROCAT..... European Registry of Congenital Abnormalities and Twins
EUROCEAN... European Ocean Association (SAUS)
EUROCEAN... European Oceanic Association [*Monaco, Monaco*] (EAIO)
EUROCEAN... European Oceanographic Association (SAUS)
EUROCENTRES... Foundation for European Language and Educational Centres (EA)
Eurochemic... European chemical processing of irradiated fuels (SAUS)
EUROCHEMIC... European Company for Chemical Processing of Irradiated Fuels (SAUS)
EURO CHEMIC... European Company for the Chemical Processing of Irradiated Fuels (DS)
EUROCHEMIC... European Organisation for the Chemical Processing of Irradiated Fuels (SAUS)
EUROCHOR... Arbeitsgemeinschaft Europaeischer Chorverbaende [*European Choral Association - ECA*] (EA)
EUROCLAMP... European Clamping Tools Association [*EC*] (ECED)
EUROCOM ... European Coal Merchants Union (SAUO)
EUROCOM ... European Communications
EUROCOM ... Union Europeenne des Negociants en Combustibles [*European Fuel Merchants Union*]
EUROCOMP... European Computing Congress
EUROCOMSAT... European Consortium Communications Satellite (MCD)
EUROCON.... European Conference (SAUS)
EUROCON.... European Conference of/on Electronics Reliability in Electrical and Electronic Components and Systems (SAUO)
EUROCON.... European Conference on Electrotechnics (SAUS)
EUROCON.... European Convention (SAUS)
EURO-CONTROL... Air Traffic Control in European NATO Countries (SAUS)
EUROCONTROL... European Agency for the Safety of Air Navigation (SAUO)
EUROCONTROL... European Organization for the Safety of Air Navigation
EURO COOP... Communaute Europeenne des Cooperatives de Consommateurs [*European Consumers' Cooperation Committee*] [*Common Market*]
EUROCOOP... European Commmunity of Cooperative Societies (PDAA)
EUROCOP-COST... European Cooperation and Coordination in the Field of Scientific and Technical Research (SAUO)
EUROCOPI ... European Computer Program Information Centre [*Databank*] (NITA)
EUROCOPI ... European Computer Program Institute (SAUO)
EUROCOR .... European Congress on Metallic Corrosion (PDAA)
EUROCORD... European Cord, Rope, and Twine Industries (SAUS)
EUROCORD... Federation des Industries de Ficellerie et Corderie de l'Europe Occidentale [*Federation of Western European Rope and Twine Industries*] (EA)
EUROCORR... European Corrosion Congress (SAUS)
EUROCOTON... Comite des Industries du Coton et des Fibres Connexes de la CEE [*Committee of the Cotton Industries of the European Economic Community*] (PDAA)
EUROCOTON... Committee of the Cotton Industries of the European Economic Community (SAUO)
EURO-CP ..... Eurocommercial Paper
EuroCr .... Europa Cruises Corp. [*Associated Press*] (SAG)
EUROCRA .... European OCR Association (SAUS)
EUROCRA .... European Optical Character Recognition Association (SAUS)
eurocrat....... European bureaucrat (SAUS)
EURODEST... European Deep Sea Transect (SAUS)
EURODICAUTOM... European Automated Dictionary
EURODICAUTOM... European Dictionary, Automatic (SAUS)
EURODIDAC... European Association of Manufacturers and Distributors of Education Materials (PDAA)
Eurodif......... European Gaseous Diffusion Uranium Enrichment Consortium (SAUS)
EURODOC.... European Documentation [*Research Service*]
EURODOC.... European Joint Documentation Service (SAUS)
EURODOC.... Joint Documentation Service of European Space Research Organisation, European Industrial Space Group and the European Organizations (SAUO)
EURODOCDEL... Document Delivery (SAUS)
EURODUCKS... European Wetland Fund (SAUO)
EURO-ENVIRON... Environmental Protection (SAUS)
EUROFAR .... European Future Advanced Rotocraft (MCD)
EuroFd .... [*The*] Europe Fund [*Associated Press*] (SAG)
EUROFED.... European Federation of Liberal and Radical Youth (SAUO)
EUROFEDAG... European Federation of Agricultural Workers (SAUO)
EUROFEDAL... European Federation of Workers in Food and Allied Industries (SAUO)
EUROFEDE... European Federation of Workers in Food and Allied Industries (SAUO)
EUROFEDOP... European Federation of Employees in Public Services (EAIO)
EUROFER..... Association of European Steel Producers (PDAA)
EUROFER..... European Confederation for/of Iron and Steel Industries (or Industry) (SAUO)
EUROFER..... European Confederation of Iron and Steel Industries [*EC*] (ECED)
EUROFER..... European Steel Federation (SAUS)
EUROFEU..... Comite Europeen des Constructeurs de Materiels d'Incendie et de Secours [*European Committee of the Manufacturers of Fire Protection and Safety Equipment and Fire Fighting Vehicles*] (EAIO)
EUROFEU..... European Committee of the Manufacturers of Fire Engines and Apparatus (SAUO)
EUROFEU..... European Committee of the Manufacturers of Fire Protection and Safety Equipment and Fire Fighting Vehicles (SAUS)
EURO-FIET... Organisation Regionale Europeenne de la Federation Internationale des Employes, Techniciens et Cadres [*European Regional Organization of the International Federation of Commercial, Clerical, Professional and Technical Employees*] [*EC*] (ECED)
EUROFIMA... European Company for the Financing of Railway Rolling Stock (SAUO)
Eurofima...... European Company for the Financing of Rolling Stock (SAUO)
EUROFINAS... European Federation of Finance Houses Association [*Belgium*] (PDAA)
EUROFINAS... European Financial Houses (SAUS)
EUROFLAG... European Future Large Aircraft Group (SAUO)
EUROFLUX EC... Project: Long-term Dioxide and Water Vapour Fluxes of European Forests and Interactions with the Climate System (SAUS)
EUROFORGE... European Committee of Forging and Stamping Industries (EAIO)
EUROFRET... European system for International Road Freight Transport Operation (SAUO)
EUROFUEL... Societe Europeene de Fabrication de Combustibles a Base d'Eranium pour Reacteursa Eau Legere [*France*] (PDAA)
EUROGI........ European Umbrella Organisation for Geographic Information (EURO)
EUROGLACES... Association des Industries de Glaces Alimentaires de la CEE [*Association of the Ice Cream Industries of the European Economic Community*]
EUROGLACES... Association for the Ice Cream Industries of the EEC (SAUO)
EuroGOOS..... European Consortium for GOOS (SAUO)
EuroGOOS.... European Global Ocean Observing System (SAUO)
EUROGRAF... Group of Federations of Graphics Industries in the European Community (SAUS)
EUROGRAF... Group of Federations of Graphics Industries in the in the European Community (SAUO)
EUROGRAPH... European Association of Manufacturers of Printing and Writing Papers (SAUO)
EUROGROPA... Union des Distributeurs de Papiers et Cartons [*European Union of Paper, Board, and Packaging Wholesalers*] (PDAA)
EUROGROUP... Informal Grouping of NATO European Defence Ministers (SAUO)
EUROGYPSUM... Working Community of the European Gypsum Industry (EAIO)
EURO-HKG... European High Temperature Nuclear Power Stations Society (EAIO)
Eurohorc...... European Heads of Research Councils
EUROHORCS... European Heads of Research Councils (SAUS)
EuroISDN..... European Integrated Services Digital Network [*Telecommunications*] (ECON)
EUROLAB..... Organisation for Testing in Europe (SAUS)
Eurolaw Com Intel... Eurolaw Commercial Intelligence [*A publication*] (DLA)
EUROLEX..... European Association for Lexicography (SAUO)
EUROLEX..... European Law Centre (SAUO)
EUROLEX..... European law database (SAUS)
Eurolex........ full-text electronic legal-research network (SAUS)
EUROLIB..... Organization of EC institutional Libraries (SAUS)
EUROLIBRI... Association of Publishers of European Legal and Economic Works (SAUO)
EUROLOC .... Locate in Europe Information Retrieval System [*University of Strathclyde*] [*Glasgow, Scotland*] [*Information service or system*] (IID)
Eurolog........ European Logistics Coordinating Group (SAUO)
EUROLOG.... European On-Line Users Group (SAUO)
EuroISPA..... European Internet Service Providers Association (SAUO)
EUROM........ European Federation for/of Optics and Precision Mechanics (SAUO)
EUROM........ European Federation of Optical and Precision Instruments Industry [*EC*] (ECED)
EUROM........ European Read Only Memory (NITA)
EUROMAISERS... Maize Industry Association Group of the EEC Countries (SAUO)
EUROMAISIERS... Groupement des Associations des Maisiers des Pays de la CEE [*Group of the Maize Processors Associations in the European Economic Community Countries*] [*Brussels, Belgium*]
EUROMALT... Comite de Travail des Malteries de la CEE [*Working Committee of European Economic Community Malters*]
EUROMALT... Working Committee of the Malt-House of the EEC (SAUO)
Euromam...... European Quaternary Mammal Research Association (SAUO)
EUROMAP.... European Committee of Machinery Manufacturers for Plastics and Rubber Industries [*EC*] (ECED)
EUROMAR ... European Marine Research and Technology Project (SAUS)
Euromarket... European Common Market (SAUO)
EUROMART... European Common Market
EUROMAT.... Federation of European Coin Machine Associations [*EC*] (ECED)
EUROMECH... European Mechanics Colloquia (PDAA)
EUROMECH... European Mechanics Colloquia, Farnborough (SAUO)
EUROMECH... European Mechanics Colloquium (SAUS)
EuroMech..... European Mechanics Committee (SAUS)
EUROMECH... European Mechanics Committee [*ICSU*]
Euromech .... European Mechanics Council (SAUO)
EUROMEDNET... European-Mediterranean Network in Marine Science and Technology (SAUS)
EUROMEDTEST... Organisation of European Laboratories Testing Medical Devices (SAUS)
EUROMICRO... European Association for Microprocessing and Microprogramming (PDAA)
EUROMICRO... European Association of Microprocessor Users (SAUO)
EUROMIL..... Europaeische Organisation der Militarverbande [*European Organization of Military Associations*] (EAIO)
EUROMINE... European Federation of the Mining Timber Associations (SAUO)
Euromissiles... European-deployed medium-range nuclear missiles (SAUS)
EUROMOT.... European Committee of Associations of Manufacturers of Internal Combustion Engines (EA)
EUROMPAP... European Committee of Machinery Manufacturers for the Plastics and Rubber Industries (PDAA)
EURONAD.... Eurogroup Committee of National Armaments Directors

EURONATUR... European Natural Heritage Fund (SAUS)
EURONEM.... European Association of Netting Manufacturers (EA)
EURONET..... European Information Network (SAUS)
EURONET..... European Network (SAUS)
EURONET..... European Network for Scientific and Technical Information (SAUO)
EURONET..... European On-Line Information Network [*Commission of the European Communities*] [*Information service or system*] (IID)
EURONET..... European Public Data Network (SAUS)
EURONET-DIANE... European Network - Direct Information Access Network for Europe [*Computer science*] (HGAA)
EURONETT... Evaluating User Reaction on New European Transport Technologies (SAUO)
EUR-OP........ EC official publications office (SAUS)
Europ........... European railway car pool (SAUS)
EUROP......... Office for Official Publications of the European Communities (SAUO)
EuroPACE.... European Programme of Advanced Continuing Education
EuroPACE.... Network of universities and their partners in education and training (SAUS)
EuroPace 2000... Professional and Academic Channel for Europe 2000 (SAUO)
EUROPAGATE... European SR-Z39.50 Gateway (SAUS)
EUROPALIA... Fondation Europalia International (SAUO)
EUROPANET... European academic network (SAUS)
EUROPARC... EUROPARC Federation (SAUS)
EuroPartners... EuroPartners Securities Corporation (SAUO)
Europea....... European Optics and Photonics Engineering Association (SAUO)
European Tele-University... European Institute for the Promotion of Long Distance Multi-media Higher Education Systems (SAUO)
EUROPEC..... European Offshore Petroleum Conference and Exhibition (PDAA)
EUROPECHE... Association des Organisations Nationales d'Entreprises de Peche de la CEE [*Association of National Organizations of Fishing Enterprises in the European Economic Community*]
EURO-PECHE... Association of National Organizations of Fishing Enterprises of the EEC (SAUO)
Europ Econ Rev... European Economic Review [*A publication*] (JLIT)
EurOpen..... European Forum for Open Systems (SAUO)
EUROPENSION... European Pension Fund (SAUO)
EUROPEX..... European Information Center for Explosion Protection (SAUS)
EUROPHOT... Association Europeenne des Photographes Professionnels [*European Association of Professional Photographers*]
EUROPHOT... European Council of Professional Photographers (SAUO)
Europhot...... European professional photographers (SAUS)
EUROPICA... European Program in Chemistry of the Atmosphere (SAUO)
EUROPILOTE... European Organization of Airline Pilots Associations (SAUS)
Europ J Devel Res... European Journal of Development Research [*A publication*] (JLIT)
Europ J Hist Econ Thought... European Journal of the History of Economic Thought [*A publication*] (JLIT)
Europ J Law Econ... European Journal of Law and Economics [*A publication*] (JLIT)
Europ J Polit Economy... European Journal of Political Economy [*A publication*] (JLIT)
EUROPLANT... European Plantmakers Committee (EA)
EUROPLATE... European Registration Plate Association (EA)
EUROPMAISERS... Groupement des Associations des Maisiers des Pays de la CEE [*Group of Associations of Maize Processors of EEC Countries*] (EAIO)
EUROPMI..... Comite de Liaison des Petites et Moyennes Entreprises Industrielles des Pays de la CEE [*Liaison Committee for Small and Medium-Sized Industrial Enterprises in the EEC*] [*Brussels, Belgium*] (EAIO)
EUROPOL.... European Police Office (SAUO)
EUROPOL.... Intra-European Air Transport Policy (SAUS)
EUROPOWERCAB... European Conference of Association of Power Cables Industries (SAUO)
EUROPOWERCAP... European Conference of Association of Power Cables Industries (SAUO)
EUROPREFAB... European Organization for the Promotion of Prefabrication and other Industralized Building (PDAA)
EUROPRESSJUNIOR... European Association of Producers of Publications for Youth (SAUO)
Europ Rev Agr Econ... European Review of Agricultural Economics [*A publication*] (JLIT)
Europ Rev Econ Hist... European Review of Economic History [*A publication*] (JLIT)
EUROPS....... European Air Operations Staff [*Military*]
Europ TS...... European Treaty Series [*Council of Europe*] [*A publication*] (DLA)
EUROPUMP... Comite Europeen des Constructeurs de Pompes [*European Committee of Pump Manufacturers*] (EAIO)
EUROPUMP... European Committee of Pump Manufacturers (EA)
EUROPUR.... Association Europeenne des Fabricants de Blocs de Mousse Souple de Polyurethane [*European Association of Flexible Foam Block Manufacturers*] (EAIO)
EUROPUR.... European Association of Flexible Polyurethane Foam Blocks Manufacturers (SAUO)
EURORAD.... European Association of Manufacturers of Radiators (EA)
EUROS......... European Register of Ships (SAUO)
EUROS......... European Retrievable Orbiting System (SAUS)
EUROSAC.... European Federation of Manufacturers of Multi-wall Paper Sacks [*France*] (PDAA)
Eurosac........ European paper sack manufacturers (SAUS)
EUROSAC.... Federation Europeenne des Fabricants de Sacs en Papier a Grande Contenance [*European Federation of Multiwall Paper Sacks Manufacturers*] (EAIO)
EUROSAM.... European Surface-to-Air Missile [*NATO*]
EUROSAT..... European Application Satellite (SAUS)
EUROSAT..... European Application Satellite Systems
EUROSAT System... European Application Satellite System (SAUS)
EUROSEP..... European Assoc. of Scientists in Environmental Pollution (SAUS)
EUROSHACK... European Expedition to the Shackleton Range (SAUS)
EUROSID..... European Side Impact Dummy [*Automotive engineering*]
EUROSITE..... European Network of Site Management Organizations (SAUS)
EUROSPACE... European Aerospace Industries Assoc. (SAUS)
EUROSPACE... European Industrial Space Research Group (SAUO)
EUROSPACE... European Industrial Space Study Group
EUROSPACE... European Space Research Group (SAUO)
EUROSPACE... European Space Study Group (SAUO)
EUROSTAR... European Communications Satellite (SAUS)
EUROSTART... European Planning Committee for START (SAUO)
EUROSTAT... European Communities. Statistical Office (SAUO)
EUROSTAT... [*The*] European Static Protection and Shielding Exhibition [*British*] (ITD)
EUROSTAT... European Statistics (SAUO)
EUROSTAT... Statistical Office of the European Communities [*Commission of the European Communities*] (EAIO)
EUROSTEP... European Association of Users of Satellites in Training and Education (SAUO)
EUROSTEP... European Association of Users of Satellites in Training and Education Programmes (AIE)
EUROSTEST... European Association of Testing Institutions (PDAA)
EUROSTRUCT... European Association of Publishers in the Field Press of Building and Design (SAUO)
eurotainer.... European-owned container (SAUS)
EUROTALC... Association Scientifique de l'Industrie Europeenne du Talc [*Scientific Association of European Talc Industry*] (EAIO)
EuroTECHNET... European Technologies Network (SAUS)
EUROTECNET... European Technical Network [*EC*] (ECED)
EUROTELCAB... European Conference of Associations of Telecommunications Cables Industries [*EC*] (ECED)
Euroterro..... European terrorism (SAUS)
Euroterro..... European terrorist (SAUS)
EUROTEST..... European Association of Testing Institutions [*Belgium*] (PDAA)
Eurotom....... European Atomic Energy Community (SAUO)
EUROTOPP... European Transport Planning Process (SAUO)
EUROTOX.... Comite Europeen Permanent de Recherches sur la Protection des Populations contreles Risques de Toxicite a Long Terme [*Permanent European Research Committee for the Protection of the Population against the Hazards of Chronic Toxicity*]
EUROTOX.... European Committee for the Protection of the Population against the Hazards of Chronic Toxicity (SAUO)
EUROTOX.... European Committee on Chronic Toxicity Hazards (SAUS)
Eurotox........ European Committee on Toxicity Hazards (SAUS)
EUROTRAC... European Experiment for Transporting and Transforming Environmentally Relevant Trace Construction in the Troposphere (SAUS)
EUROTRAC... European Experiment on Transport and Transformation of Environmentally Relevant Trace Constituents (SAUS)
EUROTRAC... European Experiment on Transport and Transformation of Environmentally Relevant Trace Constituents in the Troposphere over Europe (SAUO)
EUROTRAC... European Experiment on Transport and Transformation of over Europe (SAUS)
EUROTRAC... European Project on the Transport of Atmospheric Contaminants (SAUS)
EUROTRAC T... European Experiment on Transport and Transformation of Environmentally Relevant Trace Constituents in the Troposphere over Europe (SAUS)
EUROTRANS... European Committee of Associations of Manufacturers of Gears and Transmission Parts [*EC*] (ECED)
Eurotransplant... Eurotransplant Foundation, Leiden (SAUO)
EUROTRAP... European Transport Planning System (SAUO)
EUROTRIB... European Congress on Tribology (SAUS)
EUROVENT... European Committee of Ventilating Equipment Manufacturers (PDAA)
EUROVIS...... European vision System Economic (SAUO)
EUROVISION... European Broadcasting Union (EBF)
EUROVISION... European Television
e-urp-.......... Povolzhskii Region, RSFSR [*MARC geographic area code*] [*Library of Congress*] (LCCP)
Eur Packag Mag... European Packaging Magazine (journ.) (SAUS)
Eur Parl Deb... European Parliamentary Assembly Debates [*A publication*] (DLA)
Eur Parl Doc... European Parliament Working Documents [*A publication*] (DLA)
Eur Parl Docs... European Parliament Working Documents [*A publication*] (DLA)
EURPISO...... European Union of Public Relations - International Service Organization [*Hungary*] (EA)
Eur Pkg Mag... European Packaging Magaine (journ.) (SAUS)
Eur Plast News... European Plastics News (journ.) (SAUS)
Eur Polym J... European Polymer Journal (SAUS)
e-urr-.......... North Caucasus, RSFSR [*MARC geographic area code*] [*Library of Congress*] (LCCP)
EUR/RAN..... European Regional Air Navigation Meeting (SAUS)
EURRR......... Episcopalians United for Revelation, Renewal, and Reformation (EA)
e-ur-ru......... Russian SFSR [*MARC geographic area code*] [*Library of Congress*] (LCCP)
Eur Rubb J... European Rubber Journal (journ.) (SAUS)
e-urs-........... Siberia [*MARC geographic area code*] [*Library of Congress*] (LCCP)
Eur Semicond... European Semiconductor (journ.) (SAUS)
Eur Semicond Des Prod... European Semiconductor Design and Production (journ.) (SAUS)
Eur Semicond Prod... European Semiconductor Production (journ.) (SAUS)
EUR/SV/LDO... European Space Vehicle Launcher Development Organization (MCD)

e-ur-ta .... Tajik Soviet Socialist Republic [*MARC geographic area code*] [*Library of Congress*] (LCCP)
EUR/TFG ...... European Traffic Forecasting Group (SAUO)
e-ur-tk .... Turkmen Soviet Socialist Republic [*MARC geographic area code*] [*Library of Congress*] (LCCP)
Eur TL .... European Transport Law [*Belgium*] [*A publication*] (DLA)
EURTOA .... European Technical Operations Area [*Military*]
Eur Trans L ... European Transport Law [*Belgium*] [*A publication*] (DLA)
Eur Transp L ... European Transport Law [*Belgium*] [*A publication*] (DLA)
e-uru- .... Ural Region, RSFSR [*MARC geographic area code*] [*Library of Congress*] (LCCP)
e-ur-un .... Ukrainian Soviet Socialist Republic [*MARC geographic area code*] [*Library of Congress*] (LCCP)
e-ur-uz .... Uzbek Soviet Socialist Republic [*MARC geographic area code*] [*Library of Congress*] (LCCP)
e-urv- .... Volgo-Viatskii Region, RSFSR [*MARC geographic area code*] [*Library of Congress*] (LCCP)
e-urw- .... West Siberian Region, RSFSR [*MARC geographic area code*] [*Library of Congress*] (LCCP)
EurWtFd .... European Warrant Fund [*Associated Press*] (SAG)
EURYB .... Europa Year Book [*A publication*]
Eur YB .... European Yearbook [*A publication*] (DLA)
EURYDICE .... Education Information Network in the European Community [*Commission of the European Communities*] [*Belgium*] [*Information service or system*] (IID)
EUS .... Eastern United States
EUS .... Endoscopic Ultrasonography [*Medicine*]
EUS .... Engineering Undergraduates Society (SAUO)
EUS .... Esophageal Ultrasonography (ADWA)
Eus .... Eusebius [*Ecclesiastical historian, c. 260-340AD*] [*Classical studies*] (OCD)
EUS .... External Urethral Sphincter [*Anatomy*]
EUS .... Library Techniques, Seneca College [*EDUCATSS*] [*UTLAS symbol*]
EUSA .... Eagle USA Airfreight, Inc. [*NASDAQ symbol*] (SAG)
EUSA .... Eighth United States Army
EUSA .... Electrical Utilities Safety Organization (SAUS)
EUSA .... Evangelical Union of South America (SAUO)
EUSAK .... Eighth United States Army in Korea
EUSAMA ...... European Shock Absorber Manufacturers Association (PDAA)
EUSAR .... Eighth United States Army Rear
EUSC .... Effective United States Control Fleet
EUSC .... Effective United States Controlled Shipping (COE)
EUSC .... Effective U.S. Controlled (SAUS)
EUSEB .... European Union of Societies for Experimental Biology
EUSEB .... Eusebius [*Ecclesiastical historian, c. 260-340AD*] [*Classical studies*] (ROG)
Euseb .... Eusebius Pamphili (SAUS)
EUSEC .... Conference des Societes d'Ingenieurs de l'Europe Occidental et des Etats-Unis d'Amerique [*Conference of Engineering Societies of Western Europe and the United States of America*]
EUSEC .... Conference of Engineering Societies of Western Europe and the USA (SAUS)
EUSEC .... Conference of Representatives from European and United States Engineering Societies (SAUS)
EUSEC .... European Communication Security and Evaluation Agency (SAUS)
EUSEC .... European Communications Security Agency (SAUS)
EUSEC .... European Communications Security Agency of the Military Committee (SAUO)
EUSEC .... European Communications Security and Evaluation Agency of the Military Committee, London [*US Army*] (AABC)
EUSES .... European Union System for Evaluation of Substances (SAUO)
EUSFR .... Encyclopedia of US Foreign Relations [*A publication*]
EUSIDIC .... European Association of Information Services [*Formerly, European Association of Scientific Information Dissemination Centers*] [*Information service or system*] (IID)
EUSIDIC .... European Association of Scientific Information Dissemination Centers (SAUS)
Eusipco .... European Signal Processing Conference (SAUS)
EUSIREF ...... European Association of Science Information Referral Centres (NITA)
EUSIREF ...... European Scientific Information Referral [*EUSIDIC*] [*Information service or system*] (IID)
EUSIREF ...... European Scientific Information Retrieval Working Group (NITA)
EUSIREF ...... Network for European Scientific Information Referral Centres (SAUO)
EUSJA .... European Union of Science Journalists Associations (EAIO)
EUSM .... European Union of Social Medicine (EA)
EUSMCP .... European Union of the Social Pharmacies (SAUO)
EUSSG .... European Union for the Scientific Study of Glass (EA)
Eus Sta .... Euston Station (SAUS)
EUST .... European Starling [*North American bird banding code*] (BIBA)
Eust .... Eustacian [*Medicine*] (EDAA)
EUSX .... Exxon USA [*Private rail car owner code*]
EUT .... Einthoven University of Technology (SAUS)
EUT .... End User Terminal
EUT .... End-User Training [*Computer science*] (GART)
EUT .... Equipment under Test
EUT .... European Urology Today (SAUS)
Eut .... Euterpe [*Record label*]
EUT .... Express Update Tape (SAUS)
EUT .... Faculty of Library and Information Science, University of Toronto [*EDUCATSS*] [*UTLAS symbol*]
EU-TACIS ..... European Union Technical Assistance for the Commonwealth of Independent States (SAUO)
EUTE .... Early User Test and Evaluation [*Army*]
EUTE .... Early User Test and Experimentation [*DoD*]
eutec .... eutectic (SAUS)
eutec .... eutectoid (SAUS)
EUTECA .... European Technical Caramel Association [*EC*] (ECED)
EUTECO .... European Teleinformatics Conference (SAUS)
EUTELSAT .... European (SAUS)
EUTELSAT .... European Telecommunications Satellite [*Agency*] (BARN)
EUTELSAT .... European Telecommunications Satellite Organization [*France*] [*Telecommunications*]
euth .... Euthanase (SPVS)
euthan .... euthanasia (SAUS)
Euthphr .... Euthyphro [*of Plato*] [*Classical studies*] (OCD)
EUTO .... European Union of Tourism Executives (SAUO)
EUTO .... European Union of Tourist Officers (EAIO)
EUTOR .... European Association for Technical Orthopaedics and Orthopaedic Rehabilitation (SAUO)
EUTOW .... European Theater of War (SAUS)
EUTP .... Enhanced, Unshielded Twisted Pair (SAUS)
EUTR04 .... Eutrophication Model (SAUS)
EUTRAPLAST ... Committee of Plastic Converter Associations of Western Europe (SAUS)
EUTUG .... End-User Tool User Group (SAUO)
EUU .... Faculty of Library Science, University of British Columbia [*EDUCATSS*] [*UTLAS symbol*]
EUU .... Smithfield, NC [*Location identifier*] [*FAA*] (FAAL)
EUUG .... European Unix Systems Group [*Communications term*] (DCT)
EUUG .... European UNIX User Group [*Computer science*]
EUUG .... Extragalactic/European Unix User Group (SAUS)
EUUIG .... European Unix systems Users Group (SAUO)
EUV .... Energetic Ultra-Violet
euv .... equivalent ultraviolet (SAUS)
EUV .... Expected Utility Value
EUV .... Extreme Ultraviolet
EUV .... Extreme Ultraviolet LASER [*Medicine*] (DAVI)
EUV .... Library Technician Program, Vancouver Community College [*EDUCATSS*] [*UTLAS symbol*]
EUVE .... Extreme Ultraviolet Explorer
EUVE .... Extreme Ultraviolet Explorer satellite (SAUS)
EUVEPRO ..... European Vegetable Protein Federation (EAIO)
EUVEX .... Extreme Ultraviolet Explorer (MCD)
EUVITA .... EUV telescope (SAUO)
EUVITA .... Extreme Ultraviolet Telescope Array (SAUS)
EUVL .... Estimated Useful Vehicle Life
EUVL .... Extreme Ultraviolet Lithography
EUVP .... Extreme Ultraviolet Photometer (MCD)
EUVSH .... Equivalent Ultraviolet Solar Hour [*NASA*]
EUVT .... Extended Ultraviolet Transmission
EUVT .... Extreme Ultraviolet Telescope
EUW .... Eureka [*Washington*] [*Seismograph station code, US Geological Survey*] (SEIS)
EUW .... Euroflight Sweden, AB [*ICAO designator*] (FAAC)
EUW .... European Union of Women [*Stockholm, Sweden*]
EUW .... School of Library and Information Science, University of Western Ontario [*EDUCATSS*] [*UTLAS symbol*]
EUWEP .... European Union of Wholesale Eggs, Egg-Products, Poultry and Game [*EC*] (ECED)
EUWG .... Energy Use Working Group [*Australia*]
EUWI .... Eurasian Wigeon [*North American bird banding code*] (BIBA)
EUWO .... European Woodcock [*North American bird banding code*] (BIBA)
EUX .... European Expidite [*Belgium*] [*ICAO designator*] (FAAC)
Eux .... Euxine (SAUS)
EUX .... Saint Eustatius [*Antilles*] [*Airport symbol*] (OAG)
EUYCD .... European Union of Young Christian Democrats [*Belgium*] (EY)
EUZ .... Equatorial Upwelling Zone [*Oceanography*]
EUZ .... Euroair Transport Ltd. [*British*] [*ICAO designator*] (FAAC)
EUZ .... Exclusive Use Zone (SAUS)
EV .... Atlantic Southeast [*ICAO designator*] (AD)
EV .... Earned Value
EV .... Earned Value System (SAUS)
EV .... Eaton Vance [*NYSE symbol*] (SG)
EV .... Ebola Virus [*Medicine*] (MELL)
EV .... Echovirus [*Medicine*] (MELL)
EV .... Economic Value [*Accounting*]
EV .... Educt Vent
EV .... Efferent Vessel [*Anatomy*]
EV .... Efficient Vulcanization (SAUS)
EV .... Efficient Vulcanizing [*Rubber processing*]
EV .... Efficient Vulcanizing System (SAUS)
EV .... Eigenvalue [*Mathematics*]
EV .... Eingang Vorbehalten [*Rights reserved, i.e., copyrighted*] [*German*]
EV .... Ejected Volume [*Medicine*] (EDAA)
EV .... Electric Vehicle
EV .... Electronic Viewfinder [*Photography*]
EV .... Electron Volt (ACAE)
eV .... Electron Volt
EV .... Electrovalency (SAUS)
EV .... Electroviscosity (SAUS)
EV .... Electro Voice (SAUS)
EV .... Emergency Vehicle [*Medicine*] (DAVI)
EV .... Emissary Vein [*Medicine*] (MELL)
EV .... Emotional Violence
EV .... Enclosed and Ventilated (IAA)
EV .... End Vector (SAUS)
Ev .... energy of vibration (SAUS)
EV .... Energy Victoria [*Australia*]
EV .... Engineer Volunteers [*British military*] (DMA)
EV .... English Version

EV............... English Viscount (ROG)
EV............... Enteroviruses [*Medicine*] (MELL)
EV............... Enterprise Value [*Finance*] (ECON)
EV............... Entrained Air Volume
EV............... Environmental Viewpoints [*A publication*]
EV............... Epidermodysplasia Verruciformis (DB)
EV............... Equalizer Valve (SAUS)
EV............... Equilibrium Venography [*Medicine*] (ODA)
EV............... Equivalent (SAUS)
EV............... Erdelyi Vilagszovetseg [*Transylvanian World Federation - TWF*] (EAIO)
EV............... Ere Vulgaire [*Common Era*] [*Freemasonry*] [*French*] (ROG)
EV............... Erne Valley (SAUS)
EV............... Errata Volume [*Dialog*] [*Searchable field*] [*Information service or system*] (NITA)
EV............... Error Voltage [*Electricity*] (IAA)
EV............... Error Volume (ACAE)
EV............... Erythrocyte Volume (ODA)
EV............... Escort Vessel [*Enemy*]
EV............... Esophageal Varices [*Medicine*]
EV............... Estradiol Valerate [*Medicine*] (EDAA)
EV............... European Videotelephony (SAUO)
EV............... EuroVision [*Later, SGA*] (EA)
EV............... Evaluate
ev............... Evaluation (SAUS)
EV............... Evaluator (SAUS)
ev............... evangelical (SAUS)
EV............... Evangelist
Ev............... Evangile [*Paris*] [*A publication*] (BJA)
EV............... Evaporator Vessel (NRCH)
ev............... Evening (ADWA)
EV............... Evening
Ev............... Evenkian (SAUS)
EV............... Event (SAUS)
Ev............... Everett (SAUS)
EV............... [*The*] Everett Railroad Co. [*AAR code*]
ev............... Eversion [*Medicine*] (DAVI)
EV............... Everted [*or Eversion*] [*Medicine*]
EV............... Every
Ev............... Evidence [*Legal term*] (DLA)
EV............... Evoked Potential [*Response*] (DB)
EV............... Evoked Response [*Neurophysiology*] (MAE)
EV............... Evolution
ev............... Evolve (SAUS)
ev............... Evolvente (SAUS)
ev............... evolves (SAUS)
EV............... Excessive Ventilation [*Medicine*] (EDAA)
EV............... Exhaust Valve [*Nuclear energy*] (NRCH)
EV............... Expected Value [*Statistics*]
EV............... Expendable Vehicle (MCD)
EV............... Experimental Version (SDI)
EV............... Explosive Valve (KSC)
EV............... Exposure Value [*System*] [*Photography*]
EV............... Extended Visit (WDAA)
EV............... Extracellular Virus
EV............... Extravascular [*Anatomy*]
EV............... Extravehicular (MCD)
ev............... extremely violent (SAUS)
EV............... Exudative Vitreoretinopathy [*Ophthalmology*]
EV............... Ex Voto [*In Fulfillment of a Vow*] [*Latin*]
ev---............ Scandinavia [*MARC geographic area code*] [*Library of Congress*] (LCCP)
EV............... Entry Vehicle [*Astronautics*] (ODA)
EV1S............. Edge Vee One Side [*Lumber*] (DAC)
EV2S............. Edge V Two Sides (SAUS)
EVA.............. Early Valve Actuation [*or Actuator*] [*Nuclear energy*] (NRCH)
EVA.............. Earned Value Analysis (NASA)
EVA.............. Echo Virus Antibody [*Medicine*] (MELL)
EVA.............. Economic Value Added
EVA.............. Educational Voucher Authority (SAUS)
EVA.............. Education et vie active (projet FNRS) (SAUS)
EVA.............. Einzelsphaltrohrversuchsanlage [*Hydrogen generating reactor*]
EVA.............. Electrical Vehicle Association (SAUS)
EVA.............. Electrical Vehicle Association of Great Britain (SAUS)
EVA.............. Electric Vehicle Association of Great Britain Ltd. (BI)
EVA.............. Electronically Variable Attenuator (NITA)
EVA.............. Electronic Velocity Analyzer
EVA.............. Electronic Voice Alert [*Automotive engineering*]
EVA.............. Electronic Vote Analysis [*Election poll*]
EVA.............. Elevation Versus Amplitude (SAA)
EVA.............. Emergency Valve Assistance [*Automotive brake systems*]
EVA.............. Emissions of Volatiles into the Atmosphere (SAUS)
EVA.............. Employee Volunteer Action (SAUS)
EVA.............. Engineer Vice-Admiral [*British*]
EVA.............. English Vineyards Association (DBA)
EVA.............. English Volleyball Association
EVA.............. Enhanced Video Adapter (SAUS)
EVA.............. Equine Viral Arteritis (DB)
EVA.............. Error Volume Analysis [*Computer science*] (IBMDP)
EVA.............. Escort Vessel Administration [*World War II*]
EVA.............. Esperantlingva Verkista Asocio [*Esperanto Writers Association - EWA*] [*Netherlands*] (EA)
EVA.............. Essex Volunteer Artillery [*British military*] (DMA)
EVA.............. Ethylene Vinyl Acetate (SAUS)
EVA.............. Ethylene-Vinyl Acetate [*Copolymer*] [*Organic chemistry*]
EVA.............. Ethylene-Vinyl Acetate Polymer (EDCT)
eva.............. ethyl-vinyl acetate (SAUS)
EVA.............. Ethyl Violet-Azide [*Broth*] [*Microbiology*]
EVA.............. Europaeische Vereinigung der Allgemeinarzte [*European Union of General Practitioners*] (EAIO)
EVA.............. European Vaccine Against AIDS [*Acquired Immune Deficiency Syndrome*] [*Medicine*]
EVA.............. evacuation under anaesthesia (SAUS)
EVA.............. Evadale, TX [*Location identifier*] [*FAA*] (FAAL)
EVA.............. Evaluation Process for Road Transport Informatics (SAUO)
EVA.............. Extended Viewing Angle (SAUS)
EVA.............. Extravehicular Activity [*Aerospace*]
eva.............. extravehicular ambulation (SAUS)
EVA.............. Extravehicular Astronaut (SAA)
EVA.............. Extreme Value Engineering (SAUS)
EVAA............. Electric Vehicle Association of the Americas (EA)
EVA/ATC.......... Extra-Vehicular Activity/Air Traffic Control (SAUS)
EVAC............. Electric Vehicle Association of Canada
EVAC............. Enhanced Atrioventricular Conduction [*Medicine*] (STED)
EVAC............. Ethylene-Vinyl Acetate [*Copolymer*] [*Organic chemistry*]
EVAC............. Ethylene Vinyl Acetate Copolymer (SAUS)
EVAC............. Etoposide (VP-16), Vincristine, Adriamycin, Cyclophosphamide [*Antineoplastic drug regimen*]
evac............. evacuate (SAUS)
EVAC............. Evacuation (AFM)
evac............. Evacuation
EVAC............. Evacuation File (SAUS)
EVAC............. Evacuator (MSA)
EVA Computer... Election Vote Analysis Computer (SAUS)
EVACS............ Evacuation Hospital Semimobile (VNW)
EVACSHIP......... Evacuation Ship [*Navy*] (NVT)
EVACWP........... Exotic Vertebrate Animals Control Working Party [*Australia*]
EVADE............ Evaluation of Air Defense Effectiveness
EVAF............. International Association for Business Research and Corporate Development [*West Wickham, Kent, England*] (EAIO)
Ev Ag............ Evans on Agency [*A publication*] (DLA)
EVAL............. Earth Viewing Applications Laboratory (MCD)
EVAL............. Ethyl Vinyl Alcohol (PDAA)
EVAL............. Evaluate [*or Evaluation or Evaluator*] (AFM)
eval............. Evaluation (ADWA)
EVAL............. Evaluation
Eval Eng......... Evaluation Engineering (journ.) (SAUS)
EVALIS........... Evaluation Listing (SAUS)
EVALIS........... extended telephone simulation language evaluation listing (SAUS)
EVAN............. Electronic Verification of Account Number [*Social Security*]
EVAN............. Evangelical [*or Evangelist*]
evan............. Evangelist (ADWA)
Evan............. Evangile [*Paris*] [*A publication*] (BJA)
EVAN............. Evans, Inc. [*NASDAQ symbol*] (NQ)
EVANE............ Evans, Inc. [*NASDAQ symbol*] (SG)
EVAN-G........... End Violence Against the Next Generation (EA)
evang............ Evangelical (ADWA)
EVANG............ Evangelical [*or Evangelist*]
evang............ Evangelist (VRA)
Evangel.......... Evangelical (DIAR)
Evans............ Evans, Inc. [*Associated Press*] (SAG)
Evans............ Evans' King's Bench Reports [*1756-88*] [*A publication*] (DLA)
EVANS............ Evansville, IN [*American Association of Railroads railroad junction routing code*]
Evans............ Lord Mansfield's Decisions [*1799-1814*] [*England*] [*A publication*] (DLA)
EvansSys......... Evans Systems, Inc. [*Associated Press*] (SAG)
evap............. Evaporate (ADWA)
EVAP............. Evaporate (KSC)
EVAP............. Evaporation (SAUS)
evap............. Evaporative (SAUS)
EVAP............. Evaporative Emission (HAWK)
EVAP............. Evaporative Emission Control System [*Automotive engineering*]
EVAP............. Evaporator
evap............. evaporize (SAUS)
evap............. evapuration (SAUS)
EVAPD............ Evaporated (IAA)
evapg............ Evaporating (SAUS)
EVAPN............ Evaporation (IAA)
EVAPTR........... Evaporator [*Freight*]
E-VAR............ Environment Variable [*Computer science*] (PCM)
EVARS............ Experimental Vehicle for Avionics Research (MCD)
EVAS............. Enhanced Vortex Advisory System [*FAA*] (TAG)
EVAS............. Extravehicular Activity System (SSD)
EVAT............. Electrical Verifying Assembly Tool (SAUS)
EVATA............ Electronic-Visual-Auditory Training Aid
EVATA............ Electronic Visual Aural Training Aid (SAUS)
EVATA............ Extravehicular Activity Translational Aid (NASA)
EVATMI........... European Vinyl Asbestos Tile Manufacturers Institute (PDAA)
EVATP............ Experimental Volunteer Army Training Program (RDA)
EVATRON.......... Eccentric Variable-Angle Thermionic Rheostat
EVB.............. Esophageal Variceal Bleeding [*Medicine*] (MELL)
EVB.............. Examining and Validating Body (AIE)
EVB.............. Extruded Vinyl Bumper
EVBA............. Equivalent Vector-Boson Approximation [*Physics*] (ODA)
EVBM............. Expected Value Business Model (IAA)
EVC.............. Ecological Vegetation Class (EERA)
EVC.............. Educational Video Corporation (SAUO)
EVC.............. Election Volunteer Coordinator
EVC.............. Electric Vehicle Council [*Defunct*] (EA)

EVC Electronic Visual Communications (DNAB)
EVC Endatcom Ventures [*Vancouver Stock Exchange symbol*]
EVC Engineer Volunteer Corps [*British*]
EVC Enhanced Video Connector (VERA)
EVC Equilibrium Vapor Concentration (AAEL)
EVC Error Vector Computer (NG)
EVC Eurovision Control Center (SAUO)
EVC Executive Volunteer Corps
EVC Extravehicular Communications [*Aerospace*] (NASA)
EVC Extravehicular Communicator [*NASA*] (KSC)
e-vc- Vatican City [*MARC geographic area code*] [*Library of Congress*] (LCCP)
EVCA European Venture Capital Association
EVCAS Electronic Wide Angle Camera System (SAUS)
EVCAX EV Calif. Municipals Cl.B [*Mutual fund ticker symbol*] (SG)
EVCB Event Control Block [*Computer science*] (EECA)
EVCC Electric Vehicle Capsulated Contact [*Automotive electrical systems*]
EVCC Ex-Vessel Core Catcher [*Nuclear energy*] (NRCH)
EVC Centre Eurovision Control Centre (SAUS)
EVCD Electric Vehicle Connecting Device
EVCE Evidence
EVCI Educational Video Conferencing [*NASDAQ symbol*] (SG)
EVCI Education Video Conferencing [*NASDAQ symbol*]
EVCI Expected Value of Clinical Information [*Medicine*] (DMAA)
EVCI Ethylene-Vinyl Chloride [*Fire-retardant resin*] [*Organic chemistry*]
EVC-O Electronic Vibration Cutoff [*Aerospace*] (AAG)
evco electron vibration cutoff (SAUS)
EVCON Events Control [*Subsystem*] [*NASA*] (NASA)
EVCP Engineering Value Control Proposal (SAUS)
EVCP Event Control Block (SAUS)
EVCS Extravehicular Communications System [*NASA*]
EVCS Extruded Vinyl Chamfer Strip
EVCSG Ellis Van Creveld Support Group [*Founded in 1997*] (NRGU)
EVCT Extravehicular Crew Transfer [*NASA*] (MCD)
evctd Evacuated (SAUS)
EVCTD Extravehicular Crew Transfer Device [*NASA*] (KSC)
EVCU Extravehicular Communications Umbilical [*Aerospace*] (MCD)
EVCZ Evans [*Federal Railroad Administration identification code*]
EVD Ebola Virus Disease [*Medicine*] (MELL)
EVD Economische Voorlichtingsdienst [*Economic Information Service*] [*Information service or system*] (IID)
EVD Electrovacuum Drive
EVD Enhanced Versatile Disc
EVD Event Dispatcher [*Communications term*] (DCT)
EVD Explosive Vapor Detector (DA)
EVD Extended Voluntary Departure [*Temporary status sometimes granted by the State Department as protection against deportation*]
EVD External Visual Display (MCD)
EVDC European Veterinary Dental College (GVA)
EVDE External Visual Display Equipment [*Used in Apollo mission*] [*NASA*]
EVDF Eugene V. Debs Foundation (EA)
EVDG Electric Vehicle Development Group (SAUO)
EVDG Electric Vehicle Development Group Ltd. [*British*]
EVDL Electrically Variable Delay Line (SAUS)
EVDL Electronically Variable Delay Line (SAUS)
EVDL Electronic Variable Delay Line [*Automotive engineering*] (IAA)
EVDS Electronic Visual Display Subsystem
EVDS European Veterinary Dental Society (SAUS)
EVDS Explosive Vapor Detector Systems (MCD)
EVDT Editing Video Display Terminal (TIMI)
EVE Air Evex GmbH [*Germany*] [*ICAO designator*] (FAAC)
EVE Eagle Valley Environmentalists (EA)
EVE Economic Verification Experiments [*Marine science*] (MSC)
EVE Education, Volunteerism, Employment Opportunities
EVE Einstein Viscosity Equation
EVE Electric Vehicle Exposition (ADA)
EVE Electric, Viscous and Elastic (SAUS)
EVE Entry and Validation Equipment (SAUS)
EVE Environmental Valuation in Europe (EURO)
EVE Epoxy Vinyl Ester [*Plastics technology*]
EVE Equilibrium Vegetation Ecology (SAUS)
EVE Espace Video Europeen (EURO)
EVE Ethylene-Vinyl Ether Copolymer (EDCT)
EVE Ethyl Vinyl Ether [*Organic chemistry*]
EVE European Vacation Exchange (SAUO)
EVE European Videoconferencing Experimentation (SAUS)
EVE European Video Experiment (SAUO)
EVE European Video Telephony (SAUS)
EVE Eve, MO [*American Association of Railroads railroad junction routing code*]
EVE Evenes [*Norway*] [*Airport symbol*] (OAG)
eve Evening (ADWA)
EVE Evening
EVE Exemplary Voluntary Effort (ABAC)
EVE Expert Vax Ethernet Interface [*Work station computer-network interface*] (NITA)
EVE Extended Virtual Environment (SAUS)
EVE External Vemier Engine (IGSL)
EVE External Vernier Engine [*Space launch term*] (ISAK)
EVE Extreme Value Engineering (SAUS)
evea extravehicular engineering activities (SAUS)
EVEA Extravehicular Engineering Activity [*Aerospace*]
EVECW Extravascular Extracellular Water [*Medicine*]
EVELYN Employment of Very Low Yield Nuclear Weapons
EVEN Evening (ROG)
EVEN Evensong (ROG)
EVEN EV Environmental [*NASDAQ symbol*] (TTSB)
EV En EV Environmental, Inc. [*Associated Press*] (SAG)
EVEN EV Environmental, Inc. [*NASDAQ symbol*] (SAG)
EV Env EV Environmental, Inc. [*Associated Press*] (SAG)
EVENW EV Environmental Wrrt'A' [*NASDAQ symbol*] (TTSB)
EVER Endurance Vehicle for Extended Reconnaissance (SAUS)
EVER Everglades National Park
EVER Evergreen Resources, Inc. [*NASDAQ symbol*] (NQ)
ever Eversion [*Medicine*] (DAVI)
Everen Everen Capital Corp. [*Associated Press*] (SAG)
EverenC Everen Capital Corp. [*Associated Press*] (SAG)
EverestRe Everest Reinsurance Holdings, Inc. [*Associated Press*] (SAG)
EverJen Everest & Jennings International [*Associated Press*] (SAG)
EverMd Everest Medical Corp. [*Associated Press*] (SAG)
Everybody's LM Everybody's Law Magazine [*A publication*] (DLA)
EVERY M Everybody's Magazine [*A publication*] (ROG)
EVES Emergency Voice Evacuation System (SAUS)
EVES Environment for Verifying and Evaluating Software (SAUS)
EVESR ESADA [*Empire State Atomic Development Associates, Inc.*] Vallecitos Experimental Superheat Reactor
EVEST Experimental Valledtos Superheat Reactor (SAUS)
EVET Equal Velocity and Equal Temperature (SAUS)
Eve Trib Evening Tribune (SAUS)
EVEZ Evenson Explosives [*Federal Railroad Administration identification code*]
EVF Electromagnetic Vibrating Feeder
EVF Electronic Viewfinder [*Photography*] (WDMC)
EVF Electro-Viscous Fluid [*Electrical engineering*]
EVF Enterovaginal Fistula [*Medicine*] (MELL)
EVF Equipment Visibility File (NASA)
EVF Extracellular Volume Fraction [*Hematology*]
EVFLX EV Florida Municipals Cl.B [*Mutual fund ticker symbol*] (SG)
EVFM Evaporative Family [*Automotive emissions*]
EVFM Ex-Vessel Flux Monitor [*Nuclear energy*] (NRCH)
EVFU Electronic Vertical Format Unit (SAUS)
EVG Electrically-supported Vacuum Gyro (SAUS)
EVG Electric Vacuum Gyro
EVG Electrostatic Vector Grid
EVG Europaische Verteidigungsgemeinschaft [*European Defense Community*] [*German*] (BARN)
evg Evening (WDMC)
EVG Evening
EVG Evergold Resources [*Vancouver Stock Exchange symbol*]
EVG Evergreen Resources [*NYSE symbol*]
EVG Extravehicular Glove [*NASA*] (KSC)
EVGA Extended Video Graphics Adapter (SAUS)
EVGA Extended Video Graphics Array (PCM)
EVGM Evergreen Media Corp. [*NASDAQ symbol*] (SAG)
EVGM Evergreen Media Corp'A' [*NASDAQ symbol*] (TTSB)
EVGMP Evergreen Media $3.00 Cv Pfd [*NASDAQ symbol*] (TTSB)
EVGN Evergreen Bancorp [*NASDAQ symbol*] (TTSB)
EVGN Evergreen Bancorp, Inc. [*NASDAQ symbol*] (NQ)
EVGOX EV Government Obligs. Cl.A [*Mutual fund ticker symbol*] (SG)
EVGR Evening Grosbeak [*North American bird banding code*] (BIBA)
EvgrM Evergreen Media Corp. [*Associated Press*] (SAG)
EvgrMda Evergreen Media Corp. [*Associated Press*] (SAG)
EvgrMed Evergreen Media Corp. [*Associated Press*] (SAG)
EvgrnRs Evergreen Resources, Inc. [*Associated Press*] (SAG)
EVGRX Evergreen Fund Cl.Y [*Mutual fund ticker symbol*] (SG)
EVH Esophageal Varices Hemorrhage [*Medicine*]
EVHA English Villages Housing Association (ECON)
EVHA Europese Vereniging voor Haveninformatica [*European Port Data Processing Association*] [*Belgium*] (EA)
Ev Harr Evans' Edition of Harris' Modern Entries [*A publication*] (DLA)
EVHM Ex-Vessel Handling Machine [*Later, CLEM*] [*Nuclear energy*] (NRCH)
EVHMX EV National Municipals Cl.B [*Mutual fund ticker symbols*] (SG)
EVI Cedar Crest and Muhlenberg Colleges, Allentown, PA [*OCLC symbol*] (OCLC)
EVI Early Vendor Involvement Program [*Automotive engineering*]
EVI Eaton Vance New Jersey Municipal Income Trust [*AMEX symbol*] (NASQ)
EVI Education Voucher Institute [*Defunct*] (EA)
EVI Encapsulated Variable Inductor
EVI Energy Ventures [*NYSE symbol*] (SAG)
EVI Evacuation Immediate [*Telecommunications*] (OTD)
EVI EVent Information (SAUS)
EVI Evergreen International Corp. [*Toronto Stock Exchange symbol*]
evi evidence (SAUS)
EVI Evington, VA [*Location identifier*] [*FAA*] (FAAL)
EVI EVI Weatherford [*NYSE symbol*] [*Formerly, EVI, Inc.*]
EVI Extreme Value Index (FOTI)
EVIC Electronic Vehicle Information Center [*Automotive engineering*]
EVIC Evaluation Integrated Circuit (SAUS)
EVICT Evaluation of Intelligence Collection Tasks (SAUS)
EVID Evidence
Evid Evidences [*Paris*] [*A publication*] (BJA)
EVIDENT European Versatility in Deaf Education (EURO)
EVIF Emergency Virus Isolation Facility [*National Cancer Institute*]
EVIL Eastern Verbal Investigators League
EVIL Elevation Versus Integrated Log
EVIL Environmental Virtual Information Library (SAUO)
EVIL Extensible Video Interactive Language [*Computer science*]
EVIMEC Eastern Virginia MEDLINE Consortium (SAUS)
E VIN E Vino [*In Wine*] [*Pharmacy*]

EVIRI .... Enhanced Visible And Infrared Imager (SAUS)
EVIS .... Exchange Visitor Information System (SAUS)
evisc .... Evisceration [*Medicine*] (MAE)
EVIST .... Ethics and Values Implications of Science and Technology (SAUO)
EVIST .... Ethics and Values in Science and Technology [*National Science Foundation*]
E VIV DISC ... E Vivis Discessit [*Departed from Life*] [*Latin*] (BARN)
Ev Jud Pr ..... Evans' Practice of the Supreme Court of Judicature [*A publication*] (DLA)
EVK .... Ethyl Vinyl Ketone [*Organic chemistry*]
EVK .... Evaluation Kit [*American Microsystems Inc.*] (NITA)
EVKI .... Europaische Vereinigung der Keramik-Industrie [*Europeean Federation of the Electro-Ceramic Industry*] (PDAA)
EvKoMoe ..... Evreiskii Kommunisticheskii Soiuz Molodezhi (BJA)
EVL .... Cleveland, OK [*Location identifier*] [*FAA*] (FAAL)
EVL .... Electronic Visualization Laboratory
EVL .... Enveloping Layer
EVL .... Environment Virtual Library (SAUO)
EVL .... Everyman's Library [*A publication*]
EVLG .... European Veterinary Libraries Group (GVA)
EVLN .... Evolution (SAUS)
EVLP .... Ex Vivo Liver Perfusion (SAUS)
EVLSS .... Extravehicular Life Support System [*NASA*]
EVLTN .... Evaluation (MSA)
EVLTN .... Evolution (SAUS)
EVLW .... Extravascular Lung Water [*Medicine*]
EVM .... Earned Value Management (SAUS)
EVM .... Earth Viewing Module
evm .... earth-viewing module (SAUS)
EVM .... Eastman Visibility Meter (SAUS)
EVM .... Edatrexate, Vinblastine, Mutamycin [*Antineoplastic drug*] (CDI)
EVM .... Electronic Voltmeter (IEEE)
EVM .... Electrostatic Voltmeter (SAUS)
EVM .... Elektronno-Vychislitel'naya Mashina [*Electronic Calculating Machine*] [*Russian*]
EVM .... Energy Value of Milk (SAUS)
EVM .... Engine Vibration Monitor (MCD)
EVM .... Engine Vibration Monitoring (SAUS)
EVM .... Errors-in-Variables Model [*Statistics*]
EVM .... Ethylene Vinylacetate Copolymer (SAUS)
EVM .... Evacuation Mission [*Air Force*]
EVM .... Evaluation Module (TIMI)
EVM .... Evasive Maneuvering
EVM .... Eveleth, MN [*Location identifier*] [*FAA*] (FAAL)
EVM .... Extended Virtual Machine
EVM .... Exterior Vacuum Metallized (DICI)
evm .... extraneous vegetable matter (SAUS)
EvM .... Inscriptions of the Reigns of Evil-Merodach, Neriglissar, and Laborosoarchod (BJA)
EVMA .... Expanded Virtual Machine Assist [*Computer science*] (MHDI)
EVMC .... Enteroviral Meningitis in Childhood [*Medicine*] (MELL)
EVMD .... Everest Med [*NASDAQ symbol*] (TTSB)
EVMD .... Everest Medical Corp. [*NASDAQ symbol*] (SAG)
Ev Md Pr ..... Evans' Maryland Practice [*A publication*] (DLA)
evminfin ...... everglazed minicare fnish (SAUS)
EV Motor ..... Electric Vehicle Motor (SAUS)
EVMS .... Earned Value Management Standard (SAUS)
EVMS .... Earned Value Management System [*Army*]
EVMS .... Emil Verban Memorial Society (EA)
evmu .... extra-vehicular material unit (SAUS)
EVMU .... Extravehicular Mobility Unit [*NASA*] (NASA)
EVMV .... Electric Vapor Management Valve [*Automotive emissions*]
evn .... Electric Violin
EVN .... Erevan [*Former USSR*] [*Airport symbol*] (OAG)
EVN .... European Very-Long Baseline Interferometry Network
EVN .... European VLBI Network (SAUS)
EVN .... Evansville [*Diocesan abbreviation*] [*Indiana*] (TOCD)
EVN .... Even Resources [*Vancouver Stock Exchange symbol*]
EVNG .... Efferent Vein from Nephridial Gland (SAUS)
EVNG .... Evangeline Railway Co. [*AAR code*]
EVNG .... Evening
EVNGLCL ..... Evangelical
EVNGLST ..... Evangelist
EVNGLSTC .... Evangelstic
EVNNG .... Evening
EvnSut .... Evans & Sutherland Computer Corp. [*Associated Press*] (SAG)
EVNT .... Event
EVNTN .... Evanston, MS [*American Association of Railroads railroad junction routing code*]
Evnwth .... Evans Withycombe Residential, Inc. [*Associated Press*] (SAG)
EVNYX .... EV N.Y. Municipals Cl.B [*Mutual fund ticker symbols*] (SG)
EVO .... East Liverpool, OH [*Location identifier*] [*FAA*] (FAAL)
EVO .... Eaton Vance Ohio Municipal Income Trust [*AMEX symbol*] (NASQ)
EVO .... Eisenbahn-Verkehrsordnung [*Germany*]
EVO .... Electronic Variable Orifice [*Automotive engineering*]
EVO .... Engineering Verification Order (MCD)
EVO .... Extravehicular Operation [*Aerospace*]
EvObshchestKom ... Evreiskii Obshchestvennyi Komitet Pomoshchi Pogromlennym (BJA)
EVOC .... Excerpta Medica Vocabulary [*Elsevier Science Publishers BV*] [*Netherlands*] [*Information service or system*] (CRD)
Ev of Inf .... Evaluation of Information (SAUS)
EVOH .... Ethylene Vinyl Alcohol [*Plastics*]
EVOIL .... Economic Value of an Individual Life [*Insurance*]
EVOL .... Evolution [*or Evolutionist*] (WDAA)
evol .... evolutionary (SAUS)
evol .... evolutionist (SAUS)
EVOL .... Evolved
EVOL .... Evolving Systems [*NASDAQ symbol*] (SG)
EVOM .... Electronic Voltohmmeter (IEEE)
EVOP .... European Volcanological Project
EVOP .... Evaluation and Optimization
EVOP .... Evolutionary Operation [*Statistical technique*]
EVOS .... Electronic Variable-Orifice Steering
EVox .... English Vox [*Record label*]
EVP .... Eaton Vance Pennsylvania Municipal Trust [*AMEX symbol*] (NASQ)
EVP .... Electromagnetic Vector Potential [*Physics*] (BARN)
EVP .... Electronic Voice Phenomena [*Parapsychology*]
EVP .... End Vertical Plane (SAUS)
EVP .... Enhanced VERDIN [*Antijam Modem, Very-Low Frequency*] Processor [*Military*] (CAAL)
EVP .... Enteric Viral Pathogens [*Medicine*] (MELL)
EVP .... Episcleral Venous Pressure [*Medicine*] (MELL)
EVP .... Error-Vector Propagation (SAUS)
EVP .... Evangelische Volkspartei der Schweiz [*Swiss Evangelical People's Party*] [*Political party*] (PPW)
EVP .... Evangelische Volkspartij [*Evangelical People's Party*] [*Netherlands*] [*Political party*] (EY)
EVP .... Evoked Visual Potential [*Neurophysiology*]
EVP .... Evoked Visual Response [*Medicine*] (MELL)
EVP .... Executive Vice President (TIMI)
EVP .... Exhaust Valve Position [*Automotive engineering*]
EVP .... Experimental Version Prototype (ACAE)
EVP .... External Viewers Page (SAUO)
EVP .... Extra Value Package [*Automotive marketing*]
EVP .... Extroverted Personality (MELL)
EVP .... Protestant People's Party (Switzerland) [*Political party*] (PSAP)
EVPASSC ..... Electronic Variable Power-Assist Steering System Controller [*Automotive engineering*]
EVPC .... Even Vertical Parity Check (VLIE)
EVPD .... Evaporated
EVPHI .... Europese Vereniging voor Pediatrische Hematologie en Immunologie [*European Society for Paediatric Haematology and Immunology - ESPHI*] (EAIO)
EVPI .... Expected Value of Perfect Information [*Statistics*]
Ev Pl .... Evans on Pleading [*A publication*] (DLA)
E-VPN .... Enterprise Virtual Private Network (VLIE)
Evpn .... Evaporation (SAUS)
Ev Poth .... Evans' Translation of Pothier on Obligations [*A publication*] (DLA)
Ev Pr & Ag .... Evans on the Law of Principal and Agent [*A publication*] (DLA)
EVPREP ...... Event Preparation (VLIE)
EVPSYCA ..... European Working Group for Psychosomatic Cancer Research (SAUO)
EVR .... Electronic Vacuum Regulator [*Automotive emissions*]
EVR .... Electronic Video Recorder (SAUS)
EVR .... Electronic Video Recording [*or Recorder*] (NTCM)
EVR .... Electronic Video Reproduction (IAA)
EVR .... Environmental Voting Records (SAUO)
EVR .... Equine viral rhinopneumonitis (SAUS)
EVR .... EVEREN Capital [*NYSE symbol*] (SG)
EVR .... Everen Capital Corp. [*NYSE symbol*] (SAG)
EVR .... Everest Resources Ltd. [*Vancouver Stock Exchange symbol*]
EVR .... Evoked Response [*Neurology*] (DAVI)
EVR .... Evoked Vascular Response [*Physiology*]
EVR .... External Visual Reference [*Motion sickness*]
EVRC .... Eton Volunteer Rifle Corps [*British military*] (DMA)
EVRD .... Excellentissime Vestre Reverendissime Dominationis [*Of Your Most Excellent and Reverend Lordship*] [*Latin*] (ECON)
evrep .... event recording potential (SAUS)
EVRET .... Everett, MA [*American Association of Railroads railroad junction routing code*]
EVRGRN ...... Evergreen
EvrgrnB .... Evergreen Bancorp, Inc. [*Associated Press*] (SAG)
Ev RL .... Evans' Road Laws of South Carolina [*A publication*] (DLA)
EVRLK .... Ever-Lock
EVRM .... Envirometrics, Inc. [*NASDAQ symbol*] (SAG)
EVRMW ...... Envirometrics Inc. Wrrt [*NASDAQ symbol*] (TTSB)
EVRO .... EVRO Corp. [*NASDAQ symbol*] (TTSB)
EVRO .... EVRO Financial Corp. [*Formerly, Envirosearch Corp.*] [*NASDAQ symbol*] (NQ)
EVRPrA .... Everen Cap 13.50%'A'Ex Pfd [*NYSE symbol*] (TTSB)
EVRS .... Early Ventricular Repolarization Syndrome [*Medicine*] (MELL)
EVRS .... Electronic Video Recording System (SAUS)
EVRSN .... Everson, PA [*American Association of Railroads railroad junction routing code*]
EVRT .... Electrical Verifying Assembly Tool (SAUS)
EVRTT .... Everett, GA [*American Association of Railroads railroad junction routing code*]
EVRV .... Electronic Vacuum Regulator Valve [*Automotive engineering*]
EVRX .... Elkhorn Valley Rail Car [*Federal Railroad Administration identification code*]
EVS .... Ecumenical Voluntary Service [*Defunct*]
EVs .... Electric Vehicles (EERA)
EVS .... Electronic-optical Viewing System (SAUS)
EVS .... Electronic Valve Specification (MCD)
EVS .... Electronic Vision System [*Saab*] (NITA)
EVS .... Electronic Visual System (SAUS)
EVS .... Electronic Voice Switching (AFM)
EVS .... Electronic Voice Switching System (SAUS)
EVS .... Electro-Optical Viewing System

EVS .... Electro-Optical Visual Sensors [*Hughes Aircraft Co.*]
EVS .... Electrovisual Sensors
EVS .... Emergency Venting System
EVS .... Endoscopic Variceal Sclerosis [*Medicine*]
EVS .... Engine Vertical Scale
EVS .... Engine Vision System [*Automotive engine instrumentation*]
EVS .... Enhanced VERDIN [*Antijam Modem, Very-Low Frequency*] System [*Military*] (CAAL)
EVS .... Enhanced Videotex Service (LAIN)
EVS .... Enhanced Vision System (SAUS)
EVS .... Environmental Science (AABC)
EVS .... Environment Visualization System [*Computer science*]
EVS .... Equipment Visibility System (NASA)
EVS .... Equi Ventures, Inc. [*Vancouver Stock Exchange symbol*]
EVS .... Ethics and Values Studies (SAUS)
EVS .... Event Service (SAUS)
EVS .... Event Verification System [*Technology that encripts time and location on video recordings*]
EVS .... Expected Value Saved
E-V-S .... Expected Value-Variance-Skewness [*Statistics*]
EVS .... Extravascular Space (SAUS)
EVS .... Extravehicular Suit [*Aerospace*] (MCD)
EVS .... Extravehicular System [*Aerospace*]
EVS .... Extreme Value Statistics
EVS .... Eye-Voice Span
EVSA .... Electronic Variable Shock Absorber [*Automotive engineering*]
EVSB .... Extensible VME Subsystem Bus (SAUS)
EVSC .... Extravehicular Suit Communications [*Aerospace*]
EVSD .... Electronic Vision Systems Development
EVSD .... Energy-Variant Sequential Detection (CET)
EVSD .... European Society Veterinary Dermatology (SAUO)
EVSE .... Electronically Variable Shorting Element (SAUS)
EvSektsiia .... Evreiskaia Sektsiia (BJA)
EVSGX .... EV Strategic Income Cl.B [*Mutual fund ticker symbol*] (SG)
EVSI .... Evans Systems [*NASDAQ symbol*] (TTSB)
EVSI .... Evans Systems, Inc. [*NASDAQ symbol*] (SAG)
EVSI .... Expected Value of Sample Information [*Statistics*]
EVSN .... Elbit Vision Systems Ltd. [*NASDAQ symbol*] (SAG)
EVSP .... Employee Voluntary Support Program (SAUO)
EVSR .... Exhaust Valve Seat Recession [*Automotive engineering*]
EVSS .... Extravehicular Space Suit [*Aerospace*] (MCD)
EVSSAR .... European Veterinary Society for the Study of Small Animal Reproduction (GVA)
EVST .... Ex-Vessel Storage Tank [*Nuclear energy*] (NRCH)
Ev Stat .... Evans' Collection of Statutes [*A publication*] (DLA)
EVSTC .... Extra Vehicular Suit Telecommunications (SAUS)
EVSTC .... Extravehicular Suit Telemetry Communications [*Aerospace*]
EVSU .... Extravehicular Space Unit [*Aerospace*] (MCD)
EVSYS 599 ... Evaporative System [*Automotive emissions*]
EVT .... Earth Venus Transit [*Aerospace*]
EVT .... Economic Investment Trust Ltd. [*Toronto Stock Exchange symbol*]
evt .... educational and vocational training (SAUS)
EVT .... Education and Vocational Training [*British military*] (DMA)
EVT .... Effective Visual Transmission (NATG)
EVT .... Elasticity, Viscosity, and Thixotropy
EVT .... Electronic Valve Timing [*Automobile engine design*]
EVT .... Embedded Visual Tool (VLIE)
EVT .... Emergency Veterinary Tag
EVT .... End Viewing Tube
EVT .... Engineering Verification Test
EVT .... Equiviscous Temperature [*Chemical engineering*] (IAA)
EVT .... Evaluation Vector Table
E v T .... E van Tongeren (SAUS)
EVT .... Event (SAUS)
evt .... eventually (SAUS)
EVT .... Expect Vector To [*Aviation*] (FAAC)
EVT .... External Vacuum Therapy (MELL)
evt .... extra-value trimmed (SAUS)
EVT .... Extravehicular Transfer [*NASA*] (KSC)
EVT .... Extreme Value Theory (SAUS)
EVTC .... Environmental Technologies [*NASDAQ symbol*] (TTSB)
EVTC .... Environmental Technology Corp. [*NASDAQ symbol*] (SAG)
EVTCM .... Expected Value Terminal Capacity Matrix (SAUS)
EVTECA .... Electric Vehicle Total Energy Cycle Analysis
EVTI .... EndoVascular Technologies [*NASDAQ symbol*] (TTSB)
EVTI .... Endovascular Technologies, Inc. [*NASDAQ symbol*] (SAG)
EVTM .... Ex-Vessel Transfer Machine [*Nuclear energy*] (NRCH)
EVTMX .... EV Utilities Fund Cl.A [*Mutual fund ticker symbol*] (SG)
EVTOP .... Enhanced Tactical Vehicle Occupant Protection [*Military vehicles*]
Ev Tr .... Evans' Trial [*A publication*] (DLA)
EVTRX .... Evergreen Income & Growth Cl.Y [*Mutual fund ticker symbol*] (SG)
E/VTS .... Engine/Vehicle Test Stand
EVTV .... Extravascular Thermal Volume [*Medicine*]
Ev U .... Evaporation Unit (SAUS)
EVU .... Maryville, MO [*Location identifier*] [*FAA*] (FAAL)
EVV .... English Versions
EVV .... Environmental Safeguards [*AMEX symbol*] (SG)
EVV .... Evansville [*Indiana*] [*Airport symbol*] (OAG)
EVVA .... Europaeische Vereinigung der Veterinaranatomen [*European Association of Veterinary Anatomists - EAVA*] (EAIO)
EVVA .... Extravehicular Visor Assembly [*NASA*]
EVVTX .... Evergreen Growth & Income Cl.Y [*Mutual fund ticker symbol*] (SG)
EVW .... European Voluntary Worker
EVW .... European Voluntary Workers (SAUO)
EVW .... Evanston, WY [*Location identifier*] [*FAA*] (FAAL)
EVX .... Electric Vehicle Experimental (SAUS)
EVX .... Electronic Voice Exchange [*Commterm, Inc.*] [*Billerica, MA*] [*Telecommunications*] (TSSD)
EVY .... Eaton Vance New York Municipal Income Trust [*AMEX symbol*] (NASQ)
EVY .... Every
evythg .... everything (SAUS)
EVZS .... Edinburgh Veterinary Zoological Society (GVA)
EW .... Each Way (MSA)
EW .... Early Warning [*Air Force*]
EW .... Earthenware
EW .... Earthwatch [*United Nations Environment Program*]
ew .... earth watch (SAUS)
EW .... Earwax (MELL)
EW .... East and West [*A publication*] (ABAR)
EW .... East Washington Railway Co. [*AAR code*]
E/W .... East West (ACAE)
EW .... East-West
EW .... East-West Airlines [*ICAO designator*] (AD)
EW .... Eave-to-Eave Width [*of boxcar*]
EW .... Econoic Week (journ.) (SAUS)
EW .... Economic Warfare [*British*]
EW .... Edinger-Westphal Nucleus [*Neuroanatomy*]
EW .... Edit Word (SAUS)
EW .... Edmund Walker [*Car parts distribution company*] [*British*]
EW .... Education World
EW .... Edwards Lifesciences [*NYSE symbol*] (SG)
EW .... Effective Warmth (IAA)
EW .... Egg White
EW .... Egg Width
EW .... Eingetragenes Warenzeichen [*Registered Trademark*] [*German*]
EW .... Elastic Wave (SAUS)
EW .... Electrically Welded (SAUS)
EW .... Electrical Welding (IAA)
EW .... Electrical World (journ.) (SAUS)
EW .... Electric Windows [*Automotive accessory*]
EW .... Electronics Weekly (SAUS)
EW .... Electronics World (journ.) (SAUS)
EW .... Electronic War (SAUS)
EW .... Electronic Warfare [*Communications term*] (DCT)
EW .... Electronic Warfare Technician [*Military*] (POLM)
EW .... Electronic Welfare (CCCA)
EW .... Electronic Wholesaler (IAA)
EW .... Electronic Wholesalers Inc. (SAUO)
EW .... Electroslag Welding
EW .... Electrowinning (SAUS)
ew .... Elsewhere (MAE)
EW .... Emergency Ward
EW .... Eminent Women [*A publication*]
EW .... Empty Weight
EW .... End of Work (VLIE)
EW .... End Wall [*Of a cell*] [*Botany*]
E/W .... Energy over Weight
E/W .... Energy to Weight Ratio (SAUS)
EW .... Energy-to-Weight Ratio (MCD)
EW .... Engineer's Writer [*British military*] (DMA)
EW .... England and Wales (SAUS)
EW .... Enlisted Woman [*or Women*]
EW .... Entry Week (SAUS)
e/w .... equipped with (SAUS)
EW .... Equivalent Weapons [*Military*]
ew .... equivalent widths (SAUS)
EW .... Ether-Water (PDAA)
EW .... Euer [*Your*] [*German*]
EW .... Europaeische Wandervereinigung [*European Ramblers' Association - ERA*] [*Germany*] (EAIO)
ew--- .... Europe, Western [*MARC geographic area code*] [*Library of Congress*] (LCCP)
EW! .... Everybody Wins! [*Literacy organization*]
Ew .... Ewart (SAUS)
Ew .... Ewbanke (SAUS)
Ew .... Ewell (SAUS)
Ew .... Ewen (SAUS)
Ew .... Ewing (SAUS)
EW .... Expansion Wave (SAUS)
EW .... Extended-Wear Lenses [*Optometry*]
EW .... Extensive Wound
EW .... External Work
EW .... Extinct in the Wild (EES)
EW .... Extra White (SAUS)
EW .... Extreme Width [*of flight deck*]
EW .... Ex-Warrants [*Without Warrants*] [*Finance*]
EW .... Farly Warning (SAUS)
EW .... Sleet Shower [*Meteorology*] (BARN)
EW1 .... Electronic Warfare Technician, First Class (DNAB)
EW2 .... Electronic Warfare Technician, Second Class (DNAB)
EW3 .... Electronic Warfare Technician, Third Class (DNAB)
EWA .... Early Warning Adjunct
EWA .... Early Warning/Attack Assessment
EWA .... East and West Association (SAUO)
EWA .... East-West Acceleration
EWA .... East-West Airlines Ltd. [*Australia*] [*FAA designator*] (FAAC)
EWA .... Edgewood Arsenal [*Maryland*] [*Army*] (AABC)
EWA .... Education and World Affairs [*Later, ICED*]
EWA .... Education Writers Association (EA)

EWA............ Effective Word Address (IAA)
EWA............ Effective World Address (SAUS)
EWA............ Electrical Wholesalers Association (SAUO)
EWA............ Electronic Writing Automaton (SAUS)
EWA............ Emunah Women of America (EA)
EWA............ End Warning Area [*Computer science*] (BUR)
EWA............ Engineering Work Assignment
EWA............ Engineering Work Authorization [*Aerospace*]
EWA............ Erase/Write Alternate (VLIE)
EWA............ Esperanto Writers Association (EA)
EWA............ Estimated Warehouse Arrival (NASA)
EWA............ Europaeische Wahrungsabkommen [*European Monetary Agreement*] [*German*] (DCTA)
EWA............ European Wax Association (EAIO)
EWA............ European Welding Association (EAIO)
EWA............ Exotic Wildlife Association (NTPA)
EWA............ Foreign Fd Australia Index'WEBS' [*AMEX symbol*] (TTSB)
EWA............ Kewanee, MS [*Location identifier*] [*FAA*] (FAAL)
EWA............ WEBS, Australia Index Series [*AMEX symbol*] (SG)
EWA............ WEBS Index Fund, Inc. [*AMEX symbol*] (NASQ)
EWA............ World Equity Benchmark Shares [*AMEX symbol*] (SAG)
EW/AA........ Early Warning/Attack Assessment (ACAE)
EWAA-USA... Elsa Wild Animal Appeal - USA (EA)
EWABL/AAU... Eastern Women's Amateur Basketball League of the AAU [*Amateur Athletic Union of the United States*] (EA)
EWAC.......... Early Warning Aircraft (MCD)
EWAC.......... Electronic Warfare Anechoic Chamber
EWACS........ Electronic Warfare Analysis Centre (SAUS)
EWACS........ Electronic Wide-Angle Camera System
EWAD.......... Early Warning Air Defense (NATG)
EWAG.......... Exploding Wire Aerosol Generator [*Liquid suspension*]
EWAHA........ East West Academy of Healing Arts (EA)
EWAI.......... Eisenhower World Affairs Institute [*Later, EI*] (EA)
e-wallet...... Electronic Wallet (ADWA)
EWAMS........ Early Warning and Monitoring System (MCD)
EWAN.......... Emulator Without A Good Name (SAUS)
EWAN.......... Emulator without a Name (VLIE)
EWAN.......... Enterprise-Wide Application Network
EWAN.......... Enterprise Wide Area Network (CIST)
EW & CSq... Early Warning and Control Squadron [*Air Force*]
EW & I........ Electronic Warfare and Intelligence [*Military*]
EWAP.......... Electronic Warfare Aggressor Program [*Military*] (SEWL)
EW ARC...... Electronic Warfare Area Reprogramming Capability (SAUS)
EWARS........ Electronics Warfare Assets Reporting Systems (SAUS)
EWAS.......... Economic Warfare Analysis Section (SAUO)
EWASER...... Electromagnetic Wave Amplification by Stimulated Emission of Radiation
EWAT.......... Electronic Warfare Advanced Technology [*Military*] (SEWL)
EWAV.......... Electrical Wholesalers' Association, Victoria [*Australia*]
EWAW.......... Encyclopedia of Women's Associations Worldwide [*A publication*]
EWB............ Blanch [*E.W.*] Holdings, Inc. [*NYSE symbol*] (SPSG)
EWB............ Earl Weaver Baseball [*Computer game*]
EWB............ Embedded Wiring Board (MSA)
EWB............ Emergency Warnings Branch [*National Weather Service*]
EWB............ Emergency Waste Basin (SAUS)
EWB............ Emergency Work Bureau (SAUO)
EWB............ Encyclopedia of World Biography [*A publication*]
EWB............ Estrogen Withdrawal Bleeding [*Medicine*]
EWB............ etched wiring board (SAUS)
EWB............ E.W. Blanch Holdings [*NYSE symbol*] (TTSB)
EWB............ Fall River-New Bedford [*Massachusetts*] [*Airport symbol*] (AD)
EWB............ New Bedford [*Massachusetts*] [*Location identifier*] [*FAA*] (FAAL)
EWBA.......... English Women's Bowling Association (DBA)
EWBC.......... East West Bancorp, Inc. [*NASDAQ symbol*] (NASQ)
EWBF.......... English Women's Bowling Federation (DBA)
EWBN.......... Early Warning Broadcast Net [*DoD*]
EWBX.......... EarthWeb, Inc. [*NASDAQ symbol*] (SG)
EW/C.......... Early Warning Control [*Military*]
EWC............ Eastern Women's Center (EA)
EWC............ East-West Center (EA)
EWC............ Edward Waters College [*Jacksonville, FL*]
EWC............ Electric Water Cooler
EWC............ Electric Wire & Cable Co. of Israel Ltd. (SAUS)
EWC............ Electronic Warfare Center (MCD)
EWC............ Electronic Warfare Commander (SAUO)
EWC............ Electronic Warfare Committee (SAUO)
EWC............ Electronic Warfare Coordinator (NVT)
EWC............ Electronic Warfare/Cryptologic [*Communications term*] (DCT)
EWC............ Ellwood City, PA [*Location identifier*] [*FAA*] (FAAL)
EWC............ Episcopal Women's Caucus (EA)
EWC............ European Waste Catalogue (SAUO)
EWC............ European Weather Central (SAUO)
EWC............ Evaporative Water Chiller [*Engineering*]
EWC............ Foreign Fd Canada Index'WEBS' [*AMEX symbol*] (TTSB)
EWC............ WEBS, Canada Index Series [*AMEX symbol*] (SG)
EWC............ World Equity Benchmark Shares [*AMEX symbol*] (SAG)
EW/C3CM.... Electronic Warfare Command and Control Communications Countermeasures (SAUO)
EWCAP........ Electrical Wiring Component Application Partnership
EWCAP........ Electric Wiring Component Application Partnership (SAUS)
EWCAP........ Electronic Warfare Continuum Assessment Program [*Military*] (SEWL)
EWCAS........ Early Warning and Control Aircraft System (IEEE)
EWCAS........ Electronics Warfare-Close Air Support (ACAE)
EW/CAS...... Electronic Warfare/Close-Air Support (MCD)
EW-CAS-JTF... Electronic Warfare, Close-Air Support, Joint Task Force (MCD)
EWCB.......... Electrical Workers and Contractors' Board [*Queensland, Australia*]
EWCC.......... East-West Cultural Center (EA)
EWCC.......... Electronic Warfare Control Centre (SAUO)
EWCC.......... Electronic Warfare Coordination Center
EWCC.......... Elvis We Care Campaign [*Later, EPIAI*] (EA)
EWCC.......... Environmental Workforce Coordinating Committee [*Environmental Protection Agency*] (GFGA)
EWCD.......... Electronic Warfare Cover and Deception (MCD)
EWCDMS..... Electronic Warfare Cover and Deception Management Subsystem (MCD)
EW Change... east-west change (SAUS)
EWCI.......... East-West Communication Institute [*Later, East-West Institute of Culture and Communication*] [*Research center*] (RCD)
EWCI.......... Estonian World Council (SAUO)
EWCI.......... Evangelical Women's Caucus, International (EA)
EWCIP........ Elevated Work Cage Improvement Program (DWSG)
EWCL.......... Electromagnetic Warfare and Communications Laboratory
EW-CLI........ East-West Institute of Culture and Communication [*Research center*] (RCD)
EWCM.......... Electronic Warfare Control Module (ACAE)
EWCM.......... Electronic Warfare Coordination Module (DOMA)
EWCP.......... Early Warning Change Proposal (MCD)
EWCP.......... Electronic Warfare Control Processor [*Military*] (SEWL)
EWCP.......... EW Control Processor (SAUS)
EWCR.......... Electronic Warfare Counter Response (MCD)
EWCR.......... Elementary Well Connected Relation (SAUS)
EWCRP........ Early Warning Control and Reporting Post (SAUS)
EW/CRP...... Early Warning/Control and Reporting Post
EWCS.......... Electronic Warfare Combat System (ACAE)
EWCS.......... Electronic Warfare Concept Study (SAUO)
EWCS.......... Electronic Warfare Control Ship [*Navy*] (NVT)
EWCS.......... Electronic Warfare Coordinating Staff
EWCS.......... European Wideband Communications System [*Army*]
EWCS.......... EW Control Ship (SAUS)
EWD............ Economic Warfare Division (SAUO)
EWD............ Electric Winch Drive (DWSG)
EWD............ Electronic Warfare Department (SAUO)
EWD............ Electronic Warfare Division (SAUO)
EWD............ Elementary Wiring Diagram
EWD............ Foreign Fd Sweden Index'WEBS' [*AMEX symbol*] (TTSB)
EWD............ WEBS, Sweden Index Series [*AMEX symbol*] (SG)
EWD............ World Equity Benchmark Shares [*AMEX symbol*] (SAG)
EWDAA........ Energy and Water Development Appropriations Act (SAUS)
EWDD.......... European Wholesalers and Distributors Directory [*Pronounced "eewed"*] [*A publication*]
EW/DE........ Electronic Warfare/Directed Energy (SAUS)
EWDI.......... Electronic Wind Direction Indicator
EWDLS........ Evanescent Wave Dynamic Light Scattering [*Physics*]
EWDT.......... Early Warning Data Transmission (NATG)
EWDTC........ Electronic Warfare Design to Cost (ACAE)
EWE............ East West European [*Bulgaria*] [*ICAO designator*] (FAAC)
EWE............ Electronic Warfare Element (AABC)
EWE............ Emergency Window Escape [*NASA*] (NASA)
EWE............ Equatorial Winds Experiment (SAUS)
ewe............ Ewe [*MARC language code*] [*Library of Congress*] (LCCP)
EWE............ Extrapolated Water Elevation (PDAA)
EWEA.......... European Wind Energy Association (EAIO)
EWEB.......... Eugene Water and Electric Board (SAUO)
EWEC.......... Electromagnetic Wave Energy Conversion (SAUS)
EWEC.......... Electromagnetic Wave Energy Converter [*Solar energy conversion*]
EWEC.......... Electromagnet Wave Energy Conversion (SAUS)
EWEDF........ East West Education Development Foundation (EA)
Ewell Bl........ Ewell's Edition of Blackstone [*A publication*] (DLA)
Ewell Cas Inf... Ewell's Leading Cases on Infancy, Etc. [*A publication*] (DLA)
Ewell Ess...... Ewell's Essentials of the Law [*A publication*] (DLA)
Ewell Evans Ag... Ewell's Edition of Evans on Agency [*A publication*] (DLA)
Ewell Fix...... Ewell on the Law of Fixtures [*A publication*] (DLA)
Ewell LC...... Ewell's Leading Cases on Infancy, Etc. [*A publication*] (DLA)
EWEP.......... Electronic Warfare Evaluation Program [*Military*] (SEWL)
EWEPS........ Environmental Weapons Effects Prediction System (MCD)
EWES.......... Electronic Warfare Evaluation Simulator
EWES.......... Electronic Warfare Evaluation System [*Military*] (SEWL)
EWES.......... Engineering Waterways Experiment Station [*Army*]
EWEX.......... Electronic Warfare Exercise (NVT)
EWEXIPT..... Electronic Warfare Exercise in Port (NVT)
EWF............ Early Warning Fighter
EWF............ Early Warning Form (SAUS)
EWF............ Earth, Wind, and Fire [*Rock music group*]
EWF............ Education Without Frontiers [*An association*] (EAIO)
EWF............ Eleanor Women's Foundation (EA)
EWF............ Electrical Wholesalers Federation [*British*] (BI)
EWF............ Electromagnetic Wave Filter
EWF............ Electronic Warfare
EWF............ Elektronisches Worterbuch der Fachsprachen [*Technische Universitat Dresden*] [*Multilingual terminology bank*] (NITA)
EWF............ Equivalent-Weight Factor
ewf............ equivalent weight factor (SAUS)
EWF............ European Warrant Fund [*NYSE symbol*] (SPSG)
EWF............ European Wax Federation [*Belgium*] (EAIO)
EWF............ European Weightlifting Federation (EA)
EWF............ Wake Forest University, Winston-Salem, NC [*OCLC symbol*] (OCLC)
EWFH.......... East-West Fine, Hundreds
EWFP.......... Engineered Waste Form Program (SAUS)
EWFT.......... East-West Fine, Tens
EWFU.......... East-West Fine, Units

EWG Earth Works Group Inc. (EERA)
EWG Electron-Withdrawing Group [*Chemistry*] (MEC)
EWG Environmental Working Group [*An advocacy group*]
EWG Equipment Working Group
EWG Ernaehrungswissenschaften Giessen [*Nutrition Sciences - Giessen University*] [*Database*]
EWG Ethics Works Group (EERA)
EWG Euromissiles Working Group [*Defunct*] (EA)
EWG Europaeische Wirtschaftsgemeinschaft [*European Economic Community*]
EWG Eurowings, AG, Nurnberg [*Germany*] [*FAA designator*] (FAAC)
EWG Executive Working Group [*NATO*]
EWG Foreign Fd Germany Index'WEBS' [*AMEX symbol*] (TTSB)
EWG WEBS, Germany Index Series [*AMEX symbol*] (SG)
EWG World Equity Benchmark Shares [*AMEX symbol*] (SAG)
EWGA Executive Women's Golf Association (ADWA)
EWGAE European Working Group on Acoustic Envasion (SAUO)
EW/GCI Early Warning/Ground Control Intercept [*RADAR*]
ewgcir early-warning ground-control-intercept radar (SAUS)
EWGETS Electronic Warfare Ground Environment Threat Simulator
EWGN Economy Station Wagon (TVEL)
EWGP European Working Group in Pediatric Otorhinolaryngology (SAUO)
EWGP Excess Weapons-Grade Plutonium (FOTI)
EWGPHB Growth Planning Hearings Board for Eastern Washington (SAUO)
EWGRB European Working Group on Research and Biodiversity (EURO)
EWGS European and Pacific Weather Graphics Switch [*Air Force*] (GFGA)
EWGS European Weather Graphics System (SAUS)
EWH Expected Working Hours (IAA)
EWH Foreign Fd Hong Kong Index'WEBS' [*AMEX symbol*] (TTSB)
EWH WEBS, Hong Kong Index Series [*AMEX symbol*] (SG)
EWH World Equity Benchmark Shares [*AMEX symbol*] (SAG)
EWHA Eastern Women's Headwear Association [*Later, AMMA*] (EA)
EWHO Elbow-Wrist-Hand-Orthosis [*Medicine*]
EWHS Eli Whitney High School (SAUS)
EWHS Eli Whitney School (SAUS)
EWI Earl Warren Institute (SAUS)
EWI Economic Warfare Intelligence (CARL)
EWI Edison Welding Institute (EA)
EWI Educational Workers' International (AIE)
EWI Education with Industry
EWI Electronic Warfare Intelligence (SAUO)
EW/I Electronic Warfare/Intercept (MCD)
EWI Electronic Wiring Intercommunication
EWI Enarotali [*Indonesia*] [*Airport symbol*] (OAG)
EWI English Winter Index
EWI Entered without Inspection [*Usually applies to aliens who enter at other than a port of entry*]
EWI Executive Women International [*Salt Lake City, UT*] (EA)
EWI Experiential World Inventory [*Psychodiagnostic questionnaire*]
EWI Expert Witnesses' Institute (WDAA)
EWI Foreign Fd Italy Index'WEBS' [*AMEX symbol*] (TTSB)
EWI WEBS, Italy Index Series [*AMEX symbol*] (SG)
EWI World Equity Benchmark Shares [*AMEX symbol*] (SAG)
EWIA External Wall Insulation Association [*British*] (DBA)
EWIBA English Women's Indoor Bowling Association (DBA)
EWICB Electronic Warfare Interface Connection Box
ewicb electronic-warfare interface-connection box (SAUS)
EWICK Eastwick, PA [*American Association of Railroads railroad junction routing code*]
EWICS European Workshop for Industrial Computer Systems (SAUS)
EWICS European Workshop of Industrial Computer Systems (NITA)
EWICS European Workshop on Industrial Computer System (SAUS)
EWICST European Workshop of Industrial Computer System - Technical Committee (SAUO)
EWIF Electronic Warfare Intelligence Facility [*Fort Huachuca, AZ*] [*United States Army Electronic Proving Ground*] (GRD)
Ewing Just Ewing's Justice [*A publication*] (DLA)
EWINO East Winona, WI [*American Association of Railroads railroad junction routing code*]
EWIOC Electronic Warfare and Intelligence Operations Center [*Military*] (MCD)
EWIP Electronic Warfare Integrated Programming (SAUS)
EWIR Electronic Warfare Integrated Reprogramming [*Military*] (SEWL)
EWIRC Electronic Warfare Integrated Reprogramming Concept (MCD)
EWIRC EW Integrated Reprogramming Concept (SAUS)
EWIRDB Electronic Warfare Integrated Reprogrammable Database [*Military*] (SEWL)
EWIS Electronic Warfare Information System (MCD)
EWIS European WWMCCS Information System (SAUS)
EWITA Evaluation of Women in the Army (MCD)
EWITS Early Warning Identification Transmission System (ACAE)
EWJ Foreign Fd Japan Index'WEBS' [*AMEX symbol*] (TTSB)
EWJ WEBS, Japan Index Series [*AMEX symbol*] (SG)
EWJ World Equity Benchmark Shares [*AMEX symbol*] (SAG)
EWJC European Women's Judo Championships [*British*]
EWJT Electronic Warfare Joint Test (ACAE)
EWK Foreign Fd Belgium Index'WEBS' [*AMEX symbol*] (TTSB)
EWK Newton, KS [*Location identifier*] [*FAA*] (FAAL)
EWK WEBS, Belgium Index Series [*AMEX symbol*] (SG)
EWK World Equity Benchmark Shares [*AMEX symbol*] (SAG)
EWL Earliest Work Listed
EWL Eastern Wrestling League (PSS)
EWL Effective Wavelength
EWL Egg White Lysozyme (OA)
EWL Eigenschaftswoerterliste (DB)
EWL Electronic Warfare Laboratory [*Army*]
EWL Enterprise Workshops Ltd.
EWL Equalized Ward Leonard (SAUS)
EWL Estimated Weight Loss (MELL)
EWL European Women's Lobby [*Belgium*] (EAIO)
EWL Evaporative Water Loss
EWL Excess Weight Loss [*Morbid obesity surgical treatment*]
EWL Exchange Work List [*Telecommunications*] (TEL)
EWL Foreign Fd Switzer'd Index'WEBS' [*AMEX symbol*] (TTSB)
EWL Wake Forest University, Law Library, Winston-Salem, NC [*OCLC symbol*] (OCLC)
EWL WEBS, Switzerland Index Series [*AMEX symbol*] (SG)
EWL World Equity Benchmark Shares [*AMEX symbol*] (SAG)
EWLD Engineering Weekly Labor Distribution (AAG)
EWLP European Workshop on Lignocellulosics and Pulp (SAUO)
EWLTP Earl Warren Legal Training Program (EA)
EWLW Early Warning Lightweight (SAUS)
EWM Edgewise Meter
EWM Electrical Welding Machine
EWM End of Warning Marker (SAUS)
EWM End-of-Warning Marker (VLIE)
EWM Environmental and Waste Management (COE)
EWM Episcopal World Mission (EA)
EWM Foreign Fd Malaysia Index'WEBS' [*AMEX symbol*] (TTSB)
EWM MSU [*Michigan State University*] and WSU Union List of Serials, Detroit, MI [*Wayne State University*] [*OCLC symbol*] (OCLC)
EWM Newman, TX [*Location identifier*] [*FAA*] (FAAL)
EWM WEBS, Malaysia(Free)Index Series [*AMEX symbol*] (SG)
EWM Weintraub Music [*Publisher*]
EWM World Equity Benchmark Shares [*AMEX symbol*] (SAG)
EWMA Exponentially Weighted Moving Average [*Statistics*]
EWMB Enemy War Materials Branch [*Supreme Headquarters, Allied Expeditionary Force*] [*World War II*]
EWMC Eli Whitney Metrology Center
EWMD European Women's Management Development Network (EAIO)
EWMFC Elvis Worldwide Memorial Fan Club (EA)
EWMIS Electronic Warfare Management Information System [*Air Force*] (MCD)
EWMP Efficient Water Management Practice (ADWA)
EWMP Electronic Warfare Master Plan [*Military*] (SEWL)
EWMS Electronic Warfare Management System [*Military*] (SEWL)
EWMU Enemy Wireless Monitoring Unit (IAA)
EWMU EW Management Unit (SAUS)
EWN Early Warning Notification
EWN Foreign Fd Netherl'ds Index'WEBS' [*AMEX symbol*] (TTSB)
EWN New Bern [*North Carolina*] [*Airport symbol*] (OAG)
EWN New Bern, NC [*Location identifier*] [*FAA*] (FAAL)
EWN WEBS, Netherlands Index Series [*AMEX symbol*] (SG)
EWN World Equity Benchmark Shares [*AMEX symbol*] (SAG)
EWND Eastwind Group [*NASDAQ symbol*] (TTSB)
EWND Eastwind Group, Inc. (The) [*NASDAQ symbol*] (SAG)
EWO Educational Welfare Officer [*British*] (DI)
EWO Electrical and Wireless Operators [*Air Force*] [*British*]
EWO Electronic Warfare Office [*or Officer*]
EWO Electronic Warfare Officer [*Air Force*] (MUSM)
EWO Emergency War Operations
EWO Emergency War Order [*Air Force*]
EWO Engineering Work Order
EWO Engineer Works Organization (SAUS)
EWO Enki and the World Order [*A publication*] (BJA)
EWO Essential Work Order
EWO European Women's Orchestra (ODA)
EWO Ewo [*Congo*] [*Airport symbol*] (OAG)
EWO Foreign Fd Austria Index'WEBS' [*AMEX symbol*] (TTSB)
EWO New Hope, KY [*Location identifier*] [*FAA*] (FAAL)
EWO WEBS, Austria Index Series [*AMEX symbol*] (SG)
EWO World Equity Benchmark Shares [*AMEX symbol*] (SAG)
EWO & HP Electric Wall Oven and Hot Plates [*Classified advertising*] (ADA)
EWOBT Electronic Warfare On-Board Trainer [*Military*] (SEWL)
EWOC Eligible Worker-Owned Cooperative (SAUS)
EWODS Engineering Work Order - Drawing Summary (AAG)
EWONA Education Welfare Officers' National Association [*British*] (DI)
EWOPS Electronic Warfare Operations (NVT)
EWOS Electronic Warfare Operational System [*Air Force*]
EWOS European Workshop for Open Systems [*British*]
EWOS European Workshop for Open Systems Address (SAUS)
EWOS European Workshop in Open Systems (SAUS)
EWOS European Workshop on Open Systems (OSI) (SAUS)
EWOSE Electronic Warfare Operational Support Establishment [*Royal Air Force*] [*British*] (PDAA)
EWOS TA EWOS Technical Assembly (SAUS)
EWOT Electronic Warfare Officer Training (AFM)
EWOT EW Officer Training (SAUS)
EWOTS Early Warning Observation Teams (CINC)
E-WOW Explore the World of Work [*Vocational guidance test*]
EWP Electronic Warfare Plans [*NATO*] (NATG)
EWP Electronic White Pages [*Information service or system*] (IID)
EWP Emergency War Plan
EWP Emergency Watershed Protection (SAUO)
EWP Enhanced Winkler Processor
EWP Environmental Writing Program (SAUO)
EWP Escort Weapon Platform (ACAE)
EWP Estimates Working Party (SAUO)
EWP Expected Wire Phenomenon (SAUS)
EWP Exploding Wire Phenomena

EWP............ Foreign Fd Spain Index 'WEBS' [*AMEX symbol*] (TTSB)
EWP............ Newport, AR [*Location identifier*] [*FAA*] (FAAL)
EWP............ WEBS, Spain Index Series [*AMEX symbol*] (SG)
EWP............ World Equity Benchmark Shares [*AMEX symbol*] (SAG)
EWPA.......... Eastern Water Polo Association (PSS)
EWPA.......... Enhanced Winkler Processor Autopilot [*Military*]
EWPCA........ European Water Pollution Control Association (EAIO)
EWPE.......... Electronic Warfare Preprocessing Equipment [*Military*] (SEWL)
EWPHE........ European Working Party on High Blood Pressure in the Elderly (SAUO)
EWPHE........ European Working Party on Hypertension in the Elderly [*An association*]
EWPI........... East-West Population Institute
EWPI........... EW Prime Indicator unit (SAUS)
EWPI........... Eysenck-Withers Personality Inventory [*Psychology*]
EWPs.......... Electronic Wartare Plans (SAUS)
EWQ............ Enlisted Women's Quarters [*Military*]
EWQ............ Exceptionally Well Qualified (AFM)
EWQ............ Foreign Fd France Index 'WEBS' [*AMEX symbol*] (TTSB)
EWQ............ WEBS, France Index Series [*AMEX symbol*] (SG)
EWQ............ World Equity Benchmark Shares [*AMEX symbol*] (SAG)
EWQOS........ Environmental and Water Quality Operational Studies [*Army Corps of Engineers*]
EWQRC........ Electronic Warfare Quick Reaction Capability (MCD)
EWR............ Early Warning RADAR [*Air Force*]
EWR............ Early Warning Receiver (DWSG)
EWR............ East West Resources [*Vancouver Stock Exchange symbol*]
EWR............ Electrical Wiring Regulations (SAUS)
EWR............ Electromagnetic Wave Resistivity (SAUS)
EWR............ Electronic Word Recognizer (SAUS)
EWR............ Engineering Work Report [*or Request*]
EWR............ Engineering Work Request (SAUS)
EWR............ Environmental Web Resources (SAUO)
EWR............ Equaled World Record (SAUS)
EWR............ Erie Western Railway [*Federal Railroad Administration identification code*]
EWR............ Estimated Weight Report
EWR............ Evans Withycombe Residential, Inc. [*NYSE symbol*] (SAG)
EWR............ Newark, NJ [*Location identifier*] [*FAA*] (FAAL)
EWR............ New York [*New York*] Newark [*Airport symbol*] (OAG)
EWRA.......... Ethiopian Water Resources Authority (SAUS)
EWR & I...... Emergency Welfare Registration and Inquiry [*Civil Defense*]
EWRC.......... Eastern Women's Rowing Conference (PSS)
EWRC.......... European Weed Research Council [*Later, EWRS*]
EWRIS......... European Wire Rope Information Service [*EC*] (ECED)
EWRL.......... Electronic Warfare Reprogrammable Library [*Military*] (SEWL)
EWRL.......... Estimated Weapon Release (MCD)
EWRM.......... Electronic Warfare Response Monitor (MCD)
EWRP.......... Early Warning Reporting System (SAUS)
EWRR.......... Elkhorn & Walworth Railroad [*Federal Railroad Administration identification code*]
EWRS.......... European Weed Research Society [*See also EGH*] [*Research center*] [*Germany*] (IRC)
EW/RSTA..... Center for Electronic Warfare/Reconnaissance, Surveillance, and Target Acquisit ion [*Fort Monmouth, NJ*] [*United States Army Communications-Electronics Command*] (GRD)
EW/RSTA..... Electronic Warfare/Reconnaissance and Target Acquisition Center (SAUS)
EWRT.......... Electrical Women's Round Table (EA)
EWS............ Early Warning Signal (SAUS)
EWS............ Early Warning Station (SAUS)
EWS............ Early Warning System
EWS............ Early Wet Season (SAUO)
EWS............ East-West Speed
EWS............ East-West Stationkeeping (ACAE)
EWS............ ECOS Workstation (SAUS)
EWS............ Edgar Wallace Society (EAIO)
EWS............ Education Welfare Service [*British*] (DET)
EWS............ Eduworld Society [*Later, CFB*] (EA)
EWS............ Egg White Serum [*Immunology*]
EWS............ Electronic Warfare Supervisor [*Navy*] (DOMA)
EWS............ Electronic Warfare Support [*Military*] (SEWL)
EWS............ Electronic Warfare System (MCD)
EWS............ Electronic Weapon System (SAUO)
EWS............ Electronic Work Station (SAUS)
EWS............ Emergency Warning System (SAUS)
EWS............ Emergency Water Supply
EWS............ Emergency Weather Station (SAUS)
EWS............ Emergency Welfare Service [*Civil Defense*]
EWS............ Employee Written Software [*IBM Corp*] (VERA)
EWS............ Engineering Watch Supervisor (DNAB)
EWS............ Engineering Work Schedule (MCD)
EWS............ Engineering Work Statement (MCD)
EWS............ Engineering Work-Station [*Yokogawa Hewlett Packard Ltd.*] [*Japan*]
EWS............ Engineering Writing and Speech (MCD)
EWS............ English Westerners Society [*British*]
EWS............ Enlisted Surface Warfare Specialist (DOMA)
EWS............ Ergonomic Work Stations (SAUS)
EWS............ Estimated Will Ship
EWS............ Estimate Work Sheet (ACAE)
EWS............ European Wars Survey (SAUS)
EWS............ European Wings [*Czechoslovakia*] [*ICAO designator*] (FAAC)
EWS............ European Working Group on SGML (SAUO)
EWS............ Evelyn Waugh Society (EA)
EWS............ Ewing's Sarcoma [*Oncology*]
EWS............ Excite for Web Servers (SAUS)
EWS............ Experienced Worker Standard
EWS............ External Weapon Station (SAUS)
EWS............ Foreign Fd Singapore Index 'WEBS' [*AMEX symbol*] (TTSB)
EWS............ WEBS, Singapore(Free)Index Series [*AMEX symbol*] (SG)
EWS............ World Equity Benchmark Shares [*AMEX symbol*] (SAG)
EWSA.......... EEC Wheat Starch Manufacturers Association [*Defunct*] (EAIO)
EWSA.......... Electronic Warfare Technician, Seaman Apprentice (DNAB)
EWSA.......... European Wheat Starch Manufacturers Association (SAUO)
EWSA.......... Wheat Starch Manufacturers Association (SAUS)
EWSC.......... Eastern Washington State College (SAUS)
EWSC.......... Electric Water Systems Council
EWSC.......... European Water Sectoral Committee (SAUS)
EWSCL........ Extended-Wear Soft Contact Lens [*Optometry*]
EWSCP........ EW Systems Control Point (SAUS)
EWSD.......... Electronic Worldwide Switch Digital (VLIE)
EWSD.......... Engineering and Water Supply Department [*South Australia*]
EWSE.......... Electronic Warfare Support Element [*Army*] (DOMA)
EWSE.......... European Wide Service Exchange (SAUS)
EWSF.......... Electric Wave Section Filter
EWSF.......... European Work Study Federation (SAUO)
EWSG.......... Electronic Warfare Scenario Generator
EWSG.......... Electronic Warfare Study Group (SAUO)
EWSI........... Electronic Warfare Simulation [*Military*] (SEWL)
EWSI........... Electronic Wind Speed Indicator
EW/SIGINT... Electronic Warfare/Signal Intelligence (MCD)
EWSIP......... Electronic Warfare Standardization and Improvement Program (ACAE)
EWSL.......... Eastern Women's Swimming League (PSS)
EWSL.......... Equivalent Single Wheel Load (SAUS)
EWSLA........ East-West Sign Language Association [*Japan*] (SLS)
EWSM.......... Early-Warning Support Measures (SAUS)
EWSM.......... Electronic Warfare Support Measures [*Later, ESM*] (AABC)
EWSN.......... Electronic Warfare Technician, Seaman (DNAB)
EWSO.......... Electronic Warfare Staff Officer (SAUO)
EWSP.......... Electronic Warfare Self-Protection [*Military*] (SEWL)
EWSS.......... Electronic Warfare Support System [*Military*] (SEWL)
EWSS.......... EW Support System (SAUS)
EWST.......... Elevated Water Storage Tank [*Nuclear energy*] (NRCH)
EWST.......... Energy West [*NASDAQ symbol*] (TTSB)
EWST.......... Energy West, Inc. [*NASDAQ symbol*] (SAG)
EWSTP........ Emergency War Surgery Training Program [*Army*]
EWT............ Eastern War Time [*World War II*]
EWT............ Eastern Winter Time (SAUS)
EWT............ Eastwest Airlines, Erfurt [*Germany*] [*FAA designator*] (FAAC)
EWT............ Edible Whip Technology [*Aerosol technology*]
EWT............ Electronic Warfare Technology (MCD)
EWT............ Electronic Warfare Trainer
EWT............ Electrostatic Water Treaters (DICI)
EWT............ Elsewhere Taken (SAUS)
EWT............ Endangered Wildlife Trust (SAUS)
EWT............ Entering Water Temperature (MIST)
EWT............ Erupted Wisdom Teeth (MELL)
EWT............ Evaluation and Warning Team (CINC)
EWT............ Expandable Wing Tank
EW/TA........ Early Warning/Threat Assessment
EWTA.......... East Wind Trade Associates [*Defunct*] (EA)
EWTA.......... Expo West Trade Association (EA)
EWTAD........ Early Warning Threat Analysis Display
EWTAP........ Electronic Warfare Tactics Analysis Program [*Military*] (CAAL)
EWTAT........ Early Warning Threat Analysis Display (SAUS)
EWTBB........ Electronic Warfare Transmitter Building Block [*Military*] (SEWL)
EWTC.......... East-West Trade Council [*Defunct*] (EA)
EWTCC........ European World Trade and Convention Center (SAUO)
EWTD.......... Electronic Warfare Training Device (ACAE)
EWTD.......... EW Training Device (SAUS)
EWTES........ Electronic Warfare Tactical [*or Threat*] Environment Simulation (NG)
EWTES........ Electronic Warfare Threat Environment Simulation Facility (SAUS)
EWTGU........ Electronic Warfare Technical Guidance Unit [*Military*] (SEWL)
EWTMI........ European Wideband Transmission Media Improvement Program
EWTMIP...... European Wideband Transmission Media Improvement Program (SAUS)
EWTN.......... Eternal Word Television Network [*Cable-television system*]
EWTNGSq.... Electronic Warfare Training Squadron [*Air Force*]
EWTPC........ East-West Trade Policy Committee
EWTR.......... Electronic Warfare Test Range [*Military*]
EWTS.......... Electronic Warfare Training Squadron [*Air Force*]
EWTS.......... Electronic Warfare Training System (SAUS)
EWTS.......... Expandable Wing Tank Structure
EWTS-R....... Electronic Warfare Training System - Radar (SAUS)
EWTT.......... Electronic Warfare Tactics Trainer
EWTU.......... Except What Turns Up (DI)
EWU............ Eastern Washington University (PDAA)
EWU............ Electrical Workers Union (SAUO)
EWU............ Foreign Fd U.K. Index'WEBS' [*AMEX symbol*] (TTSB)
EWU............ WEBS, U.K. Index Series [*AMEX symbol*] (SG)
EWU............ World Equity Benchmark Shares [*AMEX symbol*] (SAG)
EWVA.......... Electronic Warfare Vulnerability Assessment [*DoD*] (RDA)
EWW............ Emery Worldwide Airlines, Inc. [*ICAO designator*] (FAAC)
EWW............ Enterprise-Wide Web (ACII)
EWW............ Extended Work Week
EWW............ Foreign Fd Mexico Index'WEBS' [*AMEX symbol*] (TTSB)
EWW............ WEBS, Mexico(Free)Index Series [*AMEX symbol*] (SG)
EWW............ World Equity Benchmark Shares [*AMEX symbol*] (SAG)
EWWA.......... Ethiopian Womens Welfare Association (SAUO)

EWWRS .... Eric's Wasted Worldwide Repair Society (EA)
EWWS .... Electronic Warfare Warning System
EWWS .... ESSA [*Environmental Science Services Administration*] Weather Wire Service
EWWW .... External World Wide Web (SAUS)
Ex .... Citation in Examiner's Decision [*Legal term*] (DLA)
Ex .... Court of Exchequer [*England*] [*Legal term*] (DLA)
EX .... Eagle Aviation [*ICAO designator*] (AD)
EX .... Eject X (SAUS)
EX .... Electronics Experimental (SAUS)
EX .... Emirates Airlines [*ICAO designator*] (AD)
Ex .... English Exchequer Reports [*A publication*] (DLA)
EX .... Exacerbate (SAUS)
Ex .... Exacerbation [*Medicine*] (EDAA)
ex .... exacting (SAUS)
ex .... exactitude (SAUS)
ex .... exactly (SAUS)
ex .... Exaggerated (DAVI)
ex .... Examination (ADWA)
Ex .... Examination (SAUS)
EX .... Examine (SAUS)
EX .... Examined
ex .... examiner (SAUS)
Ex .... Examiner's Decision [*Legal term*] (DLA)
ex .... examining (SAUS)
ex .... Example (VRA)
EX .... Example
EX .... Excalibur [*Society of Automotive Engineers auto manufacturer code for service information interchange*]
ex .... Excavate (SAUS)
EX .... Exceeding
EX .... Excellent [*Condition*] [*Deltiology*]
Ex .... Excelsior (SAUS)
EX .... Except
Ex .... Excepted (WDMC)
ex .... Excepted (WDMC)
EX .... Exception [*Communications term*] (DCT)
ex .... Exception (SAUS)
EX .... Excess (AABC)
EX .... Exchange
EX .... Exchange Key (VLIE)
EX .... Exchequer [*British*]
EX .... Exchequer Reports [*A publication*]
ex .... Excipient [*Medicine*] (EDAA)
EX .... Excise (DSUE)
ex .... Excision [*Medicine*] (MAE)
Ex .... Excitation Energy (IDOE)
Ex .... exclude (SAUS)
EX .... Excluding
EX .... Exclusive (ADA)
ex .... exclusivity (SAUS)
EX .... Excudit [*Made*] [*Latin*] (ROG)
EX .... Excursion
EX .... Excursus (ROG)
EX .... Execute
EX .... Executed Out Of [*Business term*]
ex .... executing (SAUS)
EX .... Execution (ROG)
ex .... Executive (SHCU)
EX .... Executive
EX .... Executive Level Appointments (SAUS)
EX .... Executive Management Office [*Kennedy Space Center Directorate*] [*NASA*] (NASA)
EX .... Executive Schedule [*Job classification for certain Presidentially appointed executives*]
EX .... Executor (ROG)
EX .... Exempt
ex .... Exercise (IDYL)
EX .... Exercise (NVT)
ex .... exercising (SAUS)
EX .... Exerque [*Numismatics*]
Ex .... Exerzieren (SAUS)
EX .... Exeter [*Post code*] (ODBW)
EX .... Exeunt [*They Go Out*] [*Latin*] (ROG)
EX .... Exfoliation [*Medicine*] (EDAA)
EX .... Exhaust [*Automotive engineering*]
EX .... Exhibit
EX .... Exhibition (DSUE)
EX .... Exide Corp. [*NYSE symbol*] (SAG)
EX .... Exit [*He, or She, Goes Out*] [*Latin*] (ROG)
Ex .... Exmoor (SAUS)
Ex .... Exmouth (SAUS)
Ex .... Exodus [*Old Testament book*]
ex .... Exophthalmos [*Ophthalmology*] (MAE)
Ex .... Expansion (SAUS)
EX .... Expect (DA)
ex .... expecting (SAUS)
EX .... Expedited (SAUS)
EX .... Expenditure [*Dialog*] [*Searchable field*] [*Information service or system*] (NITA)
ex .... Expenses (NTIO)
EX .... Experiment [*or Experimental*]
EX .... experimental broadcasting (SAUS)
EX .... Experimental Station [*ITU designation*] (CET)
EX .... Experimentation (SAUS)
EX .... Expert
EX .... Expiration [*Motor vehicle violation code used in state of Maryland*] (MVRD)
ex .... Expiration (NTIO)
ex .... Expires (NTIO)
EX .... Explanation
ex .... Explode (SAUS)
Ex .... Exploder (SAUS)
ex .... Explosion (SAUS)
ex .... Explosive (SAUS)
EX .... Exponent [*Mathematics*] (IAA)
ex .... exponential of x (SAUS)
EX .... Export
EX .... Exposure
ex .... Express (NTIO)
EX .... Express
EX .... Exsmoker [*Medicine*] (EDAA)
EX .... Extension (ADA)
EX .... Exterior (SAUS)
ex .... External (SAUS)
EX .... extinction (SAUS)
ex .... Extra (SHCU)
EX .... Extra
EX .... Extract (SAUS)
EX .... Extractum [*Extract*] [*Latin*]
EX .... Extra Gilt [*Bookbinding*] (ROG)
EX .... Extravaganza (ROG)
Ex .... Extraversion [*Psychology*]
Ex .... Extremadura (SAUS)
EX .... Extrusion (SAUS)
Ex .... Exuma (SAUS)
EX .... Lakeside Laboratories, Inc. [*Research code symbol*]
Ex .... Out Of (EBF)
Ex .... Without (EBF)
EXA .... Albion College, Albion, MI [*OCLC symbol*] (OCLC)
EXA .... Execaire Aviation Ltd. [*Canada*] [*ICAO designator*] (FAAC)
EXA .... Executing Agency Identifier (CINC)
EXA .... Exmar Resources Ltd. [*Vancouver Stock Exchange symbol*]
EXA .... Lehman Brothers, Inc. [*AMEX symbol*] (SAG)
Exabyte .... Exabyte Corp. [*Associated Press*] (SAG)
EXAC .... Exactech Inc. [*NASDAQ symbol*] (TTSB)
EXACCT .... Expenditure Account
exacct .... expense account (SAUS)
ExAcl .... Expanded Academic Index
EXACT .... Energy Dispersive X-Ray Analysis Computation Technique [*X-Ray fluorescence software*] [*Kevex Corp.*]
EXACT .... Exchange of Authenticated Component Performance Test Data (SAUS)
EXACT .... Exchange of Authenticated Electronic Component Performance Test Data [*European counterpart of GIDEP*]
EXACT .... Expert Adaptive Controller Tuning (NITA)
EXACT .... International Exchange of Authenticated Electronic Component Performance Tests Data (PDAA)
EX AFF .... Ex Affinis [*Of Affinity*] [*Latin*]
EXAFS .... Edge X-Ray Absorption Fine Structure
exafs .... extended X-ray-absorption final structure (SAUS)
EXAFS .... Extended X-Ray Absorption Fine Structure [*Spectrometry*]
exag .... exaggerate (SAUS)
EXAG .... Exaggerated (SAUS)
EXAG .... Exaggeration
EXAGT .... Executive Agent
EXAM .... Elemental X-Ray Analysis of Materials
ExAM .... Ex Air Ministry [*British*] (DEN)
EXAM .... Examinate (SAUS)
exam .... Examination (ADWA)
EXAM .... Examination (AFM)
Exam .... Examination (DIAR)
EXAM .... Examine
Exam .... Examiner [*Legal term*] (DLA)
EXAM .... Examining (SAUS)
EX-AM .... Expedited Air Munitions
EXAM .... Experience Analysis Mechanism [*Health insurance*] (GHCT)
EXAM .... Experimental Aerospace Multiprocessor
EXAM .... Express America Holdings [*NASDAQ symbol*] (SAG)
EXAMD .... Examined
EXAMETNET ... Experimental Inter-American Meteorological Rocket Network [*NASA*]
exametnet ... experimental meteorological sounding rocket network (SAUS)
Examg .... Examining (BARN)
EXAMIG .... Examining (SAUS)
EXAMINA .... Examination (DSUE)
EXAMN .... Examination
EXAMR .... Examiner
exams .... examinations (SAUS)
EXAMS .... Exposure Analysis Modeling System [*Environmental chemistry*]
EXAMSII .... Exposure Analysis Modeling System II [*Environmental Protection Agency*] (AEPA)
EX & AD .... Executor and Administrator (DLA)
ex & ct .... Excavate and Cart (SAUS)
EXANDIS .... Exotic Animal Disease Preparedness Consultative Committee [*Australia*]
EXAP .... Exchange Applications, Inc.
EXAPT .... Exact Automatic Programming of Tools (SAUS)
EXAPT .... Extended Automatically Programmed Tool (SAUS)
EXAPT .... Extended Subset of Automatically Programmed Tools [*Manufacturing term*]

EXAPT........ Extension of Automatically Programmed Tool language (SAUS)
EXAPT Language... Exact Automatic Programming of Tools Language (SAUS)
EXAPT Language... Extension of Automatically Programmed Tool Language (SAUS)
EX AQ......... Ex Aqua [*Out of Water*] [*Pharmacy*]
EXAR......... Exar Corp. [*NASDAQ symbol*] (NQ)
EXAS.......... Engineering Services and Safety (SAUS)
EXAS.......... Experiment on Autonomous SAR (SAUS)
EXAS.......... Experiment on Autonomous SAR Processor Calibration (SAUS)
Ex Aut......... Ex Authenticis Pandectis [*Digest of Justinian*] [*A publication*] (DSA)
EXB.......... Brazilian Army Aviation [*FAA designator*] (FAAC)
EXB.......... Grand Rapids Baptist College and Seminary, Grand Rapids, MI [*OCLC symbol*] (OCLC)
ex b.......... Ex Bonus (without Bonus) [*Finance*] (ODA)
EXBD.......... Corporate Executive Board [*NASDAQ symbol*] (SG)
EXBD.......... Corporate Executive Board Co. [*NASDAQ symbol*] (NASQ)
EXBEDCAP... Expanded Bed Capacity
EXBF.......... Exercise Hyperemia Blood Flow (MAE)
Ex B/L......... Exchange Bill of Lading (MHDW)
EXBO.......... Export Buying Offices Association [*British*] (DBA)
EXBT.......... Exabyte Corp. [*NASDAQ symbol*] (NQ)
EXBT.......... Exabyte Corporation (SAUO)
EXBT.......... External Beam Therapy
EXC.......... Calvin College and Seminary, Grand Rapids, MI [*OCLC symbol*] (OCLC)
exc.......... Escision (MELL)
EXC.......... Excalibur Aviation [*British*] [*ICAO designator*] (FAAC)
EXC.......... Excavate (MSA)
exc.......... Excavation (MIST)
EXC.......... Excavation (SAUS)
Exc.......... Excavator (SAUS)
EXC.......... Exceeding [*Weight*] [*Postage*] [*British*] (ROG)
EXC.......... Excel Industries, Inc. [*AMEX symbol*] (SPSG)
Exc.......... Excellency (WDAA)
EXC.......... Excellency
EXC.......... Excellent (AABC)
exc.......... Excellent (SHCU)
Exc.......... Excellent
exc.......... Except (SHCU)
EXC.......... Except
EXC.......... excepted (SAUS)
EXC.......... Exception (GOBB)
exc.......... Exception (SHCU)
EXC.......... Excess (SAUS)
EXC.......... Exchange
EX/C.......... Exchange Certificate [*Rate*] [*Value of the English pound*]
EXC.......... Exchange Key [*Word processing*]
EXC.......... Excision [*Medicine*]
exc.......... Excitation (IDOE)
EXC.......... Excitation (MSA)
EXC.......... excitement (SAUS)
exc.......... Exciter (IDOE)
EXC.......... Exclude
Exc.......... Excommunication (SAUS)
EXC.......... Excudit [*Made*] [*Latin*]
EXC.......... Excursion (ROG)
EXC.......... Excuse (WGA)
EXC.......... Execute (SAUS)
EXC.......... Execution (SAUS)
EXC.......... Exeption (SAUS)
EXC.......... Exitation (SAUS)
EXC.......... Experiment Computer (MCD)
EXCA.......... Excalibur Technologies [*NASDAQ symbol*] (TTSB)
EXCA.......... Excalibur Technology Corp. [*NASDAQ symbol*] (NQ)
EXCA.......... Excavate [*Technical drawings*]
exca.......... excavation (SAUS)
ExCA.......... Exchangeable Card Architecture (SAUS)
ExCA.......... Expanded Communications Electronics System (SAUS)
EXCAL.......... Excalibur (ACAE)
Excalb.......... Excalibur Technologies Corp. [*Associated Press*] (SAG)
EXCAP.......... Expanded Capability (CAAL)
excav.......... Excavate (SAUS)
Excav.......... Excavation (DIAR)
excav.......... Excavation (MIST)
EXCAVTG..... Excavating
EXCC.......... Exercise Control Center [*Military*] (AABC)
EXCD.......... Exceed (SAUS)
EXCDG.......... Exceeding (SAUS)
EXCDP.......... Expedited Combat Developments Plan (SAUO)
EXCEL.......... Corporation for Excellence in Public Education (SAUO)
EXCEL.......... Edilibe Extension to Eastern and Central European Libraries (SAUS)
Excel.......... Excel Industries, Inc. [*Associated Press*] (SAG)
excel.......... Excellent (REAL)
Excel.......... Excelsior (SAUS)
EXCEL.......... Ex-offender Coordinated Employment Lifeline (SAUS)
EXCEL.......... Expended Clinical Evaluation of Lovastatin [*Medicine*] (EDAA)
EXCEL.......... Experimental Chloride Extraction Line (SAUS)
EXCEL.......... Export Credit Enhanced Leverage
ExcelCm...... Excel Communications, Inc. [*Associated Press*] (SAG)
EXCELL.......... Excellent (ADA)
ExcelRI.......... Excel Realty Trust [*Associated Press*] (SAG)
EXCELS.......... Expanded Communications - Electronics System [*DoD*]
Excelsr.......... Excelsior Income Shares, Inc. [*Associated Press*] (SAG)
EXCEPT.......... Expert-System for Computer Aided Environmental Planing Tasks (SAUO)
EXCERP e ROT FIN... Excerpta e Rotulis Finium [*Extracts of Boundary Records*] [*A publication*] (ROG)
Excerpta Crim... Excerpta Criminologica [*A publication*] (DLA)
EXCESS.......... Extensible Expert System Shell (SAUS)
Excg.......... Exchange
EXCG.......... Exercise Control Group [*Military*] (AABC)
Exch.......... Court of Exchequer [*England*] [*Legal term*] (DLA)
Exch.......... English Exchequer Reports [*A publication*] (DLA)
Exch.......... English Law Reports, Exchequer [*1866-75*] [*A publication*] (DLA)
exch.......... Exchange (SHCU)
Exch.......... Exchange (TBD)
EXCH.......... Exchange
Exch.......... Exchequer (EBF)
EXCH.......... Exchequer [*British*]
Exch.......... Exchequer Division, High Court [*1875-80*] [*A publication*] (DLA)
Exch.......... Exchequer Reports (Welsby, Hurlstone, and Gordon) [*A publication*] (DLA)
ExchAb.......... Exceptional Child Education Abstracts
ex champ..... ex-champion (SAUS)
ex champ..... former champion (SAUS)
EXCHAR.......... Extended Character Sets for Electronic Document Delivery (SAUS)
Exch C.......... Canada Law Reports, Exchequer Court [*A publication*] (DLA)
Exch Can...... Canada Law Reports, Exchequer Court [*A publication*] (DLA)
Exch Cas...... Exchequer Cases [*Legacy duties, etc.*] [*Scotland*] [*A publication*] (DLA)
EXCH CHAM... Exchequer Chamber [*Legal term*] (DLA)
Exch CR....... Canada Law Reports, Exchequer Court [*A publication*] (DLA)
Exch Ct (Can)... Canada Law Reports, Exchequer Court [*A publication*] (DLA)
Exch Div...... Exchequer Division, English Law Reports [*A publication*] (DLA)
Exch Div (Eng)... Exchequer Division, English Law Reports [*A publication*] (DLA)
Excheq.......... exchequer (SAUS)
Ex Child.......... Exceptional Children [*A publication*]
EXCHO.......... Exchange Officer [*Air Force*]
exch oper.... exchange operator (SAUS)
EXCH P.......... Exchange of Property (DLA)
exchq.......... exchequer (SAUS)
exchr.......... extra charge (SAUS)
Exch Rep..... English Exchequer Reports [*A publication*] (DLA)
Exch Rep..... Exchequer Reports (Welsby, Hurlstone, and Gordon) [*A publication*] (DLA)
Exch Rep WH & G... Exchequer Reports (Welsby, Hurlstone, and Gordon) [*A publication*] (DLA)
exch traf bx... exchange traffic box (SAUS)
EXCIMER..... excited dimer laser (SAUS)
EXCIMER..... Excited Dimmer (IAA)
EXCIMS.......... Executive Council for Modeling and Simulation (SAUO)
EXCIPLEX.... Excited State Complex [*LASER*] (IEEE)
EXCITE.......... Expanded with Computers and Information Technology
EXCL.......... Excel
excl.......... Exclamation (WDMC)
EXCL.......... Exclamation
EXCL.......... Exclude (MSA)
excl.......... Excludes (MILB)
excl.......... Excluding (ADWA)
EXCL.......... Excluding (EY)
Excl.......... Exclusion (SAUS)
EXCL.......... Exclusive (AFM)
excl.......... Exclusive [*News media*] (WDMC)
excl.......... exclusivity (SAUS)
exclaim.......... Exclamation (ADWA)
exclam.......... exclamation (SAUS)
EXCLAM.......... Exclamatory (ROG)
EXCLASS..... Expert Job Classification Assistant (SAUS)
EXCLASS..... Extended CLASS (SAUS)
EXCLD.......... Exclude
EXCLG.......... Excluding (ROG)
Excl OR.......... Exclusive OR (SAUS)
EXCLOT.......... Executive Committee for Low Observable Technology (ACAE)
EXCLSR.......... Excelsior
exclt.......... excellent (SAUS)
ExclT.......... Excel Technology, Inc. [*Associated Press*] (SAG)
ExclTc.......... Excel Technology, Inc. [*Associated Press*] (SAG)
ExclTch.......... Excel Technology [*Associated Press*] (SAG)
EXCLU.......... Exclusive (MDG)
exclu.......... exclusivity (SAUS)
EXCLV.......... Exclusive (FAAC)
Ex Cncl.......... Executive Council (SAUO)
EXCO.......... EXCO Resources, Inc. [*NASDAQ symbol*] (NASQ)
EXCO.......... Executive Committee (IEEE)
EXCO.......... Executive Council (ADA)
EXCO.......... Exfoliation Corrosion (SAUS)
EXCOA.......... Explosives Corporation of America (SAUO)
EXCODOP.... Externally Coherent Doppler (ACAE)
EXCOM.......... Executive Committee [*National Security Council*]
EXCOM.......... Executive Committee of Board of Directors (SAUS)
EXCOM.......... Executive Component (ACAE)
EXCOM.......... Extended Communications Search [*DoD*]
EX COM.......... Extravagantes Communes [*A publication*] (DLA)
EXCOMM.......... Executive Committee (SAUS)
EXCOMM.......... Exterior Communications [*Military*] (CAAL)
EXCOMMS.... Extended Communications Search [*Navy*] (NVT)
EXCOMP..... National Executive Compensation Database [*Information service or system*] (IID)
EXCON.......... Executive Control (SSD)
EXCON.......... External Control [*Military*] (INF)

ex cont .... from contract (SAUS)
ExCOP .... Extraordinary Meeting of the Conference of the Parties (SAUO)
ExCOP .... Resumed Session on the First Extraordinary Meeting of the Conference of the Parties to Finalize and Adopt a Protocol on Biosafety (SAUO)
EXCOS .... Executive Committees (SAUS)
EXCP .... Except (SAUS)
ex cp .... ex coupon (SAUS)
EXCP .... Execute Channel Program [*Computer science*]
EXCPT .... Exception
Ex CR .... Canada Exchequer Court Reports [*1875-1922*] [*A publication*] (DLA)
Ex CR .... Canada Law Reports, Exchequer Court [*A publication*] (DLA)
excr .... excrescent (SAUS)
excr .... Excretion [*Medicine*] (EDAA)
ExcRisk .... Executive Risk, Inc. [*Associated Press*] (SAG)
Excrpt Med ... Excerpta Medica (SAUS)
ExcRsk .... Executive Risk, Inc. [*Associated Press*] (SAG)
excs .... excess (SAUS)
EXCSS .... Excess
EXCSV .... Excessive (MSA)
EXCT .... Exact
EXCT .... Execute (FAAC)
exct .... execution (SAUS)
EXCTR .... Exciter [*Electricity*]
Exctr .... Executor
EXCUR .... Excursion (KSC)
Excurs .... Excursion (DIAR)
EXCV .... Excessive (SAUS)
excv .... exclusive (SAUS)
EXCVT .... Excavate
EXCVTG .... Excavating (SAUS)
EXCVTN .... Excavation
EXCVTR .... Excavator
e(x)d .... Every (X) Days (SPVS)
Exd .... Examined (EBF)
EXD .... Examined
EXD .... Exchange Degeneracy (SAUS)
EXD .... Excluded Driver Case [*Motor vehicle violation code used in state of Maryland*] (MVRD)
ExD .... Excused from Duty (SAUS)
Ex D .... Ex Dividend [*Without dividend*] (EBF)
EX D .... Ex Dividendum [*Without the right to dividend*] [*Finance*] (ROG)
EXD .... Expeditor Resource Group Ltd. [*Vancouver Stock Exchange symbol*]
EXD .... Explained (SAUS)
EXD .... Export Air del Peru SA Cargo Air Lines [*ICAO designator*] (FAAC)
EXD .... External Degree Program [*National Court Reporters Association*]
EXD .... External Device [*Computer science*]
Ex D .... Law Reports, Exchequer Division [*England*] [*A publication*] (DLA)
EXDAMS .... Extendable Debugging and Monitoring System [*Computer science*]
EXDC .... External Data Controller (NITA)
ex det .... explosives detector (SAUS)
EXDIR .... Exercise Director (CINC)
EXDIS .... Exclusive Distribution [*Military security classification*] (AFM)
Ex Div .... Ex Dividend [*Without Dividend*] (EBF)
EX DIV .... Ex-Dividend [*Without the right to dividend*] [*Finance*]
EXDIV .... Experimental Division
Ex Div .... Law Reports, Exchequer Division [*England*] [*A publication*] (ILCA)
EXDLVY .... Expect Delivery (FAAC)
EXDOC .... Electronic Export Documentation [*Australia*]
Ex Doc .... Executive Document (BARN)
EX/DP .... Express/Direct Pack (DNAB)
EXDRONE .... Expendable Drone (ACAE)
EXDRONE .... Expendable Drone Jammer (SAUS)
EXDS .... Exodus Communications [*NASDAQ symbol*] (SG)
ExE .... Event by Event (SAUS)
EXE .... Executable [*Computer science*] (DDC)
EXE .... Executable File (SAUS)
EXE .... Executable Program File [*Computer science*]
EXE .... Execute (ROG)
EXE .... Executive Flight, Inc. [*ICAO designator*] (FAAC)
EXE .... Exeter [*British depot code*]
EXE .... Extendicare, Inc. [*NYSE symbol*] (SAG)
EXE .... Kent County Library and Kent County Library System, Grand Rapids, MI [*OCLC symbol*] (OCLC)
exe .... Self Extracting [*Computer science*]
EXEA .... Extendicare, Inc. [*NASDAQ symbol*] (SG)
EXEC .... Executable program (SAUS)
EXEC .... Execute (MSA)
exec .... execute statement (SAUS)
EXEC .... Execution (WDAA)
Exec .... Execution Executive (SAUS)
EXEC .... Execution Statement (ITCA)
Exec .... Executive (PHSD)
exec .... Executive (WDAA)
EXEC .... Executive
EXEC .... Executive Control System (SAUS)
EXEC .... Executive Extension (SAUS)
exec .... executive officer (SAUS)
EXEC .... Executive Statement (SAUS)
EXEC .... Executive System (NITA)
exec .... Executor (WDAA)
EXEC .... Executor
exec .... Executrix (WDAA)
EXEC-1 .... President on Board Civil Aircraft (FAAC)
EXEC-1F .... President's Family is Aboard Aircraft (FAAC)
EXEC-2 .... Vice President is Aboard Civil Aircraft (FAAC)
EXEC-2F .... Vice President's Family is Aboard Aircraft (FAAC)
EXECASST ... Executive Assistant (DNAB)
Exec Dir .... Executive Director (SAUS)
Exec Doc .... Executive Document [*Legal term*] (DLA)
Exec MBA .... Executive Master of Business Administration (PGP)
Exec MGA .... Executive Master of General Administration (PGP)
Exec MIM .... Executive Master of International Management (PGP)
Exec MPA .... Executive Master of Public Administration (PGP)
Exec MPH .... Executive Master of Public Health (PGP)
Exec MS .... Executive Master of Science (PGP)
ExecMSE .... Executive Master of Science in Engineering (SAUS)
EXECN .... Execution (SAUS)
EXECO .... Executive Officer
Exec Off .... Executive Officer (SAUS)
EXECORD .... Executive Order (DNAB)
Exec Order ... Executive Order of the President (AAGC)
EXEC PROD ... Executive Producer (GOBB)
execs .... executives (SAUS)
Exec Sec .... Executive Secretary (SAUS)
EXEC System ... Executive Control System (SAUS)
ExecTl .... Executive Telecard Ltd. [*Associated Press*] (SAG)
EXE Ctrl Cy ... Execute Control Cycle (SAUS)
EXECV .... Executive (SAUS)
ExecVPres ... Executive Vice President (SAUS)
EXECX .... Executrix
EXED .... Executed (ROG)
ExEF .... Ejection Fraction During Exercise (DB)
EXE file .... Executable File (CDE)
Exek .... Exekution (SAUS)
EXEL .... Exelixis, Inc. [*NASDAQ symbol*] (SG)
Exel .... EXEL Ltd. [*Associated Press*] (SAG)
EXELFS .... extended electron energy loss fine structure (SAUS)
EXELFS .... Extended Electron Loss Fine Structure [*Spectrometry*]
EXELFS .... Extended Energy-Loss Fine Structure [*Electronics*] (AAEL)
EXEMP .... Exemption (DLA)
EXEOD .... Expects to Enter on Duty (NOAA)
EXER .... Exercise (AABC)
EXERPS .... Extended Error Recovery Procedures (SAUS)
EXERSUG .... Executive Committee of Energy Research Supercomputer Users Group (SAUO)
EXES .... Electron-Induced X-Ray Emission Spectroscopy (SAUS)
EXES .... Expenses (ROG)
EXESS .... Expanded ESS (MCD)
Exe T .... Execute Time (SAUS)
Exet .... Exeter (SAUS)
EXET .... Exeter College [*Oxford University*] (ROG)
Exet Coll .... Exeter College-Oxford (SAUS)
Exeter .... Exeter College, Phillips Exeter Academy (SAUS)
EXETR .... Exeter, CA [*American Association of Railroads railroad junction routing code*]
EXEVAL .... External Evaluation [*Military*] (INF)
ExEx .... Expected Exceedance (GNE)
EXF .... Ex Factory (SAUS)
EXF .... External Function
ex f .... extremely fine (SAUS)
EXF .... Toledo, OH [*Location identifier*] [*FAA*] (FAAL)
ex fac .... ex factory (SAUS)
EXFAS .... Extended Fine Auger Structure [*Physics*]
EXFCB .... Extended File Control Block [*Computer science*] (VERA)
exfcy .... Extra Fancy
Exfil .... Exfiltration (SAUS)
EXFINCO .... Export Finance Co. [*British*]
EXFO .... EXFO Electro-Optical Engineer [*NASDAQ symbol*]
EXFOD .... Explosive Foxhole Digger [*Army*] (INF)
EXFOR .... Expeditionary Forces (SAUO)
EXFOR .... Experimental Force [*Army*] (INF)
EXFOR .... International Exchange System for Numerical Nuclear Reaction Data (SAUS)
EXFOR .... International Neutron Data Exchange System (SAUO)
exforact .... Extracted for Action (SAUS)
ex fy .... extra fancy (SAUS)
EXG .... Air Exchange, Inc. [*ICAO designator*] (FAAC)
EXG .... Cabinet Strategy Subcommittee on Expenditure Control and Government Administration (SAUO)
EXG .... Enron Corp. [*NYSE symbol*] (SAG)
EXG .... Exchange Registers (SAUS)
EXG .... Exchange Two Registers [*Computer science*]
EX G .... Exempli Gratia [*For Example*] [*Latin*] (ROG)
EX G .... Ex Grege [*Among the Rest*] [*Latin*] (ROG)
exg .... exhaust-gas donkey boiler (SAUS)
EXG .... Existing [*Technical drawings*]
EXG .... Grand Valley State College, Allendale, MI [*OCLC symbol*] (OCLC)
ex ga .... external gage (SAUS)
EXGA .... External Gauge
EXGBUS .... External Genitalia and Bartholin's, Urethral, and Skene's Glands [*Gynecology*] (DAVI)
EXGN .... Exogen, Inc. [*NASDAQ symbol*] (SAG)
EX GR .... Exempli Gratia [*For Example*] [*Latin*]
ex gr .... Ex Grupa [*Of The Group Of*] [*Latin*] (DAVI)
EX GRAF .... Extensible Language Including Graphical Operations (SAUS)
EXH .... Exhaust (KSC)
exh .... Exhaust (MIST)
exh .... Exhibit (VRA)
EXH .... Exhibit

Exh.............. exhibited (SAUS)
EXH.............. Exhibiting (SAUS)
exh.............. Exhibition (DIAR)
exh.............. Exhibitor (SAUS)
EXH.............. Hope College, Holland, MI [*OCLC symbol*] (OCLC)
EXHBN.......... Exhibition
EXHBNR........ Exhibitioner (ROG)
EXHBT.......... Exhibit
EXHBTR........ Exhibitor
EXHIB.......... Exhibeatur [*Let It Be Given*] [*Pharmacy*]
exhib.......... exhibit (SAUS)
EXHIB.......... Exhibited [*or Exhibition*]
exhib.......... exhibition (SAUS)
EXHIB.......... Exhibitioner (ROG)
EXHIB.......... Exhibitor (NTCM)
Exhibition Bull... Exhibition Bulletin (journ.) (SAUS)
EXHN.......... Exhibition
ExHPDM........ Extended High Performance Data Mover [*Computer science*] (GART)
EXHST.......... Exhaust
exh t.......... exhaust turbine (SAUS)
EXHV.......... Exhaust Vent
ex hy.......... extra heavy (SAUS)
EXI.............. Excursion Inlet [*Alaska*] [*Airport symbol*] (OAG)
EXI.............. Excursion Inlet, AK [*Location identifier*] [*FAA*] (FAAL)
ExI.............. Extropy Institute (EA)
EXI.............. Whirlpool Corp., Technical Information Center, Benton Harbor, MI [*OCLC symbol*] (OCLC)
EXIAC.......... Explosives Information and Analysis Center [*Army*] (PDAA)
ExideCp........ Exide Corp. [*Associated Press*] (SAG)
ExideEl........ Exide Electronics Group, Inc. [*Associated Press*] (SAG)
EX IDON CRASS LIQ... Ex Idoneo Crasso Liquido [*In a Suitable Thick Liquid*] [*Pharmacy*]
EX IDON LIQ... Ex Idoneo Liquido [*In a Suitable Liquid*] [*Pharmacy*]
EXIM.......... Export-Import Bank
EX-IM.......... Export-Import Bank of the US (SAUS)
EXIMBANK... Export-Import Bank
EXIMBANK... Export-Import Bank of the United States (EBF)
Eximbank.... Export-Import Bank of the United States (USGC)
EXIMBK........ Export-Import Bank
ex in.......... Ex Interest (WDAA)
exins.......... extra insurance (SAUS)
EX INT........ Excluding Interest [*Finance*] (WDAA)
Ex Int.......... Ex Interest [*Without interest*] (EBF)
EXIP.......... Execute in Place [*Computer science*] (CIST)
exis.......... existential (SAUS)
exis.......... existentialism (SAUS)
exis.......... existentialist (SAUS)
EXIS.......... Expert Information Systems Ltd. [*Information service or system*] (IID)
EXIST.......... Energetic X-ray Imaging Survey Telescope (SAUS)
EXIST.......... Existence (SAUS)
EXIST.......... Existing
EXIT.......... Ex-offenders In Transit (SAUS)
EXIT.......... Export Integrated System
EXITE.......... Energetic X-Ray Imaging Telescope Experiment (MCD)
EXIX.......... Executrix (ROG)
EXJ.............. Executive Jet Italiana SRL [*Italy*] [*ICAO designator*] (FAAC)
EXJAM.......... Expendable Communications Jammer [*Army*] (INF)
EXJAM.......... Expendable Jammer (SAUS)
EXJAM.......... Expendable Jamming System (SAUS)
exjbo.......... Extra Jumbo
EXK.............. Kalamazoo College, Kalamazoo, MI [*OCLC symbol*] (OCLC)
EXL.............. Exall Resources Ltd. [*Toronto Stock Exchange symbol*]
EXL.............. Exclusive Air P Ltd. [*South Africa*] [*FAA designator*] (FAAC)
EXL.............. Executive Control Language (SAUS)
EXL.............. Exolon-Esk Co. [*BO Symbol*] (TTSB)
EXL.............. Western Michigan University, School of Librarianship, Kalamazoo, MI [*OCLC symbol*] (OCLC)
ex lap.......... Exploratory Laparotomy (SPVS)
exlge.......... Extra Large
EX LIB.......... Ex Libris [*From the Library Of*] [*Book plate*] [*Latin*] (ROG)
EXLIB.......... Expansion of European Library systems for the visually disadvantaged (SAUS)
EXLIST........ Exit List (VLIE)
EXLITE........ Extended Life Tire (ADWA)
EXLOC.......... Expanded Localizer (PIPO)
exlong.......... Extra Long
EXLST.......... Exit List [*Computer science*]
EXLV.......... Excess Leave [*Military*]
EXM.............. CAA Flight Examiners [*British*] [*ICAO designator*] (FAAC)
EXM.............. Enterprise Messaging Exchange (SAUS)
EXM.............. Excel Maritime Carriers [*AMEX symbol*] (SG)
EXM.............. Excerpta Medica (SAUS)
EXM.............. Exempt
EXM.............. Exhaust Muffler
EXM.............. Exit Message (SAUS)
EXM.............. Expense Management and Control, Inc. [*Vancouver Stock Exchange symbol*]
EX Mag........ EX Magazine (journ.) (SAUS)
EXMAN........ Experimental Manipulation of Forest Ecosystems (SAUS)
EXMAN........ Experimental Manipulation of Forest Ecosystems in Europe (SAUO)
EXMAN........ Experimental Manipulations (SAUS)
ExMBA.......... Executive Master's of Business Administration (RDA)
EX-MER........ Ex-Meridian [*Navigation*]
EXMETNET... Experimental Meteorological Sounding Rocket Research Network (IEEE)
EXMNR........ Examiner
EXMNTN...... Examination
EXMOVREP... Expedited Movement Report [*Army*] (AABC)
EXMP.......... Expanded Metal Plate [*Technical drawings*]
EXMP.......... Experimentation Master Plan (SAUS)
EXMPT.......... Exempt
EXMPTD........ Exempted
Exmr.......... Examiner (EBF)
EXMR.......... Examiner
Ex MSE........ Executive Master of Science in Engineering (PGP)
ExMSE.......... Executive Master's of Science in Science and Technology Commercialization (RDA)
EXN.............. Andrews University, Berrien Springs, MI [*OCLC symbol*] (OCLC)
EXN.............. Europeaero Service National [*France*] [*ICAO designator*] (FAAC)
EXN.............. Exin [*Poland*] [*ICAO designator*] (FAAC)
EXNMR.......... Executive National Military Representative (SAUS)
EXNOR.......... exclusive NOR (SAUS)
EXNOR.......... Exclusive-Nor Gate (HGAA)
EXO.............. European X-Ray Observatory
EXO.............. Executive Officer
EXO.............. Executive Order (SAUS)
EXO.............. Exoatmospheric (SAUS)
Exo.............. Exodus [*Old Testament book*] (DSA)
EXO.............. Exonuclease [*An enzyme*]
EXO.............. Exophoria [*Medicine*] (MELL)
ExO.............. Experimental Officer [*Also, EO, XO*] [*Ministry of Agriculture, Fisheries, and Food*] [*British*]
EXO.............. Experiment Operator (MCD)
EXO.............. Experiment Operator (in Spacelab) (SAUS)
EXO.............. Extotal Resources, Inc. [*Vancouver Stock Exchange symbol*]
EXO.............. Olivet College, Olivet, MI [*OCLC symbol*] (OCLC)
exobio.......... exobiologist (SAUS)
exobio.......... exobiology (SAUS)
EXOBIOLOGY... Exoterrestrial Biology (SAUS)
exocrin........ exocrinologist (SAUS)
exocrin........ exocrinology (SAUS)
EXO-D.......... Exoatmospheric Discrimination (ACAE)
Exod.......... Exodus [*Old Testament book*]
EXODUS........ Object-Oriented Database [*Developed by the University of Wisconsin*] (HODG)
EXOF.......... Expanded Quota Flow [*Aviation*] (FAAC)
EX OFF........ Ex Officio [*By Virtue of Office*] [*Latin*] (ROG)
EX OFFICIN... Ex Officina [*From the Workshop Of*] [*Latin*] (ROG)
exog.......... Exogenous [*Medicine*] (EDAA)
Exogen.......... Exogen, Inc. [*Associated Press*] (SAG)
EXOIII.......... Exonuclease III [*An enzyme*]
EXOKV.......... Exoatmospheric Kill Vehicle (ACAE)
EXOLIFE........ Exoterrestrial Life (SAUS)
EXON.......... Execution (ROG)
EXON.......... Exonia [*Exeter*] [*British*]
Exon.......... Exoniensis [*Of Exeter*] [*Latin*] (ILCA)
EXON D........ Exeter Domesday Book [*A publication*] (ROG)
EXO-NNK...... Exoatmospheric Non-Nuclear Kill (ACAE)
EXOP.......... Executive Office of the President
EXOP.......... Experiment and Operations (KSC)
EXO-PAC........ Exoatmospheric Penetration Aids Concept (MCD)
EXOPORD...... Exercise Operation Order (SAUS)
EXOR.......... Exclusive Or [*Gates*] [*Computer science*]
exor.......... Executor (ADWA)
EXOR.......... Executor (ROG)
Exor.......... Executor (WDAA)
EXORCS........ Exoatmospheric Plume RADAR Cross Section (MCD)
EXORD.......... Execute Order (COE)
EXORD.......... Exercise Order [*Military*] (AFM)
EXORGATE... Exclusive OR Gate (SAUS)
EXOS.......... Executive Office of the Secretary [*Navy*]
EXOS.......... Executive Operating System [*Military*] (CAAL)
EXOS.......... Exosphere Satellite (SAUS)
EXOS.......... Exospheric Satellite [*Japan*]
EXOS.......... Extension Outside (SAUS)
EXOSAT........ European ray observatory satellite (SAUS)
Exosat.......... European Space Agencys X-ray Observatory (SAUS)
EXOSAT........ European X-Ray Observatory Satellite (MCD)
exot.......... exotic (SAUS)
exotheo........ exotheology (SAUS)
exox.......... Executrix (GEAB)
EXOX.......... Executrix
EXP.............. Business Express Delivery Ltd. [*Canada*] [*ICAO designator*] (FAAC)
EXP.............. Du Pont [*E. I.*] De Nemours & Co., Inc. [*Research code symbol*]
EXP.............. Exchange of Persons (SAUS)
EXP.............. Expand (NASA)
EXP.............. Expandable Personnel Shelter (MCD)
EXP.............. Expanded (SAUS)
EXP.............. Expanded Polystyrene (HEAS)
EXP.............. Expansion (KSC)
Exp.............. Expansion (MIST)
exp.............. Expansion (MIST)
EX P.............. Ex Parte [*One-Sided Statement*] [*Latin*] [*Legal term*] (ROG)
EXP.............. Expect
exp.............. expecting (SAUS)
exp.............. expectinged (SAUS)
EXP.............. Expectorant [*Pharmacy*] (ROG)
EXP.............. Expectorated [*Medicine*]
Exp.............. Expediatur (SAUS)
EXP.............. Expedition (ADA)

EXP .... Expend
exp .... Expenditure (MILB)
EXP .... Expense (AABC)
Exp .... Expense (EBF)
EXP .... Expensive (SAUS)
exp .... experience (SAUS)
Exp .... Experience Balance [*Used in Rorschach tests*] (DIPS)
EXP .... Experienced
exp .... Experiment (ADWA)
EXP .... Experiment (KSC)
exp .... Experimental (IDOE)
EXP .... Expert
EXP .... Expiration (SAUS)
exp .... Expiratory [*Respiration*] (DAVI)
EXP .... Expired (ROG)
EXP .... Explain (SAUS)
Exp .... Explained [*Legal term*] (DLA)
exp .... Exploration (MAE)
exp .... Explosion (SAUS)
EXP .... Explosive
EXP .... Expoloratory [*Medicine*] (MELL)
exp .... Exponent (ADWA)
EXP .... Exponent (VLIE)
exp .... Exponential (IDOE)
EXP .... Exponential
exp .... Exponential Function [*Mathematics*] (DAVI)
exp .... exponential function of (SAUS)
EXP .... Exponentiation (SAUS)
Exp .... Export (EBF)
EXP .... Export
EXP .... Exported (SAUS)
EXP .... Exporter (SAUS)
EXP .... Expose (KSC)
Exp .... Exposition (DIAR)
EXP .... Exposition of the Blessed Sacrament [*Roman Catholic*]
exp .... Exposure (VRA)
EXP .... Exposure (WGA)
EXP .... Express (AABC)
Exp .... Express (EBF)
exp .... Express (ELAL)
exp .... Expression (ELAL)
EXP .... Expressway [*Commonly used*] (OPSA)
Exp .... Expropriation [*Legal term*] (DLA)
EXP .... Expulsion (KSC)
EXP .... Expurgated
EXP .... Natural Logarithm [*Mathematics*]
EXP .... Orgue Expressif [*Swell Organ*] [*Music*]
EXP .... Portage Public Schools, Portage, MI [*OCLC symbol*] (OCLC)
EXPAC .... Explosion Prediction and Analysis Code (SAUS)
Exp Agric .... Experimental Agriculture [*A publication*] (PABS)
expamet .... Expanded Metal (SAUS)
ExPAN .... Explorer Plus Guidance Application Network [*Electronic college application*]
EXPAND .... Extensive Processing of Alpha-Numeric Data (VLIE)
Exp Appl Acarol ... Experimental and Applied Acarology (SAUS)
expat .... Expatriate (ADWA)
EXPAT .... Expatriate (DSUE)
ExpB .... [*The*] Expositor's Bible [*A publication*] (BJA)
EXP BT .... Expansion Bolt [*Technical drawings*] (DAC)
exp bt .... Expansion Bolt [*Construction term*] (MIST)
EXPC .... Expect (FAAC)
EXPC .... Experience (AABC)
Exp Cell Res ... Experimental Cell Research (journ.) (SAUS)
Exp Clin Endocrinol diabetes ... Experimental and Clinical Endocrinology and diabetes (SAUS)
Exp Clin Pharm ... Experimental and Clinical Pharmacology (MEC)
EXP/CLT .... Experta/Consultants (SAUS)
EXPD .... Expeditor
EXPD .... Expeditors International of Washington, Inc. [*NASDAQ symbol*] (NASQ)
expd .... Experienced (ADWA)
EXPD .... Expired (ROG)
EXPD .... Exposed
ExpdInt .... Expeditors International of Washington [*Associated Press*] (SAG)
expdivun .... experimental diving unit (SAUS)
EXPDIVUNIT ... Experimental Diving Unit
EXPDN .... Expedition
expdt .... expiration date (SAUS)
EXPDTN .... Expedition
EXPDTR .... Expeditor
expect .... Expectorant [*Pharmacology*] (DAVI)
EXPED .... Expedite (VLIE)
EXPED .... Expediting
exped .... expedition (SAUS)
EXPED .... Expeditionary
Expedition ... Expedition. Bulletin of the University Museum of the University of Pennsylvania [*A publication*] (ABAR)
EXPELS .... Expandable Precision Emitter Location System (MCD)
EXPEN .... Expendable (MSA)
EXPEND .... Expendable
EXPEND .... Expenditure
EXPER .... Experience (SAUS)
EXPER .... Experienced
EXPER .... Experiment [*or Experimental*] (AFM)
Exper .... Experimental Light [*Navigation signal*]
Exper Econ ... Experimental Economics [*A publication*] (JLIT)
Experim .... Experiment (AL)
Experim .... Experimental (AL)
Expermntl ... Experimental (DIAR)
EXPERT .... Expanded Program Evaluation and Review Technique
Expert Syst ... Expert Systems (journ.) (SAUS)
Expert Syst Appl ... Expert System Applications (journ.) (SAUS)
Expert Syst Rev ... Expert Systems Review (journ.) (SAUS)
Expert Syst User ... Expert Systems User (journ.) (SAUS)
Exp Eye Res ... Experimental Eye Research (journ.) (SAUS)
EXPFLDMB ... Expert Field Medical Badge [*Military decoration*] (GFGA)
Exp Fluids ... Experiments in Fluids (journ.) (SAUS)
Exp Gerontol ... Experimental Gerontology (journ.) (SAUS)
ExPGN .... Extracapillary Proliferative Glomerulonephritis [*Nephrology*]
ExpGT .... [*The*] Expositor's Greek Testament [*A publication*] (BJA)
Exp Heat J ... Experimental Heat Journal (journ.) (SAUS)
Exp Heat Transfer ... Experimental Heat Transfer (journ.) (SAUS)
Exp Hematol ... Experimental Hematology (journ.) (SAUS)
EXPHO .... Expedite Delivery by Telephone (FAAC)
expi .... export performance taxation incentive (SAUS)
EXP-IMP .... Export-Import (WDAA)
EXPIO .... Expander Input/Output [*Microprocessing*] (NITA)
EXPIR .... Expiration [*or Expiratory*] [*Medicine*]
expir .... expirationatory (SAUS)
EXPIR .... Expiratory (SAUS)
expir .... Expire [*Medicine*] (DAVI)
exp jt .... expansion joint (SAUS)
expl .... explain (SAUS)
EXPL .... Explanation
EXPL .... Explanatory (SAUS)
Expl .... Explicator [*A publication*] (ANEX)
EXPL .... Exploitation (SAUS)
expl .... Exploratory [*Surgery*] (DAVI)
EXPL .... Explorer
expl .... explosimeter (SAUS)
expl .... explosimetric (SAUS)
EXPL .... Explosion (ECII)
EXPL .... Explosive (KSC)
EXPLAN .... Exercise Plan [*Military*] (AFM)
EXPLAN .... Exercise Plan System (SAUO)
EXPLAN .... Explanatory (ADA)
Exp Lap .... Exploratory Laparatomy [*Medicine*]
EXPLD .... Explained (ROG)
EXPLD .... Explode (MSA)
EXPLET .... Expletive (ROG)
EXPLIC .... Export License (SAUS)
Expl Lap .... Exploratory Laparotomy [*Surgical procedure*] (DAVI)
EXPLN .... Explosion (MSA)
Explo .... Explosion (SAUS)
EXPLO .... Explosive (AABC)
EXPLOIT .... Exploitation (SAUS)
EXPLOIT .... Pan-European Exploitation of the Results of the Libraries Programme (SAUS)
EXPLOR .... Explicit 2-D Patterns Local Operations and Randomness [*Programming language*] [*1975*] (CSR)
EXPLOR .... Explicit Patterns, Local Operations, and Randomness (SAUS)
explor .... Exploration (DD)
Explor .... Exploration Co. [*Associated Press*] (SAG)
EXPLOR .... Exposition (SAUS)
Explorations Econ Hist ... Explorations in Economic History [*A publication*] (JLIT)
Explor Geophys ... Exploration Geophysics (journ.) (SAUS)
explos .... Explosive
Explos Anch ... Explosive Anchorage [*Buoy*]
EXPLR .... Exploder
EXPLRN .... Exploration
expls .... Explosives (SAUS)
EXPLSV .... Explosive
Exp Mech .... Experimental Mechanics (journ.) (SAUS)
Exp Med .... Experimental Medicine and Microbiology (MEC)
Exp Med Microbiol ... Experimental Medicine and Microbiology (journ.) (SAUS)
Exp Med Surg ... Experimental Medicine and Surgery (journ.) (SAUS)
Exp Mol Pathol ... Experimental and Molecular Pathology (journ.) (SAUS)
Exp Mycol .... Experimental Mycology (SAUS)
Expn .... Expansion (DIAR)
EXPN .... Expansion [*Automotive engineering*]
EXPN .... Expiration (ROG)
expn .... Expitration (SAUS)
EXPN .... Exportation
EXPN .... Exposition
EXPND .... Expenditure (AFM)
Exp Neurol ... Experimental Neurology (journ.) (SAUS)
EXPNT .... Exponent (MSA)
EXPNT .... Exponential (MSA)
EXPO .... Experimental Order (MSA)
EXPO .... Exponent (VLIE)
EXPO .... Exponent, Inc. [*NASDAQ symbol*] (NASQ)
expo .... expose (SAUS)
Expo .... Exposition (ODBW)
expo .... Exposition (VRA)
EXPO .... Exposition
EXPO .... Expressivo [*With Expression*] [*Music*] (ROG)
EXPO .... Extended-Range Poseidon [*Missile*] [*Navy*]
EXPO .... World Exposition (SAUS)
expol .... expanded polysterene (SAUS)
Export Dig ... Export Digest (journ.) (SAUS)

EXPOS .... Expenses (SAUS)
EXPOS .... Exposure (SAUS)
EXPOS .... X-Ray Spectropolarimetry Payload on Spacelab (MCD)
EXPOSE .... Ex-Partners of Servicemen (Women) for Equality (EA)
Ex-POWAA ... Ex-Prisoners of War Association of Australia
Exp Parasitol... Experimental Parasitology (journ.) (SAUS)
ExpQualBad... Expert Qualification Badge [*Military decoration*] (AABC)
EXPR .... Experiment (IAA)
EXPR .... Expert
expr .... expiration (SAUS)
EXPR .... Expire (AABC)
expr .... Exploder (SAUS)
Expr .... Express (SAUS)
expr .... Expressing (ADWA)
EXPR .... Expression
EXPR .... Expressway [*Commonly used*] (OPSA)
EXPR .... Orgue Expressif [*Swell Organ*] [*Music*]
ExprAm .... Express America Holdings [*Commercial firm*] [*Associated Press*] (SAG)
EXPRES .... Experimental Research in Electronic Submission of Scientific Documents Program [*Washington, DC*] [*National Science Foundation*]
ex-Pres .... ex-President (SAUS)
EXPRESS ..... Expanded Parts Usage Records and Structure System (VLIE)
EXPRESS ..... Expanded Pump Records and Structural System (SAUS)
EXPRESS ..... Expedite the Processing of Experiments to Space Station (SAUS)
EXPRESS ..... Expendable Parts Record and Structures System (IAA)
EXPRESS ..... Expert Requirements Expression and Systems Synthesis (SSD)
EXPRESS ..... Expressway [*Commonly used*] (OPSA)
EXPRESSNET... Express Network (VLIE)
EXPRESSO... Experiment for Regional Sources and Sinks of Oxidants (SAUO)
expressway... express highway (SAUS)
EXPRMNT .... Experiment
EXPRNC ...... Experience
EXPRO .... Experiment Procedures (KSC)
ExPro .... Exploratory Project on the Conditions of Peace [*Defunct*] (EA)
EXPROG .... Exercise Program (SAUS)
EXPRS .... Expendable Probe Receiver System (SAUS)
EXPRSS .... Express
EXPRSSN ...... Expression
EXPRT .... Export
EXPRTR .... Exporter
EXPS .... Expenses (ROG)
EXPS .... Expose
EXPS .... Express (FAAC)
EXPS .... extruded polystyrene (SAUS)
EXPSAS .... Engineering Change Proposal Service Action Status (AAG)
ExpScpt .... Express Scripts, Inc. [*Associated Press*] (SAG)
EXPSN .... Expansion
ExpSoft .... Expert Software, Inc. [*Associated Press*] (SAG)
EXPSR .... Exposure (MSA)
EXPT .... Expect (AABC)
expt .... expected (SAUS)
EXPT .... Expectorant [*Pharmacy*]
expt .... Experiment (ADWA)
EXPT .... Experiment
expt .... experimental (SAUS)
EXPT .... Expert (WGA)
EXPT .... Export (WGA)
expt .... Export
EXPTE .... Ex Parte [*One-Sided Statement*] [*Latin*] [*Legal term*] (ROG)
Exp Thernt Fluid Sci... Experimental Thermal and Fluid Science (journ.) (SAUS)
exptl .... Experimental (ADWA)
EXPTL .... Experimental
EXPTL .... Exponential (SAUS)
EXPTO .... Expedite Travel Order (NOAA)
EXPTR .... Exporter (ADA)
EXPUL .... Expulsion (SAUS)
EXPURG .... Expurgated (ADA)
Exp Val .... Experimental Values (UWER)
EXPW .... Expressway [*Commonly used*] (OPSA)
expwy .... Expressway (ADWA)
Expwy .... Expressway (TBD)
EXPWY .... Expressway (WDAA)
Expy .... Expressway (DD)
EXPY .... Expressway [*Postal Service standard*] (OPSA)
expy .... Expressway (SHCU)
EXQ .... Aquinas College, Grand Rapids, MI [*OCLC symbol*] (OCLC)
EXQ .... Execujet [*British*] [*ICAO designator*] (FAAC)
EXQ .... execute (SAUS)
exq .... ex quai (SAUS)
EXQ .... Ex Quay [*Seller's responsibility is to make goods available on the wharf at destination named*] [*"INCOTERM," International Chamber of Commerce official code*]
EXQF .... Expanded Quota Flow (FAAC)
EXQQPRI ...... Expedited Qualitative and Quantitative Personnel Requirements Information [*Army*]
ex-quay .... free on quay (SAUS)
EXR .... Exception Request [*Computer science*] (ELAL)
EXR .... Exclusive Rights (SAUO)
EXR .... Execute and Repeat
EXR .... Executor
ExR .... Exodus Rabbah (BJA)
EXR .... Express Resources Ltd. [*Vancouver Stock Exchange symbol*]
Ex R .... Ex-Rights [*Without Rights*] [*Investment term*]
ex r .... ex rights (SAUS)
EXR .... Flight Express, Inc. [*ICAO designator*] (FAAC)
EXR .... Grand Rapids Public Library, Grand Rapids, MI [*OCLC symbol*] (OCLC)
EXRAY .... Expendable Relay (SAUS)
EXRAY .... Expendable Remote Array (PDAA)
exray .... expendible relay (SAUS)
EXREDCON... Exercise Readiness Condition [*Military*] (AABC)
EX REL .... Ex Relatione [*On the Report Of*] [*Latin*] (ADA)
EXREM .... external radiation dose (SAUS)
EXREM .... External REM [*Roentgen-Equivalent-Man*] [*Radiology*]
EXREP .... Expedite Mail Reply (FAAC)
EXREQ .... Extract of Requisition
Ex Rts .... Ex Rights [*Without rights*] (EBF)
exrx .... Executrix (ADWA)
EXRX .... Executrix
EXS .... Channel Express (Air Services) Ltd. [*British*] [*ICAO designator*] (FAAC)
Exs .... De Exsecrationibus [*Philo*] (BJA)
exs .... excesses (SAUS)
ExS .... Exogenous Substance [*Biology*]
EXS .... Expenses
exs .... expropriations (SAUS)
EXS .... Ex Ship [*Seller's responsibility is to make goods available on board ship at destination named*] [*"INCOTERM," International Chamber of Commerce official code*]
ExS .... Ex-Smoker (MELL)
ExS .... Extra-Strength (MELL)
EXS .... Extrastrong [*Technical drawings*]
EXS .... Western Theological Seminary, Holland, MI [*OCLC symbol*] (OCLC)
EXSC .... Executive Standards Council (SAUO)
EX SC .... Ex Senatus Consulto [*By Decree of the Senate*] [*Latin*] (ROG)
EX SD .... Ex Senatus Decreto [*By Decree of the Senate*] [*Latin*] (ROG)
exsec .... Exsecant [*Mathematics*] (BARN)
EXSEC .... Exterior Secant (SAUS)
EXSEC .... Extra Section (FAAC)
EXSH .... Expeditionary Shelters [*Marine Corps*] (MCD)
EXSHI .... Expedite Shipment (NOAA)
Ex Ship .... Delivered Out of Ship (EBF)
ex ship .... delivered out of the ship (SAUS)
EXSL .... Exhibition of Sports and Leisure [*British*] (ITD)
EXSM .... Excessive Soil Moisture (PDAA)
EXSO .... Exsorbet Industries [*NASDAQ symbol*] (TTSB)
EXSO .... Exsorbet Industries, Inc. [*NASDAQ symbol*] (SAG)
Exsorbet ...... Exsorbet Industries, Inc. [*Associated Press*] (SAG)
EXSPEC .... Exercise Specification [*NATO*] (NATG)
EXSR .... Executive Subroutine [*NASA*] (IAA)
EXSR .... Exit Subroutine (SAUS)
EXST .... Execute Stack [*Computer science*] (IAA)
exst .... exempt sales tax (SAUS)
EXST .... Existing (MSA)
EXST .... Extra Seat [*Travel industry*] (TRID)
EXSTA .... Experimental Station
Exstar .... Exstar Financial Corp. [*Associated Press*] (SAG)
EXSTAT .... Extel Statistical Database (SAUS)
EXSUBCOM... Exploitable Subcommittee [*Military*]
EXSUBM .... Extract Submatrix (SAUS)
EXSUM .... Executive Summary (MCD)
EXSUM .... Exercise Summary (SAUS)
ex sur tr & ct... Excavate Surface Trenches and Cart (SAUS)
EXSWG .... Exploration Science Working Group [*NASA*] (EGAO)
EXSY .... exchange spectroscopy (SAUS)
ext .... entend (SAUS)
EXT .... Except (ROG)
ext .... Executor (ADWA)
EXT .... Exeter [*England*] [*Airport symbol*] (OAG)
EXT .... Experiment Terminal (MCD)
ExT .... Expository Times (SAUS)
EXT .... Extant
EXT .... Extend [*or Extension*] (AFM)
EXT .... Extende [*Spread*] [*Pharmacy*]
ext .... Extended (SHCU)
Ext .... Extension (TBD)
ext .... Extension (WDMC)
EXT .... Extension
EXT .... Extensor [*Anatomy*]
ext .... extensorion (SAUS)
ext .... extent (SAUS)
EXT .... Exterior (AABC)
ext .... Exterior (VRA)
Ext .... Exterior
EXT .... External (AABC)
ext .... External [*Therapy term*] (CTAA)
Ext .... External (DIAR)
ext .... Externus [*External*] [*Latin*]
ext .... Extinct (WDMC)
EXT .... Extinct
ext .... Extinction (DIPS)
Ext .... Extinction (UWER)
EXT .... Extinguish (KSC)
Ext .... Extinguisher (UWER)
EXT .... Extortion [*FBI standardized term*]
ext .... Extra (WDMC)
EXT .... Extra
ext .... Extract (WDMC)

EXT Extract [*or Extracted*]
Ext Extraction [*Dentistry*] (DAVI)
EXT Extractum [*Extract*] [*Latin*]
EXT Extra Executive Transport [*Germany*] [*ICAO designator*] (FAAC)
EXT Extraordinary
Ext Extrapolation [*A publication*] (BRI)
EXT Extreme
ext extremitty (SAUS)
ext Extremity (ADWA)
EXT Extremity [*Medicine*]
Ext Extrudate
EXT Night Express [*Germany*] [*FAA designator*] (FAAC)
EXTAC Experimental Tactic (NVT)
EXT AE External Aerial (SAUS)
EXTAL Extra Time Allowance
EXT ANT External Antenna (SAUS)
EXTBAT Extension Battery (IAA)
ext cav External Cavity (SAUS)
EXTCD Extension Cord (IAA)
EXTD Extend [*or Extended*] (KSC)
Extd Extended (EBF)
Ext D Extensive Damage (SAUS)
EXTD Extracted
EXTD Extrude (MSA)
EXTD Extruded (SAUS)
EXT D & C External Drug and Cosmetic [*Color*]
ext d & cc external drug and cosmetic color (SAUS)
extdiam external diameter (SAUS)
exte Exterior (BARN)
Extecp Extecapital Ltd. [*Associated Press*] (SAG)
EXTEL Exchange and Telegraph Company (SAUS)
EXTEL Exchange Telegraph [*Press agency*] [*British*] (DCTA)
EXTEL Exchange Telegraph Co Ltd (SAUS)
EXTEL Exchange Telegraph Company (SAUS)
EXTEL Company Exchange Telegraph Company (SAUO)
EXTELCOMS East African External Telecommunications Company (SAUO)
Ex Tele Exchange Telephone (WDAA)
EXTEMP Extemporaneous (WDAA)
EXTEN Extended [*Automotive advertising*]
exten extension (SAUS)
Extend Extendicare, Inc. [*Associated Press*] (SAG)
EXTEND Exercise Training for the Elderly and/or Disabled (ODA)
EXTENDEX Extended Exercise [*Navy*] (ANA)
EXTENL Extension of Enlistment [*Military*]
EXTENSION Extension [*Commonly used*] (OPSA)
EXTENSIONS Extensions [*Commonly used*] (OPSA)
EXTER External (KSC)
EXTERA Extra Terrestrial Research Agency (SAUO)
Exter Ca Lobingier's Extra-Territorial Cases [*United States Court for China*] [*A publication*] (DLA)
EXTERM Exterminating
extern external (SAUS)
extern Externally [*Medicine*] (BARN)
EXTERR Extended Error Information [*Computer science*] (UWER)
exterr exterritorial (SAUS)
EXTERRA Extraterrestrial Research Agency [*Army*] (IEEE)
EXT FHR External Fetal Heart Rate (MEDA)
ext fl extract fluid (SAUS)
Ext Fl Fluid Extract [*Pharmacology*] (DAVI)
ext flt Extension Filter (SAUS)
EXTFP Experienced Teacher Fellowship Program
EXTFREQ Extension Frequency (IAA)
EXTG Exterminating (SAUS)
EXTG Extinguish (AAG)
extg Extracting (MIST)
EXTG Extracting (MSA)
EXTGH Extinguish
EXTGR Extinguisher (AAG)
EXTHEO Extra Theoretical (SAUS)
EXTHEO Extra-Theoretical [*Telecommunications*] (TEL)
EXTIN Extinguish (ROG)
EXTING Extinguish (KSC)
exting extinguished (SAUS)
Exting Extinguished Light [*Navigation signal*]
extingd Extinguished (SAUS)
EXTL Executive Telecard Ltd. [*NASDAQ symbol*] (SAG)
EXTL External (DLA)
EXT LIQ Extractum Liquidum [*Liquid extract*] [*Latin*] [*Pharmacy*] (WDAA)
EXT LRCP Extra Licentiate of the Royal College of Physicians [*British*] (ROG)
EXTLV Extension of Leave [*Military*] (AABC)
EXTM Extended Telecommunication (SAUS)
EXTM Extended Telecommunications Module (SAUS)
EXTM Extended Telecommunications Modules
EXTM Ex Testamento [*In Accordance with the Testament Of*] [*Latin*]
EXTM Extreme (MSA)
EXT MOD FREQ External Modulation Frequency (SAUS)
Extn Extension (DIAR)
extn Extension (WDMC)
EXTN Extension
EXTN Extensity, Inc. [*NASDAQ symbol*] (SG)
Extn External (CMD)
Extn Extraction (UWER)
EXTN Extraction
Extn Extrusion (SAUS)
EXTND Extended
EXTND Extended Data Transistor (TIMI)
EXTND Extender (MSA)
EXTNL External
EXTNR Extender
extns Extension (VRA)
EXTNS Extension
EXTNSN Extension [*Commonly used*] (OPSA)
EXTON Executone Information Systems, Inc. [*Associated Press*] (SAG)
Exton Mar Dic Exton's Maritime Dicaeologie [*A publication*] (DLA)
EXTOR External Torpedo [*Formerly, DEXTOR*] (MCD)
EXTORP Exercise Torpedo (NVT)
EXTOSS Extended Range Transfer Orbit Sun Sensor (ACAE)
EXTOXNET Extension Toxicology Network (GNE)
EXT P Extra Parochial [*Geographical division*] [*British*]
EXTR Executor [*Business term*]
EXTR Exstar Financial Corp. [*NASDAQ symbol*] (SAG)
EXTR External (ROG)
EXTR Extra (ROG)
EXTR Extract
Extr Extraction (SAUS)
EXTR Extraction Code (UWER)
EXTR Extraordinary (ROG)
EXTR Extravagant (ROG)
extr Extreme
EXTR Extreme Networks [*NASDAQ symbol*] (SG)
extr Extremity (MAH)
Extr Extremum (SAUS)
EXTR Extrude (MSA)
Extr Extruder (SAUS)
EXTR Extrusion (SAUS)
EXTRA Exponentially Tapered Reactive Aerial (SAUS)
EXTRA Exponentially Tapered Reactive Antenna (SAUS)
EXTRA Exponentially-Tapered Reactive Antenna (IAA)
EXTRA Export Tender Risk Advance [*British*]
EXTRA Extended Education in Therapeutic Recreation Administration (EDAC)
extra extraordinary (SAUS)
Extra Ca Lobingier's Extra-Territorial Cases [*United States Court for China*] [*A publication*] (DLA)
EXTRACONUS Outside Continental United States [*Military*] (AFIT)
EXTRAD Extinction Of Radiation (SAUS)
EXTRAD Extradition (ADA)
EXTRADOP Extended-Range Doppler
extradop extended range doppler (SAUS)
EXTRADOVAP Extended Range Doppler Velocity and Position (SAUS)
EXTRADOVAP Extended-Range Doppler Velocity and Position (CET)
EXTRAH Extrahatur [*Draw Out*] [*Pharmacy*] (ROG)
Extra HD extra heavy duty (SAUS)
EXTRAN Expression Translator [*Computer science*] (MHDI)
EXTRAN External FORTRAN (SAUS)
EXTRAOR Extraordinary (ROG)
extrap extrapolate (SAUS)
extrap extrapolating (SAUS)
extrap extrapolation (SAUS)
extrap extrapolative (SAUS)
extrap extrapolator (SAUS)
Extra Sess Extraordinary Session [*A publication*] (DLA)
extra sess extra session (SAUS)
EXTRAV Extravaganza (ROG)
extrav Extravasation [*Medicine*] (EDAA)
Extrav Com Extravagantes Communes [*A publication*] (DSA)
Extrav Joann XXII Extravagantes Johannes XXII [*A publication*] (DSA)
EXTRC Extrication [*National Highway Traffic Safety Administration Fatal Accident Recording System code*]
Extr Comm Extravagantes Communes [*A publication*] (DSA)
EXTRCT Extract
EXTRCTR Extractor
extrd extruded (SAUS)
EXTRE Exstar Financial [*NASDAQ symbol*] (TTSB)
EXTREM External Roentgem-Equivalent-Man Dose [*Radiation therapy*] (DAVI)
Extrem Extremadura (SAUS)
Extrem Extremities (SAUS)
EXTREM Extremity [*Medicine*] (WDAA)
extrins extra insurance (SAUS)
EXTRIX Executrix
Extr Joann XXII Extravagantes Johannes XXII [*A publication*] (DSA)
EXTRM Extreme
EXTRN External (SAUS)
EXTRN External Reference (BUR)
Extrn Extraction (UWER)
EXTRN Extrusion (MSA)
extro extroversion (SAUS)
extro extrovert (SAUS)
Ext rot External Rotation (AMHC)
ext rot External Rotation [*Myology*] (MAE)
EXTR Press Extrusion Press (SAUS)
EXTRRDNRY Extraordinary
Extru Extrusion (MIST)
Extrus Extrusion (UWER)
Extrus Showc Extrusion Showcase (journ.) (SAUS)
EXTRX Executrix [*Business term*]
EXTS Extend Sign (SAUS)
EXTS Extensions [*Postal Service standard*] (OPSA)
EXTSN Extension (MDG)
EXT SPKR External Speaker (SAUS)
ExtStA Extended Stay America [*Associated Press*] (SAG)

EXT sup ALUT MOLL... Extende super Alutum Mollem [*Spread upon Soft Leather*] [*Pharmacy*] (ROG)
EXTSV.......... Extensive (FAAC)
EXT T-PHONE... Extension Telephone (SAUS)
EXT TRIG..... External Triggering (SAUS)
extub.......... Extubation [*Medicine*] (EDAA)
EXTUB......... Extubation [*Medicine*] (MELL)
EXTV.......... Extensive
EXTVE.......... Executive
EXTW.......... Extension Wire (IAA)
EXTZ.......... Explosives Technology [*Federal Railroad Administration identification code*]
EXU.......... Excretory Urogram [*Medicine*] (DMAA)
EXU.......... Execution Unit (SAUS)
EXU.......... Executive Transports [*France*] [*ICAO designator*] (FAAC)
EXU.......... Upjohn Co., Technical Library, Kalamazoo, MI [*OCLC symbol*] (OCLC)
exud.......... Edudate/tion [*Medicine*] (EDAA)
EXUD.......... Excudit [*Made*] [*Latin*] (ROG)
EXUG.......... European X Users Group (VERA)
EXUP.......... Exhaust Ultimate Power Valve [*Yamaha Motor Co.*]
exurb.......... exurban (SAUS)
exurb.......... exurbanite (SAUS)
exurb.......... exurbia (SAUS)
exurb.......... exurbian (SAUS)
EXUV.......... Extreme Ultraviolet (SAUS)
EXUV.......... Extreme Ultraviolet and X-Ray Survey Satellite (PDAA)
EXV.......... Executive Air Transport Ltd. [*Switzerland*] [*ICAO designator*] (FAAC)
EXVOC.......... Expert System Contribution to Vocational Training (SAUO)
EXW.......... Executive Airlines Services Ltd. [*Nigeria*] [*FAA designator*] (FAAC)
EXW.......... Explosion Welding
EXW.......... Extreme Width
EXW.......... Ex-Warehouse (SAUS)
Ex W.......... Ex Warrants [*Without warrants*] (EBF)
EXW.......... Ex Works [*Seller's only responsibility is to make goods available at his premises*] [*"INCOTERM," International Chamber of Commerce official code*]
EXW.......... Martinsburg, WV [*Location identifier*] [*FAA*] (FAAL)
EXW.......... Western Michigan University, Kalamazoo, MI [*OCLC symbol*] (OCLC)
Ex Warr.......... Ex Warrants [*Without warrants*] (EBF)
EXWEP.......... Exercise Weapon (NVT)
Ex Whse.......... Delivered out of Warehouse (EBF)
e(x)wks.......... Every (X) Weeks (SPVS)
EXX.......... Exador Resources, Inc. [*Toronto Stock Exchange symbol*]
EXX.......... Examples
exx.......... Executrix (GEAB)
EXX.......... Executrix
EXX.......... EXX, Inc. [*Formerly, SFM Corp.*] [*AMEX symbol*] (SAG)
EXX.......... International Air Corp. [*FAA designator*] (FAAC)
EXX.......... Lexington, NC [*Location identifier*] [*FAA*] (FAAL)
EXXA.......... EXX, Inc.'A' [*AMEX symbol*] (SG)
Exxon.......... Exxon Corp. [*Associated Press*] (SAG)
EXXPOL.......... Exxon Polymerization (UWER)
exy.......... expiry (SAUS)
Exy.......... Expressway (SAUS)
EXY.......... SA Exress Airways [*South Africa*] [*FAA designator*] (FAAC)
EXZ.......... Excessive Zeros [*Computer science*] (VERA)
EXZ.......... Exzellenz [*Excellency*] [*German*]
EXZ.......... Kalamazoo Library System, Kalamazoo, MI [*OCLC symbol*] (OCLC)
EY.......... Eastern Yiddish (BJA)
EY.......... East Yorkshire Militia [*British military*] (DMA)
EY.......... Eger's Yellow
EY.......... Egg Yolk
EY.......... Electron Yield
EY.......... Elvisly Yours [*Fan club*] (EAIO)
Ey.......... Emergency (SAUS)
EY.......... Empty [*Indian Railway*] (TIR)
EY.......... Empty Rake [*Indian Railway*] (TIR)
EY.......... Energy Yield (UWER)
EY.......... Entry Year [*Information retrieval*] (NITA)
EY.......... Epidemological Year [*Medicine*] (EDAA)
EY.......... Equilibrium Yield [*Fishery management*] (MSC)
EY.......... Essex Yeomanry [*British military*] (DMA)
EY.......... Ethyl Corp. [*NYSE symbol*] [*Toronto Stock Exchange symbol*] (SPSG)
EY.......... Europe Aero Service [*ICAO designator*] (AD)
EY.......... Execution Year
EYA.......... Ecumenical Youth Aktion (SAUO)
EYA.......... Egg Yolk-Pyruvate-Tellurite-Glycine Agar [*Medicine*] (BABM)
EYA.......... Washtenaw Community College, Ann Arbor, MI [*OCLC symbol*] (OCLC)
EYB.......... Europa Year Book [*A publication*] (MHDB)
EYB.......... Macomb County Library, Mt. Clemens, MI [*OCLC symbol*] (OCLC)
EYBSOYB.......... Examine Your Birthday Suit on Your Birthday [*To detect potentially malignant moles*] [*Skin Cancer Foundation*]
EYC.......... Eastern Yacht Club (SAUS)
EYC.......... Encinal Yacht Club (SAUS)
EYC.......... Environmental Youth Congress (SAUO)
EYC.......... European Youth Campaign
EYC.......... European Youth Centre [*Council of Europe*] (EY)
EYC.......... Michigan Library Consortium, Wayne State University, Detroit, MI [*OCLC symbol*] (OCLC)
EYCA.......... European Youth Card Association (EURO)
EYCD.......... European Young Christian Democrats [*Formerly, European Union of Young Christian Democrats*] (EA)
EYCE.......... Ecumenical Youth Council in Europe (EAIO)
EyCL.......... emitter emitter-coupled logic (SAUS)
EYCO.......... Estimated Yearly Cost of Operation [*of electrical appliance*]
EYD.......... Engineering Youth Day
EYD.......... University of Michigan, Dearborn Campus, Dearborn, MI [*OCLC symbol*] (OCLC)
EYE.......... BEC Group [*NYSE symbol*] [*Formerly, Benson Eyecare*] (SG)
EYE.......... BEC Group, Inc. [*NYSE symbol*] (SAG)
EYE.......... Benson Eyecare Corp. [*NYSE symbol*] (SAG)
EYE.......... Eastern Michigan University, Ypsilanti, MI [*OCLC symbol*] (OCLC)
EYE.......... Emerald Air [*British*] [*FAA designator*] (FAAC)
EYE.......... European Year of the Environment [*Beginning March 23, 1987*]
EYE.......... European Youth Exchange (EURO)
EYE.......... Indianapolis, IN [*Location identifier*] [*FAA*] (FAAL)
EYE.......... Visx, Inc. [*NYSE symbol*]
EYEF.......... Educated Youth for Epilepsy Foundation [*Medicine*] (EDAA)
EYES.......... Salvatori Opthalmics, Inc. [*NASDAQ symbol*] (COMM)
EYES.......... Vision Twenty-One, Inc. [*NASDAQ symbol*] (NASQ)
EYF.......... European Youth Foundation (EA)
EYF.......... Henry Ford Hospital, Medical Library, Detroit, MI [*OCLC symbol*] (OCLC)
EyFAMOS.......... electrically eras able floating-gate avalanche-injection metal-oxide semiconduct (SAUS)
EYFP.......... Enhanced Yellow Fluorescent Protein
EYG.......... General Motors Corp., Research Laboratory, Warren, MI [*OCLC symbol*] (OCLC)
EYH.......... Huron Valley Library System, Ann Arbor, MI [*OCLC symbol*] (OCLC)
EYI.......... Livonia Public Schools, Livonia, MI [*OCLC symbol*] (OCLC)
EyICs.......... Elevated Electrode Integrated Circuits (SAUS)
EYJ.......... John Wesley College Library, Owosso, MI [*Inactive*] [*OCLC symbol*] (OCLC)
EYL.......... Lawrence Institute of Technology, Southfield, MI [*OCLC symbol*] (OCLC)
EYLT.......... Eyelet (MSA)
EYM.......... Electron Yield Measurement
EYM.......... University of Michigan, Ann Arbor, MI [*OCLC symbol*] (OCLC)
EYMS.......... Electron Yield Measurement System
EYN.......... Europeaero Service National [*France*] [*FAA designator*] (FAAC)
EYOA.......... Economic and Youth Opportunity Agency (IIA)
EYOC.......... Estimated Yearly Operating Cost [*of electrical appliance*]
EYOP.......... European Year of Older People and Solidarity Between Generations
E YORK R.......... East Yorkshire Regiment [*Military unit*] [*British*] (ROG)
EYP.......... Detroit Public Library, Detroit, MI [*OCLC symbol*] (OCLC)
EYP.......... East York Public Library [*UTLAS symbol*]
EYP.......... Electronic Yellow Pages [*Dun's Marketing Services*] [*Information service or system*] (IID)
EYP.......... El Yopal [*Colombia*] [*Airport symbol*] (OAG)
EYP.......... El Yunque [*Puerto Rico*] [*Seismograph station code, US Geological Survey*] [*Closed*] (SEIS)
EYP.......... Port Huron, MI [*Location identifier*] [*FAA*] (FAAL)
EYPC.......... Eyepiece (MSA)
EyPLD.......... CMOS PLDs programmed with EyPROM switching arrays (SAUS)
EyPROM.......... electrically erasable programmable read-only memory (SAUS)
EyPROM.......... Electrically Erasable PROMs (SAUS)
EYQ.......... Detroit Cooperative Cataloging Center, Detroit, MI [*OCLC symbol*] (OCLC)
EYR.......... East Yorkshire Regiment [*Military unit*] [*British*]
EYR.......... Eyrewell [*New Zealand*] [*Geomagnetic observatory code*]
EYR.......... Oakland University, Rochester, MI [*OCLC symbol*] (OCLC)
Eyre.......... Eyre's English King's Bench Reports Tempore William III [*A publication*] (DLA)
Eyre MS.......... Eyre's Manuscript Notes of Cases, King's Bench [*New York Law Institute Library*] [*A publication*] (DLA)
EyROM.......... electrically erasable read-only memory (SAUS)
EYS.......... Board of Education for the Borough of East York [*UTLAS symbol*]
EYS.......... Ecumenical Youth Services (SAUO)
EYS.......... European Youth Centre (SAUO)
EYS.......... Experimental Yacht Society [*Defunct*] (EA)
EYS.......... St. Clair County Library System, Port Huron, MI [*OCLC symbol*] (OCLC)
EYS.......... World Council of Churches Ecumenical Youth Service (EA)
EYT.......... Detroit Institute of Arts, Research Library, Detroit, MI [*OCLC symbol*] (OCLC)
EYT.......... Europe Aero Service [*France*] [*ICAO designator*] (FAAC)
EYU.......... University of Detroit, Detroit, MI [*OCLC symbol*] (OCLC)
e-yu-.......... Yugoslavia [*MARC geographic area code*] [*Library of Congress*] (LCCP)
EYV.......... Wayne County Community College, Detroit, MI [*OCLC symbol*] (OCLC)
EYW.......... Key West [*Florida*] [*Airport symbol*] (OAG)
EYW.......... Key West, FL [*Location identifier*] [*FAA*] (FAAL)
EYW.......... Wayne State University, Detroit, MI [*OCLC symbol*] (OCLC)
EYY.......... Mercy College of Detroit, Detroit, MI [*OCLC symbol*] (OCLC)
EYZ.......... Madonna College, Livonia, MI [*OCLC symbol*] (OCLC)
EZ.......... Eastern Zone
EZ.......... Easy [*Slang*]
EZ.......... Easy Listening [*Radio*] (NTCM)
EZ.......... Economic Zone (SAUS)
Ez.......... Eczema [*Medicine*] (EDAA)
EZ.......... Eczema [*Medicine*]
EZ.......... Eineiige Zwillinge [*Monozygotic Twins*] [*Psychology*]
EZ.......... Electrical Zero
EZ.......... Emile Zola (SAUS)
EZ.......... Engagement Zone [*Army*] (ADDR)
EZ.......... Enterprise Zone [*British*]

EZ .... Enzymology [*Medicine*] (EDAA)
E/Z .... Equal Zero (MDG)
EZ .... Erogenous Zone (MELL)
EZ .... Excessive Zeros (SAUS)
EZ .... Exclusion Zone (SAUS)
EZ .... Extraction Zone [*Military*] (AFM)
Ez .... Ezekiel [*Old Testament book*]
Ez .... Ezra [*Old Testament book*]
EZ .... Sun-Air of Scandinavia [*ICAO designator*] (AD)
EZA .... Alma College, Alma, MI [*OCLC symbol*] (OCLC)
EZA .... Newark, NJ [*Location identifier*] [*FAA*] (FAAL)
EZAACMO .... Eastern Zone Army Air Corps Mail Operations (SAUO)
EZACC .... Easy Access
EZB .... Cloverland Processing Center, Escanaba, MI [*OCLC symbol*] (OCLC)
EZB .... Exclusion Zone Boundary (SAUS)
EZB .... Oakland, CA [*Location identifier*] [*FAA*] (FAAL)
EZC .... Central Michigan University, Mount Pleasant, MI [*OCLC symbol*] (OCLC)
EZC .... European Zone Charge (DS)
EZCI .... EZ Communications, Inc. [*NASDAQ symbol*] (SAG)
EZCIA .... E-Z Communications'A' [*NASDAQ symbol*] (TTSB)
EZCO .... Extraction Zone Control Officer [*Military*] (AFM)
EZCO .... Ezcony Interamerica, Inc. [*NASDAQ symbol*] (SAG)
EZCOF .... Ezcony Interamerica [*NASDAQ symbol*] (TTSB)
EZ Com .... EZ Communications, Inc. [*Associated Press*] (SAG)
Ezcony .... Ezcony Interamerica, Inc. [*Associated Press*] (SAG)
Ezcorp .... Ezcorp, Inc. [*Associated Press*] (SAG)
EZD .... Enziklopedyah shel ha-Ziyonut ha-Datit [*A publication*] (BJA)
EZ Duzit ...... Easy Does It (SAUS)
EZE .... Asociacion Protestante de Cooperacion para el Desarrollo en Alemania (SAUS)
EZE .... Buenos Aires [*Argentina*] Ezeiza [*Airport symbol*] (OAG)
EZ/EC .... Empowerment Zones/Enterprise Communities [*Medicine*]
EZECH .... Ezechiel [*Old Testament book*] [*Douay version*]
EZEE .... entectic zone electrical evaluation (SAUS)
Ezek .... Ezekiel [*Old Testament book*]
EZEM .... EXEM, Inc. [*Associated Press*] (SAG)
EZEM .... E-Z-EM, Inc. [*NASDAQ symbol*] (NQ)
EZEV .... Equivalent Zero-Emission Vehicle
EZF .... Esatzzielfunktion (SAUS)
EZF .... Ferris State College, Big Rapids, MI [*OCLC symbol*] (OCLC)
EZI .... Electrolytic Zinc Industries (SAUS)
EZI .... European Zinc Institute (EA)
EZI .... Exotic Zooplankton in Illinois (SAUO)
Ezi .... Ezias (SAUS)
Ezi .... Eziel (SAUS)
Ezi .... Eziongaber (SAUS)
EZI .... Kewanee, IL [*Location identifier*] [*FAA*] (FAAL)
EZI .... Mid-Peninsula Library Cooperative, Iron Mountain, MI [*OCLC symbol*] (OCLC)
e-zine .... Electronic Magazine [*Online newsletter*] (IGQR)
E-ZINE .... Electronic Magazine [*A publication*] (UWER)
Ezk .... Ezekiel (ADWA)
EZK .... Ezekiel [*Old Testament book*]
EZL .... Lake Superior State College, Sault Ste. Marie, MI [*OCLC symbol*] (OCLC)
EZM .... EZEM, Inc. [*AMEX symbol*] (SAG)
EZM .... Muskegon County Library, Muskegon, MI [*OCLC symbol*] (OCLC)
EZMA .... E-Z EM, Inc.'A' [*AMEX symbol*] (SG)
EZN .... Ezine [*Turkey*] [*Seismograph station code, US Geological Survey*] (SEIS)
EZN .... Northern Michigan University, Marquette, MI [*OCLC symbol*] (OCLC)
EZP .... Elliptical Zone Plate (PDAA)
EZP .... Exclusion Zone Patrol (SAUS)
EZP .... Superiorland Library Cooperative, Marquette, MI [*OCLC symbol*] (OCLC)
EZP2 .... Region 2, EZPLOT-User Operated Business Graphics Package (SAUS)
EZPERT .... Easy Programme Evaluation and Review Technic (SAUS)
EZPW .... EZCORP, Inc. [*NASDAQ symbol*] (SPSG)
EZPW .... EZCORP Inc.'A' [*NASDAQ symbol*] (TTSB)
EZR .... Easyriders, Inc. [*AMEX symbol*] (SG)
Ezr .... Ezra [*Old Testament book*]
EZR .... Gulf of Alaska/Bering Sea, AK [*Location identifier*] [*FAA*] (FAAL)
EZS .... Edgar Z. Steever IV [*Designer's mark when appearing on US coins*]
EZS .... Elazig [*Turkey*] [*Airport symbol*] (OAG)
EZS .... E-Z Serve Corp. [*AMEX symbol*] (SPSG)
EZS .... Saginaw Valley State College, University Center, MI [*OCLC symbol*] (OCLC)
EZ Serv .... EZ Serve [*Associated Press*] (SAG)
EZT .... Elizabethton, TN [*Location identifier*] [*FAA*] (FAAL)
EZT .... Michigan Technological University, Houghton, MI [*OCLC symbol*] (OCLC)
EZT .... Zenit [*Former USSR*] [*FAA designator*] (FAAC)
EZ terms ...... easy terms (SAUS)
EZV .... EZ Ventures Ltd. [*Vancouver Stock Exchange symbol*]
EZW .... White Pine Library System, Saginaw, MI [*OCLC symbol*] (OCLC)
EZY .... Elk City, OK [*Location identifier*] [*FAA*] (FAAL)
EZZ .... Michigan North Processing Center, Cadillac, MI [*OCLC symbol*] (OCLC)

F

By Acronym

f.................. Acceleration [*Symbol*] (DEN)
f.................. activity coefficient (SAUS)
f----.............. Africa [*MARC geographic area code*] [*Library of Congress*] (LCCP)
F.................. Air Force Training Category [*No inactive duty periods and 4 months minimum initial active duty training per year*]
f.................. Antiresonant Frequency (SAUS)
F.................. Atlanta [*Branch in the Federal Reserve regional banking system*] (BARN)
f.................. Atomic Orbital with Angular Momentum Quantum Number 3 [*Symbol*] (DAVI)
F.................. Bioavailability [*Medicine*] (EDAA)
F.................. Blue Second Hydrogen Line in the Solar Spectrum (BARN)
f.................. Breathing Frequency [*Medicine*] (DAVI)
f.................. Coefficient of Sliding Friction (SAUS)
F.................. College of Future Education [*British*]
F.................. Consuetudines Feudorum [*The Book of Feuds*] [*Latin*] [*A publication*] (DLA)
F.................. Dealt in Flat [*Investment term*] (DFIT)
F.................. Degrees Fahrenheit (MCD)
f.................. distribution function (SAUS)
F.................. Dominion Rubber Co. [*Research code symbol*] [*Canada*]
F.................. Eaton Laboratories, Inc. [*Research code symbol*]
F.................. Element Fluor (SAUS)
f.................. ellipsoid flattening (SAUS)
F.................. energy fluence of particles (SAUS)
F.................. Fac [*Let There Be Made*] [*Pharmacy*]
F.................. Face
F.................. Facial Rash [*Classification system used by doctors on Ellis Island to detain, re-examine, and possibly deny entry to certain immigrants*]
F.................. Facial Surface [*Dentistry*]
F.................. Facies [*Medicine*]
F.................. Facing (WDAA)
F.................. Facsimile (SAUS)
F.................. Factor (DAVI)
F.................. Faculty of Advocates Collection of Decisions, Scotch Court of Sessions [*A publication*] (DLA)
f.................. faded (SAUS)
f.................. Fah (intonic sol-fa) [*Music*] (ODA)
F.................. Fahrenheit [*German*] (EG)
F.................. Fail (ADWA)
F.................. failed (SAUS)
F.................. Failure to Appear [*Motor vehicle term used in state of Washington*] (MVRD)
F.................. Fair
F.................. Fairchild (SAUS)
F.................. Fairing (SAUS)
F.................. Fair Skiing Conditions
F.................. Falck [*When used in identifying W. F. Bach's compositions, refers to cataloging of his works by musicologist Falck*]
F.................. Falls (ROG)
F.................. False
F.................. Family
F.................. Farad [*Symbol*] [*Unit of electric capacitance*] (GPO)
F.................. Faraday (SAUS)
F.................. Faraday Constant [*Electrochemistry*]
F.................. Farce (ROG)
F.................. Farenheit (SAUS)
F.................. Farrell Lines (SAUS)
f.................. Farthing (ADWA)
F.................. Farthing [*Monetary unit*] [*British*]
F.................. Fascia (MELL)
F.................. Fast
F.................. Fasting [*Test*] [*Medicine*]
F.................. Fat
f.................. Father (GEAB)
F.................. Father
f.................. fathom (SAUS)
F.................. Fatty Acid [*Biochemistry*] (HGAA)
F.................. Fawn (WGA)
F.................. Feast
F.................. February
F.................. Feces
F.................. Fecit [*He, or She, Did It*] [*Latin*]
F.................. Federal (AAGC)
F.................. Federal League [*Major league in baseball, 1914-15*]
F.................. Federal Reporter [*A publication*] (DLA)
F.................. Feedback
F.................. Feed Rate (SAUS)
f.................. Feet [*Industrial hygiene term*] (OHS)
F.................. Feet [*or Foot*]
f.................. feet furlong (SAUS)
F.................. Feldspar Subgroup [*Orthoclase, albite, anorthite*] [*CIPW classification*] [*Geology*]
F.................. Feliciter [*Happily*]
F.................. Fell [*Horse racing*]
F.................. Fellow
F.................. Fellow of (SAUO)
F.................. Felon
f.................. Female (DD)
F.................. Female
f.................. Feminine (SHCU)
F.................. Feminine
f.................. femininum (SAUS)
F.................. Femmes [*or Feminin*] [*Initial used as title of a publication*]
f.................. Femto [*A prefix meaning divided by 10 to the 15th power*] [*SI symbol*]
F.................. Femur (MELL)
F.................. Fen [*Monetary unit*] [*China*]
F.................. Fendi [*Italian couturier*]
F.................. Fenoterol [*Pharmacology*]
F.................. Fermentation [*Biology*]
F.................. Fermi [*Later, Femtometer*] [*Unit of length*] [*Nuclear physics*]
f.................. ferroconcrete (SAUS)
F.................. Ferrosan [*Sweden*] [*Research code symbol*]
F.................. Ferrule Contact [*Lamp base type*] (NTCM)
F.................. Fertile [*Medicine*]
F.................. Fertility (SAUS)
F.................. Fertility Factor [*Genetics*]
F.................. Fertilized
F.................. Fetal [*Medicine*]
F.................. Fetch [*Computer science*]
F.................. Fever (MELL)
f.................. Fiant [*Let Them be Made*] [*Pharmacology*] (DAVI)
F.................. Fiat [*Let It Be Made*] [*Pharmacy*]
f.................. Fibers [*Industrial hygiene term*] (OHS)
f.................. Fiber Stress [*Construction term*] (MIST)
F.................. Fibre [*Classification key in textile printing*]
F.................. Fibroblast (MELL)
F.................. Fibrous
F.................. Fibula (MELL)
F.................. Fiction
F.................. Field
F.................. Field of Vision [*Medicine*]
F.................. Fighter [*Designation for all US military aircraft*]
f.................. Figured Bass [*Music*]
F.................. Fiji (BARN)
F.................. Filament (AAG)
F.................. Filaria [*Microbiology*] (MAE)
F.................. File [*Computer science*]
F.................. Filial Generation [*Biology*]
F.................. Filius [*Son*] [*Latin*]
F.................. Fill (MIST)
F.................. Filly [*Thoroughbred racing*]
f.................. filment (SAUS)
F.................. Filter
F.................. Final [*Telecommunications*] (TEL)
F.................. Final Target
f.................. final values (SAUS)
F.................. Finance [*or Financial*]
f.................. finance charge (SAUS)
f.................. Fine (MIST)
F.................. Fine [*Condition*] [*Antiquarian book trade, numismatics, etc.*]
F.................. Fine [*Designation on brandy labels*]
F.................. Fine [*End*] [*Music*]
F.................. Finger
F.................. Finish
F.................. fiord (SAUS)
F.................. Fire
F.................. Fireman [*Navy rating*]
F.................. Firm
F.................. First (SAUS)

F.................. First Class [*Airline fare code*]
F'.................. First Focal Distance [*Symbol*] [*Optics*] (ROG)
F.................. Fischer [*Rat strain*]
F.................. fishing mortality rate (SAUS)
f.................. Fission (SAUS)
F.................. fission rate (SAUS)
F.................. Fitted as Flagship [*Suffix to plane designation*]
F.................. Fitter [*Navy rating*] [*British*]
F.................. Fitzherbert's Abridgment [*1516*] [*A publication*] (DSA)
F.................. Fixed [*JETDS nomenclature*]
F.................. fixed broadcast (SAUS)
F.................. fixed broadcasting (SAUS)
f.................. Fixed Format (IAA)
F.................. Fixed Head (NITA)
F.................. Fixed Length (SAUS)
F.................. Fixed Light [*Navigation signal*]
F.................. Fixer [*Photography*] (DGA)
F.................. Fixing (SAUS)
F.................. Flag [*Computer science*]
F.................. Flagship (SAUS)
F.................. flair (SAUS)
F.................. Flame (SAUS)
F.................. Flanged Joint (DNAB)
F.................. Flap (SAUS)
F.................. Flash [*Precedence*] [*Telecommunications*] (TEL)
F.................. Flashless (SAUS)
F.................. Flat
F.................. Flat Band Metallic Armor (AAG)
F.................. Flat-Tainers [*British*] (DCTA)
F.................. Fleet
F.................. Fletcher Challenge Investments, Inc. [*Toronto Stock Exchange symbol*] [*Vancouver Stock Exchange symbol*]
F.................. Flexion (MELL)
F.................. Flied Out [*Baseball*]
F.................. Flight (SAUS)
F.................. Flint (AAG)
F.................. Floaters (MELL)
F.................. Florida State Library, Tallahassee, FL [*Library symbol*] [*Library of Congress*] (LCLS)
F.................. Florin [*Monetary unit*] [*Netherlands*]
F.................. Floryn [*Florin*] [*Monetary unit*] [*Afrikaans*]
F.................. Flow [*of blood*] [*Medicine*]
F.................. Flower
f.................. Fluency (DIPS)
F.................. Fluency [*A factor ability*] [*Psychology*]
F.................. Flugzeug [*Airplane*] [*German military*]
F.................. Fluid
F.................. Fluid Ounce
F.................. Flunk (CDAI)
F.................. Fluorescence (SAUS)
F.................. Fluoride
F.................. Fluorine [*Chemical element*]
F.................. Fluorochrome (SAUS)
F.................. Fluorouracil [*Also, FU*] [*Antineoplastic drug*]
F.................. Flush (SAUS)
F.................. Flutter Wave (MEDA)
F.................. Flux (SAUS)
F.................. Fly [*Baseball term*] (NDBD)
F.................. Flying [*Officer qualified as both pilot and observer*] [*British*]
F.................. Flyout [*Baseball term*] (NDBD)
f.................. F-Number [*Photography*] (ODA)
F.................. Focal (SAUS)
f.................. Focal Distance (NTIO)
f.................. Focal Length [*Photography*] (WDMC)
F.................. Focal Length [*Photography*]
F.................. focal length of image space (SAUS)
f.................. focal length of object space (SAUS)
f.................. focal ratio (SAUS)
F.................. Focus [*Medicine*] (EDAA)
f.................. focus of conic section (SAUS)
F.................. Foetal (SAUS)
F.................. Fog [*Meteorology*]
f.................. Foggy (SAUS)
F.................. Foil [*Dentistry*]
F.................. Folacin (MELL)
F.................. Folge [*Series*] [*Publishing*] [*German*]
F.................. Folio [*Book 30 centimeters and over in height*]
f.................. Folio [*On the Following Page*] [*Latin*]
F.................. Following [*Pages*] [*Also, FF*] (MUGU)
f.................. Following (WDMC)
f.................. following page (SAUS)
F.................. Follow-Up
F.................. Font
F.................. Fontanel (MELL)
F.................. Foord's Cape Of Good Hope Reports [*South Africa*] [*A publication*] (DLA)
F.................. Foord's Supreme Court Reports [*Cape Colony, South Africa*] [*A publication*] (DLA)
F.................. Foot [*Medicine*] (EDAA)
f.................. foot (SAUS)
F.................. For
F.................. forad (SAUS)
F.................. Foraging [*Ornithology*]
F.................. Foramen [*Anatomy*] (MAE)
F.................. Force [*Symbol*] [*IUPAC*]
f.................. fordable (SAUS)
f.................. Ford Motor [*NYSE symbol*] (TTSB)
F.................. Ford Motor Co. [*Wall Street slang names: "Tin Lizzy" or "Flivver"*] [*NYSE symbol*] (SPSG)
F.................. Forecastle
f.................. Foreground [*Computer science*] (IAA)
f.................. Foreign (ODA)
F.................. Forint [*Monetary unit*] [*Hungary*]
F.................. Form [*of*]
F.................. Form [*Rorschach*] [*Psychology*]
F.................. Form [*Letter*] [*Computer science*] [*Telecommunications*]
F.................. Forma [*Form*] [*Latin*]
F.................. Formality
F.................. Formed
F.................. Form Response [*Used in Rorschach test scoring*] (DIPS)
F.................. Formula
F.................. Formulary [*Medicine*] (EDAA)
f.................. Formulate (SAUS)
f.................. Formyl [*As substituent on nucleoside*] [*Biochemistry*]
F.................. Fornix [*Neuroanatomy*]
F.................. Fort (ROG)
F.................. Fortasse [*Perhaps*] [*Latin*]
f.................. Forte [*Loud*] [*Music*] (WA)
F.................. Forte [*Loud*] [*Music*]
F.................. [*The*] Forum (AAGC)
F.................. Forward
F.................. Forward Compartment
F.................. Forward Journey [*Indian Railway*] (TIR)
F.................. Fossa (MELL)
F.................. Foul
F.................. Foul Fly [*Baseball term*] (NDBD)
F.................. Founded (EY)
F.................. Fox [*Phonetic alphabet*] [*World War II*] (DSUE)
F.................. Foxtrot [*Phonetic alphabet*] [*International*] (DSUE)
F.................. Fraction [*Medicine*] (EDAA)
f.................. Fraction (IAA)
F.................. Fractional (MAE)
F.................. Fractional Concentration [*in dry gas phase*] (AAMN)
F.................. Fracture
F.................. Fragile
f.................. Fragment (BJA)
F.................. Fragmentation
F.................. Fragment of an Antibody (DAVI)
F.................. Frame (SAUS)
F.................. Frame Construction
F.................. Franc [*Monetary unit*] [*France*]
F.................. Francais [*French*]
F.................. France [*IYRU nationality code*]
F.................. Fraser [*James E.*] [*Designer's mark, when appearing on US coins*]
F.................. Fraser, Inc. [*Toronto Stock Exchange symbol*]
F.................. Fraser's Scotch Court of Sessions Cases, Fifth Series [*A publication*] (DLA)
F.................. Frater [*Brother*] [*Latin*]
F.................. F ratio (DIPS)
F.................. Freddy [*Phonetic alphabet*] [*Royal Navy*] [*World War I*] (DSUE)
F.................. Free [*Rate*] [*Value of the English pound*]
F.................. Freeboard (SAUS)
F.................. freedom (SAUS)
F.................. freedom, degree of (SAUS)
F.................. Free Energy [*Physics*] (BARN)
F.................. Freehold [*Legal term*] (ROG)
F.................. Freeway (ADA)
f.................. freezing (SAUS)
F.................. Fremskridtspartiet [*Progress Party*] [*Denmark*] [*Political party*] (PPE)
F.................. French [*Catheter size*] [*Medicine*] (DAVI)
F.................. frequence (SAUS)
F.................. Frequency
f.................. Frequency [*Symbol*] [*IUPAC*]
F.................. Frequency of Fading [*Broadcasting*]
F.................. Frequent [*In mention of occurrence of species*]
f.................. Frequently (DAVI)
F.................. Freshwater [*Load line mark*]
F.................. Friable (SAUS)
F.................. Friar
F.................. Friction
f.................. friction coefficient (SAUS)
f.................. friction factor (SAUS)
F.................. Friday
F.................. Frogerius [*Rogerius Beneventanus*] [*Flourished, 12th century*] [*Authority cited in pre-1607 legal work*] (DSA)
F.................. From
F.................. Front (KSC)
F.................. Frontal [*Medicine*] (DAVI)
F.................. Frontal Sinus [*Otorhinolaryngology*] (DAVI)
f.................. frost (SAUS)
f.................. frost point (SAUS)
F.................. Froude Number [*IUPAC*]
F.................. Fuchsia [*Genotype of Phlox paniculata*]
F.................. Fuel
F.................. Fueler [*Aircraft designation*]
f.................. Fugacity [*Thermodynamics*]
F.................. Full
f.................. full function (SAUS)
F.................. Full Load [*Displacement*]
F.................. Fullword (SAUS)

f .... Fully [*Expand*] [*Computer science*] [*Telecommunications*]
f .... fumble (SAUS)
f .... Function (IDOE)
F .... Function
f .... function of (SAUS)
f .... Fundamental (SAUS)
F .... Fundus (MELL)
f .... Furanose [*One-letter symbol*] [*Biochemistry*]
F .... Furlong [*Unit of distance*]
F .... Furlough [*Military*] (ADA)
F .... Furness (SAUS)
F .... Furness Lines (SAUS)
F .... Furstenau [*Medicine*] (EDAA)
F .... Fusarium Wilt [*Plant pathology*]
F .... Fuse (DEN)
F .... fusibility (SAUS)
F .... Fusiformis [*Microbiology*] (MAE)
f .... fusion (SAUS)
f .... fusion processes (SAUS)
F .... Fusobacterium [*Microbiology*] (MAE)
F .... Fuss [*Feet of organ stops*]
F .... Fuze (SAUS)
F .... Gilbert [*Unit of magnetomotive force*] (DAVI)
F .... Goals For [*Hockey*]
F .... Helmholtz Function [*Symbol*] (DEN)
F .... Inbreeding Coefficient [*Genetics*] (DAVI)
F .... Individual [*Missile launch environment symbol*]
F .... Intelligence for which the Source Reliability Cannot be Judged
F .... Interceptor [*Aircraft*]
F .... Lab. Funai [*Japan*] [*Research code symbol*]
F .... Libri Feudorum [*A publication*] (DSA)
f .... Luminous Flux (DIPS)
F .... Luminous Flux [*Physics*]
F .... Mutuel Field [*Horse racing*]
F .... Phenylalanine [*One-letter symbol*] [*Also, Phe*]
F .... Photoreconnaissance [*Aircraft designation*]
f .... Polar Flattening [*Symbol*] [*Physics*]
F .... rate of aqueous formation (SAUS)
F .... Requires Food and Water [*Search and rescue symbol that can be stamped in sand or snow*]
f .... Respiratory Frequency [*Breaths per unit of time*] [*Medicine*] (DAVI)
F" .... Second Focal Distance [*Symbol*] [*Optics*] (ROG)
F .... Society of Friends (SAUO)
F .... Upper Ionized Layer of the Ionosphere (BARN)
F .... Variance Ratio (DIPS)
F .... Vendredi [*French*] (ASC)
f .... Face Value [*Numismatics*] (ODA)
F .... Federation (ODA)
F .... Fokker [*Aircraft*] (ODA)
F .... Foolscap (ODA)
F_0 .... Frequency Emitted [*On Doppler study*] [*Cardiology*] (DAVI)
F0-F9 .... Field 0 to Field 9 (SAUS)
F_1 .... Filial Generation, First [*Biology*]
F1 .... First Folio Edition [*1623*] [*Shakespearean work*]
F1 .... Formula One [*Auto racing*]
F_1 .... Frequency Received [*On Doppler study*] [*Cardiology*] (DAVI)
F-1 .... Fury single-engine jet fighter-bomber flown from aircraft carriers (SAUS)
F_1ATPase .... F_1 Adenosine Triphosphatase [*A protein*] [*Biochemistry*] (DAVI)
F 1C .... Fireman 1st Class (SAUS)
F1C .... Fireman First Class (SAUS)
F1CL .... Fireman First-Class (SAUS)
F1S .... Finish One Side [*Technical drawings*]
F_2 .... Filial Generation, Second [*Biology*]
F2 .... Second Folio Edition [*1632*] [*Shakespearean work*]
F_2 .... Zinc Oxide-Eugenol Cement [*Dentistry*] (DAVI)
F2CL .... Fireman Second-Class (SAUS)
F 2d .... Federal Reporter, Second Series [*A publication*] (DLA)
F2F .... Face-to-Face [*Fundraising*]
F2F .... Face to Face (Slang) (SAUS)
F2F .... Frequency Double Frequency (SAUS)
F2S .... Finish Two Sides [*Technical drawings*]
F3 .... Form, Fit, Function (SAUS)
F^3 .... Form-Fit-Function [*Pronounced "f-cubed"*]
F3CL .... Fireman Third-Class (SAUS)
F 3d .... Federal Reporter, Third Series [*A publication*]
F3/FFF .... Form-Fit-Function (SAUS)
F3I .... Form-Fit-Function Interface (SAUS)
F3OEU .... Tornado F3 Operational Evaluation Unit (SAUS)
F-4 .... Phantom McDonnell Douglas [*Fighter-attack aircraft*] [*Air Force*] (POLM)
f4p .... fortran 4 plus (SAUS)
F-5A/B .... Freedom Fighter (SAUS)
F5CA .... Force 5 Class Association (EA)
F-5E/F .... Tiger II Northrop [*Fighter-training aircraft*] [*Air Force*] (POLM)
F 11 .... fluorocarbon (SAUS)
f 12 .... freon (SAUS)
F-13 .... dope (SAUS)
F-13 .... drugs (SAUS)
F1/4 .... Forequarters (SPVS)
F-14 .... Tomcat [*Fighter aircraft*] [*Navy*] (POLM)
F-15 .... Eagle Fighter Aircraft [*Air Force*] (POLM)
F-15E .... Strike Eagle Fighter-Attack Aircraft [*Air Force*] (POLM)
F-16 .... Fighting Falcon (SAUS)
F-27 .... Fokker Friendship (SAUS)
F-27M .... Fokker Troopship built in the Netherlands (SAUS)
F-28 .... Fokker turbojet aircraft (SAUS)
F50 .... Fokker 50 [*Airplane code*]
F77 .... Fortran 77 (SAUS)
F90 .... Fortran 90 (SAUS)
F-111 .... Aardvark Fighter-Attack Aircraft [*Air Force*] (POLM)
F 344 .... Fischer 344 [*Medicine*] (EDAA)
F-404 .... General Electric turbofan jet engine (SAUS)
FA .... Aeronautical Station [*ITU designation*] (CET)
fa--- .... Atlas Mountain Region [*MARC geographic area code*] [*Library of Congress*] (LCCP)
FA .... Fabrication Assembly (MCD)
FA .... Face Amount [*Business term*]
FA .... Facilitating Agency [*Business term*]
FA .... Factor Analysis [*Mathematics*]
FA .... Factory Act [*British*] (ILCA)
FA .... Factory Automation
FA .... Factury Act (SAUS)
FA .... Faculty Awards Committee (SAUS)
FA .... Faculty of Actuaries [*British*] (BI)
FA .... Faculty of Advocates [*British*] (ILCA)
Fa .... Faeroes (SAUS)
Fa .... Fahrenheit [*Temperature scale*] (DAVI)
FA .... Failed Appointment (SAUS)
FA .... Failure Analysis (AAG)
FA .... Fairchild Aircraft Ltd. [*Canada*], Fairchild/Republic [*ICAO aircraft manufacturer identifier*] (ICAO)
FA .... Fairchild Corp.'A' [*NYSE symbol*] (TTSB)
FA .... Faith Alive (EA)
FA .... Fallen Angels International (EA)
FA .... False (SAUS)
FA .... False Acceptance (SAUS)
FA .... False Alarm (ACAE)
FA .... False Aneurysm [*Cardiology*] (DAVI)
FA .... Families Anonymous (EA)
FA .... Family Agency
FA .... Family Allowance [*Navy*]
FA .... Family America [*An association*] (EA)
FA .... Famous Artists (SAUS)
FA .... Fanconi's Anemia [*Medicine*]
FA .... Fanny Adams [*Canned mutton stew*] [*Slang*] (DSUE)
FA .... Fantasy Association (EA)
FA .... Far Advanced [*Medicine*] (MAE)
FA .... Farm Advisor (SAUS)
FA .... Farm Aid (EA)
FA .... Farnesynic Acid [*Juvenile hormone analog*]
fa .... Faroe Islands [*MARC country of publication code*] [*Library of Congress*] (LCCP)
FA .... Fascicular Area [*Neurology*]
FA .... Fashion Aid (EA)
FA .... Fast Algorithm (SAUS)
FA .... Fast Axis (SAUS)
FA .... Fatal Accident [*Motor vehicle violation code used in state of Maryland*] (MVRD)
FA .... Father (DSUE)
fa .... Father (GEAB)
fa .... Fatty [*Medicine*] (EDAA)
FA .... Fatty Acid [*Biochemistry*]
FA .... Fawcett Association [*A union*] [*British*]
fa .... Fayalite [*CIPW classification*] [*Geology*]
FA .... Feasibility Assessment (COE)
FA .... Febrile Antigen [*Immunology*] (MAE)
FA .... Feet Apart [*Dance terminology*]
FA .... Felonious Assault
FA .... Femoral Artery [*Anatomy*]
fA .... Femtoampere (IEEE)
FA .... Fermi National Accelerator Laboratory (SAUO)
FA .... Ferrari Club of America (SAUO)
FA .... Ferretin-Agglutinin [*Medicine*] (EDAA)
FA .... Ferro-Alloy (SAUS)
FA .... [*The*] Ferroalloys Association (EA)
FA .... Ferrocarriles Argentinos [*Railway*] [*Argentina*] (EY)
FA .... Fertilization Antigen [*Immunology*]
FA .... Ferulic Acid [*Biochemistry*]
FA .... Fetal Age [*Obstetrics*] (DAVI)
F/A .... Fetus Active [*Obstetrics*] (DAVI)
FA .... Fibonacci Association (EA)
FA .... Fibrinolytic Activity [*Hematology*]
FA .... Fibroadenoma [*Oncology*]
FA .... Fibrosing Alveolitis [*Medicine*] (DMAA)
FA .... Field Accelerating (SAUS)
FA .... Field Accelerating Contactor or Relay [*Industrial control*] (IEEE)
F/A .... Field Activities
FA .... Field Address
FA .... Field Allowance [*British military*] (DMA)
FA .... Field Ambulance [*Military*]
FA .... Field Army
FA .... Field Artillery
FA .... Field Audit [*IRS*]
FA .... Field Availability (SAUS)
FA .... Field Goals Attempted [*Football, basketball*]
FA .... Fielding Average [*Baseball*]
FA .... Fifth Avenue Ventures [*Vancouver Stock Exchange symbol*]
FA .... Fighter Aircraft (SAUS)
FA .... Fighter Alert (NATG)

FA ... Fighter Allocator (NATG)
F-A ... fighter-attack (SAUS)
FA ... File Addressing (SAUS)
FA ... File Assignment (SAUS)
FA ... File Attribute (SAUS)
FA ... Filterable Agent [*Virology*]
FA ... filtered Air (MEDA)
FA ... Final Acceptance (SAUS)
FA ... Final Address [*Computer science*] (ECII)
FA ... Final Address Register [*Computer science*] (MDG)
FA ... Final Approach (GAVI)
FA ... Final Approval [*Automotive project management*]
FA ... Final Assembly (MSA)
FA ... Finance Act [*British*] (DCTA)
FA ... Finance and Accounting (MCD)
FA ... Financial Administrator (GART)
FA ... Financial Adviser
FA ... Financial Analysis
FA ... Fine Aggregate
FA ... Fine Alignment
FA ... Finite Automation
FA ... Fire Alarm (ROG)
F/A ... Fire and Accident [*Insurance*] (MARI)
FA ... Fireman Apprentice [*Navy rating*]
Fa ... Firma [*Legal term*] (DLA)
FA ... First Access
FA ... First Aid [*Medicine*]
FA ... First Aid/Medical Aid Station (SAUS)
FA ... First Announcement
FA ... first appearance (SAUS)
FA ... First Article
FA ... First Attack [*Men's lacrosse position*]
FA ... Fiscal Agent [*Medicaid term*] (MHCS)
FA ... Fisheries Agency (SAUO)
FA ... Fist-Allis (SAUS)
FA ... Fixed Asset [*Business term*]
fa ... Fixed assets (EBF)
FA ... Flag Allowance (CINC)
FA ... Flameless Atomizer [*Medicine*] (EDAA)
FA ... Flat Gain Amplifier (IAA)
FA ... Fleet Activity (SAUS)
FA ... Fleet Auxiliary [*British*]
FA ... Flexible Addressing (SAUS)
FA ... Flight Acceptance
FA ... Flight Accident (SAUS)
FA ... Flight Accommodation (SAUO)
FA ... Flight Aft (NASA)
FA ... Flight Attendant
FA ... Flight Critical Aft [*Aerospace*] (NAKS)
FA ... Floating Add [*Computer science*] (IAA)
FA ... Floating Address (SAUS)
FA ... Floating Airfields [*British*] [*World War II*]
FA ... Floating Asset [*Business term*]
FA ... Flora of Australia [*Commonwealth*] (EERA)
FA ... Florida (ROG)
FA ... Flourescent antibody (SAUS)
FA ... Flow alarm (SAUS)
FA ... Flowing Afterglow [*Chemical kinetic*]
FA ... Flowrate Alarm [*Engineering*]
FA ... Fluctuating Asymmetry [*Embryology*]
FA ... Fludaradine [*Medicine*] (MELL)
FA ... Fluidization Aid [*Plastics*]
FA ... Fluocinolone-Acetonide (SAUS)
FA ... Fluorenamine [*Also, AF*] [*Carcinogen*]
FA ... Fluorescein Angiogram (SAUS)
FA ... Fluorescence Assay (DB)
FA ... Fluorescent Angiography
FA ... Fluorescent Antibody [*Clinical chemistry*]
FA ... Fluoroalanine [*Organic chemistry*]
FA ... Fluorouracil and Adriamycin [*Antineoplastic drug regimen*] (DAVI)
fa ... fluvic acid (SAUS)
FA ... Folic Acid [*Also, PGA, PteGlu*] [*Biochemistry*]
FA ... Folklore Americas [*A publication*]
FA ... Food Additive
FA ... Food Administration (SAUO)
FA ... Food Allergy (MELL)
FA ... Food and Agriculture (NATG)
FA ... Football Association [*Controlling body of British soccer*]
FA ... Forage Acre
FA ... Foragers of America (EA)
FA ... For Auction (SAUS)
FA ... Forbes-Allbright [*Syndrome*] [*Medicine*] (DB)
FA ... Force account (SAUS)
FA ... Force Artillery (SAUS)
FA ... Forced Air (MSA)
FA ... Forced-Air-Cooled [*Transformer*] (IEEE)
FA ... Forced Answer (HGAA)
FA ... Ford Aerospace (SAUS)
FA ... Forearm [*Anatomy*] (DAVI)
FA ... Forecast Area (SAUS)
FA ... Forecaster Aid [*Military*]
FA ... Foreign Agent (SAUS)
FA ... Foreign Agriculture Including Foreign Crops and Markets [*A publication*]
FA ... Forestry Abstracts [*Oxford, England*] [*A publication*]
FA ... Forestry Act [*Town planning*] [*British*]
FA ... Formal Advertising (MCD)
FA ... Formamide (ACAE)
FA ... Formel Acceptance (SAUS)
FA ... Formic Acid (SAUS)
FA ... Formula Atlantic [*Class of racing cars*]
fa ... Formylaminoacyl [*As substituent on nucleoside*] [*Biochemistry*]
FA ... Fortified Aqueous [*Pharmacology*]
FA ... Forward Acquisition (ACAE)
F/A ... Forward/Aft (KSC)
FA ... Forward America [*Defunct*] (EA)
FA ... Found Abandoned
FA ... Foundation of America (EA)
FA ... Four Arrows (EA)
FA ... Fourier Analysis (SAUS)
FA ... Fracture Analysis (SAUS)
FA ... Frame Aerial (SAUS)
FA ... Frame Analyzer (MCD)
FA ... Frame Antenna (IAA)
FA ... France Auto (SAUS)
FA ... Franconi Anemia [*Medicine*] (AAMN)
FA ... Frankford Arsenal [*Pennsylvania*] [*Closed*] [*Army*]
FA ... Frater Anselm [*Pseudonym used by Anselm Baker*]
FA ... Free Acid [*Medicine*] (MAE)
FA ... Free Air (SAUS)
fa ... Free Alongside (EBF)
FA ... Free Alongside [*Shipping*]
FA ... Free America [*In the movie "Red Dawn"*]
FA ... Free Aperture [*Technical drawings*]
FA ... Free Area (OA)
FA ... Free Association [*Psychology*] (BARN)
FA ... Free Astray
FA ... Free of All Average [*Insurance*]
FA ... Freight Agent
FA ... Freight Allowal
FA ... Freight Astray
FA ... Freight Auditor
FA ... French Army (NATG)
FA ... Frente Amplio [*Broad Front*] [*Uruguay*] [*Political party*] (PD)
FA ... Frequency Adjustment (IAA)
FA ... Frequency Agility
FA ... Fresh Air (OA)
FA ... Freund's Adjuvant [*Immunology*]
FA ... Friedenwald Archives (BJA)
FA ... Friedreich's Ataxia [*Medicine*]
FA ... Friendly Aircraft
FA ... Friendship Ambassadors Foundation (EA)
FA ... Friends of Astrology (EA)
FA ... Frontal Aviation [*Soviet tactical air force*] [*World War II*]
FA ... Front Axle [*Automotive engineering*]
FA ... Frozen Asset [*Business term*]
FA ... fructional activities (SAUS)
F/A ... Fuel-Air [*Ratio*]
f/a ... fuel-air ratio (SAUS)
F/A ... Fuel Assembly (NRCH)
F/A ... Fuel-to-Air (SAUS)
FA ... Fulbright Association (EAIO)
FA ... Full Abstraction (SAUS)
FA ... Full Action
FA ... Full Adder [*Computer science*]
FA ... Full Aperture [*Photography*] (NTCM)
FA ... Full Arc (NRCH)
FA ... Fully Accessible (IAA)
FA ... Fully Automatic (KSC)
FA ... Fulvic Acid [*Organic chemistry*]
FA ... Functional Acknowledgement (SAUS)
FA ... Functional Activity [*Medicine*] (MAE)
FA ... Functional Administration (HCT)
FA ... Functional Analysis
FA ... Functional Area
FA ... Functional Assembly (MCD)
FA ... Fundamentalists Anonymous (EA)
FA ... Furfuryl Alcohol [*Organic chemistry*]
FA ... Furnace Annealing (SAUS)
FA ... Furnace Atomizer [*Medicine*] (EDAA)
f/a ... further advances (SAUS)
FA ... Further Assembly (IAA)
FA ... Fusaric Acid (MEDA)
FA ... Fuse Alarm (TEL)
FA ... Fused Alloy (SAUS)
FA ... Fuzed Alloy
FA ... Office of the Federal Inspector for the Alaska Natural Gas Transportation System (SAUO)
FA ... Fine Art (ODA)
FA1AT ... Fecal Alpha 1 - Antitrypsin [*Clinical chemistry*]
F-a2-Globulin ... fast-a2-Globulin (SAUS)
FA61 ... Factories Act 1961 (HEAS)
FAA ... Angolan Armed Forces (SAUO)
FAA ... Facility Accepted (SAUS)
FAA ... Facteur d'Anglo-Arab [*Equine term*] (TED)
FAA ... Faculty of Accountants and Auditors (SAUS)
FAA ... False Alarm Avoidance
FAA ... Family Allowance, Class A [*Navy*]
FAA ... Fatty Acid Alkanolamide [*Organic chemistry*]
FAA ... Febrile Antigen Agglutination [*Medicine*] (MELL)

FAA............ Federal Aeronautics Administration (SAUO)
FAA............ Federal Arbitration Act of 1925 (SAFN)
FAA............ Federal Aviation Act [*1958*]
FAA............ Federal Aviation Administration [*Formerly, Federal Aviation Agency*] [*Department of Transportation*]
FAA............ Federal Aviation Agency (AEBS)
FAA............ Federal Aviation Authority (SAUS)
FAA............ Fellow of the American Association for the Advancement of Science
FAA............ Fellow of the Australian Academy (WDAA)
FAA............ Field Artillery Airborne
FAA............ Fifth Avenue Association (SAUO)
FAA............ Film Artistes' Association [*A union*] [*British*] (DCTA)
FAA............ Financial Administration Act (FOTI)
FAA............ Financial Aid Administrator [*Department of Education*] (GFGA)
FAA............ Fine Art Acquisitions Ltd. (EFIS)
FAA............ Fireplace Association of America [*Later, WHA*]
FAA............ First Article Approval [*or Audit*]
FAA............ Flame Atomic Absorption (SAUS)
FAA............ Flameless Atomic Absorption
FAA............ Fleet Air Arm [*British*]
FAA............ Flexible Automatic Assembly (VLIE)
FAA............ Fluid Applied Asphalt (ABAC)
FAA............ Fluorenylacetamide [*Also, AAF, AcNHFln*] [*Organic chemistry*]
FAA............ Flying Apache Association (EA)
FAA............ Focus on Atmospheric Aerosols (SAUS)
FAA............ Folic Acid Antagonist (SAUS)
FAA............ Food Additives Amendment [*Medicine*] (EDAA)
FAA............ Forces Administrative Area (SAUS)
faa............ fore and aft (SAUS)
FAA............ Foreign Affairs Association, Pretoria (SAUO)
FAA............ Foreign Assistance Act [*1961*] (DOMA)
FAA............ Foreman's Association of America [*Defunct*] (EA)
FAA............ Forest Amendment Act (SAUS)
FAA............ Formaldehyde, Acetic Acid, and Alcohol (MELL)
FAA............ Formalin Acetic Acid (SAUS)
FAA............ Formalin-Acetic Acid-Alcohol [*Fixative*] [*Botany*]
faa............ formalin, acetic acid, alcohol (SAUS)
FAA............ formalin, acetic, alcohol (SAUS)
FAA............ Forward Assembly Area [*Army*] (DOMA)
FAA............ Foundation for American Agriculture [*Later, FAAPFF*] (EA)
FAA............ Foundation for the Advancement of Artists (EA)
FAA............ Fraternal Actuarial Association [*Defunct*] (EA)
FAA............ Fraternal Actuaries Association (SAUO)
FAA............ Free Afghanistan Alliance (SAUS)
FAA............ Free Amino Acid [*Biochemistry*]
faa............ Free of All Average (EBF)
FAA............ Free of All Average [*Insurance*]
FAA............ Fresh Acid Add [*Nuclear energy*] (NRCH)
FAA............ Friends of Africa in America [*Defunct*] (EA)
FAA............ Fuel assembly area (SAUS)
FAA............ Fulbright Alumni Association [*Later, Fulbright Association*] (EAIO)
FA/A............ Functional Analysis/Allocation (SAUS)
FAA............ Functional Analysis and its Applications (journ.) (SAUS)
FAA............ Functional Area Assessment
FAA............ National Aviation Facilities Experimental Center, Atlantic City, NJ [*OCLC symbol*] (OCLC)
FAA-1.......... SafeAir One-Federal Aviation Administration Administrator (FAAC)
FAA-2.......... SafeAir Two-Federal Aviation Administration Deputy Administrator (FAAC)
FaAA.......... Failure Analysis and Associates (RDA)
FAAA.......... Federation for American Afghan Action (EA)
FAAA.......... Fellow of the American Academy of Allergy
FAAA.......... Final Acquisition Action Approach (SAUO)
FAAA.......... Final Acquisition Action Approval (AAGC)
FAAA.......... First Allied Airborne Army [*World War II*]
FAAA.......... Flight Attendants' Association of Australia
FAA-AAF..... Federal Aviation Administration Airway Facilities Service
FAAAAI........ Fellow of the American Academy of Allergy, Asthma, and Immunology
FAA-AAP...... Federal Aviation Administration Office of Airports Programs
FAA-AAS...... Federal Aviation Administration Office of Airport Standards
FAA-AC........ Federal Aviation Administration Aeronautical Center
FA A - ADS... Federal Aviation Administranon Aircraft Development Service (SAUS)
FAA-ADS...... Federal Aviation Administration Aircraft Development Service
FAA-AEE...... Federal Aviation Administration Office of Environment and Energy
FAA-AEM...... Federal Aviation Administration Office of Systems Engineering Management
FAA-AEQ...... Federal Aviation Administration Office of Environmental Quality
FAA-AF........ Federal Aviation Administration Airway Facilities Service
FAA-AFO...... Federal Aviation Administration Flight Standards National Field Office
FAA-AFS...... Federal Aviation Administration Flight Standards Service
FAA-AFTN.... Federal Aviation Administration Aeronautical Fixed Telecommunications Network (NOAA)
FAAAL.......... Fellow of the American Academy of Arts and Letters (SAUO)
FAA-AM........ Federal Aviation Administration Office of Aviation Medicine
FAA-AP........ Federal Aviation Administration Office of Airports Programs
FAA-APO...... Federal Aviation Administration Office of Aviation Policy and Plans
FAA-ARD...... Federal Aviation Administration Systems Research and Development Service
FAA-ARP...... Federal Aviation Administration Associate Administrator for Airports
FAAARTCC... Federal Aviation Administration Area Regional Traffic Control Center (DNAB)
FAA-AS........ Federal Aviation Administration Airports Service
FAAAS.......... Fellow of the American Academy of Arts and Sciences
FAAAS.......... Fellow of the American Association for the Advancement of Science
FAA-ASF...... Federal Aviation Administration Office of Aviation Safety
FAA-ASP...... Federal Aviation Administration Office of Aviation Systems Plans
FAA-AT........ Federal Aviation Administration Air Traffic Service
FAA-ATS...... Federal Aviation Administration Air Traffic Service (NOAA)
FAA-AV........ Federal Aviation Administration Office of Aviation Policy
FAA - AV...... Federal Aviation Administration, Office of Aviation Policy and Plans (SAUS)
FAA Aviation News... Federal Aviation Agency Aviation News (journ.) (SAUS)
FAA-AVP...... Federal Aviation Administration Office of Aviation Policy and Plans
FAAB.......... Alexander Bay [*South Africa*] [*ICAO location identifier*] (ICLI)
FAAB.......... Family Allowance, Class A and B [*Navy*]
FAAB.......... Floating Add Absolute (VLIE)
FAAB.......... Frequency Allocation Advisory Board (ACAE)
FAABMS...... Forward Army Anti-Ballistic Missile System (SAUS)
FAAC.......... Airspace Control Command [*South Africa*] [*ICAO location identifier*] (ICLI)
FAAC.......... FARO [*Federation of AIDS Related Organizations*] AIDS Action Council [*Acquired Immune Deficiency Syndrome*] (EA)
FAAC.......... Fellow of the American Association of Criminology
FAAC.......... Food Additives and Contaminants Committee (SAUO)
FAAC.......... French-American Aid for Children (EA)
FAA CAP...... Federal Aviation Agency Contract Appeals Panel (AAGC)
FAA/CAS...... Federal Aviation Administration Canadian Air Services Committee
FAA/CASLO... Federal Aviation Administration Civil Aviation Security Liaison Officer
FAACB.......... Friends in Art of American Council of the Blind (EA)
FAACE.......... Forces Aeriennes Alliees Centre-Europe [*Allied Air Forces Central Europe*] [*NATO*] (NATG)
FAACIA........ Fellow, American Association of Clinical Immunology & Allergy (CMD)
FAACIA........ Fellow of the American Association of Clinical Immunology and Allergy (SAUO)
FAACS.......... Fully Automated Accounting Computer System (MCD)
FAACTS........ Free Aids Advice Counseling Treatment Support (ADWA)
FAACTS........ Free Aids Advice Counselling Treatment Support for People with or Affected by AIDS (SAUO)
FAAD.......... Adelaide [*South Africa*] [*ICAO location identifier*] (ICLI)
FAAD.......... Fellow of the American Academy of Dermatology
FAAD.......... first abundant appearance datum (SAUS)
FAAD.......... Forward Area Air Defense
FAADATS..... Forward Area Air Defense Automated Test System (SAUS)
FAADBTY..... Forward Area Air Defense Battery (DNAB)
FAADC.......... Fleet Accounting and Disbursing Center [*Navy*] (NVT)
FAAD C2...... Forward Area Air Defense Command and Control [*Military*]
FAADC2I...... Forward Area Air Defence Command, Control & Intelligence (SAUS)
FAADC2I...... Forward Area Air Defense Command and Control and Intelligence (SAUO)
FAADC^{2}I...... Forward Area Air Defense Command and Control Intelligence System [*Army*]
FAADC2I...... Forward Area Air Defense Command, Control and Intelligence (SAUS)
FAADC3I...... Forward Area Air Defence C3 Intelligence (SAUS)
FAADC3I...... Forward Area Air Defense Command, Control and Intelligence System (SAUS)
FAADC31...... Forward Area Air Defense Command, Control and Intelligence System (SAUS)
FAADCLANT... Fleet Accounting and Disbursing Center, Atlantic [*Navy*] (DNAB)
FAADCLANT BRO... Fleet Accounting and Disbursing Center, Atlantic Branch Office [*Navy*] (DNAB)
FAADCPAC... Fleet Accounting and Disbursing Center, Pacific [*Navy*] (DNAB)
FAADEZ........ Forward Area Air Defense Engagement Zone [*Army*]
FAAD-GBS... Forward Area Air Defense Ground-Based Sensor [*Army*]
FAAD-LOS.... Forward Area Air Defense - Line-of-Sight (SAUS)
FAADS.......... Federal Assistance Award Data System [*Bureau of the Census*] [*Washington, DC*] [*Information service or system*]
FAA-DS........ Federal Aviation Administration Development Services
FAADS.......... Field Army Air Defense System (MCD)
FAADS.......... Forward Air-Defense Area System (SAUS)
FAADS.......... Forward Area Air Defense System
FAADS.......... Forward Area Anti-aircraft Defence System (SAUS)
FAADW.......... Forward Area Air Defense Weapon
FAA-EE........ Federal Aviation Administration Office of Environment and Energy
FAA - EM...... Federal Aviation Administration, Office of Systems Engineering Management (SAUS)
FAA-EM........ Federal Aviation Administration-Office of Systems Engineering Management (SAUO)
FAA-EQ........ Federal Aviation Administration Office of Environmental Quality
FAAF.......... Forney Army Airfield [*Fort Leonard Wood, MO*]
FAAFP.......... Fellow, American Academy of Family Practice (CMD)
FAAFP.......... Fellow of the American Academy of Family Physicians
FAAFPRS..... Fellow of the American Academy of Facial Plastic and Reconstructive Surgery
FAA-FS........ Federal Aviation Administration Flight Standards Service
FAA-FS-NFID... Federal Aviation Administration - Flight Standards Service-National Flight Inspection Division (SAUO)
FAA-FS-NFID... Federal Aviation Administration Flight Standards Service National Flight Inspection Division
FAAG.......... Aggeneys [*South Africa*] [*ICAO location identifier*] (ICLI)
FAAG.......... First Advertising Agency Group
FAAGL.......... Foundation of the American Association of Gynecologic Laparoscopists (SAUO)
FAAH.......... Fatty Acid Amide Hydrolase [*An enzyme*]
FAAH.......... Fellow of the Australian Academy of the Humanities
FAAH.......... South African Air Force Headquarters [*ICAO location identifier*] (ICLI)
FAAHT.......... Federated Association of Australian Housewives, Tasmania

FAAI Fellow of the Institute of Administrative Accounting and Data Processing [*British*] (DCTA)
FAAI Filipinos for Affirmative Action, Inc. (SAUO)
FAAIECE Fulbright Association of Alumni of International Educational and Cultural Exchange (SAUO)
FAALC Federal Aviation Administration Logistics Center (ADWA)
FAALS Field Artillery Acoustic Locating System (MCD)
FAALS Forward Area Armored Logistic System (SAUS)
FAALS Forward Area Artillery locator System (ACAE)
FAAMC Federation des Associations d'Antiquaires du Marche Commun (EA)
FAAMD Fellow, American Association on Mental Deficiency (CMD)
FAAMS Family of Antiair Missile Systems (MCD)
FAA - MS Federal Aviation Administration, Office of Management Services (SAUS)
FAA-MS Federal Aviation Administration Office of Management Systems
FAAN Aliwal North [*South Africa*] [*ICAO location identifier*] (ICLI)
FAAN Fellow of the American Academy of Nursing
FAAN Finance and Accounts Office (SAUS)
FAAN First Advertising Agency Network [*Later, First Network of Affiliated Advertising Agencies*] [*Defunct*] (EA)
FAAN Food Allergy & Anaphylaxis Network
FAA-NA Federal Aviation Administration National Aviation Facilities Experimental Center
FAAN&OS Fellow, American Academy of Neurological & Orthopedic Surgeons (CMD)
FAANaOS Fellowship of the American Academy of Neurological and Orthopaedic Surgeons (SAUO)
FA&H Armed Forces of Haiti (SAUO)
FA&PLO Facility, analytical & post-irradiation laboratory operations (SAUS)
FA & T Final Assembly and Test (SAUS)
FAANE Forces Aeriennes Alliees Nord-Europe [*Allied Air Forces Northern Europe*] [*NATO*] (NATG)
FAA-NO Federal Aviation Administration Office of Noise Abatement
FAANQ Filipino-Australian Association of North Queensland [*Australia*]
FAA-NS Federal Aviation Administration National Airspace System Program Office
FAANTAEL Fleet Aircraft Assessment for Navy Testing and Analysis for EMP Limitations (MCD)
FAAO Federal Aviation Accounting Office (ACAE)
FAAO Federation of American Arab Organizations (EA)
FAAO Fellow, American Academy of Ophthalmology (CMD)
FAAO Fellow of the Australian Academy of Optometry
FAAO Field Artillery Aerial Observer
FAAO Finance and Accounts Office [*Army*]
FAAO Fleet Aviation Accounting Office
FAAOCAS Federal Aviation Agency's Office of the Civil Air Surgeon [*Medicine*] (EDAA)
FAA-OEE Federal Aviation Administration-Office of Environment and Energy (SAUO)
FAA-OEM Federal Aviation Administration - Office of Systems Engineering Management (SAUO)
FAAOLANT Fleet Aviation Accounting Office, Atlantic (DNAB)
FAAOM Fellow of the American Academy of Medicine (SAUS)
FAAOO Fellow, American Academy of Ophthalmology and Otolaryngology (CMD)
FAAOP Fleet Aviation Accounting Office, Pacific (DNAB)
FAAOPAC Fleet Aviation Accounting Office, Pacific (DNAB)
FAA Order Federal Aviation Administration Orders [*A publication*] (DLA)
FAAOS Fellow of the American Academy of Orthopaedic Surgeons (SAUO)
FAAOS Fellow of the American Academy of Orthopedic Surgeons
FAAP Family Assessment Adjustment Pass [*Psychology*] (DAVI)
FAAP Family Assessment Adjustment Plan [*Medicine*] (EDAA)
FAAP Federal Aid to Airports Program [*FAA*]
FAAP Fellow of the American Academy of Pediatrics (WGA)
FAAP Fellow of the Australian Academy of Paediatrics
FAAP Fixed Asset Accounting Package [*Computer science*]
FAAP Fixed Assets Accounting Package (SAUS)
FAAPFF Foundation for American Agriculture Program of the Farm Foundation [*Formerly, FAA*] (EA)
FAAPS Field Artillery Ammunition Processing System (SAUS)
FAAPS Fine Art, Antique, and Philatelic Squad [*Scotland Yard*] [*British*]
FAAQS Federal Ambient Air Quality Standards (SAUO)
FAAQS Federal Ambient Air Quality Studies
FAA-QS Federal Aviation Administration Quiet Short-Haul Air Transportation Systems Office
FAAR Arandis [*Namibia*] [*ICAO location identifier*] (ICLI)
FAAR Fellow of the American Academy in Rome (SAUO)
FAAR Feminist Alliance Against Rape [*Defunct*] (EA)
FAAR Forward Air Acquisition Radar (ACAE)
FAAR Forward Area Alerting RADAR
FAAR Friends of American Art in Religion (EA)
FAARATCF Federal Aviation Administration RADAR Air Traffic Control Facility (DNAB)
FAA-RD Federal Aviation Administration Systems Research and Development Service
FAARO Federal Aviation Administration Regional Office (NOAA)
FAARP Forward Area Aiming and Refueling Point [*Military*] (MCD)
FAAS Family of Army Aircraft System
FAAS Fellow of the Academy of Arts and Sciences
FAAS Fellow of the Australian Academy of Science (SAUO)
FAAS Field Artillery Ammunition Support [*Military*] (POLM)
FAAS Fixed Assets Accounting System (SAUS)
FAAS Flame Atomic Absorption Spectrometry
FAAS Flameless Atomic Absorption Spectrophotometry
FAAS Foreign Affairs Administrative Support System [*Department of State*]
FAAS Forward Area Alerting System (AABC)
FAAS French Association for American Studies (EAIO)
FAAS Furnace Atomic Absorption Spectrophotometry (PDAA)
FAASE Forces Aeriennes Allies Sud-Europe [*Allied Air Forces Southern Europe*] [*NATO*] (NATG)
FAAS/GFAAS Flame Atomic Absorption Spectroscopy/Graphite Furnace Atomic Absorption Spectroscopy (SAUS)
FAA SOL Formalin, Acetic, Alcohol Solution [*Medicine*] (BABM)
FAA sol Formalin, Acetic, and Alcohol Solution [*A fixative*] [*Organic chemistry*] (DAVI)
FAA-SS Federal Aviation Administration Office of Supersonic Transport Development
FAA-SST Federal Aviation Administration Office of Supersonic Transport Development
FAAST Fellow, American Academy of Surgery of Trauma (CMD)
FAA-STD Federal Aviation Administration - Standard (SAUS)
FAA-STD Federal Aviation Administration-Standard (SAUO)
FAASTU Fleet Air Arm Service Trials Unit [*British*]
FAASV Fast Attack Ammunition Support Vehicle [*Army*] (RDA)
FAASV Field Artillery Ammunition Support Vehicle
FAASVs Field Artillery Ammunition Support Vehicles (SAUS)
FAAT First Article Acceptance Test (MCD)
FAAT Fluorscent Antinuclear Antibody Test (MELL)
FAAT Fully Analytical Aerotriangulation (SAUS)
FAATC FAA Technical Center [*FAA*] (TAG)
FAATC Federal Aviation Administration Technical Center (SAUS)
FAATDC Federal Aviation Administration Technical Development Center
FAATE Fault Analyzing Automatic Test Equipment (VLIE)
FAATS Fellow, American Academy of Thoracic Surgeons (CMD)
FAAUS Field Army Airspace Utilization Study (SAUO)
FAAWC Fleet Antiair Warfare Coordinator [*Navy*] (CAAL)
FAAWC Force Anti-Air Warfare Coordinator [*Military*] (SEWL)
FAAWJ Federation of Arab Agricultural WJor (SAUS)
FAAWJ Federation of Arab Agricultural World Journal (SAUO)
FAAWTC Fleet Antiair Warfare Training Center
FAAWTC Fleet Antiair Weapon Training Center (SAUO)
FAAWTRACEN Fleet Antiair Warfare Training Center
FAB Aeronautical Broadcast Station [*ITU designation*] (CET)
Fab Antigen-Binding Fragment [*Immunology*]
FAB Antigen Binding Fragments (MELL)
Fab Fab Fragment Specific (SAUS)
Fab Fabius Accorambonus [*Deceased, 1559*] [*Authority cited in pre-1607 legal work*] (DSA)
FAB Fable (ROG)
fab Fabric (VRA)
FAB Fabric
FAB Fabricate (NAKS)
fab Fabricated (MIST)
FAB Fabrication (SAUS)
FAB Fabrication Plant (SAUS)
FAB Fabrication Plant of Computer Chips (VLIE)
FAB Fabricator
FAB Fabrichnaya [*Former USSR*] [*Seismograph station code, US Geological Survey*] [*Closed*] (SEIS)
fab fabulist (SAUS)
fab Fabulous (ADWA)
FAB Fabulous (ROG)
FAB Failure Analysis Board
FAB Families Against the Bomb [*British*] (DI)
FAB Family Allowance, Class B [*Navy*]
FAB Farm Acreage Base
FAB Fast Action Button (SEWL)
FAB Fast Atom Bombardment [*Mass spectrometry*]
FAB Features, Advantages, Benefits [*of clothing*] [*Retailing*]
FAB Feline Advisory Bureau [*British*] (CB)
FAB Feminists Against Benyon [*Pro-abortion group*] [*British*] (DI)
FAB Fibroadenoma of Breast [*Medicine*] (MELL)
FAB Field Artillery Brigade (AABC)
FAB Field Assistance Branch (SAUO)
FAB Fijian Affairs Board (SAUO)
FAB File Access Block [*Computer science*] (TIMI)
FAB Film Advisory Board (EA)
FAB Finance and Budget (SAUO)
FAB Firecracker Alternative Book [*Award Program*]
FAB First-Aid Box (AAG)
FAB First Air (Bradley Schedules) Ltd. [*Canada*] [*ICAO designator*] (FAAC)
FAB FirstFed Amer Bancorp [*AMEX symbol*] (SG)
FAB First Federal of Alabama FSB Jasper [*AMEX symbol*] (SPSG)
FAB Fixed Action Button (NVT)
FAB Fleet Air Base
FAB Fleet Air Broadcast (NATG)
FAB Florida Association of Broadcasters (SAUO)
FAB Flour Advisory Board (SAUO)
FAB Flux-Asbestos Backing (PDAA)
FAB Food Annotated Bibliography (SAUS)
FAB Forca Aerea Brasileira [*Brazilian Air Force*]
FAB Formalin-Ammonium Bromide [*Fixative*]
FAB Forward Air Base (SAUS)
FAB Forward Avionics Bay
FAB Forwarder Air Waybill [*Shipping*] (DS)
FAB Fourth Avenue Booksellers (SAUS)
FAB Fraction Actually Burned (CARB)
Fab Fragment, Antigen-Binding [*Immunochemistry*]
Fab Fragment Antigen-Binding of an Antigen [*Immunology*] (DAVI)

FAB............. Free Association Books [*Publisher*] [*British*]
FAB............. French-American-British [*Classification system for leukemia*]
FAB............. Fuel-Air Bomb (ODA)
FAB............. Functional Adhesive Bonding
FAB............. Functional Area Breakdown
FAB............. Functional Arm Brace [*Medicine*]
FABA........... Firing Attachment Blank Ammunition (MCD)
FABAC......... Fellow of the Association of Business and Administrative Computing [*British*] (DBQ)
FABAS......... Farm Amalgamations and Boundary Adjustment Schemes (SAUS)
FABAT......... Fellow, American Board of Allergy & Immunology (CMD)
FABB........... Brakpan [*South Africa*] [*ICAO location identifier*] (ICLI)
FABB........... Filene's [*Boston*] Automatic Bargain Basement
FabC........... Fabri Centers of America [*Associated Press*] (SAG)
FABC........... First Alabama Bancshares, Inc. [*NASDAQ symbol*] (NQ)
FABC........... First Alliance Bancorp (GA) [*NASDAQ symbol*] (TTSB)
FABC........... First American Bulk Carriers (SAUS)
FABCFFS...... Feline Advisory Bureau and Central Fund for Feline Studies (EAIO)
FABCOS....... Federation of African Business and Consumer Services (SAUO)
FABD........... Burgersdorp [*South Africa*] [*ICAO location identifier*] (ICLI)
FABD........... Fabricated
FABD........... Field Artillery Board (SAUS)
FABE........... Fellow of the Association of Business Executives [*British*] (DCTA)
FABER......... Flexion in Abduction and External Rotation [*Neurology and orthopedics*] (DAVI)
FABERE........ Flexion, Abduction, External Rotation, Extension [*Orthopedics*]
FABER Test... Flexion, Abduction, and External Rotation Test of the hip (SAUS)
FABF........... Fellows of the American Bar Foundation (EA)
FABF........... Femoral Artery Blood Flow [*Medicine*] (EDAA)
FABF........... Fraction of Agri-Residue Burned in Fields (CARB)
FABG........... Fabricating
FABI........... Folk Artists Bibliographical Index [*A publication*]
FabInd......... Fab Industries, Inc. [*Associated Press*] (SAG)
FABIS.......... Filmless Automatic Bond Inspection System
FABISO........ Fabrication Isometric (IAA)
FABL........... Bloemfontein/J. B. M. Hertzog [*South Africa*] [*ICAO location identifier*] (ICLI)
FABL........... Fire Alarm Bell
fabless......... Fabricationless (CDE)
FABM........... Bethlehem [*South Africa*] [*ICAO location identifier*] (ICLI)
FABM........... Fellowship of American Baptist Musicians (EA)
FABMDS...... Field Army Ballistic Missile Defense System [*Later, AADS*] [*Antimissile missile*]
FABMIDS..... Field Army Ballistic Missile Defense System [*Later, AADS*] [*Antimissile missile*]
FABMIS........ Forward Area Ballistic Missile Intercept System (PDAA)
FABMLAMSC... Fellow, American Board Medical Legal Analysis in Medicine & Surgery (CMD)
FABMS......... Fast Atom Bombardment Mass Spectroscopy
FABN........... Barberton [*South Africa*] [*ICAO location identifier*] (ICLI)
FA BN.......... Field Artillery Battalion [*Military*]
FABP........... Fatty Acid Binding Protein [*Biochemistry*]
FABP........... Folatebinding Protein [*Medicine*] (DMAA)
FABP........... Folic Acid-Binding Protein [*Biochemistry*] (DB)
FABPA......... Furniture and Bedding Publicity Association Ltd. [*British*] (BI)
FABPrevM.... Fellow, American Board of Preventive Medicine (CMD)
FABR........... Bredasdorp [*South Africa*] [*ICAO location identifier*] (ICLI)
FABR........... Fabricated
Fabr............ Fabrication (SAUS)
F Abr........... Fitzherbert's Abridgment [*1516*] [*A publication*] (DLA)
FabriC......... Fabri-Centers of America, Inc. [*Associated Press*] (SAG)
FABRIC........ Florida Architecture and Building Research Center [*University of Florida*] [*Research center*] (RCD)
FABRIC........ Frequency Assignment by Reference to Interference Charts (MCD)
FABRICS...... Fabrication of Integrated Circuits Simulator (SAUS)
FABRS......... Fabrication Reporting System (MCD)
FABS........... Brits [*South Africa*] [*ICAO location identifier*] (ICLI)
FABS........... Fast Access Btree Structure (SAUS)
FABS........... Fast-Atom Bombardment Spectroscopy (EDCT)
FABS........... Flexible Auto Body System
FABS........... Formulated Abstracting Service (SAUS)
Fab Soc........ Fabian Society (BARN)
FABTECH..... Fabrication Technology (MCD)
FABU........... Fleet Air Base Unit
FABU........... Fuel Additive Blender Unit
FABV........... Brandvlei [*South Africa*] [*ICAO location identifier*] (ICLI)
FABW........... Beaufort West [*South Africa*] [*ICAO location identifier*] (ICLI)
FABWH........ Flush Armor Balance Watertight Hatch
FABX........... Beatrix Mine [*South Africa*] [*ICAO location identifier*] (ICLI)
FABX........... Fire Alarm Box
FABY........... Beaufort West/Wes Town [*South Africa*] [*ICAO location identifier*] (ICLI)
FABYA......... Fabyan, NH [*American Association of Railroads railroad junction routing code*]
FAC............. Airport Control Station [*ITU designation*] (DEN)
fac.............. Facade (VRA)
FAC............. Face-Amount Certificate [*Banking*] (MHDB)
FAC............. Facial [*Chemistry*]
fac.............. Facilities (ADWA)
FAC............. Facilities Advisory Council (SAUS)
FAC............. Facilities Associate Contractor
FAC............. Facility (AAG)
Fac............. Facility (TBD)
FAC............. Facility Advisory Committee (SAUO)
FAC............. Facility Contract (AAGC)
FAC............. FAC Realty Trust [*NYSE symbol*] [*Formerly, FAC Realty*] (SG)
fac.............. Facsimile (SHCU)
FAC............. Facsimile
FAC............. Factor (MSA)
FAC............. Factory
FAC............. Factory Stores of America [*NYSE symbol*] (TTSB)
fac.............. Factual (ELAL)
FAC............. Factum Similis [*Facsimile*] [*Latin*]
FAC............. Faculty (AABC)
Fac............. Faculty (WDAA)
Fac............. Faculty of Advocates Collection of Decisions, Scotch Court of Sessions [*A publication*] (DLA)
FAC............. Failure Analysis Coordinator
FAC............. Familial Adenamatosis Coli [*Medicine*]
FAC............. Farm Advisory Committee [*MAFF*] [*British*]
FAC............. Fast Affinity Chromatography
FAC............. Fast as Can [*Business term*]
FAC............. Fast Attack Craft
FAC............. Fat Analysis Committee (SAUO)
FAC............. Features for Attaching Communications (VLIE)
FAC............. Federal Acquisition Circular [*DoD*]
FAC............. Federal Advisory Committee
FAC............. Federal Advisory Council [*Department of Labor*]
FAC............. Federal Aid Committee (SAUO)
FAC............. Federal Airports Corporation (SAUO)
FAC............. Federal Atomic Commission (SAUS)
FAC............. Federal Aviation Commission [*Terminated, 1935*]
FAC............. Federation of Agricultural Cooperatives [*British*] (DBA)
FAC............. Federation of Automatic Control (SAUO)
FAC............. Fellow of the American College of Radiology (SAUS)
FAC............. Femoral Ash per Centimeter
FAC............. Feral Animals Committee [*Northern Territory, Australia*]
FAC............. Ferric Ammonium Citrate [*Inorganic chemistry*]
FAC............. Field Accelerator
FAC............. File Access Channel
FAC............. File Access Code (SAUS)
FAC............. File Access Controller (SAUS)
FAC............. Film Aperture Card (SAUS)
FAC............. Filter Address Correction
FAC............. Final Acceptance Criteria (NRCH)
FAC............. Final Approach Course [*Aviation*] (DA)
FAC............. Final Assembly code [*Computer science*] (VERA)
FAC............. Final Assembly Control (SAUS)
FAC............. Financial Administrative Control (AFM)
FAC............. Financial Affairs Commission (SAUO)
FAC............. Financial Assistance Corporation (EBF)
FAC............. Fine Alignment Complete
FAC............. Firearms Acquisition Certificate [*Canada*]
FAC............. First Air Courier, Inc. [*ICAO designator*] (FAAC)
FAC............. First Alarm Code (SAA)
FAC............. First Alert Capability [*Military*]
FAC............. First Amendment Congress (EA)
FAC............. First Atlanta Corporation (SAUO)
FAC............. Fiscal Advisory Committee [*American Occupational Therapy Association*]
FAC............. Fisheries Advisory Committee (SAUO)
FAC............. Fixed Air Capacitor
FAC............. Fleet Activities Command [*Navy*]
FAC............. Fleet Air Control (SAUS)
FAC............. Fleet Analysis Center [*Corona, CA*] [*Navy*]
FAC............. Fleet Augmentation Component
FAC............. Fletcher Aviation Corp.
FAC............. Flettner Aircraft Corporation (SAUO)
FAC............. Flight Augmentation Computer (SAUS)
FAC............. Floating Accumulator
FAC............. Floating-Point Accumulator (SAUS)
FAC............. Florida Administrative Code (DEMM)
FAC............. Fluorescent Analog Cytochemistry [*Microscopic technique*]
FAC............. Fluorouracil, Adriamycin, Cyclophosphamide [*Antineoplastic drug regimen*]
FAC............. Flying Activity Category (AFM)
FAC............. Focal Adhesion Complex [*Cytology*]
FAC............. Food Advisory Committee [*New South Wales, Australia*]
FAC............. Food Aid Committee (EAIO)
FAC............. Food and Agriculture Council
FAC............. Football Association Council (SAUO)
FAC............. Football Association Cup (SAUO)
FAC............. Football Athletic Club (SAUO)
FAC............. Foothill Athletic Conference (PSS)
FAC............. Footwear and Accessories Council [*Defunct*] (EA)
FAC............. Ford Aerosports Club (EA)
FAC............. Foreign Adoption Center [*Later, FCVN*] (EA)
FAC............. Foreign Affairs Committee (SAUO)
FAC............. Foreign Agricultural Club (EA)
FAC............. Foreign Aid Committee (SAUO)
FAC............. Foreign Air Carrier [*FAA*] (TAG)
FAC............. Foreign Allowable Catch [*Fishery management*] (MSC)
fac.............. forward air cargo (SAUS)
FAC............. Forward Air Control [*or Controller*] [*Air Force*]
FAC............. Forward Air Controller [*Military*]
fac.............. Forwarding Agents Commission [*Shipping*] (DS)
FAC............. Four-Address Code (SAUS)
FAC............. Four-Address Computer (SAUS)
FAC............. Fractional Area Concentration [*Radiation therapy*] (DAVI)
FAC............. Fragments of Attic Comedy [*A publication*] (OCD)

FAC .... Free Alongside Carrier [*Business term*]
FAC .... Free Available Chlorine [*Analytical chemistry*]
FAC .... Freedom to Advertise Coalition (EA)
FAC .... Freestanding Ambulatory (ADWA)
FAC .... Freight Assembly Center (SAUS)
FAC .... French-American Committee for the Statue of Liberty [*Defunct*] (EA)
FAC .... Frequency Allocation Centre (SAUS)
FAC .... Frequency Allocation Committee
FAC .... Frequency Allotment Committee (SAUO)
FAC .... Frequency Analysis and Control
FAC .... Friday Afternoon Club (SAUS)
FAC .... Friends' Ambulance Corps (WDAA)
FAC .... Front d'Alliberament Catala [*Spain*]
FAC .... Front des Artistes Canadiens [*Canadian Artists' Representation - CAR*]
FAC .... Fuel Adjustment Clause
FAC .... Functional Account Code (SAUO)
FAC .... Functional Area Chief (SAUO)
FAC .... Functional Area Code
FAC .... Function Authority Credential [*Computer science*] (ELAL)
FAC .... Fund for Advancement of Camping (EA)
FAC .... Fund for Artists' Colonies [*Defunct*] (EA)
FAC .... Fund for the Advancement of Camping (SAUO)
FAC .... Funds at completion (SAUS)
FAC .... Fuse Arming Computer (SAUS)
FAC .... Naval Facilities Engineering Command Headquarters (AAGC)
FAC2 .... Field Artillery Command and Control (SAUS)
FACA .... Federal Advisory Committee Act
FACA .... Federal Alcohol Control Administration [*Established, 1933; abolished, 1935*]
FACA .... Fellow, American College of Allergists (CMD)
FACA .... Fellow, American College of Anesthesia (CMD)
FAcA .... Fellow of the Acupuncture Association [*British*] (DBQ)
FACA .... Fellow of the American College of Allergists (SAUO)
FACA .... Fellow of the American College of Anesthesiologists (WGA)
FACA .... Fellow of the American College of Anesthesists (SAUS)
FACA .... Fellow of the American College of Angiology
FACA .... Fellow of the American College of Apothecaries
FACA .... Fellow of the Association of Certified Accountants (SAUO)
FACA .... Florida Administrative Code Annotated (AAGC)
FAC(A) .... Forward Air Controller (Airborne) (NVT)
FAC/A .... Forward Air Controller / Airborne (SAUS)
FAC - A .... Forward Attack Coordinator - Airborne (SAUS)
FACA .... Future Attack & Combat Aircraft (SAUS)
FACA .... Monte Carlo [*South Africa*] [*ICAO location identifier*] (ICLI)
facac .... Fast As Can As Customary (SAUS)
FACACK .... facility acknowledge (SAUS)
FACADE .... Further and Adult Council for Art and Design Education (AIE)
FACAL .... Fellow of the American College of Allergists (SAUS)
FACAn .... Fellow of the American College of Anesthesiologists
FAC-ANC .... Faculty-Ancillary (SAUS)
FACAS .... Fellow of the American College of Abdominal Surgeons (DAVI)
FACAT .... First Article Capability Assessment Test (MCD)
FACATT .... Field Artillery CATT [*Army*] (RDA)
FACAY .... Friendship Among Children and Youth around the World (SAUO)
FACB .... Colesburg [*South Africa*] [*ICAO location identifier*] (ICLI)
FACB .... Fellow, American College of Biochemistry (CMD)
Facb .... Fragment, Antigen, and Complement Binding [*Medicine*] (DMAA)
FAC-BCG .... Ftorafur, Adriamycin, Cyclophosphamide, Bacille Calmette-Guerin [*Antineoplastic drug regimen*] (DAVI)
FACBOC .... Field Artillery Cannon Basic Officer's Course [*Army*]
FA-CBU .... Fuel-Air Cluster Bomb Unit [*Military*] (VNW)
FACC .... Facts About Community Colleges (SAUO)
facc .... fast as can as customary (SAUS)
FACC .... Feature and Attribute Coding Catalog (SAUS)
FACC .... Federation Africaine des Chambres de Commerce [*Federation of African Chambersof Commerce*] [*Ethiopia*] (EAIO)
FACC .... Fellow of the American College of Cardiologists (SAUO)
FACC .... Field Alterable Control Element (SAUS)
FACC .... Finnish American Chamber of Commerce (NTPA)
FACC .... Florida Association of Community Colleges (SAUO)
FACC .... Food Additives and Contaminants Committee [*British*]
FACC .... Force Associated Control Communications [*Military*] (AFM)
FACC .... Ford Aerospace and Communications Corporation (SAUO)
FACC .... Foreign Assistance Correlation Committee (SAUO)
FACC .... French-American Chamber of Commerce (EA)
FACCA .... Fellow of the Association of Certified and Corporate Accountants [*British*] (EY)
FACCC .... Faculty Association of the California Community Colleges (SAUO)
FACCC .... Federal Advisory Commision on Consolidation and Conversion [*DoD*] (RDA)
FACCE .... Family Concept of Computing Elements (SAUS)
FACCH .... Fast Associated Control Channel (SAUS)
FAC-CLIN .... Faculty-Clinical (SAUS)
FACCM .... Fast Access Charge- Coupled Memory (SAUS)
FAC/CO .... Facility Checkout
Fac Coll .... Faculty of Advocates Collection of Decisions, Scotch Court of Sessions, First and Second Series [*38 vols.*] [*A publication*] (DLA)
Fac Coll NS ... Faculty of Advocates Collection of Decisions, Scotch Court of Sessions [*A publication*] (DLA)
FACCON .... Facilities Control [*Radio Central*] [*Navy*] (CAAL)
FACCONCEN ... Facilities Control Center [*Army*] (AABC)
FACCP .... Fellow, American College of Clinical Pharmacology (CMD)
FACCP .... Fellow of the American College of Chest Physicians
FACCP .... Fellow of the American College of Clinical Pharmacology and Chemotherapy (SAUS)
FACCP&C .... Fellow, American College of Clinical Pharmacology & Chemotherapy (CMD)
FACCPC .... Fellow of the American College of Clinical Pharmacology and Chemotherapy (DAVI)
FACCS .... Flexible Assembly Cell Control System (VLIE)
FACD .... Cradock [*South Africa*] [*ICAO location identifier*] (ICLI)
FACD .... facility accepted message (SAUS)
FACD .... Failure and Consumption Data (SAUS)
FACD .... Fellow, American College of Dermatology (CMD)
FACD .... Fellow of the American College of Dentists
FACD .... Fellow of the Australian College of Dentistry (SAUO)
FACD .... Fellow of the Australian College of Dermatologists (SAUS)
FACD .... Foreign Area Consumer Dialing [*Telecommunications*]
FACD .... Foreign Area Customer Dialing (SAUS)
Fac Dec .... Faculty of Advocates Collection of Decisions, Scotch Court of Sessions, First and Second Series [*38 vols.*] [*A publication*] (DLA)
FACDIR .... Failure and Consumption Data Inspection Report (SAUS)
FACDIS .... West Virginia Consortium for Faculty and Course Development in International Studies (SAUO)
FACD Message ... Facility Accepted Message (SAUS)
FACDS .... Fellow of the Australian College of Dental Surgeons (SAUO)
FACE .... Facelifters Home Systems, Inc. [*NASDAQ symbol*] (NQ)
FACE .... Facilities and Communication Evaluation [*Army*] (AABC)
FACE .... Factory Automatic Checkout Equipment
FACE .... Families Adopting Children Everywhere (EA)
FACE .... Fatal Accident Circumstances and Epidemiology [*National Institute for Occupational Safety and Health*]
FACE .... Fatty-Acid Cellulos Esters [*Organic chemistry*]
FACE .... Federal Advertising Committee on Ethics (MCD)
FACE .... Federally Assisted Code Enforcement [*Proposed HUD program*]
FACE .... Federation des Associations Canadiennes sur l'Environnement [*Federation of Associations on the Canadian Environment*]
FACE .... Federation des Associations de Chasseurs de la CEE [*Federation of Hunters' Associations of the European Economic Community*] [*Brussels, Belgium*]
FACE .... Federation of Associations of Computer Users in Engineering, Architecture and Related Fields (SAUO)
FACE .... Federation of Associations on the Canadian Environment
FACE .... Fellow, American College of Endocrinology (CMD)
FACE .... Fellow of the Australian College of Education (WDAA)
FACE .... Fellowship of Artists for Cultural Evangelism (EA)
FACE .... Field Alterable Control Element (MDG)
FACE .... Field alterable control equipment (SAUS)
FACE .... Field Ancillary Computer Effort (SAUS)
FACE .... Field Artillery Computing Equipment (SAUS)
FACE .... Financial Advertising Committee on Ethics
Face .... Fitchburg Action to Save Energy (SAUO)
FACE .... Florida Area Cumulus Experiment [*National Science Foundation*]
FACE .... Folk Arts for Communication and Education
face .... forced-air-cooled electronics (SAUS)
FACE .... Forum for Acoustic Ecology (SAUO)
FACE .... Forward Area Collection and ECM [*Electronic Countermeasures*]
FACE .... Forward Area Collection Equipment (MCD)
FACE .... Forward Aviation Combat Engineering [*Military*] (SEWL)
FACE .... Foundation for Accredited Chiropractic Education [*Later, FCER*] (EA)
FACE .... Framed Access Command Environment [*Unix*] (VERA)
FACE .... Framework for Academic Cooperation in Europe (TELE)
FACE .... Free-Air Carbon Dioxide Enrichment (QUAC)
FACE .... Freedom of Access to Clinic Entrances Act [*1994*]
FACE .... Functional Automatic Circuit Evaluator (VLIE)
FACE .... International Federation of Associations of Computer Users in Engineering Architecture and Related Fields (EAIO)
FACE .... Saint Francis Association for Catholic Evangelism [*Defunct*] (EA)
FACEA .... Fellow of the Australian Council of Educational Administration
FACE/CARD ... Forecasting Ammunition Consumption Expenditure/Critical Assets Reporting Data Combined Subsystem (SAUO)
FACE IT .... Foreign Agents Compulsory Ethics in Trade Act [*Proposed*]
FACEL .... Feature Analysis Comparison and Evaluation Library (PDAA)
FACEM .... Federation of Associations of Colliery Equipment Manufacturers (SAUO)
FACEM .... Fellow of the American College of Emergency Medicine [*Medicine*] (EDAA)
FACEM .... Fellow of the Australian College of Emergency Medicine (SAUS)
FACENGCOM ... Facility Engineering Command
FACEP .... Fellow of American College of Emergency Physicians (DHSM)
FACEREC .... Face Recognition (SAUS)
FACES .... Family Adaptability and Cohesion Evaluation Scale [*Psychology*]
FACES .... Federal Advisory Council on Employment Security
FACES .... FORTRAN [*Formula Translating System*] Automatic Code Evaluation System [*NASA*] [*Computer science*]
FACES .... Fund for African and African-American Cultural and Educational Solidarity, Inc.
FACES .... [*The*] National Association for the Craniofacially Handicapped (PAZ)
FACET .... Faber Cost Estimating Technique (SAUS)
FACET .... Facetious
FACET .... Female Access to Careers in Engineering Technology (SAUO)
FACET .... Fluid Amplifier Control Engine Test
FACET .... Future Airborne Communications Equipment and Technology (MCD)
FACETS .... Franco American Committee for Educational Travel and Studies [*Later, FACETS Tour France*]
FACETS .... Fraud and Abuse Clearinghouse for Effective Technology Sharing [*Department of Health and Human Services*]

FACETS........ Future Anti-Air Concepts Experimental Technology Seeker [*Military aircraft research program*] [*British*]
FACF............ Facility Chief (FAAC)
FACFI........... Federal Advisory Committee on False Identification [*Department of Justice*] [*Terminated, 1976*]
FACFP.......... Fellow, American College of Forensic Psychiatry (CMD)
FACFP.......... Fellow of the American College of Family Physicians
FACFS.......... Fellow of the American College of Foot Surgeons
FACG........... Fellow of the American College of Gastroenterology
FACGD......... Federation of American Citizens of German Descent [*Later, DANK*] (EA)
FACGE......... Fellow, American College of Gastrointestinal Endoscopy (CMD)
FACGE......... Fellow of the American College of Gastroenterology (DAVI)
FACGO......... Fellow of the American College of Gastroenterology (SAUO)
FACH........... Cookhouse [*South Africa*] [*ICAO location identifier*] (ICLI)
FACH........... Forceps to After-Coming Head [*Obstetrics*]
FACHA......... Fellow of the American College of Health Administrators
FACHA......... Fellow of the American College of Hospital Administrators (SAUO)
FACHCA....... Fellow of American College of Health Care Administrators (DHSM)
FACHCA....... Foundation of American College of Healthcare Administrators (EA)
FACHE......... Fellow of the American College of Healthcare Executives (DHSM)
FACHRES-CA... Faculty for Human Rights in El Salvador and Central America (EA)
FACI............ First Article Configuration Inspection [*Gemini*] [*NASA*] (AFM)
FACI............ Folk Arts Center, Incorporated (SAUO)
facil............ Facilitation [*Therapy term*] (CTAA)
FACIL........... Facility
FACILE......... Fire and Casualty Insurance Library Edition
Facil Manager... Facilities Manager (journ.) (SAUS)
FACIM.......... Foundation for a Course in Miracles (EA)
FACIP........... Fighter Avionics / Cockpit Integration Predesign studies (SAUS)
FACISCOM... Finance and Comptroller Information System Command (SAUS)
FACISCOM... Finance and Controller Information System Command (SAUS)
FACISCOM USA... Finance and Comptroller Information Systems Command, United States Army
FACIT........... Fast Automatic Conversion with Integrated Tools [*Computer science*] (TELE)
FACL............ Carolina [*South Africa*] [*ICAO location identifier*] (ICLI)
facl............. facilitate (SAUS)
FACL............ Fellow of the Amateur Cinema League of America (SAUO)
FACLC.......... Federation of American Cultural and Language Communities (EA)
FAC-LEV...... Fluorouracil, Adriamycin, Cyclophosphamide, Levamisole [*Antineoplastic drug regimen*]
FACLM.......... Fellow of the American College of Legal Medicine (DAVI)
FACLS........... Federation of the Association of College Lecturers in Scotland (AIE)
FACLTY........ Facility
FACM........... Florida Association of Cadastral Mappers (SAUO)
FACM........... Friable Asbestos-Containing Material (GNE)
FACM........... Functional Analytic Causal Model (DIPS)
FAC MAT..... Facilities Matrix (MCD)
FACMD......... Fluoroactinomycin D [*Antineoplastic drug*]
FACMH......... Fellow of the American College of Meical Hypnotists [*Medicine*] (EDAA)
FACMN......... Fleet Chief Aircraft Mechanician [*British military*] (DMA)
FACMPE....... Fellow of the American College of Medical Practice Executives (ADWA)
FACMS......... Fellow of the American College of Sports Medicine (SAUS)
FACMS......... Foundation for Advances in Clinical Medicine and Science [*Later, FAMS*] (EA)
FACMTA....... Federal Advisory Council on Medical Training Aids
FACN........... Fellow of the American College of Nutrition (DAVI)
FACNET....... Federal Acquisition Computer Network (SAUS)
FACNET....... Federal Acquisitions Computer Network
FACNHA....... Foundation of American College of Nursing Home Administrators [*Later, FACHCA*] (EA)
FACNM......... Fellow, American College Nuclear Medicine (CMD)
FACNP.......... Fellow of the American College of Neuropsychopharmacology (DAVI)
FACNP.......... Fellow of the American College of Nuclear Physicians (ADWA)
FACO........... Copperton [*South Africa*] [*ICAO location identifier*] (ICLI)
FACO........... Fabrication and Acceptance Checkout (MCD)
FACO........... Factory Acceptance Checkout (MCD)
FACO........... Factory Assembly and Checkout
FACO........... Fellow of American College of Organists
FACO........... Fellow of the American College of Otolaryngology
FACO........... Fibromyalgia Alliance (EA)
FACO........... Final Acceptance and Checkout Facility (ACAE)
FACO........... Final Assembly Checkout [*NASA*] (NASA)
FACO........... First Alliance 'A' [*NASDAQ symbol*] (SG)
FACO........... First Alliance Corp. [*NASDAQ symbol*] (SAG)
FACO........... Food and Agriculture Organization (SAUO)
Fac/Oblig..... Facultative/Obligatory (MARI)
FACOCCP..... Fellow, American College of Occupational Physicians (CMD)
FACOG......... Fellow of the American College of Obstetricians and Gynecologists
FACOG......... Fellow of the American College of Obstetrics and Gynecology (SAUS)
FACOGAZ..... Union des Fabricants Europeens de Compteurs de Gaz [*Union of European Manufacturers of Gas Meters*] (EAIO)
FACOM......... Family of Computers (SAUS)
FACOM......... Fellow, Australian College of Occupational Medicine (CMD)
FACOM......... Fujitsu Automatic Computer (VLIE)
FACON......... Facilities Control (SAUS)
FACON......... Fellow, American College of Neuropsychopharm (CMD)
FACOR......... Failure Analysis and Close Out Report (ACAE)
FACOS......... Fellow of the American College of Orthopedic Surgeons (DAVI)
FACOSH....... Federal Advisory Committee on Occupational Safety and Health [*Department of Labor*] [*Washington, DC*]
FA/COSI....... Final Assembly and Closeout System Installation (MCD)
FACP........... Fellow of the American College of Physicians
FACP........... Fellow of the American College of Prosthodontists (SAUS)
FACP........... Fellow of the Association of Computer Professionals [*British*] (DBQ)
FACP........... Field Artillery Command Post (SAUS)
FACP........... Fire alarm control panel (SAUS)
FACP........... Forward Air Control Party [*Military*] (CAAL)
facp............ forward air control point (SAUS)
FACP........... Forward Air Control Post [*Military*] (POLM)
FACP........... Ftorafur [*Tegafur*], Adriamycin, Cyclophosphamide, Platinol [*Cisplatin*] [*Antineoplastic drug regimen*]
FACP........... Functional Assignment Control Panel (MCD)
FACP&RM.... Fellow, American College of Physical & Rehabilitation Medicine (CMD)
FACPath....... Fellow, American College of Pathology (CMD)
FACPE.......... Fellow of the American College of Physician Executives (HCT)
FACPM.......... Fellow of the American College of Preventive Medicine
FACPRM...... Fellow of the American College of Preventive Medicine (DAVI)
FACPsyA...... Fellow, American College of Psychiatry (Psychoanalysis) (CMD)
FACPT.......... Fellow, American College of Physical Therapy (CMD)
FACPTNG..... Forward Air Control Party Training [*Navy*] (ANA)
fac pwr ctl... facility power control (SAUS)
fac pwr mon... facility power monitor (SAUS)
fac pwr pnl... facility power panel (SAUS)
FACR........... Carletonville [*South Africa*] [*ICAO location identifier*] (ICLI)
FACR........... Fellow of the American College of Radiologists (SAUO)
FACR........... Fellow of the American College of Radiology
FACR........... First Article Configuration Review [*Army*] (AABC)
FACR........... Force Assessment in the Central Region [*NATO*] (NATG)
FACR........... Fourier Analysis Cyclic Reduction (SAUS)
FACRED....... Federal Advisory Council on Regional Economic Development
FAC REG...... facility register (SAUS)
FAC-REG...... Faculty-Regular (SAUS)
FAC REJ...... facility reject (SAUS)
FA Crm........ Field Artillery Crewman (SAUS)
FACRP......... Functional Analysis And Consolidation Review Panel (SAUO)
FACRS......... FORTRAN Analytical Cross Reference System (SAUS)
FACS........... Facial Action Coding System [*Psychology*] (DHP)
FACS........... Facilities (ADA)
FACS........... Facilities Assignment and Control System (VLIE)
FACS........... Facilities Control (SAUS)
FACS........... Facilities Control System
FACS........... Facility Assignment Control System (SAUS)
FACS........... Facility for Access Control and Security [*RadWare*]
facs............ Facsimile (DIAR)
FACS........... Facsimile (KSC)
FACS........... Factory Assembly Control System (SAUS)
FACS........... Failure Analysis Control System (SAUS)
FACS........... Family and Community Services (WDAA)
FACS........... Fast Atom Capillaritron Source [*Instrumentation*]
FACS........... Fast Attack Class Submarine [*Navy*]
FACS........... Feature Attribute Coding Standard (SAUS)
FACS........... Feature Attribute Coding System (SAUS)
FACS........... Federal Automated Career System
FACS........... Federation of American Controlled Shipping [*New York, NY*] (EA)
FACS........... Feedback and Analysis of Control Statistics (PDAA)
FACS........... Fellow of the American College of Surgeons
FACS........... Fellow of the Association of Certified Secretaries (SAUO)
FACS........... Fellow of the Association of Certified Secretaries of South Africa (SAUO)
FACS........... Field Army Communication System (AABC)
FACS........... Final Assembly Control System (VLIE)
FACS........... Finance and Control System (NASA)
FACS........... Financial Accounting and Control System
FACS........... Fine Attitude Control System [*Aerospace*]
FACS........... Fleet Area Control and Surveillance Facility [*Navy*] (DOMA)
FACS........... Flexible Accounting Control System [*Computer science*] (BUR)
FACS........... Flight Augmentation Control System [*Aviation*]
FACS........... Floating Decimal Abstract Coding System
FACS........... Fluid Amplifier Control System
FACS........... Fluorescence-Activated Cell Sorter [*Becton, Dickinson Electronics Laboratory*] [*Instrumentation*]
FACS........... Flurouracil, Adriamycin, Cyclophosphamide, Streptozocin [*Antineoplastic drug regimen*] (DAVI)
FACS........... Force Automation and Communications [*Military*]
FACS........... Formal Aspects of Computing Science (SAUO)
FACS........... FORTRAN Automatic Checkout System (SAUS)
FACS........... Forward Acquisition Sensor (SAUS)
FACS........... Foundation for American Communications (EA)
FACS........... Frederick A. Cook Society (EA)
FACS........... Frequency Allocation Coordinating Subcommittee (SAUS)
FACS........... Friendship Association of Chinese Students and Scholars (EA)
FACS........... Fully Automatic Compiling System
FACS........... Funds Allocation Control System
FACS........... Future Armored Combat System [*Military*]
FACSA......... Frankfurt American Community Scholarship Association (SAUO)
FACSAF....... Fleet Air Control and Surveillance Facility (SAUO)
FACSC......... Frequency Allocation Coordinating Subcommittee [*Canada*]
FACscan...... Fluorescence-Activated Cell Sorter Scan [*Medicine*] (PALA)
FAC/SCAR.... Forward Air Control / Self-Contained Airborne Reconnaissance [*Air Force*] (PDAA)
FACSFAC..... Fleet Air Control and Surveillance Facilities (SAUS)
FACSFAC..... Fleet Air Control and Survey Facility
FACSFAT..... Fleet Area Control & Surveillance Facility (SAUO)
FACSFAX..... Fleet Air Control and Surveillance Facility (MCD)

FACSI......... Fast Access Coded Small Images (SAUS)
FACSI......... Federal Advisory Committee for Scientific Information (SAUS)
FACSI......... Federal Advisory Council on Scientific Information
facsim......... Facsimile (RION)
FACSIM......... Facsimile
FACSIMILE... FAMECE [*Family of Military Engineer Construction Equipment*] Computer Simulator for Independent and Logical Evaluation [*or Simulation*] (MCD)
FACSM......... Fellow of the American College of Sports Medicine
FACSO......... Facilities Supply Office
FAC/SPC...... Fisheries Advisory Committee of the South Pacific Commission
FACSS......... Federation of Analytical Chemistry and Spectroscopy Societies (EA)
FACSSG....... Forward Area Combat Service Support Group (SAUO)
FACSTEAM... Facilities Installation Study Program [*Navy*] (NVT)
Fac Stor....... Factor Storage (SAUS)
FacStr......... Factory Stores of America, Inc. [*Associated Press*] (SAG)
FACT........... Cape Town [*South Africa*] [*ICAO location identifier*] (ICLI)
FACT........... ERL-Gulf Breeze Financial Data Management (SAUO)
FACT........... Facilitation and Coordination Therapy (SAUS)
FACT........... Facility for Automation, Control and Test (PDAA)
FACT........... Facility for the Analysis of Chemical Thermodynamics [*McGill University*] [*Information service or system*] (IID)
FACT........... Factor Analysis Chart Technique [*Business term*]
fact........... Factory (VRA)
FACT........... Factory [*Automotive engineering*]
FACT........... Factory Automation, Control, and Test Facility
FACT........... Factual Compiler
fact........... factum (SAUS)
FACT........... Faculty Access to Computing Technology (SAUS)
FACT........... Fairchild Advanced CMOS Technology [*Fairchild Semiconductor Corp.*]
FACT........... Fairchild Advanced CMOS Transistor logic (SAUS)
FACT........... Fairchild Assured Component Test (SAUO)
FACT........... Fairchild Assured Customer Test (SAUO)
FACT........... Families Against Cancer Terror (EA)
FACT........... Family Action Council of Texas (SAUO)
FACT........... Fast Access Current Text
FACT........... Fast Access Current Text Bank [*University of Missouri*] [*Electronic library*] (NITA)
FACT........... Fast Acting Control Transfer (ACAE)
FACT........... Fast-Action Computer Terminal [*Computer science*] (CIST)
FACT........... Fast Asymptotic Coherent Transmission (NVT)
FACT........... Feasibility Ascension Cape Town [*Project*] [*Marine science*] (OSRA)
FACT........... Federation Against Copyright Theft [*British*]
FACT........... Federation Automatic Coding Technologies (SAUO)
FACT........... Federation of American Consumers and Travelers (EA)
FACT........... Federation of Associations of Canadian Tamils [*Government term*] (GA)
FACT........... Federation of Automated Coding Technologies (EA)
FACT........... Feminist Anti-Censorship Task Force
FACT........... Festival of American Community Theatre [*American Community Theatre Association*]
FACT........... Field Audit and Completion Test [*Market research*]
FACT........... Field Test Analysis Correlation of Thermal Images (ACAE)
FACT........... Fighter Aircraft Code Type (SAA)
FACT........... Film and Automated Camera Technology (SAUS)
FACT........... Financial Accounting Control Technique (SAUS)
FACT........... Fingerprint Automatic Classification Technique [*Computer science*]
FACT........... First Albany Companies, Inc. [*NASDAQ symbol*] (NQ)
FACT........... First Albany Cos. [*NASDAQ symbol*] (TTSB)
FACT........... First American Congress of Theater
FACT........... Flanagan Aptitude Classification Test [*Psychology*]
FACT........... Fleet Analysis and Cost Trends (PDAA)
FACT........... Flexible Automatic Circuit Tester
FACT........... Flight Acceptance Composite Test [*NASA*]
FACT........... Focused Appendix Computed Tomography [*Medicine*]
FACT........... Focus on Alternative & Complementart Therapies [*Medicine*] (WDAA)
FACT........... Food Additive Campaign Team [*British*]
FACT........... Food Animal Concerns Trust (EA)
FACT........... Force Anti-Air Warfare Coordination Technology [*Military*] (SEWL)
FACT........... Forcecast and Control Technique (SAUS)
FACT........... Ford Anodized-Aluminum Corrosion Test (SAUS)
FACT........... Forecast and Control Technique (IAA)
FACT........... Foreign Access to Computer Technology [*USIA*]
FACT........... Foundation for Advanced Computer Technology
FACT........... Foundation for Advancement in Cancer Therapy (EA)
FACT........... Foundation for Alternative Cancer Therapies (SAUO)
FACT........... Freightliner Advanced Concept Truck [*Experimental vehicle*]
FACT........... Freshwater and Aquaculture Contents Tables (SAUS)
FACT........... Frozen Food Action Communications Team (DICI)
FACT........... fully automated compiling technique (SAUS)
FACT........... Fully Automatically Controlled Train [*British*]
FACT........... Fully Automatic Calibration Technology [*Analytical balances*]
FACT........... Fully Automatic Cataloging Technique [*Computer science*] (MCD)
FACT........... Fully Automatic Compiler [*or Computer*]-Translator [*Computer science*]
FACT........... Fully Automatic Compiling Technique [*Computer science*]
FACT........... Functional Alternating Current Tester (SAUS)
FACT........... Functional Assessment of Cancer Therapy (MELL)
FACT-90....... Film and Automated Camera Technology for 1990 (SAUS)
FACTA......... Food, Agriculture, Conservation and Trade Act of 1990
FACTA......... Frequency Agile Tactical VHF Antenna (SAUS)
FACT-AID..... Flexible Automatic Circuit Tester - Automatic Interconnection Device
FACTAN....... Factor Analysis (SAUS)
FACT Bank... Fast Access Current Text Bank (SAUS)
FactCrd....... Factory Card Outlet Corp. [*Associated Press*] (SAG)
FACTER....... Forward Air Controller Terminal
FACTEX....... Fast Asymptotic Coherent Transmission Extended (MCD)
FACT Facility... Factory Automation, Control, and Test Facility (SAUS)
FACT INIT.... Factotum Initial [*Typography*] (DGA)
FACTL......... Fellow of the American College of Trial Lawyers (DD)
FACT-LIFT.... Flexible Automatic Circuit Tester - Low Insertion Force Technique
FACTO......... Franchise Advice and Consultancy Trade Organization [*British*] (DBA)
FACTOR....... Factor Operator (SAUS)
FACTOR....... Foundation to Assist Canadian Talent on Records
FACTOR....... Fourteen-O-One Automatically-Controlled Test Optimizing Routine [*Military*] (SAA)
FACT QS...... Fairchild Advanced CMOS Transistor logic (SAUS)
FACT-QUIC... Flexible Automatic Circuit Tester - Quick Universal Interface Connector
FACTR......... Fujitsu Access and Transport System [*Computer science*] (ACRL)
FACTRO....... Factory Mechatronics (TSPED)
FACTS......... Facilities Action Control Target System [*US Postal Service*]
FACTS......... Facilities Administration Consolidated Tape System (MCD)
FACTS......... Facilities Administration Control and Time Schedule
FACTS......... Facilities and Company Tracking System [*Environmental Protection Agency*] (AEPA)
FACTS......... Facilities Assets Catalog and Tracking System [*Army*]
FACTS......... Facilities Complaint Tracking System (SAUS)
FACTS......... Facsimile Transmission System [*Telecommunications*]
FACTS......... Failure and Accident Technical Information System
FACTS......... Family and Community Treatment Services
FACTS......... Fast Access to Computerized Technical Sources [*Information service or system*] (IID)
FACTS......... Fast Action on Comments of Technical Significance
FACTS......... Fast Agricultural Communication Terminal System [*Purdue University*] [*Information service or system*]
FACTS......... Federation of Australian Commercial Television Stations (SAUO)
FACTS......... Fiche Automated Cassette Terminal System (SAUS)
FACTS......... Field Army Calibration Team Support
FACTS......... Financial Accounting and Control Techniques for Supply [*Army*]
FACTS......... Financial Analysis Capability through Scanning
FACTS......... Financing Alternative Computer Terminal System (SAUS)
FACTS......... Financing Analysis Cost and Testing Service [*LIMRA*]
FACTS......... First Amendment Consumer and Trade Society (EA)
FACTS......... FLIR [*Forward-Looking Infrared RADAR*] Augmented Cobra TOW Sight [*Tube-Launched, Optically-Tracked, Wire-Guided Weapon*]
FACTS......... Florida Atlantic Coast Transport Study [*Marine science*] (OSRA)
FACTS......... Football Association Coaching Tactics Skills [*British*] (DI)
FACTS......... Force Accounting Terminal System (SAUO)
FACTS......... FORTRAN [*Formula Translating System*] Analytical Cross Reference TabulationSystem [*Computer science*]
FACTS......... FORTRAN Analytical Cross Reference Tabulation System (SAUS)
FACTS......... Foundation for Agricultural Conservation Technology and Science (SAUS)
FACTS......... Foundation for the Advancement of Chiropractic Tenets and Science (EA)
FACTS......... Free Available Chlorine Test with Syringaldazine [*Analytical chemistry*]
FACTS......... National Food and Conservation through Swine (EA)
FactsetR....... Factset Research Systems, Inc. [*Associated Press*] (SAG)
facty........... fact filled (SAUS)
Facty........... Factory
FACUI......... Federal Advisory Council on Unemployment Insurance
FACUSJCB.... Frequency Allocation Committee United States, Joint Communicaions Board (SAUS)
FACUS JCB... Frequency Allocation Committee, United States, Joint Communication Board (SAUO)
FACV........... Calvinia [*South Africa*] [*ICAO location identifier*] (ICLI)
FACVP......... Fluorouracil, Adriamycin, Cyclophosphamide, VP-16 [*Antineoplastic drug regimen*] (DAVI)
FACW........... Clanwilliam [*South Africa*] [*ICAO location identifier*] (ICLI)
FACW........... Facultative Wetland Plant (ERG)
facw........... facultative wetlands (SAUS)
FACWA......... Familial Amyotrphic Chorea with Acanthocytosis [*Medicine*] (EDAA)
FAD............. Facility and Design (IAA)
FAD............. Facility Deactivated (SAUS)
FAD............. Faculty Author Development [*Software development program*]
FAD............. Faded [*Bookselling*] (DGA)
FAD............. Failure Activity Determination (SAUS)
FAD............. Failure Analysis Diagnostic (ACAE)
FAD............. Fairchild Aircraft Division (SAUS)
FAD............. Familial Alzheimer's Dementia (MELL)
FAD............. Familial Alzheimer's Disease [*Medicine*]
FAD............. Familial Autonomic Dysautonomia [*Medicine*] (EDAA)
FAD............. Familial Autonomic Dysfunction [*Medicine*] (DMAA)
FAD............. Families Against Drunks (SAUS)
FAD............. Family Assessment Device
FAD............. Feasible Arrival Date (COE)
FAD............. Federal Anti-Trust Decisions [*A publication*] (DLA)
FAD............. Ferrite Array Demonstration [*RADAR*]
FAD............. Fetal Activity Determination
FAD............. Field Advanced Dump (SAUS)
FAD............. Field Ammunition Depot (SAUS)
FAD............. Fighter Air Director [*Military*] (NVT)
FAD............. Filter and Detect Chip (NITA)
FAD............. Final Approach Display (MCD)
FAD............. Financial Accounting Data
FAD............. Findings and Determination (IAA)

FAD Fine Art Development [*British*]
FAD First Appearance Datum [*Geology*]
FAD First Appearance of Date (QUAC)
FAD First Article Demonstration
FAD Fish Aggregating Device [*Marine science*] (OSRA)
FAD Fish Aggregation Device (EERA)
FAD Flavinadenindinucleotid (SAUS)
FAD Flavin-Adenine Dinucleotide [*Biochemistry*]
fad flavine adenine dinucleotide (SAUS)
FAD Flea Allergy Dermatitis [*Medicine*]
FAD Fleet Air Defense (MCD)
FAD Fleet Air Detachment [*Navy*]
FAD Flexible Automatic Depot
FAD Floating Add [*Computer science*] (IEEE)
FAD Floating Add Double (SAUS)
FAD Floating And (SAUS)
FAD Fonds Africain de Developpement [*African Development Fund*]
FAD Food and Agricultural Department (SAUS)
FAD Force Activity Designation (SAUO)
F/AD Force/Activity Designator [*Military*]
FAD Forward Ammunition Depot / Dump (SAUS)
FAD Forward Ammunition Dump (SAUS)
FAD Forward Area Defense (DOMA)
FAD Fraction Actually Degrades (CARB)
FAD Fracture Analysis Diagram (PDAA)
FAD Franklin Advantage Real Estate, Inc. [*AMEX symbol*] (SPSG)
FAD Free Air Delivered
FAD Fuel Advisory Departure [*Aviation*] (FAAC)
FAD Fuerzas Armadas Democraticas [*Democratic Armed Forces*] [*Nicaragua*] (PD)
fad Full and Down (SAUS)
FAD Functional Area Description
FAD Funding Authorization Document (AABC)
FAD Rog-Air Ltd. [*Canada*] [*ICAO designator*] (FAAC)
FADA De Aar [*South Africa*] [*ICAO location identifier*] (ICLI)
FADA Federal Assets Disposition Association [*Functions transferred to FDIC and RTC, 1989*]
FADA Federation of Automobile Dealers Associations (SAUO)
FADA Fourth Armored Division Association (EA)
FADA Frequency-Amplitude Domain Analysis [*Medicine*] (EDAA)
FADA Fuerzas de Accion Armada [*Armed Action Forces*] [*Guatemala*] (PD)
FADAC Field Army Digital Artillery Computer (SAUS)
FADAC Field Army Digital Automatic Computer (SAUS)
FADAC Field Artillery Data Computer (SAUS)
FADAC Field Artillery Digital Atomic Computer (SAUS)
FADAC Field Artillery Digital Automatic Computer (IEEE)
FADAC Field Atomic Digital Automatic Computer (SAUS)
FADAC Frankfurt Area Drug Advisory Council (SAUO)
FADALA Failure Detection and Location Analysis (MCD)
FADC Douglas Colliery [*South Africa*] [*ICAO location identifier*] (ICLI)
FADC Federal Alien Detention Center (SAUS)
FADC Fighter Air Direction Center
FADC First Aid and Decontamination Centre (SAUO)
FADD Dundee [*South Africa*] [*ICAO location identifier*] (ICLI)
FADD Fan-Assisted Drug Detector
FADD Feline Attention Deficit Disorder
FADD Fight Against Dictating Designers [*Group opposing below-the-knee fashions introduced in 1970*]
FADE FAA Airline Data Exchange [*FAA*] (TAG)
FADE Fully Automatic Depot Equipment (ACAE)
FADEC Full Authority Digital Electronic Control (TIMI)
FADEC Full Authority Digital Engine Control
FADEM Flower of Friendship and Development of Macau [*Political party*] (EY)
FADES Fuselage Analysis and Design Synthesis
FADF Fluorescent Antibody Dark Field [*Clinical chemistry*] (MAE)
FADH Durnacol [*South Africa*] [*ICAO location identifier*] (ICLI)
$FADH_2$ Flavin-Adenine Dinucleotide [*Reduced*] [*Biochemistry*]
FADIC Field Artillery Digital Computer (SAUS)
FADICA Foundations and Donors Interested in Catholic Activities (EA)
FADIG First Atomic Power Industry Group (SAUO)
FADINAP Fertilizer Advisory, Development and Information Network for Asia and the Pacific (SAUS)
FADIR Flexion, Adduction, Internal Rotation [*Orthopedics*]
FADL Delareyville [*South Africa*] [*ICAO location identifier*] (ICLI)
FADM Fleet Admiral
FADM Forced Attribute Display Mhode (SAUS)
FADM Functional Area Documentation Manager [*Air Force*] (AFM)
FAdmA Fellow of the Administration Association (DD)
FADN Durban/Louis Botha [*South Africa*] [*ICAO location identifier*] (ICLI)
FADN Farm Accounting Data Network (SAUO)
FADN Flavin-Adenine Dinucleotide [*Biochemistry*] (MAE)
FADN Frente Anti-Comunista de Defensa Nacional [*Anti-Communist Front for National Defense*] [*Ecuador*]
FADO Fellow of the Association of Dispensing Opticians [*British*] (DBQ)
FADO(Hons) Fellow of the Association of Dispensing Opticians with Honours Diploma [*British*] (DBQ)
FADO(Hons)CL Fellow of the Association of Dispensing Opticians with Honours Diploma and Diploma in Contact Lens Fitting [*British*] (DBQ)
FADP Federal Automatic Data Processing (MHDI)
FADP Finish Association for Data Processing (SAUS)
FADP Finnish Association for Data Processing
FADPUG Federal ADP [*Automatic Data Processing*] Users Group
FADR Dunnottar [*South Africa*] [*ICAO location identifier*] (ICLI)
FADR Forward Area Demagnetizing Range [*Military*] (DOMA)
FADRS FM-CW Atmospheric Doppler Radar System (SAUO)
FADS Dordabis [*Namibia*] [*ICAO location identifier*] (ICLI)
FADS Fast Area Digitizing Scanner (SAUS)
FADS Fast Automatic Debugging System (SAUS)
FADS Fetal Akinesia Deformation Sequence [*Medicine*] (EDAA)
FADS Filtered Attitude Determination System (SAUS)
FADS Fixed Asset Depreciation System (PDAA)
FADS Fleet Air Defense System (ACAE)
FADS Flexible Air Data System
FADS Food Additives Data System (SAUS)
FADS Force Administration Data System [*Bell System*]
FADS FORTRAN [*Formula Translating System*] Automatic Debugging System [*Computer science*]
FADS Forward Area Deployment, Spain
FADSID Fighter-Aircraft-Delivered Seismic Intrusion Detector (NVT)
FADSN Floating Add Double Suppress Normal (SAUS)
fadsorog false and dangerous systems of religion or government (SAUS)
FADT Faecal Antigen Detection Test (SAUO)
FADU File Access Data Unit [*Telecommunications*] (OSI)
FADV Devon [*South Africa*] [*ICAO location identifier*] (ICLI)
f-ae- Algeria [*MARC geographic area code*] [*Library of Congress*] (LCCP)
FAE Dayton, OH [*Location identifier*] [*FAA*] (FAAL)
FAE Faenza [*Italy*] [*Seismograph station code, US Geological Survey*] [*Closed*] (SEIS)
Fae Faeroese (SAUS)
Fa E Far East (SAUS)
FAE Faroe Islands [*Denmark*] [*Airport symbol*] (OAG)
FAE Federal Assumed Enforcement [*State implementation plan by EPA*]
FAE Fetal Alcohol Effect [*Medicine*]
FAE Fidelity Advisor Emer'g Asia [*NYSE symbol*] (TTSB)
FAE Fidelity Advisor Emerging Asia Fund [*NYSE symbol*] (SAG)
FAE Field Advisory Element (CINC)
FAE Fighter Aircraft Establishment (SAUS)
FAE Figural After-Effect
FAE Final Approach Equipment [*Aviation*]
FAE Final Average Earnings
FAE Fine Alignment Equipment
FAE Follicle-Associated Epithelium [*Immunology*]
FAE Forward Acquisition Experiment (ACAE)
fae forward air express (SAUS)
FAE Foundation for Accounting Education (EA)
FAE Foundation of Automation and Employment Ltd. [*British*] (BI)
FAE Frei aber Einsam [*Free but Lonely*] [*Motto of Joseph Joachim, 19th century German violinist*] (ECON)
FAE Fuel adjacency effect (SAUS)
FAE Fuel Air Explosive (MCD)
FAE Fund for the Advancement of Education [*Defunct*] (EA)
FAE Merlin Express, Inc. [*FAA designator*] (FAAC)
FAE Sat-Air, Inc. [*ICAO designator*] (FAAC)
FAEA Ellisras Control Reporting Point [*South Africa*] [*ICAO location identifier*] (ICLI)
FAEA Financial and Economic Analysis
FAEC Estcourt [*South Africa*] [*ICAO location identifier*] (ICLI)
FAEC Foundation of the American Economic Council (EA)
FAEC Full Authority Electronic Control (MCD)
FAECC Fellow of the Accountants and Executives Corporation of Canada (SAUO)
FAECF Federation des Associations Europeennes des Constructeurs de Fenetres [*Federation of European Window Manufacturers Associations - FEWMA*] (EA)
FAECT Federation of Architects , Engineers , Chemists , and Technicians (SAUS)
FAECT Federation of Architects, Engineers, Chemists, and Technicians (SAUO)
FAEE Fatty Acid Ethyl Ester
FAEJ Fonds d'Action et d'Education Juridiques pour les Femmes [*Women's Legal Education and Action Fund - LEAF*] [*Canada*]
FAEL East London/Ben Schoeman [*South Africa*] [*ICAO location identifier*] (ICLI)
FAEmA Fidelity Advisor Emerging Asia Fund [*Associated Press*] (SAG)
FAEmAs Fidelity Advisor Emerging Asia Fund [*Associated Press*] (SAG)
FAEO Ermelo [*South Africa*] [*ICAO location identifier*] (ICLI)
FAEP Federation of Associations of Periodical Publishers (SAUS)
FAEPC Federation des Associations d'Editeurs de Periodiques de la CE [*Brussels, Belgium*] (EAIO)
FAER Ellisras [*South Africa*] [*ICAO location identifier*] (ICLI)
Faer Faeroe Islands (SAUS)
FAER Foreign Agricultural Economic Reports
Faeroes Faeroe Islands in the North Atlantic (SAUS)
FAERX Fidelity Advisor: Overseas Cl.T [*Mutual fund ticker symbol*] (SG)
FAES Eshowe [*South Africa*] [*ICAO location identifier*] (ICLI)
FAES Federated American Engineering Societies (SAUO)
FAES FIFRA & TSCA Enforcement System (SAUO)
FAES Flame Atomic Emission Spectrometry
FAES Foreign Affairs Executive Seminar [*Department of State*]
FAES Foundation for Appropriate Economic Solutions (SAUO)
FAESHED Fuel Air Explosive System Helicopter Delivered
FAET Elliot [*South Africa*] [*ICAO location identifier*] (ICLI)
FAET Forum for the Advancement of Educational Therapy (AIE)
FAETU Fleet Airborne Electronic Training Unit [*Navy*]
FAETUA Fleet Airborne Electronics Unit, Atlantic (SAUS)
FAETUA Fleet Airborne Electronic Training Unit, Atlantic
FAETUDET Fleet Airborne Electronic Training Unit Detachment
FAETULANT Fleet Airborne Electronic Training Unit, Atlantic
FAETUP Fleet Airborne Electronic Training Unit, Pacific (IEEE)

FAETUPAC ... Fleet Airborne Electronic Training Unit, Pacific [*Later, FASOTRAGRUPAC, F ASOTRAGRUPACFLT*]
FAEW ... Fuel Air Explosive Weapon (ACAE)
FAF ... Fafnir Bearings (SAUS)
FAF ... Families of Australia Foundation
FAF ... Family of the Americas Foundation (EA)
FAF ... Fan Air Flow [*Automotive engineering*]
FAF ... Fast Acting Fuse (SAUS)
FAF ... Fathers Are Forever [*Defunct*] (EA)
FAF ... Fatty Acid-Free [*Biochemistry*]
FAF ... Federal Armed Forces (SAUO)
FAF ... Fibroblast Activating Factor [*Biochemistry*]
FAF ... File Attribute File (SAUS)
FAF ... Film Arts Foundation (EA)
FAF ... Final Approach Fix [*Aviation*] (DA)
FAF ... Financial Accounting Foundation [*Stamford, CT*] (EA)
FAF ... Financial Aid Form [*Of College Board*]
FAF ... Financial Analysts Federation [*Later, AIMR*] (EA)
FAF ... Financing Adjustment Factor
FAF ... Fine Art Fair
FAF ... Fine Arts Foundation (EA)
FAF ... Finnish Air Force (SAUS)
FAF ... First Aerodynamic Flight (NASA)
FAF ... First Amer Finl [*NYSE symbol*] (TTSB)
FAF ... First American Financial Corp. [*NYSE symbol*] (SPSG)
faf ... first article flow (SAUS)
F/AF ... FishAmerica Foundation (EA)
FAF ... Fleet Amenities Fund [*Navy*] [*British*]
FAF ... Flyaway Factory
FAF ... Fly Away Field (SAUS)
FAF ... Fly Away Free
FAF ... Food and Agriculture Forum
faf ... forage acre factor (SAUS)
FAF ... Forces Aeriennes Francaises [*France*] [*ICAO designator*] (FAAC)
FAF ... Fort Eustis, VA [*Location identifier*] [*FAA*] (FAAL)
FAF ... Forward Air Freight (WDAA)
FAF ... Free Asia Foundation (EA)
faf ... Free at Factory (EBF)
FAF ... Free at Factory [*Business term*]
faf ... free at field (SAUS)
FAF ... French Aeronautical Federation (SAUO)
FAF ... French Air Force
FAF ... French American Foundation (SAUS)
FAF ... Fuel Adjustment Factor (SAUS)
FAF ... Fund for America's Future [*Defunct*] (EA)
FAF ... Fuzing, Arming, and Firing
FAFA ... Federation des Alliances Francaises en Australie [*Federation of Alliances Francaises (Institutes for the study of French language and culture) in Australia*]
FAFAB ... FSS [*Flight Service Station*] Assumes Flight-Plan Area [*Aviation*] (FAAC)
FAFB ... Fairchild Air Force Base [*Washington*] (AAG)
FAFB ... Ficksburg [*South Africa*] [*ICAO location identifier*] (ICLI)
FAFDOPS ... Field Artillery Fire Direction Operations (SAUS)
FAFF ... Frankfort [*South Africa*] [*ICAO location identifier*] (ICLI)
FaFiCards ... Factual Film Card System (SAUS)
FAFK ... Fisantekraal [*South Africa*] [*ICAO location identifier*] (ICLI)
FAFM ... Field Artillery Field Manual (SAUS)
FAFNAR ... Financial Aid Form Need Analysis Report
FAFnc ... First American Financial Corp. [*Associated Press*] (SAG)
FAFP ... Force and Financial Plan
FAFP ... Foreign Area Fellowship Program [*Later, SSRC*]
FAFPAS ... Federation des Associations de Fabricants de Produits Alimentaires Surgeles d e la CE [*European Federation of Quick Frozen Food Manufacturers*] [*Belgium*] (EAIO)
FAFPIC ... Forestry and Forest Products Industry Council (EERA)
FAFPS ... Five-Axis Fiber Placement System (SAUS)
FAFR ... Fatal Accident Frequency Rates (SAUS)
FAFR ... Fraserburg [*South Africa*] [*ICAO location identifier*] (ICLI)
FAFS ... Falcon Air Force Station (ACAE)
FAFS ... Farm and Food Society [*British*]
FAFS ... Flame Atomic Fluorescence Spectrometry
FAFSV ... Franco-Australian Friendly Society of Victoria [*Australia*]
FAFT ... First Article Flight Test
FAFT ... Free Air Facility Track [*Edwards Air Force Base*] (AAG)
FAFTAH ... First a Friend, Then a Host [*Safety slogan encouraging partygivers to prevent guests' overindulgence in alcohol*]
FAFTEEC ... Full Authority Fault Tolerant Electronic Engine Control (ACAE)
FAFWC ... Fuchu Air Force Weather Central (CINC)
FAFWOA ... For A Friend Without Access (SAUS)
FAG ... Faggot [*Derogatory term for male homosexual*] [*Slang*] (DSUE)
Fag ... Fagotto [*Bassoon*] [*Italian*] [*Music*] (WDAA)
FAG ... Fagotto [*Bassoon*] [*Music*]
FAG ... Failure Analysis Group (SAUO)
F-Ag ... F Antigen [*Immunochemistry*]
FAG ... Fatigue [*Slang*] (DSUE)
FAG ... Field Artillery Group (ACAE)
FAG ... Finance and Accounting Group [*Air Force*] (AFM)
FAG ... Financial Assistance Grant
FAG ... Fine Arts Gallery (SAUO)
FAG ... Finished Americans Group (SAUO)
FAG ... Fiscal Activities Guide [*Department of Labor*] (OICC)
FAG ... Fleet Assistance Group
FAG ... Forced Air Gas (SAUS)
FAG ... Forward Air Guide (NVT)
FAG ... Fraud Against the Government
FAG ... Free-Air Gradient [*Geophysics*]
FAG ... Fuerza Aerea Argentina [*ICAO designator*] (FAAC)
FAGA ... Friedreich's Ataxia Group in America [*Defunct*] (EA)
FAGA ... Full-Term Appropriate for Gestational Age [*Medicine*] (EDAA)
FAGAA ... Fellow of the Art Galleries Association of Australia
FAGAIRTRANS ... First Available Government Air Transportation [*Navy*]
FAGB ... Gobabis [*Namibia*] [*ICAO location identifier*] (ICLI)
FAGC ... Fast Automatic Gain Control
FAGC ... Federation of Arab Gulf Chamber (SAUS)
FAGC ... Forward Area Ground Control (IAA)
FAGC ... Grand Central [*South Africa*] [*ICAO location identifier*] (ICLI)
FAGCA ... Fenton Art Glass Collectors of America (EA)
FAGD ... Fellow in the Academy of General Dentistry (SAUS)
FAGE ... Factory Aerospace Ground Equipment (MCD)
FAGE ... Fluorescence Assay with Gas Expansion [*Analytical chemistry*]
FAGE ... Future Age [*A publication*] (ADA)
FAGE ... Gough Island [*South Africa*] [*ICAO location identifier*] (ICLI)
FAGF ... Grootfontein [*Namibia*] [*ICAO location identifier*] (ICLI)
FAGG ... George/P. W. Botha [*South Africa*] [*ICAO location identifier*] (ICLI)
FAGI ... False Alarm Good Intent (WDAA)
FAGI ... Fellow of the Australian Grain Institute
FAGI ... Giyani [*South Africa*] [*ICAO location identifier*] (ICLI)
FAGIX ... Fidelity Capital & Income [*Mutual fund ticker symbol*] (SG)
FAGL ... Groblersdal [*South Africa*] [*ICAO location identifier*] (ICLI)
FAGLA ... Furylacryloylglycylleucine Amide [*Biochemistry*]
FAGLANT ... Fleet Assistance Group, Atlantic [*Navy*]
FAGM ... Field Army Guided Missile (IAA)
FAGM ... Field Artillery Guided Missile (SAUS)
FAGM ... Johannesburg/Rand [*South Africa*] [*ICAO location identifier*] (ICLI)
FAGMS ... Field Artillery Guided Missile [*Air Force*]
fagms ... field artillery guided missiles (SAUS)
FAGMS-S ... Field Army Guided Missile System - Sergeant (SAA)
FAGNX ... Fidelity Advisor: Natural Resources Cl.T [*Mutual fund ticker symbol*] (SG)
FAGO ... Fellow of the Academy of Gynaecology and Obstetrics (SAUS)
FAGO ... Fellow of the American Guild of Organists
FAGOX ... Fidelity Advisor: Growth Opport. Cl.T [*Mutual fund ticker symbol*] (SG)
FAGp ... Finance and Accounting Group [*Air Force*] (AFM)
FAGPAC ... Fleet Assistance Group, Pacific [*Navy*]
FAGR ... Floating Arm Graphic Recorder (PDAA)
FAGR ... Fractional Antedating Goal Response (DIPS)
FAGR ... Graaff Reinet [*South Africa*] [*ICAO location identifier*] (ICLI)
FAGS ... Federation for Astronomical and Geophysical Services (SAUS)
FAGS ... Federation of Astronomical and Geophysical Data Analysis (SAUS)
FAGS ... Federation of Astronomical and Geophysical Permanent Services (SAUO)
FAGS ... Federation of Astronomical and Geophysical Services [*Research center*] [*France*] (IRC)
FAGS ... Fellow, American Geriatric Society (CMD)
FAGS ... Fellow of the American Geographical Society
FAGS ... ferrosilite-anorthite-garnet-silica (SAUS)
FAGT ... First Available Government Transportation
FAGT ... Functional Agricultural Thesaurus (SAUO)
FAGT ... Grahamstown [*South Africa*] [*ICAO location identifier*] (ICLI)
FAGTRANS ... First Available Government Transportation
FAGU ... Fleet Air Gunnery Unit
FAGULANT ... Fleet Air Gunnery Unit, Atlantic (SAUS)
FAGUPAC ... Fleet Air Gunnery Unit, Pacific (MUGU)
FAGV ... Gravelotte [*South Africa*] [*ICAO location identifier*] (ICLI)
FAGVX ... Fidelity Advisor: Govt. Invest. Cl.T [*Mutual fund ticker symbol*] (SG)
FAGY ... Greytown [*South Africa*] [*ICAO location identifier*] (ICLI)
FAH ... Facilitation Awards for Handicapped Scientists and Engineers Program [*Washington, DC*] [*National Science Foundation*] (GRD)
Fah ... Fahrenheit (ADWA)
FAH ... Fahrenheit (KSC)
FAH ... Failed to Attend Hearing (SAUS)
FAH ... Farner Air Transport Hungary [*FAA designator*] (FAAC)
FAH ... Farrah Resources [*Vancouver Stock Exchange symbol*]
FAH ... Federation of American Hospitals [*Later, FAHS*]
FAH ... Folklore of American Holidays [*A publication*]
FAH ... Sheboygan, WI [*Location identifier*] [*FAA*] (FAAL)
FAHA ... Fellow of the Australian Academy of Humanities (WDAA)
FAHA ... Finnish-American Historical Archives (EA)
FAHA ... Harmony [*South Africa*] [*ICAO location identifier*] (ICLI)
FAHACCS ... Fellow, American Heart Association, Council of Cardiovascular Surgery (CMD)
FAHB ... Hartebeespoortdam [*South Africa*] [*ICAO location identifier*] (ICLI)
FAHC ... First Amer Hlth Concepts [*NASDAQ symbol*] (TTSB)
FAHC ... First American Health Concepts, Inc. [*NASDAQ symbol*] (NQ)
FAHCT ... Foundation for the Accreditation of Hematopoietic Cell Therapy (ADWA)
FAHD ... Forum on Allied Health Data [*American Occupational Therapy Association*]
FAHD ... Humansdorp [*South Africa*] [*ICAO location identifier*] (ICLI)
FAHE ... Fellow of the Association of Home Economists [*British*] (DI)
FAHE ... Friends Association for Higher Education (EA)
FAHE ... Pullenshope (Hendrina) [*South Africa*] [*ICAO location identifier*] (ICLI)
FAHG ... Heidelberg [*South Africa*] [*ICAO location identifier*] (ICLI)
FAHI ... Halali [*Namibia*] [*ICAO location identifier*] (ICLI)
FAHIX ... Fidelity Advisor: Municipal Income Cl.T [*Mutual fund ticker symbol*] (SG)
FAHM ... Hermanus [*South Africa*] [*ICAO location identifier*] (ICLI)
FAHN ... Fahnestock Viner Holdings, Inc. [*NASDAQ symbol*] (NQ)

FAHN.......... Henties Bay [*Namibia*] [*ICAO location identifier*] (ICLI)
FAHNF.......... Fahnestock Viner Hldgs'A' [*NASDAQ symbol*] (TTSB)
FahnVin.......... Fahnestock Viner Holdings, Inc. [*Associated Press*] (SAG)
FAHO.......... Heilbrond [*South Africa*] [*ICAO location identifier*] (ICLI)
FAHP.......... Fellow, Association for Healthcare Philanthropy (NFD)
FAHQ.......... Pretoria [*South Africa*] [*ICAO location identifier*] (ICLI)
FAHQMI.......... fully-automatic high-quality machine translation (SAUS)
FAHQMT.......... Fully Automatic High-Quality Machine Translation [*Computer science*] (DIT)
FAHQT.......... Fully Automatic High-Quality Translation [*Computer science*]
Fahr.......... Fahrenheit (SHCU)
FAHR.......... Fahrenheit
FAHR.......... Formosan Association for Human Rights (EA)
FAHR.......... Harrismith [*South Africa*] [*ICAO location identifier*] (ICLI)
FAHRB.......... Federation of Associations of Health Regulatory Boards [*Later, FARB*] (EA)
FAHS.......... Federation of American Health Systems (EA)
FAHS.......... Federation of Australian historical Societies
FAHS.......... Franco-American Historical Society (EA)
FAHS.......... Hoedspruit [*South Africa*] [*ICAO location identifier*] (ICLI)
FAHSLA.......... Flint Area Health Sciences Libraries Association (SAUO)
FAHSLN.......... Flint Area Health Science Library Network (SAUS)
FAHSM.......... Finnish American Historical Society of Michigan (EA)
FAHSW.......... Finnish-American Historical Society of the West (EA)
FAHT.......... Hoedspruit Civil/Burgerlike [*South Africa*] [*ICAO location identifier*] (ICLI)
FAHV.......... Hendrik Verwoerddam [*South Africa*] [*ICAO location identifier*] (ICLI)
FAHYX.......... Fidelity Advisor: High Yield Cl.T [*Mutual fund ticker symbol*] (SG)
FAI.......... Facility Information (SAUS)
fai.......... Faience (VRA)
FAI.......... FAI Insurances Ltd. [*NYSE symbol*] [*Toronto Stock Exchange symbol*] (CTT)
FAI.......... FAI Insurances Ltd ADS [*NYSE symbol*] (TTSB)
FAI.......... Fail As-Is [*Nuclear energy*] (NRCH)
FAI.......... Fairbanks [*Alaska*] [*Airport symbol*] (OAG)
FAI.......... Fairbanks, AK [*Location identifier*] [*FAA*] (FAAL)
FAI.......... Falcon Air, Inc. [*ICAO designator*] (FAAC)
FAI.......... Federal Acquisitions Institute [*Formerly, FPI*] (MCD)
FAI.......... Federation Abolitionniste Internationale [*International Abolitionist Federation*] [*India*]
FAI.......... Federation Aeronautique Internationale [*International Aeronautical Federation*] [*France*]
FAI.......... Fellow of the Chartered Auctioneers' and Estate Agents' Institute [*British*]
FAI.......... Fertiliser (or Fertilizer) Association of India (SAUO)
FAI.......... Field-Aligned Irregularity (MCD)
FAI.......... Final Acceptance Inspection (SAUS)
FAI.......... Financial Accounting Institute [*Tenafly, NJ*] [*Telecommunications service*] (TSSD)
FAI.......... First-Aid Instructor [*Red Cross*]
FAI.......... First Article Inspection [*NASA*] (KSC)
FAI.......... Five-Address Instruction (SAUS)
FAI.......... Flight Anomaly Investigation [*NASA*] (KSC)
FAI.......... Fly as Is (MCD)
FAI.......... Folic Acid Injection (MELL)
FAI.......... Fonds d'Activites Internationales [*International Activities Fund*] [*Canadian Labour Congress*]
FAI.......... Food Allergy Insomnia (MELL)
FAI.......... Football Association of Ireland (DI)
FAI.......... Four-Address Instruction (SAUS)
FAI.......... Free Air Inlet (SAUS)
FAI.......... Free Androgen Index [*Medicine*] (EDAA)
FAI.......... Frequency Application Index
FAI.......... Frequency-Azimuth Intensity [*RADAR*]
FAI.......... Fresh Air Inlet (MSA)
FAI.......... Fresh Air Input
FAI.......... Fresh Air Intake (SAUS)
FAI.......... Fuel Air Incendiary Concussion Bomb (MCD)
FAI.......... Fujitsu America, Inc. [*Hillsboro, OR*]
FAI.......... Functional Aerobic Impairment [*Medicine*] (AAMN)
FAI.......... Functional Assessment Inventory [*Medicine*] (DAVI)
FAI.......... Futon Association International (NTPA)
FAIA.......... 550th Airborne Infantry Association (EA)
FAIA.......... Fellow of the American Institute of Actuaries
FAIA.......... Fellow of the American Institute of Architects
FAIA.......... Fellow of the Association of International Accountants [*British*]
FAIA.......... Florida Association of Insurance Agents (SRA)
FAIA.......... Florida Automotive Industry Association (SRA)
FAIA.......... Functional Area Information Analysis (SAUO)
FAIA.......... Fellow of the Australian Institute of Advertising (ODA)
FAIAA.......... Fellow of the American Institute of Aeronautics and Astronautics [*Formerly, FIAes,FIAS*]
FAIAT.......... Federazione delle Associazioni Italiane Alberghi e Turismo [*Hotels and Tourism Federation*] [*Italy*] (EY)
FAIAU.......... Fleet Air Intelligence Augmenting Unit (CINC)
FAIB.......... Federation des Associations Internationales Etablies en Belgique [*Federation of International Associations Established in Belgium*]
FAIB.......... Fellow of the Australian Institute of Builders (SAUS)
FAIBM.......... Finnish Section of AIBM (SAUS)
FAIC.......... Families Against Internet Censorship [*An association*] (EA)
FAIC.......... Fellow Associate of the Institute of Chemistry
FAIC.......... Fellow of Agricultural Institute of Canada
FAIC.......... Fellow of the American Institute of Chemists (SAUO)
FAIC.......... Fellow of the American Institute of Criminology
FAIC.......... Fellow of the Architectural Institute of Canada (SAUS)
FAIC.......... Fertilizer Industry Advisory Committee (SAUO)
FAICE.......... Fellow of the Institute of Civil Engineers (SAUS)
FAID.......... Factory and Agricultural Inspectorate Division (HEAS)
FAID.......... Fuel assembly integrity devices (SAUS)
FAID.......... Fund for Agricultural and Industrial Development (SAUS)
FAIDS.......... Feline Acquired Immune Deficiency Syndrome [*Pathology*]
FAIE.......... Fellow of the British Association of Industrial Editors (DBQ)
FAIEE.......... Fellow of the American Institute of Electrical Engineers
FAI Ex.......... Fellow of the Australian Institute of Export (ODBW)
FAIF.......... Field Automated Intelligence File (AFM)
FAIF.......... First Army in the Field (SAUO)
FAIFE.......... Freedom of Access to Information and Freedom of Expression
FAIGX.......... Fidelity Advisor: Growth & Inc. Cl.T [*Mutual fund ticker symbol*] (SG)
FAII.......... Fellow of the Australian Insurance Institute (ODBW)
FAI In.......... FAI Insurances Ltd. [*Associated Press*] (SAG)
FAIL.......... Failing [*Motor vehicle violation code used in state of Maryland*] (MVRD)
FAIL.......... Failure
FAIL.......... Failure Group [*NASDAQ symbol*] (TTSB)
FAIL.......... Failure Group, Inc. [*NASDAQ symbol*] (SAG)
FAIL.......... FMC [*Flight Management Computer*] Fail (GAVI)
FAILCLEA.......... Federazione Autonoma Italiana Lavoratori Cemento Legno, Edilizia, ed Affini [*Workers in Cement, Wood, Construction, and Related Industries Federation*] [*Italy*] (EY)
FAILE.......... Federazione Autonoma Italiana Lavoratori Elettrici [*Electrical Workers Federation*] [*Italy*] (EY)
FailGrp.......... Failure Group, Inc. [*Associated Press*] (SAG)
FAIM.......... Fair Market, Inc. [*NASDAQ symbol*] (SG)
FAIM.......... Fellow, Academy of Internal Medicine (CMD)
FAIM.......... Fellow of the Australian Institute of Management (ODBW)
FAIM.......... Foundation for the Advancement of Innovative Medicine (ADWA)
FAIME.......... Foreign Affairs Information Management Effort [*Computer*] [*Department of State*]
FAIMME.......... Fellow of the American Institute of Mining and Metallurgical Engineers (SAUS)
FAIMS.......... Financial Accounting and Information Management System (SAUO)
FAIMS.......... Financial and Administrative Integrated Management System [*Department of Health and Human Services*] (GFGA)
FAIMX.......... Fairmont Fund [*Mutual fund ticker symbol*] (SG)
FAIN.......... First Article Inspection Notice [*NASA*] (SAA)
fain.......... functional air index number (SAUS)
FAIN/SR.......... First Article Inspection Notice Status Report [*NASA*] (SAA)
FAIO.......... Field Artillery Intelligence Officer [*Military*] (AABC)
FAIP.......... First Assignment Instructor Pilot (SAUO)
FAIPR.......... Fellow of the Australian Institute of Parks and Recreation
FA/IPT.......... First Article/Initial Production Testing [*Army's Combat System Test Activity*] (INF)
FAIR.......... Fabrication, Assembly, and Inspection Record [*NASA*] (NASA)
FAIR.......... Failure Analysis Information Retrieval (IAA)
FAIR.......... Fair Access Coalition on Testing (SEAT)
FAIR.......... Fair Access to Insurance Requirements [*Government insurance program*]
FAIR.......... Fair Access to Insurance Requirements Plan
FAIR.......... Fair and Impartial Random Selection [*System*] [*Military draft*]
FAIR.......... Fairing
FAIR.......... Fairness and Accuracy in Reporting (EA)
FAIR.......... Family Action Information and Rescue [*British*] (DI)
FAIR.......... Fans Against Indian Racism (EA)
FAIR.......... Fast Access Information Retrieval
FAIR.......... Fast Access to Insurance Requirement (PDAA)
FAIR.......... Federal Agriculture Improvement and Reform Act
FAIR.......... Federal Assistance Information Reporting
FAIR.......... Federation for American Immigration Reform (EA)
FAIR.......... Fighter, Attack, Intercept, Reconnaissance (ACAE)
FAIR.......... Financial Assistance for Independent Rehabilitation (SAUS)
FAIR.......... Firearms and Individual Rights [*A California organization*]
FAIR.......... First-Allied Integrated Republican Party (SAUO)
FAIR.......... Fisheries, Agriculture and Industrial Research (SAUS)
FAIR.......... Fleet Air [*Wing*]
FAIR.......... Fly-Along Infrared Program [*Army*] (RDA)
FAIR.......... Focus on Arms Information and Reassurance
FAIR.......... Food Animal Integrated Research (SAUO)
FAIR.......... Forest, Agriculture, Industry, and Research
FAIR.......... Forward Acquisition Infra Red (ACAE)
FAIR.......... Free Access to Insurance Requirements (SAUS)
FAIR.......... Free from Tax, Affordable, Insured Rewarding [*Savings certificate*] [*Savings and Loan Association*]
FAIR.......... Friends in America for Independence of Rhodesia (SAUO)
FAIR.......... Full Automatic Information Retrieval (SAUS)
FAIR.......... Functional Analysis Integration Review (SAUO)
FAIR.......... Fund for Appalachian Industrial Restraining
FAIR.......... Fund for Assuring an Independent Retirement (EA)
FAIR.......... Irene [*South Africa*] [*ICAO location identifier*] (ICLI)
FAIR.......... Renaissance Entertainment Corp. [*NASDAQ symbol*] (SAG)
FAIRA.......... Foundation for Aboriginal and Island Reserve Action (SAUO)
FAIRB.......... Fairbury, IL [*American Association of Railroads railroad junction routing code*]
Fairc.......... Fairchild Industries, Inc. [*Associated Press*] (SAG)
FAIRC.......... Faircross [*England*]
FairCm.......... Fairfield Communities, Inc. [*Associated Press*] (SAG)
FairCp.......... Fairchild Corp. [*Associated Press*] (SAG)
FAIRDEX.......... Fleet Air Defense Exercise [*Navy*] (NG)
FAIREC.......... Fruits Agro-Industrie Regions Chaudes [*Institut de Recherches sur les Fruits et Agrumes*] [*Database*]
FAIRECONRON.......... Fleet Air Reconnaissance Squadron

FAIRELM ...... Fleet Air Eastern Atlantic and Mediterranean (NATG)
Fair Empl Prac Cas ... Fair Employment Practices Cases (DLA)
FAIRF .... Fairfield, IL [*American Association of Railroads railroad junction routing code*]
Fairf .... Fairfield's Reports [*10-12 Maine*] [*A publication*] (DLA)
Fairfield ...... Fairfield's Reports [*10-12 Maine*] [*A publication*] (DLA)
Fairfield U ... Fairfield University (GAGS)
Fairf (ME) .... Fairfield's Reports [*10-12 Maine*] [*A publication*] (DLA)
Fairlsc .... Fair [*Isaac*] & Co. [*Associated Press*] (SAG)
Fairleigh Dickinson U ... Fairleigh Dickinson University (GAGS)
FAIRM .... Fairmont, MN [*American Association of Railroads railroad junction routing code*]
Fair M & D ... Fairbanks' Marriage and Divorce Laws of Massachusetts [*A publication*] (DLA)
FAIRS .... Failure Analysis Information Retrieval System (SAUS)
FAIRS .... Fair and Impartial Random Selection System (SAUS)
FAIRS .... Fairchild Automatic Intercept and Response System (MCD)
Fairs .... Fairchild Automatic Interceptor and Response System (SAUS)
FAIRS .... Federal Aviation Administration (SAUS)
FAIRS .... Federal Aviation Information Retrieval System
FAIRS .... Focal Plane Array Infrared Seeker (ACAE)
FAIRS .... Food and Agriculture Organization Agricultural Information Storage and RetrievalSystem [*Operated by FAO*] (NITA)
FAIRS .... Fully Automatic Information Retrievel System [*Computer science*] (EECA)
FAIRS .... Fully Automatic Information Storage and Retrieval System (SAUS)
FAIR Selection ... Fair and Impartial Random Selection (SAUS)
FAIRSHIPS ... Fleet Airships
FAIRSHIPWING ... Fleet Airship Wing
FAIRS System ... Fair and Impartial Random Selection System (SAUS)
FairTest .... National Center for Fair & Open Testing
Fair Tr .... Fair Trade Laws [*A publication*] (DLA)
FAIRTRANS ... First Available Air Transportation
FAIRW .... Renaissance Entmt Wrrt'A' [*NASDAQ symbol*] (TTSB)
FAIRWESTPAC ... Fleet Air Wing, Western Pacific Area
FAIRWG .... Fleet Air Wing (SAUS)
FAIRWING ... Fleet Air Wing
FAIRZ .... Renaissance Entmt Wrrt'B' [*NASDAQ symbol*] (TTSB)
FAIS .... Facility Alarm and Information System (SAUS)
FAIS .... Factory Automation Interconnection System (VLIE)
FAIS .... Federation d'Associations d'Ingenieurs et de Scientifiques [*Federation of Engineering and Scientific Associations*] [*Canada*] (EAIO)
FAIS .... Fellow of the Amalgamated Institute of Secretaries (SAUO)
FAIS .... Finnish Artificial Intelligence Society (VERA)
FAIS .... Force Air Intelligence Study [*Air Force*]
FAIS .... Foreign Affairs Information System [*Department of State*] (GFGA)
FAIS .... Foreign Affairs Interdepartmental Seminar [*Military*]
FAIS .... Isithebe [*South Africa*] [*ICAO location identifier*] (ICLI)
FAISME .... Fellow of the Australian Institute of Sales and Marketing Executives
FAISR .... File Archival Image Storage and Retrieval (ACAE)
FAISS-E .... FORSCOM [*Forces Command*] Automated Intelligence Support System, Enhan ced [*Army*] (DOMA)
FAIT .... Families Against Intimidation and Terror [*An association*]
FAIT .... First Aid Instruction Trainer (SAUS)
FAIT .... First-Aid Instructor Trainer [*Red Cross*]
FAIT .... First Article Inspection Tag [*NASA*] (SAA)
FAIT .... Foreign Affairs and International Trade (FOTI)
FAITE .... Final Acceptance Inspection Test Equipment (MCD)
FAITH .... Forming and Intelligently Testing Hypotheses (VLIE)
FAITS .... Facility Action Items Tracking System (SAUS)
FAIX .... Fairways Corp. [*Air carrier designation symbol*]
FAJ .... Fajardo [*Puerto Rico*] [*Airport symbol*] (OAG)
FAJ .... Fajardo, PR [*Location identifier*] [*FAA*] (FAAL)
FAJ .... Field Artillery Journal (SAUO)
FAJ .... Fiji Air Services Ltd. [*ICAO designator*] (FAAC)
FAJ .... Final Assembly Jig (SAUS)
FAJ .... Friends of Ann Jillian (EA)
FAJ .... Frontier Adjusters of America, Inc. [*AMEX symbol*] (SAG)
FAJ .... Fused Apophyseal Joint [*Medicine*] (MELL)
FAJB .... Johannesburg [*South Africa*] [*ICAO location identifier*] (ICLI)
FAJF .... Jagersfontein [*South Africa*] [*ICAO location identifier*] (ICLI)
FAJS .... Johannesburg/Jan Smuts [*South Africa*] [*ICAO location identifier*] (ICLI)
FAK .... Fidelity Advisor Korea Fund [*NYSE symbol*] (SAG)
FAK .... File Access Key (SAUS)
FAK .... filtration artificial kidney (SAUS)
FAK .... Financial AirExpress [*ICAO designator*] (FAAC)
FAK .... Flat Rock, VA [*Location identifier*] [*FAA*] (FAAL)
FAK .... Floating Arm Keyboard (MELL)
FAK .... Fly-Away Kit (MCD)
FAK .... Focal Adhesion Kinase [*An enzyme*]
FAK .... Fondation Aga Khan [*Aga Khan Foundation*] (EAIO)
FAK .... Freight, All Kinds [*Railroad*]
fak .... freights all kinds (SAUS)
FAK .... Full-Aperture Kicker [*Synchrotron*]
FAKA .... Karibib [*Namibia*] [*ICAO location identifier*] (ICLI)
FAKB .... Karasburg [*Namibia*] [*ICAO location identifier*] (ICLI)
FAKD .... Klerksdorp [*South Africa*] [*ICAO location identifier*] (ICLI)
FAKFWSO .... Federation of Australian Kung Fu and Wun Shu Organisations
FAKG .... Komati Power Station/Kragsentrale [*South Africa*] [*ICAO location identifier*] (ICLI)
FAKH .... Kenhardt [*South Africa*] [*ICAO location identifier*] (ICLI)
FAKJ .... Kamanjab [*Namibia*] [*ICAO location identifier*] (ICLI)
FAKK .... Kakamas [*South Africa*] [*ICAO location identifier*] (ICLI)
FAKL .... Kriel [*South Africa*] [*ICAO location identifier*] (ICLI)
FAKM .... Kimberley/B. J. Vorster [*South Africa*] [*ICAO location identifier*] (ICLI)
FAKN .... Klippan Control Reporting Point [*South Africa*] [*ICAO location identifier*] (ICLI)
FA Korea ..... Fidelity Advisor Korea Fund [*Associated Press*] (SAG)
FAKP .... Komatipoort [*South Africa*] [*ICAO location identifier*] (ICLI)
fak-pak .... freight all kinds (SAUS)
FAKR .... Krugersdorp [*South Africa*] [*ICAO location identifier*] (ICLI)
FAKS .... File Access Keys (NITA)
FAKS .... Kroonstad [*South Africa*] [*ICAO location identifier*] (ICLI)
FAKT .... Keetmanshoop/J. G. H. Van Der Wath [*Namibia*] [*ICAO location identifier*] (ICLI)
FAKU .... Kuruman [*South Africa*] [*ICAO location identifier*] (ICLI)
FAKX .... Khorixas [*Namibia*] [*ICAO location identifier*] (ICLI)
FAKZ .... Kleinsee [*South Africa*] [*ICAO location identifier*] (ICLI)
FAL .... Convention on Facilitation of International Maritime Traffic (SAUO)
FAL .... Facilation of international air transport (SAUS)
FAL .... Facilitation Committee (SAUO)
FAL .... Facilitation Division (SAUO)
FAL .... Facilitation of International Air Transport [*Aviation*]
FAL .... Facilities Laboratory [*National Center for Atmospheric Research*]
FAL .... Faculty of Arts and Letters (SAUS)
FAL .... Failure Analysis Laboratory (MCD)
FAL .... Falcon Cable Sys L.P. [*AMEX symbol*] (TTSB)
FAL .... Falcon Cable Systems Ltd. [*AMEX symbol*] (SPSG)
FAL .... Fall River Gas [*AMEX symbol*] (SG)
Fal .... Falmouth (SAUS)
FAL .... Falstaff Brewing Corporation (SAUO)
F a L .... Fathers-at-Large (SAUS)
FAL .... Federal Research Institute of Agriculture (SAUS)
FAL .... File Access Listener
FAL .... Financial Analysis Language [*Computer science*] (MCD)
FAL .... Finite Automation Language [*Computer science*]
FAL .... Finite Automaton Language (SAUO)
FAL .... First Approach and Landing [*Test*] [*NASA*] (NASA)
FAL .... flexible automated line (SAUS)
FAL .... Food and Agricultural Legislation [*A publication*]
FAL .... Foodland Associates Ltd.
FAL .... Forces Armees Laotiannes [*Federated Army of Laos*]
FAL .... Fractional Allelic Loss [*Genetics*]
FAL .... France Amerique Latine [*France Latin America*] [*An association*] (EAIO)
FAL .... Frente Anti-Imperialista de Liberacion [*Peruvian guerrilla group*] (EY)
FAL .... Frequency Allocation List
FAL .... Friendship Air Alaska [*ICAO designator*] (FAAC)
FAL .... Frontier Airlines, Inc. [*Air carrier designation symbol*]
FAL .... Fuerzas Armadas de Liberacio [*Argentina*]
FAL .... Function of Astronaut Location [*NASA*] (KSC)
FAL .... Roma, TX [*Location identifier*] [*FAA*] (FAAL)
FALA .... Federation of Asian Library Associations (SAUS)
FALA .... First Amendment Lawyers Association (EA)
FALA .... Fund for Animals Ltd. Australia
FALA .... Lanseria [*South Africa*] [*ICAO location identifier*] (ICLI)
FALANA .... Fellows and Associates of the Library Association in North America (SAUO)
FALB .... Ladybrand [*South Africa*] [*ICAO location identifier*] (ICLI)
FAlban .... First Albany Companies, Inc. [*Associated Press*] (SAG)
FALC .... Armed Forces for the Liberation of Cabinda [*Angola*] (PD)
Falc .... Falconer's Scotch Court of Session Cases [*1744-51*] [*A publication*] (DLA)
FALC .... Final Assembly Logistics Control (VLIE)
FALC .... Forward Acting Linear Combiner (IAA)
FALC .... Lime Acres [*South Africa*] [*ICAO location identifier*] (ICLI)
Falc & F ...... Falconer and Fitzherbert's English Election Cases [*1835-39*] [*A publication*] (DLA)
Falc & Fitz ... Falconer and Fitzherbert's English Election Cases [*1835-39*] [*A publication*] (DLA)
FalcCbl .... Falcon Cable Systems Ltd. [*Associated Press*] (SAG)
Falc Co Cts ... Falconer's English County Court Cases [*A publication*] (DLA)
FalcDr .... Falcon Drilling Co. [*Associated Press*] (SAG)
Falc Marine Dict ... Falconer's Marine Dictionary [*A publication*] (DLA)
FalcnPr .... Falcon Products, Inc. [*Associated Press*] (SAG)
FALCON .... Fission Activated LASER Concept [*Sandia National Laboratories*]
FALCON .... Frequency-Agile Low Coverage Netted radar (SAUS)
FALCON .... Fuel / Air Line Charge Ordnance Neutraliser (SAUS)
FALCON .... Fuel-Air Line Charge Ordnance Neutralizer (SEWL)
FalconBP ...... Falcon Building Products, Inc. [*Associated Press*] (SAG)
FalconDr .... Falcon Drilling Co. [*Associated Press*] (SAG)
FalconPd .... Falcon Products, Inc. [*Associated Press*] (SAG)
FALCRI .... Federazione Autonoma Lavoratori Casse di Risparmio Italiane [*Savings Banks Workers Federation*] [*Italy*] (EY)
FALD .... Fahrenheit Agency Liaison Division (SAUO)
FALD .... Finnish American League for Democracy (EA)
FALDX .... Federated American Leaders Cl.A [*Mutual fund ticker symbol*] (SG)
FALG .... Fowl Antimouse Lymphocyte Globulin [*Immunochemistry*]
FALH .... Lohathla [*South Africa*] [*ICAO location identifier*] (ICLI)
FALI .... Lichtenburg [*South Africa*] [*ICAO location identifier*] (ICLI)
FALIA .... Fellow of the Australian Library and Information Association
FALJC .... Federal Administrative Law Judges Conference (EA)
Falk Cur .... Falkland Current (SAUS)
FALK I .... Falkland Islands (ROG)
FALK IS .... Falkland Islands (WDAA)
Falk Isl .... Falkland Islands (SAUS)
Falklands ...... Falkland Islands and Dependencies (SAUS)
FALKLD I ...... Falkland Islands (ROG)
FALL .... Fall [*Postal Service standard*] (OPSA)

fall .... fallacy (SAUS)
FALL .... Fallopian [*Gynecology*] (DAVI)
FALL .... Federal Atlantic Lake Lines (SAUS)
FALL .... Lydenburg [*South Africa*] [*ICAO location identifier*] (ICLI)
FALLEX .... Fall [*Autumn*] Exercise [*Military*] [*NATO*] (NATG)
fallex .... fall exercises (SAUS)
FAllian .... First Alliance Bancorp, Inc. [*Associated Press*] (SAG)
FALLINE .... Fedreal Atlantic-Lakes Line [*Steamship*] (MHDW)
FAlliPB .... First Alliance Premier Bancshares, Inc. [*Associated Press*] (SAG)
FALLS .... Falls [*Commonly used*] (OPSA)
Fall Warn .... Fallout Warning (SAUS)
FALM .... Falmouth [*Municipal borough in England*]
FALM .... Florida Association of Livestock Markets (SRA)
FALM .... Loraine Mine [*South Africa*] [*ICAO location identifier*] (ICLI)
FalmBk .... Falmouth Co-Operative Bank [*Associated Press*] (SAG)
FALN .... Fuerzas Armadas de Liberacion Nacional [*Armed Forces of National Liberation*] [*Venezuela*] (PD)
FALN .... Fuerzas Armadas de Liberacion Nacional Puertorriquena [*Armed Forces of Puerto Rican National Liberation*] (EA)
FALO .... Louis Trichardt [*South Africa*] [*ICAO location identifier*] (ICLI)
FALO-ALM .... Free African Liberation Organization-African Liberation Movement (EA)
FALOP .... Forward Area Limited Observing Program (MCD)
FALP .... Fluoro-Assisted Lumbar Puncture [*Medicine*] (MELL)
FALPA .... Fellow of the Incorporated Society of Auctioneers and Landed Property Agents [*British*]
FAIPHH .... Fellow of the Royal Institute of Public Health and Hygiene (SAUS)
FALPRO .... UNCTAD/ECE Special Programme for Trade Facilitation (SAUO)
FALR .... Florida Administrative Law Reports [*A publication*]
FALS .... Familial Amyotrophic Lateral Sclerosis [*Medicine*]
FALS .... Ford Authorized Leasing System (SAUS)
FALS .... Foreign Area and Language Study
FALS .... Forward Angle Light Scattering [*Analytical biochemistry*]
FALSET .... Falsetto [*Music*]
FALSIF .... Falsification (SAUS)
FALSTAF .... Forward Area LASER Systems - Tactical and Fiscal [*Military*]
FALT .... FADAC [*Field Artillery Digital Automatic Computer*] Automatic Logic Tester
FALT .... Field Artillery Logic Tester [*Army*] (AABC)
FALT .... Louis Trichardt [*South Africa*] [*ICAO location identifier*] (ICLI)
FALTRAN .... FORTRAN [*Formula Translating System*]-to-ALGOL Translator [*Algorithmic language*] [*Computer science*] (IEEE)
FALU .... Florida Association of Life Underwriters (SRA)
FALW .... Family of Air-Launched Weapons (SAUO)
FALW .... Forward Area LASER Weapon
FALW .... Langebaanweg [*South Africa*] [*ICAO location identifier*] (ICLI)
FALW-D .... Forward Area Laser Weapon-Demonstration (ACAE)
FALY .... Ladysmith [*South Africa*] [*ICAO location identifier*] (ICLI)
FALZ .... Luderitz [*Namibia*] [*ICAO location identifier*] (ICLI)
Fam .... Epistulae ad Familiares [*of Cicero*] [*Classical studies*] (OCD)
FAM .... Facilities Analysis Model [*Computer science*]
FAM .... Facility assessment methodology (SAUS)
FAM .... Factory Automation Model (VLIE)
FAM .... False Alarm Malicious (WDAA)
Fam .... Famagusta (SAUS)
FAM .... Familiar (AABC)
fam .... Familiar (SHCU)
FAM .... Familiarization (NAKS)
Fam .... familiy (SAUS)
FAM .... Family (AFM)
Fam .... Family (DIAR)
fam .... Family (GEAB)
FAM .... Family Channel (ADWA)
Fam .... Family Division, High Court, England and Wales (DLA)
FAM .... Family Finance Corporation (SAUO)
FAM .... Family of Frequencies [*Aviation*] (DA)
FAM .... Famous (WGA)
FAM .... Farmington, MO [*Location identifier*] [*FAA*] (FAAL)
FAM .... Fast Access Memory [*Computer science*] (HGAA)
FAM .... Fast Aerial Mine [*British military*] (DMA)
FAM .... Fast Air Mine (SAUS)
FAM .... Fast Auxiliary Memory (IEEE)
FAM .... Fathom Oceanology Ltd. [*Toronto Stock Exchange symbol*]
FAM .... Federal Air Mail (SAUS)
FAM .... Federal Air Marshal (SAUS)
FAM .... Federal Arab Maritime Company (SAUO)
FAM .... Federation of Apparel Manufacturers (EA)
FAM .... Feed Assembly Modification
FAM .... Fermentation Analysis Module (SAUS)
FAM .... Ferrite-Air-Metal (SAUS)
FAM .... Fiber Alarm Modem (SEWL)
FAM .... Fibrous Aerosol Monitor (SAUS)
FAM .... Field Activity Missile (MCD)
FAM .... Field Alarm Module (SAUS)
FAM .... Field Artillery Missile
FAM .... Fighter Attack Manoeuvring (SAUS)
FAM .... File Access Manager
FAM .... File Access Method (SAUS)
FAM .... Filter Assembly Machine (MCD)
FAM .... Final Address Message [*Telecommunications*] (TEL)
FAM .... Fire Apparatus Manufacturers Association (SAUO)
FAM .... First America-Tennessee [*NYSE symbol*]
FAM .... Flexible Attrition Model (SAUS)
FAM .... Flight Acceptance Meeting (SAA)
FAM .... Floating Add Magnitude [*Computer science*] (IAA)
FAM .... Fluorouracil, Adriamycin, Mitomycin [*Antineoplastic drug regimen*]
FAM .... Fluorouracil, Adriamycin, Mitomycin-C [*Antineoplastic drug*] (CDI)
FAM .... Football Association of Malaysia (SAUO)
FAM .... Foreign Affairs Manual (SAUS)
FAM .... Foreign Air Mail
fam .... foreign air mall (SAUS)
FAM .... forward address message (SAUS)
FAM .... forward air mail (SAUS)
FAM .... Free and Accepted Masons
fam .... Free at Mill (EBF)
FAM .... Free at Mill [*Business term*]
FAM .... Free Austrian Mission (or Movement) (SAUO)
FAM .... Free Austrian Movement (SAUO)
FAM .... frequency agile modem (SAUS)
FAM .... Frequency Allocation Multiplex (IAA)
FAM .... Frequency Amplitude Modulation (IAA)
FAM .... Frequency Assignment Model (SAA)
FAM .... Frequency Modulation and Advanced Memory [*Yamaha International Corp.*]
FAM .... Friable Asbestos-Containing Material (GNE)
FAM .... Friable Asbestos Material (SAUS)
FAM .... Fuel Air Munition (SAUS)
FAM .... Full Army Mobilization War Reserves (AABC)
FAM .... Fumigacion Aerea Andalusa SA [*Spain*] [*ICAO designator*] (FAAC)
FAM .... Fuzzy Associative Memory (VLIE)
FAM .... International Family Entertainment, Inc. [*NYSE symbol*] (SPSG)
FAM .... Intl Family Entert'nt 'B' [*NYSE symbol*] (TTSB)
FAMA .... Federal Agricultural (or Agriculture) Marketing Authority (SAUO)
FAMA .... Federal Association of Management Analysts [*Defunct*]
FAMA .... Fellow of the American Medical Association
FAMA .... Fire Apparatus Manufacturers Association [*Defunct*] (EA)
FAMA .... Flota Aerea Mercane Argentina
FAMA .... Fluorescent Antibody-Membrane Antigen [*Immunochemistry*]
FAMA .... Fondation pour l'Assistance Mutuelle en Afrique au Sud du Sahara [*Foundation for Mutual Assistance in Africa South of the Sahara*]
FAMA .... Forward Airhead Maintenance Area [*Military*] [*British*]
FAMA .... Matatiele [*South Africa*] [*ICAO location identifier*] (ICLI)
FAMAE .... Following Amendment Authorized Effective (FAAC)
FAMAS .... Field Artillery Meteorological Acquisition System (MCD)
FAMAS .... Financial Analysis and Management System (SAUS)
FAMAS .... Financial Analysis and Planning System (SAUO)
FAMAS .... Financial And Management Accounting System (SAUS)
FAMAS .... Flutter and Matrix Algebra System [*Computer science*]
FAMA-Test .... fluorescent antibody against membrane antigen (SAUS)
FamB .... Family Bargain Corp. [*Associated Press*] (SAG)
F Amb .... Field Ambulance [*British military*] (DMA)
FAMB .... Friends of the American Museum in Britain (EA)
FAMB .... Middelburg [*South Africa*] [*ICAO location identifier*] (ICLI)
FamBarg .... Family Bargain Corp. [*Associated Press*] (SAG)
FamBc .... Family Bancorp [*Associated Press*] (SAG)
FAMBSA .... Farmers and Manufacturers Beet Sugar Association
FAMC .... Federal Agricultural Mortgage Corporation (ADWA)
FAMC .... Fitzsimons Army Medical Center (AABC)
FAM-C .... Fluorouracil, Adriamycin, Mitomycin-C [*Antineoplastic drug regimen*] (DAVI)
FAMC .... Foreign Affairs Manual Circular [*Department of State*] [*A publication*]
FAMC .... Foreign Area Materials Center (SAUO)
FAMC .... Middelburg [*South Africa*] [*ICAO location identifier*] (ICLI)
Fam Cas Cir Ev ... Famous Cases of Circumstantial Evidence, by Phillips [*A publication*] (DLA)
Fam Cir .... Family Circle (SAUS)
FAMCK .... Federal Agricultural Mtge'C' [*NASDAQ symbol*] (TTSB)
FAMCO .... Federal Arab Maritime Company (SAUO)
Fam Code .... Family Code (SAUS)
FAMCS .... Field Army Multichannel Communications System (SAUO)
FAMD .... Malamala [*South Africa*] [*ICAO location identifier*] (ICLI)
FAMDATA .... Famulus Data Preparation Program (SAUS)
FAMDD .... Functional Area Management and Development Division [*US Army Personnel Command*] (RDA)
FamDlr .... Family Dollar Stores [*Associated Press*] (SAG)
fam doc .... Family Doctor (AAMN)
Fam Doc .... Family Doctor [*Medicine*] (EDAA)
FamDv .... Famous Daves of America, Inc. [*Associated Press*] (SAG)
FAME .... Farmers Allied Meat Enterprises (SAUS)
FAME .... Farmers Allied Meat Enterprises Cooperative (SAUS)
FAME .... Fatty Acid Methyl Ester [*Biochemistry*]
FAME .... Fellowship of Associates of Medical Evangelism (EA)
FAME .... Ferroacoustic Memory [*Electronics*] (IAA)
FAME .... Field Activity Missile Engineering (MCD)
FAME .... Filing and mailing electronically (SAUS)
FAME .... Final Approach Monitoring Equipment [*Aviation*]
FAME .... Financial Access Made Easy (SAUS)
fame .... financial accounting made easy (SAUS)
FAME .... Financial, Accounting Marketing Exercise (PDAA)
FAME .... Financial Analysis of Management Effectiveness [*Department of Agriculture*]
FAME .... Financial Assistance for Mineral Exploration (SAUS)
FAME .... Fine Arts Magnet Program (SAUS)
FAME .... [*The*] Flamemaster Corp. [*NASDAQ symbol*] (NQ)
FAME .... Flexible Automated Manufacturing Environment (VLIE)
FAME .... Florida Area Mesoscale Experiment (SAUS)
FAME .... Florida Association for Media in Education (SRA)
FAME .... Florida Association of Marine Explorers
FAME .... Fluorouracil, Adriamycin, MeCCNU [*Semustine*] [*Antineoplastic drug regimen*]

FAME .... Fluorouracil, Adriamycin, Methyl-CCNU [*Antineoplastic drug*] (CDI)
FAME .... Forecasts, Appraisals and Management Evaluations (SAUO)
FAME .... Forest Assessment and Monitoring Environment (SAUO)
FAME .... Formatting and Multiplexing Equipment (SAUS)
FAME .... FORMEX Applied to Multilingualism in Europe (SAUS)
FAME .... Framework for Achieving Managerial Excellence (EPA)
FAME .... Freeway and Arterial Management Effort [*FHWA*] (TAG)
FAME .... Frequency Assignment Management Equipment (SAUS)
FAME .... Full-sky Astrometric Mapping Explorer (SAUS)
FAME .... Fund for the Advancement of Music Education [*Defunct*] (EA)
FAME .... Fusion applications & market evaluation (SAUS)
FAME .... Future American Magical Entertainers
FAME .... Marion Island [*South Africa*] [*ICAO location identifier*] (ICLI)
FAMECE .... Family of Military Engineer Construction Equipment
FAMECE/UET... Family of Military Engineer Construction Equipment/Universal Engineer Tractor (RDA)
FAMEM .... Federation of Associations of Mining Equipment Manufacturers (MHDB)
FAMEME ..... Fellow of the Association of Mining Electrical and Mechanical Engineers (ODA)
FAMET .... Fuerzas Aeromoviles del Ejercito de Tierra (SAUS)
FAMEX .... Familiarization Exercise [*Military*] (NVT)
FAMF .... Floating Aircraft Maintenance Facility [*Army*] (AABC)
FAMFIRE ...... Familiarization Firing (DNAB)
FAMG .... Field Artillery Missile Group (SAUO)
FAMG .... Margate [*South Africa*] [*ICAO location identifier*] (ICLI)
FamGolf .... Family Golf Centers, Inc. [*Associated Press*] (SAG)
FAMH .... Maltahohe [*Namibia*] [*ICAO location identifier*] (ICLI)
FAMHEM ...... Federation of Associations of Materials Handling Equipment Manufacturers (SAUO)
fam hist .... Family History [*Medicine*] (EDAA)
FAmHlt .... First American Health Concepts [*Associated Press*] (SAG)
FAMHM .... Federation of Associations of Materials Handling Manufacturers (SAUO)
FAMHSGASSIGNSY... Family Housing Assignment Application System [*Military*] (DNAB)
FAMHSGRQMTSURVSYS... Family Housing Requirements Survey Record System (DNAB)
FAMHSGRQMTSUSY... Family Housing Requirements Survey Record System (SAUO)
FAMHW .... Federation of Associations of Mental Health Workers [*British*] (BI)
FAMI .... Australian Family and Society Abstracts (SAUO)
FAMI .... Fellow of the Australian Marketing Institute (ODBW)
FAMI .... Marble Hall [*South Africa*] [*ICAO location identifier*] (ICLI)
FAMICA .... Federal Agricultural Mtge'A' [*NASDAQ symbol*] (TTSB)
FAMID .... Field Artillery Mid-Range Concepts and Force Design Study (SAUO)
F Am IEE ..... Fellow of American Institute of Electrical Engineers (SAUS)
F Am IEE ..... Fellow of the American Institute of Electrical Engineers
Families of SMA... Families of Spinal Muscular Atrophy (NRGU)
Family Econ Nutrition Rev... Family Economics and Nutrition Review [*A publication*] (JLIT)
Family Econ Rev... Family Economics Review [*A publication*] (JLIT)
Family Law Rev... Family Law Review [*A publication*]
FAMINE .... Families Against Meat in New England [*Worcester, Massachusetts, group protesting high cost of food, 1973*]
Fam in Soc... Families in Society [*A publication*] (BRI)
FAMIS .... Factory Management Information System [*British*] (NITA)
FAMIS .... Family Assistance Management Information System [*Department of Health and Human Services*] (GFGA)
FAMIS .... Financial Accounting and Management Information System (SAUS)
FAMIS .... Financial and Management Information System [*Naval Oceanographic Office*]
FAMIS .... Full Aircraft Management/Inertial System (SAUO)
FAMK .... Mafikeng [*South Africa*] [*ICAO location identifier*] (ICLI)
FAML .... Mariental [*Namibia*] [*ICAO location identifier*] (ICLI)
FAMLIES ...... Financial Support, Advocacy, Medical Management, Love, Information, Education, Structural Support (MEDA)
Fam LQ .... Family Law Quarterly [*A publication*]
Fam L R ...... Family Law Reports [*A publication*] (SAFN)
FAMIS .... Financial And Management Information System (SAUS)
FAMM .... Families Against Mandatory Minimums Foundation (EA)
FAMM .... Fiducial Automated Measuring Machine [*Defunct*]
FAMM .... Mmabatho International [*South Africa*] [*ICAO location identifier*] (ICLI)
FAMMe .... Fluorouracil, Adriamycin, Mitomycin C, MeCCNU [*Semustine*] [*Antineoplastic drug regimen*]
Fam-Med ..... Family Medicine (SAUS)
FAMMM .... Familial Atypical Multiple Mole Melanoma [*Oncology*]
FAMMM-Syndrom... familial atypical multiple mole melanoma (SAUS)
FAMMO .... Full Ammo [*Navy*] (DOMA)
FAMMS .... Financial and Material Management System (SAA)
FAMMS .... Fixed Allowance Management Monitoring System (MCD)
FAMN .... Malalane [*South Africa*] [*ICAO location identifier*] (ICLI)
fam nov .... Familia Nova [*New Family*] [*Biology*]
FAmNucSoc ... Fellow of the American Nuclear Society (ODA)
FAMNZ .... Fellow of the Arts Galleries and Museum Association of New Zealand (SAUO)
FAMNZ .... Fellow of the Arts Galleries and Museums Association of New Zealand (SAUO)
FAMO .... Forward Airfield Maintenance Organization
FAMO .... Mossel Bay/Baai [*South Africa*] [*ICAO location identifier*] (ICLI)
FAMOS .... Fast Multitasking Operating System [*MVT Microcomputer Systems, Inc.*]
FAMOS .... Fleet Application of Meteorological Observations from Satellites (IEEE)
FAMOS .... Flight Acceleration Monitor Only System (NASA)
FAMOS .... Floating Avalanche Injection MOS (SAUS)
FAMOS .... Floating-Gate Avalanche-Injection Metal-Oxide Semiconductor [*Computer science*]
FAMOS .... floating gate avalanche injection metal oxide semiconductor (SAUS)
FAMOS .... Floating Gate Avalanche MOS (SAUS)
FAMOS-FET... floating-gate avalanche-injection MOSFET (SAUS)
FAMOSS ...... Fiberscopic Apparatus for Measurement of Surface Strain (SAUS)
FAMOST ...... Floating-Gate Avalanche-Injection Metal-Oxide Silicon Transistor (IAA)
F/A Motor .... Fully Accessible Motor (SAUS)
FAMOUS ...... File Access Maintenance Output Universal System (SAUS)
FAMOUS ...... Franco-American Mid-Ocean Undersea Study (SAUO)
FAMOUS ...... French-American Mid-Ocean Undersea Study [*Joint undersea program*]
FAMP .... Ferrite Aperture Memory Plate (VLIE)
FAMP .... Fire Alarm Monitoring Panel (IEEE)
FAMP .... Foreign Army Material Production (MCD)
FAMP .... Frontier Armed and Mounted Police [*British government*]
FAMP .... Mpacha [*Namibia*] [*ICAO location identifier*] (ICLI)
FAMPA .... Ferro Alloys and Metals Producers Association [*British*] (DBA)
FAM PER PAR... Familial Periodic Paralysis [*Medicine*] (BABM)
Fam per par... Familial Periodic Paralysis [*Neurology*] (DAVI)
fam per para... familial periodic paralysis (SAUS)
Fam Per Paralysis... Familial Periodic Paralysis (SAUS)
fam phys ...... Family Physician (CPH)
Fam Phys ..... Family Physician [*Medicine*] (EDAA)
FAMPR .... Feature Assembly Manufacturing Process Record (VLIE)
FAMR .... Family Resources
FAMR .... Mariepskop [*South Africa*] [*ICAO location identifier*] (ICLI)
FAMRA .... Fleet Air Mediterranean Repair Area (MCD)
FAMRC .... Florida Agricultural Market Research Center (SAUO)
Fam Relat ... Family Relations [*A publication*] (BRI)
famrm .... Family Room (REAL)
Fam RZ .... Zeitschrift fuer das Gesamte Familienrecht [*German*] [*A publication*] (DLA)
FAMS .... Failure Analysis of Material Systems (MCD)
FAMS .... Family of Anti-air Missile Systems (SAUS)
FAMS .... Farfield Acoustic Measuring System (KSC)
FAMS .... Fellow of the Ancient Monuments Society [*British*]
FAMS .... Fellow of the Association of Medical Secretaries, Practice Administrators, and Receptionists [*British*] (DBQ)
FAMS .... Fellow of the Indian Academy of Medical Sciences (SAUO)
FAMS .... Fellow of the Royal Microscopical Society (SAUO)
FAMS .... Field Army Messenger Service (AABC)
FAMS .... Field Artillery Missile System (RDA)
FAMS .... Field Artillery Mission Support (SAUO)
FAMS .... Field Automatic Message Switch (SAUS)
FAMS .... Fine Attitude Measurement System (ACAE)
FAMS .... Fire alarm monitoring specialist (SAUS)
FAMS .... First Article Master Schedule (MCD)
FAMS .... Flexible Automated Modelling and Scheduling (VLIE)
FAM-S .... Fluorouracil, Adriamycin (Doxorubicin), Mitomycin C, and Streptozotocin [*Antineoplastic drug regimen*]
FAMS .... Ford Academy of Manufacturing Science (SAUO)
FAMS .... Forecasting and Modeling System [*Computer science*] (BUR)
FAMS .... Forward Armored Mortar System (MCD)
FAMS .... Foundation for Advances in Medicine and Science (EA)
FAMS .... Free-Agent Market Simulator [*Computer programmed to calculate the market value of free agents in the National Basketball Association*]
FAMS .... Fuels Automated Management System [*Air Force*] (GFGA)
FAMS .... Functional Assessment of Multiple Sclerosis (SAUS)
FAMS .... Messina [*South Africa*] [*ICAO location identifier*] (ICLI)
FAMSA .... Funeral and Memorial Societies of America (NTPA)
FAmSCE .... Fellow of the American Society of Civil Engineers
FAMSCO ...... First Article Master Scheduling Committee (SAUO)
FAMSEG ...... Field Artillery Missile Systems Evaluation Group (RDA)
FAMSF .... Fine Arts Museum of San Francisco (SAUO)
FAMSIM .... Family of Automated Simulation (SAUO)
FAMSIM .... Family of Battle Simulators [*Army*]
FAMSIM .... Family of Simulations [*Computer science*] [*Army*] (RDA)
FA Msl .... Field Artillery Missile (SAUS)
FAMSL .... Fleet Aviation Material Support List [*Navy*] (AFIT)
FAMSNUB ..... Frequencies and Mode Shapes of Non-Uniform Beams (SAUS)
FAMSNUB ..... Frequencies and Mode-Shapes of Non-Union Beams (PDAA)
FamStk .... Family Steak Houses of Florida, Inc. [*Associated Press*] (SAG)
FAMSY .... Federation of Australian Muslim Students and Youth
FAMT .... Federation of Associations of Medical Technology [*British*] (DBA)
FAM-T .... Fluorouracil, Doxorubicin [*Adriamycin*], Mitomycin, Triazinate [*Antineoplastic drug regimen*]
FAMT .... Fully Automatic Machine Translation (VLIE)
FAMT .... Meyerton [*South Africa*] [*ICAO location identifier*] (ICLI)
FAMTIS .... Field Army Mapping and Terrain Information System (SAUO)
FAMTO .... First Aid Mechanical Transport Outfit [*A vehicle standard pack for immediate repairs*] [*Military*] [*British*]
FAMTOS ...... First Aid Mechanical Transport Outfits (SAUS)
FAMU .... Fleet Aircraft Maintenance Unit
FAMU .... Florida Agricultural and Mechanical University [*Tallahasse, FL*]
FAMU .... Fuel Additive Mixture Unit
FAMUS .... French-American Undersea Study (SAUS)
FAMWA .... Fellow, American Medical Writers' Association (CMD)
FAMY .... Family (ROG)
FAMY .... Malmesbury [*South Africa*] [*ICAO location identifier*] (ICLI)
FAMZ .... Msauli [*South Africa*] [*ICAO location identifier*] (ICLI)
FAN .... Family Area Network (SAUO)

FAN............. Fanatic (GOBB)
fan............. Fanatic (WDMC)
FAN............. Fanfare Horns [*Automotive engineering*]
fan............. Fang [*MARC language code*] [*Library of Congress*] (LCCP)
FAN............. Fanning Island [*Line Islands*] [*Seismograph station code, US Geological Survey*] [*Closed*] (SEIS)
fan............. fantasia (SAUS)
FAN............. Fantasy (SAUS)
FAN............. Farsund [*Norway*] [*Airport symbol*] (OAG)
FAN............. Fetal Alcohol Network (ADWA)
FAN............. Fighter Automatic Navigator
FAN............. Fixed Account Number (EPA)
FAN............. Flaming Arrow Net (SAUO)
FAN............. Food Allergy Network (SAUO)
FAN............. Forces Armees Neutralistes [*Neutralist Armed Forces*] [*Laos*]
FAN............. Forward Air Navigator (SAUO)
FAN............. Free Amino Nitrogen (PDAA)
FAN............. Frente de Avance Nacional [*National Advancement Front*] [*Guatemala*] [*Political party*]
FAN............. Fuchsin, Amido Black, and Naphthol Yellow [*Medicine*] (MAE)
FAN............. Functional Area Network (SAUO)
FAN............. Tauern Air Gesellschaft GmbH [*Austria*] [*ICAO designator*] (FAAC)
FAN 1......... frame analyzing detaction zone (SAUS)
FANA.......... Fan Association of North America (EA)
FANA.......... Federation of Australian Nurserymens Associations (SAUS)
FANA.......... Fellow of the American Neurological Association
FANA.......... Fluorescent Antinuclear Antibody Test [*Serology*]
FANA.......... Forex Association of North America (EA)
FANA.......... Futon Association of North America (EA)
FANA.......... Namatoni [*Namibia*] [*ICAO location identifier*] (ICLI)
FANAF........ Federation des Societes d'Assurances de Droit National Africains [*Federation of African National Insurance Companies*] [*Dakar, Senegal*] (EAIO)
FANC.......... First Aid Nursing Yeomanry (SAUO)
FANC.......... Newcastle [*South Africa*] [*ICAO location identifier*] (ICLI)
FANCAP....... Fluids, Aeration, Nutrition, Communication, Activity, and Pain [*Medicine*]
FANCAS....... Fluids, Aeration, Nutrition, Communication, Activity, and Stimulation [*Medicine*]
FAND.......... Fan-in Determined (SAUS)
F & A.......... February and August [*Denotes semiannual payments of interest or dividends in these months*] [*Business term*]
F & A.......... Finance and Accountability (SAUS)
F & A.......... Finance and Accounting
F & A.......... Finance and Administration (SAUS)
F & A.......... Finance and Audit Committee [*American Library Association*]
f & a.......... fire and allied (SAUS)
F & A.......... Fire and Allied Lines [*Insurance*]
f and a......... Fore and Aft (ADWA)
F & A.......... Fore and Aft
F & A.......... Free and Accepted [*Freemasonry*] (ROG)
F & ABR....... Food and Agriculture Branch [*US Military Government, Germany*]
F & ACS....... Fuel and Altitude Control System (DWSG)
F & AM........ Free and Accepted Masons
F&AO.......... Finance & Accounting Officer (SAUO)
F&AP.......... Fire and Allied Perils [*Insurance*] (MARI)
F & B.......... Fill and Bleed (SAA)
F & B.......... Fire and Bilge
F & B.......... Food and Beverage
F & B.......... Fumigation and Bath [*Military*]
F&B............ Royal Forest and Bird Protection Society Inc. (SAUO)
F&B Co........ Fumigation and Bath Company (SAUO)
F & C.......... Family and Commercial [*Hotels*] [*British*] (ROG)
F & C.......... Fever and Chills (MELL)
F & C.......... Fire and Casualty (WDAA)
f & c........... fish and chips (SAUS)
F & C.......... Foam and Condom [*Birth control methods*] (DAVI)
F&C............ Frankfort and Cincinnati Railroad (SAUO)
F and C........ Free and Clear (SAUS)
F & C.......... Full and Change (ADA)
F & CC......... Fire and Casualty Cases [*Commerce Clearing House*] [*A publication*] (DLA)
F & CD......... Failure and Consumption Data (AAG)
F & CD/IR..... Failure and Consumption Data Inspection Report (AAG)
F & CI.......... Food and Container Institute
F&CO.......... Foreign and Commonwealth Office (SAUO)
F&CT/PIT..... Fuel and control technology/postirradiation tests (SAUS)
F & D.......... Facilities and Design (KSC)
F and D........ Father and Daughter (SAUS)
F & D.......... Fill and Drain (AAG)
F & D.......... Findings and Determination (AFM)
f & d........... fire and flushing (SAUS)
F&D............ Fix & Destroy (SAUS)
F & D.......... Fixed and Dilated [*Neurology and ophthalmology*] (DAVI)
F and D........ Freight and Demurrage (SAUS)
F & D.......... Freight and Demurrage [*Shipping*]
F & DF......... Fuel and Defueling (MSA)
F & DR......... Failure and Discrepancy Reporting (KSC)
F & D Vlv..... Fill and Drain Valve (SAUS)
F and E........ Facilities and Equipment (SAUS)
F & E.......... Facilities and Equipment
F&E............ Facility and Environment [*Aerospace*] (NAKS)
F & E.......... Fearnley & Eger (SAUS)
f & e........... flood and ebb (SAUS)
F&ED.......... Facilities and Equipment Department (SAUO)
F & EDCD..... Facilities and Equipment Department's Control Division [*Navy*] (DNAB)
F & EE......... Film and Equipment Exchange [*Army*] (AABC)
F & EI.......... Fire and Explosion Index [*Hazard analysis*]
F & E Res..... F & E Resource Systems Technology, Inc. [*Associated Press*] (SAG)
F&Ex........... Fire and Explosion (HEAS)
F & F.......... Faber & Faber (SAUS)
F & F.......... Filiform and Follower [*Instruments*] [*Urology*] (DAVI)
F & F.......... Fire and Flushing (KSC)
F&F............ Fire and Forget (ACAE)
f& f............ fire-and-forget missile (SAUS)
F & F.......... Fitting and Fixtures (SAUS)
F & F.......... Fittings and Fixtures (ADA)
F&F............ Fix and Follow (SAUS)
F & F.......... Foster and Finlason's English Nisi Prius Reports [*175, 176 English Reprint*] [*A publication*] (DLA)
F&F............ Furniture and Fixtures (FOTI)
F and F........ Furniture and Fixtures (SAUS)
F & Fitz....... Falconer and Fitzherbert's English Election Cases [*1835-39*] [*A publication*] (DLA)
F & FIY........ Fife and Forfar Imperial Yeomanry [*British military*] (DMA)
FAND-FOK.... Fan-in Determined-Fan-Out Registered (SAUS)
FAND-FOR.... Fan-in-Determined-Fan-Out Registered (SAUS)
F&FP.......... Force and Financial Plan (SAUO)
F & FP........ Force and Financial Program (AFM)
f & fp.......... fraud and false pretenses (SAUS)
F & FY........ Fife and Forfar Yeomanry [*British military*] (DMA)
F & G.......... Farmers and Graziers (SAUS)
F&G............ Fish and Game (GOBB)
F & G.......... Folded and Gathered (SAUS)
F & G.......... Folded and Gathered Sheets [*Printing*]
F & GA........ Frame and Grillage Analysis [*Modray Ltd.*] [*Software package*] (NCC)
f& gc.......... failure and guilt complex (SAUS)
F & GP........ Finance and General Purposes Committee [*British*] (DCTA)
F&GPC........ Finance and General Purposes Committee (HEAS)
f & g's......... Folded And Gathered Sheets [*Publishing*] (WDMC)
F & HE........ Fridays and Holidays Excepted
F&I............. Finance and Insurance (GOBB)
F & I........... Furnished and Installed (KSC)
F&IE........... Facilities & industrial engineering (SAUS)
F & J Bank... De Gex, Fisher, and Jones' English Bankruptcy Reports [*A publication*] (DLA)
F & K RGA... Fife and Kincardine Royal Garrison Artillery [*British military*] (DMA)
F & L........... Aviation Fuels, Lubricants, and Associated Products [*NATO*] (NATG)
f & l............ fuel and lubricants (SAUS)
F & LD......... Flight and Laboratory Development (MCD)
F & M.......... Farmers & Merchants Bank
F and M........ Fire and Maneuver [*Infantry strategy*] (VNW)
F & M.......... Firm and Midline [*Uterus*] [*Gynecology and obstetrics*] (DAVI)
F&M............ First & Merchants Corp. (EFIS)
F&M............ Fischbach and Moore Inc. (SAUO)
f & m........... foot-and-mouth disease (SAUS)
F & M.......... Force and Mission
F&M............ Fortnum & Mason (WDAA)
F and M........ Franklin and Marshall College [*Pennsylvania*]
F&M............ Full and Modified [*Gunnery*]
F & M Bc...... F & M Bancorp, Inc. [*Associated Press*] (SAG)
F & M Bn...... F & M Bancorp, Inc. [*Associated Press*] (SAG)
F & M Nat..... F & M National Corp. [*Associated Press*] (SAG)
F & N.......... Fetus and Neonate (MELL)
F & NE........ Fairchild & Northeastern Railway
F&O............ Facilties and Operations (ABAC)
F & O.......... Financial and Operating Data for Investor-Owned Water Companies [*A publication*] (EAAP)
F&O............ Fisheries and Oceans (SAUS)
F&OR.......... Functional and organizational requirements (SAUS)
F & PM........ Flint & Pere Marquette Railroad
F&PR.......... functional and performance requirements (SAUS)
F and R........ Force and Rhythm (SAUS)
F & R.......... Force and Rhythm [*of Pulse*] [*Medicine*]
F&R............ Functions and Requirements (ABAC)
F & R.......... Functions and Responsibilities
F&RP.......... Free and Reduced-Price Policy (SAUO)
F and S........ Fast and Systematic [*Predicasts Inc.*] [*Set of databases*] (NITA)
F & S.......... Fatigue and Sleep (MELL)
F & S.......... Feffer & Simons [*Publisher*]
F&S............ Fire and Smoke Detection (SAUS)
F & S.......... Fox and Smith's Irish King's Bench Reports [*1822-24*] [*A publication*] (DLA)
F & S.......... Fox and Smith's Registration Cases [*1886-95*] [*A publication*] (DLA)
F & S.......... Frost & Sullivan, Inc. [*Information service or system*] (IID)
F and S........ Frost and Sullivan Inc (SAUS)
F & S.......... Funk & Scott Publishing Co. [*Detroit, MI*]
F & SA........ Engineering and Stores Association [*A union*] [*British*]
F&SAT........ Facility & systems analysis technology (SAUS)
F&SER Act.... Foreshore and Seabed Endowment Revesting Act (SAUS)
F & SF......... Fantasy and Science Fiction [*A publication*]
F & STD....... Fire and Safety Test Detachment [*Mobile, AL*] [*Coast Guard*] (GRD)
F and T........ Fire and Theft (SAUS)
F & T.......... Fire and Theft
F & T.......... Five and Thelt (SAUS)
F and T........ Frequency and Time (SAUS)
F & T.......... Fuel and Transportation [*Navy*]
FANDT......... Fuel and Transportation [*Navy*]

F & T/W .... Forest and Trees for Windows [Channel Computing, Inc.] [Computer science] (PCM)
F & U .... Flanks and Upper Quadrants [Anatomy] (DAVI)
F and V .... Flat and Vertical-up (SAUS)
F & V .... Formulation and Verification
f & w .... feed and water (SAUS)
F & W .... Feeding and Watering [Charge] [Business term]
F&W .... Food and Water [An association] (EA)
F & W .... Fortifications and Works (SAUS)
F & W .... Funk and Wagnalls (SAUS)
F & W Pr .... Frend and Ware's Precedents of Instruments Relating to the Transfer of Land to Railway Companies [2nd ed.] [1866] [A publication] (DLA)
F & WS .... Fish and Wildlife Service [Department of the Interior]
FANE .... Federation d'Action Nationale et Europeene [Federation of National and European Action] [France] [Political party] (PPE)
FANEL .... Federation for Accessible Nursing Education and Licensure (EA)
FANES .... Furnace Atomic Nonthermal Excitation Spectrometry
FANES .... Furnace Atomic Nonthermal Exitatron Spectrometry (SAUS)
FANES .... furnace atomization non-thermical excitation spectroscopy (SAUS)
FANFT .... Formamidonitrofurylthiazole [Organic chemistry]
FANG .... Fin-stabilised, Armour-piercing, Next Generation (SAUS)
FANG .... Flechette Area Neutralizing Gun
FANGIO .... feed analysis of GCMs and in observations (SAUS)
FANGIO .... Feedback Analysis for GCM Intercomparison and Observation (EERA)
FANH .... New Hanover [South Africa] [ICAO location identifier] (ICLI)
FANI .... Food, Agriculture, and Nutrition Inventory [Department of Agriculture] [Discontinued]
fan-in .... Number of independent inputs to a logic gate (SAUS)
FANK .... Forces Armees Nationales Khmeres [Cambodian National Armed Forces] [Replaced Royal Cambodian Armed Forces]
FANL .... New Largo [South Africa] [ICAO location identifier] (ICLI)
FANNDE .... Forward Addition Algorithm Using the Nearest-Neighbor Distance Error Criteria [Algorithm]
Fannie Mae .... Federal National Mortgage Association (EBF)
FANNIEMAE .... Federal National Mortgage Association (EFIS)
Fanny .... First Aid Nursing Yeomanry Service (SAUO)
FANO .... Frente Anticomunista del Nororiente [Northeastern Anticommunist Front] [Guatemala] (PD)
fan-out .... Number of inputs that can be driven by a single output (SAUS)
FANPT .... Freeman Anxiety, Neurosis, and Psychosomatic Test [Psychology]
Fan Rom Law .... Fanton's Tables of Roman Law [A publication] (DLA)
FANS .... Fellow of the American Neurological Society
FANS .... Fight to Advance the Nation's Sports [Defunct] (EA)
FANS .... Finland, Austria, Norway, and Sweden (EURO)
FANS .... Food and Nutritional System [Military] (AABC)
FANS .... Forgotten Americans Need Support (EA)
FANS .... Franchise of Americans Needing Sports (EA)
FANS .... Fresh Air for Non-Smokers (SAUS)
FANS .... Future Air Navigation Systems [Aviation]
FANS .... Nelspruit [South Africa] [ICAO location identifier] (ICLI)
FANSA .... Food and Nutrition Science Alliance
Fanshaw .... Featherstonehaugh (SAUS)
Fanstel .... Fansteel, Inc. [Associated Press] (SAG)
FANSW .... Financiers' Association of New South Wales [Australia]
FANSY .... Frequency Analysis and Synthesis [Computer program]
fant .... fantasia (SAUS)
fant .... fantasy (SAUS)
FANT .... Flight and Navigation Trainer (ACAE)
FANT .... Forces Armees Nationales Tchadiennes [Chad] (PD)
FANT .... French Atmospheric Nuclear Test (MCD)
fantabulous .... fantastic + fabulous (SAUS)
FANTAC .... Fighter Analysis Tactical Air Combat
FANTASIE .... Forecasting and Assessment of Near Technologies and Transportation Systems and Their Impacts on the Environment [Traffic management]
FANU .... Flota Argentina Navegacion Ultramar [Argentine Ship Line]
FANUC .... Fujitsu Automatic Numerical Control (SAUO)
FANUL .... Friends of the Australian National University Library
FANV .... Nieuwoudtville [South Africa] [ICAO location identifier] (ICLI)
FANX .... Friendship [Airport] Annex [National Security Agency]
FANY .... First-Aid Nursing Yeomanry [British women's organization formed to do medical transport work for the army; later did general transport work]
FANY .... Nylstroom [South Africa] [ICAO location identifier] (ICLI)
FANYS .... First Aid Nursing Yeomanry Service [British military] (DMA)
FANYS .... First-Aid Nursing Yeomanry Service (SAUO)
FANZAAS .... Fellow of the Australian and New Zealand Association for Advancement of Science (SAUO)
FANZCP .... Fellow, Australian & New Zealand College of Psychiatrists (CMD)
fanzine .... Fan Magazine (ADWA)
FANZINE .... Fan Magazine [Generic term for a publication of interest to science fiction fans]
fanzines .... fan + magazines (SAUS)
f-ao- .... Angola [MARC geographic area code] [Library of Congress] (LCCP)
FAO .... Fabrication Assembly Order (MCD)
FAO .... Facts on Aging Quiz (EDAC)
FAO .... Faro [Portugal] [Airport symbol] (OAG)
FAO .... Fatty Amine Oxide [Organic chemistry]
FAO .... Federal Approving Official (SAUO)
FAO .... Federal Assets Office (SAUO)
FAO .... Field Assessment Officer [Military] (AEBS)
fao .... filnish all over (SAUS)
FAO .... Finance and Accounting Office (SAUO)
FAO .... Finance and Account Officer (SAUS)
FAO .... Finance and Accounts Office [or Officer] [Army]
FAO .... Financial Aid Officer (SAUS)
FAO .... Finish All Over [Technical drawings]
FAO .... Flatland Atmospheric Observatory [Marine science] (OSRA)
FAO .... Fleet Accountant Officer [British]
FAO .... Fleet Account Officer (SAUS)
FAO .... Fleet Aviation Officer (SAUO)
FAO .... Flight Activities Officer [NASA]
FAO .... Food and Agricultural Organization of the United Nations (SAUS)
FAO .... Food and Agriculture Organisation (SAUS)
FAO .... Food and Agriculture Organization [United Nations] [Italy] [Information service or system] (IID)
FAO .... Foreign Agricultural Organization
FAO .... Foreign Area Officer [Army] (INF)
FAO .... For the Attention Of (ACAE)
FAO .... Forward Artillery Observer [Liaison officer] [Army] (VNW)
FAO .... Four-Address Operation (SAUS)
FAO .... Free Albania Organization (EA)
FAO .... Fumaramido Oripavine [Biochemistry]
FAOA .... Food Administrator for Occupied Area (SAUO)
FAOA .... Funk Aircraft Owners Association (EA)
FAOA .... Ondangua [Namibia] [ICAO location identifier] (ICLI)
FAOAC .... Field Artillery Officer Advanced Course [Military] (INF)
FAOAK .... Fair Oaks, AR [American Association of Railroads railroad junction routing code]
FAO/APS .... FAO [Food and Agriculture Organization of the United Nations] Association of Professional Staff [Rome, Italy] (EAIO)
FAOCP .... Food and Agriculture Organization Cooperative Programme (SAUS)
FAOD .... Odendaalsrus [South Africa] [ICAO location identifier] (ICLI)
FAO/DEES .... FAO Development Education Exchange Service (SAUS)
FAODOC .... FAO Documentation System (SAUS)
FAOE .... Federation of African Organisations of Engineers (PDAA)
FAOE .... Omega [Namibia] [ICAO location identifier] (ICLI)
FAO/ECE .... Food and Agricultural Organization/Economic Commission for Europe (SAUS)
FAO/ETAP .... FAO Expanded Technical Assistance Program (SAUS)
FAOFOG .... Fellow of the Asia-Oceania Federation of Obstetricians and Gynaecologists
FAO Food Nutr Pap .... FAO Food and Nutrition Paper (SAUS)
FAOG .... Oranjemund [Namibia] [ICAO location identifier] (ICLI)
FAOGIS .... Food and Agriculture Organization Geographic Information System [United Nations] (DUND)
FAOH .... Oudtshoorn [South Africa] [ICAO location identifier] (ICLI)
FAOIP .... French Association of On-Line Information Providers (SAUO)
FAOJ .... Outjo [Namibia] [ICAO location identifier] (ICLI)
FAOK .... Okakarara [Namibia] [ICAO location identifier] (ICLI)
FAOLU .... Federation of All Okinawan Labor Unions
FAOMA .... Fellow of the American Occupational Medicine Association (SAUO)
FAOMELU .... Federation of All Okinawan Military Employees' Labor Unions
FAOMS .... Foreign Area Officer Management System [Army]
FAON .... Okahandja [Namibia] [ICAO location identifier] (ICLI)
FAOO .... Okaukuejo [Namibia] [ICAO location identifier] (ICLI)
FAOP .... Foreign Area Officer Program [Army] (MCD)
faop .... full away on passage (SAUS)
FAOP .... Opuwa [Namibia] [ICAO location identifier] (ICLI)
FAOR .... Fighter Areas of Responsibility (SAUS)
FAOR .... Functional Analysis of Office Requirements (SAUO)
FAOR .... Olifants River Bridge [South Africa] [ICAO location identifier] (ICLI)
FAORs .... FAO Representatives (SAUS)
FAOS .... Oshakati [Namibia] [ICAO location identifier] (ICLI)
FAOSFA FAO .... State of Food and Agriculture (SAUO)
FAOTA .... Fellow of the American Occupational Therapy Association
FAOTY .... Food and Agriculture Organization of the United Nations Trade Yearbook (SAUO)
FAOU .... Fellow of the American Ornithologists Union
FAOUSA .... Finance and Accounts Office [or Officer], United States Army
FAOV .... Otavi [Namibia] [ICAO location identifier] (ICLI)
FAOW .... Friends all over the World (SAUO)
FAOW .... Otjiwarongo [Namibia] [ICAO location identifier] (ICLI)
FAO/WFP-FSA .... Field Staff Association of FAO and WFP (SAUO)
FAO/WHO/FNAf .... Joint FAO/WHO/OAU Regional Food and Nutrition Commission for Africa (SAUO)
FAOY .... Orkney [South Africa] [ICAO location identifier] (ICLI)
FAP .... Facilities Assistance Program
FAP .... Facility Analysis Plan [Telecommunications] (TEL)
FAP .... Familial Adenomatous Polyposis [Formerly, FPC] [Medicine]
FAP .... Familial Amyloid Polyneuropathy [Medicine]
FAP .... Familial Polyposis Coli Gene [Medicine]
FAP .... Family Assistance Plan [or Program] [Proposed during Nixon administration]
FAP .... Family Auto Plan
FAP .... Family Auto Policy [Insurance]
FAP .... Fast Action Procedures (NVT)
FAP .... fast arithmetic processor (SAUS)
FAP .... Fast Atmospheric Pulsation
FAP .... Fatty Acid Polyunsaturated [Medicine] (EDAA)
FAP .... Fatty Acid Poor [Medicine] (EDAA)
FAP .... Fault Analysis Process (TEL)
FAP .... Federal Art Project
FAP .... Femoral Artery Pressure [Medicine] (EDAA)
FAP .... Fibrillating Action Potential [Neurophysiology]
FAP .... Field-Activated Promotion [Marketing] (DOAD)
FAP .... Field Application Panel (IEEE)
FAP .... File Access Protocol [Telecommunications] (OSI)

FAP .... Filed a Petition [*FDA*]
FAP .... Filmmaker Assistance Program (FOTI)
FAP .... Final Abandonment Premium (EURO)
FAP .... Final Anthropic Principle [*Term coined by authors John Barrow and Frank Tipler in their book, "The Anthropic Cosmological Principle"*]
FAP .... Final Approach (SAUS)
FAP .... Final Approach Path [*or Plane*] [*Aviation*]
FAP .... Final Approach Plane (SAUS)
FAP .... Final Approach Point (PIPO)
FAP .... Finance and Accounting Policy [*Army*] (AABC)
FAP .... Financial Analysis Program [*IBM Corp.*]
FAP .... Financial Assistance Program (AFM)
FAP .... Fine Aim Positioning
FAP .... Fine Arts Philatelists (EA)
FAP .... First Aid Post (SAUS)
FAP .... First-Aid Post
FAP .... First Appearance (QUAC)
FAP .... Fixed Action Pattern
FAP .... Fixed Action Potential (MELL)
FAP .... Flexible Accelerator Path [*Economic theory*]
FAP .... Flight Acceptance Profile (KSC)
FAP .... Flight Activity Performance (SAUO)
fap .... floating arithmetic package (SAUS)
FAP .... Floating-Point Arithmetic Package [*Computer science*]
FAP .... Floating Point Arithmetic System (NITA)
FAP .... Fluorapatite (SAUS)
FAP .... Fluorouracil, Adriamycin, Cisplatin [*Antineoplastic drug regimen*] (DAVI)
FAP .... Fly Along Probe (ACAE)
FAP .... Food Additive Petition
FAP .... Food and Agriculture Program (SAUS)
FAP .... Food and Agriculture Project (SAUO)
FAP .... Force Alignment Plan [*Military*] (INF)
FAP .... Foreign Air Program
FAP .... Foreign Assistance Program (WDAA)
FAP .... FORTRAN [*Formula Translating System*] Assembly Program [*Computer science*]
FAP .... Forward Ammunition Point (SAUS)
FAP .... Fos-Associated Protein [*Biochemistry*]
FAP .... Foundation for the Arts of Peace [*Defunct*] (EA)
FAP .... Franc d'Avarie Particuliere [*Free of Particular Average*] [*Business term*] [*French*]
FAP .... Franco d'Avaria Particolare [*Free of Particular Average*] [*Business term*] [*Italian*]
FAP .... Free at Pier (SAUS)
FAP .... Freedom Attached Payloads (SAUO)
FAP .... Frequency Allocation Panel
FAP .... Frozen Animal Procedure [*Medicine*] (DMAA)
FAP .... Fuerzas Armadas Peronistas [*Argentina*]
FAP .... Full American Plan [*Hotel room rate*]
FAP .... Functional Assignment Panel (SAUS)
FAP .... functional refractory period (SAUS)
FAP .... (Furfurylamino)purine [*Plant hormone*] [*Organic chemistry*]
FAP .... Furylacryloylphenylalanine (SAUS)
FAP .... Fuse Alarm Panel [*Telecommunications*] (ITD)
FAP .... Future Anthropic Principle (SAUS)
FAP .... Parsons Airways Northern Ltd. [*Canada*] [*ICAO designator*] (FAAC)
FAPA .... F-15 Adapted Place Atlas Program (MCD)
FAPA .... Fantasy Amateur Press Association
FAPA .... Federation of Asian Pharmaceutical Associations
FAPA .... Federation of Asian Photographic Art
FAPA .... Fellow, American Pediatric Association (CMD)
FAPA .... Fellow of the American Psychiatric Association
FAPA .... Fellow of the American Psychoanalytical Association (SAUO)
FAPA .... Fellow of the American Psychoanalytic Association
FAPA .... Fellow of the American Psychological Association
FAPA .... Filipino American Political Association
FAPA .... Flight Accrual Payment Action [*Air Force*]
FAPA .... Formosan Association for Public Affairs (EA)
FAPA .... Fred Astaire Performing Arts Association
FAPA .... Future Airline Pilots of America [*BTS*] (TAG)
FAPA .... Future Aviation Professionals of America (EA)
FAPA .... Port Alfred [*South Africa*] [*ICAO location identifier*] (ICLI)
FAPA .... Fellow of the Association of Authorized Public Accountants (ODA)
FAPABS .... FORSCOM [*Forces Command*] Automatic Program and Budget System [*Army*] (MCD)
FAPAP .... Federation des Personnels Africains de Police [*Federation of African Police*]
FAPAS .... Fetch, Align, Process, Align, Store (SAUS)
FAPB .... Pietersburg [*South Africa*] [*ICAO location identifier*] (ICLI)
FAPC .... Familial Adenomatous Polyposis Coli [*Medicine*]
FAPC .... Fatty Acid Producers' Council (EA)
FAPC .... Federal Area Port Controller
FAPC .... Food and Agriculture Planning Committee [*NATO*] (NATG)
FAPC .... Food Animal Practitioners Club [*Ohio State University*] (GVA)
FAPC .... Prince Albert [*South Africa*] [*ICAO location identifier*] (ICLI)
FAPCC .... Film, Air, and Package Carriers Conference (EA)
FAPCH .... final approach (SAUS)
FAPE .... Families and Advocates Partnership for Education
FAPE .... Free Appropriate Public Education
FAPE .... Port Elizabeth/H. F. Verwoerd [*South Africa*] [*ICAO location identifier*] (ICLI)
FAPES .... Force Augmentation Planning and Execution System (DOMA)
FAPF .... Piet Retief [*South Africa*] [*ICAO location identifier*] (ICLI)
FAPG .... Fleet Air Photographic Group
FAPG .... Plettenberg Bay [*South Africa*] [*ICAO location identifier*] (ICLI)
FAPGG .... Furylacryloylphenylalanylglycylglycine (SAUS)
FAPH .... Fluoroaldehyde Pyridylhydrazone [*Organic chemistry*]
FAPH .... Phalaborwa/Hendrik Van Eck [*South Africa*] [*ICAO location identifier*] (ICLI)
FAPHA .... Fellow of the American Public Health Association
FAPHA .... Fellow of the Australian Psychology and Hypnotherapy Association
FAPHCC ...... Florida Association of Plumbing, Heating, and Cooling Contractors (SRA)
FAPHI .... Fellow of the Association of Public Health Inspectors (SAUO)
FAPI .... Family Application Program Interface (SAUS)
FAPI .... Family Application Programmer Interface [*Computer science*] (VERA)
FAPI .... Family Application Programming Interface (SAUS)
FAPI .... Fellow of the Australian Planning Institute (SAUO)
FAPI .... First Article Production Inspection (MCD)
FAPI .... Foreign Accrual Property Income (FOTI)
FAPI .... Pietersburg [*South Africa*] [*ICAO location identifier*] (ICLI)
FAPIG .... First Atomic Power Industry Group [*Japan*]
FAPIN .... Fabry-Perot Interferometer (SAUS)
FAPIP .... Fighter Airframe / Propulsion Integration Predesign (SAUS)
FAPJ .... Port St. Johns [*South Africa*] [*ICAO location identifier*] (ICLI)
FAPL .... Financial assistance policy letter (SAUS)
FAPL .... Fleet Air Photographic Laboratory (DNAB)
FAPL .... Format and Protocol Language [*IBM*] (NITA)
FAPL .... Pongola [*South Africa*] [*ICAO location identifier*] (ICLI)
FAPM .... Federation of Automotive Products Manufacturers (SAUO)
FAPM .... Fellow, Academy of Psychosomatic Medicine (CMD)
FAPM .... Functional Activity Program Manager (SAUS)
FAPM .... Pietermaritzburg [*South Africa*] [*ICAO location identifier*] (ICLI)
FAPMATC .... Fully Automated Pilot Monitored, Air Traffic Control [*Aviation*]
FAP-MS .... Formats and Protocols-Management Service (SAUS)
FAPN .... Pilansberg [*South Africa*] [*ICAO location identifier*] (ICLI)
FAPNEWDT... Financial Accounts Package New Data [*Torch Computers Ltd.*] [*Financial accounting software*] (NITA)
FAPO .... Field Army Petroleum Office (AABC)
FAPP .... Federation of Associations of Periodical Publishers (DGA)
FAPP .... Field Artillery Projectile Pallet (SAUS)
FAPP .... Fractured-Area-Projection Plot (SAUS)
FAPP .... Potgietersrus [*South Africa*] [*ICAO location identifier*] (ICLI)
FAPPEC .... Federation of Associations of Periodical Publishers in the EC (EAIO)
FAPPS .... First Article Preproduction Sample [*DoD*]
FA-PPT .... First Article - Preproduction Test (MCD)
FAPR .... Federal Aviation Procurement Regulations
FAPR .... Fellow of the Academy of Professional Reporters
FAPR .... Floydada & Plainview Railroad [*Federal Railroad Administration identification code*]
FAPR .... Formal and Applied Practical Reasoning (SAUS)
FAPR .... Pretoria [*South Africa*] [*ICAO location identifier*] (ICLI)
FAPRA .... Federation of African Public Relations Associations (SAUO)
FAPRI .... Food and Agricultural Policy Research Institute [*Iowa State University*] (RCD)
FAPRO .... Federation of ASEAN Public Relations Organizations (SAUO)
FAPRON .... Fleet Air Photo Squadron
FAPRS .... Federal Assistance Programs Retrieval System [*General Services Administration*] [*Information service or system*] (MCD)
FAPS .... Committee on the Future of the American Physical Society (SAUO)
FAPS .... Farm and Food Society (SAUO)
FAPS .... Fast-millisecond-long Atmospheric-light Pulsations (SAUS)
FAPS .... Fate of Atmospheric Pollutants Study [*National Science Foundation*]
FAPS .... Federal Aid Primary System (GNE)
FAPS .... Fellow of the American Physical Society
FAPS .... Field Automated Payroll System (SAUS)
FAPS .... Financial Aid Planning Service [*College Scholarship Service*]
FAPS .... Financial Analysis and Planning System (IAA)
FAPS .... Financial Application Preprocessor System (MHDW)
FAPS .... Foreign Affairs Programming System (CINC)
FAPS .... Freedom Attached Payloads (SAUS)
FAPS .... Potchefstroom [*South Africa*] [*ICAO location identifier*] (ICLI)
FAPSC .... Food and Agriculture Planning Committee (SAUS)
FAPSIM .... Food and Agricultural Policy Simulator
FAPT .... Fellow of the Association of Photographic Technicians (SAUO)
FAPT .... Postmasburg [*South Africa*] [*ICAO location identifier*] (ICLI)
FAPTU .... Farm Animal Practice Teaching Unit [*Royal Veterinary College*] [*British*] (IRUK)
FAPUS .... Fabrication Performance Utilization System (MCD)
FAPUS .... Frequency Allocation Panel, United States (NVT)
FAP USJCEC... Frequency Allocation Panel, United States Joint Communications Electronics Commission (SAUS)
FAP USJCEC... Frequency Allocation Panel, United States Joint Communications Electronics Committee (SAUO)
FAP USJCEC... Frequency Allocation Panel US, Joint Communications Electronics (SAUS)
FAPUSMCEB... Frequency Allocation Panel United States Military Communication Electronics Board (SAUS)
FAPUS-MCEB... Frequency Allocation Panel, United States-Military Communications Electronics Board (SAUS)
FAPV .... Petrusville [*South Africa*] [*ICAO location identifier*] (ICLI)
FAPY .... Parys [*South Africa*] [*ICAO location identifier*] (ICLI)
FAPZ .... Progress [*South Africa*] [*ICAO location identifier*] (ICLI)
FAQ .... Fair Average Quality
FAQ .... Foire Aux Questions (SAUS)
faq .... free alongside quai (SAUS)
faq .... free alongside quay (SAUS)
FAQ .... Free at Quay [*Business term*]

FAQ............ Frequently Asked Questions (ACRL)
FAQ............ Frequently asked questions file (SAUS)
FAQ file....... Frequently Asked Questions File
FAQL........... Frequent Asked Question List [*Computer science*] (NHD)
FAQS........... Fair Average Quality of Season [*Business term*]
FAQS........... Fast Queuing System [*Computer science*]
FAQT........... Queenstown [*South Africa*] [*ICAO location identifier*] (ICLI)
FAR............ African Forum for Reconstruction (Gabon) [*Political party*] (PSAP)
FAR............ Facility Audit Report (COE)
FAR............ Failure Analysis Report
FAR............ False Alarm Rate
FAR............ Family Assistance and Rehabilitation (SAUO)
FAR............ Farad [*Unit of electric capacitance*] (ROG)
Far............ Faraday (ADWA)
FAR............ Faraday (WDAA)
FAR............ Far Airlines [*Italy*] [*FAA designator*] (FAAC)
FAR............ Fargo [*North Dakota*] [*Airport symbol*] (OAG)
FAR............ Fargo, ND [*Location identifier*] [*FAA*] (FAAL)
FAR............ Farina [*Flour*] [*Pharmacy*] (ROG)
FAR............ Farmer (ROG)
FAR............ Farmington Public Library, Farmington, NM [*OCLC symbol*] (OCLC)
far............ farnery (SAUS)
FAR............ Faro [*Portugal*] [*Seismograph station code, US Geological Survey*] (SEIS)
far............ Faroese [*MARC language code*] [*Library of Congress*] (LCCP)
Far............ Farresley's Cases in Holt's King's Bench Reports [*A publication*] (DLA)
Far............ Farresley's Reports [*7 Modern Reports*] [*87 English Reprint*] [*1733-45*] [*A publication*] (DLA)
FAR............ Farrier (ROG)
FAR............ Farthing [*Monetary unit*] [*British*]
FAR............ Farymann (SAUS)
FAR............ Federal Acquisition Regulation
FAR............ Federal Air Regulations [*FAA*]
FAR............ Federal Airworthiness Regulation
FAR............ Federal Assistance Review [*Program*]
FAR............ Federal Aviation Regulation (LDOE)
FAR............ Federal Aviation Requirements (SAUS)
FAR............ Federation des Associations Roumaines du Canada [*Federation of Romanian Associations of Canada*]
FAR............ Federation of American Research (SAUO)
FAR............ Feminists for Animal Rights (EA)
FAR............ Fetus at Risk [*Medicine*] (DIPS)
FAR............ Field Action Request (CTAS)
FAR............ Field Activity Report
FAR............ Field Altering and Reconditioning (SAUS)
FAR............ Field Analysis Report
FAR............ Field Anomaly Relaxation (SAUS)
FAR............ Field Artillery Rocket (MCD)
FAR............ Field Assessment Review [*Military*]
FAR............ Fighter, Attacker, Reconnaissance [*Requirements*] [*Air Force*]
FAR............ Filament Atom Reservoir (PDAA)
FAR............ File Address Register
FAR............ Final Acceptance Review [*NASA*] (NASA)
FAR............ Financial Accounts Receivable
FAR............ Financial Accumulation and Reporting (SAUS)
FAR............ Finned Air Rocket (SAA)
FAR............ Fire Appliances Rules (SAUS)
FAR............ First Alarm Register
FAR............ First Assesment Report of the IPCC (SAUS)
FAR............ First Assessment Report (EERA)
FAR............ Fisheries and Aquacultural Research (SAUS)
FAR............ Fixed Acoustic Range
FAR............ Fixed Alternative Routing [*Computer science*] (VERA)
FAR............ Fixed Amount Reimbursement [*Agency for International Development*]
FAR............ Fixed Array RADAR
FAR............ Flight Acceptance Review (MCD)
FAR............ Flight Aptitude Rating
FAR............ Floor Area Ratio [*in office buildings*]
FAR............ Florida Association of Realtors (SAUO)
FAR............ Fluid Air Ride [*Automotive engineering*]
FAR............ Forces Armees Royales [*Royal Armed Forces*] [*Laos*]
FAR............ Foreign Affairs Research Documentation Center [*Department of State*]
FAR............ Foreign Agricultural Relations Office
FAR............ Foreign Agriculture Report [*Department of Agriculture*]
FAR............ Foreign Area Research Coordination Group [*Department of State*]
FAR............ Foreign Area Research Documentation Center [*Department of State*] (AEBS)
FAR............ Forum Africain pour la Reconstruction [*Gabon*] [*Political party*] (EY)
FAR............ Forward Acquisition RADAR
FAR............ Foundation for Administrative Research (MCD)
FAR............ Foundation for Agronomic Research [*University of Pittsburgh*] [*Research center*] (RCD)
FAR............ Foundation for Australian Resources (SAUO)
FAR............ Fowler, A. R., Saint Paul MN [*STAC*]
FAR............ Fractional Albumin Rate [*Medicine*] (EDAA)
FAR............ Franco-American Review (journ.) (SAUS)
FAR............ Free of Accident Reported (MARI)
FAR............ Fremantle Arts Review [*A publication*]
FAR............ French American Review (journ.) (SAUS)
FAR............ French Rapid Action Force (SAUO)
FAR............ Frequency Adjusting Rheostat
FAR............ Frequency Allocation Request
FAR............ Front of Associations for Renewal (Togo) [*Political party*] (PSAP)
FAR............ Fuel-Air Ratio (SAUS)
FAR............ Fuerzas Armadas Rebeldes [*Rebel Armed Forces*] [*Guatemala*]
FAR............ Functional Analysis Review (SAUO)
FAR............ Functional Area Requirement (SAUO)
FAR............ Functional Area Review [*Military*]
FAR............ Fund Availability Report (MCD)
FAR............ Fund for an American Renaissance (EA)
FAR............ Royal Armed Forces (Morocco) [*Political party*] (PSAP)
FAR............ Front Arm Rests (ODA)
FARA........... Federal Acquisition Reform Act of 1996 (AAGC)
FARA........... Federal Agents Registration Act (OICC)
FARA........... Fellow, American Rheumatism Association (CMD)
FARA........... Flexible Automation for Robotic Analysis
FARA........... Foreign Affairs Recreation Association (EA)
FARA........... Foreign Agents Registration Act of 1938
FARA........... Formula Air Racing Association (PIAV)
FARA........... French American Ridge Atlantic [*Program*] (USDC)
FARAC.......... Fuerzas Armadas Anticomunistas [*Anti-Communist Armed Forces*] [*Nicaragua*] (PD)
FARACS......... Faculty of Anaesthetists of the Royal Australian College of Surgeons (SAUS)
FARAD.......... Food Animal Residue Avoidance Databank (SAUO)
FARADA......... Failure Rate Data Program [*Navy*] (NG)
FARADA Program... Failure Rate Data Program (SAUS)
Faraday Disc Chem Soc... Faraday Discussions of the Chemical Society (journ.) (SAUS)
Faraday Discuss... Faraday Discussions (SAUS)
Faraday Discuss... FARADAY DISCUSSIONS (LONDON) (SAUS)
Faraday Symp Chem Soc... Faraday Symposia of the Chemical Society (journ.) (SAUS)
FARADS......... Fast Response Air Defense System (ACAE)
Farah.......... Farah, Inc. [*Associated Press*] (SAG)
FARA-ITMRA... Federal Acquisition Reform Act-Information Technology Management Reform Act [*Currently known as Clinger-Cohen Act*]
Farallones... Farollon Islands off San Francisco (SAUS)
FARAMC......... Field Ambulance, Royal Army Medical Corps (SAUO)
F/A Ratio...... Fuel / Air Ratio (SAUS)
FARB........... Federal Assistance Review Board (USDC)
FARB........... Federation of Associations of Regulatory Boards (EA)
FARB........... Richard's Bay [*South Africa*] [*ICAO location identifier*] (ICLI)
FARC........... Family Advancement Resources Cooperative [*Australia*]
FARC........... Farr Co. [*NASDAQ symbol*] (NQ)
FARC........... Fast Accurate Refraction Correction [*NASA*] (KSC)
FARC........... Federal Addiction Research Center (SAUO)
FARC........... Federal Archives and Records Center [*Regional depository of the National Archives and Records Service*]
FARC........... Field Artillery Replacement Center
FARC........... Field Artillery Reserve Corporation (SAUO)
FARC........... Fijian-Australian Resource Centre
FARC........... Fuerzas Armadas Revolucionarias de Colombia
FARC........... Revolutionary Armed Forces of Colombia
FARchives...... CCH FAR Archives [*Historical FARs on CD-ROM*] (AAGC)
FARCO.......... Artillery Fire Control System (ACAE)
FAR Council... Federal Acquisition Regulatory Council (AAGC)
FARCS.......... Faculty of Anaesthetists of the Royal College of Surgeons of England (SAUO)
FARD........... Action Front for Renewal and Development (Benin) [*Political party*] (PSAP)
FARD........... Foam-Breaking Apparatus with a Rotating Disk [*Chemical engineering*]
FARD........... Riversdale [*South Africa*] [*ICAO location identifier*] (ICLI)
FAR/DAR........ Functional Area Requirement/ Data Automation Requirement (SAUO)
FAR/DAR........ Functional Area Requirement/Data Automation requirement (SAUS)
Fardip......... Bizonal I.G. Farben Dispersal Panel (SAUO)
FARDRCRM... Field Artillery RADAR Crewman (IAA)
FARE........... Fatal Accident Reduction Effort [*or Enforcement*] [*Department of Transportation*]
FARE........... Federal Acquisition Regulation (SAUS)
FARE........... Federation of Alcoholic Rehabilitation Establishments [*Medicine*] (EDAA)
FARE........... Federation of Alcoholic Residential Establishments [*British*] (DI)
FARE........... Fiat Auto Recycling
FARE........... Foreign Assignment Resources Employees [*FAA*]
FARE........... Forward Area Refueling Equipment [*Army*]
FARE........... Full Access and Rights to Education Coalition
FARE........... Uniform Financial Accounting and Reporting Elements [*FTA*] (TAG)
Far East Econ Rev... Far Eastern Economic Review (journ.) (SAUS)
Far East L Rev... Far Eastern Law Review [*A publication*] (DLA)
Far East Q... Far Eastern Quarterly (journ.) (SAUS)
Far East R... Far Eastern Review (journ.) (SAUS)
Far East S... Far Eastern Survey (journ.) (SAUS)
FARE device... Fuel-Air Repetitive device (SAUS)
FAREGAZ........ Union des Fabricants Europeens de Regulateurs de Pression du Gaz [*Union of European Manufacturers of Gas Pressure Controllers*] (EAIO)
FAREGAZ........ Union of European Manufacturers of Gas Pressure Controllers (SAUO)
FARELF......... Far East Land Forces (CINC)
FarEst......... Far East National Bank [*Associated Press*] (SAG)
FARET.......... Fast Reactor Engineering Test (SAUS)
FARET.......... Fast Reactor Experiment Test [*Proposed but never built*] [*Nuclear energy*]
faret.......... fast reactor test (SAUS)
FARET.......... Fast Reactor Test Assembly (SAUS)

FARET Assembly... Fast Reactor Experiment Test Assembly (SAUS)
FarETxt........ Far Eastern Textile Ltd. [*Associated Press*] (SAG)
FAREX........ Fleet Analysis and Reconstruction of Exercise [*Navy*] (MCD)
FARF........... Fairfield-Noble Corp. [*NASDAQ symbol*] (COMM)
FARF........... Fanconi's Anemia Research Fund (EA)
FARFUL....... Feeder Analysis Route for Unbalanced Load (SAUS)
FARFUL....... Feeder Analysis Routine for Unbalanced Load (SAUO)
FARG.......... Farmington [*New Mexico*] [*Seismograph station code, US Geological Survey*] (SEIS)
FARG.......... Fluid Analogies Research Group
FARG.......... Rustenburg [*South Africa*] [*ICAO location identifier*] (ICLI)
FARGO........ Fargo, ON [*American Association of Railroads railroad junction routing code*]
FARGO........ Forty Automatic Report Generating Operation (MCD)
FARGO........ Fourteen-0-One Automatic Report Generating Operation (SAUS)
FARH.......... Rehoboth [*Namibia*] [*ICAO location identifier*] (ICLI)
FARI............ First Amendment Research Institute [*Defunct*] (EA)
FARI............ Foreign Affairs Research Institute (SAUO)
FARIB.......... Faribault, MN [*American Association of Railroads railroad junction routing code*]
FARK.......... Forces Armees Royales Khmeres [*Royal Cambodian Armed Forces*] [*Replaced by FANK*]
FARK.......... Rooikop [*South Africa*] [*ICAO location identifier*] (ICLI)
Farl............ Farley (SAUS)
FARL........... Farrel Corp. [*NASDAQ symbol*] (SAG)
FARL........... Fractions Armees Revolutionnaires Libanaise [*Lebanese Armed Revolutionary Faction*]
FARL........... Frick Art Reference Library (SAUO)
FARM.......... Farm Animal Reform Movement (EA)
FARM.......... Farmer Bros. [*NASDAQ symbol*] (TTSB)
FARM.......... Farmer Brothers Co. [*NASDAQ symbol*] (NQ)
FARM.......... Farmers Assistance Relief Mission (EA)
FARM.......... Food and Agricultural Research Mission (SAUO)
FARM.......... Food and Agriculture Regional Model (SAUO)
FARM.......... Functional Area Record Manager (SAUO)
Farmaco...... FARMACO (ROMA) (SAUS)
FARM-Africa... Food and Agricultural Research Management (SAUO)
FARMAP...... FAO Farm Analysis Package (SAUS)
FARMAP...... Farm Analysis Package (SAUS)
FARMAR...... Fighter Attack Reconnaissance Modular Adaptive Radar (ACAE)
FARMBLISS... Farm Bureau Library Serials System (SAUS)
FarmBr........ Farmer Brothers Co. [*Associated Press*] (SAG)
FARMC........ Frankfurt Army Regional Medical Center [*US Army 97th General Hospital*] [*Germany*]
FarmCB........ Farmers Capital Bank Corp. [*Associated Press*] (SAG)
FARMDOC.... Pharmaceutical Documentation [*British*] [*Patents retrieval system Derwent Publications*] (NITA)
Farmer Mac... Federal Agricultural Mortgage Corporation (USGC)
FARMERS.... Frequency Agility RADAR Modifications to Existing RADAR Systems [*DoD*]
FAR-Method... Field Anomaly Relaxation Method (SAUS)
FarmFH........ Farm Family Holdings, Inc. [*Associated Press*] (SAG)
FARMI-VISCA... Farm and Resource Management Institute-Visayas State College of Agriculture (SAUO)
Farm J......... Farm Journal (SAUS)
FarmMch...... Farmers & Mechanics Bank [*Associated Press*] (SAG)
Farmobile...... Farm Automobile (SAUS)
FARMS........ Farm Audience Readership Measurement Service [*Starch INRA Hooper, Inc.*] [*Information service or system*] (IID)
FARMS........ Financial Accounting Resource Management System
FARMS........ Foundation for Ancient Research and Mormon Studies (SAUO)
FARMS........ Future Agricultural Resources Managemt Study (SAUO)
FarmT.......... Farmstead Telephone Group, Inc. [*Associated Press*] (SAG)
FarmTel....... Farmstead Telephone Group, Inc. [*Associated Press*] (SAG)
FARMV........ Farmersville, TX [*American Association of Railroads railroad junction routing code*]
FARMWAG... Field Army Modernization War Game (SAUO)
FARN.......... Fuerzas Armadas de Resistencia Nacional [*Armed Forces of National Resistance*] [*El Salvador*] (PD)
FARN.......... Fuerzas Armadas Revolucionarias Nicaraguenses [*Nicaraguan Armed Revolutionary Forces*] (PD)
FARNET....... Federation of American Research Networks [*Computer science*] (TNIG)
FARO.......... FARO Technologies, Inc. [*NASDAQ symbol*] (NASQ)
FARO.......... Flare-Activated Radiobiological Observatory
FARO.......... Fuel Melting and Release Oven (SAUO)
FAROES....... Fleet Automatic Reconstruction and Opportunity Evaluation System [*Navy*] (CAAL)
FARP.......... Forces Afloat Repair Procedures (DNAB)
FARP.......... Forward Area Rearm Point (SAUS)
FARP.......... Forward Area Rearm/Refuel Point [*Army*] (INF)
FARP.......... Forward Area Refuel Point (SAUS)
FARP.......... Forward Area Resupply Point
FARP.......... Forward Arming and Refueling Point [*Military*] (MUSM)
FARP.......... Fuel and Rearming Point (SAUO)
FARP.......... Fully Automatic Radar Plotter (SAUS)
FARP.......... Rosh Pinah [*Namibia*] [*ICAO location identifier*] (ICLI)
FARPO........ Federal Acquisition Regulation Project Office (MCD)
Far Pom....... Farther Pomerania (SAUS)
Farq Chy....... Farquharson's Court of Chancery [*A publication*] (DLA)
FARR.......... FAA/Air Force Radar Replacement (SAUO)
FARR.......... Failure and Rejection Report (MCD)
Farr............ Farr Co. [*Associated Press*] (SAG)
Farr............ Farresley's Reports [*7 Modern Reports*] [*87 English Reprint*] [*1733-45*] [*A publication*] (DLA)
FARR.......... Federal Aviation Administration and Air Force RADAR Replacement
FARR.......... Forward Area Refuelling and Rearming
FARR.......... Frequency Agile Rain Radar (SAUS)
Farrant......... Digest of Manx Cases [*1925-47*] [*A publication*] (DLA)
Farrar.......... Farrar, Straus and Giroux (SAUS)
Farr Bill....... Farren's Bill in Chancery [*A publication*] (DLA)
Farr Const... Farrar's Manual of the United States Constitution [*A publication*] (DLA)
Farrel.......... Farrel Corp. [*Associated Press*] (SAG)
Farresley..... Farresley's Reports [*7 Modern Reports*] [*87 English Reprint*] [*1733-45*] [*A publication*] (DLA)
Farr Life Ass... Farren on Life Assurance [*A publication*] (DLA)
Farr Mas...... Farren's Masters in Chancery [*A publication*] (DLA)
Farr Med Jur... Farr's Medical Jurisprudence [*A publication*] (DLA)
FARRP......... Forward Area Rearm and Refuel Point
FARRP......... Forward-Area Rearming & Refuelling Point (SAUS)
FARRP......... Forward Area Refueling and Rearming Point (SAUS)
FARRS......... Forward Area Rearm and Refuel Site (MCD)
FARS.......... Facility for Atmospheric Remote Sensing (SAUO)
FARS.......... Failure Analysis Report Summary [*Bell System*]
Fars............ Faristan (SAUS)
FARS.......... Fast Acquisition Receiver System (SEWL)
FARS.......... Fatal Accident Reporting System [*National Highway Traffic Safety Administration*] [*Washington, DC*] (GRD)
FARS.......... Fatal Analysis Reporting System
FARs........... Federal Aviation Regulations (SAUS)
FARS.......... Field Army Replacement System (AABC)
FARS.......... Field Artillery Rocket System (SAUS)
FARS.......... Fighter Attack Reconnaissance System (ACAE)
FARS.......... File Analysis for Random Access Storage [*Computer science*] (IAA)
FARS.......... Financial Accounting and Reporting System [*Federal Emergency Management Agency*] (GFGA)
FARS.......... Forward Area RAWINSONDE [*RADAR Wind Sounding and Radiosonde*] Set [*Army*]
FARS.......... Frequency Array Radar System (SAUS)
FARS.......... Fuel and Ammunition Resupply Study
FARS.......... Robertson [*South Africa*] [*ICAO location identifier*] (ICLI)
FARt............ Field Artillery Rocket (SAUS)
FARTC........ Field Artillery Reserve and Training Center (SAUO)
FARU.......... Rundu [*Namibia*] [*ICAO location identifier*] (ICLI)
FARV.......... Future Ammunition Resupply Vehicle (SAUS)
FARV.......... Future Armored Resupply Vehicle [*Army*]
FARV.......... Riverview [*South Africa*] [*ICAO location identifier*] (ICLI)
FARV-A........ Future Armored Resupply Vehicle-Ammunition [*Army*] (RDA)
FARV-A........ Future Armored Resupply Vehicle, Artillery (SAUS)
Farwell........ Farwell on Powers [*3 eds.*] [*1874-1916*] [*A publication*] (DLA)
FARWG........ Federal Acquisition Regional Work Group [*Army*]
Farw Pow.... Farwell on Powers [*3 eds.*] [*1874-1916*] [*A publication*] (DLA)
FAS............. Archives and surveillance (SAUS)
FAS............. Facilities Automation System
FAS............. Facility Activation [*or Activity*] Schedule
FAS............. Facility Activity Schedule (SAUS)
FAS............. Facility Air Supply
FAS............. Faculty of Actuaries in Scotland (SAUO)
FAS............. Faculty of Administrative Studies (SAUS)
FAS............. Faculty of Architects and Surveyors [*British*] (DAS)
FAS............. Failure Analysis Section
FAS............. Fairbanks Air Service (SAUO)
FAS............. Fallout Assessment System
FAS............. Family Action Section (EA)
FAS............. Famous Artists Schools [*Later, FAS International, Inc.*]
FAS............. Farm Advisory Service (SAUO)
fas.............. Fascicle (ADWA)
FAS............. Fast Access Storage (SAUS)
FAS............. Fast Access Store (SAUS)
FAS............. Fast Announcement Service [*NTIS publication*]
FAS............. fast atom scattering (SAUS)
FAS............. Fasten [*Technical drawings*]
FAS............. Fastener
FAS............. Fat and Stupid (BB)
FAS............. Fatty Acid Synthase [*An enzyme*]
FAS............. Fatty Alcohol Sulfates
FAS............. Fault Alarm System (SAUO)
FAS............. Feasibility Analysis Study [*Training term*] (LPT)
FAS............. Feature Analysis System [*Image analysis*]
FAS............. Federal Advertising Services
FAS............. Federal Agricultural Service (SAUO)
FAS............. Federal Airport Service
FAS............. Federal Air Surgeon (SAUO)
FAS............. Federal Aviation Service
FAS............. Federation des Affaires Sociales, Inc. [*Federation of Social Affairs*] [*Canada*]
FAS............. Federation of American Scientists (EA)
FAS............. Federation of Astronomical Societies [*British*] (EAIO)
FAS............. Feel Augmentation System [*Helicopters*]
FAS............. Fellow of the Actuarial Society
FAS............. Fellow of the Anthropological Society [*British*] (DAS)
FAS............. Fellow of the Anthropological Society of Bombay (SAUO)
FAS............. Fellow of the Antiquarian Society [*British*]
FAS............. Fellow of the Royal Society (SAUO)
FAS............. Fellow of the Society of Actuaries in Scotland (SAUO)
FAS............. Fellow of the Society of Arts [*British*] (DAS)
FAS............. Fellows in American Studies
FAS............. Ferrous Aluminum Sulfate (SAUS)
FAS............. Fetal Alcohol Syndrome [*Medicine*]

FAS .... Fiat Auto Suisse (SAUS)
FAS .... Field Advisory Service (SAUS)
FAS .... Field Aircraft Services Ltd. [*British*] [*ICAO designator*] (FAAC)
FAS .... Field Alert Status [*Army*] (AABC)
FAS .... Field Ambulance Service (SAUO)
FAS .... Field Artillery School (MCD)
FAS .... Field Artillery Section (SAUS)
FAS .... Fielded Aircraft System
FAS .... File Access Subsystem [*Computer science*] (TEL)
FAS .... Film Availability Services [*British Film Institute*]
FAS .... Film Aviation Services (SAUO)
FAS .... Filtered Air Supply (IAA)
FAS .... Fin Actuator System (IGSL)
FAS .... Fin Acutator System [*Space launch term*] (ISAK)
FAS .... Final Approach Segment (PIPO)
FAS .... Final Assembly Schedule (SAUO)
FAS .... Final Asset Screen [*DoD*]
FAS .... Final Average Salary
FAS .... Financial Accounting Standards (SAUO)
FAS .... Financial Accounting System
FAS .... Financial Advisors Service (SAUS)
FAS .... Financial Analysis System (MHDW)
FAS .... Financial and Administrative System (ACAE)
FAS .... Finnish-American Society [*Later, LFAS*] (EA)
FAS .... Fire Alarm System
FAS .... Fire Support Aerial System
FAS .... First and Seconds [*Wood industry*] (WPI)
FAS .... First Assistant Secretary (ADA)
FAS .... Firsts and Seconds [*Lumber trade*]
FAS .... Fixed Airlock Shroud [*NASA*]
FAS .... Flame Absorption Spectroscopy
FAS .... Flank Array Sonar (SAUS)
FAS .... Fleet Attack Submarine [*Navy*] (CAAL)
FAS .... Flexible Access System
FAS .... Flexible Assembly Subsystems (SAUS)
FAS .... flexible assembly system (SAUS)
FAS .... Flight Advisory Service [*FAA*]
FAS .... Flight Analysis Section
FAS .... Flight Assistance Service
FAS .... Floating-Point Arithmetic System (SAUS)
FAS .... Florida Academy of Sciences (SAUO)
FAS .... Flow Admission Service (SAUS)
FAS .... Flow alarm switch (SAUS)
FAS .... Fluid Analysis Spectrometer (MCD)
FAS .... Flywheel Alternator Starter [*Automotive electrical systems*]
FAS .... Focusing Array Study
FAS .... Folk Art Show
FAS .... Follow-Up Alarm System
FAS .... Foras Ciseanna Saothair (ACII)
FAS .... For a Second [*Internet dialog*]
FAS .... Force Accounting Structure
FAS .... Force Accounting System [*Army*] (AABC)
FAS .... Foreign Agricultural (or Agriculture) Service (SAUO)
FAS .... Foreign Agricultural Service [*Department of Agriculture*] [*Washington, DC*]
FAS .... Foreign Aid Society [*British*]
FAS .... Foreign Area Specialist [*Army*]
FAS .... Forward Acquisition Sensor
FAS .... Forward Acquisition System
FAS .... Forward Aid Station [*Army*] (INF)
FAS .... Forward Area Sight (SAUS)
FAS .... Foundation for Aggregate Studies
FAS .... Frame Acquisition and Synchronization (LAIN)
FAS .... Frame Alignment Sequence [*Telecommunications*] (ACRL)
FAS .... Frame Alignment Signal [*Telecommunications*] (TEL)
FAS .... Frame Analysis System [*IBM UK Ltd.*] [*Software package*] (NCC)
FAS .... France Automobile Service S.A. (SAUS)
FAS .... Franciscan Apostolic Sisters (TOCD)
FAS .... Free Alongside [*Insurance*]
fas .... Free Alongside Ship (EBF)
FAS .... Free Alongside Ship [*"INCOTERM," International Chamber of Commerce official code*]
fas .... free along side ship (SAUS)
FAS .... Free Alongside Steamer (MARI)
FAS .... Free-Association Strength [*Psychometrics*]
FAS .... Frequency-Agile Subsystem (SAUS)
FAS .... Frequency Allocation [*or Assignment*] Subcommittee (AFM)
FAS .... Frequency Analysis System (SAUS)
FAS .... Frontera Audubon Society (COE)
FAS .... Fuel Advisory System (SAUO)
FAS .... Fuel Availability System (NITA)
FAS .... Fueling-at-Sea [*Navy*] (MSA)
FAS .... Full Automatic Search (SAUS)
FAS .... Functional Acquisition Specialist [*Army*]
FAS .... Functional Address Symbol [*Military*] (AFIT)
FAS .... Functional Address System (SAUO)
FAS .... Functional Analysis Sheet
FAS .... Fund for American Studies (EA)
FAS .... Funding Agency for Schools (WDAA)
FAS 106 .... Financial Accounting Standard 106 (SAUS)
FASA .... Federal Acquisition Streamlining Act of 1994 (AAGC)
FASA .... Federated Ambulatory Surgery Association (EA)
FASA .... Federation of Afghan Students Abroad (SAUO)
FASA .... Federation of ASEAN [*Association of South East Asian Nations*] Shipowners' Associations [*Kuala Lumpur, Malaysia*] (EAIO)
FASA .... Federation of Asian Shipowners Associations (SAUO)
FASA .... Fellow, American Society of Appraisers [*American Society of Appraisers*] [*Designation awarded by*]
FASA .... Fellow of the American Society of Appraisers (SAUO)
FASA .... Fellow of the American Sociological Association
FASA .... Fellow of the Australian Society of Accountants (ODBW)
FASA .... Field Army Service Area (AABC)
FASA .... Filipino Association of South Australia
FASA .... Final Approach Spacing Assignment [*Aviation*] (IAA)
FASA .... Fixed Area Scanning Alarm
FASA .... Fleet Airships, Atlantic
FASA .... Florida Association of School Administrators (SAUO)
FASA .... Freestanding Ambulatory Surgery Association (EA)
FASA .... Sani Pass [*South Africa*] [*ICAO location identifier*] (ICLI)
FASAB .... Federal Accounting Standards Advisory Board (AAGC)
FASAB .... Front Autonomiste et Socialiste Autogestionnaire Bretonne [*Breton Autonomist and Socialist Self-Rule Front*] [*France*] [*Political party*] (PPE)
FASAC .... Financial Accounting Standards Advisory Committee (SAUS)
FASAC .... Financial Accounting Standards Advisory Council [*Financial Accounting Foundation*] (EDAC)
FASAC .... Foreign Applied Sciences Assessment Center
FASAF .... Filipinas Americas Science and Art Foundation (EA)
FASA II .... Federal Acquisition Reform Act of 1996 (AAGC)
FASAS .... Federation of Asian Scientific Academies and Societies [*India*] (EY)
FASAS .... Fellow, American Society of Abdominal Surgeons (CMD)
FASB .... Fellow of the Asiatic Society of Bengal (SAUO)
FASB .... Fetch and Set BIT [*Binary Digit*] [*Computer science*] (IAA)
FASB .... Financial Accounting Standards Board [*Formerly, Accounting Principles Board*] [*American Institute of Certified Public Accountants*]
FASB .... Financial and Accounting Services Branch (AIE)
FASB .... Springbok [*South Africa*] [*ICAO location identifier*] (ICLI)
FASB 51 .... Financial Accounting Standards Board Standard 51 [*Telecommunications*] (OTD)
FASBA .... Florida Association of School Business Administrators (SAUO)
FASBI .... Financial Accounting Standards Board Interpretations (SAUS)
FASBS .... Statements of the Financial Accounting Standards Board (SAUO)
FASBT .... Financial Accounting Standards Board Technical Bulletins (SAUS)
FASC .... Concepts Statements of the Financial Accounting Standards Board (SAUO)
fasc .... Fascicle (DIAR)
FASC .... Fascicle
FASC .... Fasciculation [*Medicine*] (MELL)
Fasc .... Fascicule [*Installment*] [*A publication*] (DLA)
FASC .... Fasciculus [*Little Bundle*] [*Latin*] (ROG)
fasc .... Fascimile (VRA)
FASC .... Federation of Asian Shippers Council (SAUO)
FASc .... Fellow of the Academy of Science (SAUO)
FASC .... Field Army Support Center (SAUS)
FASC .... Financial Accounting Standards Board (SAUS)
FASC .... Fire and Air Support Center (SAUO)
FASC .... Foreign Affairs Specialist Corps [*Department of State*]
FASC .... Foreign Affairs Sub-Committee (SAUO)
FASC .... Foreign Agricultural Service Club [*Later, Foreign Agricultural Club*] (EA)
FASC .... Forward Air Support Center (SAUS)
FASC .... Forward Area Signal Center (MCD)
FASC .... Forward Area Support Center (MCD)
FASC .... Free-Standing Ambulatory Surgical Center
FASC .... Future of the Amateur Service Committee (SAUO)
FASC .... Secunda [*South Africa*] [*ICAO location identifier*] (ICLI)
FASCA .... Federation of Armenian Students Clubs of America (EA)
FASCAM .... Familiy of Scattering Mines (SAUS)
FASCAM .... Family of Scatterable Mines [*Army*] (RDA)
FASCAM .... Field Artillery Scatterable Mines (SAUS)
FASCAP .... Fast-Payback Capital Investment Program [*Air Force*]
FASCAR .... Forward Area Surveillance Command and Control Antiarmor and Reconnaissance Vehicle (SAUO)
FASCE .... Fellow of the American Society of Civil Engineers
FA Sch .... Field Artillery School (SAUO)
FASCIA .... Fixed Asset System Control Information and Accounting [*Computer science*] (MHDI)
fascic .... fascicle (SAUS)
FASCNA .... Federation of Alpine and Schuhplattler Clubs in North America (EA)
FASCO .... Fast Scan Cutoff (CAAL)
FASCO .... Forward Area Support Company [*Military*]
FASCO .... Forward Area Support Coordination Officer [*Army*] (AABC)
FASCO .... Forward Area Support Coordinator (SAUS)
FASCODE .... Fast Atmosphere (or Atmospheric) Signature Code (SAUS)
FASCOM .... Field Army Strategic Command System (SAUO)
FASCOM .... Field Army Support Command
FASCOS .... Flight Acceleration Safety Cutoff System (MCD)
FASCP .... Fellow, American Society of Clinical Pathologists (CMD)
FASCRS .... Fellow, American Society of Colon & Rectal Surgeons (CMD)
FASCS .... Federated Antisubmarine Combat System [*Navy*] (CAAL)
FASCT .... Forward Acquisition System Center Technology (ACAE)
FASCWS .... First-Aid, Small Craft, and Water Safety [*Red Cross*]
FASD .... Financial and Administrative Systems Division (SAUS)
FASD .... Flameless Alkali Sensitized Detector [*Instrumentation*]
FA/SD .... Fleet Antisubmarine Duties (SAUS)
FASD .... Saldanha [*South Africa*] [*ICAO location identifier*] (ICLI)
FASDA .... Fast Analog Scanner for Data Acquisition [*Computer science*] (PDAA)
FASDCC .... Field Army Switched Digital Communications Center (SAUS)

FASDCC....... Field Army Switched Digital Comrnunications Center (SAUS)
FASDER....... Filing And Source-Data for Easier Retrieval (SAUS)
FASDPS....... Forward Acquisition System Data Processing (ACAE)
FASDU........ Further Assignment to Duty (DNAB)
FASE.......... FASCODE for the Environment (SAUO)
FASE.......... Federation Europeenne des Societes d'Acoustique [*Federation of Acoustical Societies of Europe*] (EAIO)
FASE.......... Federation of Acoustical Societies of Europe (EAIO)
FASE.......... Fellow of the Antiquarian Society-Edinburgh (SAUS)
FASE.......... Fellow of the Antiquarian Society of Edinburgh (ROG)
FASE.......... Field Army Support Evaluation (SAUO)
FASE.......... Force at Specified Elongation (SAUS)
FASE.......... Fundamentally Analyzable Simplified English [*Computer science*]
FASE.......... Sanae [*South Africa*] [*ICAO location identifier*] (ICLI)
FASEA......... Fellow, Association of Surgeons of East Africa (CMD)
FASEB......... Federation of American Societies for/of Experimental Biology (SAUO)
FASEB......... Federation of Societies for Experimental Biology
FASEBFP...... Federation of American Societies for Experimental Biology, Federation Proceedings [*Medicine*] (EDAA)
FASEB J....... FASEB Journal (SAUS)
FASEB Journal... Federation of American Societies for Experimental Biology Journal (MEC)
FASEC......... Foundation for America's Sexually Exploited Children [*Defunct*] (EA)
FASED......... Facilitation Awards for Scientists and Engineers with Disabilities (SAUS)
FASEM......... Fabrication and Architecture of Single-Electron Memories [*Computer Science*]
FASEM......... Factor Analytic Structural Equation Modeling
FASEX......... Fastening and Mechanised Assembling Conference and Exhibition (SAUO)
FASEX......... Fleet Air Superiority Exercise (ACAE)
FASF.......... Southern Air Command [*South Africa*] [*ICAO location identifier*] (ICLI)
FASFAC....... Fast Forward-Air-Control [*Marine Corps*] (DOMA)
FAS/FAE...... Fetal Alcohol Syndrome and Fetal Alcohol Effects [*Medicine*] (NRGU)
FASFX......... Fidelity Advisor: Short Fxd.-Inc. Cl.T [*Mutual fund ticker symbol*] (SG)
FASG.......... Fanconi's Anemia Support Group (EA)
FASG.......... Fellow American Society of Genealogists (GEAB)
FASG.......... Schweizer Reneke [*South Africa*] [*ICAO location identifier*] (ICLI)
FASGROLIA... Fast Growing Language of Initialisms and Acronyms
fasgrolia...... fast-growing language of initialisms and acronyms (SAUS)
FASGX......... Fidelity Asset Manager Growth [*Mutual fund ticker symbol*] (SG)
FASH.......... fashionmall.com, Inc. [*NASDAQ symbol*] (NASQ)
fash........... forward area suport helicopter (SAUS)
FASH.......... Forward Area Support Helicopter
FASH.......... Fraternal Association of Steel Haulers [*Defunct*] (EA)
FASH.......... Full Action Switch Held (ACAE)
FASH.......... Full Acura Service History [*Automotive classified advertising*]
FASH.......... Full Audi Service History [*Automotive classified advertising*]
FASH.......... Stellenbosch [*South Africa*] [*ICAO location identifier*] (ICLI)
FA Ship....... Free Alongside Ship (SAUS)
FASHN........ Fashion
FASHNS....... Fellow of the American Society of Head and Neck Surgery (SAUO)
FASHP........ Federation of Associations of Schools of the Health Professions [*Medicine*] (EDAA)
FASHP........ Fellow of the American Society of Hospital Pharmacists [*Medicine*] (EDAA)
FashTeachCert... Fashion Teacher's Certificate
FASI........... Fellow of the Ambulance Service Institute [*British*] (DBQ)
FASI........... Friedreich's Ataxia Society of Ireland (EAIO)
FASI........... Springs [*South Africa*] [*ICAO location identifier*] (ICLI)
FASIC......... Function-Algorithm-Specific Integrated Circuit (SAUS)
FASID......... Fellow of the Society of Interior Designers
FASID......... Flywheel Alternator Starter Input Differential [*Electric vehicles*]
FASINEX...... First Air-Sea Interaction Experiment (SAUO)
FASINEX...... Frontal Air-Sea Interaction Experiment [*Marine science*] (OSRA)
FASIS......... Fully Automatic Syntactically-Based Indexing System (SAUS)
FASISMMM... Federated Associations of Scrap Iron, Steel, Metals and Machinery Merchants (SAUO)
FASIT......... Fully Automatic Syntactically-Based Indexing of Text (SAUS)
FASIT......... Fully automatic syntactically based indexing system (SAUS)
FASK.......... Swartkop [*South Africa*] [*ICAO location identifier*] (ICLI)
FASKAP....... Field Artillery Survey Knowledge Acquisition Program [*Army*]
FASL.......... Fellow of the Anthropological Society, London (ROG)
FASL.......... Fellow of the Anthropological Society of London (SAUO)
FASL.......... Fellow of the Antiquarian Society, London (ROG)
FASL.......... Florida Association of School Librarians (SAUO)
FASL.......... Sutherland [*South Africa*] [*ICAO location identifier*] (ICLI)
FASLA......... Filmstrip and Slide Laboratory
FASM.......... Fellow of the American Society for Metals (CPGU)
FASM.......... Fellow of the Australian Society of Microbiologists (SAUS)
FASM.......... Forward Air Support Munition [*Navy*] (SEWL)
FASM.......... Swakopmund [*Namibia*] [*ICAO location identifier*] (ICLI)
FAsMA......... Fellow, Aerospace Medical Association (CMD)
FASME......... Fellow of the American Society of Mechanical Engineers (SAUO)
FASMI......... Fast Analysis of Shared Multidimensional Information (SAUS)
FASMS......... Forecast/Allocation Submission Management System (SAUO)
FASMX......... Fidelity Asset Manager [*Mutual fund ticker symbol*] (SG)
FASN.......... Free Access to Selected Numbers (SAUS)
FASN.......... Senekal [*South Africa*] [*ICAO location identifier*] (ICLI)
FASO.......... Field Aviation Supply Office
FASO.......... Fleet Anti-Submarine Officer (SAUO)
FASOC......... Forward Air Support Operations Center (or Centre) (SAUO)
FASOLA....... Fa, Sol, and La [*Musical notation system*]
FASOO......... Fellow, American Society of Ophthalmologists and Otolaryngologists (CMD)
FASOR......... Forward Area SONAR Research [*Navy*]
FASOTRAGR... Fleet Aviation Specialized Operational Training Group [*Navy*] (MCD)
FASOTRAGRULANT... Fleet Aviation Specialized Operational Training Group, Atlantic [*Navy*] (DNAB)
FASOTRAGRULANTDET... Fleet Aviation Specialized Operational Training Group, Atlantic Detachment [*Navy*] (DNAB)
FASOTRAGRUPAC... Fleet Aviation Specialized Operational Training Group, Pacific [*Formerly, FAETUPAC*] [*Later, FASOTRAGRUPACFLT*] [*Navy*]
FASOTRAGRUPACDET... Fleet Aviation Specialized Operational Training Group, Pacific Detachment [*Navy*] (DNAB)
FASOTRAGRUPACFLT... Fleet Aviation Specialized Operational Training Group, Pacific Fleet (SAUO)
FASP.......... Facility for Automatic Software Production [*Computer science*] (CAAL)
FASP.......... Fault-Tolerant Array Signal Processor (SAUS)
FASP.......... Field Analytical Support Program (SAUS)
FASP.......... Fleet Airships, Pacific
FASP.......... Flexible Automation in Ship Prefabrication (EURO)
FASP.......... Future Acoustic Signal Processor (ACAE)
FASP.......... Sir Lowry's Pass [*South Africa*] [*ICAO location identifier*] (ICLI)
FASPA......... Federation Africaine des Syndicats du Petrole et Assimiles [*African Federation of Trade Unions of Oil and Petrochemicals*] [*Tripoli, Libya*] (EAIO)
FASPAC....... Ford Asia Pacific (SAUO)
faspl........... fair average sample (SAUS)
FASPX......... Fidelity Advisor: Strategic Opport. Cl.T [*Mutual fund ticker symbol*] (SG)
FASR.......... Fast Acting Shift Register [*Computer science*] (CIST)
FASR.......... Forward Acting Shift Register (MHDB)
FASR.......... Standerton [*South Africa*] [*ICAO location identifier*] (ICLI)
FASRA......... Foundation to Assist Scientific Research in Africa (EAIO)
FASRON....... Fleet Air [*or Aircraft*] Service Squadron [*Obsolete*]
FASS.......... Federation of Animal Science Societies
FASS.......... Federation of Associations of Specialists and Subcontractors [*British*] (BI)
FASS.......... Fellow of the Royal Statistical Society (SAUO)
FASS.......... Financial and Administrative Support System [*Office of Personnel Management*] (GFGA)
FASS.......... Fine Alignment Sub-System (SAUS)
FASS.......... Flight Activities Scheduling System [*NASA*]
FASS.......... Ford Aerospace Satellite Services Corporation (SAUO)
FASS.......... Fore and Aft Scanner System (PDAA)
FASS.......... Forward Acquisition Sensor (IEEE)
FASS.......... Free Air Suspension System
FASS.......... Frequency-Agile Signal Simulator (SEWL)
FASS.......... Sishen [*South Africa*] [*ICAO location identifier*] (ICLI)
FASSA......... Fellow of the Academy of Social Sciences in Australia (WDAA)
FASSA......... Fellow of the Australian Society of Sports Administrators
FASSC......... Ford Aerospace Satellite Services Corp. [*Arlington, VA*] [*Telecommunications*] (TSSD)
FASSET....... Functional Advanced Satellite-Communication System for Evaluation and Test (SAUS)
FASSN......... Fast Attack Submarine (MCD)
FASSP......... Flexible Adaptive Spatial Signal Processor (ACAE)
FASST......... Farming for Agriculturally Sustainable Systems in Tasmania (EERA)
FASST......... Federation of Americans Supporting Science and Technology
FASST......... Flexible Architecture Standard System Technology (SAUS)
FASST......... Fly America's Supersonic Transport [*Student group*]
FASST......... Fly Around Saturated Sectors and Terminals [*National Business Aircraft Association*] [*Database*]
FASST......... Forum for the Advancement of Students in Science and Technology (ACAE)
FASST......... Forward Acquisition System Sensor Technology (ACAE)
FASST......... Friends of Aerospace Supporting Science and Technology [*An association*]
FASSTER..... Federal Aviation Surveillance System for Test and Evaluation Ranges (SEWL)
FAST.......... Association for the Final Advance of Scripture Translation (SAUO)
fast........... facial affect scoring technique (SAUS)
FAST.......... Facility for Accelerated Service Testing
FAST.......... Facility for Analyzing Surface Texture [*National Bureau of Standards*] (MCD)
FAST.......... Facility for Automated Simulation Test (ACAE)
FAST.......... Facility for Automatic Sorting and Testing
FAST.......... Factor Analysis System (SAUS)
FAST.......... Factory Automated Scheduling and Tracking (TIMI)
FAST.......... Factory Automation Systems Technology [*British*]
FAST.......... Faculty and Students Together (SAUO)
fast........... failure analysis by statistical technics (SAUS)
FAST.......... Failure Analysis by Statistical Techniques [*Data processing code*]
FAST.......... Fair and Simple Tax [*Type of flat tax proposed by Rep. Jack Kemp and Sen. Bob Kasten*]
FAST.......... Fairchild Advanced Schottky T2L [*Transistor-Transistor Logic*]
FAST.......... Fairchild Advanced Schottky Technology (SAUS)
FAST.......... Fan and Supersonic Turbine (ACAE)
FAST.......... Fans Against the Strike (EA)
FAST.......... Fare Automated Search Technique [*Airline travel service information system*]
FAST.......... Farnell Adaptable System Technology (SAUS)
FAST.......... Fast Access Scan Talker [*Occupational therapy*]
FAST.......... Fast Access Stationary Tape Guide Transport (SAUO)
FAST.......... Fast Access Storage Technology [*Computer science*] (MHDB)
FAST.......... Fast Acquisition Search and Track (MCD)
FAST.......... Fast American Ship Transport Co. (SAUO)

FAST .... Fast Answers about State Taxes (SAUS)
FAST .... Fast at Sea Transfer [*Equipment*]
FAST .... Fast Auroral Snapshot Explorer
FAST .... Fast Automated Restoration System [*Communications term*] (DCT)
FAST .... Fast Automated Screen Trading [*British*] (NUMA)
FAST .... Fast Automatic Shuttle Transfer [*System*] [*Navy*]
FAST .... Fastenal Co. [*NASDAQ symbol*] (NQ)
FAST .... Fastening [*or Fastener*] [*Automotive engineering*]
FAST .... Faster Adoption of Superior Technologies
Fast .... Fasti [*of Ovid*] [*Classical studies*] (OCD)
FAST .... Fast storage technology (SAUS)
FAST .... FCES Automated Software Test (MCD)
FAST .... Federal Acquisition Services for Technology [*GSA*] (AAGC)
FAST .... Federal Advanced Superconducting Transportation Act
FasT .... Federal Assessment Team [*Department of Emergency Management*] (DEMM)
FAST .... Federal Assistance for Staff Training [*Education*]
FAST .... Federal Assistance Streamlining Taskforce [*HEW*]
FAST .... Federation Against Software Theft
FAST .... Feed and Speed Technology (SAUS)
FAST .... Fence Against Satellite Threats
FAST .... Fiduciary Activity Simulation Training [*Investment banking simulation game*]
FAST .... Field Activities Simulation Tool (VLIE)
FAST .... Field Artillery Survey Team
FAST .... Field Artillery Survey Test (MCD)
FAST .... Field Artillery System Training (ACAE)
FAST .... Field Assistance in Science and Technology Program [*US Army Materiel Command*]
FAST .... Field Assistance Support Team (MCD)
FAST .... Field Asymmetry Sensing Technique
FAST .... Field Automated Systems Test (SAUS)
fast .... field data applications, systems, and technics (SAUS)
FAST .... Field Data Applications, Systems, and Techniques [*Computer science*]
FAST .... Fighter Airborne Supply Tank (SAUO)
fast .... file analysis and selection technics (SAUS)
FAST .... File Analysis and Selection Technique [*Computer science*]
FAST .... Final Approach Spacing Tool [*FAA*] (TAG)
FAST .... Final Automated Systems Test (SAUS)
FAST .... Final Automated System Test (VLIE)
FAST .... Financial Analysis and Security Trading
FAST .... Financial Analysis System (SAUS)
FAST .... Finger Print Access and Searching Technique (SAUS)
FAST .... Fingerprint Access and Searching Technique [*Computer science*] (IAA)
FAST .... Finite Area Solids Technology (MCD)
FAST .... First Application System Test [*Computer science*] (VERA)
FAST .... First Atomic Ship Transport (SAUO)
FAST .... First Atomic Ship Transport, Inc.
FAST .... Fitness and Arthritis in Seniors Trial
FAST .... Fixed-Abrasive Sawing Technique (SAUS)
FAST .... Fixed Abrasive Slicing [*Semiconductor technology*]
FAST .... Fleet Anti-Terrorism Security Team (SEWL)
FAST .... Fleet Antiterrorist Security Team [*Marine Corps*] (DOMA)
FAST .... Fleet Attitude Status (DNAB)
fast .... fleet-sizing analysis and sensitivity technic (SAUS)
FAST .... Fleet-Sizing Analysis and Sensitivity Technique [*Bell System*]
FAST .... Flexible Ada Simulation Tool (SSD)
FAST .... Flexible Algebraic Scientific Translator [*NCR Corp.*]
FAST .... Flexible Automatic Systems Tester (SAUS)
FAST .... Flexible Automation in Shipbuilding Technology (VLIE)
FAST .... Flight Advisory Service Test [*FAA*]
FAST .... Flight Analyses System (SAUO)
FAST .... Flight Aptitude Selection Test [*Army*]
FAST .... Florida Agricultural Services and Technology (SAUO)
FAST .... Florida Association of Science Teachers (EDAC)
FAST .... Flow Actuated Sediment Trap [*Marine science*] (OSRA)
FAST .... Flow Analysis Software Toolkit (RALS)
FAST .... Flow & Analysis System For TRANSCOM (SAUS)
FAST .... Flow-Assisted, Short-Term [*Balloon catheter*] [*Cardiology*] (DAVI)
FAST .... Fluor Analytical Scheduling Technique (SAUS)
FAST .... Fluorescent Allergosorbent Test [*Medicine*] (CPH)
FAST .... Fluorescent Antibody Staining Technique [*Clinical chemistry*]
FAST .... Fluorinel dissolution process and fuel storage (SAUS)
FAST .... Fluoro-Allergo Sorbent Test [*Biochemistry*] (DAVI)
FAST .... Fly Away Satellite Terminal (SAUS)
FAST .... FMIS Applications Support Technique (SAUO)
FAST .... Focus, Aperture, Shutter, Tachometer [*Cinematography*] (NTCM)
FAST .... Folding Articulated Square Truss (SPST)
FAST .... Food Additive Suppliers and Traders [*Database from Food Association*] [*British*] (NITA)
FAST .... Food Allergy Survivors Together (ADWA)
FAST .... Food and Allied Service Trades Department [*of AFL-CIO*] (EA)
FAST .... Foolproof Auditing and Sale of Tickets [*in motion picture theaters*]
FAST .... Force and Supply Tracking System (SAUO)
FAST .... Fore-Aft Scanning Technique [*Marine science*] (OSRA)
FAST .... Forecast Analysis and Scheduling Technique (FOTI)
FAST .... Forecasting and Assessment in Science and Technology [*Commission of the European Communities program, 1978-1983*]
fast .... forecasting and scheduling technic (SAUS)
FAST .... Forecasting and Scheduling Technique
FAST .... Forecasting, Assessment and Methodology in the Field of Science and Technology (SAUS)
FAST .... Foreign Area Specialist Training [*Army*]
FAST .... Formal Auto-Indexing of Scientific Texts [*Computer science*] (IEEE)
FAST .... Formula and Statement Translator [*Computer science*] (MCD)
FAST .... Formula Automatic Scalar Translator (VLIE)
FAST .... Formula Automatic Scaler Translator (SAUS)
FAST .... Forward Airborne Surveillance and Tracking
FAST .... Forward Air Strike Task (CINC)
FAST .... Forward Area Shelterized Terminal (SAUS)
FAST .... Forward Area Support Team [*Military*] (INF)
FAST .... Foundation for Applied Science and Technology [*University of Pittsburgh*] [*Research center*] (RCD)
FAST .... Four-Address to SOAP [*Self-Optimizing Automatic Pilot*] Translator [*Computer science*] (IEEE)
FAST .... Fourier Amplitude-Sensitivity Test (CARB)
fast .... free and single tourist (SAUS)
FAST .... Freight Accounting Shipment Tracing System (MCD)
FAST .... freight accounting system tracing (SAUS)
FAST .... Freight Automated System for Traffic Management (AABC)
FAST .... French Advances in Science and Technology (SAUS)
FAST .... Frenchay Aphasia Screening Test [*Medicine*] (EDAA)
FAST .... Frequency Agile Search and Track Seeker
FAST .... Friction Assessment Screening Test [*for brake linings*]
FAST .... Fuel Aerosol Simulation Test [*Nuclear energy*] (NRCH)
FAST .... Fuel and Sensor, Tactical (MCD)
fast .... fuel and sensor tanks (SAUS)
FAST .... Fuel Assembly Stability Test (NRCH)
FAST .... Fugitive Assessment Sampling Train [*Environmental Protection Agency*] (GFGA)
FAST .... Fully Atomized Stratified Turbulence
FAST .... Fully Automated Scoring Target [*System*] (MCD)
FAST .... Fully Automated Switching Teletype (SAUS)
FAST .... Fully Automatic Scoring Target (SAUS)
FAST .... Fully Automatic Sort and Test [*Computer science*] (IAA)
FAST .... Fully Automatic Sorting and Testing (SAUS)
fast .... fully automatic switching teletype (SAUS)
FAST .... Functional Analysis Specification Tree (VLIE)
FAST .... Functional Analysis System Technique
fast .... functional assessment stages (SAUS)
FAST .... function analysis system technique (SAUS)
FAST .... Fundamentals of Application and System Training [*Course*] [*Computer science*]
FAST .... Future Aircraft Supersonic Transport (ACAE)
FAST .... Future Analytical Support Team (SAUO)
FAST .... Future Armament Systems Technology (RDA)
FAST .... Future Artillery Systems Technology (SAUS)
FAST .... Fuze-Activating Static Target (MCD)
FAST .... Somerset East [*South Africa*] [*ICAO location identifier*] (ICLI)
FASTA .... Federal Aviation Science and Technological Association [*Defunct*] (EA)
FASTA .... Federal Aviation Science and Technology Association (SAUS)
FASTAC .... Flame/Furnace Autosampling Technique with Automatic Calibration [*Spectroscopy*]
FASTAC .... Furnace Aerosol Sampling Technique with Autocalibration (SAUS)
FASTALS .... Force Analyses Simulation of Theater Administration and Logistic Support (SAUO)
FASTAR .... Family of Army Surveillance & Target Acquisition Requirements (SAUO)
FASTAR .... Forward Area Surveillance and Target Acquisition Radar (SAUS)
FASTAR .... Frequency Angle Scanning, Tracking, and Ranging
FASTBACCS .... Field Artillery System Training for the Common Battalion Command and Control System (MCD)
FASTBAC's .... First Automotive Short-Term Bonds and Certificates [*Drexel Burnham Lambert, Inc.*] [*Finance*]
FASTC .... Foreign Aerospace Science and Technology Center [*Air Force*]
FASTC .... Foreign Aerospace Science & Technology Directorate Center (SAUS)
FASTCAL .... Field Assistance Support Team for Calibration (DOMA)
FASTCAT .... Fast Catalog (SAUS)
FASTCAV .... Family Area of Subterranean Troop Carrying Vehicle (SAUO)
FASTCL .... Files for Agricultural Science and Technology Literature in Chinese (SAUS)
FastCm .... FastComm Communications Corp. [*Associated Press*] (SAG)
FASTDOC .... Fast Document Ordering and Document Delivery (TELE)
FASTEJ .... Files for Agricultural Science and Technology Research Projects (SAUS)
FASTEL .... Fast Economic Language [*Computer science*] (BUR)
FASTEL .... Files for Agricultural Science and Technology Literature [*Database*] [*Agricultural Science Information Center*] [*Information service or system*] (CRD)
FASTEL .... Files for Agricultural Science and Technology Literature in English (SAUS)
Fastenal .... Fastenal Co. [*Associated Press*] (SAG)
FASTEP .... Files for Agricultural Science and Technology Personnel [*Database*] [*Agricultural Science Information Center*] [*Information service or system*] (CRD)
FASTER .... Files for Agricultural Science and Technology Research Reports (SAUS)
FASTER .... Filing and Source-data-entry Technique for Easier Retrieval (SAUS)
FASTER .... Filing and Source Data Entry Techniques for Easier Retrieval [*Computer science*] (MHDI)
FASTEX .... Frontal and Atlantic Storm-Track Experiment [*Planned Experiment*] [*Marine science*] (OSRA)
FASTEX .... Fronts and Atlantic Storm Experiment (SAUS)
Fast Ferry Int ... Fast Ferry International (journ.) (SAUS)
FASTFIRE .... Field Artillery System Training Fire Direction Centers (MCD)
FASTI .... Fast Access to Systems Technical Information
FASTI .... Fast Access to System Test Information (SAUS)

FASTLODS... Fighter Aircraft Structural Loads [*Program*] [*Air Force*]
FASTM......... Freight Automated System for Traffic Management (SAUS)
FASTNET...... Fixed Army Strategic Telephone Network (SAUS)
Fastnr......... Fastener (SAUS)
FAST-OB....... Officer Battery Flight Aptitude Selection Test [*Military*] (INF)
FASTOP....... Flutter and Strength Optimization Program (SAUS)
FASTOP....... Flutter and Strength Optimization Program for Lifting Surface Structures (MCD)
FASTOR....... Fast Access Storage [*Computer science*] (VLIE)
FASTP......... Foreign Area Specialist Training Program [*Army*]
FAST Pack... Fuel And Sensor Tactical Package (SAUS)
FASTPACK... Fuel and Sensor Tactical Package (MCD)
FASTRACK... Force Accounting System Track [*Army*] (MCD)
FASTRAM.... Falling Sphere Trajectory Measurement (MUGU)
FASTRAM.... Fully Active Squish Turbulent Rim Air Motion [*Automotive engineering*]
FAST RIPSAW... Financial Automation Systems Team for Writing Programs for Standardized Army-Wide Applications
FASTROM.... Falling Sphere Trajectory Measurement (SAUS)
FASTRON.... Fleet Aircraft Service Squadron (MUGU)
FASTS......... Federation of Australian Scientific and Technical Societies (EERA)
FASTSUPPORT... Field Artillery System Training for the Fire Support Officer (MCD)
FASTT......... Fleet All-Source Tactical Terminal (DOMA)
FAST-TRAC... Faster and Safer Travel/Traffic Routing and Advanced Control [*FHWA*] (TAG)
FASTU......... Fleet Ammunition Ship Training Unit (DNAB)
FASTULANT... Fleet Ammunition Ship Training Unit, Atlantic
FASTUPAC... Fleet Ammunition Ship Training Unit, Pacific
FASTV......... First Artillery Ammunition Resupply Vehicle [*Army*] (RDA)
FAST-VAL.... Forward Air Strike Evaluation
FAST VISION... Facets Stereo Vision (SAUO)
FASU........... Fleet Air Support Unit (SAUO)
FASU........... Fleet Aviation Support Unit (MCD)
FASU........... Sace [*South Africa*] [*ICAO location identifier*] (ICLI)
FASUS......... Freight Assurance Storage, United States
FASV........... Field Alert Status Verification [*Army*] (MCD)
FASV........... Floral Art Society of Victoria [*Australia*]
FASV........... Silvermine [*South Africa*] [*ICAO location identifier*] (ICLI)
F/ASVS....... Fighter/Attack Simulator Visual System [*Military*]
FASW.......... Fleet Airship Wing (SAUS)
FASW.......... South West Africa Air Force Headquarters [*Namibia*] [*ICAO location identifier*] (ICLI)
FASWAC...... Food and Service Workers Association of Canada (SAUO)
FASWC........ Fleet Antisubmarine Warfare Command (IEEE)
FASWOC...... Food and Service Workers of Canada
FASWSCHOOL... Fleet Antisubmarine Warfare School
FASX........... Fairbanks Air Service [*Alaska*] [*Air carrier designation symbol*]
FASX........... Swellendam [*South Africa*] [*ICAO location identifier*] (ICLI)
FASY........... Syferfontein [*South Africa*] [*ICAO location identifier*] (ICLI)
FASZ........... Skukuza [*South Africa*] [*ICAO location identifier*] (ICLI)
Fat.............. De Fato [*of Cicero*] [*Classical studies*] (OCD)
FAT............. Factory Acceptance Test
FAT............. Factory Acceptance Trial (SAUS)
FAT............. Faithful Available and Teachable (SAUO)
FAT............. Family Adjustment Test [*Psychology*]
FAT............. Family Assessment Tool [*Kit*] [*Medicine*]
FAT............. Family Attitudes Test (DB)
FAT............. Farner Air Transport AG [*Switzerland*] [*ICAO designator*] (FAAC)
FAT............. Fast Automatic Transfer
FAT............. Fast Axonal Transport [*Neurobiology*]
FAT............. Fatalities [*Military*] (DOMA)
FAT............. Fathom (NATG)
FAT............. Fatigue (WDAA)
FAT............. Fatphobia Awareness Training
FAT............. Field Advisory Team (SAUO)
FAT............. Field Artillery Tractor [*British*]
FAT............. Field Artillery Training (SAUO)
FAT............. File Access Table [*Computer science*] (VLIE)
FAT............. File Allocation Table [*Computer science*]
FAT............. File Attribution Table [*Computer science*] (PCM)
FAT............. Filozofia Asocio Tutmonda (SAUO)
FAT............. Final Acceptance, Assembly Tests
FAT............. Final Acceptance Trial (SAUS)
FAT............. Final Aerospace Trial
FAT............. Final Approach Track [*Aviation*] (DA)
FAT............. Final Assembly Test
fat.............. fire and theft (SAUS)
FAT............. First Article Test
FAT............. Fixed Analyzer Transmission (SAUS)
FAT............. Fixed Asset Transfer [*Business term*]
FAT............. Flight Acceptance Test
FA-T............ Flight Attendant in Training (DNAB)
FAT............. Flight Attitude Table [*NASA*] (NASA)
FAT............. Flight Test Station [*ITU designation*] (CET)
FAT............. Fluorescent Antibody Technique [*Immunology*] (DAVI)
FAT............. Fluorescent Antibody Test [*Clinical medicine*]
FAT............. Folk Arts Theater (SAUS)
FAT............. Food Awareness Training
FAT............. Forces Armees Tchadiennes [*Chad Armed Forces*] (PD)
FAT............. Foreign Area Toll [*Telecommunications*] (TEL)
FAT............. Foreign Area Translation [*Telecommunications*] (TEL)
FAT............. Formula Assembler Translator [*Computer science*] (BUR)
FAT............. Forward Area Trace (MCD)
FAT............. Foundation for Anglican Traditions [*Defunct*] (EA)
FAT............. Frappe A Tort (SAUS)
FAT............. Free Air Temperature (NG)
fat.............. free alongside terminal (SAUS)
fat.............. free at terminal (SAUS)
FAT............. Fresno [*California*] [*Airport symbol*] (OAG)
FAT............. Fresno Air Terminal (SAUO)
FAT............. Friends of Appropriate Technology (EA)
FAT............. Frustration, Anxiety, and Tension
FAT............. Fuel and Transportation (IAA)
FAT............. Full Annual Toll (SAUS)
fat++........... Obese (SPVS)
FAT32......... File Allocation Table 32-Bit [*Computer science*]
FATA........... Federation of ASEAN Travel Agents (SAUO)
FATAB......... Field Artillery Target Acquisition Battalion [*Army*] (AABC)
FATACOP..... Field Artillery Tactical Operations (SAUS)
FATAG......... Field Artillery Target Acquisition Group [*Army*] (AABC)
FATAL......... FADAC [*Field Artillery Digital Automatic Computer*] Automatic Test AnalysisLanguage (IEEE)
FATAL......... Fit Anything to Anything You Like (MHDB)
FATAL......... Fully Automatic Test Algebraic Language (SAUS)
FATAR......... Fast Analysis of Tape and Recovery
FATAs......... Federally Administered Tribal Areas (Pakistan) [*Political party*] (PSAP)
FATB........... Fatbrain.com, Inc. [*NASDAQ symbol*] (NASQ)
FATB........... Floor Ataxia Test Battery
FATC........... Field Artillery Training Camp (SAUO)
FATC........... Field Artillery Training Center (SAUO)
FATC........... Field Artillery Training Centre [*British military*] (DMA)
FATC........... Fleet Area Telecommunications Center [*Navy*] (MCD)
FATC........... Tristan De Cunha [*South Africa*] [*ICAO location identifier*] (ICLI)
FATCAT....... Film and Television Correlation Assessment Technique (MCD)
FATCAT....... Frequency and Time Circuit Analysis Technique [*NASA*]
FAT CHANGE... Free All Toledoans - Committee to Help All Neglected Citizens Emigrate (SAUO)
FAT-COI...... Federation Americaine du Travail et Congres des Organisations Industrielles [*American Federation of Labor and Congress of Industrial Organizations - AFL-CIO*] [*Canada*]
FATCP......... Forum for the Advancement of Toxicology in Colleges of Pharmacy (EA)
FATD........... Federal Applied Technology Database [*National Technical Information Service*] [*Information service or system*] (CRD)
FATD(A)....... Federal Association of Teachers of Dancing (Australia)
FATDAD....... Fermanagh, Armagh, Tyrone, Derry, Antrim, Down [*The six counties of Northern Ireland*]
FATDL......... Frequency and Time-Division Data Link
FATDOC....... Film and Television Documentation Center [*State University of New York at Albany*] [*Information service or system*] (IID)
fatdog......... fatty hotdog (SAUS)
FATDS......... Field Artillery Tactical Data Systems [*Army*] (RDA)
FATE........... Federated Assessment and Targeting Enhancement (SEWL)
FATE........... Federation of Automatic Transmission Engineers [*British*] (DBA)
FATE........... Feedbacks and Arctic Terrestrial Ecosystems (SAUS)
FATE........... Field-Assisted Thermal Erasure (SAUS)
FATE........... Force Application Tactics Evaluation (SAA)
FATE........... Formation of Aerosol and their Transformation over Europe (SAUS)
FATE........... Formulating Analytical and Technical Estimate (PDAA)
FATE........... Foundation Aiding the Elderly (EA)
FATE........... Functional Attributes in Terrestrial Ecosystems (SAUO)
FATE........... Fusing and Arming Test and Evaluation (SAUS)
FATE........... Fusing and Arming Test Experiment (SAUS)
FATE........... Future Aircraft Technology Enhancement
FATE........... Fuze Arming Test Experiment
FATE........... Fuze Automatic Test Equipment (SAUS)
FATE........... Fuzing, Arming, Test and Evaluation (PDAA)
fa technique... fluorescent antibody technique (SAUS)
FATES......... FIFRA [*Federal Insecticide, Fungicide, and Rodenticide Act*] and TSCA [*Toxic Substances Control Act*] Enforcement System (GNE)
FATES......... Flow-Through Aquatic Toxicology Exposure System [*Evaluation of sediment contaminants*]
FATF........... Free Air Test Facility
fatfurters..... fat-filled frankfurters (SAUS)
FATG........... Fat Globules [*Biochemistry*] (DAVI)
FATG........... Fine Art Trade Guide [*British*] (DBA)
FATG........... Fixed Air-To-Ground (SAUS)
FATG........... Fixed Azimuth Tape Guidance (SAUS)
fath............ father (SAUS)
fath............ Fathom (SHCU)
FATH........... Fathom
FATH........... Thohoyandou [*South Africa*] [*ICAO location identifier*] (ICLI)
fath-in-law... father in-law (SAUS)
FATHOM...... Foreign Affairs Theory, Operations, and Monitoring (DNAB)
FATI............ Finance Advisers Technical Instruction (SAUO)
Fatigue Fract Eng Mater Str... Fatigue and Fracture of Engineering Materials and Structures (journ.) (SAUS)
FATIMA........ Fatigue Indicating Meter Attachment
FATIPEC...... Federation d'Associations de Techniciens des Industries de Peintures, Vernis, Emaux, et Encres d'Imprimerie de l'Europe [*Federation of the Associations of Technicians of the Paint, Varnish, and Ink Industries of Continental Europe*] (EAIO)
FATK........... Tsumkwe [*Namibia*] [*ICAO location identifier*] (ICLI)
FATLAD........ Fermanagh, Armagh, Tyrone, Londonderry, Antrim, Down [*Unionist mnemonic for the six counties of Northern Ireland*]
FAT/LOT...... First Article Test/Limited Operational Test
FATM........... Tsumeb [*Namibia*] [*ICAO location identifier*] (ICLI)
FATMA......... Frequency And Time Multiple Access (SAUS)

FATMAT .... Field Artillery Turret Maintenance Trainer (MCD)
FATMS .... Field Artillery Turret Maintenance Simulator (MCD)
FATN .... First American Corp. [*NASDAQ symbol*] (NQ)
FATN .... First Amer (Tenn) [*NASDAQ symbol*] (TTSB)
FATO .... Final Approach and Takeoff Area [*OST*] (TAG)
FATOC .... Field Army Tactical Operation Center
FATOC .... Forward Air Transport Operations Centre (SAUS)
FATOLA .... Flexible Aircraft Takeoff and Landing Analysis (MCD)
FATP .... Bloemfontein/New Tempe [*South Africa*] [*ICAO location identifier*] (ICLI)
FATP .... Factory Acceptance Test Procedure
FATP .... Field Assembly Test Point (IAA)
FATR .... Fixed Auto Transfer (MCD)
FATR .... Fixed Autotransformer
FATRACS .... Field Army Tactical Random Access Communications System
FATRANS .... First Available Transportation
FATS .... Factory Acceptance Test Specifications (SAUO)
FATS .... Facts About the States [*A publication*]
FATS .... Fast Analysis of Tape Surface [*Computer science*] (CIST)
FATS .... Field Automatic Telephone Switch (SAUS)
FATS .... Fight to Advertise the Truth about Saturates [*Student legal action organization*]
FATS .... Fiji Air Travel Service (SAUO)
FATS .... Firearms Training Systems, Inc.
FATS .... Focal Plane Array Test Station (ACAE)
FATS .... FORTRAN [*Formula Translating System*] Automatic Timing System [*Computer science*]
FATS .... Forward Area Target Surveillance System (ACAE)
FATS .... South African Air Force Tactical Support Command [*ICAO location identifier*] (ICLI)
FATSA .... Flowers Auditory Test of Selective Attention
FATSEA .... Federation of Air Traffic Safety Electronic Associations (SAUO)
FATSO .... First Aid Technical Stores Outfit [*Military*] [*British*]
FATSO .... First-Airborne Telescopic and Spectrographic Observatory (DNAB)
FATSS .... Forward Area Target Surveillance System (SAUS)
FATT .... Forward Area Tactical Teletype (MCD)
FATT .... Forward Area Tactical Teletypewriter (SAUS)
FATT .... Forward Area Tactical Typewriter (SAUS)
FATT .... Fracture Appearance Transition Temperature
FATT .... Fracture-Area Transition Temperature (SAUS)
FATT .... Friday at the Track [*Motorsports*]
FATT .... Tutuka [*South Africa*] [*ICAO location identifier*] (ICLI)
FATTCL .... Fernald Atomic Trades and Labor Council (SAUO)
FATTH .... Fiber Almost to the Home [*Telecommunications*]
FATTS .... Forward Area Tactical Teletypewriter Set
FATTY .... Forward Area Tactical Typewriter
FATU .... Fleet Air Tactical Unit
FA Tube .... French Army Tube (SAUS)
FATUREC .... Federation of Air Transport User Representatives in the European Community (DA)
FATZ .... Tzaneen [*South Africa*] [*ICAO location identifier*] (ICLI)
FAU .... Fairfield University, Fairfield, CT [*OCLC symbol*] (OCLC)
FAU .... Fairview, OK [*Location identifier*] [*FAA*] (FAAL)
FAU .... Falmouth Petroleum [*Vancouver Stock Exchange symbol*]
fau .... faucet (SAUS)
FAU .... Faucher Aviation [*France*] [*ICAO designator*] (FAAC)
FAU .... Faujasite [*A zeolite*]
FAU .... Field Action Unit (AEBS)
fau .... field action units (SAUS)
FAU .... Fine Alignment Unit
FAU .... Fixed Asset Utilization [*Business term*] (ADA)
FAU .... Flag Administrative Unit
FAU .... Flight Attendants Union (SAUO)
FAU .... Florida Atlantic University [*Boca Raton*]
fau .... forced air unit (SAUS)
FAU .... Freeport-McMoRan Gold Co. [*NYSE symbol*] (COMM)
FAU .... Frequency Allocation and Uses
FAU .... Friends Ambulance Unit [*British military*] (DMA)
FAU .... Fugitive Apprehension Unit (SAUS)
FAU .... Fundacion Arte por Uruguay [*Formerly, Relatives Committee for Uruguay*] [*Sweden*] (EAIO)
FAUC .... Ulco [*South Africa*] [*ICAO location identifier*] (ICLI)
FAUE .... Friedrich-Alexander University at Erlangen (SAUO)
FAUH .... Uitenhage [*South Africa*] [*ICAO location identifier*] (ICLI)
FAUI .... Federation of Australian Underwater Instructors
FAUK .... Usakos [*Namibia*] [*ICAO location identifier*] (ICLI)
FAUL .... Faulding, Inc. [*NASDAQ symbol*] (SAG)
FAUL .... Five Associated University Libraries [*State University of New York at Buffalo and Binghamton, Cornell University, Syracuse University, University of Rochester*]
FAUL .... Ulundi [*South Africa*] [*ICAO location identifier*] (ICLI)
Faulding .... Faulding, Inc. [*Associated Press*] (SAG)
Faunty .... Fauntleroy (SAUS)
FAUP .... Upington/Pierre Van Ryneveld [*South Africa*] [*ICAO location identifier*] (ICLI)
FAUS .... Federal Aid Urban System [*Road improvement program*] [*Federal Highway Administration*]
FAUS .... Feingold Association of the United States (EA)
FAUS .... Uis [*Namibia*] [*ICAO location identifier*] (ICLI)
FAUSA .... Fokker Aircraft USA Inc. (SAUS)
FAusPr .... First Australia Prime Income Fund [*Associated Press*]
FAUSST .... French-Anglo-United States Supersonic Transport
FAUST .... Far Ultraviolet Space Telescope
FAUST .... Fault Analysis Using Simulation and Testing (VLIE)
Faust .... Faust's Compiled Laws [*Scotland*] [*A publication*] (DLA)
FAUST .... Folkebibliotekernes Automation System [*Denmark*] [*Public libraries automation system*] (NITA)
FAUSTUS .... Frame-Activated Unified Story Understanding System (SAUS)
FAUT .... Umtata (K. D. Matanzima) [*South Africa*] [*ICAO location identifier*] (ICLI)
FAV .... Fakarava [*French Polynesia*] [*Airport symbol*] (OAG)
FAV .... Fan Air Valve (MCD)
FAV .... Fast-Acting Valve (SAUS)
FAV .... Fast Attack Vehicles (SAUS)
FAV .... Favor (WDAA)
FAV .... Favorable (AFM)
FAV .... Favorite (ADA)
FAV .... Favourite (SAUO)
FAV .... Fayetteville [*Arkansas*] [*Seismograph station code, US Geological Survey*] (SEIS)
FAV .... Feline Ataxia Virus (MAE)
FAV .... Final Acute Value (EEVL)
FAV .... Finnaviation OY [*Finland*] [*ICAO designator*] (FAAC)
FAV .... Fire Ant Venom [*Immunology*]
FAV .... Fixed-Angle Variable
FAV .... Forfar Artillery Volunteers [*British military*] (DMA)
FAV .... Frog Adenovirus
FAV .... Fuel Filtration-Additive Unit
FAVA .... Federation of Asian Veterinary (or Veterinarian) Associations (SAUO)
FAVA .... Fixed Asset Valuation Adjustment [*Business term*] (ADA)
FAVB .... Vryburg [*South Africa*] [*ICAO location identifier*] (ICLI)
FAVC .... Fleet Audio-Visual Center (DNAB)
FAVC .... Flight Attendant Volunteer Corps (EA)
FAVD .... Vrede [*South Africa*] [*ICAO location identifier*] (ICLI)
FAVDO .... Forum of African Voluntary Development Organizations
FAVE .... Faculty of Agronomy and Veterinary Sciences (SAUS)
FAVE .... Ventersdorp [*South Africa*] [*ICAO location identifier*] (ICLI)
FAVER .... Fast Virtual Export/Restore [*Computer science*] (VLIE)
FAVF .... Fleet Audio-Visual Facility (DNAB)
FAVG .... Durban/Virginia [*South Africa*] [*ICAO location identifier*] (ICLI)
FAVN .... Fluorescent-Antibody Virus Neutralization Test [*Immunology*]
FAVO .... Fleet Aviation Officer [*British*]
F Av O .... Fleet Aviation Order (SAUO)
FAVP .... Vanderbijlpark [*South Africa*] [*ICAO location identifier*] (ICLI)
FAVR .... Vredendal [*South Africa*] [*ICAO location identifier*] (ICLI)
FAVS .... Family of Army Vehicles Study
FAVS .... Fighter Attack Visual System (ACAE)
FAVS .... First Aviation Services, Inc. [*NASDAQ symbol*] (NASQ)
FAVU .... Volksrust [*South Africa*] [*ICAO location identifier*] (ICLI)
FAVV .... Vereeniging [*South Africa*] [*ICAO location identifier*] (ICLI)
FAVW .... Victoria West [*South Africa*] [*ICAO location identifier*] (ICLI)
FAVY .... Vryheid [*South Africa*] [*ICAO location identifier*] (ICLI)
FAW .... Faith at Work (EA)
FAW .... Falwell Aviation, Inc. [*ICAO designator*] (FAAC)
FAW .... Fawick Corporation (SAUO)
FAW .... Fiber Areal Weight (SAUS)
FAW .... Fighter, All Weather [*British military*] (DMA)
FAW .... First Automotive Works [*Chinese manufacturer*]
FAW .... Fixed Axial Weapon [*Military*] (MUSM)
FAW .... Fleet Air Wing [*Navy*]
FAW .... Fleet All Weather
FAW .... Florida Administrative Weekly [*A publication*] (AAGC)
FAW .... Forward Area Weapons [*Military*]
FAW .... Frame Alignment Word (SAUS)
FAW .... Free at Works (SAUS)
FAW .... Friends Around the World [*An association*] (EA)
FAW .... Friends of American Writers (EA)
FAW .... Front Art Work (SAUS)
FAW .... Northampton, MA [*Location identifier*] [*FAA*] (FAAL)
FAWA .... Factory Assist Work Authorization (SAUS)
FAWA .... Federation of Asian Women's Associations [*San Marcelino, Philippines*]
FAWA .... Warmbaths [*South Africa*] [*ICAO location identifier*] (ICLI)
FAWAC .... Farm Animal Welfare Advisory Committee (SAUS)
FAWAF .... Fleet Air Wing, Atlantic Fleet (MCD)
FAWAI .... Fishermen and Allied Workers of America, International (SAUO)
FAWB .... Pretoria/Wonderboom [*South Africa*] [*ICAO location identifier*] (ICLI)
FAWBE .... Fire Ant Whole Body Extract [*Immunology*]
FAWC .... Farm Animal Welfare Council (GVA)
Fawc .... Fawcett on Landlord and Tenant [*3 eds.*] [*1870-1905*] [*A publication*] (DLA)
FAWC .... Federation of Army Wives Clubs [*British*]
FAWC .... Franciscan Apostolate of the Way of the Cross (EA)
FAWC .... Worcester [*South Africa*] [*ICAO location identifier*] (ICLI)
FAWCE .... Farm Animal Welfare Coordinating Executive [*British*] (DI)
Fawcett .... Fawcett on Landlord and Tenant [*3rd ed.*] [*1905*] [*A publication*] (ILCA)
Fawcett .... Fawcett World Library (SAUS)
Fawc L & T .... Fawcett on Landlord and Tenant [*3 eds.*] [*1870-1905*] [*A publication*] (DLA)
FAWCO .... Federation of American Women's Clubs Overseas (EA)
Fawc Ref .... Fawcett. Court of Referees [*1866*] [*A publication*] (DLA)
FAWD .... Warden [*South Africa*] [*ICAO location identifier*] (ICLI)
FAWE .... Windhoek/Eros [*Namibia*] [*ICAO location identifier*] (ICLI)
FAWEC .... Football Association of War Emergency Committee (SAUO)
FAWEP .... Field Activity War Emergency Program [*DoD*]
FAWESP .... Field Activity War and Emergency Support Plan [*DoD*] (MCD)
FAWG .... Flight Assignment Working Group [*NASA*] (NASA)
fawg .... free at wharf gate (SAUS)
FAWH .... Windhoek/J. G. Strijdom [*Namibia*] [*ICAO location identifier*] (ICLI)

FAWI Witbank [*South Africa*] [*ICAO location identifier*] (ICLI)
FAWK Waterkloof [*South Africa*] [*ICAO location identifier*] (ICLI)
FAWL Williston [*South Africa*] [*ICAO location identifier*] (ICLI)
FAWLA Fighter Aircraft Wing Lift Augmentation (ACAE)
FAWM Welkom [*South Africa*] [*ICAO location identifier*] (ICLI)
Fawn Florida Automated Weather Network (SAUO)
FAWNA Fostering and Assistance for Wildlife Needing Aid [*Australia*]
FAWO Willowmore [*South Africa*] [*ICAO location identifier*] (ICLI)
FAWOD Furnish Assignment Instructions without Delay
FAWP Wepener [*South Africa*] [*ICAO location identifier*] (ICLI)
FAWPRA Fleet Air Western Pacific Repair Area (MCD)
FAWPS Flight and Weapons Planning System (SAUO)
FAWPSC Frequency Allocation and Wave Propagation Subcommittee (NATG)
FAWPSS Forward Area Water Point Supply System (SAUS)
FAWR front-axle weight rating (SAUS)
FAWS Federal Air Weather Service (SAUO)
FAWS Federation of African Welfare Societies (SAUO)
FAWS First Aid and Water Safety (SAUO)
FAWS Flight Advisory Weather Service
FAWSHMOTION Fast Wave Simple Harmonic Motion (SAUS)
FAWSHMOTRON Fast Wave Simple Harmonic Motion [*A microwave tube device*]
FAWT For Address, Write To
FAWT Kingwilliamstown [*South Africa*] [*ICAO location identifier*] (ICLI)
FAWTC Fleet Antiwarfare Training Center (MUGU)
FAWTU Fleet All-Weather Training Unit
FAWTULANT Fleet All-Weather Training Unit, Atlantic
FAWTUPAC Fleet All-Weather Training Unit, Pacific
FAWU Fishermen and Allied Workers Union (SAUO)
FAWU Food and Allied Workers Union (SAUO)
FAWW Windhoek [*South Africa*] [*ICAO location identifier*] (ICLI)
FAWY Wolseley [*South Africa*] [*ICAO location identifier*] (ICLI)
FAX Aeronautical Fixed Station [*ITU designation*] (CET)
Fax Electronic Facsimile (AAGC)
fax facilities (SAUS)
FAX Facsimile (AFM)
fax Facsimile (IDOE)
FAX Facsimile Authorization Transmission (SAUS)
FAX Facsimile Devices (SAUS)
fax facsimile transmission (SAUS)
fax facts (SAUS)
FAX Fast Anion Exchange [*Chromatography*]
Fax Faxon (SAUS)
FAX First Australia Prime [*AMEX symbol*] (TTSB)
FAX First Australia Prime Income Fund [*AMEX symbol*] (SPSG)
FAX fixed aeronautical station (SAUS)
FAX Friedreich's Ataxia Group (EAIO)
FAX Fuel Air Explosion (SAUS)
FAX Fuel Air Explosive
FAX Midwest Air Freighters, Inc. [*ICAO designator*] (FAAC)
Fax Telefax (TBD)
FAXCOM Facsimile (SAUS)
FAXCOM Facsimile Communication (SAUS)
FAXCOM facsimile communication service (SAUS)
FAXCOM Fascimile Communications (EECA)
FAXCOM Service Facsimile Communication Service (SAUS)
FAXDIN Facsimile Transmission over AUTODIN [*Telecommunications*]
FAXE Facsimile Equipment (SAUS)
FAXPAK Facsimile communication service provided by ITT (SAUS)
FAXPAK Facsimile Packet [*ITT*] [*Telecommunications*] (TEL)
FaxSav FaxSav Inc. [*Associated Press*] (SAG)
fax sheet facilities sheet (SAUS)
FAXT Far End Crosstalk (SAUS)
Fax-TAM Fax and Telephone Answering Machine (SAUO)
FAXTM Facsimile Transmission [*Telecommunications*] (NOAA)
FAX Transmission Facsimile Transmission (SAUS)
FAXX FaxSav Inc. [*NASDAQ symbol*] (SAG)
Fay Fagele (SAUS)
Fay Faith (SAUS)
FAY Fayban Air Services [*Nigeria*] [*FAA designator*] (FAAC)
FAY Fayetteville [*North Carolina*] [*Airport symbol*] (OAG)
FAY Fayetteville [*Arkansas*] [*Seismograph station code, US Geological Survey*] [*Closed*] (SEIS)
FAY Fayetteville, NC [*Location identifier*] [*FAA*] (FAAL)
FAY Fay's, Inc. [*NYSE symbol*] (SPSG)
FAY Field-Collected Aster Yellows [*Plant pathology*]
FAY Fleet Activities, Yokosuka Naval Base (DNAB)
FAY Friends and Associates for Yaddo (EA)
FAYA Free Asian Youth Alliance (SAUO)
Fayette Fayette County Bancshares, Inc. [*Associated Press*] (SAG)
Fayette Leg J (PA) Fayette Legal Journal [*Pennsylvania*] [*A publication*] (DLA)
Fay LJ Fayette Legal Journal [*Pennsylvania*] [*A publication*] (ILCA)
FAYP Ysterplaat [*South Africa*] [*ICAO location identifier*] (ICLI)
FaysInc Fays, Inc. [*Associated Press*] (SAG)
FAYVL Fayetteville, NC [*American Association of Railroads railroad junction routing code*]
FAZ Armed Forces of Zaire (SAUO)
FAZ Fanconi-Albertini-Zellweger [*Syndrome*] [*Medicine*] (DB)
FAZ Fish Alley [*Federal Railroad Administration identification code*]
FAZ Flint Aviation Services, Inc. [*FAA designator*] (FAAC)
FAZ foveal avascular zone (SAUS)
FAZA Zastron [*South Africa*] [*ICAO location identifier*] (ICLI)
FAZAM Full Armor Zero Administration [*Computer science*]
FAZR Zeerust [*South Africa*] [*ICAO location identifier*] (ICLI)
fb--- Africa, Sub-Saharan [*MARC geographic area code*] [*Library of Congress*] (LCCP)
FB Bartow Public Library, Bartow, FL [*Library symbol*] [*Library of Congress*] (LCLS)
FB Base Station [*ITU designation*] (CET)
Fb blanketing Frequency (SAUS)
FB Bursa Airlines, Inc. [*Turkey*] [*ICAO designator*] (ICDA)
f-b Face-Bow [*Dentistry*] (DAVI)
FB Face Brick [*Technical drawings*]
FB Facility Board [*Air Force*] (CET)
FB Faculty of Building [*British*]
FB Falcon Building Products'A' [*NYSE symbol*] (TTSB)
FB Falcon Building Products, Inc. [*NYSE symbol*] (SAG)
FB Family Bible [*Genealogy*]
FB Family Bureau [*Medicine*] (EDAA)
FB Farbenfabriken Bayer [*Germany*] [*Research code symbol*]
FB Farm Bureau [*Medicine*] (EDAA)
FB Farmers' Bulletin [*A publication*]
FB Fast Blue [*Biological stain*]
FB Fasting Blood Sugar [*Physiology*] (DAVI)
Fb February (CDAI)
FB Feedback (AAG)
f/B female Black (SAUS)
FB Fenian Brotherhood [*Irish political movement, c. 1858-1914*] (ROG)
FB Fermentation Biomass
FB Fernandina Beach (SAUS)
FB Fertiliser Board [*Tasmania, Australia*]
FB Fever Blister (MELL)
FB F-Format, Blocked Data Set (SAUS)
FB Fiber Backbone (SAUS)
FB Fiberboard [*Technical drawings*]
FB Fiber-in-Bending [*Lumber*]
FB Fiber optic Backbone (SAUS)
FB Fiberoptic Bronchoscopy [*Also, FOB*] [*Medicine*]
FB Fibre Board (SAUS)
FB Fibroblast [*Medicine*]
FB Fidelity Bond [*Business term*]
FB Fighter (SAUS)
FB Fighter Bomber
FB File Block
FB Files Busy (SAUS)
FB Film Badge (IEEE)
FB Film Bulletin
FB Final Braking (MCD)
FB Fine Business [*i.e., excellent*] [*Amateur radio*]
FB Finger Breadth [*Medicine*]
FB finger breadths (SAUS)
f/b fire and bilge (SAUS)
FB Fire Base (SAUS)
FB Fire Brigade
FB Firing Battery (AABC)
FB First Brochure
FB First National Boston Corp. (SAUO)
FB Fisheries Board (SAUS)
FB Fisheries (or Fishery) Board (SAUO)
FB Fishery Board
FB Fixed Block
FB Flag Bit (SAUS)
FB Flag Byte (SAUS)
FB Flame Black (SAUS)
FB Flanker Back [*Football*] (IIA)
FB Flashbulb [*Photography*]
F/B Flat Back [*Bookbinding*] (DGA)
FB Flat Bar [*Technical drawings*]
FB Flat Bed (SAUS)
FB Flat Bottom (OA)
FB Fleischmann Building (SAUS)
FB Flexible Benefits [*Health insurance*] (GHCT)
f/b flock book (SAUS)
F-B Florida State Library, Bureau of Book Processing, Tallahassee, FL [*Library symbol*] [*Library of Congress*] (LCLS)
FB flow base (SAUS)
FB Flow Block
FB Fluidized Bed
FB Fluorobenzene (SAUS)
FB Flying Boat
FB Flying Bomb (SAUS)
FB Fog Bell [*Navigation charts*]
FB Foldback [*Genetics*]
FB Folding Boxboard (DGA)
FB Fondation de Bellerive [*Bellerive Foundation - BF*] (EAIO)
FB Food Brokers Ltd. [*British*]
FB Football
FB Foot Bridge (SAUS)
FB Footling Breech [*Medicine*] (MELL)
FB Ford Brazil S.A. (SAUS)
FB Forebody
FB Foreground/Background (SAUS)
FB Foreign Body [*Medicine*]
FB Foreign Bond (MHDW)
FB Foreign [*or French*] Brandy [*British*] (ROG)
FB Forest Biology (SAUS)
FB Form Block (MCD)
FB Forth Bridge (SAUS)
FB Forward Base (FOTI)
FB Forward Body
fb Foul Bottom [*Navigation signal*]

FB .... Found Brothers Aviation Ltd. [*Canada*] [*ICAO aircraft manufacturer identifier*] (ICAO)
FB .... Fraction Burned Annually (CARB)
FB .... Fragmentation Bomb (SAUS)
FB .... Framing Bit (ACRL)
FB .... Free Baptists (SAUO)
FB .... Free to Bound [*Process*] (AAEL)
fb .... Freight Bill (EBF)
FB .... Freight Bill [*Business term*]
FB .... Friendship Book [*Address list circulated by Beatles fans*]
FB .... Friends of Buddhism [*Defunct*] (EA)
FB .... Fringe Benefits (WDAA)
f/b .... front to back (SAUS)
FB .... Frostbite (MELL)
fb .... full American breakfast (SAUS)
FB .... Full Back (SAUS)
FB .... Fullback [*Football*]
FB .... Full Bench
fb .... full board (SAUS)
FB .... Full Bore (SAUS)
fb .... fully bleached (SAUS)
FB .... Fumigation and Bath [*Military*]
FB .... Function Bit (SAUS)
FB .... Function Block (SAUS)
FB .... Function Button [*Computer science*]
FB .... Furnace Brazing
FB .... Fuse Block (KSC)
FB .... Fuse Box (IAA)
FB .... Promair Australia [*Airline code*]
FBA .... Factory-Built Assembly (SAUS)
FBA .... Fallbrook Annex (ACAE)
FBA .... Fanned Beam Aerial (SAUS)
FBA .... Fanned Beam Antenna
FBA .... Farbenfabriken Bayer [*Germany*] [*Research code symbol*]
FBA .... Farm Bankruptcy Act [*1933*]
FBA .... Farm Building Association (SAUO)
FBA .... Farm Buildings Association [*British*]
FBA .... FBA Pharmaceuticals Ltd. [*Great Britain*] [*Research code symbol*]
FBA .... Federal Bar Association (EA)
FBA .... Federal Bar Association: Fellow of the British Academy (SAUS)
FBA .... Federation of Bangladesh Associations (SAUO)
FBA .... Federation of Bloodstock Agents [*British*] (DBA)
FBA .... Federation of British Artists (EAIO)
FBA .... Federation of British Astrologers (SAUO)
FBA .... Federation of British Astrologers Ltd. (BI)
FBA .... Federation of British Audio (DBA)
FBA .... Fellow of Business Administration (DD)
FBA .... Fellow of the British Academy (ROG)
FBA .... Fellow of the British Arts Association (DBQ)
FBA .... Fiber (or Fibre) Box Association (SAUO)
FBA .... Fighter Aircraft (SAUS)
FB/A .... Fighter Attack (SAUS)
FBA .... Fighter Bomber Aircraft (NATG)
fba .... fighter-bomber aircraft (SAUS)
FB/A .... Fighter Bomber Attack (NATG)
fba .... fighter-bomber attack (SAUS)
FBA .... Fighter Bomber Aviation (SAUS)
FBA .... Figural Bottle Association [*Defunct*]
FBA .... Financial and Business Administration Department [*American Occupational Therapy Association*]
FBA .... Finnsheep Breeders Association (NTPA)
FBA .... First Banks America, Inc. [*NYSE symbol*] (SAG)
FBA .... First Born Approximation (SAUS)
FBA .... Fix Block Architecture (SAUS)
FBA .... Fixed Block Architecture
FBA .... Fixed-Block-Architektur (SAUS)
FBA .... Fixed Blocked ANSI-defined printer control characters (SAUS)
FBA .... Flexible Benefit Account [*Business term*]
FBA .... Florida Bandmasters Association (SRA)
FBA .... Fluorescent Brightening Agent (PDAA)
FBA .... Fluoro Butyl Acrylate (SAUS)
FBA .... Fonte Boa [*Brazil*] [*Airport symbol*] (AD)
FBA .... Forecasting by Analogy (SAUS)
FBA .... Forward-Backward Asymmetry (SAUS)
FBA .... Forward Branching Algorithm (SAUS)
FBA .... Foundation Beefmaster Association (EA)
FBA .... Four Band Award (SAUS)
FBA .... Freshwater Biological Association [*British*] (ARC)
FBA .... Functional Behavioral Assessment
FBA .... Fur Breeders Association of the United Kingdom [*British*]
FBA .... Fur Brokers Association (SAUO)
FBA .... Furnace Bottom Ash (SAUS)
FBA .... State Library of Florida, Tallahassee, FL [*OCLC symbol*] (OCLC)
FBAA .... Federation of Bloodstock Agents Australia
FBAA .... Fellow of the British Association of Accountants (WDAA)
FBAA .... Fellow of the British Association of Accountants and Auditors (EY)
FBAA .... Flying Boat Alighting Area
FBAA .... Fur Brokers Association of America (EA)
FBA-BNA .... Federal Bar Association-Bureau of National Affairs, Inc. (SAUO)
FBAC .... Fair Budget Action Campaign (EA)
FBAC .... First National Bancorp of Gainesville [*NASDAQ symbol*] (NQ)
FBACSI .... Fur Buyers Association, Coat and Suit Industry (EA)
FBAH .... Future Battlefield Attack Helicopter [*Military*] (SEWL)
FBAI .... Foodbrands America, Inc. [*NASDAQ symbol*] (SAG)
FBALX .... Fidelity Balanced [*Mutual fund ticker symbol*] (SG)
FBAN .... FNB Corp. [*NASDAQ symbol*] (NQ)
FB & D .... Ford, Bacon and Davis (SAUS)
FB&T .... FB&T Corp. [*NASDAQ symbol*] (COMM)
FB&T Fn .... Fairfax Bank & Trust Financial Corp. [*Associated Press*] (SAG)
FBANK3 .... EMSL-RTP National Filter Analysis Network (SAUO)
FBANP .... FNB Corp. 7.5% Cv'B' Pfd [*NASDAQ symbol*] (TTSB)
FBAO .... Farm Buildings Advisory Officer [*Ministry of Agriculture, Fisheries, and Food*] [*British*]
FBAP .... Federal Bureau of Advanced Paranoia [*Agency in film "Last Embrace"*]
FBAR .... Family Bargain [*NASDAQ symbol*] (TTSB)
FBAR .... Family Bargain Corp. [*NASDAQ symbol*] (SAG)
FBARP .... Family Bargain 9.5% Cv'A'Pfd [*NASDAQ symbol*] (TTSB)
FBAs .... Factory-Built Assemblies (SAUS)
FBAS .... Federation of British Aquatic Societies (DBA)
FBAS .... Fellow of the British Association of Secretaries [*British*] (DAS)
FBAS .... Fixed Base Aft Station (MCD)
FBAY .... Frisco Bay Industries [*NASDAQ symbol*] (SAG)
FBAYF .... Frisco Bay Industries [*NASDAQ symbol*] (TTSB)
FBB .... Fast-Burn Booster [*Rocketry*]
FBB .... Federal Bulletin Board (ADWA)
FBB .... Fire Brigades Board [*Queensland, Australia*]
FBB .... Fluidized-Bed Boiler (SAUS)
FBB .... Folding Boxboard (DGA)
FBB .... Frank Breech Presentation [*Medicine*] (MELL)
FBB .... Functional Breadboard System [*Skylab*] [*NASA*]
FBB .... Functional Building Block (SAUS)
FBB .... Fusion Breeder Blanket (SAUS)
FBBA .... Fishing Boat Builders Association [*British*] (BI)
FB:BC .... First Battle: Battalion through Corps [*DoD*]
FBBC .... First Bell Bancorp [*NASDAQ symbol*] (TTSB)
FBBC .... First Bell Bancorp, Inc. [*NASDAQ symbol*] (SAG)
FBBM .... Federation of Building Block Manufacturers [*British*] (BI)
FBBO .... Fellow of the British Ballet Organisation
FBBS .... Facts Bulletin Board System [*Database*] [*Fast Agricultural Communications Terminal System*] [*Information service or system*] (CRD)
FBC .... Barry College, North Miami, FL [*OCLC symbol*] (OCLC)
FBC .... Fallen Building Clause
FBC .... Family Benefit Capitalization (SAUS)
FBC .... Farm Buildings Centre (SAUO)
FBC .... Fat Binding Capacity [*Food technology*]
FBC .... Federal Broadcasting Corporation (SAUO)
FBC .... Federation of Brickwork Contractors [*British*] (DBA)
FBC .... Feedback Balanced Code (SAUS)
FBC .... Feedback Carburetor [*Automotive engineering*]
FBC .... Feedback Control [*Computer science*] (IAA)
FBC .... Filesmiths' Benefit Club [*A union*] [*British*]
FBC .... Finish Build Claims (SAUS)
FBC .... First Boston Corporation (SAUO)
FBC .... Fisons Boots Company (SAUO)
FBC .... Fixed Bathtub Capacitor
FBC .... Flexion Body Cast (MELL)
FBC .... Florence Babylonian Collection (BJA)
FBC .... Fluidized Bed Combustion (SAUS)
FBC .... Fonblanque's Bankruptcy Cases [*1849-52*] [*A publication*] (DLA)
FBC .... Foundation for Books to China (EA)
FBC .... Fox Broadcasting Co.
FBC .... Free-Binding Capacity [*Serology*]
FBC .... Friends Bible College [*Haviland, KS*]
FBC .... Friends of Books and Comics (EA)
FBC .... Frobisher Bay [*Northwest Territories*] [*Seismograph station code, US Geological Survey*] [*Closed*] (SEIS)
FBC .... Fukui Broadcasting Company (SAUO)
FBC .... Full Blood Count [*Medicine*] (ADA)
FBC .... Fully Buffered Channel
FBC .... Functional Bit Coding (SAUS)
FBCA .... Federation of British Cremation Authorities (BI)
FBCA .... Feedback Carburetor Actuator [*Automotive engineering*]
FBCA .... Fusion Bonded Coaters Association [*CRSI*] [*Absorbed by*] (EA)
FBCAEI .... Federation of Builders Contractors and Allied Employers of Ireland (BI)
FBCB^2 .... Force [*XXI*] Battle Command Brigade and Below [*Army*]
FBCB2 .... Force XXI, Battle Command, Brigade and Below [*Army*] (RDA)
FBCE .... Federation Bancaire de la Communaute Europeenne [*Banking Federation of the European Community*] (EAIO)
FBCE .... Federation de Bourses de la Communaute Europeenne [*Federation of Stock Exchanges in the European Community*] (EAIO)
FBCE .... Fellowship of British Christian Esperantists
FBCG .... First Banking Co. Southeast Georgia [*NASDAQ symbol*] (SAG)
FBCG .... First Banking S.E. Georgia [*NASDAQ symbol*] (TTSB)
FBCI .... Fidelity Bancorp [*NASDAQ symbol*] (SAG)
FBCK .... Firebrick
FBCM .... Federation of British Cutlery Manufacturers (SAUO)
FBCM .... Fellow of the Brantford Conservatory of Music (SAUO)
FBCMA .... Fiber Bonded Carpet Manufacturers Association [*British*] (DBA)
FBCN .... Federation of British Columbia Naturalists (SAUO)
FBCO .... Camp Okavango [*Botswana*] [*ICAO location identifier*] (ICLI)
FBCO .... Fellow of the British College of Ophthalmic Opticians (DBQ)
FBCOD .... foreign body cornea oculus dexter (SAUS)
FBCOD .... Foreign Body Cornea Right Eye [*Medicine*]
FBCOS .... Foreign Body Cornea Left Eye [*Medicine*]
FBCOS .... foreign body cornea oculus sinister (SAUS)
FBCP .... Familial Benign Chronic Pemphigus [*Medicine*] (MELL)
FBCP .... Fellow of the British College of Physiotherapists (SAUO)

FBCR .... Filter Bank Combiner Radiometer (CCCA)
FBCR .... Fluidized-Bed Combustion Residue (SAUS)
FBCR .... Fluidized-Bed Control Rod (PDAA)
FBCS .... Fellow of the British Computer Society
FBCS .... Fixed-Base Crew Station [*NASA*] (NASA)
FBCS .... Foreground-Background Operating System (SAUS)
FB/CSMA/CD ... feedback carrier-sense multiplex access with collision detection (SAUS)
FBCT .... Form Block Check Template (MCD)
FBCV .... 1st Bancorp Ind [*NASDAQ symbol*] (TTSB)
FBCV .... First Bancorp (Indiana) [*NASDAQ symbol*] (NQ)
FBCW .... Fallen Building Clause Waiver [*Legal term*] (DLA)
FBCW .... Federation of British Columbia Writers [*Canada*] (WWLA)
f-bd- .... Burundi [*MARC geographic area code*] [*Library of Congress*] (LCCP)
FBD .... Fibreboard Corp. [*AMEX symbol*] (CTT)
FBD .... Fibrocystic Breast Disease [*Medicine*]
FBD .... Field Base Depot (SAUO)
FBD .... Film: British Documentary
FBD .... Fischer Body Division (SAUS)
FBD .... flat belt drive (SAUS)
FBD .... Foreign Born Doctor (MELL)
FBD .... Forward Base Depot (SAUO)
FBD .... Free Board
fbd .... freeboard (SAUS)
FBD .... Full Business Day (TEL)
FBD .... Functional Block Diagram [*Telecommunications*] (TEL)
FBD .... Functional Bowel Disorder [*Medicine*] (MAE)
FBD .... Function Block Logic (ACII)
FBD .... Statens Trafikkflygerskole [*Norway*] [*ICAO designator*] (FAAC)
FBDB .... Federal Business Development Bank [*See also BFD*] [*Canada*] [*Database producer*]
FBDC .... Fiberboard, Corrugated
FBDC .... Ford County Historical Railroad Preservation Foundation [*Federal Railroad Administration identification code*]
FBDCA .... French Bulldog Club of America (EA)
FBDFCP .... Federation of Bleachers, Dyers, Finishers and Calico Printers (SAUO)
FBDS .... Fiberboard, Solid
FBE .... Federation of Bank Employers [*British*] (DCTA)
FBE .... Feeder Branch Edit (PDAA)
FBE .... Female Business Enterprise (AAGC)
FBE .... Fibrinogen Breakdown Product [*Medicine*] (PALA)
FBE .... Fleet Battle Experience [*Military*] (SEWL)
FBE .... Fluidized Bed Electrode [*Electrochemistry*]
FBE .... Folding Boat Equipment [*British military*] (DMA)
FBE .... Foreign Bill of Exchange (SAUO)
FBE .... Free Buffer Enquiry (SAUS)
FBE .... Full Blood Examination [*Medicine*] (MAE)
FBEA .... Fellow of the British Esperanto Association (DAS)
FBEA .... Funeral and Bereavement Educators Association
FBEC .... Fetal Bovine Endothelial Cell (DB)
FBEC(S) .... Fellow of the Business Education Council (Scotland) (ODBW)
FBEI .... Fellow of the Institution of Body Engineers [*British*] (DBQ)
FBEI .... First Bancorp of Indiana, Inc. [*NASDAQ symbol*] (NASQ)
FBEM .... False Best Economy Mixture (SAUS)
FBEM .... fixed beam EM (SAUS)
FBENI .... Federation of Boot Employers for Northern Ireland (SAUO)
FBER .... 1st Bergen Bancorp [*NASDAQ symbol*] (TTSB)
FBER .... First Bergen Bancorp, Inc. [*NASDAQ symbol*] (SAG)
FBergen .... First Bergen Bancorp, Inc. [*Associated Press*] (SAG)
FBETM .... Federation of British Engineers Tool Manufacturers [*British*] (DBA)
FBF .... BEA Income Fund [*NYSE symbol*] (SAG)
FBF .... Federal Buildings Fund [*General Services Administration*]
FBF .... Feedback Filter (IAA)
FBF .... Female Bowhunter Fingers [*International Bowhunting Organization*] [*Class equipment*]
FBF .... Femoral Blood Flow [*Physiology*]
FBF .... Film: British Feature
FBF .... Fine Airlines, Inc. [*ICAO designator*] (FAAC)
FBF .... First Boston Income Fund, Inc. [*Later, CS First Income Fund*] [*NYSE symbol*] (SPSG)
FBF .... FleetBoston Financial
FBF .... Folkestone-Boulogne Ferries [*English Channel ferry-boat service*] [*British*] (ECON)
FBF .... Football Finger (MELL)
FBF .... Forearm Blood Flow [*Medicine*]
FBF .... Forest Heritage Fund (SAUO)
FBF .... Frame by Frame
FBF .... Francis Bacon Foundation (EA)
FBF .... Frankfurt Book Fair (SAUO)
FBFC .... Florence Ballard Fan Club (EA)
FBFI .... Frederic Burk Foundation, Inc. [*San Francisco State University*] [*Research center*] (RCD)
FBFM .... Feedback Frequency Modulation
FBFM .... Flood Boundary Floodway Map (ADWA)
fbfm .... frequency feedback frequency modulation (SAUS)
FBFO .... Federation of British Fire Organisations
FBFR .... Fluidized-Bed Film Reactor [*For water purification*]
FBFS .... Fuel Building Filter System [*Nuclear energy*] (NRCH)
FBFT .... Flow Bias Functional Test (IEEE)
FBFT .... Francistown [*Botswana*] [*ICAO location identifier*] (ICLI)
FBG .... Faint Blue Galaxy [*Astronomy*]
FBG .... Farm Buildings Group (SAUO)
FBG .... Fasting Blood Glucose [*Physiology*] (AAMN)
FBG .... Fayetteville/Fort Bragg, NC [*Location identifier*] [*FAA*] (FAAL)
FBG .... Federal Barge Lines, Inc., St. Louis MO [*STAC*]
FBG .... Federation of British Growers (SAUO)
FBG .... Fibrinogen [*Factor 1*] [*Hematology*]
FBG .... Finsbury Group Ltd. [*Vancouver Stock Exchange symbol*]
FBG .... Flash Bang Grenade [*Military*] (MUSM)
FBG .... Fluidized-Bed Gasifier [*Coal gasification*]
FBG .... Fossil Bluff Group (SAUS)
FBG .... Fosters Brewing Group [*Australia*] [*Commercial firm*]
FBG .... Friends Burial Ground (SAUS)
FBGA .... First Bankshares (GA) [*NASDAQ symbol*] (TTSB)
FBGA .... First Bankshares, Inc. (GA) [*NASDAQ symbol*] (SAG)
FBGHA .... 483rd Bombardment Group (H) Association (EA)
FBGI .... Financial Benefit Group, Inc. [*NASDAQ symbol*] (NQ)
FBGM .... Gomare [*Botswana*] [*ICAO location identifier*] (ICLI)
FBGRX .... Fidelity Blue Chip Growth [*Mutual fund ticker symbol*] (SG)
FBGS .... Fiberglass (MIST)
FBGZ .... Ghanzi [*Botswana*] [*ICAO location identifier*] (ICLI)
FBH .... Familial Benign Hypocalciuric Hypercalcaemia [*Medicine*] (BABM)
FBH .... Familial Benign Hypocalciuric Hypercalcemia [*Nephrology*] (DAVI)
FBH .... Federal Board of Hospitalization [*Coordinated hospitalization activities of Army, Navy, and various agencies; terminated, 1948*]
FBH .... Fire Brigade Hydrant
FBH .... Flat-Bottom Hole (SAUS)
FBH .... Fluidized-Bed Hydrogenator [*Chemical engineering reactor*]
FBH .... Forced Beachhead [*Navy*] (DNAB)
FBH .... Frank B. Hall & Company, Inc. (SAUO)
fbh .... Free on Board in Harbor (EBF)
FBH .... Free on Board in Harbor [*Business term*]
FBH .... Hydroxybutyric Dehydrogenase [*Organic chemistry*] (DAVI)
FBHA .... Fellow of the British Hypnotherapy Association (DBQ)
FBHA .... Free the Battery Hen Association [*Australia*]
FBHC .... Fort Bend Hldg [*NASDAQ symbol*] (TTSB)
FBHC .... Fort Bend Holding Corp. [*NASDAQ symbol*] (SAG)
FBHC .... Fortified Benzene Hexachloride [*Insecticide*]
FBHC .... Franciscan Brothers of the Holy Cross [*See also FFSC*] [*Germany*] (EAIO)
FBHDA .... Friends and Buddies of the Hour Glass Division Association [*Later, FBHGA*] (EA)
FBHDL .... Force Beachhead Line [*Navy*]
FBHGA .... Friends and Buddies of the Hour Glass Association (EA)
FBHH .... Familial Benign Hypocalciuric Hypercalcemia [*Medicine*] (MELL)
FBHI .... Fellow of the British Horological Institute
FBHL .... Force Beachhead Line [*Navy*] (NVT)
fbhp .... flowing bottom hole pressure (SAUS)
FBHQ .... Gaborone Civil Aviation Headquarters [*Botswana*] [*ICAO location identifier*] (ICLI)
FBHS .... Fellow of the British Horse Society (DBQ)
FBHTM .... Federation of British Hand Tool Manufacturers (EAIO)
FBHVC .... Federation of British Historical Vehicle Clubs
FBHX .... Fluid Bed Heat Exchanger (PDAA)
FBI .... BEA Strategic Income Fd [*NYSE symbol*] (TTSB)
FBI .... BEA Strategic Income Fund [*NYSE symbol*] (SAG)
FBI .... Fast Boats Incorporated (SAUO)
FBI .... Federal Board of Investigation (SAUO)
FBI .... Federal Bureau of Investigation
FBI .... Federation of British Industries [*Later, CBI*]
FBI .... Filter Bank and Interrogator (SAUS)
FBI .... First Boston Strategic [*Later, CS First Boston Strategic*] [*NYSE symbol*] [*NYSE symbol*] (SPSG)
FBI .... Flossing, Brushing, and Irrigation [*Dentistry*]
FBI .... Fluidized Bed Incinerator (DOGT)
FBI .... Foodborne Illness (MELL)
FBI .... Food Business Institute (SAUS)
FBI .... Foreign Body Ingestion [*Medicine*]
FBI .... Foreign-Born Irish
FBI .... Full Bench Decisions [*India*] [*A publication*] (DLA)
FBI .... full-blooded Irishman, Icelander, Indian, Indonesian, Iranian, Iraqi, Israelite, Italian, or Ivory Coaster (SAUS)
FBIA .... Food and Beverage Importers' Association [*Australia*]
FBIAA .... Federal Bureau of Investigation Agents Association (NTPA)
FBIBA .... Fellow of the British Insurance Brokers' Association (ODBW)
FBIC .... Farm Buildings Information Centre Ltd. [*British*] (CB)
FBIC .... Firstbank of Illinois [*NASDAQ symbol*] (TTSB)
FBIC .... Firstbank of Illinois Co. [*NASDAQ symbol*] (NQ)
FBIC .... Free Beaches Information Center [*Later, The Naturists*] (EA)
FBICC .... Flow Blue International Collectors Club (EA)
FBICNSW .... Friends of Brain Injured Children of New South Wales [*Australia*]
FBID .... Fellow of the British Institute of Interior Design (DBQ)
F-BIDR .... Full-Resolution Basic Image Data Record [*RADAR mapping*]
FBIE .... Fellow of the British Institute of Embalmers (DBQ)
FBIM .... Fellow of the British Institute of Management [*Formerly, FIIA*]
FBIN .... Finnish Biodiversity Information Network (SAUS)
FBIOX .... Fidelity Select Ptfl: Biotechnology [*Mutual fund ticker symbol*] (SG)
FBIP .... Florida Institute of Phosphate Research, FIPR Library & Information Clearinghouse, Bartow, FL [*Library symbol*] [*Library of Congress*] (LCLS)
FBIPP .... Fellow of the British Institute of Professional Photography (DBQ)
FBIRA .... Federal Bureau of Investigation Recreation Association (SAUO)
FBIRE .... Fellow of the British Institution of Radio Engineers (SAUO)
FBIS .... Federal Bureau of Information Service (SAUO)
FBIS .... Fellow of the British Interplanetary Society
FBIS .... Foreign Broadcast Information Service
FBIS .... Foreign Broadcast Information System
FBIS .... Foreign Broadcast Intelligence Service [*FCC*] [*World War II*]
FBI's .... Forgotten Boys of Iceland [*Nickname for US soldiers in Iceland*] [*World War II*]

FBIST.......... Fellow of the British Institute of Surgical Technologists (DBQ)
FBIT.......... Fault Bit (SAUS)
F-Bit.......... Final Bit (SAUS)
FBIU.......... Freshwater Biological Investigation Unit [*Department of Agriculture for Northern Ireland*] [*British*] (IRUK)
FBJW.......... Jwaneng [*Botswana*] [*ICAO location identifier*] (ICLI)
FBK.......... Fairbanks [*Alaska*] [*Seismograph station code, US Geological Survey*] [*Closed*] (SEIS)
FBK.......... Fairbanks/Wainwright, AK [*Location identifier*] [*FAA*] (FAAL)
FBK.......... Fast Back (SAUS)
fbk.......... fast buck (SAUS)
FBK.......... Flat Back
FBK.......... flat bar keel (SAUS)
FBKE.......... Kasane [*Botswana*] [*ICAO location identifier*] (ICLI)
FBKG.......... Kang [*Botswana*] [*ICAO location identifier*] (ICLI)
FBkGA.......... First Bankshares, Inc. (Georgia) [*Associated Press*] (SAG)
FBKKW.......... Flugbetriebstoff-Kesselkraftwagen
FBKP.......... First Bank of Philadelphia [*NASDAQ symbol*] (NQ)
FBKP.......... First Bk Philadelphia PA [*NASDAQ symbol*] (TTSB)
FBkPhila.......... First Bank of Philadelphia [*Associated Press*] (SAG)
FBkPhl.......... First Bank of Philadelphia [*Associated Press*] (SAG)
FBKR.......... Khwai River Lodge [*Botswana*] [*ICAO location identifier*] (ICLI)
FBkS.......... First Bank System, Inc. [*Associated Press*] (SAG)
FBksAm.......... First Banks America, Inc. [*Associated Press*] (SAG)
FBKY.......... Kanye [*Botswana*] [*ICAO location identifier*] (ICLI)
FBL.......... Fantasy Bowling League
FBL.......... Faribault, MN [*Location identifier*] [*FAA*] (FAAL)
FBL.......... Fecal Blood Loss [*Medicine*]
FBL.......... Federal Barge Lines, Inc. [*AAR code*]
FBL.......... Fine Blanking (SAUS)
fbl.......... Fire Brick Lining (SAUS)
FBL.......... Fixed-Bed Loop [*Chemical engineering*]
FBL.......... Flight-by-Light [*OST*] (TAG)
FBL.......... Fly By Light (SAUO)
FBL.......... Fly-by-Light
FBL.......... Folicular Basal Lamina [*Medicine*]
FBL.......... Food Brokers Ltd. [*Canada*] [*ICAO designator*] (FAAC)
FBL.......... Foreign Bird League [*British*] (BI)
FBl.......... Forged Billet (SAUS)
FBL.......... Form Block Line (MCD)
FBL.......... Form Block Lines (SAUS)
FBL.......... Foundation for Better Living (EA)
FBL.......... Frame Burst Error Length (VERA)
FBL.......... Friction Braked Landing [*Aviation*] (IAA)
FBL.......... Functional Baseline (AAGC)
FBL.......... Furness Bermuda Line (SAUO)
FBL.......... Future Battle Laboratory (RDA)
FBLA.......... Future Business Leaders of America [*Washington, DC*] (AEBS)
FBLA-PBL.......... Future Business Leaders of America - Phi Beta Lambda [*Washington, DC*] (EA)
FBLC.......... Fibroblast-Like Cell [*Cytology*]
FBL Fn.......... FBL Financial Group [*Associated Press*] (SAG)
FBL-G.......... Freiburger Beschwerdenliste Gesamtform (DB)
FBLIM.......... Fellow, Board of Life Insurance Medicine (CMD)
FBLK.......... Functional Block (SAUS)
FBLO.......... Foreign Branch Liaison Office (SAUS)
FBLO.......... Lobatse [*Botswana*] [*ICAO location identifier*] (ICLI)
FBL Press.......... Fine Blanking Press (SAUS)
FBL-W.......... Freiburger Beschwerdenliste Wiederholungsform (DB)
FBM.......... Biscayne College, Miami, FL [*OCLC symbol*] (OCLC)
FBM.......... Feet Board Measure
FBM.......... Felbamate [*Organic chemistry*]
FBM.......... Ferber Mining Corp. [*Vancouver Stock Exchange symbol*]
FBM.......... Fetal Breathing Movements [*Gynecology*]
FB/M.......... Field Bill of Material (SAUS)
FBM.......... Fighter Battle Management (ACAE)
FBM.......... Financial and Business Management Division [*American Occupational Therapy Association*]
FBM.......... Fix Block Modus (SAUS)
FBM.......... Flavor-by-Mouth [*Sensory testing*]
FBM.......... Fleet Ballistic Missile
FBM.......... Flexible Buffer Management (VERA)
FBM.......... Fluorobenzyl(methylaminopurine) [*Biochemistry*]
FBM.......... Foot Board Measure (MSA)
FBM.......... Foreground and Background Monitor
fbm.......... forward branch mail (SAUS)
FBM.......... Four-Ball Machine [*Engineering*] (IAA)
fBm.......... Fractional Brownian Motion [*Mathematics*]
FBM.......... Fractional Brownian Movement (SAUO)
FBM.......... Frankfurt Biosphere Model (SAUO)
FBM.......... Freeboard Measure (IAA)
FBM.......... Fuzzy BIT [*Binary Digit*] Map [*Computer science*]
FBM.......... Lubumbashi [*Zaire*] [*Airport symbol*] (OAG)
FBMA.......... Food and Beverage Managers Association [*British*] (DBA)
FBMA.......... Forward Brigade Maintenance Area [*Army*]
FBMG.......... Machaneng [*Botswana*] [*ICAO location identifier*] (ICLI)
FBMInet.......... Farm Business Management Information network (SAUO)
FBML.......... Molepolole [*Botswana*] [*ICAO location identifier*] (ICLI)
FBMM.......... Makalamabedi [*Botswana*] [*ICAO location identifier*] (ICLI)
FBMN.......... Maun [*Botswana*] [*ICAO location identifier*] (ICLI)
FBMO.......... Fibrous Body-Membrane Organelle [*Biochemistry*]
FBMP.......... Fleet Ballistic Missile Program
FBMP.......... Fleet Ballistic Missile Project (SAUS)
FBMR.......... Fleet Ballistic Missile Requisition [*Navy*] (AFIT)
FBMS.......... Fleet Ballistic Missile Submarine (IAA)
FBMS.......... Fleet Ballistic Missile System
FBMS.......... FTS2000 Billing Management System [*Communications term*] (DCT)
FBMS.......... Mosetse [*Botswana*] [*ICAO location identifier*] (ICLI)
FBMSTCLANT.......... Fleet Ballistic Missile Submarine Training Center, Atlantic (DNAB)
FBMSTCPAC.......... Fleet Ballistic Missile Submarine Training Center, Pacific (DNAB)
FBMSTLL.......... Fleet Ballistic Missile Submarine Tender Load List
FBM-Supplement.......... Fleet Ballistic Missile Weapons System Supplement (SAUO)
FBMTC.......... Fleet Ballistic Missile Training Center (DNAB)
FBMTLL.......... Fleet Ballistic Missile Tender Load List (DNAB)
FBMWS.......... Fleet Ballistic Missile Weapon System
FBMWSS.......... Fleet Ballistic Missile Weapons Support System (DNAB)
FBN.......... Family Business Network [*Switzerland*]
FBN.......... Federal Base Network (SAUO)
FBN.......... Federal Bureau of Narcotics
FBN.......... Feedback Network
FBN.......... Fibronectin [*Biochemistry*]
FBN.......... Fixed Base Notation (SAUS)
FBN.......... Fly-by-Night (HLLA)
FBN.......... Food Business Network [*Information service or system*] (IID)
FBN.......... Fuel-Bound Nitrogen
FBN.......... Furniture Brands International [*NYSE symbol*] [*Formerly, INTERCO, Inc.*] (SG)
FBN.......... Furniture Brands Intl [*NYSE symbol*] (TTSB)
FBN.......... State Library of Florida, Bureau of Book Processing, Tallahassee, FL [*OCLC symbol*] (OCLC)
FBNC.......... First Bancorp (North Carolina) [*NASDAQ symbol*] (NQ)
FBNCC.......... Fall Back Network Control Center (MCD)
FBNK.......... First Banks, Inc. [*NASDAQ symbol*] (SAG)
FBNKP.......... First Banks 9% Incr Rt'C'Pfd [*NASDAQ symbol*] (TTSB)
FBNML.......... Francis Bitter National Magnet Laboratory [*MIT*]
FBNN.......... Nokaneng [*Botswana*] [*ICAO location identifier*] (ICLI)
fbnrv.......... fixed bent-nose reentry vehicle (SAUS)
FBNT.......... Nata [*Botswana*] [*ICAO location identifier*] (ICLI)
FBNW.......... Gaborone Notwane [*Botswana*] [*ICAO location identifier*] (ICLI)
FBo.......... Boca Raton Public Library, Boca Raton, FL [*Library symbol*] [*Library of Congress*] (LCLS)
FBO.......... Carroll Aircraft Corp. PLC [*British*] [*ICAO designator*] (FAAC)
FBO.......... Failing Better Offer (BB)
FBO.......... Federal Paper Board Co., Inc. [*NYSE symbol*] (SPSG)
FBO.......... Field Bake Oven [*Military*]
FBO.......... Fixed Base Operation (PIPO)
FBO.......... Fixed-Base Operator [*Provider of nonairline aviation services to users of airports*]
fbo.......... for benefit of (SAUS)
FBO.......... Foreign Building Office [*Department of State*]
f/b/o.......... For the Benefit Of (PROS)
FBO.......... For the Benefit Of
FBO.......... Full Battle Order (SAUS)
FBO.......... Furnished by Others [*Technical drawings*]
FBOA.......... Fellow of the British Optical Association
FBoC.......... College of Boca Raton, Boca Raton, FL [*Library symbol*] [*Library of Congress*] (LCLS)
FBOC.......... Figural Bottle Opener Collectors (ADWA)
FBOC.......... Figural Bottle Openers Collectors Club (EA)
FBOE.......... Frequency Band of Emission (CET)
FBOI.......... First Bank of the Internet [*Electronic commerce*]
FBOIP.......... Final Basis of Issue Plan [*Army*]
FBOK.......... Okwa [*Botswana*] [*ICAO location identifier*] (ICLI)
FBOOM.......... Fort Benning Officers' Open Mess [*Pronounced "fuhboom"*]
F/B operation.......... foreground program/background-program operation (SAUS)
FBOR.......... Orapa [*Botswana*] [*ICAO location identifier*] (ICLI)
FBOS.......... Foreground-Background Operating System (SAUS)
FBOU.......... Fellow of the British Ornithologists' Union (ROG)
FBoU.......... Florida Atlantic University, Boca Raton, FL [*Library symbol*] [*Library of Congress*] (LCLS)
FBP.......... Federal Bonding Program
FBP.......... Federal Bureau of Prisons (WDAA)
FBP.......... Federation Baden-Powell [*Canada*] (EAIO)
FBP.......... Federation of Podiatry Boards (SAUO)
FBP.......... Femoral Blood Pressure [*Medicine*]
fbp.......... fetal biophysical profile (SAUS)
FBP.......... Fibonacci Benchmark Program [*Computer science*] (BYTE)
FBP.......... Fibrin Breakdown Products [*Hematology*]
FBP.......... Fibrinogen Breakdown Products [*Hematology*] (DAVI)
FBP.......... Fibrinopeptide B [*Biochemistry*]
FBP.......... Fighter Bomber Program
FBP.......... Filtered Back-Projection [*Computer science*]
FBP.......... Final Boiling Point
FBP.......... Financial Business Package [*Computer science*]
FBP.......... First Bancorp [*NYSE symbol*] (SG)
FBP.......... FirstBank Puerto Rico [*NYSE symbol*] (TTSB)
FBP.......... Fleet Boat Pool
FBP.......... Flexible Benefits Program [*Human resources*] (WYGK)
FBP.......... Fluid-Bed Processing (SAUS)
FBP.......... Fluidized-Bed Process
FBP.......... Foam Branch Pipe (WDAA)
FBP.......... Folate-Binding Protein [*Biochemistry*]
FBP.......... Footling Breech Presentation [*Medicine*] (MELL)
FBP.......... Foreign Bases Project (EA)
FBP.......... Foreign Buyer Program (JAGO)
FBP.......... Fortschrittliche Buergerpartei [*Progressive Citizens' Party*] [*Liechtenstein*] (PPW)
FBP.......... Friends of Brazilian Philately (SAUO)
FBP.......... Fructose bisphosphate [*Also, FDP*] [*Biochemistry*]
FBP.......... Fuel Booster Pump

FBP .... Progressive Citizen's Party (Liechtenstein) [*Political party*] (PSAP)
FBPA .... Pandamatenga [*Botswana*] [*ICAO location identifier*] (ICLI)
FBPase .... Fructose bisphosphatase [*An enzyme*]
FBPC .... First Financial Bancshares Polk County [*NASDAQ symbol*] (SAG)
FBPC .... Foreign Bondholders Protective Council [*Defunct*] (EA)
FBPCS .... Federation of Behavioral, Psychological, and Cognitive Sciences (EA)
FBPI .... Federation of British Printing Ink Manufacturers (SAUO)
FBPI .... Franklin Book Programs, Incorporated (SAUO)
FBPIM .... Federation of British Printing Ink Manufacturers (SAUO)
FBPMC .... Federation of British Police Motor Clubs (SAUO)
FBPN .... Feminist Business and Professional Network (EA)
FBPP .... Federation of British Plant Pathologists (SAUO)
FBPS .... Fellow of the British Psychological Society (SAUO)
FBPS .... Forest and Bird Protection Society (SAUS)
FBPS .... Forest and Bird Protection Society of New Zealand (SAUO)
FBPsS .... Fellow of the British Psychological Society
F/BPTG .... Fuel/Blanket Properties Task Group (SAUO)
FBPY .... Palapye [*Botswana*] [*ICAO location identifier*] (ICLI)
FBQ .... Fibrequest International Ltd. [*Formerly, Trawler Petroleum Explorations Ltd.*] [*Vancouver Stock Exchange symbol*]
FBQE .... Free Block Queue Element (SAUS)
FBR .... Broward County Libraries Division, Pompano Beach, FL [*OCLC symbol*] (OCLC)
FBR .... Fabra [*Barcelona*] [*Spain*] [*Seismograph station code, US Geological Survey*] (SEIS)
FBR .... Fast Breeder Reactor [*Nuclear energy*]
FBR .... Fast Burn Rate
FBR .... Fast Burst Reactor [*Nuclear energy*]
FBR .... Feedback Report (NVT)
FBR .... Feedback Resistance (IEEE)
FBR .... Ferric-Leach Bacterial Regeneration [*Uranium extraction process*]
FBR .... Fiber (KSC)
fbr .... Fiber (VRA)
fbr .... Fibre (SAUS)
FBR .... Fireball Radius [*Military*] (AABC)
fbr .... Fire-Broken Rock [*Archaeology*] (QUAC)
FBR .... First Brands Corp. [*NYSE symbol*] (SPSG)
FBR .... Fixed Base Representation (SAUS)
FBR .... Flat Board Reach [*Test*] [*Occupational therapy*]
FBR .... Floating Point Register [*Computer science*]
FBR .... Foreign Body Reaction (MELL)
FBR .... Forschungsberichte Bundesrepublik Deutschland [*Fachinformationszentrum Karlsruhe GmbH*] [*Germany*] [*Information service or system*] (CRD)
FBR .... Forskningsbiblioteksradet [*Swedish council for research libraries*] (NITA)
FBR .... Fort Bridger, WY [*Location identifier*] [*FAA*] (FAAL)
FBR .... Foundation for Basic Research [*Russia*]
FBR .... Foundation for Biomedical Research (EA)
FBR .... Foundation for Blood Research [*Research center*] (RCD)
FBR .... Foundation for Business Responsibilities [*British*]
FbR .... Fred B. Rothman & Co., South Hackensack, NJ [*Library symbol*] [*Library of Congress*] (LCLS)
FBR .... Friedman Billings Ramsey Gp'A' [*NYSE symbol*] (SG)
FBR .... Frobisher Resources Ltd. [*Vancouver Stock Exchange symbol*]
FBR .... Full Bench Rulings [*Bengal, India*] [*A publication*] (DLA)
FBR .... Full Boiling-Range [*Fuel technology*] (PDAA)
FBR .... Full Boiling-Range fuel (SAUS)
FBr .... Manatee County Library System, Bradenton, FL [*Library symbol*] [*Library of Congress*] (LCLS)
FBR .... Engineering Fluidized-Bed Reactor [*Chemistry*] (ODA)
FBRBD .... Fiberboard
FBRC .... Fabric
FBRC .... Fabricland, Inc. [*NASDAQ symbol*] (COMM)
FBRC .... Frederick Burk Foundation Research Center
FBRCM .... Fingerbreadth Below Right Costal Margin [*Measurement*] [*Anatomy*] (DAVI)
FBRCN .... Fabrication
F/BRD .... Floor Board [*Automotive engineering*]
FBRD .... Flying Boat Repair Depot [*British military*] (DMA)
FBRE .... Full Boiling-Range Fuel (PDAA)
FBRF .... Fast Burst Reactor Facility [*Nuclear energy*]
FBRF .... Full Boiling-Range Fuel (SAUS)
FBR Fuel ...... Full Boiling-Range Fuel (SAUS)
FBRGLS .... Fiberglass
FBRIC .... Farm Based Recreation Information Centre (SAUS)
FB Rim .... Flat Bed Rim (SAUS)
FBritIRE ...... Fellow of the British Institution of Radio Engineers
FBRK .... Fire Brick [*Technical drawings*]
FBrk .... Firebrick (SAUS)
FBRK .... Rakops [*Botswana*] [*ICAO location identifier*] (ICLI)
FBRL .... Final Bomb Release Line
FBRM .... Fractional Bit Rate Modulation (SAUS)
FBrM .... Manatee Junior College, Bradenton, FL [*Library symbol*] [*Library of Congress*] (LCLS)
FBRMS .... Fixed block rotating mass storage (SAUS)
FBRNWP ...... Full Bench Rulings, Northwest Provinces [*India*] [*A publication*] (DLA)
FBro .... Frederick Eugene Lykes, Jr., Memorial County Library, Brooksville, FL [*Library symbol*] [*Library of Congress*] (LCLS)
FBroPH .... Pasco-Hernando Community College, North Campus Learning Resources Center, Brooksville, FL [*Library symbol*] [*Library of Congress*] (LCLS)
FBRS .... Farm Business Recording Scheme (SAUO)
FBRs .... Fast Breeder Reactors (SAUS)
FBRS .... Fibrous
FBRS .... Fleet Broadcast Receive Subsystem [*Navy*] (CAAL)
FBRSU .... Full-Boiling Range High-Sensitivity Unleaded [*Motor fuel*]
FBRT .... Francis Bacon Research Trust [*British*]
FBRU .... Full-Boiling Range Unleaded [*Motor fuel*]
FBRX .... Fiske Brothers Refining [*Private rail car owner code*]
f-bs- .... Botswana [*MARC geographic area code*] [*Library of Congress*] (LCCP)
FBS .... Facsimile Broadcast Service
FBS .... Failed Back Syndrome (MELL)
FBS .... Family Budget Survey (EURO)
FBS .... Fan Beam Scatterometer
FBS .... Farm Bureau Services
FBS .... Fast Blue Salt (SAUS)
FBS .... Fasting Blood Sugar [*Physiology*]
FBS .... Federal Bureau of Standards (SAUO)
FBS .... Feedback Signal
FBS .... Feedback System
FBS .... Fellow of the Botanical Society [*British*] (ROG)
FBS .... Fellow of the Building Societies Institute [*British*]
FBS .... Fetal Blood Sample [*Hematology*]
FBS .... Fetal Bovine Serum [*Medicine*]
FBS .... F-Format, Blocked Standard Data Set (SAUS)
FBS .... Fibrocystic Breast Syndrome [*Medicine*] (MELL)
FBS .... Field Broadcasting Service (SAUO)
FBS .... Fighter Bomber Squadron (SAUO)
FB/S .... Fighter Bomber Strike (NATG)
fbs .... fighterbomber strike (SAUS)
FB/S .... Fighter Strike (SAUS)
FBS .... File Backup System (SAUS)
FBS .... Film: British Series
FBS .... Fine Bearing Servo
FBS .... Finish Build Schedule (SAUS)
FBS .... Fire Brigade Society [*British*] (DBA)
FBS .... Firefighter Breathing System [*NASA*]
FBS .... First Bank System [*NYSE symbol*] (TTSB)
FBS .... First Bank System, Inc. [*NYSE symbol*] (SPSG)
FBS .... Fixed-Based Simulator (PDAA)
FBS .... Flabby Back Syndrome [*Medicine*] (MELL)
FBS .... Flare Build-Up Study [*Meteorology*]
FBS .... Flare Built-up Study (SAUS)
FBS .... Flash/Bang/Smoke (MCD)
FBS .... Flexible Bandwidth Service (SAUS)
FBS .... Flourous Biphase System [*For chemical catalysis*]
FBS .... Fly-By-Speech (SAUS)
FBS .... Focus Broadcast Satellite Corporation (NITA)
FBS .... Foetal Bovine Serum (SAUS)
FBS .... Fokes Sentence Builder [*Speech and language therapy*] (DAVI)
FBS .... Forbes Biological Station (SAUO)
FBS .... Foreign-Body Sarcoma [*Medicine*] (MELL)
FBS .... Forward-Based Systems [*US aircraft based outside the US and capable of carrying nuclear weapons to the USSR*]
FBS .... Foundry Business System [*Foundry Business Systems*] [*Software package*] (NCC)
FBS .... Francis Bacon Society (EA)
FBS .... Franco-Belgian Services (SAUS)
FBS .... Freight Billing System (SAUO)
FBS .... Frontal Boundary Study (SAUO)
FBS .... Frontal Bovine Serum [*Medicine*] (BARN)
FBS .... Fukuoka Broadcasting System (SAUO)
FBS .... Functional Bladder Syndrome [*Medicine*] (MELL)
FBSA .... Federal Boating Safety Act of 1971 [*USCG*] (TAG)
FBSA .... Filter-Band Suppressor Assembly
FB Satellite ... Fleet Broadcast Satellite (SAUS)
FBSB .... Finance Brokers Supervisory Board [*Western Australia*]
FBSB .... Forward Biased Second Breakdown (SAUS)
FBSC .... Federation of Building Specialist Contractors [*British*] (DBA)
FBSC .... Fellow of the British Society of Commerce
FBSC .... Fred Bear Sports Club (EA)
FBSComm .... Fellow of the British Society of Commerce
FBSD .... Firing Battery Status Display (SAUO)
FBSD .... Serondela [*Botswana*] [*ICAO location identifier*] (ICLI)
FBSE .... Fellow of the Botanical Society of Edinburgh (SAUO)
FBSEA .... Foreign Bank Supervision Enhancement Act [*1991*] (ECON)
FBSH .... Full Buick Service History [*Automotive classified advertising*]
FBSI .... All Indonesian Labor Federation (IMH)
FBSI .... Fellow of the Boot and Shoe Institution [*British*]
FBSI .... Fellow of the Building Societies Institute (SAUS)
FBSI .... Fellow of the National Institution of the Boot and Shoe Industry (SAUO)
FBSI .... First Bankshares [*NASDAQ symbol*] (TTSB)
FBSI .... First Bankshares of Missouri, Inc. [*NASDAQ symbol*] (SAG)
FBSI .... Furniture and Bedding Spring Institute [*Defunct*] (EA)
FBSK .... Gaborone/Sir Seretse Khama [*Botswana*] [*ICAO location identifier*] (ICLI)
FBSM .... Federal Board of Surveys and Maps (SAUO)
FBSM .... Fellow of the Birmingham and Midland Institute School of Music (SAUO)
FBSM .... Fellow of the Birmingham School of Music [*British*]
FBSMGB .... Fellow of the British Society of Master Glass Painters (SAUO)
FBSMGP .... Fellow of the British Society of Master Glass-Painters (SAUO)
FBSNSW .... French Benevolent Society of New South Wales [*Australia*]
FBSoGA .... First Banking Co. Southeast Georgia [*Associated Press*] (SAG)
FBSP .... Selebi-Phikwe [*Botswana*] [*ICAO location identifier*] (ICLI)
FBSPrX .... First Bk Sys $3.5625 Cv91A Pfd [*NYSE symbol*] (TTSB)

FBSR .... Serowe [*Botswana*] [*ICAO location identifier*] (ICLI)
FBSS .... Failed Back Surgery Syndrome [*Medicine*] (MELL)
FBSS .... Front, Back, Side-to-Side [*Lowrider vehicles*]
FBST .... Fiberstars, Inc. [*NASDAQ symbol*] (SAG)
FB Sugar ..... Fasting Blood Sugar (SAUS)
FBSV .... Savuti [*Botswana*] [*ICAO location identifier*] (ICLI)
FBSW .... First Bank System [*NASDAQ symbol*] (SAG)
FBSW .... Shakawe [*Botswana*] [*ICAO location identifier*] (ICLI)
FBSWA .... Federation of Building Societies of Western Australia
FBSWW .... First Bank Sys Wrrt [*NASDAQ symbol*] (TTSB)
FBT .... Facility Block Table (IAA)
FBT .... Feedback Technology (SSD)
FBT .... Fibertech Industries Corp. [*Formerly, Essex Petroleum Corp.*] [*Vancouver Stock Exchange symbol*]
FBT .... Flash to Bang Time [*Army*]
FBT .... Flat-Blade Turbine [*Engineering*]
FBT .... Flyback Transformer [*Electronics*] (IAA)
F/Bt .... Flying Boat [*British military*] (DMA)
FBT .... Form Block Template (MSA)
FBT .... Fort Brown, Texas (SAUS)
FBT .... Forward Ballast Tank (MSA)
FBT .... Frequent Business Traveler
FBT .... Fringe Benefits Tax
FBT .... Fuel Ballast Tank (SAUS)
FBT .... Full Berth Terms [*Shipping*]
FBT .... Functional Board Tester (SAUS)
FBTC .... Fairfax Bank & Trust Co. [*NASDAQ symbol*] (SAG)
FBTC .... Frequent Business Travellers Club (SAUO)
FBT Cps ...... Fort Belvoir Training Camps (SAUO)
FBTD .... Food and Beverage Trades Department [*of AFL-CIO*] (EA)
FBTE .... Tshane [*Botswana*] [*ICAO location identifier*] (ICLI)
FBTL .... Tuli Lodge [*Botswana*] [*ICAO location identifier*] (ICLI)
FBTPIU .... Federated Brick, Tile, and Pottery Industrial Union of Australia
FBTR .... Bederation of British Tape Recordists (DBA)
FBTR .... Fast Breeder Test Reactor [*Nuclear energy*]
FBTR .... For Better Living [*NASDAQ symbol*] (TTSB)
FBTR .... For Better Living, Inc. [*NASDAQ symbol*] (NQ)
FBTRC .... Federation of British Tape Recording Clubs (BI)
FBTS .... Form Block Template Set (MCD)
FBTS .... Tshabong [*Botswana*] [*ICAO location identifier*] (ICLI)
FBTT .... Federal Board of Tea Tasters (SAUO)
F Bty .... Field Battery (SAUS)
F Bty RA ...... Field Battery, Royal Army (SAUS)
FBU .... Federation of Bone Users and Allied Trades (SAUO)
FBU .... Federation of Broadcasting Unions [*British*]
FBU .... Field Broadcasting Unit (IAA)
FBU .... Fingers Below Umbilicus [*Measurement*] [*Anatomy*] (DAVI)
FBU .... Fire Brigades Union (SAUO)
FBU .... Fire Brigade Union
f/bu .... flowing/buildup (SAUS)
FBU .... Freie-Buerger-Union [*Free Citizens' Union*] [*Germany*] (PPW)
FBU .... Fully Built-Up [*Manufacturing*]
FBU .... Functional Business Unit (GART)
FBU .... Oslo [*Norway*] [*Airport symbol*] (AD)
FBUS .... Fisher Business Systems, Inc. [*NASDAQ symbol*] (COMM)
FBUS .... Flight Back Up System (ACAE)
FBV .... Field Base Visit (NASA)
FBV .... Friends of Bobby Vee (EA)
FBV .... Fuel Bleed Valve (NASA)
FBV .... Fuel Building Ventilation [*Nuclear energy*] (NRCH)
FBVF .... Fiberglass Backed Vacuum Forming [*Fiberglass production*]
FBW .... Fasting Blood Work [*Biochemistry*] (DAVI)
FBW .... Festbodenmulchwirtschaft (SAUO)
FBW .... Fighter-Bomber Wing (SAUO)
FBW .... Fly by Wire
FBW .... Fractional Bandwidth (SAUS)
FBW .... Full Bandwidth (SAUS)
FB WD .... Fibreboard and Wood [*Freight*]
FBWS .... Fly by Wire System (IAA)
FBW System... Fly-by-Wire System (SAUS)
FBWU .... Fire Brick Workers' Union [*British*]
FBWU .... Food and Beverage Workers' Union (SAFN)
FBWW .... International Federation of Building and Wood-Workers (SAUO)
FBX .... Fighter Bomber [*Advanced*]
FBX .... First City Bank [*AMEX symbol*] (SG)
FBX .... France, BENELUX
FBXC .... FBX Corp. [*NASDAQ symbol*] (COMM)
FBXG .... Xugana [*Botswana*] [*ICAO location identifier*] (ICLI)
FBXX .... Xaxaba [*Botswana*] [*ICAO location identifier*] (ICLI)
f-by- .... Biafra [*MARC geographic area code*] [*Library of Congress*] (LCCP)
FBY .... Fairbury, NE [*Location identifier*] [*FAA*] (FAAL)
FBY .... Future Budget Year (AFM)
FBYB .... Fly Before You Buy [*Aerospace industry slogan*]
FBypV .... United States Veterans Administration Center, Bay Pines, FL [*Library symbol*] [*Library of Congress*] (LCLS)
FBYRA .... Field Battery, Royal Army (SAUS)
FBZ .... First Brillouin Zone [*Physics*]
FBZ .... Fisher Body [*Federal Railroad Administration identification code*]
FBZ .... Forward Battle Zone [*British*]
fc--- .... Africa, Central [*MARC geographic area code*] [*Library of Congress*] (LCCP)
FC .... All India Reporter, Federal Court [*1947-50*] [*A publication*] (DLA)
FC .... British Guiana Full Court Reports (Official Gazette) [*A publication*] (DLA)
FC .... Brothers of Charity (TOCD)
fc .... Brothers of Charity (TOCD)
FC .... Canada Law Reports, Federal Court [*A publication*] (DLA)
f_c .... Carrier Frequency (IDOE)
Fc .... Central Frequency (SAUS)
FC .... Chaparral Airlines [*ICAO designator*] (AD)
FC .... Civic Forum (CAR) [*Political party*] (PSAP)
FC .... Coast Station [*ITU designation*] (CET)
FC .... Compound Fracture [*Medicine*]
FC .... Congregatio Fratrum Caritate [*Brothers of Charity*] [*Roman Catholic religious order*]
FC .... Critical Frequency (CET)
FC .... Daughters of the Cross of Liege [*Roman Catholic religious order*]
FC .... Face-Centered [*Crystallography*]
FC .... Facial Canal (MELL)
FC .... Facilitative Communication [*Autism*]
FC .... Facilities Construction (AAG)
FC .... Facilities Contract
F/C .... Facilities Control [*Military*]
FC .... Facing Concrete (SAUS)
FC .... Faciundum Curavit [*He Caused To Be Made*] [*Latin*]
FC .... Faculty of Advocates Collection of Decisions, Scotch Court of Sessions [*A publication*] (DLA)
FC .... Fail close (SAUS)
FC .... Fail Closed [*Nuclear energy*] (NRCH)
FC .... Failure Count
FC .... Fairbury College (SAUO)
FC .... Fairchild Club (EA)
fc .... Fair Condition [*Doll collecting*]
FC .... Fair Copy (SAUS)
FC .... Fair Cutting [*Brick*] (DICI)
fc .... fairly common (SAUS)
fc .... Fall Color
FC .... False Cape [*NASA*] (KSC)
FC .... False Colour (SAUS)
FC .... Family Code (SAUS)
FC .... Family Conference [*Medicine*] (EDAA)
FC .... Family Continuation of Coverage [*Health insurance*] (GHCT)
FC .... Family Contribution [*Department of Education*] (GFGA)
FC .... Faraday Cage (SAUS)
FC .... Faraday Cup (SAUS)
FC .... Farm Credit (SAUS)
FC .... Fasciculus Cuneatus (DB)
FC .... Fast Component
FC .... Fat Cell (MELL)
FC .... Fatigue Crack (SAUS)
FC .... Fault Current (SAUS)
FC .... Faulted Circuit (IAA)
FC .... fausse-couche (SAUS)
FC .... FCA International Ltd. [*Toronto Stock Exchange symbol*]
Fc .... Fc Fragment Specific (SAUS)
FC .... Feature Control (SAUS)
FC .... Feature Correlation
FC .... Feature Count [*Computer science*]
FC .... Febrile Convulsion [*Medicine*] (DMAA)
FC .... Fecal Coli [*Microbiology*]
FC .... Federal Cabinet (SAUO)
FC .... Federal Cases [*A publication*] (DLA)
FC .... Federal Conference (SAUO)
FC .... Federal Convention (SAUO)
FC .... Federalist Caucus (EA)
FC .... Federation Council (EA)
FC .... Feedback Control (VERA)
FC .... Feed the Children (EA)
FC .... Feint and Cash [*of account book rulings*]
fc .... feld champion (SAUS)
FC .... Feline Conjunctivitis [*Medicine*] (EDAA)
FC .... Fellow Craft [*Freemasonry*] (ROG)
FC .... Fenn College (SAUO)
FC .... Fermi Contact [*Physics*]
F-C .... Fermi-Curie (SAUS)
FC .... Ferric Citrate [*Medicine*] (EDAA)
FC .... Ferrite Core
FC .... Ferrocement
FC .... Ferrochelatase [*An enzyme*]
FC .... Ferromagnetic Contamination [*Medicine*]
FC .... Ferry Command [*RAF*] [*British*]
FC .... Fever and Chills [*Medicine*] (DAVI)
FC .... Fiberglass Covers (DCTA)
FC .... Fibre Channel [*Computer science*] (DCDG)
FC .... Fibro Cement (ADA)
FC .... Fibrocyte (DB)
FC .... Fidei Commissum [*Bequeathed in Trust*] [*Latin*]
FC .... Field Camera
FC .... Field Centre (SAUO)
FC .... Field Change
FC .... Field Circular [*Military*] (INF)
FC .... Field Code (SAUS)
FC .... Field Coil (SAUS)
FC .... Field Command [*Military*]
FC .... Field Commander (SAUS)
FC .... Field Compare (SAUS)
FC .... Field Completion (SAUS)
FC .... Field Component (SAUS)
FC .... Field Contactor (IAA)
FC .... Field Conversion [*Computer science*] (ECII)

FC .... Field Cooled
FC .... Field Cooling (AAEL)
FC .... Fielder's Choice [*Baseball*]
FC .... Fieri Curavit [*Caused to Be Made*] [*Latin*]
FC .... Fifth Column (ODA)
FC .... Fighter Catapult [*Ship*]
FC .... Fighter Command [*Air Force*]
FC .... Fighter Controller (SAUS)
FC .... Figures and Captions
FC .... File Cabinet (AAG)
FC .... File Chain (SAUS)
FC .... File Code [*Computer science*] (IEEE)
FC .... File Command (SAUS)
FC .... File Compare (PCM)
FC .... File Connector (SAUS)
FC .... File Control (AFIT)
FC .... File Conversion [*Computer science*] (BUR)
FC .... File Copy
f/c .... fill and check (SAUS)
FC .... Fill Code (SAUS)
FC .... Film-Coated [*Pharmacy*]
FC .... Film Comment [*A publication*] (BRI)
FC .... Film cooler (SAUS)
FC .... Films Council (SAUO)
FC .... Filson Club (EA)
FC .... Filter Center
FC .... Filter Circuit (SAUS)
FC .... Finance Charge
FC .... Finance Committee [*UN Food and Agriculture Organization*]
FC .... Finance Corps
FC .... Financial Class [*Medicine*] (EDAA)
FC .... Financial Commissioner [*Indian Railway*] (TIR)
FC .... Financial Consultant
FC .... Financial Controller
FC .... Finch College (SAUO)
FC .... Find Called [*or Calling*] Party [*Telecommunications*] (TEL)
FC .... Findlay College (SAUO)
FC .... Fine Champagne
FC .... Fine Cognac
FC .... Fine Control (DEN)
FC .... Finger Clubbing [*Medicine*] (MAE)
FC .... Finger Counting [*See also CF*]
FC .... Fire Cause [*Criminology*] (LAIN)
FC .... Fire Clay
FC .... Fire Cock [*British*] (ROG)
FC .... Fire Code (SAUS)
FC .... Fire Commander [*British military*] (DMA)
FC .... Fire Control (ADWA)
FC .... Fire Control Armourer [*British military*] (DMA)
FC .... Fire Controlman [*Navy rating*] [*Obsolete*]
FC .... Fire Cracking (SAUS)
FC .... Firing Channel [*Military*] (CAAL)
FC .... Firing Console (SAUS)
FC .... First Class (SAUS)
FC .... Fisheries (or Fishery) Council (SAUO)
FC .... Fishery Council (SAUO)
FC .... Fishmongers Company (SAUO)
FC .... Fit Check [*NASA*] (NASA)
FC .... Fitzwilliam College (SAUO)
FC .... Fixed Camera (KSC)
FC .... Fixed Capital [*Business term*]
FC .... Fixed Carbon (SAUS)
FC .... Fixed Charge [*Business term*]
f/c .... fixed contract (SAUS)
FC .... Fixed Cost [*Economics*]
FC .... Flag Captain (SAUS)
FC .... Flagellated Chamber (SAUS)
FC .... Flail Chest (MELL)
FC .... Flanged Connection [*Piping*]
F+C .... Flare and Cells [*Ophthalmology*] (DAVI)
fc .... flat cable (SAUS)
FC .... Flat Contact (SAUS)
FC .... Fleet Commander (SAUO)
FC .... fleet co-operation (SAUS)
FC .... Fleming Committee (SAUO)
FC .... Flexible Connection (OA)
FC .... Flight Capsule
F/C .... Flight Certificate
FC .... Flight Charts
FC .... Flight Commander (SAUO)
FC .... Flight Computer [*NASA*] (NASA)
FC .... Flight Control
F/C .... Flight Controller (NASA)
FC .... Flight Crew
FC .... Flight Critical (MCD)
FC .... Flip Chart (FOTI)
FC .... Flip Chip (AAEL)
FC .... Floating Capital [*Business term*]
FC .... Floating Causeway
fc .... Floating Crane (SAUS)
FC .... Flood Control
FC .... Flotilla Commander (SAUS)
FC .... Flow Chart (SAUS)
FC .... Flowchart [*Engineering*] (IAA)
FC .... Flow Coating
FC .... Flow Control (SAUS)
FC .... Flow Controller [*Nuclear energy*] (NRCH)
FC .... Flow Cytometry [*Medicine*] (MELL)
FC .... Flucytosine [*Medicine*] (EDAA)
FC .... Fluor Crowns (SAUS)
FC .... Fluoridation Committee [*Tasmania, Australia*]
FC .... Fluorocarbons [*Organic chemistry*]
FC .... Fluorocytosine [*or Flucytosine*] [*Antineoplastic drug*]
FC .... Flux Change (ELAL)
FC .... Flux Cloud (SAUS)
FC .... Flying Cadet (SAUS)
FC .... Flying Colonels [*Delta Air Lines' club for frequent flyers*] (EA)
FC .... Foam Cell (SAUS)
FC .... Foamed Concrete (SAUS)
FC .... Foaming Capacity [*Food technology*]
FC .... Foley Catheter [*Urology*]
FC .... Folin-Ciocalteau [*Clinical chemistry*]
FC .... Follicular Cell (SAUS)
fc .... Follow Copy [*Typesetting*] [*Also, Folo Copy*] (WDMC)
FC .... Follow Copy [*Printing*]
FC .... Following Copy (SAUS)
FC .... Fontbonne College (SAUO)
FC .... Font Cartridge (SAUS)
FC .... Font Change [*Computer science*] (BUR)
fc .... Font Change [*Typesetting*] (WDMC)
FC .... Font Change Character (SAUS)
FC .... Food Control (ACAE)
FC .... Food Controller [*British*] [*World War II*]
FC .... Foolscap (NTCM)
FC .... Football Club [*British*]
FC .... Football Committee [*British*]
fc .... Foot-Candle (NTIO)
FC .... Foot-Candle [*Illumination*]
fC .... foot candle (SAUS)
FC .... Foothill College (SAUO)
FC .... Footwear Caucus (EA)
FC .... Footwear Council [*Defunct*] (EA)
FC .... Forage Corps [*British military*] (DMA)
FC .... Forage Crop [*Agriculture*]
f/c .... For Cash (SAUS)
FC .... Force Control (MCD)
FC .... Forced Circulation (DICI)
FC .... Forced Convection (SAUS)
FC .... Forced Cooling (SAUS)
FC .... Ford Motor Company of Canada Ltd. [*AMEX symbol*] (COMM)
f/c .... Forecast (SAUS)
FC .... Forecast Center (SAUS)
FC .... Forecast Center Station [*Telecommunications*] (TEL)
FC .... Foreign Classics [*A publication*]
FC .... Foreign Consul (ROG)
FC .... Foreign Currency
FC .... Forest Center (SAUS)
FC .... Forestry Canada (SAUS)
FC .... Forestry Commission [*British*]
F/C .... Format Code [*Computer science*]
FC .... Format Control (SAUS)
FC .... Formula Continental [*Class of racing cars*]
FC .... Forward Cab [*Automotive engineering*]
FC .... Forward Chaining [*Psychology*]
FC .... Forward Checking (SAUS)
FC .... Forward Control [*Automotive engineering*]
FC .... Foster Care
FC .... Foundation Center (EA)
FC .... Foundation City [*Dialog*] [*Searchable field*] [*Information service or system*] (NITA)
FC .... Foundation Code [*IRS*]
FC .... Fovea Centralis (MELL)
FC .... Fowl Cholera [*Medicine*] (EDAA)
FC .... Fractionating Column (SAUS)
FC .... Fraction Collector [*Chromatography*]
FC .... Fractocumulus [*Meteorology*]
Fc .... Fractocumulus Cloud (WEAT)
Fc .... Fragment crystalline (SAUS)
Fc .... Fragment, Crystallizable [*Immunochemistry*]
FC .... Frame Control [*Computer science*] (TNIG)
FC .... Franc [*Monetary unit*] [*France*] (ROG)
FC .... Franconia College (SAUO)
FC .... Franklin Covey [*NYSE symbol*] [*Formerly, Franklin Quest*] (SG)
FC .... Frederic Chopin (SAUS)
FC .... Frederick College (SAUO)
F/C .... Free and Clear (WDAA)
FC .... Free Child [*Psychology*] (DHP)
FC .... Free Choice [*Psychology*]
FC .... Free Cholesterol [*Clinical chemistry*]
FC .... Free Church
FC .... Free Convection (SAUS)
FC .... Free Cursor (NITA)
FC .... Freedom Club
FC .... Free of Cells [*Medicine*]
FC .... French Canada (SAUS)
FC .... French Canadian (SAUS)
FC .... French Codex [*Medicine*] (EDAA)
FC .... Frequency Changer (IAA)
FC .... Frequency Control (SAUS)
FC .... Frequency Conversion (SAUS)

FC .... Frequency Converter
FC .... Frequency Counter (ACAE)
FC .... Freres de la Charite [*Brothers of Charity*] (EAIO)
FC .... Fretting Corrosion (SAUS)
FC .... Friars Club (EA)
FC .... Friction Curve [*Automotive emissions*]
FC .... Friendly Capabilities (MCD)
FC .... Friends of Community (EA)
FC .... Frontal Cortex (DB)
FC .... Front Connected (SAUS)
FC .... Front-Connected
FC .... Front Cover [*Publishing*] (WDAA)
fc .... Front Cover [*Publishing*] (WDAA)
FC .... Front-End Computer (VLIE)
FC .... Frontier Conference (PSS)
FC .... Frozen Cell
FC .... Frozen-in Conductivity (SAUS)
FC .... Frustration Clause (SAUS)
FC .... Fuel Calorimetry (SAUS)
FC .... Fuel Cell (KSC)
FC .... Fuel Consumption (SAUO)
FC .... Fuel Controller (DAS)
FC .... Fuel-Coolant Interaction (SAUS)
FC .... Fuel Cycle (NRCH)
f + c .... full and complete cargo (SAUS)
FC .... Full Cell (SAUS)
FC .... Full Charge [*Accounting*]
FC .... Full Classification Code (SAUS)
FC .... Full Color (SAUS)
FC .... Full Colour (VLIE)
FC .... Full Coordination (SAUS)
FC .... Full Corner [*Philately*]
FC .... Full Course [*Medicine*] (ODA)
FC .... Full Court (ADA)
FC .... Full Court Judgments [*Ghana*] [*A publication*] (DLA)
FC .... Full Credit [*Motor vehicle violation code used in state of Maryland*] (MVRD)
FC .... Full Custom (SAUS)
FC .... fully cellular (SAUS)
FC .... Fulton County Railroad [*Federal Railroad Administration identification code*]
FC .... Functional Character (VLIE)
FC .... Functional Checkout (SAUS)
FC .... Functional Chief [*of a civilian career program*] [*Military*]
FC .... Functional Class [*Rehabilitation*] [*Medicine*] (DAVI)
FC .... Functional Code
FC .... Function Call (IAA)
FC .... Function Code (NITA)
FC .... Fund Campaign [*Red Cross*]
FC .... Fund Code (AABC)
FC .... Funding Cycle (OICC)
FC .... Funnel Chest (MELL)
FC .... Funnel Cloud
FC .... Funny Car [*Class of racing cars*]
FC .... Furnace Container (SAUS)
FC .... Furnace Control (SAUS)
FC .... Furnace Cooled [*Engineering*] (IAA)
FC .... Furnace Cooling (SAUS)
FC .... Fuse Chamber (TEL)
FC .... Fused Chamber (SAUS)
FC .... Futures Contract [*Investment term*]
FC .... Fuze Committee [*Military*]
FC .... Hard Filled Capsules [*Pharmacy*]
FC .... Hydrofluorocarbon
FC .... ISCCP Flux Cloud (SAUO)
FC .... Selected Judgments of the Full Court, Accra and Gold Coast [*A publication*] (DLA)
FC .... Subcutaneous Fat Class
FC .... Union of Soviet Socialist Republics [*Formerly, SX*] [*License plate code assigned to foreign diplomats in the US*]
FC .... United Free Church of Scotland (SAUO)
Fc .... Crystallizable Fragment (of an Immunoglobulin) [*Immunology*] (ODA)
FC .... Fencing Club (ODA)
FC²V .... Future Command and Control Vehicle
FC '22 .... Full Court Judgments [*1922*] [*Ghana*] [*A publication*] (DLA)
FC '20-1 .... Full Court Judgments [*1920-21*] [*Ghana*] [*A publication*] (DLA)
FC '23-25 .... Selected Judgments of the Full Court [*1923-25*] [*Ghana*] [*A publication*] (DLA)
FC '26-29 .... Selected Judgments of the Full Court [*1926-29*] [*Ghana*] [*A publication*] (DLA)
FCa .... Cape Canaveral Public Library, Cape Canaveral, FL [*Library symbol*] [*Library of Congress*] (LCLS)
FCA .... Fabri Centers of America [*NYSE symbol*] (SAG)
FCA .... Fabri-Centers of America, Inc. [*NYSE symbol*] (SPSG)
FCA .... Facility Change Authorization (AAG)
FCA .... Factorial Correspondence Analysis [*Mathematics*]
FCA .... Fairlane Club of America (EA)
FCA .... Falcon Club of America (EA)
FCA .... False Claims Act (AAGC)
FCA .... Family Caregiver Alliance (SAUO)
FCA .... Family Court of Australia
FCA .... Fan Club Associates [*Later, IFCA*] (EA)
FCA .... Faraday Cup Array [*Electronics*] (OA)
FCA .... Farm Credit Administration [*Independent government agency*]
FCA .... Farm Credit Associations (SAUO)
FCA .... Fast Critical Assembly [*Nuclear reactor*] [*Japan*]
FCA .... Fault Correction Array (SAUS)
FCA .... Federal Code, Annotated [*A publication*] (DLA)
FCA .... Federal Committee on Apprenticeship [*Department of Labor*]
FCA .... Federal Communications Act
FCA .... Federal Council on the Aging [*Succeeded by President's Council on Aging, 1962*]
FCA .... Federal Credit Administration (SAUS)
FCA .... Federated Confectioners Association (SAUO)
FCA .... Federation Canadienne de l'Agriculture [*Canadian Federation of Agriculture - CFA*]
FCA .... Federation Canadienne des Archers [*Federation of Canadian Archers*]
FCA .... Federation of Canadian Archers
FCA .... Federation of Canadian Artists
FCA .... Federation of College Academics (SAUO)
FCA .... Federation of Commodity Associations (EAIO)
FCA .... Fellow of the Institute of Chartered Accountants [*British*] (ROG)
FCA .... Fellow of the Institute of Chartered Architects [*British*]
FCA .... Fellowship of Christian Athletes (EA)
FCA .... Fencing Contractors Association [*British*] (DBA)
FCA .... Ferrari Club of America (EA)
FCA .... Ferrite Control Amplifier
FCA .... Ferritin-Conjugated Antibody [*Biochemistry*] (MAE)
FCA .... Few Civilian Casualties [*Persian Gulf War*]
FCA .... Fiat Club of America (EA)
FCA .... Fibre Channel Association (DDC)
FCA .... Field Change Analysis
FCA .... Field Change Authorization [*Nuclear energy*] (NRCH)
FCA .... Fighter Control Area [*Military*]
FCA .... Fiji College of Agriculture (SAUO)
FCA .... Filipino Cultural Association [*Australia*]
FCA .... Film Council of America (SAUO)
FCA .... Films for Christ Association (EA)
FCA .... Finance Corporation of Australia (SAUO)
FCA .... Financial Corporation of America (SAUO)
FCA .... Financial Corporations Act [*Australia*]
FCA .... Fine Crushed Aggregate (SAUS)
FCA .... Finite Cellular Automaton (SAUS)
FCA .... Fire Control Area [*Army*]
FCA .... First Chair of America [*Defunct*] (EA)
FCA .... Fishing Clubs of Australia
FCA .... Fixed Coaxial Attenuator
FCA .... Fixed contamination area (SAUS)
FCA .... Fleet Chief Armourer [*British military*] (DMA)
FCA .... Flight Configuration Audit (SAUS)
FCA .... Flight Control Area (SAUS)
FCA .... Flight Control Assemblies
FCA .... Floating Channel Addressing (SAUS)
FCA .... Flood Control Act of 1936 (COE)
FCA .... Flow Control Ack (SAUS)
FCA .... Flow Control Assembly (MCD)
FCA .... Fluidized Combustor Ash (OA)
FCA .... Fluids Control Assembly (NASA)
FCA .... Fluorescence Concentration Analyzer (SAUS)
FCA .... Fluorescent Cytoprint Assay (MELL)
FCA .... Fluorocytosine Arabinoside [*Also, ara-FC*] [*Antitumor compound*]
FCA .... Flux Cored-Arc (SAUS)
FCA .... Flying Chiropractors Association (EA)
FCA .... Food Casings Association [*British*] (DBA)
FCA .... Footwear Components Association Ltd. [*British*] (BI)
FCA .... Force Cost Assessor (MCD)
FCA .... Forest Conservation Archives (SAUS)
FCA .... Formal Configuration Audit (MCD)
FCA .... Forward Controller Assembly [*Aerospace*] (NAKS)
FCA .... Foster Care Association (SAUO)
FCA .... Foundation for the Community of Artists (EA)
FCA .... Fracture, Complete, Angulated (SAUS)
FCA .... Fraternity of Canadian Astrologers
FCA .... Free Carrier (RIMS)
FCA .... Free-Carrier Absorption (SAUS)
FCA .... Free China Assistance (EA)
FCA .... Freight Claim Agent
FCA .... Freight Claim Association
FCA .... French Computing Association
FCA .... Frequency Change Approved [*Aviation*] (FAAC)
FCA .... Frequency Control and Analysis
FCA .... Freund's Complete Adjuvant [*Immunology*]
FCA .... Friendly Contacts Associates [*Defunct*] (EA)
FCA .... Fuel Capsule [*or Cell*] Assembly (MCD)
FCA .... Fuel Cell Association (EA)
FCA .... Full Circle Associates (EA)
FCA .... Full-Coverage Area [*Radio and TV*]
FCA .... Functional Compatibility Analysis (MCD)
FCA .... Functional Configuration Audit
FCA .... Fur Council of Australia
FCA .... FUTABA Corporation of America (SAUO)
FCA .... Fuzzy Cluster Analysis [*Mathematics*]
FCA .... Fuzzy Computational Acceleration (SAUS)
FCA .... Kalispell [*Montana*] [*Airport symbol*] (OAG)
FCA .... Kalispell, MT [*Location identifier*] [*FAA*] (FAAL)
FCA .... Stratford Airways Ltd. [*Canada*] [*ICAO designator*] (FAAC)
FCAA .... Federal Clean Air Act (WDAA)
FCAA .... Federal Courts Administration Act of 1992 (AAGC)
FCAA .... Fleet Chief Aircraft Artificer [*British military*] (DMA)

FCAA........... Florence Crittenton Association of America [*Later, CWLA*] (EA)
FCAA........... Foreign Correspondents' Association of Australia
FCAA........... Forest Conservation Action Alerts (SAUS)
FC/AA........... Foster Care/Adoption Assistance [*Public human service program*] (PHSD)
FCaA........... Fractional-intestinal Calcium Absorption (SAUS)
FCAA........... Frequency Control and Analysis (IAA)
FCAAA......... Federal Council of Australian Apiarists Association (SAUO)
FCAC........... Federal Council of American Churches (SAUO)
FCAC........... Field Crop Advisory Committee [*Western Australia*]
FCAC........... Folklore Studies Association of Canada
FCAC........... Forward Control and Analysis Center (MCD)
FCA(Can)...... Fellow of the Institute of Chartered Accountants in Canada
FCACMN...... Fleet Chief Aircrewman [*British military*] (DMA)
FCACS......... Federal Civil Agencies Communications System (SAUS)
FCAD........... Field Contract Administration Division [*of ONM*]
FCADD......... Fondation Canadienne sur l'Alcohol et la Dependance aux Drogues [*Canadian Foundation on Alcohol and Drug Dependencies - CFADD*]
FCAE........... Fellow of the Canadian Academy of Engineering (DD)
FCAF........... Fleet Chief Air Fitter [*British military*] (DMA)
FCAF........... Flight Crew Accommodations Facility (SAUS)
FCaF........... Florida Solar Energy Center, Cape Canaveral, FL [*Library symbol*] [*Library of Congress*] (LCLS)
FCAF........... Frequency Control Analysis Facility
FCAG........... Federal Communications Advisory Group (SAUO)
FCAI........... Fairchild Camera and Instrument (SAUS)
FCAI........... Federal Chamber of Automotive Industries (EERA)
FCAK........... Function Cable Access Kit (DWSG)
FCAL........... Fibre Channel - Arbitrated Loop (SAUS)
FC-AL........... Fibre Channel-Arbitrated Loop [*Telecommunications*] (IGQR)
Fcalc........... Calculated Structure Factor (SAUS)
FCAM........... Federation Canadienne des Amis de Musees (AC)
FCAM........... Fellow of the Communication Advertising and Marketing Education Foundation [*British*] (DBQ)
FCAM........... Fellow of the Institute of Certified Administrative Managers (DD)
FCAM........... Fellow of the Institute of CICAM [*Canadian Institute of Certified Administrative Managers*] (ASC)
FCAME......... Fellowship of Christians in the Arts, Media, and Entertainment (EA)
FCAMRT....... Fellow of the Canadian Association of Medical Radiation Technologists (SAUO)
FCAN........... Full Controller Area Network (SAUS)
FCANA......... Federation of Cambodian Associations in North America (EA)
FC & CE...... Flight Crew and Crew Equipment
FC&I........... Fairchild Camera & Instrument Corp. (SAUO)
FC&I........... Food and Container Institute (SAUO)
FC&PMS...... Fort Cumberland and Portsmouth Militaria Society (SAUO)
FC & S......... Final Command and Sequencing [*Viking lander mission*] [*NASA*]
FC and S..... Free of Capture and Seizure (SAUS)
FC & S......... Free of Capture and Seizure [*Insurance*]
fc & s and r & cc... Free of Capture and Seizure and Riots and Civil Commotion (SAUS)
fc & s and r & cc... free of capture, seizure, riots, and civil commotion (SAUS)
FC and S and R and CC... free of capture, seizure, riots, and civil commotions (SAUS)
FC & SCWSL... Fire Control and Small Caliber Weapon Systems Laboratory [*Picatinny Arsenal, Dover, NJ*] [*Army*] (RDA)
FCANSW...... Floor Coverings Association of New South Wales [*Australia*]
f cant.......... forward cant frames (SAUS)
FCA(NZ)...... Fellow Chartered Accountant of New Zealand
FCAO........... Farm Credit Administration Operations (SAUO)
FCAP........... Facility Capability Assurance Program (SAUO)
FCAP........... Fellow of the College of American Pathologists
FCAP........... Fellowship of Christian Airline Personnel (EA)
FCAP........... Flight Control Applications Program [*NASA*] (NASA)
FCAP........... Floating Point Commercial Arithmetic Processor (VLIE)
FCAP........... Fluor Chrome Arsenate Phenol [*Wood preservative*]
fcap........... Foolscap (ADWA)
FCAP........... Foolscap [*Paper*]
FCap........... French Capitol [*Record label*]
FCAP........... Fuel Cycle Advanced Project (SAUS)
FCAPO......... Fellow of the College of American Pathologists (SAUS)
FCAPS......... Fault, Configuration, Accounting, Performance, Security management areas (SAUS)
FCAR........... Field Change Activity Report (VLIE)
FCAR........... Foreign Currency Agriculture Research Program [*Department of Agriculture*]
FCAR........... Forms Control Address Register (VLIE)
FCAR........... Forrns Control Address Register (SAUS)
FCAR........... Free of Claim for Accident Reported [*Shipping*] (DS)
F Carr Cas... Federal Carriers Cases [*Commerce Clearing House*] [*A publication*] (DLA)
F Carrier Cas... Federal Carriers Cases [*Commerce Clearing House*] [*A publication*] (DLA)
F Cas........... Federal Cases [*A publication*] (DLA)
FCAS........... Federal Civil Agencies communications System (SAUS)
FCAS........... Federal Council of Agricultural Societies (SAUO)
FCAS........... Fellow, Casualty Actuarial Society
FCAS........... Fellow of the Casualty Actuarial Society [*Casualty Actuarial Society*] [*Designation awarded by*]
fcas........... free of capture and seizure (SAUS)
FCAS........... Frequency Coded Armaments System
FCAS........... Frequency Control Analysis Subsystem (MCD)
FCas........... Seminole County Public Library System, Casselberry, FL [*Library symbol*] [*Library of Congress*] (LCLS)
FCASA......... Foreign Correspondents Association of South Africa (SAUO)
FCASI.......... Fellow of the Canadian Aeronautics and Space Institute
F Cas No..... Federal Case Number [*Legal term*] (DLA)
FCAST......... Forecast [*Meteorology*] (ODA)
FCAT........... Federal Committee on Apprentice Training (SAUO)
FCAT........... Flight Composite Acceptance Test
FCAT........... Floating SI-Gate Channel Corner Avalanche Transition (MCD)
FCAT........... Florida Comprehensive Achievement Test
Fcath........... Foley Catheter [*Urology*]
FCAW........... Flux Cored Arc Welding
FCAW........... Foundation for Citizens Against Waste (EA)
FCAW-EG..... Flux Cored Arc Welding - Electrogas (SAUS)
FCb............. Cocoa Beach Public Library, Cocoa Beach, FL [*Library symbol*] [*Library of Congress*] (LCLS)
FCB............. Fabian Colonial Bureau (SAUO)
FCB............. Facility Clearance Board [*WPB*]
FCB............. Falmouth Bancorp [*AMEX symbol*] [*Formerly, Falmouth Co-Operative Bank*] (SG)
FCB............. Falmouth Co-Operative Bank [*AMEX symbol*] (SAG)
FCB............. Fast Capacitor Bank
FCB............. Feed Circuit Breaker (VLIE)
FCB............. File Cache Buffer [*Computer science*] (VLIE)
FCB............. File Control Block [*Computer science*] (BUR)
FCB............. Film Censorship Board [*Australia*]
FCB............. First Commercial Bank [*Taiwan*]
FCB............. Flight Certification Board (SAUO)
FCB............. Fluocortin Butyl [*Pharmacology*]
FCB............. Focus Control Block [*Computer science*]
FCB............. Foote, Cone & Belding Communications [*Advertising*] [*Communications*] [*Chicago, IL*] (WDMC)
FCB............. Foreign Clearance Base
FCB............. Foreign Clearing Base (SAUS)
FCB............. Forms Control Buffer [*Computer science*] (IBMDP)
FCB............. Foundation for Commercial Banks (EA)
FCB............. Free Cutting Brass
FCB............. Freight Container Bureau [*AAR*]
FCB............. Frequency Control Board [*British*] (AIA)
FCB............. Frequency Coordinating Board (SAUO)
FCB............. Frequency Coordinating Body
FCB............. Friends of Clara Barton (EA)
FCB............. Fuel Cell Battery
FCB............. Fuel Cell Bus (EURO)
FCB............. Function Control Block [*Computer science*] (IBMDP)
FCB............. Function Control Byte (SAUS)
FCB............. Marine Broadcast Station [*ITU designation*] (CET)
FCBA........... Fair Credit Billing Act
FCBA........... Federal Circuit Bar Association (AAGC)
FCBA........... Federal Communications Bar Association (EA)
FCBA........... Fellow of the Canadian Bankers' Association
FCBA........... Future Carrier-Borne Aircraft [*Military*] (SEWL)
FCBA........... Lalouila [*Congo*] [*ICAO location identifier*] (ICLI)
FCBB........... Brazzaville/Maya Maya [*Congo*] [*ICAO location identifier*] (ICLI)
FCBC........... Foreign Countries and British Colonies [*A publication*]
FCBCD......... For Carter Before Camp David [*Refers to Israeli-Egyptian agreements of 1978*]
FCBD........... Djambala [*Congo*] [*ICAO location identifier*] (ICLI)
FCBD........... Fibrocystic Breast Disease [*Medicine*] (MELL)
FCBF........... FCB Financial [*NASDAQ symbol*] (TTSB)
FCBF........... FCB Financial Corp. [*NASDAQ symbol*] (SAG)
FCBF........... Florida Customs Brokers and Forwarders Association (SRA)
FCBFL......... Feminists Concerned for Better Feminist Leadership (EA)
FCB Fn........ FCB Financial Corp. [*Associated Press*] (SAG)
FCBG........... Federation of Children's Book Groups [*British*]
FCBG........... Madingou [*Congo*] [*ICAO location identifier*] (ICLI)
FCBI........... First Commerce Bancshares, Inc. [*NASDAQ symbol*] (NQ)
FCBIA......... First Commerce Bancshares'A' [*NASDAQ symbol*] (TTSB)
FCBIB......... First Comm Bancshares 'B' [*NASDAQ symbol*] (TTSB)
FCBJS......... Federated Council of Beth Jacob Schools (EA)
FCBK........... First Charter Bank NA [*NASDAQ symbol*] (SAG)
FCBK........... Kindamba [*Congo*] [*ICAO location identifier*] (ICLI)
FCBL........... Lague [*Congo*] [*ICAO location identifier*] (ICLI)
FCBM........... Federation of Clinker Block Manufacturers [*British*] (BI)
FCBM........... Mouyondzi [*Congo*] [*ICAO location identifier*] (ICLI)
FCBN........... Fluorocarbon Co. (MHDW)
FCBO........... M'Pouya [*Congo*] [*ICAO location identifier*] (ICLI)
FCBP........... M'Passa [*Congo*] [*ICAO location identifier*] (ICLI)
FCBS........... Fayette County Bancshares, Inc. [*NASDAQ symbol*] (SAG)
FCBS........... File Control Blocks (SAUS)
FCBS........... Sibiti [*Congo*] [*ICAO location identifier*] (ICLI)
FCBSC......... Federal Council of British Ski Clubs (SAUO)
FCBSI.......... Fellow of the Chartered Building Societies Institute [*British*] (DBQ)
FCBT........... Loutete [*Congo*] [*ICAO location identifier*] (ICLI)
FCBU........... Aubeville [*Congo*] [*ICAO location identifier*] (ICLI)
FCBU........... Foreign Currency Banking Unit (WDAA)
FCBUSA....... Finance Corps Board, United States Army
FCBV........... Brazzaville [*Congo*] [*ICAO location identifier*] (ICLI)
FCBY........... N'Kay/Yokangassi [*Congo*] [*ICAO location identifier*] (ICLI)
FCBZ........... Zanaga [*Congo*] [*ICAO location identifier*] (ICLI)
FCC............. Fabrication Customer Center (TIMI)
FCC............. Face-Centered Cube (SAUS)
fcc............. Face-Centered Cubic (ABAC)
FCC............. Face-Centered Cubic [*Crystallography*]
FCC............. Faced-centred Cubic Crystal (SAUS)
FCC............. Facilities Control Console (AAG)
FCC............. Facility Communications Criteria (IAA)

FCC .... Facsimile Communication Center (SAUS)
FCC .... Fairbanks Correctional Center (SAUO)
FCC .... False color composite (SAUS)
FCC .... Falsely Claiming [*US*] Citizenship
FCC .... Familial Colonic Cancer [*Gastroenterology and oncology*] (DAVI)
FCC .... Family Communion Crusade [*Defunct*] (EA)
FCC .... Farm Credit Corp. [*Canada*]
FCC .... Farm Credit Corporation (SAUO)
FCC .... Farm Credit Council (EA)
FCC .... Farm Crisis Committee [*Defunct*] (EA)
FCC .... Federal City College [*Later, UDC*] [*Washington, DC*]
FCC .... Federal Communications Commission [*Independent government agency*]
FCC .... Federal Communications Commission, Washington, DC [*OCLC symbol*] (OCLC)
FCC .... Federal Communications Committee (SAUS)
FCC .... Federal Communications System (SAUO)
FCC .... Federal Computer Conference (VLIE)
FCC .... Federal Construction Council (EA)
FCC .... Federal Consultative Council (SAUO)
FCC .... Federal Consultative Council of South African Railways and Harbors Staff Association
FCC .... Federal Coordinating Center (SAUO)
FCC .... Federal Council of Churches
FCC .... Federal Court of Canada (SAUO)
FCC .... Federation Canadienne des Communications [*Canadian Federation of Communications Workers - CFCW*]
FCC .... Federation of Crafts and Commerce [*British*] (DBA)
FCC .... Feed Control Character (SAUS)
FCC .... Feedforward/Cascade Control (SAUS)
FCC .... Fellowship of Companies for Christ [*Later, FCCI*] (EA)
FCC .... Fellowship of Concerned Churchmen (EA)
F/CC .... Fermentation/Cell Culture [*Biology*]
FCC .... Ferntree Computer Corp.
F/cc .... Fibers per Cubic Centimeter
f/cc .... Fibers Per Cubic Centimeter of Air [*Industrial hygiene term*] (OHS)
FCC .... Field Camera Control
FCC .... Field Control Center
FCC .... Field Controller Component (MCD)
FCC .... Fighter Control Center (MUGU)
FCC .... File Carbon Copy (SAUS)
FCC .... Filipino Community Cooperative [*Australia*]
FCC .... Firearms Consultative Committee [*Australia*]
FCC .... Fire Collectors Club (EA)
FCC .... Fire Control Center (SAUS)
FCC .... Fire Control Code
FCC .... Fire Control Computer
FCC .... Fire Control Console (NATG)
FCC .... First Central Financial Corp. [*AMEX symbol*] (SPSG)
FCC .... First Central Finl [*AMEX symbol*] (TTSB)
FCC .... First Class Certificate (SAUS)
FCC .... First-Class Certificate
FCC .... First Class Commission (HGAA)
FCC .... Fixed Ceramic Capacitor
FCC .... Fixed Communications Cabinet (MCD)
FCC .... Flat Conductor Cable
FCC .... Fleet Command and Control (ACAE)
FCC .... Fleet Command Center [*Navy*] (CAAL)
FCC .... Fleet Command Control (CCCA)
FCC .... Fleet Control Center (ACAE)
FCC .... Fletcher Challenge Canada Ltd. [*Toronto Stock Exchange symbol*] [*Vancouver Stock Exchange symbol*]
FCC .... Flight Clinical Coordination (SAUO)
FCC .... Flight Communications Center
FCC .... Flight Control Center
FCC .... Flight Control Console
fcc .... flight-control console (SAUS)
FCC .... Flight Control Container
FCC .... Flight Coordination Center (AFM)
FCC .... Flight Crew Compartment (MCD)
FCC .... Florida Christian College
FCC .... Florida Citrus Commission [*Later, Florida Department of Citrus*]
FCC .... Flow Control Confirmation (SAUS)
FCC .... Fluid Catalyst Cracking (SAUS)
FCC .... Fluid Catalytic Converter [*Environmental Protection Agency*] (GFGA)
FCC .... Fluid Catalytic Cracking [*Fuel technology*]
FCC .... Fluid Cat Cracking (SAUS)
FCC .... Fluid Convection Cathode
FCC .... Fluid Cracking Catalyst (SAUS)
FCC .... Fluorochlorocarbon [*Organic chemistry*]
FCC .... Folded Capacitor Cell (SAUS)
FCC .... Follicular Center Cell [*Cytology*]
FCC .... Fontana Corrosion Center [*Ohio State University*] [*Research center*] (RCD)
FCC .... Font Change Character [*Computer science*] (ELAL)
FCC .... Food Chemicals Codex [*National Academy of Sciences*] [*A publication*]
FCC .... Food Contaminants Commission (SAUS)
FCC .... Food Control Committee (SAUO)
FCC .... Forbidden Code Combination (SAUS)
FCC .... Forbidden Combination Check
FCC .... Foreign Commerce Club of New York (EA)
FCC .... Foreign Correspondents Club (SAUS)
FCC .... Foreign Correspondents Club of Japan (NTCM)
FCC .... Forest Conservation Council (WPI)
FCC .... Forms Control Center (OICC)
FCC .... Fort Churchill [*Manitoba*] [*Seismograph station code, US Geological Survey*] (SEIS)
FCC .... Forward Carbon Copy (SAUS)
FCC .... Forward Command Channel (SAUS)
FCC .... Forward Control Channel (SAUS)
FCC .... Foundation for a Christian Civilization (EA)
FCC .... Foundation for Community Creativity (EA)
FCC .... Four Corners Club (SAUO)
FCC .... Fractional Cloud Cover (ARMP)
FCC .... Fracture, Complete, Comminuted (SAUS)
FCC .... Fracture, Compound and Comminuted [*Orthopedics*] (DAVI)
FCC .... Frame Check Character (NITA)
FCC .... Frame Code Complement (SAUS)
FCC .... Free Church Council [*British*] (DAS)
fcc .... freight control computer (SAUS)
FCC .... French Chamber of Commerce (DCTA)
FCC .... Frequency-to-Current Converter (IAA)
FCC .... Fuel Cell Catalyst
FCC .... Fuel Control Computer
FCC .... Fueled clad canister (SAUS)
FCC .... Fuels Control Center (AFIT)
FCC .... Fully Cellular Containership (DS)
FCC .... Fund Control Code
FCC .... Future Characteristics Change [*Military*] (CAAL)
FCC .... United States Federal Communication Commission (SAUS)
FCC 68 .... Federal Communications Commission Part 68 (SAUS)
FCCA .... Farmers Chinchilla Cooperative of America [*Later, ECBC*] (EA)
FCCA .... Federal Court Clerks Association (EA)
FCCA .... Fellow Chartered Association of Certified Accountants [*British*] (WA)
FCCA .... Fellow of the Association of Certified Accountants (DD)
FCCA .... Fellow of the Chartered Association of Certified Accountants (WDAA)
FCCA .... Fleet Chief Caterer [*British military*] (DMA)
FCCA .... Floor Covering Contractors' Association [*British*] (BI)
FCCA .... Florida-Caribbean Cruise Association (TRID)
FCCA .... Forestry, Conservation and Communications Association (SAUO)
FCCA .... Four Cylinder Club of America
FCCAA .... Florida Community College Athletic Association (PSS)
FCCAHA .... Fellow, Clinical Cardiology, American Health Association (CMD)
FCCB .... Field Change Control Board
FCCB .... Field Configuration Control Board [*Army*] (AABC)
FCCBMP .... Fleet Command Center Battle Management Program (SAUO)
FCCC .... Brazzaville [*Congo*] [*ICAO location identifier*] (ICLI)
FCCC .... Farm Credit Corp. Canada [*Ottawa, ON*]
FCCC .... Farming and Countryside Conservation Centre (SAUS)
FCCC .... Federal Complaint Coordinating Center [*US Office of Consumer Affairs*]
FCCC .... Federation Canadienne des Cine-Clubs [*Canada*]
FCCC .... Federation des Clubs Cooperatifs de Consommation [*Federation of Consumer Cooperative Associations*] [*Canada*]
FCCC .... Federation of Commonwealth Chambers of Commerce (BI)
FCCC .... Fire Control Control Console
fccc .... fire-control control console (SAUS)
FCCC .... Flight Coordination Control Central
FCCC .... Florida Christian College Conference (PSS)
FCCC .... Forbidden Code Combination Check (SAUS)
FCCC .... Four-Channel Communications Controller (TIMI)
FCCC .... Fox Chase Cancer Center (SAUS)
FCCC .... Fracture, Complete, Comminuted, Compound (SAUS)
FCCC .... Framework Convention on Climate Change (EERA)
FCCCA .... Federal Council of Churches of Christ in America (SAUO)
FCCD .... Florida Council on Crime and Delinquency (SAUO)
FCCD .... Fund for Co-operation (SAUS)
FCCE .... Future Combat Collaborative Environment [*Army*]
FCCEA .... Fleet Chief Control Electrical Artificer [*British military*] (DMA)
FCCEd .... Fellow of the College of Craft Education [*British*] (DI)
FCCEL .... Fleet Chief Control Electrician [*British military*] (DMA)
FCCEMN .... Fleet Chief Control Electrical Mechanician [*British military*] (DMA)
FCCFA .... Fraternite des Commis de Chemins de Fer, de Lignes Aeriennes, et de Navigation, Manutentionaires de Fret, Employes de Messageries et de Gares [*Brotherhood of Railway, Airline, and Steamship Clerks, Freight Handlers, Express and Station Employees*] [*Canada*]
FCCFF .... First Check Character Flip Flop [*Computer science*] (MHDI)
FCCH .... Frequency Correction Channel (VERA)
FCCI .... Federal Clean Car Incentive Program [*Environmental Protection Agency*] (MCD)
FCCI .... Fellowship of Companies for Christ International (EA)
FCCI .... Fuel-Cladding Chemical Interaction (ABAC)
FCCIA .... French Chamber of Commerce and Industry in Australia
FCCIM .... Federal Coordination Committee on Instrumentation and Measurement
FCCIP .... Federal Clean Car Incentive Program [*Environmental Protection Agency*]
FCCJ .... Foreign Correspondents' Club of Japan
FCCK .... Fire Control Check [*Military*] (NVT)
fcck .... fire-control check (SAUS)
FCCK .... Fleet Chief Cook [*British military*] (DMA)
FCCL .... Follicular Center Cell Lymphoma [*Medicine*] (MELL)
FCC Lattice ... Face-Centered Cubic Lattice (SAUS)
FCCM .... Facilities Capital Cost of Money (AAGC)
FCCMG .... Fellow of the Canadian College of Medical Genetics (SAUS)
FCCN .... Federal Communications Commission Network
FCC Network ... Federal Communications Commission Network (SAUS)
FCCNY .... Foreign Commerce Club of New York (SAUO)

FCCO .... Fellow of the Canadian College of Organists
FCCO .... Flight Change Control Order
FCCOM .... Facilities Capital Cost of Money (AAGC)
FCCOP .... Fire Control Computer Operational Program (MCD)
FCCP .... Carbonylcyanide p-Trifluoromethoxyphenylhydrazone (SAUS)
FCCP .... Fellow of the American College of Chest Physicians
FCCP .... Fellow of the Canadian College of Physicians (DD)
FCCP .... Fellow of the College of Chest Physicians (CMD)
FCCP .... Firm Contract Cost Proposal (NASA)
FCCP .... Friends Coordinating Committee on Peace [*Defunct*] (EA)
FCCP .... Funders Committee for Citizenship Participation (EA)
FCCP .... Trifluoromethoxycarbonylcyanide Phenylhydrazone (DB)
FCCPM .... Medical Fellow of the Canadian College of Physicians (CPGU)
FCCPO .... Federal Contract Compliance Program Office [*Department of Labor*] (IEEE)
FCCR .... Feature Customization Control Record (SAUS)
FCCS .... Federal Claims Collection Standards (OTD)
FCCS .... Federal Cost-Control Survey (SAUS)
FCCS .... Fellow of the Corporation of Certified Secretaries [*British*] (EY)
FCCS .... Flat Conductor Cables (SAUS)
FCCS .... Focusing Collimator Coincidence Scanning (SAUS)
FCCS .... Forces Correspondence Courses Scheme [*Military*] [*British*]
FCCSET .... Federal Coordinating Council for Science, Education and Technology (SAUO)
FCCSET .... Federal Coordinating Council for Science, Engineering, and Technology [*Pronounced "fix it"*] [*Office of Science and Technology Policy*]
FCCSS .... Fire Control Control Subsystem
FCCSSAT ..... Federal Council on Computer Storage Standards and Technology [*General Services Administration*]
FCCST .... Federal Coordinating Council for Science and Technology
FCCT .... Fellow of the Canadian College of Teachers
FCCT .... Field Communication Centre Terminal (SAUS)
FCCT .... Flight Controller Confidence Test (KSC)
FCCTC .... Fluid Conductors and Connectors Technical Committee
FCCTS .... Federal COBOL [*Common Business-Oriented Language*] Compiler Testing Service [*National Institute of Standards and Technology*]
FCCU .... Fluid Catalytic Cracking Unit [*Fuel technology*]
FCCUI .... Fellow of the Canadian Credit Union Institute (DD)
FCCUS .... French Chamber of Commerce of the United States [*Later, French-American Chamberof Commerce*]
FCCV .... Feline Control Council of Victoria [*Australia*]
FCCV .... Future Close Combat Vehicle
FCC-Verfahren... fluidized catalyst cracking process (SAUS)
FCCVP .... Future Close Combat Vehicle Program
FCCVS .... Future Close Combat Vehicle System (MCD)
FCCY .... Fleet Chief Communication Yeoman [*British military*] (DMA)
f-cd- .... Chad [*MARC geographic area code*] [*Library of Congress*] (LCCP)
FCD .... Failure and Consumption Data (SAUS)
fcd .... failure-correction coding (SAUS)
FCD .... Failure Correction Decoding (IAA)
FCD .... Fatal Childhood Diarrhea [*Medicine*] (MELL)
FCD .... Fecal Collection Device [*NASA*]
FCD .... Federal Consistency Determination [*Environmental application*]
FCD .... Femoral Cortical Density
FCD .... Fibrocystic Disease [*Medicine*] (DMAA)
FCD .... Field Control Division [*Military*] (LAIN)
FCD .... Fine Chemical Directory (SAUS)
FCD .... Fine Chemicals Directory Data Base [*Molecular Design Ltd.*] [*Information service or system*]
FCD .... Fine Control Damper [*Nuclear energy*] (NRCH)
FCD .... Fixed Center Distance (SAUS)
FCD .... Fixed Center Drive
FCD .... Fixed Centre Distance (SAUS)
FCD .... Fixed Centre Drive (SAUS)
FCD .... Flame Conductivity Detector (SAUS)
FCD .... Flight Control Division [*Johnson Space Center*] [*NASA*] (NASA)
FCD .... Floating Car Data (SAUS)
FCD .... Flood Control District [*Florida*]
FCD .... focal cytoplasmatic degradation (SAUS)
FCD .... Food Control Diet
FCD .... Formal Change Draft (SAA)
FCD .... Foundation for Child Development (EA)
FCD .... Foundation for Communication for the Disabled (SAUO)
FCD .... Four-Bar Cutter Device
FCD .... Fracture, Complete, Deviated (SAUS)
FCD .... Frente Civico Democratico [*Civilian Democratic Front*] [*Guatemala*] [*Political party*] (PPW)
FCD .... Frequency Compression Demodulator
FCD .... Frequency Control Division (SAA)
FCD .... Friction Curve Definition [*Automotive emissions*]
FCD .... Front Congolais pour le Restauration de la Democratie [*Belgium*] [*Political party*] (EY)
FCD .... Front Congolais pour le Retablissement de la Democratie [*Zaire*] [*Political party*] (EY)
FCD .... Fuel Cells Display (SAA)
FCD .... Fuel Cut Defenser [*Automotive engineering*]
FCD .... Functional Configuration Documentation (AAGC)
FCD .... Functional Control Diagram (NRCH)
FCD .... Function Circuit Diagram
FCD .... Function Control Document (SAUS)
FCD .... Fund of Co-operation for Development (SAUO)
FCD .... Fuze Control Device (MCD)
FCD .... Fuzzy Complex Disjunctive (SAUS)
FCD .... First Chief Directorate [*of the KGB*] (ODA)
FCDA .... Federal Civil Defense Administration [*Transferred to Office of Defense and Civilian Mobilization, 1958; to Department of Defense and Office of Emergency Preparedness, 1961*]
FCDA .... Financial Center Development Act (TBD)
FCDA .... Fire Control Decision Aid (ACAE)
FCDA .... First Cavalry Division Association (EA)
FCDA .... Fuel Control Diaphragm Assembly
FC/DASA ...... Field Command, Defense Atomic Support Agency
FCDB .... Fibrocystic Disease of the Breast [*Gynecology*] (DAVI)
FCDB .... Fibrocystic Disorder of Breast [*Medicine*] (MELL)
FCDB .... Flight Control Data Bus (MCD)
FCDC .... Final canister decontamination chamber (SAUS)
FCDC .... Fire Control Data Converter (MCD)
FCDC .... Fixed Ceramic Disk Capacitor
FCDC .... Flexible Confined Detonating Cord (SAUS)
FCDC .... Flight Control Data Recorder (SAUS)
FCDE .... Federation of Clothing Designers and Executives [*British*] (DBA)
FCDF .... Failure and Consumption Data Form (AAG)
FCDG .... Federal Civil Defense Guide
FCDivBad ..... First Class Diver Badge [*Military decoration*] (AABC)
FCDL .... Forsyth County Defense League (EA)
FCDM .... Flow Control Decision Message (DA)
FCDN .... Ferrocarril de Nacozari [*AAR code*]
FCDNA .... Field Command, Defense Nuclear Agency [*DoD*]
FCDR .... Failure and Consumption Data Report (IAA)
FCDR .... Failure Cause Data Report
FCDS .... Fleet Consolidated Data Set (SAUO)
FCDSSA .... Fleet Combat Direction Systems Support Activity [*Navy*] (MCD)
FCDSSA/SD... Fleet Combat Direction Systems Support Activity, San Diego [*California*] [*Navy*]
FCDSTC .... Fleet Combat Direction System Training Center [*Navy*] (CAAL)
FCDSTCL ..... Fleet Combat Direction System Training Center, Atlantic [*Navy*] (MCD)
FCDSTCLANT... Fleet Combat Direction System Training Center, Atlantic [*Navy*] (DNAB)
FCDSTCP ..... Fleet Combat Direction System Training Center, Pacific [*Navy*] (DNAB)
FCDSTCPAC... Fleet Combat Direction System Training Center, Pacific [*Navy*] (DNAB)
FCDT .... Fleet Clearance Diving Team (SAUS)
FCDT .... Four-Coil Differential Transformer
FCDU .... Foreign Currency Deposit Units
FCE .... Facilities Capital Employed [*DoD*]
FCE .... Factory Checkout Equipment (MCD)
FCE .... Federation Canadienne des Echecs [*Chess Federation of Canada*]
FCE .... Federation Canadienne des Enseignants [*Canadian Teachers' Federation - CTF*]
FCE .... Federation Canadienne des Etudiants [*Canadian Federation of Students*]
FCE .... Field Checkout Equipment
FCE .... Field Control Element (ACAE)
FCE .... Fire Control Electronics (MCD)
FCE .... Fire Control Element (MCD)
FCE .... Fire Control Equipment
FCE .... First Certificate in English [*Cambridge University*] [*British*] (AIE)
FCE .... Fleet Civil Engineer
FCE .... Flexible Critical Experiment
FCE .... Flight Control Electronics
FCE .... Flight Control Equipment [*NASA*] (NASA)
FCE .... Flight Crew Equipment [*NASA*] (NASA)
FCE .... Florida Citrus Exchange (SAUO)
FCE .... Fluorouracil, Cisplatin, Etoposide [*Antineoplastic drug*] (CDI)
fce .... food conversion efficiency (SAUS)
fce .... Force (SAUS)
FCE .... Foreign Currency Exchange (MHDW)
FCE .... Forest City Enterprises, Inc. [*AMEX symbol*] (SPSG)
FCE .... Forward Command Element (DOMA)
FCE .... Foundation for Character Education (EA)
FCE .... Foundation for Credit Education [*Nazareth, PA*] (EA)
FCE .... Fourier Conduction Equation (SAUS)
FCE .... French-Canadian Enterprises (SAUO)
FCE .... Frequency Converter Excitation
FCE .... Friends Council on Education (EA)
FCE .... Functional Capacities Evaluation [*Test*] [*Occupational therapy*]
Fce .... Furnace (SAUS)
FCEA .... Federal Capital Equipment Authority (SAUS)
FCEA .... Fellow of the Association of Cost and Executive Accountants [*British*] (DBQ)
FCEA .... Fleet Chief Electrical Artificer [*British military*] (DMA)
FCE & T .... Field Concept Evolution and Trials [*Army*]
FCEC .... Federation of Civil Engineering Contractors [*British*] (BI)
FCEC .... Fire Control Engagement Controller [*Military*] (CAAL)
FCED .... Fire Control Engineering Description (ACAE)
FCEE .... Federation Canadienne des Etudiantes et Etudiants (AC)
FCEF .... Flight Crew Equipment Facility [*NASA*] (NASA)
FCEH .... Federation Canadienne des Etudes Humaines [*Canadian Federation for the Humanities - CFH*]
FCEI .... Facility Contract End Item
FCEI .... Facility Contractor End Item (SAUS)
FC/EL .... Fiber Channel/Enhanced Loop (SAUS)
FCEL(A) .... Fleet Chief Electrician (Air) [*British military*] (DMA)
FCEL(AW) ..... Fleet Chief Electrician (Air Weapon) [*British military*] (DMA)
Fcelftr .... Facelifters Home Systems, Inc. [*Associated Press*] (SAG)
F Cell .... Flat Cell (SAUS)
FCELMN(A)... Fleet Chief Electrical Mechanician (Air) [*British military*] (DMA)

FCELMN(AW)... Fleet Chief Electrical Mechanician (Air Weapon) [*British military*] (DMA)
FCEM.......... Femmes Chefs d'Entreprises Mondiales [*World Association of Women Entrepreneurs*] (EAIO)
FCEM.......... Flow Control Execution Message (DA)
FCEN.......... Florida Central Railroad [*Federal Railroad Administration identification code*]
FCENA.......... Food Court Entertainment Network, Inc. [*NASDAQ symbol*] (SAG)
FCENA.......... Food Court Entmt Network'A' [*NASDAQ symbol*] (TTSB)
FCENU.......... Food Court Entertain Unit [*NASDAQ symbol*] (TTSB)
FCENW.......... Food Court Enter Wrrt 'A' [*NASDAQ symbol*] (TTSB)
FCENZ.......... Food Court Enter Wrrt 'B' [*NASDAQ symbol*] (TTSB)
FCEP.......... Florida College of Emergency Physicians (SAUO)
FCEPC.......... Flight Control Electrical Package Container
fcept.......... fire-control electrical package container (SAUS)
fcept.......... flight-control electrical package container (SAUS)
FCER.......... Foundation for Chiropractic Education and Research (EA)
FCES.......... Flight Control Electronic Set (MCD)
FCES.......... flight control electronic system (SAUS)
FCESR.......... Frequency Converter Excitation, Saturable Reactor (IAA)
FCEU.......... Fire Control Electronics Unit [*Military*] (RDA)
FCEU.......... Flight Control Engineering Description (ACAE)
FCEX.......... Fruit Growers Express (SAUS)
f-cf-.......... Congo [*MARC geographic area code*] [*Library of Congress*] (LCCP)
FCF.......... Facility Capital Funds (AAG)
FCF.......... Facsimile Control Field (SAUS)
FCF.......... Faculty Christian Fellowship [*National Council of Churches*] (AEBS)
FCF.......... Family Camping Federation [*Later, FCFA*] (EA)
FCF.......... Fasciocutaneous Flap [*Medicine*] (MELL)
FCF.......... Feline and Canine Friends (EA)
FCF.......... Fellowship of Christian Firefighters, International (EA)
FCF.......... fibroblast-chemoattractant substance factor (SAUS)
FCF.......... First Captive Flight [*NASA*] (NASA)
FCF.......... First Commonwealth Finl [*NYSE symbol*] (TTSB)
FCF.......... Fishermen's Compensation Fund [*National Oceanic and Atmospheric Administration*]
FCF.......... Flag Correlation Facility (MCD)
FCF.......... Flight Critical Forward (NASA)
FCF.......... Flow Control Function (SAUS)
FCF.......... Fluids and Combustion Facility (SAUS)
FCF.......... Footwear Components Federation [*British*] (DBA)
FCF.......... For Colouring of Food [*British*]
FCF.......... Fourier Coefficient Filter (SAUS)
FCF.......... Free Cash Flow [*Finance*] (PDAA)
FCF.......... Free China Fund for Medical and Refugee Aid
FCF.......... Frequency Compressive Feedback
fcf.......... front-end communications facility (SAUS)
FCF.......... Fuel Cycle Facility [*Nuclear energy*]
FCF.......... Functional Check Flight [*Air Force*] (AFM)
FCFA.......... Family Camping Federation of America [*Formerly, FCF*] [*Defunct*] (EA)
FCFA.......... Florida Commercial Fisheries Association (EA)
FCFC.......... Film Council Film Circuit [*Library network*]
FCFC.......... Firstcity Financial [*NASDAQ symbol*] (TTSB)
FCFC.......... First City Financial Corp. [*NASDAQ symbol*] (SAG)
FCFC.......... Free Church Federal Council
FCFC.......... Full-Coverage Film Cooling
FCFCP.......... Firstcity Finl 'B' Pfd [*NASDAQ symbol*] (TTSB)
FCFD.......... Fluorescence Capillary Fill Device [*Instrumentation*]
FCFDU.......... Federation Canadienne des Femmes Diplomees des Universites [*Canadian Federation of University Women*]
FCFI.......... Fellow of the Clothing and Footwear Institute [*British*] (DI)
FCFK.......... Fondation Canadienne de la Fibrose Kystique [*Canadian Cystic Fibrosis Foundation*]
FCFL.......... Fueled clad fabrication line (SAUS)
FCFM.......... Flight Combustion Facility Monitor [*Aerospace*] (NAKS)
FCFO.......... Full Cycling File Organization
FCFP.......... Fellow, College of Family Physicians [*Canada*] (CMD)
FCFP.......... Fueled clad fabrication process (SAUS)
FCFS.......... First Cash Financial Services, Inc. [*NASDAQ symbol*] (NASQ)
FCFS.......... First Come, First Served [*Computer science*]
FCFS.......... Frequency Coded Firing System (MCD)
FCFS.......... Fueled Clad Fabrication System (SAUS)
FCF SE.......... Facility Checking Flight - Service Evaluation [*Air Force*] (MCD)
FCFSE.......... Facility Checking Flight-Service Evaluation (SAUS)
FCFT.......... Fixed Cost, Fixed Time (IEEE)
f-cg-.......... Congo (Kinshasa) [*Zaire*] [*MARC geographic area code*] [*Library of Congress*] (LCCP)
FCG.......... Facility Change Group (KSC)
FCG.......... Facing
FCG.......... Falconbridge Gold Corp. [*Toronto Stock Exchange symbol*]
FCG.......... False Cross or Ground (SAUS)
FCG.......... Fatigue Crack Growth [*Metals*] (PDAA)
FCG.......... Faulty Connector Gate (SAUS)
FCG.......... FDDI Clock Generator (SAUS)
FCG.......... Federal Coordination Group (SAUO)
FCG.......... Federal Coordinator for Geology [*Marine science*] (OSRA)
FCG.......... Federation for Constitutional Government [*Defunct*] (EA)
FCG.......... Fernwood, Columbia & Gulf R. R. [*AAR code*]
FCG.......... Field Consultant Group (HEAS)
FCG.......... Field Coordination Group
FCG.......... Fire Control Group
FCG.......... First Communications Group, Inc. [*Coral Gables, FL*] (TSSD)
FCG.......... Fleet Composite Group [*Navy*] (CAAL)
FCG.......... Flight Control Group (MCD)
FCG.......... Florida Computer Graphics (SAUS)
FCG.......... Florida Coordinating Group (SAUO)
FCG.......... Flux Compression Generator (SEWL)
FCG.......... Foreign Clearance Guide (AFM)
FCG.......... Forest Contact Group (SAUS)
FCG.......... Fragmenta Comicorum Graecorum [*A publication*] (OCD)
FCG.......... Free Communications Group (SAUO)
FCG.......... French Catheter Gauge (MAE)
FCG.......... Friction Cam Gear
FCG.......... Fuel Contents Gauge (MSA)
FCG.......... Functional Coordinating Group (SAUO)
FCG.......... Fund for Constitutional Government (EA)
FCG1.......... FcGamma-Receptor 1 (SAUS)
fcga.......... facility gage (SAUS)
FCGA.......... Facility Gauge (AAG)
FCGA.......... Fellow of the Canadian Certified General Accountants Association (DD)
FCGA.......... Fellow of the Canadian General Accountants Association (SAUO)
FCGB.......... Forestry Committee of Great Britain (SAUO)
FCGC.......... Flight Control Gyro Container
FCGCMA.......... Federation of Cash Grain Commission Merchants Associations [*Defunct*] (EA)
FCgDH.......... Doctors Hospital, Medical Library, Coral Gables, FL [*Library symbol*] [*Library of Congress*] (LCLS)
FCGES.......... Flight Control Group Electronic System (SAA)
FCGI.......... Fellow of the City & Guilds Institute (WDAA)
FCGI.......... Fellow of the City and Guilds of London Institute [*British*] (ROG)
FCGI.......... First Consulting Group, Inc. [*NASDAQ symbol*] (NASQ)
FCGM.......... Frammenti della Commedia Greca e del Mimo nella Sicilia e nella Magna Grecia [*A publication*] (OCD)
FCgM.......... United States Department of Commerce, National Oceanic and Atmospheric Administration, Miami Branch Library, Coral Gables, FL [*Library symbol*] [*Library of Congress*] (LCLS)
FCGP.......... Fellow of the College of General Practitioners
FCGPC.......... Flight Control Gyro Package Container
fcgpc.......... flight-control gyro-package container (SAUS)
FCGR.......... Fatigue Crack Growth Rate [*Metals*]
FCGRS.......... Federation Canadienne de Gymnastique Rythmique Sportive [*Canadian Modern Rhythmic Gymnastics Federation - CMRGF*]
FCGS.......... Farm Capital Grant Scheme (SAUS)
FCGS.......... Federal Centre of Geoecological Systems (SAUS)
FCGS.......... Federal construction guide specification (SAUS)
FCGS.......... Fifth Computer Generation Systems (SAUS)
FCGS.......... Freight Classification Guide System
FCGZ.......... Farmers Cargill Elevator [*Federal Railroad Administration identification code*]
FCH.......... Familial Combined Hyperlipidemia [*Cardiology*] (DAVI)
FCH.......... Family Care Home (HCT)
FCH.......... Federal Cataloging Handbook
FCH.......... FelCor Lodging Trust [*NYSE symbol*] [*Formerly, FelCor Suite Hotels*]
FCH.......... FelCor Suite Hotels [*NYSE symbol*] (TTSB)
FCH.......... FelCor Suite Hotels, Inc. [*NYSE symbol*] (SAG)
FCH.......... Fellow of the Coopers Hill College [*British*]
FCH.......... Fetch (SAUS)
FCh.......... Field Champion [*Dog show term*]
FCH.......... Film Carrousel Handle
FCH.......... Fircrest Resources [*Vancouver Stock Exchange symbol*]
FCH.......... First Capital Holdings (EFIS)
FCH.......... Flight-Chernobyl Association [*Russian Federation*] [*ICAO designator*] (FAAC)
FCH.......... Flight Controllers Handbook
FCH.......... Foundation for Cooperative Housing [*Later, CHF*]
FCH.......... Fourier Color Hologram
FCH.......... Fourier Colour Hologram (SAUS)
fch.......... Franchise (MARI)
FCH.......... Fresno, CA [*Location identifier*] [*FAA*] (FAAL)
FCHA.......... Florence Crittenton Homes Association (SAUO)
FCHC.......... Fellow of Catherine Hall, Cambridge [*British*] (ROG)
FCHC.......... Newberry Library Family and Community History Center [*Research center*] (RCD)
FCHCA.......... Foreign Car Haters Club of America (EA)
FChemSoc.......... Fellow of the Chemical Society [*British*]
FCHG.......... Formal Change (MCD)
FCHGD.......... Feminist Center for Human Growth and Development (EA)
Fchgs.......... forwarding charges (SAUS)
FChH.......... Florida State Hospital, Chattahoochee, FL [*Library symbol*] [*Library of Congress*] (LCLS)
FChiNBD.......... First Chicago NBD Corp. [*Associated Press*] (SAG)
FCHL.......... Familial Combined Hyperlipidaemia [*Medicine*]
FCHL.......... Flight Control Hydraulics Laboratory [*NASA*] (NASA)
FCHO.......... Federation Canadienne de Handball Olympique [*Canadian Team Handball Federation - CTHF*]
FCHP.......... Feedback Controlled Heat Pipes (MCD)
FCHPrA.......... FelCor Suite Hotels $1.95 Pfd [*NYSE symbol*] (TTSB)
FCHR.......... Functional Cost Hour Report (MCD)
FChS.......... Fellow of the Society of Chiropodists [*British*]
Fchse.......... Franchise
FCI.......... Defense Foreign Counterintelligence [*Program*] [*DoD*]
FCI.......... Factors Chain International (SAUO)
FCI.......... Fairfield Communities, Incorporated (SAUO)
FCI.......... Family Care International (ADWA)
FCI.......... Family Communications, Inc. [*Public television*] (NTCM)
FCI.......... Fan Circle International (EA)
FCI.......... Fashion Coordination Institute [*Defunct*] (EA)
FCI.......... Fast Coastal Interceptor [*US Coast Guard vessel*]

FCI Fatigue Crack Initiation (SAUS)
FCI Federal Chamber of Industries (SAUS)
FCI Federal Correctional Institution (WDAA)
FCI Federal Crime Insurance
FCI Federal Crop Insurance
FCI Federation Colombophile Internationale [*International Pigeon Federation - IPF*] (EAIO)
FCI Federation Cynologique Internationale [*International Federation of Kennel Clubs*] [*Thuin, Belgium*] (EA)
FCI Fellow of the Canadian Credit Institute
FCI Fellow of the Institute of Commerce [*British*]
FCI Fertiliser Corporation of India (SAUS)
FCI Fertiliser (or Fertilizer) Corporation of India Ltd. (SAUO)
FCI Fertilizer Corporation of India, Ltd. (SAUS)
FCI Fibre Channel Interface (VERA)
FCI Finance Corporation for Industry (SAUO)
FCI Financial Consultants International (SAUO)
FCI Fire Control Information (SAUS)
FCI Fire Control Instrument (SAUS)
FCI First China Investment Corp. [*Vancouver Stock Exchange symbol*]
FCI First Communications, Inc. [*Atlanta, GA*] (TSSD)
FCI First Communications, Incorporated (SAUO)
FCI Flight Combat Instructor
FCI Flight Command Indicator (MCD)
FCI Flight Control Indicator (MCD)
FCI Flight Control Integration [*Apollo*] [*NASA*]
FCI Flight Critical Items (MCD)
FCI Florida Computer, Inc. [*Information service or system*] (IID)
FCI Florida Computer, Incorporated (SAUO)
FCI Flow Cytometric Immunophenotyping [*Medicine*] (MELL)
FCI Flowmeter components irradiation (SAUS)
FCI Fluid Conductivity Indicator
FCI Fluid Controls Institute (EA)
FCI Fluid Controls Institute, Inc.
FCI Flux Changes per Inch [*Computer science*]
FCI Folklore Canada International [*An association*] (EAIO)
FCI Food Chemical Intolerance (MELL)
FCI Food Corporation of India (SAUO)
FCI Foreign Counterintelligence
FCI Foward Cache Identifier [*Computer science*] (VERA)
FCI Framatome Connectors International [*Commercial firm*] (ECON)
FCI Franklin College of Indiana
FCI Fraud Control Institute [*Communications Fraud Control Association*] (TSSD)
FCI Freedom (SAUS)
FCI Freedom Communications International News Agency (EAIO)
FCI Fuel Cell Institute (NTPA)
FCI Fuel-Cladding Interaction (SAUS)
FCI Fuel Coolant Interaction [*Nuclear energy*] (NRCH)
FCI Full Configuration-Interaction [*Quantum chemistry*] (MCD)
FCI Functional Capacity Index [*NHTSA*] (TAG)
FCI Functional Configuration Identification (KSC)
FCI International Federation of Kennel Clubs [*Belgium*] (EAIO)
FCI2L folded collector integrated injection logic (SAUS)
FCIA Federal Courts Improvement Act (AAGC)
FCIA Federal Criminal Investigators Association (EA)
FCIA Fellow of the Canadian Institute of Actuaries
FCIA Fellow of the Corporation of Insurance Agents [*British*]
FCIA Fibre Channel Industry Association (SAUO)
FCIA Foreign Credit Insurance Association [*New York, NY*] (EA)
FCIA Franchise Consultants International Association (EA)
FCIA Freedom Council Information Abstracts (SAUO)
FCIA Friends of Cast Iron Architecture (EA)
FCIArb Fellow of the Chartered Institute of Arbitrators [*British*] (DBQ)
FCIB Fellow Chartered Institute of Bankers [*British*] (WA)
FCIB Fellow of the Chartered Institute of Bankers (WDAA)
FCIB Fellow of the Confederation of Insurance Brokers of Australia
FCIB Fellow of the Corporation of Insurance Brokers [*British*]
FCIB Foreign Credit Interchange Bureau (EA)
FCIB/NACM Foreign Credit Interchange Bureau/National Association of Credit Management (SAUO)
FCIBS Fellow of the Chartered Institution of Building Services [*British*] (DBQ)
FCIBS Fellow of the Chartered Institution of Building-Services Engineers (WDAA)
FCIBSE Fellow Chartered Institution of Building Services Engineers [*British*] (WA)
FCIC Fairchild Camera and Instrument Corporation (SAUO)
FCIC Farm Crop Insurance Corporation (SAUO)
FCIC Federal Crop Insurance Corp. [*Department of Agriculture*]
FCIC Federal Crop Insurance Corporation (SAUO)
FCIC Fellow of Chemical Institute of Canada (SAUS)
FCIC Fellow of the Canadian Institute of Chemistry (DD)
FCIC Fellow of the Chemical Institute of Canada
FCIC Fiber and Composites Information Center (SAUO)
FCIC Foreign Credit Insurance Corp. [*Business term*]
FCICA Floor Covering Installation Contractors Association (EA)
FCID Federal Court Industrial Division [*Australia*]
FCIF Flight Crew Information File (AFM)
FCIF Full Common Intermediate Format (ACRL)
FCIFPS Fellow, Canadian Institute of Facial Plastic Surgery (CMD)
FCIG Field Change Identification Guide (IAA)
FCII Federated Council of Israel Institutions (EA)
FCII Fellow of the Chartered Insurance Institute [*British*] (EY)
FCII Fibercorp Intl. [*NASDAQ symbol*] (TTSB)
FCIL Finance Corp. for Industry Ltd. [*British*]
FCILA Fellow of the Chartered Institute of Loss Adjusters [*British*] (DBQ)
FCIM Farm, Construction, and Industrial Machinery (PDAA)
FCIM Federated Council for Internal Medicine (ADWA)
FCIM Federation des Concours Internationaux de Musique [*Federation of International Music Competitions - FIMC*] (EAIO)
FCIM Fellow of the Chartered Institute of Marketing [*British*] (ODBW)
FCIM Flexible Computer-Integrated Manufacturing Program [*Army*] (RDA)
FCIM Flight Control Interface Module (MCD)
FCIN Fast Carry Iterative Network (IAA)
FCIN Fast Carry-Propagation Iterative Network (PDAA)
FCIN Flour City Intl. [*NASDAQ symbol*] (SG)
FCIN Frankfort & Cincinnati Railroad Co. [*AAR code*]
FC Inst Fire Control Instrument (SAUS)
FCIOB Fellow of the Chartered Institute of Building [*British*] (DBQ)
FCIP Federal Crime Insurance Program (WDAA)
FCIP Federal Crop Insurance Program (GNE)
FCIP Field Cable Installation Platoon [*Army*] (AABC)
FCIP Field Change Installation Program (ACAE)
FCIP Fire Company Inspection Program (SAUO)
FCIP Flight Cargo Implementation Plan (MCD)
FCIP Foreign Counterintelligence Program [*DoD*]
FCIPA Fellow of the Chartered Institute of Patent Agents [*British*]
FCIPS Fellow of the Chartered Institute of Purchasing and Supply (ODA)
FCIR Facility Chance Initiation Request (AAGC)
F-CIR Failure and Consumption Inspector's Report (AAG)
FCIR False Colour Infrared (SAUS)
FCIR Fatigue Crack Initiation Resistance (SAUS)
FCIs Federal Correctional Institutions (SAUS)
FCIS Fellow Institute of Chartered Secretaries and Administrators [*British*] (WA)
FCIS Fellow of the Chartered Institue of Secretaries & Administrators (WDAA)
FCIS Fellow of the Chartered Institute of Secretaries [*British*] (ROG)
FCIS Fire Control Interface Software (ACAE)
FCIS Flint Colon Injury Scale [*Medicine*] (MELL)
FCIS Florida Council of Independent Schools (SAUO)
FCIS Florida Crime Information Service (SAUO)
FCIS Force Cost Information System (MCD)
FCIS Foreign Counterintelligence System [*Federal Bureau of Investigation*]
FCISA Fellow of the Chartered Institute of Secretaries and Administrators (Australia) (ODA)
FCIT Fellow of the Chartered Institute of Transport [*British*]
FCIT First Citizens Financial Corp. [*NASDAQ symbol*] (NQ)
FCIT First Citizens Finl [*NASDAQ symbol*] (TTSB)
FCIT First Computer Interface Tester (NAKS)
FCIT Four Countries International Tournament [*Basketball*] (ODA)
FCIU Family Crisis Intervention Unit [*New York Police Department*]
FCIV Fellow of the Commonwealth Institute of Valuers (SAUO)
FCIyL folded collector-integrated injection logic (SAUS)
FCJ Faithful Companions of Jesus, Society of the Sisters (SAUO)
FCJ Federal Chief Justice (SAUO)
FCJ Federal Court Judgements [*Canada Department of Justice*] [*Information service or system*] (CRD)
FCJ Foreign Criminal Jurisdiction (AABC)
FCJ La Fondation Canadienne de la Jeunesse (AC)
FCJ Society of the Sisters, Faithful Companions of Jesus [*Roman Catholic religious order*]
FCJC Flit Community Junior College (SAUO)
FCJS Federal Criminal Justice System (SAUS)
FCK Field Change Kit
FCK Filter Change Kit
FCK Fuel Charge Kit
FCl Clearwater Public Library, Clearwater, FL [*Library symbol*] [*Library of Congress*] (LCLS)
FCL Facility [*Security*] Clearance
FCL Farriers Co. of London [*British*] (DI)
FCL Feedback Control Loop [*Computer science*] (BUR)
FCL Feedback Current Limiting (SAUS)
FCL Feeder Control Logic [*Computer science*] (IAA)
FCL Ferric Chloride Leach (SAUS)
FCL Fiber Composite Laminate (SAUS)
FCL Fibre Channel Loop (RALS)
FCL Film Capability Laboratories [*Bell System*]
FCL Final Coordination Line [*Military*]
FCL Fire Coordination Line [*Military*] (AABC)
FCL First Colony [*NYSE symbol*] (SPSG)
FCL Fleet Control List [*Navy*] (AFIT)
FCL Flight Control Laboratory
FCL Flight Crew Licensing (SAUO)
FCL Flightcrew Licensing (DA)
F-CL Fluorouracil, Leucovorin Calcium [*Antineoplastic drug*] (CDI)
FCL Flux Current Loop
FCL Foldback Current Limiter (ADWA)
FCL Foldback Current Limiting (SAUS)
FCL Foreign Currency Loan
FCL Format Control Language
FCL Fort Collins, CO [*Location identifier*] [*FAA*] (FAAL)
FCL Foundation for Christian Living (EA)
FCL Freon Coolant Line [*NASA*] (NASA)
FCL Freon Coolant Loop [*Space shuttle*] [*NASA*]
FCL Frick Chemical Laboratory (KSC)
fcl front connecting loop (SAUS)
FCL Fuel Cell (KSC)
FCL Fuel-Cell Energy

FCL............ Full Car Load (SAUS)
FCL............ Full Container Load [*Shipping*]
FCL............ Full Cycle Left (SAA)
FCL............ Functional Capabilities List [*Computer science*] (MHDB)
FCL............ Fuze Cavity Liner [*Projectile*] (NG)
FCL............ Sarbah's Fanti Customary Laws [*Ghana*] [*A publication*] (DLA)
FCLA............ Family Centered Learning Alternatives (EA)
FCLA............ Fisheries Council for/of Latin America (SAUO)
FCLA............ Florida Center for Library Automation [*Florida State University System*] [*Information service or system*] (IID)
FCLA............ Full Carry Lookahead Adder (SAUS)
FCLAA............ Federal Coal Leasing Amendments Act [*1976*]
FCLA Adder... Full Carry Look-Ahead Adder (SAUS)
FCLASS........ File Security Classification Codes (SAUO)
FCLAVP........ Flammable and Combustible Liquids Appeal and Variations Panel [*Queensland, Australia*]
FCLB............ Federation of Chiropractic Licensing Boards (ADWA)
FCLC............ Fibre Channel Loop Community (SAUS)
FCICC............ Clearwater Christian College, Clearwater, FL [*Library symbol*] [*Library of Congress*] (LCLS)
FCLD............ Foundation for Children with Learning Disabilities [*Later, NCLD*] (EA)
FCLE............ Forecastle Deck (IAA)
FCLI............ Fordham University School of Law, Corporate Law Institute (DLA)
FCIM............ Morton F. Plant Hospital, Clearwater, FL [*Library symbol*] [*Library of Congress*] (LCLS)
FCLO............ Flying Control Liaison Officer (SAUO)
FC/LOS........ Fire Control, Line-of-Sight
f-c los.......... fire-control line of sight (SAUS)
FCLP............ Field Carrier Landing Passes [*or Practice*]
FCLR............ First Commercial Corp. [*NASDAQ symbol*] (NQ)
FCLS............ Family Colonization Loan Society (SAUO)
FCLT............ Freeze Calculated Landing Time [*FAA*] (TAG)
FCLTY.......... Facility (AFM)
FCLTY.......... Faculty
FCLTYCHECKINGSq... Facility Checking Squadron [*Air Force*]
fcly............ Face Lying [*Medicine*] (DMAA)
f-cm-............ Cameroon [*MARC geographic area code*] [*Library of Congress*] (LCCP)
FCM............ Facilities Cost Model (AAEL)
FCM............ Faculty of Community Medicine [*British*]
FCM............ Fan Control Module [*Automotive engineering*]
FCM............ Farrier Corporal Major (SAUO)
FCM............ Farrier Corporal-Major [*British military*] (DMA)
FCM............ Fast Cyclotron Mode (SAUS)
FCM............ Fat-Corrected Milk
FCM............ Fault Control Management [*Automotive diagnostics*]
FCM............ Fault Control Module (TEL)
FCM............ FCMI Financial Corp. [*Toronto Stock Exchange symbol*]
FCM............ Feature Change Map (SAUS)
FCM............ Feature Code Master (VLIE)
FCM............ Federal Class Manager (AFIT)
FCM............ Federal Coordinator for Meteorological Services and Supporting Research (SAUO)
FCM............ Federation Canadienne des Municipalites [*Federation of Canadian Municipalities*]
FCM............ Fellowship of Christian Magicians (EA)
FCM............ Fellowship of Christian Motorcyclists [*Welwyn Garden City, England*] (EAIO)
FCM............ Fellowship of Christian Musicians (EA)
FCM............ Ferrite Core Matrix (SAUS)
FCM............ Ferrite Core Memory (SAUS)
FCM............ Ferrocarril Mexicano [*AAR code*]
FCM............ Fiber Composite Material
FCM............ Filament Composite Material
FCM............ Firestone Conservatory of Music (SAUS)
FCM............ Firmware Control Memory
FCM............ First-Class Mail [*Postal Service*]
FCM............ Flight Combustion Monitor [*NASA*] (KSC)
FCM............ Floating-Carrier Modulation (SAUS)
FCM............ Florida Agricultural and Mechanical University, Tallahassee, FL [*OCLC symbol*] (OCLC)
FCM............ Florida Citrus Mutual (EA)
FCM............ Flow Cytometry [*Analytical biochemistry*]
FCM............ Flying Cargo Private Ltd. [*Maldives*] [*ICAO designator*] (FAAC)
FCM............ Food, Clothing, Maintenance [*Red Cross*]
FCM............ Foot-Candle Meter (SAUS)
FCM............ Forged Chrom-Moly
FCM............ Framing Camera Mopper
FCM............ Franklin Telecommunications [*AMEX symbol*] (SG)
FCM............ Frequency Counter Measure (ACAE)
FCM............ Friends of Cathedral Music (EA)
FCM............ Fuel Cell Module
FCM............ Fund for a Conservative Majority (EA)
FCM............ Futures Commission Merchant
FCM............ Fuzzy Cognitive Map [*Logic*]
FCM............ Fuzzy Control Manager (SAUS)
FCM............ Minneapolis, MN [*Location identifier*] [*FAA*] (FAAL)
FCMA............ Fellow Chartered Institute of Management Accountants [*British*] (WA)
FCMA............ Fellow of the Institute of Cost and Management Accountants [*British*]
FCMA............ Fellow of the Society of Management Accountants of Canada (DD)
FCMA............ Fibre Cement Manufacturers Association [*British*] (DBA)
FCMA............ Field Cashier Military Accounts [*British military*] (DMA)
FCMA............ Finch College Museum of Art (SAUO)
FCMA............ Fishery Conservation and Management Act [*1976*] [*Also, MFCMA*]
FCMA............ Fleet Chief Medical Assistant [*British military*] (DMA)
FCMA............ Flushing Cistern Makers' Association [*British*] (BI)
FCMA............ Mavinza [*Congo*] [*ICAO location identifier*] (ICLI)
FCMAREP.... Federal Coordinator for Marine Environmental Prediction [*Marine science*] (OSRA)
FCMB............ First City Merchant Bank Ltd.
FCMB............ N'Ziba [*Congo*] [*ICAO location identifier*] (ICLI)
FCMC............ Family-Centered Maternity Care [*Obstetrics*] (DAVI)
FCMC............ Fellow of the Institute of Certified Management Consultants (DD)
FCMC............ Financial and Corporate Management Committee (SAUO)
FCMC............ Fire-Control & Monitoring Computer (SAUS)
FCmcBA........ First Commerce Bancshares, Inc. [*Associated Press*] (SAG)
FCmcBB........ First Commerce Bancshares [*Associated Press*] (SAG)
FCmcC........ First Commerce Corp. [*Associated Press*] (SAG)
FCmclCp...... First Commericial Corp. [*Associated Press*] (SAG)
FCMD............ Facilities and Construction Management Division (SAUO)
FCMD............ Fire Command (KSC)
FCMD............ Fukuyama Type Congenital Muscular Dystrophy [*Medicine*] (DMAA)
FCMD............ Vouka/Sidetra [*Congo*] [*ICAO location identifier*] (ICLI)
FCME............ First Class Marine Engineer (SAUS)
FCME............ First Coastal Corp. [*NASDAQ symbol*] (SAG)
FCMEA.......... Fleet Chief Marine Engineering Artificer [*British military*] (DMA)
FCMEM........ Fleet Chief Marine Engineering Mechanic [*British military*] (DMA)
FCMF............ Loufoula [*Congo*] [*ICAO location identifier*] (ICLI)
FCM-FF........ Fast Cyclotron Mode - Fast Forward (SAUS)
FCMG............ Gokango [*Congo*] [*ICAO location identifier*] (ICLI)
FCMI............ Federation of Coated Macadam Industries [*British*] (BI)
FCMI............ Fuel Cladding Mechanical Interaction [*Nuclear energy*] (NUCP)
FCMI............ Irogo [*Congo*] [*ICAO location identifier*] (ICLI)
FCMIdE........ Foreign & Colonial Emerging Middle East Fund, Inc. [*Associated Press*] (SAG)
FCMIE.......... Fellow of the College of Management and Industrial Engineering (SAUS)
FCMIE.......... Fellow of the Colleges of Management and Industrial Engineering (SAUO)
FCMJ............ Federation of Canadian Manufacturers in Japan (SAUO)
FCMK............ Kele/Kibangou [*Congo*] [*ICAO location identifier*] (ICLI)
FCML............ Leboulou [*Congo*] [*ICAO location identifier*] (ICLI)
FCmlBcp........ First Commercial Bancorp, Inc. [*Associated Press*] (SAG)
FCMM............ Federal Commission on Medical Malpractice [*Medicine*] (EDAA)
FCMM............ Federation Canadienne des Maires et des Municipalites [*Canadian Federation of Mayors and Municipalities*]
FCMM............ Flux Changes per Millimeter [*Computer science*] (IAA)
FCMM............ Mossendjo [*Congo*] [*ICAO location identifier*] (ICLI)
FCMN............ Family-Centered Maternity Nursing [*Obstetrics*] (DAVI)
FCMN............ N'Gongo [*Congo*] [*ICAO location identifier*] (ICLI)
FCMO............ Vouka/Mandoro [*Congo*] [*ICAO location identifier*] (ICLI)
FCMP............ Family and Community Medicine Program [*Medicine*] (EDAA)
FCMPU.......... Female Cigar Makers' Protective Union [*British*]
FCMR............ Marala [*Congo*] [*ICAO location identifier*] (ICLI)
FCMRT.......... Fellow of the Canadian Association of Medical Radiation Technologists (ASC)
FCMS............ Facilities Computer Monitoring System [*Johnson Controls, Inc.*]
FCMS............ Factory Control Management System (SAUS)
FCMS............ Fellow of the College of Medicine and Surgery [*British*]
F/CMS.......... Financial/Cost Management System (MCD)
FCMS............ Flight Crew Mission Simulator [*NASA*] (KSC)
FCMS............ Force Capability Management System [*Military*]
FCMS............ Functional Configuration Management System (SAUO)
FCMS............ Nyanga [*Congo*] [*ICAO location identifier*] (ICLI)
FCMS & SR... Federal Committee for Meteorological Services and Supporting Research (SAUO)
FCMSBR........ Federal Coal Mine Safety Board of Review [*Independent government agency*] [*Inactive, 1970*]
FCMSSR........ Federal Coordinator for Meteorological Services and Supporting Research (SAUO)
FCMT............ Bekol/Thomas [*Congo*] [*ICAO location identifier*] (ICLI)
FCMT............ Fleet Chief Medical Technician [*British military*] (DMA)
FCMT............ Flight Configuration Mode Test [*Gemini*] [*NASA*]
FCMU............ Foot-Controlled Maneuvering Unit [*Skylab*] [*NASA*]
FCMV............ Fuel Consuming Motor Vehicle
FCMVS.......... Fetal Cytomegalovirus Syndrome [*Medicine*] (MELL)
FCMW............ Foundation for Child Mental Welfare (EA)
FCmwF.......... First Commonwealth Fund, Inc. [*Associated Press*] (SAG)
FCMX............ Fort Collins Municipal Railway [*Federal Railroad Administration identification code*]
FCMY............ Mayoko/Legala [*Congo*] [*ICAO location identifier*] (ICLI)
FCMZ............ N'Zabi [*Congo*] [*ICAO location identifier*] (ICLI)
FCN............ Facilities Change Notice (ABAC)
FCN............ Falcon Aviation AB [*Sweden*] [*ICAO designator*] (FAAC)
FCN............ FC Financial Corp. [*Vancouver Stock Exchange symbol*]
FCN............ Federal Catalog Number
FCN............ Field Change Notice (SAUS)
FCN............ Field Change Notification (KSC)
FCN............ Fire Control Notes [*A publication*]
FCN............ First Chicago NBD [*NYSE symbol*] (TTSB)
FCN............ First Chicago NBD Corp. [*NYSE symbol*] (SAG)
FCN............ Florida Communities Network (SAUO)
FCN............ Friendship, Commerce, and Navigation (SAUS)
FCN............ Frijoles Canyon [*New Mexico*] [*Seismograph station code, US Geological Survey*] [*Closed*] (SEIS)
FCN............ FTI Consulting [*AMEX symbol*] (SG)
FCN............ Function (NASA)
FCN............ Treaty of Friendship, Commerce, and Navigation [*Indonesia*] (IMH)
FCNA............ Fellow of the College of Nursing Australia (SAUO)
FCNA............ Florida Citrus Nurserymen's Association (EA)

FCNA .... Foxhound Club of North America (EA)
FCNB .... FCNB Corp. [*NASDAQ symbol*]. (SAG)
FCNC .... First Citizens Bancshares, Inc. [*NASDAQ symbol*] (NQ)
FCNC .... Flavor-Changing Neutral Currents
FCNCA .... First Citizens BancShares'A' [*NASDAQ symbol*] (TTSB)
FCNI .... Flux Control Negative Inductance (SAUS)
FCNL .... French Committee of National Liberation [*World War II*]
FCNL .... Frequently-Called-Numbers List [*Bell System*]
FCNL .... Friends Committee on National Legislation (EA)
FCNP .... Fire Control Navigation Panel (IEEE)
FCNPC .... Film Culture Non-Profit Corp. (EA)
FCNPrB .... First Chi NBD Adj Div B Pfd [*NYSE symbol*] (TTSB)
FCNPrC .... First Chi NBD Adj Div C Pfd [*NYSE symbol*] (TTSB)
FCNPrE .... First Chi NBD 8.45% Dep Pfd [*NYSE symbol*] (TTSB)
FCNPrU .... First Chi NBD 7.5%PfdPurUnits [*NYSE symbol*] (TTSB)
FCNPrV .... First Chi NBD 5 3/4% Cv Dep Pfd [*NYSE symbol*] (TTSB)
FCNS .... Fairchild Communications Networks & Services Co. [*Chantilly, VA*] [*Later, FCS*] [*Telecommunications service*] (TSSD)
FCNSI .... Federation Canadienne Nationale des Syndicats Independants [*Canadian National Federation of Independent Unions - CNFIU*]
FCNSW .... Forestry Commission of New South Wales [*State*] (EERA)
FCNTL .... Function Timeline
FCNTX .... Fidelity Contrafund [*Mutual fund ticker symbol*] (SG)
FCO .... Aerofrisco [*Mexico*] [*ICAO designator*] (FAAC)
FCO .... Cleanout Flush with Finished Floor
f_{co} .... Cutoff Frequency (IDOE)
FCO .... Facility Change Order (AAG)
FCO .... Facility Control Office (CCCA)
FCO .... Facility Coordination Officer (FAAC)
FCO .... Facility Coordination Offices (SAUO)
FCO .... Fair Copy
FCO .... Federal Coordinating Officer [*Federal disaster planning*]
FCO .... Federation of Colliery Officials (SAUO)
FCO .... Fellow of the College of Optics (SAUO)
FCO .... Fellow of the College of Organists [*British*] (ROG)
FCO .... Fellow of the College of Osteopathy [*British*]
FCO .... Ferrying Control Officer (SAUO)
FCO .... Fibrocytoma of Ovary [*Medicine*] (MELL)
FCO .... Fick Cardiac Output [*Medicine*] (EDAA)
FCO .... Field Change Order
FCO .... Field Check-Out (VLIE)
F Co .... Field Company [*British military*] (DMA)
FCO .... Field Contracting Office (MCD)
FCO .... Files Control Office
FCO .... Final Checkout (SAUS)
FCO .... Finance Corps Officer (SAUO)
FCO .... Financed, Constructed and Operated (SAUS)
FCO .... Financial Control Officer [*Banking*] (TBD)
FCO .... Fire Control Officer (WDAA)
FCO .... Fire Control Operation (SAUO)
FCO .... Fire Control Operator [*Army*]
FCO .... Fire Control Order (SAUS)
FCO .... first common occurrence (SAUS)
FCO .... First Commonwealth Fund [*NYSE symbol*] (TTSB)
FCO .... First Commonwealth Fund, Inc. [*NYSE symbol*] (SPSG)
FCO .... Fixed Capital Outlay (WPI)
FCO .... Fixed Cycle Operation
FCO .... Flag Communications Officer [*Navy*]
FCO .... Fleet Communications Officer [*Navy*] [*British*]
FCO .... Fleet Construction Officer (SAUO)
FCO .... Flight Clearance Office
FCO .... Flight Communications Operator
FCO .... Flight Control Officer (SAUO)
FCO .... Flight Crew Operations [*NASA*]
FCO .... Flow Control Operator Bits (SAUS)
FCO .... Flying Control Officer [*Navy*]
FCO .... Forces Courier Office (SAUS)
FCO .... Foreign and Commonwealth Office [*British*]
FCO .... Foreign Currency Option (EBF)
FCO .... Forms Control Officer (GFGA)
FCO .... Franco [*Free of Charge*] [*Shipping*] [*Italian*]
fco .... Franco [*Free of Charge*] [*Shipping*] [*French*]
fco .... franking privilege (SAUS)
fco .... free postage (SAUS)
FCO .... Frequency-Change Oscillator (SAUS)
FCO .... Frequency Control Officer (MUGU)
FCO .... Functional Checkout
FCO .... Rome [*Italy*] Leonardo Da Vinci (Fium) Airport [*Airport symbol*] (OAG)
FCoa .... Cocoa Public Library, Cocoa, FL [*Library symbol*] [*Library of Congress*] (LCLS)
FCOA .... Federation of Chinese Organizations in America (EA)
FCOA .... Foremost Corp. of America [*NASDAQ symbol*] (NQ)
FCOA .... Foremost Corporation of America (SAUO)
FCoaB .... Brevard Community College, Cocoa, FL [*Library symbol*] [*Library of Congress*] (LCLS)
FCOAC .... Furnish Copies of Orders to Appropriate Commanders
FCOB .... Boundji [*Congo*] [*ICAO location identifier*] (ICLI)
FCOB .... First Commercial Bancorp [*NASDAQ symbol*] (NQ)
FCOB .... First Comml Bancorp, Inc. [*NASDAQ symbol*] (TTSB)
FCOB .... Flight Control Operations Branch [*NASA*] (MCD)
FCOC .... Facility Checkout Vehicle (SAUS)
FCOD .... Fire, Collision, Overturning, and Derailment [*Insurance*] (MARI)
FCOD .... Flight Crew Operations Directorate [*NASA*] (KSC)
FCOE .... Ewo [*Congo*] [*ICAO location identifier*] (ICLI)
FCOEA .... Fleet Chief Ordnance Electrical Artificer [*British military*] (DMA)
FCOEL .... Fleet Chief Ordnance Electrician [*British military*] (DMA)
FCOEMN .... Fleet Chief Ordnance Electrical Mechanician [*British military*] (DMA)
FC of C .... Foundation Company of Canada (SAUO)
FCOG .... Fellow of the British College of Obstetricians and Gynaecologists (DAS)
FCOG .... Fellow of the College of Obstetricians and Gynecologists
FCOG .... Fellow of the College of Obstetrics and Gynaecology (SAUO)
FCOG .... Fondation Canadienne d'Orientation et de Consultation (AC)
FCOG .... Gamboma [*Congo*] [*ICAO location identifier*] (ICLI)
FCOH .... Flight Controllers Operational Handbook (SAUS)
FCOH .... Flight Controllers Operations Handbook [*NASA*] (KSC)
FCOI .... Fire Control Optical Instrument
FCOI .... Impfondo [*Congo*] [*ICAO location identifier*] (ICLI)
FCOJ .... Frozen Concentrated Orange Juice
FCOK .... Kelle [*Congo*] [*ICAO location identifier*] (ICLI)
FCOL .... For Crying Out Loud (SAUS)
FCOL .... Loukolela [*Congo*] [*ICAO location identifier*] (ICLI)
FColnGp .... First Colonial Group [*Associated Press*] (SAG)
FColony .... First Colony Corp. [*Associated Press*] (SAG)
FCOM .... Federal Coordinators Office of Meteorology (SAUS)
F Com .... Fighter Command (SAUO)
FCOM .... First Commerce [*NASDAQ symbol*] (TTSB)
FCOM .... First Commerce Corp. [*NASDAQ symbol*] (NQ)
FCOM .... Flight Crew Operating Manual (MCD)
FCOM .... Focal Communications [*NASDAQ symbol*] (SG)
FCOM .... Makoua [*Congo*] [*ICAO location identifier*] (ICLI)
FComceC .... First Commerce Corp. [*Associated Press*] (SAG)
F Comm .... Full Commission
FCommA .... Fellow of Commercial Actuaries (DD)
FCommA .... Fellow of the Society of Commercial Accountants (SAUO)
FCOMP .... Federal Coordinator for Ocean Mapping and Prediction (USDC)
FCOMP .... First Commerce 7.25% Cv Pfd '92 [*NASDAQ symbol*] (TTSB)
FCONX .... Fidelity Contrafund II
FCOO .... Owando [*Congo*] [*ICAO location identifier*] (ICLI)
FCOP .... Fire Control Operator (WDAA)
FCOphth .... Fellow of the College of Ophthalmologists (ODA)
FCOPP .... Fuel cycle operation and process development (SAUS)
F Corona .... Fraunhofer Corona (SAUS)
FCOS .... Farm Cash Operating Surplus
FCoS .... Fetal Cord Serum [*Gynecology*]
FCOs .... Field Change Orders (SAUS)
FCOS .... Flight Computer Operating System [*NASA*] (NASA)
FCOS .... Flight Control Operating System [*NASA*] (NASA)
FCOS .... Flight Control Operational Software (MCD)
FCOS .... Souanke [*Congo*] [*ICAO location identifier*] (ICLI)
FCOSA .... Fellow of the Chartered Institute of Secretaries and Administrators [*Australia*] (ODBW)
FCOT .... Betou [*Congo*] [*ICAO location identifier*] (ICLI)
FCO-T .... Flight Communications Operator in Training
FCOT .... Fellow of the College of Occupational Therapists (ODA)
FCOTY award ... Fatuous Comment of the Year award (SAUS)
FCOU .... Ouesso [*Congo*] [*ICAO location identifier*] (ICLI)
FCOV .... Facility Checkout Vehicle [*NASA*] (KSC)
F/COV .... Floor Covering (ADA)
FCOZ .... Farmers Co-Operative Elevator [*Federal Railroad Administration identification code*]
FCP .... Facilities Criteria Plan (SAUO)
FCP .... Failure Correction Panel (NASA)
FCP .... Falcon Products [*NYSE symbol*] (TTSB)
FCP .... Falcon Products, Inc. [*NYSE symbol*] (SAG)
FCP .... Falls City Press, Louisville, KY [*Library symbol*] [*Library of Congress*] (LCLS)
FCP .... Family Care Program [*Insurance*] (WYGK)
FCP .... Family Circle Publications (SAUS)
FCP .... Fast Card Punch (SAUS)
FCP .... Fasting Chemistry Profile (DAVI)
FCP .... Fatigue Crack Propagation (OA)
FCP .... Federal Cataloging Program
FCP .... Federal Catalog Program (SAUO)
FCP .... Federation of Calico Printers (DGA)
FCP .... Feed Control Panel (IAA)
FCP .... Fellow of the College of Physicians (DD)
FCP .... Fellow of the College of Preceptors [*British*] (ROG)
FCP .... Ferrocarril del Pacifico, SA de CV [*AAR code*]
FCP .... Ferry Command Police [*British military*] (DMA)
FCP .... Fiber Channel Protocol (SAUS)
FCP .... Fibre Channel Protocol (VLIE)
FCP .... Field Change Package [*Nuclear energy*] (NRCH)
FCP .... Field Change Proposal
FCP .... Field Command Post
FCP .... Field control point (SAUS)
FCP .... File Control Package (NITA)
FCP .... File Control Procedure (SAUS)
FCP .... File Control Processing (SAUS)
FCP .... File Control Processor [*Computer science*] (BUR)
FCP .... File Control Program [*Computer science*]
FCP .... Final Common Pathway [*Neurology*]
FCP .... Final Control Point (PIPO)
FCP .... Fire Command Post (SAUS)
FCP .... Fire Control Panel (MCD)
FCP .... Fire Control Personnel [*Marine Corps*]
FCP .... Fire Control Platoon [*Army*]
FCP .... Fire Control Pod (ACAE)
FCP .... Fire Control Predictor (SAUS)

FCP .... Firm Cost Proposal (NASA)
FCP .... First Calgary Petroleums Ltd. [*Toronto Stock Exchange symbol*]
FCP .... First Collision Probability (SAUS)
FCP .... Fixed Code Processor
FCP .... Flat Concurrent PROLOG [*Programming in Logic*] [*Language for fifth generation computer research*] (NITA)
FCP .... Flight Control Panel (MCD)
FCP .... Flight Control Processor [*Space launch term*] (ISAK)
FCP .... Flight Control Programmer
FCP .... Flight Corp. [*New Zealand*] [*ICAO designator*] (FAAC)
FCP .... Flight Correction Proposal (MCD)
FCP .... Floating-Point Co-Processor (VLIE)
FCP .... Florida Citrus Packers (EA)
FCP .... Fluid and Chemical Processing (SSD)
FCP .... Fluorouracil, Cyclophosphamide, Prednisone [*Antineoplastic drug regimen*]
fcp .... Foolscap (ADWA)
FCP .... Foolscap [*Paper*]
FCP .... Ford Combustion Process [*Automotive engineering*]
FCP .... Foreign Corporation Project [*IRS*]
FCP .... Forest Canopy Profile (SAUS)
FCP .... Forward Command Post (NATG)
FCP .... Forward Control Post (SAUO)
FCP .... Foundation for Creative Philosophy (EA)
FCP .... Foxboro Control Package (NITA)
FCP .... Fracture Control Plan (SPST)
FCP .... Fragmented Coronoid Process [*Medicine*]
FCP .... Franck-Condon Pumping (or Principle) [*Physics*] (ODA)
FCP .... Fraud Control Plan
FCP .... Free Conducting Particle (PDAA)
FCP .... French Communist Party
FCP .... Frequency Control Panel (MCD)
FCP .... Friends of the Conservative Party [*Defunct*] (EA)
FCP .... Fuel Cell Partnership [*Automotive research*]
FCP .... Fuel Cell Plant (SAUS)
FCP .... Fuel Cell Power (SAUS)
FCP .... Fuel Cell Power Plant
FCP .... Fuel Consumption Projection (SSD)
FCP .... Fuels Cycle Plant (SAUS)
FCP .... Full Couterpoise Procedure [*Physical chemistry*]
FCP .... Functional Communication Profile
FCP .... Function Control Package [*Computer science*]
FCP .... Function Control Program (VLIE)
FCP .... Function Control Protocol [*Computer science*] (MWOL)
FCP .... Fellow of the College of Clinical Pharmacology (ODA)
FCPA .... Fabricants Canadiens de Produits Alimentaires [*Grocery Products Manufacturers of Canada - GPMC*]
FCPA .... Fellow of the Canadian Psychological Association
FCPA .... Fellow of the Institute of Certified Public Accountants [*British*] (DAS)
FCPA .... Fellow of the Institution of Certified Public Accountants (SAUO)
FCPA .... Florida Citrus Processors Association (SRA)
FCPA .... Foreign Corrupt Practices Act [*1977*]
FCPA .... Makabana [*Congo*] [*ICAO location identifier*] (ICLI)
FCPAC .... Free Congress Political Action Committee (EA)
FC Path .... Fellow of the College of Pathologists [*Later, Royal College of Pathologists*] [*British*]
FC Path .... Fellow of the College of Pathology (SAUO)
FCPB .... Bangamba [*Congo*] [*ICAO location identifier*] (ICLI)
FCPC .... Fair Campaign Practices Committee (EA)
FCPC .... Federal Committee on Pest Control
FCPC .... Field Coil Power Conversion (SAUS)
FCPC .... Fleet Computer Programming Center [*Navy*] (MUGU)
FCPC .... Flight Crew Plane Captain [*Navy*] (DNAB)
FCPCL .... Fleet Computer Programming Center, Atlantic [*Navy*]
FCPCLANT .... Fleet Computer Programming Center, Atlantic [*Navy*]
FCPCNA .... First Czechoslovak Philatelic Club of North America (EA)
FCPCP .... Fleet Computer Programming Center, Pacific [*Navy*]
FCPCPAC .... Fleet Computer Programming Center, Pacific [*Navy*] (MCD)
FCPCS .... Federal Compliance with Pollution Control Standards (COE)
FCPD .... Loudima [*Congo*] [*ICAO location identifier*] (ICLI)
FC/PDL .... Freight Classification Packaging Data List (AFIT)
FCPE .... Face Plate (SAUS)
FCPE .... [*Naval*] Force Capabilities Planning Effort (DOMA)
FCPE .... Leganda [*Congo*] [*ICAO location identifier*] (ICLI)
FCPG .... Federation of Catholic Physicians Guilds
FCPG .... Kibangou [*Congo*] [*ICAO location identifier*] (ICLI)
FC-PH .... Fibre Channel Physical [*Computer science*] (MWOL)
FCPH .... Fibre Channel PHysical and signaling interface (SAUS)
fcpi .... Flux Changes per Inch (VLIE)
FCPI .... Flux Changes per Inch [*Computer science*]
FCPI .... Vounda/Loubetsi [*Congo*] [*ICAO location identifier*] (ICLI)
FCPK .... N'Komo [*Congo*] [*ICAO location identifier*] (ICLI)
fc pl .... face plate (SAUS)
FCPL .... Loubomo [*Congo*] [*ICAO location identifier*] (ICLI)
F/CPLG .... Fluid Coupling [*Automotive engineering*]
F-C Plot .... Fermi-Curie Plot (SAUS)
FC/PM .... Facility Control / Power Management (MHDB)
FCPM .... Fellow of the Confederation of Professional Management [*British*] (DBQ)
FCPM .... Free Cuba Patriotic Movement (EA)
FCPM .... M'Baya [*Congo*] [*ICAO location identifier*] (ICLI)
FCPN .... Factory Customer Premise Network (EURO)
FCPN .... Noumbi [*Congo*] [*ICAO location identifier*] (ICLI)
FCPO .... Fellowship of Christian Peace Officers (EA)
FCPO .... First Class Post Office
FCPO .... Fleet Chief Petty Officer [*Navy*] [*British*]
FCPO .... Fuel Cycle Program Office (SAUS)
FCPO .... Pemo [*Congo*] [*ICAO location identifier*] (ICLI)
FCPO-USA ... Fellowship of Christian Peace Officers - U.S.A. (EA)
FCPP .... Fuel-Cell Power Plant (SAUS)
FCPP .... Pointe-Noire [*Congo*] [*ICAO location identifier*] (ICLI)
FCPPS .... Fuel Cell Power Plant System (KSC)
FCPR .... Fatigue Crack Propagation Rate (SAUS)
FCPR .... Fatigue Crack Propagation Resistance (SAUS)
FCPR .... Foreign Corrupt Practices Act (AAGC)
FCPRC .... Federal Cultural Policy Review Committee [*Canada*]
FCPS .... Fellow, Canadian Pediatric Society (CMD)
FCPS .... Fellow of the Cambridge Philosophical Society [*British*] (ROG)
FCPS .... Fellow of the College of Physicians and Surgeons [*British*]
FCPS .... Firewood Cutters' Protective Society [*A union*] [*British*]
FCPS .... FOSIC [*Fleet Ocean Surveillance Information Center*] Communications Processing Subsystem (MCD)
FCPS .... France and Colonies Philatelic Society (EA)
FCPs .... Free Conducting Particles (SAUS)
FCPS .... Fuel Cell Power System [*or Subsystem*]
FCPS .... Fuel-Cell Power System (SAUS)
FCPS .... Fuel Consumption Projection System (SAUO)
FCPSA .... Fellow of the College of Physicians and Surgeons South Africa (SAUS)
FCP(SA) .... Fellow of the College of Physicians of South Africa
FCPSI .... Flux Changes per Square Inch (CIST)
FCP(SoAf) ... Fellow of the College of Physicians of South Africa
FCPSO (SoAf) ... Fellow of the College of Physicians and Surgeons and Obstetricians of South Africa
FCPSSA .... Fellow of the College of Physicians and Surgeons of South Africa [*Medicine*] (EDAA)
FCPT .... Fleet Chief Physical Trainer [*British military*] (DMA)
FCPU .... Flexible Central Processing Unit [*Computer science*] (MHDB)
FCPWG .... Federal Credit Policy Working Group
FCPY .... Factory Card Outlet Corp. [*NASDAQ symbol*] (SAG)
FCPY .... Loukanyi [*Congo*] [*ICAO location identifier*] (ICLI)
FCQAS .... Financial Compliance and Quality Assurance Staff [*Environmental Protection Agency*] (GFGA)
FCR .... facilities change request (SAUS)
FCR .... Facility Capability Report [*Military*]
FCR .... Facility Capability Review
FCR .... Facility Change Request
FCR .... Falls Creek Railroad [*Federal Railroad Administration identification code*]
FCR .... False Contact Rate (CAAL)
FCR .... Family Court Reporter [*A publication*]
FCR .... Fan Control Relay [*Automotive engineering*]
FCR .... Farm Costs and Returns [*A publication*]
FCR .... Fast Ceramic-fuelled Reactor (SAUS)
FCR .... Fast Ceramic Reactor [*Program*]
FCR .... Fast Conversion Ratio (NRCH)
FCR .... Fast Cycle Resin (SAUS)
FCR .... Fast Cycling Resin (SAUS)
FCR .... Fearne on Contingent Remainders [*1722-1844*] [*A publication*] (DLA)
FCR .... Federal Contracts Reports (AAGC)
FCR .... Federal Court Reports [*Canada Department of Justice*] [*Information service or system*] (CRD)
FCR .... Federal Court Rules [*A publication*]
FCR .... Feed Conversion Ratio (SAUS)
FCR .... Fellowship of Christian Racers [*Defunct*] (EA)
FCR .... Field Change Request [*Nuclear energy*] (NRCH)
FCR .... Field Contact Report (SAUS)
FCR .... FIFO Control Register (SAUS)
FCR .... File Component Rules (VLIE)
FCR .... File Control Routine (SAUS)
FCR .... Final Configuration Review (KSC)
FCR .... Fine Crushed Rock (ADA)
FCR .... Fire Controlman, Range-Finder Operator [*Navy rating*] [*Obsolete*]
FCR .... Fire Control RADAR
FCR .... Fire Control Room (SAUS)
FCR .... First City Regiment (SAUO)
FCR .... Fixed Change Rate
FCR .... Flexor Carpi Radialis [*Anatomy*] (DMAA)
FCR .... Flight Condition Recognition [*Army aviation*]
FCR .... Flight Configuration Release (SAUS)
FCR .... Flight Configuration Review (MCD)
FCR .... Flight Control Room
FCR .... Flight Control System (SAUS)
FCR .... Flinders Chase Reserve (SAUO)
FCR .... Floating Control Regulator
FCR .... floor cavity ratio (SAUS)
FCR .... Foreign Company Representative (ACAE)
FCR .... Foreign Country Representative (SAUO)
FCR .... Foreign Currency Reserve (JAGO)
FCR .... Forward Calculation Request
FCR .... Forward Contactor (IAA)
FCR .... Forwarders Certifcate of Release (SAUS)
FCR .... Forwarders Certificate of Receipt [*Shipping*]
FCR .... Fractional Catabolic Rate [*Clinical chemistry*]
FCR .... France Cables & Radio Co. [*France*] [*Telecommunications*]
FCR .... Frederick Cancer Research Center, Frederick, MD [*OCLC symbol*] (OCLC)
FCR .... Front Communiste Revolutionnaire [*France*]
FCR .... Fruitlet Core Rot [*of pineapple*]
FCR .... Fuel consumption ratio (SAUS)

FCR .... Fuel Core Reserve [*Nuclear energy*]
FCR .... Full Cold Rolled [*Steel*]
FCR .... Functional Capability Requirement (ACAE)
FCR .... Functional Chief's Representative [*Of a civilian career program*] [*Army*] (RDA)
FCR .... Functional Configuration Review (MCD)
FCR .... Fuse Current Rating
FCR .... Fusin Coreceptor [*Medicine*] (EDAA)
FCRA .... Fabric Care Research Association [*British*] (IRUK)
FCRA .... Fair Credit Reporting Act [*1971*]
FCRA .... Fecal Collection Receptacle Assembly [*NASA*] (KSC)
FCRA .... Fellow of the College of Radiologists Australasia (SAUS)
FCRA .... Fellow of the Corporation of Registered Accountants [*British*] (DAS)
FCRAA .... Folding Chair Rental Association of America [*Later, RSA*]
FCRAM .... File Create and Maintenance [*Computer science*] (MHDI)
FC/R&D .... Federal Civilian-Oriented Research and Development (SAUO)
FCRAO .... Five College Radio Astronomy Observatory
FCRB .... Flexor Carpi Radialis Brevis [*Anatomy*] (DAVI)
FCRC .... Federal Contract Research Center
FCRC .... Federally Chartered Research Centers (AAGC)
FCRC .... Federated Computing Research Conference
FCRC .... Fort Custer Reception Center (SAUO)
FCRC .... Four Corners Regional Commission [*Department of Commerce*]
FCRC .... Frederick Cancer Research Center (RDA)
FCRD .... Feline Central Retinal Degeneration [*Animal pathology*]
FCRDC .... Frederick Cancer Research and Development Center (SAUS)
FCRDC .... Frederick Cancer Research and Development Center. National Cancer Institute (SAUS)
FCRE .... Field Company of Royal Engineers (SAUO)
FCRE .... Foundation for Cotton Research and Education [*Later, The Cotton Foundation*] (EA)
FCREA .... Fleet Chief Radio Electrical Artificer [*British military*] (DMA)
FCREF .... Free Congress Research and Education Foundation (EA)
FCREL(A) .... Fleet Chief Radio Electrician (Air) [*British military*] (DMA)
FCREMN .... Fleet Chief Radio Electrical Mechanician [*British military*] (DMA)
FCRF .... Federated China Relief Fund (SAUO)
FCRF .... Fire Control Reference Frame (MCD)
FCRF .... Frederick Cancer Research Facility [*Frederick, MD*] [*Department of Health and Human Services*] (GRD)
FC (RFC) .... Functional Capacity (Residual Functional Capacity) [*Social Security Administration*] (OICC)
FCRG .... Food Chain Research Group [*University of California*] [*Research center*] (RCD)
FCRI .... Field Crops Research Institute (SAUO)
FCRI .... Financial Control Research Institute [*British*] (DBA)
FCRL .... Fish Culture Research Laboratory [*Kearneysville, WV*] [*Fish and Wildlife Service*] [*Department of the Interior*] (GRD)
FCRL .... Flight Control Ready Light (SAUS)
FCRL .... Food, Chemical and Research Laboratories (SAUS)
FCRLI .... Food, Chemical and Research Laboratories (SAUS)
FCRLS .... Flight Control Ready Light System
FCRLSYS .... Flight Control Ready Light System (IAA)
FCRN .... Fund Classification Reference Number [*Military*] (AFIT)
FCRP .... Family Care Research Program (SAUO)
FCRP .... Fast Ceramic Reactor Program (SAUS)
FCRP .... Field Condition Report [*Aviation*] (FAAC)
FCRP .... Final CAPE [*Capability and Proficiency Evaluation*] Review Period
FCRP .... Foundation Canadienne de Recherche en Publicite (AC)
FCR-PGT .... Frente Central de Resistencia-Partido Guatemalteco del Trabajo [*Political party*] (EY)
FCRPS .... Federal Columbia River Power System
FCRR .... File Compare Relative Record (TIMI)
FCRRT .... Fundamentals Course for Radiological Response Teams (SAUO)
FCRS .... Farm Costs and Returns Survey [*Department of Agriculture*] (GFGA)
FCRS .... Flightcrew Record System (DA)
FCRSA .... Flat-Coated Retriever Society of America (EA)
FCRS(S) .... Fleet Chief Radio Supervisor (Special) [*British military*] (DMA)
FCRS(W) .... Fleet Chief Radio Supervisor (Warfare) [*British military*] (DMA)
FCRSWG .... Forestry Canada Remote Sensing Working Group (SAUO)
FCRT .... Flight Display Cathode-Ray Tube (NASA)
FCRU .... Facilities Control Relay Unit [*Army*] (AABC)
FCRV .... Family Campers and Rivers [*An association*] (EA)
FCRV .... Front Commun pour le Respect de la Vie [*Common Front for the Respect of Life*] [*Canada*]
FCS .... Facilities Chargeout System (TIMI)
FCS .... Facility Checking Squadron [*Air Force*]
FCS .... Facility Control System (SAUS)
FCS .... Facsimile Communications System [*Telecommunications*]
FCS .... Factory Control System (AAEL)
FCS .... Failure characterization subsystem (SAUS)
FCS .... Fairchild Communications Services Co. [*Washington, DC*] (TSSD)
FCS .... Fairchild Semiconductor
FC's .... False Calves [*Padding worn under tights by actors, to improve shape of their legs*]
FCS .... Farm Credit System [*of FCA*]
FCS .... Farmer Cooperative Service [*Later, ESCS*] [*Department of Agriculture*]
FCS .... Fast Circuit Switching (VERA)
FCS .... Fecal Containment System [*NASA*]
FCS .... Federal Catalog System [*of GSA*]
FCS .... Federal Communications Systems (MCD)
FCS .... Federation Costing System (DGA)
FCS .... Federation of Communication Services [*British*] (TSSD)
FCS .... Federation of Concrete Specialists (SAUO)
FCS .... Feedback Control System
FCS .... Fellow of the Chemical Society [*British*] (ROG)
FCS .... Fellow of the College of Sciences (SAUS)
FCS .... Fellowship of Catholic Scholars (EA)
FCS .... Ferrite Core Store (SAUS)
FCS .... Fetal Calf [*or Cow*] Serum [*Medicine*]
FCS .... Fetal Cocaine Syndrome [*Medicine*] (MELL)
FCS .... Fetal Cord Serum [*Embryology*]
FCS .... Fever, Chills, and Sweating (MELL)
FCS .... Fiber Channel Standard [*Computer science*] (ITCA)
FCS .... Field Centre Supervisor (SAUO)
FCS .... Field Computer System
FCS .... Field Computing Services (VLIE)
FCS .... Field Conduct Sheet (SAUS)
FCS .... Field Control Strain (SAUS)
FCS .... Field-expedient Mineclearing System (SAUS)
FCS .... Fighter Catapult Ship [*British military*] (DMA)
FCS .... Fighter Command School [*Air Force*]
FCS .... File Control Services [*Digital Equipment Corp.*]
FCS .... File Control System (NITA)
FCS .... Finance Communication System (VLIE)
FCS .... Financial Control System
FCS .... Financial Services Society [*New York, NY*] (WDMC)
FCS .... Finnish Calibration Service, Centre for Metrology & Accreditation (SAUS)
FCS .... Fire Controlman, Submarine [*Navy rating*] [*Obsolete*]
FCS .... Fire Controlman (Surface) [*U.S. Navy enlisted rating*] (AUER)
FCS .... Fire Control Simulator
FCS .... Fire Control Station (SAUO)
FCS .... Fire Control System
FCS .... First Customer Release (SAUS)
FCS .... First Customer Ship (SAUS)
FCS .... First Customer Shipment [*IBM Corp.*] [*Computer science*]
FCS .... Fish Culture Section [*American Fisheries Society*] (EA)
FCS .... Fish Culture Station (SAUS)
FCS .... Fisheries Conservation Zone
FCS .... Fixed Control Storage
FCS .... Flag Cancel Society (EA)
FCS .... Flame Control System
FCS .... Fleet Communication Satellite (ACAE)
FCS .... Flexible Clamping System (SAUS)
FCS .... Flight Command School
FCS .... Flight Command Subsystem [*Spacecraft*]
FCS .... Flight Control Set
FCS .... Flight Control Subsystem (SAUS)
F/CS .... Flight Control System (AAG)
FCS .... Flight Crew System [*NASA*] (NASA)
FCS .... Floor-Ceiling Sandwich
FCS .... Flowmeter Calibration Stand
FCS .... Fluorescence Correlation Spectroscopy
FCS .... Focus
FCS .... Foetal Calf Serum (SAUS)
FCS .... Food Containment System
FCS .... Foot Compartment Syndrome (MELL)
FCS .... Forces Courier Services [*Military*] [*British*]
FCS .... Foreign Commercial Service [*International Trade Administration*]
FCS .... Forged Carbon Steel
FCS .... Fort Calhoun Station [*Nuclear energy*] (NRCH)
FCS .... Fort Carson, CO [*Location identifier*] [*FAA*] (FAAL)
FCS .... four-crystal spectroscopy (SAUS)
fcs .... fraction charge states (SAUS)
FCS .... Frame Check/Checking Sequence (SAUS)
FCS .... Frame Check Sequence [*Computer science*] (IBMDP)
FCS .... Frame Check Sum [*Computer science*] (VERA)
FCS .... Frame Control Sequence (SAUS)
fcs .... francs (SAUS)
FCS .... Frederic Chopin Society [*Later, IFCF*] (EA)
FCS .... Free Channel Search (SAUS)
FCS .... Free Crystalline Silica
fcs .... Free of Capture and Seizure (EBF)
FCS .... Free of Capture and Seizure [*Insurance*]
FCS .... Freight Conference Services (SAUS)
FCS .... French Chemical Society [*See also SFC*] (EAIO)
FCS .... Frequency Coded System (MCD)
FCS .... Friends of Creation Spirituality (EA)
FCS .... Fuel Composition Sensor [*Automotive engineering*]
FCS .... Fuel Computer System (MCD)
FCS .... Fuel Control System (ACAE)
FCS .... Fuels Capabilities System (SAUO)
FCS .... Full Communications Service (SAUO)
FCS .... Functional Checkout Set (IAA)
FCS .... Functional Companion Standard (ACII)
FCS .... Function Control Sequence (SAUS)
FCS .... Future Combat System [*Military*] (SEWL)
FCS .... Future Combat Systems [*Military*]
FCSA .... Family and Children's Services Agency [*New South Wales, Australia*]
FCSA .... Federation Canadienne du Sport Automobile [*Canadian Automobile Sport Clubs*]
FCSA .... Fleet Chief Stores Accountant [*British military*] (DMA)
FCSA .... Flight Control Servo Assembly
FCSA .... Forest Conservation Society of America
FCSA .... Frequency Coordination System Association [*Ottawa, ON*] [*Telecommunications service*] (TSSD)
FCSAD .... Free of Capture, Seizure, Arrest, and Detainment [*Insurance*]
fcsad .... free of capture, seizure, arrest or detainment (SAUS)
FCSAIC .... Fellow, Canadian Society of Allergy & Clinical Immunology (CMD)

FCS & R & CC... free of capture, seizure riots, and civil commotions (SAUS)
FCSB... Federation Canadien des Societes de Biologie (AC)
FCSB... Federation Canadienne du Sport Boules [*An association*] (EAIO)
FCSB... Fellowship of Conservative Southern Baptists (EA)
FCSB... Fire Control Switchboard
fcsb... fire-control switchboard (SAUS)
FCSB... Fluid Circulation Storage Battery [*Automotive engineering*]
FCSC... Federal Conversion Support Center (MCD)
FCSC... Fire Control System Console [*Military*] (CAAL)
FCSC... Fire Control System Coordinator
FCSC... Fleet Command Support Center [*Navy*] (CAAL)
FCSC... Food and Civil Supplies Commissioner (SAUO)
FCSC... Foreign Claims Settlement Commission
FCSC Ann Rep... Foreign Claims Settlement Commission. Annual Report [*A publication*] (DLA)
FCSCC... Fellow of the Canadian Society of Clinical Chemists (SAUO)
FCSC Dec & Ann... Foreign Claims Settlement Commission. Decisions and Annotations [*A publication*] (DLA)
FCSCDG... Fleet Command Support Center Development Group [*Navy*] (MCD)
FCSCE... Fellow of the Canadian Society of Civil Engineers (DD)
FCSCJ... Filiae a Caritate Sacri Corde Jesus [*Daughters of Charity of the Sacred Heart of Jesus*] [*Roman Catholic religious order*]
FC (Scott)... Faculty of Advocates Collection of Decisions, Scotch Court of Sessions [*A publication*] (DLA)
FCSCUS... Federal Claims Settlement Commission of the United States
FCSCWO... Fleet Command Support Center Watch Officer [*Navy*] (MCD)
FCSD... Federal Council for Sustainable Development (SAUO)
FCSD... Flavocytochrome C Sulfide Dehydrogenase [*An enzyme*]
FCSD... Flight Crew Support Division [*NASA*] (KSC)
FCSE... Fellow, Canadian Society of Electroencephalographers (CMD)
FCSE... Fellow of the Canadian Society of Electroencephalographers (SAUO)
FCSE... Flight Control System Electronics (MCD)
FCSE... Focus Enhancements [*NASDAQ symbol*] (TTSB)
FCSE... Focus Enhancements, Inc. [*NASDAQ symbol*] (SAG)
FCSEA... Family and Consumer Science Education Association (NTPA)
FCSEW... Focus Enhancements Wrrt [*NASDAQ symbol*] (TTSB)
FCSF... Four-Conductor, Combination, Special Purpose, Flexible Cable (IAA)
FCSF Cable... Four-conductor, Combination, Special-purpose, Flexible Cable (SAUS)
FCSG... Fire Control Sensor Group
FCSG... Flight Control Sensor Group
FCSG... Focusing
FCSGE... Federation Canadienne des Services de Garde a l'Enfance [*Formerly, Canadian Child Day Care Federation*] (AC)
FCSH... Full Cadillac Service History [*Automotive classified advertising*]
FCSH... Full Chevrolet Service History [*Automotive classified advertising*]
FCSH... Full Chrysler Service History [*Automotive classified advertising*]
FCSI... FCS Labs, Inc. [*NASDAQ symbol*] (COMM)
FCSI... Fellow of the Canadian Securities Institute (DD)
FCSI... Fellow of the Construction Surveyors' Institute [*British*] (DBQ)
FCSI... Fiber Channel Systems Initiative (SAUO)
FCSI... Foodservice Consultants Society International (EA)
FCSIL... Flight Control System Integration Laboratory [*Army*]
FCSL... Fire Control System Laboratory
fcsl... Forecastle (SAUS)
FCSLA... First Catholic Slovak Ladies Association (EA)
FCSLE... Forecastle (KSC)
FCSLU... First Catholic Slovak Ladies Union [*Later, FCSLA*] (EA)
FCSM... Fire Control System Module
fcsm... fire-control system module (SAUS)
FCSM... Flight Combustion-Stability Monitor [*Apollo*] [*NASA*]
fc sm... functional simulation (SAUS)
FCSMPEUA... Federated Cold Storage and Meat Preserving Employees' Union of Australia
FCSN... Federation for Children with Special Needs (EA)
FCSNVD... Fever, Chills, Sweating, Nausea, Vomiting, and Diarrhea [*Gastroenterology*] (DAVI)
FCSO... Full Capability Sales Office (TIMI)
FCSO... Full Career Seaman Officer [*Navy*] [*British*]
FCSP... Fellow of the Chartered Society of Physiotherapy [*British*]
FCSP... final cruise sampling program (SAUS)
FCSP... Sisters of Charity of Providence [*Religious order*]
FCSPU... Flight Control System Proximity Unity (MCD)
FCSR&CC... Free of Capture, Seizure, Riots, and Civil Commotion (EBF)
FCSRCC... Free of Capture, Seizure, Riots, and Civil Commotions [*Insurance*]
fcsrcc... free of capture, selzure, riots and civil commotion (SAUS)
FCSRT... Fellow of the Canadian Society of Radiological Technicians
FCSS... Federal Civil Service System
FCSS... Federation Canadienne de Sport Scolaire [*Canadian Federation of Provincial School Athletic Associations*]
FCSS... Federation Canadienne des Sciences Sociales [*Social Science Federation of Canada - SSFC*]
FCSS... Fire Control Sight System [*Military*]
FCSS... Fire Control Sub-System (SAUS)
FCSS... Flight Control Stabilisation System (SAUS)
FCSS... Flight Control Systems Section
FCSS... Frost, Cog, and Screwmakers' Society [*A union*] [*British*]
FCSS... Fuel Cell Servicing System (MCD)
FCS(SA)... Fellow of the College of Surgeons of South Africa
FCS(SoAf)... Fellow of the College of Surgeons of South Africa
FCSSP... Federation of Crop Science Societies of the Philippines (SAUO)
FCSSRCC... Free of Capture, Seizure, Strikes, Riots, and Civil Commotions [*Insurance*] (MARI)
FCST... Federal Council for Science and Technology [*Later, FSPC, FCCSET*] [*Executive Office of President*]
FCST... Fellow of the College of Speech Therapists [*British*]
FCST... Field Controlled Thyristor [*Electronics*]
FCST... Flat Cable Stripping Tool
FCST... Flycast Communications [*NASDAQ symbol*] (SG)
FCST... Forecast (AFM)
fcst... Forecast (PIAV)
FCST-CORR... Federal Council for Science and Technology - Committee on Water Resources Research (NOAA)
FCSTD... Fleet Chief Steward [*British military*] (DMA)
FCSU... Fire Control Simulator Unit
fcsu... fire-control simulator unit (SAUS)
FCSU... Fire Control Switching Unit
FCSU... First Catholic Slovak Union of the USA and Canada (EA)
FCSU... Freon Coolant Servicing Unit (MCD)
FCSUM... Federation of Civil Service Unions of Mauritius
FCSUS... Foundation of California State University, Sacramento [*Research center*] (RCD)
FCSV... Flowering Cherry Stunt Virus (SAUS)
FCSWB... Fire Control Switchboard
FCSWBD... Fire Control Switchboard
fcswbd... fire-control switchboard (SAUS)
FCSWC... Federation of Community Sporting and Workers' Clubs [*Australia*]
FCSZ... Florida Crush Stone [*Federal Railroad Administration identification code*]
FCT... Face-Centered Tetragonal [*Crystallography*]
FCT... Facility Control Terminal (SAUS)
FCT... Factory (KSC)
FCT... Fast CMOS Technology (SAUS)
FCT... Fast Cosine Transform [*Mathematics*]
FCT... Fast Cycle Time [*Business term*]
FCT... Fatigue Cracking Test
FCT... Faucet
FCT... Federal Coordinator of Transportation [*New Deal*]
FCT... Federal Court of Canada
FCT... Federation Canadienne du Travail [*Canadian Federation of Labour - CFL*]
FCT... Fellow of the Association of Corporate Treasurers [*British*] (ODBW)
FCT... Ferric Chloride Test [*Medicine*] (MELL)
FCT... Field Controlled Thyristor (SAUS)
FCT... Field-Controlled Thyristor [*Electronics*] (IAA)
FCT... Filament Center Tap
FCT... File Control Table (RALS)
FCT... Film-Coated Tablet [*Medicine*] (DB)
FCT... Filtrate catch tank (SAUS)
FCT... Final Contract Trials [*Navy*]
FCT... Financial Correlation Table
FCT... Fire Control Technician [*Navy rating*] [*Obsolete*]
FCT... Fire Control Trainer
FCT... Firewall Configuration Tool (SAUS)
FCT... First City Bancorp, Inc. [*AMEX symbol*] (SPSG)
FCT... First City Trust Co. [*Toronto Stock Exchange symbol*]
FCT... flat crush test (SAUS)
FCT... Flight Circuit Tester (DNAB)
FCT... Flight Control Team (MCD)
FCT... Flight Crew Trainer [*NASA*] (KSC)
FCT... Florida Communities Trust (SAUO)
FCT... Flow-Controller Tester (SAUS)
FCT... Flux-Corrected Transport [*Algorithm*]
FCT... Food Composition Table
FCT... Foramen Cecum of Tongue [*Medicine*] (MELL)
fct... Forecast (SAUS)
FCT... Foreign Comparative Testing [*DoD*] (RDA)
FCT... Foreign Comparative Test programme (SAUS)
FCT... Foreign Currency Translation
FCT... Forestry Commission of Tasmania [*Australia*]
FCT... Forestry Commission Tasmania (SAUS)
FCT... Forwarding Agents' Certificate of Transport [*Insurance*] (MARI)
FCT... Foundation for Christian Theology (EA)
FCT... Four Corner Test (SAUS)
FCT... Fraction Thereof
FCT... Fragment Connection Table [*Chemistry*]
FCT... Frame Creation Terminal [*Communications term*] (DCT)
FCT... Free Convertation Test (SAUS)
FCT... Frequency Clock Trigger (IAA)
FCT... Fuel Cell Test (SAUS)
FCT... Full Cleanliness Training
FCT... Function
FCT... Functional Context Training (DNAB)
FCT... Yakima, WA [*Location identifier*] [*FAA*] (FAAL)
FCTA... Federal Central Technical Authority (SAUO)
FCTA... Flow Control Time of Arrival [*Aviation*] (FAAC)
FCTB... Featherston Camp Trumpet Band [*British military*] (DMA)
FCTB... Fellow of the College of Teachers of the Blind
FCTB... Flight Crew Training Building [*NASA*] (KSC)
FCTC... Falmouth Container Terminal Company (SAUO)
FCTC... Federal Compiler Testing Center
FCTC... Fleet Combat Training Center [*Navy*] (NVT)
FCTC... Fuel Centerline Thermocouple (SAUS)
FCTCAA... Flowers-Costello Test of Central Auditory Abilities
FCTCSC... Flue-Cured Tobacco Cooperative Stabilization Corporation (SAUO)
FCTD... Federal Court Trial Division (SAUO)
FCTE... Fire Control Test Equipment
fcte... fire-control test equipment (SAUS)
FCTF... Five Civilized Tribes Foundation [*Defunct*] (EA)
FCTF... Fuel Cell Test Facility (MCD)

FCTG........... Fast Carrier Task Group (SAUO)
FCTGA........ Flue-Cured Tobacco Growers Association (EA)
FCTN.......... Function (MSA)
FCTP.......... Field Challenge Test Plan
FCTP.......... Fire Control Test Package
FCTR.......... Factor
FCTR.......... First Charter Corp. [*NASDAQ symbol*] (NQ)
FCTRL......... Final Contractor's Trial (NVT)
FCTRY........ Factory
FCTS.......... Federal Compiler Testing Service (SAUS)
FCTS.......... Fire Control Test Set
FCTS.......... Firing Circuit Test Set
fcts............ firing-circuit test set (SAUS)
FCTS.......... Flight Controller Training System (SAUS)
FCTS.......... Flight Control Test Stand [*Aviation*]
fcts............ flight-control test stand (SAUS)
FCTS.......... Flight Crew Trainer Simulator [*NASA*] (KSC)
F Ct Sess..... Fraser's Scotch Court of Sessions Cases [*A publication*] (DLA)
FCTT........... Fuel Cladding Transient Tester [*Nuclear energy*] (NRCH)
FCTU.......... Federation of Associations of Catholic Trade Unions (SAUO)
FCTU.......... Fiji Council of Trades Unions (SAUO)
FCTX.......... Farmers Commodities Transportation [*Private rail car owner code*]
FCTY.......... Factory (MUGU)
FCTZ.......... Flower City Tissue [*Federal Railroad Administration identification code*]
FCtzBA........ First Citizens Bancshares [*Associated Press*] (SAG)
FCtzBstk...... First Citizens Bank Stock [*Associated Press*] (SAG)
FCU............ Familial Cold Urticaria (SAUS)
FCU............ Fan Coil Unit (NRCH)
fcu.............. fare calculation unit (SAUS)
FCU............ Fare Construction Unit [*Airlines*]
FCU............ Fares Calculating Unit (OA)
FCU............ Farmers Cooperative Union (SAUO)
FCU............ Federal Credit Unions (SAUO)
FCU............ Federated Clerks Union (SAUO)
FCU............ Federation of Catholic Universities (SAUO)
FCU............ Field Communication Unit [*Military*]
FCU............ Fighter Control Unit [*Military*] [*British*]
FCU............ File Control Unit
FCU............ Fire Controlman (Underwater Weapons) [*U.S. Navy enlisted rating*] (AUER)
FCU............ Fire Control Unit
FCU............ Flexor Carpi Ulnaris [*Anatomy*] (DMAA)
FCU............ Flight Command Unit (SAUS)
FCU............ Flight Control Unit
FCU............ Fluid Checkout Unit (MCD)
FCU............ Force Control Unit
FCU............ Format Conversion Unit [*Computer science*]
FCU............ Frequency Converter Unit
FCU............ Fuel Conditioning Unit (SAUS)
FCU............ Fuel Consumption / Control Unit (SAUS)
fcu.............. fuel-control unit (SAUS)
FCUA.......... Federal Credit Union Administration
FCUA.......... Fuel-Critical, Unspecified Area
FCUMS........ Federation of Computer Users in the Medical Sciences (EA)
FCUR.......... Field Change Uninstalled Report (SAUS)
FCUS.......... Federal Credit Union System [*New Deal*]
FCUS.......... FORTRAN compiler validation system (SAUS)
FCUSA........ Finance Center, United States Army
FCV............ Facility Checkout Vehicle [*NASA*] (KSC)
FCV............ Feline Calicivirus
FCV............ Fellow of College of Violinists [*British*] (ROG)
FCV............ Festuca Cryptic Virus [*Plant pathology*]
fcv.............. fill-and-check valve (SAUS)
FCV............ Fire Command Vehicle
FCV............ Flight Centre Victoria [*Canada*] [*ICAO designator*] (FAAC)
FCV............ Flight Checkout Vehicle
FCV............ Flow Control Valve
FCV............ Free-Column Volume (ABAC)
FCV............ Full Contract Value [*Insurance*] (MARI)
FCV............ Future Concept Vehicle
FCVC.......... Flow Controlled Virtual Channel (SAUS)
FCVC.......... Flow Controlled Virtual Circuit (MLOA)
FCVE.......... Foundation for Continuing Veterinary Education [*Murdoch University, Australia*]
FCVI........... Fondation Canadienne pour la Verification Integree (AC)
FCVI........... Forced-Flow Chemical Vapor Infiltration [*Materials science*]
FCVN.......... Fatal Casualties Vulnerability Number (SAA)
FCVN.......... Friends of Children of Vietnam (EA)
FCVRE........ Funders Committee for Voter Registration and Education (EA)
FCVS.......... Filtered Containment Venting System (SAUS)
FCVS.......... FORTRAN [*Formula Translating System*] Compiler Validation System [*Computer science*]
FC vsl......... fully cellular vessel (SAUS)
FCW............ Fast Cyclotron Wave [*Electromagnetism*] (IAA)
FCW............ Federal Computer Week (SAUS)
FCW............ Fire Control Workshop
FCW............ Flight Crew Workload [*Navy*]
FCW............ Flux-Cored Welding Wire (PDAA)
FCW............ Flyer Coil Winder
FCW............ Format Control Words (SAUS)
FCW............ Forward Collision Warning [*Automotive safety systems*]
FCW............ Fresh Cell Weight [*Biochemistry*]
FCW............ Paine Webber Group [*AMEX symbol*] (SAG)
FCWA.......... Family Court, Western Australia
FCWA.......... Fellow of the Chartered Institute of Cost and Work Accountants [*British*] (EY)
FCWA.......... Fellow of the Institute of Cost and Works Accountants (SAUS)
FCWA.......... Freemasons' Club of Western Australia
FCWBWU..... Fancy Cane, Wicker, and Bamboo Workers' Union [*British*]
FCWG.......... Frequency Control Working Group (SAUO)
FCWG.......... Frequency Coordinating (or Coordination) Working Group (SAUO)
FCWG.......... Frequency Coordination Working Group (MUGU)
FCWI........... First Commonwealth [*NASDAQ symbol*] (TTSB)
FCWI........... First Commonwealth, Inc. [*NASDAQ symbol*] (SAG)
FCWRENAF... Fleet Chief WREN [*Women's Royal Naval Service*] Air Fitter [*British military*] (DMA)
FCWRENCINE... Fleet Chief WREN [*Women's Royal Naval Service*] Cinema Operator [*British military*] (DMA)
FCWRENCK... Fleet Chief WREN [*Women's Royal Naval Service*] Cook [*British military*] (DMA)
FCWRENDHYG... Fleet Chief WREN [*Women's Royal Naval Service*] Dental Hygienist [*British military*] (DMA)
FCWRENDSA... Fleet Chief WREN [*Women's Royal Naval Service*] Dental Surgery Assistant [*British military*] (DMA)
FCWRENEDUC... Fleet Chief WREN [*Women's Royal Naval Service*] Education Assistant [*British military*] (DMA)
FCWRENMET... Fleet Chief WREN [*Women's Royal Naval Service*] Meteorological Observer [*British military*] (DMA)
FCWRENPHOT... Fleet Chief WREN [*Women's Royal Naval Service*] Photographer [*British military*] (DMA)
FCWRENQA... Fleet Chief WREN [*Women's Royal Naval Service*] Quarters Assistant [*British military*] (DMA)
FCWREN(R)... Fleet Chief WREN [*Women's Royal Naval Service*] (RADAR) [*British military*] (DMA)
FCWRENREG... Fleet Chief WREN [*Women's Royal Naval Service*] Regulating [*British military*] (DMA)
FCWRENREL... Fleet Chief WREN [*Women's Royal Naval Service*] Radio Electrician [*British military*] (DMA)
FCWRENRS(M)... Fleet Chief WREN [*Women's Royal Naval Service*] Radio Supervisor (Morse) [*British military*] (DMA)
FCWRENSA... Fleet Chief WREN [*Women's Royal Naval Service*] Stores Accountant [*British military*] (DMA)
FCWRENSTD... Fleet Chief WREN [*Women's Royal Naval Service*] Steward [*British military*] (DMA)
FCWRENTEL... Fleet Chief WREN [*Women's Royal Naval Service*] Telephonist [*British military*] (DMA)
FCWRENTSA... Fleet Chief WREN [*Women's Royal Naval Service*] Training Support Assistant [*British military*] (DMA)
FCWRENWA... Fleet Chief WREN [*Women's Royal Naval Service*] Weapon Analyst [*British military*] (DMA)
FCWRENWTR(G)... Fleet Chief WREN [*Women's Royal Naval Service*] Writer (General) [*British military*] (DMA)
FCWRENWTR(P)... Fleet Chief WREN [*Women's Royal Naval Service*] Writer (Pay) [*British military*] (DMA)
FCWRENWW... Fleet Chief WREN [*Women's Royal Naval Service*] Welfare Worker [*British military*] (DMA)
FCWTC......... Friends Committee on War Tax Concerns [*Defunct*] (EA)
f-cx-........... Central African Republic [*MARC geographic area code*] [*Library of Congress*] (LCCP)
FCX............ Fire Coordination Exercise [*Military*] (ADDR)
FCX............ Freeport McMoRan Copper & Gold [*NYSE symbol*] (SPSG)
FCX............ Freep't McMoRan Copper&Gold'B' [*NYSE symbol*] (TTSB)
FCx............ Frontal Cortex [*Neuroanatomy*]
FCXPr......... Freep't McMoRan Cp/Gld7%CvPref [*NYSE symbol*] (TTSB)
FCXPrA....... Freept-McMo Cp/Gld'A'Dep Pfd [*NYSE symbol*] (TTSB)
FCXPrB....... Freept-McMo Cp/Gld'B'Dep Pfd [*NYSE symbol*] (TTSB)
FCXPrC....... Freept-McMo Cp/Gld'C'Dep Pfd [*NYSE symbol*] (TTSB)
FCXPrD....... Freept-McMo Cp/Slvr'D'Dep Pfd [*NYSE symbol*] (TTSB)
fcy.............. Fancy (ADWA)
FCY............ Fancy (ROG)
FCY............ Federation Canadienne de Yachting [*Canadian Yachting Association*]
FCY............ First City Financial Corp. Ltd. [*Toronto Stock Exchange symbol*] [*Vancouver Stock Exchange symbol*]
FCY............ Forrest City, AR [*Location identifier*] [*FAA*] (FAAL)
FCY............ Furon Co. [*NYSE symbol*] (SAG)
fcy pks....... fancy packs (SAUS)
FCYR.......... Franklin County Railroad [*Federal Railroad Administration identification code*]
FcZ............. Facez, Rockford, IL [*Library symbol*] [*Library of Congress*] (LCLS)
FCZ............ Fisheries Conservation Zone (SAUO)
FCZ............ Fishery Conservation Zone
FCZ............ Forward Combat Zone (NATG)
FCZ............ Foster [*Federal Railroad Administration identification code*]
FD.............. Defender of the Faith (SAUO)
FD.............. Democratic Force (France) [*Political party*] (PSAP)
Fd............... Dilution Factor [*Also, DF*] [*Nuclear energy*] (NRCH)
fD............... Doppler frequency (SAUS)
FD.............. Fabry's Disease [*Medicine*] (MELL)
FD.............. Face of Drawing (AAG)
FD.............. Facial Dyskinesias [*Medicine*] (MELL)
FD.............. Facilities and Design (MCD)
FD.............. Facility Division [*Forecast Systems Laboratory*] (USDC)
FD.............. Facility documentation (SAUS)
FD.............. Facility Drawing
FD.............. Factory Department (SAUO)
FD.............. Faculty Department (SAUO)
fd............... faculty development (SAUS)
FD.............. Failure Definition (MCD)
FD.............. Fairbanks Dysostosis [*Medicine*] (MELL)

FD .... False Deck [*Stowage*] (DNAB)
FD .... False Dismissal (SAUS)
FD .... Familial Dysautonomia [*Medicine*]
FD .... Family Divison (SAUO)
FD .... Family Doctor (MEDA)
FD .... Fan Douche [*Medicine*]
Fd .... Fantail Darter [*Ichthyology*]
FD .... Fascia Dentata [*Brain anatomy*]
FD .... Fatal Dose
f/d .... father and daughter (SAUS)
FD .... Fault Detection (MCD)
FD .... Fault Directory
FD .... Feasibility Demonstration (TIMI)
FD .... Federal Defender (SAUS)
FD .... Federal Directive
FD .... Federal Document (AFM)
FD .... Federated Department Stores, Inc. [*NYSE symbol*] (SAG)
FD .... Federated Dept Stores [*NYSE symbol*] (TTSB)
FD .... Feed (MSA)
FD .... Feedback Decoding (SAUS)
FD .... Felxible Disk (SAUS)
FD .... Female Domination
FD .... Female Treated with DOC [*Deoxycorticosterone*]
Fd .... Ferredoxin [*Biochemistry*]
FD .... Fetal Danger [*Medicine*] (EDAA)
FD .... Fetal Death (MELL)
FD .... Fetal Distress (MELL)
FD .... Feynman Diagram (SAUS)
FD .... Fiber Duct [*Telecommunications*] (TEL)
FD .... Fibrinogen Derivative [*Hematology*] (AAMN)
FD .... Fibrous Dysplasia (MELL)
FD .... Fidei Defensor [*Defender of the Faith*] [*Latin*]
fd .... Field (MILB)
FD .... Field
FD .... Field Decelerating Contactor or Relay [*Industrial control*] (IEEE)
FD .... Field Definition (IAA)
fd .... field dependence (SAUS)
FD .... Field Depot (SAUS)
FD .... Field Description (SAUS)
FD .... Field Descriptor (SAUS)
FD .... Field Desorption [*Medicine*] (EDAA)
FD .... Field Director
fd .... field discharge (SAUS)
FD .... Field Dose (SAUS)
FD .... Field Dressing (SAUS)
FD .... Field Drum (SAUS)
FD .... Field of Drawing (AAG)
FD .... Field time waveform Distortion (SAUS)
FD .... Fighter Direction
FD .... Filatow-Dukes [*Disease*] [*Medicine*] (DB)
FD .... File Definition [*Computer science*]
FD .... File Description
FD .... File Descriptor (SAUS)
FD .... File Directory
FD .... Fill Device (SAUS)
FD .... Fill/Drain (MCD)
F/D .... Filter/Demineralizer (NRCH)
FD .... Filter Drain [*Computer science*]
FD .... Final Drive Ratio
FD .... Finance Department
FD .... Finance Direction
FD .... Finance Docket
FD .... Financial Director
FD .... Finished Dialing [*Telecommunications*] (TEL)
FD .... Finite Difference [*Metallurgy*]
fd .... fiord (SAUS)
FD .... Fire Break Door (MARI)
FD .... Fire Damper (OA)
FD .... Fire Department
FD .... Fire Department Access Point [*NFPA planning symbol*] (NFPA)
FD .... Fire Detector
FD .... Fire Direction
FD .... Fire Drop (AABC)
FD .... First Day [*Philately*]
FD .... First Defense [*Men's lacrosse position*]
FD .... First Down [*Football*]
FD .... Fisheries Department [*Western Australia*]
Fd .... Fjord [*Maps and charts*]
FD .... Flame Deflector
fd .... flame detector (SAUS)
FD .... Flange Focal Distance (IEEE)
FD .... Flange Local Distance (SAUS)
FD .... Fleet Duties [*British military*] (DMA)
FD .... Flex Density (ACAE)
FD .... flexible disc (SAUS)
FD .... Flexible Drive (SAUS)
FD .... Flight Deck (MCD)
FD .... Flight Delay (MCD)
FD .... Flight Director [*NASA*] (KSC)
FD .... Floating Decimal (SAUS)
FD .... Floating Divide (IAA)
FD .... Floating Dollar (SAUS)
FD .... Floating Dollar Sign [*Computer science*] (IAA)
FD .... Floor Drain [*Technical drawings*]
FD .... floppy disc (SAUS)
FD .... Floppy Drive [*Computer science*] (VLIE)
FD .... Flow Diagram [*Engineering*] (IAA)
FD .... Fluctuation-Dissipation [*Theorem*] [*Statistical mechanics*]
fd .... Fluid [*Medicine*] (EDAA)
FD .... Fluid Dynamics (SAUS)
FD .... Fluorescence Detection [*Spectrometry*]
FD .... Flux Delta (IAA)
FD .... Flux Density (SAUS)
FD .... Flux Drive
FD .... Flyball Dog
FD .... Flying Dutchman [*Racing dinghy*]
FD .... Focal Diameter
fd .... focal dispatch (SAUS)
FD .... Focal Distance
F/D .... Focal-length / Diameter (SAUS)
F/D .... Focal Length to Diameter Ratio (SAUS)
F/D .... Focal to Diameter ratio (SAUS)
FD .... Fog Diaphone [*Navigation charts*]
FD .... Folate Deficiency (MELL)
FD .... Fold
FD .... Folin-Denis [*Analytical chemistry*]
FD .... Follicular Diameter [*Medicine*] (DMAA)
FD .... Food
FD .... Food Distribution Division [*of AMS, Department of Agriculture*]
FD .... Food Division [*Army Natick Laboratories, MA*]
FD .... Foot Drape [*Medicine*]
FD .... Footdrop (MELL)
FD .... Forbush Decrease [*Geophysics*]
FD .... Forced (WGA)
FD .... Forced Diffusion (SAUS)
FD .... Forced Draft
FD .... Force Designator
FD .... Force Developer (SAUS)
FD .... Force Development
FD .... Force Displacement [*Sports medicine*]
FD .... Forceps Delivery [*Obstetrics*]
FD .... Ford (ROG)
FD .... Ford of Europe, Inc. [*British*] [*ICAO designator*] (ICDA)
FD .... Forest Department (SAUS)
FD .... Forestry Department (SAUS)
FD .... Forging Direction (SAUS)
FD .... Formal Decorative [*Horticulture*]
FD .... Fort Detrick [*Maryland*] [*Army*] (MCD)
FD .... Forward (ADA)
FD .... Forward Definition (SAUS)
FD .... Forward Depot (SAUS)
FD .... Found (MSA)
FD .... Foundation Damage (ADWA)
FD .... Foundation for the Disabled (SAUO)
FD .... Fourth Day (IIA)
FD .... Fourth Dimension [*Time*] (AAG)
FD .... Fractional Destraction [*Supercritical distillation*]
FD .... Fractional Distillation (SAUS)
FD .... Fraction that is dead (SAUS)
FD .... Framed [*Construction*]
FD .... Frame Difference
FD .... Frame Discard (MLOA)
FD .... Framework Density [*Crystallography*]
FD .... Franc [*Monetary unit*] [*French Somaliland*]
FD .... Franco Domicile [*Shipping*] (DS)
FD .... Free Delivery
FD .... Free Democrat (ODA)
fd .... free despatch (SAUS)
FD .... Free Discharge
FD .... Free Dispatch
FD .... Free Dock [*Business term*]
F/d .... Free Docks (EBF)
FD .... Free Drop
FD .... Free to Domicile (SAUS)
fd .... free to the door (SAUS)
FD .... Freeze-Dried
FD .... Freight Department
FD .... Frente Democratica [*Democratic Front*] [*Guinea-Bissau*] [*Political party*] (EY)
FD .... Frequency Demodulator
FD .... Frequency Detection (SAUS)
FD .... Frequency Discrimination [*Neurophysiology*]
FD .... Frequency Discriminator (SAUS)
FD .... Frequency Distance [*Telecommunications*] (TEL)
FD .... Frequency Distribution [*Mathematics*] (IAA)
FD .... Frequency Diversity
FD .... Frequency Divider [*Electronics*] (IAA)
FD .... Frequency Division
FD .... Frequency Domain (SAUS)
FD .... Frequency Doubler
FD .... Frequency Drift
FD .... Fretwell-Downing, Inc.
FD .... Frog Dose (SAUS)
FD .... Front Democratique [*Democratic Front*] [*The Comoros*] [*Political party*] (EY)
FD .... Front Door [*Shipping*]
FD .... Front of Dash [*Technical drawings*]
FD .... Fuel Demand (SAUS)
FD .... Fuel Dragster [*Class of racing cars*]
FD .... Full Development (SAUS)

FD........ Full Dress [*Colloquial reference to formal dress*]
FD........ Full Duplex [*Telecommunications*]
FD........ Functional Decomposition (VLIE)
FD........ Functional Demonstration (ACAE)
FD........ Functional Dependency (SAUS)
FD........ Functional Description
FD........ Functional Diagram [*Implementation dependant*] (ACII)
FD........ Functional Directory (HEAS)
FD........ Function Designator (NASA)
Fd........ Fund (EBF)
FD........ Fund (ROG)
FD........ Furniture Designer (SAUS)
FD........ Fuze Delay
fd---........ Sahara Desert [*MARC geographic area code*] [*Library of Congress*] (LCCP)
FD........ Winds and Temperatures Aloft Forecast [*Symbol*] [*National Weather Service*]
FD........ Wiscair [*ICAO designator*] (AD)
FD........ Fermi-Dirac [*Physics*] (ODA)
FD$_{50}$........ Median Fatal Dose [*Medicine*] (MAE)
FDA........ Angolan Democratic Forum [*Political party*] (PSAP)
FDA........ Facility Disposal Area (SAUO)
FDA........ Fast Data Acquisition (SAUS)
FDA........ Fault Detection and Annunciation (NASA)
FDA........ Feather and Down Association (EA)
FDA........ Federal Design Approval [*Nuclear energy*] (NUCP)
FDA........ Federal Domestic Assistance [*Catalog*] (OICC)
FDA........ Federal Drug Administration
FDA........ Fellowship Depressives Anonymous [*British*] (DBA)
FDA........ Fellowship Diploma of Architecture
FDA........ Ferrite Driver Amplifier
FDA........ Ferrocenedicarboxylic Acid [*Organic chemistry*]
FDA........ Fertilizer Dealers Association [*Defunct*] (EA)
FDA........ File Description Attribute (SAUS)
FDA........ File Descriptor Area (SAUS)
FDA........ Final Delivered Article
FDA........ Final Design Acceptance [*or Approval or Authorization*]
FDA........ Final Design Approval (SAUS)
FDA........ Final Design Audit (ACAE)
FDA........ Financial Data Planning
FDA........ First Division Association [*British*]
FDA........ Fisheries Development Authority (SAUO)
FDA........ Flight Deck Assembly (MCD)
FDA........ Flight Detection and Annunciation (MCD)
FDA........ Flight Direction Attitude (SAUS)
FDA........ Floating Decimal Arithmetic (SAUS)
FDA........ Florida Airlines, Inc. (SAUO)
FDA........ Florida Dental Association (SAUO)
FDA........ Florida State University, Tallahassee, FL [*OCLC symbol*] (OCLC)
FDA........ Fluorescein Diacetate [*Organic chemistry*]
FDA........ Flying Dentists Association (EA)
FDA........ Folded Dipole Antenna
FDA........ Food and Drug Act (SAUS)
FDA........ Food and Drug Administration [*Rockville, MD*] [*Department of Health and Human Services*]
FDA........ Food Distribution Administration [*Terminated, 1945*]
FDA........ Foreign Demographic Analysis Division [*Census*] (OICC)
FDA........ Formdimethylamide (SAUS)
FDA........ FORTRAN Design Aid (SAUS)
FDA........ Forum Democratico Angolana [*Political party*] (EY)
FDA........ Frenchay Dysarthria Assessment [*Speech and language therapy*] (DAVI)
FDA........ Frequency Distortion Analyzer
FDA........ Frequency-Domain Analysis (SAUS)
FDA........ Fronto-Dextra Anterior [*A fetal position*] [*Obstetrics*]
FDA........ Fuel Distribution Analyzer [*Environmental science*] (COE)
FDA........ Full-Duplex Audio (SAUS)
fda........ fully drawn account (SAUS)
FDA........ Functional Demonstration and Acceptance (AAG)
FDA........ Functional Design Activity [*Army*]
FDA........ Functional Design Agency (MCD)
FDA........ Fundacion [*Colombia*] [*Airport symbol*] (AD)
FDA........ Furniture Deliverers' Association
FDAA........ Federal Disaster Assistance Administration [*FEMA*]
FDAA........ Fluorenyldiacetamide (SAUS)
FDAAL........ Food and Drug Administration Action Level (LDOE)
FDA Cons........ FDA [*Food and Drug Administration*] Consumer [*A publication*] (DLA)
FDAD........ Full Digital Arts Display [*FAA*] (TAG)
FDAD........ Full Disk Address [*Computer science*] (VLIE)
FDAd........ Functional Data Administrator (VLIE)
FDADS........ Fault Digital Airborne Data System (ACAE)
F-DADS........ Fault-Tolerant Digital Airborne Data System (ACAE)
FDA-EDRO........ Food and Drug Administration, Office of Executive Director of Regional Operations (NRCH)
FdAgric........ Federal Agricultural Mortgage Corp. [*Associated Press*] (SAG)
FdAgricA........ Federal Agricultural Mortgage [*Associated Press*] (SAG)
FdAgricC........ Federal Agricultural Mortgage [*Associated Press*] (SAG)
FDAI........ Feather and Down Association, Inc. (SAUO)
FDAI........ Flight Direction and Altitude Indicator
FDAI........ Flight Director Attitude Indicator [*NASA*] (NASA)
Fd Amb........ Field Ambulance (SAUS)
FdAmbCo........ Field Ambulance Company (SAUO)
FDAMS........ Flight Data Acquisition and Management System (GAVI)
FD & C........ Food, Drug, and Cosmetic Act
FD&C........ Foods, Drugs, and Cosmetics Color (SAUS)
FD & CA........ Food, Drug, and Cosmetic Act (EG)
FD & C Act........ Food, Drug, and Cosmetic Act (SAUS)
FD&C act........ Food Drug Cosmetics Act (SAUO)
FD&CC........ Facilities Design & Construction Center (SAUO)
FD & D........ Freight, Demurrage, and Defense [*Shipping*] (DS)
FD&D Club........ Freight, Demurrage and Defence Club (SAUO)
FD & E........ Follow-On Development Test and Evaluation (MCD)
FD & I........ Failure Detection and Isolation
FDAP........ Frequency Domain Array Processor (SAUS)
FDAS........ Field Data Acquisition System (DWSG)
FDAS........ Field Depot Aviation Squadron [*Air Force*]
FDAS........ Flight Data Acquisition System
FDAS........ Flight Dynamics Analysis System (CIST)
FDAS........ Floppy Disk Anschaltung (SAUS)
FDAS........ Frequency Distribution Analysis Sheet
FDASM........ Floppy Disc Assembler (SAUS)
FDASM........ Floppy Disk Assembler (SAUS)
FDAT........ Final Development Acceptance Test (SAUO)
FDATC........ Flying Division, Air Training Command (SAUO)
FDAU........ Flight Data Acquisition Unit
F-Day........ Filler Day (SAUS)
FDB........ Fahrenheit Dry Bulb (KSC)
FDB........ Family Discussion Bureau [*Later, Institute of Marital Studies*] [*British*] (DI)
FDB........ Ferrari Data Bank (EA)
FDB........ Field Descriptor Block
FDB........ Field Dynamic Braking
FDB........ Fighter Dive-Bomber
FDB........ File Data Block [*Computer science*]
FDB........ File Directory Block [*Computer science*] (TIMI)
FDB........ First-Degree Burn (MELL)
FDB........ Fixed Bed (SAUS)
FDB........ Fleet Data Base [*Navy*] (CAAL)
FDB........ Flexor Digitorum Brevis (DB)
FDB........ Flight Dynamics Branch [*NASA*] (KSC)
FDB........ Foodbrands America [*NYSE symbol*] (TTSB)
FDB........ Forced Draft Blower (SAUS)
FDB........ Forestry Data Bank (SAUS)
FDB........ Form Die Bulge (MCD)
FDB........ Forte Princip [*Brazil*] [*Airport symbol*] (AD)
FDB........ Fortune Data Bank (SAUS)
FDB........ Full Data Block (KSC)
FDB........ Functional Description Block [*Telecommunications*] (TEL)
FDb........ Volusia County Public Libraries, Daytona Beach, FL [*Library symbol*] [*Library of Congress*] (LCLS)
FDbBC........ Bethune-Cookman College, Daytona Beach, FL [*Library symbol*] [*Library of Congress*] (LCLS)
FDBC........ Flight Director Bombing Computer (MCD)
FDbCC........ Daytona Beach Community College, Daytona Beach, FL [*Library symbol*] [*Library of Congress*] (LCLS)
Fd Bchy........ Field Butchery (SAUS)
FD/BE........ Finite Difference/Boundary Element (VLIE)
FDBK........ Feedback (MSA)
FDBK........ Founders Bank (SAUO)
Fd Bky........ Field Bakery (SAUS)
FDBLP........ Familial Dysbetalipoproteinemia [*Medicine*] (MELL)
FDBLR........ Frequency Doubler (MSA)
FDBM........ Functional Data Base Manager (COE)
FDBPM........ Finite-Difference Beam Propagation Method (SAUS)
FDB Press........ Fixed Bed Press (SAUS)
FDBPS........ Fleet Database Production System [*Navy*] (MCD)
Fd Bty........ Field Battery (SAUS)
FDbY........ S. Cornelia Young Memorial Library, Daytona Beach, FL [*Library symbol*] [*Library of Congress*] (LCLS)
FDC........ Daughters of Divine Charity (TOCD)
FDC........ Facility Design Criteria (AAG)
FDC........ Facsimile Data Converter [*Facilitates communication between facsimile terminal and computer*] (NITA)
FDC........ Facsimile Data Coverter (SAUS)
FDC........ Failure Diagnostic Code [*Military*] (AFIT)
FDC........ Fast Data Collecting (SAUS)
FDC........ Fathers Day Council (EA)
FDC........ Fault Detection and Classification [*Electronics*] (AAEL)
FDC........ Federacion Democrata Cristiana [*Christian Democratic Federation*] [*Spain*] [*Political party*] (PPE)
FDC........ Federal Design Council [*Defunct*] (EA)
FDC........ Federal Detention Center (BARN)
FDC........ Federal Driving Cycle (SAUS)
FDC........ Federation for a Democratic China [*Australia*]
FDC........ Federation of Dredging Contractors [*British*] (BI)
FDC........ Field Data Computer
FDC........ Field Description Card (SAUS)
FDC........ Field Discharge Chip
FDC........ Field Distribution Center (VLIE)
FDC........ File Definition Control (SAUS)
FDC........ Filiae Divinae Caritatis [*Daughters of Divine Charity*] [*Roman Catholic religious order*]
FDC........ Film Development Corporation (SAUO)
FDC........ Final Design Criteria
FDC........ Fire Department Connection (SAUS)
FDC........ Fire-Department Connection [*Technical drawings*]
FDC........ Fire Detection Center
FDC........ Fire-Detection Center (SAUS)
FDC........ Fire Direction Center [*Military*]
FDC........ Fire Direction Control

FDC.......... Fire Distribution Centre (SAUS)
FDC.......... Firing Data Computer (SAUS)
FDC.......... First Data [*NYSE symbol*] (SPSG)
FDC.......... First Data Corporation (SAUO)
FDC.......... First-Day Cover [*Philately*]
FDC.......... First-Dollar Coverage [*Insurance*] (MELL)
FDC.......... Fishery Data Center [*FAO*] (MSC)
FDC.......... Fishery Data Centre (SAUO)
FDC.......... Fixed Decade Capacitor
FDC.......... Fleur de Coin [*Mint state*] [*Numismatics*]
FDC.......... Flight Data Center (SAUO)
FDC.......... Flight Data Company (GAVI)
FDC.......... Flight Director Computer (MCD)
FDC.......... floppy disc controller (SAUS)
FDC.......... Floppy Disk Controller [*Computer science*] (MDG)
FDC.......... Floppy Drive Controller (SAUS)
FDC.......... Florida Department of Citrus (EA)
FDC.......... Fluid Die Compaction (SAUS)
FDC.......... Fluid Digital Computer
FDC.......... Fluid Dynamics Conference (SAUS)
FDC.......... Fluorosensor Data Correlator-Interactive Circuits & Systems Ltd. for CCRS (SAUS)
FDC.......... Follicular Dendritic Cell
FDC.......... Food, Drug, and Cosmetic [*Act*]
FDC.......... Food, Drug and Cosmetic Act (SAUO)
fdc.......... formation density content (SAUS)
FDC.......... Formation Drone Control [*Navy*] (NG)
FDC.......... Form Definition Component (IAA)
FDC.......... Forsyth Dental Center (SAUO)
FDC.......... Forward Direction Center [*Air Force*]
FDC.......... Frame Dependent Control (VLIE)
FDC.......... Freedom Defence Committee [*National Council for Civil Liberties*] [*British*]
FDC.......... Frequency Detection Channel (SAUS)
FDC.......... Frequency Domain Coding
FDC.......... Frequency of Dividing Cells [*Bacteriology*]
FDC.......... Front Democratique Camerounais [*Cameroon*] [*Political party*] (EY)
FDC.......... Fuel Data Center (HAWK)
FDC.......... Full Digital Correlator (SAUS)
FDC.......... Fully Distributed Costs [*Finance*] (MHDB)
FDC.......... Functional Data Coordinator (MCD)
FDC.......... Functional Design Criteria (NRCH)
FDC.......... Function Digits Code (SAUS)
FDC.......... Furniture Development Council [*British*] (BI)
FDCA.......... Fair Debt Collection Act (EBF)
FDCA.......... Federal Defense Communications Authority (SAUO)
FDCA.......... Federal Drug and Cosmetics Act (SAUS)
FDCA.......... Flying Disc Collectors Association (EA)
FDCA.......... Food, Drug, and Cosmetic Act (SAUS)
FDCB.......... Foreign and Domestic Commerce Bureau (SAUO)
FdCC.......... Canossian Daughters of Charity (TOCD)
FDCC.......... Family Day Care Centre [*Australia*]
FDCC.......... Flight [*Control*] Division-Control Criteria [*Air Force*]
FDCC.......... Fort Dodge Community College (SAUO)
FDCCC.......... First Day Cover Collectors Club (EA)
FDCD.......... Facility Design Criteria Document (AAG)
FDCD.......... Fluorescence-Detected Circular Dichroism [*Spectroscopy*]
FDCD.......... Foreign Demand & Competition Division (SAUO)
FDCDS.......... Family Day Care Development Service [*Australia*]
FDCH.......... Federal Document Clearing House
FDCH.......... Flyball Dog Champion
FDCL.......... Forschungsund Dokumentationszentrum Chile-Lateinamerika [*Germany*]
FDCL.......... Friends of the Dartmouth College Library
FDCLF.......... Friends of Dromkeen Children's Literature Foundation [*Australia*]
FDCM.......... Fluorodichloromethane (SAUS)
fd cmpt.......... Fire Direction Computer (SAUS)
FDCO.......... Defense Foreign Disclosure Coordinating Office
FDCOPY Program.......... Floppy Disc Copy Program (SAUS)
FD Cosm L Rep.......... Food, Drug, Cosmetic Law Reporter [*Commerce Clearing House*] [*A publication*] (DLA)
FDCP.......... Family Day Care Program [*Australia*]
FDCPA.......... Fair Debt Collection Practices Act
FDCPA.......... Food, Drug, and Consumer Product Agency [*Proposed successor to FDA*] [*HEW*]
FDCPX.......... Fidelity Select Ptfl: Computers [*Mutual fund ticker symbol*] (SG)
FDCR.......... Fault Detection, Correction and Recovery (SAUS)
FDCR.......... Frente Democratico contra la Represion [*Guatemala*] [*Political party*] (EY)
FdCrtE.......... Food Court Entertainment Network, Inc. [*Associated Press*] (SAG)
FDCs.......... Federal Detention Centers (SAUO)
FDCS.......... Fighter Director Control Schools [*Navy*]
FDCS.......... Flight Deck Communication System [*Navy*] (CAAL)
FDCs.......... Fluid Digital Computers (SAUS)
FDCs.......... Forces Defence Committees (Ghana) [*Political party*] (PSAP)
FDCS.......... Functionally Distributed Computing System
FDCSB.......... Federation for a Democratic China, Sydney Branch [*Australia*]
FDCT.......... Factory Data Collection Terminal (VLIE)
FDCT.......... Fast Discrete Cosine Transformation (SAUS)
FdCt.......... Food Court Entertainment Network, Inc. [*Associated Press*] (SAG)
FDCT.......... Forward Discrete Cosine Transformation (SAUS)
FDCT.......... Franck Drawing Completion Test [*Psychology*]
FDCT.......... Frequency Domain Coding Technique
FDCTB.......... Finance Director of Commodity and Technical Branches (SAUO)
FdCtE.......... Food Court Entertainment Network, Inc. [*Associated Press*] (SAG)
FDCU.......... Fire Detector Control Unit (MCD)
FDD.......... Facility design description (SAUS)
FD'd.......... Factory Damaged [*Slang*]
FDD.......... Feith Document Database [*Software*] (HODG)
FDD.......... Field Data Department (VLIE)
FDD.......... Final Delivery Date (AAGC)
FDD.......... First Digitized Division [*Army*]
FDD.......... Fixed Disk Drive (SAUS)
FDD.......... Flexible Disk Drive
FDD.......... Flight Data Document (SAUS)
FDD.......... Flight Definition Document (SAUS)
FDD.......... Flight Dynamics Division [*NASA*] (SSD)
FDD.......... Floating Digital Drive
FDD.......... Floating Dry Dock [*Navy*]
FDD.......... Floppy Disk Drive [*Computer science*]
FDD.......... Focus to Detector Distance (SAUS)
FDD.......... Food and Drug Directorate [*Canada*]
FDD.......... Foreign Document Division [*of CIA*]
FDD.......... Format Deficiency Document (MCD)
FDD.......... Formatted Data Disk (SAUS)
FDD.......... Forward Divisional Dump (SAUS)
FDD.......... Foundation Documentaire Dentaire (SAUO)
FDD.......... Franc de Droits [*Free of Charge*] [*Shipping*] [*French*]
FDD.......... Freight, Demurrage, and Defence [*Insurance*] (MARI)
FDD.......... Freight Demurrage Deadfreight (RIMS)
FDD.......... Frequency Difference Detector (IAA)
FDD.......... Frequency Divider and Distributor (SAUS)
FDD.......... Frequency Division Duplex [*Telecommunications*] (ACRL)
FDD.......... Front for Democracy and Development [*Surinam*] [*Political party*]
FDD.......... Functional Description Document (SAUS)
FDD.......... Functional Design Document (SAUS)
FDDA.......... Fiber Distributed Data Interface (SAUS)
FDDA.......... Fibre Distributed Data Interface (SAUS)
FDDA.......... four-dimensional data assimilation (SAUS)
FDDA.......... Four-dimensional data assimulation (SAUS)
FDDAMC.......... Fully Distributed Data Acquisition Monitoring and Control
FDDB.......... Function Designator Data Base (SAUS)
FDDC.......... Ferric Dimethyldithiocarbamate [*A fungicide*]
FDDC.......... Ferric Dimethyl Dithiocarbonate (SAUS)
FDDC.......... Flight Deck Debarkation Control [*Navy*] (CAAL)
FDDI.......... Fiber Data Distribution Interconnect (SAUS)
FDDI.......... Fiber Data Distribution Interface (SAUS)
FDDI.......... Fiber Digital Data Interface (SAUS)
FDDI.......... Fiber Digital Device Interface (SAUS)
FDDI.......... Fiber Distributed Data Information (AGLO)
FDDI.......... Fiber-Distributed Data Interfacce [*IBM Corp.*] (CIST)
FDDI.......... Fiber Distributed Data Interface [*Telecommunications*]
FDDI.......... Fiber Distributed Digital Interface (SAUS)
FDDI.......... Fiber Optical Data Distribution Interface (ACAE)
FDDI.......... Fiber-Optic Digital Data Interface (ACAE)
FDDI.......... Fiber-Optic Digital Device Interface [*Computer science*]
FDDI.......... Fibre Data Distributed Intelligence (SAUS)
FDDI.......... Fibre Distributed Data Interface (SAUS)
FDDI.......... File Distributed Data Interface (SAUS)
FDDI.......... Filter Distributed Data Interface (SAUS)
FDDI-II.......... FDDI supporting isochronous traffic (SAUS)
FDDip.......... Funeral Director's Diploma [*British*] (DI)
FDDITPPMD.......... FDDI Twisted Pair-Physical layer, Medium Dependend (SAUS)
FDDI TP-PMD.......... FDDI Twisted Pair Physical Layer Medium Dependent (SAUS)
FDDI/UTP.......... FDDI Unshielded Twisted Pair (SAUS)
FDDI.......... fiber distributed data interface (SAUS)
FDDL.......... Field Data Description Language (NITA)
FDDL.......... File Data Description Language (MHDI)
FDDL.......... Flight Data Entry System (SAA)
FDDL.......... Frequency-Division Data Link [*Radio*]
FDDLL.......... Find Dead Dynamic Link Library [*Computer software*] (PCM)
fddlp.......... Frequency Division Data Link Printout (SAUS)
FDDLPO.......... Frequency Division Data Link Printout (SAUS)
FDDM.......... Fire Direction Data Management (or Manager) (SAUS)
FDDM.......... Fire Direction Data Manager (SAUS)
FDDM.......... Fort Dodge, Des Moines & Southern Railway Co. [*AAR code*]
FDDM.......... Fort Dodge, Des Moines & Southern Railway Company (SAUO)
FDDM & S.......... Fort Dodge, Des Moines & Southern Railway Co.
FDDM&S.......... Fort Dodge, Des Moines & Southern Railway Company (SAUO)
FDDR.......... Field Deviation Disposition Request [*Nuclear energy*] (NRCH)
FDDRS.......... Facility Development Design and Review System [*Veterans Administration*] (GFGA)
FDDS.......... Fault Detection and Diagnosis System [*Automotive service electronics*]
FDDS.......... Federal Disability Determination Services (SAUS)
FdDS.......... Federated Department Stores, Inc. [*Associated Press*] (SAG)
FDDS.......... Federation of Dental Diagnostic Sciences [*Defunct*] (EA)
FDDS.......... Federation of Digestive Disease Societies [*Defunct*] (EA)
FDDS.......... FLAG [*FORTRAN Load and Go*] Data Display System (MCD)
FDDS.......... Flight Data Distribution System
FDDS.......... Frequency Division Discrimination Subsystem (ACAE)
FDDT.......... FDDI Full Duplex Technology (SAUS)
FDE.......... Faber Dictionary of Euphemisms (SAUS)
FDE.......... facility deactivated message (SAUS)
FDE.......... Failure Detection Electronics (ADWA)
FDE.......... Feachtas Dt-Armail Eithneach nah Eireann [*Irish Campaign for Nuclear Disarmament*] (EAIO)
FDE.......... Female-Day-Equivalent [*Entomology*]
FDE.......... Fetch-Decode-Execute (RALS)
FDE.......... Field Decelerator

FDE............. File Description Entry (SAUS)
FDE............. Final Drug Evaluation [*Pharmacology*] (DAVI)
FDE............. Finite Differential Equation (PDAA)
FDE............. Flaw Detection Equipment
FDE............. Flight Data Entry Device (IAA)
FDE............. Flight Dynamics Engineer (SSD)
FDE............. Fluid Dynamics Experiment (SAUS)
FDE............. Forde [*Norway*] [*Airport symbol*] (OAG)
FDE............. Frente Democratico Eleitoral [*Democratic Electoral Front*] [*Portugal*] [*Political party*] (PPE)
FDE............. Frequency Domain Experiment (AAEL)
FDE............. Full Duplex Ethernet [*Computer science*] (VERA)
FDE............. Functional Differential Equation
FDE............. Fund for Dental Education (SAUO)
FDEA............ Federal Drug Enforcement Administration (WDAA)
F de Ac........ Franciscus de Accursio [*Deceased, 1293*] [*Authority cited in pre-1607 legal work*] (DSA)
FDEBUG....... FORTRAN Debugging (SAUS)
FDEBUG....... FORTRAN Symbolic Debugging Package (SAUS)
FDEC............ Fluidyne Engineering Corporation (SAUO)
FDEC............ Forum for Death Education and Counseling [*Later, ADEC*] (EA)
FDEDIT........ Floppy Disc Editor (SAUS)
FDEF............ First Defiance Financial Corp. [*NASDAQ symbol*] (SAG)
FDEF............ First Defiance Fin'l [*NASDAQ symbol*] (TTSB)
FDEF............ First Federal Savings & Loan of Ohio [*NASDAQ symbol*] (SAG)
FDEG............ Democratic Forum of Guatemalan Exiles (SAUO)
FDEGX.......... Fidelity Aggressive Growth
FDEM............ Fuel Demand Evaluation Model (SAUS)
FDE Message... Facility Deactivated Message (SAUS)
FDEN............ Females, Density Of [*Ecology*]
FDEO............ Flight Development Engineering Order (MCD)
FDEOUG....... FORTRAN symbolic Debugging package (SAUS)
FDEP............ Final Draft Equipment Publication (MCD)
FDEP............ Flight Data Entry and Printout (ACAE)
FDEP............ Flight Data Entry Panel
FDEP............ Flight Data Entry Printout (SAUO)
FDEP............ Florida Department of Environmental Protection (BCP)
FDEP............ Formatted Data Entry Program [*Mohawk Data Systems*]
FDEPS.......... Fully Diluted Earnings Per Share (EBF)
FDER............ Florida Department of Environmental Regulations (DOGT)
F de Ramp... Franciscus de Ramponibus [*Deceased, 1401*] [*Authority cited in pre-1607 legal work*] (DSA)
FDES............ Framework for the Development of Environmental Statistics [*Australia*]
FDES............ Full Duplex EtherSwitch (SAUS)
F DES ASM VH... Failure to Designate an Assembled, Specially Constructed Vehicle [*Conviction term used in state of Oregon*] (MVRD)
FDESC.......... Force Description [*Military*] (DOMA)
FDESX.......... Fidelity Destiny Plan I [*Mutual fund ticker symbol*] (SG)
FDE system... Flight Data Entry system (SAUS)
FDET............ Force Development Experimentation Testing (MCD)
FDETX.......... Fidelity Destiny Plan II [*Mutual fund ticker symbol*] (SG)
FDEU............ Field Drainage Experimental Unit (PDAA)
F D EXMPT LT... Failure Display Exempt Vehicle Safety Lighting when Conditions Require [*Conviction term used in state of Oregon*] (MVRD)
FDF............. Failure Density Function
FDF............. Fast Death Factor [*Medicine*]
FDF............. Fiber Distribution Frame (SAUS)
FDF............. Fibre Distribution Frame [*Optics*] (EECA)
FDF............. File Description Files (SAUS)
FDF............. Flame Deflector Firex
FDF............. Flight Data File [*NASA*] (NASA)
FDF............. Flight Dynamics Facility (SSD)
FDF............. Flush Door Fastener
FDF............. Food and Drink Federation [*England and Belgium*]
FDF............. Food Defense Fund (EA)
FDF............. Footwear Distributors Federation [*British*] (BI)
FDF............. Foreign Disc Facility (SAUS)
FDF............. Form Die Forge (MCD)
FDF............. Forms Data Format (SAUS)
FDF............. Fort-De-France [*Martinique*] [*Airport symbol*] (OAG)
FDF............. Fort-De-France [*Martinique*] [*Seismograph station code, US Geological Survey*] (SEIS)
FDF............. Francis Drake Fellowship [*British*] (BI)
FDF............. Front Democratique des Bruxellois Francophones [*French-Speaking Democratic Front*] [*Belgium*] [*Political party*] (PPW)
FDF............. Fundamentally Different Factors [*Environmental Protection Agency*]
FDF............. Further Differentiated Fibroblast [*Cytology*]
FD Fan.......... Forced Draught Fan (SAUS)
FD-FDDI....... Full Duplex FDDI (SAUS)
FD/FF........... Flux Delta/Flux Flow (IEEE)
FDFFX.......... Fidelity Retirement Growth [*Mutual fund ticker symbol*] (SG)
FD/FI............ Fault Detection/Fault Isolation (ACAE)
FD/FL........... Fault Detection/Fault Location [*Military*] (CAAL)
FDFL............ Fluid Flow
FDFM............ Flight Data and Flow Management Group [*ICAO*] (DA)
FDFM............ Frequency Division/Frequency Modulation (SAUS)
FDFR............ Federal (SAUS)
FDFU............ Federation of Documentary Film Units [*British*] (BI)
FDG............. Feeding
FDG............. Fermi-Dirac Gas
FDG............. Fibiger-Debre-Gierki [*Syndrome*] [*Medicine*] (DB)
FDG............. Flight Director Group (MCD)
FDG............. Flight Dynamics Group [*NASA*] (KSC)
FDG............. Fluorescein Di(galactopyranoside) [*Organic chemistry*]
FDG............. Fluorodeoxyglucose [*Organic chemistry*]
FDG............. Fly Dressers Guild [*Pinner, Middlesex, England*] (EAIO)
FDG............. Fractional Doppler Gate
Fdg............. Funding (EBF)
FDG............. Funding
FDG............. Fur Dressers Guild (EA)
FDGB............ Freier Deutscher Gewerkschaftsbund [*Free German Trade Union Federation*] [*Germany*] [*Political party*] (PPE)
FDGC............ Federal Geographic Data Committee (SAUO)
FDGC............ Federated Guaranty Corporation (SAUO)
FDGD............ Nhlangano [*Swaziland*] [*ICAO location identifier*] (ICLI)
FDGE............ Fibroblast-Derived Growth Factor [*Medicine*] (DMAA)
FDGF............ Fibroblast-Derived Growth Factor (DB)
FDGL............ Lavumisa [*Swaziland*] [*ICAO location identifier*] (ICLI)
FDGM............ Final Defense Guidance Memorandum [*Navy*]
FDGRX.......... Fidelity Growth Company [*Mutual fund ticker symbol*] (SG)
FDGS............ Factory Data Gathering System (SAUS)
FDGS............ Feedings [*Medicine*] (EDAA)
FDGT............ Fluor Daniel/GTI [*NASDAQ symbol*] (TTSB)
FDGT............ Fluor Daniel GTI, Inc. [*NASDAQ symbol*] (SAG)
FDH............. Familial Dysalbuminemic Hyperthyroxinemia [*Medicine*]
FDH............. Federal Detention Headquarters (SAUO)
FDH............. Fixed Dynamical Heating [*Climatology*]
FDH............. Floating Divide or Halt
FDH............. Fluor Daniel Hanford Inc. (SAUO)
FDH............. Focal Dermal Hypoplasia [*Medicine*] (EDAA)
FDH............. Formate Dehydrogenase [*An enzyme*]
FDH............. Friedrichshafen [*Germany*] [*Airport symbol*] (OAG)
FDH............. Fully Documented History [*Automotive retailing*]
FDHD............ Floppy Disk High-Density [*Computer science*]
FDHD............ Floppy Drive High Density [*Computer science*]
FDHDB.......... Flight Deck Hazardous Duty Billet [*Navy*]
FDHDP.......... Flight Deck Hazardous Duty Pay [*Navy*]
FDHE............ Faculty Directory of Higher Education [*A publication*]
FdHL............ Federal Home Loan Mortgage Corp. [*Associated Press*] (SAG)
FdHLn........... Federal Home Loan Mortgage Corp. [*Associated Press*] (SAG)
FdHly............ Frederick's of Hollywood, Inc. [*Associated Press*] (SAG)
FDHM............ Full Duration Half Maximum [*Mathematics*]
FdHmLn........ Federal Home Loan Mortgage Corp. [*Associated Press*] (SAG)
FDHO............ Factory Department-Home Office (SAUO)
Fd Hosp....... Field Hospital (SAUS)
FDHP............ Full-Duplex Handshaking Protocol (RALS)
FDI............. Failure Detection and Identification (SAUS)
FDI............. Failure Detection and Isolation (MCD)
FDI............. Failure Detector Indicator (NASA)
FDI............. Farm Dairy Instructor (SAUO)
fdi.............. fat depth indicator (SAUS)
FDI............. Fault Detection and Identification (MCD)
FDI............. Fault Detection and Isolation (NASA)
FDI............. Federal Defense Laboratory (AAGC)
FDI............. Federal Department of Information (SAUO)
FDI............. Federal Deposit Insurance Corporation (SAUO)
FDI............. Federal Deposit Insurance Corp., Washington, DC [*OCLC symbol*] (OCLC)
FDI............. Federation Dentaire Internationale [*International Dental Federation*] [*British*] (EA)
FDI............. Feeder Distribution Interface [*Bell System*]
FD/I............. Field Dependence/Independence (EDAC)
FDI............. Field Director Indicator (OA)
FDI............. Field Discharge
FDI............. Field Displacement Isolator
FDI............. Field Disposition Instruction [*Nuclear energy*] (NRCH)
FDI............. Filmless Dental Imager (RDA)
FDI............. Fire Door Institute (SAUO)
FDI............. First Day of Issue [*Philately*]
FDI............. First Devonian Explorations [*Vancouver Stock Exchange symbol*]
FDI............. First Dorsal Interosseous Muscle [*Myology*]
fdi.............. fiteld discharge (SAUS)
FDI............. Flash Data Integrator (SAUS)
FDI............. Flight Detector Indicator (SAUS)
FDI............. Flight Direction Indicator
FDI............. Flight Direction Instrument (SAA)
FDI............. flight director indicator (SAUS)
FDI............. Fluidics Data Index (SAUS)
FDI............. Fluor Daniel, Inc. (SAUO)
FDI............. Follicle Development Index [*Gynecology*]
FDI............. Food and Disarmament International [*Belgium*] (EAIO)
FDI............. Foreign Direct Investment
FDI............. Formal Documents Issued [*Federal Power Commission*]
FDI............. Form Die Impact (MCD)
FDI............. Frequency-Domain Inequality (SAUS)
FDI............. Frequency Domain Instrument (SAUS)
FDI............. Frequency Domain Interferometer (MCD)
FDI............. Fuel Delivery Indicator (SAUS)
FDI............. Fuel Desulphurization, Inc.
FDI............. Furnish, Deliver and Install (IAA)
FDI............. Poplar Bluff, MO [*Location identifier*] [*FAA*] (FAAL)
FDI & R........ Failure Detection Identification and Control System Reconfiguration (MCD)
FDIC............ Federal Deposit Insurance Corp. [*Independent government agency*] [*Database*]
FDIC............ Fire Department Instructors Conference (EA)
FDIC............ Flying Days per Inspection Cycle [*Air Force*] (AFIT)
FDIC............ Food and Drink Industries Council [*British*]

FDIC............ Front for the Defense of Constitutional Institutions (Morocco) [*Political party*] (PSAP)
FDICA......... Foundations and Donors Interested in Catholic Activities (EA)
FDICIA........ Federal Deposit Insurance Corporation Improvement Act (ECON)
F Dict.......... Kames and Woodhouselee's Folio Dictionary, Scotch Court of Session [*A publication*] (DLA)
FDIF............ Federation Democratique Internationale des Femmes [*Women's International Democratic Federation - WIDF*] [*Germany*] (EAIO)
FDIIR.......... Fault Detection, Isolation, Identification, and Recompensation (NASA)
FDIM........... Federacion Democratica Internacional de Mujeres [*Women's International Democratic Federation*]
F-DIM......... Fluorescence Digital Imaging Microscopy
F DIM LT..... Failure to Dim Lights when Approaching on Coming Vehicle or when Following Vehicle [*Conviction term used in state of Oregon*] (MVRD)
F DIM PK VH... Failure to Dim Headlights when Vehicle is Parked [*Conviction term used in state of Oregon*] (MVRD)
FDIO........... Flight Data Input/Output [*Aviation*] (FAAC)
FDIOR......... Flight Data Input/Output Repeater [*Aviation*] (FAAC)
FDIR........... Fault Detection Identification and Recognition (SAUS)
FDIR........... Fault Detection Identification and Recovery (SAUS)
FDIR........... Fault Detection Identification/Isolation and Recovery (or Recognition) (SAUS)
FDIR........... Fault Detection Isolation and Recognition (SAUS)
FDIR........... Fault Detection Isolation and Recovery (SAUS)
FDIR........... Fronteer Directory [*NASDAQ symbol*] (TTSB)
FDIR........... Fronteer Directory Co., Inc. [*NASDAQ symbol*] (NQ)
FDIR........... Fronteer Financial Holdings Ltd. [*NASDAQ symbol*] (SAG)
FDIS............ Fault Detection and Isolation Subsystem (RDA)
FDIS............ Final Draft International Standard (RALS)
FDIS............ Flight Displays and Interface System (NVT)
FDIS............ Free Discharge (RIMS)
FDIS............ Freeway Driver Information System
FDISK......... Fixed Disk (ADWA)
FDI Substation... Furnish, Deliver, and Install Substation (SAUS)
FDI System... Failure Detection and Identification System (SAUS)
FDIT............ Federal Daily Income Trust (SAUO)
FDI Technique... Failure Detection and Identification Technique (SAUS)
FDIU........... Fetal Death in Utero [*Medicine*]
FDIU........... Flight Data Interface Unit (SAUS)
FDIUS......... Foreign Direct Investment in the United States (JAGO)
FDIUS......... Foreign Direct Investment in the U.S. (SAUO)
FDIV........... Floating Divide (SAUS)
FDIZ............ Fort Drum Industrial [*Federal Railroad Administration identification code*]
FDJ............. Filles de Jesus [*Sons of Jesus*] [*Religious order*]
FDJ............. Free Diffusion Junction [*Electrochemistry*]
FDJ............. Freie Deutsche Jugend [*Free German Youth*] [*Germany*] [*Political party*] (PPE)
FDJA........... Faroudja, Inc. [*NASDAQ symbol*] (NASQ)
FDK............. Forecastle Deck [*Naval engineering*]
FDK............. Frederick, MD [*Location identifier*] [*FAA*] (FAAL)
FDL............. FAAD [*Forward Area Air Defense*] Data Link [*Army*]
FDL............. Facility Data Link [*Computer science*] (DINT)
FDL............. Fast Deployment Logistics [*Environmental science*] (COE)
FDL............. Feature Definition Language (SAUS)
FDL............. Ferndale [*Cardiff*] [*Welsh depot code*]
FDL............. Ferrite Diode Limiter (IAA)
FDL............. Ferrite Diode Limiting (SAUS)
FDL............. Fick Diffusion Law
FDL............. Fieldbus Data Link (SAUS)
FDL............. File Definition Language [*Computer science*] (VERA)
FDL............. Final Determination Letter (GNE)
FDL............. Fish Disease Leaflet
FDL............. Fixed Delay Line
FDL............. Fleet Deployment Logistic (SAUS)
FDL............. Fleur-de-Lys [*Heraldry*]
FDL............. Flexible and Distance Learning (SAUS)
FDL............. Flexor Digitorum Longus [*Muscle or nerve*] [*Anatomy*] (DAVI)
FDL............. Flight Determination Laboratory [*WSMR*]
FDL............. Flight Director Loop (MCD)
FDL............. Food and Drug Laboratory (SAUO)
FDL............. Foremost Defence Line (SAUS)
FDL............. Foremost [*or Forward*] Defended Localities [*or Locations*] [*British*]
FDL............. Foremost Defended Locality (SAUS)
FDL............. Form Definition Language [*Xerox*] (NITA)
FDL............. Forms Description Language [*Computer science*] (MHDB)
FDL............. Forward Defended Locality [*Military*] [*British*]
FDL............. Frequency Double LASER
FDL............. Fuehrer der Luft [*Air liaison officer with Navy*] [*German military - World War II*]
FDLA........... Florida Defense Lawyers Association (SRA)
FDLA........... Florida Dental Laboratory Association (SRA)
FDLAC......... Fond Du Lac, WI [*American Association of Railroads railroad junction routing code*]
FDlb............ Delray Beach Library, Delray Beach, FL [*Library symbol*] [*Library of Congress*] (LCLS)
FDLBX......... Mgn. Stanley D. Witter Fed. Secs. Tr. Cl.B [*Mutual fund ticker symbol*] (SG)
FDLC........... Fibre Digital Loop Carrier (SAUS)
FDLD........... Federal Defense Laboratory Diversification (AAGC)
FDLD........... Frequency Doubling LASER Device
FDLDG......... Forced Landing (IAA)
FDLDP......... Federal Defense Laboratory Diversification Program (RDA)
FDLE............ Florida Department of Law Enforcement (DEMM)
FDLH........... Flight Determination Laboratory, Holloman Air Force Base
FDLI............ Food and Drug Law Institute
FdLio........... Food Lion, Inc. [*Associated Press*] (SAG)
FdLioA......... Food Lion, Inc. [*Associated Press*] (SAG)
FdLioB......... Food Lion, Inc. [*Associated Press*] (SAG)
FDLMP......... First Day of Last Menstrual Period [*Gynecology and obstetrics*] (DAVI)
FDLN........... Feedline (NASA)
FDLN........... Food Lion, Inc. [*NASDAQ symbol*] (NASQ)
FDLN........... Forced-Draft, Low-Nitrogen Oxide [*Combustion engineering*]
FDLNA......... Food Lion Inc. Cl'A' [*NASDAQ symbol*] (TTSB)
FDLNB......... Food Lion Inc. Cl'B' [*NASDAQ symbol*] (TTSB)
FDLP........... Daughters of Providence (TOCD)
FDLP........... Federal Depository Library Program (AEPA)
FD/LS......... Fault Detection/Location Subsystem
FDLS........... Fiji Department of Lands and Survey (SAUS)
FDLS........... Finite-Dimensional Linear System (SAUS)
FDL Ships.... Fast Development Logistic Ships (SAUS)
FDLUQ......... Fronte Democratica Liberale dell'Uomo Qualunque [*Liberal Democratic Front of the Common Man*] [*Italy*] [*Political party*] (PPE)
FDLV........... Fer de Lance Virus [*Medicine*] (EDAA)
f-dm-........... Dahomey [*Benin*] [*MARC geographic area code*] [*Library of Congress*] (LCCP)
FDM............ Facility Density Mapper
FDM............ Facility description manual (SAUS)
FDM............ Faraday Disc Machine
FDM............ Feasibility Demonstration Model
FDM............ Fetus of Diabetic Mother [*Medicine*] (EDAA)
FDM............ Fibrous Dysplasia of the Mandible [*Medicine*] (EDAA)
FDM............ field desorption microscopy (SAUS)
FDM............ Field Maintenance (SAUS)
FDM............ File Definition Macroinstruction (SAUS)
FDM............ Fill and Drain Module (ACAE)
FDM............ Final Draft Manuscript
FDM............ Finite Difference Method [*Mathematics*]
FDM............ Finite Differential Method (SAUS)
FDM............ First Dynasty Mines (SAUO)
FDM............ Five Digit Multiplier (SAUS)
FDM............ Fleet Demonstration Model (ACAE)
FDM............ Flight Data Manager (MCD)
FDM............ Fokker Defence Marketing (SAUS)
FDM............ Formal Development Method [*Computer science*]
FDM............ Formal Development Methodology (SAUS)
FDM............ Form Description Macro (SAUS)
FDM............ Freedom Airlines, Inc. [*ICAO designator*] (FAAC)
FDM............ Frequence Division Multiplexing (SAUS)
FDM............ Frequency Data Multiplexer (NASA)
FDM............ Frequency Demodulation (SAUS)
FDM............ Frequency Deviation Meter
FDM............ Frequency Diversity Multiplex (SAUS)
FDM............ Frequency-Division Modulation [*Telecommunications*] (IAA)
FDM............ Frequency-Division Multiplex [*or Multiplexing*] [*Telecommunications*]
FDM............ Frequency Division Multiplexor (SAUS)
FDM............ Frequency-Division Mutliplexing (SAUS)
FDM............ Full Descriptive Method
FDM............ Functional Development Model (MCD)
FDM............ Fundamental Design Method
FDM............ Fund for a Democratic Majority (EA)
FDM............ Fused Deposition Method (SAUS)
FDM............ Fused Deposition Modeling
F-DMA......... Farm-Direct Market Association (SAUO)
FDMA.......... Ferrocarril de Minatitlan al Carmen [*AAR code*]
FDMA.......... Fibre Drum Manufacturers Association [*Defunct*]
FDMA.......... Frequency Division Multiple Access [*Telecommunications*] (MCD)
FDMA.......... Frequency Division Multiple/Multiplex Access (SAUS)
FDMA.......... Frequency-Domain Multiple Access (SAUS)
FDMA.......... Full Diameter Motorized Door Assembly (SAUS)
FDMB.......... Mbabane [*Swaziland*] [*ICAO location identifier*] (ICLI)
FDMC.......... First Data Management Company (SAUO)
FDMC.......... Fiscal Director of the Marine Corps
FDMCN........ Flight Data Management and Communications Network (MCD)
FDMD.......... Foundation for Depression and Manic Depression (EA)
FDM-FM...... Frequency Division Multiplexed -- Frequency Modulated (SAUS)
FDM/FM...... Frequency Division Multiplex/Frequency Modulation [*Telecommunications*] (TEL)
FDMH.......... Mhlume [*Swaziland*] [*ICAO location identifier*] (ICLI)
FDMHA........ Frederick Douglass Memorial and Historical Association (EA)
F D MH PLT... Failure to Display Mobile Home Registration Plate [*Conviction term used in state of Oregon*] (MVRD)
FDMI........... Function Management Data Interpreter (SAUS)
FDMIS......... Force Development Management Information System [*Army*]
FDMP.......... Fault Detection Major Program (SAUO)
FDMP.......... Foundation for the Development of Medical Psychotherapy [*Switzerland*] (EAIO)
FDMR.......... Fluorescence-Detected Magnetic Resonance [*Physics*]
FDMS.......... Factory Data-Management System (SAUS)
FDMS.......... Federation of Deer Management Societies [*British*] (DBA)
FD-MS......... Field Desorption - Mass Spectrometry
FD/MS......... Field desorption mass spectrometry (SAUS)
FDMS.......... Flash Desorption Mass Spectrometry (AAEL)
FDMS.......... Flight Data Management System [*Air Force*] (AFM)
FDMS.......... Floppy Disc Management System (NITA)
FDMS.......... Floppy Disk Management System (SAUS)
FDMS.......... Force Development Management Information System [*Army*] (MCD)

FDMS.......... Frequency-Division Multiplexing System [*Radio*] (MCD)
FDMS.......... Manzini/Matsapa [*Swaziland*] [*ICAO location identifier*] (ICLI)
FDMU.......... Flight Data Management Unit (HLLA)
FDMVC.......... Frequency-Division Multiplex Voice Communication
FDN.......... Field Designator Number [*Air Force*] (AFM)
FDN.......... File Definition Name (SAUS)
Fdn.......... Fonodan [*Record label*] [*Denmark*]
FDN.......... Foreign Directory Name [*Telecommunications*] (TEL)
Fdn.......... Foundation (AL)
fdn.......... Foundation (BEE)
FDN.......... Foundation (KSC)
FDN.......... Frente Democratico Nacional [*Electoral Alliance*] [*Mexico*] (EY)
FDN.......... Fuerza Democratica Nicaraguense [*Nicaraguan Democratic Force*] (PD)
FDN.......... Future Digital Network (MCD)
FDNB.......... Fluoro-2, 4-Dinitrobenzene (ADWA)
FDNB.......... Fluorodinitrobenzene [*Also, DFB, DNFB*] [*Organic chemistry*]
FDNC.......... Frequency Dependent Negative Conductance [*Physics*]
FDND.......... Facility delayed-neutron detector (SAUS)
FDNDEA.......... Fluoro(dinitro)diethylaniline [*Organic chemistry*]
FDNET.......... Fighter Direction Net [*Navy*]
FDNG.......... Feeding
FDNG.......... New Guatemalan Democratic Front [*Political party*] (PSAP)
FDNGL.......... Flush Deck Nose Gear Launch (MCD)
FDN-Mountounchi... Nigerian Democratic Front-Mountounchi (Niger) [*Political party*] (PSAP)
FDNR.......... Florida Department of Natural Resources (BCP)
FDNR.......... Frequency Dependent Negative Resistance [*Physics*]
FDNSC.......... Daughters of Our Lady of the Sacred Heart (TOCD)
FDNW.......... Fluor Daniel Northwest (SAUS)
FDNW.......... Fluor Daniel Northwest Services (SAUS)
FDO.......... Faculty of Dispensing Opticians [*British*]
FDO.......... Family Dollar Stores [*NYSE symbol*] (TTSB)
FDO.......... Family Dollar Stores, Inc. [*NYSE symbol*] (SPSG)
FDO.......... Fee Determination Official (NASA)
FDO.......... Field Director Overseas [*Red Cross*]
FDO.......... Fighter Director Officer [*Navy*]
FDO.......... Fighter Duty Officer
FDO.......... Final Dive Order (SAUS)
FDO.......... Fire Direction Officer [*Army*] (AABC)
FDO.......... Fleet Aircraft Direction Officer [*Navy*] [*British*]
FDO.......... Fleet Dental Officer
FDO.......... Flexible Deterrent Operations (SEWL)
FDO.......... Flexible Deterrent Option [*Environmental science*] (COE)
FDO.......... Flight Deck Officer [*British military*] (DMA)
FDO.......... Flight Duty Officer [*Air Force*] (AFM)
FDO.......... Flight Dynamics Officer [*NASA*] (KSC)
FDO.......... Food Distribution Order
FDO.......... Force Direction Officer (SAUS)
FDO.......... For Declaration Purposes Only (MARI)
FDO.......... Frequency Difference Detector (SAUS)
FDO.......... Frequency Domain Oscilloscope (SAUS)
FDO.......... Fritz Darmstadt Online (SAUS)
FDO.......... Functional Device Object [*Computer science*] (MWOL)
FDO.......... Fuse Delay Override (ACAE)
FDoA.......... Flying Doctors of America [*An association*] (EA)
FDOC.......... Fire Detection Operation Center
FDOC.......... Fraction of degradable organic carbon (SAUS)
FD:OCA.......... Formatted Data: Object Content Architecture (CDE)
FDOI.......... First Day of Issue [*Philately*]
FDOMEZ.......... Frente Democratico Oriental de Mexico Emiliano Zapata [*Political party*] (EY)
FDOP.......... Filtered Detection Only Processor (CAAL)
FDOR.......... Final Design and Operations Review (SAUS)
FDOR.......... Flavoprotein Disulfide Oxidoreductase [*An enzyme*]
FDOR.......... Flight Design Operations Review (MCD)
FDOR.......... Four-Door Car (TRID)
FDOS.......... Floppy Disc Operating System (SAUS)
FDOS.......... Floppy Disk Operating System [*Computer science*] (IEEE)
FDOS.......... Franklin Computer Corp. (MHDW)
FDOS.......... Frequency Domain Optical Storage System [*Computer science*]
FDOS.......... Functional Disk Operating System [*Computer science*] (VLIE)
F D OS PLT... Failure to Display, or Improper Display of Out of State Registration Plates [*Conviction term used in state of Oregon*] (MVRD)
FDP.......... Daughters of Divine Providence (TOCD)
FDP.......... Democratic and Patriotic Forces (Rep. Of Congo) [*Political party*] (PSAP)
FDP.......... Factory Data Processing (IAA)
FDP.......... Falling Dilute-Phase (PDAA)
FDP.......... Faridpur [*Bangladesh*] [*Airport symbol*] (AD)
FDP.......... Fast Delivery Processor [*Computer science*] (EERA)
FDP.......... Fast Digital Processor [*Computer science*]
FDP.......... Fatigue Decreased Proficiency [*NASA*] (SPST)
FDP.......... FDP Corp. [*Associated Press*] (SAG)
FDP.......... Feasibility Demonstration Program (SAUO)
FDP.......... Fibrin [*or Fibrinogen*] Degradation Products [*Hematology*]
FDP.......... Fibrinogen Degradation Products (SAUS)
FDP.......... Field Data Processing
f/dp.......... field despatch (SAUS)
FDP.......... Field-Developed Program (SAUS)
FDP.......... Field Development Program [*LIMRA*]
FDP.......... Fighter Development Program (SAUS)
FDP.......... Fighter Director Post
FDP.......... Filii Divinae Providentiae [*Sons or Daughters of Divine Providence*] [*Roman Catholic religious order*]
FDP.......... Filter Drainage Protection (SAUS)
FDP.......... Final Design Presentation (NOAA)
FDP.......... Financially Disadvantaged Person
FDP.......... Firmware Development Plan
FDP.......... Fixed Dose Procedure [*Proposed toxicological standard*]
FDP.......... Fixture Data Processor
FDP.......... Flare Dispenser Pod
FDP.......... Flat Domains Propagation (VLIE)
FDP.......... flat panel display (SAUS)
FDP.......... Flexor Digitorum Profundus [*Anatomy*]
FDPIR.......... Flexor Distal Phalanx [*Anatomy*] (DAVI)
FDP.......... Flight Data Processing (KSC)
FDP.......... Flight Demonstration Program (MCD)
FDP.......... Floating Divide or Proceed (SAA)
FDP.......... Flood Damage Prevention [*Type of water project*]
FDP.......... Florida Power Corporation (SAUO)
FDP.......... Flow Diagram Processor (VLIE)
FDP.......... Fluid Dynamics Panel (SAUS)
FDP.......... Flying Duty Period (DA)
FDP.......... Food Distribution Program [*Department of Agriculture*]
FDP.......... Foreign Duty Pay
FDP.......... Form Description Program [*Computer science*] (ELAL)
FDP.......... Form Die Press (MCD)
FDP.......... Forms Description Program (VLIE)
FDP.......... FORTRAN Debug Package (SAUS)
FDP.......... Forward Defence Post (SAUS)
FDP.......... Forward Defense Post (NATG)
FDP.......... Forward Defensive Position (SAUS)
FDP.......... Forward Direction Post (SAUS)
FDP.......... Forward Director Post
FDP.......... Forward Distribution Point [*Military*]
FDP.......... Foxboro (SAUS)
FDP.......... Foxboro Display Packages (NITA)
FDP.......... Free Democrat Party [*Turkey*] [*Political party*]
FDP.......... Freedom Democratic Party [*in Mississippi*]
F/Dp.......... Free of Dispatch (SAUS)
FDP.......... Freeze Desalination Plant
FDP.......... Freie Demokratische Partei [*Free Democratic Party*] [*Germany*] [*Political party*] (EAIO)
FDP.......... Freisinnig-Demokratische Partei der Schweiz [*Radical Democratic Party of Switzerland*] (PPW)
FDP.......... Fresh Del Monte Produce [*NYSE symbol*] (SG)
FDP.......... Fronto-Dextra Posterior [*A fetal position*] [*Obstetrics*]
FDP.......... Frontul Democratic Popular [*Democratic Popular Front*] [*Romania*] [*Political party*] (PPE)
fdp.......... fructose 1,6-diphosphate (SAUS)
FDP.......... Fructose Diphosphate [*Biochemistry*]
FDP.......... Full Dog Point (MSA)
FDP.......... Full Drive Pulse (VLIE)
FDP.......... Funded Delivery Period [*DoD*]
FDP.......... Future Data Processor (IAA)
FDP.......... Sons of Divine Providence (TOCD)
fdp.......... Sons of Divine Providence (TOCD)
FDPA.......... Flood Disaster Protection Act (SAUS)
FDPA.......... Fog Dam Protected Area (SAUS)
FDPA.......... Fogg Dam Protected Area (SAUS)
FDPase.......... Fructose Diphosphatase [*An enzyme*]
FDPB.......... Fatigue-Decreased Proficiency Boundary
FDPC.......... FDP Corp. [*NASDAQ symbol*] (SAG)
FDPC.......... Financial Data Planning Corp. (EFIS)
FDPC.......... Fluorimetric Determination of Plasma Cortisol [*Clinical chemistry*]
FDPIR.......... Food Distribution Program on Indian Reservations [*Department of Agriculture*] (GFGA)
FDPL.......... Fluid Pressure Line (MSA)
F D PLT.......... Failure to Display Registration Plates [*Conviction term used in state of Oregon*] (MVRD)
FDPM.......... Final Draft, Presidential Memorandum [*DoD*]
FDPM.......... Fondation pour le Developpement de la Psychotherapie Medicale [*Foundation for t he Development of Medical Psychotherapy*] [*Switzerland*] (EAIO)
FDPM.......... Front Democratique des Patriotes Maliens [*Mali*] [*Political party*] (EY)
FDPO.......... Field Post Office [*Military*] [*British*]
FDPO.......... Floating Decimal Point Operation (SAUS)
FDPO.......... Foreign Disclosure Policy Office [*Military*] (AFIT)
FDPP.......... Framework Demonstration Projects Program (SAUS)
FDPS.......... Field Developed Programs [*Computer science*]
FDPS.......... Flight Data Processing System (DA)
FDPSI.......... Faculty Development Public Service Initiative (SAUS)
FDPSK.......... Frequency Differential Phase Shift Keyed (SAUS)
FD/PSK.......... Frequency-Differential/Phase-Shift Keyed System [*Computer science*] (TEL)
FDPSK.......... Frequency Differential Phase-Shift Keying (SAUS)
FDPSK.......... Frequency Differential PSK (SAUS)
FDQA.......... Flight Development Quality Assurance (MCD)
FDQB.......... Flexor Digiti Quinti Brevis [*Muscle or nerve*] [*Anatomy*] (DAVI)
FDR.......... Democratic Front of Renewal (Niger) [*Political party*] (PSAP)
FDR.......... Facility Data Report [*Nuclear energy*]
FDR.......... Facility Development Research (SAUS)
FDR.......... Fact, Discussion, Recommendations
FDR.......... Fahrdienstregelement [*Traffic Service Regulations*] [*German*]
FDR.......... Fairleigh Dickinson University, Rutherford, NJ [*OCLC symbol*] (OCLC)
FDR.......... Fast Dump Restore (IAA)
FDR.......... Federal Air P Ltd. [*South Africa*] [*FAA designator*] (FAAC)
FDR.......... Federal Document Retrieval [*Information service or system*] (IID)

FDR .... Federation of Drum Reconditioners [*British*] (DBA)
FDR .... Feeder
fdr .... field data recorder (SAUS)
FDR .... Field Definition Record (IAA)
FDR .... File Data Register [*Computer science*]
FDR .... File Descriptor Record [*Computer science*] (TIMI)
FDR .... Final Data Report
FDR .... Final Design Report [*Nuclear Regulatory Commission*] (GFGA)
FDR .... Finder (MSA)
FDR .... Fire Door (AAG)
FDR .... First Allied Resources Corp. [*Vancouver Stock Exchange symbol*]
FDR .... First Degree Relatives
FDR .... Fix Dump Reducer (SAA)
FDR .... Flight Data Recorder
FDR .... Floating Divide Remainder (VLIE)
FDR .... Flood Damage Reduction (SAUS)
F dr .... fluid dram (SAUS)
FDR .... Fluorogenic Drug Reagent [*Clinical chemistry*]
FDR .... Formal Design Review (POLM)
FDR .... Formal Dining Room (ADWA)
FDR .... Format Description Record (SAUS)
FDR .... Formatted Data Record (SAUS)
FDR .... Forward Dispersion Relation (SAUS)
fdr .... Founder (PROS)
FDR .... Founder
FDR .... Fractional Disappearance Rate [*Medicine*] (EDAA)
FDR .... Frame Drop Rate (SAUS)
FDR .... Framework-Determining Region [*Immunogenetics*]
FDR .... Franklin Delano Roosevelt [*US president, 1882-1945*]
FDR .... Franklin Delano Roosevelt-thirty-second President of the United States (SAUS)
FDR .... Frederick, OK [*Location identifier*] [*FAA*] (FAAL)
FDR .... Frente Democratico Contra la Represion [*Democratic Front Against Repression*] [*Guatemala*] [*Political party*] (PD)
FDR .... Frequency Dependent Rejection [*Telecommunications*] (TEL)
FDR .... Frequency Diversity RADAR
FDR .... Frequency Domain Reflectometer (SAUS)
FDR .... Frequency Domain Reflectometry
FDR .... Frequency Doubling Recording (VLIE)
F/DR .... Front Door [*Automotive engineering*]
FDR .... Full dump restore (SAUS)
FDR .... Functional Demonstration Requirement (AAG)
FDR .... Functional Design Requirements (NRCH)
FDR .... Functional Design Review (MCD)
FDR .... Future Digital Radio [*Army*]
FDRA .... Footwear Distributors and Retailers of America (EA)
FDRAKE .... First Dynamic Response and Kinematics Experiment (SAUO)
FDRAM .... Fount Description Random Access Memory (NITA)
FDRB .... Foreign Disclosure Review Board (AAGC)
FDRC .... Federal Dispute Resolution Conference (SAUO)
FDRC .... Federal Resources Corporation (SAUO)
FDRC .... Flood Damage Rehabilitation Committee (SAUO)
FDRC .... follicular dendritic reticulum cell (SAUS)
FDRC-UK .... UKs Felixstowe Dock and Railway Co. (SAUS)
FDRC-UK .... United Kingdom Felixstowe Dock and Railway Co. (SAUO)
FDRE .... Fondation Denis de Rougemont pour l'Europe [*Switzerland*] (EAIO)
FDRF .... Financial Data Records Folder (MUGU)
FDRFA .... Flight Data Recorder and Fault Analyzer [*Military*]
FDRFC .... Friends of Debbie Reynolds Fan Club (EA)
FDR-FMLN .... Frente Democratico Revolucionario - Farabundo Marti de Liberacion Nacional [*Democratic Revolutionary Front/Farabundo Marti National Liberation Front*] [*El Salvador*] [*Political party*] (EY)
FDR/FMLN .... Frente Democratico Revolucionario / Farabundo Marti para la Liberacion Nacional [*Democratic Revolutionary Front/Farabundo Marti National Liberation Front*] [*Guatemala*] [*Political party*]
FDRG .... Fluid Dynamics Research Group [*MIT*] (MCD)
FDRHS .... Franklin Delano Roosevelt High School (SAUO)
FDRI .... Family and Demographic Research Institute [*Brigham Young University*] [*Research center*] (RCD)
FDRI .... Flight Director Rate Indicator (KSC)
FDRI .... Fluid Dynamics Research Institute (SAUS)
FDRL .... Fluid Dynamics Research Laboratory [*MIT*] (MCD)
FDRL .... Franklin Delano Roosevelt Library (SAUS)
FDRL .... Franklin D. Roosevelt Library
FDRMA .... Flooring Division, Rubber Manufacturers Association (EA)
FDRMC .... Franklin Delano Roosevelt Memorial Commission (SAUO)
FDROTFL .... Falling Down Rolling on the Floor Laughing (ADWA)
FDRPS .... Franklin D. Roosevelt Philatelic Society [*Defunct*] (EA)
FDRS .... Fire Department Rescue Squad (SAUO)
FDRS .... Flight Data Recording System
FDRS .... Flight Display Research System
FDRS .... Food Distribution Research Society (EA)
FDRS .... Functional Description Requirements Specification [*Army*]
FDRT .... Flexible Digital Receiving Terminal
FDRTD .... Federated
FDRY .... Foundry (KSC)
fdry .... Foundry (MIST)
FDS .... FactSet Research Systems [*NYSE symbol*] (SG)
FDS .... Factset Research Systems, Inc. [*NYSE symbol*] (SAG)
FDS .... Failure detection subsystem (SAUS)
FDS .... Fallout Decay Simulation (OA)
FDS .... Faraday Dark Space
FDS .... Fast-access Disk Subsystem (SAUS)
FDS .... Fast Data Store (SAUS)
FDS .... Fast Diode Switch
FDS .... Fast Drive Scanner (SAUS)
FDS .... Fathometer Depth Sounder
FDS .... Fault Detection System [*Environmental science*] (COE)
FDS .... Fax Deprivation Syndrome (WDAA)
FDS .... Federated Department Stores, Inc. (SAUO)
FDS .... Fellow of Dental Surgery [*British*]
FDS .... Feminine Deodorant Spray [*Initialism used as brand name*]
FDS .... Fence Disturbance System [*Military*]
FDS .... Fermi Dirac Sommerfeld (SAUS)
FDS .... Fermi-Dirac Statistics
FDS .... Ferrite Disk Store (SAUS)
FDS .... Field Dental Section (SAUO)
FDS .... Field-Discharge Switch (SAUS)
FDS .... Field Dressing Station [*Military*] (NATG)
FDS .... Field Separator (VLIE)
FDS .... Fighter Data Storage (IAA)
FDS .... Fighter Director Ship [*Navy*]
FDS .... File Definition Statement (SAUS)
FDS .... File Description Subsystem (SAUS)
FDS .... File Description System [*Computer science*] (PDAA)
FDS .... Filter Difference Spectrometer (SAUS)
FDS .... Finance Disbursing Section [*Army*]
FDS .... Financial Data Sciences, Inc. (SAUO)
FDS .... Financial Data System (SAUS)
FDS .... Financial management Display System (SAUS)
FDS .... Finsbury Data Services Ltd. [*Database*] [*London, England*]
FDS .... Fire Detection and Suppression (SAUS)
FDS .... Fire Detection System
FDS .... Fire Direction System (SAUS)
FDS .... Fire Distribution System
FDS .... Firmware Design Specification
FDS .... First Development System (MCD)
fds .... fixed disc store (SAUS)
FDS .... Fixed Disc Stores (NITA)
FDS .... Fixed-Disk Storage (SAUS)
FDS .... Fixed Distributed Subsystem [*Antisubmarine warfare*] (MCD)
FDS .... Fixed Distribution System [*Acoustic antisubmarine warfare sensor*] (DOMA)
FDS .... Flare Detection System (KSC)
FDS .... Flash Detection Sensor (ACAE)
FDS .... Fleet Dental Surgeon [*Navy*] [*British*]
FDS .... Fleet Digital System (MCD)
FDS .... flexible disc system (SAUS)
FDS .... Flexible Disk System
FDS .... Flexible Display System
FDS .... Flexible Drive Shaft
FDS .... Flexor Digitorum Sublimis [*Muscle or nerve*] [*Anatomy*] (DAVI)
FDS .... Flexor Digitorum Superficialis [*Anatomy*]
FDS .... Flight Data Subsystem (SAUS)
FDS .... Flight Data System [*NASA*]
FDS .... Flight Design and Scheduling (MCD)
FDS .... Flight Design System (NASA)
FDS .... Flight Director System (NATG)
FDS .... Flight Dynamics Simulator (MCD)
FDS .... Flight Dynamics Software [*or System*] (MCD)
FDS .... Flight Dynamics System (ACAE)
FDS .... Float Dollar Sign (SAUS)
FDS .... floppy disc system (SAUS)
FDS .... Floppy Disk System [*Computer science*]
FDS .... Fluid Density Sensor (SAUS)
FDS .... Fluid Distribution System (KSC)
FDS .... For Duration of [*Hospital*] Stay (CPH)
FDS .... Foreign Agriculture Service (SAUS)
FDS .... Form Die-Swage
FDS .... FORTRAN [*Formula Translating System*] Deductive System [*Computer science*] (IAA)
FDs .... Forward Definitions (SAUS)
FDS .... Forward Delivery Squadron [*British military*] (DMA)
FDS .... Forward Dressing Station [*Military*] [*British*]
FDS .... Fourier Descriptor (SAUS)
FDS .... fractional diameter shortening (SAUS)
FDS .... Frame Difference Signal
FDS .... Frente Democratica Social [*Democratic Social Front*] [*Guinea-Bissau*] [*Political party*] (EY)
FDS .... Frequency Division Separator [*Multiplexing*]
FDS .... Frequency Division Switching [*Radio and television broadcasting*]
FDS .... Friends Disaster Service (EA)
FDS .... Fuels Dispensing System (SAUO)
FDS .... Functional Design Specifications (MCD)
FDS .... Functionally Distributed Simulation (SAUS)
FDS .... Function Defining Statement (SAUS)
FDS .... function definition sheet (SAUS)
FDS .... Fusion Display System (SAUS)
FDS .... Stetson University, De Land, FL [*Library symbol*] [*Library of Congress*] (LCLS)
FDSA .... Force Development System Agency [*DoD*]
FD/SC .... Failure Definitions/Scoring Criteria (AABC)
FDSC .... Flight Dynamics Simulation Complex (MCD)
FDSC .... Flight Dynamics Situation Complex (NASA)
FDSCR .... Friends of Dorothy Society of Change Ringers (WDAA)
FdScrw .... Federal Screw Works [*Associated Press*] (SAG)
FDSE .... Full-Duplex Switched Ethernet (CDE)
FDSG .... Freeze-Dried (Allogenic) Skin Graft [*Medicine*]
FDSH .... Full Dodge Service History [*Automotive classified advertising*]
FDSIS .... Flight Deck System Integration Simulator

FDS-L .... Stetson University College of Law, St. Petersburg, FL [*Library symbol*] [*Library of Congress*] (LCLS)
FDSR .... floppy disc send receive (SAUS)
FDSR .... Floppy Disk Send/Receive [*Computer science*]
FDSRCPSGlas... Fellow in Dental Surgery of the Royal College of Physicians and Surgeons of Glasgow
FDSRCPS Glasg... Fellow in Dental Surgery of the Royal College of Physicians and Surgeons of Glasgow
FDSRCS....... Fellow in Dental Surgery of the Royal College of Surgeons of England (SAUO)
FDSRCSE..... Fellow in Dental Surgery of the Royal College of Surgeons of Edinburgh
FDSRCSEd... Fellow in Dental Surgery of the Royal College of Surgeons of Edinburgh (SAUS)
FDSRCS Edin... Fellow in Dental Surgery of the Royal College of Surgeons of Edinburgh
FDSRCS Eng... Fellow in Dental Surgery of the Royal College of Surgeons of England (SAUO)
FDSS .... Fault Detection Subsystem [*Environmental science*] (COE)
FDSS .... Fine Digital Sun Sensor (SAUS)
FDSSA .... Fine Digital Sun Sensor Assembly (SAUS)
FDSSR .... Flight Dynamics Staff Support Room [*Apollo*] [*NASA*]
FDSSS .... Flight Deck Status Signaling System (MCD)
FDST........... Siteki [*Swaziland*] [*ICAO location identifier*] (ICLI)
FD Statistics... Fermi-Dirac Statistics (SAUS)
FDSU .... Flight Data Storage Unit
FDSVC .... Food Service (MSA)
Fd SVP .... Find SVP, Inc. [*Associated Press*] (SAG)
FDT............. bis-Fulvene-6.6-Dithiol (SAUS)
FDT............. Committee on Forest Development in the Tropics (SAUS)
FDT............. Failure Diagnostic Team [*Aerospace*] (AAG)
FDT............. False Doppler Target (SEWL)
FDT............. Fast Data Transmission (SAUS)
FDT............. Fault Detection Tester
FDT............. Fidelity Trust Co. [*Toronto Stock Exchange symbol*]
FDT............. Fighter Director Tender [*Navy*]
FDT............. Figure Drawing Test [*Psychology*]
FDT............. Final Dive Time (SAUS)
FDT............. First Destination Transportation [*Military*] (AFM)
FDT............. Flexible Digital Terminal
FDT............. Flight Demonstration Team (MCD)
FDT............. Floor Drain Tank [*Nuclear energy*] (NRCH)
FDT............. Florida Department of Transportation [*Federal Railroad Administration identification code*]
FDT............. Flourescent Discharge Tube [*Technology*]
FDT............. Flowing Gas Detonation Tube
FDT............. Fluorescent Discharge Tube [*Panasonic*]
FDT............. Fog Detector Unit (SAUS)
FDT............. Food, Drink, Tobacco [*Department of Employment*] [*British*]
FDT............. Forced Duction Test (MELL)
FDT............. Formal Description Technique [*Telecommunications*] (OSI)
FDT............. Formatted Data Tapes
FDT............. Frequently Discussed Topic (SAUS)
FDT............. Fronto-Dextra Transversa [*A fetal position*] [*Obstetrics*]
FDT............. Full Duplex Teletype
FDT............. Functional Description Table
FDT............. Function Data Table [*Computer science*] (ELAL)
FDTA........... Fisheries Development Trust Account Fe iron (SAUS)
FDTAA .... Federation of Democratic Turkish Associations of Australia
FDT & E....... Field Development Test and Evaluation (MCD)
FDTB........... Foreign and Domestic Teachers' Bureau [*Defunct*] (EA)
FDTC........... Fiber (or Fibre) Drum Technical Council (SAUO)
FDTC........... Finite Difference Time Domain (SAUS)
FD-TD .... Finite Difference - Time Domain [*Computer simulation*]
FDTD .... Finite Difference Time Domain (VLIE)
FDTD .... Finite-Difference Time-Domain (SAUS)
FDTE........... Final Development Test and Evaluation (MCD)
FDTE........... Force Development Test and Evaluation (SAUS)
FDTE........... Force Development Testing and Experimentation [*Military*] (AABC)
FDTF........... Federal Documents Task Force [*Government Documents Round Table*] [*American Library Association*]
FDTI........... Food, Drink and Tobacco Industry Training Board (SAUO)
FDTK........... Floating Drift Tube Klystron
FDTM........... Tambankulu [*Swaziland*] [*ICAO location identifier*] (ICLI)
FDTMDRC.... FORSCOM/DARCOM/ TRADOC Materiel Development and Readiness Council (SAUO)
FDTMDRC.... /TRADOC Material Development and Readiness Council [*Development and Readiness Communications*] [*Training and Doctrine Command*] [*Army*] (MCD)
fdtn .... Foundation (VRA)
FDTRC .... Food and Drug Toxicology Research Center (SAUS)
FDTS........... Fault Detection Test Set (SAUS)
FDTS........... Field Data Tracking System (SAUO)
FDTS........... Firing Device Test Set [*Military*] (CAAL)
FDTS........... Floor Drain Treatment System [*Nuclear energy*] (NRCH)
FDTS........... Tshaneni [*Swaziland*] [*ICAO location identifier*] (ICLI)
FDTSP .... Foreign Disclosure Technology Security Plan [*Army*]
FDTU .... Federation of Danish Trade Unions
FDTVMP ..... Frostig Developmental Test of Visual-Motor Perception [*Psychiatry*] (DAVI)
FDTVP .... Frostig Developmental Test of Visual Perception [*Psychiatry*] (DAVI)
FDU .... Bandundu [*Zaire*] [*Airport symbol*] (OAG)
FDu .... Dunedin Public Library, Dunedin, FL [*Library symbol*] [*Library of Congress*] (LCLS)
FDU .... Factory Data Utility (TIMI)
FDU .... Fairleigh Dickinson University [*New Jersey*]
FDU .... Fairleigh Dickinson University, Teaneck, NJ [*OCLC symbol*] (OCLC)
FDU .... Fidelity Union Bancorp (SAUO)
FDU .... Fire & Distribution Unit (SAUS)
FDU .... Flexible Disc Unit (NITA)
FDU .... Flexible Disk Unit (SAUS)
FDU .... Flight Data Unit (SAUS)
FDU .... Flight Development Unit (MCD)
FDU .... Fluid Distribution Unit (MCD)
FDU .... Fog Detector Unit (SAUS)
FDU .... Force Design Update [*Army*]
FDU .... Formatter and Drive Unit (SAUS)
FDU .... Form Description Utility (SAUS)
FDU .... Frequency Determining Unit
FDU .... Frequency Divider Unit [*Electronics*] (IAA)
FDU .... Frequency Doubling Unit
FDU .... United Democratic Forces (Rep. Of Congo) [*Political party*] (PSAP)
FDU(A)......... Fleet Diving Unit (Atlantic) [*Canadian Navy*]
FDUB .... Ubombo [*Swaziland*] [*ICAO location identifier*] (ICLI)
FDUNSW...... Firemen and Deckhands' Union of New South Wales [*Australia*]
FDU(P)......... Fleet Diving Unit (Pacific) [*Canadian Navy*]
FDUP .... Full Duplex (SAUS)
FDUR .... Free Democratic Union of Roma [*Political party*]
FDUX .... Full Duplex [*Computer science*] (TNIG)
FDV............. Fault Detection Verification (SAUS)
FDV............. Fault Detect Verification
FDV............. Fiji Disease Virus [*Plant pathology*]
FDV............. Flow-Diversion Valve
FDV............. Friend Disease Virus [*Also, FLV, FV*]
FDV............. Fuel Deceleration Valve [*Automotive engineering*]
FDV............. Full Duplex VOCODER [*Voice Coder*]
FDV............. Nome, AK [*Location identifier*] [*FAA*] (FAAL)
FDVLX .... Fidelity Value [*Mutual fund ticker symbol*] (SG)
FDVS .... Field Depot Veterinary Stores [*British military*] (DMA)
FDW............ Feed Water (AAG)
FDW............ Fine [*Condition*] in Dust Wrapper [*Antiquarian book trade*]
FDW............ Flat Data Wing
FDW............ Winnsboro, SC [*Location identifier*] [*FAA*] (FAAL)
FDWL........... Fiberboard, Double Wall
FD WMR...... Food Warmer (NASA)
FDX............. FDX Corp. [*NYSE symbol*] (SG)
FDX............. Federal Express [*NYSE symbol*] (TTSB)
FDX............. Federal Express Corp. [*ICAO designator*] (FAAC)
FDX............. Federal Express Corp. [*NYSE symbol*] [*Toronto Stock Exchange symbol*] (SPSG)
FDX............. Flyball Dog Excellent
FDX............. Foodex, Inc. [*Toronto Stock Exchange symbol*]
FDX............. Full Duplex
FDX Transmission... Full Duplex Transmission (SAUS)
FDY............. Atchison Casting [*NYSE symbol*] (SG)
FDY............. Atchison Casting Corp. [*NYSE symbol*] (SAG)
FDY............. Findlay, OH [*Location identifier*] [*FAA*] (FAAL)
FDY............. Foundry (SAUS)
FDYCE .... Fordyce, AR [*American Association of Railroads railroad junction routing code*]
FDYM........... First Dynasty Mines [*NASDAQ symbol*] (SAG)
FDZ............. Daughters of Divine Zeal (TOCD)
FDZ............. Fetal Danger Zone (MELL)
FDZ............. Fetal Death Zone [*Medicine*]
fe--- .... Africa, East [*MARC geographic area code*] [*Library of Congress*] (LCCP)
FE............... Assistant Secretary for Fossil Energy (SAUO)
FE............... Eustis Memorial Library, Eustis, FL [*Library symbol*] [*Library of Congress*] (LCLS)
FE............... Extended Forecasts [*Symbol*] [*National Weather Service*]
Fe............... Extended Superframe Format [*Communications term*] (DCT)
FE............... Facilities Engineer (MCD)
F/E............. Facing East [*In outdoor advertising*] (WDMC)
FE............... Failure Equation
FE............... Failure to Eject (MCD)
FE............... Far East Command (SAUO)
FE............... Farman Experimental [*British military*] (DMA)
FE............... Farm Economics Research Division [*of ARS, Department of Agriculture*]
FE............... Fat Embolism (MELL)
FE............... Fatty Ester (DB)
FE............... Feather
FE............... Feather Edge (SAUS)
fe............... feather-edged (SAUS)
FE............... Feature Extraction (SAUS)
FE............... February (ADA)
FE............... Fecal Emesis
FE............... Fecal Energy [*Nutrition*]
fe............... Fecit (maker) (SAUS)
FE............... Feliciana Eastern Railroad Co. [*Later, FERR*] [*AAR code*]
FE............... Female
fe............... female employee (SAUS)
FE............... Female with Eggs [*Pisciculture*]
FE............... Fermi Energy (AAEL)
FE............... Ferrari [*Society of Automotive Engineers auto manufacturer code for service information interchange*]
FE............... Ferroelectret (SAUS)
Fe............... Ferrum [*Iron*] [*Chemical element*]
FE............... Fertilled Egg (MELL)
FE............... Fetal Erythroblastosis [*Medicine*]

FE .... Fetal Erythrocyte (DB)
FE .... Fibrinogen Equivalent [*Hematology*]
FE .... Field Electron (SAUS)
FE .... Field Emission [*Physics*]
FE .... Field Engineer [*or Engineering*]
FE .... Field Equation (SAUS)
FE .... Field Erase (SAUS)
FE .... Field Error (SAUS)
FE .... Field Evaluation (CTAS)
FE .... Field Exit (SAUS)
FE .... Field Expedient (AABC)
FE .... Fighter Escort
FE .... File Editor (SAUS)
FE .... File Extent (SAUS)
FE .... Fine Erection
FE .... Finite Element (SAUS)
FE .... Fire Engineer (SAUS)
FE .... Fire Engineering (SAUS)
FE .... Fire Escape (DAC)
FE .... Fire Extinguisher (AAG)
FE .... First Edition (ADA)
FE .... FirstEnergy Corp. [*NYSE symbol*] [*Formerly, Ohio Edison*] (SG)
FE .... First Entry [*British military*] (DMA)
fe .... fisheye (SAUS)
FE .... Fit for Service Everywhere [*British military*] (DMA)
FE .... Fixed End (SAUS)
FE .... Flame Emission
fe .... flanged ends (SAUS)
FE .... Flash Evaporation (OA)
FE .... Fleet Engineer [*Navy*] [*British*] (ROG)
FE .... Flemish Ell [*Unit of length*] (ROG)
F/E .... Flexion/Extension [*Orthopedics*]
FE .... Flexor Exciter [*Neurology*]
FE .... Flight Engineer [*or Engineering*]
FE .... Flight Examiner [*Aeromedical evacuation*]
FE .... Flight Experiment (ACAE)
FE .... Florida Airlines and Air South [*ICAO designator*] (AD)
FE .... Flow Element [*Nuclear energy*] (NRCH)
FE .... Fluid Engineering (SAUS)
FE .... Fluid Extract [*Pharmacy*]
FE .... Fluidization Engineering (SAUS)
FE .... Fluoresceinated Estrogen [*Clinical chemistry*]
FE .... Fluorescing Erythrocyte (DB)
FE .... Fluorine-Containing Elastomer (EDCT)
FE .... Fluoroelastomer (SAUS)
FE .... Fluoroethylene (SAUS)
FE .... Fluphenazine Enanthate (SAUS)
FE .... Focusing Electrode (SAUS)
FE .... Fonetic English [*for spelling words the way they sound*]
FE .... Font Error (SAUS)
FE .... Food Engineering [*Medicine*] (EDAA)
FE .... Forced Expiration (MELL)
FE .... Force Execution (SAUO)
FE .... Foreign Editor (NTCM)
FE .... Foreign Exchange [*Investment term*]
FE .... Forest Engineer
FE .... Forest Engineering (SAUS)
FE .... For Example (ROG)
FE .... Format Effecters (SAUS)
fe .... format effective character (SAUS)
FE .... Format Effector [*Computer science*]
FE .... Format Effektor (SAUS)
f/e .... fortnight ending (SAUS)
FE .... Fossil Energy (SAUS)
FE .... Fossil Energy Program (SAUO)
FE .... Foundation Engineer (SAUS)
FE .... Foundation Engineering (SAUS)
FE .... fractional excretion (SAUS)
FE .... Frame enclosed Elevator (SAUS)
FE .... Frame/Framing Error (SAUS)
FE .... Framing Error (HGAA)
F/E .... Fraudulent Enlistment
FE .... Free Electron (ACAE)
FE .... Free End [*Dentistry*]
FE .... Free exciton (SAUS)
FE .... Free Exiton (AAEL)
FE .... Frequency Electronics Inc. (SAUO)
FE .... Friedensengel [*Angel of Peace*] [*Torpedo auxiliary equipment*] [*German military - World War II*]
FE .... Friends for Education [*Later, FFE*] (EA)
FE .... Friends of the Earth (SAUO)
FE .... Friends of the Everglades (EA)
FE .... Fries Entertainment, Inc. [*AMEX symbol*] (COMM)
FE .... Front End (ADA)
FE .... Frozen Embryo [*Medicine*] (HCT)
FE .... Fuel Economy [*In automobile model name "Honda Civic 1300 FE"*]
FE .... Fugitive Emissions [*Environmental Protection Agency*] (GFGA)
F/E .... Full/Empty (SAUS)
FE .... Functional Element (SAUS)
FE .... Functional Entity [*Telecommunications*] (TEL)
FE .... Functional Expansion (SAUS)
FE .... Fundamentals of Engineering [*Exam*]
FE .... Funding Exchange (EA)
FE .... Furnace Explosion [*Insurance*]
FE .... Further Education
FE .... Fuse Element (SAUS)
FE .... Futures Exchange [*Investment term*]
Fe .... Iron [*Chemical*] (EERA)
fe .... Iron (VRA)
FE .... Office of Fossil Energy
FE .... United Farm Equipment and Metal Workers of America (SAUO)
Fe2O3 .... Ferric Oxide (SAUS)
fe3dgw .... finite-element three-dimensional ground water (SAUS)
FE^{59} .... Radioactive Iron [*Chemistry*] (DAVI)
FEA .... Eglin Air Force Base, Eglin, FL [*OCLC symbol*] (OCLC)
FEA .... Failure Effect Analysis
FEA .... Failure Modes and Effects Analysis (SAUS)
FEA .... Family Emergency Assistance (SAUO)
FEA .... Far East (CARB)
FEA .... Far East and Australasia [*A publication*]
FEA .... Far Eastern Air Transport Corp. [*Taiwan*] [*ICAO designator*] (FAAC)
FEA .... Farmstead Equipment Association (EA)
FEA .... Fast Ethernet Alliance (SAUO)
FEA .... Feather [*Aircraft engine*] (DNAB)
FEA .... Feather Falls [*California*] [*Seismograph station code, US Geological Survey*] [*Closed*] (SEIS)
FEA .... Federal Economic Administration (SAUO)
FEA .... Federal Editors Association [*Later, NAGC*] (EA)
FEA .... Federal Education Association (NTPA)
FEA .... Federal Energy Administration [*Formerly, FEO*] [*Superseded by Department of Energy, 1977*]
FEA .... Federal Executive Association
FEA .... Federation Europeenne des Associations Aerosols [*Federation of European Aerosol Associations*] (EA)
FEA .... Federation Internationale pour l'Education Artistique
FEA .... Federation of Employment Agencies (SAUO)
FEA .... Fetlar [*Shetland Islands*] [*Airport symbol*] (OAG)
FEA .... Fiber-Embedding Approximation
FEA .... Field Effect Amplifier
FEA .... Field-Emitter Arrays
FEA .... Field Evaluation Agency [*Army*]
FEA .... Fiji Electricity Authority (SAUO)
FEA .... Filarial Excretory Antigen [*Immunology*]
FEA .... Finite Element Analysis [*Engineering*]
FEA .... Fire Extinguishing Appliances (MARI)
FEA .... Florida Education Association (SAUO)
FEA .... Fluid Experiments Apparatus (ACAE)
FEA .... Fluids Experiment Apparatus (SAUS)
FEA .... Follow-Up Error Alarm
FEA .... Foreign Economic Administration [*World War II*]
FEA .... Foreign Enlistment Act (SAUO)
FEA .... Formal Environmental Assessment (MCD)
FEA .... Fraternity Executives Association (EA)
FEA .... Free Fire Area (SAUS)
FEA .... Freelance Editorial Association (SAUO)
FEA .... French Equatorial Africa
FEA .... Front End Analysis
FEA .... Full Employment Act [*1946*] (OICC)
FEA .... Functional Economic Analysis (SEWL)
FEA .... Functional Economic Area
FEA .... Functional Entity Action (VERA)
FEA .... Future Engineers of America (EA)
FEAA .... Federal Employees' Appeal Authority [*Civil Service Commission*]
FEAA .... Fellow of the English Association of Accountants and Auditors (DD)
FeAA .... Ferric Acetylacetonate (SAUS)
FEAA .... Folk Education Association of America (EA)
FEAA .... Free Enterprise Awards Association (EA)
FEAACSREG ... Far East Airways and Air Communications Service Region (SAUS)
FEAAES .... Far East Army and Air Force Exchange Service
FEAAF .... Federation Europeenne des Associations d'Analystes Financiers [*European Federation of Financial Analysts' Societies - EFFAS*] (EAIO)
FEABL .... Finite Element Analysis Basic Library [*MIT*]
FEAC .... Fairchild Engine & Airplane Corp.
FEAC .... Far Eastern Advisory Commission (SAUO)
FEAC .... Far Eastern Advisory Council
FeAC .... Ferric Ammonium Citrate (SAUS)
FEAC .... Freelance Editors' Association of Canada
FEAC .... Full Employment Action Council [*Defunct*] (EA)
FEAC .... Further Education Advisory Council (SAUO)
FEAC .... Fusion Energy Advisory Committee
FEACCI .... Far-East-America Council of Commerce and Industry [*Defunct*] (EA)
FEACO .... Federation Europeenne des Associations de Conseils en Organisation [*European Federation of Management Consultants Associations*] [*France*]
FEAD .... Federation Europeenne des Associations de Dieteticiens [*European Federation of the Associations of Dietitians - EFAD*] (EAIO)
FEAD .... Fondo Especial de Asistencia para el Desarrollo (de la OEA) [*Organizacion de Estados Americanos*] [*Washington, DC*]
FEAD .... Front End Accessory Drive [*Automotive engineering*]
FEAF .... Far East Air Force
FEAFOC .... Far East Air Force Operations Centre (SAUO)
FEAFSUP .... Far East Air Force Supplementary (SAUO)
FEA(I) .... Federal Employees Association (Independent)
FEAICS .... Federation Europeenne des Associations d'Ingenieurs de Securite et de Chefs de Service de Securite [*European Federation of Associations of Engineers and Heads of Industrial Safety Services*]

FEAIE.......... Federation Europeenne des Associations d'Instruments a Ecrire [*Federation of European Writing Instruments Associations*] (EAIO)
FEAL.......... Far East Airlines (SAUO)
FEAL.......... Fast Data Encipherment Algorithm (SAUS)
FEAL.......... Fast data-Encryption ALgorithm (SAUS)
FEALC.......... Federacion Espeleologica de America Latina y el Caribe [*Speleological Federation of Latin America and the Caribbean*] (EAIO)
FEALD.......... Field Engineering Automated Logic Diagram (SAUS)
FEALOGFOR... Far East Air Logistical Force
FEAM.......... Foreign Exchange Accounting and Management (SAUS)
FEAMCom.... Far East Air Material Command (SAUO)
FEAMCOM... Far East Air Materiel Command
FEAMCom.... Far East Materiel Command (SAUS)
FEAMIS.......... Foreign Exchange Accounting and Management Information System
FEAN.......... Federation des Enseignants d'Afrique Noire [*Federation of Teachers of Black Africa*]
FeAn.......... Ferroan Anorthosite [*Lunar geology*]
FE & FO.......... Francis E and Freeland O Stanley of Stanley Steamer fame (SAUS)
FE & MV.......... Fremont, Elkhorn & Missouri Valley Railroad
FEANI.......... Federation Europeenne d'Associations Nationales d'Ingenieurs [*European Federation of National Engineering Associations*] (EAIO)
FEAO.......... Federation of European American Organizations (EA)
FEAOA.......... Far East Auto Owners Association (EA)
FEAP.......... Facilities Engineer Apprentice Program [*Army*] (MCD)
FEAP.......... Far East/Pacific
FEAP.......... Federation Europeenne des Associations des Psychologues [*European Federation of Professional Psychologists Associations - EFPPA*] (EA)
FEAP.......... Finite Element Analysis for Printed circuit boards (SAUS)
FEAP.......... FORTRAN [*Formula Translating System*] Executive Assembly Program [*Computer science*] (IAA)
FEAPA.......... Federation of the European Associations of Paediatric Anaesthesia (SAUO)
Fea Posth.... Fearne's Posthumous Works [*A publication*] (DLA)
FEAPW.......... Federal Emergency Administration of Public Works [*Consolidated into Federal Works Agency and administered as PWA, 1939*]
FEAR.......... Failure Effect Analysis Report (SAUS)
FEAR.......... Federal Employment Activity Report
FEAR.......... Field Engineering Assistance Request (MCD)
FEAR.......... Foreign Export Automobile Recovery [*Law enforcement*]
FEAR.......... Forfeiture Endangers American Rights (EA)
FEAR.......... Forward-Firing Aerial Rocket (IAA)
FEAREA.......... Far East Area (CINC)
FEARO.......... Federal Environmental Assessment Review Office [*Canada*]
FEARP.......... Federal Environmental Assessment Review Process (SAUO)
Fear Rem.......... Fearne on Contingent Remainders [*1722-1844*] [*A publication*] (DLA)
FEARS.......... Fourth Element Application and Rates System (SAUS)
FEAS.......... Fellow of the English Association of Corporate Secretaries (DD)
FEAS.......... Finite Element Analysis System [*IBM UK Ltd.*] [*Software package*] (NCC)
FEASIBLE..... Finite Element Analysis Sensibly Implemented by Least Effort
FEAST.......... Fab Eating at School Today [*Nutritional improvement group*] [*British*]
FEAST.......... Fast Data Encyphering Algorithm (SAUS)
FEAST.......... Food Education and Service Training
FEAST.......... Food Equipment and Additives Suppliers and Traders [*Leatherhead Food Research Association*] [*Information service or system*] (CRD)
FEAT.......... Alternate Feature Identification Code (SAUS)
FEAT.......... Feature (SAUS)
FEAT.......... Final Engineering Acceptance Test [*Apollo*] [*NASA*]
FEAT.......... Financial Evaluation and Analysis Technique (SAUS)
FEAT.......... Formal Evaluation Acceptance Test [*Apollo*] [*NASA*]
FEAT.......... Frequency of Every Allowable Term [*Computer science*]
FEAT.......... Fuel Efficiency Automobile Test (PS)
FEATA.......... Far East Air Transport Association
Feath.......... Feather (SAUS)
FEATH.......... Feathery (SAUS)
Feathers...... Featherstone (SAUS)
Featherstone... Featherstone Prison near Wolverhampton northwest of Birmingham, England (SAUS)
Feathrlte...... Featherlite Manufacturing, Inc. [*Associated Press*] (SAG)
FEATI.......... Far Eastern Air Transport Incorporation (SAUO)
FEATM.......... Far Eastern Association of Tropical Medicine (SAUO)
FEATS.......... Feasibility & Experimentation in Acquisition & Tracking Systems (SAUS)
FEATS.......... Festival of European Anglophone Theatrical Societies
FEATS.......... Firing Evaluation and Training System (SAUS)
FEATS.......... Future European Air Traffic System (GAVI)
FEAT System... Frequency of Every Allowable Term System (SAUS)
FEAU.......... Florida Education Association United (SAUO)
FEAU.......... Fluoro(ethyl)arabinosyluracil [*Biochemistry*]
FEB.......... FABS Electronic Bible [*FABS International, Inc.*] [*Information service or system*] (CRD)
FEB.......... Fair Employment Board [*of Civil Service Commission*] [*Abolished, 1955*]
FEB.......... Far Eastern Bureau of the Comintern (SAUO)
FEB.......... Far East National Bank [*AMEX symbol*] (SAG)
FEB.......... Febrifuge [*Allaying Fever Heat*] [*Pharmacy*] (ROG)
feb.......... Febrile [*Medicine*] (DAVI)
FEB.......... Febris [*Fever*] [*Pharmacy*]
FEB.......... February (EY)
Feb.......... February (ODBW)
FEB.......... Federal Executive Board
FEB.......... Fever (SAUS)
FEB.......... Field Engineering Bulletin
FEB.......... Field Engineering Bureau [*FCC*] (NTCM)
FEB.......... Financial and Economic Board (NATG)
FEB.......... Finite Elastic Body
FEB.......... Flight Evaluation Board (SAUO)
FEB.......... Flying Evaluation Board
FEB.......... Forca Expedicionaria Brasileira [*Brazilian Expeditionary Force, 1944-1955*]
FEB.......... Force Engineer Battalion [*Marine Corps*] (VNW)
FEB.......... Forward Equipment Bay (MCD)
FEB.......... Franklin Electronic Book (TELE)
FEB.......... Free Erythrocyte Protoporphyrin [*Medicine*] (MELL)
FEB.......... Functional Exploration of Bone
FEB.......... Sanfebagar [*Nepal*] [*Airport symbol*] (OAG)
FEB.......... Functional Electronic Block (ODA)
FEBA.......... Factor Eight Bypassing Activity (DB)
FEBA.......... Far East Broadcasting Association
FEBA.......... Federal Energy Bar Association (EA)
FEBA.......... Foreign Exchange Brokers Association [*British*]
FEBA.......... Forward End of the Battle Area (SAUS)
FEBA.......... Forward Engagement Battle Area (ACAE)
feb agglut.... Febrile Agglutinin [*Serology*] (CPH)
FEBANYC..... Foreign Exchange Brokers Association of New York City (SAUO)
FEBA Radio... Far East Broadcasting Association (SAUO)
Febarch.......... February and March (SAUS)
FEBC.......... Far East Broadcasting Co.
FEBC.......... Forum for European Bio-industry Coordination [*Brussels-based umbrella group*]
FEB DUR...... Febre Durante [*During the Fever*] [*Pharmacy*] (ROG)
FEBE.......... Far-End Bit Error (SAUS)
FEBE.......... Far End Block Error [*Telecommunications*] (ACRL)
FEBF.......... Far East Bridge Federation (SAUO)
FEBI.......... Front-End Bus Interface (ACAE)
FEBIA.......... Federal Employees Benefits Improvement Act of 1986
FEBMA.......... Federation of European Bearing Manufacture Associations (SAUS)
FEBMA.......... Forged Eye Bolt Manufacturers Association [*Inactive*] (EA)
FEBNO.......... Film Estimate Board of National Organizations (SAUO)
FEBNYC.......... Foreign Exchange Brokers of New York City (EA)
FEBOSCO..... Federation des Scouts du Congo
FEBP.......... Fetal Estrogen-Binding Protein (MELL)
FEBP.......... Fetoneonatal Estrogen-Binding Protein
FEBP.......... Foundation for Education Business Partnerships (AIE)
FEBRIL.......... Febrile Agglutinins [*Immunochemistry*] (DAVI)
FEBROA.......... Febrile Battery-Acute [*Medicine*] (DAVI)
FEBs.......... Federal Executive Boards (SAUS)
FEBS.......... Federation of European Biochemical Societies [*France*]
FEBS Lett..... FEBS Letters (SAUS)
FEBTC.......... Far East Bank and Trust Company (SAUO)
Feby.......... February (SAUS)
FEC.......... Denver Express, Inc. [*ICAO designator*] (FAAC)
FEC.......... Eckerd College, St. Petersburg, FL [*OCLC symbol*] (OCLC)
FEC.......... Fabrication Evaluation Chip (AAEL)
FEC.......... Facilities Engineering Command [*Also, NFEC*] [*Formerly, Bureau of Yards and Docks*] [*Navy*]
FEC.......... Faculty Exchange Center (EA)
FEC.......... Fall Electronics Conference (SAUO)
FEC.......... Famine Emergency Committee (SAUO)
FEC.......... Far East Command [*Military*]
FEC.......... Far East Conference [*Defunct*] (EA)
FEC.......... Far Eastern Commission
FEC.......... Farm Electrification Council (SAUO)
FEC.......... Fecal [*Medicine*] (DAVI)
FEC.......... Fecerunt [*They Did It*] [*Latin*] (ADA)
FEC.......... Fecit [*He, or She, Did It*] [*Latin*]
fec.......... fecit (SAUS)
fec.......... Fecit (maker) (SAUS)
fec.......... feckless (SAUS)
FEC.......... Federal Election Council (SAUO)
FEC.......... Federal Elections Commission [*Formerly, OFE*]
FEC.......... Federal Electoral Council (SAUO)
FEC.......... Federal Electric Company (SAUO)
FEC.......... Federal Electric Corporation (SAUO)
FEC.......... Federal Electronic Company (SAUO)
FEC.......... Federal Electronic Corporation (SAUO)
FEC.......... Federal Executive Committee (OICC)
FEC.......... Federal Executive Council (COE)
FEC.......... Federation Europeenne de Climatotherapie [*European Society of Climatotherapy - ESC*] [*French*] (EAIO)
FEC.......... Federation of Egalitarian Communities (EA)
FEC.......... Federation of the European Cutlery and Flatware Industries (EA)
FEC.......... Ferroelectric Ceramic
FEC.......... Field Engineering Change (KSC)
FEC.......... Field Error Correction (MCD)
FEC.......... File End Closing (SAUS)
FEC.......... final expiration capacity (SAUS)
FEC.......... Financial and Economic Committee (SAUO)
FEC.......... Fine Erection Complete
FEC.......... Finnish Employers Confederation (SAUO)
FEC.......... Fire Extinguisher Cabinet [*Technical drawings*]
FEC.......... First Edition Club (NTCM)
FEC.......... Fixed Electrolytic Capacitor
FEC.......... Floating Error Code [*Digital Equipment Corp.*]
FEC.......... Florida East Coast (SAUO)

FEC .... Florida East Coast Railway Co. [*AAR code*]
FEC .... Fondation d'Etudes du Canada [*Canada Studies Foundation - CSF*]
FEC .... Fondation Europeenne de la Culture [*European Cultural Foundation - ECF*] [*Netherlands*]
FEC .... Food and Energy Council (EA)
FEC .... Forced Expiratory Capacity [*Medicine*] (DMAA)
FEC .... Foreign Exchange Carrier (SAUS)
FEC .... Foreign Exchange Certificate [*Special currency notes sold to foreigners*] [*People's Republic of China*] (ECON)
FEC .... Foreign Exchange Cost (AFM)
FEC .... foreward error correction (SAUS)
FEC .... Format Effector Character (SAUS)
FEC .... Forward End Cap
FEC .... Forward Error Control (CCCA)
FEC .... Forward Error Correcting (SAUS)
FEC .... Forward Error Correction [*Computer code*]
FEC .... Forward Error Corrective (SAUS)
FEC .... Forward Error Corrector (SAUS)
FEC .... Forward Events Controller (MCD)
fec .... forward exchange control (SAUS)
FEC .... Foundation for Exceptional Children (EA)
FEC .... Franciscan Educational Conference [*Defunct*]
FEC .... Frederick Electronics Corporation (SAUO)
FEC .... Free Energy Change
FEC .... Free Erythrocyte Coproporphyrin [*Hematology*] (MAE)
FEC .... Free Europe Committee [*Later, RFE/RL*] (EA)
FEC .... Free-Standing Emergency Center
FEC .... Freestanding Emergency Clinic
FEC .... French Expeditionary Corps
FEC .... Friedl Expert Committee (EA)
FEC .... Friend Erythroleukemia Cell [*Medicine*] (DMAA)
FEC .... Front End Computer (SAUS)
FEC .... Front-End Computer
FEC .... Front End Control (SAUS)
FEC .... Front-End Controller (SAUS)
FEC .... Front End Control Program (IAA)
FEC .... Front End of Chest (SAUS)
FEC .... Fuel Efficiency Committee (SAUO)
FEC .... Full Economic Cost
FEC .... Henry C. Frick Educational Commission (SAUO)
FEC .... Office of Foreign Economic Coordination (SAUO)
FECA .... Facilities Engineering and Construction Agency [*HEW*]
FECA .... Federal Election Campaign Act of 1971
FECA .... Federal Employees Compensation Act [*1908*] (AFM)
FECA .... Fiji Employers Consultative Association (SAUO)
FECA .... Florida Electrical Cooperative Association (DEMM)
FECA .... Flower Export Council of Australia (SAUO)
FECA .... Fully Enclosed Covered Area (ADA)
FECAC .... Footrot Eradication Campaign Advisory Committee (SAUO)
FECAI .... Federal Electronic Commerce Acquisition Instructions (SAUS)
FECAP .... Feeder Equipment Capacity (PDAA)
FECAVA .... Federation of European Companion Animal Veterinary Associations (GVA)
FECB .... Far East Combined Bureau [*Singapore, 1940*] [*Military*]
FECB .... Federation des Employes Congolais des Banques [*Federation of Congolese Bank Clerks*]
FECB .... File Extended Control Block [*Computer science*] (BUR)
FECB .... Foreign Exchange Control Board (SAUO)
FECC .... Federal Emergency Communications Coordinator (SAUO)
FECC .... Federal Employees Coordinating Committee (EA)
FECC .... Federation Europeenne du Commerce Chimique [*Federation of European Chemical Merchants - FECM*] (EAIO)
FECDBA .... Foreign Exchange and Currency Deposit Brokers Association (MHDW)
FECEGC .... Federation Europeenne des Constructeurs d'Equipement de Grandes Cuisines [*European Federation of Catering Equipment Manufacturers - EFCEM*] (EA)
FECEP .... Federation Europeenne des Constructeurs d'Equipement Petrolier [*European Federation of Petroleum Equipment Manufacturers*]
FECES .... Forward Error Control Electronics System (IAA)
FECF .... Food Executives Club of Florida (EA)
FECG .... Far Eastern Ceramic Group (SAUO)
FECG .... Fetal Electrocardiography [*or Electrocardiogram*] [*Medicine*]
F Ech Tpt .... First Echelon Transport (SAUS)
FECI .... Fellow of the Institute of Employment Consultants [*British*] (DBQ)
FECI .... fractional chloride excretion (SAUS)
FECL .... Federal Constitutional Law
FECL .... Feedback Emitter-Coupled Logic (SAUS)
FECL .... Fleet Electronics Calibration Laboratory
FECLX .... Fortis Equity: Capital Fund Cl.A [*Mutual fund ticker symbol*] (SG)
FECM .... Federation of European Chemical Merchants (EA)
fecm .... ferret electronic countermeasures (SAUS)
FECM .... Firm Engineering Change Memo (SAA)
FECMA .... Federation of European Coin-Machine Associations (EAIO)
FECN .... Ferrocyanic acid (SAUS)
FECN .... Forward-Explicit Congestion Notification [*Computer science*]
FECN/BECN .... Forward and Backward Explicit Congestion Notification (AGLO)
FECO .... Fourth Engine Cut Off (ACAE)
FECO .... Fringes of Equal Chromatic Order [*Optics*]
FECOM .... Far East Command [*Military*]
FECOM .... Fonds Europeen de Cooperation Monetaire [*European Monetary Cooperation Fund*]
FECOMPUTPROGCENPAC .... Fleet Computer Programming Center, Pacific (SAUS)
FECOMZ .... Forward Echelon, Communications Zone [*Europe*] [*Army*]
FECONS .... Field Engineer Control System (PDAA)
FECP .... Facility Engineering Change Proposal
FECP .... Field Engineering Change Proposal
FECP .... Florida Education Computing Project (EDAC)
FECP .... Formal Engineering Change Proposal (MSA)
FECP .... Free Erythrocyte Coproporphyria [*Hematology*] (MAE)
FECR .... Far East Communications Region [*Air Force*] (MCD)
fe cr .... fernchrome (SAUS)
FeCr .... Ferrichrome Recording Tape (NTCM)
FECRO .... Federation of European Credit Reporting Organizations (SAUO)
FECS .... Federal Employees' Compensation System (GFGA)
FECS .... Federation Europeenne des Fabricants de Ceramiques Sanitaires [*European Federation of Ceramic Sanitaryware Manufacturers - EFCSM*] (EAIO)
FECS .... Federation of European Chemical Societies (EAIO)
FECS .... Foreign Exchange Counselling System (NITA)
FECS .... Front End Computer System (ACAE)
FECS .... fuel evaporation control system (SAUS)
FECT .... Factor Eight Correctional Time (DB)
FECT .... Federation of European Chemical Trade (EAIO)
FECT .... Fibroelastic Connective Tissue [*Medicine*]
FECU .... Far Eastern Container Unit (SAUS)
FECU .... Flutter Exciter Control Unit (MCD)
FECUA .... Farmers' Educational and Cooperative Union of America (EA)
FECV .... Feline Enteric Coronavirus [*Veterinary science*] (DB)
FECV .... Functional Extracellular Fluid Volume [*Medicine*] (MAE)
FECZ .... Farwell Elevator [*Federal Railroad Administration identification code*]
FECZ .... Forward Echelon, Communications Zone [*Europe*] [*Army*]
FED .... Army Engineer District, Far East
FED .... Facilities Engineering Department (SAUO)
FED .... Far End Data (SAUS)
FED .... Federal (AFM)
fed .... Federal (SHCU)
Fed .... Federal (AL)
fed .... Federal Agent [*Slang*]
FED .... Federal Building (SAUS)
FED .... Federalist
Fed .... [*The*] Federalist, by Hamilton [*A publication*] (DLA)
fed .... federal law-enforcement officer (SAUS)
fed .... federal narcotics agent (SAUS)
FED .... Federal Register (SAUS)
Fed .... Federal Reporter [*A publication*] (DLA)
Fed .... Federal Reserve Board
Fed .... Federal Reserve System (EBF)
FED .... Federal Reserve System [*Banking*]
FED .... Federal Specification
fed .... Federated (ADWA)
FED .... Federated (WDAA)
Fed .... Federation (DIAR)
FED .... Federation (EY)
FED .... ferroelectric display (SAUS)
FED .... Field Effect Device
FED .... Field Effect Diode (IAA)
FED .... Field Emission Deposition [*Coating technique*]
FED .... Field Emission Device (ADWA)
FED .... Field Emission Display (SAUS)
FED .... Field-Emission Display (ECON)
FED .... Field Emissive Display (SAUS)
FED .... Field-Emitter Display (VLIE)
FED .... Field Engineering Department (SAUS)
FED .... Field engineering directive (SAUS)
FED .... Field Experience Data (SAUS)
FED .... Final Estimation of Data [*Computer science*]
FED .... Final Evaluation Day (DB)
FED .... Finfish Excluding Device [*Fishing technology*]
FED .... FirstFed Financial [*NYSE symbol*] (TTSB)
FED .... Five-Inch Evasion Device (MCD)
FED .... Fleetwood Petroleum [*Vancouver Stock Exchange symbol*]
FED .... Flight Events Demonstration (SAUS)
FED .... Forcible Entry and Detainer (SAUO)
FED .... Foreign Engineering Department (SAUO)
FED .... Format Element Descriptor (IAA)
FED .... Form Editor (SAUS)
FED .... Forward Entry Device [*Army*] (DOMA)
FED .... Foundation for Ethnic Dance (EA)
FED .... Freeze Etching Device (SAUS)
FED .... Front-End-Processor (SAUS)
FED .... Fuel-Efficient Drive [*Tire design*]
FED .... Fuel Element Department (SAA)
FED .... Fuel Element Design (SAUS)
FED .... Fuel Examination Facility (SAUS)
FED .... Fusion Engineering Device [*Nuclear energy*]
FED .... Linea Federal Argentina SEM [*ICAO designator*] (FAAC)
Fed 2d .... Federal Reporter, Second Series [*A publication*] (DLA)
FEDA .... Farm Equipment Dealers Association (SAUO)
FEDA .... Food Service Equipment Distributors Association (SAUO)
FEDAC .... Federal Education Data Acquisition Council (OICC)
FEDAC .... Federal Executive Drug Abuse Council
FEDAC .... Forward Error Detection and Correction
FEDAI .... Foreign Exchange Dealers Association of India (SAUO)
FEDAL .... Failed Element Detection and Location [*In nuclear power reactors*]
FEDAL .... Failed Element Detection and Location Instrument (SAUS)
FEDALFARBIO .... Andean Federation for Pharmacy and Biochemistry (SAUO)
FEDALT .... Feeder Alteration (SAUS)
FEDAM .... Finite Element Data Management (SAUS)

Fed Anti-Tr Cas... Federal Anti-Trust Cases, Decrees, and Judgments [*1890-1918*] [*A publication*] (DLA)
Fed Anti-Tr Dec... Federal Anti-Trust Decisions [*A publication*] (DLA)
FEDAPT........ Foundation for the Extension and Development of the American Professional Theatre (SAUS)
FEDAS......... Federation of European Delegation Associations of Scientific Equipment Manufacturers, Importers, and Dealers (SAUS)
FEDAY......... Ferriday, LA [*American Association of Railroads railroad junction routing code*]
FEDB.......... Failure Experience Data Bank [*GIDEP*]
Fed Banking L Rep... Federal Banking Law Reports [*Commerce Clearing House*] [*A publication*] (DLA)
Fed B News & J... Federal Bar News & Journal [*A publication*] (AAGC)
FEDC........... Federal Economic Development Co-Ordinator [*Canada*]
FEDC........... Federation of Engineering Design Companies [*British*] (DBA)
FEDC........... Federation of Engineering Design Consultants (BARN)
FEDC........... Field Exercise Data Collection [*Army*] (RDA)
FEDC........... Fusion Energy Design Center (MCD)
FEDC........... Fusion Engineering Design Center (SAUO)
Fed Can M Inst J... Federated Canadian Mining Institute Journal (SAUO)
Fed Carr Cas... Federal Carriers Cases [*Commerce Clearing House*] [*A publication*] (DLA)
Fed Carr Rep... Federal Carriers Reporter [*Commerce Clearing House*] [*A publication*] (DLA)
Fed Cas....... Federal Cases [*A publication*] (DLA)
Fed Cas No... Federal Case Number [*Legal term*] (DLA)
Fed Cir........ Court of Appeals for the Federal Circuit (AAGC)
Fed Comm LJ... Federal Communications Law Journal [*A publication*] (DLA)
Fed Cont Rep (BNA)... Federal Contracts Report (Bureau of National Affairs) [*A publication*] (DLA)
FED Co-OP... Federal Employee Direct Corporate Stock Ownership Plan (GFGA)
Fed Council Bull... Federal Council of University Staff Associations. Bulletin [*A publication*]
Fed Ct......... Indian Rulings, Federal Court [*A publication*] (DLA)
Fed D.......... Federal District (SAUS)
FEDD.......... For Early Domestic Dissemination (MCD)
Fed Dist 1... Federal Reserve Bank of Boston (TBD)
Fed Dist 2... Federal Reserve Bank of New York (TBD)
Fed Dist 2 B... Federal Reserve Bank of New York - Buffalo Branch (TBD)
Fed Dist 3... Federal Reserve Bank of Philadelphia (TBD)
Fed Dist 4... Federal Reserve Bank of Cleveland (TBD)
Fed Dist 4 C... Federal Reserve Bank of Cleveland - Cincinnati Branch (TBD)
Fed Dist 4 P... Federal Reserve Bank of Cleveland - Pittsburgh Branch (TBD)
Fed Dist 5... Federal Reserve Bank of Richmond (TBD)
Fed Dist 5 B... Federal Reserve Bank of Richmond - Baltimore Branch (TBD)
Fed Dist 5 C... Federal Reserve Bank of Richmond - Charlotte Branch (TBD)
Fed Dist 6... Federal Reserve Bank of Atlanta (TBD)
Fed Dist 6 B... Federal Reserve Bank of Atlanta - Birmingham Branch (TBD)
Fed Dist 6 J... Federal Reserve Bank of Atlanta - Jackson Branch (TBD)
Fed Dist 6 M... Federal Reserve Bank of Atlanta - Miami Branch (TBD)
Fed Dist 6 N... Federal Reserve Bank of Atlanta - Nashville (TBD)
Fed Dist 6 NO... Federal Reserve Bank of Atlanta - New Orleans Branch (TBD)
Fed Dist 7... Federal Reserve Bank of Chicago (TBD)
Fed Dist 7 D... Federal Reserve Bank of Chicago - Detroit Branch (TBD)
Fed Dist 8... Federal Reserve Bank of St. Louis (TBD)
Fed Dist 8 L... Federal Reserve Bank of St. Louis - Little Rock Branch [*Arkansas*] (TBD)
Fed Dist 8 L... Federal Reserve Bank of St. Louis - Louisville Branch [*Indiana and Kentucky*] (TBD)
Fed Dist 8 M... Federal Reserve Bank of St. Louis - Memphis Branch (TBD)
Fed Dist 9... Federal Reserve Bank of Minneapolis (TBD)
Fed Dist 9 H... Federal Reserve Bank of Minneapolis - Helena Branch [*Montana*] (TBD)
Fed Dist 10... Federal Reserve Bank of Kansas City (TBD)
Fed Dist 10 D... Federal Reserve Bank of Kansas City - Denver Branch (TBD)
Fed Dist 10 O... Federal Reserve Bank of Kansas City - Omaha Branch (TBD)
Fed Dist 10 OC... Federal Reserve Bank of Kansas City - Oklahoma City Branch (TBD)
Fed Dist 11... Federal Reserve Bank of Dallas (TBD)
Fed Dist 11 E... Federal Reserve Bank of Dallas - El Paso Branch (TBD)
Fed Dist 11 H... Federal Reserve Bank of Dallas - Houston Branch (TBD)
Fed Dist 11 S... Federal Reserve Bank of Dallas - San Antonio Branch (TBD)
Fed Dist 12... Federal Reserve Bank of San Francisco (TBD)
Fed Dist 12 L... Federal Reserve Bank of San Francisco - Los Angeles Branch (TBD)
Fed Dist 12 P... Federal Reserve Bank of San Francisco - Portland Branch (TBD)
Fed Dist 12 S... Federal Reserve Bank of San Francisco - Seattle Branch (TBD)
Fed Dist 12 SL... Federal Reserve Bank of San Francisco - Salt Lake City Branch (TBD)
FEDD Programme... For Early Domestic Dissemination Programme (SAUS)
FEDE........... Federation Europeenne des Ecoles [*Later, European Schools Federation*] (EAIO)
FEDECAFE.... National Federation of Coffee Growers (Colombia) [*Political party*] (PSAP)
FEDECAME... Federacion Cafetalera de America [*Central American Coffee Growers' Federation*]
FEDECO....... Federacion de Comunidades Judias de Centroamerica y Panama [*Federation of Jewish Communities of Central America and Panama*] (EAIO)
FEDECO....... Federation of Jewish Communities of Central America and Panama (SAUO)
Fede de Sen... Federicus Petrucius de Senis [*Flourished, 1321-43*] [*Authority cited in pre-1607 legal work*] (DSA)
FEDEFAM..... Federacion Latinoamericana de Asociaciones de Familiares de Detenidos-Desaparecidos [*Federation of Associations of Families of Disappeared-Detainees*] (EAIO)
FE de las JONS... Falange Espanola de las Juntas de Ofensiva Nacional Sindicalista [*Spanish Phalange of the Syndicalist Juntas of the National Offensive*] [*Political party*] (PPE)
Fed Election Camp Fin Guide (CCH)... Federal Election Campaign Financing Guide (Commerce Clearing House) [*A publication*] (DLA)
FEDEM......... Federal Democratic Movement of Uganda (SAUO)
FEDEMO...... Federal Democratic Movement [*Uganda*] [*Political party*]
FEDEMU...... Federal Democratic Movement of Uganda [*Political party*] (PSAP)
FEDEN......... Foundation for Environmental Development and Education in Nigeria (SAUO)
FEDER......... Federal, IL [*American Association of Railroads railroad junction routing code*]
FEDER......... Fonds Europeen de Developpement Regional [*European Regional Development Fund - ERDF*] [*Belgium*] (EAIO)
FederA......... Fedders Corp. [*Associated Press*] (SAG)
Federal CAAA... Federal Clean Air Act Amendments (SAUS)
FEDERP....... Fish Estuarine-Deltaic Recruitment Project (SAUS)
Feders......... Fedders Corp. [*Associated Press*] (SAG)
FEDES......... European Flexible Packagings Industry Association (SAUS)
FEDES......... Federation Europeenne de l'Emballage Souple (EAIO)
FEDESA........ Federation Europeenne de la Sante Animale [*European Federation of Animal Health*] [*Belgium*] (ECED)
Fed Evid R... Federal Rules of Evidence [*A publication*] (DLA)
FEDEX......... [*The*] Federal Energy Data Index [*Department of Energy*] [*Information service or system*] [*Defunct*] (CRD)
FedEx.......... Federal Express [*Parcel Service*] (AAGC)
FEDEX......... Federal Express Corp. [*Service mark and trade name*]
FEDEX......... Federal Index [*Capitol Services International*] (NITA)
FEDEX......... Fujitsu Electronic Data Exchange (SAUS)
FedExp......... Federal Express Corp. [*Associated Press*] (SAG)
Fed Ex Tax Rep... Federal Excise Tax Reporter [*Commerce Clearing House*] [*A publication*] (DLA)
Fed Facil Environ J... Federal Facilities Environmental Journal [*A publication*] (PABS)
FedFOH........ Fidelity Financial of Ohio, Inc. [*Associated Press*] (SAG)
FEDFU......... Federated Engine Drivers and Firemens Union (SAUO)
FEDGE......... Finite Element Data Generation [*Computer science*]
FEDHASA..... Federated Hotel, Liquor and Catering Association (SAUO)
FEDI............ Failure Experience Data Interchange (ACAE)
FEDI............ Financial Electronic Data Exchange (GART)
FEDI............ Financial Electronic Data Interchange (HODG)
FEDIAF........ Federation Europeenne de l'Industrie des Aliments pour Animaux Familiers [*European Petfood Industry Federation*] (EAIO)
FEDIMA........ Federation des Industries de Matieres Premieres et des Ameliorants pour la Boulangerie et la Patisserie dans la CEE [*European Federation of Manufacturers of Bakers' and Confectioners' Ingredients and Additives*] [*Common Market*]
Fed Ins Counsel Q... Federal Insurance Counsel Quarterly [*A publication*] (DLA)
FEDIOL........ Federation de l'Industrie de l'Huilerie de la CEE [*EEC Seed Crushers and Oil Processors' Federation*] [*Belgium*] (EAIO)
FEDIOL........ Federation of the Oil Industry of the EEC (SAUO)
FEDIS........... Finite Element Data Interface Standard (SAUS)
FEDIS........... Front End Design Information System (SAUS)
FEDIX........... Federal Information Exchange, Inc.
FedJob.......... Federal Job Listing Reserve (SAUO)
FEDL............ Failed element detection location (SAUS)
FEDL............ Federal
Fed Law Rev... Federal Law Review [*A publication*]
FEDLEV........ Federal Low-Emission Vehicle [*Automotive engineering*]
FEDLINET.... Federal Library and Information Network (SAUS)
FEDLINK...... Federal Library and Information Network [*Formerly, FLECC*] [*Library of Congress*] [*Washington, DC*] [*Library network*]
Fed LJ......... Federal Law Journal of India [*A publication*] (DLA)
Fed LJ Ind... Federal Law Journal of India [*A publication*] (DLA)
Fed LQ......... Federal Law Quarterly [*A publication*] (DLA)
FEDM........... Field Engineering Diagram Manual (SAUS)
Fed Mal....... Federation of Malaya (SAUS)
Fed Mal....... Federation of Malaya (or Malay States) (SAUO)
Fed Mal....... Federation of Malay States (SAUS)
Fed Mal Sta... Federated Malay States (SAUO)
FEDMAP....... Federal Geologic Mapping Project (CARB)
FedMog........ Federal-Mogul Corp. [*Associated Press*] (SAG)
fedn............ Federation (ADWA)
Fedn............ Federation (AL)
FEDN........... Federation
fed narc....... federal narcotics agent (SAUS)
FEDNET........ Federal Information Network
FEDNET........ Federal Library Network (SAUS)
FEDNET........ Federal Network [*Computer network*] (NITA)
FedNM......... Federal National Mortgage Association [*Wall Street slang name: "Fannie Mae"*] [*Associated Press*] (SAG)
FEDO........... FACT Engineering and Design Organization (SAUO)
FED of A...... Federated Funeral Directors of America (SAUO)
FEDOLIVE.... Federation de l'Industrie de l'Huile d'Olive de la CEE [*Federation of the European Economic Community Olive Oil Industry*]
FEDOM......... Fonds Europeen de Developpement pour les Pays et Territoires d'Outre-Mer [*European Development Fund for Overseas Countries and Territories*]
FedOne........ Fed One Bancorp [*Associated Press*] (SAG)
FedOne........ Fed One Savings Bank [*Associated Press*] (SAG)
FEDORA........ Forum Europeen de l'Orientation Academique (AIE)
FEDORAL..... European Forum of Academic Guidance (SAUO)

FEDOSA....... Federation of Dominicans of Southern Africa (SAUO)
FEDP........... Facility and Equipment Design Plan (MCD)
FEDP........... Federal Executive Development Program [*Civil Service Commission*]
FEDP........... Fusion engineering development plan (SAUS)
FEDPAC....... Federal Pacific Lakes Lines [*Steamship*] (MHDW)
FedPB......... Federal Paper Board Co., Inc. [*Associated Press*] (SAG)
FEDPOWCOMM... Federal Power Commission (IAA)
Fed Prac...... Federal Practice and Procedure [*A publication*] (DLA)
Fed Prob...... Federal Probation [*A publication*] (BRI)
Fed Prob NL... Federal Probation Newsletter [*A publication*] (DLA)
Fed Pubs..... Federal Publications, Inc. (AAGC)
Fed R.......... Federal Reporter [*A publication*] (DLA)
FEDR.......... Full-Scale Engineering Development Phase (POLM)
FEDRAN....... Feed Drive Analysis [*Machine Tool Industry Research Association*] [*Software package*] (NCC)
Fed R App P... Federal Rules of Appellate Procedure [*A publication*] (DLA)
FEDRAT....... Feed Rate (SAUS)
FEDRC......... Forward Error Detection And Correction (SAUS)
Fed R Civil P... Federal Rules of Civil Procedure [*A publication*] (DLA)
Fed R Civ P... Federal Rules of Civil Procedure [*A publication*] (DLA)
Fed R Civ Proc... Federal Rules of Civil Procedure [*A publication*] (HGAA)
Fed R Crim P... Federal Rules of Criminal Procedure [*A publication*] (DLA)
Fed R Crim Proc... Federal Rules of Criminal Procedure [*A publication*] (HGAA)
FedrDS........ Federated Department Stores, Inc. [*Associated Press*] (SAG)
Fed Ref........ Federal Reformatory (SAUS)
Fed Reg........ Federal Register [*A publication*] (AAGC)
FEDREG........ Federal Register [*Capitol Services International*] (NITA)
FEDREG........ Federal Register Abstracts [*Capitol Services, Inc.*] [*Washington, DC*] [*Database*]
Fed Regist... Federal Register (SAUS)
Fed Rep........ Federal Reporter [*A publication*] (DLA)
FedRep........ Federal Republic of Germany
Fed Rep Nig... Federal Republic of Nigeria (SAUS)
Fed Reserve Bank Atlanta Econ Rev... Federal Reserve Bank of Atlanta Economic Review [*A publication*] (JLIT)
Fed Reserve Bank Atlanta Rev... Federal Reserve Bank of Atlanta Monthly Review [*A publication*] (JLIT)
Fed Reserve Bank Boston New Eng Econ Rev... Federal Reserve Bank of Boston New England Economic Review [*A publication*] (JLIT)
Fed Reserve Bank Bus Rev Phila... Federal Reserve Bank Business Review of Philadelphia [*A publication*] (JLIT)
Fed Reserve Bank Chicago Econ Perspect... Federal Reserve Bank of Chicago Economic Perspectives [*A publication*] (JLIT)
Fed Reserve Bank Cleveland Econ Rev... Federal Reserve Bank of Cleveland Economic Review [*A publication*] (JLIT)
Fed Reserve Bank Dallas Econ Finan Rev... Federal Reserve Bank of Dallas Economic and Financial Review [*A publication*] (JLIT)
Fed Reserve Bank Dallas Econ Rev... Federal Reserve Bank of Dallas Economic Review [*A publication*] (JLIT)
Fed Reserve Bank Kansas City Econ Rev... Federal Reserve Bank of Kansas City Economic Review [*A publication*] (JLIT)
Fed Reserve Bank Kansas City Rev... Federal Reserve Bank of Kansas City Monthly Review [*A publication*] (JLIT)
Fed Reserve Bank Minneapolis Quart Rev... Federal Reserve Bank of Minneapolis Quarterly Review [*A publication*] (JLIT)
Fed Reserve Bank New York Econ Pol Rev... Federal Reserve Bank of New York Economic Policy Review [*A publication*] (JLIT)
Fed Reserve Bank New York Quart Rev... Federal Reserve Bank of New York Quarterly Review [*A publication*] (JLIT)
Fed Reserve Bank New York Rev... Federal Reserve Bank of New York Monthly Review [*A publication*] (JLIT)
Fed Reserve Bank Philadelphia Bus Rev... Federal Reserve Bank of Philadelphia Business Review [*A publication*] (JLIT)
Fed Reserve Bank Richmond Econ Quart... Federal Reserve Bank of Richmond Economic Quarterly [*A publication*] (JLIT)
Fed Reserve Bank Richmond Econ Rev... Federal Reserve Bank of Richmond Economic Review [*A publication*] (JLIT)
Fed Reserve Bank San Francisco Econ Rev... Federal Reserve Bank of San Francisco Economic Review [*A publication*] (JLIT)
Fed Reserve Bank San Francisco Rev... Federal Reserve Bank of San Francisco Monthly Review [*A publication*] (JLIT)
Fed Reserve Bank St Louis Rev... Federal Reserve Bank of St Louis Review [*A publication*] (JLIT)
Fed Reserve Bull... Federal Reserve Bulletin [*A publication*] (JLIT)
Fed Revenue Forms (P-H)... Federal Revenue Forms (Prentice-Hall, Inc.) [*A publication*] (DLA)
Fed R Evid... Federal Rules of Evidence [*A publication*] (DLA)
Fed R Evid Serv... Federal Rules of Evidence Service [*A publication*] (DLA)
FEDRIP........ Federal Research in Progress [*NTIS*] [*Department of Commerce*] [*Information service or system*] (IID)
FedRlty........ Federal Realty Investment Trust [*Associated Press*] (SAG)
FEDRN......... Federation
Fed R Serv 2d (Callaghan)... Federal Rules Service, Second Series [*A publication*] (DLA)
FEDRT......... Federal Tax Rate
Fed Rules Civ Proc... Federal Rules of Civil Procedure [*A publication*] (DLA)
Fed Rules Cr Proc... Federal Rules of Criminal Procedure [*A publication*] (DLA)
Fed Rules Serv... Federal Rules Service [*A publication*] (DLA)
Fed Rules Serv 2d... Federal Rules Service, Second Series [*A publication*] (DLA)
FEDS............ Federal Employees for a Democratic Society [*Defunct*]
FEDS............ Federal Employment Decision Search [*Database*] [*Labor Relations Press*] [*Information service or system*] (CRD)
FEDS............ Federal Energy Data System [*Department of Energy*] (GFGA)
FEDS............ Federal Energy Decision Screening (SAUS)
Feds............ federal excise tax collectors (SAUS)
Feds............ federal law-enforcement officers (SAUS)
FEDS............ Field-Emitter Displays
FEDS............ Field Experimenter Detection [*or Detector*] Survivability (MCD)
FEDS............ Firm Enterprise Data Systems (SAUO)
FEDS............ Fixed and Exchangeable Disc Storage (NITA)
FEDS............ Fixed and Exchangeable Disk Storage (SAUS)
FEDS............ Fixed Exchangeable Disc Store (SAUS)
FEDS............ Flexible Engine Diagnostic System
FEDS............ Forced Entry Deterrent System (SAUS)
FEDS............ Foreign Economic Development Service [*Abolished 1972, functions transferred to the Economic Research Service*] [*Department of Agriculture*]
FEDSA......... Federation of European Direct Selling Associations [*Belgium*] (EAIO)
Fedsal.......... Federation of South African Labor Unions (SAUO)
FEDSEA........ Federal South East Asia Line [*Steamship*] (MHDW)
Fed Sec L Rep... Federal Securities Law Reporter [*Commerce Clearing House*] [*A publication*] (DLA)
FedSignl....... Federal Signal Corp. [*Associated Press*] (SAG)
FEDSIM........ Federal Computer Performance Evaluation and Simulation Center [*General Services Administration*]
FEDSIM........ Federal Systems Integration and Management Center (VLIE)
FEDSIM Center... Federal Computer Performance Evaluation and Simulation Center (SAUS)
FEDS/IRS..... Fourier Encoded Data Searching of Infrared Spectra (SAUS)
FEDSPEC..... Federal Specification
FED-STAN.... Standards Referenced in Federal Legislation [*Standards Council of Canada*] [*Information service or system*] (CRD)
Fed Stat Ann... Federal Statutes, Annotated [*A publication*] (DLA)
FEDSTD....... Federal Standard
FEDSTD....... Federal Telecommunications Standard (SAUO)
FED-STDS.... Federal Telecommunications Standards (AAGC)
FEDSTRIP.... Federal Standard Requisition and Issuing Procedures (SAUS)
Fed Sup....... Federal Supplement [*A publication*] (DLA)
Fed Supp..... Federal Supplement [*A publication*] (DLA)
Fed Tax Coordinator 2d (RIA)... Federal Tax Coordinator Second (Tax Research Institute of America) [*A publication*] (DLA)
Fed Tax Enf... Federal Tax Enforcement [*A publication*] (DLA)
Fed Taxes.... Federal Taxes [*Prentice-Hall, Inc.*] [*A publication*] (DLA)
Fed Taxes Est & Gift... Federal Taxes: Estate and Gift Taxes [*Prentice-Hall, Inc.*] [*A publication*] (DLA)
Fed Taxes (P-H)... Federal Taxes (Prentice-Hall, Inc.) [*A publication*] (DLA)
Fed Tr Rep... Federal Trade Reporter [*A publication*] (DLA)
FEDU........... Fluoroethyl(deoxyuridine) [*Biochemistry*]
FEDWG......... Fuel Element Development Working Group (SAUO)
FedWire....... Federal Wire Transfers (EBF)
FEDZ............ Fairfield Economic Development Association [*Federal Railroad Administration identification code*]
FEE.............. Failure Effects Evaluation (IAA)
FEE.............. Fast Exponential Experiment (SAUS)
FEE.............. Feature Extraction Environment (SAUO)
FEE.............. Field Engineering and Equipment [*Military*]
FEE.............. Fill Exit Entry [*Computer science*]
FEE.............. Final End Entry (SAUS)
FEE.............. Find End Entry [*Computer science*] (VLIE)
FEE.............. Flight Support System (SAUS)
FEE.............. Florida Employers Exchange (SRA)
FEE.............. Fondation Europeenne pour l'Economie
FEE.............. Forced Equilibrating Expiration [*Physiology*]
FEE.............. Foundation for Economic Education (EA)
FEE.............. Foundation for Environmental Education (SAUO)
FEE.............. Freeway Resources Ltd. [*Vancouver Stock Exchange symbol*]
FEE.............. Frog Embryology Experiment (SAUS)
FEEA............ Federal Employee Education and Assistance Fund
FEEA............ Federal Energy Emergency Administration (MCD)
FEE(A)......... Foundation for Economic Education (Australia)
fee add......... feeder additional (SAUS)
FEEATT........ Ferro-Electric Education Audio Tuning Tape (SAUS)
feeb............. feeble (SAUS)
feeb............. feebleminded (SAUS)
FEEB............ Fleet Electronic Effectiveness Branch (SAUO)
FEEC............ Field Enterprises Educational Corp. [*Later, World Book-Childcraft Internation al, Inc.*]
FEEC............ Foreign Exchange Entitlements Certificate (SAUS)
FEECA.......... Federation Europeenne pour l'Education Catholique des Adultes [*European Associaton for Catholic Adult Education*] (EAIO)
FEED............ Feeding (SAUS)
FEED............ Field Electron Energy Distribution (SAUS)
FEED............ Field Emission Energy Distribution (SAUS)
FEED............ Field Exploitation of Elevation Data (RDA)
FEED............ File of Evaluated and Event Data [*Nuclear energy*] (NUCP)
FEED............ Floating Electrode Effect Development (SAUS)
FEEDBAC...... Foreign Exchange (SAUS)
FEEDBAC...... Foreign Exchange, Eurodollar, and Branch Accounting (PDAA)
FEEDM.......... Federation Europeenne des Emballeurs et Distributeurs de Miel [*European Federation of Honey Packers and Distributors*] [*British*] (EAIO)
FEEDS.......... Facilities Engineering Expert and Diagnostic System (SAUO)
FEEDS.......... Fire Emergency Equipment Dispatch System
FEEE............ Foundation for Environmental Education in Europe (SAUS)
FEEF............ Federal Energy Efficiency Fund (SAUS)
FEEF............ Front End Enquiry File (SAUS)
FEEFHS........ Federation of East European Family History Societies (EA)
FEEG............ Fetal Electroencephalogram [*Medicine*] (AAMN)
FEEL............ Ferro-Electric Electro- Luminescence (SAUS)
FEEL............ Ferro-Electric Electro-Luminescent (SAUS)

FE-EL .... Ferroelectric-Electroluminescent
FEEL .... Fox Editor Enhancement Library (PCM)
FEEM .... Failure Effects and Events Management [*Automotive Diagnostics*]
FEEM .... Federation of European Explosives Manufacturers (SAUS)
FEEM .... Field Electron Emission Microscope [*or Microscopy*]
FEEMS .... Facilities Engineer Equipment Maintenance System [*Army*]
FEEOR .... Federal Equal Employment Opportunity Recruitment Program (GFGA)
FEEP .... Field Emission Electric Propulsion System (SAUS)
FEEPROM .... Flash Electrically Erasable Programmable Read Only Memory [*Electronics*]
FEER .... Far Eastern Economic Review [*A publication*] (BRI)
FEER .... Fast Eigensolution Extraction Routine [*Computer program*]
FEER .... Fundamental Equilibrium Exchange Rate [*Economics*]
FEES .... Front End Edit System (SAUO)
FEEST .... Freight Equipment Environmental Sampling Test Program [*RSPA*] (TAG)
FEET .... Just For Feet [*NASDAQ symbol*] (SAG)
feet/min .... Feet per Minute (SAUS)
FEEVA .... Federation of European Equine Veterinary Associations (GVA)
FEF .... Factory Express File (VLIE)
FEF .... Fast Extruding Furnace Black (SAUS)
FEF .... Fast Extrusion Furnace
FEF .... Feline Embryonic Fibroblast
FEF .... Film End File (SAUS)
FEF .... Flat/Exponential Filter
FEF .... Flight Engineering Facility (MCD)
FEF .... Forced Expiratory Flow [*Physiology*]
FEF .... Foundation for Educational Futures (EA)
FEF .... Foundry Educational Foundation [*Defunct*] (EA)
FEF .... Freedom of Expression Foundation (EA)
FEF .... Free Energy Function
FEF .... French Expeditionary Force
FEF .... Friends of the Earth Foundation (EA)
FEF .... Frontal Eye Field [*Neuroanatomy*]
FEF .... Frozen Equilibrium Flow
FEF .... Fuel Examination Facility [*Nuclear energy*] (NRCH)
FEF .... Fusion Energy Foundation (EA)
FEFA .... Alindao [*Central African Republic*] [*ICAO location identifier*] (ICLI)
FEFA .... Feeder Fault Analysis (PDAA)
FEFA .... Future European Fighter Aircraft project (SAUS)
FEFAC .... Federation Europeenne des Fabricants d'Aliments Composes [*European Federation of Compound Animal Feedingstuff Manufacturers*] (EAIO)
FEFANA .... European Feed Additives Manufacturers Association (GVA)
FEFANA .... Federation Europeenne des Fabricants d'Adjuvants pour la Nutrition Animale [*European Federation of Manufacturers of Feed Additives*] (EAIO)
FEFB .... Obo [*Central African Republic*] [*ICAO location identifier*] (ICLI)
FEF Black .... Fast Extruding Furnace Black (SAUS)
FEFC .... Far Eastern Freight Conference
FEFC .... Further Education Funding Council [*British*] (DET)
FEFCEB .... Federation Europeene des Fabricants de Caisses et Emballages en Bois [*European Federation of Manufacturers of Timber Crates and Packing Cases*] (PDAA)
FEFCO .... Federation Europeenne des Fabricants de Carton Ondule [*European Federation of Manufacturers of Corrugated Board*] [*France*]
FEFET .... Ferroelectric-Dielectric Field Effect Transistor (IAA)
FEFET .... Ferro-Electric Field Effect Transistor (SAUS)
FEFF .... Bangui/M'Poko [*Central African Republic*] [*ICAO location identifier*] (ICLI)
FEFG .... Bangassou [*Central African Republic*] [*ICAO location identifier*] (ICLI)
FEFGC .... Fuel Element Failure Gas Chromatograph (COE)
FEFI .... Birao [*Central African Republic*] [*ICAO location identifier*] (ICLI)
FEFI .... Flight Engineers Fault Isolation [*Aviation*]
FEFL .... Bossembele [*Central African Republic*] [*ICAO location identifier*] (ICLI)
FEFM .... Bambari [*Central African Republic*] [*ICAO location identifier*] (ICLI)
FEFM .... Federazione Europea Fabbricanti Matite [*Federation of Eraser Pencil Manufacturers Associations*] (EAIO)
FEFmax .... Forced Expiratory Flow Maximal [*Achieved during a forced vital capacity*] [*Medicine*] (DAVI)
FEFN .... N'Dele [*Central African Republic*] [*ICAO location identifier*] (ICLI)
FEFO .... Bouar [*Central African Republic*] [*ICAO location identifier*] (ICLI)
FEFO .... First-Ended, First-Out [*Computer science*]
FEFP .... Fuel Element Failure Propagation [*Nuclear energy*]
FEFPEB .... Federation Europeenne des Fabricants de Palettes et Emballages en Bois [*European Federation of Pallet and Wooden Crate Manufacturers - EFPWCM*] (EAIO)
FEFPL .... Fuel Element Failure Propagation Loop [*Nuclear energy*] (NRCH)
FEFPX .... Frontier Funds: Equity Ptfl. [*Mutual fund ticker symbol*] (SG)
FEFR .... Bria [*Central African Republic*] [*ICAO location identifier*] (ICLI)
FEFS .... Bossangoa [*Central African Republic*] [*ICAO location identifier*] (ICLI)
FEFT .... Berberati [*Central African Republic*] [*ICAO location identifier*] (ICLI)
FEFV .... Bangui [*Central African Republic*] [*ICAO location identifier*] (ICLI)
FEFV .... Forced Expiratory Flow Volume [*Medicine*] (EDAA)
FEFY .... Yalinga [*Central African Republic*] [*ICAO location identifier*] (ICLI)
FEFZ .... Zemio [*Central African Republic*] [*ICAO location identifier*] (ICLI)
f-eg- .... Equatorial Guinea [*MARC geographic area code*] [*Library of Congress*] (LCCP)
FEG .... Field Emission Gun (AAEL)
feg .... Figurative (ELAL)
FEG .... Finance and Economic Group (SAUO)
FEG .... First Canadian Energy Corp. [*Vancouver Stock Exchange symbol*]
FEG .... Fletcher Challenge Ener.ADS [*NYSE symbol*] (TTSB)
FEG .... Fletcher Challenge Energy [*NYSE symbol*] (SAG)
FEGA .... Film Editors Guild of Australia (SAUO)
FEgAD .... United States Air Force, Armament Development and Test Center, Technical Library, Eglin Air Force Base, FL [*Library symbol*] [*Library of Congress*] (LCLS)
FEGAP .... Federation Europeenne de la Ganterie de Peau [*European Federation of Leather Glove-Making*] [*EC*] (ECED)
FEGH .... Field Engineering General Handbook (SAUS)
FEGLI .... Federal Employees' Group Life Insurance
FEGO .... International Federation of Gynecology and Obstetricics [*Medicine*] (EDAA)
FEgRH .... United States Air Force, Eglin Regional Hospital, Eglin Air Force Base, FL [*Library symbol*] [*Library of Congress*] (LCLS)
FEGS .... Federation Employment and Guidance Service (EA)
FEGT .... Furnace Exit Gas Temperature
FEG TEM ...... Field Emission Gun Transmission Electron Microscope (SAUS)
FEGZ .... Bozoum [*Central African Republic*] [*ICAO location identifier*] (ICLI)
FEH .... Federation Europeenne Halterophile [*European Weightlifting Federation - EWF*] (EA)
FEH .... Fixed Established Hypertension (SAUS)
FEH .... Foundation of European Help (SAUO)
FEHA .... Federal Hall National Memorial
FEHA .... Florida Environmental Health Association (SRA)
FEHB .... Federal Employees Health Benefits
FEHBA .... Federal Employees Health Benefits Act
FEHBP .... Federal Employees Health Benefits Program (AFM)
FEHC .... Federal Emergency Housing Corp. [*New Deal*]
FEHD .... Fair Employment and Housing Department (SAUS)
FEHD .... Far Eastern Hotel Development (SAUS)
FEHE .... Feed-Effluent Heat Exchanger [*Chemical engineering*]
FEHEM .... Front-End Hardward Emulator (ADWA)
FEHO .... Federation of European Helicopter Operators (PDAA)
FEHQ .... Fluke European HeadQuarters (SAUS)
FEHVA .... Federation of European Heating and Ventilating Associations (EA)
FEI .... Facilities Engineering Items [*Military*] (AABC)
FEI .... Factor Eight Inhibitor (DB)
FEI .... Farm Equipment Institute [*Later, FIEI*] (EA)
FEI .... Federal Executive Institute
FEI .... Federation Equestre Internationale [*International Equestrian Federation*] [*Berne, Switzerland*] (EAIO)
FeI .... Ferrous Iodide [*Medicine*] (EDAA)
FEI .... Field Engineering Instruction [*British*] (DA)
FEI .... Financial Executive Institute (SAUS)
FEI .... Financial Executives Institute of Canada (DD)
FEI .... Finnish Environment Institute (SAUS)
FEI .... Firing Effectiveness Indicator [*Military*] (CAAL)
FEI .... Firing Error Indicator
FEI .... Fish Exports Inspector
FEI .... Flight Engineers International (SAUO)
FEI .... Flight Error Instrumentation [*Aerospace*] (IAA)
FEI .... Flightline Electronics Inc. (SAUS)
FEI .... Fluidic Explosive Initiator (PDAA)
FEI .... Force Effectiveness Indicator [*COEA*] (MCD)
FEI .... For Engineering Information (AAG)
FEI .... Foundation Europalia International (EAIO)
FEI .... Fourth Engine Ignition (ACAE)
FEI .... France-Europe International [*An association*] (EAIO)
FEI .... Free Enterprise Institute (SAUO)
FEI .... Free Europe, Inc. [*Later, RFE/RL*]
FEI .... Frequency Electronics, Inc. [*AMEX symbol*] (SPSG)
FEI .... Frequency Electrs [*AMEX symbol*] (TTSB)
FEI .... Frontend International Technologies, Inc. [*Vancouver Stock Exchange symbol*]
FEIA .... Financial Executives Institute of Australia
FEIA .... Flight Engineers' International Association (EA)
FEIA .... Foreign Earned Income Act [*1978*]
FEIBA .... Factor Eight Inhibitor Bypassing Activity (DB)
FEIBP .... Federation Europeenne de l'Industrie de la Brosserie et de la Pinceuterie [*European Federation of the Brush and Paint Brush Industries - EFBPBI*] (EAIO)
FEIC .... Federation Europeenne de l'Industrie du Contreplaque [*European Federation of the Plywood Industry - EFPI*] (EA)
FEIC .... FEI Co. [*NASDAQ symbol*] (SAG)
FEIC .... Fellow of the Engineering Institute of Canada
FEIC .... Fossil Energy Information Center [*ORNL*] (GRD)
FEICA .... Federation Europeenne des Industries de Colles et Adhesifs [*Association of European Adhesives Manufacturers*] (EA)
FEICA .... Federation of European Adhesives Manufacturers (SAUO)
FEICC .... Foundation for the Establishment of an International Criminal Court (EA)
FEI Co .... FEI Co. [*Associated Press*] (SAG)
FEICRO .... Federation of European Industrial Cooperative Research Organisations (or Organizations) (SAUO)
FEICUS .... Family Education and Information Council of the United States (EA)
FEID .... Flight Equipment Interface Device [*NASA*] (NASA)
FEID .... Functional Engineering Interface Device [*NASA*] (NASA)
FEIDCT .... Fellow of the Educational Institute of Design Craft and Technology (ODA)
FEIEA .... Federation of European Industrial Editors' Associations
FEIG .... Fossil Energy Information Group [*Department of Energy*] [*Information service or system*] (IID)
FEIHCCS ...... Flying Eagle and Indian Head Cent Collectors Society (EA)
FEIL .... Florida Emergency Information Line (DEMM)
FEILS .... Federal Energy Information Locator Systems

FEIM Federation Europeenne des Importateurs de Machines et d'Equipements de Bureau [*European Federation of Importers of Business Equipment*] (EAIO)
FEIN Federal Employer Identification Number
FE INC Iron Inclusion Bodies [*Hematology*] (DAVI)
FEIP Facility and Equipment Improvement Program (SAUO)
FEIP Front-end for Echographic Image Processing (SAUO)
FEIS Fellow of the Educational Institute (or Institution) of Scotland (SAUO)
FEIS Fellow of the Educational Institution of Scotland (SAUS)
FEIS Final Environmental Impact Statement
FEIS Fugitive Emissions Information System [*Environmental Protection Agency*] (GFGA)
FEIS Further Education Information Service (AIE)
FEISEAP Federation of Engineering Institutions South-East Asia and the Pacific (SAUO)
FEISM Field Engineering Instructional Systems Manual (SAUS)
FEIT Fujitsu Enhanced Imaging Technology (VERA)
FEITC Federation Europeenne des Industries Techniques du Cinema
FEITFIS FASB Emerging Issues Task Force Issue Summaries (SAUS)
FEITFM FASB Emerging Issues Task Force Minutes of Meetings (SAUS)
FEIZ Fellow of the Engineering Institution of Zambia
FEJ France Europe Avia Jet [*ICAO designator*] (FAAC)
FEJB Forum of Environmental Journalists of Bangladesh (EERA)
FEJBT Federation Europeenne des Jeunesse Bons Templiers [*European Good Templar Youth Federation*] [*Norway*] (EAIO)
FEJE Facilities Engineer Job Estimating System (SAUO)
FEJE Facility Engineering Job Estimating [*Military*] (GFGA)
FEJI Far East Job International [*Former USSR*] (ECON)
FEK File Encryption Key [*Computer science*] (MWOL)
FEK Fish Epidermal Keratocyte [*Marine science*]
FEK fractional K-excretion (SAUS)
FEK Frequency Exchange Keying
FEKG Fetal Electrocardiogram [*Medicine*]
FEL Familial Erythrophagocytic Lymphohistocytosis [*Medicine*]
FEL Family Emission Level [*Automotive engineering*]
FEL Family Emission Limit (EEVL)
FEL Faser-Elastomere- Lager (SAUS)
FEL Feldberg In Schwarzwald [*Federal Republic of Germany*] [*Seismograph station code, US Geological Survey*] (SEIS)
FEL Felicity [*Television program title*]
Fel Felinus Sandeus [*Deceased, 1503*] [*Authority cited in pre-1607 legal work*] (DSA)
FEL Fellis [*Gall*] [*Pharmacy*] (ROG)
FEL Fellow
FEL Felony [*FBI standardized term*]
Fel Felsted [*Record label*] [*Great Britain, etc.*]
FEL Felucca [*Ship's rigging*] (ROG)
FEL Fibre Elastomeric (SAUS)
FEL File End Label (SAUS)
FEL Financial Enterprises Limited (SAUO)
FEL First Element Launch (SSD)
FEL First European Airways Ltd. [*British*] [*ICAO designator*] (FAAC)
FEL Fisheries Engineering Laboratory [*Marine science*] (MSC)
FEL Flight Engineer's Licence [*British*] (AIA)
FEL Food Engineering Laboratory [*Army*]
FEL Frame Electrical System (SAUS)
FEL Frank Effect Level [*Environmental science*] (COE)
FEL Free Electron LASER
fel free-electron laser (SAUS)
FEL Frequency Engineering Laboratory (MCD)
FEL Friend Erythroleukemia Cell [*Oncology*]
FEL Fritz Engineering Laboratory [*Lehigh University*]
FEL Front End Loader (ADA)
fel front-end loader (SAUS)
fel front-end loading (SAUS)
FEL Full Employment League
FELA Federal Employers' Liability Act (Railroads) [*1906*]
FELABAN Federacion Latinoamericana de Bancos [*Latin American Banking Federation - LABF*] [*Bogota, Colombia*] (EAIO)
FELAC Latin American Federation of Surgeons (SAUO)
FELACUTI Federacion Latinoamericana de Usuarios del Transporte [*Latin American Federation of Shippers' Councils*] (EAIO)
FELAP Finite Element Analysis Program [*Nuclear energy*] (NRCH)
FELASA European Federation of Laboratory Animal Science (SAUS)
FELATRAP Federacion Latinoamericana de Trajabadores de la Prensa [*Latin American Federation of Press Workers*] (EAIO)
FELC Friend Erythroleukemia [*Medicine*] (EDAA)
FELCO Federation of English Language Course Organisation [*British*]
FelCor FelCor Suite Hotels, Inc. [*Associated Press*] (SAG)
FELCSA Federation of Evangelical Lutheran Churches in Southern Africa (SAUO)
Fel D1 Felis Domesticus 1 [*Protein found in the saliva of cats*]
FELDF Free Enterprise Legal Defense Fund [*Bellevue, WA*] (EA)
FELE Franklin Electric [*NASDAQ symbol*] (SG)
FELE Franklin Electric Co., Inc. [*NASDAQ symbol*] (NQ)
FELF Far East Land Forces [*British military*] (DMA)
FELG Far East Liaison Group (CINC)
Feli Felinus Sandeus [*Deceased, 1503*] [*Authority cited in pre-1607 legal work*] (DSA)
FELIF Feeder Length in Feet (PDAA)
Felin Felinus Sandeus [*Deceased, 1503*] [*Authority cited in pre-1607 legal work*] (DSA)
FELINE Frederick Engineering's Dataline Monitor/Protocol Analyzer [*Computer science*]
FeLINE Iron as a Limiting-Nutrient Experiment (SAUO)
felinol felinologist (SAUS)
felinol felinology (SAUS)
FELISA Fluorogenic Enzyme-Linked Immunosorbent Assay [*Biochemistry*]
Felix Felixstowe (SAUS)
FELL Federal Labor Laws
Fell Fellow (CMD)
FELL Fellow
FELL Finland, Estonia, Latvia, and Lithuania (SAUS)
FeLLC Feline lymphosarcoma-leukemia complex (SAUS)
Fell Guar Fell on Guaranty and Suretyship [*A publication*] (DLA)
FELM Felmersham [*England*]
FEL MEM Felicis Memoriae [*Of Happy Memory*] [*Latin*]
FELNET Flanders Environmental Library Network (SAUO)
FELO Far Eastern Liaison Office (SAUO)
f/e loader front-end loader (SAUS)
FELOS Feeder Load Search (PDAA)
FELP Free-Electron Laser Physics (SAUS)
FELR Feeler
FELS Field Engineering Logistics System (VLIE)
FEISM Field Engineering Instructional Systems Manual (SAUS)
Felsto Felixstowe (SAUS)
FELT Failed Element Location Team (SAUS)
FELT Fluid Encapsulated Launch Technique (PDAA)
FELT Free Electron Laser Technology (SAUS)
FEL-TIE Free Electron Laser/Technical Integration and Evaluation (ACAE)
FEL-TNO TNO Physics & Electronics Laboratory (SAUS)
FeLV Feline Leukemia Virus (ADWA)
FELV Feline Leukemia Virus [*Also, FLV*]
FEM Facility Effluent Monitoring (SAUS)
FEM Federation Europeenne de la Manutention [*European Federation of Handling Industries*] (EAIO)
FEM Federation Europeenne des Metallurgistes dans la Communaute [*European Metalworkers' Federation in the Community*] [*EC*] (ECED)
FEM Federation Europeenne des Motels [*European Motel Federation*]
FEM Female [*or Feminine*] (KSC)
fem Female (SHCU)
FEM Feminine (GOBB)
Fem Feminist (DIAR)
FEM Feministas en Marcha [*Feminists on the March*] [*Puerto Rico*] (EAIO)
FEM Femoral [*Anatomy*]
FEM femoris (SAUS)
fem femur (SAUS)
FEM Ferguson Library, Stamford, CT [*OCLC symbol*] (OCLC)
FEM Ferro-Electric Memory (SAUS)
fem field-effect mode (SAUS)
FEM Field-Effect Modified (IEEE)
FEM Field Effect Modified transistor (SAUS)
FEM Field Electron Microscope [*or Microscopy*]
FEM Field-Electron Microscope (SAUS)
FEM field electron microscopy (SAUS)
FEM Field Emission Microscope [*or Microscopy*]
FEM Field Emission Microscopy (SAUS)
FEM Field Engineering Maintenance
FEM Field engineering memo (SAUS)
FEM Field Evaluation Model
FEM Final Effluent Monitor (SAUS)
FEM Financial Evaluation Program (SAUS)
FEM Finite Element Machine (SAUS)
FEM Finite-Element Meshing [*or Modeling*] [*Computer science*] (PCM)
FEM Finite element model (SAUS)
FEM Finite Element Modeling (SAUS)
FEM Finiter Elemente (SAUS)
FEM Firmware Expansion Model [*Hewlett Packard*] (NITA)
FEM Firmware Expansion Module (SAUS)
FEM Five-level End of Message (SAUS)
FEM Fixed End Moment (SAUS)
FEM Flame Emission Spectroscopy
FEM Flexion-Extension Motion [*Orthopedics*]
F/EM Flight/Engineering Model (ACAE)
FEM Fluid Energy Mill (MCD)
FEM Flyable Engineering Model (KSC)
FEM Fondation Europeenne pour le Management [*European Foundation for Management Development*] [*Belgium*] (EAIO)
FEM Force Effectiveness Measure (SAUS)
FEM Force Effectiveness Model (ACAE)
FEM FORTRAN Enhancement Package (SAUS)
FEM Foundation for Elective Mutism, Inc. (EA)
FEM Free Electron Model [*Physical chemistry*]
FEM Front End Module (ACAE)
fem fuel efficiency monitor (SAUS)
FEMA Failure Mode and Effects Analysis (VLIE)
FEMA Farm Equipment Manufacturers Association (EA)
FEMA Federal Emergency Administration (ACAE)
FEMA Federal Emergency Management Administration (SAUS)
FEMA Federal Emergency Management Agency (ECON)
FEMA Federal Emergency Manpower Agency (SAUO)
FEMA Finite Element Model of Material Transport through Aquifers (CARB)
FEMA Fire Equipment Manufacturers Association (EA)
FEMA Flavor and Extract Manufacturers Association of the USA (EA)
FEMA Flavor Extracts Manufacturers' Association (EDCT)
FEMA Flavoring Extract Manufacturers Association of the United States (SAUO)
FEMA Food Equipment Manufacturers Association (EA)
FEMA Foundry Equipment and Materials Association [*Later, CISA*] (EA)

FEMAA......... Food Equipment Manufacturers' Association of Australia
FEMAAR...... Federal Emergency Management Agency Acquisition Regulation (AAGC)
FEMAC......... Flexible Electronic Manufacturing Assembly Cell (TIMI)
FEMALE....... Formerly Employed Mothers at the Leading Edge [*Previous name, Formerly Employed Mothers at Loose Ends*]
FEMA-M/R... Federal Emergency Management Agency Office of Mitigation and Research [*Washington, DC*]
FEMAP......... Finite Element Mold-Filling Analysis Program [*General Electric Co.*]
FEMAPR...... Federal Emergency Management Agency Procurement Regulations (AAGC)
FEMA-REP... Guidance for Developing State and Local Radiological Emergency Response Plans (SAUS)
FEMA-REP-1... Response Plans and Preparedness in Support of Nuclear Power Plants (SAUO)
FEMA-REP-5... Guidance for Developing State and Local Radiological Emergency Response Plans (SAUO)
FEMAS......... Far East Merchants Association [*Defunct*] (EA)
FEMB.......... Federation Europeenne du Mobilier de Bureau [*European Federation of Office Furniture*] [*EC*] (ECED)
FEMC.......... Finite Element Modelling Optimization (SAUS)
FEMCO........ National Federation of Export Management Companies (EA)
FEMCPL....... Facilities and Environmental Measurement Components Parts List [*NASA*] (NASA)
FEMDM........ Field Engineering Maintenance Diagram Manual (SAUS)
FEMECA....... Failure / Error Mode, Effect and Criticality Analysis (SAUS)
FEMECA....... Failure/Error Mode, Effect and Critically Analysis (SAUS)
FEMED......... Fluorouracil, Methotrexate, Cyclophosphamide, Prednisone [*Antineoplastic drug regimen*] (DAVI)
FEMEF......... Feeder Meter Flow (PDAA)
FEME-REP-2... Guidance for Developing State and Local Radiological Emergency Response Plans (SAUO)
Fem extern... Outer Side of the Thigh [*Latin*] [*Medicine*] [*Femoribus Externus*] (EDAA)
FEMF.......... Floating Electronic Maintenance Facility (MCD)
FEMF.......... Florida Emergency Medicine Foundation (SAUO)
FEMF.......... Foreign Electromotive Force (TEL)
FEM/FEA...... Finite Element Method/Finite Element Analysis (SAUS)
FEMFM........ Federation of European Manufacturers of Friction Materials (EA)
FEMGED...... Federation Internationale des Grandes et Moyennes Entreprises de Distribution [*International Federation of Retail Distributors*] [*Belgium*] (EAIO)
FEMGEN...... Finite Element Mesh Generation Program [*Fegs Ltd.*] [*Software package*] (NCC)
FemHlth....... Female Health Co. [*Associated Press*] (SAG)
FEMI........... Fernmeldeinstallateur (SAUS)
FEMI........... Field Engineering Manual of Instruction (SAUS)
FEMIB......... Federation Europeenne des Syndicats de Fabricants de Menuiseries Industrielles de Batiment [*European Federation of Building Joinery Manufacturers*] (EAIO)
FEMIC......... Fire Equipment Manufacturers Institute of Canada (SAUO)
FEMIDE....... Federacion Mundial de Instituciones Financieras de Desarrollo [*World Federation of Development Financing Institutions - WFDFI*] [*Madrid, Spain*] (EAIO)
Feminist Econ... Feminist Economics [*A publication*] (JLIT)
FEM INTERN... Femoribus Internis [*To the Inner Part of the Thigh*] [*Pharmacy*] (ROG)
FEMIPI........ Federation Europeenne des Mandataires de l'Industrie en Propriete Industrielle [*European Federation of Agents of Industry in Industrial Property*] (EAIO)
FEMIS.......... Federal Emergency Management Information System (ABAC)
FEMIS.......... Field Engineering Management Information System (SAUS)
FEMITRON.... Field Emission Microwave Device (SAUS)
FEMK........... Federation Europeenne des Masseurskinesitherapeutes Praticiens en Physiotherapie
FEMKSF....... Frauendienst der Evangelisch-Methodistischen Kirche in der Schweiz und in Frankreich [*United Methodist Women in Switzerland and in France*] (EAIO)
FEMKX......... Fidelity Emerging Markets [*Mutual fund ticker symbol*] (SG)
FEML........... Funded Environmental and Morale Leave Program [*Military*] (DOMA)
femlib.......... feminine liberationist (SAUS)
Fem LS......... Feminist Legal Studies [*A publication*]
FEMM.......... Field Engineering Maintenance Manual (SAUS)
femo............ femoral (SAUS)
FEMO.......... Finite Element Modeling Optimization
FEMO.......... Free Electron Molecular Orbital (SAUS)
Femocrat..... Feminist Bureaucrat
FEMOD........ Feature Based Modeller (VLIE)
FEMOSI....... Federation Mondiale des Syndicats d'Industries [*World Federation of Industrial Workers' Unions*]
FEMP.......... Facility Effluent Monitoring Plan (ABAC)
FEMP.......... Facility Specific Effluent Monitoring Plan (SAUS)
FEMP.......... Federal Energy Management Program [*Department of Energy*]
FEMP.......... Fernald Environmental Management Project [*Department of Energy*]
FEMP.......... Footrot Eradication Management Plan (SAUO)
FEMP.......... Free Energy Minimization Procedure [*Computer science*]
FEMP.......... Fusion Engineering Materials Program (SAUS)
Fem-pop...... Femoral Popliteal [*Medicine*] (EDAA)
fem-pop...... Femoral-Popliteal [*Bypass*] [*Cardiology*] (DAVI)
FEMPS........ Federation of Employees Membership Philatelic Societies (SAUO)
FEMPX........ Front End Multiplexer (SAUS)
FEMR.......... Femur (SAUS)
FEMR.......... Field Equipment Malfunction Report (SAUO)
FEMR.......... Fleet Electromagnetic Radiation [*Team*] [*Navy*] (NVT)
FemRx......... FemRx, Inc. [*Associated Press*] (SAG)
FEMS.......... Facilities and Environmental Measuring System [*NASA*] (KSC)
FEMS.......... Facilities Engineering Management System (MCD)
FEMS.......... Federation of European Microbiological Societies (SAUO)
FEMS.......... Field Electronic Maintenance Section [*National Weather Service*]
FEMS.......... Finite Element Modelling System (SAUS)
FEMS.......... Fleet Exercise Minelaying System (SAUS)
FEMSA........ Fire and Emergency Manufacturers and Services Association (NTPA)
FEMSA........ Fire Equipment Manufacturers and Suppliers Association (SAUO)
FEMS Immunol Med Microbiol... FEMS Immunology and Medical Microbiology (SAUS)
FEMS Microbiol Rev... FEMS Microbiology Reviews (SAUS)
FEM Transistor... Field Effect Modified Transistor (SAUS)
FEMU.......... Further Education Marketing Unit (AIE)
FEMUSI....... Federacion Mundial de Sindicatos de Industrias [*World Federation of Industrial Workers' Unions*]
FEMVIEW..... Finite Element Mesh and Result Viewing [*Fegs Ltd.*] [*Software package*] (NCC)
FEMW.......... Field Engineering and Mine Warfare (SAUO)
FEN............. Fairchild Industries, Inc. [*NYSE symbol*] (SPSG)
FEN............. Family Education Network [*Computer science*]
FEN............. Family Empowerment Network [*Support for Families Affected by FAS/FAE*] [*Organization concerned with families affected by fetal alcohol syndrome or fetal alcohol effects*] (PAZ)
FEN............. Far Eastern Network (SAUS)
FEN............. Far East Network [*US Armed Forces radio station*] [*Japan*]
FEN............. Fenfluramine [*Medicine*] (DIPS)
FEN............. Fengtien [*Hoten, Shenyang*] [*Republic of China*] [*Seismograph station code, US Geological Survey*] (SEIS)
Fen............. Fenner (SAUS)
Fen............. Fenwick (SAUS)
Fen............. Fenwood (SAUS)
FEN............. Fluid, Electrolytes, and Nutrition [*Dietetics*] [*Pharmacology*] (DAVI)
FEN............. Forest Ecology Network
FEN............. Free-Net Erlangen Nurnberg [*Information service or system*] (IID)
FEN............. Frequency Emitting Network (SAUO)
FEN............. Frequency Emphasizing Network (SAUS)
FEN............. Front-End Network (VLIE)
FE_{Na}.......... Excreted Fraction of Filtered Sodium [*Test*] (DAVI)
FENA.......... Far East News Agency (SAUO)
FENA.......... Florida Emergency Nurses Association (SAUS)
FE_{Na}.......... Fractional Extraction of Sodium [*Organic chemistry*] (DAVI)
FENa.......... fractional Na-excretion (SAUS)
FENALCO..... National Federation of Merchants (Colombia) [*Political party*] (PSAP)
FENASYCOA... Federation Nationale des Syndicats du Commerce Ouest Africain [*National Federation of Commerce Unions - West Africa*]
FENB.......... Far East National Bank [*NASDAQ symbol*] (SAG)
FENC.......... Fencing (ROG)
FENCO........ Foundation of Engineering Corporations (SAUS)
FEND.......... Federation of European Nurses in diabetes (SAUO)
FEND.......... Force End (SAUS)
fender bender... fender-bending automotive vehicle accident (SAUS)
FENDRE....... Forces to Eliminate No-Deposit/No-Return
FEND Signal... Force End Signal (SAUS)
FEng.......... Fellow [*or Fellowship*] of Engineering
FENG.......... Flight Engineer (IAA)
F Eng......... Forest Engineer
FENKN........ Fuel Supply Unknown [*Aviation*] (FAAC)
FENO.......... Far Eastern Network Okinawa (SAUO)
FENP.......... Fluoro(ethyl)norprogesterone [*Endocrinology*]
FENP.......... Front-End Network Processor (VLIE)
FENPB........ Full Employment and National Purposes Budget (OICC)
FENSA........ Film Entertainment National Service Association (SAUO)
FENSA........ Film Entertainments National Service Association (SAUO)
Fen-Scan..... Fenno-Scandia (SAUS)
Fen-Scan..... Fenno-Scandinavian (SAUS)
Fent........... Fenton's Important Judgments [*New Zealand*] [*A publication*] (DLA)
Fent........... Fenton's New Zealand Reports [*A publication*] (DLA)
FENT.......... First Enterprise Financial Group [*NASDAQ symbol*] (SAG)
FEntFn........ First Enterprise Financial Group [*Associated Press*] (SAG)
Fent Imp Judg... Fenton's Important Judgments [*New Zealand*] [*A publication*] (DLA)
FENTL........ Fuel Supply Until [*Aviation*] (FAAC)
Fent (New Zealand)... Fenton's New Zealand Reports [*A publication*] (DLA)
Fent NZ....... Fenton's New Zealand Reports [*A publication*] (DLA)
FeNTO........ Federation of the Scientific and Technical Organizations of the Socialist Countries [*Formerly, Permanent Council of Scientific and Technical Organizations of Socialist Countries*] (EA)
Fenton........ Fenton's Important Judgments [*New Zealand*] [*A publication*] (DLA)
Fenway........ Fenway Park Stadium, Boston (SAUS)
FEO............ Facility Emergency Organization [*Nuclear energy*] (NRCH)
FEO............ Federal Energy Office [*Later, FEA*]
FEO............ Federal Executive Office (SAUO)
FEO............ Federation of Economic Organizations (SAUO)
FEO............ Feodosiya [*Former USSR*] [*Seismograph station code, US Geological Survey*] [*Closed*] (SEIS)
FEO............ Field Engineering Order (KSC)
FEO............ Field Extension Office [*DoD*]
FEO............ Flag Engineering Officer [*British*]
FEO............ Fleet Engineer Officer [*Obsolete*] [*British*]
FEO............ Flora Europaea Organization [*British*]
FEO............ Fuel-Efficient Oil
FEOC.......... Farm Enterprise Organisation and Control (SAUS)
FEOC.......... Field Emergency Operations Centers (SAUO)
FEODT........ Federation Europeenne des Organisations des Detaillants en Tabacs [*European Federation of Tobacco Retail Organizations*] (EAIO)

FEOF........ Foreign Exchange Operations Fund
FEOGA........ Fonds European d'Orientation et de Garantie Agriculturel [*European Agricultural Guidance and Guarantee Fund*]
FEOGA........ Fonds Europeen d'Orientation et de Garantie Agricole [*Also known as EAGGF*]
FEOM........ Full Extraocular Motion [*or Movement*] [*Ophthalmology*] (DAVI)
FEOM........ Full Extraocular Movement (ADWA)
FEORP........ Federal Equal Opportunity Recruitment Program
FEOS........ Forward Engineering Operating Station [*Navy*] (CAAL)
FEOTC........ Federal Exporters Overseas Transport Committee (SAUS)
FEOV........ Forced End of Volume (IAA)
feov........ force end of volume (SAUS)
FEP........ Fair Employment Practice
FEP........ Fast Evening Person's
FEP........ Fast Evening Persons Report [*Nielsen Television Index*] (NTCM)
FEP........ Feature Extraction Processor (SAUS)
FEP........ Features, Events and Processes (SAUO)
FEP........ Federal Education Project [*Defunct*] (EA)
FEP........ Federal Employee Program
FEP........ Federal Employees Program (SAUS)
FEP........ Federation Europeenne de Psychanalyse [*European Psycho-Analytical Federation - EPF*] (EAIO)
FEP........ Federation of European Publishers [*Belgium*] (EAIO)
FEP........ Fermented Egg Product [*Animal repellent*]
FEP........ Fibroepithelial Polyp [*Medicine*] (MELL)
FEP........ Film Epoxypolyamide (SAUS)
fep........ final evaluation phase (SAUS)
FEP........ Financial Evaluation Program [*IBM Corp.*]
FEP........ Flash Evaporator Plant
FEP........ Flash Evoked Potential [*Behavioral science*]
FEP........ Fleet EHF Package (SAUO)
FEP........ Fleet [*Satellite Communications*] Extremely [*High Frequency*] Package (DOMA)
FEP........ Flight Evaluation Plan (SAUS)
FEP........ Flight Experiment Program (ACAE)
FEP........ Floral Ethel Propane
FEP........ Fluorethylene Propylene [*Plastics*]
FEP........ Fluorinated Ethylene-Propylene [*Copolymer*]
FEP........ Fluorinated Perfluoroethylene-Propylene Front-End Processor (SAUS)
FEP........ Fluoro Ethel Propane (SAUS)
FEP........ Foderation der Europaischen Parkettindustrieverbande [*European Federation of the Parquet Floor Industry Associations*] [*EC*] (ECED)
FEP........ Forecast Expenditure Plan (ACAE)
FEP........ Fore Edges Painted [*Paper*]
fep........ formal evaluation phase (SAUS)
FEP........ FORTRAN Enhancement Package (NITA)
FEP........ Foundation for Education with Production (EA)
FEP........ Franklin Electronic Pub [*NYSE symbol*] (TTSB)
FEP........ Franklin Electronic Publishers, Inc. [*NYSE symbol*] (SAG)
FEP........ Free Enterprise Personnel (MCD)
FEP........ Free Erythrocyte Porphyrins (SAUS)
FEP........ Free Erythrocyte Protoporphyrin [*Hematology*]
FEP........ Free Europe Press (SAUO)
FEP........ Freeport, IL [*Location identifier*] [*FAA*] (FAAL)
FEP........ Front End Package (OA)
FEP........ Front End Processing (SAUS)
FEP........ Front-End Processor [*Computer*] (NASA)
FEP........ Front-End-Prozessoren (SAUS)
FEP........ Front-End Purification [*Engineering*]
FEP........ Fully Engineered Prototype [*Automotive engineering*]
FEP........ Fuse Enclosure Package (IEEE)
FEPA........ Fair Educational Practice Act [*New York, New Jersey, Massachusetts*]
FEPA........ Fair Employment Practice Act (SAUO)
FEPA........ Fair Employment Practices Act [*1964*]
FEPA........ Far-Eastern Prehistory Association [*Later, IPPA*] (EA)
FEPA........ Federal Employees Pay Act
FEPA........ Federal Executive and Professional Association [*Defunct*] (EA)
FEPA........ Federal Executive Pay Act, 1956
FEPA........ Federation Europeenne des Fabricants de Produits Abrasifs [*European Federation of the Manufacturers of Abrasive Products*] [*France*]
FEPA........ Federation of European Producers of Abrasive Products (SAUO)
FEPA........ Florida Emergency Preparedness Association (SAUO)
FEPACE........ Federation Europeenne des Producteurs Autonomes et des Consommateurs Industrielsd'Energie [*European Federation of Autoproducers and Industrial Consumers of Energy*] (EAIO)
FEPACI........ Federation of Pan-African Cinema [*of the Organization of African Unity*]
FEPAFEM........ Federacion Panamericana de Asociacions de Facultades de Medicina [*Pan American Federation of Associations of Medical Schools - PAFAMS*] [*Caracas, Venezuela*] (EAIO)
FEPAP........ Federation of European Producers of Abrasives (PDAA)
FEPB........ Fair Employment Practices Board (SAUO)
FEPB........ Federal Express Parts Bank (TIMI)
FEPB........ Functional Electronic Peroneal Brace (DB)
FEPC........ Fair Employment Practices Code
FEPC........ Fair Employment Practices Commission (SAUO)
FEPC........ Fair Employment Practices Committee [*or Commission*]
FEPC........ Farm Employment Practices Committee (SAUO)
FE/PC........ Ferroelectric/Photoconductive (PDAA)
FE-PC........ Ferroelectric-Photoconductor (SAUS)
FEPCA........ Federal Employees Pay Comparability Act [*1990*]
FEPCA........ Federal Energy Policy and Conservation Act (GNE)
FEPCA........ Federal Environmental Pesticide Control Act [*1972*]
FEPCA........ Federal Environmental Pollution Control Act (SAUS)
FEP-CORDE........ Foundation for Education with Production Cooperative Research, Development and Education (SAUO)
FEPD........ Federation Europeenne des Parfumeurs Detaillants [*European Federation of Perfumery Retailers*] (EAIO)
FEPD........ Finance Efficiency and Planning Division (HEAS)
FEPD........ Forward Environmental Protection Device (MCD)
FEPE........ Europaeische Vereinigung der Briefumschlagfabrikanten [*European Association of Envelope Manufacturers*] (EAIO)
FEPE........ Federation Europeenne de la Publicite Exterieure [*European Federation of Outdoor Advertising*] [*France*]
FEPE........ Field-Enhanced Photo Emission (SAUS)
FEPE........ Full Energy Peak Efficiency [*Nuclear science*] (OA)
FEPEM........ Federation of European Petroleum Equipment Manufacturers [*Netherlands*]
FEPF........ European Federation of Earthenware, China and Tableware, and Ornamental Ware (EAIO)
FEPI........ Filipino Employment Policy Instruction (CINC)
FEPI........ Front End Programming Interface (VLIE)
FEPMA........ Federation of European Pencil Manufacturers Associations [*See also FEFM*] (EA)
FEPO........ For Examination Purposes Only [*Education*]
FEPO4........ fractional phosphate excretion (SAUS)
FEPOW........ Far East Prisoner of War
FEpow........ Far East prisoner of war (SAUS)
FEPP........ Facility Emergency Preparedness Program (SAUS)
FEPP........ Foreign Excess Personal Property
FEPP........ Free Erythrocyte Protoporphyrin [*Hematoloy*] (MAH)
FEPP........ Full Employment and Production Program (OICC)
FEPPD........ Federation of European Dental Laboratory Owners (SAUO)
FEP Resin........ Fluorinated Ethylene-Propylene Resin (SAUS)
FEPROM........ Flash EPROM (SAUS)
FEPS........ Facility and Equipment Planning System (SAUS)
FEPS........ Far-Encounter Planet Sensor
FEPS........ Flight Envelope Protection System [*Aviation*]
FEPSP........ Field Excitatory Postsynaptic Potential [*Neurophysiology*]
FEPTO........ Front Engine Power-Take-Off [*Automotive engineering*]
FEPU........ Frente Eleitoral do Povo Unido [*United People's Electoral Front*] [*Portugal*] [*Political party*] (PPE)
FEQ........ Failure Equation
FEQ........ Far Eastern Quarterly (journ.) (SAUS)
FEQIX........ Fidelity Equity Income [*Mutual fund ticker symbol*] (SG)
FEQL........ Food and Environmental Quality Laboratory (SAUS)
FER........ Fathers for Equal Rights (EA)
FER........ Federacion de Estudiantes Revolucionarios [*Federation of Revolutionary Students*] [*Uruguay*] (PD)
FER........ Federation des Etudiants Revolutionnaires [*Federation of Revolutionary Students*] [*France*]
FER........ Federation of Engine Re-Manufacturers [*Chigwell, Essex, England*] (EAIO)
FER........ Feed Efficiency Ratio
FER........ Feria Aviacion [*Spain*] [*ICAO designator*] (FAAC)
Fer........ Fermanagh County [*Ireland*] (BARN)
FER........ Ferndale [*California*] [*Seismograph station code, US Geological Survey*] (SEIS)
FER........ Ferrierite [*A zeolite*]
FER........ Ferrous
FER........ Ferrum [*Iron*] [*Pharmacy*]
FER........ Ferry
FER........ Field-Effect Resistor (SAUS)
FER........ Field Engineering Representative
FER........ Field Engineering Responsible (SAUS)
FER........ Final Engineering Report
FER........ Fleet Employment Reports (MCD)
FER........ Flexion, Extension, Rotation (SAUS)
FER........ Flight Effectiveness Ratio (ACAE)
FER........ Flight Experiment Review (ACAE)
FER........ Florida Environmental Reader (SAUO)
FER........ For [*Amateur radio shorthand*] (WDAA)
FER........ Force Exchange Ratio (MCD)
FER........ Forest Environment Research [*Department of Agriculture*] (GRD)
FER........ Forward Engine Room
FER........ Forward Error Correction (SAUS)
FER........ Forward Error Reporting (SAUS)
FER........ Foundation for Educational Research (SAUO)
FER........ Frame Erasure Rate (SAUS)
FER........ Frame Error Rate (ITD)
FER........ Friends of Ecological Reserves (SAUS)
FER........ Friends of Eye Research [*Formerly, FERRAT*] [*Defunct*] (EA)
FER........ Fuel Energy Ratio [*Petroleum refining*]
FER........ Fundamental Expenditure Review (HEAS)
FER........ Fusion Engineering Reactor [*Japan*]
FER........ Fusion Experimental Reactor (SAUS)
FERA........ February Eighteenth Resistance Army (SAUS)
FERA........ Federal Emergency Relief Act of 1933
FERA........ Federal Emergency Relief Administration [*Liquidated, 1937*]
FERA........ Foreign Exchange Regulation Act (SAUS)
FERA........ Formative Evaluation Research Associates [*Research center*] (RCD)
FERA........ Further Education Research Association [*British*] (DBA)
FeRAM........ Ferroelectric RAM (SAUS)
FeRAM........ Ferroelectric Random Access Memory (SAUS)
Ferard Fixt........ Amos and Ferard on Fixtures [*A publication*] (DLA)
FERAS........ Further Education Revenue Account Survey (AIE)
FERB........ Failure Evaluation and Review Board (SAUO)

FERC........ Federal Energy Regulatory Commission [*Department of Energy*]
FERC........ Foundation for Education and Research in Childbearing (SAUO)
FERC........ Franco-Ethiopian Railway Company (SAUO)
FERC........ United States Federal Energy Regulatory Commission (SAUS)
FERCAG........ Federal Energy Regulatory Commission Audit Group (SAUO)
FERCON........ Ferrule Contact [*Design engineering*] (IAA)
FERD........ Facility and Equipment Requirements Document (NASA)
FERD........ Final Evaluation Report of the Development (SAUO)
FERD........ Fuel Element Rupture Detection [*Nuclear energy*] (NRCH)
FERD........ Fuel Element Rupture Detector (SAUS)
FERDU........ Further Education Review and Development Unit (ODA)
FERES........ Federation Internationale des Instituts de Recherches Socio-Religieuses [*International Federation of Institutes for Socio-Religious Research*]
FERET........ Face Recognition Technology (GART)
FERF........ Far End Receive Failure [*Telecommunications*] (ACRL)
FERF........ Financial Executives Research Foundation (EA)
FERF........ Frost Effects Research Facility (SAUS)
FERF........ Fusion Engineering Research Facility (SAUO)
FERFA........ Federation of Epoxy Resin Formulators and Applicators (SAUO)
FERFIN........ Ferruzzi Finanziaria
Fer Fixt........ Ferard on Fixtures [*A publication*] (DLA)
Ferg........ Consistorial Decisions, Scotland, by George Ferguson, Lord Hermand [*A publication*] (DLA)
FERG........ Family Economics Research Group [*Department of Agriculture*] (GRD)
Ferg........ Fergusson's Consistorial Decisions [*Scotland*] [*A publication*] (DLA)
Ferg Cons........ Fergusson's Consistorial Reports [*Scotland*] [*A publication*] (DLA)
Ferg M & D........ Fergusson's Divorce Decisions by Consistorial Courts [*Scotland*] [*A publication*] (DLA)
Ferg Proc........ Ferguson's Common Law Procedure Act [*Ireland*] [*A publication*] (DLA)
Ferg Ry Cas........ Fergusson's Five Years' Railway Cases [*A publication*] (DLA)
FERGU........ Fergus, OH [*American Association of Railroads railroad junction routing code*]
Fergusson........ Fergusson's Consistorial Decisions [*Scotland*] [*A publication*] (DLA)
Fergusson........ Fergusson's Scotch Session Cases [*1738-52*] [*A publication*] (DLA)
FERIAS........ Forest Environment and Resource Information Analysis System (SAUO)
FERIC........ False Entries in Records of Interstate Carriers [*FBI standardized term*]
FERIC........ Florida Educational Resources Information Center (SAUO)
FERIC........ Forest Engineering Research Institute of Canada [*Vancouver, BC*]
FERIS........ Forest Environment and Resources Information System [*Queensland*] [*State*] (EERA)
FERIT........ Far East Regional Investigation Team (SAUO)
Ferllgs........ Ferrellgas Partners Ltd. [*Associated Press*] (SAG)
FERM........ Fast Escape Recallable Missile
FERM........ Fermanagh [*County in Northern Ireland*] (ROG)
FERMANH........ Fermanagh [*County in Northern Ireland*]
fermentol........ fermentology (SAUS)
FERMI........ Enrico Fermi Breeder Reactor Plant (SAUS)
Fermilab........ Fermi National Accelerator Laboratory
FERN........ Fernald Field Office (SAUS)
FERN........ Fernald Site Office (SAUO)
FERN........ Forest Ecosystem Research Network (SAUS)
FERN........ Further Education Research Network (SAUS)
Fernald Eng Synonyms... Fernald's English Synonyms [*A publication*] (DLA)
FERNS........ Federal Reserve Notes (SAUS)
FERO........ Far East Research Office
FERO........ Ferrofluidics Corp. [*NASDAQ symbol*] (NQ)
Ferofl........ Ferrofluidics Corp. [*Associated Press*] (SAG)
FEROPA........ European Federation of Fibre Board Manufacturers (SAUO)
FEROPA........ Federation Europeenne des Fabricants de Panneaux de Fibres [*European Federation of Fireboard Manufacturers*] [*EC*] (ECED)
FEROPA........ Federation Europeenne des Synicats de Panneaux de Fibres [*European Federation of Manufacturers Associations of Fiber Panels*] (PDAA)
ferp........ family educational rights and privacy (SAUS)
FERP........ Far Easten Refugee Proram (SAUS)
FERPA........ Family Educational Rights and Privacy Act [*1974*]
FERPC........ Far Eastern Research and Publications Center (SAUO)
FERPIC........ Ferroelectric Ceramic Picture Device (IEEE)
FERPIC........ Ferroelectric Photoconductor Image Camera (SAUS)
FERPIC........ ferroelectric picture (SAUS)
FERR........ Feliciana Eastern Railroad Co. [*Formerly, FE*] [*AAR code*]
FERR........ Ferrum [*Iron*] [*Pharmacy*] (ROG)
FERRAM........ Ferroelectric Random-Access Memory (GART)
FERRAT........ Friends of Eye Research, Rehabilitation, and Treatment [*Later, FER*] (EA)
FERREED........ Ferro-magnetic Reed (SAUS)
Ferriere Dict de Jr... Ferriere's Dictionary of Jurisprudence [*A publication*] (DLA)
FERRIT........ Ferritin [*Hematology*] (DAVI)
FERRO........ Far Eastern Regional Research Office (SAUS)
Ferro........ Ferro Corp. [*Associated Press*] (SAG)
FERROD........ Ferrite-Rod Antenna (IEEE)
FERROD Antenna... Ferrite Rod Antenna (SAUS)
Ferroelectr Lett... Ferroelectrics Letters (journ.) (SAUS)
Ferroelectr Lett Sect... Ferroelectrics Letters Section (journ.) (SAUS)
FERRON........ Ferry Squadron [*Navy*] (DNAB)
FERRUPS........ Galatrek trademark (SAUS)
FERRY........ Ferry [*Commonly used*] (OPSA)
FERS........ Facility Error Recognition System [*IBM Corp.*] (CIST)
FERS........ F&E Resource Systems Tech [*NASDAQ symbol*] (TTSB)
FERS........ F & E Resource Systems Technology, Inc. [*NASDAQ symbol*] (SAG)
FERS........ Federal Employees' Retirement System
FERS........ Federal Employment [*or Employees*] Retirement System
FERS........ Financial Engineering Reporting System (SAUS)
FERSA........ Federal Employees' Retirement System Act of 1986
FERSA........ Final Engineering Report and Safety Analysis (SAUO)
FERSI........ Flat Earth Research Society International (EA)
FERST........ Freight and Equipment Reporting System for Transportation [*IBM Corp.*]
FERST/VS........ Freight and Equipment Reporting System for Transportation/Virtual Storage [*IBM Corp.*]
FERT........ Failed Element Response Team (SAUS)
FERT........ Federal Emergency Response Team (DEMM)
FERT........ Fertility (WDAA)
FERT........ Fertilization (SAUS)
FERT........ Fertilize (SAUS)
FERT........ Fertilizer
FERT........ Fortitudo Eius Rhodum Tenuit [*His Strength Keeps Rhodes*] [*Motto of Lodovico family. Initials were used on gold coin struck by Duke Lodovico (1439-1465)*]
fertd........ Fertilized [*Medicine*] (DAVI)
FERTD........ Fertilized
FERTF........ Fuel Element Rupture Test Facility (SAUS)
FERTP........ Nu-West Industries [*NASDAQ symbol*] (SAG)
Fert Steril........ Fertility and Sterility (journ.) (SAUS)
FERTZ........ Fertilizer
FERUT........ Ferranti-computer at the University of Toronto (SAUO)
FERV........ Fervens [*Hot*] [*Pharmacy*]
FERV........ Foundation for Education and Research in Vision (EA)
FES........ Factor Evaluation System [*Environmental science*] (COE)
FES........ Family Endowment Society (SAUO)
FES........ Family Environment Scale
FES........ Family Expenditure Survey [*Department of Employment*] [*British*]
FES........ Far Eastern Shipping Company (SAUO)
FES........ Far-End Suppressor (IAA)
FES........ Farm Employment Scheme (SAUS)
FES........ Fast Erect System
FES........ Fat Embolism Syndrome [*Medicine*] (CPH)
FES........ Fatty Ester Sulfonate (EDCT)
FES........ Feather-Edged Spring (SAUS)
FES........ Feather-Edged Springer (SAUS)
FES........ Feature Extraction Segment (SAUS)
FES........ Federal Executive Service
FES........ Federal Expenditures by State
FES........ Federal Extension Service [*Department of Agriculture*]
FES........ Federation Europeenne de la Salmoniculture [*Federation of the European Trout and Salmon Industry*] [*Formerly, European Salmon Breeding Federation*] (EA)
FES........ Federation of Eastern Stars (EA)
FES........ Federation of the European Trout and Salmon Industry (SAUO)
FES........ Fellow of the Entomological Society [*British*]
FES........ Fellow of the Ethnological Society [*British*]
FES........ Ferroelectric Storage (SAUS)
FES........ Festus, MO [*Location identifier*] [*FAA*] (FAAL)
FES........ Field Emission Spectroscopy
FES........ Field Emitting Surface
FES........ Field Engineering Service
FES........ Field Engineering Support (ACAE)
FES........ Field Entry Standard [*Military*] (ADDR)
FES........ File Extension Specification (SAUS)
FES........ Final Environmental Statement [*Bureau of Outdoor Recreation*]
FES........ Final Environmental Survey (SAUO)
FES........ Fine Error Sensor (KSC)
FES........ Finite Element Solver (NITA)
FES........ Fire Extinguishing System
FES........ First Empire State [*AMEX symbol*] (TTSB)
FES........ First Empire State Corp. [*AMEX symbol*] (SPSG)
FES........ Fisheries Experiment Station (SAUO)
FES........ Fixed Echo Suppressor [*Electronics*] (IAA)
FES........ Flame Emission Spectrometry
FES........ Flame Emission Spectroscopy [*Medicine*] (PALA)
FES........ Flash Evaporator System (MCD)
FES........ Flat Earth Society (SAUO)
FES........ Fleet Excercise Section (SAUS)
FES........ Flight Element Set (MCD)
FES........ Flinders Earth Sciences (SAUO)
FES........ Florida Entomological Society (SAUO)
FES........ Flower Essence Society (EA)
FES........ Fluid Electric Switch (SAUS)
FES........ Fluid Experiment System (SAUS)
FES........ Fluidic Environmental Sensor (RDA)
FES........ Fluids Experiment System (SAUO)
FES........ Fluid to Electric Switch
FES........ Fluorescence Excitation Spectroscope (SAUS)
FES........ Fluorescence Excitation Spectroscopy (SAUS)
FES........ Fluorescence Excitation Spectrum
FES........ Food Education Service (SAUS)
FES........ Food Education Society [*British*]
FES........ Forced Expiratory Spirogram [*Medicine*]
FES........ Forest Extension Services (SAUS)
FES........ Forms Entry System
FES........ Front-End Screening [*DoD*]
FES........ Fuel and Electricity Survey [*Australia*]
FES........ Functional Electrical Stimulation
FES........ Fundamental Electrical Standard (IAA)
fes........ fundamental electrical standards (SAUS)

FES .... further examples see (SAUS)
FES .... Fuze/Munitions Environment Characterization Symposium (SAUS)
FES .... Federation of Engineering Societies (ODA)
FESA .... Facilities Engineering Support Agency [*Army*] (MCD)
FESA .... Federal Employees Salary Act of 1970
FESA .... Federal Employment Service Act [*1933*]
FESA .... Federal Executive Salary Act of 1964
FESA .... Federation of Engineering and Scientific Associations
FESA .... Finnish European Studies Association (SAUO)
FESA .... Fonetic English Spelling Association
FESA .... Foundry Equipment and Supplies Association [*British*] (DBA)
FESAC .... Fondation de l'Enseignement Superieur en Afrique Centrale
FESAP .... Finite Element Structures Analysis Program [*Computer science*]
FESA-TS .... Facilities Engineering Support Agency Technology Support Division [*Fort Belvoir, VA*] [*Army*]
FESB .... Federal Emergency Stabilization Board (SAUO)
FESC .... Far East Science Center
FESC .... Federal Emergency Support Coordinator (SAUO)
FESC .... Federation Europeenne des Sports Corporatifs [*European Federation for Company Sports - EFCS*] (EAIO)
FESC .... Further Education Staff College (AIE)
FESCID .... Federation Europeenne des Syndicats de la Chimie et des Industries Diverses [*European Federation of Chemical and General Workers Unions*] (EAIO)
FESCO .... Faisalabad Electric Supply Company [*Pakistan*]
FESCO .... Far Eastern Shipping Co. [*Former USSR*]
FESCO .... Foreign Enterprise Service Corp. [*China*]
FESD .... Flight Experiment Specification Document (ACAE)
FESDK .... Far East Software Development Kit (SAUS)
FESE .... Far East Stock Exchange (SAUO)
FESE .... Federation of Secondary Students of Ecuador [*Political party*] (PSAP)
FESE .... Field-Enhanced Secondary Emission
FESEM .... Field Emission Scanning Electron Microscopy
FESEM .... Forcible entry safeguards effectiveness model (SAUS)
FESFP .... Federation Europeenne des Syndicats de Fabricants de Parquets [*European Federation of Parquet Manufacturers Unions*]
FeSFV .... Feline Syncytium-Forming Virus
FESH .... Federation of Ethical Stage Hypnotists [*British*] (DBA)
FESH .... Full Eagle Service History [*Automotive classified advertising*]
FESI .... Federation Europeenne des Syndicats d'Entreprises d'Isolation [*European Federation of Associations of Insulation Contractors*] (EA)
FESIA .... Federal Employees Salary Increase Act
FESIC .... Far East Seed Improvement Conference (SAUO)
FESIP .... Fifth Estate Security Information Project (SAUS)
FESIW .... Far East Seed Improvement Workshop (SAUO)
FESL .... Failure Effects Summary List (NASA)
FESM .... Front-End Sheet Metal
FESO .... Facilities Engineering Support Office (SAUO)
FESO .... Federal Employment Stabilization Office [*Functions transferred to National Resources Planning Board, 1939*]
$FeSO_4$ .... Ferrous Sulfate [*Organic chemistry*] (DAVI)
FESP .... (Fluoroethyl)spiperone [*Biochemistry*]
Fespa .... Federation of European Screen Printers Associations (SAUO)
FESPAC .... Far East and South Pacific (SAUO)
FESPIC .... Far East and South Pacific
FESR .... Finite Energy Sum Rules [*Physics*]
FESR .... Further Education Statistical Record [*Department of Education and Science*] [*British*]
FESRR .... Field Engineering System Reference Report (SAUS)
FESS .... Facilities Engineering and Safety Services (SAUS)
FESS .... Facilities Engineering Supply System (SAUO)
FESS .... Facilities Engineer Supply System [*Army*]
FESS .... Finite Element Solution System (PDAA)
FESS .... Fleet Environmental Support System [*Navy*]
FESS .... Flight Experiment Shielding Satellite
FESS .... Flywheel Energy Storage System
FESS .... Fuel and Energy Science Series (SAUO)
Fessen Pat .... Fessenden on Patents [*A publication*] (DLA)
Fess Pat .... Fessenden on Patents [*A publication*] (DLA)
FEST .... Far East Siberia Transect (SAUS)
FEST .... Fast Erase Storage Tubes (ACAE)
FEST .... Federation for Education, Science and Technology (SAUO)
FEST .... Federation of Engineering and Shipbuilding Trades (SAUO)
FEST .... Federation of Engineering and Shipbuilding Trades of the United Kingdom (SAUO)
FEST .... Festival
Fest .... Festival [*Record label*]
fest .... festive (SAUS)
fest .... festivities (SAUS)
fest .... festivity (SAUS)
FEST .... Field Epidemiological Survey Team [*Army*] (LAIN)
FEST .... Foundation for Education Science and Technology (SAUO)
FEST .... Frankfurt English Speaking Theater (SAUO)
FEST .... Fronts Experiment Systems Test (SAUS)
FESTAC .... World Black and African Festival of Arts and Culture
FestF .... Festival (France) [*Record label*]
FESTUK .... Federation of Engineering and Shipbuilding Trades of the United Kingdom [*A union*]
FeSV .... Feline Sarcoma Virus [*Veterinary science*] (DB)
FESV .... Feline Sarcoma Virus [*Also, FeSV*]
FESW .... Federation of Eastern Stars of the World (EA)
FESWG .... Fuze Engineering Standardization Working Group [*Military*] (RDA)
FESWMS .... Finite Element Surface Water Model System (SAUS)
FESX .... First Essex Bancorp [*NASDAQ symbol*] (TTSB)
FESX .... First Essex Bancorp, Inc. [*NASDAQ symbol*] (NQ)
FESYP .... Federation Europeenne des Syndicats de Fabricants de Panneaux de Particules [*European Federation of Associations of Particleboard Manufacturers*] (EAIO)
f-et- .... Ethiopia [*MARC geographic area code*] [*Library of Congress*] (LCCP)
FET .... Far Eastern Textile Ltd. [*NYSE symbol*] (SAG)
FET .... Far Eastern Time (SAUS)
FET .... Far East Time (IAA)
FET .... Far East Trading (SAUS)
FET .... Federal Estate Tax (DLA)
FET .... Federal Excise Tax
FET .... Federation of Environmental Technologists (EA)
FET .... Field Effect Transistor
FET .... field-effect transistor (SAUS)
FET .... Field Effort Transistor (ACAE)
FET .... Field Emission Transistor (ACAE)
FET .... field-emission transistor (SAUS)
FET .... Field Evaluation Test (SAUO)
FET .... Field Exercise Test (SAUO)
FET .... Fighter Evaluation Team (ACAE)
FET .... File Enviroment Table (SAUS)
FET .... Fixed Erythrocyte Turnover [*Hematology*] (DAVI)
FET .... Fleet Evaluation Trial [*Navy*] (NG)
FET .... Flight Elapsed Time (MCD)
FET .... Flight Engineer in Training
FET .... Fluid Engineering Technology (SAUS)
FET .... Fluidic Emergency Thruster [*Aviation*]
FET .... Fluorescence Energy Transfer [*Physics*]
FET .... Foldable Elastic Tube [*Satellite hinge*]
FET .... Forced Expiratory Time [*Physiology*]
FET .... Foreign Economic Trends (JAGO)
FET .... Foreign Escorted Tour [*Travel*]
FET .... Foundation on Economic Trends (EA)
FET .... Free Endotoxin (SAUS)
FET .... Freeze-Etch Technique
FET .... Fremont, NE [*Location identifier*] [*FAA*] (FAAL)
FET .... Frozen Embryo Transfer [*Medicine*]
FET .... Full Electric Typewriter (SAUS)
FET .... Full Electronic Typewriter (SAUS)
FET .... Functional Electrical Test (ACAE)
FET .... Functional Element Test
FET .... Future and Emerging Technologies (SAUS)
FET .... Fossil-Energy Technology (ODA)
FETA .... Farm Education and Training Association (SAUS)
FETA .... Federation of Environmental Trade Associations [*British*] (DBA)
FETA .... Fire Extinguisher Trades Association [*British*] (BI)
FETAP .... Federation Europeenne des Transports Aeriens Prives [*European Federation of Independent Air Transport*]
FETAX .... Frog Embryo Teratogenesis Assay - Xenopus [*Toxicology*]
FETBB .... Federation Europeenne des Travailleurs du Batiment et du Bois [*European Federation of Building and Woodworkers - EFBWW*] (EAIO)
FETC .... Federal Energy Technology Center
FETC .... Federal Excise Tax Council [*Defunct*] (EA)
FETC .... Field-Effect-Transistor-Capacitor [*Electronics*] (PDAA)
FETCC .... Foreign Exchange and Foreign Trade Control Commission (SAUO)
FETCH .... Flight Engagement Tactical Cargo Hook (SAUO)
FET de las JONS ... Falange Espanola Tradicionalista y de las Juntas de Ofensiva Nacional Sindicalista [*Traditionalist Spanish Phalange of the Syndicalist Juntas of the NationalOffensive*] [*Political party*] (PPE)
FETDIP .... Fetlington Dual-in-Line Package (SAUS)
FETE .... Far Eastern Tick-Borne Encephalitis [*Medicine*] (DMAA)
FETE .... Federal Telecommunication (SAUS)
FETEX .... Fujitsu Electronic Telephone Exchange (SAUS)
FETF .... Flight Engine Test Facility
FETFE .... Fluorelastomer with Tetrafluoroethylene Additives (SAUS)
FETH .... Field Effect Thyristor (IAA)
FETI .... Fluorescence Energy Transfer Immunoassay [*Analytical biochemistry*]
FETIABAG .... Federation of Workers of the Food and Beverage Industry of Guatemala (SAUO)
fetin .... federation (SAUO)
FETLA .... Further Extended Three-Letter Acronym (ADWA)
FETM .... File Expansion Transport Magazine (SAA)
FETMM .... Field Engineering Theory Maintenance Manual (SAUS)
FETO .... Factory Equipment Transfer Order
FETO .... Field Engineering Theory of Operations
FETO .... Free Estimated Time of Overflight [*Aviation*] (DA)
fetol .... fetological (SAUS)
FETOL .... Fetologist (SAUS)
fetol .... fetology (SAUS)
FETOM .... Field Engineering Theory of Operation Manual (SAUS)
FETP .... Flight Experiment Test Plan (ACAE)
FETRA .... Finite Element Transport Model (EEVL)
FETS .... Far East Trade Service, Inc. (SAUO)
FETS .... Far East Training Center (SAUS)
FETS .... Far East Training School (SAUO)
FETS .... Field Evaluation and Test System (ACAE)
FETS .... Forced Expiratory Time, in Seconds [*Physiology*]
FETS/SEA .... Federal Emission Test Sequence and Selective Enforcement Audit [*General Motors Corp.*]
FETT .... Field-Effect Tetrode Transistor [*Electronics*] (OA)
FETT .... First Engine to Test
Fett Carr .... Fetter's Treatise on Carriers of Passengers [*A publication*] (DLA)

FETU .... Far Eastern Technical Unit [*World War II*]
FETU .... Federation of Entertainment Trade Unions (SAUO)
FETVM .... Field-Effect Transistorized Voltmeter (SAUS)
FETVM .... Field-Effect Transistor Volt Meter [*Electronics*] (DICI)
FET VOM .... Field-Effect Transistor Volt-Ohm-Milliammeter (IDOE)
FEU .... Compagnie Aeronautique Europeene [*France*] [*ICAO designator*] (FAAC)
FEU .... Family Education Unit [*Australia*]
FEU .... Far Eastern University, Manila (SAUS)
FEU .... Federated Engineering Union
FEU .... Fire Experimental Unit [*British Fire Service*] (IRUK)
FEU .... Fleet Expansion Unit (DNAB)
FEU .... Forty-Feet Equivalent Unit (SAUS)
feu .... forty-foot equivalent container unit (SAUS)
FEU .... Forty-Foot [*Container*] Equivalent Unit (DOMA)
FEU .... Forward Electronic Unit (SAUS)
FEU .... Fossil Energy Update [*A publication*]
FEU .... Fuel Equivalent Unit
FEU .... Functionally Equivalent Unit (SPST)
FEU .... Further Education Unit [*British*]
FEUD .... Feudal
feud .... Feudalism (ADWA)
FEUD .... Feudalism (WDAA)
feud .... feudalistic (SAUS)
Feud Lib .... Feudorum Liber [*Book of Feuds*] [*Latin*] [*A publication*] (DLA)
FEUE .... Federation of University Students of Ecuador [*Political party*] (PSAP)
FEUGRES .... Federation Europeenne des Fabricants de Tuyaux en Gre [*European Federation of Manufacturers of Salt Glazed Pipes*] (PDAA)
FEUO .... For External Use Only [*Pharmacy*] (DAVI)
FEUPF .... European Federation of Professional Florists' Unions [*Italy*] (EAIO)
FEUPF .... Federation Europeenne des Unions Professionelles de Fleuristes [*European Federation of Professional Florists' Unions*] (EAIO)
FEU/PICKUP ... Further Education Unit Professional Industrial and Commercial Updating (SAUS)
FE-UR .... Iron in Urine [*Biochemistry*] (DAVI)
FEURS .... Fabrication Equivalent Unit Reporting System (MCD)
FEUS .... File Enquiry and Update System (SAUS)
FEUS .... French Engineers in the United States (EA)
FEUTX .... Federated Utility Fund Cl.F [*Mutual fund ticker symbol*] (SG)
FEUU .... Federation of Uruguayan University Students [*Political party*] (PSAP)
FEV .... Eaton Vance Florida Municipal Income Trust [*AMEX symbol*] (NASQ)
FEV .... Familial Exudative Vitreoretinopathy [*Ophthalmology*]
FEV .... Far End Voice (SAUS)
FeV .... Feline Leukemia Virus [*Veterinary medicine*]
FEV .... Fever (WDAA)
fev .... Fevrier [*February*] [*French*] (ASC)
FEV .... Field Force, Vietnam (SAUO)
FEV .... Forced Expectorant Volume [*Medicine*]
FEV .... Forced Expiratory Volume [*Physiology*]
FEV .... Forced Expired Volume (SAUS)
FEV .... Functional Evaluator (SAUS)
FEV .... Future Electric Vehicle [*Nissan Corp.*] (PS)
fev 1 .... forced expiratory volume in 1 second (SAUS)
FEV1 .... Forced Expiratory Volume-one second (SAUS)
FEV1 .... Front End Volatility Index (SAUS)
FEV_1/VC .... Forced Expiratory Volume (In One Second)/Vital Capacity [*Physiology*] (MAE)
fev2 .... forced expiratory volume in 2 seconds (SAUS)
fev3 .... forced expiratory volume in 3 seconds (SAUS)
FEVA .... Federal Employees Veterans Association [*Later, NAGE*] (EA)
FEVAC .... Ferroelectric Variable Capacitor
FEVB .... Frequency Ectopic Ventricular Beat (DB)
FEVE .... Federation Europeenne du Verre d'Emballage [*European Container Glass Federation - ECGF*] (EA)
Feversham Cttee ... Committee on Human Artificial Insemination. Report [*1960*] [*A publication*] (ILCA)
FEVI .... Front End Volatility Index [*Environmental Protection Agency*] (GFGA)
FEVIR .... Federation of European Veterinarians (or Veterinaries) in Industry and Research (SAUO)
FEVR .... Familial Exudative Vitreoretinopathy [*Medicine*] (MELL)
FEVR .... Freemont & Elkhorn Valley Railroad [*Federal Railroad Administration identification code*]
FEVs .... Functional Evaluators (SAUS)
FEVSD .... Federation Europeenne pour la Vente et le Service a Domicile [*European Direct Selling Federation*] [*Brussels, Belgium*] (EA)
FEVt .... Forced Expiratory Volume (Timed) [*Medicine*] (DAVI)
FEVt/FVC .... Forced Expiratory Volume (Timed) to Forced Vital Capacity Ratio [*Expressed as a percentage*] [*Medicine*] (DAVI)
FEW .... Cheyenne, WY [*Location identifier*] [*FAA*] (FAAL)
FEW .... Far Eastern Cargo Airlines [*Former USSR*] [*FAA designator*] (FAAC)
FEW .... Feather-Edge Wear [*Tire maintenance*]
FEW .... Federally Employed Women (EA)
FEW .... Fighter Escort Wing (SAUS)
FEWA .... Farm Equipment Wholesalers Association (EA)
FEWA .... Finite Element of Water Flow through Aquifers (SAUS)
Few Body Syst ... Few-Body Systems (journ.) (SAUS)
Few Body Syst Suppl ... Few-Body Systems Supplementum (journ.) (SAUS)
FEWC .... Force Electronic Warfare Coordinator (NVT)
fewd .... Ironwood (VRA)
FEWEC .... Further Education Work Experience Co-Ordinator (AIE)
FEWG .... Flight Evaluation Working Group (MCD)
FEWIA .... Federation of European Writing Instruments Associations [*See also FEAIE*] (EA)
FEWITA .... Federation of European Wholesale and International Trade Associations [*Common Market*] [*Belgium*]
FEWMA .... Federation of European Window Manufacturers Associations (EA)
FEWO .... Fund for Education in World Order [*Later, FFP*] (EA)
FEWQ .... Federation of English-Writers in Quebec [*Canada*] (WWLA)
FEWS .... Famine Early Warning System [*US Agency for International Development*]
FEWS .... Famine Early Warning System Project (SAUS)
FEWS .... Feature Extraction Workstation (SAUS)
FEWS .... Follow-on Early Warning System [*Satellite*] (DOMA)
FEWSG .... Fleet Electronic Warfare Support Group
FEWT .... Functional Equipment Withholding Tab [*Obsolete*]
FEWTS .... Force Electronic Warfare/Tactical SIGINT
FEX .... Fabien Exploration, Inc. [*Toronto Stock Exchange symbol*]
FEX .... Feature Extractor (ACAE)
FEX .... Fleet Exercise [*Navy*]
FEX .... Flightexec Ltd. [*Canada*] [*ICAO designator*] (FAAC)
FEX .... Foreign Exchange [*Telecommunications*] (TEL)
FEX .... Foreign Exchange Service (SAUS)
FEX .... Fort Worth, TX [*Location identifier*] [*FAA*] (FAAL)
FEX .... Fueled experiment (SAUS)
FEX .... Funding Exchange [*An association*] (EA)
FEXC .... First Executive Corporation (SAUO)
FExF .... Forced Expiratory Flow (GNE)
FEXHA .... Fuel Supply Exhausted [*Aviation*] (FAAC)
FEXT .... Far-End Crosstalk [*Telecommunications*]
FEXT .... Fire Extinguisher
FEXT .... Frame Time for Extrapolation (SAA)
FEY .... Forever Yours
FEYI .... Fey Industries (SAUO)
FEZ .... Federation Europeenne de Zootechnie [*European Association for Animal Production - EAAP*] [*France*] (ASF)
FEZ .... Fez [*Morocco*] [*Airport symbol*] (OAG)
FEZ .... Fighter Aircraft Engagement Zone (SAUS)
FEZ .... Fighter Engagement Zone [*Military*] (NVT)
ff--- .... Africa, North [*MARC geographic area code*] [*Library of Congress*] (LCCP)
FF .... Air Link [*ICAO designator*] (AD)
ff .... and the following pages, sections, etc. (SAUS)
FF .... Degree of Fineness of Abrasive Particles [*Medicine*] (EDAA)
FF .... Fabric Filter (EEVL)
FF .... Face Flange (SAUS)
F-F .... Face to Face
FF .... Facility Forecast (MCD)
FF .... Factitious Fever [*Medicine*] (CPH)
FF .... Factory Finish [*Technical drawings*]
FF .... Failure Factor (NG)
FF .... Failure to Feed (MCD)
FF .... Fairness Fund (EA)
FF .... Faith and Freedom (SAUS)
FF .... Falk Foundation (SAUO)
FF .... Fanfare [*A publication*] (BRI)
FF .... Fan Fold (SAUS)
FF .... Fanny Fern [*Pseudonym used by Sara Payson Parton*]
FF .... Far Field (MCD)
FF .... Farm Foundation (EA)
FF .... Fast-Fast Wave (SAUS)
FF .... Fast Fatigue [*Type of muscle contraction*]
FF .... Fast Flow
FF .... Fast Forward [*Audio-visual technology*]
FF .... Fatal Facts
f/f .... fat and forward (SAUS)
FF .... Fat Fraction [*Medicine*] (DB)
FF .... Fat Free [*Biochemistry*]
FF .... Father Factor [*Medicine*] (MAE)
Ff .... Fatigue Correction Factor [*Environmental science*] (COE)
FF .... Fatigue Factor (MELL)
FF .... Fatigue Fracture (MELL)
FF .... Fear of Failure [*Medicine*] (EDAA)
FF .... Fecal Frequency (MAE)
FF .... Fecerunt [*They Did It*] [*Latin*]
FF .... Federal Facilities (EEVL)
FF .... Federal Facility (GFGA)
FF .... Federal Funds (EBF)
FF .... Federated Farmers (SAUO)
FF .... Federations of Federations (SAUO)
FF .... Feed Form (SAUS)
FF .... Feed Forward (IAA)
FF .... Fee Factor (MCD)
FF .... Felicissimi Fratres [*Most Fortunate Brothers*] [*Latin*]
FF .... Felicissimus [*Most Happy*] [*Latin*] (ROG)
fF .... Femtofarad [*One quadrillionth of a farad*]
FF .... Ferguson Formula [*Four-wheel drive system*] [*Automotive engineering*] [*British*]
FF .... Fertlity Factor [*Medicine*] (DAVI)
FF .... Fetch and Follow (SAUS)
FF .... Fianna Fail [*Warriors of Destiny*] [*Political party*] [*Ireland*]
FF .... Fiat France S.A. (SAUS)
FF .... Fiber Forming (SAUS)
FF .... Fibula Fracture (MELL)
FF .... Fieldbus Foundation (SAUS)
FF .... Field File (LAIN)
FF .... Field Forces [*Military*]
FF .... Field Format
FF .... Field Foundation (SAUO)
FF .... Field Frequency [*Computer science*] (ELAL)
FF .... Field Function [*Telecommunications*] (TEL)

FF ... Field of Fire (SAUS)
FF ... Fields of Forel (DB)
FF ... Fieri Fecit [*Caused to Be Made*] [*Latin*]
FF ... Fifty-Fifty (SAUS)
FF ... Fighting French
FF ... Fight or Flight [*Medicine*] (EDAA)
ff ... Figures Finished (SAUS)
FF ... File Field (SAUS)
FF ... File Finish (MSA)
FF ... File Format (SAUS)
FF ... Filene Foundation (SAUO)
FF ... Fill Factor [*Photovoltaic energy systems*]
F/F ... Fill/Full [*or Full/Fill*] (MCD)
FF ... Filmfacts (journ.) (SAUS)
FF ... Filterable [*Filtration*] Fraction [*Medicine*] (EDAA)
FF ... Filter Factor (NRCH)
FF ... Filtration Factor [*Physiology*] (DAVI)
FF ... Filtration Fraction [*Physiology*]
FF ... Fimbria-Fornix [*Neuroanatomy*]
FF ... Finagle-Factor
FF ... Financial Federation, Inc. (EFIS)
FF ... Fine Fiber [*Medicine*] (EDAA)
FF ... Fine Furnace (SAUS)
FF ... Finger Flexion (SAUS)
FF ... Finger to Finger [*Medicine*]
FF ... Fining Furnace (SAUS)
FF ... Finlandia Foundation (EA)
FF ... Fire and Forget (ACAE)
Ff ... Firefighter (WDAA)
FF ... Fire Fighting (MSA)
FF ... Firefinder
FF ... Firefinder radar (SAUS)
FF ... Fir-Fast [*Forestry*]
FF ... First Fail (Principle) (SAUS)
FF ... First Families [*i.e., the aristocracy*] [*Slang*]
FF ... First Fandom (EA)
FF ... First Financial Fund [*NYSE symbol*] (TTSB)
FF ... First Financial Fund, Inc. [*NYSE symbol*] (SPSG)
FF ... First Fit (SAUS)
FF ... First Fit Algorithm (IAA)
FF ... first flight (SAUS)
FF ... Fixation Fluid [*Medicine*] (DMAA)
FF ... Fixed Fee [*Business term*] (AAG)
FF ... Fixed Focus [*Photography*]
FF ... Fixed Format (SAUS)
FF ... Fixed Frequency (SAUS)
FF ... Fixing Fluid [*Histology*]
FF ... Flash Filament (SAUS)
FF ... Flat Face [*Diamonds*]
FF ... Flat Feet
FF ... Flat Film (SAUS)
FF ... Flat filter (SAUS)
FF ... Fleet Fighter [*Air Force*]
FF ... Fleet Frigate (SAUO)
ff ... Fleurs [*Flowers*] [*Pharmacy*]
FF ... Flexible-Fueled [*Automotive engineering*]
FF ... Flight Ferry [*Navy*] (ANA)
FF ... Flight Forward (MCD)
FF ... Flip-Flop (IDOE)
F-F ... Flip-Flop [*Computer science*]
FF ... Flip-Flop latch (SAUS)
FF ... Florida Facility [*NASA*] (KSC)
FF ... Fluid Flow (SAUS)
FF ... Fluorescent Foci (DB)
FF ... Fluorine Facility [*Nuclear energy*] (NRCH)
FF ... Flush Fitting
FF ... Flux Flow (IAA)
FF ... Focus on the Family [*An association*] (EA)
FF ... Fog Factor
FF ... Fog Fever (MELL)
FF ... Folded File
FF ... Folded Flat [*Freight*]
FF ... Folding Fin (SAA)
FF ... Folgende [*And the Following Pages, Verses, etc.*] [*German*] (ROG)
ff ... Folios (ADWA)
FF ... Folios [*Leaves*]
FF ... Follicular Fluid (MELL)
ff ... Following [*Copyediting*] (WDMC)
FF ... Following [*Pages*] [*Also, F*]
FF ... Foot Flat (SAUS)
ff ... Force(d) Fluids [*Medicine*] (EDAA)
FF ... Force Feed (MSA)
FF ... Force Field
FF ... Force Flagship
FF ... Force [*or Forced*] Fluid [*Medicine*]
FF ... Ford Foundation
ff ... Ford Foundation
FF ... Ford France S.A. (SAUS)
FF ... Fordyce-Fox [*Disease*] [*Medicine*] (DB)
FF ... Forearm Flow [*Cardiology*] (DAVI)
FF ... Foreign Flag
FF ... Foreign Friend (SAUS)
FF ... Foremanship Foundation [*Defunct*] (EA)
FF ... Form (SAUS)
FF ... format feed (SAUS)
FF ... Formation Flying (MCD)
FF ... Formel Ford (SAUS)
FF ... Form Factor (IAA)
FF ... Form Feed [*Communications term*] (DCT)
ff ... form feed character (SAUS)
FF ... Formula Ford [*Class of racing cars*]
FF ... Formular Feed (SAUS)
ff ... Fortissimo (SHCU)
FF ... Fortissimo [*Very Loud*] [*Music*]
FF ... Forward Flexion (SAUS)
FF ... Forward Fuselage
FF ... Fossil Fuels
FF ... Foster Father
FF ... Foul Fly [*Baseball*]
FF ... Fraction of Fill (ACAE)
FF ... Francs Francais [*French Francs*] [*Monetary unit*]
FF ... Franklin Foundation (SAUO)
FF ... Franklin Furnace (EA)
F-F ... Frasnian-Famennian [*Boundary*] [*Geophysics*]
FF ... Fratres [*Brothers*] [*Latin*]
FF ... Fredspolitisk Folkeparti [*People's Peace Policy Party*] [*Denmark*] (PPE)
FF ... Freedom Federation [*Defunct*] (EA)
FF ... Freedom Front (SAUS)
FF ... Freedom Fund [*An association*] [*Defunct*] (EA)
FF ... Freedom's Friends (EA)
FF ... Free-Fall
FF ... Free Fat [*Biochemistry*] (DAVI)
FF ... Free Flight
FF ... Free Float (VLIE)
FF ... Free Flood
FF ... Free Flow [*Automotive engineering*]
FF ... Free Flyaround (SAA)
FF ... Free Flyer (MCD)
FF ... Free Form [*Automotive engineering*]
FF ... Free Format (CARB)
FF ... Free Fraction
FF ... Free French [*World War II*]
FF ... Free the Fathers (EA)
FF ... Freeze Fracture (SAUS)
FF ... Freeze-Fracturing (MELL)
FF ... Freight Forwarder
FF ... French Fourragere [*Military decoration*]
FF ... French Franc [*Monetary unit*]
FF ... French Fried
FF ... Frequency Feedback (SAUS)
FF ... Frequency Filter (SAUS)
FF ... Fresh Frozen
FF ... Frie Folkevalgte [*Freely Elected Representatives*] [*Norway*] (PPE)
FF ... Friendship Force (EA)
FF ... Friends of the Farm [*An association*] (EA)
FF ... Frigate [*Navy symbol*]
FF ... Front Engine, Front Drive [*Automotive engineering*]
ff ... front focal (SAUS)
FF ... Front Focal Length [*Optics*]
ff ... front focus (SAUS)
F/F ... Front Frame (SAUS)
FF ... Frontier Force (ODA)
FF ... Front of Democratic Forces (Djibouti) [*Political party*] (PSAP)
FF ... Froth Flotation (SAUS)
FF ... Fruit Frost (NOAA)
FF ... Fuel fabrication (SAUS)
FF ... Fuel Flow (AAG)
FF ... Fuller Fund (SAUO)
FF ... Full Face [*Photography*]
FF ... Full-Fashioned
ff ... full fashioned (SAUS)
FF ... Full Field
FF ... Full Floating [*Automotive engineering*]
f/f ... full force (SAUS)
FF ... Fully Factored (SAUS)
FF ... Functional Food
FF ... Function of a Quantity [*Mathematics*] (ROG)
FF ... Fundus Firm [*Obstetrics*] (DAVI)
FF ... Furon Formaldehyde [*Organic chemistry*]
FF ... Further Flexion [*Neurology and orthopedics*] (DAVI)
ff ... page following (SAUS)
ff ... pages following (SAUS)
FF ... Thick Fog [*Navigation*]
FF ... Fellows (ODA)
f/f ... Fully Furnished (ODA)
FFA ... Air-Cushion Vehicle built by Flygtekniska Forsoksanstalen [*Sweden*] [*Usually used in combination with numerals*]
FFA ... Factory Flow Analysis (VLIE)
FFA ... Failed fuel assembly (SAUS)
FFA ... Fast Fourier Analysis (SAUS)
FFA ... Fast Fourier Analyzer (MCD)
ffa ... fat-free acid (SAUS)
FFA ... Federal Facilities Agreement
FFA ... Federal Facility Agreement (BCP)
FFA ... Federal Firearms Act
FFA ... Federal Fisheries Act (SAUS)
FFA ... Feed Freight Assistance adjustement fund (SAUO)
FFA ... Fellow Institute of Financial Accountants [*British*] (WA)
FFA ... Fellow of the Faculty of Actuaries [*British*]

FFA .... Fellow of the Faculty of Actuaries in Scotland (SAUO)
FFA .... Fellow of the Faculty of Anesthetists [*British*]
FFA .... Fellow of the Institute of Financial Accountants [*British*] (ODBW)
FFA .... Fellows of the Faculty of Anesthetists (SAUS)
FFA .... Female-Female Adaptor (MEDA)
FFA .... Fiberglass Fabrication Association (EA)
FFA .... Field Failure Analysis (VLIE)
FFA .... Field Firing Area (SAUS)
FFA .... Field Force Automation (GART)
FFA .... Finite Fuzzy Automaton (SAUS)
FfA .... Fire Fighters Association (SAUS)
FFA .... Fire for Adjustment (SAUS)
FFA .... Flammability Fabrics Act (SAUS)
FFA .... Flammable Fabrics Act [*1953*]
FFA .... Flash Flood Watch [*Telecommunications*] (OTD)
FFA .... Flexible Factory Automation
FFA .... Florida Foliage Association (EA)
FFA .... Florida Forestry Association (WPI)
FFA .... Fluorescein Fundus Angiogram [*Ophthalmology*] (CPH)
FFA .... Folding Fin Aircraft (SAUS)
FFA .... Forces Francaises en Allemagne [*French Forces in Germany*]
FFA .... Foreign Freight Agent
FFA .... Forest Farmers Association (EA)
FFA .... For Further Assignment
FfA .... Forum Fisheries Agency (SAUS)
FFA .... Foundation for Foreign Affairs (EA)
FFA .... Franchise Finance Corp. of America [*NYSE symbol*] (SAG)
FFA .... Franchise Finance Cp Amer [*NYSE symbol*] (TTSB)
FFA .... Frankford Arsenal [*Pennsylvania*] [*Army*] [*Closed*] (AABC)
FFA .... free fat acid (SAUS)
FFA .... Free Fatty Acid [*Biochemistry*]
FFA .... Free Field Analysis
FFA .... Free Fire Area (AABC)
FFA .... Free-for-All (ADA)
ffa .... free for all (SAUS)
FFA .... Free Foreign Agency [*or Agent*] [*Business term*]
ffa .... Free from Alongside (EBF)
FFA .... Free from Alongside [*Shipping*]
FFA .... Free from Average [*Insurance*]
FFA .... Free from Foreign Agency (SAUS)
FFA .... Free of Fatty Acid (SAUS)
ffa .... free of foreign agency (SAUS)
FFA .... Fretz Family Association (EA)
FFA .... Friends of Frank Ashmore [*Defunct*] (EA)
FFA .... Friends of French Art (EA)
F/FA .... Fuel and Fuel Additives [*Gasoline*] [*Automotive emissions*]
FFA .... Full Freight Allowance (MIST)
FFA .... Full Freight Allowed
FFA .... Function to Function Architecture [*Computer science*] (ELAL)
FFA .... Function-to Function Architecture (SAUS)
FfA .... Fund for Animals (SAUS)
FFA .... Funds Flow Analysis
FFA .... Future Families of America (SAUO)
FFA .... Future Farmers of America [*Later, NFFAO*] (EA)
FFA .... Future Farmers of Australia
FfA .... Future Fuels of America (SAUS)
FFA .... Kill Devil Hills, NC [*Location identifier*] [*FAA*] (FAAL)
FFAA .... 4th Field Artillery (Pack) Association (EA)
FFAA .... Flavour and Fragrance Association of Australia
FFA&CO .... Federal Facility Agreement & Consent Order (SAUS)
FFAC .... Federal Food Advisory Committee [*Cost of Living Council*]
FFAC .... Forest Farmers Association Cooperative (SAUO)
FFAC .... Forward Forward Air Controller [*Military*]
FFAC .... Freshwater Fisheries Advisory Council (SAUO)
FFAC .... Friends For All Children [*Medicine*] (EDAA)
FFACCRR .... Freedom of Faith: A Christian Committee for Religious Rights (EA)
FFA/CO .... Federal Facility Agreement/Consent Order (SAUS)
FFACT .... Fiber, Fabric, and Apparel Coalition for Trade (EA)
FFACT .... Frozen Foods Action Communications Team (EA)
F Factor .... Fertility Factor (SAUS)
FFACTS .... Flammable Fabric Accident Case and Testing System [*National Institute of Standards and Technology*]
FFADV .... Frozen Food Association of Delaware Valley (SRA)
FFAG .... Fixed-Field Alternating Gradient [*Accelerator*] [*Nuclear energy*]
FFAG .... Fixed Frequency Alternating Gradient (SAUS)
FFAG Accelerator ... Fixed Field Alternating Gradient Accelerator (SAUS)
FFAG Cyclotron ... Fixed Frequency Alternating Gradient Cyclotron (SAUS)
FFAGHS .... Federation of Franco-American Genealogical and Historical Societies [*Defunct*] (EA)
FFA/HERO .... Future Homemakers of America/Home Economics Related Occupations (SAUO)
FFAI .... South Pacific Forum Fisheries Agency (SAUO)
FFAIR .... Freight Forwarder-Air
FFAIS .... Full Frontal Area Impact Switch (MCD)
FFALA .... Fund For Animals Ltd. Australia [*Commercial firm*]
FFAM .... First Family Group, Inc. (MHDW)
FFAMIS .... Florida Fiscal Accounting Management Information System (SAUO)
FF & E .... Furniture, Fixtures, and Equipment [*Insurance*]
FF & P .... Falsification, Fabrication, and Plagiarism [*Scientific misconduct*]
FF & V .... Fresh Fruits and Vegetables
FF& VPC .... Flower, Fruit & Vegetable Publicity Council (SAUO)
FF & W .... Furnish Fuel and Water (SAUS)
FFANE .... Frozen Food Association of New England (SRA)
FFANY .... Fashion Foot Wear Association
FFAP .... Free Fatty Acid Phase [*Biochemistry*] (DAVI)
FFAP .... Full Face Air Purifying (SAUS)
FFAPI .... File Format API (SAUS)
FFAR .... Folding-Fin Aerial Rocket (SEWL)
FFAR .... Folding Fin Aircraft Rocket
FFAR .... Folding Fin Air Rocket (SAUS)
FFAR .... Forward Fighting Aircraft Rocket
ffar .... forward-fighting aircraft rocket (SAUS)
FFAR .... Forward-Fin Aircraft Rocket [*Military*] (MUSM)
FFAR .... Forward Firing Aerial Rocket (SAUS)
FFAR .... Forward Firing Aircraft
FFAR .... Forward-Firing Aircraft Rocket (SAUS)
FFAR .... Free Flight Aerial Rocket [*Military*] (INF)
FFAR .... Free-Flight Aircraft Rocket (SAUS)
FFAR .... Fuel and Fuel Additive Registration [*Environmental Protection Agency*] (GFGA)
FFARACS .... Fellow of the Faculty of Anaesthetists of the Royal Australasian College of Surgeons (SAUS)
FFARACS .... Fellow of the Faculty of Anaesthetists, Royal Australasian College of Surgeons (SAUO)
FFARCS .... Fellow, Faculty of Anesthesia, Royal College of Surgeons [*British*] (CMD)
FFARCS Eng ... Fellow of the Faculty of Anaesthetists of the Royal College of Surgeons of England
FFARCSI .... Fellow of the Faculty of Anaesthetists of the Royal College of Surgeons in Ireland (SAUO)
FFARCSIrel ... Fellow of the Faculty of Anaesthetists of the Royal College of Surgeons in Ire land [*British*] (DBQ)
FFARM .... Failed fuel assembly receiving mechanism (SAUS)
FFARP .... Fleet Fighter Acoustic Countermeasures Readiness Program [*Navy*] (MCD)
FFARP .... Fleet Fighter Air [*Combat*] Readiness Program [*Navy*] (DOMA)
FFARS .... Fuel and Fuel Additives Registration System (SAUO)
FFAS .... Farm and Foreign Agricultural Service
FFAS .... Fellow Incorporated Architect of the Faculty of Architects and Surveyors (SAUO)
FFAS .... Fellow of the Faculty of Actuaries in Scotland (SAUO)
FFAS .... Fellow of the Faculty of Architects and Surveyors, London [*British*]
FFAS .... Flash Flood Alarm System [*National Weather Service*]
FFAS .... Flickinger Foundation for American Studies (EA)
FFAS .... Free Flight Air Space (SAUS)
FFAS .... Free Flight Analysis Section
FFAS .... Full Face Air Supplied (SAUS)
FFAST .... Fire and Forget Antitank System Technology (MCD)
FFAST .... Forest Fire Advanced System Technology (SAUO)
FFAUS .... Federation of French Alliances in the United States [*Later, FIAF*] (EA)
FFAUSC .... Federation of French Alliances in the United States and Canada (SAUO)
FFAWC .... Fur Farm Animal Welfare Coalition (EA)
FFB .... Africair Service [*Senegal*] [*ICAO designator*] (FAAC)
FFB .... Fact-Finding Bodies
FFB .... Fat-Free Body
FFB .... Federal Farm Board [*Name changed to Farm Credit Administration, 1933*]
FFB .... Federal Financing Bank
FFB .... Fellow of the Faculty of Building (SAUO)
FFB .... Filter-Fan-Battery (SAUS)
FFB .... First Fidelity Bancorp. [*NYSE symbol*] (SPSG)
FFB .... First Fidelity Bancorp, Inc. [*Associated Press*] (SAG)
FFB .... First Fidelity Bancorporation (SAUO)
FFB .... Fixed-Film Biological [*Process for wastewater treatment*]
FFB .... Fixed Frequency Pulsed (SAUS)
FFB .... Flexible Fiber-Optic Bronchoscopy [*Medicine*]
FFB .... Fluid Film Bearing
FFB .... Folding Float Bridge [*Military*] (RDA)
FFB .... Food from Britain
FFB .... Foundation Fighting Blindness (ADWA)
FFB .... Free-Fall Bomb (SAA)
FFB .... French Forces Broadcasting (SAUS)
FFB .... Frequency Feedback (SAUS)
FFB .... Frequent Flier Bonus (BARN)
FFB .... Friends of Fritz Busch [*Record label*]
FFB .... Functional Flow Block
FFBA .... Fellow of the Corporation of Executives and Administrators [*British*] (DBQ)
FFBA .... First Colorado Bancorp [*NASDAQ symbol*] (TTSB)
FFBA .... First Colorado Bancorp, Inc. [*NASDAQ symbol*] (SAG)
FFBA .... First Federal Savings Bank Colorado [*NASDAQ symbol*] (SAG)
FFBA .... First Fidelity Bancorporation (SAUO)
FFBA .... Foundation of the Federal Bar Association (EA)
FFBA .... New York Foreign Freight & Brokers Association (SAUO)
FFBArk .... First Federal Bancshares of Arkansas, Inc. [*Associated Press*] (SAG)
FFBB .... Form Factor Brassboard
FFBC .... First Financial Bancorp [*NASDAQ symbol*] (NQ)
FFBC .... First Financial Bancorp OH [*NASDAQ symbol*] (SAG)
FFBC .... First Finl Bancorp(OH) [*NASDAQ symbol*] (TTSB)
FFBD .... Functional Flow Block Diagram
FFBG .... First Federal Savings Bank of Brunswick [*NASDAQ symbol*] (SAG)
FFBG .... First Fed Svg (GA) [*NASDAQ symbol*] (TTSB)
FFBH .... First Fed Bancshares (AR) [*NASDAQ symbol*] (TTSB)
FFBH .... First Federal Bancshares of Arkansas, Inc. [*NASDAQ symbol*] (SAG)
FFBI .... First Financial Bancorp, Inc. [*NASDAQ symbol*] (SAG)
FFBI .... First Finl Bancorp [*NASDAQ symbol*] (TTSB)
FFBI .... Foundation for Blood Irradiation (EA)
FFBJ .... Federation of Free Byelorussian Journalists (EA)

FFBK First Florida Banks, Inc. (SAUO)
ff black fine furnace black (SAUS)
FFBM Fat-Free Body Mass
FFBM Field Feature Bill of Material (SAUS)
ffbp free-fall bomb pod (SAUS)
FFBS FFBS Bancorp [*NASDAQ symbol*] (TTSB)
FFBS FFBS Bancorp, Inc. [*NASDAQ symbol*] (SAG)
FFBT Forward Fuel Ballast Tank
FFBZ First Fed Bancorp [*NASDAQ symbol*] (TTSB)
FFBZ First Federal Bancorp, Inc. [*NASDAQ symbol*] (SAG)
FFC Fabric FIFO Controller (SAUS)
FFC Family Fitness Council
FFC Farmers Federation Cooperative
FFC Fault and Facility Control (IAA)
FFC Federal Facilities Corp. [*Dissolved, 1961*]
FFC Federal Fire Council [*Defunct*] (EA)
FFC Federation of Fire Chaplains (EA)
FFC Feed Forward Compensation (ACAE)
FFC Feed Forward Control (IAA)
FFC Fellowship of Fire Chaplains (EA)
FFC Ferret Fanciers Club (EA)
FFC Field file custodian (SAUS)
FFC Film Finance Corporation (SAUO)
FFC Films for Christ Association
FFC Final Flight Certification [*Aerospace*]
FFC Financial Funds Control
FFC Fire Force Commander (SAUO)
FFC Firemans Fund Corporation (SAUO)
FFC Firm Fan Club [*Defunct*] (EA)
FFC First Families of Carolina [*See also FFV*]
FFC First Flight Cover [*Philately*]
FFC Firstfund Capital Corp. [*Vancouver Stock Exchange symbol*]
FFC Fiscal and Financial Commission (SAFN)
FFC Fixed Film Capacitor
FFC Fixed Flexion Contracture [*Neurology and orthopedics*] (DAVI)
FFC Flagler College, St. Augustine, FL [*OCLC symbol*] (OCLC)
FFC Flat Field Conjugate (IAA)
FFC Flat Flexible Cable (VLIE)
FFC Flexible Flatness Control (SAUS)
FFC Flin Flon [*Manitoba*] [*Seismograph station code, US Geological Survey*] (SEIS)
FFC Flip-Flop Circuit (SAUS)
FFC Flip-Flop Complementary [*Computer science*] (MSA)
FFC Fluorescence Flow Cytometry [*Medicine*] (EDAA)
FFC Food Freezer Committee (SAUO)
FFC Ford Forestry Center [*Michigan Technological University*] [*Research center*] (RCD)
ffC foreign friend of China (SAUS)
FFC Foreign Funds Control
FFC For Further Clearance [*Aviation*] (FAAC)
FFC Form Feed Character (SAUS)
FFC Forum Fisheries Committee [*Australia*]
FFC Foundation for Cure [*Defunct*] (EA)
FFC Freedom Football Conference (PSS)
FFC Free from Chlorine
FFC Free from Foreign Capture (ROG)
ffc free of foreign capture (SAUS)
FFC Full Faith and Credit [*Finance*]
FFC Full Function Crew station (SAUS)
FFC Fully Formed Character (VERA)
FFC Functional Flow Chart (ACAE)
FFC Fund Amer Enterpr Hldgs [*NYSE symbol*] (TTSB)
FFC Fund American Enterprise Holdings [*Formerly, Fireman's Fund Corp.*] [*NYSE symbol*] (SPSG)
FFC Fund for the Future Committee (EA)
FFC Fuse Factor Correction (SAUS)
FFC Futures for Children (EA)
FFC Fuze Firing Circuit (RDA)
FFC Fuze Function Control (DNAB)
FFCA Carolina Bancorp, Inc. [*NASDAQ symbol*] (COMM)
FFCA Federal Facilities Compliance Agreement (COE)
FFCA Federal Facility Compliance Act
FFCA Federal Facility Compliance Act of 1992 (GAAI)
FFCA Federal Facility Compliance Agreement (DOGT)
FFCA Federal Farm Credit Administration (SAUO)
FFCA Florida Fire Chiefs Association (SAUO)
FFC-A Forward Forces Command-Army (DOMA)
FFCA Freight Forwarders Council of America (SAUO)
FFCAA Federation Francaise des Cooperatives Agricoles d'Approvisionnement
FFCAC Federation Francaise des Cooperatives Agricoles de Cereales
FFCAct Federal Facilities Compliance Act (SAUS)
FFCB Federal Farm Credit Bank (EBF)
FFCB Federal Farm Credit Board [*of FCA*]
FFCBB Fred's Fan Club - Burstein's Buffalos [*Defunct*] (EA)
FFCC Federal Free Church Council (SAUO)
FFCC Ford Four Car Club [*Australia*]
FFCC Forward-Face-Crew-Cockpit (SAUO)
FFCC Forward-Facing Crew Cockpit (SAUO)
FFCC Free-Flyer Control Centre (SAUS)
FFCDA Federal Food, Drug, and Cosmetic Act (SAUS)
FFCDPA Federal Field Committee for Development Planning in Alaska (SAUO)
FFCF Federation des Femmes Canadiennes-Francaises [*Federation of French-Canadian Women*]
FFCH First Financial Holdings, Inc. [*NASDAQ symbol*] (NQ)
FFCH First Finl Hldgs [*NASDAQ symbol*] (TTSB)
FFCI Fairfield Communities, Inc. [*NASDAQ symbol*] (SAG)
FFCI Fellow of the Faculty of Commerce and Industry [*British*] (DBQ)
FFCM Fellow of the Faculty of Community Medicine [*British*]
FFCMH Federation of Families for Children's Mental Health (EA)
FFcMN First Federal Bancorporation Minnesota [*Associated Press*] (SAG)
FFCNMR fastfield-cycling NMR (SAUS)
FFCP Farm Financial Counselling Program [*of Queensland*] (EERA)
FFCP Forme Fruste of Chickenpox (MELL)
FFCP Founders Financial Corp. [*NASDAQ symbol*] (SAG)
FFCPsy Fellow of the Faculty of Child and Adolescent Psychiatry
FFCR Freight Forwarders Certificate of Receipt [*Shipping*] (DS)
FFC Resonator Flat Field Conjugate Resonator (SAUS)
FFCRS Front-Facing Child-Restraint System [*Automotive safety*]
FFCS Federal Facilities Compliance Staff [*Office of External Affairs*] (COE)
FFCS Federal Farm Credit System
FFCS Fellow of the Faculty of Secretaries [*British*] (DBQ)
FFCS Food Facilities Consultants Society [*Later, FCSI*] (EA)
FFCS Free-Fall Control System (SAUS)
FFCSA Florida Fresh Citrus Shippers Association [*Later, FCP*] (EA)
FFCT Forest Farm and Community Tree Network (NTPA)
FFCZ Funk Farmers Co-Op [*Federal Railroad Administration identification code*]
FFD Failure Flux Density (SAUS)
FFD Fairfield Communities [*NYSE symbol*] (TTSB)
FFD Fairfield Minerals Ltd. [*Vancouver Stock Exchange symbol*]
FFD Fat-Free Diet (MELL)
FFD Fat-Free Dry (SAUS)
FFD Fellow in the Faculty of Dentistry [*British*]
FFD Fellow of the Faculty of Dental Surgeons (SAUS)
FFD Field Forcing (Decreasing)
FFD Film: Foreign Documentary
FFD Fire Fighting Department (SAUO)
FFD First Flowering Date [*Botany*]
FFD Fitness for duty (SAUS)
FFD Fixed Format Display (MCD)
FFD Flange Focal Distance (MCD)
FFD Fluid Flow Dynamics (SAUS)
FFD Focus Film Distance [*Radiology*]
FFD Formal Functional Description (LAIN)
FFD Formation Flight Display
FFD Forward Floating Depot [*Army*]
FFD Fraction of Failures Detected (ACAE)
FFD Free Fishing Days (SAUO)
FFD Free Flight Data
ffd free free domicile (SAUS)
FFD Free From Disability (SAUS)
FFD Friendly Forward Disposition
FFD Fuel Failure Detection
FFD Functional Flow Diagram
FFDA Family Farm Development Act (SAUO)
FFDA Federated Funeral Directors of America [*Commercial firm*] (EA)
FFDA Fiber Fineness Distribution Analyzer (ADA)
FFDA Flying Funeral Directors of America (EA)
FFDB Friendly Facilities Data Base (SAUS)
FFDB Friendly Forces Data Base (SAUS)
FFDB Friendly Forces/Facilities Data Base (SAUO)
FFdBrun First Federal Savings Bank of Brunswick [*Associated Press*] (SAG)
FFDC First Failure Data Capture [*IBM Corp.*] [*Computer science*] (PCM)
FFDCA Federal Food, Drug, and Cosmetic Act
FFDE Fit for Duty Evaluation (DIPS)
FFdEH First Federal Savings & Loan Association, East Hartford [*Associated Press*] (SAG)
FFDF FFD Financial [*NASDAQ symbol*] (TTSB)
FFDFinl FFD Financial Corp. [*Associated Press*] (SAG)
FFDG Farm Forestry Development Group (SAUO)
FFDI Fast Fiber Data Interface (ITD)
FF distance Front Focal distance (SAUS)
FFDK Fixed Flexion Deformity of the Knee [*Orthopedics*]
FFDLR Families and Friends for Drug Law Reform (SAUS)
FFDM Failed fuel dismantling machine (SAUS)
FFdMN First Federal Bancorp. MN [*Associated Press*] (SAG)
FFDO Fellow of the Faculty of Dispensing Opticians [*British*] (DBQ)
FFDO Force Fighter Director Officer
FFD of A Federated Funeral Directors of America [*Commercial firm*]
FFDP Firstfed Bancshares [*NASDAQ symbol*] (TTSB)
FFDP FirstFed Bancshares, Inc. [*NASDAQ symbol*] (SAG)
FFDRCS Fellow of the Faculty of Dental Surgery of the Royal College of Surgeons (SAUS)
FFDRCS Fellow of the Faculty of Dental Surgery Royal College of Surgeons (SAUO)
FFDRCSI Fellow of the Faculty of Dentistry of the Royal College of Surgeons in Ireland (SAUO)
FFDRCS Irel Fellow of the Faculty of Dentistry of the Royal College of Surgeons in Ireland
FFDS Fleet Flag Data System [*Navy*] (MCD)
FFDSRCS Fellow of the Faculty of Dental Surgery, Royal College of Surgeons [*British*] (DAVI)
FFDT FDDI Full Duplexing Technology (SAUS)
FFDT FDDI Full Duplex Technology (SAUS)
FFDW Fat-Free Dry Weight
FFE Failed Fuel Element [*Environmental science*] (COE)
FFE Falling Film Evaporation
FFE Fecal Fat Excretion [*Medicine*] (EDAA)
FFE Ferric-Ferrous Electrode (SAUS)

FFE .... Ferroelectric Field Effect (SAUS)
FFE .... Fife (SAUS)
FFE .... Fight for Free Enterprise (SAUS)
FFE .... Finished Floor Elevation [*Technical drawings*]
FFE .... Fire Fighting Equipment (SAUS)
FFE .... Fire-Fighting Equipment (AAG)
FFE .... Fire for Effect [*Army*] (INF)
FFE .... Flexible-Fuel Engine [*Automotive engineering*]
FFE .... Forced Fault Entry [*Computer science*]
FFE .... Free Flow Electrophoresis [*Analytical biochemistry*]
FFE .... Free From Explosives (SAUS)
FFE .... Free Front Endpapers (DGA)
FFE .... Friends for Education (EA)
FFE .... Furniture, Fittings, and Equipment (VLIE)
FFE(A) .... Fire Fighting Enterprises (Australia) Ltd. [*Commercial firm*]
FF EauCl .... First Federal Bancshares of Eau Claire, Inc. [*Associated Press*] (SAG)
FFEC .... Femtosecond Field Emission Camera [*Physics*]
FFEC .... Field-Free Emission Current
FFEC .... Firestone Firehawk Endurance Championship [*Auto racing*]
FFEC .... First Federal Bancshares of Eau Claire, Inc. [*NASDAQ symbol*] (SAG)
FFEC .... First Fed of Eau Clair [*NASDAQ symbol*] (TTSB)
FFED .... Ferroelectric Field Effect Device (SAUS)
FFED .... Fidelity Fed Bancorp [*NASDAQ symbol*] (TTSB)
FFED .... Fidelity Federal Bancorp [*NASDAQ symbol*] (NQ)
FFedKY .... First Federal Financial Corp. [*Associated Press*] (SAG)
FFEF .... FFE Financial Corp. [*NASDAQ symbol*] (SAG)
FFE Fn .... FFE Financial Corp. [*Associated Press*] (SAG)
FFEII .... Federal Facility Environmental Improvement Initiatives (SAUO)
FFEJWW .... Future Farm Experts of the Junior Woodchucks of the World [*Subgroup of Junior Woodchucks organization mentioned in Donald Duck comic by Carl Barks*]
FFEL .... Federal Family Education Loan [*Program*]
FFEM .... Freeze-Fracture Electron Microscopy
FFEP .... Finlands Folks Enhetsparti [*Finnish People's Unity Party*] (PPE)
FFEPW .... Federation of Far Eastern Prisoners of War (WDAA)
FFER .... Federal Facility Environmental Restoration (AAGC)
FFERD .... Ferroelectric Field Effect Radiation Detector (SAUS)
FFERDC .... Federal Facilities Environmental Restoration Dialogue Committee
FFES .... First Fed. S & L Association of East Hartford [*NASDAQ symbol*] (NASQ)
FFES .... First Fed S & L (CT) [*NASDAQ symbol*] (TTSB)
FFES .... Food Facilities Engineering Society [*Later, FFCS*] (EA)
FFES .... Fossil Free Energy System (SAUO)
FFEX .... Field Firing Exercise [*Military*] (NVT)
FFEX .... Frozen Food Express [*NASDAQ symbol*] (TTSB)
FFEX .... Frozen Food Express Industries, Inc. [*NASDAQ symbol*] (SAG)
FFEZ .... Finley Farmers Elevator [*Federal Railroad Administration identification code*]
FFF .... Fairly Fearless Flier
FFF .... Family of Faith Foundation [*Later, FFM*] (EA)
FFF .... Famous Fone Friends (EA)
FFF .... Farm Film Foundation [*Later, Grange-Farm Film Foundation*] (EA)
FFF .... Fast Fission Factor
FFF .... Fast Freeform Fabrication (SAUS)
fff .... fat, forty, and female (SAUS)
FFF .... Federation of Fly Fishers (EA)
FFF .... Federation of Free Farmers [*Philippines*]
FFF .... Feed Forward Filter (IAA)
FFF .... Fellowship of First Fleeters
FFF .... Ferro-Resonant Flip-Flop (VLIE)
FFF .... Field-Flow Fractionation [*Chemical separation method*]
FFF .... Fighting French Forces (SAUO)
FFF .... Film: Foreign Feature
FFF .... Find, Fix and Finish [*Military slang*] (VNW)
FFF .... Fine French Furniture
FFF .... Firm Financial Facility (COE)
FFF .... First Fall (SAUS)
FFF .... First Free First (SAUS)
FFF .... Fission-Fusion-Fission [*Bomb*] (DEN)
FFF .... Fitness for the Future [*Nursing Services Course*] [*Red Cross*]
FFF .... Five Freedoms Foundation (SAFN)
FFF .... Flat or Folded Flat [*Freight*]
FFF .... Flexible File Finder [*Computer science*] (PCM)
FFF .... Flicker Fusion Frequency [*Ophthalmology*]
FFF .... Flight Facilities Flight
FFF .... Flight Freedoms Foundation (EA)
FFF .... Form, Fit, and Function (MCD)
fff .... Fortissississimo (ADWA)
FFF .... Fortississimo [*As Loud as Possible*] [*Music*]
FFF .... Foundation for a Future [*Defunct*] (EA)
FFF .... Foundation for Fluency (NRGU)
FFF .... Foundry Educational Foundation (SAUO)
FFF .... Four Freedoms Foundation (SAUO)
FFF .... Freedom Fellowship Foundation (EA)
FFF .... free-fall funnel (SAUS)
FFF .... Free Farmers Federation (SAUO)
FFF .... Free Flight Facility (MCD)
FFF .... Free Float Facility (SSD)
FFF .... Free-Form Fabrication (ECON)
FFF .... Free French Forces [*World War II*]
FFF .... Frozen Food Foundation (SAUO)
FFF .... Fuel Failure Fraction [*Nuclear energy*] (NRCH)
FFF .... Full-Flow Filter [*Automotive engineering*]
FFF .... Furnishing Fabrics Federation (SAUO)
FFF .... Future Fisherman Foundation (EA)
FFF .... Future of Freedom Foundation (EA)
FFFA .... Federation Feminine Franco-Americaine [*Federation of French American Women*] (EA)
FFFA .... Federation of French American Women (EA)
FFFC .... FFVA Financial [*NASDAQ symbol*] (TTSB)
FFFC .... FFVA Financial Corp. [*NASDAQ symbol*] (SAG)
FFFC .... Franklin First Financial Corp. [*NASDAQ symbol*] (COMM)
FFFC .... Freddy Fender Fan Club (EA)
FFFCA .... Fabulous Fifties Ford Club of America (EA)
FFFD .... First Federal Savings Bank Fort Dodge [*Iowa*] [*NASDAQ symbol*] (SAG)
FFFD .... North Central Bancshares [*NASDAQ symbol*] (TTSB)
FFFD .... North Central Bancshares, Inc. [*NASDAQ symbol*] (SAG)
FFFE .... Friends for Free Enterprise (EA)
FFFF .... Fast Free-Form Fabrication [*Engineering design and modeling*]
FFFF .... Food, Family, Friendship, Freedom (SAUO)
FFFF .... Fusion-Fission Fuel Factory (SAUS)
FF/FFG .... Frigate/Frigate Guided Missile (ACAE)
FFFFM .... Full-Face Fire-Fighters' Mask (MCD)
FFFG .... F.F.O. Financial Group [*NASDAQ symbol*] (TTSB)
FFFG .... FFO Financial Group, Inc. [*NASDAQ symbol*] (CTT)
FFFI .... Frozen Food Foundation Inc. (SAUS)
FFFI .... Frozen Food Foundation, Incorporated (SAUO)
FFFL .... Fidelity Bankshares, Inc. [*NASDAQ symbol*] (NASQ)
FFFL .... Fidelity Federal Savings Bank [*NASDAQ symbol*] (SAG)
FFFL .... Fidelity Fedl Svgs Bk Fla [*NASDAQ symbol*] (TTSB)
FFFn .... FirstFederal Financial Services Corp. [*Associated Press*] (SAG)
FFFP .... Film-Forming Fluoroprotein Formulation [*Organic chemistry*]
FFFP .... Fuel-Flexible Fuel Processor [*Vehicle power systems*]
FFFS .... First Federal Financial Services [*Associated Press*] (SAG)
FFFSG .... Fossil Fuel Fired Steam Generator (GNE)
FFFTP .... Fuel Fab Facilities Transition Project (SAUS)
FFFU .... Federal Fire Fighters' Union [*Australia*]
FFG .... FBL Financial Group [*NYSE symbol*] (SAG)
FFG .... FBL Financial Group'A' [*NYSE symbol*] (SG)
FFG .... Fine-Fine Grain (SAUS)
FFG .... First Families of Georgia 1733-1797 (EA)
FFG .... Fiscal and Force Capability Guidance (DNAB)
FFG .... Flora and Fauna Guarantee Act (SAUO)
FFG .... Flora and Fauna Guarantee Act 1988 [*Victoria*] [*State Act*] (EERA)
FFG .... Flugdienst Fehlhaber GmbH [*Germany*] [*ICAO designator*] (FAAC)
FFG .... Forcing Function Generator (SAUS)
FFG .... Form and Finish Grinding
FFG .... Foundation Faith of God (EA)
FFG .... Foundation for Future Generations (EA)
FFG .... Free-Fall Grab [*Marine geology*]
FFG .... Free Fat Graft [*Medicine*] (DMAA)
FFG .... Freshbake Foods Group [*British*]
FFG .... Friendly Foreign Government
FFG .... Functional Feeding Groups [*Ecology*]
FFG .... Guided Missile Frigate [*Navy symbol*]
FFGA .... 1st Fighter Association (EA)
FFGA .... Full Funding Grant Agreement (AAGC)
FFGI .... Food and Feed Grain Institute [*Kansas State University*] [*Research center*] (RCD)
FFGI .... Food and Feel Grain Institute (SAUS)
FFGI .... ForeFront Group [*NASDAQ symbol*] (TTSB)
FFGI .... ForeFront Group, Inc. [*NASDAQ symbol*] (SAG)
ffGn .... Fast Fractional Gaussian Noise [*Mathematics*]
FFGT .... Fire Fighter (SAUS)
FFGT .... Firefighter [*Army*] (AABC)
FFGT .... Fire Fighting (SAUS)
FFGT .... First Federal S&L Assn. of Georgetown [*NASDAQ symbol*] (COMM)
FFGZ .... Fisher Farmers Grain [*Federal Railroad Administration identification code*]
FFH .... Fairfax Financial Holdings Ltd. [*Toronto Stock Exchange symbol*]
FFH .... Families for the Homeless (EA)
FFH .... Farm Family Holdings [*NYSE symbol*] (SG)
FFH .... Farm Family Holdings, Inc. [*NYSE symbol*] (SAG)
FFH .... Fast-Frequency Hopping (MCD)
FFH .... Fauna-Flora-Habitats Directive (SAUS)
FFH .... Fellow of the Faculty of Homoeopathy (SAUO)
FFH .... Female Family Household [*Bureau of the Census*] (GFGA)
FFH .... Fixed Flight Hours (ACAE)
FFH .... For Further Headings (DA)
FFH .... Formerly Fat Housewife [*Weight Watchers, International; advertising*]
ffh .... formerly-fat housewife (SAUS)
FFH .... Formerly-Fat Husband (SAUS)
FFH .... Foundation for Health (EA)
FFH .... Freedom from Hunger Foundation [*UN Food and Agriculture Organization*] (EA)
FFH .... Frigate, Helicopter (SAUS)
FFH-AD .... Freedom from Hunger - Action for Development (SAUO)
FFH/AD .... Freedom from Hunger/Action for Development (SAUO)
FFHC .... Federation of Feminist Health Centers (SAUO)
FFHC .... First Financial Corp. [*NASDAQ symbol*] (NQ)
FFHC .... First Finl Corp Wis [*NASDAQ symbol*] (TTSB)
FFHC .... Foam-Filled Honeycomb Core
FFHC .... Freedom from Hunger Campaign [*UN Food and Agriculture Organization*]
FFHC/AD .... Freedom from Hunger Campaign - Action for Development [*UN Food and Agriculture Organization*]
FFHH .... FSF Financial [*NASDAQ symbol*] (TTSB)

FFHH .... FSF Financial Corp. [*NASDAQ symbol*] (SAG)
FFHHS .... Farm Family Health and Hazard Surveillance
FFHMA .... Full-Fashioned Hosiery Manufacturers of America (SAUO)
FFHom .... Fellow of the Faculty of Homeopathy (SAUS)
FF Hom .... Fellow of the Faculty of Homoeopathy [*British*]
FFHom .... Fellow of the Facuty of Homeopathy (SAUS)
FFHP .... First Federal S&L Assn. of Harrisburg [*NASDAQ symbol*] (COMM)
FFHP .... First Harrisburg Bancorp, Inc. [*NASDAQ symbol*] (NQ)
FFHR .... Fatigue, fracture, and high rate (SAUS)
FFHR .... Fusion-Fission Hybrid Reactor
FFHS .... Federation of Family History Societies (EA)
FFHS .... First Franklin Corp. [*NASDAQ symbol*] (NQ)
FFHS .... Forby Family Historical Society (EA)
FFHT .... Fast Fourier-Hadamard Transform (PDAA)
FFI .... Fairmont Financial, Incorporated (SAUO)
FFI .... Family Farm Income (EURO)
FFI .... Family Firm Institute (NTPA)
FFI .... Family Functioning Index
FFI .... Fatal Familial Insomnia [*Medicine*]
FFI .... Fauna and Flora International
FFI .... Feature File Index (VLIE)
FFI .... Fellow of the Faculty of Insurance [*French Forces of the Interior*] (DAS)
FFI .... Fiber Fuels Institute (WPI)
FFI .... Field Feature Index (SAUS)
FFI .... Field Forcing (Increasing)
FFI .... Fiji Forest Industry (SAUO)
FFI .... Film Four International [*Commercial firm*] [*British*]
FFI .... Finance for Industry [*Later, Investors in Industry International - 3I*] [*British*]
FFI .... Financial Federation, Incorporated (SAUO)
FFI .... Fit for Issue [*Navy*]
F FI .... fixed and flashing (SAUS)
FFI .... Fixed Fee Incentive (SSD)
FFI .... Flanders Filters Incorporated (SAUO)
FFI .... Flexible Film Isolator (HEAS)
FFI .... Fluid Flow Indicator
FFI .... Flying Fifteen International (EA)
FFI .... Forces Francaises de l'Interieur [*French Forces of the Interior*] [*World War II*]
FFI .... Foreign Function Interface (SAUS)
FFI .... Forest Future Initiative (SAUS)
FFI .... For Further Information
FFI .... For Further Instructions (DS)
FFI .... Formation Flight Trainer (SAUS)
FFI .... Foundation for Fluency (EA)
FFI .... Fraction of Failures Isolated (ACAE)
FFI .... Franciscan Friars of the Immaculate (TOCD)
ffi .... Franciscan Friars of the Immaculate (TOCD)
FFI .... Fraunhofer Filling In (SAUS)
FFI .... Free Fluid Index (SAUS)
FFI .... free-fluid index log (SAUS)
FFI .... Free from Infection [*Medicine*]
FFI .... Freeman Fox International [*Commercial firm*] [*British*]
FFI .... Freight Forwarders Institute [*Defunct*] (EA)
FFI .... French Forces of the Interior (SAUO)
FFI .... Freshwater Fish of Illinois (SAUO)
FFI .... Friend Finders International [*Defunct*] (EA)
FFI .... Frozen Food Institute
FFI .... Frozen Foods Industries (SAUO)
FFI .... Fuel Flow Indicator
FFI .... Full Field Investigation (NRCH)
FFI .... Full Force Integration (SEWL)
FFI .... Fundamental Frequency Indicator [*Medicine*] (DMAA)
FFIA .... Fellow, Fundraising Institute-Australia, Inc. (NFD)
FFIA .... Fellow of the Federal Institute of Accountants (SAUO)
FFIC .... Fairbanks Family Investment Center (SAUO)
FFIC .... Flushing Financial [*NASDAQ symbol*] (TTSB)
FFIC .... Flushing Financial Corp. [*NASDAQ symbol*] (SAG)
fFIDA .... Fringe Festival of Independent Dance Artists [*Canada*]
FFIDX .... Fidelity Fund [*Mutual fund ticker symbol*] (SG)
FFIEC .... Federal Financial Institutions Examination Council (OICC)
FFIEI .... Foundation in Favour of the International Economic Information (SAUO)
FFIH .... Familial Fat-Induced Hyperlipemia [*Medicine*] (MELL)
FFII-MS .... Fission Fragment-Induced Ionization - Mass Spectroscopy
FFILH .... Flat Fillister Head [*Screws*]
F/FILT .... Fuel Filter [*Automotive engineering*]
ffim .... far-field image maximizer (SAUS)
FFIN .... First Financial Bankshares [*NASDAQ symbol*] (SAG)
ff ind .... fact-finding index (SAUS)
FFinFd .... First Financial Fund, Inc. [*Associated Press*] (SAG)
FFIN-L .... Nova University, Law Library, Fort Lauderdale, FL [*Library symbol*] [*Library of Congress*] (LCLS)
FF International... World Federation of Flying Fifteen Owners Associations (SAUO)
FFinWM .... First Financial Corporation Western Maryland [*Associated Press*] (SAG)
FFIP .... Firm Fixed Incentive Price [*Government contracting*]
FFIR .... Foundation for Financial Institutions Research [*Defunct*] (EA)
FFIR .... Friendly Forces Information Requirements [*Military*] (INF)
FFIRN .... Field Format Index Reference Number
FFIS .... Federal Facilities Information System (EPA)
FFIS .... Foreign Fisheries Information Service (SAUO)
FFIS .... Forests and Forest Industries Strategy (EERA)
FFIT .... Fluorescent Focus Inhibition Test [*Medicine*] (BABM)
FFJ .... Franciscan Familiar of Saint Joseph (SAUO)
FFJ .... Friends for Jamaica (EA)
FFJF .... Federation of Former Jewish Fighters (EA)
FFK .... Fixed Function Key [*Computer science*] (ECII)
FFK .... Fixed Function Keyboard (MCD)
FFKT .... Farmers Capital Bank [*NASDAQ symbol*] (TTSB)
FFKT .... Farmers Capital Bank Corp. [*NASDAQ symbol*] (NQ)
FFKY .... First Federal Financial Corp. [*NASDAQ symbol*] (SAG)
FFKY .... First Federal Savings Bank of Elizabethtown (Kentucky) [*NASDAQ symbol*] (COMM)
FFKY .... First Fed Finl (KY) [*NASDAQ symbol*] (TTSB)
FFKZ .... First Federal S&L of Kalamazoo [*NASDAQ symbol*] (COMM)
FFL .... Fairfield, IA [*Location identifier*] [*FAA*] (FAAL)
FFL .... Family Friendly Libraries
FFL .... Fast Freight Line [*Shipping*]
FFL .... Federal Firearms License
FFL .... Federal Fiscal Liability
FFL .... Federation of Free Labor [*Philippines*]
FFL .... Female Flared
FFL .... Feminists for Life (SAUO)
FFL .... Feminists for Life of America (EA)
FFL .... Field Failure (AAG)
FFL .... Fiji Federation of Labor
FFL .... Finished Floor (SAUS)
FFL .... Finished Floor Line [*Technical drawings*]
FFL .... Firearm from a Licensed Dealer
FFL .... First Financial Language [*Computer science*]
FFL .... Fitness for Life [*An association*] (EA)
FFL .... Fixed and Flashing Light [*Navigation signal*]
FFL .... Flip-Flop Latch [*Computer science*] (MSA)
FFL .... Floral Variant of Follicular Lymphoma [*Medicine*] (MELL)
FFL .... Forces Francaises Libres [*Free French Forces*]
FFI .... Fort Lauderdale Public Library, Fort Lauderdale, FL [*Library symbol*] [*Library of Congress*] (LCLS)
FFL .... Front Focal Length [*Optics*]
FFL .... Fuel Fill Line (AAG)
FFL .... Full Funding Limit (AAGC)
FFL .... Intavia Ltd. [*British*] [*FAA designator*] (FAAC)
FFL .... Light Frigate
FFLA .... Federal Farm Loan Act [*1916*]
FFLA .... Federal Farm Loan Association (SAUO)
FFLA .... Fellow of the Faculty of Fire Loss Adjusters [*British*] (DAS)
FFLA .... Ferromagnetic Fluid Levitation Accelerometer
FFIAI .... Art Institute of Fort Lauderdale, Fort Lauderdale, FL [*Library symbol*] [*Library of Congress*] (LCLS)
FFIB .... Broward Community College, Fort Lauderdale, FL [*Library symbol*] [*Library of Congress*] (LCLS)
FFLB .... Federal Farm Loan Board (SAUO)
FFIBL .... Broward County Libraries Division, Fort Lauderdale, FL [*Library symbol*] [*Library of Congress*] (LCLS)
FFLC .... FFLC Bancorp [*NASDAQ symbol*] (SAG)
FFLC .... Freight Forwarder Location Code (AAGC)
FFLC Bc .... FFLC Bancorp [*Associated Press*] (SAG)
FF Length .... Front Focal Length (SAUS)
FFLG .... Guided missile light frigate or corvette (SAUS)
FFLI .... Frozen Food Locker Institute (SAUO)
FFIN .... Nova University, Fort Lauderdale, FL [*Library symbol*] [*Library of Congress*] (LCLS)
FFIN-O .... Nova University, Physical Oceanographic Laboratory Library, Dania, FL [*Library symbol*] [*Library of Congress*] (LCLS)
FFLOP .... Field Fresnel Lens Optical Platform
FFLS .... Failed Fuel Location Subsystem [*Nuclear energy*] (NRCH)
FFLSC .... Feed-Forward Linear Sequential Circuit (SAUS)
FFLT .... Familiarization Flight (FAAC)
FFlt .... Free Flight (SAUS)
FFLY .... Faithfully
FFM .... Family Farm Movement (EA)
FFM .... Family of Faith Ministries (EA)
FFM .... Fast File Manager (NITA)
FFM .... Fat-Free Mass (MAE)
FFM .... [*The*] Fellowship for Freedom in Medicine [*British*]
FFM .... Fergus Falls, MN [*Location identifier*] [*FAA*] (FAAL)
FFM .... File-on-File Mounting File System (SAUS)
FFM .... Fire-and-Forget Missile (SEWL)
FFM .... First Financial Management Corp. [*NYSE symbol*] (SPSG)
FFM .... Fixed Format Message (VLIE)
FFM .... Fixed Freqency Mode (SAUS)
FFM .... Fixed Frequency Modem (SAUS)
FFM .... Flat Film Memory (VLIE)
ffm .... floating fecal material (SAUS)
FFM .... Foundation for Microbiology (EA)
FF/M .... Fracture Frequency per Meter [*Mining technology*]
FFM .... Free-Flying [*Experiment*] Module [*NASA*] (NASA)
FFM .... Friction Force Microscope
FFM .... Fuel fabrication modification (SAUS)
FFM .... Fuel Failure Mock-Up [*Nuclear energy*]
FFM .... Fuel failure monitoring (SAUS)
FFM .... Fuel Fill to Missile [*Aerospace*] (AAG)
FFM .... Full Face Mask [*Military*] (CAAL)
FFM .... Fulton Fish Market (SAUS)
FFM .... Fundamental Frequency Modulator (VLIE)
FFM .... Fund for the Feminist Majority (EA)
FFm .... Lee County Public Library, Fort Meyers, FL [*Library symbol*] [*Library of Congress*] (LCLS)
FFMA .... Fidelity Federal Savings Bank (MHDW)

FFMA .... Field Force Maintenance Area (SAUS)
FFMA .... Foundry Facings Manufacturers Association (SAUO)
FFMA .... Fraternal Field Managers' Association [*Appleton, WI*] (EA)
FFMAS .... Furniture Factories' Marketing Association of the South [*Later, IHFMA*] (EA)
FFMC .... Faceted Fixed Mirror Concentrator (PDAA)
FFMC .... Federal Farm Mortgage Corp. [*Established, 1934; assets transferred to Secr etary of the Treasury, 1961*]
FFMC .... Federal Financial Managers Council
FFMC .... Fine Fuel Moisture Code (SAUS)
FFMC .... First Financial Management Corporation (SAUO)
FFMC .... Freshwater Fish Marketing Corp. [*See also OCPED*]
FFmE .... Edison Community College, ECC/USF Learning Resources, Fort Meyers, FL [*Library symbol*] [*Library of Congress*] (LCLS)
FFMED .... Fixed Format Message Entry Device (SAUS)
FFMED .... Fixed Former Message Entry Device (MCD)
FFMG .... Foundry Facings Manufacturers Group [*Later, FSMG*] (EA)
FFMIA .... Federal Financial Management Improvement Act (SAUS)
FFMIP .... Foreign Military Sales Financial Management Improvement Program (MCD)
FFML .... First Family Bank Florida [*NASDAQ symbol*] (SAG)
FFML .... First Family Finl [*NASDAQ symbol*] (TTSB)
FFML .... Franklin Ferguson Memorial Library (SAUO)
FFmL .... Lee County Library System, Fort Myers, FL [*Library symbol*] [*Library of Congress*] (LCLS)
FFMN .... Fixed Federal Monitoring Network (FAAC)
FF Model .... Free Flight Model (SAUS)
FFMOP .... Freshwater Fisheries Management Plans (SAUS)
FFMS .... Fast Fourier Mass Spectrometry (SAUS)
FFMS .... Free Flight Melt Spinning (SAUS)
FFMSPAC .... Farm Financial Management Skills Program Advisory Committee [*Australia*]
FFMY .... First Federal S&L Assn. of Fort Myers [*NASDAQ symbol*] (COMM)
FFMZ .... Fisher Flour Mill [*Federal Railroad Administration identification code*]
FFN .... Fetal Fibronectin [*Medicine*] (MELL)
FFN .... Field Format Name
FFN .... Fleet Flash Network [*Navy*]
FFN .... Fly-Fishing Network [*Information service or system*]
FFN .... Folded Flat or Nested [*Freight*]
ffn .... free-floating nozzle (SAUS)
FFN .... FreeLance Finders Network (EA)
FFN .... Friend, Foe, or Neutral (MCD)
FFN .... Full-Frontal Nudity (WDAA)
FFN .... Full Function Node (MHDB)
FFnBcp .... First Financial Bancorp, Inc. [*FL*] [*Associated Press*] (SAG)
FFNC .... First Fix Not Converted
FFncOH .... First Financial Bancorp Ohio [*Associated Press*] (SAG)
FFnCpRI .... First Financial Corp. (Providence, RI) [*Associated Press*] (SAG)
FF-NM .... Flip-Flop - National Module [*Computer science*] (AAG)
FFNM .... Fort Frederica National Monument (SAUO)
FFNPA .... Fund for New Priorities in America (EA)
FFNSW .... Filipino Forum in New South Wales [*Australia*]
FFO .... Dayton, OH [*Location identifier*] [*FAA*] (FAAL)
FFO .... Forces Francaises de l'Ouest
FFO .... Formation Flight Operation
FFO .... Forward Firing Ordnance (MCD)
FFO .... Fraction of oxidized (SAUS)
FFO .... French Family Association (EA)
FFO .... Fullam Family Organization (EA)
FFO .... Furnace Fuel Oil (NATG)
FFOA .... Association of Farmer FAO and WFP Staff Members (SAUO)
FFOA Rome .... Association of Former FAO and WFP Staff Members (SAUO)
FFOB .... Flexible Fiber Optic Borescope (SAUS)
FFOB .... Flexible Fiber Optics Bundle (ACAE)
FFOB .... Forward Fighting Operating Base [*Military*] (AFM)
FFOB .... Front Face of Block [*Automotive engineering*]
FFOB .... Frontiers Foundation Operation Beaver [*Canada*] (EAIO)
FFOC .... Farm Enterprise Organisation and Control (SAUS)
FFOF .... Foreign Fishing Observer Fund [*National Oceanic and Atmospheric Administration*]
FFO Fn .... FFO Financial Group, Inc. [*Associated Press*] (SAG)
FFOH .... Fidelity Financial of Ohio, Inc. [*NASDAQ symbol*] (SAG)
FFOH .... Fidelity Finl Ohio [*NASDAQ symbol*] (TTSB)
FFOL .... FDDI Follow-On LAN (SAUS)
FFOL .... Fuel Facility Operating License (FOTI)
FFOM .... Fellow of the Faculty of Occupational Medicine (DAVI)
FFOM .... First Federal of Michigan (SAUO)
FFOP .... Failure Free Operating Period (ACAE)
FFOPA .... Federal Firearms Owners Protection Act (SAUS)
FFORCEV .... Field Force, Vietnam (CINC)
F for L .... Feminists for Life (SAUO)
FFOS .... Facilities Forecast Obligations Summary
FFOS .... Forward Flying Observation System (SAUO)
FFOT .... Fast Frequency on Target
FFOX .... Firefox Communications [*NASDAQ symbol*] (TTSB)
FFOX .... Firefox Communications, Inc. [*NASDAQ symbol*] (SAG)
FFP .... Consolidated First Fund [*Vancouver Stock Exchange symbol*]
FFP .... Failure Free Period (ACAE)
FFP .... False Force Presentation (SEWL)
FFP .... Far-Field Pressure
FFP .... Farm Forestry Program (EERA)
FFP .... Fast Floating Point [*Computer science*]
FFP .... Federal Financial Participation
FFP .... Federation for Progress [*Defunct*] (EA)
FFP .... Feminists Fighting Pornography (EA)
FFP .... FFP Partners L.P. [*AMEX symbol*] (TTSB)
FFP .... FFP Partners Ltd. [*AMEX symbol*] (SPSG)
FFP .... Field Forcing, Protective (IAA)
FFP .... Filiform Papilla [*Medicine*] (MELL)
FFP .... Finite Flat Plate
ffp .... Fireplace (REAL)
FFP .... Firm-Fixed Price [*Government contracting*]
FFP .... First Focal Point (SAUS)
FFP .... Fistful of Prisms [*Opthalmology*] (DAVI)
FFP .... Fixed Fee Procurement (ACAE)
FFP .... Fixed Frequency Pulse (IAA)
FFP .... Flat Field Program (SAUS)
FFP .... flat-file processor (SAUS)
FFP .... Floating Foundation of Photography
FFP .... Food for Peace [*Overseas food donation program*]
FFP .... Food for Poland [*Later, Food for Peace*] (EA)
FFP .... Forest Fires Prevention (SAUS)
FFP .... Forte Piano [*Loud, then Soft*] [*Music*]
FFP .... Foundation for Peace (EA)
FFP .... Founding Fathers Papers (EA)
FFP .... Free Flight Plan [*Northwest Airlines, Inc.*]
FFP .... Frequent Flier Program (BARN)
FFP .... Fresh Frozen Plasma [*Medicine*]
FFP .... Friends of Family Planning (EA)
FFP .... Friends of the Filipino People (EA)
FFP .... Frozen Food Product (SAUS)
FFP .... Fuel Fabrication Plant [*Nuclear energy*] (NRCH)
FFP .... Fuel Fill to Fuel Prefab (AAG)
FFP .... [*The*] Fund for Peace [*An association*] (EA)
FFP .... Fungiform Papilla [*Medicine*] (MELL)
FFp .... Saint Lucie-Okeechobee Regional Library, Fort Pierce, FL [*Library symbol*] [*Library of Congress*] (LCLS)
FFPA .... Farmland Protection Policy Act (EEVL)
FFPA .... Fast Fuzzy Processor Architecture (SAUS)
FFPA .... Free From Prussic Acid (SAUS)
FFPAF .... Forest and Forest Products Policy Advisory Forum (EERA)
FFPB .... First Palm Beach Bancorp [*NASDAQ symbol*] (TTSB)
FFPB .... First Palm Beach Bancorp, Inc. [*NASDAQ symbol*] (SAG)
FFPB .... Flora and Fauna Protection Board (EERA)
FFPB .... Free-Fall Practice Bomb (SAUS)
FFPC .... Firm-Fixed Price Contract
FFPC .... Florida First Bancorp [*NASDAQ symbol*] (TTSB)
FFPC .... Florida First Bancorp, Inc. [*NASDAQ symbol*] (SAG)
FFPC .... Florida First Federal Savings Bank [*NASDAQ symbol*] (NQ)
FFPE .... Federation de la Fonction Publique Europeenne [*European Civil Service Federation*] (EAIO)
FFPEPA .... Firm Fixed Price with Economic Price Adjustment [*Government contracts*]
FFPh .... Fellow of the Faculty of Physiotherapists
FFPHM .... Fellow Faculty of Public Health Medicine [*British*] (WA)
FFPI .... Firm Fixed Price Incentive (ACAE)
FFPI .... Fixed-Fee-plus-Incentive [*Business term*] (MCD)
FFPI .... Flip-Flop Position Indicator [*Computer science*]
FFpI .... Indian River Community College, Fort Pierce, FL [*Library symbol*] [*Library of Congress*] (LCLS)
FFPIC .... Forestry and Forest Products Industry Council [*Australia*]
FFPLE .... Firm-Fixed Price Letter [*Government contracting*] (MCD)
FFPLO .... Frequency Feedback Phase-Locked Oscillator (SAUS)
FFPLOE .... Firm-Fixed-Price Level of Effort [*Type of contract*] (AAGC)
FFPLRM .... Firmed Fixed Price Labor Reimburseable Materials (ACAE)
FFPM .... Fellow of the Faculty of Pharmaceutical Medicine (ODA)
FFPR .... First Federal Savings Bank of Puerto Rico [*NASDAQ symbol*] (COMM)
FFPRI .... Forestry and Forest Product Research Institute (SAUS)
FF Product .... Frozen Food Product (SAUS)
FFPS .... Fauna and Flora Preservation Society (EA)
FFPS .... Fauna Flora Preservation Society (SAUS)
FFPS .... Fellow of the Faculty of Physicians and Surgeons [*British*]
FFPS .... Fellow of the Royal Faculty of Physicians and Surgeons (SAUO)
FFPS .... Flora and Fauna Preservation Society (EERA)
FFPS .... Fuel Flow Power Supply (ACAE)
FFPS .... Functional Force Planning System (SAUO)
FFPSG .... Fellow of the Faculty of Physicians and Surgeons (SAUS)
FFPSG .... Fellow of the Faculty of Physicians and Surgeons Glasgow (SAUO)
FFPVE .... Firm Fixed Price Value Engineering (ACAE)
FFQ .... ferrosilite-fayalite-quartz (SAUS)
FFR .... Failure Frequency Report [*Military*] (AFIT)
FFR .... Falfurrias, TX [*Location identifier*] [*FAA*] (FAAL)
FFR .... False-Flag Recruitment [*CIA*] (LAIN)
FFR .... Fauna and Flora Reserve [*State*] (EERA)
FFR .... Fellow of the Faculty of Radiologists [*British*]
FFR .... FERD-loop flow reduction (SAUS)
FFR .... Field Forcing, Reversing (IAA)
FFR .... Film Forum Review (journ.) (SAUS)
FFR .... Fission-Fusion Ratio
FFR .... Fit for Role [*Military*] [*British*]
FFR .... Fitted for Radar (SAUS)
FFR .... Fitted for Radio [*Military*] [*British*]
FFR .... Fixed Frequency Receiver
FFR .... Flash Format Program (SAA)
FFR .... Flat Face Rolling System (SAUS)
FFR .... Fleet Fighter Reconnaissance [*Air Force*]
FFR .... Flight Feasibility Review (ACAE)
FFR .... Flux Fraction Ratio (SAUS)
FFR .... Folded Flow Reactor

FFR .... Foreign Force Reduction (NATG)
FFR .... For Future Reference [*Internet dialog*]
FFR .... Fosterlaendska Folkroerelsen [*Patriotic People's Movement*] [*Finland*] (PPE)
FFR .... Foundation for Field Research (EA)
FFR .... Four-Frequency Radar (SAUS)
F Fr .... (Frater) Johannes de Freiburg [*Deceased, 1314*] [*Authority cited in pre-1607 legal work*] (DSA)
FFR .... Freedom from Relapse (MELL)
FFR .... Free Field Room
FFR .... Free Flight Rocket (NATG)
FFR .... Free Flooding Projector (SAUS)
FFR .... Free-Form Reflector [*Automotive lighting*]
FFR .... Free French [*World War II*]
FFr .... French Franc [*Monetary unit*]
FFR .... Frequency-Following Response [*Neurophysiology*]
ffr .... frequency following response (SAUS)
FFR .... Front Engine, Front and Rear Drive [*Automotive engineering*]
FFR .... Frontier Force Rifles [*British military*] (DMA)
FFR .... RADAR Picket Frigate [*Navy symbol*] (NVT)
FFRATS .... Full Flight Regime Auto Throttle System (ADA)
FFRB .... Field Failure Review Board (ACAE)
FFRC .... Food Freezer Research Council (SAUO)
FFRC .... Fossil Fuel Research Committee (SAUO)
FFRC .... Fossil Fuel Resources Committee
FFRD .... Federally Funded Research and Development (SAUO)
FFRD .... Flip-Flop Relay Driver [*Computer science*]
FFRDC .... Federally Funded Research and Development Center [*National Science Foundation*]
F/FRED .... Forestry/Fuel-wood Research and Development Project (GNE)
FFRF .... Freedom from Religion Foundation (EA)
FFrHQ .... Free French Headquarters (SAUO)
FFRI .... Finnish Forest Research Institute (SAUO)
FFRI .... Fruit and Food Research Institute (SAUS)
FFRIBA .... Fellows of the Royal Institute of British Architects (SAUO)
FFROM .... Free and Full Range of Motion (MELL)
FFRP .... Fans and Friends of Ray Price [*An association*] (EA)
FFRR .... First Flight Readiness Review (SSD)
FFRRCSIrel ... Fellow of the Faculty of Radiologists, Royal College of Surgeons of Ireland [*British*] (DBQ)
FFRR System ... Full Frequency Range Records System (SAUS)
FFRS .... Fast Fleet Replenishment Ship
FFRS .... Federal Forest Research Station (SAUS)
FFRV .... Fidelity Federal Savings Bank [*NASDAQ symbol*] (NQ)
FFRV .... Fidelity Financial Bankshares Corp. [*NASDAQ symbol*] (SAG)
FFRV .... Fidelity Finl Bancshares [*NASDAQ symbol*] (TTSB)
FFS .... Fallback Fault-tolerant Server (SAUS)
FFS .... Family Financial Statement
FFS .... Fast File System [*Computer science*] (VERA)
FFS .... Fast Filing System (SAUS)
FFS .... Fat-Free Solids
FFS .... Fat-Free Supper [*Medicine*]
FFS .... Feeder Fault Sensing (MCD)
FFS .... Fee for Service [*Equivalency*]
FFS .... Fee For Service Reimbursement (SAUS)
FFS .... Fellow of the Faculty of Architects and Surveyors [*British*] (DBQ)
FFS .... Fellow of the Faculty of Secretaries (SAUO)
FFS .... Fellow of the Franklin Society [*British*]
FFS .... Feminism and Family Studies Section of the National Council on Family Relations (EA)
FFS .... Fight for Sight [*An association*] (EA)
FFS .... Film: Foreign Series
FFS .... Financial Forecasting System (SAUS)
FFS .... Fine-Blanking and Finishing System [*Metal stamping*]
FFS .... Finite Fermi System (SAUS)
FFs .... First Families (SAUS)
FFS .... First Flight Society (EA)
FFS .... Fixed Frequency Sampling [*for water quality assessment*]
FFS .... Flame Fluorescence Spectroscopy
FFS .... Flash File System (SAUS)
FFS .... Flash Flood Statement [*Telecommunications*] (OTD)
FFS .... Fletcher Challenge Forest [*NYSE symbol*] (SPSG)
FFS .... Fletcher Challenge Forest ADS [*NYSE symbol*] (TTSB)
FFS .... Flexible Fiberoptic Sigmoidoscopy [*Medicine*] (MELL)
FFS .... Flight Facilities Survey (SAUS)
FFS .... Flight Following Service [*FAA*]
FFS .... Flip-Flop Storage (SAUS)
FFS .... Florida Department of Agriculture and Consumer Services, Division of Forestry [*FAA designator*] (FAAC)
FFS .... Focused feasibility study (SAUS)
FFS .... Food Fair Stores, Inc. (SAUO)
FFS .... For Free Server (SAUS)
FFS .... For Further Study (ACRL)
FFS .... Formated File System (SAUS)
FFS .... Formation Flying Simulator
FFS .... Formatted File System [*Computer science*]
FFS .... Foundation for Fire Safety [*Defunct*] (EA)
FFS .... Frame Floor System [*Automotive engineering*]
FFS .... Free-Fall Sensor
FFS .... Free Floating Silicone (SAUS)
FFS .... Free-Flying System (SAUS)
FFS .... Frequently-Found Substructure (SAUS)
FFS .... Front des Forces Socialistes [*Front of Socialist Forces*] [*Algeria*] [*Political party*] (PD)
FFS .... Frost-Free Season (QUAC)
FFS .... Fruit Frost Service (SAUO)
FFS .... Health Promotion Foundation (SAUO)
FFSA .... Federation Francaise du Sport Automobile [*French Federation of Motorsport*]
FFSA .... Field Functional System Assembly and Checkout
FFSA .... Fund Family Shareholder Association Incorporated (SAUO)
FFSA & C ..... Field Functional System Assembly and Checkout (KSC)
FFSAC .... Field Functional Systems Assembly and Checkout (IAA)
FFS & FP ..... Five-Year Force Structure and Financial Program [*Navy*] (AFIT)
FFSB .... Federation des Foires et Salons du Benelux [*Federation of Fairs and Trade Shows of BENELUX - FFTSB*] (EA)
FFSB .... First Federal Savings Bank (SAUO)
FFSBern .... First Federal Savings & Loan Association, San Bernardino [*Associated Press*] (SAG)
FFSC .... Failed fuel shipping container (SAUS)
FFSc .... Fellow of the Faculty of Sciences (SAUO)
FFSC .... Franciscan Brothers of the Holy Cross (TOCD)
ffsc .... Franciscan Brothers of the Holy Cross (TOCD)
FFSCC .... Full-Flow Staged Combustion Cycle
FFSCUG .... Formatted File System Commercial Users' Group [*Computer science*]
FFSD .... Free Foil Switching Device
FFSF .... Fossil Fired Steam Plant (SAUS)
FFSF .... Full Fat Soy Flour (OA)
FFSH .... Full Ford Service History [*Automotive classified advertising*]
FFSI .... Financing for Science International, Inc. [*NASDAQ symbol*] (SAG)
FFSI .... Financing for Science Intl [*NASDAQ symbol*] (TTSB)
FFSIW .... Financing for Science Intl Wrrt [*NASDAQ symbol*] (TTSB)
FFSK .... Fast Frequency Shift Keying (MCD)
FFSL .... First Independence Corp. [*NASDAQ symbol*] (SAG)
FFSL .... First Independence Del [*NASDAQ symbol*] (TTSB)
FFSM .... Fast Fourier Synoptic Mapping (SAUS)
FFSM .... Federation des Fondations pour la Sante Mondiale [*Federation of World Health Foundations - FWHF*] [*Geneva, Switzerland*] (EA)
FFSM .... First Federal Savings Bank of Montana (SAUO)
FFSP .... Fossil Fired Steam Plant (IEEE)
FFSP .... Full Function Signal Processor (SAUS)
FFSR .... Feed-Forward Signal Regeneration (PDAA)
FFSR .... Fund for Stockowners Rights (EA)
FFSS .... Full-Frequency Stereophonic Sound (DEN)
FFSSiou .... First Federal Savings Bank Siouxland [*Associated Press*] (SAG)
FFST .... 4 Front Software Intl [*NASDAQ symbol*] (TTSB)
FFST .... First Failure Support Technology (SAUS)
FFST .... Free Floating Silicon Technology (SAUS)
FFST2 .... First Failure Support Technology /2 (SAUS)
FFSTA .... Federated Furnishing Trades Society [*Australia*]
FFSvFD .... First Federal Savings Bank Fort Dodge IA [*Associated Press*] (SAG)
FFSW .... FirstFederal Financial Services [*NASDAQ symbol*] (SAG)
FFSW .... First Federal S&L Assn. of Wooster (Ohio) [*NASDAQ symbol*] (COMM)
FFSW .... Firstfed Finl Svcs [*NASDAQ symbol*] (TTSB)
FFSWO .... FirstFederal Finl 6.5% Cv'B' Pfd [*NASDAQ symbol*] (TTSB)
FFSWP .... FirstFederal Finl 7% Cv'A'Pfd [*NASDAQ symbol*] (TTSB)
FFSX .... First Federal Bankshares, Inc. [*NASDAQ symbol*] (NASQ)
FFSX .... First Federal Savings Bank Siouxland [*NASDAQ symbol*] (SAG)
FFSX .... First Fed Svgs Bk Siouxland [*NASDAQ symbol*] (TTSB)
FFT .... Fast Formula Translation (ACAE)
FFT .... Fast Fourier Transform [*Mathematics*]
FFT .... Fast Fourier Transformation [*Noise reduction technique*] (NITA)
FFT .... Fast-Fourier Transforms (DAVI)
FFT .... Fast Freight Train
FFT .... Fat Free Tissue (SAUS)
FFT .... File Format Table (SAUO)
FFT .... final form text (SAUS)
FFT .... Finger-to-Finger Test [*Medicine*] (MELL)
FFT .... Finite Fourier Transform
FFT .... Fixture Functional Test (ACAE)
FFT .... Flash Fusion Technology (SAUS)
FFT .... Flicker Fusion Threshold [*Cardiology*] (DAVI)
FFT .... Floor-to-Floor Time [*Engineering*]
FFT .... For Further Transfer [*to*] [*Military*]
FFT .... Formation Fighter Trainer (ACAE)
FFT .... Formation Flight Trainer [*Air Force*]
FFT .... Forward Flexion: fingertips to Toes (SAUS)
FFT .... Frankfort, KY [*Location identifier*] [*FAA*] (FAAL)
FFT .... Frankfurt [*Kentucky*] [*Airport symbol*] (AD)
FFT .... Free-Fall Test (SAA)
FFT .... Free-Floating Thrombus [*Medicine*]
FFT .... Freight Forwarders Tariff Bureau, Inc., New York NY [*STAC*]
f-ft- .... French Territory of the Afars and Issas [*Djibouti*] [*MARC geographic area code*] [*Library of Congress*] (LCCP)
FFT .... Frontier Airlines, Inc. [*FAA designator*] (FAAC)
FFT .... Fuel Flow Totalizer [*Aerospace*]
FFT .... Full Free Triple [*Lift truck*]
FFT .... Training Frigate [*Navy symbol*]
FFTA .... Fast Fourier Transform Analyzer (SAUS)
FFTA .... Foundation of the Flexographic Technical Association [*Later, FTA*] (EA)
FFTA .... Frozen Fish Trades Association (EA)
FFT-analyzer ... fast Fourier-transformation analyzer (SAUS)
FFTB .... Freight Forwarders Tariff Bureau [*Defunct*] (EA)
FFTC .... Fixed Feed Through Capacitor
FFTC .... Food and Fertilizer Technology Center (SAUS)
FFTC/ASPAC ... Food and Fertilizer Technology Center (or Centre) for the Asian and Pacific Region (SAUO)
FFTCom .... Fellow of the Faculty of Teachers in Commerce [*British*] (DBQ)

FF-TEM Freeze-Fracture Transmission Electron Microscopy

FF/Test Forward-Flow-Test (SAUS)

FFTF Fast Flux Test Facility [*Nuclear energy*]

FFTF Future Framework Task Force [*Environmental science*] (COE)

FFTFPO Fast Flux Test Facility Project Office [*Nuclear energy*] (GFGA)

FFTFPO FFTF Project Office (SAUS)

FFTFPR FFTF periodic report (SAUS)

FFTG Firefighting [*Army*] (AABC)

FFTI 4Front Technologies, Inc. [*NASDAQ symbol*] (NASQ)

FFTO Free-Flying Teleoperator [*Program*] [*Electronics*]

FFTO Program Free-Flying Tele-Operator Program (SAUS)

FF/TOT Fuel Flow Totalizer [*Aerospace*] (AAG)

FFTP Fast Food Transfer Protocol (SAUS)

FFTP Fast Fourier Transformations Processor (SAUS)

FFTP Fast Fourier Transform Processor [*Mathematics*] (IAA)

FFTP Fast Fourier Transform Pruning (SAUS)

FFTP First Full-Term Pregnancy [*Medicine*] (EDAA)

FFTQ Four Factor Theory Questionnaire (EDAC)

FFTR Fast Flux Test Reactor [*Nuclear energy*] (OA)

FFTR Federal Fuel Tax Rebate (SAUS)

FFTR Firefighter (AFM)

FFTRI Fruit and Food Technology Research Institute (SAUO)

FFTs fast-Fourier transforms (SAUS)

FFTS Fire Fighting Training Systems [*Army*]

FFTS Fixed Frequency Topside Sounder (SAA)

FFTSB Federation of Fairs and Trade Shows of BENELUX [*Formerly, Federation of Fairs and Exhibitions in BENELUX - FFSB*] (EA)

FFTSO File Transfer Time Sharing Option [*Communications term*] (DCT)

FFTU Fast Fourier Transform Unit (SAUS)

FFTV Free Flight Test Vehicle

FFU Federation of Film Unions [*British*]

FFU Feminist Free University (SAUO)

FFU Ferranti PLC [*British*] [*ICAO designator*] (FAAC)

FFU Field Follow-up (SAUS)

FFU Fire Fighters Union (SAUO)

FFU Fish Farmers Union (SAUO)

FFU Focus-Forming Unit [*Medical/biochemical research*]

FFU Futaleufu [*Chile*] [*Airport symbol*] (AD)

FFU GEC Marconi Avionics Ltd. [*British*] [*FAA designator*] (FAAC)

FFU Provo, UT [*Location identifier*] [*FAA*] (FAAL)

FFUR Failure Factor Update Request

F/FURN Fully Furnished (ADA)

FFUSS Flat Field Unaberrated Source System (SAUS)

FFV Far-Field Visibility [*Aviation*]

FFV Fast Flying Vestibule [*Old railroad term for a deluxe coach*]

FFV Field Failure Voltage (IEEE)

FFV Field Force, Vietnam

FFV Finest Foods of Virginia [*Brand name*]

FFV First Families of Virginia (BARN)

FFV Flexible-Fuel Vehicle [*Operable by either gasoline or methanol*] [*Ford Motor Co.*]

FFV Foreign Fishing Vessel

FFVA Florida Fruit and Vegetable Association (EA)

FFVA Fn FFVA Financial Corp. [*Associated Press*] (SAG)

FFVF Freedoms Foundation at Valley Forge (EA)

FFVIB Fresh Fruit and Vegetable Information Bureau [*British*] (CB)

FFVMA Fire Fighting Vehicles Manufacturers Association [*British*] (DBA)

FFV's First Families of Virginia [*Supposedly elite society*] [*Slang*]

FFVS Free Field Voltage Sensitivity

FFVUR Front Feed Visual Unit Record (SAUS)

FFW Failure Free Warranty [*Military*] (AFIT)

ffw fast flood watch (SAUS)

FFW Fat-Free Weight (DB)

FFW Federation of Free Workers [*Philippines*]

FFW Feed Forward (ECII)

FFW Feet of Fresh Water

FFW Filoil Free Workers [*Philippines*]

FFW Fitted for Wireless [*British military*] (DMA)

FFW Flash Flood Warning [*Telecommunications*] (OTD)

FFW Foreign Free World (MCD)

FFWC FFW Corp. [*NASDAQ symbol*] (SAG)

FFWC Fractional Free Water Clearance [*Medicine*] (EDAA)

FFWCB Federation of Flatmen, Watermen, and Canal Boatmen [*A union*] [*British*]

FFW Cp FFW Corp. [*Associated Press*] (SAG)

FFWD Fast Forward [*Audio-visual technology*]

ffwd full-speed forward (SAUS)

FFWD Wood Bancorp [*NASDAQ symbol*] (TTSB)

FF-Weite front focal distance (SAUS)

FFWHC Federation of Feminist Women's Health Centers (EA)

FFWM First Financial Corp., Western Maryland [*NASDAQ symbol*] (SAG)

FFWM First Finl (MD) [*NASDAQ symbol*] (TTSB)

FFWM Free Floating Wavemeter (SAUS)

FFWS Fuel Filter Water Separator [*Automotive engineering*]

FFWT Final Feedwater Temperature [*Nuclear energy*] (NRCH)

FFWV Federation of French War Veterans (EA)

FFWW Fat-Free Wet Weight

FFY Faithfully

FFY Fanny Farmer Candy Shops (SAUO)

FFY Federal Fiscal Year (SAUO)

FFY Fife and Forfar Yeomanry (SAUO)

FFYF FFY Financial [*NASDAQ symbol*] (TTSB)

FFYF FFY Financial Corp. [*NASDAQ symbol*] (SAG)

FFY Fn FFY Financial Corp. [*Associated Press*] (SAG)

FFYQ Federal Fiscal Year Quarters (OICC)

FFY/SH Fife and Forfar Yeomanry/Scottish Horse [*British military*] (DMA)

FFZ Fiji Fracture Zone [*Geology*]

FFZ Forzatissimo [*Extremely Loud*] [*Music*] (ROG)

FFZ Free Fire Zone [*Army*] (AABC)

FG Ariana Afghan Airlines [*ICAO designator*] (AD)

fg--- Congo River and Basin [*MARC geographic area code*] [*Library of Congress*] (LCCP)

FG Facility generator (SAUS)

FG Facility Ground

FG Fallschirmjaeger-Gewehr [*Parachutist's rifle*] [*German military - World War II*]

FG Family Groups [*Aid to Families with Dependent Children*] (OICC)

FG Fasciculus Gracilis (DB)

FG Fashion Group [*Later, TFG*] (EA)

FG Fast Glycolytic [*Muscle*]

FG Feature Group

FG February Group [*An association*] (EA)

FG Federal Government (WDAA)

F-G Feeley-Gorman [*Agar*] [*Microbiology*]

FG Feldenkrais Guild [*An association*] (EA)

fg Felsic Granulite [*Geology*]

FG Female Groove

fg Femtogram (SAUS)

fg femtogramm (SAUS)

fg fencing (SAUS)

FG Ferrosan [*Sweden*] [*Research code symbol*]

FG Festinant Gait [*Medicine*] (EDAA)

F-G Feynman-Gellman Theory [*Nuclear physics*]

FG Fiberglass (ADA)

FG Fiberguide [*Medicine*] (EDAA)

FG Fibrin Glue [*Medicine*] (EDAA)

Fg Fibrinogen [*Factor 1*] [*Hematology*]

FG Fidelity Guarantee [*Insurance*] (MARI)

FG Field Gain (IAA)

FG Field Goal [*Football, basketball*]

FG Field Grade

FG Field Gun

FG Fifth-Generation (FOTI)

FG Fighter Group (SAUO)

FG Filament Ground (MSA)

FG File Gap [*Computer science*] (BUR)

FG Filter Gate

FG Final Grid (IAA)

FG Finanzgericht [*Tax Court*] [*German*] (ILCA)

FG Fine Grain

FG fine grind (SAUS)

FG Finished Goods (AAEL)

FG Finished Grain [*Construction term*] (MIST)

FG Finite Geometry (SAUS)

FG Fire Glaze (SAUS)

FG Firegreen Ltd. [*Food-processing and distributing company*] [*British*]

FG Fire Guardsman [*British*] [*World War II*]

FG Fiscal Guidance (AABC)

FG Fisher Graphics (SAUS)

FG Fission Gas (NRCH)

FG Fitzroy Gardens (SAUS)

F/G Flag/General Officer (SAUO)

FG Flashgun [*Photography*]

FG Flat Grain [*Lumber*]

FG Flemish Giant Rabbit [*Medicine*] (DMAA)

FG Flint Glazed [*Paper*] (DGA)

FG Floated Gyro [*Aerospace*] (AAG)

FG Floating Gate (SAUS)

FG Floor Gypsum (SAUS)

FG Flow Gage (SAUS)

FG Flow Gauge

FG Flue Gas (SAUS)

FG Foam Generator (WDAA)

FG Fog

FG Fog Gong [*Navigation charts*]

FG Fog Gun [*Navigation charts*]

FG Folding

FG Foodservice Group [*Atlanta, GA*] (EA)

FG Football Grounds [*Public-performance tariff class*] [*British*]

FG Foot Groove

FG Foot Guards [*British*]

fg Foreground (ELAL)

FG Foreground [*Film arts*]

FG Foreground [*Computer science*]

FG Foreign Geneva [*Alcohol*] (ROG)

FG Foreign Government (AAGC)

FG Forging (SAUS)

FG Forgotten Generation (EA)

f/g Form/Genre

FG Formula Grants [*Vocational education*] (OICC)

FG Forward Gate

FG Foundation for Grandparenting (EA)

FG Fourth Generation (SAUS)

FG Fracture Gradient

FG Frame Ground [*Computer science*] (BUR)

FG Framework Ground (SAUS)

FG Frank Gasperro [*Designer's mark, when appearing on US coins*]

FG Free Gingiva (MELL)

FG Free Gyroscope (SAA)

fg French Guiana [*MARC country of publication code*] [*Library of Congress*] (LCCP)
FG Frequency Generator (SAUS)
FG Frog [*Engineering*]
FG Fuel Gage (SAA)
FG Fuel Gas
FG Fuel grade (SAUS)
FG Full Gilt [*Bookbinding*] (ADA)
FG Fully Good
FG Functional Group
FG Function Generator [*Computer science*] (IEEE)
FG Fundamentals Graduate
FG Funding Greater Than [*Dialog*] [*Searchable field*] (NITA)
FG Future Generations [*An association*] (EA)
FG Gainesville Public Library, Gainesville, FL [*Library symbol*] [*Library of Congress*] (LCLS)
Fg Gravitational Force (SAUS)
FG USF & G Corp. [*NYSE symbol*] (SPSG)
FGA Family Grocer Alliance Ltd. [*British*] (BI)
FGA Fasting Glycocholic Acid [*Clinical chemistry*]
FGA Feature Group A (SAUO)
FGA Fellow of the Gemmological Association [*British*]
FGA Field Goals Attempted [*Football, basketball*]
FGA Fighter Ground Attack (NATG)
FGA Fine Gravel Aggregate (SAUS)
FGA First General Resources Co. [*Vancouver Stock Exchange symbol*]
FGA Floating-Gate Amplifier (PDAA)
FGA Font Graphics Accelerator [*Toshiba*]
FGA Foreign General Agent [*Insurance*]
FGA Foreign General Average [*Insurance*]
FGA Fort Garland, CO [*Location identifier*] [*FAA*] (FAAL)
fga Free General Average (EBF)
FGA Free of General Average
FGA Freer Gallery of Art (SAUS)
FGA Fresh Garlic Association [*Defunct*] (EA)
F/GA Fuel Gage [*Automotive engineering*]
FGA Future Graphics Adapter (SAUS)
FGAA Federal Government Accountants Association [*Later, AGA*] (EA)
FGAC Federation of German-American Clubs (SAUO)
FGAH First-Generation Antihistamine [*Medicine*] (MELL)
FGAJ Fellow of the Guild of Agricultural Journalists [*British*] (DGA)
FGAN Fertiliser Grade Ammonium Nitrate (SAUS)
FGAN Fertilizer Grade Ammonium Nitrate
FG&B Fungal Genetics and Biology (SAUO)
FG&CW Federal Grants & Contracts Weekly [*Capital Publications*] (AAGC)
FG&E Fitchburg Gas & Electric Light Company (SAUO)
FG&FWFC Florida Game & Fresh Water Fish Commission (SAUO)
FGANSW Flower Growers' Association of New South Wales [*Australia*]
FGAR Foreign Governments or Their Authorized Representatives (MCD)
FGAR Formylglycinamide Ribonucleotide (MAE)
FGAS Forcenergy Gas Exploration, Inc. [*NASDAQ symbol*] (SAG)
FGAS Forcenergy, Inc. [*NASDAQ symbol*] [*Formerly, Forcenergy Gas Exploration*] (SG)
FGB Fast Gunboat [*Navy*] [*British*]
FGB Feature Group B (SAUO)
FGB Fiber Glass Brush (SAUS)
FGB Fiber Glass Bundle (SAUS)
FGB Fireclay Grate Back Association (SAUO)
FGB Foliage-Gleaning Bat [*Zoology*]
FGB Foundation for Global Broadcasting (EA)
FGB Fully Granulated Basophil (SAUS)
FGB Functional Cargo Block
FGBA Fireclay Grate Back Association [*British*] (BI)
FGBI Federation of Soroptimist Clubs of Great Britain and Ireland (BI)
FGBI First Granite Bancorporation, Incorporated (SAUO)
FGBMFI Full Gospel Business Men's Fellowship International (EA)
FGBT Bata [*Equatorial Guinea*] [*ICAO location identifier*] (ICLI)
FGC Departamento de Agricultura de la Generalitat de Cataluna [*Spain*] [*ICAO designator*] (FAAC)
FGC Facility Group Control [*Military*] (AFM)
FGC Fast Gas Cooled Reactor (SAUS)
FGC Feature Group C (SAUO)
FGC Federal Group Code (MCD)
FGC Federation Generale du Congo [*Congolese General Federation*]
FGC Fiber Glass Curtain (SAUS)
FGC Fifth Generation Computer (NITA)
FGC fine-grained clays (SAUS)
fgc finegrained concrete (SAUS)
FGC Finished Goods Control
FGC First Global Commerce (SAUO)
FGC Fiscal Guidance Category [*Military*] (CAAL)
FGC Fish and Game Code (SAUS)
FGC Fixed Gain Control
FGC Fixed Glass Capacitor
FGC Flat Glass Council [*British*] (DBA)
FGC Flight Guidance and Control (SAUS)
FGC Florida Gulf Coast Railroad Museum [*Federal Railroad Administration identification code*]
FGC Flue gas cleaning (SAUS)
FGC Food and Grains Committee (SAUO)
FGC Foundation for Global Community (EA)
FGC Freemont Gold [*Vancouver Stock Exchange symbol*]
FGC Friends General Conference (EA)
FGC Friends of Guy Clark (EA)
FGC Functional Group Code (MCD)
FGCA Ford Galaxie Club of America (EA)
FGCAA Federal Grant and Cooperative Agreement Act (AAGC)
FGCB Fiber Glass Cone Brush (SAUS)
FGcC Clay County Public Library, Green Cove Springs, FL [*Library symbol*] [*Library of Congress*] (LCLS)
FGCC Federal Geodetic Control Committee [*Department of Commerce*]
FGCC Foundation for Gifted and Creative Children [*Defunct*] (EA)
FGCH Full Gas Central Heating [*Real Estate*] (ODA)
FGCI Family Golf Centers [*NASDAQ symbol*] (TTSB)
FGCI Family Golf Centers, Inc. [*NASDAQ symbol*] (SAG)
FGCL Fellow of the Guild of Cleaners and Launderers [*British*] (DBQ)
FGCL Florida Center for Library Automation, Gainesville, FL [*Library symbol*] [*Library of Congress*] (LCLS)
FGCM Field General Court-Martial
FGCR Fast Gas-Cooled Reactor [*Nuclear energy*] (NUCP)
FGCS Federal Geodetic Control Subcommittee (SAUS)
FGCS Flight Guidance and Control Systems
FGCS Future Generation Computer Systems (NITA)
FGCS Future Ground Combat Systems [*Army*]
FGCSO Florida Gulf Coast Symphony Orchestra (SAUO)
Fg-cy frequency (SAUS)
FGD Fatal Granulomatous Disease (MAE)
FGD Feature Group D (SAUO)
FGD Ferri-Gas Duplexer
FGD Fine Grain Data [*Equipment*] [*RADAR*]
FGD Fish and Game Department (SAUS)
FGD Fishguard [*Goodwick*] [*British depot code*]
FGD Flue Gas Desulfurization (SAUS)
FGD Flue-Gas Desulfurization
FGD Flue Gas Desulphurisation (SAUS)
FGD Forged
FGD Formaldehyde-Glutaraldehyde-Dichromate [*Fixative*]
FGD Ft. Derik [*Mauritania*] [*Airport symbol*] (AD)
FGD Fuel Gas Desulfurization
FGDAC Function Generating Digital-to-Analog Converter [*Computer science*] (IAA)
FGDC Federal Geographic Data Commission (SAUO)
FGDC Federal Geographic Data Committee
FGDC Federal Geographic Data Products (SAUO)
FGDC Federal Geospatial Data Clearinghouse (SAUO)
FGDCh Flyball Grand Champion
FGD Equipment Fine Grain Data Equipment (SAUS)
FGDF Fidelco [*Fidelity Cooperative*] Guide Dog Foundation (EA)
FGDI Forging Die [*Tool*] (AAG)
FGDIS Flue Gas Desulfurization Information System (SAUS)
FGDIS Fuel Gas Desulfurization Information System (SAUO)
FGDP Federal Geographic Data Products (SAUO)
FgDP Fibrin(ogen) Degradation Product(s) [*Medicine*] (EDAA)
FGDS Fibergastroduodenoscope (DB)
FGE Factory Ground Equipment (KSC)
FGE Federation of Gas Employers (SAUO)
FGE Fine Guidance Electronics (SAUS)
FGE Fitchburg Gas & Electric Light Co. (SAUO)
FGE Fractographic Examination [*Metallurgy*]
FGEA Full Gospel Evangelistic Association (EA)
FGEF Federal Geographic Exchange Format (SAUO)
FGEIU Federated Gas Employees' Industrial Union [*Australia*]
FGEP Feral Goat Eradication Program (SAUO)
FGEPR field-gradient EPR (SAUS)
FGETR Federal Gasoline Excise Tax Refund (SAUS)
FGETS Food and Gill Exchange of Toxic Substances [*Environmental Protection Agency*] (AEPA)
FGEX Fruit Growers Express [*Private rail car owner code*]
FGF Father's Grandfather (MAE)
FGF Fibroblast Growth Factor [*Cytochemistry*]
FGF fibroblast growth factors (SAUS)
FGF Filament-Wound Glass Fiber
FGF Filament-Wound Glass Fibre (SAUS)
FGF Fishermen's Guarantee Fund [*National Oceanic and Atmospheric Administration*]
FGF Fresh Gas Flow
FGF Froimovich Geriatric Formula [*Medicine*] (EDAA)
FGF Fully Good, Fair [*Business term*]
FGF Future Germany Fund (EFIS)
FGF-2 Fibroblast Growth Factor-2
FGFA Fibroblast Growth Factor Receptor [*Biochemistry*]
FGFA Field and Game Federation of Australia
FGFC Fixed Gas-Filled Capacitor
FGFR Fibroblast Growth-Factor Receptor [*Biochemistry*]
FGFRI Finnish Game and Fisheries Research Institute
FGFSA Florida Gift Fruit Shippers Association (EA)
FGG Fowl Gamma-Globulin (DB)
FGG Fruit Growers' Group [*Australia*]
FGG-1 First-Generation Fuelcell System (SAUS)
FGGE First GARP [*Global Atmospheric Research Program*] Global Experiment [*National Academy of Sciences*]
FGGE SOP FGGE Special Observing Period (SAUO)
FGGM Federation of Gelatine and Glue Manufacturers [*British*] (BI)
FGGM Field General Court-Martial (SAUO)
FGGM Fort George G. Meade [*Maryland*]
FGH Fans of General Hospital (EA)
FGH Fiber Glass Hull (SAUS)
FGH Flameless Gas Heater
FGH Flexible Gyro Header
FGH Fort Garry Horse [*Military unit*] [*World War I*] [*Canada*]

f-gh-............ Ghana [*MARC geographic area code*] [*Library of Congress*] (LCCP)
FGHA............ Flexible Gyro Header Assembly
FGHC............ First Georgia Holding [*NASDAQ symbol*] (TTSB)
FGHC............ First Georgia Holding, Inc. [*NASDAQ symbol*] (NQ)
FGH-JWB..... Florence G. Heller - JWB [*Jewish Welfare Board*] Research Center [*Research center*] (RCD)
FGHT............ Fight
FGHTR......... Fighter
FGI.............. Fashion Group International (EAIO)
FGI.............. Federation Graphique Internationale [*International Graphical Federation - IGF*] [*Berne, Switzerland*] (EAIO)
FGI.............. Federation of German Industries (EA)
FGI.............. Fellow of the Greek Institute [*British*] (DI)
FGI.............. Fellow of the Institute of Certificated Grocers [*British*]
FGI.............. Finish Goods Inventory (SAUS)
FGI.............. Finnish Geodetic Institute (SAUO)
FGI.............. Foothill Group, Incorporated (SAUO)
FGI.............. Friede Goldman International [*NYSE symbol*]
FGI.............. Friede Goldman Intl. [*NYSE symbol*] (SG)
FGIC............ Financial Guaranty Insurance Corp.
FGIM............ Figures or Images [*Freight*]
FGIP............ Finished Goods in Process (TIMI)
FGIPC.......... Federal Government Information Processing Council (ACAE)
FGIPCI......... Federation of Government Information Processing Councils, Inc. (EA)
FGIS............ Federal Grain Inspection Service [*Department of Agriculture*]
FGJ.............. Freezing Gas Jet
FGJA............ Flat Glass Jobbers Association [*Later, FGMA*]
FGJS............ Farm Groups Joint Secretariat (SAUO)
FGL.............. Fasting Gastrin Level [*Medicine*] (MELL)
FGL.............. Fiberglass [*Technical drawings*]
FGL.............. Financial General Ledger
FGL.............. FMC Gold [*NYSE symbol*] (SPSG)
FGL.............. Force Generation Level (SAUO)
FGL.............. Fourth Generation Language (SAUO)
FGL.............. Fox Glacier [*New Zealand*] [*Airport symbol*] (AD)
FGL.............. Francis Galton Laboratory (SAUO)
f/glass......... fiberglass (SAUS)
FGLF............ Renaissance Golf Products [*NASDAQ symbol*] (TTSB)
FGLK............ Finger Lakes Railway [*Federal Railroad Administration identification code*]
FGLS............ Florida Glass Industries, Inc. (SAUO)
FGLS............ Force Generation Levels [*Military*] (NVT)
FGLU............ Fasting Glucose [*Endocrinology*] (DAVI)
FGLX............ Factor Gas Liquids [*Private rail car owner code*]
FGM............. Father's Grandmother (MAE)
FGM............. Female Genital Mutilation
FGM............. Field Goals Made [*Football, basketball*]
fgm.............. field guided missile (SAUS)
FGM............. First General Mine Management & Gold Corp. [*Vancouver Stock Exchange symbol*]
FGM............. Fiscal Guidance Memo (SAUS)
FGM............. Fiscal Guidance Memorandum [*Navy*]
FGM............. Fission Gas Monitor (NRCH)
FGM............. Florida Atlantic University, Boca Raton, FL [*OCLC symbol*] (OCLC)
FGM............. Fluxgate Magnetometer
FgM.............. Foreign Mission Section [*Diocesan abbreviation*] (TOCD)
FGM............. Foundation for Genetic Medicine (SAUO)
FGM............. Freunde Guter Musik Club [*Record label*] [*Germany*]
FGM............. Functionally Gradient Material [*Materials science and technology*]
f-gm-............ Gambia [*MARC geographic area code*] [*Library of Congress*] (LCCP)
FGM-77........ Dragon [*Military*] [*Man-portable assault missile for use against armor and bunkers*] (POLM)
FGMA............ Flat Glass Manufacturers Association [*British*] (DBA)
FGMA............ Flat Glass Marketing Association (EA)
FGMAX......... Federated GNMA Trust [*Mutual fund ticker symbol*] (SG)
FGMC............ Federal Government Micrographic Council (SAUS)
FGMC............ Federal Government Micrographics Council (SAUO)
FGMD............ Fairchild Guided Missile Division (SAA)
FGMDSS....... Future Global Maritime Distress and Safety System
FGMM............ Fluxgate Magnetometer (SAUS)
FGMS............ Fission Gas Monitoring System (SAUS)
FGMT............ Functional Group Management Team (TIMI)
FGN.............. Family Group Number
FGN.............. Federal German Navy
FGN.............. First Generation Resources Ltd. [*Vancouver Stock Exchange symbol*]
FG n............. fixed green (SAUS)
FGN.............. Flow General, Inc. [*NYSE symbol*] (COMM)
FGN.............. Focal Glomerulonephritis (DB)
FGN.............. Foreign (AFM)
FGN.............. Foreigner (SAUS)
FGN.............. Gendarmerie Nationale [*France*] [*ICAO designator*] (FAAC)
FGNCC.......... Foreign Claims Commission [*Canada*]
FGND............ Frame Ground [*Computer science*] (HGAA)
FGNR............ Flaming Gorge National Recreation Area (SAUS)
FGNRA.......... Flaming Gorge National Recreation Area (SAUO)
FGO.............. Fellow of the Guild of Organists [*British*]
FGO.............. Finance Group Office
FGO.............. Flag Gunnery Officer
FGO.............. Fleet Gunnery Officer [*Obsolete*] [*British*]
FGO.............. Fuego [*Guatemala*] [*Seismograph station code, US Geological Survey*] (SEIS)
f-go-............ Gabon [*MARC geographic area code*] [*Library of Congress*] (LCCP)
Fg Off........... Flying Officer [*British military*] (DMA)
FGOG............ Foregoing (ROG)
FGOIX.......... Federated Govt. Income [*Mutual fund ticker symbol*] (SG)
FGOLF.......... Federation des Gynecologues et Obstetriciens de Langue Francaise [*Federation of French-Language Gynaecologists and Obstetricians*] [*Paris, France*] (EAIO)
FGORC.......... Flower Gardens Ocean Research Center [*Marine Biomedical Institute, University of Texas*] (PDAA)
FGOS............ Flag and General Officers Seminar (SAUO)
FGOVX.......... Fidelity Govt. Inc. [*Mutual fund ticker symbol*] (SG)
FGP.............. Ferrellgas Partners L.P. [*NYSE symbol*] (TTSB)
FGP.............. Ferrellgas Partners Ltd. [*NYSE symbol*] (SAG)
FGP.............. Fetch, Generate [*or Generalize*], and Project [*Computer Program*]
FGP.............. First Guardian [*Vancouver Stock Exchange symbol*]
FGP.............. Fixed Gear Pump [*Hydraulics*]
FGP.............. Fixed Gerotor Pump [*Hydraulics*]
FGP.............. Foreground Program [*Computer science*] (IAA)
FGP.............. Foster Grandparent Program (SAUS)
FGP.............. Frontal Groove of Pinnule
FGP.............. Fuerza de Guerrilleros de los Pobres [*Guerrilla group*] [*Guatemala*] (EY)
FGP.............. Fundic Gland Polyposis [*Medicine*]
FGP.............. General Purpose Frigate
FGPFL.......... Fixed and Group Flashing Light [*Navigation signal*]
FGPFL.......... Fixed Group Flashing (SAUO)
FGPFL Lt...... Fixed and Group Flashing Light (SAUO)
FGPSS.......... FORTRAN General Purpose System Simulator (SAUS)
FGPT............ Fellow of the Guild of Professional Toastmasters [*British*] (DI)
FGR.............. Fast Gas-cooled Reactor (SAUS)
FGR.............. Feline Gardner-Rasheed Virus
FGR.............. Fellowship of the Golden Rule (EA)
FGR.............. Fertility and Genetics Research (SAUS)
FGR.............. Fighter Ground Attack Reconnaissance (SAUO)
fgr............... Fine Grained (SAUS)
FGR.............. Finger (MSA)
FGR.............. Floating-Gate Reset (IAA)
FGR.............. Flue Gas Recirculation [*Combustion engineering*]
FGR.............. Foundation for Giraffe Rescue
FGR.............. Foundation for Glaucoma Research (EA)
FGR.............. Franklin Game Reserve (SAUO)
FGR.............. Freehold Ground Rent (ROG)
FGRA............ Family Group Record Archives [*Genealogy*] (GEAB)
FGRAAL........ FORTRAN [*Formula Translating System*] Extended Graph Algorithmic Language [*1972*] [*Computer science*] (CSR)
FGRAL.......... FORTRAN Graph Algorithmic Language (SAUS)
FGREP.......... Fixed Global Regular Expression Print [*Unix*] (VERA)
fgrep............ Fixed grep (SAUS)
FGRF............ Forest Genetics Research Foundation (EA)
FGrH............ Fragmente der Griechischen Historiker [*A publication*] (OCD)
FGRI............ Fixed Ground Radio Installations
FGRIX.......... Fidelity Growth & Income [*Mutual fund ticker symbol*] (SG)
FGRN............ Finely Granular [*Laboratory*] (DAVI)
FGRP............ Farmers Group, Inc. (SAUO)
FGRP............ fiber-glass reinforced plastic (SAUS)
FGRWX......... Fortis Growth Fund Cl.A [*Mutual fund ticker symbol*] (SG)
FGS.............. Fancy Goods Store [*British military*] (DMA)
FGS.............. Fashion Glamour Set
FGS.............. Fatstock Guarantee Scheme (SAUS)
FGS.............. Federal German Ship (SAUS)
FGS.............. Federation of Genealogical Societies (EA)
FGS.............. Fellow of the Geographical Society
FGS.............. Fellow of the Geological Society [*British*]
FGS.............. Fibergastroscope (DB)
FGS.............. Fine Guidance Sensor (PDAA)
FGS.............. Fine Guidance System (SAUS)
FGS.............. Finished Goods Store
FGS.............. Flight Guidance System (MCD)
FGS.............. Florida Geological Survey (SAUS)
FGS.............. Flowing Gas Stream
FGS.............. Focal Glomerulosclerosis [*Medicine*]
FGS.............. Fort Greely Station (SAA)
FGS.............. Francis Grose Society [*Defunct*] (EA)
FGS.............. Friends of George Sand (EA)
FGS.............. Friends of Georges Sadoul (EAIO)
FGS.............. Friends of the Golden State
FGS.............. Fulton Generating Station [*Nuclear energy*] (NRCH)
FGS.............. Palmer, AK [*Location identifier*] [*FAA*] (FAAL)
FGS.............. Santa Fe Community College, Gainesville, FL [*Library symbol*] [*Library of Congress*] (LCLS)
FGSA............ Fellow of the Geographical Society of America
FGSA............ Fellow of the Geological Society of America
FGSA............ Fostoria Glass Society of America (EA)
FGSB............ FFS [*Flight Service Station*] Guarding Service B [*Aviation*] (FAAC)
FGS/C.......... Flight Guidance System/Computer (GAVI)
FGSE............ field-gradient spin-echo (SAUS)
FGSF............ Full Gospel Student Fellowship (EA)
FGSL............ Malabo, Isla De Macias, Nguema Biyoga [*Equatorial Guinea*] [*ICAO location identifier*] (ICLI)
FGSM............ Fellow of Guildhall School of Music [*British*] (EY)
FGSP............ Fractal Geometry and Spatial Phenomena (SAUO)
FGSS............ Flexible Guidance Software System (MCD)
FGST............ First Grade Screening Test [*To detect learning disabilities*]
FG Structure... Floating-Gate Structure (SAUS)
FG-Struktur... floating gate structure (SAUS)
FGT.............. Fairflight Ltd. [*British*] [*ICAO designator*] (FAAC)
FGT.............. Farmington, MN [*Location identifier*] [*FAA*] (FAAL)
FGT.............. Federal Geographic Technology (SAUS)
FGT.............. Federal Gift Tax (DLA)

FGT .... Female Genital Tract [*Medicine*] (PALA)
FGT .... Floating Gate Transistor (SAUS)
FGT .... Flue-Gas Treatment
FGT .... Fluorescent Gonorrhea Test [*Medicine*] (DMAA)
FGT .... Foreground Table (MHDB)
FGT .... fractional glow technique (SAUS)
FGT .... Freight
FGT-H .... Fluorescence Gonorrhea Test - Heated [*Medicine*] (DB)
FGTO .... French Government Tourist Office
FGTS .... Flammable Gas Tank Safety (ABAC)
FGTSA .... Fur Garment Traveling Salesmen's Association
FGTT .... Flue-Gas-through-the-Tubes [*Incinerator*]
FGU .... Fangatau [*French Polynesia*] [*Airport symbol*] (OAG)
FGU .... Fellow of Guelph University (CPGU)
FGU .... Flaming Gorge [*Utah*] [*Seismograph station code, US Geological Survey*] [*Closed*] (SEIS)
FGU .... Floating Point/Graphics Unit (VLIE)
FGU .... Forearm Glucose Uptake [*Clinical chemistry*]
FGU .... From the Ground Up (MARI)
FGU .... Fuel Geoscience Unit (SAUS)
FGUG .... Federal Government Users Group (SAUO)
FGULS .... Florida Union List of Serials, Gainesville, FL [*Library symbol*] [*Library of Congress*] (LCLS)
FGV .... Fasting Glucose Value [*Medicine*] (MELL)
FGV .... Field-Gradient Voltage (PDAA)
FGV .... Free Gas Volume
FGV .... Future Growth Value
f-gv- .... Guinea [*MARC geographic area code*] [*Library of Congress*] (LCCP)
FGV .... United States Veterans Administration Hospital, Gainesville, FL [*Library symbol*] [*Library of Congress*] (LCLS)
FGW .... Floor Ground Window (SAUS)
FGWC .... First Greatwest Corp. [*NASDAQ symbol*]
FGWE .... First Global Weather Experiment (SAUO)
FGX .... Flemingsburg, KY [*Location identifier*] [*FAA*] (FAAL)
FGY .... Foggy (MSA)
FGY .... NewWest Airlines, Inc. [*FAA designator*] (FAAC)
FH .... C. H. Boehringer Sohn, Ingelheim [*Germany*] [*Research code symbol*]
FH .... Clin-Byla [*France*] [*Research code symbol*]
fh--- .... East African Horn [*MARC geographic area code*] [*Library of Congress*] (LCCP)
FH .... Faculty of Homoeopathy (SAUO)
FH .... Fair Haven (SAUS)
FH .... Familial Hypercholesteremia [*or Hypercholesterolemia*] [*Medicine*]
fh .... familial hypercholesterolemia (SAUS)
FH .... Family Health (AMHC)
FH .... Family History [*Medicine*]
FH .... Family of Humanists [*An association*] (EA)
FH .... Fanconi-Hegglin [*Syndrome*] [*Medicine*] (DB)
FH .... Fane's Horse [*British military*] (DMA)
FH .... Far Hills (SAUS)
FH .... Fashion Hills (SAUS)
FH .... Fasteners and Hardware (SAA)
FH .... Fasting Hemoglobin [*Medicine*] (MELL)
FH .... Fasting Hyperbilirubinemia [*Medicine*] (DMAA)
FH .... Federation of Homemakers (EA)
FH .... Feed Hopper (SAUS)
f h .... feet per hour (SAUS)
FH .... Fellowship Homes (SAUO)
FH .... Femoral Hernia [*Medicine*] (MELL)
FH .... Fetal Head [*Medicine*]
FH .... Fetal Heart [*Medicine*]
FH .... Fetal Hemoglobin [*Medicine*] (MELL)
FH .... Fiat Haustus [*Let a Drink Be Made*] [*Pharmacy*]
FH .... Fiber Hub
FH .... Fibromuscular Hyperplasia [*Medicine*] (DMAA)
FH .... Ficoll-Hypaque [*Clinical hematology*]
FH .... Field Handler (MHDB)
FH .... Field Headquarters (SAUO)
FH .... Field Hospital [*British military*] (DMA)
FH .... Field Howitzer [*British military*] (DMA)
FH .... Fighter (NATG)
FH .... File Handler [*Computer science*] (ELAL)
FH .... Fillister Head (SAUS)
FH .... Filter housing (SAUS)
FH .... Fire Hose (AAG)
FH .... Fire Hydrant
FH .... First Half [*of month*] (DCTA)
FH .... Fishtailed Hole (SAUS)
FH .... Fixed Head [*Computer science*] (MHDB)
FH .... Fixed Hub [*Rotary piston meter*]
FH .... Flag Hoist
FH .... Flat Head [*Screw*]
FH .... Flex Hose (MCD)
FH .... Flight Hour
FH .... Floating Hospital (EA)
FH .... Flying Hour
fh .... Flying Hours (SAUS)
FH .... Fog Horn [*Navigation charts*]
FH .... Follicular Hyperplasia [*Medicine*] (PALA)
FH .... Food for the Hungry (ADWA)
FH .... Force Headquarters [*Allied forces*] [*World War II*]
FH .... Fore Hatch [*Shipping*]
FH .... Foundation for Health (EA)
FH .... Foundation Health [*NYSE symbol*] (TTSB)
FH .... Foundation Health Corp. [*NYSE symbol*] (SPSG)
FH .... Frame Handler [*Telecommunications*] (ACRL)
FH .... Frankfort Horizontal [*Eye-ear plane*] [*Anatomy*]
FH .... Freedom House (EA)
FH .... Freeholder [*Real estate*] (BARN)
FH .... French Horn
FH .... Frequency Hop (GART)
FH .... Frequency Hopping [*Modulation*]
FH .... Friendship House (EA)
FH .... Friends of Hibakusha (EA)
FH .... Fuji Heavy Industries Ltd. [*Japan*] [*ICAO aircraft manufacturer identifier*] (ICAO)
FH .... Full Hard (MSA)
fh .... full hole (SAUS)
FH .... Full-Hole Mining (SAUS)
FH .... Fulminant Hepatitis [*Medicine*]
FH .... Fumarate Hydratase [*An enzyme*]
FH .... Fundal Height [*Obstetrics*] (DAVI)
F_H .... Heeling Force [*Sailing terminology*]
FH .... Mall Airways [*ICAO designator*] (AD)
FH .... Fly-Half (ODA)
FH-1100 .... Fairchild-Hiller observation helicopter (SAUS)
FHA .... Fair Housing Act (EBF)
FHA .... Familial Hypoplastic Anemia [*Medicine*] (DB)
FHA .... Family Heart Association [*British*] (DBA)
FHA .... Family History of Alcoholism (SAUS)
FHA .... Farmers Home Administration [*Later, FmHA*] [*Department of Agriculture*]
FHA .... Fault Hazard Analysis [*Hazard quantification method*]
FHA .... Federal Highway Administration [*Department of Transportation*]
FHA .... Federal Home Administration (SAUS)
FHA .... Federal Housing Administration [*HUD*]
FHA .... Federal Housing Authority (TDOB)
FHA .... Fellow of the Australian Institute of Hospital Administrators (SAUO)
FHA .... Fellow of the Institute of Health Service [*formerly, Hospital*] Administrators [*British*]
FHA .... Fellowship Holidays Association (SAUO)
FHA .... Field Headspace Analysis (SAUO)
FHA .... Fiji Hotel Association (EY)
FHA .... Filamentous Hemagglutinin [*Medicine*]
FHA .... Filterable Haemolytic Anaemia (SAUS)
FHA .... Filterable Hemolytic Anemia [*Medicine*] (DB)
FHA .... Finance Houses Association [*British*]
FHA .... Fine Hardwoods Association [*Later, FHAWA*] (EA)
FHA .... Flexible Header Assembly
FHA .... Flight Hardware Availability (SAUS)
FHA .... Floating Homes Association (EA)
FHA .... Florida Hospital Association (SAUS)
FHA .... Foundation for Humanities Adulthood [*Australia*]
FHA .... Free-Heave Amplitude
FHA .... French Holden Algorithm (SAUS)
FHA .... Friends Historical Association (EA)
FHA .... Future Homemakers of America (EA)
FHA .... Future Horsemen of America
FHAA .... Field Hockey Association of America (EA)
FHAAO .... Force Headquarters, Antiaircraft [*World War II*]
FHAEB .... Force Headquarters, North African Economic Board [*World War II*]
FHAG .... Force Headquarters, Adjutant General [*World War II*]
FHAGG .... Force Headquarters, Adjutant General, Executive [*World War II*]
FHAGM .... Force Headquarters, Adjutant General, Miscellaneous [*World War II*]
FHAGP .... Force Headquarters, Adjutant General, Personnel [*World War II*]
FHAGR .... Force Headquarters, Adjutant General, Mail and Records [*World War II*]
FHA (HERO) ... Future Homemakers of America (Home Economics Related Occupations) (OICC)
FHAI .... Federal Housing Authority Insurance (AABC)
FHAIR .... Force Headquarters, Air Commander-in-Chief, Mediterranean [*World War II*]
FHAM .... Federal Housing Administration Matters [*FBI standardized term*]
FH & C .... Faith, Hope, and Charity [*Freemasonry*] (ROG)
FH&MA .... Florida Hotel and Motel Association (SRA)
FH & RM ..... Fuel Handling and Radioactive Maintenance (NRCH)
FH&RM .... Fuel handling and remote maintenance (SAUS)
FH & SL .... Furnished Hardware and Services List (MCD)
F; H and V ... Flat, Horizontal-vertical and Vertical-up (SAUS)
FHANG .... Federation of Heathrow Anti-Noise Groups [*British*] (DI)
F-H Annual ... Fitzgerald-Hemingway Annual [*A publication*] (ANEX)
FHAP .... Fair Housing Assistance Program [*HUD*]
FHAR .... Fire Hazard Analysis Report [*Environmental science*] (COE)
FHarBc .... First Harrisburg Bancor, Inc. [*Associated Press*] (SAG)
FHARM .... Fuel Handling and Radioactive Maintenance (IAA)
FHAS .... Federation of Hellenic American Societies of Greater New York (EA)
FHAS .... Fellow of the Highland and Agricultural Society of Scotland (SAUO)
FHAW .... Wideawake [*Ascension Island*] [*ICAO location identifier*] (ICLI)
FHAWA .... Fine Hardwoods American Walnut Association (EA)
FH-AWA .... Fine Hardwoods-American Walnut Association (SAUO)
FHB .... Family Hold Back [*Indicates family should take small portions at a meal where guests are present*]
FHB .... Federal Home Bank
FHB .... Fine Homebuilding [*A publication*] (BRI)
FHB .... Flat Head Brass [*Screw*] (IAA)
FHB .... Fuel-Handling Building [*Nuclear energy*] (NRCH)
FHBC .... Federation of Historical Bottle Clubs (ADWA)
FHBM .... Floodway Hazard Boundary Map (ADWA)
FH/B USA ..... Freedom House/ Books USA (SAUS)

FHBVI .... Fuel-Handling Building Ventilation Isolation [*Nuclear energy*] (NRCH)
FHC .... Fairchild-Hiller Corp. [*Later, Fairchild Industries, Inc.*] (KSC)
FHC .... Fairchild Hiller Corporation (SAUO)
FHC .... Faith, Hope, and Charity [*Freemasonry*]
FHC .... Familial Hypertrophic Cardiomyopathy [*Medicine*]
FHC .... Familial Hypocalcemia [*Medicine*] (DB)
FHC .... Familial Hypocalciuria [*Medicine*] (DB)
FHC .... Family History Center [*Genealogy*] (GEAB)
FHC .... Federal Hospital Council (SAUO)
FHC .... Federal Housing Commission [*HUD*] (OICC)
FHC .... Federal Housing Commissioner (SAUS)
FHC .... Federal Housing Corporation (SAUO)
FHC .... Female Health [*AMEX symbol*] (TTSB)
FHC .... Female Health Co. [*AMEX symbol*] (SAG)
FHC .... Fickle Hill [*California*] [*Seismograph station code, US Geological Survey*] (SEIS)
FHC .... Ficoll-Hypaque Centrifugation [*Medicine*] (DMAA)
FHC .... Fire Hose Cabinet (KSC)
FHC .... First Hospitality [*Vancouver Stock Exchange symbol*]
FHC .... Fish Creek, AK [*Location identifier*] [*FAA*] (FAAL)
FHC .... Fixed-Head Coupe [*Automobile design*]
FHC .... Flight Half Coupling (MCD)
FHC .... Fluid Hydrostatic Cell (SAUS)
FHC .... Fluorhydrocarbon (SAUS)
FHC .... Four-Horse Club [*British*]
FHC .... Freed-Hardeman College [*Tennessee*]
FHC .... Friends' Health Connection (EA)
FHC .... Fuel-Handling Cell [*Nuclear energy*] (NRCH)
FHC .... University of South Florida, Sarasota Campus, Sarasota, FL [*OCLC symbol*] (OCLC)
FHC .... Wisconsin Pharmacal Co., Inc. [*AMEX symbol*] (SAG)
FHCAO .... Force Headquarters, Chief Administrative Officer [*World War II*]
FHCAS .... Federal Highway Cost Allocation Study [*Also, HCAS*]
FHCC .... First Health Group [*NASDAQ symbol*] (SG)
FHCCH .... Force Headquarters, Claims and Hirings [*World War II*]
FH-CDMA .... Frequency Hopped CDMA (SAUS)
FH/CDMA .... Frequency-Hopping - Code Division Multiple Access (SAUS)
FHCE .... Foundation for Health Care Evaluation (EA)
FHCI .... Fellow of the Hotel and Catering Institute (SAUO)
FHCIC .... Force Headquarters, Commander-in-Chief [*World War II*]
FHCIMA .... Fellow of the Hotel, Catering, and Institutional Management Association [*British*] (DBQ)
FHCIV .... Force Headquarters, Civil Affairs [*World War II*]
fhcm .... familial hypertrophic cardiomyopathy (SAUS)
FHCOS .... Force Headquarters, Chief of Staff [*World War II*]
FHCP .... Forum for Health Care Planning (NTPA)
FHCQ .... Foundation for Health Care Quality (ADWA)
FHCRC .... Fred Hutchinson Cancer Research Center [*University of Washington*] [*Research center*] (RCD)
FHCS .... Fellow, Hungarian College of Surgeons (CMD)
FHCS .... First Hebrew Christian Synagogue (SAUO)
FHCSFST .... Fuel handling cell spent fuel storage tank (SAUS)
FHCW .... Force Headquarters, Chemical Warfare (SAUO)
FHCWS .... Force Headquarters, Chemical Warfare [*World War II*]
FHD .... Family History of Diabetes [*Medicine*] (DB)
FHD .... Family Housing Division [*Army*] (AABC)
FHD .... Feline heartworm disease (SAUS)
FHD .... First-Hand Distribution
FHD .... First Harmonic Distortion [*Electronics*] (IAA)
FHD .... Fixed Head Disc (SAUS)
FHD .... Fixed-Head Disk [*Computer science*]
FHD .... Flat Head (SAUS)
FHD .... Foundation for Human Development [*Australia*]
FHD .... Friends of Holly Dunn (EA)
FHD .... Fund for Human Dignity (EA)
FHDA .... Fir and Hemlock Door Association [*Defunct*] (EA)
FHDCC .... Force Headquarters, Deputy Allied Commander-in-Chief [*World War II*]
FHDCS .... Force Headquarters, Deputy Chief of Staff (SAUO)
FHD Fluid .... Ferrohydrodynamic Fluid (SAUS)
FHDHC .... Force Headquarters, Director of Harbor Craft [*World War II*]
FHDMS .... Force Headquarters, Military Secretary Section [*World War II*]
FHDMSS .... Force Headquarters, Military Secretary Section (SAUO)
FHDO .... Field Handling Design Objective
FHDS .... Farm and Horiticulture Development Scheme (SAUS)
FHDS .... Fixed Head Disk / Drum Store [*Computer science*] (MHDI)
FHDS .... Fixed-Head Disk Storage (SAUS)
FHDSC .... Force Headquarters, Deputy Chief of Staff [*World War II*]
FHD-Speicher ... fixed head disk store (SAUS)
FHD Store .... Fixed Head Disk Store (SAUS)
FHDTC .... Fixed Head Disc Transfer Channel (SAUO)
FHE .... Family Home Entertainment [*Division of International Video Entertainment*]
FHE .... Fast Hydrofoil Escort
FHE .... Fatal Hyponatremic Encephalopathy [*Medicine*] (MELL)
FHE .... First Harmful Event [*National Highway Traffic Safety Administration Fatal Accident Recording System code*]
FHE .... Forward Headquarters Element
FHE .... Foundation for Handgun Education [*Later, EFEHV*] (EA)
FHE .... Fuel-Handling Equipment [*Nuclear energy*] (NRCH)
FHEFI .... Force Headquarters, Expeditionary Forces Institute [*World War II*]
FHENG .... Force Headquarters, Engineer [*World War II*]
FHENW .... Force Headquarters, Works [*World War II*]
FHEO .... Fair Housing and Equal Opportunity [*HUD*] (OICC)
FHEPFC .... For the Heart Elvis Presley Fan Club (EA)
FHES .... Fuel-Handling Equipment System [*Nuclear energy*] (NRCH)
FHEx .... Fridays and Holidays Excepted (DS)
FHF .... Federation of Health Funds - International [*British*] (EAIO)
FHF .... fetal heart frequency (SAUS)
FHF .... First Horizontal Flight [*NASA*] (KSC)
FHF .... Fixed Head File [*Computer science*] (MHDB)
FHF .... Friendly Hand Foundation (EA)
FHF .... Fulminant Hepatic Failure [*Medicine*]
FHF .... University of South Florida, Fort Myers Campus, Fort Myers, FL [*OCLC symbol*] (OCLC)
FHFA .... Florida Housing Finance Agency (DEMM)
FHFA .... Four-Conductor, Heat-and-Flame-Resistant, Armor [*Cable*]
FHFA .... Four-conductor, Heat and Flame-resistant, Armoured (SAUS)
FHFB .... Federal Housing Finance Board [*Pronounced "foof-ba"*]
FHFC .... Farm House Foods Corporation (SAUO)
FHFC .... Fast-Handling Flexibox Carrier (SAUS)
FHFF .... Fleet Hurricane Forecast Facility
FHFLD .... Force Headquarters, Field Artillery Section [*World War II*]
FH/FNN .... Freedom House/National Forum Foundation (SAUO)
FHFS .... Foundation Health Federal Services
FHFTA .... Four-Conductor, Heat and Flame Resistant, Thin Walled, Armored [*Cable*] (IAA)
FHFTA .... Four-conductor, Heat and Flame-resistant, Thin-walled, Armoured (SAUS)
FHFW .... Federation of High Frequency Welders [*British*] (DBA)
FHG .... Fellow of the Institute of Heraldic and Genealogical Studies [*British*] (DBQ)
FHG .... Female Health [*AMEX symbol*] [*Formerly, Wisconsin Pharmacal*] (SG)
FHG .... Flat Head Galvanized [*Screw*] (IAA)
FHG .... Fragmenta Historicorum Graecorum [*A publication*] (OCD)
FHGA .... Fellow of the Horological Guild of Australia
FHGDM .... Force Headquarters, Movements and Transportation [*World War II*]
FHGDQ .... Force Headquarters, "Q" Maintenance [*World War II*]
FHGDT .... Force Headquarters, Supply and Transport [*World War II*]
FHG Screw ... Flat Head Galvanized Screw (SAUS)
FHH .... Familial Hypocalciuric Hypercalcemia [*Medicine*]
FHH .... Family History of Hirsutism [*Medicine*] (DB)
FHH .... Female Headed Household
FHH .... Fetal Heart Heard [*Medicine*]
FHH .... Foundation for Hospice and Homecare (EA)
FHHDC .... Force Headquarters, Headquarters Commandant [*World War II*]
FHI .... Fair Housing, Incorporated (SAUO)
FHI .... Family Health International (EA)
FHI .... Federation Halterophile Internationale [*International Weightlifting Federation - IWF*] (EAIO)
FHI .... Fellow of the Ontario Hostelry Institute [*Canada*] (DD)
FHi .... Florida Historical Society, University of South Florida, Tampa, FL [*Library symbol*] [*Library of Congress*] (LCLS)
FHI .... Folk Heritage Institute (EA)
FHI .... Food for the Hungry, Inc. (EA)
FHI .... Food for the Hungry, Incorporated (SAUO)
FHI .... Food for the Hungry International (ADWA)
FHI .... Ford Holdings, Inc. [*NYSE symbol*] (SPSG)
FHI .... Fraser-Hickson Institute (SAUO)
FHI .... Freedom House, Incorporated (SAUO)
FHI .... Fritz-Haber Institute (SAUS)
FHI .... Fuch's Heterochromic Iridocyclitis [*Ophthalmology*] (DAVI)
FHI .... Fuji Heavy Industries Ltd. (SAUS)
FHI .... Institute of Marine Research (SAUO)
FHiaC .... Coulter Diagnostics, Inc., Hialeah, FL [*Library symbol*] [*Library of Congress*] (LCLS)
FHIC .... Flying Hours per Inspection Cycle [*Air Force*] (AFIT)
FHIC .... Franciscan Hospitaller Sisters of the Immaculate Conception [*Roman Catholic religious order*]
FHIF .... Fibroblast Human Interferon (DB)
FHIF .... Frequenting House of Ill Fame
FHIGX .... Fidelity Spartan Muni Income [*Mutual fund ticker symbol*] (SG)
FHIID .... Fast Heavy Ion Induced Desorption [*Analytical chemistry*]
FHI/IFRP .... Family Health International [*Family Health International/International Fe rtility Research Program*] [*Acronym is based on former name,*] (EA)
FHIMA .... Fellow of the Hotel and Catering International Management Association (DD)
FHINC .... Force Headquarters, Information and Censorship [*World War II*]
FHINC .... Force Headquarters, Office of Intelligence and Censorship (SAUO)
FHINC .... Friday Holidays Included (RIMS)
Fhinc .... Fridays and Holidays included (SAUS)
FHIP .... Fair Housing Initiatives Program [*Department of Housing and Urban Development*] (GFGA)
FHIP .... Family Health Insurance Plan
FHIP .... Federal Health Insurance Plan [*Proposed*] (DHSM)
FHIT .... Fragile Histidine Triad Protein [*Biochemistry*]
FHK .... Fachhochschulkommission (SAUO)
FHK .... Fourier-Hermite Kernel (SAUS)
FHKSC .... Fort Hays Kansas State College (SAUO)
FHL .... Family History Library [*Genealogy*] (GEAB)
FHL .... File Header Label (SAUS)
FHL .... Forest Hydrology Laboratory [*Forest Service*]
FHL .... Forward Half-Line [*Feed*]
FHL .... Fraser's House of Lords Reports [*Scotland*] [*A publication*] (DLA)
FHL .... Friends Historical Library (SAUO)
FHLB .... Federal Home Loan Bank
FHLB .... Federal Home Loan Bank System (AGLO)
FHLBA .... Federal Home Loan Bank Administration (IIA)

FHLBB .... Federal Home Loan Bank Board [*Functions transferred to Office of Thrift Supervision, 1989*]
FHLBs .... Federal Home Loan Banks (SAUS)
FHLBS .... Federal Home Loan Bank System
FHLC .... Forest Hill Learning Centre (SAUO)
FHLD .... Freehold [*Legal term*]
FHLIA .... Force Headquarters, Liaison [*World War II*]
FHLMC .... Federal Home Loan Mortgage Association (SAUS)
FHLMC .... Federal Home Loan Mortgage Corp. [*Federal Home Loan Bank Board*] [*Nickname: "Freddie Mac"*]
FHLS .... First Hungarian Literary Society (EA)
FHLT .... Force (Fleet) High-Level Terminal [*Navy*] (CAAL)
FHM .... Faith Mines Ltd. [*Vancouver Stock Exchange symbol*]
FHM .... Familial Hemiplegic Migraine [*Medicine*]
FHM .... Fargo House Movement [*Trinidad and Tobago*] [*Political party*] (PPW)
FHM .... Fat Head Minnow
FHM .... Feed Water Heater Management
FHM .... Franciscan Handmaids of the Most Pure Heart of Mary [*Roman Catholic religious order*]
FHM .... Franciscan Sisters Daughters of Mercy (TOCD)
FHM .... Fuel handling machine (SAUS)
FHM .... University of South Florida, Tampa, FL [*OCLC symbol*] (OCLC)
FHM .... For Him Magazine (ODA)
FHMA .... Family Housing Management Account [*Army*] (AABC)
FHMA .... Family Housing Management Appropriation
FHMA .... Federal Home Mortgage Association (SAUO)
FHMA .... Frequency-Hopping Multiple Access (IAA)
FHMED .... Force Headquarters, Surgeon [*World War II*]
FHMGS .... Force Headquarters, Military Government Section [*World War II*]
FHMO .... Federal Hazard Mitigation Officer (DEMM)
FHMO .... Friends of the Hop Marketing Order [*Defunct*] (EA)
FHMO .... Fully Hydrogenated Menhaden Oil [*Food science*]
FHMS .... Flat Head Machine Screw [*Technical drawings*]
FHMUX .... Frequency-Hopping Multiplexer (DWSG)
FHN .... Fund for Human Need [*British*]
FHNC .... Fermi Hypernetted Chain (SAUS)
FHNH .... Fetal Heart Not Heard [*Medicine*]
FHNL .... Far Horizons Newsletter [*A publication*]
FHNP .... United States National Park Service, Everglades National Park, Homestead, FL [*Library symbol*] [*Library of Congress*] (LCLS)
FHNWR .... Flint Hills National Wildlife Refuge (SAUO)
FHO .... Failed Handover [*NASA*] (NASA)
FHO .... Family Hands Off [*Indicates that a certain dish is not to be eaten by members of the family at a meal where guests are present*]
FHO .... Family Hold Off [*Indicates that a certain dish is not to be eaten by members of the family at a meal where guests are present*]
FHO .... Family Housing Officer
FHO .... Frederick's of Hollywood, Inc. [*AMEX symbol*] (COMM)
FHOB .... Ford House Office Building [*U.S. House of Representatives*] [*Washington, D.C.*]
FHOD .... Flexible Hydroactive Occlusive Dressing [*Equine term*] (TED)
FHOF .... Four Conductor, Heat, Oil, and Flame Resistant [*Cable*] (IAA)
FHOF Wire ... Four-conductor, Heat-, Oil-, and Flame-resistant Wire (SAUS)
f-holes .... f-shaped sound holes in tops of stringed instruments such as violins, violas, cellos, double basses (SAUS)
FHONF .... Facing History and Ourselves National Foundation (EA)
FHORD .... Force Headquarters, Ordnance [*World War II*]
FHP .... Family Health Plan (SAUS)
FHP .... Federal Highway Projects [*Department of Transportation*]
FHP .... FHP International Corp. [*Associated Press*] (SAG)
FHP .... Fixed Header Prefix [*Computer science*] (ELAL)
FHP .... Flash hydropyrolysis (SAUS)
FHP .... Florida Highway Patrol (DEMM)
FHP .... Fluid Hydrostatic Pressure (SAUS)
FHP .... Flying Hour Program [*Army*]
FHP .... Fort Howard Paper Co. (SAUO)
FHP .... Fractional Horsepower (MSA)
FHP .... Free Hepatic Venous Pressure [*Medicine*]
FHP .... frictional horse-power (SAUS)
fhp .... Friction Horsepower (ADWA)
FHP .... Friction Horsepower
FHP .... Friends of Historical Pharmacy (EA)
FHP .... Fuel Handling Procedure [*Nuclear energy*] (NRCH)
FHP .... Fuel High Pressure (NASA)
FHPC .... FHP International Corp. [*NASDAQ symbol*] (NQ)
FHPC .... FHP Int'l Corp. [*NASDAQ symbol*] (TTSB)
FHPC .... Fuel-Handling and Preparation Cell [*Nuclear energy*] (NRCH)
FHPCA .... FHP Intl $1.25 Cv Pfd'A' [*NASDAQ symbol*] (TTSB)
FHPET .... Force Headquarters, Petroleum [*World War II*]
FHP Motor ... Fractional Horsepower Motor (SAUS)
FHP motor ... Fractional-Horsepower Motor (MED)
FHPRO .... Force Headquarters, Public Relations [*World War II*]
FHPRP .... Family Housing Program Review Panel (SAUO)
FHPS .... Federal Health Programs Service [*Health Services and Mental Health Administration, HEW*]
FHPSGI .... Funeral Home Public Service Group International [*Defunct*] (EA)
FHPSM .... International Federation for Hygiene, Preventive and Social Medicine (SAUO)
FHPWO .... Force Headquarters, Psychological Warfare Office [*World War II*]
FHPZ .... Fort Howard Plant [*Federal Railroad Administration identification code*]
FHQ .... Fleet Headquarters [*Australia*]
FHQ .... Florida Historical Quarterly (journ.) (SAUS)
FHQAE .... Force Headquarters, "Q" Army Equipment Branch [*World War II*]
FHR .... Familial Hypophosphatemic Rickets
FHR .... Fetal Heart Rate [*Medicine*]
FHR .... Fetal Heart Rhythm [*Medicine*] (ADWA)
FHR .... Fire Hose Rack
FHR .... Fire Hose Reel
FHR .... Fisher Foods, Inc. [*NYSE symbol*] (COMM)
FHR .... Fixed Head Recorder (SAUS)
FHR .... Fixed Head Recording (SAUS)
FHR .... fixed head video recorder (SAUS)
FHR .... Foundation for Hand Research (EA)
FHR .... Foundation for Homeopathic Research [*Defunct*] (EA)
FHR .... Frequency-agile, High-resolution Radar (SAUS)
FHR .... Friends of Haitian Refugees [*Defunct*] (EA)
FHR .... Fund for Human Rights [*Later, WDL*] (EA)
FHR .... Further
FHR .... Federal House of Representatives [*Australia*] (ODA)
FHRA .... Fetal Heart Rate Acceleration (MELL)
FHRA .... Foundation for Human Rights in Asia (SAUO)
FH-RDC .... Family History-Research Diagnostic Criteria [*Medicine, Psychiatry*]
FHRDC .... Foundation for Human Rights and Democracy in China (EA)
FHR FNSHD T PRMD ... Further Finished Than Primed [*Freight*]
FHR FNSHD T RGH ... Further Finished Than Rough [*Freight*]
FHRI .... Full House Resorts [*NASDAQ symbol*] (SAG)
FHRIW .... Full House Resorts Wrrt [*NASDAQ symbol*] (TTSB)
FHRNA .... Force Headquarters, Commander-in-Chief, Mediterranean [*World War II*]
FHRO .... International Federation of Health Records Organizations (SAUO)
FHRR .... Ferdinand & Huntingburg Railroad [*Federal Railroad Administration identification code*]
FHS .... Facial Hemispasm [*Medicine*] (EDAA)
FHS .... Family and Health Section (EA)
FHS .... Family and Health Section of the National Council on Family Relations [*Formerly, Family and Health Section*] (EA)
FHS .... Fan Heat-Sink (SAUS)
FHS .... Farm Household Support Scheme [*Australia*]
FHS .... Fatal Heart Sound [*Medicine*] (DHSM)
FHS .... Federal Hazardous Substances Act (SAUS)
FHS .... Fellow Heraldry Society [*British*] (WA)
FHS .... Fellow of the Heraldry Society (WDAA)
FHS .... Fellow of the Historical Society (SAUO)
FHS .... Fellow of the Horticultural Society [*British*]
FHS .... Feminine Hygiene Spray
FHS .... Fetal Heart Sounds [*Medicine*]
FHS .... Fetal Hydantoin Syndrome [*Medicine*]
FHS .... File Handling System (SAUS)
FHS .... Fire Hose Station [*Technical drawings*]
FHS .... Fixed head sampler (SAUS)
FHS .... Flame Hardness Standard (MCD)
FHS .... Flat Head Steel [*Screw*] (IAA)
FHS .... Flintshire Historical Society (SAUO)
FHS .... Florida Online High School
FHS .... Football Hall of Shame [*Defunct*] (EA)
FHS .... Forces Help Society [*British*] (BI)
FHS .... Forest History Society (EA)
FHS .... Format Handling System (IAA)
FHS .... Forward Head Shield (SAUS)
FHS .... Forward Heat Shield [*NASA*] (KSC)
FHS .... Foundation Health Systems'A' [*NYSE symbol*] (SG)
FHS .... Foundling Hospitals Schools (SAUO)
FHS .... Framingham Heart Study (SAUS)
FHS .... French Historical Studies (journ.) (SAUS)
FHS .... Frequency Hopping Signal
FHS .... Fuel-Handling System [*Nuclear energy*] (NRCH)
FHS .... Furniture History Society (EA)
FHS .... University of South Florida, St. Petersburg Campus, St. Petersburg, FL [*OCLC symbol*] (OCLC)
FHSA .... Family Health - Service Authority [*British*] (ECON)
FHSA .... Federal Hazardous Substances Act
FHSAA .... Florida High School Athletics Association (EDAC)
FHSC .... Fellow of the Heraldry Society of Canada
FHSCNA .... Federation of Home and Southern Counties Newspaper Associations (SAUO)
FH Screw ..... Flat Head Screw (SAUS)
FHSF .... Fixed-Head Storage Facility [*Computer science*]
FHSG .... Family Housing [*Army*] (AABC)
FHSGS .... Force Headquarters, Secretary General Staff [*World War II*]
FHSH .... Full Honda Service History [*Automotive classified advertising*]
FHSIG .... Force Headquarters, Signal [*World War II*]
FHSIG .... Force Headquarters, Signal Officer (SAUO)
FHSM .... Fellow Institute of Health Service Management [*British*] (WA)
FHSM .... Fellow of the Institute of Health Service Management (WDAA)
FHSP .... Frank Holten State Park (SAUO)
FHSR .... Final Hazards Summary Report [*Nuclear energy*] (NRCH)
FHSR .... Foundation for Health Services Research (EA)
FHSRB .... File History Selection Request Block (VLIE)
FHSS .... Family Housing Survey System (SAUO)
FHSS .... Forward Heat-Shield Separation [*NASA*] (KSC)
FHSS .... Frequency-Hopping Spread Spectrum [*Computer science*] (PCM)
FHST .... Fixed Head Star Trackers
FHSUP .... Force Headquarters, Quartermaster [*World War II*]
FHSV .... Federation of Housing Societies of Victoria [*Australia*]
FHT .... Fast Haar Transform (SAUS)
FHT .... Fast Hadamard Transform (SAUS)
FHT .... Fast Hartley Transform (BYTE)
FHT .... Federation of Holistic Therapists [*British*]

FHT .... Fellowship Houses Trust (SAUO)
FHT .... Fetal Heart [*Medicine*] (MAE)
FHT .... Fetal Heart Tone [*Obstetrics*]
FHT .... Field Handling Trainer [*Army*] (INF)
FHT .... Fingerhut Companies [*NYSE symbol*] (TTSB)
FHT .... Fingerhut Companies, Inc. [*NYSE symbol*] (SPSG)
FHT .... Finite Hilbert Transform (PDAA)
FHT .... Fisher-Hirschfelder-Taylor [*Molecular model*]
FHT .... Fourier-Hadamard Transform [*Medicine*] (EDAA)
FHT .... Free-Heave Test
FHT .... Friedrich Technologies, Inc. [*Vancouver Stock Exchange symbol*]
FHT .... Fuel handling transporter (SAUS)
FHT .... Fully Heat Treated (IEEE)
FHTB .... Flax and Hemp Trade Board (SAUO)
FHTC .... Fixed High-Temperature Capacitor
FHTE .... Fachhochschule Esslingen - Hochschule fuer Technik [*Business Management Program*] [*Germany*]
FHTE .... Flight Hardware Test Equipment [*Aviation*] (IAA)
FHTFX .... Federated Municipal Opport. [*Mutual fund ticker symbol*] (SG)
FHTG .... Familial Hypertriglyceridemia [*Medicine*] (DMAA)
FHTL .... First-Class Hotel (TRID)
FHTNC .... Fleet Home Town News Center
FHTTA .... Fellow of the Highway and Traffic Technicians Association [*British*] (DBQ)
FHTV .... Family of Heavy Tactical Vehicles [*MTMC*] (TAG)
FHTV .... Heavy Tactical Vehicle (AAGC)
FHU .... Force Helicopter Unit (SAUO)
FHU .... Fort Huachuca/Sierra Vista [*Arizona*] [*Airport symbol*] (OAG)
FHU .... Fort Huachuca/Sierra Vista, AZ [*Location identifier*] [*FAA*] (FAAL)
FHU .... Foundation for Human Understanding (SAUS)
FHU .... Foundation of Human Understanding (EA)
FH-UFS .... Femoral Hypoplasia-Unusual Facies Syndrome [*Medicine*] (DMAA)
FHUSN .... Force Headquarters, United States Naval Staff [*World War II*]
FHV .... Fahnestock Viner Holdings, Inc. [*Toronto Stock Exchange symbol*] [*Vancouver Stock Exchange symbol*]
FHV .... Falcon Herpes Virus [*Medicine*] (EDAA)
FHV .... Flockhouse Virus
FHVA .... Fine Hardwood Veneer Association (NTPA)
FHVA/AWMA ... Fine Hardwood Veneer Association/American Walnut Manufacturers Association (SAUO)
F; H; V and O ... Flat, Horizontal-vertical, Vertical-up and Overhead (SAUS)
FHVC .... Fixed High-Volt Capacitor
FHVDRR .... Familial Hypophospatemic Vitamin-D Resistant Rickets [*Medicine*] (EDAA)
FHVMA .... Flowers and Hughes Values for Marriage Analysis (SAUS)
FHVP .... Free Hepatic Venous Pressure [*Medicine*]
FHW .... Foundation of the Hellenic World (SAUO)
FHW .... Freeman, Hardy & Willis (WDAA)
FHWA .... Federal Highway Administration [*Department of Transportation*]
FHWA .... Federal Highway Administration Office of Highway Safety
FH-WC .... Fellow of Heriot-Watt College, Edinburgh
FHWC .... Fellow of the Heriot-Watt College (SAUS)
FHWN .... First Hawaiian [*NASDAQ symbol*] (TTSB)
FHWN .... First Hawaiian, Inc. [*NASDAQ symbol*] (NQ)
FHWS .... Flat Head Wood Screw [*Technical drawings*]
FHWU .... Federated Hotel Workers Union (SAUO)
FHx .... Family History (DAVI)
FHY .... Fire Hydrant
FI .... Daughters of Jesus [*Roman Catholic religious order*]
FI .... Fabrication Instruction (NG)
FI .... Face Immersion (DNAB)
FI .... Facilities Item
FI .... Facility Investigation (SAUO)
FI .... Factories Inspectorate [*British*] (NUCP)
FI .... Factor of Inertia (SAUS)
FI .... Factory Installed (SAUO)
FI .... Factory Integration (AAEL)
FI .... Factory Invoice (SAUS)
FI .... Fade In [*Films, television, etc.*]
F/I .... Failed Item (AAG)
FI .... Fail in Place [*Nuclear energy*] (NRCH)
FI .... Fairchild Industries, Inc. (SAUO)
FI .... Fairplay Information [*Fairplay Publications Ltd.*] [*Information service or system*] (IID)
FI .... Falkland Islands
FI .... False Information (SAUS)
fi .... family interview (SAUS)
FI .... Fan In [*Electronics*] (IAA)
FI .... Farm Index (journ.) (SAUS)
FI .... Farmitalia [*Italy*] [*Research code symbol*]
FI .... Farmland Industries (EA)
FI .... Faroe Islands
FI .... Fatigue Index [*Aircraft strain/fatigue scale*] [*British*]
FI .... Fault Identification (MCD)
FI .... Fault Isolation
FI .... Feature Interaction (SAUS)
FI .... Federal Ibgul (SAUS)
FI .... felsic index (SAUS)
fi .... female impersonator (SAUS)
FI .... Fertilization Inhibitor (SAUS)
FI .... [*The*] Fertilizer Institute
FI .... Fever Caused by Infection (MAE)
F/I .... Fever due to Infection (SAUS)
FI .... Fibrinogen Factor 1 [*Hematology*] (MAE)
FI .... Fibula (MELL)
FI .... Fictitious [*Motor vehicle violation code used in state of Maryland*] (MVRD)
Fi .... Fidel (SAUS)
FI .... Fidelity [*to Living Condition*] Index [*Botany*]
Fi .... Fidell's Precedents [*A publication*] (DLA)
fi .... field independence (SAUS)
FI .... Field Independent (EDAC)
FI .... Field Inspection
FI .... Field Intensity
FI .... Field Interrogation
FI .... Field Interview
FI .... Field Ionization
FI .... Field Item (DNAB)
FI .... Fieseler [*Germany*] [*ICAO aircraft manufacturer identifier*] (ICAO)
Fi .... Fighter (SAUS)
FI .... Fighter Interceptor
FI .... Figure of Insensitiveness (SAUS)
FI .... Fiji Islands (SAUS)
FI .... File Identification (SAUS)
FI .... File Identifier (SAUS)
FI .... File Initialization (SAUS)
FI .... File Interchange (VLIE)
FI .... File Interlock (SAUS)
FI .... File Identifier (SAUS)
FI .... Films, Inc.
FI .... Films, Incorporated (SAUO)
FI .... Filterability Index (AAEL)
FI .... Fina, Inc. [*AMEX symbol*] (SPSG)
FI .... FINA,Inc. Cl'A' [*AMEX symbol*] (TTSB)
F/I .... Final Inspect [*Electronics*] (AAEL)
FI .... Final Issue
FI .... Financial Institution (GART)
FI .... Finished Intelligence (MCD)
FI .... Finland [*ANSI two-letter standard code*] (CNC)
fi .... Finland [*MARC country of publication code*] [*Library of Congress*] (LCCP)
Fi .... Finnie (SAUS)
Fi .... Finnish (SAUS)
FI .... Firearm Injury (MELL)
FI .... Fireball International [*Axminster, Devonshire, England*] (EAIO)
fi .... fire insurance (SAUS)
FI .... First Idaho Resources [*Vancouver Stock Exchange symbol*]
FI .... Fiscal (AFIT)
FI .... Fiscal Intermediary (DNAB)
FI .... Fisheries Department (SAUS)
FI .... Fisher Institute [*Dallas, TX*] (EA)
FI .... Fixed Interface (ACAE)
FI .... Fixed Internal (MAE)
FI .... Fixed Interval [*Reinforcement schedule*]
FI .... Flame Ionization [*Medicine*] (EDAA)
FI .... Flexible Interconnect (SAUO)
FI .... Flight Idle (DNAB)
FI .... Flight Instructor
FI .... Flight Instrumentation (MCD)
FI .... Flood Insurance [*HUD*]
FI .... flos (SAUS)
FI .... flow-in (SAUS)
FI .... flow indicated (SAUS)
FI .... Flow Indicator
FI .... Flow Injection [*Chemical processing*]
FI .... Flow instability (SAUS)
FI .... Flowrate Indicating [*Engineering*]
FI .... Flugfelag-Icelandair [*ICAO designator*] (AD)
FI .... fluid (SAUS)
FI .... Fog Index (SAUS)
FI .... Follicle Lysis [*Medicine*] (PALA)
FI .... Follicular Involution [*Medicine*] (EDAA)
FI .... Foodbanking, Inc. [*An association*] (EA)
FI .... Food Intolerance (MELL)
FI .... Forced Inspiration [*Medicine*] (MAE)
FI .... Force Integration (SAUO)
FI .... Force Integrator [*DoD*]
FI .... Forecasting International Ltd. [*Information service or system*] (IID)
FI .... Foreign Intelligence (MCD)
FI .... Foreign Investment [*Business term*]
FI .... Foresight Institute (EA)
FI .... For Instance
FI .... Formaldehyde Institute (EA)
FI .... Formal Inspection (MCD)
FI .... Format Identifier [*Computer science*] (ELAL)
FI .... Format Item (SAUS)
FI .... Form Interpreter (SAUS)
FI .... Formula Internationale [*Agreement of Unification of Formulae*] [*Medicine*] (ROG)
FI .... Forum Institute [*Defunct*] (EA)
FI .... Forward Italy [*Political party*] (PSAP)
FI .... Fourier Integral (SAUS)
FI .... Fourth International (SAUS)
FI .... France Info [*Radio France*]
FI .... Franco-Iberian (SAUS)
FI .... Franklin Institute (SAUS)
FI .... Fraunhofer Institute (SAUS)
FI .... Freedom International (SAUO)
FI .... Free In [*Shipping*] (ADA)
FI .... Freemen Institute (EA)

FI .... Friden, Incorporated (SAUO)
FI .... Front-End Processor Interface [*Computer science*] (VLIE)
FI .... Frontiers International (EA)
FI .... Front Independantiste [*Independence Front*] [*New Caledonia*] [*Political party*] (PPW)
FI .... Frontoiliac [*Medicine*] (EDAA)
FI .... Fructose Intolerance (MELL)
FI .... Fuel Injection [*Automotive engineering*]
fi .... fuel inspection (SAUS)
FI .... Full Interchangeability (SAUS)
FI .... Fulminating Infection [*Medicine*] (MELL)
FI .... Functional Inquiry (SAUS)
FI .... Functional Iteration (SAUS)
FI .... Function Instruction (SAUS)
FI .... Function Interpreter (VLIE)
FI .... Fungal Infection (MELL)
FI .... Future Interest [*Legal shorthand*] (LWAP)
FI .... Fuze, Instantaneous (SAUS)
fi--- .... Niger River and Basin [*MARC geographic area code*] [*Library of Congress*] (LCCP)
FI .... Faeroe Islands (ODA)
FIA .... Facility Inventory Assessment (ABAC)
FIA .... Factory Insurance Association [*Later, Industrial Risk Insurers*] (EA)
FIA .... Faculty Insurance Association (SAUO)
FIA .... Families in Action [*Later, NFA*] (EA)
FIA .... Family and Intimate Assault [*Criminology*]
FIA .... Fasteners Institute of Australia
FIA .... Fault Isolation Analysis (MCD)
FIA .... Federacion Interamericana de Abogados [*Washington, DC*]
FIA .... Federal Insurance Administration [*HUD*]
FIA .... Federal Intelligence Agency (SAUO)
FIA .... Federal Inventory Accounting
FIA .... Federal Investigators Association (NTPA)
FIA .... Federation Internationale de l'Artisanat [*International Federation of Master-Craftsmen*]
FIA .... Federation Internationale de l'Automobile [*International Automobile Federation*] (EAIO)
FIA .... Federation Internationale des Acteurs [*International Federation of Actors*] (EAIO)
FIA .... Federation Internationale des Aveugles [*International Federation of the Blind*]
FIA .... Feline Infectious Anemia (ADWA)
FIA .... Fellow of the Institute of Actuaries [*British*]
FIA .... Fellow of the Institute of Auctioneers [*British*]
FIA .... Fellow of the Institute of Auctioners (SAUO)
FIA .... Fiat SpA [*NYSE symbol*] (CTT)
FIA .... Fiat SpA ADR [*NYSE symbol*] (TTSB)
FIA .... Fiberoptic Industry Association (VERA)
FIA .... Field Image Alignment (CIST)
FIA .... Field Information Agency (SAUS)
FiA .... Fighter Aviation (SAUS)
FIA .... Financial Institutions Act (FOTI)
FIA .... Financial Inventory Accounting
FIA .... Fire Island Association
FIA .... Fiscal Impact Analysis (PA)
FIA .... Fixed Income Account
FIA .... Flame Ionization Analysis (ACAE)
FIA .... Flatware Importers Association [*Defunct*]
FIA .... Flight Information Area
FIA .... Floating-Point Instruction Address [*Computer science*]
FIA .... flow injection analysis (SAUS)
FIA .... Flow Injection Analyzer [*Chemical analyses*]
FIA .... Flowrate Indicating Alarm [*Engineering*]
FIA .... fluorescence immuno-assay (SAUS)
FIA .... Fluorescence Indicator Adsorption (SAUS)
FIA .... Fluorescence Indicator Analysis
FIA .... Fluorescent Immunoassay [*Analytical biochemistry*]
FIA .... Fluorescent Indicated Analysis (SAUS)
FIA .... fluorescent indication analysis (SAUS)
FIA .... Fluorescent Indicator Absorption (SAUS)
FIA .... Fluoroimmunoassay (DB)
FIA .... Footwear Industries of America (EA)
FIA .... Force Integration Analysis [*DoD*]
FIA .... Forest Inventory and Analysis (WPI)
FIA .... Forging Industry Association (EA)
FIA .... Formal Interaction Analysis (VLIE)
FIA .... Four Island Air Ltd. [*Antigua and Barbuda*] [*ICAO designator*] (FAAC)
FIA .... Fraser Island Association [*Australia*]
FIA .... Freedom in Advertising [*British*] (DI)
FIA .... Freedom of Information Act [*1966*] (AFM)
FIA .... Free Interstitial Atom
FIA .... Freund's Incomplete Adjuvant [*Immunology*]
FIA .... Friends in Adoption [*An association*] (EA)
FIA .... Friends of Israel Association [*British*] (DBA)
FIA .... Fruit Importers Association [*British*] (DBA)
FIA .... Fuel Inlet Adapter [*Automotive emissions*]
fia .... Full Interest Admitted (EBF)
FIA .... Full Interest Admitted
FIA .... Functional Interoperability Architecture (SAUO)
FI-A .... Fundraising Institute-Australia, Inc. (NFD)
FIA .... Futures Industry Association (EA)
FIA .... Socorro, NM [*Location identifier*] [*FAA*] (FAAL)
FIAA .... Federation Internationale d'Athletisme Amateur [*International Amateur Athletic Federation - IAAF*] [*British*] (EAIO)
FIAA .... Fellow, International Association of Allergists (CMD)
FIAA .... Fellow of the Incorporated Association of Architects and Surveyors [*British*] (DBQ)
FIAA .... Fellow of the Institute of Actuaries of Australia (ODBW)
FIAA & S .... Fellow of the Incorporated Association of Architects and Surveyors [*British*]
FIAAS .... Fellow of the Incorporated Association of Architects and Surveyors (SAUO)
FIAAS .... flow injection AAS (SAUS)
FIAB .... Federation Internationale des Associations de Bibliothecaires [*International Federation of Library Associations*]
FIAB .... Fellow of the International Association of Bookkeepers [*British*] (DCTA)
FIAB .... Foreign Intelligence Advisory Board (CINC)
FIABCI .... Federation Internationale des Professions Immobilieres [*International Real Estate Federation*] (EAIO)
FIAC .... FAO/Fertizer Industry Advisory Committe of Experts (SAUS)
FIAC .... Federation Internationale Amateur de Cyclisme [*International Amateur Cycling Federation*] [*Rome, Italy*] (EA)
FIAC .... Federation of Independent Advice Centres [*British*] (DBA)
FIAC .... Federation of International Amateur Cycling (SAUO)
FIAC .... Federation of International American Clubs [*Oslo, Norway*] (EAIO)
FIAC .... Fellow, Institut des Assurances du Canada (CPGU)
FIAC .... Fellow, International Academy of Cytology (CMD)
FIAC .... Fellow of the Institute of Company Accountants [*British*] (DAS)
FIAC .... Fialcytosine [*Medicine*]
FIAC .... Fishing Industry Advisory Committee [*Australia*]
FIAC .... Flanders Interaction Analysis Categories (EDAC)
FIAC .... Flight Information Advisory Committee [*Terminated, 1977*] [*FAA*]
FIAC .... Fluorodeoxyiodoara-C [*An antiviral compound*]
FIAC .... Fluoroiodoarabinosylcytosine
FIAC .... Foundries Industry Advisory Committee (HEAS)
FIAC .... Industrial Forum of Central Africa (SAUO)
FIACAT .... Federation Internationale de l'Action des Chretiens pour l'Abolition de la Torture [*International Federation of Action of Christians for the Abolition of Torture*] (EAIO)
FIACC .... Five International Associations Coordinating Committee [*Hungary*] (EAIO)
FIACHA .... First Interstate Automated Cleaning House Association (TBD)
FIACS .... Fellow, International Academy Cosmetic Surgery (CMD)
FIACTA .... Federation Internationale des Associations de Controleurs du Trafic Aerien [*International Federation of Air Traffic Controllers' Associations*] (EAIO)
FIACTC .... Federation Internationale des Associations des Chimistes du Textile et da la Couleur
FIAD .... Federation Internationale des Associations de Distributeurs de Films [*International Federation of Associations of Film Distributors*] (EAIO)
FIAD .... Flame Ionization Analyzer and Detector (SAUS)
FIAEA .... Fellow of the Institute of Automotive Engineer Assessors [*British*] (DBQ)
FIAEM .... Federation Internationale des Associations d'Etudiants en Medecine [*International Federation of Medical Students Associations - IFMSA*] [*Vienna, Austria*] (EAIO)
FIAEP .... Federation Internationale des Associations d'Entrepots Publics [*International Federation of Public Warehousing Associations - IFPWA*] (EAIO)
FIAeS .... Fellow of the Institute of Aeronautical Sciences [*Later, FAIAA*] [*British*] (EY)
FIAES .... Initiative for the Americas Debt Reduction Fund (SAUO)
FIAESTA .... Federation Internationale des Associations de l'Electronique de Securite du Trafic Aerien [*International Federation of Air Traffic Safety Electronic Associations*] (EAIO)
FIAF .... Federation Internationale des Archives du Film [*International Federation of Film Archives*] (EAIO)
FIAF .... French Institute/Alliance Francaise (EA)
FIAgrE .... Fellow of the Institution of Agricultural Engineers [*British*]
FIAI .... Federation Internationale des Associations d'Instituteurs [*International Federation of Teachers' Associations - IFTA*] (EAIO)
FIAI .... Fellow of the Institute of Arbitrators Incorporated (SAUO)
FIAI .... Fellow of the Institute of Industrial and Commercial Accountants [*British*]
FIAJ .... Federation Internationale des Auberges de la Jeunesse [*International Youth Hostel Federation - IYHF*] [*Welwyn Garden City, Hertfordshire, England*] (EAIO)
FIAJF .... Federation Internationale des Amies de la Jeune Fille
FIAJY .... Fellowship in Israel for Arab-Jewish Youth (EA)
FIAL .... Fellow of the Institute of Arts and Letters (SAUS)
FIAL .... Fine Imaging Algorithm (SAUS)
FIAM .... Fellow of the Institute of Administrative Management [*British*] (ODBW)
FIAM .... Fellow of the International Academy of Management
FIAMA .... Fellow of the Incorporated Advertising Managers Association [*British*] (DAS)
FIAMC .... Federation Internationale des Associations Medicales Catholiques [*International Federation of Catholic Medical Associations*] (EA)
FIAMS .... Fellow of the Indian Academy of Medical Sciences
FIAMS .... Flinders Institute for Atmospheric and Marine Sciences [*Australia*] [*Marine science*] (OSRA)
FIAMS .... Flinders Institute of Atmospheric and Marine Sciences (SAUS)
FIAN .... Foodfirst Information and Action Network (SAUO)
FIAN .... Food International Action Network (SAUO)
FIANA .... File Analyzer and Report Generator (DNAB)
FIANATM .... Federation Internationale des Associations Nationales de Negociants en Aciers, Tubes, et Metaux [*International Federation of Associations of Steel, Tube, and Metal Merchants*] (EAIO)

FIANDIC....... Families in Action National Drug Information Center [*Later, NFA*] (EA)
FI and O...... Free In and Out (SAUS)
FI&SC.......... Freight, Insurance, and Shipping Charges (SAUS)
FI & SS........ Foreign Intelligence and Security Service (MCD)
FIANEI......... Federation Internationale des Associations Nationales d'Eleves Ingenieurs [*International Federation of National Associations of Engineering Students*]
FIANG.......... Federal Inspector for Alaska Natural Gas (COE)
FIANZ.......... Fellow of the Institute of Actuaries of New Zealand
FIA/ORA/TOD/PCB/FEMA... Federal Insurance Administration, Office of Risk Assessment, Technical Operations Division, Production Control Branch of the Federal Emergency Management Agency (SAUO)
FIAP............ Federation Internationale de l'Art Photographique [*International Federation of Photographic Art*] (EAIO)
FIAP............ Fellow of the Institution of Analysts and Programmers [*British*] (DBQ)
FIAPA........... Federation Internationale des Associations de Chefs de Publicite d'Annonceurs [*International Federation of Advertising Managers Associations*]
FIAPF........... Federation Internationale des Associations de Producteurs de Films [*International Federation of Film Producers' Associations*]
FIAPL........... Federation Internationale des Associations de Pilotes de Ligne
FIAPN........... Federation Internationale des Associations de Patrons de Navires [*International Federation of Shipmasters Associations*] (EAIO)
FIAPr........... Fiat SpA Preference ADR [*NYSE symbol*] (TTSB)
FIAPrA.......... Fiat SpA Savings ADR [*NYSE symbol*] (TTSB)
FIAPS........... Federation Internationale des Associations de Professeurs de Sciences [*International Council of Associations for Science Education - ICASE*] (EAIO)
FIAR............ European aviation partnership (SAUS)
FIAR............ Fabbrica Italiana Apparecchiature Radioelettriche (SAUS)
FIAR............ Failed Item Analysis Report (MCD)
FIAR............ Failure Investigation Action Report [*NASA*] (NASA)
FIAR............ Fault Isolation Analysis Routine (VLIE)
FIArb........... Fellow of the Institute of Arbitrators
FIARBC.......... Federal Interagency River Basin Committee (SAUO)
FIARE........... Flight Investigation of Apollo Reentry Environment (MUGU)
FIAS............ Federacion Interamericana de Asociaciones de Secretarias [*Inter-American Federation of Secretaries*] [*San Salvador, El Salvador*] (EAIO)
FIAS............ Federation Internationale Amateur de Sambo [*Anglet, France*] (EAIO)
FIAS............ Federation Internationale des Assistantes Sociales [*International Federation of Social Workers*] [*Switzerland*] (EAIO)
FIAS............ Fellow of the Incorporated Association of Architects and Surveyors [*British*] (DBQ)
FIAS............ Fellow of the Institute of Aeronautical Sciences [*Later, FAIAA*] [*British*]
FIAS............ Fellow of the Institute of the Aerospace Sciences (SAUO)
FIAS............ Financial Information and Accounting System
FIAS............ Flanders Interaction Analysis System (EDAC)
FIAS............ Flow Impedance Analysis System (SAUS)
FIAS............ Flow indicator alarm switch (SAUS)
FIAS............ Flow-Injection Analysis System (ABAC)
FIAS............ Forging Industry Association
Fias............ Free in and Stowed [*Shipping*] (DS)
FIASC........... Federal Inter-Agency Sedimentation Conference [*Department of Agriculture*]
FIASI........... Fixed Income Analysts Society (NTPA)
FIAT............ Fabbrica Italiana Automobile, Torino [*Italian automobile manufacturer*] [*Facetious translations: "Fix It Again, Tony"; "Futile Italian Attempt at Transportation"*]
FIAT............ Facility for Independent Acquisition & Tracking (SAUO)
FIAT............ Federation Internationale des Archives de Television [*International Federation of Television Archives - IFTA*] (EAIO)
FIAT............ Federation Internationale des Associations de Thanatopraxie [*International Federation of Thanatopractic Associations*]
FIAT............ Fellow of the Institute of Animal Technicians [*British*] (DBQ)
FIAT............ Fellow of the Institute of Asphalt Technology [*British*] (DBQ)
Fiat............ Fiat SpA [*Associated Press*] (SAG)
FIAT............ Field Information Agency, Technical [*Under G-2, SHAEF*]
FIAT............ Film Inspection Apply Template (MCD)
FIAT............ First Installed Article, Tests [*NATO*] (NATG)
FIAT............ Fishing Industry Appeals Tribunal [*Australia*]
FIAT............ Floating Interpretive Automatic Translator (SAUS)
FIAT............ Food Industry Association of Tasmania [*Australia*]
FIAT............ Forest Industries Association of Tasmania (EERA)
FIAT............ Fraternity International Apostolic Team (SAUO)
FIAT............ free fatty acids incorporation in adipose tissue trigiycerides (SAUS)
FIATA........... Federation Internationale des Associations de Transitaires et Assimilies [*International Federation of Freight Forwarders Associations*] [*Zurich, Switzerland*] (EAIO)
FIATA........... International Federation of Forwarding Association (SAUS)
FIATA........... International Federation of Freight Forwarders (SAUS)
FIATA-FBL...... FIATA-Combined Transport Bill of Lading (SAUS)
FIATA-FCR...... FIATA-Certificate of Receipt (SAUS)
FIATA-FCT...... FIATA-Certificate of Transport (SAUS)
FIATC........... Federation Internationale des Associations Touristiques de Cheminots [*International Federation of Railwaymen's Travel Associations - IFRTA*] [*France*]
FIATC........... Florida International Agricultural Trade Council (SRA)
FIATE........... Federation Internationale des Associations de Travailleurs Evangeliques
FIAT Report... Field Information Agency, Technical Report (SAUS)
FIATS........... Freedom of Information Action Tracking System (SAUO)
Fiat-USA....... Fiat Auto USA, Inc. (SAUO)
FIAU............ Fialuridine [*Medicine*]
FIAU............ Fluorodeoxyiodoara-U [*An antiviral compound*]
FIAV............ Federation Internationale des Agences de Voyages [*International Federation of Travel Agencies*]
FIAV............ Federation Internationale des Associations de Vexillologie [*International Federation of Vexillological Associations*] (EA)
FIAWOL.......... Fandom Is a Way of Life [*Science-fiction-fan slogan*]
FIAWS........... Fellow of the International Academy of Wood Sciences
FIAX............ Fiesta-Air [*Air carrier designation symbol*]
FIB............. Far-Infrared Background [*Astronomy*]
FIB............. Fast Ion Bombardment
FIB............. Federation Internationale de Badminton [*International Badminton Federation - IBF*] (EA)
FIB............. Federation Internationale de Baseball [*International Baseball Federation*]
FIB............. Federation Internationale de Boules [*International Bocce Federation*] [*Turin, Italy*] (EAIO)
FIB............. Federation of Insurance Brokers (SAUO)
FIB............. Fellow of the Institute of Bankers [*British*] (EY)
FIB............. Fellow of the Institute of Biology (DAVI)
FIB............. Fellow of the Institute of Builders [*British*]
FIB............. Fiber
FIB............. Fibre (SAUS)
Fib............. Fibrillation [*Medicine*] (AMHC)
fib............. Fibrillation [*Medicine*]
FIB............. Fibrin [*Hematology*] (DAVI)
FIB............. Fibrinogen [*Factor 1*] [*Hematology*]
Fib............. Fibroblastic (QSUL)
fib............. fibro cement (SAUS)
FIB............. Fibrosing Interstitial Pneumonitis [*Medicine*] (CPH)
FIB............. Fibrositis [*Medicine*]
FIB............. Fibula [*Medicine*]
FI B............ Fide Bona [*In Good Faith*] [*Latin*] (ROG)
FIB............. File Information Block
FIB............. File Interface Block (ACAE)
FIB............. Fire Indicator Board
FIB............. First Interstate Bank (SAUS)
FIB............. Fisherman's Information Bureau [*Chicago, IL*]
FIB............. Fish Industry Board (SAUO)
FIB............. Fishing Industry Board (SAUO)
FIB............. Fixed Interim Baseline
FIB............. Fleet Installation Budget [*Navy*]
FIB............. fleet torpedo bomber (SAUS)
FIB............. Flight Information Bulletin (AABC)
FIB............. Fluidics Inertial Bomb
FIB............. Focused Ion Beam [*Photonics*]
FIB............. Food Investigation Board (SAUO)
FIB............. Force-in-Being (ADA)
FIB............. Foreground Initiated Batch [*Computer science*]
FIB............. Forestry and Timber Bureau (SAUS)
FIB............. FORTRAN [*Formula Translating System*] Information Bulletin [*Computer science*] (IEEE)
FIB............. Forward Indicator BIT [*Binary Digit*] (TEL)
FIB............. Forwarding Information Base (VLIE)
FIB............. Franchise Tax Board (SAUS)
FIB............. Franklin Institute of Boston (SAUS)
FIB............. Free into Barge [*Shipping*]
fib............. free into bond (SAUS)
fib............. Free into Bunker [*or Barge*] (EBF)
FIB............. Freeway Iberica SA [*Spain*] [*ICAO designator*] (FAAC)
FIB............. International Concrete Federation (SAUO)
FIB............. Kodiak, AK [*Location identifier*] [*FAA*] (FAAL)
FIBA............ Federation Internationale de Basketball Amateur [*International Amateur Basketball Federation*] [*Germany*] (EA)
FIBA............ Federazione Italiana Bancari e Assicuratori [*Italy*] (EY)
FIBA............ Fellow of the Institute of Banking Associations
FIBA............ Fellow of the Institute of Business Administration [*British*]
FIBAS........... Field Installation Branch Adaption Section (SAA)
Fibb............ fibroblast (SAUS)
FIBC............ Federal Interagency Broadcast Committee
Fibc............ fibrocyte (SAUS)
FIBC............ Financial Bancorp [*NASDAQ symbol*] (TTSB)
FIBC............ Financial Bancorp, Inc. [*NASDAQ symbol*] (SAG)
FIBC............ Flexible Intermediate Bulk Container [*Shipping*]
FIBCA........... Fellow of the Institute of Burial and Cremation Administration (SAUO)
FIBCA........... Flexible Intermediate Bulk Container Association (EA)
FIBCC........... Federal Interagency Broadcast Committee (SAUO)
Fibchm.......... Fiberchem, Inc. [*Associated Press*] (SAG)
FIBCM........... Fellow of the Institute of British Carriage and Automobile Manufacturers (SAUO)
FIBCO........... Fellow of the Institution of Building Control Officers (DBQ)
FIBCS........... Field Installation Branch Control Section (SAA)
FIBCs........... Flexible Intermediate Bulk Containers (SAUS)
FIBD............ Fellow of the Institute of British Decorators
fibd............ Fiberboard (VRA)
FIBD............ Ford International Business Development [*Ford Motor Co.*]
FIBE............ Fellow of the Institute of Building Estimators (SAUO)
FIBEC........... Federal Industrial Boiler Emission Control (SAUS)
FIBEP........... Federation Internationale des Bureaux d'Extraits de Presse [*International Federation of Press Cutting Agencies - IFPCA*] (EAIO)
FIBER........... Fund for Integrative Biomedical Research
Fiber Integr Opt... Fiber and Integrated Optics (journ.) (SAUS)
Fiber Opt Mag... Fiber Optics Magazine (journ.) (SAUS)
fiberoptronics... Fiberoptics and Optoelectronics (VLIE)

FIBETRAC .... Firing Error Trajectory Recorder and Computer (SAUS)
FIBEX .... First International Biological Experiment (SAUS)
FIBEX .... First International BIOMASS Experiment [*ICSU*] (MSC)
FIBF .... Fellow of the Institute of British Foundrymen (DBQ)
fibgl .... Fiberglass (VRA)
FIBI .... Filed but Impracticable to Transmit [*NWS*] (FAAC)
FIBI .... First International Bank of Israel Ltd. (BJA)
FI Bio .... Fellow of the Institute of Biology (SAUS)
FI Biol .... Fellow of the Institute of Biology [*Formerly, FInstBiol*] [*British*]
FIBL .... Focused Ion-Beam Lithography (SAUS)
FIBM .... Fellow of the British Institute of Management (SAUO)
FIBMA .... Federation of Ironmongers and Builders Merchants Staff Associations (SAUO)
FIBO .... Federation of Independent British Optometrists (DBA)
FIBOR .... Frankfurt Inter-Bank Offered Rate [*Germany*] [*Finance*]
FIBOT .... Fair Isle Bird Observatory Trust (SAUS)
FIBP .... Federal Industrial Boiler Program (FOTI)
FIBP .... Fellow of the Institute of British Photographers
FIBR .... American Fiber Optics Corp. [*NASDAQ symbol*] (COMM)
FIBR .... Fiber
fibr .... fibrillation (SAUS)
FIBR .... Osicom Technologies, Inc. [*NASDAQ symbol*] (SAG)
Fibrbd .... Fibreboard Corp. [*Associated Press*] (SAG)
fibrd .... fiberboard (SAUS)
FIBRD .... Fibreboard [*Freight*]
Fibre Sci Technol... Fibre Science and Technology (journ.) (SAUS)
FIBRGN .... Fibrinogen [*Hematology*] (DAVI)
fibril .... fibrillation (SAUS)
fibrill .... Fibrillation [*Medicine*] (DAVI)
fibrin .... Fibrinogen [*Factor 1*] [*Hematology*]
FIBRIN .... Fibrinolysin (SAUS)
Fibrstrs .... Fiberstars, Inc. [*Associated Press*] (SAG)
FIBS .... Field by Information Blending and Smoothing [*Marine science*] (OSRA)
FIBS .... Flight Information Billing System (DA)
FIB(Scot) ..... Fellow of the Institute of Bankers in Scotland [*British*] (DBQ)
FIBST .... Fellow of the Institute of British Surgical Technicians (SAUO)
FIBT .... Federation Internationale de Bobsleigh et de Tobogganing [*International Bobsledding and Tobogganing Federation*] [*Milan, Italy*] (EAIO)
FIBTP .... Federation Internationale du Batiment et des Travaux Publics
FIBUA .... Fighting in Built-Up Areas [*Military*] (INF)
FIBV .... Federation Internationale des Bourses de Valeurs [*International Federation of Stock Exchanges*] (EAIO)
FIC .... Brothers of Christian Instruction (TOCD)
FIC .... Congregatio Fratrum Immaculatae Conceptionis Beatae Mariae Virginis [*Brothers of the Immaculate Conception of the Blessed Virgin Mary*] (EAIO)
FIC .... Factory Inspectorate Circular (HEAS)
FIC .... Fair Isaac & Co. [*NYSE symbol*] (TTSB)
FIC .... Family Information Centre (SAUO)
FIC .... Family Investment Center (SAUO)
FIC .... Fasting Intestinal Contents [*Gastroenterology*] (DAVI)
FIC .... Fast Ion Conduction (PDAA)
FIC .... Fast-Moving Industrializing Country
FIC .... Fault Isolation Code
FIC .... Federal Ibgul Corp. (SAUO)
FIC .... Federal Information Center (COE)
FIC .... Federal Insurance Contribution (MHDW)
FIC .... Federal Insurance Counsel (SAUS)
FIC .... Federal Interagency Committee on Transportation of Radioactive Materials (SAUO)
FIC .... Federation Internationale de Canoe [*International Canoe Federation - ICF*] [*Florence, Italy*] (EAIO)
FIC .... Federation Internationale de Cremation [*International Cremation Federation*] (EAIO)
FIC .... Federation Internationale des Chronometreurs [*Rome, Italy*] (EAIO)
FIC .... Federation of Insurance Counsel (EA)
FIC .... Federation of Irish Cyclists (EAIO)
FIC .... Fellow of Imperial College, London (ODA)
FIC .... Fellow of the Institute of Chemistry [*Later, FRIC*] [*British*]
FIC .... Fellow of the Institute of Chemists (SAUS)
FIC .... Fellow of the Institute of Commerce
FIC .... Fellowship for Intentional Community (EA)
fic .... fiction (SAUS)
FIC .... Field Installation Charge (SAUS)
FIC .... Field Installed Connector
FIC .... Film Integrated Circuit
FIC .... Filter Integrated Color (SAUS)
FIC .... Financial Inventory Control
FIC .... Fire Industry Council [*British*] (DBA)
FIC .... First-in-Chain [*Computer science*]
FIC .... First International Computer, Inc. (VERA)
FIC .... Fleet Intelligence Center [*Navy*] (NVT)
FIC .... Fleet Issue Control [*Navy*] (NVT)
FIC .... Flight Information Center
FIC .... Flight Inspection Center [*Military*] (DOMA)
FIC .... Flow Indicator Controller [*Electronics*] (ECII)
FIC .... Fluidics Information Center (SAUS)
FIC .... Fluid Integrated Circuit [*Electronics*] (AAEL)
FIC .... Fluoriodocarbon [*Fire extinguishing compound*]
FIC .... Flying Instructor Course (DA)
FIC .... Foam Inhibiting Conjugate [*Chemical engineering*]
FIC .... Focus-Inducing Cell [*Population*] [*Immunochemistry*]
FIC .... Fogarty International Center [*National Institutes of Health*]
FIC .... Food Industries Center [*Ohio State University*] [*Research center*] (RCD)
FIC .... Food Instrument Corporation (SAUO)
FIC .... Force Indicator Code (MCD)
FIC .... Forest Industries Council (EA)
FIC .... Foundation for International Cooperation (EA)
FIC .... Fractal Image Compression (SEWL)
FIC .... Fractional Inhibitory Concentration (SAUS)
FIC .... Fraternal Insurance Counselor [*Fraternal Field Managers' Association*] [*Designation awarded by*]
FIC .... Fratrum Instructionis Christianae [*Brothers of Christian Instruction*] [*La Mennais Brothers*] [*Roman Catholic religious order*]
FIC .... Freedom of Information Center (SAUS)
FIC .... Freedom of Information Clearinghouse [*An association*] (EA)
FIC .... Freedom of Information Committee (SAUO)
FIC .... Free Insurance and Carriage [*Shipping*] (DS)
fic .... freight (SAUS)
FIC .... Freight, Insurance, Carriage
FIC .... Frequency Interference Control
FIC .... Frequency Interval Counter (ACAE)
FIC .... Friends of Imperial Cancer [*British*]
FIC .... Funding Information Center [*Spokane Public Library*] [*Information service or system*] (IID)
FIC .... Fur Institute of Canada
FIC .... Falkland Islands Company (ODA)
FICA .... Factory Inspectorate and Canteen Advisers (SAUO)
FICA .... Federal Insurance Compensation Act
FICA .... Federal Insurance Contributions Act [*1954*] [*Under which collections are made from employers and employees for OASDI benefits*]
FICA .... Federation Internationale des Cheminots Antialcooliques [*International Railway Temperance Union*]
FICA .... Fellow of the Commonwealth Institute of Accountancy
FICA .... Fellow of the International College of Anesthetists (SAUS)
FICA .... flow indicated controlled alarmed (SAUS)
FICA .... Flowrate Indicating Controlling Alarm [*Engineering*]
FICA .... Food Industries Credit Association (SAUO)
FICA .... Food Industry Council of Australia
FICA .... Foreign Intelligence Surveillance Act (SAUS)
FICA .... Forest Industries Campaign Association (EERA)
FICA .... Fraternal Insurance Counsellors Association [*Later, NAFIC*] (EA)
FICA .... Fur Information Council of America
FICA(An) ...... Fellow, International College of Anatomists (CMD)
FICA(Ang) .... Fellow, International College of Angiology (CMD)
FICAC .... Federation Internationale des Corps et Associations Consulaires [*Federation of International Consular Corps and Associations*] (EAIO)
FICAI .... Fellow of the Institute of Chartered Accountants in Ireland (ODBW)
FICAP .... Federation of International Country Air Personalities [*Defunct*] (EA)
FICAP .... Furniture Industry Consumer Action Panel (SAUO)
FICAP .... Furniture Industry Consumer Advisory Panel [*Defunct*] (EA)
FICB .... Federal Intermediate Credit Bank
FICB .... Federation Internationale de la Croix-Bleue [*International Federation of the Blue Cross*] [*Switzerland*] (EAIO)
FICB .... Federation of International Commercial Broadcasters (SAUO)
FICB .... Fellow of the Institute of Canadian Bankers (DD)
FICB .... File Identification Control Block [*Computer science*] (IAA)
FICC .... Federal Interagency Coordinating Council
FICC .... Federation Internationale de Camping et de Caravanning [*International Federation of Camping and Caravanning*] [*Brussels, Belgium*] (EA)
FICC .... Federation Internationale de Chimie Clinique [*International Federation of Clinical Chemistry*]
FICC .... Federation Internationale des Cine-Clubs [*International Federation of Film Societies*]
FICC .... Federation of Insurance and Corporate Counsel [*Marblehead, MA*] (EA)
FICC .... Fixed Income Consumer Counseling [*ACTION*]
FICC .... Freon Isopropyl Circuit Cleaner (SAUS)
FICC .... Frequency Interference Control Center [*Air Force*]
FICCA .... False Identification Crime Control Act of 1982
FIC/CAF .... FID Commission for Africa (SAUS)
FIC CATIS .... Fleet Intelligence Center Computer-Aided Tactical Information System [*Navy*] (DNAB)
FICCC .... Federation Internationale des Clubs de Camping-Cars [*Montreuil, France*] (EAIO)
FICCDC .... Federal Inter-Agency Coordinating Committee on Digital Cartography
FICCDC/SWG... Federal Interagency Coordinating Committee on Digital Cartography/Standards Working Group (SAUO)
FICCDC/SWG... FICCDC /Standards Working Group (SAUS)
FICCI .... Federation of the Indian Chambers of Commerce and Industry (SAUS)
FICCIA .... Federation Internationale des Cadres de la Chimie et des Industries Annexes
FICCIM .... First International Congress on the Conservation of Industrial Monuments (SAUO)
FICCS .... Functional Inventory of Cognitive Communication Strategies (EDAC)
FICD .... Fellow of the Indian College of Dentists
FICD .... Fellow of the Institute of Canadian Dentists
FICD .... Fellow of the Institute of Civil Defence [*British*]
FICD .... Fellow of the International College of Dentists
FICE .... Federal Interagency Committee on Education
FICE .... Federation Internationale des Choeurs d'Enfants [*International Federation of Children's Choirs*] (EA)
FICE .... Federation Internationale des Communautes d'Enfants [*International Federation of Children's Communities*]

FICE .... Federation Internationale des Communautes Educatives [*International Federation of Educative Communities*] [*Zurich, Switzerland*] (EAIO)
FICE .... Fellow of the Institute of Civil Engineers (SAUS)
FICE .... Fellow of the Institution of Civil Engineers [*British*]
FICEA .... Fellow of the Association of Industrial and Commercial Executive Accountants (SAUO)
FICEM .... Federcion Interamericana del Cemento [*Inter American Cement Federation*] [*Colombia*] (EAIO)
FICEMEA .... Federation Internationale des Centres d'Entrainement aux Methodes d'Education Active [*International Federation of Training Centres in Methods of Active Education*] (EAIO)
FICEP .... Federation Internationale Catholique d'Education Physique et Sportive [*Catholic International Federation for Physical and Sports Education - CIFPSE*] [*Paris, France*] (EAIO)
FICeram .... Fellow of the Institute of Ceramics [*British*]
FICEUR .... Fleet Intelligence Center, Europe [*Navy*]
FICEURLANT ... Fleet Intelligence Center, Europe and Atlantic [*Navy*] (MCD)
FICF .... Federation Internationale Culturelle Feminine [*Women's International Cultural Federation - WICF*] (EAIO)
FICFR .... FORUM for International Cooperation in Fire Research (SAUO)
FICG .... Federation Internationale des Choeurs de Garcons (EAIO)
FIChemE .... Fellow of the Institution of Chemical Engineers [*British*]
FIC/HEW .... Fogarty International Center-HEW (SAUS)
FIChor .... Fellow of the Benesh Institute of Choreology [*British*] (DBQ)
FICI .... Failed Instrument Component Inspection [*Environmental science*] (COE)
FICI .... Fair [*Isaac*] & Co., Inc. [*NASDAQ symbol*] (NQ)
FICI .... Fair, Isaac & Company, Inc. [*NASDAQ symbol*] (COMM)
FICI .... Federation of Irish Chemical Industries (SAUS)
FICI .... Fellow of the Institute of Chemistry of Ireland
FICI .... Fellow of the International Colonial Institute [*British*]
fi/ci .... foreign intelligence/counterintelligence (SAUS)
FICIA .... Fellow of the Guild of Industrial, Commercial, & Institutional Accounts (DD)
FICIC .... Federation Internationale du Commerce et des Industries du Camping
FICICA .... Federation Internationale du Personnel d'Encadrement des Industries et CommercesAgricoles et Alimentaires [*International Federation of Managerial Staff of Agricultural and Alimentary Industry and Commerce*] (EAIO)
Fic Int .... Fiction International [*A publication*] (BRI)
FICJA .... Fellow of the International Criminal Justice Association
FICJF .... Federation Internationale des Conseils Juridiques et Fiscaux [*International Federation of Legal Fiscal Consultants*]
FICL .... Fellow of Trinity College of Music-London (SAUS)
FICL .... Financial Inventory Control Ledger (DNAB)
FIC-Index .... fractional inhibitory concentration-Index (SAUS)
FICM .... Federation Internationale des Cadres des Mines
FICM .... Federation of International Music Competitions (EA)
FICM .... Fellow of the Institute of Credit Management [*British*] (DCTA)
FICM .... Fleet Intelligence Collection Manual (MCD)
FICM .... Fluidic Industrial Control Module (IAA)
FICMA .... Fellow of the Institute of Cost and Management Accountants [*British*] (ODBW)
FICMX .... Federated Income Trust [*Mutual fund ticker symbol*] (SG)
FICN .... Federal Interagency Communication in Nutrition (SAUO)
FICO .... Fair, Issac and Co.
FICO .... Fellow of the Institute of Careers Officers [*British*] (DBQ)
FICO .... Field Installation Change Order (MCD)
FICO .... File Control [*Microfilm*] (MCD)
FICO .... File under Control (SAUS)
FICO .... Financing Corp. [*Created by the Reagan administration in 1987 for the Fede ral Savings and Loan Insurance Corp.*]
FICO .... Financing Corporation (SAUO)
FICO .... Flight Information and Control of Operations
FICO .... Ford Instrument Company (SAUO)
FICO .... Franchiseit Corp. [*NASDAQ symbol*] (COMM)
$FICO_2$ .... Fraction of Inspired Carbon Dioxide [*Medicine*] (DAVI)
FICOA .... Film Instruction Company of America (SAUO)
FICOD .... Force Identification Code [*Military*]
FICON .... Fiber Connectivity [*Telecommunications*] (DINT)
FICON .... Fibre Channel Connectivity (GART)
FICON .... Fighter Conveyor
FICON .... File Conversion [*Computer science*]
FICorrST .... Fellow of the Institution of Corrosion Science and Technology [*British*] (DBQ)
FICO System ... File under Control System (SAUS)
FICP .... Federal Information Centers Program (SAUS)
FICP .... Federation Internationale des Clubs de Publicite [*International Federation of Advertising Clubs*] [*Lille, France*] (EAIO)
FICP .... Federation Internationale du Cyclisme Professionel [*International Federation of Professional Cycling*]
FICP .... Fellow, International College of Pediatricians (CMD)
FICP .... Freres de l'Instruction Chretienne de Ploermel [*Brothers of Christian Instruction of Ploermel*] [*Rome, Italy*] (EAIO)
FICPAC .... Fleet Intelligence Center, Pacific [*Navy*] (CINC)
FICPACFAC ... Fleet Intelligence Center, Pacific Facility [*Navy*]
FICPI .... Federation Internationale des Conseils en Propriete Industrielle [*International Federation of Industrial Property Attorneys*] (EAIO)
FICPM .... Fellow, International College of Physical Medicine (CMD)
FICPSM .... Fellow, International College of Psychosomatic Medicine (CMD)
FICR .... Fidelcor, Inc. (SAUO)
FICR .... Financial Inventory Control Report
FICS .... Facility Information and Control System (SAUS)
FICS .... Facsimile Intelligent Communications System (SAUS)
FICS .... Factory Information Control System (MHDB)
FICS .... Fault Isolation Checkout System
FICS .... Federation Internationale des Chasseurs de Son [*International Federation of Sound Hunters - IFSH*] (EAIO)
FICS .... Fellow, International College of Surgery (CMD)
FICS .... Fellow of the Institute of Chartered Shipbrokers [*British*]
FICS .... Fellow of the International College of Surgeons
FICs .... Film Integrated Circuits (SAUS)
FiCS .... Financial Clearing and Services Ltd. [*Information service or system*] (IID)
FICS .... Financial Information and Control Software (SAUS)
FICS .... Financial Information and Control System (SAUS)
FICS .... Fire Control Simulation (MCD)
FICS .... Forecasting and Inventory Control System
FICS .... Free Internet Chess Server
FICS .... Freshman Issues and Concerns Survey (EDAC)
FICSA .... Federation of International Civil Servants' Associations [*Geneva, Switzerland*] (EA)
FICT .... Federation Internationale de Centres Touristiques [*International Federation of Tourist Centres*] (EAIO)
FICT .... Fictilis [*Made of Pottery*] [*Latin*]
Fict .... Fiction (AL)
fict .... Fiction (SHCU)
FICT .... Fiction
FICT .... Fictional (WDAA)
fict .... Fictitious (ADWA)
FICT .... Fictitious (WDAA)
FICT .... Forest Industry Council on Taxation (WPI)
FICTIONZINE ... Fiction Magazine [*Generic term for a publication covering science fiction*]
FICU .... Fetal Intensive Care Unit [*Neonatology*] (DAVI)
FICU .... Fonds Internationale de Cooperation Universitaire [*International Fund for University Cooperation*] [*Canada*] (EAIO)
FICUS .... Florida Internet Center for Understanding Sustainability
FICW .... Fellow of the Institute of Clerks of Works of Great Britain, Inc. (DBQ)
FICWA .... Fellow of the Institute of Cost and Work Accountants (SAUS)
FICWA .... Floricultural Industry Council of Western Australia
FICZ .... Farm & Industrial Chemical [*Federal Railroad Administration identification code*]
FID .... Failure Identification (MCD)
FID .... Falkland Islands Dependency (SAUS)
FID .... Far-Infrared Detector
FID .... Fault Insertion Device (ACAE)
FID .... Fault Isolation Detection (MCD)
FID .... Fault Isolation Diagnostics (MCD)
FID .... Federacion Internacional de Documentacion [*International Federation for Documentation - IFD*] [*Spanish*] [*Information service or system*] (ASF)
FID .... Federation Internationale d'Information et de Documentation [*International Federation for Information and Documentation*] [*Netherlands*] [*Information service or system*] (IID)
FID .... Federation Internationale du Diabete [*International Diabetes Federation - IDF*] [*Brussels, Belgium*] (EAIO)
FID .... Federation of International Documentation (SAUO)
FID .... Fellow of the Institute of Directors [*British*]
FID .... Fidata Corp. (SAUO)
fid .... Fidelity (ADWA)
Fid .... Fidelity (EBF)
FID .... Fidelity (WGA)
FID .... Fides [*Faith*] [*Latin*] (ROG)
FID .... Fiduciary (ADA)
Fid .... Fiduciary (EBF)
FID .... Field Identifier [*Computer science*]
FID .... Field-Induced Delay [*Astrophysics*]
FID .... Field Instrumentation Division (SAA)
FID .... Field Intelligence Department
FID .... Field Intelligence Division (SAUS)
FID .... Field Ionization Detector (SAUS)
FID .... File Identification (TIMI)
FID .... File Identifier Descriptor (SAUS)
FID .... Flame Ionization Detector
FID .... Flight Implementation Directive (MCD)
FID .... Flight Instrumentation Division [*Langley*]
FID .... Floating Input Distortion
FID .... Food Ingredients Division (SAUS)
FID .... Foolproof Identification [*System*]
FID .... Force Identification [*Military*] (NVT)
FID .... Forecasts-in-Depth (MHDB)
FID .... Foreign Internal Defense
FID .... Format Identification [*Computer science*] (IBMDP)
FID .... Format Identifier (SAUS)
FID .... Free Indirect Discourse
FID .... Free Induction Decay [*Physics*]
FID .... Free into Container Depot [*Business term*]
FID .... Friends in Deed [*An association*]
FID .... Fuel Injector Driver [*Automotive engineering*]
FID .... Fungal Immunodiffusion [*Medicine*] (MELL)
FID .... Fuze, Instantaneous Detonating (SAUS)
FID .... Port Fidalgo [*Alaska*] [*Seismograph station code, US Geological Survey*] (SEIS)
FID4 .... Format Indicator 4 [*Communications term*] (DCT)
FIDA .... Federal Independent Democratic Alliance [*South Africa*] [*Political party*] (EY)
FIDA .... Federation of Industrial Development Associations (SAUO)

FIDA Federation of Industrial Development Organizations (SAUS)
FIDA Fellow of the Institute of Directors, Australia (ODBW)
FID/A FID Committee on Copyright in Connection with Reproduction (SAUS)
FIDA Fondo Internacional de Desarrollo Agricola [*International Fund for Agricultural Development*] [*Spanish*] [*United Nations*] (DUND)
FIDA Fonds International de Developpement Agricole [*International Fund for Agricultural Development*] [*French*] [*United Nations*] (DUND)
FIDA Formyliminodiacetic Acid [*Organic chemistry*]
FIDA French Investment Development Association (SAUO)
FIDA Palestinian Democratic Union Party [*Political party*] (PSAP)
FIDAC Federation Interalliee des Anciens Combattants [*World War I*] [*French*]
FIDAC Film Input to Digital Automatic Computer
FIDACSYS FIDAC [*Film Input to Digital Automatic Computer*] System (NITA)
FIDA Estimator Full Information Dynamic Autoregressive Estimator (SAUS)
FIDAF Federacion Internacional de Asociaciones de Ferreteros y Almacenistas de Hierros [*International Federation of Ironmongers and Iron Merchants Associations*]
FIDAL Fixed-wing Insecticide Dispersal Apparatus, Liquid (SAUS)
FIDAP Fluid Dynamics Analysis Package [*Computer-assisted engineering*]
FIDAPS Forest Inventory Data Processing System (SAUS)
FIDAQ Federation Internationale des Associations de Quincailliers et Marchands de Fer [*International Federation of Ironmongers and Iron Merchants Associations - IFIA*] (EAIO)
FIDAR Futures in Drug Abuse Research (SAUS)
FIDAS Forms oriented interactive data base system (SAUS)
FIDAS Formularorientiertes Interaktives Datenbanksystem [*Forms-Oriented Interactive Database System*] [*Germany*]
FIDASE Falkland Islands and Dependencies Aerial Survey Expedition [*1955-57*]
FIDB Facility Interface Data Bus [*Communications term*] (DCT)
FID/B FID Committee on Bibliography and Abstracting (SAUS)
FID/BCC FID Conference Board of Committee Chairmen (SAUS)
FidBcp Fidelity Bancorp [*Associated Press*] (SAG)
FidBnCh Fidelity Bancorp [*Associated Press*] (SAG)
FID/BSO Panel Board System of Ordering (SAUS)
FID/C 2 Religion FID/C Revision Committee for 2 Religion (SAUS)
FID/CA FID Committee on General Theory of Classification (SAUS)
FID/CAO FID Commission for Asia and Oceania (SAUS)
FID/CAO/AG FID/CAO Agricultural Information and Documentation (SAUS)
FID/CAO/II FID/CAO Information for Secondary Industry (SAUS)
FID/C-AUX FID/C Revision Committee for Auxiliaries (SAUS)
FID/CC FID Committee on Committees (SAUS)
FID/CCC FID Central Classification Committee (SAUS)
FID/CCC/BME FID/CCC Basic Medium Edition of UDC (SAUS)
FID/CCC-D FID/CCC Subcommittee on Development of UDC (SAUS)
FID/CCC/DD FID/CCC Drastic Development of UDC (SAUS)
FID/CCC-EG FID/CCC Executive Group (SAUS)
FID/CCC-F FID/CCC Subcommittee on UDC Fundamentals (SAUS)
FID/CCC/IME FID/CCC International Medium Edition of UDC (SAUS)
FID/CCC-M FID/CCC Subcommittee on Mechanization and UDC (SAUS)
FID/CCC/P FID/CCC Proposals Editing Subcommittee (SAUS)
FID/CCC/RG FID/CCC Rules and Guidelines for UDC (SAUS)
FID/CCC/SN FID/CCC Structure and Notation of UDC (SAUS)
FID/CCC/SRC FID/CCC Standard Reference Code (SAUS)
FID/CCC-UDC FID/CCC Universal Decimal Classification (SAUS)
FID/CLA FID Latin American Commission (SAUS)
FID/CLA FID Regional Commission for Latin America (SAUS)
FID/CN FID Committee on Notation Principles (SAUS)
FID/CNC FID Canadian National Committee (SAUS)
FIDCO Farmers Independent Ditch Co.
FIDCR Federal Interagency Day Care Requirements
FID/CR FID Committee on Classification Research (SAUS)
FID/DC FID Committee for Developing Countries (SAUS)
FID/DC FID Committee on Developing Countries (SAUS)
FID/DE FID Ad Hoc Committee on Multilingual Dictionary of Economics (SAUS)
FID DEF Fidei Defensor [*Defender of the Faith*] [*Latin*] (ROG)
FIDDI Fiber-Distributed Data Interface [*Computing*] (ODA)
FIDD Shearer Fully Integrated Double Drum Shearer (SAUS)
FID/DT FID Committee on the Terminology of Information and Documentation (SAUS)
FIDE Federation de l'Industrie Dentaire en Europe [*Federation of the European Dental Industry*]
FIDE Federation Internationale des Echecs [*International Chess Federation*] [*Switzerland*]
FIDE Federation Internationale pour le Droit Europeen [*International Federation for European Law*] [*Benelux*] (EAIO)
FIDE Formally Integrated Data Environment (EURO)
FIDE Fuzzy Inference Development Environment [*Computer science*]
FIDEGEP Federation Interalliee des Evades de Guerre et des Passeurs
Fidel Fidel Castro (SAUS)
fidel Fidelity (GEAB)
FidelFin Fidelity Financial Corp. [*Associated Press*] (SAG)
FidelNtl Fidelity National Corp. [*Associated Press*] (SAG)
FIDEM Federation Internationale des Editeurs de Medailles [*International Federation of Medal Producers*]
FIDEM Federation Internationale d'Etudes Medievales (EAIO)
FIDER Foundation for Interior Design Education Research (EA)
FIDES Fisheries Data Exchange System (EURO)
FIDES Fonds d'Investissement pour le Developpement Economique et Social [*Investment Fund for Economic and Social Development*] [*United Nations*] (AF)
FIDES Forecaster's Intelligent Discussion Experiment System (USDC)
FIDESY Fire Detection System (SAUO)
FIDESZ Federation of Young Democrats [*Hungary*] [*Political party*] [*Acronym is based on foreign phrase*] (ECON)
FID/ET FID Committee on Education and Training (SAUS)
FIDEX Floating Ice Detection Experiment (SAUO)
FIDF Financial Institutions Data File [*Rand McNally & Co.*] [*Information service or system*] (CRD)
FIDF Fuel Improvement Demonstration Facility (SAUO)
FidFdB Fidelity Federal Bancorp [*Associated Press*] (SAG)
FID/FDC FID/DC Working Group on Film Information (SAUS)
FidFdlSv Fidelity Federal Savings Bank [*Associated Press*] (SAG)
FidFdVA Fidelity FSB [*Associated Press*] (SAG)
FidFnVA Fidelity Financial Bankshares Corp. [*Associated Press*] (SAG)
FIDH Federation Internationale des Droits de l'Homme [*International Federation for Human Rights*] [*Paris, France*] (EA)
FIDI FAO Fishery Information, Data and Statistics Service (SAUS)
FIDI Federation Internationale des Demenageurs Internationaux [*International Federation of International Furniture Removers - IFIFR*] (EAIO)
FID/I FID Committee on Information Services (SAUS)
FIDI Fishery Information, Data and Statistics Service [*Marine science*] (OSRA)
FIDI Forward Intra-Target Data Indicator (ACAE)
FIDIA Federation Internationale des Intellectuels Aveugles
FIDIC Federation Internationale des Ingenieurs Conseils [*International Federation of Consulting Engineers*] (EAIO)
FIDIC International Federation of Consulting Engineers (SAUS)
FIDICS Fujitsu Integrated Digital Communications System (SAUO)
FID/II FID Committee on Information for Industry (SAUS)
FID/IM FID Committee on Informetrics (SAUS)
FID/IS/NW FID Task Force on Information Systems and Network Design and Management (SAUS)
fidivan fiber-diameter video analyzer (SAUS)
FIDJC Federation Internationale des Directeurs de Journaux Catholiques
Fid L Chron Fiduciary Law Chronicle [*A publication*] (DLA)
FID/LD FID Committee on Linguistics in Documentation (SAUS)
FIDLE FIFE Doppler Lidar Experiment (SAUO)
FID/LP FID Committee for Linguistic Problems (SAUS)
FIDLTY Fidelity
FID/MD FID Committee on Medical Documentation (SAUS)
FID/MSR FID Committee on Mechanized Storage and Retrieval (SAUS)
FIDNet Federal Intrusion Detection Network (SEWL)
FIDO Face Information Digested Online (NITA)
FIDO Facility for Integrated Data Organization
FIDO Fallout Intensity Detector Oscillator
FIDO Federal Island Development Organization (SAUO)
FIDO Fighter Interceptor Duty Officer (SAUO)
FIDO Film Industry Defence Organisation [*British*] (DI)
FIDO Film Industry Defence Organization (SAUO)
FiDO Filter Device Object (MWOL)
FIDO Fire Incident Data Organization (SAUO)
FIDO Flame Ionization Detector Optimization [*Automotive emissions*]
FIDO Flight Dynamics Officer [*NASA*]
FIDO Flight Inspection District Office [*FAA*]
FIDO Fluxes in the Deep Ocean Instrument (SAUS)
FIDO Fog Dispersal equipment (SAUS)
FIDO Fog, Intense, Dispersal Of [*NASA*]
FIDO Fog Investigation and Dispersal Operation [*System used on airfield landing strips*] [*World War II*]
FIDO Forget It and Drive On (BB)
FIDO Forklift Independent Distributors Organization (SAUO)
FIDO Frazer Island Defenders Organisation (EERA)
FIDO Freaks, Irregulars, Defects, and Oddities [*Numismatics*]
FIDO Fugitive Information Data Organizer [*Database*]
FIDO Fully Integrated Discovery Organization [*Business term*]
FIDO Function Input Diagnostic Output (SAUS)
FIDOAO Federation Internationale des Diffuseurs d'Oeuvres d'Art Originales [*International Federation of Original Art Diffusors*] [*France*] (EAIO)
FIDOC Firing Doctrine (ACAE)
FIDOF Federation Internationale des Organisateurs de Festivals [*International Federation of Festival Organizations*] (EAIO)
FID/OM FID Committee on Operational Machines Techniques and Systems (SAUS)
FID/OM FID committee on operational machine techniques (SAUS)
FID/OM FID Committee on Operational Machine Techniques and Systems (SAUS)
FIDOR Fibre Building Board Development Organisation Ltd. [*British*] (BI)
FIDP Farm Income Disaster Program (FOTI)
FIDP Fellow of the Institute of Data Processing (WDAA)
FIDP Foreign Internal Defense Plan (MCD)
FIDP Foreign International Defense Policy (SAUO)
FID/PD FID Committee on Patent Information and Documentation (SAUS)
FID/R FID Committee on Technical Means of Documentation (SAUS)
FID/RI FID Committee on Research on the Theoretical Basis of Information (SAUS)
FID/RRS FID Research Referral Service (SAUS)
FIDRS Facilities Interface Data Requirements Sheets (MCD)
FIDS Facility Intrusion Detection System (RDA)
FIDS Falkland Islands Dependencies Survey [*1943-62*]
FIDS Fast Interbroker Delivery Service [*Australian Stock Exchange*]
FID/S FID Committee on Selection (SAUS)
FIDS Flight Information Data System [*United Airlines*]
FIDS Flight Information Display System [*Information service or system*] (IID)

FIDS............ Foolproof Identification System (SAUS)
FID/SD......... FID Committee on Social Sciences Documentation (SAUS)
FID/SRC....... FID Working Group for Standard Reference Code (SAUO)
FID/SUN....... FID Task Force on the Study of User Needs (SAUS)
FID System... Foolproof Identification System (SAUS)
FIDT............ Forced Incident Destiny Testing (IAA)
FIDTA.......... Fellow of the International Dance Teachers' Association [*British*] (DBQ)
FID/TD......... FID Committee for Training of Documentalists (SAUS)
FID/TI.......... FID Committee for Technical Information for Industry (SAUS)
FID/TM......... FID Committee on Theory and Methods of Systems, Cybernetics and Information Networks (SAUS)
FID/TM......... FID Committee on the Theory of Machine Techniques and Systems (SAUS)
FID/TMO...... FID Committee on Theory, Methods and Operation of Information Systems and Networks (SAUS)
FID/TMO...... FID Committee on Theory, Methods and Operations of Information Systems and Networks (SAUS)
FID/TU......... FID Task Force on User Needs and Habits (SAUS)
Fiduciary..... Fiduciary Reporter [*Pennsylvania*] [*A publication*] (DLA)
Fiduciary R (PA)... Fiduciary Reporter [*Pennsylvania*] [*A publication*] (DLA)
Fiduciary Rptr... Fiduciary Reporter [*Pennsylvania*] [*A publication*] (DLA)
Fiduc Rep.... Fiduciary Reporter [*Pennsylvania*] [*A publication*] (DLA)
FIDWV......... Friends of Israel Disabled War Veterans (EA)
FIE.............. Fair Isle [*Scotland*] [*Airport symbol*] (OAG)
FIE.............. Fault Isolation Equipment (MCD)
FIE.............. Federal Information Exchange (SAUS)
FIE.............. Federation Internationale d'Escrime [*International Fencing Federation*]
FIE.............. Federation Internationale des Echecs [*International Chess Federation*]
FIE.............. Feline Infectious Enteritis (SAUS)
FIE.............. Fellow of the Institute of Engineers [*British*]
FIE.............. Feuerstein's Instrumental Enrichment [*Education*] (AEE)
FIE.............. Field Aviation GmbH & Co. [*Germany*] [*ICAO designator*] (FAAC)
FIE.............. Flight Instrumentation Engineer (MCD)
FIE.............. Florida Industries Exposition
FIE.............. Fluoride Ion Electrode (PDAA)
FIE.............. Fly-In Echelon [*Navy*] (ANA)
FIE.............. Foundation for Integrative Education (EA)
FIE.............. Fourier Integral Estimate
FIE.............. Friends of International Education [*An association*] (EA)
FIE.............. Fuel Injection Equipment [*Diesel engines*]
FIEA............ Federation Internationale des Experts en Automobiles [*International Federation of Automobile Experts*] [*Rhode St. Genese, Belgium*] (EAIO)
FIEAust........ Fellow of the Institution of Engineers of Australia (SAUO)
FIEC............ Canadian Classical association (SAUO)
FIEC............ European Construction Industry Federation (SAUS)
FIEC............ Federation de l'Industrie Europeenne de la Construction [*European Construction Industry Federation*] (EAIO)
FIEC............ Federation Internationale des Associations d'Etudes Classiques [*International Federation of the Societies of Classical Studies*] (EAIO)
FIEC............ Fellowship of Independent Evangelical Churches
FIEC............ FORUM for International Cooperation in Fire Research (SAUO)
FIED............ Fellow of the Institution of Engineering Designers [*British*] (DBQ)
FIED............ Field Ionization Energy Distribution (SAUS)
FIEDA.......... Fondation Internationale pour l'Enseignement du Droit des Affaires [*Canada*]
FIEE............ Fellow of the Institute of Electrical Engineers [*British*]
FIEE............ Fellow of the Institution of Electrical Engineers (SAUO)
FIEEE.......... Fellow of the Institute of Electrical and Electronic Engineers
FIEF............ Federation Internationale pour l'Economie Familiale [*International Federation for Home Economics - IFHE*] (EAIO)
FIEFS.......... Funnel Ion-Exchange Fallout Sampler (SAUS)
FIEG............ Federazione Italiana Editori Giornali [*Italian Federation of Newspaper Publishing*] (EY)
FIEGA.......... Federation Internationale d'Eutonie Gerda Alexander [*International Federation for Gerda Alexander Eutony*] [*Belgium*] (EAIO)
FIEI............. Farm and Industrial Equipment Institute (EA)
FIEI............. Fellow of the Institution of Engineering Inspection [*British*]
FIEI............. Fraser Island Environmental Inquiry [*Australia*]
FIElecIE...... Fellow of the Institution of Electronic Incorporated Engineers (ODA)
FIE(India).... Fellow of the Institution of Engineers, India
FIEJ............ Federation Internationale des Editeurs de Journaux [*International Federation of Newspaper Publishers*] [*Paris, France*] (EAIO)
FIELD.......... Field [*Commonly used*] (OPSA)
FIELD.......... First Integrated Experiment for Lunar Development (SAUS)
Field Anal.... Field's Analysis of Blackstone's Commentaries [*A publication*] (DLA)
Field & D Ch Pr... Field and Dunn's Chancery Practice [*A publication*] (DLA)
Field & S..... Field & Stream (journ.) (SAUS)
FIELDATA.... Field Data Computers (SAUS)
Field Com Law... Field on the Common Law of England [*A publication*] (DLA)
Field Corp... Field on Corporations [*A publication*] (DLA)
Field Crops Res... Field Crops Research [*A publication*] (PABS)
Field Cur..... Field on Protestant Curates and Incumbents [*A publication*] (DLA)
Field Dam.... Field on the Law of Damages [*A publication*] (DLA)
Field Ev....... Field's Law of Evidence in British India [*A publication*] (DLA)
Field Int Code... Field's International Code [*A publication*] (DLA)
Fieldistor..... Field Effect Transistor (SAUS)
Field Nat..... Field Naturalist (journ.) (SAUS)
Field on Inh... Field on the Hindu and Mohammedan Laws of Inheritance [*A publication*] (DLA)
Field Pen L... Field's Penal Law [*A publication*] (DLA)
Field Pr Cor... Field on Private Corporations [*A publication*] (DLA)
FIELDS......... Fields [*Commonly used*] (OPSA)
FIELecIE...... Fellow of the Institution of Electrical and Electronics Incorporated Engineers [*British*] (DBQ)
FIELS........... Foreign Information Exchange for Life Scientists (SAUO)
FIEM............ Federation Internationale de l'Enseignement Menager
FIEM............ Fellow of the Institute of Executives and Managers [*British*] (DBQ)
FIEO............ Federation of Indian Export Organisations (or Organizations) (SAUO)
FIEP............ Federation Internationale d'Education Physique [*International Federation for Physical Education*] (EAIO)
FIEP............ Federation Internationale des Etudiants en Pharmacie
FIEP............ Federation Internationale pour l'Education des Parents [*International Federation for Parent Education - IFPE*] [*Sevres, France*] (EAIO)
FIEP............ Forest Industry Energy Program (HGAA)
FIEP............ Foundation for International Economic Policy (EA)
FIER............ Federation Internationale des Enseignants de Rythmique [*International Federation of Teachers of Rhythmics - IFTR*] (EA)
FIER............ Fieramente [*Boldly*] [*Music*] (ROG)
FIER............ Foundation for Instrumentation Education and Research [*Defunct*]
FIERA.......... Ferrous Industry Energy Research Association (SAUO)
FIERE.......... Fellow of the Institution of Electronic and Radio Engineers [*British*]
FIERF.......... Forging Industry Educational and Research Foundation (EA)
FIES............ Federal Information Exchange System (DNAB)
FIES............ Fellow of the Illuminating Engineering Society [*Later, FIllumES*] [*British*]
FIESP.......... Federation Internationale des Etudiants en Sciences Politiques
FIET............ Federation Internationale des Employes, Techniciens, et Cadres [*International Federation of Commercial, Clerical, Professional, and Technical Employees*] [*Geneva, Switzerland*] (EAIO)
FIET............ Field Integration Engineering Test (MCD)
FIEWS.......... Food Information and Early Warning System [*FAO*] [*United Nations*]
FIEx............ Fellow of the Institute of Export [*British*] (DCTA)
FIExE.......... Fellow of the Institute of Executive Engineers and Officers [*British*] (DBQ)
FIEZ............ Fisher Elevator [*Federal Railroad Administration identification code*]
FIF.............. Facsimile Information Field (SAUS)
FIF.............. Failure Indicating Fuse
FIF.............. Family Information Facility (MHDB)
FIF.............. Federation Internationale de la Filterie [*International Thread Federation*] [*EC*] (ECED)
FIF.............. Feedback Inhibition Factor [*Immunochemistry*]
FIF.............. Ferric Ion Free
FIF.............. Fibroblast Interferon [*Genetics*]
FIF.............. Fibroblast-Migration Inhibitory Factor [*Immunochemistry*]
FIF.............. Fifteen [*Lawn tennis*] (DSUE)
FIF.............. Financial Federal [*NYSE symbol*] (SG)
FIF.............. Financial Federal Corp. [*AMEX symbol*] (SPSG)
FIF.............. Financial Information File (SAUS)
FIF.............. First Investment Fund (SAUO)
FIF.............. First Irish Families
FIF.............. Forced Inspiratory Flow [*Physiology*]
FIF.............. Foreign Investment Fund
FIF.............. Forest Industries Federation [*Australia*]
FIF.............. Formaldehyde-Induced Fluorescence
FIF.............. Fractal Image Format [*Computer graphics*] (PCM)
FIF.............. Fractal Interchange Format [*Computer science*] (VERA)
FIF.............. fractionally integrated flux (SAUS)
FIF.............. Frifly SpA [*Italy*] [*ICAO designator*] (FAAC)
FIF.............. Fund of Intellectual Freedom (SAUO)
f-if-............ Ifni [*MARC geographic area code*] [*Library of Congress*] (LCCP)
FIFA............ Federation Internationale de Football Association [*International Federation of Association Football*] [*Zurich, Switzerland*] (EA)
FIFA............ Federation Internationale du Film sur d'Art [*International Federation of Films on Art*]
FI FA........... Fieri Facias [*Cause to Be Made*] [*A writ commanding the sheriff to execute judgment*] [*Legal term*] [*Latin*]
FIFA............ Fissions per Initial Fissile Atom [*Nuclear energy*]
FIFA............ Fissions per Initial Fissionable Atoms (SAUS)
FIFC............ First Fincorp, Inc. (SAUO)
FIFC............ Fur Information and Fashion Council (EA)
FIF Cable.... Foam Insulated Filled Cable (SAUS)
FIFCJ.......... Federation Internationale des Femmes des Carrieres Juridiques [*France*]
FIFCLC........ Federation Internationale des Femmes de Carrieres Liberales et Commerciales [*International Federation of Business and Professional Women*]
FIFCQ.......... Festival International du Film de la Critique Quebecoise [*International Festival of Quebec Film Critics*] [*Canada*]
FIFDA.......... Fellow of the International Furnishings and Design Association (SAUO)
FIFDU.......... Federation Internationale des Femmes Diplomees des Universites [*International Federation of University Women - IFUW*] (EAIO)
FIFE............ American Institute of Fellows in Free Enterprise [*Houston, DE*] (EA)
FIFE............ Federation Internationale des Associations de Fabricants de Produits d'Entretien [*International Federation of Associations of Manufacturers of Household Products*] (EAIO)
FIFE............ Fellow of the Institution of Electrical Engineers [*Canada*] (ASC)
Fife............. Fifeshire (SAUS)
FIFE............ First International Satellite Land Surface Climatology Project (ISLSCP) Field Experiment (SAUS)
FIFE............ First ISLSCP [*International Satellite Land Surface Climatology Project*] Field Experiment [*NASA*]
FIFE............ International Federation of Associations of Cleaning Products Manufacturers (SAUO)
FIFES.......... Fifeshire [*County in Scotland*]

FIFF .... Fellow of the Institute of Freight Forwarders [*British*] (ODBW)
FIFF .... First In First Fit [*Computer science*] (ELAL)
FIFF .... First-In, First-Fit (SAUS)
FIFG .... Financial Instrument for Fisheries Guidance (EURO)
FIFI .... Field Image Feature Interface [*Photovoltaic energy systems*]
FiFI .... Fire Fighting (RIMS)
FIFI .... Flexible Ideal Format for Information
FIFirE .... Fellow of the Institution of Fire Engineers [*British*] (DCTA)
FIFIS .... Fire Fighting Systems (SAUO)
FIFM .... Fellow of the Institute of Factory Managers (SAUO)
FI-FMD .... Function Interpreter for Function Management Data (VLIE)
FIFO .... Fade In, Fade Out [*Films, television, etc.*]
FI/FO .... Fan-In, Fan-Out (SAUS)
fifo .... first in (SAUS)
FIFO .... First In, First Out [*Accounting*]
FIFO .... First In-First Out (SAUS)
FIFO .... Flight Inspection Field Office [*FAA*]
FIFO .... Floating Input - Floating Output [*Computer science*]
FIFO-H .... Flight Inspection Field Office High Altitude (FAAC)
FIFO-I .... Flight Inspection Field Office, Intermediate Altitude [*FAA*] (SAA)
FIFO/LIFO .... First-in-first-out/ Last-in-first-out (SAUS)
FIFOR .... flight forecast (SAUS)
FIFR .... Fasting Intestinal Flow Rate (MAE)
FIFR .... FORUM for International Cooperation in Fire Research (SAUS)
FIFR .... Region 7 FIFRA Neutral Inspection Selection System (SAUO)
FIFRA .... Federal Insecticide, Fungicide, and Rodenticide Act [*1947*] [*Department of Agriculture*]
FIFS .... First Investors Financial Services Group, Inc. [*NASDAQ symbol*] (SAG)
FIFS .... First Investors Finl Svcs Grp [*NASDAQ symbol*] (TTSB)
FIFSP .... Federation Internationale des Fonctionnaires Superieurs de Police [*International Federation of Senior Police Officers*] [*France*]
FIFST .... Fellow of the Institute of Food Science and Technology [*British*]
FifthDim .... Fifth Dimension, Inc. [*Associated Press*] (SAG)
FifthT .... Fifth Third Bancorp [*Associated Press*] (SAG)
FIFV .... Future Infantry Fighting Vehicle [*Army*] (RDA)
FIF(WA) .... Forest Industries Federation, Western Australia
FIFZ .... Fisher Farmer Elevator [*Federal Railroad Administration identification code*]
FIG .... Falkland Islands Government (SAUS)
FIG .... Farmers Group Capital II [*NYSE symbol*] (SAG)
FIG .... Farmers Group Captial [*NYSE symbol*] (SAG)
FIG .... Farmers Insurance Group (SAUO)
FIG .... Federation Internationale de Genetique [*International Genetics Federation*] (EAIO)
FIG .... Federation Internationale de Gymnastique [*International Gymnastic Federation - IGF*] [*Lyss, Switzerland*] (EAIO)
FIG .... Federation Internationale des Geometres [*International Federation of Surveyors - IFS*] [*Edmonton, AB*] (EAIO)
FIG .... Fiber Interferometer Gyroscope (MCD)
FIG .... Fighter Intercepter Group (MCD)
Fig .... Figur (SAUS)
fig .... figurativ (SAUS)
Fig .... Figurative (DIAR)
fig .... Figurative (WDMC)
FIG .... Figurative
fig .... Figuratively (ADWA)
FIG .... Figure (AFM)
fig .... Figure (VRA)
fig .... figures (SAUS)
FIG .... Fishing Industry Grants [*Marine science*] (OSRA)
FIG .... Flight Inspection Group [*FAA*]
FIG .... Floated Integrating Gyro [*Aerospace*] (AAG)
FIG .... Formiminoglyxin (SAUS)
FIG .... Forth Interest Group (SAUS)
FIG .... Fraud Investigation Group [*Serious Fraud Office*] [*British*]
FIG .... Fria [*Guinea*] [*Airport symbol*] (AD)
FIG .... Friends of Internet in Greece [*Discussion list*]
FIG .... International Federation of Surveyors (SAUO)
FIGA .... Fellow, International Geriatric Association (CMD)
FIGA .... Fretted Instrument Guild of America (EA)
FIGA .... Iberian Federation of Anarchist Groups [*Spain*] (PD)
FIGAS .... Falkland Islands Government Air Service (EY)
FIGasE .... Fellow of the Institution of Gas Engineers [*British*]
FIGAT .... Fiberglass Aerial Target (DNAB)
FIGAT .... Fiberglass Optical Target (ACAE)
FIGCM .... Fellow of the Incorporated Guild of Church Musicians [*British*]
FIGD .... Familial Idiopathic Gonadotropin Deficiency [*Medicine*] (DMAA)
FIGD .... Fellow of the Institute of Grocery Distribution [*British*] (DBQ)
FIGE .... Federation de l'Industrie Granitiere Europeenne [*Federation of the European Granite Industry*] (EAIO)
FIGE .... Field Inversion Gel Electrophoresis [*Analytical biochemistry*]
FIGED .... Federation Internationale des Grandes et Moyennes Entreprises de Distribution [*International Federation of Retail Distributors*] (EAIO)
FIGeol .... Fellow of the Institution of Geologists [*British*] (DBQ)
FigEtym .... Figura Etymologica [*A publication*] (BJA)
Figgie .... Figgie International, Inc. [*Associated Press*] (SAG)
FiggieA .... Figgie International [*Associated Press*] (SAG)
FiggieB .... Figgie International [*Associated Press*] (SAG)
FIGHT .... Family Interest Group - Head Trauma (EA)
FIGHT .... Freedom, Independence, God, Honor, Today (IIA)
FIGHTRON .... Fighting Squadron
FIGI .... Figgie International, Inc. [*NASDAQ symbol*] (NQ)
FIGI .... Figgie Intl Cl'B' [*NASDAQ symbol*] (TTSB)
FIGIA .... Figgie Intl Cl'A' [*NASDAQ symbol*] (TTSB)
FIGIEFA .... Federation Internationale des Grossistes, Importateurs, et Exportateurs Fournitures Automobiles [*International Federation of Wholesalers, Importers, and Exporters in Automobile Fittings*] (EAIO)
FIGIJ .... Federation Internationale de Gynecologie Infantile et Juvenile [*International Federation of Infantile and Juvenile Gynecology - IFIJG*] [*Sierre, Switzerland*] (EAIO)
FIGIT .... Follett Implementation Group for Information Technology (SAUO)
FIGLU .... Formiminoglutamic Acid (WDAA)
FIGLU .... Formimino-L-glutamic Acid [*Organic chemistry*]
FIGLU .... Formimino-L-Glutamic Acid Transferase (SAUS)
FIGLU Acid .... Formiminoglutamic Acid (SAUS)
FIGM .... Friends of Israel Gospel Ministry (EA)
FIGO .... Federation Internationale de Gynecologie et d'Obstetrique [*International Federation of Gynecology and Obstetrics*] [*British*] (EAIO)
FIGO .... International Federation of Gynecology and Obstetrics (SAUO)
FIGPrA .... Farmers Grp Cap 8.45% 'QUIPS' [*NYSE symbol*] (TTSB)
FIGPrB .... Farmers Grp Cap II 8.25% 'QUIPS' [*NYSE symbol*] (TTSB)
FIGR .... Faeroe-Iceland-Greenland Ridge (SAUS)
FIGRS .... Fellow of the Irish Genealogical Research Society (SAUO)
FIGS .... Fabray-Perot Infrared Grating Spectrometer [*Chemistry*]
FIGS .... Fellow, International Gastroenterologist's Society (CMD)
figs .... Figures (DIAR)
FIGS .... Figure Shift (SAUS)
FIGS .... Figures Shift [*Teleprinters*]
FIGS .... Fully Integrated Groups (ADWA)
FIGS .... Future Income Growth Security [*Finance*]
figt .... fully inclusive group tour (SAUO)
FIH .... Fat-Induced Hyperglycemia [*Medicine*]
FIH .... Federation Internationale de Handball [*International Handball Federation*]
FIH .... Federation Internationale de Hockey [*International Hockey Federation*] [*Brussels, Belgium*] (EA)
FIH .... Federation Internationale des Hopitaux [*International Hospital Federation*]
FIH .... Fellow of the Institute of Housing [*British*] (DBQ)
FIH .... Fellow of the Institute of Hygiene [*British*]
FIH .... Free in Harbor [*Navigation*]
FIH .... Kinshasa [*Zaire*] [*Airport symbol*] (OAG)
FIH .... Focused-Imaged Holography (ODA)
FIHBJO .... Federation Internationale des Horlogers, Bijoutiers, Joailliers, Orfevres Detaillants de la CE [*International Federation of Retailers in Horology, Jewellery, Gold and Silverware of the EC*] (ECED)
FiHBWE .... National Board of Water and the Environment, Urho Kekkosen Katu, Helsinki, Finland [*Library symbol*] [*Library of Congress*] (LCLS)
FIHC .... Federation Internationale des Hommes Catholiques [*International Council of Catholic Men - ICCM*] [*Vatican City, Vatican City State*] (EAIO)
FIHC .... Federation Internationale Halterophile et Culturiste
FiHCRN .... Finnish Center for Radiation and Nuclear Safety [*Sateilyturvakeskus*], H elsinki, Finland [*Library symbol*] [*Library of Congress*] (LCLS)
FIHE .... Fellow of the Institute of Health Education [*British*]
FIHE .... Fellow of the Institute of Highway Engineers (SAUO)
FIHE .... Foundation for Independent Higher Education (EA)
FiHK .... Kauppakorkeakoulu [*Helsinki School of Economics*], Helsinki, Finland [*Library symbol*] [*Library of Congress*] (LCLS)
FIHM .... Fellow of the Institute of Housing Managers [*Formerly, FIHsg*] [*British*]
FiHMR .... Institute of Marine Research, Helsinki, Finland [*Library symbol*] [*Library of Congress*] (LCLS)
FIHospE .... Fellow of the Institute of Hospital Engineering [*British*] (DI)
FIHP .... Filter-High Pass (SAUS)
FIHR .... Foundation for International Human Relations (EA)
FiHR .... Oy Rekolid, Mikrofilmipalvelu, Helsinki, Finland [*Library symbol*] [*Library of Congress*] (LCLS)
FIHS .... Fellow of the Institute of Hospital Secretaries [*British*]
FIHsg .... Fellow of the Institute of Housing [*Later, FIHM*] [*British*]
FIHT .... Fellow of the Institution of Highway Engineers [*British*] (DBQ)
FiHT .... Valtion Teknillinen Tutkimuskeskus, Helsinki, Finland [*Library symbol*] [*Library of Congress*] (LCLS)
FIHU .... Federation Internationale de l'Habitation et de l'Urbanisme
FiHU .... Helsingin Yliopisto [*University of Helsinki*], Helsinki, Finland [*Library symbol*] [*Library of Congress*] (LCLS)
FiHU-A .... Helsinki University, Library of Agriculture, Viikki, Helsinki, Finland [*Library symbol*] [*Library of Congress*] (LCLS)
FIHUAT .... Federation Internationale pour l'Habitation, l'Urbanisme et l'Amenagement des Territoires [*International Federation for Housing and Planning - IFHP*] [*The Hague, Netherlands*] (EA)
FiHU-F .... Helsinki University Library of Forestry [*Helsingin Yliopiston Metsakirjaston*], Helsinki, Finland [*Library symbol*] [*Library of Congress*] (LCLS)
FIHVE .... Fellow of the Institution of Heating and Ventilating Engineers [*British*]
FII .... FARMS International, Inc. (EA)
FII .... Federal Item Identification
FII .... Federated Investors 'B' [*NYSE symbol*] (SG)
FII .... Federation of Irish Industries (SAUS)
FII .... Federation of Irish Industries, Ltd. (SAUO)
FII .... Fellow of the Imperial Institute [*British*] (DAS)
FII .... Field Installation Instruction (VLIE)
FII .... Fisheries Industries Institute (SAUS)
FII .... Fletcher Challenge Investments II [*Toronto Stock Exchange symbol*] [*Vancouver Stock Exchange symbol*]

FII .... Food Industry Institute [*Michigan State University*] [*Research center*] (RCD)
FII .... Foreign Investment Institute (SAUO)
FII .... Franked Investment Income [*Accounting*]
FIIA .... Fellow of the Institute of Industrial Administration [*Later, FBIM*] [*British*]
FIIA .... First Interstate of Iowa, Inc. (SAUO)
FIIAL .... Fellow of the International Institute of Arts and Letters (SAUO)
FIIC .... Federacion Interamericana de la Industria de la Construccion [*Inter-American Federation of the Construction Industry - IAFCI*] (EAIO)
FIIC .... Fellow of the Insurance Institute of Canada
FIIC .... Field Impact Insulation Class (DAC)
FIIC .... Flight Inspector in Charge
FIICPI .... Federation Internationale des Ingenieurs-Conseils en Propriete Industrielle
FIICU .... Federation of Independent Illinois Colleges and Universities (SAUO)
FIID .... Federation Internationale d'Information et de Documentation [*International Federation for Information and Documentation - IFID*] (EAIO)
FIIF .... Florafax International, Inc. [*NASDAQ symbol*] (COMM)
FIIG .... Federal Item Identification Guides
FIIG .... Federal Item Inventory Group
FIIG .... Federation des Institutions Internationales Semi-Officielles et Privees Etabliesa Geneve [*Federation of Semi-Official and Private International Institutions Established in Geneva*] [*Switzerland*] (EA)
FIIG .... Flight Instructions Indoctrination Group (SAUO)
FIIGMO .... Forget It, I've Got My Orders [*Bowdlerized version*] [*Military slang*]
FIIGS .... Federal Item Identification Guide System
FIIGSC .... Federal Item Identification Guides for Supply Cataloging (AABC)
FIIHE .... Federation Internationale des Instituts de Hautes Etudes [*International Federation of Institutes for Advanced Study*] (EAIO)
FIIIV .... Full Information Iterated Instrumental Variable (SAUS)
FIIIX .... Invesco Industrial Income [*Mutual fund ticker symbol*] (SG)
FIILS .... Full Integrity Instrument Landing System
FIIM .... Federation Internationale de l'Industrie du Medicament [*International Federation of Pharmaceutical Manufacturers Associations - IFPMA*] (EAIO)
FIIM .... Federation Internationale des Ingenieurs Municipaux [*International Federation of Municipal Engineers - IFME*] (EAIO)
FIIM .... Fellow of the Institute of Industrial Managers (SAUS)
FIIM .... Fellow of the Institution of Industrial Managers [*British*] (DCTA)
FIIN .... Federal Item Identification Number
FIInfSc .... Fellow of the Institute of Information Scientists [*British*]
FIInst .... Fellow of the Imperial Institute [*British*]
FIIP .... Federation Internationale de l'Industrie Phonographique
FIIRO .... Federal Institute of Industrial Research Oshodi (SAUO)
FIIS .... Food Industry Information System (SAUS)
FIISE .... Fellow of the International Institute of Social Economics [*British*] (DBQ)
FIISec .... Fellow of the Institute of Industrial Security [*British*] (DBQ)
FIIT .... Fault Isolation Interface Test (VLIE)
FIIT .... Federal Individual Income Tax (SAUS)
FIIT .... Flash Internal Information Transfer (SAUO)
FIJ .... Federation Internationale de Judo [*International Judo Federation*]
FIJ .... Federation Internationale des Journalistes [*International Federation of Journalists - IFJ*] [*Brussels, Belgium*] (EAIO)
FIJ .... Fellow of the Institute of Journalists [*British*]
FIJ .... Fund for Investigative Journalism (EA)
FIJA .... Fully Informed Jury Association (EA)
FIJB .... Fondation Internationale Jacques Brel [*International Jacques Brel Foundation - IJBF*] (EA)
FIJBT .... Federation Internationale des Jeunesse Bons Templiers [*International Good Templar Youth Federation*] (EAIO)
FIJC .... Federation Internationale de la Jeunesse Catholique
FIJET .... Federation Internationale des Journalistes et Ecrivains du Tourisme [*World Federation of Travel Journalists and Writers*] [*Paris, France*] (EA)
Fiji .... Dominion of Fiji (SAUS)
Fiji LR .... Fiji Law Reports [*A publication*] (DLA)
Fijis .... Fiji islanders (SAUS)
Fijis .... Fiji Islands (SAUS)
FIJL .... Federation Internationale des Journalistes Libres [*International Federation of Free Journalists*]
FIJM .... Federation Internationale des Jeunesses Musicales [*International Federation of Jeunesses Musicales*] (EAIO)
FIJPA .... Federation Internationale des Journalistes Professionnels de l'Aeronautique
FIJU .... Federation Internationale des Producteurs de Jus de Fruits [*International Federation of Fruit Juice Producers - IFFJP*] (EAIO)
Fik .... Families Including Kids [*Lifestyle classification*]
FIK .... Field Ionization Kinetics
FIL .... Avia Filipines International, Inc. [*Philippines*] [*ICAO designator*] (FAAC)
FIL .... Father-in-Law (ADWA)
FIL .... Federal Industries Ltd. [*Toronto Stock Exchange symbol*]
FIL .... Federation Internationale de Laiterie [*International Dairy Federation - IDF*] (EAIO)
FIL .... Federation Internationale de Luge de Course [*International Luge Federation - ILF*] [*Rottenmann, Austria*] (EA)
FIL .... Fellow of the Institute of Linguists [*British*] (EY)
fil .... Filament (IDOE)
FIL .... Filament (KSC)
fil .... Filamentous (SAUS)
FIL .... Filigree [*Jewelry*] (ROG)
FIL .... Fillet (MSA)
FIL .... Filling (SAUS)
FIL .... Fillister
Fil .... Fillmore (SAUS)
fil .... filltrate (SAUS)
FIL .... Film (SAUS)
Fil .... Filmore (SAUS)
Fil .... Filpot (SAUS)
Fil .... Filpotts (SAUS)
FIL .... Filter (AABC)
FIL .... Filtrate (SAUS)
FIL .... financial intermediary loan (SAUS)
FIL .... Firearm Image Library (SAUO)
FIL .... Firestone Indy Lights [*Auto racing*]
FIL .... Florida Instructional League [*Baseball*]
FIL .... Foreign Insurance Legislation (SAUS)
FIL .... Foreign Investment Law
FIL .... Formal Intermediate Language (SAUS)
FIL .... Forum for Interlending (SAUS)
FIL .... Franklin Institute Laboratories (MUGU)
FIL .... Fuel Injection Line (MSA)
FIL .... Fuzzy Interface Language (SAUS)
FIL .... National Film Archives, Film Canadiana [*UTLAS symbol*]
FIL .... Sanifill, Inc. [*NYSE symbol*] (SPSG)
FILA .... Farm Improvement Loans Act [*Canada*]
FILA .... Federation Internationale de Lutte Amateur [*International Amateur Wrestling Federation*] [*Lausanne, Switzerland*] (EAIO)
FILA .... Federation of Indian Library Association (SAUS)
FILA .... Federation of Indian Library Associations (SAUO)
FILA .... Fellow of the Institute of Landscape Architects [*British*]
FILA .... Fighting Intruders at Low Altitude (SAUS)
FILA .... Filament (SAUS)
Fil Act Tst .... Filament Activity Test (SAUS)
FilaHold .... Fila Holdings SA [*Associated Press*] (SAG)
FILAM .... Fellow of the Institute of Leisure and Amenity Management [*British*] (DBQ)
Fil-Am .... Filipino-American (SAUS)
FILAN .... Fibronics Integrated Local Area Network (SAUS)
FILAR .... Filariasis [*Infectious disease*] (DAVI)
FILBAS .... Philippine Base [*Army*] [*World War II*]
FILBDLP .... Fondation Internationale Lelio Basso pour le Droit et la Liberation des Peuples [*International Lelio Basso Foundation for the Rights and Liberation of Peoples - ILBFRLP*] (EA)
FilBsmt .... Filenes Basement Corp. [*Associated Press*] (SAG)
FILCEN .... Filter Center
FILCO .... Film Coalition [*Defunct*] (EA)
FILD .... Federal Item Logistics Data
FILD .... Fumeless In-Line Degassing (PDAA)
FILDIR .... Federation Internationale Libre des Deportes et Internes de la Resistance [*International Free Federation of Deportees and Resistance Internees*]
Fil Dr .... Doctor of Philology
FILDR .... Federal Item Logistics Data Record
FILE .... Family Inventory of Life Events and Changes
FILE .... Fast Index Location Educators
FILE .... Feature Identification and Landmark Experiment [*NASA*]
FILE .... Fellow of the Institute of Legal Executives [*British*] (DLA)
FILE .... FileNet Corp. [*NASDAQ symbol*] (NQ)
FILE .... Florida Institute for Law Enforcement [*St. Petersburg Junior College*] [*Research center*] (RCD)
FILE .... Future Identification and Location Experiment [*NASA*] (NASA)
FILE .... On STS-2 Feature Identification and Location Experiment (SAUO)
FILEM .... File Management System (SAUS)
FileNet .... FileNet Corp. [*Associated Press*] (SAG)
FILER .... File Information Language Executive Routine [*Computer science*]
FIL et HOER .... Filius [*or Filia*] et Hoeres [*Latin*] (ROG)
FILEX .... File Exchange
FILFP .... Forum International de Liaison des Forces de la Paix [*International Liaison Forum of Peace Forces - ILF*] [*Moscow, USSR*] (EAIO)
FILG .... Filing (ROG)
FI IGO .... Floating Input To Ground Output (SAUS)
FILH .... Fillister Head [*Screws*]
FILHB .... Fillister Head Brass [*Screw*] (IAA)
fil hd .... fillister head (SAUS)
FILHS .... Fillister Head Steel [*Screw*] (IAA)
FILIP .... Florida Interlibrary Loan Improvement Project (SAUS)
Fil Kand .... Candidate in Philosophy
FILL .... Fillet (VLIE)
FILL .... Filling
FILL .... Fleet Issue Load List [*Navy*]
Fil Lic .... Licentiate in Philosophy
FILLM .... Federation Internationale des Langues et Litteratures Modernes [*International Federation for Modern Languages and Literatures*] (EAIO)
FILLS .... Fast Inter-Library Loans and Statistics [*MacNeal Hospital*] [*Information service or system*] (IID)
FILLS .... fast library loans and statistics (SAUS)
FILLS .... Federated Inter-Library Loan Service (SAUS)
FIllumES .... Fellow of the Illuminating Engineering Society [*Formerly, FIES*] [*British*]
FILM .... Children's Broadcasting [*NASDAQ symbol*] (SG)
FILM .... CSIRO [*Commonwealth Scientific and Industrial Research Organisation*] Films [*Database*]
FILM .... Federal Land Manager (GNE)

FILM .... For Illustrating Legal Methods [*Student legal action organization*] (EA)
FILM .... Hollywood Productions, Inc. [*NASDAQ symbol*] (SAG)
Film Cr .... Film Criticism [*A publication*] (BRI)
Film Libr Q... Film Library Quarterly (journ.) (SAUS)
Filmnet .... Film Users Network [*Cine Information*] [*Information service or system*] (IID)
FilmRm......... Film Roman, Inc. [*Associated Press*] (SAG)
FILMSORT ... Microfilm Sorter [*Electronics*]
filn .... Filtration (SAUS)
filo .... first in (SAUS)
FILO .... First In, Last Out [*Accounting*]
FILOS .... Far-Infrared Limb Observing Spectrometer (SAUS)
FILOS-process... full implantation local oxidation of silicon process (SAUS)
FILOS Process... Full Implementation Local Oxidation of Silicon Process (SAUS)
FILOS-Prozea... full implantation local oxidation of silicon process (SAUS)
FILP .... Fiscal Investment and Loan Programme [*Japan*]
FILRAP .... Formal Integrate Long Range Planning (PDAA)
FILS .... Federal Government Information Locator System (SAUS)
FILS .... Federal Information Locator System
FILS .... field ionization LASER spectroscopy (SAUS)
FILS .... Flarescan Instrument Landing System
FILS .... Foreign Intelligence Literary Scene (CARL)
FILS .... Fujitsu Image Library System (SAUO)
FILSCAF....... Family of Improved Lightweight, Secure Storage Containers for the Army in the Field (SAUO)
FILSCAF....... Family of Improved Lightweight, Secure Storage Containers for the Army in the Fire (SAUS)
FILSG........... Fels Institute of Local and State Governments [*University of Pennsylvania*]
FILSUP .... Filament Supply (IAA)
FILSYS......... File Handling Subsystem (SAUO)
FILSYS......... File System (VLIE)
FILT .... Federation Internationale de Lawn Tennis [*International Lawn Tennis Federation*]
FILT .... Filtra [*Filter*] [*Pharmacy*]
filt.............. filtrate (SAUS)
FILT .... Filtration (SAUS)
FILt .... flashing light (SAUS)
FILTAN......... Filter Analysis (SAUS)
FILTAN......... Passive Filter Analysis (SAUS)
FILTH........... For Improved Labeling to Terminate Hazards [*Student legal action organization*]
Fil Tr .... Filament Transformer (SAUS)
FILTR........... Filter (SAUS)
Filtr Sep ...... Filtration and Separation (journ.) (SAUS)
FILU............. Federation of Information Users (SAUO)
FILU............. Florida International University (SAUO)
FILU............. Forward Interpretation Unit (SAUS)
FILU............. Four-BIT [*Binary Digit*] Interface Logic Unit
FILUP........... Franklin Institute Laboratories Universal Pulser (KSC)
FILU Pulser... Franklin Institute Laboratories Universal Pulser (SAUS)
FIM.............. Fabric Insulation Material
FIM.............. Facility inspection methodology (SAUS)
FIM.............. Facing Identification Mark [*Postal Service*]
FIM.............. Factory Inspectorate Minute (HEAS)
FIM.............. Fairness in Media (EA)
FIM.............. Far-Infrared MASER [*Microwave Amplification by Stimulated Emission of Radiation*]
FIM.............. Fault Isolation Meter (MCD)
FIM.............. Fault Isolation Module (CAAL)
FIM.............. Federation Internationale des Mineurs [*Miners' International Federation - MIF*] [*Brussels, Belgium*] (EAIO)
FIM.............. Federation Internationale des Musiciens [*International Federation of Musicians*] [*Zurich, Switzerland*] (EAIO)
FIM.............. Federation Internationale Motocycliste [*International Motorcycle Federation*] [*Geneva, Switzerland*] (EAIO)
FIM.............. Fellow of the Institute of Materials (DD)
FIM.............. Fellow of the Institute of Metallurgists [*British*] (EY)
FIM.............. Fellow of the Institute of Metals [*British*]
FIM.............. Fellow of the Institute of Mining (SAUO)
FIM.............. Fellow of the Institute of Mining and Metallurgy (SAUS)
FIM.............. Fellow of the Institution of Metallurgists (SAUO)
FIM.............. Fellowship International Mission (EA)
FIM.............. Fellowship of Independent Missions (EA)
FIM.............. Fetch Immediate (SAUS)
FIM.............. Fiber Interface Module (VLIE)
FIM.............. Field Induction Model (SAUS)
FIM.............. Field Inspection Manual (NRCH)
FIM.............. Field Instruction Memorandum
FIM.............. Field Intensity Meter
FIM.............. Field Ion Microscope [*or Microscopy*]
FIM.............. Fillmore, CA [*Location identifier*] [*FAA*] (FAAL)
FIM.............. Finnish Institute of Management (SAUO)
FIM.............. Finnish Mark (SAUS)
FIM.............. Finnmark [*Finnish Mark*] [*Monetary unit*]
FIM.............. Firing Instruction Manual (ACAE)
FIM.............. Flame Ionization Method (PDAA)
FIM.............. Flexible Intelligent Manufacturing (VLIE)
FIM.............. Flight Information Manual
FIM.............. Flight Information Memorandum (ACAE)
FIM.............. Flight Integrity Management (MCD)
FIM.............. Flight Interruption Manifest [*Travel industry*] (TRID)
FIM.............. Food Industries Manual (SAUO)
FIM.............. Foundation for Innovation in Medicine (EA)
FIM.............. Foundation for International Meetings (EA)
FIM.............. frequency intermodulation (SAUS)
FIM.............. Friable Insulation Material (GNE)
FIM.............. Front Interface Module [*Computer science*]
FIM.............. Full Indicator Movement (MSA)
FIM.............. Functional Independence Measure [*Occupational therapy*]
FIM.............. Independent Clean Government Front (Peru) [*Political party*] (PSAP)
FIMA............ Fault Isolation Maintainability Analysis (MCD)
FIMA............ Fellow, Industrial Medical Association (CMD)
FIMA............ Fellow of the Industrial Medical Association (SAUO)
FIMA............ Fellow of the Institute of Mathematics and its Application [*British*]
FIMA............ Fellow of the Institute of Municipal Administration (SAUO)
FIMA............ Fellow of the Institute of Municipal Treasurers and Accountants [*British*]
FIMA............ Financial Institutions Marketing Association [*Chicago, IL*] (EA)
FIMA............ Financial Management System (USDC)
FIMA............ Fission Initial Metal Atom [*Nuclear energy*] (NRCH)
FIMA............ Fissions per Initial Metal Atoms (SAUS)
FIMA............ Future International Medium Aircraft (SAUS)
FIMA............ Future International Medium Airlifter (SAUS)
FIMA............ Future International Military/Civil Airfighter [*British*]
FIMACO .... Financial Management Co.
FIManf......... Fellow of the Institute of Manufacturing [*British*] (DBQ)
FIMARC .... Federation Internationale des Mouvements d'Adultes Ruraux Catholiques [*International Federation of Adult Rural Catholic Movements*]
FIMarE......... Fellow of the Institute of Marine Engineers [*British*]
FIMAS.......... Financial Institution Message Authentication Standard (VERA)
FIMATE........ Factory-Installed Maintenance Automatic Test Equipment
FIMATE........ Field-Installed Maintenance Automatic Test Equipment (SAUO)
FIMBE.......... Focused Ion Molecular Beam Epitaxy (VLIE)
FIMBI........... Fellow of the Institute of Medical and Biological Illustration [*British*] (DBQ)
FIMBM......... Fellow of the Institute of Municipal Building Management [*British*] (DBQ)
FIMBRA .... Financial Intermediaries, Managers, and Brokers Association [*British*] (ECON)
FIMBRA .... Financial Intermediaries Managers and Brokers Authority (SAUS)
FIMC............ Federal Interagency Media Committee (EGAO)
FIMC............ Fellow of the Institute of Management Consultants [*British*]
FIMC............ Forest Industries Management Center (SAUS)
FIMCAP........ Federation Internationale de Communautes de Jeunesse Catholique Paroissiales [*International Federation of Catholic Parochial Youth Communities*] [*Antwerp, Belgium*] (EAIO)
FIMCEE........ Federation de l'Industrie Marbriere de la Communaute Economique Europeenne [*Federation of the Marble Industry of the European Economic Community*] (EAIO)
FIMCLA........ Farm Improvement and Marketing Co-Operatives Loans Act (FOTI)
FIMD............ Fluorescence-Imaged Microdeformation [*Analytical chemistry*]
FIMD............ Foot-In-Mouth Disease (SAUS)
FIME............ Federation Internationale des Maisons de l'Europe [*International Federation of Europe Houses - IFEH*] (EAIO)
FIME............ Fellow of the Institute of Marine Engineers [*British*] (DCTA)
FIME............ Fellow of the Institute of Mechanical Engineers (SAUO)
FIME............ Fluorouracil, ICRF-159 [*Razoxane*], MeCCNU [*Semustine*] [*Antineoplastic drug regimen*]
FIMechE ...... Fellow of the Institute of Mechanical Engineers (SAUS)
FI Mech E.... Fellow of the Institution of Mechanical Engineers [*British*]
FIMEM......... Federation Internationale des Mouvements d'Ecole Moderne (EAIO)
FIMF............ Federacion Internacional de Medecina Fisica [*International Federation of Physical Medicine*]
FIMF............ Fellow of the Institute of Metal Finishing [*British*] (DBQ)
FIMG............ Facilities Installation Monitoring Group (MUGU)
FIMG............ Fischer Imaging [*NASDAQ symbol*] (TTSB)
FIMG............ Fisher Imaging Corp. [*NASDAQ symbol*] (SPSG)
FIMgt........... Fellow of the Institute of Management (DD)
FIMGTechE... Fellow of the Institution of Mechanical and General Technician Engineers [*British*] (DBQ)
FIMH............ Fellow of the Institute of Materials Handling [*British*] (DBQ)
FIMI............. Fellow of the Institute of the Motor Industry [*Formerly, FIMT*] [*British*]
FIMIG-CEE ... Federation of the Marble Industry of the European Economic Community (EAIO)
FIMinE......... Fellow of the Institution of Mining Engineers [*British*]
FIMIS........... Financial Management Information System [*Army*]
FIMIS........... Fishery Management Information System [*Marine science*] (OSRA)
FIMIT........... Fellow of the Institute of Instrument Technology (SAUS)
FIMIT........... Fellow of the Institute of Musical Instrument Technology (SAUO)
FIMIT........... Fellow of the Institute of Music Instrument Technology [*British*]
FIMITIC........ Federation Internationale des Mutiles, des Invalides du Travail, et des Inval ides Civils [*International Federation of Disabled Workmen and Civilian Handicapped*] (EAIO)
FIML............ Full-Information Maximum Likelihood [*Econometrics*]
FIM L........... Full-Information Maximum Likelihood (SAUS)
FIMLS.......... Fellow of the Institute of Medical Laboratory Sciences [*British*] (DBQ)
FIMLT.......... Fellow of the Institute of Medical Laboratory Technology [*British*] (DI)
FIMM........... Federation Internationale de Medicine Manuelle [*International Federation of Manual Medicine*] [*Zurich, Switzerland*] (EAIO)
FIMM........... Fellow of the Institute of Mining and Metallurgy (SAUS)
FIMM........... Fellow of the Institution of Mining and Metallurgy [*British*] (DBQ)
FIMM........... Finite Input Memory Machine (SAUS)
FIMM........... Flexible Intelligent Microelectronics Manufacturing (VLIE)
FIMM........... Mauritius Flight Information Center [*ICAO location identifier*] (ICLI)
FIMOC .... Federation Internationale des Mouvements Ouvriers Chretiens [*International Federation of Christian Workers Movements*]
FIMOS .... Floating-Gate Ionization Injection Metal-Oxide Semiconductor (SAUS)

FIMP .... Fault Isolation Major Program (SAUO)
FIMP .... Federation Internationale de Medecine Physique [*International Federation of Physical Medicine*]
F Imp .... Field Imprisonment [*British military*] (DMA)
FIMP .... Mauritius/Sir Seewoosagur Ramgoolam International [*ICAO location identifier*] (ICLI)
FIMPACS ..... Fashion Integrated Merchandising Planning and Control System (BUR)
FIMPS .... Federation Internationale de Medecine Preventive et Sociale [*International Federation for Preventive and Social Medicine*] (EAIO)
FIMR .... Federal Information Resource Management Regulations Interagency Advisory Council [*Information Resources Management Service*] [*General Services Administration*]
FIMR .... Finnish Institute of Marine Research (SAUO)
FIMR .... Rodriguez Island/Plaine Corail [*Mauritius*] [*ICAO location identifier*] (ICLI)
FIMS .... Facility Information Management System (MCD)
FIMS .... Fault Isolation and Monitoring System [*NGT*] (MCD)
FIMS .... Federation Internationale Medecine Sportive [*International Federation of Sportive Medicine*]
FIMS .... Fellow of the Institute of Management Specialists [*British*] (DBQ)
FIMS .... Fellowship of Interdenominational Missionary Societies
FIMS .... Ferranti Integrated Mine Countermeasures System (SAUS)
FIMS .... Field Intensity Measuring System
FIMS .... Field Ionization Mass Spectrometry [*Air-pollutant detector*]
FIMS .... Financial Information Management System [*Computer science*] (EERA)
FIMS .... Fine-Split Infrared Multispectral Scanner (SAUS)
FIMS .... Firestone Inventory Management System (SAUO)
FIMS .... Fluorescence Imaging MicroSpectrophotometer
FIMS .... Form In-Mold Surfacing [*Plastics technology*]
FIMS .... Forms Integration Management Standard (SAUO)
FIMS .... Forms Interface Management System (RALS)
FIMS .... Friendly Iron Moulders Society [*A union*] [*British*]
FIMS .... Functionally-Identifiable Maintenance System [*Computer science*] (EECA)
FIMS .... Functionally Identification Maintenance System (SAUO)
FIMS .... Functionally Identified Maintenance System (SAUO)
FIMS .... Fellow of the Institute of Mathematical Statistics (ODA)
FIMT .... Fellow of the Institute of Motor Trade [*Later, FIMI*] [*British*]
FIMT .... Firefinder Intermediate Maintenance Trainer (DWSG)
FIMTA .... Fellow of the Institute of Municipal Treasurers and Accountants [*British*]
FIMunE .... Fellow of the Institution of Municipal Engineers [*British*]
FIMV .... Figwort Mosaic Virus [*Plant pathology*]
FIN .... Ad Finem [*At or To the End*] [*Latin*] (ADA)
Fin .... De Finibus [*of Cicero*] [*Classical studies*] (OCD)
FIN .... facility information message (SAUS)
FIN .... Factory Inspectorate Note (HEAS)
FIN .... Federal Identification Number
FIN .... Federal Information Network (SAUS)
FIN .... Federal Item Name
FIN .... Federated Information Network (SAUS)
FIN .... Fellow of the Institute of Navigation [*British*]
FIN .... Fetch Indirect (SAUS)
FIN .... Fiduciary Identification Number [*IRS*]
FIN .... Field Information Notice (SAUS)
FIN .... Final (WDAA)
FIN .... Finance [*or Financial*] (AFM)
fin .... Finance (DD)
Fin .... Finance (EBF)
FIN .... Finance Department (SAUS)
FIN .... Finance Department of AHFC (SAUO)
FIN .... Finance Division (SAUS)
Fin .... Financial (AAGC)
fin .... Financial (WDMC)
FIN .... Financial plan (SAUS)
FIN .... Financial Responsibility [*Motor vehicle violation status code used in state of Arkansas*] (MVRD)
FIN .... Financier (WDAA)
Fin .... Finch's English Chancery Reports [*1673-81*] [*A publication*] (DLA)
FIN .... Findlay College, Findlay, OH [*OCLC symbol*] (OCLC)
FIN .... Fine Intestinal Needle [*Medicine*] (DMAA)
Fin .... Finger
FIN .... Finis [*The End*] [*Latin*]
fin .... Finish (ADWA)
FIN .... Finish (KSC)
Fin .... Finish (MIST)
fin .... Finished (VRA)
Fin .... Finish this Treatment (SPVS)
FIN .... Finland [*ANSI three-letter standard code*] (CNC)
Fin .... Finland (SHCU)
Fin .... Finlay's Irish Digest [*A publication*] (DLA)
FIN .... Finnair OY [*Finland*] [*ICAO designator*] (FAAC)
Fin .... Finnic (SAUS)
Fin .... Finnish (DIAR)
FIN .... Finnish (SAUS)
fin .... Finnish [*MARC language code*] [*Library of Congress*] (LCCP)
FIN .... Finschhafen [*Papua New Guinea*] [*Airport symbol*] (OAG)
FIN .... Firearm Identification Number (FOTI)
FIN .... Fish Information Network (CARB)
FIN .... Fishmeal Information Network (GVA)
FIN .... Fleet Identification Number [*Automobile sales*]
FIN .... Flexible Interface Network (SAUS)
FIN .... Flight Interneuron [*Zoology*]
FIN .... FOCI Interactive Network (SAUS)
FIN .... Focused Information Network (EERA)
FIN .... Food Irradiation Network (SAUO)
FIN .... Franklin Real Estate Income Fund [*AMEX symbol*] (SPSG)
FIN .... Frente de Integracion Nacional [*Front for National Integration*] [*Guatemala*]
FIN .... Futures Information Network [*Defunct*] (EA)
FINA .... Federation Internationale de Natation Amateur [*International Amateur Swimming Federation*] [*Vancouver, BC*]
Fina .... Fina, Inc. [*Associated Press*] (SAG)
FINA .... Following Items Not Available
FINABEL ...... France, Italy, Netherlands, Allemagne, Belgium, Luxembourg [*Army Chiefs of Staff Joint Committee*] (PDAA)
FINAC .... Fast Interline Nonactivate Automatic Control [*AT & T*]
FINAC .... Field Notice to Airmen is Current (SAUS)
FinAF .... Finnish Air Force
FINAFRICA... Centre for Financial Assistance to African Countries (SAUO)
FINAL .... Financial Analysis Language [*Computer science*]
FINALCL ...... Final Coordination Line [*Military*]
FINAN .... Financial
Finance Devel... Finance and Development [*A publication*] (JLIT)
Finance Trade Rev... Finance and Trade Review [*A publication*] (JLIT)
FinancSci .... Financing for Science International, Inc. [*Associated Press*] (SAG)
Financ Times... Financial Times (journ.) (SAUS)
Financ World... Financial World (journ.) (SAUS)
FINANDAS ... Contractor Financial Data Retrieval and Analysis System (SAUS)
Fin & Dul..... Finnemore and Dulcken's Natal Law Reports [*A publication*] (DLA)
Finan Hist Rev... Financial History Review [*A publication*] (JLIT)
Finan Industry Stud... Financial Industry Studies [*A publication*] (JLIT)
Finan Manage... Financial Management [*A publication*] (JLIT)
Finan Markets, Inst Instruments... Financial Markets, Institutions and Instruments [*A publication*] (JLIT)
Finan Practice Educ... Financial Practice and Education [*A publication*] (JLIT)
Finan Rev.... Financial Review [*A publication*] (JLIT)
FINANSAT.... Financial Satellite Corp. [*Washington, DC*] [*Telecommunications service*] (TSSD)
FINAR .... Financial Analysis and Reporting (MHDB)
FINART .... Feria Internacional de Artesania
FINASA .... Financiera Nacional Azucarera, SNC [*Mexico*] (EY)
FINAST .... First National Stores, Inc.
FINAST .... First National Supermarkets, Inc. (EFIS)
FINAT .... Federation Internationale des Fabricants et Transformateurs d'Adhesifs et Thermocollants sur Papiers et Autres Supports [*International Federation of Manufacturers and Converters of Pressure-Sensitive and Heatseals on Paper and Other Base Materials*] (EAIO)
FINAT .... International Federation of Manufacturers and Converters of Pressure-Sensitive and Heatseal Materials on Paper and other (SAUO)
FINBIN .... Finnish Biodiversity Information Network (SAUS)
Fin C........... Financial Code (DLA)
FINCA .... Foundation for International Community Assistance (EA)
FINCC .... Familial Idiopathic Nonarteriosclerotic Cerebral Calcification [*Medicine*] (EDAA)
FINCEN .... Financial Crimes Enforcement Network [*Federal task force*]
Finch .... English Chancery Reports Tempore Finch [*A publication*] (DLA)
Finch .... Finch's Precedents in Chancery [*England*] [*A publication*] (DLA)
Finch Cas Cont... Finch's Cases on Contract [*1886*] [*A publication*] (DLA)
Finch Cas Contr... Finch's Cases on Contract [*1886*] [*A publication*] (DLA)
Finch (Eng)... English Chancery Reports Tempore Finch [*A publication*] (DLA)
Finch (Eng)... Finch's Precedents in Chancery [*England*] [*A publication*] (DLA)
Finch Ins Dig... Finch's Insurance Digest [*A publication*] (DLA)
Finch LC..... Finch's Land Cases [*A publication*] (DLA)
Finch Nomot... Finch's Nomotechnia [*A publication*] (DLA)
Finch Prec... Precedents in Chancery, Edited by Finch [*A publication*] (DLA)
Finch Sum CL... Finch's Summary of the Common Law [*A publication*] (DLA)
Finci .... Financial (BARN)
FINCISCOM... Finance and Comptroller Information Systems Command [*Army*]
fincl .... financial (SAUS)
FinclBcp ...... Financial Bancorp, Inc. [*Associated Press*] (SAG)
FIN CLK ...... Finance Clerk (SAUS)
FinclSec ...... Financial Security Corp. [*Associated Press*] (SAG)
FINCO .... Field Intelligence Non-Commissioned Officer [*British military*] (DMA)
FINCO .... Finance Committee (SAUS)
FINCOM .... Finance Committee [*Institute of Electrical and Electronics Engineers*] (IEEE)
F INC ST...... Fellow of the Incorporated Shorthand Teachers [*British*] (ROG)
FIND .... Facility Index Directory [*Office of Information Resources Management*] (COE)
FIND .... Facsimile Information Network Development
FIND .... Fault Isolation by Nodal Dependency (MCD)
FIND .... Federal Item Name Directory
FIND .... Festival International de Nouvelle Danse
FIND .... Filed/Indexed Documents (SAUS)
FIND .... File Interrogation of Nineteen-Hundred Data [*Computer science*] (DIT)
FIND .... File of Industrial Data [*Computer science*]
FIND .... Flight Information Display
FIND .... Flow Information Display
FIND .... Food Ingredient Network Development (NTPA)
FIND .... Forecasting Institutional Needs for Dartmouth (SAUO)
FIND .... Freshwater Institute Numeric Database (SAUS)

FIND .... Friendless, Isolated, Needy, Disabled [*Project of National Council on the Aging - acronym used as name of New York City coffeehouse*]
FIND .... Fugitive Intercept Net Deployment [*Philadelphia police program*]
FINDAR........ Facility for Interrogating the National Directory of Australian Resources (EERA)
FINDB .... Financial Institution Data Base [*Cates Consulting Analysts, Inc.*] [*Information service or system*] (CRD)
FINDE .... Flight Information Display Electronics (SAUS)
fin dec......... final decree (SAUS)
FINDER........ Fingerprint Reader
FINDER........ Functional, Integrated, Designating, and Referencing (MCD)
FINDEX .... Faced-oriented Indexing System for Architecture and Construction Engineering (SAUS)
Fin Dig .... Finlay's Irish Digest [*A publication*] (DLA)
FINDL .... Findlay, OH [*American Association of Railroads railroad junction routing code*]
FINDS.......... Facility Indexing System
FINDS.......... Facility Index System [*Environmental Protection Agency*] (EPA)
FINDS.......... Fault Inferring Nonlinear Detection System [*NASA*]
FINE............. European Federation of Nurse Educators (SAUS)
FINE............. Fighter Inertial Navigation System
FINE............. Financial Institutions in the Nation's Economy [*Study initiated by House of Representatives*]
FINE............. Fine Hose Corp. [*NASDAQ symbol*] (SAG)
FINE............. FINE Is Not Emacs (SAUS)
FINE............. Fixed Installation Naiad Equipment (ACAE)
fine b........... fine boomerang (SAUS)
FINEBEL....... France, Italy, Netherlands, Belgium, and Luxembourg [*Economic agreement*]
fined .... finished (SAUS)
FINEFTA....... Finland-European Free Trade Association Treaty
Fine Gard .... Fine Gardening [*A publication*]
FineHost...... Fine Host Corp. [*Associated Press*] (SAG)
FINER .... Fingerprint-Reader (SAUS)
fines .... fine particulates (SAUS)
FINES.......... furnace ionization non-thermical excitation spectroscopy (SAUS)
fine scr........ Fine Screening (SAUS)
FINESS .... Fichier National des Etablissements Sanitaires et Sociaux
FINESSE ...... Fusion Integral Nuclear Experiments Strategy Study Effort (SAUS)
FINESSE ...... Fusion Integrated Nuclear Experiment Strategy Study Effort (SAUS)
FINEX........... Financial Instrument Exchange of the NY Cotton Exchange (EBF)
FINEX........... Financial Investments Exchange [*New York*]
FINEX........... Finish Exercise [*Military*] (NVT)
FINF............. Firmen- und Marktinformationen [*Company and Market Information Data Base*] [*Society for Business Information*] [*Information service or system*] (IID)
FinFdl .... Financial Federal Corp. [*Associated Press*] (SAG)
fin fl............. finished floor (SAUS)
F Infm.......... False Information (SAUS)
FINFO .... First In Not Used First Out [*Processing procedure*] (NITA)
FINFO .... Flight Inspection National Field Office [*FAA*]
FING............. Financing
fing............... finishing (SAUS)
FINGAL .... Fixation in Glass of Active Liquid [*British*] (NUCP)
Fingerht....... Fingerhut Companies, Inc. [*Associated Press*] (SAG)
FINGIS .... Finnish Geographical Information System (SAUO)
FINGLA .... Fission Products in Glass (SAUS)
FINI.............. Financial Industry Information Service [*Database*] [*Bank Marketing Association*] [*Information service or system*]
FINIC .... Food and Nutrition Information and Educational Materials Center (SAUO)
FINID .... Finnish International Development Assistance (SAUO)
FINIDA......... Finnish International Development Assistance (SAUO)
FINIF........... Field-Induced Negative Ion Formation
fin indep...... Financially Independent (ADWA)
FININFO....... Financial Information Services Project (SAUS)
FINIS .... Financial Industry Information Service [*Database*] [*Bank Marketing Association*] [*Information service or system*] (CRD)
FINISH .... Finisher (SAUS)
FINISH .... Finishing
Finish Ind.... Finishing Industries (journ.) (SAUS)
Finish Manage... Finishers Management (journ.) (SAUS)
FINISTRAT... Finishing Strategies (SAUS)
Finite Elem News... Finite Elements News (journ.) (SAUS)
F/INJ........... Fuel Injection [*Automotive engineering*]
FINJX........... First Investors MSITF New Jersey Cl.A [*Mutual fund ticker symbol*] (SG)
FINK............ Flying Infantrymen with Naval Knowledge (SAA)
Finkel Medical Cyc... Finkel, et Alia. Lawyers' Medical Cyclopedia [*A publication*] (DLA)
Fink Ev .... Fink's Indian Evidence Act [*A publication*] (DLA)
finl.............. Financial (DD)
Finl.............. Financial (TBD)
FINL............ Financial
FINL............ Finish Line 'A' [*NASDAQ symbol*] (TTSB)
FINL............ Finish Line, Inc. [*NASDAQ symbol*] (SAG)
Finl.............. Finland (VRA)
FinLAS......... Finnish Laboratory Animal Scientists (GVA)
Finlay .... Finlay Enterprises, Inc. [*Associated Press*] (SAG)
Finl Ch Tr.... Finlason on Charitable Trusts [*A publication*] (DLA)
Finl Com...... Finlason on Commons [*A publication*] (DLA)
Finl Dig .... Finlay's Irish Digest [*A publication*] (DLA)
FinlInd......... Financial Industries Corp. [*Associated Press*] (SAG)
FinLine .... Finish Line, Inc. [*Associated Press*] (SAG)
Finl Jud Sys... Finlason's Judicial System [*A publication*] (DLA)
Finl LC......... Finlason's Leading Cases on Pleading [*A publication*] (DLA)
Finl Ld Ten... Finlason's History of Law of Tenures of Land [*1870*] [*A publication*] (DLA)
Finl Mar L ... Finlason's Commentaries on Martial Law [*A publication*] (DLA)
FinlMgmt..... Financial Management (DD)
Finl Rep ...... Finlason's Report of the Gurney Case [*A publication*] (DLA)
Finl Riot ...... Finlay on Repression of Riot or Rebellion [*A publication*] (DLA)
Finl Ten....... Finlason's History of Law of Tenures of Land [*1870*] [*A publication*] (DLA)
FinlTrust...... Financial Trust Corp. [*Associated Press*] (SAG)
FINMAN........ Financial Management (MHDB)
FINMARC..... Finnish MARC (SAUS)
FIN Message... Facility Information Message (SAUS)
FINMIS .... Financial Management and Information System
Finn .... Finnish (ADWA)
FINN .... Finnish
FINNAIR....... Aero O/Y [*Finnish airline*]
FINNAIR....... FINNAIR Aero O/Y (SAUO)
FINNARP...... Finnish Antarctic Research Program (SAUS)
Finn Chem Lett... Finnish Chemical Letters (journ.) (SAUS)
FINNFUND ... Finnish Fund for Industrial Development Cooperation (SAUO)
Finnglish ..... Finnish + English (SAUS)
FINNIDA....... Finnish International Development Agency (International) (EERA)
FINNRET ...... Feminist International Network on the New Reproductive Technologies (SAUS)
FINO .... Federation of Independent Nursing Organization (DICI)
FINO .... Finance Officer [*Army*]
FINO .... Weather Report Will Not be Filed for Transmission [*NWS*] (FAAC)
Fi-No-Tro..... Finmark-Nord-Troms (SAUS)
Finova .... Finova Group, Inc. Finance Trust [*Associated Press*] (SAG)
FinovaGp ..... Finova Group, Inc. [*Associated Press*] (SAG)
FINP............ Aboriginal freehold/National Park (SAUO)
FINP............ Finnish Periodicals Index in Economics and Business [*Helsinki School of Economics Library*] [*Information service or system*]
FIN Plan ...... financial plan (SAUS)
FINPLT Program... Finite-element Field-Plotting Program (SAUS)
Fin Pr .... Finch's Precedents in Chancery [*England*] [*A publication*] (DLA)
Fin Prec....... Finch's Precedents in Chancery [*England*] [*A publication*] (DLA)
FINQ .... Final Queue (IAA)
FINR .... Financier
FINRACS...... File of Normalized Radar Cross Sections (SAUS)
FINRAE .... Ferranti Intertial Rapid Alignment Equipment (SAUO)
FINRAGE...... Feminist International Network of Resistance to Reproductive and Genetic Engineering (SAUO)
Fin Ren........ Finlay on Renewals [*A publication*] (DLA)
FINREP .... Final Reply (SAUS)
FINREP .... Final Report
FIN RESP..... Financial Responsibility [*Motor vehicle violation code used in state of Maryland*] (MVRD)
Fin Rev......... Australian Financial Review [*A publication*]
FINRS .... Far Infrared Noncoherent Radiating Systems (ACAE)
FINS............ Fire Island National Seashore
FINS............ Fishing Industry News Service (SAUS)
FINS............ Forensically Informative Nucleotide Sequencing [*Technique for tracing genetic origin*]
FINS............ Freight Information System [*BTS*] (TAG)
FINSAP .... Financial Sector Adjustment Program [*West Africa*]
FinSci .... Financing for Science International, Inc. [*Associated Press*] (SAG)
fin sec .... Financially Secure (ADWA)
Fin Sec .... Financial Secretary (WGA)
FINSHG........ Finishing (SAUS)
FINSIN .... Finlandia Sinfonietta (SAUS)
FinsMst........ Finishmaster, Inc. [*Associated Press*] (SAG)
F Inst .... Fellow of the Institute (SAUO)
F Inst .... Fellow of the Institution (SAUO)
FINST........... Final Instruction Station (SAUS)
FINST........... Final Station [*Computer science*]
FInstAEA...... Fellow of the Institute of Automotive Engineer Assessors [*British*] (DBQ)
F Inst AM..... Fellow of the Institute of Administrative Management [*British*] (ODBW)
FInstArb....... Fellow of the Institute of Arbitrators (SAUS)
Finstat .... Financial Times Database of Key Statistical Information (MHDB)
FInstBB........ Fellow of the Institute of British Bakers (DBQ)
FInstBCA...... Fellow of the Institute of Burial and Cremation Administration [*British*] (DBQ)
FInstBiol...... Fellow of the Institute of Biology [*Later, FI Biol*] [*British*]
FInstBRM..... Fellow of the Institute of Baths and Recreation Management [*British*] (DBQ)
FInstBTM ..... Fellow of the Institute of Business and Technical Management [*British*] (DBQ)
FInstC .... Fellow of the Institute of Commerce [*British*]
FInstCh .... Fellow of the Institute of Chiropodists [*British*]
F Inst CM..... Fellow of the Institute of Commercial Management [*British*] (DCTA)
F Inst D .... Fellow of the Institute of Directors [*British*] (ODBW)
F Inst Dir..... Fellow of the Institute of Directors [*British*]
FInstE .... Fellow of the Institute of Energy [*British*] (DBQ)
FInstF .... Fellow Institute of Fuel [*British*] (WA)
F Inst F........ Fellow of the Institute of Fuel [*British*]
F Inst FF...... Fellow of the Institute of Freight Forwarders [*British*] (ODBW)
FInstHE........ Fellow of the Institution of Highway Engineers (SAUS)
F Inst L Ex... Fellow of the Institute of Legal Executives [*British*] (DCTA)
FInstM .... Fellow of the Institute of Marketing [*British*]
FInstM .... Fellow of the Institute of Meat [*British*]

FInstMC .... Fellow of the Institute of Measurement and Control [*British*] (DBQ)
FInstMet ...... Fellow of the Institute of Metals [*British*]
F Inst MSM... Fellow of the Institute of Marketing and Sales Management [*Formerly, FSMA*] [*British*]
FInstNDT...... Fellow of the British Institute of Non-Destructive Testing (DBQ)
FInstP .... Fellow Institute of Physics [*British*] (WA)
F Inst P........ Fellow of the Institute of Physics and the Physical Society [*British*] (EY)
FInstPC .... Fellow of the Institute of Public Cleaning (SAUS)
F Inst Pet...... Fellow of the Institute of Petroleum [*British*]
F Inst Pl .... Fellow of the Institute of Patentees and Inventors [*British*] (EY)
FInstPkg ...... Fellow of the Institute of Packaging [*British*] (DI)
FInstPRA...... Fellow of the Institute of Park and Recreation Administration [*British*] (DI)
F Inst PS ..... Fellow of the Institute of Purchasing and Supply [*British*] (ODBW)
FInstR.......... Fellow of the Institute of Refrigeration [*British*] (DBQ)
FInstRE........ Fellow of the Institute of Radio Engineers (SAUS)
FInstRE Aust... Fellow of the Institute of Radio Engineers Australia (SAUS)
FInstRM....... Fellow of the Institute of Recreation Management [*British*] (DI)
FInstSM....... Fellow of the Institute of Sales Management [*British*] (DI)
F Inst SMM... Fellow of the Institute of Sales and Marketing Management [*British*] (ODBW)
FInstSMM .... Fellow of the Institute of Sales Management [*British*] (DBQ)
FInstSP........ Fellow of the Institute of Sewage Purification (DAVI)
F INST ST.... Fellow of the Institute of Shorthand Teachers [*British*] (ROG)
FInstT .... Fellow of the Institute of Transport (SAUS)
F Inst TA...... Fellow of the Institute of Transport Administration [*British*] (DCTA)
FInstW......... Fellow of the Institute of Welding [*British*]
FInstWM...... Fellow of the Institute of Wastes Management [*British*] (DBQ)
FInstWM(Hon)... Honorary Fellowship of the Institute of Wastes Management [*British*] (DBQ)
F-insulin...... fibrous insulin (SAUS)
FINSUPSCOL... Finance and Supply School [*Coast Guard*]
Fin-Syn........ Federal Communications Commission-Financial and Syndication (SAUS)
FIN-SYN....... Financial Interest and Syndication Rules [*FCC*]
FIN System... Finance System (SAUS)
FInt............. First Interstate Bancorp [*Associated Press*] (SAG)
Fin T............ T. Finch's Precedents in English Chancery [*1689-1722*] [*A publication*] (DLA)
Fin Tax & Comp L... Finance Taxation and Co. Law [*Pakistan*] [*A publication*] (DLA)
FinTech........ Financial Technology [*Publisher*] [*British*]
FINTEL......... Financial Times Company Information Database [*Financial Times Business Information Ltd. and Predicasts*] [*Bibliographic database*] [*British*]
FINTEL......... Financial Times Electronic Publishing [*Financial Times*] [*British*] (NITA)
FINTEL......... Financial Times Publishing Group (SAUO)
FINTEL......... Financial Timnes electronic publishing (SAUS)
FINTOR........ Frascali-Ispra-Naples Torus (MCD)
Fin Tot......... Final Total (SAUS)
FINTR .... Financial Transaction (SAUS)
FInste .... First Interstate Bancorp [*Associated Press*] (SAG)
FINU .... Finance Unit (HEAS)
Fl Nucl E ..... Fellow of the Institution of Nuclear Engineers [*British*]
FINUC-P...... Finnish Union Catalogue (SAUO)
FINUFO........ First-In/Not-Used/First-Out [*Replacement algorithm*] [*Computer science*] (BYTE)
Fin-Ug .... Finno-Ugric (SAUS)
FINX............. Fingermatrix, Inc. [*NASDAQ symbol*] (COMM)
FINX............. Finley [*Private rail car owner code*]
FINZ............. Fund Raising Institute of New Zealand (NFD)
FIO............... Far Infrared Observation (SAUS)
FIO............... Federacion Internacional de Oleicultura [*International Olive Oil Federation*] [*Rome, Italy*] [*Defunct*] (EA)
FIO............... Federation Internationale d'Oleiculture [*International Olive Growers Federation*]
FIO............... Fellow of the Institute of Ophthalmic Opticians [*British*]
FIO............... Fibrogenesis Imperfecta Ossium [*Medicine*] (EDAA)
FIO............... Field Input/Output [*Computer science*] (ECII)
FIO............... Field Intelligence Officer [*British military*] (DMA)
FIO............... Fleet In and Out (DNAB)
FIO............... Fleet Information Office (SAUO)
FIO............... Fleet Instruction Officer [*Navy*] [*British*]
FIO............... Fleet Intelligence Officer
FIO............... Florida Institute of Oceanography
FIO............... Food Investigation Organization (SAUO)
FIO............... Force XXI Integration Office (SAUS)
FIO............... Foreign Intelligence Office
FIO............... For Information Only (AAG)
FIO............... Fraction Inspired Oxygen [*Physiology*]
FI/O............. Frame Input / Output (SAUS)
fio................ Free In and Out [*Business term*] (EBF)
FIO............... Free In and Out [*Shipping*]
FIO............... Frequency In and Out (SAUS)
FIO............... Furnished and Installed by Others (SAUS)
FIO............... Paducah, KY [*Location identifier*] [*FAA*] (FAAL)
FIO_2.............. Forced Inspiratory Oxygen [*Physiology*]
FIO_2.............. Fractional Concentration of Inspired Oxygen [*Physiology*] (DAVI)
FiO2............. fraction of inspiratory oxygen concentration (SAUS)
FIOA............. File Input/Output Area (SAUS)
FIOB............. Fellow of the Institute of Builders [*British*]
FIOC............. Fellow of the Institute of Carpenters [*British*] (DBQ)
FIOC............. Final Initial Operational Capability [*Aerospace*] (AAG)
FIOC............. Frame Input/Output Controller [*Computer science*] (VERA)
FIOCC .... Federation Internationale des Ouvriers de la Chaussure et du Cuir [*International Shoe and Leather Worker's Federation*]
FIOCES .... Federation Internationale des Organisations de Correspondances et d'Echanges Scolaires [*International Federation of Organizations for School Correspondence and Exchange*] [*Paris, France*] (EA)
FIODS .... Federation Internationale des Organisations de Donneurs de Sang Benevoles [*International Federation of Blood Donor Organizations - IFBDO*] [*Dole, France*] (EAIO)
FIOE............. Fraternite Internationale des Ouvriers en Electricite [*International Brotherhood of Electrical Workers - IBEW*] [*Canada*]
fio ex trim... fioextrim (SAUS)
FIO EXTRIM... Free in and out Excluding Trimming (SAUS)
fiograbtrim... free in & out and free grab trimmed (SAUS)
FIOHX.......... First Investors MSITF Ohio Cl.A [*Mutual fund ticker symbol*] (SG)
FIOM............ Federation Internationale des Organisations de Travailleurs de la Metallurgie [*International Metalworkers Federation - IMF*] [*Geneva, Switzerland*] (EAIO)
FIOM............ Federation Internationale des Ouvriers sur Metaux [*International Metalworkers' Federation*]
FIOM............ Fellow of the Institute of Office Management (SAUS)
FIOP............. Fellow of the Institute of Plumbing [*British*] (DBQ)
FIOP............. Fellow of the Institute of Printing [*British*] (DBQ)
FIOP............. FORTRAN [*Formula Translating System*] Input-Output Package [*Computer science*] (IEEE)
FIOPM .... Federation Internationale des Organismes de Psychologie Medicale [*International Federation of the Psychological-Medical Organizations - IFPMO*] (EAIO)
FIOR .... Fluid Iron Ore direct Reduction (SAUS)
FIOR .... Fluid Iron Ore Reduction (SAUS)
FIOR .... Fluidized Iron Ore Reduction (SAUS)
Fiordland..... Fiordland National Park (SAUS)
FIORE .... Funding and Investment Objectives for Road Transport Informatics in Europe (SAUO)
FIORH.......... Federation Internationale pour l'Organisation de Rencontres de Handicapes [*International Federation for the Organization of Meetings for the Handicapped*]
FIOR-Verfahren... fluidized iron ore reduction process (SAUS)
fios .... free in and out and free stowed (SAUS)
FIOS............ Free In and Out and Stowed [*Shipping*]
fios .... free in and out stowage (SAUS)
FIOSc.......... Fellow of the Institute of Optical Science (SAUS)
FIOSH .... Fellow of the Institution of Occupational Safety and Health [*British*] (DCTA)
FIOSS .... Federation Internationale des Organisations de Sciences Sociales [*International Federation of Social Science Organizations - IFSSO*] (EAIO)
fio ss trimming... free in and out (SAUS)
FIOST.......... Federation Internationale des Organisations Syndicales du Personnel des Transporte [*International Federation of Trade Unions of Transport Workers - IFTUTW*] (EAIO)
fios/t........... free in and out (SAUS)
FIOST.......... Free In and Out Stowed and Trimmed (RIMS)
FIO S/T .... Free in and out Stowed / Trimmed (SAUS)
FIOT............ Fellow of the Institute of Operating Theatre Technicians [*British*]
fiot.............. free in and out and free trimmed (SAUS)
FIOT............ Free In and Out and Trimmed [*Shipping*]
FIOT............ Free In and Out of Trucks [*Business term*]
fiot.............. free in and out trimmed (SAUS)
FiOTV.......... Tuula Vauhkonen [*Regional Institute of Occupational Health*], Oulv, Finland [*Library symbol*] [*Library of Congress*] (LCLS)
FIOU .... Film Input/Output Unit
FiOU .... Oulun Yliopisto [*Oulu University*], Oulu, Finland [*Library symbol*] [*Library of Congress*] (LCLS)
FIP.............. Facility Interface Processor (VERA)
FIP.............. Fact Issue Paper
FIP.............. Factory Information Protocol (SAUS)
FIP.............. Factory Instrumentation Protocol (VERA)
FIP.............. Fail-in-place (SAUS)
fip............... fair in place (SAUS)
FIP.............. Fairly Important Person
FIP.............. Falcon Improvement Program (ACAE)
FIP.............. Familial Intestinal Polyposis [*Medicine*] (MELL)
FIP.............. Family Involvement Process [*Used to encourage parental support in the education of handicapped children*]
FIP.............. Far-Infrared Pointer
FIP.............. Fastener Installation Procedure [*Manual*] (MCD)
FIP.............. Fault Isolation Plan (ACAE)
FIP.............. Fault Isolation Procedure
FIP.............. FDDI Interface Processor (SAUS)
FIP.............. Federacion Internacional de Periodistas [*International Federation of Journalists*]
FIP.............. Federal Identity Program [*Canada*]
FIP.............. Federal Implementation Plan [*Environmental Protection Agency*] (ERG)
FIP.............. Federal Independence Party (SAUO)
FIP.............. Federal Information Plan (COE)
FIP.............. Federal Information Processing [*ANSI*] (EECA)
FIP.............. Federal Information Processing Standards (SAUS)
FIP.............. Federation Internationale de la Precontrainte [*International Federation of Prestressed Concrete*] (EAIO)
FIP.............. Federation Internationale de Philatelie [*International Federation of Philately*] (EAIO)
FIP.............. Federation Internationale de Podologie [*International Federation of Podology*]

FIP Federation Internationale des Phonotheques [*International Federation of Record Libraries*]
FIP Federation Internationale des Pietons [*International Federation of Pedestrians*] [*Netherlands*]
FIP Federation Internationale Pharmaceutique [*International Pharmaceutical Federation*] [*The Hague, Netherlands*] (EAIO)
FIP Feline Infectious Peritonitis
FIP Fellow of the Institute of Physics [*British*]
FIP Fellowship in Prayer (EA)
FIP Field Inspection Procedure (NRCH)
FIP File Processor Buffering (SAUS)
FIP Final Implementation Plan (EPA)
FIP Finance Image Processing (SAUS)
FIP Finance Image Processor [*Computer science*] (IBMDP)
FIP Fire Insurance Policy [*Legal shorthand*] (LWAP)
FIP First Ionization Potential [*Physical chemistry*]
fip first job program (SAUS)
FIP Fit in Place (SAUS)
FIP fixed interconnection pattern (SAUS)
FIP Fleet Improvement Program [*Navy*]
FIP Fleet Indoctrination Program [*Navy*] (MCD)
FIP Fleet Information Program [*Navy*]
FIP Fleet Introduction Program [*Navy*]
FI/P Flight Inspection / Permanent (SAUS)
FIP Flight Instruction Program [*Air Force*] (AFM)
FIP floating instrument platform (SAUS)
FIP Flow impedance phenomena (SAUS)
FIP flow injection potentiometry (SAUS)
FIP Fluorescence Indicator Panel (IAA)
FIP Foamed-in-Place [*Plastics technology*]
FIP Foam-in-Place (SAUS)
FIP Force Improvement Plan (MCD)
FIP Forestry Incentive Program [*US Forest Service*]
FIP Forestry Inceptive Program (SAUS)
FIP Formed-in-Place
FIP Free Instrument Package
FIP Frente de Izquierda Popular [*Popular Left Front*] [*Argentina*] [*Political party*] (PPW)
FIP Fuel Improvement Program (SAUO)
FIP Fuel Injection Pressure (KSC)
FIP Fuel Injection Pump (MSA)
FIP Fully-Ionized Plasma (SAUS)
FIP Future Impact Point (MCD)
FIP Vacuum Fluorescent Indicator Panel (SAUS)
FIPA Farm Income Protection Act (FOTI)
FIPA Federation Internationale des Producteurs Agricoles [*International Federation of Agricultural Producers*]
FIPA Federation of International Poetry Associations (EA)
FIPA Fellow, International Psychiatric Association (CMD)
FIPA Fellow of the Institute of Practitioners in Advertising [*British*]
FIPA Fellow of the Institute of Public Administration [*British*]
FIPA Festival International de Programmes Audiovisuels
FIPA Foundation for Intelligent Physical Agents (SAUS)
FIPAC Forest Industry Political Action Committee (WPI)
FIPACE Federation Internationale des Producteurs Auto-Consommateurs Industriels d'Electricite [*International Federation of Industrial Producers of Electricity for Own Consumption*]
FIPAD Fondation Internationale pour un Autre Developpement [*International Foundation for Development Alternatives - IFDA*] [*Nyon, Switzerland*] (EAIO)
FIPAGO Federation Internationale des Fabricants de Papiers Gommes [*International Federation of Manufacturers of Gummed Paper*] (EAIO)
FIPAH Federation des Importateurs et Producteurs d'Adjuvants et Additifs pour Coulis Mortier et Beton de Ciment [*Association of Importers and Producers of Admixtures*] (EAIO)
FIPAPA Flame Ionization-Pulse Aerosol Particle Analyzer (SAUS)
FIPAPA Flame Ionization-Pulse Aerosol Particle Analyzer (SAUS)
FIPAS Flight Information Publication, Alaska Supplement [*Air Force*] (DNAB)
FipaSS Falklands Interim Port and Storage System (SAUS)
FIPC Federation Internationale des Pharmaciens Catholiques [*International Federation of Catholic Pharmacists*] [*Eupen, Belgium*] (EAIO)
FIPC Fellow of the Institute of Production Control [*British*] (DBQ)
FIPC Fishing Industry Policy Council [*Australia*]
FIPCO Fully Integrated Pharmaceutical Company [*Business term*]
FIPD Fellow of the Institute of Professional Designers
FIPE Fund for the Improvement of Postsecondary Education [*Department of Education*] (EGAO)
FIPESO Federation Internationale des Professeurs de l'Enseignement Secondaire Officiel [*International Federation of Secondary Teachers*] (EAIO)
FIPET Federacion Interamericana de Periodistas y Escritores de Turismo [*Interamerican Federation of Journalists and Writers in the Tourist Trade*]
FIPet Fellow of the Institute of Petroleum (SAUS)
FIPF Federation Internationale des Professeurs de Francais [*International Federation of Teachers of French - IFTF*] (EAIO)
FIPFP Federation Internationale des Petits Freres des Pauvres [*International Federation of the Little Brothers of the Poor - IFLBP*] (EAIO)
FIPG Formed-in-Place Gasket [*Automotive engineering*]
FIPG Formed in Place Gaskets (SAUS)
FIPG Formed-in-Place Plastic Gasket [*Automotive engineering*]
FIPHE Fellow of the Institution of Public Health Engineers [*British*]
FIPI Fellow of the Institute of Professional Investigators [*British*] (DBQ)
FIPIS Fishery Project Information System [*FAO*] [*United Nations*] (DUND)
FIPJF Federation Internationale des Producteurs de Jus de Fruits [*International Federation of Fruit Juice Producers - IFFJP*]
FIPJP Federation Internationale de Petanque et Jeu Provencal [*Marseille, France*] (EAIO)
FIPL Fuel Injection Pump Lever [*Automotive term*] (HAWK)
FIPlantE Fellow of the Institution of Plant Engineers [*British*] (DBQ)
FIPLF Federation Internationale de la Presse de Langue Francaise (EA)
FIPLV Federation Internationale des Professeurs de Langues Vivantes [*International Federation of Modern Language Teachers*] [*Switzerland*]
FIPM Federation Internationale de la Philatelie Maritime [*International Federation of Maritime Philately - IFMP*] (EA)
FIPM Federation Internationale de Psychotherapie Medicale [*International Federation for Medical Psychotherapy*]
FIPM Fellow of the Institute of Personnel Management [*Later, CIPM*] [*British*]
FIPMEC Federation Internationale des Petites et Moyennes Entreprises Commerciales [*International Federation of Small and Medium-Sized Commercial Enterprises*]
FIPMT Fraunhofer Institute of Physical Measurement Techniques (SAUS)
FiPo Fire and Police (SAUS)
FIPOL Fonds International d'Indemnisation pour les Dommages dus a la Pollution par lesHydrocarbures [*International Oil Pollution Compensation Fund*] (EAIO)
FIPOS full isolation by porous oxidized silicon (SAUS)
FIPP Far Infrared Pointer Package (SAUS)
FIPP Federation Internationale de la Presse Periodique [*International Federation of the Periodical Press*] (EAIO)
FIPP Federation Internationale pour la Protection des Populations
FIPP Fondation Internationale Penale et Penitentiaire [*International Penal and Penitentiary Foundation - IPPF*] [*Bonn, Federal Republic of Germany*] (EAIO)
FIPR Fellow of the Institute of Public Relations [*British*]
FIPR Foreign Intelligence Production Requirement [*Army*] (RDA)
FIPR Foundation for International Potash Research [*Later, PI*] (EA)
FIPRA Federation Internationale de la Presse Agricole
FIPRECAN Fire Prevention Canada Association
FIPREGA Federation Internationale de la Presse Gastronomique et Vinicole [*International Federation of Gastronomical and Vinicultural Press*]
FIPRESCI Federation Internationale de la Presse Cinematographique [*International Federation of the Cinematographic Press - IFCP*] (EAIO)
FIProdE Fellow of the Institute of Production Engineers (SAUS)
FIProdE Fellow of the Institution of Production Engineers [*British*]
FIPS Facilities Inventory and Planning System (SAUO)
FIPS Federal Information Procedures System [*Environmental Protection Agency*] (ERG)
FIPS Federal Information Processing Standards [*Gaithersburg, MD*] [*National Institute of Standards and Technology*]
FIPS Federal Information Processing Standards Publications
FIPS Federal Item Procurement Specification (SAUS)
FIPS Fellow of the Incorporated Phonographic Society [*British*] (ROG)
fips female iron-pipe size (SAUS)
FIPS First Independent Political Success [*Political campaigning*]
FIPS Fisheries Image Processing System (SAUO)
FIPS Flagstaff Image Processing System (SAUS)
FIPS Flight Inspection Positioning System
FIPS Floating-point Interpretation System (SAUS)
FIPS Foreign Interest Payment Security [*Investment term*]
FIPS Freiburg Image Processing System (SAUO)
FIPSCAC Federal Information Processing Standards Coordinating and Advisory Committee [*National Institute of Standards and Technology*]
FIPSCAC FIPS [*Federal Information Processing Standard*] Coordinating and Advis ory Committee (NITA)
FIPSE Fund for the Improvement of Postsecondary Education [*Department of Education*]
FIPSG Falkland Islands Philatelic Study Group [*of the American Philatelic Society*] [*Fordingbridge, Hampshire, England*] (EAIO)
FIPS-PUB Federal Information Processing Standards Publication [*National Institute of Standards and Technology*]
FIPS/PUB Federal Information Processing Standards Publications (SAUS)
FIPS-PUBS Federal Information Processing Standards-Publications (SAUS)
FIPSR Federal Information Processing Standards Register [*National Institute of Standards and Technology*]
FIPT Fuel Inlet Pressure Test [*Automotive emissions*]
FI PTG M Fellow of the Institute of Printing Management [*British*] (DGA)
FIPTP Federation Internationale de la Presse Technique et Periodique [*International Federation of the Technical and Periodical Press*]
FIPUB Flight Information Publication [*Air Force*] (NVT)
FIPV Federacion Internacional de Pelota Vasca [*International Federation of Pelota Vasca - IFPV*] (EA)
FIPV Feline Infectious Peritonitis Virus
FIQ Fast Interrupt Request (SAUS)
FIQ Federation Internationale des Quillieurs [*International Federation of Bowlers*] [*Espoo, Finland*] (EA)
FIQ Fellow of the Institute of Quarrying [*British*] (DBQ)
FIQ Flow indicator integrator (SAUS)
FIQ Frequently Invented Questions (VLIE)
FIQ Full-Scale Intelligence Quotient [*Medicine*] (EDAA)
FIQ Morganton, NC [*Location identifier*] [*FAA*] (FAAL)
FIQA Fellow of the Institute of Quality Assurance [*British*] (DBQ)
FIQPS Fellow of the Institute of Qualified Private Secretaries [*British*] (DI)
FIQS Fellow of the Institute of Quantity Surveyors [*British*] (DI)
FIR Fabrication Information Report (SAUS)
FIR Faeroe-Iceland Ridge (SAUS)

FIR.............. Failed Item Report
FIR.............. Far Infrared
FIR.............. Far-Infrared Radiometer
FIR.............. Fast Information Retrieval (SAUS)
FIR.............. Fast Infrared (MWOL)
FIR.............. Fast Infrared Communication (SAUS)
FIR.............. Fault Interrupt Routine (SAUS)
FIR.............. Fault Isolation Routine
FIR.............. Federation Internationale des Resistants [*International Federation of Resistance Movements*]
FIR.............. Fellow of the Institute of Population Registration [*British*] (DBQ)
FIR.............. Field Information Release (MCD)
FIR.............. Field Information Report [*CIA*]
FIR.............. Field Intensity Receiver
FIR.............. Field Interrogation Record (SAUS)
FIR.............. Fiji Infantry Regiment (SAUO)
FIR.............. File Indirect Register
FIR.............. File Information Record (TIMI)
FIR.............. Films in Review [*A publication*] (BRI)
FIR.............. Final Inspection Record [*Army*]
FIR.............. Financial Inter-Relations Ratio
FIR.............. Financial Inventory Report
FIR.............. Finite Duration Impulse Response (SAUS)
FIR.............. Finite Impulse Response [*Filter*] (MCD)
FIR.............. Finnish Reactor
FIR.............. Fired (MSA)
FIR.............. Firenze Ximeniano [*Florence*] [*Italy*] [*Seismograph station code, US Geological Survey*] (SEIS)
FIR.............. Firkin
FIR.............. First (SAUS)
FIR.............. First Citizens BancStock (SPSG)
FIR.............. First Citizens Bank Stock [*AMEX symbol*] (SAG)
FIR.............. First City Trustco, Inc. [*Vancouver Stock Exchange symbol*]
FIR.............. Fixed Interface Ratio (ACAE)
FIR.............. Flight Incident Recorder (SAUS)
FIR.............. Flight Information Region [*FAA*]
FIR.............. Flight Information Report
FIR.............. Flight Information Requirement (NVT)
FIR.............. Flight Inspection Report (NG)
FIR.............. Floating-In Rates
FIR.............. flow indicated registrated (SAUS)
FIR.............. Flow Indicator Recorder [*Electronics*] (ECII)
FIR.............. Fluids Integrated Rack (SAUS)
FIR.............. Fluorescent Ionic Resin (MCD)
FIR.............. Fold Increase in Resistance (DB)
FIR.............. Food Irradiation Reactor
FIR.............. Frente de Izquierda Revolucionaria [*Peru*]
FIR.............. Freshwater Institute Report [*United Nations*]
FIR.............. Fuel Indicating Reading [*Aerospace*] (NAKS)
FIR.............. Fuel Indicator Reading (SAUS)
FIR.............. Full Indicator Reading
FIR.............. Full Inspection Report (MCD)
FIR.............. Functional Input Report (MCD)
FIR.............. Functional Item Replacement [*Program*] [*Navy*] (NG)
FIR.............. Future Issue Requirement
FIRA............ Falciparum Interspersed Repeat Antigen [*Genetics*]
FIRA............ Federal Investment Review Agency (SAUS)
FIRA............ Federation Internationale de Football-Rugby Amateur [*International Amateur Rugby Foundation*] (EA)
FIRA............ Fontes Iuris Romani ante Iustiniani [*A publication*] (OCD)
FIRA............ Foreign Investment Review Act [*1973*] [*Canada*] (IMH)
FIRA............ Foreign Investment Review Agency [*Canada*]
FIRA............ Freedom of Information Reform Act of 1986
FIRA............ Furniture Industry Research Association [*Research center*] [*British*] (IRC)
FIRAA.......... Fire Insurance Research and Actuarial Association [*Later, ISO*] (EA)
FIRA(Ind)..... Fellow of the Institute of Railway Auditors and Accountants (India)
FIRAMS....... Flight Incident Recorder and Aircraft Monitoring System (MCD)
FIRAS.......... Far-Infrared Absolute Spectrophotometer
FIRAV.......... First Available [*Military*]
FIRAVF........ First Available Flight (SAUS)
FIRAVV........ First Available Vessel (SAUS)
FIRB............ Fire Insurance Rating Bureau (SAUO)
FIRB............ Flight Information Region Boundary (FAAC)
FIRB............ Florida Inspection and Rating Bureau (SAUO)
FIRC............ Far Infra Red Camera (ACAE)
FIRC............ Fishing Industry Research Council (EERA)
FIRC............ Flow Indicator Recorder Controller [*Electronics*] (ECII)
FIRC............ Foreign Investment Review Corporation (JAGO)
FIRC............ Forest Industries Radio Communications [*Later, FIT*] (EA)
FIRCAP........ Foreign Intelligence Requirements, Capabilities, and Priorities (COE)
FIR/CPL....... Flight Incident Recorder/Crash Position Locator [*Navy*] (RDA)
FIRD............ Far-Infrared Detector
FIRD............ Fast-Induced Radioactivity Decay (SAUS)
FIRD............ Fault Isolation Requirement Document (MCD)
FIRDA.......... Frontal, Intermittent Delta Activity [*Medicine*] (DMAA)
FIRDC.......... Fishing Industry Research and Development Corporation (SAUO)
FIRDC.......... Fishing Industry Research and Development Council (EERA)
FIRDC.......... Forest Industry Research and Development Corp. [*Commercial firm*] [*Australia*]
FIRE............ Factor Information Retrieval Data System [*Information service or system*] (IID)
FIRE............ Factor Information Retrieval System (SAUS)
FIRE............ Fairchild Integrated Real-time Executive (SAUS)
FIRE............ Far Infrared Experiment (SAUO)
FIRE............ Fast Imaging Ranicon Experiment (SAUS)
FIRE............ Feedback Information Request Evidence (DNAB)
FIRE............ Fellow of the Institute of Radio Engineers (SAUS)
FIRE............ Fellow of the Institution of Radio Engineers [*British*]
FIRE............ Film Image Recorder (SAUS)
FIRE............ Finance, Insurance, and Real Estate [*Insurance*]
FIRE............ Financial Institutions Insurance Group Ltd. [*NASDAQ symbol*] (SAG)
FIRE............ Financial Reporting System
FIRE............ Fingerprint Reader
FIRE............ Finl Institutions Insur Grp [*NASDAQ symbol*] (TTSB)
FIRE............ Fire Pond, Inc. [*NASDAQ symbol*] (SG)
FIRE............ First International Radiation Experiment [*Climatology*]
FIRE............ First ISCCP Radiation Experiment (SAUS)
FIRE............ First ISLSCP Regional Experiment (SAUS)
FIRE............ Flame Infrared Emission
FIRE............ Flexible Intelligent Routing Engine (SAUS)
FIRE............ Flight in a Radiation Environment
FIRE............ Flight Investigation of the Reentry Environment
FIRE............ Forest Industry Renewable Energy Program (SAUS)
FIRE............ Forwarding Indian Resposibility in Education [*Bureau of Indian Affairs*] [*Department of the Interior*] (AEBS)
FIRE............ Foundation for Insurance Reform and Education
FIRE............ Fully Integrated Robotized Engine [*FIAT*]
Fire & Cas Cas... Fire and Casualty Cases [*A publication*] (DLA)
fire bottle..... Electron tube (SAUS)
FIREC.......... Federation Internationale des Redacteurs en Chef
FireE........... Fire Engineer (SAUS)
Fire Flammabl Bull... Fire and Flammability Bulletin (journ.) (SAUS)
FIREFLEX..... Flexible Fire Support System (SAUS)
Firefox......... Firefox Communications, Inc. [*Associated Press*] (SAG)
Fire Mater... Fire and Materials (journ.) (SAUS)
FIREMEN..... Fire Resistant Materials Engineering (PDAA)
FIRE PLAN.... Fleet Improved Readiness by Expediting Procurement, Logistics, and Negotiations [*Navy*] (NG)
fireplc.......... Fireplace (ADWA)
Fire Prev...... Fire Prevention [*A publication*] (CABS)
fires............ firearms (SAUS)
FIRES.......... Fire Inspection Reporting and Evaluation System (SAUS)
FIRES.......... Fire Insurance Reporting and Evaluation System (SAUS)
FIRES.......... Fuel Information Reporting and Engineering System (SAUS)
Fire Saf J.... Fire Safety Journal (journ.) (SAUS)
FIRESCAN.... Fire Research Campaign Asia - North (SAUS)
FIRESCAN.... Fire Research Campaign Asia-North (SAUO)
FIRES-T....... Fire Response of Structures-Thermal (SAUS)
Firestone T & R... Firestone Tire & Rubber Comp. (SAUS)
Firetct.......... Firetector, Inc. [*Associated Press*] (SAG)
FIRETRAC.... Firing Error Trajectory Recorder and Computer
FIRE USA..... Finance, Insurance, and Real Estate USA [*A publication*]
fir ex........... fire extinguisher (SAUS)
FIREX........... Fire Extinguisher [*or Extinguishing*] System (AAG)
FIREX........... Firing Exercise (NVT)
FIREX........... Free-Flying Imaging Radar Experiment (SAUO)
FIREX/SAMEX... Free-Flying Imagine RADAR Experiment/Soviet-American Microwave Experiment (MCD)
FIRFD.......... Finite-Impulse Response Filter Design (SAUS)
FIR Filter..... Finite-duration Impulse Response Filter (SAUS)
FIR Filter..... Finite Impulse Response Filter (SAUS)
FIRFLT......... First Fleet [*Pacific*] [*Navy*]
FIRFT........... fast inversion-recovery Fourier transform (SAUS)
FIRG............ Firing (FAAC)
FIRI............. Fellow of the Institute of Rubber Industry (SAUS)
FIRI............. Fishing Industry Research Institute (SAUO)
FIRIA........... Financial Institutions Regulatory and Interest Rate (EBF)
FIRIRCA....... Financial Institutions Regulatory and Interest Rate Control Act of 1978
FIRIV........... Arrival Report Will be Filed With [*Aviation*] (FAAC)
FIRL............. Faceted Information Retrieval for Linguistics (PDAA)
FIRL............. Fiber-Optic Inter-Repeater Link (VLIE)
FIRL............. Fleet Issue Requirements List [*Navy*]
FIRL............. Franklin Institute Research Laboratories
FIRL/SG....... Fleet Issue Requirements List/Shopping Guide [*Navy*] (MCD)
FIRM............ Far Infrared Radiation Measurements (ACAE)
FIRM............ Federation Internationale des Reconstructeurs de Moteurs [*International Federation of Engine Reconditioners - IFER*] (EAIO)
FIRM............ Financial Information for Resources Management (AFM)
FIRM............ Financial Institutions Resource Management [*Online database*]
FIRM............ Firstmark Corp. [*NASDAQ symbol*] (SAG)
FIRM............ Fleet Induction Replacement Model [*Navy*]
FIRM............ Fleet Intensified Repairables Management (DNAB)
FIRM............ Fleet Introduction of Replacement Models (SAUS)
FIRM............ Flood Insurance Rate Map
FIRM............ Flowcharting is Realistic Management (SAUS)
FIRM............ Flowcharting Realistic Management (VLIE)
FIRM............ Forum on Information Resources and Microcomputers (NITA)
FIRMA.......... Firepower and Maneuver [*Army*] (AABC)
FIRMCO....... Federal Information Requirements Management Council
FIRMN......... Fireman
FIRMR......... Federal Info Resources Management Regulation (SAUS)
FIRMR......... Federal Information Resources Management Regulation [*A publication*] (AAGC)
FIRMR......... Federal Information Resources Management Regulation Interagency Advisory Council [*Information Resources Management Service*] [*General Services Administration*] (EGAO)
FIRMS.......... Flood Rate Insurance Maps (SAUS)

FIRMS .... Forecasting Information Retrieval of Management System (IEEE)
FIRMS .... Foreign Intelligence Relations Management System (MCD)
FIRMS .... Forest Information Resource Management System (SAUO)
FIRMS .... Fourier Ion Resonance Mass Spectrometer
FIRN .... Florida Information Resource Network (EDAC)
FIRO .... Far-Infrared Observation
FIRO .... First In, Random-Out (FOTI)
FIRO .... Fundamental Interpersonal Relations Orientation [*Psychology*]
FIRO-B .... Fundamental Interpersonal Relations Orientation - Behavior
FIRO-BC .... Fundamental Interpersonal Relations Orientation - Behavior Characteristics [*Personality development test*] [*Psychology*]
FIRO-F .... Fundamental Interpersonal Relations Orientation - Feelings [*Personality development test*] [*Psychology*]
FIRP .... Far-Infrared Pointer
FIRP .... Federal Internet Requirements Panel (SAUO)
FIRP .... Federal Internetworking Requirements Panel [*Telecommunications*] (ACRL)
FIRP .... Functional Item Replacement Program [*Navy*]
FIRPP .... Far-Infrared Pointer Package
FIRPRECAN ... Fire Prevention Association of Canada (SAUO)
FIR Program ... Functional Item Replacement Program (SAUS)
FIRP Scheme ... Foreign Inward Remittance Payment Scheme (SAUS)
FIRPTA .... Foreign Investment in Real Property Tax Act of 1980
FIRQ .... Fast Interrupt Request (IAA)
FIRR .... Failure and Incidents Report Review Committee (SAUS)
FIRR .... Federal Institute for Reactor Research (SAUS)
FIRR .... Federation for Industrial Retention and Renewal (CROSS)
FIRRE .... Financial Institutions Reform, Recovery, and Enforcement Act [*1989*] [*Also, FIRREA*] [*Pronounced "Fire"*]
FIRREA .... Financial Institutions Reform, Recovery, and Enforcement Act [*1989*] [*Pronounced "fi-ree-a"*]
FIRS .... Fairplay International Records and Statistics (SAUS)
FIRS .... Far-Infrared Spectrometer
FIRS .... Federal Information Relay Service (USGC)
FIRS .... Federation Internationale de Roller-Skating [*International Roller Skating Federation*] (EAIO)
FIRS .... Field Incident Radio System [*Nuclear energy*] (NRCH)
FIRS .... File Interrogation and Reporting System [*Computer science*]
FIRS .... Flats Industrial Railroad [*Federal Railroad Administration identification code*]
FIRS .... Forest Inventory and Regeneration System
FIRS .... Forest Inventory Reconnaissance System (SAUO)
FIRS .... Fourier Transform Infrared Sounder (SAUS)
FIRS .... Framing Infra Red Sensor (ACAE)
FIRS .... Free-Text Information Retrieval System (SAUS)
FIRS .... Full Input Record Storage (SAUS)
FIRS .... Future Information Retrieval System (SAUS)
FIRSDIMS .... Flexible Interactive Remote Sensing Data Information and Management System (SAUO)
FIRSE .... Fellow of the Institute of Railway Signal Engineers [*British*] (DBQ)
FIRSE .... Field Reference Scene Equipment (MCD)
FIRS Method ... Full Input Record Storage Method (SAUS)
FIRST .... Fabrication of Inflatable Reentry Structures for Testing (SAUS)
FIRST .... Faculty Information and Research Service for Texas (SAUS)
FIRST .... Far Infrared and Submillimeter Space Telescope [*Proposed European*]
FIRST .... Far Infrared and Submillimeter Telescope
FIRST .... Far Infrared Search and Track (SAUS)
FIRST .... Far-Infrared Search and Track
FIRST .... Far Infrared Space Telescope
FIRST .... Far Infrared Spectroscopy Telescope (SEWL)
FIRST .... Fast Implementation of Real Time Signal Transforms [*University of Edinburgh*] [*Silicone compiler*] [*British*] (NITA)
FIRST .... Fast Information Retrieval for Surface Transportation [*IBM Corp.*]
FIRST .... Fast Interactive Radio System Tool (SAUS)
FIRST .... Fast Interactive Retrieval System Technology
FIRST .... Federal Information Research Science and Technology (DICI)
FIRST .... Federal Information Research Science and Technology Network (NITA)
FIRST .... Feeding Interaction Report, Scale, and Treatment [*Occupational therapy*]
FIRST .... File Integration and Retrieval System through Terminals (SAUS)
FIRST .... Financial Information Reporting System [*Computer science*]
FIRST .... Financial Information Retrieval System (SAUS)
FIRST .... FIRST - Foundation for Ichthyosis and Related Skin Types (EA)
FIRST .... First Independent Research Support and Transition Award [*National Institutes of Health*]
FIRST .... Fisheries Imaging Radar Surveillance Test (SAUO)
FIRST .... Fleet Input and Reserve Support Training
FIRST .... Flexible Information Retrieval System for Text (SAUS)
FIRST .... Flexible Infra Red Search and Track (ACAE)
FIRST .... Food Information Retrieval by Selected Terms (SAUS)
FIRST .... For Inspiration and Recognition of Science and Technology (VLIE)
FIRST .... Forum of Incident Response and Security Teams (DDC)
FIRST .... Foster Initial Reading Skills in Time (SAUS)
FIRST .... Foundation for Ichthyosis and Related Skin Types (PAZ)
FIRST .... Foundation for Individual Responsibility and Social Trust (SAUO)
FIRST .... Fourier Infrared Software Tools
FIRST .... Fourier Interferometer for Random Source Transient (ACAE)
FIRST .... Fragment Information Retrieval of Structures (SAUS)
FIRST .... Frequent Importer Release System (FOTI)
FIRST .... Friendly Interactive Robot for Service Tasks (EURO)
FIRST .... Fully Integrated Road Safety Technology [*Automotive safety*]
FIRST .... Fund for the Improvement and Reform of Schools and Teaching [*Department of Education*] (GFGA)
FIRST .... Futures Information Retrieval System [*Congressional Research Service*]
FIRSTA .... Fund for the Improvement and Reform of Schools and Teaching Act [*1988*]
Firstar .... Firstar Corp. [*Associated Press*] (SAG)
FIRSTASKFLT ... First Task Fleet
First Bk Judg ... First Book of Judgments [*1655*] [*England*] [*A publication*] (DLA)
First Book Judg ... First Book of Judgments [*1655*] [*England*] [*A publication*] (DLA)
FIRSTCHA .... First Access Channel (CGWS)
FIRSTCHP .... First Paging Channel (CGWS)
First D .... First Diploma (WDAA)
Firstier .... FirsTier Financial, Inc. [*Associated Press*] (SAG)
FirstInv .... First Investors Financil Services Group, Inc. [*Associated Press*] (SAG)
FIRST Network ... Federal Information Research Science and Technology Network (SAUS)
First Pt Edw III ... Part II of the Year Books [*A publication*] (DLA)
First Pt H VI ... Part VII of the Year Books [*A publication*] (DLA)
FIRSTS .... Floating-Interest-Rate Short-Term Securities [*Shearson Lehman Brothers, Inc.*]
FIRST-UP ..... Financial Information Register Satellite Terminal Users Package (SAUO)
FIRT .... Federation Internationale pour la Recherche Theatrale [*International Federation for Theatre Research - IFTR*] (EAIO)
FIRT .... Fertilizer Industry Round Table (EA)
FIRTA .... Far-Infrared Technical Area [*Night Vision Laboratories*] [*Army*] (RDA)
FIRTA .... Fishing Industry Research Trust Account (EERA)
FIRTE .... Fellow of the Institute of Road Transport Engineers [*British*]
FIRTI .... Far Infrared Target Indicator [*Military*]
FIRTO .... Fire Insurers Research and Testing Organisation (SAUS)
FIRTO .... Fire Insurers Research and Testing Organization (SAUS)
Firton .... Girton College, Cambridge (SAUS)
FIRTS .... Following Individual Reported This Station [*Army*] (AABC)
FiRUL-A .... University of Lapland, Lapland Artic Center, Rovaniemi, Lapland [*Library symbol*] [*Library of Congress*] (LCLS)
firwd .... Firwood (VRA)
FIS .... Fachinformationssystem [*Information service or system*] [*Germany*] (NITA)
FIS .... Facilities Inventory Study
FIS .... Facility Interface Sheet
FIS .... Facility Interface Sheets (SAUS)
FIS .... Factory Information System (VLIE)
FIS .... Factory Information Systems (TIMI)
FIS .... Factory Installation Software (SAUS)
FIS .... Fairy Investigation Society [*Inactive*] (EA)
FIS .... Family Income Supplement (ODBW)
FIS .... Family Interaction Scale [*Medicine*] (EDAA)
FIS .... Farallon Islands (GAAI)
FIS .... Far Infrared Search (SAUS)
FIS .... Far-Infrared Search
FIS .... Far Infrared Spectrometer (SAUS)
FIS .... Farm Improvement Scheme (SAUO)
FIS .... Farm Income Situation
FIS .... Farm Income Statistics (SAUO)
FIS .... Fast Information System (SAUO)
FIS .... Fault Isolation Software (CAAL)
FIS .... Fauna Impact Statement
FIS .... Feasible Ideal System (MHDI)
FIS .... Federal Information Service (SAUS)
FIS .... Federal Inspection Service (SAUO)
FIS .... Federal interim storage (SAUS)
FIS .... Federated Information System (VLIE)
FIS .... Federation Internationale de Sauvetage Aquatique [*Germany*]
FIS .... Federation Internationale des Centres Sociaux et Communautaires [*International Federation of Settlements and Neighborhood Centers*]
FIS .... Federation Internationale de Ski [*International Ski Federation*] [*Gumlingen, Switzerland*] (EA)
FIS .... Federation Internationale du Commerce des Semences [*International Federation of the Seed Trade*]
FIS .... Federation Internationale pour la Sante [*International Federation for Health*] [*France*] (EAIO)
FIS .... Fellow of the Institute of Statisticians [*British*]
FIS .... Fellow of the Institution of Surveyors [*British*]
FIS .... Fellowship of Independent Schools [*British*]
FIS .... Fennoscandian Ice Sheet
FIS .... Fictitious Illness Syndrome [*Medicine*] (EDAA)
FIS .... Field Information System [*Computer science*]
FIS .... Field Infrared Spectrometer
FIS .... Field Installation Simulator
FIS .... Field Instruction System
FIS .... Field Integration Services (ACAE)
FIS .... Fighter Identification System
fis .... Fighter Interceptor Squadron (SAUS)
FIS .... Fighter-Interceptor Squadron [*Air Force*]
FIS .... File Identification Statement (SAUS)
FIS .... Financial Information System
FIS .... Financial Inventory Subsidiary
FIS .... Finite Intermediate Storage [*Industrial engineering*]
FIS .... FINSAP Implementation Secretariat [*West Africa*]
FIS .... Fire Island [*Alaska*] [*Seismograph station code, US Geological Survey*] [*Closed*] (SEIS)
FIS .... Fiscal
FIS .... Fiscal Information System
FIS .... Fiscal Service (SAUO)

FIS............ Fischbach Corp. (SAUO)
FIS............ Fishing (SAUS)
FIS............ Fixed Instruction System (VLIE)
FIS............ Fleet Indoctrination Site [*Navy*]
FIS............ Fleet Information Service [*Navy*]
FIS............ Fleet Introduction Site (SAUO)
FIS............ Flexible Inspection System
FIS............ Flexible Instuction System (SAUS)
FIS............ Flight Identification System (SAUO)
FIS............ Flight Information Section (SAUO)
FIS............ Flight Information Service (AFM)
FIS............ Floating Instruction Set (SAUS)
FIS............ Floating-Point Instruction Set [*Computer science*] (MSA)
FIS............ Flood Insurance Study (ADWA)
FIS............ Floppy Infant Syndrome [*Medicine*] (MELL)
FIS............ Flow indicator switch (SAUS)
FIS............ Fluid Induction System [*Automotive engineering*]
FIS............ Fluoroimmunosensor [*Analytical chemistry*]
FIS............ Flying Instrument School [*British military*] (DMA)
FIS............ Foam in Salvage (SAUS)
FIS............ Foam in System
FIS............ Fondation Internationale pour la Science [*International Foundation for Science - IFS*] (EAIO)
FIS............ Forced Inspiratory Spirogram [*Medicine*] (MELL)
FIS............ Force Information Service [*Military*] (NVT)
FIS............ Force Information System (SAUO)
FIS............ Forces Information Service (SAUO)
FIS............ Foreign Information Service (SAUS)
FIS............ Foreign Information System (SAUO)
FIS............ Foreign Instrumentation Signals (MCD)
FIS............ Foreign Intelligence Service (SAUS)
FIS............ Forest Industry Strategy (EERA)
FIS............ FORSCOM [*Forces Command*] Information System [*DoD*] (GFGA)
FIS............ Foundation for Infinite Survival (SAUO)
FIS............ Foundation for/of International Studies (SAUO)
FIS............ Foundations of Information Science [*American Society for Information Science*]
FIS............ Fourier Interferometric Stimulation [*Instrumentation*]
FIS............ Four-Impinging-Stream Reactor [*Chemical engineering*]
FIS............ Freedom Information Service (EA)
FIS............ Free in Store [*Business term*]
FIS............ freight (SAUS)
FIS............ Freight, Insurance, and Shipping Charges [*Business term*]
FIS............ Friendly Information System [*Military*] (RDA)
FIS............ Frontier Inspections Service (SAUO)
FIS............ Front Islamique de Salut [*Algeria*] [*Political party*]
FIS............ Fuel Injection System [*Automotive engineering*]
FIS............ Functional Interface Specification [*Telecommunications*] (TEL)
FIS............ Functional Interference Specification (SAUS)
FIS............ Islamic Salvation Front [*Algeria*] [*Political party*] (ECON)
FIS............ Key West, FL [*Location identifier*] [*FAA*] (FAAL)
Fis............ Physicist
FISA............ Automated Flight Information Service [*ICAO designator*] (FAAC)
FISA............ Federation Internationale des Semaines d'Art
FISA............ Federation Internationale des Societes Aerophilateliques [*International Federation of Aero-Philatelic Societies*] [*Zurich Airport, Switzerland*] (EAIO)
FISA............ Federation Internationale des Societes d'Aviron [*International Rowing Federation*] [*Neuchatel, Switzerland*] (EAIO)
FISA............ Federation Internationale du Sport Automobile [*Paris, France*] (EAIO)
FISA............ Federation of Insurance Staffs Associations (SAUO)
FISA............ Fellow of the Incorporated Secretaries Association (SAUO)
FiSa............ fibrosarcoma (SAUS)
FISA............ Financial Information Services Agency
FISA............ Financial Institutions Supervisory Act of 1966
FISA............ Fisheries Society of Africa (SAUO)
FISA............ Flexible Integrated Solar Array (ACAE)
FISA............ Fondation Internationale pour le Saumon de l'Atlantique [*International Atlantic Salmon Foundation*] [*Canada*]
FISA............ Food Industries Suppliers Association (EA)
FISA............ Foreign Intelligence Surveillance Act of 1978
FISA............ Forest Industries Safety Association (SAUO)
FISA............ Foundation for International Scientific Coordination (SAUO)
FISAA............ Fellow of the Incorporated Society of Accountants and Auditors [*British*] (DAS)
FISAA............ Fellow of the Institute of Shops Acts Administration (SAUO)
FISAC............ Fellow of the Incorporated Society of Advertisement Consultants [*British*] (DAS)
FISAE............ Federation Internationale des Societes d'Amateurs d'Exlibris [*British*] (EAIO)
FISAIC............ Federation Internationale des Societes Artistiques et Intellectuelles de Cheminots [*International Federation of Railwaymen's Art and Intellectual Societies*]
FISAP............ Fiscal Operations Report and Application to Participate [*Department of Education*] (GFGA)
FISAR............ Federal Institute for Snow and Avalanche Research
FISAR............ Fleet Information Storage and Retrieval [*Navy*]
FISARS............ Fleet Information Storage and Retrieval System (SAUS)
FISB............ Federal Internal Security Board [*Formerly, Subversive Activities Control Board*]
FISB............ Federation Internationale de Skibob [*Germany*] (EAIO)
FISB............ First Indiana Corp. [*NASDAQ symbol*] (NQ)
FISC............ Federal Information Systems Corp. (IID)
FISC............ Federation of Infant School Clubs (SAUO)
FISC............ Financial Industries Service Corporation (SAUO)
FISC............ Fiscal (MUGU)
FISC............ Fleet and Industrial Supply Center [*Formerly, Naval Supply Center, Norfolk, VA.; changed in 1993*] (DOMA)
FISC............ Fleet Intelligence Support Center (SAUO)
FISC............ Flight Instrumentation Signal Converter (SAUS)
FISC............ Flight Instrument Signal Converter (MCD)
FISC............ Foreign Intelligence Surveillance Court (CARL)
FISC............ Foundation for International Scientific Coordination (SAUO)
FISC............ freight inventory control system (SAUS)
FISC............ Fuel Inspection and Sampling Cell [*Nuclear energy*] (NRCH)
FISC............ Fund for International Student Cooperation (SAUO)
FISC............ Fur Industry Salvage Commission [*New Deal*]
FISCA............ Flexible Integrated Solar Cell Assembly
FISCC............ Fruit Industry Sugar Concession Committee (SAUO)
FISCETCV.... Federation Internationale des Syndicats Chretiens d'Employes, Techniciens, Cadres, et Voyageurs de Commerce [*International Federation of Christian Trade Unions of Salaried Employees, Technicians, Managers, and Commercial Travellers*]
FischIm........ Fischer Imaging Corp. [*Associated Press*] (SAG)
fisc irre........ fiscal irresponsibility (SAUS)
FISCIT........ Foundation for International Exchange of Scientific and Cultural Information by Telecommunications (SAUO)
FISCM........ Federation Internationale des Syndicats Chretiens de la Metalurgie [*International Federation of Christian Metalworkers Unions*]
FISCO........ Fuji International Speedway Co. [*Automobile racing*]
FISCO........ Fuji International Speedway Co. Ltd. (SAUO)
FISCOA........ Federation Internationale des Syndicats Chretiens d'Ouvriers Agricoles [*International Federation of Christian Agricultural Workers Unions*]
FISCOBB...... Federation Internationale des Syndicats Chretiens d'Ouvriers du Batiment et du Bois [*International Federation of Christian Trade Unions of Building and Wood Workers*]
FIS countries... France, Ivory Coast, Senegal (SAUS)
FIS-COV...... Fire Survivability for Ground Combat Vehicles (MCD)
Fisc Stud...... Fiscal Studies [*A publication*] (JLIT)
FISCTTH...... Federation Internationale des Syndicats Chretiens des Travailleurs du Textile etde l'Habillement [*International Federation of Christian Trade Unions of Textile and Clothing Workers*]
FISC YR...... Fiscal Year (SAUS)
FISD............ Federation Internationale de Stenographie et de Dactylographie [*International Federation of Shorthand and Typewriting*]
FISDO.......... Flight Standards District Office [*FAA*]
FISDW.......... Field-Induced Spin Density Wave [*Physics*]
FISE............ Emergency Social Investment Fund (SAUO)
FISE............ Federation Internationale Syndicale de l'Enseignement [*World Federation of Teachers' Unions*] [*Berlin, Federal Republic of Germany*] (EAIO)
FISE............ Fellow of the Institution of Sanitary Engineers [*British*]
FISE............ Fonds International de Secours a l'Enfance [*Also known as Fonds des Nations Unies pour l'Enfance*] [*Canada*]
FISEC.......... Federation Internationale Sportive de l'Enseignement Catholique
FISEL.......... Fluorescent In Situ End-Labelling [*Analytical biochemistry*]
FIS-ELF........ German Information System on Food, Agriculture, and Forestry [*Bonn*] [*Information service or system*] (IID)
FISEM.......... Federation Internationale des Societes d'Ecrivains-Medecins
FISEMA........ Federation Internationale et Syndicale des Employes de Madagascar [*International Federation and Union of Malagasy Employees*] [*WFTU affiliate*]
Fiserv.......... Fiserv, Inc. [*Associated Press*] (SAG)
FISF............ Family Interaction Summary Format
FISGV.......... Federazione Internazionale della Stampa Gastronomica e Vinicola [*International Federation of Gastronomical and Vinicultural Press*]
FISH............ Fellow, International Society of Hematology (CMD)
FISH............ First In, Stays Here (SAUS)
FISH............ First-In, Still-Here [*Facetious extension of FIFO definition*] [*Accounting*]
FISH............ Fisheries
Fish............ Fisher's United States Patent Cases [*A publication*] (DLA)
Fish............ Fisher's United States Prize Cases [*A publication*] (DLA)
FISH............ Fishery (SAUS)
fish............ fishes (SAUS)
fish............ fishing (SAUS)
FISH............ Fluorescence In Situ Hybridization [*Analytical biochemistry*]
FISH............ Forensic Information System for Handwriting (VLIE)
FISH............ Friends in Service Here
FISH............ Friends in Service to Humanity (SAUO)
FISH............ Friends Involved in Sportfishing Heritage
FISH............ Full Infiniti Service History [*Automotive classified advertising*]
FISH............ Full Isuzu Service History [*Automotive classified advertising*]
FISH............ Fully Instrumented Submersible Housing [*An oceanographic instrument*]
FISH............ Smalls Oilfield Services [*NASDAQ symbol*] (SAG)
Fish & GC.... Fish and Game Code [*A publication*] (DLA)
Fish & L Mort... Fisher and Lightwood on Mortgages [*9th ed.*] [*1977*] [*A publication*] (DLA)
Fish Bull...... Fishery Bulletin [*A publication*] (PABS)
FISHC.......... Federation Internationale des Societes d'Histochimie et de Cytochimie [*International Federation of Societies for Histochemistry and Cytochemistry*] (EAIO)
Fish Cas...... Fisher's Cases, United States District Courts [*A publication*] (DLA)
Fish CL Dig... Fisher's Digest of English Common Law Reports [*A publication*] (DLA)
Fish Const... Fisher on the United States Constitution [*A publication*] (DLA)
Fish Cop...... Fisher on Copyrights [*A publication*] (DLA)
Fish Crim Dig... Fisher's Digest of English Criminal Law [*A publication*] (DLA)

Fish Dig....... Fisher's Digest of English Common Law Reports [*A publication*] (DLA)
Fisher.......... Fisher on Mortgages [*A publication*] (DLA)
Fisher.......... Fisher's United States Prize Cases [*A publication*] (DLA)
Fisher & Lightwood... Fisher and Lightwood on Mortgages [*9th ed.*] [*1977*] [*A publication*] (DLA)
Fisher Pat Cas (F)... Fisher's United States Patent Cases [*A publication*] (DLA)
Fisher Pr Cas (F)... Fisher's United States Prize Cases [*A publication*] (DLA)
Fisher Pr Cas (PA)... Fisher. Pennsylvania Prize Cases [*A publication*] (DLA)
Fisher's Pat Cas... Fisher's United States Patent Cases [*A publication*] (DLA)
Fish Fish..... Fish and Fisheries [*A publication*] (PABS)
fishg............ Fishing (SAUS)
Fish Manage Ecol... Fisheries Management and Ecology [*A publication*] (PABS)
Fish Mort..... Fisher on Mortgages [*A publication*] (DLA)
Fish Mortg... Fisher on Mortgages [*A publication*] (DLA)
Fish Pat....... Fisher's United States Patent Cases [*A publication*] (DLA)
Fish Pat Cas... Fisher's United States Patent Cases [*A publication*] (DLA)
Fish Pat Dig... Fisher's Digest of Patent Law [*A publication*] (DLA)
Fish Pat R... Fisher's United States Patent Reports [*A publication*] (DLA)
Fish Pat Rep... Fisher's United States Patent Reports [*A publication*] (DLA)
FISHPATS.... Fisheries Patrols [*Canadian Navy*]
Fish Pr Cas... Fisher's United States Prize Cases [*A publication*] (DLA)
Fish Prize.... Fisher's United States Prize Cases [*A publication*] (DLA)
Fish Prize Cas... Fisher's United States Prize Cases [*A publication*] (DLA)
Fish Res (Amst)... Fishery Research (Amsterdam) (SAUS)
FISHROD..... Fiche Information Selectively Held and Retrieved on Demand [*Computer science*] (PDAA)
FishrSci....... Fisher Scientific International [*Associated Press*] (SAG)
FISHSTATS... Fishery Statistics Data Base [*National Marine Fisheries Service*] [*Information service or system*] (CRD)
FISHTEM P... National Compendium of Freshwater Fish & Water Temperature Data (SAUO)
Fish WA....... Fisher on the Will Act [*A publication*] (DLA)
fishwich....... fish sandwich (SAUS)
FISI............. Fault Insertion Simulation (ACAE)
FISI............. Friends of India Society International (EA)
FISICAL........ Freedom in Sport International Committee and Lobby [*British*] (DI)
FISIER......... Federation Internationale des Societes et Instituts pour l'Etude de la Renaissance [*International Federation of Societies and Institutes for the Study of the Renaissance*] (EA)
FISINT......... FIS [*Foreign Instrumentation Signals*] Intelligence (MCD)
FISINT......... Foreign Instrumentation Signals Intelligence (SAUO)
FISITA......... Federation International des Societes d'Ingenieurs des Techniques de l'Automobile
FISITA......... Federation Internationale des Societes d'Ingenieurs des Techniques de l'Automobile [*International Federation of Automobile Engineers' and Technicians' Associations*]
Fisk Anal..... Fisk's Analysis of Coke on Littleton [*1824*] [*A publication*] (DLA)
Fiskeridir Skr Ser Havunders... Fiskeridirektoratets Skrifter Serie Havundersokelser (SAUS)
Fisk U.......... Fisk University (GAGS)
FISL............ Federally-Insured Student Loan [*Medicine*] (EDAA)
FISLIB......... FORTRAN [*Formula Translating System*] Interactive Subroutine Library [*Computer science*]
FISLP........... Federal Insured Student Loan Program
FISLP........... Federally Insured Student Loan Program (SAUO)
FISM............ Factory Inspectorate Specialist Minute (HEAS)
FISM............ Federation Internationale des Societes Magiques [*International Federation of Magical Societies - IFSM*] [*Paris, France*] (EAIO)
FISM............ Fellow of the Institute of Supervisory Management [*British*] (DBQ)
FISM............ International Federation of Sports Medicine (EA)
FISMARC..... Federation Internationale du Sport Medical pour l'Aide a la Recherche Cancerologique [*International Medical Sports Federation for Aid to Cancer Research*] [*Beziers, France*] (EAIO)
FISN............ Fisons Ltd. [*NASDAQ symbol*] (NQ)
FISNY.......... Fisons plc [*NASDAQ symbol*] (COMM)
FISO............ Force Informational Services Officer (SAUO)
FISO............ Force Integration Staff Officer [*Army*] (RDA)
FISOB.......... Fellow of the Incorporated Society of Organ Builders [*British*] (DI)
Fisons.......... Fisons Ltd. [*Associated Press*] (SAG)
FISP............ Family Income Security Plan
FISP............ Fast Imaging with Steady Precision [*Medicine*] (EDAA)
FISP............ Federation Internationale des Societes de Philosophie [*International Federation of Philosophical Societies - IFPS*] (EAIO)
FISP............ Fellow of the Institute of Sewage Purification (SAUO)
FISPO.......... Fischer & Porter Co. (EFIS)
FISPPMA..... Franklin Institute of the State of Pennsylvania for the Promotion of the Mechanic Arts (SAUO)
FISPPMA..... Franklin Institute of the State of Pensylvania for the Promotion of the Mechanic (SAUS)
FISq............ Fighter-Interceptor Squadron [*Air Force*] (AFM)
FISR............ Financial Interest and Syndication Rules [*FCC*]
FISRO.......... Federation Internationale des Societes de Recherche Operationelle [*International Federation of Operational Research Societies*] [*Denmark*] (EAIO)
FISS............ Federation Internationale des Societes Scientifiques (EERA)
FISS............ Finance Inter-System Support (VLIE)
FISS............ Foreign Intelligence Security Service (COE)
FISS............ Free Text Synthesis System (SAUS)
FISSG.......... Fleet Issue Ship Shopping Guide [*Navy*] (NVT)
FISSL.......... Finite State Specification Language [*Computer science*] (MHDI)
FISSO.......... Foreign Intelligence Special Security Office (MCD)
FIST............ Facility for Infantry Situation Training (SAUS)
FIST............ facility installation software team (SAUS)
FIST............ Fault Isolation by Semiautomatic Techniques [*National Institute of Standards and Technology*]
FIST............ Feasible Ideal System Target (MHDI)
FIST............ Federal Information Processing Standards (DOMA)
FIST............ Federal Investigative Strike Team
FIST............ Federation of Interstate Truckers [*Acronym is title of film*]
FIST............ Fellow of the Institute of Science Technology [*British*]
FIST............ Field Artillery Fire Support Team [*Army*] (RDA)
FIST............ Field Intelligence Signal Terminal (SAUO)
FIST............ Field Intelligence Simulation Test (NATG)
FIST............ Fighter Interceptor Slaved Telescope (ACAE)
FIST............ Final Integration System Test (ACAE)
FIST............ Fire Integration Support Team
FIST............ Fire Support Team [*Military*] (INF)
FIST............ First-In, Still-There [*Facetious extension of FIFO definition*] [*Accounting*]
FIST............ First Intelligence Simulative Test (SAUO)
FIST............ Fistula
FIST............ Flagship International Sports Television [*Phony TV station used as bait to capture fugitives*] [*Canada*]
FIST............ Fleet Imagery Satellite Terminal [*Navy*] (ANA)
FIST............ Fleet Imagery Support Terminal (SEWL)
FIST............ Flight Information Scheduling and Tracking System (MCD)
FIST............ Free Indian Socially-Traditionally [*India*] [*Political party*]
FIST............ Fugitive Investigative Strike Team [*Operation conducted jointly by the US Marshals Service and local police*]
FIST............ Full Integral Simulation Test [*Nuclear energy*] (NRCH)
FIST............ Functional Integrated Systems Trainer (MCD)
FISTA.......... Federation Internationale des Syndicats des Travailleurs Audiovisuel [*International Federation of Audio-Visual Workers Unions - IFAVWU*] (EAIO)
FISTA II....... Flying Infrared Signature Technology Aircraft [*Air Force*]
FIST ARM.... Fistula Armata [*Clyster-Pipe and Bladder Fitted for Use*] [*Pharmacy*] (ROG)
FISTC.......... Fellow of the Institute of Scientific and Technical Communicators [*British*] (DBQ)
FISTC.......... Fellow of the International Institute of Sports Therapy [*British*] (DBQ)
FISTD.......... Fellow of the Imperial Society of Teachers of Dancing [*British*] (DBQ)
fisteg.......... fiscal integrity (SAUS)
FISTM.......... Fellow of the Institute of Sales Technology and Management [*British*] (DBQ)
FI-STM......... Field Ion-Scanning Tunneling Microscopy
FI Struct E... Fellow of the Institute of Structural Engineers (SAUS)
FIStructE...... Fellow of the Institution of Structural Engineers [*British*]
FIST-V......... Fire Integration Support Team Vehicle [*Military*] (POLM)
FISTV.......... Fire Support Team Vehicle [*Army*] (RDA)
FISU............ Federation Internationale du Sport Universitaire [*International University Sports Federation*] [*Brussels, Belgium*] (EAIO)
FISU............ filling in signal unit (SAUS)
FISU............ Filling Signal Units (SAUS)
FISU............ Fill-In Signal Unit (SAUS)
FISU............ Westinghouse Federation of Independent Salaried Unions
FISV............ FIserv, Inc. [*NASDAQ symbol*] (NQ)
FISW............ Fellow of the Institute of Social Welfare [*British*] (DBQ)
fis yr........... Fiscal Year (SAUS)
FISYS.......... Fairplay Information Systems Ltd. (IID)
FISYS.......... Fisheries System Management Model (SAUO)
FIT.............. Aero Fiesta Mexicana SA de CV [*Mexico*] [*FAA designator*] (FAAC)
FIT.............. Fab Indus [*AMEX symbol*] (TTSB)
FIT.............. Fab Industries, Inc. [*AMEX symbol*] (SPSG)
FIT.............. Fabrication, Integration, and Test
FIT.............. Fabrication in Transit (ADA)
FIT.............. Failure in Time [*Telecommunications*] (TEL)
FIT.............. Failures in Test [*Electronics*]
FIT.............. Failure Unit [*Electronics*] (AAEL)
FIT.............. Families In Touch (SAUS)
FIT.............. Far-Infrared Track
FIT.............. Fashion Institute of Technology
FIT.............. Fast Installation Technique (SAUS)
FIT.............. Fault Isolation Test
FIT.............. Fault Isolation Time (MCD)
FIT.............. Fault Isolation Tree (SAUS)
FIT.............. Federal Income Tax
FIT.............. Federal Information Technologies, Inc. (SAUO)
FIT.............. Federal Institute of Technology (SAUO)
FIT.............. Federal Insurance Tax (DLA)
FIT.............. Federation Internationale des Traducteurs [*International Federation of Translators - IFT*] (EAIO)
FIT.............. Federation Internationale de Trampoline [*International Trampoline Federation*] (EA)
FIT.............. Federation International Triathlon (EA)
FIT.............. Feedback reactivity code using magnitudes of integrals (SAUS)
FIT.............. Fellow of the Institute of Transport (SAUO)
FIT.............. Fentanyl Isothiocyanate [*Biochemistry*]
FIT.............. Field Installation and Test
FIT.............. Field Installation Time (IAA)
FIT.............. Field Investigation Team [*Environmental Protection Agency*] (ERG)
FIT.............. Fighter
FIT.............. Fight Inflation Together [*Group opposing high food prices in 1973*]
FIT.............. File enquiry technique (SAUS)
FIT.............. File Information Table [*Computer science*]
FIT.............. File Inquiry Technique
FIT.............. Finance for Innovative Technology (EURO)
FIT.............. Finding in Transit
FIT.............. Fingerprint Identification Technology (SAUS)

FIT .... Fire Investigation Team (WDAA)
FIT .... First Computer Interface Tester (MCD)
FIT .... First Indication of Trouble
FIT .... Fit and Independent Traveler (TAG)
FIT .... Fitchburg [*Massachusetts*] [*Airport symbol*] (AD)
FIT .... Fitchburg, MA [*Location identifier*] [*FAA*] (FAAL)
FIT .... Fitness, Intensity, Time [*Exercise*]
Fit .... Fitting (SAUS)
FIT .... Fixed Individual Tariff (SAUS)
FIT .... Fixed Interval Timer
FIT .... Flame and Incendiary Technology Program [*Chemical Research, Development, and Engineering Center*] [*Army*] (INF)
FIT .... Flanagan Industrial Tests [*Aptitude and skills test*]
FIT .... Fleet Indoctrination Team (MCD)
FIT .... Fleet Introduction Team [*Navy*] (NVT)
FIT .... Flexible Infrared Transmission
FIT .... Flexible Interface Technique (PDAA)
FIT .... Flexible Interface Tool (SAUS)
FI/T .... Flight Inspection, Temporary (SAUS)
FIT .... Flight Instrument Trainer (AFM)
FIT .... Flight Technical Tolerance [*Aviation*] (DA)
FIT .... Floating Input Transistor [*Electronics*]
FIT .... Florida Institute of Technology [*Melbourne*]
FIT .... Flow Indicator Transmitter [*Nuclear energy*] (NRCH)
FIT .... Fluorescein Isothiocyanate [*Organic chemistry*] (DAVI)
FIT .... Food Intolerance Testing (MEDA)
FIT .... Footscray Institute of Technology (SAUO)
fit .... foreign inclusive tour (SAUS)
FIT .... Foreign Independent Tours (SAUO)
FIT .... Foreign Independent [*or Individual*] Travel [*Air travel term*]
fit .... foreign independent traveler (SAUS)
FIT .... Foreign Independent Trip (SAUS)
FIT .... Forest Industries Telecommunications [*Eugene, OR*] (EA)
fit .... formation interval tester (SAUS)
FIT .... Forward Inspection Team [*Military*]
FIT .... Foundation to Improve Television (EA)
FIT .... Fourier Integral Transform [*Physics*]
FIT .... Frame Interline Transfer (SAUS)
FIT .... Franchise Industry Training [*High school dropout program*] [*Department of Labor*]
FIT .... Free and Independent Traveller (EERA)
fit .... free from income tax (SAUS)
FIT .... Free in Trimmed (RIMS)
fit .... Free in Truck (EBF)
FIT .... Free in Truck [*Business term*]
fit .... freely independent traveller (SAUS)
FIT .... Free of Income Tax
FIT .... Frequency, Intensity, and Time [*Exercise formula*] [*Army*]
FIT .... Frequent Independent Traveler
FIT .... Frequent International Traveler (ADWA)
FIT .... Front Intertropical (SAUS)
fit .... fully inclusive tour (SAUS)
FIT .... Fully Independent Traveller
FIT .... Functional Industrial Training (SAUS)
FIT .... Functional Integration Technology (SAUS)
FIT .... Functional Integration Test
FIT .... Fusion at the Inferred Threshold [*Test*] [*Medicine*]
FiTA .... Abo Akademi [*Swedish University of Abo*], Turku, Finland [*Library symbol*] [*Library of Congress*] (LCLS)
FITA .... Fault Isolation Test Adapter (MCD)
FITA .... Federation Internationale de Tir a l'Arc [*International Archery Federation*] [*Milan, Italy*] (EA)
FITA .... Federation of International Trade Associations (EA)
FITA .... Foreign Investors Tax Act of 1966
FITAC .... Federacion Interamericana de Touring y Automovil Clubes [*Inter-American Federation of Touring and Automobile Clubs - IFTAC*] (EAIO)
FITAC .... Film Industry Training and Apprenticeship Council (SAUO)
FITAKTRON ... Fighter Attack Squadron (DNAB)
FITAL .... Financial Terminal Application Language (IAA)
FITAP .... Federation Internationale des Transports Aeriens Prives [*International Federation of Private Air Transport*]
FITASC .... Federation Internationale de Tir aux Arms Sportives de Chasse [*International Federation for Sport Shooting*] [*Paris, France*] (EAIO)
FITB .... Federation Internationale des Techniciens de la Bonneterie [*International Federation of Knitting Technologists - IFKT*] (EAIO)
FITB .... Fifth Third Bancorp [*NASDAQ symbol*] (NQ)
FITB .... Fill in the Blank [*Online dialog*]
FITB .... Fluorospar International Technical Bureau (EAIO)
FITBB .... Federation Internationale des Travailleurs du Batiment et du Bois [*International Federation of Building and Woodworkers*]
FITBT .... Fishing Industry Training Board of Tasmania [*Australia*]
FITC .... Fiber to the Curb [*Telecommunications*] (ITD)
FITC .... Financial Trust Corp. [*NASDAQ symbol*] (NQ)
FITC .... Financial Trust Corporation (SAUO)
FITC .... Fishery Industrial Technology Center (SAUS)
FITC .... Fleet Intelligence Training Center [*Navy*] (DNAB)
FITC .... Flight Instructor Training Course [*Navy*] (DNAB)
FITC .... Fluorescein Isothiocyanate [*Organic chemistry*]
FITC .... Fluoreszeinthiocyanat (SAUS)
FITC .... Foundation for International Technological Cooperation (DICI)
FITC .... Foundry Industry Training Committee [*British*] (BI)
FITCAL .... Feel, Inspect, Tighten, Clean, Adjust, Lubricate [*A keyword representing operations in preventive maintenance of communications equipment*] [*Military*]
FITCE .... Federation des Ingenieurs des Telecommunications de la Communaute Europeenne [*Federation of Telecommunications Engineers in the European Community*]
FITC-gARGG ... Fluorescein Isothiocyanate Conjugated Goat Antiserum to Rabbit Gamma Globulin [*Immunology*]
FITCH .... Fitchburg, MA [*American Association of Railroads railroad junction routing code*]
Fitchburg ..... Fitchburg Gas & Electric Light Company (SAUO)
Fitchburg St C ... Fitchburg State College (GAGS)
Fitch RE Ag ... Fitch on Real Estate Agency [*A publication*] (DLA)
FITCLANT .... Fleet Intelligence Training Center, Atlantic [*Navy*] (DNAB)
FITCPAC ...... Fleet Intelligence Training Center, Pacific [*Navy*] (DNAB)
FITD .... Far-Infrared Target Detector
FITD .... Fellow of the Institute of Training and Development [*British*] (DBQ)
FITDC .... Footwear Industry Traffic and Distribution Council (EA)
FITE .... Fair International Trade Employment Committee
FITE .... Federacion Interamericana de Trabajadores del Espectaculo [*Interamerican Federation of Entertainment Workers*]
FITE .... Forward Interworking Telephony Event [*Telecommunications*] (TEL)
FITEC .... Fair International Trade Employment Committee (SAUO)
FITEC .... Federation Internationale du Thermalisme et du Climatisme [*International Federation of Thermalism and Climatism*]
FITEC .... Forest Industry Training and Education Council (WPI)
FITFIMS ...... Federal Interagency Task Force on Inadvertent Modification of the Stratosphere (SAUO)
FITGO .... Floating Input to Ground Output
FITH .... Federation Internationale des Travailleurs de l'Habillement
FITH .... Fiber to the House [*Telecommunications*] (ITD)
FITH .... Fire-in-the-Hole [*Burn*] [*NASA*]
FITH .... First-in-the-Hole (MCD)
FITI .... Fabric Inspection Testing Institute (SAUS)
FITI .... Far-Infrared Target Indicator
FITIM .... Federacion Internacional de Trabajadores de las Industrias Metalurgicas [*International Metalworkers' Federation*]
FITITHC .... Federation Internationale des Travailleurs des Industries du Textile, de l'Habillement, et du Cuir [*International Textile, Garment, and Leather Workers' Federation*] [*Brussels, Belgium*]
FITITV .... Federacion Interamericana de Trabajadores de la Industria Textil, Vestuario , y Cuero [*Interamerican Textile, Garment, and Leather Workers Federation*]
FITITVCC ...... Federacion Interamericana de Trabajadores de la Industria Textil, Vestuario, Cuero, y Calzado [*Interamerican Textile, Leather, Garment, and Shoe Workers Federation - ITLGSWF*] (EA)
FITJ .... Fellow of the Institute of Technical Journalists [*British*] (DGA)
FiTK .... Turun Yliopiston Kirjasto [*Turku School of Economics*], Turku, Finland [*Library symbol*] [*Library of Congress*] (LCLS)
FITL .... Fiber in The Loop (ACRL)
FITL .... Flight Increment Training Load [*NASA*] (SPST)
FITLOG .... Foundation for Information Technology in Local Government (AIE)
FITNGSq ...... Fighter Interceptor Training Squadron [*Air Force*]
FITNR .... Fixed In The Next Release (SAUS)
FITNS .... Fitness
FITP .... Federation Internationale des Travailleurs des Plantations
FITP .... Federation Internationale des Travailleurs du Petrole
FITPASC ...... Federation Internationale des Travailleurs des Plantations, de l'Agriculture, etdes Secteurs Connexes [*International Federation of Plantation, Agricultural, and Allied Workers*]
FITPC .... Federation Internationale des Travailleurs du Petrole et de la Chimie [*International Federation of Petroleum and Chemical Workers*]
FITPQ .... Federacion Internacional de Trabajadores Petroleros y Quimicos [*International Federation of Petroleum and Chemical Workers*]
FITR .... Final Integrated Technology Reviews (ACAE)
FITR .... Flight Instrument Test Report (ACAE)
FITR .... Foundation for International Trade Research (EA)
FITREP .... Officer Fitness Report [*Navy*] (NVT)
FITRON .... Fighter Squadron [*Navy*] (MUGU)
FITRONDET ... Fighter Squadron Detachment (DNAB)
FITS .... Falkland Islands Trunk System (SAUS)
FITS .... Federation Internationale du Tourisme Social [*International Social Travel Federation - ISTF*] (EAIO)
FITS .... Fighter Interceptor Training Squadron [*Air Force*]
FITS .... Flexible Image Transport System [*Computer science*]
FITS .... Flexible Interchange Transport Standard (SAUS)
FITS .... Flexible Interchange Transport System (SAUS)
FITS .... Flying Instructors Training School (SAUO)
fits .... foreign individual travellers (SAUS)
FITS .... Fourteen-O-One Input-Output Tape System [*Military*] (SAA)
FITS .... Functional Individual Training System [*Navy*] (NVT)
FITS .... Functional Interpolating Transformational System [*HSC Software Co.*] (PCM)
FITS .... Functional Interpolating Transformation System (SAUS)
FITSA .... Fellow of the Institute of Trading Standards Administration [*British*] (DBQ)
F-I-T-T .... Fearful, Irritable, Tense, and Tremulous [*Combat behavior disorder*] [*Military*] (INF)
FITT .... Federation Internationale des Travailleurs de la Terre
FITT .... Federation Internationale de Tennis de Table [*International Table Tennis Federation*]
FITT .... Food Integrated Tech, Inc. [*NASDAQ symbol*] (SAG)
FITT .... Frequency, Intensity, Time, and Type [*Exercise formula*] [*Army*] (INF)
FITTC .... Federation of International Trampoline Technical Committee (EA)
FIT Test ...... Fusion at the Inferred Threshold Test (SAUS)

FITTHC .... Federation Internationale des Travailleurs des Industries du Textile, de l'Habillement, et du Cuir [*International Textile, Garment, and Leather Workers' Federation - ITGLWF*] (EAIO)
FITTS .... Fittings (ADA)
FITU .... Federation of Independent Trade Unions [*Lebanon*]
FITW .... Federal Income Tax Withholding
FITWEPSCOL... Fighter Weapons School [*Topgun*] [*Navy*] (DOMA)
fitwh .... federal income tax withholding (SAUS)
FITWING ...... Fighter Wing [*Navy*] (NVT)
Fitz .... Fitzgibbon's King's Bench Reports [*England*] [*A publication*] (DLA)
Fitz .... Fitzherbert's Abridgment [*1516*] [*A publication*] (DSA)
Fitz Abridg ... Fitzherbert's Abridgment [*1516*] [*A publication*] (DLA)
Fitzad Jud Act... Fitzadams on the Judicature Act [*A publication*] (DLA)
Fitzg .... Fitzgibbon's Irish Land Reports [*A publication*] (DLA)
Fitzg .... Fitzgibbon's Irish Registration Appeals [*A publication*] (DLA)
Fitzg .... Fitzgibbon's King's Bench Reports [*England*] [*A publication*] (DLA)
Fitzg Land R... Fitzgibbon's Irish Land Reports [*A publication*] (DLA)
Fitzg LG Dec... Fitzgibbon's Irish Local Government Decisions [*A publication*] (DLA)
Fitzg Pub H... Fitzgerald on the Public Health [*A publication*] (DLA)
Fitzg Reg Ca... Fitzgibbon's Irish Registration Appeals [*A publication*] (DLA)
Fitzh .... Fitzherbert's Abridgment [*1516*] [*A publication*] (DLA)
Fitzh Abr ...... Fitzherbert's Abridgment [*1516*] [*A publication*] (DLA)
Fitzh Nat Brev... Fitzherbert's Natura Brevium [*A publication*] (DLA)
Fitzh NB .... Fitzherbert's Natura Brevium [*A publication*] (DLA)
Fitzh N Br .... Fitzherbert's Natura Brevium [*A publication*] (DLA)
Fitz LG Dec... Fitzgibbon's Irish Local Government Decisions [*A publication*] (DLA)
Fitz Nat Brev... Fitzherbert's Natura Brevium [*A publication*] (DLA)
Fitzw .... Fitzwilliam Library (SAUS)
Fitzw .... Fitzwilliam Library, Cambridge (SAUO)
Fitzw Coll .... Fitzwilliam College-Cambridge (SAUS)
FIU .... Facilities Interface Unit (SAUS)
FIU .... Facility Interface Unit [*Telecommunications*]
FIU .... Federal Information Users (SAUS)
FIU .... Federation of Information Users [*Defunct*] (EA)
FIU .... Field Insertion Unit [*Rational, California*] (NITA)
FIU .... Field Intelligence Unit (MUGU)
FIU .... Fighter Interception Unit [*RAF*] [*British*]
FIU .... Fingerprint Identification Unit [*Sony Corp.*]
fiu .... Finno-Ugrian [*MARC language code*] [*Library of Congress*] (LCCP)
FIU .... Fire Investigation Unit (WDAA)
FIU .... Flight Interim Unit (ACAE)
FIU .... Florida International University [*Miami*]
FIU .... Forward Interpretation Unit [*Military*]
FIU .... Frequency Identification Unit (IAA)
FIUC .... Federation Internationale des Universites Catholiques [*International Federation of Catholic Universities - IFCU*] (EAIO)
FIUGX .... Fortis Inc: U.S. Govt. Secs. Cl.E [*Mutual fund ticker symbol*] (SG)
FIUIX .... Fidelity Utilities Fund [*Mutual fund ticker symbol*] (SG)
FIUL .... Fleet Issue Unit Load (DNAB)
FIUO .... For Internal Use Only (KSC)
FIUP .... Foundation for Indiana University of Pennsylvania [*Research center*] (RCD)
FIUS .... Flax Institute of the United States [*Defunct*] (EA)
FIUS .... French Institute in the United States [*Later, FIAF*] (EA)
FIUV .... Federation Internationale Una Voce (EA)
FIV .... Federation Internationale de la Vieillesse [*International Federation on Ageing - IFA*] (EAIO)
FIV .... Feline Immunodeficiency Virus
FIV .... Fellow of the Institute of Valuers [*British*]
FIV .... Fitness Institute of Victoria [*Australia*]
FIV .... Forced Inspiratory Volume (MELL)
FIV .... Fuel Insolation Valves (MCD)
FIV .... Future Infantry Vehicle [*Army*] (INF)
FIV .... Interface Group, Inc. [*ICAO designator*] (FAAC)
f-iv- .... Ivory Coast [*MARC geographic area code*] [*Library of Congress*] (LCCP)
FIV 1 .... Forced Inspiratory Volume in 1 sec. (SAUS)
FIVA .... Federation Internationale des Vehicules Anciens (EA)
FIVA .... Fluid Inject Valve Actuator
FIVB .... Federation Internationale de Volleyball [*International Volleyball Federation*] [*Switzerland*]
FIVC .... Festival International du Video-Clip [*The first festival entirely devoted to pop-music video, at San Tropez, October, 1984*]
FIVC .... First Valley Corporation (SAUO)
FIVC .... Forced Inspiratory Vital Capacity [*Medicine*]
FIVD .... Fifth Dimension [*NASDAQ symbol*] (TTSB)
FIVD .... Fifth Dimension, Inc. [*NASDAQ symbol*] (NQ)
FIVE .... Feature Interactive Verification Environment [*Communications term*] (DCT)
FIVEATAF ..... Fifth Allied Tactical Air Force, Southern Europe (NATG)
FIVER .... Five-Year Treasury Note Futures Contract (EBF)
FIVGV .... Fan Inlet Variable Guide Vanes (MCD)
FIVRS .... Financial Information Variance Reporting System (SAUS)
FIVRS .... Financial Information Variance System (SAUS)
FIVS .... Federation Internationale des Vins et Spiritueux [*International Federation of Wines and Spirits - IFWS*] (EAIO)
FiVTRC .... Technical Research Centre of Finland, Information Service, Espoo, Vuorimiehentie, Finland [*Library symbol*] [*Library of Congress*] (LCLS)
FIVU .... Federacion Internacional de Vivienda y Urbanismo [*International Federation for Housing and Planning*]
FIVV .... Federation Internationale de Vo Viet Nam [*An association*] (EAIO)
FIVZ .... Federation Internationale Veterinaire de Zootechnie
FIW .... Fellow of the Welding Institute [*British*]
FIW .... Fiberglass-Insulated Wire
FIW .... Fighter-Interceptor Wing (MCD)
FIW .... Flight Input Workstation (DA)
FIW .... Free in Wagon [*Business term*]
FIWC .... Fiji Industrial Workers' Congress
FIWC .... Food Industry War Committee (SAUO)
FIWES .... Fellow of the Institution of Water Engineers and Scientists [*British*] (DI)
FIWG .... Financial Issues Working Group (EURO)
FIWHTE .... Fellow of the Institution of Works and Highways Technician Engineers [*British*] (DBQ)
FIWM .... Fellow of the Institution of Works Managers [*British*]
FIWMA .... Fellow of the Institute of Weights and Measures Administration (SAUO)
FIWSc .... Fellow of the Institute of Wood Science [*British*]
FIWT .... Fellow of the Institute of Wireless Technology [*British*] (DAS)
FIX .... Comfort Systems USA [*NYSE symbol*] (SG)
FIX .... Factor IX [*Hematology*]
FIX .... Fault Isolater and Exercizer [*Honeywell*] (NITA)
FIX .... Federal Internet Exchange (TNIG)
FIX .... Ferndale Internet Experiment [*Computer science*]
FIX .... Financial Information Exchange (GART)
FIX .... Firing in Extension [*Missiles*]
fix .... Fixation (SAUS)
FIX .... Fixture
FIXBLK .... Fixed Blocked [*Computer science*] (MHDB)
FIXe .... Fix Error, Navigational [*Environmental science*] (COE)
fixed .... fixed-rate (SAUS)
FIXExpE .... Fellow of the Institute of Explosives Engineers [*British*] (DBQ)
FIXIT .... Fighting, Innovations and Experiment in Teaching (SAUS)
FIXIT .... Flexible Information Exploitation Interpretive Transfer [*Software engineering tool*] (NITA)
FIXIT .... Fostering, Innovations, and Experiment in Teaching (SAUS)
FIXIT .... Fostering, or Fighting, Innovations and Experiment in Teaching [*Game*]
FIXMI .... Financial Information Exchange Markup Language (GART)
FIXN .... Fixation
FIXRES .... Fixtures (ROG)
FIXS .... Fixtures (SAUS)
Fixt .... Fixture (MIST)
FIXT .... Fixture
FIXUNB .... Fixed Unblocked [*Computer science*] (MHDB)
FIXWEX .... Fixed-Wing Evaluation Exercise [*Aviation*]
f-i-y kit .... Fit It Yourself kit (SAUS)
FIYTO .... Federation of International Youth Travel Organizations [*Copenhagen, Denmark*] (EAIO)
FIZ .... Dritte Welt Frauensinformationszentrum [*Information Center for Third World Women*] [*Zurich, Switzerland*] (EAIO)
FIZ .... Fachinformationszentrum [*Information centre*] [*Germany*] (NITA)
FIZ .... National Beverage Corp. [*AMEX symbol*] (SAG)
FIZ .... Natl Beverage [*AMEX symbol*] (TTSB)
FIZ-technik... Fachinformationszentrum Technik [*Germany*] (NITA)
FIZ-W .... Fachinformationszentrum Werkstoffe [*Information Center for Materials*] [*Information service or system*] (IID)
FJ .... Air Pacific [*ICAO designator*] (AD)
FJ .... Congregation of Daughters of Jesus [*Roman Catholic religious order*]
FJ .... Congregation of St. John (TOCD)
fj .... Congregation of St. John (TOCD)
FJ .... Farm Journal (SAUS)
FJ .... Fast Jet (SAUS)
FJ .... Fedders Corp. [*NYSE symbol*] (SAG)
FJ .... Federal Judge (SAFN)
FJ .... Field Judge [*Football*]
FJ .... Fighter Jet
FJ .... Fiji [*ANSI two-letter standard code*] (CNC)
fj .... Fiji [*MARC country of publication code*] [*Library of Congress*] (LCCP)
FJ .... Fiji Airways (SAUS)
FJ .... Filles de Jesus de Kermaria [*Daughters of Jesus of Kermaria - DJK*] [*Paris, France*] (EAIO)
FJ .... First Judge [*Legal term*] (DLA)
F-J .... Fisher-John (SAUS)
FJ .... Fisher-Johns [*Melting point method*]
FJ .... Fixed Jack [*Electronics*] (IAA)
FJ .... Fjord (WDAA)
FJ .... Flush Joint [*Diamond drilling*]
FJ .... Flying Junior [*Boating*] (DICI)
FJ .... Formula Junior [*Class of racing cars*]
FJ .... Fort James [*NYSE symbol*] [*Formerly, James River Corp.*] (SG)
FJ .... Freeman's Journal [*A publication*]
FJ .... Friends for Jamaica [*An association*] (EA)
FJ .... Friends of Jerusalem [*An association*] (EA)
fj .... From Japan (SAUS)
FJ .... Fuel-Jet (DA)
FJ .... Fuji Heavy Industries (Subaru) [*Society of Automotive Engineers auto manufacturer code for service information interchange*]
FJ .... Fused Junction
FJ .... Jacksonville Public Library System, Jacksonville, FL [*Library symbol*] [*Library of Congress*] (LCLS)
FJA .... Fedders Corp. [*NYSE symbol*] (SAG)
FJA .... Fedders Corp'A' [*NYSE symbol*] (TTSB)
FJA .... Fluid Jet Amplifier
FJA .... Functional Job Analysis
FJA .... Future Journalists of America [*Defunct*] (EA)
FJAA .... Fashion Jewelry Association of America (EA)
FJAP .... Federal and Judicial Appointments Project [*Defunct*] (EA)

Fj-Ar .... Central Archives of Fiji, Suva, Fiji [*Library symbol*] [*Library of Congress*] (LCLS)
FJB .... West Jefferson, NC [*Location identifier*] [*FAA*] (FAAL)
FJbF .... Florida Institute of Technology, Jensen Beach Campus, Jenson Beach, FL [*Library symbol*] [*Library of Congress*] (LCLS)
FJC .... Fairbury Junior College [*Nebraska*]
FJC .... Falcon Jet Centre [*British*] [*ICAO designator*] (FAAC)
FJC .... Falcon Jet Corporation (ACAE)
FJC .... Fedders Corp. [*NYSE symbol*] (SAG)
FJC .... Federal Judicial Center
FJC .... Ferrum Junior College (SAUO)
FJC .... Fisher Junior College [*Boston, MA*]
FJC .... Flint Junior College [*Michigan*]
FJC .... Fraser's Reports, Justiciary Court [*Scotland*] [*A publication*] (DLA)
FJC .... Freely Jointed Chain [*Model of a polymer*] [*Organic chemistry*]
FJC .... Freeman Junior College [*South Dakota*]
FJC .... Friendship Junior College [*South Carolina*]
FJC .... Fullerton Junior College [*Later, Fullerton College*] [*California*]
FJCC .... Fall Joint Computer Conference [*Replaced by National Computer Conference - NCC*]
FJCE .... Forum Jeunesse des Communautes Europeennes [*Youth Forum of the European Communities - YFEC*] (EAIO)
FJCEE .... Federation des Jeunes Chefs d'Entreprises d'Europe [*European Federation of Young Managers*]
FJCF .... Federation des Jeunes Canadiens-Francais [*Federation of French-Canadian Youth*]
FJCNY .... Furriers Joint Council of New York (EA)
FJCT .... Freedom and Justice for Cyprus Trust (EA)
FJD .... Florida Junior College at Jacksonville, DTC, Jacksonville, FL [*OCLC symbol*] (OCLC)
FJDG .... Diego Garcia [*British Indian Ocean Territory*] [*ICAO location identifier*] (ICLI)
FJE .... Free Jet Expansion
FJF .... Farmworker Justice Fund (EA)
FJF .... Federal Junior Fellowship [*Army*] (RDA)
FJF .... Florida Junior College at Jacksonville, Jacksonville, FL [*Library symbol*] [*Library of Congress*] (LCLS)
FJG .... Fonda, Johnstown & Gloversville Railroad Co. [*AAR code*]
FJGS .... Church of Jesus Christ of Latter-Day Saints, Genealogical Society Library, Jacksonville Branch, Jacksonville, FL [*Library symbol*] [*Library of Congress*] (LCLS)
FJI .... Air Pacific Ltd. [*Fiji*] [*ICAO designator*] (FAAC)
FJI .... Federal Job Information (SAUS)
FJI .... Fellow of the Journalists' Institute [*British*] (ROG)
FJI .... Fidjii (SAUS)
FJI .... Fiji [*ANSI three-letter standard code*] (CNC)
Fji .... Fiji (MILB)
FJI .... Frequency Jumper Identification
FJI .... Friends of Julio International (EA)
FJIC .... Federal Job Information Center (SAUO)
FJK .... Florida Junior College at Jacksonville, Kent, Jacksonville, FL [*OCLC symbol*] (OCLC)
FJL .... Frente Juventil Lautaro [*Chile*] [*Political party*] (EY)
FJM .... Friedman, John M., Hurricane WV [*STAC*]
FJM .... Friends of Johnny Mathis [*Defunct*] (EA)
FJMC .... Federation of Jewish Men's Clubs (EA)
FJN .... Familial Juvenile Nephrophthisis [*Medicine*]
FJN .... Florida Junior College at Jacksonville, North, Jacksonville, FL [*OCLC symbol*] (OCLC)
FJN .... Front Jednosci Narodowej [*Polish Front of National Unity*]
FJNA .... Front des Jeunes Nationalistes Africains [*National African Youth Front*]
FJNC .... First Jersey National Corporation (SAUO)
FJNF .... Foundation for the Jewish National Fund (EA)
FJNM .... Fort Jefferson National Monument (SAUO)
FJO .... Ft. Johnson [*Malawi*] [*Airport symbol*] (AD)
FJO .... Offshore Power Systems, Jacksonville, FL [*Library symbol*] [*Library of Congress*] (LCLS)
FJOL .... Federal Job Opportunity List (SAUS)
FJP .... Familial Juvenile Polyposis [*Medicine*] (MELL)
FJP .... Federation of Jewish Philanthropies of New York (EA)
FJPC .... Federation des Jeunes Progressistes-Conservateurs du Canada [*Progressive Conservative Youth Federation of Canada*]
FJPTFCG .... Federation of Jewish Philanthropies Task Force on Compulsive Gambling (SAUO)
FJPX .... Fort James Pennington [*Federal Railroad Administration identification code*]
FJR .... Factories Journal Reports [*India*] [*A publication*] (DLA)
FJR .... Friends of James Rogers (EA)
FJRM .... Full Joint Range of Movement [*Orthopedics*]
FJS .... Facet Joint Syndrome (MELL)
FJS .... Finger Joint Size (MELL)
FJS .... First Jersey Securities
FJS .... Florida Junior College at Jacksonville, South, Jacksonville, FL [*OCLC symbol*] (OCLC)
FJS .... Fort Jones, CA [*Location identifier*] [*FAA*] (FAAL)
FJS .... Fulton J Sheen (SAUS)
FJSH .... Full Jaguar Service History [*Automotive classified advertising*]
FJSH .... Full Jeep Service History [*Automotive classified advertising*]
FJSRL .... Frank J. Seiler Research Laboratory [*US Air Force Academy, CO*]
FJSTO .... Federation of Jewish Student Organizations [*Defunct*] (EA)
FJT .... Familiarization Job Training (AFIT)
FJT .... Flush Joint [*Technical drawings*]
FJT .... Free Jet Test
FJU .... Chicago, IL [*Location identifier*] [*FAA*] (FAAL)
FJU .... Jacksonville University, Jacksonville, FL [*Library symbol*] [*Library of Congress*] [*OCLC symbol*] (LCLS)
FJUNF .... University of North Florida, Jacksonville, FL [*Library symbol*] [*Library of Congress*] (LCLS)
FJUS .... FJ United States [*An association*] (EA)
FJUS .... International FJ Class Organization (EA)
FJW .... Friends of Jackie Wilson (EA)
FJWO .... Federation of Jewish Women's Organizations (EA)
FK .... 5,000 [*Film*] (WDMC)
FK .... Faker Track (MUGU)
FK .... Falkirk [*Postcode*] (ODBW)
FK .... Falkland Islands [*ANSI two-letter standard code*] (CNC)
fk .... Falkland Islands [*MARC country of publication code*] [*Library of Congress*] (LCCP)
FK .... Falkland Islands [*Internet country code*]
FK .... Feil-Klippel [*Syndrome*] [*Medicine*] (DB)
F-K .... Feynman-Kak Formula [*Particle physics*]
FK .... Fish Kill [*Environment term*] (EGA)
FK .... Fixture Key (SAUS)
FK .... Flamenco Airlines [*ICAO designator*] (AD)
FK .... Flat Keel [*Shipbuilding*]
FK .... Flat Knob [*Gunnery*]
FK .... Fluid Kinetics (SAUS)
FK .... Fokker-VFW BV [*Netherlands*] [*ICAO aircraft manufacturer identifier*] (ICAO)
FK .... Foreign Key [*Computer science*] (PCM)
FK .... Fork (MSA)
FK .... Foster-Kennedy [*Syndrome*] [*Medicine*] (DB)
FK .... Foundation Kit (SAUS)
FK .... Friends of Karen (EA)
FK .... Fujisawa Pharmaceutical Co. [*Japan*] [*Research code symbol*]
FK .... Fujita Airways (SAUS)
FK .... Function Key (MCD)
FK .... Geelong Air Travel [*ICAO designator*] (AD)
fka .... Formerly Known As (ADWA)
FKA .... Formerly Known As (TBD)
FKAB .... Banyo [*Cameroon*] [*ICAO location identifier*] (ICLI)
FKAF .... Bafia [*Cameroon*] [*ICAO location identifier*] (ICLI)
FKAG .... Abong-M'Bang [*Cameroon*] [*ICAO location identifier*] (ICLI)
FKAL .... Lomie [*Cameroon*] [*ICAO location identifier*] (ICLI)
FKAM .... Meiganga [*Cameroon*] [*ICAO location identifier*] (ICLI)
FKAN .... N'Kongsamba [*Cameroon*] [*ICAO location identifier*] (ICLI)
FKAO .... Betare-Oya [*Cameroon*] [*ICAO location identifier*] (ICLI)
FKAV .... Free Kindergarten Association of Victoria [*Australia*]
FKAY .... Yoko [*Cameroon*] [*ICAO location identifier*] (ICLI)
FKB .... Flight Display Keyboard [*NASA*] (NASA)
FKB .... Fredericksburg, TX [*Location identifier*] [*FAA*] (FAAL)
FKB .... Function Key Button (IAA)
FKBC .... First-Knox Banc Corp. [*NASDAQ symbol*] (TTSB)
FKBC .... First Knox Bancorp [*NASDAQ symbol*] (SAG)
FKBD .... Fort Knox Bullion Depository (SAUS)
FKBG .... Fourdrinier Kraft Board Group (SAUO)
FKBG-API .... Fourdrinier Kraft Board Group of American Paper Institute (SAUO)
FKBI .... Fourdrinier Kraft Board Institute [*Later, CKPG*] (EA)
FKC .... Fellow of King's College [*London*]
FKC .... Friends of the Kennedy Center (EA)
FKC .... Function Key Calling (SAUS)
FKCBS .... Frantisek Kmoch Czech Bands Society [*British*] (DBA)
FKCL .... Fellow of King's College, London
FKCM .... Franklin Cons Mng [*NASDAQ symbol*] (TTSB)
FKCM .... Franklin Consolidated Mining Co., Inc. [*NASDAQ symbol*] (NQ)
FKD .... Forked
Fkd .... Frankford (SAUS)
FKE .... Federation of Kenya Employers (SAUO)
FKE .... Full Knee Extension (MELL)
f-ke- .... Kenya [*MARC geographic area code*] [*Library of Congress*] (LCCP)
FKES .... First Keystone Financial [*NASDAQ symbol*] (TTSB)
Fkey .... Function Key [*Computer science*]
FKF .... Finlands Kristliga Foerbund [*Finnish Christian League*] (PPE)
FKF .... Flight Kits Facility (SAUS)
FKF .... Franklin Bluffs, AK [*Location identifier*] [*FAA*] (FAAL)
FKFC .... First Kent Financial Corp. [*NASDAQ symbol*] (SAG)
FKFS .... First Keystone Financial, Inc. [*NASDAQ symbol*] (SAG)
FKG .... Feldkanonengeschoa (SAUS)
FKgP .... Fueggetlen Kisgazda-, Foeldmunkas- es Polgari Part [*Independent Smallholders' Party*] [*Hungary*] [*Political party*] (EY)
FKI .... Fachverband Klebstoffindustrie [*Association of European Adhesives Manufacturers*] (EAIO)
FKI .... Kisangani [*Zaire*] [*Airport symbol*] (OAG)
FKII .... Federation of Korea Information Industries (SAUO)
FKJ .... Fukue [*Japan*] [*Seismograph station code, US Geological Survey*] (SEIS)
FKJC .... Florida Keys Junior College (SAUS)
FKK .... Freie-Koerper-Kultur [*Nudism, a pre-NAZI fad in Germany*]
FKK .... Fukuoka [*Japan*] [*Seismograph station code, US Geological Survey*] (SEIS)
FKKA .... Maroua/Ville [*Cameroon*] [*ICAO location identifier*] (ICLI)
FKKB .... Kribi [*Cameroon*] [*ICAO location identifier*] (ICLI)
FKKC .... Tiko [*Cameroon*] [*ICAO location identifier*] (ICLI)
FKKD .... Douala [*Cameroon*] [*ICAO location identifier*] (ICLI)
FKKE .... Eseka [*Cameroon*] [*ICAO location identifier*] (ICLI)
FKKF .... Mamfe [*Cameroon*] [*ICAO location identifier*] (ICLI)
FKKG .... Bali [*Cameroon*] [*ICAO location identifier*] (ICLI)
FKKH .... Kaele [*Cameroon*] [*ICAO location identifier*] (ICLI)
FKKI .... Batouri [*Cameroon*] [*ICAO location identifier*] (ICLI)

FKKJ .... Yagoua [*Cameroon*] [*ICAO location identifier*] (ICLI)
FKKK .... Douala [*Cameroon*] [*ICAO location identifier*] (ICLI)
FKKL .... Maroua/Salak [*Cameroon*] [*ICAO location identifier*] (ICLI)
FKKM .... Foumban/Nkounja [*Cameroon*] [*ICAO location identifier*] (ICLI)
FKKN .... N'Gaoundere [*Cameroon*] [*ICAO location identifier*] (ICLI)
FKKO .... Bertoua [*Cameroon*] [*ICAO location identifier*] (ICLI)
FKKR .... Garoua [*Cameroon*] [*ICAO location identifier*] (ICLI)
FKKS .... Dschang [*Cameroon*] [*ICAO location identifier*] (ICLI)
FKKT .... Tibati [*Cameroon*] [*ICAO location identifier*] (ICLI)
FKKU .... Bafoussam [*Cameroon*] [*ICAO location identifier*] (ICLI)
FKKV .... Bamenda [*Cameroon*] [*ICAO location identifier*] (ICLI)
FKKW .... Ebolowa [*Cameroon*] [*ICAO location identifier*] (ICLI)
FKKY .... Frankfort First Bancorp [*NASDAQ symbol*] (TTSB)
FKKY .... Frankfort First Bancorp, Inc. [*NASDAQ symbol*] (SAG)
FKKY .... Yaounde [*Cameroon*] [*ICAO location identifier*] (ICLI)
FKL .... Franklin [*Pennsylvania*] [*Airport symbol*] (OAG)
FKL .... Franklin Capital Corp. [*AMEX symbol*] (NASQ)
FKL .... Franklin Corp. [*AMEX symbol*] (SPSG)
FKL .... Franklin Hldg Corp. [*AMEX symbol*] (TTSB)
FKL .... Franklin, PA [*Location identifier*] [*FAA*] (FAAL)
FKL .... V. Kelner Airways Ltd. [*Canada*] [*FAA designator*] (FAAC)
FKLN .... Franklin Ophthalmic Instruments [*NASDAQ symbol*] (TTSB)
FKLT .... Fast Karhunen-Loeve Transform (SAUS)
FKM .... Fluoroelastomer [*Plastics*]
FKM .... fluoro rubbers (SAUS)
FKM .... Fort Knox Minerals Ltd. [*Vancouver Stock Exchange symbol*]
FKN .... Field-Koros-Noves [*Physical chemistry*]
Fkn .... Franklin (SAUS)
FKN .... Franklin, VA [*Location identifier*] [*FAA*] (FAAL)
FKN .... Fraunhofer Knowledge Network (VLIE)
FKNMS .... Florida Keys National Marine Sanctuary
FKO .... Family Keep Off [*Food, in presence of company*] [*British*] (DI)
FKP .... Finlands Kommunistiska Parti [*Finnish Communist Party*] (PPE)
FKP .... Francia Kommunista Part [*French Communist Party*] [*Political party*]
FKP .... Fratsuzskaia Kommunisticheskaia Partiia [*Political party*]
FKP .... French Communist Party [*Political party*]
FKP .... Fueggetlen Kisgazda Part [*Independent Smallholders' Party*] [*Hungary*] (PPE)
FKP .... Hopkinsville, KY [*Location identifier*] [*FAA*] (FAAL)
FKQ .... Fak-Fak [*Indonesia*] [*Airport symbol*] (OAG)
FKQCP .... Fellow of the King's and Queen's College of Physicians, Ireland
FKQCPI .... Fellow of the King's and Queen's College of Physicians, Ireland [*Later, FRCPI*] (ROG)
Fkr .... Faeroese Krone [*Monetary unit*] (ODBW)
FKR .... Frankfort, IN [*Location identifier*] [*FAA*] (FAAL)
F KR .... Krona [*Crown*] [*Monetary unit*] [*Faroe Islands*]
FKRX .... Flintkote [*Private rail car owner code*]
Fks .... Fredrikstad (SAUS)
FKS .... Friends of Kate Smith [*Later, Kate Smith/God Bless America Foundation*] (EA)
FKS .... Fukushima [*Japan*] [*Seismograph station code, US Geological Survey*] (SEIS)
FKSB .... Florida Kindergarten Screening Battery (DHP)
FKSBG .... Fredericksburg, VA [*American Association of Railroads railroad junction routing code*]
FKscNA .... National Aeronautics and Space Administration, John F. Kennedy Space Center, Kennedy Space Center, FL [*Library symbol*] [*Library of Congress*] (LCLS)
FKSII .... Fresh Kills, Staten Island, Incinerator (SAUS)
FKSNS .... Fort Kent State Normal School (SAUO)
FKT .... Field Kitchen Trailer (MCD)
FKT .... Filtrate kill tank (SAUS)
FKT .... Friends of Kristoffer Tabori [*Defunct*] [*Defunct*] (EA)
FK Track .... Faker Track (SAUS)
FKTU .... Federation of Korean Trade Unions [*South Korea*]
FKU .... Feminist Karate Union (EA)
FKV .... Gainesville, GA [*Location identifier*] [*FAA*] (FAAL)
FKw .... Monroe County Public Library, Key West, FL [*Library symbol*] [*Library of Congress*] (LCLS)
FKWBRC .... Florida Keys Wild Bird Rehabilitation Center (EA)
FKwC .... Florida Keys Community College, Key West, FL [*Library symbol*] [*Library of Congress*] (LCLS)
FKwH .... Ernest Hemingway Home, Key West, FL [*Library symbol*] [*Library of Congress*] (LCLS)
FKwHi .... Key West Art and Historical Society, Key West, FL [*Library symbol*] [*Library of Congress*] (LCLS)
FKWR .... Florida Keys Wildlife Refuge (SAUS)
FKWR .... Florida Keys Wildlife Refuges (SAUO)
FKZ .... Sacramento, CA [*Location identifier*] [*FAA*] (FAAL)
FL .... Face Lift (MELL)
FL .... Fail (NASA)
FL .... Falconbridge Limited (SAUO)
FL .... Falconbridge Ltd. [*Toronto Stock Exchange symbol*] [*Vancouver Stock Exchange symbol*]
FL .... Fall
FL .... Falsa Lectio [*False Reading, in a text*] [*Latin*]
FL .... Fan Lift
FL .... Farmer's Lung (MELL)
fl .... farmland (SAUS)
FL .... Fastest Lap [*Auto racing*]
FL .... Fatigue Limit
FL .... Fatty Liver (DB)
FL .... Fault Localization (CAAL)
FL .... Fault Location (SAUS)
FL .... Federal League [*Major league in baseball, 1914-15*]
FL .... Feed Lines (NASA)
Fl .... Feldspar [*A mineral*]
FL .... Feline Lung (Cell) [*Cytology*]
fl .... Femtoliter [*One quadrillionth of a liter*]
FL .... Fetch Load (SAUS)
F/L .... Fetch/Load [*Computer science*] (MDG)
FL .... Fiber Link (SAUS)
FL .... Fiberoptic Link (SAUS)
FL .... fibre lisse (SAUS)
FL .... Field Length
FL .... Field Lens (SAUS)
FL .... Field Loss Contactor or Relay [*Industrial control*] (IEEE)
FL .... Fiessinger-Leroy [*Syndrome*] [*Medicine*] (DB)
FL .... Fight Level (PDAA)
FL .... File (SAUS)
FL .... File Label (VLIE)
FL .... File Limit (SAUS)
FL .... Filler (VLIE)
F/L .... Film Load (KSC)
FL .... Filter (CET)
FL .... Filtered Load (MAE)
FL .... Finished Lower Level (ADWA)
FL .... First Lady [*Imelda Marcos of The Philippines*]
FL .... First Level (VLIE)
FL .... First Light (SAUS)
FL .... Fiscal Letter (OICC)
FL .... Fish Lake [*Pisciculture*]
FL .... Fixed Length (VLIE)
FL .... fixed light (SAUS)
FL .... Fixed Line (SAUS)
FL .... fixing letter (SAUS)
FL .... Flag [*British naval signaling*]
FL .... Flag Lieutenant [*Navy*]
fl .... Flake (SAUS)
FL .... Flame (AAG)
FL .... Flammable
FL .... Flanders [*Belgium*] (WDAA)
FL .... Flange (WGA)
FL .... Flank (SAUS)
FL .... Flanker [*Football*]
Fl .... Flash (DAS)
FL .... Flash Advisory [*Meteorology*] (FAAC)
FL .... Flashing (DAC)
FL .... Flashing Lamp (SAUS)
FL .... Flashing Light [*Navigation signal*]
FL .... Flash Lamp
FL .... Flat (MSA)
FL .... flat ledge (SAUS)
FL .... Flauto [*Flute*] [*Music*] (ROG)
FL .... flavin mononucleotide (SAUS)
FL .... Flawless [*Diamond clarity grade*]
Fl .... Fleet (SAUS)
FL .... Fleischner Society (SAUO)
FL .... Flemish [*Language, etc.*] (ROG)
FL .... Flexible (SAUS)
FL .... Flexileave (HEAS)
FL .... Flexion [*Medicine*]
Fl .... Flight (SAUS)
FL .... Flight Leader (SAUS)
FL .... Flight Level
FL .... Flight Lieutenant
F/L .... Flintlock [*British military*] (DMA)
FL .... Flip Latch (VLIE)
FL .... Float (IAA)
fl .... floating (SAUS)
FL .... Floating Landing (ROG)
FL .... Flood (MSA)
fl .... floodable length (SAUS)
Fl .... Flooding (SAUS)
FL .... Floodlight (SAUS)
Fl .... Floor (PROS)
fl .... Floor (SHCU)
FL .... Floor
FL .... Floor Level (SAUS)
FL .... Floor Line (MSA)
Fl .... Floorline [*Construction term*] (MIST)
FL .... Flores [*Flowers*] [*Latin*]
FL .... Florida [*Postal code*]
FL .... Florin [*Monetary unit*] [*Netherlands*]
FL .... Floruit [*He Flourished*] [*Latin*]
FL .... Flotilla Leader [*British*]
FL .... Flour (WGA)
fl .... flourish (SAUS)
fl .... Flourished (VRA)
FL .... Flow (MSA)
fl .... Flower [*Botany*]
FL .... Flow Line [*Technical drawings*]
fl .... Fluid (IDYL)
FL .... Fluid (KSC)
fl .... Fluid (MIST)
fl .... fluid loss (SAUS)
FL .... Fluidus [*Fluid*] [*Pharmacy*]
FL .... Fluorescence [*or Fluorescent*]
FL .... Fluorescent Lamp (SAUS)
fl .... fluorescent level (SAUS)

FL .... Fluorescent Light (SAUS)
FL .... Fluorine [*Symbol is F*] [*Chemical element*] (ROG)
FL .... Fluorite [*Mineral*]
fl .... Fluoro [*As substituent on nucleoside*] [*Biochemistry*]
FL .... Fluoroleucine (SAUS)
Fl .... Fluorometric [*or Fluorometry*]
FL .... Flush (MSA)
FL .... Flush Left [*Graphic arts*] (DGA)
fl .... Flush Left [*Typography*] (WDMC)
fl .... Flute (GROV)
FL .... Flute
FL .... Flute Lead (MSA)
FL .... Fluvio-Lacustrine Sandstone [*Geology*]
fl .... flyleaf (WDAA)
FL .... Focal Length [*Photography*]
FL .... Focal Line (SAUS)
FL .... Follicular Lymphoma [*Oncology*]
FL .... Foodborne Listeriosis [*Medicine*] (MELL)
FL .... Food Laboratory [*Army*]
FL .... Football League (ODA)
FL .... Foothills Laboratory (SAUS)
fL .... Foot-Lambert (IDOE)
FL .... Foot-Lambert [*Illumination*]
FL .... Foot Lumen (SAUS)
FL .... Forced Lubrication (SAUS)
FL .... Foreign Language
FL .... Foreign Listing [*Telecommunications*] (TEL)
fl .... forklift (SAUS)
FL .... For Life [*An association*] (EA)
FL .... Formal Language (SAUS)
FL .... Formal Logic (SAUS)
FL .... Format List (SAUS)
FL .... Form Letter
FL .... Formula Language (SAUS)
FL .... Formula Libre [*Automotive competition*]
FL .... Forrnat List (SAUS)
FL .... Forward Link (NAKS)
FL .... Fraction that live (SAUS)
FL .... France-Louisiane [*Later, FLFADDFA*] [*France*] (EAIO)
FL .... Fraunhofer Line (PDAA)
FL .... Freedom League (EA)
F/L .... Free Lance
FL .... Free Length (SAUS)
fl .... free loading (SAUS)
FL .... Freie Liste [*Free List*] [*Liechtenstein*] [*Political party*] (EY)
F/L .... Freight Liner [*British Railways Board*] (DS)
FL .... Frenkel and Ladd Method (SAUS)
Fl .... Frequency-Shift Keying (IDOE)
FL .... Friend Erythroleukemia [*Medicine*] (DB)
FL .... Friend Leukemia [*Cytology*] (DMAA)
FL .... Frontal Lobe [*Brain anatomy*]
FL .... Frontier Airlines, Inc. [*ICAO designator*]
FL .... Front Lay [*Printing*] (DGA)
FL .... front left (SAUS)
FL .... Front Line (SAUS)
FL .... Fuel (KSC)
FL .... Full Lift (KSC)
FL .... Full Liquid [*Medicine*]
FL .... Full Load (EEVL)
FL .... Functional Learning (VLIE)
FL .... Function Language (SAUS)
FL .... Function Libraries (SAUS)
FL .... funding less than (SAUS)
FL .... Funnel Length
FL .... Fusible Link (EECA)
FL .... Fuzzy Language (SAUS)
FL .... Fuzzy Logic (AAEL)
FL .... Guilder [*Florin*] [*Monetary unit*] [*Netherlands*]
FL .... Land Station [*ITU designation*] (CET)
FL .... Languages and Linguistics [*Educational Resources Information Center (ERIC) Clearinghouse*] [*Center for Applied Linguistics*] (PAZ)
FL .... Liechtenstein [*IYRU nationality code*] (IYR)
fl--- .... Nile River and Basin [*MARC geographic area code*] [*Library of Congress*] (LCCP)
FL1 .... first flight model (SAUS)
FL/1 .... Function Language 1 (SAUS)
FL1 .... Function Language One
FL2 .... second flight model (SAUS)
FLA .... Air Florida [*ICAO designator*] (FAAC)
FLA .... Fabric Laminators Association [*Defunct*]
FLA .... Fair Labor Association
FLA .... Family Law Act (FOTI)
FLA .... Family Lodging Allowance (SAUO)
FLA .... Federal Librarians Association [*Defunct*]
FLA .... Federal Loan Administration
FLA .... Federal Loan Agency [*Abolished 1947, records transferred to Reconstruction Finance Corp.*]
FLA .... Federation of Local Authorities (SAUO)
FLA .... Fellow of the Library Association [*British*]
FLA .... Fellowship of the Library Association (SAUO)
FLA .... Feminists for Life of America [*Later, FFL*] (EA)
FLA .... Fiat Lege Artis [*Let It Be Done According to the Rules of the Art*] [*Pharmacy*]
FLA .... Film Laboratory Association Ltd. [*British*] (BI)
FLA .... Finance and Leasing Association [*British*] (EAIO)
FLA .... Firearms Lobby of America [*Later, CCRKBA*] (EA)
fla .... firn-line altitude (SAUS)
FLA .... First Lord of the Admiralty [*British*]
FLA .... Flake (SAUS)
Fla .... Flare Stack (at sea) [*Nautical term*] (HRNC)
FLA .... Flats [*Utah*] [*Seismograph station code, US Geological Survey*] [*Closed*] (SEIS)
FLA .... Flight Article [*Army*] (AABC)
FLA .... Flood Watch [*Telecommunications*] (OTD)
FLA .... Florencia [*Colombia*] [*Airport symbol*] (OAG)
FLA .... Florida (AFM)
Fla .... Florida (ODBW)
FLA .... Florida East Coast Indus [*NYSE symbol*] (TTSB)
FLA .... Florida East Coast Industries, Inc. [*NYSE symbol*] (SPSG)
FLA .... Florida East Coast Railway (SAUS)
FLA .... Florida Library Association (SAUO)
Fla .... Florida Reports [*A publication*] (DLA)
Fla .... Floridian (SAUS)
FLA .... Fluid Levitation Accelerometer
FLA .... Fluid Loss Additive (SAUS)
FLA .... Fluorescent-Labeled Antibody [*Medicine*] (MELL)
FLA .... Fluorescent Lighting Association (EA)
FLA .... Foam Laminators Association (EA)
FLA .... Foothills Library Association (SAUO)
FLA .... Foreign Language Acquisition (ADWA)
FLA .... Foreign Language Assistant (SAUO)
FLA .... Foreign Language Associates
FLA .... Foreign Launch Assessment (SAUO)
FLA .... Four-Conductor, Lighting, Armor [*Cable*] (IAA)
FLA .... Four Letter Acronym (SAUS)
FLA .... France Latin America [*An association*] (EAIO)
FLA .... Free Luggage Allowance (SAUS)
FLA .... Freustrum Location Addition
FLA .... Frontline Ambulance [*Army*] (INF)
FLA .... Front Line Assembly (SAUS)
FLA .... Fronto-Laeva Anterior [*A fetal position*] [*Obstetrics*] (MAE)
FLA .... Fuel-Air (SAUS)
FLA .... Full Load Ampere (SAUS)
FLA .... Full Look Ahead (SAUS)
FLA .... Future Large Aircraft [*Cooperative manufacturing effort of France, Germany, Britain, Italy, Portugal, Spain and Turkey*] (ECON)
FLA .... Future Large Airlifter (SAUO)
FLA .... Librairies Flammarion [*ACCORD*] [*UTLAS symbol*]
FLAA .... Fellow, London Association of Accountants
FLAA .... Fellow of the Library Association of Australia (SAUO)
FLAA .... Fellow of the London Association of Certified Accountants (SAUO)
FLAA .... Fellow of the London Associaton of Certified and Corporate Accountants (DAS)
FLAA .... Liberation Front of Air and Azaouad (Niger) [*Political party*] (PSAP)
Fla A&M U ... Florida Agricultural and Mechanical University (GAGS)
FLAAC .... Florida Lime and Avocado Administrative Committee (EA)
Fla Admin Code ... Florida Administrative Code [*A publication*] (DLA)
Fla Admin Code Weekly ... Florida Administrative Code Weekly [*A publication*] (AAGC)
Fla & K .... Flanagan and Kelly's Irish Rolls Court Reports [*1840-42*] [*A publication*] (DLA)
FLAAR .... Foundation for Latin American Anthropological Research (EA)
Fl-AAS .... Flame Atomic Absorption Spectroscopy (SAUS)
Fla Atlantic U ... Florida Atlantic University (GAGS)
F Lab .... Field Laboratory (SAUS)
flab .... flabby (SAUS)
FLAB .... Flag Lieutenant to the Admiralty Board (SAUS)
FLAB .... Florida East Coast Ind "B" [*NYSE symbol*]
fl abwth .... flush armor balanced watertight hatch (SAUS)
FLAC .... Federation of Latin American Clubs, Europe (SAUO)
FIAC .... Fellow of the International Academy of Cytology (SAUS)
FLAC .... Flaccid
FLAC .... Florida Automatic Computer [*Air Force*]
FLAC .... Flutter Analysis by a Collocation Method (ACAE)
Flac .... In Flaccum [*of Philo Judaeus*] (BJA)
Flac .... Pro Flacco [*of Cicero*] [*Classical studies*] (OCD)
FLACC .... Full Language ALGOL Checkout Compiler (SAUS)
FLACC .... Full Level Algol Checkout Compiler [*Computer science*] (VERA)
FLACCS .... Florida Climate and Control System (SAUS)
FLAC-H .... Fuzzy Logic Adaptive Controller - Helicoptor [*Army*] (RDA)
FLACSO .... Facultad Latinoamericana de Ciencias Sociales [*Latin American Faculty of Social Sciences*] [*San Jose, Costa Rica*]
FLACT .... Forward Looking Active Classification Technology (ACAE)
FLACTO .... Frequency-Locked Automatic Computing Transfer Oscillator (PDAA)
Fla Cur .... Florida Current (SAUS)
FLACV .... Future Light Armor Combat Vehicle (ACAE)
FLAD .... Fluorescence Activated Display (SAUS)
Fla Dig .... Thompson's Digest of Laws [*Florida*] [*A publication*] (DLA)
FLAE .... Fatigue Life Assessment Expert [*Automotive engineering*]
FlaEC .... Florida East Coast Industries, Inc. [*Associated Press*] (SAG)
Fla Entomol ... Florida Entomologist (journ.) (SAUS)
FLAER .... Foundation for Latino-American Economic Research [*Argentina*] (EAIO)
FlaFst .... Florida First Bancorp, Inc. [*Associated Press*] (SAG)
FlaFst .... Florida First Federal Savings Bank [*Associated Press*] (SAG)
FLAG .... Family Liaison Action Group [*Inactive*] (EA)
FLAG .... Federal Lesbians and Gays (EA)
FLAG .... Federation of Leisure Activity Groups [*Australia*]
FLAG .... Female Liberal Arts Graduate

FLAG........... Fiber Link Around the Globe (GART)
FLAG........... Fiberoptic Link Around the Globe [*Undersea communications cable*]
FLAG........... Firm Level Assistance Group (SAUO)
FLAG........... First Federal S&L Assn. of LaGrange [*NASDAQ symbol*] (COMM)
FLAG........... Fixed Link Aerospace to Ground (SAA)
FLAG........... Flageolet [*Music*]
FLAG........... Flag Financial [*NASDAQ symbol*] (SAG)
FLAG........... Flagstaff National Park Service Group
FLAG........... Fleet Locating and Graphics (SAUS)
FLAG........... Flemish Aerospace Group (SAUS)
FLAG........... Flexible Hours Action Group [*British*]
FLAG........... Flexible Lightweight Agile Guided experiment programme (SAUS)
FLAG........... Florida-Alabama-Georgia League [*Old baseball league*]
FLAG........... Foreign Language Arts in the Grades (EDAC)
FLAG........... FORTRAN [*Formula Translating System*] Load and Go [*Xerox Corp.*] [*Computer science*]
FLAG........... Forward Looking Air to Ground (ACAE)
FLAG........... Foundation for Law and Government [*Organization on television series "Knight Rider"*]
FLAG........... Four London Airport Group [*British*]
FLAG........... Parents, Families, and Friends of Lesbians and Gays (PAZ)
FlaGam.......... Florida Gaming Corp. [*Associated Press*] (SAG)
FLAGCENT... Flag Officer, Central Europe
FLAGE.......... Flexible Lightweight Agile Guide Experiment (SAUO)
FlagFncl..... Flag Financial [*Associated Press*] (SAG)
FLAGRP....... Florida Group [*Navy*]
FLAGS......... Far North Liquids and Associated Gas System (SAUS)
FLAGS......... Far North Liquids and Associated Gas Systems (SAUS)
Flagstar....... Flagstar Companies, Inc. [*Associated Press*] (SAG)
FLAGU......... Flammables and Gas Policy Unit (HEAS)
FLAI........... Fellow of the Library Association of Ireland (SAUO)
FLAIEUA...... Federated Liquor and Allied Industries Employees Union of Australia
Fla Inst Tech... Florida Institute of Technology (GAGS)
FLAIR.......... Factory Liaison and Inspection Resources (ACAE)
FLAIR.......... Field Low Altitude Intermediate-range Radar (SAUS)
FLAIR.......... Fleet Location and Information Reporting [*Police term*]
FLAIR.......... Floating Airport (SAUS)
FLAIR.......... Florida Leader Active in Research
FLAIR.......... Food-Linked Agricultural Industrial Research [*EC*] (ECED)
FLAIR.......... Food-Linked Agro-Industrial Research (SAUS)
FLAIR.......... FORTRAN [*Formula Translation*] Language in Core Rapid Translator [*Xerox*] (NITA)
FLAIR.......... Fundamental Land-Air Integrated Research (SAA)
FLAIR.......... Research Library Automated Information Retrieval Service (SAUS)
FLAIRS........ Fleet Locating and Information Reporting System (SAUS)
FLAIRS........ Food Launch Awareness in the Retail Sector [*Leatherhead Food Research Association*] [*Information service or system*] (CRD)
FLAIR System... Fleet Location and Information Reporting System (SAUS)
Fla Jur......... Florida Jurisprudence [*A publication*] (DLA)
FLAK........... Fliegerabwehrkanone [*German word for antiaircraft gun; acronym used in English for antiaircraft fire and as a slang term for dissension*]
FLAK........... Fondest Love and Kisses [*Correspondence*]
Fla LJ.......... Florida Law Journal [*A publication*] (DLA)
Fla L Rev..... Florida Law Review [*A publication*] (DLA)
FLAM........... Fault Location and Monitoring (AABC)
Flam............ Flamininus [*of Plutarch*] [*Classical studies*] (OCD)
FLAM........... Flammable (DNAB)
FLAM........... Flutter Analysis by a Model Method (ACAE)
FLAM........... Forces de Liberation Africaine de Mauritanie [*Political party*] (EY)
flamby......... Flamboyant (VRA)
FLAME......... Facility Laboratory for Ablative Materials Evaluation (SAA)
FLAME......... Facts and Logic about the Middle East [*An association*]
FLAME......... Family Life and Maternity Education (ADWA)
FLAME......... Fault Location Automated by Monitored Emulation (VLIE)
FLAME......... Fighter Launched Advanced Materials Experiment (SAUS)
FLAME......... Fire Logistics Airborne Mapping Equipment (SAUO)
FLAME......... Flame-Launched Advance Material Experiment (DNAB)
FLAME......... Flexible Application Program Interface for Module-based Environments (SAUS)
FLAME......... Foundation of Light and Metaphysical Education [*Defunct*] (EA)
FLAME......... Friendship Loans to Latin American Endeavors, Inc.
FlamelT....... Flamel Technologies [*Associated Press*] (SAG)
FLAMES....... Fabrication Labour and Material Estimating Service (SAUO)
FLAMES....... Family of Lightweight Advanced Mobile-Mounted Electronic-Attack Systems [*Military*] (SEWL)
FLAMR......... Flores Assembly Program (SAUS)
FLAMR......... Forward-Looking Advanced Multimode RADAR
Flamst......... Flamemaster Corp. [*Associated Press*] (SAG)
FLAMTI........ Forward-Looking Airborne Moving Target Indication (NG)
FLAN........... Factory Layout Analysis [*PERA*] [*Software package*] (NCC)
flan............ Flannel (VRA)
FLAN........... Flying Local Area Network (SEWL)
Flan & K...... Flanagan and Kelly's Irish Rolls Court Reports [*1840-42*] [*A publication*] (DLA)
Flan & Ke.... Flanagan and Kelly's Irish Rolls Court Reports [*1840-42*] [*A publication*] (DLA)
Flan & Kel... Flanagan and Kelly's Irish Rolls Court Reports [*1840-42*] [*A publication*] (DLA)
Fla NBA....... Flather's New Bankrupt Act [*A publication*] (DLA)
Fland.......... Flanders (VRA)
Fland Ch J... Flanders' Lives of the Chief Justices of the United States [*A publication*] (DLA)
Fland Const... Flanders on the United States Constitution [*A publication*] (DLA)
FL & DI........ Food Law and Drug Institute (SAUO)
Flanders...... Flanders Corp. [*Associated Press*] (SAG)
Fland Fire Ins... Flanders on Fire Insurance [*A publication*] (DLA)
Fl & K.......... Flanagan and Kelly's Irish Rolls Court Reports [*1840-42*] [*A publication*] (DLA)
Fland Mar L... Flanders' Maritime Law [*A publication*] (DLA)
Fland Sh...... Flanders on Shipping [*A publication*] (DLA)
FLANG......... Florida Air National Guard (ACAE)
FLANG......... Flowchart Language (SAUS)
Fl Ang......... Fluorescein Angiography [*Cardiology*] (DAVI)
FLANI.......... Flanigan, NV [*American Association of Railroads railroad junction routing code*]
Flanign........ Flanigan's Enterprises, Inc. [*Associated Press*] (SAG)
Fl Ant.......... Fluorescent Antibody [*Biochemistry*] (DAVI)
FLAP........... Failure Location Analysis Program (SAUS)
FLAP........... Fear, Love, Anger, and Pain [*Cognitive system*]
FLAP........... Federacion Latinoamericana de Parasitologos
FLAP........... Five-Lipoxygenase Activating Protein [*Biochemistry*]
FLAP........... flap setting (SAUS)
FLAP........... Flight Application Software [*NASA*] (NASA)
FLAP........... Flores Assembly Program [*Computer science*]
FLAP........... Flores Assembly Programme (SAUO)
FLAP........... Flow Analysis Program [*Computer science*]
FLAP........... FOKTRAN List Array Processor (SAUS)
FLAP........... Formula Algebraic Processor [*Computer science*] (CSR)
FLAP........... Light from the Ancient Past, the Archeological Background of Judaism and Christianity [*Jack Finegan*] [*A publication*] (BJA)
FLAPHO....... Flame Photometer (SAUS)
FlaProg........ Florida Progress Corp. [*Formerly, Florida Power Corp.*] [*Associated Press*] (SAG)
FLAPS.......... Flexibility Analysis of Piping System (SAUS)
FLAPS.......... Flight Application Software [*NASA*] (NASA)
FLAPS.......... Force Level Automated Planning System (SAUO)
FlaPUt......... Florida Public Utilities Co. [*Associated Press*] (SAG)
FLAPW......... Full-Potential Linear Augmented Plane Wave [*Physical chemistry*]
FLAPW......... Full potential Linearized APW (SAUS)
FLAR........... Fault Location and Repair (AABC)
FLAR........... Flare, Inc. [*NASDAQ symbol*] (COMM)
Fla R.......... Florida Reports [*A publication*] (DLA)
FLAR........... Forward-Looking Airborne RADAR
FlaRck......... Florida Rock Industries, Inc. [*Associated Press*] (SAG)
FLARE......... Fault Locating and Reporting Equipment (SAUS)
FLARE......... Flight Anomalies Reporting (KSC)
FLARE......... Florida Aquanaut Research Expedition [*National Oceanic and Atmospheric Administration*]
FLARE......... Florida Lightning and Radar Experiment (SAUO)
Fla Rep........ Florida Reports [*A publication*] (DLA)
FLAREX....... Flare Exercises [*Navy*]
FLAS........... Federal Library Advisory Service (SAUS)
FLAS........... Fellow of the Chartered Land Agents' Society [*British*]
FLAS........... FlashNet Communications [*NASDAQ symbol*] (SG)
FLAS........... Foreign Language and Area Studies
FLAS........... Fuels Logistical Area Summary (SAUO)
Fla SBA Jo... Florida State Bar Association. Journal [*A publication*] (DLA)
Fla SBALJ.... Florida State Bar Association. Law Journal [*A publication*] (DLA)
Fla Sci......... Florida Scientist [*A publication*] (PABS)
FLASER....... Forward Looking Infrared Laser Radar (ADWA)
Fla Sess Law Serv... Florida Session Law Service (West) [*A publication*] (DLA)
FLASH......... Facts Location and Summarized History [*General Motors Corp.*] [*Computer science*]
FLASH......... Factual Lines about Submarine Hazards (DNAB)
FLASH......... Fast Low-Angle Shots
FLASH......... Fast Luciferase Automated Assay of Specimens for Hospitals [*Bacteria analysis*] [*NASA*]
FLASH......... Fault Location and Simulation Hybride (SAUS)
FLASH......... Feeder Lighter Aboard Ship
FLASH......... First edition of List of Australian Subject Heading (SAUS)
FLASH......... Flame Launched Assault Shoulder or Hip-Fired Weapon [*Army*]
flash........... Flashing [*Construction term*] (MIST)
FLASH......... Flash Lights and Send Help [*Florida highway driving aid*]
FLASH......... Folding Light Acoustic Sonar for Helicopters (DOMA)
FLASH......... Folding Light Acoustic System for Helicopters (SAUS)
FLASH......... Force Level Alerting System (SAUO)
FLASH......... Foreign Fishing Vessels Licensing and Surveillance Hierarchical Information System (SAUS)
Flash........... Foundation Life, Adoption Service and Happiness (SAUO)
FLASH......... Function Library for ASN. 1 Syntax Handlers (SAUS)
FLASHA....... Florida Language, Speech, and Hearing Association (SRA)
FLASH FIRE... Flash Financial Report [*for prospective overruns*] [*Navy*]
FLASH P...... Flash Point (SAUS)
FLASH PT.... Flash Point (SAUS)
FLASHWESS... Flash Weapon Effect Signature Simulator [*Military*]
FLASP......... Flight Plan Support Specialist [*NASA*]
Fla Stat........ Florida Statutes [*A publication*] (DLA)
Fla Stat Ann... Florida Statutes, Annotated [*A publication*] (DLA)
Fla Stat Anno... Annotations to Official Florida Statutes [*A publication*] (DLA)
Fla State LJ... Florida State Law Journal [*A publication*] (DLA)
Fla St U....... Florida State University (GAGS)
Fla Supp...... Florida Supplement [*A publication*] (DLA)
FLAT........... Fellow Lady Astronaut Trainee
FLAT........... Flat [*Commonly used*] (OPSA)
FLAT........... Flight-Aided Tracking (SAUS)
FLAT........... Flight Plan Aided Tracking [*Aviation*] (IAA)
FLAT........... Flight-Plane-Aid Tracking (MCD)
FLAT........... Foreign Language Aptitude Test
FLAT........... Full Look at Turbulent Kinetic Energy (SAUS)

FLAT .... Katete [*Zambia*] [*ICAO location identifier*] (ICLI)
FLATPLAN ... Latin American Plantation Workers Federation (SAUO)
FLATS .... Flats [*Commonly used*] (OPSA)
FLAUK .... Fellow of the Library Association of the United Kingdom (SAUO)
Fla Univ ...... University of Florida (SAUO)
FLAUS .... Latin-American Federation of Societies for Ultrasound in Medicine and Biology (SAUO)
FLAV .... Family of Light Armoured Vehicles (SAUS)
FLAV .... Flavus [*Yellow*] [*Pharmacy*]
FLAVA .... Food and Libations Association of Virginia (SRA)
FLAW .... Fleet Logistic Air Wing
FLAW .... Foreign Languages at Work (AIE)
FLAWP .... French-Language Association of Work Psychology [*Viroflay, France*] (EAIO)
FLAWS .... Fault Location Aerial Warning System (SAUO)
FLAX .... Fleming International Airways, Inc. [*Air carrier designation symbol*]
FLAX .... Flexsys America [*Private rail car owner code*]
Flax Reg ...... Flaxman's Registration of Births and Deaths [*1875*] [*A publication*] (DLA)
FLB .... Brittany Revolutionary Front [*France*]
FLB .... Family Life Bureau (EA)
FLB .... Federal Land Bank
FLB .... Federal Loan Bank
FLB .... First Line Battleship (SAUS)
FLB .... Fixed-Length Block (SAUS)
FLB .... Fletcher Challenge Bldg ADS [*NYSE symbol*] (TTSB)
FLB .... Fletcher Challenge Building [*NYSE symbol*] (SAG)
FLB .... Flight Line Bunker (NATG)
flb .... flight-line bunker (SAUS)
FLB .... Floriano [*Brazil*] [*Airport symbol*] (AD)
FLB .... Flow Brazing
FLB .... Fluorescently Labelled Bacteria [*Microbiology*]
FIB .... Flying Boat (SAUS)
flb .... foot-lambert (SAUS)
FLB .... Foreign Language Bulletin
FLB .... Funny Looking Beat [*Cardiology*]
f-lb- .... Liberia [*MARC geographic area code*] [*Library of Congress*] (LCCP)
FLBA .... Family Law Bar Association [*British*] (DBA)
FLBA .... Federal Land Bank Association
FLB-ARB ...... Front de Liberation de la Bretagne - Armee Republicaine Bretonne [*Liberation Front of Brittany - Breton Republican Army*] [*France*] (PD)
FLBAs .... Federal Land Bank Associations (SAUO)
FL BDG .... Flexible Binding (DGA)
FLBE .... Filter Band Eliminator (SAUS)
FL-BE .... Filter-Band Eliminator (MUGU)
FLBE .... Filter for Band Elimination (SAUS)
FLBH .... Filter-Band High (IAA)
FLBIN .... Floating-Point Binary [*Computer science*]
FIBiol .... Fellow of the Institute of Biology (SAUS)
FLBL .... Filter, Band Low (SAUS)
FLB-LNS ...... Front de Liberation de la Bretagne pour la Liberation Nationale et le Socialisme [*Liberation Front of Brittany for National Liberation and Socialism*] [*France*] (PD)
flbm .... fleet-launched ballistic missile (SAUS)
FL-BP .... Filter-Bandpass (MUGU)
FLBR .... Facility Laser Beam Recorder (SAUS)
FLBR .... Film and Literature Board of Review [*Australia*]
FLBR .... Fusible Link Bottom Register (SAUS)
fl bs .... filter, band-suppression (SAUS)
FLC .... Aviation Standards National Field Office [*ICAO designator*] (FAAC)
flc .... Brothers of Christian Instruction (TOCD)
FLC .... Falcon Drilling Co. [*NYSE symbol*] (SAG)
FLC .... Family Law Council (EA)
FLC .... Farm Labor Coalition (EA)
FLC .... Fatty Liver Cell (MELL)
FLC .... Fault Locator Cable
FLC .... Federal Laboratory Consortium
FLC .... Federal Laboratory Consortium for Technology Transfer
FLC .... Federal Library Committee [*Later, FLICC*] [*Library of Congress*] [*Washington, DC*]
FLC .... Federation of Lutheran Clubs (EA)
FLC .... FEDLINK [*Federal Library and Information Network*], Washington, DC [*OCLC symbol*] (OCLC)
FIC .... Fellow of the Institute of Chemistry (SAUS)
FLC .... Fenway Library Consortium/Abbot Memorial Library [*Library network*]
FLC .... Ferroelectric
FLC .... Ferroelectric Liquid Crystal [*Physical chemistry*]
FLC .... Fetal Liver Cell [*Medicine*] (EDAA)
FLC .... Fiber Loop Carrier (SAUS)
FLC .... Fibrolamellar Carcinoma [*Oncology*]
FLC .... File Label Card (SAUS)
FLC .... File Location Code [*Computer science*]
FLC .... First Line Check
FLC .... Five Level Code (SAUS)
FLC .... Fixed Length Computer (SAUS)
FLC .... Flag-Lieutenant-Commander [*Navy*] [*British*]
FLC .... Flat Load Cell
FLC .... Fleet Loading Center
FLC .... Fletcher Challenge ORD [*NYSE symbol*] (SPSG)
FLC .... Flexible Learning Centre (SAUS)
FLC .... Flight Crew (KSC)
FLC .... Force Level Commander (SAUS)
FLC .... Force Logistics Command [*Marine Corps*] (NVT)
FLC .... Forming Limit Curve [*Steel sheet fabrication*]
FLC .... Forward Load Control (MCD)
FLC .... Foundation Library Center (SAUO)
FLC .... Freightliner Corporation (SAUO)
FLC .... Frequency and Load Controller
FLC .... Friend Leukemia Cells [*Cytology*]
FLC .... Frontal Lobe of Cerebrum [*Medicine*] (MELL)
FLC .... Funny Looking Child [*Medical slang*]
FLC .... Fuzzy-Logic Controller [*Engineering*]
FICA .... Fellow of the International College of Anesthetists (SAUS)
FLCA .... Folk Lore Council of Australia
FLCA .... Forward Load Control Assembly (MCD)
FLCA .... Front Lower Control Arm
FLC-Anzeige ... ferroelectric liquid crystal display (SAUS)
FLCB .... Frequency and Load Control Box (MCD)
FLCBE .... Federation of London Clearing Bank Employers (SAUO)
FICBs .... Federal Intermediate Credit Banks (SAUS)
FLCC .... Field and Laboratory Coordination Council (SAUO)
FLCC .... Flight Control Computer (ACAE)
flcc .... flight-control computer (SAUS)
FLCCU .... FIREX [*Fire Extinguisher*] and Launch Coolant Control Unit [*Aerospace*] (AAG)
FICD .... Fellow of the International College of Dentists (SAUS)
FLCD .... Ferroelectric Liquid Crystal Display (SAUS)
FLCD .... Forestry for Local Community Development Programme (SAUS)
FLCDG .... Flow Control Data Generator (SAUS)
FLC Display ... Ferroelectric Liquid Crystal Display (SAUS)
FLCDSSACT ... Fleet Combat Direction System Support Activity (SAUO)
FLCH .... Choma [*Zambia*] [*ICAO location identifier*] (ICLI)
FLCH .... Flechette (SAUS)
FLCH .... Fletchers Fine Foods Ltd. [*NASDAQ symbol*] (SAG)
FLCH .... Flight Level Change (GAVI)
FLCI .... Functional Linguistic Communication Inventory [*Test*] (TMMY)
FLCK .... Flock
FLCL .... Family Life Communications Line
FLCM .... Fellow of the London College of Music [*British*]
FLCN .... Falcon Drilling [*NASDAQ symbol*] (TTSB)
FLCN .... Falcon Drilling Co. [*NASDAQ symbol*] (SAG)
FLCN .... Field Length Condition Register (MHDB)
FLCNAVJUSMAG ... Field Logistics Center, Navy Joint United States Military Assistance Group (DNAB)
FLCO .... Chocha [*Zambia*] [*ICAO location identifier*] (ICLI)
FLCO .... Fellow of the London College of Osteopathy (SAUO)
FLCO .... Finalco Group, Inc. [*NASDAQ symbol*] (COMM)
FLCO .... Floor Cleanout [*Technical drawings*]
FLCON .... Flight Control (SAUS)
FLCP .... Chipata [*Zambia*] [*ICAO location identifier*] (ICLI)
FLCP .... Falcon Products, Inc. [*NASDAQ symbol*] (NQ)
FLCR .... Fixed Length Cavity Resonance
FLCRA .... Farm Labor Contractor Registration Act [*1963*] [*US Employment Service*] [*Department of Labor*]
FL CRS .... Flat Cars [*Freight*]
FLCS .... Chinsali [*Zambia*] [*ICAO location identifier*] (ICLI)
FICS .... Fellow of the International College of Surgeons (SAUS)
FLCS .... Fiber optics Low Cost System (SAUS)
Flcs .... Flight Control System (SAUS)
FLCS .... Force Level Control System
FLCS .... Front de Liberation de la Cote des Somalis [*Front for the Liberation of the Somali Coast*] [*Djibouti*]
FLCSP .... Fellow of the London and Counties Society of Physiologists [*British*]
FLCT .... Federation of Lutheran Churches of Tanganyika (SAUO)
FLCT .... Flow Control (SAUS)
FLCT .... Friends of Libraries Charitable Trust [*British*]
FLCTN .... Fluctuation (FAAC)
FLcV .... United States Veterans Administration Hospital, Lake City, FL [*Library symbol*] [*Library of Congress*] (LCLS)
fld .... failed (SAUS)
FLD .... Fairchild Gold [*Vancouver Stock Exchange symbol*]
FLD .... Fairlead (MSA)
FLD .... Family Law Division (New South Wales Supreme Court) [*Australia*]
FLD .... Fatty Liver Disease [*Medicine*] (EDAA)
FLD .... Fault Logic Diagram
FLD .... Ferret LASER Detector
FLD .... Fibrotic Lung Disease (MELL)
Fld .... Fiducary [*Banking*] (TBD)
fld .... Field (ELAL)
Fld .... Field (POLM)
FLD .... Field
FLD .... Fieldair Freight Ltd. [*New Zealand*] [*ICAO designator*] (FAAC)
FLD .... Fieldcrest Cannon [*NYSE symbol*] (TTSB)
FLD .... Fieldcrest Cannon, Inc. [*NYSE symbol*] (SPSG)
FLD .... Field Division [*Census*] (OICC)
FLD .... Field Liaison Division [*Military*]
FLD .... First Level Destination (SAUS)
FLD .... Flood (MCD)
fld .... Flowered [*Botany*]
FLD .... Fluid (AAG)
Fld .... Fluid (AMHC)
FLD .... Fluid Dynamics (SSD)
FLD .... Flutamide and Leuprolide Depot [*Medicine*] (EDAA)
FLD .... Flux Lattice Dislocation (PDAA)
FLD .... Fond Du Lac, WI [*Location identifier*] [*FAA*] (FAAL)
FLD .... Forming Limit Diagram [*Manufacturing term*]
FLD .... Fraunhofer Line Discriminator [*Physics*]
FLD .... Friends of the Lake District (EERA)
FLD .... Fuel Loading Data [*Nuclear energy*] (NRCH)

FLD............ Full Lower Denture (MELL)
FLD............ Fund for Labor Defense (EA)
FLD............ L.A.T. Sportswear [*AMEX symbol*] (SG)
FLD............ Newfoundland Tracking Station
FLDA............ Federal Land Development Authority [*Malaysia*]
FLDACTYSq... Field Activity Squadron [*Air Force*]
Fld Amb....... Field Ambulance [*British military*] (DMA)
FLDARTYGRU... Field Artillery Group
FLDBR......... Field Branch
FLDBRBUMED... Field Branch, Bureau of Medicine and Surgery [*Navy*] (DNAB)
FLDC............ Fieldcrest Cannon [*NASDAQ symbol*] (SAG)
FldCH............ Field Champion [*Dog show term*]
FLDCK......... Field Cook [*Marine Corps*]
FLDCK(B)..... Field Cook (Baker) [*Marine Corps*]
FLDCK(C)..... Field Cook (Commissary) [*Marine Corps*]
Fld Com....... Field Command (SAUS)
FLDCOMDASA... Field Command, Defense Atomic Support Agency (AABC)
FLDCOMDNA... Field Command, Defense Nuclear Agency [*DoD*] (AABC)
Fld Comm.... Field Communication (SAUS)
FldCoRE....... Field Company, Royal Engineers (SAUO)
FLDCP......... Fieldcrest Cannon $3 Cv [*NASDAQ symbol*] (TTSB)
Fldcrst......... Fieldcrest Cannon [*Associated Press*] (SAG)
Fldcrst......... Fieldcrest Cannon, Inc. [*Associated Press*] (SAG)
Fld Def........ Field Definition (SAUS)
fld dr........... field drum (SAUS)
FLDE............ Delkin (Lusiwasi) [*Zambia*] [*ICAO location identifier*] (ICLI)
FLDEC.......... Floating-Point Decimal [*Computer science*]
FIDEN.......... Flight Data Entry (SAUS)
Fld Err.......... Field Error (SAUS)
fld ext.......... Fluid Extract [*Pharmacology*] (DAVI)
FLDEXT........ Fluidextractum [*Fluidextract*] [*Pharmacy*]
FLDG............ Folding (MSA)
FLDGM......... Folding Map [*Publishing*]
Fld Hosp...... Field Hospital (SAUS)
FLDI............ Flare Die
FL DIAG....... Functional Line Diagram (SAUS)
FLDK............ Flight Deck
FLDL............ Field Length (IAA)
FLDLE.......... Fieldale, VA [*American Association of Railroads railroad junction routing code*]
FLDMAINTSq... Field Maintenance Squadron [*Air Force*]
FLDMEDSERVSCOL... Field Medical Service School (DNAB)
FLDMS.......... Field Maintenance Shop [*Army*] (AABC)
FLDMSLMAINTSq... Field Missile Maintenance Squadron [*Air Force*]
FLDNG.......... Flooding
FLDO............ Field Officer
FLDO............ Final Limit, Down
FIDO............ Flight Dynamics Officer (SAUS)
Fld Off.......... Field Officer (SAUS)
FLDOL.......... Floating Dollar (SAUS)
FLDOP.......... Field Operation (SAUS)
fldop............ field operations (SAUS)
FLD OPS....... Field Operations (SAUS)
FLDOT.......... Florida Department of Transportation (DEMM)
FLDP............ Federation of Liberal and Democratic Parties (PPE)
FLDR............ Flanders Corp. [*NASDAQ symbol*] (TTSB)
FLDR............ Flight Loads Data Recorder (ACAE)
fl dr............. Fluid Drachm (SAUS)
fldr.............. Fluid Dram (SHCU)
FLDR............ Fluid Dram
FLD RATS..... Field Rations (DNAB)
fld rest......... Fluid Restriction [*Dietetics*] (DAVI)
FLDS............ Fault Locating Diagnostics (SAUS)
FLDS............ Fields [*Postal Service standard*] (OPSA)
FLDS............ Fixed-Length Distinguishing Sequence [*Computer science*] (IAA)
FLDST.......... Flood Stage [*NWS*] (FAAC)
FLDSUPPACT... Field Support Activity [*Military*] (DNAB)
FLD SWBD... Field Switchboard (SAUS)
FLDT............ Fast Linear Displacement Transducer [*Electronics*]
FLDT............ Floodlight
FLDTG.......... Field Training Group [*Military*]
FLDTNS........ Field Trains
FLDTS.......... Field Training Squadron
FldUrd.......... Fluorodeoxyuridine [*Floxuridine*] [*Also, FUDR*] [*Antineoplastic drug*]
FLDX............ Fieldston Transportation Services [*Private rail car owner code*]
FLDXT.......... Fluid Extract (SAUS)
FLDXT.......... Fluidextractum [*Fluidextract*] [*Pharmacy*]
FLE............... Fatigue Life Expectancy [*or Expended*] (MCD)
FLE............... Fire (SAUS)
FLE............... Fire, Lightning, and Explosion [*Insurance*] (AIA)
FLE............... Fixed Leading Edge (MCD)
FLE............... Fleet [*Navy*]
FLE............... Fleetwood Enterpr [*NYSE symbol*] (TTSB)
FLE............... Fleetwood Enterprises, Inc. [*NYSE symbol*] (SPSG)
FLE............... Fletcher [*Vermont*] [*Seismograph station code, US Geological Survey*] (SEIS)
FLE............... Flight Engineer (SAUO)
FLE............... Forward Logistical Element [*Military*]
FLE............... Free List Exhausted (VLIE)
FLe............... Leesburg Public Library, Leesburg, FL [*Library symbol*] [*Library of Congress*] (LCLS)
FLE............... Telemetering Land Station [*ITU designation*] (CET)
FLEA............ East One [*Zambia*] [*ICAO location identifier*] (ICLI)
FLEA............ Farm Level Economic Analysis (FOTI)
FLEA............ Flux Logic Element Array
FLEA............ Flux Logic Evaluation Assembly (SAUS)
FLEA............ Four Letter Extended Acronym (VERA)
FLEACT........ Fleet Activities
FleActy......... Fleet Activity (SAUS)
FLEASWSCOL... Fleet Antisubmarine Warfare School (MUGU)
FLEASWTACSCOL... Fleet Antisubmarine Warfare Tactical School
FLEASWTRACENLANT... Fleet Antisubmarine Warfare Training Center, Atlantic (DNAB)
FLEASWTRACENLPAC... Fleet Antisubmarine Warfare Training Center, Pacific (DNAB)
FLEASWTRAGRU... Fleet Antisubmarine Warfare Training Group (DNAB)
FLEAVNACCTO... Fleet Aviation Accounting Office (DNAB)
FLEAVNACCTOLANT... Fleet Aviation Accounting Office, Atlantic (DNAB)
FLEAVNACCTOPAC... Fleet Aviation Accounting Office, Pacific (DNAB)
FLEAVNMATOPAC... Fleet Aviation Material Office, Pacific (DNAB)
FLEB............ East Two [*Zambia*] [*ICAO location identifier*] (ICLI)
FLEB............ Flebile [*Pensive*] [*Music*] (ROG)
FLEBALMISTRACEN... Fleet Ballistic Missile Training Center (DNAB)
FLEBALMISUBTRACEN... Fleet Ballistic Missile Submarine Training Center
FLEBALMISUBTRACENLANT... Fleet Ballistic Missile Submarine Training Center, Atlantic (DNAB)
FLEBALMISUBTRACENPAC... Fleet Ballistic Missile Submarine Training Center, Pacific (DNAB)
FLEC............ East Three [*Zambia*] [*ICAO location identifier*] (ICLI)
FLEC............ Frente de Libertacao do Enclave de Cabinda [*Front for the Liberation of the Cabinda Enclave*] [*Angola*] (PD)
FLECC.......... Federal Libraries' Experiment in Cooperative Cataloging [*Later, FEDLINK*]
FLECC.......... Federal Libraries Experiment in Cooperative Cataloguing (SAUS)
FLECHT........ Full Length Emergency Cooling Heat Transfer [*Nuclear energy*] (NRCH)
FLECHT Test... Full Length Emergency Cooling Heat Transfer Test (SAUS)
FLECOMBDIRSYSTRACEN... Fleet Combat Direction System Training Center [*Navy*] (DNAB)
FLECOMBDIRSYSTRACENLANT... Fleet Combat Direction System Training Center, Atlantic [*Navy*] (DNAB)
FLECOMBDIRSYSTRACENPAC... Fleet Combat Direction System Training Center, Pacific [*Navy*] (DNAB)
FLECOMPRON... Fleet Composite Squadron [*Navy*]
FLECOMPRONDET... Fleet Composite Squadron Detachment [*Navy*] (DNAB)
FLECOMPUT... Fleet Computer Programming Center [*Navy*] (MCD)
FLECOMPUTPROGCEN... Fleet Computer Programming Center [*Navy*] (MCD)
FLECOMPUTPROGCENLANT... Fleet Computer Programming Center, Atlantic [*Navy*]
FLECOMPUTPROGCENPAC... Fleet Computer Programming Center, Pacific [*Navy*] (DNAB)
FLED............ East Four [*Zambia*] [*ICAO location identifier*] (ICLI)
FLEDR.......... Foreign Language Entrance and Degree Requirements (EDAC)
FLEE............ East Five [*Zambia*] [*ICAO location identifier*] (ICLI)
FLEE............ Fast Linkage Editor [*Computer science*] (MHDI)
FLEEP.......... Feeble Beep (SAUS)
FLEEP.......... Flying Lunar Excursion Experimental Platform [*NASA*]
FLEET.......... Freight and Logistics Efforts for European Traffic (SAUO)
FleetEn......... Fleetwood Enterprises, Inc. [*Associated Press*] (SAG)
FLEETEX....... Fleet Exercise [*Navy*] (NVT)
FleetFnc....... Fleet Financial Group [*Associated Press*] (SAG)
FLEETSAT.... Fleet Communications Satellite [*Navy*] (MCD)
FLEETSATCOM... Fleet Satellite Communications System [*DoD*]
FLEETSATCOM System... Fleet Satellite Communications System (SAUS)
FLEF............ East Six [*Zambia*] [*ICAO location identifier*] (ICLI)
FLEG............ East Seven [*Zambia*] [*ICAO location identifier*] (ICLI)
FLEGX.......... Flag Investors Emerging Growth Cl.A [*Mutual fund ticker symbol*] (SG)
FLEH............ East Eight [*Zambia*] [*ICAO location identifier*] (ICLI)
FLEHOSPSUPPOFF... Fleet Hospital Support Office (DNAB)
FLEINTROTM... Fleet Introduction Team [*Navy*] (DNAB)
FLeL............ Lake-Sumter Community College, Leesburg, FL [*Library symbol*] [*Library of Congress*] (LCLS)
FLELO.......... Fleet Liaison Officer (DNAB)
FLELOGSUPPRON... Fleet Logistics Support Squadron (DNAB)
FLELOGSUPPRONDET... Fleet Logistics Support Squadron Detachment (DNAB)
Flem............ Fleming (SAUS)
Flem............ Flemish (VRA)
FLEM............ Flemish
FLEM............ Flyby-Landing Excursion Mode [*Aviation*]
FLEMARFOR... Fleet Marine Force [*Navy*] (DNAB)
FLEMARFORLANT... Fleet Marine Force, Atlantic [*Navy*] (DNAB)
FLEMARFORPAC... Fleet Marine Force, Pacific [*Navy*] (DNAB)
FLEMATSUPPO... Fleet Material Support Office [*Navy*]
FLEMATSUPPODET... Fleet Material Support Office Detachment [*Navy*] (DNAB)
FLEMATSUPPOFAGLANT... Fleet Material Support Office, Fleet Assistance Group, Atlantic [*Navy*]
FLEMATSUPPOFAGPAC... Fleet Material Support Office, Fleet Assistance Group, Pacific [*Navy*]
FlemgBT....... [*The*] Flemington National Bank & Trust [*Associated Press*] (SAG)
FLEMINWARTRACEN... Fleet Mine Warfare Training Center (DNAB)
FLEMIS......... Flexible Management Information System (DNAB)
Flemng......... Fleming Companies, Inc. [*Associated Press*] (SAG)
FLEND.......... Flendist [*England*]
FLE network... follow-the-Teader-feedback network (SAUS)
FLENUMOCEANCEN... Fleet Numerical Oceanography Center (DNAB)
FLENUMWEAFAC... Fleet Numerical Weather Facility (MUGU)
FLEOA.......... Federal Law Enforcement Officers Association (EA)
FLEOPINTRACEN... Fleet Operational Intelligence Training Center [*Navy*]
FLEOPINTRACENLANT... Fleet Operational Intelligence Training Center, Atlantic [*Navy*] (DNAB)

FLEOPINTRACENPAC... Fleet Operational Intelligence Training Center, Pacific [*Navy*] (DNAB)
FLEP........... Funded Legal Education Program (SAUO)
FLEPOW...... Fletcher-Powell (SAUS)
FLEPOW Program... Fletcher-Powell Program (SAUS)
FLER........... Fractional Loss Exchange Ratio (MCD)
FLEREADREP... Fleet Readiness Representative [*Navy*] (AFIT)
fles............ foreign language in elementary school (SAUS)
FLES........... Foreign Languages in Elementary Schools
FLESCOP....... Flexible Signal Collection and Processing (DNAB)
FLESONARSCOL... Fleet SONAR School [*Navy*]
FleSonarScol... Fleet Sonar School (SAUS)
FLESUBTRAFAC... Fleet Submarine Training Facility [*Navy*]
FLET........... Forward Line of Enemy Troops (SAUS)
FLETAC........ Fleet Tactical Field Office (DNAB)
FLETACSUPPRON... Fleet Tactical Support Squadron [*Navy*]
FletBld........ Fletcher Challenge Building [*Associated Press*] (SAG)
FLETC......... Federal Law Enforcement Training Center [*Department of the Treasury*]
Fletcher Corporations... Fletcher's Cyclopedia of Corporations [*A publication*] (DLA)
Fletcher Cyc Corp... Fletcher's Cyclopedia of Corporations [*A publication*] (DLA)
Fletch Tr...... Fletch on Trustees of Estates [*A publication*] (DLA)
FLETECHSUPPCENDET... Fleet Technical Support Center Detachment (DNAB)
FletEgy........ Fletcher Challenge Energy [*Associated Press*] (SAG)
FletFD.......... Fletcher Challenge ADR ORD [*Associated Press*] (SAG)
FletOD.......... Fletcher Challenge ADR ORD [*Associated Press*] (SAG)
FletPap......... Fletcher Challenge Paper [*Associated Press*] (SAG)
FLETRABASE... Fleet Training Base
FLETRACEN.... Fleet Training Center [*Navy*]
FLETRAGRU.... Fleet Training Group (SAUO)
FLETRAGRUDET... Fleet Training Group Detachment [*Navy*] (DNAB)
FLETRAGRUWATE... Fleet Training Group and Underway Training Element
FLETRAGRUWESTPAC... Fleet Training Group, Western Pacific [*Navy*] (DNAB)
FLETRAN..... Fleet Training Unit (DNAB)
FLEUROSELECT... European Organization for Testing New Flowerseeds (SAUO)
Fleury Hist... Fleury's History of the Origin of French Laws [*1724*] [*A publication*] (DLA)
FLEWEACEN... Fleet Weather Center [*or Central*] [*NATO*] (NATG)
FLEWEAFAC... Fleet Weather Facility [*NATO*] (NATG)
FLEWORKSTUDYGRULANT... Fleet Work Study Group, Atlantic [*Navy*]
FLEX........... Federal Licensing Examination [*for physicians*]
FLEX........... Federation Licensing Examination (SAUO)
FLEX........... Federation Licensure Examination (SAUO)
FLEX........... Fladden Ground Experiment [*Oceanography*] (MSC)
FLEX........... Flaw Examination (SAUS)
FLEX........... Fleet Exercise [*Navy*] [*British*]
FLEX........... Fleet Life Extension (MCD)
FLEX........... Flexible (AABC)
FLEX........... Flexible Extendable Language (SAUS)
FLEX........... Flexible Universal Character Code (SAUS)
Flex............ Flexion (AMHC)
flex............ Flexion (IDYL)
FLEX........... Flexion [*Medicine*]
flex............ Flexor [*Anatomy*] (DAVI)
FLEX........... Flexowriter Equipment (AABC)
FLEX........... Flextronics Intl. [*NASDAQ symbol*] (SG)
FLEX........... Flexure [*Mechanics*]
FLEX........... Force Level Execution (SAUS)
FLEX........... Free Learning Exchange [*An association*] [*Defunct*] (EA)
FLEXAR....... Flexible Adaptive RADAR (MCD)
FLEXBL....... Flexible (BARN)
FLEXEM....... Flexible Energy Management (MCD)
FLEXER....... Fundamental Loop Exerciser (SAUS)
FLEXF......... Flextronics International [*NASDAQ symbol*] (SAG)
FLEXF......... Flextronics Intl [*NASDAQ symbol*] (TTSB)
FLEXIMIS..... Flexible Management Information System (MHDI)
FLEXIS........ Federal Library Extension Instructional System (SAUS)
FLEX Language... Flexible Extendable Language (SAUS)
FLEX LAVR... Flexible Large Area Vulnerability Report (SEWL)
flexo........... flexographic (SAUS)
FLEXOPS...... Flexible Operations (DNAB)
flex sig....... Flexible Sigmoidoscopy [*Gastroenterology*] (DAVI)
Flexstl......... Flexsteel Industries, Inc. [*Associated Press*] (SAG)
Flextrn......... Fletronics International [*Associated Press*] (SAG)
Flextrn......... Flextronics International [*Associated Press*] (SAG)
FLF............. Fast Landing Force (SAUS)
FLF............. Fault Location Facility [*Aircraft*]
FLF............. Final Limit, Forward
FLF............. Fisheries Loan Fund [*National Oceanic and Atmospheric Administration*]
FLF............. Fixed Length Field (SAUS)
FLF............. Fixed-Length Field [*Computer science*] (BUR)
FLF............. Flin Flon Mines [*Vancouver Stock Exchange symbol*]
FLF............. Flip Flop (SAUS)
FLF............. Flip-Flop [*Computer science*] (DEN)
FLF............. Follow-the-Leader Feedback [*Circuit theory*] (IEEE)
FLF............. Follow-the-Leader Filter (SAUS)
FLF............. Four Lucky Fellows [*In company name, FLF Associates*] [*Investment group comprised of four sons of Lawrence Tisch*]
FLF............. Fran Lee Foundation (EA)
FLF............. Freedom Leadership Foundation (EA)
FLF............. Friendly Laotian Forces (CINC)
FLFADDFA... France-Louisiane/Franco-Americaine - Defense et Developpement de la FrancophonieAmericaine (EAIO)
FLFC........... First Liberty Financial Corp. [*NASDAQ symbol*] (NQ)
FLFC........... First Liberty Financial Corporation (SAUO)
FLFCO......... First Liberty Fin'l 6% Cv Pfd [*NASDAQ symbol*] (TTSB)
FLFI............ Lusaka [*Zambia*] [*ICAO location identifier*] (ICLI)
f/l FL.......... Front Legs (SPVS)
FLFM........... Federation of London Flour Millers (SAUO)
FLFN........... Free Lance Finders Network (EA)
FLF Network... Follow-the-Leader Feedback Network (SAUS)
FLFT........... Forklift (AABC)
FLFT........... Full Load Frame Time [*Term used in SAGE operations*]
FLFW........... Fiwila [*Zambia*] [*ICAO location identifier*] (ICLI)
FLG............. Express Airlines I, Inc. [*ICAO designator*] (FAAC)
flg.............. failing (SAUS)
FLG............. Falling [*NWS*] (FAAC)
FLG............. Flag [*Computer science*] (MDG)
FLG............. Flag Flange (MCD)
flg.............. flagging (SAUS)
FLG............. Flagship [*Navy*] (NVT)
FLG............. Flagstaff [*Arizona*] [*Airport symbol*] (OAG)
FLG............. Flagstaff [*Arizona*] [*Seismograph station code, US Geological Survey*] [*Closed*] (SEIS)
FLG............. Flagstaff, AZ [*Location identifier*] [*FAA*] (FAAL)
FLG............. Flange (MSA)
FLG............. Flashing
FLG............. Fletcher Leisure Group, Inc. [*Toronto Stock Exchange symbol*]
flg.............. Floating (SAUS)
FLG............. Flong [*Printing*] (DGA)
FLG............. Flooring (KSC)
Flg.............. Flooring (WPI)
FLG............. Florida Gas Co. (SAUO)
flg.............. Flugelhorn
FLG............. Flying (AABC)
FLG............. Focal Length [*Photography*] (IAA)
FLG............. Following
FLG............. Forward Landing Ground (SAUS)
FLG............. Franciscan Sisters of Our Lady of Grace (TOCD)
FLG............. Friends of Little Gidding (EA)
FLG............. Front de Libertacao de Guinee [*Guinean Liberation Front*] [*Portuguese Guinea*]
FLG............. Full Load Governed [*Hydraulics*]
FLGA........... Fellow of Local Government Association (SAUO)
FLGA........... Fellow of the Local Government Association [*British*]
FLGA........... Florida Lychee Growers Association (EA)
FLGA........... Full-Term Large for Gestational Age [*Medicine*] (EDAA)
FLGB........... Federal Loan Guarantee Board (SAUS)
FLGC........... Friends for Lesbian and Gay Concerns (EA)
FlgCl........... Floating clause (SAUS)
flgd............ flanged (SAUS)
flge............ Flange (SAUS)
FLGE........... Mukinge [*Zambia*] [*ICAO location identifier*] (ICLI)
FLGed.......... Flanged (SAUS)
FlghtSf......... Flightsafety International, Inc. [*Associated Press*] (SAG)
flgit............ floating light (SAUS)
FLGLA......... Flagler Bank Corp. (Class A) [*NASDAQ symbol*] (COMM)
Flg Lt.......... Floating Light (SAUS)
Flg Off......... Flying Officer (SAUS)
FLGS........... Flagstar Bancorp [*NASDAQ symbol*] (SG)
FLGSTF....... Flagstaff
FLGSTN....... Flagstone
Flgstr.......... Flagstar Companies, Inc. [*Associated Press*] (SAG)
FLGT........... Flight
FLGW.......... Mpongwe [*Zambia*] [*ICAO location identifier*] (ICLI)
flh.............. familial lefthandedness (SAUS)
FLH............. Federacion Latinoamericana de Hospitales [*Latin American Hospital Federation*] (EAIO)
FLH............. Fife Light Horse [*British military*] (DMA)
FLH............. Fila Holdings [*NYSE symbol*] (SPSG)
FLH............. Fila Holdings ADS [*NYSE symbol*] (TTSB)
FLH............. Final Limit, Hoist
FLH............. Flash
FLH............. Flat Head (MSA)
FLH............. Fluorescence Line Height (SAUS)
FLH............. Land Hydrological and Meteorological Station [*ITU designation*] (DEN)
FLH............. Skybus, Inc. [*ICAO designator*] (FAAC)
fl hd........... flathead (SAUS)
FLHLS......... Flashless [*NASA*] (KSC)
Flhls-Smkls... Flashless-Smokeless (SAUS)
FLHO........... Federal Lands Highway Office (SAUS)
FL-HP.......... Filter-High Pass (MUGU)
FLHQ........... Lusaka [*Zambia*] [*ICAO location identifier*] (ICLI)
FLHS........... Fellow of the London Historical Society [*British*]
FLHS........... Flashless
FLHV........... Fife Light Horse Volunteers [*British military*] (DMA)
FLI.............. American Eagle Group [*NYSE symbol*] (SAG)
FLI.............. Atlantic Airways, PF (Faroe Islands) [*Denmark*] [*ICAO designator*] (FAAC)
FLI.............. Farm and Land Institute [*Later, RLI*] (EA)
FLI.............. Farm Labor Information [*US Employment Service*] [*Department of Labor*]
FLI.............. Fault Location Indicator
FLI.............. Federation Lainiere Internationale [*International Wool Textile Organization - IWTO*] (EAIO)
FLI.............. Fellow of the Landscape Institute [*British*] (DBQ)
FLI.............. Field Lane Institution (SAUO)

FLI ..... Field Length Indication (SAUS)
FLI ..... Field Length Indicator (SAUS)
FLI ..... Flateyri [*Iceland*] [*Airport symbol*] (OAG)
FLI ..... Flick [*A motion-video format*]
FLI ..... Flight Leader Identification (SAUS)
FLI ..... Flight Leader Identity [*RADAR*]
FLI ..... Flint Rock Mines [*Vancouver Stock Exchange symbol*]
FLI ..... Fluorescence-Line Imager [*Instrumentation*]
FLI ..... Flying Line Indoctrination (SAUO)
FLI ..... Font Library (SAUS)
FLI ..... Food Law Institute [*Later, FDLI*] (EA)
FLI ..... Foodservice and Lodging Institute (EA)
FLI ..... Former Live-In
FLI ..... Forward-Looking Infrared
FLI ..... Free Language Indexing [*Information retrieval*] (NITA)
FLI ..... Friend Laboratory, Inc. (EFIS)
FLI ..... Front for the Liberation of Iran (CARL)
FLI ..... Full Length Instruction (SAUS)
FLI ..... Funnel Length Index
FLIA ..... Federation Life Insurance of America [*Milwaukee, WI*] (EA)
FLIA ..... Fellow of the Life Insurance Association [*British*] (ODBW)
FLIC ..... Fault Location Indicating Console (AABC)
FLIC ..... Film Library Information Council [*EFLA*] [*Absorbed by*] (EA)
FLIC ..... Film Library Inter-College Cooperative of Pennsylvania [*Library network*]
FLIC ..... First Long Island [*NASDAQ symbol*] (TTSB)
FLIC ..... [*The*] First of Long Island Corp. [*NASDAQ symbol*] (NQ)
FLIC ..... Flaw Locating and Imaging Computer (PDAA)
FLIC ..... Foreign Languages for Industry and Commerce [*British*] (DBQ)
FLICC ..... Federal Library and Information Center Committee [*Library of Congress*] [*Also, an information service or system*] (IID)
FLICON ..... Flight Control [*or Controller*]
Fli Con C ..... Flight Control Centre (SAUO)
FLICR ..... Fluid Logic Industrial Control Relay
FLICS ..... Farm Labor Interstate Clearance System [*US Employment Service*] [*Department of Labor*]
FLICS ..... Flight Command Simulation (ACAE)
FLICS ..... Foreign Language Innovative Curricula Study [*University of Michigan*] (AEBS)
FLID ..... Find or List the Identifications (SAA)
FLID ..... Front de la Lutte pour l'Independence du Dahomey [*Battle Front for the Independence of Dahomey*]
FLIDAP ..... Flight Data Position
FLIDAR ..... Fluorescence Lidar (SAUS)
FLIDEN ..... Flight Data Entry [*Device*] [*SAGE*]
FLIDEN Device ..... Flight Data Entry Device (SAUS)
FLIDEPEC ..... Federation of Liberal and Democratic Parties in the European Community (SAUO)
FLIDIT ..... Flight Line Detection and Isolation Techniques
FLIDRAS ..... Flight Data Replay and Analysis System (GAVI)
FLIER ..... Fast, Low-Ionization Emission-Line Region [*Planetary science*]
FLIFO ..... Flight Information
FLIGA ..... Forced Landing Incidents - Ground Accidents
FLIH ..... First Level Interrupt Handler [*Computer science*]
FLIK ..... Isoka [*Zambia*] [*ICAO location identifier*] (ICLI)
FLIM ..... Faithful Library about Internet Message (SAUS)
FLIM ..... Fast Library Maintenance
FLIM ..... Fast Library Management (SAUO)
FLIM ..... Flight Mechanics Internal Memorandum (SAUS)
FLIM ..... Fluoresence Lifetime Imaging Microscopy
FLIM ..... Forest-Light Interaction Model (SAUO)
FLIMAN ..... Flight Information Manual (SAUS)
FLIMBAL ..... Floated Inertial Measurement Ball
FLIN ..... Florida Library Information Network [*Florida State Library*] [*Tallahassee, FL*] [*Library network*]
FLINBAL ..... Fluid Inertial Balance (MCD)
Flinders ..... Flinders Ranges of South Australia (SAUS)
FLING ..... Frente da Luta pela Independencia Nacional da Guine "Portuguesa" [*Front for the Fight for Guinea-Bissau's National Independence*] (PD)
FLING ..... Frente para a Libertacao e Independencia de Guine [*Front for the Liberation and Independence of Guinea*]
FLINK ..... Flash/Wink Signal [*Telecommunications*] (TEL)
FLINKS ..... Front de Liberation Nationale Kanake Socialiste [*National Liberation Front ofSocialist Kanakes*] [*New Caledonia*] [*Political party*]
FLINN ..... Fiducial Laboratory for an International Science Network (ACAE)
FLIN-NSW ..... Federal Libraries Information Network - New South Wales [*Australia*]
FLIN-NT ..... Federal Libraries Information Network - Northern Territory [*Australia*]
FLIN-QLD ..... Federal Libraries Information Network - Queensland [*Australia*]
FLINT ..... Facilities Loading Investigation New Technique (SAUS)
FLINT ..... Flint, MI [*American Association of Railroads railroad junction routing code*]
Flint ..... Flintshire [*Former county in Wales*] (WGA)
FLINT ..... Floating Interpretative Language (SAUS)
FLINT ..... Floating Interpretive Language [*Princeton University*]
Flint Conv ..... Flintoff's Introduction to Conveyancing [*A publication*] (DLA)
Flint R Pr ..... Flintoff's Real Property [*1839-40*] [*A publication*] (DLA)
FLINTS ..... Flintshire [*Former county in Wales*]
FLIN-VIC ..... Federal Libraries Information Network - Victoria [*Australia*]
FLIN-WA ..... Federal Libraries Information Network - Western Australia
FLINX ..... Flag Investors Intermed. Term Inc. Cl.A [*Mutual fund ticker symbol*] (SG)
FLIOP ..... Flight Operations Planner
FLIP ..... Family Life Income Patterns [*Economics simulation game*]
FLIP ..... Family Limited Partnership
FLIP ..... Film Library Instantaneous Presentation [*Computer science*]
FLIP ..... Financially Limited Plan (NATG)
FLIP ..... Flat Linear Induction Pump (SAUS)
FLIP ..... Flexible Image Processing Computer System (SAUO)
FLIP ..... Flexible Loan Insurance Program
FLIP ..... Flight Information Plan
FLIP ..... Flight Information Publication [*Air Force*]
FLIP ..... Flight Launched Infrared Probe
Flip ..... Flippin's Circuit Court Reports [*United States*] [*A publication*] (DLA)
FLIP ..... Floated Inertial Platform (SAUS)
FLIP ..... Floated Lightweight Inertial Platform
FLIP ..... Floating Indexed Point Arithmetic [*Computer science*]
FLIP ..... Floating Instrument Platform [*Navy*] (NG)
FLIP ..... Floating Laboratory Instrument Platform [*Movable oceanographic research station*]
FLIP ..... Floating-Point Interpretive Program [*Computer science*]
FLIP ..... Fluorescence Loss in Photobleaching [*Analytical biochemistry*]
FLIP ..... Format Directed List Processor [*Computer science*] (IAA)
FLIP ..... Free-Form Language for Image Processing (PDAA)
FLIP ..... French Language Intensive Program [*Illinois*] (EDAC)
FLIP ..... Fuzzy Logic Inferences per Second [*Computer chip technology*]
FLIP Arithmetic ..... Floating Indexed Point Arithmetic (SAUS)
FLIPCO ..... Flight Plan and Coordination (SAUS)
FLIPCO System ..... Flight Plan and Coordination System (SAUS)
Flipp (F) ..... Flippin's Circuit Court Reports [*United States*] [*A publication*] (DLA)
FLIPPG ..... French-Language Infant Pneumology and Phthisiology Group [*Yerres, France*] (EAIO)
FLIPPY ..... Double sided floppy disc (SAUS)
FLIPS ..... Flight Information Processing System (SAUO)
FLIPs ..... Flight Information Publications (SAUO)
FLIPs ..... Floating Instrument Platforms (SAUS)
FLIPS ..... Future Language Information Processing System (BUR)
FLIPS ..... Fuzzy Logical Inferences per Second [*Computer chip technology*]
flips ..... Fuzzy Logic Inferences per Second (VLIE)
FLIPSIM ..... Firm Level Income and Policy Simulator Model (SAUO)
FLIR ..... Flight Low-Level Image Receiver
FLIR ..... FLIR Systems [*NASDAQ symbol*] (TTSB)
FLIR ..... FLIR Systems, Inc. [*NASDAQ symbol*] (SAG)
FLIR ..... Forward-Loading Infrared (RDA)
flir ..... forward-look infrared (SAUS)
FLIR ..... Forward-Looking Infrared (AFM)
FLIR ..... Forward Looking Infrared RADAR [*Military*] (INF)
FLIR ..... Forward-looking infrared radar (SAUS)
FLIR ..... Forward-Looking Infrared Sensor (VNW)
FLIRAS ..... Forward-Looking Infrared Attack Set
FLIR Radar ..... Forward Looking Infrared Radar (SAUS)
FLIRS ..... Forward Looking Infrared Radar System (ACAE)
FLIRS ..... Forward-Looking Infrared System
FLIRT ..... Federal Librarians Round Table [*American Library Association*]
FLIRT ..... First Ladies' International Racing Team [*Group of women racing at Le Mans, France*]
FLIRT ..... Free Language Information Retrieval Tool [*Netherlands*] (NITA)
FLIRT ..... Free Language Retrieval Tool (SAUS)
FLIRTS ..... Forward-Looking Infrared Thermovision System (MCD)
FLIS ..... Faculty of Library and Information Science (SAUS)
FLIS ..... Federal Logistics Information System (VLIE)
FLIS ..... Flexible Interruption System (VLIE)
FLIS ..... Florida Lumber Inspection Service (WPI)
FLIS ..... Free-Legal Information Service (SAUS)
FLiS ..... Suwannee River Regional Library, Live Oak, FL [*Library symbol*] [*Library of Congress*] (LCLS)
FLIST ..... File List Processor [*Computer science*]
FLIT ..... Fault Location by Interpretive Testing (VLIE)
FLIT ..... Fault Location through Interpretive Testing [*Computer science*]
FLIT ..... Flexowriter Interrogation Tape
FLIT ..... Free Limiting Internal Truss [*Nuclear energy*] (NRCH)
FLIT ..... Frequency Line Tracker [*Military*] (CAAL)
FLIT ..... Functional Literacy [*Program to provide marginally literate soldiers with minimal literacy skills*] [*Army*] (RDA)
FLITE ..... Federal Legal Information through Electronics [*Air Force*] (IID)
FLITE ..... Federal legal inforrnation through electronics (SAUS)
FLITE ..... Flight Information Test Element (VLIE)
FLITE ..... Future Lawyers Investigating Transportation Employment [*Student legal action organization*] (EA)
FLITT ..... Frigate LAMPS [*Light Airborne Multipurpose System*] Integrated Team Training [*Navy*] (ANA)
fliv ..... flivver (SAUS)
FLIWR ..... Functional Listing and Interconnection Wiring Record
FLIX ..... Farmland Industries [*Federal Railroad Administration identification code*]
FLIXS ..... Fleet Information Exchange System [*Navy*] (MCD)
FLIZ ..... F-Layer Irregularity Zone [*Geophysics*]
FLJ ..... Canada Fortnightly Law Journal [*A publication*] (DLA)
FLJ ..... Federal Law Journal [*1939*] [*A publication*] (DLA)
FLJ ..... Federal Law Journal of India [*A publication*] (DLA)
FLJ ..... Freelance Journalist (DGA)
FLJ (Can) ..... Fortnightly Law Journal (Canada) [*A publication*] (ILCA)
FLJ Ind ..... Federal Law Journal of India [*A publication*] (ILCA)
FLJTC ..... Freeland League for Jewish Territorial Colonization [*Later, LYI*] (EA)
FLK ..... Falcks Redningskorps Beldringe AS [*Denmark*] [*ICAO designator*] (FAAC)
FLK ..... Falkland Islands [*ANSI three-letter standard code*] (CNC)
FLK ..... Fetal Lamb Kidney [*A cell line*]
FLK ..... Fleck Resources Ltd. [*Vancouver Stock Exchange symbol*]
FLK ..... Fluke Corp. [*NYSE symbol*] (SAG)

Flk Folk (DIAR)

FLK Funny Looking Kid [*Syndrome*] [*Medical slang*]

FLKB Kawambwa [*Zambia*] [*ICAO location identifier*] (ICLI)

FLKD Fluked [*Naval architecture*]

FLKD Kalundu [*Zambia*] [*ICAO location identifier*] (ICLI)

FLKE Kasompe [*Zambia*] [*ICAO location identifier*] (ICLI)

FLKG Kalengwa [*Zambia*] [*ICAO location identifier*] (ICLI)

FLKJ Kanja [*Zambia*] [*ICAO location identifier*] (ICLI)

FLKK Kakumbi [*Zambia*] [*ICAO location identifier*] (ICLI)

FLKL Kalabo [*Zambia*] [*ICAO location identifier*] (ICLI)

Fklore Folklore (DIAR)

FLKM Kapiri Mposhi [*Zambia*] [*ICAO location identifier*] (ICLI)

FLKO Kaoma [*Zambia*] [*ICAO location identifier*] (ICLI)

flkprt flock printed (SAUS)

Flks Falkland Islands (SAUS)

FLKS Fatty Liver and Kidney Syndrome (MELL)

FLKS Kasama [*Zambia*] [*ICAO location identifier*] (ICLI)

FLKU Kanyau [*Zambia*] [*ICAO location identifier*] (ICLI)

FLKW Kabwe/Milliken [*Zambia*] [*ICAO location identifier*] (ICLI)

FLKY First Lancaster Bancshares, Inc. [*NASDAQ symbol*] (SAG)

FLKY Kasaba Bay [*Zambia*] [*ICAO location identifier*] (ICLI)

FLKZ Lukuzi [*Zambia*] [*ICAO location identifier*] (ICLI)

FLL Federal Airlines [*Sudan*] [*FAA designator*] (FAAC)

FLL Field Length for Large core memory (SAUS)

FLL Final Limit, Lower

FLL Finanglia Line Ltd (SAUS)

FLL Fixed Loss Loop (VLIE)

FLL Flash Lamp Life (ACAE)

FLL Flow Line

FLL Flux-Line Lattice [*Superconductivity*] [*Physics*]

FLL Flux-Locked Loop (SAUS)

FLL Folch Lower Layer (SAUS)

FLL Fort Lauderdale [*Florida*] [*Airport symbol*] (OAG)

FLL FoxPro Link Library [*Microsoft Corp.*] [*Computer science*] (PCM)

FLL Frequency Locked Loop (IAA)

FLL Friends Library, London (SAUO)

FLL Harvard University, Frances Loeb Library, Cambridge, MA [*OCLC symbol*] (OCLC)

Fll Lakeland Public Library, Lakeland, FL [*Library symbol*] [*Library of Congress*] (LCLS)

FLLA Luanshya [*Zambia*] [*ICAO location identifier*] (ICLI)

FLLAP Foreign Languages for Lower Attaining Pupils [*Project*] (AIE)

FLLAR Forward Looking Light Attack Radar (SAUS)

FLLASH Full Level Light Aircraft System Hardware (MCD)

FLLC Lusaka [*Zambia*] [*ICAO location identifier*] (ICLI)

FLLD Familial Lipoprotein Lipase Deficiency [*Medicine*] (MELL)

fl ld floor load (SAUS)

FLLD Full Load

FLLD Lundazi [*Zambia*] [*ICAO location identifier*] (ICLI)

FlLE Flandra Ligo Esperantista (SAUO)

FLLI Livingstone [*Zambia*] [*ICAO location identifier*] (ICLI)

FLLK Frustum Lifting Lug Kit (SAUS)

FLLK Lukulu [*Zambia*] [*ICAO location identifier*] (ICLI)

FLLLTV Forward Looking Low Light Television (ACAE)

FlINAC Fast Interline Nonactivate Automatic Control (SAUS)

FlIND Facsimile Information Network Development (SAUS)

FLLO Kalomo [*Zambia*] [*ICAO location identifier*] (ICLI)

FL-LP Filter-Low Pass (MUGU)

FLLS Family Location and Legal Service [*Formerly, FLS*] (EA)

FLLS Finger Lakes Library System [*Library network*]

FlS Florida Southern College, Lakeland, FL [*Library symbol*] [*Library of Congress*] (LCLS)

FLLS Focused LASER Lithographic System

FLLS Frequency-Locked Loops (SAUS)

FLLS Fuel Low Level Sensor (IAA)

FLLS Lusaka/International [*Zambia*] [*ICAO location identifier*] (ICLI)

FLLS Waterfalls [*Board on Geographic Names*]

FlSC Southeastern College of the Assemblies of God, Lakeland, FL [*Library symbol*] [*Library of Congress*] (LCLS)

Fl Lt Flashing Light (SAUS)

FLLU Federation of Libyan Labor Unions

FLLU Luampa [*Zambia*] [*ICAO location identifier*] (ICLI)

FLLWSHP Fellowship

FLLY Lilayi [*Zambia*] [*ICAO location identifier*] (ICLI)

FLM Falmouth, KY [*Location identifier*] [*FAA*] (FAAL)

FLM Family Life Mission [*An association*] (EAIO)

FLM Fasciculus Longitudinalis Medialis [*Medicine*] (DMAA)

FLM Federal Land Manager [*Department of the Interior*] (GFGA)

FLM Federation Lutherienne Mondiale [*Lutheran World Foundation - LWF*] [*Geneva, Switzerland*] (EAIO)

FLM Fetal Lung Maturity [*Physiology*]

FLM Fibre Loop Multiplexer (SAUS)

FLM Film

FLM Finished Lens Molding

FLM Flame (MSA)

FLM Fleming Co., Inc. (SAUO)

FLM Fleming Companies, Inc. [*NYSE symbol*] (SPSG)

FLM Fleming Cos. [*NYSE symbol*] (TTSB)

Flm Flemish (SAUS)

FLM Flight Line Maintenance

FLM Flight-Weighted LASER Module (SEWL)

FLM Fluidic Logic Module

FLM Fraction of Labeled Mitoses [*Measurement of cell labeling*]

FLM Free Library Movement (SAUO)

FLM Friends of the Louvre Museum (EA)

FLM Frightened Little Man

FLM Functional Level Management

flm functional-level manager (SAUS)

FLM Funny Little Man [*Recognizable graphic type*]

FLM Fur, Leather and Machine (SAUO)

FLMA Family Life Movement of Australia

FLMA Mansa [*Zambia*] [*ICAO location identifier*] (ICLI)

flmb Film Bagged

FLMB Flammable (MSA)

FLMB Maamba [*Zambia*] [*ICAO location identifier*] (ICLI)

FLMC Full Load Motor Current [*Kraus & Naimer Microelectronics*]

FLMD Musonda Falls [*Zambia*] [*ICAO location identifier*] (ICLI)

FLME Fatigue Life Modification Expert [*Automotive engineering*]

FLMECH Fluid Mechanical (MCD)

FL MECH Fluid Mechanical (SAUS)

FL MECH Fluid Mechanics (SAUS)

FLMEM Floppy Disc Memory (NITA)

FLMF Mfuwe [*Zambia*] [*ICAO location identifier*] (ICLI)

FLM-FJC Fur, Leather and Machine Workers Unions - Furriers Joint Council (EA)

FLMG Mongu [*Zambia*] [*ICAO location identifier*] (ICLI)

FLMI Fellow, Life Management Institute [*Life Office Management Association*] [*Designation awarded by*]

FLMI Fellow of the Life Management Institute (DD)

FLMI Mukonchi [*Zambia*] [*ICAO location identifier*] (ICLI)

FLMK Foilmark, Inc. [*NASDAQ symbol*] (SAG)

FLMK Mkushi [*Zambia*] [*ICAO location identifier*] (ICLI)

FLML Flamel Technologies [*NASDAQ symbol*] (SAG)

FLML Flight Line Memory Loader (ACAE)

FLML Mufulira [*Zambia*] [*ICAO location identifier*] (ICLI)

FIMLT Fellow of the Institute of Medical Laboratory Technology (SAUS)

FLMM Mwami [*Zambia*] [*ICAO location identifier*] (ICLI)

FLMMAR Forward Looking Multi-Mode Attack Radar (ACAE)

FLMMX Flag Investors Managed Munic. [*Mutual fund ticker symbol*] (SG)

FLMNAG Fulminating (ABBR)

FLMNAN Fulmination (ABBR)

FLMNC Flamboyance (ABBR)

FLMNGY Flamingly (ABBR)

FLMNS Filminess (ABBR)

FLMNT Flamboyant (ABBR)

FLMNTY Flamboyantly (ABBR)

FLMO Monze [*Zambia*] [*ICAO location identifier*] (ICLI)

FLMP Mpika [*Zambia*] [*ICAO location identifier*] (ICLI)

FLMPRF Flameproof (MSA)

FLMPRS Film Processing

FLMPTS Future Land Mobile Personal Telephone Service

FLMR Filmier (ABBR)

F/LMR First and Last Month's Rent (ADWA)

FLM RES Flame Resistant (MSA)

FLM RTD Flame Retardant (MSA)

FLMRY Flummery (ABBR)

FLMSD Film Sound

FLMSNS Flimsiness (ABBR)

FLMSR Flimsier (ABBR)

FLMSST Flimsiest (ABBR)

FLMST Filmiest (ABBR)

FLMSY Flimsily (ABBR)

FLMSY Flimsy (ABBR)

FLMT Flash Mount (SAUS)

FLMT Flush Mount

FLMT Mutanda [*Zambia*] [*ICAO location identifier*] (ICLI)

FLMTHR Flamethrower (AABC)

flmthwr flame thrower (SAUS)

FLMTO Film Linearized Muffin-Tin Orbital [*Physics*]

FL/MTR Flow Meter (AAG)

FLMTT Flame Tight

FLMTT Flametight (SAUS)

FLMU Mulobezi [*Zambia*] [*ICAO location identifier*] (ICLI)

flmw Film Wrapped

FLMW Mwinilunga [*Zambia*] [*ICAO location identifier*] (ICLI)

flmwrpd Film Wrapped

FLMY Filmy (ABBR)

FLMZ Mazabuka [*Zambia*] [*ICAO location identifier*] (ICLI)

FLN Fallen (ABBR)

FLN Feline (ABBR)

FLN Felon (ABBR)

FLN Flanders Airlines [*Belgium*] [*ICAO designator*] (FAAC)

FLN Flatten (MSA)

FLN Florianopolis [*Brazil*] [*Airport symbol*] (OAG)

FLN Flourescence Line Narrowing (SAUS)

FLN Flown

Fln Fluorene [*Biochemistry*]

FLN Fluorescence-Line Narrowed [*Spectrometry*]

FLN Following Landing Numbers [*Shipping*]

FLN Freelance Network (EA)

FLN Frente de Liberacion Nacional [*National Liberation Front*] [*Venezuela*] [*Political party*] (PD)

FLN Frente de Liberacion Nacional [*National Liberation Front*] [*El Salvador*] [*Political party*]

FLN Frente de Liberacion Nacional [*National Liberation Front*] [*Chile*] [*Political party*]

FLN Frente de Liberacion Nacional [*National Liberation Front*] [*Peru*] [*Political party*]

FLN Front de Liberation Nationale [*National Liberation Front*] [*Algeria*] [*Political party*] (PPW)

FLN............ Front de Liberation Nationale [*National Liberation Front*] [*France*] [*Political party*]
FLN............ Front de Liberation Nationale [*National Liberation Front*] [*South Vietnam*] [*Use NFLSV*] [*Political party*]
FLN............ Fuel Line
FLN............ Functional Link Net (VLIE)
FLN............ La Foliniere [*France*] [*Seismograph station code, US Geological Survey*] (SEIS)
FLNA............ Ngoma [*Zambia*] [*ICAO location identifier*] (ICLI)
FLNB............ [*The*] Flemington National Bank & Trust [*NASDAQ symbol*] (SAG)
FLNC............ Front de Liberation Nationale Congolais [*Congolese National Liberation Front*] [*Zaire*] [*Political party*] (PD)
FLNC............ Front de Liberation Nationale de la Corse [*Corsican National Liberation Front*] [*Political party*] (PD)
FLNCD............ Flounced (ABBR)
FLNCG............ Flouncing (ABBR)
FLND............ Ndola [*Zambia*] [*ICAO location identifier*] (ICLI)
FLNDR............ Flounder (ABBR)
FLNDRD............ Floundered (ABBR)
FLNDRG............ Floundering (ABBR)
FLNF............ Front de Liberation Nationale Francaise [*French National Liberation Front*] (PD)
flng............ falling (SAUS)
FLNG............ Florida National Guard (DEMM)
FLNG............ Fueling
FLNGG............ Flinging (ABBR)
FLNH............ Flinch (ABBR)
FLNHGY............ Flinchingly (ABBR)
FLNHR............ Flincher (ABBR)
FLNK............ Flank (ABBR)
FLNK............ Force de Liberation Nationale Kamerunaise [*National Cameroonian Liberation Force*] [*Political party*]
FLNKD............ Flanked (ABBR)
FLNKG............ Flanking (ABBR)
FLNKR............ Flanker (ABBR)
FLNKS............ Kanak Socialist National Liberation Front (SAUS)
FLNKY............ Flunky (ABBR)
FLNL............ Namwala [*Zambia*] [*ICAO location identifier*] (ICLI)
FLNM............ Fort Laramie National Monument (SAUO)
FLNPP............ Federal Library Network Prototype Project (NITA)
FLNS............ Fluidness (ABBR)
FLNS............ Fluorescence Line-Narrowing Spectroscopy
FINSystem............ Finance System (SAUS)
FLNT............ Felinity (ABBR)
FLNT............ Flint (ABBR)
FLNTEST............ Flauntiest (ABBR)
FLNTNS............ Flintiness (ABBR)
FLNTR............ Flintier (ABBR)
FLNTST............ Flintiest (ABBR)
FLNTY............ Flinty (ABBR)
FLNTYNS............ Flintiness (ABBR)
FLNTYY............ Flintily (ABBR)
FLNUS............ Felonious (ABBR)
FLNUSNS............ Feloniousness (ABBR)
FLNUSY............ Feloniously (ABBR)
FLNY............ Felinely (ABBR)
FLNY............ Felony (ABBR)
FLNY............ Nyimba [*Zambia*] [*ICAO location identifier*] (ICLI)
FLO............ Falcon Airlines [*Yugoslavia*] [*ICAO designator*] (FAAC)
FLO............ Family Liaison Office
FLO............ Fast Light-Off [*Automotive emissions*]
FLO............ Fault-Location Oscillator [*Bell System*]
FLO............ Film Liaison Officer [*Army*]
FLO............ First Lunar Observatory (SAUS)
FLO............ Fleet Electrical Officer [*British military*] (DMA)
FL O............ Flight Officer (WDAA)
Flo............ Floodlight (DA)
FLO............ Florence [*South Carolina*] [*Airport symbol*] (OAG)
FLO............ Florence, SC [*Location identifier*] [*FAA*] (FAAL)
Flo............ Florentinus [*Flourished, 2nd century*] [*Authority cited in pre-1607 legal work*] (DSA)
Flo............ Florianus de Sancto Petro [*Deceased, 1441*] [*Authority cited in pre-1607 legal work*] (DSA)
Flo............ Florilege [*Record label*] [*France*]
FLO............ Florin [*Monetary unit*] [*Netherlands*] (ROG)
FLO............ Florissant [*Missouri*] [*Seismograph station code, US Geological Survey*] [*Closed*] (SEIS)
FLO............ Flowers Indus [*NYSE symbol*] (TTSB)
FLO............ Flowers Industries, Inc. [*NYSE symbol*] (SPSG)
Fl/O............ Flying Officer [*British*] (DMA)
FLO............ Foreign Liaison Office [*Military*] (AABC)
FLO............ Frederick Law Olmsted [*American landscape architect, 1822-1903*]
FLO............ Fuel Lube Oil
FLO............ Functional Line Organization
f-lo-............ Lesotho [*MARC geographic area code*] [*Library of Congress*] (LCCP)
FLOA............ Federal Licensed Officers Association (EA)
FLOA............ Frederick Law Olmsted Association (EA)
FLOAG............ Front of the Liberation of the Occupied Arabian Gulf (SAUO)
FLOAT............ Floating Offshore Attended Terminal (SAUS)
Floatainer............ Floating Container (SAUS)
floatel............ floating motel (SAUS)
FLOC............ Farm Labor Organizing Committee (EA)
FLOC............ Fault Localization
FLOC............ Fault Locator (SAUS)
FLoC............ Federated Logic Conference (VLIE)
floc............ Flocculated (SAUS)
floc............ Flocculation (SAUS)
FLOC............ Floccule (ABBR)
FLOC............ Flocculent (ABBR)
FLOC............ Floccus (ABBR)
FLOC............ For Love of Children
FLOCC............ Flocculation
FLOCCPAC............ Fleet Operational Control Center, Pacific (SAUO)
flo-chip............ Flowchart-building Chip (SAUS)
FLOCOM............ Floating Commutator
FLOCON............ Floating Container (PDAA)
FLOCON............ Floor Control (SAUS)
FLOD............ Flood (ABBR)
FLODAC............ Fluid-Operated Digital Automatic Computer [*Sperry UNIVAC*]
FLODD............ Flooded (ABBR)
FLODG............ Flooding (ABBR)
FLOF............ Full Level One Feature (SAUS)
Fl Offr............ Flying Officer [*British*] (DMA)
FLO/FLO............ Float On/Float Off
FLOG............ Fleet Logistics
FLOG............ Fleet Logistics Air Wing (SAUS)
FLOGAIR............ Fleet Logistics Air Wing [*Navy*]
FLOGEN............ Flow Generator [*Air Force*] (DOMA)
FLOGRAP............ Fuels Logistics Readiness Assessment Program (SAUO)
FLOGWING............ Fleet Logistics Air Wing [*Obsolete*] [*Navy*]
FLOGWINGLANT............ Fleet Logistics Air Wing, Atlantic [*Navy*]
FLOGWINGPAC............ Fleet Logistics Air Wing, Pacific [*Navy*]
Flojo............ Florence Griffith Joyner [*American track athlete and Olympic gold medalist*]
flok............ Flocked (VRA)
FLOLS............ Fresnel Lens Optical Landing System [*Navy*]
FLOM............ Fractional Low-Order Moments (SAUS)
FLOOD............ Fleet Observation of Oceanographic Data [*Navy*]
Flood El Eq............ Flood. Equitable Doctrine of Election [*1880*] [*A publication*] (DLA)
Flood Lib............ Flood. Slander and Libel [*1880*] [*A publication*] (DLA)
FLOODS............ Florida Object-Oriented Device Simulator (AAEL)
Flood Wills............ Flood on Wills of Personal Property [*A publication*] (DLA)
FLOOPS............ Florida Object-Oriented Process Simulator (AAEL)
FLOP............ Floating Octal Point [*IBM Corp.*]
FLOP............ Floating Point [*Electronics*] (ECII)
FLOP............ Floating Point Operation [*Computer science*]
flop............ Floating-Point Operation (ADWA)
FLOP............ Foreign Liaison Officer Program
FIOP............ FORTRAN input/output package (SAUS)
FLOP............ Fresnel Lens Optical Practice [*Navy*]
FLOPAC............ Flight Operations Advisory Committee (SAUO)
FLOPC............ Floating Point Operations Needed per Cycle (AAEL)
FLOPD............ Flopped (ABBR)
FLOPF............ Fresnel Lens Optical Practice, Fleet [*Navy*]
FLOPG............ Flopping (ABBR)
FLOPLY............ Floppily (ABBR)
FLOPNS............ Floppiness (ABBR)
FLOPP............ Floating Power Platform (PDAA)
floppy............ Floppy disk (SAUS)
FLOPR............ Flopper (ABBR)
FLOPR............ Floppier (ABBR)
FLOPS............ Flight Optimization System [*Aerospace engineering*]
flops............ Floating-Point Operations per Second (ADWA)
FLOPS............ Floating-Point Operations per Second [*Computer science*]
FLOPS............ floating point operations per second (SAUS)
FLOPST............ Floppiest (ABBR)
Floptical............ Floppy Optical [*Computer science*]
FLOPY............ Floppy (ABBR)
FLOPYR............ Floppier (ABBR)
FLOPYST............ Floppiest (ABBR)
FLOR............ Florence [*Italy*] (ROG)
FLOR............ Florence, AL [*American Association of Railroads railroad junction routing code*]
FLOR............ Flores [*Flowers*] [*Latin*] (ROG)
Flor............ Florianus de Sancto Petro [*Deceased, 1441*] [*Authority cited in pre-1607 legal work*] (DSA)
FLOR............ Floriculture
Flor............ Florida [*of Apuleius*] [*Classical studies*] (OCD)
Flo R............ Florida Reports [*A publication*] (DLA)
Flor............ Florida Reports [*A publication*] (DLA)
FLOR............ Florist (ROG)
FLOR............ Floruit [*He Flourished*] [*Latin*]
FLOR............ Flourished (SAUS)
FLORA............ Fire Location RADAR (NG)
FLORA............ Flora, IL [*American Association of Railroads railroad junction routing code*]
Flore............ Florentinus [*Flourished, 2nd century*] [*Authority cited in pre-1607 legal work*] (DSA)
Florence............ Federal Detention Headquarters at Florence, Arizona (SAUS)
FLORENT............ Florentia [*Florence*] [*Latin*] (ROG)
FloresRk............ Flores & Rucks, Inc. [*Associated Press*] (SAG)
FLOREX............ Technical Exhibition for Florists [*Brussels International Trade Fair*]
FLORG............ Flooring (ABBR)
Flori............ Florianus de Sancto Petro [*Deceased, 1441*] [*Authority cited in pre-1607 legal work*] (DSA)
Floria............ Florianus de Sancto Petro [*Deceased, 1441*] [*Authority cited in pre-1607 legal work*] (DSA)
Floribbean............ Floridian-Caribbean (SAUS)
FLORICO............ Florida-Puerto Rico Submarine Cable (SAUS)
Florida............ Florida Reports [*A publication*] (DLA)

FLORIDA COMCAT... Florida Computer Catalog of Monographic Holdings [*Library network*]
Florida R..... Florida Reports [*A publication*] (DLA)
Florida Rep... Florida Reports [*A publication*] (DLA)
FLORKAT..... Datenbank Floristische Kartierung (SAUS)
FLORL....... Fluorescent Runway Lighting
FLORR......... Flourier (ABBR)
FLORSENT... Fluorescent [*Freight*]
FlorshGp...... Florsheim Group [*Associated Press*] (SAG)
FlorshSh...... [*The*] Florsheim Shoe Co. [*Associated Press*] (SAG)
FLORST....... Flouriest (ABBR)
FLOR-WKR... Floorwalker (ABBR)
FLORY......... Floury (ABBR)
FLOS........... Fixed Line of Sight (KSC)
FLOS........... Flight Level Orientation System (SAUS)
FLOSOST..... Fluorine One-Stage Orbital Space Truck (KSC)
floss............. flossing (SAUS)
FLOSY......... Front for the Liberation of Occupied South Yemen (PD)
FLOT............ Float (ABBR)
FLOT............ Flotation (KSC)
FLOT............ Flotilla (AABC)
FLOT............ Flotsam (ABBR)
FLOT............ Forward Line of Own Troops (MCD)
FLOT............ Forward Line Of Troops (SAUS)
FLOT............ Front Line of Troops (ACAE)
FLOTD......... Floated (ABBR)
FloTech........ Florida Institute of Technology (SAUS)
flotel........... floating hotel (SAUS)
FLOTG......... Floating (ABBR)
FLOTGE........ Floatage (ABBR)
FLOTL.......... Flotilla (ABBR)
FLOTM......... Flotsam (ABBR)
FLOTN......... Flotation (ABBR)
FLOTOX....... Floating Gate Tunnel Oxide [*Electronics*] (EECA)
FLOTR.......... Floater (ABBR)
FLOTRAN..... Flowcharting FORTRAN [*Computer science*] (IEEE)
FLOTRONCOM... Flotilla or Squadron Commander (DNAB)
FLOT STOR... Floating Storage (DNAB)
FLOTUS....... First Lady of the United States
FLOU........... Flourish (WGA)
flour............ Flourescent (VRA)
FLOV........... Federation of Latvian Organisations of Victoria [*Australia*]
FLOVTH....... Flush Oiltight Ventilation Hole
FLOW........... Flow International [*NASDAQ symbol*] (TTSB)
FLOW........... Flow International Corp. [*NASDAQ symbol*] (NQ)
FLOW........... Flow Systems, Inc. [*NASDAQ symbol*] (COMM)
FLOW........... Flow Welding (SAUS)
Flower......... Flowers Industries, Inc. [*Associated Press*] (SAG)
FLOWGEN.... Flowchart Generator (VLIE)
FlowInt........ Flow International Corp. [*Associated Press*] (SAG)
Flow Meas Instrum... Flow Measurement and Instrumentation [*A publication*] (CABS)
FLOWS......... Faa-Lincoln Laboratory Operational Weather Studies (SAUO)
FLOWSIM.... Traffic Flow Planning Simulation [*FAA*] (TAG)
FLOX........... Flex Leasing [*Private rail car owner code*]
flox............. flourine + liquid oxygen (SAUS)
FLOX........... Fluorine/Liquid Oxygen Mixture (SAUS)
FLOYD......... Floydada, TX [*American Association of Railroads railroad junction routing code*]
Floy Proct Pr... Floyer's Proctors' Practice [*A publication*] (DLA)
fl oz............ fluid once (SAUS)
fl oz............ Fluid Ounce (SHCU)
FLOZ........... Fluid Ounce
FLP............. Bristol & Wessex Aeroplane Club Ltd. [*British*] [*ICAO designator*] (FAAC)
FLP............. Facility Location Planner (SAUS)
FLP............. Family Limited Partnership
FLP............. Fast Link Pulse (SAUS)
FLP............. Fault Location Panel [*Aerospace*] (AAG)
FLP............. Featherly Pass [*Alaska*] [*Seismograph station code, US Geological Survey*] (SEIS)
FLP............. Federal Labor Party (SAUO)
FLP............. Fermi Level Pinning (AAEL)
FLP............. Festlegepunkt [*Reference point, a gunnery term*] [*German military - World War II*]
FLP............. Few Large Platelets [*Hematology*] (DAVI)
FLP............. Field Landing Practice
FLP............. Fighting Landplane
FLP............. Fiji Labour Party [*Political party*] (FEA)
FLP............. Fillip (ABBR)
FLP............. Filter Low Pass (SAUS)
FLP............. Finlands Landsbygdsparti [*Finnish Rural Party*] [*Political party*] (PPE)
FLP............. Fisheries Licensing Panel [*Victoria, Australia*]
FLP............. Flame Leak Proof
FLP............. Flameproof (HEAS)
FLP............. Flap (NASA)
flp............. Flash Point [*Industrial hygiene term*] (OHS)
FLP............. Flashpoint (GNE)
FLP............. Fletcher Challenge Paper [*NYSE symbol*] (SAG)
FLP............. Fletcher Challenge Paper ADS [*NYSE symbol*] (TTSB)
FLP............. Flight Line Printer
FLP............. Flippin, AR [*Location identifier*] [*FAA*] (FAAL)
FLP............. Floating Point [*Computer science*]
FLP............. Florida Law and Practice [*A publication*] (DLA)
Flp............. Fluorescent Pseudomonad
FLP............. Free Library of Philadelphia (SAUS)
F/LP........... Freight/Luggage Panniers [*Hovercraft*]
FLP............. Frente de Liberacion de los Pobres [*Liberation Front of the Poor*] [*Ecuador*] [*Political party*] (PD)
FLP............. Friends of Luna Park [*Sydney, New South Wales, Australia*]
FLP............. Frog-Leg Position [*Medicine*] (MELL)
FLP............. Front de Liberation de la Polynesie [*Political party*] (EY)
FLP............. Front de Liberation Populaire [*Quebec separatist group*]
FLP............. Fronto-Laeva Posterior [*A fetal position*] [*Obstetrics*] (MAE)
FLPA........... Flight Level Pressure Altitude
FLPA........... Foreign Language Press of America
FLPA........... Kasempa [*Zambia*] [*ICAO location identifier*] (ICLI)
FLPanth....... Florida Panthers Holdings, Inc. [*Associated Press*] (SAG)
FLPAQ......... Family Law Practitioners' Association of Queensland [*Australia*]
FLPAU......... Floating Point Arithmetic Unit (SAUS)
FLPB........... First Leesport Bancorp [*NASDAQ symbol*] (SAG)
FLPC........... Federal Local Port Controller
FLPC........... Film Layer Purifying Chamber (SAUS)
FLPC........... Flat Line Powder Coating [*Metal finishing*]
FLPD........... Flapped (ABBR)
FLPDC......... Floppy Disc Controller (NITA)
FLPE........... Petauke [*Zambia*] [*ICAO location identifier*] (ICLI)
FL PF.......... Flat Proof [*Graphic arts*] (DGA)
FLPG........... Flapping (ABBR)
FLPK........... Mporokoso [*Zambia*] [*ICAO location identifier*] (ICLI)
FLPKG......... File Package (SAUS)
flpl............. Flore Pleno [*With Double Flowers*] [*Botany*] [*Latin*] (BARN)
flpl............. fortran-compiled list-processing language (SAUS)
FLPL........... FORTRAN [*Formula Translating System*] List Processing Language [*Computer science*] (IEEE)
FLPMA......... Federal Land Policy and Management Act [*1976*]
FLPNC......... Flippancy (ABBR)
FLPNT......... Flippant (ABBR)
FLPNTY....... Flippantly (ABBR)
FLP Number... Floating Point Number (SAUS)
FLPO........... Kabompo [*Zambia*] [*ICAO location identifier*] (ICLI)
FLPOL......... Floating-Point On-Line (SAUS)
FLPP........... Foreign Language Proficiency Pay [*Army*] (INF)
FLPP/CWS... Family Life and Population Program/Church World Service [*Defunct*] (EA)
fl pr............ Flameproof (SAUS)
FLPR........... Flapper
FLPRF......... Flameproof (IAA)
FLPS........... First Lot Procurement Status (AAG)
FLPS........... Flight Load Preparation System [*NASA*] (NASA)
FIPS-PUBS.... Federal Information Processing Standards- Publications (SAUS)
FLPSX......... Fidelity Low Priced Stock [*Mutual fund ticker symbol*] (SG)
FL PT.......... Flash Point [*Graphic arts*] (DGA)
FLPT........... Flash Point [*Chemistry*] (IAA)
FL PT.......... Fluid Pint (WDAA)
FLPT........... Fork Lift Pallet Trailer (SAUS)
FLPTREGS... Floating Point Registers (SAUS)
FLPw........... Florida Power & Light Co. [*Associated Press*] (SAG)
FLPw25........ Florida Power & Light [*Associated Press*] (SAG)
FLPZ........... Fruitland Louisa Power Plant [*Federal Railroad Administration identification code*]
FLQ............. Dallas-Fort Worth, TX [*Location identifier*] [*FAA*] (FAAL)
FLQ............. Families Leaving Quebec [*Humorous interpretation for Front de Liberation du Quebec*]
FLQ............. Front de Liberation de Quebec [*Quebec Liberation Front*] [*Separatist group*]
FLQX........... Juvancourt [*France*] [*ICAO location identifier*] (ICLI)
FLR............. Failure (MSA)
FLR............. Fall River [*Massachusetts*] [*Seismograph station code, US Geological Survey*] (SEIS)
FLR............. Fall River, MA [*Location identifier*] [*FAA*] (FAAL)
FLR............. Family Law Reform Party [*Political party*] [*Australia*]
FLR............. Family Law Reports [*A publication*]
FLR............. Fast Liner Reactor (MCD)
FLR............. Field Level Repair (NVT)
FLR............. Field Loss Relay
FLR............. Fiessinger-Leroy-Reiter [*Syndrome*] [*Medicine*] (DB)
FLR............. Fiji Law Reports [*A publication*] (DLA)
FLR............. File Label Record (SAUS)
FLR............. Filler (AABC)
FLR............. Final Limit, Reverse
flr............. firkin (SAUS)
FLR............. First-Light-Readiness [*Military alert*] (VNW)
FLR............. Fixed-Length Record (SAUS)
FLR............. Fixed Loan Rate [*Business term*]
FLR............. Flag Register (SAUS)
flr............. flame resistant (SAUS)
FLR............. Flares
FLR............. flar rate (SAUS)
FLR............. Flight Line Recorder (SAUS)
FLR............. Flight Line Reference (NVT)
FLR............. Flight Load Recorder
FLR............. Floating-point Register (SAUS)
Flr............. Floor (MIST)
flr............. Floor (VRA)
FLR............. Floor
FLR............. Flora Reserve [*State*] (EERA)
FLR............. Florence [*Italy*] [*Airport symbol*] (OAG)
FLR............. Florence, Italy Airport (SAUS)
FLR............. Florin [*Monetary unit*] [*Netherlands*]

FLR .... Flower
FLR .... Flow Rate (AAG)
FLR .... Fluor Corp. [*NYSE symbol*] (SPSG)
FLR .... Fluor Corporation, Ltd. (SAUO)
FLR .... Fluoroleucine Resistant (SAUS)
FLR .... Flyair [*Spain*] [*FAA designator*] (FAAC)
flr .... Flyer (SAUS)
FLR .... Folder (SAUS)
FLR .... Folder (file name extension) (SAUS)
FLR .... Forward-Looking RADAR
FLR .... Funny Looking Rash [*Medicine*] (EDAA)
FLRA .... Family Law Reform Association [*Australia*]
FLRA .... Federal Labor Relations Authority [*Independent government agency*]
FLRA .... Flora (ABBR)
FLRAL .... Floral (ABBR)
FLRANSW .... Family Law Reform Association of New South Wales [*Australia*]
FLRC .... Farm Labor Research Committee [*Defunct*] (EA)
FLRC .... Federal Labor Relations Council [*Later, FLRA*]
FLRC .... Feminist Library and Resource Centre [*British*] (EAIO)
FLRCLTR .... Floriculture (ABBR)
FLRCLTRL .... Floricultural (ABBR)
FLRCLTRST .... Floriculturalist (ABBR)
FLRCVG .... Floorcovering
FLRD .... Flared
FLRD .... Floored (ABBR)
FLRD .... Flurried (ABBR)
FLRD .... Front de Liberation et de Rehabilitation du Dahomey [*Dahomey Liberation and Rehabilitation Front*] [*Benin*] [*Political party*] (PD)
FLRDA .... Flouridate (ABBR)
FLRDAD .... Flouridated (ABBR)
FLRDAG .... Flouridating (ABBR)
FLRDN .... Flouridation (ABBR)
FlrDnlGTI .... Fluor Daniel GTI, Inc. [*Associated Press*] (SAG)
FLREN .... Florence, VT [*American Association of Railroads railroad junction routing code*]
FLRev .... Federal Law Review [*A publication*]
FLRFA .... Federation of Land Reform Farmers Associations (SAUO)
FLRFX .... Invesco Growth Fund [*Mutual fund ticker symbol*] (SG)
FLRG .... Flaring
FLRG .... Flooring (ABBR)
FLRG .... Flurrying (ABBR)
FLRG .... Rusangu [*Zambia*] [*ICAO location identifier*] (ICLI)
FLRH .... Flourish (ABBR)
FLRHG .... Flourishing (ABBR)
FLRID .... Florid (ABBR)
FLRIDNS .... Floridness (ABBR)
FLRIDT .... Floridity (ABBR)
FLRIDY .... Floridly (ABBR)
FLRL .... Floral
FLRMP .... Forest Land and Resource Management Plan [*US Forest Service*]
FLRNE .... Florence, CO [*American Association of Railroads railroad junction routing code*]
FLRNG .... Flash Ranging
FLRNG .... Flooring
FLRO .... FluoroScan Imaging Sys [*NASDAQ symbol*] (TTSB)
FLRO .... FluoroScan Imaging Systems, Inc. [*NASDAQ symbol*] (SAG)
FLRO .... Rosa [*Zambia*] [*ICAO location identifier*] (ICLI)
FLROW .... Fluoroscan Imaging Sys Wrrt [*NASDAQ symbol*] (TTSB)
FLRP .... Farm Labor Research Project (EA)
FLRR .... Federal Labor Relations Reporter (SAUS)
flrs .... flares (SAUS)
flrs .... flowers (SAUS)
FLRS .... Forward-Looking RADAR Set (NVT)
FLRSH .... Full Land Rover Service History [*Automotive classified advertising*]
FLRSNC .... Flourescence (ABBR)
FLRSNT .... Flourescent (ABBR)
FLRST .... Florist (ABBR)
FLRT .... Factory Layout/Relayout Tool (AAEL)
FLRT .... Fat Lip Readers Theater (EA)
FLRT .... Federal Librarians Round Table [*American Library Association*] (EA)
FLRT .... Flexible, Longwave Radiative Transfer (SAUS)
FLRT .... Floret (ABBR)
FL/RT .... Flow Rate (AAG)
FLRTN .... Flirtation (ABBR)
FLRTU .... Flirtatious (ABBR)
FLRU .... Rufansa [*Zambia*] [*ICAO location identifier*] (ICLI)
FLRY .... Flurly (SAUS)
FLRY .... Flurry [*NWS*] (FAAC)
FLS .... Faculty of Library and Information Science, University of Toronto [*UTLAS symbol*]
FLS .... Faculty of Library Science (SAUS)
FLS .... Fair Labor Standards (SAUS)
FLS .... Fairlines, BV [*Netherlands*] [*FAA designator*] (FAAC)
FLS .... Falls
FLS .... False [*FBI standardized term*]
FLS .... Family Location Service [*Later, FLLS*] (EA)
FLS .... Farm Labor Service [*of USES*]
FLS .... Fatty Liver Syndrome [*Medicine*] (EDAA)
FLS .... Fault Locator System (AABC)
FLS .... Fellow of the Linnaean Society [*British*]
FLS .... Fibrous Long-Spacing Collagen
FLS .... Field Length for Small Core Memory (IAA)
FLS .... Field Logistics System (SAUO)
FLS .... Fighter Leader School [*British military*] (DMA)
FLS .... Final Line of Sight (SAUS)
FLS .... Finance Ledger System [*Economics*]
FLS .... Financial Listing Service [*Prime Rating, Inc.*] [*Defunct*] [*Information service or system*] (CRD)
FLS .... Flashing Lights and/or Scotoma [*Neurology and ophthalmology*] (DAVI)
FLS .... Flashing Light System (AAG)
FLS .... Flashless
FLS .... Fleet Logistics Support Department [*Naval Weapons Support Center*]
FLS .... Flight Surgeon (MCD)
FLS .... Flinders Island [*Australia*] [*Airport symbol*] (OAG)
FLS .... Floating License Server (SAUS)
FLS .... Flood Statement [*Telecommunications*] (OTD)
fls .... floors (SAUS)
FLS .... Florida Specialized Carriers Rate Conference, Inc., Jacksonville FL [*STAC*]
FLS .... Florida State University, School of Library Science, Tallahassee, FL [*OCLC symbol*] (OCLC)
FLS .... Florida Steel Corp. (SAUO)
FLS .... Florida Supplement [*A publication*] (DLA)
FLS .... Flowserve Corp. [*NYSE symbol*] (SG)
FLS .... Flow Switch
FLS .... Fluid Level Sensor [*Engineering*]
fl s .... Fluid Scruple (SAUS)
Fls .... Flushing (SAUS)
FLS .... Flushing, NY (ABBR)
F-LS .... Folk-Lore Society (SAUO)
FLS .... Force Level Simulation (SAUS)
FLS .... Forward Light Scatter
FLS .... Forward Logistics Site [*Navy*]
fls .... forward-looking sonar (SAUS)
fls .... Forward Looking Strategy
FLS .... Forward Look SONAR
FLS .... Foundation for Life Sciences [*Australia*]
FLS .... Foundation of Law and Society [*Defunct*] (EA)
FLS .... Free Line Signal [*Telecommunications*] (TEL)
FLS .... Freight Logistics System (TIMI)
FLS .... Front Line States
FLS .... Full Length Shot (SAUS)
FLS .... Functional Language Survey (EDAC)
FLS .... Fundamentals of Land Surveying (SAUS)
FLS .... Future Launching System [*Space flight*]
FLS .... New Air Ltd. [*British*] [*ICAO designator*] (FAAC)
FLSA .... Fair Labor Standards Act [*1938*]
FLSA .... Federal Labor Standard Act [*Marine science*] (OSRA)
FLSA .... Federal Labor Standards Act (AAGC)
FLSA .... Follicular Lymphosarcoma [*Oncology*]
FLSA .... Frankie Laine Society of America (EA)
FLSA .... St. Anthony [*Zambia*] [*ICAO location identifier*] (ICLI)
FLSASP .... Florida State Agency for Surplus Property (DEMM)
FLSC .... Federal Lake Survey Center
FLSC .... Fixed Laboratory Standard Capacitor
FLS/C .... Fleet Logistics Support Department/Crane, IN [*Naval Ammunition Depot*]
FLSC .... Flexible Linear Shaped Charge
flsc .... flight shape charge (SAUS)
FLSC .... Florsheim Group, Inc. [*NASDAQ symbol*] (NASQ)
FLSC .... Florsheim Shoe [*NASDAQ symbol*] (TTSB)
FLSC .... [*The*] Florsheim Shoe Co. [*NASDAQ symbol*] (SAG)
FLSCK .... Falls Creek, PA [*American Association of Railroads railroad junction routing code*]
FLSCL .... Fullscale (ABBR)
FLSCP .... Flouroscope (ABBR)
FLS-CP .... Foolscap (ABBR)
FLSCY .... Falls City, NE [*American Association of Railroads railroad junction routing code*]
FLSD .... Fleet Logistics Support Department (SAUO)
FLSD .... Fleet Logistics Support Detachment [*Naval Weapons Support Center*] (DNAB)
FISDO .... Flight Standards District Office (SAUO)
FLSE .... Serenje [*Zambia*] [*ICAO location identifier*] (ICLI)
FISEA .... Florida Society of Enrolled Agents (SAUO)
FLSEP .... Family Life and Sex Education Program (SAUO)
FLS EXMPT FR ... False Certification of Exemption from Financial Responsibility [*Conviction term used in state of Oregon*] (MVRD)
FLSFCAN .... Falsification (ABBR)
FLSFD .... Falsified (ABBR)
FLSFG .... Falsifying (ABBR)
FLSFN .... Falsification (ABBR)
FLS FR .... Falsification of Financial Responsibility [*Conviction term used in state of Oregon*] (MVRD)
FLSFR .... Falsifier (ABBR)
FLSFY .... Falsify (ABBR)
FLSG .... Force Logistics Support Group [*Marine Corps*] (NVT)
FLSH .... Flash (ABBR)
FLSH .... Full Lexus Service History [*Automotive classified advertising*]
FLSH .... Full Lincoln Service History [*Automotive classified advertising*]
FLSH .... Shiwan'Gandu [*Zambia*] [*ICAO location identifier*] (ICLI)
FLSH-BK .... Flash-Back (ABBR)
FLSHD .... Flashed (ABBR)
FLSHD .... Flashehood (ABBR)
flshd .... fleshed (SAUS)
FLSHF .... M-Sys Flash Disk Pioneers Ltd [*NASDAQ symbol*] (TTSB)
FLSHG .... Flashing (ABBR)
FLSHLT .... Flashlight (ABBR)
FLSHLY .... Flashily (ABBR)

FLSHNS....... Flashiness (ABBR)
FLSH-PTS.... Fleshpots (ABBR)
FLSHR......... Flasher (ABBR)
FLSHR......... Flashier (ABBR)
FLSHST........ Fleshiest (ABBR)
FLSHY......... Flashy (ABBR)
FLSHY......... Fleshly (ABBR)
FLSHYNS..... Flashiness (ABBR)
FLSHYR....... Flashier (ABBR)
FLSHYST...... Flashiest (ABBR)
FLSHYY....... Flashily (ABBR)
FLS INFO INS... Giving False Information about Liability Insurance to a Police Officer [*Conviction term used in state of Oregon*] (MVRD)
FLS INFO PLC... Giving False Information to a Police Officer [*Conviction term used in state of Oregon*] (MVRD)
FLSIP.......... Fleet Logistic Support Improvement Program [*Navy*] (NG)
FLSIP-COSAL... Fleet Logistics Support Improvement Program Consolidated Stock Allowance List (SAUO)
FLSJ........... Sakeji [*Zambia*] [*ICAO location identifier*] (ICLI)
flslk........... Feels Like [*A term used by weather forecasters*] (WDMC)
FLSLY.......... Falsely (ABBR)
FLSM........... Fulsome (ABBR)
FLSM........... St. Mary's [*Zambia*] [*ICAO location identifier*] (ICLI)
FLSMNS...... Fulsomeness (ABBR)
FLSMP........ French-Language Society of Medical Psychology (EA)
FLSMY........ Fulsomely (ABBR)
FLSN........... Senanga [*Zambia*] [*ICAO location identifier*] (ICLI)
FLSNS......... Falseness (ABBR)
FLSO........... Fort Lauderdale Symphony Orchestra (SAUO)
FLSO........... Southdowns [*Zambia*] [*ICAO location identifier*] (ICLI)
FLSOA........ Frankie Laine Society of America (EA)
FLSP........... Flame Spraying [*Welding*]
FLSP........... Flight Space
FLSP........... Fluorescein-Labeled Serum Protein [*Clinical chemistry*]
FLSP........... Fort Lincoln State Park (SAUO)
FLSPT......... Fellowship of the London School of Polymer Technology [*British*] (DBQ)
FLSR........... Falser (ABBR)
FLSR........... Flossier (ABBR)
FLSS........... Falcon Launching Saber System
FLSS........... Flight Level Sensing System [*or Subsystem*] (MCD)
FLSS........... Sesheke [*Zambia*] [*ICAO location identifier*] (ICLI)
FLSST......... Falsest (ABBR)
FLSST......... Flossiest (ABBR)
FLS SWR DL... False Swearing to Receive a Driver License [*Conviction term used in state of Oregon*] (MVRD)
FLS SWR FM... False Swearing on Farm Registration or Renewal [*Conviction term used in state of Oregon*] (MVRD)
FLS SWR REG... False Swearing Relating to Registration of Vehicle [*Conviction term used in state of Oregon*] (MVRD)
FLS SWR TTL... False Swearing Relating to Titling of Vehicle [*Conviction term used in state of Oregon*] (MVRD)
FLST........... Falsest (ABBR)
FLST........... Falsity (ABBR)
FLST........... Flagstar Companies [*NASDAQ symbol*] (TTSB)
FLST........... Flagstar Companies, Inc. [*NASDAQ symbol*] (SAG)
FLST........... Flautist (ABBR)
FLST........... Flutist (ABBR)
FLSTP......... Flagstar Cos $2.25 Cv Ptd [*NASDAQ symbol*] (TTSB)
FLSTR......... Fluster (ABBR)
FLSTY......... Falsity (ABBR)
FLSU........... Florida State University (SAUO)
FLSU........... Force Logistics Support Unit [*Marine Corps*] (NVT)
FLSW........... Fleet Logistic Support Wing [*Navy*]
FLSW........... Flow Switch
FLSW........... Solwezi [*Zambia*] [*ICAO location identifier*] (ICLI)
FL Switch.... Float Switch (SAUS)
FL Switch.... Flow Switch (SAUS)
FLSY........... Falsely (ABBR)
FLSY........... Flossy (ABBR)
FLSZ........... Florida Steel [*Federal Railroad Administration identification code*]
FLT............. Faculty of Library and Information Science (Teaching), University of Toronto [*UTLAS symbol*]
FLT............. Faster-than-Light Travel (SAUS)
FLT............. Fault
FLT............. Fault Locating Test (SAUS)
FLT............. Fault Location Technique (SAUS)
FLT............. Fault Location Technology [*or Test*] (IEEE)
FLT............. Fault Location Test (IAA)
FLT............. Federacion Latinoamericana de Termalismo [*Latin American Federation of Thermalism and Climatism - LAFTC*] [*Buenos Aires, Argentina*] (EAIO)
flt............... Felt (VRA)
FLT............. Fermat's Last Theorem [*Mathematics*]
FLT............. Fermet's Last Theorem [*Mathematics*]
FLT............. Fermi Liquid Theory [*Physics*]
FLT............. Field Level Training
FLT............. Figure Location Test (EDAC)
FLT............. Filing Time [*Time a message is presented for transmission*]
FLT............. Filter
FLT............. Finance Leadership Team (TIMI)
FLt.............. Fixed Light (SAUS)
FLT............. Flashlight (MSA)
Flt.............. Flat [*Business term*] (EBF)
FLT............. Flat [*Alaska*] [*Airport symbol*] (OAG)
flt............... Flat
FLT............. Flat, AK [*Location identifier*] [*FAA*] (FAAL)
FLT............. Flats
FLT............. Fleet (CINC)
FLT............. Fleet Aerospace Corp. [*Toronto Stock Exchange symbol*]
FLT............. Fleet Financial Group [*Later, FNG*] [*NYSE symbol*] (SPSG)
FLT............. Fleet/Norstar Financial Group, Inc. (MHDW)
FLT............. Fleetwood [*Alabama*] [*Seismograph station code, US Geological Survey*] (SEIS)
FLT............. Flex-Lead Torque
FLT............. Flight (AFM)
flt............... Flight (MILB)
F/LT............ Flight Lieutenant (ADA)
FLT............. Flightline [*British*] [*ICAO designator*] (FAAC)
FLT............. Flight Line Taxi
FLT............. Flight Line Tester
FLT............. Florida Institute of Technology, Melbourne, FL [*OCLC symbol*] (OCLC)
FLT............. Flotation (SAUS)
FLT............. Fluidity (ABBR)
FLT............. Fluorodeoxythymidine [*Antiviral*]
FLT............. Fluorothimidine [*A nucleoside analog*] [*Medicine*] (TAD)
FLT............. force-length-time system (SAUS)
FLT............. Foreign Labor Trends [*Department of Labor*] [*A publication*]
FLT............. Foreign-Language Teaching (SAUS)
FLT............. Forklift Truck
FLT............. Foss Launch & Tug [*AAR code*]
FLT............. Front for the Liberation of Tamoust (SAUS)
FLT............. Front Load Tape (SAUS)
FLT............. Fronto-Laeva Transversa [*A fetal position*] [*Obstetrics*] (MAE)
flt............... frontolaeva transverse (SAUS)
FLT............. Full Line Terminal [*Computer science*] (DINT)
FLT............. Functional Logic Trend (SAUS)
FLTA........... French Lawn Tennis Association (SAUO)
FLTA........... Fullerton Language Test for Adolescents (DAVI)
FLTAC......... Fisher-Logemann Test of Articular Competence [*Speech and language therapy*] (DAVI)
FLTAC......... Fleet Analysis Center [*Navy*] (CAAL)
FLTACFO..... Fleet Analysis Center Field Office [*Navy*] (DNAB)
FLTACREP... Fleet Analysis Center Representative [*Navy*] (DNAB)
FLTACT....... Fleet Activities
FltActy......... Fleet Activity (SAUS)
FLT ADM..... Fleet Admiral [*Navy*] (WDAA)
FltAllWeaTraU... Fleet All-Weather Training Unit (SAUS)
FltAllWeaTraULant... Fleet All-Weather Training Unit, Atlantic (SAUS)
FltAllWeaTraUPac... Fleet All-Weather Training Unit, Pacific (SAUS)
FLTAN......... Flotation (ABBR)
FLTASWTRACEN... Fleet ASW [*Antisubmarine Warfare*] Training Center [*Navy*]
FLTAVCEN... Fleet Audio-Visual Center (DNAB)
FLTAVCENEUR... Fleet Audio-Visual Center, Europe (DNAB)
FLTAVCENLANT... Fleet Audio-Visual Center, Atlantic (DNAB)
FLTAVCENPAC... Fleet Audio-Visual Center, Pacific (DNAB)
FLTAVCOMLANT... Fleet Audio-Visual Command, Atlantic (DNAB)
FLTAVCOMLANTDET... Fleet Audio-Visual Command, Atlantic Detachment (DNAB)
FLTAVCOMPAC... Fleet Audio-Visual Command, Pacific (DNAB)
FLTAVCOMPACDET... Fleet Audio-Visual Command, Pacific Detachment (DNAB)
FLTAVFAC.... Fleet Audio-Visual Facility (DNAB)
FLTAVFACLANT... Fleet Audio-Visual Facility, Atlantic (DNAB)
FLTAVFACPAC... Fleet Audio-Visual Facility, Pacific (DNAB)
FLTB........... Floatable (ABBR)
FLTBCST...... Fleet Broadcast [*Navy*] (NVT)
FLTBDCST... Fleet Broadcast [*Navy*] (NVT)
FLTBRG....... Float Bridge
FLTCAL........ Flight Calibration Procedure [*Aviation*] (DA)
FLTCERT...... Flight Certificate
Fltcher C...... Fletcher College (SAUS)
FltchFF........ Fletchers Fione Foods Ltd. [*Associated Press*] (SAG)
FLTCINC....... Fleet Commander in Chief [*Military*] (DOMA)
FLTCINCS..... Fleet Commanders in Chief (SAUO)
FLTCK......... Flight Check [*Aviation*]
Flt Comdr.... Flight Commander (DAS)
FLTCON....... Fleet Control
FLTCON....... Flight Control
FLTCONT..... Flight Control [*Aerospace*] (IAA)
FLTCOORDGRU... Fleet Coordinating Group (DNAB)
FLTCORGRU... Fleet Composite Operational Readiness Group [*Navy*] (CAAL)
FLT CQ........ Fleet Carrier Qualification (DOMA)
FLT-CR........ Flat-Car (ABBR)
FLTD........... Flatted (ABBR)
FLTD........... Fluted (MSA)
FLTDECGRU... Fleet Deception Group (SAUO)
FLTDECGRULANT... Fleet Deception Group Atlantic (SAUS)
FLTDEMO.... Fleet Demonstration [*Navy*] (NVT)
FLTDESGW... Flight Design Gross Weight (MCD)
FLTE........... Film Library for Teacher Education (SAUS)
FLTEX......... Fleet Exercise [*Navy*] (NVT)
FLTF........... Field Lysimeter Test Facility (SAUS)
FltFn.......... Fleet Financial Group [*Associated Press*] (SAG)
FLT-FT........ Flat-Foot (ABBR)
FLTG........... Flatting (ABBR)
FLTG........... Fleeting (ABBR)
FLTG........... Floating (AABC)
FLTGNS....... Fleetingness (ABBR)
FLTGUNSCH... Fleet Gunnery School
FLTGUNSCOL... Fleet Gunnery School

FLTGY........ Fleetingly (ABBR)
FLTHNS....... Filthiness (ABBR)
FLTHR........ Filthier (ABBR)
FLTHST....... Filthiest (ABBR)
FLTHY........ Filthy (ABBR)
FLTINTSUPPCEN... Fleet Intelligence Support Center [*Navy*] (DNAB)
FLTIO........ Fellatio (ABBR)
FLTK........ Flight Line Test Kit (ACAE)
FLTL........ Flight Line
FLTLA........ Flotilla (ABBR)
flt ld sim..... flight-load simulator (SAUS)
Flt Lieut....... Flight Lieutenant [*British military*] (DMA)
FLTLOSCAP... Fleet Liaison Officer, Supreme Commander Allied Powers [*World War II*]
Flt Lt........ Flight Lieutenant [*Military*] (WDAA)
FLTMINWARTRACEN... Fleet Mine Warfare Training Center (DOMA)
FLTMOD...... Fleet Modernization [*Navy*] (DNAB)
FLT MTNCE... Fleet Maintenance (SAUS)
FLTN........ Flatten (ABBR)
FLTN........ Floatation (ABBR)
FLTND........ Flattened (ABBR)
FLTNES........ Flatness (ABBR)
FLTNG........ Flattening (ABBR)
Flt No........ Flight Number (SAUS)
FLTNS........ Flatness (ABBR)
FLTNS........ Fleetness (ABBR)
FLTO........ Flight Officer [*Air Force*] (AFM)
FLTO........ Flight Orders [*Aviation*] (FAAC)
FLTOPS........ Fleet Operations (CCCA)
FLTOPS........ Flight Test Oriented Pre-Compiler System (ACAE)
FL/TOT........ Flow Totalizer
fltp........ flight template (SAUS)
FLTP........ Flush Type
FLTP........ Foreign Language Training Program [*Air Force*]
FLT/PG........ Flight Programmer (AAG)
FLT PLN...... Flight Plan (MSA)
FLTPrB........ Fleet Fin'l 10.12% Dep Pfd [*NYSE symbol*] (TTSB)
FLTPrC........ Fleet Fin'l 9.375% Dep Pfd [*NYSE symbol*] (TTSB)
FLTPrD........ Fleet Fin'l 9.30% Dep Pfd [*NYSE symbol*] (TTSB)
FLTPrE........ Fleet Fin'l9.35% Dep Pfd [*NYSE symbol*] (TTSB)
FLTPrF........ Fleet Fin'l 7.25% Dep Pfd [*NYSE symbol*] (TTSB)
FLTPrG........ Fleet Fin'l 6.75% Dep Pfd [*NYSE symbol*] (TTSB)
FLTR........ Filter (MSA)
FLTR........ Flatter (ABBR)
FLTR........ Floater (ABBR)
FLTR........ Flutter (ABBR)
FLTR........ Fusible Link-Top Register (OA)
FLTRACKCEN... Fleet Tracking Center [*Navy*]
FLTRASUPPRON... Fleet Training Support Squadron (DNAB)
FLTRD........ Flattered (ABBR)
FLTREADREP... Fleet Readiness Representative [*Navy*] (MCD)
FLTRELSUPPACT... Fleet Religious Support Activity (DNAB)
FLTRELSUPPACTLANT... Fleet Religious Support Activity, Atlantic (DNAB)
FLTRELSUPPACTPAC... Fleet Religious Support Activity, Pacific (DNAB)
FLTRG........ Flattering (ABBR)
FLTRG........ Fluttering (ABBR)
FLTRGY...... Flatteringly (ABBR)
FLTRGY...... Flutteringly (ABBR)
FLTRIR........ Flutterier (ABBR)
FLTRIST........ Flutteriest (ABBR)
FLTRK........ Flat Rock, MI [*American Association of Railroads railroad junction routing code*]
FLTRNR....... Flattener (ABBR)
FLTRR........ Flattered (ABBR)
FLTRY........ Flattery (ABBR)
FLTRY........ Fluttery (ABBR)
FLTS........ FASTER [*Filing and Source Data Entry Techniques for Easier Retrieval*] Language Translation System (MHDI)
FLTS........ Flats [*Postal Service standard*] (OPSA)
FLTS........ Flight Line Test Set [*Military*] (CAAL)
flts........ flights (SAUS)
FLTSAT........ Fleet Satellite [*Navy*] (MCD)
FLTSATCOM... Fleet Satellite Communications System [*DoD*]
FLTSATCOMSYS... Fleet Satellite Communications System [*DoD*] (DNAB)
FLTSATSEVCOM... Fleet Satellite Secure Voice Communications (MCD)
FLTSERVSCOL... Fleet Service School [*Navy*]
FLTSEVO........ Fleet Secure Voice (SAUO)
FLTSEVOCOM... Fleet Secure Voice Communications [*Navy*] (NVT)
Flt Sgt Nav... Flight Sergeant Navigator (SAUO)
FLTSIP........ Fleet Support Improvement Program [*Navy*] (DNAB)
FLTSM........ Flotsam (ABBR)
FLTSOUNDSCOL... Fleet Sound School
FLTST........ Flattest (ABBR)
FLTST........ Flautist (ABBR)
FLTST........ Flight Steward
Flt Str........ Flight Strip (SAUS)
fltstrikex...... full general-emergency striking force (SAUS)
FLTSTRIKEX... Full General-Emergency Striking Force Exercise [*Navy*] (NVT)
FltSubTraFa... Fleet Submarine Training Facility (SAUS)
FLTSUPPO... Fleet Support Office [*Navy*] (DNAB)
FLTSURBAD... Flight Surgeon Badge [*Military decoration*] [*Army*]
FltSurg........ Fleet Surgeon (SAUS)
FLTSURG........ Flight Surgeon
FltSurgBad... Flight Surgeon Badge [*Military decoration*] [*Army*] (AABC)
FLTSX........ Flag Invest. Total Return U.S. Treas. Cl.A [*Mutual fund ticker symbol*] (SG)
FLTTACREDGRU... Fleet Tactical Readiness Group (SAUS)
FLTTRACEN... Fleet Training Center [*Navy*]
FLTTRACKCEN... Fleet Tracking Center (SAUO)
FLTTRAGRU... Fleet Training Group [*Navy*]
FLTWEACEN... Fleet Weather Center (SAUO)
FLTWEPCEN... Fleet Weapons Center [*Navy*]
FLTWO........ Flight Watch Outlet [*Aviation*] (FAAC)
FLTWR........ Flatware (ABBR)
FLTx........ Fork Lift Truck (DS)
FLTX........ Fort Lincoln Trolley [*Federal Railroad Administration identification code*]
FLTY........ Flatly (ABBR)
FLTY........ Fleetly (ABBR)
FLTZ........ Floyd Timber [*Federal Railroad Administration identification code*]
FLU........ Fault Location Unit [*Aerospace*] (AAG)
FLU........ Federation of Labor Unions [*Lebanon*]
FLU........ Final Limit, Up
FLU........ First Line Unit (MCD)
FLU........ Flight Loads Unit (MCD)
flu........ Florida [*MARC country of publication code*] [*Library of Congress*] (LCCP)
FLU........ Fluid (SAUS)
FLU........ Flunitrazepam [*A hypnotic*]
FLU........ Fluoxetine (SAUS)
FLU........ Front for Liberation and Unity [*Western Sahara*]
FLU........ Front Line Units (ACAE)
FLU........ Full Line-Up (SAUS)
flu........ Influenza [*Medicine*] (DAVI)
FLU........ New York/Flushing, NY [*Location identifier*] [*FAA*] (FAAL)
FLUB........ First language under bootstrap (SAUS)
fluc........ fluctuant (SAUS)
FLUC........ Fluctuate
fluc........ fluctuating (SAUS)
FLUC........ Fluctuation (SAUS)
FLUCD........ Fluctuated (ABBR)
FLUCG........ Fluctuating (ABBR)
FLUCN........ Fluctuation (ABBR)
FLUCNT....... Fluctuant (ABBR)
FLUD........ Fluid
FLUFD........ Fluffed (ABBR)
FLUFG........ Fluffing (ABBR)
FLUFY........ Fluffy (ABBR)
FLUFYNS...... Fluffiness (ABBR)
FLUFYR........ Fluffier (ABBR)
FLUFYST........ Fluffiest (ABBR)
FLUFYY........ Fluffily (ABBR)
FLUG........ Flugfelag Islands H.F. [*Iceland Airways Ltd.*]
FLUID........ Facility for Listing, Updating and Interpreting Deck (SAUS)
FLUID........ Formed Lines Using Interactive Data (MCD)
FLUIDEX...... Fluid Engineering Index (SAUS)
FLUIDEXTER... Fluidextractum [*Fluidextract*] [*Pharmacy*] (ROG)
FLUIDEXTR... Fluidextractum [*Fluidextract*] [*Pharmacy*] (ROG)
FLUIDICS...... Fluid Dynamics (SAUS)
Fluidics...... Fluid Logics (SAUS)
Fluid/Particle Sep J... Fluid/Particle Separation Journal (journ.) (SAUS)
Fluid Phase Equilib... Fluid Phase Equilibria [*A publication*] (CABS)
FLUK........ Fluke (ABBR)
Fluke........ Fluke Corp. [*Associated Press*] (SAG)
FLUL........ Federation of Labor Unions in Lebanon
FLULC........ Forest Land Use Liaison Committee (SAUS)
FLUNC........ Fluency (ABBR)
FLUNCI....... Foreign Language Use in Northern Commerce and Industry (AIE)
FLUNT........ Fluent (ABBR)
FLUNTY........ Fluently (ABBR)
fluor........ fluor-apatite (SAUS)
Fluor........ Fluor Corp. [*Associated Press*] (SAG)
Fluor........ Fluoresce (SAUS)
fluor........ fluorescence (SAUS)
FLUOR........ Fluorescent [*or Fluoresces or Fluorescence*] (KSC)
FLUOR........ Fluoridation (SAUS)
FLUOR........ Fluoride [*or Fluoridation*] (WDAA)
FLUOR........ Fluorine (SAUS)
FLUOR........ Fluorite (SAUS)
fluor........ Fluorometry (DAVI)
FLUOR........ Fluoroscope (SAUS)
FLUOR........ Fluoroscopy
fluor........ fluorspar (SAUS)
fluor........ fluotaramite (SAUS)
FLUORES...... Fluorescent (ABBR)
FLUORO....... Fluoroscopy [*Radiology*] (DAVI)
FLU Press...... Fluid Press (SAUS)
FLUR........ Fluorescent [*Technical drawings*]
FLURAM...... Fluorescamine [*Biochemical analysis*] [*Acronym is trademark of Roche Diagnostics*]
FLUREX....... Fluorescence Experiment (SAUO)
FluroS........ FluoroScan Imaging Systems, Inc. [*Associated Press*] (SAG)
FluroScn...... FluoroScan Imaging Systems, Inc. [*Associated Press*] (SAG)
FlushF........ Flushing Financial Corp. [*Associated Press*] (SAG)
Flush mtd..... Flush Mounted (SAUS)
Flush mtg..... Flush Mounting (SAUS)
FLUSOC....... Fluted Socket
FLUSOCH..... Fluted Socket Head
FLUT........ Flute (ABBR)

FLUT .... Flutter (MSA)
FLUTD .... Feline Lower Urinary Tract Disease [*Veterinary Science*]
FLUTD .... Feline Lower Urinary Tract Disorder
FLUTD .... Fluted (ABBR)
FLUTG .... Fluting (ABBR)
FLUTR .... Flouter (ABBR)
FLUTR .... Flutter (ABBR)
FLUTRD .... Fluttered (ABBR)
FLUTRG .... Fluttering (ABBR)
FLUTRR .... Flutterer (ABBR)
FLUTRY .... Fluttery (ABBR)
FLUTST .... Flutist (ABBR)
FLUVIS .... Fluid Dynamics Visualization in a Virtual Windtunnel (SAUS)
FLUX .... Flux (ABBR)
FLUXD .... Fluxed (ABBR)
FLUXG .... Fluxing (ABBR)
FLUXN .... Fluxion (ABBR)
FLUXNET .... Long-term Carbon and Water Flux Network (SAUS)
FLV .... Feline Leukemia Virus [*Also, FELV*]
FLV .... Finite Logical View (MHDB)
FLV .... Flat Limb Virus (SAUS)
FLV .... Foreign Leave [*Military*] (AABC)
FLV .... Friend Leukemia Virus [*Also, FDV, FV*]
FLV .... Leavenworth, KS [*Location identifier*] [*FAA*] (FAAL)
FLVBX .... Flag Investors Value Builder Cl.A [*Mutual fund ticker symbol*] (SG)
FLVD .... Fine Line Velocity Discriminator (SAUS)
FLVFD .... Front Luminous Vacuum Fluorescence Display (IAA)
FLVR .... Flavor (ABBR)
FLVR .... Flavour (SAUS)
FLVRD .... Flavored (ABBR)
FLVRFL .... Flavorful (ABBR)
FLVRFLY .... Flavorfully (ABBR)
FLVRG .... Flavoring (ABBR)
FLVRLS .... Flavorless (ABBR)
FLVRR .... Flavorer (ABBR)
FLVRSM .... Flavorsome (ABBR)
FLVRUS .... Flavorous (ABBR)
FLVS .... Florida Virtual High School
FLVV .... Fill-Limit Vent Valve [*Automotive emissions*]
FLW .... Fault Location Word (MCD)
FLW .... Feedlot Waste
FLW .... Fellows (SAUS)
FLW .... Fellows, CA [*Location identifier*] [*FAA*] (FAAL)
FLW .... Fixed-Length Word (SAUS)
FL/W .... Flash Welding [*Metallurgy*]
FLW .... Flat Washer
FLW .... Fleet Logistics Wing [*Navy*]
Flw .... Fliegerwerkstoff (SAUS)
FLW .... Flood Warning [*Telecommunications*] (OTD)
flw .... Flower
FLW .... Flow Resources Ltd. [*Vancouver Stock Exchange symbol*]
FLW .... Follow
FLW .... Forced Longitudinal Wave (MCD)
FLW .... Fort Leonard Wood Utility Railroad [*Federal Railroad Administration identification code*]
FLW .... Foulwind [*New Zealand*] [*Seismograph station code, US Geological Survey*] [*Closed*] (SEIS)
FLW .... Frank Lloyd Wright [*American architect*] (IIA)
FLW .... International Fur and Leather Workers Union of United States and Canada (SAUO)
FLw .... Lake Worth Public Library, Lake Worth, FL [*Library symbol*] [*Library of Congress*] (LCLS)
FLW .... Santa Cruz, Flores [*Azores*] [*Airport symbol*] (OAG)
FLWA .... Frank Lloyd Wright Association [*Later, FLWN*] (EA)
FLWA .... West One [*Zambia*] [*ICAO location identifier*] (ICLI)
FLWB .... West Two [*Zambia*] [*ICAO location identifier*] (ICLI)
FLWC .... West Three [*Zambia*] [*ICAO location identifier*] (ICLI)
flwd .... followed (SAUS)
FLWD .... West Four [*Zambia*] [*ICAO location identifier*] (ICLI)
FLWE .... West Five [*Zambia*] [*ICAO location identifier*] (ICLI)
FLWF .... Feedlot Waste Filtrate
FLWF .... Feetlot Waste Fiber (SAUS)
FLWF .... Frank Lloyd Wright Foundation (EA)
FLWF .... West Six [*Zambia*] [*ICAO location identifier*] (ICLI)
FLWFEA .... Fort Leonard Wood Facilities Engineer Activity
FLWG .... Following
FLWG .... West Seven [*Zambia*] [*ICAO location identifier*] (ICLI)
FLWGA .... Finger Lakes Wine Growers Association (EA)
FLWHSF .... Frank Lloyd Wright Home and Studio Foundation (EA)
FLWIS .... Flood Warnings Issued
FLWK .... Flat Work
FLWL .... Flower Length [*Botany*]
FLWN .... Federation of London Wholesale Newsagents (SAUO)
FLWN .... Frank Lloyd Wright Newsletter (EA)
FLWND .... Federation of London Wholesale Newspaper Distributors (SAUO)
FLWO .... Fred Lawrence Whipple Observatory [*Amado, AZ*] [*Smithsonian Institution*] (GRD)
flwop .... forced landing without power (SAUS)
FLWP .... Follow-Up
FLwP .... Palm Beach Junior College, Lake Worth, FL [*Library symbol*] [*Library of Congress*] (LCLS)
FLWR .... Celebrity, Inc. [*NASDAQ symbol*] (SAG)
FLWR .... Flower
FLWR .... French Lick, West Baden & Southern Railway [*Federal Railroad Administration identification code*]
FLWs .... Fault Location Words (SAUS)
FLW TOO CLS ... Following Too Closely [*Conviction term used in state of Oregon*] (MVRD)
FLWW .... Waka Waka [*Zambia*] [*ICAO location identifier*] (ICLI)
FLWY .... Secretariat for Family, Laity, Women, and Youth [*An association*] (EA)
FLX .... Fallon, NV [*Location identifier*] [*FAA*] (FAAL)
FLX .... Flavex Industries Ltd. [*Vancouver Stock Exchange symbol*]
FLX .... Flexible [*Technical drawings*]
FLX .... Flexion (SAUS)
FLX .... Florida Express, Inc. [*ICAO designator*] (FAAC)
FLX .... Flxible Historic Association [*Defunct*] (EA)
FLXS .... Flexsteel Indus [*NASDAQ symbol*] (TTSB)
FLXS .... Flexsteel Industries, Inc. [*NASDAQ symbol*] (NQ)
FLY .... Airlease Ltd. [*NYSE symbol*] (SPSG)
FLY .... Airlease Ltd L.P. [*NYSE symbol*] (TTSB)
FLY .... CHC Helicopter Corp. [*Toronto Stock Exchange symbol*]
fly .... Flinty [*Quality of the bottom*] [*Nautical charts*]
Fly .... Flying [*A publication*] (BRI)
FLY .... Flying
FLY .... Flying Enterprise AB [*Sweden*] [*FAA designator*] (FAAC)
FLY .... Flying Tiger Corporation (SAUO)
FLY .... Flying Tiger Line (SAUS)
fly .... flyweight (SAUS)
FLY .... Flywheel [*Automotive engineering*]
f-ly- .... Libya [*MARC geographic area code*] [*Library of Congress*] (LCCP)
FLYA .... CHC Helicopter [*NASDAQ symbol*] (SAG)
FLYA .... Samfya [*Zambia*] [*ICAO location identifier*] (ICLI)
FLYAF .... CHC Helicopter Cl'A' [*NASDAQ symbol*] (TTSB)
fly butr .... Flying Buttress (VRA)
FLYCO .... Commander, Flying [*British military*] (DMA)
FLYCO .... Flying Control [*Position*] [*British*]
FLYCON .... Flight Control
Flyers .... Fun-Loving Youth En Route to Success [*Title of book by Lawrence Graham an d Lawrence Hamdan*] [*Lifestyle classification*]
Fly Needle ... Flying Needle [*A publication*] (BRI)
FLYOBRPT ... Flying Object Report [*Air Force*]
FLYP .... Fax Like You Print [*3X USA*] (PCM)
FLYR .... Navigant International [*Stock market symbol*]
FLYRT .... Flying RADAR Target (SEWL)
fly stat .... Flying Status [*Military*]
FLYT .... Flight Dynamics, Inc. [*NASDAQ symbol*] (COMM)
FLYT .... Interactive Flight Tech'A' [*NASDAQ symbol*] (TTSB)
FLYT .... Interactive Flight Technologies, Inc. [*NASDAQ symbol*] (SAG)
FLYT .... Interactive Flight Technologies, Inc. Cl.A [*NASDAQ symbol*] (SAG)
FLYTAF .... Flying Training Air Force
FLYTU .... Interactive Flight Tech Unit [*NASDAQ symbol*] (TTSB)
FLYTW .... Interactive Flight Wrrt'A' [*NASDAQ symbol*] (TTSB)
FLYTZ .... Interactive Flight Wrrt'B' [*NASDAQ symbol*] (TTSB)
FLYWHL .... Flywheel
FLYWT .... Flyweight [*Boxing*]
FLZ .... Flurazepam Hydrochloride [*Medicine*] (MELL)
FLZ .... Furman Lumber [*Federal Railroad Administration identification code*]
FLZB .... Zambezi [*Zambia*] [*ICAO location identifier*] (ICLI)
FLZO .... Farband Labor Zionist Order [*Later, Labor Zionist Alliance*] (EA)
FM .... Face Mask [*Medicine*] (DAVI)
FM .... Face Measurement
FM .... Facial Measurement (SAUS)
FM .... Facilities Maintenance
FM .... Facilities Management
FM .... Facility/Fault/Function Management (SAUS)
FM .... Facility Management (SAUS)
FM .... Facility Manager
FM .... Facility Mapping (PA)
fm .... facing matter (SAUS)
FM .... Factory Manual
FM .... Factory material (SAUS)
FM .... Factory Mutual Engineering Association [*Industrial hygiene term*] (OHS)
FM .... Factory Mutual Laboratories
FM .... Factory Mutual System [*Formerly, AFMFIC*] [*Group of four insurance companies and an engineering organization*]
FM .... Faience Mosaics (DICI)
FM .... Failure Mechanics (SAUS)
FM .... Failure Mode (MCD)
FM .... Fair Merchandise (SAUS)
fm .... fair merchantable (SAUS)
FM .... Familial Melanoma [*Medicine*] (MELL)
FM .... Fan Marker [*Aviation*]
F/M .... Farads per Meter
FM .... Farm
FM .... Farm to Market
FM .... Farnsworth-Munsell [*One hundred hue test*] [*Ophthalmology*] (DAVI)
FM .... Fashion Merchandising, Fashion Design, and/or Interior Design Programs [*Association of Independent Colleges and Schools specialization code*]
FM .... Fast Memory (IAA)
FM .... Fast Multiply
FM .... Fathom
FM .... Fathometer (SAUS)
FM .... Fault Management (SAUS)
FM .... Fault Modelling (SAUS)
FM .... Fault Monitor (TEL)
FM .... Faulty Magazine [*Military*] (MCD)
FM .... FDTE Master (MCD)

F-M .... Federal-Mogul
FM .... Federated States of Micronesia [*ANSI two-letter standard code*] (CNC)
FM .... Fed Mart (SAUS)
FM .... Feedback Mechanism
FM .... Feeder Monitor (SAUS)
f/m .... Feet Per Minute [*Industrial hygiene term*] (OHS)
F/M .... Feet per Minute (ADA)
f/M .... female Mexican (SAUS)
fm .... female white (SAUS)
FM .... Feminist Majority [*An association*] (EA)
FM .... Femtometer [*Formerly, Fermi*] (MCD)
FM .... Ferdinand Marcos [*Former Philippine president*]
Fm .... Fermi (SAUS)
FM .... Fermium (LDT)
Fm .... Fermium [*Chemical element*]
FM .... Ferranti Ltd (SAUS)
FM .... Ferrite Memory (SAUS)
FM .... Ferrite Metal
FM .... Ferritenmental (SAUS)
FM .... Ferritic and Martensitic [*Metallurgy*] (ODA)
FM .... Ferromagnet [*Physics*]
FM .... Ferro Magnetic (SAUS)
FM .... Ferromagnetic Memory (SAUS)
FM .... Ferromagnetism (SAUS)
FM .... Fetal Medicine (MELL)
FM .... Fetal Membranes (MELL)
FM .... Fetal Monitor (MELL)
FM .... Fetal Movement [*Gynecology*]
FM .... Fetal Movements [*Obstetrics*] (DAVI)
FM .... Fiat Mistura [*Let a Mixture Be Made*] [*Pharmacy*]
FM .... Fibrin Monomer [*Hematology*] (DAVI)
FM .... Fibrious Material (SAUS)
FM .... Fibromuscular (DB)
FM .... Fibromyalgia
FM .... Fibrous Material
FM .... Field Magnet (ROG)
FM .... Field Main (AAG)
FM .... Field Maintenance (MCD)
FM .... Field Manager (SAUS)
FM .... Field Manual [*Military*]
FM .... Field Manufacture (AFIT)
FM .... Field Mark (SAUS)
FM .... Field Marshal
FM .... Field Marshall (SAUO)
FM .... Field Memorandum
FM .... Field Modification (AAG)
FM .... Field Moist Soil [*Agronomy*]
FM .... Field Music [*Marine Corps*]
FM .... Fighting Method (SAUS)
FM .... Figure of Merit
FM .... Filament Mid (SAUS)
FM .... Filament Mid-tap (SAUS)
FM .... Filament Midtop
FM .... File Maintenance [*Computer science*] (BUR)
FM .... File Management
FM .... File Manager [*Computer science*] (ELAL)
FM .... File Mark (ACAE)
FM .... File Memory (SAUS)
FM .... File Merge (SAUS)
FM .... Film Microelectronics (SAUS)
FM .... Financial Management
FM .... Financial Manager (SAUS)
FM .... Finder Matrix (IAA)
FM .... Fine Measurement
FM .... Fine Motor
FM .... Fineness Modulus (DICI)
FM .... Fire Main (AAG)
Fm .... Fireman (SAUS)
FM .... Fire Marshal (SAUS)
FM .... Fire Mission (SAUS)
FM .... Firm [*Horse racing*]
FM .... First Main [*Firefighting*] (ROG)
F/M .... First Motion (KSC)
FM .... Fish Meal
FM .... Fissile Material
FM .... Fixed Memory (SAUS)
FM .... Flavin Mononucleotide [*Biochemistry*] (AAMN)
FM .... Flea Market
FM .... Fleet management (SAUS)
FM .... Flexible Manufacturing (FOTI)
FM .... Flexural Moment (SAUS)
FM .... Flight Manual (MCD)
FM .... Flight Mechanic
FM .... Flight Mishap (SEWL)
FM .... Flight Model
FM .... Flight Monitor
FM .... Flint's Murmur [*Medicine*] (MELL)
FM .... Floating Multiply (IAA)
FM .... Floor Manager (DEN)
FM .... Flour Milling (OA)
FM .... Flow Manufacturing (GART)
FM .... Flow Meter (KSC)
FM .... Flowmeter (SAUS)
FM .... Fluid Mechanics (SAUS)
FM .... Fluorescein Maleimide
FM .... Fluorescence Microphotolysis
FM .... Fluorescence Microscope (SAUS)
FM .... Fluorescent Microscopy [*Biochemistry*] (DAVI)
FM .... Flyball Master
fm .... Foam (VRA)
FM .... Foam Monitor (DS)
FM .... Focolare Movement (EA)
FM .... Focusing Mount [*Photography*]
FM .... fonte mince (SAUS)
FM .... Food Chain Multipliers (EEVL)
FM .... Food Machinery (SAUS)
FM .... Foodmaker, Inc. [*NYSE symbol*] (SPSG)
F/M .... Food to Microorganism Ratio (EPA)
FM .... Foramen Magnum (DB)
FM .... Force Modernization (SAUO)
FM .... force module (SAUS)
FM .... Ford Motor Co. [*Toronto Stock Exchange symbol*]
FM .... Ford Museum [*Federal Railroad Administration identification code*]
FM .... Foreign Material (MCD)
FM .... Foreign Military
FM .... Foreign Minister [*or Ministry*]
FM .... Foreign Ministry (SAUO)
FM .... Foreign Mission
FM .... Foreman (SAUS)
FM .... Forensic Medicine (DAVI)
FM .... Forest Management (SAUS)
FM .... Form
FM .... Formation [*Lithology*]
FM .... Format Management (SAUS)
FM .... Format Manager [*Computer science*] (ELAL)
FM .... Formerly Married
FM .... Forms Management
FM .... Fort Major [*British*] (ROG)
FM .... Forward Motion
FM .... Foster Mother
FM .... Fouling Mark [*Indian Railway*] (TIR)
FM .... Foundation Member
FM .... Fracture Mechanics (SAUS)
FM .... Frame (IAA)
f/m .... Frames per Minute (SAUS)
FM .... France Moto (SAUS)
FM .... France Motors S.A. (SAUS)
FM .... Franc Macon [*Freemasonry*] [*French*] (ROG)
FM .... Franc Mali [*Monetary unit*] [*Mali*]
FM .... Franklin and Marshall College (SAUO)
FM .... Franklin Mint
FM .... Fraternite Mondiale [*World Brotherhood*]
FM .... Freemason (ROG)
FM .... Free Men [*Defunct*] (EA)
FM .... Free Minds [*An association*] (EA)
FM .... Freezing Mixture (SAUS)
FM .... freight management (SAUS)
FM .... Freimaurer [*Freemason*] [*German*] (ROG)
FM .... Frequency Management [*Aviation*] (DA)
FM .... Frequency Meter
FM .... Frequency Minute (SAUS)
FM .... Frequency Modulation (Modulated) (SAUS)
FM .... Frequency Modulator [*Amateur radio Shorthand*] (WDAA)
FM .... Frequency Multiplex
fm .... frequency multiplier (SAUS)
FM .... Frequenz Modulation (SAUS)
FM .... Fresh Mortar (SAUS)
FM .... Friable Material (GNE)
FM .... Friars Minor (ODA)
FM .... Friend-Moloney (DB)
FM .... Friends of Mineralogy
FM .... Frisker-Monitor [*Radiation detection*]
FM .... From (MUGU)
fm .... From (SHCU)
FM .... Front Matter [*Publishing*]
FM .... Fuels Manufacturing (SAUS)
FM .... Full Moon [*Astronomy*]
FM .... Fulminate of Mercury (SAUS)
fm .... fumigation (SAUS)
FM .... Functional Manager (MCD)
FM .... Functional Mathematical Programming System [*Computer science*] (MCD)
FM .... Functional Megaspore [*Botany*]
FM .... Functional Module (VLIE)
FM .... Function Management (ACRL)
FM .... Function manager (SAUS)
FM .... Function Multiplier (SAUS)
FM .... Furnace Module (SAUS)
FM .... Furuncular Myiasis [*Medicine*] (MELL)
FM .... Fusarium Multiformis [*A fungus*]
FM .... Fused to Metal [*Dentistry*]
FM .... Fusobacteria [*or Fusobacterium*] Micro-Organism [*Medicine*]
FM .... Libya [*License plate code assigned to foreign diplomats in the US*]
FM .... Miami-Dade Public Library, Miami, FL [*Library symbol*] [*Library of Congress*] (LCLS)
FM .... Micronesia [*Internet country code*]
f_m .... Modulation Frequency (IDOE)
FM .... Shippers Forecasts [*Symbol*] [*National Weather Service*]
FM .... Titanium Tetrachloride [*Inorganic chemistry*]

FMA............ Average Female Mass [*Ecology*]
FMA............ Daughters of Mary, Help of Christians [*Salesian Sisters of St. John Bosco*] [*Roman Catholic religious order*]
FMA............ Fabricating Machinery Association (SAUO)
FMA............ Fabricating Manufacturers Association (SAUO)
FMA............ Fabricators and Manufacturers Association
FMA............ Fabricators and Manufacturers Association, International (EA)
FMA............ Facilities Management Analysis
FMA............ Factory Materials Association
FMA............ Failure Mode Analysis
FMA............ Family Mediation Association (EA)
FMA............ Fan Manufacturers Association [*British*] (DBA)
FMA............ Farm Management Association [*British*]
FMA............ Fault Modus Analysis (VLIE)
FMA............ Federal Managers Association (EA)
FMA............ Federal Maritime Adminstration (WDAA)
FMA............ Federated Management Architecture (VLIE)
FMA............ Federation Mondiale des Annonceurs [*World Federation of Advertisers - WFA*] [*Brussels, Belgium*] (EAIO)
FMA............ Federation of British Port Wholesale Fish Merchants Associations (SAUO)
FMA............ Federation of Management Associations (SAUO)
FMA............ Fein-Marquart Associates [*Chemical Information Systems, Inc.*] [*Information service or system*] (IID)
FMA............ Fellow of the Museums Association [*British*] (EY)
FMA............ Felt Manufacturers Association (SAUO)
FMA............ Ferrite Manufacturers Association
FMA............ Ferrite Modulator Assembly (ACAE)
FMA............ Fertiliser Manufacturers Association [*British*]
FMA............ Fertilizer Manufacturers Association Ltd. (SAUO)
FMA............ Fibromyalgia Syndrome [*Medicine*]
FMA............ Field Maintenance Activity (MCD)
FMA............ File Manufacturers Association [*Defunct*] (EA)
FMA............ Final Marker Aid [*FAA*] (TAG)
FMA............ Financial Management Association [*Tampa, FL*] (EA)
FMA............ Financial Marketing Association (EA)
FMA............ Fire Marshals Association of North America (NTPA)
FMA............ First Medical Management [*Vancouver Stock Exchange symbol*]
FMA............ First Mercantile American Bank (SAUO)
FMA............ Flexicore Manufacturers Association (EA)
FMA............ Flight Manual Allowance
FMA............ Flight Mode Annunciator (MCD)
FMA............ Floral Marketing Association (NTPA)
FMA............ Florida Medical Association (SAUO)
FMA............ Flour Mills of America (SAUO)
FMA............ Fluorescein Mercury Acetate [*Analytical chemistry*]
FMA............ Fogg Museum of Art (SAUO)
FMA............ Fonds Monetaire Andin [*Andean Monetary Fund*] (PDAA)
FMA............ Food Machinery Association [*British*] (BI)
FMA............ Food Management Area (MCD)
FMA............ Food Merchandisers of America (EA)
FMA............ Ford Motor Argentina (SAUO)
FMA............ Foreign Marriages Act (SAUO)
FMA............ Foreign Media Analysis (SAUO)
FMA............ Foreign Military Assistance (SAUO)
FMA............ Foremost Aviation Ltd. [*Nigeria*] [*ICAO designator*] (FAAC)
FMA............ Forest Management Area (SAUS)
FMA............ Forging Manufacturers Association [*Later, ODFI*]
FMA............ Formosa [*Argentina*] [*Airport symbol*] (OAG)
FMA............ Forum for Medical Affairs [*Formerly, CPOSMA*] (EA)
FMA............ Forward Maintenance Area (NATG)
FMA............ Foxon-Maddocks Associates (IID)
FMA............ Fracmaster Ltd. [*NYSE symbol*] [*Formerly, Canadian Fracmaster Ltd.*]
FMA............ Fracture mechanics assembly (SAUS)
FMA............ Fragrance Materials Association (SAUO)
FMA............ Fragrance Materials Association of the US (EA)
FMA............ Frankfort-Mandibular Plane Angle [*Medicine*] (DMAA)
FMA............ Frequency Measurement Adapter (VLIE)
FMA............ Frequency Modulation Altimeter (IAA)
FMA............ Frequency Modulation Association (SAUO)
FMA............ Frequency Modulator Altimeter (SAUS)
FMA............ Fulfillment Management Association (EA)
FMA............ Fundamental Mode Asynchronous (IAA)
FMA............ Furniture Manufacturers Association (SAUO)
FMA............ Future Mailing Address
FMAA............ Federal Managers Financial Integrity Act (SAUO)
FMAA............ Fleet Master-at-Arms [*British military*] (DMA)
FMAA............ Footwear Manufacturers' Association of Australia
FMAA............ Furniture Manufacturers' Association of Australia (EERA)
FMaC............ Chipola Junior College, Marianna, FL [*Library symbol*] [*Library of Congress*] (LCLS)
FMAC............ Fabricators and Manufacturers Association International (SAUO)
FMAC............ Facility Maintenance and Control (VLIE)
FMAC............ Federation Mondiale des Anciens Combattants [*World Veterans Federation - WVF*] [*Paris, France*] (EAIO)
FMAC............ fetal movement acceleration test (SAUS)
FMAC............ Finance Member of the Army Council (SAUO)
FMAC............ Financial Management Advisory Committee
FMAC............ First Merchants Acceptance [*NASDAQ symbol*] (TTSB)
FMAC............ First Merchants Acceptance Corp. [*NASDAQ symbol*] (SAG)
FMAC............ Frequency Division Multiplexed Analogue Components [*Colour TV broadcasting method*] (NITA)
FMAC............ Frequency Management Advisory Council [*Department of Commerce*] [*Washington, DC*] (EGAO)
FMACC............ Foreign Military Assistance Coordinating Committee [*Department of State*] [*Terminated, 1950*]
FMACCU...... Federation Mondiale des Associations, Centres, et Clubs UNESCO [*World Federation of UNESCO Clubs and Associations*] [*France*] (EAIO)
FMacn............ Macnaghten's Hindu Law [*India*] [*A publication*] (DLA)
FMAD............ Flight Mission Assignments Document (KSC)
FMAD............ Fluid Management and Distribution (SSD)
F-MADE............ Forum for the Military Applications of Directed Energy (SEWL)
FMadN............ North Florida Junior College, Madison, FL [*Library symbol*] [*Library of Congress*] (LCLS)
FMA/F/S............ Foreign Military Assistance/Financing/Sales (MILB)
FMAG............ Fleet Maintenance Assistance Group [*Navy*] (NVT)
FMAG............ Fluxgate Magnetometer (MCD)
FMAG CRUDESLANT CHAR... Fleet Maintenance Assistance Group for Cruiser-Destroyer Force, Atlantic, Charleston, South Carolina [*Navy*] (DNAB)
FMAG CRUDESLANT MPT... Fleet Maintenance Assistance Group for Cruiser-Destroyer Force, Atlantic, Mayport, Florida [*Navy*] (DNAB)
FMAG CRUDESLANT NORVA... Fleet Maintenance Assistance Group for Cruiser-Destroyer Force, Atlantic, Norfolk, Virginia [*Navy*] (DNAB)
FMAGPAC.... Fleet Maintenance Assistance Group, Pacific (SAUO)
FMAGR............ Furniture Manufacturers Association of Grand Rapids [*Later, GRAFMA*] (EA)
FMAG SERVLANT NORVA... Fleet Maintenance Assistance Group for Service Forces, Atlantic, Norfolk, Virginia [*Navy*] (DNAB)
FMAGX............ Fidelity Magellan Fund [*Mutual fund ticker symbol*] (SG)
FMAHTS...... Flight Manifest and Hardware Tracking System (MCD)
FMAI............ Fabricators and Manufacturers Association, International (EA)
FMAI............ Financial Management for Administrators Institute (SAUO)
FMAIN............ File Maintenance [*Computer science*] (IAA)
F MAINT S/BL... Failure to Maintain Seat Belts in Working Order [*Conviction term used in state of Oregon*] (MVRD)
FMaJ............ Jackson County Public Library, Marianna, FL [*Library symbol*] [*Library of Congress*] (LCLS)
FMAL............ Funds Management Audit List (AFIT)
FMAM............ Federation Mondiale des Amis de Musees [*World Federation of Friends of Museums - WFFM*] (EAIO)
FMAM............ Frequency Modulation - Amplitude Modulation (IAA)
FMAN............ February, May, August, November [*Denotes quarterly payments of interest or dividends in these months*] [*Business term*]
FMAN............ Foreman (AABC)
FMANA............ Fire Marshals Association of North America (EA)
FM & C............ Factory Management and Control [*Computer Automation Ltd.*] [*Software package*] (NCC)
FM & M............ Fibber McGee and Molly [*Radio program*]
FM & P............ Force Management and Personnel (DOMA)
FM&P............ Force Management and Personnel [*Military*] (POLM)
FMANTS............ Flight Manifest [*Aerospace*] (NAKS)
FMANU............ Federation Mondiale des Associations pour les Nations Unies [*World Federation of United Nations Associations - WFUNA*] [*Geneva, Switzerland*] (EA)
FMAP............ Fan Marker Approach [*Aviation*]
FMAP............ Father Moriarty Asylum Project [*Defunct*] (EA)
FMAP............ Federal Medical Assistance Percentage [*Department of Health and Human Services*] (GFGA)
FMAP............ Financial Management Assistance Project [*Environmental Protection Agency*] (EPAT)
FMAP............ Flood Mitigation Assistance Program (DEMM)
FMAR............ Ferromagnetic Antiresonance (SAUS)
FMAR............ First Mariner Bancorp [*NASDAQ symbol*] (SAG)
FMAS............ Federation of Manufacturers of Artificial Stone (SAUO)
FMAS............ Federation of Midland Art Societies (SAUO)
FMAS............ Financial Management Accounting System (HEAS)
FMAS............ Florida Marine Aquarium Society
FMAS............ Flush Mounted Antenna System (ACAE)
FMAS............ Foreign Marriage Advisory Service (SAUO)
FMAS............ Foreign Medial Analysis Subsystem [*Environmental science*] (COE)
FMAS............ Fundamental Mode Asynchronous Sequential (SAUS)
FMASC............ Foreign Military Assistance Steering Committee
FMAT............ Food Management Assistance Team [*Army*] (INF)
FMAT............ Frequency Modulation Anticipation Time (ACAE)
FMATH............ Federation Mondiale de Travailleurs des Industries Alimentaires, du Tabac, et del'Hotellerie [*World Federation of Workers in Food, Tobacco, and Hotel Industries - WFFTH*] (EAIO)
FMAU............ Fluoro(methyl)arabinosyluracil [*Biochemistry*]
FMAW............ First Marine Aircraft Wing
FMAW............ Fleet Marine Air Wing
FMAX............ Franchise Mortgage Acceptance Co. [*NASDAQ symbol*] (NASQ)
FMAX............ Franchise Mtge Acceptance [*NASDAQ symbol*] (SG)
FMAZ............ Froedert Malt [*Federal Railroad Administration identification code*]
FMB............ Biscayne Chemical Laboratories, Inc., Miami, FL [*Library symbol*] [*Library of Congress*] (LCLS)
FMB............ Factory Mutuals' Combined Fire-Boiler Policy [*Insurance*]
FMB............ Farmers Marketing Board (SAUS)
FMB............ Fast Missile Boat [*Navy*]
FMB............ Federal Maritime Board [*1950-1961; functions transferred to FMC*]
FMB............ Federal Maritime Board Reports [*United States Maritime Administration, Department of Commerce*] [*A publication*] (DLA)
FMB............ Federal Mortgage Bank [*Nigeria*]
FMB............ Federation of Master Builders [*British*] (DAS)
FMB............ Field Maintenance Bulletin [*Army*]
FMB............ File Mask Bit (SAUS)
FMB............ Financial Management Board [*Air Force*] (AFIT)
FMB............ First Maryland Bancorp [*NYSE symbol*] (SPSG)

FMB .... First Merchant Bank (SAUS)
FMB .... First Michigan Bank Corp. (EFIS)
FMB .... First Mortgage Bonds (EBF)
FMB .... Fishing Motorboat (SAUS)
FMB .... Flag Motorboat (SAUS)
FMB .... Foreign Materiel Branch [*Military*]
FMB .... Forward Mounting Base (SAUS)
FMB .... Foundation for Microbiology (SAUO)
FMB .... Frequency Management Branch [*White Sands Missile Range*]
FMB .... frequency modulation band (SAUS)
FMB .... Frequency Modulation Broadcasters
FMB .... Full Maternal Behavior [*Physiology*]
FMB .... Fuze Management Board [*Army*]
FMBA .... 51st Medical Battalion Association (EA)
FMBA .... Financial Management & Business Analysis (SAUO)
FMBC .... Biscayne College, Miami, FL [*Library symbol*] [*Library of Congress*] (LCLS)
FMBC .... First Michigan Bank [*NASDAQ symbol*] (TTSB)
FMBC .... First Michigan Bank Corp. [*NASDAQ symbol*] (NQ)
FMBC-L .... Biscayne College, St. Thomas University Law School, Miami, FL [*Library symbol*] [*Library of Congress*] (LCLS)
FMBD .... First Mutual Bancorp [*NASDAQ symbol*] (TTSB)
FMBD .... First Mutual Bancorp, Inc. [*NASDAQ symbol*] (SAG)
FMBH .... Baptist Hospital of Miami, Health Sciences Library, Miami, FL [*Library symbol*] [*Library of Congress*] (LCLS)
FMBI .... First Midwest Bancorp [*NASDAQ symbol*] (TTSB)
FMBI .... First Midwest Bancorp, Inc. [*NASDAQ symbol*] (NQ)
fmbid .... firm bid (SAUS)
FMBK .... F & M Bancorp, Inc. [*NASDAQ symbol*] (SAG)
FMBK .... F&M Bancorporation, Inc. [*NASDAQ symbol*] (TTSB)
FMbMS .... Mount Sinai Medical Center, Media Center, Miami Beach, FL [*Library symbol*] [*Library of Congress*] (LCLS)
FMBN .... F&M Bancorp [*NASDAQ symbol*] (TTSB)
FMBN .... F & M Bancorp, Inc. [*NASDAQ symbol*] (SAG)
FMBPr .... First Maryland Banc 7.875% Pfd [*NYSE symbol*] (TTSB)
FMBRA .... Flour Milling and Baking Research Association [*British*] (IRUK)
FMBS .... Forward Mobile Base Stockage (MCD)
FMBS .... Frame-Mode Bearer Service (VLIE)
FMBSA .... Farmers and Manufacturers Beet Sugar Association (EA)
FMBT .... Future Main Battle Tank (NATG)
FMbW .... Wolfsonian Foundation, Miami Beach, FL [*Library symbol*] [*Library of Congress*] (LCLS)
FMC .... Decisions of the Federal Maritime Commission [*United States*] [*A publication*] (DLA)
FMC .... Facilities Management Contract
FMC .... Failure Mode Center (SAUO)
FMC .... Family Mediation Centre [*Australia*]
FMC .... Farm Mortgage Corp. [*New Deal*]
FMC .... Fatstock Marketing Corp. [*British*]
FMC .... Fatstock Marketing Corporation, Ltd. (SAUO)
FMC .... Federal Management Circular
FMC .... Federal Manufacturers Code (MCD)
FMC .... Federal Maritime Commission [*Independent government agency*]
FMC .... Federal Micrographic Council (SAUO)
FMC .... Federal Mogul Corporation (SAUO)
FMC .... Federated Mountain Clubs (SAUO)
FMC .... Federation of Mothers Clubs (SAUO)
FMC .... Fellow of the Institute of Management Consultants (DD)
FMC .... Fellow of the Medical Council [*British*]
FMC .... Felt Manufacturers Council (EA)
FMC .... Ferrite Memory Core
FMC .... Fetal Movement Count [*Obstetrics*] (DAVI)
FMC .... Field Medical Card [*Army*] (AABC)
FMC .... Fighter Mission Coordinator (SAUS)
FMC .... Fighter Mode Command (ACAE)
FMC .... File Management Computer (SAUS)
FMC .... File Mask Command (SAUS)
FMC .... Film Magnetic Counter
FMC .... Film-Makers' Cooperative (EA)
FMC .... Filter Manufacturers Council (EA)
FMC .... Final Moisture Content (IAA)
FMC .... Financial Management Center (USDC)
FMC .... Fine Motor Coordination (IDYL)
FMC .... Finite Memory Channel (SAUS)
FMC .... Finnish Management Council (SAUO)
FMC .... Fireball Mode of Combustion [*Combustion in engines*]
FMC .... Fire Mark Circle [*Liverpool, England*] (EAIO)
FMC .... Fire Mission Control (SAUS)
FMC .... First Ministers' Conference [*Canada*]
FMC .... Fisheries Management Committee [*Victoria, Australia*]
FMC .... Fishery Management Council [*National Oceanic and Atmospheric Administration*] (GFGA)
FMC .... Fixed Message Code (SAUS)
FMC .... Fixed Message Cycle [*Telecommunications*] (TEL)
FMC .... Fixed Mica Capacitor
FMC .... Fixed Mirror Concentrator
FMC .... Fixed Mobile Convergence (SAUS)
FMC .... Fixed Mylar Capacitor
FMC .... Flatness Measuring and Control (SAUS)
FMC .... Fleet Maintenance Council (SAUO)
FMC .... Fleet Management Center (DNAB)
FMC .... Flexible Machining Cell (SAUS)
FMC .... Flexible Machining Center [*Manufacturing technology*]
FMC .... Flexible Manufacturing Cell [*Industrial engineering*]
FMC .... Flexible Manufacturing Center (SAUS)
FMC .... Flexible Molding Composite [*Plastics*]
FMC .... Flexible Monte Carlo [*Computer science*]
FMC .... Flexible Motor Coupling
FMC .... Flight Management Computer
FMC .... Flight Medicine Clinic
FMC .... Flinders Medical Centre [*Australia*]
FMC .... Florida Memorial College, Miami, FL [*OCLC symbol*] (OCLC)
FMC .... Flow Microcalorimeter (SAUS)
FMC .... Fluid Momentum Controller (SSD)
FMC .... Flutter Mode Control [*Aviation*]
FMC .... FMC Corp. [*Formerly, Food Machinery Corp.*] [*Associated Press*] (SAG)
FMC .... Focal Macular Choroidopathy [*Medicine*] (MELL)
FMC .... Focus on Micronesia Coalition [*Later, MC*] (EA)
FMC .... Food Machinery & Chemical Corp., New York (SAUS)
FMC .... Food Machinery Corporation (NAKS)
FMC .... Food Management Compartment (MCD)
FMC .... Food Media Club [*Australia*]
FMC .... Force Missile Coordinator [*Navy*] (CAAL)
FMC .... Force Mobile (Canadian Forces)
FMC .... Forces Mobile Command [*Canada*] (DD)
FMC .... Forces Motoring Club [*British military*] (DMA)
FMC .... Ford Motor Company Ltd. (SAUO)
FMC .... Ford Motor Co. of Canada Ltd. [*Toronto Stock Exchange symbol*]
FmC .... Forman Co., Monmouth, IL [*Library symbol*] [*Library of Congress*] (LCLS)
FMC .... Former Members of Congress [*US*] [*Later, AFMC*]
FMC .... Forum Managed Care (SAUS)
FMC .... Forward Motion Compensation
FMC .... Foundation for Medical Care [*Generic term*] (DHSM)
FMC .... Foundation for Mideast Communication [*Later, FMEC*] (EA)
FMC .... Four Mile Canyon [*Oregon*] [*Seismograph station code, US Geological Survey*] (SEIS)
FMC .... Franklin and Marshall College [*Pennsylvania*]
FMC .... Free Man of Color [*Term of reference for blacks after the Civil War*]
FMC .... Frequency Management Center (SAUO)
FMC .... Frequency-Modulated Cyclotron
FMC .... Friele-MacAdam-Chickering (SAUS)
FMC .... Fuel Management Computer (NG)
FMC .... Full Metal Case [*Ammunition*] (DICI)
FMC .... Full Mission Capable (SAUO)
FMC .... Fully Mission Capable (MCD)
FMC .... Fulminating Meningococcemia [*Medicine*] (MELL)
FMC .... Fundamental Material Controls
FMC .... Fund for Modern Courts (EA)
FMCA .... Failure Mode Criticality Analysis (VLIE)
FMCA .... Family Motor Coach Association (EA)
FMCA .... Federated Music Clubs of Australia
FMCA .... Fire Mark Circle of the Americas (EA)
FMCA .... Flour Millers Council of Australia
FMCA .... Ford Mercury Club of America [*Defunct*] (EA)
FMCA .... [*The*] Forensic Medicine Consultant-Advisor [*Program*]
fmca .... forming cam (SAUS)
FM Can .... Ford Motor of Canada (SAUO)
FM-Card .... field medical card (SAUS)
FMCARP .... Father Moriarty Central American Refugee Program [*Later, FMAP*] (EA)
FMCC .... Cordis Corp. Library, Miami, FL [*Library symbol*] [*Library of Congress*] (LCLS)
FMCC .... Force Movement Control Center [*Marines*] (ANA)
FMCC .... Ford Motor Credit Company (SAUO)
FMCC .... Fulton-Montgomery Community College (SAUO)
FMCCS .... Force Modernization Command and Control System (SAUO)
FMCDET .... Fleet Management Center Detachment (DNAB)
FMCDU .... Flight Management Control and Display Unit (HLLA)
FMCE .... Federacion Mundial Cristiana de Estudiantes [*World Student Christian Federation*]
FMCE .... Federation of Manufacturers of Construction Equipment (SAUO)
FMCEC .... Federation of Manufacturers of Construction Equipment and Cranes [*British*] (EAIO)
FMCF .... First Manned Captive Flight [*NASA*] (NASA)
FMC/FMS .... Flexible Manufacturing Cell / Flexible Manufacturing [*Industrial engineering*] (BTTJ)
FMCG .... Fast-Moving Consumer Goods (DS)
FMCG .... Freeport McMoRan Copper & Gold [*Associated Press*] (SAG)
FMC Gd .... FMC Gold Co. [*Associated Press*] (SAG)
FMCh .... Flyball Master Champion
FMCH .... Moroni/Hahaia [*Comoros*] [*ICAO location identifier*] (ICLI)
FMcHNM .... Fort McHenry National Monument (SAUO)
FMCI .... Forms Manufacturers Credit Interchange (EA)
FMCI .... Moheli/Bandaressalam [*Comoros*] [*ICAO location identifier*] (ICLI)
FMCIM .... Federation Mondiale des Concours Internationaux de Musique [*World Federation of International Music Competitions - WFIMC*] (EAIO)
FMC-in-C .... Field Marshal Commanding-in-Chief [*British military*] (DMA)
FMCL .... Fleet Mechanical Calibration Laboratory
FM/CM .... Frequency Modulated Continuous Wave (SAUS)
FMCMA .... Fraternal and Military Club Managers Association [*Defunct*] (EA)
FMCMS .... F. Marion Crawford Memorial Society (EA)
FMCN .... Mexico Conservation Fund (SAUO)
FMCN .... Moroni/Iconi [*Comoros*] [*ICAO location identifier*] (ICLI)
FMCO .... FMS Financial [*NASDAQ symbol*] (TTSB)
FMCO .... FMS Financial Corp. [*NASDAQ symbol*] (CTT)
FMCORP .... Field Music Corporal [*Marine Corps*]
FMCPL .... Field Music Corporal [*Marine Corps*]
FMCR .... Fleet Marine Corps Reserve

FMCS .... Facilities Management Control System (SAUS)
FMCS .... Facility/Process Monitor & Control System (SAUS)
FMCS .... Factory Monitoring and Control System [*Computer science*]
FMCS .... Federal Mediation and Conciliation Service [*Independent government agency*]
FMCS .... Fighter Management Computer System (SAUO)
FMCS .... Fleet Management Control Systems, Inc. [*Software*]
FMCS .... Flight Management Computer System
FMCS .... Flight Mission Control Study (ACAE)
FMCS .... Franklin Mint Collector's Society (EA)
FMCS .... Freight Movement Control System [*MTMC*] (TAG)
FMCS .... FSIS [*Food Safety and Inspection Service*] Management and Communication System [*Department of Agriculture*] (GFGA)
FMCS .... Fuels Management Capabilities System (SAUO)
FMCSR .... Federal Motor Carrier Safety Regulation
FMCT .... Farmers & Mechanics Bank [*NASDAQ symbol*] (SAG)
FMCT .... Federation of Moulders and Collateral Trades [*A union*] [*British*]
FMCTY .... Farmer City, IL [*American Association of Railroads railroad junction routing code*]
FMCU .... File Memory Control Unit [*Computer science*] (VLIE)
FMCU .... Form Cutter
FMCV .... Anjouan/Ouani [*Comoros*] [*ICAO location identifier*] (ICLI)
FMCVC .... Federation Mondiale des Communautes de Vie Chretienne [*World Federation of Christian Life Communities - WFCLC*] [*Rome, Italy*] (EAIO)
FM-CW .... frequency-modulated continous wave (SAUS)
FM-CW .... Frequency Modulated Continuous Wave (SAUS)
FMCW .... Frequency-Modulated Continuous-Wave [*RADAR*] (KSC)
FM/CW .... Frequency Modulation/Continuous Wave (SAUS)
FMCWR .... Frequency Modulated Carrier Wave Radar (NITA)
FMCZ .... Dzaoudzi/Pamanzi [*Mayotte*] [*ICAO location identifier*] (ICLI)
FMCZ .... Ford Motor Company [*Federal Railroad Administration identification code*]
FMD .... Familial Metaphyseal Dysplasia [*Medicine*] (MELL)
FMD .... Family Medical Doctor (DAVI)
FMD .... Federated Metals Division-American Smelting and Refining (SAUS)
FMD .... Feline Miliary Dermatitis (SPVS)
FMD .... Ferrous Metal Detector
FMD .... Ferry Movement Directives (SAUO)
FMD .... Fibromuscular Dysplasia [*Medicine*]
FMD .... Financial Management Division [*Environmental Protection Agency*] (EPA)
FMD .... Financial Markets Development
FMD .... Fisheries Management Division (SAUO)
FMD .... Fixtures Manufacturers and Dealers (EA)
FMD .... Fluorescence Multilayer Disk (SAUS)
FMD .... Fluorescent Multilayer Disc
FMD .... Foot-and-Mouth Disease [*Veterinary medicine*]
FMD .... Force Modernization Division [*Military*] (MCD)
FMD .... Forest Management Division (SAUO)
FMD .... Form Molding Die (MCD)
FMD .... Forward Metro Denver (SAUS)
FMD .... Frequency Management Division [*White Sands Missile Range*]
FMD .... Frequency-Modulated Demodulator [*Telecommunications*] (IAA)
FMD .... Frequency Modulation Discriminator
FMD .... Frequency Modulation Distortion (SAUS)
FMD .... Frequency Multiplexing Division (SAUS)
FMD .... Frequency of Minimum Delay
FMD .... Friends of Medieval Dublin [*Irish*]
FMD .... Front Militant Departementaliste [*Militant Departmentalist Front*] [*Reunion*] (PD)
FMD .... Fulcrum Development Ltd. [*Vancouver Stock Exchange symbol*]
FMD .... Function Management Data (IBMDP)
FMDA .... 1st Marine Division Association (EA)
FMDA .... 4th Marine Division Association WWII (EA)
FMDA .... FM Development Association [*Later, NRBA*]
FMDA .... Frequency Modulation Development Association (SAUO)
FMDA .... Futuremedia Ltd. [*NASDAQ symbol*] (SAG)
FMDAA .... Farm Machinery Dealers' Association of Australia
FMD & C .... Flight Mechanics, Dynamics, and Control (KSC)
FmDaves .... Famous Daves of America, Inc. [*Associated Press*] (SAG)
FMDAY .... Futuremedia PLC ADS [*NASDAQ symbol*] (TTSB)
FMDC .... First Medical Devices Corporation (SAUO)
FMDC .... Franciscan Missionaries of the Divine Child (TOCD)
FMDC .... Franciscan Missionary Sisters of the Divine Child [*Roman Catholic religious order*]
FMDCAS .... Farm Management Data Collection and Analysis System (SAUS)
FMDCS .... Fleet Maintenance Data Collection System (DNAB)
fmdf .... fixed mirror-distributed focus (SAUS)
FMDI .... Form Die
FMDLE .... Farmdale, IL [*American Association of Railroads railroad junction routing code*]
FMDM .... Flex Multiplexer/Demultiplexer (MCD)
FMDM .... Franciscan Missionaries of the Divine Motherhood [*Roman Catholic religious order*]
FMDM .... Frequency Modulation Deviation Meter
FMDN .... Farm Machinery Development Network (SAUO)
FMDP .... Financial Management for Data Processing [*An association*] (EA)
FMDP .... Fuel manufacturing development plan (SAUS)
FMDR .... Final Missile Deviation Report [*Aerospace*] (AAG)
FMDRI .... Foot- and Mouth Disease Research Institute (SAUS)
FMDRI .... Foot-and-Mouth Disease Research Institute (SAUO)
FMD-ROM .... Fluorescent Multilayer Disk
FMDS .... Failure Management Design System (ACAE)
FMDS .... Field Maintenance Data System (SAUO)
FMDS .... Fleet Management Demonstration System (SAUS)
FMDS .... Flight Management Data System (ACAE)
FMDS .... Flight Management Display System (ACAE)
FMDS .... Flight Model Discharge System (BARN)
FMDS .... Fresno Madera Dental Society (SAUS)
FMDU .... Fast Multiply/Divide Unit (NITA)
FMDV .... Foot-and-Mouth Disease Virus [*Veterinary medicine*]
FMDY .... Futuremedia Ltd. [*NASDAQ symbol*] (SAG)
FMDYW .... Futuremedia PLC Wrrt [*NASDAQ symbol*] (TTSB)
FMDZ .... Forward Missile Deployment Zone (SAUS)
FME .... Failure Mode and Effects
FME .... Fairbanks Mining Engineering (SAUO)
FME .... Farnesyl Methyl Ether [*Juvenile hormone analog*]
FME .... Feature Manipulation Engine (SAUS)
FME .... Federal Manufacturing & Engineering Corporation (SAUO)
FME .... Fetal-Maternal Exchange [*Medicine*] (MELL)
FME .... Field Maintenance Equipment [*Military*]
FME .... Field Modification Engineering (ACAE)
FME .... Field Moisture Equivalent (SAUS)
FME .... Finished with Main Engines [*Navy*]
FME .... Fixed Mobile Experiment (MCD)
FME .... Foreign Materials Exclusion (SAUS)
FME .... Foreign Materiel Exploitation (RDA)
FME .... Foreign Military Equipment (SEWL)
FME .... Forensic Medical Examiner (WDAA)
FME .... Fort Meade, MD [*Location identifier*] [*FAA*] (FAAL)
FME .... Foundation for Management Education [*British*]
FME .... Frequency-Measuring Equipment
FME .... Full Mouth Extraction [*Dentistry*]
FMe .... Melbourne Public Library, Melbourne, FL [*Library symbol*] [*Library of Congress*] (LCLS)
FMEA .... Failure Mode and Effects Analysis
FMEA .... Failure Mode Effects Analysis (SAUS)
FMEA .... Fault Modes and Effect Analysis (SAUS)
FMEA .... Florida Municipal Electric Association (SRA)
FMEA .... Florida Music Educators Association (SRA)
FMEA .... Flour Millers Export Association (EA)
FMEA/CIL .... Failure Mode Effects Analysis/Critical Items List (SAUS)
FMEA-CIL .... Failure Modes and Effects Analyses/Critical Items List (SAUS)
FMEC .... Failure Modes, Effects, and Criticality Analyses (ACAE)
FMEC .... Forward Master Events Controller [*NASA*] (NASA)
FMEC .... Foundation for Mideast Communication (EA)
FMEC .... Fur Merchants Employers Council (EA)
FMECA .... Failure Mode Effects and Criticality Analysis
FMECA .... Failure Modes Effects and Critical Analysis (SAUS)
FMED .... Forward Medical Equipment Depot [*Military*] [*British*]
FMED .... Foster Medical Corp. (SAUO)
FMeE .... Eau Gallie Public Library, Melbourne, FL [*Library symbol*] [*Library of Congress*] (LCLS)
FMEE .... Saint-Denis/Gillot [*Reunion*] [*ICAO location identifier*] (ICLI)
FMeF .... Florida Institute of Technology, Melbourne, FL [*Library symbol*] [*Library of Congress*] (LCLS)
FMEF .... forced mid-expiratory flow (SAUS)
FMEF .... Fuels and Materials Examination Facility [*Department of Energy*]
FMeH .... Harris Government Systems Sector, Engineering Library, Melbourne, FL [*Library symbol*] [*Library of Congress*] (LCLS)
FMEI .... Farm Management Extension Initiative (EERA)
F-MEL .... Friend Murine Erythroleukaemia [*Cell line*]
FMEL .... Fuels & Materials Examination Lab (SAUS)
FMEL .... Fuels and Materials Examination Laboratory (SAUS)
FMEM .... Failure Mode and Effects Management [*Engineering*]
FMEM .... Federation Mondiale pour l'Enseignement Medical [*World Federation for Medical Education - WFME*] (EA)
FMeM .... Meadowlane Community Library, Melbourne, FL [*Library symbol*] [*Library of Congress*] (LCLS)
FMEN1 .... Familial Multiple Endocrine Neoplasia Type 1 [*Medicine*] [*A rare genetic disorder*] (NRGU)
FMEO .... Fleet Marine Engineering Officer [*Navy*] [*British*]
FMEP .... Foreign Material Exploitation Program (CARL)
FMEP .... Foundation for Middle East Peace (EA)
FMEP .... Friction Mean Effective Pressure [*Automotive engineering*]
FMEP .... Saint-Pierre-Pierrefonds [*Reunion*] [*ICAO location identifier*] (ICLI)
FMEPS .... Family of Mobile Electric Power Sources (SAUO)
FMER .... Factory Mutual Engineering and Research
FMER .... FirstMerit Corp. [*NASDAQ symbol*] (SAG)
FMer .... French Mercury [*Record label*]
FMerAcc .... First Merchants Acceptance Corp. [*Associated Press*] (SAG)
FMERC .... Factory Mutual Engineering & Research Corp.
FMERO .... Factory Mutual Engineering and Research Organization (EA)
FMES .... Failure Modes Effects and Analysis (SAUS)
FMES .... Federal Ministry for Education and Science (SAUO)
FMES .... Ferry Mission Equipment Store (MCD)
FMES .... Full Mission Engineering Simulator (KSC)
fMet .... Formylmethionyl [*Biochemistry*]
FMET .... Functional Management Engineering Team (MUSM)
FMETA .... Foreign Material Exploitation Tactical Air [*Military*] (CAAL)
fmet-N .... formylmethionine (SAUS)
FMETO .... Fleet Meteorological Officer [*Navy*] [*British*]
F-MET-PHE .... Formyl-Methionyl-Phenylalanine (SAUS)
fMet-tRNA .... Formyl-Methionyl-Transfer Ribonucleic Acid (SAUS)
fMet-tRNA .... Ribonucleic Acid, Transfer - Formylmethionyl [*Biochemistry, genetics*]
FMEVA .... Floating-Point Means and Variance [*Biochemistry, genetics*]
FMEW .... Financial Management Executive Workshop
FMF .... Fairmont Foods Co. (SAUO)
FMF .... Familial Mediterranean Fever

FMF .... Farm Management and Finance [*British*]
FMF .... Fetal Movement Felt [*Medicine*]
fmf .... field maintenance factor (SAUS)
FMF .... Fiji Military Forces (ODA)
FMF .... Financial Markets Foundation
FMF .... First Mercantile Currency Fund, Inc. [*Toronto Stock Exchange symbol*]
FMF .... Flagler Memorial Library, Miami, FL [*Library symbol*] [*Library of Congress*] (LCLS)
FMF .... Fleet Marine Force [*Navy*]
FMF .... Flexible Manufacturing Factory (SAUS)
FMF .... Florida Mango Forum (EA)
FMF .... Flow Microfluorometer [*Instrumentation*]
FMF .... Fluid Modeling Facility [*Environmental Protection Agency*] (GRD)
FMF .... Food Manufacturers' Federation [*British*]
FMF .... Forced Midexpiratory Flow [*Medicine*] (DAVI)
FMF .... Foreign Military Financing (DOMA)
FMF .... Foreign Military Funding (SAUS)
FMF .... Francis Marion National Forest [*South Carolina*] [*Seismograph station code, US Geological Survey*] [*Closed*] (SEIS)
FMF .... Free Molecular Flow
FMF .... Fudan Museum Foundation (EA)
FMF .... Fuel Manufacturing Facility
FMF .... Fuel Material Facility (SAUO)
FMF .... Fuel Melt Fraction [*Nuclear energy*] (NRCH)
FMFATL .... Fleet Marine Force Atlantic (ACAE)
FM FAX .... Frequency-Modulated Facsimile (SAUS)
FMFB .... Frequency Modulated Feedback (SAUS)
FMFC .... First M & F Corp. [*NASDAQ symbol*] (SAG)
FMFC .... Francisco Morazan Frente Constitucional [*Honduras*] [*Political party*] (EY)
FMFD .... Frequency Modulation Feedback Discriminator
FMF-E UCE .... Fleet Marine Force (SAUS)
FMF-E UCE .... Fleet Marine Force-End User Computing Equipment (SAUO)
FMFEUR .... Fleet Marine Force, Europe (SAUO)
FMFF .... Frequency Modulation Feed Forward (PDAA)
FMFIA .... Federal Managers Financial Integrity Act [*1982*]
FMFIC .... Federation of Mutual Fire Insurance Companies (EA)
FMFIU .... Florida International University, Miami, FL [*Library symbol*] [*Library of Congress*] (LCLS)
FMFLANT .... Fleet Marine Force, Atlantic [*Navy*] (MCD)
FMFM .... Fleet Marine Force Manual [*Marine Corps*] (MCD)
FMFM .... Florida Memorial College, Miami, FL [*Library symbol*] [*Library of Congress*] (LCLS)
FM-FM .... Frequency Modulation - Frequency Modulation
FM/FM .... Frequency Modulation/Frequency Multiplexing (SAUS)
FMF-P .... Fleet Marine Force-Pacific (SAUO)
FMFP .... Foreign Military Financing Program [*DoD*]
FMFPAC .... Fleet Marine Force, Pacific Fleet [*Navy*]
FMFR .... Fuel Mass Flow Rate [*Automotive engineering*]
FMFRP .... FLeet Marine Force Reference Publication (COE)
fmfs .... fat in the moisture-free substance (SAUS)
FMFS .... Full Mission Fighter Simulator [*Air Force*] (PDAA)
FMFT .... forced mid-expiratory flow time (SAUS)
FMFT .... four-minus-five test (SAUS)
FMFWESTPAC ... Fleet Marine Force, Western Pacific [*Navy*]
FMG .... Fabricated Metal Goods
FMG .... Federal Military Government (Nigeria) [*Political party*] (PSAP)
FMG .... Fine Mesh Gauze [*Surgery*] (DAVI)
FMG .... Flakmessgerat [*Antiaircraft, gun-laying RADAR*] [*German*]
FMG .... Fleet Maintenance Group (SAUS)
FMG .... Fluorescein Mono(galactopyranoside) [*Organic chemistry*]
FMG .... Food Machinery Group [*British*] (DBA)
FMG .... Foreign Medical Graduate [*doing residency in US hospital*]
FMG .... Foreign Medical Graduation (SAUS)
FMG .... Foundry Marketing Group (SAUO)
Fmg .... Framing [*Construction term*] (MIST)
FMG .... Franc [*Monetary unit*] [*Malagasy Republic*]
FMG .... Frequency Manager (ACAE)
FMG .... Frequency Modulation Generator
f-mg- .... Malagasi Republic [*Madagascar*] [*MARC geographic area code*] [*Library of Congress*] (LCCP)
FMG(A) .... Fleet Maintenance Group (Atlantic) [*Canada*]
FMGC .... Flight Management Guidance Computer (GAVI)
FMGEC .... Flight Management Guidance Envelope Computer (HLLA)
FMGEMS .... Foreign Medical Graduate Examination in Medical Sciences
FMGF .... Factorial Moment Generating Function [*Statistics*]
FMGJ .... Federation of Master Goldsmiths and Jewelers (SAUO)
FMGM .... French MGM [*Record label*]
FMG(P) .... Fleet Maintenance Group (Pacific) [*Canada*]
FMGP .... Fungal Mitochondrial Genome Project
FMGS .... Church of Jesus Christ of Latter-Day Saints, Genealogical Society Library, MiamiBranch, Miami, FL [*Library symbol*] [*Library of Congress*] (LCLS)
FMGS .... Flight Management and Guidance System (DA)
FMH .... County Fermanagh (SAUS)
FMH .... Falling Mass Hazard
FMH .... Falmouth, MA [*Location identifier*] [*FAA*] (FAAL)
FMH .... Family Medical History [*Medicine*] (HGAA)
FMH .... Fan Marker Located with Radio Beacon [*Aviation*] (FAAC)
FMH .... Fat-Mobilizing Hormone [*Medicine*]
FMH .... Federal Meteorological Handbook
FMH .... Federation Mondiale de l'Hemophilie [*World Federation of Hemophilia*] (EAIO)
FMH .... Federation of Master Hairdressers (SAUO)
FMH .... Fetal Maternal Hemorrhage [*Medicine*]
FMH .... Fibromuscular Hyperplasia [*Neurology*] (DAVI)
FMH .... Fluoromethylhistidine [*Biochemistry*]
FMH .... Foederatio Medicorum Helveticorum [*Federation of the Swiss Physicians*] (CMD)
FMH .... Freemasons' Hall [*Freemasonry*] (ROG)
FMH .... Free Motion Headform [*Automotive safety systems*]
FMH .... Friends Meeting House [*Quakers*]
FMH .... Function Management Header (ACRL)
FMH-1 .... Federal Meteorological Handbook, Volume 1 (SAUS)
FmHA .... Department of Agriculture/Rural Economic & Community Development/Rural Housing Services (SAUO)
FmHA .... Farmers Home Administration [*Formerly, FHA*] [*Department of Agriculture*]
FMHC .... Federation of Mental Health Centers [*Defunct*] (EA)
FMHCA .... Florida Mental Health Counselors Association (SEAT)
FMHCSS .... Federal Mobile Home Construction and Safety Standard (SAUS)
FMHHS .... Fort McHenry Historic Shrine (SAUO)
FMHiS .... Historical Association of Southern Florida, Miami, FL [*Library symbol*] [*Library of Congress*] (LCLS)
FMHO .... Federal Hazard Mitigation Officer (SAUO)
FMHR .... Federal Hazardous Materials Regulations (TAG)
FMHS .... Faximile Message Handling System (SAUS)
FMHS .... Flexible Materials Handling System (SAUS)
FMHS .... Formal Message Handling System (SAUO)
FMHS .... Freely Moving Human Subject
FMHSU .... Federated Miscellaneous and Hospital Service Union [*Australia*]
FMHW .... Federation of Mental Health Workers [*British*]
FMI .... Daughters of Mary Immaculate [*Marianist Sisters*] [*Roman Catholic religious order*]
FMI .... Failure Mode Indicator (MUGU)
FMI .... Farmers Mutual Insurance (SAUS)
FMI .... Federation of Malta Industries (SAUO)
FMI .... Federation of Music Industries [*British*] (DBA)
FMI .... Fellow of the Motor Industry (SAUO)
FMI .... Fellowship of the Motor Industry [*British*] (BI)
FMI .... Fermilab Main Injector
FMI .... Fiber Materials Inc (SAUS)
FMI .... Fiber (or Fibre) Materials Incorporated (SAUO)
FMI .... Fibre Materials Inc. (SAUS)
FMI .... Fils de Marie Immaculee [*Sons of Mary Immaculate*] [*Saint Fulgent, France*] (EAIO)
FMI .... Financial Management Initiative [*British*]
FMI .... Finnish Meteorological Institute [*Helinski, Finland*]
FMI .... First Market Intelligence Ltd. [*Information service or system*] (IID)
FMI .... Fixed Mobile Integration (SAUS)
FMI .... Flann Microwave Instruments (SAUS)
FMI .... Flexible Modular Interface
FMI .... Flow Measurement and Indication (DEN)
FMI .... Fluid Metering, Incorporated (SAUO)
FMI .... Fondo Monetario Internacional [*International Monetary Fund*] [*Spanish*] [*United Nations*] (DUND)
FMI .... Food Marketing Institute (EA)
FMI .... Force Module Identifier (DOMA)
FMI .... Ford Marketing Institute
FMI .... Forest Management Institute (SAUO)
FMI .... Franciscan Sisters of Mary Immaculate of the Third Order of St. Francis of Assisi [*Roman Catholic religious order*]
FMI .... Franklin McLean Memorial Research Institute [*University of Chicago*] [*Research center*] (RCD)
FMI .... Franklin Multi-Income Tr [*NYSE symbol*] (TTSB)
FMI .... Free Motion Impedance
FMI .... Freeport-McMoran, Inc. (EFIS)
FMI .... Frequency Modulation Index (SAUS)
FMI .... Frequency Modulation Intercity Relay Broadcasting
FMI .... Friedrich Miescher Institute [*Switzerland*]
FMI .... Fujitsu Microelectronics, Incorporated (SAUO)
FMI .... Functional Management Inspection [*Military*]
FMI .... Functional Management Inspection system (SAUS)
FMI .... Future Manned Interceptor [*Military*]
FMI .... Kalemi [*Zaire*] [*Airport symbol*] (OAG)
FMi .... Merritt Island Public Library, Merritt Island, FL [*Library symbol*] [*Library of Congress*] (LCLS)
FMIA .... Federal Meat Inspection Act
FMIAA .... Fitness Motivation Institute of America Association (EA)
FMiB .... Brevard County Library System, Merritt Island, FL [*Library symbol*] [*Library of Congress*] (LCLS)
FMIC .... Flight Manual Interim Changes
FMIC .... Frequency Monitoring and Interference Control [*Radio*]
FMIC .... Front Malaysian Islamic Council [*Political party*] (FEA)
FMIC .... Fund Management Identification Code [*Military*] (AFM)
FMICS .... Financial Management Information and Control System [*Navy*]
FMICW .... Frequency-Modulated Intermittent Continuous Wave [*Electronics*] (OA)
FMID .... Florida Midland Railroad [*Federal Railroad Administration identification code*]
FMID .... Function Modification Identification [*IBM Corp.*] (CIST)
FMidBc .... First Midwest Bancorp [*Associated Press*] (SAG)
FMIG .... Farmers Mutual Insurance Group (SAUO)
FMIG .... Food Manufacturers Industrial Group (SAUO)
FMIJ .... Franciscan Missionaries of the Infant Jesus (TOCD)
FMILS .... Force Modernization Integrated Logistics Support
f/min .... Feet per Minute (SAUS)
FMIN .... Function, Minimum value (SAUS)
FMIP .... Financial Management Improvement Program

FMIR........... Frustrated Multiple Internal Reflectance
FMIR........... Frustrated Multiple Internal Reflections (SAUO)
FMIRA......... Fighter Multifunctional Inertial Reference Assembly (MCD)
FMIS........... Facilities Management Information System (SAUO)
FMIS........... Farm Market Infodata Service [*Department of Agriculture*] [*Database*]
FMIS........... Field Management Information System (AAGC)
FMIS........... Financial Management Information System
FMIS........... Fiscal Management Information System
FMIS........... Fleet Management Information System [*Software*]
FMIS........... Force Management Information System (SAUO)
FMIS........... Force Modernization Information System (MCD)
FMIS........... Forms Management Information System (SAUS)
FMIS........... Functional Management Inspection System (SAUS)
FMISC......... Field Measurement Information System Center (SAUS)
F MIST........ Fiat Mistura [*Let a Mixture Be Made*] [*Pharmacy*] (ROG)
FMIT........... Fusion Materials Irradiation Test Facility [*Proposed*]
FMITACTIVLIB... FMIT Neutron Activation Library (SAUS)
FMIV........... Forced Mandatory Intermittent Ventilation [*Medicine*] (DAVI)
FMJ............ Financial Mail (Johannesburg) [*A publication*]
FMJ............ Full Metal Jacket [*Ammunition*] (DICI)
fmj............ The Monastic Fraternity of Jerusalem (TOCD)
FMJBT........ Full Metal Jacket Boat Tail [*Weaponry*] [*Military*] (INF)
FMJC.......... Federation Mondiale de Jeunesse Catholique [*World Federation of Catholic Youth*]
FMJD.......... Federation Mondiale de la Jeunesse Democratique [*World Federation of Democratic Youth - WFDY*] [*Budapest, Hungary*] (EAIO)
FMJD.......... Federation Mondiale du Jeu de Dames [*World Draughts (Checkers) Federation - WDF*] [*Dordrecht, Netherlands*] (EAIO)
FMJFC......... Federation Mondiale des Jeunesses Feminines Catholiques
FMJLR......... Federation Mondiale des Jeunesses Liberales et Radicales [*World Federation of Liberal and Radical Youth*]
FMK............ FiberMark, Inc. [*NYSE symbol*] (SG)
FMK............ Field Modification Kit (SAUS)
Fmk............ Finmark (SAUS)
Fmk............ Finnmark (SAUS)
fmk............ full-mouth radiograph (SAUS)
F MK........... Markka [*Monetary unit*] [*Finland*]
F MK END LD... Failure to Mark End of Load with Light or Flag when Required [*Conviction term used in state of Oregon*] (MVRD)
FMKR.......... Fan Marker [*Aviation*] (IAA)
FML............ Factory Mutual Laboratories (SAUO)
FML............ Fault Message Line (MCD)
FML............ Feedback, Multiple Loop
FML............ Ferguson Memorial Library [*Presbyterian Church, Sydney, New South Wales, Australia*]
FML............ Fermi National Laboratory (SAUO)
FML............ Fiber-Metal Laminate [*Plastics*]
FMI............ Field Maintenance Instructions (SAUS)
FML............ File Manipulation Language
FML............ Final Materials List [*NASA*] (NASA)
FML............ Flail Mitral Leaflet (DB)
FML............ Flexible Membrane Liner [*For waste containment*]
FML............ Flight Mechanics Laboratory [*Texas A & M University*] [*Research center*] (RCD)
FML............ Fluid Mechanics Laboratory [*MIT*] [*Research center*]
FML............ Fluorometholone [*Anti-inflammatory drug*]
FML............ FM Resources Ltd. [*Vancouver Stock Exchange symbol*]
FML............ Force Module Library (DOMA)
fml............ formal (SAUS)
FML............ Fort Mill, SC [*Location identifier*] [*FAA*] (FAAL)
FML............ French Men of Letters [*A publication*]
FML............ Frequency Memory Loops (SAUS)
FML............ Front Mounting Light
FML............ Major Force List (SAUO)
f-ml-........... Mali [*MARC geographic area code*] [*Library of Congress*] (LCCP)
FML............ University of Miami, Law Library, Coral Gables, FL [*OCLC symbol*] (OCLC)
FMLA.......... Family and Medical Leave Act of 1993 (WYGK)
FMLA.......... Family Medical Leave Act (ADWA)
FMLA.......... Florida Medical Library Association (SAUO)
FMLC.......... Fetal Mouse Liver Cell [*Bioassay*]
F/MLDG....... Finish Moulding [*Automotive engineering*]
fml dr......... Formal Dining Room (ADWA)
FMLF.......... File Management Loading Facility
FMLF.......... File management loading language (SAUS)
FMLH.......... Frente Morazanista para la Liberacion de Honduras [*Guerrilla forces*] (EY)
FMLI........... Forms and Menu Language Interpreter (SAUS)
FMLIN......... Farabundo Marti National Liberation Front (SAUS)
FMLIS......... Federal Mineral Lands Information System (SAUS)
FMLIS......... Fuzzy Multispectral Landcover Information System (SAUO)
FMLM.......... French Military Liaison Mission [*World War II*]
FMLN.......... Farabundo Marti National Liberation Front [*Brazil*] [*Political party*] (ECON)
FMLN.......... Frente Farabundo Marti de Liberacion Nacional [*Farabundo Marti National Liberation Front*] [*El Salvador*] (ECON)
FMLN.......... Frente Morazanista de Liberacion Nacional [*Morazanista National Liberation Front*] [*Honduras*] [*Political party*] (PD)
FMLNH........ Frente Morazanista de Liberacion Nacional de Honduras [*Honduran Morazanist National Front*] [*Political party*]
Fm Lo.......... Farm Loan Officer Banking (TBD)
FMLP.......... Field Mirror Landing Practice
FMLP.......... Formyl(methionyl)(leucyl)phenylalanine [*Biochemistry*]
FMLS.......... Fleet Maintenance and Logistics Support (DNAB)
FMLS.......... Force Module Logistics Sustainability (SAUO)
FMLS.......... Forum for Modern Language Studies (journ.) (SAUS)
FMLS.......... Full-Matrix Least Squares [*Statistics*] (PDAA)
FMLSM........ Force Module Logistics Sustainability Model (DOMA)
FMLT.......... FORCE, Mass, Length, and Time [*Rocket dynamics*] (BARN)
FMLT System... Force Mass Length Time System (SAUS)
FMLY.......... Family
FMLY.......... Family Bancorp [*NASDAQ symbol*] (NQ)
FMLY.......... Formerly
fmly k a....... formerly known as (SAUS)
FMM........... Brothers of Mercy (TOCD)
fmm............ Brothers of Mercy (TOCD)
FMM........... Fast Multipole Method [*Physics*]
FMM........... Federation of Malay Manufacturers (SAUO)
FMM........... Ferromagnetic Material
FMM........... FFP Marketing [*AMEX symbol*] (SG)
FMM........... Financial Management for Managers (SAUO)
FMM........... Financial Management Manual [*NASA*]
FMM........... Finite Message Machine [*Telecommunications*]
FMM........... First Maritime Mining Corp. Ltd. [*Toronto Stock Exchange symbol*]
FMM........... First Moment Model (SAUS)
FMM........... Flash Memory Manager (SAUS)
FMM........... Flight Management Module (MCD)
FMM........... Flowmeter Method (SAUS)
FMM........... Fort Morgan, CO [*Location identifier*] [*FAA*] (FAAL)
FMM........... Framework Molecular Models
FMM........... Franciscan Missionaries of Mary [*Roman Catholic women's religious order*]
FMM........... French Military Mission (NATG)
FMM........... Front Motor Mount [*Automotive term*]
FMM........... Fuel motion monitor (SAUS)
FMM........... Missionary Fraternity of Mary (TOCD)
FMM........... University of Miami, Music Library, Coral Gables, FL [*OCLC symbol*] (OCLC)
FMMA......... Antananarivo/Arivonimamo [*Madagascar*] [*ICAO location identifier*] (ICLI)
FMMA......... Ferrocenylmethyl Metacrylate (SAUS)
FMMA......... Ferrocenylmethyl Methacrylate (SAUS)
FMMA......... Finite-Memory Moving- Average (SAUS)
FMMA......... Floor Machine Manufacturers Association
FMMA......... Floor Machine (or Machinery) Manufacturers Association (SAUO)
FMMA......... Floor Machinery Manufacturers Association (SAUS)
FMMAA....... Federated Mining Mechanics Association of Australia
FMMAF........ Fusion Material Microstructural Analysis Facility (SAUS)
FM Magazine... Frequency Modulation Magazine (journ.) (SAUS)
FMMC......... Factory Material Movement Component (AAEL)
FMMC......... Fixed Mylar Metallized Capacitor
FMMC......... Foundation for MultiMedia Communications [*Japan*] (DDC)
FMMC......... Malaimbandy [*Madagascar*] [*ICAO location identifier*] (ICLI)
FMMD......... Antananarivo [*Madagascar*] [*ICAO location identifier*] (ICLI)
FMMD......... Form Mandrel [*Tool*] (AAG)
FMMD......... Miami-Dade Community College, Miami, FL [*Library symbol*] [*Library of Congress*] (LCLS)
FMME......... Antsirabe [*Madagascar*] [*ICAO location identifier*] (ICLI)
FMME......... Fund for Multinational Management Education (EA)
FMME......... Racal-Milgo, Inc., Miami, FL [*Library symbol*] [*Library of Congress*] (LCLS)
FMMF......... Flexure Monitor Mounting Fixture
FMMG......... Antsalova [*Madagascar*] [*ICAO location identifier*] (ICLI)
FMMGEUA... Federated Millers and Manufacturing Grocers' Employees' Union of Australia
FMMH......... Mahanoro [*Madagascar*] [*ICAO location identifier*] (ICLI)
FMMI.......... Antananarivo/Ivato [*Madagascar*] [*ICAO location identifier*] (ICLI)
FMM Inductance... Flush Moebius Mutual Inductance (SAUS)
FMMJ.......... Ambohijanahary [*Madagascar*] [*ICAO location identifier*] (ICLI)
FMMK......... Ankavandra [*Madagascar*] [*ICAO location identifier*] (ICLI)
FMML......... Belo-Sur-Tsiribihina [*Madagascar*] [*ICAO location identifier*] (ICLI)
FMMM........ Antananarivo [*Madagascar*] [*ICAO location identifier*] (ICLI)
FMMN......... Miandrivazo [*Madagascar*] [*ICAO location identifier*] (ICLI)
FMMO......... Maintirano [*Madagascar*] [*ICAO location identifier*] (ICLI)
FMMOPS..... Federal Milk Markerting Order Policy Simulator (SAUO)
FMMP......... Amparafaravola [*Madagascar*] [*ICAO location identifier*] (ICLI)
FMMP......... Federal Master Mobilization Plan (SAUO)
FMMP......... Force Modernization Master Plan (MCD)
FMMP......... Formylmethionyl (sulfonyl) Methyl Phosphate [*Biochemistry*]
FMMQ......... Ilaka-Est [*Madagascar*] [*ICAO location identifier*] (ICLI)
FMMR......... Morafenobe [*Madagascar*] [*ICAO location identifier*] (ICLI)
FMMRI........ Franklin McLean Memorial Research Institute [*University of Chicago*] [*Research center*]
FMMRS........ Force Modernization Milestone Reporting System [*Army*] (RDA)
FMMS......... Field Missile Maintenance Squadron [*Air Force*]
FMMS......... Functionalized Monolayers on Mesoporous Supports [*Organic chemistry*]
FMMS......... Sainte-Marie [*Madasgascar*] [*ICAO location identifier*] (ICLI)
FMMT......... Toamasina [*Madagascar*] [*ICAO location identifier*] (ICLI)
FMMU......... Tambohorano [*Madagascar*] [*ICAO location identifier*] (ICLI)
FMMV......... Finger Millet Mosaic Virus [*Plant pathology*]
FMMV......... Morondava [*Madagascar*] [*ICAO location identifier*] (ICLI)
FMMX......... Tsiroanomandidy [*Madagascar*] [*ICAO location identifier*] (ICLI)
FMMY......... Vatomandry [*Madagascar*] [*ICAO location identifier*] (ICLI)
FMMZ......... Ambatondrazaka [*Madagascar*] [*ICAO location identifier*] (ICLI)
F/M/N......... Faith-Man-Nature [*from F/M/N Papers, National Council of Churches*]
FMN........... F & M National Corp. [*NYSE symbol*] (SAG)
FMN........... Farmington [*New Mexico*] [*Airport symbol*] (OAG)
FMN........... Farmington, NM [*Location identifier*] [*FAA*] (FAAL)
FMN........... Federation Mondiale de Neurologie [*World Federation of Neurology*]

FMN Flavin Mononucleotide [*Biochemistry*]
FMN Flexible Machining Network [*Automotive engineering*]
FMN Flight Motor Neuron [*Entomology*]
FMN FMC Corp., Princeton, NJ [*OCLC symbol*] (OCLC)
FMN Ford Motor Norge A/s (SAUS)
FMN Formation
FMN France Marine Nationale [*ICAO designator*] (FAAC)
F MN Full Moon [*Astronomy*] (ROG)
FMN United States Department of Commerce, National Oceanic and Atmospheric Administration, Miami, FL [*Library symbol*] [*Library of Congress*] (LCLS)
FMNA Antsiranana/Arrachart [*Madagascar*] [*ICAO location identifier*] (ICLI)
FMNBNA Frequency Modulation and Narrowband Noise Analyzer (MCD)
FMNC Mananara-Nord [*Madagascar*] [*ICAO location identifier*] (ICLI)
FMND Andapa [*Madagascar*] [*ICAO location identifier*] (ICLI)
FMNE Ambilobe [*Madagascar*] [*ICAO location identifier*] (ICLI)
FMNF Befandriana Nord [*Madagascar*] [*ICAO location identifier*] (ICLI)
FMNG Port Berge [*Madagascar*] [*ICAO location identifier*] (ICLI)
FMNH Antalaha [*Madagascar*] [*ICAO location identifier*] (ICLI)
FMNH Field Museum of Natural History [*Chicago, IL*]
FMNH Finnish Museum of Natural History (SAUS)
FMNH Flavin Mononucleotide [*Reduced*] [*Biochemistry*]
FMNH Florida Museum of Natural History (SAUO)
FMNJ Ambanja [*Madagascar*] [*ICAO location identifier*] (ICLI)
FMNL Analalava [*Madagascar*] [*ICAO location identifier*] (ICLI)
FMNLF Farabundo Marti National Liberation Front (SAUO)
FMNM Fort Matanzas National Monument (SAUO)
FMNM Mahajanga/Amborovy [*Madagascar*] [*ICAO location identifier*] (ICLI)
FMNN Nosy-Be/Fascene [*Madagascar*] [*ICAO location identifier*] (ICLI)
FMNO Soalala [*Madagascar*] [*ICAO location identifier*] (ICLI)
FMNP Farmers Market Nutrition Program
FMNP Mampikony [*Madagascar*] [*ICAO location identifier*] (ICLI)
FMNQ Besalampy [*Madagascar*] [*ICAO location identifier*] (ICLI)
FMNR Maroantsetra [*Madagascar*] [*ICAO location identifier*] (ICLI)
FMNS Sambava [*Madagascar*] [*ICAO location identifier*] (ICLI)
FMNT F&M National Corp. (EFIS)
FMNT Tsaratanana [*Madagascar*] [*ICAO location identifier*] (ICLI)
FMNV Vohemar [*Madagascar*] [*ICAO location identifier*] (ICLI)
FMNW Antsohihy/Ambalabe [*Madagascar*] [*ICAO location identifier*] (ICLI)
FMNW-Mu New World School of Arts, Music Library, Miami, FL [*Library symbol*] [*Library of Congress*] (LCLS)
FMNX Mandritsara [*Madagascar*] [*ICAO location identifier*] (ICLI)
FMO Facilities Maintenance Operations and Computerized Systems Show (TSPED)
FMO Fast Moving Object
FMO Fax/Modem (SAUS)
FMO Federal Management Officer (GFGA)
FMO Federal-Mogul [*NYSE symbol*] (TTSB)
FMO Federal-Mogul Corp. [*NYSE symbol*] (SPSG)
FMO Federation of Manufacturing Opticians [*British*] (BI)
FMO Federation of Mobile Home Owners (EA)
FMO Field Movement Officer (SAUO)
FMO Financial Management Office (KSC)
FMO Financial Management Officer (EAGT)
FMO Fiscal Management Office (SAUO)
FMO Flatland Meteorological Observatory [*Marine science*] (OSRA)
FMO Flavin Monooxygenases
FMO Fleet Mail Office [*British*]
FMO Fleet Maintenance Office [*or Officer*]
FMO Fleet Medical Officer
FMO Flight Management Office [*Air Force*] (AFM)
FMO Flight Medical Officer [*Air Force*]
FMO Force Modernization Office [*Army*] (RDA)
fmo Former Owner [*MARC relator code*] [*Library of Congress*] (LCCP)
FMO Forms Management Officer [*Army*] (AABC)
FMO Forward Medical Officer (SAUO)
FMO Free-Electron Molecular Orbital (SAUS)
FMO Frequency Management Office (DOMA)
FMO Frequency Multiplier Oscillator (IAA)
FMO Frontier Molecular Orbital Theory [*Physical chemistry*]
FMO Fuels Management Officer [*Air Force*] (AFIT)
FMO Full Marching Order [*British military*] (DMA)
FMO Functional Microoperation (SAUS)
FMO Fundamentals of Machine Operation [*John Deere Service Publications*] [*Moline, IL*] [*A publication*]
FMO Fuze Management Organization [*Army*]
FMOB Federation of Master Organ Builders [*British*] (BI)
FMOC Fluorenylmethyloxycarbonyl [*Organic chemistry*]
FMOCC Fleet Mobile Operations Command Center (DOMA)
FMOD Federal Ministry of Defence (SAUO)
FMOD File Modify (SAUS)
FMOF First Manned Orbital Flight [*NASA*]
FMOFEV First Manned Orbital Flight with EVA [*Extravehicular Activity*] (MCD)
FMOFPL First Manned Orbital Flight with Payload (MCD)
fmofr firm offer (SAUS)
FMOGDS Field Medical Oxygen Generation/Distribution System (DOMA)
FMOI Federation Mondiale des Organisations d'Ingenieurs [*World Federation of Engineering Organizations*]
FMOI First Moment of Inertia (SAUS)
fmol Femtomole (MAE)
F Moore English King's Bench Reports [*72 English Reprint*] [*A publication*] (DLA)
FMOP Field office management plan (SAUS)
FMOP Frequency Modulation On Pulse (SAUS)
FMOR First Mortgage [*NASDAQ symbol*] (TTSB)
FMOR First Mortgage Corp. [*NASDAQ symbol*] (SAG)
FMOs Functional Microoperations (SAUS)
FMOZ Ford Motor Company-Monroe [*Federal Railroad Administration identification code*]
FMP Facility Management Plan (COE)
FMP Faculty of Mining and Petroleum (SAUO)
FMP Fairbanks Morse Pump (SAUS)
FMP Fair Market Price (AAGC)
FMP Family Medicine Program (SAUS)
FMP Family Member Prefix (DNAB)
FMP Family Nurse Practitioner (SAUS)
FMP Fannie Major Pool [*FNMA*] [*Business term*] (EMRF)
FMP Fast-access Memory Parity Error (SAUS)
FMP Fasting Metabolic Panel [*Biochemistry*] (DAVI)
FMP Fault Modeling Procedures (SAUS)
FMP Federation of Malaya Police (SAUO)
FMP Ferrite Memory Plane (SAUS)
FMP Ferrous Metal Powder
FMP Field Maintenance Party [*Aviation*]
FMP Field Maintenance Processor (SAUS)
FMP Field Marching Pack
FMP Field Pack Mobile Professional (SAUS)
FMP File Merge Phase (SAUS)
FMP Final Management Plan (SAUS)
FMP Financial Management Plan
FMP Financial Modeling Program (SAUO)
FMP First Menstrual Period [*Medicine*]
FMP Fisheries Management Plan [*Marine science*] (OSRA)
FMP Fishery Management Plan
FMP Fleet Modernization Plan [*Navy*]
FMP Fleet Modernization Program (MCD)
FMP Flight Mechanic's Panel
FMP Flight Mode Panel [*Aviation*]
FMP Florida Marine Patrol (DEMM)
FMP Flow Management Position [*ICAO*] (DA)
FMP Flow Management Protocol (SAUS)
FMP Flow Model Processor (SAUS)
FMP Fluid Motion Panel [*of the British Aeronautical Research Council*] (MCD)
FMP Force Modernization Program
FMP Force Module Package (SAUO)
FMP Foreign Materiel Program [*Military*] (RDA)
FMP Formable Metallized Plastics [*Industrial technology*]
FMP Formation Pressure (SAUS)
FMP FORSCOM [*Forces Command*] Mobilization Plan [*DoD*]
FMP Fourth Malaysia Plan (SAUS)
FMP Frontier Mounted Police (SAUO)
FMP Fructose Monophosphate [*Biochemistry*]
FMP Fuel Maintenance Panel (AAG)
FMP Fuel Management Panel (SAUS)
FMP Fuels and Mining Practice Division [*Department of Mines and Technical Surveys*] [*Canada*]
FMP Full Marching Pack [*Military*]
FMP Functional Maintenance Procedure
FMP Functional Multiprocessing (SAUS)
FMP Function Management Protocol (TIMI)
fmp funny-man prop (SAUS)
FMPA Federation Mondiale pour la Protection des Animaux [*World Federation for the Protection of Animals*] [*Also known as WFPA and WTB*]
FMPA Fellow of the Master Photographers Association [*British*] (DBQ)
FMPC Federation of Motion Picture Councils (EA)
FMPC Feed Materials Processing Center (SAUS)
FMPC Feed Materials Production Center [*AEC*]
FMPCert Family Medicine Program Certificate
FMPD Fort Monmouth Procurement Division
FMPE Fast Access Memory Parity Error (SAUS)
FMPE Fast Memory Parity Error (IAA)
FMPE Federation of Master Process Engravers [*British*] (BI)
FMPEC Financial Management Plan for Emergency Conditions [*Army*]
FMPM Family Manned Planetary Mission
FM-PM Frequency Modulation - Phase Modulation [*RADAR*]
FM PM Frequency Modulation Phase Modulation (SAUS)
FMPMIS Fleet Maintenance Program Management Information System (SAUO)
FMPMIS Fleet Modernization Program Management Information System [*Navy*] (GFGA)
FMPO FM Properties [*NASDAQ symbol*] (TTSB)
FMPO FM Properties, Inc. [*NASDAQ symbol*] (SAG)
FMPO Fort Monmouth Procurement Office
FMPP Familial Male Precocious Puberty [*Medicine*]
FMPP Federal Merit Promotion Program
FMPP Federation of Motion Picture Pioneers (SAUO)
FMPP Flexible Multi-Pipeline Processor (SAUS)
FMPP Foundation of Motion Picture Pioneers (EA)
FM Prop FM Properties, Inc. [*Associated Press*] (SAG)
FMPROT Fine Mesh Cover Protected (IAA)
FMPS Fairbanks Morse Power Systems (SAUS)
FMPS Fast Multidimensional Processing System (SAUO)
FMPS Federation of Modern Painters and Sculptors (EA)
FMPS Form Pads [*Tool*] (AAG)
FMPS FORTRAN [*Formula Translating System*] Mathematical Programming System [*Computer science*] (IEEE)
FMPSA Federation of Master Painters and Signwriters of Australia
FMPT First Material Processing Test [*Japan*]

FMPTE......... Federation of Municipal Passenger Transport Employers [*British*] (BI)
FMPT-Experinient... first materials processing technology experiment (SAUS)
FMQ............ Fayalite Magnetite Quartz (Buffer) [*Geophysics*]
FMQ............ Fichier MARC [*Machine-Readable Cataloging*] Quebecois [*Source file*] [*UTLAS symbol*]
FMQ............ Frequency-Modulated Quartz
FMQ............ frequency-modulated quartz oscillator (SAUS)
FMQB........... Friday Morning Quarterback [*In title FMQB Album Report*]
FMQ Circuit... Frequency-Modulated Quartz Circuit (SAUS)
FMR............ Facility Management Reporting (SAUS)
FMR............ Failure and Malfunction Report [*NASA*] (KSC)
FMR............ Fairbourne Miniature Railway [*Wales*]
FMR............ Fair Market Rent (GFGA)
fmr............ farmer (SAUS)
FMR............ Fasting Metabolic Rate (PDAA)
fmr............ fast metabolic rate (SAUS)
FMR............ Fellow of the Association of Health Care Information and Medical Records Officers [*British*] (DBQ)
FMR............ Female-to-Male Ratio (SAUS)
FMR............ Ferromagnetic Resonance
FMR............ Fetal Movement Record [*Medicine*] (EDAA)
FMR............ Field Maintenance Reliability (SAUS)
FMR............ Field Maintenance Request
FMR............ Field Marketing Representative (SAUS)
FMR............ Field material requisition (SAUS)
FMR............ Field Materials Request (SAUS)
FMR............ Field Miniature Range (SAUS)
FMR............ Field Modification Report
FMR............ Field Modification Request [*Military*]
FMR............ Fife Mounted Rifles [*British military*] (DMA)
FMR............ File Mask Register (SAUS)
FMR............ Final Meteorological Radiation
FMR............ Financial Management Report (AABC)
FMR............ Financial Management Review (ACAE)
Fmr............ Firemaster (WDAA)
FMR............ Fire Movement Range (MCD)
FMR............ Flamingo Air, Inc. [*FAA designator*] (FAAC)
FMR............ Flanagan McAdam Resources, Inc. [*Toronto Stock Exchange symbol*]
FMR............ Former
FMR............ Foundation for Moral Restoration (EA)
FMR............ Freeport McMoRan O/G Rlty [*NYSE symbol*] (TTSB)
FMR............ Freeport-McMoRan Oil & Gas Royalty Trust [*NYSE symbol*] (SPSG)
FMR............ Frequency Modulated Radar (SAUS)
FMR............ Frequency-Modulated RADAR
FMR............ Frequency-Modulated Ranging (MCD)
FMR............ Frequency-Modulated Receiver [*Telecommunications*]
FMR............ Friend-Moloney-Rauscher [*Virus*] (AAMN)
FMR............ Frontier Mounted Rifles [*British military*] (DMA)
FMR............ Functional Management Review (SAUO)
FMR............ Function Maximum Rate (NASA)
FMR............ Function Max Rate (SAUS)
FMR............ Funds Management Record [*Military*] (AFM)
FMR............ Les Fusiliers Mont Royal [*British military*] (DMA)
f-mr-.......... Morocco [*MARC geographic area code*] [*Library of Congress*] (LCCP)
FMR-1......... Fragile Mental Retardation [*A gene*] (PAZ)
FMRA........... Foreign Media Representatives Association
FMRAAM..... Future Medium-Range AAM (SAUS)
FMRAAM..... Future Medium-Range Air-to-Air Missile (WDAA)
FM range..... frequency modulation range (SAUS)
FMRC........... Farmrail [*Federal Railroad Administration identification code*]
FMRC........... Fibrous Materials Research Center (SAUS)
FMRC........... Financial Management Research Center (SAUO)
FMRC........... Fixed Motor Run Capacitor
FMR Corp.... Fidelity Management & Research Corporation (SAUO)
FM-RD......... Farm-to-Market Road (SAUO)
FMRD.......... Flight Mission Rules Document [*NASA*] (KSC)
FMREC......... Force Mobilization Review and Evaluation Committee [*Military*] (MCD)
FM-Relation... female-male relation (SAUS)
FMRF........... Femarfarmamide [*Biochemistry*]
F MRG DR Y... Failure to Merging Driver to Yield Right of Way [*Conviction term used in state of Oregon*] (MVRD)
FMRI........... Functional Magnetic Resonance Imaging
fMRI........... Functional Magnetic Resonance Imaging
FMRL........... Ford Motor Research Laboratories (SAUS)
FMRL........... Form Roll
FMRL........... Functional Machine Representation Language [*Computer science*] (CSR)
FMRLY......... Formerly (EY)
FMRM.......... Field Management Reference Manual (SAUS)
FM RoyT....... Freeport-McMoran Oil & Gas Royalty Trust [*Associated Press*] (SAG)
FMRP........... Freeport McMoRan Resource Partners Ltd. [*Associated Press*] (SAG)
FMRR........... Financial Management Rate of Return [*Business term*]
FMRS........... Federal Mediation and Reconciliation Service (MHDB)
FMRS........... Force Movement Requirements System (SAUO)
FMRS........... Forecast Movement Requirements System (SAUO)
FMRS........... Foreign Member of the Royal Society [*British*] (BARN)
FMRS........... Fuels Management Requirements System (SAUO)
FMR-T......... Field Material-Handling Robot Technology [*US Army Human Engineering Laboratory*] (RDA)
FMRT........... Final Meteorological Radiation Tape
FMRT........... Frequency Modulation Real Time (ACAE)
FMRU.......... Farm Machinery Research Unit (SAUS)
FMRX........... FemRx, Inc. [*NASDAQ symbol*] (SAG)
FMS............ ERL-Ada Financial System Management (SAUO)
FMS............ Facilities Management System
FMS............ Facility Management System (SAUS)
FMS............ Facility Mapping Systems Inc. (SAUO)
FMS............ Facility Monitoring System (SAUS)
FMS............ Facsimile Mail System (SAUS)
FMS............ Factory Management System [*General Electric Co.*]
FMS............ Factory Mutual System [*Formerly, AFMFIC*] [*Group of four insurance companies and an engineering organization*]
FMS............ Fallout Monitoring Station [*Civil Defense*]
FMS............ False Memory Syndrome (SAUS)
FMS............ Famous
FMS............ Farm Management Service (SAUS)
FMS............ Farm Management System (SAUS)
FMS............ Fathoms (RIMS)
FMS............ Fatigue Monitoring System (MCD)
FMS............ Fat-Mobilizing Substance [*Medicine*]
FMS............ Fecal Management System [*NASA*] (KSC)
FMS............ Federal Management System (GFGA)
FMS............ Federal Mining and Smelting Co. (SAUO)
FMS............ Federal Music Society (EA)
FMS............ Federated Malay States
FMS............ Federation Mondiale des Sourds [*World Federation of the Deaf - WFD*] [*Rome, Italy*] (EA)
FMS............ Federation of Malay States (SAUO)
FMS............ Federation of Materials Societies (EA)
FMS............ Feline McDonough Sarcoma [*Virus*]
FMS............ Fellow of the Institute of Management Services [*British*] (DBQ)
FMS............ Fellow of the Medical Society [*British*]
FMS............ Fellow of the Meteorological Society [*British*]
FMS............ Ferranti Modular Sonar (SAUS)
FMS............ fetal monitoring system (SAUS)
FMS............ Fibromyalgia Syndrome [*Medicine*]
FMS............ Fieldbus Message Specification (SAUS)
FMS............ Field Maintenance Shop [*Army*] (NATG)
FMS............ Field Maintenance Squadron [*Air Force*] (MCD)
FMS............ Field Maintenance System
FMS............ Field Marketing Specialist (TIMI)
FMS............ Field Music School [*Marine Corps*]
FMS............ Fighter Missile System
FMS............ File Maintenance System (MCD)
FMS............ File Management Supervisor [*Honeywell, Inc.*]
FMS............ File Management System [*Computer science*] (HODG)
FMS............ Final Multiple Score (NVT)
FMS............ Financial Management System
FMS............ Financial Managers Society (EA)
FMS............ Financial Managers' Statement [*Financial Managers' Society*] [*A publication*]
FMS............ Fire Marking System (SAUS)
FMS............ First Marathon, Inc. [*Toronto Stock Exchange symbol*]
FMS............ First Melt Sample (SAUS)
FMS............ Fleet Management System [*Arrencross Ltd.*] [*Software package*] (NCC)
FMS............ Fleet Material Support [*Navy*]
FMS............ Fleet Medical School (DOMA)
FMS............ Fleet Mine Sweeper (SAUS)
FMS............ Fleet Music School
FMS............ Flexible Machine System [*Industrial engineering*]
FMS............ Flexible Machining System (DOMA)
FMS............ Flexible Manufacturing System (SEWL)
FMS............ Flexible Measuring System (SAUS)
FMS............ Flexible Modular Scheduling (EDAC)
FMS............ Flight Managing System (SAUS)
FMS............ Flight Mission Simulation Test (MCD)
FMS............ Flight Motion Simulator
FMS............ Floating Machine Shop
FMS............ Floating Maintenance Shop (MCD)
FMS............ Floating Marine Repair Shop [*Army ship designation*] (POLM)
FMS............ Flow Measuring System
FMS............ Fluid Management System (SSD)
FMS............ Fluorouracil, Mutamycin, Streotozocin [*Antineoplastic drug*] (CDI)
fms............ flush metal saddle (SAUS)
FMS............ Flux Monitoring System [*Nuclear energy*] (NRCH)
FMS............ Flying Medical Samaritans (SAUS)
FMS............ Food Management System [*or Subsystem*] (MCD)
FMS............ Foramen Magnum Syndrome [*Medicine*] (EDAA)
FMS............ Force Management System [*Air Force*] (GFGA)
FMS............ Force Measuring System (KSC)
FMS............ Force Module Subsystem (DOMA)
FMS............ Ford Motor Sport (SAUS)
FMS............ Foreign Military Sales (AFM)
FMS............ Foreign Military Service (MCD)
FMS............ Formal Message Service (SAUO)
FMS............ formation microscanner logging tool (SAUS)
FMS............ Forms Management System [*Computer science*]
FMS............ Fort Myers Southern (SAUO)
FMS............ Fort Myers Southern Railroad Co. [*AAR code*]
FMS............ FORTRAN [*Formula Translating System*] Monitor System [*Computer science*]
FMS............ Frankfurt-Marburg Syndrome [*Medicine*] (DB)
FMS............ Franklin Mint Society (SAUO)
FMS............ Fratres Maristae Scholarum [*Marist Brothers of the Schools*] [*Also known as Little Brothers of Mary*] (EAIO)
FMS............ Free-Machining Steel

FMS .... Freeway Management System
FMS .... French Meteorological Society (SAUS)
FMS .... Frequency Management System [ITU] [United Nations] (DUND)
FMS .... Frequency Mixer Stage
FMS .... Frequency Monitoring System (SAUS)
FMS .... Frequency-Multiplexed Subcarrier
fms .... frequency multiplexed subcarrier (SAUS)
FMS .... Frequency Multiplier Storer
FMS .... Fresenius Medical AG ADS [NYSE symbol] (SG)
FMS .... Fresenius Medical Care AG [NYSE symbol] (SAG)
FMS .... Friends Mission Society (SAUO)
FMS .... Fuel Management System (SAUS)
FMS .... Fuel-Monitoring System [Cheshire County Council] [Software package] (NCC)
FMS .... Full Mouth Series [Dentistry]
FMS .... Future Management Services [A Lebanese arms company] (ECON)
FMS .... Fuze Maintenance Spares (NG)
FMS .... Hadison Aviation [Sudan] [ICAO designator] (FAAC)
fms .... Marist Brothers (TOCD)
FMSA .... Ambalavao [Madagascar] [ICAO location identifier] (ICLI)
FMSA .... Federal Managers Support Agency (SAUS)
FMSA .... Fellow of the Mineralogical Society of America
FMSA .... Foreign Military Sales Act (AFIT)
fmsa .... frequency measuring spectrum analyzer (SAUS)
FMSA .... Future Military Systems Authority
FMSAEG .... Fleet Missile Systems Analysis and Evaluation Group [Navy]
FMSAEGA .... Fleet Missile Systems Analysis and Evaluation Group Annex [Navy] (MCD)
FMSAEGANX... Fleet Missile Systems Analysis and Evaluation Group Annex [Navy] (DNAB)
FMSAEL .... Fleet Missile Systems Analysis and Evaluation Laboratory (MCD)
FMsB .... Barry College, Miami Shores, FL [Library symbol] [Library of Congress] (LCLS)
FMSB .... Beroroha/Antsoa [Madagascar] [ICAO location identifier] (ICLI)
FMSB .... First Mutual Savings Bank [NASDAQ symbol] (NQ)
FMSB .... First Mutual Svgs (WA) [NASDAQ symbol] (TTSB)
FMSBA .... Farmers and Manufacturers Beet Sugar Association (SAUO)
FMSC .... Federal Manual for Supply Cataloging (AABC)
FMSC .... Federation Mondiale des Societes de Cuisiniers [World Association of Cooks Societies - WACS] (EA)
FMSC .... Film Magazine Stowage Container (MCD)
FMSC .... Fixed Motor Starting Capacitor
FMSC .... Flexible Manufacturing System Complex (SAUS)
FMSC .... Franciscan Missionary Sisters of the Sacred Heart [Roman Catholic religious order]
FMSC .... Mandabe [Madagascar] [ICAO location identifier] (ICLI)
FMSCEUA .... Federated Municipal and Shire Council Employees' Union of Australia
FMSCL .... Flexible Manufacturing System Complex provided with Laser (SAUS)
FMSCR .... Foreign Military Sales Credit [Financing]
FMSCSEL........ Foreign Military Sales Consolidated Support Equipment List (MCD)
FMSD .... Facilities Management and Services Division [Environmental Protection Agency] (GFGA)
FMSD .... Tolagnaro [Madagascar] [ICAO location identifier] (ICLI)
FMSE .... Betroka [Madagascar] [ICAO location identifier] (ICLI)
FM-SE .... International Falcon Movement - Socialist Educational International (SAUO)
FMSF .... False Memory Syndrome Foundation (SAUS)
FMSF .... Fianarantsoa [Madagascar] [ICAO location identifier] (ICLI)
FMSF .... Foreign Military Sales Financing
FMS Fn .... FMS Financial Corp. [Associated Press] (SAG)
FMSG .... Farafangana [Madagascar] [ICAO location identifier] (ICLI)
FMSGT .... Field Music Sergeant [Marine Corps]
FMSH .... Federal Mine Safety and Health (SAUO)
FMSH .... Full Mazda Service History [Automotive classified advertising]
FMSH .... Full Mercury Service History [Automotive classified advertising]
FMSH .... Full Mitsubishi Service History [Automotive classified advertising]
FMSHRC .... Federal Mine Safety and Health Review Commission (EG)
FMSHRD .... Federal Mine Safety and Health Review Decisions [A publication] (DLA)
FMSI .... Filii Mariae Salutis Infirmorum [Sons of Mary, Health of the Sick] [Roman Catholic religious order]
FMSI .... Folk Music Society of Ireland (EAIO)
FMSI .... Food Machinery Service Institute (EA)
FMSI .... Friction Materials Standards Institute (EA)
FMSI .... Ihosy [Madagascar] [ICAO location identifier] (ICLI)
FMSI .... Sons of Mary Missionary Society (TOCD)
fmsi .... Sons of Mary Missionary Society (TOCD)
FM signal .... frequency-modulated signal (SAUS)
FMS II .... Financial Management System (SAUO)
FMSJ .... Franciscan Missionaries of St. Joseph [Mill Hill Sisters] [Roman Catholic religious order]
FMSJ .... Manja [Madagascar] [ICAO location identifier] (ICLI)
FMSJ .... Mill Hill Sisters (TOCD)
Fm Sk .... Form Skip (SAUS)
FMSK .... Manakara [Madagascar] [ICAO location identifier] (ICLI)
FMSL .... Bekily [Madagascar] [ICAO location identifier] (ICLI)
FMSL .... Fort Monmouth Signal Laboratory [Army]
FMSLGR .... Federation of Master Saddlers and Leather Goods Retailers (SAUO)
FMSM .... Federation Mondiale pour la Sante Mentale [World Federation for Mental Health]
FMSM .... Mananjary [Madagascar] [ICAO location identifier] (ICLI)
FMSMG .... Financial Management System Management Group (SAUO)
FMSMP .... Foreign Military Sales Management Plan (AFIT)
FMSN .... Tanandava-Samangoky [Madagascar] [ICAO location identifier] (ICLI)
FMSO .... Fleet Material Support Office [Navy]
FMSO .... Foreign Military Sales Order [Army] (AABC)
FMSO .... Foreign Military Studies Office
FMSO .... Ranohira [Madagascar] [ICAO location identifier] (ICLI)
FMSP .... Facility Management and Site Planning (SAUS)
FMSP .... [A] Fool and His Money Are Soon Parted (ROG)
FMSP .... Foreign Military Sales Program [Army] (AABC)
FMSP .... Foundation for Social and Preventive Medicine (SAUO)
FMSP .... Frequency Modulation Signal Processor (NASA)
FMSPA .... Fish and Meat Spreadable Products Association [British] (DBA)
FMSq .... Field Maintenance Squadron [Air Force] (AFM)
FMSR .... Daughters of Our Lady of Holy Rosary (TOCD)
FMSR .... Facilities Management System (SAUO)
FMSR .... Fast Mixed Spectrum Reactor (SAUS)
FMSR .... Federated Malay States Reports [A publication] (DLA)
FMSR .... Federation des Mouvements Socialistes Regionalistes de la Reunion [Federation of Socialist Regionalist Movements of Reunion] [Political party] (PPW)
FMSR .... Final Mission and Systems Review (ACAE)
FMSR .... Finite Mass Sum Rule [Nuclear science] (OA)
FMSR .... Morombe [Madagascar] [ICAO location identifier] (ICLI)
FMSS .... Financial and Merchandising Service System (SAUS)
FMSS .... Financial Management Systems [A publication]
FMSS .... Financial Management Systems Software (AAGC)
FMSS .... Five-Minute Speech Sample (SAUS)
FMSS .... Fleet Medical Service School (DNAB)
FMSS .... Force Module Subsystem (SAUO)
FMST .... Field Missile Specification Test
FMST .... Field Missile System Test
FMST .... Finishmaster, Inc. [NASDAQ symbol] (SAG)
FMST .... Foreign Military Sales Training
FMST .... Frequency Mass Spectrometer Tube
FMST .... Toliara [Madagascar] [ICAO location identifier] (ICLI)
FMSTI .... FMS Transaction Input System (SAUO)
FMSTIU .... FMS Transaction Input & Update System (SAUO)
FMSU .... Forward Mobile Support Unit
FMSV .... Betioky [Madagascar] [ICAO location identifier] (ICLI)
FMSVR .... Federated Malay Straits Volunteer Reserve [British military] (DMA)
FMSWR .... Flexible Mild Steel Wire Rope
FMSY .... Ampanihy [Madagascar] [ICAO location identifier] (ICLI)
FMSZ .... Ankazoabo [Madagascar] [ICAO location identifier] (ICLI)
FMT .... Facilities Maintenance Team [Military]
FMT .... Factory Marriage Test
FMT .... Farrer Memorial Trust [Australia]
FMT .... Feature Machine Type (SAUS)
FMT .... Federation of Merchant Tailors of Great Britain, Inc. (BI)
FMT .... Fetal Maturity Test [Medicine] (EDAA)
FMT .... Field Maintenance Technician
FMT .... Field Modification Task (MCD)
FMT .... Field Modulation Technique (SAUS)
FMT .... File Management Task (TIMI)
FMT .... Firemont Genl [NYSE symbol] (TTSB)
FMT .... Firmware Measurement Tool (SAUS)
FMT .... Flight Management Team [Skylab] [NASA]
FMT .... Flour-Milling Technology (OA)
FMT .... Fluoro-meta-tyrosine [Organic chemistry]
FMT .... Flush Metal Threshold [Technical drawings]
FMT .... Force Modernization Training [Military]
FMT .... Foreign Material for Training (MCD)
FMT .... Foreign Military Training (CINC)
FMT .... Foremost Energy Corp. [Vancouver Stock Exchange symbol]
FMT .... Format
FMT .... format error (SAUS)
FMT .... Foundation for Medical Technology (EA)
FMT .... Frankfurt Main Terminal (SAUS)
FMT .... Freemasons Tavern [Freemasonry] (ROG)
FMT .... Free Memory Table (SAUS)
FMT .... Freiberg Mining and Technology (SAUO)
FMT .... Fremont General Corp. [NYSE symbol] (SPSG)
FMT .... Fremont Genl [NYSE symbol] (SG)
FMT .... Frequency-Modulated Transmitter [Telecommunications]
FMT .... Friction Measurement Test
FMT .... Full Mission Trainer (SAUS)
FMT .... Functional Message Type [Communications]
FMTA .... Farm Machinery and Tractor Trade Association (SAUO)
FMTA .... Federal Mass Transportation Act (SAUS)
FMTA .... Federation Mondiale de Travailleurs Agricoles [World Federation of Agricultural Workers - WFAW] (EAIO)
FMTA .... Flash Mass Thermal Analysis (KSC)
FMTAG .... Foreign Military Training Affairs Group (SAUS)
FMTB .... Force Mobilization Troop Bases (SAUO)
FMTB .... Foreign Military Training Board (AAGC)
fmtb .... frequency-modulation feedback (SAUS)
FMTC .... Familial Medullary Thyroid Carcinoma [Oncology]
FMTC .... Farm Mechanization Training Centre (SAUS)
FMTE .... Field Maintenance Test Equipment
FMTM .... Frequency Modulation Team (IAA)
FMTM .... Friction Materials Test Machine
FMTMF .... Foreign Military Training Management Flight
FMTNM .... Federation Mondiale des Travailleurs Non-Manuels [World Federation of Trade Unions of Non-Manual Workers - WFNMW] [Antwerp, Belgium] (EAIO)
FMTO .... Form Tool
FMTP .... File Management Transaction Processor
FMTPr .... Fremont Genl Fin 1 9%'TOPrS' [NYSE symbol] (TTSB)

FMTR.......... Florida Missile Test Range (MUGU)
FMTR.......... Formatter (MCD)
FMTS.......... Federation Mondiale des Travailleurs Scientifiques [*World Federation of Scientific Workers - WFSW*] (EAIO)
FMTS.......... Field Maintenance Test Set
FMTS.......... Field Maintenance Test Station [*Military*] (AFIT)
FMTS.......... Flat Moving Target Screen [*Weaponry*] (INF)
FMTT.......... Forward Medical Treatment Team [*Army*] (INF)
FMTV.......... Family of Medium Tactical Vehicles [*Military*] (RDA)
FM-TV.......... Frequency Modulation-Television (SAUS)
FMTZ.......... Ford Motor Track [*Federal Railroad Administration identification code*]
FMU.......... Farm Machinery Unit (SAUS)
FMU.......... Federated Mining Union (SAUO)
FMU.......... Field Management Unit (HEAS)
FMU.......... Field Medical Unit (SAUS)
FMU.......... Files Management Unit [*Computer science*]
FMU.......... Financial Management Unit [*LIMRA*]
FMU.......... First-Morning Urine (MELL)
FMU.......... Flow Management Unit [*Aviation*] (FAAC)
FMU.......... Force Measurement Unit
FMU.......... Force Measuring Unit (SAUS)
FMU.......... Forecasting and Monitoring Unit (SAUO)
FMU.......... Forms Management Utility [*Computer science*] (HODG)
FMU.......... Freight Multiple Unit (SAUS)
FMU.......... Fuel Management Unit (SAUS)
FMU.......... Functional Mock-Up (KSC)
FMU.......... Function Memory Unit
FMU.......... Fundus Monitoring Unit (SAUS)
FMU.......... Fuze Munition Unit (ACAE)
f-mu-.......... Mauritania [*MARC geographic area code*] [*Library of Congress*] (LCCP)
FMU.......... University of Miami, Coral Gables, FL [*Library symbol*] [*Library of Congress*] (LCLS)
FMU-L.......... University of Miami, Law Library, Coral Gables, FL [*Library symbol*] [*Library of Congress*] (LCLS)
F-MuLV.......... Friend Murine Leukemia Virus
FMU-M.......... University of Miami, Medical Library, Miami, FL [*Library symbol*] [*Library of Congress*] (LCLS)
FMU-Mu.......... University of Miami, Music Library, Coral Gables, FL [*Library symbol*] [*Library of Congress*] (LCLS)
FM Unit.......... Forecasting and Monitoring Unit (SAUS)
FMU-R.......... University of Miami, Rosenstiel School of Marine and Atmospheric Sciences, Miami, FL [*Library symbol*] [*Library of Congress*] (LCLS)
FMUSIC.......... Federation of Military and United Services Institutes of Canada
FMUX.......... Flexible Multiplexer (SAUS)
FMV.......... Fair Market Value [*Bargaining term*]
FMV.......... Fluorouracil, Methyl-CCNU, Vincristine [*Antineoplastic drug*] (CDI)
FMV.......... Foreign Market Value [*Business term*]
FMV.......... Formation Volume Factor (SAUS)
FMV.......... Frangipani Mosaic Virus [*Plant pathology*]
FMV.......... Full Motion Video (BARN)
FMV.......... United States Veterans Administration Hospital, Miami, FL [*Library symbol*] [*Library of Congress*] (LCLS)
FMVCP.......... Federal Motor Vehicle Control Program (GNE)
FMVE.......... Perfluoro Methyl Vinyl Ether (SAUS)
FMVEME.......... Federation of Malaya Volunteer Electrical and Mechanical Engineers [*British military*] (DMA)
FMVFT.......... Frequency Modulation Voice Frequency Telegraph (VLIE)
FM-VFT System... Frequency-Modulated Voice-Frequency-Telegraphy System (SAUS)
FMVJ.......... Federation Mondiale des Villes Jumelees-Cites Unies [*United Towns Organisation - UTO*] (EA)
FMVP.......... Framework Member Validation Project (AAEL)
FMVRC.......... Federation of Malaya Volunteer Reconnaissance Corps [*British military*] (DMA)
FMVSS.......... Federal Motor Vehicle Safety Standard
FMVT.......... Failure Mode Verification Testing (VLIE)
FMVTPS.......... Federal Motor Vehicle Theft Prevention Standard [*Automotive engineering*]
FMW.......... Fast Magnetosonic Wave (PDAA)
FMW.......... Federation of Masons of the World (EA)
FMW.......... First Main Watch
f-mw-.......... Malawi [*MARC geographic area code*] [*Library of Congress*] (LCCP)
FMW.......... Mount Fremont [*Washington*] [*Seismograph station code, US Geological Survey*] (SEIS)
FMW.......... World University-Miami, Miami, FL [*Library symbol*] [*Library of Congress*] (LCLS)
FMWA.......... First Mutual Savings Bank of Washington [*Associated Press*] (SAG)
FMWA.......... Fixed Momentum Wheel Assembly (SAUS)
FMWA.......... Florida Movers and Warehousemen's Association (SRA)
FMWC.......... Federation of Medical Women of Canada (SAUO)
FMWF.......... Free Methodist World Fellowship (EA)
FMWG.......... Fuels and Materials Working Group (SAUO)
FMWOS.......... Facility Management Work Order System (SAUO)
FMWS.......... Fairbanks Morse Weighing Systems (SAUS)
FMW T.......... Field Merge by World Trade (SAUS)
FMWTC.......... Fleet Mine Warfare Training Center (DNAB)
FMWU.......... Federated Miscellaneous Workers' Union of Australia
FMWWR.......... Fire, Mildew, Water, and Weather Resistant (MCD)
FMWX.......... Fillmore & Western [*Federal Railroad Administration identification code*]
FMX.......... Fire & Manoeuvre Exercise (SAUS)
FMX.......... Flexible Multiplexer (SAUS)
FMX.......... Flyball Master Excellent
FMX.......... FM Transmitter (SAUS)
FMX.......... Fomento Economico ADS [*NYSE symbol*] (SG)
FMX.......... Frequency-Modulated Transmitter [*Telecommunications*] (KSC)
FMX.......... Frequency Modulation Transmitter (SAUS)
FMX.......... Full Mouth Radiograph (SAUS)
FMX.......... Full Mouth Radiography (SAUS)
FMX.......... Full Mouth X-Ray [*Dentistry*]
FMXI.......... Foamex International [*NASDAQ symbol*] (SAG)
FMY.......... Foreign Missons of Yarumal [*Colombia*] (EAIO)
FMY.......... Fort Myers [*Florida*] [*Airport symbol*] (OAG)
FMY.......... Fort Myers, FL [*Location identifier*] [*FAA*] (FAAL)
FMY.......... Meyer [*Fred*], Inc. [*NYSE symbol*] (SPSG)
FMYX.......... FM Yorke and Son [*Private rail car owner code*]
f-mz-.......... Mozambique [*MARC geographic area code*] [*Library of Congress*] (LCCP)
FN.......... Air Carolina [*ICAO designator*] (AD)
FN.......... Facilities north (SAUS)
F/N.......... Facing North [*In outdoor advertising*] (WDMC)
Fn.......... Factonimbus (SAUS)
FN.......... False Negative [*Medicine*]
FN.......... Family Name (SAUS)
FN.......... Fault Management (SAUS)
Fn.......... Female (Neutered) (SPVS)
FN.......... Fence [*Technical drawings*]
FN.......... Fenley & Nicol Co., Inc. (EFIS)
FN.......... Fernald Area Office (SAUS)
FN.......... Ferrite Number (SAUS)
FN.......... Fiber Node
FN.......... Fibronectin [*Biochemistry*]
FN.......... Field Manager (SAUS)
fn.......... Filemame (SAUS)
FN.......... File Name (SAUS)
FN.......... File Number (SAUS)
FN.......... Filter Network (SAUS)
FN.......... Financial [*Rate*] [*Value of the English pound*]
FN.......... Find Number (MSA)
fn.......... Fine (SAUS)
FN.......... Finger Nail [*Medicine*] (EDAA)
F-N.......... Finger to Nose Test [*Neurology*]
FN.......... Finish (SAUS)
FN.......... Fireman [*Nonrated enlisted man*] [*Navy*]
FN.......... First Name
FN.......... First Nation (FOTI)
FN.......... First National Corp. (California) [*AMEX symbol*] (COMM)
FN.......... First Nucleotide (DB)
F/N.......... Fixing Note (RIMS)
FN.......... Flange Nut (SAUS)
FN.......... Flat Nose [*Projectile*]
FN.......... Flat Nose Projectile (SAUS)
FN.......... Flat or Nested [*Freight*]
FN.......... Flight Nurse
FN.......... Flip Number [*Number of times an animal can right itself when placed on its back*] [*Veterinary science*] (DB)
FN.......... Fluoride Number (MAE)
FN.......... Fog Nautophone [*Navigation charts*]
FN.......... Fog Nozzle (EEVL)
FN.......... Foil Normal (SAUS)
fn.......... Footnote (WDMC)
FN.......... Footnote
fn.......... foot note (SAUS)
FN.......... Foreign National (ADWA)
FN.......... Foreign Patent Number (NITA)
fn.......... formerly nested (SAUS)
FN.......... Form Number (VLIE)
FN.......... Foundation Name [*Dialog*] [*Searchable fields*] [*Information service or system*] (NITA)
FN.......... Franco-Nevada Mining Corp. [*Toronto Stock Exchange symbol*]
FN.......... Frazer Nash [*Automobile manufacturer*] [*British*]
FN.......... Freelance Network [*Defunct*] (EA)
FN.......... Freenet (SAUS)
f/n.......... freight note (SAUS)
FN.......... French Navy (NATG)
FN.......... Fridtjof Nansen (SAUS)
FN.......... Friends of Nature (EA)
FN.......... Front National [*Belgium*] [*Political party*] (EY)
FN.......... Front National [*Gabon*] [*Political party*] (EY)
FN.......... Front National [*France*] [*Political party*] (PPW)
Fn.......... Froude number (SAUS)
FN.......... Fruitarian Network (EA)
FN.......... Full Employment [*Economics*]
fn.......... Function (AAMN)
FN.......... Function (GOBB)
FN.......... Functional Network
FN.......... Function Name (SAUS)
FN.......... Fusion (WGA)
FN.......... Futures Network [*Ormskirk, Lancashire, England*] [*Defunct*] (EA)
Fn.......... [*The*] Holy Bible in Modern English (1903) [*Ferrar Fenton*] [*A publication*] (BJA)
FN.......... Night First Class [*Airline fare code*]
fn---.......... Sudan (Region) [*MARC geographic area code*] [*Library of Congress*] (LCCP)
FNA.......... Federation of National Associations (EA)
FNA.......... Fellow of the Indian National Science Academy [*Formerly, FNI*]
FNa.......... Filtered Sodium (MAE)
FNA.......... Final Approach [*Aviation*]

FNA............ Final Network Acceptance (SAUS)
FNA............ Fine-Needle Aspiration [*Medicine*]
FNA............ Firing Needle Assembly (SAUS)
FNA............ Flora North America Program [*Defunct*] (EA)
FNA............ Florenville, LA [*Location identifier*] [*FAA*] (FAAL)
FNA............ Florida Nurses Association (SAUO)
FNA............ Flugfelag Nordurlands [*Iceland*] [*ICAO designator*] (FAAC)
FNA............ Following Named Airmen
FNA............ For Necessary Action (ADA)
FNA............ Free Network Addresses (SAUS)
FNA............ Free Network Architecture (VLIE)
FNA............ Freetown [*Sierra Leone*] [*Airport symbol*] (OAG)
FNA............ French North Africa
FNA............ Frequency Network Analyzer
FNA............ Fujitsu Network Architecture [*Fujitsu Ltd.*] [*Japan*]
FNA............ Fuming Nitric Acid (KSC)
FNA............ Functional Name Addresses
FNAA............ Fast Neutron Activation Analysis [*Analytical chemistry*]
FNAA............ Fellow of the National Association of Auctioneers (SAUO)
FNAA............ Fellow of the National Association of Auctioneers, House Agents, Rating Surveyors and Valuers (SAUO)
FNAB............ Fine-Needle Aspiration Biopsy [*Medicine*]
FNaC............ Collier County Free Public Library, Naples, FL [*Library symbol*] [*Library of Congress*] (LCLS)
FNAC............ Federation Nationale d'Achats des Cadres [*Initials alone now used as name of discount-store chain in France*] [*Pronounced "f-nak"*]
FNAC............ Fine Needle Aspiration Cytology (DAVI)
FNADT............ Fuel and Transportation (SAUS)
FNAEA............ Fellow of the National Association of Estate Agents [*British*] (DBQ)
FNAF............ Front National pour l'Algerie Francaise [*National Front for French Algeria*] [*Political party*]
FNAI............ Florida Natural Areas Inventory [*Information service or system*] (IID)
FNAL............ Fermi National Accelerator Laboratory [*Also, FERMILAB*] [*Batavia, IL*] [*Department of Energy*]
fnal............ Functional (SAUS)
FNAM............ Ambriz [*Angola*] [*ICAO location identifier*] (ICLI)
FNAM............ Fishes of the North-eastern Atlantic and the Mediterranean (SAUS)
FNAN............ Luanda [*Angola*] [*ICAO location identifier*] (ICLI)
FNAO............ Fellow of the National Association of Opticians [*British*] (DAS)
FNAOE............ Federation of National AFS Organizations in Europe [*Brussels, Belgium*] (EAIO)
FNAOO............ Fellow of the National Association of Optometrists and Opticians (SAUO)
FNAP............ FORTRAN Network Analysis Program (SAUS)
FNAP............ FORTRAN Network-Analysis Program (SAUO)
FNAP............ FORTRAN Network-Analysis Programme (SAUS)
FNAR............ Financial Need Analysis Report
FNARS............ Federal National Radio System (DEMM)
FNARS............ FEMA [*Federal Emergency Management Agency*] National Radio System (GFGA)
FNASR............ First North American Serial Rights (ADWA)
FNAT............ First National Entertainment Corp. [*NASDAQ symbol*] (SAG)
FNAT............ First National Entmt [*NASDAQ symbol*] (TTSB)
FNATS............ Federal National Teletype System (DEMM)
F/Nav............ Flight Navigator (AIA)
FNAVS............ Federal National Voice System (DEMM)
FNAWS............ Foundation for North American Wild Sheep (EA)
FNB............ Falls City, NE [*Location identifier*] [*FAA*] (FAAL)
FNB............ False Negative Rate [*Medicine*] (DAVI)
FNB............ Federation Nationale du Batiment [*France*] (NITA)
FNB............ File Name Block [*Computer science*] (MHDB)
FNB............ First Chicago Corp. [*NYSE symbol*] (SPSG)
FNB............ First National Bank (EFIS)
FNB............ Fitzherbert's Natura Brevium [*A publication*] (DLA)
FNB............ FNB Corp. [*Associated Press*] (SAG)
FNB............ Food and Nutrition Bibliography (SAUS)
FNB............ Food and Nutrition Board (EA)
FNB............ Fort Necessity National Battlefield, Farmington, PA [*OCLC symbol*] (OCLC)
FNB............ Free National Block (SAUO)
FNBA............ Fellow of the North British Academy (DAS)
FNBA............ First National Bancorp of Allentown (SAUO)
FNBB............ First National Bank of Boston (SAUO)
FNBC............ Fellow of the National Board for Certification (SAUO)
FNBC............ First National Bank of Chicago (SAUO)
FNBC............ Four Nations Beef Conference (SAUO)
FNBC............ Franklin Bancorp [*NASDAQ symbol*] (SAG)
FNBC............ Franklin Bancorporation [*NASDAQ symbol*] (TTSB)
FNBC............ M'Banza-Congo [*Angola*] [*ICAO location identifier*] (ICLI)
FNBDT............ Future Narrow Band Digital Terminal (SEWL)
FnBen............ Financial Benefit Group, Inc. [*Associated Press*] (SAG)
FNBF............ Florida National Banks of Florida, Inc. (SAUO)
FNBF............ FNB Financial Services Corp. [*NASDAQ symbol*] (SAG)
FNBF............ FNB Financial Svcs [*NASDAQ symbol*] (TTSB)
FNB FS............ FNB Financial Services Corp. [*Associated Press*] (SAG)
FNBG............ Benguela [*Angola*] [*ICAO location identifier*] (ICLI)
FNBN............ FNB Corp. [*North Carolina*] [*NASDAQ symbol*] (SAG)
FNBP............ Far North Bicentennial Park (SAUO)
FNBP............ FNB Corp. [*NASDAQ symbol*] (NASQ)
FNB PA............ FNB Corp. (Pennsylvania) [*Associated Press*] (SAG)
FNBR............ Fast Neutron Breeder Reactor [*Nuclear energy*] (DEN)
FNBR............ FNB Rochester Corp. [*NASDAQ symbol*] (SAG)
FNBRo............ FNB Rochester Corp. [*Associated Press*] (SAG)
FNC............ Family Nurse Clinician [*Medicine*] (EDAA)
FNC............ Fast Neutron Cavity
FNC............ Fatty Nutritional Cirrhosis (DB)
FNC............ Federal National Council (United Arab Emirates) [*Political party*] (PSAP)
FNC............ Federal Networking Council [*Computer science*] (TNIG)
FNC............ Federal Networking Council, USA (SAUS)
FNC............ Federation Nationale des Communications [*National Federation of Communication*] [*Canada*] (EAIO)
FNC............ Fence
FNC............ Ferritic Nitrocarburizing (SAUS)
FNC............ Ferrocarriles Nacionales de Colombia [*National Railways of Colombia*] (EY)
fnc............ finance (SAUS)
FNC............ Fine-Needle Cholangiography [*Gastroenterology*]
FNC............ Finlay Fork [*British Columbia*] [*Seismograph station code, US Geological Survey*] [*Closed*] (SEIS)
FNC............ Finnish National Committee of the IEC (SAUO)
FNC............ First National City Corporation (SAUO)
FNC............ First National Corp. [*AMEX symbol*] (SG)
FNC............ Fixed Niobium Capacitor
FNC............ Flexible Numerical Control [*Manufacturing engineering*] [*Computer science*]
FNC............ Flexible Nylon Coupling
FNC............ Focus National Mortgage Corp. [*Toronto Stock Exchange symbol*]
FNC............ Food and Nutrition Collection (SAUS)
FNC............ Fox News Channel
FNC............ Frente Nacional Constitucionalista [*National Constitutionalist Front*] [*Ecuador*] [*Political party*] (PPW)
FNC............ Frente Nacional Opositora [*National Opposition Front*] [*Panama*] [*Political party*] (PPW)
FNC............ Friends of Nicaraguan Culture (EA)
FNC............ Front National de Concertation [*Haiti*] [*Political party*] (EY)
FNC............ Funchal [*Portugal*] [*Airport symbol*] (OAG)
FNC............ Future Naval Capability
FNC............ Future Nurses Clubs [*National League for Nursing*] (AEBS)
FNCA............ Cabinda [*Angola*] [*ICAO location identifier*] (ICLI)
FNCA............ Federation of Nordic Commercial Agents [*Stockholm, Sweden*] (EA)
FNCB............ Camembe [*Angola*] [*ICAO location identifier*] (ICLI)
FNCB............ First National City Bank [*Later, Citibank*] [*New York City*]
FNCC............ Cacolo [*Angola*] [*ICAO location identifier*] (ICLI)
FNCC............ Federation Nationale des Cooperatives de Cereales
FNCC............ Foreign Claims Commission (SAUS)
FNCD............ Front National pour le Changement et la Democratie [*Haiti*] [*Political party*] (EY)
FNCETA............ Federation Nationale des Centres d'Etudes Techniques Agricoles
fncg............ financing (SAUS)
FNCH............ Chitato [*Angola*] [*ICAO location identifier*] (ICLI)
FNCI............ Financial News Composite Index [*Pronounced "fancy"*] [*Financial News Network*]
FNCJ............ Fine Needle Catheter Jejunostomy [*Medicine*] (DMAA)
fncl............ financial (SAUS)
FnclSec............ Financial Security Assurance Holdings [*Associated Press*] (SAG)
FnclSvcs............ Financial Services Acquisition Corp. [*Associated Press*] (SAG)
FNCM............ Camabatela [*Angola*] [*ICAO location identifier*] (ICLI)
FNCM............ Fellow, National College of Music [*London, England*] (ADA)
FNCM............ Fellow of the National College of Music (SAUO)
FNCM............ Finet.com, Inc. [*NASDAQ symbol*] (SG)
FNCO............ Funco, Inc. [*NASDAQ symbol*] (SAG)
FNCRT............ Fellow of the National College of Rubber Technology [*British*]
FNCS............ Food, Nutrition, and Consumer Services
FncSv............ Financial Svcs. Acquisition Corp. [*Associated Press*] (SAG)
FNCTN............ Function (FAAC)
FNCUMA............ Federation Nationale des Cooperatives d'Utilisation de Materiel Agricole
FNCV............ Cuito Cuanavale [*Angola*] [*ICAO location identifier*] (ICLI)
FNCX............ Camaxilo [*Angola*] [*ICAO location identifier*] (ICLI)
FNCY............ Fancy
FNCZ............ Cazombo [*Angola*] [*ICAO location identifier*] (ICLI)
FND............ Baltimore, MD [*Location identifier*] [*FAA*] (FAAL)
FND............ Facility Need Date (NASA)
FND............ Fast Neutron Dose
FND............ Febrile Neutrophilic Dermatosis [*Medicine*] (EDAA)
FND............ Fender [*s*] [*Freight*]
FND............ Finnemore's Notes and Digest of Natal Cases [*A publication*] (DLA)
FND............ First Chicago Corp. [*NYSE symbol*] (SAG)
FND............ First Chi NBD 5.50% 'DECS'97 [*NYSE symbol*] (TTSB)
FND............ First Northern Capital [*NYSE symbol*] [*Formerly, First Northern Savings Bank*] (SG)
FND............ Focal Neurological Deficit [*Medicine*] (EDAA)
FND............ Fonds National de Developpement [*Mauritania*] (EY)
FND............ Found
FND............ Foundation [*Technical drawings*]
fnd............ foundered (SAUS)
FND............ Frank Nelson Doubleday [*American publisher*]
FND............ Friends of Neil Diamond (EA)
FND............ Frontul National Democratic [*National Democratic Front*] [*Romania*] [*Political party*] (PPE)
fnd............ Funder/Sponsor [*MARC relator code*] [*Library of Congress*] (LCCP)
FNDAT............ Foundation Directory (SAUO)
FNDB............ Damba [*Angola*] [*ICAO location identifier*] (ICLI)
FNDD............ Founded
FNDD............ Funded (ROG)
FNDF............ Federal National Democratic Front [*Myanmar*] [*Political party*] (PD)
FNDG............ Finding
FNDG............ Founding
FNDG............ Funding (KSC)

FNDH .... Foreign National Direct Hire [*Military*]
FNDI .... First Nations Development Institute (EA)
FNDMNTLST ... Fundamentalist
FNDN .... Foundation
FNDNG .... Funding
fndobj .... Found Object (VRA)
FNDP .... Frente Nacional Democratico Popular [*Popular National Democratic Front*] [*Mexico*] (PD)
FNDR .... Fender [*Automotive engineering*]
FNDR .... Founder
FNDR .... National Front for the Defense of the Revolution (Madagascar) [*Political party*] (PSAP)
FndrFn .... Founders Financial Corp. [*Associated Press*] (SAG)
fndrs .... fenders (SAUS)
Fndry .... Foundry (BARN)
FNDRY .... Foundry
FNDT .... Fundtech, Ltd. [*NASDAQ symbol*] (NASQ)
fndtn .... Foundation (MIST)
fndtn .... Foundation (RION)
FNDTN .... Foundation
FNE .... Faisceaux Nationalistes Europeens [*European Nationalist Alliances*] [*France*] (PD)
FNE .... Fane [*Papua New Guinea*] [*Airport symbol*] (OAG)
FNE .... Fear of Negative Evaluation Scale (EDAC)
fne .... Fine [*Quality of the bottom*] [*Nautical charts*]
FNE .... Finnsnes [*Norway*] [*Airport symbol*] (AD)
FNE .... Following Named Enlisted Personnel
FNE .... Free Nerve Ending [*Anatomy*]
FNEA .... Federation of National Electrolysis Associations [*Defunct*] (EA)
FNEA .... First Nations Environmental Assessment (SAUO)
FNECInst ...... Fellow of the North East Coast Institution of Engineers and Shipbuilders [*British*]
FNEG .... False Negative [*Medicine*]
FNEORID ...... Following Named Enlisted Member Organization Indicated
FNEP .... Federal Nuclear Emergency Plan (FOTI)
FNERAS ...... Following Named Enlisted Members Are Relieved Assignment
FNERP .... Federal Nuclear Emergency Response Plan (FOTI)
FNES .... Field Network Evaluation Study [*Survey*]
FNESA .... Federation of New England Surveyors Associations (SAUS)
FNET .... Fuzzy Network (PDAA)
FNEUC .... Federation Nationale des Etudiants des Universites Canadiennes [*National Federation of Canadian University Students*]
FNF .... Families Need Fathers [*British*] [*An association*] (DBA)
FNF .... Fidelity Financial Corp. [*NYSE symbol*] (SAG)
FNF .... Fidelity Natl Finl [*NYSE symbol*] (SG)
FNF .... Finger-Nose-Finger [*Test*] [*Neurology*] (DAVI)
FNF .... Finnish Air Force Headquarters [*ICAO designator*] (FAAC)
FNF .... First Normal Form (MHDB)
FNF .... Flash Non-Fragmentation (SAUS)
FNF .... Flying Needle Frame (SAUS)
FNF .... Foundation for the New Freeman (EA)
FNF .... Friday-Night Fracas (WDAA)
FNF .... Friedrich Naumann Foundation (SAUO)
FNFA .... Fellow of the National Federation of Accountants [*British*] (DAS)
FNFC .... First National Finance Corporation (SAUO)
FNFC .... First National Financial Co. [*British*]
FNFHFTM .... Federation of Needle Fish Hook and Fishing Tackle Makers [*British*] (BI)
FNFL .... Forces Navales Francaises Libres [*Free French Naval Forces*] [*World War II*]
FNFP .... First Nations Financial Project (EA)
FNG .... Fada N'Gourma [*Burkina Faso*] [*Airport symbol*] (OAG)
FNG .... Firan Corp. [*Toronto Stock Exchange symbol*]
FNG .... Frontier Guard, Finland [*FAA designator*] (FAAC)
FNG .... Furnishing (SAUS)
f-ng- .... Niger [*MARC geographic area code*] [*Library of Congress*] (LCCP)
FNGAA .... Federation Nationale des Groupements Agricoles d'Approvisionnement
FNGB .... First Northen Capital [*NASDAQ symbol*] (TTSB)
FNGB .... First Northern Capital Corp. [*NASDAQ symbol*] (SAG)
FNGB .... First Northern Savings Bank SA [*NASDAQ symbol*] (NQ)
FNGC .... Frontier Natural Gas [*NASDAQ symbol*] (SAG)
FNGCP .... Frontier Nat Gas $1.20 Cv Ptd [*NASDAQ symbol*] (TTSB)
FNGCW .... Frontier Natural Gas Wrrt [*NASDAQ symbol*] (TTSB)
FNGDA .... Farmers National Grain Dealers Association (SAUO)
FNGI .... N'Giva [*Angola*] [*ICAO location identifier*] (ICLI)
FNGIREA ...... First National Group of Independent Real Estate Agents Ltd. [*Australia*]
FNGP .... Federation Nationale des Gaullistes de Progres [*National Federation of Progressive Gaullists*] [*France*] [*Political party*] (PPW)
FNGS .... Fellow, National Gastroenterologists Society (CMD)
FNGS .... Fellow, National Genealogical Society (SAUS)
FNGU .... N'Gunza [*Angola*] [*ICAO location identifier*] (ICLI)
FNH .... Familial Neonatal Hypoglycemia [*Medicine*] (MELL)
FNH .... First National Bankshares, Inc. [*AMEX symbol*] (SAG)
FNH .... First Natl Bankshares(LA) [*AMEX symbol*] (TTSB)
FNH .... Flashless Nonhygroscopic [*Gunpowder*]
FNH .... Focal Nodular Hyperplasia [*Medicine*]
FNH Gunpowder ... Flashless Nonhygroscopic Gunpowder (SAUS)
FNHO .... Forum of National Hispanic Organizations (EA)
FNHP .... Federation of Nurses and Health Professionals (EA)
FNHR .... Febrile Nonhemolytic Reaction [*Medicine*] (MELL)
FNHS .... Fairbanks Neighborhood Housing Services (SAUO)
FNHU .... Huambo [*Angola*] [*ICAO location identifier*] (ICLI)
FNI .... Facial Nerve Involvement [*Medicine*]
FNI .... Fan In
FNI .... Federation Naturiste Internationale [*International Naturist Federation*]
FNI .... Fellow of the National Institute of Sciences in India [*Later, FNA*]
FNI .... Fellow of the National Institute of Sciences of India (SAUO)
FNI .... FNI Fashion, Inc. [*Vancouver Stock Exchange symbol*]
FNI .... Following Named Individuals
FNI .... Foreign National Indirect (NVT)
FNI .... Nimes [*France*] [*Airport symbol*] (OAG)
FNIAL .... Fellow of the National Institute of Arts and Letters [*British*]
FNIC .... Food and Nutrition Information and Educational Materials Center (SAUS)
FNIC .... Food and Nutrition Information and Educational Materials Centre (SAUS)
FNIERC .... Food & Nutrition Information & Educational Resources Center (SAUO)
FNIF .... Florence Nightingale International Foundation [*Defunct*] (EA)
FNIH .... Fellow of the National Institute of Hardware [*British*] (DBQ)
FNILP .... Fellow of the National Institute of Licensing Practitioners (SAUO)
FNIMC .... Florida Normal and Industrial Memorial College (SAUO)
FNIMH .... Fellow of the National Institute of Medical Herbalists [*British*]
FNIN .... Financial Inds [*NASDAQ symbol*] (TTSB)
FNIN .... Financial Industries Corp. [*NASDAQ symbol*] (NQ)
FNiO .... Okaloosa-Walton Junior College, Niceville, FL [*Library symbol*] [*Library of Congress*] (LCLS)
FNIS .... Fellow of the National Institute of Sciences of India (SAUO)
FNJ .... Feng Yang-Pyongyang [*North Korea*] [*Airport symbol*] (AD)
FNJ .... Fort Gordon, GA [*Location identifier*] [*FAA*] (FAAL)
FNJ .... Front National de la Jeunesse [*National Youth Front*] [*France*] (PD)
FNJ .... National Front for Justice (Comoros) [*Political party*] (PSAP)
FNJ .... Pyongyang [*North Korea*] [*Airport symbol*] (OAG)
FNJ FDC ...... United States Food and Drug Administration. Notices of Judgment: Foods [*A publication*] (DLA)
FNK .... Fin Creek, AK [*Location identifier*] [*FAA*] (FAAL)
Fn key .... Function Key (CDE)
FNKFI .... Frankfort, KS [*American Association of Railroads railroad junction routing code*]
FNKU .... Kuito/Bie [*Angola*] [*ICAO location identifier*] (ICLI)
FNL .... Fansteel, Inc. [*NYSE symbol*] (SPSG)
FNL .... Final (NASA)
FNL .... Five New Laender [*Lands*] [*Name given to former East German territory after unification*]
FNL .... Flight Navigator's Licence [*British*] (AIA)
FNL .... Fort Collins/Loveland, CO [*Location identifier*] [*FAA*] (FAAL)
FNL .... Friends of the National Libraries [*British*]
FNL .... Fund for New Leadership [*Defunct*] (EA)
FNLA .... Front National de Liberation de l'Angola [*Angolan National Liberation Front*] (PD)
FNLB .... Front National de Liberation de Bretagne [*National Liberation Front of Brittany*] [*France*] (PD)
FNLB .... Lobito [*Angola*] [*ICAO location identifier*] (ICLI)
FNLG .... Front National de Liberation Guyanais [*Guiana National Liberation Front*] [*French Guiana*] (PD)
FNLLP .... Formyl(norleucyl)(leucyl)phenylalanine [*Biochemistry*]
FNLM .... Friends of the National Library of Medicine (ADWA)
fnl qtr .... filnal quarter (SAUS)
FNLU .... Luanda/4 De Fevereiro [*Angola*] [*ICAO location identifier*] (ICLI)
FNLW .... Foundation for Non-Lethal Warfare [*Defunct*] (EA)
fnly .... finally (SAUS)
FNLY .... Finlay Enterprises [*NASDAQ symbol*] (TTSB)
FNLY .... Finlay Enterprises, Inc. [*NASDAQ symbol*] (SAG)
fnlz .... finalize (SAUS)
FNM .... Fancamp Resources Ltd. [*Vancouver Stock Exchange symbol*]
FNM .... Federal National Mortgage Association [*Wall Street slang name: "Fannie Mae"*] [*NYSE symbol*] (SPSG)
FNM .... Federal Natl Mtge [*NYSE symbol*] (TTSB)
FNM .... Ferrocarriles Nacionales de Mexico [*National Railways of Mexico*]
FNM .... Financial Network Manager (BUR)
FNM .... Free National Movement [*Bahamas*] [*Political party*] (PPW)
FNMA .... Federal National Mortgage Administration (PA)
FNMA .... Federal National Mortgage Association
FNMA .... Front National Martiniquais pour l'Autonomie [*Martinique National Front for Autonomy*] [*Political party*] (PPW)
FNMA .... Malanje [*Angola*] [*ICAO location identifier*] (ICLI)
FNMA SPCL ... Fannie Mae Special (SAUO)
FNmB .... Barry College, North Miami, FL [*Library symbol*] [*Library of Congress*] (LCLS)
FNME .... Menongue [*Angola*] [*ICAO location identifier*] (ICLI)
FNMI .... FN Manufacturing Inc. (SAUS)
FNMO .... Mooamedes/Yuri Gagarin [*Angola*] [*ICAO location identifier*] (ICLI)
FNMOC .... Fleet Numerical Meteorology and Oceanography Center (SAUO)
FNMP .... Foreign Newspaper Microfilm Project (SAUS)
FNMPrA ...... Federal Natl Mtge 6.41% Pfd [*NYSE symbol*] (TTSB)
FNMPrB ...... Federal Natl Mtge 6.50% Pfd [*NYSE symbol*] (TTSB)
FNMQ .... Maquela [*Angola*] [*ICAO location identifier*] (ICLI)
F-NMR .... Fluorinated Nuclear Magnetic Resonance (SAUS)
FNMRI .... flow NMR imaging (SAUS)
FNMS .... Foundation for Nager and Miller Syndromes (NRGU)
FNN .... Feed-Forward Neural Network (AAEL)
FNN .... Fiji News Network (SAUO)
FNN .... Financial News Network [*Cable-television system*]
FNN .... Franconia Notch [*New Hampshire*] [*Seismograph station code, US Geological Survey*] [*Closed*] (SEIS)
FNNG .... Finnigan Corp. [*NASDAQ symbol*] (COMM)
FNNG .... Negage [*Angola*] [*ICAO location identifier*] (ICLI)
FNNH .... Fabrique Nationale Nouvelle Herstal (SAUS)

FNNI .... Financial News Network, Incorporated (SAUO)
FNNPE .... Federation of Nature and National Parks of Europe (EERA)
FNNPE .... Federation of Nature and Natural Parks of Europe (SAUO)
FNNWR .... Fort Niobrara National Wildlife Refuge (SAUO)
FNO .... Clinton, IA [*Location identifier*] [*FAA*] (FAAL)
FNO .... Fan Out
FNO .... Following Named Officers
FNO .... Foreign Namespace Object (MWOL)
FNO .... Frente Nacional de Oposicion [*National Opposition Front*] [*Guatemala*] [*Political party*]
FNO .... Frente Nacional de Oposicion [*National Opposition Front*] [*Venezuela*] [*Political party*]
FNOA .... Following Named Officers and Airmen
FNOC .... Fleet Numerical Oceanographic (or Oceanography) Center (SAUO)
FNOC .... Fleet Numerical Operations Center (SAUS)
FNOIO .... Fleet Naval Ordnance Inspecting Officer
FNOR .... Florida Northern Railroad [*Federal Railroad Administration identification code*]
F NOT CND VH... Failure to Notify a Subsequent Purchaser of the Condition of a Vehicle [*Conviction term used in state of Oregon*] (MVRD)
FNOW .... [*The*] Future Now, Inc. [*NASDAQ symbol*] (SPSG)
FNP............. Family Nurse Practitioner
FNP............. Fijian Nationalist Party [*Political party*] (PPW)
FNP............. Fjordland National Park (SAUS)
FNP............. Floating Nuclear Plant [*or Powerplant*] [*ERDA*]
FNP............. Floating Nuclear Power Plant (SAUS)
FNP............. Fonds Non Publics (SAUO)
FNP............. Force, Net Propulsive
FNP............. Foreign Newspaper Project (SAUS)
FNP............. Foundation for National Progress (EA)
FNP............. Frente Nacional de Panama [*Panamanian National Front*] [*Political party*] (PD)
FNP............. Friends of the National Parks (SAUO)
FNP............. Front-End Network Processor
FNP............. Front Network Processor (SAUS)
FNP............. Fundy National Park (SAUO)
FNP............. Fusion Point
FNP............. National Progressive Force (Dominican Rep.) [*Political party*] (PSAP)
FNP............. University of North Florida, Jacksonville, FL [*OCLC symbol*] (OCLC)
FNPA .... Foreign Numbering Plan Area [*AT & T*] [*Telecommunications*] (TEL)
FNPA .... Porto Amboim [*Angola*] [*ICAO location identifier*] (ICLI)
FNPB .... Sanza Pombo [*Angola*] [*ICAO location identifier*] (ICLI)
FNPF........... Fiji National Provident Fund (SAUO)
FNPH .... Foreningen Nordiska Pappershistoriker [*Association of Nordic Paper Historians - NPH*] [*Stockholm, Sweden*] (EAIO)
FNPLT......... Front Nationaliste Progressiste pour la Liberation de la Tunisie [*Progressive Nationalist Front for the Liberation of Tunisia*] [*Political party*] (PD)
FNPOR........ Federation of National Professional Organizations for Recreation (EA)
FNPP .... Floating Nuclear Power Plant Study [*Marine science*] (MSC)
FNPR........... Federation of Independent Trade Unions of Russia (ECON)
FNPR........... Friends of National Public Radio [*Defunct*] (EA)
FN Projectile... Flat Nose Projectile (SAUS)
FNprP .... Pasco County Library System, New Port Richey, FL [*Library symbol*] [*Library of Congress*] (LCLS)
FNPT........... Fusion Point
FNQ .... Franklin Quest [*NYSE symbol*] (TTSB)
FNQ .... Franklin Quest Co. [*NYSE symbol*] (SAG)
FNQR........... Far North Queensland Regiment [*Australia*]
FNR .... Ferromagnetic Nuclear Resonance (SAUS)
FNR .... File Next Register
FNR .... Flexible Nuclear Response (SAUO)
FNR .... Flores & Rucks [*NYSE symbol*] (TTSB)
FNR .... Flores & Rucks, Inc. [*NYSE symbol*] (SAG)
FNR .... Ford Nuclear Reactor
FNR .... Foundations Resources [*Vancouver Stock Exchange symbol*]
FNR .... Foward Neutral Reverse
FNR .... Front National de Renouvellement [*Algeria*] [*Political party*] (EY)
FNR .... Funter Bay [*Alaska*] [*Airport symbol*] (OAG)
FNR .... Funter Bay, AK [*Location identifier*] [*FAA*] (FAAL)
FNR .... National Reconstruction Front (Ecuador) [*Political party*] (PSAP)
f-nr- .... Nigeria [*MARC geographic area code*] [*Library of Congress*] (LCCP)
FNRA .... Federal National Railroad Association [*Proposed railroad corporation*] [*Nickname: Fannie Rae*]
FNRA .... First Nations Responsible Authority (SAUO)
FNRC .... Federal Nuclear Regulatory Commission (SAUO)
FNRC .... Federated Natural Resources Corporation (SAUO)
FNRC .... Financial Network Readiness Consortium (VLIE)
FNRC .... Food and Nutrition Research Center (SAUO)
FNREB .... Food and Nutrition Research and Engineering Board [*Military*] (RDA)
FNRI .... Federation Nationale des Republicains Independants [*National Federation of Independent Republicans*] [*France*] [*Political party*] (PPW)
FNRI .... Flores & Rucks, Inc. [*NASDAQ symbol*] (SAG)
FNRL .... Funeral
FNRM .... Friends of the National Rail Museum [*Indian Railway*] (TIR)
FNRS .... Finite Number Representation System (SAUS)
FNS............. Factory Network System (SAUS)
FNS............. Failure Notification Sheet (KSC)
FNS............. Family and Neighborhood Services
FNS............. Federal News Service [*Database*] (IID)
FNS............. Federated Naming Service (VLIE)
FNS............. Federation of Netherlands Societies [*Australia*]
FNS............. Feedback Node Set
FNS............. Feminist News Service
FNS............. File-Nesting Store [*Computer science*] (OA)
FNS............. First National State Bancorporation (SAUO)
FNS............. Flash-Nitrogen Supply
fns .... flask-nitrogen supply (SAUS)
FNS............. Food and Nutrition Service [*Department of Agriculture*]
FNS............. Foreign Nation Support (COE)
FNS............. Forever Nonstatic (IAA)
FNS............. formule normale du sang (SAUS)
FNS............. Frame Network Server [*Tylink Corp.*]
FNS............. Frontier Nursing Service (EA)
FNS............. Full NAEGIS Site (SAUS)
FNS............. Functional Neuromuscular Stimulation [*Physiotherapy*]
FNS............. Functional Neuromuscular Stimulator (SAUS)
FNS............. Functional Nomenclature Signal
FNS............. Functional Signal (SAUS)
FNS............. Fusion Neutron Source (SAUS)
FNS............. Fuzzy Neuron Syndrome
FNS............. USDA Food and Nutrition Service (SAUS)
FNSA .... Frente Nacional Socialista Argentino [*Argentinian National Socialist Front*] [*Political party*] (PD)
FNSA .... Saurimo [*Angola*] [*ICAO location identifier*] (ICLI)
FNSAE .... Fellow of the National Society of Art Education (SAUO)
FNSBB .... Federation Nationale des Syndicats du Batiment et du Bois, Inc. [*National Federation of Shipyard and Woodworkers Unions*]
FNSC .... Federation pour une Nouvelle Societe Caledonienne [*Federation for a New Caledonian Society*] [*Political party*] (PPW)
FNSC .... Financial Security Corp. [*NASDAQ symbol*] (SAG)
FNSCC .... Federation of Nuclear Shelter Consultants and Contractors [*British*] (DBA)
FNSF........... Fast Night Striking Force [*British military*] (DMA)
FNSH .... Finish (MSA)
FNSH .... Full Nissan Service History [*Automotive classified advertising*]
fnshd .... finished (SAUS)
fnshg .... finishing (SAUS)
fnshr........... finisher (SAUS)
FNSH SPEC... Finish Specification (SAUS)
FNSI............ Finding of No Significant Impact
FNSID .... Fellow of the National Society of Interior Designers
FNSII .... Federation Nationale des Syndicats d'Infirmieres et d'Infirmiers [*National Federation of Nurses' Unions - NFNU*]
FNSL............ Fixed Nozzle Slow [*or Short*] Landing (MCD)
FNSM........... Faculty of Natural Sciences and Mathematics (SAUS)
FNS Nomenclature... Functional Signal Nomenclature (SAUS)
FNSO .... Soyo [*Angola*] [*ICAO location identifier*] (ICLI)
FNSRO .... Food and Nutrition Service Regional Office [*Department of Agriculture*] (GFGA)
FNSS .... FMC-Nurol Savunma Sanayii (SAUS)
FNSSC .... Franciscan Sisters of Our Lady of the Sacred Heart (TOCD)
FNST............ Finest
fnstr............ Fenestration (VRA)
FNT.............. Aerostar Airlines, Inc. [*ICAO designator*] (FAAC)
FNT.............. Failure Notification Telex (MCD)
FNT.............. False Neurochemical Transmitter [*Medicine*] (DMAA)
FNT.............. Fenestra, Inc. (SAUO)
FNT.............. Fermat Number Transform (SAUS)
FNT.............. File Name Table [*Computer science*] (MHDB)
FNT.............. Finger-to-Nose Test (MELL)
FNT.............. First Nations Tax (FOTI)
FNT.............. Flint [*Michigan*] [*Airport symbol*] (OAG)
FNT.............. Flint, MI [*Location identifier*] [*FAA*] (FAAL)
Fnt.............. Fonit [*Record label*] [*Italy*]
fnt.............. Font (VLIE)
FNT.............. Fort Nelson [*Hobart*] [*Tasmania*] [*Seismograph station code, US Geological Survey*] [*Closed*] (SEIS)
FNT.............. Fowler-Nordheim tunneling (SAUS)
fnt.............. Front (VRA)
FNT.............. Frontline Communications [*AMEX symbol*] (SG)
FNT.............. Fusion Nuclear Technology (SAUS)
FNT.............. National Worker's Front (Nicaragua) [*Political party*] (PSAP)
FNTA............ Farnesyltransferase [*An enzyme*]
FNTBB .... Federation Nordique des Travailleurs du Batiment et du Bois [*Nordic Federation of Building and Wood Workers - NFBWW*] (EAIO)
FNtBsh......... First National Bankshares, Inc. [*Associated Press*] (SAG)
FNTC............ Frente Nacional de Trabajadores y Campesinos [*National Workers' and Peasants' Front*] [*Peru*] [*Political party*] (PPW)
FNtGa .... First National Bancorp of Gainesville [*Associated Press*] (SAG)
FNTGNS....... Frontogenesis [*NWS*] (FAAC)
FNthCap....... First Northern Capital Corp. [*Associated Press*] (SAG)
FNthSB .... First Northern Savings Bank SA [*Associated Press*] (SAG)
FNTL............ FINTEL (SAUS)
FNTLYS........ Frontolysis [*NWS*] (FAAC)
FNTMH .... Flush Non-Tight Manhole (SAUS)
FNTO .... Finnish National Travel Office (SAUO)
FNTO .... Toto [*Angola*] [*ICAO location identifier*] (ICLI)
fntpc .... Frontispiece (VRA)
FNT Pr......... Frontline Commun. Cv'B' Pfd. [*AMEX symbol*] (SG)
FNTS............ France Telecom Network Services (SAUO)
FNTS............ Fujitsu Network Transmission Systems, Inc. (SAUO)
FNTSTIC ...... Fantastic
FNTSY .... Fantasy
FNTT............ Femoral Nerve Traction Test [*Medicine*] (MELL)
F-N tunneling... Fowler-Nordheim Tunneling (SAUS)
FNU .... Family Nursing Unit
FNU .... First Name Unknown

FNU .... Forces des Nations Unies [*United Nations Forces*]
FNU .... Foreningarna Nordens Ungdomsrepresentation (SAUO)
FNU .... Front National Uni [*United National Front*] [*The Comoros*]
FNUA .... Luau [*Angola*] [*ICAO location identifier*] (ICLI)
FNUAP .... Fondo de Poblacion de las Naciones Unidas [*United Nations Population Fund*] [*Spanish*] (DUND)
FNUAP .... Fonds des Nations Unies pour la Population [*United Nations Population Fund*] [*French*] (DUND)
FNUB .... Lubango [*Angola*] [*ICAO location identifier*] (ICLI)
FNUDD .... Front for National Unity, Democracy and Development (SAUS)
FNUE .... Fonds des Nations Unies pour l'Enfance [*United Nations Children's Fund*] (EAIO)
FNUE .... Luena [*Angola*] [*ICAO location identifier*] (ICLI)
FNUG .... Uige/Vige [*Angola*] [*ICAO location identifier*] (ICLI)
FNUI .... Fellow of the National University of Ireland (DI)
FNUK .... Front National Uni des Komores [*National United Front of the Comoros*] [*Political party*] (PD)
f-number...... diameter of a lens aperture in relation to its focal length (SAUS)
f number...... focal length of a lens (SAUS)
F Number .... Fraction Number (SAUS)
FNUR .... Fonds des Nations Unies pour les Refugies [*United Nations Funds for Refugees*]
FNV............. Festuca Necrosis Virus [*Plant pathology*]
FNV............. Field Not Valid (SAUS)
FNV............. FINOVA Group [*NYSE symbol*] (TTSB)
FNV............. Finova Group, Inc. [*NYSE symbol*] (SAG)
FNV............. Frame Not Valid (SAUS)
FNV............. Partido Federacion Nacional Velasquista [*National Velasquista Federation*] [*Ecuador*] [*Political party*] (PPW)
FNVA .... Farm Net Value-Added (EURO)
FNW............. First Nationwide Bank A Federal Savings Bank [*NYSE symbol*] (SAG)
FNWA .... Federal Noxious Weed Act
FNWA .... Foreign National Weather Agency
FNWC .... Fleet Numerical Weather Center [*Monterey, CA*] [*Navy*]
FNWF........... Fleet Numerical Weather Facilities (SAUS)
FNWF........... Fleet Numerical Weather Facility
FNWK .... Wako-Kungo [*Angola*] [*ICAO location identifier*] (ICLI)
FNWPr .... First Nationwide Bk 11.50% Pfd [*NYSE symbol*] (TTSB)
FNX............. Fenix Airways [*Latvia*] [*FAA designator*] (FAAC)
FNX............. Fort Knox Gold Resources, Inc. [*Toronto Stock Exchange symbol*]
FNXA .... Xangongo [*Angola*] [*ICAO location identifier*] (ICLI)
FNY............. French Navy
FNYFS .... Florida Network of Youth and Family Services (SRA)
FNYFX .... First Investors N.Y. Insured Tax Free [*Mutual fund ticker symbol*] (SG)
FNZ............. Friends of the National Zoo (EA)
FNZ............. Huntingburg, IN [*Location identifier*] [*FAA*] (FAAL)
FNZDT .... Federation of New Zealand Dancing Teachers (SAUO)
FNZE............ N'Zeto/N'Zeto [*Angola*] [*ICAO location identifier*] (ICLI)
FNZIA........... Fellow of the New Zealand Institute of Architects
FNZIAS .... Fellow of the New Zealand Institute of Agricultural Science
FNZIC........... Fellow of the New Zealand Institute of Chemistry
FNZIE........... Fellow of the New Zealand Institution of Engineers
FNZLA........... Fellow of the New Zealand Library Association
FNZP............ Flunitrazepam [*A hypnotic*]
FNZSA .... Fellow of the New Zealand Society of Accountants (SAUO)
FNZSID .... Fellow of the New Zealand Society of Industrial Designers (SAUO)
FO.............. Alon, Inc. [*ICAO aircraft manufacturer identifier*] (ICAO)
FO.............. Fabrication Order (MCD)
FO.............. Fabrication Outline (MCD)
fo............... faced only (SAUS)
FO.............. Facilities Office (COE)
FO.............. Factory Order
FO.............. Faculty Of (SAUS)
FO.............. Faculty of Ophthalmologists [*British*]
FO.............. Faculty of Ophthalmology (SAUO)
FO.............. Fade Out [*Films, television, etc.*]
FO.............. Fail Open [*Nuclear energy*] (NRCH)
FO.............. Fail Operation [*NASA*] (KSC)
FO.............. Fail Operational (SAUS)
FO.............. Fails Open (SAUS)
FO.............. Fairest One [*Genotype of Phlox paniculata*]
FO.............. Fallout (IIA)
FO.............. Familiarization and Orientation (SAUS)
F/O............. Families within Orders (DICI)
FO.............. Fan Out
FO.............. Faroe Islands [*ANSI two-letter standard code*] (CNC)
FO.............. Fast Operate (SAUS)
FO.............. Fast Operating [*Relay*]
f/o.............. father of (SAUS)
FO.............. Fatty Oil
F/O............. Feature Film Only (ADA)
f/O.............. female Oriental (SAUS)
FO.............. Fiber Optic [*Data transmission*] (TEL)
FO.............. Fibre Optics (SAUS)
FO.............. Field-Grade Officer (ADWA)
FO.............. Field Office [*or Officer*]
FO.............. Field Officer (SAUO)
FO.............. Field Operational [*Test*] (NATG)
FO.............. Field Operations (SAUS)
FO.............. Field Order
FO.............. File Organization (VLIE)
FO.............. File Output (SAUS)
FO.............. Filter Output (AAG)
FO.............. Finance Officer [*Army*]
FO.............. Fine Old
FO.............. Firing Order
FO.............. Firm Offer [*Business term*]
FO.............. Firm Order [*Business term*]
FO.............. first occurrence (SAUS)
FO.............. First Officer (ADA)
FO.............. First Open [*First class train compartment*] (DCTA)
FO.............. Fishery Officer [*Ministry of Agriculture, Fisheries, and Food*] [*British*]
FO.............. Fitting Out [*Navy*] (NG)
FO.............. Fixed Oil
FO.............. Flag Officer [*Navy*]
FO.............. Flank Observation (SAUS)
FO.............. Flash Operate Relay
FO.............. Flashover (SAUS)
FO.............. Flash Override [*Telecommunications*] (TEL)
FO.............. Flat Oval [*Technical drawings*]
FO.............. Fleet Operations [*Navy*] (MCD)
FO.............. Fleet Order (SAUS)
FO.............. Flight Officer [*Air Force*]
FO.............. Flight operations (SAUS)
FO.............. Flight Order
FO.............. Flight Orderly
FO.............. Flintkote Co. (SAUO)
FO.............. Fluoroorotate [*Organic chemistry*]
FO.............. Flying Officer [*British*]
F/O............. Flyout
FO.............. Foam System [*NFPA pre-fire planning symbol*] (NFPA)
FO.............. Foldout (MSA)
fo............... Folio (WA)
FO.............. Folio
FO.............. Follow On (ACAE)
F-O............. Follow-On (ACAE)
fo............... Fomentation [*Pharmacology*] (DAVI)
FO.............. Font (DNAB)
FO.............. Foot Orthosis [*Medicine*]
FO.............. For (SAUS)
FO.............. Foramen Ovale [*Anatomy*]
FO.............. Forced-Oil (SAUS)
FO.............. Forced Oscillation (SAUS)
F/O............. Force Objective (CINC)
FO.............. Force Out [*Baseball*]
F/O............. For Credit Of (WDAA)
FO.............. Forecast Order (SAUS)
FO.............. Foreign Object
FO.............. Foreign Office
FO.............. Foreign Order (ADA)
FO.............. Foreign to Occupation [*Insurance*]
fo............... formal offer (SAUS)
Fo.............. Formation (SAUS)
Fo.............. Fornax (SAUS)
fo............... For Orders (EBF)
FO.............. For Orders
fo............... Forsterite [*CIPW classification*] [*Geology*]
FO.............. Fortissimo [*Very Loud*] [*Music*] (ROG)
FO.............. Fortune Brands [*NYSE symbol*] [*Formerly, American Brands*] (SG)
FO.............. Forwarding Order (SAUS)
FO.............. Forward Oblique (CAAL)
FO.............. Forward Observation (SAUS)
FO.............. Forward Observer [*Military*]
FO.............. Fouled Out [*Sports*] (IIA)
Fo.............. Fourier Number [*IUPAC*]
FO.............. Fraction Optimizing
FO.............. Fragmented Order [*Military*] (VNW)
FO.............. Fragment Offset (SAUS)
FO.............. Frame Offset (SAUS)
FO.............. Frame Outstanding (VLIE)
FO.............. Free Out [*Shipping*]
FO.............. Free Overside
fo............... freight on (SAUS)
FO.............. Frente Obrero [*Workers' Front*] [*Nicaragua*] [*Political party*] (PD)
fo............... Frequency of the carrier (SAUS)
FO.............. Fridays Only [*British railroad term*]
FO.............. Friends Outside [*An association*] (EA)
FO.............. Fronto-Occipital [*Anatomy*]
FO.............. Fuel Oil
FO.............. Fuels operations (SAUS)
F/O............. Fuel to Oxidizer [*Ratio*]
FO.............. Full Organ [*Music*]
FO.............. Full Out [*Typesetting*]
F/O............. Full Out Terms [*Business term*] [*British*] (ROG)
FO.............. Functional Objective (KSC)
FO.............. furnace oil (SAUS)
FO.............. Oil-Immersed Forced-Oil-Cooled [*Transformer*] (IEEE)
Fo.............. orbital Frequency (SAUS)
FO.............. Orlando Public Library, Orlando, FL [*Library symbol*] [*Library of Congress*] (LCLS)
FO.............. Southern Nevada [*ICAO designator*] (AD)
FO.............. Worker's Force (France) [*Political party*] (PSAP)
FO .... Federal Official (ODA)
FOA............ Faculty of Advocates [*British*] (DAS)
FOA............ Failure to Obtain Action (AAG)
FOA............ Farmers Organization Authority (SAUO)
FOA............ Federation of Orthodontic Associations (EA)
FOA............ Fellow of Advertising [*British*]

FOA............. Fiber Optic Association (DDC)
FOA............. Field office accounting (SAUS)
FOA............. Field Office Assistant [*Red Cross*]
FOA............. Field Operating Activity (AAGC)
FOA............. Field Operating Agency (MCD)
FOA............. Filipinas Orient Airways, Inc. [*Philippines*] [*ICAO designator*] (FAAC)
FOA............. Financial Operations Association (EA)
FOA............. First of America Bank [*NYSE symbol*] (SPSG)
FOA............. First of America Bk [*NYSE symbol*] (TTSB)
FOA............. Fitting Out Availability [*Navy*]
FOA............. Fleet Operational Assets (ACAE)
FOA............. Flora, IL [*Location identifier*] [*FAA*] (FAAL)
FOA............. Fluoroorotic Acid [*Organic chemistry*]
FOA............. Foam (SAUS)
FOA............. FOB Airport [*"INCOTERM," International Chamber of Commerce official code*]
FOA............. Focus on Africa [*A publication*]
FOA............. Football Officials Association
FOA............. Forced Oil and Air (MSA)
FOA............. Forced-Oil and Forced-Air Cooling (SAUS)
FOA............. Foreign Operations Administration [*Later, ICA*]
FOA............. Foreign Operations Agency (SAUO)
FOA............. Foreign-Owned or Affiliated [*Business term*]
FOA............. Foresters of America
FOA............. Forsvarets Forskningsanstalt [*Research Institute of National Defense*] [*Information service or system*] (IID)
foa............. free of average (SAUS)
FOA............. Free on Aircraft [*Cargo delivery term for export traffic*] (DCTA)
FOA............. Freezer Owners Association of America, Inc. (SAUO)
FOA............. Friends of Animals (EA)
FOA............. Fugitive Other Authorities [*FBI standardized term*]
FOA............. Full Operational Assessment (ADWA)
FOA............. Fund of America (SAUO)
FOA............. Oil-Immersed Forced-Oil-Cooled with Forced-Air Cooler [*Transformer*] (IEEE)
FOA............. Weather Forecasting Office Advanced (SAUS)
FOAA........... Flying Optometrists Association of America (EA)
FOAC........... Federal Office Automation Center (SAUS)
FOAC........... Federal Office Automation Conference (HGAA)
FOAC........... Flag Officer, Aircraft carrier (SAUS)
FOAC........... Flag Officer, Aircraft Carriers (SAUS)
FOAC........... Flag Officer, Atlantic Coast [*Canada*]
FOAD........... Field Operations Analysis Digest (ACAE)
FOAE........... Finding of Adverse Effect [*Environmental science*] (COE)
FOAF........... Friend of a Friend [*Urban folklore term coined by Rodney Dale*]
FOAFB......... Forbes Air Force Base [*Kansas*] (AAG)
FOAFOAG..... Father Of A Friend Of A Girlfriend (SAUS)
FOAG........... father of a girlfriend (SAUS)
FOAIB.......... Flag Officer, Admiralty Interview Board [*Navy*] [*British*]
FOALLS........ Far Off Axis LASER Location System (SEWL)
FOAM........... Fast Ocean-Atmosphere Model (SAUS)
FOAM........... Fates of Aromatic Model (SAUS)
FOAM........... Fluorouracil, Oncovin [*Vincristine*], Adriamycin, Mitomycin C [*Antineoplastic drug regimen*]
FOAM........... Forecasting Ocean-Atmosphere Model (SAUS)
FOAM........... Fragmenting Offensive Aerial Mine (MCD)
FOAM........... Texstyrene Corp. [*NASDAQ symbol*] (COMM)
Foamex......... Foamex International [*Associated Press*] (SAG)
FOAMP......... Foreign Aerospace Material Production (MCD)
FOAMP......... Fraternal Order of Air Mail Pilots [*Defunct*] (EA)
FOAMS......... Forecasting, Order Administration, and Master Scheduling (PDAA)
FO & R......... Fleet Operations and Readiness
Fo-An-Si....... Forsterite-Anorthite-Silica [*Lunar geology*]
FOAP........... Foreign Aircraft Production (MCD)
FOAPH......... Federation Ouest Africaine des Associations pour la Promotion des Personnes Handicapees [*West African Federation of Associations for the Advancement of Handicapped Persons - WAFAH*] [*Bamako, Mali*] (EAIO)
Foard Mer Sh... Foard on Merchant Shipping [*A publication*] (DLA)
FOAS........... Akerman, Senterfitt, Eidson, Law Library, Orlando, FL [*Library symbol*] [*Library of Congress*] (LCLS)
FOAS........... Field Operating Agencies [*Air Force*] (DOMA)
FOAS........... Fleet Operational Analysis Staff (SAUS)
FOAS........... Future Offensive Air System [*Military*] (SEWL)
FOAVF......... Failure of All Vital Forces (MAE)
FOB............. Facilities Operations Branch (SAUS)
FOB............. Faculty of Building (PDAA)
FOB............. Fan-out Branch (SAUS)
FOB............. Fans of Bentsen [*Treasury Secretary, Lloyd Bentsen*] (ECON)
FOB............. fast oxide breeder (SAUS)
FOB............. Father of Baby (DAVI)
FOB............. Fecal Occult Blood [*Medicine*] (MAE)
FOB............. Federal Office Building
FOB............. Feet Out of Bed
FOB............. Fetal Occult Blood [*Medicine*]
FOB............. Fiberoptic Bronchoscopy [*Also, FB*] [*Medicine*]
FOB............. Fiber Optics Board (MCD)
FOB............. Fiber Optics Bundle (SAUS)
FOB............. Fibre Optics Board (SAUS)
FOB............. Field Operations Bureau [*FCC*] (NTCM)
FOB............. Fine Old Blend [*Wines and spirits*]
FOB............. First Overtone Band
FOB............. Flatpack On Board (SAUS)
FOB............. Flight Operations Building [*NASA*] (KSC)
FOB............. Foot of Bed (CPH)
FOB............. Foot Overbridge [*Indian Railway*] (TIR)
FOB............. Ford Motor Co. Ltd. [*ICAO designator*] (FAAC)
FOB............. Ford of Britain [*Corporate subsidiary*]
FOB............. Foreign Body (ADWA)
FOB............. Foreign Office Branch of the Secret Service (SAUO)
FOB............. Form Overlay Buffer (SAUS)
FOB............. Forward Observation (SAUS)
FOB............. Forward Observer Bombardment [*Military*]
FOB............. Forward Operating Base [*Air Force*] (AFM)
FOB............. Forward Operating (or Operations) Base (SAUO)
FOB............. Fractional Orbital Bombardment (MCD)
fob............. Free on Board [*Shipping*] (WA)
FOB............. Free on Board [*"INCOTERM," International Chamber of Commerce official code*] [*Shipping*]
fob............. freight on (SAUS)
FOB............. Freight on Board (AAG)
FOB............. Fresh off the Boat (SAUS)
FOB............. Friends of Bill [*Political network built by President Bill Clinton*]
FOB............. Friends of Blue [*British*] [*An association*] (DBA)
FoB............. Friends of the Bureau (SAUO)
FOB............. Front of Board (MSA)
fob............. front of body (SAUS)
FOB............. Fuel-Oil Blend (ABAC)
FOB............. Fuel on Board [*Aviation*]
fob............. full of baloney (SAUS)
FOB............. Full of Brooklyns [*Coined by baseball broadcaster Red Barber, initialism refers to bases loaded with Brooklyn Dodgers*] [*Obsolete*]
FOB............. Full Operational Base (SAUO)
FOB............. Functional Observational Battery [*Toxicology*]
FOB............. Function Operation Block (SAUS)
FOb............. Ormond Beach Public Library, Ormond Beach, FL [*Library symbol*] [*Library of Congress*] (LCLS)
FOBA........... Free on Board Airport [*Business term*]
FOBAA......... Flag Officer, British Assault Area
FOB & T...... Free on Board and Trimmed (SAUS)
FOBB........... First Oak Brook Bancshares, Inc. [*NASDAQ symbol*] (NQ)
FOBBA......... First Oak Brook Bancshrs'A' [*NASDAQ symbol*] (TTSB)
FOBBS......... Federation of British Bonsai Societies (DBA)
FOBC........... Fed One Bancorp [*NASDAQ symbol*] (TTSB)
FOBC........... Fed One Savings Bank [*NASDAQ symbol*] (SAG)
FOBC........... Fibre Optic Bus Components (SAUS)
fobcnlf......... free on board cars, named point, lighterage free (SAUS)
fobcnp......... free on board cars, named point (SAUS)
FOBES......... Fiber Optics Borehole Earth Strainmeter [*Geology*]
fob ex stowage... free on board except stowage (SAUS)
fob ex stowage/trimming... free on board excluding stowage/trimming (SAUS)
fob ex trim... free on board excluding trimming (SAUS)
FOBFO......... Federation of British Fire Organisations (BI)
FOBFO......... Federation of British Fire Organizations (SAUS)
fob/fob......... free on board/free of board (SAUS)
FOB/FOB..... Free on Board / Free off Board (SAUS)
FOBID.......... Federation of Library, Documentation and Information Organisations (SAUS)
FOBID.......... Federation of Library Information and Documentation Organisations (SAUO)
FOBO........... Fort Bowie National Historic Site
fobot........... free on board (SAUS)
FoBOT.......... Free on Board, Owners Trim (SAUS)
FObP........... Forward Observation Post (SAUS)
FOBS........... Fiber Optics Borescope
F Obs........... Forward Observer (SAUS)
FOBS........... Fractional Orbital Bombardment System
FOBS........... Fractional-Orbit Bombardment System (SAUS)
fobse........... free on board. sacks extra (SAUS)
fobsi........... free on board, sacks included (SAUS)
FOBSR......... Forward Observer [*Military*]
fob ss trimming... free on board (SAUS)
fobst........... free on board and free stowed (SAUS)
FOBT........... Fecal Occult Blood Test [*Medicine*]
fobtrim......... free on board and free trimmed (SAUS)
FoB Trim...... Free on Board and Trimmed (SAUS)
FOBTSU....... Forward Observer Target Survey Unit [*Military*]
FO Bty......... Forward Observation Battery (SAUS)
FOBW.......... Frequencies of Occurrence of Binary Words [*Computer science*] (PDAA)
FOC............. 505th Ordnance Company (EA)
FOc............. Central Florida Regional Library, Ocala, FL [*Library symbol*] [*Library of Congress*] (LCLS)
FOC............. Chemical Flux Cutting (SAUS)
FOC............. Face of Concrete [*Technical drawings*]
FOC............. Factor of Cooperation (SAUS)
FOC............. Faint-Object Camera [*Astronomy*]
FOC............. Farthest-On Circle (NVT)
FoC............. Father of Chapel [*Shop steward*] [*British*] (ODBW)
FOC............. Father of Chapel [*Shop steward*] [*British*]
FOC............. Father of Child (DAVI)
FoC............. Father of the Chapel (WDAA)
FOC............. Federation Organization Committee (SAUO)
FOC............. Ferrari Owners Club (EA)
FOC............. Fiber Optic Cable (SAUS)
FOC............. Fiber-Optic Cable (SSD)
FOC............. fiberoptic catheter (SAUS)
FOC............. Fiber Optic Converter (SAUS)
FOC............. Fiber Optics Communications [*Data transmission*] (TEL)

FOC .... Fibre-Optic Communications (SAUS)
FOC .... Field Officer Commanding (SAUS)
FOC .... Final / Full Operational Capability (SAUS)
FOC .... Final Operational Capability [*Military*] (AFM)
FOC .... Final Operational Capacity
FOC .... Final Operation Capability (SAUS)
FOC .... Fire Offices Committee [*British*] (AIA)
FOC .... First Class Operators' Club [*Amateur radio shorthand*] (WDAA)
FOC .... First Of Chain (SAUS)
FOC .... First of Class (DOMA)
FOC .... First Operational Capability (ACAE)
FOC .... First Operators Club (SAUO)
FOC .... Fixed Oil Capacitor
FOC .... Flag of Convenience
FOC .... Flag Officer Commanding
FOC .... Fleet Operational Center (CCCA)
FOC .... Fleet Operations Center (SAUS)
FOC .... Fleet Operations Commitment (SAUO)
FOC .... Flight of Colors test (SAUS)
FOC .... Flight Operating Costs
FOC .... Flight Operations Center
FOC .... Focal (MSA)
FOC .... Focsani [*Romania*] [*Seismograph station code, US Geological Survey*] (SEIS)
FOC .... Focus (KSC)
FOC .... focus electrode (SAUS)
FOC .... Focus of Contraction [*Motion perception*]
FOC .... Folding Operation Code (SAUS)
FOC .... Follow-On Contract
FOC .... Foreign Object Check (MCD)
FOC .... Foreign Operating Committee [*World War II*]
FOC .... Formula One Constructors Association (SAUO)
FOC .... Forward Observer COLIDAR [*Coherent Light Detecting and Ranging*]
FOC .... Forward Operations Center (SAUO)
FOC .... Freedom of Choice [*Insurance*] (DHP)
foc .... Free of Charge (EBF)
FOC .... Free of Charge [*Business term*]
FOC .... Free of Claims [*Insurance*] (MARI)
foc .... free of costs (SAUS)
FOC .... Free Offices Committee (SAUO)
FOC .... Free on Car [*Shipping*]
FOC .... Friends of Community (EA)
FOC .... From Own Correspondent
FOC .... Fuel Oil Cooler
FOC .... Full and Open Competition [*Government contracting*]
FOC .... Full Operational Capability Program [*Navy*] (NVT)
FOC .... Fully Operating Capacity (SAUS)
FOC .... Furthest-On Circle [*Navy*] (ANA)
FOC .... Fuzhou [*China*] [*Airport symbol*] (OAG)
FOC .... Office Federal de l'Aviation Civile [*Sweden*] [*ICAO designator*] (FAAC)
FOCA .... Federal Office for Civil Aviation (SAUO)
FOCA .... Federation of Citizens Associations (SAUO)
FOCA .... Fibre Optic Cable Assembly (NITA)
FOCA .... Field Offices of Contract Administration (SAUO)
FOCA .... Field Operating Cost Agency [*Army*]
FOCA .... Fiero Owners Club of America (EA)
FOCA .... Font Object Content Architecture (CDE)
FOCA .... Formula One Constructors Association (SAUO)
FOCA .... Formula-One Constructors Association (SAUS)
FOCA .... Fort Caroline National Memorial
FOCA .... Free and Open Church Association [*British*]
FOCA .... Freedom of Choice Act [*Abortion-rights bill*] (ECON)
FOCA .... Friends of the Origami Center of America (EA)
FOCAL .... Formula Calculation [*Pharmacology*] (DAVI)
FOCAL .... Formula Calculator [*Digital Equipment Corp.*] (CSR)
FOCAL .... Formulating Online Calculations in Algebraic Language [*Computer science*] (IAA)
FOCAL .... Foundations of Communication and Language (AIE)
FOCAL .... French Ocean-Climat Atlantique Equatorial [*Program*] [*Marine science*] (OSRA)
FOCAL .... French Program Ocean-Climat Atlantique Equatorial (USDC)
FOCAP .... Federacion Odontologica Centro America y Panama [*Odontological Federation of Central America and Panama*]
FOCAP .... Fiber Optics Cost Analysis Program (ACAE)
FOCAS .... Faint-Object Classification and Analysis System [*Astronomy*]
FOCAS .... Fiber Optic Communications for Aerospace Systems (MCD)
FOCAS .... Fibre Optical Communications for Aerospace Systems (SAUS)
FOCAS .... Flag Officer, Carriers and Amphibious Ships [*Navy*] [*British*]
FOCAS .... Force Capability Assessment System (SAUO)
FOCAS .... Ford [*Automobile*] Operating Cost Analysis System
FOCAS .... Forward Crash Avoidance Systems [*NHTSA*] (TAG)
FOCAS .... Foundation of Compassionate American Samaritans (EA)
FOCAS .... Fuji Juken, Ogisaka, Kawabe, Asahi Juken and Sueno Kosan [*Group of Japanese development companies located in Osaka, Japan*] (ECON)
Fo-castle ..... Forecastle (SAUS)
FOCB .... Federal Oil Conservation Board (SAUO)
FOcC .... Central Florida Community College, Ocala, FL [*Library symbol*] [*Library of Congress*] (LCLS)
FOCC .... Fiber Optic Coordinating Committee [*American National Standards Institute*] [*Telecommunications*]
FOCC .... Fleet Operational Control Center (SAUS)
FOCC .... Fleet Operations Control Center [*Navy*]
FOCC .... Flight Operations Control Center (SAUS)
FOCC .... Forward Analog Control Channel (CGWS)
FOCC .... Forward Optimistic oriented Concurrency Control (SAUS)
FOCC .... Friends of China Club (SAUO)
FOCCEUR ..... Fleet Operations Control Center, Europe [*Navy*]
FOCCLANT ... Fleet Operations Control Center, Atlantic [*Navy*] (DNAB)
FOCCPAC ..... Fleet Operations Control Center, Pacific Fleet [*Navy*]
FOCFAR .... Free of Claim for Accident Reported (SAUS)
FOCFC .... Friends of the Cassidys [*An association*] (EA)
FOC/FCC ...... Flight Operations Center/Flight Coordination Center (MCD)
FOCH .... Forward Channel [*Telecommunications*]
fochr .... free of charge (SAUS)
FOCI .... Farrand Optical Co., Inc.
FOCI .... First Operational Computer Installation (IAA)
FOCI .... Fisheries-Oceanography Cooperative Investigations [*National Oceanic and Atmospheric Administration*] (USDC)
FOCI .... Fisheries-Oceanography Cooperative Users System [*Marine science*] (OSRA)
FOCI .... Fisheries Oceanography Coordinated Investigations (SAUO)
FOCI .... Foreign Ownership, Control, or Influence
FOCIA .... Fibre-Optics-Coupled Image Amplifier (PDAA)
FOCI BP .... Fisheries-Oceanography Cooperative Investigations Biophysical Platform [*Marine science*] (OSRA)
FOCI BP .... FOCI [*Fisheries-Oceanography Cooperative Investigations*] Biophysical Platform (USDC)
FOCIS .... Fiber Optic Communication and Information Society (MHDI)
FOCIS .... Fibre Optic Communication and Information Society (SAUS)
FOCIS .... Financial On-Line Central Information System [*Computer science*] (MHDB)
FOCIS .... Financial Online Customer Information System (SAUS)
FOCIS .... Forest Classification and Inventory System (SAUO)
FOCL .... Focal, Inc. [*NASDAQ symbol*] (NASQ)
FOCL .... Fort Clatsop National Memorial
FOCLA .... Federation of Country Local Associations (SAUO)
FOC/LAN ...... Fiber Optic Commanications/Local Area Networks (SAUS)
FOC/LAN ...... International Fiber Optics and Communications Exposition and Show on Local Area Networks
FOCLEARN ... Teaching Program for FOCAL (SAUS)
FOCM .... Feminists on Children's Media [*Defunct*] (EA)
FOCMA .... Feline Orcornavirus-Associated Cell Membrane Antigen [*Immunology*]
focmg .... forthcoming (SAUS)
FOCNAS .... Flag Officer Commanding, North Atlantic Station [*British military*] (DMA)
FOCOA .... Fiero Owners Club of America (EA)
FOCOBANK .... Foreign Commerce Bank [*Switzerland*]
FOCOHANA .... Fourier Coefficient Harmonic Analyzer
FOCOL .... Federation of Coin Operated Launderettes (SAUS)
FOCOL .... Fox Communities Online [*Computer science*]
FOCON .... Fibre Cone Optics (SAUS)
FOCON System... Floor Control System (SAUS)
FOCOS .... Foam Overhead Cover Support System (SAUS)
FOCOS .... FORDAC [*FORTRAN Data Acquisition and Control*] Conversational System [*Computer science*] (IAA)
FO/COT .... Firing Out/Consolidate Operability Tests (MCD)
FOCP .... Fluid-Operated Card Processor (SAUS)
FOCP .... Foreign Officer Contract Program (SAUO)
FOC Program... Full Operation Capability Program (SAUS)
FOCPX .... Fidelity O-T-C [*Mutual fund ticker symbol*] (SG)
FOCR .... Final Operational Concept Review (ACAE)
FOCRIN .... Flag Officer Commanding, Royal Indian Navy [*British military*] (DMA)
FOCS .... Factory Operation Control System (TIMI)
FOCS .... Federation of Old Cornwall Societies [*British*] (DBA)
FOCS .... Fiberchem, Inc. [*NASDAQ symbol*] (NQ)
FOCS .... Fiber Optic Cable System (DWSG)
FOCS .... Fiber-Optic Chemical Sensor [*Analytical chemistry*]
FOCS .... Flag Officer's Command System [*Military*] (SEWL)
FOCS .... Foundations of Computer Science [*Symposium*] (VERA)
FOCS .... Freight Operation Control System (PDAA)
FOCSI .... Fiber Optic Control System Integration (ACAE)
FOCSL .... Fleet Oriented Consolidated Stock List [*Navy*]
FOCSL .... Forecastle
FO'C'SLE ...... Forecastle (ROG)
FOCSY .... foldover-corrected spectroscopy (SAUS)
FOCT .... Flag Officer, Carrier Training [*British military*] (DMA)
FOCUS .... Federation of Community United Services (SAUO)
FOCUS .... Federation of Computer Users in the Medical Sciences (SAUO)
FOCUS .... Federation on Computing in the US (CDE)
FOCUS .... Field Operations Computer System (HEAS)
FOCUS .... Financial and Operations Combined Uniform Single Report
FOCUS .... Financially-Oriented Computer Updating Service (IAA)
FOCUS .... Fire Operational Characteristics Using Simulation [*System for comparing organizations for wildland fire protection services in cost-effective terms*] [*Department of Agriculture, Forest Services*]
FOCUS .... Fisheries Oceanography Cooperative Users System [*Marine science*] (OSRA)
FOCUS .... Florida On-line Coordinate Index (SAUS)
Focus .... Focus Enhancements, Inc. [*Associated Press*] (SAG)
FOCUS .... Food Operational Cellular Unit Source (SAUS)
FOCUS .... Forecasting Control and Updating Schedule (MCD)
FOCUS .... Formal Officer Career Utilization Structure [*Military*]
FOCUS .... Form of Control Users System (MCD)
FOCUS .... For On-Line Computer Users (SAUS)
FOCUS .... For Our Children's Unpaid Support [*Defunct*] (EA)
FOCUS .... For Our Christian Understanding [*Program*]
FOCUS .... FORTRAN-Oriented Control and Universal System (SAUS)

FOCUS Forum of Control Data Users [*Later, VIM, Inc.*]
FOCUS Forum of Control Users System (SAUS)
FocusEn Focus Enhancements, Inc. [*Associated Press*] (SAG)
FOCWA Flag Officer Commanding West Africa [*British*]
FOD Factory on Dock (SAA)
FOD Familial Osseous Dystrophy [*Medicine*] (MELL)
FOD Fax on Demand (ITD)
FOD Fear of Death
FOD Field Officer of the Day [*Army*] (AABC)
FOD Field Operations Department
FOD Field Operations Directorate (HEAS)
FOD Field Operations Division (EERA)
FOD Finger of Death [*Fantasy gaming*] (NHD)
FOD first occurrence of date/datum (SAUS)
FOD First Occurrence of Date (or Datum) (SAUO)
FOD Flag Officer, Denmark (NATG)
FOD Flashblindness Orientation Device
FOD Flexible Optical Disk (SAUS)
FOD Flies-Odors-Ducts [*Veterinary science*] (OA)
FOD Flight Operations Department (SAUS)
FOD Flight Operations Directorate [*or Division*] [*Apollo*] [*NASA*]
FOD Fluidic Output Device
fod fodder (SAUS)
FOD follow-on destroyer (SAUS)
FOD Foreign Object Damage
FOD For Onward Dispatch (SAUS)
FOD Fort Dodge [*Iowa*] [*Airport symbol*] (OAG)
FOD Fort Dodge, IA [*Location identifier*] [*FAA*] (FAAL)
fod Free of Damage (EBF)
FOD Free of Damage [*Business term*]
FOD Free of Disease [*Medicine*]
FOD Front de l'Opposition Democratique [*Togo*] [*Political party*] (EY)
FOD Front of Dash [*Automotive design*]
FOD Functional Operational Design
FOD Function Operational Design (SAUS)
FODA Formal specification of ODA document structures (SAUS)
FODA Fort Davis National Historic Site
FODAAP Fleet Operational Data Acquisition and Analysis Program (SAUO)
FODAAS Field Online Data Acquisition and Analysis System
FODabs Free of Damage Absolutely [*Insurance*] (MARI)
FODB Fiber Optic Data Bus (SSD)
FODC Friends of David Cassidy [*Defunct*] (EA)
FODCCIS Flag Officer Denmark Command, Control and Information System (SAUO)
FOD FREE Free of Dirt (SAUS)
F-O Dis Feeling-Oriented Discussion
FODL Fiber Optics Data Link (MCD)
FODLM Fiber Optics Data Link Missile (ACAE)
FODMS Fiber-Optic Data Multiplex System (SEWL)
FODO Federation of Ophthalmic and Dispensing Opticians [*British*] (DBA)
FODO Fort Donelson National Military Park
FODO Foundations of Data Organization and Algorithms [*Conference*] (VERA)
fo/do fuel oil/diesel oil (SAUS)
FODOF Flag Officer Danish Operational Forces (SAUO)
FoDokAB Forschungsdokumentation zur Arbeitsmarkt- und Berufsforschung [*Deutsche Bundesanstalt fuer Arbeit*] [*Germany*] [*Information service or system*] (CRD)
FODS Fiber Optic Distributed System (ACAE)
FODS Fraud and Overservicing Detection System (ADA)
FODS Front-Office Decision Support (GART)
FODW Friends of Dennis Wilson (EA)
FOE Factory Overall Efficiency (SAUO)
FOE Federal Energy Office (SAUS)
FOE Females Opposed to Equality
FOE Ferro Corp. [*NYSE symbol*] (SPSG)
FOE Field Operational Evaluation
FOE Figure-of-Eight (SAUS)
FOE File of Enemies [*British*] [*An association*] (DBA)
FOE Final Operational Evaluation (ACAE)
FOE Flight Operations Engineer (MCD)
FOE Focus of Expansion [*Motion perception*]
FOE Follow On Engine (ACAE)
FOE Follow On Equipment (ACAE)
FOE Follow-On Evaluation
FoE Ford of Europe, Inc. (SAUO)
FOE Foreign-Object Elimination [*Manufacturing*]
FOE Fraternal Order of Eagles (BARN)
FOE Friends of Europe (SAUO)
FOE Friends of the Earth (EA)
FoE Friends of the Earth (WDAA)
FOE Fuel Oil Equivalent (BARN)
FOE Functional & Organizational Evaluation (SAUO)
FOE Functional and Organizational Experimentation (SAUO)
FOE Grand Aerie, Fraternal Order of Eagles (EA)
FOE Topeka [*Kansas*] Forbes [*Airport symbol*] (OAG)
FOE Topeka, KS [*Location identifier*] [*FAA*] (FAAL)
FOEB Fuel Oil Equivalent Barrel
FOEC First-Order Elastic Constant (SAUS)
FOEC Fourth-Order Elastic Constant (SAUS)
FOEF Freedom of Expression Foundation (EA)
FOEI Friends of the Earth International
Foel Dr Int Foelix. Droit International Prive [*A publication*] (DLA)
FoEng Fellowship of Engineering [*British*] (DBA)
FOENIC Foeniculum [*Fennel*] [*Pharmacy*] (ROG)
FOEP Frog Otolith Experiment Package [*NASA*]
FOES Fine Old Extra Special
FOESR flow orientation ESR (SAUS)
FOET Follow-On Evaluation Test
FOEU Foreign Organizations' Employees Union
FOF Face of Finish [*Technical drawings*]
FOF Factor Out Failure (SAUS)
FOF Factory-of-the-Future
FOF Facts on File, Inc.
FoF Feed of Frame (SAUS)
FOF Field Observing Facility [*National Center for Atmospheric Research*]
FOF Field of Fire [*Military*] (MCD)
FOF Field Of View (SAUS)
FOF Firm-on-Firm Review (SAUS)
FOF First Operational Flight (MCD)
FOF First Orbital Flight [*NASA*] (NASA)
FOF Fish Oil Film
FOF Flag Officer, Flotilla [*British military*] (DMA)
FOF Flight Operations Facility
FOF Force On Force (SAUS)
FOF Force-on-Force Performance Test [*Environmental science*] (COE)
FoF Foto File Systems, Inc., Kansas City, KS [*Library symbol*] [*Library of Congress*] (LCLS)
FOF Fred Olsen Flyselskap AS [*Norway*] [*FAA designator*] (FAAC)
fof free on field (SAUS)
FOF Freund oder Feind (SAUS)
FOF Friends of Families [*Defunct*] (EA)
FOF Friends of Freddy (EA)
FOF Friends of the FBI (EA)
FOF Fukuoka Occupation Force
FOF Full Octave Filter
FOF Fund of Funds
FOF Futures and Options Fund [*Investment term*] (ECON)
FO-F 9 Field O to Field 9 (SAUS)
FOFA Follow-On Forces Attack
F of A Foresters of America (SAUS)
F of A Freethinkers of America (SAUS)
FOFA Friends of Free Asia [*Defunct*]
FO/FAC Forward Observer - Forward Air Controller [*Military*] (INF)
FOFATUSA Federation of Free African Trade Unions of South Africa
FOFAX Forecast Office Facsimile [*National Weather Service*]
FOFC Friends of Free China (EA)
FOFCC Federal Oceanographic Fleet Coordination Council
F of E Friends of the Earth (SAUS)
FOFEBA Forward of the FEBA [*Forward Edge of the Battle Area*] [*Military*]
FOFF 50-Off Stores [*NASDAQ symbol*] (TTSB)
F of F Field of Fire [*Military*] (AABC)
FOFF Fifty Off Stores [*NASDAQ symbol*] (SAG)
F of F Firth of Forth (DAS)
FOffr Field Officer (SAUS)
FOffr Flying Officer (SAUS)
F of JR Fourth of July Road
F of L Friends of the Library (SAUO)
FOFM Fog Foam
FO/FO/FS Fail Operational, Fail Operational, Fail Safe (SAUS)
F of R Fellowship of Reconciliation (SAUO)
fofr firm offer (SAUS)
FOFR Fort Frederica National Monument
FO/FS Fail-Operational, Fail-Safe (NASA)
FO/FS Flight Operational/Fail Safe (MCD)
F of S Foreman of Signals [*Military*] [*British*]
FOFT Flag Officer Flying Training (SAUO)
FOFT Florida Technological University, Orlando, FL [*Library symbol*] [*Library of Congress*] (LCLS)
FOFT Force-on-Force Trainer
FOG Fast Oxidative Glycolytic [*Fibers*] [*Neuroanatomy*]
FOG Fats, Oils, and Grease [*Food plant effluent*]
FOG Fiber Optic Gyro (ADWA)
FOG Fiber-Optic Gyroscope [*Automotive navigation systems*]
FOG Fiber Optics Guidance (MCD)
FOG Fibre Optics Guidance (SAUS)
FOG Field Operations Group
FOG Fineness of Grind [*Materials science*]
FOG First Osborne Group (SAUO)
FOG Fishing/Fisheries/Vessel Obligation Guarantee (USDC)
FOG Flag Officer, Germany (NATG)
FOG Flight Operations Group
FOG Florida Orange Growers (SAUO)
FOG Flow of Gold
FOG Fluothane, Oxygen, and Gas [*Nitrous oxide*] [*Anesthesiology*] (DAVI)
FOG Foggia [*Italy*] [*Airport symbol*] (AD)
FOG FOG [*First Osborne Group*] International Computer Users Group (EA)
FOG Forecast Generator [*Canadian natural language generation system*] (IDAI)
FOG Foreign Operating Group (LAIN)
FOG For Our Guidance (RIMS)
FOG Frequency Offset Generator
FoG Friends of Gill (SAUO)
FOG Shreveport, LA [*Location identifier*] [*FAA*] (FAAL)
FOGA Akieni [*Gabon*] [*ICAO location identifier*] (ICLI)
FOGA Fair and Open Grants Act (SAUO)
FOGA Fashion Originators Guild of America [*Defunct*] (EA)
FOGB Booue [*Gabon*] [*ICAO location identifier*] (ICLI)
FOGCO Federal Oil & Gas Corp.

FOGCO .... Federal Oil-Gas Company (SAUO)
FOGD .... Fiber Optics Guidance Demonstration (RDA)
Fog Det Lt ... Fog Detector Light [*Nautical charts*]
FOGE .... N'Dende [*Gabon*] [*ICAO location identifier*] (ICLI)
FOGF .... Fougamou [*Gabon*] [*ICAO location identifier*] (ICLI)
FOGG .... Feed-Only-Good Generator [*Nuclear energy*] (NRCH)
Fogg .... Fogg's Reports [*32-35 New Hampshire*] [*A publication*] (DLA)
FOGG .... Mbigou [*Gabon*] [*ICAO location identifier*] (ICLI)
FOGI .... Moabi [*Gabon*] [*ICAO location identifier*] (ICLI)
FOGJ .... Ndjole [*Gabon*] [*ICAO location identifier*] (ICLI)
FOGK .... Koula-Moutou/Mabimbi [*Gabon*] [*ICAO location identifier*] (ICLI)
FOGL .... Leconi [*Gabon*] [*ICAO location identifier*] (ICLI)
FOGM .... Fiber Optic Guidance Missile (SAUS)
FOG-M .... Fiber Optic Guided Missile [*Army*] (RDA)
FOGM .... Mouila [*Gabon*] [*ICAO location identifier*] (ICLI)
FOGMA .... Flag Officer, Gibraltar Mediterranean Area [*British*]
FOGO .... Oyem [*Gabon*] [*ICAO location identifier*] (ICLI)
FOGQ .... Okondja [*Gabon*] [*ICAO location identifier*] (ICLI)
FOGR .... Lambarene [*Gabon*] [*ICAO location identifier*] (ICLI)
FOGRMA .... Federal Oil and Gas Royalty Management Act
FOGS .... Church of Jesus Christ of Latter-Day Saints, Genealogical Society Library, Orlando Branch, Orlando, FL [*Library symbol*] [*Library of Congress*] (LCLS)
FOGS .... Faint-Object Grism Spectrograph [*Astronomy*]
FOGs .... Fiber Optic Gyros (SAUS)
FOGS .... Functioning of the GATT [*General Agreement on Tariffs and Trade*] System
FOGS .... Function-on-Generator-Stop (RDA)
Fog Sig .... fog signal (SAUS)
FOGSIG .... Fog Signal Station [*Nautical charts*]
Fog Sig Stn ... Fog Signal Station (SAUS)
FOGT .... First Order Gradient Technique
FOGU .... Moupoupa [*Gabon*] [*ICAO location identifier*] (ICLI)
FOGV .... Minvoul [*Gabon*] [*ICAO location identifier*] (ICLI)
FOGW .... Wonga-Wongue [*Gabon*] [*ICAO location identifier*] (ICLI)
Fog WIT .... fog wireless Telegraph or radio fog signal (SAUS)
Fog WT .... Fog Wireless Telegraph (SAUS)
FOH .... Columbia, MS [*Location identifier*] [*FAA*] (FAAL)
FOH .... Familial Orthostatic Hypotension [*Medicine*] (MELL)
FOH .... Forced Outage Hours [*Electronics*] (IEEE)
FOH .... Frederick's of Hollywood, Inc. [*NYSE symbol*] (SPSG)
FOH .... Friends of Haiti (EA)
FOH .... Friends of Hibakusha [*An association*] (EA)
FOH .... Front of House (ADA)
FoH .... Front of House (WDAA)
FOH .... Front of House Spot [*Theatrical lighting*] (NTCM)
FOHBC .... Federation of Historical Bottle Clubs (EA)
FOHBC .... Federation of Historical Bottle Collectors (EA)
FOHC .... Free of Heart Center (DAC)
FOHC .... Friends of Helix Club (EA)
FOHMD .... Fiber Optic Helmet Mounted Display [*Computer generated imagery*]
FOHO .... For Oily Hair Only [*Trademark of The Gillette Co.*]
FOHS .... Foundation for Osteopathic Health Services (EA)
FOI .... Faulty Operator Intervention (SAUS)
FOI .... Fiber-Optic Interface (SAUS)
FOI .... Field Operations Intelligence
FOI .... Fighter Officer for Interceptors [*Member of the SAGE Command Post staff*]
FOI .... Final Opinion Inventory [*Psychometrics*]
FOI .... First-Order Interpolator (IAA)
FOI .... Fleet Operational Investigation [*NOO*]
FOI .... Flight of Ideas [*Psychiatry*] (DAVI)
FOI .... Flight Ops International [*FAA designator*] (FAAC)
FOI .... Fluffy Opaque Inclusions [*In a meteorite*]
FOI .... Follow-On Interceptor [*Military*]
FOI .... Forced Oil Injection
FOI .... Foreign Object Inspection [*or Investigation*] (MCD)
FOI .... Foreign Object Investigation
FOI .... Freedom of Information [*Army*]
FOI .... Freedom of Information Act
foi .... Free of Interest (EBF)
FOI .... Free of Interest [*Business term*]
FOI .... Fuels Operating Instruction (AFIT)
FOI .... Functional Operating Instruction
FOIA .... Freedom of Information Act [*1966*]
FOIA .... Fund for Open Information and Accountability [*Defunct*] (EA)
FOIA .... OWPE Freedom of Information Act System (SAUO)
FOIA/PA .... Freedom of Information Act/Privacy Act (SAUS)
FOIC .... Field Office International Coordinator (SAUO)
FOIC .... Flag Officer-in-Charge [*British-controlled port*]
FOIC .... Freedom of Information Center (SAUS)
FOIC .... Freedom of Information Clearinghouse (EA)
FOICR .... Freedom of Information Center. Reports [*A publication*] (DLA)
FOI Dig .... FOI [*Freedom of Information*] Digest [*A publication*] (DLA)
FOIDRS .... FNWF Ocean History Information Retrieval System (SAUS)
FOIDS .... Fiber Optic Intelligence and Detection System (SEWL)
FOIF .... Free Oceanographic Instrument Float
FOIH .... Flight Operations Integration Handbook (MCD)
FOIL .... Field Oil Identification Laboratory [*Marine science*] (MSC)
FOIL .... File-Oriented Interpretive Language [*1969*] [*Computer science*]
FOIL .... First, Outer, Inner, Last [*Mathematical term used in factoring second degree trinomials*]
FOIL .... First Outside, Inside Last (VLIE)
FOIL .... Fleet Optimum Inventory Level [*Navy*]
FOIL .... Foil on Incandescent Light (VLIE)
FOIL .... Forest Oil [*NASDAQ symbol*] (TTSB)
FOIL .... Forest Oil Corp. [*NASDAQ symbol*] (NQ)
FOIL .... Freedom of Information Legislation (SAUS)
Foilmark .... Foilmark, Inc. [*Associated Press*] (SAG)
FOILO .... Forest Oil $0.75 Cv Pfd [*NASDAQ symbol*] (TTSB)
FOILW .... Forest Oil Wrrt [*NASDAQ symbol*] (TTSB)
FOIMS .... Field Office Information Management System (VLIE)
FOINTRACEN ... Fleet Operational Intelligence Training Center [*Navy*] (DNAB)
FOINTRACENLANT ... Fleet Operational Intelligence Training Center, Atlantic [*Navy*] (DNAB)
FOINTRACENPAC ... Fleet Operational Intelligence Training Center, Pacific [*Navy*] (DNAB)
FOIO .... Freedom of Information Act (TDOB)
FOIP .... Fax Over Internet Protocol (SAUS)
FOIP .... Follow-On In-Plant [*Test*] (MCD)
FOIPA .... Freedom of Information and Privacy Act
FOIPO .... Freedom of Information/Privacy Office (SAUO)
FOIR .... Field of Interest Register (SAUS)
FOIR .... Field-of-Interest Register [*DoD*]
FOIRL .... Fiber Optic Inter-Repeater Link (GART)
FOIRL .... Fiber Optic Inter Repeater Link Standard [*Institute of Electrical and Electronics Engineers*]
FOIS .... First Overseas Investment Service (SAUO)
FoiS .... Foika Systems Services, Inc., Moscow, PA [*Library symbol*] [*Library of Congress*] (LCLS)
fois .... folios (SAUS)
fois .... follows (SAUS)
FOIS .... Freight Operation Information System [*Indian Railway*] (TIR)
FOIS .... Friends of Iris Society [*An association*]
FOISD .... Fiber Optic Isolated Spherical Dipole Antenna (EEVL)
foit .... Free of Income Tax (SAUS)
FOITC .... Fleet Operational Intelligence Training Center [*Navy*]
FOITCL .... Fleet Operational Intelligence Training Center, Atlantic [*Navy*] (DNAB)
FOITCP .... Fleet Operational Intelligence Training Center, Pacific [*Navy*] (DNAB)
FOIU .... Fiber Optic Interface Unite (COE)
FOIU .... Flowmeter Ordering and Indicating Unit
FOJ .... Fremont, MI [*Location identifier*] [*FAA*] (FAAL)
FOJ .... Friends of the Jessup [*An association*] (EA)
FOJ .... Fuse on Jam (MCD)
FOJE .... Fort Jefferson National Monument
FOJI .... Friends of Julio International (EA)
FOJT .... Formal On-the-Job Training
FOK .... Fill or Kill [*Stock options*] [*Investment term*]
FOK .... Free of Knots
FOK .... Westhampton Beach, NY [*Location identifier*] [*FAA*] (FAAL)
FOKEU .... Foreign Organizations Korean Employees' Union [*South Korea*]
FOKN .... Fixation Optokinetic Nystagmus [*Eye movement*]
FOL .... Facility Operating License [*Nuclear energy*] (NRCH)
FOL .... [*The*] Facts of Life [*NBC television program*]
FOL .... Federal Office of Languages (SAUO)
FOL .... Federation of Labor (SAUS)
FOL .... Federation of Labour [*New Zealand*] (WDAA)
FOL .... Festival of Lights [*Hanukkah*] [*Commemoration of the rededication of the Temple by Judas Maccabeus in 165BC*] (ADA)
FOL .... Fiber Optic Link (ACAE)
FOL .... Fiber Optics LASER
FOL .... Fiber Optics Light
FOL .... Field Operations Leader (VLIE)
FOL .... First-Order Language (SAUS)
FOL .... First Order Logic
FOL .... Flight Over Land (ACAE)
FOL .... Fly-Off Lever (SAUS)
Fol .... Foley's English Poor Law Cases [*1556-1730*] [*A publication*] (DLA)
FOL .... Folia [*Leaves*]
FOL .... Foligno [*Italy*] [*Seismograph station code, US Geological Survey*] [*Closed*] (SEIS)
Fol .... Folio (EBF)
fol .... Folio (ELAL)
FOL .... Folio
fol .... folios (SAUS)
fol .... Folium (WDAA)
FOL .... Folium [*or Foliorum*] [*Leaf (or Leaves)*] [*Pharmacy*] (ROG)
fol .... follow (SAUS)
Fol .... Following [*Business term*] (EBF)
FOL .... Following [*Business term*]
fol .... follows (SAUS)
FOL .... Folsom State Prison (SAUS)
FOL .... Foreign Office Library (SAUO)
FOL .... Forest Airline South Africa [*ICAO designator*] (FAAC)
FOL .... Forward Operating Location [*Military*]
FoL .... Foundations of Language (journ.) (SAUS)
fol .... free on lorry (SAUS)
fol .... free-on-lorry oil and lubricants (SAUS)
FOL .... Frente Obrero de Liberacion [*Workers' Liberation Front*] [*Netherlands Antilles*] [*Political party*] (PPW)
FOL .... Friends of the Land [*Later, IWLA*]
FOL .... Fuel, Oil, and Lubricants (PDAA)
FOL .... Function of Lines (ELAL)
FOLA .... Fort Laramie National Historic Site
FOLA .... Friends of Libraries Australia
FOLACL .... Federation of Local Authority Chief Librarians [*British*] (TELE)
FO-LAN .... Fibre Optical Local Area Network (SAUS)
FOLAN .... Fibre Optic Local Area Network [*Telecommunications*] (PDAA)
FOLAN .... Flight Operations Local Area Network (ADWA)

FOLAV .... Family of Light-Armed Vehicle [*Saudi Arabian National Guard*] (DWSG)
FOLC .... Further Outlook Little Change (SAUS)
FOLC .... Office of the Foreign Liquidation Commissioner (SAUO)
FOLD .... Federally-Owned Landsat Data (SAUO)
FOLD .... Fibre Optic Line Dividers (NITA)
fold .... folding (SAUS)
FOLD .... Forward Observer Laser Designator (SAUS)
Fol Dic .... Kames and Woodhouselee's Folio Dictionary, Scotch Court of Session [*A publication*] (DLA)
Fol Dict .... Kames and Woodhouselee's Folio Dictionary, Scotch Court of Session [*A publication*] (DLA)
Folding Carton Ind ... Folding Carton Industry (journ.) (SAUS)
FOLDOB .... Forward Operating Location Dispersed Operating Base (SAUO)
FOLDOC .... Free On-Line Dictionary of Computing [*Computer science*]
fold pl .... Folded Plate (SAUS)
FOLDS .... Formal Language Definition System (SAUS)
FOLEM .... Flag Officer, Levant and Eastern Mediterranean [*British Marines*] [*World War II*]
FOLG .... Fiber Optics LASER Gyro (MCD)
folg .... folgend(e) (SAUS)
FOLG .... Following (ROG)
FOLIS .... Following Information Is Submitted [*Army*] (AABC)
Folkes .... Folkestone (SAUS)
Folkl .... Folklore [*A publication*] (BRI)
Folk Pl .... Folkard's Loans and Pledges [*2nd ed.*] [*1876*] [*A publication*] (DLA)
Folk St Sl .... Folkard's Edition of Starkie on Slander and Libel [*A publication*] (DLA)
foll .... followed by (SAUS)
FOLL .... Following
foll .... following (SAUS)
folld .... Followed (SAFN)
FOLLG .... Following (ROG)
FOLNOAVAL ... Following Items Not Available
FOLP .... Fitting-Out of Leased Premises
FOLPEN .... Foliage Penetration [*RADAR*] (MCD)
FOLPES .... Foliage Penetration System [*Military*]
Fol PLC .... Foley's English Poor Law Cases [*1556-1730*] [*A publication*] (DLA)
Fol PL Cas ... Foley's English Poor Law Cases [*1556-1730*] [*A publication*] (DLA)
FOLQ .... Foam Liquid
FOLR .... Foreign Ownership Land Register [*Queensland*] [*State*] (EERA)
FOLR .... Forward Observer LASER Range-Finder
FOLRP .... Field office long-range plan (SAUS)
fols .... folios (SAUS)
FOLS .... Follows (NVT)
FOLS .... Fort Larned National Historic Site
FOLS .... Fresnel Lens Optical Landing System (SAUO)
FOLUP .... Follow-Up
FOL USA .... Friends of Libraries USA (EA)
FOLUSA .... Friends of Libraries USA [*American Library Association*]
FOLZ .... First-Order Laue Zone (AAEL)
FOM .... Face of Masonry [*Technical drawings*]
FOM .... Factor of Merit [*Telecommunications*] (TEL)
fom .... fat off mothers (SAUS)
FOM .... Fault of Management
FOM .... Federation Object Model (SAUO)
FOM .... Fellowship of Missions (EA)
FOM .... Fiber Optic MODEM [*Modulator-Demodulator*]
FOM .... Fibre Optic Modem (SAUS)
FOM .... Field Operations Manual
FOM .... Field Operations Memorandum
FOM .... Fighter Officer for Missiles [*Member of the SAGE Command Post staff*]
FOM .... Figure of Merit
FOM .... Finnish Options Market (NUMA)
FOM .... Flag Officer, Malta (SAUS)
FOM .... Flag, Ownership, or Management (MARI)
FOM .... flight operation manual (SAUS)
FOM .... Flight Operations Memorandum (ACAE)
FOM .... Floor of Mouth [*Medicine*] (EDAA)
FOM .... Folding Outside Mirrors [*Automotive engineering*]
FOM .... Foreign Materiel Number [*Weapons*] (INF)
FOM .... Foremost Corp.Amer [*NYSE symbol*] (TTSB)
FOM .... Formula One Management
FOM .... Fortnightly Operational Minute (HEAS)
FOM .... Forum Resources Ltd. [*Vancouver Stock Exchange symbol*]
FOM .... Foumban [*Cameroon*] [*Airport symbol*] (AD)
FOM .... Fractional Orbiting Missile (SAA)
FOM .... Functional Operating Module (VLIE)
FOMA .... Foreign Military Assistance (MCD)
FOMA .... Foreign Military Assistance File (SAUS)
FOMA .... Fort Matanzas National Monument
FOMAD .... Food Market Awareness Databank [*Leatherhead Food Research Association*] [*Information service or system*] (CRD)
FOMAE .... Follow-On Management Application and Evaluation (SAUO)
fomaj .... force majeure (SAUS)
FOMAU .... Fiber Optic MAU (SAUS)
FOMAU .... Fiber Optic Medium Access Unit (SAUS)
FOMAU .... fiber optic medium attachment unit (SAUS)
FOMAU .... Fibre Optic Medium Attachment Unit (SAUS)
FOMC .... Federal Open Market Commission (SAUS)
FOMC .... Federal Open Market Committee [*Also, OMC*] [*Federal Reserve System*]
FOMC .... Fort McHenry National Monument
FOMCAT .... Foreign Material Catalog
FOMENTO .... Venezuelan Development Ministry (SAUO)
FOMi .... Fluorouracil, Oncovin [*Vincristine*], Mitomycin C [*Antineoplastic drug regimen*]
FOMi/CAP .... Fluorouracil, Oncovin, Mitomycin-C, Cytoxan, Adriamycin, Platinol [*Antineoplastic drug*] (CDI)
FOMIN .... Foreign Minister (CINC)
FOMINPI .... Fomento Industrial do Piani, SA
FOMIS .... Fitting Out Management Information System [*Navy*] (CAAL)
FOMIS .... Fossil Operations and Maintenance Information Service (IID)
FOMM .... Finite Output-Memory Machine (SAUS)
FOMM .... Functional-Oriented Maintenance Manual (MCD)
FOMMS .... Flight Operations Maintenance Management System [*NASA*] (SPST)
FoMoCo .... Ford Motor Company (SAUS)
Fomoco .... Ford Motor Company
FOMOT .... Four Mode Ternary (SAUS)
FOMOT .... Four Mode Ternary Code (VLIE)
FOMOT Code ... Four Mode Ternary Code (SAUS)
FOMP .... Fiber Optic Mortar Projectile [*Boeing Co.*] [*Military*]
FOMP .... Field office management plan (SAUS)
FOMP .... First Order Magnetization Process (AAEL)
FOMP .... Foreign Missile Production (MCD)
FOMP .... Fuel and Oil Metering Pump [*Engine design*]
FOMR .... First-Order Moment Reorientation (SAUS)
FOMR .... Flight Operations Management Room [*NASA*] (KSC)
FoMRHI .... Fellowship of Makers and Researchers of Historical Instruments [*Formerly, Fellowship of Makers and Restorers of Historical Instruments*] (EA)
FOMRP .... Fiber Optic Material Research Program [*Rutgers University*]
FOMS .... Fiber Optic Myocardium Stimulator (VLIE)
FOMS .... Functionally Oriented Maintenance Manual (ACAE)
FOMS .... Future Operational Microwave Sounder (MCD)
fomth .... for one month (SAUS)
FOMTR .... Formatter (MCD)
FOMV .... Foxtail Mosaic Virus [*Plant pathology*]
FON .... Federation of Ontario Naturalists [*Canada*]
FON .... Fiber Optic Network (VLIE)
FON .... Fiber Optics Network (SAUS)
FON .... Fibre Optic Network (SAUS)
FON .... Fire Order Number (ACAE)
FON .... Flag Officer, Norway (SAUO)
fon .... Fon [*MARC language code*] [*Library of Congress*] (LCCP)
FON .... Font (SAUS)
FON .... Freedom of Navigation (DOMA)
FON .... front octane number (SAUS)
FON .... Phone Directory (SAUS)
FON .... Sprint Corp. [*NYSE symbol*] (SAG)
FON .... United States Navy, Naval Training Equipment Center, Orlando, FL [*Library symbol*] [*Library of Congress*] (LCLS)
FONA .... Flag Officer, Naval Aviation (SAUS)
FONA .... Friends of the National Arboretum (SAUS)
FONA .... Friends of the US National Arboretum (EA)
FONAC .... Flag Officer, Naval Air Command [*British*]
FONAE .... Finding of No Adverse Effect [*Environmental science*] (COE)
FONAP .... Flag Officer, Naval Air, Pacific [*British*]
FONAR .... Field Focusing Nuclear Magnetic Resonance
Fonar .... Fonar Corp. [*Associated Press*] (SAG)
FONAS .... Flag Officer, Naval Air Stations [*British military*] (DMA)
FONASBA .... Federation of National Associations of Ship Brokers and Agents (SAUS)
Fon BC .... Fonblanque's Bankruptcy Cases [*1849-52*] [*A publication*] (DLA)
Fonb Eq .... Fonblanque's Equity [*England*] [*A publication*] (DLA)
Fonbl .... Fonblanque on Medical Jurisprudence [*A publication*] (DLA)
Fonbl .... Fonblanque's Equity [*England*] [*A publication*] (DLA)
Fonbl .... Fonblanque's New Reports, English Bankruptcy [*1849-52*] [*A publication*] (DLA)
Fonbl (Eng) ... Fonblanque's Equity [*England*] [*A publication*] (DLA)
Fonbl Eq (Eng) ... Fonblanque's Equity [*England*] [*A publication*] (DLA)
Fonbl Med Jur ... Fonblanque on Medical Jurisprudence [*A publication*] (DLA)
Fonbl NR .... Fonblanque on Medical Jurisprudence [*A publication*] (DLA)
Fonbl NR .... Fonblanque's English Cases in Chancery [*A publication*] (DLA)
Fonbl NR .... Fonblanque's Equity [*England*] [*A publication*] (DLA)
Fonbl NR .... Fonblanque's New Reports, English Bankruptcy [*1849-52*] [*A publication*] (DLA)
Fonbl R .... Fonblanque's Bankruptcy Cases (or New Reports) [*1849-52*] [*A publication*] (DLA)
Fonbl R & Wr ... Fonblanque's Rights and Wrongs [*1860*] [*A publication*] (DLA)
FONCON .... Telephone Conversation (MCD)
FOND .... Font family descriptor (SAUS)
FOND .... Foreign Office News Department (SAUO)
FONDA .... Fonda, NY [*American Association of Railroads railroad junction routing code*]
FONDEM .... Inter-American Emergency Aid Fund (SAUO)
Fond P & S Div ... Fond Parts & Service Division (SAUS)
FONE .... Farmstead Telephone Group, Inc. [*NASDAQ symbol*] (NQ)
FONE .... Farmstead Tel Group [*NASDAQ symbol*] (TTSB)
FONE .... Fort Necessity National Battlefield
FONE .... Intellicell Corp. [*NASDAQ symbol*] (SAG)
FONE .... Telephone [*Amateur radio shorthand*] (WDAA)
FONECON .... Telephone Conference [*or Conversation*]
FONEW .... Farmstead Tel Group Wrrt [*NASDAQ symbol*] (TTSB)
F on F .... Facts-on-File (SAUS)
FONF .... Flag Officer, Newfoundland [*British*]
FONFT .... Flag Officer Naval Flying Training (SAUO)
FONHEP .... Haitian Private School Foundation (SAUO)
FONL .... Flag Officer's Newsletter [*A publication*] (DNAB)

FonMin........ Foreign Minister
FONN........... Flag Officer, Northern Norway (SAUO)
FONOFF....... Foreign Office
FonOff......... Foreign Office
FONPLATA... Fondo Financiero para el Desarrollo de la Cuenca del Plata [*Financial Fund for the Development of the Plata Basin*] (EAIO)
FONPr......... Sprint Corp. $1.50 CV Ser 1 Pfd [*NYSE symbol*] (TTSB)
FONPrA........ Sprint Corp. $1.50 Cv Ser 2 Pfd [*NYSE symbol*] (TTSB)
FONR........... Fonar Corp. [*NASDAQ symbol*] (NQ)
FONR........... Fund for Objective News Reporting (EA)
FONS........... Foundation of Nursing Studies (SAUS)
FONSI.......... Finding of No Significant Impact [*Office of Surface Mining*]
Font............. Fontes Iuris Romani Antiqui [*A publication*] (OCD)
Font............. Pro Fonteio [*of Cicero*] [*Classical studies*] (OCD)
Fontanka...... Fontanka Canal linking Leninport with the main section of Leningrad and the Neva River (SAUS)
FONX........... Fonix Corp. [*NASDAQ symbol*] (SG)
Fony............. Fund of New York (SAUO)
FONZ............ Friends of the National Zoo
FOO............. Fairness of Opportunity [*Competitive bidding*]
FOO............. Family of Origin (SEAT)
FOO............. Fear of Obesity
FOO............. Field Ordering Officer [*Army*] (RDA)
FOO............. Field Ordnance Officer (SAUO)
FOO............. Fire Observation Officer (SAUO)
FOO............. Fleet Operations Officer [*Navy*] [*British*]
FOO............. Flight Operations Officer (SAUO)
FOO............. Forward Observation Officer [*Military*]
FOO............. Fraternal Order of Orioles (EA)
FOO............. Frequency of Optimum Operation (SAA)
FOO............. Fundamental Order of Operation [*Mathematics game*]
FOO............. Noemfoor [*New Guinea*] [*Airport symbol*] (AD)
FOO............. Numfor [*Indonesia*] [*Airport symbol*] (OAG)
FOOA........... Mouila [*Gabon*] [*ICAO location identifier*] (ICLI)
FOOB........... Bitam [*Gabon*] [*ICAO location identifier*] (ICLI)
FOOB........... Fell Out of Bed [*Medicine*] (DMAA)
FOOB........... Firing Out of Battery [*Military*] (PDAA)
foob............. firing out of the battery (SAUS)
FOOBAR....... Fouled up beyond all recognition (SAUS)
FOOBAR....... FTP Operation Over Big Address Records (SAUS)
FOOC........... Cocobeach [*Gabon*] [*ICAO location identifier*] (ICLI)
FOOD........... Foodservice Organization of Distributors (EA)
Food............. Foodweek [*A publication*]
FOOD........... Forum et infos on reactions Due to foods (SAUS)
FOOD........... Fresh Foods [*NASDAQ symbol*] [*Formerly, WSMP, Inc.*]
FOOD........... International Fast Food Corp. [*NASDAQ symbol*] (SAG)
FOOD........... Moanda [*Gabon*] [*ICAO location identifier*] (ICLI)
FOODAP....... Food Distributors Application (SAUS)
Foodbrnd..... Foodbrands America, Inc. [*Associated Press*] (SAG)
Food Chem Toxicol... Food and Chemical Toxicology [*A publication*] (PABS)
Food Drug Cos L Rep... Food, Drug, Cosmetic Law Reporter [*Commerce Clearing House*] [*A publication*] (DLA)
Food Drug Cosm L Rep (CCH)... Food, Drug, Cosmetic Law Reporter (Commerce Clearing House) [*A publication*] (DLA)
Food Drug Packag... Food and Drug Packaging (journ.) (SAUS)
FOOD ENG... Food Engineer (SAUS)
FOOD ENG... Food Engineering (SAUS)
FoodIn......... Food Integrated Tech, Inc. [*Associated Press*] (SAG)
FoodIntg...... Food Integrated Tech, Inc. [*Associated Press*] (SAG)
Food Manuf... Food Manufacture (journ.) (SAUS)
Foodmk........ Foodmaker, Inc. [*Associated Press*] (SAG)
Food Pol...... Food Policy [*A publication*] (JLIT)
Food Process... Food Processing (journ.) (SAUS)
Foodq.......... Foodquest, Inc. [*Associated Press*] (SAG)
Foodqust...... Foodquest, Inc. [*Associated Press*] (SAG)
Food Res Inst Stud... Food Research Institute Studies [*A publication*] (JLIT)
Food Rev..... Food Review [*A publication*] (PABS)
Foodrm........ Foodarama Supermarkets, Inc. [*Associated Press*] (SAG)
FoodSc........ Food Science (DD)
Foodst.......... Foodstuff (SAUS)
FoodTch....... Food Technology Service, Inc. [*Associated Press*] (SAG)
Food Tech... Food Technology (MEC)
Food Technol Aust... Food Technology in Australia (journ.) (SAUS)
FOOE........... Mekambo [*Gabon*] [*ICAO location identifier*] (ICLI)
FOOF........... Fanout-Observed Output Function (MHDB)
FOOG........... Port Gentil [*Gabon*] [*ICAO location identifier*] (ICLI)
FOOH........... Fell on Outstretched Hand [*Medicine*] (WDAA)
FOOH........... Omboue [*Gabon*] [*ICAO location identifier*] (ICLI)
FOOI............ Iguela [*Gabon*] [*ICAO location identifier*] (ICLI)
FOOK........... Makokou/Epassengue [*Gabon*] [*ICAO location identifier*] (ICLI)
FOOL........... Libreville/Leon M'Ba [*Gabon*] [*ICAO location identifier*] (ICLI)
FOOM........... Mitzic [*Gabon*] [*ICAO location identifier*] (ICLI)
FOON........... Franceville/Mvengue [*Gabon*] [*ICAO location identifier*] (ICLI)
FOOO........... Libreville [*Gabon*] [*ICAO location identifier*] (ICLI)
FOOP........... First Order Polynomial Predictor (SAUS)
FOOQ........... Foodquest, Inc. [*NASDAQ symbol*] (SAG)
FOOQW........ Foodquest Inc. Wrrt [*NASDAQ symbol*] (TTSB)
FOOR........... Lastourville [*Gabon*] [*ICAO location identifier*] (ICLI)
Foord........... Foord's Supreme Court Reports [*Cape Colony, South Africa*] [*A publication*] (DLA)
FOOS........... Fail-Operational-Fail-Safe (SAUS)
FOOS........... Field Officer, Ordnance Service (SAUO)
FOOS........... Force Out of Service [*Telecommunications*] (TEL)
FOOS........... Function-Oriented Organizational Structure (AAG)
FOOS........... Sette-Cama [*Gabon*] [*ICAO location identifier*] (ICLI)
FOOSH......... Fell Onto Outstretched Hand [*Medicine*] (EDAA)
FOOSP......... Fourteen-O-One Statistical Program [*Military*] (SAA)
FOOT........... Follow-On Operational Test
FOOT........... Foothill Independent Banc [*NASDAQ symbol*] (TTSB)
FOOT........... Foothill Independent Bancorp [*NASDAQ symbol*] (NQ)
FOOT........... Forum for Object Oriented Technology (VERA)
FOOT........... Tchibanga [*Gabon*] [*ICAO location identifier*] (ICLI)
Foote & E Incorp Co... Foote and Everett's Law of Incorporated Companies Operating under Municipal Franchises [*A publication*] (DLA)
Foote B & B... Foote's Bench and Bar of the South and Southwest [*A publication*] (DLA)
Foote Highw... Foote's Law of Highways [*A publication*] (DLA)
Foote Int Jur... Foote on Private International Jurisprudence [*A publication*] (DLA)
FootInd......... Foothill Independent Bancorp [*Associated Press*] (SAG)
FOOTL......... Foot Lambert (SAUS)
Footstr......... Footstar, Inc. [*Associated Press*] (SAG)
FOOV........... Libreville [*Gabon*] [*ICAO location identifier*] (ICLI)
FOOW........... Finding Our Own Ways [*An association*] (EA)
FOOY........... Mayumba [*Gabon*] [*ICAO location identifier*] (ICLI)
FOP.............. Faculty of Procurators (SAUO)
FOP.............. falling object protection (SAUS)
FOP.............. Farthest on Point
FOP.............. feminization of poverty (SAUS)
FOP.............. Festschrift fuer Otto Procksch (1934) [*A publication*] (BJA)
FOP.............. Fiber Optics Probe
FOP.............. Fibre Optics Probe (SAUS)
FOP.............. Fibrodysplasia Ossificans Progressiva [*Medicine*]
FOP.............. Financial Operating Plan
F/OP............ Firing/Observation Port
FOP.............. First Off Production (SAUS)
FOP.............. First Order Predictor (SAUS)
FOP.............. Fleet Operations Programme (SAUS)
FOP.............. Flight Operations Panel
FOP.............. Flight Operations Plan (MCD)
FOP.............. Floating Octal Point (SAUS)
FOP.............. Fokker Flight Operations [*Netherlands*] [*ICAO designator*] (FAAC)
FOP.............. Follow on Production (SAUS)
FOP.............. Forced Oscillation Program [*Military*]
FOP.............. Forensic Pathology [*Medicine*] (DHSM)
FOP.............. Form of Payment (TRID)
FOP.............. Forward Observation Post [*Military*]
FOP.............. Forward Operating Pad (SAUS)
FOP.............. Frame Oriented Protocol (SAUS)
FOP.............. Fraternal Order of Police (WDAA)
FOP.............. Fraternal Order of Police, Grand Lodge (EA)
FOP.............. Free on Plane (SAUS)
FOP.............. Friendship Oil Pipeline [*Eastern Europe*]
FOP.............. Friends of Photography (EA)
FoP.............. Friends of the Pleistocene (SAUO)
FOP.............. Friends of the Poor (SAUO)
FOP.............. Fuel Oil Pump (MSA)
FOP.............. Grand Lodge, Ladies Auxiliary, Fraternal Order of Police (EA)
FOPA........... Firearms Owners' Protection Act
FOPBRPIC.... Association for the Development of Further Professional Training in the Foundry and Related Industries (SAUO)
FOPC........... First Order Predicate Calculus (MHDB)
FOPC........... Flag Officer, Pacific Coast [*Canada*]
FOPC........... Flag Officer, Pacific Command (SAUO)
FOPC........... Formosa Plastics [*Federal Railroad Administration identification code*]
FOPC Machine... Fluid-Operated Punched Card Machine (SAUS)
FOPDAC....... Federation of Overseas Property Devlopers, Agents, and Consultants [*British*] (DBA)
FOPEN......... Foliage Penetration [*RADAR*] (MCD)
FOPG........... Flight Operations Planning Group [*NASA*] (NASA)
FOPI............ First Order Polynomial Interpolator (SAUS)
FOPINTRACENLANT... Fleet Operational Intelligence Training Center, Atlantic [*Navy*] (DNAB)
FOPINTRACENPAC... Fleet Operational Intelligence Training Center, Pacific [*Navy*] (DNAB)
FOPL............ First Order Predicate Logic (SAUS)
FOPP........... Fiber Optics Photo Pickup
FOPP........... First Order Polynomial Predictor (SAUS)
FOPP........... Follow-On Parts Production (NASA)
FOPPA......... First-Order Polarization Propagator Approach [*Physics*]
FOP-PT........ Front Oubangais Patriotique - Parti du Travail [*Oubangian Patriotic Front - Party of Labor*] [*Central Africa*] (PD)
FOPR........... Full Outpatient Rate (AFM)
FOPR........... Society of Friends of Puerto Rico (EA)
FOPRA......... Federation of Private Residents Associations (SAUO)
FOPREP....... Force Packaging Report [*Military*]
FOPS........... Fair Organ Preservation Society [*British*]
FOPS........... Falling Object Protection Standards (WPI)
FOPS........... Falling Object Protective Structure [*For mining machines*]
FOPS........... Federation of Playgoers Societies [*British*] (BI)
FOpS............ Fellow of the Optical Society (SAUO)
FOPS........... Field Oriented Programming System (SAUS)
FOPS........... File-Oriented Programming System [*Computer science*] (PDAA)
FOPS........... First Orbit Penetration System (MCD)
FOPS........... Flight Operations and Planning Scheduling (MCD)
FOPS........... Flight Operations and Scheduling (SAUS)
FOPS........... Flight Operations Planning Schedule (SAUS)
FOPS........... Forecast Operating System (SAUO)
FOPSA......... Federation of Productivity Services Association (SAUS)
FOPSA......... Federation of Productivity Services Associations (SAUO)
FOPT........... Fiber Optic Photo Transfer (SAUS)

fopt .... fiber-optics photon transfer (SAUS)
FOPT .... Fiber Optics Photo Transfer
FOPT .... Fibre Optic Photo Transfer (SAUS)
FOPU .... Fort Pulaski National Monument
FOPV .... Outboard-Passenger Vehicle [*Automotive safety*]
FOPW .... Federation of Organizations for Professional Women (EA)
FOPZ .... Formosa Plant [*Federal Railroad Administration identification code*]
foq .... free on quai (SAUS)
foq .... Free on Quay [*Business term*] (ODBW)
FOQ .... Free on Quay [*Business term*]
FOQA .... Flight Operations Quality Assurance [*FAA*] (TAG)
FOQCV .... Fuel Oil Quick Closing Valve (NVT)
FOR .... Boyds Collection [*NYSE symbol*] (SG)
FOR .... Faculty of Radiologists (SAUO)
FOR .... Faculty of Reconstruction (SAUO)
FOR .... Failure Outage Rate [*Electronics*] (IAA)
FOR .... Falloff Ratio (SAUS)
FOR .... Family of Operational Rations [*Army*]
FOR .... Fan-Out Registered (SAUS)
FOR .... Farmer-Owned Reserve [*Business term*]
FOR .... Farm O' Road [*Crosley vehicle*]
FOR .... Federacion Obrera Revolucionaria [*Mexican political party*]
FOR .... Federation of Outdoor Recreationists [*Defunct*] (EA)
FOR .... Fellow of Operational Research [*British*] (DBQ)
FOR .... Fellowship of Reconciliation (EA)
FOR .... Fellowship of Riders (Motorcyclists) [*British*] (BI)
FOR .... Field of Regard
FOR .... Final Outturn Report (SAUS)
FOR .... Flight Operations Review (MCD)
FOR .... Flying Objects Research (SAUS)
For .... Foramen (SAUS)
FOR .... Force (NVT)
FOR .... Forced Outage Rate [*Electronics*] (IEEE)
FOR .... Force Resources Ltd. [*Vancouver Stock Exchange symbol*]
FOR .... Ford Foundation Library, New York, NY [*OCLC symbol*] (OCLC)
FOR .... Fordham [*New York*] [*Seismograph station code, US Geological Survey*] [*Closed*] (SEIS)
For .... Foreign (AL)
for .... Foreign (ELAL)
FOR .... Foreign
FOR .... Foreigner (SAUS)
FOR .... Forel Parchment [*Bookbinding*] (ROG)
FOR .... Foremost-McKesson, Inc. (SAUO)
for .... Forensic (SAUS)
FOR .... Forensic Pathology [*Medicine*]
FOR .... Fore River Railroad Corp. [*AAR code*]
FOR .... Forest
FOR .... Forester (SAUS)
FOR .... Forestry
FOR .... Forestry Resources (SAUS)
for .... Forging (SAUS)
FOR .... Forma Orbis Romanae. Carte Archeologique de la Gaule Romaine [*A publication*] (OCD)
FOR .... Formation (SAUS)
FOR .... Former (SAUS)
FOR .... Formica Corp. [*NYSE symbol*] (COMM)
For .... Fornax [*Constellation*]
For .... Forrester's English Chancery Cases Tempore Talbot [*A publication*] (DLA)
For .... Forrest's English Exchequer Reports [*A publication*] (DLA)
FOR .... Forskolin [*Also, FSK*] [*Organic chemistry*]
FOR .... Forsyth, MT [*Location identifier*] [*FAA*] (FAAL)
FOR .... Fortaleza [*Brazil*] [*Airport symbol*] (OAG)
FOR .... Forte [*Loud*] [*Music*]
FOR .... Fortis Securities [*Formerly, AMEV Securities*] [*NYSE symbol*] (SPSG)
FOR .... Fortran source code (SAUS)
FOR .... Fortune SRL [*Italy*] [*ICAO designator*] (FAAC)
For .... Forum [*Record label*]
FOR .... Forward [*Business term*]
FOR .... Forward Motion [*Indian Railway*] (TIR)
FOR .... Foundation for Ocean Research (SAUO)
FOR .... Free on Rail (ADWA)
FOR .... Free on Rail/Free on Truck [*"INCOTERM," International Chamber of Commerce official code*]
for .... Free on Rails (EBF)
for .... free on road (SAUS)
FOR .... Friends of Rafferty (SAUO)
FOR .... Friends of the River (EA)
FOR .... Fuel Oil Return (AAG)
FORA .... Families of Resisters for Amnesty (EA)
FORA .... Flag Officer Reserve Aircraft (SAUO)
FORA .... Fort Raleigh National Historic Site
FORAC .... Fisheries and Oceans Research and Advisory Council (SAUO)
FORAC .... Fleet Operational Readiness Accuracy Check (SAUO)
FORAC .... For Action
FORACS .... Fleet Operational Readiness Accuracy & Check System (SAUS)
FORACS .... Fleet Operational Readiness Accuracy Check Sites [*Navy*]
FORACS .... Fleet Operational Readiness and Calibration Systems (SAUO)
FORACS .... Force Accuracy Standards
FO RAF .... Flying Officer, Royal Air Force (SAUO)
For Aff .... Foreign Affairs [*A publication*] (BRI)
FORAM .... Foraminiferal [*Geology*]
ForAm .... Foremost Corp. of America [*Associated Press*] (SAG)
for & cc .... free of riots and civil commotion (SAUS)
For&ColBks ... Foreign and Colonial Banks (SAUO)
FORAST .... Forest Responses to Anthropogenic Stress [*Project sponsored by university and governmental research groups*]
FORAST .... Formula Assembler Translator [*Computer science*]
F/O Ratio ..... Fuel to Oxidizer Ratio (SAUS)
FORATOM .... European Atomic Forum (SAUS)
FORATOM .... Forum Atomique Europeen [*Association of European Atomic Forums*] (EAIO)
Forb .... Forbes' Cases in St. Andrews Bishop's Court [*A publication*] (DLA)
Forb .... Forbes' Court of Session Decisions [*Scotland*] [*A publication*] (DLA)
Forb .... Forbes' Journal of the Session [*1705-13*] [*Scotland*] [*A publication*] (DLA)
FORBAK .... Front [*End*]/Back [*End*]
For Bal .... Forensic Balistics (SAUS)
for bal .... forensic ballistics (SAUS)
Forb Bills ..... Forbes on Bills of Exchange [*A publication*] (DLA)
Forbes .... Forbes' Journal of the Session [*1705-13*] [*Scotland*] [*A publication*] (DLA)
ForBetr .... For Better Living, Inc. [*Associated Press*] (SAG)
Forb Inst ..... Forbes' Institutes of the Law of Scotland [*A publication*] (DLA)
FORBIS .... FORTRAN Bibliotheks-System (SAUS)
FORBLOC ..... FORTRAN [*Formula Translating System*] Compiled Block-Oriented Simulation Language [*Computer science*] (IEEE)
for bod .... foreign body (SAUS)
Forb Tr .... Forbes on Trustees and Post Office Savings Banks [*A publication*] (DLA)
FORC .... Fluorinator Off-Gas Recycle Compressor [*Nuclear energy*] (NRCH)
FORC .... Force-Optimized Recoil Control (MCD)
FORC .... Foreclose [*Legal shorthand*] (LWAP)
FORC .... Formula Coder [*Computer science*]
FORCAP .... Force Application Processor (MCD)
FORCAP .... Force Combat Air Patrol [*Military*] (NVT)
forcap .... forward combat air patrol (SAUS)
For Cas & Op ... Forsyth's Cases and Opinions on Constitutional Law [*A publication*] (DLA)
FORCAST ..... Flexible Operational Resolution for Combat Air Support [*Model*] (MCD)
FORCE .... Forecast of Conflict Environment (SAUO)
FORCE .... FORTRAN [*Formula Translating System*] Conversational Environment [*Computer science*]
FORCE .... Western Federation of Regional Construction Employees (SAUO)
FORCE .... Western Federation of Regional Construction Employers
FORCEFLO ... Force Flow [*Model*] [*Army*]
FORCEM .... Force Evaluation Model [*Army*] (RDA)
Forcen .... Forcenergy Gas Exploration, Inc. [*Associated Press*] (SAG)
FORC ENT .... Forcible Entry and Detainer [*Legal term*] (DLA)
FORCK .... Format Checking (SAUS)
FORCL .... Foreclosure [*Legal shorthand*] (LWAP)
FORCOL .... Fourteen Column (SAUS)
For Comp ..... Forsyth on Composition with Creditors [*A publication*] (DLA)
For Cons Law ... Forsyth's Cases and Opinions on Constitutional Law [*A publication*] (DLA)
FORCOPEXOS ... Forward Copy of Orders with Endorsements to Administrative Office, Executive Office of the Secretary of the Navy (DNAB)
FOR CORP .... Foreign Corp. [*Legal term*] (DLA)
FORCORS .... Forestry Committee on Remote Sensing (SAUO)
FORCY .... Forrest City, AR [*American Association of Railroads railroad junction routing code*]
FOrD .... Dickinson Memorial Library, Orange City, FL [*Library symbol*] [*Library of Congress*] (LCLS)
FORD .... Families Opposed to Revolutionary Destruction (SAUO)
FORD .... Fix or Repair Daily [*Reference to the alleged defects of Ford automobiles*]
FORD .... Flight Operations Requirements Document (SAUS)
FORD .... Flip Over and Read Directions (VLIE)
FORD .... Floating Ocean Research and Development [*Station*]
FORD .... Ford [*Commonly used*] (OPSA)
FORD .... Fordham [*England*]
Ford .... Ford Motor Co. [*Detroit, MI*] [*Associated Press*] (SAG)
FORD .... Ford Motor Company
FORD .... Foreign Office Research Department [*British*]
FORD .... Forum for the Restoration of Democracy [*Kenya*] [*Political party*] (ECON)
FORD .... Forward
FORD .... Forward Industries, Inc. [*NASDAQ symbol*] (SAG)
FORD .... Forward Industries(NY) [*NASDAQ symbol*] (TTSB)
FORD .... Found on Road Dead [*Reference to the alleged defects of Ford automobiles*]
FORD .... Found On the Road Dead (SAUO)
FORD .... Fraternal Order of Restored DeSotos (SAUO)
FORDAC .... FORTRAN Data Acquisition and Control (SAUS)
FORDAC .... FORTRAN Data Application and Control (SAUS)
FORDACS .... Fuel Oil Route Delivery and Control System [*Computer-based system*]
FORDAD ...... Foreign Disclosure Automated Data [*System*]
FORDAP .... FORTRAN [*Formula Translating System*] Debugging Aid Program [*Computer science*]
FORDAP .... FORTRAN Dynamic Analyzer Program (SAUS)
Ford-BR .... Ford Brazil S.A. (SAUS)
FORDEX .... Formula Index [*Molecular formula indexing*]
Ford-F .... Ford France S.A. (SAUS)
Fordham Corp Inst ... Proceedings. Fordham Corporate Law Institute [*A publication*] (DLA)
Fordham U ... Fordham University (GAGS)
Ford-I .... Ford Italiana S.p.A. (SAUS)
FORDIM .... Force Distribution Model (SAUO)

FORDIMS..... Force Development Integrated Management System [*Military*]
FORDIMS..... Force Development Management Information System (SAUO)
FORDIO........ Forecast of Radio Propagation Conditions (SAUS)
FordM.......... Ford Motor Co. [*Associated Press*] (SAG)
Ford Oa....... Ford on Oaths [*8th ed.*] [*1903*] [*A publication*] (DLA)
FORDS......... Floating Ocean Research and Development Station
FORDS......... Fords [*Commonly used*] (OPSA)
FORD Station... Floating Ocean Research and Development Station (SAUS)
FORDTIS...... Foreign Disclosure and Technical Information System
FORDU......... For Duty [*Military*]
FORE.......... FORE Systems [*NASDAQ symbol*] (TTSB)
FORE.......... Fore Systems, Inc. [*NASDAQ symbol*] (SAG)
fore............ Forward [*Publishing*] (WDMC)
FORE.......... Foundation for Oceanographic Research and Education
FORE.......... Foundation for Oregon Research and Education (EDAC)
FORE.......... Foundation of Record Education (SAUO)
FORE.......... Fraternity of Recording Executives (EA)
fore............ Front (WDMC)
FORE.......... Fundamental Operations Resources (SAUS)
FORE.......... Future of Ocean Research (SAUO)
fore 1/4s...... fore-quarters (SAUS)
FORECAST... Airlift Requirements Forecast System (SAUO)
FORECAST... Force Accounting System (SAUO)
For Ecol Manage... Forest Ecology and Management [*A publication*] (PABS)
FORECON.... Forward Reconnaissance (NVT)
FORECONCO... Force Reconnaissance Company [*Marine Corps*]
ForeFrt......... ForeFront Group, Inc. [*Associated Press*] (SAG)
FOREG......... Foregoing (ROG)
FOREGE....... Food Regulation Enquiries [*Leatherhead Food Research Association*] [*Information service or system*] (CRD)
Foreign Aff... Foreign Affairs [*A publication*] (JLIT)
FO Relay..... Fast Operating Relay (SAUS)
Foreld......... Foreland Corp. [*Associated Press*] (SAG)
Forelnd........ Foreland Corp. [*Associated Press*] (SAG)
FOREM........ File organisation evaluation model (SAUS)
FOREM........ File Organization and Evaluation Modeling (SAUS)
FOREM........ File Organization Evaluation Model
FOREM........ Force Requirements and Methodology [*Military*]
FOREMAN.... Form Retrieval and Manipulation Language
FOREMAN Language... Form Retrieval and Manipulation Language (SAUS)
foren........... forensic medicine (SAUS)
FORENA....... Forests of Eastern North America (SAUO)
Forensic Eng... Forensic Engineering (journ.) (SAUS)
FORESDAT... Formerly Restricted Data [*Military*]
foresh.......... Foreshorten (VRA)
FOREST....... [*The*] Ancient Order of Foresters [*Freemasonry*] (ROG)
FOREST....... Fast Order Radiation Effects Sampling Technique
FOREST....... Forest [*Commonly used*] (OPSA)
FOREST....... Forestry Sectoral Research and Technology (SAUO)
FOREST....... Freedom Organisation for the Right to Enjoy Smoking Tobacco [*British*] (DI)
Forest AIDS... Forest Products Abstract Information Digest Service [*Database*] [*Germany*] (NITA)
Forest Ecol Manage... Forest Ecology Management (journ.) (SAUS)
Forester....... Chancery Cases Tempore Talbot [*England*] [*A publication*] (DLA)
Forest Ind.... Forest Industries (journ.) (SAUS)
ForestO........ Forest Oil Corp. [*Associated Press*] (SAG)
Forest Prod J... Forest Products Journal (SAUS)
Forestry Abstr... Forestry Abstracts (journ.) (SAUS)
FORESTS..... Forest [*Commonly used*] (OPSA)
ForeSys........ Fore Systems, Inc. [*Associated Press*] (SAG)
FORET......... Forest of East Tennessee (SAUS)
FORET......... Forests of East Tennessee (SAUS)
ForeTch........ Forensic Technologies International Corp. [*Associated Press*] (SAG)
FOREWAS.... Force and Weapon Analysis System (AABC)
FOREWAS.... Force and Weapon on Analysis System (SAUS)
FOREWON... Forces and Weapons
Forex........... Foreign Exchange (TBD)
FOREX......... Foreign Exchange [*Investment term*]
For Exch Bull... Foreign Exchange Bulletin [*A publication*] (DLA)
Forex Club... International Association of Exchange Dealers (SAUO)
forf.............. forfeit (SAUS)
FORF.......... Forfeiture (AFM)
FORF.......... Fortune Financial Group, Inc. [*NASDAQ symbol*] (COMM)
FORF & P.... Forfeiture and Penalties [*Legal term*] (DLA)
FOR/FOT..... Free on Rail/Free on Truck [*Business term*]
FORFTR....... Forfeiture of Pay (DNAB)
FORG.......... Fiber Optic Rate Gyro (SEWL)
FORG.......... Forge [*Commonly used*] (OPSA)
forg............ Forged (VRA)
forg............ forger (SAUS)
Forg............ Forgery (EBF)
FORG.......... Forgery [*Business term*]
FORG.......... Forging (MSA)
F ORG......... Full Organ [*Music*]
FORGE........ File Organization Generator
FORGE........ Funds for Overseas Research Grants for Education (SAUS)
FORGEN....... Force Generation [*Military*] (SAA)
FORGEN....... Force Generation Report (SAUO)
FORGES....... Forges [*Commonly used*] (OPSA)
FORGN........ Foreign
FORGN........ Fourgon
FORGNG...... Forgoing
FORGO........ FORTRAN Load and Go (SAUS)
FORGO........ FORTRAN [*Formula Translating System*] Load and Go System [*University of Wisconsin*] [*Computer science*] (IEEE)
FORGO-77... Compiler language [*Computer science*] (HODG)
FORGOV...... Foreign Government (AFIT)
forgr............ Foreground (VRA)
Forg Top...... Forging Topics (journ.) (SAUS)
For Hort....... Forsyth's Hortensius [*A publication*] (DLA)
FORI............ Forest Research Institute (SAUO)
FORIMS....... FORTRAN [*Formula Translating System*]-Oriented Information Management System [*Computer science*]
FORINDECO... Forest Industries, Development and Consulting Company (SAUO)
For Inf......... Forsyth's Custody of Infants [*A publication*] (DLA)
FORIS.......... Forest Information Resource System (SAUS)
FORIS.......... Forest Resources Information System [*Global Environmental Monitoring System*]
FORIS.......... Forschungsinformationssystem Sozialwissenschaften [*Informationszentrum Sozialwissenschaften*] [*Database*]
FORIS.......... Tropical Forest Resources Information System (SAUS)
FORIV.......... Forest River, ND [*American Association of Railroads railroad junction routing code*]
FORJ........... Fellowship of Religious Journalists (EA)
FORJC......... Forest Junction, WI [*American Association of Railroads railroad junction routing code*]
For Jury Tr... Forsyth's Trial by Jury [*A publication*] (DLA)
FORK.......... Fork [*Commonly used*] (OPSA)
FORKS......... Forks [*Commonly used*] (OPSA)
FORL........... Foreland Corp. [*NASDAQ symbol*] (NQ)
FOR LANG... Foreign Language (WDAA)
FORLL......... Foreland Corp.Wrrt 'L' [*NASDAQ symbol*] (TTSB)
FORLOGMD... Force Logistics Command [*Marine Corps*] (NVT)
FORM.......... Ferromagnetic Object Recognition Matrix
FORM.......... Food Operations Reference Manual (DNAB)
form............ Form (VRA)
FORM.......... Formaline (ACAE)
Form............ Forman's Reports [*1 Scammon, 2 Illinois*] [*A publication*] (DLA)
form............ format (SAUS)
form............ Formation [*Medicine*] (EDAA)
FORM.......... Formation (MSA)
FORM.......... Formerly (ROG)
FORM.......... Formula
form............ formula [*Medicine*] (EDAA)
Form............ Formular (SAUS)
FORM.......... Forum Re Group, Inc. [*NASDAQ symbol*] (COMM)
FORM.......... JetForm Corp. [*NASDAQ symbol*] (NASQ)
FORMA........ FORTRAN [*Formula Translating System*] Matrix Analysis [*Computer science*]
FORMAC...... Fiber-Optic Ring Medium Access Controller (AGLO)
FORMAC...... Formula Assembler Compiler (SAUS)
FORMAC...... Formula Assembler Translator (SAUS)
FORMAC...... Formula Manipulation Compiler [*Programming language*] [*1962*] [*Computer science*]
formal.......... formaldehyde (SAUS)
FORMAL...... Formula Manipulation Language [*1970*] [*Computer science*] (MDG)
Forman........ Forman's Reports [*1 Scammon, 2 Illinois*] [*A publication*] (DLA)
Forman (Ill)... Forman's Reports [*1 Scammon, 2 Illinois*] [*A publication*] (DLA)
FORMAS....... Feedback to Oral Reading Miscues Analysis System (EDAC)
FORMAT...... Foreign Material (MCD)
FORMAT...... FORTRAN [*Formula Translating System*] Matrix Abstraction Technique [*Computer science*] (MCD)
FORMAT-FORTRAN... FORTRAN [*Formula Translating System*] Matrix Abstraction Technique-FORTRAN [*Computer science*] (CSR)
FORMATS.... FDF Orbital and Mission Aids Transformation System (SAUS)
FORMDEPS... FORSCOM [*Forces Command*] Mobilization and Deployment Planning System (MCD)
FORMECU.... Forestry Management, Evaluation, and Co-Ordinating Unit [*Nigeria*] [*World Bank Assisted Project*] [*Federal Department of Rural Development*]
for med........ forensic medicine (SAUS)
FORMERLYRESDAT... Formerly Restricted Data (SAUS)
FORMETS.... NATO Message Test Formatting System (SAUO)
FORMEX...... Formal Executor (IAA)
FORMEX...... Formalized Exchange of Electronic Publications (VERA)
FORMEX...... Format Executor (SAUS)
FORMEX...... Format for the Exchange of Electronic Publications (SAUS)
FORMF........ Jet Form Corp. [*NASDAQ symbol*] (SAG)
FORMICA..... Foreign Military Intelligence Collection Activities [*Navy*] (ANA)
For Min........ Foreign Minister (SAUS)
FORMIS....... FORTRAN Oriented Information Management System (SAUO)
FORML........ FORTH Modification Laboratory (SAUS)
FORMN........ Foreman (WDAA)
FORMN........ Formation
FORMOST.... Force Mobilization Steering Committee [*Army*] (MCD)
FORMPATPAC... Formosa Patrol Force, US Pacific Fleet
Form Pla...... Brown's Formulae Bene Placitandi [*A publication*] (ILCA)
FORMS........ Federation of Rocky Mountain States (SAUO)
FORMS........ Field Office Reporting-Management System [*HUD*]
FORMS........ File Organization and Modeling System (SAUS)
FORMS........ File Organization Modelling System (SAUS)
FORMS........ Form Matrix from Scalar (SAUS)
FORMS........ Forms Management System (SAUS)
FORMS........ Forward Observer's Ranging and Marking Scope (SEWL)
FORMSA...... Force Command Standards Activity
FORMTL...... Form Tool (SAUS)
FORMUL...... Formulary
Forn............ Fornax [*Constellation*]

FORN .... Fornication [*FBI standardized term*]
FORNDY ...... Foreign Duty (DNAB)
FORNN......... Forenoon (FAAC)
Foro Nap ..... Foro Napoletano [*A publication*] (ILCA)
FORPA......... Force Planning System
FORPAC........ Forecasting Passenger and Cargo (MCD)
FORPAC........ Forecasting Passengers and Cargo (SAUS)
For Pathol ... Forest Pathology [*A publication*] (PABS)
FORPC .... Frozen Onion Ring Packers Council [*AFFI*] [*Absorbed by*] (EA)
FORPORT .... Forward Port Capabilities [*Navy*]
For Pr .... Foran. Code of Civil Procedure of Quebec [*A publication*] (DLA)
FOR Press ... Forging Press (SAUS)
FORPRIDECOM... Forest Products Research and Industries Development Commission
FORPRIDECOM... Forest Products Research Industries Development Commission (SAUS)
For Prod J ... Forest Products Journal [*A publication*] (PABS)
FORR .... Forrester Research [*NASDAQ symbol*] (SG)
Forr.............. Forrester's English Chancery Cases Tempore Talbot [*A publication*] (DLA)
Forr.............. Forrest's English Exchequer Reports [*A publication*] (DLA)
ForRel .... Foreign Relations of the United States (SAUO)
For Res........ Forest Research [*A publication*] (PABS)
Forrest......... Forrest's English Exchequer Reports [*A publication*] (DLA)
Forrester...... Forrester's English Chancery Cases Tempore Talbot [*A publication*] (DLA)
FORRK......... Fiber Optic Radar Remoting Kit (SAUO)
FORRS......... Forrest, IL [*American Association of Railroads railroad junction routing code*]
FOR RTS...... Foreign Rights (WDAA)
FORRUM...... Foundation for Objective Research and Reporting on the Unexplained Mysterious (ADWA)
FORS .... Fabrication Operations Requirements System (MCD)
FORS .... Faint Object Red Spectrograph [*Astronomy*]
FORS .... Fiber Optic Rate Sensors [*Instrumentation*]
FORS .... Field Office Reporting System (SAUS)
FORS .... Forensic Science Database [*British Home Office Forensic Science Service*] [*Reading, Berkshire, England*] [*Information service or system*] (IID)
FORS .... Forestry
FORS .... Forschungsprojekte, Raumordnung, Stadtebau, Wohnungswesen [*Regional Planning, Town Planning, Housing, Research Projects Database*] [*Fraunhofer Society*] (IID)
FORS .... ForSoft Ltd.
FORS .... Fully Optimized Reaction Space
FORSCAP..... Force Capability System (SAUO)
Fors Cas & Op... Forsyth's Cases and Opinions on Constitutional Law [*A publication*] (DLA)
Forsch .... [*The*] Forschner Group, Inc. [*Associated Press*] (SAG)
FORSCI......... Federation of Remote Sensing Companies of India (SAUO)
For Sci......... Forest Science [*A publication*] (PABS)
FORSCOM.... Army Forces Command (SAUS)
FORSCOM.... Forces Command [*Formerly, CONARC*] [*Army*]
FORSCOM.... US Army Forces Command (SAUS)
Fors Comp... Forsyth on Composition with Creditors [*A publication*] (DLA)
ForServ........ Foreign Service (DD)
FORSERVSUPPGRU... Force Service Support Group [*Military*] (DNAB)
FORSERVSUPPGRUDET... Force Service Support Group Detachment [*Military*] (DNAB)
FORSGHT .... Foresight
Fors Hor ...... Forsyth's Hortensius [*A publication*] (DLA)
FORSIC........ Forces Intelligence Center (AABC)
FORSIG........ FORSCOM [*Forces Command*] Intelligence Group [*Army*]
Fors Inf........ Forsyth's Custody of Infants [*A publication*] (DLA)
FORSIZE....... Force Sizing Exercise [*Military*]
FORST .... Forestry (SAUS)
FORST .... Foundation for Research, Science and Technology (SAUS)
FORSTAR..... Force Status and Identity Report
FORSTAT ..... Force Status and Identity Report (SAUS)
FORSTAT ..... Force Status and Identity Report System (SAUO)
FORSTAT ..... Force Status Report [*Military*]
ForstC.......... Forest City Enterprises, Inc. [*Associated Press*] (SAG)
Forst Cust.... Forster's Digest of the Laws of Customs [*A publication*] (DLA)
ForstLb .... Forest Laboratories, Inc. [*Associated Press*] (SAG)
ForstO.......... Forest Oil Corp. [*Associated Press*] (SAG)
Fors Tr......... Forsyth on Trusts and Trustees in Scotland [*A publication*] (DLA)
Fors Tr Jur... Forsyth's History of Trial by Jury [*A publication*] (DLA)
FORSTRY..... Forestry
FORSUM...... Force Summary System (SAUO)
FORT .... Fish Oil Restenosis Trial [*Cardiology*]
Fort.............. Flying Fortress (SAUS)
FORT .... Formal Operational Reasoning Test (EDAC)
FORT .... Formula Systems (1985), Ltd. [*NASDAQ symbol*] (NASQ)
FORT .... Formula Translation (VLIE)
FORT .... Fort [*Commonly used*] (OPSA)
Fort.............. Fortescue's English King's Bench Reports [*92 English Reprint*] [*1695-1738*] [*A publication*] (DLA)
FORT .... Fort Howard [*NASDAQ symbol*] (TTSB)
FORT .... Fort Howard Corp. [*NASDAQ symbol*] (SAG)
FORT .... Fortification
fort.............. Fortified [*Nutrition*]
fort.............. Fortify (SAUS)
FORT .... Fortis [*Strong*] [*Pharmacy*]
FORT .... Fortran (VLIE)
Fort.............. Fortress (SAUS)
fort.............. free out (SAUS)
FORT .... Free out, Rye Terms (SAUS)
fort.............. full out (SAUS)
FORT .... Full Out Rye Terms [*Grain trade*]
FORTACOM... FORTRAN Algebraic Compiler (SAUS)
Fort Ar......... Fortified Area (SAUS)
For Tax Bull... Foreign Tax Law Bi-Weekly Bulletin [*A publication*] (DLA)
For Tax L S-W Bull... Foreign Tax Law Semi-Weekly Bulletin [*A publication*] (DLA)
For Tax LS Weekly Bull... Foreign Tax Law Semi-Weekly Bulletin [*A publication*] (DLA)
For Tax LW Bull... Foreign Tax Law Weekly Bulletin [*A publication*] (DLA)
FORTE .... fast on-orbit recording of transient events (SAUS)
FORTE .... Fast Orbital Recording of Transient Events Satellite [*Department of Energy*]
FORTE .... File Organization Technique (BUR)
FORTE .... Formal Description Techniques (VLIE)
FORTE .... Formal Description Techniques for Distributed Systems and Communication Protocols (SAUS)
FORTE .... FRAM [*Ferroelectric RAM*]-Oriented Real-Time Environment
FORTEL........ Formatted Teletypewriter (CET)
Fortes.......... Fortescue's English Courts Reports [*A publication*] (DLA)
Fortesc .... Fortescue's English King's Bench Reports [*92 English Reprint*] [*1695-1738*] [*A publication*] (DLA)
Fortescue..... Fortescue's English King's Bench Reports [*92 English Reprint*] [*1695-1738*] [*A publication*] (DLA)
Fortescue (Eng)... Fortescue's English King's Bench Reports [*92 English Reprint*] [*1695-1738*] [*A publication*] (DLA)
ForteSft........ Forte Software, Inc. [*Associated Press*] (SAG)
Fortes Rep... Fortescue's English King's Bench Reports [*92 English Reprint*] [*1695-1738*] [*A publication*] (DLA)
FOR TFLAC... Fellowship of Reconciliation Task Force of/on Latin American and the Caribbean (SAUO)
FORTFLAC ... Fellowship of Reconciliation Task Force on Latin America and Caribbean (EA)
FortGrp .... Fortress Group, Inc. (The) [*Associated Press*] (SAG)
FORTH......... Compiler language (HODG)
FORTH......... Fort Worth, TX [*American Association of Railroads railroad junction routing code*]
FORTH......... Foundation for/of Research and Technology-Hellas (SAUO)
FORTH......... [*The*] Foundation for Research and Technology Hellas [*Greece*]
FORTH......... Fourth-Generation Language [*Programming language created by Charles Moore*] (CDE)
Fort Hays St U... Fort Hays State University (GAGS)
Forthcoming Int Sci Tech Co... Forthcoming International Scientific and Technical Conferences (journ.) (SAUS)
Forth Dimens... Forth Dimension (journ.) (SAUS)
Forth Worth... Federal Correctional Institution at Fort Worth, Texas (SAUS)
FORTIS........ Fortissimo [*Very Loud*] [*Music*]
FORTIS........ Forward Observation and Reconnaissance Thermal Imaging System (SEWL)
FORTISS...... Fortissimo [*Very Loud*] [*Music*] (ROG)
FORTISS...... Fortissimus [*Strongest*] [*Pharmacy*] (ROG)
FortisSc........ Fortis Securities [*Associated Press*] (SAG)
Fort Jeff....... Fort Jefferson National Monument on the Dry Tortugas in the Gulf of Mexico west-northwest of Key West (SAUS)
FORTL .... Force Requirement Troop List Reporting System (AABC)
Fort Laramie... Fort Laramie National Monument on the Oregon Trail in southeastern Wyoming (SAUS)
Fort LJ......... Fortnightly Law Journal [*A publication*] (DLA)
fortly............ fortnightly (SAUS)
Fort Matanzas... Fort Matanzas National Monument near St Augustine, Florida, built by the Spaniards in 1736 (SAUS)
Fort McHenry... Fort McHenry National Monument in Baltimore Harbor where the Star Spangled Banner was written (SAUS)
FORTN......... Forreston, IL [*American Association of Railroads railroad junction routing code*]
FORTN......... Fortnightly
Fortnightly LJ... Fortnightly Law Journal [*A publication*] (DLA)
Fortn LJ........ Fortnightly Law Journal [*A publication*] (DLA)
Fortn Rev Chicago Dent Soc... Fortnightly Review of the Chicago Dental Society (journ.) (SAUS)
FORTOCOM... FORTRAN [*Formula Translating System*] Compiler [*Computer science*] (SAA)
for tox.......... forensic toxicology (SAUS)
FortPet......... Fortune Petroleum Corp. [*Associated Press*] (SAG)
FortPt........... Fortune Petroleum Corp. [*Associated Press*] (SAG)
Fort Pulaski... Fort Pulaski National Monument at the mouth of the Savannah River (SAUS)
FORTRA....... Federation of Radio and Television Retailers Association (MHDB)
FORTRA....... Federation of Radio and Television Retailers Associations (SAUS)
FORTRAN .... formular translation (SAUS)
FORTRAN .... Formular Translator (SAUS)
FORTRAN .... Formula Translating Language (SAUS)
FORTRAN .... Formula Translating System [*Programming language*] [*1953-54*] (CSR)
FORTRAN .... Formula Translation [*Computer science*] (NAKS)
Fortran......... Formula Translation [*A computer programming language*] (WDMC)
FORTRAN .... Formula Translation Computer Language (IDOE)
FORTRAN .... formula translation language (SAUS)
FORTRAN .... Formula Translator [*Computer science*] (GART)
FORTRAN D... Fortran for Distributed-memory systems (SAUS)
For-Trans..... Ford Foundation Transfer Student Project (SAUO)
FORTRANS... Formula Translating System (SAUS)
fortransit...... formula translator internal translator (SAUS)

FORTRANSIT... FORTRAN [*Formula Translating System*] and Internal Translator System [*Computer science*] (IEEE)
For Trees Livelihoods... Forests, Trees and Livelihoods [*A publication*] (PABS)
FORTRPS..... Force Troops
FORTRUNCIBLE... FORTRAN [*Formula Translating System*] Style Runcible [*Computer science*]
FORTSIM..... FORTRAN Simulation (SAUS)
FORTSK....... For Task Force [*Military*] (AABC)
Fortu........... Fortunius Garcia de Erzila [*Flourished, 16th century*] [*Authority cited in pre-1607 legal work*] (DSA)
FORTUNE..... FORTRAN [*Formula Translating System*] Tuner [*Computer science*]
Fort Union... Fort Union National Monument near Santa Fe (SAUO)
Fort Union... Fort Union National Monument near Santa Fe, New Mexico (SAUS)
Fort Valley St C... Fort Valley State College (GAGS)
FORUM........ Federation Of Retired Union Members (SAUS)
FORUM........ Formula for Optimizing through Realtime Utilization of Multiprogramming (SAUS)
Forum.......... Forum: Bench and Bar Review [*A publication*] (DLA)
Forum.......... Forum. Dickinson School of Law [*A publication*] (DLA)
FORUM........ Forum for Medical Affairs (EA)
Forum.......... Forum Group, Inc. [*Associated Press*] (SAG)
Forum.......... Forum Law Review [*A publication*] (DLA)
Forum.......... The Forum for Health Care Planning (EA)
Forum Devel Stud... Forum for Development Studies [*A publication*] (JLIT)
Forum LR.... Forum Law Review [*A publication*] (DLA)
ForumR........ Forum Retirement Partners Ltd. [*Associated Press*] (SAG)
Forum Rev... Forum Law Review [*A publication*] (ILCA)
Forum Soc Econ... Forum for Social Economics [*A publication*] (JLIT)
FORVR......... Forever
FORWAARD... Foundation of Rehabilitation with Aboriginal Alcohol Related Difficulties [*Australia*]
FORWARD... Feedback Of Repair, Workshop And Reliability Data (SAUS)
FORWARD... Forces Organized Ready for War and Able to Rapidly Deploy (MCD)
Forward....... Forward Industries, Inc. [*Associated Press*] (SAG)
forwd........... Forward (SAUS)
FORWEPCON... Forward Weapons Controller [*Military*] (NVT)
FORWEPCORD... Force Weapons Coordinator [*Navy*] (NVT)
For Whom... For Whom The Bell Tolls (SAUS)
forwn........... forewoman (SAUS)
Forwrd......... Forward Industries, Inc. [*Associated Press*] (SAG)
FORY........... Flag Officer, Royal Yachts [*Navy*] [*British*]
FORZ........... Forzato [*Strongly Accented*] [*Music*]
FOS............. Face of Studs [*Technical drawings*]
FOS............. Factor of Safety (IAA)
fos............. faint object spectography (SAUS)
FOS............. Faint Object Spectrograph [*Astronomy*]
FOS............. Fall of Shot (NVT)
FOS............. Family of Services (SAUS)
FOS............. Family of Small Arms [*Military*] (MCD)
FOS............. Fats and Oils Situation
FOS............. Ferrite Disk Store (SAUS)
FOS............. Festival of Sydney [*Australia*]
FOS............. Fiber-Optic Scintillating [*Plate*]
FOS............. Fiber Optic Sensor (IAA)
FOS............. Fiber Optic Sigmoidoscope [*Medicine*] (MELL)
FOS............. Fiberoptic Sigmoidoscopy [*Medicine*] (MELL)
FOS............. Fiber-Optic System (SAUS)
FOS............. Fibre Optical Sensor (SAUS)
FOS............. Fibreoptic and Optoelectronics Scheme (SAUS)
FOS............. Field Officers School [*Formerly, AOS*] [*LIMRA*]
FOS............. Field of Science (EERA)
FOS............. Field Oriented Support (SAUS)
FOS............. Filed Oriented Support (VLIE)
FOS............. File Operating System (VLIE)
FOS............. File Organization System (DIT)
FOS............. Final Offer Selection (SAUS)
FOS............. Final Operating System (MCD)
FOS............. Finish One Side [*Technical drawings*] (IAA)
FOS............. Fire of Savannas (SAUO)
FOS............. First-Order Spectrum (SAUS)
FOS............. First Order Subroutine (SAUS)
FOS............. Fisheries Organisation (or Organization) Society (SAUO)
FOS............. Fisheries Organization Societies (SAUS)
FOS............. Fisheries Organization Society (COE)
FOS............. Fissura Orbitalis Superior (DB)
FOS............. Flight Operations Segment (SAUS)
FOS............. Flight Operations Support (KSC)
FOS............. Floppy Operating System [*Computer science*] (IAA)
FOS............. Florida Orthopaedic Society (SAUS)
FOS............. Follow-On Satellite (SAUS)
FOS............. Follow-On Spares (AFM)
FOS............. FORTRAN [*Formula Translating System*] Operating System [*Computer science*]
fos............. fossil (SAUS)
FOS............. Fractional Osteoid Surface [*Medicine*] (EDAA)
FOS............. Fragmentary Order System (SAUO)
FOS............. Frank Orthogonal System [*Medicine*] (MELL)
FOS............. Freedom Of Speech (SAUS)
FOS............. Free on Ship [*or Steamer*] [*Shipping*]
FOS............. Free on Station
FOS............. Free on Steamer (ADWA)
fos............. Free on Steamer (EBF)
FOS............. free on steamer or ship (SAUS)
F-o-S.......... Frinton-on-Sea (SAUS)
FOS............. Fructooligosaccharides [*Type of carbohydrate*]
FOS............. Fuel Oil Supply (SAUS)
FOS............. Fuel Oil Supply Co. (SAUO)
FOS............. Fuel-Oxygen Scrap (PDAA)
FOS............. Full Operational Status
FOS............. Functional Operational Specification [*Military*] (CAAL)
FOS............. Function Operational Specification (SAUS)
FOS............. Fundamental Operating System (SAUS)
fos............. Free of Stamp [*Finance*] (ODA)
FOSA........... Family of Small Arms [*Military*]
FOSA........... Federation of Spine Associations (SAUO)
FOSA........... Fixed Orifice Sound Attenuator (DNAB)
FOSA........... Flight Operations Support Annex (SSD)
FOSA........... Formula One Spectators Association (EA)
FOSAMS...... Fleet Optical Scanning Ammo. Marking System (SAUO)
FOSAT......... Fitting Out Supply Assistance Team [*Navy*]
FOSAT......... Fleet Outfitting Supply Assistance Team (SAUO)
FOSATLANT... Fitting Out Supply Assistance Team, Atlantic [*Navy*]
FOSATPAC... Fitting Out Supply Assistance Team, Pacific [*Navy*]
FOSATS....... Fleet Outfitting Supply Assistance Teams (SAUO)
FOSBel........ Belgian Fund for Development Cooperation (SAUO)
FOSC........... Federal On-Scene Commander (DNAB)
FOSC........... Federation of Sidecar Clubs [*British*] (DBA)
FOSC........... From Other Service Centers [*IRS*]
FOSC........... Full Overlap Slotted Container [*Packaging*]
FOSCAN....... Food News Scanning Database [*Leatherhead Food Research Association*] [*Information service or system*] (CRD)
FOSCAN....... Food Scan [*Database from Food Research Association*] [*British*] (NITA)
FOSCAS....... Foreign Ship Construction and Shipyards (MCD)
FOSCO......... Foreign Officer Supply Corps (DNAB)
FOSCO......... Foreign Officer Supply Course (SAUO)
FOSCOD....... Federation of Special Care Organizations in Dentistry (SAUS)
FOSD........... Field Operations and Support Division [*Environmental Protection Agency*]
FO/SD.......... Foreign Office, State Department (SAUO)
FOSD........... Functional Operational Sequence Diagram
FOSDIC........ Field Optical Sending Device (SAUS)
FOSDIC........ Film Optical Scanning Device for Input to Computer (NITA)
FOSDIC........ Film Optical Sensing Device for Input to Computer (SAUO)
FOSDIC........ Film Optical Sensing Device for Input to Computers [*National Institute of Standards and Technology*]
FOSE........... Federal Office Systems Expo [*National Trade Productions*] (TSPED)
FOSE........... Federal Office Systems Exposition (SAUO)
FOSF........... Field Observing Support Facility [*National Center for Atmospheric Research*]
FOSF........... Flag Officer, Surface Flotillas (SAUS)
FOSF........... Friends of Old St. Ferdinand (EA)
FOSF........... Friends of Sinn Fein (SAUS)
FOSFA......... Federation of Oils, Seeds and Fats Association Ltd. (SAUO)
FOSFA......... Federation of Oils, Seeds, and Fats Associations [*British*]
fos fls.......... fossil fuels (SAUS)
FOSFX......... Fidelity Overseas [*Mutual fund ticker symbol*] (SG)
FOSG........... Factory Outlet Shopping Guide (SAUS)
FOSGEN....... Fog Oil Smoke Generator
FOSH........... Full Oldsmobile Service History [*Automotive classified advertising*]
FOSI............ Florida Ocean Sciences Institute (SAUO)
FOSI............ Format Option Specification Instance (SAUS)
FOSI............ Format Output Specification Instance (SAUS)
FOSI............ Formatting Output Specification Instance [*Computer science*]
Fo-Si........... Forsterite-Silica [*Lunar geology*]
FOSIC.......... Fleet Ocean Surveillance Center [*Military*] (POLM)
FOSIC.......... Fleet Ocean Surveillance Information Center [*Navy*] (CAAL)
FOSIC.......... Fleet Ocean Surveillance Information Centre (SAUS)
FOSICPAC.... Fleet Ocean Surveillance Information Center, Pacific [*Navy*] (DNAB)
FOSIF........... Fleet Ocean Surveillance Facility [*Military*] (POLM)
FOSIF........... Fleet Ocean Surveillance Information Facilities [*Navy*]
FOSIF........... Fleet Ocean Surveillance Information Facility (SAUO)
FOSIF........... Fleet Operational Support Intelligence Facility (SAUO)
FOSIFWESTPAC... Fleet Ocean Surveillance Information Facility, Western Pacific [*Navy*] (DNAB)
FOSIL........... FOCAL Simulator Language (SAUS)
FOSIL........... Formulating On-Line Calculations in Algebraic Language Simulator Language (PDAA)
FOSKOR....... Phosphate Development Corporation (SAUO)
FOSL........... Finding of Suitabilty to Lease (BCP)
FOSL........... Focal Simulator Language (SAUS)
FOSL........... Fossil, Inc. [*NASDAQ symbol*] (SAG)
FOSM........... Flag Officer, Submarines [*Navy*] [*British*]
FOSM........... Fort Smith National Historic Site
FOSMA......... Function-Oriented Symbolic Macromodelling Algorithm (PDAA)
FOSMEF....... Flag Officer, Soviet Middle East Forces
FOSN........... Fabrication Order Special Number
FOSNI.......... Flag Officer, Scotland & Northern Ireland (SAUS)
FOSO........... Flight Operations Scheduling Office [*NASA*] (MCD)
FOSO........... Flight Operations Scheduling Officer [*NASA*] (NASA)
FOSOL......... Florian's Own Statistically Oriented Language [*Computer science*] (CSR)
FOSP........... Fabrication Outline Special Purpose
FOSP........... Flight Operations Support Personnel (MCD)
Fo-Sp-Crd-Pl... Forsterite-Spinel-Cordierite-Plagioclase [*Lunar geology*]
FOSPLAN..... Formal Space Planning Language [*Computer science*] (PDAA)
FOSPLAN..... Format Space Planning Language (SAUS)
FOSPSL....... Follow-On Spare Parts Selection List (MCD)
FOSS........... Family of Systems Studies [*Military*] (RDA)
foss............ fear-of-success syndrome (SAUS)

FOSS .... Fiber Optic Sensor System (MCD)
FOSS .... Fiber Optics SONAR System (MCD)
FOSS .... Fiber-Optic Strain Sensor (SAUS)
FOSS .... Field Operations Support System (SAUS)
FOSS .... Fred Olsen Seaspeed Service (SAUS)
FOSS .... Fred Olssen/Seaspeed/Svedel (SAUS)
FOSS .... Functional Operation Simulation System
FOSSCS .... Field Office Sales and Service Costs Study [*LIMRA*]
FOSSIL .... Fido Opus Seadog Standard Interface Layer (SAUS)
FOSSIL .... Fido/Opus/Seadog Standard Interface Layer (VLIE)
FOSSIL .... Fido/Opus/Seadog Standard Interface Level (SAUS)
Fossil .... Fossil, Inc. [*Associated Press*] (SAG)
FOSSIL .... Frame Orientated System for Spectroscopic Inductive Learning [*Data analysis*]
FOSSL .... Follow-On Spares Support List (AFIT)
FOST .... Finding of Suitability to Transfer
FOST .... Flag Officer, Sea Training [*Navy*] [*British*]
FOST .... Flight Operations Support Team (MCD)
Fost .... Foster's English Crown Law Cases [*168 English Reprint*] [*1743-61*] [*A publication*] (DLA)
Fost .... Foster's Legal Chronicle Reports [*Pennsylvania*] [*A publication*] (DLA)
Fost .... Foster's New Hampshire Reports [*A publication*] (DLA)
Fost .... Foster's Reports [*5, 6, and 8 Hawaii*] [*A publication*] (DLA)
FOST .... Fostoria, OH [*American Association of Railroads railroad junction routing code*]
Fost & F ...... Foster and Finlason's English Nisi Prius Reports [*175, 176 English Reprint*] [*A publication*] (DLA)
Fost & F (Eng)... Foster and Finlason's English Nisi Prius Reports [*175, 176 English Reprint*] [*A publication*] (DLA)
Fost & Fin ... Foster and Finlason's English Nisi Prius Reports [*175, 176 English Reprint*] [*A publication*] (DLA)
Fost CL .... Foster's English Crown Law Cases [*168 English Reprint*] [*1743-61*] [*A publication*] (DLA)
Fost CL (Eng)... Foster's English Crown Law Cases [*168 English Reprint*] [*1743-61*] [*A publication*] (DLA)
Fost Cr Law... Foster's English Crown Law Cases [*168 English Reprint*] [*1743-61*] [*A publication*] (DLA)
Fost Doct Com... Foster on Doctors' Commons [*A publication*] (DLA)
Fost El Jur... Foster's Elements of Jurisprudence [*1853*] [*A publication*] (DLA)
Foster .... Foster [*L. B.*] Co. [*Associated Press*] (SAG)
Foster .... Foster's English Crown Law Cases [*168 English Reprint*] [*1743-61*] [*A publication*] (DLA)
Foster .... Foster's New Hampshire Reports [*A publication*] (DLA)
Foster .... Legal Chronicle Reports, Edited by Foster [*Pennsylvania*] [*A publication*] (DLA)
Foster Fed Pr... Foster on Federal Practice [*A publication*] (DLA)
Foster (PA)... Foster's Legal Chronicle Reports [*Pennsylvania*] [*A publication*] (DLA)
Fost Fed Prac... Foster's Treatise on Pleading and Practice in Equity in Courts of the United States [*A publication*] (DLA)
FOSTG .... Freedom of Ocean Science Task Group [*NAS-NRC*] (NOAA)
Fost (Haw)... Foster's Reports [*5, 6, and 8 Hawaii*] [*A publication*] (DLA)
Fost Jt Own... Foster on Joint Ownership and Partition [*A publication*] (DLA)
Fost (NH)... Foster's New Hampshire Reports [*A publication*] (DLA)
Fost on Sci Fa... Foster on the Writ of Scire Facias [*1851*] [*A publication*] (DLA)
Fost Sci Fa... Foster on the Writ of Scire Facias [*1851*] [*A publication*] (DLA)
FOSTTA .... Forum on State and Tribal Toxics Action [*Environmental Protection Agency*] (EGAO)
FostWh .... Foster Wheeler Corp. [*Associated Press*] (SAG)
FOSU .... Fort Summer National Monument (SAUO)
FOSU .... Fort Sumter National Monument
FOSWAC ...... Family of special weapons atomic contractor (SAUS)
FOSWAC ...... Family of Special Weapons Atomic Contractors
FOT .... Face of Template (MCD)
FOT .... Faint Object Telescope (PDAA)
FOT .... Fecal-Oral Transmission [*Medicine*] (EDAA)
FOT .... Fiber-Optics-printing Tube (SAUS)
FOT .... Fiber Optics Technology (SAUS)
FOT .... Fiber Optic Terminal [*Electric*] (ACRL)
FOT .... Fiber Optic Transceiver (VERA)
FOT .... Field Operational Test (SAUS)
FOT .... Fifth-Order Theory
FOT .... Final on Trajectory (SAUS)
FOT .... Flight Operations Team (MCD)
FOT .... Flow Object Tree (SAUS)
FoT .... Foam Tender (WDAA)
FOT .... Follow-On Operational Test (AFM)
FOT .... Follow-On Operational Test and Evaluation (ACAE)
FOT .... Forster [*Airport symbol*]
FOT .... Fortuna, CA [*Location identifier*] [*FAA*] (FAAL)
FOT .... Forward Ordnance Team (SAUS)
FOT .... Forward Transfer [*Telecommunications*] (TEL)
FOT .... forward transfer signal (SAUS)
FOT .... Fourier Optical Transform (SAUS)
FOT .... Franchise Operations Team [*Automobile sales and marketing*]
FOT .... Fraternal Order of Police (SAUO)
FOT .... Free of Tax
FOT .... Free of Turn (SAUS)
fot .... free on train (SAUS)
fot .... Free on Truck (EBF)
FOT .... Free on Truck [*See also FOR*] [*Business term*]
FOT .... Frequence Optimum de Travail [*Optimum traffic frequency*] [*Telecommunications*] (NITA)
FOT .... Frequency for Optimum Traffic (SAUS)
FOT .... Frequency of Optimum Operation (MCD)
FOT .... frequency of optimum traffic (SAUS)
FOT .... Frequency of Optimum Transmission (SAUS)
FOT .... Frequency on Target
FOT .... Frequency Optimum Traffic
FOT .... Fuel Oil Tank (MSA)
FOT .... Fuel Oil Transfer
FOTA .... Fuel open test assembly (SAUS)
FOTA .... Fuels Open Test Assembly [*Nuclear energy*] (NRCH)
FOTACS .... Fleet Operational Telecommunications Automated Control System (ACAE)
FOTALI .... Flag Officer, Taranto and Adriatic and for Liaison
FOT&E .... Follow-on Operational Test and Evaluation (SAUO)
FOT & E .... Follow-On Test and Evaluation (MCD)
FOT&E .... Full Operational Test and Evaluation (ACAE)
FOTARS .... Follow-On Tactical Reconnaissance System (SEWL)
FOTAS .... Forward Observer Target Acquisition System (ACAE)
FOTC .... Force Over-the-Horizon Tactical Coordination (SAUS)
FOTC .... Force Over-the-Horizon Targeting Coordinator [*Navy*] (ANA)
FOTC .... Force Over the Horizon Track Commander (SAUS)
FOTC .... Forward Observer Training Center [*Army*] (INF)
FOTC .... Friends of Terra Cotta (EA)
FOTCL .... Falling off the Chair Laughing (ADWA)
FOTCLANT .... Fleet Operational Training Command, Atlantic (SAUO)
FOTCPAC ..... Fleet Operational Training Command, Pacific (SAUO)
FOTD .... Fiber-Optic Towed Device (SEWL)
FOTE .... Follow-On Operational Test and Evaluation
FOTEGLLD ... Forward Observer Team Equipped with Ground LASER Locator Designator (MCD)
FOTELSYS ... Foreign Telecommunications Systems (MCD)
FOTF .... Fellow of the Ontario Teachers' Federation [*Canada*] (DD)
FOTF .... Folded Other Than Flat [*Freight*]
FOTFL .... Falls on the Floor Laughing (VLIE)
FOTJ .... Formal On-the-Job
FOTL .... Follow-On to Lance [*Army*]
F o t L .... Friends of the Library (SAUS)
FOTLAN .... Fiber-Optics Tactical Local Area Network [*Army*]
FOTLU .... Federation of Organized Trades and Labor Unions (SAUO)
FOTLU .... Federation of Organized Trades and Labor Unions of the United States and Canada (SAUS)
FOTM .... Field office traffic managers (SAUS)
FOTM .... Friends of Old-Time Music [*Later, Society for Traditional Music*] (EA)
FOTMH .... Flush Oil-Tight Manhole (SAUS)
FOTO .... Forced Oscillation in a Tightening Oscillator [*Chemical kinetics*]
FOTO .... Seattle FilmWorks [*NASDAQ symbol*] (SAG)
Fotoball .... Fotoball USA, Inc. [*Associated Press*] (SAG)
Fotobl .... Fotoball USA, Inc. [*Associated Press*] (SAG)
FOTP .... Fiber Optic Test Procedure
FOTP .... Fibre Optic Test Procedure (SAUS)
FOTP .... Fleet Operational Telecommunications Program (DNAB)
FOTP .... Friends of the Prisoners [*Australia*]
FOTR .... Follow-On Tactical Fighter (ACAE)
FOTR .... Follow-On Tactical Reconnaissance (SAUS)
FOTR .... Friends of Old-Time Radio (EA)
FOTR .... Friends of the River (EA)
FOTRS .... Follow-On Tactical Reconnaissance System [*Air Force*] (DOMA)
FOTS .... Fiber-Optic Terminal System (SAUS)
FOTS .... Fiber Optic Transmission System [*Consists of modulated light signals sent through glass fibers and demodulated by photo-diodes*] [*Data transmission*]
FOTS .... fibre optics transmission system (SAUS)
FOTS .... Fibre-Optic Transmission System (SAUS)
FOT Signal... Forward-Transfer Signal (SAUS)
FOTS-LH ...... Fibre Optic Transmission System - Long Haul (SAUS)
fotsu .... forward observer target survey unit (SAUS)
FOTU .... Fotus [*A Fermentation*] [*A publication*] (ROG)
FOU .... Field Operating Unit (VLIE)
FOU .... Forward Oberservation Unit (SAUO)
FOU .... Forward Observation Unit (SAUS)
FOU .... Forward Observer Unit (SAUO)
FOU .... Fougamou [*Gabon*] [*Airport symbol*] (OAG)
Foulk Act ..... Foulke's Action at Law [*A publication*] (DLA)
FOUN .... Fort Union National Monument
FOUND .... Finding of Unstructured Documents (SAUS)
Found .... Foundation (AAGC)
FOUND .... Foundation
FOUND .... Founding (SAUS)
found .... foundling (SAUS)
found .... foundry (SAUS)
Found Econ Educ... Foundation for Economic Education (SAUO)
FOUNDEX ..... International Foundry Exhibition
FoundH .... Foundation Health Corp. [*Associated Press*] (SAG)
Found L Rev... Foundation Law Review [*A publication*] (DLA)
Foundly Trade J... Foundry Trade Journal (journ.) (SAUS)
FOUNDN ...... Foundation
Found Phys... Foundations of Physics (journ.) (SAUS)
Found Phys Lett... Foundations of Physics Letters (journ.) (SAUS)
Foundry Manage Technol... Foundry Management and Technology (journ.) (SAUS)
Foundry Pract... Foundry Practice (journ.) (SAUS)
Foundry Technol... Foundry Technology (journ.) (SAUS)
Foun Mot Dent... Foundation for Motivation in Dentistry (SAUO)
fount .... Fountain (VRA)
Fount .... Fountainhall's Decisions, Scotch Court of Session [*1678-1712*] [*A publication*] (DLA)

Fount Dec.... Fountainhall's Decisions, Scotch Court of Session [*1678-1712*] [*A publication*] (DLA)
Foun Than... Foundation of Thanatology (SAUO)
FountO...... Fountain Oil, Inc. [*Associated Press*] (SAG)
FountPw...... Fountain Powerboat Industries, Inc. [*Associated Press*] (SAG)
FOUO.......... For Official Use Only [*Army*]
FOUP.......... Front Opening Unified Pod (AAEL)
FOUR.......... Federation of Union Representatives (BARN)
FOUR.......... Forum Group [*NASDAQ symbol*] (TTSB)
FOUR.......... Forum Group, Inc. [*NASDAQ symbol*] (NQ)
FOUR.......... Four Media Co. [*NASDAQ symbol*] (NASQ)
FOURA......... Forward Observation Unit, Royal Artillery (SAUO)
FOURATAF... Fourth Allied Tactical Air Force (SAUS)
FOURATAF... Fourth Allied Tactical Air Force, Central Europe
Four Cs...... Community-Coordinated Child Care (SAUS)
FOURS........ Focus, Organize, Understand, Rehearse, and Simplify [*Business Term*]
FOUS.......... Fort Union Trading Post National Historic Site
FOUSA........ Finance Officer, United States Army
FOV............ Family Of Vehicles (SAUS)
fov............. feld of view (SAUS)
FoV............ Field of View (ADWA)
FOV............ Field of View [*or Vision*]
FOV............ Field-of-Vision (SAUO)
FOV............ First Orbital Vehicle [*NASA*] (NASA)
FOV............ Flyable Orbital Vehicle
FOV............ Forward Observer Vehicle [*Military*] (MCD)
FOV............ Friends of Opera in Victoria [*Australia*]
FOV............ Valencia Community College, Orlando, FL [*Library symbol*] [*Library of Congress*] (LCLS)
FOVA.......... Fort Vancouver National Historic Site
FOVEANT..... Foveantur [*Let Them Be Fermented*] [*Pharmacy*] (ROG)
FOVES......... Fine Old Very Extra Special [*Designation on brandy labels*]
FOVH.......... Flush Oiltight Ventilation Hole (MSA)
FOVI........... Field of Vision Intact [*Ophthalmology*] (DAVI)
FOVISSSTE... Fondo de la Vivienda del Instituto de Seguridad y Servicios Sociales de los Trabajadores del Estado (SAUO)
FOW............ Family Of Weapons (SAUS)
FOW............ Fenestration Oval Window [*Otology*]
FOW............ First Open Water [*Shipping*]
fow............. first open water chartering (SAUS)
FOW............ Forced-Oil and Forced-Water (SAUS)
FOW............ Forge Welding
FOW............ Formation Ordnance Workshop [*British military*] (DMA)
FOW............ Free on Wagon [*Business term*]
fow............. Free on Wagons [*or Water*] (EBF)
fow............. free on warehouse (SAUS)
FOW............ Free on Water [*Business term*]
FOW............ Free on Wharf [*Business term*] (ROG)
FOW............ Free on Wheels (SAUS)
FOW............ Friends of the Wilderness [*Defunct*] (EA)
FOW............ Morristown, MN [*Location identifier*] [*FAA*] (FAAL)
FOW............ Oil-Immersed Forced-Oil-Cooled with Forced-Water Cooler [*Transformer*] (IEEE)
FOWABPF.... Flag Officer, Western Area, British Pacific Fleet
FOWCIS....... Forest and Wildlands Conservation Information System [*FAO*] [*United Nations*] (DUND)
FOWHM....... Fuel Oil and Water Heater Manufacturers Association (EA)
Fowl Col...... Fowler. Collieries and Colliers [*4th ed.*] [*1884*] [*A publication*] (DLA)
Fowl L Cas... Fowler's Leading Cases on Collieries [*A publication*] (DLA)
Fowl Pews... Fowler on Church Pews [*A publication*] (DLA)
Fowl Pr........ Fowler's Exchequer Practice [*A publication*] (DLA)
FOWM......... Fibre Optic Well Monitoring System (SAUO)
FOWP.......... Fertilisers from Organic Wastes Program (EERA)
FOWP.......... Field office work plan (SAUS)
FOWSAB...... Federation of Women Shareholders in American Business [*New York, NY*] (EA)
FOWW......... Follow On Wild Weasel (ACAE)
FOX............ Fiber Optic Extension (SAUS)
FOX............ fiber optic transceiver (SAUS)
FOX............ Fibre Optic Transceiver (SAUS)
FOX............ Fidelity Online Express [*Trading and investment tracking program*] (PCM)
FOX............ Field Operational X.500 (SAUS)
FOX............ Field Oxide (AAEL)
FOX............ Fishery-Oceanography Experiment (USDC)
FOX............ Fox, AK [*Location identifier*] [*FAA*] (FAAL)
FOX............ Foxboro Co. (SAUO)
FOX............ Fox Entertainment Grp 'A' [*NYSE symbol*] (SG)
FOX............ Foxmeyer Corp. [*NYSE symbol*] (SPSG)
FOX............ FoxMeyer Health [*NYSE symbol*] (TTSB)
Fox............. Fox's Circuit and District Court Decisions [*United States*] [*A publication*] (DLA)
Fox............. Fox's Patent, Trade Mark, Design, and Copyright Cases [*Canada*] [*A publication*] (DLA)
Fox............. Fox's Registration Cases [*England*] [*A publication*] (DLA)
FOX............ Futures and Options Exchange [*British*]
FOX............ Jetair APS [*Denmark*] [*ICAO designator*] (FAAC)
FOX............ London Futures and Options Exchange (SAUO)
Fox & S....... Fox and Smith's Irish King's Bench Reports [*1822-24*] [*A publication*] (DLA)
Fox & S (Ir)... Fox and Smith's Irish King's Bench Reports [*1822-24*] [*A publication*] (DLA)
Fox & Sm.... Fox and Smith's Irish King's Bench Reports [*1822-24*] [*A publication*] (DLA)
Fox & Sm.... Fox and Smith's Registration Cases [*1886-95*] [*A publication*] (DLA)
Fox & Sm RC... Fox and Smith's Registration Cases [*1886-95*] [*A publication*] (DLA)
Fox & S Reg... Fox and Smith's Registration Cases [*1886-95*] [*A publication*] (DLA)
Fox Dig Part... Fox's Digest of the Law of Partnership [*A publication*] (DLA)
Foxes.......... Fox Islands off southwestern tip of Alaska (SAUS)
Foxi............ Fibre Optic Taxi (SAUS)
FOXI............ Foxmoor Inds Ltd [*NASDAQ symbol*] (TTSB)
FOXI............ Foxmoor Industries Ltd. [*NASDAQ symbol*] (SAG)
FOXI............ Foxmoor International Films Ltd. [*NASDAQ symbol*] (COMM)
Foxm........... Foxmeyer Health Corp. [*Associated Press*] (SAG)
FoxMHlt....... FoxMeyer Health Corp. [*Formerly, National Intergroup*] [*Associated Press*] (SAG)
Foxmor........ Foxmoor Industries Ltd. [*Associated Press*] (SAG)
Fox Pat C..... Fox's Patent, Trade Mark, Design, and Copyright Cases [*Canada*] [*A publication*] (DLA)
Fox Pat Cas... Fox's Patent, Trade Mark, Design, and Copyright Cases [*Canada*] [*A publication*] (DLA)
Fox PC......... Fox's Patent, Trade Mark, Design, and Copyright Cases [*Canada*] [*A publication*] (DLA)
FOXPr......... FoxMeyer Health $5 Cv Pfd [*NYSE symbol*] (TTSB)
FOXPrA....... FoxMeyer Hlth $4.20 Ex'A'Pfd [*NYSE symbol*] (TTSB)
Fox Reg Ca... Fox's Registration Cases [*England*] [*A publication*] (DLA)
FOXY.......... Fraction-Optimizing X-Y Collector [*Spectroscopy*]
FOY............ Fellowship of Youth [*British*] (BI)
FOY............ Fellowship of Youth, Cambridge (SAUO)
FOY............ FGGE [*First Global Atmospheric Research Program Global Experiment*] Operational Year [*Marine science*] (MSC)
Foy............. Fowey (SAUS)
FOY............ Foya [*Liberia*] [*Airport symbol*] (OAG)
FOY............ Foyer (MSA)
FOzM.......... Ozona Microfilm, Inc., Ozona, FL [*Library symbol*] [*Library of Congress*] (LCLS)
FP.............. Fabry-Perot [*Etalon on interferometer*] [*Optics*]
FP.............. Face Plate (SAUS)
FP.............. Faceplate (IEEE)
FP.............. Facial Pain (MELL)
FP.............. Facing Point (SAUS)
FP.............. Factory Pass (AAG)
FP.............. Failure potential (SAUS)
FP.............. Fair Play [*Signature used on warning letters sent by George Metesky, the "Mad Bomber" of New York City in 1940's and 1950's*]
FP.............. Faithful Performance
FP.............. Falk Project for Economic Research in Israel (SAUO)
FP.............. False Positive [*Medicine*]
FP.............. False Pretenses
FP.............. Familial Polyposis [*Medicine*] (MELL)
FP.............. Family Physician (MELL)
FP.............. Family Planning
FP.............. Family Practice [*or Practioner*]
FP.............. family practitioner (SAUS)
FP.............. Family Product (SAUS)
FP.............. Fanconi-Petrassi [*Syndrome*] [*Medicine*] (DB)
FP.............. Far Point (SAUS)
FP.............. Fascist Party (SAUO)
FP.............. Fast Path (ACAE)
fp............... fast peak (SAUS)
FP.............. Fast Processor [*Instrumentation*]
FP.............. Fatherhood Project (EA)
FP.............. Fat Pad (MELL)
FP.............. Fecal Pellet
FP.............. Federacion Progresista [*Spain*] [*Political party*] (EY)
FP.............. Federal Parliament (DLA)
FP.............. Federal Party [*Namibia*] (PPW)
F/P............. Federal/Provincial (FOTI)
FP.............. Federal Publication (SAUO)
FP.............. Feedback Positive [*Computer science*]
FP.............. Feedback Potentiometer
FP.............. Feeding Point (SAUS)
FP.............. Feeding Pump (MELL)
FP.............. Feed Pump (SAUS)
FP.............. Fee Paid [*Classified advertising*]
fp............... feld punishment (SAUS)
FP.............. Fellowship in Prayer [*An association*] (EA)
FP.............. Fellowship Party [*British*]
FP.............. Female Penitentiary [*British*] (ROG)
FP.............. Female Protein [*Biochemistry*]
FP.............. Feminist Press [*An association*] (EA)
F-P............. Femoral-Popliteal [*Medicine*] (MAE)
FP.............. Ferriprotoporphyrin [*Biochemistry*]
FP.............. Fertilization Product (SAUS)
FP.............. Festpunkt [*Reference point, a surveying term*] [*German military - World War II*]
FP.............. Fetal Presentation [*Medicine*] (MELL)
FP.............. Fiat Pilula [*Let a Pill Be Made*] [*Pharmacy*]
FP.............. Fiat Potio [*Let a Potion Be Made*] [*Pharmacy*]
FP.............. Fiber Passive (SAUS)
FP.............. Fibrinopeptide
FP.............. Fibrous Plaster (ADA)
FP.............. Fielding Percentage [*Baseball term*] (NDBD)
FP.............. Field Park (SAUS)
FP.............. Field Portable
FP.............. Field Potential [*Neuroelectricity*]

FP Field Printing (SAUS)
FP Field Protective (AAG)
FP Field Punishment [*Military*]
FP Fighter Prop
FP Filament Power Supply (SAUS)
FP File Packing (SAUS)
FP File Parameter (SAUS)
FP File Processing (SAUS)
FP File Processor [*Computer science*] (BUR)
FP File Protect
FP Film Pack [*Photography*]
Fp Filtered Phosphate (MAE)
FP Filter Paper
FP Filter Pump (SAUS)
FP Final Payment (TVEL)
FP Final Plan (DNAB)
FP Financial Plan
FP Financial planning (SAUS)
FP Fine Paper
FP Fine Particle (SAUS)
FP Fine Particulate (GFGA)
FP Fine Particulate Matter (SAUS)
FP Fine Pointing (MCD)
fp fine print (SAUS)
FP Finger Pin (SAUS)
FP Finger Pulse (SAUS)
fp Fin Prochain [*At the End of Next Month*] [*Business term*] [*French*]
fp Fireplace (ADWA)
FP Fireplace [*Real estate*]
fp Fireplace (MIST)
FP Fire Plug
FP Fire Point (SAUS)
F/P Fire Policy [*Insurance*]
FP Fire Prevention (WDAA)
FP Fire Proof (SAUS)
Fp Fireproof (DAS)
FP Fire Protection (SAUS)
FP Fire Protection Equipment [*Nuclear energy*] (NRCH)
FP Fire Pump Room [*NFPA pre-fire planning symbol*] (NFPA)
FP Firing Point [*Military*] (INF)
FP Firing Position [*Army*] (DOMA)
FP First Monthly Payment
FP First Paragraph
FP First Performance [*Music*]
fp first performed (SAUS)
FP FIRSTPLUS Financial Group [*NYSE symbol*]
FP First Proof (ADA)
FP Fischer & Porter Co. (EFIS)
FP fishery protection (SAUS)
FP Fission Product
FP Fixation Protein [*Biochemistry*] (DB)
FP Fixed Part (SAUS)
FP Fixed Pitch (SAUS)
FP Fixed Point (MCD)
FP Fixed Price
FP Fixed Price contract (SAUS)
fp fix point (SAUS)
FP Flag Plot
FP Flagpole
FP Flag Post (MCD)
FP Flame Photography (SAUS)
FP Flame Photometry (SAUS)
FP Flame Proof (SAUS)
FP Flameproof (AAG)
FP Flame Protected (SAUS)
FP flanged plate (SAUS)
FP Flashless Propellant (SAUS)
FP Flash Photolysis [*Chemical kinetics*]
FP Flash Point
FP Flash pot (SAUS)
FP Flash Profile (EURO)
FP Flat Pack (IAA)
FP flat package (SAUS)
FP Flat Pad
FP Flat Panel [*Computer science*]
FP Flat Paper (DAVI)
F/P Flat Pattern
FP Flat Plate [*Medicine*]
FP Flat Point [*Technical drawings*]
FP Flavin Phosphate [*Biochemistry*]
FP Flavoprotein [*Biochemistry*]
FP Flavor Profile [*Sensory test method developed by A. D. Little, Inc.*]
FP Fleet Paymaster [*Navy*] [*British*] (ROG)
FP Flexible Pavements (SAUS)
FP Flexible Programming (SAUS)
FP Flight Pay
FP Flight Plan [*Aviation*]
FP Flight Planning (SAUS)
FP Flight Position [*Aerospace*] (IAA)
F/P Flight Programmer (AAG)
FP Flight Progress (KSC)
FP Floating Open Marine Policy [*Insurance*] (DS)
FP Floating Point [*Computer science*] (BUR)
FP Floating Policy [*Insurance*]
FP Flood-Prone Rice Program (SAUO)
FP Florid Papillomatosis [*Medicine*]
fp flower people (SAUS)
F/P Fluid/Plasma Ratio [*Biochemistry*] (DAVI)
FP Fluid Pressure [*Spinal fluid pressure*] [*Medicine*] (DAVI)
FP Fluorescence Polarization
FP Fluorescent Particle
FP Fluorescent Pseudomonad spp.
FP Fluorochrome/Protein (SAUS)
FP Fluorophosphate (SAUS)
FP Fluoropolymers [*Organic chemistry*]
FP Flying Psychologists [*Defunct*] (EA)
FP Focal Plane [*Photography*]
FP Focal Point (SAUS)
FP Fokker-Planck Equation [*Mathematics*]
FP Food Poisoning [*Medicine*]
FP Food Policy [*British*]
FP Food Processing (SAUS)
FP Food Processor (SAUS)
FP Food Production [*British*]
FP Foot Pad (MELL)
FP Foot Path (SAUS)
FP Footpath (ADA)
FP Foot Patrol (AFM)
FP Foot Pound (SAUS)
FP Foot-Pound [*Unit of work*]
FP Forbidden Planet [*Bookstore chain*] [*British*]
FP Force Package (SAUS)
FP Fordyce & Princeton Railroad Co. [*AAR code*]
fp Forearm Pronated [*Medicine*]
FP Foreground Program (SAUS)
FP Foreign Policy
FP Foreign Program [*FCC*] (NTCM)
FP Forensic Pathologist (ODA)
fp fore part (SAUS)
FP Forepeak [*Naval architecture*]
Fp fore peak (SAUS)
FP Fore Perpendicular
FP Forest Park [*State*] (EERA)
FP Forest Patrol [*Activity of Civil Air Patrol*]
FP Forfeiture of Pay
FP Formal Parameter (SAUS)
FP Format Primary (SAUS)
FP Former Priest
FP Former Pupil [*Alumnus*] [*British*]
FP For Private Use (ROG)
FP Forte Piano [*Loud, then Soft*] [*Music*]
fp Fortepiano (GROV)
FP Forward Peak (DNAB)
FP Forward Perpendicular
FP Fouling Point [*Indian Railway*] (TIR)
FP Four-Pole (SAUS)
FP Fowl Pest (SAUS)
FP FoxPro (SAUS)
FP Frame Period [*Computer science*] (IAA)
FP Frame Pointer [*Computer science*]
FP Frame Protected [*Insurance classification*]
FP Framework Programme (SAUS)
FP Franklin Pierce [*US president, 1804-1869*]
FP Franklin Planner [*Annual organizer*]
FP Free Pardon (ADA)
FP Free Piston [*Machinery*] (DS)
FP Free Play [*Military*] (CAAL)
FP Free Port [*Shipping*]
f P free pratique (SAUS)
FP Free Presbyterian (SAUO)
FP Free Press (SAUS)
FP Free Propellers (AAG)
fp Freezing Point (SHCU)
FP Freezing Point
FP freight and passengers (SAUS)
FP Freight and Passenger Vessels [*Army*]
fp freight paid (SAUS)
fp Freight Prepaid (SAUS)
FP Fremskrittspartiet [*Progress Party*] [*Norway*] [*Political party*] (PPE)
FP French Patent
fp French Polynesia [*MARC country of publication code*] [*Library of Congress*] (LCCP)
FP Fresh Paragraph (ADA)
FP Friendly Peersuasion [*Girls Club of America*] (EA)
FP [*The*] Friends Program (EA)
FP Friends' Provident Life Office [*Insurance*] [*British*]
FP Frog Pond - Frog Collectors Club (EA)
Fp Frontispiece (NTCM)
fp Frontispiece [*Publishing*] (WDAA)
FP Fronto-Parietal [*Anatomy*] (MAE)
FP Front Panel [*Navy Navigation Satellite System*] (DNAB)
FP Front Populaire [*Burkina Faso*] [*Political party*] (EY)
FP Front Projection (NTCM)
FP Frozen Plasma [*Medicine*]
FP Fructose Phosphate (SAUS)
FP Fruition Project (EA)
FP Fuel (Petroleum) (DA)
FP Fuel Pressure (NASA)
FP Fuel Pump (HAWK)
FP Fuel Pump Gasket [*Automotive engineering*]

fp ... full page (SAUS)
FP ... Full Parole (FOTI)
FP ... Full Pay [*Military*] [*British*] (ROG)
FP ... Full Pension [*Hotel rate*]
FP ... Full Period
FP ... Full Point (SAUS)
FP ... Full Power
FP ... Full Price (ADA)
FP ... Fully Paid [*Business term*]
FP ... Functional Path (NASA)
FP ... Functional Programming (RALS)
FP ... Functional Proponent
FP ... Function Part (SAUS)
FP ... Function Path (NAKS)
FP ... Function Point (GART)
FP ... Function Procedure (SAUS)
FP ... Function Processor (NITA)
FP ... Fundal Pressure (MAE)
FP ... Fundamental Parameter (SAUS)
FP ... Fungiform Papilla [*Medicine*] (MELL)
FP ... Fungus Proof
FP ... Fuse Plug (SAUS)
FP ... Fusible Plug [*Engineering*] (IAA)
FP ... Fusing Point
FP ... Fusion Point (SAUS)
FP ... fusion power (SAUS)
FP ... Liberal Party (Sweden) [*Political party*] (PSAP)
FP ... Patriotic Front (D. Rep. Congo) [*Political party*] (PSAP)
FP ... Pipefitter [*Navy*]
fp ... plasma frequency (SAUS)
F_p ... Power-Loss Factor (IDOE)
FP ... Progress Party (Denmark) [*Political party*] (PSAP)
FP ... Public Forecasts [*Symbol*] [*National Weather Service*]
FP ... Shipfitter [*Navy symbol*]
FP ... Simmons [*ICAO designator*] (AD)
FP ... Sub-committee on Fire Protection (SAUO)
fp ... Foolscap (ODA)
fp ... Forward Pass (ODA)
FP1 ... Floating Platform No. 1 [*English bilingual film made in Germany with actor Conrad Veidt, 1933*]
FP-1 ... Force Package One (SAUS)
fp4c ... full page four colors (SAUS)
FP-25 ... People's Forces of 25 April [*Portugal*] (PD)
FP-31 ... Frente Popular 31 de Enero [*31st January Popular Front*] [*Guatemala*] (PD)
FPA ... Facilities Procurement Application (AAG)
FPA ... Facility Pattern Array (SAUS)
FPA ... Failure Print Address (SAUS)
FPA ... Failure Probability Analysis (MCD)
FPA ... Families for Private Adoption (EA)
FPA ... Family Planning Association
FPA ... Family Planning Australia (SAUO)
FPA ... Far Point of Accommodation [*Ophthalmology*]
FPA ... Fast-Pass Algorithm
FPA ... Feature Protection Area [*Conservation*] [*Australia*]
FPA ... Federal Party of Australia [*Political party*]
FPA ... Federal Pesticide Act (GNE)
FPA ... Federal Physicians Association (EA)
FPA ... Federal Power Act (SAUO)
FPA ... Federal Powers Act (GNE)
FPA ... Federal Preparedness Agency [*FEMA*]
FPA ... Federal Professional Association [*Later, FEPA*]
FPA ... Federal Property Assistance [*Department of Health and Human Services*]
FPA ... Federation of Motion Picture Producers in Asia (SAUO)
FPA ... Federation of Professional Athletes [*Later, NFLPA*] (EA)
FPA ... FedEx Pilots Association
FPA ... Fibrinopeptide A [*Biochemistry*]
fpa ... fibrinopeptide-A (SAUS)
FPA ... Field Profit Analysis
FPA ... Fill Producers' Association
FPA ... Film Production Association of Great Britain (BI)
FPA ... Filter Paper Activity
FPA ... Final Power Amplifier
FPA ... Financial Printers Association (EA)
FPA ... Fire Protection Association [*British*]
FPA ... Fire Protection Association [*Australia*]
FPA ... First Pennsylvania Corp. (SAUO)
FPA ... First Point of Aries [*Navigation*]
FPA ... First Production Article (MCD)
FPA ... Fixed Plant Adapter (DWSG)
FPA ... Fixed Point Addition (SAUS)
FPA ... Fixed Point Arithmetic (SAUS)
FPA ... Fixed Price with Adjustment (ACAE)
FPA ... Fixed Principal Axes [*Hypothesis describing forces in a sand-pile*]
FPA ... Flat Plate Aerial (SAUS)
FPA ... Flat-Plate Antenna [*or Array*]
FPA ... Flexible Packaging Association (EA)
FPA ... Flexible Premium Annuity (PDAA)
FPA ... Flight Path Accelerometer
FPA ... Flight Path Analysis
FPA ... Flight Path Angle (MCD)
FPA ... Flight Plan Approval [*Aviation*] (AFM)
FPA ... Flight Plan Area [*Aviation*] (FAAC)
FPA ... Floating Point Accelerator (SAUS)
FPA ... Floating-Point Accelerator [*Computer science*] (BYTE)
FPA ... Floating Point Accumulator (SAUS)
FPA ... Floating Point Addition (SAUS)
FPA ... Floating Point Arithmetic (SAUS)
FPA ... Flowers and Plants Association [*British*] (DBA)
fpa ... fluorescent pen aerosol (SAUS)
FPA ... Fluorophenylalanine [*Biochemistry*]
FPA ... Flying Pharmacists of America [*Defunct*] (EA)
FPA ... Flying Physicians Association (EA)
FPA ... Focal Plane Array (SAUS)
FPA ... Focal Plane Assembly (ACAE)
FPA ... Food and Environmental Protection Act (HEAS)
FPA ... Food Production Administration [*World War II*]
FPA ... Force Planning Analysis [*Army*] (AABC)
FPA ... Foreign Policy Association (EA)
FPA ... Foreign Press Association (EA)
FPA ... Forest Practice Act (SAUS)
FPA ... Forest Practices Act [*Tasmania*] [*State legislation*] (EERA)
FPA ... Forest Products Abstracts [*Oxford, England*] [*A publication*]
FPA ... Forest Products Association (EERA)
FPA ... Forests Production Association [*Australia*]
FPA ... Formalin-Propionic Acid-Alcohol [*Fixative*] [*Botany*]
FPA ... Formula Pricing Agreement (AAGC)
FPA ... Forward Pitch Amplifier (MCD)
FPA ... Forward Planning Activity (SAUO)
FPA ... Foundation for Public Affairs (EA)
FPA ... FPA Corp. [*Associated Press*] (SAG)
FPA ... Franklin Pierce Adams [*1881-1960*] [*American newspaper columnist*]
FPA ... Freemantle Port Authority (SAUO)
fpa ... Free of Particular Average (EBF)
FPA ... Free of Particular Average [*Insurance*]
FPA ... Free of Particular Average Unless Caused By (MARI)
FPA ... Free Pacific Association (EA)
FPA ... Free Press Association (EA)
FPA ... Freestyle Players Association
FPA ... Freethought Press Association (SAUO)
FPA ... Friends of the Peaceful Alternatives [*Defunct*] (EA)
FPA ... Full Performance Antenna (SAUS)
FPA ... Function point analysis (SAUS)
FPA ... Fundamental Planning Analysis (MCD)
FPA ... Funding Program Advice [*Military*] (AABC)
FPA ... Fused Polyethylene Aluminium
FPA ... Fusion Power Associates (EA)
FPa ... Larimer Memorial Library, Palatka, FL [*Library symbol*] [*Library of Congress*] (LCLS)
FPA71 ... Fire Precautions Act 1971 (HEAS)
FPAA ... Federacion Panamericana de Asociaciones de Arquitectos [*Panamerican Federation of Architects' Associations*] (EA)
FPAA ... Field Programmable Analog Array (AAEL)
FPAA ... Final Procurement Action Approval (MCD)
FPAA ... First Printings of American Authors [*A publication*]
FPAA ... Flat Plate Array Aerial (SAUS)
FPAA ... Flat Plate Array Antenna (SAUS)
FPAA ... Flight Path Analysis Area [*Space Flight Operations Facility, NASA*]
FPAA ... Fort Polk Army Airfield [*Fort Polk, LA*]
fpaa ... free from particular average, absolutely (SAUS)
FPAA ... Fresh Produce Association of the Americas (NTPA)
FPA Abs ... Free of Particular Average Absolutely (MARI)
fpaac ... Free of Particular Average American Conditions (EBF)
FPAAC ... Free of Particular Average, American Conditions [*Insurance*]
FPAB ... Forest Practices Appeals Board (SAUO)
FPAC ... Flight Path Analysis and Command [*Team*] [*NASA*]
FPAC ... Food Services Purchasing Association of Canada (SAUO)
FPAC ... Fusion Policy Advisory Committee [*Department of Energy*]
FPACCP ... Foundation for the Preservation of Antique and Contemporary Cup Plates (EA)
FPAD ... Field Programmable Address Decoder (SAUS)
FPAD ... Fret Payable a Destination [*Freight Payable at Destination*] [*French*] [*Business term*]
FPAD ... Fund for Peaceful Atomic Development [*Defunct*]
FPAEC ... Free of Particular Average, English Conditions [*Insurance*]
FPAF ... Fixed Price Award Fee [*Contract*]
FPAF ... Fixed Price Award Free (SAUS)
FPAG ... Flight Path Analysis Group (ACAE)
FPA/GSA ... Federal Preparedness Agency/General Services Administration
FPAH ... Foundation for Preservation of the Archeological Heritage (EA)
FPAK ... Family Planning Association of Kenya (EERA)
FPAL ... Field Programmable Array Logic (SAUS)
FPAL ... Floating-Point Arithmetic Library [*Computer science*] (MHDI)
FPAL ... Florida Power and Light (SAUS)
FPAL ... Full-Term Deliveries, Premature [*Preterm*] Deliveries, Abortions, and Living Children [*Gynecology and obstetrics*] (DAVI)
FPAM ... FPA Medical Management [*NASDAQ symbol*] (SAG)
FPAM ... FPA Medical Mgmt [*NASDAQ symbol*] (TTSB)
FPA Md ... FPA Medical Management [*Associated Press*] (SAG)
FP&A ... Freight Prepaid and Allowed (SAUS)
FP&C ... Financial planning and control (SAUS)
FP & D ... Facility Planning and Design (KSC)
FP & DB ... Facilities Planning and Development Branch [*BUPERS*]
FP & E ... Food Products and Equipment [*A publication*]
FP&GPC ... Finance, Publications and General Purposes Committee (SAUS)
FPANSW ... Family Planning Association of New South Wales [*Australia*]
FPANY ... Film Producers Association of New York [*Defunct*] (EA)
FPANZ ... Fellow, Public Accountant, New Zealand
FPAP ... Family Planning Association of Pakistan (SAUO)

FPap........... Federal Paper Board Co., Inc. [*Associated Press*] (SAG)
FPAP........... Floating Point Arithmetic Processor (SAUS)
FPAP........... Floating-Point Array Processor [*Computer science*]
FPAPA......... Forest Products Accident Prevention Association (SAUO)
FPAPWG...... Fluid Processes in Accretionary Prisms Working Group (SAUO)
FPAR........... Fraction of PAR Absorbed by the Plant Canopy (SAUS)
FPAS........... Fail-Passive Autoland System [*Aviation*]
FPAs........... Family Planning Agencies
FPAS........... Federal Property and Administrative Services (SAUO)
FPAS........... Fellow of the Pakistan Academy of Sciences
FPAS........... Focal-Plane Array Seeker (SAUS)
FPAS........... Foreign Purchase Acknowledgement Statements (EPAT)
FPAS........... Front for Popular Armed Struggle [*Iraq*]
FPASA......... Federal Property and Administrative Services Act [*1949*]
FPA - Suchkopf... Focal Plane Array (SAUS)
FPAT........... Family Planning Association of Tasmania (SAUO)
FPAT........... Fuel pin accident transient (SAUS)
fpaucb......... free from particular average unless caused by (SAUS)
FPAucb........ free of particular average unless caused by (SAUS)
FPAX........... Formosa Transrail [*Private rail car owner code*]
FPB............. Farm Practices Board (FOTI)
FPB............. Fast Patrol Boat [*Navy*] (NVT)
FPB............. Federal Petroleum Board [*Department of the Interior*]
FPB............. Federation of Podiatry Boards [*Later, FPMB*] (EA)
FPB............. Femoral Popliteal Bypass [*Medicine*]
FPB............. Fibrino-Peptide B [*Biochemistry*] (DMAA)
FPB............. Fire Prevention Bureau (SAUS)
FPB............. First Philson Financial Corp. [*AMEX symbol*] (NASQ)
FPB............. Fixed-Price Basis (SAUS)
FPB............. Flexor Pollicis Brevis [*Anatomy*]
FPB............. Flight Progress Board [*Aviation*]
FPB............. Floating-Point Board [*Computer science*] (MHDI)
FPB............. Foreign Policy Briefs
FPB............. Forum of Private Business [*British*]
FPB............. Fuel Preburner (KSC)
FPB............. Fuel Preburner (Space Shuttle Main Engine) (SAUS)
FPB............. Pipefitter (Coppersmith) [*U.S. Navy enlisted rating*] (AUER)
FPBA........... Folding Paper Box Association (DGA)
FPBAA......... Folding Paper Box Association of America [*Later, PPC*] (EA)
FPBCCA....... Famous Personalities' Business Card Collectors of America [*Defunct*] (EA)
FP Bcp......... FP Bancorp, Inc. [*Associated Press*] (SAG)
FPBD........... Fibrous Plasterboard
FPBD........... Functional Plan Block Diagram (DOMA)
FPBG........... Final Program and Budget Guidance
FPBG........... Fingerprick Blood Glucose [*Medicine*] (MELL)
fpbg............ Fast Patrol Boat with Guided Missiles (ODA)
FPBK........... First Patriot Bankshares [*NASDAQ symbol*] (SAG)
FPBN........... FP Bancorp [*NASDAQ symbol*] (TTSB)
FPBN........... FP Bancorp, Inc. [*NASDAQ symbol*] (SAG)
FPBOV......... Fuel Preburner and Oxidizer Valve (NASA)
FPBRS......... Fels Parent Behavior Rating Scales [*Psychology*]
FPBT........... Fountain Powerboat Industries, Inc. [*NASDAQ symbol*] (COMM)
FPBX........... FPB Leasing [*Private rail car owner code*]
FPc............. Bay County Public Library, Panama City, FL [*Library symbol*] [*Library of Congress*] (LCLS)
FPC............. Facilities projects control (SAUS)
FPC............. Facility Power Control (AAG)
FPC............. Faculty and Promotions Committee (SAUS)
FPC............. Fall Planting Council (EA)
FPC............. Familial Polyposis Coli [*Later, FAP*] [*Medicine*]
FPC............. Family Personal Computer (PCM)
FPC............. Family Planning Center (WDAA)
FPC............. Family Planning Clinic [*British*]
FPC............. Family Practice Center (MEDA)
FPC............. Family Practice Clinic (ADWA)
FPC............. Family Practitioner Committee [*British*]
FPC............. Family Proceedings Court (SAUO)
FPC............. fast patrol craft (SAUS)
FPC............. Fast Positive Complex (SAUS)
FPC............. Fast Pursuit Craft (SAUS)
FPC............. Federal Pacifc Electric (SAUS)
FPC............. Federal Pacific Electric Company (SAUO)
FPC............. Federal Personnel Council [*Abolished, 1954*] [*Civil Service Commission*]
FPC............. Federal Petroleum Commission (SAUS)
FPC............. Federal Power Commission [*Superseded by Department of Energy, 1977*]
FPC............. Federal Power Commission Reports [*A publication*] (DLA)
FPC............. Federal Prison Camp (SAUO)
FPC............. Federal Property Council [*Terminated, 1977*]
FPC............. Federal Publishers Committee (SAUO)
FPC............. Federal US Power Commission (SAUS)
FPC............. Federation of Painting Contractors Ltd. (SAUO)
FPC............. Fellow of Pembroke College [*British*] (ROG)
FPC............. Feminist Party of Canada
FPC............. Ferrite Pot Core
FPC............. Field Petroleum Corp. [*Vancouver Stock Exchange symbol*]
FPC............. Field Petroleum Corporation (SAUO)
FPC............. Field Police Camp (SAUO)
FPC............. Field Press Censorship
FPC............. Fiji Pine Commission (SAUO)
FPC............. File Parameter Card (SAUS)
FPC............. Final Processing Center
FPC............. Final procurement and construction (SAUS)
FPC............. Financial Print & Communications Ltd. [*British*]
FPC............. Financial Programs Committee (SAUO)
FPC............. Fine Pumice Concrete (SAUS)
FPC............. Finisher/Preserver/Cleaner (DGA)
FPC............. Fire Permit Computer (ACAE)
FPC............. Fire Pump Control (IEEE)
FPC............. Firestone Plastics Company (SAUO)
FPC............. Firestone Polyvinyl Chloride
FPC............. Fiscal Policy Council (EA)
FPC............. Fishery Protection Cruiser (SAUS)
FPC............. Fish Protein Concentrate [*For use in antistarvation programs*]
FPC............. Fish Protein Content (SAUS)
FPC............. Fixed Paper Capacitor
FPC............. Fixed Partial Charge [*Physical chemistry*]
FPC............. Fixed Photoflash Capacitor
FPC............. Fixed Point Calculation
FPC............. Fixed Point Computation (SAUS)
FPC............. Fixed Point Computer (SAUS)
FPC............. Fixed Polycarbonate Capacitor
FPC............. Fixed Precision Capacitor
FPC............. Fixed Price Call
fpc.............. fixed price contract (SAUS)
FPC............. Fixed Price Contracts
FPC............. Fixed Program Computer
fp-C............ flash point-Celsius (SAUS)
FPC............. Flat Plate Collector [*Engineering*] (BARN)
FPC............. Flexible Printed Circuit
FPC............. Flexible Program Computer (SAUS)
FPC............. Flexible Program Control (SAUS)
FPC............. Flight Path Control
FPC............. Flight Programmer Computer
fpc.............. flight progress chart (SAUS)
FPC............. Flight Purpose Code (DNAB)
FPC............. Floating Point Calculation (SAUS)
FPC............. Floating-Point Calculation
FPC............. Floating Point Computation (SAUS)
FPC............. Floating Point Constant (SAUS)
FPC............. Floating Point Coprocessor (SAUS)
FPC............. Florida Portland Cement [*Federal Railroad Administration identification code*]
FPC............. Florida Power Corporation (SAUO)
FPC............. Florida Presbyterian College [*Later, Eckerd College*]
FPC............. Florida Progress [*NYSE symbol*] (TTSB)
FPC............. Florida Progress Corp. [*Formerly, Florida Power Corp.*] [*NYSE symbol*] (SPSG)
FPC............. Florida Progress Corporation (SAUO)
FPC............. Flowers and Plants Council (SAUO)
FPC............. Flowers Publicity Council (SAUO)
FPC............. Flowers Publicity Council Limited, London (SAUO)
FPC............. Flowers Publicity Council Ltd. [*British*] (BI)
FPC............. Fluid Power Centre [*University of Bath*] [*British*] (CB)
FPC............. Fluids Pressure Control (NASA)
FPC............. Focal Plane Camera (ROG)
FPC............. Food Packaging Council (EA)
FPC............. Food Priority Countries (SAUO)
FPC............. Food Protein Concentrate (PDAA)
FPC............. Food Protein Council [*Later, SPC*] (EA)
FPC............. Forced Pair Copulation [*Sociobiology*]
FPC............. Forest Products Council [*Western Australia*]
FPC............. For Private Circulation
FPC............. Forty Pound Charge (SAA)
FPC............. Forward Power Controller (MCD)
FPC............. Foundation for Philosophy of Creativity (EA)
FPC............. Foundation for Psychotherapy and Counselling (SAUO)
FPC............. Frank Phillip College (SAUO)
FPC............. Frank Phillips College [*Texas*]
FPC............. Free Polymer-Derived Carbon [*Chemistry*]
FPC............. Free-Programmable Controller (SAUS)
FPC............. French Petroleum Company (SAUO)
FPC............. French Pressure Cell
FPC............. Frente Popular Costarricense [*Costa Rican Popular Front*] [*Political party*] (PPW)
FPC............. Frequency Parent Coefficient (SAUS)
FPC............. Frequency Plane Correlator (IAA)
FPC............. Friends Peace Committee (EA)
FPC............. Front Panel Control
FPC............. Frozen Pea Council [*Defunct*]
FPC............. Fuel Pool Cooling [*Nuclear energy*] (NRCH)
FPC............. Functional Processor Cluster (SAUS)
FPC............. Functional Progression Chart [*Telecommunications*] (TEL)
FPC............. Fusion Power Core (SAUS)
FPC............. Future Physicians Clubs (EA)
FPC............. United States Federal Power Commission Opinions and Decisions [*A publication*] (DLA)
FPCA........... Family Planning Councils of America (SAUO)
FPCA........... Federal Pay Comparability Act (SAUS)
FPCA........... Federal Pay Comparability Act of 1970
FPCA........... Federal Pollution Control Act (SAUO)
FPCA........... Federal Post Card Application [*For an absentee ballot*] (AABC)
FPCA........... Fiber Producers Credit Association (EA)
FPCA........... Forward Power Control Assembly (MCD)
FPCA........... Forward Power Controller Assembly [*Aerospace*] (NAKS)
FPCA........... Foundation of Pharmacists and Corporate America for AIDS Education (EA)

FPCANSW.... Federation of Parents and Citizens' Associations of New South Wales [*Australia*]
FP-CART...... Federal/Provincial Committee on Atlantic Region Transportation [*Canada*]
FPCC........... Fair Play for Cuba Committee [*Defunct*]
FPCC........... Federal Potato Co-ordinating Committee [*Australia*]
FPCC........... First Portuguese Canadian Club
FPCC........... Fixed Polycarbonate Capacitor
FPCC........... Fixed Printed Circuit Capacitor
FPCC........... Flight/Propulsion Control Coupling [*Air Force*]
FPCC........... Fluid Power Coordinating Council (SAUO)
FPCC........... Forest Park Chamber of Commerce (SAUS)
FPCC........... Fuel Pool Cooling and Cleanup [*Nuclear energy*] (NRCH)
FPCCI.......... Federation of Pakistan Chambers of Commerce and Industry (ECON)
FPCCM......... Flight Planning and Cruise Control Manual (MCD)
FPCCS......... Fuel Pool Cooling and Cleanup System [*Nuclear energy*] (NRCH)
FPCD........... Federal Personnel and Compensation Division (AAGC)
FPCDE......... Freight/Postage Code (SAUS)
FPCE........... Fission Products Conversion and Encapsulation [*Plant*] [*Nuclear energy*]
FPCE........... Floating-Point C Extension [*Computer science*]
FPCE........... Floating-Point C Extension (specification) (SAUS)
FPCEA......... Fibreboard Packaging Case Employers Association (SAUO)
FPCEA......... Fibreboard Packing Case Employers Association (SAUO)
FPcG........... United States Department of Commerce, National Oceanic and Atmospheric Administration, Gulf Coastal Fisheries Center, Panama City, FL [*Library symbol*] [*Library of Congress*] (LCLS)
FPCH........... Foreign Policy Clearing House [*Defunct*]
FPCH........... Foreign Policy Clearinghouse (SAUS)
FPCI........... Federal Penal and Correctional Institution (WDAA)
FPCI........... Federal Penal and Correctional Institutions (SAUO)
FPCI........... Fluid Power Consultants International (EA)
FPCL........... Front Paisanu di Liberazione [*Corsica*]
FPCLANT..... Fleet Programming Center, Atlantic
FPCM........... Fibroblast Populated Collagen Matrix [*Biology*]
FPCM........... Floor Plate-Conditioned Culture Medium
FPCMA......... Fibreboard Packing Case Manufacturers' Association [*British*] (BI)
FPcN........... Northwest Regional Library, Panama City, FL [*Library symbol*] [*Library of Congress*] (LCLS)
FPcNM......... United States Navy, Mine Defense Laboratory, Technical Library, Panama City, FL [*Library symbol*] [*Library of Congress*] (LCLS)
FPCO........... Facilities Procuring Contracting Officer [*Military*] (AFIT)
FPCO........... Florida Partners Corporation (SAUO)
FPCORP....... Financial Post Canadian Corporate Database [*Financial Post Corporation Service Group*] [*Information service or system*] (CRD)
FPCP........... Ferrocene Polymer Cure Process
FPCP........... Floating Point Co-Processor [*Motorola*] (NITA)
FPCR........... Federal Power Commission Reports
FPCR........... Fluid Poison Control Reactor (IAA)
FPCS........... Farm Planning Computer Service (SAUO)
FPCS........... Felixstowe Port Consultrng Services (SAUS)
FPCS........... File & Program Catalog System (SAUO)
FPCS........... Fire Power Control Subsystem (SAUS)
FPCS........... Focal-Plane Crystal Spectrometer
FPCS........... Free Polar Corticosteroids [*Endocrinology*]
FPCS........... Freezing Point Calibration Standard
FPCS........... Fuel Pool Cooling System [*Nuclear energy*] (IEEE)
FPCS........... Full-Page Composition System [*Computer science*]
FPC's.......... Functions/Parameters/Characteristics (MCD)
FPCSTL....... Fission Product Control Screening Test Loop [*Nuclear energy*] (NRCH)
FPCU........... Fuel Pump Control Unit (MCD)
FPCZ........... Florida Power [*Federal Railroad Administration identification code*]
FPD............. Facilities Planning and Design (SAUS)
FPD............. Facilities Planning Document (ACAE)
FPD............. Federacion Popular Democratica [*Popular Democratic Federation*] [*Spain*] [*Political party*] (PPE)
FPD............. Federal Court Procurement Decisions [*A publication*] (AAGC)
FPD............. Federal Pattern Description (AAG)
FPD............. Federal Public Defender (SAUO)
fpd.............. Feet per Day (SAUS)
FPD............. Ferrite Phase Driver
FPD............. Feto-Pelvic Disproportion [*Medicine*] (DMAA)
FPD............. Field Petrol Depot (SAUS)
FPD............. Field Plated Diode (PDAA)
FPD............. First Part Done [*Computer science*] (CIST)
FPD............. Fixed Partial Denture [*Dentistry*] (DAVI)
FPD............. flame photometric detection (SAUS)
FPD............. Flame Photometric Detector
FPD............. Flat Pack Diode
FPD............. Flat-Panel Display [*Instrumentation*]
FPD............. Flat Plate Display (SEWL)
FPD............. Flight Projects Directorate (SAUS)
FPD............. Floating Point Data (SAUS)
FPD............. Floating Point Device (SAUS)
FPD............. Floating Point Division (SAUS)
FPD............. Florida P&L 8.75% 'QUIDS' [*NYSE symbol*] (TTSB)
FPD............. Florida Power & Light [*NYSE symbol*] (SAG)
FPD............. Flush Plate Diode (PDAA)
FPD............. Flush Plate Dipole (PDAA)
FPD............. Focal-Plane Deviation (AAEL)
FPD............. Foreign Publicity Department (SAUO)
FPD............. Fort Peck District (SAUO)
FPD............. FoxPro for DOS (SAUS)
FPD............. Free Democrats (Germany) [*Political party*] (PSAP)
FPD............. Friction Pressure Drop
FPD............. Front for Democracy (Angola) [*Political party*] (PSAP)
FPD............. Full Page Display (BYTE)
FPD............. Full Paid [*Stock exchange term*] (SPSG)
FPD............. Full Power Days [*Nuclear energy*] (NRCH)
FPD............. Full-power days (SAUS)
FPD............. Full-power delays (SAUS)
Fpd.............. Fully Paid (EBF)
FPD............. Functional planning document (SAUS)
FPDA........... Finnish Plywood Development Association
FPDA........... Five Power Defence Agreement (SAUS)
FPDA........... Five Power Defence Arrangement (SAUO)
FPDA........... Fluid Power Distributors Association (EA)
FPDB........... Force Planning Data Base (SAUO)
FPDC........... Federal Procurement Data Center [*Database*]
FPDD........... Familial Pure Depressive Disease
FPDD........... Final Project Design Description (NRCH)
FP/DF.......... Fluid Physics/Dynamics Facility (SSD)
FPDG........... Foreign Policy Discussion Group (EA)
FPDI............ Flat Panel Display Interface [*Computer science*] (VERA)
FPDI............ Flight Path Deviation Indicator [*Navigation*]
FPDI............ Food Processing Development Irradiator
FPDL........... Federacion de Partidos Democraticas y Liberales [*Federation of Democratic and Liberal Parties*] [*Spain*] [*Political party*] (PPE)
FPDL........... Fission Products Development Laboratory [*ORNL*]
FPDL........... Flashlamp-Pumped Dye LASER
FPDM.......... Fault/Pattern Data Merger (ACAE)
FPDP........... Flight Path Design Program
FPDP........... Follow-On Program Development Plan (SAA)
FPDP........... Front Panel Data Port (SAUS)
FPDR........... Flight proof design release (SAUS)
FPDS........... Federal Procurement Data System [*Database*] (IID)
FPDS........... Fission Product Detection System (SAUS)
FPDS........... Fleet Probe Data System [*Navy*] (NG)
FPDS........... Fleet Problem Data System (SAUS)
FPDT........... Federal Police Disciplinary Tribunal [*Australia*]
FPDU........... FTAM [*File Transfer, Access, and Management*] Protocol Data Unit [*Telecommunications*] (OSI)
FPDVP......... Frostig Program for the Development of Visual Perception [*Psychiatry*] (DAVI)
FPE............. Fairport, Painesville & Eastern Railway Co. [*AAR code*]
FPE............. False-Positive Error [*Medicine*] (MELL)
FPE............. Fatal Pulmonary Embolism [*Medicine*] (MELL)
FPE............. Federal Pacific Electric (SAUS)
FPE............. Federal Pacific Electric Co. (SAUO)
FPE............. Federal Pioneer Ltd. [*Toronto Stock Exchange symbol*]
FPE............. Federal Procurement Eligibility
FPE............. Federation des Pecheurs de l'Est [*Eastern Fishermen's Federation - EFF*] [*Canada*]
FPE............. File Protection Function (SAUS)
FPE............. Final Prediction Error [*Statistics*]
FPE............. Final Predictor Error (SAUS)
FPE............. Fire Protection Engineer (SAUS)
FPE............. Fire Pump Engine [*Auto racing engine model designation*] [*British*]
FPE............. First-pass-Effekt (SAUS)
FPE............. Fixed Potential Electrode [*Electrochemistry*]
FPE............. Fixed Price with Escalation
FPE............. Flight Planning Element (ACAE)
FPE............. Floating Point Engine (VERA)
FPE............. Foam PolyEthylene (SAUS)
FPE............. Foot-Pounds of Energy
FPE............. Force and Plan Execution (SAUO)
FPE............. Force Planning Estimate (MCD)
FPE............. Force-Producing Element (SAUS)
FPE............. FORTRAN [*Formula Translating System*] Programming Environment [*Computer science*] (HGAA)
FPE............. Foundation for Personality Expression (SAUO)
FPE............. Friends Peace Exchange (EA)
FPE............. Fruit & Produce Exchange (SAUO)
FPE............. Fuel pin elevator (SAUS)
FPE............. Full Personality Expression (SAUS)
FPE............. Functional Program Elements [*NASA*]
FPE............. Fundamental Phenomena Experimentation (SSD)
FPe............. Pensacola Public Library, Pensacola, FL [*Library symbol*] [*Library of Congress*] (LCLS)
FPEA........... Fellow of the Physical Educatian Association (SAUO)
FPEA........... Ford Philpot Evangelistic Association (EA)
FPEB........... Family Planning Evaluation Branch [*Public Health Service*] (IID)
FPEB........... Fuel Pool Exhaust Blower [*Nuclear energy*] (NRCH)
FPEBT......... Fire Prevention and Engineering Bureau of Texas (SAUO)
FPEC........... Federal Pacific Electrical Company (SAUO)
FPEC........... Federal Pacific Electric Co. (KSC)
FPEC........... Fixed Porcelain Enamel Capacitor
fpec............ four-pile-extended cantilever (SAUS)
FPeC........... Pensacola Junior College, Pensacola, FL [*Library symbol*] [*Library of Congress*] (LCLS)
FPeCC......... Pensacola Christian College, Pensacola, FL [*Library symbol*] [*Library of Congress*] (LCLS)
FPEC Platform... Four-Pile Extended Cantilever Platform (SAUS)
FPED........... Family Planning Evaluation Division [*HEW*] (IID)
FPED........... Fann Production Economics Division (SAUS)
FPED........... Farm Production Economics Division (SAUO)
FPED III....... Force Protection Equipment Demonstration III
FPEE........... Fuel pin examination equipment (SAUS)

FPEEPM....... Floor Proximity Emergency Escape Path Marking [*Aviation*] (DA)
FPEG....... Fast Pulse Electron Gun (MCD)
FPeGS....... Church of Jesus Christ of Latter-Day Saints, Genealogical Society Library, Pensacola Branch, Pensacola, FL [*Library symbol*] [*Library of Congress*] (LCLS)
FPeHiP....... Historic Pensacola Preservation Board, Pensacola, FL [*Library symbol*] [*Library of Congress*] (LCLS)
FPEIS....... Fine Particulate Emissions Information System [*Environmental Protection Agency*] (GFGA)
FPeJC....... Pensacola Junior College, Pensacola, FL [*Library symbol*] [*Library of Congress*] (LCLS)
FPEM....... Force and Plan Execution Monitoring (SAUO)
FPeN....... United States Naval Air Station, Pensacola, FL [*Library symbol*] [*Library of Congress*] (LCLS)
FPeN-M....... United States Navy, Naval Aerospace Medical Institute, Pensacola, FL [*Library symbol*] [*Library of Congress*] (LCLS)
FPEPA....... Fixed Price with Economic Price Adjustment (SAUS)
FPEPA....... Fixed-Price with Economic Price Adjustment [*Type of contract*] (AAGC)
F-P equations... Fokker-Planck equations (SAUS)
FPerCC....... Taylor County Court House, Perry, FL [*Library symbol*] [*Library of Congress*] (LCLS)
FPERR....... Field Personnel Record
FPES....... Femtosecond Photoelectron Spectroscopy
FPeU....... University of West Florida, Pensacola, FL [*Library symbol*] [*Library of Congress*] (LCLS)
FPeW....... West Florida Regional Library, Pensacola, FL [*Library symbol*] [*Library of Congress*] (LCLS)
FPF....... Fail to Pay Fine [*Motor vehicle violation code used in state of Maryland*] (MVRD)
FPF....... Familial Pulmonary Fibrosis
FPF....... Fast Path Feature (VLIE)
FPF....... Feathered Pipe Foundation (EA)
FPF....... Federal Packaging Facility (SAUS)
FPF....... Feed Per Foot (SAUS)
FPF....... Fibroblast Pneumonocyte Factor [*Biochemistry*]
FPF....... File Protection Function (SAUS)
FPF....... Final Protective Fire [*Artillery term*]
FPF....... Final Protective Firetask (SAUS)
FPF....... Fine Pointing Facility [*NASA*] (KSC)
FPF....... Fire Protective Fire (SAUS)
FPF....... First Philippine Fund, Inc. [*NYSE symbol*] (SAG)
FPF....... First Phillipine Fund [*NYSE symbol*] (TTSB)
FPF....... Fish Promotional Fund [*National Oceanic and Atmospheric Administration*] (GFGA)
FPF....... Fixed Price Firm (AFM)
FPF....... Flexible Polyurethane Foam
FPF....... Floating Production Facility
FPF....... Fluid Physics Facility (SSD)
FPF....... Force Package File (SAUO)
FPF....... Frames Per Foot of Film (WDMC)
FPF....... Fuel Packaging Facility [*Nuclear energy*]
FPF....... Fuels Processing Facility (SAUO)
FPF....... Full Power Frequency
FPFA....... Family Planning Federation of Australia Inc. (EERA)
FPFA....... Flexible Polyurethane Foam Association (SAUO)
FPFC....... Fixed Photoflash Capacitor
FPFC....... Flight Patrol Fan Club (EA)
FPFC....... Fresh Produce and Floral Council (NTPA)
FPFGBI....... French Polishers' Federation of Great Britain and Ireland [*A union*]
FPFL....... Flight Plan Fuel Load (SAUS)
FPFM....... Fuel pin failure mechanisms (SAUS)
FPFN....... Fast Pulse Forming Network (ACAE)
FPFSG....... Federation of Prisoners' Families' Support Groups (WDAA)
FPG....... Aeroleasing SA [*Switzerland*] [*ICAO designator*] (FAAC)
FPG....... Fasting Plasma Glucose [*Medicine*]
FPG....... Federal Pecan Growers
FPG....... Federated Pecan Growers of the United States of America (SAUO)
FPG....... Film Producers Guild Limited (SAUO)
FPG....... Fire Philatelic Group (EA)
FPG....... Firing Pulse Generator (IAA)
FPG....... Flat Package of Glas (SAUS)
FPG....... Flat-Pulse Generator (SAUS)
FPG....... Fluorescence plus Giemsa [*Cell-staining technique*]
FPG....... Focal Proliferative Glomerulonephritis [*Medicine*] (DMAA)
FPG....... Force Planning Guide [*Army*] (AABC)
FPG....... Fragmenta Philosophorum Graecorum [*A publication*] (OCD)
FPG....... Frank Porter Graham Child Development Center [*University of North Carolina at Chapel Hill*] [*Research center*] (RCD)
FPG....... Freelance Photographers Guild (SAUS)
FPG....... Pipefitter (Shipboard) [*U.S. Navy enlisted rating*] (AUER)
f-pg-....... Portuguese Guinea [*Guinea-Bissau*] [*MARC geographic area code*] [*Library of Congress*] (LCCP)
FPGA....... Field Programmable Gate Array [*Computer science*]
FPGAUS....... Federated Pecan Growers' Associations of the United States (EA)
FPGEC....... Foreign Pharmacy Graduate Examination Commission (EA)
FPGEC....... Foreign Pharmacy Graduate Examination Committee [*Formerly, Foreign Pharmacy Graduate Examination Commission*] (EA)
FPGEE....... Foreign Pharmacy Graduate Equivalency Examination
FPGL....... Flight Plan Gas Load [*Air Force*]
FPGN....... Focal Proliferative Glomerulonephritis [*Medicine*]
FPGT....... Free Piston Gas Turbine (SAUS)
FPGT Machinery... Free Piston Gas Turbine Machinery (SAUS)
FPH....... Failures per Hour [*Military*]
FPH....... Federal Pacific Hotels (SAUO)
FPH....... Feet per Hour (WDAA)
FPH....... Female Pseudohermaphroditism [*Medicine*] (EDAA)
FPH....... First Pilot Hours (SAUS)
FPH....... Fish Protein Hydrolysate
FPH....... Flavin Phosphate [*Medicine*] (EDAA)
FPH....... Floating-Point Hardware [*Computer science*]
FPH....... Fondation pour le Progrès de l'Homme [*France*] (EERA)
FPH....... Fredericks Place Holdings [*British*]
FPH....... Freephone Supplementary Service [*Telecommunications*] (DOM)
FPH....... Frente Patriotico Hondureno [*Honduran Patriotic Front*] [*Political party*] (PD)
FPH....... Friends of Patrick Henry (EA)
FPH....... Full Power Hours [*Nuclear energy*] (DEN)
FPH_2....... Flavin Phosphate, Reduced [*Biochemistry*] (MAE)
FPHA....... Federal Public Housing Administration (SAUO)
FPHA....... Federal Public Housing Authority [*Functions transferred to Public Housing Administration, 1947*]
FPHA....... Florida Public Health Association (SAUO)
FPharmS....... Fellow of the Pharmaceutical Society [*British*]
FPHB....... Flight Procedures Handbook (MCD)
FPHC....... Fast-Pass Hydrocarbons [*Automotive emissions*]
FPHC....... Foreign Personal Holding Co.
FPHE....... Formaldehyde-Treated Pyruvaldehyde-Stablized Human Erythrocytes [*Medicine*] (EDAA)
FPHE....... Formalin-Treated Pyruvaldehyde-Stabilized Human Erythrocytes [*Immunology*]
FPhilologSoc... Fellow of the Philological Society (SAUO)
FPHNH....... Federation of Private Hospitals and Nursing Homes [*Australia*]
FPHS....... Fallout Protection in Homes (SAUS)
FPHS....... Fallout Protection in Houses
FPhS....... Fellow Philosophical Society [*British*] (WA)
FPhS Eng....... Fellow of the Philosophical Society of England (SAUO)
FPHx....... Family Psychiatry History [*Medicine*] (EDAA)
F Phy S....... Fellow of the Physical Society (SAUS)
F Phys S....... Fellow of the Physical Society [*British*]
F PHYS SOC... Fellow of the Physical Society (SAUO)
FPI....... Fabry-Perot Interferometer
FPI....... Faded Prior to Interception [*RADAR*]
FPI....... Family Pitch In [*Indicates family may eat freely of a certain dish at a meal where guests are present*]
FPI....... Family Programming Interface (VLIE)
FPI....... Fast Probability Integration (VLIE)
FPI....... Fast Processor Interface [*Computer chip*]
FPI....... Federal Personnel Intern [*Program*] [*Civil Service Commission*]
FPI....... Federal Prison Industries (COE)
FPI....... Federal Prison Industries, Inc. [*Department of Justice*]
FPI....... Federal Procurement Institute [*Later, FAI*] (MCD)
FPI....... Federal procurement instruction (SAUS)
FPI....... Federal Publications, Inc. (AAGC)
FPI....... Federation Prohibitionniste Internationale [*International Prohibition Federation*]
FPI....... Fellow of the Plastics Institute [*British*]
FPI....... Femoral Pulsatility Index [*Medicine*] (EDAA)
FPI....... Field Presence Indicator
FPI....... Fins per Inch [*Heat exchangers*]
FPI....... Firing Point Instructor (SAUS)
FPI....... First Periodic Inspection (AAG)
FPI....... Fisheries Products International [*Canada*]
FPI....... Fishmongers and Poulterers Institution (SAUS)
FPI....... Fixed Price Incentive
FPI....... Flexible Pavements (EA)
FPI....... Flexion Producing Interneuron [*Neurology*]
FPI....... Flight Path Indicator [*Aviation*] (AIA)
FPI....... Floating Point Instruction (SAUS)
FPI....... Flossing Performance Index [*Medicine*] (EDAA)
FPI....... Fluorescent Penetrant Inspection (MSA)
FPI....... Flux Changes per Inch (SAUS)
FPI....... Food Processors Institute (EA)
FPI....... Foodservice and Packaging Institute (EA)
FPI....... Food Service Packaing Institute (SAUS)
FPI....... Foot Pedal Interface
FPI....... Forest Products Industry
FPI....... Forest Products Insurance (SAUS)
FPI....... Fountain Powerboat Industries, Inc. [*AMEX symbol*] (SPSG)
fpi....... Frames per Inch (VLIE)
FPI....... Frames per Inch [*Computer science*]
FPI....... Free Press International (SAUO)
FPI....... Friends of Pioneering Israel
FPI....... Front Populaire Ivoirien [*Ivorian Popular Front*] [*The Ivory Coast*] [*Political party*] (EY)
FPI....... fuel indicator (SAUS)
FPI....... Fuel Pressure Indicator
FPI....... Functional Process Improvement (SAUO)
FPI....... Fuzzy Prime Implicant (SAUS)
FPi....... Pinellas Park Public Library, Pinellas Park, FL [*Library symbol*] [*Library of Congress*] (LCLS)
FPIA....... 504th Parachute Infantry Regiment Association (EA)
FPIA....... Family Planning International Assistance (EA)
FPIA....... Fluorescence Polarization Immunoassay
FPIAA....... Fire Protection Industry Association of Australia (EERA)
FPIAR....... Federal Prison Industries Acquisition Regulation (AAGC)
FPIB....... Food Production Inspection Branch (SAUS)
FPIC....... Field-Programmable Interconnect Chip (SAUS)
FPIC....... Field Programmable Interconnect Circuit (SAUS)
FPIC....... Field-Programmable Interconnect Component [*Computer science*]

FPIC............ Financial Post Information Centre [*MacLean-Hunter Ltd.*] [*Information service or system*] (IID)
FPIC............ Fixed Price Incentive Contract
FPIC............ FPIC Insurance Group, Inc. [*NASDAQ symbol*] (SAG)
FPIC............ FPIC Insurance Grp [*NASDAQ symbol*] (SG)
FPIC............ Fuel and Power Industries Committee [*British*] (DCTA)
FPIC Ins...... FPIC Insurance Group, Inc. [*Associated Press*] (SAG)
FPID............ Field-Programmable Interconnect Device (SAUS)
FPID............ Fixed Price Incentive with Delay Firm Target (SAA)
FPIECE........ Frontispiece [*Publishing*] (ROG)
FPIF............ Fixed Price Incentive (SAUS)
FPIF............ Fixed Price Incentive Fee
FPIF............ Fixed Price Incentive Firm [*Award*] [*Government contracting*]
fpif............ fixed-price-incentive firm (SAUS)
FPIF............ Fixed Price Incentive Force (AFM)
FPIFP.......... Fixed Price Incentive Fee Performance (ACAE)
FPIFV.......... Fixed-Price Incentive Fee Contract Value Engineering (AAGC)
FPIG............ Fonds Professionel des Industries Graphiques (SAUS)
F PIL............ Fiat Pilula [*Let a Pill Be Made*] [*Pharmacy*]
FPIL............ Fixed Premium if Lost (SAUS)
FPIL............ Full Premium If Lost [*Insurance*] (MHDW)
FPILIP......... full premium (SAUS)
FPILPIA....... full premium (SAUS)
FPIM............ Fine Particulate Inorganic Matter (EES)
FP-IMS........ Fixed-Point Ion Mobility Spectrometer (SAUS)
F/P-INT........ Fabry-Perot Interferometer (SAUO)
FPI Program... Federal Personnel International Program (SAUO)
FPI Program... Federal Personnel Intern Program (SAUS)
FPIQ............ Freiburger Personality Identification Questionnaire [*Medicine*] (EDAA)
FPIS............ Family Planning and Information Service
FPIS............ Fixed Price Incentive Successive (SAUS)
FPIS............ Fixed Price Incentive Successive Targets
FPIS............ Fixed Price Incentive with Successive Targets (SAUS)
FPIS............ Force Planning Information System (SAUO)
FPIS............ Forward Propagation by Ionospheric Scatter [*Radio communications technique*]
FPIS............ Forward Propagation Ionospheric Scatter (SAUS)
FPIS............ Fuel pin identification system (SAUS)
FPITC.......... Food Processing Industry Training Council [*Australia*]
FPITS.......... Fabry-Perot Inverse Transform Spectrometer (SAUS)
FPIX............ Ferriprotoporphyrin IX [*Biochemistry*]
FPJ.............. Pensacola Junior College, Pensacola, FL [*OCLC symbol*] (OCLC)
FPJMC......... Four-Power Joint Military Commission (SAUO)
FPJMT......... Four Party Joint Military Team [*Established March, 1973 as part of the Paris Peace Accords*] (VNW)
FPJPA.......... Fully Proceduralized Job Performance Aid (MCD)
FPJU............ Fonds Special pour la Jeunesse de l'UNESCO [*UNESCO Special Fund for Youth*] (EAIO)
F Pk............. Field Park (SAUS)
FPK.............. Fixed Position Keyboard
FPK.............. Flash Pack Ltd. [*Vancouver Stock Exchange symbol*]
FPK.............. Folding Pocket Kodak [*Photography*] (ROG)
FPKC............ Fair Public Key Cryptosystem [*Telecommunications*]
F-P-K Equation... Fokker-Planck-Kolmogorow Equation (SAUS)
fpl............... Face Plate (SAUS)
FPL.............. Faceplate [*Electronics*] (IAA)
FPL.............. Facing Point Lock (SAUS)
FPL.............. Family Protection Law (SAUS)
FPL.............. Family Protection League of USA [*Defunct*] (EA)
FPL.............. Fasting Plasma Lipids [*Medicine*] (MELL)
FPL.............. Fatherland Party of Labor [*Bulgaria*] [*Political party*]
FPL.............. Federal Public Library (SAUO)
FPL.............. feline panleukopaenia (SAUS)
FPL.............. Feline Panleukopenia
FPL.............. Ferry-Porter Law [*Physics*]
FPL.............. Field Flight Plan
FPL.............. Field Processing Language (IAA)
FPL.............. Filed Flight Plan (DA)
FPL.............. Filed Flight Plan Message [*Aviation code*]
FPL.............. File Parameter List [*Computer science*] (IAA)
FPL.............. Final Parts List (MCD)
FPL.............. Final Protective Line [*Military*]
FPL.............. Findlay-Hancock County District Public Library, Findlay, OH [*OCLC symbol*] (OCLC)
fpl............... Fireplace (ADWA)
FPL.............. Fireplace [*Real estate*]
FPL.............. Fire Plug (AAG)
FPL.............. Fisons Pharmaceuticals Limited (SAUO)
FPL.............. Flexor Pollicis Longus [*Anatomy*]
FPL.............. Flight Plan (SAUO)
FPL.............. Flight Propulsion Laboratory
FPL.............. Floor Plate [*Technical drawings*]
FPL.............. Florida Power and Light (SAUS)
FPL.............. Florida Power & Light Co. [*NYSE symbol*] (SPSG)
FPL.............. Fluid Power Laboratory [*Ohio State University*] [*Research center*] (RCD)
FPL.............. Food Quality Laboratory (SAUS)
FPL.............. Forced-Choice Preferential Looking
FPL.............. Foreign Parts List (ACAE)
FPL.............. Forest Pest Leaflets
FPL.............. Forest Products Laboratory [*Department of Agriculture*]
FPL.............. Formal Parameter List (SAUS)
FPL.............. Foxboro Programming Language (SAUS)
FPL.............. Fox Programming Language
FPL.............. FPI Ltd. [*Toronto Stock Exchange symbol*]
FPL.............. FPL Group [*NYSE symbol*] (TTSB)
FPL.............. FPL Group, Inc. [*NYSE symbol*] (SPSG)
FPL.............. Fragmenta Poetarum Latinorum Epicorum et Lyricorum [*A publication*] (OCD)
FPL.............. Freelance Programmers Limited (SAUS)
FPL.............. Frente Popular de Liberacion, Nueve de Mayo [*Honduras*] [*Political party*] (EY)
FPL.............. Frequency Phase Lock
FPL.............. Fuerzas Populares de Liberacion Farabundo Marti [*Farabundo Marti Popular Liberation Forces*] [*El Salvador*] (PD)
FPL.............. Full Performance Level [*Aviation*] (FAAC)
FPL.............. Full Power Level [*NASA*] (NASA)
FPL.............. Functional Problem Log [*Computer science*] (OA)
FPL.............. Functional Problem Logging (SAUS)
FPL.............. Functional Programming Language [*Computer science*]
FPLA............ Fair Packaging and Labeling Act [*1966*]
FPLA............ Fair Packaging and Labelling Act (SAUS)
FPLA............ Field Programmable Logic Array [*Computer science*]
fpla.............. Fireplace [*Real estate*]
F (Plan)....... Fiber Plan [*Used in title of book advocating a high-fiber diet*]
FPL Array.... Field Programmable Logic Array (SAUS)
FPLAs.......... Field Programmable Logic Arrays (SAUS)
FPLC............ Fast Performance Liquid Chromatography [*Analytical chemistry*]
FPLC............ Fast Protein Liquid Chromatography (ADWA)
FPLC............ Fast Protein, Peptide, and Polynucleotide Liquid Chromatography
FPLC............ Federal-Provincial Liaison Committee (SAUS)
FPLC............ Franklin Pierce Law Center (SAUS)
FPLC............ Full Power Level Certification (SAUS)
FPLCE.......... Fireplace [*Real estate*] (WDAA)
FPL Controller Contact... Facing Point Locking Controller Contact (SAUS)
FPLD............ Field Programmable Logic Device (AEBE)
FPLE............ Field-Programmable Logic Element [*Military*]
FPLET.......... Fixed-Price Level of Effort Term (AAGC)
FPLF............ Field Programmable Logic Family (TEL)
FPLF............ field-programmable logic family (SAUS)
FPL-FM........ Fuerzas Populares de Liberacion-Farabundo Marti [*El Salvador*]
FPL Gp........ FPL Group, Inc. [*Associated Press*] (SAG)
FPLIF........... Field Pack, Large, with Internal Frame [*Army*] (INF)
FPLMTS....... Future Public Land Mobile Telecommunications System
FPLMTS....... Future Public Land Mobile Telephone System (SAUS)
fpln.............. Flight Plan (SAUS)
FPLN............ Frente Patriotica de Libertacao Nacional [*Portugal*]
FPLOE.......... Fixed-Price Level of Effort (SAUO)
FPLP............ Frente Patriotico de Libertacao de Portugal [*Patriotic Front for the Liberation of Portugal*] [*Political party*] (PPE)
FPLPrA........ Fla Pwr&Lt $2 Pfd'A' [*NYSE symbol*] (TTSB)
FPLS............ Federal Parent Locator Service [*HEW*]
FPLS............ Field Programmable Logic Sequencer [*Computer science*] (HGAA)
FPLS............ Field-Programmable Logic Switch [*Electronics*] (AAEL)
FPLS............ Patriotic Front of Liberation of the Sahara (Niger) [*Political party*] (PSAP)
F Plsk.......... Feuerplanskizze (SAUS)
FPLX............ Florida Power & Light [*Federal Railroad Administration identification code*]
FPM............. Facilities Planning Module (SAUO)
FPM............. Facility Power Monitor (AAG)
FPM............. Facsimile Posting Machine (SAUS)
FPM............. Family Practice Management (SAUS)
FPM............. Fast Packet Multiplexing (AGLO)
FPM............. Fast-Page-Mode [*Computer science*] (PCM)
FPM............. Federal Personnel Manual
FPM............. Federal Personnel Manuals (SAUS)
FPM............. Federal Procurement Manual (SAUO)
fpm.............. Feet per Minute (PIAV)
FPM............. Ferrite Plate Memory (SAUS)
FPM............. FFTF Preventive Maintenance (SAUS)
FPM............. Fiber Pulling in Microgravity (SAUS)
FPM............. Field Programmable Microcontroller (SAUS)
FPM............. File Protect Memory [*Computer science*] (BUR)
FPM............. File Protect Mode (SAUS)
FPM............. Filter Paper Microscopic [*Test*] [*Medicine*]
FPM............. Financial Planning Model (SAUS)
FPM............. Fine Particulate Matter [*Pisciculture*]
FPM............. First Pennsylvania Mortgage Trust (SAUO)
FPM............. First Polar Platform Mission (SAUO)
FPM............. Fissions per Minute
FPM............. Fixed-Payment Mortgage (DFIT)
FPM............. Fixed Piston Motor [*Hydraulics*]
FPM............. Flashes per Minute (SAUS)
FPM............. Flexible Payment Mortgage
FPM............. Flexual Plate Mode (AAEL)
FPM............. Flight Path Marker
FPM............. Floating Point Method (SAUS)
FPM............. Floating-Point Multiplexer (VLIE)
FPM............. Floating Point Multiplication (SAUS)
FPM............. Floppy Disc Processor Module [*Transdata*] (NITA)
FPM............. Floppy-Disk Processor Mode (SAUS)
FPM............. Fluid Phase Marker
FPM............. Fluorocarbon elastomer [*Plastics technology*]
FPM............. Focal Plane Module (ADWA)
FPM............. Folding Platform Mechanism (MCD)
FPM............. Force Packaging Methodology [*Military*]
FPM............. Force Projection Model (SAUS)
FPM............. Forest Pest Management [*Program*] [*Forest Service*]
FPM............. Four Phase Modulation (VLIE)

FPM FoxPro for Macintosh (SAUS)
FPM Frames per Minute [*Telecommunications*] (IAA)
FPM Fratres Presentationis Mariae [*Presentation Brothers - PB*] (EAIO)
FPM Free Papau Movement [*Indonesia*] [*Political party*]
FPM Frequency Position Modulation [*Telecommunications*] (IEEE)
fpm frequency pulse modulation (SAUS)
FPM Fuel Pump Monitor [*Automotive engineering*]
FPM Full Passive Movements (SAUO)
FPM Functional Planning Matrices (IEEE)
FPM Functional Project Manager (SAUO)
FPM Presentation Brothers (TOCD)
FPMA Focal Point for Mountain Activities (SAUO)
FPMA Law for Federal Marine Protection (SAUO)
FPM&SA Food Processing Machinery and Suppliers Association (SAUS)
FPM & SA Food Processing Machinery and Supplies Association (EA)
FPMB Federation of Podiatric Medical Boards (EA)
FPMC Fixed Paper Metallized Capacitor
FPMCS Facility Process Monitoring and Control System (SAUS)
FPMD Facilities Project Management Division (SAUO)
FPMD Family Planning Management Development (SAUO)
FPMDC Federal/Provincial Market Development Council (SAUO)
FPME FFTF Plant Maintenance Engineering (SAUS)
FPMG-38 Facilities projects management (SAUS)
FPMH Failures per Million Hours [*Telecommunications*] (TEL)
FPMI Fellow of the Pensions Management Institute [*British*] (DBQ)
FPMI Forest Pest Management Institute [*Environment Canada*] [*Research center*] (RCD)
FPMI Frequency Position Modulation with phase Increments (SAUS)
FPMIS Federal Personnel Management Information System [*Civil Service Commission*]
FPML Federal Personnel Management Letters [*Office of Personnel Management*] (GFGA)
FPML Field Programmable Macro Logic (SAUS)
FpML Financial Products Markup Language
FPML Forest Products Marketing Laboratory [*Forest Service*]
FPMO Free of Poundage Money Order
FPMPI Frequency Position Modulation with Phase Increments (SAUS)
FPMPMA Fountain Pen and Mechanical Pencil Manufacturers Association (SAUO)
FPMR Federal Procurement Management Regulations (SAUS)
FPMR Federal Property Management Regulations
FPMR Fixed-Price Material Reimbursable (AAGC)
FPMR Frente Patriotico Manuel Rodriguez [*Manuel Rodriguez Patriotic Front*] [*Chile*] [*Political party*]
FPM RAM Fast Page Mode RAM (SAUS)
FPMS Factory Performance Modeling Software (AAEL)
FPMS Federal Personnel Manual Systems (OICC)
FPMS Federal Productivity Measurement System [*Bureau of Labor Statistics*] (GFGA)
FPMS Flood Plain Management Services [*Army*]
FPMS Fueled Prototype Mock-Up System
FPMSA Food Processing Machinery and Supplies Association (SAUO)
FPM System Functional Planning Matrices System (SAUS)
FPMT Field Post Motor Transport (SAUS)
FPMT Filter Paper Microscopic Test (SAUS)
FPMT Foundation for the Preservation of the Mahayana Tradition (SAUO)
FPMT Fund for the Preservation of the Mahyana Tradition [*An association*]
FPM Test Filter Paper Microscopic Test (SAUS)
F/Pn Factor of Production [*Economics*]
FPN Fairview Park [*Nevada*] [*Seismograph station code, US Geological Survey*] [*Closed*] (SEIS)
FPN Falange Patria Nova [*New Fatherland Phalange*] [*Brazil*] (PD)
fpn fine print note (SAUS)
FPN Fixed Pattern Noise [*Electronics*] (OA)
FPN Fixed Point Number (SAUS)
FPN Floating Point Number (SAUS)
FPN Foreign Pendant Numbers Files (SAUO)
FPN Frederick Point, AK [*Location identifier*] [*FAA*] (FAAL)
FPN Frente Patriotico Nacional [*National Patriotic Front*] [*Nicaragua*] [*Political party*] (PPW)
FPN Friends of Peace Now (EA)
FPNA First-Pass Nuclear Angiocardiography [*Cardiology*] (DAVI)
FPNA Free Pacific News Agency (SAUO)
FPND Fission product nuclear data (SAUS)
FPNE First Phone of New England [*Telecommunications service*] (TSSD)
FPNIX FPA New Income [*Mutual fund ticker symbol*] (SG)
FPNM Fort Pulaski National Monument (SAUO)
FPNO Field Punishment, Number One (SAUS)
FPNOR Flight Plan not Received (SAUS)
FPNW File and Print Service for NetWare [*Computer science*] (VERA)
FPNX First Pacific Networks [*NASDAQ symbol*] (TTSB)
FPNX First Pacific Networks, Inc. [*NASDAQ symbol*] (SAG)
FPO Fabricated Parts Order (TIMI)
FPO Federal Protective Officer [*General Services Administration*]
FPO Federation of Professional Organisations [*British*] (DBA)
FPO Federation of Prosthodontic Organizations (EA)
FPO Field / Forces Post Office (SAUS)
FPO Field Placement Officer
FPO Field Post Office [*Military*] [*British*]
FPO Field Project Office (SAUS)
FPO Field Project Officer
FPO Field Purchase Order (SAUO)
FPO Final Public Oral (SAUS)
FPO Fire Prevention Officer [*British*]
FPO Firm Planned Order (SAUO)
FPO Fission Products Operations (SAUS)
FPO Fixed Path of Operation
FPO Fixed Point Operation
FPO Fixed Post Office (SAUS)
FPO Fixed Price Open
FPO Fleet Photographer Officer (SAUO)
FPO Fleet Postal Organization (SAUO)
FPO Fleet Post Office [*Navy*]
FPO Flight Projects Office (ACAE)
FPO Floating Point Operation (SAUS)
FPO Florida Philharmonic Orchestra (SAUS)
FPO Force Performance Objective (SEWL)
FPO Forces Post Office [*Military*] [*British*]
FPO For Placement Only (SAUS)
FPO For Positioning Only (SAUS)
FPO For Position Only (WDAA)
FPO For-Profit Organization (FOTI)
FPO Foundation Pedigree Option [*Equine term*] (TED)
FPO FPA Corp. [*AMEX symbol*] (SPSG)
FPO Freeport [*Bahamas*] [*Airport symbol*] (OAG)
FPO Free Post Office (SAUS)
fpo free post office (SAUS)
FPO Freezing Point Osmometer
FPO Freiheitliche Partei Oesterreichs [*Liberal Party of Austria (or Austrian Freedom Party)*] [*Political party*] (PPW)
FPO Frequency Planning Organisation [*Telecommunications*] [*British*]
FPO Fuel Pressure Out
FPO Fuerza Popular Organizada [*Organized Popular Force*] [*Guatemala*] [*Political party*] (PPW)
FPO fusion point (SAUS)
FPO Future Projects Office [*NASA*]
FPOA Federal Probation and Pretrial Officers Association (EA)
FPOA Federal Probation Officers Association (EA)
FPOA Federation of Professional Officers Association (AIE)
FPOA Fentanyl/Pancuronium/Oxygen Anesthesia
FPOA Florida Peace Officers Association (SRA)
FPOC Field Purchase Order Correction (SAUO)
FPoCG Charlotte-Glades Library System, Port Charlotte, FL [*Library symbol*] [*Library of Congress*] (LCLS)
FPODA Fixed Assignment PODA (SAUS)
FPODA Fixed Priority Orientated Demand Assignment (SAUS)
FPODA Fixed Priority Oriented Demand Assignment [*Telecommunications*] (OSI)
FPOE First Port of Entry (AFM)
fpoh food prepared outside the home (SAUS)
F/POL Fire Policy [*Insurance*] (DCTA)
FPOM Fine Particulate Organic Matter
FPONJ Fresh Pond Junction, NY [*American Association of Railroads railroad junction routing code*]
FPOP Family Planning Organization of the Philippines (SAUO)
FPOP Floating Parallel Output Port (SAUS)
FPOR Ferrite Post Open Resonator (SAUS)
FPORT Freeport, IL [*American Association of Railroads railroad junction routing code*]
FPOS Formalized Plant Opportunity Survey [*Vendor marketing*]
FPOSO Federation of Post Office Supervision Officers (SAUO)
FPOT Facility Power Out Test (KSC)
FPOT Feedback Potentiometer (MSA)
FPOV Fuel Preburner and Oxidizer Valve (MCD)
FPOV Fuel Preburner Oxidizer Valve (SAUS)
FPOW Friendly Prisoner of War (SAUO)
FPP Facility Power Panel (AAG)
FPP Family Planning Perspectives (SAUO)
FPP Family Planning Program (WDAA)
FPP Farnesyl Pyrophosphate [*Biochemistry*]
FPP Fast Parallel Port (SAUS)
FPP Fast Prepotential [*Neurophysiology*]
FPP Feral Pests Program (EERA)
FPP Fetal Protection Policy [*Insurance*] (WYGK)
FPP Fibreboard Paper Products Corp. (SAUO)
FPP Fine Particle Processing (SAUS)
FPP Firepower Potential (AABC)
FPP First Principal Plane (SAUS)
FPP Fisher-Price, Inc. (EFIS)
FPP Fixed Path Control (SAUS)
FPP Fixed Path Protocol (SAUS)
FPP Fixed-Path Protocol [*Telecommunications*]
FPP Fixed Piston Pump [*Hydraulics*]
FPP Fixed Pitch Propeller (SAUS)
FPP Fixed-Pitch Propeller (PDAA)
FPP Fixed Point Protocol (NITA)
FPP Fleet Planning & Programming (SAUS)
FPP Flight Preparation Ltd. [*British*] [*ICAO designator*] (FAAC)
FPP Flight Purpose Plans (ACAE)
FPP Floating Point Package (TIMI)
FPP Floating Point Process (NITA)
FPP Floating Point Processing (SAUS)
FPP Floating Point Processor (ACAE)
FPP Floating Point Programming (SAUS)
FPP Food Processing and Packaging (IMH)
FPP Force Planning Package [*Military*] (RDA)
FPP Formal Parameter Part (SAUS)
FPP FORTRAN Pre-Processor (SAUS)
FPP Foster Parents Plan (SAUS)
FPP Foster Parents Program (SAUS)

FPP............ Freon Pump Package (MCD)
FPP............ Friendly Peoples Proviso (SAUS)
FPP............ Friends of Palestinian Prisoners (EA)
FPP............ Friends of Peace Pilgrim (EA)
FPP............ From Present Position (SAUS)
FPP............ Funder-Purchaser-Provider (SAUO)
FPP............ Panama Public Forces
FPP............ Patriotic Front for Progress (Central African Republic) [*Political party*] (PSAP)
FPP............ Pipefitter (Plumber) [*U.S. Navy enlisted rating*] (AUER)
FPPA........... Farmland Protection Policy Act (GNE)
FPPA........... Federal Pollution Prevention Act (EEVL)
FPPA........... Foster Parents Plan of Australia
FPPA........... Porto Alegre [*Sao Tome*] [*ICAO location identifier*] (ICLI)
FPPB........... Family Planning and Population Board (SAUO)
FPPB........... Fiscal Policies and Procedures Branch (SAUO)
FPPC........... Fair Political Practices Commission (OICC)
FPPC........... Flight Plan Processing Center [*Aviation*] (IAA)
FPPC........... Float Program Planning Committee (SAUO)
FPPCA.......... Fuel and Purchased Power Cost Adjustment
fppe........... fluorescent pen-post emulsified (SAUS)
FPPFX.......... FPA Perennial Fund [*Mutual fund ticker symbol*] (SG)
FPPH........... Fire Protection Pumphouse [*Nuclear energy*] (NRCH)
FPPI........... Frozen Potato Products Institute (EA)
FPPIG.......... Family Presence Patient Interview Guide
FPPO........... Federation of Postal Police Officers [*Defunct*] (EA)
FPPOD.......... Financial Planners and Planning Organizations Directory [*A publication*]
FPPP........... Fuel pin photo positioner (SAUS)
FPPPH.......... Foundation for the Preservation and Protection of the Przewalski Horse (SAUO)
FPPR........... Fishpaper [*Insulation*]
FPPR........... Fixed Price, Price Redetermination [*or Revision*]
FPPR........... Fixed Price with Price Revision (NAKS)
FPPR........... Fluorescence Pattern Photobleaching Recovery [*for study of surfaces*]
FPPR........... Principe [*Principe*] [*ICAO location identifier*] (ICLI)
FPPS........... Flight Plan Progressing System (OA)
FPPs........... Floating Point Packages (SAUS)
FPPs........... Floating Point Processors (SAUS)
FPPS........... Full-Page Phototypesetting System (DGA)
FPPT........... Fuel pin pressurization test (SAUS)
FPPTE.......... Federation of Public Passenger Transport Employees [*British*] (DCTA)
FPPTX.......... FPA Capital Fund [*Mutual fund ticker symbol*] (SG)
FPPU........... Floating Point Processor Unit [*Computer science*] (CIST)
FPPU........... Food Preservation and Processing Unit (SAUS)
FPPVS.......... Fuel Pool Pump Ventilation System [*Nuclear energy*] (NRCH)
FPPWS.......... Front Page Personal Web Server (AGLO)
FPQA........... Fixed Portion Queue Area [*Computer science*]
FPQFP.......... Fine-Pitch Quad Flat Pack (SAUS)
FPQI........... Federal Plant Quarantine Inspectors National Association [*Later, NAAE*]
FPQINA......... Federal Plant Quarantine Inspectors National Association [*Later, NAAE*] (EA)
FPR............ Fabry-Perot Resonator (SAUS)
FPR............ Factory Problem Report (SAUS)
FPR............ Failure/Problem Report
FPR............ Fair Pressure Ratio (SAUS)
FPR............ False Positive Rate (MELL)
FPR............ Familial Polyposis Registry (MELL)
FPR............ Fan Pressure Ratio [*Aviation*]
FPR............ Farm Publications Report (SAUS)
FPR............ Farm Publications Reports (EA)
FPR............ Federal Procurement Regulations
FPR............ Feet per Revolution
FPR............ Fibre Reinforced Plastic (SAUS)
FPR............ Field Personnel Record
FPR............ Field Problem Report (ACAE)
FPR............ File Protection Ring (VLIE)
FPR............ Final Progress Report
FPR............ Financial Public Relations Consultants Retained
FPR............ Fire Protection Relay (SAUS)
FPR............ Fishing Ports Registration (SAUS)
FPR............ Fission Product Release [*Nuclear energy*] (NUCP)
FPR............ Fixed Point Representation
FPR............ Fixed Price Redeterminable (NG)
FPR............ Fixed Price Repair (TIMI)
FPR............ Fixed Problem Report (MCD)
FPR............ Fixed Program Receive (VLIE)
FPR............ Flat Plate Radiometer (SAUS)
FPR............ Flexible Plastic Reactor (NRCH)
FPR............ Flight Performance Propellant Reserve (MCD)
FPR............ Flight Performance Reserve
FPR............ Flight Planned Route (PIPO)
FPR............ Floating Point Register (SAUS)
FPR............ Floating Point Representation (SAUS)
FPR............ Floating Point Routine (SAUS)
FPR............ Fluid Properties Research, Inc.
FPR............ Fluorescence Photobleaching Recovery
FPR............ Foliage Penetration RADAR
FPR............ Folin Phenol Reagent [*For protein assay*]
FPR............ Force Program Review [*DoD*]
FPr............ Ford Motor 8.40% Cv Dep Pfd [*NYSE symbol*] (TTSB)
FPR............ Forest Penetrating Radar (SAUS)
FPR............ Forms Printing Requisition (VLIE)
FPR............ Fort Pierce, FL [*Location identifier*] [*FAA*] (FAAL)
fpr............ forward parcels rail (SAUS)
FPR............ Fractional Proximal Resorption [*Medicine*] (DMAA)
FPR............ Fragmenta Poetarum Romanorum [*A publication*] (OCD)
FPR............ Frente Patriotico para la Revolucion [*Patriotic Front for the Revolution*] [*Nicaragua*] [*Political party*] (PPW)
FPR............ Frente Popular Contra la Represion [*Popular Front Against Repression*] [*Honduras*] [*Political party*] (PD)
FPR............ Friends of Parks and Recreation (SAUO)
FPR............ Fuel Pressure Regulator (SAUS)
FPR............ Fuel processing restoration (SAUS)
FPR............ Fuel Pump Relay [*Automotive engineering*]
FPR............ Fuerza Aerea del Peru [*ICAO designator*] (FAAC)
FPR............ Fuerzas Populares Revolucionarias Lorenzo Zelaya [*Lorenzo Zelaya Popular Revolutionary Forces*] [*Honduras*] [*Political party*] (PD)
FPR............ Full Power Response
FPR............ Full Propellant Requirement
FPR............ Functional and Performance Requirements (MCD)
FPR............ Purchasing Module of FRS (SAUS)
FPR............ Rwanda Patriotic Front [*Political party*] (PSAP)
FPRA........... Federation of Private Residents' Associations [*British*] (DBA)
FPRA........... Fifty-Plus Runners Association (EA)
FPRA........... Financial Public Relations Association [*Later, BMA*] (EA)
FPRA........... First-Pass Radionuclide Angiogram [*Medicine*]
FPRA........... Fixed Price Redeterminable Article
FPRA........... Florida Public Relations Association (SRA)
FPRA........... Forward Pricing Rate Agreement
FPRAC.......... Federal Prevailing Rate Advisory Committee [*Washington, DC*] (EGAO)
FPRAX.......... FPA Paramount Fund [*Mutual fund ticker symbol*] (SG)
FPRB........... Food Prices Review Board
FPrB........... Ford Motor Dep'B'Pfd [*NYSE symbol*] (TTSB)
FPRC........... Fair Play for Rhodesia Committee (SAUO)
FPRC........... Fixed Price Redetermination Contract
FPRC........... Fluid Power Research Center [*Oklahoma State University*] [*Research center*] (RCD)
FPRC........... Flying Personnel Research Committee [*British*] (MCD)
FPRC........... For Possible Reclearance [*Aviation*] (FAAC)
FPRC........... Fuel Pressure Regulator Circuit [*Automotive term*] (HAWK)
FPRD........... Fouling Prevention Research Digest (SAUS)
FPRDC.......... Food Protein Research and Development Center [*Texas A & M University*]
FPRDI.......... Forest Products Research and Development Institute (SAUO)
FPRF........... Fats and Proteins Research Foundation (EA)
FPRF........... Fireproof (AABC)
FP-RF.......... Flash Photolysis-Resonance Fluorescence Technique [*Physics*]
FPRF........... Forest Products Research Foundation (SAUO)
FPRF........... Fusion Plasma Research Facility [*Department of Energy*]
FPRI........... Fellow of the Plastics and Rubber Institute [*British*] (DBQ)
FPRI........... Fire Protection Research International (SAUO)
FPRI........... Foreign Policy Research Institute (SAUO)
FPRI Technical Note... Forest Products Research Institute Technical Note (SAUS)
FPRL........... Fish Pesticide Research Laboratory [*Department of the Interior*]
FPRL........... Forest Products Research Laboratory [*British*]
FPRM........... Flexible Parts Repair Material [*Automotive engineering*]
FPRO........... Federal-Provincial Relations Office [*Canada*]
FPRO........... Forest Products Library (SAUS)
FPROM.......... Field Programmable Read Only Memory (SAUS)
F-PROM......... Field-Programmable Read-Only Memory [*Computer science*] (MCD)
FPROM.......... field programmable ROM (SAUS)
FPRP........... Field Programmable Read-Only Memory Patch [*Computer science*] (VLIE)
FPRP........... Fixed-Price-Redeterminable-Prospective (MCD)
FPRR........... Fire Protection Repeating Relay (SAUS)
FPRR........... Fixed-Price-Redeterminable-Retroactive (MCD)
FPRRE.......... Foundation for Public Relations Research and Education (EA)
FPRS........... Fabry-Perot Recycling Spectrometer (PDAA)
FPRS........... Federal Program Resources Statement (COE)
FPRS........... Federal Property Resources Service [*General Services Administration*]
FPRS........... Federation of Professional Railway Staff [*A union*] [*British*]
FPRs........... Floating Point Registers (SAUS)
FPRS........... Forest Products Radio Service
FPRS........... Forest Products Research Society (EA)
FPRS........... Formal Planning and Reporting System (SAUO)
FPRS........... Formal Planning and Supporting System (SAUS)
FPRS News Digest... Forest Products Research Society News Digest (SAUO)
FPRY........... First Federal Savings Bank of Perry [*NASDAQ symbol*] (COMM)
FPRY........... First Financial Bancorp, Inc. Florida [*NASDAQ symbol*] (SAG)
FPRY........... First Finl Bancorp [*NASDAQ symbol*] (TTSB)
FPS............ Fabry-Perot spherical (SAUS)
FPS............ Faceplate Starter (SAUS)
FPS............ Facilities Planning System (SAUO)
FPS............ Faculty of Physicians and Surgeons [*British*] (ROG)
FPS............ Farm Placement Service (SAUO)
fps............ fast packet switch (SAUS)
FPS............ Fast Packet Switching [*Telecommunications*]
FPS............ Fast-Pass Standard [*Automotive emissions*]
FPS............ Fast Payback System (SAUO)
FPS............ Fauna Preservation Society [*Later, FFPS*] (EA)
FPS............ Favorite Picture Selection [*Photo CD feature*] (PCM)
FPS............ Favorite Play Sequence (SAUS)
FPS............ Federal Prison System (MCD)
FPS............ Federal Protection Service (SAUO)

FPS .... Federal Protective Service [*General Services Administration*]
FPS .... Federated Programming System (SAUS)
FPS .... Federation of Personnel Services of Great Britain (SAUO)
FPS .... Federation of Piling Specialists [*British*] (DBA)
fps .... Feet per Second (IDOE)
FPS .... Feet per Second
fps .... feet-pound-second (SAUS)
FPS .... Fellow of the Pathological Society (SAUS)
FPS .... Fellow of the Pathological Society of Great Britain
FPS .... Fellow of the Pharmaceutical Society [*British*]
FPS .... Fellow of the Philological Society [*British*]
FPS .... Fellow of the Philosophical Society [*British*]
FPS .... Fellow of the Physical Society [*British*]
FPS .... Fell Pony Society [*British*] (BI)
FPS .... Fence Protection System (SAUS)
FPS .... Ferrite Phase Shifter
FPS .... Ferrite Plate Store (SAUS)
FPS .... Fiber Placement System (SAUS)
FPS .... Field Power Supply
FPS .... Field Printing Squadron
FPS .... Field Programming System (SAUS)
FPS .... Film Performance Score (SAUS)
FPS .... Financial Planning Simulator (SAUO)
FPS .... Financial Planning System [*IBM Corp.*]
FPS .... Fine Particle Society (EA)
FPS .... Finger Print Sheet (FOTI)
FPS .... Finite Population Sampling (SAUS)
FPS .... Fire Protection Specialist (SAUS)
FPS .... Fire Protection System [*Nuclear energy*] (NRCH)
FPS .... First Person Shooter (SAUS)
FPS .... First Preferred Stock [*Investment term*]
FPS .... Fiscal Pay Services of Armies [*World War II*]
FPS .... Fishery Protection Squadron (SAUS)
FPS .... Fission product source (SAUS)
FPS .... Fixed Pattern Signal [*Optics*]
FPS .... Fixed Plasma Sheath
FPS .... Fixed Point Station [*RADAR*]
FPS .... Fixed-Point Station (SAUS)
FPS .... Fixed Point Subtraction (SAUS)
FPS .... Fixed Point System
FPS .... Fixed Price Supply
FPS .... Flashes per Second (IAA)
FPS .... Flash Photolysis System
FPS .... Fleet Patrol Ship (MILB)
FPS .... Flight Path Stabilization (MCD)
FPS .... Flight per Second (NASA)
FPS .... Flight Power Subsystem
FPS .... Flight Preparation Sheet (MCD)
FPS .... Flight Progress Strip [*Aviation*]
FPS .... Floating Point Subroutine (SAUS)
FPS .... Floating Point System (SAUO)
FPS .... Floating Point Systems (SAUS)
FPS .... Floating Point Systems GmbH (SAUO)
FPS .... Floating Point Systems, Incorporated (SAUS)
FPS .... Flocculated Polystyrene (SAUS)
FPS .... Florida Psychiatric Society (SAUS)
FPS .... Fluid Power Society (EA)
FPS .... Fluid Power Supply
FPS .... Fluid Power System
FPS .... Fluid Purification System
FPS .... Fluor Power Services, Inc. (NRCH)
FPs .... Flying Physicians (SAUO)
FPs .... Flying Psychologists (SAUO)
FPS .... Focal Plane Structure (SAUS)
FPS .... Focus Projection and Scanning
fps .... Foot per Second (SAUS)
FPS .... Foot, Pound, Second (SAUS)
FPS .... Foot-Pound-Second [*System*]
fps .... Foot-Pound-Second (IDOE)
fps .... foot-pound second system of measurements (SAUS)
FPS .... Forces Postal Service [*British*]
FPS .... Ford Performance Solutions (SAUS)
FPS .... Foreground Program Start (SAUS)
FPS .... Forest Products Society (NTPA)
FPS .... For Pay Server (SAUS)
FPS .... For Pay Server, Fast Packet Switching (SAUS)
FPS .... FORTRAN Processing System (SAUS)
FPS .... Forward Power Supply (MCD)
FPS .... Foundation for the Private Sector [*San Diego, CA*] (EA)
fps .... Frame per Second (IDOE)
fps .... Frames Per Second (WDMC)
FPS .... Frames per Second [*Computer science*]
FPS .... Franciscan Preparatory Seminary
FPS .... Francophone Primatological Society [*See also SFDP*] [*Plelan Le Grand, France*] (EAIO)
FPS .... Friction Pendulum System [*for earthquake protection*]
FPS .... Front Populaire Soudanais [*Sudanese Popular Front*]
FPS .... Fuel Planning System (SAUO)
FPS .... Full Pressure Suit [*Aerospace*]
FPS .... Functional Performance Structure (ACAE)
FPS .... Fusion Power Systems (MCD)
FPS .... Future Programming System (SAUS)
FPS .... Military Primary Radar [*FAA*] (TAG)
FPS .... Pipefitter (Steamfitter) [*U.S. Navy enlisted rating*] (AUER)
FPS2 .... Feet per Second Squared (NAKS)
FPS1117 .... Federal Procurement Disc [*Alde Publishing*] [*Information service or system*] (IID)
FPSA .... Fellow of the Photographic Society of America (SAUO)
FPSA .... Finnish Political Science Association (SAUO)
FPSA .... Florida Pool and Spa Association (SRA)
FPSA .... Flowering Plants of South Africa (SAUO)
FPSAA .... Federated Public Service Assistants Association (SAUO)
FPS-APs .... Floating Point System - Architectural Principles (SAUS)
FPSB .... Federation of Performance Sheep Breeders [*Australia*]
FPSB .... Financial Products Standards Board (EA)
FPSB .... Fisheries Prices Support Board (SAUS)
FPSC .... Family Policy Studies Centre [*British*] (CB)
FPSC .... Foreign Petroleum Supply Committee [*Terminated, 1976*]
FPSC .... Forest Products Safety Conference (EA)
FPSC .... Forum Public Speaking Clubs [*Australia*]
FPSC .... Fuel pin shipping container (SAUS)
FPSE .... Federation of Public Service Employees (SAUO)
FPSE .... Fellow of the Philosophical Society of England (SAUO)
FPSE .... Foot-Pound-Second Electrostatic (SAUS)
FPSE .... Foot-Pound-Second Electrostatic System (SAUS)
FPSE .... Free Piston Stirling Engine (SAUS)
fpsec .... Feet per Second (SAUS)
FPSE System ... Foot-Pound-Second Electrostatic System (SAUS)
FPSG .... Focus Policy Study Group [*British*]
FPSG .... Food Processors and Suppliers Group (EAIO)
F(PS)G .... Forum (Public Speaking) Group [*Australia*]
FPSH .... Full Plymouth Service History [*Automotive classified advertising*]
FPSH .... Full Pontiac Service History [*Automotive classified advertising*]
FPSH .... Full Porsche Service History [*Automotive classified advertising*]
FPSI .... Fellowship of Progressive Societies and Institutions (SAUO)
FPSK .... Frequency and Phase Shift Keying
FPSL .... Fellow of the Physical Society of London (SAUO)
FPSL .... Fission Product Screening Loop [*Nuclear energy*] (NRCH)
FPSLA .... Free Piston Stirling Linear Alternator (SAUS)
FPSLST .... Fluharty Preschool Speech and Language Screening Test (DAVI)
FPSM .... Fleet Program Support Material
FPSM .... Foot-Pound-Second Electromagnetic System (SAUS)
FPSM .... Foot Pound Second Magnetic (SAUS)
FPSM .... Foot-Pound-Second Magnetic System (IAA)
FPSNW .... File and Print Service for NetWare [*Computer science*]
FPSO .... Fleet Publication Supply Office (SAUO)
FPSO .... Flight Project Support Office [*Jet Propulsion Laboratory*]
FPSO .... Floating Production, Storage and Offloading Facility (SAUO)
FPSO .... Floating Production, Storage, and Offloading System [*Petroleum technology*]
FPSO .... Forms and Publications Supply Office [*Military*] (CINC)
FPSP .... Federal Power Support Program (SAUS)
FPSP .... Federation of Postal Security Police [*Later, FPPO*] (EA)
FPSP .... (Fluoropropyl)spiperone [*Organic chemistry*]
FPSP .... Future Problem Solving Program (EA)
FPSP .... Future Programmable Signal Processor (ACAE)
FPSPS .... Feet per Second per Second
FPSR .... Field Problem Summary Report (ACAE)
FPSR .... Fire Protection Stick Relay (SAUS)
FPS/S .... Feet per Second per Second
FPSS .... Fine Pointing Sun Sensor (ADWA)
F-P SSAR .... Fluor Pioneers Standard Safety Analysis Report (SAUO)
FPS System ... Foot-Pound-Second System (SAUS)
FP-ST .... Flash Photolysis-Shock Tube Experiment [*For study of chemical kinetics*]
FPST .... Sao Tome [*Sao Tome*] [*ICAO location identifier*] (ICLI)
FPSTU .... Full Pressure Suit Training Unit [*Military*]
FPSU .... Foot-Pound-Second Unit (SAUS)
FPSV .... Fixed Platform Supply Vessel
FPSV .... Flow Path Selector Valve (MCD)
FPT .... Failure of Passive Transfer [*Equine term*] (TED)
FPT .... Fan-Powered Terminal (DAC)
FPT .... Fast Polynomial Transform (SAUS)
FPT .... Feedwater Pump Turbine [*Nuclear energy*] (NRCH)
FPT .... Female Pipe Thread (MSA)
FPT .... Fighter Plot Table (SAUS)
FPT .... File Parameter Table (IAA)
fpt .... fill, puddle, and tamp (SAUS)
FPT .... Fine Pitch Technology [*Engineering*]
FPT .... Finite Perturbation Theory [*Physics*]
FPT .... Finnish Paper and Timber (SAUO)
FPT .... Fire Protection Technician (SAUS)
FPT .... First Pass Trigger (SAUS)
FPT .... First Preferred Trust [*Vancouver Stock Exchange symbol*]
FPT .... Fitted Parts Tag (SAA)
FPT .... Fixed Parenchymal Turnover [*Physiology*] (DAVI)
FPT .... Fixed Pattern Tester (SAUS)
FPT .... Fixed Price Tender (SAUS)
FPT .... Fixed Price Tenders [*Commerce*] (BARN)
FPT .... Fleet Project Team (DNAB)
FPT .... Flight Plan Talker [*Aviation*] (SAA)
FPT .... Floating Point Trap (SAUS)
FPT .... Fluidic Proportional Thruster
FPT .... Forced Perfect Termination [*Computer science*]
FPT .... Force/Forced Perfect Termination (SAUS)
FPT .... Fore Peak Tank (SAUS)
FPT .... Forward Peak Tank [*On ships*]
FPT .... Foundation for Physical Therapy (EA)
FPT .... Four Picture Test [*Psychology*]
FPT .... Frame Paperfeed Transport (SAUS)

FPT .... Franklin Principal Maturity [*NYSE symbol*] (SPSG)
FPT .... Free Plasma Trytophan (PDAA)
FPT .... Freight Pass-Through [*Publishing*]
FPT .... Fruit Pressure Test (SAUS)
FPT .... Fruit Pressure Tester
FPT .... Full Period Termination (CAAL)
FPT .... Full Power Trial
FPT .... Full Production Training (SAUO)
FPT .... Functional Performance Time
FPT .... Functional Program Translator [*Computer science*]
FPT .... Fundamental Parameters Technique
FPT .... Ivorian Popular Front (Ivory Coast) [*Political party*] (PSAP)
FPTA .... Forest Products Traffic Association (EA)
FPTA .... Fully Proceduralized Troubleshooting Aids [*Military*]
FPTC .... Forest Products Trucking Council (EA)
FPTD .... Focal Plane Technology Demonstration (ACAE)
FPTE .... Facility Portable Test Equipment (AAG)
FPTF .... Fuel Performance Test Facility (IAA)
FPTG .... Free Patellar Tendon Graft [*Sports medicine*]
fptm .... fluorescent pen-tank method (SAUS)
FPTO .... Fluid Power Take-Off [*Hydraulic transmissions*]
FPTO .... Forest Products Trucking Council (SAUO)
FPTP .... First Past the Post [*Electoral system*] [*British*] (ECON)
FPTP .... Flight Proof Test Plan (AAG)
FPTPEC .... France Pacific Territories National Committee for Pacific Economic Cooperation
FPTPI .... Fiberglass Petroleum Tank and Pipe Institute (EA)
FPTS .... Fire Protection Tracking System [*Environmental science*] (COE)
FPTS .... Fixed Point Test Site [*Military*] (CAAL)
FPTS .... Forward Propagation by Tropospheric Scatter [*Radio communications technique*]
FPTU .... Federation of Progressive Trade Unions [*Zanzibar*]
fpu .... field pickup unit (SAUS)
FPU .... File Processing Unit (SAUS)
FPU .... Film Production Unit [*British military*] (DMA)
FPU .... Filter Paper Units [*Pulp and paper technology*]
FPU .... Finance and Planning Unit (HEAS)
FPU .... First Production Unit
FPU .... Fixed Point Unit (SAUS)
FPU .... Floating Point Processor Unit (SAUS)
FPU .... Floating Point Underflow (SAUS)
FPU .... Floating-Point Unit [*Computer science*] (MCD)
FPU .... Florida Public Utilities [*AMEX symbol*] (TTSB)
FPU .... Florida Public Utilities Co. [*AMEX symbol*] (SPSG)
FPU .... Folkepartiets Ungdomsforbund [*Liberal Youth*] [*Political party*] (EAIO)
FPU .... Food Preservers Union (SAUO)
FPU .... Food Production Unit (SAUS)
FPU .... Forwarding Participating Unit (SAUO)
FPU .... Francis Peak [*Utah*] [*Seismograph station code, US Geological Survey*] (SEIS)
FPU .... Frente del Pueblo Unido [*Bolivia*] [*Political party*] (EY)
FPU .... Fuel Purification Unit [*Aerospace*] (AAG)
FPU .... Future Publication Uncertain
FPUA .... Food Preservers' Union of Australia
FPUB .... Femoral Propliteal Vein Bypass (SAUS)
FPUO .... For Personal Use Only
FPUP .... Federal Photovoltaics Utilization Program [*Department of Energy*]
FPUR .... For the Purpose Of
FPURX .... Fidelity Puritan [*Mutual fund ticker symbol*] (SG)
FPUSA .... Federation of Petanque U.S.A. (EA)
FPUT .... Florida Public Utilities Co. (SAUO)
FPUWA .... Food Preservers' Union of Western Australia
FPV .... Fast Patrol Vessel (SAUS)
FPV .... Federation of Paint and Varnish Production Clubs (SAUO)
FPV .... Feed Water Regulation Valve (IEEE)
FPV .... Feline Panleukopenia Virus
FPV .... Financial Planning Volume
FPV .... Fishery Protection Vessel
FPV .... Fixed Point Value (SAUS)
FPV .... Fixed Point Variable (SAUS)
fpv .... fixed-price vendor (SAUS)
FPV .... Flow Proportioning Value (MCD)
FPV .... Force Projection Vehicle (SAUO)
FPV .... Fowl Pest Virus [*Veterinary science*] (DB)
FPV .... Fowl Plague Virus
FPV .... Free Piston Vessel (GFGA)
FPV .... French Polydor Variable Micrograde [*Record label*]
FPV .... Front Progressiste Voltaique [*Upper Volta Progressive Front*] [*Political party*] (PPW)
FPV .... Functional Proofing Vehicle
FPVB .... Femoral Popliteal Vein Bypass [*Medicine*]
FPVC .... Flexible Polyvinyl Chloride [*Plastics*]
FPVN .... Vila Das Neves [*Sao Tome*] [*ICAO location identifier*] (ICLI)
FPVPC .... Federation of Paint and Varnish Production Clubs [*Later, FSCT*]
FPV/S .... Floating Production Vessel/System (DS)
FPW .... Fields Point [*Washington*] [*Seismograph station code, US Geological Survey*] (SEIS)
FPW .... Firing Port Weapon
FPW .... Fixed Point Word (SAUS)
FPW .... Flat Pack Welder
FPW .... Flexural Plate Wave (SAUS)
FPW .... Floating Point Word (SAUS)
FPW .... Focused Pressure Wave (SEWL)
FPW .... FoxPro for Windows (SAUS)
FPW .... Free Progressive Wave
FPWA .... Federation of Professional Writers of America (EA)
FPWA .... Federation of Protestant Welfare Agencies (EA)
FPWA .... Forest Products Wholesalers Association (SAUO)
FPWA .... Further Particulars When Available
FPWP .... Female Prisoners' Welfare Project (WDAA)
FPWR .... Fountain Powerboat Ind [*NASDAQ symbol*] (SG)
FPWR .... Fountain Powerboats [*NASDAQ symbol*] (SAG)
FPWS .... Flat Pack Welder System
FPWSAC .... Fluoridation of Public Water Supplies Advisory Committee [*New South Wales, Australia*]
FPWT .... Fire Protection Water Tank (IEEE)
FPWT .... Flight Plan Weight (SAUS)
FPWT .... Fuel Pool Water Treatment [*Nuclear energy*] (NRCH)
FPX .... Flash Pix (Format) (SAUS)
FPX .... Fortune Natural Res [*AMEX symbol*] (SG)
FPX .... Fortune Petroleum [*AMEX symbol*] (TTSB)
FPX .... Fortune Petroleum Corp. [*AMEX symbol*] (SPSG)
FPX .... Kodak Flashpix Image Format
FPY .... Failures per Year [*Telecommunications*] (TEL)
FPY .... First-Pass Yield (SAUS)
FPY .... Perry, FL [*Location identifier*] [*FAA*] (FAAL)
FPZ .... Federal Paper [*Federal Railroad Administration identification code*]
FPZ .... Fluphenazine [*Tranquilizer*]
FPZ .... Free Port Zone [*Shipping*] (DS)
FPZ .... Frontage Protection Zone (PA)
FPZ-D .... Fluphenazine Decanoate [*Tranquilizer*] (DAVI)
fq--- .... Africa, Equatorial [*MARC geographic area code*] [*Library of Congress*] (LCCP)
FQ .... Air Aruba [*ICAO designator*] (AD)
FQ .... Compagnie Aerienne du Languedoc [*ICAO designator*] (AD)
FQ .... Fare Quotation [*Airline*]
FQ .... Film Quarterly [*A publication*] (BRI)
FQ .... First Quarter [*Moon phase*]
FQ .... Fiscal Quarter (AFM)
FQ .... Flight Qualification
FQ .... Flight Quality (ACAE)
FQ .... Fore Quarters (SPVS)
FQ .... Formal Qualification
FQ .... French Quarter (SAUO)
FQ .... Frequency [*Online database field identifier*]
FQ .... Frequency Equalizer (SAUS)
FQ .... Fused Quartz
FQ .... Fuse, Quick (SAUS)
FQ .... Fuze, Quick (SAUS)
FQA .... Field Quality Audit (IAA)
FQA .... Fixed Quality Area (AAEL)
FQA .... Floor Quarry Association (SAUO)
FQA .... Following Question/Answer (SAUO)
FQAG .... Angoche [*Mozambique*] [*ICAO location identifier*] (ICLI)
FQ & P .... Flight Qualities and Performance
FQAWT .... Flush Quick-Acting Watertight (SAUS)
FQBE .... Beira [*Mozambique*] [*ICAO location identifier*] (ICLI)
FQBI .... Bilene [*Mozambique*] [*ICAO location identifier*] (ICLI)
FQBR .... Beira [*Mozambique*] [*ICAO location identifier*] (ICLI)
FQC .... Foret Quality Class (EERA)
FQCB .... Cuamba [*Mozambique*] [*ICAO location identifier*] (ICLI)
FQCH .... Chimoio [*Mozambique*] [*ICAO location identifier*] (ICLI)
FQCY .... Frequency (WGA)
FQDN .... Fully-Qualified Domain Name [*Internet*]
FQE .... Free Queue Element (IAA)
FQE .... Fuqua Enterprises [*NYSE symbol*] (SAG)
FQES .... Estima [*Mozambique*] [*ICAO location identifier*] (ICLI)
FQF .... Front du Quebec Francais
FQFU .... Furancungo [*Mozambique*] [*ICAO location identifier*] (ICLI)
FQG .... University of Miami, Coral Gables, FL [*OCLC symbol*] (OCLC)
FQGI .... Fully Qualified Generic Identifier
FQH .... Filled Quartz Helix
FQHC .... Federally Qualified Health Center
FQHE .... Fractional Quantum Hall Effect [*Solid-state physics*]
FQI .... Federal Quality Institute [*Office of Management and Budget*] (GFGA)
FQI .... File Quality Index (SAUS)
FQI .... Flight Qualification Instrumentation (MCD)
FQI .... Fuel Quantity Indicator
FQIA .... Inhaca [*Mozambique*] [*ICAO location identifier*] (ICLI)
FQIL .... Fused Quartz Incandescent Lamp
FQIL .... Fuzed Quartz Incandescent Lamp (SAUS)
FQIN .... Inhambane [*Mozambique*] [*ICAO location identifier*] (ICLI)
FQIS .... Fuel Quantity Indicating System [*Aviation*]
FQIS .... Fuel Quantity Indication System (SAUS)
FQK .... Fully Qualified Key (VLIE)
FQL .... Food Quality Laboratory (SAUO)
FQL .... Formal Query Language (NITA)
FQL .... Functional Querry Language (SAUS)
FQL .... Functional Query Language [*1978*] [*Computer science*] (CSR)
FQLC .... Lichinga [*Mozambique*] [*ICAO location identifier*] (ICLI)
FQLU .... Lumbo [*Mozambique*] [*ICAO location identifier*] (ICLI)
FQM .... Four Quadrant Multiplier (SAUS)
FQM .... Four-Quadrant Multiplier
FQM .... University of Miami, School of Medicine, Miami, FL [*OCLC symbol*] (OCLC)
FQMA .... Maputo [*Mozambique*] [*ICAO location identifier*] (ICLI)
FQMD .... Mueda [*Mozambique*] [*ICAO location identifier*] (ICLI)
FQML .... Fort Worth Qualified Material List [*NASA*] (KSC)
FQMP .... Mocimboa Da Praia [*Mozambique*] [*ICAO location identifier*] (ICLI)
FQMR .... Marrupa [*Mozambique*] [*ICAO location identifier*] (ICLI)

FQMS .... Farrier Quartermaster-Sergeant [*British military*] (DMA)
FQMU .... Mutarara [*Mozambique*] [*ICAO location identifier*] (ICLI)
FQN .... Family Quarters, Navy (DNAB)
FQNC .... Nacala [*Mozambique*] [*ICAO location identifier*] (ICLI)
FQNP .... Nampula [*Mozambique*] [*ICAO location identifier*] (ICLI)
FQO .... Federation of Quarry Owners (SAUS)
FQOGB .... Federated Quarry Owners of Great Britain (SAUO)
FQP .... Fundamental Questions Program (EERA)
FQPA .... Flight Quality Photomultiplier Assembly
FQPA .... Food Quality Protection Act [*1996*]
FQPB .... Pemba [*Mozambique*] [*ICAO location identifier*] (ICLI)
FQPCID .... Fully Qualified Procedure Correlation Identifier (ACRL)
FQPO .... Ponta Do Ouro [*Mozambique*] [*ICAO location identifier*] (ICLI)
FQPR .... Frequency Programmer (IEEE)
FQQL .... Quelimane [*Mozambique*] [*ICAO location identifier*] (ICLI)
FQQPRI .... Final Qualitative and Quantitative Personnel Requirements Information
FQR .... Fabrication Quality Record
FQR .... Final Qualification Review (SAUS)
FQR .... Flight Qualification Recorder (KSC)
FQR .... Flight Qualification Review (SAUS)
FQR .... Flight Qualification Reviews (MCD)
FQR .... Formal Qualification Review (SAUO)
FQR .... Formal Qualification Reviews (MCD)
FQR .... Functional Qualification Review
FQS .... Federal Quarantine Service (BARN)
FQS .... Flight Qualified System (MCD)
FQS .... Flight Quality Simulator (SAUS)
FQS .... Friendly Query System [*IBM*] (NITA)
FQSEBT .... Fixed Quantum Shortest Expected Burst Time (SAUS)
FQSERBT .... Fixed Quantum Shortest Expected Remaining Burst Time (SAUS)
FQSG .... Songo [*Mozambique*] [*ICAO location identifier*] (ICLI)
FQT .... Formal Qualification Test (KSC)
FQT .... Frequent
FQT .... Functional Qualification Test (VLIE)
FQT .... Fused Quartz Tubing
FQTE .... Tete [*Mozambique*] [*ICAO location identifier*] (ICLI)
FQTR .... Flight Qualification Tape Recorder [*NASA*] (KSC)
FQTT .... Tete/Chingozi [*Mozambique*] [*ICAO location identifier*] (ICLI)
FQTV .... Frequent Traveler (TVEL)
FQUG .... Ulongwe [*Mozambique*] [*ICAO location identifier*] (ICLI)
FQV .... Plattsburgh, NY [*Location identifier*] [*FAA*] (FAAL)
FQVL .... Vilanculos [*Mozambique*] [*ICAO location identifier*] (ICLI)
FQXA .... Xai-Xai [*Mozambique*] [*ICAO location identifier*] (ICLI)
FR .... Fabric Reinforced (SAUS)
FR .... Facilities Report [*or Request*]
FR .... Facilities Request (SAUS)
FR .... Faculty of Radiologists
FR .... Faculty of Radiology (SAUS)
FR .... Faculty Rating
F/R .... Failure and Recovery (VLIE)
FR .... Failure Rate
FR .... Failure Report
FR .... Fair (ROG)
Fr .... Fair [*Numismatic term*]
fr .... Fair
fr .... Faire Reporter [*Carry Over*] [*Stock exchange term*] [*French*]
f/r .... Fair Rate
FR .... Fall River [*Diocesan abbreviation*] [*Massachusetts*] (TOCD)
FR .... False Rejection (SAUS)
FR .... Family Registry (GEAB)
FR .... Family Room [*Real estate*]
FR .... Family Rosary (EA)
FR .... Fanaroff-Riley [*Radio galaxy*]
FR .... Fargo Resources Ltd. [*Vancouver Stock Exchange symbol*]
FR .... Fast Reactor (SAUS)
FR .... Fast Recovery
FR .... Fast Register (SAUS)
FR .... Fast Release [*Relay*]
FR .... Fast-release Relay (SAUS)
Fr .... Father (SHCU)
fr .... father (SAUS)
FR .... Father
FR .... Fatigue Resistant
FR .... Favre-Racouchot [*Syndrome*] [*Medicine*] (DB)
FR .... Feather River [*AAR code*]
FR .... Federal Reformatory (SAUS)
FR .... Federal Region [*Dialog*] [*Searchable field*] [*Information service or system*] (NITA)
FR .... Federal Register [*A publication*]
FR .... Federal Regulation (OTD)
FR .... Federal Reporter [*A publication*] (DLA)
FR .... Federal Representative [*Job Training and Partnership Act*] (OICC)
FR .... Federal Republic (EY)
FR .... Federal Reserve
FR .... Feed Reel (SAUS)
FR .... Felicity Ratio (SAUS)
FR .... Ferroresonance (SAUS)
FR .... Ferry Range (MCD)
FR .... Fiber Reinforced (MCD)
FR .... Fibrinogen-Related [*Hematology*] (DAVI)
FR .... Fibron-Related [*Hematology*] (DAVI)
FR .... Field Regulator (SAUS)
FR .... Field Relay (IAA)
FR .... Field Report
FR .... Field Reporting (SAUS)
FR .... Field Requisition (VLIE)
FR .... Field Resistance (DEN)
FR .... Field Retrofit (MCD)
FR .... Field Reversing (AAG)
FR .... Field Rheostat (SAUS)
FR .... Fighter Reconnaissance [*Air Force*]
FR .... File Register
FR .... File Revision (SAUS)
FR .... Filing Requirement [*IRS*]
FR .... Filmless Radiography (MCD)
FR .... Film Recording
FR .... Film Report (AFM)
FR .... Final Release (AAG)
FR .... Final Report
FR .... Final Review (SAUS)
FR .... Final Rule [*RSPA*] (TAG)
FR .... Final Rulemaking (COE)
FR .... Finance Regulation [*Economics*]
F/R .... Financial Responsibility
FR .... Fineness Ratio
fr .... fire (SAUS)
FR .... Fireman Recruit [*Navy rating*]
Fr .... Fire Rating [*Construction term*] (MIST)
FR .... Fire Request (SAUS)
FR .... Fire Resistance (SAUS)
FR .... Fire Resistant [*or Retardant*]
FR .... Fire Resistive
fr .... fire retardant (SAUS)
FR .... Firestone Radial [*Tire design*]
FR .... Firing Room [*NASA*] (KSC)
FR .... First Industrial Realty Trust, Inc. [*NYSE symbol*] (SAG)
FR .... First Industrial Rlty Tr [*NYSE symbol*] (TTSB)
FR .... First Reader
FR .... First Renewal
FR .... Fisher-Race Notation [*Medicine*] (MAE)
FR .... Fixed Ratio
FR .... Fixed-Ratio Schedule of Reinforcement (DIPS)
FR .... Fixed Red (SAUS)
FR .... Fixed Resistor (SAUS)
F/R .... Fixed Response (WDAA)
FR .... Flag Register (ACAE)
FR .... Flame Resistance (SAUS)
FR .... Flame Resistant (SARE)
FR .... Flame Retardancy (SAUS)
FR .... Flame Retardant
F/R .... Flared Rudder (NASA)
fr .... flaring and retracting (SAUS)
FR .... Flash Radiography (SAUS)
FR .... Flash Ranging
FR .... Flash Red (SAUS)
FR .... flash red-enemy aircraft nearby (SAUS)
f/r .... flat rack (SAUS)
FR .... Flat Rack Container [*Shipping*] (DS)
FR .... Flat Rate (SAUS)
FR .... Fleet Readiness [*Navy*] (AFIT)
FR .... Fleet Reserve [*Navy*]
FR .... Fleet Reservist (SAUS)
FR .... Flight Readiness
FR .... Flight Recorder (MCD)
FR .... Flight Refueling (MCD)
FR .... Flight Reliability (MCD)
fr .... flight request (SAUS)
FR .... Flight Rule (MCD)
FR .... Floating-Point Register (VLIE)
FR .... Floating Register (SAUS)
FR .... Floating Regulator (SAUS)
FR .... Flocculation Reaction [*Obsolete test for liver function*]
FR .... Flood Relief Punt [*Coast Guard*]
FR .... Flow Rate
FR .... Flow Recorder
FR .... Flow Regime
FR .... Flow Regulator [*Nuclear energy*] (NRCH)
FR .... Fluid Resistant
FR .... Fluid Restriction (MELL)
FR .... Fluid Retention (MELL)
FR .... Fluorescence
FR .... Fluorescent Radiation (SAUS)
fr .... Fluorite [*CIPW classification*] [*Geology*]
fr .... Folio Recto [*Right-hand page number*] [*Right-hand page*] [*Publishing*] (WDMC)
FR .... Folio Recto [*Right-Hand Page*] [*Latin*]
FR .... Folkways Records (SAUS)
FR .... Food Ratio
FR .... Food Research (SAUO)
FR .... Food Research Association Computerized Information Service (SAUO)
FR .... Food Research (journ.) (SAUS)
FR .... Foot Ratio (SAUS)
fr .... Foot Run (SAUS)
FR .... For [*Telecommunications*] (ADDR)
fr .... for (SAUS)
Fr .... Foraminifera [*Quality of the bottom*] [*Nautical charts*]
FR .... forced release (SAUS)
FR .... Forced Removal

FR............... Force Release [*Telecommunications*] (TEL)
FR............... Foreign [*Searchable field*] (NITA)
FR............... Foreign Relations (DLA)
FR............... Foreign Relations Committee [*US Senate*]
FR............... Foreign Requirements
FR............... fore peak (SAUS)
FR............... Forest Rangers [*British military*] (DMA)
FR............... Forest Reserve [*State*] (EERA)
FR............... Formation Pennant [*Navy*] [*British*]
fr............... Former (SAUS)
FR............... Forming Rolls (MCD)
FR............... Fort (ROG)
FR............... Fortnightly Review (journ.) (SAUS)
FR............... Forum Romanum [*The Roman Forum*]
FR............... forward peak (SAUS)
FR............... Forward Reference (SAUS)
FR............... Fossil Record
fr............... Fraction (ADWA)
FR............... Fractional Reabsorption [*Biochemistry*] (DAVI)
Fr............... Fraction of liquid waste treated anaerobically (SAUS)
FR............... Fraction of Reads (SAUS)
fr............... Fracture [*Orthopedics*] (DAVI)
FR............... Fragipan [*Soil biology*] (QSUL)
fr............... Fragment (SAUS)
Fr............... Fragmenta [*of Aristotle*] [*Classical studies*] (OCD)
fr............... Fragmentation (SAUS)
FR............... Fragmentum [*Fragment*] [*Latin*] (ROG)
FR............... Frame (MSA)
fr............... Frame (WDMC)
FR............... Frame Rate (SAUS)
FR............... Frame Recognition (SAUS)
FR............... Frame Relay (ACRL)
FR............... Frame Reprint (SAUS)
FR............... Frame Reset [*Telecommunications*] (TEL)
FR............... Frames Recovered (SAUS)
FR............... Framework Region [*Genetics*]
FR............... Franc [*Monetary unit*] [*France*] (EY)
Fr............... France (CMD)
FR............... France [*ANSI two-letter standard code*] (CNC)
fr............... France [*MARC country of publication code*] [*Library of Congress*] (LCCP)
FR............... France Routiers (SAUS)
Fr............... Franciscus de Telese [*Flourished, 1270-82*] [*Authority cited in pre-1607 legal work*] (DSA)
Fr............... Francium [*Chemical element*]
Fr............... Franco- (SAUS)
Fr............... Franklin [*Also, sC, statC*] [*Unit of electric charge*]
fr............... Frankline (IDOE)
fr............... franko (SAUS)
fr............... franline (SAUS)
FR............... Frater [*Brother*] [*Latin*]
FR............... Fraud [*Legal shorthand*] (LWAP)
fr............... frayed (SAUS)
FR............... Free (ADA)
Fr............... Free (AL)
Fr............... Freeman's English King's Bench and Chancery Reports [*A publication*] (DLA)
FR............... Free Radical (DB)
FR............... Free Response
FR............... Free Ribosomes [*Cytology*]
FR............... Freight Release
Fr............... French (BEE)
Fr............... French [*Catheter gauge*] [*Medicine*] (DAVI)
FR............... French
FR............... French Research [*Satellite*]
FR............... French Review [*A publication*] (BRI)
FR............... French Rite [*Freemasonry*] (ROG)
FR............... Frequency (SAUS)
FR............... Frequency Measuring Devices [*JETDS nomenclature*] [*Military*] (CET)
FR............... frequency meter (SAUS)
FR............... Frequency of Respiration (SAUS)
FR............... Frequency Range
FR............... Frequency Rate (WDAA)
FR............... Frequency Received (ACAE)
FR............... Frequency Recorder (SAUS)
FR............... Frequency Response
FR............... Frequent
FR............... Fresh
FR............... Fresnel (SAUS)
FR............... Friar
F_r............... Frictional Force (DA)
FR............... Friday
FR............... Friden (SAUS)
FR............... Friden, Inc. (SAUO)
FR............... Frigate
fr............... Frigorie [*Unit of rate of extraction of heat*] [*Thermodynamics*]
FR............... From (AFM)
fr............... From (VRA)
FR............... Front
FR............... Front Engine, Rear Drive [*Automotive engineering*]
Fr............... frontier set of (SAUS)
FR............... Frontispiece [*Publishing*]
F/R............... Front/Rear
FR............... front right (SAUS)
f/r............... front to rear (SAUS)
Fr............... Froude number (SAUS)
FR............... Fructus [*Fruit*] [*Latin*] (ROG)
fr............... Fruit
FR............... Fuel Remaining [*Aviation*]
FR............... Fuel Research (SAUO)
FR............... Fuerza Republicana [*Argentina*] [*Political party*] (EY)
FR............... Full Range (MCD)
FR............... Full Rate (SAUS)
FR............... Full-Rate [*Telegrams and cables*]
FR............... Fully Registered
FR............... Functional Requirements
FR............... Function Reference (SAUS)
FR............... Functions of Reads (VLIE)
FR............... Fundamental Research (SAUS)
FR............... Fundamental Resonance (MCD)
FR............... Fund for the Republic [*Later, Robert Maynard Hutchins Center for the Study of Democratic Institutions*] (EA)
FR............... Funding Request
FR............... Fund Raising [*Red Cross*]
FR............... Furlough Rations [*Army*]
FR............... Furness Railway [*Scotland*]
FR............... Furness Railway Co. (SAUO)
FR............... Fusion Reactor (SAUS)
fr---............... Rift Valley [*MARC geographic area code*] [*Library of Congress*] (LCCP)
FR............... Susquehanna [*ICAO designator*] (AD)
FR............... Fluorine Rubber (ODA)
F/R............... Folio Reference (ODA)
FR-2............... Flame-Retardant paper substrate material for cheap electronic circuits (SAUS)
FR-4............... Fire-Retardant glass laminate substrate material for electronic circuits (SAUS)
FR-6............... Fire-Retardant glass-and-polyester substrate material for electronic circuits (SAUS)
FR-172............... French-built four-place rocket-launching counterin-surgency aircraft (SAUS)
FRA............... Farah, Inc. [*NYSE symbol*] (SPSG)
FRA............... Farah Manufacturing Co., Inc. (SAUO)
FRA............... Father's Rights of America (EA)
FRA............... Federal Radio Act (NITA)
FRA............... Federal Railway Administration [*DOT*] (AAGC)
FRA............... Federal Register Act (GFGA)
FRA............... Federal Regular Army [*Federation of South Arabia*]
FRA............... Federal Reports Act (DLA)
FRA............... Federal Reserve Act [*1913*]
FRA............... Fellow of the Royal Academy (SAUO)
FRA............... Fibrinogen-Related Antigen [*Immunology*]
FRA............... File Recovery Area [*Computer science*] (ECII)
FRA............... Film Research Associates (SAUO)
FRA............... Financial Research Associates
FRA............... Financial Responsibility Action
FRA............... Financial Restructuring Authority [*Thailand*]
FRA............... Financial Sector Restructuring Authority
FRA............... Fire Retarding Additive
FRA............... First Run Attack (SAUS)
FRA............... Fixed Radio Access (SAUS)
FRA............... Flap Retraction Altitude (GAVI)
FRA............... Fleet Readiness Assistants (SAUO)
FRA............... Fleet Reserve Association (EA)
FRA............... Floating Reset Add (VLIE)
FRA............... Florida Redevelopment Association (SRA)
FRA............... Flowrate Recording Alarm [*Engineering*]
FRA............... Flow Recorder and Alarm [*Nuclear energy*] (NRCH)
FRA............... Fluorescent Rabies Antibody [*Immunology*]
FRA............... Food Retailers Association (SAUO)
FRA............... Footwear Research Association (SAUO)
FRA............... Footwear Retailers of America [*Later, FDRA*] (EA)
FRA............... Force Recon Association (EA)
FRA............... Foreign Resources Associates
FRA............... Forest Resource Assessment (SAUS)
FRA............... Forward Rate Agreement [*Banking*]
FRA............... Forward Refueling Area
FRA............... Fos-Related Antigens [*Biochemistry*]
Fra............... Fragrant
fra............... Frame (VRA)
FRA............... Framycetin [*Neomycin B*] [*Antibacterial compound*]
FRA............... France [*ANSI three-letter standard code*] (CNC)
FRA............... France-Reunion-Avenir [*Political party*] (EY)
Fra............... Franciscus de Telese [*Flourished, 1270-82*] [*Authority cited in pre-1607 legal work*] (DSA)
Fra............... Francis' Maxims of Equity [*1722-46*] [*A publication*] (DLA)
FRA............... Frankfurt [*Germany*] [*Airport symbol*] (OAG)
FRA............... FR Aviation Ltd. [*British*] [*ICAO designator*] (FAAC)
FRA............... Frente Radical Alfarista [*Radical Alfarista Front*] [*Ecuador*] [*Political party*] (PPW)
FRA............... Frequency Response Analyzer (SAUS)
FRA............... Friant, CA [*Location identifier*] [*FAA*] (FAAL)
FRA............... Friction Reducing Agent [*Chemicals*]
FRA............... Functional Residual Air (ADA)
FRA............... Funded Reimbursable Authority (SAUO)
FRA............... Funded Reimburseable Authority (MCD)
FRA............... Fuzzy Rule Approximation (IDAI)
fra............... Flame Retardant Additive (ODA)
FRAA............... Fleet Repairables Assistance Agent (MCD)

FRAA .... Fleet Reserve Association Auxiliary
FRAA .... Furniture Rental Association of America (EA)
FRAACA .... Foundation for Research in the Afro-American Creative Arts (EA)
Fra Ac F ...... Franciscus de Accursio (Filius) [*Deceased, 1293*] [*Authority cited in pre-1607 legal work*] (DSA)
FRAB .... Banque Franco-Arabe d'Investissements Internationaux
FRAB .... Financial Reports and Analysis Branch (SAUO)
FRAB .... Fuel Receiving Air Blowers [*Nuclear energy*] (NRCH)
FRAC .... Arts Foundation for Research in the Afro-American Creative Arts (SAUO)
FRAC .... Food Research and Action Center (EA)
FRAC .... Fractal Design [*NASDAQ symbol*] (TTSB)
FRAC .... Fractal Design Corp. [*NASDAQ symbol*] (SAG)
FRAC .... Fraction (SAUS)
FRAC .... Fractional (MSA)
FRAC .... Fractionation (SAUS)
FRAC .... Fractionator Reflux Analog Computer
FRAC .... Fracture [*Medicine*]
FRAC .... Franchise Rights Action Committee (SAUO)
frac .... frationator reflux analog computer (SAUS)
FRACA .... Failure Reporting, Analyses, and Corrective Action (MCD)
FRACAS .... Failure Rating Analysis and Corrective Action System [*Environmental science*] (COE)
FRACAS .... Failure Reporting, Analysis, and Corrective Action System (SAUO)
FRACAS .... Failure Reporting and Corrective Action System (MCD)
FRACAS .... Filter Response Analysis for Continuously Accelerating Spacecraft [*NASA*]
FRACD .... Form Row from Array Components in principal Diagonal (SAUS)
FRACGP .... Fellow of the Royal Australasian College of General Practitioners [*Medicine*] (DMAA)
FRACGP .... FelloW of the Royal Australian College of General Practitioners (SAUS)
FRACHE .... Federation of Regional Accrediting Commissions of Higher Education [*Later, COPA*] (EA)
FRACI .... Fellow of the Royal Australian Chemical Institute (SAUO)
FRACI .... Form Row from Array Components with given Index (SAUS)
FRACO .... Fellow of the Royal Australasian College of Ophthalmologists [*Medicine*] (DMAA)
FRACO .... Fellow of the Royal Australian College of Ophthalmologists (SAUS)
FRACO .... Framycetin [*Neomycin B*], Colistin [*Antineoplastic drug regimen*]
FRACOG .... Fellow of the Royal Australian College of Obstetricians and Gynecologists (CMD)
F Racon .... Fixed Frequency Radar Transponder Beacon [*Nautical term*] (HRNC)
FRACON .... Framycetin [*Neomycin B*], Colistin, Nystatin [*Antineoplastic drug regimen*]
FRACP .... Fellow of the Royal Australasian College of Physicians
FRACP .... Fellow of the Royal Australian College of Physicians (SAUS)
FRACR .... Fellow of the Royal Australasian College of Radiologists
FRACS .... Fellow of the Royal Australasian College of Surgeons
FRACS .... Fellow of the Royal Australian College of Surgeons (SAUO)
fract .... Fraction [*Medicine*] (EDAA)
FRACT .... Fraction
fract .... Fractionate (SAUS)
fract .... Fracture [*Medicine*] (EDAA)
FRACT .... Fracture [*Medicine*]
Fractal .... Fractal Design Corp. [*Associated Press*] (SAG)
FRACTAL ..... Fractional (VLIE)
FRACT DOS... Fracti Dosi [*In Divided Doses*] [*Pharmacy*]
fractn .... Fractionation (SAUS)
fractnl .... Fractional (SAUS)
FRACTS .... Fractitional Urines [*Medicine*] (EDAA)
FRAD .... Fellow of the Royal Academy of Dancing [*British*]
FRAD .... Frame Relay Access Device [*Plantronics Futurecomms, Inc.*]
FRAD .... Frame Relay Assembler/Disassembler [*Communications*]
FRAD .... Frame Relay Assembler/Dissassembler [*Telecommunications*] (IGQR)
FRADA .... Factice Research and Development Association (SAUO)
Fra de Sax... Franciscus de Saxolinis [*Flourished, 13th century*] [*Authority cited in pre-1607 legal work*] (DSA)
Fra de Saxolis... Franciscus de Saxolinis [*Flourished, 13th century*] [*Authority cited in pre-1607 legal work*] (DSA)
Fra de Te..... Franciscus de Telese [*Flourished, 1270-82*] [*Authority cited in pre-1607 legal work*] (DSA)
Fra de Tels... Franciscus de Telese [*Flourished, 1270-82*] [*Authority cited in pre-1607 legal work*] (DSA)
FRADU .... Fleet Requirements and Aircraft Direction Unit [*Navy*] (MCD)
FRADU .... Fleet Requirements & Air Detection Unit (SAUS)
FRADU .... Fleet Requirements & Air Direction Unit (SAUS)
Fr Adv Sci Technol... French Advances in Science and Technology (journ.) (SAUS)
FrAE .... French Antarctic Expedition [*1903-05,1908-10,1948-*]
FRAeS .... Fellow of the Royal Aeronautical Society [*British*] (EY)
FRAF .... Fuel Receiving Air Filters [*Nuclear energy*] (NRCH)
FRAG .... Fragile
FRAG .... Fragment [*Military*] (AFM)
frag .... Fragment (VRA)
FRAG .... Fragment [*Used in correcting manuscripts, etc.*]
FRAG .... Fragmentary (SAUS)
Frag .... Fragmentation [*Weapon*] (DOMA)
frag .... Fragmented (SAUS)
FRAG .... French Fragrances [*NASDAQ symbol*] (TTSB)
FRAG .... French Fragrances, Inc. [*NASDAQ symbol*] (SAG)
FrAg .... Frequency Agility (SAUS)
FRAGBOMB... Fragmentation Bomb
FRAG II .... Fragmentary Order Processing System (SAUO)
FRAGM .... Fragmentation (SAUS)
FRAGM .... Fragments
FRAGNET..... Fragmented Network (SAUS)
FRAGO .... Fragmentary Order [*Military*]
FRAGO .... Fragmentation Order [*Army*]
frago .... fragmented order (SAUS)
Fra Gon .... Franciscus Gonzaga [*Authority cited in pre-1607 legal work*] (DSA)
FRAG PREP... Fragmentary Order Preparation System (SAUO)
FRAGROC .... Fragmenting Warhead Rocket
FRAgS .... Fellow of the Royal Agricultural Societies (SAUS)
FRAgSs .... Fellow of the Royal Agricultural Societies [*British*]
FRAH .... Fluid Regenerative Air Heater (PDAA)
FRAIC .... Fellow of the Royal Architectural Institute of Canada
fraid .... afraid (SAUS)
FRAIN .... Front Revolutionnaire Africain pour l'Independence Nationale des Colonies Portugaises [*African Revolutionary Front for the National Independence of Portuguese Colonies*]
FrAipNA .... Centre d'Etudes Nord-Americaines, Aix-En-Provence, France [*Library symbol*] [*Library of Congress*] (LCLS)
FRAK .... Flak RADAR Automatic Kanon
FRAKL .... Franklin, VA [*American Association of Railroads railroad junction routing code*]
FRALINE ...... Fast Reaction Automatic Lightweight Inertial North-Seeking Equipment (PDAA)
FRAM .... Failure Rate Assessment Machine (PDAA)
FRAM .... Fellow of the Royal Academy of Medicine (SAUS)
FRAM .... Fellow of the Royal Academy of Music [*British*]
FRAM .... Fellow, Royal Academy of Medicine [*British*] (CMD)
FRAM .... ferroelectrical random-access memory (SAUS)
FRAM .... Ferroelectric/Ferromagnetic Random Access Memory (SAUS)
FRAM .... Ferroelectric RAM (SAUS)
FRAM .... Ferroelectric Random Access Memory [*Computer science*]
FRAM .... Ferroelectronic RAM [*Random-Access Memory*] [*Ramtron*]
FRAM .... Ferromagnetic Random Access Memory (SAUS)
FRAM .... Fine Resolution Antarctic Model [*Oceanography*]
FRAM .... Fleet Modernization and Repair Program [*Navy*]
FRAM .... Fleet Rehabilitation and Maintenance
FRAM .... Fleet Rehabilitation And Modernisation programme (SAUS)
FRAM .... Fleet Rehabilitation and Modernization [*Navy*] (MCD)
FRAM .... Fleet Replacement and Modernization [*Military*] (USDC)
Fra M .... Francis' Maxims of Equity [*1722-46*] [*A publication*] (DLA)
FRAM .... Fusible Random Access Memory [*Computer science*] (PDAA)
FRAM2 .... Field Records Administration Microform Mode
FRAMATOME... Societe Franco-Americaine de Constructions Atomiques (NRCH)
FraMCoS ...... Fracture Mechanics of Concrete Structures (SAUS)
FRAME .... Failure Rate Analysis and Modeling (AAEL)
FRAME .... Frame Relay and Mux Expander [*Computer science*]
FRAME .... Fund for the Replacement of Animals in Medical Experiments
FRAME .... Fund for the Replacement of Animals in Medical Research (SAUS)
FRAMEWORK... Formal Risk Assessment, Millennium Engineers, Workaround Options, Replacement Policy, Keep Going (VLIE)
FRAMG .... Framing
Framingham St C... Framingham State College (GAGS)
FRAMME .... Facilities Rule-Based Model Management Environment
FRAMP .... Fleet Readiness Aircraft Maintenance Personnel [*Navy*] (MCD)
FRAMP .... Fleet Readiness Aviation Maintenance Personnel [*Navy*]
FRAMP .... Fleet Rehabilitation and Modernization Program [*Navy*]
FRAMP .... Fleet Replacement Aviation Maintenance Program (ACAE)
FRAMP .... Frampton [*England*]
FRAMPO ...... Frente Amplio Popular [*Broad Popular Front*] [*Panama*] [*Political party*] (PPW)
FRAM Program... Fleet Rehabilitation and Modernization Program (SAUS)
FramS .... Framingham Savings Bank [*Associated Press*] (SAG)
FramSv .... Framingham Savings Bank [*Associated Press*] (SAG)
FRAN .... Fleet Readiness Analysis [*NORRS*]
FRAN .... Framed structure Analysis (SAUS)
FRAN .... Frame Structure Analysis (IAA)
Fran .... France (SAUS)
fran .... franchise (SAUS)
Fran .... Franciscan (SAUS)
Fran .... Franciscus de Telese [*Flourished, 1270-82*] [*Authority cited in pre-1607 legal work*] (DSA)
Fran .... Franciscus Vercellensis [*Flourished, 13th century*] [*Authority cited in pre-1607 legal work*] (DSA)
Fran .... Franciscus Zabarella [*Deceased, 1417*] [*Authority cited in pre-1607 legal work*] (DSA)
FRAN .... Franklin Institute Journal (SAUS)
Fran Anz ...... Franciscus Anzolellus [*Authority cited in pre-1607 legal work*] (DSA)
Fran Anzol... Franciscus Anzolellus [*Authority cited in pre-1607 legal work*] (DSA)
Fran Aret ..... Franciscus de Accoltis de Aretio [*Deceased, 1486*] [*Authority cited in pre-1607 legal work*] (DSA)
FRANC .... Franciscan [*Religious order*] (WDAA)
Franc .... Franciscus de Telese [*Flourished, 1270-82*] [*Authority cited in pre-1607 legal work*] (DSA)
Franc Ac ...... Franciscus de Accursio [*Deceased, 1293*] [*Authority cited in pre-1607 legal work*] (DSA)
FRANC AD MOEN... Francofurtum Ad Moenum [*Frankfort-On-The-Main*] [*Imprint*] [*Latin*] (ROG)
Franc Anz .... Franciscus Anzolellus [*Authority cited in pre-1607 legal work*] (DSA)
Franc Conn... Franciscus Connanus [*Deceased, 1551*] [*Authority cited in pre-1607 legal work*] (DSA)
Franc de Are... Franciscus de Accoltis de Aretio [*Deceased, 1486*] [*Authority cited in pre-1607 legal work*] (DSA)
Franc de Rampo... Franciscus de Ramponibus [*Deceased, 1401*] [*Authority cited in pre-1607 legal work*] (DSA)

Franc de T... Franciscus de Telese [*Flourished, 1270-82*] [*Authority cited in pre-1607 legal work*] (DSA)
Franc de Tel... Franciscus de Telese [*Flourished, 1270-82*] [*Authority cited in pre-1607 legal work*] (DSA)
France......... France Growth Fund [*Associated Press*] (SAG)
France......... France's Reports [*3-11 Colorado*] [*A publication*] (DLA)
France......... French Republic (SAUS)
France (Colo)... France's Reports [*3-11 Colorado*] [*A publication*] (DLA)
Fran Char.... Francis' Law of Charities [*2nd ed.*] [*1855*] [*A publication*] (DLA)
Franchise LJ... Franchise Law Journal [*A publication*] (DLA)
FRANCIS...... Fichier de Recherches Automatisees sur les Nouvautes, la Communication et l'Information en Sciences Sociales et Humaines [*French Retrieval Automated Network for Current Information in Social and Human Sciences*] [*Database*]
FRANCIS...... Food Research Association Computerized Information Service [*Food Research Association*] [*Database*] (NITA)
Francis Bald... Franciscus Balduinus [*Deceased, 1572*] [*Authority cited in pre-1607 legal work*] (DSA)
FRANCIS: DOGE... FRANCIS: Documentation Automatisee en Gestion des Entreprises [*Database*]
Francis Duar... Franciscus Duarenus [*Deceased, 1559*] [*Authority cited in pre-1607 legal work*] (DSA)
Francis Max... Francis' Maxims of Equity [*1722-46*] [*A publication*] (DLA)
FRANCIS: RESHUS... FRANCIS: Reseau Documentaire en Sciences Humaines de la Sante [*Database*] [*French*]
Francis Sonsb... Franciscus Sonsbeccius [*Flourished, 16th century*] [*Authority cited in pre-1607 legal work*] (DSA)
Franc Judg... Francillon's County Court Judgments [*England*] [*A publication*] (DLA)
FRANCOF..... Francofortium [*Frankfort*] [*Imprint*] [*Latin*] (ROG)
Fran Coll LJ... Franciso College Law Journal [*A publication*] (DLA)
Franc Viv..... Franciscus Vivius [*Flourished, 16th century*] [*Authority cited in pre-1607 legal work*] (DSA)
Franc Zoannet... Franciscus Zoannettus [*Deceased, 1586*] [*Authority cited in pre-1607 legal work*] (DSA)
FRAND......... Fractionally Anded (ACAE)
FR and AS... Fellow of the Royal and Antiquarian Society (SAUO)
FR and ASS... Fellow of the Royal and Antiquarian Societies [*British*]
fr & cc......... free of riots and civil commotion (SAUS)
FR&CC......... Free of Riots and Civil Commotions (SAUS)
FR & CC........ Free of Riots and Civil Commotions [*Insurance*]
Fran de Are... Franciscus de Accoltis de Aretio [*Deceased, 1486*] [*Authority cited in pre-1607 legal work*] (DSA)
Fran de Rampo... Franciscus de Ramponibus [*Deceased, 1401*] [*Authority cited in pre-1607 legal work*] (DSA)
FR & RC....... Family Resource and Referral Center [*National Council on Family Relations*] [*Information service or system*] (IID)
Fran Duar.... Franciscus Duarenus [*Deceased, 1559*] [*Authority cited in pre-1607 legal work*] (DSA)
Fr & W Prec... Frend and Ware's Precedents of Instruments Relating to the Transfer of Land to Railway Companies [*2nd ed.*] [*1866*] [*A publication*] (DLA)
Fran Eng Law... Francillon's Lectures on English Law [*1860-61*] [*A publication*] (DLA)
FRANF......... Frankford, DE [*American Association of Railroads railroad junction routing code*]
FranFin........ Franchise Finance Corp. of America [*Associated Press*] (SAG)
Frank........... Frankford (SAUS)
Frank........... Frankfort (SAUS)
FRANK......... Frankfort, IN [*American Association of Railroads railroad junction routing code*]
Frank........... Frankfurt (SAUS)
Frank........... Frankish (ADWA)
FRANK......... Frequency Regulation and Networking Keying (SAUS)
FRANK......... Frequency Regulation and Network Keying (IEEE)
FrankF......... Frankfort First Bankcorp, Inc. [*Associated Press*] (SAG)
Franklin Pierce Law Sch... Franklin Pierce Law School (GAGS)
Fran Max..... Francis' Maxims of Equity [*1722-46*] [*A publication*] (DLA)
Fran Prec..... Francis' Common Law Precedents [*A publication*] (DLA)
FRANS......... Family Resource and Network Support [*Australia*]
Frans........... Francis (SAUS)
FRANS......... Franciscan
FRANSW...... Food Retailers' Association of New South Wales [*Australia*]
FRANSW...... Footwear Repairers' Association of New South Wales [*Australia*]
FRANTIC...... Formal Reliability Analysis Including Normal Testing, Inspection and Checking
Fran Vercell... Franciscus Vercellensis [*Flourished, 13th century*] [*Authority cited in pre-1607 legal work*] (DSA)
FRANY......... Fashion Reporters Award - New York
FRANZ......... Fellow Registered Accountant Member of the New Zealand Society of Accountants (SAUO)
FRANZ......... Fellow, Registered Accountant, New Zealand
FRANZ......... Franz, ON [*American Association of Railroads railroad junction routing code*]
FRANZCP..... Fellow of the Royal Australian and New Zealand College of Psychiatrists (SAUS)
FRAP.......... Fast Response Action Potential [*Psychology*]
FRAP.......... Federal Rules of Appellate Procedure [*A publication*]
FRAP.......... Fellow of the Royal Academy of Physicians [*British*]
FRAP.......... Fire Rescue Air Pack [*NASA*]
FRAP.......... Flat Response Audio Pickup
FRAP.......... Fleet Readiness Assistance Program (MCD)
FRAP.......... Fleet Reliability Assessment Program [*Navy*] (MCD)
FRAP.......... Fluorescence Recovery [*or Redistribution*] after Photobleaching [*Analytical biochemistry*]
FRAP.......... Fluoride-Resistant Acid Phosphatase [*An enzyme*]
FRAP.......... Forest Resources Assessment Program Unit (SAUO)
FRAP.......... Frente de Accion Popular [*Popular Action Front*] [*Chile*]
FRAP.......... Frente Revolucionario Antifascista Patriotica [*Anti-Fascist and Patriotic Revolutionary Front*] [*Spain*]
FRAP.......... Front d'Action Politique
FRAP.......... Front Revolutionnaire d'Action Proletarienne [*Terrorist organization*] [*Belgium*] (EY)
FRAP.......... Fuel Rod Analysis Program [*Nuclear energy*] (NRCH)
FRAP.......... Fuerzas Revolucionarias Armadas Populares [*People's Revolutionary Armed Forces*] [*Mexico*] (PD)
FRAPA......... Forest Products Accident Prevention Association
FRAPA......... Forest Resources Assessment and Policy Act (SAUO)
FRAPC......... French Argos Processing Centre (SAUS)
FRAPH......... Front for the Advancement and Progress of Haiti [*Political party*]
FRAPRU....... Front d'Action Populaire en Reamenagement Urbain [*Canada*]
FRAPS......... Farm Record Analysis Pilot Scheme (SAUS)
FRAPS......... Fixed Rate Auction Preferred Stock (EBF)
FRAP-S........ Fuel Rod Analysis Program - Steady-State [*Nuclear energy*] (NRCH)
FRAP-T........ Fuel Rod Analysis Program - Transient [*Nuclear energy*] (NRCH)
FRAQ.......... Footwear Repairers' Association of Queensland [*Australia*]
FRARM......... Firearm
Fr Ar Rev..... Fremantle Arts Review [*A publication*]
FRAS........... Feature Ratio Analysis System (VLIE)
FRAS........... Fellow of the Royal Asiatic Society (SAUO)
FRAS........... Fellow of the Royal Astronomical Society [*British*]
Fras............ Fraser's English Election Cases [*1776-77*] [*A publication*] (DLA)
FRAS........... Free-Rocket Anti-Submarine (SAUS)
FRASA......... Footwear Repairers' Association of South Australia
FRASB......... Fellow of the Royal Asiatic Society of Bengal
FRASCO....... Foundation for Religious Action in the Social and Civil Order (EA)
FRASCO....... Foundation for the Religious Action in the Social and Civil Order (SAUO)
Fras Div....... Fraser's Conflict of Laws in Cases of Divorce [*A publication*] (DLA)
Fras Dom Rel... Fraser on Personal and Domestic Relations [*Scotland*] [*A publication*] (DLA)
FRASE......... Factor Relationship and Sequence of Events [*Environmental science*] (COE)
FRASE......... Fellow of the Royal Agricultural Society of England
Fras Elec Cas... Fraser's English Election Cases [*1776-77*] [*A publication*] (DLA)
Fraser.......... Fraser's English Cases of Controverted Elections [*1776-77*] [*A publication*] (DLA)
Fraser.......... Fraser's Husband and Wife [*1876-78*] [*Scotland*] [*A publication*] (DLA)
Fraser.......... Fraser's Scotch Court of Sessions Cases, Fifth Series [*A publication*] (DLA)
Fraser (Scot)... Fraser's English Cases of Controverted Elections [*1776-77*] [*A publication*] (DLA)
Fraser (Scot)... Scotch Court of Session Cases, Fifth Series, by Fraser [*A publication*] (DLA)
FRASM......... Frame Relay Access Service Module (DINT)
Fras M & S... Fraser on Master and Servant in Scotland [*A publication*] (DLA)
Fras Par & Ch... Fraser's Parent and Child [*Scotland*] [*A publication*] (DLA)
FRASTA....... Fracture-Surface Topography Analysis (SAUS)
FRAT........... Facilities Relative Allocation Technique (SAUS)
FRAT........... Fiber-Reinforced Advanced Titanium (MCD)
FRAT........... First Recorded Appearance Time (SAA)
frat............. Fraternity (ADWA)
FRAT........... Fraternity
FRAT........... Fraternize (DSUE)
FRAT........... Free Radical Assay Technique [*Clinical chemistry*]
FRATADD..... Foundation for Research and Treatment of Alcoholism and Drug Dependence (SAUO)
FRATE......... Formulae for Routes and Technical Equipment (SAUS)
frate........... formula for routes and technical equipment (SAUS)
frater.......... fraternity brother (SAUS)
frats........... fraternities (SAUS)
FRATS......... Frequency, Recency, Amount and Type [*Direct marketing*] (WDMC)
fratting........ fraternizing (SAUS)
FRATU......... Fleet Requirements and Aircraft Training Unit [*British military*] (DMA)
FRAU.......... Field Replaceable Unit (SAUS)
FRAUD......... Fraudulent (MSA)
fraud........... Fraudulently (SAUS)
FrAv........... Bibliotheque Calvet, Avignon, France [*Library symbol*] [*Library of Congress*] (LCLS)
FRAV.......... First Available (TVEL)
FRAV.......... Footwear Repairers' Association of Victoria [*Australia*]
FRAWA........ Footwear Repairers' Association of Western Australia
fra(X)......... Fragile X [*Chromosome*] [*Genetics*] (DAVI)
FRAX.......... Fragile X [*Medicine*] (EDAA)
FRAXA........ Fragile X Locus (HGEN)
FRAXA........ Fragile X Syndrome Research Foundation (ADWA)
FRAX-MR..... Fragile X-Mental Retardation [*Medicine*] (EDAA)
Fraz........... Frazer's Admiralty Cases, Etc. [*Scotland*] [*A publication*] (DLA)
Fra Za......... Franciscus Zabarella [*Deceased, 1417*] [*Authority cited in pre-1607 legal work*] (DSA)
Fraz Adm..... Frazer's Admiralty Cases, Etc. [*Scotland*] [*A publication*] (DLA)
FRB............ FABS Reference Bible [*FABS International, Inc.*] [*Information service or system*] (CRD)
FRB............ Failure Review Board [*NASA*] (NASA)
FRB............ Failure to Return to Battery [*Study*] (MCD)
FRB............ Fair Rents Board [*New South Wales, Australia*]
FRB............ Fast Rise Balloon
FRB............ Faultsman's Ring Back [*Telecommunications*] (NITA)
FRB............ Federal Reserve Bank (SAUO)
FRB............ Federal Reserve Banks [*of FRS*]

FRB............ Federal Reserve Board [*Later, BGFRS*]
FRB............ Federation of Radical Booksellers [*British*]
FRB............ Fiberglass Rotor Blade (MCD)
FRB............ Fireball Resources [*Vancouver Stock Exchange symbol*]
Frb............ Fire Boat (SAUS)
FRB............ Fire-Resistant Brick [*Technical drawings*]
FRB............ First Republic Bank (SAUO)
FRB............ Fisheries Research Board of Canada [*Marine science*] (MSC)
FRB............ Fitness Reports Branch [*BUPERS*]
FRB............ Flight Rated Bioinstrumentation
FRB............ Forbes [*Australia*] [*Airport symbol*] (OAG)
FRB............ Forschungs-Reaktor Berlin
FRB............ Frobisher [*Northwest Territories*] [*Seismograph station code, US Geological Survey*] (SEIS)
FRB............ Functional Review Board (SAUO)
Fr Baldui..... Franciscus Balduinus [*Deceased, 1572*] [*Authority cited in pre-1607 legal work*] (DSA)
Fr Bank........ Frank on the United States Bankrupt Act of 1867 [*A publication*] (DLA)
Fr BB.......... Fracture of Both Bones [*Medicine*] (MAE)
frbb............ free room, board, and beverages (SAUS)
FRBC.......... First Republic Bancorp, Inc. (SAUO)
FRBC.......... Fisheries Research Board of Canada (SAUO)
fr bel.......... from below (SAUS)
FRBFC......... Foggy River Boys Fan Club (EA)
FRBFX......... Hancock(J) Inv. II Regional Bank Cl.B [*Mutual fund ticker symbol*] (SG)
FRBK.......... Fairfield 1st Bank & Trust Co. [*NASDAQ symbol*] (COMM)
FR Bk.......... Federal Reserve Bank (SAUO)
FRBk.......... Federat Reserve Bank (SAUS)
FRBK.......... First Republic Bancorp [*NASDAQ symbol*] (SAG)
FRBNY......... Federal Reserve Bank of New York (SAUO)
FRBR.......... Functional Requirements of Bibliographic Records
FRBRC......... Fondation de Recherches sur les Blessures de la Route au Canada (EAIO)
FRBs........... Federal Reserve Banks (SAUO)
FRBS.......... Fellow of the Royal Botanical Society (SAUS)
FRBS.......... Fellow of the Royal Botanic Society [*British*]
FRBS.......... Fellow of the Royal Society of British Sculptors
FRBS.......... Frame Relay Bearer Service (ACRL)
FRBTMRAIL... front bottom rail (SAUS)
FRBW.......... Federal Reserve Board Weekly [*Database*] [*I. P. Sharp Associates*] [*Information service or system*] (CRD)
FRC............ Control of Rents and Furnished Lets [*British*]
FRC............ Fabric-Reinforced Ceramics (SAUS)
FRC............ Facilities Review Committee (SAUO)
FRC............ Facility Review Committee
FRC............ Failure Recurrence Control (SAA)
FRC............ Fairchild Research Center (SAUS)
FRC............ Family Reading Center (SAUS)
FRC............ Family Research Council (EA)
FRC............ Family Resource Coalition (EA)
FRC............ Family Rosary Crusade [*Later, FR*] (EA)
FRC............ Famine Relief Committee (SAUO)
FRC............ Fasteners Research Council [*Defunct*] (EA)
FRC............ Fast Reaction Concept (SAUS)
FRC............ Fast Rescue Craft (SAUS)
FRC............ Fatah Revolutionary Council [*Libyan-based terrorist organization*]
FRC............ Federal Radiation Council [*Defunct*] (EA)
FRC............ Federal Radio Commission [*Functions transferred to FCC, 1934*]
FRC............ Federal Ranch [*British Columbia*] [*Seismograph station code, US Geological Survey*] [*Closed*] (SEIS)
FRC............ Federal Records Center [*General Services Administration*] (AABC)
FRC............ Federal Records Council
FRC............ Federal Regional Center [*Office of Civil Defense*]
FRC............ Federal Regional Council [*for federal-state-local interchange*] [*Abolished, 1983*]
FRC............ Federal Region Council (EBF)
FRC............ Federal Relief Commission (SAUO)
FRC............ Federal Republic of Cameroon (SAUO)
FRC............ Federal Reserve Bank of Philadelphia, Philadelphia, PA [*OCLC symbol*] (OCLC)
FRC............ Federal Response Center (COE)
FRC............ Federation of Rambling Clubs (SAUO)
FRC............ Federation Radiation Council [*Medicine*] (EDAA)
FRC............ Fellow of the Royal College (SAUO)
FRC............ Fiber-Reinforced Cement (SAUS)
FRC............ Fiber-Reinforced Ceramics (SAUS)
FRC............ Fiber Reinforced Composite (SAUS)
FRC............ Fiber-Reinforced Composite
FRC............ Fiber-Reinforced Concrete (SAUS)
FRC............ Fibre Reinforced Composite (SAUS)
FRC............ Field Reversed Configuration
FRC............ Filipino Rehabilitation Commission [*Post-World War II*]
FRC............ Film Reorganization Committee (SAUO)
FRC............ Final Routing Center [*Telecommunications*] (TEL)
FRC............ Financial Reconstruction Commission
FRC............ Financial Reporting Council (ODBW)
FRC............ First Republic Bancorp [*NYSE symbol*] (TTSB)
FRC............ First Republic Bancorp, Inc. [*NYSE symbol*] (SAG)
FRC............ First Republic Bank [*NYSE symbol*] [*Formerly, First Republic Bancorp*] [*California*] (SG)
FRC............ Fishery Research Craft
FRC............ Fixed Radio Communication
FRC............ Flag Research Center (EA)
FRC............ Flare Remote Control (SAUS)
FRC............ Flat Rock Consultants, Inc. [*Information service or system*] (IID)
FRC............ Fleet Resources Office (SAUO)
FRC............ Fletcher Challenge Finance Canada, Inc. [*Toronto Stock Exchange symbol*]
FRC............ Flight Research Center [*Later, DFRC*] [*NASA*]
FRC............ Flight Rule Computer [*Aviation*] (IAA)
FRC............ Flight Rules Computer (SAUS)
FRC............ Flowers' Roguish Cultivator
FRC............ Flow Recorder Controller
FRC............ Flow-recording Ratio Controller (SAUS)
FRC............ Follmer, Rudzewicz & Co.
FRC............ Food Research Centre (SAUS)
FRC............ Force
FRC............ Forced (HAWK)
FRC............ Forced Rerouting Control (SAUS)
FRC............ Foreign Relations Council (SAUO)
FRC............ Forest Resources Committee [*Australia*]
FRC............ FORSCOM [*Forces Command*] Redistribution Center [*Army*]
FRC............ Forward Report Centre (SAUO)
FRC............ Fram Corporation (SAUO)
FRC............ Frame Rate Control
FRC............ Franca [*Brazil*] [*Airport symbol*] (OAG)
FRC............ Franklin Research Center [*Research center*] (RCD)
FRC............ Frederick Research Center (KSC)
FRC............ Free Carrier [*Followed by a named point*] [*"INCOTERM," International Chamber of Commerce official code*]
FRC............ Free of Reported Casualty [*Insurance*] (MARI)
FRC............ Free Radical Chemistry (SAUS)
FRC............ Free Radio Campaign (SAUS)
FRC............ Free Radio Campaign, London (SAUO)
FRC............ Free Residual Chlorine
FRC............ Frequency Recommendation Committee (SAUO)
FRC............ Frequency Response Curve
FRC............ Fresnel Reflection Coefficient [*Optics*]
FRC............ Front-Range Consortium (USDC)
FRC............ Frozen Red Cells [*Medicine*]
FRC............ Fuels Research Council [*Defunct*]
FRC............ Full Rate Channel (SAUS)
FRC............ Full Route Clearance [*Aviation*] (PIPO)
FRC............ Functional Redundancy Check [*Computer science*]
FRC............ Functional Reserve [*or Residual*] Capacity [*of the lungs*] [*Physiology*]
FRC............ Functional Residual Capacity (MELL)
FRC............ Functional Residue Capacity (SAUS)
FRC............ Future Requirements Committee (SAUS)
FRC............ Request Full Route Clearance [*FAA*] (TAG)
FRC............ Spokane, WA [*Location identifier*] [*FAA*] (FAAL)
FRCA.......... Family Research Council of America [*Later, FRC*] (EA)
FRCA.......... Farming and Rural Conservation Agency (GVA)
FRCA.......... Fellow of the Royal College of Art [*British*]
FRCA.......... Fellow Royal College of Anesthetists [*British*] (WA)
FRCA.......... Fire Retardant Chemicals Association (EA)
FRCA.......... First Republic Corp. of America (EFIS)
FRCAA......... Fellow of the Royal Cambrian Academy of Art (SAUO)
FRC-AAP..... Freedom-to-Read Committee-Association of American Publishers (SAUO)
FRCAB......... Felt Roofing Contractors' Advisory Board [*British*] (BI)
FRCAB......... Flat Roofing Contractors Advisory Board [*British*] (DBA)
FR CAN........ French-Canadian (WDAA)
FR Card....... Field Requisition Card (SAUS)
FRCAT......... Fellow of the Royal College of Advanced Technology (SAUO)
FRCATS....... Fellow of the Royal College of Advanced Technology, Salford [*British*]
FRCB.......... Financial Recap Contract Brief (ACAE)
FRCC.......... Federal Research Contract Center
FRCC.......... First Financial Caribbean [*NASDAQ symbol*] (TTSB)
FRCC.......... First Financial Caribbean Corp. [*NASDAQ symbol*] (CTT)
FRCC.......... Fisheries Resource Conservation Council (SAUS)
FRCC.......... Free of Riots and Civil Commotions [*Insurance*]
FRCC.......... Front Range Community College (COE)
FRCD.......... Family Resource Center on Disabilities [*Formerly, Coordinating Council for Handicapped Children*] (NRGU)
FRCD.......... Fellow of the Royal College of Dentists [*British*]
FRCD.......... fixed ratio combination drug (SAUS)
FRCD.......... Floating Rate Certificate of Deposit
FRCD(C)...... Fellow of the Royal College of Dentists (Canada)
FRCF.......... Federation of Reconstructionist Congregations and Fellowships [*Later, FRCH*] (EA)
FRCG.......... Free Radio Campaign Germany (SAUO)
FRCGA......... Fletcher-Reeves Conjugate Gradient Algorithm (SAUS)
FRCGP......... Fellow of the Royal College of General Practitioners [*British*]
FRCGP......... Fellow, Royal College of General Practice [*British*] (CMD)
FRCGS......... Fellow of the Royal Canadian Geographical Society (DD)
FRCH.......... Federation of Reconstructionist Congregations and Havurot (EA)
FR CH.......... Free Church (ROG)
Fr Ch........... Freeman's English Chancery Reports [*A publication*] (DLA)
Fr Ch........... Freeman's Mississippi Chancery Reports [*A publication*] (DLA)
FRCHS......... Franchise (SAUS)
Fr Chy......... Freeman's English Chancery Reports [*A publication*] (DLA)
Fr Chy......... Freeman's Mississippi Chancery Reports [*A publication*] (DLA)
FRCI........... Fellow of the Royal Colonial Institute [*British*]
FRCI........... Fibrous Refractory Composite Insulation
FRCJ........... Fiber-Reinforced Composite Junction
FRCM.......... Fellow of the Royal College of Medicine [*Canada*] (DD)
FRCM.......... Fellow of the Royal College of Music [*British*]

FRCM .... Fellow, Royal College of Medicine [*British*] (CMD)
FRCM .... FEMA Regional Communications Manager (SAUO)
FRCM .... Firecom, Inc. [*NASDAQ symbol*] (COMM)
FRCMC .... Fiber-Reinforced Ceramic Matrix Composite [*Organic chemistry*]
FRCMO .... Floating Rate Collateralized Mortgage Obligation
FRCO .... Fellow of the Royal College of Ophthalmologists (SAUS)
FRCO .... Fellow of the Royal College of Organists [*British*]
FRCOA .... Fruit Color (No Green to Mostly Green) [*Botany*]
FRCOB .... Fruit Color (Greenish Red to Dark Red) [*Botany*]
FRCO(CHM)... Fellow of the Royal College of Organists (Choir-Training Diploma) [*British*]
FRCOG .... Fellow of the Royal College of Obstetricians and Gynaecologists [*British*]
FRCOG .... Fellow, Royal College of Obstetrics & Gynecology [*British*] (CMD)
Fr Cosci .... Franciscus Coscius [*Deceased, 1556*] [*Authority cited in pre-1607 legal work*] (DSA)
FRCOUSA .... Federation of Russian Charitable Organizations of the United States of America (SAUO)
FRCP .... Facility Remote Control Panel (AAG)
FRCP .... Federal Rules of Civil Procedure [*A publication*] (DLA)
FRCP .... Fellow of the Royal College of Physicians [*British*]
FRCP .... Fellow of the Royal College of Preceptors [*British*]
FRCP .... Fiber Reinforced Composite Propellant (ACAE)
FRCPA .... Fellow of the Royal College of Pathologists of Australia (SAUS)
FRC Path ..... Fellow of the Royal College of Pathologists [*British*]
FRCPath ...... Fellow of the Royal College of Pathology (SAUS)
FRCPath ...... Fellow Royal College of Pathologists [*British*] (WA)
FRCPath ...... Fellow, Royal College of Pathology [*British*] (CMD)
FRCP(C) .... Fellow of the Royal College of Physicians (Canada)
FRCPC .... Fellow of the Royal College of Physicians of Canada (DD)
FRCPC .... Fellow, Royal College of Physicians Canada (CMD)
FRCPCan ..... Fellow of the Royal College of Physicians of Canada
FRCPE .... Fellow of the Royal College of Physicians of Edinburgh
FRCPEd .... Fellow of the Royal College of Physicians of Edinburgh
FRCP Edin ... Fellow of the Royal College of Physicians of Edinburgh
FRCPGlas .... Fellow of the Royal College of Physicians and Surgeons of Glasgow
FRCPGlas .... Fellow of the Royal College of Physicians of Glasgow (SAUS)
FRCPI .... Fellow of the Royal College of Physicians, Ireland (ROG)
FRCP Irel ..... Fellow of the Royal College of Physicians of Ireland
FRCP Lond... Fellow of the Royal College of Physicians of London [*British*]
FRCPSG .... Fellow of the Royal College of Physicians & Surgeons of Glasgow [*Scotland*] (WDAA)
FRCPS(Hon)... Honorary Fellow of the Royal College of Physicians and Surgeons [*Glasgow*]
FRC Psych ... Fellow of the Royal College of Psychiatrists [*British*]
FRCPsych .... Fellow Royal College of Psychiatrists [*British*] (WA)
FRCR .... Fellow of the Royal College of Radiologists [*British*]
FRCR .... Fellow, Royal College of Radiology [*British*] (CMD)
FRCR .... Free Recall-Controlled Recall Test [*Psychology*] (AEBS)
FRCrP .... Federal Rules of Criminal Procedure (SAUS)
FRCS .... Feature Ratio Control System (SAUS)
FRCS .... Feature Ration Control System (SAUS)
FRCs .... Federal Regional Councils (SAUO)
FRCS .... Federal Register Chargeback System (SAUO)
FRCS .... Federal Reserve Communications (SAUS)
FRCS .... Federal Reserve Communications System
FRCS .... Federation of Rabbit Clearance Societies (SAUO)
FRCS .... Fellow of the Royal College of Surgeons [*British*]
FRCS .... Fellow of the Royal College of Surgeons of England (SAUO)
FRCS .... Flow Recording Controller Switch [*Nuclear energy*] (NRCH)
FRCS .... Forged Radius Clamp Straps (SAUS)
FRCS .... Forward Reaction Control Subsystem [*NASA*] (NASA)
FRCS .... Forward Reaction Control System [*Aerospace*] (NAKS)
FRCS .... Francs [*Monetary units*] (ROG)
FRCSA .... Furniture Retailers Council of South Australia
FRCSc .... Fellow of the Royal College of Science (SAUO)
FRCS(C) .... Fellow of the Royal College of Surgeons (Canada)
FRCSC .... Fellow of the Royal College of Surgeons of Canada (DD)
FRCSCan ..... Fellow of the Royal College of Surgeons of Canada
FRCScI .... Fellow of the Royal College of Science in Ireland (SAUS)
FRCScI .... Fellow of the Royal College of Science of Ireland (SAUO)
FRCSE .... Fellow of the Royal College of Surgeons of Edinburgh
FRCS Ed ...... Fellow of the Royal College of Surgeons of Edinburgh
FRCSEd(C/Th)... Fellow of the Royal College of Surgeons of Edinburgh, Specialising in Cardiothoracic Surgery [*British*] (DBQ)
FRCS Edin ... Fellow of the Royal College of Surgeons of Edinburgh
FRCSEd(Orth)... Fellow of the Royal College of Surgeons of Edinburgh, Specialising in Orthopaedic Surgery [*British*] (DBQ)
FRCSEd(SN)... Fellow of the Royal College of Surgeons of Edinburgh, Specialising in Surgical Neurology [*British*] (DBQ)
FRCS Eng .... Fellow of the Royal College of Surgeons of England
FRCSGlas .... Fellow of the Royal College of Surgeons of Glasgow
FRCS(Glasg)... Fellow of the Royal College of Physicians and Surgeons of Glasgow [*British*] (BABM)
FRCS(Glasg)... Fellow of the Royal College of Physicians and Surgeons of Glasgow qua Surgeon (DAVI)
FRCSI .... Fellow of the Royal College of Surgeons in Ireland
FRCS Irel ..... Fellow of the Royal College of Surgeons in Ireland
FRCSL .... Fellow of the Royal College of Surgeons of London
FRCSoc .... Fellow of the Royal Commonwealth Society [*British*]
Frcst .... Forecast (SAUS)
FRCSTNG ..... Forecasting
FRCT .... Factor-Referenced Cognitive Tests [*Medicine*] (EDAA)
FRCT .... Fixed Record Communications Teletypewriter (SAUO)
FRCTF .... Fast Reactor Core Test Facility [*Nuclear energy*]
FRCTN .... Friction
FRCTS .... Fast Reactor Core Test Facility (SAUO)
FRCU .... Fractocumulus [*Meteorology*]
FRCUS .... Fellow of the Royal College of University Surgeons [*Denmark*]
FRCV .... Fellow of the Royal College of Veterinary Surgeons (SAUO)
FRCV .... Furniture Retailers' Council of Victoria [*Australia*]
FRCVS .... Fellow of the Royal College of Veterinary Surgeons [*British*]
FRCZ .... Florida Rock [*Federal Railroad Administration identification code*]
FRD .... Facilities Requirements Documents (MCD)
FRD .... Facility Requirements Division [*Environmental Protection Agency*] (EPA)
FRD .... Failure Rate Data (KSC)
FRD .... Fast Reaction Dynamics (SAUS)
FRD .... Fast Recovery Diode (SAUS)
FRD .... Fat-Restricted Diet (MELL)
FRD .... Federal Research Division [*Library of Congress*] (GFGA)
FRD .... Federal Reserve Bank of Dallas, Dallas, TX [*OCLC symbol*] (OCLC)
FRD .... Federal Reserve District
FRD .... Federal Rules Decisions (SAUO)
FRD .... Fiber Resin Development (SAUS)
FRD .... Fiber-Rich Diet (MELL)
FRD .... Field Remount Depot [*British military*] (DMA)
FRD .... Field Research Division [*Marine science*] (OSRA)
FRD .... Field Reset Device [*Army*]
frd .... Fired (VRA)
FRD .... Fire RetarDant (SAUS)
F/RD .... Fixed and Roll Down (ACAE)
FRD .... Flight Readiness Demonstration
FRD .... Flight Requirements Document (MCD)
FRD .... Floating Round (SAUS)
FRD .... Fluid Rate Damper
Frd .... Ford (SAUS)
FRD .... Ford Motor Co. [*ICAO designator*] (FAAC)
FRD .... Forecast Research Division [*Forecast Systems Laboratory*] (USDC)
FRD .... Foreign Relations Department (SAUO)
FRD .... Forest Resources Division (SAUS)
FRD .... Formerly Restricted Data [*Military*]
FRD .... Forum for the Restoration of Democracy (Comoros) [*Political party*] (PSAP)
FRD .... Foundation for Research and Development (SAUS)
FRD .... Foundation for Research Development [*South Africa*]
FRD .... Fraction Reliability Deviation
frd .... Framed (BARN)
FRD .... Fraud [*FBI standardized term*]
FRD .... Fredericksburg [*Virginia*] [*Geomagnetic observatory code*]
FRD .... Free Rural Delivery [*British*]
FRD .... Friday Harbor [*Washington*] [*Airport symbol*] (OAG)
FRD .... Fried
FRD .... Friedman Indus [*AMEX symbol*] (TTSB)
FRD .... Friedman Industries, Inc. [*AMEX symbol*] (SPSG)
FRD .... Friend (AABC)
FRD .... Functional Referenced Device (SAUS)
FRD .... Functional Reference Device (IEEE)
FRD .... Functional Requirement Diagram [*Implementation dependant*] (ACII)
FRD .... Functional Requirement Document (SAUS)
FRD .... Functional Requirements Description (SAUO)
FRD .... Functional Requirements Document (SSD)
FRDA .... Forest Resource Development Agreement (SAUS)
FRDA .... Friedreich's Ataxia [*Medicine*]
FRDB .... Failure Rate Data Bank [*GIDEP*]
FRDB .... Fisheries Research and Development Board (SAUS)
FRDC .... Fisheries Research and Development Corporation [*Commonwealth*] (EERA)
FRDC .... Fusion Research and Development Center (SAUS)
FRDD .... federal resource decision document (SAUS)
FRDD .... Front for the Restoration and Defense of Democracy (Niger) [*Political party*] (PSAP)
FRDE .... Front for the Restoration of Right and Equality (Djibouti) [*Political party*] (PSAP)
FRDENL .... Fraudulent Enlistment (DNAB)
Fr de T .... Franciscus de Telese [*Flourished, 1270-82*] [*Authority cited in pre-1607 legal work*] (DSA)
FRDF .... Fonds de Recherches et de Developpement Forestier [*Forest Research and Development Foundation*] [*Canada*]
FRDF .... Forest Research and Development Foundation [*Canada*]
FRDF .... Forest Research Development Foundation (SAUS)
FrdH .... Ford Holdings, Inc. [*Associated Press*] (SAG)
FRDI .... Faculty of Royal Designs for Industry (SAUO)
FRDI .... Flight Research and Development Instrumentation (KSC)
FR DIST .... Federal Reserve District (MHDB)
FR Dist .... Federal Reserve District (SAUS)
FR-DLP .... Frame Recognition - Data Link Processor (SAUS)
FR-DLP .... Frame Recognition-Data Link Processor (NITA)
FRDLT .... Fraudulent (ROG)
FRDM .... Fast Retrieval and Data Manipulator (MCD)
FRDM .... Friedmans, Inc. [*NASDAQ symbol*] (SAG)
FRDM .... Friedman's Inc.'A' [*NASDAQ symbol*] (TTSB)
FRDN .... Ferdinand Railroad Co. [*AAR code*]
FRDN .... Ferdinand Railroad Company (SAUO)
FRDR .... Fixed Reserve Deposit Ratio [*Finance*]
FRDRK .... Frederick, OK [*American Association of Railroads railroad junction routing code*]
FRDS .... Failure Resistant Disk System (SAUS)
FRDS .... Federal Reporting Data System (EPA)

FRDS .... Fellow of the Royal Dublin Society for Promoting Natural Knowledge (SAUO)
FRDS .... Flight Record Data System (SAUO)
FRDS .... Fords [*Postal Service standard*] (OPSA)
FRDT .... Facility Requirements Definition Team (SAUS)
FRDT .... Flexion-Rotation Drawer Test (MELL)
FRE .... Aviation Services Ltd. [*Guam*] [*ICAO designator*] (FAAC)
FRE .... Facteur Respiratoire Equilibre [*Ingredient in a cosmetic by Chanel*]
FRE .... Facture [*Invoice*] [*Business term*] [*French*]
FRE .... Fault-Removal Efficiency (SAUS)
FRE .... Federal Home Loan [*NYSE symbol*] (TTSB)
FRE .... Federal Home Loan Mortgage [*NYSE symbol*] (SPSG)
FRE .... Federal Rules of Evidence
FRE .... Fera Island [*Solomon Islands*] [*Airport symbol*] (OAG)
FRE .... Field Representative, Europe (SAUS)
FRE .... Fischer Rat Embryo [*Medicine*] (DMAA)
FRE .... Flight Readiness Element (ACAE)
FRE .... Flight Related Element (MCD)
FRE .... Food and Resource Economics Department (SAUS)
FRE .... Format Request Element (MCD)
FRE .... Frederick Community College, Frederick, MD [*OCLC symbol*] (OCLC)
fre .... free energy region (SAUS)
Fre .... Freemantle (SAUS)
fre .... French [*MARC language code*] [*Library of Congress*] (LCCP)
FRE .... French
Fr E .... French Ell (SAUS)
FRE .... Frequency
FRE .... Frequently Requested Enhancement (SAUS)
FRE .... Fresno [*California*] [*Seismograph station code, US Geological Survey*] [*Closed*] (SEIS)
FRE .... Friends of R. [*Ralph*] Emery (EA)
FRE .... Full Regular Expression (SAUS)
FRE .... Functional Requirements Envelope (SSD)
FRE2001 .... Faculty Research Endowment Campaign 2001 (SAUS)
FREARF .... Forward Rearm and Refuel Point [*Military*] (VNW)
FREAVY .... Frequency Availability (SAUS)
FREB .... Federal Real Estate Board [*Abolished, 1951*]
FREB .... Federal Real Estate Bord (SAUS)
FREB .... Field Repairable - Expendable Rotor Blade (RDA)
FREC .... Federal Radio Education Committee
FREC .... Fertilizer Research Education Council (SAUO)
FREC .... Forestry Research and Education Center (SAUS)
Fr EC .... Fraser's English Election Cases [*1776-77*] [*A publication*] (DLA)
FRECoIl .... Forest Resources and Environment Collective (EERA)
Frecon .... frequency-controlled (SAUS)
FREconS .... Fellow of the Royal Economical Society (SAUS)
FR Econ S .... Fellow of the Royal Economic Society [*British*]
FREconS .... Fellow Royal Economic Society [*British*] (WA)
FR Econ Soc .... Fellow of the Royal Economic Society [*British*] (ROG)
FR Ec S .... Fellow of the Royal Economic Society [*British*]
FRED .... Faceted Region Editor [*Software package*] [*Military*] (RDA)
FRED .... Fantastically Reliable Electronic Device (SAUS)
FRED .... Fare Reduction Enhancement Device [*Travel industry software*] [*CompuCheck Corp.*]
FRED .... Fast Random Enquiry Display (SAUS)
FRED .... Fast-Rate Electro-Deposition Plating [*Automotive engineering*]
FRED .... Fast Reactivity Exclusion Device [*Nuclear energy*]
FRED .... Fast Reading Electronic Digitizer (SAUS)
FRED .... Fast Realistic Editor [*Word processing program*] (ADA)
FRED .... Fast-Recovery Diode (SAUS)
FRED .... fast recovery epitaxial diode (SAUS)
FRED .... Fast Reference for Engineering Drawings (IAA)
FRED .... Fast Relocatable Editing Dump (SAA)
FRED .... Federal Reserve Economic Data [*A publication*]
FRED .... Field Recovery Epitaxial Diode (SAUS)
FRED .... Field Reset Device [*Army*]
FRED .... Fiendishly Rapid Electronic Device
fred .... figure-reader electronic device (SAUS)
FRED .... Figure Reading Device (SAUS)
FRED .... Figure Reading Electronic Device [*Information retrieval*]
FRED .... fiigure reading electronic device (SAUS)
FRED .... Flaming Ridiculous Electronic Device (SAUS)
FRED .... Flashing Rear End Device
FRED .... Flexible Recreational and Educational Device (SAUS)
FRED .... Flexible Red (ACAE)
FRED .... Flexible Repository Engineering Data (ACAE)
FRED .... Foolish Rear End Device [*Electronic caboose replacement*] [*Bowdlerized version*]
FRED .... FORTRAN Routines for the Elliott Display (SAUS)
FRED .... Forward RADAR Enhancement Device
FRED .... Fractionally Rapid Electronic Device
FRED .... Fragmentation and Reassembly Engine with DMA (SAUS)
FRED .... Frame Editor (SAUS)
FRED .... Fredericton [*City in Canada*] (ROG)
Fred .... Fredonia [*Record label*]
FRED .... Fred Resembles Emacs Deliberately (SAUO)
FRED .... Freds, Inc. [*NASDAQ symbol*] (SAG)
FRED .... Fred's Inc.'A' [*NASDAQ symbol*] (TTSB)
FRED .... Friendly Recoton Entertainment Decoder [*Television stereo adapter*]
FRED .... Friendly Robot Educational Device [*Androbot, Inc.*]
FRED .... Front End for Databases [*GTE usage*]
FRED .... Front-End to Dish (SAUS)
FRED .... Front-End to Disk (SAUS)
FRED .... Fund for Rural Economic Development [*Canada*]
FRED .... Space Station Freedom (SAUO)
FRED .... Financial Reporting Exposure Draft (ODA)
FREDA .... Fredonia, KS [*American Association of Railroads railroad junction routing code*]
FREDA .... Fully Remote Data Acquisition (SAUS)
FREDA System .... Fully Remote Data Acquisition System (SAUS)
FredBrw .... Frederick Brewing Co. [*Associated Press*] (SAG)
FREDD .... Free Resources for Educating the Developmentally Disabled (SAUS)
FREDDIE MAC .... Federal Home Loan Mortgage Corp. (ECON)
Freddie Mac .... Federal Home Loan Mortgage Corporation (EBF)
FREDEMO .... Frente Democratico [*Peru*] [*Political party*] (EY)
FRED FET .... Fast Recovery Epitaxial Diode FET [*Field Effect Transistor*] (NITA)
FRED-FET .... Field Recovery Epitaxial Diode Field-Effect Transistor (SAUS)
FREDI .... Flight Range and Endurance Data Indicator
FREDS .... Flexible Regional Emissions Data System (GNE)
FREDS .... Flexible Regional Emissions Data Systems (SAUO)
FREDS .... Flight Readiness Evaluation Data System (MCD)
Freds .... Freds, Inc. [*Associated Press*] (SAG)
FREE .... Fabric Retailers, Etc., Etc. [*Trade group*]
FREE .... Fathers Rights and Equality Exchange (EA)
FREE .... Feasibility of Rocket Energy Employment (MCD)
FREE .... Federal Resources for Educational Excellence
FREE .... Fellowship for Racial and Economic Equality [*Later, Southeast Institute*] (EA)
FREE .... Feminist Resources on Energy and Ecology [*Defunct*] (EA)
FREE .... Florida Resources in Education Exchange (SAUO)
FREE .... Foundation for Rational Economics and Education (EA)
FREE .... Foundation for Research on Economics and the Environment [*Research center*] (RCD)
Free .... Freeman's English Chancery Reports [*A publication*] (DLA)
Free .... Freeman's English King's Bench Reports [*89 English Reprint*] [*1670-1704*] [*A publication*] (DLA)
Free .... Freeman's Reports [*31-96 Illinois*] [*A publication*] (DLA)
FREE .... Freeserve plc ADS [*NASDAQ symbol*] (SG)
Free .... Freeway (SAUS)
FREE .... Fund for Renewable Energy and the Environment (EA)
FREE .... Fund to Restore an Educated Electorate [*Defunct*] (EA)
FREEBD .... Freeboard (KSC)
freebies .... free services (SAUS)
freebies .... free things (SAUS)
freebies .... free tickets (SAUS)
FreeCATS .... Free Catecholamines Column Test
Free CC .... Freeman's English Chancery Reports [*A publication*] (ILCA)
Free Ch .... Freeman's English Chancery Reports [*A publication*] (DLA)
Free Ch .... Freeman's Mississippi Chancery Reports [*A publication*] (DLA)
FREED .... Foundation for Research and Education in Eugenics and Dysgenics (SAUO)
FREEDOM .... Freedom for Russia and Emerging Eurasian Democracies and Open Markets Support Act (SAUO)
Free Ex Ins .... Free of any Extra Insurance (RIMS)
Free KB .... Freeman's English King's Bench Reports [*89 English Reprint*] [*1670-1704*] [*A publication*] (DLA)
Free Lib Phila .... Free Library of Philadelphia (SAUS)
freem .... Freeman (GEAB)
Freem .... Freeman's English Chancery Reports [*A publication*] (DLA)
Freem .... Freeman's Mississippi Chancery Reports [*A publication*] (DLA)
Freeman Ch R .... Freeman's Mississippi Chancery Reports [*A publication*] (DLA)
Freeman's (Miss) Rep .... Freeman's Mississippi Chancery Reports [*A publication*] (DLA)
Freem CC .... Freeman's English Chancery Cases [*A publication*] (DLA)
Freem Ch .... Freeman's English Chancery Reports [*A publication*] (DLA)
Freem Chan .... Freeman's Mississippi Chancery Reports [*A publication*] (DLA)
Freem Ch (Eng) .... Freeman's English Chancery Reports [*A publication*] (DLA)
Freem Ch (Miss) .... Freeman's Mississippi Chancery Reports [*A publication*] (DLA)
Freem Ch R .... Freeman's Mississippi Chancery Reports [*A publication*] (DLA)
Freem Compar Politics .... Freeman. Comparative Politics [*A publication*] (DLA)
Freem Cot .... Freeman on Cotenancy and Partition [*A publication*] (DLA)
Freem Eng Const .... Freeman's Growth of the English Constitution [*3rd ed.*] [*1876*] [*A publication*] (DLA)
Freem Ex .... Freeman on Executors [*A publication*] (DLA)
Freem (Ill) .... Freeman's Reports [*31-96 Illinois*] [*A publication*] (DLA)
Freem Judgm .... Freeman on Judgments [*A publication*] (DLA)
Freem KB .... Freeman's English King's Bench and Common Pleas Reports [*89 English Reprint*] [*A publication*] (DLA)
Freem (Miss) .... Freeman's Mississippi Chancery Reports [*A publication*] (DLA)
Freem Pr .... Freeman's Practice [*Illinois*] [*A publication*] (DLA)
Free-O .... Freemantle, Western Australia (SAUS)
FREEP .... Freeport, PA [*American Association of Railroads railroad junction routing code*]
FREEP .... Los Angeles Free Press [*A publication*]
FREES .... File Retrieval and Editing Systems (SAUS)
Free Soc .... Freethinkers Society (SAUO)
FREE-TH .... Free-Thinker [*or Free-Thinking*] (ROG)
freeture .... freedom, the wave of the future (SAUS)
FREEWAY .... Freeway [*Commonly used*] (OPSA)
FREEWY .... Freeway [*Commonly used*] (OPSA)
FREF .... Force Record Extract File [*Military*] (DOMA)
FREFAL .... Floating-point Regula Falsi (SAUS)
FRegBc .... First Regional Bancorp [*Associated Press*] (SAG)
FREGG .... Free Range Egg Association (ODA)
FREI .... Fellow of the Real Estate and Stock Institute of Australia (SAUO)
FREIDA .... Fellowship and Residency Electronic Interactive Database Access System (ADWA)
FREIR .... Federal Research on Biological and Health Effects of Ionizing Radiations
FREIT .... Finite-Life Real Estate Investment Trust

FREJID........ Frequency Jumper Identification
FREL........... Feltman Research and Engineering Laboratory [*Picatinny Arsenal*] [*Army*]
FRELATOR... Frequency Translator
FRELIMO..... Frente da Libertacao de Mocambique [*Mozambique Liberation Front*] [*Political party*] (PPW)
FRELIS......... Frequency List (SAUS)
FRELP.......... Flexible Real Estate Loan Plan
FREM........... Fleet Readiness Enlisted Maintenance [*Trainees*] [*Navy*]
Frem............ Fremantle (SAUS)
FREM........... Fremington [*England*]
FREM........... Fremitus Vocalis [*Vocal Fremitus*] [*Medicine*]
FREMD......... Farm Real Estate Market Developments (SAUO)
FREMEC....... Frequent Traveller Medical Card (SAUS)
Fremnt......... Fremont General Corp. [*Associated Press*] (SAG)
Fremont....... Fremont General Corp. [*Associated Press*] (SAG)
FREMT......... Fremont, NE [*American Association of Railroads railroad junction routing code*]
FREN........... French (DNAB)
FREN........... Frente Revolucionario Nacionalista [*Chile*] [*Political party*] (EY)
FRENA......... Frequency and Amplitude (IAA)
FRENAC....... Frequency and Amplitude Coded (IAA)
FRENATRACA... Frente Nacional de Trabajadores y Campesinos [*National Workers' and Peasants' Front*] [*Peru*] [*Political party*] (PD)
French Can... French Canadian (SAUS)
FrenchF....... French Fragrances, Inc. [*Associated Press*] (SAG)
French (NH)... French's Reports [*6 New Hampshire*] [*A publication*] (DLA)
FREND......... Federal Register Electronic News Delivery
FREND......... Flow Regime from Experimental and Network Data (SAUS)
Frend & W Prec... Frend and Ware's Precedents of Instruments Relating to the Transfer of Land to Railway Companies [*2nd ed.*] [*1866*] [*A publication*] (DLA)
FRENDS....... Floating Rate Certificate of Deposit (EBF)
FRENDS....... Floating Rate Enhanced Debt Securities (TDOB)
Frenglish..... frenchified English (SAUS)
Freno........... Frente Nacional Opositora [*National Opposition Front*] [*Panama*] [*Political party*] (PPW)
FRENSIT....... Friendly Situation (MCD)
FR Ent S...... Fellow of the Royal Entomological Society [*British*]
FRENU......... Frente Nacional de Unidad [*National Unity Front*] [*Guatemala*] [*Political party*] (PPW)
Freon........... Fluorine, Refrigerant [*and the suffix-On*] [*Trademarked name of a gaseous inert chlorofluorocarbon used in refrigerants, aerosol propellants, and plastic foams*]
FREP........... Faculty Rep to the ASUC (SAUS)
FREP........... Fleet Return Evaluation Program
FREPAS....... Forest Range Environmental Production Analytical System (MCD)
Frepaso....... Front for a Country in Solidarity (Argentina) [*Political party*] (PSAP)
FRepBcp...... First Republic Bancorp [*Associated Press*] (SAG)
FREPr.......... Fed'l Home Ln Mtg 7.90% Pfd [*NYSE symbol*] (TTSB)
FREPrA........ Fed'l Home Ln Mtg 6.72% Pfd [*NYSE symbol*] (TTSB)
FREPrB........ Fed'l Home Ln Mtg Var Rt Pfd [*NYSE symbol*] (TTSB)
FREPSOG..... Free Play Scenario Generator (MCD)
FREQ........... Frequency [*or Frequent*] (AFM)
freq............. Frequency (WDMC)
FREQ........... Frequency Management (SAUS)
freq............. frequent (SAUS)
freq............. Frequentative (BEE)
freq............. Frequently (WDMC)
FrEqAfr........ French Equatorial Africa (SAUS)
FREQCH....... Frequency Changer (IAA)
FREQCONV... Frequency Converter (MCD)
FREQDIV...... Frequency Divider (MCD)
FREQ DIV..... Frequency Divider (SAUS)
FreqEL......... Frequency Electronics, Inc. [*Associated Press*] (SAG)
FREQIND...... Frequency Indicator (IAA)
FREQLY....... Frequently (ROG)
FREQM........ Frequency Meter
FREQMULT... Frequency Multimeter (SAUS)
FREQMULT... Frequency Multiplier (KSC)
FREQN........ Frequency (IAA)
FREQ OCC... Frequenter Occurrit [*It Occurs Frequently*] [*Latin*] (ROG)
FREQSCANRA... Frequency Scan RADAR (MCD)
FREQT......... Frequent (ROG)
frequ............ Frequency (SAUS)
FRERP......... Federal Radiological Emergency Response Plan [*Environmental science*] (COE)
FRES........... Federal Regulation of Employment Service [*A publication*] (DLA)
FRES........... Federation of Recruitment and Employment Services [*British*] (EAIO)
FRES........... Fellow of the Royal Economic Society [*British*]
FRES........... Fellow of the Royal Empire Society [*British*] (EY)
FRES........... Fellow of the Royal Entomological Society [*British*] (ROG)
FRES........... File Retrieval and Editing System (SAUS)
FRES........... Fire Resistant
FRES........... Forest Range Environmental Study (GNE)
FRES........... Forward Recoil Spectrometry [*Measurement method*]
FRES........... Freres [*Brothers*] [*French*]
FRES........... Fresh America [*NASDAQ symbol*] (TTSB)
FRES........... Fresh America Corp. [*NASDAQ symbol*] (SAG)
FRESCA....... Fermi-Level Referenced Electron Spectroscopy for Chemical Analysis
FRESCA....... Field-Emitter Referenced Electron Spectroscopy for Chemical Analysis
FRESCAN..... Frequency Scanning
FRESCANAR... Free Scanning Radar (ACAE)
frescanar..... frequency scan radar (SAUS)
FRESCANNAR... Frequency Scanning RADAR
FRESCANNAR... Frequency Scan Radar (SAUS)
FRESCANNER... Frequency Scanner (SAUS)
FreSCn......... Free State Consolidated Gold Mines Ltd. [*Associated Press*] (SAG)
FRESCO....... Frequency Stability Code (PDAA)
Fresenius..... Fresenius USA, Inc. [*Associated Press*] (SAG)
Fresenius Environ Bull... Fresenius Environmental Bulletin [*A publication*] (PABS)
Fresenius J Anal Chem... Fresenius, Journal of Analytical Chemistry [*A publication*] (PABS)
FresenM...... Fresenius Medical Care AG [*Associated Press*] (SAG)
FRESH......... Foam Removal for Environmentally Safe Housing (SAUS)
FRESH......... Foil Research Hydrofoil (SAUS)
FRESH......... Foil Research Supercavitating Hydrofoil
FRESH......... Force Readiness Expert System (SAUO)
FRESH......... Force Requirements Expert System [*Navy*]
FRESH......... Freshman [*or Freshmen*] (WDAA)
fresh........... freshmen (SAUS)
FreshAm...... Fresh America Corp. [*Associated Press*] (SAG)
Freshst........ Freshstart Venture Capital Corp. [*Associated Press*] (SAG)
FRESHW...... Freshwell [*England*]
Freshwat Biol... Freshwater Biology [*A publication*] (PABS)
Freshwater Biol... Freshwater Biology (journ.) (SAUS)
FresM.......... FDresenius Medical Care AG [*Associated Press*] (SAG)
FRESN......... Fresno, CA [*American Association of Railroads railroad junction routing code*]
FRESS......... file retrieval and editing system (SAUS)
FRESSCAN... Frequency Scan [*Radar*] (DOMA)
FRESTAR..... Frequency Scanned Typhon Array Radar (ACAE)
FRET........... Fluorescence Resonance [*or Resonant*] Energy Transfer [*Analytical biochemistry*]
FRET........... Freezing Rain Endurance Test [*Aviation*] (DA)
FRET........... Functional Reliability End Test (SAUS)
FRET........... Functional Reliability Evaluation Technique (SAUS)
FRET-ANON... Family-Related Emotional Trauma - Anonymous
FRETILIN..... Frente Revolucionaria Timorense de Libertacao e Independencia [*Revolutionary Front for the Liberation and Independence of Timor*]
FRETT......... Fleet Readiness Emergency Travel Team (ACAE)
Fretter......... Fretter, Inc. [*Associated Press*] (SAG)
FRETURN..... Function Return [*Computer science*]
Freud........... Freudian (SAUS)
frev............. fast reverse (SAUS)
FREV........... Favorable Reversal [*Social Security Administration*] (DHP)
F REV......... Further Review (DNAB)
FREWCAP.... Flexible Reworkable Chip Attachment Process (IAA)
FREZ........... Freeze
FRF............. Faraday-Rotation Feature [*Astrophysics*]
FRF............. Fertility Research Foundation (EA)
FRF............. Field Record Form (ABAC)
FRF............. Field Research Facility [*Army*]
FRF............. Filter Replacement Fluid
FRF............. Filtration Replacement Fluid [*Medicine*] (EDAA)
FRF............. Fire-Resistant Fuels (RDA)
frf............... flight-readiness filring (SAUS)
FRF............. Flight Readiness Firing [*NASA*] (NASA)
FRF............. Flight Readiness Firing Test [*NASA*] (AFM)
FRF............. Floating Point Register File [*Computer science*] (VERA)
FRF............. Florida Retail Federation (SRA)
FRF............. Follicle-Stimulating Hormone Releasing Factor [*Also, FSH-RF, FSH-RH*] [*Endocrinology*]
FRF............. Fragrance Research Fund (EA)
FRF............. Frame Relay Forum (ACRL)
FRF............. France Growth Fund [*NYSE symbol*] (SPSG)
FRF............. Freedom to Read Foundation
FRF............. Free French [*World War II*]
FRF............. Free Running Frequency
fr-f............. french-fried (SAUS)
FRF............. Frequency Response Function [*Statistics*]
FRF............. Fringe Reduction Facility (SAUS)
FRF............. FSLIC [*Federal Savings and Loan Insurance Corp.*] Resolution Fund [*Administ ered by the Federal Deposit Insurance Corp.*]
FRF............. Fuel Reprocessing Facility [*Nuclear energy*] (NRCH)
FRF............. Functional Renal Failure [*Medicine*]
FRFA........... Federal Regulatory Flexibility Act (IEEE)
FRFAB......... FSS [*Flight Service Station*] Returns Flight-Plan Area and Service B [*Aviation*] (FAAC)
FRFDS......... Fund Raising and Financial Development Section [*Library Administration and Management Association*]
FRFE........... Field Representative, Far East (SAUO)
FRFID.......... Fast Response Flame Ionization Detector [*Automotive emissions testing*]
FRFOURRA... French Fourragere [*Military decoration*]
FRFP........... Fellow of the Royal Faculty of Physicians (SAUO)
FRFPI.......... Friends of Radio for Peace International (EA)
FRFPS......... Fellow of the Royal Faculty of Physicians and Surgeons [*British*]
FRFPS(G).... Fellow of the Royal Faculty of Physicians and Surgeons of Glasgow
FRFPSGlas... Fellow of the Royal Faculty of Physicians and Surgeons of Glasgow
FRFS........... Fast Reaction Fighting System (NATG)
FRFS........... Fellow of the Royal Faculty of Surgeons (SAUO)
FRFT........... Flight Readiness Firing Test (MCD)
FRFV........... Four by Five Inches (VRA)
FRG............ Emerging Germany Fund [*NYSE symbol*] (SPSG)
FRG............ Faculty Review Group [*Education*] (AIE)
FRG............ Family Rights Group [*British*] (DBA)
FRG............ Farmingdale, NY [*Location identifier*] [*FAA*] (FAAL)

FRG .... Federal Republic of Germany (AABC)
FRG .... Federal Reserve System, Board of Governors, Washington, DC [*OCLC symbol*] (OCLC)
FRG .... Fergana [*Former USSR*] [*Seismograph station code, US Geological Survey*] (SEIS)
FRG .... Field Review Group [*Army*] (RDA)
FRG .... Filtration-Resistant Glaucoma (MELL)
FRG .... Fisher Research Group (SAUO)
FRG .... Floated Rate Gyro [*Aerospace*] (AAG)
FR(g) .... Flow Rate of Sparge Gas
FRG .... Force Requirements Generator
FRG .... Forge
frg .... Forger [*MARC relator code*] [*Library of Congress*] (LCCP)
FRG .... Forward Repair Group (SAUS)
FRG .... Freight Runners Express, Inc. [*ICAO designator*] (FAAC)
FrG .... French Guiana (SAUS)
FRG .... Frente Republicano Guatemalteco [*Political party*] (EY)
FRG .... Frigate with missiles (SAUS)
Frg .... Frog [*Medicine*] (EDAA)
FRG .... Functional Related Groups (SAUS)
FRG .... Long Island Republic [*New York*] [*Airport symbol*] (OAG)
FRGB .... First Regional Bancorp [*NASDAQ symbol*] (NQ)
FRGDWG ..... Federal Republic of Germany Documentation Working Group (SAUO)
FRGHT .... Freight
FRGMI .... Federal Republic of Germany Ministry of the Interior (SAUO)
FRGMRT ...... Federal Republic of Germany Ministry of Research and Technology (SAUO)
FRGN .... Flashless Grain (SAUS)
FRGN .... Foreign
FRGNC .... Fragrance
FRGO .... Fargo Electronics [*NASDAQ symbol*] (SG)
Fr Gon .... Franciscus Gonzaga [*Authority cited in pre-1607 legal work*] (DSA)
FRGp .... Field Record Group [*Air Force*] (AFM)
FRGR .... Frozen Granular Snow [*Skiing condition*]
FrGrALP .... Bibliotheque Americaine, Universite de Grenoble III, Domaine Universitaire, Grenoble, France [*Library symbol*] [*Library of Congress*] (LCLS)
FrGrU .... Universite de Grenoble, Bibliotheque Droit-Lettres, St.-Martin d'Heres, France [*Library symbol*] [*Library of Congress*] (LCLS)
FRGRX .... Founders Growth [*Mutual fund ticker symbol*] (SG)
FRGS .... Fellow of the Royal Geographical Society [*British*] (ROG)
FRGS .... Force Reports Generation System (SAUO)
FRGS .... Forges [*Postal Service standard*] (OPSA)
FRGS .... Forked River Generating Station [*Nuclear energy*] (NRCH)
FRGSA .... Fellow of the Royal Geographical Society of Australia (SAUO)
FRGS(C) ...... Fellow of the Royal Geographical Society (Canada)
FRGSC .... Fellow of the Royal Geographical Society of Canada (SAUS)
FRGSS .... Fellow of the Royal Geographical Society, Scotland (ROG)
FRGT .... Fast Response Gamma Thermometer [*Environmental science*] (COE)
FRGT .... Freight (WDAA)
FRGTN .... Farmington, MN [*American Association of Railroads railroad junction routing code*]
Fr Gu .... French Guiana (SAUS)
FRGZ .... Froedert Grain [*Federal Railroad Administration identification code*]
FRH .... Fellowship of Religious Humanists (EA)
FRh .... Fetal Rhesus Monkey Kidney Cell [*Medicine*] (DMAA)
FRH .... Fire Resistant Hydraulics (SAUS)
FRH .... Flameless Ration Heater [*Army*] (RDA)
FRH .... Fly Runway Heading [*Aviation*] (FAAC)
FRH .... Follicle-Stimulating Hormone-Releasing Hormone [*Endocrinology*] (DAVI)
FRH .... follicle stimulating hormone releasing hormone (SAUS)
FRH .... Follitropin-Releasing Hormone (ADWA)
FRH .... French Lick, IN [*Location identifier*] [*FAA*] (FAAL)
FRH .... Frequency Response Histogram [*Biometrics*]
FRH .... Fruehauf Canada, Inc. [*Toronto Stock Exchange symbol*]
FRH .... Fuller, R. H., Los Angeles CA [*STAC*]
f-rh- .... Rhodesia [*Southern Rhodesia*] [*MARC geographic area code*] [*Library of Congress*] (LCCP)
FRHB .... Federation of Registered House Builders (SAUO)
FRHB .... Federation of Registered Housebuilders (SAUO)
FRHB .... Foundation for Research on Human Behavior (EA)
FRHGT .... Free Height
Fr Hist .... Fragmenta Historica [*of Aristoxenus*] [*Classical studies*] (OCD)
FRHistS .... Fellow of the Royal Historical Society [*British*] (ROG)
FRHistSoc .... Fellow of the Royal Historical Society [*British*]
FRHortS .... Fellow of the Royal Horticultural Society [*British*]
FRHQMT ...... Fully Automatic High Quality Machine Translation (SAUS)
Fr hr .... French horn (SAUS)
Fr hrn .... French horn (SAUS)
FRHS .... Fast-Repeat High Sequence (DB)
FRHS .... Fellow of the Royal Historical Society [*British*] (ROG)
FRHS .... Fellow of the Royal Horticultural Society [*British*] (ROG)
FRI .... American Family Restaurants, Inc. [*AMEX symbol*] (SAG)
FRI .... Central Fuel Research Institute, Bihar (SAUO)
FRI .... Family Relationship Inventory [*Psychology*]
FRI .... Family Relationships Institute [*Australia*]
FRI .... Family Relations Indicator [*Psychology*]
FRI .... Family Research Institute (EA)
FRI .... Federal Relighting Initiative (SAUS)
FRI .... Feeling Rough Inside [*Slang*]
FRI .... Fellow of the Canadian Institute of Realtors
FRI .... Fellow of the Institute of Realtors (SAUO)
FRI .... Fellow of the Real Estate Institute (DD)
FRI .... Fellow of the Royal Institution [*British*]
FRI .... Fels Research Institute (SAUO)
FRI .... Fermentation Research Institute [*Japan*] (DB)
FRI .... Financial Real Estate Insurance
FRI .... Firearm-Related Injury (MELL)
FRI .... First Rate Investments (DICI)
FRI .... Fisheries Research Institute [*Australia*]
FRI .... Fisheries Research Institute [*University of Washington*] [*Research center*]
FRI .... Flandre Air International [*France*] [*ICAO designator*] (FAAC)
FRI .... Flight Refueling, Incorporated (SAUO)
FRI .... Flux Reversals/Inch [*Magnetic storage measure*] (NITA)
FRI .... Flux Reversals per Inch (SAUS)
FRI .... Focal Region Investigation
FRI .... Food Research Institute [*Canada*] (ARC)
FRI .... Food Research Institute [*University of Wisconsin - Madison*] [*Research center*] (RCD)
FRI .... Food Research Institute [*Australia*]
FRI .... Forest Research Institute
FRI .... Forest Research Institute Herbarium International Acronym (SAUS)
FRI .... Formal Reading Inventory [*Educational test*]
FRI .... Fort Riley, KS [*Location identifier*] [*FAA*] (FAAL)
FRI .... Freeport Resources, Inc. [*Vancouver Stock Exchange symbol*]
FRI .... Frente Revolucionaria de Izquierda [*Left Revolutionary Front*] [*Bolivia*] [*Political party*] (PPW)
fri .... Friable (SAUS)
FRI .... Friant [*California*] [*Seismograph station code, US Geological Survey*] (SEIS)
FRI .... Friday (EY)
Fri .... Friday (ODBW)
FRI .... Friendly Initiated [*Incident*] [*Vietnam*]
FRI .... Friends of Rhodesian Independence (SAUO)
fri .... Frisian [*MARC language code*] [*Library of Congress*] (LCCP)
FRI .... Fuel Research Institute (SAUS)
FRI .... Fully Read Index [*Publishing*]
FRI .... Fulmer Research Institute (AAG)
FRIA .... Fellow of the Royal Irish Academy (SAUO)
FRIA .... Finnish Radio Industries Association
FRIA .... Finnish Radio Industries (or Industry) Association (SAUO)
FRIA .... Finnish Radio Industry Association (SAUS)
FRIA .... Firearms Research and Identification Association (EA)
FRIA .... Foreign Investment Review Agency (SAUO)
FRIAI .... Fellow of the Royal Institute of Architects of Ireland
FRIAI .... Fellow of the Royal Institution of Architects of Ireland (SAUS)
FRIAS .... Fellow of the Royal Incorporation of Architects in/of Scotland (SAUO)
FRIAS .... Fellow of the Royal Incorporation of Architects in Scotland (SAUS)
FRIAS .... Fellow of the Royal Incorporation of Architects of Scotland (DI)
FRIAS .... Fellow of the Royal Incorporation or Architects of Scotland (SAUS)
FRIAS .... Fellow of the Royal Institute of Architects in Scotland (SAUO)
FRIAS .... Fellow of the Royal Institute of Architects of Scotland
FRIBA .... Fellow of the Royal Institute of British Architects (ROG)
FRIC .... Fellow of the Royal Institute of Chemistry [*Formerly, FIC*] [*British*]
FRIC .... Forest Research Institute of Canada (SAUS)
fric .... frication (SAUS)
fric .... Fricative (BARN)
fric .... fricatrix (SAUS)
fric .... fricatruce (SAUS)
FRIC .... Friction [*or Frictional*] (WDAA)
FRICAND ...... Fricandus [*To Be Rubbed*] [*Pharmacy*] (ROG)
FRICC .... Federal Research Internet Coordinating Committee [*National Science Foundation*]
FRICENT ...... Fricentur [*Let Them Be Rubbed*] [*Pharmacy*] (ROG)
Frick .... Frick Collection (SAUS)
FRICS .... Fellow of the Royal Institute of Chartered Surveyors [*Canada*] (DD)
FRICS .... Fellow of the Royal Institution of Chartered Surveyors [*Formerly, FSI*] [*British*]
frict .... Friction [*Medicine*] (EDAA)
FRICT .... Friction
FRID .... Friday (ADA)
FRIDA .... Fund for Research and Investment for the Development of Africa Ltd (SAUO)
fridg .... frigidaire (SAUS)
fridge .... Refridgerator (REAL)
FRIED .... Friedman Test [*for pregnancy*] [*Obstetrics*]
FRIEDA .... Flourescence Radiation Induced Energy Dispersive Analyzer (SAUS)
FRIEDA .... Fluorescence Radiation Induced Energy Dispersive Analyzer (SAUS)
Friedm .... Friedman Industries, Inc. [*Associated Press*] (SAG)
Friedmn .... Friedmans, Inc. [*Associated Press*] (SAG)
Fried Test .... Friedman Test (SAUS)
FRIEND .... Fast Running Interpreter Enabling Natural Diagnosis (VLIE)
FRIEND .... Flow Regimes from International Experiments and Network Data (SAUO)
FRIENDS ...... Flow Regimes from International Experimental and Network Data Sets (SAUS)
FRIENDS ...... Flow Regimes from International Experiments and Network Data Sets (SAUS)
Friends .... Society of Friends (SAUO)
Friends Meet ... Friends Meeting (SAUS)
FRIES .... Fast Rope Insertion/Extraction System [*for rappeling*] [*Military*] (RDA)
FRIES .... Friesian [*Language, etc.*] (ROG)
Fries .... Friesic (SAUS)
Friesn .... Friesian (SAUS)
Fries Tr. .... Trial of John Fries (Treason) [*A publication*] (DLA)
FRIET .... Finite Real Estate Investment Trust
FRIF .... Field Reporting Information Forms (SAUO)
FRIF .... Furnished Recurring Intelligence File (MCD)

FRIG........... Floated Rate Integrating Gyro (SAUS)
Frig........... Frigidity [*Medicine*] (EDAA)
FRIG........... Frigidus [*Cold*] [*Pharmacy*]
FRIGS........... Fellow of the Royal Imperial Geographical Society (SAUO)
FRIH........... Fellow of the Royal Institute of Horticulture [*New Zealand*]
FRIIA........... Fellow of the Royal Institute of International Affairs [*British*] (DI)
FRIIA........... Fellow of the Royal Institution of International Affairs (SAUO)
FRIL........... Fuzzy Relational Inference Language (NITA)
FRIM........... Forest Research Institute of Malawi (SAUS)
FRIMP........... Flexible Reconfigurable Interconnected Multiprocessor
FRIMP System... Flexible Reconfigurable Interconnected Multiprocessor System (SAUS)
FRIN........... Fellow of the Royal Institution of Navigation [*British*] (DBQ)
FRIN........... Firing Research Investigation, Navy
FRINA........... Fellow of the Royal Institute of Naval Architects [*British*]
FRINA........... Fellow of the Royal Institution of Naval Architects (SAUO)
FRINGE........... File and Report Information Processing Generator [*Computer science*]
FRINGE........... File and Report Information System (SAUS)
Fringlish........... French + English (SAUS)
FRIP........... Fleet Readiness Improvement Plan
FRIP........... Fleet Readiness Improvement Program (SAUO)
FRIP........... Fushun Research Institute of Petrochemistry (SAUS)
FRIPA........... Fellow of the Royal Institute of Public Administration [*British*] (ADA)
FRIPA........... Fellow of the Royal Institution of Public Administration (SAUS)
FRIPH........... Fellow of the Royal Institute of Public Health [*British*] (ADA)
FRIPHH........... Fellow of the Royal Institute of Public Health and Hygiene [*British*]
FRIR........... File Access Interface Routines (SAUS)
FRIS........... fayalite-rutile-ilmenite-silica (SAUS)
FRIS........... Fire Research Information Services [*National Institute of Standards and Technology*] (IID)
FRIS........... Forest Resource Information System (SAUO)
FRIS........... Friesland [*County in the Netherlands*] (ROG)
Fris........... Frisia (SAUS)
Fris........... Frisian (ADWA)
FRIS........... Frisian [*Language, etc.*]
FRISA........... Fuel Research Institute of South Africa (SAUO)
FRISB........... Flathead River International Study Board (SAUS)
FrisBay........... Frisco Bay Industries [*Associated Press*] (SAG)
FRISC........... Formally Reduced Instruction Set Computer (VLIE)
FRISC........... Frisco, TN [*American Association of Railroads railroad junction routing code*]
Frischs........... Frisch's Restaurants, Inc. [*Associated Press*] (SAG)
FRISCO........... Fast Reaction Integrated Submarine Control [*Navy*]
FRISCO........... Framework for Integrated Symbolic/Numeric Computation (VLIE)
Frisco........... San Francisco (ADWA)
FRISCO........... San Francisco [*California*] (ROG)
Frisians........... Frisian islanders or the Frisian Islands in the North Sea (SAUS)
FRISP........... Filchner-Ronne Ice Shelf Programme (SAUS)
FRITA........... Friend of a Resistor-in-the-Army [*Peace movement slang during the Vietnam War*] (VNW)
Fritalux........... France, Italy, and Benelux nations (SAUS)
FRITALUX........... France, Italy, Benelux Economic Union (SAUO)
FRITALUX........... Union Economique France, Italie, Benelux
Frith........... United States Opinions Attorneys-General (Frith) [*Pt. 2., Vol. 21*] [*A publication*] (DLA)
FRITS........... Free Reservation, Information and Travel Service (SAUO)
frits........... fritters (SAUS)
Fritz........... Fritz Companies, Inc. [*Associated Press*] (SAG)
FRIVOL........... Frivolous (DSUE)
FRIVOLS........... Frivolities [*Slang*] (DSUE)
FRIZ........... Fremont Industries [*Federal Railroad Administration identification code*]
FRJ........... Facility Reject (SAUS)
FRJ........... facility rejected message (SAUS)
FRJ........... File Return Jump (SAUS)
FRJ........... Frejus [*France*] [*Airport symbol*] (AD)
FRJ........... Oklahoma City, OK [*Location identifier*] [*FAA*] (FAAL)
FRJD........... Forward Reaction Jet Driver (MCD)
FRJM........... Full Range Joint Movement [*Occupational therapy*]
FRJM........... Full range of joint movement (SAUS)
FRJ Message... Facility Rejected Message (SAUS)
FrJuice........... [*The*] Fresh Juice Co., Inc. [*Associated Press*] (SAG)
FRK........... Federal Reserve Bank of Kansas City, Kansas City, MO [*OCLC symbol*] (OCLC)
FRK........... Florida Rock Indus [*NYSE symbol*] (SG)
FRK........... Florida Rock Industries, Inc. [*AMEX symbol*] (SPSG)
FRK........... Folkstone Resources Ltd. [*Vancouver Stock Exchange symbol*]
FRK........... Fork
Frk........... Frankfort (SAUS)
FRK........... Fregate Island [*Seychelles Islands*] [*Airport symbol*] (OAG)
FrkBncp........... Franklin Bancorp [*Associated Press*] (SAG)
FrkCon........... Franklin Consolidated Mining Co., Inc. [*Associated Press*] (SAG)
FrkEPb........... Franklin Electronic Publishers, Inc. [*Associated Press*] (SAG)
FRKLFT........... Forklift
FrkMul........... Franklin Multi-Income Trust [*Associated Press*] (SAG)
FRKPK........... Franklin Park, IL [*American Association of Railroads railroad junction routing code*]
FrkPr........... Franklin Principal Maturity Trust [*Associated Press*] (SAG)
FrkQst........... Franklin Quest Co. [*Associated Press*] (SAG)
FRKS........... Forks [*Postal Service standard*] (OPSA)
FrkUnv........... Franklin Universal Trust [*Associated Press*] (SAG)
Frl........... El Ferrol (SAUS)
FRL........... Fabric Research Laboratories (SAUS)
FRL........... Facility Restriction Level [*Communications term*] (DCT)
FRL........... Faculty Research Lecture Committee (SAUS)
FRL........... Family Resource Library (NRGU)
FRL........... Feltman Research Laboratories (SAUS)
FRL........... Feltman Research Laboratory [*Picatinny Arsenal*] [*Army*] (RDA)
FRL........... Field Requirements List
FRL........... Filter, Regulator and Lubricator Unit (SAUS)
FRL........... Fire Resistance Level
FRL........... Fisheries Radiobiological Laboratory [*British*] (NUCP)
FRL........... Fisheries Research Laboratory (SAUO)
FRL........... Fisher Radio Laboratory (SAUS)
FRL........... Fisher Radio Laboratory Inc. (SAUO)
FRL........... Fixed Record Length (SAUS)
FRL........... Flame Retardant Latex (SAUS)
FRL........... Flight Research Laboratory [*University of Kansas*] [*Research center*] (RCD)
FRL........... Food Research Laboratories (SAUO)
FRL........... forced release signal (SAUS)
FRL........... Forest Research Laboratory [*Oregon State University*] [*Research center*] (RCD)
FRL........... Forest Resources Laboratory [*Pennsylvania State University*] [*Research center*] (RCD)
FRL........... Forli [*Italy*] [*Airport symbol*] (AD)
FRL........... Forum Retirement Partnership Ltd. [*AMEX symbol*] (SPSG)
FRL........... Fractional (WGA)
FRL........... Fraeulein [*Miss*] [*German*]
FRL........... Frame Reference Line (MCD)
FRL........... Frame Representation Language [*Computer science*]
FRL........... Free Recall Learning (PDAA)
FRL........... Fuel Research Laboratory (SAUS)
FRL........... Full Reservoir Level (SAUS)
FRL........... Fuselage Reference Line [*Aviation*]
FRL........... Jackson, MS [*Location identifier*] [*FAA*] (FAAL)
FRL........... Maria Elisa Gonzales Farelas [*Mexico*] [*FAA designator*] (FAAC)
FRL........... Mobil Research & Development Corp., Dallas, TX [*OCLC symbol*] (OCLC)
FRL........... Full Repairing Lease (ODA)
FRLA........... Federal Regulation of Lobbying Act
FRLA........... Federation of Right to Life Associations [*Australia*]
FRLAB........... Front Range Lidar, Aircraft, and Balloon (SAUS)
FRIC........... Fellow of the Royal Institute of Chemistry (SAUS)
FRLD........... Foreland
FrLemU........... Universite du Maine, Le Mans, France [*Library symbol*] [*Library of Congress*] (LCLS)
FRL-EWSIN... Forest Research Literature and the Evolving World Science Information Network (SAUS)
FrLimU........... Universite de Limoges, Limoges, France [*Library symbol*] [*Library of Congress*] (LCLS)
FrLimU-L..... Universite de Limoges, Bibliotheque des Lettres, Limoges, France [*Library symbol*] [*Library of Congress*] (LCLS)
FrLiU........... Universite de Lille, Bibliotheque de Section Droit-Lettres, Domaine Universitaire, Litteraire, et Juridique, Lille, France [*Library symbol*] [*Library of Congress*] (LCLS)
FRLL........... Farrell Lines (SAUS)
FRLM........... Fixed Reference Lung Model (SAUS)
FRL Newsletter... Fabric Research Laboratories Newsletter (SAUS)
FRIPHH........... Fellow of the Royal Institute of Public Health and Hygiene (SAUS)
FRL Signal... Forced Release Signal (SAUS)
FrLy........... Bibliotheque Municipale de Lyon, Lyon, France [*Library symbol*] [*Library of Congress*] (LCLS)
FrLyU........... Universite de Lyon, Bibliotheque Centrale, Lyon, France [*Library symbol*] [*Library of Congress*] (LCLS)
FRM........... Fairmont [*Minnesota*] [*Airport symbol*] (OAG)
FRM........... Fairmont, MN [*Location identifier*] [*FAA*] (FAAL)
FRM........... Farm (ADA)
FRM........... Fast Resource Management (SAUS)
FRM........... Fault Reporting Module (TEL)
FRM........... Federal Armored Service, Inc. [*ICAO designator*] (FAAC)
FRM........... Federal Reference Method
FRM........... Federal Reference Methods (SAUO)
FRM........... Federal Reformatory for Men (SAUO)
FRM........... Federation of Retail Merchants [*Defunct*] (EA)
frm........... fiberglass-reinforced metal (SAUS)
FRM........... Fiber-Reinforced Material
FRM........... Fiber-Reinforced Metal [*Materials science*]
FRM........... fiber reinforced metal (SAUS)
FRM........... fibre-reinforced metal (SAUS)
FRM........... Field Reversed Mirror (MCD)
FRM........... Film Reading Machine
FRM........... Final Rulemaking [*Federal government*] (GFGA)
FRM........... Fire Room
frm........... fireroom (SAUS)
FRM........... First America Mining Corp. [*Vancouver Stock Exchange symbol*]
FRM........... First Mississippi [*NYSE symbol*] (TTSB)
FRM........... First Mississippi Corp. [*NYSE symbol*] (SPSG)
FRM........... Fixed Range Marks (VLIE)
FRM........... Fixed Rate Mortgage
FRM........... Flat River [*Missouri*] [*Seismograph station code, US Geological Survey*] [*Closed*] (SEIS)
FRM........... Flight-Related Mishap (SEWL)
FRM........... Floating Roof Mixer (SAUS)
FRM........... Flow Rate Meter (SAUS)
FRM........... Fluid Resupply Module (SAUS)
FRM........... Force Reaction Motor
FRM........... Foucault Rotating Mirror [*Physics*]
FRM........... Frame

frm .... framing (SAUS)
FRM .... Framingham Public Library, Framingham, MA [*OCLC symbol*] (OCLC)
Fr M .... Francis' Maxims of Equity [*1722-46*] [*A publication*] (DLA)
FRM .... Free Running Multivibrator (SAUS)
frm .... French, Middle [*MARC language code*] [*Library of Congress*] (LCCP)
FRM .... Frequency Meter
FRM .... Frequency Response Method (SAUS)
FRM .... From
FRM .... Full Range of Motion [*Orthopedics*] (DAVI)
FRM .... Functional Requirements Model (VLIE)
FRMA .... Floor Rug Manufacturers' Association [*British*] (BI)
FRMAC .... Federal Radiological Management Assessment Center (USDC)
FRMAC .... Federal Radiological Monitoring and Assessment Center [*Department of Energy*]
FRMAP .... Federal Radiological Monitoring and Assessment Plan [*Environmental science*] (COE)
FRMAP .... Foreign Rights Marketing Assistance Program [*Australia*]
FRMB .... Fast Ramp Mini Batch (AAEL)
FRMC .... Frame Counter (SAA)
FrMC .... Institut National de la Propriete Industrielle, Centre Regional, Marseilles, France [*Library symbol*] [*Library of Congress*] (LCLS)
FRMCM .... Fellow of the Royal Manchester College of Music [*British*]
FRMCS .... Fellow of the Royal Medico-Chirurgical Society (SAUO)
FRMCSL .... Fellow of the Royal Medical and Chirurgical Society, London (ROG)
FRMD .... Formed
FRMD .... Framed
FRME .... First Merchants Corp. [*NASDAQ symbol*] (NQ)
FRME .... Frequency Response Measuring Equipment (PDAA)
FRMedSoc .... Fellow of the Royal Medical Society [*British*]
FR Meter .... Frequency Meter (SAUS)
FR Met S .... Fellow of the Royal Meteorological Society [*British*]
FRMetS .... Fellow Royal Meteorological Society [*British*] (WA)
FR Met Soc .... Fellow of the Royal Meteorological Society [*British*] (ROG)
FrMeyer .... Meyer [*Fred*], Inc. [*Associated Press*] (SAG)
FrmG .... Farmers Group Capital [*Associated Press*] (SAG)
FrmG .... Farmers Group Capital II [*Associated Press*] (SAG)
FRMG .... FirstMiss Gold [*NASDAQ symbol*] (TTSB)
FRMG .... FirstMiss Gold, Inc. [*NASDAQ symbol*] (NQ)
FRMG .... Forming (FAAC)
FRMG .... Framing [*of a ship*] (DS)
frmg .... Framing [*Construction term*] (MIST)
FRMIT .... Fellow of the Royal Melbourne Institute of Technology (SAUO)
FRML .... Formal
FRML .... Freymiller Trucking, Inc. [*NASDAQ symbol*] (NQ)
FRMM .... Flux Reversals/Millimeter (SAUS)
FRMM .... flux reversals/millimetre (SAUS)
FRMN .... Foreman (SAUS)
FRMN .... Formation (FAAC)
FRMNG .... Farming
FRMNTN .... Fermentation
FRMO .... Fleet Royal Marines Officer [*Navy*] [*British*]
FrMpALP .... Bibliotheque Americaine, Universite Paul-Valery, Montpellier, France [*Library symbol*] [*Library of Congress*] (LCLS)
FRMR .... Farmer
FRMR .... Field Reversed Mirror Reactor (SAUS)
FRMR .... Former (MSA)
FRMR .... Frame Reject
FRMR .... Frame Reject (frame) (SAUS)
Frms .... Farms (SAUS)
FRMS .... Federation of Recorded Music Societies [*British*] (EAIO)
FRMS .... Federation of Rocky Mountain States
FRMS .... Fellow of the Royal Meteorological Society [*British*]
FRMS .... Fellow of the Royal Meterological Society [*Canada*] (ASC)
FRMS .... Fellow of the Royal Microscopical Society [*British*] (ROG)
FRMS .... Financial Resources Management System (SAUS)
FRMS .... Flow Reactor Mass Spectroscopy (MCD)
FRMS .... Frequency Record Management System (SAUO)
FRMS .... Frequency Resource Management System (SAUO)
FRMT .... Format
FRMT .... Fremont General Corp. [*NASDAQ symbol*] (COMM)
FRM Technique .... Foam Reservoir Moulding Technique (SAUS)
FRMTN .... Formation
FRMV .... Free Running Multivibrator (PDAA)
FRMWG .... Floodplain and River Management Working Group [*Australia*]
FRMWRK .... Framework
FrN .... Bibliotheque Municipale, Nantes, France [*Library symbol*] [*Library of Congress*] (LCLS)
FRN .... Federal Register Notice (NRCH)
FRN .... Federal Reserve Note
FRN .... Federation of Rhodesia and Nyassaland (SAUO)
FRN .... Feed Rate Number (MCD)
FRN .... Feedrate Number (SAUS)
FRN .... Feminist Radio Network [*Defunct*] (EA)
FRN .... Fernie [*British Columbia*] [*Seismograph station code, US Geological Survey*] [*Closed*] (SEIS)
FRN .... File Reference Number (ACAE)
FRN .... Final Rulemaking Notice [*Federal government*] (GFGA)
FRN .... Fixed Radix Notation (VLIE)
FRN .... Floating Rate Note
FRN .... Floating Round
FRN .... Food Ratio Normal (SAUS)
FRN .... Force Requirement Number [*Army*] (AABC)
FRN .... Fort Richardson, AK [*Location identifier*] [*FAA*] (FAAL)
FRN .... Fredonia Oil & Gas [*Vancouver Stock Exchange symbol*]
FRN .... Frente de Reconstruccion Nacional [*Ecuador*] [*Political party*] (EY)
FRN .... Fresenius USA [*AMEX symbol*] (TTSB)
FRN .... Fresenius USA, Inc. [*AMEX symbol*] (SAG)
FRN .... Friendly Ice Cream [*AMEX symbol*]
FRN .... Frontul Renasterii Nationala [*Front of National Rebirth*] [*Romania*] [*Political party*] (PPE)
FRN .... Full-Round Nose [*Diamond drilling*]
FRN .... Furniture (SAUS)
FRN .... Swedish Council for Planning and Coordination of Research (SAUS)
FRNA .... Foreign Rations Not Available (AABC)
FrNALP .... Bibliotheque Americaine de Nantes, Universite de Nantes Chemin du Tertre, Nantes, France [*Library symbol*] [*Library of Congress*] (LCLS)
FrNanALP .... Bibliotheque Americaine, Universite de Nancy II, Nancy, France [*Library symbol*] [*Library of Congress*] (LCLS)
FrNanU .... Universite de Nancy, Bibliotheque Centrale, Nancy, France [*Library symbol*] [*Library of Congress*] (LCLS)
FrNanU-L .... Universite de Nancy, Bibliotheque des Lettres-Droit-Sciences, Nancy, France [*Library symbol*] [*Library of Congress*] (LCLS)
FrNb .... Fractonimbus (SAUS)
FRNC .... Furnace
FRNCH .... French
FRNCHS .... Franchise
FRNCHSNG .... Franchising
FRNCM .... Fellow of the Royal Northern College of Music [*British*] (DBQ)
FRND .... Friend
FRND .... Friendly Ice Cream Corp. [*NASDAQ symbol*] (NASQ)
FRNDLY .... Friendly
FRNG .... Firing
FRNG .... Fringe (MSA)
FRNHS .... Fort Raleigh National Historic Site (SAUO)
FrNiU-D .... Universite de Nice, Bibliotheque de Droit, Nice, France [*Library symbol*] [*Library of Congress*] (LCLS)
FrNiU-S .... Universite de Nice, Bibliotheque des Sciences, Nice, France [*Library symbol*] [*Library of Congress*] (LCLS)
FRNK .... Frequency Regulation and Network Keying [*Computer science*] (IAA)
FrnkAdv .... Franklin Advantage Real Estate, Inc. [*Associated Press*] (SAG)
FrnkBk .... Franklin Bank NA [*Associated Press*] (SAG)
FrnkEl .... Franklin Electric Co., Inc. [*Associated Press*] (SAG)
FRNKF .... Frankfort, KY [*American Association of Railroads railroad junction routing code*]
Frnkln .... Franklin Corp. [*Associated Press*] (SAG)
FrnkRE .... Franklin Real Estate Income Fund [*Associated Press*] (SAG)
FrnkRs .... Franklin Resources, Inc. [*Associated Press*] (SAG)
FrnkSel .... Franklin Select Real Estate Income Fund [*Associated Press*] (SAG)
FrnkSup .... Franklin Supply Co. Ltd. [*Associated Press*] (SAG)
FRNM .... Foundation for Research on the Nature of Man (EA)
FRNP .... Federal Radio Navigation Plan (SAUS)
FRNS .... Family Respite and Network Support [*Australia*]
FRNS .... Fellow of the Royal Navy School of Architects (SAUO)
FRNS .... Fellow of the Royal Numismatic Society [*British*] (EY)
FRNT .... Front
FRNT .... Frontier Airlines [*NASDAQ symbol*] (TTSB)
FRNT .... Frontier Airlines, Inc. [*NASDAQ symbol*] (SAG)
FrntDir .... Fronteer Directory Co., Inc. [*Associated Press*] (SAG)
FrntN .... Frontier Natural Gas [*Associated Press*] (SAG)
FrntNat .... Frontier Natural Gas [*Commercial firm*] [*Associated Press*] (SAG)
FrntNt .... Frontier Natural Gas [*Commercial firm*] [*Associated Press*] (SAG)
FRNTR .... Frontier
FrntrFin .... Fronteer Financial Holdings Ltd. [*Associated Press*] (SAG)
FrntrIns .... Frontier Insurance Group [*Associated Press*] (SAG)
FRNTW .... Frontier Airlines Wrrt [*NASDAQ symbol*] (TTSB)
FrNU .... Universite de Nantes, Section Droit-Lettres, Nantes, France [*Library symbol*] [*Library of Congress*] (LCLS)
FrNU-M .... Universite de Nantes, Section Medecine, Nantes, France [*Library symbol*] [*Library of Congress*] (LCLS)
Fr Number .... Froude Number (SAUS)
FrNU-S .... Universite de Nantes, Section Sciences, Nantes, France [*Library symbol*] [*Library of Congress*] (LCLS)
FRNWC .... French Naval War College
FRNZIH .... Fellow of the Royal New Zealand Institute of Horticulture (SAUO)
FRO .... Failure Requiring Overhaul (SAUS)
FRO .... Faroe Islands [*ANSI three-letter standard code*] (CNC)
FRO .... Federal Register Office [*National Archives and Records Administration*] (GFGA)
FRO .... Feed Rate Override [*Mechanical engineering*] (IAA)
FRO .... Fire Research Organization (SAUO)
FRO .... Fire Risk Only [*Insurance*] (MARI)
FRO .... Fleet Records Office [*Navy*]
FRO .... Fleet Recreational Officer (SAUS)
FRO .... Fleet Recreation Officer (SAUO)
FRO .... Fleet Recruiting Officer (SAUO)
FRO .... Fleet Resources Office
FRO .... Flexible Response Option (SAUO)
FRO .... Flight Radio Officer [*Aviation*]
FRO .... Floro [*Norway*] [*Airport symbol*] (OAG)
FRO .... Food Rationing Order [*British*]
FRO .... Force Routine Order (SAUO)
FRO .... Free-Running Oscillator [*Instrumentation*]
fro .... French, Old [*MARC language code*] [*Library of Congress*] (LCCP)
FRO .... Frequency Reference Oscillator (ACAE)
FRO .... Friends Religious Order (SAUO)
FRO .... Frobisher NV (European Airlines) [*Belgium*] [*ICAO designator*] (FAAC)
FRO .... Front

FRO .... Frontier Corp. [*Formerly, Rochester Telephone*] [*NYSE symbol*] (SAG)
FRO .... Front Receiver On (ACAE)
FRO .... Frozya Industries [*Vancouver Stock Exchange symbol*]
FROA .... Fellow of the British Optical Association (SAUO)
FROB .... Flash Radar Order of Battle (SAUS)
FROC .... Federated Russian Orthodox Clubs (EA)
FROD .... Functionally Related Observable Difference [*between weapons*]
FROD .... Functionally Related Observable Differences (SAUS)
FRODEBU .... Front for a Democratic Burundi (SAUS)
frof .... Fire Risk on Freight [*Insurance*] (MARI)
FROF .... Fire Risk on Freight [*Insurance*]
FROF .... Freight Office
FROG .... Fast RHIC Oscillation Grabber (SAUS)
FROG .... Finished Room over Garage
Frog .... Free flight Range Over Ground (SAUS)
FROG .... Free Ranging on Grid [*Computer-controlled transport system*]
FROG .... Free Rocket over Ground [*USSR missile*]
FROG .... Friends of Research and Odd Gadgets (SAUS)
Frog .... Frogerius [*Rogerius Beneventanus*] [*Flourished, 12th century*] [*Authority cited in pre-1607 legal work*] (DSA)
FROGIE .... Fellowship to Resist Organized Groups Involved in Exploitation (SAUO)
FROGS .... Fund Raising Organization Graphics Service
FROKA .... First Republic of Korea Army
FROLIC .... File Room Online Information Control (SAUS)
FROLIC .... Formal Retrieval Oriented Language for Indexing Content (SAUS)
FROLIC .... Formal Retrieval Oriented Language for Indexing Context (VLIE)
FROLINAT .... Front de Liberation Nationale [*Chad*]
Froliswa .... Front for the Liberation of Swaziland (SAUS)
FROLIZI .... Front for the Liberation of Zimbabwe
FROM .... Factory Programmable Read Only Memory [*Computer science*] (IAA)
FROM .... factory programmable read-only memory (SAUS)
FROM .... Factory Read Only Memory (SAUS)
FROM .... Factory ROM (SAUS)
FROM .... Field Programmable Read-Only Memory [*Computer science*] (EECA)
FROM .... Field programmable read -only memory (SAUS)
FROM .... Force Reception and Onward Movement System (SAUO)
FROM .... Full Range of Motion [*or Movement*] [*Occupational therapy*]
FROM .... Fusable Read-Only Memory [*Computer science*] (MDG)
fron .... frontal (SAUS)
fron .... frontalis (SAUS)
FRON .... Frontier
FRON .... Frontline, Ltd. [*NASDAQ symbol*] (NASQ)
FRONASA .... Front for National Salvation [*Uganda*]
Front .... Frontier (SAUS)
front .... Frontispiece (ADWA)
FRONT .... Frontispiece [*Publishing*]
FrontA .... Frontier Airlines, Inc. [*Associated Press*] (SAG)
FrontAdj .... Frontier Adjusters of America, Inc. [*Associated Press*] (SAG)
FRONTAL .... frontal process studies (SAUS)
Frontera Girls ... California Institution for Women at Frontera (SAUS)
FRONTIERS ... Forecasting Rain Optimized using New Techniques of Inter- Actively Enhanced Radar and Satellite (SAUS)
Frontin .... Frontinus [*First century AD*] [*Classical studies*] (OCD)
FRONTIS .... Frontispiece [*Publishing*]
FrontrAir .... Frontier Airlines, Inc. [*Associated Press*] (SAG)
FrontrCp .... Frontier Corp. [*Associated Press*] (SAG)
FROOM .... Features and Relations Used in Object Oriented Modelling (VLIE)
FROPA .... Frontal Passage [*NWS*] (FAAC)
FR ORD .... French Ordinances [*A publication*] (DLA)
FROS .... Fleet Resources Office Subsystem (MCD)
FROSFC .... Frontal Surface [*NWS*] (FAAC)
frosh .... Freshman (ADWA)
FROSS .... Fast Read Cinly Storage Simulation (SAUS)
FROSS .... Fast Read Only Storage Simulation (SAUS)
FROSS .... Fast Read-Only Storage Simulator (VLIE)
FROST .... First Regional Observational Study of the Troposphere (SAUO)
FROST .... Floating Repair and Oil Storage Terminal
FROST .... Food Reserve on Space Trip (SAUS)
FROST .... Food Reserves on Space Trips
Frostburg St U ... Frostburg State University (GAGS)
FROSTI .... Food RA Online Scientific and Technical Information [*Leatherhead Food Research Association*] [*Information service or system*] (CRD)
FROZ .... Franklin Coal [*Federal Railroad Administration identification code*]
FROZ .... Frozen (SAUS)
FrozenFd .... Frozen Food Express [*Associated Press*] (SAG)
FrozFd .... Frozen Food Express [*Associated Press*] (SAG)
FRP .... Facility Requirements Panel (SAUO)
FRP .... Faculty Research Participation [*National Science Foundation program*]
FRP .... F-Air AS [*Denmark*] [*ICAO designator*] (FAAC)
FRP .... Fairfield Public Library, Supervisor of Technical Services, Fairfield, CT [*OCLC symbol*] (OCLC)
FRP .... Famous Records of the Past [*Record label*]
FRP .... Fares and Rates Panel (SAUS)
FRP .... Fast Response Processing (VLIE)
FRP .... Fast Retinal Potential (SAUS)
FRP .... Fast Rise Pulse
FRP .... Fault Report Point (TEL)
FRP .... Feather River Project
FRP .... Feature Recognition Processor
FRP .... Federal Radio Navigation Plan (SAUS)
FRP .... Federal Regulatory Plan [*Database*] (IID)
FRP .... Federal Response Plan (DEMM)
FRP .... Federation des Republicains de Progres [*Federation of Progressive Republicans*] [*France*] [*Political party*] (PPW)
FRP .... Ferritin Repressor Protein [*Biochemistry*]
FRP .... Fiberglass-Reinforced Plastic
frp .... fiberglass reinforced plastic (SAUS)
FRP .... Fiberglass-Reinforced Plywood
FRP .... fiberglass reinforced plywood (SAUS)
FRP .... Fiberglass-Reinforced Polyester [*Organic chemistry*]
FRP .... fiber reinforced plastic (SAUS)
FRP .... fiber reinforced plastics (SAUS)
FRP .... Fiber-Reinforced Polyester (SAUS)
FRP .... Fiber-Reinforced Polymer
FRP .... fibre-glas reinforced plastic (SAUS)
FRP .... Fibre-glass Reinforced Plastic (SAUS)
frp .... fibre-glass reinforced plastics (SAUS)
FRP .... fibre-glass reinforced polyester (SAUS)
FRP .... fibre-reinforced plastic (SAUS)
FRP .... Filament-Reinforced Plastic
FRP .... File Retention Period (SAUS)
FRP .... File Rules Pointer (SAUS)
FRP .... Flag Register Processing
FRP .... Flame-Retardant Polyethylene [*Communications term*] (DCT)
FRP .... Fleet Replacement Pilot [*Navy*] (NVT)
FRP .... Flight Release Point (SAUS)
FRP .... Follicle Regulatory Protein [*Endocrinology*]
frp .... follicular regulatory protein (SAUS)
FRP .... Force Rendezvous Point [*Military*] (AFM)
FRP .... Forest Response Program [*USA*] (EERA)
FRP .... For Record Purposes (ACAE)
frp .... forward refueling area (SAUS)
FRP .... Forward Refueling Point
FRP .... Fragmentation Bomb, Parachute
FRP .... Fragmentation Protocol [*Telecommunications*] (ACRL)
FRP .... Freeport McmoRan Res LP [*NYSE symbol*] (TTSB)
FRP .... Freeport-McMoRan Resource Partnership LP [*NYSE symbol*] (SPSG)
FRP .... Free Radical Photography
FRP .... Free-Radical Polymerization (SAUS)
FRP .... Free Romanian Press [*British*]
FRP .... Fremont Peak [*California*] [*Seismograph station code, US Geological Survey*] (SEIS)
FrP .... French Patent (SAUS)
FrP .... French Pharmacopeia [*Medicine*] (EDAA)
FRP .... Frequency Reference Protection
FRP .... Frequency Response Plotter
FRP .... Fresh Water Bay [*Alaska*] [*Airport symbol*] (OAG)
FRP .... Fuel Reprocessing Plant [*Nuclear energy*] (NRCH)
FRP .... Fuel Restoration Project
FRP .... Fuerzas Populares Revolucionarias [*Guerrilla forces*] [*Honduras*] (EY)
FRP .... Full-Rate Production (DOMA)
FRP .... Fully Refined Paraffinic Wax [*Petroleum technology*]
FRP .... Functional Refractory Period [*Neurophysiology*]
FRP .... Functional Review Process (SAUS)
FRP .... Fundamental Research Press (SAUS)
FRP .... Fur Renewing Process (SAUO)
FRP .... Fuselage Reference Plane [*Aviation*] (MCD)
FRP .... Parachute Fragmentation Bomb [*Air Force*]
FRPA .... Family Rights and Privacy Act [*1974*] (OICC)
FRPA .... Feather River Project Association (BARN)
FRPA .... Fiberglass Reinforced Panel Association [*Defunct*] (EA)
FRPA .... Fixed Radiation Pattern Antenna
FRPA .... Fixed Reception Pattern Antenna (SAUS)
FrPALP .... American Library in Paris, Paris, France [*Library symbol*] [*Library of Congress*] (LCLS)
FrPAUP .... American University in Paris, Paris, France [*Library symbol*] [*Library of Congress*] (LCLS)
FRP-AVN .... functional refractory period of atrioventricular node (SAUS)
FrPBA .... Bibliotheque de l'Arsenal, Paris, France [*Library symbol*] [*Library of Congress*] (LCLS)
FrPBN .... Bibliotheque Nationale, Paris, France [*Library symbol*] [*Library of Congress*] (LCLS)
FRPC .... Fast Reaction Procedure Card (SAUO)
FRPCC .... Federal Radiological Preparedness Coordinating Committee (SAUO)
FrPCF .... College de France, Paris, France [*Library symbol*] [*Library of Congress*] (LCLS)
FRPD .... Finitely Repeated Prisoner's Dilemma [*Psychology*]
FRPE .... Fellow of the Royal Society of Painter-Etchers and Engravers [*British*] (ROG)
FrPE-C .... Ecole Normale Superieure, Laboratoire de Chimie, Paris, France [*Library symbol*] [*Library of Congress*] (LCLS)
FrPED .... Institut National d'Etudes Demographiques, Paris, France [*Library symbol*] [*Library of Congress*] (LCLS)
FRPERC .... Food Refrigeration and Process Engineering Research Centre (SAUS)
FR-PET .... Fiber-Reinforced Polyethylene Terephthalate [*Glass*]
frpf .... fireproof (SAUS)
FRPG .... Fantasy Role Playing Game (SAUS)
FRPH .... Fiber-Reinforced Polymer Honeycomb
FRPharmS ... Fellow Royal Pharmaceutical Society [*British*] (WA)
frpi .... flux reversals per inch (SAUS)
FRPipe .... Fire-Retardant Pipe (SAUS)
FrPJO .... Direction des Journaux Officiels Service de Microfiches, Paris, France [*Library symbol*] [*Library of Congress*] (LCLS)
FRPL .... Fireplace [*Real estate*] (WGA)

FRPL .... Fuerzas Rebeldes y Populares Lautaro [*Chile*] [*Political party*] (EY)
FRPLC .... Fireplace [*Classified advertising*]
FRPMM .... Flux Reversals/Millimeter (SAUS)
frpng .... fireproofing (SAUS)
FRPO .... Front-Panel Operation [*Computer science*] (PCM)
Fr Pol .... French Polynesia (SAUS)
FrPoU .... Universite de Poitiers, Bibliotheque de Droit-Lettres, Poitiers, France [*Library symbol*] [*Library of Congress*] (LCLS)
FRPP .... Flame Retardant Phosphonitratic Polymer
FRPP .... FRP Properties [*NASDAQ symbol*] (TTSB)
FRPP .... FRP Properties, Inc. [*NASDAQ symbol*] (NQ)
FRP Pr .... FRP Properties, Inc. [*Associated Press*] (SAG)
FRPR .... Australian Financial Review Property Review [*A publication*] (ADA)
FRPrA .... First Indl Rlty Tr 9.50% Pfd [*NYSE symbol*] (TTSB)
FRPS .... Fellow of the Royal Photographic Society [*British*] (ROG)
FRPS .... Flux Reversals Per Second (NITA)
FrPS .... Sirco-France, Paris, France [*Library symbol*] [*Library of Congress*] (LCLS)
FRPSL .... Fellow of the Royal Philatelic Society of London (SAUO)
FrptMc .... Freeport McMoRan, Inc. [*Associated Press*] (SAG)
FRPTNG .... Fleet Replacement Pilot Training [*Navy*] (NVT)
FrPU .... Universite de Paris a la Sorbonne, Bibliotheque de la Faculte des Lettres et de la Faculte des Sciences, Paris, France [*Library symbol*] [*Library of Congress*] (LCLS)
FrPU-AL .... Institut des Hautes Etudes de l'Amerique Latine, Universite de Paris, Paris, France [*Library symbol*] [*Library of Congress*] (LCLS)
FrPU-M .... Universite de Paris a la Sorbonne, Faculte de Medecine, Paris, France [*Library symbol*] [*Library of Congress*] (LCLS)
FrPU-OS .... Universite de Paris, Faculte des Sciences, (Orsay), Orsay, France [*Library symbol*] [*Library of Congress*] (LCLS)
FrPU-P .... Universite de Paris a la Sorbonne, Faculte des Sciences Pharmaceutiques et Biologiques de Paris-Luxembourg, Paris, France [*Library symbol*] [*Library of Congress*] (LCLS)
FRPV .... Full-Range Picture Vocabulary Test [*Intelligence test*]
FRPVT .... Full-Range Picture Vocabulary Test [*Education*]
FRQ .... facility request message (SAUS)
FRQ .... Flush Rush Quarterly (SAUS)
FRQ .... Frequent
FRQ Message ... Facility Request Message (SAUS)
FRQMULT .... Frequency Multiplier (KSC)
FRR .... Facilities and Rearrangement Request (SAUS)
FRR .... Failure and Rejection Report
FRR .... Failure and Replacement Report (SAUS)
FRR .... Failure Reporting Review (KSC)
FRR .... Fair Round-Robin (SAUS)
FRR .... Falls Road Railroad [*Federal Railroad Administration identification code*]
FRR .... False Rejection Rate (SAUS)
FRR .... False Removal Rate (CAAL)
FRR .... Fast Recovery Rectifier (IAA)
FRR .... fast repetition rate (SAUS)
FRR .... Federal Register Reprint
FRR .... Federal Research Report [*Business Publishers, Inc.*] [*Information service or system*] (CRD)
FRR .... Federal Reserve Bank of Richmond, Richmond, VA [*OCLC symbol*] (OCLC)
FRR .... Federal Reserve Regulation (EBF)
FRR .... Financial Reporting Releases [*Securities and Exchange Commission*] (EBF)
FRR .... Firariana [*Madagascar*] [*Seismograph station code, US Geological Survey*] (SEIS)
FRR .... Fitchburg Railroad
FRR .... fixed retarding ratio (SAUS)
FRR .... Flight Readiness Review (KSC)
FRR .... Force Readiness Report [*DoD*]
FRR .... Foreign Receiving Report (MCD)
FRR .... Foreign Research Reactor (GAAI)
FRR .... Forester Resources, Inc. [*Vancouver Stock Exchange symbol*]
FRR .... Front Royal, VA [*Location identifier*] [*FAA*] (FAAL)
FRR .... Full Reimbursement Rate (AFM)
FRR .... Functional Recovery Routine [*Computer science*] (BUR)
FRR .... functional recovery routines (SAUS)
FRR .... Functional Requirement Review (SAUS)
FRR .... Royal Irish Fusiliers Reserve Regiment [*Military unit*] [*British*] (DMA)
FRRA .... Facilities and Rearrangement Request and Authorization (SAUS)
FRRA .... Fashoda Relief and Rehabilitation Association (SAUO)
FRRA .... Federal Regional Reconstitutional Area
FRRB .... Fast Rise Reflective Balloon
FRRC .... Flow Recording Ratio Controller (IAA)
FRRE .... Field and Reservoir Reserve Estimate [*US Geological Survey*]
FR Relay .... Fast Release Relay (SAUS)
FR Resin .... Flame Retardant Resin (SAUS)
FRRID .... Flight Readiness Review Item Description [*NASA*] (NASA)
FRRID .... Flight Readiness Review Item Disposition [*NASA*] (NASA)
FRRIO .... Fleet Replacement RADAR Intercept Officer [*Navy*] (NVT)
FRRP .... Financial Reporting Review Panel
FRRPA .... Forest and Rangeland Renewable Planning Act (SAUO)
FRRPP .... Free Radical Retrograde Precipitation Polymerization [*Organic chemistry*]
FRRRB .... Fast Rise RADAR Reflective Balloon
FRRRPA .... Forest and Rangeland Renewable Resources Planning Act (COE)
FRRS .... Frequency Resource Records System
FRRS .... Frequency Resource Record System (SAUO)
FRRS .... Full Remaining Radiation Service [*Unit*] [*Military*]
FRRU .... Freight Receiving and Redistribution Unit
FRRV .... Fast-Response Relief Valve (MCD)
FRRY .... Ferry [*Commonly used*] (OPSA)
FRS .... Face Recognition System [*Automotive safety system*]
FRS .... Facilities Requirements Study
FRS .... Facilities Restoral System [*Communications term*] (DCT)
FRS .... Failure Reporting System (MCD)
FRS .... Fall Reaction Spheres (AAG)
FRS .... Family Radio Service
FRS .... Fashion Reporter System (SAUS)
FRS .... Fast Reactor Safety [*Nuclear energy*] (NRCH)
FRS .... Fast Retrieval Storage [*Computer science*]
FRS .... Fault Repair Service [*Telecommunications*] [*British*]
FRS .... Feature Recognition System (SAUS)
FRS .... Fecal Reducing Substance [*Medicine*] (MELL)
FRS .... Federal Relay Service (SAUO)
FRS .... Federal Reserve Bank of St. Louis, St. Louis, MO [*OCLC symbol*] (OCLC)
FRS .... Federal Reserve System [*Independent government agency*]
FRS .... Federal Service System (SAUO)
FRS .... Fellow of the Royal Society [*British*] (ROG)
FRS .... Fellow of the Royal Society of London [*1660*] (NGC)
FRS .... Female Reproductive System (MELL)
FRS .... Ferredoxin-Reducing Substance [*Biochemistry*] (MAE)
FRS .... Ferrite Resonance Switch
FRS .... Festiniog Railway Society (SAUO)
FRS .... Fetal Radiation Syndrome [*Medicine*] (MELL)
FRS .... Fetal Rubella Syndrome [*Medicine*] (MELL)
FRS .... Fiber-Reinforced Superalloy (SAUS)
FRS .... Fighter, Reconnaissance, Strike (SAUO)
FRS .... File Replication Service [*Computer science*] (MWOL)
FRS .... Financial Records System (SAUS)
FRS .... Financial Relations Society [*Defunct*] (EA)
FRS .... Financial Reporting System (MHDW)
FRS .... Financial Results Simulator (MHDB)
FRS .... Fire Research Station [*Research center*] [*British*] (IRC)
FRS .... Firmware Requirement Specification
FRS .... First Rank Symptoms [*Medicine*] (MEDA)
FRS .... First Readiness State (AAG)
FRS .... First Remove Subroutine (SAUS)
FRS .... First Repository States (SAUS)
FRS .... Fisheries Research Society (SAUO)
FRS .... Fisheries Research Station [*British*]
FRS .... Fixed Radial Shield [*Nuclear energy*] (NRCH)
FRS .... Flandre Air Service [*France*] [*ICAO designator*] (FAAC)
FRS .... Flash Ranging System
FRS .... Fleet Readiness Squadron [*Navy*] (NVT)
FRS .... Fleet Repair Service [*Navy*] (NVT)
FRS .... Fleet Replacement Squadron [*Military*]
FRS .... Fleet Replenishment Squadron (SAUO)
FRS .... Flexible Route Selection [*Computer science*] (VERA)
FRS .... Flexible Routing Selection (SAUS)
FRS .... Flight Radio Subsystem
frs .... flight reference selector (SAUS)
FRS .... Floating Report Sign (SAUS)
FRS .... Flood Relief Services (SAUO)
FRS .... Flores [*Guatemala*] [*Airport symbol*] (OAG)
FR(s) .... Flow Rate of Sample
FRS .... Fluidic Rate Sensor (MCD)
FRS .... Fluid Recycling Service, Inc. (EFIS)
FRS .... Flux Reversals per Second (SAUS)
FRS .... Flying Relay Station
FRS .... Folding Roadway System (SAUS)
FRS .... Font Resource (SAUS)
FRS .... Forced Response Simulation [*Computer science*]
FRS .... Forest Resource Survey [*Australia*]
FRS .... Formal Reporting System [*Environmental science*] (COE)
FRS .... Formatted Read Statement (SAUS)
FRS .... Fortress Resources [*Vancouver Stock Exchange symbol*]
FRS .... Forward RADAR Sensor
FRS .... Forward Ready Signal [*Telecommunications*] (TEL)
FRS .... Foundation Research Service
FRS .... Fractal Representation of Sets [*Genetics*]
FRS .... Fragility Response Spectrum (IEEE)
FRS .... Fragility Response System (IAA)
FRS .... Frame Relay Service [*Computer science*] (VERA)
FRS .... Frame Relay Switch [*Newbridge Networks Corp.*]
frs .... frames (SAUS)
frs .... francs (SAUS)
FRS .... Franz Rosenzweig Society (EA)
FRS .... Fraternitatis Regiae Socius [*Fellow of the Royal Society*] [*Latin*]
FRS .... Free-Running Speed (SAUS)
FRS .... Freethought Reprint Series (SAUS)
Fr S .... French Somaliland (SAUS)
FRS .... Frente Republicana e Socialista [*Republican and Socialist Front*] [*Portugal*] [*Political party*] (PPW)
FRS .... Frente Revolucionaria Sandinista [*Nicaragua*] [*Political party*] (EY)
FRS .... Frequency Response Survey (CET)
FRS .... Fresno [*Diocesan abbreviation*] [*California*] (TOCD)
FRS .... Frisch's Restaurants [*AMEX symbol*] (TTSB)
FRS .... Frisch's Restaurants, Inc. [*AMEX symbol*] (SPSG)
Frs .... Frisian (ADWA)
FRS .... Frisian [*or Frisic*] [*Language, etc.*]
FRS .... Fruit Research Station (SAUO)
frs .... Fruits
FRS .... Fuel Receiving Station [*Nuclear energy*] (NRCH)

FRS............ Fulton Recovery System (SAUO)
FRS............ Functional Requirement Specification (AAG)
FRS............ Functional Requirements Summary (SSD)
FRS............ Fundamental Reference System (SAUS)
FRS............ Furosemide [*Pharmacology*] (DAVI)
FRS............ Future Rifle System (SAUO)
FRS .... Fuel Research Station (ODA)
FRSA .... Fellow of the Royal Society of Arts [*British*] (EY)
FRSA .... Fellow of the Royal Society of Arts, London [*1909, founded 1754 as Society of Arts*] (NGC)
FRSA .... Fellow of the Royal Swedish Academy (SAUO)
FRSAI .... Fellow of the Royal Society of Antiquaries of Ireland
FRSAIrel...... Fellow of the Royal Society of Antiquaries, Ireland (ROG)
FRSAMD...... Fellow of the Royal Scottish Academy of Music and Drama [*British*] (DI)
FRSanI........ Fellow of the Royal Sanitary Institute [*Later, FRSH*] [*British*]
FRSAS .... Fast-Response Solar Array Simulator
FRSB .... Federal Reserve System Bank
FRSB .... Frequency-Referenced Scanning Beam [*Aviation*] (OA)
FRSB .... FSS [*Flight Service Station*] Returns Service B [*Aviation*] (FAAC)
FRSBY......... Friendly, Round Robin, Special, Bee and Yoke Tracks (SAA)
FRSC .... Fellow of the Royal Society of Canada (SAUS)
FRSC .... Fellow of the Royal Society of Chemistry [*British*] (DBQ)
frsc .... Fresco (VRA)
frsc .... full range source code (SAUS)
FRSCan........ Fellow of the Royal Society of Canada
FRSCM........ Fellow of the Royal School of Church Music [*British*]
FRSE........... Fellow of the Royal Society, Edinburgh (ROG)
FRSEC .... Frames per Second [*Telecommunications*] (IAA)
FRSEd......... Fellow of the Royal Society of Edinburgh (SAUS)
FRS Edin ...... Fellow of the Royal Society of Edinburgh
FRS et AS.... Fraternitatis Regiae Socius et Associatus [*Fellow and Associate of the Royal Society*] [*Latin*] (ROG)
FRSF........... Fuel Receiving and Storage Facility [*Nuclear energy*] (NRCH)
FRSGS......... Fellow of the Royal Scottish Geographical Society (ROG)
FRSH .... Fellow of the Royal Society for the Promotion of Health (SAUS)
FRSH .... Fellow of the Royal Society of Health [*Formerly, FRSanI*] [*British*]
FRSH .... Fresh
FRSH .... [*The*] Fresh Juice Co., Inc. [*NASDAQ symbol*] (NQ)
FRSH .... Fresh Juice Inc. [*NASDAQ symbol*] (TTSB)
FrshChc .... Fresh Choice, Inc. [*Associated Press*] (SAG)
FRSI............ Farm-Related Service Industries [*FHWA*] (TAG)
FRSI............ Fellow of the Royal Sanitary Institute [*British*] (ROG)
FRSI............ Felt Reusable Surface Insulation (MCD)
FRSI............ Flexible Reusable Surface Insulation (MCD)
FRSIS .... Fuzzy Relational Soil Information System (SAUO)
FRSL........... Fellow of the Royal Society, London (SAUO)
FRSL........... Fellow of the Royal Society of Literature [*British*] (ROG)
FRSL........... Forestry Remote Sensing Laboratory
FRSM.......... Fellow of the Royal School of Mines (SAUS)
FRSM.......... Fellow of the Royal Society of Medicine [*British*]
FRSM.......... Ferroresonance Servo Motor (PDAA)
FRSM.......... Force and Resource Status Monitoring (SAUO)
FRSM.......... Future Radionavigation Systems Mix (SAUO)
FRSNA......... Fellow of the Royal School of Naval Architects [*British*] (ROG)
FRSNZ......... Fellow of the Royal Society of New Zealand
FRSocMed.... Fellow of the Royal Society of Medicine [*British*]
Fr Som .... French Somaliland (SAUS)
Fr Soma ...... French Somaliland (VRA)
frsp .... frame spacing (SAUS)
FRSP .... Fredericksburg and Spotsylvania County Battlefield Memorial National Military Park
FRSPC .... Free Space (SAUS)
FRSPS .... Fellow of the Royal Society of Physicians and Surgeons (SAUO)
FRSS .... Fast Response Survey System [*Washington, DC*] [*Department of Education*] (GRD)
FRSS .... Federal Register Search System [*Chemical Information Systems, Inc.*] [*Information service or system*] (CRD)
FRSS .... Fellow of the Royal Statistical Society [*British*] (ROG)
FRSS .... Financial Results Simulator System (MHDB)
FRSs........... Fire Research Stations (SAUS)
FRSS .... Fire-Retardant and Smoke-Suppressant [*Chemicals*]
FRSS .... Flight Reference Stabilization System (SAUO)
FRSS .... Flight Reference Stabilization Systems (KSC)
FRSSA......... Fellow of the Royal Scottish Society of Arts (ROG)
FRSSA......... Fellow of the Royal Society of South Africa (SAUO)
FRSSACS..... Free Reaction Sphere Satellite Attitude Control System (DNAB)
FRSSAf........ Fellow of the Royal Society of South Africa
FRSSI.......... Fellow of the Royal Statistical Society of Ireland (SAUO)
FRSSS.......... Fellow of the Royal Statistical Society of Scotland (ROG)
FRST........... Fellow of the Royal Society of Teachers [*British*]
FRST........... FirsTier Finance, Inc. [*NASDAQ symbol*] (NQ)
FRST........... Forest [*Postal Service standard*] (OPSA)
FrSt............ Fractostratus (SAUS)
Fr St .... French Studies (journ.) (SAUS)
FRST........... Frost [*Meteorology*] (DA)
FrstAll.......... First Alliance Corp. [*Associated Press*] (SAG)
FRSTAT........ Fringe Software System (SAUS)
FrstCstl........ First Coastal Corp. [*Associated Press*] (SAG)
FrstCtz......... First Citizens Corp. [*Associated Press*] (SAG)
FrstLanc .... First Lancaster Bancshares, Inc. [*Associated Press*] (SAG)
FRSTM......... Fellow of the Royal Society of Tropical Medicine and Hygiene (SAUO)
FRSTM & H... Fellow of the Royal Society of Tropical Medicine and Hygiene [*British*]
FrstMar........ First Mariner Bancorp [*Associated Press*] (SAG)
FrstMF......... First M & F Corp. [*Associated Press*] (SAG)
FRSTP .... Fire-Refined Tough Pitch Copper with Silver (SAUS)
FrstVrtl .... First Virtual Holdings, Inc. [*Associated Press*] (SAG)
FRSTY .... Forestry School (SAUS)
FrSU .... Bibliotheque Nationale et Universitaire, Affaires Generales, Strasbourg, France [*Library symbol*] [*Library of Congress*] (LCLS)
FRSWG........ Fast Reactor Safety Working Group (EURO)
FRSZ........... Freezer Service [*Federal Railroad Administration identification code*]
FRT............. Facial Recognition Technology (SEWL)
FRT............. Fairbanks Rhyme Test [*Hearing*]
FRT............. Family Relations Test [*Psychology*]
FRT............. Fantasy Relaxation Technique [*Psychology*] (DHP)
FRT............. Faratahi [*Tuamotu Archipelago*] [*Seismograph station code, US Geological Survey*] (SEIS)
FRT............. Fast Reaction Team (SAUO)
FRT............. Fast Reorg Facility [*Computer science*] (HODG)
FRT............. Federal Radio and Telephone Company (SAUO)
FRT............. Federal Realty Investment Trust SBI [*NYSE symbol*] (SPSG)
FRT............. Federal Rlty Inv Tr SBI [*NYSE symbol*] (TTSB)
FRT............. Federation of Retail Tobacconists (SAUO)
FRT............. Figure Reading Test (SAUS)
FRT............. Figure Reasoning Test (SAUS)
FRT............. Fine Range Tuning [*Military*] (CAAL)
FRT............. Finish-Rolling Temperature (SAUS)
FRT............. Fire Retardant [*Technical drawings*]
FRT............. Fire-Retardant Treated
FRT............. First Response Team [*Environmental science*] (COE)
FRT............. Fixed Radar Tracking (SAUS)
FRT............. Fixed Roof Tank [*Engineering*]
FRT............. Flight Rating Test
FRT............. Flight Readiness Test
FRT............. Flight Readiness Training (MCD)
FRT............. Flow Recording Transmitter
FRT............. Fort [*Commonly used*] (OPSA)
FRT............. Fortnight
Frt.............. Fortress (SAUS)
FRT............. Forward Repair Team [*Military*] [*British*]
frt............... free return trajectory (SAUS)
FRT............. Freight (AFM)
Frt.............. Freight (EBF)
frt............... Freight (WDAA)
Frt.............. Freightage (SAUS)
frt............... Freight Ton (SAUS)
FRT............. Frequency Response Test (MCD)
FRT............. Frequency Response Tracer (SAUS)
FRT............. Front [*Telecommunications*] (TEL)
FRT............. Front [*Automotive engineering*]
FRT............. Fruit
FRT............. Full Recovery Time [*Medicine*]
FRT............. Functional Requirements Test (SAUO)
FRT............. Spartanburg, SC [*Location identifier*] [*FAA*] (FAAL)
FRTC........... Fast Reactor Training Center [*Nuclear energy*] (NUCP)
FRTC........... Finance Replacement Training Center [*World War II*]
FRTE........... Forte Software [*NASDAQ symbol*] (TTSB)
FRTE........... Forte Software, Inc. [*NASDAQ symbol*] (SAG)
FRTEF.......... Fast Reactor Thermal Engineering Facility [*Nuclear energy*] (NRCH)
FRTF........... Fixed Radio Transmission Facility
Frt Fwd........ Freight Forward [*Shipping*] (DS)
FRT FWDR... Freight Forwarder (MCD)
frt-fwdr-type MTO... freight-forwarder-type Multi-modal Transport Operator (SAUS)
frtfwt........... freight forward (SAUS)
FRTG .... Fortress Group [*NASDAQ symbol*] (TTSB)
FRTG .... Fortress Group, Inc. (The) [*NASDAQ symbol*] (SAG)
FRTH .... Fourth Financial Corp. [*NASDAQ symbol*] (NQ)
FrthF........... Fourth Financial Corp. [*Associated Press*] (SAG)
FrthFn.......... Fourth Financial Corp. [*Associated Press*] (SAG)
FrthShift ...... Fourth Shift Corp. [*Associated Press*] (SAG)
FRTIB........... Federal Retirement Thrift Investment Board (GFGA)
FRTIG .... Federal Retirement Thrift Investment Board (COE)
FRTISO .... Floating-Point Root Isolation [*Computer science*] (MDG)
FrTIALP........ Bibliotheque Americaine, Universite de Toulouse-Le Mirail, Toulouse, France [*Library symbol*] [*Library of Congress*] (LCLS)
FRTM........... Functional Requirements Traceability Matrix (ADWA)
frtn............. Fortification (SAUS)
FRTN .... Fortune
FRTN .... Front End
FRTN .... Frontend (SAUS)
FrtNt........... Frontier Natural Gas [*Commercial firm*] [*Associated Press*] (SAG)
FRTO .... Federated Road Transport Organization (SAUO)
frto.............. flight radio telephone operator (SAUS)
FRTO .... Flight Radio Telephony Operator (DA)
FRTO .... French Togoland
FRTP........... Fiberglass-Reinforced Thermoplastic
FRTP........... Fiber-Reinforced Thermoplastic (SAUS)
FRTP........... Fiber-Reinforced Thermosetting Plastic (SAUS)
FRTP........... Fire-Refined Tough Pitch Copper (SAUS)
FRTP........... Fraction of Rated Power (IEEE)
FRTPI.......... Fellow of the Royal Town Planning Institute [*British*]
Frt Ppd .... Freight Prepaid [*Business term*] (MHDW)
Frt ppd......... Freight Prepaid (WDAA)
frtr .... freighter (SAUS)
FRTR .... Frontier Insurance Group, Inc. [*NASDAQ symbol*] (COMM)
FRTRA......... Federation of Radio and Television Retailers Association (SAUS)
FRTRA......... Federation of Radio and Television Retailers Associations (SAUS)

FrtrCp .... Frontier Corp. [*Formerly, Rochester Telephone*] [*Associated Press*] (SAG)
FrtrIns......... Frontier Insurance Group, Inc. [*Associated Press*] (SAG)
FRTRNL......... Fraternal
FRTRNTY..... Fraternity
FRTS........... Fellow of the Royal Television Society (SAUO)
FRTS........... Forward Propagation by Tropospheric Scatter (SAUS)
FRTS........... Frame Relay Traffic Shaping [*Computer science*] (DINT)
FRTSAP....... Federation of Radio and Television Service Associations of Pennsylvania (SAUO)
Frt Ton......... Freight Ton (SAUS)
FRTV........... Forward Repair and Test Vehicle (SAUS)
FRTW........... Federation of Revolutionary Trade Workers (SAUO)
FRTX........... Farm City Transport [*Private rail car owner code*]
FRTX........... Fox River Trolley Museum [*Federal Railroad Administration identification code*]
FRTX........... Frontier Texas Corp. [*NASDAQ symbol*] (COMM)
FRTZ........... Fritz Companies [*NASDAQ symbol*] (TTSB)
FRTZ........... Fritz Companies, Inc. [*NASDAQ symbol*] (SAG)
FRU............ Failing-field Replaceable Unit (SAUS)
FRU............ Field Replaceable Unit [*IBM Corp.*]
FRU............ Fiji Rugby Union (SAUO)
FRU............ Fleet Radio Unit
FRU............ Fleet Requirements Unit (SAUS)
FRU............ Fleet Requirements Units [*Aircraft*]
FRU............ Forwarding Reporting Unit (SAUO)
FRU............ Free Representation Unit [*Legal term*] (DLA)
Fru............ Fructose [*A sugar*]
FRU............ Fruit
fru............ fruit sugar (SAUS)
FRU............ Frunze [*Former USSR*] [*Airport symbol*] (OAG)
FRU............ Frunze [*Former USSR*] [*Seismograph station code, US Geological Survey*] (SEIS)
FRU............ Grand Junction, CO [*Location identifier*] [*FAA*] (FAAL)
FRU............ Transportadora Fruyleg, SA de CV [*Mexico*] [*FAA designator*] (FAAC)
FRUCOM...... European Federation of Importers of Dried Fruits, Preserves, Spices and Honey (SAUO)
FRUCOM...... Federation Europeenne des Importateurs de Fruits Secs, Conserves, Epices et Miels [*European Federation of Importers of Dried Fruits, Preserves, Spices, and Honey*]
FRUCT......... Fructus [*Fruit*] [*Latin*] (ROG)
FRUD........... Front for Restoration of Unity & Democracy (SAUS)
FRUD........... Front pour la Restauration de l'Unite et de la Democratie [*Djibouti*] [*Political party*] (EY)
FRUGAL....... FORTRAN [*Formula Translating System*] Rules Used as a General Applications Language [*Computer science*]
FRUI........... Fellow of the Royal University of Ireland (ROG)
FruitL......... Fruit of the Loom, Inc. [*Associated Press*] (SAG)
FRUM........... Forum
FRUM........... Fratrum [*Of the Brothers*] [*Latin*] (ADA)
FRUMEL...... Fleet Radio Unit, Melbourne [*World War II*]
FRUMP........ Fast Reading and Understanding Memory Program [*Computer science*]
FRUMP........ Fast Reading Understanding and Memory Program (SAUS)
frumpie........ formerly-radical upwardly-mobile professional in elections (SAUS)
FRUMPS...... Frugal Responsible Unpretentious Mature Persons
FRUPAC....... Fleet Radio Unit, Pacific
FRUS........... Foreign Relations of the United States [*1900-1918*] [*A publication*]
FRUSA......... Flexible Rolled-Up Solar Array [*Air Force*]
FRUSA......... Flexible Roll-Up Solar Array (SAUS)
FRUST......... Frustillatim [*In Little Pieces*] [*Pharmacy*] (ROG)
FRUSTUM..... Frame-Based Unified Story-Understanding Model (SAUS)
FruTrail........ Fruehauf Trailer Corp. [*Associated Press*] (SAG)
frutwd.......... Fruitwood (VRA)
fru veg......... fruits and/or vegetables (SAUS)
FRU VEG...... Fruits or Vegetables [*Freight*]
FRV............ Feedwater Regulation Valve (SAUS)
FRV............ Final Rendezvous (SAUS)
FRV............ First Response Vehicle [*Emergency vehicles*]
FRV............ Fishing Research Vessel
FRV............ Flight Readiness Vehicle
frv............ flight-readiness vehicle (SAUS)
FRV............ Force Rendezvous (SAUO)
FRV............ Formant Restoring Vocoder (SAUS)
FRV............ Fur Vault, Inc. (MHDW)
FRV............ Future Reconnaissance Vehicle [*Army*]
FRVA........... Fellow of the Rating and Valuation Association [*British*] (DBQ)
FRVC........... Fellow of the Royal Veterinary College [*British*] (DI)
FRVIA......... Fellow of the Royal Victorian Institute of Architects [*British*] (ROG)
FRVP........... Fernald Residues Vitrification Plant (SAUS)
FRW............ Faraway Gold Mines Ltd. [*Vancouver Stock Exchange symbol*]
FRW............ Federal Reformatory for Women (SAUO)
FRW............ Federation of Rural Workers (SAUO)
FRW............ First Wash Realty Trust [*NYSE symbol*] (SG)
F/RW........... Flow per Relative Weight (SAUS)
FRW............ Francistown [*Botswana*] [*Airport symbol*] (OAG)
FRW............ Friction Welding
FRW............ Friedman-Robertson-Walker Theory [*Cosmology*]
f-rw-........... Rwanda [*MARC geographic area code*] [*Library of Congress*] (LCCP)
Fr wa........... Fresh Water (RIMS)
FrWAfr......... French West Africa
FRWAY........ Freeway [*Commonly used*] (OPSA)
FRWD........... Foreword
FRWF........... Forecast Wind Factor [*NWS*] (FAAC)
Fr Wf........... Fresh Wharf (SAUS)
FRWG........... Fleet Requirements Working Group (DOMA)
FRWI........... Framingham Relative Weight Index [*Cardiology*]
FRWID......... Fruit Width [*Botany*]
FRWIS......... Frost Warnings Issued (NOAA)
FRWK........... Framework [*Also, FR*] [*Genetics*] (MSA)
FRWL........... Forest, Range, and Watershed Laboratory [*Laramie, WY*] [*Department of Agriculture*] (GRD)
FRWRK........ Firework
frwy............ Freeway (MIST)
Frwy............ Freeway (TBD)
FRWY........... Freeway
FRX............ Financial Reporting Extender [*Computer science*]
frx............ firex (SAUS)
FRX............ Forest Laboratories, Inc. [*AMEX symbol*] (SPSG)
FRX............ Forest Labs [*AMEX symbol*] (TTSB)
Frx............ Fracture [*Medicine*] (EDAA)
FRXD........... Five-Level Reperforator Transmitter Distributor (ACAE)
FRXD........... Fully automatic reperforator transmitter (SAUS)
FRXD........... Fully Automatic Reperforator Transmitter Distributor [*Telecommunications*] (TEL)
FRXO........... Front Transmitter On (ACAE)
FRY............ Fairlady Energy [*Vancouver Stock Exchange symbol*]
FRY............ Federal Army of Yugoslavia (SAUS)
FRY............ Federal Republic of Yugoslavia (MILB)
FRY............ Ferry
FRY............ Fore River Railroad [*Federal Railroad Administration identification code*]
FRY............ Former Republic of Yugoslavia (SAUS)
Fry............ Freeway (SAUS)
FRY............ Friary
FRY............ Fryeburg, ME [*Location identifier*] [*FAA*] (FAAL)
Fry............ Fry on Specific Performance of Contracts [*A publication*] (DLA)
FRYA........... Frey Associates, Inc. (SAUO)
FRYC........... Fall River Yacht Club (SAUO)
Fry Lun........ Fry on Lunacy [*A publication*] (DLA)
fr yr gdnce... for your guidance (SAUS)
Fry Sp Per... Fry on Specific Performance of Contracts [*A publication*] (DLA)
Fry Vac......... Fry on the Vaccination Acts [*A publication*] (DLA)
FRZ............ Freeze [*NWS*] (FAAC)
frz............ Frieze (VRA)
FRZ............ Frozen
Fr Zabar...... Franciscus Zabarella [*Deceased, 1417*] [*Authority cited in pre-1607 legal work*] (DSA)
FRZER......... Freezer (DNAB)
FRZG........... Freezing
FRZLVL........ Freezing Level [*NWS*] (FAAC)
FRZN........... Frozen
FRZR........... Freezer (MSA)
FRZS........... Fellow of the Royal Zoological Society [*British*] (DI)
FRZSI.......... Fellow of the Royal Zoological Society of Ireland (SAUO)
FRZSScot..... Fellow of the Royal Zoological Society of Scotland
fs---........... Africa, Southern [*MARC geographic area code*] [*Library of Congress*] (LCCP)
FS............ Fabian Society [*British*] (ILCA)
FS............ Facility Status (SAUS)
F/S............ Facing South [*In outdoor advertising*] (WDMC)
FS............ Facsimile (ADA)
FS............ Factor of Safety
FS............ Factor Storage (IAA)
FS............ Fail-Safe (NASA)
FS............ Fail to Synchronize (MCD)
FS............ faint object spectrograph (SAUS)
FS............ Fairbairn-Sykes [*British military*] (DMA)
FS............ Fairchild Semiconductor (SAUS)
FS............ Faire Suivre [*Please Forward*] [*French*]
FS............ Fallschirm [*Parachute*] [*German military*]
FS............ Family Services (SAUO)
FS............ Family Stability [*Medicine*] (EDAA)
FS............ Family Status (OICC)
FS............ Famous Sayings [*Psychological testing*]
FS............ Famous Scots [*A publication*]
FS............ Fanconi Syndrome [*Medicine*] (DMAA)
FS............ Farm Sanctuary (EA)
FS............ Far Side (VLIE)
FS............ Fast-Scan [*Medicine*] (EDAA)
FS............ Fast Screening
FS............ Fast Set [*Adhesives*]
FS............ Fast Slew
FS............ Fast-Slow Wave (SAUS)
FS............ Fast-Spiking
FS............ Fast Store [*Computer science*] (TEL)
FS............ Fast Supply [*Ships*]
FS............ Father of Sion [*Roman Catholic*]
FS............ Fathers of Sion [*An association*] [*British*] (BI)
FS............ Fault Sequence (SAUS)
FS............ Fault Summary (MCD)
FS............ Feasibility Study
FS............ Federal Specification
FS............ Federal Specifications (SAUO)
FS............ Federal Standard
FS............ Federal Supplement [*A publication*] (DLA)
FS............ Federal Survey Division (SAUS)
FS............ Feedback, Stabilized
fs............ fee simple (SAUS)

FS .... Feet per Second
FS .... Felix Schlag [*Designer's mark, when appearing on US coins*]
FS .... Female Servant
FS .... Female Soldered (MSA)
FS .... Female, Spayed
FS .... Femininity Study [*Psychology*]
fs .... Femtosecond (ABAC)
FS .... Femtosecond [*One quadrillionth of a second*]
F-S .... Fenno-Shipping (SAUS)
FS .... Fermi Surface (SAUS)
FS .... Fernschreiben [*or Fernschreiber*] [*Teletype Message or Teletype*] [*German military - World War II*]
FS .... Ferrite Store (SAUS)
FS .... Ferromagnetic Storage (SAUS)
FS .... Ferromagnetic Store (SAUS)
fs .... Ferrosilite [*CIPW classification*] [*Geology*]
FS .... Ferrovie dello Stato [*Italian State Railways*]
FS .... Ferry Service (SAUS)
Fs .... Festschrift [*A publication*] (BJA)
F/S .... Fetch and Send [*Telecommunications*] (TEL)
FS .... Fiber Society (EA)
FS .... Fiberstock [*Firearms*]
FS .... Fibrosarcoma [*Medicine*] (DB)
FS .... Fichtel & Sachs [*Auto industry supplier*] [*German*]
FS .... Field of Science [*Dialog*] [*Searchable field*] [*Information service or system*] (NITA)
FS .... Field Security [*British Army detective police - a branch of Intelligence*]
FS .... Field Separator
FS .... Field Sequential (IAA)
FS .... Field Service
FS .... Field Sparrow [*Ornithology*]
FS .... Field Specification (SAUS)
FS .... Field Standard (SAUS)
FS .... Field Station
FS .... Field Stimulation [*Medicine*] (EDAA)
FS .... Field Stop (ACAE)
FS .... Field Strength (SAUS)
FS .... Field Switch (IAA)
FS .... Fighter, Single (SAUS)
FS .... Fighter Squadron (SAUO)
FS .... Fight for Sight [*Also known as NCCB*] (EA)
FS .... Figure Shift (SAUS)
FS .... Figure Switching (SAUS)
FS .... File Save [*Computer science*]
FS .... File Section (SAUS)
FS .... File Segment [*Searchable field*] (NITA)
FS .... File Separator [*Computer science*]
fs .... file separator character (SAUS)
FS .... File Server [*Computer science*] (AGLO)
FS .... File Services (SAUS)
FS .... File Source [*Computer science*]
FS .... File Store (SAUS)
FS .... File Structure (SAUS)
FS .... File System [*Computer science*] (VERA)
FS .... Filing Status [*IRS*]
FS .... Filing System (SAUS)
FS .... Filler for Smoke Shells [*Weaponry*] (NATG)
F/S .... Film and Sheet [*Plastics technology*]
fs .... Filmstrip (VRA)
FS .... Filmstrip
FS .... Filtration Society (EA)
FS .... Final Sector (SAUS)
FS .... Final Selecto (SAUS)
FS .... Final Selector [*Telecommunications*]
FS .... Final Settlement
FS .... Final Splice (SAUS)
F/S .... Final Statement [*Army*]
FS .... Finance Section (SAUO)
FS .... Financial Scribe [*Freemasonry*] (ROG)
FS .... Financial Secretary
F/S .... Financial Statement
FS .... Fine Sand (SAUS)
FS .... fine shine (SAUS)
fs .... Fine Structure (SAUS)
FS .... Finishers' Society [*A union*] [*British*]
FS .... Finish Specification
FS .... Finite State (SAUS)
FS .... Fin-Stabilised (SAUS)
FS .... Fin Stabilized [*Rocketry*]
FS .... Fire and Safety [*Technician*] [*Coast Guard*] (DOMA)
FS .... Fire Service
FS .... Fire Station [*Maps and charts*]
FS .... Firestone [*Tire casing code*]
FS .... Fire Support
FS .... Fire Suppression (MCD)
FS .... Fire Switch (KSC)
FS .... Firing Section (SAUS)
FS .... Firing Set (NG)
FS .... Firing Station (MUGU)
FS .... First Scan
FS .... First Stage [*Aerospace*]
FS .... First Step (MUGU)
FS .... First Sunday (EA)
FS .... Fiscal Service (IEEE)
FS .... Fisher Sientific Co. (SAUO)
Fs .... Fission (SAUS)
FS .... Fixed Sequence (SAUS)
FS .... Fixed Side (SAUS)
FS .... Fixed Storage (SAUS)
FS .... Fixed Store (SAUS)
FS .... Flagstaff
FS .... flag staff (SAUS)
FS .... Flameless, Smokeless [*Gunpowder*]
FS .... Flame Shielding
FS .... Flame Spectrum (SAUS)
FS .... Flammable Solid [*Medicine*] (EDAA)
FS .... Flashes per Second [*Telecommunications*] (IAA)
FS .... Flash Source (SAUS)
FS .... Flash Spotting (SAUS)
FS .... Flat Seam (DNAB)
FS .... Flat Slip (OA)
F/S .... Fleet Status [*Navy*] (MCD)
FS .... Fleet Support [*Navy*]
FS .... Fleet Surgeon
FS .... Fleischner Society (EA)
FS .... Flexible Sigmoidoscopy [*Proctoscopy*]
FS .... Flexible Sustainment (SAUS)
FS .... Flexi-Soft
FS .... Flexspline (SAUS)
FS .... Flight Safety (AFM)
FS .... Flight Security (SAUO)
FS .... Flight Segment (SAUS)
FS .... Flight Sergeant [*RAF*] [*British*]
FS .... Flight Service
FS .... Flight Simulator (AFM)
FS .... Flight Standards Service (SAUO)
FS .... Flight Surgeon
FS .... Flight System (MCD)
FS .... Floating Sign
FS .... Floating Subtract (IAA)
FS .... Float Switch [*Aerospace*] (AAG)
FS .... Flood Stage
FS .... Floor Shift
FS .... Floppy System [*Computer science*] (TIMI)
FS .... Florida Southern College (SAUO)
FS .... Florida Statute (SAUO)
FS .... Flow Switch
FS .... Fluid Statics (SAUS)
FS .... Fluid Switch
FS .... Fluorescence Spectroscopy
FS .... Fluorescent Screen (SAUS)
FS .... Flying Scholarship [*British military*] (DMA)
FS .... Flying Status
FS .... Flying Surgeon (NUJO)
FS .... Foamed Slag (SAUS)
FS .... Foaming Stability [*Food technology*]
FS .... fog over sea (SAUS)
FS .... Fog Signal [*Station*] [*Maps and charts*]
FS .... Fog Siren [*Navigation charts*]
FS .... Folio Society [*British*] (EAIO)
FS .... Follow Sender [*Telecommunications*] (TEL)
FS .... Follow Shot [*Photography*] (NTCM)
FS .... Fomant Synthesis [*Speech synthesis*] (NITA)
FS .... Font Server (SAUS)
FS .... Food Service [*Medicine*] (EDAA)
FS .... Food Supply (SAUS)
FS .... Foot-Second (ADA)
fs .... foot second (SAUS)
FS .... Foot Shock [*Biometrics*]
FS .... Foramen Spinosum [*Neuroanatomy*]
FS .... Force Structuring (MCD)
FS .... Forearm Supinated [*Medicine*]
FS .... Forecast/Surface (NATG)
FS .... Foreign Service [*Department of State*]
FS .... Foresight (AAG)
F/S .... Forest/Savanna Soils [*Agronomy*]
FS .... Forest Service [*Later, Department of Natural Resources*] [*Department of Agriculture*]
FS .... Forged Steel
FS .... Format Secondary (SAUS)
FS .... Format Selector (SAUS)
FS .... Format Specification (SAUS)
FS .... Format Statement (IAA)
FS .... Form Separator [*Computer science*] (PCM)
FS .... For Sale
FS .... Fortune Society (EA)
FS .... Forward Scatter
FS .... Forward Segment (ACAE)
FS .... Forward Support
FS .... Foundation Seed (SAUO)
FS .... Foundation State [*Dialog*] [*Searchable field*] [*Information service or system*] (NITA)
FS .... Fourier Series (SAUS)
FS .... Four Seasons Hotels [*NYSE symbol*] (SG)
FS .... Fourth Section [*of Interstate Commerce Act*]
FS .... Fractional Shortening [*Cardiology*]
FS .... Fractostratus [*Meteorology*]
Fs .... Fractostratus Cloud (WEAT)
FS .... Fracture, Simple [*Medicine*]

FS .... Fracture Site (MELL)
FS .... Fragile Site [*Medicine*] (DMAA)
FS .... frame spacing (SAUS)
F/S .... Frames per Second (NTCM)
FS .... Frame Status (ACRL)
FS .... Franklin Simon & Co. [*Retail clothing stores*]
FS .... Fred Society (EA)
FS .... Free by Servitude (ADA)
FS .... Freedom School (SAUO)
FS .... Freeman-Sheldon [*Syndrome*] [*Medicine*] (DB)
FS .... Free Safety [*Football*]
FS .... Free Sale (TVEL)
FS .... Free Standing (ADA)
FS .... Freestanding System (SAUS)
FS .... Free State (SAUO)
FS .... Free Sterol [*Biochemistry*] (OA)
FS .... Free Stock (FOTI)
FS .... Freestone (ADA)
FS .... Freeze Substitution (OA)
FS .... Freighter, Small (SAUS)
FS .... Freight Ship
FS .... Freight Supply (SAUS)
FS .... Freight Supply Vessel [*Obsolete*] [*Navy*]
FS .... French Ship (SAUS)
fs .... French Southern and Antarctic Lands [*MARC country of publication code*] [*Library of Congress*] (LCCP)
FS .... French Studies (journ.) (SAUS)
FS .... Freon Service (SAUO)
FS .... Freon Servicer (MCD)
FS .... Frequency Stability
FS .... Frequency Standard
FS .... Frequency Synthesizer [*Electronics*] (OA)
FS .... Fresno State College (SAUO)
FS .... Friendly Society [*British*] (ILCA)
FS .... Friendly Status (MCD)
FS .... Friends of Solidarity (EA)
FS .... Friends of the Shakers (EA)
FS .... Friends Society (SAUO)
FS .... Friesinger's Score (DB)
FS .... Frigate Squadron (SAUO)
fs .... front scalloped (SAUS)
FS .... Front Spar (SAUS)
FS .... Frozen Section [*Medicine*]
FS .... Frozen Shoulder (MELL)
FS .... Fruitarian Society (SAUO)
FS .... Fuel Saver [*Automotive engineering*]
FS .... fuel ship (SAUS)
FS .... Fuel Storage Subsystem (MCD)
FS .... Full and Soft [*Dietetics*]
FS .... Fullrack System
FS .... Full Scale [*Analog computers*]
FS .... Full-Scale [*Intelligence quotient*] [*Psychology*] (DAVI)
fs .... Full Score [*Music*] (GROV)
FS .... Full Service (SAUO)
FS .... Full Shot [*Photography*] (NTCM)
FS .... Full Size (MSA)
FS .... full speed (SAUS)
FS .... Full Stop (ADA)
FS .... Full Strength [*Medicine*] (EDAA)
FS .... Full Subtractor (SAUS)
FS .... Full Sun
FS .... Functional Schedules (MCD)
FS .... Functional Schematic
FS .... Functional Section
FS .... Functional Selector
FS .... Functional Specification [*Telecommunications*] (TEL)
FS .... Functional Substitution (SAUS)
FS .... Functional Symbol (SAUS)
FS .... Function Select (NITA)
FS .... Function Set
FS .... Function Specification (SAUS)
FS .... Function Statement (SAUS)
FS .... Function Study [*Medicine*] (MAE)
FS .... Function Switch (ACAE)
FS .... Function Symbol (IAA)
FS .... Furnace Sensitize (PDAA)
FS .... Furnace Slag (SAUS)
FS .... Furnace Soldering
FS .... Fuse
FS .... Fuselage Station [*Aviation*]
FS .... fusible link (SAUS)
FS .... Future Series (IAA)
FS .... Futures Spread [*Investment term*]
FS .... Future System [*IBM Corp.*] [*Computer science*]
FS .... Graduate of the Royal Air Force Staff College [*British*]
FS .... Key Airlines [*ICAO designator*] (AD)
FS .... Registry of Friendly Societies [*British*]
FS .... Sarasota Public Library, Sarasota, FL [*Library symbol*] [*Library of Congress*] (LCLS)
Fs .... Signal Framing Bits [*Telecommunications*] (ACRL)
FS .... Small Freighter (SAUS)
FS .... Sound Frequency (SAUS)
FS .... Sulfur Trioxide Chlorsulfonic Acid [*Inorganic chemistry*]
FS .... Faraday Society (ODA)
fs .... Flying Saucer (ODA)
FS³ .... Future Strategic Strategy Study [*Military*] (SDI)
FS5 .... Firing Squad Synchronization, Simulation, and Solution System (SAUS)
FSA .... Fabless Semiconductor Association (SAUO)
FSA .... Fabric Salesmen's Association (EA)
FSA .... Faculty Student Association (SAUO)
FSA .... Failing Storage Address (SAUS)
FSA .... Fallout Shelter Analysis [*or Analyst*] [*Civil Defense*]
FSA .... Family Separation Allowance [*Military*] (AABC)
FSA .... Family Service America (EA)
FSA .... Family Setzekorn Association (EA)
FSA .... Family Support Act of 1988 (WYGK)
FSA .... Family Support Administration [*Department of Health and Human Services*]
FSA .... Farm Safety Association (SAUO)
FSA .... Farm Security Administration [*Succeeded by Farmers Home Administration, 1946*]
FSA .... Farm Service Agency
FSA .... Federal Savings Association (TBD)
FSA .... Federal Securities Act (SAUO)
FSA .... Federal Security Administration (SAUO)
FSA .... Federal Security Agency [*Functions and units transferred to HEW, 1953*]
FSA .... Federal Statutes, Annotated [*A publication*] (DLA)
FSA .... Federal Student Aid
FSA .... Federal Supply Classification (SAUS)
FSA .... Federation of Schools of Accountancy (SAUS)
FSA .... Federation of South Arabia (SAUO)
FSA .... Fellesradet for det Sorlige Afrika [*Norway*]
FSA .... Fellow of the Society of Actuaries [*Society of Actuaries*] [*Designation awarded by*]
FSA .... Fellow of the Society of Antiquaries [*British*]
FSA .... Fellow of the Society of Arts [*British*]
FSA .... Fellow, Society of Actuaries
fsa .... fetal sulfoglyco-protein (SAUS)
FSA .... Fetal Sulfoglycoprotein Antigen [*Oncology*]
FSA .... Fiat Secundum Artem [*Let It Be Done According to Art*] [*Pharmacy*]
FSa .... Fibrosarcoma [*Oncology*]
FSA .... Field Safety Activity (MCD)
FSA .... Field Safety Agency (MCD)
FSA .... Field Sales Assistant (TIMI)
FSA .... Field Search Argument (VLIE)
FSA .... Field Service Addition (MCD)
FSA .... Field Specification Analysis (ACAE)
FSA .... Field Staff Association (SAUO)
FSA .... Field Support Activity [*Military*] (NVT)
FSA .... Field Support office (SAUS)
FSA .... Field Survey Association (BARN)
FSA .... File System Agent [*Telecommunications*] (PCM)
FSA .... Final Site Acceptance (NATG)
FSA .... Final System Acceptance (SAUS)
FSA .... Finance Service, Army
FSA .... Financial Sec Assurance Hldg [*NYSE symbol*] (TTSB)
FSA .... Financial Security Assurance
FSA .... Financial Security Assurance Holdings [*NYSE symbol*] (SAG)
FSA .... Financial Services Act [*British*]
FSA .... Financial Services Agreement (FOTI)
FSA .... Financial Services Authority
FSA .... Financial Stationers Association (EA)
FSA .... Financial Supervisory Agency [*Japan*]
FSA .... Financial Suppliers Association [*Later, FSF*] (EA)
FSA .... Fine Sand Aggregate (SAUS)
FSA .... Fine Slag Aggregate (SAUS)
FSA .... Fine Structure Analysis (IAA)
FSA .... Finite State Acceptor (SAUS)
FSA .... Finite State Automation (HGAA)
FSA .... Finnish Society of Adelaide [*South Australia*]
FSA .... Fire Science Abstracts [*Department of the Environment*] [*Information service or system*] (IID)
FSA .... Fire Site Assembly (MCD)
FSA .... Fire Support Area [*Military*]
FSA .... Fixed Savings Account [*Software*] (HODG)
FSA .... Fixed Slot Acknowledgement [*Telecommunications*] (OSI)
FSA .... Fixed Starting Address (SAUS)
FSA .... Flared Slot Antenna
FSA .... Flat-Plate Solar Array
FSA .... Flax Spinners Association (SAUO)
FSA .... Flexible Solar Array
FSA .... Flexible Spending Account [*Employer distribution of nontaxable income to employees*]
FSA .... Floating Storage Addressing (SAUS)
FSA .... Florida Statutes, Annotated [*A publication*] (DLA)
FSA .... Florida Student Association (SAUO)
FSA .... Fluidic Self-Assembly [*Allied Technology*]
FSA .... Fluid Sealing Association (EA)
FSA .... Flux Switch Alternator
FSA .... Food Security Act [*of 1985*]
FSA .... Food Standards Agency (GVA)
FSA .... Force Structure Allowance [*DoD*]
FSA .... Foreign Service Act
FSA .... Foreign Service Allowances [*British*]
FSA .... Foreign Service Availability [*Military*]
FSA .... Foreign Statesmen [*A publication*]
FSA .... Foreign Systems Acquisition [*Army*]
FSA .... Forensic Science Agency (WDAA)

FSA .... Formal Safety Assessment (WDAA)
FSA .... Formatter Sense Amplifier (IAA)
FSA .... Formosa Resources Corp. [*Vancouver Stock Exchange symbol*]
FSA .... Forward Sale Agreement [*EXFINCO*]
FSA .... Forward Skirt Adapter
FSA .... Forward Sortation Area [*Mailing technique*]
FSA .... Forward Spread Agreement (NUMA)
FSA .... Forward Support Area [*Military*]
FSA .... Foster Aviation [*ICAO designator*] (FAAC)
FSA .... Fracture Surface Analysis (SAUS)
FSA .... Framed Structure Analysis (VLIE)
FSA .... Fraternal Scholastic Association (SAUO)
FSA .... Fraternity Scholarship Association [*Later, College Fraternity Scholarship Officers Association*] (EA)
FSA .... Freedom Support Act (SAUO)
FSA .... Free Selectors Association (SAUO)
FSA .... Free Support Area (MUGU)
FSA .... Freethinkers Society of America (SAUO)
FSA .... French Society of Acoustics [*Formerly, Group of French-Speaking Acousticians*] (EA)
FSA .... Frequency Selective Amplifier (IAA)
FSA .... Frequency Stability Analyzer
FSA .... Friendly Societies Act [*British*] (ILCA)
FSA .... Front Suspension Arm
FSA .... Fuel Storage Area (AAG)
FSA .... Full-Scale Accuracy (IAA)
FSA .... Full-State Assumption [*Education*] (AEE)
FSA .... Fuming Sulfuric Acid (SAUS)
FSA .... Functional System Analyzer (SAUO)
FSA .... Functional Systems Audit (SAUS)
FSA .... Fuse Safe/Arm
FSA .... Future Scientists of America [*Defunct*] (EA)
FSA .... Future Surface-to-Air (SAUS)
f-sa- .... South Africa [*MARC geographic area code*] [*Library of Congress*] (LCCP)
FSA .... Federation of Small Businesses (ODA)
FSAA .... Family Service Agency of America (SAUO)
FSAA .... Family Service Association of America [*Later, FSA*] (EA)
FSAA .... Fellow of the Society of Accountants and Actuaries (SAUO)
FSAA .... Fellow of the Society of Accountants and Auditors (DD)
FSAA .... Fellow of the Society of Incorporated Accountants and Auditors [*British*] (EY)
FSAA .... Flat Slips All Around (OA)
FSAA .... Flight Simulator for Advanced Aircraft [*NASA*]
FSAA .... Folk-School Association of America [*Later, FEAA*] (EA)
FSAB .... Floating Subtract Absolute (VLIE)
FSAC .... Federal Safety Advisory Council [*Later, FACOSH*]
FSAC .... Film Studies Association of Canada
FSAC .... Finnish Society of Automatic Control (SAUO)
FSAC .... Fire Support Ada Conversion (SAUS)
FSAC .... Fire Support Armament Center [*Dover, NJ*] [*Army*] (GRD)
FSAC .... First South Africa Corp. Ltd. [*NASDAQ symbol*] (SAG)
FSAC .... Food Safety Advisory Centre (HEAS)
FSAC .... Fourth Stowage Adapter Container
FSAC .... Freight Station Accounting Code [*Railroad term*]
FSAC .... From the Stone Age to Christianity [*A publication*] (BJA)
FSACF .... First South Africa [*NASDAQ symbol*] (TTSB)
FSA/CM .... Foundation for the Study of the Arts and Crafts Movement at Roycroft (EA)
FSAD .... Female Sexual Arousal Disorder (SEAT)
FSAE .... Fellow of the National Society of Art Education [*British*]
FSAE .... Fellow of the Society of Antiquaries, Edinburgh
FSAE .... Fellow of the Society of Antiquaries of Edinburgh (SAUO)
FSAE .... Fellow of the Society of Automotive Engineers (SAUO)
FSaF .... Flagler College, St. Augustine, FL [*Library symbol*] [*Library of Congress*] (LCLS)
FSAF .... Frequency Shift Audio Frequency [*Telecommunications*] (IAA)
FSAF .... Future Scientists of America Foundation [*Defunct*]
FSAG .... Fellow of the Society of Australian Genealogists (SAUO)
FSAG .... Free Software Association Germany (SAUS)
FSaHi .... St. Augustine Historical Society, St. Augustine, FL [*Library symbol*] [*Library of Congress*] (LCLS)
FSA-HSC .... Formal Safety Assessment of High-Speed Craft (EURO)
FSAI .... Fellow of the Society of Antiquaries, Ireland (ROG)
FSAI .... Fellow of the Society of Antiquaries of Ireland (SAUO)
FSAI .... Fellow of the Society of Architectural Illustrators (ODA)
F(SA)ICE .... Fellow of the South African Institution of Civil Engineers
FSAICU .... Federation of State Associations of Independent Colleges and Universities (SAUO)
F(SA)IEE .... Fellow of the South African Institute of Electrical Engineers
F(SA)IME .... Fellow of the South African Institution of Mechanical Engineers
FSAIS .... Federation of Science Abstracting and Indexing Services (SAUO)
FSAK .... Franklin Savings Assn. (Kansas) [*NASDAQ symbol*] (COMM)
FSAL .... Fellow of the Society of Antiquaries of London (SAUO)
FSAL .... financial sector adjustment loan (SAUS)
FSALA .... Fellow of the South African Library Association
FSAM .... Federated Storage Area Management
FSAM .... Fellow of the Society of Art Masters [*British*]
FSAM .... Fellow, Society of Adolescent Medicine (CMD)
FSAM .... Flying Swiss Ambulance Maldives (SAUS)
FSAM .... Free South Africa Movement (EA)
FSAN .... Full Services Access Network (SAUS)
FSan .... Sanford Public Library, Sanford, FL [*Library symbol*] [*Library of Congress*] (LCLS)
FS & G .... Farrar, Straus & Giroux [*Publisher*]
fs & q .... functions, standards, and qualifications (SAUS)
FS & R .... Filling, Storage, and Remelt System [*Nuclear energy*] (NRCH)
FS&S .... Field Service and Support Division (ACAE)
FS & T Section ... Food Science and Technology Section (SAUS)
FsanLC .... Central Florida Library Consortium, Sanford, FL [*Library symbol*] [*Library of Congress*] (LCLS)
FSanS .... Seminole Community College, Sanford, FL [*Library symbol*] [*Library of Congress*] (LCLS)
FSANSW .... Family Support Association of New South Wales [*Australia*]
FSAO .... Family Services and Assistance Officer (AABC)
FSAO .... Fellow of the Scottish Association of Opticians (DAS)
FSAO .... Fellowship Diploma of the Scottish Association of Opticians (SAUO)
FSAP .... Factory Space Allocation Plan (MCD)
FSAP .... Federal Student Aid Program [*Department of Education*] (GFGA)
FSAP .... Field Sampling and Analysis Plan (SAUO)
FSAP .... Fleet Ships Assistance Program (SAUO)
FSAP .... Food Security Action Programme (SAUS)
FSAP .... Full Spectrum Active Protection (SEWL)
FSAPO .... Fade Sound and Picture Out [*Cinematography*] (NTCM)
FSA-R .... Family Separation Allowance (Restricted Station) [*Military*] (DNAB)
FSAR .... Fiat Secundum Artem Reglas [*Let It Be Done According to the Rules of the Art*] [*Pharmacy*]
FSAR .... Filling, Storage, and Remelt System [*Nuclear energy*] (IAA)
FSAR .... Final Safety Analysis Report [*NASA*] (KSC)
FSAR .... Final Safety Assessment Report (SAUO)
FSAR .... Forest Service Acquisition Regulation [*A publication*] (AAGC)
FSAR .... Fuel Systems Analysis Report (SAA)
FSArc .... Fellow of the Society of Architects [*British*]
FSArch .... Fellow of the Society of Architects [*British*]
FSA-S .... Family Separation Allowance (Shipboard Operations) [*Military*] (DNAB)
FSAS .... Fellow of the Society of Antiquaries of Scotland
FSAS .... Flight Service Automation System [*FAA*] (TAG)
FSAS .... Fluidic Stability Augmentation System [*for helicopters*]
FSAS .... Force Structure Assessment System [*Model*] [*Army*]
FSAS .... Fuel Savings Advisory Systems (SAUS)
FSA Scot .... Fellow of the Society of Antiquaries of Scotland
FSAS/INS .... Fuel Savings Advisory System / Inertial Navigation System [*Air Force*]
FSASM .... Fellow of the South African School of Mines (SAUS)
FSA-T .... Family Separation Allowance (Temporary Duty) [*Military*] (DNAB)
FSAT .... Financial Svcs. Acquisition Corp. [*NASDAQ symbol*] (SAG)
FSAT .... Full-Scale Aerial [*or Afterburning*] Target
FSAT .... FutureSat Industries, Inc. (SAUO)
FSATE .... Futuresat Industries, Inc. [*NASDAQ symbol*] (COMM)
FSAU .... First South Africa Corp. Ltd. [*NASDAQ symbol*] (SAG)
FSAUF .... First South Africa Unit [*NASDAQ symbol*] (TTSB)
FSAVC .... Free-Standing Additional Voluntary Contribution [*Pension fund payment option*] [*British*]
FSAW .... First Savings Association of Wisconsin (SAUO)
FSAW .... First South Africa Corp. Ltd. [*NASDAQ symbol*] (SAG)
FSAWF .... First South Africa Wrrt'A' [*NASDAQ symbol*] (TTSB)
FSAZ .... First South Africa Corp. Ltd. [*NASDAQ symbol*] (SAG)
FSAZF .... First South Africa Wrrt'B' [*NASDAQ symbol*] (TTSB)
FSB .... Falange Socialista Boliviana [*Bolivian Socialist Phalange*] [*Political party*] (PPW)
FSB .... Fallout Studies Branch [*AEC*]
FSB .... Family Services Branch [*Australian Capital Territory*]
Fsb .... Federal Savings Bank (TBD)
FSB .... Federal Savings Bank
FSB .... Federal Security Council (Russia) [*Political party*] (PSAP)
FSB .... Federal Specification Board
FSB .... Federal Supplemental Benefits
FSB .... Federation of Small Businesses (WDAA)
FSB .... Female Sexual Biomass [*Botany*]
FSB .... Fetal Scalp Blood [*Fetal monitoring*] (CPH)
FSB .... Field Selection Board [*Military*]
FSB .... Field Service Bulletin (AAG)
FSB .... Final Selection Board (SAUO)
FSB .... Final Staging Base (AFM)
FSB .... Financial Corporation of Santa Barbara (SAUO)
FSB .... Financial Systems Branch (SAUO)
FSB .... Fire-control Switchboard (SAUS)
FSB .... Fire Support Base [*Army*] (AABC)
FSB .... Flat Slip on Bottom (OA)
FSB .... Fleet Satellite Broadcast (SAUO)
FSB .... Fleet Satellite Broadcasting [*Navy*] (MCD)
FSB .... Floating Subtract [*Computer science*] (IAA)
FSB .... Floating Supply Base [*Military*] (PDAA)
FSB .... Food Supply Board [*Ministry of Food*] [*British*] [*World War II*]
FSB .... Foreign Science Bulletin
FSB .... For Small Business (SAUS)
FSB .... Forward Space Block (CMD)
FSB .... Forward Staging Base (SAUO)
FSB .... Forward Support Base
FSB .... Forward Support Battalion [*Army*] (INF)
FSB .... Fractional Sampling Bit (VLIE)
FSB .... Free Storage Block [*Computer science*] (IAA)
FSB .... Front Side Bus (SAUS)
FSB .... Front Striker Bulletin [*An association*] (EA)
FSB .... Fuel Storage Basin [*Nuclear energy*]
FSB .... Functional Specification Block [*Telecommunications*] (TEL)
FSB .... Functional System Block (SAUS)
FSb .... Satellite Beach Public Library, Satellite Beach, FL [*Library symbol*] [*Library of Congress*] (LCLS)

FSBA........ Federal and State Business Assistance Database [*National Technical Information Service*] [*Information service or system*] (CRD)
FSBA........ Finnsheep Breeders Association (EA)
FSBA........ Florida School Boards Association (SAUO)
FSBA........ Fluorosulfonylbenzoyl Adenosine [*Biochemistry*]
FSBA........ Food Service Brokers of America [*Defunct*] (EA)
FSBC........ 1st State Bancorp, Inc. [*NASDAQ symbol*] (NASQ)
FSBC........ First Savings Bank [*NASDAQ symbol*] (NQ)
FSBC........ First SB Clovis N Mex [*NASDAQ symbol*] (TTSB)
FSBC........ Foreign Service Buildings Commission (SAUO)
FSBF........ First Savings Bank of Florida (SAUO)
FSBF........ FSB Financial Corp. [*NASDAQ symbol*] (SAG)
FSB Fin........ FSB Fiancial Corp. [*Associated Press*] (SAG)
FSBG........ Finger-Stick Blood Gas (MEDA)
FSBG........ Fingerstick Blood Glucose [*Medicine*] (MELL)
FSBG........ First Federal Savings Bank of Georgia [*NASDAQ symbol*] (COMM)
FSBI........ Falange Socialista Boliviana de Izquierda [*Bolivian Socialist Phalange of the Left*] [*Political party*] (PPW)
FSBI........ Fellow of the Savings Bank Institute [*British*] (ODBW)
FSBI........ Fidelity Bancorp [*NASDAQ symbol*] (SAG)
FSBI........ Fisheries Society of the British Isles
FSBIC........ First Stop Business Information Center (SAUO)
FSBkNJ........ First Savings Bank FSLA Perth Amboy NJ [*Associated Press*] (SAG)
FSBL........ Feasible (MSA)
FSBL........ Fusible (MSA)
FSBL CUT........ Fusible Cut-out (SAUS)
fsbly........ feasibility (SAUS)
FSBM........ Full-Strength Breast Milk [*Neonatology*] (DAVI)
FSBO........ For Sale by Owner [*Real estate ads*] [*Pronounced "fizz-bo"*]
FSBPRT........ Free Storage Block Pointer (HGAA)
FSBR........ Financial Statement and Budget Report [*British*]
FSBR........ fractional solar broadband radiometer (SAUS)
FSBS........ First Ashland Financial [*NASDAQ symbol*] (TTSB)
FSBS........ First Ashland Financial Corp. [*NASDAQ symbol*] (SAG)
FSBS........ Fixed Submarine Broadcast System (SAUO)
FSBS........ Fleet Satellite Broadcast System (SAUO)
FSBS........ Front Supply Base Sections (MCD)
FSBSEM........ Free Storage Block Semaphore [*Computer science*] (IAA)
FSBT........ First State [*NASDAQ symbol*] (TTSB)
FSBT........ First State Corp. [*NASDAQ symbol*] (SAG)
FSBT........ Fowler Single Breath Test [*Medicine*] (DMAA)
FSBTh........ Fellow of the Society of Health and Beauty Therapists [*British*] (DBQ)
FSBW........ Frame Space Bandwidth Product (IAA)
FSBWA........ First Savings Bank Washington Bancorp, Inc. [*Associated Press*] (SAG)
FSBW Product... Frame Space Bandwidth Product (SAUS)
FSBX........ Framingham Savings Bank [*NASDAQ symbol*] (SAG)
FSBX........ Framingham Svgs Bank (MA) [*NASDAQ symbol*] (TTSB)
FSC........ Brothers of the Christian Schools (TOCD)
fsc........ Brothers of the Christian Schools (TOCD)
FSC........ Fabricated Steel Construction [*Bethlehem Steel Corp.*]
FSC........ Facilities Service Center (SAUO)
FSC........ Facility Security Clearance (ACAE)
FSC........ Fairmont State College [*West Virginia*]
FSC........ Family Services Bureau (SAUS)
FSC........ Family Services Center [*Military*]
FSC........ Farm Safety Council (SAUO)
FSC........ Fatigue Safety Coefficient [*Durability testing*]
FSC........ Fat-Storing Cell [*Liver anatomy*]
FSC........ Fault Simulation Comparator
FSC........ Federal Safety Council
FSC........ Federal Salary Commission (SAUS)
FSC........ Federal Science Council (SAUO)
FSC........ Federal Simulation Center
FSC........ Federal Sports Club [*Australia*]
FSC........ Federal Stock [*or Supply*] Catalog (NG)
FSC........ Federal Stock Class (SAUO)
FSC........ Federal Stock [*or Supply*] Classification [*Army*]
FSC........ Federal Stock Code (SAUS)
FSC........ Federal Stock Control
FSC........ Federal Supplemental Compensation [*Unemployment insurance*] (OICC)
FSC........ Federal Supply Catalog (MCD)
FSC........ Federal Supply Category (SAUS)
FSC........ Federal Supply Classification [*DoD*] (MCD)
FSC........ Federal Supply Code (MCD)
FSC........ Federal Systems Center (SAUS)
FSC........ Federation of Southern Cooperatives [*Later, FSC/LAF*] (EA)
FSC........ Federation Socialiste Caledonienne [*Caledonian Socialist Federation*] [*Political party*] (PPW)
FSC........ Fellow of the Society of Chiropodists (ODA)
FSC........ Fellowship of Southern Churchmen [*Later, Committee of Southern Churchmen*] (EA)
FSC........ Fest Resources [*Vancouver Stock Exchange symbol*]
FSC........ Fibrous Sausage Casing
FSC........ Field Separator Character (SAUS)
FSC........ Field Standard C (SAUS)
FSC........ Field Studies Council [*British*] (ARC)
FSC........ Field Study Coordinator [*Military*] (MCD)
FSC........ Field Support Center [*Military*] (IAA)
FSC........ Field Survey Company [*British military*] (DMA)
FSC........ Field System Center (VLIE)
FSC........ Figari [*Corsica*] [*Airport symbol*] (OAG)
FSC........ File Server Control [*Computer science*] (DOMA)
FSC........ File Structure Common [*Computer science*] (TIMI)
FSC........ File System Control [*Computer science*]
FSC........ Filing Status Code [*IRS*]
FSC........ Film Stowage Container
FSC........ Final Subcircuit [*An enzyme*] (IAA)
FSC........ Final Systems Check [*NASA*] (KSC)
FSC........ Financial Services Council (NTPA)
FSC........ Finite State Channel (IAA)
FSC........ Fire Service College [*British*]
FSC........ Fire Service Council (SAUO)
FSC........ Fire Support Center [*Army*] (DOMA)
FSC........ Fire Support Coordination [*Military*]
FSC........ Fire Support Coordinator [*Environmental science*] (COE)
FSC........ First-Stage Conduit [*Aerospace*]
FSC........ Five Star Corporation (SAUO)
FSC........ Fixed Satellite Communications (DNAB)
FSC........ Fixed Self Contacting (VLIE)
FSC........ Fixed Self-Contacting (SAUS)
FSC........ Fixed Silicon Capacitor
FSC........ Flame-Sprayed Coating (SAUS)
FSC........ Flame Spread Classification [*For polymers*]
FSC........ Fleet Satellite Communications [*DoD*]
FSC........ Fleet Systems Capable (NVT)
FSC........ Flexible Shielded Cable
FSC........ Flight Safety Committee (SAUS)
FSC........ Flight Security Controller [*Military*]
FSC........ Flight Sensor Computer (ACAE)
FSC........ Flight Service Center
FSC........ Florida Southern College, Lakeland, FL [*OCLC symbol*] (OCLC)
FSC........ Florida Sun Conference (PSS)
FSC........ Florida Supreme Court (SAUO)
F-SC........ Florida Supreme Court, Tallahassee, FL [*Library symbol*] [*Library of Congress*] (LCLS)
FSC........ Fluid Storage Container
FSC........ Flying Status Code (AFM)
FSC........ Food Safety Consortium (ADWA)
FSC........ Food Safety Council [*Defunct*] (EA)
FSC........ Food Standards Code [*Australia*]
FSC........ Food Standards Committee [*British*]
FSC........ Food Storage Cell
FSC........ Food Supplement Co. [*British*]
FSC........ Foolscap (NTCM)
FSC........ Force Structure Committee (AFM)
FSC........ Foreign Sales Corp. [*See also Domestic International Sales Corp. - DISC*]
FSC........ Foreign Service Commission (SAUO)
fsc........ foreign service credit (SAUS)
FSC........ Foreign Service Credits [*Military*]
FSC........ Foreign Staff College [*British*]
FSC........ Forer Sentence Completion Test [*Psychology*] (DAVI)
FSC........ Forestry Safety Council (SAUO)
FSC........ Forest Stewardship Council
FSC........ Forward Scatter (NATG)
FSC........ Forward Support Company [*Military*]
FSC........ Foundation for Student Communication [*Princeton, NJ*] (EA)
FSC........ Foundation for the Study of Cycles (EA)
FSC........ Four Star Aviation, Inc. [*Virgin Islands*] [*ICAO designator*] (FAAC)
FSC........ Fracture, Simple Comminuted [*Orthopedics*] (DAVI)
FSC........ Franklin Stores Corporation (SAUO)
FSC........ Fratres Scholarum Christianarum [*Institute of the Brothers of the Christian Schools*] [*Also known as Christian Brothers*] (EAIO)
FSC........ Free Secreting Component [*Immunology*]
FSC........ Frequency Shift Converter
FSC........ Fresno Service Center [*IRS*]
FSC........ Fresno State College [*Later, California State University, Fresno*]
FSC........ Friends of the Superior Court (EA)
FSC........ Friends Service Committee (SAUO)
FSC........ Friends Service Council [*Quakers*]
FSC........ Frostburg State College (SAUS)
FSC........ Fuel Savings Computer (SAUS)
FSC........ Fuel Scheduling Computer (MCD)
FSC........ Fuel System Controller (HLLA)
FSC........ Fuel Systems Capability (MCD)
FSC........ Full Scale
FSC........ Full Scale range (SAUS)
FSC........ Full-Service Contractor (SEWL)
FSC........ Full Systems Capable [*Military*] (CAAL)
FSC........ Fully Self-Contained (ADA)
FSC........ Funding Sources Clearinghouse, Inc. (IID)
FSC........ Fuscaldo [*Italy*] [*Seismograph station code, US Geological Survey*] (SEIS)
FSC........ Future Studies Centre [*British*] (CB)
FSC........ Selected Judgments of the Federal Supreme Court [*1956-61*] [*Nigeria*] [*A publication*] (DLA)
FSC........ Subcarrier Frequency (SAUS)
FSC........ Federal Supreme Court (ODA)
FSCA........ Fellow of the Society of Company and Commercial Accountants [*British*] (DCTA)
FSCA........ Full Systems Capable Aircraft (ACAE)
FSCAIS........ Family Services Center Automated Information System (SAUO)
F scan........ F Scanner (SAUS)
f/scap........ foolscap (SAUS)
FSCAP........ Funeral Service Consumer Assistance Program (EA)
FSCATT........ Fire Support Combined Arms Tactical Trainer [*Army*] (RDA)
FSCB........ Fielded Software Control Board [*Army*]
FSCB........ File System Control Block [*Computer science*] (IBMDP)

FSCC........... Federal Supply Classification Code
FSCC........... Federal Surplus Commodities Corp.
FSCC........... Ferrous Scrap Consumers Coalition (EA)
FSCC........... Field Service Communications Center (TIMI)
FSCC........... Figure Skating Coaches of Canada [*See also EPAC*]
FSCC........... Financial Services Call Center (GART)
FSCC........... Fire Support Control Center (ACAE)
FSCC........... Fire Support Coordination Center [*Military*]
FSCC........... Fire Support Co-ordination Centre (SAUS)
FSCC........... First Federal Savings Bank of Charlotte County (Florida) [*NASDAQ symbol*] (COMM)
FSCC........... First-Stage Conduit Container [*Aerospace*]
FSCC........... Food Surplus Commodities Corp.
FSCC........... Fracture, Simple, Complete, Comminuted (SAUS)
FSCE........... Fire Support Coordination Element [*Military*]
FSCE........... Free-Solution Capillary Electrophoresis [*Physical chemistry*]
fsce........... fre-support coordination element (SAUS)
FSCEA........... French-Speaking Comparative Education Association [*See also AFEC*] [*Sevres, France*] (EAIO)
FSCEH........... Fellow, Society for Clinical & Experimental Hypnosis (CMD)
FSCEN........... Flight Service Center
FSCFC........... Friends of Shaun Cassidy Fan Club (EA)
FSCG........... Federal Supply Classification Group (AFM)
FSCGN........... Federal Supply Classification Group Number (SAUO)
FSCH........... Form and Structure of Corporate Headings [*Cataloguing*] [*Association for Library Collections and Technical Services*]
FSCH........... Fulbright Scholarship
FSCI........... Frequency Space Characteristic Impedance
FSCIL........... Federal Supply Catalog Identification List (MSA)
FSCJ........... Congregatio Filiorum Sacratissimi Cordis Jesu [*Sons of the Sacred Heart*] [*Verona Fathers*] [*Roman Catholic religious order*]
FSCJ........... Friendly Society of Carpenters and Joiners [*A union*] [*British*]
FSCK........... File System Check [*Computer science*] (VLIE)
fsck........... File System Check and repair (SAUS)
FSCK........... File System Consistency Check [*Unix*] (VERA)
FSCL........... Federal Supply Classification Listing
FSCL........... Fire Support Control Line (SAUO)
FSCL........... Fire Support Coordination Line [*Military*] (AABC)
FSC/LAF........... Federation of Southern Cooperatives and Land Assistance Fund (EA)
FSCM........... Federal Standard Codes of Manufacturers (ACAE)
FSCM........... Federal Stock Code for Manufacturers (AAEL)
FSCM........... Federal Supply Code for Manufacturers
FSCM........... Fire Support Coordinating Measure (SAUS)
FSCM........... Fire Support Coordination Measure [*Military*] (INF)
FSC/MMAC........... Federal Supply Classification/Material Management Aggregation (MCD)
FSCN........... Free State Consolidated Gold [*NASDAQ symbol*] (SAG)
FSCNHA........... Federal Service Campaign for National Health Agencies [*Later, National Health Agencies for the Combined Federal Campaign*] (EA)
FSC (Nig)........... Judgments of the Federal Supreme Court [*1956-61*] [*Nigeria*] [*A publication*] (DLA)
FSCNM........... Federal Supply Code for Non-Manufacturers
FSCNY........... Free St Con Gld Mines ADR [*NASDAQ symbol*] (TTSB)
FSCO........... Federation of Straight Chiropractic Organizations (EA)
FSCO........... Federation of Straight Chiropractors and Organizations [*Formerly, Federation of Straight Chiropractic Organizations*] (EA)
FSCO........... First Security [*NASDAQ symbol*] (TTSB)
FSCO........... First Security Corp. [*NASDAQ symbol*] (NQ)
FS/COLS........... Fire Support Team and Combat Observation Lasing System [*Army*]
FSCOORD........... Fire Support Coordinator [*Military*] (AABC)
FSCP........... Feasibility Study Change Proposal (MCD)
FSCP........... Federal/State Cooperative Program for Population Estimates and Projections (OICC)
FSCP........... Fellow of the Society of Certified Professionals [*British*] (DBQ)
FSCP........... Fire Sensor Control Panel (MCD)
FSCP........... Firing Site Command Post [*Army*] (AABC)
FSCP........... Foolscap [*Paper*] (ROG)
FSCP........... Full Spectrum Color Projector (ACAE)
FSCR........... Federal Screw Works [*NASDAQ symbol*] (NQ)
FSCR........... Field Select Command Register
FSCR........... Filed Select Command Register (SAUS)
FSCR........... Final System Concept Review (ACAE)
FSCR........... First Ship Configuration Review [*Navy*]
FSCR........... Fuel Storage Control Room [*Nuclear energy*] (NRCH)
FSCRC........... Follow-on Small Computer Requirements Contract (SAUO)
FSCS........... Federal-State Cooperative System for Public Library Data Collection (SAUO)
FSCS........... Federal Supply Classification System
FSCS........... Fire Support Coordination Section [*Military*]
FSCS........... Fleet Satellite Communications System [*DoD*] (DNAB)
FSCS........... Foresight Sierra Communications System (MCD)
FSCS........... Forged Straight Clamp Strap (SAUS)
FSCS........... Frequency Shift Communications System
FSCS........... Fuel Storage Cable Spread [*Nuclear energy*] (NRCH)
FSCS........... Functional Standard Conformance Statement [*Telecommunications*]
FSCS........... Future Scout and Cavalry System [*Army*]
FSCS........... Future Scout Combat System [*Army*]
FSCSI........... Fast SCSI (SAUS)
FSCSS........... Flexible Satellite Communications Systems Simulator (CCCA)
FSCT........... Federation of Societies for Coatings Technology (EA)
FSCT........... Fellow of the Society of Cardiological Technicians [*British*] (DBQ)
FSCT........... Fellow of the Society of Commercial Teachers [*British*] (DBQ)
FSCT........... Fire Support Control Terminal (SAUS)
FSCT........... Five-Soldier Crew Tent
FSCT........... Floyd Satellite Communications Terminal
FSCTT........... Fire Support Coordination Team Trainer (DOMA)
FSCU........... Fire Support Coordination Unit (SAUS)
FSCU........... Frequency Select Control Unit (MCD)
FSCUSA........... Flying Senior Citizens of United States of America [*Defunct*] (EA)
FSCV........... Fire Support Combat Vehicle (MCD)
FSCW........... Fast Space Charge Wave (IAA)
FSCW........... Florida State College for Women (SAUO)
FSCWC........... Florida Space Coast Writers Conference (EA)
FSCX........... FastComm Communications [*NASDAQ symbol*] (TTSB)
FSCX........... FastComm Communications Corp. [*NASDAQ symbol*] (NQ)
FSD........... Fabrication Support Division (SAUO)
FSD........... Federal Systems Division (SAA)
FSD........... Federation des Socialistes Democrates [*Federation of Democratic Socialists*] [*France*] [*Political party*] (PPE)
FSD........... Female Sexual Disorder (SEAT)
FSD........... Female Sexual Dysfunction
FS/D........... Field Service/Dispatch (GART)
FSD........... Field Services Division (SAUO)
FSD........... Field Supply Depot (SAUS)
FSD........... Field Support Diagram (IAA)
FSD........... File Search Device (SAUS)
FSD........... File-Set Description [*Computer science*]
FSD........... File System Driver (PCM)
FSD........... Finance and Secretarial Department (SAUO)
FSD........... Financial Sector Deepening
FSD........... Financial Services Division (SAUS)
FSD........... Financial Systems Development (TIMI)
FSD........... Fire Service Department (SAUO)
FSD........... First-Degree Stochastic Dominance [*Statistics*]
FSD........... First Ship Delivered (DNAB)
FSD........... Fisher Significant Difference (PDAA)
FSD........... Flight Service Director (SAUO)
FSD........... Flight Simulation Division [*Johnson Space Center*] [*NASA*] (NASA)
FSD........... Flight Situation Display
FSD........... Flight Support Division (SAUO)
FSD........... Flue Gas Desulfurization (SAUS)
FSD........... Fluidic Setting Device
FSD........... Fluid System Design [*NASA*] (SPST)
FSD........... Flying Spot Device (SAUS)
FSD........... Flying Spot Digitizer
FSD........... Focal Skin Distance [*Radiology*]
FSD........... Focus to Source Distance (SAUS)
FSD........... Force Spectral Density
FSD........... Forecast Support Date
FSD........... Foreign Sea Duty
FSD........... Formal Syntax Definition [*Aviation*]
FSD........... Forum for Sustainable Development (SAUS)
FSD........... Foster-Seeley Discriminator
FSD........... Foundation for Science and Disability (PAZ)
FSD........... Frequency Ship Demodulator (DNAB)
FSD........... Fuel Supply Depot [*Military*]
FSD........... Full-Scale Deflection [*Instrumentation*]
FSD........... Full Scale Development (SAUO)
fsd........... full-scale development (SAUS)
FSD........... Full Size Detail (SAUS)
FSD........... Functional Sequence Diagram [*Computer science*]
FSD........... Functional Statement Document (SAUO)
FSD........... Functional System Description (SAUO)
FSD........... Functional System Design (ACAE)
FSD........... Funky Site of the Day (SAUO)
FSD........... Fuzzy Simple Disjunctive (SAUS)
FSD........... Sioux Falls [*South Dakota*] [*Airport symbol*] (OAG)
FSD........... Sioux Falls, SD [*Location identifier*] [*FAA*] (FAAL)
FSDA........... Frequency Spectral Density Analysis (PDAA)
FSDB........... Fishery Statistics Data Base [*National Marine Fisheries Service*] [*Information service or system*] (MSC)
FSDC........... Federal Statistical Data Center (IEEE)
FSDC........... Fellow of the Society of Dyers and Colourists [*British*]
FSDC........... Fiber Supported Droplet Combustion (SAUS)
FSDE........... Fission Suppressed Direct Enrichment (SAUS)
FSDET........... Field System Design Evaluation Test (SAUO)
FSDH........... Fondation de la Sante et des Droits de l'Homme [*Foundation for Health and Human Rights*] (EA)
FSDH........... Forsyth School for Dental Hygienists (SAUO)
FSDI........... Four-Stroke, Direct-Injection [*Automotive engineering*]
FSDL........... Foreign Service Drafting Leave (SAUO)
FSDLWG........... Fundamental Standard Data Link Working Group [*NATO*] (NATG)
FSDM........... Financial Services Data Model (GART)
FSDM........... First Stage Digital Multiplexer (CCCA)
FSDM........... Free Surface Deformation Measurement System (SAUO)
FSDM........... Full-Scale Development Model (MCD)
FSDO........... Flight Safety District Office (SAUS)
FSDO........... Flight Standards District Office [*FAA*]
FSDP........... Full-Scale Development Phase (MCD)
FSDPANSW........... Friendly Societies', Dispensaries, and Pharmacies Association of New South Wales [*Australia*]
FSDPS........... Flight Service Data Processing System [*FAA*] (TAG)
FSDR........... Final Site Design Review (SAUO)
FSDR........... Final Software Design Review
FSDR........... Final System Design Review (SAUS)
FSDR........... Functional System Design Requirement (SAUO)
FSDS........... Fin Stabilized Discarding Sabot (MCD)
FSDS........... Flagship Data System (MCD)

FSDT........... Fiscal Service of the Department of Treasury (SAUO)
FSDT........... Functional System Design Team (SAUO)
FSDU........... Full Scale Demonstration Unit (ACAE)
FSDU........... Fur Skin Dressers' Union [*British*]
FSDVP......... Freiheitlich Soziale Deutsche Volkspartei [*Liberal Social German People's Party*] [*Germany*] [*Political party*] (PPW)
FSDWS......... Fixed Site Detection and Warning System (ACAE)
FSE............. Brothers of the Holy Eucharist (TOCD)
fse.............. Brothers of the Holy Eucharist (TOCD)
FSE............. Facilities System Engineer
FSE............. Facility Support Equipment
FSE............. Faculty of Surgeons of England
FSE............. Faculty of Surveyors of England (SAUO)
fse.............. False (SAUS)
FSE............. Family Stop Eating [*A table signal at a meal where guests are present*]
FSE............. Farm Sanctuary-East [*An association*] (EA)
FSE............. Fat-Specific Element [*Genetics*]
FSE............. Federation of Stock Exchanges (WDAA)
FSE............. Federation of Swaziland Employers (SAUO)
FSE............. Feline Spongiform Encephalopathy (SAUS)
FSE............. Fellow of the Society of Engineers [*British*]
FSE............. Fetal Scalp Electrode [*Obstetrics*] (DAVI)
FSE............. Field Sales Engineer (TIMI)
FSE............. Field Scanned (SAUS)
FSE............. Field Scanned Electron Nuclear Double Resonance (AAEL)
FSE............. Field Service Engineer [*Military*]
FSE............. Field Service Engineering (SAUS)
FSE............. Field Support Engineer (SAUO)
FSE............. Field Support Engineering
FSE............. Field Support Equipment [*Military*]
FSE............. File Scan Equipment (SAUS)
FSE............. File Server Ethernet (ADWA)
FSE............. Filles du Saint Esprit [*Institute of the Franciscan Sisters of the Eucharist*] [*Roman Catholic religious order*]
FSE............. Fill Start Entry [*Computer science*]
FSE............. Fini Sec Assurance 6.95%Sr'QUIDS' [*NYSE symbol*] (SG)
FSE............. Fire Support Element [*Military*] (AABC)
FSE............. First Star Energy [*Vancouver Stock Exchange symbol*]
FSE............. Fleet Supportability Evaluation (MCD)
FSE............. Flight Simulation Engineer (MCD)
FSE............. Flight Support Equipment (KSC)
FSE............. Florida Solar Energy Center, Cape Canaveral, FL [*OCLC symbol*] (OCLC)
FSE............. Fluid Shaft Encoder
FSE............. Formerly Socialist Economy (ECON)
FSE............. Forward Security Element [*Soviet military force*]
FSE............. Forward Support Element
FSE............. Fosston, MN [*Location identifier*] [*FAA*] (FAAL)
FSE............. Frankfurt Stock Exchange (SAUS)
FSE............. Full Screen Editor [*Computer science*] (IAA)
FSE............. [*The*] Institute of the Franciscan Sisters of the Eucharist (TOCD)
FSEA........... Foil Stamping and Embossing Association (NTPA)
FSEA........... Food Service Executives' Association [*Later, IFSEA*] (EA)
FSEA........... Full Shear Energy Absorption (PDAA)
FSEB........... Fire Services Examination Board (WDAA)
FSEB........... Fuel Storage Exhaust Blower [*Nuclear energy*] (NRCH)
FSEC........... Faculty Senate Executive Committee (SAUS)
FSEC........... Fairchild Space and Electronics Company (ACAE)
FSEC........... Federal Securities and Exchange Commission [*New Deal*]
FSEC........... Federal Software Exchange Center
FSEC........... Federal Specifications Executive Committee
fsec............ Femtosecond [*One quadrillionth of a second*]
FSEC........... Florida Solar Energy Center [*University of Central Florida*] [*Research center*] (RCD)
FSecCp........ First Security Corp. [*Associated Press*] (SAG)
FSECO......... First-Stage Engine Cutoff [*Aerospace*]
FSED........... Full-Scale Engineering Development (MCD)
FSEE........... Federal Service Entrance Examination [*Later, PACE*] [*Civil Service*]
FSEE........... Field-Stimulated Exoelectron Emission [*Physics*]
FSEE........... Flying Service Engineering & Equipment (SAUO)
FSEEEC....... Federation of Stock Exchanges in the European Community [*Belgium*] (EAIO)
FSEF........... Foreign Service Educational Foundation (SAUO)
FSEI............ First Seismic (EFIS)
FSEI............ Food Service Equipment Industry [*Later, FEDA*] (EA)
FSELX.......... Fidelity Select Ptfl: Electronics [*Mutual fund ticke symbol*] (SG)
FSEO........... Flight Systems Engineering Order (MCD)
FSEOG......... Federal Supplemental Educational Opportunity Grants (SAUS)
FSEP........... Federal Software Exchange Program (AAGC)
FSER........... Field Service Engineering (AAG)
FSER........... Field Service Engineering Report (SAUS)
FSERA......... Fellow of the Scientific and Experimental Research Association (SAUO)
FSERI.......... Federal Solar Energy Research Institute [*Energy Research and Development Administration*]
FSERT......... Fellow of the Society of Electronic and Radio Technicians [*British*] (DBQ)
F-SERT........ Forward State Emergency Response Team (SAUO)
FSES........... Federal-State Employment Service (SAUO)
FSES........... Federation of Swiss Employees' Societies
FSES........... Fire Safety Evaluation System [*National Institute of Standards and Technology*]
FSES........... Friendly Society of Engravers and Sketchmakers [*Later, MPEA*]
FSETP......... Food Stamp Employment and Training Program [*Department of Agriculture*] (GFGA)
FSEUCA....... Federal-State Emergency Unemployment Compensation Act [*1970*]
FSF............. Fading Safety Factor [*Telecommunications*] (TEL)
FSF............. Federal Security Forces
FSF............. Fellow of the Institute of Shipping and Forwarding Agents [*British*] (ODBW)
FSF............. Fibrin-Stabilizing Factor [*Factor XIII*] [*Also, LLF*] [*Hematology*]
FSF............. Field Site Facility
FSF............. Financial Services Industry (TDOB)
FSF............. Financial Suppliers Forum (EA)
FSF............. Financial Suspense File [*Army*]
FSF............. First Static Firing (MCD)
FSF............. Fixed Sequence Format
FSF............. Flash Smelting Furnace (SAUS)
FSF............. Fleet Servicing Facility (SAUO)
FSF............. Fleet Sweeping Flotilla (SAUS)
FSF............. Flight Safety Foundation (EA)
FSF............. Folder-staging Facility (SAUS)
FSF............. Forensic Sciences Foundation (EA)
FSF............. Forward Space File (CMD)
FSF............. Free Software Foundation (DDC)
FSF............. Front of Socialist Forces (SAUO)
FSF............. Fuel Storage Facility [*Nuclear energy*] (NRCH)
FSF............. Fuel Supply Facility (COE)
FSF............. Fully Submerged Foil [*Hydrofoil craft*]
f-sf-........... Sao Tome and Principe [*MARC geographic area code*] [*Library of Congress*] (LCCP)
FSFA........... Farm Sector Financial Accounts (SAUO)
FSFA........... Federal Student Financial Aid [*Department of Education*] (GFGA)
FSFA........... Federation of Specialised Film Associations [*British*] (BI)
FSFA........... Federation of Specialized (or Specialised) Film Associations (SAUO)
FS/FB.......... Free Store/Food Bank (EA)
FSFC........... Federal Services Finance Corporation (SAUO)
FSFC........... Federal, State and Farm Credit (SAUS)
FSFC........... First Security Financial Corporation (SAUO)
FSFC........... First Southeast Financial Corp. [*NASDAQ symbol*] (SAG)
FSFC........... First Southeast Finl [*NASDAQ symbol*] (TTSB)
FSFC........... Florida State Fire College (DEMM)
FSFC........... Forester Sisters Fan Club (EA)
FSFCS......... Federal State Facilities Compliance Agreement (SAUO)
FS/FD.......... Flux System/Flux Delta (SAUS)
FSFE........... Flash Smelting Furnace with Electrodes (SAUS)
FSF Fin........ FSF Financial Corp. [*Associated Press*] (SAG)
FSFI............ First State Financial Services, Inc. [*NASDAQ symbol*] (NQ)
FSFL........... First State Finl Svcs [*NASDAQ symbol*] (TTSB)
FSFLP......... Farm Storage Facility Loan Program
FSFM........... Full Screen Full Motion (TELE)
FSFO........... Failsave Failover (SAUS)
FSFS........... Family Security Friendly Society [*Australia*]
FSFT........... Fourth Shift [*NASDAQ symbol*] (TTSB)
FSFT........... Fourth Shift Corp. [*NASDAQ symbol*] (SAG)
FS/FW......... Flow of Steam/Flow of Water (SAUS)
FSG............. Factoring Services Group [*British*] (DBA)
FSG............. Family Support Group [*Military*] (INF)
FSG............. Fasting Serum Glucose [*Clinical chemistry*]
FSG............. Federal Sentencing Guidelines (LDOE)
FSG............. Federal Stock Group
FSG............. Federal Supply Group [*Air Force*]
FSG............. Fellow of the Society of Genealogists [*British*]
FSG............. Field Supply Group
FSG............. Field Support Group (SAUO)
FSG............. Finite State Grammar
FSG............. Fire Support Group (SAUO)
FSG............. First Stage Graphitization (PDAA)
FSG............. Fiume Study Group (EA)
FSG............. Flexible Space Garment
FSG............. Flight Strip Generator (IAA)
FSG............. Flight Study Group (SAUO)
FSG............. Florida Sea Grant College [*University of Florida*] [*Research center*] (RCD)
FSG............. Fluorinated Silicate Glass (AAEL)
FSG............. Focal and Segmental Glomerulosclerosis [*Nephrology*] (DAVI)
FSG............. Foodservice Group (NTPA)
FSG............. Foreign Services Group [*British*]
FSG............. Format Standard Generalized Markup Language [*Computer science*] (VLIE)
FSG............. Fortress Study Group (EAIO)
FSG............. Forward Support Group (SAUS)
FSG............. Free Standards Group (VLIE)
FSG............. Frequency of Signal Generator (IAA)
FSG............. Freres de Saint Gabriel [*Brothers of Christian Instruction of St. Gabriel*] [*Rome, Italy*] (EAIO)
FSG............. Friends School Group (SAUO)
f-sg-........... Senegal [*MARC geographic area code*] [*Library of Congress*] (LCCP)
FSGA........... Four-Wire, Shipboard, General Use, Armored [*Cable*]
FSGA........... Four-wire Shipboard, General use, Armoured (SAUS)
FSGB........... Foreign Service Grievance Board [*Department of State*]
FSGBI.......... Federation of Sailmakers of Great Britain and Ireland [*A union*]
FSGD........... Feasibility Guidance Document
FSGD........... Federation of Sports Goods Distributors [*British*] (DCTA)
FSGHS......... Focal Segmental Glomerular Hyalinosis and Sclerosis [*Medicine*] (DMAA)
FSGM........... Forward Sector Ground Mapping (ACAE)
FSGN........... Focal Sclerosing Glomerulonephritis (DB)

FSGO.......... Floating Spherical Gaussian Orbitals [*Atomic physics*]
FSGp.......... Federal Supply Group [*Air Force*] (AFM)
FSGS.......... Flare/Shallow Glide Slope (MCD)
FSGS.......... Focal Segmental Glomerulosclerosis [*Nephrology*]
FSGT.......... Federation Sportive et Gymnique du Travail
FSGT.......... Fellow of the Society of Glass Technology [*British*]
F Sgt.......... First Sergeant (SAUS)
F/Sgt.......... Flight Sergeant [*RAF*] [*British*] (DMA)
FSgt.......... Flight Sergeant (ODA)
FSGTR-NC... Forest Service General Technical Reports of the North Central Forest (SAUS)
FS Gunpowder... Flameless, Smokeless Gunpowder (SAUS)
FSH.......... Fascioscapulohumeral [*Medicine*]
FSH.......... Federacion de Sociedades Hispanas [*Defunct*] (EA)
FSH.......... Federation of Sterea Hellas (EA)
FSH.......... Final Shift (SAUS)
FSH.......... First-Stage Hydraulics [*Aerospace*]
FSH.......... Fisher Scientific International [*NYSE symbol*] (SPSG)
FSH.......... Fisher Scientific Intl. [*NYSE symbol*] (TTSB)
Fsh.......... Fishing (SAUS)
FSH.......... Flame-Shaped Hemorrhage (SAUS)
FSH.......... Flash Airline Ltd. [*Nigeria*] [*ICAO designator*] (FAAC)
FSH.......... Flight Services Handbook
FSH.......... Follicle-Stimulating Hormone [*Endocrinology*]
FSH.......... Forest Service Handbook [*Department of Agriculture, Forest Service*] [*A publication*]
FSH.......... Foundation for Science and the Handicapped (EA)
FSH.......... Four Seasons Hotels, Inc. [*Toronto Stock Exchange symbol*]
FSH.......... Fuel Sleeve Housing (COE)
FSH.......... Full Hyundai Service History [*Automotive classified advertising*]
FSH.......... Full Mercedes-Benz Service History [*Automotive classified advertising*]
FSH.......... Full Service History [*Automotive retailing*]
f-sh-.......... Spanish Territories in Northern Morocco [*Spanish North Africa*] (LCCP)
FSHAA.......... Fellow of the Society of Hearing Aid Associations (SAUO)
FSHAA.......... Fellow of the Society of Hearing Aid Audiologists [*British*] (DBQ)
FSHB.......... Follicle-Stimulating Hormone Beta Subunit [*Endocrinology*]
FSHC.......... Federal Subsistence Homesteads Corp. [*New Deal*]
FSHC.......... Federation of State Humanities Councils (NTPA)
FSHC.......... Financial Services Holding Co.
FSHD.......... Facioscapulohumeral Muscular Dystrophy (HGEN)
FSHDB.......... Fishing Catch Database (SAUS)
FSHDB.......... World Fishing Catch Database (SAUS)
FSHDB.......... Worldfishing catch database (SAUS)
FSHEW.......... Federal Security Agency, Health, Education, and Welfare
FSHG.......... Fisher Scientific Group, Inc. [*NASDAQ symbol*] (COMM)
FSHIP.......... Fellowship
FSH-LH.......... Follicle-Stimulating Hormone-Luteinizing Hormone [*Endocrinology*] (DAVI)
FSH/LH-RH... Follicle-Stimulating Hormone and Luteinizing Hormone-Releasing Hormone [*Endocrinology*] (MAE)
FSHLPS.......... File System Helpers (PCM)
FSHM.......... Fellow of the Society of Housing Managers (SAUO)
FSHMD.......... Facioscapulohumeral Muscular Dystrophy [*Neurology*] (DAVI)
FSHN.......... Food Science and Human Nutrition
FSHNG.......... Fishing
FSHPAC.......... Frequency-Agile Solid-State High-Frequency Power Amplifier Coupler [*Army*]
FSHPC.......... Fort Sam Houston Purchasing and Contracting Office (SAUO)
FSHRBI.......... Follicle-Stimulating Hormone Receptor Binding Inhibitor [*Endocrinology*]
FSH-RF.......... Follicle-Stimulating Hormone Releasing Factor [*Also, FRF, FSH-RH*] [*Endocrinology*]
FSH-RH.......... Follicle-Stimulating Hormone Releasing Hormone [*Also, FRF, FSH-RF*] [*Endocrinology*]
FSHRY.......... Fishery
FSHS.......... Florida State Horicultural Society (SAUS)
FSHS.......... Florida State Horticultural Society (SAUO)
FSHS.......... Friendly Societies Health Services (SAUO)
fsh stk.......... fish steak (SAUS)
Fsh stks.......... Fishing Stakes [*Nautical charts*]
FSHV.......... Full-Scale Hydrodynamic Vehicle (MCD)
FSI.......... Faggan Studio Industries [*Database producer*] (IID)
FSI.......... Family Suffering Index [*Economic measurement based on unemployment rate, plus costs of food, fuel, and housing*]
FSI.......... Famous Schools International (SAUO)
FSI.......... Fastbreak Syndicate Incorporated (SAUO)
FSI.......... Fastening Systems International Inc. (SAUS)
FSI.......... FDDI System Interface (SAUS)
FSI.......... Federal Stock Item
FSI.......... Federation of Sussex Industries, Ltd. (SAUO)
FSI.......... Federation of Swedish Industries (SAUO)
FSI.......... Federation Spirite Internationale [*International Spiritualist Federation*]
FSI.......... Felec Services Incorporated (SAUO)
FSI.......... Fellow of Sanitary Institute (SAUO)
FSI.......... Fellow of the Sanitary Institute [*British*] (ROG)
FSI.......... Fellow of the Surveyors' Institute [*Later, FRICS*] [*British*]
FSI.......... Fellow of the Surveyors' Institution (DD)
FSI.......... Final Systems Installation [*NASA*] (NASA)
FSI.......... Financial Services Industry (EBF)
FSI.......... Fire Service Inspectorate [*British*]
FSI.......... Fire Service Instructors
FSI.......... Fish and Shellfish Immunology [*A publication*]
FSI.......... Flight Safety International, Inc. (SAUO)
FSI.......... Flightsafety International, Inc. [*Aerospace*] [*NYSE symbol*] (SPSG)
FSI.......... Flightsafety Intl. [*NYSE symbol*] (TTSB)
FSI.......... Flight Simulator Instructor (SAUO)
FSI.......... Flight System Integration (ACAE)
FSI.......... Fluid Structure Interaction [*Nuclear energy*] (NRCH)
FSI.......... Fluorinated Silicone (EDCT)
FSI.......... Flutter Speed Index [*Aerodynamics*]
FSI.......... Foam Stability Index [*Chemistry*]
FSI.......... Food Sanitation Institute (EA)
FSI.......... Forces Services International (SAUO)
FSI.......... Force Structure Increase [*Military*]
FSI.......... Foreign Science Information Program (SAA)
FSI.......... Foreign Service Institute [*Department of State*]
FSI.......... Foreign Services Institute [*Australia*]
FSI.......... Foreign Substance Inhalation [*Medicine*] (MELL)
FSI.......... Forensic Science International (ADWA)
FSI.......... Forest Survey of India (SAUO)
FSI.......... Formed Steel Institute
FSI.......... Fort Sill, OK [*Location identifier*] [*FAA*] (FAAL)
FSI.......... Foundation for Savings Institutions [*Defunct*] (EA)
FSI.......... Foundation Sciences Incorporated (SAUO)
FSI.......... Freedom Securities [*NYSE symbol*] (SG)
FSI.......... Freedom System Integrators (SAUS)
FSI.......... Freedom Systems Integrators (SAUS)
FSI.......... Freelance Syndicate, Inc. (EA)
FSI.......... Free Sons of Israel (EA)
FSI.......... Freestanding Insert [*Advertising*]
FSI.......... Free Swelling Index (SAUS)
FSI.......... Functionally Significant Items (MCD)
FSI.......... Functional Simulation Installation (SAUS)
FSI.......... Functional Surveillance Inspection (SAUO)
FSI.......... Fuzzy Singleton Inference (IDAI)
FSI.......... International Society of Fire Service Instructors (EA)
FSI.......... Sub-Committee on Flag State Implementation (SAUO)
FSIA.......... Fellow of the Society of Industrial Artists [*British*] (EY)
FSIA.......... Fellow of the Society of Investment Analysts [*British*] (DBQ)
FSIA.......... Foot Shock-Induced Analgesia [*Neurology*] (DAVI)
FSIA.......... Foreign Sovereign Immunities Act of 1976 (AAGC)
FSIA.......... Foreign Sovereign Immunity Act (SAUS)
FSIAD.......... Fellow of the Society of Industrial Artists and Designers [*British*]
FSIB.......... Flight Safety Information Bulletin [*NASA*]
FSIC.......... Feature Space Iterative Clustering (SAUS)
FSIC.......... Federal Savings Insurance Corporation (SAUO)
FSIC.......... Foreign Service Inspection Corps [*Department of State*]
FSIC.......... Forward Sensor Interface & Control module (SAUS)
FSIC.......... Forward Sensor Interface Control [*Army*] (RDA)
FSIC.......... Franciscan Sisters of the Third Order of the Immaculate Conception [*Roman Catholic religious order*]
F/SICC.......... Federal/State Initiative Coordinating Committee [*Department of Commerce*] (GFGA)
FSICIT.......... Education for International Exchange of Scientific and Cultural Information by Telecommunications (SAUO)
FSID.......... Foundation for the Study of Infant Deaths [*British*] (DBA)
FSIDA.......... Fund for Support of International Development Activities (SAUO)
FSIF.......... Flight Suit with Integrated Flotation
FSIF.......... Friendly Society of Ironfounders of England, Ireland, and Wales [*A union*]
FSIG.......... Franklin Signal Corp. (SAUO)
FSIGBN.......... Field Signal Battalion (IAA)
F SIG LT RQ... Failure to Signal with Lights when Required [*Conviction term used in state of Oregon*] (MVRD)
F SIGN REG... Failure to Sign Registration Card [*Conviction term used in state of Oregon*] (MVRD)
FSIGT.......... Frequently Sampled Intravenous Glucose Tolerance (Test) [*Clinical chemistry*]
FSIH.......... Fellow of the Society of Industrial Hygiene (SAUO)
FSIH.......... Fellow, Society of Industrial Hygiene (CMD)
FSII.......... FSI International [*NASDAQ symbol*] (TTSB)
FSII.......... FSI International, Inc. [*NASDAQ symbol*] (CTT)
FSII.......... Fuel System Icing Inhibitor [*Aviation*] (AFIT)
FSI Int.......... FSI International, Inc. [*Associated Press*] (SAG)
FSIM.......... Functional Simulator (NASA)
FSIMS.......... Fire Service Incident Management System Consortium (SAUO)
FSIMT.......... Foundation for the Support of International Medical Training (EA)
FS-INFO.......... Forest Service Information Network - Forestry Online [*US Forest Service*] [*Information service or system*] (IID)
FSIO.......... Foreign Service Information Officer [*Department of State*]
FSIOP.......... File System Input/Output Processor [*Communications term*] (DCT)
FSIP.......... Fast Serial Interface Processor (VLIE)
FSIP.......... Federal Service Impasses Panel
FSIP.......... Federal Shelter Incentive Program
FSIP.......... Fire Service in Philately [*An association*]
FSIP.......... Full-Scale Input (MWOL)
FSIPR.......... Federation of Unions of Pre-University Educators [*Bucharest, Romania*]
FSIR.......... Force Status Identity Report (MCD)
FSIRR.......... Filter Scanning Infrared Radiometer (SAUS)
FSIS.......... Fast Sample Insertion System (SAUS)
FSIS.......... First-Stage Ignition System [*Aerospace*] (MCD)
FSIS.......... Flight Safety Information System (SAUO)
FSIS.......... Food Safety and Inspection Service [*Formerly, FSQS*] [*Department of Agriculture*]
FSISI.......... Foundation for the Study of Independent Social Ideas (EA)
FSISWG.......... Flight System Interface Working Group
FSIT.......... First Spanish Investment Trust [*London Stock Exchange*]

FSIT .... Flat Screen Image Tube [*Computer science*] (IAA)
FSIWA .... Federation of Sewage and Industrial Wastes Associations [*Later, Water PollutionControl Federation*]
FSIWG .... Flight System Interface Working Group (MCD)
FSJ .... Faculte Saint-Jean Library, University of Alberta [*UTLAS symbol*]
FSJ .... Feedback Summing Junction [*Computer science*]
FSJ .... Fellowship of St. James (EA)
FSJ .... Fort St. James [*British Columbia*] [*Seismograph station code, US Geological Survey*] (SEIS)
FSJ .... Fratres Sancti Joseph [*Brothers of St. Joseph*] [*Roman Catholic religious order*]
FSJ .... Free Supersonic Jet
FSJ .... Fuel Society of Japan (SAUO)
FSJ .... Religious Daughters of St. Joseph (TOCD)
f-sj-............. Sudan [*MARC geographic area code*] [*Library of Congress*] (LCCP)
FSJC .... Fort Scott Junior College [*Kansas*]
FSJC .... Fort Smith Junior College [*Arkansas*]
FSJM .... Society of Franciscan Servants of Jesus and Mary [*Anglican religious community*]
FSK............. Fatigue Scales Kit [*Psychology*]
FSK............. Figure Shift Key (SAUS)
FSK............. Fisk University, Nashville, TN [*OCLC symbol*] (OCLC)
FSK............. Forskolin [*Also, FOR*] [*Organic chemistry*]
FSK............. Fort Scott, KS [*Location identifier*] [*FAA*] (FAAL)
FSK............. Frequency Shift Key (SAUS)
FSK............. Frequency Shift Keyed (SAUS)
FSK............. Frequency Shift Keying [*Telecommunications*]
fsk.............. Frequency-Shift Keying
FSKLF.......... Frequency Shift Keying Low-Frequency [*Converter*] (NATG)
fsklf .... frequency shift keying low frequency (SAUS)
fskof............ for the sake of (SAUS)
FSL .... Fail-Safe Logic (SAUS)
FSL .... Family Strike Light [*Indicates family should take small portions at a meal where guests are present*]
FSL .... Federal Society of Linguists (SAUO)
FSL .... Federal Stock Listings
FSL .... Federation des Syndicats Libres des Travailleurs Luxembourgeois [*Free Luxembourg Workers' Federation*]
FSL .... Field Storage List (MCD)
FSL .... Field Storage Location (SAUS)
FSL .... Finite State Language
FSL .... Fire Control and Small Caliber Weapon Systems Laboratory [*Picatinny Arsenal, Dover, NJ*] [*Army*] (INF)
fsl .... fire services levy (SAUS)
FSL .... First Sea Lord [*British*] (DI)
FSL .... First Standard Mining Ltd. [*Vancouver Stock Exchange symbol*]
FSL .... Fixed Safety Level
FSL .... Flexible Satellite Link (SAUS)
FSL .... Flexible System Link (SAUS)
FSL .... Flight Safety Ltd. [*British*] [*ICAO designator*] (FAAC)
FSL .... Flight Simulation Laboratory [*NASA*] (NASA)
FSL .... Flight Systems Laboratory (MCD)
FSL .... Florida State League [*Baseball*]
FSL .... Florida State University, Law Library, Tallahassee, FL [*OCLC symbol*] (OCLC)
FSL .... Folger Shakespeare Library (SAUO)
FSL .... Food Science Laboratory (SAUO)
FS/L .... Food Service/Lodging
FSL .... Forecast Science Laboratory, Boulder (SAUS)
FSL .... Forecast Systems Laboratory [*Environmental Research Laboratories*] (USDC)
FSL .... Foreign Service Leave [*British military*] (DMA)
FSL .... Foreign Service Local (CINC)
FSL .... Foreign Study League, Stuttgart (SAUO)
FSL .... Forestry Sciences Laboratory [*US Forest Service*] [*Research center*] (RCD)
FSL .... Formal Semantic Language [*Computer science*]
FSL .... Forward Supply Locations (SAUO)
fsl .... Fossil (VRA)
FSL .... Franklin Supply Co. Ltd. [*AMEX symbol*] (SPSG)
FSL .... Free Shear Layer
FSL .... French as a Second Language (SAUS)
FSL .... French Sign Language
FSL .... Frequency Selective Limiter (IAA)
FSL .... Friends of the Sea Lion (SAUO)
FSL .... Full Shallow Learning (SAUS)
FSL .... Full Stop Landing [*Aviation*]
FSL .... Full Supply Level (ADA)
FSL .... Full System Listing (SAUO)
FSL .... Functional Solution Language (SAUS)
FSL .... Future State List (SAUS)
f-sl-............. Sierra Leone [*MARC geographic area code*] [*Library of Congress*] (LCCP)
FSLA .... Federal Sales and Loan Association (SAUO)
FSLA .... Federal Savings and Loan Association [*New Deal*]
FSLA .... Fibroblast Somatomedin-Like Activity (DB)
FSLA .... First Savings Bank FSLA Perth Amboy NJ [*NASDAQ symbol*] (SAG)
FSLA .... First Savings Bank of New Jersey [*NASDAQ symbol*] (SAG)
FSLA .... First Savings Bk(Perth Amboy) [*NASDAQ symbol*] (TTSB)
FSLA .... Franklin Savings and Loan Association (SAUO)
FSLAC.......... Federal Savings and Loan Advisory Committee (EBF)
FSLAC.......... Federal Savings and Loan Advisory Council (SAUO)
FSLAET........ Fellow of the Society of Licensed Aircraft Engineers and Technologists [*British*]
FSLAs .... Federal Savings and Loan Associations (SAUO)
FSIC............ Saint Leo College, Saint Leo, FL [*Library symbol*] [*Library of Congress*] (LCLS)
FSLIC.......... Federal Savings & Loan Insurance Corp. [*of FHLBB*] [*Pronounced "FIZ-lick"*] [*Functions transferred to SAIF, 1989*]
FSLIC.......... Federal Savings and Loan Insurance Corporation (EBF)
FSLMMC...... Friends of the Sea Lion Marine Mammal Center (EA)
FSLN........... Frente Sandinista de Liberacion Nacional [*Sandinista National Liberation Front*] [*Nicaragua*] [*Political party*] (PPW)
FSLO........... First Spacelab Payload [*Aerospace*] (NAKS)
FSLP........... First Spacelab Payload [*NASA*]
FSLPPS....... Federalist Society for Law and Public Policy Studies (EA)
FSLSTE....... Flight Line System Level Special Test Equipment (ACAE)
FSLT........... First Sea Level Test [*NASA*] (NASA)
FSLUPC....... Federal/State Land Use Planning Commission for Alaska (SAUS)
F SLW DR RT... Failure of Slow Driver to Drive on Right [*Conviction term used in state of Oregon*] (MVRD)
F SLW DR Y... Failure of a Slow Driver to Yield to Overtaking Vehicle [*Conviction term used in state of Oregon*] (MVRD)
FSM .... Fabryka Samochodow Malolotia [*Polish affiliate of Fiat Motors*]
FSM .... Factory Service Manual
FSM .... Failure Strength Minimum (SAUS)
FSM .... Fast Settle Mode
FSM .... Fast Steering Mirror [*Optical instrumentation*]
FSM .... Federacion Socialista Madrilena [*Spain*] [*Political party*] (EY)
FSM .... Federated States of Micronesia [*ANSI three-letter standard code*] (CNC)
FSM .... Federation Sephardite Mondiale [*World Sephardi Federation - WSF*] [*Geneva, Switzerland*] (EAIO)
FSM .... Federation Socialiste de la Martinique [*Socialist Federation of Martinique*] [*Political party*] (PPW)
FSM .... Federation Syndicale Mondiale [*World Federation of Trade Unions - WFTU*] [*French*] (EAIO)
FSM .... Fellow of the Society of Metaphysicians [*British*]
FSM .... Fellowship Recorded Libraries of Sacred Music [*Record label*] [*Atlanta, GA*]
FSM .... Female Sexual Medicine
FSM .... Field Service Manual [*British military*] (DMA)
FSM .... Field Strength Meter
FSM .... Fiji School of Medicine (SAUO)
FSM .... Final Stage Marker (IAA)
FSM .... Financial Systems Manager (SAUS)
FSM .... Fine Scale Modeler [*A publication*]
FSM .... Finite State Machine
FSM .... Finite Strip Method (SAUS)
FSM .... Fire Support Matrix (SAUS)
FSM .... Firmware Support Manual
FSM .... First-Stage Motor [*Aerospace*]
FSM .... First Surface Mirror
FSM .... Flight Simulation Monitor [*FAA*] (TAG)
FSM .... Flight Simulator Model (SAUO)
FSM .... Flight Synchronizer Module (ADWA)
FSM .... Flight System Mockup
FSM .... Floating Subtract Magnitude [*Computer science*] (IAA)
FSM .... Fluid System Module (SAUS)
FSM .... Flying Spot Microscope (ADA)
FSM .... Folded Sheets Mesoporous-Material [*Inorganic chemistry*]
FSM .... Folded Sideband Modulation
FSM .... Foodarama Suermkts [*AMEX symbol*] (TTSB)
FSM .... Foodarama Supermarkets, Inc. [*AMEX symbol*] (SPSG)
FSM .... Formatted Screen Manager (SAUS)
FSM .... Fort Smith [*Arkansas*] [*Airport symbol*] (OAG)
FSM .... Fort Smith, AR [*Location identifier*] [*FAA*] (FAAL)
FSM .... Forward Scatter Meter (SAUS)
FSM .... forward set up message (SAUS)
FSM .... Forward Support Manual (SAUS)
FSM .... Frame-Scanning Mode [*Microscopy*]
FSM .... Franciscan Sisters of Mary (TOCD)
FSM .... Free Space Management (SAUS)
FSM .... Free Speech Movement [*University of California, Berkeley*]
FSM .... Frequency Shift Modulation [*Radio*]
FSM .... Friendly Society of Mechanics [*A union*] [*British*]
FSM .... Fuel Supply Module (MCD)
FSMA.......... Families of SMA [*Spinal Muscular Atrophy*] [*An association*] (EA)
FSMA.......... Farm Store Merchandising Association [*Defunct*] (EA)
FSMA.......... Fashion Sales and Marketing Association [*Australia*]
FSMA.......... Fellow of the Incorporated Sales Managers' Association [*Later, F Inst MSM*] [*British*]
FSMA.......... Frame Screen Manufacturers Association (SAUO)
FSMA.......... Friendly Societies Medical Association (SAUO)
FSMA.......... Full Service Maintenance Agreement (SAUS)
FSMAA........ Fire Support Mission Area Analysis (SAUS)
FSMAC........ Fellow of the Society of Management Accountants of Canada (DD)
FSMAMS...... Field Service Manual for Army Medical Services (SAUO)
FSMAO .... Field Supply and Maintenance Analysis Office (DNAB)
FSMAWA ..... Fashion Sales and Marketing Association of Western Australia
FSMB.......... Federation of State Medical Boards of the United States (EA)
FSMBUS ...... Federation of State Medical Boards of the United States (EA)
FSMC.......... Federal Supply Manufacturers' Code [*DoD*]
FSMC.......... Fellow of the Spectacle Makers Company (SAUO)
FSMC.......... First-Stage Motor Container [*Aerospace*]
FSMC.......... Fixed Silver Mica Capacitor
FSMC.......... Flora Stone Mather College (SAUO)
FSMC.......... Forward Support Medical Company [*Military*] (INF)
FSMER........ Foundation for Sports Medicine Education and Research (SAUO)
FS Method... Federal Standard Method (SAUS)

FSMF.......... Furnishing Springmakers Federation [*British*] (BI)
FSMG.......... Foundry Supply Manufacturers Group (EA)
FSMGB........ Federation of Small Mines of Great Britain (SAUO)
FSMGDOS.... Graphics Device Operating System (SAUS)
FSMI.......... Food Service Marketing Institute (EA)
FSMIP......... Federal State Marketing Improvement Program
FSML.......... Fleet Support Material List [*Navy*]
FSMNS........ Federal State Market News Service (SAUO)
FSMO.......... Field Service Marching Order [*British military*] (DMA)
FSMR.......... Field Station Materiel Requirements
FSMR.......... Fixed Simultaneous Multibeam Radar (SAUS)
FSMS.......... Firing Set Maintenance Spares (NG)
FSMS.......... Flight Structural Monitoring System (SAUO)
FSMS.......... Florida Surveying and Mapping Society (SAUS)
FSMSC........ Federal Software Management Support Center (SAUO)
FSMSI......... Fire Support Modeling and Simulations Institute
FSMT.......... Feed System Maintenance Transfer (MCD)
FSMT.......... Fleet Service Mine Test [*Navy*] (NG)
FSMT.......... Full-Size Maneuverable Target (SAUS)
FSMTC........ Full-Size Moving Tank Target Carrier (SAUS)
fsmtc.......... full-size moving target carrier (SAUS)
FS MVMT COORD... FS Movement Coordination (SAUS)
FSMWI......... Free Space Microwave Interferometer
FSMWO....... Field Service Modification Work Order
FSN............. Factory Serial Number (MCD)
FSN............. Federal Stock Number [*Later, NSN*]
FSN............. FEMA [*Federal Emergency Management Agency*] Switched Network (GFGA)
FSN............. File Sequence Number [*Computer science*] (IAA)
FSN............. File Serial Number (SAUS)
FSN............. File System Navigator (SAUS)
FSN............. Filler Sensor Nozzle
FSN............. Financial Satellite Network
FSN............. Fiscal Station Number [*Military*]
FSN............. Foreign Service National (JAGO)
FSN............. Foreign State National
FSN............. Forward Sequence Number [*Telecommunications*] (TEL)
FSN............. Forward Specification Number (SAUS)
FSN............. Franklin Select Real Estate Income Fund [*AMEX symbol*] (SPSG)
FSN............. Franklin Select Realty Trust [*AMEX symbol*] [*Formerly, Franklin Select R.E., Inc. Fd.*] (SG)
FSN............. Franklin Select R.E. Inc.Fd'A' [*AMEX symbol*] (TTSB)
FSN............. French-Speaking Nations [*NATO*]
FSN............. Fuel Service Nozzle (MSA)
FSN............. Full Serial Number (SAUS)
FSN............. Full Service Network [*Television broadcasting*]
FSN............. National Salvation Front [*Romania*] [*Political party*]
FSN............. New College, Sarasota, FL [*Library symbol*] [*Library of Congress*] (LCLS)
FSNA.......... Fellow of the Society of Naval Architects (SAUO)
FSNC.......... Federal Steam Navigation Company (SAUO)
FSNE........... Flower-Spray Nerve Ending (MELL)
FSNet.......... Food Safety Network (SAUS)
FSNFO........ Flight Standards National Field Office (SAUO)
FSNJ........... First Savings Bank(N.J.) [*NASDAQ symbol*] (TTSB)
FSNJ........... First Savings Bank of New Jersey [*NASDAQ symbol*] (SAG)
FSNM.......... First Savings Bank [*Associated Press*] (SAG)
FSNM.......... First State Bancorp [*NASDAQ symbol*] (SAG)
FSNM.......... First State Bancorporation [*NASDAQ symbol*] (TTSB)
FSNM.......... Fort Sumter National Monument (SAUO)
FSNMDR...... Federal Stock Number [*later, NSN*] Master Data Record
FSNO.......... Federation of Sunday Newspaper Owners (DGA)
FSNOx......... Fuel-Specific Nitrogen Oxide Emissions [*Air pollution*]
FSNP.......... Famous Spock Neck Pinch [*From television show "Star Trek"*]
FSNP.......... Fuyot Spring National Park (SAUO)
FSNR.......... [*The*] Forschner Group, Inc. [*NASDAQ symbol*] (NQ)
FSNS.......... French-Speaking Neuropsychological Society [*Paris, France*] (EAIO)
FSNWR........ Fish Springs National Wildlife Refuge (SAUO)
FSNY.......... Free Synagogue of New York (SAUO)
FSO............. Fabryka Samochodow Osobowych [*Polish automobile manufacturer*]
FSO............. Facility Security Officer
FSO............. Fast Settle Operation
FSO............. Fast Shift Operation (SAUS)
FSO............. Fearing Surname Organization (EA)
FSO............. Field Sales Office (TIMI)
FSO............. Field Service Operations (NATG)
FSO............. Field Support Office (ACAE)
FSO............. Fire Safety Officer (HEAS)
FSO............. Fire Support Officer [*Military*]
FSO............. Fleet Signal Officer (SAUS)
FSO............. Fleet Signals Officer [*Navy*]
FSO............. Fleet Supply Officer [*Navy*]
FSO............. Fleet Support Operations (NVT)
FSO............. Flight Safety Officer (MCD)
FSO............. Flight Services Officer (ADA)
FSO............. Flint Symphony Orchestra (SAUO)
FSO............. Florida Society of Ophthalmology (SRA)
FSO............. Florida Symphony Orchestra (SAUO)
FSO............. Flotilla Staff Officer (SAUO)
FSO............. Flying Safety Officer [*Air Force*] (AFM)
FSO............. Force Supply Officer
FSO............. Foreign Service Office (ADWA)
FSO............. Foreign Service Officer [*Department of State*]
FSO............. Frequency Sweep Oscillator
FSO............. Friars' Society Orchestra (WDAA)
FSO............. Friends of the Sea Otter (EA)
FSO............. Fuel Supply Office [*Military*]
FSO............. Full Scale Output (SAUS)
FSO............. Full-Scale Output
FSO............. Full Screen Output (SAUS)
FSO............. Fulltext Sources Outline [*A publication*]
FSO............. Functional Supplementary Objective (MCD)
FSO............. Fund for Special Operations [*Inter-American Development Bank*]
FSO............. Funding Services Officer (FOTI)
f-so-........... Somali [*MARC geographic area code*] [*Library of Congress*] (LCCP)
FSO............. Field Security Officer (ODA)
FSOB.......... Friendly Society of Operative Bricklayers [*A union*] [*British*]
FSOC.......... European Space Operations Centre (SAUS)
FSOC.......... Fairchild Satellite Operation Center (SAUO)
FSOC.......... Fairchild Satellite Operations Complex (MCD)
FSOC.......... Fixed Stand-Off Capacitor
FSOC.......... Free Serbian Orthodox Church [*Australia*]
FSOCM........ Friendly Society of Operative Cabinet Makers [*A union*] [*British*]
FSOCOM..... First Special Operations Command (DOMA)
FSOF........... Forward Special Operations Facility (SAUO)
FSOFC......... Federal Service Overseas Fund Campaign (SAUO)
FSOH.......... Flight Support Operations Handbook (MCD)
FSOHNS...... Florida Society of Otolaryngology-Head and Neck Surgery (SRA)
FSOL........... Franciscan Sisters of Our Lady (TOCD)
FSOLF......... Forasol-Foramer NV [*NASDAQ symbol*] (TTSB)
FSOMA........ Florida State Oriental Medical Association (SAUS)
FSON.......... Fusion Medical Technologies, Inc. [*NASDAQ symbol*] (SAG)
FSOP.......... Field Standard Operating Procedure (SAUO)
FSOP.......... Field Standing Operating Procedures (SAUS)
FSOP.......... Flying Standing Operations Procedures (SAUO)
FSOP.......... Free-Standing Surgical Outpatient Facility (HCT)
FSOP.......... Full-Scale Output (MWOL)
FSor........... French Cetra-Soria [*Record label*]
FSOs........... Foreign Service Officers (SAUS)
FSOS.......... Free-Standing Operating System [*General Automation, Inc.*]
FSOSEIW..... Friendly Society of Operative Stonemasons of England, Ireland, and Wales [*A union*]
FSOT........... Friendly Society of Operative Tobacconists [*A union*] [*British*]
FSOTS......... Foreign Service Officers Training School (SAUO)
FSouth......... First South Africa Corp. Ltd. [*Associated Press*] (SAG)
FSP............. Brothers of St. Patrick (TOCD)
fsp.............. Brothers of St. Patrick (TOCD)
FSP............. Facility Security Profile [*Military*] (GFGA)
FSP............. Facility Security Program [*World War II*]
FSP............. Facility Support Plan [*Military*]
FSP............. Familial Spastic Paraplegia [*Medicine*] (DMAA)
FSP............. Family Services Program [*Military*]
FSP............. Family Support Plan
FSP............. Family Survival Project (SAUS)
FSP............. Fault Servicing Process (TEL)
FSP............. Fault Summary Page (MCD)
FSP............. Federal/State Programs [*Social Security Administration*] (OICC)
FSP............. Federation of Sub-Postmasters (SAUO)
FSP............. Fellow of Sheffield Polytechnic [*British*]
FSP............. Fellow of the Society of Philology (SAUO)
FSP............. Fellowship and Stipends for the Professionals [*Medicine*] (EDAA)
FSP............. Fellowship of St. Paul (EA)
FSP............. Fiber Saturation Point [*Of drying lumber*] (BARN)
FSP............. Fibre Saturation Point (SAUS)
FSP............. fibrinogen split product (SAUS)
FSP............. Fibrinogen-Split Products [*Hematology*]
FSP............. Fibrinolytic Split Products (SAUS)
FSP............. Fibrin [*or Fibrinolytic*] Split Products (DAVI)
FSP............. Field Sampling Plan (BCP)
FSP............. Field Security Personnel
FSP............. Field Security Police
FSP............. Fighter Seaplane (SAUS)
FSP............. Figlie de San Paolo [*Pious Society of the Daughters of Saint Paul - PSDSP*] [*Rome, Italy*] (EAIO)
FSP............. File Server Processes (SAUS)
FSP............. File Service Process (SAUS)
FSP............. File Service Protocol (Internet) (SAUS)
FSP............. File Slurping Protocol [*Computer science*] (VERA)
FSP............. Fine Suspended Particles [*Medicine*] (EDAA)
FSP............. Finger Sweat Print [*Psychometrics*]
FSP............. Fire Support Planning (SAUS)
Fsp.............. Fischerella Species (SAUS)
FSP............. Fixed Sample-Size Procedure
FSP............. Fixed Silo Price [*Wheat*]
FSP............. Fixed Store Procedure (SAUS)
FSp............. Flash Spotting (SAUS)
FSP............. Flat Salary Payroll (AAG)
FSP............. Fleet Scheduling Program [*DoD*] (IAA)
FSP............. Flight Safety Foundation (SAUO)
FSP............. Flight Scheduling Precedence
FSP............. Flight Screening Program (SAUS)
FSP............. Flight Strip Printer [*Aviation*] (FAAC)
FSP............. Floating Stock Platform (DNAB)
FSP............. Food Safety Panel (WDAA)
FSP............. Food Stamp Program
FSP............. Force Sensing Probe
FSP............. Ford Satellite Plan [*Telecommunications*]
FSP............. Foreign Service Pay
FSP............. Forest Stewardship Program (WPI)
F-SP........... Forma Specialis [*Taxonomy*] (DB)

f sp .... Forma Specialis [*Special Form*] [*Biology*]
FSP .... Forward Staging Post (SAUS)
FSP .... Forward Supply Point [*Military*] (AFM)
FSP .... Foundation for the Peoples of the South Pacific (EA)
FSP .... Fragment Simulator Projectile (SAUS)
FSP .... Franciscan Sisters of Peace (TOCD)
FSP .... Freedom Socialist Party (EA)
FSP .... Freeway Service Patrol (SAUS)
FSP .... French Socialist Party
FSP .... Frente Socialista Popular [*Portugal*]
FSP .... Frente Social Progresista [*Progressive Social Front*] [*Ecuador*] [*Political party*] (PPW)
FSP .... Frequency Shift Pulsing
FSP .... Frequency Standard, Primary
FSP .... Fuel Storage Pool [*Nuclear energy*] (NRCH)
FSP .... Full-Scale Production
FSP .... Full-Scale Prototype [*Military*] (CAAL)
FSP .... Full Screen Package (SAUS)
FSP .... Full Screen Processing (SAUS)
FSP .... Full-Screen Processing [*Computer science*]
FSP .... Full Screen Product (SAUS)
FSP .... Full Service Provider
FSP .... Full Spectrum Processing (SAUS)
FSP .... Full-Time Equivalent Software Personnel
FSP .... Functional Sentence Perspective (SAUS)
FSP .... Functional Specification Package [*Computer science*]
FSP .... Functional System Plan [*Military*]
FSP .... Pious Society Daughters of St. Paul (TOCD)
FSp .... St. Petersburg Public Library, St. Petersburg, FL [*Library symbol*] [*Library of Congress*] (LCLS)
FSPA .... Farm Shop and Pick Association (SAUO)
FSPA .... Fellow, Society of Pension Actuaries [*American Society of Pension Actuari es*] [*Designation awarded by*]
FSPA .... Florida State Pharmaceutical Association (SAUO)
FSPA .... Former Spouse Protection Act
FSPA .... Fuel Storage Personnel Area [*Nuclear energy*] (NRCH)
FSPA .... Sisters of the Third Order of St. Francis of the Perpetual Adoration [*Roman Catholic religious order*]
FS-PAL .... Field Sequential Phase Alternation Line (SAUS)
FSPB .... Field Service Pocket Book [*British military*] (DMA)
FSPB .... Fire Support Primary Base (DNAB)
FSPB .... Food Safety Promotion Board [*Ireland*] (GVA)
FSPB .... Forward Support Patrol Base
FSPB .... Fuel Storage Processing Building [*Nuclear energy*] (NRCH)
FSPBC .... For a Separate Peace Before Carter [*Refers to Israeli-Egyptian agreements of 1978*]
FSPC .... Federal Science Policy Council [*Later, FCCSET*]
FSPC .... Field-Site Production Capability (SAA)
FSPC .... Foundation for the Study of Primitive Culture
FSPC .... Frontispiece [*Publishing*] (WGA)
FSpC .... St. Petersburg Junior College, St. Petersburg, FL [*Library symbol*] [*Library of Congress*] (LCLS)
FSPCM .... Flight Strip Printer Control Module (MCD)
FSPCT .... Foundation for the Study of Presidential and Congressional Terms (EA)
FSPD .... Freeze Speed Parameter [*FAA*] (TAG)
FSPDUA .... Federated Ship Painters and Dockers' Union of Australia
FSpE .... Eckerd College, St. Petersburg, FL [*Library symbol*] [*Library of Congress*] (LCLS)
FSPE .... Fellow of the Society of Plastics Engineers (SAUO)
FSPER .... Finances of Selected Public Employee Retirement System [*Bureau of the Census*] (GFGA)
FSpFP .... Florida Power Corp., St. Petersburg, FL [*Library symbol*] [*Library of Congress*] (LCLS)
FSPG .... First Home Bancorp, Inc. [*NASDAQ symbol*] (SAG)
FSPG .... First Home Savings Bank [*NASDAQ symbol*] (NQ)
FSPG .... First Home Savings Bk [*NASDAQ symbol*] (TTSB)
FSPG .... Force Structure Planning Group [*Marine Corps*] (DOMA)
FSPHX .... Fidelity Select Ptfl: Health Care [*Mutual fund ticker symbol*] (SG)
FSPL .... First Spacelab Payload (ACAE)
FS PLAN .... FS Plan (SAUS)
FSPLS .... Florida Society of Professional Land Surveyors (SAUO)
FSPM .... Foundation for Social and Preventive Medicine (SAUO)
FSPMA .... Federal Services Podiatric Medical Association (EA)
FSPO .... Force Structure Planning Objective (MUGU)
FS/PP .... Feasibility Study/Proposed Plan (SAUS)
FSPP .... Fiske-Subbarow Positive Phosphorus [*Analytical chemistry*]
FSPPR .... Fast Supercritical Pressure Power Reactor
FSPRR .... Fast Supercritical Pressure Power Reactor (SAUS)
FSPRS .... Field-Site Production and Reduction System (SAA)
FSPS .... Federation of Sailing and Powerboat Schools (SAUO)
FSPS .... Ferranti Sonobuoy Processing System (MCD)
FSPS .... Field-Site Production System (SAA)
FSPS .... Foundation for the Study of Plural Societies (EA)
FSPSC .... Field-Site Production Study Committee (SAA)
FSPSG .... Freeman-Sheldon Parent Support Group (EA)
FSPSO .... Federal Statistical Policy and Standards Office (OICC)
FSPT .... Federation of Societies for Paint Technology [*Later, FSCT*] (EA)
FSPT .... FirstSpartan Financial [*NASDAQ symbol*] (SG)
FSpW .... Jim Walter Research Corp., St. Petersburg, FL [*Library symbol*] [*Library of Congress*] (LCLS)
FSQ .... Atlanta, GA [*Location identifier*] [*FAA*] (FAAL)
FS/Q .... Directorate of Flight Standards and Qualification Research [*St. Louis, MO*] [*Army*]
FSQ .... Flat Sqare (SAUS)
FS/Q .... Flight Standards and Qualification [*Army*]
FSq .... Flying Squadron
f-sq- .... Swaziland [*MARC geographic area code*] [*Library of Congress*] (LCCP)
FSQS .... Food Safety and Quality Service [*Later, FSIS*] [*Department of Agriculture*]
FSQW .... Free-standing Quantum Well (SAUS)
FSR .... Air Link Charters [*Canada*] (FAAC)
FSR .... Brothers of the Congregation of Our Lady of the Holy Rosary (TOCD)
fsr .... Brothers of the Congregation of Our Lady of the Holy Rosary (TOCD)
FSR .... Facility Siting Requests (SAUO)
FSR .... False Signal Recognition [*RADAR technology*]
FSR .... Farming Systems Research
FSR .... Fast Slew Rate
FSR .... Fast Sodium-Cooled Reactor (SAUS)
FSR .... fast source reactor (SAUS)
FSR .... Feedback Shift Register
FSR .... Fellow of the Royal Society of Radiographers
FSR .... Fellow of the Society of Radiographers (SAUO)
FSR .... Female Seniors [*International Bowhunting Organization*] [*Class Equipment*]
FSR .... Fermi Selection Rules
FSR .... Fiberglass Stain Remover [*Cleaning product*] [*Jamie Industries*]
FSR .... Fielded System Review
FSR .... Field Sales Representative (TIMI)
FSR .... Field Service Regulations [*Army*]
FSR .... Field Service Report
FSR .... Field Service Representative (AFM)
FSR .... Field Strength Radio
FSR .... Field Strength Ratio (SAUS)
FSR .... Fighter Strategic Reconnaissance (SAUS)
FSR .... File Space Rules (SAUS)
FSR .... File Storage Region [*Digital Equipment Corp.*]
FSR .... Film Society Review [*A publication*]
FSR .... Final Shift Register (SAUS)
FSR .... Final System Release (MCD)
FSR .... Final System Run (KSC)
FSR .... Financial Services Recorder [*Telecommunications*] [*British*]
FSR .... Financial Status Report (OICC)
FSR .... Fin Stabilized Rockets
FSR .... Firstar Corp. [*NYSE symbol*] (SPSG)
FSR .... First Soviet Reactor
FSR .... First Surrey Rifles [*Military unit*] [*British*]
FSR .... Fixed Sample Rate
FSR .... Fleet Spotter Reconnaissance [*British military*] (DMA)
FSR .... Fleet Street Reports [*A publication*]
FSR .... Fleet Street Reports of Patent Cases [*England*] [*A publication*] (DLA)
FSR .... Flight Safety Region (SAUS)
FSR .... Flight Safety Research
FSR .... Flight Safety Rules (MCD)
FSR .... Flight Simulation Report
FSR .... Flight Solar Reflectometer
FSR .... Flight Specific Requirements (MCD)
FSR .... Flight Summary Report (SAUS)
FSR .... Flight Support Request (KSC)
FsR .... Floating Point Register (SAUS)
FSR .... Flood Search Routeing (SAUS)
FSR .... Floor Space Ratio
FSR .... Flowable Solids Reactor (SAUS)
FSR .... Flux Sensitive Resistor
FSR .... Flying Selection Squadron (SAUS)
FSR .... Force Sensing Resistor [*Maxell*] [*Electronics*]
FSR .... Force Service Regiment [*Marine Corps*] (NVT)
FSR .... Foreign Separate Rations (AABC)
FSR .... Foreign Service Reserve (CARL)
FSR .... Foreign Service Reservists (MUGU)
FSR .... Fort Smith Railroad [*Federal Railroad Administration identification code*]
FSR .... Forward Space Record
FSR .... Foundation for Scientific Relaxation
FSR .... Four Seasons Resources Ltd. [*Vancouver Stock Exchange symbol*]
FSR .... Fragmented Sarcoplasmic Reticulum (DB)
FSR .... Franciscan Sisters of Ringwood [*Roman Catholic religious order*]
fsr .... free of strikes and riots (SAUS)
FSR .... Free Space Reactor (SAUS)
FSR .... Free Spectral Range
FSR .... Free System Resource [*Computer science*] (PCM)
FSR .... Freight and Supply Vessel, Refrigerated [*Army ship designation*] (POLM)
FSR .... Frequency Scan RADAR
FSR .... Frequency Selective Relay
FSR .... Frequency Shift Ratio (SAUS)
FSR .... Frequency Shift Receiver
FSR .... Frequency Shift Reflector
FSR .... Full-Scale Range [*Military*] (IAA)
FSR .... Full-Scale Reading (SAUS)
FSR .... Full Scale Record (SAUS)
FSR .... Full-Scale Record [*Instrumentation*]
fsr .... full-scale repository (SAUS)
FSR .... Full-Scale Review
FSR .... Full Systems Ready (DNAB)
FSR .... Functional Stretch Reflex [*of muscles*]
FSR .... Functional Support Requirement (ACAE)
FSR .... Function Status Review (MCD)
FSR .... Fundamental System Reliability (SAUS)

FSR............ Fund for Stockowners Rights [*Later, FFSR*] (EA)
FSR............ Fund Summary Record [*Military*] (AFIT)
FSR............ Fusiform Skin Revision [*Medicine*] (MAE)
FSR............ Future Safety Research [*Honda experimental vehicle*]
FSR............ John and Mable Ringling Museum of Art, Sarasota, FL [*Library symbol*] [*Library of Congress*] (LCLS)
FSR-3.......... Isoniazid [*Pharmacology*] (DAVI)
FSRA........... Federal Sewage Research Association [*Later, Federal Water Quality Association*]
FSRAM........ Fast Static RAM (SAUS)
FSRAMIS..... Forest Service Range Management Information System (SAUS)
FSR&CC...... Free of Strikes, Riots, and Civil Commotion [*Insurance*] (MARI)
FSRB........... Flight Safety Review Board
FSRB........... Forest Service Research Bulletins (SAUS)
FSRC........... Foreign Supplies & Requirements Committee (SAUO)
FSRC........... Foreign Systems Research Center
FSRC........... Frontier Science Research Conferences
FSRC........... Ringling Museum of the Circus, Sarasota, FL [*Library symbol*] [*Library of Congress*] (LCLS)
FSRD........... Fighting Services Research Departments (SAUO)
FSRDC......... Full Straps Roosevelt Dime Club (EA)
FSRDF......... Foreign Service Retirement and Disability Fund (SAUO)
FSRG........... Fellow of the Society of Remedial Gymnasts [*British*]
FSRI............ Farming Systems Research Institute (SAUO)
FSRI............ Foreign Services Research Institute (EA)
FSRM........... First-Stage Rocket Motor [*Aerospace*]
FSRN........... Forest Service Research Notes
FSRP........... Firstar Corp. [*NASDAQ symbol*] (SAG)
FSRP........... Forest Service Research Paper
FS/RPNL...... Function Safe-Release Panel [*Aerospace*] (AAG)
FSRPZ......... Firstar Corp. $1.75 Cv Dep Pfd [*NASDAQ symbol*] (TTSB)
FSRQ........... Flat-Spectrum Radio Quasar [*Galaxy*]
FSRR........... Ferrocarriles del Sureste [*Federal Railroad Administration identification code*]
FSRR........... Flight Software Readiness Review (MCD)
FSRR........... Flight System Readiness Review (NASA)
FSRs........... Feedback Shift Registers (SAUS)
FSRS........... Flight System Recording System (MCD)
FSRS........... Force Structure Requirements Study [*Military*]
FSRS........... Forms Supplies Request System (TIMI)
FSRS........... Frequency Selective Receiver System (MCD)
FSRS........... Functional Security Requirements Specification (SAUS)
FSRT........... Firm Scheduled Return Time (SAUO)
FSRT........... Flight Systems Redundancy Test (MCD)
FSRU........... Foreign Service Reserve (Unlimited) [*Department of State*]
FSRV........... FirstService Corp. [*NASDAQ symbol*] (SAG)
FSRVF......... FirstService Corp.(Mfg) [*NASDAQ symbol*] (TTSB)
FSS............. Fabrication Statusing System (MCD)
FSS............. Facilities Support Services (SAUS)
FSS............. Facility Security Supervision (MCD)
FSS............. Facility Status Sheet (EEVL)
FSS............. Fail Safe System (SAUO)
FSS............. Family Security Service
FSS............. Family Self-Sufficiency (SAUO)
FSS............. Family Support Service [*Australia*]
FSS............. Fast Sealift Ship [*Navy*] (DOMA)
FSS............. Fast System Switch [*Unix*] (VERA)
FSS............. Fatigue Striation Spacing (SAUS)
FSS............. Fear Survey Schedule [*Psychology*]
FSS............. Federal Signal [*NYSE symbol*] (TTSB)
FSS............. Federal Signal Corp. [*Formerly, Federal Sign & Signal Corp.*] [*NYSE symbol*] (SPSG)
FSS............. Federal Supply and Services (SAUO)
FSS............. Federal Supply Schedule
FSS............. Federal Supply Service (USGC)
FSS............. Fellow of the Royal Statistical Society [*British*]
FSS............. Fellow of the Statistical Society (SAUO)
FSS............. Fetal Scalp Sampling [*Medicine*] (MELL)
FSS............. Fetal Solvent Syndrome [*Medicine*] (MELL)
FSS............. Fetal Syphilis Syndrome [*Medicine*] (MELL)
FSS............. Field Security Section (SAUO)
FSS............. Field Security Service (SAUO)
FSS............. Field Sequential System [*Military*] (IAA)
FSS............. Field Service Section [*Military*]
FSS............. Field Spectrometer System (MCD)
FSS............. Field Storage Site (SAUO)
FSS............. Field Support Subsystem (SAUS)
FSS............. Field Support System
FSS............. Field System Support (VLIE)
FSS............. Financial Self-Sufficiency (FOTI)
FSS............. Financial Status Summary (OICC)
FSS............. Financial Supervisory Service
FSS............. Fine Sun Sensor [*NASA*]
FSS............. Finite Solution Set [*Mathemetics*] (WDAA)
FSS............. Finnish Sauna Society [*British*] (DBA)
FSS............. Finnish Society of Sydney [*New South Wales, Australia*]
FSS............. Fire Sensing & Suppression system (SAUS)
FSS............. Fire Sprinkler System (SAUS)
FSS............. Fire Support Section (SAUS)
FSS............. Fire Support Ship
FSS............. Fire Support Station [*Navy*] (NVT)
FSS............. Fire Support System (ACAE)
FSS............. Fire Suppression System (MCD)
FSS............. First-Stage Separation [*Aerospace*]
FSS............. Fixed Satellite Service
FSS............. Fixed-Service Satellite (SAUS)
FSS............. Fixed Service Structure (MCD)
FSS............. Flap-Slat-Spoiler [*Aviation*] (MCD)
FSS............. Fleet Service School [*Navy*]
FSS............. Fleet Supply Ship (SAUS)
FSS............. Flight Safety System
FSS............. Flight Screening Squadron (SAUO)
FSS............. Flight Security Supervisor [*Military*]
FSS............. Flight Sensor System (ACAE)
FSS............. Flight Service Station (ACAE)
FSS............. Flight Standards Service [*FAA*] (MCD)
FSS............. Flight Support Station [*For manned maneuvering unit*] (NASA)
FSS............. Flight Support Structure (MCD)
FSS............. Flight Support System (MCD)
FSS............. Flight Systems Simulator [*NASA*] (NASA)
FSS............. Floor Service Station (SAUS)
FSS............. Floor Service Stations (NRCH)
FSS............. Fluid Supply System (MCD)
FSS............. Flutter Suppression System [*Aviation*]
FSS............. Flying Spot Scanner [*Optical character recognition*]
FSS............. Focal Segmental Sclerosis [*Medicine*] (MELL)
FSS............. Fog Signal Station [*Coast Guard*]
FSS............. Food Service System (SAUO)
FSS............. Force Status System (SAUO)
FSS............. Force Stratification System
FSS............. Force Structure Subsystem [*Military*]
FSS............. Foreign Shore Service
FSS............. Foreign Student Service (SAUO)
FSS............. Forensic Science Service [*British*]
FSS............. Forensic Science Society (EAIO)
FSS............. Foreward Scatter System (SAUS)
FSS............. Formatted System Services (SAUS)
FSS............. Forward Scattering Spectroscopy
FSS............. Forward Scatter System (NATG)
FSS............. Forward Supply Support
FSS............. Forward Supply System (SAUO)
FSS............. Forward Support System (ACAE)
FSS............. Fossil Stromgen Sphere (PDAA)
FSS............. Foundation for Shamanic Studies (EA)
FSS............. Four Sigma Society (EA)
FSS............. Frame Storage System [*Television*]
FSS............. Franco-Scottish Society
FSS............. Freeman-Sheldon Syndrome [*Medicine*] (EDAA)
FSS............. Free Space Simulator (ACAE)
FSS............. French Steel Sound [*Medicine*] (DMAA)
FSS............. Frequency-Selective Saturation [*Medicine*] (MELL)
FSS............. Frequency Selective Surface (SAUS)
FSS............. Frozen Semen Storage [*Medicine*] (EDAA)
FSS............. Full Scale Scanner (SAUS)
FSS............. Full-Scale Section (DNAB)
FSS............. Full Scale Span (AAEL)
FSS............. Full Screen Support (TIMI)
FSS............. Fully Separated Subsidiary
FSS............. Functional System Specification (SAUO)
FSS............. Seminole Community College, Sanford, FL [*OCLC symbol*] (OCLC)
f-ss-........... Spanish Sahara [*Western Sahara*] [*MARC geographic area code*] [*Library of Congress*] (LCCP)
FSSA........... Federation des Syndicats du Secteur de l'Aluminium, Inc. [*Federation of Aluminum Sector Unions, Inc.*] [*Canada*]
FSSA........... Fellow of the Society of Science and Art [*British*]
FSSA........... Fine Sun Sensor Assembly (SAUS)
FSSA........... Fire Suppression Systems Association (EA)
FSSA........... Flight Service Station Automation (VLIE)
FSSA........... Flying Scot Sailing Association (EA)
FSSANSW.... Family Support Services Association of New South Wales [*Australia*]
FSSB........... Fire Support Surveillance Base [*Military*] (VNW)
FSSB........... First Federal Savings & Loan Association, San Bernardino [*NASDAQ symbol*] (SAG)
FSSB........... First Fed Svgs & Ln Assn [*NASDAQ symbol*] (TTSB)
FSSB........... Flight Status Selection Board (DNAB)
FSSC........... Federal Standard Stock Catalog
FSSC........... Federation of Serbian Sisters Circle [*Australia*]
FSSC........... Fielded Software Support Center
FSSC........... Foreign Student Service Council (EA)
FSSC........... Franciscan Sisters of St. Clare (Pious Union) (TOCD)
FSScA......... Fellow of the Society of Science and Art of London (SAUO)
FSSCA......... Fellow of the Society of Science and Arts, London [*British*] (ROG)
FSSCOM...... Flight Services Station Operations and Procedures Committee (FAAC)
FSSCT......... Forer Structured Sentence Completion Test [*Psychology*]
FSSD........... Facilities and Support Service Division [*Environmental Protection Agency*] (GFGA)
FSSD........... Federal Supply Storage Depot
FSSD........... First-Stage Separation Device [*Aerospace*]
FSSD........... Foreign Service Selection Date
FSSE........... Federation des Societes Suisses d'Employes [*Federation of Swiss Employees' Societies*]
FSSE........... Foreign Service Sales Expense
FSSE........... Forward Service Support Element (AABC)
FSSE........... Franciscan Sisters of St. Elizabeth [*Roman Catholic religious order*]
FSSE........... Fuzzy System Standard Environment (SAUS)
FSSec......... Field Security Section (SAUO)
FSSF........... First Special Service Force (MCD)
FSSFA......... First Special Service Force Association (EA)
FSSG........... Field Service Support Group [*USMC*] (MCD)

FSSG .... Fleet Service Support Group [*Military*]
FSSG .... Force Service Support Group [*Military*] (NVT)
FSSGDET .... Force Service Support Group Detachment [*Military*] (DNAB)
FSSH .... Full Saab Service History [*Automotive classified advertising*]
FSSH .... Full Saturn Service History [*Automotive classified advertising*]
FSSH .... Full Subaru Service History [*Automotive classified advertising*]
FSSH .... Full Suzuki Service History [*Automotive classified advertising*]
FSSI .... Fellow of the Statistical Society of Ireland (ROG)
FSSI EE .... Functional Skills Screening Inventory: Employment Edition [*Test*] (TES)
FSS II .... Fear Survey Schedule II [*Psychology*] (DIPS)
FSSIre .... Fellow of the Statistical Society of Ireland (SAUO)
FSSI TPE ..... Functional Skills Screening Inventory: Training Program Edition (TES)
FSSJ .... Franciscan Sisters of St. Joseph [*Roman Catholic religious order*]
FSSLA .... Financial Security Savings & Loan Association (SAUO)
FSSM .... Flying Spot Scanner Memory (SAUS)
FSSM .... Flying-Spot Scanner Memory (VLIE)
FSSM .... Franciscan Sisters of the Sorrowful Mother (TOCD)
FSSN .... Fission (MSA)
FSSO .... Flight Science Support Office (SAUO)
FSSO .... Foreign Service Staff Officer (SAUO)
FSSP .... Facility Security and Safety Plan (SAUS)
FSSP .... Families of Structurally Similar Proteins [*A database*]
FSSP .... Fellowship of St. Paul (EA)
FSSP .... Film Strip Sound Projector
FSSP .... Foreign Student Summer Project (SAUO)
FSSP .... Forward-Scattering Spectrometer Probe [*Aerosol measurement device*]
FSSP .... Forward-Scattering Spectroscopic Probe (SAUS)
FSSP .... Fraternite Sacerdotale Saint Pie X [*International Sacerdotal Society Saint Pius X - ISSSP*] (EAIO)
FSSP .... Friendly Sons of Saint Patrick (SAUO)
FSSP .... Fuel System Supply Point
FSSP .... Priestly Fraternity of St. Peter (TOCD)
FSSpJ .... Franciscan Sisters of the Spirit of Jesus (TOCD)
FSSPX .... International Sacerdotal Society Saint Pius X [*Switzerland*] (EAIO)
FSSR .... Fellow of the Royal Statistical Society [*British*]
FSSR .... Flight Systems Software Requirement (MCD)
FSSR .... Functional Subsystem Software Requirements (NASA)
FSSRI .... Farming Systems and Soil Resources Institute (SAUO)
FSSRP .... Fast Simple Server Redundancy Protocol [*Computer science*] (DINT)
FSSRS .... Farm Structure Survey Retrieval System [*Information service or system*] (IID)
FSSRS .... Fixed Step Size Random Search (IAA)
FSS/S .... Fine Sun Sensor/Signal Conditioner [*NASA*] (MCD)
FSSS .... Fire Support Subordinate System (SAUO)
FSSS .... Flying Spot Scanner System [*Optical character recognition*] (IAA)
FSSS .... Fuel Set Subsystem (SAUS)
FSSS .... Fuse Set Subsystem
FSSS .... Future Security Strategy Study (ACAE)
FSSS .... Mahe/Seychelles International (ICLI)
FSST .... Fastnet Corp. [*NASDAQ symbol*] (SG)
FSST .... Flying Scot Scanner Tube (PDAA)
FSSTMUK .... Friendly Society of Spade Tree Makers of the United Kingdom [*A union*]
FSSU .... Federated Superannuation Scheme for Universities [*British*]
FSSU .... Field Scientific Support Unit (HEAS)
FSSWT .... Full-Scale Subsonic Wind Tunnel
FST .... Factory Service Tape (SAUS)
FST .... Far Eastern Resources Corp. [*Vancouver Stock Exchange symbol*]
FST .... Farming Systems Trial (GNE)
FST .... Fast [*Horse racing*]
FST .... Fast Air Ltda. [*Chile*] [*ICAO designator*] (FAAC)
FST .... Federal Sales Tax [*Canada*]
FST .... Field Sampling Team [*Environmental science*] (COE)
FST .... Field Service Technician (MCD)
FST .... Field Sobriety Test (SARE)
FST .... Field Suitability Test
FST .... Field Supply Technician (MCD)
FST .... Field Support Teams (SAUS)
FST .... Field Support Terminal (EOSA)
FST .... field surgery team (SAUS)
FST .... Field Surgical Team [*Military*] [*British*]
FST .... Field Survey Team
FST .... File Status Table [*Computer science*] (IBMDP)
FST .... File Systems Tree [*Computer science*]
FST .... Film Supertwist
FST .... Financial Secretary to the Treasury (SAUO)
FST .... Finger Skin Temperature (HEAS)
FST .... Finite Sampling Time
FST .... Fire Safety Technology (SSD)
FST .... Fire Safety Toxicity
FST .... Fire Situation Trainer (SAUS)
FST .... Fire, Smoke, and Toxicity [*Materials science*]
FST .... Fire Support Team (MCD)
FST .... Fire Support Terminal (ACAE)
FST .... First
FST .... First Class or Saloon Passengers [*Shipping*] [*British*]
FST .... First National Stores, Inc. (SAUO)
FST .... Fixed Service Tower
FST .... Flame Smoke Toxicity
FST .... Flat Seam Tin [*Construction term*] (MIST)
FST .... Flat Slip on Top (OA)
FST .... Flat Square Technology (SAUS)
FST .... Flat Square Tube [*IBM Corp.*] (PCM)
FST .... Flat Square Tube (monitor) (SAUS)
FST .... Flatter, Squarer Tube [*Television picture tube*]
FST .... Flavonol 3-Sulfotransferase (SAUS)
FST .... Fleurs Synthesis Telescope
FST .... Flight Support Tapes
FST .... Foam Stability Test
FST .... Follow-On Soviet Tank [*In FST-1, model name of a Russian "supertank" having improved armor and a 135-mm gun*] [*Introduced in the late 1980's*]
FST .... Foreign Service Tour [*Military*]
FST .... Forest Oil [*NYSE symbol*] (SG)
FST .... Forged Steel [*Technical drawings*]
FST .... Forstmann & Company, Inc. [*AMEX symbol*] (COMM)
FST .... Fort Stockton, TX [*Location identifier*] [*FAA*] (FAAL)
FST .... Forward Support Team (MCD)
FST .... Forward Surgical Team (SAUS)
FST .... Framingham State College, Framingham, MA [*OCLC symbol*] (OCLC)
FST .... Franciscan School of Theology (SAUS)
FST .... Free Southern Theater
FST .... Free Space Transfer (MCD)
FST .... Free Stowed and Trimmed (SAUS)
fs/t .... free stowed/trimmed (SAUS)
FST .... Frequency Shift Telegraphy
FST .... Frequency Shift Transmission
FST .... Frit Slurry Transport (ABAC)
FST .... Full-Scale Tunnel [*Aerospace*]
FST .... full square tube (SAUS)
FST .... Full System Test (SAUS)
FST .... Functional Simulator and Translator [*Computer science*] (CSR)
FST .... Functional Subassembly Tester (SAUS)
FST .... Functional System Test (ACAE)
FST .... Funkstelle [*Radio Station*] [*German military - World War II*]
FST .... Future Soviet Tank (SAUS)
FST .... Future Strategic Targets (MCD)
FST .... Fuzed Silica Tube
FST .... Society of Swedish Composers (SAUO)
FSTA .... Fellow of the Swimming Teachers' Association [*British*] (DBQ)
FSTA .... Food Science and Technology Abstracts [*Database*] (NITA)
FSTA .... Food Science and Technology Abstracts (journ.) (SAUS)
FSTA .... Force Structure Trade-Off Analysis (MCD)
FStaB .... Bradford County Public Library, Starke, FL [*Library symbol*] [*Library of Congress*] (LCLS)
FSTACOE ..... Fleet Special Test and Checkout Equipment
FSTAD .... Fire Support and Target Acquisition Division [*Human Engineering Laboratory*] [*Army*]
FstAlert .... First Alert, Inc. [*Associated Press*] (SAG)
FstAm .... First of America Bank Corp. [*Associated Press*] (SAG)
FstARwy ...... First American Railways, Inc. [*Associated Press*] (SAG)
FstBell .... First Bell Bancorp, Inc. [*Associated Press*] (SAG)
FstbkIll .... Firstbank of Illinois Co. [*Associated Press*] (SAG)
FstbkPR .... Firstbank Puerto Rico [*Associated Press*] (SAG)
FstBks .... First Banks, Inc. [*Associated Press*] (SAG)
FstBkshs ...... First Bankshares of Missouri, Inc. [*Associated Press*] (SAG)
FstBrnd .... First Brands Corp. [*Associated Press*] (SAG)
FSTBSGB ..... Feeding Stuffs Trade Benevolent Society of Great Britain (SAUO)
FSTC .... Farmington State Teachers College [*Merged with University of Maine*]
FSTC .... Fayetteville State Teachers College [*Later, Fayetteville State University*] [*North Carolina*]
FSTC .... Federal Software Testing Center (ACAE)
FSTC .... Field Sound Transmission Class (DAC)
FSTC .... Financial Services Technical Consortium
FSTC .... First Citizens Corp. [*NASDAQ symbol*] (SAG)
FSTC .... Foreign Science and Technology Center [*Army*]
FstChi97 ...... First Chicago Corp. [*Associated Press*] (SAG)
FstChic .... First Chicago Corp. [*Associated Press*] (SAG)
FstCity .... First City Bancorp, Inc. [*Associated Press*] (SAG)
FstCity .... First City Financial Corp. [*Associated Press*] (SAG)
FST Code ...... Field Start Code (SAUS)
FstCom .... First Commonwealth, Inc. [*Associated Press*] (SAG)
Fstcrp .... Firstcorp, Inc. (MHDW)
FstCsh .... First Cash, Inc. [*Associated Press*] (SAG)
FstCtzF .... First Citizens Financial Corp. [*Associated Press*] (SAG)
FstCwlth ...... First Commonwealth Financial Corp. [*Associated Press*] (SAG)
FSTD .... Feedback Subsequence Transition Diagram (SAUS)
FSTD .... Fellow of the Society of Typographic Designers [*British*] (DI)
FSTD .... Fire Support Test Directorate (SAUS)
FSTD .... Flight Simulation Test Data
FstData .... First Data Corp. [*Associated Press*] (SAG)
FstDefiFn ...... First Defiance Financial Corp. [*Associated Press*] (SAG)
FSTDS .... Flight Station Tactical Display Set (ACAE)
FSTDY .... Final Semester Temporary Duty [*Air Force*] (AFM)
FSTE .... Factory Special Test Equipment (NASA)
FSTE .... Federation of Unions of Workers in the Service of the State (Mexico) [*Political party*] (PSAP)
FSTE .... Field Support Test Equipment
FSTE .... Fixed Systems Test Equipment (SAA)
FSTE .... Foreign Service Tour Extension (INF)
FstEnter .... First Entertainment, Inc. [*Associated Press*] (SAG)
FstEntr .... First Entertainment, Inc. [*Associated Press*] (SAG)
FstFed .... FirstFed Financial [*Associated Press*] (SAG)
FstFedFn ...... FirstFederal Financial Services [*Associated Press*] (SAG)
FstFnHld ...... First Financial Holdings, Inc. [*Associated Press*] (SAG)

FstFnIN........ First Financial Corp. [*Associated Press*] (SAG)
FSth........ First South Africa Corp. Ltd. [*Associated Press*] (SAG)
FSTH........ First Southern Bancshares [*NASDAQ symbol*] (TTSB)
FSTH........ First Southern Bancshares, Inc. [*NASDAQ symbol*] (SAG)
FstHmBcp........ First Home Bancorp, Inc. [*Associated Press*] (SAG)
FstHmSv........ First Home Savings Bank SLA [*Associated Press*] (SAG)
FSTI........ Federal Council for Science and Technology (SAUO)
FSTI........ Federal Scientific and Technical Information (SAUS)
FSTI........ Formed Steel Tube Institute [*Later, WSTI*]
FSTI........ Free Search Terminal Interface [*Telecommunications*]
Fstln Cp........ First Indiana Corp. [*Associated Press*] (SAG)
FstInRt........ First Industrial Realty Trust, Inc. [*Associated Press*] (SAG)
FST/IP........ Fast Sequenced Transport Encapsulation for IP Networks [*Communications term*] (DCT)
FSTIS........ Federal Scientific and Technical Information System (SAUS)
FSTI System... Federal Scientific and Technical Information System (SAUS)
FstKent........ First Kent Financial Corp. [*Associated Press*] (SAG)
FSTK/SUP........ Friendly Strike or Support [*Military*] (NVT)
FSTL........ Foreign Salable Technology and Licence [*South Korea*] [*Information service or system*] (IID)
FSTL........ Future Strategic Target List
FstLI........ First of Long Island Corp. [*Associated Press*] (SAG)
FSTM........ Fort Smith Trolley Museum [*Federal Railroad Administration identification code*]
FSTMA........ Firearm and Security Trainers Management Association (EA)
Fstmark........ Firstmark Corp. [*Associated Press*] (SAG)
FSTMB........ Bolivian Mineworkers Syndical Federation [*Political party*] (PSAP)
FstMerit........ FirstMerit Corp. [*Associated Press*] (SAG)
FstMtge........ First Mortagage Corp. [*Associated Press*] (SAG)
FstMutl........ First Mutual Bancorp, Inc. [*Associated Press*] (SAG)
FSTN........ Film Compensated STN [*Super Twisted Nematic*] (CDE)
FSTN........ Financial Services Technology Network (NTPA)
FSTNR........ Fastener
FstNtw........ First Nationwide Bank A Federal Savings Bank [*Associated Press*] (SAG)
FSTP........ Foiled Shielded Twisted Pair [*Cable*] (VERA)
F/STP........ Foil STP (SAUS)
FstPalm........ First Palm Beach Bancorp, Inc. [*Associated Press*] (SAG)
F STP DRVWY... Failure to Stop when Emerging from an Alley, Driveway, or Building [*Conviction term used in state of Oregon*] (MVRD)
FSTPP........ Foreign Service Team Preceptorship Program (SAUS)
F STP PAS LD... Failure to Stop for Passenger Loading of Public Transit Vehicle [*Conviction term used in state of Oregon*] (MVRD)
F STP RR........ Failure to Stop for a Railroad Signal [*Conviction term used in state of Oregon*] (MVRD)
FSTPW........ Friendly Society of Tin Plate Workers [*A union*] [*British*]
FSTR........ Fallschirmtruppen [*Parachute Troops*] [*German military*]
FSTR........ Field Service Technical Report (AAG)
FSTR........ Foster
FSTR........ Foster [*L.B.*] Co. [*NASDAQ symbol*] (NQ)
FSTRA........ Foster (LB)Cl'A' [*NASDAQ symbol*] (TTSB)
F STR BUS... Failure to Stop for Bus Safety Lights [*Conviction term used in state of Oregon*] (MVRD)
FSTRE........ Field Service Trouble Report
FSTS........ Federal Secure Telephone Service [*or System*] [*DoD*]
FSTS........ Federal Secure Telephone System (SAUO)
FSTS........ Financial Services Terminals Support [*IBM Corp.*]
FSTS........ Fire Service Training School (SAUO)
FSTS........ Fire Support Training Strategy (SAUS)
FSTS........ Fitting Shop Trade Society [*A union*] [*British*]
FSTS........ Flight Simulated Training System [*Military*]
FStS........ Forward Storage Site (SAUS)
FSTS........ Future Space Transportation System
FSTS........ Fuze Set Test Set
FstSouth........ First South Africa Corp. Ltd. [*Associated Press*] (SAG)
FstStBc........ First State Bancorp (NM) [*Associated Press*] (SAG)
FstSvc........ FirstService Corp. [*Associated Press*] (SAG)
FstSvNJ........ First Savings Bank of New Jersy [*Associated Press*] (SAG)
FSTT........ Floating Shuttle Tape Transport (PDAA)
FSTTC........ Flight Safety Training and Test Center
FstTenn........ First Tennessee National Corp. [*Associated Press*] (SAG)
FSTU........ Fluid Sealing Technology Unit (SAUS)
FstUC........ First Union Corp. [*Associated Press*] (SAG)
FStuM........ Martin County Public Library, Stuart, FL [*Library symbol*] [*Library of Congress*] (LCLS)
Fst USA........ First USA, Inc. [*Associated Press*] (SAG)
FstUtdCp........ First United Corp. [*Associated Press*] (SAG)
FSTV........ Fast Scan Television [*Computer science*] (IAA)
FSTV........ Flat-Square Television (SAUS)
FSTV........ Full-Scale Test Vehicle [*NASA*]
FstVict........ First Victoria National Bank [*Associated Press*] (SAG)
FstWash........ First Washingtn Bancorp, Inc. [*Associated Press*] (SAG)
FSTWP........ Fellow of the Society of Technical Writers and Publishers (SAUO)
FstWV........ First West Virginia Bancorp, Inc. [*Associated Press*] (SAG)
FSTX........ Fuel Supply Trust [*Private rail car owner code*]
fsty........ firstly (SAUS)
FstYears........ [*The*] First Years, Inc. [*Associated Press*] (SAG)
FSU........ Facsimile Switching Unit
FSU........ Factor of Safety Ultimate (ACAE)
FSU........ Fail Sheer Ultimate (MCD)
FSU........ Family Service Unit [*Medicine*] [*British*]
FSU........ Fast Scan Utility (TIMI)
FSU........ Fellowship for Spiritual Understanding (EA)
FSU........ Ferrite Store Unit (SAUS)
FSU........ Ferry Service Unit
FSU........ Field Select Unit
FSU........ Field Service Uniform (SAUS)
FSU........ Field Storage Unit [*Military*]
FSU........ Field Support Unit (SAUS)
FSU........ Field Surgical Unit (SAUS)
FSU........ File Support Utility [*Computer science*] (VLIE)
FSU........ Final Signal Unit [*Telecommunications*] (TEL)
FSU........ Fire and Safety Unit [*Coast Guard*] (DOMA)
FSU........ Fleet Support Unit (SAUS)
FSU........ Flightline Support Unit (MCD)
FSU........ Flight Service Unit (ADA)
FSU........ Florida State University, Tallahassee (SAUS)
FSU........ Food Service Unit (SAUS)
FSU........ Former Soviet Union (RDA)
fsu........ Former Soviet Union
FSU........ Fort Sumner, NM [*Location identifier*] [*FAA*] (FAAL)
FSU........ Forward Studies Unit (EURO)
FSU........ Forward Support Unit (SAUS)
fsu........ freak student union (SAUO)
FSU........ Free Software Union (SAUO)
FSU........ Freisoziale Union - Demokratische Mitte [*Free Social Union - Democratic Center*] [*Germany*] [*Political party*] (PPW)
FSU........ Freon Servicing Unit (NASA)
FSU........ Frequency Set on Unit (SAUS)
FSU........ Friedrich Schiller University (SAUS)
FSU........ Friends of the Soviet Union (SAUO)
FSU........ Full-Scale Unit (KSC)
FSU........ Fusion Splicer Unit [*Telecommunications*] (NITA)
FSUA........ Finance Sector Union of Australia
FSUC........ Federal Statistics Users' Conference [*Defunct*] (EA)
FSUD........ Fort Street Union Depot Company (SAUO)
FS/UEG........ Fleet Staff/Unit Expansion Group (DNAB)
FSuH........ Fridays, Sundays, Holidays (SAUS)
FSUJPM........ Friendly Society of United Journeymen Platers and Moulders [*A uniôn*] [*British*]
FSupp........ Federal Supplement (SAFN)
F Supp........ Federal Supplement Reporter [*West*] [*A publication*] (AAGC)
FSURAM........ Functional Storage Unit Random Access Method [*Computer science*] (VLIE)
FSUROS........ Functional Storage Unit Read Only Storage (SAUS)
FSUROS........ Functional Storage Unit Read-Only Storage [*Computer science*] (VLIE)
FSUS........ Florida State University Studies (SAUO)
FSUs........ Food Service Units (SAUS)
FSUSA........ Finance School, United States Army
FSUWG........ Facility Science Users Working Group (SAUS)
FSV........ Falciparum Sporozoite Vaccine [*Antimalarial*]
FSV........ Fat-Soluble Vitamins (MELL)
FSV........ Feline Fibrosarcoma Virus
FSV........ Ferry Supply Vehicle
FSV........ Final Stage Vehicle
FSV........ Final Storage Vehicle (SAUS)
FSV........ Fire Service Valve (IEEE)
FSV........ Fire Support Vehicle [*Military*] (MCD)
FSV........ Floating point Status Vector (SAUS)
FSV........ Floating-Point Status Vector (VLIE)
FSV........ Formula Super Volkswagen [*Class of racing cars*]
FSV........ Fort Smith & Van Buren Railway [*Federal Railroad Administration identification code*]
FSV........ Fort St. Vrain [*Nuclear plant*] (NRCH)
FSV........ Free Steered Vehicle (HEAS)
FSV........ Frequency Selective Voltmeter
FSV........ Fujinami Sarcoma Virus
FSV........ Future Scout Vehicle [*Military*]
FSVA........ Fellow of the Incorporated Society of Valuers and Auctioneers [*British*] (DBQ)
FSVA........ Fellow of the Society of Valuers and Auctioneers (SAUO)
FSVB........ Fort Smith & Van Buren Railway Co. [*AAR code*]
FSVB........ Franklin Bank NA [*NASDAQ symbol*] (SAG)
FSvBkNJ........ First Savings Bank FSLA Perth Amboy NJ [*Associated Press*] (SAG)
FSVC........ Financial Services Volunteer Corps [*An association*] (EA)
FSVC........ Freshstart Venture Capital Corp. [*NASDAQ symbol*] (SAG)
FSVDR........ File Structure Volume Descriptor Record (NTCM)
FSVM........ Frequency Selective Voltmeter (IAA)
FSVNGS........ Fort St. Vrain Nuclear Generating Station (NRCH)
FSVP........ Find SVP [*NASDAQ symbol*] (TTSB)
FSVP........ FIND/SVP, Inc. [*New York, NY*] [*NASDAQ symbol*] (NQ)
FSVR........ Fort St. Vrain Reactor [*Platteville, CO*] (GAAI)
FSVS........ Future Secure Voice System (LAIN)
FSW........ Feet of Salt Water (SAUS)
FSW........ Feet of Seawater [*Deep-sea diving*]
fsw........ feet of sea water (SAUS)
FSW........ Field Service Worker [*Social Services*] (DAVI)
FSW........ Field Switch
FSW........ Final Status Word [*Computer science*] (IAA)
FSW........ Fire Team Support Weapon (MCD)
FSW........ Fletcher Sutcliffe Wild [*Commercial firm*] [*British*]
FSW........ Flexible Steel Wire
FSW........ flightserv.com [*AMEX symbol*] (SG)
FSW........ Flight Software (MCD)
FSW........ Fork Status Word (SAUS)
FSW........ Forward Swept Wing
FSW........ Frame Synchronization Word (MSA)
FSW........ Friendly Society of Watermen [*A union*] [*British*]
FSWA........ Federation of Sewage Works Associations (COE)

FSWD .... Foundation for the Study of Wilson's Disease [*Later, NCSWD*] (EA)
FSWD .... Full-Scale Weapons Delivery [*Military*]
FSWEC .... Federal Software Exchange Center
FSWEP .... Federal Student Work Experience Program (FOTI)
FSWFS .... Field Standard Weight and Force System (AAG)
FSWMA .... Fine and Specialty Wire Manufacturers Association [*Later, Specialty Wire Association*] (EA)
FSWO .... Financial Secretary to the War Office [*British*]
FSWR .... Flexible Steel Wire Rope
FSWT .... Free Surface Water Tunnel
FSWU .... Federation of Sudanese Workers Unions (SAUO)
FSWW .... First Society of Whale Watchers [*Defunct*] (EA)
FSX .... Fighter Support Experiment (SAUS)
FSX .... Fighter Support Experimental [*Military*]
FSX .... Fire Support Execution (SAUS)
FSX .... Flagship Express Services, Inc. [*ICAO designator*] (FAAC)
FSX .... Future Shock Experimental [*Mountain bike*] (PS)
FS-X .... Future Sports-Sedan Experimental [*Concept car*]
f-sx- .... South West Africa [*Namibia*] [*MARC geographic area code*] [*Library of Congress*] (LCCP)
FSY .... Factor of Safety Yield (ACAE)
FSY .... Fassey Aviation Ltd. [*Nigeria*] [*FAA designator*] (FAAC)
FSYO .... Fleet Security Officer [*Navy*] [*British*]
FSZ .... Fully Stabilized Zirconia (SAUS)
FT .... Factory Test
FT .... Faience Tile (DICI)
FT .... Failed Test [*Motor vehicle violation code used in state of Maryland*] (MVRD)
FT .... Fail Type [*Military*] (AFIT)
FT .... Faint
FT .... False Transmitter [*Neurology*] (DAVI)
FT .... Family Therapy
FT .... Fanconi-De Tari [*Syndrome*] [*Medicine*] (DB)
FT .... Fan Tek (EA)
FT .... Fashion Technology
FT .... Fashion Television [*TV program*]
FT .... Fast [*Track condition*] [*Thoroughbred racing*]
FT .... Fast Track [*Insurance*]
FT .... Fast-Twitch (DB)
FT .... Fatigue Testing (SAUS)
FT .... Fatigue Time [*Sports medicine*]
FT .... Fault Tolerance (SAUS)
FT .... Fault Tolerant (HGAA)
FT .... Fault Tree (MCD)
FT .... Feature Translation (VLIE)
FT .... Fecal Trypsin [*Medicine*] (MELL)
FT .... Federal Triangle [*Washington, DC*]
FT .... Feet [*or Foot*] (AAG)
ft .... Feet
FT .... Feet Together [*Dance terminology*]
FT .... Feint [*of account book rulings*]
Ft .... Ferritin [*Biochemistry*] (AAMN)
FT .... Ferroresonant Transformer (SAUS)
FT .... Fiant [*Let Them Be Made*] [*Pharmacy*] (ROG)
FT .... Fiat [*Make*] [*Pharmacy*]
FT .... Fiat SpA [*Italy*] [*ICAO aircraft manufacturer identifier*] (ICAO)
FT .... Fibrous Tissue [*Medicine*]
FT .... Field Target (SAUS)
FT .... Field Terminator (SAUS)
FT .... Field Test (AAG)
FT .... Field Training [*AFROTC*] (AFM)
FT .... Field Transfer (SAUS)
FT .... Field Trip
FT .... File Transfer (VLIE)
FT .... File Transporter (SAUS)
FT .... Filing Time [*Time a message is presented for transmission*]
FT .... Film Thickness (SAUS)
FT .... Filum Terminale [*Medicine*] (MELL)
FT .... Final Test (AAEL)
FT .... Final Total (SAUS)
FT .... Financial Times [*A publication*] (ODBW)
FT .... Fine Thermal [*Furnace*]
FT .... Fine Thermal Black (SAUS)
FT .... Fine Turned (SAUS)
FT .... Finger Tip (MELL)
FT .... Fire Control Technician [*Navy rating*]
FT .... Fire-control Technician (SAUS)
FT .... Fire Team [*Marine Corps*]
FT .... Fire Technologist (SAUS)
FT .... Fire Technology (SAUS)
FT .... Fire Thermostat (AAG)
FT .... Fire Trench (SAUS)
FT .... Fire-Tube (SAUS)
FT .... Fire-Tube Boiler
ft .... firing table (SAUS)
FT .... Firing Tables [*Military*]
FT .... Firing Temperature [*Military*] (IAA)
FT .... First Telecast (DOAD)
FT .... First Trust (SAUO)
FT .... Fischer-Tropsch Synthesis [*Organic chemistry*]
FT .... Fisher Test building (SAUS)
FT .... Fission Track [*Geological age dating*]
FT .... Fissured Tongue (MELL)
FT .... Fitter and Turner [*Navy rating*] [*British*]
FT .... Fixation and Transfer [*of text*] (DNAB)
ft .... fixed tannin (SAUS)
FT .... Fixed Tone
FT .... Flagon and Trencher (EA)
FT .... Flame Thrower (SAUS)
FT .... Flamethrower [*Engineering*] (IAA)
FT .... Flame Tight
FT .... Flame-Tint (SAUS)
FT .... Flanging Tube
FT .... Flat [*Paper*]
FT .... Flat Template
FT .... Flat Top (SAUS)
FT .... Flat-Topped [*Frames*] [*Optometry*]
Ft .... Fleet (SAUS)
FT .... Flexible Trunk [*Hovercraft*]
Ft .... Flight (SAUS)
FT .... Flight Team (MCD)
FT .... Flight Termination
F/T .... Flight Test (KSC)
FT .... Flight Time (SAUS)
FT .... Float Time (VLIE)
FT .... Flow Through
FT .... Flow Time (SAUS)
FT .... Flow Transducer [*Instrumentation*]
FT .... Flow Transformer (SAUS)
FT .... Flow Transmitter [*Nuclear energy*] (NRCH)
FT .... Fluorescent Target
FT .... Fluoride Treatment (MELL)
FT .... Flushometer Tank
FT .... Flush Threshold [*Technical drawings*]
FT .... Flying Test (SAUS)
FT .... Flying Tiger Line, Inc. [*ICAO designator*]
FT .... Flying Tiger Lines (SAUS)
FT .... FM Broadcast Translator [*FCC*] (NTCM)
FT .... Foam Tape
FT .... Foden Trucks (SAUS)
FT .... Fog Trumpet [*Navigation charts*]
FT .... Follow-On Test
F-T .... Follow Through
FT .... Food Technologist (SAUS)
FT .... Food Technology (SAUS)
ft .... Food Technology (journ.) (SAUS)
ft .... Foot (AAMN)
FT .... Foot (GOBB)
ft .... foot or feet (SAUS)
FT .... Force Terminal (SAUS)
FT .... Foreign Theater
FT .... Foreign Tourist [*Indian Railway*] (TIR)
FT .... Foreign Transaction (AFM)
FT .... Forest Trust [*An association*] (EA)
FT .... Foretop [*Obsolete*]
FT .... fore top (SAUS)
Ft .... Forint [*Florin*] [*Monetary unit*] [*Hungary*] (GPO)
FT .... Forklift Truck (DCTA)
FT .... Formal Test (SAUS)
FT .... Formal Toxoid [*Medicine*]
FT .... Formal Training [*Military*] (AFM)
FT .... Format Tape (SAUS)
FT .... Formula Translation (SAUS)
FT .... Formula Translator (SAUS)
FT .... Fort (AFM)
Ft .... Fort (PROS)
FT .... Fortean Times [*A publication*]
FT .... Fortification (ROG)
ft .... Fortification (VRA)
ft .... Fortified (SAUS)
FT .... For Trade
FT .... Forward-in-Time (SAUS)
FT .... Forward Transfer [*Telecommunications*] (TEL)
FT .... Foundation of Thanatology (EA)
FT .... Foundation Type [*Dialog*] [*Searchable field*] [*Telecommunications*] (NITA)
FT .... Fourier Tachometer (SAUS)
FT .... Fourier Transform
FT .... Fourier Transformation (EDCT)
FT .... Fourier-transform techniques (SAUS)
FT .... Frame Transfer (SAUS)
FT .... Franciscus Tigrini de Pisis [*Flourished, 13th-14th century*] [*Authority cited in pre-1607 legal work*] (DSA)
FT .... Franklin Universal Tr [*NASDAQ symbol*] (TTSB)
FT .... Franklin Universal Trust [*NYSE symbol*] (CTT)
FT .... Free Term (SAUS)
FT .... Free Testosterone (MELL)
FT .... Freethought Today (SAUS)
FT .... Free Throw [*Basketball*]
FT .... Free Thyroxine [*Also, FT$_4$*] [*Endocrinology*]
ft .... free trade (SAUS)
FT .... Free Trader (ROG)
FT .... Free Troposphere (CARB)
FT .... Free Turbine (AAG)
FT .... Free Turn
FT .... Freight (SAUS)
FT .... Freight Ton
FT .... Freight Transport
FT .... French Telefunken [*Record label*]

ft .... French Territory of the Afars and Issas [*Djibouti*] [*MARC country of publication code*] [*Library of Congress*] (LCCP)
FT .... French Title [*Online database field identifier*]
FT .... Frequency and Time (IEEE)
FT .... Frequency Tolerance
FT .... Frequency Tracker (MSA)
FT .... Frequent Traveler [*on airlines*]
ft .... frequent traveller (SAUS)
FT .... Fresh Target (SAUS)
FT .... Friends of the Tango (EA)
FT .... Front [*Deltiology*]
FT .... Fruit (SAUS)
FT .... Ftorafur [*Analog of 5-fluorourical deoxyribose*] [*Soviet anticancer drug*]
FT .... fuel tank (SAUS)
FT .... Fuel Tanking [*Aerospace*] (AAG)
FT .... Fuel Terms (DS)
FT .... Fuel Trim (HAWK)
FT .... Fuller Transmission (SAUS)
FT .... Full Term [*Pregnancy*] [*Medicine*]
ft .... full terms (SAUS)
ft .... full ternis (SAUS)
F/T .... Full Throttle (SAUS)
FT .... Full Tilt Container (DCTA)
FT .... Full Time [*Employment, education*]
ft .... full time (SAUS)
FT .... Fully Tracked (NATG)
FT .... Fume-Tight [*Technical drawings*]
FT .... Functionally Terminated (MCD)
FT .... Functional Test [*Computer science*]
FT .... Functional Tester [*Mars Electronics*] (NITA)
FT .... Functional Type (SAUO)
FT .... Function Table (SAUS)
FT .... Function Translator (SAUS)
FT .... Fundic Type [*of epithelium*] [*Medicine*]
FT .... Fund Type [*Military*] (AFIT)
FT .... Fusion Technology (SAUS)
FT .... Tampa-Hillsborough County Public Library, Tampa, FL [*Library symbol*] [*Library of Congress*] (LCLS)
FT .... Terminal Forecasts [*Symbol*] [*National Weather Service*]
Ft .... Terminal Framing Bits [*Telecommunications*] (ACRL)
FT1 .... Fire Control Technician, First Class [*Navy rating*]
FT-1 .... Fractional T-1 (SAUS)
FT1 .... fractional T1, common carrier transmission in multiples of 64 kb/s (SAUS)
FT2 .... Fire Control Technician, Second Class [*Navy rating*]
ft2 .... Square Feet
FT^2 .... Square Foot
FT^2/H .... Square Feet per Hour
FT^2/MIN .... Square Foot per Minute (WDAA)
FT^2/S .... Square Feet per Second
FT^3 .... Cubic Feet (EG)
ft3 .... Cubic Feet
FT3 .... Fire Control Technician, Third Class [*Navy rating*]
FT_3 .... Free Triiodothyronine [*Endocrinology*] (DAVI)
FT^3/(FT D) .... Cubic Feet per Foot Day
FT_3IX .... Free Triiodothyronine Index
ft3/min .... Cubic Foot per Minute (SAUS)
FT^3/MIN .... Cubic Foot per Minute (WDAA)
ft3/min/min .... Cubic Feet per Minute (SAUS)
FT^3/S .... Cubic Feet per Second
ft3/sec .... Cubic Feet per Second (SAUS)
FT_4 .... Free [*Unbound*] Thyroxine [*Endocrinology*] (DAVI)
FT4 .... Free Thyroxine T4 (SAUS)
FT_4F .... Serum Free Thyroxine Fraction [*Endocrinology*] (DAVI)
FT4IX .... Free Thyroxine Index [*Endocrinology*]
FT-30 .... Financial Times Ordinary Share Index (ODBW)
FTA .... European Throwsters Association [*Italy*] (EAIO)
FTA .... Failed to Arrive (WDAA)
FTA .... Failed to Attend (ADA)
FTA .... Failure to Agree (FOTI)
FTA .... Failure to Appear [*Court case*]
FTA .... Fairchild Tenants Association (SAUO)
FTA .... Fast Time Analysis
FTA .... Fast Turnaround (SAUS)
FTA .... Fatigue Test Article (NASA)
FTA .... Fault Tree Analysis (NASA)
FTA .... Federal Transit Act (COE)
FTA .... Federal Transit Administration [*Formerly, UMTA*] [*Department of Transportation*]
FTA .... Federated Tanners' Association of Australia
FTA .... Federation of Tax Administrators (EA)
FTA .... Federation of Trade Associations [*Republic of Ireland*] (BI)
FTA .... Feed Test Algorithm (ABAC)
FT/A .... Feet per Year
FTA .... Fernsehteilnehmeranschlua (SAUS)
FTA .... Field Technical Authority (NVT)
FTA .... Field Test Administration (AAG)
FTA .... Field to Advice (SAUS)
FTA .... Field to Advise [*Telecommunications*] (TEL)
FTA .... File Trade Association [*British*] (BI)
FTA .... File Transfer Agent (SAUS)
FTA .... Film Training Aid
FTA .... Final Type Approval (SAUS)
FTA .... Financial Times Actuaries (ODBW)
FTA .... Financial Transfer Agreement (FOTI)
FTA .... Finnish Travel Association (SAUO)
FTA .... Fire Control Technician (Automatic Directors) [*U.S. Navy enlisted rating*] (AUER)
FTA .... Fire Technology Abstracts (SAUS)
FTA .... Fire Training Area (BCP)
FTA .... Fitness Trade Association (NTPA)
FTA .... Fixed Term Agreement
FTA .... Fixed Time of Arrival [*Aviation*]
FTA .... Flexographic Technical Association (EA)
FTA .... Flight Test Article (KSC)
FTA .... Floatation Tank Association (NTPA)
FTA .... Floptical Technology Association (SAUO)
FTA .... Florida Trail Association (EA)
FTA .... Florida Transit Association (SRA)
FTA .... Florida Trucking Association (SRA)
FTA .... Fluid Transpiration Arc
FTA .... Fluorescent Titer Antibody [*Clinical chemistry*]
FTA .... Fluorescent Treponemal Antibody [*Clinical chemistry*]
FTA .... Fluorescent Treponemal Antibody Test [*Medicine*] (IDYL)
FTA .... Food, Tobacco, Agricultural and Allied Workers of America (SAUO)
FTA .... Food Tray Association [*Defunct*]
FTA .... Forced Transpiration Arc (SAUS)
FTA .... Foreign Technology Assessment (SEWL)
FTA .... Foreign Trade Association [*Cologne, Federal Republic of Germany*] (EAIO)
FTA .... Forward Transfer Admittance
FTA .... Foundation of the Twelve Apostles (EA)
FTA .... Free the Army [*Barracks graffiti; also, title of antimilitary play*] [*Bowdlerized version*]
FTA .... Free Theater Associates (SAUO)
FTA .... Free Thought Association (EA)
FTA .... Free Throws Attempted [*Basketball*]
FTA .... Free Trade Agreement [*or Arrangement*]
FTA .... Free Trade Area
FTA .... Free Trade Association [*European*]
FTA .... Free Transport Association (SAUO)
FTA .... Freight Transport Association [*British*]
FTA .... Freight Transport Association Ltd. (SAUO)
FTA .... Frontier Flying Service, Inc. [*ICAO designator*] (FAAC)
FTA .... Fuel Treatment Apparatus
fta .... full-throttle altitude (SAUS)
FTA .... Full-Time Attendance (GFGA)
FTA .... Fun, Travel, Adventure [*Sarcastic alternate to FTA - Free the Army*]
FTA .... Fur Takers of America (EA)
FTA .... Future Teachers of America [*Later, SAE*] (EA)
FTA .... Hot Springs, SD [*Location identifier*] [*FAA*] (FAAL)
FTaA .... Apalachee Community Mental Health Services, Inc., Tallahassee, FL [*Library symbol*] [*Library of Congress*] (LCLS)
FTAA .... Federated Tanners' Association of Australia
FTAA .... Federation of Turkish-American Associations
FTAA .... Free Trade Agreement of the Americas [*Proposed*]
FTAA .... Free Trade American Area (SAUS)
FTAA .... Free Trade Area of the Americas [*NAFTA*] (ECON)
FTA-AB .... Fluorescent Treponemal Antibody-Absorption Syphilis Test [*Medicine*] (MAH)
FTA-ABS .... Fluorescent Treponemal Antibody - Absorption [*Test for syphilis*]
FTA-Abs .... Fluorescent Treponemal Antibody Absorption (DB)
FTA--ABS .... fluorescent treponemal antibody absorption test (SAUS)
FTA-ABS Test ... Fluorescent Treponemal Antibody-Absorption Test (SAUS)
FTAAE .... Failure to Avoid Adverse Effects [*Environmental science*] (COE)
FTAAT .... Fluorescent Treponemal Antibody Absorption Test [*Medicine*] (MELL)
FTAB .... Field Tab (SAUS)
FTAB .... Focused Technical Advisory Board (SAUS)
FTAB .... Focus Technical Advisory Board (AAEL)
FTAC .... Foreign Trade Arbitration Commission (SAUO)
FTAC .... Functional Test and Calibration (IAA)
FTACCC .... Florida Technical Advisory Committee on Citrus Canker (EA)
FTACH .... Fourier Tachometer (SAUS)
FTACS .... Future Tactical Air Control System (ACAE)
FTACT .... Financial Times Actuaries Share Indices [*Database*] [*Financial Times Business Enterprises Ltd.*] [*Information service or system*] (CRD)
FT/ADIRS .... Fault Tolerant/Air Data Inertial Reference System (SAUO)
FTAF .... Flying Training Air Force
FTaFA .... Florida A & M University, Tallahassee, FL [*Library symbol*] [*Library of Congress*] (LCLS)
F-TAG .... Fast-Binding Target-Attaching Globulin [*Medicine*] (MEDA)
FTaL .... Leon-Jefferson-Wakulla County Public Library, Tallahassee, FL [*Library symbol*] [*Library of Congress*] (LCLS)
FTAM .... File Telecommunications Access Method (SAUS)
FTAM .... File Transfer, Access, and Management [*Telecommunications*] (TSSD)
FTAM .... File Transfer Access Management [*Computer science*] (EERA)
FTAM .... File Transfer Access Method [*Computer science*]
FTAM .... File Transfer and Access Management (SAUS)
FTAM .... File Transfer and Access Method (ADWA)
FTAM .... File Transfer and Management (ACAE)
FTAM .... File Transfer and Manipulation (NITA)
FT & A .... Field Tests and Applications (SAUS)
FT & C .... Feint and Cash [*of account book rulings*]
FT & C .... Formal Training and Certification (MCD)
FT & C .... Functional Test and Calibration (IEEE)
FT&E .... Florida Testing & Engineering, Inc. (EFIS)
FT & E .... Follow-On Test and Evaluation (MCD)
FT & IR .... Flight Taxiing and Ingestion Risks [*Insurance*] (AIA)

FT & SA ...... Fuel Transfer and Storage Assembly [*Nuclear energy*] (NRCH)
FT&TW ...... Combination Flat Top and Typewriter (SAUS)
FT & TW ...... Desk, Combination Flat Top and Typewriter
FTAO ...... Foreign Technology Activity Office [*or Officer*] (AFM)
FTAR ...... Following Transmitted as Received (SAUS)
FTAS ...... Division of Fluid Thermal and Aerospace Sciences (SAUO)
FTAS ...... Fast Time Analysis System (SAUS)
FTAS ...... Fast Time Analyzer System
FTAS ...... Federation of Turkish-American Societies (EA)
FTAS ...... Fluid Thermal and Aerospace Sciences (SAUS)
FTAS ...... Future Theater Airlift Studies (SAUS)
FTaS ...... Sunland Center, Tallahassee, FL [*Library symbol*] [*Library of Congress*] (LCLS)
FTASB ...... Faster Than a Speeding Bullet (ADWA)
FTASB ...... Faster Than A Speeding Bullet (Slang) (SAUS)
FTase ...... Farnesyltransferase [*An enzyme*]
FtAshld ...... First Ashland Financial Corp. [*Associated Press*] (SAG)
FTASI ...... Financial Times Actuaries All-Share Index (ODBW)
FTaSU ...... Florida State University, Tallahassee, FL [*Library symbol*] [*Library of Congress*] (LCLS)
FTaSU-L ...... Florida State University, Law Library, Tallahassee, FL [*Library symbol*] [*Library of Congress*] (LCLS)
FTAT ...... Facilities Technology Application Test [*Army*] (RDA)
FTAT ...... Field Turn-Around Time (MCD)
FtAT ...... First American Corp. [*Associated Press*] (SAG)
FTAT ...... Fluorescent Treponemal Antibody Test [*for syphilis*]
FTAT ...... Furniture, Timber, and Allied Trades Union [*British*]
FTaT ...... Tallahassee Community College, Tallahassee, FL [*Library symbol*] [*Library of Congress*] (LCLS)
FTA Test ...... Fluorescent Treponemal Antibody Test (SAUS)
FtATn ...... First American Corp. [*Associated Press*] (SAG)
FTATU ...... Furniture, Timber, and Allied Trades Union [*British*]
FtAust ...... First Australia Fund, Inc. [*Associated Press*]
FTAWA ...... Food Technology Association of Western Australia
FT-AWI ...... Financial Times-Actuaries World Indices [*British*]
FTB ...... Fade To Black (SAUS)
FTB ...... Fails to Break
FTB ...... Fast Torpedo Boat [*NATO*]
FTB ...... Field Team Bulletin [*Military*] (CINC)
FTB ...... Fighter Bomber [*Obsolete*]
FTB ...... Film Transfer Boom [*NASA*]
FTB ...... Fingertip Blood [*Medicine*]
FTB ...... Fire Control Technician, Ballistic Missile [*Navy rating*]
FTB ...... Fire-Tube Boiler (DS)
FTB ...... First Time Borrower (SAUO)
FTB ...... First-Time-Buy (MCD)
FTB ...... Fitchburg State College, Fitchburg, MA [*OCLC symbol*] (OCLC)
FTB ...... Fleet Torpedo Bomber
FTB ...... Flight Test Bed (SAUS)
FTB ...... Flying Test Bed (SAUS)
FTB ...... Forestry and Timber Bureau (SAUO)
FTB ...... Fort Bragg Range Control Project (SAUO)
FTB ...... For the Birds [*Slang*] (IAA)
FTB ...... Frame Time Base (SAUS)
FTB ...... Franchise Tax Board (SAUO)
FTB ...... Freight Tariff Bureau
FTB ...... Freight Traffic Bureau
FTB ...... Frequency Time Base (DEN)
FTB ...... Front to Back
FTB ...... Front To Back Algorithm (SAUS)
FTB ...... Ft Bragg Range Control Project (SAUS)
FTB ...... Fukui Television Broadcasting (SAUO)
FTB ...... Full-Thickness Burn (MELL)
FTB ...... Full-Tilt Boogie [*Hot-rod slang for wide-open throttle*]
FTB ...... Full to Bursting [*Reply to question, "Have you had enough to eat"*]
FTB ...... Functional Test Bulletin [*Computer science*] (IAA)
FTB ...... Functional Training Branch [*BUPERS*]
FTB ...... Fur Trade Board (SAUO)
FTB1 ...... Fire Control Technician, Ballistic Missile Fire Control, First Class [*Navy rating*] (DNAB)
FTB2 ...... Fire Control Technician, Ballistic Missile Fire Control, Second Class [*Navy rating*] (DNAB)
FTB3 ...... Fire Control Technician, Ballistic Missile Fire Control, Third Class [*Navy rating*] (DNAB)
F-TBA ...... Fasting-Total Bile Acids [*Physiology*]
FTBA ...... Food Tray and Board Association [*Later, SSI*]
FTBA ...... Furniture Trades Benevolent Association [*British*] (BI)
FT BAL ...... Football [*Freight*]
FTBC ...... Fire Control Technician, Ballistic Missile Fire Control, Chief [*Navy rating*] (DNAB)
FtBcIN ...... First Bancorp (IN) [*Associated Press*] (SAG)
FtBcIN ...... First Bancorp of Indiana, Inc. [*Associated Press*] (SAG)
FTBD ...... Fit to Be Detained [*Medicine*]
FTBD ...... Full Term Born Dead [*Medicine*]
FTBE ...... Focal Tick-Borne Encephalitis [*Medicine*] (EDAA)
FtBend ...... Fort Bend Holding Corp. [*Associated Press*] (SAG)
FTBF ...... Frequency Tuned Bandpass Filter
FTBI ...... Financial Times Business Information [*British*]
FTBK ...... Frontier Financial Corp. [*NASDAQ symbol*] (NASQ)
FtBkSy ...... First Bank System, Inc. [*Associated Press*] (SAG)
FT black ...... Fine Thermal Black (EDCT)
FTBLL ...... Football
FT BM ...... Board Foot Meter (SAUS)
FTBM ...... Family Trustees of the British Museum (SAUO)
ft bm ...... Fast Time Constant (SAUS)
ft bm ...... Fault Tolerant Compiler (SAUS)
ft bm ...... Federal Trade Commission (SAUS)
ftbm ...... foot board measure (SAUS)
ft bm ...... Frequency Time Control (SAUS)
ft bm ...... Fusion Technology Commission (SAUS)
FtBNC ...... First Bancorp North Carolina [*Associated Press*] (SAG)
ftbrg ...... footbridge (SAUS)
FtBrnd ...... First Brands Corp. [*Associated Press*] (SAG)
FTBS ...... Family Therapists Behavioral Scale [*Medicine*] (EDAA)
FTBS ...... Fire-Tube Boiler Survey (DS)
FTBS ...... forced thermical Brillouin scattering (SAUS)
FTBS ...... Forces Travel Booking Service (SAUO)
FTBS ...... Free Throwers Boomerang Society (EA)
FTBSA ...... Fire Control Technician, Ballistic Missile Fire Control, Seaman Apprentice [*Navy rating*]
FTBSN ...... Fire Control Technician, Ballistic Missile Fire Control, Seaman [*Navy rating*]
FTC ...... Facilities Technical Criteria (SAUO)
FTC ...... Facility Terminal Cabinet (AAG)
FTC ...... Fair Trade Commission [*Japan*] (ECON)
FTC ...... Fallopian Tube Carcinoma [*Medicine*] (MELL)
FTC ...... False Target Can [*Navy*] (NVT)
FTC ...... Farmers Trading Company (SAUO)
FTC ...... Fast Time Constant [*RADAR*]
FTC ...... Fast Time Control (IAA)
FTC ...... Fault Tolerant Compiler (NITA)
FTC ...... Fault Tolerant Computer (SAUS)
FTC ...... Fault-Tolerant Computing
FTC ...... Fault Tolerant Controller. (SAUS)
FTC ...... Fax Transfer Centre (SAUS)
FTC ...... Federal Telecommunications Center (NUCP)
FTC ...... Federal Telecommunications Laboratories (SAUS)
FTC ...... Federal Telecommunications System [*of GSA*] (NOAA)
FTC ...... Federal Trade Commission [*Independent government agency*] [*OCLC symbol*]
FTC ...... Federal Trade Commission Decisions [*A publication*] (DLA)
FTC ...... Federal Trade Commission, USA (SAUS)
FTC ...... Federation of Translation Companies (SAUO)
FTC ...... Feed the Children [*An association*] (EA)
FTC ...... Fiat [*Federal Railroad Administration identification code*]
FTC ...... Field Training Command [*Military*]
FTC ...... Field Trial Champion [*Sporting dogs*] (IIA)
FTC ...... File Transmission Control (SAUS)
FTC ...... Final Turn Collision (SAUS)
FTC ...... Financial Trustco Capital Ltd. [*Toronto Stock Exchange symbol*]
FTC ...... Fine Tar Concrete (SAUS)
FTC ...... Fire Control Technician, Chief [*Navy rating*]
FTC ...... Fixed Tantalum Capacitor
FTC ...... Flame Traversing the Charge
FTC ...... Flanked, Towed, Classification (SAUS)
FTC ...... Fleet Training Center [*Navy*]
FTC ...... Flight Crew (SAUS)
FTC ...... Flight Test Center
FTC ...... Flight Test Centre (SAUS)
FTC ...... Flight Test Conductor (NASA)
FTC ...... Flight Time Capability (SAUS)
FTC ...... Flight Time Constant
FTC ...... Flight Training Command (SAUO)
FTC ...... Float Trend Chart (PDAA)
FTC ...... Florida Test Center [*NASA*] (KSC)
FTC ...... Fluid-Bed Thermal Cracking [*A chemical process developed by the Institute of Gas Technology*]
FTC ...... Flying Training Command [*Air Force*]
FTC ...... Flying Training Course (SAUS)
ftc ...... Foot Candle [*Medicine*] (EDAA)
ft-c ...... Foot-Candle (SHCU)
FT-C ...... Foot-Candle [*Illumination*]
FTC ...... Force Track Coordinator [*Navy*] (NVT)
FTC ...... Fordson Tractor Club (EA)
FTC ...... Foreign Tax Credit
FTC ...... Foreign Trade Council (SAUO)
FTC ...... Forestry Training Council (AIE)
FTC ...... Forest Tent Caterpillars
FTC ...... Forrestal Telecommunications Center (SAUO)
FTC ...... Fort Collins [*Colorado*] [*Airport symbol*] (OAG)
FTC ...... Fort Tejon [*California*] [*Seismograph station code, US Geological Survey*] [*Closed*] (SEIS)
FTC ...... Frames to Come [*Optometry*]
FTC ...... Freighter Travel Club of America (EA)
FTC ...... Freon Tank Container
FTC ...... Frequency Threshold Curve
FTC ...... Frequency Time Control
FTC ...... Frequency Transfer Control
FTC ...... Fruehauf Trailer [*NYSE symbol*] (SPSG)
FTC ...... Fuel Transfer Canal [*Nuclear energy*] (NRCH)
FTC ...... Fuji Telecasting Company (SAUS)
FTC ...... Fuji Telecasting Company Ltd. (SAUO)
FTC ...... Full Technological Certificate [*British*]
FTC ...... Full-Time Care [*Pet-adoption terminology*]
FTC ...... Full to Confrontation (SAUS)
FTC ...... Future Technology Communications [*Distributor and networking specialist*] [*British*] (NITA)
FTCA ...... Federal Tort Claims Act
FTCA ...... Fire-control Technicians Class (SAUS)
FTCA ...... French Central Technical Armament Establishment (ACAE)

FTCA........... Future Tactical Combat Aircraft (SAUS)
FTC&H......... Fishbeck, Thompson, Carr & Huber, Inc. (EFIS)
FTCAP......... Freshman Testing, Counseling and Advising Program (SAUS)
FT CAT........ Fiat Cataplasma [*Let a Poultice Be Made*] [*Pharmacy*]
ft cataplasm... Fiat Cataplasma [*Let a Poultice Be Made*] [*Pharmacy*] (DAVI)
FTCC........... Fellow of Trinity College, Cambridge [*British*] (ROG)
FTCC........... Fixed Temperature Compensating Capacitor
FTCC........... Flight Test Coordinating Committee [*Air Force*]
FTCC........... French Telegraph Cable Company (SAUO)
FTCC........... FTC Communications, Inc. [*New York, NY*] (TSSD)
FTCCD......... Field Transfer Charge-Coupled Device [*Instrumentation*]
FTCCD......... Frame Transfer Charge Coupled Device (SAUS)
FTCD........... Fellow of Trinity College, Dublin
FTCD........... Fellow of Trinity College-Dublin (SAUS)
FT CD......... Foot-Candela [*Foot-Candle*] [*Illumination*] (ADA)
ft cd............ foot candela (SAUS)
FTCD........... Foot-Candle (SAUS)
ft-cdl........... Foot-Candle (SAUS)
FTCE........... Florida Teacher Certification Examination (EDAC)
FTC Element... Fast Time Constant Element (SAUS)
FT CERAT.... Fiat Ceratum [*Let a Cerate Be Made*] [*Pharmacy*]
FTCG........... First Colonial Group [*NASDAQ symbol*] (SAG)
FT CHART.... Fiat Chartula [*Let a Powder Be Made*] [*Pharmacy*]
FtChi............ First Chicago NBD Corp. [*Associated Press*] (SAG)
FtChrt........... First Charter Corp. [*Associated Press*] (SAG)
FtChrtBk....... First Charter Bank NA [*Associated Press*] (SAG)
FT-CIDEC..... Fourier Transform - Chemically Induced Dynamic Electron Polarization (SAUS)
FTCL........... Fellow of the Trinity College, London (SAUS)
FTCLR......... Financial Times Commercial Law Reports [*A publication*] [*British*]
FTCM........... Fire Control Technician, Master Chief [*Navy rating*]
FTCM........... Foundation for Traditional Chinese Medicine (ADWA)
FTCMS......... File Transfer Customer Monitor System [*Communications term*] (DCT)
FTCN........... Fleet Teletype Conferencing Network (SAUO)
FtCntrl......... First Central Financial Corp. [*Associated Press*] (SAG)
FTCO........... Foreign Trade Central Office (SAUO)
FTCO........... Franklin Telecommunications Corp. [*NASDAQ symbol*] (COMM)
ft col........... fast color (SAUS)
FTCOL......... Fort Collins, CO [*American Association of Railroads railroad junction routing code*]
FT COLLYR... Fiat Collyrium [*Let an Eyewash Be Made*] [*Pharmacy*]
FtColoBcp.... First Colorado Bancorp, Inc. [*Associated Press*] (SAG)
ftcolovprt..... fast color overprint (SAUS)
FTCP........... Field Trains Command Post [*Army*] (INF)
FTCP........... Flight Test Change Proposal (MCD)
Ft CP........... Fort Command Post (SAUS)
FTCR........... Functional Test Change Request
FTCS........... Fault-Tolerant Computing Symposium (SAUS)
FTCS........... Fire Control Technician, Senior Chief [*Navy rating*]
FTCS........... Foreign Tax Credit System
FTCS........... International Symposium on Fault-Tolerant Computing (SAUO)
FTCSS......... Flight Trace Contaminant Sensor System [*NASA*] (KSC)
FTC Symposium... Fault Tolerant Computing Symposium (SAUS)
FTC-TLTR.... Freight Traffic Committee - Trunk Line Territory Railroads
FTCWU........ Federated Tobacco and Cigarette Workers' Union [*Australia*]
FTCX........... Fort Campbell Military Railroad [*Federal Railroad Administration identification code*]
FTCZ........... Farmers Terminal [*Federal Railroad Administration identification code*]
FTD............. Fails to Drain
FTD............. Fails to Drive (DNAB)
FTD............. Failure to Descend [*Obstetrics and urology*] (DAVI)
FTD............. Familiarization Training Data (MCD)
FTD............. Fastener Testing Development (MCD)
FTD............. Fastest Time of the Day [*Auto racing*]
FTD............. Federal Tax Deposit [*IRS*]
FT/D............ Feet per Day
FTD............. Femoral Total Density
FTD............. Field Terminated Diode [*Electronics*]
FTD............. Field Training Detachment [*Program*] [*Air Force*]
FTD............. Fight Test Division Flight (ACAE)
FTD............. Fine Test Dust [*Automotive engineering*]
FTD............. Fire Control Tracking and Designation (ACAE)
FTD............. Fire Technology Division [*National Institute of Standards and Technology*]
FTD............. First Target Detection (SAUS)
FTD............. First Tier Debt [*Economics*]
FTD............. First Tridon Industry [*Vancouver Stock Exchange symbol*]
FTD............. Fitted (MSA)
FTD............. Fixed Threshold Detector (ACAE)
FTD............. Flight Test Direction [*or Directive*] (AAG)
FTD............. Flight Test Directive (SAUS)
FTD............. Flight Test Drawing (MCD)
FTD............. Flight Training Device [*Aviation*] (DA)
FTD............. Florists Transworld Delivery (SAUO)
FTD............. Folded Triangular Dipole [*Electronics*] (OA)
FTD............. Folic Acid and Thymidine [*Medium*] [*Biochemistry*] (DB)
FTD............. Force, Type, District Code (DNAB)
FTD............. Foreign Technical Department [*Navy*] (NVT)
FTD............. Foreign Technology Directorate (DOMA)
FTD............. Foreign Technology Division [*Wright-Patterson Air Force Base, Ohio*] [*Air Force*]
FTD............. Foreign Trade Definitions (SAUO)
FTD............. Foreign Trade Division [*Census*] (OICC)
FTD............. Formal Technical Documents
FTD............. Formal Thought Disorder (SAUS)
FTD............. Fort Dearborn Income Securities, Inc. [*NYSE symbol*] (SPSG)
FTD............. Fort Dearborn Inc.Sec [*NYSE symbol*] (TTSB)
FTD............. Fortified
FTD............. Freight Traffic Department
FTD............. Freight Traffic Division [*Army*]
FTD............. Frequency Translation Distortion
FTD............. Frontotemporal Dementia [*Medicine*]
FTD............. Fuel Testing Department (SAUO)
FTD............. Full-Time Duty (ADA)
FTD............. Functional Test Data
FTD............. Functional Test Demonstration (SAUO)
FTD............. Functional Training Detachment (SAUO)
FTD............. Fuze Time Difference (SAUS)
FTD............. Fuze-Triggering Device (MCD)
FTDA........... Fellow of the Theatrical Designers and Craftsmen's Association [*British*]
FTDA........... Fleurop Transworld Delivery Association (SAUO)
FTDA........... Florists' Transworld Delivery Association (EA)
FTDAS......... Flight Test Data Acquisition System (SAUO)
FTDC........... Fellow of the Society of Typographic Designers of Canada (DGA)
FTDC........... Field Testing and Development Center
FTDC........... Food Technology Development Center (SAUS)
FTDD........... Fishery Technological Development Division (SAUS)
FTD-E.......... Freight Traffic Division - Export [*MTMC*] (TAG)
FtDear......... Fort Dearborn Income Securities, Inc. [*Associated Press*] (SAG)
FtDefFn........ First Defiance Financial Corp. [*Associated Press*] (SAG)
FTDGE......... Fort Dodge, IA [*American Association of Railroads railroad junction routing code*]
ft di............. flattening die (SAUS)
FTD-I........... Freight Traffic Division - Import [*MTMC*] (TAG)
FTDIP.......... Flight Test Division, Internal Project [*Navy*] (MCD)
FTDMA......... Fixed Time Division Multiple Access (CCCA)
FTDMA......... Frequency and Time-Division Multiple Access (MCD)
FTDP-17...... Frontotemporal Dementia and Parkinsonism Linked to Chromosome 17 [*Medicine*]
FTDR........... Flight Test Data Recorder (MCD)
ftdr.............. friction-top drum (SAUS)
FTDS........... Failure Tolerant Disk System (SAUS)
FTDS........... Flag Tactical Data System (MUGU)
FTDS........... Formal Training Data System (NVT)
FTD-S.......... Freight Traffic Division - Inspection [*MTMC*] (TAG)
FTDV........... Function Table Development and Verification (SAUS)
FtDynM........ First Dynasty Mines [*Associated Press*] (SAG)
FTE............. Facility Training Equipment
FTE............. Factory Test Equipment (MCD)
FTE............. FFTF [*Fast Flux Test Facility*] Test Engineering [*Nuclear energy*] (NRCH)
FTE............. Flight Technical Error [*Aviation*] (DA)
FTE............. Flight Test Encoder
FTE............. Flight Test Engineer (MCD)
FTE............. Flight Test Equipment
FTE............. Flight Test Evaluation
FTE............. Florida Tomato Exchange (EA)
FTE............. Flux Transfer Event [*Planetary physics*]
FTE............. Follett, TX [*Location identifier*] [*FAA*] (FAAL)
FTE............. Foote Mineral Co. (SAUO)
FTE............. Forced Test End (NASA)
fte............... foreign trade enterprise (SAUS)
FTE............. For Enterprise (SAUS)
FTE............. For The Enterprise (SAUS)
FTE............. Fotografia F3 SA [*Spain*] [*ICAO designator*] (FAAC)
FTE............. Foundation for Teaching Economics (EA)
FTE............. Fracture Transition Elastic Temperature (MCD)
FTE............. Frame Table Entry [*Computer science*] (IBMDP)
FTE............. France Telecom ADS [*NYSE symbol*] (SG)
FTE............. Free the Eagle [*Washington, DC*] (EA)
FTE............. Free Thyroxine Equivalent [*Endocrinology*]
FTE............. Freeze-Thaw/Evaporation
FTE............. Frequency Tracks Error (ACAE)
FTE............. Full-Time Education
FTE............. Full-Time Employee
fte............... full-time equivalence (SAUS)
FTE............. Full Time Equivalent (SAUS)
FTE............. Full-Time Equivalent
FTE............. Full-time Equivalent Student (SAUO)
FTE............. Functional Test Equipment
FTE............. Fund for Theological Education (EA)
FTEC........... Federal Trial Examiners Conference [*Later, FALJC*] (EA)
FTEC........... Feminist Teacher Editorial Collective (EA)
FTEC........... Firetector, Inc. [*NASDAQ symbol*] (NQ)
FTEC........... Free Territory of Ely-Chatelaine [*An association*] (EA)
FTECS......... Field Training Equipment Concentration Site [*Army*] (AABC)
FTEE........... Full-Time Equivalency Enrollment [*Education*]
FTEF........... Fair Tax Education Fund (EA)
FTEG........... Flight Test and Engineering Group [*Navy*] (DOMA)
FTEKF......... Fuel Tech [*NASDAQ symbol*] (SAG)
FTEKF......... Fuel Tech N.V. [*NASDAQ symbol*] (TTSB)
FTEM........... Factory Test Equipment Manufacturing
FtEmp.......... First Empire State Corp. [*Associated Press*] (SAG)
FT EMULS.... Fiat Emulsio [*Let an Emulsion Be Made*] [*Pharmacy*]
FTEN........... First Tennessee National Corp. [*NASDAQ symbol*] (NQ)
FTEN........... First Tenn Natl [*NASDAQ symbol*] (TTSB)

ft enem .... Fiat Enema [*Let an Injection (per Rectum) be Made*] [*Pharmacy*] (DAVI)
FTEO .... Flight Test Engineering Order
FTEPS .... Fault-Tolerant Electrical Power System (SEWL)
FTERE .... Fort Erie, ON [*American Association of Railroads railroad junction routing code*]
FTESA .... Foundry Trades Equipment and Supplies Association (SAUS)
FTESA .... Foundry Trades Equipment and Supplies Association, Ltd. (SAUO)
FTESE .... Fourier transform ESE (SAUS)
FtEsex .... First Essex Bancorp, Inc. [*Associated Press*] (SAG)
FTESR .... Fourier transform ESR (SAUS)
FTE staff .... Full-Time Equivalent staff (SAUS)
FTET .... First Entertainment, Inc. [*NASDAQ symbol*] (SAG)
FTET .... Full-Time Equivalent Terminals [*Computer science*]
FTETD .... First Entertainment [*NASDAQ symbol*] (TTSB)
FTEWA .... Force Threat Evaluation and Weapon Assignment [*Military*] (SEWL)
FTF .... Face to Face
FTF .... Factory Terminal Facility (SAUS)
FTF .... Factory Test Facility (ACAE)
FTF .... Failure To File (SAUS)
FTF .... Fair Tax Foundation [*Defunct*] (EA)
FTF .... Farmer to Farmer Program (SAUO)
FTF .... fault transfer facility (SAUS)
FTF .... Fibre Trade Federation [*British*] (BI)
FTF .... Field Test Facility (SAUS)
FTF .... Field Training Flight (MCD)
FTF .... File-to-File (SAUS)
FTF .... File Transfer Facility [*Telecommunications*] (OSI)
FTF .... Finger-to-Finger [*Neurology*] (DAVI)
FTF .... Fisheries Task Force
FTF .... Fixed Time Firing (ACAE)
FTF .... Flame Thrower Fluid (SAUS)
FTF .... Flared Tube Fitting
FTF .... Flux Transition Frequency (VLIE)
FTF .... Forward Transfer Function [*Telecommunications*] (IAA)
FTF .... Freedom of Thought Foundation (EA)
FTF .... Free Thyroxine Fraction [*Endocrinology*] (DAVI)
FTF .... Functional Test Flight (AFM)
FTF .... Fundamental Train Frequency [*Machinery*]
FTF .... Texarkana First Financial Corp. [*AMEX symbol*] (NASQ)
FTFA .... Filipino Task Force on AIDS (SAUO)
FtFAla .... First Federal of Alabama FSB [*Jasper, AL*] [*Associated Press*] (SAG)
FT-FAM .... Fourier Transform-Faradic Admittance Measurements [*Spectrometry*]
FtFamFL .... First Family Financial Corp. [*Associated Press*] (SAG)
FTFC .... Fabulous Thunderbirds Fan Club (EA)
FTFC .... Field Training Feedback Components (MCD)
FTFC .... First Federal Capital [*NASDAQ symbol*] (TTSB)
FTFC .... First Federal Capital Corp. [*NASDAQ symbol*] (NQ)
FTFC .... Florida College, Tampa, FL [*Library symbol*] [*Library of Congress*] (LCLS)
FTFC .... Fourier Transform Flow Cytometer (SAUS)
FTFC .... Functional Test Flight Checklist
FtFCap .... First Federal Capital Corp. [*Associated Press*] (SAG)
FtFCrb .... First Financial Caribbean Corp. [*Associated Press*] (SAG)
FTFCS .... Foreign Tank Fire Control System (ACAE)
FTFD .... Field Test Force Director (ACAE)
FtFdBc .... First Federal Bancorp, Inc. [*Associated Press*] (SAG)
FtFdBcp .... First Federal Bancorp [*Associated Press*] (SAG)
FtFedBn .... FirstFed Bancshares, Inc. [*Associated Press*] (SAG)
FtFedCO .... First Federal Savings Bank Colorado [*Associated Press*] (SAG)
FTFET .... Four-Terminal Field-Effect Transistor (IEEE)
FTFF .... Formaldehyde Task Force Fund [*Defunct*] (EA)
FTFFA .... Florida Tropical Fish Farms Association (EA)
FTFGS .... Flared Tube Fitting Gasket Seal (MSA)
FT/FH .... Flight Time/Flight Hour (MCD)
FTFI .... Florida Tropical Fish Industries (SAUO)
f-t fibers .... fast-switch musclecell fibers (SAUS)
FTFL .... Fixed-to-Fixed-Length (in FTFL Code) [*Computing*] (ODA)
FTFLSU .... Fairy Tale-Folklore Study Unit [*American Topical Association*] (EA)
FTFM .... Florida Mental Health Institute, Tampa, FL [*Library symbol*] [*Library of Congress*] (LCLS)
FTFN .... First Financial [*NASDAQ symbol*] (TTSB)
FTFN .... First Financial Corp. (Providence, RI) [*NASDAQ symbol*] (SAG)
FtFnBcp .... First Financial Bancorp [*Associated Press*] (SAG)
FtFnBk .... First Financial Bankshares [*Associated Press*] (SAG)
FtFnCp .... First Financial Corp. [*Associated Press*] (SAG)
FtFnCrb .... First Financial Caribbean Corp. [*Associated Press*] (SAG)
FtFnPlk .... First Financial Bancshares Polk County [*Associated Press*] (SAG)
FTFO .... Fixed Terminal Fuel-Optimal (SAUS)
FtFrnk .... First Franklin Corp. [*Associated Press*] (SAG)
FTFRS .... Fort Frances, ON [*American Association of Railroads railroad junction routing code*]
FTFSU .... Fairy Tale-Folklore Study Unit [*American Topical Association*] (EA)
FTG .... Fairchild Tropical Garden
FTG .... False Target Generator (SAUS)
FTG .... Farmstead Telephone Group [*AMEX symbol*] (SAG)
FTG .... Field Technical Guidelines (SAUO)
FTG .... Filtering (SAUS)
FTG .... Final Trunk Group (VLIE)
FTG .... Fire Control Technician, Gun [*Navy rating*]
FTG .... Fitting (MSA)
FTG .... Fleet Training Group [*Navy*]
FTG .... Fluid Thioglycolate [*Medium*] [*Microbiology*]
FTG .... Footing (KSC)
FTG .... Free Tendon Graft [*Medicine*] (MELL)
FTG .... Fuji Texaco Gas (SAUO)
FTG .... Full Thickness Graft [*Medicine*]
FTG .... Function Timing Generator (IAA)
FTG .... Servicios Aereos y Fotograficos, SA de CV [*Mexico*] [*FAA designator*] (FAAC)
f-tg- .... Togo [*MARC geographic area code*] [*Library of Congress*] (LCCP)
FTG1 .... Fire Control Technician, Gun Fire Control, First Class [*Navy rating*] (DNAB)
FTG2 .... Fire Control Technician, Gun Fire Control, Second Class [*Navy rating*] (DNAB)
FTG3 .... Fire Control Technician, Gun Fire Control, Third Class [*Navy rating*] (DNAB)
FTGA .... Florida Turfgrass Association (SRA)
FtGaHd .... First Georgia Holding, Inc. [*Associated Press*] (SAG)
FT GARG .... Fiat Gargarisma [*Let a Gargle Be Made*] [*Pharmacy*]
FTGBG .... Flareout and Terminal Glide Beam Guidance [*Aerospace*] (AAG)
FTGC .... Fire Control Technician, Gun Fire Control, Chief [*Navy rating*] (DNAB)
FTGDV .... Footage Dives [*Military*] (AABC)
FTGS .... Church of Jesus Christ of Latter-Day Saints, Genealogical Society Library, TampaBranch, Tampa, FL [*Library symbol*] [*Library of Congress*] (LCLS)
FTGSA .... Fire Control Technician, Gun Fire Control, Seaman Apprentice [*Navy rating*] (DNAB)
FTGSN .... Fire Control Technician, Gun Fire Control, Seaman [*Navy rating*] (DNAB)
FTGSVC .... Fleet Training Group Services (NVT)
FTGWP .... Fleet Training Group, Western Pacific [*Navy*] (DNAB)
FTH .... Faith
fth .... Fathom (NTIO)
FTH .... Fathom
FTH .... Feedback Threshold (CCCA)
FT/H .... Feet per Hour
FTH .... Ferritin Heavy Chain [*Medicine*] (EDAA)
FTH .... Fetch (VLIE)
FTH .... Fourier Transform Holographic
FTH .... Fuel Tank Helicopter
FTH .... Full Tree Harvesting (SAUS)
FTHA .... Fork Truck Hire Association [*British*] (DBA)
Ft Haust .... Fiat Haustus [*Let a Drink Be Made*] [*Pharmacy*]
FtHaw .... First Hawaiian, Inc. [*Associated Press*] (SAG)
FTHB .... First-Time Home Buyer (FOTI)
ft hd .... flathead (SAUS)
ft hd .... Foot Head (SAUS)
FTHF .... Formyltetrahydrofolate [*Biochemistry*]
FTHil .... Hillsborough Community College, Tampa, FL [*Library symbol*] [*Library of Congress*] (LCLS)
FTHL .... Flag Telecom Hldgs. [*NASDAQ symbol*] (SG)
FTHM .... Fathom (ROG)
FTHM .... Full to Hand Motion (SAUS)
FTHMA .... Frequency Time-Hopping Multiple Access [*Electronics*] (OA)
fthp .... flowing tubing head pressure (SAUS)
FTHR .... Featherlite, Inc. [*NASDAQ symbol*] (NASQ)
FTHR .... Featherlite Manufacturing, Inc. [*NASDAQ symbol*] (SAG)
FTHR .... Featherlite Mfg [*NASDAQ symbol*] (TTSB)
ft/hr .... feet per hour (SAUS)
FTHRD .... Feathered [*Aviation*] (FAAC)
FTHRD .... Female Thread (SAUS)
fthrs .... Feathers (VRA)
FTHRX .... Fidelity Intermed. Bond [*Mutual fund ticker symbol*] (SG)
FtHwrd .... Fort Howard Corp. [*Associated Press*] (SAG)
FTI .... Dansk Fiskeriteknologisk Institut [*Danish Institute of Fisheries Technology*] [*Information service or system*] (IID)
FTI .... Facing Tile Institute (EA)
FTI .... Fast Tactical Imagery (SEWL)
FTI .... Fatigue Technology Inc. (SAUS)
FTI .... Fatigue Technology Incorporated (SAUO)
FTI .... Federal Tax Included
FTI .... Fellow of the Textile Institute [*British*]
FTI .... Fellow of Trust Institute (DD)
FTI .... Ferranti Technologies Incorporated (SAUO)
FTI .... File Trailer Identifier (SAUS)
FTI .... Film and Television Group [*Western Australia*]
FTI .... Film Thickness Indicator
FTI .... Financial Times Index [*A publication*] (CDAI)
FTI .... Finished Terminal Inventory [*Computer science*] (TIMI)
FTI .... First Flight Test in Flight Experiment Program (ACAE)
FTI .... Fixed Target Imagery (SAUS)
FTI .... Fixed Target Indication (SAUS)
FTI .... Fixed Target Indicator (ACAE)
FTI .... Fixed Target Information [*Army*] (AABC)
fti .... fixed time indicator (SAUS)
FTI .... Fixed Time Interval (PDAA)
FTI .... Flanders Technology International [*European technology fair*]
FTI .... Fluorescent Tagging of Infiltrator [*Surveillance system*]
FTI .... Flux Transitions per Inch (SAUS)
FTI .... Foreign Trade Institute [*Mexico*]
FTI .... Foreign Traders Index [*Department of Commerce*] [*Washington, DC*] [*Information service or system*] (IID)
FTI .... Forest Trees of Illinois (SAUO)
FTI .... Forval Turbo Interface [*Computer science*]
FTI .... Fourier Transform Infrared (SAUS)
FTI .... France Telecom International, Inc. [*Telecommunications service*] (TSSD)
FTI .... Free Testosterone Index [*Endocrinology*]

FTI .... Free Thyroxine Index [*Endocrinology*]
FTI .... free thyroxin index (SAUS)
FTI .... Frequency Time Indicator [*RADAR*]
FTI .... Frequency Time Intensity [*RADAR*]
FTI .... Frustration Tolerance Index [*Psychology*]
FTI .... FTI Foodtech International, Inc. [*Vancouver Stock Exchange symbol*]
FTi .... North Brevard Public Library, Titusville, FL [*Library symbol*] [*Library of Congress*] (LCLS)
f-ti- .... Tunisia [*MARC geographic area code*] [*Library of Congress*] (LCCP)
FTIA .... Family Therapy Institute of Australia
FTIA .... Financial Times Institute of Actuaries [*A publication*] (BARN)
FTIA .... Florida Telecommunications Industry Association (SRA)
FTIAP .... Footwear and Tanning Industry Adjustment Program (SAUS)
FtIber .... First Iberian Fund, Inc. [*Associated Press*]
FTIC .... Firm Time in Commission (DNAB)
FTIC .... Forensic Technologies International Corp. [*NASDAQ symbol*] (SAG)
FTIC .... Forensic Technologies Intl [*NASDAQ symbol*] (TTSB)
FT-ICP .... Fourier Transform Inductively-Coupled Plasma [*Spectrometry*]
FTICR .... Fourier Transform Ioncyclotron Resonance (HGEN)
FT-ICR .... Fourier Transform-Ion Cyclotron Resonance [*Spectrometry*]
FT-ICRMS .... Fourier Transform Ion Cyclotron Resonance Mass Spectrometry
FTID .... Flame Thermionic Ionization Detector [*Instrumentation*]
FTID .... Flight Test Information Drawing (MCD)
FTIG .... Fort Indiantown Gap [*Army*] (AABC)
FTII .... Fellow of the Taxation Institute, Inc. [*British*] (DBQ)
FTIL .... First Illinois Corp. (SAUO)
FTIM .... Frequency and Time Interval Meter (DNAB)
FTIMA .... Federal Tobacco Inspectors Mutual Association
FtIn .... First Interstate Bancorp [*Associated Press*] (SAG)
FT Index .... Financial Times Index (SAUS)
FtIndp .... First Independence Corp. [*Associated Press*] (SAG)
FT INFUS .... Fiat Infusum [*Let an Infusion Be Made*] [*Pharmacy*]
FtInRt .... First Industrial Realty Trust, Inc. [*Associated Press*] (SAG)
FTIO .... Fast Tuned Local Oscillator (SAUS)
FTIO .... Foreign Technical Intelligence Office (SAUO)
FTIR .... Fourier transformed infrared (SAUS)
FT-IR .... Fourier Transform Infrared [*Spectroscopy*]
FTIR .... Fourier Transform Infrared Radiometer [*Marine science*] (OSRA)
FTIR .... Fourier Transform Infrared Spectroscopy [*Environment term*] (EGA)
FTIR .... Fourier Transform Interferometer (SAUS)
FTIR .... Frustrated Total Internal Reflection
FTIR .... Functional Terminal Innervation Ratio [*Psychiatry*]
FT-IR .... International Fourier Transform Infra-Red Conference (SAUO)
FT-IRAS .... Fourier Transform-Infrared Reflection Absorption Spectroscopy
FTIR-PAS .... Fourier Transform Infrared Photoacoustic Spectroscopy
FTIR-RAS .... Fourier Transform Infrared Reflection Absorption Spectroscopy
FTIRS .... Fourier Transform Infrared Spectroscopy (EDCT)
FTIR Spectroscopy ... Fourier Transform Infrared Spectroscopy (SAUS)
FTIS .... Flight Test Instrumentation System (NASA)
FtIsrl .... First Israel Fund Corp. [*Associated Press*] (SAG)
FTIT .... Fan Turbine Inlet Temperature (MCD)
FTIT .... Fellow of the Institute of Taxation [*British*] (DCTA)
FTITB .... Furniture and Timber Industry Training Board [*British*] (BI)
FTIU .... Fault Transient Interface Unit (SAUS)
FTIV .... Flight Test Instrumentation Van (ACAE)
FTIWA .... Film and Television Institute (Western Australia)
FTJS .... Frequency Tracking Jitter Suppressor (SAUS)
FTK .... Facility Tape Loading (SAUS)
FTK .... Faster than Light (SAUS)
F Tk .... Fast Tank (SAUS)
FTK .... Fast Transit Link (SAUS)
FTK .... Field Test Kit
FTK .... Flying Thread Loom (SAUS)
FTK .... Force, Time, Length (SAUS)
FTK .... Formal Technical Literature (SAUS)
FTK .... Forschungsinstitut fuer Telekommunikation [*Research Institute for Telecommunications*] [*Germany*] (DDC)
FTK .... Fort Knox, KY [*Location identifier*] [*FAA*] (FAAL)
FTK .... Forward Track Kill (SAUS)
FTK .... Fuel Tank
FTK .... Futurtek Communications, Inc. [*Toronto Stock Exchange symbol*]
FTKA .... Failed to Keep Appointment (MELL)
FtKeyst .... First Keystone Financial, Inc. [*Associated Press*] (SAG)
FtKnox .... First Knox Bancorp [*Associated Press*] (SAG)
FTL .... Facility Tape Loading (SAA)
FTL .... Faster Than Light [*Science fiction*] (AAG)
ftl .... Faster than Light (SHCU)
FTL .... Fast Trailer Label (SAUS)
FTL .... Fast Transient Loader
FTL .... Fast Transit Link [*Rapid-transit term*]
FTL .... Federal Telecomm (ACAE)
FTL .... Federal Telecommunications Laboratory [*Air Force*]
FTL .... Ferritin Light Chain [*Medicine*] (EDAA)
FTL .... Field Transmission Loss (SAUS)
FTL .... File Trailer Label (SAUS)
FTL .... File Translation Language (SAUS)
FTL .... Flash Transition Layer (AAEL)
FTL .... Flash Translation Layer (VLIE)
FTL .... Flexible Transfer Line (VLIE)
FTL .... Flightline [*Spain*] [*FAA designator*] (FAAC)
FTL .... Flight Test Letter (SAUS)
FTL .... Flight Time Limitation [*Aviation*] (DA)
FTL .... Flight Transportation Laboratory (SAUO)
FTL .... Flying Thread Loom
FTL .... Flying Tiger Line, Inc.
FTL .... Flying Tiger Line, Incorporated (SAUO)
ft-L .... Foot-Lambert (ABAC)
ftl .... Foot-Lambert (DIPS)
FT-L .... Foot-Lambert [*Illumination*]
FTL .... Foreign Theological Library [*A publication*]
FTL .... Formal Technical Literature
FTL .... Format Tape Loop (SAUS)
FTL .... Freeze Thaw Lysate [*Cytology*]
FTL .... Fruit of The Loom'A' [*NYSE symbol*] (TTSB)
FTL .... Fruit of the Loom, Inc. [*NYSE symbol*] (SPSG)
FTL .... Full Term License [*For nuclear power plant*] (NRCH)
FTL .... Full Truck Loads
FTL .... Future Temporal Logic (SAUS)
FTLA .... Foot-Lambert [*Illumination*] (IAA)
ft-lam .... Foot-Lambert (SAUS)
FTLB .... Flight Time Limitations Board (SAUS)
ft-Lb .... foot-lambert (SAUS)
FT-LB .... Foot-Pound [*Unit of work*] (AAG)
ft-lb .... Foot-Pound (SHCU)
ft lb .... foot pound (SAUS)
ft-lb .... foot pound force (SAUS)
FTLB .... Full Term Living Birth [*Medicine*] (MAE)
ft-lbf .... Foot Pound-Force (SAUS)
FT LBF .... Foot-Pound Force
FT LB/H .... Foot-Pounds per Hour
ft-lb/hr .... Foot-Pound per Hour (SAUS)
ft-lb/min .... Foot-Pound per Minute (SAUS)
FT LB/MIN .... Foot-Pounds per Minute
FT LB/S .... Foot-Pounds per Second
Ft Lbt .... Foot-Lambert (SAUS)
FtLbty .... First Liberty Financial Corp. [*Associated Press*] (SAG)
ft lb wt .... Foot Pound Weight (SAUS)
ft lb wt/s .... Foot Pound-Weight per Second (SAUS)
ft lb wt/sec .... Foot Pound-Weight per Second (SAUS)
FTLC .... Tampa Bay Library Consortium, Tampa, FL [*Library symbol*] [*Library of Congress*] (LCLS)
FTLD .... Faster-than-Light Drive (SAUS)
Ftle .... Fremantle (SAUS)
FtLesprt .... First Leesport Bancorp [*Associated Press*] (SAG)
FTLFC .... Full-Term Living Female Child [*Obstetrics*] (DAVI)
FT LINIM .... Fiat Linimentum [*Let a Linament Be Made*] [*Pharmacy*]
FTLMC .... Full-Term Living Male Child [*Obstetrics*] (DAVI)
FTLO .... Fast Tuned Local Oscillator (SAUS)
FTLP .... Final Turn Lead Pursuit (SAA)
FTLP .... Fixed Term Lease Plan [*Business term*] (IAA)
FTLR .... Fallopian Tube Ligation Ring [*Medicine*] (MELL)
FTLR .... Financial Times Law Report [*A publication*] (DLA)
FTLS .... Final Top Level Statistics (SAUO)
FTLS .... Formal Top-Level Specification (SAUS)
FTLV .... Feline T-Lymphotropic Lentivirus [*Later, FIV*]
FTLX .... Flying Tiger Line, Inc. [*Air carrier designation symbol*]
FTM .... Facilitated Transport Membrane [*Separation of chemicals*]
FTM .... Failed to Make (IAA)
FTM .... Fan-Type Marker
FTM .... Fault Tolerant Multiprocessor System [*Computer science*] (HGAA)
FTM .... File Transfer Manager [*Computer science*] (TIMI)
FTM .... File Transfer Method (VLIE)
FTM .... Film Thickness Monitor
FTM .... Fire Control Technician, Surface Missile [*Navy rating*]
FTM .... Flat Technology Monitor [*Zenith*]
FTM .... Flat Tension Mask (VLIE)
FTM .... Fleet Training Missile (MUGU)
FTM .... Flexible Theatre Missile (AFM)
FTM .... Flight Test Manual
FTM .... Flight Test Matrix (MCD)
FTM .... Flight Test Memo (SAUS)
FTM .... Flight Test Missile [*Air Force*]
FTM .... Flight Test Model (ACAE)
FTM .... Flight Training Mission (MCD)
FTM .... Fluid Thioglycolate Medium [*Microbiology*]
FTM .... Flying Training Manual (SAUS)
FTM .... Folded Triangular Monopole [*Electronics*] (OA)
FTM .... Force/Torque Module [*NASA*]
FTM .... Fourier Transform Mass Spectroscopy (ACAE)
FTM .... Fourier Transform Microwave
FTM .... Fractional Test Meal [*Medicine*]
FTM .... Free Throws Made [*Basketball*]
FTM .... Free to Member
FTM .... Freight Traffic Manager
FTM .... French Training Mission [*Military*] (CINC)
FTM .... Frequency Time Modulation (DEN)
FTM .... FTM Resources, Inc. [*Vancouver Stock Exchange symbol*]
FTM .... Full-Time Manning (MCD)
FTM .... Full Travel Membrane (PDAA)
FTM .... Full-Travel-Membrane (SAUS)
FTM .... Functional Test Manager [*Hewlett-Packard Co.*]
FTM .... Furnace Translation Mechanism (SAUS)
FTM1 .... Fire Control Technician, Missile Fire Control, First Class [*Navy rating*] (DNAB)
FTM2 .... Fire Control Technician, Missile Fire Control, Second Class [*Navy rating*] (DNAB)
FTM3 .... Fire Control Technician, Missile Fire Control, Third Class [*Navy rating*] (DNAB)
FTMA .... Federated Textile Managers Associations (SAUO)
FTMA .... Federation of Textile Manufacturers Associations (SAUO)

FTMAD......... Fort Madison, IA [*American Association of Railroads railroad junction routing code*]
FT MAS........ Fiat Massa [*Let a Mass Be Made*] [*Pharmacy*]
FT MAS DIV in PIL... Fiat Massa et Divide in Pilulae [*Let a Mass Be Made and Divided into Pills*] [*Pharmacy*]
FTMC........... Fire Control Technician, Missile Fire Control, Chief [*Navy rating*] (DNAB)
FTMC........... Frequency and Time Measurement Counter
FTMCC......... Flight Test Mission Control Complex (ACAE)
FtMchBk...... First Michigan Bank Corp. [*Associated Press*] (SAG)
FTMCP......... Fort McPherson, GA [*American Association of Railroads railroad junction routing code*]
FtMD........... First Maryland Bancorp [*Associated Press*] (SAG)
ft md........... flattening mandrel (SAUS)
FTMD........... Flight Torque Measurement Demonstration (SAUS)
FtMdwF........ First Midwest Financial [*Associated Press*] (SAG)
FtMerc......... First Merchants Corp. [*Associated Press*] (SAG)
FTMI............ Flight Operations and Air Traffic Management Integration [*FAA*] (TAG)
FtMichBk..... First Michigan Bank Corp. [*Associated Press*] (SAG)
FT/MIN......... Feet per Minute
ft/min.......... Foot per Minute (SAUS)
FtMiss......... First Mississippi Corp. [*Associated Press*] (SAG)
FtMissG....... FirstMiss Gold, Inc. [*Associated Press*] (SAG)
FT MIST....... Fiat Mistura [*Let a Mixture Be Made*] [*Pharmacy*]
FTMIX.......... First Investors MSITF Michigan Cl.A [*Mutual fund ticker symbol*] (SG)
FTML........... Folded-Tape Meander Line (IAA)
FTMP........... Fault Tolerant Multiprocessor System [*Computer science*]
FTMS........... Fabrication Tracking and Management System (MCD)
FTMS........... Federal Test Method Standards (MCD)
FTMS........... Fluid Transfer Management System (SSD)
FTMS........... Fourier Transform Mass Spectrometry (SAUS)
FT/MS.......... Fourier Transform/Mass Spectrometry
FTMS........... Fourier Transform Microwave Spectroscopy
FTMSA......... Fire Control Technician, Missile Fire Control, Seaman Apprentice [*Navy rating*] (DNAB)
FTMSN......... Fire Control Technician, Missile Fire Control, Seaman [*Navy rating*] (DNAB)
FTMT........... Fantom Technologies, Inc. [*NASDAQ symbol*] (NASQ)
FTMT........... Final Thermomechanical Treatment (MCD)
FTMTF......... Fantom Technologies [*NASDAQ symbol*] (SG)
FT-MW......... Fourier Transform-Microwave [*Spectroscopy*]
FTN............. Aviation Charter & Management [*British*] [*ICAO designator*] (FAAC)
FTN............. Facsimile Transmission Network (SAUS)
FTN............. Family Therapy Network (EA)
FTN............. Federacion de Trabajadores Nicaraguenses [*Political party*] (EY)
FTN............. Fido Technology Network (SAUS)
F Tn............ Field Train (SAUS)
FTN............. Field Transfer Notice (SAUS)
FTN............. Film Twisted Nematic (SAUS)
FTN............. Finger to Nose [*Medicine*] (DMAA)
FTN............. First Tenn Natl [*NYSE symbol*] (SG)
FTN............. Flocculus Target Neuron [*Neuroanatomy*]
FTN............. Fortification (AABC)
FTN............. FOTC Track Number (SAUS)
FTN............. Fountain
Ftn............. Freetown (SAUS)
FTN............. Full-Term Nursery [*Neonatology*] (DAVI)
FtNatEnt...... First National Entertainment Corp. [*Associated Press*] (SAG)
FTNB........... Fulton Bancorp, Inc. [*NASDAQ symbol*] (NASQ)
FTNC........... Fault Tolerant Network Computing (SAUS)
FTNC........... First National Corporation (SAUO)
FTND........... Full Term Normal Delivery [*Medicine*]
FTNIR......... Fourier Transform Near Infrared (SAUS)
FTNMR........ Fourier Transform Nuclear Magnetic Resonance (SAUS)
FT-NMR....... Fourier Transform-Nuclear Magnetic Resonance [*Spectrometry*]
FTNS........... Fast Transient Noise Simulator
FTNS........... Flight Track Navigation System (ACAE)
FTNT........... NEC/TAMPA Technology Institute, Tampa, FL [*Library symbol*] [*Library of Congress*] (LCLS)
FTO............. Failed to Open (IEEE)
FTO............. Field Test Office (MCD)
FTO............. Field Test Operations [*Aerospace*] (KSC)
FTO............. Field Training Officer (SAUO)
FTO............. First Toronto Capital Corp. [*Toronto Stock Exchange symbol*]
FTO............. Flameless Thermal Oxidation
FTO............. Fleet Torpedo Officer [*British*]
FTO............. Fleet Training Officer (SAUO)
FTO............. Flexible and Selective Targeting Options [*DoD*]
fto.............. flexible time off (SAUS)
FTO............. Flight Test Objective (SAUS)
FTO............. Flight Test Operations
FTO............. Flight Test Release Order (SAUS)
FTO............. Flying Training Organisation (PIAV)
FTO............. Flying Training Organization (SAUS)
FTO............. Ford Tractor Operations (SAUS)
FTO............. Foreign Technology Office [*Army Tank-Automotive Command*]
FTO............. Foreign Trade Organization
FTO............. Foreign Training Officer [*Military*]
FTO............. Fort Yukon, AK [*Location identifier*] [*FAA*] (FAAL)
FTO............. Fourier Transform Operator
FTO............. Franciscan Third Order (SAUS)
FTO............. Frontier Oil [*NYSE symbol*] [*Formerly, Wainoco Oil*]
FTO............. Fructose-Terminated Oligosaccharide (DB)
FTO............. Fruit Traffic Organization (SAUS)
FTO............. Full-Time Officer [*of an organization*]
FTO............. Functional Test Objective (KSC)
FtOakBrk..... First Oak Brook Bancshares [*Associated Press*] (SAG)
FTOC........... Fetal Thymic Organ Cultures [*Biochemistry*]
FTOC........... Fleet Tactical Operations Center (SAUO)
F to F.......... Face to Face [*Technical drawings*]
f to f........... foe to foe (SAUS)
f to f........... friend to friend (SAUS)
F to G.......... Fair to Good (SAUS)
FTOH........... Flight Team Operations Handbook (NASA)
FTOH........... Flight Test Operations Handbook (NASA)
FTOL........... Full Term Operating License (NRCH)
FT/OLTP....... Fault Tolerant/Online Transaction Processing (NITA)
F to N.......... Finger to Nose Test [*Neurology*]
FTOP........... Femtosecond Time-Resolved Optical Polarigraphy
FTOP........... First Trimester of Pregnancy (MELL)
Ft OP........... Fort Observation Post (SAUS)
FT/OPAS...... Funds-in-Trust / Operational Assistance Scheme (SAUS)
FTOR-MIM-BCG... Ftorafur, Adriamycin, Cyclophosphamide, Bacille Calmette-Guerin [*Antineoplastic drug regimen*] (DAVI)
FTOS........... FGGE Tropical Observing System (SAUS)
FTOS........... Field Test Operations Support [*Aerospace*] (AAG)
FTOs........... Field Training Officers (SAUS)
FTOS........... File Transfer Open System [*Computer science*] (VERA)
FTOS........... File Transfer OSI Support (SAUS)
FTOS........... Flight Termination Ordnance System [*Small intercontinental ballistic missile*] (DWSG)
FTOs........... Foreign Terrorist Organizations [*Government term*] (GA)
FTOS........... Full-Time Outservice (MELL)
F-TOSS........ Fighter Time Ordered Spread Spectrum (ACAE)
F-town......... Frenchtown (SAUS)
F-town......... Funtown (SAUS)
FTP............. Factor/Test Procedure (MCD)
FTP............. Failure to Pay [*IRS*]
FTP............. Failure to Progress [*In labor*] [*Obstetrics*] (DAVI)
FTP............. Falling to Pieces [*Slang*]
FTP............. Fallopian Tube Papilloma [*Medicine*] (MELL)
FTP............. Fast Tape Perforator (SAUS)
FTP............. Fast Tape Punch (SAUS)
FTP............. Fault-Tolerant Processing (RALS)
FTP............. Fear, Tension, Pain [*Syndrome*] [*Psychology*] (BARN)
FTP............. Federal Theater Project
FTP............. FFTF [*Fast Flux Test Facility*] Test Procedure [*Nuclear energy*] (NRCH)
FTP............. Field Task Proposal (ABAC)
ftp.............. field terminal platform (SAUS)
FTP............. Field Test Operational Procedures [*Aerospace*] (AAG)
FTP............. Field Test Plan (SAUS)
FTP............. Field Test Program [*Aerospace*] (IAA)
FTP............. Field Transport Pack (DNAB)
FTP............. File Tranfer Protocol (SAUS)
FTP............. File Transfer Packet [*Computer science*] (IAA)
FTP............. File Transfer Program [*or Protocol*] [*Computer science*]
ftp.............. File Transfer Protocol
FTP............. File Transfer Protocol (Internet) (SAUS)
FTP............. File Transmission Protocol (SAUO)
FTP............. File Transport Protocol (SAUS)
FTP............. Final Technical Proposal (NATG)
FTP............. Final Turn Pursuit (SAUS)
FTP............. Finger-Trap Phenomenon [*Medicine*] (MELL)
FTP............. Firmware Test Plan [*Military*]
FTP............. First Temple Period (SAUS)
FTP............. Fixed Term Plan (BUR)
FTP............. Fixed Throttle Point [*NASA*]
FTP............. Fixed Throttle Position (SAUS)
FTP............. Flash Temperature Parameter (IAA)
FTP............. Fleet Training Publication [*Navy*]
FTP............. Flight Test Plan [*or Procedure or Program*]
FTP............. Flight Test Procedure (SAUS)
FTP............. Flight Test Program (SAUS)
FTP............. Florida Test Procedure [*Aerospace*] (AAG)
FTP............. Fluorocarbons Technical Panel [*of Manufacturing Chemists Association*]
FTP............. Fluorothermoplastic
FTP............. Fly-to-Point (NVT)
FTP............. Foiled Twisted Pair [*Cable*] (VERA)
FTP............. Folded, Trimmed, Packed [*Books*]
FTP............. Fourier Transform Processor (SAUS)
FTP............. Fracture Toughness Parameter
FTP............. Fructose Triphosphate (SAUS)
FTP............. Fuel Tanking Panel [*Aerospace*] (AAG)
FTP............. Fuel Transfer Pool [*Nuclear energy*] (NRCH)
FTP............. Fuel Transfer Port [*Nuclear energy*] (NRCH)
FTP............. Fuel Transfer Pump (MSA)
FTP............. Full-Term Pregnancy (MELL)
FTP............. Full Throttle Position (KSC)
FTP............. Full-Time Permanent [*Employment*]
FTP............. Full Time Personnel (SAUS)
FTP............. Full-Time Personnel [*Employment*]
FTP............. Full Transport Pack [*Military*]
FTP............. Functional Test Procedure [*or Program*]
FTP............. Functional Test Program (SAUS)
FTP............. Functional Test Progress (SAUS)
FTP............. Function Test Procedure [*or Progress*] (NASA)
FTP............. Funds Transfer Pricing (EBF)

FTP .... Fusion Track Processor (SAUS)
FTPA .... Family Therapy Practice Academy (SAUO)
FTPA .... Federal Timber Purchasers Association (EA)
FTPA .... Fellow of the Town and Country Planning Association (SAUO)
FTPA .... Fellow of the Town Planning Association [*British*]
FTP/A .... field task proposal/agreement (SAUS)
FTPAA .... Film and Television Production Association of Australia (SAUO)
FTP & E .... Flight Test Planning and Evaluation
FtPatBn .... First Patriot Bankshares [*Associated Press*] (SAG)
FTPAX .... First Investors MSITF Penn. Cl.A [*Mutual fund ticker symbol*] (SG)
FTPC .... Francs-Tireurs et Partisans Corses [*Corsican Guerrillas and Partisans*] (PD)
FtPcNtw .... First Pacific Networks, Inc. [*Associated Press*] (SAG)
FTPCS .... Failure to Pay Child Support
FTPD .... File Transfer Protocol Daemon (SAUS)
FT PDL .... Foot-Poundal [*Unit of work*]
ft-pdl .... foot poundal (SAUS)
ft pdl/s .... Foot-Poundal per Second (SAUS)
FTPF .... Federation des Travailleurs du Papier et de la Foret [*Federation of Paper and Forest Workers*] [*Canada*]
ft/pf .... foot-pound force (SAUS)
FtPhil .... First Philippine Fund, Inc. [*Associated Press*] (SAG)
FTPI .... Fiberglass Tank and Pipe Institute (NTPA)
FTPI .... Flux Transitions per Inch
FTPI .... Future Time Perspective Inventory [*Psychology*]
FT PIL .... Fiat Pilulae [*Let Pills Be Made*] [*Pharmacy*] (ROG)
FTPL .... Fourier Transform Photo Luminescence (AAEL)
FTPLE .... Fourier-Transform Photoluminescence Excitation (SAUS)
ftpm .... Feet per Minute (SAUS)
FTPM .... Fixed Time Printing Mode [*Photography*]
FTPMM .... Flux Transitions per Millimeter (IAA)
ft/pnl .... fuel-tanking panel (SAUS)
ftpo .... for testing purposes only (SAUS)
FTPO .... For the President Only (WPI)
FTPP .... Fault-Tolerant Parallel Processing (RALS)
FTPP .... Fault-Tolerant Parallel Processor (SAUS)
FTPR .... Federacion del Trabajo de Puerto Rico [*Puerto Rican Federation of Labor*]
FTPRP .... Federal Test Procedure Revision Project
ftps .... feet per second (SAUS)
FTPS .... Fellow of the Technical Publishing Society
FTPS .... Food Trades Protection Society Ltd. [*British*] (BI)
FTPS .... FTP Software [*Commercial firm*] [*NASDAQ symbol*] (SAG)
FTP Sft .... FTP Software [*Commercial firm*] [*Associated Press*] (SAG)
ftpss .... feet per second squared (SAUS)
FT PULV .... Fiat Pulvis [*Let a Powder Be Made*] [*Pharmacy*]
FT PULV SUBTIL ... Fiat Pulvis Subtilis [*Let a Fine Powder Be Made*] [*Pharmacy*]
FTQ .... Federation des Travailleurs et Travailleuses du Quebec [*Canada*] (CROSS)
FTQ .... Monterey/Fort Ord, CA [*Location identifier*] [*FAA*] (FAAL)
FTQG .... Family of Tactical Quiet Generators (SEWL)
FTR .... Australian Federal Tax Reporter [*A publication*]
FTR .... Factor (KSC)
FTR .... Failed to Return [*British military*] (DMA)
FTR .... Fails to Reproduce
FTR .... Fails to Respond (DNAB)
FTR .... False Target Rate [*Military*] (CAAL)
FTR .... False Target Rejection (SAUS)
FTR .... Fan Thrust Reverser
FTR .... Fast Test Reactor
FTR .... Fault Transfer Facility (NITA)
FTR .... Feather (MSA)
FTR .... Federacion de Trabajadores Revolucionarios [*Revolutionary Workers' Federation*] [*El Salvador*] (PD)
FTR .... Federal Telephone and Radio
FTR .... Federal Telephone and Radio Company (SAUS)
FTR .... Federal Telephone and Radio Corporation (SAUS)
FTR .... Federal Travel Regulations (NRCH)
FTR .... Federal Trial Reports [*Maritime Law Book Co. Ltd.*] [*Canada*] [*Information service or system*] (CRD)
FTR .... Feed per Tooth per Revolution (SAUS)
FTR .... Fighter (AABC)
ftr .... Fighter (MILB)
FTR .... Filestore Transfer Routine [*Computer science*] (PDAA)
FTR .... File Transfer Facility (NITA)
FTR .... Film, Photography, Television and Reprography (SAUS)
FTR .... Film Tracing Reproduction
FTR .... Final Technical Report
FTR .... Final Test Rack (KSC)
FTR .... Finist' Air [*France*] [*ICAO designator*] (FAAC)
FTR .... Fixed Target Rejection [*Military*] (IAA)
FTR .... Fixed Transom (AAG)
FTR .... Flag Tower [*Maps and charts*]
FTR .... Flash Triangulation Reduction
FTR .... Flat-Tile Roof (AAG)
FTR .... Flight Tape Recorder (SAUS)
FTR .... Flight Test Report
FTR .... Flight Test Requirements [*NASA*] (NASA)
FTR .... Flight-Test Round (SEWL)
FTR .... Floating Time Recording (SAUS)
FTr .... Foam Trailer (WDAA)
FTR .... Foreign Trade Reports
FTR .... Formation Temperature Ratio (PDAA)
FTR .... For the Record (DAVI)
FTR .... Fractional Tubular Reabsorption [*Medicine*] (MELL)
FTR .... Fractional Turn-Over Rate [*Medicine*] (EDAA)
FTR .... Free-Text Retrieval [*Computer system alternative to Content-Addressable File Store*]
FTR .... Frontier Insurance Group, Inc. [*NYSE symbol*] (SPSG)
FTR .... Fruehauf (SAUS)
FTR .... Frustrated Total Reflection
FTR .... Full Text Retrieval (NITA)
FTR .... Full-Time Regular [*Civil Service employee category*]
FTR .... Functional Test Report
FTR .... Functional Test Request (SAUS)
FTR .... Functional Test Requirement (IEEE)
FTR .... functional throughput rate (SAUS)
FTR .... Funds Transfer [*Banking*] (MHDW)
ftr .... fusion test reactor (SAUS)
F Tr .... Fusion Treaty [*European Communities*] [*1965*] (ILCA)
FTR .... Future Technology Requirements (ACAE)
FTRAC .... Full-Tracked (SAUS)
FTRAC .... Full-Tracked Vehicle
FTRAC Vehicle ... Full-Tracked Vehicle (SAUS)
FT RA-IR .... Fourier Transform Reflectance-Absorbtion Infra Red (SAUS)
FT RA-IR .... Fourier Transform Reflectance-Absorbtion Infra-Red (SAUS)
FTRB .... Flight Test Review Board (MCD)
FTRC .... Federal Telecommunications Records Center (NRCH)
FTRCA .... Finite Turn Repetitive Checking Automata (SAUS)
FTRD .... Flight Test Requirements Document [*NASA*] (NASA)
FTRD .... Functional Test Requirements Document (NASA)
FTRF .... Freedom to Read Foundation (EA)
FT/RF .... Frequency Translator/Recursive Filter (CAAL)
FTRF .... Full-Time Recruiting Force [*DoD*]
FTR Filter .... Fixed Target Rejection Filter (SAUS)
FTRFLT .... Fighter Flight (SAUO)
FTRFME .... Flight Test Rocket Facilities Mechanical Engineering (AAG)
FTRG .... Fleet Tactical Readiness Group (COE)
FTRG .... Flight Test Report Guide (MCD)
FTRIA .... Flow and Temperature Removable Instrument Assembly [*Nuclear energy*] (NRCH)
Ftr-Intcp .... Fighter-Interceptor (SAUS)
FTrk .... Fast Truck (SAUS)
FTRM .... Flight Test Request Memorandum (MCD)
FTRN .... First American Railways, Inc. [*NASDAQ symbol*] (SAG)
FTRNX .... Fidelity Trend [*Mutual fund ticker symbol*] (SG)
FTRO .... Fellow of the Toastmasters for Royal Occasions [*British*] (DI)
FTRO .... Fighter Operations
FTRO .... Flight Test Release Order (SAUS)
FTRP .... Fighter Plans
FTRP .... Future of Tropical Rainforest Peoples (SAUS)
FtRpBc .... First Republic Bancorp, Inc. [*Associated Press*] (SAG)
FTRR & I .... For Their Respective Rights and Interests [*Insurance*] (AIA)
FTRS .... Fourier transform RS (SAUS)
FTRS .... Fruit Tree Research Station (SAUS)
FTRS .... Full-Text Retrieval System (MELL)
FTRT .... Flight Test Release Ticket (MCD)
FTRU .... Food Technology Research Unit (SAUS)
FTRW .... Flight Test Reports Writer (MUGU)
FTRWPNSSq ... Fighter Weapons Squadron [*Air Force*]
FTS .... African Transair [*Nigeria*] [*FAA designator*] (FAAC)
FTS .... Facsimile Test Society
FTS .... Facteur Thymique Serique [*Synthetic Serum Thymic Factor*] [*Immunochemistry*] [*French*]
FTS .... Factory-based Test Stand (SAUS)
FTS .... Factory Test Set
FTS .... Factory Test System (SAUS)
FTS .... Factory Training School
FTS .... Failure to Surrender (WDAA)
FTS .... Faith Theological Seminary
FTS .... Fallopian Tube Sarcoma [*Medicine*] (MELL)
FTS .... Family Tracking System [*Medicine*] (EDAA)
FTS .... Fault Tolerance System
fts .... favorite-track selection (SAUS)
FTS .... Federal Technology Service
FTS .... Federal Telecommunications System [*of GSA*]
FTS .... Federal Telecommunication System (SAUS)
FTS .... Federal Telephone System (KSC)
FTS .... Federal Teleprocessing Service [*GSA*]
ft/s .... Feet per Second (ABAC)
FT/S .... Feet per Second
FTS .... Fellow of Technological Sciences
FTS .... Feminizing Testis Syndrome [*Medicine*] (DMAA)
FTS .... Femtosecond Transition-State Spectroscope
FTS .... Fetal Tobacco Syndrome [*Medicine*] (MELL)
FTS .... Fidonet Technical Standard (SAUO)
FTS .... Fidonet Transport Standard (SAUO)
FTS .... Field Computer Test Set
FTS .... Field Target Screen
FTS .... field task simulator (SAUS)
FTS .... Field Test Set (SAUS)
FTS .... Field Test Support [*Aerospace*] (AAG)
FTS .... Field Training Services [*Army*] (AABC)
FTS .... Field Transfer Service (SAUS)
FTS .... Field Transfer System (SAUS)
FTS .... Fighter Training Squadron (SAUS)
FTS .... File Transfer Server (SAUS)
FTS .... File Transfer Service (DOMA)
FTS .... File Transfer Special (SAUS)
FTS .... File Transfer Spooler (SAUS)

FTS File Transfer System (SAUS)
FTS Filled Thermal System [*Temperature sensor*]
FTS Financial Terminal System (SAUS)
FTS Financial Tracking System (ACAE)
FTS Financial Transaction System (SAUS)
FTS Fine Track Sensor
FTS Finish Two Sides [*Technical drawings*] (IAA)
FTS Fischer-Tropsch Synthesis [*Organic chemistry*]
FTS Fissured Tongue Syndrome [*Medicine*] (MELL)
FTS Fixed Tail Stock (SAUS)
FTS Fixed Task Supervisor (SAUS)
FTS Fleet Training Squadron [*Navy*]
FTS Flexible Test Station
FTS Flexible Track System [*Aviation*] (DA)
FTS Flexible Turret System (MCD)
FTS Flight Safety (SAUS)
FTS Flight Telemetry Subsystem [*Spacecraft*]
FTS Flight Telemetry System (SAUS)
FTS Flight Telerobotic Servicer [*NASA*]
FTS Flight Termination System (AFM)
FTS Flight Test Sketch (MCD)
FTS Flight Test Standard
FTS Flight Test Station (MCD)
FTS Flight Test Support
FTS Flight Test System (NASA)
FTS Flight Traffic Specialist (SAA)
FTS Flight Training School (SAUO)
FTS Flight Training Squadron (SAUO)
FTS Flight Training Target Simulator (ACAE)
FTS Float Switch [*Aerospace*] (IAA)
FTS Flying Target Simulator (SAUS)
FTS Flying Traffic Specialist (SAUS)
FTS Flying Training School
FTS Flying Training Squadron [*Air Force*]
FTS Footstar, Inc. [*NYSE symbol*] (SAG)
FTS Foot Switch [*Industrial control*] (IEEE)
FTS Force Tracking System (SAUO)
FTS Ford's Theatre Society (EA)
FTS Foreign Trade Statistics [*Bureau of Census*]
FTS Forged Tool Society (SAUO)
FTS Fortis, Inc. [*Toronto Stock Exchange symbol*]
FTS Foundation for Traffic Safety
FTS Fourier Transform Spectrometer [*or Spectroscopy*]
FTS Fourier Transform Spectrophotometer (SAUS)
FTS Fourier Transform System
FTS Frame-Supported Tension Structure [*Tent*] [*Navy*]
FTS Frame Transfer Sensor (SAUS)
FTS Free-Time System [*GE/PAC*] (IEEE)
FTS Frequency and Timing Subsystem [*Deep Space Instrumentation Facility, NASA*]
FTS Frequency Time Schedule (NVT)
FTS Frequency Time Standard
FTS Fuel Transfer System [*Nuclear energy*] (NRCH)
FTS Full-Time Support
FTS Full Turbulence Simulation (CARB)
FTS Fulmer Technical Services [*Research center*] [*British*] (IRC)
FTS Functional Test Specification (KSC)
FTS Funds Transfer System
FTS Funeral Telegraph Service
FTS Furnishing Trades Society (SAUO)
FTS Future Tank Study (SAUS)
FTS Future Technology Systems (NITA)
FTS University of South Florida, Tampa, FL [*Library symbol*] [*Library of Congress*] (LCLS)
FTS Fellow of the Tourism Society (ODA)
FTS2000 Federal Telecommunications Services - 2000 (SAUS)
FTS 2000 Federal Telecommunications System 2000 [*A digital fiber-optic network*] (IGQR)
FTSA Fault Tolerant System Architecture [*Computer science*]
FTSA Seaman Apprentice, Fire Control Technician, Striker [*Navy rating*]
FTSB Fort Thomas Financial Corp. [*NASDAQ symbol*] (SAG)
FTSB Fort Thomas Finl [*NASDAQ symbol*] (TTSB)
FTSC Fako Transport Shipping Lines [*Joint venture between Cameroon and the US*] [*Shipping line*] (EY)
FTSC Fault Tolerant Spaceborne Computer
FTSC Federal Telecommunications Standards Committee
FTSC Fellow in the Technology of Surface Coatings [*British*] (DBQ)
FTSC Fellow of the Tonic Sol-fa College (WDAA)
FTSC Fidonet Technical Standard Conference (SAUO)
FTSC Fidonet Technical Standards Committee (SAUS)
FTSC First Federal S&L Assn. of South Carolina [*NASDAQ symbol*] (COMM)
FTSC FSL Technical Steering Committee (SAUS)
FTSCDET Fleet Technical Support Center Detachment (DNAB)
FTSCO Fort Scott, KS [*American Association of Railroads railroad junction routing code*]
FTSD Full-Term Spontaneous Delivery [*Medicine*] (MELL)
FT-SE Financial Times - Stock Exchange [*Stock index*] [*Pronounced "footsie"*] [*British*]
FT-SE 100 Financial Times-Stock Exchange 100 (ODBW)
FTSE-100 Financial Times Stock Exchange 100 stock index (SAUS)
FT/SEC Feet per Second (MCD)
ft sec foot second (SAUS)
FT-Sensor frame transfer sensing element (SAUS)
FTSG Full Thickness Skin Graft [*Medicine*] (DMAA)
FTSH Full Toyota Service History [*Automotive classified advertising*]
FtShengo First Shenango Bancorp, Inc. [*Associated Press*] (SAG)
FTSI Fisher Transportation Services, Inc. [*NASDAQ symbol*] (COMM)
ft sm Feet Surface Measure [*Construction term*] (MIST)
FTS-M University of South Florida, College of Medicine, Tampa, FL [*Library symbol*] [*Library of Congress*] (LCLS)
FTSMC Full-Time Support Management Center [*Army*] (INF)
FTS-MC University of South Florida, Media Center, Tampa, FL [*Library symbol*] [*Library of Congress*] (LCLS)
FTSMI Fort Smith, AR [*American Association of Railroads railroad junction routing code*]
FTSMS Flying Training Student Management System [*Air Force*]
FTSN Seaman, Fire Control Technician, Striker [*Navy rating*]
FTSNCFR Family Therapy Section of the National Council on Family Relations (EA)
FTSNSW Furnishing Trades Society of New South Wales [*Australia*]
ft solut Fiat Solutio [*Let a Solution Be Made*] [*Pharmacy*] [*Latin*] (MAE)
FtSouest First Southeast Financial Corp. [*Associated Press*] (SAG)
FTSP First Team Sports [*NASDAQ symbol*] (TTSB)
FTSP First Team Sports, Inc. [*NASDAQ symbol*] (NQ)
FTSPS Field Technical Support Programming System (SAUS)
FTSq Flying Training Squadron [*Air Force*]
FTSR Flight Termination System Report (ACAE)
FTSR Foreign Trade Statistical Regulation (SAUS)
FTSR Foreign Trade Statistics Regulations
FTSS Ferranti-Thomson Sonar Systems Ltd. (SAUS)
FTSS Flight Test Simulation Station
FTSS Free Text Synthesis System (SAUS)
FtStateCp First State Corp. [*Associated Press*] (SAG)
FtSteCp First State Corp. [*Associated Press*] (SAG)
FtStFin First State Financial Services, Inc. [*Associated Press*] (SAG)
FtSthnB First Southern Bancshares, Inc. [*Associated Press*] (SAG)
FTSTP Flexible Test Station Test Procedure
ftsup Foot Superficial (SAUS)
ft suppos Fiat Suppositorium [*Let a Suppository Be Made*] [*Pharmacy*] (DAVI)
FtSvBanc First Savings Bank of Moore County [*Associated Press*] (SAG)
FTT Failure to Thrive [*Syndrome*] [*Medicine*]
FTT Failure to Train (SAUS)
FTT Fat Tolerance Test [*Medicine*] (MELL)
FTT Fault Test (SAUS)
FTT Fever Therapy Technician [*Navy*]
FTT- Fiber To The (SAUS)
FTT Field Tactical Trainer [*Army*] (INF)
FTT Field Test Telescope (ACAE)
FTT Field Training Team [*Military*] (CINC)
FTT field transfusion team (SAUS)
FTT Financial Transaction Terminal [*Banking*] (MHDW)
FTT Finning Intl. [*Toronto Stock Exchange symbol*] (SG)
FTT Finning Ltd. [*Toronto Stock Exchange symbol*] [*Vancouver Stock Exchange symbol*]
FTT Fischer-Tropsch Type [*Class of chemical reaction*]
FTT Five Task Test [*Psychology*]
FTT Fixed Target Track (MCD)
FTT Fixed Tissue Turnover [*Laboratory and physiology*] (DAVI)
FTT Flanged Tongue Terminal
FTT Flat Trim Template (MSA)
FTT Flight Technical Tolerance (SAUS)
ftt Foot Ton (SAUS)
ftt formation tester tool (SAUS)
ftt framed timber trestle (SAUS)
FTT Free Territory of Trieste
FTT Free Tissue Transfer [*Medicine*] (MELL)
FTT French Teaching Theatre (SAUO)
FTT Fructose Tolerance Test (SAUS)
FTT Fuel Transfer Tool
FTT Full-Time Temporary [*Civil Service employee category*]
FTT Fulton, MO [*Location identifier*] [*FAA*] (FAAL)
ftt functional test tool (SAUS)
FTTA Federal Technology Transfer Act (AUEG)
FTTA Fertile Thoughts To All (SAUS)
FTTA Sarh [*Chad*] [*ICAO location identifier*] (ICLI)
FTTB Bongor [*Chad*] [*ICAO location identifier*] (ICLI)
FTTB Fiber To The Bridger (SAUS)
FTTB Fiber To The Building (SAUS)
FTTC Abeche [*Chad*] [*ICAO location identifier*] (ICLI)
FTTC Fiber to the Curb [*Telecommunications*]
FTTC Fleet Tactical Training Course (DOMA)
FTTD Fiber To The Desk (SAUS)
FTTD Fiber-to-the-Desk (AAEL)
FTTD Fiber to the Desktop [*Materials science*]
FTTD Fiber To The Distribution frame (SAUS)
FTTD Full-Time Training Duty [*Army*] (AABC)
FTTD Moundou [*Chad*] [*ICAO location identifier*] (ICLI)
FTTE Biltine [*Chad*] [*ICAO location identifier*] (ICLI)
FtTeam First Team Sports, Inc. [*Associated Press*] (SAG)
FTTERM File Transfer and Terminal Emulator Program [*Communications term*] (DCT)
FTTF Fada [*Chad*] [*ICAO location identifier*] (ICLI)
FTTF Fiber-to-the Feeder [*Telecommunications*]
FTtF Florida College, Temple Terrace, FL [*Library symbol*] [*Library of Congress*] (LCLS)
FTTF Freedom through Truth Foundation (EA)
FTTG Fiber To The Galaxy (SAUS)
FTTG Goz-Beida [*Chad*] [*ICAO location identifier*] (ICLI)
FTTH Fiber to the Home [*Telecommunications*]

FTTH .... Lai [*Chad*] [*ICAO location identifier*] (ICLI)
FtThom .... Fort Thomas Financial Corp. [*Associated Press*] (SAG)
FTTI .... Ati [*Chad*] [*ICAO location identifier*] (ICLI)
FT-TIPS .... Fourier Transform Of The Time-Interval Probability (SAUS)
FTTJ .... N'Djamena [*Chad*] [*ICAO location identifier*] (ICLI)
FTTK .... Bokoro [*Chad*] [*ICAO location identifier*] (ICLI)
FTTK .... Fibre To The Kerb (SAUS)
FTTL .... Bol [*Chad*] [*ICAO location identifier*] (ICLI)
FTTM .... Few-Tube Test Model [*Nuclear energy*] (NRCH)
FTTM .... Mongo [*Chad*] [*ICAO location identifier*] (ICLI)
FTTN .... Am-Timan [*Chad*] [*ICAO location identifier*] (ICLI)
FTTO .... Fiber to the Office (VLIE)
FTTP .... Fiber to the Pedestal [*Telecommunications*]
FTTP .... Fibre To The Building (SAUS)
FTTP .... Full-Time Temporary Personnel [*Employment*]
FTTP .... full-time training position (SAUS)
FTTP .... Pala [*Chad*] [*ICAO location identifier*] (ICLI)
FTTPP .... Federation of Trainers and Training Programs in PsychoDrama (EA)
fttr .... filter (SAUS)
FTTR .... Fretter, Inc. [*NASDAQ symbol*] (SAG)
FTTR .... Zouar [*Chad*] [*ICAO location identifier*] (ICLI)
FT TROCH .... Fiat Trochisci [*Make Lozenges*] [*Pharmacy*]
FTTS .... Bousso [*Chad*] [*ICAO location identifier*] (ICLI)
FTTS .... Failure to Thrive Syndrome [*Medicine*] (MELL)
FTTS .... FIFRA/TSCA Tracking System (SAUO)
FTTS .... Flow-Through Tube Sampler [*Nuclear energy*] (NRCH)
FTTT .... N'Djamena [*Chad*] [*ICAO location identifier*] (ICLI)
FTTU .... Field Technical Training Unit (MCD)
FTTU .... Mao [*Chad*] [*ICAO location identifier*] (ICLI)
FTTV .... N'Djamena [*Chad*] [*ICAO location identifier*] (ICLI)
FTTY .... Faya-Largeau [*Chad*] [*ICAO location identifier*] (ICLI)
FTTZ .... Bardai-Zougra [*Chad*] [*ICAO location identifier*] (ICLI)
FTU .... Factory Training Unit (KSC)
FTU .... Fail Tension Ultimate (MCD)
FTU .... Federation of Theatre Unions [*British*] (DCTA)
FTU .... Federation of Trade Unions [*British*] (DAS)
FTU .... Ferry Training Unit [*British*]
FTU .... Field Torpedo Unit
ftu .... field transfer unit (SAUS)
FTU .... Field Transfusion Unit [*Military*] [*British*]
FTU .... Fire Control Technician (Underwater) [*U.S. Navy enlisted rating*] (AUER)
FTU .... First Time Use
FTU .... First Training Unit
FTU .... First Union Corp. [*NYSE symbol*] (SPSG)
FTU .... Fixed Treatment Unit [*Engineering*]
FTU .... Fleet Training Unit
FTU .... Flight Test Unit (KSC)
FTU .... Florida Technology University (DAVI)
FTU .... Fluorescein Thiourea [*Organic chemistry*]
FTU .... Fluorescence Thiourea [*Organic chemistry*] (DAVI)
FTU .... Formal Training Unit (SAUS)
FTU .... Formazin Turbidity Unit [*Analytical chemistry*]
FTU .... Fort Dauphin [*Madagascar*] [*Airport symbol*] (OAG)
FTU .... Frascati Tokamak Upgrade (SAUS)
FTU .... Freeman Time Unit [*Psychology*]
FTU .... Free Trade Union (SAUO)
FTU .... Frequency Transfer Unit
FTU .... Fuel Tanking Unit (SAUS)
FTU .... Fuel Transfer Unit [*NASA*] (KSC)
FTU .... Functional Test Unit [*Computer science*] (IAA)
FTU .... University of Central Florida, Orlando, FL [*OCLC symbol*] (OCLC)
FTU .... University of Tampa, Tampa, FL [*Library symbol*] [*Library of Congress*] (LCLS)
FTUB .... Free Trade Unions of Burma
FTUC .... Federal Trade Union Congress [*European*]
FTUC .... Trade Union Congress of the Federation of Rhodesia and Nyasaland (SAUO)
FTUC of AFL .... Free Trade Union Committee of the A.F.L. (SAUO)
FT UNG .... Fiat Unguentum [*Make an Ointment*] [*Pharmacy*]
FTUnH .... University Community Hospital, Medical Library, Tampa, FL [*Library symbol*] [*Library of Congress*] (LCLS)
FTUP .... Free Trade Unions of the Philippines
FTUPrB .... First Union $2.15 Cv B Pfd [*NYSE symbol*] (TTSB)
FTUPrD .... First Union Adj D Pfd [*NYSE symbol*] (TTSB)
FTUPrF .... First Union 10.64% Dep Pfd [*NYSE symbol*] (TTSB)
FTUR .... Flight Test Unsatisfactory Report (SAUS)
FTURE .... Furniture (ROG)
FTUS .... Factory 2-U Stores [*Formerly, Family Bargain*] [*NASDAQ symbol*]
FTUS .... Full-Time Unit Support [*Army Reserve*] (INF)
FtUSA .... First USA, Inc. [*Associated Press*] (SAG)
FTUSWAW .... Federation of Trade Unions of Salt Workers, Alkali Workers, etc. (SAUO)
FtUtd .... First United Bancshares, Inc. [*Associated Press*] (SAG)
FtUtdBcp .... First United Bancorp [*Associated Press*] (SAG)
FtUtdBs .... First United Bancshares [*Associated Press*] (SAG)
FTUV .... Federated Teachers' Union of Victoria [*Australia*]
FT-UV/Vis .... Fourier-Transform Ultraviolet/Visible [*Spectrophotometer*]
FTV .... Fashion Television [*Video sales technique in the apparel industry*]
FTV .... Flight Television [*NASA*] (KSC)
FTV .... Flight Test Validation (ACAE)
FTV .... Flight Test Vehicle [*Air Force*]
FTV .... Flow-Through Ventilation
FTV .... Foxtail Mosaic Virus
FTV .... Fukushima Television (SAUO)
FTV .... Functional Technical Validation (SDI)
FTV .... Functional Technology Vehicle [*Army*]
FTV .... Functional Test Vehicle (ACAE)
FTV .... Functional Test Verification (SAUS)
FTV .... Fuze Test Vehicle (SAUS)
FTV .... Masvingo [*Zimbabwe*] [*Airport symbol*] (OAG)
FTV .... United States Veterans Administration Hospital, Tampa, FL [*Library symbol*] [*Library of Congress*] (LCLS)
FtVaBks .... First Virginia Banks, Inc. [*Associated Press*] (SAG)
FTVL .... Fixed-to-Variable-Length (in FTVL Code) [*Computing*] (ODA)
FTVSP .... Flight Test Vehicle Safety Plan [*Air Force*] (MCD)
FTW .... Fairmont [*Washington*] [*Seismograph station code, US Geological Survey*] (SEIS)
FTW .... Federation of Telephone Workers
FTW .... Fighter Tactical Wing (MCD)
FTW .... File Tree Walk (SAUS)
FTW .... Fizean Toothed Wheel
FTW .... Flying Training Wing [*Air Force*]
FTW .... Footwall Exploration [*Vancouver Stock Exchange symbol*]
FTW .... Fort Wayne-South Bend [*Diocesan abbreviation*] [*Indiana*] (TOCD)
FtW .... Fort Worth (SAUS)
FTW .... Fort Worth, TX [*Location identifier*] [*FAA*] (FAAL)
FTW .... Forward Traveling Wave
FTW .... Free Trade Wharf
FTW .... Friends of the Third World (EA)
FtWayne .... Fort Wayne National Corp. [*Associated Press*] (SAG)
FtWBc .... First Western Bancorp [*Associated Press*] (SAG)
FTWG .... Flight Test Working Group
FTWIAD .... Fort Wingate Army Depot [*New Mexico*]
FTWO .... Flight Test Work Order (MCD)
FTWOAD .... Fort Worth Army Depot [*Texas*]
FTWR .... Footwear
FTWS .... Federal Train Wreck Statute
FtWstnBc .... First Western Bancorp [*Associated Press*] (SAG)
FTWUA .... Federated Tobacco Workers' Union of Australia
FTWYN .... Fort Wayne, IN [*American Association of Railroads railroad junction routing code*]
FTX .... Fault Tolerance Extension (SAUS)
FTX .... Fault Tolerant UNIX (CDE)
FTX .... Federal Tax Code (SAUS)
FTX .... Field Test Exercise [*Military*]
FTX .... Field Training Exercise [*Army*] (INF)
FTX .... Fleet Training Exercise
FTX .... Fort Riley, KS [*Location identifier*] [*FAA*] (FAAL)
FTX .... Four Transistors (SAUS)
FTX .... Freeport-McMoRan, Inc. [*NYSE symbol*] (SPSG)
FTX .... Freeport McMoRan(New) [*NYSE symbol*] (TTSB)
FTX .... Free Text Retrieval (NITA)
FTX .... Free Text System (SAUS)
FTX .... Ft. Rousset [*Congo*] [*Airport symbol*] (AD)
FTX .... Funnel-Web Spider Toxin
FTX .... Owando [*Congo*] [*Airport symbol*] (OAG)
FTX Module .... Four Transistor Module (SAUS)
FTX System .... Free Text System (SAUS)
FTY .... Atlanta, GA [*Location identifier*] [*FAA*] (FAAL)
Fty .... Factory (SAUS)
FTY .... Futurity Oils Ltd. [*Vancouver Stock Exchange symbol*]
FTyAF-T .... United States Air Force, Technical Library, Tyndall AFB, FL [*Library symbol*] [*Library of Congress*] (LCLS)
FTYP .... Fuel Type [*Automotive emissions*]
FTYPE .... Feature Type (SAUS)
F-type .... Jungian feeling type (SAUS)
FTZ .... Federal Trade Zone
FTZ .... Foreign Trade Zone [*New York City docks area*]
FTZ .... Foristell, MO [*Location identifier*] [*FAA*] (FAAL)
FTZ .... Free Trade Zone (IMH)
FTZ .... Fushi Tarazu [*Not Enough Segments*] [*Genetics*] [*Japan*]
f-tz- .... Tanzania [*MARC geographic area code*] [*Library of Congress*] (LCCP)
FTZB .... Foreign Trade Zone Board
FTZ-Board .... Federal Trade Zone Board (SAUO)
FTZ-SZ .... Free Trade Zone-Subzone (JAGO)
FTZ-SZ .... FTZ-Subzone (SAUO)
FU .... Air Littoral [*ICAO designator*] (AD)
FU .... Faecal Urobilinogen (SAUS)
FU .... Fairfield University (SAUO)
FU .... Farmacopea Ufficiale [*Italy*] (DB)
FU .... Fecal Urobilinogen [*Clinical chemistry*]
FU .... Federal Union (DAS)
FU .... Federal Union, Inc. (SAUO)
FU .... Feed Unit (ODA)
FU .... Feministas Unidas [*An association*] (EA)
FU .... Ferry Unit (SAUS)
FU .... Fetal Urobilinogen (DB)
FU .... Field Unit (SAUS)
f/u .... fine used (SAUS)
Fu .... fining upward (SAUS)
Fu .... Finsen Unit [*for ultraviolet light*]
FU .... Finsen Unit (UV) Unit of Ultraviolet Light [*Medicine*] (EDAA)
FU .... Fire Unit (SAUS)
FU .... Firing Unit [*Military*]
FU .... Fisk University (SAUO)
FU .... Flight Unit (MCD)
FU .... Floating University (SAUO)
FU .... Fluorouracil [*Also, F*] [*Antineoplastic drug*]

fu flux unit (SAUS)
FU Flying Unit (SAUS)
FU Foederalistische Union [*Federal Union*] [*Germany*] [*Political party*] (PPE)
FU Folkuniversitetet
F/U Follow-Up [*Medicine*] (EDAA)
FU Follow-Up
FU Fordham University (SAUO)
FU Forecast Unit
FU Forecast Upper Air (NATG)
FU Forming-up (SAUS)
FU Fouled Up [*To describe a confused, mixed-up situation, person, or action*] [*Bowdlerized version*]
FU Fractional Urinalysis [*Medicine*]
FU Frame Unprotected [*Insurance classification*]
FU Franklin University (SAUO)
FU Frederick Ungar [*Publisher*]
FU Freeman Time Unit [*Psychology*]
FU Freeman Unit (SAUS)
FU Freie Union in Niedersachsen [*Free Union in Lower Saxony*] [*Germany*] [*Political party*] (PPW)
FU Freie Universitaet (Berlin) [*Free University (Berlin)*] [*Information retrieval*] [*Germany*]
FU Friends University (SAUO)
Fu Fucus [*Quality of the bottom*] [*Nautical charts*]
FU Fudan University [*China*]
FU Fuel (NASA)
FU Fukui University (SAUO)
FU Fukuoka University (SAUO)
FU full (SAUS)
FU Fumarate Concentration (OA)
FU Fume Concentration (SAUS)
FU Functional Unit [*Computer science*]
FU Function Unit (SAUS)
FU Funding (NITA)
F/U Fundus at Umbilicus [*Obstetrics*] (DAVI)
FU Furman University (SAUO)
FU Fuse (MSA)
FU Fuze (SAUS)
fu--- Suez Canal [*MARC geographic area code*] [*Library of Congress*] (LCCP)
FU University of Florida, Gainesville, FL [*Library symbol*] [*Library of Congress*] (LCLS)
FU Farmers' Union (ODA)
FUA Compania Hispano Irlandesa de Aviacion [*Spain*] [*ICAO designator*] (FAAC)
FUA Farm Underwriters Association [*Defunct*]
FUA Federal Unemployment Account [*Unemployment insurance*]
FUA Fire Unit Analyzer [*Military*]
FUA Flexible Use of Airspace (SAUS)
FUA Follow-Up Amplifier
FUA Frente Unita Angolana [*Angolan United Front*]
FUA Fuel Use Act
FUA Future Urban Area (SAUS)
f-ua- United Arab Republic [*Egypt*] [*MARC geographic area code*] [*Library of Congress*] (LCCP)
FU-A University of Florida, Agricultural Experiment Station, Gainesville, FL [*Library symbol*] [*Library of Congress*] (LCLS)
FUA University of Florida, Agricultural Library, Gainesville, FL [*OCLC symbol*] (OCLC)
FUAA Filmmakers United Against Apartheid (EA)
FUAAV Federation Universelle des Associations d'Agences de Voyages [*Universal Federation of Travel Agents' Associations - UFTAA*] (EAIO)
FUACE Federation Universelle des Associations Chretiennes d'Etudiants [*Universal Federation of Christian Students Associations*]
FUAI Front Uni pour l'Autonomie Interne [*United Front for Internal Autonomy*] [*French Polynesia*] [*Political party*] (PPW)
FUAM Freie und Angenommene Maurer [*Free and Accepted Mason*] [*Freemasonry*] [*German*]
FUB Facility Utilization Board (AFM)
FUB Forward Utility Bridge (NASA)
FUB Free University of Berlin (SAUO)
FUB Front de l'Unite Bangala [*Bangala United Front*]
FUB Fube [*Japan*] [*Seismograph station code, US Geological Survey*] (SEIS)
FUB Fulleborn [*Papua New Guinea*] [*Airport symbol*] (OAG)
FUB Functional Uterine Bleeding [*Medicine*]
FUB University of Florida, Law Library, Gainesville, FL [*OCLC symbol*] (OCLC)
FUBA Federal Unemployment Benefit and Allowance Account [*Unemployment insurance*]
FUBAR Failed UNI BUS Address Register [*Computer science*] (NHD)
FUBAR Fangmeyer's Utility, a Basic Algorithm for Revision (PDAA)
FUBC 1st United Bancorp(FL) [*NASDAQ symbol*] (TTSB)
FUBC First United Bancorp [*NASDAQ symbol*] (SAG)
FUBS Fido Used Book Squad (SAUS)
FUBU For Us By Us
FUBX Fuse Box
FUC Filipiniana Union Catalogue (SAUO)
fuc Fucose (ADWA)
Fuc Fucose (DB)
FUC Fucose (SAUS)
fuc full usable capacity (SAUS)
FUCA Federal Unemployment Compensation Act (SAUS)
FUCA Front Upper Control Arm
FUCCO First (United States Army Reserve) Company Chaplain Office
FUCG Fetal Ultrasonic Cardiography [*Medicine*] (EDAA)
FUCI Fire Unit Control Indicator (SAUS)
FUCL Fellow of University College, London [*British*] (ROG)
fucm full-utility cruise missile (SAUS)
FUCO Fellow of University College, Oxford [*British*] (ROG)
FU_{co} Functional Uptake of Carbon Monoxide [*Medicine*] (DAVI)
FU-CP University of Florida, Chemistry-Pharmacy Library, Gainesville, FL [*Library symbol*] [*Library of Congress*] (LCLS)
FUCT Failed under Continuous Testing (VLIE)
FUCUA Federation of University Conservative and Unionist Associations (SAUO)
FUD Fear, Uncertainty, and Doubt [*Factors hindering sales of lesser-known products*]
FUD Fellow of the University of Dublin (ROG)
FUD Field Use Data (SAUS)
FUD Field Use Date (VLIE)
FUD File Update Database (SAUS)
FUD Fire Unit Deployed
FUD Fire Up Decoder
FUD First Use Date [*NASA*] (NASA)
FUD Force Unit Designator (SAUS)
FUD Frente Voluntario de Defensa [*Voluntary Defense Front*] [*Guatemala*] (PD)
FUD Full Upper Denture (MELL)
FUDD Frequently Updated Distributed Data [*Computer science*] (VLIE)
FUDD Fuddruckers, Inc. [*NASDAQ symbol*] (COMM)
FUD factor Fear Uncertainty Doubt Factor [*Marketing*]
FUDR Failure and Usage Data Report (IEEE)
FUDR Fluorodeoxyuridine [*Floxuridine*] [*Also, FldUrd*] [*Antineoplastic drug*]
FUDR United Front for Democracy and the Republic (Burkina Faso) [*Political party*] (PSAP)
FUDS Federal Urban Driving Schedule
FUDS Fluids Utility Distribution System [*NASA*] (SPST)
FUDS Formerly Used Defense Site [*DoD*]
FUDT Forensic Urine Drug Testing [*Analytical chemistry*]
FUDT Newsletter Forensic Urine Drug Testing Newsletter (SAUS)
FUE Farmers Union Elevator [*Federal Railroad Administration identification code*]
FUE Federated Union of Employers [*Ireland*] (IMH)
FUE Fever of Uncertain Etiology [*Medicine*] (EDAA)
FUE Fever of Undetermined Etiology [*Medicine*] (DAVI)
FUE Fire Unit Effectiveness (MCD)
FUE First Unit Equipped (MCD)
FUE Fuerteventura [*Canary Islands*] [*Airport symbol*] (OAG)
FUE Full Unit-Equipped (SEWL)
FUED First Unit Equipped Date (MCD)
FUEL Fuel Use Efficiency Level [*Automotive engineering*]
FUEL Fuel Users Emergency Line [*Pennsylvania*]
FUEL Griffith Consumers Co. [*NASDAQ symbol*] (COMM)
FUEL Streicher Mobile Fueling, Inc. [*NASDAQ symbol*] (SAG)
FUELDB Fuels Inspection Data Base (SAUO)
Fuel Econ 1925-1936 Fuel Economist (1925-1936) [*A publication*]
Fuel Process Technol Fuel Processing Technology (journ.) (SAUS)
FUELS Aviation Fuels Management System (SAUO)
Fuel Sci Tecbnol Int Fuel Science and Technology International (journ.) (SAUS)
Fuel Sci Technol Fuel Science and Technology (journ.) (SAUS)
FuelTch Fuel Tech [*Commercial firm*] [*Associated Press*] (SAG)
FUEMR Federalist Union of European Minorities and Regions (SAUO)
FUEMSSO Federation of United Kingdom and Eire Malaysian and Singaporean Students [*British*]
FUEN Federal Union of European Nationalities [*Political party*] (PPW)
FUES Follow-up and Evaluation Section (EERA)
FUEV Foederalistische Union Europaeischer Volksgruppen [*Federal Union of European Nationalities*]
FUF Facing the Uncertain Future (ADWA)
FUF Federation des Unions de Familles [*Federation of Family Unions*] [*Canada*]
FUF Federation for Universal French (EAIO)
FUF French Union Forces (VNW)
FUFA Free Volatile Fatty Acid [*Medicine*] (EDAA)
FUFO Fly-Under, Fly-Out (MCD)
FUFO Fuel-Fusing Option [*Nuclear energy*] (GFGA)
FUFO Full Fusing Option bomb (SAUS)
FUFO Full Fuzing Option [*Air Force*]
FUFO Bomb Full Fuzing Option Bomb (SAUS)
FUFOR Fund for UFO [*Unidentified Flying Object*] Research (EA)
FUFS First United Financial Services, Inc. (SAUO)
FUFTB Full-Up/Fit-to-Bust [*Slang*] [*British*] (DI)
Fug De Fuga et Inventione [*Philo*] (BJA)
FUG Fuyang [*China*] [*Airport symbol*] (OAG)
f-ug- Uganda [*MARC geographic area code*] [*Library of Congress*] (LCCP)
FUG University of Florida, Gainesville, FL [*OCLC symbol*] (OCLC)
FUGA Fellow, Utah Genealogical association (SAUS)
FUGB Federation of Ukrainians in Great Britain (DBA)
FUGE Federation of Unions of Government Employees (SAUO)
FUH University of Florida, Health Center Library, Gainesville, FL [*OCLC symbol*] (OCLC)
FU-HC University of Florida, J. Hillis Miller Health Center Library, Gainesville, FL [*Library symbol*] [*Library of Congress*] (LCLS)
FUHLR Fuse Holder
FUI Fake User Interface
FUI File Update Information [*Computer science*] (VLIE)
FUI Friendly Unit Information Functional Area (SAUO)

FUIB .... Fire Underwriters Inspection Bureau (SAUS)
FUIF .... Fire Unit Integration Facility [*Military*]
FUINCA .... Fundacion de la Red de Informacion Cientifica Automatizada [*Spain*] (NITA)
FUINCA .... Fundacion para el Fomento de la Informacion Automatizada [*Foundation for the Promotion of Automated Information*] [*Information service or system*] (IID)
FuiszT .... Fuisz Technologies [*Associated Press*] (SAG)
FUJ .... Front Upset Jaw (MSA)
FUJ .... Fujairah Aviation Centre [*United Arab Emirates*] [*ICAO designator*] (FAAC)
FUJ .... Fujitsu [*Japan*] (NITA)
FUJ .... Fukue [*Japan*] [*Airport symbol*] (OAG)
FU-J .... University of Florida, Health Sciences, JHEP Processing Center, Gainesville, FL [*Library symbol*] [*Library of Congress*] (LCLS)
Fuji .... Fujinoyama, Fujisan, or Mount Fuji (SAUS)
FUJI .... Fuji Photo Film Co. Ltd. [*NASDAQ symbol*] (NQ)
FujiPh .... Fuji Photo Film Co. Ltd. [*Associated Press*] (SAG)
Fujitsu Sci and TechJ... Fujitsu Scientific and Technical Journal (SAUS)
FUJIY .... Fuji Photo Film ADR [*NASDAQ symbol*] (TTSB)
FUJOPS .... FORSCOM Unique JOPS (SAUS)
FUK .... Fukui [*Japan*] [*Seismograph station code, US Geological Survey*] (SEIS)
FUK .... Fukuoka [*Japan*] [*Airport symbol*] (OAG)
FUL .... Florida Union List of Serials, Gainesville, FL [*Inactive*] [*OCLC symbol*] (OCLC)
FUL .... Folch Upper Layer (SAUS)
FUL .... Forming-up Line (SAUS)
FUL .... Frente de Unidad Liberal [*Honduras*] [*Political party*] (EY)
FUL .... Front Uni Liberateur de la Guinee Portuguesa et des Isles du Cap Vert [*United Liberation Front of Portuguese Guinea and Cape Verde*] [*Political party*]
Ful .... Fulcran (SAUS)
FUL .... Fulcrum (MSA)
Ful .... Fulgence (SAUS)
Ful .... Fulgencio (SAUS)
Ful .... Fulke (SAUS)
Ful .... Fuller (SAUS)
FUL .... Fullerton [*California*] [*Airport symbol*] (OAG)
FUL .... Fullerton, CA [*Location identifier*] [*FAA*] (FAAL)
Ful .... Fulton (SAUS)
Ful .... Fulvia (SAUS)
Ful .... Fulvius (SAUS)
FUL .... Funchal [*Madeira Island*] [*Seismograph station code, US Geological Survey*] (SEIS)
FU-L .... University of Florida, Law Library, Gainesville, FL [*Library symbol*] [*Library of Congress*] (LCLS)
Fulb Par .... Fulbeck's Parallel [*A publication*] (DLA)
Fulb St Law... Fulbeck's Study of the Law [*A publication*] (DLA)
FULC .... First Unit Loading Cost
Fulc .... Fulcrum (SAUS)
FULC .... Fulcrum Tech, Inc. [*NASDAQ symbol*] (SAG)
FULCF .... Fulcrum Technologies [*NASDAQ symbol*] (TTSB)
Fulcrum .... Fulcrum Tech, Inc. [*Associated Press*] (SAG)
fulg .... Fulguration [*Medicine*] (DAVI)
FULICO .... Fidelity Union Life Insurance Co.
FULK .... Front Uni de Liberation Kanake [*New Caledonia*] [*Political party*] (FEA)
FULL .... Fuller [*H.B.*] Co. [*NASDAQ symbol*] (NQ)
FULL .... Fuller (HB) [*NASDAQ symbol*] (TTSB)
FULL .... Fulltext Sources Online [*Information service or system*] (IID)
Full BR .... Bengal Full Bench Rulings [*North-Western Provinces, India*] [*A publication*] (DLA)
Full Ch Hist... Fuller's Church History [*A publication*] (DLA)
Fuller .... Fuller's Reports [*59-105 Michigan*] [*A publication*] (DLA)
Fuller (Mich)... Fuller's Reports [*59-105 Michigan*] [*A publication*] (DLA)
FullHs .... Full House Resorts [*Associated Press*] (SAG)
FullHse .... Full House Resorts [*Associated Press*] (SAG)
Fulmer Newsl... Fulmer Newsletter (journ.) (SAUS)
fulnm .... full name (SAUS)
FulrHB .... Fuller [*H. B.*] Co. [*Associated Press*] (SAG)
FULRO .... Front Unifie de la Lutte de la Race Opprime [*United Front for the Struggle of Oppressed Races*] (CINC)
FULS .... Florida Union List of Serials
FULT .... Formation/Unit Loading Table (SAUS)
FULT .... Fulton Financial [*NASDAQ symbol*] (TTSB)
FULT .... Fulton Financial Corp. [*NASDAQ symbol*] (NQ)
Fult .... Fulton's Supreme Court Reports, Bengal [*1842-44*] [*India*] [*A publication*] (DLA)
Fulton .... Fulton Financial Corp. [*Associated Press*] (SAG)
Fulton .... Fulton's Supreme Court Reports, Bengal [*1842-44*] [*India*] [*A publication*] (DLA)
FULTYPE .... Fuel Type [*Automotive emissions*]
FUM .... Familial Uveal Melanoma [*Oncology*]
FUM .... Fluorouracil, Methotrexate [*Antineoplastic drug regimen*]
FUM .... Freiberg University of Mining (SAUO)
FUM .... Friendly Union of Mechanics [*British*]
FUM .... Friends United Meeting
FUM .... Fumarase (SAUS)
Fum .... Fumarate [*Medicine*] (EDAA)
FUM .... Fumarate
FUM .... Fumaroid (SAUS)
FUM .... Fumigate [*or Fumigation*] (AABC)
fum .... Fuming (SAUS)
FUM .... Functional User's Manual (AABC)
FUMAR .... Fumaroid (SAUS)
FUME .... Foam Upholstery Must End [*Royal Society for the Prevention of Accidents*] [*British*] (DI)
fumi .... fumigant (SAUS)
fumi .... fumigate (SAUS)
fumi .... fumigation (SAUS)
FUMIST .... Fellow of the University of Manchester Institute of Science and Technology [*British*]
FUMM .... [*The*] Fellowship of United Methodist Musicians (EA)
FUMMWA .... Fellowship of United Methodists in Music and Worship Arts (NTPA)
FUMP .... Flurouridine Monophosphate [*Medicine*] (EDAA)
FUMT .... Freiberg University of Mining and Technology (SAUO)
FUN .... Atlanta, GA [*Location identifier*] [*FAA*] (FAAL)
FUN .... Cedar Fair LP [*NYSE symbol*] (SAG)
FUN .... Fantasy Unrestricted Network [*Cable-television system*]
FUN .... Feminist Uniting Women [*Australia*]
FUN .... Follow-Up Note [*Medical records*] (DAVI)
FUN .... Forty Upward Network [*Defunct*] (EA)
FUN .... Fractional and Unknown Nuclear [*Material in meteorites*]
FUN .... Free University Network [*Later, LERN*] (EA)
FUN .... Frente de Unidad Nacional [*National Unity Front*] [*Guatemala*] [*Political party*] (PPW)
FUN .... Frente Unido Nacionalista [*Nationalist United Front*] [*Venezuela*] [*Political party*] (PPW)
FUN .... Friends of the Unied Nations (SAUO)
FUN .... Frye Utilities for Network [*Frye Computer Systems*] [*Telecommunications*] (PCM)
FUN .... Funafuti Atol [*Tuvalu*] [*Airport symbol*] (OAG)
FUN .... Funatsu [*Kawaguchuko*] [*Japan*] [*Seismograph station code, US Geological Survey*] (SEIS)
FUN .... Function (MDG)
FUN .... Functional Unit Number (SAUS)
FUN .... Function Bits Sent to Periphere for Control [*Computer science*] (ECII)
FUN .... Fundament [*Slang*] [*British*] (DSUE)
fun .... funeral (SAUS)
fun .... funerary (SAUS)
FUN .... Funtshi Aviation Service [*Zaire*] [*ICAO designator*] (FAAC)
FUNA .... Former Uganda National Army (SAUS)
FUNA .... Front d'Union Nationale de l'Angola [*National Union Front of Angola*]
funamb .... funambulation (SAUS)
funamb .... funambulist (SAUS)
FUNAP .... Federation of Staff Associations of United Nations and its Specialized Agencies in the Philippines (SAUO)
FUNBIO .... Brazilian Fund for Biodiversity (SAUO)
FUNC .... First Union Corporation (SAUO)
FUNC .... First United Corp. [*NASDAQ symbol*] (SAG)
FUNC .... Force de l'Union National Cambodge [*Cambodia*] [*Political party*]
FUNC .... Function (AABC)
FUNC .... Functional (ACAE)
Func .... Functional (AMHC)
func .... Functional [*Therapy term*] (CTAA)
func .... Functioning [*Therapy term*] (CTAA)
FUNCINPEC... Front Uni National pour Cambodge Independant, Neutre, Pacifique et Cooperatif [*National United Front for an Independent National, Peaceful, and Cooperative Cambodia*] [*Political party*] (PD)
Funco .... Funco, Inc. [*Associated Press*] (SAG)
FUNCT .... Function (KSC)
FUNCT .... Functional (NASA)
funct .... functionally (SAUS)
FUNCTL .... Functional
FUNCTLINE... Functional Line Diagram Funding (SAUS)
FUND .... All Seasons Global Fund [*NASDAQ symbol*] (TTSB)
FUND .... Family Violence Prevention Fund
FUND .... Fund (SAUS)
FUND .... Fundamental (MSA)
fund .... fundamentalism (SAUS)
FUND .... Fundamentalist (WDAA)
FUND .... Funding (NITA)
FUND .... International Convention on the Establishment of an International Fund for Compensation for Oil Pollution Damage (SAUO)
FUND .... Royce Focus Trust, Inc. [*NASDAQ symbol*] (NASQ)
FundA .... Fund American Enterprises Holdings, Inc. [*Associated Press*] (SAG)
FundAm .... Fund American Enterprises Holdings, Inc. [*Formerly, Fireman's Fund Corp.*] [*Associated Press*] (SAG)
Fundam Cosm Phys... Fundamentals of Cosmic Physics (journ.) (SAUS)
FUNDE .... Foundation for Economic Development (SAUO)
FUNDEA .... Mexican Foundation for Environmental Education (SAUO)
FUNDESCO... Fundacion para el Desarrollo de la Funcion Social de las Comunicaciones (IID)
FUNDFREQ... Fundamental Frequency (IAA)
fundies .... fundamentalists (SAUS)
FUNDWI .... Fund for the United Nations for the Development of West Irian
Fundy .... Bay of Fundy (SAUS)
Fundy .... Fundy National Park on the north shore of the Bay of Fundy in New Brunswick, Canada (SAUS)
FUNET .... [*The*] Finnish University Network [*Finland*] [*Computer science*] (TNIG)
FUNG-C .... Fungus Culture [*Medicine*] (EDAA)
fungi .... fungicide (SAUS)
FUNGIC .... Fungicide
FUNG-S .... Fungus Smear [*Medicine*] (EDAA)
FUNI .... Frame based User Network Interface (SAUS)
FUNI .... Frame Relay User Network Interface (SAUS)
FUNI .... Frame User-to-Network Interface [*Telecommunications*] (ACRL)
F Univ .... Fordham University (SAUO)

Funk.......... Funk & Wagnalls (SAUS)
Funk & W.... Funk & Wagnalls (SAUS)
FUNL.......... Federation of Unions of Workers and Employees of North Lebanon
FUNL.......... Funnel (MSA)
FUNLIS........ Fundamentals of Library and Information Science [*Drexel University*] (NITA)
FUNLOC....... Function Location (VLIE)
FUNLOG....... Functional Programming and Prolog
FUNM.......... Fort Union National Monument (SAUO)
FUNN.......... Mountasia Entertainment [*NASDAQ symbol*] (TTSB)
FUNN.......... Mountasia Entertainment International, Inc. [*NASDAQ symbol*] (SAG)
FUNNs......... For Your Nieces and Nephews (SAUS)
FUNOP......... Full Normal Plot [*Computer science*]
FUnRI.......... First Union Real Estate Equity & Mortgage Investments [*Associated Press*] (SAG)
FUNSA......... Fabrica Uruguaya de Neumaticos, Sociedad Anonima [*A tire manufacturer*]
FUNT.......... French Underground Nuclear Test (MCD)
F-U-N trio.... flourine, uranium, nitrogen tests for relative dating (SAUS)
FUNU.......... Force d'Urgence des Nations Unies
FUNY.......... Free University of New York
FUO........... Fever of Undetermined [*or Unknown*] Origin [*Medicine*]
FUO........... Fever of Unknown Origin (ADWA)
FUO........... Final Used On (VLIE)
FUO........... Follow-Up Output (NASA)
FUOP.......... Fix Up on Printer [*Have technician add or change an effect by means of optical printing*] [*Motion-picture production*]
FUOV.......... Follow-Up Office Visit [*Medicine*] (EDAA)
FUP........... Facilities Use Pass (SAUO)
FUP........... Facility Utilization Plan (AFM)
FUP........... Falciparum Uganda - Palo Alto [*Plasmodium strain causing malaria*]
FUP........... File Utility Program (SAUS)
F/UP.......... Follow Up (WDAA)
FUP........... Forca de Unidade Popular [*Terrorist group*] [*Portugal*] (EY)
FUP........... Forming Up Place (MCD)
FUP........... Form-Up Point (SAUS)
FUP........... Forward Unity Periscope
FUP........... Frente por la Unidad del Pueblo [*United Popular Front*] [*Colombia*] [*Political party*] (PPW)
FUP........... Friends United Press (DGA)
FUP........... Furman University Press (DGA)
FUP........... Fusion Point
FUPAC......... Federacion de Universidades Privadas de America Central
FUPCD......... Fonds un Pour Cent pour le Developpement [*One Percent for Development Fund*] (EAIO)
FUPL.......... Field Use Parts List (SAUS)
FUPOSAT...... Follow-Up on Supply Action Taken
FUPP.......... Full-Up Powerpack [*Military*]
Fuppy.......... Female Urban Professional [*Lifestyle classification*]
FUPRO......... Future Production (MCD)
FUQ........... Fuquene [*Colombia*] [*Seismograph station code, US Geological Survey*] (SEIS)
FuquaEn...... Fuqua Enterprises [*Associated Press*] (SAG)
FUR........... Failure and Unsatisfactory Report (SAUO)
FUR........... Failure or Unsatisfactory Report
FUR........... Failure, Unsatisfactory or Removal (SAUS)
FUR........... File Utility Routines [*Computer science*]
FUR........... First Union RE EqSBI [*NYSE symbol*] (TTSB)
FUR........... Florida University Reactor (SAUO)
FUR........... Fluorouracil, Riboside [*Antineoplastic drug regimen*] (MAE)
FUR........... Follow-Up Report
FUR........... Forma Urbis Romae [*Rome*] [*A publication*] (OCD)
FUR........... Frente Unido de la Revolucion [*United Revolutionary Front*] [*Guatemala*] [*Political party*] (PPW)
FUR........... Fuerstenfeldbruck [*Germany*] [*Seismograph station code, US Geological Survey*] (SEIS)
fur............ Furlong (SHCU)
FUR........... Furlong [*Unit of distance*]
FUR........... Furlough [*Military*] (WGA)
FUR........... Furnace (MSA)
FUR........... Furnished
FUR........... Furred [*Technical drawings*]
FUR........... Furrier
FUR........... Furring (SAUS)
FUR........... Further (AABC)
FUR........... Future Utility Rotorcraft (SAUS)
FUR-30........ Frente Universitario Revolucionario 30 de Julio [*30th July Revolutionary University Front*] [*El Salvador*]
FURA.......... Federal Utility Regulation, Annotated [*A publication*] (DLA)
FUra........... French Urania [*Record label*]
FURAM........ Ftorafur [*Tegafur*], Adriamycin, Mitomycin C [*Antineoplastic drug regimen*]
FURAN......... Furfuryl Alcohol Aniline (SAUS)
FURAS......... For Further Assignment
FURASPERS... For Further Assignment by the Commander Naval Military Personnel Command to (Duty Indicated) (DNAB)
FURASUB...... For Further Assignment to Duty in Submarine [*Navy*] (DNAB)
FURB.......... Facilities Utilization Review Board (SAUS)
FurB........... Furr's/Bishop's Cafeteria Ltd. [*Associated Press*] (SAG)
FurBish........ Furr's/Bishop's Cafeteria Ltd. [*Associated Press*] (SAG)
FurBsh......... Furrs Bishops [*Associated Press*] (SAG)
FUREPT....... Further Report to (SAUS)
FURF.......... Federation des Unions Royalistes de France [*Federation of Royalist Unions of France*] (PPW)
FURL.......... Furlough [*Military*] (ROG)
Furl L & T.... Furlong on the Irish Law of Landlord and Tenant [*A publication*] (DLA)
furlong........ furrow long (SAUS)
Furman U..... Furman University (GAGS)
furmr.......... furthermore (SAUS)
Furm Univ.... Furman University (SAUO)
furn............ Furnace (REAL)
FURN.......... Furnace
FURN.......... Furnish (AFM)
Furn............ Furnish (MIST)
furn............ Furnished (SHCU)
furn............ Furnishing (BEE)
Furn............ Furniture (DIAR)
furn............ Furniture (VRA)
FURN.......... Furniture
FURNASER... Furnish Full Names, Rates, and Social Security Numbers of Men Transferred in Accordance with This Directive (DNAB)
FurnBrds...... Furniture Brands Intl., Inc. [*Associated Press*] (SAG)
FURNG......... Furnishing
furngs......... furnishings (SAUS)
FURNIDEC... International Fair of Furniture, Decoration, Lighting Fixtures, Machinery, and Equipment [*Hellexpo*]
furnit.......... furniture (SAUS)
FURN PTS... Furniture Parts [*Freight*]
FURO.......... Furioso [*Furiously*] [*Music*] (ROG)
FUROF......... Working Group on the Future Role and Functions of the Commission (SAUO)
FUROL......... Fuel and Road Oil (SAUS)
Furon.......... Furon Co. [*Associated Press*] (SAG)
FURORDMOD... Orders Further Modified [*Navy*] (DNAB)
FUROX-technology... fully recessed oxide technology (SAUS)
FURPO......... Full Utilization of Rural Program Opportunities (EA)
FURPS......... Functionality, Usability, Reliability, Performance, and Support (GART)
FURPSI........ Functionality, Usability, Reliability, Performance, Supportability, Integratability (VLIE)
FURPUR...... File Utility Routines, Program Utility Routines [*Computer science*]
FURR.......... Furrier
FURR.......... Further
FURS.......... Failure or Unsatisfactory Report System
FURS.......... Federal Underground Injection Control Reporting System [*Environmental Protection Agency*] (ERG)
FURS.......... Follow-Up Reporting System (MCD)
FURS.......... Functional Urban Regions (EURO)
FURSA......... Antonovich, Inc. (Class A) [*NASDAQ symbol*] (COMM)
Fur Seals..... Fur Seal Islands (SAUS)
FURST......... FORTRAN Unit Record Simulation Technique (SAUS)
FURST......... FORTRAN Utility System (SAUS)
FURTH......... Further
FURTH C..... Further Care [*Medicine*]
FURTS......... Furnished This Station [*Army*] (AABC)
FURX.......... First Union Rail [*Private rail car owner code*]
FUS........... Far Ultraviolet Spectrometer [*NASA*]
FUS........... Feline Urologic Syndrome
FUS........... Film Unit Secretary
FUS........... Firing Unit Simulator
FUS........... First USA [*NYSE symbol*] (SPSG)
FUS........... Focused Ultrasonic Surgery
FUS........... FORTRAN [*Formula Translating System*] Utility System [*Computer science*]
FUS........... Forward Support Unit (DOMA)
FUS........... Frontul Unitatii Socialiste [*Front of Socialist Unity*] [*Romania*] [*Political party*] (PPE)
FUS........... Full Use Standard (SAUS)
FUS........... Functional Unit Scan (SAUS)
FUs........... Function Units (SAUS)
FUS........... Fusa [*Let It Be Fused*] [*Pharmacy*] (ROG)
fus............ Fuse (VRA)
FUS........... Fuselage [*Aviation*] (AABC)
Fus............ Fusible (DAC)
fus............ Fusible (MIST)
FUS........... Fusilier
fus............ fusing (SAUS)
FUSA.......... First United States Army
FUSA.......... Fotoball USA, Inc. [*NASDAQ symbol*] (SAG)
FUSA.......... United Front for the Salvation of Angola [*Political party*] (PSAP)
FUSAC......... Finno-Ugrian Studies Association of Canada [*See also ACEFO*]
FUSAG......... First United States Army Group
FUSAW........ Fotoball USA Wrrt [*NASDAQ symbol*] (TTSB)
FUSB.......... First Utd SB Greencastle Ind [*NASDAQ symbol*] (TTSB)
FUSC.......... First United Bancorp [*NASDAQ symbol*] (SAG)
FUSE.......... Far Ultraviolet Satellite Experiment (MCD)
FUSE.......... Far Ultraviolet Spectroscopic Explorer (SAUS)
FUSE.......... Far Ultraviolet Spectroscopy Explorer [*NASA*] (SSD)
FUSE.......... Federation for United Science Education (SAUO)
FUSE.......... Fuisz Technologies [*NASDAQ symbol*] (TTSB)
FUSE.......... Fuisz Technologies, Ltd. [*NASDAQ symbol*] (NASQ)
FUSED......... Field Unit System Engineering Document (SAUS)
FUSES......... Flinders University School of Earth Sciences (SAUO)
FUSES......... Fordham Urban Solar Eco-System
FUSF.......... Fortsetzung und Schluss Folgen [*To Be Continued and Concluded*] [*German*]
FUSGX......... Federated Fund for U.S. Govt. Secs. Cl.A [*Mutual fund ticker symbol*] (SG)
FUSIM......... Functional Simulator (TIMI)
Fusion Eng Des... Fusion Engineering and Design (journ.) (SAUS)

FusionSy...... Fusion Systems Corp. [*Associated Press*] (SAG)
Fusion Technol... Fusion Technology [*A publication*] (CABS)
FUSL............ Fusil
FUSLA......... Friends of the United States of Latin America (EA)
FUS/LF......... Fuselage, Lower Forward (MCD)
FUSLG......... Fuselage [*Aviation*] (MSA)
FUSMX........ Fremont US Micro-Cap
FUSN........... Fusion
FUSN........... Fusion Systems [*NASDAQ symbol*] (TTSB)
FUSN........... Fusion Systems Corp. [*NASDAQ symbol*] (SAG)
FusnMed...... Fusion Medical Technologies, Inc. [*Associated Press*] (SAG)
FUSOB......... Friendly United Society of Operative Brickmakers [*A union*] [*British*]
FUSOD......... Future of Scientific Ocean Drilling [*Marine science*] (MSC)
FUS Pay...... First USA Paymentech, Inc. [*Associated Press*] (SAG)
FUSPr.......... First USA 6.25% 'PRIDES' [*NYSE symbol*] (TTSB)
FUSRAP....... Formerly Used Sites Remedial Action Plan (SAUO)
FUSRAP....... Formerly Utilized Sites Remedial Action Program [*Department of Energy*]
FUSS........... Fleet Undersea Surveillance System [*CIA terminology*]
FUS Station... Functional Unit Scan Station (SAUS)
FUST........... Full-Up System Test (RDA)
FUS/UF........ Fuselage, Upper Forward (MCD)
FuSV........... Fujinami sarcoma virus (SAUS)
FUT............. Federal Unemployment Tax (MCD)
FUT............. Federation Under Test (SAUO)
FUT............. Fibrinogen Uptake Test (DB)
FUT............. Fire Until Touchdown [*Apollo*] [*NASA*]
FUT............. Fleet Utility [*Navy*]
FUT............. Function Under Test (ACAE)
FUT............. Futura Airlines Ltd. (SAUO)
fut.............. Future (SHCU)
FUT............. Future
fut.............. Futures [*Finance*] (ODBW)
Fut.............. Futurist [*A publication*] (BRI)
FUT............. Unitary Workers Front (Ecuador) [*Political party*] (PSAP)
FUT............. University of Tampa, Tampa, FL [*OCLC symbol*] (OCLC)
FUTA........... Federal Unemployment Tax Act [*1954*]
FUTA........... Friends United through Astronomy [*Defunct*] (EA)
FUTB........... Futbol Internacional [*Ministerio de Cultura*] [*Spain*] [*Information service or system*] (CRD)
FUTC........... Federacion Unica de Trabajadores Campesinos [*Single Federation of Peasant Workers*] [*Bolivia*] (PD)
FUTC........... Fidelity Union Trust Co. (MHDB)
FUtdBcp....... First United Bancorporation [*Associated Press*] (SAG)
FUTIL.......... File Utility (TIMI)
Futmd.......... Futuremedia Ltd. [*Associated Press*] (SAG)
futr............ Futurism (VRA)
FUTR........... Jack Carl 312 Futures [*NASDAQ symbol*] (SAG)
FUTR........... Jack Carl 312 Futures Inc. [*NASDAQ symbol*] (TTSB)
Futrbi.......... Futurebiotics, Inc. [*Associated Press*] (SAG)
Futrmdia...... Futuremedia Ltd. [*Associated Press*] (SAG)
FUTS........... Firing Unit Test Set
FUTSAGA..... Frente Unitario de Trabajadores del Sector Agricola, Ganaderia y Alimentaci"n (SAUO)
FUTU........... Futures Information Service [*Institute for Futures Studies*] [*Information service or system*] [*Defunct*]
Futur........... Futurism (DIAR)
Futurbio....... Futurebiotics, Inc. [*Associated Press*] (SAG)
FUTURE....... Friends United Toward Understanding, Rights, and Equality
Futurebio..... Futurebiotics, Inc. [*Associated Press*] (SAG)
Future Comput Syst... Future Computing Systems (journ.) (SAUS)
Future Gener Comput Syst... Future Generation Computer Systems [*A publication*] (CABS)
FUTZ........... Fundamental Test Zone (SAUS)
FUTZ........... Futorian [*Federal Railroad Administration identification code*]
FUU............ Federacion de Universitarios de Uruguay [*Federation of University Students of Uruguay*] (PD)
FUU............ Foundation of Universal Unity (EA)
FUUNCTRY... Functionary
FUV............ Far Ultraviolet (SAUS)
FUV............ Far-Ultraviolet [*Spectra*]
FUV............ For Ultraviolet
FUV............ Fraction of Unexplained Variance (ACAE)
f-uv-........... Upper Volta [*MARC geographic area code*] [*Library of Congress*] (LCCP)
FUVD.......... Far Ultraviolet Detector
FUW............ Farmers' Union of Wales (BI)
FUW............ Federation of University Women
FUW............ Virginia Gildersleeve International Fund for University Women (SAUO)
FUWG.......... Forest Use Working Group [*Australia*]
FUWOB........ Forward Unconventional Warfare Operations Base (MCD)
FUWPM....... Free University, Washington-Paris-Moscow [*An association*] (EA)
FUWW......... Federal Union of Wire Weavers of the United Kingdom
FUY............ Fury Exploration Ltd. [*Vancouver Stock Exchange symbol*]
FUZ............ Frente Urbana Zapatista [*Mexico*]
Fuzzy Sets Syst... Fuzzy Sets and Systems [*A publication*] (CABS)
FV............... Face Value (ADA)
fv................ Face Velocity (MIST)
FV............... Facial Vein (MELL)
FV............... Fahr-Volhard [*Disease*] [*Medicine*] (DB)
FV............... Fair Value (JAGO)
FV............... Family Viewing Time [*FCC rule*] (NTCM)
FV............... Family Voices, Inc. (NRGU)
FV............... Fantasy Violence (ADWA)
FV............... Fashion Victim [*Women's Wear Daily*]
Fv............... Femoral Vein [*Anatomy*]
FV............... Femtovolt (MDG)
FV............... Fenestra Vestibuli [*Anatomy*]
FV............... Fiber Volume (SAUS)
FV............... Field Vehicle (SAUS)
FV............... Fighting (SAUS)
FV............... Fighting Vehicle [*Bradley*] [*Army*]
FV............... Final Value
FV............... Finite Volume [*Metallurgy*]
FV............... Fired Vessel [*Insurance*]
fv................ Fire Vent (BARN)
FV............... Firing Velocity
FV............... Firm Verification (SAUS)
FV............... Fishing Vessel [*Nautical term*] (NTA)
fv................ flats vacant (SAUS)
FV............... Flight Vehicle
FV............... Flight Version (MCD)
FV............... Flight Visibility (PIPO)
FV............... Floodable Volume (SAUS)
FV............... Floor Valve (NRCH)
F-V............. Flow Volume [*Measurement*] [*Cardiology*] (DAVI)
FV............... Fluid Volume
FV............... Flush Valve [*Technical drawings*]
FV............... Flux Valve
fv................ Folio Verso [*The left-hand page number*] [*The left-hand page*] [*Publishing*] (WDMC)
FV............... Folio Verso [*On the Back of the Page*] [*Latin*]
FV............... Forced Value (SAUS)
FV............... Forced Vibration (SAUS)
FV............... Formal Validation
FV............... Formel V (SAUS)
FV............... Formula Vee [*Class of racing cars*]
FV............... Formula Volkswagen [*Class of racing cars*]
FV............... Forward Visibility
FV............... Freeze Voter (EA)
FV............... French RCA (Victor) [*Record label*]
F/V.............. Frequency to Voltage (IEEE)
F/V.............. Frequency to Voltage converter (SAUS)
FV............... Friend Virus [*Also, FDV, FLV*]
FV............... Frisia Luftverkehr [*ICAO designator*] (AD)
FV............... Front View (MSA)
FV............... Fruit and Vegetable Division [*of Agricultural Research Service*] [*Department of Agriculture*]
FV............... Fuel Valve (AAG)
FV............... Full Above the Eaves (ROG)
FV............... Full Voltage (MSA)
F-V............. Fussell-Vesely (SAUS)
FV............... Future Value [*Finance*]
Fv............... Vertical Force (SAUS)
FV............... Vision Frequency (SAUS)
fv---............ Volta River and Basin [*MARC geographic area code*] [*Library of Congress*] (LCCP)
FV-1609....... Advanced Model of the FV-432 (SAUS)
FVA............. Avair, Inc. [*ICAO designator*] (FAAC)
FVA............. Fellow of the Valuers' Association [*British*] (DAS)
FVA............. Fighting Vehicle Armament (RDA)
FVA............. Film/Video Arts (EA)
FVA............. Finnish Veterinary Association (GVA)
FVA............. Floor Valve Adapter (NRCH)
FVA............. Flying Veterinarians Association (EA)
FVA............. Food and Veterinary Agency (EURO)
FVA............. Four Valve Type A [*Cosworth racing engines*]
FVA............. Fredonia Veterans Association (EA)
FVA............. Friend Virus Anemia [*Medicine*] (DMAA)
FVAA........... Federal Voting Assistance Act (SAUO)
FVAP........... Federal Voting Assistance Program
FVAP........... Filtration Ventilation Anti-Pollution (SAUS)
FVB............. Fiji Visitors Bureau (SAUO)
FVB............. First Virginia Banks [*NYSE symbol*] (TTSB)
FVB............. First Virginia Bankshares Corp. [*NYSE symbol*] (SPSG)
FVB............. Fitzwilliam Virginal Book
FVB............. Future Villain Band [*Evil rock music group in 1978 film "Sgt. Pepper's Lonely Hearts Club Band"*]
FVBB........... Beit Bridge [*Zimbabwe*] [*ICAO location identifier*] (ICLI)
FVBD........... Bindura [*Zimbabwe*] [*ICAO location identifier*] (ICLI)
FVbF........... Florida Medical Entomology Laboratory, Vero Beach, FL [*Library symbol*] [*Library of Congress*] (LCLS)
FVBG........... Free Vascularized Bone Graft [*Medicine*] (MELL)
FVBU........... Bulawayo/Bulawayo [*Zimbabwe*] [*ICAO location identifier*] (ICLI)
FVC............. Filtered Vented Containment [*Environmental science*] (COE)
FVC............. Fixed Vacuum Capacitor
FVC............. Florida Virtual Campus
FVC............. Forced Vital Capacity [*Physiology*]
FVC............. Forward Analog Voice Channel (CGWS)
FVC............. Franciscan Vocation Conference [*Formerly, AFSV*] [*Defunct*] (EA)
FVC............. Fraser Valley College Learning Resources Centre [*UTLAS symbol*]
FVC............. Frequency to Voltage Converter (CIST)
FVC............. Frozen Vegetable Council (EA)
FVC............. Valencia Community College, Orlando, FL [*OCLC symbol*] (OCLC)
FVC-1.......... Forced Vital Capacity-One Second [*Industrial hygiene term*] (OHS)
FVCH........... Chipinge [*Zimbabwe*] [*ICAO location identifier*] (ICLI)
FVCM.......... Fellow of the Victoria College of Music [*London*] [*British*] (ROG)
F/V converter... Frequency-to-Voltage Converter [*Electronics*] (MED)
FVCP........... Harare/Charles Prince [*Zimbabwe*] [*ICAO location identifier*] (ICLI)

FVCQFRA..... Fruit and Vegetable Canning and Quick Freezing Research Association (SAUO)
FVCV............ Chiredzi/Buffalo Range [*Zimbabwe*] [*ICAO location identifier*] (ICLI)
FVCX............ FVC.com, Inc. [*NASDAQ symbol*] (SG)
FVD............. Forward Vehicle Depot (SAUS)
FVD............. Friction Volume Damper (OA)
FVD............. Front Vertex Back Focal Distance
FVD............. Front Vortex Distance (SAUS)
FVD............. Fuel Vapor Detector
FVD............. Fuel Vapour Detector (SAUS)
FVD............. Full Vision Drive (SAUS)
fvd & w........ firearms, venereal disease, and whiskey (SAUS)
FVDE............ Fighting Vehicles Design Establishment [*British military*] (DMA)
FVE............. Federation of Veterinarians of the EEC (EAIO)
FVE............. Forced Volume, Expiratory [*Physiology*]
FVE............. Frenchville, ME [*Location identifier*] [*FAA*] (FAAL)
F VENOES.... Fiat Venaesectio [*Let the Patient Be Bled*] [*Pharmacy*] (ROG)
F-VF............ Fine to Very Fine [*Philately*]
FVF............. Finevest Foods, Inc. [*NYSE symbol*] (COMM)
FVF............. First Vertical Flight [*NASA*] (NASA)
FVF............. Flexible Vertex Format (SAUS)
FVFA............ Friedmann Visual Field Analyzer (SAUS)
FVFA............ Victoria Falls/Victoria Falls [*Zimbabwe*] [*ICAO location identifier*] (ICLI)
FVG............. Frevag Airlines [*Belgium*] [*ICAO designator*] (FAAC)
FV/GCE........ Fighting Vehicle / Gun Control Equipment (SAUS)
FVGDCF....... Fishing Vessel and Gear Damage Compensation Fund [*National Oceanic and Atmospheric Administration*]
FVGO........... Gokwe [*Zimbabwe*] [*ICAO location identifier*] (ICLI)
FVGR........... Free Vehicle Grab Respirometer (NUCP)
FVGR........... Mutare/Grand Reef [*Zimbabwe*] [*ICAO location identifier*] (ICLI)
FVGW........... Gweru/Gweru [*Zimbabwe*] [*ICAO location identifier*] (ICLI)
FVH............. Fahnestock Viner Hldgs'A' [*NYSE symbol*] (SG)
FVH............. Focal Vascular Headache [*Cardiology and neurology*] (DAVI)
FVH............. Fulminant [*or Fulminating*] Viral Hepatitis [*Medicine*]
FVH............. Fulminating Viral Hepatitis (SAUS)
FVHA........... Harare/Harare [*Zimbabwe*] [*ICAO location identifier*] (ICLI)
FVHI............ First Virtual Holdings, Inc. [*NASDAQ symbol*] (SAG)
FVHQ........... Harare [*Zimbabwe*] [*ICAO location identifier*] (ICLI)
FVI.............. Final Voluntary Indefinite [*Status*] [*Army*] (INF)
FVI.............. First Volar Interosseous Muscle [*Myology*]
FVI.............. Flow Velocity Integral [*Cardiology*]
FVI.............. Forage Value Index [*Agriculture*]
FVIF............ Future Value Interest Factor [*Finance*]
FVIN............ Bulawayo/Induna [*Zimbabwe*] [*ICAO location identifier*] (ICLI)
FVIP............ Fishing Vessel Insurance Plan [*Canada*]
FVIRL.......... Fruit and Vegetable Insects Research Laboratory [*Closed 1985*] [*Vincennes, IN*] [*Department of Agriculture*] (GRD)
FVKA............ Karoi [*Zimbabwe*] [*ICAO location identifier*] (ICLI)
FVKB............ Kariba/Kariba [*Zimbabwe*] [*ICAO location identifier*] (ICLI)
FVKK............ Kwekwe [*Zimbabwe*] [*ICAO location identifier*] (ICLI)
FVL.............. Femoral Vein Ligation [*Medicine*]
FVL.............. Flexible Video Laparoscope [*Medicine*] (MELL)
FVL.............. Flow Volume Loop [*Hemodialysis*]
FVLC............ Fox Valley Library Council (SAUO)
FVLF............ Fixed VLF Station (MCD)
FVM............. Five-Mile Camp, AK [*Location identifier*] [*FAA*] (FAAL)
FVM............. Fluid Vacancy Model
FVM............. French Village [*Missouri*] [*Seismograph station code, US Geological Survey*] (SEIS)
FVMA........... Marondera [*Zimbabwe*] [*ICAO location identifier*] (ICLI)
FVMF........... Friends of Vieilles Maisons Francaises (EA)
FVMMA........ Floor and Vacuum Machinery Manufacturers' Association [*Defunct*] (EA)
FVMP........... Federal Visibility Monitoring Program (GNE)
FVMS........... Fluid Volume Measurement System (MCD)
FVMT........... Mutoko [*Zimbabwe*] [*ICAO location identifier*] (ICLI)
FVMU........... Mutare/Mutare [*Zimbabwe*] [*ICAO location identifier*] (ICLI)
FVMV........... Masvingo/Masvingo [*Zimbabwe*] [*ICAO location identifier*] (ICLI)
FVN............. Failed Vector Number (OA)
FVN............. Familial Visceral Neuropathy [*Medicine*] (MELL)
FVN............. File Version Number (VLIE)
FVNB........... First Victoria National Bank [*NASDAQ symbol*] (SAG)
FVNB........... First Victoria Natl Bank [*NASDAQ symbol*] (TTSB)
FVNB........... FVNB Corp. [*NASDAQ symbol*] (NASQ)
FVNC........... Fondation Vietnam-Canada [*Vietnam-Canada Foundation*]
FVNM........... Fort Vancouver National Monument (SAUO)
FVNR........... Full Voltage Non-Reversing Motor (DICI)
FVO............. Farm Verified Organic
FVO............. Femoral Valgus Osteotomy [*Medicine*] (MELL)
FVO............. Fluidic Valve Operator
FVO............. Food and Veterinary Office (EURO)
FVO............. For Valuation Only [*Business term*]
FVOC........... Facel Vega Owners Club [*Defunct*] (EA)
FVOG........... Fishing Vessel Obligation Guarantee [*Program*] [*Marine science*] (OSRA)
FVOP........... Finger Venous Opening Pressure [*Medicine*] (EDAA)
FVP............. Feasibility Validation Program
FVP............. Fixed Vane Pump [*Hydraulics*]
FVP............. Flash-Vacuum Pyrolysis
FVP............. Flight Verification Payload (SAUS)
FVP............. Fluid Velocity Potential
FVP............. Freie Volkspartei [*Free People's Party*] [*Germany*] [*Political party*] (PPE)
FVP............. Friend Virus Polycythemia [*Medicine*] (DMAA)
FVPA........... Flat Veneer Products Association (SAUO)
FVPB........... Flight Vehicle Power Branch
FVPD........... Film/Video Producers and Distributors [*National Film Board of Canada*] [*Information service or system*] (CRD)
FVPE........... Fighting Vehicles Proving Establishment (SAUS)
FVPPA......... Families of Vietnamese Political Prisoners Association (EA)
FVPR........... Fluor Vinylidene Propylene Rubber (SAUS)
FVPRA......... Fruit and Vegetable Preservation Research Association (SAUO)
fvq............... full variable quality (SAUS)
FVR............. Feline Viral Rhinotracheitis [*Vaccine*]
FVR............. Fiber Volume Ratio
FVR............. Flexible Vocabulary Recognition (SAUS)
FVR............. Forearm Vascular Resistance [*Medicine*]
FVR............. Free Voluntary Reading
FVR............. Fuels and Vehicles Research (COE)
FVR............. Functional Vestibular Reserve [*Orientation*]
FVR............. Fuse Voltage Rating
fvrbl............ favorable (SAUS)
FVRC........... Foreign Vehicle Resource Center [*Tank-Automotive Command*] [*Army*]
FVRCP......... Feline viral rhinotracheitis, calicivirus, panleukopenia (SAUS)
FVRDE......... Fighting Vehicles Research and Development Establishment [*British*]
FVRDEs....... Fighting Vehicles Research and Development Establishments (SAUS)
fvrl gls........ Favrile Glass (VRA)
FVRU........... Rusape [*Zimbabwe*] [*ICAO location identifier*] (ICLI)
FVR Vaccine... Feline Viral Rhinotracheitis Vaccine (SAUS)
FVS............. Fetal Valproate Syndrome [*Medicine*] (DMAA)
F VS............. Fiat Venaesectio [*Let the Patient Be Bled*] [*Pharmacy*]
FVS............. Fighting Vehicle Systems (RDA)
FVS............. Flight Vehicle Simulation (ACAE)
FVS............. Flight Vehicles Systems (MCD)
FVS............. Flight Vehicle Structure (SAUS)
FVS............. Floppy Valve Syndrome [*Medicine*] (MELL)
FVS............. Forer Vocational Survey [*Psychology*]
FVS............. Forest, MS [*Location identifier*] [*FAA*] (FAAL)
FVS............. Fraser Videotex Services [*Information service or system*] (IID)
FVSA........... Federation of Victorian School Administrators [*Australia*]
FVSC........... Fighting Vehicle Systems Carrier (SAUS)
FVSC........... Flight Vehicle System Committee (SAUO)
FVSC........... Fort Valley State College [*Georgia*]
FVSF........... Flight Vehicle Simulation Facility (ACAE)
FVSH........... Full Volvo Service History [*Automotive classified advertising*]
FVSH........... Zvishavane [*Zimbabwe*] [*ICAO location identifier*] (ICLI)
FVSNA......... Friends Vegetarian Society of North America (EA)
FVSV........... Victoria Falls/Spray View [*Zimbabwe*] [*ICAO location identifier*] (ICLI)
fvt............... family vewing time (SAUS)
FVT............. Family Viewing Time [*Television*]
FVT............. Field Validation Test
FVT............. Flash-Vacuum Thermolysis
FVT............. Follicular-Variant-Translocation [*Medicine*] (DMAA)
FVT............. Full Video Translation (VLIE)
FVT............. Functional Validation Test [*Army*]
FVTL........... Gweru/Thornhill [*Zimbabwe*] [*ICAO location identifier*] (ICLI)
FVTP........... Formal Validation Test Program [*Military*]
FVTS........... Field Verification Test Set (MCD)
FVTS........... Function Verification Test Set (SAUS)
FVTT........... Fishing Vessel Transmit Terminal (PDAA)
FVU............. File Verification Utility [*Computer science*]
FVU............. First Voided Urine [*Medicine*] (CPH)
FVU............. Functional Verification Unit [*Photography*]
FVV............. Facility Verification Vehicle
FVV............. Fossa of Vestibule of Vagina [*Medicine*] (MELL)
FVV............. Functional Venous Volume [*Medicine*] (EDAA)
FVVM........... Friends of the Vietnam Veterans Memorial (EA)
FVW............. Forward Volume Wave [*Telecommunications*] (TEL)
FVW............. Fox Valley & Western [*Federal Railroad Administration identification code*]
FVWC........... Federation of Victorian Walking Clubs [*Australia*]
FVWM........... Feeble Virtual Window Manager (VLIE)
FVWN........... Hwange/Hwange National Park [*Zimbabwe*] [*ICAO location identifier*] (ICLI)
FVWS........... Female Voice Warning System (MCD)
FVWSH......... Full Volkswagen Service History [*Automotive classified advertising*]
FVWT........... Hiwange Town [*Zimbabwe*] [*ICAO location identifier*] (ICLI)
FVWU........... Free Visayan Workers' Union [*Philippines*]
FVX............. Farmville, VA [*Location identifier*] [*FAA*] (FAAL)
FVZC........... Zisco [*Zimbabwe*] [*ICAO location identifier*] (ICLI)
fw---............ Africa, West [*MARC geographic area code*] [*Library of Congress*] (LCCP)
FW............... Face Width (MSA)
F/W............. Facing West [*In outdoor advertising*] (WDMC)
FW............... Failure Warning (SAUS)
FW............... Fairbanks Whitney Corp. (SAUO)
FW............... Falconer-Wadell [*Syndrome*] [*Medicine*] (DB)
FW............... Fascinating Womanhood [*Title of book by Helen Andelin and of antifeminist seminars*]
FW............... Feed Water (KSC)
FW............... Felix-Weil [*Reaction*] [*Clinical chemistry*]
f/W.............. female White (SAUS)
FW............... Field Weakening
FW............... Field Weld (NRCH)
FW............... Field Welded (SAUS)
FW............... Field Welding (SAUS)
FW............... Field Well (SAUS)
FW............... Field Width (SAUS)

FW............. Field Winding [*Electromagnetism*] (IAA)
FW............. Field Wire [*Communications term*] (DCT)
fw............. fieldworker (SAUS)
FW............. Field Worship [*Army*] [*British*]
FW............. Fighter Weapons (MCD)
FW............. Fighter Wing [*Military*] (POLM)
FW............. Filament Winding (SAUS)
FW............. Filament Wound
FW............. Filled Weight (SAUS)
FW............. Fillet Weld (SAUS)
FW............. filter wheel (SAUS)
FW............. Filter Wheels
FW............. Financial Weekly [*A publication*]
FW............. Fire Wall [*Technical drawings*]
FW............. Firmware [*Computer science*]
FW............. First Wachovia Corp. [*NYSE symbol*] (COMM)
FW............. First Word
FW............. Fiscal Week [*Business term*] (IAA)
FW............. Fish Waste (SAUS)
FW............. Fixed-Length Word [*Computer science*] (IAA)
FW............. Fixed Wavelength [*Electronics*]
FW............. Fixed Width (SAUS)
FW............. Fixed Wing [*Aircraft*]
FW............. Flag Word (MCD)
FW............. Flash Welding [*Metallurgy*]
FW............. Flat Washer (SAUS)
FW............. Flight Weight
FW............. Floor Waste
F/W............. Fly Wheels
FW............. Focke-Wulf [*A German fighter plane*]
FW............. Focke-Wulf GmbH [*Germany*] [*ICAO aircraft manufacturer identifier*] (ICAO)
FW............. Fog Whistle [*Navigation charts*]
FW............. Folin and Wu's Method [*Medicine*] (MAE)
FW............. Folin-Wu Reaction [*Medicine*] (DMAA)
FW............. footwall (SAUS)
FW............. Foot Wide
FW............. Forced Whisper [*Medicine*]
FW............. Foreign War (SAUS)
fw............. forewing (SAUS)
FW............. Formula Weight [*Chemistry*]
fw............. Formula Weight
FW............. Fort Worth (SAUO)
FW............. Forward of Wing [*Aerospace*] (AAG)
FW............. Forward Wave [*Electronics*] (IAA)
FW............. Foster Wheeler Corp. (MCD)
FW............. Fragment Wound [*Medicine*] (DAVI)
FW............. Frame Synchronization Word (MUGU)
FW............. Framework
FW............. Franklin Watts Group [*Publishers*] [*British*]
FW............. Frank Williams [*Racing car model designation prefix, indicating principal of company*] [*British*]
FW............. Freeware (SAUS)
FW............. Free Wheel (ADA)
fw............. Fresh Water (MELL)
FW............. Fresh Water [*Technical drawings*]
FW............. Freshwater [*Load line mark*]
FW............. Fresh Weight [*of fruit*] [*Botany*]
FW............. Friderichsen-Waterhouse [*Syndrome*] [*Medicine*] (DB)
FW............. Fringeworthy (SAUS)
fw............. front wiring (SAUS)
FW............. Fuel Wasting (MCD)
FW............. Full Wave
FW............. full-wave rectifier (SAUS)
FW............. Full Weight (IAA)
FW............. Full Word (SAUS)
FW............. Function Word (SAUS)
fw............. Funk & Wagnalls (SAUS)
FW............. Furness, Withy & Co. [*Steamship line*] (MHDW)
Fw............. F Wave [*Medicine*] (EDAA)
FW............. Isles of Scilly Skybus [*ICAO designator*] (AD)
FW............. Le Point Air [*France*] [*ICAO designator*] (ICDA)
FWA............. Factories and Workshops Act (SAUO)
FWA............. Factories and Workshops Acts [*Law*] [*British*] (ROG)
FWA............. Family Welfare Association [*British*] (ILCA)
FWA............. Farmers and World Affairs [*An association*] [*Defunct*] (EA)
FWA............. Farm Workers Association (SAUO)
FWA............. Far West Airlines, Inc. [*ICAO designator*] (FAAC)
FWA............. Feather Weight Automotive [*Auto racing engine model designation*] [*British*]
FWA............. Federal Works Agency [*Abolished, 1949*]
FWA............. Federation of Women Clerks [*A union*] [*British*]
FWA............. Fellow of the World Academy of Arts and Sciences
FWA............. File Work Application (SAUS)
FWA............. File Work Area (SAUS)
FWA............. Filler Wire Addition
FWA............. Film Weekly Award [*British*]
FWA............. Final Writing Amplifier (SAUS)
FWA............. Financial Women's Association of New York [*New York, NY*] (EA)
FWA............. Financial Working Arrangement
FWA............. First Word Address [*Computer science*]
FWA............. Fixed Wing Aircraft (SAUS)
FWA............. Fixed Word Address [*Computer science*] (IAA)
FWA............. Fleet Weapon Acceptance (SAUS)
FWA............. Flow Weighted Average (COE)
FWA............. Fluorescent Whitening Agent [*Detergent*]
FWA............. Forest Workers Association (SAUO)
FWA............. Fort Wayne [*Indiana*] [*Airport symbol*] (OAG)
FWA............. Fort Wayne, IN [*Location identifier*] [*FAA*] (FAAL)
FWA............. Forward Wave Amplifier
FWA............. Fraud, Waste, and Abuse
FWA............. Free Wales Army (SAUO)
FWA............. French West Africa
FWA............. Fresh Water Allowance (DS)
FWA............. Full-Wave Amplifier
FWA............. Future Weapons Agency [*Army*]
FWA............. University of West Florida, Pensacola, FL [*OCLC symbol*] (OCLC)
FWAA............. Fiji-West Australian Association
FWAA............. Football Writers Association of America (EA)
FWAA............. Fur Wholesalers Association of America (EA)
FWAC............. Far West Agents Conference
FWAC............. Full-Wave Alternating Current
FWACS............. Fellow of the West African College of Surgeons (CMD)
FWAD............. Fort Wingate Army Depot [*New Mexico*] (AABC)
FWAD............. Fresh Water Arrival Draft (RIMS)
FWAF............. Free World Armed Forces
FWAG............. Farming and Wildlife Advisory Group [*British*] (DI)
FWAIS............. Free World Air Intelligence Study (MCD)
FWAIT............. Floating-Point Wait [*Computer science*]
FWAM............. Fleet Weapon Armament Maintenance [*Navy*] (MCD)
FWAM............. Full Width Attack Mine
FW & C............. Furners, Withy & Company (SAUS)
FW&C............. Furness, Withy & Company (SAUO)
FW&D............. Fort Worth & Denver Railway Company (SAUO)
FW & DC............. Fort Worth & Denver City Railway Co.
FW&DC............. Fort Worth and Denver City Railway Company (SAUO)
FW & JC............. Fine Wheel and Jet Controller (SAUS)
FWAOB............. Free World Air Order of Battle (MCD)
FWAPSA............. Federation of West African Pharmaceutical Students Associations (SAUO)
FWAS............. Failure Warning and Analysis System
FWAS............. Flight Warning and Analysis System (SAUS)
FWAS............. Fort Wayne Art School (SAUO)
FWAT............. Fish and Wildlife Advisory Team (SAUO)
FWAT............. Flexwatt Corp. [*NASDAQ symbol*] (COMM)
FWAT............. Forest Workers Association of Tasmania (EERA)
FWB............. Fahrenheit Wet Bulb (KSC)
FWB............. First Wisconsin Bankshares (SAUO)
FWB............. First Wisconsin Corp. [*NYSE symbol*] (COMM)
FWB............. First Women's Bank [*New York City*]
FWB............. Fort Worth Belt Railway Co. [*AAR code*]
FWB............. Fort Worth Belt Railway Company (SAUO)
FWB............. Forum for Women in Bridge [*Defunct*] (EA)
FW/B............. Forward Toward the Bow [*Stowage*] (DNAB)
FWB............. Four-Wheel Brake
fwb............. fourwheel braking (SAUS)
FWB............. Free-Wheel Bicycle
FWB............. Free-Will Baptists
FWB............. Fresh Water Ballasting
fwb............. front-wheel bicycle (SAUS)
FWB............. Full Weight Bearing [*Medicine*]
FWB............. Full Word Boundary (SAUS)
fwb............. furnished with bed (SAUS)
FWB............. University of Minnesota, Freshwater Biological Institute, Navarre, MN [*OCLC symbol*] (OCLC)
FWBA............. Full-Wave Balanced Amplifier
fw ball............. freshwater ballast (SAUS)
FWBC............. Fort Wayne Bible College [*Indiana*]
FW-BF............. Foster Wheeler-Bergbau Forschung [*Flue gas treatment*]
FWBG............. Bangula [*Malawi*] [*ICAO location identifier*] (ICLI)
FWBI............. First Western Bancorp, Inc. [*NASDAQ symbol*] (NQ)
FWBO............. Friends of the Western Buddhist Order (EA)
FW Boiler............. Foster-Wheeler Boiler (SAUS)
FWBPA............. Free Will Baptist Press Association (EA)
FWBR............. Full-Wave Bridge Rectifier
FWBS............. Farm Writers and Broadcasters' Society [*Australia*]
FWC............. Fairfield, IL [*Location identifier*] [*FAA*] (FAAL)
FWC............. Fair Weather Current
FWC............. Farmers Wholesale Cooperative (SAUS)
FWC............. Fault Warning Computer [*Aviation*] (DA)
FWC............. Federal Warning Center (NATG)
FWC............. Federal Warning Centre (SAUO)
FWC............. Federation of Working Communities (SAUO)
FWC............. Feedwater Control [*Nuclear energy*] (NRCH)
FWC............. Filament-Wound Case (MCD)
FWC............. Filament-Wound Cylinder (SAUS)
FWC............. Filipino Women's Council [*Australia*]
FWC............. Fleet Weapons Center [*Navy*] (MCD)
FWC............. Fleet Weather Center [*Navy*] (NVT)
FWC............. Flight Warning Computer (MCD)
FWC............. Flying Wheel Casting [*Metallurgy*]
FWC............. Foil Wound Coil
FWC............. Force Weapons Coordinator [*Navy*] (NVT)
FWC............. Foster Wheeler [*NYSE symbol*] (TTSB)
FWC............. Foster Wheeler Corp. [*NYSE symbol*] (SPSG)
FWC............. Foster Wheeler Corporation (SAUO)
FWC............. Fourdrinier Wire Council (EA)
FWC............. Free Wallenberg Committee (EA)
FWC............. Freeway Air BV [*Netherlands*] [*ICAO designator*] (FAAC)
fwc............. free woman of color (SAUS)

FWC.......... Freshwater Cooling
FWC.......... Friends World College [*Huntington, NY*] (EA)
FWC.......... Full-loaded Weight and Capacity (SAUS)
FWC.......... Full-Wave Circuit (SAUS)
fwc.......... full weight contents (SAUS)
FWC.......... Full Well Capacity (MCD)
FWC.......... Fully Loaded Weight and Capacity [*Shipping*]
FWC.......... Functional Work Center (COE)
FWCA.......... Fish and Wildlife Conservation Act of 1980 (COE)
FWCA.......... Fish and Wildlife Coordination Act (GFGA)
FWCC.......... Chintheche [*Malawi*] [*ICAO location identifier*] (ICLI)
FWCC.......... Fine Weave Carbon Carbon (ACAE)
FWCC.......... Friends of the World Council of Churches (EA)
FWCC.......... Friends' Work Camp Committee [*British*] (BI)
FWCC.......... Friends World Committee for Consultation [*British*] (EAIO)
FWCC.......... Full Word Channel Control [*Computer science*] (TIMI)
FWCCANZ.......... Federation of Wall and Ceiling Contractors of Australia and New Zealand
FWCD.......... Chelinda [*Malawi*] [*ICAO location identifier*] (ICLI)
FWCF.......... Fellow of the Worshipful Company of Farriers [*British*] (DI)
FWCH.......... First World Cheese, Inc. (SAUO)
FWCI.......... Feedwater Coolant Injection [*Nuclear energy*] (NRCH)
FWCI.......... Foundation of the Wall and Ceiling Industry (EA)
FWCI.......... Foundation of the Wall and Ceiling Institute (SAUO)
FWCL.......... Blantyre/Chileka [*Malawi*] [*ICAO location identifier*] (ICLI)
FWCL.......... Field Wire Command Link [*Army*] (AABC)
FWCM.......... Makokola Club [*Malawi*] [*ICAO location identifier*] (ICLI)
FWCNG.......... Florida West Coast Nuclear Group
FWCR.......... Florida West Coast Railway [*Federal Railroad Administration identification code*]
FWCS.......... Feedwater Control System [*Nuclear energy*] (NRCH)
FWCS.......... Flight Watch Control Station (SAUO)
FWCS.......... Ntchisi [*Malawi*] [*ICAO location identifier*] (ICLI)
FWCT.......... Chitipa [*Malawi*] [*ICAO location identifier*] (ICLI)
FWCW.......... Fourth World Conference on Women (SAUO)
FWD.......... Falling Weight Deflectometer [*FHWA*] (TAG)
FWD.......... Fast Wide Differential (SAUS)
FWD.......... Federation of Wholesalers and Distributors [*British*] (DBA)
fwd.......... Foreword (BJA)
FWD.......... Fort Worth & Denver Railway Co. [*AAR code*]
fwd.......... Forward (ADWA)
FWD.......... Forward (AFM)
Fwd.......... Forward (EBF)
fwd.......... Four Wheel Drive (MIST)
FWD.......... Four-Wheel Drive [*Vehicle*]
FWD.......... Four Wheel Drive Auto Company (SAUO)
FWD.......... Free Water Damage (ADA)
FWD.......... Free Wheeling Diode (IAA)
FWD.......... Free Working Distance (SAUS)
fWd.......... freight forward (SAUS)
fwd.......... Fresh Water Damage [*Insurance*] (MARI)
FWD.......... Fresh Water Damage
FWD.......... freshwater draught (SAUS)
FWD.......... Front Wheel Drive
fwd.......... Front-Wheel Drive (FOTI)
FWD.......... Functional Workload Demonstration (AAGC)
FWDA.......... Federal Wholesale Druggists Association [*Later, DWA*] (EA)
FWDA.......... Federated Wire Drawers' Association [*A union*] [*British*]
FWDA.......... Food Waste Disposer Association (SAUO)
FWDA.......... Fort Wingate Depot Activity [*New Mexico*] [*Army*]
FWDB.......... Fort Worth & Dallas Belt Railroad [*Federal Railroad Administration identification code*]
FW/DB.......... Forward Warning and Deployment Base (SAUO)
FWDBAA.......... Forward Brigade Administrative Area [*British*]
FWDBL.......... Forward Bomb Line
FWDC.......... Flemings in the World Development Cooperation [*Belgium*] (EAIO)
FWDC.......... Forward Collect (FAAC)
FWDC.......... Full-Wave Direct Current
FWDCT.......... Fresh Water Drain Collecting Tank
FWDD.......... Forwarded
FWDD.......... Fresh Water Departure Draft (RIMS)
Fwd Ech.......... Forward Echelon [*Army*]
FWDG.......... Forwarding
FWDHTSHLD... Forward Heat Shield (MCD)
FWD HT SHLD... Forward Heat Shield (SAUS)
Fwd Ob.......... Forward Observer (SAUS)
Fwd Obsvr... Forward Observer (SAUS)
FWDP.......... Family Worker Development Program [*Australia*]
FWDP.......... Force Command WWMCCS Development Plan (SAUO)
FWDP.......... Foreign Weapon Development Program (NG)
FWDP.......... Fourth World Documentation Project [*Center for World Indigenous Studies*] [*Internet resource*]
FWDR.......... Fort Worth & Dallas Railroad [*Federal Railroad Administration identification code*]
FWDR.......... Forwarder
FwdScEndSt... Forward-Scatter- Endstelle (SAUS)
FWDT.......... Flight Worthiness Demonstration Test (KSC)
FWDW.......... Dwanga [*Malawi*] [*ICAO location identifier*] (ICLI)
FWDZ.......... Dedza [*Malawi*] [*ICAO location identifier*] (ICLI)
FWE.......... Federation of Woman's Exchanges (EA)
FWE.......... Finished with Engines
FWE.......... Foreign Weapons Evaluation
FWE.......... Freshwater Ecosystems (SAUO)
FWE.......... Friends of Waycross Express [*Defunct*] (EA)
FWEA.......... Finnish Workers' Educational Association [*Defunct*] (EA)
FWEA.......... International Federation of Workers Educational Associations (SAUO)
FWEC.......... Fort Worth Electronics Club (SAUO)
FWEC.......... Foster Wheeler Energy Corporation (SAUO)
FWED.......... Fleet Weapons Engineering Department (DNAB)
FWeldI.......... Fellow of the Welding Institute [*British*] (DBQ)
FWEO.......... Fleet Weapons Engineering Officer [*Navy*] [*British*]
FWERAT.......... Fourth World Educational and Research Association Trust (EA)
FWES.......... First Western Financial Corp. [*NASDAQ symbol*] (COMM)
FWETE.......... Foreign Weapons, Equipment, and Technology Evaluation (MCD)
FWETE.......... Foreign Weapons Equipment Technology Evaluation (SAUS)
FWE Valve... Front Wheel Emergency Valve (SAUS)
FWF.......... Far West Financial Corp. (SAUO)
FWF.......... Felicidades Wildlife Foundation (EA)
FWF.......... Firewall Forward (PIPO)
FWF.......... Fleet Weather Facility [*Navy*]
FWF.......... Fly without Fear [*Commercial firm*] (EA)
FWF.......... Forderung der Wissenschaftlichen Forschung [*Austrian science foundation*]
FWF.......... Free World Military Forces [*Group of countries which provided military aid to South Vietnam*] [*Also, FWMF*] (VNW)
FWF.......... Fresh Water Flux (SAUS)
FWF.......... Fund for the Advancement of Scientific Research (SAUS)
FWFAA.......... From within funds already authorized (SAUS)
FWFHC.......... Farm Workers Family Health Center
FWFM.......... Federation of Wholesale Fish Merchants (SAUO)
FWFWA.......... Fresh Water Fish Wholesalers Association (EA)
FWG.......... Facility Working Group
FWG.......... Factory Work Group
FWG.......... Factory Working Group (SAUO)
FWG.......... Feminist Writers' Guild [*Defunct*] (EA)
FWG.......... Financial Working Group [*Military*] (AFIT)
FWG.......... Flexible Wave Guide (SAUS)
FWG.......... Flexible Waveguide
fwg.......... following (SAUS)
FWG.......... FREDDIE MAC 6.688%'98 Debs [*NYSE symbol*] (SG)
FWG.......... French Wire Gage (IAA)
FWG.......... French Wire Gauge (SAUS)
FWG.......... Fresh Water Generator (SAUS)
FWGE.......... Forth Worth Grain Exchange (SAUS)
FWGE.......... Fort Worth Grain Exchange (EA)
FWGE.......... FREE [*Federated Republics of Earth and Its Environs*] World Government (EA)
FWGIP.......... Federation of Workers of Government of India Presses (SAUO)
FWGPM.......... Federal Working Group on Pest Management (SAUO)
FWGS.......... Fort Worth Geological Society (SAUO)
FWH.......... Fast Weekly Household Audience Report [*Nielsen Television Index*] (NTCM)
FWH.......... Firmware Hub (SAUS)
FWH.......... Flexible Working Hours
FWH.......... Folklore of World Holidays [*A publication*]
FWH.......... Fort Worth, TX [*Location identifier*] [*FAA*] (FAAL)
FWH.......... Frank W. Horner Ltd. [*Research code symbol*] [*Canada*]
fwh.......... free-wheeling hubs (SAUS)
FWHC.......... Feminist Women's Health Center [*Later, FWHC/WCC*] (EA)
FWHC/WCC... Feminist Women's Health Center/Women's Choice Clinic [*Defunct*] (EA)
FWHF.......... Federation of World Health Foundations (EA)
FWHH.......... Full Width at Half Height [*Spectrometry*] (DB)
FWHM.......... Full Wave Half Modulation (SAUS)
FWHM.......... Full Width at Half Maximum [*Spectroscopy*]
FWHMA.......... Feed Water Heater Manufacturers Association (EA)
FWHP.......... Flywheel Horsepower (SAUS)
FWHP.......... Full Width at Half Peak [*Spectroscopy*] (DEN)
FWhP.......... Polk Community College, Winter Haven, FL [*Library symbol*] [*Library of Congress*] (LCLS)
FWHQ.......... Lilongwe [*Malawi*] [*ICAO location identifier*] (ICLI)
FWHS.......... Fort Wayne Historical Society [*Federal Railroad Administration identification code*]
FWHT.......... Fast Walsh-Hadamard Transform (SAUS)
FWI.......... Families and Work Institute (EA)
FWI.......... Federation of West Indies
FWI.......... Federation of Women's Institutes [*British*] (DI)
FWI.......... Fellow of the Institute of Welfare Officers [*British*]
FWI.......... Field Widened Interferometer (ACAE)
FWI.......... Financial Women International (NTPA)
FWI.......... Fire Weather Index (QUAC)
FWI.......... Fixed-Weight Indexes
FWI.......... Focused What If [*Method for hazard analysis*]
FWI.......... French West Indies
FWI.......... Frequently Wanted Information (SAUO)
FWI.......... Fresh Water Institute [*Rensselaer Polytechnic Institute*] [*Research center*] (RCD)
FWI.......... Freshwater Institute [*Federal Department of Fisheries and Oceans*] [*Canada*] (IRC)
FWI.......... Roslyn, NY [*Location identifier*] [*FAA*] (FAAL)
FWIB.......... Federal Women's Interagency Board (EA)
FWIC.......... Federated Women's Institutes of Canada
FWIC.......... Fighter Weapons Instructor Course [*Military*]
FWID.......... Federation of Wholesale and Industrial Distributors (SAUO)
F wire.......... Financial Wire [*Wire service term*] (WDMC)
FWIS.......... First World Communic 'B' [*NASDAQ symbol*] (SG)
FWISU.......... Federation of Westinghouse Independent Salaried Unions (EA)
FWIT.......... Federated Women in Timber (EA)
FWIT.......... Fighter Weapons Instructors Training (SAUO)
FWIT.......... Fixed-Wing Tactical Transport [*Aviation*] (MUGU)

FWIW........... For What It's Worth
FWK........... Field Weakening
FWK........... Framework
FWKA........... Karonga [*Malawi*] [*ICAO location identifier*] (ICLI)
FWKB........... Katumbi [*Malawi*] [*ICAO location identifier*] (ICLI)
FWKG........... Kasungu/Kasungu [*Malawi*] [*ICAO location identifier*] (ICLI)
FWKI........... Kamuzu International [*Malawi*] [*ICAO location identifier*] (ICLI)
FWKK........... Nkhotakota [*Malawi*] [*ICAO location identifier*] (ICLI)
FWKT........... Fast Walsh-Kaczmarz Transform (SAUS)
FWL........... Fantasy Wrestling Leagues
FWL........... Farewell [*Alaska*] [*Airport symbol*] (OAG)
FWL........... Farewell, AK [*Location identifier*] [*FAA*] (FAAL)
FWL........... Far West Laboratory for Educational Research and Development [*San Francisco, CA*] [*Department of Education*] (GRD)
FWL........... Federation of Women Lawyers', Judicial Screening Panel [*Defunct*] (EA)
FWL........... Finite World Length (SAUS)
FWL........... Fixed Word Length [*Computer science*]
FWL........... Florida West Airlines [*ICAO designator*] (FAAC)
FWL........... Foilborne Water Line
fwl........... foilborne waterline (SAUS)
FWL........... Foreign Workers Levy (SAUS)
FWL........... Fort Worth Livestock [*Federal Railroad Administration identification code*]
FWL........... Foundation for World Literacy [*Defunct*]
FWL........... Foundation of World Literacy (SAUO)
FWL........... Fraternity of the Wooden Leg [*Inactive*] (EA)
FWL........... Furness Warren Line [*Steamship*] (MHDW)
FWLC........... Free World Labour Confederation (SAUO)
FWLERD........... Far West Laboratory for Educational Research and Development [*Department of Education*]
FWLK........... Likoma [*Malawi*] [*ICAO location identifier*] (ICLI)
FWLL........... Lilongwe [*Malawi*] [*ICAO location identifier*] (ICLI)
FWLP........... Kasungu/Lifupa [*Malawi*] [*ICAO location identifier*] (ICLI)
FWLS........... Fever Without Localizing Signs (MELL)
FWM........... Feather Weight Marine [*Auto racing engine model designation*] [*British*]
FWM........... Food Web Model (SAUO)
FWM........... Fort William [*Scotland*] [*Airport symbol*] (OAG)
FWM........... Fourier Wave Mixing (SAUS)
FWM........... Fourth World Movement [*Later, NI/FWM*] (EA)
FWMA........... Feather Weight Marine Automotive [*Auto racing engine model designation*] [*British*]
FWMA........... Free World Military Assistance (CINC)
FWMAC........... Free World Military Assistance Council
FWMAF........... Free World Military Assistance Forces [*Vietnam*]
FWMAO........... Free World Military Assistance Organization (MCD)
FWMB........... Federation of Wholesale and Multiple Bakers [*British*] (BI)
FWMC........... Feather Weight Marine Twin Cam [*Auto racing engine model designation*] [*British*]
FWMC........... Mchinji [*Malawi*] [*ICAO location identifier*] (ICLI)
FW Method... Free-Wilson Method (SAUS)
FWMF........... Free World Military Forces [*Group of countries which provided military aid to South Vietnam*] [*Also, FWF*] (VNW)
FWMG........... Mangochi [*Malawi*] [*ICAO location identifier*] (ICLI)
FWMQC........... Fixed-Wing Multiengine Qualification Course [*Aviation*]
FWMU........... Fire-Weather Mobile Unit [*National Weather Service*] (NOAA)
FWMY........... Monkey Bay [*Malawi*] [*ICAO location identifier*] (ICLI)
FWMZ........... Mzimba [*Malawi*] [*ICAO location identifier*] (ICLI)
FWN........... Futures World News [*Information service or system*] (CRD)
FWN........... Futures World News Network [*Information service or system*] (IID)
FWNC........... Fort Wayne National Corp. [*NASDAQ symbol*] (NQ)
FWNC........... Fort Wayne National Corporation (SAUO)
FWNEOFAP... Funds Will Not Be Entrusted to Others for Any Purpose [*Army*] (AABC)
FWO........... Facilities Work Order (SAUS)
FWO........... Federation of Wholesale Organisations (or Organizations) (SAUO)
FWO........... Federation of Wholesale Organizations (SAUO)
FWO........... Field Works Officer (SAUO)
FWO........... Fire-Weather Office [*National Weather Service*] (NOAA)
FWO........... Fleet Wireless Officer [*British*]
FWOA........... Fort Worth Opera Association (SAUO)
FWOC........... Federation of Western Outdoor Clubs (EA)
FWOC........... Fleet Weather & Oceanographic Centre (SAUS)
FWOC........... Fleet Weather & Oceanographic Computer (SAUS)
FWOC........... Forward Wing Operations Centre (SAUO)
FWONA........... Free World Outside North America (SAUO)
FWOP........... Federal Women's Program Committee/Coordinator (AABC)
FWOP........... Furloughed without Pay
FWOS........... Free Will Offering Scheme (ROG)
FWOSR........... Flight Work Orders - Ships Records (MCD)
FWOTSC........... First Woman on the Supreme Court [*Sandra Day O'Connor*]
FWOTY........... Four-Wheeler of the Year [*Automotive promotion*]
FWP........... Faculty White Pages [*A publication*]
FWP........... Fair-Witness Project (EA)
FWP........... Feather Weight Pump [*Auto racing engine model designation*] [*British*]
FWP........... Federal Water Policy (SAUS)
FWP........... Federal Women's Program
FWP........... Federal Writers' Project [*Obsolete*]
FWP........... Feed Water Pump (MSA)
FWP........... Field-Work Proposal (ABAC)
FWP........... Filament-Wound Plastic (PDAA)
FWP........... First Word Pointer [*Computer science*] (MHDB)
FWP........... Flight Watch Point [*Aviation*] (FAAC)
FWP........... Fresh Water Pump (MSA)
FWP........... Fulcrum, Weight, Power
FWP........... Full Write Pulse (SAUS)
FWp........... Winter Park Public Library, Winter Park, FL [*Library symbol*] [*Library of Congress*] (LCLS)
FWPAC........... Federal Women's Program Advisory Committee (GFGA)
FWPAC........... FWP Advisory Committee (SAUO)
FWPB........... Feedwater Pipe Break [*Nuclear energy*] (NRCH)
FWpb........... West Palm Beach Public Library, West Palm Beach, FL [*Library symbol*] [*Library of Congress*] (LCLS)
FWpbC........... Palm Beach Atlantic College, West Palm Beach, FL [*Library symbol*] [*Library of Congress*] (LCLS)
FWpbG........... Good Samaritan Hospital, Medical Library, West Palm Beach, FL [*Library symbol*] [*Library of Congress*] (LCLS)
FWpbP........... Palm Beach County Public Library System, West Palm Beach, FL [*Library symbol*] [*Library of Congress*] (LCLS)
FWPCA........... Federal Water Pollution and Control Act (SAUS)
FWPCA........... Federal Water Pollution and Control Administration (SAUS)
FWPCA........... Federal Water Pollution Contral Administration (SAUS)
FWPCA........... Federal Water Pollution Control Act [*1972*] (CARB)
FWPCA........... Federal Water Pollution Control Act [*1965*] (NRCH)
FWPCA........... Federal Water Pollution Control Administration [*Later, OWP*] [*Department of the Interior*]
FWP J........... FWP Journal (journ.) (SAUS)
FWPLN........... Fairwater Planes
FWPO........... Federal Wildlife Permit Office [*Department of the Interior*]
FWPO........... Fort Wayne Philharmonic Orchestra (SAUO)
FWPP........... Fremont, West Point & Pacific Railway [*Federal Railroad Administration identification code*]
FWPR........... Field Work Performance Report
FWpR........... Rollins College, Winter Park, FL [*Library symbol*] [*Library of Congress*] (LCLS)
FWPRDC........... Forest and Wood Products Research and Development Corporation (EERA)
FWpR-S........... Rollins College, Bush Science Library, Winter Park, FL [*Library symbol*] [*Library of Congress*] (LCLS)
FWPT........... Fast Walsh-Paley Transform (SAUS)
FWQ........... Flight West Airlines [*Australia*] [*ICAO designator*] (FAAC)
FWQA........... Federal Water Quality Administration [*Later, OWP*] [*Environmental Protection Agency*]
FWQA........... Federal Water Quality Association (EA)
FWQC........... Federal Water Quality Criteria (EEVL)
FWR........... Federal Waste Repository (NUCP)
FWR........... Felix-Weil Reaction [*Clinical chemistry*] (AAMN)
FWR........... First Washington Realty Trust [*AMEX symbol*] (SAG)
FWR........... Fitted With Radio
FWR........... Folin-Wu Reaction [*Medicine*] (DMAA)
FWR........... Forest, Wildlife, and Range Experiment Station [*University of Idaho*] [*Research center*] (RCD)
FWR........... Free-Wheel Rectifier
FWR........... Full-Wave Rectification (SAUS)
FWR........... Full Wave Rectifier (SAUS)
FWR........... Full-Wave Reflector (SAUS)
FWR........... Functional Work Recording (HEAS)
FWRAP........... Federal Water Resources Assistance Program (EERA)
FWRC........... Federal Water Resources Council
FWRD........... Fairmont & Western Railroad [*Federal Railroad Administration identification code*]
FWRD........... Forward Air Corp. [*NASDAQ symbol*] (NASQ)
FW Rectifier... Full-Wave Rectifier (SAUS)
FWREL........... Far West Regional Educational Laboratory [*San Francisco, CA*] [*Department of Education*] (AEBS)
FWRM........... Federation of Wire Rope Manufacturers (SAUO)
FWRMGB........... Federation of Wire Rope Manufacturers of Great Britain (BI)
FWRNG........... Fire Warning (FAAC)
FWRRC........... University of Florida Water Resources Research Center [*Research center*] (RCD)
FWRS........... Fish and Wildlife Reference Service [*Fish and Wildlife Service*] [*Information service or system*] (MSC)
FWRS........... Flexible Wing Recovery System [*Aerospace*] (AAG)
FWRTTC........... Far West Regional Technology Transfer Center [*University of Southern California*]
FWRU........... Full-Wave Rectified Unfiltered
FWRX........... Field Works, Inc. [*NASDAQ symbol*] (NASQ)
FWS........... Famous Writers School (SAUS)
FWS........... FAS [*Fixed Airlock Shroud*] Work Station
FWS........... Federal Wage Systems [*DoD*]
FWS........... Fighter Weapons School [*Military*]
FWS........... Fighter Weapons Squadron [*Air Force*]
FWS........... Filament-Wound Structure
FWS........... Filter Wedge Spectrometer
FWS........... Final Work Statement (MCD)
FWS........... Fire Water Service
FWS........... Fish and Wildlife Service [*Department of the Interior*]
FWS........... Fixed Wireless Station (IAA)
FWS........... Fleet Work Study [*Navy*] (NG)
FWS........... Flight and Weapons Simulator (MCD)
FWS........... Flight Warning System (MCD)
FWS........... Flight Watch Specialist [*Aviation*] (FAAC)
FWS........... Fluid Wetting and Spreading [*Lubrication*]
FWS........... Fly Wire Screen (ADA)
FWS........... Formatted Write Statement (SAUS)
FWS........... Forward Swept Wing (SAUO)
FWS........... Furtwangen [*Schwarzwald*] [*Federal Republic of Germany*] [*Seismograph station code, US Geological Survey*] (SEIS)

FWSAB .... Federation of Women Shareholders in American Business (EA)
FWSCH .... Fighter Weapons School [*Military*]
FWSDR .... Final Working System Design Review [*Nuclear energy*] (NRCH)
FWSG .... Fann Water Supply Grant (SAUS)
FWSG .... Fleet Work Study Group [*Navy*]
FWSGLANT... Fleet Work Study Group Atlantic [*Norfolk, VA*] [*Navy*]
FWSGPAC.... Fleet Work Study Group Pacific [*San Diego, CA*] [*Navy*]
FWSH .... First Washington Realty Trust [*NASDAQ symbol*] (SAG)
FWSH .... First Wash Realty Trust [*NASDAQ symbol*] (TTSB)
FWSH .... Fresh Water Supply Header [*Nuclear energy*] (NRCH)
FWSHP .... First Wash Rlty 9.75% Cv Pfd [*NASDAQ symbol*] (TTSB)
FWshR........ First Washington Realty Trust [*Associated Press*] (SAG)
F Wshr........ Flat Washer (SAUS)
FWshRT....... First Washington Realty Trust [*Associated Press*] (SAG)
FWSI........... Fairchild-Weston Systems, Inc. (SAUS)
FW/SIFR ...... Fixed-Wing Special Instrument Flight Rules [*Aviation*]
FWSJ........... Nsanje [*Malawi*] [*ICAO location identifier*] (ICLI)
FWSM........... Salima [*Malawi*] [*ICAO location identifier*] (ICLI)
FWSO .... Fort Worth Symphony Orchestra (SAUO)
FWS/OBS..... Fish and Wildlife Service/Office of Biological Services [*Department of the Interior*]
FWSRSA...... Farmington Wild and Scenic River Study Act (COE)
FWSSUSA.... Federation of Workers' Singing Societies of the USA (EA)
FWSU .... Nchalo/Sucoma [*Malawi*] [*ICAO location identifier*] (ICLI)
FWSV........... Funnel-Web Spider Venom
FW/SVFR ..... Fixed-Wing Special Visual Flight Rules [*Aviation*]
fwt .... Fair Wear and Tear (ODBW)
FWT............ Fair Wear and Tear
FWT............ Farming and Wildlife Trust [*British*] (DBA)
FWT............ Far West Industries, Inc. [*Toronto Stock Exchange symbol*] [*Vancouver Stock Exchange symbol*]
FWT............ Fast Walsh Transform [*Spectrometry*]
FWT............ Fast Wavelet Transformation (SAUS)
fwt .... feather-weight (SAUS)
FWT............ Fine Wear and Tear (SAUS)
FWT............ Fixed-Wing Transport Company, [*Army aviation company*] (VNW)
FWT............ Fleetwork Trainer (SAUS)
FWT............ Forward Wave Tube
FWT............ Free World Trade (SAUO)
FWT............ Fresh Water Tank (SAUS)
FWT............ Friends of the World Treasures Network (SAUO)
FWT............ FW Capital I [*AMEX symbol*] (NASQ)
FWT & GD... fair wear (SAUS)
FWTAO .... Federation of Women Teachers Associations of Ontario (SAUO)
FWTC........... Far and Wide Tape Club (EA)
FWTC........... Fighter Weapons Training Command (MCD)
FWTH........... Flush Water-Tight Hatch (SAUS)
FWTK........... Fire Wall Tool Kit [*Computer science*] (HODG)
FW Tk.......... Fresh Water Tank (SAUS)
FWTM........... Full Width at Tenth Maximum (IEEE)
FWTMH......... Flush Water-Tight Manhole (SAUS)
FWTs .... Fast Walsh Transforms (SAUS)
FWTT........... Fixed-Wing Tactical Transport [*Aviation*] (MCD)
FWTUC .... Free Workers' Trade Union Congress [*Aden*]
FWU............ Fixed-Wing Utility Company, [*Army aircraft company*] (VNW)
FWu............ Flight Watch Unit [*Aviation*] (FAAC)
FWU............ Food Workers Union (SAUO)
FWU............ Fort Wayne Union [*AAR code*]
FWUU .... Mzuzu [*Malawi*] [*ICAO location identifier*] (ICLI)
FWV............ Farmerville, LA [*Location identifier*] [*FAA*] (FAAL)
FWV............ First West Virginia Bancorp [*AMEX symbol*] (TTSB)
FWV............ First West Virginia Bancorp, Inc. [*AMEX symbol*] (SAG)
FWV............ Fixed-Wing Vehicle (ADWA)
FWVA........... Finnish War Veterans in America (EA)
FWW............ Federation of Wholefood Wholesalers [*British*]
FWW............ Fighter Weapons Wing
FWW............ First Western Communications Corp. [*Vancouver Stock Exchange symbol*]
FWW............ First World War (DMA)
FWW............ Follow-on Wild Weasel (SAUS)
FWW............ Food, Water, and Waste [*NASA*] (MCD)
FWW............ Forestry, Wildlife And Wildland Working Group (SAUS)
FWW............ Friends of Workshop Way (EA)
FWW............ Front Wheel Walker [*Rehabilitation*] (DAVI)
FWWB .... First Savings Bank Washington Bancorp, Inc. [*NASDAQ symbol*] (SAG)
FWWB .... First Svgs Bk Wash Bancorp [*NASDAQ symbol*] (TTSB)
FWWM.......... Food, Water, and Waste Management [*NASA*] (NASA)
FWWMR ...... Fire, Water, Weather, Mildew Resistant (MCD)
FWWMS ...... Food, Water, and Waste Management Subsystem [*NASA*] (NASA)
FWWMS ...... Food, Water, and Waste Management System (SAUS)
FWWR .... Fort Worth & Western Railroad [*Federal Railroad Administration identification code*]
FWWS .... Fire-Weather Warning Service (SAUO)
FWWSU .... Fiji Waterside Workers and Seamens Union (SAUO)
FWWTA........ Fraction of Waste Water Treated Anaerobically (CARB)
FWWU .... Food Beverage Workers Union (SAUO)
FWY............ Fairways Corp. [*ICAO designator*] (FAAC)
FWY............ Fenway Resources Ltd. [*Vancouver Stock Exchange symbol*]
fwy.............. Freeway (ADWA)
Fwy............. Freeway (DD)
FWY............ Freeway (MCD)
FWZI........... Full Width at Zero Intensity [*Spectroscopy*]
F/X.............. Effects [*Filmmaking and television*] [*Also title of a movie about special effects*]
FX............... Export Fighter (SAUS)
FX............... Express Air [*ICAO designator*] (AD)
FX............... Facsimile (KSC)
FX............... Factory Experimental [*Class of drag racing cars*]
FX............... Fast Crosstalk (SAUS)
FX............... Field Exchange [*Computer science*] (PCM)
FX............... Field Exercise [*Military*] (MCD)
FX............... Fighter Experimental (MCD)
FX............... Fighter Export [*Military*]
FX............... Fix [*Navigation*]
fx............... fixed (SAUS)
FX............... Fixed Area [*of magnetic disk*]
FX............... Fixed-point (SAUS)
FX............... Fixed Station [*ITU designation*] (CET)
FX............... Fluoroscopy [*Medicine*] (DMAA)
FX............... Forecastle [*Navy*] [*British*]
FX............... Foreign Exchange [*ADP Network Services, Inc.*] [*Information service or system*]
FX............... Foreign Exchange [*Investment term*]
FX............... Foreign Exchange Rate Service [*Refco, Inc.*] [*Information service or system*] (IID)
FX............... Fornix [*Medicine*] (DMAA)
fx............... Fornix [*Medicine*] (EDAA)
FX............... Foxed (WGA)
Fx............... Fractional Urine [*Biochemistry*] (DAVI)
fx............... Fractional Urine [*Medicine*] (EDAA)
fx............... Fracture (ADWA)
Fx............... Fracture (MELL)
FX............... Fracture [*Medicine*]
fx............... fractured (SAUS)
FX............... Fracture Frozen Section [*Medicine*] (DMAA)
fx............... fractures (SAUS)
FX............... France, Metropolitan [*Internet country code*]
FX............... Francis Xavier (SAUS)
FX............... Freight Traffic Concurrence
FX............... Frozen Section [*Medicine*] (EDAA)
fx............... Frozen Section [*Medicine*] (MAE)
FX............... Mountain West Airlines [*ICAO designator*] (AD)
FX............... Special Effects
FXA............. Express Air, Inc. [*ICAO designator*] (FAAC)
FXA............. Fleet Exercise Area (SAUS)
FXA............. Foreign Exchange Agreement (NUMA)
FX-ALPHA.... FSL [*Forecast Systems Laboratory*] X-Window AWIPS-Like Prototype for Hydrometeorological Applications (USDC)
FXBASE........ International Interest and Exchange Rate Database [*Citicorp Database Services*] [*Information service or system*] (IID)
FXBB........... Bobete [*Lesotho*] [*ICAO location identifier*] (ICLI)
Fx BB........... Fracture of Both Bones [*Medicine*]
FXBC........... ExecuFirst Bancorp [*NASDAQ symbol*] (SAG)
FXBIN .... Fixed Binary (DEN)
FXC............. Ferrox Cube [*Telecommunications*] (TEL)
FXC............. FerroxCube (SAUS)
FXC............. Fortunair Canada [*FAA designator*] (FAAC)
FXC............. Francis X. Curzio [*In company name FXC Investors Corp.*]
FX-CCSA...... Foreign Exchange-Common Control Switching Arrangement (SAUS)
FXD............. Ferroxdure (SAUS)
FXD............. Fixed (AAG)
Fxd............. Fixed (EBF)
FXD............. Flash X-ray Device (SAUS)
fxd .... foxed (SAUS)
FX Database... Foreign Exchange Rates Database [*Databank produced by Conticurrency*] (NITA)
fxd frt......... fixed freight (SAUS)
Fx-Dis.......... Fracture-Dislocation [*Orthopedics*] (DAVI)
Fx-dis .... Fracture-Dislocation [*Medicine*] (DMAA)
FXE .... Ferrocarril Mexicano [*Federal Railroad Administration identification code*]
FXE .... Fort Lauderdale, FL [*Location identifier*] [*FAA*] (FAAL)
FXE .... Telemetering Fixed Station [*ITU designation*] (CET)
FXEN........... FX Energy, Inc. [*NASDAQ symbol*] (SAG)
FX Ener........ FX Energy, Inc. [*Associated Press*] (SAG)
FXER........... Foreign Exchange Encashments Receipts [*Finance*]
FXF .... Flash X-ray Facility (SAUS)
FXF .... Fragile X Foundation (MELL)
FXF .... VIP Air Charter, Inc. [*FAA designator*] (FAAC)
FXG............. Fixing (ADA)
FXG............. Florida International University, Miami, FL [*OCLC symbol*] (OCLC)
FXG............. Tatonduk Outfitters Ltd. [*FAA designator*] (FAAC)
FXGL........... Foreign Exchange Gains and Losses
FXH............. Hydrological and Meteorological Fixed Station [*ITU designation*] (CET)
FXKB........... Kolberg [*Lesotho*] [*ICAO location identifier*] (ICLI)
fxle .... forcecastle (SAUS)
Fxle .... Forecaste (SAUS)
FXLE .... Forecastle
FXLK........... Lebakeng [*Lesotho*] [*ICAO location identifier*] (ICLI)
FXLR........... Leribe [*Lesotho*] [*ICAO location identifier*] (ICLI)
FXLS........... Lesobeng [*Lesotho*] [*ICAO location identifier*] (ICLI)
FXLT .... Letseng [*Lesotho*] [*ICAO location identifier*] (ICLI)
FXM............. Flaxman Island, AK [*Location identifier*] [*FAA*] (FAAL)
FXM............. Fox Movies (SAUS)
FXMA........... Matsaile [*Lesotho*] [*ICAO location identifier*] (ICLI)
FXMF........... Mafeteng [*Lesotho*] [*ICAO location identifier*] (ICLI)
FXMH........... Mohales'Hoek [*Lesotho*] [*ICAO location identifier*] (ICLI)
FXMK........... Mokhotlong [*Lesotho*] [*ICAO location identifier*] (ICLI)

FXML Malefiloane [*Lesotho*] [*ICAO location identifier*] (ICLI)
FXMM Maseru Moshoeshoe International [*Lesotho*] [*ICAO location identifier*] (ICLI)
FXMN Mantsonyane [*Lesotho*] [*ICAO location identifier*] (ICLI)
FXMP Mohlanapeng [*Lesotho*] [*ICAO location identifier*] (ICLI)
FXMS Mashai Store [*Lesotho*] [*ICAO location identifier*] (ICLI)
FXMT Matabeng Store [*Lesotho*] [*ICAO location identifier*] (ICLI)
FXMU Maseru/Leabua Jonathan [*Lesotho*] [*ICAO location identifier*] (ICLI)
FXMV Matabeng Village [*Lesotho*] [*ICAO location identifier*] (ICLI)
FXN Florida International University, North Campus, North Miami, FL [*OCLC symbol*] (OCLC)
FXN Function (DAVI)
FXN Sprint Corp. [*NYSE symbol*] (SAG)
FXN Sprint Corp 8.25%'DECS' 2000 [*NYSE symbol*] (TTSB)
FXNH Nohanas [*Lesotho*] [*ICAO location identifier*] (ICLI)
FXNK Nkaus [*Lesotho*] [*ICAO location identifier*] (ICLI)
FXO Foreign Exchange Office [*Telecommunications*] (ITD)
FXO Nova Freixo [*Mozambique*] [*Airport symbol*] (AD)
FXP Fixed Point
FXP Fleet Exercise Publication [*Navy*]
FXPALU Fixed Point Address Arithmetic Logic Unit [*Computer science*] (MHDB)
FXPCU Fixed Point Unit (SAUS)
FXPG Pelaneng [*Lesotho*] [*ICAO location identifier*] (ICLI)
FXPLU Fixed Point address arithmetic Logic Unit (SAUS)
FXPU Fixed Point Unit (SAUS)
FXQG Quthing [*Lesotho*] [*ICAO location identifier*] (ICLI)
FXQN Qachas' Nek [*Lesotho*] [*ICAO location identifier*] (ICLI)
fxr fixer (SAUS)
FXR Flash X-Ray
FXR Foxair Ltd. [*British*] [*ICAO designator*] (FAAC)
FXR Foxer [*Navy*] [*British*]
FXR Fox Resources Ltd. [*Vancouver Stock Exchange symbol*]
FXR Fracture [*Orthopedics*] (DAVI)
FXS Fine-Focus X-Ray Series (SAUS)
FXS Foreign Exchange Station (SAUO)
FXS Foreign Exchange Subscriber (SAUO)
FXS Fox Sparrow [*Ornithology*]
FXS Fragile X Syndrome [*Genetics*]
FXSE Sehlabathebe [*Lesotho*] [*ICAO location identifier*] (ICLI)
FXSH Sehonghong [*Lesotho*] [*ICAO location identifier*] (ICLI)
FXSK Sekake [*Lesotho*] [*ICAO location identifier*] (ICLI)
FXSM Semongkong [*Lesotho*] [*ICAO location identifier*] (ICLI)
FXSR Foreign Exchange Sale Receipts [*Finance*]
FXSS Seshote [*Lesotho*] [*ICAO location identifier*] (ICLI)
FXST St. Theresa [*Lesotho*] [*ICAO location identifier*] (ICLI)
FXSTA Fixed Station (IAA)
fxt Fixative (VRA)
FXT Fixed Time Call [*Telecommunications*] (NITA)
FXTA Thaba Tseka [*Lesotho*] [*ICAO location identifier*] (ICLI)
FXTB Tebellong [*Lesotho*] [*ICAO location identifier*] (ICLI)
FXTK Tlokoeng [*Lesotho*] [*ICAO location identifier*] (ICLI)
FXTR Fixture (MSA)
FXU Fixed-Point Unit
FXU F. W. Faxon Co. [*ACCORD*] [*UTLAS symbol*]
FXV Appleton, WI [*Location identifier*] [*FAA*] (FAAL)
FXV Future Experimental Vehicle [*Toyota Motor Co.*]
FXX Foxx Industry, Inc. [*Vancouver Stock Exchange symbol*]
FXXILW Force XXI Land Warrior [*Military*]
FXY Flexair BV [*Netherlands*] [*ICAO designator*] (FAAC)
FXY Forest City, IA [*Location identifier*] [*FAA*] (FAAL)
Fy Duffy [*Blood group*]
FY Fall Yearling [*Pisciculture*]
FY Feng Yun Satellite (SAUS)
Fy Ferry [*Nautical charts*]
F-Y Fibrinogen Qualitative Test [*Hematology*] (DAVI)
FY Final Year (SAUO)
FY Financial Year (EERA)
FY Fiscal Year [*Business term*]
FY Fishery Flag [*Navy*] [*British*]
FY Flashing Yellow (SAUS)
FY Fort Yukon [*Alaska*] [*Seismograph station code, US Geological Survey*]
FY Full Year
FY Future Value [*Business term*] (EBF)
FY Metroflight Airlines and Great Plains Airline [*ICAO designator*] (AD)
FY South Africa [*Later, BL*] [*License plate code assigned to foreign diplomats in the US*]
FY-2 Feng Yun - 2 [*Chinese geostationary satellite*] (EERA)
FYA Duffy A Positive [*Blood type*] [*Hematology*] (DAVI)
FYA Faya Largeau [*Chad*] [*Airport symbol*] (AD)
FYA First-Year Algebra [*National Science Foundation project*]
FYA For Your Action (TIMI)
FYA For Your Advice (SAUO)
FYA For Your Amusement [*Computer hacker terminology*] (NHD)
FYA For Your Approval (TIMI)
FYA For Your Attention [*Business term*]
FYAN Duffy A Negative [*Blood type*] [*Hematology*] (DAVI)
FYB Albert Lea, MN [*Location identifier*] [*FAA*] (FAAL)
FYB Duffy B Positive [*Blood type*] [*Hematology*] (DAVI)
FYBN Duffy B Negative [*Blood type*] [*Hematology*] (DAVI)
FYBR Critical Industries, Inc. [*NASDAQ symbol*] (COMM)
FYC Federal Youth Center (SAUO)
FYC Fine Young Canibals (SAUS)
FYC Fission Yield Curve
FYC Florida Yacht Club (SAUO)
FYC For Your Consideration (VLIE)
FYC Family and Youth Concern (ODA)
FYCP Five Year Corporate Plan (SAUO)
FYCP Future Years Corporate Plan (SAUS)
FYD Federation of Young Democrats [*Hungary*] [*Political party*] (EY)
FYD Fellowship of Youth Development [*British*] (DBQ)
FYD Frayed [*Bookselling*] (DGA)
FYDA Associate Fellowship of Youth Development [*British*] (DBQ)
FYDO Fiscal Year Design Objective
FYDO Five-Year Design Objective
FYDP First-Year Development Program (SAUS)
FYDP Fiscal Year Defense Program (ACAE)
FYDP Fiscal Year Development Plan (MCD)
FYDP Five-Year Defence Programme (SAUS)
FYDP Five-Year Defense Plan [*or Program*] [*Military*]
FYDP Five Year Defense Program (SAUS)
FYDP Future Year Defense Plan (SAUS)
FYDP Future Year Defense Program (SAUO)
FYDS Fiscal Year Data Summary
FYDSP Five-Year Defense Standardization Plan (MCD)
FYE First-Year Experience (SAUS)
FYE Fiscal Year End (NFD)
FYE Fiscal Year Ending
FYE For Your Entertainment (VLIE)
FYE For Your Eyes (BARN)
FYE Full Year Equivalent (EERA)
FYEO For Your Eyes Only (ADWA)
FYF For Your Files
FYFC Faron Young Fan Club (EA)
FYFSFP Five-Year Force Structure and Financial Program [*Navy*] (KSC)
FYG For Your Guidance (RIMS)
FYG Friends of Yesh Gvul (EA)
FYI For Your Information
FYI For Your Interest [*Internet language*] [*Computer science*]
FYI News/Retrieval for Your Information [*Dow Jones & Co., Inc.*] [*Information service or system*] (CRD)
FYIG For Your Information and Guidance
FYII F.Y.I., Inc. [*NASDAQ symbol*] (NASQ)
FYIP Five Year Instrumentation Program (SAUO)
FYIP Five Year Intelligence Program [*Military*]
FYK First York Corp. (SAUO)
FYM Farm Yard Manure (SAUS)
FYM Fayetteville, TN [*Location identifier*] [*FAA*] (FAAL)
FYM Fiscal Year Month
FYM Miami-Dade Community College, Miami, FL [*OCLC symbol*] (OCLC)
FYMCP Five Year Master Construction Plan [*DoD*]
FYMOP Five Year Master Objectives Program (CCCA)
FYMOPP Five Year Master Objectives Plan Program [*Military*]
FYMP Five-Year Materiel Program [*Military*]
FYMP Five-Year Methodology Program (SAUO)
FYMS Fourth-Year Medical Student (DMAA)
FYN Fuyun [*China*] [*Airport symbol*] (OAG)
FYO Federation of Youth Organizations (SAUO)
FYO Fiscal Year Option
FYP Five-Year Plan [*Military*]
FYP Five Year Program (CCCA)
FYP Four-Year Plan
FYPB Five-Year Planning Base [*Military*] (AABC)
Fy pd Fully Paid (EBF)
fypi for your personal information (SAUS)
FYPP Five-Year Procurement Program [*Military*] (AABC)
FYPP Five-Year Program Plan
FYQ Rome, NY [*Location identifier*] [*FAA*] (FAAL)
F Yr Fiscal Year (SAUS)
fyr for your reference (SAUS)
fyrace for your account (SAUS)
FYRM Former Yugoslav Republic of Macedonia
FYROM Former Yugoslav Republic of Macedonia [*Temporary name*] (ECON)
FYS Five-Year Survival (MELL)
FYS For Your Signature (VLIE)
FYSA Foundation for Youth and Student Affairs [*Defunct*] (EA)
FYT Force Year Total Model (SAUO)
FYTD Fiscal Year to Date (ABAC)
FYTDP Five-Year Training Development Plan [*Army*]
FYTDY Final Year Temporary Duty [*Military*] (AFM)
FYTP Five-Year Test Plan (SAUO)
FYTP Five-Year Test Program [*Military*] (AABC)
FYTQ Fiscal Year Transition Quarter
FYU Fort Yukon [*Alaska*] [*Airport symbol*] (OAG)
FYU Fort Yukon [*Alaska*] [*Seismograph station code, US Geological Survey*] (SEIS)
FYU Fort Yukon, AK [*Location identifier*] [*FAA*] (FAAL)
FYV Fayetteville [*Arkansas*] [*Airport symbol*] (OAG)
FYV Fayetteville, AR [*Location identifier*] [*FAA*] (FAAL)
FYWP Fiscal Year Work Plan (ABAC)
FYY Finningley FTU [*British*] [*ICAO designator*] (FAAC)
Fyz Fyzabad (SAUS)
FZ Air Chico [*ICAO designator*] (AD)
FZ Farmaco [*Federal Railroad Administration identification code*]
FZ fault zone (SAUS)
FZ Fetal Zone [*Medicine*]
FZ Fire Zone [*Bulkhead*] (DNAB)
FZ Floating Zone (SAUS)
FZ Float Zone [*Crystallization process*]

FZ Flow Zone [*Environmental science*] (COE)
FZ Fluoresceinated Zymosan [*Clinical chemistry*]
FZ Fluorozirconate (SAUS)
FZ Flurazepam [*Organic chemistry*]
FZ Focal Zone [*Medicine*] (MAE)
Fz Forzando [*or Forzato*] [*Strongly Accented*] [*Music*]
fz Forzato [*Forced*] [*Italian*] [*Music*] (WDAA)
FZ Fracture Zone [*Geophysics*]
FZ Franc Zone
fz freeze (SAUS)
FZ Freezing
FZ Free Zone (SAUS)
FZ French Zone (SAUS)
FZ Frigid Zone (ROG)
Fz Frontal Midline Placement of Electrodes in Electroencephalography [*Medicine*] (EDAA)
FZ Frozen Zone (VLIE)
FZ Frugal Zealot (SAUS)
FZ Furazolidone [*Antimicrobial drug*]
FZ Fusion Zone (SAUS)
FZ Fuze (MSA)
fz--- Zambezi River and Basin [*MARC geographic area code*] [*Library of Congress*] (LCCP)
FZA Fellow of the Zoological Academy
FZA Fellow of the Zoological Association (SAUO)
FZA Free Zone Authority (EA)
f-za- Zambia [*MARC geographic area code*] [*Library of Congress*] (LCCP)
FZAA Kinshasa/N'Djili [*Zaire*] [*ICAO location identifier*] (ICLI)
FZAB Kinshasa/N'Dolo [*Zaire*] [*ICAO location identifier*] (ICLI)
FZAD Celo-Zongo [*Zaire*] [*ICAO location identifier*] (ICLI)
FZAE Kimpoko [*Zaire*] [*ICAO location identifier*] (ICLI)
FZAF Nsangi [*Zaire*] [*ICAO location identifier*] (ICLI)
FZAG Muanda [*Zaire*] [*ICAO location identifier*] (ICLI)
FZAH Tshela [*Zaire*] [*ICAO location identifier*] (ICLI)
FZAI Kitona-Base [*Zaire*] [*ICAO location identifier*] (ICLI)
FZAJ Boma [*Zaire*] [*ICAO location identifier*] (ICLI)
FZAL Luozi [*Zaire*] [*ICAO location identifier*] (ICLI)
FZAM Matadi [*Zaire*] [*ICAO location identifier*] (ICLI)
FZAN Inga [*Zaire*] [*ICAO location identifier*] (ICLI)
FZAP Lukala [*Zaire*] [*ICAO location identifier*] (ICLI)
FZAR Nkolo-Fuma [*Zaire*] [*ICAO location identifier*] (ICLI)
FZAS Inkisi [*Zaire*] [*ICAO location identifier*] (ICLI)
FZAU Konde [*Zaire*] [*ICAO location identifier*] (ICLI)
FZAW Kwilu-Gongo [*Zaire*] [*ICAO location identifier*] (ICLI)
FZAX Luheki [*Zaire*] [*ICAO location identifier*] (ICLI)
FZAY Mvula-Sanda [*Zaire*] [*ICAO location identifier*] (ICLI)
FZAZ Kinshasa [*Zaire*] [*ICAO location identifier*] (ICLI)
FZB Mansa [*Zambia*] [*Airport symbol*] (AD)
FZBA Inongo [*Zaire*] [*ICAO location identifier*] (ICLI)
FZBB Bongimba [*Zaire*] [*ICAO location identifier*] (ICLI)
FZBC Bikoro [*Zaire*] [*ICAO location identifier*] (ICLI)
FZBD Oshwe [*Zaire*] [*ICAO location identifier*] (ICLI)
FZBE Beno [*Zaire*] [*ICAO location identifier*] (ICLI)
FZBF Bontika [*Zaire*] [*ICAO location identifier*] (ICLI)
FZBG Kempa [*Zaire*] [*ICAO location identifier*] (ICLI)
FZBI Nioki [*Zaire*] [*ICAO location identifier*] (ICLI)
FZBJ Mushie [*Zaire*] [*ICAO location identifier*] (ICLI)
FZBK Bosobe-Boshwe [*Zaire*] [*ICAO location identifier*] (ICLI)
FZBL Djokele [*Zaire*] [*ICAO location identifier*] (ICLI)
FZBN Malebo [*Zaire*] [*ICAO location identifier*] (ICLI)
FZBO Bandundu [*Zaire*] [*ICAO location identifier*] (ICLI)
FZBP Ngebolobo [*Zaire*] [*ICAO location identifier*] (ICLI)
FZBQ Bindja [*Zaire*] [*ICAO location identifier*] (ICLI)
FZBS Semendua [*Zaire*] [*ICAO location identifier*] (ICLI)
FZBT Kiri [*Zaire*] [*ICAO location identifier*] (ICLI)
FZBU Ibeke [*Zaire*] [*ICAO location identifier*] (ICLI)
FZBV Kempili [*Zaire*] [*ICAO location identifier*] (ICLI)
FZBW Bokote/Basengele [*Zaire*] [*ICAO location identifier*] (ICLI)
FZCA Kikwit [*Zaire*] [*ICAO location identifier*] (ICLI)
FZCB Idiofa [*Zaire*] [*ICAO location identifier*] (ICLI)
FZCD Vanga [*Zaire*] [*ICAO location identifier*] (ICLI)
FZCE Lusanga [*Zaire*] [*ICAO location identifier*] (ICLI)
FZCF Kahemba [*Zaire*] [*ICAO location identifier*] (ICLI)
FZCG Float Zone Crystal Growth (SSD)
FZCGF Float Zone Crystal Growth Facility (SAUS)
FZCI Banga [*Zaire*] [*ICAO location identifier*] (ICLI)
FZCK Kajiji [*Zaire*] [*ICAO location identifier*] (ICLI)
FZCL Banza-Lute [*Zaire*] [*ICAO location identifier*] (ICLI)
FZCO Boko [*Zaire*] [*ICAO location identifier*] (ICLI)
FZCP Popokabaka [*Zaire*] [*ICAO location identifier*] (ICLI)
FZCR Busala [*Zaire*] [*ICAO location identifier*] (ICLI)
FZ Crystal Float Zone Crystal (SAUS)
FZCS Kenge [*Zaire*] [*ICAO location identifier*] (ICLI)
FZCT Fatundu [*Zaire*] [*ICAO location identifier*] (ICLI)
FZCU Ito [*Zaire*] [*ICAO location identifier*] (ICLI)
FZCV Masi-Manimba [*Zaire*] [*ICAO location identifier*] (ICLI)
FZCW Kikongo Sur Wamba [*Zaire*] [*ICAO location identifier*] (ICLI)
FZCX Kimafu [*Zaire*] [*ICAO location identifier*] (ICLI)
FZCY Yuki [*Zaire*] [*ICAO location identifier*] (ICLI)
FZDA Malanga [*Zaire*] [*ICAO location identifier*] (ICLI)
FZDB Kimbau [*Zaire*] [*ICAO location identifier*] (ICLI)
FZDC Lukuni [*Zaire*] [*ICAO location identifier*] (ICLI)
FZDD Wamba-Luadi [*Zaire*] [*ICAO location identifier*] (ICLI)
FZDE Tono [*Zaire*] [*ICAO location identifier*] (ICLI)
FZDF Nzamba [*Zaire*] [*ICAO location identifier*] (ICLI)
FZDG Nyanga [*Zaire*] [*ICAO location identifier*] (ICLI)
FZDH Ngi [*Zaire*] [*ICAO location identifier*] (ICLI)
FZDJ Mutena [*Zaire*] [*ICAO location identifier*] (ICLI)
FZDK Kipata' Katika [*Zaire*] [*ICAO location identifier*] (ICLI)
FZDL Kolokoso [*Zaire*] [*ICAO location identifier*] (ICLI)
FZDM Masamuna [*Zaire*] [*ICAO location identifier*] (ICLI)
FZDN Mongo Wa Kenda [*Zaire*] [*ICAO location identifier*] (ICLI)
FZDO Moanda [*Zaire*] [*ICAO location identifier*] (ICLI)
FZDP Mukedi [*Zaire*] [*ICAO location identifier*] (ICLI)
FZDS Flood Zone Determination Services (SAUS)
FZDS Yasa-Bonga [*Zaire*] [*ICAO location identifier*] (ICLI)
FZDT Matari [*Zaire*] [*ICAO location identifier*] (ICLI)
FZDU Kimpangu [*Zaire*] [*ICAO location identifier*] (ICLI)
FZDY Misay [*Zaire*] [*ICAO location identifier*] (ICLI)
FZDZ Freezing Drizzle [*Meteorology*]
FZEA Mbandaka [*Zaire*] [*ICAO location identifier*] (ICLI)
FZEB Monieka [*Zaire*] [*ICAO location identifier*] (ICLI)
FZEG Lokolela [*Zaire*] [*ICAO location identifier*] (ICLI)
FZEI Ingende [*Zaire*] [*ICAO location identifier*] (ICLI)
FZEM Yembe-Moke [*Zaire*] [*ICAO location identifier*] (ICLI)
FZEN Basankusu [*Zaire*] [*ICAO location identifier*] (ICLI)
FZEO Beongo [*Zaire*] [*ICAO location identifier*] (ICLI)
FZEP Mentole [*Zaire*] [*ICAO location identifier*] (ICLI)
FZER Kodoro [*Zaire*] [*ICAO location identifier*] (ICLI)
FZES Float Zone Experiment System
FZF Float Zone Furnace (SAUS)
FZFA Libenge [*Zaire*] [*ICAO location identifier*] (ICLI)
FZFB Imasse [*Zaire*] [*ICAO location identifier*] (ICLI)
FZFD Gbadolite [*Zaire*] [*ICAO location identifier*] (ICLI)
FZFE Abumumbazi [*Zaire*] [*ICAO location identifier*] (ICLI)
FZFF Bau [*Zaire*] [*ICAO location identifier*] (ICLI)
FZFG Bokada [*Zaire*] [*ICAO location identifier*] (ICLI)
FZFG Freezing Fog [*Meteorology*]
FZFH Mokaria-Yamoleta [*Zaire*] [*ICAO location identifier*] (ICLI)
FZFJ Goyongo [*Zaire*] [*ICAO location identifier*] (ICLI)
FZFK Gemena [*Zaire*] [*ICAO location identifier*] (ICLI)
FZFL Kala [*Zaire*] [*ICAO location identifier*] (ICLI)
FZFN Lombo [*Zaire*] [*ICAO location identifier*] (ICLI)
FZFP Kotakoli [*Zaire*] [*ICAO location identifier*] (ICLI)
FZFQ Mpaka [*Zaire*] [*ICAO location identifier*] (ICLI)
FZFS Karawa [*Zaire*] [*ICAO location identifier*] (ICLI)
FZFT Tandala [*Zaire*] [*ICAO location identifier*] (ICLI)
FZFU Bumba [*Zaire*] [*ICAO location identifier*] (ICLI)
FZFV Gbado [*Zaire*] [*ICAO location identifier*] (ICLI)
FZFW Gwaka [*Zaire*] [*ICAO location identifier*] (ICLI)
FZG Federation of Zoological Societies of Great Britain and Northern Ireland (SAUO)
FZG Fitzgerald, GA [*Location identifier*] [*FAA*] (FAAL)
FZG Fluorozirconate Glass (SAUS)
FZGA Lisala [*Zaire*] [*ICAO location identifier*] (ICLI)
FZGB Bosondjo [*Zaire*] [*ICAO location identifier*] (ICLI)
FZGB Federation of Zoological Gardens of Great Britain and Ireland (SAUO)
FZGBI Fellow of the Zoological Gardens of Great Britain and Ireland (SAUO)
FZGD Bokenge [*Zaire*] [*ICAO location identifier*] (ICLI)
FZGF Bokungu [*Zaire*] [*ICAO location identifier*] (ICLI)
FZGG Mondombe [*Zaire*] [*ICAO location identifier*] (ICLI)
FZGH Wema [*Zaire*] [*ICAO location identifier*] (ICLI)
FZGI Yalingimba [*Zaire*] [*ICAO location identifier*] (ICLI)
FZGN Boende [*Zaire*] [*ICAO location identifier*] (ICLI)
FZGT Boteka [*Zaire*] [*ICAO location identifier*] (ICLI)
FZGV Ikela [*Zaire*] [*ICAO location identifier*] (ICLI)
FZGY Yemo [*Zaire*] [*ICAO location identifier*] (ICLI)
FZI Fostoria, OH [*Location identifier*] [*FAA*] (FAAL)
FZIA First Zen Institute of America (EA)
FZIA Kisangani [*Zaire*] [*ICAO location identifier*] (ICLI)
FZIC Kisangani/Bangoka [*Zaire*] [*ICAO location identifier*] (ICLI)
FZIF Ubundu [*Zaire*] [*ICAO location identifier*] (ICLI)
FZIK Katende [*Zaire*] [*ICAO location identifier*] (ICLI)
FZIR Yangambi [*Zaire*] [*ICAO location identifier*] (ICLI)
FZIZ Lokutu [*Zaire*] [*ICAO location identifier*] (ICLI)
FZJA Isiro [*Zaire*] [*ICAO location identifier*] (ICLI)
FZJB Doko [*Zaire*] [*ICAO location identifier*] (ICLI)
FZJF Aba [*Zaire*] [*ICAO location identifier*] (ICLI)
FZJH Isiro/Matari [*Zaire*] [*ICAO location identifier*] (ICLI)
FZJI Watsha [*Zaire*] [*ICAO location identifier*] (ICLI)
FZJK Faradje [*Zaire*] [*ICAO location identifier*] (ICLI)
FZJR Kerekere [*Zaire*] [*ICAO location identifier*] (ICLI)
FZKA Bunia [*Zaire*] [*ICAO location identifier*] (ICLI)
FZKB Bambili-Dingila [*Zaire*] [*ICAO location identifier*] (ICLI)
FZKC Mahagi [*Zaire*] [*ICAO location identifier*] (ICLI)
FZKF Kilomines [*Zaire*] [*ICAO location identifier*] (ICLI)
FZKI Yedi [*Zaire*] [*ICAO location identifier*] (ICLI)
FZKJ Buta Zega [*Zaire*] [*ICAO location identifier*] (ICLI)
FZKN Aketi [*Zaire*] [*ICAO location identifier*] (ICLI)
FZKO Ango [*Zaire*] [*ICAO location identifier*] (ICLI)
FZKP Bondo [*Zaire*] [*ICAO location identifier*] (ICLI)
FZL Freezing Level (ARMP)
FZM Floating Zone Melting
FZMA Bukavu/Kavumu [*Zaire*] [*ICAO location identifier*] (ICLI)
FZMB Butembo [*Zaire*] [*ICAO location identifier*] (ICLI)
FZMC Mulungu [*Zaire*] [*ICAO location identifier*] (ICLI)
FZMK Bulonge-Kigogo [*Zaire*] [*ICAO location identifier*] (ICLI)
FZMP Kimano II [*Zaire*] [*ICAO location identifier*] (ICLI)
FZMW Shabunda [*Zaire*] [*ICAO location identifier*] (ICLI)

FZNA........... Goma [*Zaire*] [*ICAO location identifier*] (ICLI)
FZNC........... Rutshuru [*Zaire*] [*ICAO location identifier*] (ICLI)
FZNF........... Lubero [*Zaire*] [*ICAO location identifier*] (ICLI)
FZNI........... Ishasha [*Zaire*] [*ICAO location identifier*] (ICLI)
FZNK........... Katanda Sur Rutshuru [*Zaire*] [*ICAO location identifier*] (ICLI)
FZNM........... Mweso [*Zaire*] [*ICAO location identifier*] (ICLI)
FZNP........... Beni [*Zaire*] [*ICAO location identifier*] (ICLI)
FZNR........... Ruindi [*Zaire*] [*ICAO location identifier*] (ICLI)
FZNT........... Mutwanga [*Zaire*] [*ICAO location identifier*] (ICLI)
FZOA........... Kindu [*Zaire*] [*ICAO location identifier*] (ICLI)
FZOB........... Tingi-Tingi [*Zaire*] [*ICAO location identifier*] (ICLI)
FZOC........... Kalima-Kamisuku [*Zaire*] [*ICAO location identifier*] (ICLI)
FZOD........... Kalima [*Zaire*] [*ICAO location identifier*] (ICLI)
FZOE........... Kampene [*Zaire*] [*ICAO location identifier*] (ICLI)
FZOF........... Kiapupe [*Zaire*] [*ICAO location identifier*] (ICLI)
FZOG........... Lulingu-Tshioka [*Zaire*] [*ICAO location identifier*] (ICLI)
FZOH........... Moga [*Zaire*] [*ICAO location identifier*] (ICLI)
FZOJ........... Obokote [*Zaire*] [*ICAO location identifier*] (ICLI)
FZOK........... Kasongo [*Zaire*] [*ICAO location identifier*] (ICLI)
FZOO........... Kailo [*Zaire*] [*ICAO location identifier*] (ICLI)
FZOP........... Punia [*Zaire*] [*ICAO location identifier*] (ICLI)
FZOS........... Kasese [*Zaire*] [*ICAO location identifier*] (ICLI)
FZP............ Fresnel Zone Plate (PDAA)
FZPB........... Kamituga [*Zaire*] [*ICAO location identifier*] (ICLI)
FZQA........... Lubumbashi/Luano [*Zaire*] [*ICAO location identifier*] (ICLI)
FZQC........... Pweto [*Zaire*] [*ICAO location identifier*] (ICLI)
FZQD........... Mulungwishi [*Zaire*] [*ICAO location identifier*] (ICLI)
FZQF........... Fungurume [*Zaire*] [*ICAO location identifier*] (ICLI)
FZQG........... Kasenga [*Zaire*] [*ICAO location identifier*] (ICLI)
FZQH........... Katwe [*Zaire*] [*ICAO location identifier*] (ICLI)
FZQI........... Kamatanda [*Zaire*] [*ICAO location identifier*] (ICLI)
FZQJ........... Mwadingusha [*Zaire*] [*ICAO location identifier*] (ICLI)
FZQM........... Kolwezi [*Zaire*] [*ICAO location identifier*] (ICLI)
FZQN........... Mutshatsha [*Zaire*] [*ICAO location identifier*] (ICLI)
FZQO........... Lubumbashi/Karavia [*Zaire*] [*ICAO location identifier*] (ICLI)
FZQP........... Kisenge [*Zaire*] [*ICAO location identifier*] (ICLI)
FZQU........... Lubudi [*Zaire*] [*ICAO location identifier*] (ICLI)
FZQV........... Mitwaba [*Zaire*] [*ICAO location identifier*] (ICLI)
FZQW........... Luishi [*Zaire*] [*ICAO location identifier*] (ICLI)
fzr............ freezer (SAUS)
FZR............ Freezing Rain (SAUS)
FZRA........... Freezing Rain [*Meteorology*]
FZRA........... Manono [*Zaire*] [*ICAO location identifier*] (ICLI)
FZRB........... Moba [*Zaire*] [*ICAO location identifier*] (ICLI)
FZRC........... Frozen Red Blood Cells [*Hematology*] (DAVI)
FZRC........... Mukoy [*Zaire*] [*ICAO location identifier*] (ICLI)
FZRD........... Kabombo [*Zaire*] [*ICAO location identifier*] (ICLI)
FZRF........... Kalemie [*Zaire*] [*ICAO location identifier*] (ICLI)
FZRG........... Kania-Sominka [*Zaire*] [*ICAO location identifier*] (ICLI)
FZRJ........... Pepa [*Zaire*] [*ICAO location identifier*] (ICLI)
FZRK........... Kansimba [*Zaire*] [*ICAO location identifier*] (ICLI)
FZRL........... Lusinga [*Zaire*] [*ICAO location identifier*] (ICLI)
FZRM........... Kabalo [*Zaire*] [*ICAO location identifier*] (ICLI)
FZRN........... Nyunzu [*Zaire*] [*ICAO location identifier*] (ICLI)
FZRO........... Luvua [*Zaire*] [*ICAO location identifier*] (ICLI)
FZRQ........... Kongolo [*Zaire*] [*ICAO location identifier*] (ICLI)
FZS............ Fellow of the Zoological Society [*British*]
FZS............ Frontozygomatic Suture [*Medicine*] (MELL)
FZSA........... Kamina-Base [*Zaire*] [*ICAO location identifier*] (ICLI)
FZSB........... Kamina-Ville [*Zaire*] [*ICAO location identifier*] (ICLI)
FZSC........... Songa [*Zaire*] [*ICAO location identifier*] (ICLI)
FZSD........... Sandoa [*Zaire*] [*ICAO location identifier*] (ICLI)
FZSE........... Kanene [*Zaire*] [*ICAO location identifier*] (ICLI)
FZSI........... Dilolo [*Zaire*] [*ICAO location identifier*] (ICLI)
FZ Silicon.... Floating-Zone Silicon (SAUS)
FZSJ........... Kasaji [*Zaire*] [*ICAO location identifier*] (ICLI)
FZSK........... Kapanga [*Zaire*] [*ICAO location identifier*] (ICLI)
FZSL........... Fellow of the Zoological Society, London [*British*] (ROG)
FZSScot....... Fellow of the Zoological Society of Scotland (SAUO)
FZSTO.......... Frozen Storage
FZT............ United States Fish and Wildlife Service, Laurel, MD [*OCLC symbol*] (OCLC)
FZTK........... Kaniama [*Zaire*] [*ICAO location identifier*] (ICLI)
FZTL........... Luena [*Zaire*] [*ICAO location identifier*] (ICLI)
FZTS........... Kasese/Kaniama [*Zaire*] [*ICAO location identifier*] (ICLI)
FZU............ St. Louis, MO [*Location identifier*] [*FAA*] (FAAL)
FZU............ United States Fish and Wildlife Service, Slidell, LA [*OCLC symbol*] (OCLC)
FZUA........... Kananga [*Zaire*] [*ICAO location identifier*] (ICLI)
FZUE........... Lubondaie [*Zaire*] [*ICAO location identifier*] (ICLI)
FZUF........... Kasongo [*Zaire*] [*ICAO location identifier*] (ICLI)
FZUG........... Luisa [*Zaire*] [*ICAO location identifier*] (ICLI)
FZUH........... Moma [*Zaire*] [*ICAO location identifier*] (ICLI)
FZUI........... Mboi [*Zaire*] [*ICAO location identifier*] (ICLI)
FZUJ........... Muambi [*Zaire*] [*ICAO location identifier*] (ICLI)
FZUK........... Tshikapa [*Zaire*] [*ICAO location identifier*] (ICLI)
FZUL........... Bulape [*Zaire*] [*ICAO location identifier*] (ICLI)
FZUM........... Mutoto [*Zaire*] [*ICAO location identifier*] (ICLI)
FZUN........... Luebo [*Zaire*] [*ICAO location identifier*] (ICLI)
FZUO........... Musese [*Zaire*] [*ICAO location identifier*] (ICLI)
FZUR........... Tshibala [*Zaire*] [*ICAO location identifier*] (ICLI)
FZUS........... Tshikaji [*Zaire*] [*ICAO location identifier*] (ICLI)
FZUT........... Katubwe [*Zaire*] [*ICAO location identifier*] (ICLI)
FZUU........... Lutshatsha [*Zaire*] [*ICAO location identifier*] (ICLI)
FZUV........... Kalonda [*Zaire*] [*ICAO location identifier*] (ICLI)
FZV............ Fraserfund Venture Capital Corp. [*Vancouver Stock Exchange symbol*]
FZV............ United States Fish and Wildlife Service, National Fishery Research Laboratory, La Crosse, WI [*OCLC symbol*] (OCLC)
FZVA........... Lodja [*Zaire*] [*ICAO location identifier*] (ICLI)
FZVC........... Kole Sur Lukenie [*Zaire*] [*ICAO location identifier*] (ICLI)
FZVD........... Dingele [*Zaire*] [*ICAO location identifier*] (ICLI)
FZVE........... Lomela [*Zaire*] [*ICAO location identifier*] (ICLI)
FZ-Verfahren... floating-zone melting (SAUS)
FZVF........... Kutusongo [*Zaire*] [*ICAO location identifier*] (ICLI)
FZVG........... Katako, Kombe [*Zaire*] [*ICAO location identifier*] (ICLI)
FZVH........... Shongamba [*Zaire*] [*ICAO location identifier*] (ICLI)
FZVI........... Lusambo [*Zaire*] [*ICAO location identifier*] (ICLI)
FZVJ........... Tshumbe [*Zaire*] [*ICAO location identifier*] (ICLI)
FZVK........... Lukombe-Batwa [*Zaire*] [*ICAO location identifier*] (ICLI)
FZVL........... Wasolo [*Zaire*] [*ICAO location identifier*] (ICLI)
FZVM........... Mweka [*Zaire*] [*ICAO location identifier*] (ICLI)
FZVN........... Wembo-Nyama [*Zaire*] [*ICAO location identifier*] (ICLI)
FZVO........... Bena-Dibele [*Zaire*] [*ICAO location identifier*] (ICLI)
FZVP........... Dikungu [*Zaire*] [*ICAO location identifier*] (ICLI)
FZVR........... Basongo [*Zaire*] [*ICAO location identifier*] (ICLI)
FZVS........... Ilebo [*Zaire*] [*ICAO location identifier*] (ICLI)
FZVT........... Dekese [*Zaire*] [*ICAO location identifier*] (ICLI)
FZVU........... Idumbe [*Zaire*] [*ICAO location identifier*] (ICLI)
FZW............ United States Fish and Wildlife Service, Denver, CO [*OCLC symbol*] (OCLC)
FZWA........... Mbuji-Mayi [*Zaire*] [*ICAO location identifier*] (ICLI)
FZWB........... Bibanga [*Zaire*] [*ICAO location identifier*] (ICLI)
FZWC........... Gandajika [*Zaire*] [*ICAO location identifier*] (ICLI)
FZWE........... Mwene-Ditu [*Zaire*] [*ICAO location identifier*] (ICLI)
FZWF........... Kipushia [*Zaire*] [*ICAO location identifier*] (ICLI)
FZWI........... Kashia [*Zaire*] [*ICAO location identifier*] (ICLI)
FZWR........... Kisengwa [*Zaire*] [*ICAO location identifier*] (ICLI)
FZWS........... Lubao [*Zaire*] [*ICAO location identifier*] (ICLI)
FZWT........... Kabinda/Tunta [*Zaire*] [*ICAO location identifier*] (ICLI)
FZX............ Columbia National Fisheries Research Laboratory, Columbia, MO [*OCLC symbol*] (OCLC)
FZY............ Federation of Zionist Youth (SAUO)
FZY............ United States Fish and Wildlife Service, Portland, OR [*OCLC symbol*] (OCLC)
FZZ............ United States Fish and Wildlife Service, Atlanta, GA [*OCLC symbol*] (OCLC)
FZZA........... Zaire Fir [*Zaire*] [*ICAO location identifier*] (ICLI)

G
By Acronym

g ..... acceleration due to gravity (SAUS)
G ..... Acceleration Force (DMAA)
g ..... Acceleration of Free Fall [*Symbol*]
G ..... Acceleration of Gravity Force (PIPO)
g ..... Acoustical Conductance (SAUS)
G ..... Air Force Training Category [*12 training periods and zero days active duty training per year*]
G ..... Application for Writ of Error Granted [*Legal term*] (DLA)
G ..... Chicago [*Branch in the Federal Reserve regional banking system*] (BARN)
G ..... Ciba-Geigy AG [*Switzerland*] [*Research code symbol*]
g ..... Conductance (VLIE)
G ..... Conductance [*Symbol*] [*IUPAC*]
G ..... Deflection Factor (VLIE)
G ..... Dividends and Earnings in Canadian Dollars [*Investment term*] (DFIT)
G ..... Federal Republic of Germany [*IYRU nationality code*] (IYR)
G ..... Fire Control [*JETDS nomenclature*]
G ..... Force [*Pull of gravity*] (STED)
G ..... Gage (IAA)
G ..... Gain
G ..... Gale [*Meteorology*]
G ..... Gale's English Exchequer Reports [*A publication*] (DLA)
G ..... Galliot [*Ship's rigging*] (ROG)
g ..... Gallon(s) (ODA)
G ..... Gallop [*Cardiology*] (DAVI)
G ..... Gambia [*Country in West Africa*] (ROG)
G ..... Game
G ..... Games Played [*Sports statistics*]
G ..... Gamma
G ..... Gamut [*Music*] (ROG)
G ..... Gandulphus [*Flourished, 1160-85*] [*Authority cited in pre-1607 legal work*] (DSA)
G ..... Ganglion [*Medicine*]
G ..... Ganz [*White Blot*] [*Rorschach*] [*Psychology*]
G ..... Gaon (BJA)
G ..... Gap in Cell Cycle [*Cytology*]
G ..... Garage
G ..... Gas (STED)
G ..... Gas Oil
G ..... Gas Shutoff [*NFPA pre-fire planning symbol*] (NFPA)
g ..... Gastralia [*Osteology*]
G ..... Gastrin [*Biochemistry*]
G ..... Gastrulation (MELL)
g ..... Gate (IDOE)
G ..... Gate [*Electronics*]
G ..... Gauche [*Left*] [*French*]
g ..... Gauche [*Chemical conformation*]
G ..... Gauge [*Of needle*] (STED)
g ..... Gauge (WDMC)
g ..... Gauss (ABAC)
G ..... Gauss [*Unit of magnetic flux density*] [*Preferred unit is T, Telsa*]
G ..... Gear (AAG)
G ..... Ge'ez (BJA)
G ..... Gelaendegaengig [*Having cross-country mobility*] [*German military - World War II*]
G ..... Gelding [*Thoroughbred racing*]
g ..... Gemeisamer Faktor [*General Factor*] [*Rorschach*] [*Psychology*]
G ..... Gemini Airline [*British*]
g ..... Gender (MELL)
G ..... Gender
G ..... General Ability (DIPS)
G ..... General Admission (NTIO)
G ..... General Audiences [*All ages admitted*] [*Movie rating*]
G ..... General Duties [*Ranking title*] [*British Women's Royal Naval Service*]
G ..... General Exhibition (ODA)
G ..... General Factor (ADA)
G ..... General Intelligence
G ..... Generalist [*Ecology*]
G ..... Generalized Feeder [*Ichthyology*]
G ..... General List [*Navy*] [*British*]
G ..... Generally Labeled [*Radioactive compounds*]
G ..... General Procedures
G ..... General-Purpose Freight Container (DCTA)
G ..... General Staff Branch [*Army*] [*British*]
G ..... Generate (VLIE)
G ..... Generating Item [*Military*]
g ..... Generator (IDOE)
G ..... Generators, Power [*JETDS nomenclature*] [*Military*] (CET)
G ..... Genitive [*Case*] [*Grammar*]
g ..... Genome [*Genetics*]
G ..... Geography [*Secondary school course*] [*British*]
G ..... Geometric Efficiency (DMAA)
G ..... Geometry (SAUS)
G ..... Geonic (BJA)
G ..... George [*Phonetic alphabet*] [*Royal Navy*] [*World War I*] [*Pre-World War II*] [*World War II*] (DSUE)
G ..... George (King of England) (DLA)
G ..... Georgia State Library, Atlanta, GA [*Library symbol*] [*Library of Congress*] (LCLS)
G ..... Georgics [*of Vergil*] [*Classical studies*] (OCD)
G ..... Gericht [*Court*] [*German*] (ILCA)
G ..... German [*or Germanic*]
G ..... Germanischer Lloyd [*Shipping*] (ROG)
G ..... Germany (WDAA)
G ..... Gerontology [*American Occupational Therapy Association*]
G ..... Geschichte [*History*] [*German*] (ILCA)
G ..... Gesetz [*Law*] [*German*] (ILCA)
G ..... Ghost
G ..... Giant Slalom [*In Olympics event, Super-G*]
G ..... Gibbs Energy [*Symbol*] [*IUPAC*]
G ..... Gibbs Free Energy (STED)
G ..... Gibbs Function [*Preferred term is Gibbs Energy*]
G ..... Giemsa [*Method*] [*Chromosome stain*]
g ..... GIF [*Graphics Interchange Format*] [*Computer science*] [*Telecommunications*]
G ..... Gift Tax (DLA)
G ..... Giga [*A prefix meaning multiplied by* 10^9] [*SI symbol*]
G ..... Gigabyte
G ..... Gilbert [*A unit of magnetomotive force*]
G ..... Gilbertus [*Flourished, 13th century*] [*Authority cited in pre-1607 legal work*] (DSA)
G ..... Gillette Co. [*NYSE symbol*] (SAG)
G ..... Gilt [*Bookbinding*]
G ..... Gingiva (DMAA)
G ..... Gingival [*Dentistry*]
G ..... Girder [*Technical drawings*]
G ..... Girls School [*British*]
g ..... Girth [*Construction term*] (MIST)
G ..... Givenchy [*Couturier*]
G ..... GKSS (SAUS)
G ..... Glabella [*Medicine*] (DMAA)
G ..... Gladstonian [*Politics, 1868-1894*] [*British*] (ROG)
G ..... Gland (MELL)
G ..... Glasgow [*Postcode*] (ODBW)
G ..... Glass (AAG)
G ..... Gleason's Score
G ..... Glider
G ..... Gliding (SAUS)
G ..... Glimpse [*Optics*]
G ..... Globular [*Referring to proteins*] [*Biochemistry*] (DAVI)
G ..... Globulin
G ..... Glossy Photographic Prints of Source
G ..... Glucinium [*Also, Gl*] [*Old name for chemical element beryllium*]
G ..... Glucose [*Also, Glc, GLUC*] [*A sugar*]
g ..... Gluon (ODA)
G ..... Glycine [*One-letter symbol; see Gly*] [*An amino acid*]
G ..... Glycogen [*Biochemistry*]
G ..... Glycolic Acid (SAUS)
g ..... Go [*to*] [*Computer science*] [*Telecommunications*]
G ..... Goal [*A position in lacrosse, soccer, hockey, etc.*]
G ..... Goalkeeper [*Sports*] (BARN)
G ..... Goals (SHCU)
G ..... Goat [*Veterinary medicine*]
G ..... Gofredus de Trano [*Deceased, 1245*] [*Authority cited in pre-1607 legal work*] (DSA)
G ..... Gold
G ..... Goldcorp Investments Ltd. [*Toronto Stock Exchange symbol*]
G ..... Gold Inlay [*Dentistry*]
G ..... Golf [*Phonetic alphabet*] [*International*] (DSUE)
G ..... Gonidial [*With reference to colonies of bacteria*]
g ..... Good (WDMC)
G ..... Good [*Condition*] [*Antiquarian book trade, numismatics, etc.*]

G........ Good Skiing Conditions
G........ Goose (STED)
g........ G-Orbital (MEC)
G........ Gourde [*Monetary unit*] [*Haiti*]
G........ Government
G........ Government Expenditure [*Economics*]
G........ Government Purchases
G........ Government Spending (SAUS)
G........ Grade (ADA)
G........ Grafenberg Spot [*Medicine*] (DMAA)
g........ Graft (Polymer) [*Organic chemistry*]
G........ Grain
g........ grain capacity (SAUS)
g........ grain cubic capacity (SAUS)
g........ grain space (SAUS)
G........ Gram [*Stain*] (STED)
g........ Gram
G........ Grammar School [*British*]
g........ grammes (SAUS)
g%........ Gram Percent [*Meaning grams per deciliter*] [*Measurement*] (DAVI)
G........ Grand [*Slang term for 1,000 dollars*]
G........ Grand-Orgue [*Great Organ*] [*Music*]
G........ Granite
G........ Granted [*Legal term*] (ILCA)
G........ Granular
G........ Granulocyte (MELL)
G........ Graph (OA)
G........ Graphed [*Quilting*]
G........ Graphics (VLIE)
G........ Graphite
G........ Grass [*Botany*]
g........ Grav (ODA)
G........ Gravel
G........ Gravida [*Obstetrics*]
G........ Gravitational Constant [*or Newtonian Constant*] [*Physics*] (DAVI)
g........ Gravitational Constant (MELL)
g........ Gravity (IDOE)
G........ Gravity [*or the force or acceleration produced by it*]
g........ Great (GEAB)
G........ Great
G........ Great Lakes Aircraft Corp. (SAUO)
G........ Greek
G........ Green
G........ Greenhouse Plant [*Botany*]
G........ Green Line (SAUS)
G........ Greenwich Meridian [*Upper branch*]
g........ Greenwich Meridian [*Lower branch*]
G........ Greenwich Time
G........ Gregarious [*Biology*]
G........ Gregorowski's Reports of the High Court [*A publication*] (DLA)
g........ Grey (ODA)
G........ Greyhound Corp. (SAUO)
g........ Grid (IDOE)
G........ Grid [*Electronics*]
G........ Grin (SAUS)
G........ Grinding (SAUS)
G........ Grog [*i.e., entitled to draw a daily rum ration and doing so*] [*See also, T, UA*] [*Obsolete*] [*Navy*] [*British*]
G........ Grondwet [*Constitution*] [*Netherlands*] (ILCA)
G........ Gros [*Large*] [*French*]
G........ Groschen [*Monetary unit*] [*Austria*]
G........ Gross [*Leukemia antigen*] [*Immunochemistry*]
G........ Groszy [*Monetary unit*] [*Poland*]
G........ Ground
G........ Ground Control [*Aviation*] (DA)
G........ Grounded [*Electronics*]
G........ Ground Foraging [*Ecology*]
G........ Ground, General [*JETDS nomenclature*]
G........ Ground Swell
g........ Group (MELL)
G........ Group
G........ Growth [*Business term*]
G........ Grumman American Aviation [*ICAO aircraft manufacturer identifier*] (ICAO)
g........ grunting (SAUS)
G........ Gruppenfuehrer [*Squad Leader*] [*German military - World War II*]
G........ Guanidine [*Biochemistry*] (DAVI)
G........ Guanine [*Also, Gua*] [*Biochemistry*]
G........ Guanosine [*One-letter symbol; see Guo*]
G........ Guarani [*Monetary unit*] [*Paraguay*]
G........ Guard [*Position in football, basketball, etc.*]
G........ Guardian
G........ Guarnerius [*Irnerius*] [*Flourished, 1113-18*] [*Authority cited in pre-1607 legal work*] (DSA)
G........ Gucci [*Designer*]
G........ Guide
G........ Guided Tour [*On a bus*] [*British*]
G........ Guido de Baysio [*Deceased, 1313*] [*Authority cited in pre-1607 legal work*] (DSA)
G........ Guido de Suzaria [*Deceased, 1293*] [*Authority cited in pre-1607 legal work*] (DSA)
G........ Guilder [*Modification of gulden*] [*Monetary unit*] [*Netherlands*]
G........ Guillelmus de Tocco [*Authority cited in pre-1607 legal work*] (DSA)
G........ Guilty
G........ Guinea [*Monetary unit*] [*Obsolete*] [*British*]
G........ Guirsh [*Monetary unit*] [*Saudi Arabia*]
G........ Guitar [*Music*]
g........ Guitar
G........ Guizzardinus [*Deceased, 1222*] [*Authority cited in pre-1607 legal work*] (DSA)
G........ Gulden [*Monetary unit*] [*Netherlands*]
G........ Gules [*Heraldry*]
G........ Gulf [*Maps and charts*]
G........ Gun
g........ Gunnery [*Navy*] [*British*]
G........ Guttae [*Drops of liquid*] [*Pharmacy*] (CPH)
G........ Gutter Ball [*Bowling*]
G........ Gynecology (STED)
G........ Gynoecium [*Botany*]
G........ Gyromagnetic Ratio
G........ Halls (Noncommercial) [*Public-performance tariff class*] [*British*]
G........ HMV [*His Master's Voice*], Gramophone Co. [*Record label*] [*Great Britain, Europe, etc.*]
G........ Immunoglobulin G (STED)
G........ Longitude
G........ Obstetrics and Gynaecology [*Medical Officer designation*] [*British*]
G........ Permanently Grounded [*Aircraft classification letter*]
G........ Promoted to Glory [*Salvation Army*]
G........ Ranger [*Army skill qualification identifier*] (INF)
G........ Reports of the High Court of Griqualand [*1882-1910*] [*South Africa*] [*A publication*] (DLA)
G........ Shear Modulus [*Symbol*] [*IUPAC*]
G........ Shunt Conductance [*Communications term*] (DCT)
g........ Statistical Weight [*Symbol*] [*IUPAC*]
G........ Surface Attack [*Missile mission symbol*]
G........ Symbol for Storm [*Meteorology*] (ODA)
G........ Telegraph [*JETDS nomenclature*]
G........ Teletype [*JETDS nomenclature*]
G........ Unit of Acceleration [*Military*]
G........ Unit of Force of Acceleration (STED)
G........ Unit of Gravitational Force (NASA)
G........ Weight [*Symbol*] [*IUPAC*]
G........ Workout from Starting Gate [*Horse racing*]
g........ Degeneracy (ODA)
g........ General (ODA)
G........ Guernsey (ODA)
g0........ normal gravity acceleration at sea-level (SAUS)
G1........ General Staff, Personnel (SAUS)
G1........ Government Current Expenditure [*Economics*]
G-1........ Gulfstream-1 (SAUS)
G-1........ Personnel Section [*of an Army or Marine Corps division general staff, or Marine brigade or aircraft wing general staff; also, the officer in charge of this section*]
G1........ Primigravida [*Medicine*] (EDAA)
G^1........ Staff Officer for Personnel [*Army*] [*Marine Corps*] (DOMA)
G-1........ US Army General Staff level, Assistant Chief of Staff for Personnel (CARL)
G1P........ Glucose-1-phosphate [*Biochemistry*]
G-2........ Army Intelligence Network [*Guatemala*] (BUAC)
G-2........ Army Intelligence Unit [*Panama*] (BUAC)
G2........ General Staff, Intelligence & Security (SAUS)
G2........ Government Capital Expenditure [*Economics*]
G-2........ Group of Two (BUAC)
G-2........ Military Intelligence Section [*of an Army or Marine Corps division general staff, or Marine brigade or aircraft wing general staff; also, the officer in charge of this section*]
G2........ Secundigravida [*Medicine*] (EDAA)
G^2........ Staff Officer for Intelligence [*Army*] [*Marine Corps*] (DOMA)
G-2........ US Army General Staff level, Assistant Chief of Staff for Intelligence (CARL)
G2B........ Government-to-Business (VLIE)
G2C........ Government-to-Citizen (VLIE)
G2S........ Good Two Sides (SAUS)
G2W........ Glaube in der 2. Welt [*Faith in the Second World - FSW*] [*An association*] [*Switzerland*] (EAIO)
G3........ Gadolinium, Gallium, Garnet
G3........ General Staff, Operations & Training (SAUS)
G3........ [*The*] Godfather Part III [*Motion picture*]
G-3........ Group of Three (BUAC)
G-3........ Operations and Training Section [*of an Army or Marine Corps division general staff or Marine brigade or aircraft wing general staff; also, the officer in charge of this section*]
G^3........ Staff Officer for Operations [*Army*] [*Marine Corps*] (DOMA)
G3........ Tertigravida [*Medicine*] (EDAA)
G-3........ Treaty of the Group of Three among the United States of Mexico, the Republic of Colombia, and the Republic of Venezuela
G3 FAX........ Group 3 Facsimile (SAUS)
G3OS........ Global Observing Systems of GCOS, GOOS and GTOS (SAUO)
G3OS........ Sponsors Group for the Global Observing Systems (SAUO)
G-3-P........ Glyceraldehyde-3-Phosphate [*Biochemistry*] (DAVI)
G-3-P........ Glycerol-3-Phosphate (SAUS)
G3PD........ Glyceraldehyde 3-P Dehydrogenase (SAUS)
G4........ Logistics Officer/Section (SAUO)
G-4........ Logistics Section [*of an Army or Marine Corps division general staff, or Marine brigade or aircraft wing general staff; also, the officer in charge of this section*]
G^4........ Staff Officer for Supply/Logistics [*Army*] [*Marine Corps*] (DOMA)
G-5........ Civil Affairs Section [*of an Army division or brigade general staff; the officer in charge of this section*]
G5........ General Staff, Civil/Military Co-operation (SAUS)

G5............... Group of Five [*United States, Japan, West Germany, France, and Britain*]
G⁵............... Staff Officer for Planning [*Army*] [*Marine Corps*] (DOMA)
G-6............... Group of Six (BUAC)
G6P............... Glucose-6-Phosphate (LDT)
G-6-Pase..... Glucose-6-Phosphatase [*Organic chemistry*] (DAVI)
G6PD............ Glucose-6-phosphate Dehydrogenase [*Also, GPD, G6PDH*] [*An enzyme*]
G6PD............ Glucose-6-Phosphate Dehydrogenase Deficiency [*Inherited enzyme deficiency*] [*Medicine*] (TAD)
G6PDA.......... Glucose-6-Phosphate Dehydrogenase, Varient A (STED)
G-6-PDH...... Gluclose-6-Phosphate Dehydrogenase (SAUS)
G6PDH.......... Glucose-6-phosphate Dehydrogenase [*Also, GPD, G6PD*] [*An enzyme*]
G-6-PDHA.... Glucose-6-Phosphate Dehydrogenase Enzyme Variant A [*Organic chemistry*] (DAVI)
G-7............... Group of Seven [*United States, Japan, West Germany, France, Britain, Italy, and Canada*]
G7............... Grumpy Seven [*Facetious translation for the Group of Seven: United States, Japan West Germany, France, Britain, Italy, and Canada*] (ECON)
G7 ENRM project... G7 Environment and Natural Resources Management Project (SAUS)
G7 GELOS.... G7 Global Environmental Information Locator Service (SAUS)
G-8............... Group of Eight [*Nations*] (EERA)
G-9............... Group of Nine (BUAC)
G10............... Group of Ten [*United States, Japan, West Germany, France, Britain, Italy, Canada, Sweden, Holland, Belgium, and Switzerland*] [*There are actually eleven member countries*]
G-11............. Gulfstream 11 [*Shuttle Training Aircraft*] (NAKS)
G-15............. Group of Fifteen (SAUS)
G18 IYRA..... Geary 18 International Yacht Racing Association (EA)
G24............... Group of 24 [*A clearinghouse for monetary aid to Eastern Europe*] (ECON)
G30............... Group of Thirty [*Financial think-tank*] (ECON)
G-33............. Group of Thirty-Three (BUAC)
G-77............. Group of 77 [*Coalition of environmentalists representing developing countries*]
G77/China.... Group of 77 and China (SAUO)
G 115........... Ginseng Standard Extract [*Medicine*] (EDAA)
G 5668......... Prethecamide [*Medicine*] (EDAA)
G 24480....... Diazinon [*Medicine*] (EDAA)
G 25766....... Clorindione [*Medicine*] (EDAA)
G/A............... Air General Staff (SAUO)
Ga............... Airway Conductance [*Medicine*] (DAVI)
GA............... Atlanta Public Library, Atlanta, GA [*Library symbol*] [*Library of Congress*] (LCLS)
GA............... Decisions of General Appraisers [*United States*] [*A publication*] (DLA)
GA............... Gabon [*ANSI two-letter standard code*] (CNC)
GA............... Gage
GA............... Gain of Antenna (IEEE)
GA............... Galatians [*New Testament book*]
Ga............... Galatians [*New Testament book*]
GA............... Galea Aponeurotica (MELL)
Ga............... Galileo Number
GA............... Gallic
Ga............... Gallium [*Chemical element*]
GA............... Galvanizers Association [*British*] (EAIO)
GA............... Gamblers Anonymous (EA)
GA............... Games Abroad [*Baseball*]
GA............... Games Ahead [*Baseball*]
GA............... Games Away [*Sports*] (GOBB)
GA............... Gamma Alpha (EA)
Ga............... Gandulphus [*Flourished, 1160-85*] [*Authority cited in pre-1607 legal work*] (DSA)
GA............... Gardens for All [*Later, National Association for Gardening*] (EA)
GA............... Garin Arava (EA)
GA............... Garrison Adjutant [*Military*] [*British*]
GA............... Garrison Artillery [*British military*] (DMA)
GA............... Garuda Indonesia [*Airline flight code*] (ODBW)
GA............... Garuda Indonesian Airways [*ICAO designator*] (AD)
GA............... Gas Amplification
GA............... Gas Analysis (NRCH)
GA............... Gasoline Stowage and Fuel System Man [*Navy*]
GA............... Gas or Air [*Transportation*]
GA............... Gastric Acid (MELL)
GA............... Gastric Analysis
GA............... Gastric Antrum [*Medicine*] (DMAA)
GA............... Gate
GA............... Gated Attenuation [*Computer science*]
GA............... Gauge (AAG)
ga............... Gauge [*of needles*] [*Measurement*] (DAVI)
GA............... Gauge Man [*Navy*]
GA............... Gear Assembly
GA............... Gelbray Association [*Later, GI*] (EA)
GA............... Gemini Agena [*NASA*] (KSC)
GA............... Gemmological Association [*British*] (DBA)
GA............... Gemmological Association of Great Britain (BUAC)
GA............... General Accident [*British insurance organization*]
GA............... General Accounting (AAG)
GA............... General Activities (ADA)
GA............... General Adjutant (SAUO)
GA............... General Agent [*Insurance*]
GA............... General Aircraft Ltd.
GA............... General Alert (NATG)
GA............... General American [*A type of spoken American English*] (BARN)
GA............... General Anesthesia [*Medicine*]
GA............... General Appearance [*On physical examination*] [*Medicine*] (DAVI)
GA............... General Appraisers' Decisions [*A publication*] (DLA)
GA............... General Arrangement (MCD)
GA............... General Assembly
GA............... General Assembly of the United Nations (BUAC)
GA............... General Assignment (ADA)
GA............... General Assistance [*A form of public charity*]
GA............... General Atomic Corp. (SAUO)
GA............... General Atomic Europe (SAUO)
GA............... General Atomics [*Division of General Dynamics Corp.*]
GA............... General Atomics Corporation
GA............... General Attention [*Medicine*]
GA............... General Automation, Inc. [*AMEX symbol*]
GA............... General Availability (SAUO)
GA............... General Average [*Insurance*]
GA............... General Avia SpA [*Italy*] [*ICAO aircraft manufacturer identifier*] (ICAO)
GA............... General Aviation (EA)
GA............... General of the Air Force (SAUO)
GA............... General of the Army (AABC)
GA............... Genetic Algorithm [*Computer science*]
GA............... Genl Automation [*NYSE symbol*] (TTSB)
GA............... Genome Analysis (MELL)
GA............... Gentisic Acid [*Analgesic drug*]
GA............... Geographic access (SAUS)
GA............... Geographical Association [*British*] (DBA)
GA............... Geographic Analysis (SAUO)
GA............... Geological Abstracts
GA............... Geological Association (SAUO)
GA............... Geologic Associates (EFIS)
GA............... Geologists' Association [*British*]
GA............... Geometrical Acoustics
GA............... Georgia [*Postal code*] (AFM)
Ga............... Georgia (ODBW)
GA............... Georgia Railroad Co. [*AAR code*]
GA............... Georgia Supreme Court Reports [*A publication*] (DLA)
GA............... Geriatric Assessment (MELL)
GA............... Geriatric Authority (DICI)
GA............... German Army (NATG)
GA............... Germanium Alloy (IAA)
GA............... Gesammelte Abhandlungen [*A publication*] (BJA)
GA............... Gesellschaft fuer Arzneipflanzenforschung [*Society for Medicinal Plant Research*] (EA)
GA............... Gestational Age [*Medicine*]
GA............... Getting Along [*Psychological testing*]
GA............... Giant Axon [*Neurology*]
GA............... Gibberellic Acid [*Also, GA_3*] [*Plant growth hormone*]
GA............... Giftware Association (BUAC)
Ga............... Gigayear
GA............... Gimbal Angle (KSC)
GA............... Gimbal Assembly
GA............... Ginger Ale [*Medicine*] (EDAA)
ga............... Ginger Ale
GA............... Gingivoaxial [*Dentistry*]
GA............... Gland Anlage
GA............... Glen Alden (SAUS)
GA............... Glen Alden Corporation (SAUO)
GA............... Glide Angle [*Aviation*]
G/A............... Gliding Angle (SAUS)
GA............... Global Address
GA............... Global Advisor
GA............... Global Assessment [*Psychiatric evaluation test*]
GA............... Global Auto [*Computer science*]
G/A............... Globulin/Albumin [*Ratio*] [*Medicine*] (DMAA)
GA............... Glucoamylase [*An enzyme*]
GA............... Glucose/Acetone [*Biochemistry*] (DAVI)
GA............... Glucuronic Acid [*Also, GlcUA*] [*Biochemistry*]
GA............... Glutamic Acid [*See also Glu*] [*An amino acid*]
GA............... Glutamin Acid (SAUS)
GA............... Glutaraldehyde [*Biochemistry*]
GA............... Glyoxylic Acid [*Biochemistry*] (OA)
GA............... Gnomes Anonymous [*New Malden, Surrey, England*] (EA)
GA............... Go Ahead [*or resume sending*] [*Communications*]
GA............... Go Ahead Signal (SAUS)
GA............... Goal Attack [*Netball*]
GA............... Goals Against [*Hockey*]
GA............... Go Around (MCD)
GA............... Golfing Association (SAUO)
GA............... Golgi Apparatus [*Medicine*] (DMAA)
GA............... Golgi Axons (SAUS)
GA............... Good Afternoon [*Amateur radio shorthand*] (WDAA)
GA............... Gouty Arthritis (MELL)
GA............... Government Actuary [*Australia*]
GA............... Government Agency (AAG)
GA............... Governmental Affairs (DLA)
GA............... Government Architect (ADA)
GA............... Grade Age [*Education*]
GA............... Gradient Angle (PIPO)
GA............... Graduate Assistant
GA............... Graduate in Agriculture
G/A............... Grains per Anther [*Botany*]
GA............... Gramicidin A [*Antibiotic*]

GA ..... Grand Admiral [*Freemasonry*] (ROG)
GA ..... Grand Almoner [*Freemasonry*]
GA ..... Grand Architect [*Freemasonry*]
GA ..... Grand Award [*Record label*]
GA ..... Grands Arrets de la Jurisprudence Civile [*A publication*] (ILCA)
GA ..... Grant Agreement (COE)
GA ..... Grant Aid [*Military*] (AFM)
GA ..... Grant Application [*Job Training and Partnership Act*] (OICC)
GA ..... Grant Award [*Job Training and Partnership Act*] (OICC)
GA ..... Granulocyte Adherence (DB)
Ga ..... Granulocyte Agglutination (STED)
GA ..... Granulocyte Agglutination [*Hematology*]
GA ..... Granuloma Annulare [*Medicine*] (EDAA)
GA ..... Granulomatous Angiitis [*Medicine*]
GA ..... Graphic Acquisition (SAUS)
GA ..... Graphic Adapter (ELAL)
GA ..... Graphic Addition (SAUS)
GA ..... Graphic Ammeter (MSA)
GA ..... Graphic Artists Guild (EA)
GA ..... Graphics and Administration [*Military*] (GFGA)
G-A ..... Graphite-Adhesive (SAUS)
GA ..... Grapple Adapter [*Nuclear energy*] (NRCH)
GA ..... Grate Area (SAUS)
GA ..... Great Artists [*A publication*]
GA ..... Great Attractor [*Galactic science*]
GA ..... Green Alliance (BUAC)
GA ..... Green Alliance Senate - New South Wales [*Political party*] [*Australia*]
GA ..... Green Alternatives (Austria) [*Political party*] (PSAP)
GA ..... Green Arrow
GA ..... Greenhouse Annual [*Horticulture*] (ROG)
GA ..... Greening Australia (EERA)
GA ..... Gross Asset [*Business term*]
GA ..... Gross Average (SAUS)
G/A ..... Ground/Air (SAUS)
GA ..... Ground Alert (SAUS)
GA ..... Ground Attack [*Military*]
GA ..... Ground Attacker Aircraft
G/A ..... Ground to Air (PIPO)
G-A ..... Ground-to-Air [*Communications, weapons*] (MSA)
GA ..... Group Addressing (SAUS)
GA ..... Group Advance (SAUS)
GA ..... Group Adviser (SAUO)
GA ..... Group Army (MILB)
GA ..... Group Atmosphere (PDAA)
GA ..... Guajaretic Acid (SAUS)
GA ..... Guanosine Triphosphatase Activating [*Biochemistry*]
GA ..... Guard Army (SAUS)
GA ..... Guardian Angels (EA)
GA ..... Guardian Association (EA)
GA ..... Guessed Average
GA ..... Guidance Amplifier (IAA)
GA ..... Guidance Assembly (ACAE)
GA ..... Gun Assembly (SAUS)
GA ..... Gunlayer Armourer [*British military*] (DMA)
GA ..... Gut-Associated [*Medicine*]
GA ..... Gyn Anamnese (SAUS)
GA ..... Gypsum Association (EA)
GA ..... Gyrate Atrophy [*Medicine*]
GA ..... Gyro Assembly (NASA)
GA ..... L-Glutamic [*acid*] and L-Alanine [*Copolymer*]
GA ..... Tabun [*Nerve gas*] [*Army symbol*]
GA ..... Gaelic Athletic (Club) (ODA)
GA ..... Graphic Arts (ODA)
GA_3 ..... Gibberellin A_3[*Also, GA*] [*Plant growth hormone*]
GA3PD ..... Glyceraldehyde-3-Phosphate Dehydrogenase (SAUS)
GAA ..... Atlanta College of Art Library, Atlanta, GA [*OCLC symbol*] (OCLC)
GAA ..... Atlanta School of Art, Atlanta, GA [*Library symbol*] [*Library of Congress*] (LCLS)
GAA ..... Business Express [*ICAO designator*] (FAAC)
GAA ..... Gaelic Athletic Association
GAA ..... Gaelic Athletic Association of Australia
GAA ..... Gain Adjuster Adapter
GAA ..... Gale Auto Annual [*A publication*]
GaA ..... Gallium Arsenide [*Semiconductor*]
GAA ..... Gamblers Anonymous Association (SAUO)
GAA ..... Gastroenterology Administration Assembly (ADWA)
GAA ..... Gay AA (EA)
GAA ..... Gay Activists' Alliance [*Defunct*]
GAA ..... General Account of Advances
GAA ..... General Agency Agreement [*Navy*] (AABC)
GAA ..... General Aviation Authority [*FAA*] (TAG)
GAA ..... Geographic Areas of Affinity (TAD)
GAA ..... Georgia Apartment Association (SRA)
GaA ..... Georgia Appeals Reports [*A publication*] (DLA)
GAA ..... German Agro Action (SAUO)
GAA ..... Gift Association of America (EA)
GAA ..... Girls Athletic Association [*Local school affiliates of National Girls Athletic Association*] [*Defunct*]
GAA ..... Glacial Acrylic Acid [*Organic chemistry*]
GAA ..... Global Aircraft Appraisals (SAUO)
GAA ..... Gospel and the Age Series [*A publication*]
GAA ..... Gossypol Acetic Acid (DMAA)
GAA ..... Government Administrators Association (SRA)
GAA ..... Government Advertising Agency [*New South Wales, Australia*]
GAA ..... Grand National Resources, Inc. [*Vancouver Stock Exchange symbol*]
GAA ..... Grandparents Association of America (EA)
GAA ..... Grants for Aboriginal Advancement [*Australia*]
GAA ..... Graphic Arts Association (SRA)
GAA ..... Gravure Association of America (EA)
GAA ..... Grease, Artillery/Automotive [*Military*] (INF)
GAA ..... Greehouse Action Australia (SAUS)
GAA ..... Greek Agrochemical Association (SAUS)
GAA ..... Greenhouse Action Australia (EERA)
GAA ..... Greening Australia Action
GAA ..... Grenfell Association of America (EA)
GAA ..... Gross Average Audience [*Nielsen rating*] [*Television*] (WDMC)
GAA ..... Ground-Aided Acquisition
GAA ..... Ground-Air-Air (SAUS)
GAA ..... Ground Area Attainable
GAA ..... GTO [*Gran Torismo Omologato*] Association of America (EA)
GAA ..... Guanine Adenine Adenine [*A triplet of bases coding for the amino acid, glutamic acid*] (EES)
GAAA ..... General Aviation Activity and Avionics [*FAA*] (TAG)
GAAA ..... General Aviation Association Australia
GAAA ..... Greek Advertising Agencies Association (BUAC)
GAAAP ..... Gallerie Amrad African Art Publications (SAUS)
GAAB ..... Alston & Bird, Law Library, Atlanta, GA [*Library symbol*] [*Library of Congress*] (LCLS)
GAAB ..... Georgia & Alabama Division [*Federal Railroad Administration identification code*]
GAAB ..... Graphic Alphanumeric Attributes Block (SAUS)
GAAC ..... General Aviation Awareness Campaign (PIAV)
GAAC ..... German-American Academic Council (SAUS)
GAAC ..... German-American Advisory Council (SAUO)
GAAC ..... Government Accounting and Auditing Committee (SAUO)
GAAC ..... Graphic Arts Advertisers Council [*Later, GAAEC*]
GAAC ..... Graphics Arts Advisers Council (SAUS)
GA Admin Comp ..... Official Compilation of the Rules and Regulations of the State of Georgia [*A publication*] (DLA)
GAADV ..... Graphic Arts Association of the Delaware Valley (SAUO)
GAAE ..... Georgia Association of Alternative Educators (SAUO)
GAAE ..... Graphic Arts Association Executives [*Defunct*] (EA)
GAAEC ..... Graphic Arts Advertisers and Exhibitors Council [*Defunct*] (EA)
GAAEF ..... Grupo de Abogados Argentinos en el Exilio en Francia
GAAFOFY ..... Go Away and Find Out for Yourself (BB)
GAAFR ..... Governmental Accounting, Auditing and Financial Reporting (SAUO)
GAAG ..... Gross Actual Generation (SAUS)
GAAG ..... Guerrilla Art Action Group
GAAI ..... Atlanta Art Institute, Atlanta, GA [*Library symbol*] [*Library of Congress*] (LCLS)
GAAIASA ..... Georgia Association of American Industrial Arts Student Association (SAUO)
GaAIN ..... Gallium-Aluminum Nitride (ACAE)
GaAIAs ..... Gallium Aluminum Arsenide (SSD)
GAAM ..... Ghana Association for the Advancement of Mangement (BUAC)
GAAM ..... Guided Antiaircraft Missile [*Military*] (IAA)
GA&AW ..... GA/AW General Aviation and Aerial Work (SAUS)
GA & CS ..... Ground Acquisition and Command Station (MCD)
GA&ES ..... Georgia Architectural and Engineering Society (SAUO)
GA&L ..... General Aircraft and Leasing (SAUO)
GAAO ..... Ansongo [*Mali*] [*ICAO location identifier*] (ICLI)
GAAP ..... Gateway Army Ammunition Plant
GAAP ..... Generally Accepted Accounting Principles [*or Procedures*]
GAAP ..... Geological Analysis Aid Package (SAUS)
GAAP ..... German Army Assistance Plan (SAUO)
GAAP ..... Guided Anti-armor Artillery Projectile (SAUS)
GAAP ..... UNITA Cabinet for the Implementation of the Lusaka Protocol (SAUO)
GA App ..... Georgia Appeals Reports [*A publication*] (DLA)
Ga App ..... Georgia Court of Appeals Reports [*A publication*] (AAGC)
GA App (NS) ..... Georgia Appeals Reports [*A publication*] (DLA)
GAAR ..... General Anti-Avoidance Rule (FOTI)
GAAR ..... Graphic Attention Analysis Routine (SAUS)
GAARC ..... German-American Amateur Radio Club (SAUO)
GAARD ..... General Automation Automatic Recovery Device (IAA)
GAAREX ..... Global Atmospheric Aerosol Radiation Experiment (SAUO)
GAARS ..... Global Atmospheric and Aerosol Radiation Study
GAARS ..... Global Atmospheric and Aerosol Radiation Supply (SAUS)
GAART ..... Government Astronomy Administration Round Table
GaAs ..... Galliumarsenid (SAUS)
GaAs ..... Gallium Arsenide [*Semiconductor*] (IEEE)
GAAS ..... Generally Accepted Auditing Standards
GAAS ..... German Association for American Studies (EAIO)
GAAS ..... Goldberg Anorectic Attitude Scale [*Medicine*] (DMAA)
GAAS ..... Ground Airborne Avionics System (SAUS)
GAAS ..... Guangdong Academy of Agricultural Sciences [*China*] (BUAC)
GAAS ..... Guangxi Academy of Agricultural Sciences [*China*] (BUAC)
GAAS ..... Gun-bore Alignment & Analysis System (SAUS)
GAASD ..... Gallium Arsenide [*Phosphide Semiconductor*]
GAASEET ..... Gallium Arsenide Field Effect Transistor (ACAE)
GaAs FET ..... Gallium Arsenide Field-Effect Transistor [*Electronics*] (LAIN)
GaAsP ..... Gallium Arsenide Phosphide [*Semiconductor*] (IEEE)
GAASS ..... Government Agency Arbitrage and Swap System (MHDW)
GAAT ..... Glacial Acetic Acid Test (MELL)
GAAT ..... Gunner-Assisted Autotracking
GAATS ..... Gander Automated (or Automatic) Air Traffic System (SAUO)
GAATV ..... Gemini Atlas/Agena Target Vehicle [*NASA*] (MCD)
GAAWD ..... Gunnery and Anti-Aircraft Warfare Division (SAUO)
GAB ..... Gabbs [*Nevada*] [*Seismograph station code, US Geological Survey*] [*Closed*] (SEIS)

GAB .... Gabbs, NV [*Location identifier*] [*FAA*] (FAAL)
GAB .... Gabbs Resources Ltd. [*Vancouver Stock Exchange symbol*]
GAB .... Gabelli Equity Trust, Inc. [*NYSE symbol*] (SPSG)
GAB .... Gable
GAB .... Gabon [*ANSI three-letter standard code*] (CNC)
GAB .... Games and Amusement Board (SAUO)
GAB .... Gas Adapter Beam (SAUS)
GAB .... Gendall Air Ltd. [*Canada*] [*ICAO designator*] (FAAC)
GAB .... General Adjustment Bureau [*Insurance*]
GAB .... General Agreements to Borrow [*International Monetary Fund*] (EBF)
GAB .... General Agreement to Borrow [*Business term*] (EBF)
GAB .... General Arrangements to Borrow [*United Nations*] (EY)
GAB .... Georgia Academy for the Blind (SAUO)
GAB .... Georgia Association of Broadcasters (SRA)
GAB .... Gospel Association for the Blind (EA)
GAB .... Government Affairs Branch [*European Theater of Operations*] [*World War II*]
GAB .... Graphic Adapter Board
GAB .... Graphic Adapter (or Adaptor) Board (SAUS)
GAB .... Great Artesian Basin [*Australia*]
GAB .... Great Australian Bight [*Region*] (EERA)
GAB .... Ground Analog Box (SAUS)
GAB .... Group Announcement Bulletin [*Defense Documentation Center*]
GAB .... Group Audio Bridging (SAUO)
GAB .... Guardianship and Administration Board [*Victoria, Australia*]
GAB .... Gusseted Angle Bracket (SAUS)
GABA .... Gambling and Betting Addiction
GABA .... Gamma-Aminobutyric Acid [*Biochemistry*]
GABA .... German American Business Association (NTPA)
GABA .... Global Agricultural Biotechnology Association (BUAC)
GABA-Ch ...... Gamma-Aminobutyrylcholine (DB)
GA Back .... Great American Backrub Store, Inc. [*Associated Press*] (SAG)
GABA-T .... Gamma-Aminobutyric Acid Transaminase [*Pharmacology*] (DMAA)
Gabb Cr Law... Gabbett's Criminal Law [*A publication*] (DLA)
Gabb Stat L... Gabbett. Abridgment of Statute Law [*1812-18*] [*A publication*] (ILCA)
GABC .... GAB Bancorp [*NASDAQ symbol*] (SAG)
GABC .... German Amer Bancorp [*NASDAQ symbol*] (TTSB)
GABC .... German American Bancorp [*NASDAQ symbol*] (SAG)
GABCC .... Great Artesian Basin Consultative Committee (SAUO)
GABCC .... Great Australian Bight Consultative Committee
GA Bcp .... Great American Bancorp, Inc. [*Associated Press*] (SAG)
GabCv .... Gabelli Convertible Securities Fund [*Associated Press*] (SAG)
GABD .... Bandiagara [*Mali*] [*ICAO location identifier*] (ICLI)
GABD .... Gauge Board
Gabeli .... Gabelli Equity Trust [*Associated Press*] (SAG)
Gabelli .... Gabelli Equity Trust, Inc. [*Associated Press*] (SAG)
GABEX .... Georgia Bight Experiment (SAUO)
GABF .... Bafoulabe [*Mali*] [*ICAO location identifier*] (ICLI)
GABG .... Bougouni [*Mali*] [*ICAO location identifier*] (ICLI)
GabGloM ..... Gabelli Global Multimedia Trust, Inc. [*Associated Press*] (SAG)
GabGM .... Gabelli Global Multimedia Trust, Inc. [*Associated Press*] (SAG)
GABH .... Georgia Baptist Hospital, Medical Library, Atlanta, GA [*Library symbol*] [*Library of Congress*] (LCLS)
GABH-N .... Georgia Baptist Hospital, School of Nursing, Atlanta, GA [*Library symbol*] [*Library of Congress*] (LCLS)
GABHS .... Group A a-Hemolytic Streptococci (SAUS)
GABHS .... Group A Beta-Hemolytic Streptococcus [*Pathology*]
GABIA .... Great Australian Bight Industry Association (EERA)
GablRsd ...... Gables Residential Trust [*Associated Press*] (SAG)
GABN .... Ground-to-Air Broadcast Network
GaBnd .... Georgia Bonded Fibers, Inc. [*Associated Press*] (SAG)
GABOA .... Gamma-Amino-Beta-Hydroxybutyric Acid (DMAA)
GABOB .... Gamma-Amino-beta-hydroxybutyric Acid [*Pharmacology*]
GABR .... Bourem [*Mali*] [*ICAO location identifier*] (ICLI)
GABRA .... Gamma-Aminobutyric Acid Alpha Receptor (DMAA)
Gabriel .... Gateway and Bridge to Europe's National Libraries [*Internet science*]
GABRIELA .... General Assembly Binding Women for Reforms, Integrity, Equality, Leadership and Action [*Philippines*] (BUAC)
GABS .... Bamako/Senou [*Mali*] [*ICAO location identifier*] (ICLI)
GABS .... Group A Beta-Hemolytic Streptococcus (STED)
GABTX .... Gabelli Global Telecommunications
GABU .... Greater Antillean Bullfinch [*North American bird banding code*] (BIBA)
GA Bus Law... Georgia Business Lawyer (DLA)
GABV .... Bamako [*Mali*] [*ICAO location identifier*] (ICLI)
GABVX .... Gabelli Value Fund [*Mutual fund ticker symbol*] (SG)
GAC .... Armstrong State College, Savannah, GA [*OCLC symbol*] (OCLC)
GAC .... Clark College, Atlanta, GA [*Library symbol*] [*Library of Congress*] (LCLS)
GAC .... GAC Corporation (SAUO)
GAC .... Galvanized Aircraft
GAC .... Geac Computer Corp. Ltd. [*Toronto Stock Exchange symbol*]
GAC .... General Acceptance Corp. (MHDW)
GAC .... General Access Copy (MHDI)
GAC .... General Advisory Committee [*to the AEC, later, the Energy Research and Development Administration*]
GAC .... General Advisory Committee of the Commission (SAUS)
GAC .... General Agency Check [*Army*]
GAC .... General Air Cargo [*Venezuela*] [*ICAO designator*] (FAAC)
GAC .... General American Corporation
GAC .... General Analytics Corporation
GAC .... General Apprenticeship Committee (SAUO)
GAC .... General Areas of Competence [*Education*] (AIE)
GAC .... General Atomic Company (SAUO)
GAC .... General Average Certificate [*Business term*] (DS)
GAC .... General Aviation Center (SAUS)
GAC .... General Avionics Computer
GAC .... Generic Artificial Consciousness
GAC .... Geological Association of Canada (BUAC)
GAC .... Georgia Accrediting Commission (SAUO)
GAC .... Georgia Association of Colleges (SAUO)
GAC .... Georgia Athletic Conference (PSS)
GAC .... Get a Clue (SAUS)
GAC .... Ghost in Addition to Crew [*Sailing*]
GAC .... Gimbal Angle Change
GAC .... Gimbal Angle Controller
GAC .... Giordano Automation Corp.
GAC .... Gippsland Agriculture Centre [*Australia*]
GAC .... Global Area Coverage [*Meteorology*]
GAC .... Global Atmospheric Chemistry (SAUS)
GAC .... Gloster Aircraft Company (SAUO)
GAC .... Goodyear Aerospace Corporation (SAUO)
GAC .... Goodyear Aircraft Corporation (SAUO)
GAC .... Government Administrative Council (SAUO)
GAC .... Government Advisory Committee on International Book and Library Programs [*Terminated, 1977*] (EGAO)
GAC .... Government Advisory Council (SAUO)
GAC .... Government Art Collection (BUAC)
GAC .... Grand Assistant Conductor [*Freemasonry*] (ROG)
GAC .... Granular Activated Carbon
GAC .... Granular Activated Carbon (LDOE)
GAC .... Granular Activated Carbon Absorption
GAC .... Graphic Art Club, Toronto [*c.1903, SGA from 1912, CSGA from 1923*] [*Canada*] (NGC)
GAC .... Graphic Art Communications (SAUS)
GAC .... Great American Country
GAC .... Great American Crab Company, Inc. (SAUO)
GAC .... Grilled American Cheese Sandwich
GAC .... Gross Available Capacity [*Electronics*] (IEEE)
GAC .... Ground Assault Convoy
GAC .... Ground Attitude Control (MCD)
GAC .... Groundwater Activated Carbon (EPA)
GAC .... Group Access Capabilities [*Library automation*]
GAC .... Groups Advisory Council (SAUO)
GAC .... Grumman Aerospace Corp. [*of Grumman Corp.*]
GAC .... Guangxi Agricultural College [*China*] (BUAC)
GAC .... Guanine Adenine Cytosine [*A triplet of bases coding for the amino acid, aspartic acid*] (EES)
GAC .... Guidance and Control [*Military*] (IAA)
G Ac .... Guillelmus de Accursio [*Deceased, 1314*] [*Authority cited in pre-1607 legal work*] (DSA)
GAC .... Gulf Aviation Company (SAUO)
GAC .... Gulfstream Aeorspace [*NYSE symbol*] (SG)
GAC .... Gustavus Adolphus College [*St. Peter, MN*]
GACA .... American College of Applied Arts, Atlanta, GA [*Library symbol*] [*Library of Congress*] (LCLS)
GACAC .... Gateway Collegiate Athletic Conference (PSS)
GACB .... Graphic Attention Control Block (SAUS)
GACC .... Atlanta Chamber of Commerce, Atlanta, GA [*Library symbol*] [*Library of Congress*] (LCLS)
GACC .... General Acceptance Corp. [*NASDAQ symbol*] (SAG)
GACC .... Genl Acceptance [*NASDAQ symbol*] (TTSB)
GACC .... German American Chamber of Commerce (NTPA)
GACC .... Great American Communications Co. [*NASDAQ symbol*] (COMM)
GACC .... Ground Attack Control Capability (ACAE)
GACC .... Ground Attack Control Center (ACAE)
GACC .... Ground Attack Control Centre (SAUS)
GACC .... Guidance Alignment and Checkout Console (IAA)
GACC .... Guidance and Control Coupler (IAA)
GACCB .... Government Agency Configuration Control Board (SAUO)
GACCC .... Coca-Cola Co., Technical Information Services, Atlanta, GA [*Library symbol*] [*Library of Congress*] (LCLS)
GACCLC ...... Cooperative College Library Center, Inc., Atlanta, GA [*Library symbol*] [*Library of Congress*] (LCLS)
GACCP .... Georgia Agricultural Commodity Commission for Peanuts (SRA)
GACD .... General Administration for Cooperation and Development (SAUS)
GACDC .... Center for Disease Control, Main Library, Atlanta, GA [*Library symbol*] [*Library of Congress*] (LCLS)
GACDC-FP ... Center for Disease Control, Family Planning Evaluation Division, Atlanta, GA [*Library symbol*] [*Library of Congress*] (LCLS)
GACDL .... Georgia Association of Criminal Defense Lawyers (SRA)
GACE .... Gamma-Site Amyloid Precursor Protein-Cleaving Enzyme
GACE .... Georgia Advisory Council on Education (SAUO)
GACE .... Georgia Association for Community Education (SAUO)
GACEP .... Guidance and Control Equipment Performance (IAA)
GAC/GAI ...... General Atomic Company/ General Atomic International (SAUO)
GACHA .... Georgia Automated Clearing House Association
GACI .... Geographic Area Code Index [*Bureau of Census*]
GACIA .... Guidance and Control Information [*DoD*] (MCD)
GACIAC .... Guidance and Control Information Analysis Center [*Chicago, IL*] [*DoD*] [*Also, an information service or system*]
GACIAC .... Guidance and Control Information and Analysis Center (SAUO)
GACIC .... German Australian Chamber of Industry and Commerce [*Australia*]
GACIS .... Georgia Association of Curriculum and Instructional Supervisors (SAUO)
GACL .... Crawford W. Long Memorial Hospital, Atlanta, GA [*Library symbol*] [*Library of Congress*] (LCLS)
GACL .... Georgia Advisory Council on Libraries (SAUO)
GACL .... Guernsey Aero Club, Limited (SAUO)
GACNA .... Graphic Arts Council of North America (EA)

GACo .... Coca-Cola Co., Marketing Information Center, Atlanta, GA [*Library symbol*] [*Library of Congress*] (LCLS)
GACO .... Garden America Corp. [*NASDAQ symbol*] (COMM)
GACO .... Graphic Attention Control Block (SAUS)
GACOA .... Groupe Commercial Africain [*Central Africa*] (BUAC)
GA Code ...... Code of Georgia [*A publication*] (DLA)
GA Code Ann... Georgia Code, Annotated [*A publication*] (DLA)
G/A COMM... Ground-to-Air Communications (MCD)
GaCOMO...... Georgia Library Association/Council of Media Organizations
G/A Con ...... General Average Contribution [*Marine insurance*] (DS)
GA Const ..... Georgia Constitution [*A publication*] (DLA)
GACP .... Gunner's Accuracy Control Panel (MCD)
GACRI.......... Guangdong Arts and Crafts Research Institute [*China*] (BUAC)
GACS .... General Assembly of the Church of Scotland (SAUO)
GACS .... Georgia Association of Christian Schools (SRA)
GACS .... Georgia Association of Convenience Stores (SRA)
GACS .... Gun Alignment and Control System (MCD)
GACS .... Gun Alignment Control System (SAUS)
GACSC .... Contel Service Corp., Atlanta, GA [*Library symbol*] [*Library of Congress*] (LCLS)
GACSU .... Singapore Government Administrative and Clerical Services' Union
GACT .... Generally Available Control Technology [*Environmental chemistry*]
GACT .... Granular Activated Carbon Treatment (EPAT)
GACT .... Graphic Analysis and Correlation Terminal (MCD)
GACT .... Greenwich Apparent Civil Time [*Astronomy*] (IAA)
GACTAI .... General Arbitration Council of the Textile and Apparel Industries (EA)
GACTFOSIF... Graphic Analysis and Correlation Terminal Fleet Ocean Surveillance Information Facility (DNAB)
GACTI .... General Arbitration Council of the Textile Industry [*Later, GACTAI*] (EA)
GACU .... Ground Air Conditioning Unit (MCD)
GACU .... Ground Avionics Cooling Unit
GACVS .... German-American Center for Visiting Scholars (SAUO)
GAD .... Action Group for Democracy (Dominican Rep.) [*Political party*] (PSAP)
GAD .... Gadabout (DSUE)
GAD .... Gadsden [*Alabama*] [*Airport symbol*] (OAG)
GAD .... Gallium Arsenide Diode
GAD .... Galvanized and Dipped Metal (IAA)
GAD .... Gender and Development
GAD .... General Anthropology Division (EA)
GAD .... General Assembly Data
GAD .... General Average Deposit (MARI)
GAD .... Generalized Anxiety Disorder [*Medicine*] (DMAA)
GAD .... Germanium Alloy Diffused (IAA)
GAD .... Germersheim Army Depot (MCD)
GAD .... Gieaen Army Depot (SAUO)
GAD .... Gladstone Resources [*Vancouver Stock Exchange symbol*]
GAD .... Glutamate Acid Decarboxylase [*An enzyme*]
GAD .... Glutamate Decarboxylase [*An enzyme*]
GAD .... Glutamic Acid Decarboxylase (SAUS)
GAD .... Government Actuary's Department
GAD .... Government Archives Division [*National Archives of Canada*] [*Information service or system*] (IID)
GAD .... Graduate Assistantship Directory [*A publication*]
GAD .... Grand Alliance for Democracy [*Philippines*] [*Political party*]
GAD .... Grants Administration Division [*Environmental Protection Agency*]
GAD .... Graphic Active Device [*Computer science*] (MHDI)
GAD .... Great American Desert (SAUS)
GAD .... Great American Dream
GAD .... Gross Air Dried
GAD .... Guards' Armoured Division [*Military unit*] [*British*]
GAD .... Guards Artillery Division [*British*]
GAD .... Guide to American Directories [*A publication*]
GADA .... Dioila [*Mali*] [*ICAO location identifier*] (ICLI)
GADA .... General Aviation Distributors Association (SAUO)
GADAR .... Guild of Antique Dealers and Restorers [*British*] (DBA)
GADC .... General Audio and Data Communications Ltd. (NITA)
GADDR .... Group Address (SAUS)
GA Dec .... Georgia Decisions [*A publication*] (DLA)
GA Dec (Dudley)... Dudley's Georgia Reports [*A publication*] (DLA)
GADEF .... Groupement des Associations Dentaires Francophones [*Group of Francophone Dentists' Associations*] [*Paris, France*] (EAIO)
G/A Dep .... General Average Deposit [*Marine insurance*] (DS)
GADES .... Gun Air Defense Effectiveness Studies (SAUS)
GADES .... Gun Air Defense Effectiveness Study (MCD)
GADG .... Global Application Data Group [*Computer science*] (TIMI)
GADGES .... German Air Defense Ground Environment System (SAUO)
GADGET .... Grievance and Discipline Great Event Tracking (SAUS)
GADH .... Gastric Alcohol Dehydrogenase [*An enzyme*]
GADH .... Glutamic Acid Dehydrogenase [*Medicine*] (EDAA)
GADL .... Ground-to-Air Data Link
GADMIS .... Grants Administration Division Management Information System (SAUO)
GADNA .... Gduei Noar [*Youth Battalions*] [*Israel*]
GADNPH ...... Glycolic Aldehyde Dinitrophenylhydrazone [*Organic chemistry*]
GADO .... General Aviation District Office [*FAA*]
GADOSAG .... Georgia DOSAG (SAUO)
GADPET .... Graphic Data Presentation and Edit (PDAA)
GADPET Program... Graphic Arts Data Presentation and Edit Program (SAUS)
GA-DPR .... General Atomic Demonstration Power Reactor (SAUO)
GADPS .... Graphic Automatic Data Processing System (MCD)
GADR .... Guided Air Defense Rocket
GADS .... garnet-anorthite-diopside-silica (SAUS)
GADS .... Gate-Assignment and Display System [*United Air Lines, Inc.*]
GADS .... Geographic Analysis and Display System (SAUO)
GADS .... Geographic and Alphanumeric Display System (MCD)
GADS .... Gonococcal Arthritis/Dermatitis Syndrome [*Medicine*]
GADS .... Goose Air Defense Sector
GADSCO ...... Gages Documentation Scheduling Committee
GADT .... Graded Assessment in Design and Technology (AIE)
GADT .... Ground/Air Defense Threat (MCD)
GADV .... Gross Arrived Damaged Value (MARI)
GADW .... Gadwall [*North American bird banding code*] (BIBA)
GADZ .... Douentza [*Mali*] [*ICAO location identifier*] (ICLI)
GADZ .... Gadzooks, Inc. [*NASDAQ symbol*] (SAG)
Gadzks .... Gadzooks, Inc. [*Associated Press*] (SAG)
gae .... Gaelic (Scots) [*MARC language code*] [*Library of Congress*] (LCCP)
GAE .... Gale Environmental Almanac [*A publication*]
GAE .... Gallic Acid Equivalent [*Wine analysis*]
GAE .... GAO [*General Accounting Office*] Denver Regional Office, Denver, CO [*OCLC symbol*] (OCLC)
GAE .... Gaslite Petroleum [*Vancouver Stock Exchange symbol*]
GAE .... General Administrative Expense [*A budget appropriation title*]
GAE .... General Air Express
GAE .... General American English
GAE .... General Analytical Evaluation
GAE .... General Classification Test/Arithmetic Test/Electronics Technician Selection Test [*Military*] (DNAB)
GAE .... Generate Airlift Requirement (SAUO)
GAE .... Generic Application Environment (SAUS)
GAE .... Georgia Association of Educators (SAUO)
GAE .... German Application Environment (SAUO)
GAE .... Gibbs Adsorption Equation [*Physical chemistry*]
GAE .... Graphic Arts Employers of America (EA)
GAE .... Grupos Armados Espanoles [*Armed Spanish Groups*] [*Political party*] (PD)
GAE .... Gummed All Edges [*Envelopes*] (DGA)
GAE .... Gunner Aiming Error (MCD)
GAEA .... Georgia Art Education Association (SAUO)
GAE-BPH ...... Georgia State Department of Education, Division of Public Library, Library for the Blind and Physically Handicapped, Atlanta, GA [*Library symbol*] [*Library of Congress*] (LCLS)
GAEC .... Ghana Atomic Energy Commission (BUAC)
GAEC .... Goodyear Aircraft and Engineering Corp.
GAEC .... Greek Atomic Energy Commission
GAEC .... Grumman Aircraft Engineering Corp. [*Later, Grumman Corp.*]
GAEI .... Equifax, Inc., Atlanta, GA [*Library symbol*] [*Library of Congress*] (LCLS)
Gael .... Gaelic (BEE)
GAEL .... Gaelic [*Language, etc.*]
GAEL .... Georgia Association of Educational Leaders (SRA)
GAEL .... Greater Antillean Elaenia [*North American bird banding code*] (BIBA)
GAELIC .... Gauteng and Environs Library Consortium
GAELIC .... Grumman Aerospace Engineering Language for Instructional Checkout
GAEO .... Galileo Corp. [*NASDAQ symbol*] (NASQ)
GAEO .... Galileo Electro-Optics [*NASDAQ symbol*] (TTSB)
GAEO .... Galileo Electro-Optics Corp. [*NASDAQ symbol*] (NQ)
GAE-P .... Georgia State Department of Education, Division of Public Library Services, Atlanta, GA [*Library symbol*] [*Library of Congress*] (LCLS)
GAER .... Gay Alliance for Equal Rights (SAUO)
GAERF .... Graphic Arts Education and Research Foundation (DGA)
GAES .... garnet-anorthite-enstatite-silica (SAUS)
GAES .... Gas Appliance Engineers Society [*Later, ASGE*] (EA)
GAESD .... Graphic Arts Equipment and Supply Dealers (SAUS)
GAESDA .... Graphic Arts Equipment and Supply Dealers Association [*Defunct*] (EA)
GAESP .... Georgia Association of Elementary School Principals (SAUO)
GAESRE .... Genealogical Association of English-Speaking Researchers in Europe (EAIO)
GAF .... GAF Corp. [*NYSE symbol*] (COMM)
GAF .... GA Financial [*AMEX symbol*] (TTSB)
GAF .... GA Financial, Inc. [*AMEX symbol*] (SAG)
GAF .... Gamma-Activated Factor [*Biochemistry*]
GAF .... GAO [*General Accounting Office*] Boston Regional Office, Boston, MA [*OCLC symbol*] (OCLC)
GAF .... Gay Asian Female (ADWA)
GAF .... German Air Force [*ICAO designator*] (FAAC)
GAF .... Ghana Air Force (SAUO)
GAF .... Giant Axon Formation (STED)
GAF .... Global Assessment of Functioning Scale (SAUS)
GAF .... Government Affairs Foundation [*Defunct*] (EA)
GAF .... Government Aircraft (SAUS)
GAF .... Government Aircraft Facilities
GAF .... Grafton, ND [*Location identifier*] [*FAA*] (FAAL)
GAF .... Greek Armed Forces (SAUO)
GAF .... Greek Armed Forces Radio Station (SAUS)
GAF .... Growth of the American Family [*A study*]
GAF .... Gummed Across the Flap (SAUS)
GAFA .... General Merchandise, Apparel, Furniture, and Appliances (FOTI)
GAFA .... German-American Film Association (SAUO)
GAFA .... German-American Football Association [*Later, CSL*]
GAFACOOPS... Ghana Federation of Agricultural Cooperatives (SAUO)
GAFADS .... German Air Force Air Defense School (MCD)
GAFB .... George Air Force Base [*California*] (MCD)
GAFB .... Goodfellow Air Force Base [*Texas*]
GAFB .... Griffiss Air Force Base [*New York*]

GAFC .... Fulton County Court House, Atlanta, GA [*Library symbol*] [*Library of Congress*] (LCLS)
GAFC .... Government Assessment Facilitation Committee (SAUO)
GAFCOR .... Gas and Fuel Corp. [*Victoria, Australia*] [*Commercial firm*]
GAFD .... Faladie [*Mali*] [*ICAO location identifier*] (ICLI)
GAFD .... Guild of American Funeral Directors [*Defunct*]
GAFD .... United States Food and Drug Administration, Atlanta, GA [*Library symbol*] [*Library of Congress*] (LCLS)
GAFET .... Gallium Arsenide Field-Effect Transistor (MCD)
GAFG .... General Aviation Flight Guide [*British*] (AIA)
GAFG .... Goal Attainment Follow-Up Guide (DMAA)
GAFI .... Garfield, WA [*American Association of Railroads railroad junction routing code*]
GAFIA .... German Armed Forces Intelligence Agency (MCD)
GAFICA .... Advisory Group for Central American Economic Integration (SAUS)
GA Fighter ... Ground Attack Fighter (SAUS)
GAFL .... Fulton County Law Library, Atlanta, GA [*Library symbol*] [*Library of Congress*] (LCLS)
GAFLAC .... General Accident Fire and Life Assurance Corporation (SAUO)
GAFLT .... German Air Force Liaison Team (SAUO)
GAFM .... Fulton County Medical Society, Atlanta, GA [*Library symbol*] [*Library of Congress*] (LCLS)
GAFM .... Get Away From Me (SAUS)
GA Fncl .... GA Financial, Inc. [*Associated Press*] (SAG)
GAFOR .... General Aviation forecast (SAUS)
GAFOR .... General Aviation Visual Flight Forecast (PIAV)
GAFP .... German Air Force Planning (SAUO)
GAFPG .... General Aviation Facilities Planning Group
GAFR .... Federal Reserve Bank of Atlanta, Research Library, Atlanta, GA [*Library symbol*] [*Library of Congress*] (LCLS)
GAFRO .... Ghana Association for Research on Women (BUAC)
GAFS .... garnet-anorthite-ferrosilite-silica (SAUS)
GAFS .... General Accounting and Finance System Base Level (SAUO)
GAFS .... Gentile Air Force Station [*Ohio*]
GAFS .... United States Forest Service, Atlanta, GA [*Library symbol*] [*Library of Congress*] (LCLS)
GAFSC .... Fernbank Science Center, Atlanta, GA [*Library symbol*] [*Library of Congress*] (LCLS)
GAFSC .... German Air Force Southern Command (MCD)
GAFSSC .... German Air Force Southern Support Command (SAUO)
GAFTA .... Grain and Feed Trade Association (BUAC)
GAFTA .... Grain and Food Trade Association [*British*]
GAFTAC .... German Air Force Tactical Air Command (MCD)
GAFTO .... Germany Air Force Technical Order (MCD)
GAFW .... United States Fish and Wildlife Service, Atlanta, GA [*Library symbol*] [*Library of Congress*] (LCLS)
GAFY .... Grazing-Angle Fluorescence Yield (SAUS)
GAG .... Cologne Air Transport [*Germany*] [*FAA designator*] (FAAC)
GAG .... Gage, OK [*Location identifier*] [*FAA*] (FAAL)
GAG .... Gallant Gold Mines Ltd. [*Vancouver Stock Exchange symbol*]
GAG .... GAO [*General Accounting Office*] Philadelphia Regional Office, Philadelphia, PA [*OCLC symbol*] (OCLC)
GAG .... Gays Against Genocide [*An association*] (BUAC)
GAG .... General Affairs Group (EURO)
GAG .... Glycosaminoglycan [*Biochemistry*]
GAG .... Glyoxal Bis(guanylhydrazone) [*Organic chemistry*]
GAG .... Grand Aleph Godol (BJA)
GAG .... Graphic Artists Guild (EA)
GAG .... Gridding Accuracy Group (ACAE)
GAG .... Gross Available Generation [*Electronics*] (IEEE)
GAG .... Gross Gradability [*Truck specification*]
G/A/G .... Ground/Air/Ground (SAUO)
G/A/G .... Ground-to-air and Air-to-Ground communication (SAUS)
GAG .... Ground-to-Air-to-Ground [*Aviation*]
GAG .... Group-Specific Antigen Gene (DMAA)
GAG .... Guanine Adenine Guanine [*A triplet of bases coding for the amino acid, glutamic acid*] (EES)
GAGAS .... Generally Accepted Government Auditing Standards [*A publication*] (AAGC)
GAGB .... Gemmological Association of Great Britain (BI)
GAGB .... General Association of General Baptists (EA)
GAGDT .... Ground-to-Air-to-Ground Data Terminal [*Air Force*] (MCD)
GAGE .... Global Atmosphere Gases Experiment (EERA)
GAGE .... Global Atmospheric Gases Experiment [*Environmental science*]
GAGE .... Gulf-Stream Atmospheric Gradient Exchange (SAUS)
GAGF .... Graphic Artists Guild Foundation (EA)
GAGI .... Goethe Institute, German Culture Institute, Atlanta, GA [*Library symbol*] [*Library of Congress*] (LCLS)
GAGK .... Graphic Arts Guidance Kit
GAGL .... Aguelhoc [*Mali*] [*ICAO location identifier*] (ICLI)
GAGM .... Georgia Mental Health Institute, Atlanta, GA [*Library symbol*] [*Library of Congress*] (LCLS)
GAGM .... Goundam [*Mali*] [*ICAO location identifier*] (ICLI)
GAGN .... Graphic Artists Guild National (NTPA)
GAGO .... Gao [*Mali*] [*ICAO location identifier*] (ICLI)
GAGP .... Georgia Power Co., Atlanta, GA [*Library symbol*] [*Library of Congress*] (LCLS)
GAGR .... Courma-Rharous [*Mali*] [*ICAO location identifier*] (ICLI)
GAGR .... Georgia Retardation Center, Atlanta, GA [*Library symbol*] [*Library of Congress*] (LCLS)
GAGR .... Greater Antillean Grackle [*North American bird banding code*] (BIBA)
GAGR .... Group Automatic Gain Regulator (SAUS)
GAGS .... Geological and Geophysical Sciences (SAUO)
GAGS .... Greek Army Geographic Service (SAUO)
GAGTh .... Gammon Theological Seminary, Atlanta, GA [*Library symbol*] [*Library of Congress*] (LCLS)
GAGTL .... Gemmological Association and Gem Testing Laboratory of Great Britain (BUAC)
GaGulf .... Georgia Gulf Corp. [*Associated Press*] (SAG)
GAH .... Games at Home [*Baseball*]
GAH .... Gayndah [*Australia*] [*Airport symbol*] (OAG)
GAH .... Grand American Handicap [*Shooting competition*]
GAH .... Wren's Nest [*Joel Chandler Harris Home*], Atlanta, GA [*Library symbol*] [*Library of Congress*] (LCLS)
GAHB .... Hombori [*Mali*] [*ICAO location identifier*] (ICLI)
GAHF .... Grapple Adapter Handling Fixture [*Nuclear energy*] (NRCH)
GAHH .... Good American Helping Hands (EA)
GAHi .... Atlanta Historical Society, Atlanta, GA [*Library symbol*] [*Library of Congress*] (LCLS)
GAHM .... High Museum of Art, Atlanta, GA [*Library symbol*] [*Library of Congress*] (LCLS)
GAHoM .... Home Mission Board of the Southern Baptist Convention, Atlanta, GA [*Library symbol*] [*Library of Congress*] (LCLS)
GAHR .... Georgia Department of Human Resources, Atlanta, GA [*Library symbol*] [*Library of Congress*] (LCLS)
GAHRS .... Gyrocompassing Attitude and Heading Reference System (ACAE)
GAHS .... Galactorrhea-Amenorrhea Hyperprolactinemia Sydrome [*Medicine*] (EDAA)
GAHS .... Galway Archaeological and Historical Society (SAUO)
GAHS .... garnet-anorthite-hedenbergite-silica (SAUS)
GAHS .... German-American Historical Society (SAUO)
GAHSC .... Georgia Association of Homes and Services for Children (SRA)
GAHu .... Hurt, Richardson, Garner, Law Library, Atlanta, GA [*Library symbol*] [*Library of Congress*] (LCLS)
GAI .... Gaithersburg, MD [*Location identifier*] [*FAA*] (FAAL)
GAI .... Gate Alarm Indicator [*RADAR*]
GAI .... Gay American Indians (EA)
GAI .... General Accounting Instructions
GAI .... General & Administrative Instruction (SAUS)
GAI .... General Atomic International (SAUO)
GAI .... Generalized Area of Intersection (OA)
GAI .... Geophysical Associates International
GAI .... Gibbs Adsorption Isotherm [*Physical chemistry*]
GAI .... Gilbert Associates, Inc.
GAI .... Global-Tech Appliances [*NYSE symbol*] (SG)
GAI .... [*A*] Glossary of the Aramaic Inscriptions [*A publication*] (BJA)
GAI .... Golder Associates, Inc. (SAUS)
GAI .... Golder Associates Incorporated (SAUO)
GAI .... Governmental Affairs Institute [*Later, VPS*] (EA)
GAI .... Grand Auto, Incorporated (SAUO)
GAI .... Guaranteed Annual Income
GAI .... Guided Affected Imagery (DIPS)
GAI .... Guild of Architectural Ironmongers [*British*] (BI)
GAI .... Gurr & Associates, Inc. (EFIS)
GAIA .... Galactic Census Project (SAUS)
GAIA .... Global Astrometric Interferometer for Astrophysics (SAUS)
GAIA .... Go and Inspect Aircraft (SAUS)
GAIA .... Graphic Arts Industries Association
GAIA .... Graphic Arts Information Association (SAUS)
GAIC .... Gallium Arsenide Integrated Circuit [*Computer chip*]
GAIC .... Graphic Arts International Union (SAUO)
GAIC .... Guizhou Aviation Industry Corp. (SAUO)
GAICO .... Gilbert Associates, Inc. (EFIS)
GAIF .... General Arab Insurance Federation [*Egypt*] (BUAC)
GAIF .... General Assembly of International Sports Federations [*Later, GAISF*] (EA)
GAIF .... Gimbal Angle Information Failure
GAIFC .... Gene Autry International Fan Club (EA)
Gaii .... Gaii Institutionum Commentarii [*Gaius' Institutes*] [*A publication*] (DLA)
GAIIA .... Global Alliance of International Information Industry Associations (BUAC)
Gai Inst .... Gaius, Institutiones [*Second century AD*] [*Classical studies*] (OCD)
GAIL .... Gas Authority of India Ltd. (ECON)
GAIL .... Gate Array Interface Language (NITA)
GAIL .... General Atomic In-Pile Loop (SAUO)
GAIL .... General Atomic In-Pool Loop (SAA)
GAIL .... Glide Angle Indicator Light [*Aviation*] (DNAB)
GAILL .... Groupement des Allergologistes et Immunologistes de Langues Latines [*Latin Languages Speaking Allergists - LLSA*] (EAIO)
GAIM .... Global Analyses, Interpretation, and Modeling [*Task Force*] [*Marine science*] (OSRA)
GAIM .... Global Analysis, Interpretation and Modelling [*Climate*] (EERA)
GAIM .... Group Achievement Identification Measure [*Test*] [*Sylvia B. Rimm*] (TES)
GAIMH .... German-speaking Association of Infant Mental Health (SAUO)
GAIN .... Federal and State Governments Assistance Programs [*Database*] [*Australia*]
GAIN .... Gas Appliance Improvement Network
GAIN .... German Advanced Integrated Network (SAUO)
GAIN .... Gifted Advocacy Information Network [*Defunct*] (EA)
GAIN .... Giftware Associates Interchange (NTPA)
GAIN .... Global Automation Information Network [*An association*]
GAIN .... Graphic Aids for Investigating Networks [*NASA*] (NASA)
GAIN .... Graphic Arts Information Notation (SAUS)
GAIN .... Greater Avenues for Independence (SAUS)
GainAs .... Gallium Indium Arsenide (MED)
GainP .... Gallium Indium Phosphide (MED)
GAINS .... Gimballess Analytic Inertial Navigation System

GAINS Global Airborne Integrated Navigation System [*Military*] (IAA)
GAINS Global Air-ocean in-situ System (SAUS)
GAINS Graphic Administrative Information System (DNAB)
GAINS Growth And Income Securities (SAUS)
GAINS Growth and Income Security [*Finance*]
GAINS Guaranteed Annual Income System
Gainsco Gainsco, Inc. [*Associated Press*] (SAG)
GAInv General American Investors Co., Inc. [*Associated Press*] (SAG)
GAIPAS General Adult Inpatient Psychiatric Assessment Scale [*Medicine*] (EDAA)
GAIPS Graphic and Inter-Program Structure (ACAE)
GAIS Gallium Arsenide Illuminator System
GAIS General Aviation Inspection Aids Summary [*FAA*]
GAIS Georgia Association of Independent Schools (SAUO)
GAISER Generic Airborne Interceptor Search RADAR [*Military*] (SEWL)
GAISF General Assembly of International Sports Federations (SAUO)
GAISF General Association of International Sports Federations [*Formerly, GAIF*] (EA)
GAISO Gam-Anon International Service Office (EA)
GAISSAR Gilbert Associates, Incorporated, Standard Safety Analysis Report [*Nuclear energy*] (NRCH)
GAIT Government and Industry Team
G/AIT Ground/Airborne Integrated Terminal [*Air Force*] (DOMA)
GAIT GSM MAP Network/ANSI-41 Interoperability Team (SAUO)
GAIT Langer Biomechanics Group [*NASDAQ symbol*] (SAG)
GAITh Interdenominational Theological Center, Atlanta, GA [*Library symbol*] [*Library of Congress*] (LCLS)
GAIU Graphic Arts International Union [*Later, GCIU*]
Gaius Gaius' Institutes [*A publication*] (DLA)
Gaius Inst Gaius' Institutes [*A publication*] (DLA)
GAJ Atlanta Junior College, Atlanta, GA [*Library symbol*] [*Library of Congress*] (LCLS)
GAJ Gaseous Axisymmetric Jet
GAJ Guild of Agricultural Journalists
GAJ Yamagata [*Japan*] [*Airport symbol*] (OAG)
GAJC Georgia Association of Junior Colleges (SAUO)
GAJC Jimmy Carter Library, Atlanta, GA [*Library symbol*] [*Library of Congress*] (LCLS)
GAK Gakona, AK [*Location identifier*] [*FAA*] (FAAL)
GaK Gakushuin University, Tokyo (SAUS)
GAK Galactokinase [*Also, GALK*] [*An enzyme*]
GAK Garlock, Inc. (SAUO)
GAK Government Access to Keys (SAUO)
GAKA Kenieba [*Mali*] [*ICAO location identifier*] (ICLI)
GAKL Kidal [*Mali*] [*ICAO location identifier*] (ICLI)
GAKM Ke-Macina [*Mali*] [*ICAO location identifier*] (ICLI)
GAKN Kolokani [*Mali*] [*ICAO location identifier*] (ICLI)
GAKO Koutiala [*Mali*] [*ICAO location identifier*] (ICLI)
GAKT Kita [*Mali*] [*ICAO location identifier*] (ICLI)
GAKY Kayes [*Mali*] [*ICAO location identifier*] (ICLI)
GAI Albany Public Library, Albany, GA [*Library symbol*] [*Library of Congress*] (LCLS)
GAL Anti-Terrorist Liberation Group [*Undercover anti-Basque terrorist interior-ministry network*] [*Acronym is based on foreign phrase*] [*Spain*] (ECON)
GAL Galactic (KSC)
gal Galactose [*Medicine*] (EDAA)
Gal Galactose [*A sugar*]
GAL Galactosyl [*Biochemistry*] (DAVI)
Gal Galatians [*New Testament book*]
Gal Galen [*Second century AD*] [*Classical studies*] (OCD)
GAL Galena [*Alaska*] [*Airport symbol*] (OAG)
GAL Galerazamba [*Colombia*] [*Seismograph station code, US Geological Survey*] (SEIS)
gal Galileo [*Unit of acceleration*]
gal Galla [*MARC language code*] [*Library of Congress*] (LCCP)
Gal Gallery (WDAA)
GAL Gallery
Gal Gallison's United States Circuit Court Reports [*A publication*] (DLA)
GAL Gallium Arsenide LASER
GAL Gallon (AAG)
gal Gallon (ODBW)
Gal Gallon
GAL Gallons (SAUS)
GAL Gallons of Fuel [*"Energy equivalent" abbreviation - biomass agriculture and conversion*] [*Fuel chemistry*]
GAL Gallop [*Music*] (ROG)
GAL Gallup Public Library, Gallup, NM [*OCLC symbol*] (OCLC)
GAL Gallus-adeno-like [*Avian virus*]
GAL Galoob (Lewis) Toys [*NYSE symbol*] (TTSB)
GAL Galoob [*Lewis*] Toys, Inc. [*NYSE symbol*] (SPSG)
gal Galvanized Iron (ADA)
GAL Galveston-Houston [*Diocesan abbreviation*] [*Texas*] (TOCD)
GAL Galveston Resources Ltd. [*Toronto Stock Exchange symbol*] [*Vancouver Stock Exchange symbol*]
GAL Galway [*County in Ireland*] (ROG)
GAL Gas-Analysis Laboratory [*NASA*]
GAL Gate Array Logic (AAEL)
GAL Gate/Generic Array Logic (SAUS)
GAL Gemini Airlines Ltd. [*Ghana*] [*ICAO designator*] (FAAC)
GAL General Administration Letter (OICC)
GAL General Assembly Library (SAUO)
GAL General Average Loss (MARI)
GAL General George A. Lincoln [*World War II*]
GAL Generalized Assembly Language [*Computer science*] (MHDB)
GAL Generic Array Cell (SAUS)
GAL Generic Array Logic [*Computer science*]
GA L Georgia Lawyer [*A publication*] (DLA)
GA L Georgia Sessions Laws [*A publication*] (DLA)
GAL German Atlantic Line [*Steamship*] (MHDB)
GAL Get a Life
GAL Gibraltar Airways Limited (SAUO)
GAL Gideon-Anderson Lumber [*Federal Railroad Administration identification code*]
GAL Gimbal Angle Loss
GAL Global Address List
GAL Glucuronic Acid Lactone (DB)
GAL Goods Avoiding Line [*Indian Railway*] (TIR)
GAL Governmental Articulation List (SAUO)
GAL Graphics Application Language (BYTE)
GAL Greening Australia Limited (EERA)
GAL Ground Optical Analysis Of Lens Systems (SAUS)
GAL Grupos Armados Libertarios [*Armed Libertarian Groups*] [*Spain*] [*Political party*] (PD)
Gal Gualcosius [*Flourished, 11th-12th century*] [*Authority cited in pre-1607 legal work*] (DSA)
GAL Guaranteed Access Level [*Foreign Trade*]
GAL Guardian Ad Litem [*Social services*] (PAZ)
GAL Guggenheim Aeronautical Laboratory [*California Institute of Technology*]
GAL Guild of American Luthiers (EA)
GAL Guinea Airways, Limited (SAUO)
GAL Guinea Airways Ltd.
gal-1-P Galactose-1-Phosphate [*Organic chemistry*] (DAVI)
GALA Gallium Aluminum Arsenide (CIST)
GALA Gate Array Layout Automation (ACAE)
GALA Gay and Lesbian Atheists [*Defunct*] (EA)
GALA Gay Atheist League of America (SAUO)
GALA Geoscience Airborne Laser Altimeter (SAUS)
GALA Global Access to Local Applications (EURO)
GALA Graduated Audio Level Adjustment
GALA Graphic Arts Literature Abstracts [*A publication*]
GALA Graphic Arts Literature Abstracts (journ.) (SAUS)
GALA Greek Applied Linguistics Association (BUAC)
GALA Grupo de Artistas Latino Americanos [*An association*]
GALA Guidance and Learner Autonomy [*Project*] (AIE)
GALAC Gay and Lesbian Association of Choruses (EA)
GALAF Galagraph Ltd. [*NASDAQ symbol*] (COMM)
GalaGen GalaGen, Inc. [*Associated Press*] (SAG)
Gal & Dav Gale and Davison's English Queen's Bench Reports [*1841-43*] [*A publication*] (DLA)
GALAP Graphic Arts Literacy Action Program (SAUS)
GA Law Reporter Georgia Law Reporter [*A publication*] (DLA)
GALAXY General Automatic Luminosity and X-Y [*Engine technology*] (PDAA)
GALAXY Package from Concurrent Computer Corp. (SAUO)
GALB Galbanum [*Agum*] [*Pharmacology*] (ROG)
Galb Galbraith's Reports [*9-11 Florida*] [*A publication*] (DLA)
G-ALB Globulin-Albumin [*Biochemistry*] (DAVI)
Galb & M Galbraith and Meek's Reports [*9-12 Florida*] [*A publication*] (DLA)
Galb & M (Fla) Galbraith and Meek's Reports [*9-12 Florida*] [*A publication*] (DLA)
GALBG Galesburg, IL [*American Association of Railroads railroad junction routing code*]
Galbraith Galbraith's Reports [*9-12 Florida*] [*A publication*] (DLA)
GALC European Booksellers Association (BUAC)
GalC Galactocerebroside [*Biochemistry*]
GALC Galactosylceramidase [*An enzyme*]
GALC Groupement des Associations de Librairies de la CEE [*Group of Booksellers Associations in the EEC*] (ECED)
GAL CAP Gallon Capacity (WDAA)
GALCF Galactic Resources Ltd. [*NASDAQ symbol*] (COMM)
GALCIT Graduate Aeronautical Laboratories - California Institute of Technology [*Research center*] (RCD)
GALCIT Guggenheim Aeronautical Laboratory-California Institute of Technology (SAUO)
gal/cycle Gallons per Cycle (ADWA)
GAlD Dougherty County Court House, Albany, GA [*Library symbol*] [*Library of Congress*] (LCLS)
gal/d Gallons per Day (ABAC)
GALD Greatest Axial Linear Dimension
GAlDC Darton College, Albany, GA [*Library symbol*] [*Library of Congress*] (LCLS)
Gale Gale on Easements [*A publication*] (DLA)
GALE Galerias de Arte y Salas de Exposiciones [*Ministerio de Cultura*] [*Spain*] [*Information service or system*] (CRD)
Gale Gale's English Exchequer Reports [*A publication*] (DLA)
Gale Gale's New Forest Decisions [*England*] [*A publication*] (DLA)
GALE Gaseous and Liquid Effluent [*Nuclear energy*] (NRCH)
GALE Genesis of Atlantic Lows (SAUS)
GALE Genesis of Atlantic Lows Experiment (USDC)
GALE Genesis of Atlantic Tropical Lows Experiment [*National Oceanic and Atmospheric Administration*]
GALE Genesis of Atmosphere Lows Experiment (SAUO)
Gale & D Gale and Davison's English Queen's Bench Reports [*1841-43*] [*A publication*] (DLA)
Gale & Dav Gale and Davison's English Queen's Bench Reports [*1841-43*] [*A publication*] (DLA)
Gale & D (Eng) Gale and Davison's English Queen's Bench Reports [*1841-43*] [*A publication*] (DLA)

Gale & Whatley Easem... Gale and Whatley [*later, Gale*] on Easements [*A publication*] (DLA)
Gale & Wh Eas... Gale and Whatley [*later, Gale*] on Easements [*A publication*] (ILCA)
Gale Eas .... Gale on Easements [*A publication*] (ILCA)
GALEN .... Generalised Architecture for Languages, Encyclopaedias, and Nomenclatures in Medicine (SAUS)
GALEN .... Generalized Architecture for Languages, Encyclopaedias, and Nomenclatures (ADWA)
Gale's St .... Gale's Statutes [*A publication*] (DLA)
Gale Stat .... Gale's Statutes [*A publication*] (DLA)
GALEX .... Galaxy Evolution Explorer
GaleyL .... Galey & Lord, Inc. [*Associated Press*] (SAG)
GALF .... Global Assessment of Leisure Functioning (IDYL)
GALF .... Groupement des Acousticiens de Langue Francaise [*Group of French-Speaking Acousticians*] (EA)
GAL/(FT² D)... Gallons per Square-Foot per Day
GAL/(FT D)... Gallons per Foot per Day
GAL/H .... Gallons per Hour (MCD)
GALH .... General Association of Ladies Hairdressers [*British*] (BI)
GALHA .... Gay and Lesbian Humanist Association (BUAC)
GAL/(HP H)... Gallons per Horsepower-Hour
GALIC .... General American Life Insurance Co.
Galileo .... Galileo Electro-Optics Corp. [*Associated Press*] (SAG)
GALILEO .... Georgia Library Learning Online
GA LJ .... Georgia Law Journal [*A publication*] (DLA)
GAIJC .... Albany Junior College, Albany, GA [*Library symbol*] [*Library of Congress*] (LCLS)
GALK .... Galactokinase [*Also, GAK*] [*An enzyme*]
GALL .... Gallae [*Nut Galls*] [*Pharmacology*] (ROG)
GALL .... Gallery (MSA)
gall .... Gallery (VRA)
Gall .... Gallison's United States Circuit Court Reports [*A publication*] (DLA)
gall .... Gallon (ODBW)
GALL .... Gallon
GALL .... Galloway [*District in Scotland*] (ROG)
Gallagr .... Gallagher [*Arthur J.*] & Co. [*Associated Press*] (SAG)
Gallaudet U... Gallaudet University (GAGS)
Gall CCR .... Gallison's United States Circuit Court Reports [*A publication*] (DLA)
Gall Cr Cas... Gallick's Reports (French Criminal Cases) [*A publication*] (DLA)
GALLEX .... Gallium Experiment
GallHist .... Gallery of History, Inc. [*Associated Press*] (SAG)
Gall Int L .... Gallaudet on International Law [*A publication*] (DLA)
Gallison .... Gallison's United States Circuit Court Reports [*A publication*] (DLA)
Gallison's Rep... Gallison's United States Circuit Court Reports [*A publication*] (DLA)
GALLSMIN... Gallons per Minute (IAA)
GALLY .... Gallery (ROG)
GALM .... Gains and Lee Memory (SAUO)
gal/min .... Gallons per Minute (ABAC)
GAL/MIN .... Gallons per Minute
GalN .... Galactosamine [*Biochemistry*]
GALNA .... Galena, KS [*American Association of Railroads railroad junction routing code*]
GalNac .... N-Acetylgalactosamine
Galob .... Galoob [*Lewis*] Toys, Inc. [*Associated Press*] (SAG)
Galoob .... Galoob [*Lewis*] Toys, Inc. [*Associated Press*] (SAG)
GALOP .... Gay London Policing (BUAC)
GALOVAL .... Grappling and Lock-On Validation
GALP .... Galapagos Penguin [*North American bird banding code*] (BIBA)
GALP .... Good Automated Laboratory Practice [*Environmental Protection Agency*]
GALPAT .... Galloping Pattern Memory
GALPO .... Gallipolis, OH [*American Association of Railroads railroad junction routing code*]
GA L Rep .... Georgia Law Reporter [*A publication*] (DLA)
Gals .... Galleries (DIAR)
gal/s .... Gallons per Second (ABAC)
GAL/S .... Gallons per Second
GALS .... General Aerodynamic Lifting Surface (KSC)
GALS .... Generalized Assembly Line Simulator [*General Motors Corp.*]
GALS .... Geographic Adjustment by Least Squares (PDAA)
GALS .... Gravity Anomaly Location System (SAUS)
GAISC .... Albany State College, Albany, GA [*Library symbol*] [*Library of Congress*] (LCLS)
GALSFC .... Ginger Alden "Lady Superstar" Fan Club (EA)
GALT .... Galactotransferase [*Cell strain deficient in galactose-1-phosphate uridyltransferase*]
GALT .... Galileo Technology [*NASDAQ symbol*] (SG)
GALT .... Galt, ON [*American Association of Railroads railroad junction routing code*]
GALT .... Gut-Associated Lymphoid Tissue [*Medicine*]
GALTS .... Generated Author Language Teaching System (EDAC)
Galv .... Galvanic [*Medicine*] (EDAA)
GALV .... Galvanic [*or Galvanized*]
galv .... Galvanized (VRA)
GALV .... Galvanometer
GALV .... Galveston [*Texas*]
GALV .... Galveston Terminal [*Federal Railroad Administration identification code*]
GALV .... Gibbon Ape Leukemia Virus
GALVA .... Gay and Lesbian Veterinary Association [*Australia*] (GVA)
GALVE .... Galveston, TX [*American Association of Railroads railroad junction routing code*]
GALVI .... Galvanized Iron
GALVND .... Galvannealed
GALVNM .... Galvanometer
galvo .... Galvanometer [*An instrument for detecting and measuring an electric current*] (WDMC)
GALVS .... Galvanized Steel
GALV TND... Galvanized or Tinned [*Freight*]
GALVWG .... Gemini Agena Launch Vehicle Working Group [*NASA*] (KSC)
GALW .... Galway [*County in Ireland*]
GALX .... Galaxy Foods [*NASDAQ symbol*] (TTSB)
GALX .... Galaxy Foods Co. [*NASDAQ symbol*] (SAG)
GALX .... Gas Liquids [*Private rail car owner code*]
GalxCbl .... Galaxy Cablevision Ltd. [*Associated Press*] (SAG)
GALXY .... Galaxy
GALY .... Galley (MSA)
GALZ .... Gays and Lesbians of Zimbabwe [*An association*]
GAM .... Air-to-Surface Missile (SAUS)
GAM .... Gambell [*Alaska*] [*Airport symbol*] (OAG)
Gam .... Gambia (MILB)
GAM .... Gambia
GAM .... Gameness (DSUE)
GAM .... Gamin Resources, Inc. [*Vancouver Stock Exchange symbol*]
GAM .... Gamma (NASA)
Gam .... Gamma Biologicals, Inc.
GAM .... Gamut [*Music*] (ROG)
GAM .... Gay Asian Male (ADWA)
GAM .... General Accounting Material (DNAB)
GAM .... General Accounting Office, Los Angeles Region, Los Angeles, CA [*OCLC symbol*] (OCLC)
GAM .... General Aeronautical Material
GAM .... General American Investors Co., Inc. [*NYSE symbol*] (SPSG)
GAM .... General American Investors Company, Inc. (SAUO)
GAM .... General Audit Manual
GAM .... Generalized Additive Model (IDAI)
GAM .... Genl Amer Investors [*NYSE symbol*] (TTSB)
GAM .... Geographical Analysis Machine
GAM .... Georgia Motor Trucking Association [*STAC*]
GAM .... Geostationary Airglow Monitor (SAUO)
GAM .... German Army [*ICAO designator*] (FAAC)
GAM .... Global Account Management (SAUO)
GAM .... Global Asset Management [*Commercial firm*] [*British*] (ECON)
GAM .... Globe and Mail [*Newspaper databank*] [*Canada*] (NITA)
GAM .... Globe and Mail Data Base [*Info Globe*] [*Information service or system*] (CRD)
GAM .... Goal Automated Manufacturing (SAUS)
GAM .... Golf Association of Michigan (SRA)
GAM .... GPS-Aided Munitions (SAUS)
GAM .... Graduate Aerospace Mechanical Engineering
GAM .... Grants Administration Manual [*HEW*]
GAM .... Graphic Access Method (SAUS)
GAM .... Graphic Arts Machine (SAUS)
GAM .... Graphic Arts Monthly [*A publication*] (DGA)
GAM .... Graphics Access Method (BUR)
GAM .... Graz Applied Mineralogy (SAUO)
GAM .... Great Adductor Muscle [*Medicine*] (MELL)
GAM .... Ground-to-Air Missile (AAG)
GAM .... Groupement des Associations Meunieres des Pays de la CEE [*Flour Milling Associations Group of the EEC Countries*] (EAIO)
GAM .... Grupo de Apoyo Mutuo [*Group for Mutual Support*] [*Mexico*] [*Political party*]
GAM .... Guaranteed Annual Minimum
GAM .... Guest Aerovias Mexico, SA
GAM .... Guided Aircraft Missile [*Obsolete*]
GAM .... Guided Air Missile (AAGC)
GAM .... Guided Artillery Munition (SAUS)
GAM .... Morehouse College, Atlanta, GA [*Library symbol*] [*Library of Congress*] (LCLS)
Gam .... Republic of The Gambia (NTIO)
GAMA .... Game Manufacturers Association (EA)
GAMA .... Gamma Biologicals, Inc. [*NASDAQ symbol*] (COMM)
GAMA .... Gas Appliance Manufacturers Association (EA)
GAMA .... General Agents & Managers Association [*Insurance*]
GAMA .... General Aircraft Manufacturers Association (SAUO)
GAMA .... General Aviation Manufacturers Association (EA)
GAMA .... Graphic Arts Machinery Association (DGA)
GAMA .... Graphic Arts Marketing Associates (SAUS)
GAMA .... Graphics-Assisted Management Application [*Computer science*] (BUR)
GAMA .... Groupe d'Analyse Macroeconomique Appliquee [*Group for Applied Macroeconomic Analysis*] [*University of Paris - Nanterre*] [*Information service or system*] (IID)
GAMA .... Guam Air Materiel Area (SAUS)
GAMA .... Guitar and Accessory Manufacturers Association [*Formerly, NAMMM*]
GAMA .... Guitar and Accessory Manufacturers Association of America (BUAC)
GAMA .... Markala [*Mali*] [*ICAO location identifier*] (ICLI)
GAMAA .... Graphic Arts Merchants' Association of Australia
GAMAA .... Guitar and Accessories Manufacturers Association of America (SAUO)
GamaB .... Gamma Biologicals, Inc. [*Associated Press*] (SAG)
Gam-Anon ... Gamblers (WDAA)
GAMARTA .... Metropolitan Atlanta Rapid Transit Authority, Atlanta, GA [*Library symbol*] [*Library of Congress*] (LCLS)
GAMAS .... Gamma Activation Materials Assay System [*Mobile laboratory*]
GAMAS .... General Atomic Material Assay System [*Nuclear energy*] (NRCH)
GAMAS .... Gulf Atomic Mobile Assay System
GAMAST .... Girls and Mathematics and Science Teaching

GAMB .... Gambro [*A.B.*], Inc. [*NASDAQ symbol*] (NQ)
GAMB .... Mopti/Barbe [*Mali*] [*ICAO location identifier*] (ICLI)
GAMB .... Morris Brown College, Atlanta, GA [*Library symbol*] [*Library of Congress*] (LCLS)
Gamb & Barl... Gamble and Barlow's Digest [*Ireland*] [*A publication*] (DLA)
GAMBICA..... Association for the Instrumentation Control and Automation Industry in the United Kingdom (BUAC)
GAMBICA..... Group of Associations of Manufacturers of British Instrumentation; Control and Automation (SAUS)
GAMBIT....... Gate-Modulated Bipolar Transistor (MCD)
Gambit....... General Anti-Material Bomblet with Improved Terminal effects (SAUS)
Gamboa....... Gamboa's Introduction to Philippine Law [*A publication*] (DLA)
Gamboa Philippine Law... Gamboa's Introduction to Philippine Law [*A publication*] (DLA)
GAMBOG...... Gambogia [*Gamboge*] [*Pharmacology*] (ROG)
Gambro....... Gambro [*A. B.*], Inc. [*Associated Press*] (SAG)
GAMBY........ Gambro AB [*NASDAQ symbol*] (COMM)
GAMC......... General Agents and Managers Conference
GAMC......... General Agents and Managers Conference of NALU [*Washington, DC*] (EA)
GAMC......... General Agents and Managers Conference of the National Association of Life Underwriters (SAUO)
GAMD......... Gallium Arsenide Microwave Diode
GAME.......... Gametek, Inc. [*NASDAQ symbol*] (SAG)
GAME.......... GEWEX [*Global Energy and Water Cycle Experiment*] [*Marine science*] (OSRA)
GAME.......... GEWEX Asian Monsoon Experiment (SAUS)
GAME.......... GEWEX -related Asian Monsoon Experiment (SAUS)
Game Coin... Game Conservation International (BUAC)
GAMECOIN... Game Conservation International (EA)
GameFn....... Game Financial Corp. [*Associated Press*] (SAG)
GAM Engineering... Graduate Aerospace Mechanical Engineering (SAUO)
GAMES........ General Architecture for Medical Expert Systems (SAUO)
Games Econ Behav... Games and Economic Behavior [*A publication*] (JLIT)
GAMET........ Gyro Accelerometer Misalignment Erection Test
GAMETAG.... Global Atmospheric Measurements Experiment on Tropospheric Aerosols and Gases [*National Science Foundation*]
Gametek...... Gametek, Inc. [*Associated Press*] (SAG)
GAmG......... Georgia Southwestern College, Americus, GA [*Library symbol*] [*Library of Congress*] (LCLS)
GAMG......... Goat Anti-Mouse Immunoglobulin G (STED)
GAMHTE...... General Association of Municipal Health and Technical Experts (EA)
GAMI.......... Gorham Advanced Materials Institute (SAUS)
GAMI.......... Great American Management & Investment, Inc. [*NASDAQ symbol*] (NQ)
GAMIC......... Gamma Incomplete [*Chemistry*] (IAA)
GAMIg......... Goat Anti-Mouse Immunoglobulin [*Immunology*]
GAMIN......... General Activity, Ascendence-Submission, Masculinity-Femininity, Inferiority Feelings, Nervousness [*Psychology*] (AEBS)
GamingW.... Gaming World International, Inc. [*Associated Press*] (SAG)
GAMIS......... General Analytical Methods Information Service [*Laboratory of the Government Chemist*] [*British*] (NITA)
GAMIS......... Graphic Arts Marketing and Information Service (SAUO)
GAMIS......... Graphic Arts Marketing Information Service (EA)
GAMK.......... Martin Luther King, Jr., Memorial Center, Atlanta, GA [*Library symbol*] [*Library of Congress*] (LCLS)
GAMK.......... Menaka [*Mali*] [*ICAO location identifier*] (ICLI)
GAMLOGS.... Gamma Ray Logs (IEEE)
GamLott....... Gaming Lottery Corp. [*Associated Press*] (SAG)
GAMM.......... Generalized Air Mobility Model (ACAE)
GAMM.......... German Association for Applied Mathematics and Mechanics
GAMM.......... Gimbal Angle Matching Monitor
GAM-M........ Morehouse College, School of Medicine, Atlanta, GA [*Library symbol*] [*Library of Congress*] (LCLS)
GAMMA....... Gender and Mathematics Association (BUAC)
GAMMA....... Generalized Automatic Method of Matrix Assembly [*Computer science*] (IAA)
GAMMA....... Graphically-Aided Mathematical Machine
GAMMA....... Guitar and Accesories Music Marketing Association (EA)
GAMMA....... Guns and Magnetic Material Alarm [*Weapon-detecting device to prevent skyjacking*]
GAMMA....... Institute of Advanced Research Long-Range Planning (BUAC)
GAMNA........ Gambia News Agency (EY)
Gamng......... Gaming Corporation of America [*Associated Press*] (SAG)
GamngCp..... Gaming Corporation of America [*Associated Press*] (SAG)
GAMO.......... German Army Material Office
GAMO.......... Ground and Amphibious Military Operations [*Army*]
GAMP.......... General Administration Ministry of Pensions (SAUO)
GAMP.......... Global Atmospheric Measurements Program [*National Science Foundation*]
GAMP.......... Group Agromet Monitoring Project (SAUO)
GAMP.......... Guided Antiarmor Monitor Projectile (ACAE)
GAMP.......... Guided Antiarmor Mortar Projectile (INF)
GAMPS........ Gander Automated Message Processing System [*ICAO*] (DA)
GAMRA........ Graphic Arts Manufacturers' Representative Association
GAMS.......... Gas Analysis Modeling System [*Department of Energy*] (GFGA)
GAMS.......... Girls Against More Skirt (SAUO)
GAMS.......... Groupement pour l'Avancement des Methodes Spectroscopiques et Physio-Chimiques d'Analyse [*Group for the Advancement of Spectroscopic Methods and Physicochemical Analysis*] [*Information service or system*] (IID)
GAMS.......... Group for the Advancement of Spectroscopic and Physiochemical Analysis Methods (BUAC)
GAMS.......... Guide to Available Mathematical Software [*Internet resource*]
GAMSA........ Glutamylaminomethylsulfonic Acid [*Biochemistry*]
GAMSA........ Management Science America, Inc., Atlanta, GA [*Library symbol*] [*Library of Congress*] (LCLS)
GAMSC........ German-American Motor Sport Club (SAUO)
GAMSP........ Georgia Association of Middle School Principals (SAUO)
GAM/SP....... Graphics Access Method/System Product [*IBM Corp.*]
GAMTA........ General Aviation Manufacturers' and Traders' Association [*British*] (DA)
GAMU.......... Mercer University, Atlanta, GA [*Library symbol*] [*Library of Congress*] (LCLS)
GAMU-P....... Mercer University, Southern School of Pharmacy, Atlanta, GA [*Library symbol*] [*Library of Congress*] (LCLS)
GAMV.......... Galinsoga Mosaic Virus [*Plant pathology*]
GamW.......... Gaming World International, Inc. [*Associated Press*] (SAG)
GAMZ.......... Gardinier Mine [*Federal Railroad Administration identification code*]
GAN............ Federal Nuclear and Radiation Safety Authority of the Russian Federation (SAUO)
GAN............ Galactic Area Network (SAUS)
GaN............ Gallium Nitride (AAEL)
GAN............ Gandalf Technologies, Inc. [*Toronto Stock Exchange symbol*]
GAN............ Gander Aviation Ltd. [*Canada*] [*ICAO designator*] (FAAC)
Gan............ Gandulphus [*Flourished, 1160-85*] [*Authority cited in pre-1607 legal work*] (DSA)
GAN............ GAO [*General Accounting Office*] Norfolk Regional Office, Virginia Beach, VA [*OCLC symbol*] (OCLC)
GAN............ Garan, Inc. [*AMEX symbol*] (SPSG)
GAN............ Gaseous Nitrogen (PDAA)
GAN............ Generalized Activity Network (IEEE)
GAN............ Generating and Analyzing Networks [*Computer science*]
GAN............ Generating and Assembly Networks (NITA)
GAN............ Giant Axon Neuropathy [*Medicine*] (DMAA)
GAN............ Global Alignment Network (SAUS)
GAN............ Global Area Network (IAA)
GAN............ Goldfields Air Navigation [*Australia*]
GAN............ Grant Anticipation Note (EBF)
GAN............ Green Academic Network (BUAC)
GAN............ Greenwich Apparent Noon (ROG)
GAN............ Ground Attack Night (MCD)
GAN............ Guidance and Navigation
GAN............ Gyro-Compass Automatic Navigation [*System*] (RDA)
GAN............ Net Gradability [*Truck specification*]
GANA.......... Gem Artists of North America
GANA.......... Glass Association of North America (NTPA)
Ganatra........ Ganatra's Criminal Cases [*India*] [*A publication*] (DLA)
Ganc........... Ganciclovir [*Medicine*] (EDAA)
Gand........... Gandulphus [*Flourished, 1160-85*] [*Authority cited in pre-1607 legal work*] (DSA)
G and A....... Gas and Air [*Medicine*]
G&A........... General and Administrative (ACAE)
G & A.......... General and Administrative
G&A........... General and Administrative Cost (EEVL)
G&A........... Geophysics and Astronomy (SAUO)
G&A/CSP..... General and administrative/common support pool (SAUS)
G&AE......... General and Administrative Expense [*Accounting*] (ODA)
GANDALF..... General Alpha-Numeric Direct Access Library Facility [*Search system*]
G&A PAN..... Gyroscope and Accelerometer Panel (SAUS)
G & B.......... Gloucester and Bristol [*Diocese*] (ROG)
G & B.......... Gordon & Breach [*Publisher*] [*British*]
G and B....... Grafton and Belington Railroad [*Initialism refers to a settlement of Indians who lived near this railroad*]
G&BS.......... Greek and Byzantine Studies (SAUO)
G&BS.......... Greek and Byzantine Studies (journ.) (SAUS)
G&C........... G & C Music Corporation
G&C........... Glass & Ceramic Division (ACII)
G & C.......... Gonville and Caius College [*Cambridge University*] (ROG)
G & C.......... Goodrich and Clincher (ROG)
G&C........... Guidance and Command (SAUS)
G&C........... Guidance and Control (ACAE)
G & C.......... Guidance and Control [*Military*] (CAAL)
G&CC.......... Gonville and Caius College (SAUO)
G & CC......... Guidance and Control Coupler (KSC)
G&CC.......... Guidance and Coordinating Council (SAUO)
G & CEP....... Guidance and Control Equipment Performance (KSC)
G & CS........ Guidance and Control System
G & D.......... Gale and Davison's English Queen's Bench Reports [*1841-43*] [*A publication*] (DLA)
G&D........... Galvanized and Dipped (SAUS)
G & D.......... Grosset & Dunlap [*Publisher*]
G & D.......... Growth and Development [*Pediatrics*] (DAVI)
G and D....... Growth and Development (STED)
G and D....... Guts and Determination (DSUE)
G&E........... Gift and Exchange
G & E.......... Ground and Environmental (KSC)
G&EI........... Gilbert and Ellice Islands (SAUS)
G&EIC......... Gilbert and Ellice Islands Colony (SAUO)
Gander........ Gander Mountain, Inc. [*Associated Press*] (SAG)
GANDER...... Guidance and Navigation Development and Evaluation Routine (PDAA)
GANDF........ Gandalf Technologies [*NASDAQ symbol*] (TTSB)
GANDF........ Gandalf Technologies, Inc. [*NASDAQ symbol*] (NQ)
G&F........... Georgia and Florida Railroad Co. (SAUO)
G & F.......... Georgia & Florida R. R.
G&FTEA....... Glazed and Floor Tile Export Association (SAUO)
G&FTHA....... Glazed and Floor Tile Home Trade Association (SAUO)
G & G.......... Gems & Gemology [*A publication*] (EAAP)

G & G......... Goldsmith and Guthrie's Appeals Reports [*Missouri*] [*A publication*] (DLA)
G & G......... Gyandoh and Griffiths. Sourcebook of the Constitutional Law of Ghana [*A publication*] (ILCA)
G&GBR........ Geologists and Geophysicists Board of Registration (SAUS)
G & G (MO)... Goldsmith and Guthrie's Appeals Reports [*Missouri*] [*A publication*] (DLA)
G & H......... Gavin and Hord's Indiana Statutes [*A publication*] (DLA)
G & H......... Gibbs & Hill, Inc. (NRCH)
G & J......... Gill and Johnson's Maryland Court of Appeals Reports [*1829-42*] [*A publication*] (DLA)
G & J......... Glyn and Jameson's English Bankruptcy Reports [*1821-28*] [*A publication*] (DLA)
G & J......... Gruner & Jahr AG & Co. [*Magazine publisher*] [*Germany*]
G & J (MD)... Gill and Johnson's Maryland Reports [*A publication*] (DLA)
G & Jo......... Gill and Johnson's Maryland Reports [*A publication*] (DLA)
G & John..... Gill and Johnson's Maryland Reports [*A publication*] (DLA)
G & K......... G & K Services, Inc. [*Associated Press*] (SAG)
Gandlf......... Gandalf Technologies, Inc. [*Associated Press*] (SAG)
G & L Rty.... G & L Realty Corp. [*Associated Press*] (SAG)
G & M......... General and Municipal
G&M........... Geography and Map (SAUS)
G&M........... Geography and Map Division (SAUO)
G & M......... Geraghty & Miller, Inc.
G & M......... Girth and Mirth (EA)
G&M........... Globe and Mail (SAUS)
G & M......... Gulf & Mississippi Railroad
G&MW......... General & Municipal Workers (SAUO)
G&N........... Gippsland and Northern (SAUS)
G & N......... Greenville & Northern Railway Co. (IIA)
G & N......... Guidance and Navigation [*System*] [*Apollo*] [*NASA*]
G&N Coop.... G & N Cooperator (SAUS)
G&NS.......... Guidance and Navigation Subsystem [*Aerospace*] (NAKS)
G&NS.......... Guidance and Navigation System (SAUO)
G & O......... Gas and Oxygen [*Medicine*]
G & OA....... Glycerine and Oleochemicals Association (EA)
G & PA....... Girls and Physical Activity National Newsletter [*A publication*]
G&PA.......... Girls and Physical Activity National Newsletter (journ.) (SAUS)
G & P RR Laws... Gregg and Pond's Railroad Laws of the New England States [*A publication*] (DLA)
G & R......... Geldert and Russell's Nova Scotia Reports [*A publication*] (DLA)
G&R........... Greece and Rome (journ.) (SAUS)
G&R........... Greek and Roman (SAUS)
G & RS....... Guidance and Reporting System [*Army*]
G&S........... General and Standard (ACAE)
G & S......... Gilbert and Sullivan
G&SA.......... Goods and Service Allowance (SAUS)
G&SA.......... Gulf and South American (SAUS)
G & Sh RR... Godefroi and Shortt's Law of Railway Companies [*A publication*] (DLA)
G&Sh RR..... Godefroi and Shortts Law of Railway Companies (journ.) (SAUS)
G&SI.......... Gulf and Ship Island (SAUS)
G & SI......... Gulf & Ship Island Railroad Co.
G&SJ.......... Gilbert and Sullivan Journal (journ.) (SAUS)
G & SS....... Gilbert and Sullivan Society [*Australia*]
G&SSEL....... General and Standard Support Equipment List (ACAE)
G & SW....... Glasgow & South-Western [*Railway*] [*Scotland*]
G & SWR..... Glasgow & South-Western Railway [*Scotland*]
G&SWR....... Glasgow and South Western Railway (SAUO)
G&SWR....... Great Southern and Western Railway (SAUO)
G & T......... Gin and Tonic
G&T........... Goals and Timetables (AAGC)
G & T......... Gould and Tucker's Notes on Revised Statutes of United States [*A publication*] (DLA)
G & T......... Gowns and Towels [*Medicine*] (DMAA)
G and TC..... Game and Tsetse Control Department (SAUO)
G & U......... Grafe & Unzer [*Publisher*] [*German*]
G & W......... Genesee & Western Railroad (IIA)
G&W........... Glycerine and Water (STED)
G&W........... Graham & Whiteside
G & W......... Gulf & Western Industries, Inc.
G & Wh Eas... Gale and Whatley [*later, Gale*] on Easements [*A publication*] (ILCA)
G & WI........ Gulf & Western Industries, Inc.
G & W New Tr... Graham and Waterman on New Trials [*A publication*] (DLA)
Gane........... Eastern District Court Reports [*South Africa*] [*A publication*] (DLA)
GANEFO....... Federation of the Games of the New Emerging Forces (SAUO)
GANEFO....... Games of the New Emerging Forces [*A counter-attraction to the Olympic Games*] [*Indonesia*]
GANF.......... Ganfield [*England*]
GANF.......... Niafunke [*Mali*] [*ICAO location identifier*] (ICLI)
gang........... Ganglion (STED)
GANG.......... Ganglion [*Medicine*]
gangl.......... Ganglion [*or Ganglionic*] [*Neurology*] (DAVI)
GANH.......... Northside Hospital, Atlanta, GA [*Library symbol*] [*Library of Congress*] (LCLS)
GAN/HQ....... GANs headquarters (SAUO)
GANIL......... Grand Accelerator National A Ions Lourds (SAUS)
GANIP......... Graphic Approach to Numerical Information Processing (IAA)
GANK.......... Nara/Keibane [*Mali*] [*ICAO location identifier*] (ICLI)
GAN/NED...... GANs regional office North Eastern District (SAUO)
GANNET....... General Administrative Network [*Computer linkup*] [*British*]
Gannett....... Gannett Co., Inc. [*Associated Press*] (SAG)
Gannon U..... Gannon University (GAGS)
GANO.......... [*The*] Georgia Northern Railway Co. [*AAR code*]
GANO.......... Georgia Northern Railway Company (SAUO)
GA-NOC....... General Assembly, National Olympic Committees (BUAC)
GA-NOC....... General Assembly of the National Olympic Committees (SAUO)
GANPAC....... German American National Political Action Committee (EA)
GANR.......... Nioro [*Mali*] [*ICAO location identifier*] (ICLI)
GANS.......... Geomatics Association of Nova Scotia (SAUO)
GANS.......... Global Access, Navigation, and Safety (SEWL)
GANS.......... Granulomatous Angiitis of the Nervous System [*Medicine*] (DMAA)
GANS.......... Guidance and Navigation System [*Apollo*] [*NASA*] (IAA)
GANSAT....... Gannett Satellite Information Network
Gantos......... Gantos, Inc. [*Associated Press*] (SAG)
Gantt Dig..... Gantt's Digest of Arkansas Statutes [*A publication*] (DLA)
Gantts Dig... Gantt's Digest of Arkansas Statutes [*A publication*] (DLA)
ganz............ Ganzlich [*Complete*] [*German*] (BARN)
GANZ.......... Gas Association of New Zealand (SAUO)
GAO............ GARP Activities Office [*Marine science*] (MSC)
GAO............ General Accounting Office [*of the US government*]
GAO............ General Accounting Office, Technical Information Sources and Service, Washington, DC [*OCLC symbol*] (OCLC)
GAO............ General Administrative Order
GAO............ General Agricultural Officer [*Ministry of Agriculture, Fisheries, and Food*] [*British*]
GAO............ General Alert Order (NATG)
GAO............ General American Oil Co. of Texas (SAUO)
GAO............ General American Overseas Corp. (SAUO)
GAO............ General Auditing Office (SAUO)
GAO............ German Army Office
GAO............ Glycolic Acid Oxidase [*An enzyme*]
GAO............ Golden Air Commuter AB [*Sweden*] [*ICAO designator*] (FAAC)
GAO............ Government Accounting Office (MCD)
GAO............ Guantanamo [*Cuba*] [*Airport symbol*] (OAG)
GAO............ Gummed All Over [*Envelopes*] (DGA)
GAO............ United States General Accounting Office (SAUS)
GAOC.......... Oglethorpe University, Atlanta, GA [*Library symbol*] [*Library of Congress*] (LCLS)
GAO/CED...... General Accounting Office/Community and Economic Development Division
GAOF.......... Gummed All Over Flap [*Envelopes*]
GAO/FGMSD... General Accounting Office/Financial and General Management Studies Division
GAO/FPCD... General Accounting Office/Federal Personnel and Compensation Division
GAO/GGD..... General Accounting Office General Government Division
GAOHP........ General Alliance of Operative House Painters [*A union*] [*British*]
GAO/HRD...... General Accounting Office Human Resources Division
GAO/LCD...... General Accounting Office/Logistics and Communications Division
GAO Let Rep... General Accounting Office Letter Report [*A publication*] (DLA)
GAO/MASAD... General Accounting Office Mission Analysis and Systems Acquisition Division
GAO NOTE... General Accounting Office, Notice of Execution (DNAB)
GAO/NSIAD... General Accounting Office National Security and International Affairs Division
GAO/PAD...... General Accounting Office Program Analysis Division
GAO/PEMD... General Accounting Office Program Evaluation and Methodology Division
GAO/PSAD... General Accounting Office/ Procurement and Systems Acquisition Division (SAUO)
GAO/PSAD... General Accounting Office/Procurement and Systems Acquisition Division
GAOR.......... General Accounting Office Review
GAOR.......... General Assembly Official Record [*United Nations*] [*A publication*] (DLA)
GAOS.......... German Association for Political Science (SAUO)
GAOTU........ Grand Architect of the Universe [*Freemasonry*] (ROG)
GAOW.......... General Accounting Office, Washington DC (SAUO)
GAP............ Atlanta Public Library, Atlanta, GA [*OCLC symbol*] (OCLC)
GAP............ Atlanta Public Schools, Professional Library, Atlanta, GA [*Library symbol*] [*Library of Congress*] (LCLS)
GAP............ Gadolinium Aluminium Perovskite [*Inorganic chemistry*]
GaP............ Gallium Phosphide (AAEL)
GAP............ Gap Analysis Program (SAUS)
Gap............ Gap, Inc. [*Formerly, Gap Stores, Inc.*] [*Associated Press*] (SAG)
GAP............ Gardner Analysis of Personality [*Survey*] [*Medicine*] (STED)
GAP............ Garmisch-Partenkirchen [*Federal Republic of Germany*] [*Seismograph station code, US Geological Survey*] (SEIS)
GAP............ Gastric and Peptic Ulcer [*A laboratory test kit*] [*Medicine*]
GAP............ GATE Advisory Panel (SAUS)
GAP............ General Accounting Package (IAA)
GAP............ General Accounts Payments (FOTI)
GAP............ General and Practical Energy Information Data Base (MCD)
GAP............ General Antenna Package [*COMSAT*]
GAP............ General Application Plan (AFIT)
GAP............ General Assembly Program [*Computer science*]
GAP............ Generalized Availability Program (ACAE)
GAP............ Generic Access Profile (SAUS)
GAP............ Generic Address Parameter [*Computer science*] (DDC)
GAP............ Generic Electro-Optical Auto Processor (ACAE)
GAP............ Geographic Applications Program [*United States Geological Survey*] (IID)
GAP............ Georgia Assessment Project (SAUO)
GaP............ Georgia Power [*Associated Press*] (SAG)
GAP............ Georgia Power [*Federal Railroad Administration identification code*]
GAP............ Geostationary Atmospheric Profiler (SAUO)
GAP............ Ghetto Arts Program [*Later, Urban Arts Corps*] (EA)
GAP............ Girls Alone Project (BUAC)
GAP............ Glaciology of the Antarctic Peninsula Project (SAUO)

GAP .... Global Action Plan for the Earth (BUAC)
GAP .... Glyceraldehyde Phosphate [*Biochemistry*]
GAP .... Glycidyl Azide Polymer [*Chemistry*]
GAP .... GnRH [*Gonadotropin Releasing Hormone*] Associated Peptide [*Endocrinology*]
GAP .... GOAL [*Ground Operations Aerospace Language*] Automatic Procedure [*NASA*] (NASA)
GAP .... Good Agricultural Practice [*Toxicology*]
GAP .... Goodyear Associative Processor [*Computer science*]
GAP .... Government Accountability Project (EA)
GAP .... Government Aircraft Plant
GAP .... Government-Assured Program [*Medicine*] (EDAA)
GAP .... Government Available Property (SAUO)
GAP .... Government of Alberta Publications [*Alberta Public Affairs Bureau*] [*Canada*] [*Information service or system*] (CRD)
GAP .... Graduate Academic Program (SAUO)
GAP .... Grand Anatolia Project [*Dam system*] [*Turkey*] (ECON)
GAP .... Grandparents As Parents (SAUS)
GAP .... Grant Air Program [*DoD*] (MCD)
GAP .... Graphical Automatic Programming [*Computer science*]
GAP .... Graphic Arts Professionals (NTPA)
GAP .... Graphics Adapter Processor [*Baytec*]
GAP .... Graphics Application Program
GAP .... Great American Public (SAUO)
GAP .... Great Ape Project (SAUO)
GAP .... Great Atl & Pac Tea [*NYSE symbol*] (TTSB)
GAP .... Great Atlantic & Pacific Co. (SAUO)
GAP .... Great Atlantic & Pacific Tea Co., Inc. [*NYSE symbol*] (SPSG)
GAP .... Greater Access to Publishing [*British*]
GAP .... Greenwood, Archer, and Pine [*Major streets in Tulsa, OK*] [*In musical group "The GAP Band"*]
GAP .... Gross Agricultural Product (WDAA)
GAP .... Group Attainment Program
GAP .... Group for Aquatic Primary Productivity [*ICSU*]
GAP .... Group for the Advancement of Psychiatry (EA)
GAP .... Growth-Associated Protein [*Cytochemistry*]
GAP .... Growth Associated Proteins (SAUS)
GAP .... Grupo de Auto-Defensa [*Self-Defense Group*] [*Uruguay*] [*Political party*] (PD)
GAP .... Guanosine Triphosphatase Activating Protein [*Medicine*] (EDAA)
GAP .... Guanosine Triphosphatase Activating Protein [*Biochemistry*]
GAP .... Guidance Autopilot (SAUS)
GAP .... Guided Antitank Projectile (MCD)
GAP .... Guide for Application Programming (SAUS)
GAP .... Guildhall Automation Project (TELE)
GAP .... Gun Aiming Point (SAUS)
GAP .... Gun-Fired Antitank Projectile (ACAE)
GAP .... Gusap [*Papua New Guinea*] [*Airport symbol*] [*Obsolete*] (OAG)
GAP .... Southeast Anatolia Project [*Turkey*] (BUAC)
GAPA .... Greek American Progressive Association (EA)
GAPA .... Ground-to-Air Pilotless Aircraft [*Early US test missiles*]
GAPA .... International Geological/Geophysical Atlases of the Atlantic and Pacific Oceans (SAUS)
GaPac .... Georgia-Pacific Corp. [*Associated Press*] (SAG)
GAPAN .... Guide to Air Pilots and Air Navigation [*A publication*]
GAPAN .... Guild of Airline Pilots and Navigators (SAUS)
GAPAN .... Guild of Air Pilots and Air Navigators (MCD)
GAPAN .... Guild of Air Pilots and Navigators (SAUO)
GAPB .... General Aptitude Test Battery (DNAB)
GaPC .... Georgia Power Capital Ltd. [*Associated Press*] (SAG)
GaPC .... Georgia Power Capital Trust I [*Associated Press*] (SAG)
GAPC .... Global Alternative Propulsion Center [*Automotive industry*]
GAPC .... Ground Attitude and Positioning Control (ACAE)
GAPCE .... General Assembly of the Presbyterian Church of England (DAS)
GAP CON .... Gap Conductance (GAAI)
Ga-PD .... Gallium Arsenide Phosphide Photodiode
GAPD .... Garrett Auxiliary Power Division [*Military contractor*] (RDA)
GAPD .... Geiger-mode avalanche photo diode detector (SAUS)
GAPD .... Glyceraldehyde-3-Phosphate Dehydrogenase (STED)
GAPD .... Glyceraldehyde Phosphate Dehydrogenase [*Organic chemistry*] (MAH)
GAPD .... Government and Aeronautical Products Division [*Honeywell, Inc.*]
GAPDH .... Glyceraldehydephosphate Dehydrogenase [*Also, GPDH*] [*An enzyme*]
GAPE .... General Aviation Pilot Education [*Safety project*]
GAPE .... Geographical Association Package Exchange (AIE)
GAPE .... Global Agricultural Productivity Estimation (SAUO)
GAPE .... Graphic Acids to Packaging Equipment (PDAA)
GAPE .... Graphic Aids to Packaging Engineers (SAUS)
GAPE .... Ground Anchor Placement Equipment
GAPEA .... Graphic Arts Platemakers Employers' Federation (DGA)
GAPEWS .... Graphic Air Picture Early Warning System (SAUO)
GAPEX .... General Agricultural Products Export Corp. [*Tanzania*] (BUAC)
GAPEX .... Ground-Based Atmospheric Profiling Experiment (SAUO)
GAPh .... Southern School of Pharmacy, Mercer University, Atlanta, GA [*Library symbol*] [*Library of Congress*] (LCLS)
GAPHYOR .... Gaz-Physique-Orsay Database [*Universite de Paris-Sud*] [*Information service or system*]
GAPI .... Gateway Application Programming Interface (SAUS)
GAPIE .... Georgia Partners in Education (SAUO)
GAPie .... Piedmont Hospital, Atlanta, GA [*Library symbol*] [*Library of Congress*] (LCLS)
GAPL .... Ground Assembly Parts List (ACAE)
GAPL .... Group Assembly Parts List (MCD)
GAPL .... Group Assembly Provisioning List (MCD)
GAPM .... Generalized Access Path Method [*Computer science*] (MHDB)
GAPM .... Global Atmospheric Prediction Model (SAUO)
GAPMB .... Ghana Agriculutural Produce Marketing Board (BUAC)
GAPO .... Gorilla Armpit Odor (SAUS)
GAPO .... Growth Retardation, Alopecia, Pseudo-Anodontia, and Optic Atrophy Syndrome [*Medicine*] (DMAA)
GAPP .... Geometric Arithmetic Parallel Processor [*Computer science*]
GAPR .... Grant Application Request (WDAA)
GA Prac .... Stand's Georgia Practice [*A publication*] (DLA)
GA-PROGRAM ... Geographic Application Program (SAUO)
GAPS .... Billions of Actions Per Second (SAUS)
GAPS .... Geo-Assimilated Positioning System [*Navigation systems*]
GAPS .... German Association for Political Science (BUAC)
GAPS .... Global Assimilation and Prognosis System (SAUO)
GAPS .... Government Accountability Property System (MCD)
GAPSALS .... Give a Pint, Save a Life Society [*World War II organization which encouraged donating blood*]
GAPSAT .... Gap-Filler Satellite [*RADAR*] (NVT)
GAPSAT .... Tactical Communications Satellite System (SAUO)
GAPSATCOM ... Gap-Filler Satellite Communication System (MCD)
GA PSC .... Georgia Public Service Commission Reports [*A publication*] (DLA)
GAPSF .... Government Agricultural Policy and Services for Farmers [*British*]
GAPSFAS .... Graduate and Professional School Financial Aid Service (GAGS)
GAPSFAS .... Graduate and Professional Students Financial Statement (SAUS)
GAPSS .... Graphical Analysis Procedures for System Simulation (PDAA)
GAPT .... Generalized Atomic Polar Tensor [*Physical chemistry*]
GAPT .... Georgia Association for Pupil Transportation (SAUO)
GAPT .... Graphical Automatically Programmed Tools [*Computer science*]
GAPT .... Guild of Anatomical Pathology Technicians (BUAC)
GAP UK .... Global Action Plan [*United Kingdom*] (BUAC)
GaPw .... Georgia Power Co. [*Associated Press*] (SAG)
GAQ .... Gao [*Mali*] [*Airport symbol*] (OAG)
GAQ .... Geotechnical Aquifer Test (SAUO)
GAQ .... Golfe Air Quebec Ltd. [*Canada*] [*ICAO designator*] (FAAC)
GAQ .... Good Average Quality (ADA)
GAQ .... Graphic Arts Quality (DGA)
GAQA .... Government Acquisition Quality Assurance (MCD)
GAR .... Commodore Aviation [*Australia*] [*ICAO designator*] (FAAC)
GAR .... GAO [*General Accounting Office*] San Francisco Regional Office, San Francisco, CA [*OCLC symbol*] (OCLC)
GAR .... Garage [*Classified advertising*]
GAR .... Garaged [*Automobile*]
GAR .... Garaina [*Papua New Guinea*] [*Airport symbol*] (OAG)
GAR .... Garamond [*Typography*] (DGA)
gar .... Garden (BEE)
GAR .... Garden Lake Resources [*Vancouver Stock Exchange symbol*]
GAR .... Garm [*Former USSR*] [*Seismograph station code, US Geological Survey*] (SEIS)
GAR .... Garrett Corporation (SAUO)
GAR .... Garrison (MUGU)
GAR .... Gate Acceptance Rate (CTAS)
GAR .... General Adverse Reaction [*Noise*]
GAR .... Generic Airborne Radar (SAUS)
GAR .... Genitoanorectal [*Syndrome*] [*Medicine*] (DB)
GAR .... Geologic Aspects of Rivers (SAUO)
GAR .... George assembly routine (SAUS)
GaR .... Georgia Reports [*A publication*] (DLA)
Ga R .... Georgia Review [*A publication*] (BRI)
G-Ar .... Georgia State Department of Archives and History, Atlanta, GA [*Library symbol*] [*Library of Congress*] (LCLS)
GAR .... German Air Force (SAUS)
GAR .... German Army
GAR .... Gimbal Angle Rate
GAR .... Gimbal Angle Readout
GAR .... Glass Accumulation Rate [*Oceanography*]
GAR .... Global Atmospheric Research (NOAA)
GAR .... Glycinamidribotid (SAUS)
GAR .... Go-Around (GAVI)
GAR .... Goat Anti-Rabbit [*Also, GARb*] [*Immunology*]
GAR .... Golden Age Records [*Record label*]
GAR .... Government Analysis Report (SAUO)
GAR .... Government Authorized Representative
GAR .... Governors Authorized Representative (SAUO)
GAR .... Grand Army of the Republic (GPO)
GAR .... Graphics Action Request (MCD)
GaR .... Greece and Rome [*A publication*] (ABAR)
GAR .... Gross Annual Return (SAUS)
GAR .... Gross as Received
GAR .... Ground Accident Report (MCD)
GAR .... Ground Avoidance Radar (SAUS)
GAR .... Group Advisory Representative (SAUO)
GAR .... Growth Analysis and Review (BUR)
GAR .... Gruppi Armati Radicali per il Comunismo [*Armed Radical Groups for Communism*] [*Italy*] (PD)
GAR .... Guangxi Research and Design Institute of Architectural Science [*China*] (BUAC)
GAR .... Guaranteed Annuity Rates
GAR .... Guided Aerial Rocket
GAR .... Guided Airborne Rocket (SAUS)
GAR .... Guided Aircraft Rocket
GAR .... Guided Aircraft Rocket. Examples (SAUO)
GAR .... Guided Antiarmor Rocket
GAR .... Gummed All Round [*Envelopes*] (DGA)
GARA .... Garamond [*Typography*] (WDAA)
Garan .... Garan, Inc. [*Associated Press*] (SAG)

garb.......... Garbage (BARN)
GARB.......... Garment and Allied Industries Requirements Board (SAUO)
GARb.......... Goat Anti-Rabbit [*Also, GAR*] [*Immunology*]
GARB.......... Green, Amber, Red, Blue [*Priority of the airways*]
GARB.......... Guided Antiradiation Bomb
Garbage....... Garbage: The Independent Environmental Quarterly [*A publication*] (BRI)
GARBC......... General Association of Regular Baptist Churches (EA)
GARBD......... Garboard [*Naval architecture*]
GARC.......... General Astronautics Research Corporation (SAUO)
GARC.......... Graphic Arts Research Center [*Later, T & E Center*] [*Rochester Institute of Technology*]
GARC.......... Great Atlantic Radio Conspiracy (EA)
GARC.......... Retail Credit Co., Atlanta, GA [*Library symbol*] [*Library of Congress*] (LCLS)
GARCH......... Generalized Auto-Regressive Conditional Heteroskedacity [*Business term*] (ECON)
GARCH......... Generalized Autoregressive Conditional Heteroskedasticy Process
G Arch........ Graduate in Architecture
GARD.......... Denning Mobile Robotics, Inc. [*NASDAQ symbol*] (COMM)
GARD.......... Gamma Atomic Radiation Detector
gard.......... Garden (VRA)
GARD.......... Gardener (ROG)
Gard.......... Gardens (BARN)
GARD.......... General Address Reading Devices [*Computer science*]
GARD.......... General American Research Division (SAUO)
GARD.......... General Aviation Recovery Device
GARD.......... Gimbal Angle Runaway Detector
GARD.......... Graphic Analyzation (or Analyzer) of Resistance Defects (SAUS)
GARD.......... Graphic Analyzer of Resistance Defects
GARD.......... Graphic Arts Research Department (SAUS)
GARD.......... Grumman-Alderson Research Dummy [*Aircraft ejection seats*]
GARDAE........ Gathers Alarms, Reports, Displays, and Evaluates
GardDen....... Gardner Denver Machinery, Inc. [*Associated Press*] (SAG)
GARDE......... Gather, Alarm, Report, Display, and Evaluate (IAA)
GARDEN........ Garden [*Commonly used*] (OPSA)
GARDENEX...... Federation of Garden and Leisure Equipment Exporters (BUAC)
Gardenhire.... Gardenhire's Reports [*14, 15 Missouri*] [*A publication*] (DLA)
GARDENS....... Gardens [*Commonly used*] (OPSA)
Gard Ev....... Garde on Evidence [*1830*] [*A publication*] (DLA)
GARDIAN....... GBL Point Defense System (SAUS)
GARDIAN....... General Area Defense Integrated Anti-Missile LASER System (SEWL)
GARDN......... Garden [*Commonly used*] (OPSA)
GardnFr....... Garden Fresh Restaurant Corp. [*Associated Press*] (SAG)
Gardn PC...... Gardner's Peerage Case, Reported by Le Marchant [*A publication*] (DLA)
GardnR........ Garden Ridge Corp. [*Associated Press*] (SAG)
Gard NY Rep... Gardenier's New York Reporter [*A publication*] (DLA)
Gard NY Rept... Gardenier's New York Reporter [*A publication*] (DLA)
Gard NY Rptr... Gardenier's New York Reporter [*A publication*] (DLA)
Gard Pl....... Garde's First Principles of Pleading [*A publication*] (DLA)
GARDS......... Global Atmospheric Radionuclide Detection System (SAUO)
GardStat...... Garden State Bancshares [*Associated Press*] (SAG)
GARDTRAK...... Gamma Absorption and Radiation Detection Tracking (IAA)
GARE.......... Guidelines for Authority and Reference Entries [*Cataloguing*] [*Association for Library Collections and Technical Services*]
GA Rep........ Georgia Reports [*A publication*] (DLA)
GA Rep Ann.... Georgia Reports, Annotated [*A publication*] (DLA)
GAREX......... Ground Aviation Radio Exchange (SAUS)
GAREX......... Ground Aviation Radio Exchange System (MCD)
GAREX System... Ground Aviation Radio Exchange System (SAUS)
GARF.......... Goddard Antenna Research Facility (SAUS)
GARF.......... Graphic Arts Research Foundation (EA)
GARF.......... Ground Approach Radio Fuse (IAA)
GARF.......... Guam Acoustic Range Facility [*Military*] (CAAL)
GARG.......... Garganey [*North American bird banding code*] (BIBA)
GARG.......... Gargarisma [*Gargle*] [*Pharmacy*]
Garg.......... Gargle (STED)
GarG.......... Garment Graphics, Inc. [*Associated Press*] (SAG)
GARGAR........ Gargarisma [*Gargle*] [*Pharmacy*] (ROG)
GARGD......... Garaged [*Automotive advertising*]
GARGG......... Goat Anti-Rabbit Gamma Globulin (STED)
GARGG......... Goat Antiserum to Rabbit Gamma-Globulin [*Immunology*]
GARH.......... Georgia Regional Hospital at Atlanta, Atlanta, GA [*Library symbol*] [*Library of Congress*] (LCLS)
GARI.......... Goat Anti-Rabbit Immunoglobulin [*Immunochemistry*]
GAR/I......... Ground Acquisition Receiver/Interrogator (SAUS)
GARI.......... Groupe d'Action Revolutionnaire Internationaliste [*International Revolutionary Action Group*] [*France*] [*Political party*] (PD)
GARI.......... Grupo de Accion Revolucionaria Internacional [*International Revolutionary Action Group*] [*Spain*] [*Political party*]
GARIM......... Air Group Headquarters (SAUO)
GARIOA........ Government Aid and Relief in Occupied Areas (SAUS)
GARIOA........ Government and Relief in Occupied Areas [*Post-World War II*]
GARIOA........ Government Appropriations for Relief in Occupied Areas (SAUO)
Garkreba...... Garantie- und Kreditbank [*Guaranty and Credit Bank*] [*Germany*] (EG)
GARLD......... Garland, TX [*American Association of Railroads railroad junction routing code*]
GarmGph....... Garment Graphics, Inc. [*Associated Press*] (SAG)
GARMI......... General Aviation Radio Magnetic Indicator
GArmO......... Group Armaments Officer [*British military*] (DMA)
GARN.......... Garneau, PQ [*American Association of Railroads railroad junction routing code*]
GARN.......... Garnet Resources [*NASDAQ symbol*] (TTSB)
GARN.......... Garnet Resources Corp. [*NASDAQ symbol*] (NQ)
GARN.......... Garnish [*Automotive engineering*]
GARN.......... Garnishee Order (DCTA)
GARNEE........ Garnishee [*Legal shorthand*] (LWAP)
Garnet........ Garnet Resources Corp. [*Associated Press*] (SAG)
GARNOR........ Garnishor [*Legal shorthand*] (LWAP)
GARNT......... Garnett, KS [*American Association of Railroads railroad junction routing code*]
GARP.......... Generic Attribute Registration Protocol (SAUS)
GARP.......... Global Atmosphere Research Programme (SAUS)
GARP.......... Global Atmospheric Research Program [*Terminated*] [*National Science Foundation*]
GARP.......... Globally optimized Alternating phase Rectangular Pulse (SAUS)
GARP.......... Group Address Resolution Protocol (SAUO)
GARP.......... Growth at the Right Price
GARP-I........ GARP First Objective (SAUS)
GARS.......... Generic Airborne Radar Simulator (SAUS)
GARS.......... Generic Airborne RADAR System (DWSG)
GARS.......... Gilliam Autism Rating Scale [*Test*] (TMMY)
GARS.......... Glycine Amide Phosphoribosyl Synthetase (DMAA)
GARS.......... Grand Assistant Recording Scribe [*Freemasonry*] (ROG)
GARS.......... Guided Accelerated Random Search (SAUS)
GARS.......... Gyrocompassing Attitude Reference System (SAUS)
GART.......... Gartner Group'A' [*NASDAQ symbol*] (TTSB)
GART.......... Gartner Group, Inc. [*NASDAQ symbol*] (NQ)
GART.......... Graphics Address Relocation Table (SAUS)
GART.......... Graphics Address Remapping Table (SAUS)
GARTEur....... Group for Aeronautical Research and Technology in Europe (BUAC)
Gartner....... Gartner Group, Inc. [*Associated Press*] (SAG)
GARY.......... Gary, IN [*American Association of Railroads railroad junction routing code*]
GAS........... Autonomous Anarchist Groups [*Spanish*] (PD)
GAS........... Gach Saran [*Iran*] [*Airport symbol*] (AD)
GAS........... Galactorrhea-Amenorrhea Syndrome [*Medicine*] (DMAA)
GAS........... Galena Air Services, Inc. [*ICAO designator*] (FAAC)
GAS........... Gallipolis, OH [*Location identifier*] [*FAA*] (FAAL)
GAS........... Gallium Arsenide [*Semiconductor*]
GAS........... Gamma-Activated Site [*Biochemistry*]
GAS........... Garissa [*Kenya*] [*Airport symbol*] (OAG)
GAS........... Gas Acquisition System
GAS........... Gas Anti-Solvent [*Chemical engineering*]
GAS........... Gas-Insulated Switchgear
GAS........... Gasoline (AFM)
GAS........... Gastric Acid Secretion [*Medicine*] (DMAA)
GAS........... Gastroenterology [*Medicine*]
GAS........... Gauss [*Later, GTT*] [*Federal Republic of Germany*] [*Geomagnetic observatory code*]
GAS........... General Adaptation Syndrome [*Medicine*]
GAS........... General Adaptation to Stress (SAUS)
GAS........... general adaption syndrome (SAUS)
GAS........... General Air Situation (SAUS)
GAS........... General Air Staff (NATG)
GAS........... General Aptitude Series [*Test*]
GAS........... General area services (SAUS)
GAS........... General Automotive Support
GAS........... General Aviation Services [*Canada*] (BUAC)
GAS........... General Aviation Simulator [*Computer science*] [*NASA*]
GAS........... Generalized Arteriosclerosis [*Medicine*]
GAS........... Generalized Audit Software [*Computer science*]
GAS........... Genetic Algorithm (SEWL)
GAS........... Genome Automation System (HGEN)
GAS........... Geometric Analysis Section
GAS........... Georgia Academy of Science (SAUO)
GAS........... Get Away Special (MCD)
GAS........... Giant Air Shower
GAS........... Giant Attribute Survey
GAS........... Glasgow Archaeological Society [*Scotland*] (BUAC)
GAS........... Glasgow Assessment Schedule [*Medicine*] (EDAA)
GAS........... Glass Art Society (EA)
GAS........... Global Address Space (MHDI)
GAS........... Global Analysis Systems [*Information service or system*] (IID)
GAS........... Global Anxiety Score [*Medicine*] (DMAA)
GAS........... Global Assessment Scale [*Psychiatric evaluation test*]
GAS........... Goal Attainment Scale
GAS........... Goilala Air Services [*Australia*]
GAS........... Goods Acquisition System (SAUS)
GAS........... Government Accounting Service [*British*]
GAS........... Government Accounting System (SAUO)
GAS........... Governmental Accounting Standards (SAUO)
GAS........... Government-Assisted Students
GAS........... Government of American Samoa (MUGU)
GAS........... Government Payroll System (SAUO)
GAS........... Gradient Accentuated Spectroscopy (SAUS)
GAS........... Grand Annual Sojourner [*Freemasonry*] (ROG)
GAS........... Grants Acronymical Shorthand (SAUS)
GAS........... Graphics Application Program [*Computer science*] (MHDI)
GAS........... Graphics Attachment Support (IAA)
GAS........... Gray Area Systems (MCD)
GAS........... Great American Smokeout (SAUO)
GAS........... Group Analytic Society (BUAC)
GAS........... Group Apprenticeship Scheme (SAUS)
GAS........... Group A Streptococci [*Medicine*]
GAS........... Group Autonomous Specialised Working Party (SAUO)
GAS........... Growth Arrest-Specific Gene [*Medicine*] (DMAA)

GAS .... Guild of All Saints [*British*] (ROG)
GAS .... Guild of All Souls [*British*]
GAS .... Gun Accessory System (MCD)
GAS .... Gun Aiming Sensor (MCD)
GAS .... Gunner's Auxiliary Sight (MCD)
GAS .... Gust Alleviation System [*Aviation*] (MCD)
GAS .... NICOR, Inc. [*Formerly, Northern Illinois Gas Co.*] [*NYSE symbol*] (SPSG)
GAS .... Northern Illinois Gas Co. (SAUO)
GAS .... Southern Technical Institute, Marietta, GA [*OCLC symbol*] (OCLC)
GASA .... Georgia Aeronautics and Space Administration (SAUO)
GASA .... German Australian Society of Australia
GASA .... Growth-Adjusted Sonographic Age [*Obstetrics*] (DMAA)
GASA .... Guinness Awards for Scientific Achievement (SAUO)
GASAC .... Garden State Athletic Conference (PSS)
GASAD .... Gate and Source and Drain (AAEL)
GA S&L .... Great American Savings & Loan (SAUS)
GASANSW ... Graphic Arts Services Association of New South Wales [*Australia*]
GASAV .... Graphic Arts Services Association of Victoria [*Australia*]
GaSb .... Gallium Antimonide (SAUS)
GASB .... Governmental Accounting Standards Board [*Stamford, CT*] (EA)
GASBC .... Concepts Statements of the Governmental Accounting Standards Board (SAUO)
GASB-COD ... Governmental Accounting Standards Board Codification (SAUO)
GASBEND .... Good and Safe Port Both Ends (RIMS)
GASBI .... Governmental Accounting Standards Board Interpretations (SAUO)
GASBIINDO... Gabungan Serikat Buruh Islam Indonesia [*Federation of Indonesian Islamic Trade Unions*]
GASBO .... Georgia Association of School Business Officials (SAUO)
GASBOC .... Governmental Accounting Standards Board Organizing Committee (SAUO)
GASBS .... Statements of the Governmental Accounting Standards Board (SAUO)
GASBT .... Governmental Accounting Standards Board Technical Bulletions (SAUO)
GASC .... Gas-Analysis Sample Container [*Apollo*] [*NASA*]
GASC .... Georgia, Ashburn, Sylvester & Camilla R. R. [*AAR code*]
GASC .... German-American Securitie Corporation, Boston (SAUO)
GASC .... German-American Securities Corp. (BARN)
GASC .... Graphic and Software Communication System (SAUS)
GASC .... Graphic Arts Show Co., Inc. (DGA)
GASC .... Ground Air Support Command (SAUS)
GASC .... Guggenheim Aviation Supply Control (SAUO)
GASC .... Gurkha Army Service Corps [*British military*] (DMA)
Ga scan .... Gallium Scan [*Medicine*] (EDAA)
GAS Can ...... Get-Away-Special Canister (SAUS)
GAS Can ...... Get-Away-Special Cannister [*NASA*]
GASCD .... Georgia Association for Supervision and Curriculum Development (SAUO)
GASCO .... Abu Dhabi Gas Industries Ltd. (BUAC)
GASCO .... General Aviation Safety Commission (SAUO)
GASCO .... General Aviation Safety Committee (BUAC)
GASCO .... Ground Air Support Command (SAUS)
GASCOFIL .... Gas Correlation Filter Spectrometer (SAUS)
GASCS .... Graphic and Software Communication System (SAUS)
GASD .... Government Aerospace Systems Division [*Harris Corp.*]
GASDA .... Gasoline and Automotive Service Dealers Association (EA)
Gas de Cal... Gaspar de Calderinis [*Deceased, 1390*] [*Authority cited in pre-1607 legal work*] (DSA)
Gas de Cald... Gaspar de Calderinis [*Deceased, 1390*] [*Authority cited in pre-1607 legal work*] (DSA)
GASDSAS .... Gust Alleviation and Structural Dynamic Stability Augmentation [*Aviation*]
Gas Eng Manage... Gas Engineering and Management [*A publication*] (CABS)
GASEQ .... Graziers' Association of South East Queensland [*Australia*]
GASER .... Gamma Ray LASER (NATG)
GASERBUN... Gabungan SB2 Non-Vakcentral [*Federation of Non-Affiliated Trade Unions*] [*Indonesia*]
GASERC .... Gulf Arab States Educational Research Center [*Kuwait*] (BUAC)
GASES .... Gravity-Anchored Space Experiments Satellite (MCD)
GAS-EUROSOUD... European Committee of Manufacturers of Gas-Welding Equipment (BUAC)
GASF .... Graphic Arts Sales Foundation (EA)
GASFET .... Gallium Arsenide Field-Effect Transistor
GASG .... Segou [*Mali*] [*ICAO location identifier*] (ICLI)
GASGA .... Group for Assistance on Storage of Grains in Africa (SAUO)
GASGA .... Group for Assistance on Systems Relating to Grain Afterharvest [*Netherlands*] (BUAC)
GASGASGAS... Guild of Ancient Suppliers of Gas Appliance, Skills, Gins, Accessories and Substances (SAUS)
GASH .... Group Administration Shell (SAUO)
GASH .... Guanidine Aluminum Sulfate Hexahydrate [*Insecticide*]
GASH .... Guanidine Aluminum Sulfate Hydrate [*Ferroelectrics*]
GASHA .... Golden American Saddlebred Horse Association (EA)
GASI .... Greenwich Air Services, Inc. [*NASDAQ symbol*] (SAG)
GASIA .... Greenwich Air Services 'A' [*NASDAQ symbol*] (TTSB)
GASIB .... Greenwich Air Svcs'B' [*NASDAQ symbol*] (TTSB)
GASIL .... General Aviation Safety Information Leaflet (PIAV)
GASJ .... Saint Joseph's Infirmary, Atlanta, GA [*Library symbol*] [*Library of Congress*] (LCLS)
GASK .... Sikasso [*Mali*] [*ICAO location identifier*] (ICLI)
GASKET .... Graphic Surface Kinetics [*Computer program*] (KSC)
GASL .... General Activity Simulation Language [*Computer science*]
GASL .... General Applied Science Laboratories (SAUO)
GASL .... General Applied Science Laboratory
GASL .... Southeastern Library Network [*SOLINET*], Atlanta, GA [*Library symbol*] [*Library of Congress*] (LCLS)
GASLAB .... Global Atmospheric Sampling Laboratory (EERA)
GASM .... Graphic Arts Spray Manufacturers [*Defunct*] (EA)
GASMAP ...... Gallium Arsenide Model Analysis Program (SAUS)
GASMAP ...... Gas Analysis System for Metabolic Analysis of Physiology [*NASA*] (SPST)
GAS-MOP .... Gulf of Alaska Mesoscale Oceanographic Processes
GASMPA ...... Group for the Advancement of Spectroscopic Methods and Physicochemical Analysis (SAUS)
GASMS .... Ground Aircraft Services and Maintenance Support (ACAE)
GASN .... San [*Mali*] [*ICAO location identifier*] (ICLI)
GASNET .... Global Anesthesiology Server Network (ADWA)
GASO .... Gasoline
GASOHOL .... Gasoline/Ethanol [*Automotive fuel*]
Gasonics ...... Gasonics International Corp. [*Associated Press*] (SAG)
GASP .... Galloping Acronyms Save Paper
GASP .... Gamma-Ray Astronomy at the South Pole (SAUS)
GASP .... garnet-aluminosilicate-silica-plagioclase (SAUS)
GASP .... Gas Accumulation Over Spreading Pools (HEAS)
GASP .... Gas Annulus Sizing Program
GASP .... Gas Plasma Display (HGAA)
GASP .... Gas Properties [*NASA computer program*]
GASP .... General Activity Simulation Program [*Programming language*] [*1970*] [*Computer science*] (BUR)
GASP .... General ADP Support-PDP 11/70 (SAUO)
GASP .... General All-Purpose Simulation Package [*McDonnell Douglas Automation Co.*] (MCD)
GASP .... General Analysis of System Performance (IAA)
GASP .... General and Annual Survey Processing (SAUS)
GASP .... General Assembly to Stop the Powerline (EA)
GASP .... Generalized Academic Simulation Program [*Computer science*] (IEEE)
GASP .... Generalized Aerospace Program (KSC)
GASP .... Generalized Antisymmetric Potential
GASP .... Generalized Audit Software Package [*Computer science*] (MHDI)
GASP .... Georgia Association of School Psychologists (SAUO)
GASP .... Gevic Arithmetic Simulation Program
GASP .... Global Assimilation and Prediction (SAUO)
GASP .... Global Assimilation and Prognosis System (EERA)
GASP .... Global Atmospheric Sampling Program [*NASA*]
GASP .... Goldfields Against Serious Pollution [*Australia*]
GASP .... Graded Assessment in Science Project (AIE)
GASP .... Grand Accelerated Space Platform
GASP .... Graph Algorithm Software Package (SAUS)
GASP .... Graphic Applications Subroutine Package [*Computer science*] (BUR)
GASP .... Gravity and Sun Pointing (SAUS)
GASP .... Gravity-Assisted Space Probe [*NASA*]
GASP .... Greater [*name of city*] Alliance to Stop Pollution
GASP .... Grip, Aim, Stance, and Posture [*Golf*]
GASP .... Ground Avoidance Simulation Program (MCD)
GASP .... Group Against Smog and Pollution (SAUO)
GASP .... Group Against Smokers' Pollution (EA)
GASP .... Group Against Smoking in Public (ADWA)
GASP .... Group Against Smoking Pollution (SAUS)
GASP .... Group Against Steroid Prescription (WDAA)
GASP .... Groups Against Sewage Pollution [*Australia*]
Gaspar .... Gaspar's Small Cause Court Reports [*Bengal*] [*A publication*] (DLA)
Gasp de Cald... Gaspar de Calderinis [*Deceased, 1390*] [*Authority cited in pre-1607 legal work*] (DSA)
GASPE .... Gated Spin Echo [*Nuclear magnetic resonance*]
GASPEC .... Gas Filter Correlation Spectrometer (SAUS)
GASPI .... Guidance Attitude Space Position Indicator (MCD)
GASPILS ...... Gas Pipeline Leak Sensor (SAUS)
GASPT .... Generalized Axially-Symmetrical Potential Theory (PDAA)
GASR .... Graphic Attention Service Routine (SAUS)
GASR .... Guided Air-Ground Rocket (SAUS)
GASR .... Guided Air-to-Surface Rocket (IAA)
GASS .... American Resources, Inc. [*NASDAQ symbol*] (SAG)
GASS .... Amer Resources Del [*NASDAQ symbol*] (TTSB)
GASS .... General Air & Surface Situation (SAUS)
GASS .... Generalized Assembly System [*Computer science*] (IEEE)
GASS .... Generic Acoustics Stimulation System [*Navy*] (SEWL)
GASS .... Geomagnetic Airborne Survey System
GASS .... Gimbal Assembly Storage System
GASS .... Great American Shoe Store [*Advertising slogan of Kinney Shoe Corp.*]
GASS .... Great Analog Signal Saver
GASS .... Ground Analysis Sub-System (SAUO)
GASS .... Guidance Accuracy Study for SPRINT [*Missile*] [*Army*] (AABC)
GASSAR .... Gilbert Associates [*or General Atomic*] Standard Safety Analysis Report [*Nuclear energy*] (NRCH)
GASSER .... Geographic Aerospace Search RADAR
GASSER .... Graphic Aerospace Search Radar (SAUS)
GASSP .... Gas Source Seismic Section Profiler
GASSP .... Georgia Association of Secondary School Principals (SAUO)
GASSW .... Amer Res Del Wrrt [*NASDAQ symbol*] (TTSB)
GASSWF ...... Geological Assistance for Siting Solid Waste Facilities (SAUO)
GAST .... Gastric (WDAA)
GAST .... Gastronomia Espanola [*Ministerio de Cultura*] [*Spain*] [*Information service or system*] (CRD)
GAST .... Geraeteausgabestelle [*Equipment distributing point*] [*German military - World War II*]
GAST .... Globally Averaged Surface Temperature (EERA)
GAST .... Greenwich Apparent Sidereal Time (PDAA)

GASTA .... Gimbal Angle Sequencing Transformation Assembly (KSC)
GASTO .... Gastonia, NC [*American Association of Railroads railroad junction routing code*]
GASTRN .... Gastrin [*Gastroenterology*] (DAVI)
GASTRNTRLGST... Gastroenterologist
GASTRNTRLY... Gastroenterology
Gastro .... Gastroenterology (DAVI)
Gastro .... Gastrointestinal [*Gastroenterology*] (DAVI)
Gastroc .... Gastrocnemius [*Medicine*] (EDAA)
GASTROC .... Gastrocnemius [*Muscle*] [*Anatomy*]
GASU .... Georgia State University, Atlanta, GA [*Library symbol*] [*Library of Congress*] (LCLS)
GASU-D .... Georgia State University, Documents Library, Atlanta, GA [*Library symbol*] [*Library of Congress*] (LCLS)
GASU-I......... Georgia State University, Instructional Resource Center, Atlanta, GA [*Library symbol*] [*Library of Congress*] (LCLS)
GASU-L........ Georgia State University, Law Library, Atlanta, GA [*Library symbol*] [*Library of Congress*] (LCLS)
GA Sup .... Georgia Reports, Supplement [*A publication*] (DLA)
GA Supp ...... Georgia Reports, Supplement [*A publication*] (DLA)
GASV .... Gross Arrived Sound Value (MARI)
GAS/W .... Gas Weld
GASWOA...... Great American Station Wagon Owner's Association [*Defunct*] (EA)
GASZ .... Pargas [*Federal Railroad Administration identification code*]
GAt............... Athens Regional Library, Athens, GA [*Library symbol*] [*Library of Congress*] (LCLS)
GAT.............. Gabon Air Transport (BUAC)
GaT .... Galactosyltransferase (SAUS)
GAT.............. Gate-Associated Transistor (MCD)
GAT.............. Gateway Industries, Inc. (SAUO)
Gat............... Gattung (SAUS)
GAT.............. Geek of All Trades (SAUS)
GAT.............. Geek of All Trades, Generic Application Template (SAUS)
GAT.............. Gelatin-Agglutination Test [*Clinical chemistry*]
GAT.............. Gemini Agena Target [*NASA*]
GAT.............. General Air Traffic [*Europe-Asia*]
GAT.............. General Air Training
GAT.............. General American Transportation Corp. (SAUO)
GAT.............. General Analysis Technique
GAT.............. General Aptitude Test [*Psychometrics*]
GAT.............. General Aviation Terminal (SAUS)
GAT.............. General Aviation Trainer
GAT.............. General Aviation Transponder
GAT.............. Generalized Algebraic Translator [*Computer science*]
GAT.............. Generic Application Template (SAUS)
GAT.............. Genetic Algorithm Technology (SEWL)
GAT.............. Geography Association of Thailand (SAUS)
GAT.............. Georgetown Automatic Translator [*Computer science*]
GAT.............. Georgia Institute of Technology (SAUO)
GAT.............. Georgia Institute of Technology, Atlanta, GA [*Library symbol*] [*Library of Congress*] [*OCLC symbol*] (LCLS)
GAT.............. Geriatric Assessment Team [*Medicine*] (DMAA)
GAT.............. Gerontological Apperception Test [*Medicine*] (DMAA)
GAT.............. Gonorrhea Antibody Test [*Medicine*] (DB)
GAT.............. Goodyear Atomic Corp. (KSC)
GAT.............. Government Acceptance Test (MCD)
g-at.............. gram-atom (SAUS)
GAT.............. Graphic Arts Terminal [*Phototypesetting*] (NITA)
GAT.............. Great American Trials [*A publication*]
GAT.............. Greenwich Apparent Time
GAT.............. Ground-Air Transmitter (SAUS)
GAT.............. Ground Attack Tactics [*for air delivery of weapons against a ground target*]
GAT.............. Ground-to-Air Transmitter
GAT.............. Ground-to-Air Transmitter Gate (MCD)
GAT.............. Group Adjustment Therapy [*Psychology*] (DAVI)
GAT.............. Gulf Air, Inc. [*ICAO designator*] (FAAC)
GAT.............. Guyane Air Transport [*Airline*] [*French Guiana*]
GAT_{10}.......... Glutamic Acid-Alanine-Tyrosine [*Biopolymer*]
GATA .... Glass and Allied Traders' Association [*British*] (DBA)
GATA .... Glass and Allied Trades Association (BUAC)
GATA .... Graphic Arts Technical Association (SAUO)
GATAC .... General Assessment Tridimensional Analog Computer (IEEE)
GATAE .... Graphic Arts Trade Association Executives [*Later, GAAE*]
GAtAR .... United States Department of Agriculture, Russell Agriculture Research Center, Athens, GA [*Library symbol*] [*Library of Congress*] (LCLS)
GATB .... General Aptitude Test Battery
GATB .... General Avionics Testbed [*Military*]
GATB .... Graphical Articulated Total Body
GATB .... Tombouctou [*Mali*] [*ICAO location identifier*] (ICLI)
GATBY .... General Aptitude Test Battery
GATC .... Gay Airline and Travel Club (EA)
GATC .... General American Transportation Corporation (SAUO)
GATC .... General Aviation Technology Conference
GATC .... Graphic Arts Technical Committee (SAUO)
GATCO......... Guild of Air Traffic Control Officers [*British*]
GATD .... Graphic Analysis of Three-Dimensional Data
GATE............ GARP [*Global Atmospheric Research Program*] Atlantic Tropical Experiment [*National Oceanic and Atmospheric Administration*]
GATE............ Gateway 2000 [*NASDAQ symbol*] (TTSB)
GATE............ Gateway 2000, Inc. [*NASDAQ symbol*] (SAG)
GATE............ General Access Transportation Extention [*Telecommunications*] (TSSD)
GATE............ Generalized Algebraic Translator Extended [*Computer science*]
GATE............ General-Purpose Automatic Test Equipment [*Army*] (RDA)
GATE............ Generic Automatic Test Equipment (ACAE)
GATE............ Germany Appropriate Technology Exchange (BUAC)
GATE............ Get Away Tether Experiment (SAUS)
GATE............ Gifted and Taleted Education Program [*California*] (EDAC)
GATE............ Global Acoustic Transmission Experiment (SAUO)
GATE............ Global Alliance for Transnational Education (SAUO)
GATE............ Global Atmosphere Tropical Experiment (SAUO)
GATE............ Graduate Aid to Employment (OICC)
GATE............ Ground Activity Target Elimination (ACAE)
GATE............ Group to Advance Total Energy (SAUO)
Gate2000..... Gateway 2000, Inc. [*Associated Press*] (SAG)
GATEC .... Government Acquisition through Electronic Commerce
GATEOR....... Gas-Assisted Thermal-Enhanced Oil Recovery
GATERS....... Ground-Air Telerobotic Systems [*Marine Corps*] (DOMA)
GATES .... Generic Access to Electronic Services (SAUS)
GATEWAY.... Gateway [*Commonly used*] (OPSA)
Gateway ...... National Federation of Gateway Clubs (BUAC)
GATEWY ...... Gateway [*Commonly used*] (OPSA)
GATF............ Graphic Arts Technical Foundation (EA)
GATF............ Graphics Arts Technical Foundation (SAUS)
GATH .... Gatha [*Language, etc.*] (ROG)
GAThS .... Theosophical Society, Atlanta, GA [*Library symbol*] [*Library of Congress*] (LCLS)
GATI............. Gaming and Technology, Incorporated (SAUO)
GAtL............. Athens Regional Library, Athens, GA [*Library symbol*] [*Library of Congress*] (LCLS)
GATM........... Global Air Traffic Management (SEWL)
GATN .... Taoudenni [*Mali*] [*ICAO location identifier*] (ICLI)
GAT-NUMERICAL... General Ability Tests: Numerical (TES)
GATO .... Greater Atlantic Treaty Organization (SAUO)
GATORS....... Ground Air Telerobotics System (ACAE)
GATP .... Ground Acceptance [*or Article*] Test Procedure (MCD)
GATP .... Ground Article Test Procedure (SAUS)
GATPCO....... German-American Trade Promotion Company (SAUO)
GAT PERCEPTUAL... General Ability Tests: Perceptual (TES)
GATPRO-CO... German-American Trade Promotion Company (BUAC)
GATR .... Great American Truck Racing (EA)
GATR .... Gross Average Tax Rate
GATR .... Ground-to-Air Transmitter-Receiver (SAUS)
GATR .... Ground-to-Air Transmitting-Receiving [*Station*]
GATRI........... Gamma Technology Research Irradiator (ADA)
GATS .... General Acceptance Test Software
GATS .... General Agreement on Trade in Services
GATS .... Global Automotive Telematics Standard [*Transportation management*]
GATS .... GPS [*Global Positioning System*] Aided Targeting System [*Army*] (DOMA)
GATS .... Guidance Acceptance Test Set
GATS .... Gulf Applied Technologies, Inc. (SAUO)
GATS .... Tessalit [*Mali*] [*ICAO location identifier*] (ICLI)
GATSA .... Georgia Association of the Technology Student Association (SAUO)
GAtT............. Athens Are Technical Institute, Athens, GA [*Library symbol*] [*Library of Congress*] (LCLS)
GATT............ Gate Assisted Turnoff Thyristor [*NASA*] (NASA)
Gatt.............. Gattung (SAUS)
GATT............ General Agreement on Tariffs and Trade [*Organization, and the concept it represents, concerned with adjustment of tariffs among 73 member nations*] [*See also AGTDC*] [*Switzerland*] [*Also, an information service or system*]
GATT............ General Agreement on Trade and Tariffs (SAUS)
GATT............ General Agreement on Traffic and Trade (SAUS)
GATT............ Graphics Address Translation Table (SAUS)
GATT............ Ground-to-Air Transmitter Terminal
GATTC .... General Aviation Technical Training Conference
GATTIS .... Georgia Institute of Technology and Technical Information Science (HGAA)
GATTIS .... Georgia Institute of Technology Technical Information Service (NITA)
GATTS .... General Area Time-Based Train Simulator (PDAA)
GATU .... Geophysical Automatic Tracker Unit
GATV .... Gemini Agena Target Vehicle [*NASA*]
GAT VERBAL... General Ability Test: Verbal (TES)
GATW .... Gateway Federal S&L Assn. (Ohio) [*NASDAQ symbol*] (COMM)
GATWAY .... Gateway [*Commonly used*] (OPSA)
G AT WT...... Gram Atomic Weight (WDAA)
GATX .... GATX Corp. [*Formerly, General American Transportation Corp.*] [*Associated Press*] (SAG)
GATX .... General American Transportation Corp. (SAUO)
GAU .... Atlanta University, Atlanta, GA [*Library symbol*] [*Library of Congress*] (LCLS)
GAu.............. Augusta-Richmond County Library, Augusta, GA [*Library symbol*] [*Library of Congress*] (LCLS)
GAU .... Gauhati [*India*] [*Airport symbol*] (OAG)
Gau.............. Gauss [*Unit of magnetic flux density*]
GAU .... gauze (SAUS)
GAU .... Gay Academic Union [*Defunct*] (EA)
GAU .... General Accounting Unit (SAUS)
gau .... Georgia [*MARC country of publication code*] [*Library of Congress*] (LCCP)
GAU .... Geriatric Assessment Unit [*Australia*]
GAU .... Glen Auden Resources Ltd. [*Toronto Stock Exchange symbol*]
GAU .... Glucoamylase Unit [*Of hydrolytic enzyme activity*]
GAU .... Grupos de Accion Unificadora [*Groups for Unified Action*] [*Uruguay*] (PD)

GAU .... Guanine Adenine Uracil [*A triplet of bases coding for the amino acid, aspartic acid*] (EES)
GAU .... Gun Aircraft Unit (SAUS)
GAU .... Gun Automatic (MCD)
GAuA .... Augusta College, Augusta, GA [*Library symbol*] [*Library of Congress*] (LCLS)
GAuACH .... Augusta Chronicle-Herald, Augusta, GA [*Library symbol*] [*Library of Congress*] (LCLS)
GAuAH .... Aquinas High School, Augusta, GA [*Library symbol*] [*Library of Congress*] (LCLS)
GAuAR .... Academy of Richmond County, Augusta, GA [*Library symbol*] [*Library of Congress*] (LCLS)
GAuBH .... Butler High School, Augusta, GA [*Library symbol*] [*Library of Congress*] (LCLS)
GAUBR .... Gauley Bridge, WV [*American Association of Railroads railroad junction routing code*]
GAuCL .... Augusta-Richmond County Library, Augusta, GA [*Library symbol*] [*Library of Congress*] (LCLS)
GAUD .... Region 4 Grants Audit System (SAUS)
GAUFCC .... General Assembly of Unitarian and Free Christian Churches (BUAC)
GAUGE .... General Automation Users Group Exchange [*Defunct*] (EA)
Gauh .... University of Gauhati (SAUO)
GAuJ .... T. W. Josey High School, Augusta, GA [*Library symbol*] [*Library of Congress*] (LCLS)
GAUK .... Gamekeepers' Association of the United Kingdom (BI)
Gaul .... Gaulish [*Language*] (BARN)
GAuL .... Lucey C. Laney High School, Augusta, GA [*Library symbol*] [*Library of Congress*] (LCLS)
GAUM .... General Areas Unsuitable for Mining (SAUO)
GAuM .... Medical College of Georgia, Augusta, GA [*Library symbol*] [*Library of Congress*] (LCLS)
GA (UN) .... General Assembly of the United Nations
Ga Univ .... Georgia University (SAUO)
GAuP .... Paine College, Augusta, GA [*Library symbol*] [*Library of Congress*] (LCLS)
GAuRC .... Richmond County Law Library, Augusta, GA [*Library symbol*] [*Library of Congress*] (LCLS)
GAUSA .... Georgian Association in USA (EA)
GAUSS .... Geophex Airborne Unmanned Survey System (SAUO)
GAUSS .... Gravity Association for Universal Scientific Study
GAuT .... Augusta Technical Institute, Augusta, GA [*Library symbol*] [*Library of Congress*] (LCLS)
GAuU .... University Hospital, Augusta, GA [*Library symbol*] [*Library of Congress*] (LCLS)
GAuV-F .... United States Veterans Administration Hospital, Forest Hills Division, Augusta, GA [*Library symbol*] [*Library of Congress*] (LCLS)
GAuV-L .... United States Veterans Administration Hospital, Lenwood Division, Augusta, GA [*Library symbol*] [*Library of Congress*] (LCLS)
G/AV .... General Average (WDAA)
GAV .... Geschichte des Alten Vorderasien [*A publication*] (BJA)
GAV .... Glen Avon [*California*] [*Seismograph station code, US Geological Survey*] (SEIS)
GAV .... Granada Aviacion [*Spain*] [*ICAO designator*] (FAAC)
GAV .... Gravity Accelerated Vehicle (ACAE)
GAV .... Gross Annual Value [*Accounting*] (ODBW)
GAV .... Gustavus, AK [*Location identifier*] [*FAA*] (FAAL)
GAVA .... Gavotto [*Gavotte*] [*Music*] (ROG)
GAvA .... Guild of Aviation Artists [*British*] (DBA)
GAVA .... United States Veterans Administration Hospital, Atlanta, GA [*Library symbol*] [*Library of Congress*] (LCLS)
Gav & H Rev St ... Gavin and Hord's Revised Indiana Statutes [*A publication*] (DLA)
GAVRS .... Ground Attitude Vertical Reference System [*Aviation*]
GAVRS .... Gyrocompass Attitude Vertical Reference System (SAUS)
GAVRS .... Gyrocompassing Attitude and Velocity Reference System (SAUS)
GAW .... Airway Conductance [*The reciprocal of airway resistance*] [*Medicine*] (DAVI)
GAW .... Gambia Airways [*ICAO designator*] (FAAC)
GAW .... Gangaw [*Myanmar*] [*Airport symbol*] (OAG)
GAW .... Gay Authors Workshop (BUAC)
GAW .... Global Atmosphere Watch [*Marine science*] (OSRA)
GAW .... Global Atmospheric Watch (EERA)
GAW .... Gram Atomic Weight [*Chemistry*]
GAW .... Green Acres Woodland [*Federal Railroad Administration identification code*]
GAW .... Guaranteed Annual Wage
GAW .... Guided Atomic Warhead
GAWA .... Geographical Association of Western Australia
GAWAM .... Great American Wife and Mother [*Slang*]
GAWBS .... Guided Acoustic Wave Brillouin Scattering [*Physics*]
GAWF .... General Arab Women Federation (EA)
GAWF .... Greek Animal Welfare Fund (BUAC)
GAWH .... Global Alliance for Women's Health (ADWA)
GAWI .... German Corporation for Technical Assistance to Developing Countries (SAUO)
GAWR .... Gross Axle Weight Rating [*Auto safety*]
GAWRF .... Gross Axle Weight Rating Front [*Auto safety*]
GAWRR .... Gross Axle Weight Rating Rear [*Auto safety*]
GAWS .... German American World Society (EA)
GAWS .... Grandmothers of America in War Service [*World War II*]
GAWS .... Westminster School, Carlyle Fraser Library, Atlanta, GA [*Library symbol*] [*Library of Congress*] (LCLS)
GAWTS .... Genetic Amplification with Transverse Sequencing [*Genetics*]
GAWTS .... Genomic Amplification with Transcript Sequencing [*Genetics*]
GAWU .... General Agricultural Workers' Union [*Kenya*]
GAWU .... General and Allied Workers Union (SAUO)
GAWU .... Guyana Agricultural Workers Union (BUAC)
GAW/V_1 .... Specific Conductance [*Expressed per liter of lung volume at which G is measured*] [*Medicine*] (DAVI)
GAWW .... Woodrow Wilson College of Law, Atlanta, GA [*Library symbol*] [*Library of Congress*] (LCLS)
GAX .... Gamba [*Gabon*] [*Airport symbol*] (OAG)
GAX .... GAO [*General Accounting Office*] Seattle Regional Office, Seattle, WA [*OCLC symbol*] (OCLC)
GAY .... Galvasay [*Former USSR*] [*Seismograph station code, US Geological Survey*] [*Closed*] (SEIS)
GAY .... Gaylord [*Diocesan abbreviation*] [*Michigan*] (TOCD)
GAY .... German-American Youth Center (SAUO)
GAY .... Government Accumulation Yard
Gayarre .... Gayarre's Annual Reports [*25-28 Louisiana*] [*A publication*] (DLA)
GAYC .... Georgia Association of Young Children (SAUO)
GAYC .... German-American Youth Club (SAUO)
GAYE .... Yelimane [*Mali*] [*ICAO location identifier*] (ICLI)
GAYIG .... Gallium Substituted Yttrium Iron Garnet
Gay (LA) .... Gayarre's Annual Reports [*25-28 Louisiana*] [*A publication*] (DLA)
GaylC .... Gaylord Container Corp. [*Associated Press*] (SAG)
GaylCn .... Gaylord Container Corp. [*Associated Press*] (SAG)
GaylEnt .... Gaylord Entertainment [*Associated Press*] (SAG)
Gaylord .... Gaylord Companies, Inc. [*Associated Press*] (SAG)
Gaylrd .... Gaylord Companies, Inc. [*Associated Press*] (SAG)
GAYZ .... Gaylord Mill [*Federal Railroad Administration identification code*]
GAZ .... GAO [*General Accounting Office*] Atlanta Regional Office, Atlanta, GA [*OCLC symbol*] (OCLC)
gaz .... Gazeteer (WDAA)
Gaz .... Gazette (DIAR)
GAZ .... Gazette [*or Gazetteer*]
GAZ .... General Allied Oil [*Vancouver Stock Exchange symbol*]
GAZ .... Gesamtverzeichnis Auslaendischer Zeitschriften [*Cumulative List of Foreign Periodicals*]
GAZ .... Globe, AZ [*Location identifier*] [*FAA*] (FAAL)
GAZ .... Gruene Aktion Zukunft [*Green Action for the Future*] [*Germany*] (PPW)
Gaz .... Weekly Law Gazette [*Ohio*] [*A publication*] (DLA)
Gaz & BC Rep ... Gazette and Bankrupt Court Reporter [*New York*] [*A publication*] (DLA)
GAZ B .... Gazette of Bankruptcy [*A publication*] (ROG)
Gaz Bank ..... Gazette of Bankruptcy [*A publication*] (DLA)
Gaz Bank Dig ... Gazzam's Digest of Bankruptcy Decisions [*A publication*] (DLA)
Gaz Bankr .... Gazette of Bankruptcy [*A publication*] (DLA)
Gaz LR .... Gazette Law Reports [*New Zealand*] [*A publication*] (DLA)
Gaz LR (NZ) ... New Zealand Gazette Law Reports [*A publication*] (DLA)
Gaz L Soc of Upper Can ... Gazette. Law Society of Upper Canada [*A publication*] (DLA)
GAZS .... Gesamtverzeichnis Auslaendischer Zeitschriften und Serien [*Cumulative List of Foreign Periodicals and Serials*]
Gaz Zan EA ... Gazette for Zanzibar and East Africa [*A publication*] (ILCA)
GB .... Air Inter Gabon [*ICAO designator*] (AD)
GB .... Barrel Racing [*Rodeo term*]
GB .... Der Grosse Brockhaus [*A publication*]
GB .... Gain Bandwidth (DEN)
GB .... Galaxy Books [*Oxford University Press*]
GB .... Gall Bladder [*or a patient with an affliction of this organ*] [*Medicine*]
GB .... Games Behind [*Baseball*]
GB .... G & B Automated Equipment Ltd. [*Toronto Stock Exchange symbol*]
GB .... Gangbusters (SAUS)
GB .... Ganzer Bogen [*Full Bow*] [*Music*]
GB .... Garanti Bankasi [*Guarantee Bank*] [*Turkey*]
GB .... Gardner's Books Ltd. [*British*]
GB .... Gas Board (SAUO)
GB .... Gemeinde Berlin (BJA)
GB .... Gemini B
GB .... Gene Bank (SAUO)
GB .... General Background
GB .... General Board [*Military judicial or investigative body*]
GB .... General Bronze Corp. (MCD)
GB .... General Business (MHDI)
GB .... Generation Breakdown
GB .... Generic Behaviour (SAUS)
GB .... Germplasm Bank (SAUO)
GB .... Geschichtsbetrachtung und Geschichtliche Ueberlieferung bei den Vorexilischen Propheten [*A publication*] (BJA)
GB .... Gettysburg [*Civil War term*]
Gb .... Gibbsite [*A mineral*]
Gb .... GigaBIT [*Binary Digit*] [*10^9 BITs*]
Gb .... Gigabits (SAUS)
Gb .... Gigabyte [*Computer science*] (EERA)
gb .... Gigabyte (ELAL)
GB .... Gigabyte [*10^9 bytes*]
GB .... Gigabytes (SAUS)
Gb .... Gilbert [*A unit of magnetomotive force*] (CET)
GB .... Gilbert-Behcet [*Syndrome*] [*Medicine*] (DB)
gb .... Gilbert Islands [*gn (Gilbert and Ellice Islands) used in records cataloged before October 1978*] [*MARC country of publication code*] [*Library of Congress*] (LCCP)
GB .... Ginzburg's Bible [*New Massoretico-Critical Text of the Hebrew Bible*] [*A publication*] (BJA)
GB .... Girls Brigade [*British*] (BI)
GB .... Glass Beads [*Composites*]
GB .... Glass Block (DAC)
GB .... Glass Bowl

GB............ Glial Bundle [*Medicine*] (DMAA)
GB............ Glide Bomb [*Air Force*]
GB............ Glovebox (SAUS)
GB............ Gold Black [*Ultrafine gold metal particles*]
GB............ Gold Bond [*Bond payable in gold coin*]
GB............ [*The*] Golden Bough [*A publication*] (OCD)
GB............ Good-By [*Amateur radio*]
GB............ Good Bye (SAUS)
GB............ Goofball [*Barbiturate pill*]
GB............ Gougerot-Blum [*Syndrome*] [*Medicine*] (DB)
GB............ Goulburn-Broken (SAUS)
GB............ Gould Belt [*Galactic science*]
GB............ Governing Body
G/B............ Government Boat
GB............ Government Bunkers
GB............ Grab Bar [*Technical drawings*]
GB............ Grain Boundary (SAUS)
GB............ Granby Mining Co., Ltd. (SAUO)
GB............ Grand Bounce [*Suspension or dismissal*] [*Slang*]
GB............ Grassland Biome [*Ecological biogeographic study*]
GB............ Gravity Bomb (ACAE)
GB............ Great Barrier Airlines [*Airline code*] [*Australia*]
GB............ Great Books
GB............ Great Britain [*International automobile identification tag*]
GB............ Green Bag (SAUS)
GB............ Green Bay [*Diocesan abbreviation*] [*Wisconsin*] (TOCD)
GB............ Green Belt Act [*Town planning*] [*British*]
GB............ Greenhouse Biennial [*Horticulture*] (ROG)
GB............ Greenish Blue
GB............ Greif Bros. (EFIS)
GB............ Grid Base [*Electronics*] (EECA)
GB............ Grid Bearing [*Navigation*]
GB............ Grid Bias (DEN)
GB............ Griffiths & Bedell's [*System of stud tramways*] [*British*] (ROG)
GB............ Grouded Base (SAUS)
GB............ Ground Beacon [*Navigation*] (IAA)
GB............ Grounded Base
GB............ Group Buffer (COE)
GB............ Grundbuch [*Land Register*] [*German*] (ILCA)
GB............ Guaranteed Bond [*Business term*]
GB............ Guard Book (DGA)
GB............ Guardbridge Papers [*Manufacturer*] [*British*]
GB............ Guardian Bancorp [*AMEX symbol*] (SPSG)
GB............ Guardianship Board [*Tasmania, Australia*]
GB............ Guidebook
GB............ Guided Bomb (SAUS)
GB............ Guild of Bricklayers [*British*] (BI)
GB............ Guillain-Barre [*Syndrome*] [*Medicine*]
GB............ Gun Board [*British*]
GB............ Gunboat [*Naval*]
GB............ Gun Branch [*Electronics*] (OA)
GB............ Gun-Bus [*Gun-carrying plane*] [*Air Force*] [*British*]
GB............ Sarin [*Nerve gas*] [*Army symbol*]
GB............ United Kingdom [*ANSI two-letter standard code*] (CNC)
GB .... Government and Binding (ODA)
GBA............ Alderney [*International vehicle registration*] (ODBW)
GBA............ Association of Governing Bodies of Public Schools (SAUO)
GBA............ Association of Government Bodies of Public Schools (SAUO)
GBA............ Ganglionic-Blocking Agent [*Medicine*]
GBA............ Gas Bridge Assembly (SAUS)
GBA............ Gauribidanur Array [*India*] [*Seismograph station code, US Geological Survey*] (SEIS)
GBA............ George Butler Associates, Inc. (EFIS)
GBA............ Georgian Bay Airways [*Canada*] [*ICAO designator*] (FAAC)
GBA............ Gingivobuccoaxial [*Dentistry*]
GBA............ Girls' Brigade Australia
GBA............ Give Better Address [*Communications*]
GBa............ Glioblastoma (SAUS)
GBA............ Global Alert System [*Vancouver Stock Exchange symbol*]
GBA............ Global Biodiversity Assessment [*Book*] (EERA)
GBA............ Governing Bodies Association [*Organization of school officials*] [*British*]
GBA............ Grain Boundary Allotriomorph (SAUS)
GBA............ Grammatik des Biblische-Aramaeischen [*A publication*] (BJA)
GBA............ Great Britain Alderney (SAUS)
GBA............ Gross Building Area (ADA)
GBA............ Grundbuchamt [*Land Registry*] [*German*] (ILCA)
GBA............ Gurkha Brigade Associatin (WDAA)
GBA............ Gustin-Bacon Manufacturing Co. (SAUO)
GBaB............ Bainbridge Junior College, Bainbridge, GA [*Library symbol*] [*Library of Congress*] (LCLS)
GBAD............ Great Britain Allied and Dominion (SAUO)
GBAD............ Groundbased Air Defense [*Military*]
GBAN............ Gateway Bancorp, Inc. (SAUO)
GBAN............ Groove-Billed Ani [*North American bird banding code*] (BIBA)
GB & A............ Grosvenor Barber and Associates (IID)
GB&C............ General Battery and Ceramic Corp. (SAUO)
GB and I............ Great Britain and Ireland (SAUS)
GB & I............ Great Britain and Ireland
GB & W............ Green Bay & Western Railroad Co.
GBAO............ Graham Bond Appreciators Organization [*Defunct*] (EA)
GBAPS............ Governing Bodies Association of Public Schools [*British*]
GBARC............ Great Britain Aeronautical Research Committee (BUAC)
GBAS............ Ground Based Augmentation System (SAUO)
GBaS............ Southwest Georgia Regional Library, Bainbridge, GA [*Library symbol*] [*Library of Congress*] (LCLS)
GBASE............ Genome Database of the Mouse (HGEN)
GBAT............ Graduate Business Administration Test (WDAA)
GBAT............ Graduate Business Admission Test
GBB............ General Banner Bearer [*Freemasonry*] (ROG)
GBB............ Generic Blackboard System (SAUO)
GBB............ Group for Biology Information [*Medicine*] (EDAA)
GBB............ Guild of British Butlers [*British*] (EAIO)
GBBA............ Glass Bottle Blowers Association of the United States and Canada [*Later, GPPAW*]
GBBCS............ Ground Based Beam Control System (ACAE)
GBBerG............ Grundbuchbereinigungsgesetz vom 20.12.1993 (SAUS)
GBBG............ Great Black-Backed Gull [*North American bird banding code*] (BIBA)
GBBHS............ Group B Beta-Hemolytic Streptococcus [*Bacteriology*] (DAVI)
GBBK............ Greater Bay Bancorp [*NASDAQ symbol*] (NASQ)
GBBM............ Ground Based Battle Manager (ACAE)
GBBS............ Great Bay Bankshares, Inc. [*NASDAQ symbol*] (COMM)
GBBS............ Group B Beta-Hemolytic Streptococcus [*Medicine*] (MEDA)
GBC............ Berry College, Mount Berry, GA [*OCLC symbol*] (OCLC)
GBC............ GBI Capital Management [*AMEX symbol*] (SG)
GBC............ General Binding Company (SAUO)
GBC............ General Binding Corp.
GBC............ General Biscuit Company (SAUO)
GBC............ General Board of Control (SAUO)
GBC............ Ghana Broadcasting Corp. (BUAC)
GBC............ Gibraltar Broadcasting Corporation (SAUO)
GBC............ Glassblower's Cataract (MELL)
GBC............ Globe Air Cargo [*Antigua and Barbuda*] [*ICAO designator*] (FAAC)
GBC............ Gold-Braid Chaser [*Refers to a woman who dates only officers*] [*Slang*] [*British*] (DSUE)
GBC............ Green Bag Charge (SAUS)
GBC............ Green Belt Council of Greater London (SAUO)
GBC............ Greenland Base Command
GBC............ Ground-Based Computer
GBC............ Guantanamo Bay [*Cuba*] [*Seismograph station code, US Geological Survey*] [*Closed*] (SEIS)
GBCB............ GBC Bancorp [*NASDAQ symbol*] (NQ)
GBC Bc............ GBC Bancorp [*Associated Press*] (SAG)
GBCC............ Beijing Computer Center [*China*] (BUAC)
GBCC............ Great Britain Collectors Club (EA)
GBCC............ Great Britain Correspondence Club (SAUO)
GBCC............ Ground Based Control Center (ACAE)
GBCE............ Global Biodiversity Calendar of Events (SAUO)
GBCI............ Glacier Bancorp, Inc. [*NASDAQ symbol*] (SPSG)
GBCL............ Glacier Bancorp [*NASDAQ symbol*] (TTSB)
GBCO............ Greif Brothers Corp. [*NASDAQ symbol*] (SAG)
GBCOA............ Grief Bros Cl'A' [*NASDAQ symbol*] (TTSB)
GBCOB............ Greif Bros 'B' [*NASDAQ symbol*] (TTSB)
GB COLL............ George Brown College (SAUO)
GB Contact............ Gold Bonded Contact (SAUS)
GBCRMWU............ Grand Bahama Construction, Refinery, and Maintenance Workers' Union (BUAC)
GBCS............ General Board of Church and Society of the United Methodist Church (EA)
GBCS............ Global Business Communications Systems (SAUO)
GBCS............ Global Casinos [*NASDAQ symbol*] (SAG)
GBCS............ Ground-Based Common Sensor
GBCSCMC............ General Board of Christian Social Concerns of the Methodist Church (EA)
GBCS-H............ Ground-Based Common Sensor for Heavy divisions (SAUS)
GBCS-L............ Ground Based Common Sensor-Light (SEWL)
GBCS-L/H............ Ground Based Common Sensor-Light/Heavy [*Military*]
GBCS-LT............ Ground Based Common Sensor-Light (SAUS)
GBCT............ GBC Technologies, Inc. [*NASDAQ symbol*] (SAG)
GBCT............ Guild of British Camera Technicians (DBA)
GBC Tch............ GBC Technologies, Inc. [*Associated Press*] (SAG)
GBCW............ Governing Body of the Church in Wales (DAS)
GBD............ Gale's Business Directory [*A publication*]
GBD............ Gallbladder Disease [*Gastroenterology*] (DAVI)
GBD............ Gamma Ray Burst Detector [*Instrumentation*]
GBD............ General Board
GBD............ Geometric Data Base (DOMA)
GBD............ Glass-Blowers' Disease [*Medicine*] (DB)
GBD............ Global Burden of Disease
GBD............ Grain Boundary Dislocation
GBD............ Great Bear Development [*Vancouver Stock Exchange symbol*]
GBD............ Great Bend [*Kansas*] [*Airport symbol*] (OAG)
GBDC............ Grand Bahama Development Company (SAUO)
GBDe............ Global Business Dialog on electronic commerce (SAUO)
GBDLS............ Ground-Based Doppler Lidar System (SAUS)
GBDO............ Guild of British Dispensing Opticians (BI)
GBDV............ Gate Breakdown Voltage
GBE............ Dame Grand Cross of the Order of the British Empire (ADA)
GBE............ Gaborone [*Botswana*] [*Airport symbol*] (OAG)
GBE............ GEBCO Bathymetric Editor (SAUS)
GBE............ Gilt Beveled Edges [*Bookbinding*]
GBE............ Ginkgo Biloba Extract [*Biochemistry*]
GBE............ Goal-Based Evaluation
GBE............ Ground-Based Element (SAUS)
GBE............ Groupement Belge des Banques d'Epargne [*Banking association*] [*Belgium*] (EY)
GBE............ Grubb & Ellis [*NYSE symbol*] (TTSB)
GBE............ Grubb & Ellis Co. [*NYSE symbol*] (SPSG)
GBE............ Knight Grand Cross of the [*Order of the*] British Empire

GBERL .... Gulf Breeze Environmental Research Laboratory [*Environmental Protection Agency*] (MSC)
GBESM .... Ground Based Electronic Support Measures (ACAE)
GBEU .... Grand Bahama Entertainers' Union (BUAC)
GBEV .... Ground Based Experimental Version (SAUS)
GBF .... Gay Black Female [*Classified advertising*] (CDAI)
GBF .... Geographic Base File [*Civil Defense*]
GBF .... Geographic Base Files (SAUO)
GBF .... Gesellschaft fuer Biotechnologische Forschung mbH [*Germany*]
GBF .... Global Biodiversity Forum (SAUO)
GBF .... Grand Ballon [*France*] [*Seismograph station code, US Geological Survey*] [*Closed*] (SEIS)
GBF .... Great Bear Foundation (EA)
GBF .... Great Books Foundation (EA)
GBF .... Ground-Based Field
GBFC .... GB Foods [*NASDAQ symbol*] (TTSB)
GBFC .... GB Foods Corp. [*NASDAQ symbol*] (SAG)
GBF/DIME .... Geographic Base File/Dual Independent Map Encoding [*BTS*] (TAG)
GBF-DIME .... Geographic Base File/Dual Independent Map Encoding File (SAUS)
GB Fds .... GB Foods [*Associated Press*] (SAG)
GBFE .... Golden Books Family Ent [*NASDAQ symbol*] (TTSB)
GBFE .... Golden Books Family Entertainment [*NASDAQ symbol*] [*Formerly, Western Publishing*] (SG)
GBFE .... Golden Books Family Entertainment, Inc. [*NASDAQ symbol*] (SAG)
GBFE .... Guild of British Film Editors (BUAC)
GBFEL .... Ground Based Free Electron Laser (SAUS)
GBFEL .... Ground-Based Free Electron Laser (SAUO)
GBFEL .... Ground Based Free Electron LASER Proposal
GBFEL/TIE .... Ground Based Free-Electron Laser/Technology Integration Experiment (SAUS)
GBFH .... Georgia Bonded Fibers, Inc. [*NASDAQ symbol*] (COMM)
GB for M .... Guidebook for Marines (SAUS)
GBF/PL .... Government-Furnished Baseline/Parts List (SEWL)
GBG .... Galesburg [*Illinois*] [*Airport symbol*] (OAG)
GBG .... Garbage (MSA)
GBG .... General Baking Company (SAUO)
gBg .... Gigabecquerel, 1 E9 Bq [*Industrial hygiene term*] (OHS)
GBG .... Glycine-Rich Beta-Globulin [*Immunology*]
GBG .... Gonadal Steroid-Binding Globulin [*Medicine*] (DMAA)
GBG .... Gordon Junior College, Barnesville, GA [*Library symbol*] [*Library of Congress*] (LCLS)
GBG .... Governor's Bodyguard [*British military*] (DMA)
GBG .... Great Britain Guernsey (SAUS)
GBG .... Greensboro [*Georgia*] [*Seismograph station code, US Geological Survey*] (SEIS)
GBG .... Greensburg [*Diocesan abbreviation*] [*Pennsylvania*] (TOCD)
GBG .... Guernsey [*International vehicle registration*] (ODBW)
GBGB .... Gaming Board for Great Britain (SAUO)
GBGB .... Gastric Bypass Gone Bad
GBGB .... Graded Band Gap Base (SAUS)
GBGM .... General Board of Global Ministry (SAUO)
GBGSA .... Association of Governing Bodies of Girls Public Schools (SAUO)
GBGSA .... Governing Body of Girls' Schools Association [*British*]
GBH .... Galbraith Lake, AK [*Location identifier*] [*FAA*] (FAAL)
GBH .... Gamma Benzene Hexachloride [*Also, BHC, HCH*] [*Insecticide*]
GBH .... Garbell Holdings Ltd. [*Toronto Stock Exchange symbol*]
GBH .... Gas Bath Heater [*Classified advertising*] (ADA)
GBH .... Girth Breast Height (WGA)
gbh .... Grams per Brake Horsepower Hour (COE)
GBH .... Graphite-Benzalkonium-Heparin [*Medicine*] (MAE)
GBH .... Great British Holiday [*Television movie*]
GBH .... Grievous Body Harm
GBH .... Group Busy Hour [*Telecommunications*] (TEL)
GBHA .... Glyoxal Bis(o-hydroxyanil) [*An indicator*] [*Chemistry*]
GBH&K .... Great Big Hugs & Kisses (SAUS)
GBH&KB .... Greak Big Hugs & Kisses Back (SAUS)
GBHC .... Governor Bacon Health Center (SAUO)
GBHE .... Great Blue Heron [*North American bird banding code*] (BIBA)
GBHE .... Ground-Based Hypervelocity Experiment (SAUS)
GBHP .... Gross Brake Horsepower (MCD)
GBHRG .... Ground-Based Hypervelocity Rail Gun [*Military*] (SDI)
GBHRS .... Granite Belt Horticultural Research Station [*Australia*]
GBI .... BioLabs, Inc. [*AMEX symbol*]
GBI .... Bufete Industrial SA [*NYSE symbol*] (SPSG)
GBI .... Buffalo, NY [*Location identifier*] [*FAA*] (FAAL)
GBI .... Gable Industries, Inc. (SAUO)
GBI .... Gabriel Resources, Inc. [*Vancouver Stock Exchange symbol*]
GBI .... Gained by Inventory (DNAB)
GBI .... Georgia Bureau of Investigation (SAUO)
GBI .... Gesellschaft fuer Betriebswirtschaftliche Information mbH [*Society for Business Information*] [*Germany*] [*Database producer*]
GBI .... Global Brain Ischemia
GBI .... Globulin-Binding Insulin [*Medicine*] (DMAA)
GBI .... Globulin-Bound Insulin [*Medicine*] (STED)
GBI .... Governesses Benevolent Institute [*British*] (AIE)
GBI .... Government Benevolent Institution (SAUS)
GBI .... Grace Bible Institute [*Nebraska*]
GBI .... Grand Bahama Island (KSC)
GBI .... Great Barrier Island (SAUS)
GBI .... Green Biomass Index (SAUS)
GBI .... Gridlays Bank International Zambia Ltd.
GBI .... Ground Backup Instrument (MUGU)
GBI .... Ground-Based Interceptor [*Army*] (DOMA)
GBI .... Guanidinebenzimidazole [*Biochemistry*]
GBIA .... Guthrie Bacterial Inhibition Assay [*Medicine*] (MAE)
GBIB .... Gorsedd of Bards of the Isle of Britain (SAUO)
GBIF .... Global Biodiversity Information Facility (SAUO)
GBIGAS .... Institute of Geochemistry, Guangzhou Branch, Academia Sinica [*China*] (BUAC)
GBII .... GBI International Industries, Inc. [*NASDAQ symbol*] (COMM)
GBII .... Ground-Based Infrared Instrumentation
GBIIS .... Ground-Based Infrared Instrumentation System
GBIP .... General Purpose Interface Bus (SAUS)
GBiP .... German Books in Print [*A publication*]
GBIRET .... Germplasm Bank Information Retrieval (SAUO)
GBIS .... Geo-Based Information System (SAUS)
GBIS .... Geographic Base Information System (VLIE)
GBIS .... Global Business Intelligence Solutions (SAUO)
GBIS .... Grimes Business Information System (SAUS)
GBIT .... Gigabit (MHDB)
GBIT .... Global Intellicom [*NASDAQ symbol*] (TTSB)
GBIT .... Global Intellicom, Inc. [*NASDAQ symbol*] (SAG)
GBIU .... Geoballistic Input Unit
GBIX .... Globix Corp. [*NASDAQ symbol*] [*Formerly, Bell Tech Group Ltd.*]
GBI-X .... Ground Based Interceptor-Exoatmospheric (SAUS)
GBI-X .... Ground-Based Interceptor-Experiment [*US Army Strategic Defense Command*] (RDA)
GBIZ .... Goldberg [*Federal Railroad Administration identification code*]
GBIZ .... Grow Biz International [*NASDAQ symbol*] (TTSB)
GBIZ .... Grow Biz International, Inc. [*NASDAQ symbol*] (SAG)
GBJ .... Glass Bell Jar
GBJ .... Graph Based Backjumping (SAUS)
GBJ .... Great Britain Jersey (SAUS)
GBJ .... Ground Based Jammer (SAUS)
GBJ .... Jersey [*Great Britain*]
GBJ .... Marie Galante [*French Antilles*] [*Airport symbol*] (OAG)
GBK .... Gbangbatok [*Sierra Leone*] [*Airport symbol*] (OAG)
GBL .... Gabelli Asset Management'A' [*NYSE symbol*] (SG)
GBL .... Gable Mountain [*Washington*] [*Seismograph station code, US Geological Survey*] (SEIS)
GBL .... Games behind Leader [*Baseball*]
GBL .... Gamma Biologicals [*AMEX symbol*] (TTSB)
GBL .... Gamma Biologicals, Inc. [*AMEX symbol*] (SPSG)
GBL .... Gamma-Butyrolactone [*Organic chemistry*]
GBL .... GB Airways Ltd. [*British*] [*ICAO designator*] (FAAC)
GBL .... General Bearing Line [*Navy*] (NVT)
GBl .... Gesetzblatt [*Gazette*] [*German*] (DLA)
GBL .... Glomerular Basal Lamina [*Medicine*] (DAVI)
GBL .... Glucose-Blood Level [*Medicine*] (MELL)
GBL .... Goebel Brewing Company (SAUS)
GBL .... Goldenbell Resources, Inc. [*Toronto Stock Exchange symbol*] [*Vancouver Stock Exchange symbol*]
GBL .... Goulburn Island [*Australia*] [*Airport symbol*] [*Obsolete*] (OAG)
GBL .... Government Bill of Lading
GBL .... Ground-Based Laboratory (SAUS)
GBL .... Ground Based Laser (SAUS)
GBL .... Ground-Based LASER (MCD)
GBL .... Ground Based Launcher (ACAE)
GBL .... Guide to Baseball Literature [*A publication*]
GBLA .... Great Bitter Lake Association (SAUO)
GBLADING .... Government Bill of Lading
GBLADING .... Government Bill of Loading (SAUO)
GBLD .... General Building Products Corp. [*NASDAQ symbol*] (COMM)
GBLE .... Green Barley Leaf Extract (TAD)
GBLIC .... Gaussian Band Limited Channel (NITA)
GBLNF .... Goldenbell Resources, Inc. [*NASDAQ symbol*] (COMM)
GBLOC .... Government Bill of Lading Office Code (AFIT)
GBLOC .... Government Bill of Loading Office Code (SAUO)
GBLV .... Grapevine Bulgarian Latent Virus [*Plant pathology*]
GBLX .... Global Crossing Ltd. [*NASDAQ symbol*] (SG)
GBM .... Gain Band Merit
GBM .... Galilean Baptist Mission (EA)
GBM .... Garfinckel, Brooks Brothers, Miller & Rhodes, Inc. (SAUO)
GBM .... Gay Black Male [*Classified advertising*] (CDAI)
GBM .... General Bookkeeping Machine (VLIE)
GBM .... Generalized Bridge Method (VLIE)
GBM .... Gesellschaft Fuer Biochemie Und Molekularbiologie [*Germany*]
GBM .... Gibraltar Mines Ltd. [*Toronto Stock Exchange symbol*] [*Vancouver Stock Exchange symbol*]
GBM .... Glass-Bonded Mica
GBM .... Glioblastoma Multiforme [*Medicine*] (RAWO)
GBM .... Global Battle Manager (ACAE)
GBM .... Glomerular Basement Membrane [*Medicine*] (STED)
GBM .... Glycerine Ball Memory
GBM .... Grain Boundary Migration (SAUS)
GBM .... Granite Butte [*Montana*] [*Seismograph station code, US Geological Survey*] [*Closed*] (SEIS)
GBM .... Grape Berry Moth
GBM .... Great Britain Man (SAUS)
GBM .... Greater Britain Movement [*British*]
GBM .... Ground Based Manager (ACAE)
GBM .... Ground-Based Measurement (MCD)
GBM .... Gulf Building Materials (BUAC)
GBM .... Isle Of Man (Great Britain)
GBMA .... Garden Building Manufacturers Association (BUAC)
GBMA .... Golf Ball Manufacturers Association (EA)
GBMA .... Gray-Breasted Martin [*North American bird banding code*] (BIBA)
GBMA .... Great Britain Ministry of Aviation
GBMC .... Golf Ball Manufacturers' Conference [*British*] (BI)
GBMC .... Grain Bin Manufacturers Council [*Later, GEMC*] (EA)

GBMC .... Greater Baltimore Medical Center (SAUO)
GBMD .... Global Ballistic Missile Defense
GBMI .... Ground-Based Midcourse Interceptor [*Military*] (SDI)
GBMI .... Guilty-but-Mentally-Ill [*Legal term*]
GBMP .... General Benchmark Program (MHDB)
GBMPC .... Great Britain Map Postcard Club (BUAC)
GBM-rAb .... Glomerular Basement Membrane-Reactive Antibodies [*Immunology*]
Gbn .... Gabon (MILB)
GBN .... Gila Bend, AZ [*Location identifier*] [*FAA*] (FAAL)
GBN .... Gila Bend special upper-air observing site (SAUS)
GBN .... Global Business Network (SAUO)
GBN .... Golden Band Resources [*Vancouver Stock Exchange symbol*]
GBN .... Graphite Boron Nitride [*Chemistry*] (ODA)
GBNC .... Guaranty Bancshares Corp. [*NASDAQ symbol*] (COMM)
GBND .... General Binding Corp. [*NASDAQ symbol*] (NQ)
GBND .... Genl Binding [*NASDAQ symbol*] (TTSB)
GBNE .... Global Net, Inc. [*NASDAQ symbol*]
GBNE .... Guild of British Newspapers Editors (BI)
GBNK .... Gaston Federal Bancorp, Inc. [*NASDAQ symbol*] (NASQ)
GBNM .... Glacier Bay National Monument (SAUO)
GBO .... Geo-Biosphere Observatories (SAUS)
GBO .... Geosphere-Biosphere Observatories (QUAC)
GBO .... Geosphere-Biosphere Observatory (SAUS)
GBO .... Gissel Bargaining Order [*Labor relations*] (WYGK)
gbo .... Goods in Bad Order (MARI)
GBO .... Goods in Bad Order
GBO .... Ogooue Air Cargo [*Gabon*] [*ICAO designator*] (FAAC)
GBOA .... Gale Book of Averages [*A publication*]
GBOE .... Georgia Board of Education (SAUO)
G-Bomb .... Gravitational Bomb (SAUS)
GbOse3cer .... Globotriaosylceramide,E.-coli-verocytotoxin-R (SAUS)
GboSidek .... Grupo Sidek SA de CV [*Associated Press*] (SAG)
GBOT .... Garden Botanika [*NASDAQ symbol*] (TTSB)
GBOTA .... Greyhound Breeders, Owners, and Trainers Association (SAUO)
GBowdC .... Bowdon College, Bowdon, GA [*Library symbol*] [*Library of Congress*] [*Obsolete*] (LCLS)
GBP .... Gables Residential Trust [*NYSE symbol*] (SPSG)
GBP .... Gain-Bandwidth Product
GBP .... Galactose-Binding Protein [*Biochemistry*]
GBP .... Gas Bearing Part
GBP .... Gastric Bypass [*Surgery*]
GBP .... Gated Blood Pool [*Hematology*] (DMAA)
GBP .... Gay Bereavement Project (BUAC)
GBp .... Gigabytes per Second (DCOM)
GBP .... Glutamate-Binding Protein [*Biochemistry*]
GBP .... Glycophorin Binding Protein [*Biochemistry*]
GBP .... Great Britain Pound [*Banking*]
GBP .... Great British Public
GBP .... Guanylate-Binding Protein [*Biochemistry*]
GBP .... Guinea-Bissau Peso [*Monetary unit*]
GBPA .... Gettysburg Battlefield Preservation Association [*Defunct*] (EA)
GBPC .... Gold Bondholders Protective Council (EA)
GBPLM .... Benishangul Peoples Liberation Movement (SAUO)
GBPR .... Grain-Burning Pattern Regulation (MCD)
GBPS .... Gallbladder Pigment Stones [*Medicine*] (STED)
GBPS .... Gemini B Procedures Simulator (MCD)
GBPS .... GigaBIT [*Binary Digits*] per Second [*Transmission rate*] [*Computer science*] (TSSD)
Gbps .... Gigabits per Second (EERA)
GBps .... Gigabytes per Second [*Computer science*] (DCDG)
GBPU .... G.B. Pant University (SAUO)
GBPW .... Great Bay Power [*NASDAQ symbol*] (TTSB)
GBPW .... Great Bay Power Corp. [*NASDAQ symbol*] (SAG)
GBq .... Gigabecquerel (NUCP)
Gbq .... giga becquerel (SAUS)
GBQ .... Good, Bad, Questionable (ACAE)
GBR .... Gas-Cooled Breeder Reactor [*Nuclear energy*] (NRCH)
GBR .... Give Better Reference [*Communications*]
GBR .... Glass Bead Rating (MCD)
GBR .... Global Business Research
GBR .... Glutathione Bicarbonate Ringer [*Solution mixture*]
GBR .... Golden Bear Resources Ltd. [*Vancouver Stock Exchange symbol*]
GBR .... Grain-Boundary Reaction (SAUS)
GBR .... Grain Boundary Relaxation
GBR .... Great Barrier Reef (EERA)
GBR .... Great Barrington, MA [*Location identifier*] [*FAA*] (FAAL)
GBR .... Greenbriar Corp. [*AMEX symbol*] (SAG)
GBR .... Ground-Based RADAR [*Military*]
GBR .... Ground-Based Radiometer
GBR .... Gun, Bomb, and Rocket
GBR .... Gun Boosted Rocket (ACAE)
GBR .... Rader Aviation, Inc. [*ICAO designator*] (FAAC)
GBR .... United Kingdom [*ANSI three-letter standard code*] (CNC)
GBRA .... Gas Breeder Reactor Association (BUAC)
GBRA .... Gas-cooled Breeder Reactor Association (SAUO)
GBRCC .... Great Barrier Reef Consultative Committee [*Australia*]
GBRE .... General Board of Religious Education (SAUO)
GBRF .... Great Britain Racquetball Federation (BUAC)
GBRF .... Ground Based Radio Frequency (ACAE)
GBRG .... Ground Based Rail Gun (ACAE)
GBRMP .... Great Barrier Reef Marine Park [*Region*] (EERA)
GBRMPA .... Great Barrier Reef Marine Park Authority [*Commonwealth*] (EERA)
GBRP .... General Bending Response Program [*Computer*] [*Navy*]
GBR-P .... Ground-Based RADAR Prototype [*Military*]
GBR-PO .... Ground-Based RADAR Project Office [*Military*] (RDA)
GBRS .... Generic Block Recording System (ADWA)
GBRT .... Ground-Based Radar Terminal (SAUS)
GBru .... Brunswick Regional Library, Brunswick, GA [*Library symbol*] [*Library of Congress*] (LCLS)
GBruJC .... Brunswick Junior College, Brunswick, GA [*Library symbol*] [*Library of Congress*] (LCLS)
GBruM .... MAP International, Brunswick, GA [*Library symbol*] [*Library of Congress*] (LCLS)
GBR-X .... GBR-Experimental (SAUS)
GBR-X .... Ground Based RADAR-Experimental [*Army*]
GBRY .... Gettysburg Railroad [*Federal Railroad Administration identification code*]
GBS .... British Guillain Barre Syndrome Support Group (BUAC)
GBS .... Gall Bladder Series [*Radiography*]
GBS .... Gallbladder Stone [*Medicine*]
GBS .... Gas Bearing System (KSC)
GBS .... Gas Bioassay System [*NASA*]
GBS .... Gas-Bloat Syndrome [*Medicine*] (MELL)
GBS .... Gas Bridge System (SAUS)
GBS .... Gastric Bypass Surgery (MELL)
GBS .... General Bancshares Corp. (SAUO)
GBS .... General Business System (MHDW)
GBS .... Geographic Base System (SAUS)
GBS .... George Bernard Shaw [*Irish-born playwright, 1856-1950*]
GBS .... Gifu Broadcasting System (SAUO)
GBS .... GigaBIT [*Binary Digit*] per Second [*Computer science*] (IAA)
Gb/s .... Gigabits per Second (VLIE)
GBS .... Global Biodiversity Strategy (SAUS)
GBS .... Global Broadcasting System (SAUS)
GBS .... Global Broadcast Services
GBS .... Glycerine-Buffered Saline [*Medicine*] (STED)
GBS .... Glycine-Buffered Saline [*Microbiology*]
GBS .... Government Bureau of Standards
GBS .... Grain Boundary Segregation [*Metallurgy*]
GBS .... Granular Boundary Segregation [*Petrology*]
GBS .... Great Big Star [*in the movies*]
GBS .... Ground Based Scanner (SAUS)
GBS .... Ground Based Sensor [*Radar*]
GBS .... Ground Based Software (SAUS)
GBS .... Ground Based System (SAUS)
GBS .... Ground Beacon System (MCD)
GBS .... Group Bridging Service (SAUO)
GBS .... Group B Streptococci [*Medicine*]
GBS .... Group Busy Signal (SAUS)
GBS .... Guidance Test Battery for Secondary Pupils (TES)
GBS .... Guillain-Barre Syndrome [*Medicine*]
GBS .... Guyana Broadcasting System (SAUO)
GBSA .... Group B Strep Association (NRGU)
GBSAS .... Ground Based Scanning Aerial System (SAUO)
GBSAS .... Ground-Based Scanning Antenna System (IAA)
GBSCA .... Greater Blouse and Skirt Contractors Association [*Later, GBSUA*] (EA)
GBSE .... Gibbs Construction [*NASDAQ symbol*] (TTSB)
GBSE .... Gibbs Construction, Inc. [*NASDAQ symbol*] (SAG)
GBSEW .... Gibbs Construction Wrrt [*NASDAQ symbol*] (TTSB)
GBSFCS .... Ground Based Surveillance and Fire Control System (SAUS)
GBSFI .... Guillain-Barre Syndrome Foundation International (EA)
GBSM .... Graduate of Birmingham & Midland Institute School of Music (SAUO)
GBSM .... Graduate of the Birmingham & Midland Institute School of Music (SAUO)
GBSM .... Graduate of the Birmingham School of Music [*British*] (DBQ)
GBSM .... Guild of Better Shoe Manufacturers
GBSP .... Gray-Backed Storm-Petrel [*North American bird banding code*] (BIBA)
GBSR .... Gaekwar's Baroda State Railway [*Indian Railway*] (TIR)
GBSR .... Graphite-Moderated Boiling and Superheating Reactor
GBSRN .... Global Baseline Surface Radiation Network (ADWA)
GBSS .... Gey's Balanced Salt Solution [*Medium*] [*Cell culture*]
GBSS .... Governesses' Benevolent Society of Scotland (BUAC)
GBSS .... Grey's Balanced Saline Solution [*Medicine*] (STED)
GBSS .... Ground Based Surveillance System (SAUS)
GBSS .... Guillain-Barre-Strohl Syndrome [*Medicine*] (STED)
GBSSG .... Guillain-Barre Syndrome Support Group [*Later, GBSFI*] (EA)
GBSSGI .... Guillain-Barre Syndrome Support Group International [*Later, GBSFI*] (EA)
GBST .... Georgia Basic Skills Test (SAUO)
GBST .... Global Blood Safety Initiative [*Switzerland*] (BUAC)
GBST .... Grass Block Substitution Test (SAUS)
GBST .... Grassi Block Substitution Test [*Psychology*]
GBST .... Ground-Based Software Tool (HLLA)
GBSTC .... General Beadle State Teachers College (SAUO)
GBSTS .... Ground Based Surveillance Tracking System (ACAE)
GBSUA .... Greater Blouse, Skirt, and Undergarment Association (EA)
GBSVC .... General Broadcast Signaling Virtual Channel [*Telecommunications*] (ACRL)
GBSX .... Great Bear Spring Co. (SAUS)
GBT .... Der Babylonische Talmud [*Goldschmidt*] [*A publication*] (BJA)
GBT .... Generalized Burst Trapping
GBT .... Global Ballistic Transport [*Military*]
GBT .... Global Light Telecommun. [*AMEX symbol*] (SG)
GBT .... Gold Belt Air Transport, Inc. [*Canada*] [*ICAO designator*] (FAAC)
GBT .... Gordon's Biological Test (MELL)
GBT .... Graded Base Transistor
GBT .... Great Big Table (VLIE)
GBT .... Great Bustard Trust [*An association*] (EA)

GBT .... Green Bank Telescope (ROAS)
GBT .... Ground-Based Telemetry
GBT .... Ground-Based Test (SAUS)
GBT .... Gunboat
GBTA .... Guild of Business Travel Agents [*British*] (DBA)
GBTB .... GB&T Bancshares, Inc. [*NASDAQ symbol*] (NASQ)
GBTBC .... Graham Brothers Truck and Bus Club (EA)
GBTC .... Generalized Burst Trapping Code (PDAA)
GBTCU .... Grand Bahama Telephone and Telecommunications Union (BUAC)
GBTE .... Gull-Billed Tern [*North American bird banding code*] (BIBA)
GBTEWS .... General Based Tactical Electronic Warfare System (ACAE)
GBTI .... Gray-Body Temperature Index [*for thermal ecology of lizards*]
GBTS .... General Banking Terminal System (MHDW)
GBTS .... Gold Beaters' Trade Society [*A union*] [*British*]
GBTS .... Ground Based Surveillance and Tracking System (ACAE)
GBTS .... Ground-Based Training System (SAUO)
GBTSF .... Great Britain Target Shooting Federation (BUAC)
GBTV .... Granite Broadcasting Corp. [*NASDAQ symbol*] (SPSG)
GBTVK .... Granite Broadcasting [*NASDAQ symbol*] (TTSB)
GBTVP .... Granite Brdcst $1.9375 Cv Pfd [*NASDAQ symbol*] (TTSB)
GBU .... Geschichtsbetrachtung und Geschichtliche Ueberlieferung bei den Vorexilischen Propheten [*A publication*] (BJA)
GBU .... Glide Bomb Unit [*Air Force*] (MCD)
GBU .... Graphics Business Unit (VLIE)
GBU .... Greenland Botanical Survey (SAUO)
GBU .... Ground Backup (DNAB)
GBU .... Groupes Bibliques Universitaires [*University Biblical Groups*] [*Canada*]
GBU .... Guided Bomb Unit (MCD)
GBU .... Khasm el Girba [*Sudan*] [*Airport symbol*] (AD)
GBU .... Transports Aeriens de la Guinee-Bissau [*Guinea-Bissau*] [*ICAO designator*] (FAAC)
GBUR .... Gardenburger, Inc. [*NASDAQ symbol*] [*Formerly, Wholesome & Hearty Foods*] (SG)
GBUV .... Geostationary Backscatter Ultraviolet (SAUO)
GBV .... Gate Breakdown Voltage
GBV .... Gibb River [*Australia*] [*Airport symbol*] [*Obsolete*] (OAG)
GBV .... Globe Ball Valve
GBV .... Green Bank [*West Virginia*] [*Seismograph station code, US Geological Survey*] (SEIS)
GB vis .... Gallbladder Visualization [*Medicine*] (EDAA)
GBviz .... Gall Bladder Visualization [*Medicine*]
GBW .... Gain Bandwidth
GBW .... General Body Weakness (MELL)
GBW .... Good Bears of the World (EA)
GBW .... Green Bay & Western Railroad Co. [*AAR code*]
GBW .... Guild of Book Workers (EA)
GBWA .... Georgia Beer Wholesalers Association (SRA)
GBX .... GBX Resources [*Vancouver Stock Exchange symbol*]
GBX .... Ginkgo Biloba Extract [*Biochemistry*]
GBX .... Glovebox (SAUS)
GBX .... [*The*] Greenbrier Companies, Inc. [*NYSE symbol*] (SAG)
GBX .... Greenbrier Cos. [*NYSE symbol*] (TTSB)
GBX .... Ground Branch Exchange (DNAB)
GBY .... General Battery Corporation (SAUO)
GBY .... Giant Bay Resources Ltd. [*Toronto Stock Exchange symbol*]
G-B-Y .... God Bless You
GBY .... Greate Bay Casino [*AMEX symbol*] (SAG)
GBYD .... Banjul [*Gambia*] [*ICAO location identifier*] (ICLI)
G by Pos .... Games by Position [*Baseball*]
GBYSO .... Greater Boston Youth Symphony Orchestras (ROAS)
GBYTE .... Gigabyte (VLIE)
GBZ .... Gibraltar
GBZ .... Glass-Bonded Zeolite
GBZ .... Great Barrier [*New Zealand*] [*Seismograph station code, US Geological Survey*] (SEIS)
GBZ .... Great Barrier Island [*Australia*] [*Airport symbol*] (OAG)
GBZ .... Tampa, FL [*Location identifier*] [*FAA*] (FAAL)
GC .... Gain Control
GC .... Galactic Center
GC .... Galactocerebroside [*Biochemistry*]
GC .... Gallaudet College (SAUO)
GC .... Galvanized Corrugated [*Metal industry*]
GC .... Game Computer (SAUS)
GC .... Game Conservancy [*British*]
GC .... Game Conservancy Trust (BUAC)
GC .... Ganglion Cell [*Medicine*]
GC .... Gannon College (SAUO)
GC .... Garbage Collect (SAUS)
GC .... Garbage Collection [*Slang*] [*Computer science*]
GC .... Garden Council (SAUO)
GC .... Garrisan Company (SAUO)
GC .... Garrison Co. [*British military*] (DMA)
gc .... gas check (SAUS)
GC .... Gas Chromatograph [*or Chromatography*]
gc .... gas controller (SAUS)
GC .... Gas Cooler (EEVL)
GC .... Gas Council [*British*]
G/C .... Gas-to-Cloth [*Ratio*] (FFDE)
GC .... Gaston College (SAUO)
GC .... Gastrocnemius [*A muscle*]
Gc .... Gate Circuit (SAUS)
GC .... Gate Connector (VLIE)
GC .... Gavel Clubs (EA)
GC .... Geiger Counter (SAUS)
GC .... Geiger-Mueller Counter [*Nucleonics*] (IAA)
GC .... Gel Chromatography
GC .... Gen Circular (SAUS)
GC .... General Cable (IAA)
gc .... general cargo (SAUS)
GC .... General Catalogue [*Astronomy*] (ODA)
G-C .... General Ceramics (SAUO)
GC .... General Cinema Theatres, Inc. (EFIS)
GC .... General Circular
GC .... General Circulation [*Medicine*] (EDAA)
GC .... General Code [*A publication*] (DLA)
GC .... General Computer (SAUS)
GC .... General Condition [*Medicine*]
GC .... General Construction (SAUO)
GC .... General Contractor [*Technical drawings*]
GC .... General Control
GC .... General Council (IAA)
GC .... General Counsel
GC .... General Cover [*Insurance*]
GC .... General Cueing
GC .... General Motors [*Society of Automotive Engineers auto manufacturer code for service information interchange*]
GC .... Generative Cell [*Botany*]
GC .... Generic Code (AFM)
GC .... Genetic Code (MELL)
GC .... Genetic Counseling (MELL)
GC .... Geneva College (SAUO)
GC .... Geneva Convention (COE)
GC .... Geneva Convention Relative to Protection of Civilian Persons in Time of War [*Army*] (AABC)
GC .... Gentleman Cadet [*British*]
Gc .... Geochemist (SAUS)
Gc .... Geochemistry (SAUS)
Gc .... Geochronology (SAUS)
gc .... geographical coordinates (SAUS)
GC .... Geopolitical Code [*Military*] (AFIT)
GC .... George Cross [*British*]
GC .... Georgetown College (SAUO)
GC .... Georgia Central Railroad [*Federal Railroad Administration identification code*]
GC .... Geriatric Care [*Medicine*] (EDAA)
GC .... Geriatric Chair (DAVI)
GC .... Germinal Center [*Immunochemistry*]
GC .... Gettysburg College (SAUO)
GC .... Gigacycle (ACAE)
Gc .... Gigacycle [*Measurement*]
GC .... Gigacycles (NAKS)
gc .... gigacyle (SAUS)
GC .... Gimbal Case (KSC)
GC .... Gin Cocktail [*Slang*]
GC .... Girls' College (ADA)
GC .... Girton College (SAUO)
GC .... Glandular Cancer (MELL)
GC .... Glass Capillary
Gc .... Glass Ceramics (SAUS)
GC .... Glassy Carbon
GC .... Glendale College (SAUO)
GC .... Glial Cells (SAUS)
GC .... Gliding Club [*British*] (ADA)
GC .... Global Catalog (SAUO)
GC .... Global Control (IAA)
GC .... Globular Cluster [*Astrophysics*]
GC .... Glomar Challenger (SAUS)
GC .... Glucocorticoid [*Endocrinology*]
GC .... Glucorticoid (SAUS)
GC .... Glutamate-Citrate (SAUS)
GC .... Glycocalyx [*Medicine*] (MELL)
GC .... Gnome Club (EA)
GC .... Goblet Cells [*Medicine*] (MELL)
GC .... Goddard College (SAUO)
gc .... going concern (SAUS)
GC .... Gold Coast [*Later, Ghana*] (ROG)
GC .... Gold Corp. [*Western Australia*] [*Commercial firm*]
GC .... Golden Companions [*An association*] (EA)
GC .... Goldsmith's College [*London, England*]
GC .... Golf Club
GC .... Gonococcal [*Clinical chemistry*]
gc .... Gonococcus [*Medicine*] (IDYL)
GC .... Gonococcus (SAUS)
GC .... Gonorrhea Case [*Medical slang*]
gc .... Good Condition [*Doll collecting*]
GC .... Good Conduct [*Military decoration*]
GC .... Gordon College (SAUO)
GC .... Goshen College (SAUO)
GC .... Goucher College (SAUO)
GC .... Gougerot-Carteaud [*Syndrome*] [*Medicine*] (DB)
GC .... Governing Council (EERA)
GC .... Government Chemist (SAUO)
GC .... Government Communications (TEL)
GC .... Government Contractor
GC .... Government Contribution
Gc .... Government of Canada (SAUS)
GC .... Governors' Conference
GC .... Graceland College (SAUO)
Gc .... Gradational, Calcareous [*Soil*]

GC .... Grade Crossing (SAUS)
GC .... Graduate Council (SAUO)
GC .... Graduated Cylinder (SAUS)
GC .... Graham Center [*An association*] (EA)
GC .... Graham County Railroad Co. [*AAR code*]
GC .... Grain Count [*Measurement of cell labeling*]
GC .... Grain Cube (SAUS)
GC .... Grain Cubic (DS)
GC .... Grambling College (SAUO)
G-C .... Gram-Negative Cocci [*Clinical chemistry*] (DAVI)
G+C .... Gram-Positive Cocci [*Clinical chemistry*] (DAVI)
GC .... GranCare, Inc. [*NYSE symbol*] (SPSG)
GC .... Grand Canyon [*Arizona*]
GC .... Grand Chancellor
GC .... Grand Chaplain
GC .... Grand Chapter
GC .... Grand Commander
GC .... Grand Conductor
GC .... Grand Council [*Freemasonry*] (ROG)
GC .... Grand Cross
GC .... Grantsmanship Center (EA)
GC .... Granular Cast [*Medicine*]
GC .... Granular Cyst [*Medicine*] (MAE)
GC .... Granulocyte Cytotoxic [*Hematology*]
GC .... Granulomatous Colitis [*Medicine*] (DB)
GC .... Granulosa Cells [*Cytology*]
GC .... Graphic Code (SAUS)
GC .... Graphic Console (SAUS)
GC .... Graphic Context (SAUS)
GC .... Graphics Conferencing (MCD)
GC .... Graphics Context (SAUS)
GC .... Gravimetric Calibrator (AAEL)
GC .... Grazing Capacity [*Agriculture*]
GC .... Great Central Railway [*British*] (ROG)
GC .... Great Churchmen [*A publication*]
GC .... Great Circle
Gc .... Great tropic range (SAUS)
GC .... Greek Church (ROG)
GC .... Green Cheeked Conure [*Bird*]
GC .... Green Concrete (SAUS)
GC .... Green Currency [*EEC*]
GC .... Greene Committee (SAUO)
GC .... Greenhouse Corps [*Australia*]
GC .... Greenland Cruiser
GC .... Greensboro College (SAUO)
GC .... Greenville College (SAUO)
GC .... Grey Code (SAUS)
GC .... Grid Course [*Navigation*]
GC .... Grid Current (SAUS)
GC .... Grinnell College (SAUO)
GC .... Grip Clutch (SAUS)
GC .... Grolier Club (EA)
GC .... Ground Clearance (SAUS)
GC .... Ground Contamination (SAUS)
GC .... Ground Control (AFM)
GC .... Ground Controlled (SAUS)
GC .... Ground Crew (SAUS)
GC .... Grounded Collector
GC .... Group Captain
GC .... Group Code [*Dialog*] [*Searchable field*] [*Information service or system*] (NITA)
GC .... Group Cohesiveness [*Psychological testing*]
GC .... Group Command (SAUO)
GC .... Group Connector (SAUS)
GC .... Group Control (SAUO)
GC .... Groupe de Chasse [*French aircraft fighter unit*] [*World War II*]
GC .... Group-Specific Component [*Medicine*] (EDAA)
Gc .... Group-Specific Component [*A serum group*]
GC .... Grouting Concrete (SAUS)
G+C .... Guanine and Cytosine (SAUS)
GC .... Guanine Cystine (SAUS)
GC .... Guanine, Cytosine [*Type*] [*Biochemistry*]
Gc .... Guanine-Plus-Cytosine (SAUS)
GC .... Guanylcyclase (DB)
GC .... Guidance Computer
GC .... Guidance Control [*NASA*] (NASA)
GC .... Guide Catheter [*Medicine*] (MELL)
GC .... Guild of Cleaners (SAUO)
GC .... Guilford College (SAUS)
GC .... Gun Camera (MCD)
GC .... Gun Capital (DNAB)
GC .... Gun Captain
GC .... Gun Carriage
GC .... Gun Clear (SAUS)
GC .... Gun Control
GC .... Gun Controller (SAUS)
Gc .... Gun Cotton (SAUS)
GC .... Guyon's Canal [*Medicine*] (EDAA)
GC .... Gyro Caged (ACAE)
GC .... Gyro Compass
GC .... Gyrocompassing [*Aerospace*] (NAKS)
GC .... Gyro Control
GC .... Gyroscopic Compass (SAUS)
GC .... Lina-Congo [*ICAO designator*] (AD)
GC .... Office of General Council (SAUO)
GC .... Southwire Co. (SAUO)
GC4A .... Global Command, Control, Communications and Computers Assessment (SAUO)
GCA .... Gain Control Amplifier
GCA .... Gain Control Driver (SAUS)
GCA .... Gallocyanin-Chrome Alum (SAUS)
GCA .... Garden Centers of America (EA)
GCA .... Garden Centre Association (BUAC)
GCA .... Garden Centres of Australia
GCA .... Garden Club of America (EA)
GCA .... Garden Club of Australia
GCA .... Gasket Cutters' Association (BUAC)
GCA .... Gastric Cancer Area [*Medicine*] (DMAA)
GCA .... Gauge Control Analyzer
GCA .... GCA Corp. (SAUO)
GCA .... Gearbox Controller Automatic (SAUS)
GCA .... Genealogy Club of America [*Defunct*] (EA)
GCA .... General Claim Agent
GCA .... General Combining Ability
GCA .... General Communications Architecture (SAUS)
GCA .... General Control Approach
GCA .... General Council Audit (SAUO)
GCA .... Geneva Convention Act (SAUO)
GCA .... Geophysics Corp. of America
GCA .... Geophysics Corporation of America (SAUO)
GCA .... Giant Cell Arteritis [*Medicine*]
GCA .... Girls Clubs of America [*Later, GI*] (EA)
GCA .... Glass Crafts of America [*Defunct*] (EA)
GCA .... Glazing Contractors Association (SAUO)
GCA .... Glen Canyon [*Arizona*] [*Seismograph station code, US Geological Survey*] (SEIS)
GCA .... Global Citizens Association [*Quebec, PQ*] (EAIO)
GCA .... Global Coalition for Africa (SAUO)
GCA .... Glycosphingolipid Sorbent Assay (SAUS)
GCA .... Gold Clause Agreement [*Shipping*] (DS)
GCA .... Golf Course Association (EA)
GCA .... Government Contract Advisor [*CD-ROM*] [*Published by Clark Boardman*] (AAGC)
GCA .... Government Contract Awards (SAUS)
GCA .... Government Contract Committee (SAUO)
GCA .... Grains Council of Australia (EERA)
GCA .... Grand Central Association (SAUO)
GCA .... Graphic Communications Association (EA)
GCA .... Great China Airlines [*Taiwan*] [*ICAO designator*] (FAAC)
GCA .... Green Coffee Association (SAUO)
GCA .... Green Coffee Association of New Orleans (SAUO)
GCA .... Green Coffee Association of New York City (EA)
GCA .... Greeting Card Association (EA)
GCA .... Greyhound Club of America (EA)
GCA .... Ground Communication Activities (SAUS)
GCA .... Ground Communication Activity (IAA)
GCA .... Ground Control Approach (SAUS)
GCA .... Ground Control Center (SAUO)
GCA .... Ground-Controlled Aircraft (AFM)
GCA .... Ground-Controlled Apparatus [*RADAR*]
GCA .... Ground-Controlled Approach [*for lateral and vertical guidance of landing aircraft through use of ground RADAR and radio communications*]
GCA .... Grounded Cathode Amplifier
GCA .... Group Capacity Analysis [*or Assessment*]
GCA .... Group Capacity Assessment (SAUO)
GCA .... Guacamayas [*Colombia*] [*Airport symbol*] (OAG)
GCA .... Guanine Cytosine Adenine [*A triplet of bases coding for the amino acid, alanine*] (EES)
GCA .... Guatemala (SAUS)
GCA .... Guidance and Control Assembly (NG)
GCA .... Guidance Control and Adapter Section (MCD)
GCA .... Guidance Coupler Assembly (SAUO)
GCA .... Gulf Coast Aluminium Corp. (SAUO)
GCA .... Gulf General Atomic (SAUO)
GCA .... Gun Control Act [*1968*]
GCA .... Gun Control Australia
GCA .... Gunite Contractors Association (EA)
GCA .... Gyro Control Assembly
GCA .... WHO Global Commission on AIDS (SAUO)
GCAA .... Ghana Civil Aviation Authority (SAUS)
GCAA .... Golf Coaches Association of America (EA)
GCAA .... Government Corporations Athletic Association (SAUO)
GCAA .... Guidance, Control, and Airframe (IAA)
GCAB .... Global Community Advisory Board (HVTR)
GCABY .... General Cable PLC [*NASDAQ symbol*] (SAG)
GCABY .... Genl Cable plc.ADS [*NASDAQ symbol*] (TTSB)
GCAC .... Gulf Coast Athletic Conference (PSS)
GCA-CTS .... Ground-Controlled Approach - Controller Training System (MCD)
GCAD .... Geographical Computer Aided Design System (SAUO)
GCAD .... Granite City Army Depot (AABC)
GCADA .... Governor's Council on Alcoholism and Drug Abuse [*New Jersey*]
GC/AFID .... Gas Chromatography/Alkali Flame Ionization Detector (EEVL)
GCAGS .... Gulf Coast Association of Geological Societies (SAUO)
GCAHS .... Guggenheim Center for Aviation Health and Safety (SAUO)
GCai .... Roddenbery Memorial Library, Cairo, GA [*Library symbol*] [*Library of Congress*] (LCLS)
GCAL .... Gram Calorie
g-cal .... Gram-Calorie (IDOE)
GCAL .... Gramme Calorie (SAUS)

GCAM .... Gaming Corp. of America [*NASDAQ symbol*] (SAG)
GCAM .... Groupement de la Caisse des Depots Automatisation pour le Management [*Bank Group for Automation in Management*] [*Information service or system*] (IID)
GC & A .... Guidance, Control, and Airframe
GC&CS .... Government Code and Cipher School (SAUO)
GC & O .... Guidance, Control, and Ordnance
GC & SF ...... Gulf, Colorado & Santa Fe Railway Co.
GC&TPA ...... Garden Cities and Town Planning Association (SAUO)
GCanS .... Sequoyah Regional Library, Canton, GA [*Library symbol*] [*Library of Congress*] (LCLS)
GCA of NO ... Green Coffee Association of New Orleans (EA)
GCAP .... General Circuit Analysis Program (SAUS)
GCAP .... Generalized Circuit Analysis Problem (SAUS)
GCAP .... Generalized Circuit Analysis Program (IEEE)
GCAP .... Germ-Cell Alkaline Phosphatase (DMAA)
GCAP .... Gold Co. of America (SAUO)
GCAPEF .... Grace Contrino Abrams Peace Education Foundation (EA)
G/Capt .... Group Captain [*British military*] (DMA)
GCARA .... Greater Cincinnati Amateur Radio Association (SAUO)
GCarrS .... Southwire Co., Carrollton, GA [*Library symbol*] [*Library of Congress*] (LCLS)
GCarrWG ..... West Georgia College, Carrollton, GA [*Library symbol*] [*Library of Congress*] (LCLS)
GCAS .... Generic Configuration Accounting System (SAUO)
GCAS .... Ground Collision Avoidance System [*Army*]
G-CASE .... Georgia Council of Administrators of Special Education (SAUO)
GCAT .... Guidance and Control Analysis Team [*Space Flight Operations, NASA*]
GCATE .... Global Change and Terrestrial Ecosystems (SAUO)
GCatO .... Group Catering Officer [*British military*] (DMA)
GCATT .... Georgia Center for Advanced Telecommunications Technology (SAUS)
GCAU .... General Commission Agents Union (SAUO)
GCAU .... Grain-Consuming Animal Unit [*Agricultural Statistics*] (BARN)
GCAutrey ..... Grupo Casa Autrey [*Associated Press*] (SAG)
GCAW .... Gas Carbon Arc Welding (SAUS)
GCB .... Dame Grand Cross of the Order of the Bath [*British*] (ADA)
GCB .... General Circuit Breaker (MHDI)
GCB .... General Council of the Bar (SAUO)
GCB .... Generator Control Breaker
GCB .... German Convention Bureau (EA)
GCB .... Ghana Commercial Bank
GCB .... Ghanian Cocoa Butter
GCB .... Giro Central Bank (SAUO)
GCB .... Glen Canyon Bridge (SAUS)
GCB .... Gonococcal Base [*Broth*] [*Growth medium*]
GCB .... Good Conduct Badge [*British*]
GCB .... Grand Cross of the Bath (SAUS)
GCB .... Grand Cross of the Order of the Bath (SAUS)
GCB .... Graphic Control Byte (SAUS)
GCB .... Graphitized Carbon Black
GCB .... Graphitizes Carbon Black (SAUS)
GCB .... Gravity Cutback (NRCH)
GCB .... Great-Circle Bearing [*Navigation*] (IAA)
GCB .... Greyhound Consultative Body (BUAC)
GCB .... Ground Control Byte (SAUS)
GCB .... Group Circuit Breaker (SAUO)
GCB .... Guernsey Cattle Breeders' Association (BUAC)
GCB .... Gun Control Box (SAUS)
GCB .... Guthrie, C. B., Tariff Bureau Inc., Washington DC [*STAC*]
GCB .... Knight Grand Cross of the [*Order of the*] Bath [*British*]
GCB .... Lignes Nationales Aeriennes - Linacongo [*Congo*] [*ICAO designator*] (FAAC)
GCBA .... Golf Course Builders of America (EA)
GCBAA .... Golf Course Builders Association of America (NTPA)
GCBC .... Goucher College Babylonian Collection (BJA)
GCBDS .... Gonococcal Broth Defined Supplement [*Medicine*] (EDAA)
GCBK .... Great Country Bank [*NASDAQ symbol*] (NQ)
GCBM .... Gas Chromatography in Biology and Medicine [*British*]
GCBR .... Gas-Cooled Breeder Reactor [*Nuclear energy*]
GCBS .... General Council of British Shipping
GCBS .... Ground-Control Bombing System (NG)
GCBT .... Gray-Cheeked/Bicknell's Thrush [*North American bird banding code*] (BIBA)
GCBW .... General Committee for Bahrain Workers (BUAC)
GCBW .... Global Cooperation for a Better World [*Australia*]
GCC .... Arab Gulf Co-operation Council (SAUS)
GCC .... Coca-Cola Co., Business Information, Atlanta, GA [*OCLC symbol*] (OCLC)
GCC .... Cooperation Council for the Arab States of the Gulf (SAUO)
GCC .... Game Conservancy Council (BUAC)
GCC .... Garden Cat Club (EA)
GCC .... Gas Chromatograph Column (SAUS)
GCC .... Gas Consumers Council (BUAC)
GCC .... Gasification Combined Cycle (SAUS)
GCC .... General Channel Coordinator (SAUS)
GCC .... General Cinema Corp. [*Chestnut Hill, MA*]
GCC .... General Commission on Chaplains and Armed Forces Personnel [*Later, NCMAF*] (EA)
GCC .... General Conditions of Contract for Works of Civil Engineering Construction (SAFN)
GCC .... General construction contractor (SAUS)
GCC .... General Contracting Company (SAUO)
GCC .... General Council of Congress (SAUO)
GCC .... Generic Cell Controller (AAEL)
GCC .... Generic Conference Control (SAUO)
GCC .... Geodetic Coordinate Conversion (SAUO)
GCC .... Georgian Court College [*Lakewood, NJ*]
GCC .... Geoscience Conference Calendar (SAUO)
GCC .... German Computer Club (SAUS)
GCC .... German Concentration Camp (SAUO)
GCC .... German Control Center (SAUO)
GCC .... Germ Cell Cancer (MELL)
GCC .... Giannini Controls Corp. (AAG)
GCC .... Giannini Controls Corporation (SAUO)
GCC .... Gillette [*Wyoming*] [*Airport symbol*] (OAG)
GCC .... Girton College [*Cambridge University*] (DAS)
GCC .... Glassy Cell Carcinoma (MELL)
GCC .... Global Change Category (EOSA)
GCC .... Global Climate Change (SAUS)
GCC .... Global Climate Change Program (SAUO)
GCC .... Global Climate Coalition [*A US lobby group*]
GCC .... Global Climate Convention (SAUO)
GCC .... Global Climatic Change [*Marine science*] (OSRA)
GCC .... Global Collecting Centre (SAUO)
GCC .... Global Command Center (ACAE)
GCC .... Global Community Center (SAUS)
GCC .... Global Competitiveness Council [*Defunct*] (EA)
GCC .... Glove Collector Club (EA)
GCC .... GNU C-Compiler (SAUS)
GCC .... Goddard Communications Center [*NASA*]
GCC .... Goddard Computing Center [*NASA*]
GCC .... Goebel Collectors' Club [*Later, MIHC*] (EA)
GCC .... Gogebic Community College [*Ironwood, MI*]
GCC .... Golden Concord Mining [*Vancouver Stock Exchange symbol*]
GCC .... Gonville and Caius College [*Cambridge University*] (ROG)
GCC .... Good Counsel College [*New York*]
GCC .... Gore-Chernomyrdin Commission (SAUO)
GCC .... Government Chemistry Centre (SAUO)
GCC .... Government Contract Committee [*Later, OFCCP*] [*Department of Labor*]
GCC .... Graduated Combat Capability [*Military*]
g/cc .... Grams per Cubic Centimeter (SAUS)
g/cc .... Grams per Cubic Centimetre (SAUS)
GCC .... Grand Canyon College [*Phoenix, AZ*]
GCC .... Grand Council of the Crees (SAUO)
GCC .... Granite Creek [*California*] [*Seismograph station code, US Geological Survey*] (SEIS)
GCC .... Graphic Control Center [*Touch-activated CRT display*]
GCC .... Great Council of Chiefs [*Fiji*] (BUAC)
GCC .... Greenfield Community College [*Massachusetts*]
GCC .... Greyhound Computer Corporation (SAUO)
GCC .... Grid Control Center (SAUS)
GCC .... Grid Cooperating Centre (EERA)
GCC .... Ground Calcium Carbonate [*Inorganic chemistry*]
GCC .... Ground Communications Controller
GCC .... Ground Communications Coordinator [*NASA*] (NASA)
GCC .... Ground Component Command (SAUO)
GCC .... Ground Computer Controller
GCC .... Ground-Control Center
GCC .... Group Change Control
GCC .... Group Control Center (or Centre) (SAUO)
GCC .... Grove City College [*Pennsylvania*]
GCC .... Guanine Cytosine Cytosine [*A triplet of bases coding for the amino acid, alanine*] (EES)
GCC .... Guidance and Control Computer
GCC .... Guidance Checkout Computer
GCC .... Gulf Coast College (SAUO)
GCC .... Gulf Cooperation Council [*Consists of Saudi Arabia, Bahrain, Kuwait, Oman, Qatar, and the United Arab Emirates*]
GCC .... Gulf Cooperative Council (EERA)
GCC .... Gun Control Console [*Military*] (CAAL)
GCCA .... Gambling Chip Collectors Association (EA)
GCCA .... G-Cat Class Association (EA)
GCCA .... Graphic Communication Computer Association (SAUS)
GCCA .... Graphic Communications Computer Association [*Printing Industries of America*] [*Later, GCA*]
GCCA .... Greater Clothing Contractors Association (EA)
GCCA .... Greeting Card and Calendar Association [*British*]
GCCB .... Government Change Control Board (SAUS)
GCCC .... Canarias [*Canary Islands*] [*ICAO location identifier*] (ICLI)
GCCC .... General Computer Corp. (SAUS)
GCCC .... General Computer Corporation (SAUO)
GCCC .... General Council of County Councils [*Eire*] (BUAC)
GCCC .... Georgia Commodity Classification Code (SAUO)
GCCC .... Goshen County Community College (SAUO)
GCCC .... Ground Communications, Command, and Control (ACAE)
GCCC .... Ground Control Computer Center [*Aerospace*] (NAKS)
GCCCOONS ... Geese Command, Control and Communication Operations, Navigation and Security (SAUO)
GCCD .... Glass-Passivated Ceramic Chip Diode (SAUS)
GCCD .... Global Climate Change Digest [*A publication*]
GCCEA .... General Committee of the Comite Europeen des Assurances [*France*] (EAIO)
GCCF .... Governing Council of the Cat Fancy [*British*] (BI)
GCCG .... German Colonies Collectors Group (EA)
GCCIP .... Global Climate Change Information Programme (BUAC)
GCCL .... Gas-cooled closed loop (SAUS)
GCCM .... Glasgow Chamber of Commerce and Manufactures (SAUO)

GCCM .... Global Carbone Cycle Modeling (SAUS)
GCCNI .... General Consumer Council for Northern Ireland (BUAC)
GCCNPIP ...... General Conference Committee of the National Poultry Improvement Plan [*Department of Agriculture*] (EGAO)
GCCO .... Granite Construction [*NASDAQ symbol*] (TTSB)
GCCO .... Granite Construction, Inc. [*NASDAQ symbol*] (SAG)
GCCO .... Ground Control Checkout (SAUS)
GC Cos .... GC Companies [*Associated Press*] (SAG)
GCCP .... Global Climate Change Program (SAUO)
GCCS .... Geneva Convention on the Continental Shelf (NOAA)
GCCS .... Global Change Catalog System (SAUS)
GCCS .... Global Command and Control System
GCCS .... Government Code and Cypher School [*Later, GCHQ*] [*Sometimes facetiously translated as Golf, Chess, and Cheese Society*] [*British*]
GCCS-A .... Global Command and Control System-Army (SEWL)
GCCVF .... Golden Concord Mining (SAUS)
GCCW .... United Gas, Coke, and Chemical Workers of America [*Later, OCAW*]
GCCZ .... Gibson County Co-Operative [*Federal Railroad Administration identification code*]
GCD .... DeKalb Community College, Clarkston, GA [*OCLC symbol*] (OCLC)
GCD .... Gain Control Driver (CET)
GCD .... Gas Chromatography Distillation (AAEL)
GCD .... Gate-Controlled Diode (IAA)
GCD .... General and Complete Disarmament
GCD .... General and Comprehensive Disarmament (FOTI)
GCD .... General System Division (SAUS)
GCD .... Geometric Correction Data (SAUO)
GCD .... Gold Coupling Dendrite
GCD .... Golden Cadillac Resources Ltd. [*Vancouver Stock Exchange symbol*]
GCD .... Good Conduct Discharge
GCD .... Graft Coronary Disease [*Cardiology*] (DMAA)
GCD .... Graphic Codepoint Definition [*Telecommunications*]
GCD .... Great Circle Distance
GCD .... Great Circle Distance Calculator (SAUO)
GCD .... Greater Confinement Disposal (SAUS)
gcd .... Greatest Commom Divisor (NTIO)
GCD .... Greatest Common Denominator
gcd .... Greatest Common Divisor (SHCU)
GCD .... Greatest Common Divisor
GCD .... Ground Controlled Descent (ROAS)
GCD .... Ground-Controlled Descent (SAUS)
GCD .... Gyro-Compass, Desired Cluster Orientation (MCD)
GCDA .... Gulf Canada Resources Ltd. (SAUO)
GCDB .... Geographic Coordinate Data Base (SAUS)
GCDB .... Geographic Coordinates Data Base (SAUS)
GCDB .... Global Change Database (SAUS)
GCDC .... Gas Chromatography Data Committee (SAUO)
GCDC .... Global Change Data Center (SAUS)
GCDC .... Gold Coast Divisional Court Reports [*A publication*] (DLA)
GCDC .... Grace Cancer Drug Center [*Roswell Park Memorial Institute*] [*Research center*] (RCD)
GCDC .... Ground Checkout Display and Control [*NASA*] (NASA)
GCDCS .... Ground Checkout Display and Control System (MCD)
GC/DD .... Gas Chromatography/Dual Detector (EEVL)
GCDFP .... Gross Cystic Disease Fluid Protein (DAVI)
GCDI .... Galacticomm Custom Device Interface [*Galacticomm, Inc.*] [*Telecommunications*]
GCDIS .... Global Change Data and Information System [*Marine science*] (OSRA)
GC Div C ...... Selected Judgments of the Divisional Courts [*Ghana*] [*A publication*] (DLA)
GC Div Ct ..... Gold Coast Selected Judgments of the Divisional Courts [*A publication*] (DLA)
GCDMWG .... Global Change Data Management Working Group (SAUO)
GCDP .... Global Change Database Project (EERA)
GCDP .... Gunner's Control and Display Panel [*Military*] (RDA)
GCDR .... Gulf Canada Resources Ltd. (SAUS)
GCDRA .... Green Crop Driers Research Association (SAUO)
GCDR PR ..... Gulf Canada Resources Ltd. Preferred (SAUS)
GCDS .... Gamma Dose Detector System (SAUS)
GCDU .... Grupo de Convergencia Democratica en Uruguay [*Group of Democratic Convergence in Uruguay*] (EA)
GCDU .... Gunner Control & Display Unit (SAUS)
GCE .... Commission for Geographical Education (EA)
GCE .... Galveston Cotton Exchange and Board of Trade (SAUS)
GCE .... Gas City Empire (SAUO)
GCE .... General Certificate of Education [*British*]
GCE .... General Consulting & Engineering Srl. (SAUS)
GCE .... General Consumers Electronics (NITA)
GCE .... General Control Equipment (SAUS)
GCE .... Glassy Carbon Electrode
GCE .... Global Change Encyclopedia (SAUS)
GCE .... Gordon Consulting Engineers Ltd. (SAUO)
GCE .... Government Capital Expenditure [*Finance*]
GCE .... Government Computer Expo (HGAA)
GCE .... Great Canadian Cider [*Vancouver Stock Exchange symbol*]
GCE .... Greenwood Cotton Exchange (EA)
GCE .... Ground Checkout Equipment [*Aerospace*] (AAG)
GCE .... Ground Combat Element [*Marine Corps*] (DOMA)
GCE .... Ground Communication Equipment (SAUS)
GCE .... Ground Communications Equipment
GCE .... Ground Control Equipment (SAUS)
GCE .... Ground-Control Equipment
GCE .... Ground Cooperational Equipment (SAUS)
GCE .... Ground Crew Ensemble (ACAE)
GCE .... Group Control Entry (SAUO)
GCE .... Group Control Exit (SAUO)
GCE .... Gun Control Equipment (DNAB)
GCE .... Gun Controlled Equipment (SAUS)
GCEBT .... Galveston Cotton Exchange and Board of Trade (EA)
GC-EC .... Gas Chromatography with Electron Capture
GCEC .... Global Change and Ecological Complexity (SAUO)
GCEC .... Gold Coast Environment Centre (EERA)
GCEC .... Greater Colombo Economic Community (SAUS)
GC/ECD .... Gas Chromatograph/Electron Capture Detector (SAUS)
GC/ECD .... Gas Chromatograph with Electron Capture Detector [*Chemical analysis*]
GC/ECD .... Gas Chromatography/Electrolytic Conductivity Detector (EEVL)
GC/ECD .... Gas Chromatography using Electron-Capture Detection (SAUS)
GC-ECD .... Gas Chromatography with an Electron Capture Detector (SAUS)
GCECEE .... Groupement des Caisses d'Epargne de la CEE [*Savings Bank Group of the European Economic Community*]
GCE Examination ... General College Entrance Examination (SAUS)
GCEG .... Grid-Controlled Electron Gun
GCEI .... Gold C Enterprises, Inc. (SAUS)
GCEI .... Gold C Enterprises, Incorporated (SAUO)
GCEL .... Georgia Compensatory Education Leaders (SAUO)
GCEL .... Ground Control Experiment Laboratory (SAUO)
GCEM .... Geographic Correlator Exploration Machine (SAUO)
GCEM .... Goddard Cumulus Ensemble Model (SAUO)
GC ENV .... Government of Canada (SAUS)
GC ENV .... Government of Canada, Environment Canada (SAUS)
GCEOS .... Group Contribution Equation of State
GCEP .... Gas Centrifuge Enrichment Plant [*Department of Energy*]
GCEP .... Global Change Education Program (SAUO)
GCEP .... Governing Council for Environmental Programs [*United Nations*]
GCER .... General Ceramics, Inc. (SAUO)
GCER .... Growth Environmental, Inc. [*NASDAQ symbol*] (SAG)
GCertClinInstr ... Graduate Certificate in Clinical Instruction [*Australia*]
GCertEd .... Graduate Certificate in Education [*Australia*]
GCertEdStudies ... Graduate Certificate in Educational Studies [*Australia*]
GCertMaths & MathEd ... Graduate Certificate in Mathematics and Mathematics Education [*Australia*]
GCertMusMgmt ... Graduate Certificate of Museum Management [*Australia*]
GCertSc & TechWriting ... Graduate Certificate of Scientific and Technical Writing [*Australia*]
GCertSocAdmin ... Graduate Certificate in Social Administration [*Australia*]
GCES .... Generalized Constant Elasticity of Substitution (PDAA)
GCES .... Geodetic Communications and Electronia Squadron (SAUS)
GCES .... Glen Canyon Environmental Studies [*Department of the Interior*]
GCES .... Green Creek Elementary School (SAUO)
GCESq .... Geodetic Communications and Electronics Squadron [*Air Force*] (AFM)
G-CEU .... General Certified End User [*Department of Commerce export license*]
GCF .... General Contract Finance Corporation (SAUO)
GCF .... General Control Function (SAUS)
GCF .... Generation Control Function [*Telecommunications*] (TEL)
gcf .... Greatest Common Factor (SHCU)
GCF .... Greatest Common Factor
GCF .... Greenhouse Crisis Foundation (EA)
GCF .... Gross Capacity Factor (IEEE)
GCF .... Ground Command Facility
GCF .... Ground Communications Facility [*NASA*]
GCF .... Growth-Rate-Controlling Factor [*Medicine*] (DMAA)
GCF .... Gynecologic Cancer Foundation (SAUO)
GCFA .... Gridded Crossed Field Amplifier (IAA)
GCFAP .... Guidance and Control Flight Analysis Program [*Aerospace*]
GCFBE .... Gas-Cooled Fast Reactor Experiment (SAUS)
GCFBR .... Gas Cooled Fast Breeder (EDCT)
GCFBR .... Gas Cooled Fast Breeder Reactor (SAUS)
GCFC .... Glen Campbell Fan Club (EA)
GCFC .... Gold Coast Full Court Selected Judgments [*A publication*] (DLA)
GCFC .... Gulf Coast Fisheries Center
GCF-CS .... Ground Communications Facility - Communications Switcher [*NASA*]
GCFGA .... Georgia Commercial Flower Growers Association Inc. (SAUO)
GCFI .... Gulf and Caribbean Fisheries Institute (EA)
GC/FID .... Gas Chromatography/Flame Ionization Detector (EEVL)
GC-FID .... Gas Chromatography with Flame Ionization Detection
GCFL .... Great Crested Flycatcher [*North American bird banding code*] (BIBA)
GCFLH .... Grand Cross of the French Legion of Honour
gc-FPD .... Gas Chromatographic-Flame Photometric Detector (SAUS)
GC-FPD .... Gas Chromatography-Flame Photometric Detector (LDOE)
GCFR .... Gas-Cooled Fast Reactor
GCFRC .... Gulf Coastal Fisheries Research Center (SAUO)
GCFRE .... Gas-Cooled Fast-breeder Reactor Experiment (SAUS)
GCFRE .... Gas-Cooled Fast Reactor Experiment (IEEE)
GCFT .... Gonorrhea Complement Fixation Test [*Medicine*]
GC/FTIR .... Gas Chromatography plus Fourier Transform Infrared Spectrometry
GCFU .... Germinal Center-Forming Unit (DNAB)
GC Full Ct .... Gold Coast Full Court Selected Judgments [*A publication*] (DLA)
GC Full Ct .... Gold Coast Full Court Selected Judgments (journ.) (SAUS)
GCFV .... Puerto Del Rosario/Fuerteventura [*Canary Islands*] [*ICAO location identifier*] (ICLI)
GCFX .... Alsthon Canada [*Private rail car owner code*]
gcg .... gas-chamber green (SAUS)
GCG .... General Electric Capital Exchange [*AMEX symbol*] (SAG)
GCG .... Genl Chemical Group [*NYSE symbol*] (TTSB)
GCG .... Geocartographics Subdivison (SAUS)

GCG .... Geological Curators Group (SAUO)
GCG .... Glucagon (DMAA)
GCG .... Gorham Collectors' Guild [*Defunct*] (EA)
GCG .... Grand Captain General [*Freemasonry*]
GCG .... Grand Captain of the Guard [*Freemasonry*]
GCG .... Gravity-Controlled Gyro
GCG .... Greenhouse Coordinating Group [*Australia*]
GCG .... Ground Command Guidance
GCG .... Group Clock Generator (SAUS)
GCG .... Guanine Cytosine Guanine [*A triplet of bases coding for the amino acid, alanine*] (EES)
GCG .... Guardian Capital Group Ltd. [*Toronto Stock Exchange symbol*]
GCG .... Guatemala City [*Guatemala*] [*Seismograph station code, US Geological Survey*] [*Closed*] (SEIS)
GCG .... Guidance Control Group [*Military*]
GCG .... Gyro Control Gunsight
GCGB .... Gas-Cooled Graphite-Moderated Reactor (SAUS)
GCGC .... Golden Cycle Gold Corp. (SAUS)
GCGC .... Golden Cycle Gold Corporation (SAUO)
GCGGA .... Gulf Coast Association of Geological Societies. Field Trip Guidebook (journ.) (SAUS)
GCGI .... Geneve Capital Group, Incorporated (SAUO)
GCGLD .... Grants, Contracts, and General Law Division [*Environmental Protection Agency*] (GFGA)
GCGR .... Gas-Cooled Graphite-Moderated Reactor (SAUS)
GCGR .... Glucagon Receptor (DMAA)
GCGR .... Glucocorticoid Receptor (DMAA)
GCGS .... Gravity-Controlled Gyro System
G CH .... [*The*] Gardeners' Chronicle [*A publication*] (ROG)
GCH .... Gas Collection Header (NRCH)
GCH .... Generalized Continuum Hypothesis [*Logic*]
GCH .... Germinal Center Hyperplasia [*Medicine*]
GCH .... Gigacharacter (SAUS)
GCH .... Gigacharacters
GCH .... Global Change Climate and History (SAUS)
GCH .... Global Community Health
GCH .... Glucocorticoid Hormone [*Endocrinology*]
GCH .... Golden Chance Resources, Inc. [*Vancouver Stock Exchange symbol*]
GCH .... Grand Captain of the Host [*Freemasonry*]
GCH .... Grand Chapter of Harodim [*Freemasonry*]
gch .... Grandchildren (GEAB)
GCH .... Grand Cross of the Hanoverian Order (SAUS)
GCH .... [*The*] Greater China Fund [*NYSE symbol*] (SAG)
GCH .... Guidance Capsule Handling
GCH .... Knight Grand Cross of the Guelphic Order of Hanover [*British*]
GCHC .... Gulf Coast Hydroscience Center [*Department of the Interior*] [*National Space Technology Laboratories Station, MS*] (GRD)
GC/HECD ..... Gas Chromatography/Hall Electrolytic Conductivity Detector (EEVL)
GCHI .... Giant Cement Holding [*NASDAQ symbol*] (TTSB)
GCHI .... Giant Cement Holding, Inc. [*NASDAQ symbol*] (SAG)
GCHI .... Hierro [*Canary Islands*] [*ICAO location identifier*] (ICLI)
GChM .... Global Chemistry Model (SAUS)
GCHQ .... Government Code Headquarters [*Formerly, GCCS*] [*British*] (INF)
GCHQ .... Government Communications Headquarters [*British*]
GCHR .... Guard Committee for Human Rights (SAUS)
GCHR .... Guatemala Committee for Human Rights (EAIO)
GCHWR .... Gas-Cooled Heavy Water Moderated Reactor (SAUS)
GCHWR .... Gas-Cooled, Heavy-Water-Moderated Reactor [*Nuclear energy*] (NRCH)
GCHWR .... Gas-Cooled Heavy Water Reactor (SAUS)
GCHWR .... Gas-Cooled Hot Water Reactor (SAUS)
GCHX .... Grand Cypress Resort Hyatt Hotel [*Federal Railroad Administration identification code*]
GCHX .... Ground Cooling Heat Exchanger [*NASA*] (NASA)
GCI .... Gannett Co. [*NYSE symbol*] (TTSB)
GCI .... Gannett Co., Inc. [*NYSE symbol*] (SPSG)
GCI .... Gas Chromatograph Intoximeter [*Measure-of-intoxication test for drunk drivers*]
GCI .... General Capital Increase [*Banking*]
GCI .... General Circuit Interface
GCI .... General Cognitive Index [*Medicine*] (DMAA)
GCI .... General Communication, Inc. [*Anchorage, AK*] [*Telecommunications*] (TSSD)
GCI .... Generalised Communication Interface (SAUS)
GCI .... Generalized Communication Interface
GCI .... Genetics Citation Index (SAUS)
GCI .... Genie Climatique International (EA)
GCI .... Georgia Correctional Industries (SAUO)
GCI .... Gestational Carbohydrate Intolerance [*Medicine*] (MELL)
GCI .... Getty Conservation Institute [*Database producer*] (IID)
GCI .... Global Change Institute (SAUO)
GCI .... Global Commons Institute (SAUS)
GCI .... Globetrotter Communications, Inc. (SAUS)
GCI .... Gnostic Concepts, Inc. [*San Mateo, CA*] [*Database producer*] [*Information service or system*] [*Telecommunications*] (TSSD)
GCI .... Gossman Consulting, Inc. (EFIS)
GCI .... Grand Canary Island (SAUO)
GCI .... Grand China Resources Ltd. [*Vancouver Stock Exchange symbol*]
GCI .... Granulosa Cell Islands (SAUS)
GCI .... Graphic Communications, Inc. [*Computer science*]
GCI .... Graphic Converter Interface [*Computer science*] (DGA)
GCI .... Graphics Command Interpreter (IAA)
GCI .... Gray Cast Iron
GCI .... Green Chemistry Institute
GCI .... Green Cross International (SAUO)
GCI .... Ground Clearance Intercept [*System similar to US commercial RADAR for ground control of aircraft*] [*North Vietnam*]
GCI .... Ground Control Intercept [*Military*] (MUSM)
GCI .... Ground Control Interception (SAUS)
GCI .... Ground Control Interceptor (SAUS)
GCI .... Ground-Controlled Interception [*RADAR*]
GCI .... Ground-Controlled Interjection (SAUS)
GCI .... Ground Control of Interception (SAUS)
GCI .... Group Control Interruption (SAUO)
GCI .... Groupe des Communications Informatiques [*Computer Communications Group*] [*Canada*]
GCI .... Guernsey [*Channel Islands*] [*Airport symbol*] (OAG)
GCI .... Gulf Communications, Inc. [*Melbourne, FL*] [*Telecommunications service*] (TSSD)
GCIA .... Granite Cutters' International Association [*Later, Tile, Marble, Terrazzo, Finishers, Shopworkers, and Granite Cutters International Union*]
GCIAA .... Granite Cutters' International Association of America (DICI)
GCI/ADC ..... Ground-Controlled Intercept/Air Defense Center (DNAB)
GCIB .... German Commercial Information Bureau (SAUO)
GCIC .... Gifted Children's Information Centre [*British*] (CB)
GCIC .... Groupement Cinematographique International de Conciliation (EA)
GCICU .... German Chamber of Industry and Commerce in the United Kingdom (EAIO)
GCID .... Global Call Identifier (SAUO)
GCID-IE ...... Global Call Identifier-Information Element (SAUS)
GCIE .... Grand Commander of the Order of the Indian Empire (SAUS)
GCIE .... Knight Grand Commander of the [*Order of the*] Indian Empire [*British*]
GCIIG .... Glass and Ceramics Industry Instrumentation Group (ACII)
GCIIS .... Glucose Controlled Insulin Infusion System [*Medicine*] (DMAA)
GCIL .... Ground Command Interface Logic (NAKS)
GCIL .... Ground-Control Interface Logic (MCD)
GCILC .... Ground Command Interface Logic Controller (SAUS)
GCILC .... Ground-Control Interface Logic Controller (MCD)
GCILU .... Ground-Control Interface Logic Unit (MCD)
GCIP .... GEWEX [*Global Energy and Water Cycle Experiment*] Continental-Scale International Project [*World Climate Research Program*] [*Geoscience*]
GCIP .... Global Continental-Scale International Project (SAUS)
GCIP .... Guidance Correction Input Panel
GC-IR .... Gas Chrnmatography Infrared (SAUS)
GC/IR .... Gas Chromatography/Infrared
GC/IR .... Gas Chromatography/Infrared Absorption Spectrometer (EEVL)
GC-IR .... Gas Chromatography - Infrared Spectroscopy (SAUS)
GCIRC .... Glass Container Industry Research Corp. [*An association*] (EA)
GCIRC .... Groupe Consultatif International de Recherche sur le Colza [*International Consultative Research Group on Rape Seed*] (EAIO)
GC-IRMS ..... Gas Chromatography - Isotope-Ratio Mass Spectrometry [*Chemistry*]
GCIS .... German Criminal Investigation Section (SAUO)
GCIS .... Germany Counter Intelligence Service (SAUO)
GCIS .... Grade Crossing Inventory System [*BTS*] (TAG)
GCIS .... Ground Combat Identification System (SAUS)
GCIS .... Ground Combat Information System (SAUS)
GCIS .... Ground Control Interception Station (SAUS)
GCISD .... Guidance, Control, and Information Systems Division [*NASA*]
GC-ISS .... Gas Chromatography Isotope Separation System (SAUS)
GCIT .... Ground Control Interception Team (IAA)
GCIT .... Ground-Controlled Interception Team (SAUS)
GCITING ..... Ground-Control Intercept Training [*Navy*] (ANA)
GCITNG ...... Ground-Control Intercept Training (NVT)
GCIU .... Graphic Communications International Union (EA)
GCJ .... Gastric Cancer Secretions [*Medicine*] (EDAA)
GCJB .... Ground Crew Jack Box (SAUS)
GCJB .... Guidance Checkout Junction Box
GCJB .... Guidance Computer Junction Box (SAUS)
GCJC .... Gulf Coast Junior College (SAUO)
GCJLU .... General Council of Japanese Labour Unions (SAUO)
GCK .... Garden City [*Kansas*] [*Airport symbol*] (OAG)
GCK .... Glomerulocystic Kidney [*Nephrology*]
GCK .... Grid-Controlled Klystron
GCK .... Grocka [*Yugoslavia*] [*Geomagnetic observatory code*]
GCKI .... Golden-Crowned Kinglet [*North American bird banding code*] (BIBA)
GCKP .... Grand Commander of the Knights of Saint Patrick
GCL .... Columbia Theological Seminary, Decatur, GA [*OCLC symbol*] (OCLC)
GCL .... Galactic Center Lobe
GCL .... Ganglion Cell Layer [*Neuroanatomy*]
GCL .... Gas Cooled Loop (SAUS)
GCL .... Gas-Cooled Loop [*Nuclear energy*] (NRCH)
GCL .... Gas Flow and Chemical Lasers (SAUS)
GCL .... Gastrocolic Ligament [*Medicine*] (MELL)
GCL .... Gate Circuit Logic (SAUS)
GCL .... General Confederation of Labour (SAUO)
G C L .... General Control Language (SAUS)
GCL .... Generic Control Language [*Computer science*] (TEL)
GCL .... Geosciences Computing Laboratory (SAUO)
GCL .... Globoid Cell Leukodystrophy [*Medicine*] (DMAA)
GCL .... GNU Common LISP (SAUS)
GCL .... Golden Circle Ltd. [*Australia*] [*Commercial firm*]
GCL .... Grade Cooling Level [*Automotive engineering*]
GCL .... Grand Cross (of the Order) of Leopold (ROG)
GCL .... Graphics Card Language (SAUS)
GCL .... Graphics Command Language (SAUS)

GCL.......... Great Cameron Lake Resources, Inc. [*Vancouver Stock Exchange symbol*]
GCL.......... Greenclose Aviation Services Ltd. [*British*] [*ICAO designator*] (FAAC)
GCL.......... Ground Control Landing (SAUS)
GCL.......... Ground-Control Landing
GCL.......... Ground-Controlled Landing (SAUS)
GCL.......... Ground Coolant Loop (MCD)
GCL.......... Guidance Control Laboratory (AAG)
GCL.......... Guide to Catholic Literature (SAUS)
GCL.......... Guide to Computing Literature [*A publication*] (IT)
GCL.......... Guild of Catholic Lawyers (EA)
GCL.......... Guild of Cleaners and Launderers [*British*] (DBA)
GCL.......... Gulf Canada Ltd. [*UTLAS symbol*]
GCL.......... Gulf Caribbean Lines (SAUO)
GCLA.......... Group Carry Look-Ahead (MHDI)
GCLA.......... La Palma [*Canary Islands*] [*ICAO location identifier*] (ICLI)
GCLC.......... Greater Cincinnati Library Consortium [*Library network*]
GCLC.......... Guidance Control Launch Console (IAA)
GC/LC/MS.......... Gas Chromatography/Liquid Chromatography/Mass Spectroscopy (SAUS)
GCLCS.......... Groundcrew Liquid Cooling System
GCLF.......... Globular-Cluster Luminosity Function (SAUS)
GCLH.......... Grand Cross of the Legion of Honour (SAUS)
GCLH.......... Knight Grand Cross of the Legion of Honour [*British*]
GCLI.......... Grand Court Lifestyles, Inc. [*NASDAQ symbol*] (NASQ)
GC LISP.......... Golden Common LISP [*List Processor*] [*Artificial intelligence language*]
GCLJ.......... Grand Cross, St. Lazarus of Jerusalem (DD)
GCLLM.......... Groupement Canadien des Locataires des Logements Municipaux [*Canadian Organization of Public Housing Tenants*]
GCLO.......... German Civil Labour Organization (SAUO)
GCLP.......... Gran Canaria [*Canary Islands*] [*ICAO location identifier*] (ICLI)
GC/LRMS.......... Gas Chromatography/Low Resolution Mass Spectrometry
GCIV.......... General Circulation Model (SAUS)
GCLWD.......... Gulf Coast Low Water Datum
gcm.......... gas-cut mud (SAUS)
GCM.......... Gaussian Cosine Modulation (PDAA)
GCM.......... Gay Christian Movement [*British*]
GCM.......... General Circulation Model [*Meteorology*] [*Computer science*]
GCM.......... General Classification of Merchandise (SAUO)
GCM.......... General Climate Model
GCM.......... General Command of Mapping (SAUS)
GCM.......... General Counsel's Memorandum [*Internal Revenue Service*]
GCM.......... General Court Martial (SAUS)
GCM.......... General Court-Martial
GCM.......... General George C. Marshall [*World War II*]
GCM.......... Generator Coordinate Method [*Physics*]
GCM.......... Genetic Control of Mosquitoes (SAUS)
GCM.......... Geriatric-Care Manager
GCM.......... German Christian Movement (SAUO)
GCM.......... Glazed Ceramic Mosaic (DICI)
GCM.......... Global Change Model (SAUS)
GCM.......... Global Circulation Model [*National Center for Atmospheric Research*]
GCM.......... Global Circulation Models [*Climate*] (EERA)
GCM.......... Global Climate Model
GCM.......... Global Computer Model (WEAT)
GCM.......... Good, Central and Maintained (SAUS)
GCM.......... Good Company Man [*Theater term*] (DSUE)
GCM.......... Good Conduct Medal [*Military decoration*]
GCM.......... Graduate Certificate in Mining (SAUO)
g-cm.......... gram-centimeter (SAUS)
GCM.......... Grand Cayman [*West Indies*] [*Airport symbol*] (OAG)
GCM.......... Great Central Mines [*Vancouver Stock Exchange symbol*]
GCM.......... Greatest Common Measure
GCM.......... Greatest Common Multiple (ADA)
GCM.......... Greenwich Street California Municipal Fund, Inc. [*AMEX symbol*] (SAG)
GCM.......... Greenwich Street CA Muni Fd [*AMEX symbol*] (TTSB)
GCM.......... Ground Check Monitor (SAUS)
GCM.......... Ground-Control Message (MCD)
GCM.......... Groupement Carte a Memoire [*Group promoting use of 'smart' credit cards*] [*France*] (NITA)
GCM.......... Guidance and Control Module (ACAE)
GCM.......... Guildhall College of Music (SAUO)
GCM.......... Guild of Church Musicians [*British*] (DBA)
GCM.......... Gyro-Compass Module (SAUS)
G/CM².......... Grams per Square Centimeter
G/CM³.......... Grams per Cubic Centimeter
GCMA.......... General Court-Martial Authority
GCMA.......... Glazed Cement Manufacturers Association Ltd. [*British*] (BI)
GCMA.......... Government Contract Management Association (AAGC)
GCMAPA.......... Gay Caucus of Members of the American Psychiatric Association [*Later, AGLP*] (EA)
gc-mass spec.......... Gas Chromatography-Mass Spectrometry (MEC)
GCMC.......... Glass Ceramic Matrix Composite (SAUS)
GCMC.......... Global Climate Modeling Group (SAUO)
GCMC.......... Good Conduct Medal Clasp
GCMCA.......... General Court-Martial Convening Authority [*DoD*]
GCMD.......... Gaining Command (SAUO)
GCMD.......... Global Change Master Director (EERA)
GCMD.......... Global Change Master Directory (ADWA)
GCMDL.......... Good Conduct Medal [*Military decoration*] (AABC)
GCMED.......... Good Conduct Medal (SAUO)
GCMER.......... General Council of Medical Education and Registration (SAUO)
GCMES Detector.......... Gas Chromatography with Microwave Emission Spectrometric Detector (SAUS)
GCMF.......... George C. Marshall Foundation (EA)
GCMG.......... Dame Grand Cross of the Order of Saint Michael and Saint George [*British*] (ADA)
GCMG.......... Dante Grand Cross of the Order of Saint Michael and Saint George (SAUS)
GCMG.......... Global Climate Modeling Group (SAUO)
GCMG.......... Grand Cross of the Order of St. Michael and St George (SAUS)
GCMG.......... Knight Grand Cross of St. Michael and St. George [*Facetiously translated "God Calls Me God"*] [*British*]
GCMI.......... Glass Container Manufacturers Institute [*Later, GPI*] (EA)
GCMJ.......... General Court-Martial Jurisdiction
GCMO.......... General Court-Martial Order
GCMP.......... General Court-Martial Prisoner
GCMP.......... Greater Cleveland Mathematics Program [*Education*]
GCMPC.......... General Chairman-Member Pickwick Club [*From "The Pickwick Papers" by Charles Dickens*]
GCMPP.......... Global Current Meter Pilot Project (SAUS)
GCMPS.......... Gyro Compass
GCMPS.......... Gyroscope Compass (SAUS)
GCMR.......... Ground-Control Message Request (MCD)
GCMRF.......... George C. Marshall Research Foundation (EA)
GCMRGlc.......... Global Cerebral Metabolic Rate for Glucose [*Brain research*]
GCMRJS.......... Great Central Midland [*or Metropolitan*] Joint Stock [*Railroad*] [*British*] (ROG)
GCM-RTM.......... GCM-class radiative transfer model (SAUS)
GCMRU.......... General Control of Mosquitoes Research Unit (SAUS)
G C -M S.......... Gas Chromatograph linked with a Mass Spectrometer (SAUS)
GC/MS.......... Gas Chromatograph/Mass Spectrograph (SAUS)
GCMS.......... Gas Chromatograph Mass Spectromenter (SAUS)
G C M S.......... Gas Chromatograph Mass Spectrometer (SAUS)
GCMS.......... Gas Chromatography and Mass Spectroscopy
GC-MS.......... Gas Chromatography linked with a Mass Spectrometer (SAUS)
GC/MS.......... Gas Chromatography/Mass Spectrometry
GC/MS.......... Gas Chromatography - Mass Spectroscopy (SAUS)
GC/MS.......... Gas Chromatography / Mass Spectrum (SAUS)
g/cms.......... Grams per Square Centimeter (SAUS)
GCMSC.......... George C. Marshall Space Flight Center [*Also known as MSFC*] [*NASA*]
GCMSFC.......... George C. Marshall Space Flight Center [*Also known as MSFC*] [*NASA*]
GCMSS.......... gas-chromatography-mass-spectrometry studies (SAUS)
GCMTW.......... Guild of Canadian Musical Theatre Writers [*Canada*] (WWLA)
GCMU.......... Genetic Control of Mosquito Unit (SAUS)
GCMU.......... Glazed Concrete Masonry Units [*Technical drawings*]
GCMV.......... Grapevine Chrome Mosaic Virus [*Plant pathology*]
GCN.......... Gage Code Number (SAUS)
GCN.......... Gamma-Ray Burst Coordinates Network
GCN.......... Garden City Northern Railway [*Federal Railroad Administration identification code*]
GCN.......... Gas-cooled Carbon-moderated Nuclear (SAUS)
GCN.......... Gauge Code Number
GCN.......... Gay Community News (journ.) (SAUS)
GCN.......... General Cinema Corp. (SAUO)
GCN.......... Generalized Connection Network (SAUS)
GCN.......... Geometric Constraint Network (DMAA)
GCN.......... Giant Cerebral Neuron [*Brain anatomy*]
GCN.......... Global Challenge Network (SAUO)
GCN.......... Gold Canyon Mines, Inc. [*Vancouver Stock Exchange symbol*]
GCN.......... Gospel Communications Network (SAUS)
GCN.......... Government Computer News
GCN.......... Grand Canyon [*Arizona*] [*Airport symbol*] (OAG)
GCN.......... Greenwich Civil Noon
GCN.......... Ground Communications Network
GCN.......... Ground-Control Network [*NASA*] (NASA)
GCN.......... Gulf Central Airlines, Inc. [*ICAO designator*] (FAAC)
GCNA.......... Guild of Carillonneurs in North America (EA)
GCNA.......... Guild of Carillonneurs in North America. Bulletin (journ.) (SAUS)
GCNED.......... Government Computer News (journ.) (SAUS)
GCNET.......... Global Change Network (SAUO)
GcNM.......... GCN/Microfilm, Boston, MA [*Library symbol*] [*Library of Congress*] (LCLS)
GCNM.......... Good, Central, not Maintained (SAUS)
GCNM.......... Grand Canyon National Monument (SAUO)
GCNP.......... Grand Canyon National Park (SAUO)
GC-NPD.......... Gas Chromatography-Nitrogen Phosphorus Detector
GCNPP.......... Gay Community News Prisoner Project [*An association*] (EA)
GCNPP.......... Greene County Nuclear Power Plant (NRCH)
GCNR.......... Gas Core Nuclear Rocket
GCNRA.......... Glen Canyon National Recreation Area (SAUO)
GCN Reactor.......... Gas-cooled Carbon-moderated Nuclear Reactor (SAUS)
GCNS.......... Knight Grand Cross of the Royal Northern Star (SAUO)
GCNSMS.......... Global Coastal and Near-Shore Monitoring System (SAUO)
GCNSMS.......... System of Long-term Monitoring of Coastal and Near-shore Phenomena related to Climate Change (SAUS)
GCNSW.......... Gas Council of New South Wales [*Australia*]
GCNVF.......... Gold Coast Naval Volunteer Force (SAUO)
GCN-X.......... Ground Communications Network III Residual (SAUO)
GCO.......... Columbus College, Library, Columbus, GA [*OCLC symbol*] (OCLC)
GCO.......... GC Optronics, Inc.
GCO.......... General Commanding Officer (SAUO)
GCO.......... General counsel office (SAUS)
GCO.......... General Counteroffensive (SAUS)
GCO.......... Generation Certification Official (SAUO)

GCO .... GENESCO, Inc. [*NYSE symbol*] (SPSG)
GCO .... Georgetown College Observatory (MCD)
GCO .... Glenco International Corp. [*Vancouver Stock Exchange symbol*]
GCO .... Government Concept of Operations (RDA)
GCO .... Governor's Commissioned Officer [*British military*] (DMA)
GCO .... Grand Chapter of Officers (SAUO)
GCO .... Greater Coin Operators (SAUS)
GCO .... Ground Checkout [*NASA*] (NASA)
GCO .... Ground Cutout
GCO .... Guidance Control Officer (AAG)
GCO .... Guidance Cut-Off (SAUS)
GCO .... Gun Control Officer [*Navy*]
GCO .... Gunfire Control Officer (SAUS)
gCO2 .... Grams of Carbon Dioxide Equivalent (EERA)
GCOC .... General Conditions of Contract
GCOC .... Gun Control Officer Console [*Military*] (CAAL)
GCocM .... Middle Georgia College, Cochran, GA [*Library symbol*] [*Library of Congress*] (LCLS)
GCOE .... Ground Check-Out Equipment (SAUS)
GCOE .... Ground-Control Operational Equipment (IAA)
GCola .... W. C. Bradley Memorial Library, Columbus (SAUS)
GColu .... W. C. Bradley Memorial Library, Columbus, GA [*Library symbol*] [*Library of Congress*] (LCLS)
GColuC .... Columbus College, Columbus, GA [*Library symbol*] [*Library of Congress*] (LCLS)
GColuGS .... Church of Jesus Christ of Latter-Day Saints, Genealogical Society Library, MaconBranch, Columbus, GA [*Library symbol*] [*Library of Congress*] (LCLS)
GCOM .... Globecomm Systems, Inc. [*NASDAQ symbol*] (NASQ)
GCom .... Grand Commander [*or Commandery*] [*Freemasonry*]
GCOM .... Gray Communications Systems, Inc. (SAUO)
GCON .... Grand Cross, Order of the Niger [*British*]
GConT .... Monastery of the Holy Ghost, Conyers, GA [*Library symbol*] [*Library of Congress*] (LCLS)
GCOR .... Gencor Industries, Inc. [*NASDAQ symbol*] (NQ)
GCOS .... General Comprehensive Operating Supervisor [*Computer science*]
GCOS .... General Comprehensive Operating System (NITA)
GCOS .... General Comprehensive Operating Systems (SAUS)
GCOS .... General Comprehensive Operation Supervisor (SAUS)
GCOS .... General Computer Operational System [*NASA*]
GCOS .... Generalized Comprehensive Operating System (SAUS)
GCOS .... GEWEX Cloud System Study (SAUS)
GCOS .... Global Change Observation (or Observing) System (SAUO)
GCOS .... Global Change Observation System (VLIE)
GCOS .... Global Climate Observing System [*Marine science*] (OSRA)
GCOS .... Great Canadian Oil Sands Ltd.
GCOS .... Great Canadian Sands News (journ.) (SAUS)
GCOS .... Ground Computer Operating System [*NASA*] (NASA)
GCOSF .... Global Climate Observing System Fund (SAUO)
G Counter .... Geiger Counter (SAUS)
GCOVE .... Georgia Council of Vocational Education (SAUO)
GCOX .... Miller Compressing [*Private rail car owner code*]
GCOZ .... Greenway Co-Operative [*Federal Railroad Administration identification code*]
GCP .... Gain Control Pulse (IAA)
GCP .... Gaining Command Program (MCD)
GCP .... General Circuit Parameter (SAUS)
GCP .... General Control Processor (SAUS)
GCP .... Generalized Computer Program
GCP .... Generator Control Panel (DNAB)
GCP .... Geometrically Close-Packed (SAUS)
GCP .... GEWEX Continental-Scale Project (SAUS)
GCP .... Ghana Congress Party (SAUO)
GCP .... Giant Cell Pneumonia [*Medicine*] (MELL)
GCP .... Gift Coupon Programme [*Later, Co-Action*] [*UNESCO*]
GCP .... Glareshield Control Panel (HLLA)
GCP .... Global Change Program (SAUS)
GCP .... Global Chemistry Program (SAUS)
GCP .... Global Control Point (SAUS)
GCP .... GLOBEC Core Programme (SAUS)
GCP .... Goddard Corporate Park (SAUS)
GCP .... Golden CommPass [*Front-end computer processor*] (PCM)
GCP .... Good Clinical Practice [*Medicine*]
GCP .... Good Combustion Practices (EEVL)
GCP .... Government Contracts Program [*George Washington University Law Center*] (DLA)
GCP .... Grancamp Resources [*Vancouver Stock Exchange symbol*]
GCP .... Granulocytopenia [*Medicine*] (MELL)
GCP .... Graphics Control Program [*IBM Corp.*] (PCM)
GCP .... Green Circle Program (EA)
GCP .... Gross Community Product (SAUS)
GCP .... Gross Criminal Product
GCP .... Ground Contact Pressure (SAUS)
GCP .... Ground Control Point
GCP .... Ground Control Processor (SAUO)
GCP .... Ground Correlator and Processor (ACAE)
GCP .... Guidance and Control Panel (SAUS)
GCP .... Guidance Checkout [*or Control*] Package (NG)
GCP .... Guidance Computer (VLIE)
GCP .... Guidance Control Package (SAUS)
GCP .... Guild of Catholic Psychiatrist (SAUS)
GCP .... Guild of Catholic Psychiatrists [*Later, National Guild of Catholic Psychiatrists*] (EA)
GCP .... Guild of Computer Practitioners [*British*] (DBA)
GCPA .... Grammatik des Christlich-Palaestinischen Aramaeisch [*A publication*] (BJA)
GCPB .... BLs General Catalogue of Printed Books (SAUS)
GCPBL .... Ground Control Point Build Library (ACAE)
GCPCAC .... Gun Groupment Command Post, Coast Artillery Corps (SAUO)
GCPD .... Grade Crossing Protection Device
GCPI .... Cape Grim Photochemical Intensive (SAUO)
GC/PID .... Gas Chromatography/Photoionization Detector (EEVL)
GCPL .... Glasgow Corporation Public Libraries (SAUO)
GCPL .... Glasgow Corporation Public Library (SAUS)
GCPPD .... Global Committee of Parliamentarians on Population and Development (EA)
GCPPI .... Gifted Children's Pen Pals International (EA)
GCPR .... General Ceiling Price Regulation (DLA)
GCPR .... Gigacycles per Second (SAUS)
GCPS .... Gigacycles per Second (MUGU)
GCPS .... Global Climate Perspectives System [*Marine science*] (OSRA)
GCPS .... Greig Cephalopolysyndactyly Syndrome [*Medicine*]
GCPS .... Greig Cephalopolysyndadyry Syndrome (SAUS)
GCPS .... Ground Claims Processing System
GCPS .... Ground Control and Processing Station (SAUS)
GCPS .... Group Claims Processing System [*McAuto*]
G Cpt .... Group Captain (SAUO)
GCPW .... General Conditions for the Performance of Work (SAUS)
GCQ .... Group Climate Questionnaire [*Occupational therapy*]
GCQBD .... Geo-Heat Center. Quarterly Bulletin (journ.) (SAUS)
GCQZ .... Granite Canyon Quarry [*Federal Railroad Administration identification code*]
GCR .... Gain Control Range
GCR .... Galactic Cosmic Radiation [*or Ray*]
GCR .... Galactic Cosmic Ray [*Astronomy*]
GCR .... Galvanocutaneous Reaction
GCR .... Gamma Cosmic Ray [*Geophysics*]
GCR .... Gas-Cooled Graphite-Moderated (SAUS)
G C R .... Gas-cooled Graphite-moderated Reactor (SAUS)
GCR .... Gas Cooled Power Reactor (EDCT)
GCR .... Gas-Cooled Reactor
GCR .... Gas Cycle Reactor (SAUS)
GCR .... Gaseous Core Reactor (SAUS)
GCR .... Gaylord Container'A' [*AMEX symbol*] (TTSB)
GCR .... Gaylord Container Corp. Class A [*AMEX symbol*] (SPSG)
GCR .... General Cargo Rates [*Business term*]
GCR .... General Cigar Co., Inc. (SAUO)
GCR .... General Commodity Rate [*Shipping*] (DS)
GCR .... General Component Reference (IEEE)
GCR .... General Control Register (SAUS)
GCR .... General Control Relay (SAUS)
GCR .... General Control Room (SAUS)
GCR .... Generator Control Relay [*Electronics*] (OA)
GCR .... Geneva Consultants Registry [*Alpha Systems Resource*] [*Database*]
GCR .... Geological Characterization Report (SAUS)
GCR .... German Canadian Review (journ.) (SAUS)
GCR .... Ghost Canceling Reference [*Television technology*]
GCR .... Ghost Cancellation Reference (SAUS)
GCR .... Glencair Resources, Inc. [*Toronto Stock Exchange symbol*]
GCR .... Glomerular Complement Receptor [*Immunology*]
GCR .... Glucocorticoid Receptor (DMAA)
GCR .... Glucose Consumption Rate
GCR .... Glucuronidase [*An enzyme*]
GCR .... Glycinecresol Red [*An indicator*] [*Chemistry*]
GCR .... Gold Coast Railroad [*Federal Railroad Administration identification code*]
GCR .... Gold Coast Regiment [*British military*] (DMA)
GCR .... Good Conduct Ribbon (SAUS)
GCR .... Government Contracts Reporter [*A publication*] (AAGC)
GCR .... Grand Central Rocket Co. (AAG)
GCR .... Grandparents'/Children's Rights (EA)
GCR .... Graphics Code Recording [*Computer science*]
GCR .... Gray-Component Replacement [*Color reproduction technology*]
GCR .... Grayling Creek [*Montana*] [*Seismograph station code, US Geological Survey*] (SEIS)
GCR .... Great Central Railway [*British*]
GCR .... Great Circle Route (WDAA)
GCR .... Grey Component Removal (SAUS)
GCR .... Grignard's Chemical Reaction
GCR .... Ground Clutter Reduction (SAUS)
GCR .... Ground-Controlled RADAR
GCR .... Ground Control Radar (SAUS)
GCR .... Group Coded Recording [*Computer science*] (BUR)
GCR .... Group Code Recording [*Data storage method*] (NITA)
GCR .... Group Conformity Rate (DB)
GCR .... Group Conformity Rating (DMAA)
GCR .... Group Encoded Recording (NITA)
GCR .... Guerrilleros de Cristo Rey [*Warriors of Christ and King*] [*Revolutionary Group*] [*Spain*]
GCR .... Gulf Coast Repository at TAMU (SAUO)
GCRA .... Gas-Cooled Reactor Associates (NRCH)
GCRA .... Generic Cell Rate Algorithm (MLOA)
GCRA .... Geographic and Cartographic Research and Applications Section (SAUS)
GCRA .... Giant Chinchilla Rabbit Association (EA)
GCRA .... Global Coral Reef Alliance (EA)
GCRA .... Golden Corral Realty Corp. (SAUO)
G+C ratio .... Fraction of nucleic acid base pairs that are guanine and cytosine (SAUS)

GCRC .... General Clinical Research Center [*University of Alabama in Birmingham*] (RCD)
GCRC .... General Clinical Research Center [*Stanford University*] (RCD)
GCRC .... General Clinical Research Center [*University of Virginia*] (RCD)
GCRC .... General Clinical Research Center [*Scripps Clinic and Research Foundation*]
GCRCH .... General Council and Register of Consultant Herbalists [*British*] (DBA)
GCRCPB .... General Clinical Research Center Program Branch [*National Institutes of Health*]
GCRE .... Gas-Cooled Reactor Experiment (NRCH)
GCREF .... GCR Hldgs Ltd [*NASDAQ symbol*] (TTSB)
GCRES .... Ground Combat-Readiness Evaluation Squadron
GCRF .... Gray-Crowned Rosy-Finch [*North American bird banding code*] (BIBA)
GCRF .... Greensboro Civil Rights Fund [*Defunct*] (EA)
GCRFPA .... General Content Requirements for Permit Applications (SAUO)
GCRG .... Giant Cell Reparative Granuloma [*Oncology*]
GCRG .... Gun Carriage
GCRI .... Georgetown Clinical Research Institute [*FAA*]
GCRI .... German Carpet Research Institute [*See also TFI*] (EAIO)
GCRI .... Gillette Co. Research Institute
GCRI .... Glasshouse Crops Research Institute (SAUO)
GCRI .... Grain Crack Resistance Index (SAUS)
GCRI .... Greenhouse Climate Response Index (SAUO)
GCRIO .... Global Change Research Information Office
GCRL .... Glass House Crops Research Institute [*Agricultural Research Council*] (PDAA)
GCRL .... Gulf Coast Research Laboratory [*Ocean Springs, MS*]
GCRMN .... Global Coral Reef Monitoring Network (SAUO)
GCRN .... General Council and Register of Naturopaths [*British*] (DBA)
GCRO .... General Council and Register of Osteopaths (SAUO)
GCRO .... General Council and Register of Osteopaths Ltd. [*British*]
GCRO .... Golden Cat Railroad [*Federal Railroad Administration identification code*]
GCRO .... Grand Council and Register of Osteopaths (SAUO)
GCRP .... Galactic Cosmic Ray Particle
GCRP .... Global Change Research Plan [*Program*] [*Marine science*] (OSRA)
GCRR .... Arrecife/Lanzarote [*Canary Islands*] [*ICAO location identifier*] (ICLI)
GCRR .... Graham County Railroad [*Federal Railroad Administration identification code*]
GCRRAE .... Glasshouse Crops Research Institute. Annual Report (journ.) (SAUS)
GCRs .... Gas-Cooled Reactors (SAUS)
GCRS .... Gulf Centre for Remote Sensing (SAUO)
GCRV .... Ground Cruising Recreational Vehicle [*Owosso Motor Car Co.*] [*Owosso, MI*]
GCRWS .... Gaylord Container Wrrt [*AMEX symbol*] (TTSB)
GCRX .... Grand Canyon Railway [*Federal Railroad Administration identification code*]
GCRY .... Grand Canyon Railway [*Federal Railroad Administration identification code*]
GCS .... Game Conservation Society (SAUO)
GCS .... Gas Chemical Sterlization (MELL)
GCS .... Gas Cleaning System [*Combustion technology*]
GCS .... Gas Cylinder System
GCS .... Gate Controlled Switch (SAUS)
GCS .... GCS Air Service (SAUS)
GCS .... Geek of Computer Science (SAUO)
GCS .... General Clearing Station (SAUS)
GCS .... General Clinical Service (MAE)
GCS .... General Communications System [*Sperry Univac*] (NITA)
GCS .... General Communication Subsystem [*Computer science*]
GCS .... General Computer Systems (NITA)
GCS .... General Computer Systems, Inc.
GCS .... General Computing Services (SAUS)
GCS .... Generalized Computer Systems (SAUS)
GCS .... Generalized Computer Systems Incorporated (SAUS)
GCS .... Generalized Contentment Scale (STED)
GCS .... Generator Control Switch (MCD)
GCS .... Geo-Common Subsystem [*Environmental Protection Agency*] (AEPA)
GCS .... Geophysical Consulting Services (SAUO)
GCS .... Georgia Consumer Services (SAUO)
GCS .... Geostationary Communications Satellite [*WARC*]
GCS .... Geosynchronous Communication Satellites (SAUO)
GCS .... Ghana Customs Service (SAUS)
GCS .... Giant-Cell Sarcoma (MELL)
GCS .... Gifted Child Society (EA)
Gc/s .... Gigacycles per Second [*IEEE*]
GCS .... Glasgow Coma Scale [*Medicine*] (WDAA)
gcs .... Glasgow Coma Scale [*Medicine*]
GCS .... Glasgow Coma Score [*Medicine*]
GCS .... Global Change Science (SAUS)
GCS .... Global Conceptional Scheme (SAUS)
GCS .... Global Coordinate System (SAUS)
GCS .... Glucocorticosteroid [*Biochemistry*] (DB)
GCS .... Glutamylcysteine Synthetase (STED)
GCS .... Gluteus Compartment Syndrome (MELL)
GCS .... Golden Crown Resources Ltd. [*Vancouver Stock Exchange symbol*]
GCS .... Golf Collectors' Society (EA)
GCS .... Government Contractors Subcontractors
gcs .... gram-centimeter-second (SAUS)
GCS .... Grand Commander (of the Order) of Spain (ROG)
GCS .... Grant and Contract Service (SAUS)
GCS .... Graphic Compatibility System [*US Military Academy*] (NITA)
GCS .... Graphics Capability System (SAUO)
GCS .... Graphics Compatibility Standard [*For image processing*]
GCS .... Graphics Compatibility System (SAUS)
GCS .... Graphics Control System (SAUO)
GCS .... Graphite Cooling Shield (SAUS)
GCS .... Graphite Cooling System (SAUS)
GCS .... Gray Communications Systems [*NYSE symbol*] (SAG)
GCS .... Green Cross Society (SAUO)
GCS .... Ground Checkout Station (SAUS)
GCS .... Ground Command System
GCS .... Ground Communications System
GCS .... Ground Control Squadron (ACAE)
GCS .... Ground Control Station (SAUO)
GCS .... Ground-Control Station (MCD)
GCS .... Ground Control System (SAUS)
GCS .... Ground radio Control Station (SAUS)
GCS .... Ground Water Council (SAUO)
GCS .... Group Control System (VLIE)
GCS .... Guidance and Control Section (SAUS)
GCS .... Guidance and Control System (ACAE)
GCS .... Guidance Command Shutdown [*Space launch term*] (ISAK)
GCS .... Guidance Control Section (SAUS)
GCS .... Guidance Control System (SAUS)
GCS .... Guidance Cutoff Signal [*NASA*] (NASA)
GCS .... Gun Control System (ACAE)
GCS .... Gyroless Control System
GCS .... Portland, ME [*Location identifier*] [*FAA*] (FAAL)
GCSA .... Galloway Cattle Society of America (EA)
GCSA .... Gross Cell-Surface Antigen [*Immunology*]
GCSAA .... Golf Course Superintendents Association of America (EA)
GCSA/NJ ...... Golf Course Superintendents Association of New Jersey (SRA)
GCSAS .... Global Configuration Status Accounting System (SAUO)
GCSB .... Government Communications Security Bureau of New Zealand (CARL)
GCSC .... Graphic Control and Sequencing Computer (SAUS)
GCSC .... Guidance Control and Sequencing Computer
GCSD .... Government Communications Systems Department (SPST)
GCSDIDS ..... Global Conference on the Sustainable Development of Small Island Developing States (SAUS)
GCSE .... General Certificate of Secondary Education [*British*]
GCSE .... Generalized Convulsive Status Epilepticus [*Medicine*] (CPH)
Gc/sec .... Gigacycles per Second [*AIP*]
GCSF .... Granulocyte Cell-Stimulating Factor (STED)
G-CSF .... Granulocyte-Colony Stimulating Factor [*Hematology*]
GCSF .... Gulf, Colorado & Santa Fe Railway Co. [*AAR code*]
GCSG .... Graphic Communications Societies Group [*British*] (NITA)
GCSG .... Knight Grand Cross of St. Gregory the Great [*British*]
GCS/GTV ...... Guidance and Control Simulator/Ground Test Verification (ACAE)
GCSI .... Government Computer Sales, Inc.
GCSI .... Grand Commander of the Order of the Star of India (SAUS)
GCSI .... Knight Grand Commander of the [*Order of the*] Star of India [*British*]
GC-SICM ...... Gas Chromatography - Single Ion Current Monitoring (PDAA)
GCSJ .... Grand Cross of Justice of the Order of St. John of Jerusalem (SAUS)
GCSM .... Glandless Cottonseed Meal [*Animal feed*]
GCSM .... Ground Composite Signal Mixer
GCSMP .... Graphic Continuous System Modelling Program (VLIE)
GCSOLAR .... Green Cross Solar (AEPA)
GCSP .... Government Communications Staff Federation (SAUO)
GCSP .... Guidance and Control Set Processor
GCSPC Section... Graphic Communications Special Projects Section (SAUS)
GCSR .... Global Control & Status Resister (SAUS)
GCSR .... Gulf, Colorado & San Saba Railway [*Federal Railroad Administration identification code*]
GCSRW - UMC... General Commission on the Status and Role of Women - United Methodist Church (EA)
GCSS .... GEWEX [*Global Energy and Water Cycle Experiment*] Cloud System Study (EERA)
GCSS .... Global Cloud Systems Study (SAUO)
GCSS .... Global Combat Support System [*Military*] (SEWL)
GCSS .... Global Communications Satellite System
GCSS .... Global energy and Water Cycle Experiment Cloud System Study (SAUS)
GCSS .... Ground-Controlled Space System
GCSS .... Ground Control Space System (SAUS)
GCSS .... Guidance Counseling Support System (SAUS)
GCSS .... Knight Grand Cross of St. Sylvester [*British*]
GCSS-A .... Global Combat Service Support-Army
GCSSOLAR... Green Cross Solar [*Version 1.1*] [*Environment term*] (EGA)
GCStJ .... Bailiff Grand Cross of [*the Order of*] Saint John of Jerusalem [*British*] (ADA)
GCStJ .... Dame Grand Cross of [*the Order of*] Saint John of Jerusalem [*British*] (ADA)
GCStJ .... Grand Cross of the Most Venerable Order of the Hospital of St. John of Jerusalem (SAUS)
GCStJ .... Knight Grand Cross of [*the Order of*] St. John of Jerusalem [*British*]
GCSU .... Government Clerical Services' Union [*Ceylon*]
GCSV .... Groundnut Chlorotic Spot Virus
GCSW .... Graduate Certificate of Social Work
GCSX .... National Steel [*Private rail car owner code*]
GCSZ .... Gulf Central Systems [*Federal Railroad Administration identification code*]
GCT .... Coca-Cola Co., Technical Information Services, Atlanta, GA [*OCLC symbol*] (OCLC)
GCT .... Galactic Center Transient [*Astronomy*]
GCT .... Gamma Correction Table (SAUS)
GCT .... Gate Controlled Thyristor (SAUS)
GCT .... General Care and Treatment (STED)

GCT .... General Classification Test [*Military*]
GCT .... General Clerical Test (TES)
GCT .... Germ-Cell Tumor [*Medicine*] (RAWO)
GCT .... Gesture Comprehension Test [*Occupational therapy*]
GCT .... Giant Cell Thyroiditis [*Medicine*] (DB)
GCT .... Giant Cell Tumor [*Oncology*]
GCT .... Giro [*Money Order*] Credit Transfer (DI)
GCT .... Glamorgan College of Technology (SAUO)
GCT .... Glasgow College of Technology (AIE)
GCT .... Glass Cloth Tape
GCT .... Government Competitive Testing
GCT .... Grand Cadence de Tir [*Self-propelled howitzer*] (RDA)
GCT .... Grand Cadencede Tir (SAUS)
GCT .... Grand Canyon Trust
GCT .... Graphics Communications Terminal
GCT .... Great Circle Test (SAUS)
GCT .... Great Circle Track
GCT .... Greenwich Central Time [*Astronomy*] (IAA)
GCT .... Greenwich Civil Time
GCT .... Greenwich Conservatory Time
GCT .... Ground Checkout and Test [*Aerospace*]
GCT .... Guard Control System (SAUS)
GCT .... Guidance and Control Technology Integration (ACAE)
GCT .... Guidance Command Test
GCT .... Guidance Computer Test
GCT .... Gun Compatibility Test
GCT .... Gun Control Tower [*British military*] (DMA)
GCT .... Gyro-Compass Trial (IAA)
GCTA .... Ground Commanded [*or Controlled*] Television Assembly [*Apollo*] [*NASA*]
gctbr .... gas-cooled fast breeder reactor (SAUS)
GCTC .... Giant Cell Tumor Cells [*A cell line*]
GCTC .... Green County Teachers College (SAUO)
GC/TCD .... Gas Chromatography/Thermal Conductivity Detector (EEVL)
GCTE .... Global Change and/in Terrestrial Ecosystems Program of the IGBP (SAUO)
GCTE .... Global Change in Terrestrial Ecosystems (SAUS)
GCTE .... Guidance Computer Test Equipment
GCTE-SSC .... GCTE Scientific Steering Committee (SAUO)
GCTEV .... Garland Chrysanthemum Temperate Virus [*Plant pathology*]
GCTF .... Gold Coast Territorial Force [*British military*] (DMA)
GCTI .... Genesys Telecommunications [*NASDAQ symbol*] (SG)
GCTI .... Genesys Telecommunications Laboratories, Inc. [*NASDAQ symbol*] (NASQ)
GCTM .... Global Chemical Transport Model [*Marine science*] (OSRA)
GCTOA .... Greek Cultural and Theatrical Organisation of Australia
GCTP .... General Coordinate Transformation Package (SAUS)
GCTP .... Generic construction test procedure (SAUS)
GCTP .... Geo-Coordinate Transformation Package (SAUS)
GCTP .... Geographic Coordinate Transformation Package (SAUS)
GCtryB .... Great Country Bank [*Associated Press*] (SAG)
GCTS .... Gas Component Test Stand (MCD)
GCTS .... Tenerife-Reina Sofia [*Canary Islands*] [*ICAO location identifier*] (ICLI)
GC/TSD .... Gas Chromatography/Thermionic Specific Detector (EEVL)
GCTTS .... Giant Cell Tumor of the Tendon Sheath [*Medicine*] (RAWO)
GCTU .... Great Consolidated Trade Union (SAUO)
GCTW .... Gross Combination Test Weight [*Automotive engineering*]
GCTY .... Geo Cities [*NASDAQ symbol*] (NASQ)
GCU .... Gas-Cooled Unit
GCU .... General Communications Unit (SAUS)
GCU .... General Control Unit (MCD)
GCU .... Generation Control Unit (SAUS)
GCU .... Generator Control Unit [*Aviation*] (NASA)
GCU .... Generator/Converter Unit
GCU .... Global Control Unit (SAUS)
GCU .... God Command Universe (SAUS)
GCU .... Gold Canyon Resources [*Vancouver Stock Exchange symbol*]
GCU .... Gonococcal Urethritis [*Medicine*] (DMAA)
GCU .... Graphic Control Unit (SAUS)
GCU .... Ground Checkout Unit [*Aerospace*] (MCD)
GCU .... Ground Control Unit (SAUS)
GCU .... Ground-Control Unit (AAG)
GCU .... Ground Cooling Unit [*NASA*] (NASA)
GCU .... Guidance and Control Unit (NATG)
GCU .... Guidance Coupler Unit
GCU .... Gunner's Control Unit
GCU .... Gyro Coupling Unit (KSC)
GCU .... Gyroscope Coupling Unit (SAUS)
GCuA .... Andrew College, Cuthbert, GA [*Library symbol*] [*Library of Congress*] (LCLS)
g/cucm .... Grammes per Cubic Centimetre (SAUS)
g/cucm .... Grams per Cubic Centimeter (SAUS)
GCUGA .... Grounded Current Unity-Gain Amplifier
g/cum .... Grammes per Cubic Metre (SAUS)
g/cum .... Grams per Cubic Meter (or Metre) (SAUS)
GCUS .... Generic Cryogenic Upper Stage [*Space launch term*] (ISAK)
GCUUSA .... Greek Catholic Union of the USA (EA)
GCV .... Chattahoochee Valley Regional Library, Columbus, GA [*OCLC symbol*] (OCLC)
GCV .... Gabelli Convertible Securities Fund [*NYSE symbol*] (SAG)
GCV .... Gabelli Conv Securities Fd [*NYSE symbol*] (TTSB)
GCV .... Gaseous Oxygen Control Valve (NASA)
GCV .... Granulose Cell Tumor (MELL)
GCV .... Great Cardiac Vein [*Medicine*] (DMAA)
GCV .... Great Cephalic Vein [*Medicine*] (MELL)
GCV .... Green Crinkle Virus (SAUS)
GCV .... Gross Caloric Value
GCV .... Leakesville, MS [*Location identifier*] [*FAA*] (FAAL)
GCVF .... Great Cardiac Vein Flow [*Medicine*] (DMAA)
GCVO .... Dame Grand Cross of the Royal Victorian Order [*British*] (ADA)
GCVO .... Grand Cross of the Royal Victorian Order (SAUS)
GCVO .... Knight Grand Cross of the Royal Victorian Order [*British*]
GCVO .... Knight or Dame Grand Cross of the Royal Victorian Order (SAUO)
GCVS .... General Catalog of Variable Stars [*Astronomy*] (OA)
GCVTC .... Grand Canyon Visibility Transport Commission (EPAT)
GCVW .... Gross Combination Vehicle Weight [*Automotive engineering*]
GCW .... Coca-Cola Co., Law Library, Atlanta, GA [*OCLC symbol*] (OCLC)
GCW .... [*The*] Garden City Western Railway Co. [*AAR code*]
GCW .... General Continuous Wave (IAA)
GCW .... Generative Cell Wall [*Botany*]
GCW .... Gerber Childrenswear [*NYSE symbol*] (SG)
GCW .... Global Chart of the World [*Air Force*]
GCW .... Global Conventional War (SEWL)
GCW .... Glomerular Capillary Wall [*Anatomy*]
GCW .... Grand Coulee [*Washington*] [*Seismograph station code, US Geological Survey*] [*Closed*] (SEIS)
GCW .... Gridiron Club of Washington, DC (EA)
GCW .... Gross Carrying Weight (GOBB)
GCW .... Gross Combination Weight [*for tractor and loaded trailer*]
GCWC .... Governor and Constabler of Windsor Castle (SAUO)
GCWDA .... Gulf Coast Waste Disposal Authority [*Governmental industrial waste disposal system*]
GCWIU .... General Cigarette Workers' Industrial Union [*British*]
GCWM .... General Conference on Weights and Measures
GCWOD .... Graphic Communications World (journ.) (SAUS)
GCWR .... Global Congress of the World's Religions (EA)
GCWR .... Gross Combination Weight Rating [*Environmental Protection Agency*]
GCW theorem ... Gibbs-Curie-Wulff theorem (SAUO)
GCX .... GC Companies [*NYSE symbol*] (SAG)
GCXO .... Tenerife [*Canary Islands*] [*ICAO location identifier*] (ICLI)
GCY .... Gastroscopy [*Medicine*] (DMAA)
GCY .... General Cybernetics Corp. [*Vancouver Stock Exchange symbol*]
GCY .... Glen Cove [*New York*] [*Seismograph station code, US Geological Survey*] (SEIS)
GCY .... Greeneville, TN [*Location identifier*] [*FAA*] (FAAL)
GCYF .... Grantmakers for Children, Youth, and Families (NFD)
GCyMS .... Ground Command and Control Mobile Seek Talk Radio Set (SAUS)
GCZ .... Governor of the Canal Zone (SAUO)
GD .... Air Antilles [*Airline*] (MHDB)
GD .... Air North [*ICAO designator*] (AD)
GD .... Chemical Agent/Soman (SAUS)
GD .... Defence Guide (SAUS)
GD .... DeKalb County Library System, Regional Service-Rockdale and Newton Counties, Decatur, GA [*Library symbol*] [*Library of Congress*] (LCLS)
GD .... Diganglioside [*Chemistry*]
Gd .... Gadolinium [*Chemical element*]
g/d .... gallons per day (SAUS)
GD .... Gaol Delivery [*Legal*] [*British*] (ROG)
GD .... Gap Detector
GD .... Gap Digit (SAUS)
GD .... Gas Detector (SAUS)
GD .... Gas Discharge (SAUS)
GD .... Gas Dragster [*Class of racing cars*]
GD .... Gas Drainage
GD .... Gas Dynamics (SAUS)
GD .... Gastroduodenal (STED)
GD .... Gate Driver
GD .... Gaucher's Disease (MELL)
GD .... Gaussian Distribution (SAUS)
GD .... Gauze Dressing (MELL)
GD .... Gave Delivery
GD .... Gear Down [*Aviation*]
GD .... Gel Destainer [*Analytical chemistry*]
GD .... Gel Dryer [*Chromatography*]
GD .... General Delivery
GD .... General Department (SAUO)
GD .... General Depot (SAUS)
GD .... General Design (AAG)
GD .... General Development
GD .... General Diagnostics [*Medicine*] (STED)
GD .... General Diagram
GD .... General Discharge
GD .... General Dispensary [*Military*]
GD .... General Division (SAFN)
GD .... General Duties (STED)
GD .... General Duty
GD .... General Dynamics Corp. [*NYSE symbol*] (SPSG)
G-D .... General Dynamics Corporation (SAUS)
GD .... Genetic Disorder (MELL)
GD .... Genl Dynamics [*NYSE symbol*] (TTSB)
GD .... Geographic Digest [*A publication*] [*British*]
GD .... Geographic Distribution
GD .... Geologic Division (ADWA)
GD .... Geospatial Data (SAUS)
GD .... Gestational Day
GD .... Gestational Diabetes (MELL)
GD .... Gianotti Disease [*Medicine*] (STED)
gd .... gilt edges (SAUS)
GD .... Given Data (SAUS)

GD .... Glass Door (ADA)
GD .... Global Data (ELAL)
GD .... Global Data Graphics Display (SAUS)
GD .... Global Data Systems [*Vancouver Stock Exchange symbol*]
GD .... Global Digest (journ.) (SAUS)
GD .... Glow Discharge [*Photovoltaic energy systems*]
GD .... Glutamate Dehydrogenase [*An enzyme*]
GD .... Glutaraldehyde-Dichromate [*Fixative*]
GD .... Glyceryl Distearate [*Organic chemistry*]
GD .... Goal Defence [*Netball*]
GD .... Goal Delivery (SAUS)
GD .... God Damn
GD .... Golden Dawn [*In occult society name, Hermetic Order of the Golden Dawn*]
GD .... Gonadal Dysgenesis [*Endocrinology*]
GD .... Good [*Track condition*] [*Thoroughbred racing*]
GD .... Good Day [*Amateur radio shorthand*] (WDAA)
GD .... Good Delivery [*Business term*]
GD .... Good for the Day [*Investment term*] (NUMA)
GD .... Good Grade (SAUS)
GD .... Governing Document (SAUO)
Gd .... Government Expenditure [*Economics*]
GD .... Grade [*Technical drawings*]
GD .... Graduate Diploma
GD .... Graduate in Divinity
GD .... Granddaughter
GD .... Grand Deacon [*Freemasonry*]
GD .... Grand Division
GD .... Grand Duchy
GD .... Grand Duke (WGA)
GD .... Grandes Decisions de la Jurisprudence Administrative [*A publication*] (ILCA)
GD .... Graphic Data (SAUS)
GD .... Graphic Demand Meter
GD .... Graphic Digitization (SAUS)
GD .... Graphic Display
GD .... Graphics Database tool (SAUS)
GD .... Grave's Disease [*Endocrinology*]
GD .... Gravimetric Density
Gd .... Greenside Darter [*Ichthyology*]
GD .... Greenwich Date
GD .... Grenada [*ANSI two-letter standard code*] (CNC)
gd .... Grenada [*MARC country of publication code*] [*Library of Congress*] (LCCP)
GD .... Grinding Direction (SAUS)
GD .... Gross Debt [*Business term*]
GD .... Ground
GD .... Ground Defence (or Defense) (SAUS)
GD .... Ground Detector (MSA)
GD .... Ground Directional (IAA)
GD .... Group Delay (ELAL)
GD .... Group Delay Distortion (LAIN)
GD .... Grouping Distance [*Industrial engineering*]
GD .... Grove Dictionary of Music and Musicians [*A publication*]
GD .... Grown Diffused
GD .... Growth and Development (STED)
GD .... Guard (AABC)
gd .... Guard (MILB)
GD .... Guard Digit (SAUS)
GD .... Gudermannian Amplitude
GD .... Guidance Document (EEVL)
GD .... Guide (VLIE)
GD .... Gum Disturbance (SAUS)
GD .... Gundeck
GD .... Gun Director (SAUS)
GD .... Gun Drill (SAUS)
GD .... Gunnery Division [*British military*] (DMA)
GD .... Guntersville Dam [*TVA*]
GD .... Gyrodynamics (SAUS)
GD .... Nerve Gas [*US Chemical Corps symbol*]
GD .... Soman [*Nerve gas*] [*Army symbol*]
GDA .... Galvo-Drive Amplifier
GDA .... Gas Distributation Administration (SAUS)
G D A .... Gas Distribution Administration (SAUS)
GDA .... Gastroduodenal Artery [*Medicine*] (MELL)
GDA .... General Development Agreement (SAUS)
GDA .... General Disposal Authority
GDA .... General Dynamics Ardmore (SAUO)
GD/A .... General Dynamics / Astronautics (SAUS)
GDA .... General Dynamics Astronautics
GD/A .... General Dynamics/Astronautics (SAUO)
GDA .... Geocentric Datum of Australia (SAUO)
GDA .... Georgia Dental Association (SAUS)
GDA .... Georgia Dietetic Association (SAUO)
GDA .... Germin-3.16-Diacetat (SAUS)
GDA .... Germine Diacetate [*Medicine*] (DMAA)
GDA .... Gimbal Dish Antenna (SAUO)
GDA .... Gimbal Drive Actuator [*or Assembly*] (KSC)
GDA .... Gimbaled Dish Antenna (CCCA)
GDA .... Global Data Administrator (MHDI)
GDA .... Global Data Area
GDA .... Global Dialog Association (SAUO)
GDA .... Global Directory Agent
GDA .... Glycidyldiisopropylidenearabitol [*Organic chemistry*]
GDA .... Glycol Diacetate (SAUS)
GDA .... Goat Dairymen's Association [*Australia*]
GDA .... Goldera Resources, Inc. [*Vancouver Stock Exchange symbol*]
GDA .... Good Data Area (SAUS)
GDA .... Graduate Diploma in Administration
Gda .... Granddaughter
GDA .... Graphic Data Acquisition (SAUS)
GDA .... Ground Defence Area (SAUS)
GDA .... Guide Dogs of America (EA)
GDA .... Gun Damage Assessment (NVT)
GDA .... Gun-Defended Area
GDA .... Gunned Accelerator (SAUS)
GDAA .... Gift and Decorative Accessories Association of America [*Later, GAA*] (EA)
GDAAC .... Goddard Distributed Active Archive Center (SAUO)
Gdag Ill .... Gardening Illustrated (journ.) (SAUS)
GDahN .... North Georgia College, Dahlonega, GA [*Library symbol*] [*Library of Congress*] (LCLS)
GDAIS .... Atlanta Information Services, Decatur (SAUS)
GDAIS .... Atlanta Information Services, Decatur, GA [*Library symbol*] [*Library of Congress*] (LCLS)
GDAJA .... Journal. Georgia Dental Association (journ.) (SAUS)
GDal .... Dalton Regional Library, Dalton, GA [*Library symbol*] [*Library of Congress*] (LCLS)
GDalC .... Dalton College, Dalton, GA [*Library symbol*] [*Library of Congress*] (LCLS)
GDAM .... General Data Access Method (SAUS)
GDAM .... Graduate Division of Applied Mathematics
GD&H .... Grinning, Ducking & Hiding (SAUS)
GD & R .... Grinning, Ducking, and Running (CDE)
GD & T .... Geometric Dimensioning and Tolerancing
GD&T .... Guidance Dimensioning and Tolerancing (SAUS)
GD&W .... Grinning, Ducking & Weaving (SAUS)
GDanH .... Heritage Papers, Danielsville, GA [*Library symbol*] [*Library of Congress*] (LCLS)
GDAP .... Generic Digital Autopilot (ACAE)
GDAP .... GEOS [*Geodetic Earth-Orbiting Satellite*] Data Adjustment Program
GDAP .... Government Document Application Profile [*Telecommunications*] (OSI)
GDAP .... Growing Danger of Acronym Proliferation (SAUO)
GDAS .... Geokinetic Data Acquisition System (PDAA)
GDAS .... Global Data Assimilation System (SAUS)
GDAS .... Ground Data Acquisition System
GDAS .... Groundwater Data Analysis System (SAUS)
GDAU .... General Data Acquisition Unit (MCD)
GDAY .... Generic Decomposition And Yield (SAUS)
GDB .... Gas Density Balance [*Medicine*] (DMAA)
GDB .... Genome Data Base [*Genetics*]
GDB .... Geometric Database (MCD)
GDB .... Global Database
GDB .... Gnu Debugger (SAUS)
GDB .... Government Development Bank of Puerto Rico
GDB .... Graphic Data Base (SAUS)
GDB .... Graphic Data Byte (SAUS)
GDB .... Guide Dogs for the Blind (EA)
GDBA .... Guide Dogs for the Blind Association [*British*] (EAIO)
GDBM .... GNU Data Base Manager (SAUS)
GDBMS .... Generalized Data Base Management System (VLIE)
GDBMS .... Generalized Data Base Management Systems [*Air Force*]
GDBMS .... Generalized Date Base Management System (SAUS)
GDB/OMIM ... Genome Database/Online Mendelian Inheritance in Man (SAUO)
GDBS .... Generalized Database System (NASA)
GDBS .... Geo facilities Data Base Support (SAUS)
GDBS .... Geofacilities Data Base Support (VLIE)
GDBS .... Global Data Base System (SAUS)
GDBTG .... Generalized Data Base Task Group (SAUO)
GDBusAd ..... Graduate Diploma in Business Administration
GDC .... Columbia Theological Seminary, Decatur, GA [*Library symbol*] [*Library of Congress*] (LCLS)
GDC .... Gamma-Ray, Density and Caliper Survey (SAUS)
GDC .... Garage Door Council (EA)
GDC .... Gardener-Denver Company (SAUO)
GDC .... GARP Data Center (SAUS)
GDC .... Gas Discharge Counter
GDC .... Gas Displacement Chromatography
GDC .... Gated Digital Correlator (SAUS)
GDC .... Gated Diode Crosspoint (SAUS)
GDC .... Gel Dryer with Clamps [*Chromatography*]
GDC .... Gel Drying Cart [*Chromatography*]
GDC .... General Data Comm (NITA)
GDC .... General DataComm Industries (SAUS)
GDC .... General DataComm Industries, Inc. [*NYSE symbol*] (SPSG)
GDC .... General Data Communications (SAUS)
GDC .... General Data Corporation (SAUO)
GDC .... General Defense Corp. (SAUO)
GDC .... General Dental Council [*British*]
GDC .... General Design Criteria (NRCH)
GDC .... General Development Corp. (AAG)
GDC .... General [*Purpose*] Digital Computer
GDC .... General Dynamics, Convair
GD/C .... General Dynamics/Convair (SAUS)
GDC .... General Dynamics Corp.
GDC .... General Dynamics Corporanon (SAUS)
GDC .... Generalized Dynamic Charge (SAUS)
GDC .... General-purpose Digital Computer (SAUS)
GDC .... Genl DataComm Ind [*NYSE symbol*] (TTSB)

GDC .... Geocentric Dust Cloud
GDC .... Geocentric Dust Converter (SAUS)
GDC .... Geodetic Data Center [*Environmental Science Services Administration*]
GDC .... Geographic Data Committee (SAUO)
GDC .... Geographic Data Council (SAUO)
GDC .... Geological Data Center [*University of California, San Diego*] (IID)
GDC .... Geomagnetic Data Center [*National Oceanic and Atmospheric Administration*]
GDC .... Geophysical Data Center
GDC .... Geosciences Data Center (SAUO)
GDC .... Geospatial Data Clearinghouse (SAUO)
GDC .... German Data Center (SAUS)
GDC .... Gettysburg College, Gettysburg, PA [*OCLC symbol*] (OCLC)
GDC .... Giant Dopamine-Containing Cell [*Medicine*] (DMAA)
GDC .... Global Data Centre (SAUO)
GDC .... Global Drifter Center (or Centre) (SAUO)
GDC .... Glow Discharge Cleaning (SAUS)
GDC .... Glow Discharge Condition (SAUS)
GDC .... Good Door Closer
GDC .... Governmental Defence Council [*British*]
GDC .... Governmental Defence (or Defense) Council (SAUO)
GDC .... Grand-Dad's Day Council [*Defunct*] (EA)
GDC .... Grand Deacon of Ceremonies [*Freemasonry*] (ROG)
GDC .... Granduc Mines Ltd. [*Toronto Stock Exchange symbol*] [*Vancouver Stock Exchange symbol*]
GDC .... Graphic Designers of Canada (SAUS)
GDC .... Graphic Display Console (MCD)
GDC .... Graphic Display Controller (SAUS)
GDC .... Gravity Die-Cast [*Automotive engineering*]
GDC .... Gross Dependable Capacity [*Electronics*] (IEEE)
GDC .... Ground Digit Control (IAA)
GDC .... Guglielmi Detachable Coil [*Medicine*] (RAWO)
GDC .... Guidance Data Converter [*Aerospace*] (AAG)
GDC .... Guidance Display Computer (DNAB)
GDC .... Guild of Dyers and Cleaners [*British*] (BI)
GDC .... Gun Direction Computer
GDC .... Gyro Display Coupler (MCD)
GDC .... Society of Graphic Designers of Canada (EAIO)
GDCA .... Great Dane Club of America (EA)
GDCA .... Gypsum Drywall Contractors Association (SAUO)
GD/CD .... General Dynamics/Convair Division (SAUS)
Gd-CDTA .... Gadolinium Cyclohexanediaminetetraacetic Acid [*Medicine*] (RAWO)
GDCH .... Glycerol Dichlorohydrin [*Organic chemistry*]
GDCH .... Graduate Diploma in Community Health
GDCI .... Gypsum Drywall Contractors International [*Later, AWCI*]
GDCL .... General Dynamics Canadair Limited (SAUO)
GDCL .... General Dynamics Candair Limited (SAUS)
GDCLS .... General Dynamics Commercial Launch Services (SAUS)
Gd Co .... Guard Company (SAUO)
GD/Convair... General Dynamics/Convair (SAUO)
GDCP .... Geostationary Data Collection Platform (SAUO)
GDCR .... Glacial Debris Conjugate Region [*Oceanography*]
GDCS .... Government Documents Catalog Service [*Information service or system*] (IID)
GDCS .... Ground Distributed Control System (SSD)
GD/CV .... General Dynamics/Convair Division (MCD)
GDCX .... Growth Development Corp. (SAUO)
GDD .... DeKalb Historical Society, Decatur, GA [*Library symbol*] [*Library of Congress*] (LCLS)
GDD .... Gas Discharged Display (SAUS)
GDD .... Gas Discharge Display (IAA)
GDD .... Gay Disaster Disease [*Also called AIDS*] (DAVI)
GDD .... Geddes Resources Ltd. [*Toronto Stock Exchange symbol*]
GDD .... General Design Document [*Computer science*] (MHDI)
GD/D .... General Dynamics/Daingerfield (SAA)
GDD .... GIS Data Depot (SAUO)
GDD .... Global Developmental Delay
GDD .... Graphics Data Display Manager (SAUS)
GDD .... Gridded (SAUS)
GDD .... Group Display Device (MCD)
GDD .... Growing Degree Day [*Agriculture*] (PDAA)
GDDL .... Graphical Data Definition Language
GDDM .... Graphical Data Display Manager [*Computer science*]
Gd-DOTA ...... Gadolinium Tetraazacyclododecanetetraacetic Acid [*Medicine*] (RAWO)
GDDQ .... Group Dimensions Descriptions Questionnaire [*Psychology*]
GDDS .... DeKalb County School System, Decatur, GA [*Library symbol*] [*Library of Congress*] (LCLS)
GDDS .... Gamma Dose Detector System
GD/DS .... Generalized Dictionary/Directory System [*Computer science*] (MHDB)
GDE .... Beaumont, TX [*Location identifier*] [*FAA*] (FAAL)
GDE .... Gage Deviation (SAUS)
GDE .... General Dynamics Electronics (SAUO)
GD/E .... General Dynamics/Electronics (SAA)
GDE .... Generalized Data Entry (ADA)
GDE .... Generalized Entry (SAUS)
GDE .... Generic Data Exemption (EPAT)
GDE .... Generic Decryption Engine (SAUS)
GDE .... Genetic Data Environment (SAUO)
GDE .... Georgia Department of Education (SAUO)
GDE .... Gibbs-Duhem Equation [*Physical chemistry*]
GDE .... Gilt Deckled Edge [*Bookbinding*]
gde .... gilt deckle edging (SAUS)
GDE .... Gimbal Drive Electronics (ACAE)
GDE .... Gode [*Ethiopia*] [*Airport symbol*] (OAG)
GDE .... Golden Dawn Explorations Ltd. [*Vancouver Stock Exchange symbol*]
GDE .... Gourde [*Monetary unit*] [*Haiti*]
GDE .... Graduate Dental Education (SAUO)
GDE .... Graduate Diploma in Educational Studies
GDE .... Graduate Diploma in Extension (ADA)
GDE .... Granular Diatomaceous Earth (DB)
GDE .... Graphics Differential Engine (SAUS)
GDE .... Gross Domestic Expenditure (WDAA)
GDE .... Ground Data Equipment [*Electronics*]
GDE .... Guide [*or Guided*] (MSA)
GDE .... Guided (SAUS)
GDE .... Servicios Aereos Gadel SA de CV [*Mexico*] [*ICAO designator*] (FAAC)
GD/EB .... General Dynamics/Electric Boat (SAUS)
GD/EB .... General Dynamics/Electric Boat Division (KSC)
G de Bay ..... Guido de Baysio [*Deceased, 1313*] [*Authority cited in pre-1607 legal work*] (DSA)
G de Ca .... Guillelmus de Cabriano [*Deceased, 1201*] [*Authority cited in pre-1607 legal work*] (DSA)
G de Cal ...... Gaspar de Calderinis [*Deceased, 1390*] [*Authority cited in pre-1607 legal work*] (DSA)
G de Cu .... Guillelmus de Cuneo [*Deceased, 1335*] [*Authority cited in pre-1607 legal work*] (DSA)
GDED .... General Dynamics Electro Dynamic (SAUS)
GDED .... General Dynamics/Electro Dynamic (SAUO)
Gd-EDTA ...... Gadolinium Ethylenediaminetetraacetic Acid [*Medicine*] (RAWO)
G de Fr .... Guillelmus de Ferreriis [*Deceased, 1295*] [*Authority cited in pre-1607 legal work*] (DSA)
GDEJ .... Green Disk Environmental Journal (SAUO)
G de Mon .... Guillelmus de Monte Lauduno [*Deceased, 1343*] [*Authority cited in pre-1607 legal work*] (DSA)
G de Mon Lau... Guillelmus de Monte Lauduno [*Deceased, 1343*] [*Authority cited in pre-1607 legal work*] (DSA)
G de Mon Laud... Guillelmus de Monte Lauduno [*Deceased, 1343*] [*Authority cited in pre-1607 legal work*] (DSA)
GDemP .... Piedmont College, Demorest, GA [*Library symbol*] [*Library of Congress*] (LCLS)
GDES .... Governmental Department for Electrical Specification (SAUO)
GDES .... Governmental Department for Electrical Specifications (SAUS)
GDES .... Governmental Department for Electronical Specification (SAUS)
GDES .... Government Department Electrical Specification (SAUS)
GDES .... Government Department Electrical Specifications (SAUS)
GDest .... General Destillation (SAUS)
G-Dest .... General Destination
G de Suz ...... Guido de Suzaria [*Deceased, 1293*] [*Authority cited in pre-1607 legal work*] (DSA)
GDEU .... Guidance Digital Evaluation Unit
GDEUT .... Guidance Digital Evaluation Test (SAUS)
GDEX .... Gold Express Corp. (SAUO)
GDF .... Gas Dynamic Facility [*Air Force*]
GDF .... Gas Dynanmic Facility (SAUS)
GDF .... Gel Diffusion Precipitin [*Medicine*] (MELL)
GDF .... General Defence Plan (SAUS)
GDF .... Geographic Data File [*LPC, Inc.*] [*Information service or system*] (IID)
GDF .... Geographic Data Format (SAUO)
GDF .... Geophysical Data Facility
GDF .... Gibraltar Defence Force [*British military*] (DMA)
GDF .... Global Partners Income Fd [*NYSE symbol*] (TTSB)
GDF .... Global Partners Income Fund [*NYSE symbol*] (SPSG)
GDF .... Goldfarb Corp. [*Toronto Stock Exchange symbol*]
GDF .... Granular Diffusion Flame (MCD)
GDF .... Graphical Display File (SAUS)
GDF .... Graphics Data Form (SAUS)
GDF .... Ground Decommutation Facility
GDF .... Ground Defense Forces
GDF .... Ground Diverted Force [*Military*] (CINC)
GDF .... Group Distribution Frame [*Telecommunications*] (NITA)
GDF .... Grout Disposal Facility (SAUS)
GDF .... Growth Differentiation Factor [*Embryology*]
GDF .... Guidaut Defibrillator [*Medicine*] (MELL)
GDF .... Guyana Defence Force (SAUS)
GDF .... Guyanese Defense Force
GDFB .... Guide Dog Foundation for the Blind [*Also known as Second Sight Guiding Eyes - Guide Dog Foundation*] (EA)
GDFCF .... Gross Domestic Fixed Capital Formation (EERA)
GDFE .... Gas-Jet Diffusion Flames Experiment (SAUS)
GDFF .... Geographic Distribution of Federal Funds Information System [*Comptroller General of the United States*]
GD Fort Worth... General Dynamics Fort Worth (SAUS)
GD Fort Worth... General Dynamics/Fort Worth (SAUO)
GDFT .... Generalized Discrete Fourier Transform (SAUS)
GD/FW .... General Dynamics/Fort Worth (KSC)
GDFY .... Godfrey Co. (SAUO)
GDG .... Gas Discharge Gage (SAUS)
GDG .... Gas Discharge Gauge
GDG .... General Data Gap (SAUS)
GD(G) .... General Duties (Ground) [*British military*] (DMA)
GDG .... Generation Data Gap (SAUS)
GDG .... Generation Data Group [*Computer science*] (ITCA)
GDG .... Golden Glory [*Vancouver Stock Exchange symbol*]
GDG .... Graphic Display Generator (SAUS)
GDG .... Group Display Generator
GDG .... Guarding [*Bookbinding*] (DGA)

GDGA.......... Garment Dyers Guild of America (EA)
GD/GA.......... General Dynamics/General Atomic (KSC)
GDGIP.......... Gas-Driven Gyro Inertial Platform [*Aerospace*] (AAG)
GDGS.......... Guidance Digital Ground Station (IAA)
GDH.......... DeKalb General Hospital, Decatur, GA [*Library symbol*] [*Library of Congress*] (LCLS)
GDH.......... Glucose Dehydrogenase
GDH.......... Glutamate Dehydrogenase [*An enzyme*]
GDH.......... Glycerin-3-phosphatdehydrogenase (SAUS)
GDH.......... Glycerophosphate Dehydrogenase (MAE)
GDH.......... Glycol Dehydrogenase (DB)
GDH.......... Godhavn [*Greenland*] [*Seismograph station code, US Geological Survey*] (SEIS)
GDH.......... Goldsearch, Inc. [*Vancouver Stock Exchange symbol*]
GDH.......... Gonadotropic Hormone [*Endocrinology*]
GDH.......... Goods on Hand (DS)
GDH.......... Government Distribution HUB (SAUS)
GDH.......... Grand Ducal Highness (ROG)
GDH.......... Ground Data Handling
GDH.......... Growth and Development Hormone (SAUS)
GDH.......... Growth and Differentiation Hormone [*Endocrinology*]
GdH.......... Guard House (SAUS)
GDH.......... Guidance During Homing (SAUS)
GDH.......... Sargodha [*Pakistan*] [*Airport symbol*] (AD)
GDHA.......... Garage Door Hardware Association (NTPA)
GDHC.......... Ground Data Handling Centre [*Canada*]
Gd House..... Good Housekeeping (journ.) (SAUS)
GDHP.......... Galveston District Home Page (SAUO)
GDHS.......... Ground Data Handling System (MCD)
GDHSE.......... Guardhouse (AABC)
GDHSWT.......... General Dynamics High-Speed Wind Tunnel
GDH-TPI...... Glycerophosphate Dehydrogenase-Triosephosphate Isomerase (SAUS)
GDI.......... Gardner Denver [*NYSE symbol*] (SG)
GDI.......... Gas-Driven Intensifier Pump (MCD)
GDI.......... Gasoline Direct Injection
GDI.......... Gender-related Development Index (SAUS)
GDI.......... General DataComm Industries, Incorporated (SAUS)
GDI.......... General Dissemination of Information (SAUS)
GDI.......... General Dynamics International (SAUO)
GDI.......... Generalized Data Base Interface (SAUS)
GDI.......... Generalized Database Interface [*Computer science*] (MHDB)
GDI.......... Generic Device Interface [*Automotive electronics*]
GDI.......... German Development Institute (SAUO)
GDI.......... Global Defense Initiative
GDI.......... God Damned Independent [*College slang for student not affiliated with a fraternity or sorority*]
GDI.......... Gordon Diagnostic System (TES)
GDI.......... Graphical Device Interface (SAUS)
GDI.......... Graphical Display Interface (SAUS)
GDI.......... Graphic Data Input (SAUS)
GDI.......... Graphic Datakits International (SAUS)
GDI.......... Graphic Device Interface (SAUS)
GDI.......... Graphic Display Interface (MCD)
GDI.......... Graphics Device Interface
GDI.......... Graphics Display Interface (SAUS)
GDI.......... Gross Domestic Income (GOBB)
GDI.......... Gross Domestic Investment (SAUS)
GDI.......... Ground Detector Indicator
GDI.......... New York, NY [*Location identifier*] [*FAA*] (FAAL)
GDI.......... Sammlung der Griechischen Dialektinschriften [*A publication*] (OCD)
GDIAN.......... Guardian (ROG)
GDIC.......... General Devices, Incorporated (SAUO)
GDIC.......... Government Departmental Industrial Council (SAUO)
GDID.......... General Defense International Division (SAUS)
GDID.......... Genetically Determined Immunodeficiency Disease (MELL)
GDIFS.......... Gray and Ductile Iron Founders' Society [*Later, Iron Castings Society - ICS*]
GdIG.......... Gadolinium Iron Garnet (IEEE)
GDIM.......... Graduate Diploma in Industrial Management [*Australia*]
GDIN.......... Global Defense Information Network (SEWL)
GDIP.......... Gale Directory of International Publications [*A publication*]
GDIP.......... General Defence Intelligence Programme office (SAUS)
GDIP.......... General Defense Intelligence Program [*DoD*]
GDip.......... Graduate Diploma (DD)
GDipA(Couns)... Graduate Diploma in Arts (Counselling)
GDipCD.......... Graduate Diploma in Child Development
GDipCh.......... Graduate Diploma in Chiropractic
GDipClinSc... Graduate Diploma in Clinical Science
GDipCompSt... Graduate Diploma in Computer Studies
GDipEc.......... Graduate Diploma in Economics
GDipErg....... Graduate Diploma in Ergonomics
GDipExerSpSc... Graduate Diploma in Exercise and Sport Science
GDipHA.......... Graduate Diploma in Health Administration
GDipHC.......... Graduate Diploma in Health Counselling
GDipHSM..... Graduate Diploma in Health Services Management
GDipHumNut... Graduate Diploma in Human Nutrition
GDipLS.......... Graduate Diploma in Legal Studies
GDipM.......... Graduate Diploma in Management
GDipMLS..... Graduate Diploma in Medical Laboratory Science
GDIPP.......... General Defense Intelligence Proposed Program [*DoD*] (MCD)
GDipPEC.......... Graduate Diploma in Parent Education and Counselling
GDipPHC...... Graduate Diploma in Primary Health
GDipPrfMgt... Graduate Diploma in Professional Management
GDipPubL.... Graduate Diploma in Public Law
GDIS.......... General Dynamics International Service (SAUO)
GDIS.......... Gier-Dunkle Integrating Sphere
GDIS.......... Graphic Device Interface Standard (SAUS)
GDIS.......... Guam Data Interface System (SAUS)
Gdk.......... Gdansk [*Poland*] (BARN)
GDK Azat..... Freedom Civil Movement of Kazakhstan "Azat" [*Political party*] (PSAP)
GDKKD2....... Annual Report. Faculty of Education. Gunma University. Art, Technology, Health and Physical Education and Science of Human Living Series (journ.) (SAUS)
GDKYA7....... Annual Report. Faculty of Education. Gunma University. Art and Technology Series (journ.) (SAUS)
GDL.......... Gas Discharge Lamp
GDL.......... Gas Dynamic LASER
G D L.......... Gas-Dynamic Laser (SAUS)
GDL.......... Gas Dynamics Laboratory
GDL.......... Gladstone-Dale Law
GDL.......... Glas Development Laser system (SAUS)
GDL.......... Glass Delay Line
GDL.......... Glass Development LASER
GDL.......... Global Data Link
GDL.......... Glow-Discharge Lamp [*Spectrometry*]
GDL.......... Glucono-delta-Lactone [*Organic chemistry*]
GDL.......... Graduate Driver Licensing
g/dl.......... Grams per Deciliter [*Medicine*] (EDAA)
GDL.......... Graphic Display Library
GDL.......... Graphic Drawing Library [*Graphic Data Ltd.*] [*Software package*] (NCC)
GDL.......... Graphics Display List [*Graphic Data Ltd.*] [*Software package*] (NCC)
GDL.......... Ground Dynamic Laser (SAUS)
GDL.......... Guadalajara [*Mexico*] [*Airport symbol*] (OAG)
GDLB.......... Glendale Federal Bank FSB [*NASDAQ symbol*] (SAG)
GDLC.......... General Dynamics Liquid Carbonic (SAUO)
GDLC.......... Generic Data Link Control (SAUS)
GDLE.......... Graduate Diploma in Land Economy
GDLEW.......... Glendale Fed Bk FSB Wrrt [*NASDAQ symbol*] (TTSB)
GDLK.......... Grid Leak
gd lkg.......... Good-Looking (ADWA)
GDLP.......... Grenada Democratic Labour Party [*Political party*] (EY)
GDLP.......... Ground Data Link Processor (GAVI)
GDLs.......... Gas Dynamic Lasers (SAUS)
GDLS.......... General Dynamics [*Corp.*] Land Systems Division
GDLS.......... General Dynamics Land Systems Inc. [*A publication*] (AAGC)
GDLS.......... Generals Dynamics Land Systems
GDLS.......... Glow-Discharge Lamp Source [*Spectrometry*]
GDLS.......... Graduate Diploma in Library Science (ADA)
GDLST.......... General Dynamics Low-Speed Tunnel (SAUS)
GDM.......... Gardner (SAUS)
GDM.......... Gardner, MA [*Location identifier*] [*FAA*] (FAAL)
GDM.......... General Design Memorandum [*US Army Corps of Engineers*]
GDM.......... General Development Map [*or Model*]
GDM.......... General Dynamics Manufacturing (SAUS)
GDM.......... Generalized Development Model (ACAE)
GDM.......... Geodetic Distance Measurement
gdm.......... Geodynamic Meter (SAUS)
GDM.......... Geospatial Data Management (SAUO)
GDM.......... Gestational Diabetes Mellitus [*Medicine*]
GDM.......... Ghana Democratic Movement [*Political party*] (EY)
GDM.......... Gibraltar Democratic Movement [*Political party*] (PPE)
GDM.......... Glass Disk Memory (SAUS)
GDM.......... Global Data Manager
GDM.......... Goldome [*NYSE symbol*] (COMM)
GDM.......... Graphic Display Monitor (SAUS)
GDM.......... Gravitational Dipole Moment (PDAA)
GDM.......... Grenada Democratic Movement [*Political party*] (EAIO)
GDM.......... Grid-Dip Meter (IAA)
GDM.......... Grid-Dip Modulator
GDM.......... Group on Defence Matters (SAUO)
GDM.......... Guidance Design Manager (MCD)
GDMA.......... Glycol Dimethacrylate (MCD)
GDManTher... Graduate Diploma in Manipulative Therapy
GdmCl.......... Guanidinium Chloride [*Biochemistry*]
GDMCN.......... Ground Data Management and Communications Network (MCD)
GDME.......... Glycol Dimethyl Ether [*Organic chemistry*]
GDME.......... Graduate Degrees for Minorities in Engineering (SAUS)
GD Meter..... Graphic Demand Meter (SAUS)
GDMI.......... Gardner Denver Machinery [*NASDAQ symbol*] (TTSB)
GDMI.......... Gardner Denver Machinery, Inc. [*NASDAQ symbol*] (SAG)
GDMI.......... Generic Definition of Management Information (SAUS)
GDMK.......... GoodMark Foods [*NASDAQ symbol*] (TTSB)
GDMK.......... GoodMark Foods, Inc. [*NASDAQ symbol*] (NQ)
GDML.......... Gas Dynamic Mixing LASER [*Navy*]
GDMO.......... General Duties Medical Officer
GDMO.......... General Duty Medical Officer (SAUS)
GDMO.......... Group Data Management Office (ACAE)
GDMO.......... Guidelines for the Definition of Managed Objects (SAUO)
GDMS.......... General Dynamics Material Service (SAUO)
GDMS.......... Generalized Data Management System [*Computer science*] (BUR)
G D M S.......... Generalized Data Management Systems (SAUS)
GDMS.......... Geographic Data Management System [*Computer science*]
GDMS.......... Geophysical Data Management System (SAUO)
GDMS.......... Global Data Management System
GDMS.......... Glow-Discharge Mass Spectroscopy [*or Spectrometry*]
GDMS.......... Graphics Display Management System (MCD)
GDMS.......... Ground Data Management System (SAUS)

GDMT .... Gemini Detailed Maneuver Table (IAA)
GDN .... Garden
GDN .... Gdansk [*Poland*] [*Airport symbol*] (OAG)
GDN .... Giant Descending Neuron [*Neurology*]
GDN .... Glycol Dinitrate [*Organic chemistry*]
Gdn .... Godown (SAUS)
GDN .... Golden News Resources Corp. [*Vancouver Stock Exchange symbol*]
GDN .... Government Data Network [*Telecommunications*] (OSI)
Gdn .... Graduation (SAUS)
GDN .... Group Dispatch Number (CGWS)
Gdn .... Guanidine [*Biochemistry*]
gdn .... Guardian (GEAB)
GDN .... Guardian
GDNC .... Guidance (MSA)
GDNCE .... Guidance (AFM)
GDNCY .... Garden City, KS [*American Association of Railroads railroad junction routing code*]
GDNF .... Glial-Derived Growth Factor [*Biochemistry*]
Gdn J NY Bot Gdn ... Garden Journal. New York Botanical Garden (journ.) (SAUS)
GdNPF .... Glia-Derived Neurite-Promoting Factor (DB)
gdnr .... gardener (SAUS)
GDNRJ .... Gardiner Junction, OR [*American Association of Railroads railroad junction routing code*]
Gdns .... Gardens (DD)
GDNS .... Gardens (MCD)
Gdns Bull ..... Gardens Bulletin (journ.) (SAUS)
GDNT .... Gradient (SAUS)
GDNVW .... Gardenview Room (TVEL)
GDO .... Garage Door Opener (NG)
G/DO .... Gas / Diesel Oil (SAUS)
gdo .... Gate-Dip Oscillator (IDOE)
GDO .... General Development Order [*Town and country planning*] [*British*]
GDO .... Geraldton District Office (SAUO)
GDO .... Graphic Data Output (SAUS)
GDO .... Grid Dip Oscillator (SAUS)
gdo .... Grid-Dip Oscillator (IDOE)
GDO .... Grid-Dip Oscillator
GDO .... Gross Domestic Output [*Economics*]
GDO .... Guasdualito [*Venezuela*] [*Airport symbol*] (OAG)
GDO .... Guidance Officer (KSC)
GDO .... Guild of Dispensing Opticians (SAUS)
GDO .... Gun Direction Officer (NATG)
GDO .... Gunn Diode Oscillator [*Electronics*] (PDAA)
GDOA .... Georgia DARE Officers Association (SAUO)
GDOA .... Graphic Data Output Area (CMD)
GDO(A) .... Guild of Dispensing Opticians (Australia)
GDOC .... University of Guelph Document Holdings [*Database*] [*No longer available online*]
GDOccHlth ... Graduate Diploma in Occupational Health
GDOES .... Glow-Discharge Optical Emission Spectroscopy
GDOFA .... Guide Dog Owners and Friends' Association [*Australia*]
GDOP .... Geometric Degradation of Position [*Aerospace*]
GDOP .... Geometric Dilution of Precision
GDOS .... General Dynamics Ordnance Systems
GDOS .... Graphic Device Operating System (VLIE)
GDOS .... Graphics Device Operating System (SAUS)
GDoS .... South Georgia College, Douglas, GA [*Library symbol*] [*Library of Congress*] (LCLS)
GDOT .... Georgia Department of Transportation [*Federal Railroad Administration identification code*]
GDOUG .... Greater Detroit OS/2 User Group (SAUO)
GDP .... Gaede Diffusion Pump
GDP .... Gale Directory of Publications [*Later, GDPBM*] [*A publication*]
GDP .... Gallium Photo Diode
GDP .... Galvanostatic Double-Pulse (SAUS)
GDP .... GARP Data Processing (SAUS)
GDP .... Gas Discharge Panel (VLIE)
GDP .... Gaseous Diffusion Plant [*Nuclear energy*] (NUCP)
GDP .... Gaseous Discharge Principle
GDP .... Gel Diffusion Precipitin [*Biochemistry*] (DAVI)
GDP .... General Defence Plan (SAUS)
GDP .... General Defense Plan [*Formerly, EDP*] [*NATO*] (NATG)
GDP .... General Defensive Position (SAUS)
GDP .... General Development Plan (MUGU)
GDP .... General Dynamics Pomona (SAUO)
GDP .... General Dynamics Procedure (SAUS)
GDP .... Generalized Data Base Processor [*Computer science*] (MHDI)
GDP .... Generalized Data Processor (SAUS)
GDP .... Generalized Distributor Program [*Computer science*]
GDP .... Generalized Documentation Processor (NASA)
GDP .... Generalized Drawing Primitive
GDP .... Geographic Data Products (SAUO)
GDP .... Geometric Data Processing (VLIE)
GDP .... Geometric Design Processor (VLIE)
GDP .... Gesamtdeutsche Partei [*All-German Party*] [*Political party*] (PPE)
GDP .... Giant Depolarizing Potential [*Neurophysiology*]
GDP .... Giant Depolarizing Synaptic Potential [*Neurochemistry*]
GDP .... Global Dataset Project (SAUO)
GDP .... Global Drifter Programme (SAUS)
GDP .... Gloria Dei Press [*An association*] (EA)
GDP .... Glow Discharge Polymer (SAUS)
GDP .... Goal-Directed Programming
GDP .... Golden Pond Resources [*Vancouver Stock Exchange symbol*]
GDP .... Good Design Practice (DB)
GDP .... Goodrich Petroleum [*NYSE symbol*] (SAG)
GDP .... Government Data Publications [*Information service or system*] (IID)
GDP .... Government Development Platform [*Marine science*] (OSRA)
GDP .... Graphic Data Processing (VLIE)
GDP .... Graphic Display Processor
GDP .... Graphic Display Program (VLIE)
GDP .... Graphic Draw Primitive (VLIE)
GDP .... Grid Driving Power
GDP .... Gross Domestic Product [*Economics*]
GDP .... Ground Data Processor (SAUS)
GDP .... Grounded into Double Plays [*Baseball*]
GDP .... Groupe des Democrates Patriotes [*Burkina Faso*] [*Political party*] (EY)
GDP .... Guadalupe Pass, TX [*Location identifier*] [*FAA*] (FAAL)
GDP .... Guanosin-5-diphosphat (SAUS)
GDP .... Guanosine Diphosphate [*Biochemistry*]
GDP .... Guanosine Dyphosphate [*Biochemistry*]
GDP .... Guanosintriphosphat (SAUS)
GDP .... Gun Defence Position [*Navy*] [*British*]
GDP .... Gun Director Pointer [*Naval gunnery*]
GDP .... Guyana Democratic Party [*Political party*] (PSAP)
GDPA .... General Dental Practitioner's Association [*British*]
GDPA .... Graduate Diploma in Public Accountancy (DD)
GDPA .... Graduate Diploma in Public Accounting (DD)
GDPA .... Graduate Diploma in Public Administration (PGP)
GDP (A) .... Gross Domestic Product (Average) [*Economics*]
GDPAP .... Goodrich Petrol 8% Cv'A'Pfd [*NASDAQ symbol*] (TTSB)
GDPAP .... Goodrich Petroleum [*NASDAQ symbol*] (SAG)
GDPBM .... Gale Directory of Publications and Broadcast Media [*Formerly, GDP*] [*A publication*]
GDP(CL) ...... Gun Director Pointer (Cross Leveler) [*Naval gunnery*]
GD/PD .... General Dynamics, Pomona Division
GDP (E) .... Gross Domestic Product (Expenditure) [*Economics*]
GDPG .... Guanosine Diphosphoglucose (SAUS)
GDPGM .... Ground Delay Program [*Aviation*] (FAAC)
GDPH .... Geogia Division of Public Health (SAUO)
GDPI .... GeoData Products Index (SAUO)
GDP (I) .... Gross Domestic Product (Income) [*Economics*]
GDP(L) .... Gun Director Pointer (Leveler) [*Naval gunnery*]
GDPMan .... Guanosine Biphosphomannose (SAUS)
GDPMan .... Guanosine Diphosphomannose [*Biochemistry*]
GDPO .... General Development Procedure Order (HEAS)
GDP (P) .... Gross Domestic Product (Production) [*Economics*]
GDP(P) .... Gun Director Pointer (Pointer) [*Naval gunnery*]
GDPS .... General Disk Programming System [*Computer science*] (IAA)
GDPS .... Generalized Disk Programming System (SAUS)
GDPS .... Geographically Dispersed Parallel Sysplex (GART)
GDPS .... Georgia Department of Public Safety (SAUO)
GDPS .... Global Data Processing System [*World Meteorological Organization*]
GDPS .... Government Document Publishing Service
GDP(SS) .... Gun Director Pointer (Sight Setter) [*Naval gunnery*]
GDP System ... Generalized Data Processor System (SAUS)
GDPT .... Graphical Database Presentation Tool (VLIE)
GDP(T) .... Gun Director Pointer (Trainer) [*Naval gunnery*]
GDQ .... Golden Dragon Resources [*Vancouver Stock Exchange symbol*]
GDQ .... Gondar [*Ethiopia*] [*Airport symbol*] (OAG)
GDQ .... Lincoln, Nebraska Air National Guard [*FAA designator*] (FAAC)
GDQF .... Graphical Display and Query Facility [*IBM Corp.*]
GDR .... Gaol Delivery Roll (ROG)
GDR .... Gaucher's Disease Registry [*National Gaucher Foundation - NGF*] [*Superseded by*] (EA)
GDR .... General Design Requirements (SAUS)
GDR .... Generalized Data Retrieval System (SAUO)
GDR .... Geodetic Data Reduction
GDR .... Geodyne Resources, Inc. (SAUO)
GDR .... Geophysical Data Record
GDR .... German Democratic Republic [*East Germany*]
GDR .... Giant Dipole Resonance
GDR .... Global Data Router (SAUO)
GDR .... Goal Delivery Roll (SAUS)
GDR .... Goldstack Resources (SAUO)
GDR .... Graphic Depth Recorder
GDR .... Grid Dead Reckon [*Military*] (CAAL)
GDR .... Ground Delay Response [*Telecommunications*] (OA)
GDR .... Ground Detection Radarmeteorology (SAUS)
GDR .... Group Decision Room (VLIE)
GDR .... Group Delay Response (IAA)
GDR .... Groupement des Democrates Revolutionnaires [*Burkina Faso*] [*Political party*] (EY)
GDR .... Guard Rail (AAG)
GDRAP .... Grand Rapids, MI [*American Association of Railroads railroad junction routing code*]
GDRC .... Ground Defence Reporting Cell (SAUS)
GDRC .... Gyro Drift Rate Compensation
GdrcCa .... Goodrich, BF Capital [*Associated Press*] (SAG)
GDRCT .... Gardner Denver Rework Command Tape (SAUS)
GDRDA .... Genetically Directed Representational Difference Analysis
GDRE .... Graduate Diploma in Religious Education (PGP)
GD Relay ..... Ground Directional Relay (SAUS)
Gdrich .... [*The*] Goodrich [*B.F.*] Co. [*Associated Press*] (SAG)
GDRL .... Government Data Requirement List (ACAE)
GDRO .... Government Defence Regulations and Orders (SAUO)
GDRP .... Ghana Democratic Republican Party (SAUO)
GDRPG .... Greater Davis Research and Planning Group (SAUO)
GDR Review ... German Democratic Republic Review (journ.) (SAUS)
GDRS .... Geoscience Data Referral System (SAUS)

GDS .... Agnes Scott College, Decatur, GA [*Library symbol*] [*Library of Congress*] (LCLS)
GDS .... Gas Deployed Skirt (MCD)
GDS .... Gas Dynamic System
GDS .... Gated Diode Switch (SAUS)
GDS .... GDP [*Guanosine Diphosphate*] Dissociation Stimulator [*Biochemistry*]
GDs .... Gel Destainers (SAUS)
GDS .... Gel Drying System [*Chromatography*]
GDS .... Gendis, Inc. [*Toronto Stock Exchange symbol*]
GDS .... General Data Stream [*Computer science*]
GDS .... General Data Systems (SAUS)
GDS .... General Declassification Schedule (MCD)
GDS .... General Drafting System [*Applied Research of Cambridge Ltd.*] [*Software package*] (NCC)
GDS .... General Dynamics Specification (SAUS)
GDS .... Generalized Database Subsystem (SAUS)
GDS .... Generalized Data Stream (VLIE)
GDS .... Generation Dataset (SAUS)
GDS .... Geo-Data System (SAUO)
GDS .... Geodetic Data Site
GDS .... Geographically Disadvantaged States (SAUO)
GDS .... Geographic Data Service (SAUS)
GDS .... Geriatric Depression Scale [*Medicine*] (DMAA)
GDS .... Gesell Developmental Schedules [*Education*]
GDS .... Glass Disk Store (SAUS)
GDS .... Glenmore Distilleries Co. (SAUO)
GDS .... Global Data-processing System (SAUO)
GDS .... Global Deterioration Scale [*Medicine*]
GDS .... Global Directory Service
GDS .... Global Distribution Systems
GDS .... Global Dynamics Section (SAUS)
GDS .... Glow-Discharge Spectrometry
GDS .... GNC [*Guidance and Navigation Computer*] Dynamic Simulator [*NASA*] (NASA)
GDS .... Going Down Swinging (journ.) (SAUS)
GDS .... Goldstone, CA [*Spaceflight tracking and data network*] [*NASA*] (NASA)
gds .... Goods (WDAA)
GDS .... Goods
GDS .... Gordon Diagnostic System (EDAC)
GDS .... Government Disclosure Service [*A publication*] (AAGC)
GDS .... Gradual Dosage Schedule [*Medicine*] (DMAA)
GDS .... Graphical Design Software (AAEL)
GDS .... Graphical Design System (SAUS)
GDS .... Graphical Display System [*Station control and data acquisition*] (IEEE)
GDS .... Graphic Data Set (SAUO)
GDS .... Graphic Data Syntax (SAUS)
GDS .... Graphic Data System
GDS .... Graphic Data Systems Corp. (SAUO)
GDS .... Graphic Design System
GDS .... Graphic Display Segment
GDS .... Graphic Display System (SAUS)
GDS .... Grapple Drive System (SAUS)
GDS .... Great Dark Spot [*Image on Neptune*] [*Astronomy*]
GDS .... Great Dark Spot on Neptune [*Astronomy*]
GDS .... Greater Danube Society (SAUO)
GDS .... Gross Debt Service (FOTI)
GDS .... Ground Data System
GDS .... Ground Development System (SAUO)
GDS .... Ground Display System
GDS .... Grumman Data Systems (SAUO)
Gds .... Guards [*British military*] (DMA)
GDS .... Gun Defense Simulation (SAUS)
GDS .... Gun Display System (MCD)
GDSA .... Goal-Directed Serial Alternation
GDSA .... Ground Data Systems Assurance (SAUS)
GDSafH .... Graduate Diploma in Safety and Health
GDSafS .... Graduate Diploma in Safety Science
GDSBFC .... Good Day Sunshine Beatles Fan Club (EA)
GDSC .... Gateway Data Sciences [*NASDAQ symbol*] (TTSB)
GDSC .... Gateway Data Sciences Corp. [*NASDAQ symbol*] (SAG)
GDSC .... General Dynamics Services Company (SAUO)
GDSC .... Geodesic
GDSC .... Graduate Diploma in Social Communication (ADA)
GDSCC .... Goldstone Deep Space Communications Complex [*NASA*]
GDSD .... Ground Data Systems Divsion [*NASA*] (NASA)
GDSDF .... Generalized Data Structure Definition Facility [*Computer science*] (MHDB)
GDSF .... Generalized Data Structure Definition Facility (SAUS)
GDSI .... Global Development Studies Institute (SAUO)
GDSIB .... Global Digital Sea Ice Data Bank (USDC)
GDSIDB .... Global Digital Sea Ice Data Bank [*Marine science*] (OSRA)
GDSL .... Graduate Diploma in School Librarianship (ADA)
GDSM .... Ground Data Systems Manager (MCD)
GDSM .... Guardsman [*Military*]
GDSM .... Gun Defence Simulation Model (SAUS)
GDSN .... Global Digital Seismic Network
GDSN .... Global Digital Seismograph Network [*Earthquake study*]
GDSO .... Ground Data Systems Officer (MCD)
GDSP .... Georgia Department of Public Safety (SAUO)
GDSS .... General Dvnamics Space Systems (SAUS)
GDSS .... Global Decision Support System (MCD)
GDSS .... Group Decision Support System [*Army*]
GDSSc .... Graduate Diploma in Sport Science
GDSSR .... GDSD [*Ground Data Systems Division*] Staff Support Room [*NASA*] (NASA)
GDSU .... Global Digital Service Unit (SAUS)
GDT .... Gas Decay Tank (NRCH)
GDT .... Gas Discharge Tube
GD/T .... General Dynamics/Telecommunications
GDT .... Generator Development Tools [*Silicon Design Laboratories*] (NITA)
GDT .... Geographic Data Technology, Inc. [*Information service or system*] (IID)
GDT .... Geometric Dimensioning and Tolerancing (SAUO)
GDT .... Global Descriptor Table [*Computer science*]
GDT .... Glow Discharge Tube (SAUS)
GDT .... Golden Diamond Travel and Tourism Agency [*Saudi Arabia*]
GDT .... Graduate Diploma in Taxation (PGP)
GDT .... Graduate Diploma in Theology (PGP)
GDT .... Grand Turk [*British West Indies*] [*Airport symbol*] (OAG)
GDT .... Graphic Display Terminal
GDT .... Graphics Development Toolkit (SAUS)
GDT .... Ground Data Terminal
GDT .... Ground Delay Time (IAA)
GDT .... Group Delay Time (SAUO)
GDT .... Guidant Corp. [*NYSE symbol*] (SAG)
GDTE .... Graduate Diploma in Technological Entrepreneurship (PGP)
GDTI .... General Database Technology (SAUS)
Gd Times ...... Good Times (journ.) (SAUS)
GDTL .... Graduate Diploma in Teacher Librarianship (ADA)
GDTR .... Global Descriptor Table Register [*Computer science*] (PCM)
GDTRC .... Global Descriptor Table Register Cache (SAUS)
GDTS .... Gliding Deceleration Technology System
GDTSS .... Group Dynamic Traffic Safety School (SAUO)
GDU .... Gamo Democratic Union [*Ethiopia*]
GDU .... Garbage Disposal Unit (ADA)
GDU .... Gastroduodenal Ulcer [*Medicine*] (DMAA)
GDU .... Gastroduodenal ulceration (SAUS)
GDU .... Gelatine Digestive Unit (SAUS)
GDU .... Glendale Resources, Inc. [*Vancouver Stock Exchange symbol*]
GDU .... Graphic Display Unit
GDU .... Guide Dog Users (EA)
GDU .... Gun Display Unit (SAUS)
GDUI .... Guide Dog Users, Inc. (EA)
GDunGS .... Church of Jesus Christ of Latter-Day Saints, Genealogical Society Library (SAUO)
GDunGS .... Church of Jesus Christ of Latter-Day Saints, Genealogical Society Library, SandySprings Georgia Branch, Dunwoody, GA [*Library symbol*] [*Library of Congress*] (LCLS)
G Dur .... Guillelmus Durandi [*Deceased, 1296*] [*Authority cited in pre-1607 legal work*] (DSA)
G Duran .... Guillelmus Durandi [*Deceased, 1296*] [*Authority cited in pre-1607 legal work*] (DSA)
GDurng .... Grupo Industrial Durango SA de CV [*Associated Press*] (SAG)
GDuV .... United States Veterans Administration Center, Dublin, GA [*Library symbol*] [*Library of Congress*] (LCLS)
GDV .... Gastric Dilatation Volvulus
GDV .... General Development Corp. (SAUO)
GDV .... Geomagnetic Daily Variations
GDV .... Glendive [*Montana*] [*Airport symbol*] (OAG)
GDV .... Graphic Deflection Vector (SAUS)
GdVP .... Grossdeutsche Volkspartei [*Pan-German People's Party*] [*Austria*] [*Political party*] (PPE)
GDVS .... Greater Delaware Valley Savings Bank [*NASDAQ symbol*] (SAG)
GDVS .... Greater Del Valley Svgs [*NASDAQ symbol*] (TTSB)
GDW .... General Direction of Workshops (SAUO)
GDW .... Gladwin, MI [*Location identifier*] [*FAA*] (FAAL)
GDW .... Glass-Distilled Water [*Medicine*] (DMAA)
GDW .... Golden West Financial Corp. [*NYSE symbol*] (SPSG)
GDW .... Golden West Finl [*NYSE symbol*] (TTSB)
GDW .... Goldwest Resources Ltd. [*Vancouver Stock Exchange symbol*]
GDW .... Grin, Duck and Weave (SAUS)
GDWDA .... Glaciological Data. World Data Center A (journ.) (SAUS)
GDWDCA .... Glaciol Data World Data Center A (journ.) (SAUS)
GDWND .... Gradient Wind (NOAA)
GDX .... Gated-Diode Crosspoint [*Electronics*] (PDAA)
GDX .... General Data Expansion [*Computer science*] (HODG)
GDX .... Genovese Drug Stores, Inc. [*AMEX symbol*] (SPSG)
GDX .... Glycidydiisopropylidenexylitol [*Organic chemistry*]
GDX .... Goldstone, California [*Spaceflight Tracking and Data Network*] [*NASA*]
GDX .... Grandex Resources Ltd. [*Vancouver Stock Exchange symbol*]
GDX .... Gun Direction Exercise [*British military*] (DMA)
GDX .... Upperville, VA [*Location identifier*] [*FAA*] (FAAL)
GDXA .... Genovese Drug Str'A' [*AMEX symbol*] (TTSB)
GDxCI .... German Dx-Club International (SAUO)
GDXM .... Goldex Mines Ltd. (SAUO)
GDXY .... Gonadal Dysgenesis [*Medicine*] (EDAA)
GDY .... Grundy, VA [*Location identifier*] [*FAA*] (FAAL)
GdyFam .... Goody's Family Clothing [*Associated Press*] (SAG)
GDYL .... Great Dictionary of the Yiddish Language [*Columbia University Department of Linguistics*] [*Information service or system*] (IID)
GDYN .... Geodynamics Corp. [*NASDAQ symbol*] (NQ)
GDYS .... Goody's Family Clothing [*NASDAQ symbol*] (SPSG)
GE .... Ecological Generation (France) [*Political party*] (PSAP)
GE .... Federal Republic of Germany [*NATO*]
GE .... Gaensslen-Erb [*Syndrome*] [*Medicine*] (DB)
GE .... Gainfully Employed [*Medicine*] (EDAA)
GE .... Gamma-Endorphin (DB)

GE .... Gamson Engineer (SAUS)
GE .... Garnson Engineer (SAUS)
GE .... Garrison Engineer [*British military*] (DMA)
GE .... Garrison Extracts [*Army*]
GE .... Gas Ejection [*Opening*] [*Technical drawings*]
GE .... Gas Engine (SAUS)
GE .... Gas Engineer (SAUS)
GE .... Gas Engineering (SAUS)
GE .... Gas Examiner [*British*]
GE .... Gasoline Engine (SAUS)
GE .... Gastric Emptying [*Medicine*] (DB)
GE .... Gastroemotional [*Medicine*] (MAE)
GE .... Gastroenteritis [*Medicine*] (DB)
GE .... Gastroenterology [*Medicine*]
GE .... Gastroenterostomy [*Medicine*]
GE .... Gastroesophageal [*Medicine*] (CPH)
GE .... Gateway Exchange [*Telecommunications*]
GE .... Gauge
GE .... Gaussian Elimination (IEEE)
Ge .... Gecelinus [*Zenzelinus de Cassanis*] [*Deceased, 1334*] [*Authority cited in pre-1607 legal work*] (DSA)
GE .... Geek of Engineering (SAUO)
GE .... Gel Electrophoresis [*Analytical chemistry*]
GE .... Gelundic [*Soil biology*] (QSUL)
GE .... Gender Equity (FOTI)
GE .... General Eastern (SAUS)
GE .... General Education (SAUS)
GE .... General Election
GE .... General Electric (NITA)
GE .... General Electric Co. [*NYSE symbol*] (SPSG)
GE .... General Electric Corp. (SAUO)
GE .... General Electric Vallecitos Nuclear Center (DOGT)
GE .... General Electronic (SAUS)
GE .... General Emergency (COE)
GE .... General Engineer (ACAE)
GE .... General Engineering (SAUS)
GE .... General Examination
GE .... General Expenses
GE .... Generalized Epilepsy [*Medicine*] (EDAA)
GE .... Generator of Excitation [*Medicine*] (DMAA)
GE .... Generic Element (SAUS)
GE .... Genetically Engineered (FOTI)
GE .... Genetic Engineer (SAUS)
GE .... Gentamicin [*Antibacterial compound*] [*Generic form*]
GE .... Geographic equivalent (SAUS)
GE .... Geological Engineer (SAUS)
GE .... Geological Engineering (SAUS)
GE .... Georgia [*Internet country code*]
GE .... Geoscience Electronics (MCD)
GE .... Geothermal Engineer (SAUS)
GE .... Geothermal Engineering (SAUS)
Ge .... Gerbich [*Red cell antigen*] (STED)
Ge .... German (SAUS)
GE .... German Cargo Services (SAUS)
Ge .... Germanium [*Chemical element*]
GE .... Germaniunm (SAUS)
Ge .... Germany (MILB)
GE .... Germany (NATG)
ge .... Germany, East [*MARC country of publication code*] [*Library of Congress*] (LCCP)
GE .... Gigabit Ethernet (SAUS)
GE .... Gilbert Islands [*ANSI two-letter standard code*] [*Obsolete*] (CNC)
ge .... Gild Edged (SAUS)
GE .... [*The*] Gilgamesh Epic and Old Testament Parallels [*A publication*] (BJA)
GE .... Gilgamesh Epic and Old Testament Parallels (journ.) (SAUS)
ge .... Gilt-Edge (WDMC)
GE .... Gilt Edges [*Bookbinding*]
GE .... Gimbal Electronics
GE .... glacio-eustatic (SAUS)
GE .... Glandular Epithelium [*Medicine*] (EDAA)
GE .... Glass Electrode (SAUS)
GE .... Global Engagement (SEWL)
GE .... Global Relation Object (SAUS)
GE .... Gnome Engine [*Hovercraft*]
GE .... Good Evening [*Amateur radio*]
GE .... Gradient-Enhanced (SAUS)
GE .... Graduate Engineer (SAUS)
GE .... Grand Earl [*Freemasonry*] (ROG)
GE .... Grand East [*Freemasonry*] (ROG)
GE .... Grand Encampment [*Freemasonry*]
GE .... Grand Expert [*Freemasonry*] (ROG)
GE .... Grand Ezra [*Freemasonry*] (ROG)
G/E .... Granulocyte-Erythroid (Ratio) [*Hematology*]
GE .... Graphic Escape [*Computer science*] (DCDG)
G/E .... Graphite Epoxy (NASA)
GE .... Gravissimam Educationis [*Declaration on Christian Education*] [*Vatican II document*]
G-E .... Gravity Eliminated (DAVI)
GE .... Great Educators [*A publication*]
GE .... Greater than or Equal To [*FORTRAN*]
GE .... Great Exuma [*Bahama Islands*]
GE .... Gripper Edge [*Bookbinding*] (DGA)
GE .... Gross Earnings [*Business term*]
GE .... Gross Energy (SAUS)
GE .... Grounded Emitter
GE .... Ground Environment (ACAE)
GE .... Ground Equipment
GE .... Group Engineer
GE .... Group Equipment (SAUO)
GE .... Group of Experts (NATG)
GE .... Gsell-Erdheim [*Syndrome*] [*Medicine*] (DB)
GE .... Guanidoethyl (SAUS)
GE .... Guernsey Airlines [*ICAO designator*] (AD)
GE .... Gyro Error
GE .... Gyroscope Error (SAUS)
GE .... Greatest Elongation [*Astronomy*] (ODA)
GEOS .... Geoscope (SAUS)
GEA .... Farbenfabriken Bayer [*Germany*] [*Research code symbol*]
GEA .... Gale Environmental Almanac [*A publication*]
GEA .... Gamma Energy Analysis [*Nuclear energy*] (NUCP)
GEA .... Garage Equipment Association (EAIO)
GEA .... Gas Evolution Analysis (DICI)
GEA .... Gastric Electrical Activity [*Medicine*] (DMAA)
GEA .... General Electric-ARSD, Sunnyvale, CA [*OCLC symbol*] (OCLC)
GEA .... Georgia Air [*Czechoslovakia*] [*ICAO designator*] (FAAC)
GEA .... Georgia Air Freight (SAUS)
GEA .... Geothermal Energy Association (NTPA)
GEA .... Germana Esperanto-Asocio (SAUO)
GEA .... German East Africa [*Obsolete*] (ROG)
GEA .... Ghana Employers Association (SAUO)
GEA .... Gigabit Ethernet Alliance [*Telecommunications*] (ACRL)
GEA .... Global Education Associates (EA)
GEA .... Glossary of EPA [*Environmental Protection Agency*] Acronyms [*A publication*] (EPA)
GEA .... Gravure Engravers Association (EA)
GEA .... Greater East Asia [*Used by Japanese in such terms as War of Greater East Asia and Greater East Asia Co-Prosperity Sphere*] [*World War II*]
GEA .... Greater Ecosystem Alliance (EA)
GEA .... Greek Electrotechnical Association (SAUO)
GEA .... Gross External Area
GEA .... Group on Educational Affairs (SAUO)
GEA .... Grupo de Economistas y Asociados [*Provides economic analysis in Mexico and abroad*] (CROSS)
GEA .... Noumea [*New Caledonia*] Magenta Airport [*Airport symbol*] (OAG)
GEAAE .... Groupement Europeen des Artistes des Ardennes et de l'Eifel [*European Group of Artists of the Ardennes and the Eifel*] (EAIO)
Gea Appl Entomol... General and Applied Entomology (journ.) (SAUS)
GEAB .... Geophysical Abstracts [*A publication*]
GEAC .... Dutch computer supplier of GLIS (SAUS)
GEACS .... Great East Asia Coprosperity Sphere (SAUO)
GEADGE .... German Air Defence (or Defense) Ground Environment (SAUO)
GEADGE .... German Air Defense Ground Environment
GEAE .... GE Aircraft Engines
GEAE .... General Electric Aircraft Engines (SAUS)
GEAEGIS .... German Airborne Environment (SAUS)
GEAEGIS .... Ground Integration System (SAUS)
Geaet Princ Perspect... Genetics, Principles and Perspectives (journ.) (SAUS)
GEAG .... Gastroepiploic Artery Graft [*Medicine*] (MELL)
GEAG .... General Electric Airborne Guidance (AAG)
GEAM .... Gale Encyclopedia of Alternative Medicine [*A publication*]
GE AMERICOM... GE American Communications Inc. (SAUS)
GEAMR .... Groupement Europeen des Associations des Maisons de Reforme [*EC*] (ECED)
GE&D .... General Engineering and Development (SAUO)
GE & JR .... Great Eastern & Joint Railway [*British*] (ROG)
GE-ANPD .... General Electric Aircraft Nuclear Propulsion Department (SAA)
GE-ANPD .... General Electric Aircraft Nuclear Propulsion Development (SAUS)
G E A N S .... Gimbaled Electrostatic Gyro Aircraft Navigation System (SAUS)
GEANS .... Gimbaled Electrostatic-Gyro Aircraft Navigation System [*Air Force*]
GEANS .... Gimbaled ESG Aircraft Navigation System (SAUS)
GEANS .... Gimballed Electrostatic Airborne (SAUS)
GEANS .... Gimballed Electrostatic Aircraft Navigation System (SAUS)
GEaO .... Ocmulgee Regional Library System, Eastman, GA [*Library symbol*] [*Library of Congress*] (LCLS)
GEAOS .... Grain Elevator and Processing Society (SAUO)
GEAP .... General Electric Atomic Power [*or Products*]
GEAP .... General Electric Atomic Products (SAUS)
GEAP .... Groupe Europeen d'Administration Publique [*European Group of Public Administration - EGPA*] [*Brussels, Belgium*] (EAIO)
GE-APO .... General Electric-Advanced Products Operation (SAUS)
GE-APO .... General Electric Company, Advanced Products Operation (SAUO)
GEAPS .... Grain Elevator and Processing Society (EA)
gear .... gearing (SAUS)
GEAR .... Geometric External Amplification Ratio (SAUO)
GEAR .... Get Excited about Reading
GEAR .... Glasgow Eastern Area Renewal (SAUO)
GEAR .... Great Eastern Australian Rally [*Cycling*]
GEAR .... Growth, Employment & Redistribution [*Economic program*] [*South Africa*]
GEARA .... Georgia Agricultural Research (journ.) (SAUS)
Gear Landl & T... Gear on Landlord and Tenant [*A publication*] (DLA)
Gear Landl&T... Gear on landlord and Tenant (journ.) (SAUS)
GEARS .... Global Entomology Agricultural Research Server (SAUO)
GEAR UP .... Gaining Early Awareness and Readiness for Undergraduate Programs [*U.S. Department of Education*]
GEASCOP .... General Asymptotic Composition Program [*Computer science*]
GE/ASD .... General Electric/Apollo Support Division (KSC)
GEASO .... General Electric Aviation Service Operation (SAUS)

GEATP .... Group of Experts on Air Transport Policies (SAUO)
GEAU .... Groupe d'Etudes et d'Actions Urbaines [*Canada*]
GEAV .... Guidance Error Analysis Vehicles [*Air Force*]
GEAX .... Trinity Rail Management [*Private rail car owner code*]
GEB .... Geboren [*Born*] [*German*]
GEB .... Gebrueder [*Brothers*] [*German*]
GEB .... Gebunden [*Bound*] [*Publishing*] [*German*]
GEB .... General Education Board (SAUO)
GEB .... General Engine Bulletin
GEB .... General Executive Board (SAUO)
GEB .... Genetronics Biomedical [*Toronto Stock Exchange symbol*] (SG)
GEB .... Gerber Products (SAUS)
GEB .... Gerber Products Co. (SAUO)
GEB .... Grain Elevators Board (SAUO)
GEB .... Gross Expenditure Base (FOTI)
GEB .... Guiding Eyes for the Blind (EA)
GEBA .... Global Energy Balance Archive [*A publication*]
GEBA .... Government Excess Baggage Authorization
GEBCO .... General Bathymetric Chart of the Oceans [*International Hydrographic Bureau*]
GEBEP .... Generalized Equipment Beliability Evaluation Procedure (SAUS)
GEBOS .... Generalized Exploratory Base Operations (ACAE)
GEBPA .... Gale Encyclopedia of Business and Professional Associations [*A publication*]
GEC .... European Group of Curietherapy (SAUO)
GEC .... Galactose Elimination Capacity
GEC .... Gaseous Electronics Conference
GEC .... Geauga County Public Library, Chardon, OH [*OCLC symbol*] (OCLC)
GEC .... GEICO Corp. [*NYSE symbol*] (SPSG)
GEC .... GEICO Corporation (SAUO)
GEC .... General Electric Capital Exchange [*Associated Press*] (SAG)
GEC .... General Electric Co.
GEC .... General Electric Company (SAUS)
GEC .... General Electric Company Ltd. (SAUO)
GEC .... General Electric Corporation (SAUO)
GEC .... General Electrodynamics Company (SAUO)
GEC .... General Electrodynamics Corp. (MCD)
GEC .... General Electronic Company (SAUO)
GEC .... General Equipment Command [*Army*]
GEC .... Generalized Equivalent Cylinder (OA)
GEC .... Genetics Education Center
GEC .... Geneva Executive Centre (SAUS)
GEC .... Geneva Executives Club (EA)
GEC .... Georgia Electrification Council (SAUO)
GEC .... German Cargo Services [*ICAO designator*] (FAAC)
GEC .... Global Environmental Change [*Marine science*] (OSRA)
GEC .... Glomerular Epithelial Cell [*Medicine*] [*Medicine*] (DMAA)
GEC .... Government Employees Council [*Later, PED*] (EA)
GEC .... Graphic Export Center [*Netherlands*]
GEC .... Graphite Epoxy Composite (SAUS)
GEC .... Grolier Educational Corp. (AEBS)
GEC .... Ground Environment Complex (MCD)
GEC .... Guyana Electricity Corp.
GEC .... Lufthansa Cargo, AG [*Germany*] [*FAA designator*] (FAAC)
GECA .... Government Employees' Compensation Act [*1908*]
GEC-AEL ...... General Electric Company - Applied Electronics Laboratories (SAUS)
GEC-AEL ...... General Electric Company-Applied Electronics Laboratories (or Laboratory) (SAUO)
GECAL .... General Electric Caliber [*Gatling Gun*]
GECAL .... General Electric Credit Auto Lease, Inc.
GECC .... Gasoline Engine, Close-Coupled
GECC .... General Electric Capital Corp.
GECC .... General Electric Credit Corp. (SAUS)
GECC .... General Electric Credit Corporated (SAUS)
GECC .... General Electric Credit Corporation (SAUO)
GECC .... Golf Entertainment [*NASDAQ symbol*] (SG)
GECC .... Government Employees Clinic Center [*British*]
GECCAP .... General Election Coordinating Committee for Animal Protection (SAUO)
GECCMSEF... Group to Establish Criteria for Certifying Munitions Systems to Electromagnetic Fields [*DoD*] (RDA)
GECCS .... General Electric Company Computer Services [*British*] (NITA)
GECE .... Groupement Europeen des Caisses d'Epargne [*European Savings Bank Group*] [*EC*] (ECED)
GECECS .... General Electric Chemical Engineering Calculation System
Gecel .... Gecelinus [*Zenzelinus de Cassanis*] [*Deceased, 1334*] [*Authority cited in pre-1607 legal work*] (DSA)
GE-Cellulose... Guanidino-Ethyl-Cellulose (SAUS)
GECEP .... General Civil Engineering Package (IAA)
GECHB .... Geochemistry (journ.) (SAUS)
GECHD .... Geochronique (journ.) (SAUS)
GECHS .... Global Environmental Change and Human Security (SAUS)
GECIS .... General Electric Co. Information Systems (SAUO)
GECLO .... German Civil Labour Organization (SAUO)
GECM .... GENICOM Corp. [*NASDAQ symbol*] (NQ)
GECO .... General Aero Products Corporation (SAUO)
GECO .... General Electric Company Ltd. (SAUO)
GECO .... Geophysical Company of Norway (SAUO)
GECO .... Guidance Engine Cutoff [*NASA*] (KSC)
GECOM .... General Compiler (NITA)
GECOM .... General Electric Compiler (SAUS)
GECOM .... Generalized Compiler [*Computer science*]
GECOM .... Generalized Computer (SAUS)
GECOMIN..... General Congolese Ore Company (SAUO)
GECOR .... General Communication Routine (IAA)
GECOS .... General Comprehensive Operating Supervisor [*Computer science*]
GECOS .... General Comprehensive Operating System
GECOS .... General Electric Comprehensive Operating Supervisor (SAUO)
GECOS .... General Electric Comprehensive Operating Supervisory System (SAUS)
GECOS .... General Electric Comprehensive Operating System [*Computer science*] (NHD)
GECOS System... General Electric Comprehensive Operating Supervisory System (SAUS)
GECOT .... Group of Experts on Costs and Tariffs (SAUO)
GECP .... Global Environmental Change Programme (SAUO)
GECR .... Global Environmental Change Report (SAUS)
GECR .... Global Environment Change Report (EERA)
GECRD .... General Electric Corporate Research and Development (SAUS)
GECREF .... Geographic Reference (SAUS)
GECRL .... General Electric Corporation Research Laboratories (SAUO)
GECS .... Gemini Environmental Control System (SAUO)
GECS .... Geostationary Earth Climate Sensor (SAUO)
GECS .... Gold Exchange Currency System (SAUO)
GECS .... Graphite-Epoxy Composite Structure (PDAA)
GECS .... Ground Environmental Control System (IAA)
GEC Telecommun... GEC Telecommunications (journ.) (SAUS)
GECX .... Gulf Exploration Consultants, Inc. (SAUO)
GED .... Gasoline Engine Driven
GED .... Gas-Phase Electron Diffraction [*Physics*]
Ged .... Gedaagde [*Defendant*] [*Netherlands*] (ILCA)
GED .... Gedampft [*Muted*] [*Music*]
GED .... Gedeh [*Java*] [*Seismograph station code, US Geological Survey*] [*Closed*] (SEIS)
GED .... Genelal Equivalency Diploma (SAUS)
GED .... General Educational Development [*Test*]
GED .... General Education Degree (DIPS)
GED .... General Education Development (SAUS)
GED .... General Education Diploma (AGLO)
GED .... General Energy Development Ltd. (SAUO)
GED .... General Equivalency Diploma [*For nongraduates*]
GED .... Generic Expendable Decoy (ACAE)
GED .... Genetically Engineered Drug (MELL)
GED .... Geo-Data International [*Vancouver Stock Exchange symbol*]
GED .... Georgetown [*Delaware*] [*Airport symbol*] (AD)
GED .... Georgetown, DE [*Location identifier*] [*FAA*] (FAAL)
GED .... Global Ecosystem Dynamics (SAUS)
GED .... Global Engineering Documents [*Santa Ana, CA*] [*Information service or system*]
GED .... Gluten-Free Diet (DB)
GED .... Government Electronics Division
GED .... Graduate Equivalency Degree (SAUS)
GED .... Graduate Equivalency Diploma (SAUS)
GED .... Great Energy Debate (SAUO)
GED .... Gross Earnings Deflator [*Economics*] (BARN)
GED .... Ground Environmental Development (SAUS)
GED .... Group on Electronic Devices
GED .... Guanidoethyl Disulfide (SAUS)
GED .... Gunn Effect Device
GEDA .... General Education Development Agency (SAUO)
GEDA .... GNU Electronic Design Automation (SAUS)
GEDA .... Goldfields Esperance Development Authority [*Australia*]
GEDA .... Goodyear Electronic Differential Analyzer (IAA)
GEDAC .... General Electric Detection and Automatic Correction (NASA)
GEDAG .... German Decartelization Agency (SAUO)
GEDAN .... General Data Analyzer (IAA)
GEDC .... Ghanaian Enterprices Development Commission (SAUS)
GEDCOM ...... Genealogical Data Communications [*Computer science*]
GEDD .... Gunn-Effect Digital Device (SAUS)
GEDEC .... German Decartelization Commission (SAUO)
GEDED .... General Dentistry (journ.) (SAUS)
GEDEMON.... Geometrics, Derivatives, Moments and Noise (SAUS)
GEDEX .... Greenhouse Effect Detection Experiment (EOSA)
GED-GB .... Gulf Ecology Division-Gulf Breeze [*Environmental Protection Agency*] (AEPA)
GEDI .... General Educational Development Institute (EA)
GEDI .... Groupe d'Etudes en Developpement International [*International Development Studies Group*] [*Canada*]
GEDI .... Group of/on Electronic Document Interchange (SAUO)
GEDI .... Guided Electromagnetic Defensive Interceptor (SAUS)
GEDID2 .... Gerbil Digest (journ.) (SAUS)
GEDIS .... Geological, Exploration and Development Information System [*Australia*]
GEDIS .... Groupement Europeen des Enterprises de Distribution Integrees [*European Multiple Retailers Association*] [*Belgium*] [*EC*] (ECED)
GEDIT .... General-Purpose Text Editor [*Computer science*] (MHDB)
GEDITS .... Edit/Update Program (SAUO)
GEDL .... General Electric Data Link (SAUS)
GEdO .... Group Education Officer [*British military*] (DMA)
GEDP .... General Educational Development Program [*Army*] (AABC)
GEDP .... General Education Development Program (SAUO)
GEDP .... Global Ecosystems Database Project (SAUO)
GEDPD .... Gallaudet Encyclopedia of Deaf People and Deafness [*A publication*]
GEDRT .... Group European d'Echange d'Experience sur la Direction de la Recherche Textil e [*European Group for the Exchange of Information on Textile Research*] (PDAA)
GEDS .... Gaseous Emissions Data System [*Environmental Protection Agency*] (GFGA)
GEDS .... Gaseous Emissons Data System (SAUS)
GEDS .... General Environmental Data Base System (SAUS)

GEDS .... Global Engineering Documentation Services, Incorporated (SAUO)
GEDT .... General Educational Development Test
GED Test ..... General Educational Development Test (SAUS)
GEDU .... Gun Elevation Displacement Unit (DNAB)
GEDY .... Genetic Dynamics Corp. (SAUO)
GEE .... Geehi [*Australia*] [*Seismograph station code, US Geological Survey*] [*Closed*] (SEIS)
GEE .... Geeseair [*Canada*] [*ICAO designator*] (FAAC)
GEE .... General Education in Engineering (SAUS)
GEE .... General Estimating Equation [*Mathematics*]
GEE .... General Evaluation Equipment
GEE .... Generalized Estimating Equation (DMAA)
GEE .... Generic Environmental Evaluation (SAUS)
GEE .... Geneseo (SAUS)
GEE .... Geneseo, NY [*Location identifier*] [*FAA*] (FAAL)
GEE .... Geoelectric Effect (SAUS)
GEE .... Glycine Ethyl Ester (MAE)
GEE .... Gross Ecosystem Exchange [*Biology*]
GEE .... Ground Electronics Engineering (ACAE)
GEE .... Ground Environment Equipment (SAUS)
GEE .... Ground Exploration System (SAUS)
GEE .... Group for Environmental Education
GEE .... Group of Economic Experts (EERA)
GEE .... Grupo de Edukistoj Esperantistaj (SAUO)
GEEAS .... Geostatistical Environmental Exposure Assessment Software (SAUO)
GEEB .... Geerlings & Wade [*NASDAQ symbol*] (TTSB)
GE economic forecasts... General Economic Forecasts [*Databank*] (NITA)
G E E D A.... Groundnut Extractions Export Development Association (SAUO)
GEEI .... General Electric Electronic Installation (SAUS)
GEEI .... General Electric Electronic Instaltation (SAUS)
GEEIA .... General Electronics Engineering Installation (SAUS)
GEEIA .... General Electronics Engineering Installation Agency (SAUS)
GEEIA .... Ground Electronics Engineering Installation Agency [*Air Force*]
GEEK .... Geomagnetic Electrokinetograph [*Equipment for exploring ocean depths*]
GEEK .... Internet America, Inc. [*NASDAQ symbol*] (NASQ)
GEEL .... General Election Expenditure Limit [*Federal Election Commission*]
GEEL .... General Electric experimental loop (SAUS)
GEEN .... Genetic Engineering, Inc. (SAUO)
GEENET .... Global Environment Epidemiology Network (ADWA)
GE ENG .... Geological Engineer (WDAA)
Ge Engr .... Geological Engineer
GEEP .... General Electric Electronic Evaluator (SAUS)
GEEP .... General Electric Electronic Processor
GEEP .... Group of Experts on Effects of Pollutants (SAUO)
GEEP .... Group of Experts on Environmental Pollutants (EERA)
GEER .... Geerlings & Wade, Inc. [*NASDAQ symbol*] (SAG)
GeerlWd .... Geerlings & Wade, Inc. [*Associated Press*] (SAG)
GEESE .... General Electric Electronic System Evaluation (SAUS)
GEESE .... General Electric Electronic System Evaluator
GEF .... Air GEFCO [*France*] [*ICAO designator*] (FAAC)
GEF .... Gas Evaporation Experiment Facility (SAUS)
GEF .... Gastroesophageal Fundoplication [*Medicine*] (EDAA)
GEF .... Gauss Error Function [*Mathematics*]
GEF .... Gel Electrofocusing [*Analytical chemistry*]
GEF .... General Electric Co. and Fanuc Automation Corp.
GEF .... Global Environment Facility [*Implemented jointly by the World Bank, the United Nations Environment Program, and the United Nations Development Program*]
GEF .... Global Environment Fund [*of the World Bank*] (EERA)
GEF .... Glossoepiglottic Fold (STED)
GEF .... Glycosylation-Enhancing Factor (QSUL)
GEF .... Gonadotropin Enhancing Factor [*Endocrinology*]
GEF .... Gradient Elution Fractionation
GEF .... Granule, Effervescent (SAUS)
GEF .... Gravure Education Foundation (EA)
GEF .... Greenville, FL [*Location identifier*] [*FAA*] (FAAL)
GEF .... Ground Equipment Failure [*Air Force*]
GEF .... Guanine-Nucleotide-Exchange Factor [*Biochemistry*]
GEF .... Guanine-Nucleoxide Exchange Factor [*Biochemistry*]
GEF .... Nicholas-Applegate Group (SAUS)
GEFA .... Gulf-European Freight Association [*Defunct*] (EA)
GEFACS .... Groupement des Fabricants d'Appariels Sanitaires en Ceramique de la CEE [*Group of Manufacturers of Ceramic Sanitary Ware of the European Economic Community*] (PDAA)
GEFAP .... Groupement Europeen des Associations Nationales des Fabricants de Pesticides [*European Group of National Pesticide Manufacturer' Associations*] [*Common Market*]
GE-FBRD .... General Electric Fast Breeder Reactor Division (SAUO)
GE-FBRD .... General Electric-Fast Breeder Reactor Division (SAUS)
GEFD .... Geographical Engineering Field Division (SAUO)
GEFD .... Geophysical and Environmental Fluid Dynamics
GEFDU .... Groupe Europeen des Femmes Diplomees des Universites [*University Women of Europe - UWE*] (EA)
GEFFEN .... Gay Extremists Fighting Fascistic Entertainment Normalcy [*Focus group of Queer Nation*]
GEFO .... General Electric follow on (SAUS)
GEFO .... Geoforum (journ.) (SAUS)
GEFOAMS .... General Electric Foams Optimized through Analysis and Materials Selection (SAUS)
GEFP .... Guild of Ethical Funeral Practice (EA)
GEFR .... George Eliot Fellowship Review (journ.) (SAUS)
GEFRC .... General File/Record Control [*Honeywell, Inc.*]
GEFS .... General Electric Financial Services [*Australia*] [*Commercial firm*]
GEFS .... General Electric Flame Site (MUGU)
GEFSE .... General Electric Electronic System Evaluator (SAUS)
GEFT .... Group Embedded Figure Test [*Education*]
GEF/UNDP ... Global Environment Facility/ UNDP as the Implementing Agencie (SAUO)
GEF/UNDP ... Global Environment Facility/UNDP as the Implementing Agency (SAUS)
GEG .... Gamma Eta Gamma [*Fraternity*]
GEG .... Gegechkori [*Former USSR*] [*Seismograph station code, US Geological Survey*] [*Closed*] (SEIS)
GEG .... General Euclidian Geometry (SAUS)
GEG .... Generalized Euclidian Geometry (OA)
GEG .... Geotechnical Engineering Groups (SAUO)
GEG .... Grace Energy Corp. (EFIS)
GEG .... Grange Gold Corp. [*Vancouver Stock Exchange symbol*]
GEG .... Gravure Engraving Group [*British*] (DBA)
GEG .... Groundwater and Environmental Geology (SAUO)
GEG .... Gun Evaluation Group [*Military*] (CAAL)
GEG .... Spokane [*Washington*] [*Airport symbol*] (OAG)
GEGAS .... General Electric Gas [*Process*]
GEGB .... General Electricity-Generating Board (OA)
GEGG .... Geological Enginneering Geology and Geophysics (SAUO)
GEGID .... Global Spill Mgmt [*NASDAQ symbol*] (TTSB)
GE/GLOSS .... Group of Experts on Global Sea-Level Observing System (SAUO)
GE-GLOSS ... Group of Experts on the Global Sea-Level Observing System [*Marine science*] (OSRA)
GE-GLOSS ... IOC Group of Experts on the Global Sea-Level Observing System (SAUS)
GEGP .... Golden Eagle Group [*NASDAQ symbol*] (TTSB)
GEGP .... Golden Eagle Group, Inc. [*NASDAQ symbol*] (SAG)
GEGPW .... Golden Eagle Group Wrrt [*NASDAQ symbol*] (TTSB)
GEGR .... General Grant National Memorial
GEGS .... General Electric Guidance System [*Aerospace*] (AAG)
Geh .... Gehalt [*Contents*] [*German*] (ILCA)
Geh .... Geheimrat [*Privy Councillor*] [*German*] (ILCA)
GEH .... George Eastman House [*Rochester, NY*]
GEH .... Glycerol Ester Hydrolase (DB)
GEHA .... Government Employees Housing Accommodation (SAUO)
GEHA .... Government Employees Housing Authority (SAUO)
GE-HAPO ..... General Electric Company, Hanford Atomic Products Operation (SAUO)
GE-HAPO ..... General Electric Hanford Atomic Products Operation (SAA)
GEHB .... Genessee Brewing Company, Inc. (SAUO)
GEHL .... Gehl Co. [*NASDAQ symbol*] (NQ)
GEHME .... General Electric Heavy Military Electronics (IAA)
GEHP .... George Eastman House of Photography (SAUO)
GEHP .... Global Ecology Honors Program (SAUO)
GEHS .... Gamma Energy Analysis System (SAUS)
GEI .... Geisinger Medical Center, Medical Library, Danville, PA [*OCLC symbol*] (OCLC)
GEI .... Gender Equality Indicator [*Australia*]
GEI .... General Electric Information Serices Proprietary Limited (SAUS)
GEI .... Geographic Enforcement Initiative [*Environmental Protection Agency*] (EPA)
GEI .... Geotechnical Engineers, Inc. (EFIS)
GEI .... Graphics Engine Interface [*Computer science*]
GEI .... Graymoor Ecumenical Institute (EA)
GEI .... Grenlock Energy, Inc. [*Vancouver Stock Exchange symbol*]
GEI .... Gruppo Esponenti Italiani (EA)
GEIA .... Generic Environmental Impact Assessment (SAUS)
GEIA .... Global Emissions Inventory Activity (SAUO)
GEIA .... Ground Equipment Electronics Installations Agency (SAUS)
GEIAC .... Georgia Division, Lockheed Aircraft Corporation (SAUO)
GEIAO .... German Export-Import Advisory Office (SAUO)
GEIAO .... German Export-Import Asvisory Office (SAUS)
Geibank .... Government Employees Industrial Bank (SAUO)
GEIC .... Gilbert and Ellice Islands Colony (SAUS)
GEICO .... GEICO Corp. [*Associated Press*] (SAG)
GEICO .... Government Employees Insurance Co.
GEICO .... Government Employees Insurance Corp. (SAUS)
GEIDC .... Greater Erie Industrial Development Corp. [*Pennsylvania*]
Geiger .... Geiger-Muller Counter (SAUS)
GEII .... Graymoor Ecumenical and Interreligious Institute (EA)
GEII .... Great Eastern International, Incorporated (SAUO)
GEIL .... Greenfield Industries [*NASDAQ symbol*] (TTSB)
GEIMS .... General Electric Inventory Management System (IAA)
GEIN .... German Environmental Information Network (SAUO)
GEIP .... Greenhouse Education and Information Program (EERA)
GEIPS .... General Electric Industrial and Power Systems [*Australia*] [*Commercial firm*]
GEIR .... GPETE End Item Replacement (NVT)
GEIS .... GE [*General Electric Co.*] Information Services [*Information service or system*] (IID)
GEIS .... General Electric Information System (SAUS)
GEIS .... General Electric Inventory System (SAUO)
GEIS .... General Experiment Interface Specification (ACAE)
GEIS .... General Export Incentive Scheme (SAFN)
GEIS .... Generalized Environmental Impact Statement
GEIS .... Generic Environmental Impact Statement [*or Study*] [*Nuclear energy*] (NRCH)
GEIS .... Generic Environmental Impact Study (SAUS)
GEIS .... Guild Economic Information Service (SAUS)
GEISA .... Gestion et Etude des Informations Spectroscopiques Atmospheriques [*Database*] [*Laboratoire de Meteorologie Dynamique du CNRS*] [*French*] [*Information service or system*] (CRD)

GEISCO........ General Electric Information Services Co. [*General Electric Co.*] [*Software manufacturer*] [*Information service or system*] [*Telecommunications*] (IID)
GEISHA........ Geodetic Inertial Survey and Horizontal Alignment (IEEE)
GEISHA........ Gun Electron Induced Semiconductor Hybrid Amplifier (SAUS)
GEISHA........ Gun Electron-Induced Semiconductor Hybrid Amplifier
GEISI........ General Electric Information Systems Italy (SAUO)
GEIST........ German Encyclopedic Internet Service Terminal (SAUS)
GEIZ........ Geiger Industries [*Federal Railroad Administration identification code*]
GEJ........ Gaseous Ejection (KSC)
GEJ........ Gastroesophageal Junction [*Anatomy*] (DAVI)
GEJ........ Germana Esperanto-Junularo (SAUO)
GEJ........ Group of Experts on Jurisdiction (SAUO)
GEJO........ Geographical Journal (journ.) (SAUS)
GEJOBE........ Geochemical Journal (journ.) (SAUS)
GEJODG........ Geomicrobiology Journal (journ.) (SAUS)
GEK........ Ganes Creek, AK [*Location identifier*] [*FAA*] (FAAL)
GEK........ Geoelectrokinetograph (SAUS)
GEK........ Geomagnetic Electrokinetograph [*Equipment for exploring ocean depths*]
Gekap........ Gelatin-Coated Capsule (SAUS)
GE-KAPL........ General Electric Company, Knolls Atomic Power Laboratory (SAUO)
GE-KAPL........ General Electric-Knolls Atomic Power Laboratory (SAUS)
GEKTUSA........ Grand Encampment of the Knights Templar of the United States of America (SAUO)
GEL........ Gambcrest Enterprises Ltd. [*Gambia*] [*ICAO designator*] (FAAC)
gel........ Gelatin (ADWA)
GEL........ Gelatin
gel........ gelatine (SAUS)
GEL........ Gelco Corp. (SAUO)
gel........ gelding (SAUS)
GEL........ General Electric Laboratory
GEL........ General Electric Lighting [*Australia*] [*Commercial firm*]
GEL........ General Electric, Limited (SAUS)
GEL........ General Emulation Language
GEL........ General Engineering Laboratory (SAUO)
GEL........ General Export License (JAGO)
GEL........ Genesis Energy LP [*NYSE symbol*] (SAG)
GEL........ Geotechnical Engineering Laboratory (SAUS)
GEL........ Gilbert Islands [*ANSI three-letter standard code*] [*Obsolete*] (CNC)
GEL........ Golden Eagle Airlines (SAUS)
GEL........ Goldenlode Resources Ltd. [*Vancouver Stock Exchange symbol*]
GEL........ Great Eastern Line (SAUO)
GEL........ Groupement Europeen de Lymphologie [*European Lymphology Group - ELG*] [*Brussels, Belgium*] (EAIO)
GEL........ Guaranteed Employment Level
GEL........ Santo Angelo [*Brazil*] [*Airport symbol*] (OAG)
GELA........ Georgia Education Leadership Academy (SAUO)
GELAC........ Georgia Division, Lockheed Aircraft Corp.
Gel and Glue Res Assoc... Gelatin and Glue Research Association (journ.) (SAUS)
GELAP........ General Electric Computer Analysis Program
GELC........ Groupe des Editeurs de Livres de la CEE [*Book Publishers Group of EEC*] (EAIO)
Gelcap........ Gelatin-Coated Capsule [*Pharmacy*]
GELCINA........ German Evangelical Lutheran Conference in North America (EA)
GELCO........ General Electric Co. (EFIS)
Geld & M........ Geldart and Maddock's English Chancery Reports [*6 Maddock's Reports*] [*A publication*] (DLA)
Geld & O........ Nova Scotia Decisions, by Geldert and Oxley [*A publication*] (DLA)
Geld & Ox........ Nova Scotia Decisions, by Geldert and Oxley [*A publication*] (DLA)
Geld & R........ Geldert and Russell's Nova Scotia Reports [*A publication*] (DLA)
Geldart........ Geldart and Maddock's English Chancery Reports [*6 Maddock's Reports*] [*A publication*] (DLA)
GElektr........ Grupo Elektra SA de CV [*Associated Press*] (SAG)
GELFAC........ Gel Frontal Analysis Chromatography
GELIS........ Ground Emitter Location and Identification System [*Army*]
GELIS-H........ Ground Emitter Location and Identification System - High [*Army*]
GELME........ General Electric Light Military Electronics (IAA)
GELME........ Group of Experts on Large Marine Ecosystems (SAUO)
GELMS........ Gelman Sciences, Inc. (SAUO)
GelmSci........ Gelman Sciences, Inc. [*Associated Press*] (SAG)
GELNET........ Global Health and Environment Library Network (ADWA)
GELO........ Geographic Locator (SAUS)
GELOAD........ General Loader [*Honeywell*] (NITA)
GELOC........ Geolocation (DOMA)
GELOS........ G7 Global Environmental Information Locator Service (SAUO)
GEL QUAV... Gelatina Quavis [*In Any Kind of Jelly*] [*Pharmacy*] (ROG)
GelTex........ GelTex Pharmaceuticals, Inc. [*Associated Press*] (SAG)
GELTSPAP... Group of Experts on Long-Term Scientific Policy and Planning [*UNESCO*]
GELX........ GelTex Pharmaceuticals [*NASDAQ symbol*] (TTSB)
GELX........ GelTex Pharmaceuticals, Inc. [*NASDAQ symbol*] (SAG)
GEM........ Bristol BAE [*British*] [*ICAO designator*] (FAAC)
GEM........ Galileo Europa Mission (SAUO)
GEM........ Galileo Extended Mission
GEM........ Gamma-Electron-Muon [*Particle detector*]
GEM........ Gas Energy Management
GEM........ Gas Engine Management [*Alternative fuel conversion equipment*]
GEM........ Gas Equipment Manufacturers' Group (IIA)
GEM........ Gas Exchange Module [*Cell culture*]
GEM........ Gas expansion module (SAUS)
GEM........ Gateway to Educational Materials
Gem........ Gemara (BJA)
GEM........ Geminal (SAUS)
Gem........ Geminatae (BJA)
gem........ Geminate [*Chemistry*]
GEM........ Gemini (SHCU)
Gem........ Gemini [*Constellation*]
GEM........ Gemini Fund Inc. (SAUO)
GEM........ General Ecosystem Model (SAUO)
GEM........ General Education Model (SAUS)
GEM........ General Effectiveness Model (DNAB)
GEM........ General Electric Motors [*Australia*] [*Commercial firm*]
GEM........ General Electric Music (SAUO)
GEM........ General Electronics Module (SAUS)
GEM........ General Enrollment Manual
GEM........ General Epitacial Monolith (SAUS)
GEM........ General Epitaxial Monolith (IEEE)
GEM........ General Evaluation Model (SAUS)
GEM........ General Event Monitor (SAUS)
GEM........ General Experimental Monitor (SAUS)
GEM........ General Expression Manipulation (SAUS)
GEM........ Generalized Effectiveness Method (SAUS)
GEM........ Generalized Emulation Microcircuit (SAUO)
GEM........ Generalmusic (SAUS)
GEM........ Generic Electronic Module (SSD)
GEM........ Generic Entity Model (SAUS)
GEM........ Generic Equipment Model [*Electronics*] (AAEL)
GEM........ Generic Experiment Module
GEM........ Genetically Engineered Machine (ABAC)
GEM........ Genetically Engineered Microorganism
GEM........ Genetically Modified Organism
GeM........ Geograpbical Magazine (journ.) (SAUS)
GeM........ Geographical Magazine (journ.) (SAUS)
GEM........ Geospace Environment Modeling (CARB)
GEM........ Geospace Environment Modeling program (SAUS)
GEM........ Geostatistical Evaluation of Mines (SAUS)
gem........ Germanic [*MARC language code*] [*Library of Congress*] (LCCP)
GEM........ GeV Electron Microtron [*Atomic accelerator*] [*Proposed*]
GEM........ Giant Earth Mover [*Machine*]
GEM........ Gimbal Electronics Module (ACAE)
GEM........ Giotto Extended Mission [*European Space Agency*]
GEM........ Global Electric Motor Cars LLC (STAH)
GEM........ Global Electrodynamics Monitor (SAUO)
GEM........ Global Electronic Marketplace (GART)
GEM........ Global Enterprise Management (SAUO)
GEM........ Global Environmental Monitoring (FOTI)
GEM........ Goddard Earth Model [*NASA*]
GEM........ Governmental Energy and Minerals Committee (SAUS)
GEM........ Government Education and Medical (SAUS)
GEM........ Government Education and Mining (SAUO)
GEM........ Government-Education-Medical
GEM........ Government Electronics Market (IAA)
GEM........ Government Electronics Market (journ.) (SAUS)
GEM........ GPS Embedded Module (SAUS)
GEM........ Graduated [*or Growing*] Equity Mortgage
GEM........ Graff Electronic Machines Ltd. [*British*]
GEM........ Grafical Environment Manager (SAUS)
GEM........ Grand Eagle Mining (SAUO)
GEM........ Graphical Environment Manager (RALS)
GEM........ Graphic Engine Monitor (DA)
GEM........ Graphic Expression Machine (VLIE)
GEM........ Graphics Environment Manager [*Computer science*]
GEM........ Graphite Electrode Contouring Machine (PDAA)
GEM........ Graphite Epoxy Motor (MCD)
GEM........ Grey Entertainment & Media (EFIS)
GEM........ Ground Effect Machine (NG)
GEM........ Ground Electronics Maintenance
GEM........ Ground Elevation Meter (PDAA)
GEM........ Ground Exploitation Module
GEM........ Groupes Evangile et Mission [*Institute of the Heart of Jesus - IHJ*] [*France*] (EA)
GEM........ Growing Equity Mortgage [*Real estate*]
GEM........ Growth with Equity in Mindano [*A USAID backed organization*] [*Philippines*]
GEM........ Grupo Embotellador de Mexico [*NYSE symbol*] (SAG)
GEM........ Grupo Embotellador Mex GDS [*NYSE symbol*] (TTSB)
GEM........ Guild of Experienced Motorists [*British*] (DBA)
GEM........ Gulf Energy & Minerals Co.
GEM........ Gun Effectiveness Model
GEM........ Gunn Effect Material
GEM........ Gyro Energy & Minerals Corp. [*Vancouver Stock Exchange symbol*]
GEM........ Miami, FL [*Location identifier*] [*FAA*] (FAAL)
GEM........ National Consortium for Graduate Degrees for Minorities in Engineering (EA)
GEM........ Ventura/GEM drawing image format (SAUS)
GEM........ Guidance Evaluation Missile (ODA)
GEMA........ Gale Encyclopedia of Multicultural America [*A publication*]
GEMA........ General Electric Measurement and Control (SAUS)
GEMA........ Geographical Magazine (journ.) (SAUS)
GEMA........ Grain Equipment Manufacturers Association (EA)
GEMA........ Gymnastic Equipment Manufacturers' Association [*British*] (BI)
GE/MAC........ General Electric Measurement and Control
GEMAG........ General Electric Mobile Air Defense Gun (SAUS)
GEMAGS........ General Electric Magnetically Anchored Gravity System
GEMAN........ General Electric Miniature Aerospace Navigator (SAUS)
GEMAP........ General Electric Macro Assembly Program (SAUS)
GEMAP........ Geocoded Emissions Modeling and Projections (SAUS)

GEMAS .... Groupement Europeen des Maisons d'Alimentation et d'Approvisionnement a Succursales [*European Group of Food and Provision Chain Stores*] [*Common Market*] [*Brussels, Belgium*]
GEMBITS ..... Generic Electro-Mechanical Burn in Test System (VLIE)
GEmbMx ...... Grupo Embotellador de Mexico [*Associated Press*] (SAG)
GEMC .... Geriatric & Medical Centers, Inc. (SAUO)
GEMC .... Geriatric & Medical Companies [*NASDAQ symbol*] (NQ)
GEMC .... Geriatric & Medl Cos. [*NASDAQ symbol*] (TTSB)
GEMC .... Grain Equipment Manufacturers Council (SAUO)
GEMCO .... Gemco National, Inc. (SAUO)
GEMCO .... Global Electronic Markets Co. [*Joint venture of Citicorp and McGraw-Hill, In c. to provide computerized buying, selling, shipping, and insuring services for commodities traders*]
GEMCO .... Global Electronic Markets Company (SAUO)
GEMCO .... Grazing Export Meat Company (SAUO)
GEMCO .... Groote Eylandt Mining Co. [*Australia*] [*Commercial firm*]
GEMCO .... Groot Eylandt Mining Company (SAUO)
GEMCOS ...... Generalized Message Control System (BUR)
GEMCS .... General Engineering and Management Computation System (SAUO)
GEMD .... Ground Electronics Maintenance Division (SAUS)
GEMDES ...... Government Electronic Messaging and Document Exchange Service (VLIE)
GEMEC .... Chemical Comments of the General Metallurgical and Chemical Company (SAUO)
GEMEE2 .... Genitourinary Medicine (journ.) (SAUS)
GEMFET .... Gain-Enhanced MOSFET (SAUS)
GEMGA4 ...... Geological Magazine (journ.) (SAUS)
GEMH .... Gemcraft, Inc. (SAUO)
Gemi .... Gemini [*Constellation*]
Gemi .... Geminiano [*Flourished, 1407-09*] [*Authority cited in pre-1607 legal work*] (DSA)
GEMI .... Global Environmental Management Initiative [*Environmental science*]
GEMI .... Global Environmental Management Institute (LDOE)
GEMI .... Grating Efficiency Measurement Instrument (SAUS)
GemII .... Gemini II Fund, Inc. [*Associated Press*] (SAG)
GEMIM .... Group of Experts on Marine Information Management [*Marine science*] (OSRA)
GEMINI .... General Excitation Mechanisms in Nightglow (SAUO)
GEMINI .... Government Expert Systems Method Initiative (VLIE)
GEML .... Melilla [*Spain*] [*ICAO location identifier*] (ICLI)
G E M M ...... Generalized Electronic Maintenance Model (SAUS)
GEMM .... Generalized Electronics Maintenance Model
GEMM .... Generic Missile Model (MCD)
GEMM .... Gilt-Edged Market Maker [*London Stock Exchange*] [*England*]
GEMM .... Granulocyte, Erythroid, Macrophage, Megakaryocyte [*Hematology*]
GEMMA .... Gilt-Edged Market Makers' Association [*London Stock Exchange*] [*England*]
Gemmol Soc Jap J... Gemmological Society of Japan. Journal (journ.) (SAUS)
GEMMS .... Geophysical Exploration Manned Mobile Submersible
GEMMS .... Global Enterprise Manufacturing Management System (HODG)
GEMMSS ..... Ground Emplaced Mine Scattering System [*Military*] (RDA)
Gemntol Abstr... Gerontological Abstracts (journ.) (SAUS)
GEMO .... Ground Electronic Maintenance Officer [*NASA*] (NG)
GEMOS .... Generalized Message Control System (SAUS)
GEMP .... Government Energy Management Program [*Australia*]
GEMPAK ...... General Meteorology Package (SAUO)
GEMS .... Electronic Specialty Products, Inc. [*NASDAQ symbol*] (COMM)
GEMS .... Gamma Ray Environmental Mapping Spectrometer (SAUS)
GEMS .... Gender Equality in Mathematics and Science
GEMS .... General Education Management System [*Computer science*] (IEEE)
GEMS .... General Electrical and Mechanical System (SAUS)
GEMS .... General Electrical and Mechanical Systems (IAA)
GEMS .... General Electric Manufacturing Simulator (IEEE)
GEMS .... General Electric Medical Systems [*Australia*] [*Commercial firm*]
GEMS .... General Electric Multispectral Information System (SAUO)
GEMS .... General Energy and Materials Balance System [*Chemical engineering*] [*Computer science*]
GEMS .... General Engine Management System
GEMS .... General Equipment Maintenance System [*Software*] [*Diagonal Data Corp.*] [*Automotive engineering*]
GEMS .... Generalized Evaluation Model Simulator [*NASA*]
GEMS .... Generic Missile Simulation (SAUS)
GEMS .... Geographic Monitoring System (SAUO)
GEMS .... Geological Exploration and Mapping System (SAUO)
GEMS .... Geostationary European Meteorological Satellite
GEMS .... German Mass Spectrometer
GEMS .... Glass with Embedded Metal and Sulphide [*In interplanetary dust particles*]
GEMS .... Glenayre Technologies [*NASDAQ symbol*] (TTSB)
GEMS .... Glenayre Techs, Inc. [*NASDAQ symbol*] (SAG)
GEMS .... Global Enterprise Management of Storage (SAUS)
GEMS .... Global Environmental Monitoring Service (SAUS)
GEMS .... Global Environment Monitoring System [*UNEP*] [*Database producer*] (IID)
GEMS .... Good Emergency Mother Substitute [*Pediatrics*] (DAVI)
GEMS .... Goodyear Electronic Mapping System (SAUO)
GEMS .... Government Equipment Monitoring System (SAUO)
GEMS .... Government Expenditure Management System [*Australia*]
GEMS .... Graphical Exposure Modeling System [*For estimating pollutants*]
GEMS .... Graphic Exposure Modeling System (SAUS)
GEMS .... Graphics Engineering and Mapping System [*Navy*] (GFGA)
GEMS .... Gravity Environment Measurement System (ACAE)
GEMS .... Ground Electromagnetic Survey (SAUS)
GEMS .... Ground Emplaced Mine Scattering System [*Military*] (AABC)
GEMS .... Ground Equipment Maintenance Squadron
GEMS .... Group Export Marketing Scheme (SAUO)
GEMS .... Growth, Economy, Management, and Customer Satisfaction [*Procedure for establishing management goals*]
GEMSA .... Guanidinoethylmercaptosuccinic Acid [*Biochemistry*]
GeMSAEC .... General Medical Sciences and Atomic Energy Commission
GEMSAT ...... Girls' Education in Mathematics, Science, and Technology (AIE)
GEMSCOPE... General Multipurpose Simulation and Control Package (SAUS)
GE-MSD .... General Electric Missile and Space Vehicle Department (SAUO)
GE-MSD .... General Electric-Missile and Space-vehicle Department (SAUS)
GEMSERVICE... Global Electronic Mail Service [*Electronic Mail Corp. of America*] [*Old Greenwich, CT*] [*Telecommunications*] (TSSD)
Gems Gemol... Gems and Gemology. Gemological Institute of America (journ.) (SAUS)
GEMSI .... Group of Experts on Methods, Standards, and Intercalibration [*Oceanography*] (MSC)
GEMSIP .... Gemini Stability Improvement Program [*NASA*]
Gems Miner... Gems and Minerals (journ.) (SAUS)
GEMS/PAC... Global Environmental Monitoring Service / Programme Activity Centre (SAUS)
GEMSS .... Ground Emplaced Mine Scattering System [*Military*] (RDA)
Gem State News Lett... Gem State News Letter (journ.) (SAUS)
Gem Statte RN News Lett... Gem State RN News Letter (journ.) (SAUS)
Gemstr .... Gemstar International Group Ltd. [*Associated Press*] (SAG)
GEMSVD ...... General Electric Missile and Space Vehicle Department [*Military*] (IAA)
GEMSVD ...... General Electric Missile Space Vehicle Department (SAUS)
GEMS/WATER... Global Water Quality Monitoring Programme (SAUO)
GEMT .... Group of European Metallurgical Thermodynamicists [*National Physical Laboratory*] [*Databank*] (NITA)
GEMU .... German Economic and Monetary Union
GEMVS .... GEM verification system (SAUS)
GEMVS .... Generic Equipment Model Verification System [*Electronics*] (AAEL)
GEMWU .... General Engineering and Metalworkers Union (SAUO)
GEMx .... German Equity Market Index (NUMA)
Gemy .... General Motors Corporation (SAUO)
GEN .... Business Operations Support Services [*British*] [*FAA designator*] (FAAC)
Gen .... Gecelinus [*Zenzelinus de Cassanis*] [*Deceased, 1334*] [*Authority cited in pre-1607 legal work*] (DSA)
Gen .... Genava (journ.) (SAUS)
GEN .... Genavco Air Ltd. [*British*] [*ICAO designator*] (FAAC)
gen .... Gender (SHCU)
GEN .... Gender
Gen .... Genealogical (SAUS)
GEN .... Genealogy
gen .... genera (SAUS)
GEN .... General (AABC)
gen .... General (ELAL)
Gen .... General (ODBW)
GEN .... General Court Martial [*Court type found in state of Virginia*] (MVRD)
GEN .... General Electric Network [*Computer science*]
GEN .... General Telephone & Electronics Corp. (SAUO)
gen .... Generate [*News media*] (WDMC)
GEN .... Generate
GEN .... Generate, Generator (SAUS)
gen .... generating (SAUS)
GEN .... Generation (MSA)
GEN .... Generator [*Computer science*] (AAG)
gen .... Generator (IDOE)
GEN .... Generic
Gen .... Genesis [*Old Testament book*]
Gen .... Genetic(s) [*Medicine*] (EDAA)
GEN .... Genetics
GEN .... Geneva [*City in Switzerland*]
gen .... Genital [*Medicine*] (DMAA)
GEN .... Genital
GEN .... Genitive [*Case*] [*Grammar*]
GEN .... Genoa [*Italy*] [*Seismograph station code, US Geological Survey*] [*Closed*] (SEIS)
Gen .... Genoese (SAUS)
GEN .... GenRad, Inc. [*NYSE symbol*] (SPSG)
gen .... gentian (SAUS)
GEN .... Genuine (ADA)
GEN .... Genus [*Biology*]
GEN .... Gerin, Inc. [*Toronto Stock Exchange symbol*]
GEN .... Gilgamesh, Enkidu, and the Netherworld (BJA)
GEN .... Global European Network (EURO)
GEN .... Government Equipment News (journ.) (SAUS)
GEN .... Greater Lenora Resources Corp. [*Toronto Stock Exchange symbol*] [*Vancouver Stock Exchange symbol*]
GEN .... Group of European Nutritionists (SAUO)
GEN .... Oslo [*Norway*] Ardermoen Airport [*Airport symbol*] (OAG)
GenA .... General Assembly (SAUO)
GENA .... German Extended Network Access (SAUS)
GENA .... Great Eastern Numismatic Association (SAUO)
GENA .... Ground Environment and Navigational Aid (PDAA)
Gen Abr Cas Eq... General Abridgment of Cases in Equity [*Equity Cases Abridged*] [*1677-1744*] [*A publication*] (DLA)
Gen AF .... General of the Air Force (WGA)
GENAGRO ... Gestion Environnement Agronomie (SAUO)
GENALERT... Generate Alert (SAUS)
Gen An .... De Generatione Animalium [*of Aristotle*] [*Classical studies*] (OCD)
Gen An .... Generation Animalium (SAUS)
Gen Anes..... General Anesthesia [*Medicine*] (AMHC)

Gen Arm...... Generals of the Army and the Air Force and Admirals of the Navy (journ.) (SAUS)
GENASIS...... Generalised Avionics Simulation / Integration System (SAUS)
GEN AV........ General Average (WDAA)
GENB........... [*The*] Genesee Brewing Co., Inc. [*NASDAQ symbol*] (NQ)
GENB........... Genesee Corp. [*NASDAQ symbol*] (NASQ)
GENB........... Genessee Brewing [*NASDAQ symbol*] (SAG)
GENBANK.... Genetic Sequences Databank [*Intelligenetics, Inc.*] [*Information service or system*] (IID)
GENBB......... Genesee Corp. 'B' [*NASDAQ symbol*] (TTSB)
GENC........... General Electric Nose Cone [*Aerospace*] (AAG)
GEN CAR..... General Cargo [*Shipping*] (DS)
Gen C Endoc... General and Comparative Endocrinology (journ.) (SAUS)
GENCHEM.... General Chemical Indicators [*Database*] [*Probe Economics, Inc.*] [*Information service or system*] (CRD)
GENCMM..... Generic Enterprise Change Management Methodology (VLIE)
Gen Comp Endncrinol Suppl... General and Comparative Endocrinology. Supplement (journ.) (SAUS)
Gen Comp Endocrinol... General and Comparative Endocrinology (SAUS)
GenCompEndocrinol... General and Comparative Endocrinology (journ.) (SAUS)
GenCon........ General Control (SAUS)
Gen Con...... General Counsel (AAGC)
GEN CONT... general contract (SAUS)
GEN CONT... general contractor (SAUS)
Gen Contract... General Contracting (journ.) (SAUS)
GENCONV.... Geneva Conventions [*Military*] (NVT)
Gencor......... Gencor Industries, Inc. [*Associated Press*] (SAG)
GENCOR...... General Mining Union Corp. (SAUO)
Gen Corr...... De Generatione et Corruptione [*of Aristotle*] [*Classical studies*] (OCD)
Gen Corr...... Generation and Corruption (SAUS)
GenCrp........ GenCorp, Inc. [*Associated Press*] (SAG)
Gen Cytochem Methods... General Cytochemical Methods (journ.) (SAUS)
GEND........... General Electric Nuclear Division (SAUO)
GEND........... General Expenses (SAUS)
GEND........... Generated Data File [*Computer science*]
GENDA......... General Data Analysis (SAUS)
GENDA......... General Data Analysis and Simulation (IAA)
GENDARE.... Generalized Data Reduction Evalution (SAUS)
GENDARME... Generalized Data Reduction (SAUS)
GENDARME... Generalized Data Reduction, Evaluation (SAUS)
GENDARME... Generalized Data Reduction, Manipulation and Evaluation (SAUS)
GENDAS....... General Data Analysis and Simulation (SAUS)
GEN DEL...... General Delivery
Gen Dent..... General Dentistry (journ.) (SAUS)
GENDEP....... General Depot [*Military*]
GENDET....... General Detail [*Coast Guard*]
GENDEX....... General Index (SAUS)
GENDEX....... General Indexer (SAUS)
Gen Dig....... General Digest [*A publication*] (DLA)
Gen Dig....... General Digest (journ.) (SAUS)
Gen Dig NS... General Digest, New Series [*A publication*] (DLA)
GENDIS........ General Distribution [*Pentagon security classification code*]
GenDisch...... General Discharge (SAUS)
GENDISP...... General Dispensary [*Military*]
GENDRA...... GENeralized Data Reduction + Analysis (SAUS)
GENDRA...... Generalized Data Reduction and Analysis (VLIE)
GENDYN...... General Dynamics
Gene........... GENE (AMSTERDAM) (SAUS)
GENE........... Genome Therapeutics [*NASDAQ symbol*] (TTSB)
GENE........... Genome Therapeutics Corp [*NASDAQ symbol*] (SAG)
Geneal......... Genealogist (DIAR)
GENEAL....... Genealogy
GENEAL MAG... Genealogical Magazine (journ.) (SAUS)
Genealogical Period Annv Index... Genealogical Periodical Annual Index (journ.) (SAUS)
Geneal Per Ind... Genealogical Periodical. Annual Index (journ.) (SAUS)
Gene Anal T... Gene Analysis Techniques (journ.) (SAUS)
Gene Anal Tech... Gene Analysis Techniques (journ.) (SAUS)
Gene Expression Dev Proc Int Congr Isozyrnes... Gene Expression and Development. Proceedings. International Congress on Isozymes (journ.) (SAUS)
Gene Expression Its Regal Proc Int Lat Am Symp... Gene Expression and Its Regulation. Proceedings. International Latin American Symposium (journ.) (SAUS)
Gen Electr Co Ltd J... General Electric Company Limited. Journal (SAUO)
Gen Electr Co Ltd J... General Electric Company Limited. Journal (journ.) (SAUS)
genel........... genealogy (SAUS)
GenEl........... General Electric Co. [*Associated Press*] (SAG)
GenELC........ General Electric Company (SAUS)
Gen Electr Co Ltd J Sci Tecbnol... General Electric Company Limited. Journal of Science and Technology (SAUO)
Gen Electr Co Ltd J Sci Tecbnol... General Electric Company Limited. Journal of Science and Technology (journ.) (SAUS)
Gen El Rev... General Electric Review (journ.) (SAUS)
GeneLTc...... GeneLabs Technologies, Inc. [*Associated Press*] (SAG)
GeneMed...... GeneMedicine, Inc. [*Associated Press*] (SAG)
GENENG....... Generalized Engine [*Computer science*]
Gen EngTrans... General Engineering Transactions (journ.) (SAUS)
Genentc........ Genentech, Inc. [*Associated Press*] (SAG)
General Ed... General Education (journ.) (SAUS)
General Topology and Appl... General Topology and Its Applications (journ.) (SAUS)
Generation... Generations [*A publication*] (BRI)
GENERIC...... Generation of Integrated Circuits (SAUS)
GENES......... Geneseo, KS [*American Association of Railroads railroad junction routing code*]
Genes Chromosomes Cancer... Genes, Chromosomes and Cancer (SAUS)
GENESCO..... General Shoe Corp. [*Acronym now official name of firm*]
GenesCp...... [*The*] Genessee Brewing Company, Inc. [*Associated Press*] (SAG)
Genes Dev... Genes and Development (journ.) (SAUS)
GENESIS...... Generation Simulation System [*Power systems*]
Genesis....... Genesis Health Ventures, Inc. [*Associated Press*] (SAG)
GENESIS...... Georgia Educational Network Exchanging School Information State-Wide (SAUO)
GENESIS...... Global Ecosystem Numerical Estimation Using Satellite Imaging Systems (SAUO)
GENESIS...... Global Environmental and Ecological Simulation of Interactive System (CARB)
GENESIS...... Global Environmental and Ecological Simulation of Interactive Systems (SAUO)
GenesisH...... Genesis Health Ventures, Inc. [*Associated Press*] (SAG)
GENESSIS.... Generic Scene Simulation Software (EERA)
Genes Tumor Genes Workshop Conf Hoechst... Genes and Tumor Genes. Workshop Conference Hoechst (journ.) (SAUS)
GENESYS..... General Engineering System
GENESYS..... Generalized System [*Computer program*] (NITA)
GENESYS..... Generalized System of Structural Engineering (SAUO)
GENESYS..... Graduate Engineering Education System
Genet........... Genetic (SAUS)
GENET......... Genetics
Genet Abstr... Genetics Abstracts (journ.) (SAUS)
Genet Biol Drosophila... Genetics and Biology of Drosophila (journ.) (SAUS)
Genet Breed... Genetics and Breeding (journ.) (SAUS)
Genet Cell Technol... Genetic and Cellular Technology (journ.) (SAUS)
Genet Dev Evol Stadler Genet Symp... Genetics, Development and Evolution. Stadler Genetics Symposium (journ.) (SAUS)
Genet Eng Biotechnol Yearb... Genetic Engineering and Biotechnology Yearbook (journ.) (SAUS)
Genet Eng Lett... Genetic Engineering Letter (journ.) (SAUS)
Genet Eng News... Genetic Engineering News (journ.) (SAUS)
Genet Epidemiol... Genetic Epidemiology (journ.) (SAUS)
Genet Epidemiol Suppl... Genetic Epidemiology. Supplement (SAUS)
GenetI.......... Genetics Institute, Inc. [*Associated Press*] (SAG)
Genetics Suppl... Genetics. Supplement (journ.) (SAUS)
GenetInst..... Genetics Institute, Inc. [*Associated Press*] (SAG)
Genet Lect... Genetics Lectures (journ.) (SAUS)
Genet Maps... Genetic Maps (journ.) (SAUS)
GENETOX..... Genetic Toxicity [*Database*] [*Environmental Protection Agency*] [*Information service or system*] (CRD)
GENE-TOX.... Genetic Toxicology (ADWA)
Genet Physiol Notes... Genetics and Physiology Notes (journ.) (SAUS)
Genet Plant Breed... Genetics and Plant Breeding (journ.) (SAUS)
GenetPsycholMonogr... Genetic Psychology Monographs, Child Behavior, Animal Behavior, and Comparative (SAUS)
Genet Sel Evol... Genetique, Selection, Evolution (journ.) (SAUS)
Genet Soc Gen Psychol Monogr... Genetic, Social and General Psychology Monographs (journ.) (SAUS)
gen et sp nov... Genus et Species Nova [*New Genus and Species*] [*Latin*] (DMAA)
Geneva Association... International Association for the Study of Insurance Economics (SAUO)
GenevaMAN... Geneva Metropolitan Area Network (SAUO)
GENFAP....... General Nonlinear Frame Analysis Program [*Structures & Computers Ltd.*] [*Software package*] (NCC)
Gen Fish Counc Mediten Sess Rep... General Fisheries Council for the Mediterranean. Session Report (journ.) (SAUS)
Gen Fish Counc Mediterr Proc Tecb Pap... General Fisheries Council for the Mediterranean. Proceedings and Technical Papers (journ.) (SAUS)
GENG........... Gasoline Engine
GENG........... General Genetics Corp. (SAUO)
GEngr........... Garrison Engineer (SAUS)
Gen Heterocyd Chem Ser... General Heterocyclic Chemistry Series (journ.) (SAUS)
Gen Hosp..... General Hospital (SAUO)
Gen Hosp Psychiatry... General Hospital Psychiatry (journ.) (SAUS)
GENI........... Genetics Institute, Inc. [*NASDAQ symbol*] (NQ)
GENI........... Global Employer's Network, Inc.
GENI........... Global Energy Network International
Genicm........ GENICOM Corp. [*Associated Press*] (SAG)
GEnie........... General Electric Network for Information Exchange [*General Electric Co.*] [*Online information service*] (IID)
GENIE.......... General Information Environment [*Data Dynamics, Inc.*] [*Portland, OR*] [*Telecommunications service*] (TSSD)
GENIE.......... General Information Extractor
GENIE.......... Global Environmental Network for Information Exchange (SAUO)
GENII........... Generation II Model For Environmental Dose Calculations (SAUS)
GEN II.......... Second Generation (SAUS)
Gen Index.... General Index (journ.) (SAUS)
Gen Index Publ Reports... General Index to Published Reports. Mineral Resources Group (journ.) (SAUS)
Gen Int Dep... General Intermediate Depot (SAUS)
GENIP.......... Geographic Education National Implementation Project [*National Geographic Society*]
GENIRAS....... General Information Retrieval and Application System (PDAA)
GENIRAS....... Generalized Information Retrieval System (SAUS)
Genisco........ Genisco Technology Corp. (SAUO)
GENISIS....... General Imaging Spectrometry Interpretation Systems (SAUO)
GENISYS...... General Inferencing System
GENISYS...... Generalized Information System (VLIE)
GENIT.......... Genitalia [*Medicine*]

genit .... Genitive (SHCU)
GENIT .... Genitive [*Case*] [*Grammar*]
Genitourin ... Genitourinary (SAUS)
Genitourin Med... Genitourinary Medicine (journ.) (SAUS)
GENIUS .... Genetic Interactive Unix System (SAUS)
GENIZ .... Genetics Institute Dep Shrs [*NASDAQ symbol*] (TTSB)
GenKinet...... General Kinetics, Inc. [*Associated Press*] (SAG)
genl .... General (SHCU)
GENL .... General
GEN L .... General Licence [*British*] (ROG)
GENL .... Genetic Laboratories, Inc. (SAUO)
GENLEAF ..... generic models of leaf response (SAUS)
Gen Led....... General Ledger (EBF)
GENLED....... General Ledger
genlock......... Generator Lock (CDE)
GENLOCK..... Generator Locking (SAUS)
GenlRe .... General Re Corp. [*Associated Press*] (SAG)
GENLY .... Generally (ROG)
Genlyte........ Genlyte Group, Inc. [*Associated Press*] (SAG)
GenManCert... General Management Certificate
Gen M As Que J... General Mining Association of the Province of Quebec. Journal (journ.) (SAUS)
GEN MGR .... General Manager (WDAA)
GENMIN....... General Mining, Metals and Minerals (SAUS)
GENMISH...... US Military Mission with the Iranian Gendarmerie
GENMO......... Generalissimo [*Commander-in-Chief*] [*Spanish*] (ROG)
GENMOD...... General Model (RDA)
Gen Mot Corp Res Lab Res Publ... General Motors Corporation. Research Laboratories. Research Publication (journ.) (SAUS)
Gen Mot Eng J... General Motors Engineering Journal (journ.) (SAUS)
GE-NMPO .... General Electric Company, Nuclear Materials and Propulsion Operation (SAUO)
GE-NMPO .... General Electric-Nuclear Materials and Propulsion Operation (SAUS)
Gen Mtge..... General Mortgage [*Bond*] (MHDW)
GenN .... General Notice (SAFN)
Gen No .... General Number (SAUS)
gen nov .... Genus Novum [*New Genus*] [*Latin*] (DAVI)
GenNutr .... General Nutrition Co. [*Associated Press*] (SAG)
genoc.......... genocide (SAUS)
Genome....... Genome Therapeutics Corp. [*Associated Press*] (SAG)
GENOPAUSE... Geodetic Satellite in Polar Geosynchronous Orbit (NAKS)
Gen Ord Ch... General Orders of the English High Court of Chancery [*A publication*] (DLA)
GENOS......... Generate Operating System [*Computer program*]
GENOT .... General Notice
GENOTES ..... General Notices (SAUS)
GENOUT....... Generalized Output Program for Nuclear Science Reference Data (SAUS)
GENP .... General Publication (SAUS)
GENP .... General Purpose (SAUS)
GENP .... Gentamicin Peak [*Level*] [*Immunology*] (DAVI)
GENPDTS...... Generate Pack Definition Tables (SAUS)
GEN PRAC ... General Practice (WDAA)
Gen Pract Clin... General Practice Clinics (journ.) (SAUS)
GENPRL....... General Precision Laboratory
GEN PROC ... General Procedure (BABM)
GENPS.......... Genital Neoplasm-Papilloma Syndrome [*Medicine*] (DMAA)
Gen Psych Mon... Genetic Psychology Monographs (journ.) (SAUS)
gen pub .... general public (SAUS)
Gen Pub ...... General Publication (journ.) (SAUS)
GEN PUR ..... general purpose (SAUS)
GENR........... Generate (AABC)
genr............ Generation (BARN)
genr............ Generator (SAUS)
GenR .... Genesis Rabbah (BJA)
GENRA8....... Genetical Research (journ.) (SAUS)
GenRabb...... Genesis Rabbah (BJA)
Gen Rad Exp... General Radio Experimenter (journ.) (SAUS)
GENRB......... Genie Rural (journ.) (SAUS)
GEN REL...... General Release (SAUO)
Gen Relativ Gravit... General Relativity and Gravitation (journ.) (SAUS)
Gen Relativity Gravitation... General Relativity and Gravitation (journ.) (SAUS)
Gen Rep ...... General Repair (SAUS)
GENREP....... General Reports [*Military*]
Gen Rep Dep Archit Sci Syd Univ... General Report. Department of Architectural Science. University of Sydney (journ.) (SAUS)
Gen Rep Minist Mines Prov Que... General Report. Minister of Mines. Province of Quebec (journ.) (SAUS)
Gen Repos... General Repository (journ.) (SAUS)
Gen Res ...... Genetical Research (journ.) (SAUS)
genrl .... general (SAUS)
GENS .... General Soviet [*Later, A Group*] [*Division of National Security Agency*]
GENS .... Genetic Systems Corp. (SAUO)
GENSA......... Journal. Georgia Entomological Society (journ.) (SAUS)
GenSAA....... Generic Spacecraft Analyst Assistant (IDAI)
GENSAL....... Generic Structure Language
GenScan...... General Scanning, Inc. [*Associated Press*] (SAG)
Gen Sci Index... General Science Index (journ.) (SAUS)
Gensco .... Genesco, Inc. [*Associated Press*] (SAG)
GENSER....... General Service [*Military*] (MCD)
GENSER....... General Service Communications (SAUO)
GENSER....... General Services Intelligence [*Military*] (CAAL)
Gen Ser Colo State Agr Exp Sta... General Series. Colorado State University. Agricultural Experiment Station (journ.) (SAUS)
GenServ....... General Service (SAUS)
GENSESS..... General Sessions (ADA)
GENSET .... Generator Set (SAUO)
GENSH......... Generate Shell [*Computer science*] (PCM)
Gensia......... Gensia Pharmaceuticals, Inc. [*Associated Press*] (SAG)
GenSignl...... General Signal Corp. [*Associated Press*] (SAG)
GensisE....... Genesis Energy LP [*Associated Press*] (SAG)
GENSIT .... General Situation [*Military*] (NVT)
GENSLA....... Generic Structure Language (SAUS)
GENSM........ Generate Shell (SAUS)
GENSPECS... General Specifications (DNAB)
Gen SriQ...... General Science Quarterly (journ.) (SAUS)
GenSS .... General Screw Steam Navigation Company (SAUO)
GENST .... Standard Goods Nomenclature for Transport Statistics (SAUO)
gen sta .... generating station (SAUS)
GENSTAN...... Generalized Data Standardizer [*Bureau of the Census*] (GFGA)
GENSTAT Program... General Statistical Program (SAUS)
GEN STOR ... General Storage (SAUS)
GENSUP...... General Supplies (SAUS)
GENSUP...... General Support [*Army*]
GENSUPSP... General Supply Specialist (SAUS)
Gen Supt ..... General Superintendent (SAUO)
GENSUR ...... National Survey of Hazardous Waste Generators (SAUO)
GENSURG.... General Surgery (AABC)
GenSurg ...... General Surgical Innovations, Inc. [*Associated Press*] (SAG)
GENSV......... General Service [*Military*]
GENSYM...... Generated Symbol [*Computer science*] (NHD)
GENT .... General Technologies Group Ltd. (SAUO)
Gen T........... General Term (DLA)
GENT .... Gentamicin [*Antibacterial compound*]
GENT .... Gentamicin Trough [*Level*] [*Immunology*] (DAVI)
GENT .... Gentleman
Gent............. Gentlemen (DIAR)
gent .... Gentlemen (ELAL)
Genta........... Genta, Inc. [*Associated Press*] (SAG)
GENTAE .... Genetics (journ.) (SAUS)
GENTEC .... Genetic Technology Databank (SAUS)
Gen Tech Rep FPL US Dep Agric For Serv For Prod La... General Technical Report FPL. United States Department of Agriculture. Forest Service. Forest Products Laboratory (journ.) (SAUS)
Gen Tech Rep RM Rocky Mt For Range Exp Stn US For... General Technical Report. RM. Rocky Mountain Forest and Range Experiment Station. United States Forest Service (journ.) (SAUS)
GENTEL........ General Intelligence (SAUS)
GENTEL........ General Telephone & Electronics Corp.
Gen Tel&El... General Telephone and Electric (SAUS)
Gen Tel & EL... General Telephone and Electric Corp. (SAUO)
GENTEX .... General Telegraph Exchange (IAA)
Gentex......... Gentex Corp. [*Associated Press*] (SAG)
GENTEXT ..... General Text (COE)
GENTHES..... generierbarer Thesaurus (SAUS)
GENTN .... Gentleman [*or Gentlemen*] (ROG)
Gentnr .... Gentner Communications Corp. [*Associated Press*] (SAG)
GENTRAS..... General Training System (MHDB)
GENTS .... Generic Test System (SAUS)
Gents........... Gentelmen (SAUS)
gents .... gentlemen (SAUS)
GENU .... General Nutrition, Inc (SAUS)
GENU .... Generated Non-Elementary Unit (VLIE)
GENU .... Genuity, Inc. 'A' [*NASDAQ symbol*]
GenuPrt .... Genuine Parts Co. [*Associated Press*] (SAG)
Genus.......... Genus, Inc. [*Associated Press*] (SAG)
GenvDr .... Genovese Drug Stores, Inc. [*Associated Press*] (SAG)
Gen View Cr L... Stephen's General View of the Criminal Law [*2nd ed.*] [*1890*] [*A publication*] (DLA)
GENVST....... General Public Visiting [*Navy*] (NVT)
genvst.......... general visiting (SAUS)
GenWyo....... Genessee and Wyoming, Inc. [*Associated Press*] (SAG)
GENX .... General Electric Railcar Services [*Private rail car owner code*]
Gen-X .... Generation X (ADWA)
GEN-X.......... Generic Expendable (SAUS)
GEN-X.......... Generic Expendable Active Decoy (SAUS)
GENX .... Generic Expendable Decoy (SAUO)
GENX .... Genset [*NASDAQ symbol*] (NASQ)
GENXY......... Genset ADR [*NASDAQ symbol*] (SG)
GENY .... General Energy Resources & Technology Corp (SAUS)
GENY .... Generally
GENZ .... Genzyme Corp. [*NASDAQ symbol*] (NQ)
GENZ .... Genzyme Corp.-Genl Div [*NASDAQ symbol*] (TTSB)
GENZL .... Genzyme Corp.-Tissue Repair [*NASDAQ symbol*] (TTSB)
GENZL .... Geothermal Energy New Zealand Limited (SAUO)
Genzy.......... Genzyme Corp. [*Associated Press*] (SAG)
Genzym....... Genzyme Corp. [*Associated Press*] (SAG)
GenzyT........ Genzyme Corp. [*Associated Press*] (SAG)
GenzyTis..... Genzyme Corp. [*Associated Press*] (SAG)
GenzyTr ...... Genzyme Transgenics Corp. [*Associated Press*] (SAG)
GENZZ .... Genzyme Corp. Wrrt [*NASDAQ symbol*] (TTSB)
GEO .... Air Georgia [*Former USSR*] [*FAA designator*] (FAAC)
GEO .... Central of Georgia Railway Co. (SAUO)
G E O........... Gas and Electric Operations (SAUS)
GEO .... Genetically Engineered Organism
geo .... geocentric (SAUS)
geo .... geochemistry (SAUS)
geo .... geodesy (SAUS)
geo .... geodetic (SAUS)

geo .... geodynamics (SAUS)
geo .... geognosy (SAUS)
geo .... Geographer (SAUS)
GEO .... Geographic
GEO .... Geographic Division [*Census*] (OICC)
GEO .... Geographic or true (SAUS)
geo .... geography (SAUS)
GEO .... Geography Division (SAUS)
GEO .... Geologist
geo .... geology (SAUS)
GEO .... Geomaque Explorations [*TS, exchange symbol*] (TTSB)
GEO .... Geometry
GEO .... Geophysical Report [*Oil industry term*] (DSUE)
geo .... geophysics (SAUS)
geo .... geopolitics (SAUS)
Geo .... George (SAFN)
GEO .... Georgetown [*Guyana*] [*Airport symbol*] (OAG)
GEO .... Georgetown [*District of Columbia*] [*Seismograph station code, US Geological Survey*] (SEIS)
Geo .... Georgetown Law Journal (journ.) (SAUS)
GEO .... Georgetown, OH [*Location identifier*] [*FAA*] (FAAL)
GEO .... Georgia [*Obsolete*] (ROG)
geo .... Georgian [*MARC language code*] [*Library of Congress*] (LCCP)
Geo .... Georgia Reports [*A publication*] (DLA)
GEO .... Geoscience Electronics (MCD)
GEO .... Geosciences Directorate (SAUS)
geo .... geostatic (SAUS)
GEO .... Geostationary Earth Observation (CARB)
GEO .... Geostationary Earth Observatory (SAUO)
GEO .... Geostationary Earth Orbit
GEO .... Geostationary Earth Orbiter (SAUS)
GEO .... Geostationary Orbit (SAUS)
GEO .... Geosynchronous [*Satellite orbit*] (CDE)
GEO .... Geosynchronous Earth Orbit
GEO .... Geotech Capital [*Vancouver Stock Exchange symbol*]
geo .... geothermal (SAUS)
GEO .... Geothermal Resources International, Inc. (SAUO)
GEO .... Global Earth Orbit
GEO .... Glosa Education Organisation (EAIO)
GEO .... Grandview, PA [*American Association of Railroads railroad junction routing code*]
GEO-1 .... Global Environment Outlook-1 (SAUO)
Geo1 Surv Iran Rep... Geological Survey of Iran. Report (SAUS)
GEO-2 .... Global Environment Outlook-2 Process (SAUO)
GeoAb .... Geographical Abstracts (journ.) (SAUS)
Geo Abs&Indexes... Geo Abstracts and Indexes (journ.) (SAUS)
Geo Abstr .... Geographical Abstracts (journ.) (SAUS)
Geo Abstr B Climatol Hydrol... Geo Abstracts. B. Climatology and Hydrology (journ.) (SAUS)
Geo Abstr C Econ Geog... Geo Abstracts. C. Economic Geography (journ.) (SAUS)
Geo Abstr D Soc Hist Geog... Geo Abstracts. D. Social and Historical Geography (journ.) (SAUS)
Geo Abstr E Sedimentology... Geo Abstracts. E. Sedimentology (journ.) (SAUS)
Geo Abstr F Reg Com Plan... Geo Abstracts. F. Regional and Community Planning (journ.) (SAUS)
Geo Abstr G Remote Sensing Pho Cartogr... Geo Abstracts. G. Remote Sensing, Photogrammetry and Cartography (journ.) (SAUS)
GEOALERT.... Geophysical Alert (ACAE)
GEOARCHIVE... Geology Archive [*Database on earth science*] [*British*] (NITA)
Geoastrophys... Geoastrophysics (SAUS)
GeoB .... Geography Database for the United States (SAUS)
GEOBASE ..... Geographic Cross-Reference Data [*Claritas LP*] [*Information service or system*] (CRD)
GEOBD2 .... Geobotany (journ.) (SAUS)
Geobot sel... Geobotanica selecta (SAUS)
GEOC .... General Estate and Orphan Chamber (SAUO)
GEOC .... GeoTel Communications Corp. [*NASDAQ symbol*] (SAG)
GEO-CAT ...... Geographic Catalog of political and statistical areas (SAUO)
GEOCD .... Geochimica (journ.) (SAUS)
GEOCEIVER... Geodetic Receiver
GEOCHEM.... Geochemical
GEOCHEM.... Geochemist (SAUS)
GEOCHEM.... Geochemistry (SAUS)
Geochem Geochem Methods Data... Geochemie. Geochemical Methods (SAUS)
Geochem J... Geochemical Journal [*A publication*] (PABS)
Geochem Soc India Bull... Geochemical Society of India. Bulletin (journ.) (SAUS)
Geochim Cosmochim Acta... Geochimica et Cosmochimica Acta (journ.) (SAUS)
GEOCODES... Geographic Codes (COE)
GEOCOMP.... Geocoding and Compositing (SAUS)
Geocorr........ Geographic Correspondence Engine (SAUS)
GE/OD .... General Electric / Ordnance Department (SAUS)
geod .... Geodesic (SAUS)
GEOD .... Geodesist (SAUS)
GEOD .... Geodesy [*Science of measuring the earth*] (ROG)
GEOD .... Geodetic
GEOD .... Geodyne Resources, Inc. [*NASDAQ symbol*] (COMM)
GEODAS .... Geology Oriented Database System (SAUS)
GEODAS .... Geophysical Data System (EERA)
GEODAT .... Geological Survey Analytical Data Sorage and Retrieval System (SAUS)
GEODAT .... Geosciences data analysis toolkit (SAUS)
Geo Dat Pt... Geodetic Datum Point (SAUS)
Geod E......... Geodetic Engineer
Geo Dec ...... Georgia Decisions [*A publication*] (DLA)
GEODES .... Ground-based Electro-Optical Deep Space Surveillance (DICI)
Geodes Mapp Photogramm... Geodesy, Mapping and Photogrammetry (journ.) (SAUS)
GEODIAL ...... Geoscience Data Index for Alberta [*Alberta Research Council*] [*Information service or system*] (IID)
Geo Dig .... George's Mississippi Digest [*A publication*] (DLA)
GEODIS .... Geographic Design and Implementation System [*Australian Capital Territory*] (EERA)
GeoDIS .... Geographic Districting Information System for (SAUS)
GeoDIS .... Geographic Districting Information System for Maryland [*Maryland State Department of State Planning*] [*Baltimore*] [*Information service or system*] (IID)
Geod Mapp Photogram... Geodesy, Mapping and Photogrammetry (journ.) (SAUS)
Geod Mapp Photogramm Engl Transl... Geodesy, Mapping and Photogrammetry. English Translation (journ.) (SAUS)
GEODOM...... Geographic Data, Overlay and Manipulation System (SAUO)
GEODRS ...... Geodyne Resources (SAUS)
GEODRS ...... Geodyne Resources, Inc. (SAUO)
GEODS .... Ground Based Electro-Optical Deep-Space Surveillance (ACAE)
GEODS .... Ground Electro-Optical Deep Space Surveillance System (CCCA)
Geod Soc Jap J... Geodetic Society of Japan. Journal (journ.) (SAUS)
GEODSS....... Ground-Based Electro-Optical Deep Space Surveillance [*Satellite-tracking network*]
GEODSS....... Ground-based Electro-optical Deep-space Surveillance System (SAUO)
GEODSS....... Ground-based Electro-Optics Deep Space Surveillance (SAUS)
GEODSS....... Ground Electro-Optical Deep Space System (SAUS)
GEODSSS .... Ground Based Electro Optical Deep Space Surveillance System (ACAE)
Geodyn .... Geodynamics Corp. [*Associated Press*] (SAG)
GEO-EAS...... Geostatistical Environmental Assessment Software [*US Environmental Protection Agency*]
geoelectr ..... Geoelectric (SAUS)
Geoelectr..... Geoelectricity (SAUS)
GEOF .... Geological Editor of Field Notes (SAUS)
GEOFILE ...... Geographic File [*DoD*]
GEOFILE ...... Geographic Location File (COE)
GEOFILE ...... Geographic Locations Code File System (SAUO)
GEOFILE ...... Standard Specified Geographic Location File (POLM)
GEOFIZ .... Geosciences Information Center [*Federal Institute for Geosciences and NaturalResources*] [*Information service or system*] (IID)
GEOG .... Geografia (journ.) (SAUS)
geog .... geographer (SAUS)
Geog .... Geographia [*of Ptolemy*] [*Classical studies*] (OCD)
Geog .... Geographic
Geog .... Geographical [*A publication*] (BRI)
GEOG .... Geography [*or Geographer*] (AFM)
Geog .... Geography (AL)
geog .... Geography (NTIO)
Geog Bull .... Geographical Bulletin (journ.) (SAUS)
Geog Map Dir Bull... Geography and Map Division Bulletin (journ.) (SAUS)
GeogMapDivBull... Geography & Map Division Bulletin (journ.) (SAUS)
GEOGNOS .... Geognosy [*A knowledge of the structure of the earth*] (ROG)
GEOGR......... Geographer (SAUS)
Geogr........... Geographical (SAUO)
geograph ..... geographical (SAUS)
GEOGRAPHY... George Emerson's Old Grandmother Rode a Pig Home Yesterday [*Mnemonic guide for spelling "geography"*]
Geogr Ed ..... Geographical Education [*A publication*]
GEOGRID ..... Geographical Information Display System (SAUS)
Geog R Ind... Geographical Review of India (journ.) (SAUS)
Geogr J........ Geographical Journal, The (SAUS)
Geogrph....... Geographics, Inc. [*Associated Press*] (SAG)
Geogr Rev ... Geographical Review, The (SAUS)
Geogr Teach... Geography Teacber (journ.) (SAUS)
Geog Soc Chicago B... Geographic Society of Chicago. Bulletin (journ.) (SAUS)
Geog Soc Phila... Geographical Society of Philadelphia (SAUO)
Geog Soc Phila B... Geographical Society of Philadelphia. (SAUS)
GEOG T........ Geographical Teacher [*A publication*] (ROG)
GEOG T........ Geographical Teacher (journ.) (SAUS)
Geohem Soc India Bull... Geochemical Society of India (SAUO)
geohy........... geohygiene (SAUS)
GEOI .... Georesources, Inc. [*NASDAQ symbol*] (NQ)
GEOI .... Georesources, Incorporated (SAUO)
Geol Assoc Can... Geological Association of Canada (journ.) (SAUS)
GEO-IRS ...... Geostationary Orbit - Infrared Sensor (SAUS)
GEOIS .... Geographic Information System [*Computer science*]
Geol Soc S Afr Trans... Geological Society of South Africa. Transactions (journ.) (SAUS)
Geol Surv W Aust Bull... Geological Survey of Western Australia. Bulletin (journ.) (SAUS)
Geol Surv West Malaysia Dist Mem... Geological Survey of West Malaysia. District Memoir (journ.) (SAUS)
GEOJA .... Geophysical Journal. Royal Astronomical Society (journ.) (SAUS)
GEOK .... Geokinetics (SAUS)
GEOK .... Geokinetics, Inc. (SAUO)
Geokhim Mineral Petrol... Geokhimiya (SAUS)
GeoL............ Geographica (SAUS)
geol .... geologic (SAUS)
Geol............. Geological (SAUO)
GEOL .... Geologist
GEOL .... Geology [*or Geologist*] (AFM)
Geol............. Geology (BEE)
geol .... Geology (SHCU)
GEOL .... Georesources Inc. [*NASDAQ symbol*] (TTSB)
Geol Assoc Canada Proc... Geological Association of Canada. (SAUS)

Geol Assoc Canada Proc... Geological Association of Canada. Proceedings (journ.) (SAUS)
Geol Assoc Can Cordilleraa Sect Programme Abstr... Geological Association of Canada. Cordilleran Section. Programme and Abstracts (journ.) (SAUS)
Geol Assoc Can Spec Pap... Geological Association of Canada. (SAUS)
Geol Assoc Can Spec Pap... Geological Association of Canada. Special Paper (journ.) (SAUS)
Geol Assoc Can Spec Pap... Geological Association of Canada. Special Papers (SAUO)
Geol Astrophys Fluid Dyn... Geophysical and Astrophysical Fluid (SAUS)
Geol Bull Natl Geol Surv China... Geological Bulletin. (SAUS)
Geol Bull Univ Peshawar... Geological Bulletin. University (SAUO)
Geol Bull Univ Peshawar... Geological Bulletin. University of Peshawar (journ.) (SAUS)
Geol Center Res Ser... Geological Center. Research Series (journ.) (SAUS)
Geol Correl... Geological Correlation (journ.) (SAUS)
Geol E......... Geological Engineer
Geol Explor Min BC... Geology. Exploration and Mining in British Columbia (journ.) (SAUS)
GEOLGCL..... Geological
Geol Geophys... Geology and Geophysics (journ.) (SAUS)
GEOLGY....... Geology
Geo Lib........ George on Libel [*1812*] [*A publication*] (DLA)
GEOLIN........ Geology Digital Inventory (SAUS)
Geol Invest Ser Geol Surv Pak... Geological (SAUS)
Geol Invest Ser Geol Surv Pak Interim Geol Rep... Geological Investigation Series. Geological Survey of Pakistan. Interim Geological Report (journ.) (SAUS)
Geol J.......... Geological Journal (journ.) (SAUS)
Geo LJ......... Georgetown Law Journa1 (SAUS)
Geo LJ......... Georgetown Law Journal (journ.) (SAUS)
Geol J Queen Mary Coll... Geological Journal of Queen Mary (SAUS)
Geol J Queen Mary Coll... Geological Journal of Queen Mary College (journ.) (SAUS)
GeolM.......... Geological Magazine (SAUO)
GeolMag........ Geological Magazine (SAUO)
Geol Map Deputy Minist Miner R... Geologic (SAUS)
Geol Map Miner Resour Summ Nor... Geology (SAUS)
Geol Map Miner Resour Summ North Carolina Geol Sur... Geology Map and Mineral Resources Summary. North Carolina Geological Survey (journ.) (SAUS)
Geol Map Montana Bur Mines Geol... Geologic Map. Montana Bureau of Mines and Geology (journ.) (SAUS)
Geol Mem Geol Surv China Ser B... Geological Memoirs. Geological Survey of China.Series B (journ.) (SAUS)
Geol Mem Geol Surv Cbina Ser B... Geological Memoirs. Geological (SAUS)
Geol Mem Geol Surv China Ser A... Geological Memoirs. Geological (SAUS)
Geol Mem Geol Surv China Ser A... Geological Memoirs. Geological Survey of China. Series A (journ.) (SAUS)
Geol Min Metall Soc India Q J... Geologial, Mining and Metallurgical Society of India. Quarterly Journal (journ.) (SAUS)
Geol Min Metall Soc India Q J... Geological (SAUS)
Geol Min Metall Soc Liberia Bu... Geological (SAUS)
Geol Min Met Soc Liberia Bull... Geological (SAUS)
Geol Notes Local De 1:10000 Sheets Inst Geol Sci... Geological Notes and Local Details for 1:10,000 Sheets. Institute of Geological Sciences (journ.) (SAUS)
GEOLOC....... Geographical Location [*Military*] (AABC)
GEOLOC....... Geographic Location Code (COE)
Geology Club Puerto Rico Bull... Geology Club of Puerto Rico. Bulletin (journ.) (SAUS)
Geol Palaeontol Southeast Asia... Geology and Palaeontology of Southeast Asia (journ.) (SAUS)
Geol Palaeontol Southeast Asia... Geology and Palaeontology of Southeast Asia (journ.) (SAUS)
Geol Pap Carleton Univ Dep Geo... Geological Paper. Carleton (SAUS)
Geol Pap Carleton Univ Dep Geol... Geological Paper. Carleton University. Department of Geology (journ.) (SAUS)
Geol Pap Geol Surv Malaysia... Geological Papers. Geological (SAUS)
Geol Pap Geol Surv Malaysia... Geological Papers. Geological Survey of Malaysia (journ.) (SAUS)
Geol Rep Hiroshima Univ... Geological Report. Hiroshima (SAUS)
Geol Rep Hiroshima Univ... Geological Report. Hiroshima University (journ.) (SAUS)
Geol Rep Shimane Unir... Geologial Reports. Shimane Univetsity (SAUS)
Geol Rep Shimane Univ... Geological Reports. Shimane University (journ.) (SAUS)
Geol Rep State Alaska Dep Nat Resour... Geologic Report. State of Alaska Department of Natural Resources (journ.) (SAUS)
GeolSci........ Geological Science (DD)
Geol Sect Bull Libya Minist In... Geological Section. Bulletin. (SAUS)
Geol Sect Bull Libya Minist Ind... Geological Section. Bulletin. Libya Ministry of Industry (journ.) (SAUS)
Geol Soc Am Abst Programs... Geological Society of America. Abstracts with Programs (journ.) (SAUS)
Geol Soc Am Abstr Programs... Geological Society of America. Abstracts Programs (SAUO)
Geol Soc Am Annu Meet Field Trip Guideb... Geological Society of America. Annual Meeting. Field Trip Guidebook (journ.) (SAUS)
Geol Soc Am Cordilleran Sect Annu Meet Guideb... Geological Society of America. Cordilleran Section. Annual Meeting Guidebook (journ.) (SAUS)
Geol Soc Amer Bull... Geological Society of America, Bulletin (journ.) (SAUS)
Geol Soc Amer Eng Geol Case Hist... Geological Society of America. Engineering Geology Case Histories (journ.) (SAUS)
Geol Soc America Abs with Prog... Geological Society of America. Abstracts with Programs (journ.) (SAUS)
Geol Soc America Spec Paper... Geological Society of America. Special Paper (SAUO)
Geol Soc America Spec Paper... Geological Society of America. Special Papers (journ.) (SAUS)
Geol Soc Amer Spec Pap... Geological Society of America, Special Paper (journ.) (SAUS)
Geol Soc Am Map Chart Ser... Geological Society of America. Map and Chart Series (journ.) (SAUS)
Geol Soc Am Mem... Geological Society ofAmerica. Memoir (SAUS)
Geol Soc Am Mem... Geological Society of America. Memoirs (SAUO)
Geol Soc Am Microform Publ... Geological Society of America. Microform Publica1ion (journ.) (SAUS)
Geol Soc Am Spec Pap... Geological Society of America. Special (SAUS)
Geol Soc Australia J... Geological Society of Australia Journal (journ.) (SAUS)
Geol Soc Bull... Geological Socety of America. Bulletin (SAUS)
Geol Soc Bull... Geological Society of America. Bulletin (journ.) (SAUS)
Geol Soc China Proc... Geological Society of China. Proceedings (journ.) (SAUS)
Geol Soc Egypt Annu Meet Abstr... Geological Society of Egypt. (SAUS)
Geol Soc Egypt Annu Meet Abstr... Geological Society of Egypt. Annual Meeting. Abstracts (journ.) (SAUS)
Geol Soc India Jour... Geological Society of India Journal (SAUO)
Geol Soc Jam J... Geological Society of Jamaica Journal (SAUO)
Geol Soc Korea J... Geological Society of Korea. Journal (journ.) (SAUS)
Geol Soc India J... Geological Society ofIndia Journal (SAUS)
Geol Soc Lond Misc Pap... Geological Society of London. (SAUS)
Geol Soc Lond Misc Pap... Geological Society of London. Miscellaneous Paper (journ.) (SAUS)
Geol Soc Lond Q J... Geological Society of London. Quarterly (SAUO)
Geol Soc Lond Q J... Geological Society of London. Quarterly Journal (journ.) (SAUS)
Geol Soc Lond Spec Rep... Geological Society of London. Special (SAUS)
Geol Soc Lond Spec Rep... Geological Society of London. Special Report (journ.) (SAUS)
Geol Soc Malays Bull... Geologial Society of Malaysia. Bulletin (SAUO)
Geol Soc Malays Bull... Geological Society of Malaysia Bulletin (journ.) (SAUS)
Geol Soc Malays Newsl... Geological Society of Malaysia. (SAUS)
Geol Soc Malays Newsl... Geological Society of Malaysia. Newsletter (journ.) (SAUS)
Geol Soc NZ Newsl... Geological Society of New Zealand. (SAUS)
Geol Soc NZ Newsl... Geological Society of New Zealand. Newsletter (journ.) (SAUS)
Geol Soc Oregon Country Newsl... Geological Society of the Oregon Country. Newsletter (SAUO)
Geol Soc Oregon Country News Letter... Geological Society of the Oregon Cou:ntry. News Letter (journ.) (SAUS)
Geol Soc Philipp J... Geological Society of the Philippines. Journal (journ.) (SAUS)
Geol Soc S Afr Congr Abstr... Geological Society of South (SAUO)
Geol Soc S Afr Congr Abstr... Geological Society of South Africa. Congress Abstracts (journ.) (SAUS)
Geol Soc S Afr Q News Bull... Geological Society of South Africa. Quarterly News Bulletin (journ.) (SAUS)
Geol Soc S Afr Spec Publ... Geological Society of South Africa. (SAUS)
Geol Soc S Afr Spec Publ... Geological Society of South Africa. Special Publication (journ.) (SAUS)
Geol Soc S Afr Trans... Geological Socielv of South Africa. Transactions (SAUS)
Geol Soc So Africa Trans... Geological Society of South Africa. (SAUS)
Geol Soc So Africa Trans... Geological Society of South Africa. Transaction (SAUO)
Geol Soc So Africa Trans... Geological Society of South Africa. Transactions and Proceedings (journ.) (SAUS)
Geol Soc Zimbabwe Spec Publ... Geological Society of Zimbabwe. (SAUS)
Geol Soc Zimbabwe Spec Publ... Geological Society of Zimbabwe. Special Publication (journ.) (SAUS)
Geol Surr Irel Bull... Geological Survey of Ireland. Bulletin (journ.) (SAUS)
Geol Surr Tanzania Bull... Geological Survey of Tanzania. Bulletin (journ.) (SAUS)
Geol Surv.... Geological Survey (SAUS)
Geol Surv Br Guiana Bull... Geological Survey of British Guiana. (SAUS)
Geol Surv Br Guiana Bull... Geological Survey of British Guiana. Bulletin (journ.) (SAUS)
Geol Surv Bull... Geological Survey Bulletin (journ.) (SAUS)
Geol Surv Can Econ Geol Rep... Geological Survey of Canada. (SAUS)
Geol Surv Can Econ Geol Rep... Geological Survey of Canada. Economic Geology Report (journ.) (SAUS)
Geol Surv Can Pap... Geological Survey of Canada. Paper (journ.) (SAUS)
Geol Surv Den III Ser... Geological Survey of Denmark. III (SAUS)
Geol Surv Den III Ser... Geological Survey of Denmark. III Series (journ.) (SAUS)
Geol Surv GA Bull... Geological Survey of Georgia Bulletin (SAUS)
Geol Surv India Misc Publ... Geological Survey of India. Miscellaneous Publication (journ.) (SAUS)
Geol Surv India News... Geological Survey of India News (journ.) (SAUS)
Geol Surv Iran Rep... Geological Survey of Iran. Report (journ.) (SAUS)
Geol Surv Jap Hydrogeol Maps J... Geological Survey of Japan. Hydrogeological Maps of Japan (journ.) (SAUS)
Geol Surv Jap Hydrogeol Maps Jap... Geological Survey of Japan. Hydrogeological Maps of Japan (journ.) (SAUS)
Geol Surv Jap Rep... Geological Survey of Japan. Report (journ.) (SAUS)
Geol Surv Jpn Rep... Geological Survey of Japan. Report (journ.) (SAUS)
Geol Surv Korea Tech Pap... Geological Survey of Korea. Technical Paper (journ.) (SAUS)
Geol Surv Malays Annu Rep... Geological Survey of Malaysia. Annual Report (journ.) (SAUS)
Geol Surv Malays Dist Mem... Geological Survey of Malaysia. District Memoir (journ.) (SAUS)

Geol Surv Malays Geol Pap... Geological Survey of Malaysia. Geological Papers (journ.) (SAUS)
Geol Surv NSW Bull... Geological Survey of New South Wales. Bulletin (journ.) (SAUS)
Geol Surv NSW Geol Surv Rep... Geological Survey of New South Wales. Geological Survey Report (journ.) (SAUS)
Geol Surv NSW Rep... Geological Survey of New South Wales. Geological Survey Report (journ.) (SAUS)
Geol Surv of NSW Miner Ind NSW... Geological Survey of New South Wales. Department of Mines. The Mineral Industry of New South Wales (journ.) (SAUS)
Geol Surv Pap Tas Dep Mines... Geological Survey Paper. Department of Mines. Tasmania (journ.) (SAUS)
Geol Surv Queensl Pub... Geological Survey of Queensland. Publication (journ.) (SAUS)
Geol Surv Queensl Publ... Geological Survey of Queensland. Publication (journ.) (SAUS)
Geol Surv Queensl Rep... Geologial Survey of Queensland. Report (SAUS)
Geol Surv Queensl Rep... Geological Survey of Queensland. Report (journ.) (SAUS)
Geol Surv Sierra Leone Bull... Geological Survey of Sierra Leone. Bulletin (journ.) (SAUS)
Geol Surv Tanzania Bull... Geological Survey of Tanzania. Bulletin (journ.) (SAUS)
Geol Surv Victoria Bull... Geological Survey of Victoria. Bulletin (journ.) (SAUS)
Geol Surv W Aust Bull... Geological Survey of Western Australia. Bulletin (journ.) (SAUS)
Geol Surv West Aust Bull... Western Australia. Geological Survey. Bulletin (SAUS)
Geol Surv West Malaysia Dist M... Geological Survey of West Malaysia. District Memoir (journ.) (SAUS)
Geol Surv Wyo C Resour Ser... Geological Survey of Wyoming County Resource Series (journ.) (SAUS)
Geol Surv Wyo Prelim Rep... Geological Survey of Wyoming. Preliminary Report (journ.) (SAUS)
Geol Surv Wyo Rep Invest... Geological Survey of Wyoming. Report of Investigations (journ.) (SAUS)
geom.......... geometric (SAUS)
GEOM.......... Geometrician (SAUS)
Geom.......... Geometry (BEE)
geom.......... Geometry (SHCU)
GEOM.......... Geometry [*or Geometric*]
GEOMADJ.......... Geometry Adjustment (SAUS)
Geom Aeron... Geomagnetism and Aeronomy (journ.) (SAUS)
GEOMAG...... Geomagnetism
Geomagn..... Geomagnetism (SAUS)
Geomagn Aeron... Geomagnetism and Aeronomy (journ.) (SAUS)
Geomagn and Aeron... Geomagnetism and Aeronomy (journ.) (SAUS)
Geomagn Bull Inst Geol Sci... Geomagnetic Bulletin. Institute of Geological Sciences (journ.) (SAUS)
GEOMAN...... Global Energy Operations & Management Co.
GEOMAP...... Geographic Information For Multiple Application (SAUO)
GEOMAR...... FRG Research Center for Marine Geosciences (SAUS)
Geo-Mar Lett... Geo-Marine Letters [*A publication*] (PABS)
Geo Mason U... George Mason University (GAGS)
Geo Mason UL Rev... Geolge Mason University. Law Review (journ.) (SAUS)
GEOMATE.... Geographic Map Attribute Enhancement (SAUS)
GEOMAUD... Geoscience Expedition to Dronning Maud Land (SAUS)
Geomech Comput... Geomechania Computing Programme (journ.) (SAUS)
Geomech Comput Progm... Geomechanica Computing Programme (SAUS)
G E O M E D... Geometric Editor (SAUS)
GEOMER...... Geostationary Multispectral Electroscanning Radiometer (SAUO)
Geometep.... Geothermal Metallogenesis East Pacific (SAUO)
Geomicrobiol J... Geomicrobiology Journal [*A publication*] (PABS)
GEOMIPS..... Geographic Data Management and Image Processing System (SAUO)
GEOMOD...... Geometric Modeller [*GE CAE International*] [*Software package*] (NCC)
geomorph.... geomorphologist (SAUS)
geomorph.... geomorphology (SAUS)
GEOMPAK.... Geometric Manipulation Package (SAUS)
GEOMULTI... Geocodage Multivarie (SAUS)
GEON.......... Gyro Erected Optical Navigation
GEONAMES... Geologic Names of the United States [*US Geological Survey*] [*Information service or system*] (IID)
GEONAV....... Geographic Navigation [*Navy*] (CAAL)
Geon Co...... [*The*] Geon Co. [*Associated Press*] (SAG)
GEONDS...... Ground Electromagnetic Pulse & Optical Nuclear Detonation Detection System (SAUS)
GEONESS..... Geostationary Earth Orbiting Nadir Etalon Sounding Spectrometer (SAUS)
GEON System... Gyro-Erected Optical Navigation System (SAUS)
GEOP.......... General Emergency Operations Plan (CINC)
GEOPAUSE... Geodetic Satellite in Polar Geosynchronous Orbit [*NASA*] (NASA)
Geopbys J R... Geophysical Journal. Royal Astronomical Society (SAUO)
Geopbys J R... Geophysical Journal. Royal Astronomical Society (journ.) (SAUS)
GE-OPC.......... Group of Experts on Ocean Processes and Climate [*Marine science*] (OSRA)
Geo Peabody C... George Peabody College for Teachers of Vanderbilt University (GAGS)
Geoph.......... Geophysics (DD)
geophy......... geophysical (SAUS)
geophy......... geophysics (SAUS)
GEOPHYS.... Geophysical
GEOPHYS.... Geophysicist (SAUS)
GEOPHYS.... Geophysics (SAUS)
Geophys Astrophys Fluid Dyn... Geophysical and Astrophysical Fluid Dynamics (journ.) (SAUS)
Geophys Astrophys Monogr... Geophysics and Astrophysics Monographs (journ.) (SAUS)
Geophysical... American Geophysical Union (SAUS)
Geophys J Int... Geophysical Journal International (journ.) (SAUS)
Geophys J R Astronom Soc... Geophysical Journal. Royal Astronomical Society (journ.) (SAUS)
Geophys J R Astron Soc... Geophysical Journal. Royal Astronomical Society (journ.) (SAUS)
Geophys J R Astr Soc... Geophysical Journal. Royal Astronomical Society (journ.) (SAUS)
GeophysJRoyAstronSoc... Geophysical Journal of the Royal Astronomical Society (SAUO)
Geophys J Roy Astron Soc... Geophysical Journal. Royal Astronomical Society (journ.) (SAUS)
Geophys Mag... Geophysical Magazine (journ.) (SAUS)
Geophys Norr... Geophysica Norvegica (SAUS)
Geophys Prospecting... Geophysical Pospecting (SAUS)
Geophys Res Lett... Geophysical Research Letters [*A publication*] (PABS)
Geophys Soc Tulsa Proc... Geophysical Society of Tulsa (SAUO)
Geophys Soc Tulsa Proc... Geophysical Society of Tulsa Proceedings (journ.) (SAUS)
Geophys Tecton Abstr... Geophysics and Tectonia Abstracts (journ.) (SAUS)
geopol......... geopolitical (SAUS)
geopol......... Geopolitics (BARN)
Geopol......... Geopolities (SAUS)
Geopp.......... Geopposserde [*Defendant*] [*Netherlands*] [*Legal term*] (DLA)
Geo-Process... Geo-Processing (journ.) (SAUS)
GEOPROPS... geophysical properties tool (SAUS)
GEOPS......... Geodetic Estimates from Orbital Perturbation of Satellites (IAA)
GEOPS......... Geodetic Estimates from Orbital Perturbations of Satellites
GEOPS......... Goedesy Program System (SAUS)
GEOQ........... Geos. Canada Department of Energy, Mines and Resources (journ.) (SAUS)
Geo R.......... Geographical Review (SAUS)
Geor............ Georgian (SAUS)
GEOREF....... Geographical Reference (SAUS)
GEOREF....... Geographical Reference Grid System (SAUS)
GEOREF....... Geographic Reference (SAUS)
GEOREF....... Geographic Reference Grid System (SAUO)
GEOREF....... Geographic Reference System [*Civil Defense*]
GEO-REF...... Geological Reference (SAUS)
GEOREF....... Geological Reference File [*American Geological Institute*] [*Bibliographic database*] [*Information service or system*] (IID)
GEOREF....... Geological Reference System (SAUO)
GEOREF....... World Geographic Reference System (SAUS)
GEOREF System... Geographic Reference System (SAUS)
Geo Rep...... Geological Reports (journ.) (SAUS)
Geo Rep...... Georgia Reports [*A publication*] (DLA)
GEOREQ....... Relocation Request [*Code*] [*Military*] (MCD)
Geo Rer....... Georgia Law Review (journ.) (SAUS)
Geores......... Georesources, Inc. [*Associated Press*] (SAG)
GEORG......... Georgetown, DE [*American Association of Railroads railroad junction routing code*]
Georg........... Georgian (DIAR)
GEORG......... Georgics [*Poetry*] (ROG)
GEORGE....... General Organizational Environment [*Computer science*] (BUR)
GEORGE....... General Organization and Environment (SAUS)
George......... George's Reports [*30-39 Mississippi*] [*A publication*] (DLA)
GEORGE-3D... Geoscience Research Graphics Environment - 3 Dimensional (SAUS)
GEORGE-3D... Geoscience Research Graphics Environment-3 Dimensional (SAUO)
Georgebwn LT... Georgetown Law Journal (journ.) (SAUS)
George Partn... George on Partnership [*A publication*] (DLA)
GEORGETN... Georgetown (ROG)
Georgetown C... Georgetown College (Kentucky) (GAGS)
Georgetown IJ... Georgetown Law Journal (SAUS)
Georgetown Med Bull... Georgetown Medical Bulletin (journ.) (SAUS)
Georgetown U... Georgetown University (District of Columbia) (GAGS)
Georgetown Univ Sch Dent Mirror... Georgetown University. School of Dentistry. Mirror (journ.) (SAUS)
Georgetowrn Dent J... Georgetown Dental Journal (journ.) (SAUS)
George Wash... George Washington Law Review (journ.) (SAUS)
George Washington J Internat Law and Econ... George Washington Journal of International Law and Economics (journ.) (SAUS)
George Washington Law R... George Washington Law Review (journ.) (SAUS)
George Washington U... [*The*] George Washington University (GAGS)
George Washington Univ Bull... George Washington University. Bulletin (journ.) (SAUS)
George Wash L Rev... George Washington Law Review (journ.) (SAUS)
George Wash Univ Bull... George Washington University. Bulletin (journ.) (SAUS)
Georgia........ Georgia Reports [*A publication*] (DLA)
Georgia C Milledgeville... Georgia College of Milledgeville (GAGS)
Georgia Inst Tech... Georgia Institute of Technology (GAGS)
Georgia J Int Comp L... Georgia Journal of International and Comparative Law (journ.) (SAUS)
Georgia Rep... Georgia Reports [*A publication*] (DLA)
Georgia So U... Georgia Southern University (GAGS)
Georgia St U... Georgia State University (GAGS)
Georg Nat.... Georgius Natta [*Flourished, 1477-95*] [*Authority cited in pre-1607 legal work*] (DSA)
GEOROT....... Geographical Rotation (RIMS)
GEOS........... Generator Earth Orbital Scene (SAUS)

GEOS .... Geodetic Earth Orbiting or Geodynamic Experimental Ocean Satellite (SAUS)
GEOS .... Geodetic Earth Orbiting Satellite (SAUO)
GEOS .... Geodetic Earth-Orbiting Satellite
GEOS .... Geodetic Observation Satellite
GEOS .... Geodetic Orbiting Satellite (SAUS)
GEOS .... Geodetic Satellite (SAUS)
GEOS .... Geodynamic Experimental Ocean Satellite
GEOS .... Geological (Research) Satellite
GEOS .... Geosciences group (SAUO)
GEOS .... Geoscope (journ.) (SAUS)
GEOS .... Geos Corp. (SAUO)
GEOS .... Geostationary Earth Observation Satellite (SAUO)
GEOS .... Geostationary Earth-Orbiting Satellite (SAUS)
GEOS .... Geostationary Environmental Operational Satellite (SAUS)
GEOS .... Geostationary Operational Environmental Satellite (SAUO)
GEOS .... Geosynchronous Earth Observation System (IEEE)
GEOS .... Geosynchronous Earth Orbit Satellites (ACRL)
GEOS .... Geoworks Ensemble Operating System (SAUO)
GEOS .... Goddard Earth Observing System (SAUO)
GEOS .... Graphic Environment Operating System [*Commodore 64*]
Geos-3 .... Geodetic Satellite Mission (SAUO)
GEOS-3 .... Geodynamics Experimental Ocean Satellite (SAUS)
GEOSAR .... Geologic Synthetic Aperture Radar (SAUS)
GEOSAR .... Geostationary Search and Rescue (SAUO)
GEOSAR .... Geosynchronous Earth Orbit Synthetic Aperture Radar (SAUS)
GEOSAR .... Geosynchronous Synthetic Aperture RADAR (IEEE)
Geosat .... Geodesy Satellite (CARB)
GEOSAT .... Geodesy Satellite
GEOSAT .... Geodetic/Geophysical Satellite (SAUS)
GEOSAT .... Geodetic Satellite (ADWA)
Geosat .... Geodetic Satellite
GEOSAT .... Geodynamic Experimental Ocean Satellite (MCD)
Geosat .... Geologic Satellite (SAUS)
GEOSAT .... Geopotential Satellite (SAUO)
GEOSAT .... Geostationary Environmental Operational Satellite (SAUO)
GEOSAT .... Geostationary Satellite (SAUS)
GEOSAT .... Geosynchronous Satellite (SEWL)
GEOSAT .... US Navy Geodetic Satellite (SAUS)
Geosc .... Geoscience (SAUS)
GEOSCAN .... Geographic Scanning (SAUS)
GEOSCAN .... Geological Survey of Canada (SAUS)
GEOSCAN .... Ground Based Communications Antenna (SAUS)
GEOSCAN .... Ground-Based Electronic Omnidirectional Satellite Communications Antenna
Geosci .... Geoscience (DIAR)
Geosci Doc... Geoscience Documentation (journ.) (SAUS)
Geoscience Inf Soc Proc... Geoscience Information Society. Proceedings (journ.) (SAUS)
Geoscience Ini Soc Proc... Geoscience Information Society. Proceedings (journ.) (SAUS)
GEOSEC .... Geographic Security (SAUS)
GEOSECS ..... Geochemical Ocean Sections (SAUS)
GEOSECS ..... Geochemical Ocean Sections Study [*Submarine ocean exploration by US for International Decade of Ocean Exploration*]
GEOSECS ..... Geochemical Oceans Section Study (SAUS)
GEOSECS ..... Geochemical Sections Study (USDC)
GEOSEM ...... Global Electro-Optical Systems Environment Matrix (SAUS)
GEOSEPS ..... General Summary Edit Program (NAKS)
GEOSEPS ..... Geosynchronous Solar Electric Propulsion Stage [*NASA*] (NASA)
GEO/SIT .... Geographical Situation (MCD)
GEO/SIT .... Geographical Situation (SAUS)
GEOSS .... Geophysical Survey System [*Naval Oceanographic Office*]
GEOSS .... Integrated Geophysical Survey System (SAUS)
GeoSSR .... Georgian Soviet Socialist Republic
Geosynchron... Geosynchronous Operational Environmental Satellite (NAKS)
GE/OTA .... IGOSS Group of Experts on Operations and Technical Applications (SAUO)
GEOTAIL ...... Geomagnetic Tail Laboratory (ADWA)
Geotech Abstr... Geotechnical Abstracts (journ.) (SAUS)
Geotech Geol Eng... Geotechnical and Geological Engineering [*A publication*] (PABS)
GEOTECHNIQ... GEOTECHNIQUE (SAUS)
Geotherm Hot Line... Geothermal Hot Line (journ.) (SAUS)
Geotherm Res Counc Trans... Geothermal Resources Council. Transactions (journ.) (SAUS)
Geotherm Resouces Counc Trans... Geothermal Resources Council Transactions (SAUS)
Geotherm Resour Counc Bull... Geothermal Resources Council Bulletin [*A publication*] (CABS)
Geotherm Technol... Geothermal Technology (journ.) (SAUS)
Geo time ..... Geological Time [*Medicine*] (EDAA)
GeoTk .... Geotek Communications, Inc. [*Associated Press*] (SAG)
GeoTICo .... GeoTel Communications Corp. [*Associated Press*] (SAG)
GeoTMS .... Geographic Town Management System (SAUS)
GEOTN .... Georgetown, LA [*American Association of Railroads railroad junction routing code*]
GEOTp .... Geographic Township (SAUS)
GEOU .... Graphics Entity and Operation Unification [*Computer science*]
GEOW .... Geothermal Resources International, Inc. (SAUO)
GEOW .... GeoWaste, Inc. [*NASDAQ symbol*] (SPSG)
Geo Wash J Int L... George Washington Journal of International (SAUS)
Geo Wash L Rev... George Washington Law Review (journ.) (SAUS)
Geo Williams C... George Williams College (GAGS)
Geoworks..... GeoWorks [*Associated Press*] (SAG)
GeoWste ...... GeoWaste, Inc. [*Associated Press*] (SAG)
GEOX .... Geonest Corp. (SAUO)
GEOX .... Geonex Corp. (SAUO)
GEP .... Gastroenteropancreatic System [*Medicine*]
GEP .... General Electric Plastics [*Australia*] [*Commercial firm*]
GEP .... General Enrollment Plan [*Insurance*]
GEP .... General Entry Permit
GEP .... General Equivalence Point (SAUS)
GEP .... Geological Echo Profiler [*Oceanography*] (MSC)
GEP .... Geologie Echo Profiler (SAUS)
GEP .... Goddard Experimental Package [*NASA*]
GEP .... Good Engineering Practice (EG)
GEP .... Graduate Education Program
GEP .... Graduate Education Programme [*Dialog*]
GEP .... Graduate English Papers (journ.) (SAUS)
GEP .... Grasslands Ecology Program (EERA)
GEP .... Great Pacific Resources [*Vancouver Stock Exchange symbol*]
GEP .... Grolier Electronic Publishing, Inc. [*Information service or system*] (IID)
GEP .... Gross Energy Product
GEP .... Ground Effects Phenomenon
GEP .... Ground Entry Point (NVT)
GEP .... Ground Entry Points (SAUO)
GEP .... Ground Environment Program (SAUO)
GEP .... Group Employment Plan (MCD)
GEP .... Grupos Especiais de Paraquedistas [*Mozambique*]
GEP .... Gulf Environmental Measurements Program (MCD)
GEP .... Gustatory Evoked Potential [*Medicine*] (DMAA)
GEP .... Minneapolis, MN [*Location identifier*] [*FAA*] (FAAL)
GEPA .... General Education Provisions Act [*1970*]
GEPA .... Grade Eight Proficiency Assessment
GEPA .... Gulf-European Freight Association (SAUO)
GEPAC .... General Electric Process Automation Computer
GEPAC .... General Electric Programmable Automatic Comparator [*or Computer*]
GEPAC .... General Purpose Automatic Checkout (SAUS)
GEPB .... Grievance and Employment Policy Board [*Army*]
GEPC .... German External Property Commission (SAUO)
GEPC .... German External Property Control Commission [*Minden*] [*Allied German Occupation Forces*]
GEPCA .... GP. Journal of the American Academy of General Practice (journ.) (SAUS)
GEPDS .... General Electric Process Design System
GEPE .... GATE [*GARP Atlantic Tropical Experiment*] Equatorial Profiling Experiment [*Marine science*] (MSC)
GEPE .... Groupe d'Etudes Politiques Europeennes (EA)
GEPEXS .... General Electric Parts Explosion System
GEpFAR .... Federal Archives and Records Center, General Services Administration, Atlanta Region (SAUS)
GEpFAR .... Federal Archives and Records Center, General Services Administration, Atlanta Region, East Point, GA [*Library symbol*] [*Library of Congress*] (LCLS)
GEPFR .... General Electric Prototype Fast Reactor (SAUO)
GEPG .... Gastroesphageal Pressure Gradient [*Medicine*] (EDAA)
GEPH .... Gestational Edema with Proteinuria and Hypertension [*Medicine*] (MELL)
GEPI .... Gestioni e Partecipazioni Industriali [*Industrial Management and Participation*] [*Italian government-sponsored agency to aid ailing companies*]
GEPL .... General Equipment and Packaging Laboratory [*Army*]
GEPLACEA ... Grupo de Paises Latinoamericanos y del Caribe Exportadores de Azucar [*Group of Latin American and Caribbean Sugar Exporting Countries - GLACSEC*] (EAIO)
GEPM .... General Electric Company, Physical Metallurgy (SAUO)
GEPM .... General Electric Physical Metallurgy (SAUS)
GEPOD .... General Electric Pod (SAUS)
GEPOL .... Generalized Processor for Command-Oriented Language (DNAB)
GEPROC .... German External Property Commission (SAUO)
GEPS .... Geostationary Earth Processes Spectrometer (SAUS)
GEPURS .... General Electric General Purpose
GEPVP .... Groupement Europeen des Producteurs de Verre Plat [*European Group of Flat Glass Manufacturers*] (EAIO)
GEPX .... Trinity Rail Management [*Private rail car owner code*]
GEPZ .... Gen Park [*Federal Railroad Administration identification code*]
g-eq .... Gram Equivalent [*Industrial hygiene term*] (OHS)
G-EQ .... Gram-Equivalent (EEVL)
GEQ .... Moline, IL [*Location identifier*] [*FAA*] (FAAL)
GEQUIV .... Gram Equivalent [*Chemistry*] (IAA)
GER .... Gardiner Resources [*Vancouver Stock Exchange symbol*]
GER .... Gastric Emptying Rate [*Medicine*] (EDAA)
GER .... Gastroesophageal Reflux [*See also GERD*] [*Medicine*]
GER .... Gene Expression Regulation [*Medicine*] (MELL)
GER .... General Engineering Research
GER .... Generat Engineering Research (SAUS)
GER .... Geomagnetic Electrorinetograph
Ger .... Gerard Pucelle [*Deceased, 1184*] [*Authority cited in pre-1607 legal work*] (DSA)
GER .... Geriatric Core Study (SAUO)
GER .... Geriatrics
Ger .... Gerim (BJA)
ger .... German [*MARC language code*] [*Library of Congress*] (LCCP)
Ger .... German (SHCU)
GER .... German [*Language, etc.*]
GER .... German Educational Reconstruction (SAUS)
GER .... German Education Reconstruction (SAUO)
Ger .... Germanic (DIAR)

Ger.............. Germany (VRA)
GER.............. Germany
GER.............. Germany Fund [*NYSE symbol*] (TTSB)
GER.............. Germany Fund, Inc. [*NYSE symbol*] (SPSG)
Ger.............. Germnania (SAUS)
GER.............. Gerontology [*American Occupational Therapy Association*]
GER.............. GE Rosenberger [*Federal Railroad Administration identification code*]
ger.............. Gerund (SHCU)
GER.............. Gerund
ger.............. gerundial (SAUS)
ger.............. gerundival (SAUS)
ger.............. gerundive (SAUS)
GER.............. Global Environmental Research
GER.............. Global Environment Research Office (SAUS)
GER.............. Goodyear Engineering Report (MCD)
GER.............. Gran Enciclopedia Rialp [*A publication*]
GER.............. Granular Endoplasmic Reticulum (DB)
GER.............. Granule, Extended Release (SAUS)
GER.............. Great Eastern Railway [*British*]
GER.............. Gross Energy Requirement (SAUS)
GER.............. Group of European Radiotherapists (SAUO)
GER.............. Guernsey Airlines Ltd. [*British*] [*ICAO designator*] (FAAC)
GER.............. Guide to Environmental Resources (SAUO)
GER.............. Guilde Europeenne du Raid [*European Expedition Guild - EEG*] (EAIO)
GER.............. Nueva Gerona [*Cuba*] [*Airport symbol*] (OAG)
GERA.............. Georgia Educational Research Association (SAUO)
gera.............. geratologist (SAUS)
gera.............. geratology (SAUS)
GERA.............. Guard's Expense in Returning Absentee [*Army*]
GerABcp.............. German American Bancorp [*Associated Press*] (SAG)
GerAE.............. German Antarctic Expedition [*1901-03,1911-12,1938-39*]
GERB.............. Geostationary Earth Radiation Budget (SAUO)
GERB.............. Global Earth Radiation Budget
GERBIL.............. Great Education Reform Bill [*British*]
GerbSc.............. Gerber Scientific, Inc. [*Associated Press*] (SAG)
GERC.............. Geophysical and Environmental Research Corporation (SAUO)
GERD.............. Gastroesophageal Reflux Disease [*Gastroenterology*] (DAVI)
GERD.............. Gross Domestic Expenditure on Research and Development (SAUO)
GERD.............. Gross Expenditure on Research Development
Gerda.............. Gyro Equipped Road Data Analyser (SAUO)
GERDA.............. Gyro Equipped Road Data Analyser (or Analyzer) (SAUS)
GERDAT.............. Groupement d'Etudes et de Recherche pour le Developpement de l'Agronomie Tropicale [*Group for the Study and Research of Tropical Agronomy*] [*International Cooperation Center of Agricultural Research for Development*] [*Information service or system*] (IID)
GER DEM REP... German Democratic Republic (WDAA)
GERD/GDP... Gross Expenditure on Research and Development/Gross Domestic Product [*Ratio*]
GERE.............. Government Employees Real Estate (SAUO)
Ger Ec Bul... Economic Bulletin (SAUS)
Ger Ec Bul... Economic Bulletin (journ.) (SAUS)
GEREP.............. Generalized Equipment Reliability Evaluation Procedure
Gereq.............. Gerequireerde [*Defendant*] [*Netherlands*] (ILCA)
GERES.............. Geometric Rectification Expert System (SAUO)
GE ResLab... General Electric Research Laboratory, Schenectady (SAUO)
GerFd.............. Germany Fund, Inc. [*Associated Press*] (SAG)
GERG.............. Global Environment Research Group (SAUO)
GERG.............. Grassy Ecosystems Reference Group (SAUO)
GERG.............. Groupe Europeen de Recherches Gazieres [*European Gas Research Group*] (EAIO)
ger grndng... gerund grinding (SAUS)
GERI.............. Geriatric
geri.............. Geriatrics [*Medicine*] (DAVI)
GERI.............. Greenland Environmental Research Institute (SAUO)
GERIACT.............. Great Education Reform Act [*1988*] (AIE)
GERIAT.............. Geriatrics
GeriMed.............. Geriatric & Medical Companies, Inc. [*Associated Press*] (SAG)
GERIS.............. Geophysical And Environmental Research Imaging Spectrometer (SAUS)
GERIS.............. Graphic Expression Reading Improvement System
GERIS.............. Group on Evaluation of Research in Information Science (SAUO)
GERL.............. Golgi-Associated Endoplasmic Reticulum Lysosomes
Ger L&L.............. German Life and Letters (journ.) (SAUS)
Ger Life L... German Life and Letters (journ.) (SAUS)
GERM.............. Generalized Entity-Relationship Model (HGAA)
Germ.............. German (NTIO)
GERM.............. German [*Language, etc.*] (ROG)
Germ.............. Germania [*of Tacitus*] [*Classical studies*] (OCD)
Germ.............. Germany (CMD)
GERM.............. Global Error Recovery Mechanism (SAUS)
GERM.............. Ground Effect Research Machine
GERMA.............. Germantown, WI [*American Association of Railroads railroad junction routing code*]
GERMA.............. Groupe d'Etude des Ressources Maritimes [*Universite du Quebec a Rimouski*] [*Canada*] [*Research center*]
German.............. Germanicus [*15BC-19AD*] [*Classical studies*] (OCD)
Germanan Chem Engng... German Chemica1 Engineering (SAUS)
German Chem Engng... German Chemical Engineering (journ.) (SAUS)
German DR... German Democratic Republic (SAUO)
German Fct... Facts and Figures (journ.) (SAUS)
German Int... German International (SAUS)
German Med Monthly... German Medical Monthly (SAUS)
German Q.... German Quarterly (journ.) (SAUS)
German Tb Q... German Tribune Quarterly Review (journ.) (SAUS)
German Yb Int'l L... German Yearbook of International Law [*A publication*] (DLA)
Germany FR... Federal Republic of Germany (SAUO)
GERMDF.............. German Ministry of Defense
GERM DIO... Germanium Diode (SAUS)
GERME.............. Groupe d'Etude en Regulation Metabolique [*University of Quebec at Rimouski*] [*Research center*] (RCD)
Germed.............. German Medicament (SAUO)
GerMedMon... German Medical Monthly (journ.) (SAUS)
Germfask.............. Grant, Edge, Robinson, Mead, French, Ackley, Shephard, and Knaggs [*Founders of a town in Michigan's Upper Peninsula that derived its name from the initial letters of their surnames*]
germi.............. germicide (SAUS)
GermJud.............. Germania Judaica [*A publication*] (BJA)
Germ R.............. Germanic Review (journ.) (SAUS)
GERN.............. Geron Corp. [*NASDAQ symbol*] (SAG)
GerNew.............. Germany Fund New [*Associated Press*] (SAG)
GERNORSEA... German Naval Forces in the North Sea (SAUS)
GERNORSEA... German Naval Forces, North Sea Subarea [*NATO*] (NATG)
GERO.............. George Rogers Clark National Historical Park
GERO.............. GE [*General Electric Co.*] Robot
GERO.............. Global Environmental Research Organization
Gerodontolo... Gerodontology (journ.) (SAUS)
Geron.............. Geronimo (SAUS)
GeronCp.............. Geron Corp. [*Associated Press*] (SAG)
Gerontol.............. Gerontology [*or Gerontologist*] [*Geriatrics*] (DAVI)
Gerontol Abstr... Gerontological Abstracts (journ.) (SAUS)
Gerontol Clin... Gerontotogia Clinica (journ.) (SAUS)
Gerontol Geriatr Educ... Gemntology and Geriatrics Education (journ.) (SAUS)
GEROS.............. General Routing Optimization System (IAA)
GEROS.............. Geological Resource Study (SAUO)
Ger P.............. German Pharmacopeia [*Medicine*] (EDAA)
GERPAT.............. German Patent (IAA)
Ger Plast.............. German Plastics (journ.) (SAUS)
Ger Q.............. German Quarterly [*A publication*] (BRI)
Ger Q.............. German Quarterly (journ.) (SAUS)
GERR.............. Government Employee Relations Report (journ.) (SAUS)
Ger Rev.............. Germanic Review (journ.) (SAUS)
GERRI.............. Geriatric Evaluation by Relative Rating Instrument [*Medicine*] (DMAA)
GERRI.............. Geriatric Evaluation by Relative's Rating Instrument
Gerrity.............. Gerrity Oil & Gas [*Associated Press*] (SAG)
GERS.............. Geophysical Environmental Research Inc. Spectroradiometer (SAUO)
GERSAL.............. General Electric Symbolic Assembly Language (IAA)
GERSIS.............. General Electric Range Safety Instrumentation System [*Aerospace*]
Ger Slav.............. Germano-Slavica (journ.) (SAUS)
GERT.............. General Employee Radiation Training (SARE)
GERT.............. Graphical Evaluation and Review Technique
Gertherm Rep... GeothermalReport (journ.) (SAUS)
GERTIE.............. GEORGE [*General Organizational Environment*] Remote Terminal Interrogative Environment [*Computer science*] (IAA)
Ger Tit.............. Gerard's Titles to Real Estate [*A publication*] (DLA)
GERTS.............. General Electric Radio [*or Range*] Tracking System [*Aerospace*]
GERTS.............. General Electric Remote Terminal Supervisor
GERTS.............. General Electric Remote Terminal System (IEEE)
GERTS.............. General Electric Remote Transmission Supervisor (SAUS)
GERTS.............. General Remote Terminal Supervisor (SAUS)
GERTS.............. General Remote Terminal System (NITA)
GERV.............. General Electric Reentry Vehicle [*Aerospace*] (AAG)
GERY.............. Georgia Eastern Railroad [*Federal Railroad Administration identification code*]
GES.............. Gale Environmental Sourcebook [*A publication*]
GES.............. Gamma European System (IAA)
GES.............. Gateway Earth Station (SEWL)
GES.............. General and Estimates Section (SAUO)
GES.............. General Edit System [*Computer science*] (IAA)
GES.............. General Educational Services Corp.
GES.............. General Education Services (SAUS)
GES.............. General Electric Semiconductor
GES.............. General Electric Silicones [*Australia*] [*Commercial firm*]
GES.............. General Engineering Service (SAUS)
GES.............. General Engineering Squadron
GES.............. General Estimates System [*NHTSA*] (TAG)
GES.............. Generalized Edit System (SAUS)
GES.............. Generalized Expectancies Scale (SAUS)
GES.............. General Santos [*Philippines*] [*Airport symbol*] (OAG)
GES.............. Generic Environmental Statement [*Nuclear energy*] (NRCH)
GES.............. Generic Equipment Simulator [*Electronics*] (AAEL)
GES.............. Genesis Resource Corp. [*Vancouver Stock Exchange symbol*]
GES.............. Genisco Technology Corp. (SAUO)
GES.............. Geographical Enforcement System (SAUO)
GES.............. Geographic Entry System (SAUO)
GES.............. Gesellschaft [*Company*] [*German*]
Ges.............. Gesellschaft [*Company*] [*German*] (ODBW)
ges.............. Gesso (VRA)
GES.............. Gestair Executive Jet [*Spain*] [*ICAO designator*] (FAAC)
GES.............. Gilt-Edged Securities [*Business term*]
GES.............. Global External Scheme (SAUS)
GES.............. Gloucestershire Engineering Society (SAUO)
GES.............. Glucose Electrolyte Solution [*Medicine*]
GES.............. Goddard Experiment Support System [*NASA*] (MCD)
GES.............. Gold Exchange Standard
GES.............. Goliath Edison Screw
GES.............. Goode Environmental Services (EFIS)
GES.............. Gordon, E. S., Joplin MO [*STAC*]
GES.............. Government Economic Service [*British*]

GES............ Government Evacuation Scheme [*British*] [*World War II*]
GES............ Grand Exploitation System (SAUS)
GES............ Great Eastern Shipping (SAUS)
GES............ Green Extension System [*Traffic signal*] (DICI)
GES............ Grips Strong and Equal [*Medicine*] (MEDA)
GES............ Ground Earth Station [*Telecommunications*]
GES............ Ground Electronics System (SAUO)
GES............ Ground Electronic System
GES............ Ground Engineering System (ACAE)
GES............ Ground Entry Station (MCD)
GES............ Ground Environment Installation (SAUS)
GES............ Ground Equipment Storage (SAUS)
GES............ Ground Equipment System
GES............ Ground Exploitation System (SAUS)
GES............ Groupe d'Etudes Sartriennes (EAIO)
GES............ Group Encounter Survey
GES............ Group Environment Scale [*Personality development test*] [*Psychology*]
GES............ Group E streptococcus (SAUS)
GES............ Guess, Inc. [*NYSE symbol*] (SG)
GES............ Gulf Electronics System (SAUS)
GES............ Gulf Environmental Systems Inc. (SAUO)
GES............ WHO Global Epidemiological Surveillance and Health Situation Assessement SP (SAUS)
GESAANP/NW... GE [*General Electric Co.*] Stockholders' Alliance Against Nuclear Power/Nuclear Weapons (EA)
Ges Abh....... Gesammelte Abhandlungen zur Roemischen Religions- und Stadtgeschichte [*A publication*] (OCD)
GESAC........ General Electric Self Adaptive Control (SAUS)
GESAC........ General Electric Self-Adaptive Control System
GESAC System... General Electric Self Adaptive Control System (SAUS)
GESAG........ GIPME Expert Scientific Advisory Group (SAUO)
GESAL........ General Electric Symbolic Assembly Language (IAA)
GESAL........ General Symbolic Assembly Language (SAUS)
GESAMP...... Group of Experts on the Scientific Aspects of Marine Environmental Protection [*Marine science*] (OSRA)
GESAMP...... Group of Experts on the Scientific Aspects of Marine Pollution [*ICSU*] (EAIO)
GESAMP...... IMO-FAO-UNESCO-WMO-WHO-IAEA-UN-UNEP Joint Group of Experts on the Scientific Aspects of Marine Environmental Protection (SAUS)
GESAMP...... Joint Group of Experts on the Scientific Aspects of Marine Environmental Protection (SAUS)
GESASA........ Greek Ex-Servicemen's Association of South Australia
GESASNFF.... General Electric Stockholders' Alliance for a Sustainable Nuclear-Free Future (EA)
GESB.......... General Export Services Branch [*Department of Trade*] [*British*]
GesB.......... Hebraeisches und Aramaeisches Handwoerterbuch ueber das Alte Testament [*W. Gesenius and F. Buhl*] [*A publication*] (BJA)
GESBT........ Generic Expert System Building Tool
GESC.......... Government EDP [*Electronic Data Processing*] Standards Committee [*Canada*]
GESC.......... Govenoment EDP Standards Committee (SAUS)
Gesch.......... Geschichte [*of Germanicus*] [*Classical studies*] (OCD)
GESCH........ Geschichte [*History*] [*German*]
GESCO........ General Electric Supply Corp.
GESCOM..... General Electric Scientific Color Matching (IAA)
Ge Se.......... Germanium Selenide (SAUS)
GESEM........ Groupement Europeen des Sources d'Eaux Minerales Naturelles [*European Group ofNatural Mineral Water Sources*] (EAIO)
GESEP........ Centre for European Social and Economic Policy (SAUO)
GESG.......... Communications Electronics Security Group (SAUO)
GESH.......... Grain Effect Screenless Halftone [*Printing technique*]
GESHUA...... General Electric Six Hundred Users' Association [*Later, HLSUA*] [*Computer science*]
GeSi............ Germanium Silicide (SAUS)
GESIFLOG.... Generalized Signal Flow Graph (SAUS)
GESIMA....... Geesthacht Simulation Model of the Atmosphere (SAUS)
GE-SJ.......... General Electric Company-San Jose (SAUO)
GESM.......... Group for Educational Services in Museums (SAUO)
GESMAR...... Geodetic Survey Marks Register [*of Western Australia*] [*State*] (EERA)
GESMO........ General Environmental Impact Statement on the Use of Mixed Oil Fuel (SAUO)
GESMO........ Generic environment statement on mixed oxide (SAUS)
Gesnerus Suppl... Gesnerus. Supplement (SAUS)
GESO.......... Geodetic Earth-Orbiting Satellite (SAUS)
GESO.......... Group Equipment Staff Officer [*British military*] (DMA)
GESO.......... Gurkha Ex-Servicemen's Organisation
GESOC........ General Electric Satellite Orbit Control [*Aerospace*]
GESP.......... Gas entrainment suppressor plates (SAUS)
GESP.......... General Extrasensory Perception [*Parapsychology*]
G-ESP.......... Greens-Ecological Social Party [*Slovenia*] [*Political party*] (BUAC)
GESPL.......... General Edit System Programming Language (IAA)
G E S P L...... Generalised Edit System Programming Language (SAUS)
GESPL.......... Generalized Edit System Programming Language [*Computer science*] (PDAA)
GESREM...... Group of Experts on Standards and Reference Materials (SAUO)
GESS.......... Generator Exhaust Signature Suppression (PDAA)
GESS.......... Geostationary Environmental Satellite System (SAUO)
GESS.......... GE Solid State (SAUS)
GESS.......... Graphics Executives Support System (ADWA)
GESS.......... Grinding Energy Saving System (SAUS)
GESSAR........ General Electric Standard Safety Analysis Report (SAUS)
Ges Schr..... Gesammelte Schriften [*A publication*] (OCD)
GesStud....... Gesammelte Studien [*A publication*] (BJA)
GEST.......... Gas Explosive Simulation Technique [*Air Force*]
GEST.......... Gemini Slowscan Television [*NASA*]
GEST.......... General Systems Theory
GEST.......... Gestation [*Medicine*] (EDAA)
gest............ Gestation (STED)
GEST.......... Gestational [*Pediatrics*]
GEST.......... Gestorben [*Died*] [*German*]
gest............ Gesture [*Theater*] (WDMC)
GEST.......... Grants for Education Support and Training [*British*] (DET)
GEST.......... Guest Supply [*NASDAQ symbol*] (TTSB)
GEST.......... Guest Supply, Inc. [*NASDAQ symbol*] (NQ)
GESTA........ Gesetzgebungsstand [*Database*] [*Deutscher Bundestag*] [*German*] [*Information service or system*] (CRD)
GESTAPO..... Geheime Staats Polizei [*Secret State Police*] [*Germany*]
GESTAPU.... Gerkang, September, Tigapuluh [*See also GESTOK*] [*Plot against the government of Indonesia beginning on September 30, 1965*]
GESTEC........ Genome Science and Technology Center (HGEN)
GESTI.......... General System Theory Implementar (SAUS)
GESTI.......... General System Theory Implementer (SAUS)
GESTOK........ Gerkang Oktober [*See also GESTAPU*] [*Plot against the government of Indonesia which began on September 30, 1965 and continued into October*]
GET............ Gaming Entertainment Television [*Interactive-gambling TV station*] (ECON)
GET............ Gas, Electric, Telephones [*of GET, Inc., a consumer group*]
GET............ Gas Evaporation Technique (SAUS)
GET............ Gastric Emptying Time [*Medicine*]
GET............ Gaylord Entertainment [*NYSE symbol*] (SPSG)
GET............ Gaylord Entertainment 'A' [*NYSE symbol*] (TTSB)
GET............ General Employee Training (COE)
GET............ General Equivalence-Point Titration (SAUS)
GET............ General Ethiopian Transport (SAUO)
GET............ Generator Environmental Tester
GET............ Genetic Engineering Technologist (SAUS)
GET............ Genetic Engineering Technology (SAUS)
GET............ Geological Engineering Technologist (SAUS)
GET............ Geological Engineering Technology (SAUS)
GET............ Geophysical Exploration Technology (SAUO)
GET............ Geraldton [*Australia*] [*Airport symbol*] (OAG)
GET............ Germanium Transistor [*Electronics*] (IAA)
Get............ Geteilt [*Divided*] [*Music*]
GET............ Get Execute Trigger (SAUS)
GET............ Getty Oil (SAUS)
GET............ Getty Oil Co. (SAUO)
GET............ Gilchrist Educationalist Trust (SAUO)
GET............ GOSIP Engineering Test Bed (SAUO)
GET............ Graded Treadmill Exercise Test [*Medicine*] (DMAA)
GET............ Graduate Employment and Training [*British*]
GET............ Graduate Employment and Training Survey (AIE)
GET............ Graphics Editing of Text (SAUS)
GET............ Great Eastern Television (SAUS)
GET............ Ground Elapsed Time [*Aerospace*]
GET............ Ground Engaging Tool (SAUS)
GET............ Ground Entry Terminal (MCD)
$GET_{1/2}$.......... Gastric Emptying Half-Time [*Gastroenterology*] (DAVI)
GETA.......... GeneralEndotracheal Anesthesia [*Medicine*] (DAVI)
GETA.......... General Equipment Test Activity [*Army*]
GETA.......... Government Employees Training Act [*1966*]
GETAB........ General Electric BWR [*Boiling Water Reactor*] Thermal Analysis Branch (NRCH)
GETAC........ General Electric Telemetering and Control
GETADE...... Group of Experts on Technical Aspects of Data Exchange (SAUO)
GETB.......... General Electric Test Reactor (SAUS)
GETC.......... Gemtec Corp. (SAUO)
GETC.......... Gurkha Engineering Training Centre (SAUO)
GetchGld...... Getchell Gold Corp. [*Associated Press*] (SAG)
GETD.......... General Equipment Testing Directorate (SAUO)
GETE.......... Geotel (SAUS)
GETE.......... Geotel, Inc. (SAUO)
Ge Te.......... Germanium Telluride (SAUS)
GETEL........ General Electric Test Engineering Language [*Computer science*] (IEEE)
GETEL........ General Test Engineering Language (SAUS)
GETEL........ General Test Engineer Language (SAUS)
GETEN........ Research & Development Centre (SAUS)
GETF.......... Global Environmental Trust Fund [*GEF-Core Fund*] (EERA)
GET FIT...... Georgia Educators Training for the Integration of Technology
GETh.......... [*The*] Epic of Gilgamesh [*R. C. Thompson*] [*A publication*] (BJA)
GETI.......... Ground Elapsed Time of Ignition [*Aerospace*] (KSC)
GETIL.......... Ground Elapsed Time of Landing
GETIS.......... Ground Environmental Team of the International Staff (SAUO)
GETIS.......... Ground Environment Team of the International Staff (SAUS)
GETIS.......... Ground Environment Technical Information System (SAUS)
GETIS.......... Ground Environment Technical Installation System [*NATO*] (NATG)
GETL.......... Ground Elapsed Time of Landing [*NASA*] (GFGA)
getlo.......... get locally (SAUS)
GETLO........ Obtain by Local Purchase [*Military*]
GETMA........ German Traffic Management Agency (SAUO)
getma.......... get from local manufacturer (SAUS)
GETMA........ Obtain by Local Manufacture [*Military*]
GETMS........ Geostationary Experimental Temperature and Moisture Sounder (SAUS)
GETO.......... Ground Equipment Turn Off (KSC)
GETO.......... Ground Equipment Turn Office (SAUS)

GETOL .... General Electric Training Operational Language (MCD)
GETOL .... General Electric Training Operational Logic [*Computer science*] (IEEE)
GETOL .... Ground Effect Takeoff and Landing
getontol .... gerontology (SAUS)
GETR .... General Electric Test Reactor
GETR .... General employee training records (SAUS)
GETR .... Group of European Manufacturers for the Advancement of Turbine Technology (SAUO)
GETS .... Gabriel Extended Travel Services (TVEL)
GETS .... General Electric Transportation Systems [*Australia*] [*Commercial firm*]
GETS .... Generalized Electronic Troubleshooting (IAA)
GETS .... General Track Simulation [*NASA*] (KSC)
GETS .... Generic ESM Test Set (SAUS)
GETS .... Global Emergency Telemedicine Service (EURO)
GETS .... Glucose Enzymatic Test Strip [*Medicine*] (EDAA)
GETS .... Government Emergency Telecommunications Service (SEWL)
GETS .... Government Emergency Telecommunications System (SAUO)
GETS .... Ground Equipment Test Set
GETS .... Groundwater Extraction and Treatment System [*Environmental science*] (BCP)
GETS .... Group Estimating Techniques System (ACAE)
GETS .... Gunnery Electronic Training Simulator (SAUS)
GETSC .... General Electric Technical Services Company
GETSCO .... General Electric Technical Services Co. (NRCH)
GETSCO .... General Electric Technical Services Company (SAUS)
GETSCO .... General Electric Technical Services Company Inc. (SAUO)
GETS Program... General Track Simulation Program (SAUO)
GETSS .... General Electric Time Sharing System (IAA)
GE-TSS .... General Electronic-Time-Sharing System (SAUS)
GETT .... German Tactical Truck (MCD)
GETT .... Gettysburg National Military Park
GETT .... Grants Equal to Taxes
GETT .... Group of European Manufacturers for the Advancement of Turbine Technology (SAUO)
GETTY .... Getty Communications [*NASDAQ symbol*] (SAG)
Getty .... Getty Petroleum Corp. [*Associated Press*] (SAG)
GettyCo .... Getty Communications [*Associated Press*] (SAG)
Getty Mus J... J. Paul Getty Museum. Journal (journ.) (SAUS)
Getuig .... Getuigenis [*Roermond/Maaseik*] (BJA)
GETVIS .... GET Virtual Storage (SAUS)
GETWS .... Get Word from String (SAUS)
GETY .... Getty Images, Inc. [*NASDAQ symbol*] (NASQ)
GETY .... Gettysburg Railroad Co. [*AAR code*]
GETYB .... Gettysburg, PA [*American Association of Railroads railroad junction routing code*]
GETZ .... General Tire [*Federal Railroad Administration identification code*]
Getz F .... Getz's Forms in Conveyancing [*A publication*] (DLA)
GEU .... Emory University, Atlanta, GA [*Library symbol*] [*Library of Congress*] (LCLS)
GEU .... Genetic Evaluation and Utilization (PDAA)
GEU .... Geothermal Energy Update [*A publication*]
GEU .... Geriatric Evaluation Unit [*Veterans Administration*] (GFGA)
GEU .... Gestation, Extrauterine (STED)
GEU .... Grosse Extra-Uterine (SAUS)
GEU .... Grossesse Extra-Uterine [*Medicine*]
GEU .... Ground Electro-Optic Unit
GEU .... Gun Electric Unit (SAUS)
GEU .... Gyroscope Electronics Unit (ADWA)
GEU-B .... Emory University, School of Business Administration, Atlanta, GA [*Library symbol*] [*Library of Congress*] (LCLS)
GEU-D .... Emory University, School of Dentistry (SAUO)
GEU-D .... Emory University, School of Dentistry, Atlanta, GA [*Library symbol*] [*Library of Congress*] (LCLS)
GEUEP .... General Electonic Utility Engineering Program (SAUS)
GEU-L .... Emory University (SAUS)
GEU-L .... Emory University, Lamar School of Law, Atlanta, GA [*Library symbol*] [*Library of Congress*] (LCLS)
GEU-LS .... Emory University, Division of Librarianship, Atlanta, GA [*Library symbol*] [*Library of Congress*] (LCLS)
GEU-M .... Emory University, A. W. Calhoun Medical Library (SAUO)
GEU-M .... Emory University, A. W. Calhoun Medical Library, Atlanta, GA [*Library symbol*] [*Library of Congress*] (LCLS)
GEU-S .... Emory University, Special Collections Department, Atlanta, GA [*Library symbol*] [*Library of Congress*] (LCLS)
GEU-T .... Emory University, Candler School of Theology, Atlanta, GA [*Library symbol*] [*Library of Congress*] (LCLS)
GEU-Y .... Emory University, Yerkes Primate Research Center (SAUO)
GEU-Y .... Emory University, Yerkes Primate Research Center, Atlanta (SAUS)
GEU-Y .... Emory University, Yerkes Primate Research Center, Atlanta, GA [*Library symbol*] [*Library of Congress*] (LCLS)
GeV .... Billion Electron Volts (SAUS)
GEV .... Gallivare [*Sweden*] [*Airport symbol*] (OAG)
Gev .... Giga Electron Volt (STED)
GeV .... Giga Electron Volt
GEV .... Gravure Education Foundation (SAUO)
GEV .... Ground Effect Vehicle
GEV .... Groundnut Eyespot Virus
GEVIC .... General Electric Variable Increment Computer
GE-VNC .... General Electric Company-Vallecitos Nuclear Center (SAUO)
GEVNC .... General Electric Vallecitos Nuclear Center [*Vallecitos, CA*] (GAAI)
GEVS .... General Environmental Verification Specification (SAUO)
GEVST .... Gordon Environmental Studies Laboratory [*University of Montana*] [*Research center*] (RCD)
GEW .... Gas Electricity (SAUS)
GEW .... Gas, Electricity, Water [*Department of Employment*] [*British*]
GEW .... Gewoy (SAUS)
GEW .... Gewoya [*Papua New Guinea*] [*Airport symbol*] (OAG)
GEW .... Glazed Earthenware
GEW .... Gram Equivalent Weight
GEW .... Ground Effect Wing (PDAA)
GEWA .... George Washington Birthplace National Monument
GEWEX .... Continental-Scale Project (SAUS)
GEWEX .... Global Energy (SAUS)
GEWEX .... Global Energy and Water Cycle Experiment [*World Climate Research Program*] [*Geo science*]
GEWEX .... Global Energy and Water Experiment (ARMP)
GEWP .... George Washington Memorial Parkway [*National Park Service designation*]
GEWS .... Gianturco Expandable Wire Stent [*Medicine*] (EDAA)
GEWS .... Group on Engineering Writing and Speech (SAUO)
GEX .... Gas Exchange
GEX .... Gas Exchange Experiment (SAUO)
GEX .... Government Employees Exchange
GEX .... Granges Exploration Ltd. [*Toronto Stock Exchange symbol*]
GEXA .... GEXA Gold Corp. (SAUO)
GEXR .... Goderich-Exeter Railway [*Federal Railroad Administration identification code*]
GEY .... Getty Resources Ltd. [*Toronto Stock Exchange symbol*]
GEY .... Geuserland Airways Ltd. [*New Zealand*] [*ICAO designator*] (FAAC)
GEY .... Greybull (SAUS)
GEY .... Greybull, WY [*Location identifier*] [*FAA*] (FAAL)
GEZ .... Garretson - Elmendorf- Zinov (SAUS)
GEZ .... Garretson - Elmendorf - Zinov, Architects and Engineers [*San Francisco, CA*] [*Telecommunications service*] (TSSD)
GEZ .... Garretson - Elmendorf- Zinov, Architects and Engineers (SAUS)
GEZ .... General Electric Canada, Inc. [*Toronto Stock Exchange symbol*]
Gez .... Gezira (SAUS)
GEZ .... Goldberg Elevator [*Federal Railroad Administration identification code*]
GEZ .... Gosudarstvennoe Knigoizdatelstvo [*State Publishing House*] [*Former USSR*]
GEZERD .... Alfarbandishe Gezelshaft far Ainordenen Yidn af Erd in FSSR [*A publication*] (BJA)
Gezira Res Stn Substn Annu Rep... Gezira Research Station and Substations. Annual Report (journ.) (SAUS)
GF .... America First Guaranteed Income Fund [*AMEX symbol*] (COMM)
GF .... Aviation Guided Missileman [*U.S. Navy enlisted rating*] (AUER)
GF .... French Guiana [*ANSI two-letter standard code*] (CNC)
GF .... Gage Factor [*Aerospace*] (NAKS)
GF .... Gain Factor [*Computer science*]
GF .... Galois Field [*Mathematics*] (IAA)
GF .... Galvanized Steel Fastenings
GF .... Games Finished [*Baseball*]
GF .... G and A Factor
GF .... Gap Filler [*RADAR*]
GF .... Gap Filter (SAUS)
GF .... Garage Forecourts [*Public-performance tariff class*] [*British*]
GF .... Gas Filled (MSA)
GF .... Gas Flow (SAUS)
GF .... Gas Focusing (SAUS)
GF .... Gas-Freeing System
GF .... Gasoline-Fueled [*Automotive engineering*]
GF .... Gastric Fistula [*Gastroenterology*] (DAVI)
GF .... Gastric Fluid [*Medicine*] (MAE)
GF .... Gaudeamus Foundation [*Netherlands*] (EAIO)
GF .... Gauge Factor (MCD)
GF .... Gelatinous Fiber [*Botany*]
GF .... General File (COE)
GF .... General Files (SAUS)
GF .... General Fireproofing (SAUS)
GF .... General Foods (SAUS)
GF .... General Foods Corp. (CDAI)
GF .... General Foods, Ltd (SAUS)
G/F .... General within Families (DICI)
GF .... Generating Function (SAUS)
GF .... Generator Field
GF .... Generic Failure
GF .... Gentleman Friend
GF .... Georgia and Florida Railroad Co. (SAUO)
GF .... Georgia & Florida R. R. [*AAR code*]
GF .... Germfree [*Medicine*]
GF .... Giant Food, Inc. (EFIS)
GF .... gigaflops (SAUS)
GF .... Gingival Fibromatosis [*Medicine*] (MELL)
GF .... Girl Friend [*Slang*]
GF .... girlfriend (SAUS)
GF .... Girl Friends (EA)
GF .... Glaciofluvial Soil [*Agronomy*]
GF .... Glandular Fever [*Medicine*] (MELL)
GF .... Glass Factor [*Tissue culture*]
GF .... Glass Fiber
GF .... Glass Fibre (SAUS)
GF .... Glenoid Fossa [*Medicine*] (MELL)
G-F .... Globular-Fibrous [*Protein*] (STED)
GF .... Globular-Fibrous [*Biochemistry*]
GF .... Globule Fibril (STED)
GF .... Glomerular Filtrate [*Medicine*]
GF .... Glomerular Filtration (STED)

GF Gluten-Free [*Diet*]
GF Goals For [*Hockey*]
GF Gold Field
gf Gold Filled [*Watch*]
GF Gold Filling (SAUS)
GF Goldfinch [*Ornithology*]
GF Goldflow (AFM)
GF Gonococcus Filus [*A microorganism*]
GF Good Faith [*Legal shorthand*] (LWAP)
GF Gordon Fraser [*Publisher*] [*British*]
GF Gorilla Foundation (EA)
GF Governmental Finances (SAUO)
GF Government Form
GF Government Funded (BABM)
GF Government Furnished (SAUS)
GF Gradient Freezing (SAUS)
GF Gradient Furnance (SAUS)
GF Gram Force (IAA)
gf Gram-Force (DMAA)
GF Grand Fast (SAUS)
GF Grandfather
GF Grand Fleet [*British military*] (DMA)
GF Grand Format [*Graphic arts*] (DGA)
GF Grant Foundation (SAUO)
GF Graphite Furnace (SAUS)
GF Grapple Fixture (SPST)
GF Gravimetric Factor (SAUS)
GF Grayson Foundation [*Later, GJC*] (EA)
GF Great Falls-Billings [*Diocesan abbreviation*] [*Montana*] (TOCD)
GF Great Fire [*of London, 1666*]
GF Green Feed (SAUS)
GF Green Function (SAUS)
GF Greens Function (SAUS)
GF Greenstick Fracture [*Medicine*] (MELL)
GF Greensward Foundation (EA)
GF Grief Facilitation [*Psychology*] (DHP)
GF Grinding Fixture (MCD)
GF Griseofulvin (STED)
GF Ground Face [*Technical drawings*]
GF Ground Fault (SAUS)
G/F Ground/Flight Test
GF Ground Fog [*Meteorology*]
GF Ground Foraging [*Ecology*]
GF Ground Forces [*Military*]
GF Ground Frost (WEAT)
GF Group of Fourteen [*NATO countries minus France*] (NATG)
GF Growth Factor [*Endocrinology*] (DAVI)
GF Growth Failure (STED)
GF Growth Fraction [*Endocrinology*]
GF Guggenheim Foundation (BARN)
GF Guided Flight (ACAE)
gf guiltfree (SAUS)
GF Guinean Franc [*Monetary unit*] (ODBW)
GF Gulf Air [*ICAO designator*] (AD)
GF Gulf Aviation Ltd. (SAUO)
GF Gunfired (SAUS)
GF Gunnery Flight
GF New Germany Fund [*NYSE symbol*] (SPSG)
GF3 General Format No. 3 (SAUS)
GFA Federal Aviation Administration (SAUS)
GFA Federal Aviation Administration, Southern Region, East Point (SAUS)
GFA Federal Aviation Administration, Southern Region, East Point, GA [*OCLC symbol*] (OCLC)
GFA Game Fishing Association (SAUO)
GFA Gardens For All (SAUO)
GFA Gasket Fabricators Association (EA)
GFA General Fitness Assessment
GFA General Forestry Assistance
GFA General Freight Agent
GFA Geophysical Focus Area (ARMP)
GFA Georgia Forestry Association (SAUO)
GFA Giddens Family Associates (EA)
GFA Gideon Family Association (EA)
GFA Glass Formation Ability (SAUS)
GFA Glial Fibrillary Acidic Protein [*Also, GFAP*] [*Biochemistry*]
GFA Glider Flying Area (SAUS)
GFA Gloucester Fisheries Association (EA)
GFA Gold Filled Association [*Defunct*] (EA)
GFA Goodenow Family Association (EA)
GFA Good Fair Average [*Insurance*]
GFA Good Freight Agent (SAUS)
GFA Government Furnished Accessories (SAUS)
GFA Government Furnished Accessory (ACAE)
GFA Government-Furnished Ammunition (MCD)
GFA Government-Furnished Articles (KSC)
GFA Grain Futures Act (FOTI)
GFA Grain Futures Administration [*Superseded by Commodity Exchange Administration, 1936*]
GFA Graphite Furnace Atomizer (SAUS)
GFA Graves Family Association
GFA Great Falls, MT [*Location identifier*] [*FAA*] (FAAL)
GFA Gross Floor Area (ADA)
GFA Group Feedback Analysis
GFA Guitar Foundation of America (EA)
GFA Gulf Air [*United Arab Emirates*] [*ICAO designator*] (FAAC)
GFA Gun Fire Area (SAUS)
GFA Gunfire Area
GFA Gust Front Algorithm (USDC)
GFAA Game Fishing Association of Australia (EERA)
GFAA Graphite-Furnace Atomic Absorption [*Spectroscopy*] [*Physics*]
GFAAS Graphite Furnace Atomic Absorption Spectrometry (AAEL)
GFAAS Graphite Furnace Atomic Absorption Spectroscopy [*Physics*]
GFAC Ghana Federation of Agricultural Cooperatives (SAUO)
GFAC Glucose-Fatty Acid Cycle (MELL)
GFAC Ground Forward Air Controller (MCD)
g factor general factor (SAUS)
GFADS Grand Forks Air Defense Sector [*North Dakota*] (SAA)
GFAE Government-Furnished Accessory Equipment
GFAE Government-Furnished Aeronautical Equipment (AFM)
GFAE Government-Furnished Aerospace Equipment
GFAE Government Furnished Airborne Equipment (SAUS)
GFAE Government-Furnished Aircraft Equipment
GFAE Government Furnished Avionics Equipment (SAUS)
GFAEL Government Furnished Aeronautical Equipment List (MCD)
GFAEL Government Furnished Aircraft Equipment List (SAUS)
GFAGE Government Furnished Aerospace Ground Equipment (SAUS)
GFAK Go Fly a Kite (SAUS)
GFAM Graphics Flutter Analysis Methods [*Computer science*]
GF & A Gulf Florida & Alabama Railway
GF & P Gases, Fluids, and Propellants [*NASA*] (NASA)
GFAP Glial Fibrillary Acidic Protein [*Also, GFA*] [*Biochemistry*]
GFAPA Glycerine and Fatty Acid Producers Association (SAUO)
gFARAD Global Food Animal Residue Avoidance Databank (GVA)
GFAX General Facts (TVEL)
GFB Gas-Forming Bacteria (MELL)
GFB Gastroscope for Biopsy [*Medicine*] (EDAA)
GFB Georgia Factory for the Blind (SAUO)
GFB GF Corp. (SAUO)
GFB Go for Broke [*Slang*]
GFB Government Facilities Brochure
GFB Government-Furnished Baseline
GFBA Graduate Fellowships for Black Americans (EA)
GFBI Grand Fleet Battle Instructions [*British military*] (DMA)
GFbIS United States Army, Infantry School, Fort Benning, GA [*Library symbol*] [*Library of Congress*] (LCLS)
GFBN Bonthe [*Sierra Leone*] [*ICAO location identifier*] (ICLI)
GFBO Grand Fleet Battle Orders [*British military*] (DMA)
GfBV Gesellschaft fuer Bedrohte Voelker [*Society for Threatened Peoples*] (EAIO)
GFC Gas-Filled Cable (SAUS)
GFC Gas Filled Counter (SAUS)
GFC Gas-Filled Counter
GFC Gas Filter Correlation [*NASA*] (KSC)
GFC Gas Frontal Chromatography
GFC Gateway Football Conference (PSS)
GFC Gel Filtration Chromatography
GFC General Failure Criteria
GFC Generic Flow Control [*Telecommunications*] (ACRL)
GFC Genstar Financial Corp. [*Toronto Stock Exchange symbol*]
GFC George Fost College (SAUS)
GFC George Fox College [*Oregon*]
GFC Get Fresh Crew [*Rap recording group*]
GFC Gibraltar Financial Corporation (SAUS)
GFC Glass Filter Covers
GFC Global Forcing Contribution [*Environmental science*]
GFC Going for Coffee [*Computer hacker terminology*]
GFC Goldwing Flyers Club (EA)
GFC Gorilla Foundation of California (SAUO)
GFC Government Furnished Concept (SAUS)
GFC Grand Falls Central Railway Co. Ltd. [*AAR code*]
GFC Grand Fascist Council (SAUO)
GFC Graphite Fiber Composite
GFC Gulf Coast Aviation, Inc. (SAUO)
GFC Gun Feed Control (MCD)
GFC Gunfire Control (DOMA)
GFCA Golf Products and Components Association (SAUO)
GFCB Ground Fault Circuit Breaker [*Electronics*]
GFCBS Glassy-Film-Coated Boundaries (SAUS)
GFCC Guarantee Financial Corporation of California (SAUO)
GFCC Gunfire Control Center (SAUO)
GFCC Gun Fire Control Computer [*Military*] (CAAL)
GFCC Gunners Fire Control Console (SAUS)
GFCE Government-Furnished Capital Equipment (MCD)
GFCE Gross Fixed Capital Expenditure
GFCES Glider Flight Control Electronics Subsystem
GFCF Gross Fixed Capital Formation
GFCFEDA General Federation of Colliery Firemen, Examiners and Deputies Associations (SAUO)
GFCG Government Fluidic Coordinating Group
GFCG Government Fluidics Coordination Group (SAUO)
gfci gas-flow indicator (SAUS)
GFCI Gay Fathers Coalition International [*Later, GLPCI*] (EA)
GFCI Ground Fault Circuit Interrupter [*Electronics*]
GFCL Giant Follicular Cell Lymphoma [*Medicine*] (MELL)
GFCL Guild of Freemen of the City of London (SAUO)
GFCM General Fisheries Council for the Mediterranean [*ICSU*]
GF/CM^2 Gram Force per Square Centimeter
GF/CMy Gram Force per Square Centimeter (SAUS)
gf/cmy Gramme-Force per Square Centimetre (SAUS)
GFCO Glenway Financial Corp. [*NASDAQ symbol*] (SAG)

GFCO .... Glenway Fin'l [*NASDAQ symbol*] (TTSB)
GFCO .... Good Faith Charitable Organization (EA)
GFCO .... Group Fire Control Officer (WDAA)
GFCP .... Gross Fixed Capital Formation [*Medicine*] (EDAA)
GFCR .... Gas Filter Correlation Radiometer [*NASA*]
GF/CRP .... Gap Filler Control and Reporting Post (SAUS)
GFCRP .... Gap-Filler Control and Reporting Post [*RADAR*] (IAA)
GFCS .... Gaseous Flowmeter Calibration Stand
GFCS .... Gun Filter Control System (SAUS)
GFCS .... Gun Fire Control System (SAUS)
GFCS .... Gunfire Control System
GFCS .... Gun Fired Contol System (SAUS)
GFCS-B .... Gunfire Control System-Backup (DNAB)
GFCSMT ...... Generalized Fire-Control System Maintenance Trainer [*Spacecraft*] [*Navy*]
GFCSS .... Gunfire Control Subsystem (DNAB)
GFCS SATSIM... Gun Fire Control System Satellite Simulation [*Military*] (CAAL)
GFCSX .... Gun Fire Control System, Experimental (ACAE)
GFCT .... Greenwich Finance Corp. (SAUS)
GFCV .... Gas and Fuel Corp. of Victoria [*Australia*]
GFD .... Galeazzi Fracture-Dislocation [*Medicine*] (MELL)
GFD .... Gallons per Square-Foot per Day
GFD .... Gap-Filler Data [*RADAR*]
GFD .... Gemini Food Corp. [*Toronto Stock Exchange symbol*]
GFD .... General Freight Department
GFD .... General Funclional Description (SAUS)
GFD .... General Functional Description [*Military*] (AABC)
GFD .... Geographical Fluid Dynamics (SAUS)
GFD .... Geophysical Fluid Dynamics Laboratory [*National Oceanic and Atmospheric Administration*]
GFD .... Gesellschaft fur Flugzieldarstellung GmbH [*Germany*] [*ICAO designator*] (FAAC)
GFD .... Gingival Fibromatosis-Progressive Deafness Syndrome [*Medicine*] (DMAA)
GFD .... Glucose-Free Dialysate [*Nephrology*]
GFD .... Gluten-Free Diet
GFD .... Gone for the Day
GFD .... Goodenough Figure Drawing [*Psychology*] (DAVI)
GFD .... Government-Furnished Data (NASA)
GFD .... Government Furnished Design (SAUS)
GFD .... Government-Furnished Documentation (KSC)
GFD .... Greenfield, IN [*Location identifier*] [*FAA*] (FAAL)
GFD .... Ground Fault Detector (SAUS)
GFD .... Ground Forces Training Devices (Provisional) [*Army*] (RDA)
GFD .... Ground Futures Administration (SAUS)
GFD .... Group Finance Department
GFD .... Guilford Mills [*NYSE symbol*] (SAG)
GFDA .... Gust Front Detection Algorithm (USDC)
GFDC .... Group Fire Distribution Center [*Army*] (AABC)
GFDD .... Gun Fire Detection Device (SAUS)
GFDD .... Gunfire Detection Device
GFDE .... Global Force-Displacement Equation (SAUS)
GFDEP .... Ground Fog Estimated Feet Deep (SAUS)
GFDI .... Geophysical Fluid Dynamics Institute (SAUO)
GFDL .... Geophysical Fluid Dynamics Laboratory [*Princeton, NJ*] [*National Oceanic and Atmospheric Administration*]
GFDL .... Geophysics Fluid Dynamics Laboratory (SAUO)
GFDL .... Goddard Fluid Dynamics Laboratory (SAUO)
GFDNA .... Grain and Feed Dealers National Association [*Later, NGFA*] (EA)
GFDP .... Geophysical Fluid Dynamics Program [*National Oceanic and Atmospheric Administration*] (GFGA)
GFDS .... Goldfelds Flying Doctor Service (SAUS)
GFE .... Gas Fluid Exchange (SAUS)
GFE .... Gays for Equality
GFE .... Gibbs Free Energy [*Physical chemistry*]
GFE .... Goal-Free Evaluation [*Education*] (AEE)
GFE .... Government Furnished Engines (SAUS)
GFE .... Government-Furnished Equipment
GFE .... Govett Far East Investments Ltd. (SAUO)
GFE .... Greater Fuel Economy
GFE .... Gross Feasibility Estimator (MCD)
GFE .... Grout Failed Equipment (SAUS)
GFEAM .... Government-Furnished Equipment and Material (IAA)
GFE&D .... Government-Furnished Equipment and Data (SAUS)
GFE & D .... Government-Furnished Equipment and Data
GFE&M .... Government Furnished Equipment and Material (SAUS)
GFE & M .... Government-Furnished Equipment and Material (NRCH)
GFEC .... General Egyptian Electricity Corporation (SAUO)
GFEC .... Graphite-Fiber Epoxy-Composite
GFEC .... Gulf Energy Corporation (SAUO)
GFED .... Guaranty Federal Bancshares, Inc. [*NASDAQ symbol*] (NASQ)
GFED .... Guaranty Federal Savings Bank [*NASDAQ symbol*] (SAG)
GFED .... Guaranty Fedl Svgs [*NASDAQ symbol*] (TTSB)
GFE/GFAE .... Government-Furnished Equipment / Government-Furnished Aircraft Equipment (SAA)
GFE/I .... Government-Furnished Equipment/Information (AAGC)
GFE II .... Gross Feasibility Estimator II (SAUO)
GFEL .... Government-Furnished Equipment List (MCD)
GFEM .... Graphics Finite Element Module [*McDonnell-Douglas Automation Corp.*]
GFEMO .... Generalized Free-Electron Molecular Orbital (SAUS)
GFER .... Government-Furnished Equipment Records
GFERC .... Grand Forks Energy Research Center [*Energy Research and Development Administration*]
GFERR .... Government-Furnished Equipment Requirements Request
GFETC .... Grand Forks Energy Technology Center [*Later, University of North Dakota Energy Research Center*] [*Department of Energy*] (GRD)
GFEZ .... Galesburg Farmers Elevator [*Federal Railroad Administration identification code*]
GFF .... Geology Facts on File (SAUO)
GFF .... Glass-Fiber Filter [*Separation technology*]
GFF .... Government Furnished Facilities (or Facility) (SAUS)
GFF .... Granolithic Finish Floor [*Technical drawings*]
GFF .... Graphic Firing Fan [*Weaponry*] (INF)
GFF .... Griffith [*Australia*] [*Airport symbol*] (OAG)
GFF .... Griffon Corp. [*NYSE symbol*] (SAG)
GFFAPA .... Grain, Feed and Fertilizer Accident Prevention Association (SAUO)
GFFAR .... Guided Folding Fin Aircraft Rocket (SAUS)
GFFAR .... Guided Folding-Fin Aircraft Rocket
GFFC .... Geophysical Fluid Flow Cell [*Instrumentation*]
GFFC .... Geophysical Fluid Flow Cell Experiment (SAUS)
GFFC .... Gibb Family Friendship Club (EA)
GFFD .... Gross Failed Fuel Detector [*Nuclear energy*] (NRCH)
GFFE .... Global Fossil Fuel Emissions (SAUO)
GFFIL .... Groupement Francais des Fournisseurs d'Information en Ligne [*French Association of Online Information Providers*] [*Paris*] [*Information service or system*] (IID)
GFFPrI .... Griffon Corp. 2nd Cv Pfd [*NYSE symbol*] (TTSB)
GFFS .... Glycogen and Fat-Free Solid (DMAA)
GFFSA .... German Federal Flight Security Agency (SAUO)
GFG .... Geographical Field Group [*British*]
GFG .... Glare Free Gloss [*Paper*]
GFG .... Going for Growth
GFG .... [*The*] Good Food Guide [*A publication*] [*British*]
GFG .... Good Food Guide (journ.) (SAUS)
GFG .... Governor's Foot Guard
GFG .... Grafton Group Ltd. [*Toronto Stock Exchange symbol*]
GFG .... Leesburg, VA [*Location identifier*] [*FAA*] (FAAL)
GFGA .... Gippsland Fruit Growers' Association [*Australia*]
GFGC .... Great Falls Gas Company (SAUO)
GFgC .... United States Army, Civil Affairs School, Fort Gordon, GA [*Library symbol*] [*Library of Congress*] (LCLS)
GFGCA .... Gympie Fruit Growers' Cooperative Association [*Australia*]
GFGF .... Group Fore Golf Foundation (EA)
GFGK .... Gbangbatok [*Sierra Leone*] [*ICAO location identifier*] (ICLI)
GFgML .... United States Army, Medical Library, Fort Gordon, GA [*Library symbol*] [*Library of Congress*] (LCLS)
GFgMP .... United States Army, Military Police School, Fort Gordon, GA [*Library symbol*] [*Library of Congress*] (LCLS)
GFgS .... United States Army, Special Services Library, Fort Gordon, GA [*Library symbol*] [*Library of Congress*] (LCLS)
GFgSS .... United States Army, Southeastern Signal School, Fort Gordon, GA [*Library symbol*] [*Library of Congress*] (LCLS)
GFH .... Gifford-Hill & Co. Inc. (SAUO)
GFH .... Glucose-Free Hanks [*Solution*] [*Cell incubation medium*]
GFH .... Group Financial Holdings, Pty. Ltd. (SAUS)
GFHA .... Gaelic Football and Hurling Association [*Australia*]
GFHA .... Hastings [*Sierra Leone*] [*ICAO location identifier*] (ICLI)
GFHR .... Gas-Filled Hydrophobic Region
GFI .... Gap-Filler Input [*RADAR*]
GFI .... Gas Flow Indicator [*NASA*]
GFI .... General Felt Industries (SAUO)
GFI .... General Format Identifier [*Computer science*] (TNIG)
GFI .... Global Finance Information [*Information service or system*] (IID)
GFI .... Glucagon-Free Insulin [*Medicine*] (DMAA)
GFI .... Gmelin Formula Index [*Gmelin-Institut fuer Anorganische Chemie und Grenzgebiete*] [*Germany*] [*Information service or system*] (CRD)
GFI .... Government Final Inspection
GFI .... Government Free Issue (AABC)
GFI .... Government-Furnished Information
GFI .... Government Furnished Instructions (ACAE)
GFI .... Government Furnished Issue (SAUS)
GFI .... Government-Furnished Items [*DoD*]
GFI .... Government-Owned Financial Institution (ADA)
GFI .... Graham-Field Health [*NYSE symbol*] (TTSB)
GFI .... Graham Field Health Products [*NYSE symbol*] (SAG)
GFI .... Graham-Field Health Products, Inc. (SAUO)
GFI .... Graphics Function Interface (SAUS)
GFI .... Greyvest Financial Services, Inc. [*Toronto Stock Exchange symbol*]
GFI .... Ground-Fault Circuit Interrupter (LDOE)
GFI .... Ground Fault Indicator (SAUS)
GFI .... Ground-Fault Interceptor (SAUS)
GFI .... Ground Fault Interrupter [*Electronics*]
gfi .... Ground-Fault Interrupter (IDOE)
GFI .... Ground Fuel Injection (SAUS)
GFI .... Group Fault Interrupter [*Computer science*] (ELAL)
GFI .... Group Format Identifier [*Communications term*] (DCT)
GFI .... Group Fuel Injection [*Automotive engineering*]
GFI .... Group Functional Instruction (ACAE)
GFI .... Guided Fault Isolation
GFI .... Gun Filter Input (SAUS)
GFIC .... Georgia Foundation for Independent Colleges (SAUO)
GFID .... General Format Identifier (VLIE)
GFII .... Greenfield Industries, Inc. [*NASDAQ symbol*] (SAG)
GFIML .... Gap Filler Input Message Label (VLIE)
GFIN .... Game Financial Corp. [*NASDAQ symbol*] (SAG)
GFIN .... Gam Financial [*NASDAQ symbol*] (TTSB)
GFinSerf .... Grupo Fnanciero Serfin SA [*Associated Press*] (SAG)
GFIP .... Gross Fault Indicator Panel (SAA)
GFIT .... Glass-Fiber Insulation Tubing

GFIV .... Generation 5 Technology (SAUS)
GFIV .... Generation 5 Technology, Inc. (SAUO)
GfK .... Glassfibre-reinforced plastic (SAUS)
GFK .... Grand Forks [North Dakota] [Airport symbol] (OAG)
GFK .... Grand Forks Mines [Vancouver Stock Exchange symbol]
GFKB .... Kabala [Sierra Leone] [ICAO location identifier] (ICLI)
GFKE .... Kenema [Sierra Leone] [ICAO location identifier] (ICLI)
Gfl .... Genfle (SAUS)
GFL .... Geoffrion (SAUS)
GFL .... Geoffrion, Leclerc, Inc. [Toronto Stock Exchange symbol]
GFL .... German Film Library, London (SAUO)
GFL .... Germ-Free Life (MELL)
GFL .... Giant Follicular Lymphoma [Medicine] (DMAA)
GFL .... Glens Falls [New York] [Airport symbol] (AD)
GFL .... Glens Falls, NY [Location identifier] [FAA] (FAAL)
GFL .... Glossary Function List
GFL .... Government-Furnished List
GFL .... Green Forest Lumber Ltd. [Canada] [ICAO designator] (FAAC)
GFL .... Green-Fuel Loading (SAUS)
GFL .... Ground Fire Locator
GFL .... Guide to Football Literature [A publication]
GFLA .... Growth Fund of Florida, Inc. (SAUO)
GFLAAL .... Gesellschaft zur Foerderung der Literatur aus Afrika, Asien, und Lateinamerika (EAIO)
GFLD .... Generator Field
GFLI .... General Federation of Labour in Israel (SAUO)
GFLI .... GFLOPS (SAUS)
GFLL .... Freetown/Lungi [Sierra Leone] [ICAO location identifier] (ICLI)
GFLOP .... Gigaflop (DCOM)
gflop .... Gigaflop (HODG)
GFLOPS .... Billions of Floating Point Instructions Per Second (SAUS)
GFLOPS .... Giga Floating Operations per Second [Computer science]
GFLOPS .... Gigaflops (SAUS)
GFLOPS .... One Billion Floating Point Operations per Second (ACRL)
GFLP .... General Facility Layout Problem (VLIE)
GFLS .... Gaffsail (SAUS)
GFLS .... Greater Community Bancorp [NASDAQ symbol] (NASQ)
GFLS .... Ground Fire Locating System
GFLU .... General Federation of Labor Unions [Syria]
GFLV .... Grapevine Fan Leaf Virus [Plant pathology]
GFM .... Gas Flowmeter (SAUS)
GFM .... Gel Filtration Medium [Medicine] (EDAA)
GFM .... Gertsch Frequency Multiplier (ACAE)
GFM .... Glass-Fiber Material
GFM .... Goldfinch Mineral Ltd. [Vancouver Stock Exchange symbol]
GFM .... Good Fetal Movement [Medicine] (EDAA)
GFM .... Government-Furnished Material
GFM .... Government-Furnished Missile
GFM .... Gradient Decent Based Fiduccia-Mattheyses (VLIE)
GFM .... Graphics Function Monitor [Tektronix] (NITA)
GFM .... Gravitational Field Measurements (SAA)
GFM .... Greyhound Food Management
GFMA .... Gold-Filled Manufacturers Association [Later, GFA] (EA)
GFmA .... United States Army, Fort McPherson Post Library, Fort McPherson, GA [Library symbol] [Library of Congress] (LCLS)
GFMD .... Gold Film Mercury Detector [Spectrometry]
GFME .... Government-Furnished Missile Equipment (AAG)
GFML .... United States Army, Medical Library, Fort Gordon (SAUS)
GFMM .... Gaussian Fast Multipole Method [Physics]
GFMP .... Guaranteed Fair Market Price (FOTI)
GFMP .... Marampa [Sierra Leone] [ICAO location identifier] (ICLI)
GFMPL .... Geophysical Fleet Mission Program Library (SAUO)
GFMS .... Gaseous Flow Measuring System
GFMS .... Generalized File Maintenance System (ADA)
GFMS .... Generalized File Management System [Computer science] (VLIE)
GFMS .... Graseus Flow Measuring System (SAUS)
GFMVT .... General Foods Moisture Vapor Test (SAUO)
GFMVT .... General Foods Moisture Vapor Transmission
GFMZ .... Great Falls Milling [Federal Railroad Administration identification code]
GFN .... Ganglion of Facial Nerve [Medicine] (MELL)
GFN .... General Finance Corp. of Delaware (SAUO)
GFN .... Genitofemoral Nerve [Medicine] (MELL)
GFN .... Glass-Filled Nylon (SAUS)
GFN .... Global Futures Network [India] [India]] (EAIO)
GFN .... Grafton [Australia] [Airport symbol] (OAG)
GFN .... Grafton [New York] [Seismograph station code, US Geological Survey] [Closed] (SEIS)
GFN .... Growth to Full NADGE System (SAUS)
GFNL .... Granite Financial, Inc. [NASDAQ symbol] (SAG)
GFO .... Bartica [Guyana] [Airport symbol] (OAG)
GFO .... Gap-Filler Output [RADAR]
GFO .... Gas-Fired Oven
GFO .... General Freight Office
GFO .... GEOSAT [Geodetic Satellite] Follow On [Marine science] (OSRA)
GFO .... German Foreign Office [British] [World War II]
GFO .... Golden Field Office (SAUS)
GFO .... Goodwin Family Organization (EA)
GFO .... Grant Funding Order (EPAT)
GFO .... Ground Forward Observer (ACAE)
GFO .... Gulf, Mobile & Ohio Railroad [Later, Illinois Central Gulf Railroad] (IIA)
GFO .... Gulf, Mobile & Ohio R.R. Co. (SAUO)
GFOA .... Government Finance Officers Association of United States and Canada (EA)
GFOAR .... Global Family of Operational [Plan] Assessment Report (DOMA)
GFoF .... Fort Valley State College, Fort Valley, GA [Library symbol] [Library of Congress] (LCLS)
GFOF .... Geared Futures and Options Fund [Investment term] (NUMA)
GFOFB .... Geared Futures and Options and Funds (SAUS)
GFOG .... Government Fluidics Coordination Group (SAUO)
GFOM .... General Fisheries Council for the Mediterranean (SAUO)
G forces .... Acceleration forces (SAUS)
GForsT .... Tift College, Forsyth, GA [Library symbol] [Library of Congress] (LCLS)
GFOV .... Gunn Flange Oscillator; Voltage-tunable (SAUS)
GFP .... Gamma-Fetoprotein (DB)
GFP .... Gas Flow Programmer [Chromatography]
GFP .... Geeneralized File Processor (SAUS)
GFP .... Geheime Feldpolizei [Secret Police] [German]
GFP .... Gel-Filtered Platelet [Medicine] (EDAA)
GFP .... General Forecasting Program (BUR)
GFP .... General Foreign Policy [A publication]
GFP .... Generalized Fiile Policy (SAUS)
GFP .... Generalized File Processor
GFP .... Generations for Peace (EA)
GFP .... German Freedom Party (SAUO)
GFP .... Glass-Fiber Pulling [Materials processing]
GFP .... Glass-Fibre Plastic (SAUS)
GFP .... Glass Filler Pulling (SAUS)
GFP .... Global Functional Plane (SAUO)
GFP .... Glomerular Filtered Phosphate [Medicine] (EDAA)
GFP .... Government Full Period (SAUS)
GFP .... Government-Funded Procurement
GFP .... Government-Funded Program
GFP .... Government-Furnished Parts (AFM)
GFP .... Government-Furnished Property
GFP .... Green Fluorescent Protein [Biochemistry]
GFP .... Ground Fault Protector (PDAA)
GFP .... Ground Fine Pitch (AIA)
GFP&S .... Government Furnished Property and Services (SAUS)
GFP & S .... Government-Furnished Property and Services (MSA)
GFPBBD .... Groupement Francais des Producteurs de Bases et Banques de Donnees [French Federation of Data Base Producers] [Information service or system] (IID)
GFP/E .... Government Furnished Property/Equipment (ACAE)
GF-PET .... Glass-Fiber Polyethylene Terephthalate [Plastics technology]
GFPI .... Gregory Forest Products [Federal Railroad Administration identification code]
GFPIAW .... Ghana. Council for Scientific and Industrial Research. Forest Products Research Institute. Annual Report (journ.) (SAUS)
GFPL .... Government-Furnished Property List (MCD)
GFPLAW .... Ghana. Council for Scientific and Industrial Research (SAUO)
GFPM .... Gas Fission Products Monitor
GFPM .... Gated Frequency Position Modulation (SAUS)
GFPM .... Gate Frequency Position Modulation (IAA)
GFP/M .... Government-Furnished Property and Material
GFPO .... Grand Forks Project Office [Grand Forks, ND] [Terminated] [Department of Energy] (GRD)
GFPO .... Port Loko [Sierra Leone] [ICAO location identifier] (ICLI)
GFPP .... Global Forest Policy Project (SAUO)
GFPP .... Guide for the Preparation of Proposals (ACAE)
GFPS .... Globally Finite-Pulse Stable (SAUS)
GFPZ .... Granite Falls Pit [Federal Railroad Administration identification code]
GFQ .... Austin, TX [Location identifier] [FAA] (FAAL)
GFR .... Federal Reserve Bank of Atlanta (SAUS)
GFR .... Federal Reserve Bank of Atlanta, Atlanta, GA [OCLC symbol] (OCLC)
gfr .... gap-filled radar (SAUS)
GFR .... Gap-Filler RADAR
GFR .... Gas Filled Rectifier (SAUS)
GFR .... Gas-Filled Rectifier
GFR .... Gas-Filled Relay (SAUS)
GFR .... General Flight Rules [CAB] [A publication] (DLA)
GFR .... General Functional Requirements
GFR .... Generator Field Regulator (IAA)
GFR .... Geotechnical Fabrics Report [A publication] (EAAP)
GFR .... German Federal Railroad (SAUO)
GFR .... German Federal Republic [West Germany]
GFR .... Glass and Fiber Resin
GFR .... Glass-Fiber Reinforced
GFR .... Glomerular Filtrate Rate (SAUS)
GFR .... Glomerular Filtration Rate [Nephrology]
GFR .... Government Facilities Request (AAG)
GFR .... Government Flight Representative
GFR .... Government of France (SAUS)
GFR .... Grand Forks Railway [Federal Railroad Administration identification code]
GFR .... Granville [France] [Airport symbol] (AD)
GFR .... Grim File Reaper [Computer hacker terminology] (NHD)
GFR .... Gromerular Filtration Rate
GFR .... Ground Fault Monitor (SAUS)
GFR .... Group Feeding Ration (SAUO)
GFR .... Growth Factor Receptors (MELL)
GFR .... Guaranteed Frame Rate (VLIE)
GFRC .... Gas Flow Radiation Counter [Nucleonics] (IAA)
GFRC .... General File/Record Control [Honeywell, Inc.] (IAA)
gfrc .... glass-fiber reinforced cement (SAUS)
GFRC .... Glass Fiber Reinforced Concrete
GFRHS .... Germans-from-Russia Heritage Society (EA)

GFRI .... Greenland Fisheries Research Institute (SAUO)
GF/RP .... Gap-Filler/Reporting Post [*RADAR*]
GFRP .... Glass-Fiber-Reinforced Plastic [*Also, GIFRP*]
GFRP .... Glass Fiber Reinforced Plastics (SAUS)
GFRP .... Glass-Fibre-Reinforced Plastic (SAUS)
GFRP .... Government Furnished Repair Parts
GFRP .... Graphite-Fiber-Reinforced Plastic [*Also, GrFRP*] (NASA)
GFRR .... Georgia & Florida Railroad [*Federal Railroad Administration identification code*]
GFRS .... Ground Forces Replacement Service [*World War II*]
GFRT .... Gas-Filled Rectifying Tube
GFRTP .... Glass-Fiber-Reinforced Thermoplastic (MCD)
GFRX .... Western Refrigerator Line [*Private rail car owner code*]
GFS .... Fernbank Science Center, Atlanta, GA [*OCLC symbol*] (OCLC)
GFS .... Gap-Filler Sonar (SAUS)
GFS .... General Electric Semiconductor (SAUS)
GFS .... General Financial System (SAUO)
GFS .... Geometry of Fractal Sets (SAUO)
GFS .... G. Frederick Smith Chemical Company (SAUO)
GFS .... Giant Foods [*AMEX symbol*] (SAG)
GFS .... Girls' Friendly Society of the USA (EA)
GFS .... Global Financial Studies
GFS .... Global Focal Sclerosis [*Medicine*] (DMAA)
GFS .... Global Forecast System (SAUS)
GFS .... Goffs, CA [*Location identifier*] [*FAA*] (FAAL)
GFS .... Government Finance Statistics (NITA)
GFS .... Government Finance Statistics Yearbook (journ.) (SAUS)
GFS .... Government Flying Service (SAUS)
GFS .... Government-Furnished Services (KSC)
GFS .... Government Furnished Software [*Military*] (POLM)
GFS .... Government Furnished Support (SAUS)
GFS .... Government-Furnished Support (SAUO)
GFS .... Gower Federal Service [*Rocky Mountain Mineral Law Foundation*] [*Information service or system*] (CRD)
GFS .... Grandfather-Father-Son [*Computer science*] (PCM)
GFS .... Grand Financial Scribe [*Freemasonry*] (ROG)
GFS .... Ground Equipment System (SAUS)
GFS .... Group Final Selector (IAA)
GFS .... Guernsey Freight Services [*British*]
GFS .... Gulfstream Airlines, Inc. [*ICAO designator*] (FAAC)
GFS .... Gunfire Support (NVT)
GFSA .... Goldfish Society of America (EA)
GFSB .... GFS Bancorp [*NASDAQ symbol*] (SAG)
GFSB B .... GFSB Bancorp, Inc. [*Associated Press*] (SAG)
GFS Bcp .... GFS Bancorp [*Associated Press*] (SAG)
GFSC .... Goddard Flight Space Center [*NASA*] (AAGC)
GFSE .... Government-Furnished Support Equipment (MCD)
GFSF .... Gas-Cooled Fuel Storage Facility (SAUS)
GFsH .... United States Army, Fort Stewart/Hunter AAF Library, Fort Stewart, GA [*Library symbol*] [*Library of Congress*] (LCLS)
GFSK .... Gaussian Frequency Shift Keying (SAUS)
GFSL .... Gaffsail [*Ship's rigging*] (ROG)
GFSM .... Government-Furnished Surplus Material (MCD)
GFSMO .... General Environmental Statement for Missed Oxide Fuel (SAUS)
GFSP .... Government-Furnished Support Property (KSC)
gf/sqcm .... Gramme-Force per Square Centimetre (SAUS)
GFSR .... General Function System Requirement
GFSR .... Generalized Feedback Shift Register [*Mathematics*]
GFSS .... Global Forecasting and Supply System (SAUO)
GFSS .... Gunfire Support Ship
GFST .... Ground Fuel Start Tank (AAG)
GFSUSA .... Girls' Friendly Society of the USA (EA)
GFSY .... Government Finance Statistics [*International Monetary Fund*] [*Information service or system*] (CRD)
GFT .... Gas-Filled Tube (SAUS)
GFT .... General Flying Test (PIAV)
GFT .... Generalized Fast Transform (PDAA)
GFT .... Geographical Full-Time (SAUS)
GFT .... Glass Fabric Tape
GFT .... Glass-Forming Tendency [*Materials science*]
GFT .... (Glucopyranosyl)fluorothymine [*Biochemistry*]
GFT .... Grant Functional Transmission (VLIE)
GFT .... Graphical Firing Tables
GFT .... Graphic Firing Table [*Weaponry*] (NATG)
GFT .... Green Forest Lumber Corp. [*Toronto Stock Exchange symbol*]
GFT .... Gruppo Finanziario Tessile [*Commercial firm*]
GFT .... Guided Flight Test (MCD)
GFT .... Gulfstream International Airlines, Inc. [*ICAO designator*] (FAAC)
GFT .... Gun-Fired Target (SAUS)
G/FT² .... Grams per Square Foot
GFTA .... Goldman-Fristoe Test of Articulation [*Education*]
GFTANSW .... Grain and Feed Trade Association of New South Wales [*Australia*]
GFTC .... Goldman-Fristoe Test of Articulation (SAUS)
GFTC-ER .... General Freight Traffic Committee - Eastern Railroads
GFTD .... Global Forces Trends Data Base (SAUO)
GFTM .... General Familiarization Training Manual (SAUS)
GFTMP .... Groundwater Flow and Transport Modelling Page (SAUO)
GFTNAX .... Ghana. Council for Scientifc and Industrial Research. (SAUO)
GFTNAX .... Ghana. Council for Scientifc and Industrial Research. Forest Products Research Institute. Technical Newsletter (journ.) (SAUS)
GFTO .... Tongo [*Sierra Leone*] [*ICAO location identifier*] (ICLI)
GFTU .... General Federation of Trade Unions [*Various countries*]
GFTWR .... Giftwear
g/fty .... Grams per Square Foot (SAUS)
GFU .... Glazed Facing Unit (SAUS)
GFU .... Glazed Facing Units [*Technical drawings*]
G Function .... Gibbs Function (SAUS)
GFUT .... Ground Fuel Ullage Tank (AAG)
GFV .... Fort Valley State College, Fort Valley, GA [*OCLC symbol*] (OCLC)
GFV .... Goldfever Resources Ltd. [*Vancouver Stock Exchange symbol*]
GfV .... Gueterfernverkehr [*Carriage of Goods*] [*German*] [*Business term*] (ILCA)
GFV .... Guided Flight Vehicle
GFW .... General Flight Work
GFW .... Gesellschaft fuer Weltraumforschung [*Society for Space Research*] [*Germany*]
GFW .... GFW Aviation [*Australia*] [*FAA designator*] (FAAC)
GFW .... Glass Filament Wound (IAA)
G-F-W .... Goldman-Fristoe-Woodcock Test of Auditory Discrimination [*Education*]
GFW .... Gram Formula Weight [*Chemistry*]
GFW .... Great French Writers [*A publication*]
GFW .... Ground-Fault Warning (IEEE)
GFWC .... General Federation of Women's Clubs (EA)
GFWI .... Greek Food and Wine Institute (NTPA)
GFWO .... Gulfwest Oil Co. [*NASDAQ symbol*] (SAG)
GFX .... Ghuraf [*South Arabia*] [*Airport symbol*] (AD)
GFX .... Government Furnished Other (SAUS)
GFX .... Grandfield, OK [*Location identifier*] [*FAA*] (FAAL)
GFX .... PLM Equipment Growth Fund I Ltd. [*AMEX symbol*] (SPSG)
gf x cm .... Gramme-Force times Centimetre (SAUS)
gf x mm .... Gramme-Force times Millimetre (SAUS)
GFY .... Government Fiscal Year (MCD)
GFY .... Grootfontein [*South-West Africa*] [*Airport symbol*] (OAG)
GFY .... PLM Equipment Growth Fund II Ltd. [*AMEX symbol*] (SPSG)
GFYE .... Yengema [*Sierra Leone*] [*ICAO location identifier*] (ICLI)
GFZ .... General Foods [*Federal Railroad Administration identification code*]
GFZ .... Greenfield, IA [*Location identifier*] [*FAA*] (FAAL)
GFZ .... PLM Equipment Growth Fund III Ltd. [*AMEX symbol*] (SPSG)
GG .... Galloping Gourmet [*TV program*]
GG .... Gamma Globulin [*Medicine*]
GG .... Gamma Globulinemia [*Medicine*] (MELL)
Gg .... Garage (SAUS)
GG .... Gas Gangrene (MELL)
GG .... Gas Generator (AAG)
gg .... gas genera tor (SAUS)
GG .... Gatling Gun
gg .... Gauge (SAUS)
GG .... Gdynia or Gdansk (SAUS)
GG .... Gem State Airlines [*ICAO designator*] (AD)
GG .... Gender Gap [*Refers to women's tendency to vote for Democratic over Republican candidates, a phenomenon noticed by pollsters beginning with the 1980 election*]
GG .... Generator Gas [*System*] [*Nuclear energy*] (NRCH)
GG .... Genito-Genital [*Medicine*]
GG .... Georgia (SAUS)
Gg .... Georgian (SAUS)
GG .... German Government (SAUO)
GG .... Gestational Glaucoma (MELL)
GG .... Gewehrgranate [*Rifle Grenade*] [*German military - World War II*]
Gg .... Gigagram
GG .... Girl Guides (BARN)
GG .... glaciogenic (SAUS)
GG .... Glasgow (SAUS)
GG .... Glass Glover [*Commercial firm*] [*British*]
GG .... Glazing Glas (SAUS)
GG .... Gleason's Grade
Gg .... Glucagon [*Endocrinology*]
GG .... Glyceryl Guaiacolate [*Expectorant*] (AAMN)
GG .... Glycylglycine [*Organic chemistry*]
GG .... Goal Gradient [*Psychology*]
GG .... Going [*Amateur radio shorthand*] (WDAA)
GG .... Goldcorp [*NYSE symbol*] (SAG)
GG .... Golden Globe (SAUO)
GG .... Golden Gloves Association of America [*Later, GGA of A*]
GG .... Golden Goose (journ.) (SAUS)
GG .... Government Gazette (SAFN)
GG .... Government Girl
GG .... Government Grade [*Followed by a number, 1-18; National Security Agency Employee Grade*]
GG .... Government Guaranteed (EBF)
GG .... Governor General
GG .... Grain Growth (SAUS)
GG .... Grand Guardian [*Freemasonry*]
GG .... Grant Greater Than [*Dialog*] [*Searchable field*] [*Information service or system*] (NITA)
GG .... Gravity Gradient (KSC)
GG .... Great Gatsby [*Describes clothing style modeled after the type worn by characters in F. Scott Fitzgerald's novel, "The Great Gatsby"*]
GG .... Great Gross [*144 dozen*] [*Also, GGR*]
GG .... Green Giant Co. (SAUO)
G-G .... Green-Green (SAUS)
GG .... Grenadier Guards [*Military*] [*British*]
GG .... Groove Gauge
GG .... Grounded Grid [*Valve*] (DEN)
G/G .... Ground/Ground (SAUO)
GG .... Ground Guidance [*Aerospace*] (AAG)
GG .... Ground Gunner [*Air Force*] [*British*]
G-G .... Ground-to-Ground [*Communications, weapons, etc.*] (MSA)
GG .... Guaifenesin [*An expectorant*] [*Pharmacology*] (DAVI)

GG .... Guided Missile Cruiser (SAUS)
GG .... Guinea Gulf Line [*Steamship*] (MHDB)
GG .... Gutenberg Gesellschaft (EA)
GGA .... Gale Global Access [*Also, GGAEA*]
GGA .... General Gonadotropic Activity [*Endocrinology*] (MAE)
GGA .... Generalized Gradient Approximation [*Mathematics*]
GGA .... Ghana Geographical Association (SAUO)
GGA .... Girl Guides Association [*British*]
GGA .... Global Gecko Association (GVA)
GGA .... Golden Glacier [*Vancouver Stock Exchange symbol*]
GGA .... Good Gardeners' Association [*British*]
GGA .... Grounded Grid Amplifier
GGA .... Group Gross Assets (ADA)
GGA .... Guanine Guanine Adenine [*A triplet of bases coding for the amino acid, glycine*] (EES)
GGA .... Guernsey Growers Association [*British*] (DBA)
GGA .... Gulf General Atomic [*Commercial firm*]
GGAA .... Girl Guides Association of Australia
GGAA .... Golden Gloves Association of America [*Later, GGA of A*] (EA)
GGaB .... Brenau College, Gainsville, GA [*Library symbol*] [*Library of Congress*] (LCLS)
GGAB .... Ghana Geographical Association. Bulletin [*A publication*]
GGaC .... Gainesville Junior College, Gainesville, GA [*Library symbol*] [*Library of Congress*] (LCLS)
GGAC .... Gulf General Atomic Company (SAUO)
GGaCL .... Chestatee Regional Library System, Gainsville, GA [*Library symbol*] [*Library of Congress*] (LCLS)
GGADP .... German-Ghanaian Agricultural Development Project (SAUO)
GGAE .... Gulf General Atomic Europe (SAUO)
GGAEA .... Gale Global Access, Encyclopedia of Associations [*Also, GGA*]
GGAO .... Goddard Geophysical and Astronomical Observatory (SAUO)
GGA of A .... Golden Gloves Association of America (EA)
GGAR .... Gas-Guided Aircraft Rocket
GGAWA .... Grape Growers' Association of Western Australia
GGB .... Gerdau S.A. ADS [*NYSE symbol*] (SG)
GGB .... Golden Gate Bridge (SAUS)
Ggb .... Gorilla Gorilla Beringei (SAUS)
GGB&HD .... Golden Gate Bridge and Highway District (SAUS)
GGBB .... Bambadinca [*Guinea-Bissau*] [*ICAO location identifier*] (ICLI)
GGBE .... Bedanda [*Guinea-Bissau*] [*ICAO location identifier*] (ICLI)
GGBF .... Bafata [*Guinea-Bissau*] [*ICAO location identifier*] (ICLI)
GGBG .... Governor-General's Bodyguard [*British military*] (DMA)
GGBI .... Bissora [*Guinea-Bissau*] [*ICAO location identifier*] (ICLI)
GGBO .... Bolama [*Guinea-Bissau*] [*ICAO location identifier*] (ICLI)
GGBU .... Bubaque [*Guinea-Bissau*] [*ICAO location identifier*] (ICLI)
GGC .... Gamma-Glutamyl Carboxylase (DMAA)
GGC .... General Grand Chapter [*Freemasonry*]
GGC .... Generalized Genetic Code (SAUS)
GGC .... Georgia College, Milledgeville, GA [*OCLC symbol*] (OCLC)
GGC .... Georgia Gulf Corp. [*NYSE symbol*] (SPSG)
GGC .... Glossary of Genetics and Cytogenetics (SAUS)
GGC .... Gobar Gas Company (SAUO)
GGC .... Golden Gate College [*California*]
GGC .... Goo Goo Cluster (SAUS)
GGC .... Grey Goose Corp. Ltd. [*Toronto Stock Exchange symbol*]
GGC .... Grey Goose Corporation Ltd. (SAUO)
GGC .... Ground Guidance Computer [*Aerospace*]
GGC .... Guanine Guanine Cytosine [*A triplet of bases coding for the amino acid, glycine*] (EES)
GGC .... Gun Group Commander [*British military*] (DMA)
GGCA .... German Governmental Construction Agency (SAUO)
GGCC .... Cacine [*Guinea-Bissau*] [*ICAO location identifier*] (ICLI)
GGCC .... Grand Gaming Corp. [*NASDAQ symbol*] (SAG)
GGCCW .... Grand Gaming Wrrt [*NASDAQ symbol*] (TTSB)
GGCF .... Cufar [*Guinea-Bissau*] [*ICAO location identifier*] (ICLI)
GGCG .... Cantchungo [*Guinea-Bissau*] [*ICAO location identifier*] (ICLI)
GGCS .... Gamma-Glutamyl Cysteine Synthetase [*Medicine*] (EDAA)
GGCST .... Gleb-Goldstein Color Sorting Test [*Psychology*]
GGCT .... Catio [*Guinea-Bissau*] [*ICAO location identifier*] (ICLI)
GGCV .... Caravela [*Guinea-Bissau*] [*ICAO location identifier*] (ICLI)
GGCX .... Georgia Gulf [*Private rail car owner code*]
GGCZ .... Graham Grain [*Federal Railroad Administration identification code*]
GGD .... General Government Division [*GAO*] (AAGC)
G G D .... Generalized Gamma Distribution (SAUS)
GGD .... Gold Bridge Development [*Vancouver Stock Exchange symbol*]
GGD .... Great Granddaughter
GGD .... Gregory Downs [*Australia*] [*Airport symbol*] [*Obsolete*] (OAG)
GGDA .... Geocentric Datum of Australia [*Geographic*] (EERA)
GGDBMS .... Generalized Data Base Management System (SAUS)
GGDC .... G. G. Drayton Club (EA)
GGDF .... Gas Gathering Data File [*Phillips Petroleum*]
GGDPAC .... Government Geologists Database Policy Advisory Committee (SAUO)
GGDPAC .... Government Geoscience Database Policy Advisory Committee [*Commonwealth*] (EERA)
gge .... garage (SAUS)
GGE .... Gauge
G G E .... General Graphical Editing (SAUS)
GGE .... Generalized Glandular Enlargement [*Medicine*]
gge .... generalized grandular enlargement (SAUS)
GGE .... Georgetown (SAUS)
GGE .... Georgetown, SC [*Location identifier*] [*FAA*] (FAAL)
GGE .... Golden Group Explorations, Inc. [*Vancouver Stock Exchange symbol*]
GGE .... Gospelrama Gospel Expo [*An association*] (EA)
GGE .... Gradient Gel Electrophoresis
GGE .... Griffin Gaming & Entertainment [*AMEX symbol*] (SAG)
GGE .... Ground Guidance Equipment [*Aerospace*]
G-GE .... Group on Geoscience Electronics (SAUO)
GGEM .... Gravity Gradiometer Explorer Mission (SAUO)
GGEN .... GalaGen Inc. [*NASDAQ symbol*] (TTSB)
GGE-OSNLR ... Guiding Group of Experts on the Programme of Ocean Science in Relation to Non-Living Resources, short name: Guiding Group of Experts on (SAUO)
GGEP .... Empada [*Guinea-Bissau*] [*ICAO location identifier*] (ICLI)
GGF .... Glass and Glazing Federation [*British*]
GGF .... Glial Growth Factor [*Biochemistry*]
GGF .... Global Government Plus Fund Ltd. [*Toronto Stock Exchange symbol*]
GGF .... Global Growth & Income Fund, Inc. (SAUO)
GGF .... Granges-Gontardes [*France*] [*Seismograph station code, US Geological Survey*] [*Closed*] (SEIS)
GGF .... Grant, NE [*Location identifier*] [*FAA*] (FAAL)
GGF .... Ground Gained Forward [*Aerial photography*]
GGFC .... Girl Groups Fan Club (EA)
GGFC .... Go Go's Fan Club [*Defunct*] (EA)
GGFO .... Formosa [*Guinea-Bissau*] [*ICAO location identifier*] (ICLI)
GGFR .... Farim [*Guinea-Bissau*] [*ICAO location identifier*] (ICLI)
GGFR .... Geosynchronous Gas Filter Radiometer (SAUS)
G/G/FRIS .... Gal/Guy Fridays [*Classified advertising*]
GGFRJ .... Gas Generator Fueled Ramjet (MCD)
GGFU .... Fulacunda [*Guinea-Bissau*] [*ICAO location identifier*] (ICLI)
GGG .... Gadolinium (SAUS)
GGG .... Gadolinium, Gallium, Garnet [*Also, G3*] [*Substrate for magnetic film*]
GGG .... Giggle (SAUS)
GGG .... Gladewater-Kilgore-Longview [*Texas*] [*Airport symbol*] (AD)
GGG .... Glycine-Rich Gamma-Glycoprotein [*Immunology*]
GGG .... Goat Gamma-Globulin [*Immunology*]
GGG .... Good and Green Georgetown (Guyana) [*Political party*] (PSAP)
GGG .... Gorilla Gorilla Gorilla (SAUS)
GGG .... Graco, Inc. [*NYSE symbol*] (SPSG)
GGG .... Guanine Guanine Guanine [*A triplet of bases coding for teh amino acid, glycine*] (EES)
GGG .... Gummi Guttae Gambiae [*Gamboge*] [*Pharmacology*] (ROG)
GGG .... Gunnar Gold, Inc. [*Toronto Stock Exchange symbol*]
GGG .... Longview [*Texas*] [*Airport symbol*] (OAG)
GGGA .... Galinhas [*Guinea-Bissau*] [*ICAO location identifier*] (ICLI)
GGGB .... Gabu [*Guinea-Bissau*] [*ICAO location identifier*] (ICLI)
GGGG .... 4G Data Systems, Inc. (SAUO)
GGGG and H-B ... Gamo, Gardula, Gofa, Geleb and Hamer-Bako Peoples Democratic Organization (SAUS)
GGH .... Generalized geometry hold-up (SAUS)
GGHNP .... Golden Gate Highlands National Park (SAUO)
GGHP .... General Grand High Priest [*Freemasonry*]
GGHP .... Geomagnetism Group Home Page (SAUO)
GGHP .... Governor-Generals Honorary Physician (SAUS)
GGHY-A .... Geography (journ.) (SAUS)
GGI .... General Graphics Interface (SAUS)
GGI .... Generalized Graphical Input (VLIE)
GGI .... Generic Graphical Interface (SAUS)
GGI .... Geodesy and Geographic Information (SAUO)
GGI .... Geology and Geophysics Index (SAUO)
GGI .... GPS Geoscience Instrument (SAUO)
GGI .... Greenhouse Gas Index
GGI .... Guided Group Interaction (SAUO)
GGIA .... Georgia Green Industry Association (SAUO)
GGIA .... Granite Grit Institute of America (EA)
GGIF .... Federal Law Enforcement Training Center (SAUS)
GG-IR .... Gas Chromatography Infrared (SAUS)
G-GIS .... Gulf Geographic Information System (SAUO)
GGISS .... Gas Chromatography Isotope Separation System (SAUS)
GGIT .... Geographics Inc. [*NASDAQ symbol*] (TTSB)
GGJOA .... Geographical Journal (SAUS)
GGK .... Gaigokugo Caigoku Bungaku Kenkyu (SAUS)
GGK .... Goldstein Golub Kessler [*Commercial firm*]
GGL .... Gain Guided LASER (IAA)
GGL .... Geodesy and Geodynamics Laboratory (SAUO)
GGL .... Gerle Gold Ltd. [*Vancouver Stock Exchange symbol*]
GGL .... Gissing (SAUS)
GGL .... Gissing, Glen L., Evansville WI [*STAC*]
GGL .... Gravity-Gradient Libration [*Damper*]
GGL .... Ground Glass
GGL .... Guild of Guide Lecturers [*British*]
GGL .... Titusville, FL [*Location identifier*] [*FAA*] (FAAL)
GGIF .... Federal Law Enforcement Training Center, Glynco, GA [*Library symbol*] [*Library of Congress*] (LCLS)
GGLF .... Georgia Gulf Corp. (SAUO)
GGM .... Geographici Graeci Minores [*A publication*] (OCD)
GGM .... Girl Guide Movement (SAUO)
GGM .... Glacial Geomorphology (SAUS)
GGM .... Glitter Gold Mines [*Vancouver Stock Exchange symbol*]
GGM .... Glucose/Galactose Malabsorption [*Medicine*]
GGM .... Gravity Gradiometer Mission [*NASA*]
GGM .... Ground-to-Ground Missile
GGMA .... Glassine and Greaseproof Manufacturers Association [*Later, API*] (EA)
GGMA .... Government Gold Mining Areas
GGMJ .... German Geological Mission in Jordan (SAUO)
GGMK .... Great, Grand Master Key [*Locks*] (ADA)
GGMMA .... Gabriel Garcia Moreno Memorial Association (EA)
GGMS .... Mansoa [*Guinea-Bissau*] [*ICAO location identifier*] (ICLI)
GGMWA .... Grace of God Movement for the Women of America [*Later, GGMWW*] (EA)

GGMWW...... Grace of God Movement for the Women of the World (EA)
GGMX......... Golden Gate Railroad Museum [*Federal Railroad Administration identification code*]
GGMX......... Goodpasture Grain and Milling [*Private rail car owner code*]
GGN............ Air Georgian [*Canada*] [*FAA designator*] (FAAC)
GGN............ Gagnoa [*Ivory Coast*] [*Airport symbol*] (OAG)
GGN............ Global Geophysical Network (ACAE)
GGN............ Golden Globe Nomination (SAUO)
GGN............ Gotta Go Now (VLIE)
GGNCF......... Geology and Geophysics Number Crunchers Forum (SAUO)
GGNG........... Gelatin Glass Negative (VRA)
GGNI........... Governor-General of Northern Ireland (DAS)
GGNRA......... Golden Gate National Recreation Area (SAUO)
GGNRA......... Golden Gate National Recreation Area Advisory Commission [*National Park Service*] [*San Francisco, CA*] (EGAO)
GGNRAAC.... Golden Gate National Recreation Area Advisory Commission (SAUO)
GGNRACAC... Golden Gate National Recreation Area Advisory Commission [*National Park Service*] [*San Francisco, CA*] (EGAO)
GGNS........... Genus (SAUS)
GGNS........... Genus, Inc. [*NASDAQ symbol*] (CTT)
GGNS........... Grand Gulf Nuclear Station (NRCH)
GGO............ Getchell Gold Corp. [*AMEX symbol*] (SAG)
GGO............ Glavnaya Geofizicheskaya Observatory [*Main Geophysical Observatory*] [*Former USSR*]
GGO............ Governor-General's Order [*British military*] (DMA)
GGO............ Greater Greensboro [*North Carolina*] Open [*Golf tournament*]
GGO............ Ground-Glass Opacification [*Medicine*] (RAWO)
GGO............ Guiglo [*Ivory Coast*] [*Airport symbol*] (OAG)
GGOA........... Generalized Geometric Optics Approximation (SAUS)
GGOC........... Goldovsky Grand Opera Company (SAUO)
GGOP........... Gun Group Observation Post (SAUO)
GGOR........... Gross Gas-Oil Ratio (SAUS)
GG or S....... Glands, Goiter, or Stiffness [*Medicine*]
GGOV........... Bissau/Oswaldo Vieira International [*Guinea-Bissau*] [*ICAO location identifier*] (ICLI)
GGP............ Gas-Gathering Pipeline
GGP............ Gateway-Gateway Protocol (SAUS)
GGP............ Gateway-to-Gateway [*Communications term*] (DCT)
GGP............ Gateway-to-Gateway Protocol [*Computer science*] (TNIG)
GGP............ General Growth Properties [*NYSE symbol*] (SPSG)
GGP............ Genl Growth Properties [*NYSE symbol*] (TTSB)
GGP............ George Resources Co. [*Vancouver Stock Exchange symbol*]
GGP............ Global Geodynamics Project (SAUO)
GGP............ Golden Gate Productions [*San Francisco, CA*] [*Telecommunications*] (TSSD)
GGP............ Good Gay Poets (EA)
GGP............ Good Guidance Practice [*Drug evaluation*]
GGP............ GPS [*Global Positioning System*] Guidance Package
GGP............ Gross Global Product
GGP............ Logansport, IN [*Location identifier*] [*FAA*] (FAAL)
GGPA........... Graduate Grade-Point Average [*Higher education*]
GGPAS......... General Performance Appraisals System (SAUS)
GGPC........... Pecixe [*Guinea-Bissau*] [*ICAO location identifier*] (ICLI)
GGPD........... Gross Gas Produced (SAUS)
GGPF........... Glial Growth Promoting Factor [*Neurology*]
GGPL........... Glycine, Glycine Phenylalanine, Leucine [*A synthetic peptide*]
GGPNA......... Gamma-Glutamyl-P-Nitroanilide (SAUS)
GGPP........... Giant Gaseous Protoplanet [*Planetary science*]
GGPR........... Pirada [*Guinea-Bissau*] [*ICAO location identifier*] (ICLI)
G-GPRF........ Gradient General Purpose Rocket Furnace (SAUS)
GGQ............ Gagnoa [*Ivory Coast*] [*Airport symbol*] (AD)
GGR............ Gallagher Explorations Ltd. [*Vancouver Stock Exchange symbol*]
GGR............ Gambill Goose Refuge (SAUO)
GGR............ Gas-cooled Graphite-moderated Reactor (SAUS)
GGR............ Gas Graphite Reactor (SAUS)
GGR............ Geschichte der Griechischen Religion [*A publication*] (OCD)
GGR............ Great Gross [*144 dozen*] [*Also, GG*]
GGR............ Greenes Iowa Reports (journ.) (SAUS)
GGR............ Ground Gunnery Range
GGRA........... Gelatine and Glue Research Association [*British*] (BI)
G Gracch..... Gaius Gracchus [*of Plutarch*] [*Classical studies*] (OCD)
GGraG.......... Gracewood State School and Hospital, Gracewood, GA [*Library symbol*] [*Library of Congress*] (LCLS)
GG rate....... Guaranteed Group Rate [*Travel industry*] (TRID)
GGriEx........ University of Georgia, Experiment Station, Griffin, GA [*Library symbol*] [*Library of Congress*] (LCLS)
GGS............ Gates-Gaudin-Schuhmann [*Particle size distribution*]
GGS............ Gdynia, Gdansk or Szczecin (SAUS)
GGS............ Generalized Gradient Search (SAUS)
GGS............ Georgia Geologic Survey (SAUO)
GGS............ Georgia Great Southern [*Federal Railroad Administration identification code*]
GGS............ German General Staff (SAUO)
GGS............ Girls' Grammar School (ADA)
GGS............ Glands, Goiter, or Stiffness [*Of neck*] [*Medicine*] (STED)
GGS............ Global Geospace Science
GGS............ Global Geospace Science Program (SAUO)
GGS............ Global Geospace Study [*Proposed*] [*United States, Japan, and Europe*]
GGS............ Global Geosynchronous Science (SAUS)
GGS............ Gobernador Gregores [*Argentina*] [*Airport symbol*] (OAG)
GGS............ Graphic Generator System
GGS............ Gravity Gradient Satellite (SAUS)
GGS............ Gravity-Gradient Satellite
GGS............ Gravity Gradient Sensor (SAUS)
GGS............ Gravity-Gradient Sensor
GGS............ Gravity Gradient Stabilization (SAUS)
GGS............ Great Grandson
G Gs........... Grenadier Guards (SAUO)
GGS............ Ground Gained Sideways [*Aerial photography*]
GGS............ Ground Guidance System [*Aerospace*] (AAG)
GGS............ Gyro Gunsight (SAUO)
GGS............ Gyroscopic Gun Sight (SAUS)
GGSA........... German Genealogical Society of America (EA)
GGSD........... Sao Domingos [*Guinea-Bissau*] [*ICAO location identifier*] (ICLI)
GGSE........... Gravity-Gradient Stabilization Experiment
GGSM........... Graduate Diploma of the Guildhall School of Music [*British*] (DBQ)
GGSP........... Giant-to-Giant Interneuron Synaptic Potential [*Neurochemistry*]
GGSPFWFH... Goose and Gander, Society for the Preservation of First Wives and First Husbands (SAUO)
GGSTIDE...... Global Geosynchronous Science Thermal Ions Dynamics Experiment (SAUS)
GGS-Wind.... Global Geospace Science satellite Wind (SAUS)
GGT............ Gabelli Global Multimedia Tr [*NYSE symbol*] (TTSB)
GGT............ Gabelli Global Multimedia Trust, Inc. [*NYSE symbol*] (SAG)
GGT............ Gamma-Glutamyltransferase [*Also, GGTP, GT*] [*An enzyme*]
GGT............ Gamma-Glutamyl Transpeptidase [*Also, GGT, GT*] [*An enzyme*] (DAVI)
gGT............ gamma-Glutamyl-Transpeptidase (SAUS)
GGT............ Gas Guzzler Tax
GGT............ George Town [*Bahamas*] [*Airport symbol*] (OAG)
GGT............ Georgetown, NY [*Location identifier*] [*FAA*] (FAAL)
GGT............ Gerber Garment Technology (SAUS)
GGT............ Global Geoscience Transects (SAUO)
GGT............ Gravitational Gradient Torque (SAUS)
GGT............ Gravity-Gradient Torque
GGT............ Greater Temagami [*Vancouver Stock Exchange symbol*]
GGTI........... GTI Corp. [*NASDAQ symbol*] (SAG)
GGTP........... Gamma-Glutamyl Transpeptidase [*Also, GGT, GT*] [*An enzyme*]
GGTS........... Gravity-Gradient Test Satellite [*NASA*]
GGTT........... Tite [*Guinea-Bissau*] [*ICAO location identifier*] (ICLI)
GGU............ Geological Survey of Greenland (SAUS)
GGU............ Giant Gastric Ulcer [*Medicine*]
GGU............ Guanine Guanine Uracil [*A triplet of bases coding for the amino acid, glycine*] (EES)
GGUALE....... Golden Gate University Advanced Legal Education Program (DLA)
GGUGA......... Grounded Grid Unity-Gain Amplifier (SAUS)
GGUN........... Uno [*Guinea-Bissau*] [*ICAO location identifier*] (ICLI)
GGUY........... [*The*] Good Guys, Inc. [*NASDAQ symbol*] (NQ)
GGV............ Gabriel Gonzalez Videla [*Antarctica*] [*Seismograph station code, US Geological Survey*] [*Closed*] (SEIS)
GGV............ Gas Generator Valve (KSC)
GGV............ Kwigillingok, AK [*Location identifier*] [*FAA*] (FAAL)
GGVB........... Gelatin, Glucose, and Veronal Buffer [*Medicine*] (DMAA)
GGVR........... Varela [*Guinea-Bissau*] [*ICAO location identifier*] (ICLI)
GGW............ Geology Gems from Winona (SAUO)
GGW............ Glasgow [*Montana*] [*Airport symbol*] (OAG)
GGWSU......... Geology Gems from Winona State University (SAUO)
GGX............ Golden Gate Explorations [*Vancouver Stock Exchange symbol*]
GGY............ Clanton, AL [*Location identifier*] [*FAA*] (FAAL)
GGY............ Compagnie Genl Geophy ADS [*NYSE symbol*] (SG)
GGY............ Greentree Energy [*Vancouver Stock Exchange symbol*]
GGZ............ Akron, OH [*Location identifier*] [*FAA*] (FAAL)
GH.............. Gaseous Hydrogen (KSC)
GH.............. Gate House (NRCH)
GH.............. Gee-Herter [*Disease*] [*Medicine*] (DB)
GH.............. Gemini Hatch [*NASA*]
GH.............. General Headquarters [*Military*] (CDAI)
GH.............. General Health (DMAA)
GH.............. General Hospital [*Initialism also refers to a TV program*]
GH.............. General Host Corp. [*NYSE symbol*] (SPSG)
GH.............. Genetically Hypertensive [*Rat*] (STED)
GH.............. Genetic Hypertension [*Medicine*] (DB)
GH.............. Geniohyoid (STED)
GH.............. Genl Host [*NYSE symbol*] (TTSB)
GH.............. George Horne [*Refers to old news*] [*Slang*] (DSUE)
GH.............. Gestational Hypotension [*Medicine*] (MELL)
GH.............. Ghana [*ANSI two-letter standard code*] (CNC)
gh.............. Ghana [*MARC country of publication code*] [*Library of Congress*] (LCCP)
GH.............. Ghana Airways [*ICAO designator*] (AD)
GH.............. Gilford-Hutchinson [*Syndrome*] [*Medicine*] (STED)
GH.............. Gilt Head [*Bookbinding*] (ROG)
GH.............. Gingival Hyperplasia [*Medicine*] (MELL)
GH.............. Glenohumeral [*Joint*] [*Anatomy*] (DAVI)
GH.............. Glenohumeral Joint [*Anatomy*] (DAVI)
G-H............ Goodenough-Harris Drawing Test [*Education*]
GH.............. Good Health (STED)
GH.............. Good Housekeeping (journ.) (SAUS)
GH.............. Gordon Highlanders (SAUO)
GH.............. Gougerot-Hailey [*Syndrome*] [*Medicine*] (DB)
GH.............. Government House [*Canada*]
GH.............. Gradient Heating Facility (SAUS)
GH.............. Gray Herbarium [*Harvard University*] [*Cambridge, MA*]
GH.............. Greenwich Hospital (ODA)
GH.............. Grid Heading [*Navigation*]
Gh.............. Grosvenor House (SAUS)
GH.............. Ground Handling [*Aerospace*]
GH.............. Growth Hormone [*Somatotrophin*] [*Also, SH, STH*] [*Endocrinology*]
GH.............. Guardhouse

GH .... Guest House
GH .... Gun Howitzer (SAUS)
GH .... Gyro Horizon (SAUS)
GH .... Green Howards [*Military*] (ODA)
GH_2 .... Gaseous Hydrogen [*NASA*] (KSC)
GHA .... Gay and Homosexually Active
GHA .... General Agency Agreement (SAUO)
GHA .... General Housekeeping Area [*NASA*] (NASA)
GHA .... Georgia Hospital Association [*Atlanta*] (TSSD)
GHA .... Georgia Southwestern College (SAUS)
GHA .... Georgia Southwestern College, Americus, GA [*OCLC symbol*] (OCLC)
GHA .... Gesneriad Hybridizers Association (EA)
GHA .... Ghana [*ANSI three-letter standard code*] (CNC)
Gha .... Ghana (MILB)
GHA .... Ghana Airways Corp. [*ICAO designator*] (FAAC)
GHA .... Ghardaia [*Algeria*] [*Airport symbol*] (OAG)
GHA .... Glashutten [*Austria*] [*Seismograph station code, US Geological Survey*] (SEIS)
GHA .... Global Health Action (EA)
GHA .... Glucoheptanoic Acid [*Biochemistry*] (DAVI)
GHA .... Glucoheptanoic Acid [*Medicine*] (RAWO)
GHA .... Golden Hat Resources [*Vancouver Stock Exchange symbol*]
GHA .... Grassland Heritage Association (SAUO)
GHA .... Grassland Husbandry Adviser [*Ministry of Agriculture, Fisheries, and Food*] [*British*]
GHA .... Green Hills Aviation Ltd. (SAUO)
GHA .... Greenwich Hour Angle
GHA .... Ground Hazard Area (MUGU)
GHA .... Gyro Header Assembly
GHAA .... Greenwich Hour Angle of Aries (SAUS)
GHAA .... Group Health Association of America (EA)
GhAF .... Ghanaian Air Force
GhAF .... Ghanian Air Force (SAUS)
GHAF .... Grosvenor House Antiques Fair [*British*] (ITD)
GHAI .... Greater Horn of Africa Initiative (SAUO)
Ghan .... Afghan Express (SAUS)
GHANA .... Ghana Airways (SAUS)
Ghana Anim Res Inst Annu Rep... Ghana. Animal Research Institute. Annual Report (journ.) (SAUS)
GHANABATT... Ghana Battalion [*Military*]
Ghana B Theol... Ghana Bulletin of Theology (journ.) (SAUS)
Ghana Bull Theol... Gbana Bulletin of Theology (journ.) (SAUS)
Ghana Bull Theol... Ghana Bulletin of Theology (journ.) (SAUS)
Ghana Counc Sci Ind Res For Prod Res Inst Tech New... Ghana. Council for Scientific and Industrial Research. Forest Products Research Institute. Technical Newsletter (journ.) (SAUS)
Ghana CSIR For Prod Res Inst Annu Rep... Ghana. Council for Scientific and Industrial Research. Forest Products Research Institute. Annual Report (journ.) (SAUS)
Ghana CSIR For Prod Res Inst Tech Newsl... Ghana. Council for Scientifc and Industrial Research. Forest Products Research Institute. Technical Newsletter (journ.) (SAUS)
Ghana Fish Res Unit Inf Rep... Ghana. Fishery Research Unit. Information Report (journ.) (SAUS)
Ghana Fish Res Unit Ma Fish Res Rep... Ghana. Fishery Research Unit. Marine Fishery Research Reports (journ.) (SAUS)
Ghana Fish Res Unit Mar Fish R... Ghana. Fishery Research Unit. Marine Fishery Research Reports (journ.) (SAUS)
Ghana For J... Ghana Forestry Journal (journ.) (SAUS)
Ghana J Agric Sci... Ghana Journal of Agricultural Science (journ.) (SAUS)
Ghana J Sci... Ghana Journal of Science (journ.) (SAUS)
Ghana LRC... Ghana Law Reform Commission (SAUS)
GHANASO .... Ghana National Students Organization (SAUO)
GH&H .... Galveston, Houston & Henderson (SAUS)
GHAQ .... General High Altitude Questionnaire (PDAA)
GHARS .... Gyroscopic Heading and Altitude Reference System (SAA)
GHAT .... Ground Handling and Transportation [*Aerospace*] (KSC)
GHATS .... Greenwich Hour Angle of the The Sun (SAUS)
GHB .... Gamma Hydroxy Butyrate [*Steroid*]
GHB .... Gamma-Hydroxybutyric Acid [*Organic chemistry*]
G H B .... General Hospital, Birmingham (SAUS)
GHB .... Glycohemoglobin (SAUS)
GHb .... Glycohemoglobin [*Biochemistry, medicine*]
GHB .... Glycosylated Hemoglobin [*Clinical chemistry*]
GHB .... Goddard Handbook (SAUS)
GHB .... Good Housekeeping Bureau (SAUO)
GHB .... Governor's Harbour [*Bahamas*] [*Airport symbol*] (OAG)
GHB .... GSFC Handbook (SAUS)
GHBA .... Galiceno Horse Breeders Association (EA)
GHBP .... Growth Hormone Binding Protein (DMAA)
GHBZ .... G. Heileman Brewing [*Federal Railroad Administration identification code*]
GHC .... Gating Half-Cycle [*Computer science*]
GHC .... Generalized Hyperbolic Class
GHC .... German High Command (SAUO)
GHC .... Ghanian Cedi (SAUS)
GHC .... Global Heritage Center (SAUO)
GHC .... Gold Hill [*California*] [*Seismograph station code, US Geological Survey*] (SEIS)
GHC .... Gray Harbor College (SAUO)
GHC .... Grays Harbor College [*Washington*]
GHC .... Great Harbour Cay [*Bahamas*] [*Airport symbol*] (OAG)
GHC .... Greyhound Computer of Canada Ltd. [*Toronto Stock Exchange symbol*]
GHC .... Ground Half Coupling (KSC)
GHC .... Group Health Cooperative (DMAA)
GHC .... Guidance Heater Control
GHC .... Guidance, Homing, Control (ACAE)
GHC .... Gulf Life Holding Company (SAUO)
GHC .... Halic Havacilik, AS [*Turkey*] [*FAA designator*] (FAAC)
GHC&EA .... General Hazard Cause & Effect Analysis (SAUO)
GHCD .... Growth Hormone Concentrations and Distribution (SAUS)
GHCH .... Giant Hepatic Cavernous Hemangioma [*Medicine*] (RAWO)
GHCl .... Guanidine Hydrochloride (SAUS)
GHCIMA .... Graduate of the Hotel Catering and Institutional Management Association (SAUO)
GHCl .... Guanidine Hydrochloride [*Organic chemistry*]
GHCN .... Global Historical Climate Network [*Marine science*] (OSRA)
GHCN .... Global Historical Climate (or Climatology) Network (SAUO)
GHCP .... Georgia Hospital Computer Group
GHCR .... Gross Henle Chromoreaction [*Clinical chemistry*]
GHCS .... Good Housekeeping Check Sheet (AAG)
GHD .... Generalized Hamming Distance (SAUS)
GHD .... Growth Hormone Deficiency [*Endocrinology*]
GHD .... Guest-Host Dichroic (SAUS)
GHDNet .... Global Health Disaster Network (ADWA)
GHDT .... Goodenough-Harris Drawing Test [*Psychology*] (DAVI)
GHDV .... Gasoline-Engine Heavy-Duty Vehicle
GHDVHS .... Grace H. Dodge Vocational High School (SAUO)
GHE .... Gable House Estates Ltd. [*British*]
GHE .... Garachine [*Panama*] [*Airport symbol*] (OAG)
GHE .... Gaseous Helium (KSC)
GHe .... Gaseous Helium (NAKS)
GHE .... Gauss Hypergeometric Equation [*Mathematics*]
GHE .... Gibbs-Helmholtz Equation [*Physical chemistry*]
GHE .... Ginn, Herbert E., South Portland ME [*STAC*]
GHE .... Golden Hemlock [*Vancouver Stock Exchange symbol*]
GHE .... Ground Handling Equipment [*Aerospace*]
G Heb .... Gospel of the Hebrews [*Apocryphal work*]
GHEF .... Givat Haviva Educational Foundation (EA)
GHEN .... Global Hindu Electronic Network
GHER .... Greater Heritage Corp. (SAUO)
GHF .... Gauss Hypergeometric Function [*Mathematics*]
GHF .... Gay Hispanic Female (ADWA)
GHF .... Generalized Hartree-Fock (SAUS)
GHF .... Government Hospitality Fund (SAUO)
GHF .... Gradient Heating Facility
GHF .... Gradient Heating Furnace (SAUS)
GHF .... Grassland Heritage Foundation (EA)
GHF .... Growth Hormone Transcription Factor [*Endocrinology*]
GHFC .... Gebhardt-Heriot Foundation for All Cats (EA)
GHFC .... Gunilla Hutton Fan Club (EA)
GHFF .... George Hamilton IV and Friends [*Defunct*] (EA)
GHF-NO-CI... Generalized Hartree-Fock/Natural Orbital/ Configuration Interactions (SAUS)
GHG .... Galactic Hitchhiker's Guild (EA)
GHG .... [*The*] Good Hotel Guide [*A publication*] [*British*]
GHG .... Governor's Horse Guard
GHG .... Greenhouse Gas [*Climatology*]
GHG .... Greenhouse Gases
GHG .... Grosshandelsgesellschaft [*Wholesale Business Establishment*] [*German*]
GHGB .... Good Health is Good Business (HEAS)
GHH .... Galveston, Houston & Henderson Railroad Co. [*AAR code*]
GHi .... Georgia Historical Society, Savannah (SAUS)
GHi .... Georgia Historical Society, Savannah, GA [*Library symbol*] [*Library of Congress*] (LCLS)
GHI .... German Historical Institute (EA)
GHI .... German Hydrographic Institute (SAUO)
GHI .... GHI Mortgage Investors [*Vancouver Stock Exchange symbol*]
GHI .... Gilbert Hill [*Idaho*] [*Seismograph station code, US Geological Survey*] [*Closed*] (SEIS)
GHI .... Global High Inc. Dollar Fd [*NYSE symbol*] (TTSB)
GHI .... Global High Income Dollar Fund [*NYSE symbol*] (SPSG)
GHI .... Group Health Insurance [*British*]
GHI .... Growth Hormone Insufficiency
GHI .... Good Housekeeping Institute (ODA)
GHIA .... Genealogical and Heraldic Institute of America (EA)
GHIH .... Growth Hormone Inhibiting Hormone (MELL)
GHIID .... Geothermal Hot Line (journ.) (SAUS)
GHIS .... GOES High Resolution Interferometer Sounder (SAUS)
GHIUD .... Global Human Information Use per Decade (SAUS)
GHIX .... Gifford Hill [*Federal Railroad Administration identification code*]
GHJ .... Gastonia, NC [*Location identifier*] [*FAA*] (FAAL)
GHJSA .... Ghana Journal of Science (journ.) (SAUS)
GHK .... Greyhawk Resources Ltd. [*Vancouver Stock Exchange symbol*]
GHK .... Grosshandelskontor [*Wholesale Business Office*] [*German*]
GHK .... Handkommentar zum Alten Testament (Goettingen) [*A publication*] (BJA)
GHL .... Gatwick Handling Ltd. [*British*] [*ICAO designator*] (FAAC)
GHL .... George Henry Lewes [*Initials used as pseudonym*]
GHL .... Grammar of the Human Language (journ.) (SAUS)
GHL .... [*A*] Grammar of the Hurrian Language [*A publication*] (BJA)
GHL .... Greyhound Lines of Canada Ltd. [*Toronto Stock Exchange symbol*]
GHL .... Growth-Hormone Loaded (SAUS)
GHL .... Guardhouse Lawyer [*Military slang*]
GH/LCD .... Guest-Host/Liquid Crystal Display [*Telecommunications*] (TEL)
GHLI .... Guilford-Holley L Inventory [*Psychology*]
GHM .... Aero Service Bolivia [*ICAO designator*] (FAAC)

GHM .... Centerville, TN [*Location identifier*] [*FAA*] (FAAL)
GHM .... Gay Hispanic Male (ADWA)
GHM .... General Hydrological Model (SAUO)
GHM .... generalized Hall model (SAUS)
GHM .... Geniohyoid Muscle (MELL)
GHM .... Going-Home Money
GHM .... Graham Corp. [*AMEX symbol*] (SPSG)
GHM .... Group-to-Highway Multiplexer (SAUO)
GHM .... Guaranteed Hourly Minimum
GHMA .... Greek Hellenic Mapping Agency (SAUO)
GH-MATRIX... Generalized Hadamand Matrix
GHMC .... Good Harvest Marine Company (SAUO)
GHME .... Gott Hilf Mir Elenden [*God Help Miserable Me*] [*Motto of Eleonore, Electress of Brandenburg (1583-1607)*] [*German*]
GHMI .... Generalized Human-Machine Interface (MCD)
GHMS .... Graduate in Homeopathic Medicine and Surgery (SAUO)
GHMS .... Home Mission Sisters of America (Glenmary) (TOCD)
GHN .... Generalized Hypertrophic Neuropathy
GHN .... Get Hold Next (SAUS)
GHN .... Ghana Navy
GHN .... Goldhaven Resources Ltd. [*Vancouver Stock Exchange symbol*]
GHN .... Groupe Hygiene Naturelle [*European Natural Hygiene Society - ENHS*] (EAIO)
GHN .... Gun Howitzer NORICUM (SAUS)
GHNet .... Global Health Network (ADWA)
GHNP .... Get Hold Next within Parent (SAUS)
GHNWP .... Get Hold Next With Parent (SAUS)
GHO .... General Health Questionnaire (SAUS)
GHO .... General Homes Corp. (SAUO)
GHO .... Grahamstown [*South Africa*] [*Airport symbol*] (AD)
GHO .... Greater Hartford [*Connecticut*] Open [*Golf tournament*]
Ghose Mort... Ghose on Mortgages in India [*A publication*] (DLA)
GHOST .... Global Hierarchical Observing Strategy (SAUO)
GHOST .... Global Horizontal Sounding Technique [*Meteorology*]
GHOST .... Goal Hierarchy and Objectives Structuring Technique (SAUS)
GHOST .... Golf Head Optical Speed Trap [*Golf self-improvement program*]
GHOW .... Great Horned Owl [*North American bird banding code*] (BIBA)
GHP .... Gas High Pressure
GHP .... GEWEX Hydrometeorological Panel (SAUS)
GHP .... Grand High Priest [*Freemasonry*]
GHP .... Greater Hartford Process [*An association*] (EA)
GHP .... Great Hungarian Plain [*Geology*]
GHP .... Greenwich Hospital Pension [*British military*] (DMA)
GHP .... Gross Horsepower [*Engineering*]
GHP .... Group Health Program (SAUO)
GHP .... Guild of Hospital Pharmacists [*British*] (DBA)
GHPC .... Geothermal Heat Pump Consortium (SAUO)
GHPD .... Grated High Power Decoupling (SAUS)
g/hphr .... gallons per horsepower hour (SAUS)
GHPM .... General Health Policy Model
GHPP .... Genetically Handicapped Persons Program (MEDA)
GHPR .... Gliding Horse and Pony Registry (EA)
GHQ .... General Headquarters [*Military*]
GHQ .... General Health Questionnaire [*Personality development test*] [*Psychology*]
GHQ AATps... General Headquarters, Antiaircraft Troops (SAUS)
GHQAF .... General Headquarters Air Force
GHQC .... GH [*General Hospital*] Questionnaire Club [*Defunct*] (EA)
GHQF .... General Headquarters File [*Army*]
GHQ-FEC .... General Headquarters (SAUS)
GHQ-FEC .... General Headquarters, Far East Command (SAUS)
GHQS .... General Headquarters Exercise
g/hr .... gallons per hour (SAUS)
GHR .... Golden Hope Resources, Inc. [*Vancouver Stock Exchange symbol*]
GHR .... Granulomatous Hypersensitivity [*Medicine*] (DMAA)
GHR .... Gross Heat Rate (DNAB)
GHR .... Growth Hormone Receptor [*Biochemistry*]
GHRC .... Global Hydrology Resource Center
GHRC/USA ... Guatemala Human Rights Commission/United States of America (EA)
GHRD .... Green Hills Rural Development [*Federal Railroad Administration identification code*]
GHREA .... Guys Hospital Reports (journ.) (SAUS)
GH-RF .... Growth Hormone Releasing Factor [*Somatoliberin*] [*Also, GH-RH, GRF*] [*Endocrinology*]
GHRF .... Growth Hormone-Releasing Factor (ADWA)
GHRF .... Guardians of Hydrocephalus Research Foundation (EA)
GHRH .... Growth Hormone Realising Hormone (SAUS)
GHRI .... Guidance System, Hybrid Radio-Inertial (SAUS)
GH-RIF .... Growth Hormone Release Inhibiting Factor [*Also, GH-RIH, GRIF, SRIF, SS*] [*Endocrinology*]
GH-RIH .... Growth Hormone Release Inhibiting Hormone [*Also, GH-RIF, GRIF, SRIF, SS*] [*Endocrinology*]
GHRIH .... Growth Hormone-Releasing Inhibiting Hormone (SAUS)
GH-RIH .... Growth Hormone Release Inhibiting Hormone (SAUS)
GHRP .... Growth Hormone Releasing Peptide [*Endocrinology*]
GHRS .... Goddard High-Resolution Spectrograph
GHRSP .... Guatemalan Health Rights Support Project (EA)
GHR/USA .... Guatemalan Human Rights Commission (SAUS)
GHR/USA .... Guatemalan Human Rights Commission/USA (EA)
GHS .... Galileo High School (SAUO)
GHS .... Garden History Society [*British*]
GHS .... Gatari Hutama Air Services PT [*Indonesia*] [*ICAO designator*] (FAAC)
GHS .... Genealogical and Historical Society (SAUO)
GHS .... General Health Services, Inc. (EFIS)
GHS .... General Household Survey [*Office of Population Census and Surveys*] [*British*]
GHS .... Getchell Resources, Inc. [*Vancouver Stock Exchange symbol*]
GHS .... Getchell Resourees, Inc. (SAUO)
GHS .... Gill Hematoxylin Solution (SAUS)
GHS .... Gilroy Hot Springs [*California*] [*Seismograph station code, US Geological Survey*] (SEIS)
GHS .... Girls High School (SAUO)
GHS .... Glamorgan History Society (SAUO)
GHS .... Global Health Sciences Fd [*NYSE symbol*] (TTSB)
GHS .... Global Health Sciences Fund [*NYSE symbol*] (SPSG)
GHS .... Ground Handling System [*Aerospace*] (AAG)
GHS .... Group Health Service (GHCT)
GHS .... Growth Hormone Secretagogue [*Biochemistry*]
GHS .... Grunberg Hydrofoil System
GHSA .... Georgia Head Start Association (SAUO)
GHSA .... Georgia High School Association (SAUO)
GH Scale ..... Gardner-Holdt Scale (SAUS)
GHSE .... Ground Handling and Servicing Equipment [*Aerospace*] (IAA)
GHSG .... Guest Housing [*Army*] (AABC)
GHSGT .... Georgia High School Graduation Test (SAUO)
GHSI .... GHS (SAUS)
GHSI .... GHS, Inc. [*Formerly, Global Health Systems, Inc.*] [*NASDAQ symbol*] (NQ)
GHS Inc .... GHS, Inc. [*Associated Press*] (SAG)
GHSLA .... Georgia Health Sciences Library Association (SAUO)
GHSP .... Great High Schools Program (SAUO)
GHSR .... Governors Highway Safety Representative (SAUS)
GHSV .... Gas Hour Space Velocity [*Chemical engineering*]
GHSWT .... Georgia High School Writing Test (SAUO)
GHT .... Gas Holding Tank (SAUS)
GHT .... Ghat [*Libya*] [*Airport symbol*] (OAG)
Ght .... Ghent (SAUS)
GHT .... Golden Hour Tango
GHT .... Goldhurst Resources [*Vancouver Stock Exchange symbol*]
GHT .... Ground Handling Test
GHTSTN .... Guest Host Technique Supertwisted Nematic (SAUS)
GHU .... Get Hold Unique (SAUS)
GHU .... Gualeguaychu [*Argentina*] [*Airport symbol*] (OAG)
Ghub .... Ghubba (SAUS)
GHV .... Genesis Health Ventures [*NYSE symbol*] (SPSG)
GHV .... Genesis Hlth Ventures [*NYSE symbol*] (TTSB)
GHV .... Golden Hind Ventures Ltd. [*Vancouver Stock Exchange symbol*]
GHV .... Goose Hepatitis Virus [*Medicine*] (DMAA)
GHV .... Gross Heating Value (SAUS)
GHV .... Growth Hormone Variant [*Medicine*] (DMAA)
GHVI .... Genesis Health Ventures (SAUS)
GHVL .... Groot Hertog von Luxemberg [*Grand Duke of Luxemburg*] [*Numismatics*] (ROG)
GHVM .... Global High-Visibility Mast
GHW .... Garrison Hill [*Washington*] [*Seismograph station code, US Geological Survey*] (SEIS)
GHW .... General Housewares Corp. [*NYSE symbol*] (SPSG)
GHW .... Generalized Hamming Weight (SAUS)
GHW .... Generators of hazardous waste (SAUS)
GHW .... Genl Housewares [*NYSE symbol*] (TTSB)
GHW .... Guaranteed Hourly Wage
GHWP .... Greenhouse Warming Potential [*Environmental chemistry*]
GHWS .... Gas Hot Water Service [*Classified advertising*] (ADA)
GHX .... Galveston-Houston Co. (SAUO)
GHX .... Graham, TX [*Location identifier*] [*FAA*] (FAAL)
GHX .... Ground Heat Exchange (SAUS)
GHX .... Ground Heat Exchanger
GHYD .... General Hydrocarbons of Minnesota (SAUS)
GHz .... Gigahertz [*1,000 megahertz*]
GHZ .... Golden Horizon [*Vancouver Stock Exchange symbol*]
GI .... Air Guinee [*ICAO designator*] (AD)
GI .... Galleries Index (SAUS)
GI .... Galvanized Iron
GI .... Gas Injection (SAUS)
GI .... Gas Instructor (SAUS)
GI .... Gas Insufflation (MELL)
GI .... Gastroenterology (DAVI)
GI .... Gastrointestinal [*Medicine*]
GI .... Gelatin Infusion [*Medium*] [*Biochemistry*] (DAVI)
GI .... Gelatin Infusion Medium [*Medicine*] (BABM)
GI .... Gelation Index [*Lubricants*]
GI .... Gelbray International (EA)
GI .... Gemeinschaft der Ikonenfreunde [*Society of Friends of Icons - SFI*] (EAIO)
GI .... Gender Identity (DIPS)
GI .... Genealogical Institute (EA)
GI .... General Index
GI .... General Indication (SAUS)
GI .... General Indulgence (ROG)
GI .... General Infantry [*Soldier*] [*Army*] (DAVI)
GI .... General Information (IAA)
GI .... General Input [*Computer science*] (IAA)
GI .... General Inspection [*Military*] (AABC)
GI .... General Instrument (SAUS)
GI .... General Instrument Corporation (SAUS)
GI .... General Instruments
GI .... General Issue
gi .... generation interval (SAUS)
GI .... Generic Identifier [*Telecommunications*] (TEL)

GI............... Genesis Information (EA)
GI............... Genesis Institute [An association] (EA)
GI............... Genetics Institute, Inc.
GI............... Genito-Intestinal [Medicine] (EDAA)
GI............... Genomic Imprinting (MELL)
GI............... Genral Instrument Corp. (SAUS)
GI............... Geodesic Isotensoid (IEEE)
GI............... Geodetic Institute (SAUS)
GI............... Geodic Isotensoid (SAUS)
GI............... Geographically Impossible (ADA)
GI............... Geographic Information (SAUO)
GI............... Geological Institute (SAUO)
GI............... Geometric Intelligence
GI............... Geon International Corp. (EFIS)
GI............... Geophysical Institute [University of Alaska, Fairbanks] [Research center]
GI............... Gerson Institute (EA)
GI............... Giant Industries [NYSE symbol] (SPSG)
GI............... Giant Interneurons [Neurology]
GI............... Gibraltar [ANSI two-letter standard code] (CNC)
gi............... Gibraltar [MARC country of publication code] [Library of Congress] (LCCP)
GI............... Gideons International (EA)
Gi............... Gilbert [A unit of magnetomotive force]
Gi............... Giles (SAUS)
GI............... Gilgai [Soil biology] (QSUL)
gi............... Gill (NTIO)
GI............... Gill
GI............... Gimbel Brothers (SAUS)
GI............... Gingival Index [Dentistry]
GI............... Girls, Inc. (EA)
GI............... Glasgow Institute (SAUS)
GI............... Glaucoma (SAUS)
GI............... Glazed Interior [Title] (DICI)
GI............... Glider Infantry (SAUS)
GI............... Global Indexing System (SAUO)
GI............... Global Indicator (TVEL)
GI............... Global Intelligence (SAUS)
GI............... Globigerina (SAUS)
GI............... Globin Insulin
GI............... Globulin Insulin (SAUS)
GI............... Globus (SAUS)
GI............... Glomerular Index [Medicine] (AAMN)
GI............... Glomus intraradices [A fungus]
GI............... Glovebox Investigations (SAUS)
GI............... Glucose Intolerance (MELL)
GI............... Glucose Isomerase (EDCT)
GI............... Glycemic Index
GI............... Goethe Institute (EA)
GI............... Gold Inlay (MELL)
GI............... Gold Institute [Also known as L'Institut de l'Or] (EA)
GI............... Governmental and Industrial (SAUS)
GI............... Government and Industrial (IEEE)
GI............... Government Initiated (IEEE)
GI............... Government Issue [Army]
GI............... Government of India
GI............... Graded Index [Optics]
GI............... Grain Iron (SAUS)
GI............... Grand Island [Diocesan abbreviation] [Nebraska] (TOCD)
GI............... Granuloma Inguinale [Endocrinology] (DAVI)
GI............... Grassroots International (EA)
GI............... Gravida I [Gynecology and obstetrics] (DAVI)
GI............... Gray Iron (MSA)
GI............... Gray's Inn [London] [One of the Inns of Court]
GI............... Great Indulgence
GI............... Green Island [Plant pathology]
GI............... Greenpeace International (EA)
GI............... Grid Interval (IAA)
GI............... Gross Impression [Television ratings] (NTCM)
GI............... Gross Income
GI............... Gross Inventory (MHDB)
GI............... Gross Investment
G/I............... Ground Idle (SAUS)
GI............... Ground Insulation (ELAL)
GI............... Ground Interception (IAA)
GI............... Group Identification (SAUO)
GI............... Group Indicate (SAUO)
GI............... Group Insurance
GI............... Group Item (SAUO)
GI............... Growth and Income [Business term]
GI............... Growth Index
GI............... Growth Inhibiting
GI............... Growth Inhibitor (SAUS)
GI............... Guardian Independent [A publication]
GI............... Guest Investigator
GI............... Guidance Inventory [Psychology]
GI............... Guided Imagery [Psychology]
Gi............... Guido de Suzaria [Deceased, 1293] [Authority cited in pre-1607 legal work] (DSA)
GI............... Gunner Instructor [Navy] [British]
GI............... Gym Itch (MELL)
GI............... Gyro International (EA)
GI............... Royal Glasgow Institute of Fine Arts [Scotland]
GI............... Soldier [Slang, probably from Government Issue]
GI .... Generic Issue (ODA)
GIO............... Gas Identifcation Officer (SAUS)
GIO............... Giocossamente (SAUS)
GI1T............... Glucose Insulin Tolerance Test (SAUS)
GIA............... Armed Islamic Group [Anti-government faction] [Algeria] [Acronym is based on foreign phrase] (ECON)
GIA............... Garber International Associates Inc. (SAUS)
GIA............... Garden Industry of America [Inactive] (EA)
GIA............... Garuda Indonesian Airways Ltd.
GIA............... Garuda Indonesia PT [ICAO designator] (FAAC)
GIA............... Gastrointestinal Anastomosis [Medicine] (DAVI)
GIA............... Gastrointestinal Anthrax [Medicine] (MELL)
GIA............... Gemological Institute of America (EA)
GIA............... General Industrial Application (SAUS)
GIA............... General International Agreement [Legal term] (DLA)
GIA............... General Ledger Account (SAUS)
GIA............... Geographical Information Analysis (EERA)
GIA............... Geographic information analysis (SAUS)
GIA............... Geographic information and analysis (SAUS)
GIA............... Geophysical Institute, University of Alaska [Alaska] [Seismograph station code, US Geological Survey] [Closed] (SEIS)
GIA............... Glacial Isostatic Adjustment [Geophysics]
GIA............... Global Industry Analysts'
GIA............... Goldale Investments (SAUS)
GIA............... Goodwill Industries of America (EA)
GIA............... Government Information and Advertising [New South Wales, Australia]
GIA............... GPC [General Purpose Computer] Interface Adapter (NASA)
GIA............... GPS International Association (SAUS)
GIA............... Grants-in-Aid
GIA............... Graphic Information Acquisition (SAUS)
GIA............... Gregorian Institute of America (SAUO)
GIA............... Gross Internal Area
GIA............... Group Interaction Analysis
GIA............... Gummed Industries Association (EA)
GIAA .... Geometrics Industry Association of America (SAUO)
GIABS .... Gastrointestinal Absorption Database [Environmental Protection Agency] [Information service or system] (CRD)
GIAC .... General Industry Advisory Committee
GIAC .... Geomatics Industry Association of Canada (SAUS)
GIAC .... Graphical Input Aggregate Control (SEWL)
GIAD .... Gladiator Fighter Aircraft (SAUS)
GIAHA............... Gilcrease Institute of American History and Art (SAUO)
GIAKF .... Goldale Investments (SAUS)
GIAL............... Geographic Information and Analysis Laboratory (SAUS)
GIAM .... Conference on Global Impacts of Applied Microbiology (SAUS)
GIAM .... Global Impact of Application Microbiology (SAUS)
GIAM .... Global Impacts of Applied Microbiology [International conferences]
GIAM .... Global Integrated Assessment Models (SAUO)
GIAM .... International Conference on Global Impacts of Applied Microbiology (SAUO)
GIANB............... Geomatics Industry Association of New Brunswick (SAUO)
GIANT .... Genealogical [or Geological] Information and Name Tabulating System [Computer science] (IEEE)
GIANT .... Genealogical Information and Name Tabulation (SAUO)
GIANT .... General Information and Analysis Tool
GIANT .... General Instrument Advanced Nitride Technology (IAA)
GIANT .... General Integrated Analytical Triangulation Program [National Oceanic and Atmospheric Administration]
GIANT .... General Intgrated Analytical Triangulation Program (SAUS)
GIANT .... Geodetic Infrastructure for Antarctica (SAUS)
GIANT .... Geographic Intelligence and Topographic System
GIANT .... Geological Information and Name Tabulating System (SAUS)
GIANT .... Giant Group Ltd. [Associated Press] (SAG)
GIANT .... Graphic Interactive Analytic Network Technique (MCD)
GiantCmt .... Giant Cement Holding, Inc. [Associated Press] (SAG)
GiantFd............... Giant Foods [Associated Press] (SAG)
GiantIn............... Giant Industries [Associated Press] (SAG)
GIANTS............... General Instrument Advanced Nitride Technology Shift-register (SAUS)
Giants............... Giants Stadium (SAUS)
Giants............... Giardiasis diarrhea (SAUS)
GIANTS............... Greater Independent Association of National Travel Services (EA)
GIANT System... Geological Information and Name Tabulating System (SAUS)
GIAO .... Gauge Invariant Atomic Orbital (SAUO)
GIAO .... Gauge-Invariant Atomic Orbital [NASA]
GIAPP .... Geological Image Analysis Program Package (SAUO)
GIAPPAR............... General Ledger, Accounts Payable and Accounts Receivable (SAUS)
GIAR .... Grants-in-Aid of Research
GIAS .... Global Integration and Synthesis [Climate change] (EERA)
Giauq El .... Giauque's Election Laws [A publication] (DLA)
GIAWA............... Gas Industry Association of Western Australia
GIB............... Air Guinea [Guinea] [ICAO designator] (FAAC)
GIB............... CGI Group [NYSE symbol] (SG)
GIB............... Gastric Ileal Bypass [Medicine] (DAVI)
GIB............... Gastrointestinal Bleeding [Medicine] (DMAA)
GIB............... General Information Book (SAUO)
GIB............... General Information Booklet [Navy]
GIB............... General Instruction Book
GIB............... Geographic Information Board (SAUO)
GIB............... Geomagnetic Indices Bulletin (SAUS)
Gib............... Gibbon's Reports, New York Surrogate Court [A publication] (DLA)
GIB............... Gibilmanna [Sicily] [Seismograph station code, US Geological Survey] (SEIS)
GIB............... Gibraltar [ANSI three-letter standard code] (CNC)
GIB............... Gibraltar [Airport symbol] (OAG)

Gib .... Gibraltar (ODBW)
Gib .... Gibraltarian (SAUS)
GIB .... Gibson (SAUS)
GIB .... Glass in Barrels (SAUS)
GIB .... Good in Bed (DSUE)
GIB .... Goods in Bond (SAUS)
GIB .... GPS [*Global Positioning System*] Integrity Broadcast [*Navigation systems*]
GIB .... Greal Lakes Freight Bureau Inc. (SAUO)
GIB .... Gulf International Bank [*Bahrain*] (EY)
GIB .... Guy in the Back [*Copilot*] [*Air Force slang*]
GIBA .... Gastrointestinal Bleeding from Aspirin (MELL)
Gib Aids .... Gibson's Aids to the Examinations [*A publication*] (DLA)
GIBAIR .... Gibraltar Airways (SAUS)
GIBAIR .... Gibraltar Airways Ltd.
Gib & Na Eq Jur ... Gibbons and Nathans' Equitable Jurisdiction of County Courts [*A publication*] (DLA)
GIBAPA .... Guild of International Butler Administrators and Personal Assistants [*British*] (EAIO)
Gibbon .... Gibbon on Nuisances [*A publication*] (DLA)
Gibbon Rom Emp ... Gibbon's History of the Decline and Fall of the Roman Empire [*A publication*] (DLA)
Gibbons .... Gibbon's Reports, New York Surrogate Court [*A publication*] (DLA)
Gibbons (NY) ... Gibbon's Reports, New York Surrogate Court [*A publication*] (DLA)
Gibb Rom Emp ... Gibbon's History of the Decline and Fall of the Roman Empire [*A publication*] (DLA)
GIBBS .... Gibbs, ID [*American Association of Railroads railroad junction routing code*]
Gibbs .... Gibbs' Reports [*2-4 Michigan*] [*A publication*] (DLA)
GibbsC .... Gibbs Construction, Inc. [*Associated Press*] (SAG)
GibbsCn .... Gibbs Construction, Inc. [*Associated Press*] (SAG)
Gibbs F .... Gibbs' Practical Forms [*A publication*] (DLA)
Gibbs' Jud Chr ... Gibbs' Judicial Chronicle [*A publication*] (DLA)
GIBBSSAR ... Gibbs & Hill, Inc., Standard Safety Analysis Report [*Nuclear energy*] (NRCH)
Gibb Sur .... Gibbon's Reports, New York Surrogate Court [*A publication*] (DLA)
Gibb Surr .... Gibbon's Reports, New York Surrogate Court [*A publication*] (DLA)
Gibb Surv .... Gibbon s Reports (SAUS)
Gib Civ L .... Gibbons on the Civil Law [*A publication*] (DLA)
GIBCO .... Grand Island Biological Company (SAUO)
Gib Cod .... Gibson's Codex Juris Ecclesiastia Anglicani [*A publication*] (DLA)
Gib Cont .... Gibbons on Contracts (journ.) (SAUS)
GIBCY .... Gibson City, IL [*American Association of Railroads railroad junction routing code*]
Gib Dec .... Gibson's Scottish Decisions [*A publication*] (DLA)
Gib Dec .... Gibson's Scottish Decisions (SAUS)
Gib Dil .... Gibbon's Dilapidations and Nuisances [*2nd ed.*] [*1849*] [*A publication*] (DLA)
GIBF .... Gastrointestinal Bacterial Flora [*Medicine*] (MEDA)
Gib Fix .... Gibbon's Law of Fixtures [*1836*] [*A publication*] (DLA)
Gibfo .... Gibraltar for Orders (SAUS)
GIBG .... Gibson Greetings [*NASDAQ symbol*] (TTSB)
GIBG .... Gibson Greetings, Inc. [*NASDAQ symbol*] (NASQ)
GIBH .... Gibson-Homans Co. (SAUO)
GI (Bill) .... Veterans Benefits Act, Public Law 345, 1944
GIBIS .... Graphical IBIS [*Issue-Based Information System*] [*Computer science*] (BYTE)
Gib Lim .... Gibbons' Lex Temporis, Limitations and Prescription [*A publication*] (DLA)
Gib LN .... Gibson's Law Notice [*1882-84*] [*A publication*] (DLA)
Gib LN .... Gibson's Law Notice (SAUS)
GIBLOCN .... Global Ocean Camers Ltd (SAUS)
Gib Lynd .... Gibson's Memoir of Lord Lyndhurst [*A publication*] (DLA)
GIBMED .... Gibraltar Mediterranean Area (SAUS)
GIBMED .... Gibraltar Mediterranean Command [*NATO*] (NATG)
GIBN .... Global Interoperability for Broadband Networks (SAUO)
Gib Nui .... Gibbon's Dilapidations and Nuisances [*2nd ed.*] [*1849*] [*A publication*] (DLA)
Gibo Res Dev Headquarters Jpn ... Giho.Research and Development Headquarters.Japan Defense Agency (journ.) (SAUS)
GibPack .... Gibraltar Packaging Group [*Associated Press*] (SAG)
Gibr .... Gibraltar
GibrStl .... Gibraltar Steel Corp. [*Associated Press*] (SAG)
GIBS .... C.R. Gibson Co. [*AMEX symbol*] (COMM)
Gibs .... Gibraltarians (SAUS)
GIBS .... Guy in the Backseat [*Copilot*] [*Air Force slang*]
GIBsAR .... Gibbs & Hill, Inc., Standard Safety Analysis Report (SAUO)
Gibs Code .... Gibson's Codex [*A publication*] (DLA)
Gibs LN .... Gibson's Law Notes [*1882-84*] [*A publication*] (DLA)
GIBSN .... Gibson, IN [*American Association of Railroads railroad junction routing code*]
GibsnG .... Gibson Greetings, Inc. [*Associated Press*] (SAG)
Gibson .... Gibson Desert of east-central Western Australia (SAUS)
Gibson .... (Gibson of) Durie's Decisions, Scotch Court of Session [*1621-42*] [*A publication*] (DLA)
Gib-tv .... Gibraltar television (SAUS)
GIBUS .... Belgian PC package (SAUS)
GIBYD .... Gilbert Yard, WV [*American Association of Railroads railroad junction routing code*]
GIC .... Compagnie de Bauxites de Guinee [*Guinea*] [*ICAO designator*] (FAAC)
GIC .... Galit Resource Corp. [*Vancouver Stock Exchange symbol*]
GIC .... General Immunocompetence [*Immunology*] (DAVI)
GIC .... General Impedance Converter (SAUS)
GIC .... General Improvement Contractors Association (EA)
GIC .... General Industries Corporation (SAUO)
GIC .... General Input Channel (NITA)
GIC .... General Input/Output Channel
GIC .... General Instrument [*NYSE symbol*] [*Formerly, Nextlevel Systems*] (SG)
GIC .... General Instrument Corp. [*NYSE symbol*] (SPSG)
GIC .... General Instrument Corporation (SAUO)
GIC .... General Investment Corporation (SAUO)
GIC .... General Investment Corporation of Quebec (SAUO)
GIC .... Generalised Immittance Converter (SAUS)
GIC .... Generalised Impedance Converter (SAUS)
GIC .... Generalized Immittance [*or Impedance*] Converter (IEEE)
GIC .... Generalized Impedance Converter (SAUS)
GIC .... Genl Instrument [*NYSE symbol*] (TTSB)
GIC .... Geomagnetically Induced Current
GIC .... German Information Center [*Information service or system*] (IID)
GIC .... German-Iran-Corporation, Teheran (SAUO)
GIC .... Ghana Investment Center (SAUS)
GIC .... Glass Industry Club (SAUO)
GIC .... Glass-Ionomer Cement [*Dental material*]
GIC .... Glatzer Industries Corp. (SAUS)
GIC .... Global Instructional Chemistry (SAUS)
GIC .... Global Interdependence Center (EA)
GIC .... Goods in Custody (ADA)
GIC .... Government Information Center (SAUO)
GIC .... GPS [*Global Positioning Systems*] Integrity Channel [*Navigation systems*]
GIC .... Graduate Induction Campaign [*Australia*]
GIC .... Grains Industry Council [*Australia*]
GIC .... Graphite Intercalation Compound [*Inorganic chemistry*]
GIC .... Graphite Intercalculation Compound (SAUS)
GIC .... Greenland Ice Sheet (SAUS)
GIC .... Ground Intercept Control (SAUS)
GIC .... Group Indicate Clause (SAUO)
GIC .... Group Indicate Cycle (SAUO)
GIC .... Guaranteed Income Contract
GIC .... Guaranteed Investment Certificate (SAUS)
GIC .... Guaranteed Investment Contract
GIC .... Guarantee Investment Contract (SAUS)
GIC .... Gulf Intercoastal Conference
GICA .... Gastrointestinal Cancer Antigen [*A tumor marker*] (CDI)
GICA .... Goat Industry Council of Australia
GICA .... Green Island Coral Atoll (SAUO)
GICAS .... Greenland Ice Cap Aeromagnetic Survey (SAUO)
GICC .... Geographic Information Coordinating Committee (SAUS)
GICC .... Glazing Industry Code Committee (NTPA)
GICC .... Government-Industry Coordinating Committee
GICCW .... Government-Industry Conference against Chemical Weapons (EERA)
GI Ceram .... Glass and Ceramics (journ.) (SAUS)
GICG .... Gila Cliff Dwellin National Monument (SAUS)
GICG .... Glase Icing (SAUS)
GICG .... Glaze Icing (SAUS)
GICL .... Gila Cliff Dwellings National Monument
GICL .... Graphics Language [*Computer science*] (HGAA)
GICLDC .... Civil Liberties Defense Committee (SAUS)
GICLDC .... GI Civil Liberties Defense Committee
GICLE .... Institute of Continuing Legal Education in Georgia [*University of Georgia School of Law*] (DLA)
GICO .... Gilat Communications, Ltd. [*NASDAQ symbol*] (NASQ)
GICORP .... Government Industry Cooperative Oyster Research Program (SAUO)
GICORP .... Government-Industry Cooperative Oyster Research Program
GICQ .... General Investment Corporation of Quebec (SAUO)
GICQA .... Gifted Child Quarterly (journ.) (SAUS)
GICR .... Goodwin Institute for Cancer Research [*Nova University*] [*Research center*] (RCD)
GICS .... Generic Intelligence Control System (ABAC)
GICS .... Geocoded Image Correction System (SAUO)
GICS .... Geographic Identification Code Scheme [*Bureau of the Census*] (GFGA)
GICS .... Global Instrumentation Control System (IAA)
GICS .... Grant Information and Control System [*Environmental Protection Agency*] (GFGA)
GICS .... Graphic Identification Code Scheme (SAUS)
GICWG .... Government Interface Control Working Group [*Military*]
GICZ .... Gibson Co-Operative [*Federal Railroad Administration identification code*]
GID .... Channel Aviation Ltd. [*British*] [*ICAO designator*] (FAAC)
GID .... Gastrointestinal Dialysis [*Medicine*]
GID .... Gastrointestinal Disease (MELL)
GID .... Gastrointestinal Disorder (MELL)
GID .... Gender Identity Disorder [*Medicine*] (DMAA)
GID .... General Improvement District (ADWA)
GID .... General Installation Dolly
GID .... General Intelligence Division (SAUO)
GID .... Gesellschaft fuer Information und Dokumentation mbH [*Society for Information and Documentation*] [*Information service or system*] (IID)
GID .... Giddings & Lewis Inc. (SAUO)
GID .... Gitega [*Burundi*] [*Airport symbol*] (OAG)
GID .... Group Identification (SAUO)
GID .... Group Identifier(or Identity) (SAUS)
GID .... Grupo Indl Durango ADS [*NYSE symbol*] (TTSB)
GID .... Grupo Industrial Durango SA de CV [*NYSE symbol*] (SAG)
GID .... Guilde International du Disque [*Record label*] [*France*]
GID .... Sud Air Transport SA [*Guinea*] [*ICAO designator*] (FAAC)

GIDA International Group for Agricultural Development in Latin America (SAUO)
GIDAANT Gender Identity Disorder of Adolescence or Adulthood, NonTranssexual type (SAUS)
GIDAP Government Industry Data Exchange Program (CIST)
GIDAP Guidance Inertial Data Analysis Program
GIDAS Geoanomaly Interactive Data Analysis System (MCD)
GIDB Geographic Information Database (SAUO)
GIDC Georgia Information Dissemination Center (SAUO)
GIDC Gujarat Industrial Development Corporation (SAUO)
GIDE Grupo Industrial des Defensa Europeo (SAUS)
GIDEL General Input Device Emulation Interface [*Computer science*] (MWOL)
GIDEON Global Infectious Disease and Epidemiology Network
GIDEP Government-Industry Data Exchange Program [*Formerly, IDEP*] [*Navy*] [*Information service or system*]
GIDFLD Goldfield Corp. (SAUO)
gi distress gastro-intestinal distress (SAUS)
GID-IZ Gesellschaft fuer Information und Dokumentation - Informationszentrum fuer Informationswissenschaft und -Praxis [*Information Center for Information Science and Information Work*] [*Society for Information and Documentation*] (IID)
GID-IZ GID (SAUS)
GIDL Gate-Induced Drain Leakage (SAUS)
GIDL Giddings & Lewis [*NASDAQ symbol*] (TTSB)
GIDL Giddings & Lewis, Inc. [*NASDAQ symbol*] (NQ)
GidLew Giddings & Lewis, Inc. [*Associated Press*] (SAG)
GIDP Gale International Directory of Publications [*A publication*]
GIDP Grounded into Double Plays [*Baseball*]
GIDS Generic Intelligent Driver Support System (SAUO)
GIDS Georgia Information Dissemination Center (SAUS)
GIDW General Inverse-Distance Weighted interpolation model (SAUS)
GIE Galapagos Islands [*Ecuador*] [*Seismograph station code, US Geological Survey*] (SEIS)
GIE General Image Engineering (SAUS)
GIE Global Information Environment (SAUS)
GIE Glycerinisopropylidene Ether [*Organic chemistry*]
GIE Graduate of the Institute of Engineers and Technicians (SAUS)
GIE Ground Instrumentation Equipment
GIE Group Indication Elimination (SAUO)
GIE Grupo Interamericano de Editores [*Interamerican publishers group*] (NITA)
GIE Guinee Inter Air [*Guinea*] [*ICAO designator*] (FAAC)
GIE Gyro Interface Electronics (ACAE)
GIEA General Industrial Electric Automation (SAUS)
GIEA German-American Information and Education Association (EA)
GIER General Industrial Equipment Reserve
GIEUS Guide to International Education in the US [*A publication*]
GIE VI Groupe International Postal d'Echanges d'Information et d'Experience [*International Group for the Exchange of Information and Experience Among Postal Savings Institutions*] (EAIO)
GIEWS Global Information and Early Warning System [*FAO*] [*United Nations*] (DUND)
GIEWSP Global Information and Early Warning System on Food and Agriculture (SAUO)
GIF Compuserve Graphics Interchange Format (SAUS)
GIF Gastrointestinal Fistula [*Medicine*] (MELL)
GIF Gatan Imaging Filter (AAEL)
GIF Gaussian Lens Formula (SAUS)
GIF General Image Format [*Marine science*] (OSRA)
GIF General Information File (SAUS)
GIF General Insurance Fund [*Federal Housing Administration*]
GIF German-Israeli Foundation [*US and Israel*]
GIF Gesellschaft fuer Informationsmarkt-Forschung [*Society for Information-Market Research*] [*Database producer*] (IID)
GIF Giant Intestinal Fluke [*Medicine*] (MELL)
Gif Giffard's English Vice-Chancellors' Reports [*65-66 English Reprint*] [*A publication*] (DLA)
GIF Gift (SAUS)
GIF Gifu [*Japan*] [*Seismograph station code, US Geological Survey*] (SEIS)
GIF Global Income Fund, Inc. [*AMEX symbol*] (NASQ)
GIF Glucosylisoflavonoid (DB)
GIF Glycosylation-Inducing Factor (QSUL)
GIF Glycosylation Inhibition Factor [*Medicine*] (MELL)
GIF Gonadotropin-Inhibitory Factor [*Somatostatin*] (STED)
GIF Graphical Information Format [*Satellite*]
GIF Graphical Interchange Format (SAUS)
gif Graphic Interchange Format [*Computer science*]
GIF Graphics Image Format (SAUS)
GIF Graphics Interchange File [*Computer science*] (ITCA)
GIF Graphics Interchange Format [*Computer technology*]
GIF Gravito-Inertial Force
GIF Growth Hormone-Inhibiting Factor (STED)
GIF Growth-Hormone Release-Inhibiting Factor [*Medicine*] (DB)
GIF Growth Inhibiting Factor [*Endocrinology*] (MAE)
GIF Guardian International Income Fund Units [*Toronto Stock Exchange symbol*]
GIF Guinee Air Lines SA [*Guinea*] [*ICAO designator*] (FAAC)
GIF Gulf It to FORTRAN [*Translator*] [*Computer science*]
GIF Guy in the Front Seat [*Pilot*] [*Slang*] (DSUE)
GIF Winter Haven (SAUS)
GIF Winter Haven, FL [*Location identifier*] [*FAA*] (FAAL)
GIFA General Iron Fitters Association [*A union*] [*British*]
GIFA Geneva Infant Feeding Association
GIFA German Interregional Food Allocation (SAUO)
GIFA Governing International Fishing Agreement (MSC)
GIFAP Groupement International des Associations Nationales de Fabricants de Produits Agrochimiques [*International Group of National Associations of Manufacturers of Agrochemical Products*] (EAIO)
GIFAP International Group of National Associations of Agrochemical Manufacturers (SAUS)
GIFAP International Group of National Associations of Manufacturers of Agrochemical Products (SAUO)
GIFC Gilligan's Island Fan Club (EA)
Giff Giffard's English Vice-Chancellors' Reports [*65-66 English Reprint*] [*A publication*] (DLA)
Giff & H Giffard and Hemming's English Chancery Reports [*A publication*] (DLA)
Giff (Eng) Giffard's English Vice-Chancellors' Reports [*65-66 English Reprint*] [*A publication*] (DLA)
GIFFI Group Inventory for Finding Interests [*Educational test*]
GIFFTS Gravitational Influences on Flammability and Flamespread (SAUO)
GIFH Golden Isles Financial Holdings, Inc. [*NASDAQ symbol*] (SAG)
GIFH Golden Isles Finl Hldg [*NASDAQ symbol*] (TTSB)
GIFHU Golden Isles Finl Hldg Unit [*NASDAQ symbol*] (TTSB)
GIFI General Information File Interrogation (PDAA)
GIFL Gilded Flicker [*North American bird banding code*] (BIBA)
GI for SS Goddard Institute for Space Studies [*NASA*]
GIFOV Ground Instantaneous Field-of-View (MCD)
GIFRP Glass-Fiber-Reinforced Plastic (SAUS)
GIFS Generalized Interrelated Flow Simulation (IEEE)
GIFS Gospel-in-Film Service [*Australia*]
GIFS Gray Iron Founders Society (EA)
GIFT Gamete Intrafallopian Transfer [*Fertilization technique*]
GIFT Gamete Intrafallopian Tube Transfer (ADWA)
GIFT Gas-Insulated Flow Tube (NRCH)
GIFT General Information File Tester (SAUS)
GIFT General Internal FORTRAN Translator [*Computer science*] (IEEE)
GIFT Geometric Information for Targets (MCD)
GIFT Gerald Stevens, Inc. [*NASDAQ symbol*] (NASQ)
GIFT Glasgow International Freight Terminal [*Scotland*] (DS)
GIFT Gneral Information File Tester (SAUS)
GIFT Granulocyte Immunofluorescence Test (STED)
GIFT Ground and In Flight Training (ACAE)
GIFT Group Inventory for Finding Creative Talent [*Educational test*]
Gift Child Gifted Child Quarterly (journ.) (SAUS)
GiftCh Q Gifted Child Quarterly (journ.) (SAUS)
GIFTPOOL Datenbank ueber Gifte und Vergiftungen [*Databank for Poisons and Poisoning*] [*German*]
GIFTS Geostationary Imaging Fourier Transform Spectrometer [*NASA's proposed launch date is 2003*]
GIFTS Gift Information and Fund-raising Tasks System (SAUS)
GIFTS Graphics-Oriented Interactive Finite Element Time-Sharing System (PDAA)
GIFUN Guardian International Income Fund Units (SAUO)
GIFY Grazing Incidence x-ray Fluorescence Yield (SAUS)
Gig De Gigantibus [*Philo*] (BJA)
GIG Genetia Interest Group (SAUO)
GIG Genetics Interest Group [*British*]
GIG Geographical Information Group (SAUO)
GIG Geological Information Group (SAUO)
GIG Geologic Inquiries Group (SAUS)
GIG Geometric Interpolation Grid (SAUO)
GIG Gesellschaft fuer Internationale Geldgeschichte (EAIO)
gig Gigabyte (ADWA)
GIG Gigi Resources Ltd. [*Vancouver Stock Exchange symbol*]
GIG Global Information Grid (SEWL)
GIG Gluten Intolerance Group [*Later, GIGNA*] (EA)
GIG Glycidylisopropylideneglycerol [*Organic chemistry*]
GIG Rio De Janeiro [*Brazil*] [*Airport symbol*] (OAG)
GIG Scottsbluff, NE [*Location identifier*] [*FAA*] (FAAL)
GIGA Giga-Tronics, Inc. [*NASDAQ symbol*] (NQ)
giga One Billion (WDMC)
GigaInfo Giga Information Group, Inc. [*Associated Press*] (SAG)
GigaTr Giga-Tronics, Inc. [*Associated Press*] (SAG)
GIGI Gamma Inspection of Grain Integrity
GIGI General Imaging Generator and Interpreter (IAA)
GIGL Gale Information Guide Library [*Publication series*]
GIGM Giga Media Ltd. [*NASDAQ symbol*] (SG)
GIGNA Gluten Intolerance Group of North America (EA)
GIGO Garbage In (SAUS)
gigo Garbage In Garbage Out [*Computer science*] (ODBW)
GIGO Garbage In, Garbage Out [*Computer science*]
GIGO Garbage In Gospel Out (SAUS)
Gigo Garbarge in Gararge out (SAUS)
GIGPP Green Institute of Geophysics and Planetary Physics (SAUO)
GIGS Gemini Inertial Guidance System [*NASA*] (KSC)
GIGS Gravity-Gradient Test Satellite
GIGX Giga Information Group, Inc. [*NASDAQ symbol*] (SAG)
GIH Gastric Inhibitory Hormone [*Medicine*] (STED)
GIH Gastrointestinal Hemorrhage [*Medicine*] (DMAA)
GIH Gastrointestinal Hormone [*Endocrinology*]
GIH Groupe International Hachette [*France*]
GIH Growth Hormone Inhibiting Hormone (ADWA)
GIH Growth Inhibiting Hormone [*Endocrinology*] (MAE)
GIH United States Geological Survey, Water Resources Division, Helena, MT [*OCLC symbol*] (OCLC)
GIHC Ghana Industrial Holding Corporation (SAUO)

Giho Res Dev Hdqrters Jpn Defease Agency... Giho.Research and Development Headquarters.Japan Defense Agency (journ.) (SAUS)
GIHS............ Genealized Information Handling System (SAUS)
GIHS............ General Information Handling System (SAUS)
GIHS............ Generalized Information Handling System (SAUS)
GIHX............ Gifford Hill [*Private rail car owner code*]
GII............... Gastrointestinal Infection [*Medicine*]
GII............... General Industrial Insulation, Inc. (EFIS)
GII............... Geographic Information Index (SAUO)
GII............... Global Information Infrastructure
GII............... Goods Inwards Inspection (SAUS)
GII............... Goodwill Industries International (EA)
GII............... Government Information Infrastructure (SAUS)
GII............... Government Information on the Internet
GII............... Graphic Interface Indicator (SAUS)
GII............... Greiner Engineering, Inc. [*NYSE symbol*] (SPSG)
GII............... Guillevin International, Inc. [*Toronto Stock Exchange symbol*]
G-II............. Gulfstream II [*Shuttle training aircraft*] [*NASA*] (NASA)
GII............... Siguiri [*Guinea*] [*Airport symbol*] (AD)
GIIC............ Generic Item Indicator Code (ACAE)
GIIC............ Global Information Infrastructure Commission (DDC)
GIID............ GENSER Integration Information Display (MCD)
GIIGNL......... Groupe Internationale des Importateur du Gaz Natural Liquefie
GIII.............. G-III Apparel Group Ltd. [*NASDAQ symbol*] (NQ)
G-III............ GThree Apparel Group Ltd. [*Associated Press*] (SAG)
GIILS........... Guide to Integrated Information Literacy Skills [*A publication*]
GIIP............. Groupement International de l'Industrie Pharmaceutique des Pays de la CEE [*International Pharmaceutical Industry Group for the EEC Countries*]
GIIR............. Government Idle Industrial Reserve (AAG)
GIIR............. Grazing Incidence Infrared (ABAC)
GIIS............. Graduate Institute of International Studies (SAUO)
GIITS........... General Imagery Intelligence Training System (SAUO)
GIIV............. Gated Image Intensifier Viewer
GIJ............... Government Issue Jane (SAUO)
GIJ............... Guild of Irish Journalists (SAUO)
GIK.............. Glucose, Insulin, and Potassium [*Solution*] [*Medicine*]
GIK.............. Great Lakes Chemical Corp. (SAUO)
GIKA............ Gifts In Kind America (NFD)
GIL............... Gaseous Ion LASER
GIL............... General Instruction Logic (SAUS)
GIL............... General Leaseholds Limited (SAUS)
GIL............... General-Purpose Interactive Programming Language [*Computer science*] (MHDB)
Gil................ Gilbert [*A unit of magnetomotive force*]
GIL............... Gilbert Felxi-Van Corp. (SAUO)
Gil................ Gilbert's Cases in Law and Equity [*A publication*] (DLA)
Gil................ Gilbert's English Chancery Reports [*1705-27*] [*A publication*] (DLA)
GIL............... Gildan Activewear'A' [*AMEX symbol*] (SG)
Gil................ Gilfillan's Reports [*1-20 Minnesota*] [*A publication*] (DLA)
GIL............... Gilgit [*Pakistan*] [*Airport symbol*] (AD)
GIL............... Gill Aviation Ltd. [*British*] [*ICAO designator*] (FAAC)
GIL............... Gilley Airways Corp. (SAUO)
Gil................ Gilman's Reports [*6-10 Illinois*] [*A publication*] (DLA)
Gil................ Gilmer's Virginia Reports [*21 Virginia*] [*A publication*] (DLA)
GIL............... Gilmore Creek [*Alaska*] [*Seismograph station code, US Geological Survey*] (SEIS)
GIL............... Grain Isolation Liner (MCD)
GIL............... Graphics Interface Language [*Computer science*] (TIMI)
GIL............... Green Indicating Lamp
GIL............... Green Indicating Light (SAUS)
GIL............... Gross Installing Load (SAUS)
GIL............... Group Investment-Linked (ADA)
GIL............... Guide to Internet Libraries (SAUO)
Gil................ Guillelmus Durandi [*Deceased, 1296*] [*Authority cited in pre-1607 legal work*] (DSA)
GIL............... GULL, Inc. (SAUO)
GIL............... United States Geological Survey, Metairie, LA [*OCLC symbol*] (OCLC)
GILA............ Gila, AZ [*American Association of Railroads railroad junction routing code*]
Gil & Fal..... Gilmour and Falconer's Cases, Scotch Court of Session [*A publication*] (DLA)
GilatSat....... Gilat Satellite Networks Ltd. [*Associated Press*] (SAG)
GILB............ Gilbert Associates (SAUS)
GILB............ Gilbert Associates, Inc. [*NASDAQ symbol*] (NQ)
Gilb............. Gilbert's Cases in Law and Equity [*A publication*] (DLA)
Gilb............. Gilbert's English Chancery Reports [*1705-27*] [*A publication*] (DLA)
GILBA.......... Gilbert Assoc'A' [*NASDAQ symbol*] (TTSB)
Gilb Bank..... Gilbert on Banking [*A publication*] (DLA)
Gilb Cas...... Gilbert's Cases in Law and Equity [*A publication*] (DLA)
Gilb Cas L & Eq... Gilbert's Cases in Law and Equity [*A publication*] (DLA)
Gilb Cas L&Eq... Gilbert's Cases in Law and Equity (SAUS)
Gilb Cas L & Eq (Eng)... Gilbert's Common Pleas [*93 English Reprint*] [*A publication*] (DLA)
Gilb Ch........ Gilbert's English Chancery Reports [*1705-27*] [*A publication*] (DLA)
Gilb Ch........ Gilbert's English Chancery Reports (SAUS)
Gilb Com Pl... Gilbert's Common Pleas [*93 English Reprint*] [*A publication*] (DLA)
Gilb CP........ Gilbert's Common Pleas [*93 English Reprint*] [*A publication*] (DLA)
Gilb CP........ Gilbert's Common Pleas (SAUS)
Gilb Debt..... Gilbert on the Action of Debt [*A publication*] (DLA)
Gilb Dev...... Gilbert's Law of Devises [*A publication*] (DLA)
Gilb Dis....... Gilbert on Distress and Replevin [*A publication*] (DLA)
Gilb Ej......... Gilbert on Ejectments [*A publication*] (DLA)
Gilb Eq........ Gilbert's English Equity Reports [*25 English Reprint*] [*1705-27*] [*A publication*] (DLA)
Gilb Eq (Eng)... Gilbert's English Equity Reports [*25 English Reprint*] [*1705-27*] [*A publication*] (DLA)
Gilb Eq Rep... Gilbert's English Equity Reports [*1705-27*] [*A publication*] (DLA)
Gilbert Ev.... Gilbert's Law of Evidence [*A publication*] (DLA)
Gilberts........ Gilbert and Ellice Islands (SAUS)
Gilbert Uses by Sugd... Gilbert's Uses and Trusts by Sugden [*A publication*] (DLA)
Gilb Ev......... Gilbert's Law of Evidence [*A publication*] (DLA)
Gilb Ex......... Gilbert's Executions [*A publication*] (DLA)
Gilb Exch..... Gilbert's English Exchequer Reports [*A publication*] (DLA)
Gilb Exch Pr... Gilbert's History and Practice of the Exchequer [*A publication*] (DLA)
Gilb For Rom... Gilbert's Forum Romanum [*A publication*] (DLA)
Gilb Forum Rom... Gilbert's Forum Romanum [*A publication*] (DLA)
Gilb Hist CP... Gilbert's History of Common Pleas [*A publication*] (DLA)
Gilb KB........ Gilbert's Cases in Law and Equity [*A publication*] (DLA)
Gilb Lex Pr... Gilbert's Lex Praetoria [*A publication*] (DLA)
Gilb PC........ Gilbert's Common Pleas [*93 English Reprint*] [*A publication*] (DLA)
Gilb Rem..... Gilbert's Remainders [*A publication*] (DLA)
Gilb Rents..... Gilbert's Treatise on Rents [*A publication*] (DLA)
Gilb Rents... Gilbert's Treatise on Rents (SAUS)
Gilb Rep...... Gilbert's English Chancery Reports [*1705-27*] [*A publication*] (DLA)
Gilb Repl..... Gilbert on Replevin [*A publication*] (DLA)
Gilb RR........ Gilbert's Railway Law of Illinois [*A publication*] (DLA)
GilbtA........... Gilbert Associates, Inc. [*Associated Press*] (SAG)
Gilb Ten...... Gilbert on Tenures [*A publication*] (DLA)
Gilb Uses..... Gilbert on Uses and Trusts [*A publication*] (DLA)
GILC............ Global Internet Liberty Campaign (RALS)
Gilchr.......... Gilchrist's Local Government Cases [*A publication*] (DLA)
GILCU.......... Gradual Increase in Length and Complexity of Utterance (STED)
GILD............ Gas Immersion LASER Doping (AAEL)
Gild.............. Gildersleeve's Reports [*New Mexico*] [*A publication*] (DLA)
GILD............ Gilead Sciences [*NASDAQ symbol*] (TTSB)
GILD............ Gilead Sciences, Inc. [*NASDAQ symbol*] (SPSG)
Gildersleeve... Gildersleeve's Reports [*New Mexico*] [*A publication*] (DLA)
Gildersleeve (N Mex)... Gildersleeve's Reports [*New Mexico*] [*A publication*] (DLA)
Gildr............ Gildersleeve's Reports [*New Mexico*] [*A publication*] (DLA)
Gil Dur......... Guillelmus Durandi [*Deceased, 1296*] [*Authority cited in pre-1607 legal work*] (DSA)
Gilead.......... Gilead Sciences, Inc. [*Associated Press*] (SAG)
Gilfillan....... Gilfillan's Reports [*1-20 Minnesota*] [*A publication*] (DLA)
Gilg............. Gilgames (BJA)
gill............... gill (SAUS)
GILL............. Gillingham [*Municipal borough in England*]
Gill.............. Gill's Maryland Court of Appeals Reports [*1843-51*] [*A publication*] (DLA)
Gill & J........ Gill and Johnson's Maryland Reports [*A publication*] (DLA)
Gill and J (Maryland)... Gill and Johnson's Maryland Reports [*A publication*] (DLA)
Gill & J (MD)... Gill and Johnson's Maryland Reports [*A publication*] (DLA)
Gill & Johns... Gill and Johnson's Maryland Reports [*A publication*] (DLA)
GILLBT......... Ghana Institute of Linguistics, Literacy and Bible Translation (SAUO)
Gillete......... Gillette Co. [*Associated Press*] (SAG)
Gillett Cr Law... Gillett's Treatise on Criminal Law and Procedure in Criminal Cases [*A publication*] (DLA)
GILLLL.......... Gull Laboratories, Inc. (SAUO)
Gill (MD)..... Gill's Maryland Reports [*A publication*] (DLA)
Gill Pol Rep... Gill's Police Court Reports [*Boston, MA*] [*A publication*] (DLA)
GILM............ German Language and Literature Monographs (SAUS)
Gilm............. Gilman's Reports [*6-10 Illinois*] [*A publication*] (DLA)
GILM............ Gil-Med Industries (SAUS)
GILM............ Gil-Med Industries, Inc. (SAUO)
Gilm............. Gilmer's Virginia Reports [*21 Virginia*] [*A publication*] (DLA)
Gilm............. Gilmour's Reports, Scotch Court of Session [*A publication*] (DLA)
Gilman......... Gilman's Reports [*6-10 Illinois*] [*A publication*] (DLA)
Gilm & F...... Gilmour and Falconer's Decisions, Scotch Court of Session [*1961-66*] [*A publication*] (DLA)
Gilm & Fal... Gilmour and Falconer's Decisions, Scotch Court of Session [*1961-66*] [*A publication*] (DLA)
Gilm & Falc... Gilmour and Falconer's Reports, Scotch Court of Session [*A publication*] (DLA)
GilmC........... Gilman & Ciocia, Inc. [*Associated Press*] (SAG)
Gilm Dig...... Gilman's Illinois and Indiana Digest [*A publication*] (DLA)
Gilmer......... Gilmer's Virginia Reports [*21 Virginia*] [*1820-21*] [*A publication*] (DLA)
GILMER........ Guardian of Impressive Letters and Master of Excellent (SAUS)
GILMER........ Guardian of Impressive Letters and Master of Excellent Replies
Gilmer (VA)... Gilmer's Virginia Reports [*21 Virginia*] [*A publication*] (DLA)
Gilm (Ill)..... Gilman's Reports [*6-10 Illinois*] [*A publication*] (DLA)
Gil (Minn).... Gilfillan's Edition [*1-20 Minnesota*] [*A publication*] (DLA)
GILMJ.......... Gilmore Junction, NE [*American Association of Railroads railroad junction routing code*]
GILMN......... Gilman, IL [*American Association of Railroads railroad junction routing code*]
GilmnCio...... Gilman & Ciocia, Inc. [*Associated Press*] (SAG)
GILN............ Glosa International Language Network (EAIO)
GILO............ German Industry Liaison Office (SAUO)
Gilp............. Gilpin's United States District Court Reports [*A publication*] (DLA)
Gilp Opin..... Gilpin's Opinions of the United States Attorneys-General [*A publication*] (DLA)
GILS............ Global Information Locator Service
GILS............ Government Information Locator Service [*Internet*] (AAGC)
GILSP.......... Good Industrial Large-Scale Practice
GILT............ General Inertial Logic Test (SAUS)
GILT............ General Internal Logic Test (PDAA)

GILT............ Get Interconnected Local Text Systems (SAUO)
GILT............ Gilat Satellite Networks Ltd. [*NASDAQ symbol*] (SAG)
GILTF.......... Gilat Satellite Networks [*NASDAQ symbol*] (TTSB)
GIM............ Gaining Inventory Managers (AFM)
GIM............ Gas Injection Molding [*Plastic fabrications*]
GIM............ Gastrointestinal Myiasis [*Medicine*] (MELL)
GIM............ Geldermann Investment Management [*Finance*] [*British*]
GIM............ General Information Management (SAUS)
GIM............ General Information Manual (SAUS)
GIM............ General Instrument Microelectronics [*British*] (NITA)
GIM............ Generic Interface Module (SAUS)
GIM............ Geneva Informal Meeting [*of International Non-Governmental Organizations*] [*British*]
GIM............ Geneva Informal Meeting of International Non-Governmental Youth Organizations (SAUO)
GIM............ Geophysical Investigations Maps (SAUO)
GIM............ Glashow-Iliopoulos-Maiani [*Theory in particle physics*]
GIM............ Glas Insulation Material (SAUS)
GIM............ Glass Insulation Material
GIM............ Global Internet Marketing (SAUO)
GIM............ Glock Image Map (SAUO)
GIM............ Gonadotropin-Inhibitory Material [*Endocrinology*] (MAE)
GIM............ Governor Impulse Method [*Automotive engineering*]
GIM............ Grace's Insect [*Growth*] Medium [*Microbiology*]
GIM............ Graphical Information Map (SAUO)
GIM............ Graphic Integrated Manual (VLIE)
GIM............ Gross Income Multiplier [*Business term*]
GIM............ Ground Influence Mine (SAUS)
GIM............ Group Information Mark (VLIE)
GIM............ Gruppe Internationale Marxisten [*International Marxist Group*] [*Germany*] [*Political party*] (PPW)
GIM............ Gulf International Minerals [*Vancouver Stock Exchange symbol*]
GIM............ Miele Mimbale [*Gabon*] [*Airport symbol*] (AD)
GIM............ Templeton Global Income [*NYSE symbol*] (SPSG)
GIM-1.......... Generalized Information Management (SAUS)
GIMA.......... Garden Industry Manufacturers Association [*British*] (DBA)
GIMA.......... Geodesy Intelligence and Mapping Research and Development Agency (SAUS)
Gima............ Grupo Independente de Macau [*Independent Group of Macao*] [*Political party*] (PPW)
GIMAD........ Generic Integrated Maintenance and Diagnostic (ACAE)
GIMADS...... Generic Integrated Maintenance and Diagnostic (SAUS)
GIMADS...... Generic Integrated Maintenance and Diagnostic System (MCD)
GIMADS...... Generic Integrated Maintenance Diagnostics Research and Development Agency (SAUS)
GIMADS...... Generic Integrated Maintenance Diagnostic System (SAUS)
GIMB.......... Gimbal (KSC)
GIMBADA..... Geodesy Intelligence and Mapping Research and Development Agency (SAUS)
GIMC.......... Grinding of Industrial Minerals Conference (SAUS)
GIMEC........ GI Motility Education Centre (SAUO)
GI Mech E... Graduate of the Institution of Mechanical Engineers [*British*]
GIMI............ Graduate of the Institute of the Motor Industry [*British*] (DBQ)
GIM-IC........ Genetics of Industrial Microorganisms - International Commission (SAUS)
GIMIC.......... Guard-ring Implanted Monolithic Integrated Circuit (SAUS)
GIMIC.......... Guardring Isolated Molitic IC (SAUS)
GIMIC.......... Guard-ring Isolated Monolithic Integrated Circuit (SAUS)
GIML............ Generalized Information Management Language (SAUS)
GIMLCS....... Generalized Information Management Language and Computer System (SAUS)
GIMMIS....... G-I Manpower Management Information System
GIMMS........ Geographic Information Mapping and Management System (EERA)
GIMMS........ Global Inventory Modeling and Monitoring Study (EERA)
GIMMS........ Global Inventory Mounting Modeling and Simulation (SAUO)
GIMP.......... General Image Manipulation Program (SAUS)
GIMP.......... Gimbal Positioning
GIMP.......... Global Inventorying and Monitoring Programme (SAUO)
GIMP.......... GNU Image Manipulation Program (SAUS)
GIMPAP....... GOES Product Assurance Plan (SAUS)
GIMPE......... Global Investigation of Pollution in the Marine Environment (SAUO)
GIMPEX....... Guyana Import-Export (SAUO)
GIMPS......... Great Internet Mersenne Prime Search
GIMPY......... Growing, Improving, Maturing - Puppy of the Year [*Canine award*]
GIMR.......... Garvan Institute of Medical Research [*Australia*]
GIMRADA.... Geesy, Intelligence and Mapping Research and Development Agency (SAUS)
GIMRADA.... Geodesy (SAUS)
GIMRADA.... Geodesy, Intelligence, and Mapping Research and Development Agency [*Army*]
GIMS.......... Generalized Information Management System (SAUO)
GIMS.......... Geographic-Based Information Management System (PDAA)
GIMS.......... Geographic Information and Modeling System (SAUO)
GIMS.......... Geographic Information Management Systems Committee (SAUS)
GIMS.......... Georgia Initiative in Math and Science (SAUO)
GIMS.......... Global Information Management System (SEWL)
GIMS.......... Global Integrated Monitoring System (EERA)
GIMS.......... Graduates of Italian Medical Schools (EA)
GIMS.......... Ground Identification of Missions in Space
GIMSOT....... Gimbal System for Optical Tracker (ACAE)
GIM System... Generalized Information Management System (SAUO)
GIMT........... Geographic Information Management Technology (SAUO)
GIMT........... Gott Ist Mein Teil [*God Is My Portion*] [*Motto of Friedrich IV, Duke of Liegnitz (1552-96)*] [*German*]
GIMT........... Gott Ist Mein Trost [*God Is My Comfort*] [*Motto for a number of 16th and 17th century German and Bavarian rulers*]
GIMTACS..... GOES I-M Telemetry and Command System (SAUO)
GIMTB4....... Italian Journal of Chest Diseases (journ.) (SAUS)
GIMU.......... Gimballess Inertial Measuring Unit
GIMX.......... GATX Capital [*Private rail car owner code*]
GIN............ Association de Recherche et d'Exploitation de Diamant et de l'Or [*Guinea*] [*ICAO designator*] (FAAC)
GIN............ Galilean Resources Corp. [*Vancouver Stock Exchange symbol*]
GIN............ General Information Notice (SAUS)
GIN............ GeoInfo Network (SAUO)
GIN............ Gimbaled Integral Nozzle
GIN............ Gimbaled Intel Nozzle (SAUS)
GIN............ Global Imaging Networks (DGA)
GIN............ Global Information Network (EA)
gin............. Glutamine [*Also, Q*] [*An amino acid*] (DOG)
GIN............ Glutamine (STED)
GIN............ Gold Coin Mining, Inc. (SAUO)
GIN............ Graphics Input (VLIE)
GIN............ Green Index Number (SAUO)
GIN............ Greenland-Iceland-Norway [*Gap*] (DOMA)
GIN............ Guinea [*ANSI three-letter standard code*] (CNC)
GIN............ Stromboli-Ginostra [*Italy*] [*Seismograph station code, US Geological Survey*] (SEIS)
G I N A....... Gas Industries Network Analyser (SAUS)
GINA.......... Gas Industries Network Analyzer (PDAA)
GINA.......... Girls in National Alliance [*An association*]
GINA.......... Global Integrated Network Access [*Communications term*] (DCT)
GINA.......... Global Inventory in the Northern Hemisphere (SAUO)
GINA.......... GPS Inertial Navigation system Assembly (SAUS)
GINA.......... Graphical Identification and Authentication [*Computer science*] (MWOL)
GINA.......... Graphical Input for Network Analysis (SAUS)
GINA.......... Graphical Interactive NMR Analysis [*Computer science*]
GINA.......... Graphical Interactive Nuclear Magnetic Resonance Analysis System (SAUS)
GINAS......... GPS Integrated Navigation and Attitude-Determination System (SAUO)
G-in-C......... General Officer-in-Chief (WDAA)
GINC.......... Global Information Network on Chemicals (ADWA)
GINETEX...... Groupement International d'Etiquetage pour l'Entretien des Textiles [*International Association for Textile Care Labelling*] [*Barcelona, Spain*] (EA)
G Infy......... Glider Infantry (SAUS)
GING.......... Gingiva [*Gum*] [*Latin*]
Ging............ Gingival (STED)
ging............ gingivitis (SAUS)
GINHIE MAE... Government National Mortgage Association (SAUO)
GINI............ Gazette International Networking Institute (EA)
GINI............ GOES-I Ingest NOAAPort Interface (SAUS)
GINIF.......... Gain to Noise Figure (Ratio) (SAUS)
G I N I F..... GINO FORTRAN IV (SAUS)
gink............ ginkitis (SAUS)
gink............ ginkitology (SAUS)
GINLC......... Grosse Ile Nature and Land Conservancy
G in N......... Graduate in Nursing
GINNI.......... Generic Interactive Neural Network Interpreter
GINNIEMAE... Government National Mortgage Association (SAUO)
GINNIE MAE... Government National Mortgage Association [*See also GNMA*]
GINO.......... Garbage-In, Nothing-Out (SAUS)
GINO.......... Graphical Input and Output (SAUS)
GINO.......... Graphical Input/Output
GINO.......... Graphics Input/Output (SAUS)
G I N O - F... GINO FORTRAN IV (SAUS)
GINO-F........ Graphical Input and Output in FORTRAN [*GST Computer Systems Ltd.*] [*Software package*] [*Computer science*] [*British*]
G Inst.......... Institutes of Gaius (journ.) (SAUS)
GInstAEA...... Graduate of the Institute of Automotive Engineer Assessors (SAUS)
GInstM......... Graduate of the Institute of Marketing [*British*] (DBQ)
GInstT......... Graduate of the Institute of Transport (SAUS)
GInstT......... Graduate of the Institute of Transportation (SAUO)
GINTRAP...... European Guide to Industrial Trading Regulations and Practice [*EC*] (ECED)
GINTRAP...... Guide to Industrial Trading Regulations and Practice (SAUO)
GINucE........ Graduate of the Institute of Nuclear Engineers (SAUO)
GIO............ Gas Identification Officer
GIO............ Gastrointestinal Obstruction [*Medicine*] (MELL)
GIO............ Generalist Intelligence Officer
GIO............ Generic Interface for Operations [*Telecommunications*] (ACRL)
GIO............ Geographic Information Officer (SAUO)
GIO............ Geographic Investigations Office (SAUS)
GIO............ Geograpic Investigations Office (SAUS)
GIO............ Giocossamente [*Humorously*] [*Music*] (ROG)
GIO............ Glucocorticoid-Induced Osteoporosis [*Medicine*]
GIO............ Golden Trio Minerals [*Vancouver Stock Exchange symbol*]
GIO............ Government Information Organization [*Later, NAGC*]
GIO............ Group Intelligence Officer [*British military*] (DMA)
GIO............ Guaranteed Insurability Option
GIO............ Guarantee Insurability Option (SAUS)
GIO............ Guild of Insurance Officials [*British*] (BI)
GIO............ Regionnair, Inc. [*Canada*] [*ICAO designator*] (FAAC)
GIOA.......... Gregorian Institute of America [*Record label*]
GIOC.......... General Input/Output Channel (SAUS)
GIOC.......... General Input/Output Computer (SAUS)
GIOC.......... General Input/Output Controller (SAUS)

GIOC .... Generalized Input/Output Controller [*Computer science*] (IEEE)
GIOC .... Gulf Organization for Industrial Consulting (SAUO)
g-ion .... Gram-Ion (STED)
gion .... gram ion (SAUS)
GIOP .... General Inter-ORB Protocol (SAUS)
GIOP .... Generalized Inter-ORB Protocol (SAUS)
GIOP .... General-Purpose Input/Output Processor [*Computer science*]
GIOR .... GPETE Initial Outfitting Requirement [*Military*] (CAAL)
GIP .... Galvanized Improved Plow [*Steel*]
GIP .... Galvanized iron pipe (SAUS)
gip .... gas in place (SAUS)
GIP .... Gastric Gastrin Inhibitory Principle (SAUS)
GIP .... Gastric Inhibitory Peptide [*Gastroenterology*] (DAVI)
GIP .... Gastric Inhibitory Polypeptide (ADWA)
GIP .... Gastric [*or Gastrin*] Inhibitory Principle [*or Polypeptide*] [*Medicine*]
GIP .... Gastrin Inhibitory Polypeptide (SAUS)
GIP .... Gastrin Inhibitory Principle (SAUS)
GIP .... Gaussian Image Point [*Optics*]
GIP .... General Implementation Plan
GIP .... General Insertion Protein [*Genetics*]
GIP .... General Insurance Policy (SAUO)
GIP .... General Internal Process [*Computer science*] (IAA)
GIP .... Generic implementation procedure (SAUS)
GIP .... Genetic Improvement Programs [*Queensland*] (EERA)
GIP .... Giant-Cell Interstitial Pneumonia (SAUS)
GIP .... Gibraltar Pound (SAUS)
GIP .... Gileppe [*Belgium*] [*Seismograph station code, US Geological Survey*] (SEIS)
GIP .... Glazed Imitation Parchment
GIP .... Global Industry Profile
GIP .... Global Internet Project (TELE)
GIP .... Global Inventory Project (TELE)
GIP .... Glucose Dependent Insulinotropic Peptide [*Medicine*] (EDAA)
GIP .... Glucose-Dependent Insulinotropic Polypeptide (QSUL)
GIP .... Gonorrheal Invasive Peritonitis [*Medicine*] (DMAA)
GIP .... Good Import Practice (DB)
GIP .... Graphic Input Program (VLIE)
GIP .... Graphic Interactive Processing (VLIE)
GIP .... Great Indian Peninsular railway (SAUO)
GIP .... Great Indian Peninsular R. R.
GIP .... Great Irish Painter [*Reference to Jack B. Yeats, ca. 1905*]
GIP .... Gross Internal Product
GIP .... Ground Instructor Pilot (DNAB)
GIP .... Ground Instrumentation Plan (ACAE)
GIP .... Group Interface Processor (SAUS)
GIP .... Gun Improvement Program (ACAE)
GIP .... Gunnery Improvement Program [*Military*] (CAAL)
GIP .... Gunter Industrial Park (SAUO)
GIPB .... General-Purpose Instrument Bus (SAUS)
GIPD .... B. F. Goodrich Institute for Personnel Development
GIPD .... General Intelligence Production Division (SAUO)
GIPE .... Generation of Interactive Programming Environments (SAUO)
GIPE .... State Institute of Applied Ecology (SAUO)
GIPEC .... Groupe d'Etudes International pour l'Utilization de Profils Creux dans la Construction [*International Study Group on the Use of Hollow Sections in Construction*] [*Switzerland*] (PDAA)
GIPEIE .... Groupe International Postal d'Echanges d'Information et d'Experience [*International Group for the Exchange of Information and Experience among Postal Savings Institutions - IGEIEPSI*] (EAIO)
GIPGS .... Greenhouse Information Program Grants Scheme (EERA)
GI/PI .... General Inspection/Procurement Inspection (MCD)
GIPL .... Glycoinositolphospholipid [*Biochemistry*] (QSUL)
GIPLACED .... Grupo Informal de Paises Latinoamericanos y del Caribe Exportadores de Crudo (SAUO)
GIPLD .... Gippsland (SAUS)
GIPME .... Global Investigation of Pollution in the Marine Environment [*National Science Foundation*]
GIPME .... Working Committee for the Global Investigation of Pollution in the Marine Environment (SAUO)
GIPND .... General Information Programme-UNISIST Newsletter (SAUS)
Gipps .... Gippsland (SAUS)
GIPPS .... Gippsland Database (SAUS)
GIPR .... Great Indian Peninsula Railway (SAUO)
GIPS .... Billions of Instructions per Second (SAUS)
GIPS .... Gastrointestinal Pathology Society (NTPA)
GIPS .... Generalized Image Processing Sytstem (SAUS)
GIPS .... Geographical Information Processing System (EERA)
GIPS .... Giga-Instructions per Second [*Computer science*] (NHD)
GIPS .... Government Imprinted Penalty Stationery Society (EA)
GIPS .... Ground Information Processing System
GIPS .... Ground Information Programming System (SAUS)
GIPSA .... Grain Inspection, Packers, and Stockyards Administration
GIPSE .... Gravity Independent Photosynthetic Gas Exchanger
G I P S S Y ... Generalised Interactive Programme for the Simulation of Systems (SAUS)
GIPSSY .... Generalized Interactive Programme for the Simulation of Systems (SAUO)
GIPSY .... General Image Processing System (SAUO)
GIPSY .... Geographic Incremental Plotting System (SAUO)
GIPSY .... Geoscan Image Processing System (SAUO)
GIPSY .... Graphic Information Presentation System (SAUO)
GIPSY .... Ground Information Processing System (SAUS)
GIQ .... Giant Imperial Quart [*of beer*]
GIR .... Gastrointestinal Reflux [*Medicine*] (EDAA)
GIR .... General Improvement Rate [*Medicine*] (EDAA)
GIR .... Generalized Information Retrieval (SAUS)
GIR .... Girder [*Technical drawings*]
GIR .... Global Improvement Rating (DMAA)
GIR .... Glucose Infusion Rate [*Physiology*]
GIR .... Golden Lion Resources Ltd. [*Vancouver Stock Exchange symbol*]
GIR .... Graduated Interest Rate [*Finance*] (BARN)
GIR .... Greens in Regulation Golf (BARN)
GIR .... Gulf Interior Region (SAUS)
GIR .... Resource Appraisal Group Library, United States Geological Survey, Denver, CO [*OCLC symbol*] (OCLC)
GIRA .... Gallups Island Radio Association (EA)
GIRA .... Geographic Information Retrieval and Analysis (SAUO)
GIRA .... Gordon Institute Research Association (SAUO)
GIRA .... Groupement Independant de Reflexion et d'Action [*Independent Grouping of Reflection and Action*] [*Central Africa*] (PD)
GIRA .... Group Individual Retirement Account
GIRACO .... Gray Company (SAUO)
GIRAFFE ...... Graphic Interface for Finite Elements [*Graphics data processing*]
GIRAS .... Geographic Information (SAUS)
GIRAS .... Geographic Information Retrieval and Analysis System [*Department of the Interior*]
GIRAS .... Graphic Information Retrieval and Analysis System (SAUS)
GIRAST .... Groupe Interdisciplinaire de Recherche pour l'Amelioration des Situations de Travail [*University of Quebec at Rimouski*] [*Canada*] [*Research center*] (RCD)
GIRB .... Georgia Inspection and Rating Bureau (SAUO)
GIRC .... Global Issues Resource Center (EA)
GIRCE .... Gecaga Institute of Tropical Comparative Endocrinology (SAUS)
GIRCFF .... Government Industry Research Committee on Flammable Fabrics (SAUS)
GIRCFF .... Government/Industry Research Committee on Flammable Fabrics (SAUO)
GIRD .... General Incentive for Research and Development [*Canada*]
GIRD .... Good Industrial Relations Directors [*Meetings sponsored by Master Printers of America*]
GIRD .... Grants for Industrial (or Industry) Research and Development (SAUS)
GIRD .... Grants for Industrial Research and Development (EERA)
GIRD .... Ground-Installed Recording Data (SAUS)
GIRD .... Ground Integration Requirements Document (MCD)
GIRDHS .... Ground Installation Reconnaissance Data Handling System (SAUS)
GIREP .... International Group for the Advancement of Physics Teaching (AIE)
GIRF .... Gastro-Intestinal Research Foundation (NRGU)
GIRGV .... Groupe International des Ressources Genetiques Vegetales [*International Board for Plant Genetic Resources - IBPGR*] (EA)
GIRI .... Gray Iron Research Institute (SAUS)
GIRIN .... Government Industrial Research Institute at Nagoya (SAUS)
GIRIS .... Generalized Information Retrieval and Listing System (SAUS)
GIRL .... General Information Report Language (SAUO)
GIRL .... Generalized Information Retrieval Language [*US Defense Nuclear Agency*]
GIRL .... German Infrared Laboratory (SAUO)
GIRL .... Graphic Information Report Language (SAUS)
GIRL .... Graphic Information Retrieval Language (SAUS)
GIRL .... Graph Information Report Language (SAUO)
GIRL .... Graph Information Retrieval Language [*1970*] [*Computer science*] (CSR)
GIRLS .... General Indexing in Reciprocal Lattice Space (KSC)
GIRLS .... General Information Retrieval and Listing System (SAUS)
GIRLS .... Generalized Information Retrieval and Listing System
GIRLS .... Global Interrogation Recording and Location System (MCD)
GIRLS .... Graphical data Interpretation and Reconstruction in Local Satellite (SAUS)
GIRM .... Generalized Internal Reference Method [*Statistical procedure*]
GIRM .... Generalized International Reference Metbod (SAUS)
GIRMS .... Geographical Inter-University Resource Management Seminar
GIRO .... General Instructions for Routing and Reporting Officers
GIROQ .... Groupe Interuniversitaire des Recherches Oceanographiques du Quebec [*Interuniversity Group for Oceanographic Research of Quebec*] [*Laval University*] [*Canada*] [*Research center*] (RCD)
GIRPB .... Groupe International de Recherches sur la Preservation du Bois [*Sweden*] (EAIO)
GIRS .... Gallaudet Information Retrieval Service
GIRS .... Generalized Information Retrieval System (SAUS)
GIRS .... Gimballess Inertial Reference System
GIRS .... Graphic Information Retrieval System (SAUS)
GIRS .... Graph Information Retrieval System (SAUS)
GIRSO .... Groupement International pour la Recherche Scientifique en Stomatologie et Odontologie [*International Group for Scientific Research on Stomato-Odontology*] (EA)
GIRSS .... General Information Retrieval System (SAUS)
GIRSS .... General Information Retrieval System Simulation
GIRSTERM ... Groupe Interdisciplinaire de Recherche Scientifique et Appliquee en Terminologie [*INFOTERM*]
GIRTC .... Geographic Information and Resource Technology Conference (SAUO)
GIRTS .... Generic Infrared Training System (ACAE)
GIRU .... General Intelligence and Reconnaissance Unit (SAUO)
Gir WC .... Girard's Will Case Report [*A publication*] (DLA)
GIS .... Gamma Iota Sigma [*An association*] (NTPA)
GIS .... Gas Imaging Spectrometer
GIS .... Gas in Stomach (MAE)
GIS .... Gas Insulated Substation (SAUS)
GIS .... Gas Insulated Switchgear (SAUS)
GIS .... Gas Insulated System (SAUS)

GIS Gas-Scintillation Imaging Spectrometer
GIS Gastrointestinal Series [*Radiology*]
GIS Gastrointestinal System [*Gastroenterology*] (DAVI)
GIS Gaylord Circulation Control System (SAUS)
GIS Gaylord Information Services
GIS Gaylord Information Systems
GIS General Information System (SAUS)
G I S General Initalization System (SAUS)
GIS General Inquiry System (SAUS)
GIS General Installation Subcontractor
GIS General Instrument Specification (ACAE)
GIS Generalized Information System [*IBM Corp.*]
GIS Generalized Initialization Sequencer (SAUS)
GIS Generalized Inquiry System [*Computer science*]
GIS General Lighting Service (SAUS)
GIS General Mills, Inc. [*NYSE symbol*] (SPSG)
GIS Genl Mills [*NYSE symbol*] (TTSB)
GIS Geographical Informations System (SAUS)
GIS Geographic Information System (EERA)
GIS Geographic Information Systems [*Fish and Wildlife Service*] (IID)
GIS Geohydrologic Information System (SAUO)
GIS Geological Information Systems [*University of Oklahoma*] [*Information service or system*] (IID)
GIS Geophysical Incentive System (SAUS)
GIS Geoscience Information Society (EA)
GIS German Industrial Standard (SAUO)
GIS Gisborne [*New Zealand*] [*Airport symbol*] (OAG)
GIS Gismondine [*A zeolite*]
GIS Gissar [*Former USSR*] [*Seismograph station code, US Geological Survey*] [*Closed*] (SEIS)
GIS Global Indexing System (GNE)
GIS Global Information Services, Inc. [*Flushing, NY*] [*Telecommunications*] (TSSD)
GIS Global Information Solutions (SAUO)
GIS Global Information System (SAUS)
GIS Global Ionospheric Studies
GIS Global Issues [*Program*] [*Department of State*]
GIS Golden Iskut Resources [*Vancouver Stock Exchange symbol*]
GIS Government Information Service (WDAA)
GIS Government Information Services [*Republic of Ireland*]
GIS Government Information Subcommittee [*American Library Association*]
GIS Government Information System (SAUS)
GIS Government Issued Soldiers (SAUO)
GIS Grain Inventory System [*Department of Agriculture*] (GFGA)
GIS Grand Inside Sentinel [*Freemasonry*] (ROG)
GIS Grant Information System [*Oryx Press*] (IID)
GIS Graphical Information System (SAUO)
GIS Graphic Information System [*Computer databases*]
GIS Graphic Input System
GIS Grazing-Incidence Spectrometer (PDAA)
GIS Greater India Society (SAUO)
GIS Great Ideas System database (SAUS)
GIS Greatness Is Simplicity [*See also SIG*]
GIS Greenland Ice Sheet
GIs Gross Impressions [*Advertising*] (WDMC)
GIS Ground Instrumentation System (IAA)
GIS Growth-Initiating Substance (SAUS)
GIS Guaranteed Income Stream [*UAW program included in the union's 1982 contract with General Motors Corp.*]
GIS Guaranteed Income Supplement [*Program*] [*Canada*]
GIS Guidance Information System [*Houghton Mifflin Co.*] [*Information service or system*] (IID)
GIS Guidelines Implementation Staff [*Environmental Protection Agency*] (GFGA)
GIS Guild for Infant Survival [*Later, ICIS*]
GIS Guild of the Infant Saviour [*Defunct*] (EA)
GIS Guinee Air Service [*Guinea*] [*ICAO designator*] (FAAC)
GIS Gypsy Lore Society, North American Chapter (SAUO)
GIS United States Department of the Interior, United States Geological Survey, Reston, VA [*OCLC symbol*] (OCLC)
GISA General Ledger Subsidiary Account (SAUS)
GISA Geochemical Interactive Systems Analysis (SAUO)
GISA Government in the Sunshine Act [*1976*]
GISA Guidance Set Architecture (SAUS)
GISAT Ground Identification of Satellites (MCD)
GISC Generic Intelligent Control System
GISC Generic Intelligent System Controller (SAUO)
GISC Global; Industrial; and Systematic Cooperation (SAUS)
GISC Government Information Services Committee [*Special Libraries Association*]
GISC Grail International Student Center [*Defunct*] (EA)
GISCO Geographic Information System of the European Commission (EURO)
GISD General Intermediate Stores Depot (SAUS)
GISD Geographic Information Systems Division (SAUS)
GISDEX Federal Geographic Information and Spatial Data Exposition and Conference (SAUO)
GISE Generalized Integrated Square Error [*Aeronautics*]
GI Sec General Inspectorate Section [*European Theater of Operations*] [*World War II*]
GISGE Good Intent Society of Galvanizers and Enamellers [*A union*] [*British*]
GISH Gish Biomedical [*NASDAQ symbol*] (TTSB)
GISH Gish Biomedical, Inc. [*NASDAQ symbol*] (NQ)
GishBi Gish Biomedical, Inc. [*Associated Press*] (SAG)
GISIG Geographic Information System Interest Group (SAUO)
GISL Geographic Information System Laboratory (SAUO)
GISL Graphic Imaging Specification Language [*Printing technology*]
GISM GeoInfo Systems Magazine (SAUO)
GISMO General Interpretative System for Matrix Operations [*Data processing system used in engineering*] [*Navy*]
GISMO Geographic Information System-Mobile
GISMO Graphic Information System Modeling (SAUS)
GISMOS Global Incoherent Scatter Measurements of Substorms (SAUS)
GISNET Geographic Information Systems Bulletin Board (SAUO)
GISOF Gas Industry Salaried Officers' Federation [*Australia*]
GISP General Information System for Planning (IAA)
GISP Government Information Sharing Project [*Internet resource*]
GISP Grain Income Stabilization Plan
GISP Greenland Ice Sheet Program (SAUO)
GISP Greenland Ice Sheet Project [*National Science Foundation*]
GISP Guided Independent Study Program (SAUO)
GISP2 Greenland Ice Sheet Project (SAUO)
GISP-2 Greenland Ice Sheet Project-2 (SAUO)
GISPA Geoscience Information Society. Proceedings (journ.) (SAUS)
GISPA Guide to International Scientific Publications and Associations [*A publication*]
gi spasm gastro-intestinal spasm (SAUS)
GISPB Government Information Services Policy Board (SAUO)
GISP II Second Greenland Ice Sheet Project (SAUO)
GISPRI Global Industrial and Social Progress Research Institute
GIS-R Geospatial Information System Repository
GISRA Guyana Institute for Social Research and Action (SAUO)
GISS Goddard Institute for/of Space Studies (SAUO)
GISS Goddard Institute for Space Sciences (SAUO)
GISS Goddard Institute for Space Studies [*NASA*]
GISSA Great Lake Seaplane Association (SAUO)
GISS-ISURSL Goddard Inst. for Space Studies-Indiana State University Remote Sensing Laboratory (SAUO)
GISSL Glaciers, Ice Sheets and Sea Level (SAUS)
GISST Global Sea Ice and Sea Surface Temperature (SAUS)
GIST GARP International Sea Trial [*National Science Foundation*]
GIST Gastrointestinal Stromal Tumor [*Medicine*] (RAWO)
GIST GCIP Integrated Systems Test (SAUS)
GIST General Intelligence Ship Terminal (SAUS)
GIST Genome Informatics System of Transputers (HGEN)
GIST Geographic Information System for Transportation (SAUO)
GIST Geographic Information System Toolkit (SAUO)
GIST Geographic Information System Tutorial (SAUO)
GIST Georgia Interactive Statewide Telecommunications (SAUO)
GIST GEWEX Integrated System Test (SAUS)
GIST Girls into Science and Technology [*British*] (DI)
GIST Global Information System Technology, Inc. (PCM)
GIST Gochnour Idiom Screening Test
GIST Government Information Systems Technology (SAUS)
GISTA Gruppo Italiano di Studio Tubercolosi e AIDS
GISTARS Geographic Information Starter System (SAUO)
GISTI Groupe d'Information et de Soutien des Travailleurs Immigres [*Information and Support Group for Immigrant Workers*] [*France*] (EAIO)
GISTYE Gochnour Idiom Screening Test (SAUS)
GIS/VS Generalized Information System - Virtual Storage (SAUS)
GISVS Generalized Information System Virtual Storage (IAA)
GISX Global Imaging Systems, Inc. [*NASDAQ symbol*] (NASQ)
GIT Gain to Temperature (Ratio) (SAUS)
GIT Gas Injection Technique (SAUS)
GIT Gastrointestinal Test (SAUS)
GIT Gastrointestinal Tract [*Medicine*]
GIT Gease Interceptor Trap (SAUS)
GIT Gene Immunotherapy (for Cancer) [*Medicine*] (EDAA)
GIT General Industrial Training (SAUS)
GIT General Information Test
GIT Georgia Institute of Technology [*Atlanta*]
GIT Geospace Interorbital Transportation (SAUS)
GIT Gilgit [*Pakistan*] [*Geomagnetic observatory code*]
GIT Gitano Group, Inc. (SAUO)
Git Gittin (BJA)
GIT Global Information Technology (SAUO)
GIT Global Interface Table (RALS)
GIT Glucose Infusion Test [*Diabetes detection*] (CPH)
GIT Glutathione-Insulin Transhydrogenase [*An enzyme*] (MAE)
GIT GNU Interactive Tools (SAUS)
GIT Goods Intermodal Transshipment [*Indian Railway*] (TIR)
GIT Goods in Transit (MARI)
GIT Graduate Institute of Technology [*University of Arkansas at Little Rock*] [*Research center*] (RCD)
GIT Grand Illinois Trail (SAUO)
GIT Granton Institute of Technology (SAUS)
GIT Graph Isomorphism Tester
GIT Grease Interceptor Trap
GIT [*The*] Great Ideas Today [*A publication*]
GIT Great Ideas Today (journ.) (SAUS)
GIT Grit Resources, Inc. [*Vancouver Stock Exchange symbol*]
GIT Grooved for Iron Tongues
GIT Group Inclusive Tour [*Travel industry*] (TRID)
GIT Guaranteed Income Contract (FOTI)
GIT Guitar (SAUS)
GITA Geospatial Information & Technology Association (SAUS)
GITARA German Italian Aeromagnetic Research in Antarctica (SAUS)
GITB Gas Industry Training Board (SAUO)

GITC............ Glucopyranosyl Isothiocyanate (SAUS)
GITC............ Goodrich International Tire Technical Center (SAUO)
GITC............ Government of Israel Trade Center (EA)
GITCE.......... Gecaga Institute of Tropical Comparative Endocrinology (SAUO)
GITEC.......... CEC Project on Genesis and Impact of Tsunamis on European Coasts (SAUS)
GITG............ Ground Interface Technical Group [*NASA*] (NASA)
GITI............ Global Information and Telecommunications Industries
GITI............ Government Issue Technical Inspection (INF)
GITIC.......... Guangdong International Trust & Investment Corp. [*China*]
GITIS.......... Georgia Institute of Technology (SAUS)
GITIS.......... Georgia Institute of Technology School of Information Science [*Report series code*] (NITA)
GITIS.......... Ground Integrated Target Identification System (SEWL)
GITL............ Gas Insulated Transmission Line (SAUS)
GITL............ Government/Industry Technical Liaison Committee [*Australia*]
GITM............ Global Information Technology Management (SAUO)
GITM............ Golden Isles Terminal Railroad [*Federal Railroad Administration identification code*]
Gitmo.......... Guantanamo Naval Base (SAUS)
GI tract....... Gastro-Intestinal Tract [*Medicine*] (WDAA)
GITS............ Gastrointestinal Therapeutic System [*Medicine*]
GITS............ GM Hughes Electronics Integrated TOW Sight (SAUS)
GITS............ Government Information Technology Services
GITSG.......... Gastrointestinal Tumor Study Group [*Oncology*] (DAVI)
GITSIS........ Georgia Institute of Technology School of Information Science (SAUS)
GITT............ Gastrointestinal Transit Time [*Medicine*] (EDAA)
GITT............ Glucose Insulin Tolerance Test [*Medicine*]
GITU............ Gastrointestinal Transcription Unit [*Medicine*]
GIU............ Gateway Interface Unit (DGA)
GIU............ General Importers Union (SAUO)
GIU............ General Intelligence Unit [*US, London*]
GIU............ Geoballistic Input Unit
GIU............ Government Information Unit (SAUO)
GIU............ Guidance Integration Unit (MCD)
GIU............ Guidance Interface Unit (SAUS)
GIU............ Union Guineene de Transports [*Guinea*] [*ICAO designator*] (FAAC)
GIUAC.......... Geophysical Institute. University of Alaska.Contribution Series (journ.) (SAUS)
GIUAG R...... Geophysical Institute. University of Alaska. UAG (SAUO)
GIUAG R...... Geophysical Institute.University of Alaska.UAG Report Series (journ.) (SAUS)
Giude to Computer L... Guide to Computer Law (SAUS)
GIUK............ Greenland-Iceland-United Kingdom [*NATO naval defense line*]
GIUK Early Warning... Greenland-Iceland United Kingdom Early Warning (SAUS)
Gluscll......... Grupo Iusacell SA de CV [*Associated Press*] (SAG)
Gluscl IL...... Grupo Iusacell SA de CV [*Associated Press*] (SAG)
GIV............ Geographic Information Visualization (SAUO)
GIV............ Geologic Information Visualisation (or Visualization) (SAUO)
giv............ Given [*Medicine*] (EDAA)
GIV............ Given
GIV............ Grivco International Ltd. [*Romania*] [*FAA designator*] (FAAC)
G-IV............ Gulfstream IV (SAUS)
GIVE............ Government's Involvement in Volunteer Efforts Programs
Givhans....... Ferry Givhans Feny State Park (SAUS)
GIVN............ Given (DAVI)
GIVS............ Goodwill Industries Volunteer Services (EA)
GIW............ Glass-Insulated Wire
GIW............ Greenwood, SC [*Location identifier*] [*FAA*] (FAAL)
GIW............ Gulf Intracoastal Waterway
GIWA.......... Global Inland Waters Assessment programme (SAUO)
GIWA.......... Global International Water Assessment (SAUS)
GIWG.......... Ground Interface Working Group
GI Wire....... Galvanized Iron Wire (SAUS)
GIWIST........ Gee, I Wish I'd Said That (VLIE)
GIWO.......... Gila Woodpecker [*North American bird banding code*] (BIBA)
GIWW.......... Gulf Intracoastal Waterway
GIX............ Global Industrial Tech [*NYSE symbol*] (TTSB)
GIX............ Global Industrial Technologies [*NYSE symbol*] (SAG)
GIX............ Global Internet Exchange (SAUO)
GIX............ Goldex Mines Ltd. (SAUO)
GIX............ Government Information Exchange [*Internet*] (AAGC)
GIXD.......... Grazing-Incidence X-Ray Diffraction
GIXF.......... Grazing Incidence X-ray Fluorescence (SAUS)
GIXS.......... G-Incidence X-ray Scattering (SAUS)
GIXS.......... Grazing-Incidence X-Ray Scattering [*Imaging technique*]
GIXU.......... Grain Inspection X-Ray Unit (IAA)
GIY............ Glamorgan Imperial Yeomanry [*British military*] (DMA)
GIZ............ Gerber Industries [*Federal Railroad Administration identification code*]
GIZ............ Gizan [*Saudi Arabia*] [*Airport symbol*] (OAG)
GIZ............ Gizo [*Solomon Islands*] [*Seismograph station code, US Geological Survey*] (SEIS)
GIZ............ Glaze (SAUS)
GIZ............ Marshfield, WI [*Location identifier*] [*FAA*] (FAAL)
GIZH.......... Gosudarstvennyi Institut Zhurnalistiki
GJ............ Ansett Airlines of South Australia [*ICAO designator*] (AD)
GJ............ British Guiana General Jurisdiction (Official Gazette) [*1899-*] [*A publication*] (ILCA)
GJ............ Gap Junction [*Cytology*]
GJ............ Gastric Juice [*Medicine*] (DMAA)
GJ............ Gastrojejunostomy [*Surgery*] (DAVI)
GJ............ Genealogical Journal (SAUS)
GJ............ General Journal [*Accounting*]
GJ............ Geographical Journal [*A publication*] (BRI)
GJ............ Germania Judaica (BJA)
GJ............ German Jewish (BJA)
GJ............ Gigajoule
GJ............ Gill and Johnson's Maryland Reports [*A publication*] (DLA)
GJ............ Goldreich-Julian [*PULSAR theory*]
GJ............ Graduate Jeweller
GJ............ Grand Junction Operations Office (SAUO)
GJ............ Grand Junction Project Office (SAUO)
GJ............ Grand Jury
GJ............ Grapefruit Juice [*Restaurant slang*]
GJ............ Graphic Job (SAUS)
GJ............ Greenwich & Johnsonville Railway Co. [*AAR code*]
GJ............ Group Junction (MCD)
GJ............ Grown Junction (IEEE)
G+J............ Gruner + Jahr [*A publisher*] [*Hamburg, Germany*] (WDMC)
GJAB.......... Groups Joint Administration Board (SAUO)
GJAC.......... Groups Joint Administration Committee (SAUO)
GJACS........ Gas Jet Attitude Control System (ACAE)
GJAP.......... Grand Junction Remedial Action Program (SAUS)
GJASA........ Ghana Journal of Agricultural Science (journ.) (SAUS)
GJB............ George Jackson Brigade (SAUO)
GJB............ Marie-Galante Island [*Guadeloupe*] [*Airport symbol*] (AD)
GJB............ Trans-Air Link Corp. [*ICAO designator*] (FAAC)
GJC............ Gainesville Junior College [*Later, Cooke County Junior College*] [*Texas*]
GJC............ Gang Job Card (SAUS)
GJC............ Gas Jet Controlled (SAUS)
GJC............ Gibbs Junior College (SAUO)
GJC............ Grand Junction Canal (SAUS)
GJC............ Grayson-Jockey Club Research Foundation (EA)
GJCAA........ Georgia Junior College Athletic Association (PSS)
GJCFC........ George Jones Country Fan Club (EA)
GJCO.......... Gaylord Companies, Inc. [*NASDAQ symbol*] (SAG)
GJCO.......... Gaylord Cos. [*NASDAQ symbol*] (TTSB)
GJCOW........ Gaylord Cos. Wrrt [*NASDAQ symbol*] (TTSB)
GJD............ Channel Aviation Ltd. [*British*] [*FAA designator*] (FAAC)
GJD............ Germanium Junction Diode (IDOE)
GJD............ Global Jewish Database [*Bar-Ilan University*] [*Information service or system*] (CRD)
GJD............ Grand Junior Deacon [*Freemasonry*]
GJE............ Gauss-Jordan Elimination (IEEE)
GJEN.......... Glen Jean, OH [*American Association of Railroads railroad junction routing code*]
GJF............ Gay Jewish Female (ADWA)
GJF............ Greensboro Justice Fund (EA)
GJFC.......... George Jones Fan Club (EA)
GJG............ Augusta College, Augusta, GA [*OCLC symbol*] (OCLC)
GJI............ Ghetto Job Information [*US Employment Service*] [*Department of Labor*]
GJL............ Geographical Journal (London) [*A publication*]
GJL............ Jijel [*Algeria*] [*Airport symbol*] (OAG)
GJM............ Gay Jewish Male (ADWA)
GJM............ Guajara Mirim [*Brazil*] [*Airport symbol*] (AD)
GJNT.......... Gas Jet Nose Tip (SAUS)
GJO............ Grand Junction Office [*Grand Junction, CO*] [*Department of Energy*]
GJO............ Greater Jacksonville [*Florida*] Open [*Golf tournament*]
GJOA.......... G. J. Orphan & Associates [*Telecommunications service*] (TSSD)
G-JOBS........ Jobs for Georgia Graduates (SAUO)
GJP............ Galactic Jupiter Probe [*NASA*]
GJP............ Grand Jury Project (EA)
GJP............ Graphic Job Processor (MCD)
GJPA.......... Grammatik des Juedisch-Palaestinischen Aramaeisch [*A publication*] (BJA)
GJPO.......... Grand Junction Project Office [*Department of Energy*]
GJPORAP.... Grand Junction Project Office Remedial Action Project (SAUO)
GJR............ Gjogur [*Iceland*] [*Airport symbol*] (OAG)
GJRAP........ Grand Junction Remedial Action Project [*Department of Energy*] [*Colorado*] (GAAI)
GJS............ Ghana Journal of Sociology [*A publication*]
GJT............ Grand Junction [*Colorado*] [*Airport symbol*] (OAG)
GJTA.......... Goldsmiths' and Jewellers' Trade Association [*A union*] [*British*]
GJV............ Geschichte des Juedischen Volkes im Zeitalter Jesu Christi [*A publication*] (BJA)
GJW............ Grand Junior Warden [*Freemasonry*]
GJW............ Great Jurists of the World (SAUO)
GJW............ Great Jurists of the World, by Sir John MacDonnel and Edward Manson [*1913*] [*A publication*] (DLA)
GJW............ Great Jurists of the World (journ.) (SAUS)
GK............ Gasser-Karrer [*Syndrome*] [*Medicine*] (DB)
GK............ General Knowledge
GK............ GenTek, Inc. [*NYSE symbol*] (SG)
GK............ Geographenkalender (BJA)
GK............ Ginze Kedem (BJA)
gk............ Glauconite (SAUS)
GK............ Glycerol Kinase [*An enzyme*] (MAE)
GK............ Goal Keeper [*Netball*]
GK............ Grand King [*Freemasonry*]
GK............ Granular Kidney [*Medicine*] (ROG)
G-K............ Grate-Kiln (SAUS)
Gk............ Greek (BEE)
GK............ Greek
Gk............ Grundkurs (SAUS)
GK............ Guy America Airways, Inc. (SAUO)
GK............ Hebraeische Grammatik Voellig Umgearbeitet [*Gesenius and E. Kautzsch*] [*A publication*] (BJA)

GK .... Laker Airways [*ICAO designator*] (AD)
GK-101 .... N-Monochloroglycine [*Dental caries treatment named for patent holders, Goldman and Kronman*]
GKA .... Garter King of Arms
GKA .... Goroka [*Papua New Guinea*] [*Airport symbol*] (OAG)
GKA .... Goroka [*Papua New Guinea*] [*Seismograph station code, US Geological Survey*] [*Closed*] (SEIS)
GKA .... Government Key Access (ADWA)
GKA .... Grounded Kathode Amplifier
GKa .... Hebraeische Grammatik Voellig Umgearbeitet [*Gesenius and E. Kautzsch*] [*A publication*] (BJA)
GKA .... US Army Aeronautical Services [*ICAO designator*] (FAAC)
GKABL .... George Khoury Association of Baseball Leagues (EA)
GKAP .... Georgia Kindergarten Assessment Program
GKB .... Garantie- und Kreditbank [*Guaranty and Credit Bank*] [*Germany*] (EG)
GKBZH .... Glowna Komisja Badania Zbrodni Hitlerowskich [*A publication*] (BJA)
GKB Zt .... GKB (SAUS)
GKC .... Gilbert Keith Chesterton [*British journalist and author*]
GKC .... Gold King Construction [*Vancouver Stock Exchange symbol*]
GKC .... Gold King River [*Alaska*] [*Seismograph station code, US Geological Survey*] (SEIS)
GKC .... Hebrew Grammar Gesenius, Kautzsch, Cowley [*A publication*] (BJA)
GKCA .... Go-Kart Club of America (SAUO)
GKCI .... Gold King Consolidated, Inc. (SAUS)
GKCI .... Gold King Consolidated, Incorporated (SAUO)
GKCS .... G. K. Chesterton Society (EA)
GKD .... Glycerol Kinase Deficiency [*Medicine*]
GKDC .... Group Key Distribution Centre (SAUO)
GKD-notation... Gordon-Kendall-Davison notation for chemical formulas (SAUS)
GKEP .... Guided Kinetic Energy Penetrator (SAUS)
GKF .... Florence (SAUS)
GKF .... Florence, SC [*Location identifier*] [*FAA*] (FAAL)
GKFS .... Grand Forks, BC [*American Association of Railroads railroad junction routing code*]
GKH .... G. K. Hall Co. [*Publisher*]
GKhI .... Hydrochemical Institute (SAUO)
GKI .... General Kinetics, Inc. [*AMEX symbol*] (SPSG)
GKI .... Genl Kinetics [*AMEX symbol*] (TTSB)
GKI .... GK Intelligent Systems, Inc. [*AMEX symbol*] (NASQ)
GKI .... Glon Kristy Resources [*Vancouver Stock Exchange symbol*]
GkI .... Greek Isles (SAUS)
GKIE .... General Kinetics, Inc. [*NASDAQ symbol*] (COMM)
GKIN .... Green Kingfisher [*North American bird banding code*] (BIBA)
GKIS .... Great Kiskadee [*North American bird banding code*] (BIBA)
GKJ .... Kennesaw College, Marietta, GA [*OCLC symbol*] (OCLC)
GKJ .... Meadville, PA [*Location identifier*] [*FAA*] (FAAL)
GKL .... Great Keppel Island [*Australia*] [*Airport symbol*] (OAG)
GKLC .... Law Companies Group, Inc., Kennesaw, GA [*Library symbol*] [*Library of Congress*] (LCLS)
GKLL .... Garage Keeper's Legal Liability [*Insurance*]
GKMDT .... Graham-Kendall Memory for Designs Test [*Psychology*] (DAVI)
GKMP .... Group Key Management Protocol (SAUO)
GKN .... Guest (SAUS)
GKN .... Guest, Kean & Nettlefolds [*Steel-forging company*] [*British*]
GKN .... Gulkana [*Alaska*] [*Airport symbol*] (OAG)
GKN .... Gulkana, AK [*Location identifier*] [*FAA*] (FAAL)
GKNHS .... Golden Key National Honor Society (EA)
GKNT .... Gosudarstvennyy Komitet po Nauki i Teknologii [*State Committee for Science and Technology*] [*Former USSR*] (LAIN)
GKO .... Gosudarstvennyi Komitet Oborony [*State Defense Committee*] [*Former USSR*] [*World War II*]
GKO .... Kongo Boumba [*Gabon*] [*Airport symbol*] (AD)
GkOd .... Greek Odeon [*Record label*]
GKQ .... Newark, NJ [*Location identifier*] [*FAA*] (FAAL)
GKR .... Goddard Kay Rogers Ltd. [*British*]
GKR .... Golden Knight Resources, Inc. [*Toronto Stock Exchange symbol*] [*Vancouver Stock Exchange symbol*]
GKR .... Government of the Khmer Republic [*Anticommunist government of Cambodia during the early seventies*] (VNW)
GKRV .... Golden Knight Resources, Inc. [*NASDAQ symbol*] (NQ)
GKRVE .... Golden Knight Res [*NASDAQ symbol*] (TTSB)
GKRVF .... Golden Knight Resources, Inc. [*NASDAQ symbol*] (COMM)
GKS .... Gesamtverzeichnis der Kongressschriften [*Union List of Conference Proceedings*] [*Deutsches Bibliotheksinstitut*] [*Germany*] [*Information service or system*] (CRD)
GKS .... Grand Keeper of the Seals [*Freemasonry*]
GKS .... Graphical Kernel Standard (SAUS)
GKS .... Graphical Kernel System [*International Standards Organization*] [*Computer science*]
GKS .... Graphics Kernel System (SAUS)
GK-SGB IV... Gemeinschaftskommentar zum Sozialgesetzbuch-Gemeinsame Vorschriften zur Sozialversicherung (SAUO)
GKSM .... GKS Metafile (SAUS)
GKSR .... G & K Service, Inc. (SAUO)
GKSR .... G & K Services (SAUS)
GKSRA .... G & K Services Cl'A' [*NASDAQ symbol*] (TTSB)
GKSS .... Formerly an abbreviation, now a logo (SAUS)
GKSS .... GKSS-Research Center Geesthacht Ltd. (SAUO)
GKSS .... Graphics Kernel System Standard (SAUS)
GKT .... Gasket [*Technical drawings*]
GKT .... General Knowledge Test
GKT .... Goldteck Mines Ltd. [*Toronto Stock Exchange symbol*]
GKTU .... Ngizim Karekare Tribal Union (SAUO)
GKTW .... Give Kids the World (EA)
GKW .... God Knows What
GKWHR .... Grams per Kilowatt Hour (EEVL)
GKY .... Golden Key Resources Ltd. [*Vancouver Stock Exchange symbol*]
GL .... Gage Length (SAUS)
Gl .... Galatians [*New Testament book*] (BJA)
GL .... Galeries Lafayette [*Department store*] [*Paris, France*]
Gl .... Galleon [*Spanish vessel*] (DS)
GL .... Gallon (MCD)
Gl .... Galvanized [*Metallurgy*]
GL .... Galvanoluminescence (SAUS)
GL .... Gas Lamp (SAUS)
GL .... Gas LASER
GL .... Gasoline Lean-Burn [*Automotive engineering*]
GL .... Gastric Lavage [*Medicine*] (MELL)
Gl .... Gastrointestinal (SAUS)
GL .... Gate Leads (IEEE)
GL .... Gauge Length
GL .... Gear Lubricant [*Automotive engineering*]
GL .... General Laws [*A publication*] (DLA)
GL .... General Laws of Massachusetts (SAUS)
GL .... General Ledger (AABC)
GL .... General Letter
GL .... General Liability [*Insurance*]
GL .... General Licence to Officate (SAUS)
GL .... General Linear [*Group theory, mathematics*]
GL .... General List [*Navy*] [*British*] (DMA)
GL .... Generator Lorry [*British*]
GL .... Genius Loci [*Genius of the Place*] [*Latin*] (ROG)
GL .... Genomic Library (MELL)
GL .... Geodesic Line (SAUS)
GL .... Geographic Location (NITA)
GL .... Geophysics Laboratory (SAUO)
GL .... Germanischer Lloyd [*German ship classification society*] (DS)
GL .... Germ Line [*Medicine*] (MELL)
Gl .... Glagolitic (SAUS)
GL .... Gilbert Lereboullet [*Syndrome*] [*Medicine*] (DB)
gl .... Gill [*Oceanography*] (DAVI)
GL .... Gill [*Unit of weight*]
GL .... Gilt Leaves [*Bookbinding*] (ROG)
GL .... Gilt Lines [*Bookbinding*] (ROG)
GL .... Gimbal Limit (SAUS)
GL .... Gimbal Limit Prearming Inhibiting Signal
GL .... Ginsburg-Landau Theory (SAUS)
GL .... Giustizia e Liberta [*Italy*] [*Political party*]
GL .... Glabella [*Anatomy*] (ROG)
GL .... Glacier (ROG)
GL .... Gladstonian Liberal [*British*] (ROG)
GL .... Gland (MELL)
gl .... Gland
GL .... Glass
GL .... Glass-type Loctal tube (SAUS)
GL .... Glaucolacustrine Soil [*Agronomy*]
GL .... Glaxo Laboratories (SAUO)
GL .... Glaze
GL .... Glazed (SAUS)
gl .... Glazing [*Construction term*] (MIST)
Gl .... Gleaver's Reports [*Jamaica*] [*A publication*] (ILCA)
GL .... Glebe [*Ecclesiastical*] (ROG)
GL .... Global Learning (EA)
GL .... Global Utility Fund (SAUS)
Gl .... Globe (journ.) (SAUS)
Gl .... Globigerina [*Quality of the bottom*] [*Nautical charts*]
Gl .... Globus (BJA)
Gl .... Gloria (GROV)
GL .... Gloria [*Glory*] [*Latin*]
Gl .... Gloss (DSA)
gl .... Gloss (WDMC)
GL .... Glossary (ROG)
gl .... Glossy (WDMC)
Gl .... Glucinium [*Also, G*] [*Old name for chemical element beryllium*]
GL .... Gluconolactone (SAUS)
GL .... Glycolipid (DB)
GL .... Glycosphingolipid [*Biochemistry*]
GL .... Gold Lease (ADA)
GL .... Gold Line [*Automotive tires*]
GL .... Goldstar Lines (SAUO)
GL .... Go Long [*Investment term*]
GL .... Good Luck (MHDB)
GL .... Gothic Letter
GL .... Government Laboratory (BARN)
GL .... Grade Line
GL .... Graduate in Law
g/l .... gram/liter (SAUS)
g/l .... Grams per Liter (MEC)
G/L .... Grams per Liter
GL .... Grand Larceny
GL .... Grand Lodge [*Freemasonry*]
GL .... Grand Lot
GL .... Grant Less Than [*Dialog*] [*Searchable fields*] [*Information service or system*] (NITA)
GL .... Graphic Language (SAUS)
GL .... Graphic Library
GL .... Graphics Language (SAUS)
GL .... Graphics Library (SAUS)
GL .... Gravitational Lens (SAUS)

GL............... Greater London [*England*]
GL............... Greatest Length
GL............... Great Lakes [*Vessel load line mark*]
GL............... Great Lakes Dredge & Dock Co. (SAUO)
GL............... Great Lakes Forest Products Ltd. [*Toronto Stock Exchange symbol*]
GL............... Great Lakes REIT [*NYSE symbol*] (SG)
GL............... Greek Line (SAUS)
GL............... Greenland [*ANSI two-letter standard code*] (CNC)
gl............... Greenland [*MARC country of publication code*] [*Library of Congress*] (LCCP)
GL............... Green Lantern
GL............... Green Library [*See also BVM*] [*France*] (EAIO)
GL............... Green Light (MSA)
GL............... Grenade Launcher (AABC)
GL............... Grid Leak
GL............... Gronlandsfly [*ICAO designator*] (AD)
GL............... Gronlandsfly Ltd. (SAUO)
GL............... Gross Leak (SAUS)
GL............... Gross Line [*Insurance*]
GL............... Ground Level
GL............... Ground Line (SAUS)
GL............... Ground Location (SAUS)
GL............... Growth Ledge (SAUS)
G/L............... Guideline (SAUS)
GL............... Guidelines (ADWA)
GL............... Guiding Light [*Television program title*]
GL............... Guild Library [*Church of Scotland*] [*A publication*]
GL............... Guild Library (journ.) (SAUS)
GL............... Gun Lay [*or Laying*] [*RADAR*]
GL............... Gun Laying (SAUS)
GL............... Gun Licence [*British*] (DAS)
GL............... Gunnery Lieutenant [*British military*] (DMA)
GL............... Gustatory Lacrimation [*Medicine*] (DMAA)
GL............... Lanier Lake Regional and Gwinnett County Library, Lawrenceville, GA [*Library symbol*] [*Library of Congress*] (LCLS)
GL............... L-Glutamic [*acid*] and L-Lysine [*Copolymer*]
GLA............... Gamma-Linoleic Acid [*Organic chemistry*]
GLA............... Gamma-Linolenic Acid
GLA............... Gate Logic Array (SAUS)
GLA............... Generalized Lehmann Alternatives (SAUS)
GLA............... General Laboratory Associates
GLA............... General Learning Ability
GLA............... General Ledger Account (AFM)
GLA............... General Lighthouse Authority [*British*]
GLA............... Georgia Library Association (SAUO)
GLA............... Giant Left Atrium (DB)
gla............... gingiovolinguo-axial (SAUS)
GLA............... Gingivolinguoaxial [*Dentistry*]
GLA............... Ginvolinguoaxial (SAUS)
GLA............... Glamis [*California*] [*Seismograph station code, US Geological Survey*] (SEIS)
GLA............... Glasgow [*Scotland*] [*Airport symbol*] (OAG)
GLA............... Glass [*Automotive engineering*]
Gl-a............... Glioma (SAUS)
GLA............... Goddard Laboratory for Atmospheres (SAUO)
GLA............... Gold Star Resources, Inc. [*Vancouver Stock Exchange symbol*]
GLA............... Grain Legume Association [*Australia*]
GLA............... Great Lakes Aviation Ltd. [*ICAO designator*] (FAAC)
GLA............... Gross Leasable Area
GLA............... Groupe de Liberation Armee [*Armed Liberation Group*] [*Guadeloupe*] (PD)
GLA............... Group Life Assurance [*British*]
GLA............... Guadeloupe Liberation Army
GLA............... Gulkana, AK [*Location identifier*] [*FAA*] (FAAL)
GLA............... Gust Load Alleviation [*Aviation*]
GLAA............... Greater London Arts Association (SAUO)
GLAAD............... Gay and Lesbian Alliance Against Defamation (EA)
GLAAD............... Global Learning at a Distance [*An association*]
GLAAD/NY... Gay and Lesbian Alliance Against Defamation/New York (EA)
GLAADS............... Gun Low-Altitude Air Defense System (NASA)
GLAAF............... Greater Los Angeles Area Facility (ACAE)
GLAASE............... Greater Los Angeles Area Security Facility (ACAE)
glab............... Glabrous [*Botany*] (BARN)
GLAB............... Greater London Arts Board (SAUS)
GLAC............... Gay and Lesbian Association of Choruses (EA)
GLAC............... General Ledger Account Code
glac............... Glacial [*Chemistry*] (DAVI)
GLAC............... Glacial
GLAC............... Glacier National Park
GLAC............... Grain Legume Advisory Committee [*Australia*]
GLAC............... Greek Library Association of Cyprus (SAUO)
Glacier............... Glacier Bay National Monument (SAUS)
Glacier............... Glacier Highway (SAUS)
Glacier............... Glacier Island (SAUS)
Glacier............... Glacier Mountain (SAUS)
Glacier............... Glacier National Park (SAUS)
Glacier............... Glacier Peak (SAUS)
Glacier Nat History Assoc Spec... Glacier Natural (SAUS)
Glacier Nat History Assoc Special Bull... Glacier Natural History Association.Special Bulletin (journ.) (SAUS)
glaciol............... glaciolography (SAUS)
glaciol............... glaciology (SAUS)
GLACSEC.... Group of Latin American and Caribbean Sugar Exporting Countries [*See also GEPLACEA*] [*Mexico City, Mexico*] (EAIO)
GLACT............... General Ledger Account (SAUS)
G L A D............... GALS LESA-A-A AGILE Dialogue (SAUS)
GLAD............... Gay and Lesbian Advocates and Defenders (EA)
GLAD............... Gladiator Fighter Aircraft [*British*] (DSUE)
GLAD............... Gladiolus (DSUE)
GLAD............... Glancing Angle Deposition [*Coating technology*]
GLAD............... GLOTRAC [*Global Tracking*] Adjustment
GLAD............... Gold-labelled Antigen Detection [*Medicine*] (DMAA)
GLAD............... Government and Legal Affairs Division [*American Occupational Therapy Association*]
GLAD............... Gradient Light Analytical Detector (ACAE)
GLAD............... Greater London Association for the Disabled (SAUO)
GLAD............... Grenade Launcher Attachment Development (MCD)
GLAD............... Group Learning about Drugs
GLADIATOR... Global Aerospace Defense Interceptor and Terrestrial Ordnance (ACAE)
GLADIS............... General Library Automated Database Information System (SAUS)
GLADIS............... Ground-LASER Attack Designator/Identification System (MCD)
glads............... gladiolas (SAUS)
GLADS............... Gladstone, MB [*American Association of Railroads railroad junction routing code*]
GLADS............... Great Falls Air Defense Sector [*Montana*] (SAA)
GLADS............... Gun Low-Altitude Air Defense System
GLADS............... Long-range Gun Low-altitude Air Defence System (SAUO)
GLAEX............... Glass Technology and Fabrication Exhibition (SAUS)
GLAFAMS.... Grand Lodge of Ancient Free and Accepted Masons of Scotland (SAUO)
GLAFLI............... Graded Levels of Achievement in Foreign Language Learning (AIE)
GLAG............... Ginzburg-Landau-Abrikosov-Gorkov [*Superconductivity theory*]
GLagC............... La Grange College, La Grange, GA [*Library symbol*] [*Library of Congress*] (LCLS)
GLagCM............... Callaway Mills Co. (SAUS)
GLagCM............... Callaway Mills Co., Technical Library (SAUO)
GLagCM............... Callaway Mills Co., Technical Library, LaGrange, GA [*Library symbol*] [*Library of Congress*] (LCLS)
GLagTAr............... Troup County Archives, La Grange, GA [*Library symbol*] [*Library of Congress*] (LCLS)
GLAI............... Green Leaf Area Index (MCD)
GLAKES............... Great Lakes (MUGU)
GLAL............... German Life and Letters (journ.) (SAUS)
GLAM............... Glamor (GOBB)
Glam............... Glamorgan (GROV)
GLAM............... Glamorganshire [*County in Wales*]
GLAM............... Greying, Leisured, Affluent, and Married [*Lifestyle classification*] [*British*]
Glam Hist.... Glamorgan Historian (journ.) (SAUS)
Glamis............... Glamis Gold Ltd. [*Associated Press*] (SAG)
GLAMIS............... Grant/Loan Accounting and Management Information System [*Department of Commerce*] (GFGA)
GLAMO............... Great Lakes Association of Marine Operators (SAUO)
Glamorgan... Glamorganshire (SAUS)
Glamorgan Hist... Glamorgan Historian (journ.) (SAUS)
Glams............... Glamorganshire (DIAR)
GLAMS............... Glamorganshire [*County in Wales*]
GLAN............... Global LAN (SAUS)
GLANCE............... Global Lightenergy weight Airborne Navigation Computer Equipment (SAUS)
GLANCE............... Global Lightweight Airborne Navigation Computer Equipment
GLANCE............... Global Lightweight Air Navigation Computing Equipment (SAUS)
GLAND............... Gibsland, LA [*American Association of Railroads railroad junction routing code*]
gland............... Glandula [*Gland*] [*Endocrinology*] (DAVI)
gland............... Glandular (STED)
Gl & J............... Glyn and Jameson's English Bankruptcy Reports [*1821-28*] [*A publication*] (DLA)
GL&L............... German Life and Letters (journ.) (SAUS)
Glan El Cas... Glanville's English Election Cases [*A publication*] (DLA)
Glanv El Cas... Glanville's English Election Cases [*A publication*] (DLA)
GLAP............... Gay Legal Advice Project [*British*] (DI)
GLAP............... Greater Los Angeles Plans, Inc. (SAUO)
GLAPPAR.... General Ledger, Accounts Payable, and Accounts Receivable [*Accounting*]
GLAR............... Glas-Aire Indus Grp Ltd [*NASDAQ symbol*] (TTSB)
GLAR............... Glas-Aire Industries Group Ltd. [*NASDAQ symbol*] (SAG)
GLARE............... Glass Reinforced [*Organic chemistry*]
GLARE............... Ground-Level Attack, Reconnaissance, and Electronic Countermeasures (MCD)
GLaRGG............... Great Lakes Regional Genetics Group (HGEN)
GLARP............... Grupo Latinoamericano de Rehabilitacion Profesional [*Latin American Vocational Rehabilitation Group*] [*Bogata, Colombia*] (EAIO)
GLARS............... Geoscience Laser Altimetry/ Ranging System (SAUO)
GLARS............... Geoscience Laser Altimetry/Ranging System (SAUS)
GLAS............... General Logic Analysis Simulator (SAUS)
GLAS............... General Logic Analysis System (SAUS)
GLAS............... Geoscience Laser Altimeter System (EOSA)
Glas............... Glascock's Reports in All the Courts of Ireland [*A publication*] (DLA)
GLAS............... Glasgal Communications [*NASDAQ symbol*] (TTSB)
GLAS............... Glasgal Communities [*NASDAQ symbol*] (SAG)
GLAS............... Glasgow [*Scotland*]
Glas............... Glaswegian (SAUS)
GLAS............... Global Land AVHRR Sampled (SAUS)
GLAS............... Goddard Laboratory for Atmospheric Sciences (MCD)
GLAS............... Goddard Laboratory of Atmospheric Sciences [*Marine science*] [*Army*] (OSRA)
GlasAire............... Glas-Aire Industries Group Ltd. [*Associated Press*] (SAG)
GLAS & SW... Glasgow & South-Western [*Railway*] [*Scotland*] (ROG)

Glas Aust..... Glass in Australia (journ.) (SAUS)
Glasc.......... Glascock's Reports in All the Courts of Ireland [*A publication*] (DLA)
Glascock...... Glascock's Reports in All the Courts of Ireland [*A publication*] (DLA)
GLASG......... Glasgow [*Scotland*] (ROG)
GLASG......... Glasgow, VA [*American Association of Railroads railroad junction routing code*]
Glasgal........ Glasgal Communities [*Associated Press*] (SAG)
GlasgOrTrans... Glasgow University (SAUO)
GlasgOrTrans... Glasgow University. Oriental Society.Transactions (journ.) (SAUS)
Glasgow AJ... Glasgow Archaeological Journal (journ.) (SAUS)
Glasgow Archaeol J... Glasgow Archaeological Journal (journ.) (SAUS)
Glasgow Arch J... Glasgow Archaeological Journal (journ.) (SAUS)
Glasgow Art R... Glasgow Art Gallery and Museums Association (SAUO)
Glasgow Art R... Glasgow Art Gallery and Museums Association.Review (journ.) (SAUS)
Glasg Univ Publ... Glasgow University. Publications (journ.) (SAUS)
GLAS H........ Glasgow Highlanders, Territorial Army (SAUO)
GLASLA....... Great Lakes - St. Lawrence Association
Glas Math J... Glasgow Mathematical Journal (journ.) (SAUS)
Glasock........ Glascock's Reports in All the Courts of Ireland (SAUS)
GLASOD....... Global Assessment of/on Soil Degradation (SAUO)
glasphalt..... glass and asphalt (SAUS)
GLASS......... Geodetic LASER Survey System
GLASS......... Germanium-Lithium Argon Scanning System (NRCH)
GLASS......... Gernmanium-Lithium Argon Scanning System (SAUS)
GLASS......... Glaciology of the South Shetland Islands (SAUO)
GLASS......... Global Area Strike System [*Military*] (SEWL)
GLASS......... Globally Accessible Services (SAUO)
GLASS......... Good Luck and Smooth Sailing [*Slang*] [*Military*] (DNAB)
GLASS......... Greater London Audio Specialization Scheme (SAUS)
Glass Aust... Glass in Australia (journ.) (SAUS)
Glassboro St C... Glassboro State College (GAGS)
GLASSEX..... Glass Technology and Fabrication Exhibition (TSPED)
Glassf Ev..... Glassford on Evidence [*A publication*] (DLA)
Glasshouse Crops Res Inst Annu... Glasshouse Crops Research Institute. Annual Report (journ.) (SAUS)
Glasshouse Crops Res Inst Annu Rep... Glasshouse Crops Research Institute. Annual Report (journ.) (SAUS)
glassie......... glass playing marble (SAUS)
Glass Ind..... Glass Industry (journ.) (SAUS)
Glass Int...... Glass International (journ.) (SAUS)
Glassmst..... Glassmaster Co. [*Associated Press*] (SAG)
Glass Technol... Glass Technology [*A publication*] (CABS)
glassteel...... glass and steel (SAUS)
Glass Wkrs News... Glass Workers News (journ.) (SAUS)
GLAST......... Gamma Large Array Space Telescope [*A collaboration of physics groups*]
GLAST......... Gamma-Ray Large Area Space Telescope
Glastech...... Glastechnik (SAUS)
GLASU......... Glasgal Communications Unit [*NASDAQ symbol*] (TTSB)
GLASW........ Glasgal Communications Wrrt [*NASDAQ symbol*] (TTSB)
GLAT............ Glutamic Acid, Lysine, Alanine, and Tyrosine (STED)
GLAT............ Government Lot Acceptance Test [*Military*] (CAAL)
GLAT............ Guidance Level Acceptance Test (ACAE)
GLATC......... Graphics and Languages Agreement Group for Testing and Certification (SAUO)
Glatflt.......... Glatfelter [*P.H.*] Co. [*Associated Press*] (SAG)
GLAU........... General Labourers' Amalgamated Union [*British*]
glau............. Glaucous [*Botany*] (BARN)
Glauberite... Calcium Sodium Sulfate (SAUS)
glauc........... glaucoma (SAUS)
GLAVATOM... Chief Directorate to the Council of Ministries for the Utilisation of Atomic Energy [*British*] (NUCP)
GlaxcWeL.... Glaxo Wellcome PLC [*Associated Press*] (SAG)
GLAZ............ Great Lakes Industries [*Federal Railroad Administration identification code*]
GLB.............. Galactosidase Beta (DMAA)
GLB.............. Gas [*or Grease*] Lubricated Bearing
GLB.............. Ghana Library Board (SAUS)
GLB.............. Gilbues [*Brazil*] [*Airport symbol*] (AD)
GLB.............. Girls' Life Brigade [*British*]
GLB.............. Girls' Life Brigade (SAUS)
GLB.............. Glass Block (AAG)
GLB.............. Glass in Barrels [*Freight*]
GLB.............. Glenborough Realty Trust [*NYSE symbol*] (TTSB)
GLB.............. Glenborough Realty Trust, Inc. [*NYSE symbol*] (SAG)
GLB.............. Global Air [*Bulgaria*] [*ICAO designator*] (FAAC)
GLB.............. Globe-Union, Inc. (SAUO)
GLB.............. Grease Lubricated Bearing (SAUS)
GLB.............. Greater London Borough (SAUS)
GLB.............. Great Lakes Freight Bureau Inc., Cleveland OH [*STAC*]
GLB.............. Gay, Lesbian, Bisexual (ODA)
GLBA........... Glacier Bay National Monument
GLBA........... Great Lakes Booksellers Association (EA)
GLBBX......... Mgn. Stanley D. Witter Global Divd. Growth [*Mutual fund ticker symbol*] (SG)
GLBC........... Great Lakes Bancorp (EFIS)
GLBC........... Great Lakes Basin Commission [*Terminated, 1981*] (EGAO)
GLBC........... Great Lakes Bioregional Congress (SAUO)
GlbCasn....... Global Casinos [*Associated Press*] (SAG)
GlbDir.......... Global Directmail Corp. [*Associated Press*] (SAG)
GLBE........... Globe Business Resources [*NASDAQ symbol*] (TTSB)
GLBE........... Globe Business Resources, Inc. [*NASDAQ symbol*] (SAG)
GlbeBus....... Globe Business Resources, Inc. [*Associated Press*] (SAG)
GlbGvt......... Global Government Plus Fund, Inc. [*Associated Press*] (SAG)
GlbHlt.......... Global Health Sciences Fund [*Associated Press*] (SAG)
GLBIN.......... Global Ocean Carriers Ltd. (SAUO)
GLBK........... Glendale Co-Operative Bank [*NASDAQ symbol*] (SAG)
GLBK........... Glendale Co. Operative Bk [*NASDAQ symbol*] (TTSB)
GLBL............ Global
GLBL............ Global Industries [*NASDAQ symbol*] (TTSB)
GLBL............ Global Industries Ltd. [*NASDAQ symbol*] (SAG)
GlblOcn....... Global Ocean Carriers Ltd. [*Associated Press*] (SAG)
GlblOne....... Global One Distribution & Merchandising, Inc. [*Associated Press*] (SAG)
GLBM........... Ground-Launched Ballistic Missile
GlbMktl........ Global Market Information, Inc. [*Associated Press*] (SAG)
GlbRsc......... Global Resources, Inc. [*Associated Press*] (SAG)
GLBS........... Globes [*Freight*]
GLBSA......... Greater London Building Surveyors Association (SAUO)
GlbSpill....... Global Spill Management [*Associated Press*] (SAG)
GLBT............ Glastonbury Bank & Trust Co. [*NASDAQ symbol*] (SAG)
GlbTel.......... Global Telecommunications Solutions, Inc. [*Associated Press*] (SAG)
GLB TRG...... Global Trigger
GLBTRT........ Gay, Lesbian, Bisexual & Transgendered Round Table
GLBU........... Buchanan [*Liberia*] [*ICAO location identifier*] (ICLI)
GlbVilag...... Global Village Communictions, Inc. [*Associated Press*] (SAG)
GLC.............. Galactic Resources Ltd. (SAUO)
GLC.............. Galileo Intl. [*NYSE symbol*] (SG)
GLC.............. Gas Liquid Chromatogram (SAUS)
glc............... gas-liquid-chromatographic (SAUS)
GLC.............. Gas-Liquid Chromatography [*Analytical chemistry*]
GLC.............. Gas-Liquid Chronomatography (SAUS)
GLC.............. Gate Leakage Current
GLC.............. Gay and Lesbian Caucus (EA)
GLC.............. Genealogical Library Catalog (GEAB)
GLC.............. General Learning Corp. [*of Time, Inc.*]
GLC.............. Generator Line Contractor (NASA)
GLC.............. Geographic Location Code (ACAE)
GLC.............. German Language Club (EA)
GLC.............. German Library Conference (SAUS)
GLC.............. G-force-induced Loss of Consciousness (SAUS)
GLC.............. Glace
GLC.............. Glass Industry Standards Committee (SAUO)
Glc............... Glaucoma [*Medicine*] (EDAA)
glc............... Glaucoma (STED)
GLC.............. Glaucoma
GLC.............. Global LORAN Navigation Chart [*Air Force*]
Glc............... Glucose [*Also, G, GLUC*] [*A sugar*]
GLC.............. Granulosa Lutein Cell [*Medicine*] (MELL)
GLC.............. Grat Lakes Commission (SAUS)
GLC.............. Gray Level Co-Occurrence (SAUS)
GLC.............. Greater London Councellor (SAUO)
GLC.............. Greater London Council [*Information service or system*] (IID)
GLC.............. Great Lakes Carbon Corporation (SAUO)
GLC.............. Great Lakes Club (EA)
GLC.............. Great Lakes Colleges (SAUO)
GLC.............. Great Lakes Commission (EA)
GLC.............. Great Little Car [*Mazda Motors of America*]
GLC.............. Ground Level Concentration (EG)
GLC.............. Grupo Logistico de Combati (SAUS)
GLC.............. Guild of Lettering Craftsmen (SAUO)
GLC.............. Gun Lay Computer (SAUS)
GLC.............. Philadelphia, PA [*Location identifier*] [*FAA*] (FAAL)
GLCA........... Gallery of Living Catholic Authors [*Defunct*] (EA)
GLCA........... Glen Canyon National Recreation Area
GlcA............ Gluconic Acid [*Biochemistry*]
GLCA........... Great Lakes Colleges Association (EA)
GLCB........... Globo Cabo S.A. [*NASDAQ symbol*] (NASQ)
GLCBY......... Globo Cabo ADS [*Formerly, Multicanal Participacoes ADS*] [*NASDAQ symbol*]
GLCC........... Gas Light and Coke Company (SAUO)
GLCC........... Greater London County Council [*England*] (WDAA)
GLCCF......... Gaming Lottery [*NASDAQ symbol*] (TTSB)
GLCCF......... Gaming Lottery Corp. [*NASDAQ symbol*] (SAG)
GLCCF......... GLC Ltd. [*Formerly, Gaming Lottery*] [*NASDAQ symbol*]
GLCES......... Great Lakes Coastal Forecasting System [*Marine science*] (OSRA)
GLCFS......... Great Lakes Coastal Forecasting System (USDC)
glcl............. Glacial (SAUS)
GLCM.......... Graduate Diploma of the London College of Music [*British*] (DBQ)
GLCM.......... Graduate of the London College of Music (SAUO)
GLCM.......... Grey Level Co-Occurrence Matrix (SAUS)
GLCM.......... Ground-Launched Cruise Missile [*Pronounced "glick-em"*]
GLCM.......... Ground-Launched surface-to-surface Cruise Missile (SAUS)
GLCM.......... Robertsport/Cape Mount [*Liberia*] [*ICAO location identifier*] (ICLI)
GLCM/LCC... Ground Launched Cruise Missile/Launch Control Center (SAUS)
GLC/MS...... Gas-Liquid Chromatography/Mass Spectrometry (STED)
Glcn............ Glucosamin (SAUS)
GlcN........... Glucosamine [*Biochemistry*]
GLCN.......... Gold Coin Mining, Inc. (SAUO)
GLCNA........ German Lutheran Conference of North America (EA)
GlcNac........ N-Acetylglucosamine
GLCNSW...... Gem and Lapidary Council of New South Wales [*Australia*]
GLCOE......... Glencoe, ON [*American Association of Railroads railroad junction routing code*]
GLCP........... Harper/Cape Palmas [*Liberia*] [*ICAO location identifier*] (ICLI)
GlcrBc......... Glacier Bancorp, Inc. [*Associated Press*] (SAG)
GLC/SBS...... Great Little Computer/Small Business System [*Business software*] [*Cumulus Computer Corp.*] (PCM)
GLCSC......... Gay and Lesbian Community Service Center (SAUO)

GLCSNSW.... Gay and Lesbian Counselling Service of New South Wales [*Australia*]
GLCSSA....... Gay and Lesbian Counselling Service of South Australia
GLCTS......... Global Land Cover Test Sites [*Remote sensing*] (EERA)
GlcUA.......... Glucuronic Acid [*Also, GA*] [*Biochemistry*]
GlcWatr....... Glacier Water Services, Inc. [*Associated Press*] (SAG)
GLCZ............ Great Lakes Cotton [*Federal Railroad Administration identification code*]
GLD............ Cases in the Griqualand West Local Division of the Supreme Court [*1910-46*] [*South Africa*] [*A publication*] (DLA)
GLD............ Gas Leak Detector
GLD............ Gasoline Lean-Burn Draw-Through [*Automotive fuel systems*]
GLD............ Generalized Logic Diagram (IDAI)
GLD............ General Learning Disability
GLD............ General Logistics Department (SAUS)
gld............ gilded (SAUS)
GLD............ Glad [*Amateur radio shorthand*] (WDAA)
GLD............ Glider
GLD............ Glide Slope [*Aviation*] (NASA)
GLD............ Globoid Leukodystrophy [*Medicine*] (DB)
GLD............ Glutamate Dehydrogenase (DMAA)
GLD............ Gold (MSA)
GLD............ Golden [*Colorado School of Mines*] [*Colorado*] [*Seismograph station code, US Geological Survey*] (SEIS)
GLD............ Golden Star Air Cargo Co. Ltd. [*Sudan*] [*ICAO designator*] (FAAC)
GLD............ Goodland [*Kansas*] [*Airport symbol*] (OAG)
GLD............ Goodland Weather Forecast Office (SAUS)
GLD............ Gould (SAUS)
GLD............ Granulomatous Lung Disease (MELL)
GLD............ Gross Logical Design
GLD............ Ground-LASER Designators (RDA)
GLD............ Guided Land Development (SAUS)
GLD............ Guild
Gld............ Guilder [*Modification of gulden*] [*Monetary unit*] [*Netherlands*]
GLD............ Santa Fe Pacific Gold Corp. [*NYSE symbol*] (SAG)
GLD............ Sante Fe Pacific Gold [*NYSE symbol*] (TTSB)
GLDA.......... Gay and Lesbian Democrats of America [*Defunct*] (EA)
GLDB.......... Gold Banc Corp., Inc. [*NASDAQ symbol*] (SAG)
GldBear....... Golden Bear Golf, Inc. [*Associated Press*] (SAG)
GLDC.......... Glutamic Decarboxylase (SAUS)
GLDC.......... Golden Enterprises [*NASDAQ symbol*] (TTSB)
GLDC.......... Golden Enterprises, Inc. [*NASDAQ symbol*] (NQ)
GLDC.......... Great Lakes Data Center (SAUS)
Gld Cst........ Gold Coast (SAUS)
GldEagl........ Golden Eagle Group, Inc. [*Associated Press*] (SAG)
GldEg.......... Golden Eagle Group, Inc. [*Associated Press*] (SAG)
GLDF.......... Gold Fields of South Africa Ltd. [*NASDAQ symbol*] (NQ)
GldFld.......... Goldfield Corp. [*Associated Press*] (SAG)
GLDFY......... Gold Fields S. Africa ADR [*NASDAQ symbol*] (TTSB)
GLDH.......... Glutamate Dehydrogenase [*Organic chemistry*]
GLDH.......... Glutamic Dehydrogenase (SAUS)
GldKngt........ Golden Knight Resources, Inc. [*Associated Press*] (SAG)
GLDMS........ Groupe de Liaison de Docimologues en Milieu Scolaire [*Canada*]
GLDN.......... Golden
gldn............ Golden [*Philately*]
GLDN.......... Golden Systems, Inc. [*NASDAQ symbol*] (SAG)
GldnSyst....... Golden Systems, Inc. [*Associated Press*] (SAG)
GLDP.......... Ginn Language Development Program (EDAC)
GLDP.......... Glutamic Dephosphatase (SAUS)
GLD PLTD.... Gold Plated [*Freight*]
GldPoul........ Golden Poultry Co., Inc. [*Associated Press*] (SAG)
GldQual........ Golden Quail Resources Ltd. [*Associated Press*] (SAG)
GLDR.......... Glider (FAAC)
GLDR.......... Gold Reserve [*NASDAQ symbol*] (TTSB)
GLDR.......... Gold Reserve Corp. [*NASDAQ symbol*] (NQ)
GLDR.......... Groupe Liberal (SAUO)
GLDR.......... Groupe Liberal, Democratique, et Reformateur (EAIO)
GLDS.......... Gemini Launch Data System [*NASA*] (MCD)
GLDS.......... Ground LASER Designator Station (PDAA)
GLDS.......... Guidance Laser Designator Station (ACAE)
GLDSAM...... Goldwyn Co. (SAUO)
GLDSB......... Goldsboro, NC [*American Association of Railroads railroad junction routing code*]
GldStarR...... Golden Star Resources Ltd. [*Associated Press*] (SAG)
GldStd......... Gold Standard, Inc. [*Associated Press*] (SAG)
GLDT.......... Gas LASER Discharge Tube
GLDTR......... Gladiator
GldWF......... Golden West Financial Corp. [*Associated Press*] (SAG)
GldwSam..... Goldwyn [*Samuel*] Co. [*Associated Press*] (SAG)
GLDX.......... Glades Gas [*Private rail car owner code*]
GLE............ Gainesville (SAUS)
GLE............ Gainesville, TX [*Location identifier*] [*FAA*] (FAAL)
GLE............ Gallium Light Emitting (SAUS)
GLE............ Gemini LASER Experiment [*NASA*] (IAA)
GLE............ General Electric, Ltd. (SAUO)
GLE............ Generative Language Environment (HODG)
GLE............ Gleason Corp. [*NYSE symbol*] (SPSG)
GLE............ Glenmuick [*New Zealand*] [*Seismograph station code, US Geological Survey*] [*Closed*] (SEIS)
GLE............ GLE Resources Ltd. [*Vancouver Stock Exchange symbol*]
GLE............ Gloss Low Emission [*Ink*] (DGA)
GLE............ Government-Loaned Equipment (MSA)
GLE............ Grade Level Equivalent [*Educational testing*]
GLE............ Grand Larousse Encyclopedique [*A publication*]
GLE............ Ground-Level Event [*Geophysics*]
GLE............ Ground Liaison Element (MCD)
GLE............ Gummed Long Edge [*Envelopes*] (DGA)
GLEAM........ Graphic Layout and Engineering Aid Method
GleasC......... Gleason Corp. [*Associated Press*] (SAG)
GLEDIC........ Great Lakes Environmental Data and Information Center (SAUS)
GLEDIC........ Great Lakes Environmental Information Center [*Ann Arbor, MI*]
GLEEP......... Graphite Low-Energy Experimental Pile [*Nuclear reactor*] [*British*]
GLEF........... Gay and Lesbian Emergency Fund (SAUO)
GLEF........... Geothermal Loop Experimental Facility [*Department of Energy*]
GLEI............ Georgia Leadership Evaluation Instrument (SAUO)
GLEIS.......... Great Lakes Environmental Information Sharing
GLEMEDS.... Great Lakes Embryo Mortality, Edema, and Deformities Syndrome [*Marine birds*]
GLEN........... Glen [*Commonly used*] (OPSA)
GLEN........... Global Environmental Corp. (SAUO)
Glenayr........ Glenayre Techs, Inc. [*Associated Press*] (SAG)
Gl Ency........ Globe Encyclopaedia [*A publication*] (ROG)
GLENDAL..... Glendalough [*Valley in Ireland*] (ROG)
GlendCo....... Glendale Co-Operative Bank [*Associated Press*] (SAG)
GlenF........... Glendale Federal Bank Federal Savings Bank [*Associated Press*] (SAG)
GlenF........... Glendale Federal Bank FSB [*Associated Press*] (SAG)
GlenFed........ Glendale Federal Bank Federal Savings Bank [*Associated Press*] (SAG)
Glen High.... Glen's Highway Laws [*A publication*] (DLA)
Glenn........... Glenn's Annual Reports [*16-18 Louisiana*] [*A publication*] (DLA)
Glen Pub H... Glen on the Public Health Laws [*A publication*] (DLA)
Glen Pub H... Glen on the Public Health Laws (journ.) (SAUS)
Glen Reg..... Glen on Registration of Births and Deaths [*A publication*] (DLA)
GlenRT......... Glenborough Realty Trust, Inc. [*Associated Press*] (SAG)
GLENS......... Glens [*Commonly used*] (OPSA)
GLENW........ Glenwood, PA [*American Association of Railroads railroad junction routing code*]
Glenway...... Glenway Financial Corp. [*Associated Press*] (SAG)
GLEP........... Group for Lunar Exploration and Planning (MCD)
GLER........... General Electric Co. Ltd. (SAUO)
GLERL......... Great Lakes Environmental Research Laboratory [*Ann Arbor, MI*] [*National Oceanic and Atmospheric Administration*] (GRD)
GLERR......... Great Lakes Ecosystem Restoration and Rehabilitation [*Canada*] (ASF)
GLES........... Great Lakes Forecasting System [*Marine science*] (OSRA)
GLESS......... Gearless (RIMS)
GLET........... Government Logistics Evaluation and Testing (MCD)
GLEW........... Great Lakes Environmental Wire (SAUO)
GLEX........... General Ledger and Expense system (SAUS)
GLEX System... General Ledger and Expense System (SAUS)
GLF............ Gates Library Foundation
GLF............ Gaussian Lens Formula [*Optics*]
GLF............ Gay Liberation Front
GLF............ Generalized Lambda Family [*Statistics*]
GLF............ General Telephone Co. of Florida [*NYSE symbol*] (SPSG)
GLF............ Glass Fiber [*Technical drawings*]
GLF............ Golfito [*Costa Rica*] [*Airport symbol*] (OAG)
GLF............ Great Lakes Fisheries Laboratory (SAUO)
GLF............ Great Lakes Fisheries Laboratory, Ann Arbor, MI [*OCLC symbol*] (OCLC)
GLF............ GTE Florida, Inc. [*NYSE symbol*] (SAG)
GLF............ Gulf (SAUS)
GLF............ Gulfstream Aerospace Corp. [*ICAO designator*] (FAAC)
GLF............ McGill University, Law Library [*UTLAS symbol*]
GLFA........... Gays and Lesbians in Foreign Affairs [*An association*] (EA)
GLFALSK..... Gulf of Alaska (FAAC)
GLFB........... Greater London Fund for the Blind (SAUO)
GLFC........... Georganne LaPiere Fan Club (EA)
GLFC........... Ginger Lynn Fan Club [*Defunct*] (EA)
GLFC........... Gloria Loring Fan Club [*Defunct*] (EA)
GLFC........... Graphite Lunar-module Fuel Cask (SAUS)
GLFC........... Great Lakes Fisheries Commission (SAUO)
GLFC........... Great Lakes Fishery Commission [*Canada and United States*] (NOAA)
GLFC........... Great Lakes Football Conference (PSS)
GLFC........... Guiding Light Fan Club (EA)
GLFCAL....... Gulf of California (FAAC)
GlfCda......... Gulf Canada Resources Ltd. [*Associated Press*] (SAG)
GLFD........... Guilford Pharmaceuticals [*NASDAQ symbol*] (TTSB)
GLFD........... Guilford Pharmaceuticals, Inc. [*NASDAQ symbol*] (SAG)
GLFDCC....... Great Lakes Fish Disease Control Committee [*Canada*] (ASF)
GLFE........... Golf Enterprises [*NASDAQ symbol*] (TTSB)
GLFE........... Golf Enterprises, Inc. [*NASDAQ symbol*] (SAG)
GLFFF......... Great Lakes Fly Fishing Federation (SAUO)
GL/FICS....... General Ledger / Financial Information and Control System
GL/FICS....... Greater Ledger/Financial Information and Control System (SAUO)
GLFL........... Great Lakes Fishery Laboratory [*Department of the Interior*] (GRD)
GLFMEX....... Gulf of Mexico (FAAC)
Glfmrk......... Gulfmark International [*Associated Press*] (SAG)
GLFPrA........ GTE Fla $1.25 Pfd [*NYSE symbol*] (TTSB)
GLFPrB........ GTE Fla $1.30cm B Pfd [*NYSE symbol*] (TTSB)
GLFPrC........ GTE Fla 8.16% Pfd [*NYSE symbol*] (TTSB)
GLFRB......... Great Lakes Fisheries Research Branch [*Canadian Department of Fisheries and Oceans*] [*Research center*] (RCD)
GLFRC......... Great Lakes Forest Research Centre [*Environment Canada*] [*Research center*] (RCD)
GlFRP......... Glass-Fiber-Reinforced Plastic [*Also, GFRP*]
GLFS........... Great Lakes Federal Savings & Loan Association (SAUO)
GLFS........... Great Lakes Forecasting System (USDC)

GLFS........... Grenade Launcher Fighting System (SAUS)
GLFSTLAWR... Gulf of St. Lawrence (FAAC)
Glf Str........ Gulf Stream (SAUS)
GlfSU.......... Gulf States Utilities Co. [*Associated Press*] (SAG)
GLFT........... Gas-Insulated Flow Tube (SAUS)
GLFT........... Great Lakes Fishery Trust
GLG............ Glamis Gold Ltd. [*Toronto Stock Exchange symbol*] [*NYSE symbol*]
GLG............ Glengyle [*Australia*] [*Airport symbol*] (OAG)
GLG............ La Grange College, La Grange, GA [*OCLC symbol*] (OCLC)
GLGC.......... Gene Logic, Inc. [*NASDAQ symbol*] (NASQ)
GLGE.......... Greenville/Sinoe [*Liberia*] [*ICAO location identifier*] (ICLI)
GLGH.......... Good Luck and Good Hunting (SAUS)
GLGL.......... Gwinnett County Law Library, Lawrenceville, GA [*Library symbol*] [*Library of Congress*] (LCLS)
GLGS.......... GOES Local Groundstation System (SAUS)
GLGS.......... Gwinnett County Public Schools, Lawrenceville, GA [*Library symbol*] [*Library of Congress*] (LCLS)
GLGST......... Geologist (SAUS)
GLGT.......... Germ-Line Gene Therapy [*Medicine*] (EDAA)
GLGT.......... Gwinnett Technical Institute, Lawrenceville, GA [*Library symbol*] [*Library of Congress*] (LCLS)
GLGU.......... Glaucous Gull [*North American bird banding code*] (BIBA)
GLGV.......... Glamis Gold Ltd. (SAUO)
GLGYB......... Geolagy (journ.) (SAUS)
GLH............ Gallaher Group ADS [*NYSE symbol*] (SG)
GLH............ Generalized Lymphoid Hyperplasia [*Medicine*] (MELL)
GLH............ Gentleman's Left Handed [*Golf club*]
GLH............ Germinal Layer Hemorrhage [*Medicine*] (EDAA)
GLH............ Giant Lymph Node Hyperplasia [*Medicine*] (DMAA)
GlH............ Glass Hill (journ.) (SAUS)
GLH............ Glue Line Heating
GLH............ Go Like Hell [*In model name Omni GLH, proposed for Dodge car designed by Carroll Shelby*]
GLH............ Greenville [*Mississippi*] [*Airport symbol*] (OAG)
GLH............ Ground Launched Hellfire (SAUS)
GLH............ Gwent Local History (journ.) (SAUS)
GLHA.......... Great Lakes Harbor Association (EA)
GLH-H......... Ground-Launched Hellfire-Heavy (SAUS)
GLHISC........ Gay and Lesbian History on Stamps Club (SAUS)
GLHK.......... Granato-Luecke Theory for High Kelvin Temperatures (SAUS)
GLH-S......... Goes Like Hell - Some More [*In model "GLH-S," Dodge car designed by Carroll Shelby*] [*Facetious translation: "Goes Like Hell - Squared"*]
GLHS.......... Great Lakes Historical Society (EA)
GLHS.......... Ground-Launched HELLFIRE System (MCD)
GLHSC......... Gay and Lesbian History on Stamps Club (EA)
GLHSC......... Gay and Lesbian History Stamp Club (EA)
GLI............ Gale's Literary Index [*CD-ROM*]
GLI............ Gallic Aviation [*France*] [*ICAO designator*] (FAAC)
GLI............ Gamma LINAC Instrumentation
GLI............ General Time (SAUS)
GLI............ Genetic Linkage (analysis) [*Medicine*] (EDAA)
GLI............ Glass Industry (journ.) (SAUS)
GLI............ Glen Innes [*Australia*] [*Airport symbol*] (OAG)
GLI............ Glicentin [*Biochemistry*]
GLI............ Glider
GLI............ Global Imager (EOSA)
GLI............ Global Income Plus Fund, Inc. (SAUO)
GLI............ Glucagon-Like Immunoreactant (SAUS)
GLI............ Glucagon-Like Immunoreactive (SAUS)
GLI............ Glucagon-Like Immunoreactivity [*or Immunoreactant*] [*Endocrinology*]
GL-I........... Glyoaxalase I (SAUS)
gli............ Grams per Liter [*Medicine*] (EDAA)
GLI............ Grand Lodge of Ireland (SAUO)
GLI............ Grandma Lee's, Inc. [*Toronto Stock Exchange symbol*]
GLI............ Great Lakes Institute (SAUO)
GLI............ Greyhound Lines, Inc. (EFIS)
GLI............ Gurkha Light Infantry [*British military*] (DMA)
GLIA........... Gliatech, Inc. [*NASDAQ symbol*] (SAG)
GLIAC.......... Great Lakes Intercollegiate Athletic Conference
GLIAS.......... Greater London Industrial Archaeology Society (SAUO)
Gliatech....... Gliatech, Inc. [*Associated Press*] (SAG)
GLIB........... Gay and Lesbian Information Bureau (IID)
GLIB........... Glossy Ibis [*North American bird banding code*] (BIBA)
GliBad......... Glider Badge [*Military decoration*]
GLIC........... General Ledger Identification Code (AFM)
GLICP.......... Great Lakes Initiative Contract Program (EEVL)
GLID........... Ground Laser Locator Designator (SAUS)
GLIDER P..... Glider Pilot Regiment (SAUO)
GLIFWC........ Great Lakes Indian Fish and Wildlife Commission (EA)
GLIJ........... Greater London Intelligence Journal (journ.) (SAUS)
GLIM........... Generalised Linear Interactive Modelling System [*Software*] (EERA)
GLIM........... General Light Inter-Reflection Model (PDAA)
GLIM........... General Linear Modeling Program [*Computer science*]
GlimchRt...... Glimcher Realty Trust [*Associated Press*] (SAG)
GLIMPCE...... Great Lakes International Multidisciplinary Program on Crustal Evolution [*Geophysics*]
GLIMPSE...... Global Limb Photometric Scanning Experiment (MCD)
GLIMR......... Great Lakes Information Management Resource (SAUO)
GLIN........... Georgia Library Information Network [*Library network*]
GLIN........... Global Legal Information Network (SAUO)
GLIN........... Great Lakes Information Network
G-Line........ Goubau Line (SAUS)
GLINN......... Gay/Lesbian International News Network
GLINN......... Government Libraries Information Network in New South Wales [*Australia*]
GLINT.......... Gated Laser Illuminator for Night Television (SAUS)
GLINT.......... Global Intelligence (IEEE)
GLINT.......... Gospel Literature International (EA)
glio........... Glioma [*Neurology*] (DAVI)
GLIP........... Glide and Skip [*Bombing mission*]
GLIPAR........ Guide Line Identification Program for Antimissile Research [*ARPA*]
GLIPAR........ Guideline Identification Program for Anti-missile Research (SAUS)
GLIPAR........ Guide Lines for Investigation, Planning and Research (SAUO)
GLIPAR........ Guidelines for Investigation, Planning, and Research
GLIPS.......... Giga Logical Inferences per Second (CIST)
GLIR........... Gunfire Locating Infra-Red (SAUS)
GLIR........... Gunfire Locating Infrared System (SAUS)
GLIS........... GEAC Library Information System (SAUS)
GLIS........... Geographic and Land Information Society (SAUO)
GLIS........... Geographic Land Information System (SAUS)
GLIS........... Gleaner Life Insurance Society [*Adrian, MI*] (EA)
GLIS........... Glissando [*Gliding*] [*Music*] (ROG)
GLIS........... Global Land Information System (EERA)
GLISA.......... Government Losses in Shipment Act [*1937*]
GLISCAC...... Government Library and Information Service Computer (SAUS)
GLISP.......... Great Lakes International Surveillance Plan (SAUS)
gliss........... Glissando (SHCU)
Gliss........... Glissando [*Gliding*] [*Music*]
glit............ Glitter (VRA)
glit............ glittering (SAUS)
GLIT........... Ground Loop Impedance Tester (VLIE)
GLITCH........ Goblin Loose in the Computer Hut [*Computer science*]
GLJ............ Gates Lear Jet Corp. (SAUO)
GLJ............ Global Getra Ltd. [*Bulgaria*] [*ICAO designator*] (FAAC)
GLK............ Golden Lake Resources Ltd. [*Vancouver Stock Exchange symbol*]
GLK............ Great Lakes Chemical [*NYSE symbol*] (TTSB)
GLK............ Great Lakes Chemical Corp. [*NYSE symbol*] (SPSG)
GLL............ Galileo [*NASA*]
GLL............ Gay and Lesbian Literature
GLL............ General Leaholds Limited (SAUS)
GLL............ General Leaseholds Ltd. [*Toronto Stock Exchange symbol*]
GLL............ Gilgames and the Land of the Living (BJA)
GLL............ Gill (SAUS)
GLL............ Gill, CO [*Location identifier*] [*FAA*] (FAAL)
Gll............ Glass Industry (journ.) (SAUS)
GLL............ Great Lakes Laboratory [*State University College at Buffalo*] [*Research center*] (RCD)
GLL............ Laidlaw Global [*AMEX symbol*]
GLL............ McGill University Library [*UTLAS symbol*]
Glla........... Guerilla (SAUS)
GLLB........... Buchanan [*Liberia*] [*ICAO location identifier*] (ICLI)
GLLD........... Ground Laser Location Designator (SAUS)
GLLD........... Ground Laser Locator Designator (SAUO)
GLLD........... Ground-LASER Locator Designator (MCD)
GLLD-E........ Ground-LASER Locator Designator-Evaluator (MCD)
GLLD-TNS.... Ground-LASER Locator Designator-Thermal Night Sight (MCD)
GLLD-VLLD... Ground Laser Locator Designator-Vehicular Laser Locator Designator (SAUS)
GLLD/VLLD... Ground-LASER Locator Designator/Vehicular LASER Locator Designator (MCD)
GLLKA......... Great Lakes Lighthouse Keepers Association (EA)
GLLM........... Gerrnan Language and Literature Monographs (journ.) (SAUS)
GLLO........... Great Lakes Licensed Officers' Organization
GLLRY......... Gallery
glm............ Gallons per Minute [*Medicine*] (EDAA)
GLM............ Gay Liberation Movement (SAUO)
GLM............ Generalized Lagrange Multipliers (SAUS)
GLM............ Generalized Lagrangian Multiplier [*Military*] (AFIT)
GLM............ Generalized Langrangian Multiplier (SAUS)
GLM............ Generalized Linear Model [*Statistics*]
GLM............ Generalized Linear Models [*Computer science*] (EERA)
GLM............ Generalized Markup Language (SAUS)
GLM............ General Linear Model (ACAE)
GLM............ General Linear Models (VLIE)
GLM............ Genetic Linkage Map [*Medicine*] (MELL)
GLM............ Gigabit Link Module [*Computer science*]
GLM............ Gilmore [*Alaska*] [*Also, GLN*] [*Seismograph station code, US Geological Survey*] (SEIS)
GLM............ Gimbal Latch Mechanism (SAUS)
GLM............ Global Marine [*NYSE symbol*] (TTSB)
GLM............ Global Marine, Inc. [*NYSE symbol*] (SPSG)
GLM............ Gold Life-Saving Medal [*Military decoration*] (GFGA)
GLM............ Government-Loaned Material
GLM............ Graduated Learning Method (SAUS)
GLM............ Graduated Length Method [*of learning to ski*] [*Later, Accelerated Length Method*]
GLM............ Grand Livre du Mois [*Best-selling book of the month*] [*French*]
GLM............ Graphics Lathe Module [*McDonnell-Douglas Automation Co.*]
GLM............ Great Lakes Megalopolis [*Proposed name for possible "super-city" formed by growth and mergers of other cities*]
GLM............ Growth-Limiting Medium [*For microorganisms*]
GLM............ McGill University, Medical Library [*UTLAS symbol*]
GLMA.......... Gay and Lesbian Medical Association (SAUO)
GLMA.......... Glassmaster Co. [*NASDAQ symbol*] (SAG)
GLMA.......... Great Lakes Mink Association (EA)
GLMC.......... Gay and Lesbian Media Coalition (EA)
GLMC.......... Monrovia City [*Liberia*] [*ICAO location identifier*] (ICLI)
GLMI........... Great Lakes Maritime Institute (EA)

GlMkt Global Market Information, Inc. [*Associated Press*] (SAG)
GLML Great Lakes Maritime Institute (SAUS)
GLMMM Grand Lodge of Mark Master Masons [*Freemasonry*]
GLMMS Groupement Latin et Mediterraneen de Medecine du Sport [*Latin and Mediterranean Group for Sport Medicine - LMGSM*] (EAIO)
GLMR Monrovia/Spriggs Payne [*Liberia*] [*ICAO location identifier*] (ICLI)
GLMRB Great and Little Miami River Basins (SAUS)
GlmRS Glutaminyl-RNA Synthetase [*An enzyme*]
GLMV Ground Launched Miniature Vehicle (ACAE)
GLMWC Great Lakes and Marine Waters Center [*University of Michigan*] [*Research center*] (RCD)
Glmy [*The*] Glenmary Home Missioners (TOCD)
glmy [*The*] Glenmary Home Missioners (TOCD)
GLMZ Glenmore [*Federal Railroad Administration identification code*]
GLN Gastric Lymph Node [*Medicine*] (MELL)
GLN Gilmore [*Alaska*] [*Also, GLM*] [*Seismograph station code, US Geological Survey*] (SEIS)
GLN Glen
GLN Glenayre Electronics Ltd. [*Toronto Stock Exchange symbol*]
GLN Glendale Federal Bank [*NYSE symbol*] (SPSG)
GLN Glenfed, Inc. (SAUO)
GLN Glidden Company (SAUO)
Gln Glucagon [*Medicine*] (DMAA)
Gln Glutamine [*or Glu(NH_2)*] [*Also, Q*] [*An amino acid*]
Gln Glutaminyl (SAUS)
GLN Great Lakes National Program Office (SAUS)
GLN Group Level Number (SAUO)
GLN Lennox Airways, Gambia Ltd. [*ICAO designator*] (FAAC)
GLNA Nimba [*Liberia*] [*ICAO location identifier*] (ICLI)
GLNH Giant Lymph Node Hyperplasia [*Medicine*] (DMAA)
GLNMR Glenmore Distilleries Co. (SAUO)
GLNPO Great Lakes National Program Office [*Environmental Protection Agency*]
GLNPrE Glendale Fed Bk Cv'E'Prd [*NYSE symbol*] (TTSB)
GlnRS Glutamine-Transfer Ribonucleic Acid Synthetase
GLNS Glens [*Postal Service standard*] (OPSA)
GLNSW Gould League of New South Wales [*Australia*]
GLNTC Great Lakes Naval Training Center
GLO Cheltenham-Gloucester [*England*] [*Airport symbol*] (AD)
GLO Clovis, NM [*Location identifier*] [*FAA*] (FAAL)
GLO General Land Office [*Became part of Bureau of Land Management, 1946*]
GLO Get the Lead Out [*Of GLO week, sponsored by American Oil Co.*]
GLO Gland Leak-Off (SAUS)
Glo Global
GLO Global Ocean Carriers [*AMEX symbol*] (TTSB)
GLO Global Ocean Carriers Ltd. [*AMEX symbol*] (CTT)
GLO Gloria [*Kyrgyzstan*] [*FAA designator*] (FAAC)
glo Gloss (VRA)
GLO Gloucester [*Massachusetts*] [*Seismograph station code, US Geological Survey*] (SEIS)
GLO Gloucester [*British depot code*]
Glo Glyoxalase (DB)
GLO Glyoxalase [*An enzyme*]
GLO Goddard Launch Operations [*NASA*]
GLO Gospel literature Outreach [*Australia*]
GLO Gottdard Launch Operations (SAUS)
G LO Grand Lodge [*Freemasonry*] (ROG)
GLO Great Lakes Only (SAUS)
GLO Greens in Lowe [*Political party*] [*Australia*]
GLO Ground Liaison Officer [*Military*]
GLO Ground Logistics Operations [*NASA*] (KSC)
GLO Guaiacol-Linoleic Acid Hydroperoxide Oxidoreductase [*An enzyme*]
GLO Gun Launched Orbiter (ACAE)
GLO Gunnery Liaison Officer [*Navy*]
GLO GVN [*Government of Vietnam*] Liaison Officer
GLO GVN Liason Officer (SAUS)
GLO L-Gulanolactone Oxidase [*An enzyme*]
GLO Ultra Glow Cosmetics [*Vancouver Stock Exchange symbol*]
GLO2T Ground Liquid-Oxygen Tank (SAUS)
GLOAD General Loader (SAUS)
Gloag & Henderson Gloag and Henderson's Introduction to the Law of Scotland [*7th ed.*] [*1968*] [*A publication*] (DLA)
GLOAS German Liaison Office for the Armament Sector [*Military*]
GLOB Glare Obstructor (ACAE)
GLOB Globular
Glob Globulin [*Therapy term*] (CTAA)
GLOB Globulin
GLOB Guidance and Launch Operation Building (SAUS)
Global Anal Pure Appl Adv Global Analysis Pure and Applied. Advanced (journ.) (SAUS)
Global ATmos Ocean Syst Global Atmosphere and Ocean System [*A publication*] (PABS)
Global Atmos Res Programme Pub Global Atmospheric (SAUS)
Global Atmos Res Programme Publ Ser Global Atmospheric Research Programme. Publications Series (journ.) (SAUS)
Global Biodivers Global Biodiversity [*A publication*] (PABS)
Global Bus Econ Rev Global Business and Economics Review [*A publication*] (JLIT)
Global Change Biol Global Change Biology [*A publication*] (PABS)
Global Commun Global Communications (journ.) (SAUS)
Global Econ Rev Global Economic Review [*A publication*] (JLIT)
Global Environ Change Global Environmental Change [*A publication*] (PABS)
Global Environ Polit Global Environmental Politics [*A publication*] (PABS)
Global Finance J Global Finance Journal [*A publication*] (JLIT)
Global One Global 2000. Report to the President. Volume I (SAUS)
Global One Global 2000. Report to the President. Volume I (journ.) (SAUS)
GlobalPh Global Pharmaceutical Corp. [*Associated Press*] (SAG)
Global Planet Change Global and Planetary Change [*A publication*] (PABS)
Globalstr Globalstar Telecommunications Ltd. [*Associated Press*] (SAG)
Global Two Global 2000. Report to the President. Volume 2 (journ.) (SAUS)
Glob Biogeochem Cycles Global Biogeochemical Cycles (SAUS)
GLOBE Gay, Lesbian, or Bisexual Employees [*An association*]
GLOBE Global Backscatter Experiment [*NASA/MSFC*]
GLOBE Global Land One kilometer (or One-kilometre) Base Elevation (SAUO)
GLOBE Global Learning and Observations to Benefit the Environment [*NASA*]
GLOBE Global Legislators Organization for a Balanced Environment [*International coalition*]
GLOBE Global Lending and Overseas Banking Evaluator [*Chase Econometrics*] [*Database*]
GLOBE Global Observations to Benefit the Environment (EERA)
GLOBEC Global Marine Ecosystem Dynamics Program
GLOBEC Global Ocean-Ecosystem Coupling (SAUS)
Globec Global Ocean Ecosystem Dynamics or Global Ocean-Ecosystem Coupling (USDC)
GLOBEC-INT International Global Ocean Ecosystem Dynamics Programme (SAUS)
Glob Ecol Biogeogr Lett Global Ecology and Biogeography Letters (SAUS)
GLOBECOM Global Communications System [*Air Force*]
GLOBE Europe Global Legislators Organization for a Balanced Environment (SAUO)
Globe Mail Rep Bus Globe Mail Ltd Globe and Mail Report on Business. Globe and Mail Limited (journ.) (SAUS)
GlobeSAR Globe SAR (SAUS)
GLOBEX Global Electronic Exchange (NUMA)
GlobHi Global High Income Dollar Fund [*Associated Press*] (SAG)
GlobIndl Global Industrial Technologies [*Associated Press*] (SAG)
GLOBIS Global Change and Biodiversity in Soils (SAUS)
GLOBIXS Global Information Exchange System (POLM)
GloblInd Global Industries Ltd. [*Associated Press*] (SAG)
Globlink Globalink, Inc. [*Associated Press*] (SAG)
GloblInt Global Intellicom, Inc. [*Associated Press*] (SAG)
Globlstr Globalstar Telecommunictions Ltd. [*Associated Press*] (SAG)
GlobM Global Marine, Inc. [*Associated Press*] (SAG)
GlobNR Global Natural Resources, Inc. [*Associated Press*] (SAG)
GlobOut Global Outdoors, Inc. [*Associated Press*] (SAG)
GlobPart Global Partners Income Fund [*Associated Press*] (SAG)
GlobSml Global Small Cap Fund, Inc. [*Associated Press*] (SAG)
GlobTele Global Telecommunications Solutions, Inc. [*Associated Press*] (SAG)
GlobTR Global Total Return Fund [*Associated Press*] (SAG)
GLOBUS Global Budget of the Stratosphere (SAUO)
G Loc Geographical Location (SAUS)
GLOC G - Induced Loss of Conscioness (SAUS)
G-LOC G-induced Loss Of Consciousness (SAUS)
G-LOC Gravity-Induced Loss of Consciousness [*Aviation*]
GLOCARB Global Tropospheric Carbon Dioxide Network (SAUO)
GLOCHANT Global Change and/in the Antarctic (SAUO)
GLOCHANT Global Change Research in the Antarctic (SAUS)
GLOCHANT Group of Specialists on Global Change and the Antarctic (SAUO)
GLOCHEM Global Atmospheric Chemical (or Chemistry) Survey (SAUO)
GLOCK Glockenspiel [*Music*]
glock Glockenspiel
GLOCOM Global Communications System [*Air Force*]
GLOCOM Symposium on Global Communications (SAUO)
GLOCOPH Global Continental Palaeohydrology Project (SAUO)
GLODIR Global Directory of Marine Scientists (SAUS)
GLODIS General Language-Operated Decision Implementation System (PDAA)
GLODISL General Language Operated Decision Implementation System Language (SAUS)
GLOE Gay and Lesbian Outreach to Elders (SAUO)
GloED Global Emissions Database (SAUO)
GLOL Goday Logic Language (SAUS)
GLOM Gross Lift-Off Mass [*NASA*] (KSC)
GLOMAC Global Modelling of Atmospheric Chemistry (SAUO)
GLOMAGS Global Magnetic Survey Satellite (ACAE)
GLOMAR Global Maximum Array Radar (ACAE)
GLOMB Glide Bomb [*Air Force*]
GLOMEX Global Meteorological Experiment (SAUS)
GLOMEX Global Oceanographic and Meteorological Experiment [*Marine science*] (MSC)
GloMo Global Mobile information systems (SAUS)
GLOMR Global Low-Orbiting Message Relay [*Astronomy term*]
GLONASS Global Navigation Satellite System [*Military*]
GLONET Global Ozone Observing System (SAUS)
GLONET Global Tropospheric Ozone Network (SAUO)
GLOOP Ground Launched Optical Observation Platform (SAUO)
GLOP Gevic Logic Operation Program
GLOP Guidance and Launch Operation [*Aerospace*] (IAA)
GLOPAC Gyroscopic Low-Power Attitude Control
GLOPC Gyroscopic Lower Power Control (IAA)
GLOPC Gyroscopic Low Power Controller (SAUS)
GLOPR Goday Logic Processor (SAUS)
GLOPR Golay Logic Processor (SAUS)
GLOPS Giga Logical Operations per Second (SAUS)
Gl Ord Glossa Ordinaria [*A publication*] (DSA)
GLORI Global And Local Radar Imager (SAUS)
GLORI Global Land-Ocean River Inputs database (SAUO)

GLORIA........ Geologic Long-Range Inclined Asdic system (SAUO)
GLORIA........ Global Observation Research Initiative in Alpine Environments (SAUO)
GLOS........... General Ledger Operating System (VLIE)
GLOS........... Glossary
Glos............ Gloucestershire (DIAR)
GLOS........... Gloucestershire [*County in England*]
GLOS........... Gun Line of Site [*Tank*] [*Army*]
GLOSIS........ General Language Operated Decision Implementation System (SAUS)
GLOSS......... Global Observation Surveillance System (SAUO)
GLOSS......... Global Ocean Surveillance System (IEEE)
GLOSS......... Global Ocean Surveillance System Glossary (SAUS)
GLOSS......... Global Sea Level Observing System [*Marine science*] (OSRA)
gloss........... Glossary (ELAL)
Gloss........... Glossary (SAUO)
GLOSS......... Glossary
Gloss........... Glossopharyngeal (SAUS)
Glossary Acarol Terminol... Glossary of Acarological Terminology (journ.) (SAUS)
Gloss Lat..... Glossaria Latina [*A publication*] (OCD)
GLOSS-LTT... Tide Gauges for Long Term Sea Level Trends (SAUS)
GLOSS-OC... Tide Gauges for Ocean Circulation Monitoring (SAUS)
GLOSTER..... Gloucester [*City in England*] (ROG)
GLOSTER H... Royal Gloucestershire Hussars (SAUO)
GLOTOS....... Graphical Representation of Language for Temporal Ordering Specification [*Telecommunications*] (OSI)
GLOTRAC..... Global Tracking [*RADAR*]
GLOUC......... Gloucester [*City in England*] (ROG)
GLOUC......... Gloucestershire [*County in England*] (ROG)
Gloucester... Gloucestershire [*County in England*] (BARN)
GLOUC R..... Gloucestershire Regiment [*Military*] [*British*] (ROG)
GLOUCS....... Gloucestershire [*County in England*]
GLOV........... Gays and Lesbians Opposing Violence [*An association*]
GLOVE......... Glover, IL [*American Association of Railroads railroad junction routing code*]
Glov Mun Cor... Glover's Municipal Corporations [*A publication*] (DLA)
GLOW.......... Giving and Learning Our Way [*An association*]
GLOW.......... Global RADAR for Ocean Waves
Glow............ Glow International (journ.) (SAUS)
GLOW.......... Greater Leadership Opportunity for Women (SAUO)
GLOW.......... Great Lakes of the World (SAUO)
GLOW.......... Gross Lift-Off Weight [*NASA*]
GLOW.......... Ground Lift-Off Weight [*NASA*] (NASA)
GLOWATS.... Global War Avoidance Telecommunications System (MCD)
GLOXAC....... Gloxinian (journ.) (SAUS)
GLP.............. Gallup [*Diocesan abbreviation*] [*New Mexico*] (TOCD)
GLP.............. Gambro Liendia Plate [*Medicine*] (EDAA)
GLP.............. Gelled Liquid Propellant
GLP.............. Generalized Lattice-Point
GLP.............. General Layout Plan (NATG)
GLP.............. General Letter Package (PDAA)
glp............... general letter packet (SAUS)
GLP.............. General Linguistic Processor (SAUS)
GLP.............. Gibraltar Labour Party (SAUS)
GLP.............. Glucagon-Like Peptide [*Biochemistry*]
GLP.............. Glucose L-Phosphate (DB)
GLP.............. Glycolipoprotein (DMAA)
GLP.............. GOAL Language (SAUS)
GLP.............. GOAL [*Ground Operations Aerospace Language*] Language Processor (MCD)
GLP.............. Golden Princess [*Vancouver Stock Exchange symbol*]
GLP.............. Golpazari [*Turkey*] [*Also, GPA*] [*Seismograph station code, US Geological Survey*] (SEIS)
GLP.............. Good Laboratory Practice [*FDA*]
GLP.............. Gospel Light Publications [*British*]
GLP.............. Gould Investors Ltd. (SAUO)
GLP.............. Government-Lent Property (NG)
GLP.............. Government Loaned Property (SAUO)
GLP.............. Gradient Linear Prediction (SAUS)
GLP.............. Graphic Language Processor (VLIE)
GLP.............. Greek Literary Papyri [*A publication*] (OCD)
GLP.............. Gross Lawyer Product [*Term for measurement of the income of attorneys*]
GLP.............. Group-Living Program (DAVI)
GLP.............. Guadeloupe [*ANSI three-letter standard code*] (CNC)
GLP.............. Guide Line Paper [*of Washington Standardization Officers*] [*Military*]
GLP.............. Gurgura Liberation Front (SAUS)
GLP.............. Guyana Labour Party [*Political party*] (EY)
GLPA............ Gay and Lesbian Press Association (EA)
GLPA............ Great Lakes Pilotage Administration [*Department of Transportation*]
GLP-AACR... Gibraltar Labour Party - Association for the Advancement of Civil Rights [*Political party*] (PPW)
GLPC............ Gas-Liquid Partition Chromatography
GLPC............ Gas-Liquid Phase Chromatography [*Medicine*] (RAWO)
GLPC............ Global Pharmaceutical Corp. [*NASDAQ symbol*] (SAG)
GLPCI.......... Gay and Lesbian Parents Coalition International (EA)
GLPF............ Great Lakes Protection Fund (SAUS)
GLPG............ Glow Plug
GLPIAC........ Great Lakes Physical Information Analysis Center
GLP Method... Gradient Linear Prediction Method (SAUS)
GLPO............ Good Laboratory Practice Office (SAUS)
GLPP............ Glucose, Post Prandial [*Clinical chemistry*]
GLPPS.......... Graphical Lathe Part Programming System (VLIE)
GLPR............ Goldstone Predict [*Orbit identification*] [*NASA*]
GLPS............ Gun Laying & Positioning System (SAUS)
GL-PTC........ Gas Liquid Phase Transfer Catalysis [*Physical chemistry*]
GLPU............ Gasline Planning Update. Northwest Alaska Pipeline Company. Manpower and Impact Planning Department (SAUO)
GLPU............ Gasline Planning Update. Northwest Alaska Pipeline Company. Manpower and Impact Planning Department (journ.) (SAUS)
GLPZ............ Golden Pump [*Federal Railroad Administration identification code*]
GLQ.............. Golden Adit Resources [*Vancouver Stock Exchange symbol*]
GLQ.............. Greater-than-Lot Quantities
GLR.............. Central Mountain Air Ltd. [*Canada*] [*ICAO designator*] (FAAC)
GLR.............. G & L Realty Corp. [*NYSE symbol*] (SPSG)
GLR.............. Gas / Liquid Ratio (SAUS)
GLR.............. Gaylord (SAUS)
GLR.............. Gaylord, MI [*Location identifier*] [*FAA*] (FAAL)
GLR.............. Gazette Law Reports [*New Zealand*] [*A publication*] (DLA)
G L R........... Generalized Likelihood Ratio (SAUS)
GLR.............. General Line Rate [*Advertising*]
GLR.............. Gladiator Resources Ltd. [*Vancouver Stock Exchange symbol*]
glr................ glare (SAUS)
GLR.............. Glass LASER Rod
GLR.............. Golden Lion Resources Ltd. (SAUS)
GLR.............. Government Land Register [*of Western Australia*] [*State*] (EERA)
GLR.............. Graphic Level Recorder
GLR.............. Greater London Radio (WDAA)
GLR.............. Great Lakes Rules [*Boating*] (DICI)
GLR.............. Grolier, Inc. (SAUO)
GLR.............. Groom Lake Road [*Nevada*] [*Seismograph station code, US Geological Survey*] (SEIS)
GLR.............. Gujarat Law Reporter (journ.) (SAUS)
GLR.............. Gwalior Light Railway [*Indian Railway*] (TIR)
GLR.............. McGill University Rare Books [*UTLAS symbol*]
GLRA............ Gun-Launched/Rocket-Assisted (MCD)
GL RADAR... Gun Laying RADAR
GLRAFN....... German Logistic Representative AFNORTH Area (SAUO)
GLR-AV........ Grapevine Leafroll-Associated Virus [*Plant pathology*]
GLRB............ Monrovia/Roberts International [*Liberia*] [*ICAO location identifier*] (ICLI)
GLRBAT....... Great Britain. Land Resources Division. Land Resourcé (SAUS)
GLRBAT....... Great Britain. Land Resources Division. Land Resource Bibliography (journ.) (SAUS)
GLRC............ Gas-Liquid Radiochromatography [*Analytical chemistry*]
GLRC............ Geneva Lake Radio Club (SAUO)
GLRC............ Grain Legumes Research Council [*Australia*]
GLRC............ Great Lakes Regional Conference
GLRC............ Great Lakes Research Center (SAUO)
GLRD............ Great Lakes Research Division (SAUO)
GLRE............ Geniki Laiki Rizospastiki Enosis [*General Union of Populists and Radicals*] [*Greek*] (PPE)
GLRev.......... Great Lakes Review (journ.) (SAUS)
GLR (NZ)..... Gazette Law Reports [*New Zealand*] [*A publication*] (DLA)
GLRS............ Geodynamics LASER Ranging System [*NASA*]
GLRS............ Georgia Learning Resources System (SAUO)
GLRS............ Geoscience Laser Ranging System (ACAE)
GLRS............ Global Outdoors, Inc. [*NASDAQ symbol*] (SAG)
GLRS............ Global Res [*NASDAQ symbol*] (TTSB)
GLRS............ Global Resources, Inc. [*NASDAQ symbol*] (SAG)
GLRS-A........ Geoscience Laser Ranging System-Altimeter (EOSA)
GLRSAC....... Great Britain. Land Resources Development Centre. Land Resource Study (journ.) (SAUS)
GLRSHLD.... Glare Shield (MCD)
GLRS-R........ Geoscience Laser Ranging System-Ranger (EOSA)
GLS.............. Freemasonry Grand Lodge of Scotland (SAUS)
GLS.............. Galveston [*Texas*] [*Airport symbol*] (OAG)
GLS.............. Gaylord Circulation Control System [*Information service or system*] (IID)
GLS.............. Generalized Least Squares [*Statistics*]
GLS.............. Generalized Logic Simulator (VLIE)
GLS.............. Generalized Lymphadenopathy Syndrome [*Medicine*] (DMAA)
GLS.............. General Ledger System [*Accounting*] (IAA)
GLS.............. General License Symbol Corps (JAGO)
GLS.............. General Lighting Service
GLS.............. General Lighting System [*Incadescent lighting*]
GLS.............. General Line School
GLS.............. Geological Society of London (SAUO)
GLS.............. Georgetown Law School (SAUO)
GLS.............. Geotechnical Logging Society (SAUO)
GLS.............. Giles [*Australia*] [*Seismograph station code, US Geological Survey*] (SEIS)
Gls............... Glasgow (SAUS)
gls............... Glass (VRA)
GLS.............. Glass
GLS.............. Glide Slope [*Aviation*] (MSA)
GLS.............. Global International Ltd. [*Bulgaria*] [*ICAO designator*] (FAAC)
GLS.............. GlobalLearningSystems
GLS.............. Global Leasing Services (SAUO)
GLS.............. Global Logistics System (SAUS)
GLS.............. Golden Shield Resources Ltd. [*Toronto Stock Exchange symbol*] [*Vancouver Stock Exchange symbol*]
GLS.............. GOMR Limb Sounder (SAUS)
GLS.............. Government Launch Service (SSD)
GLS.............. GPS Landing System (SAUO)
GLS.............. Graduate Library School
GLS.............. Grand Lodge of Scotland [*Freemasonry*]
GLS.............. Grand Lodge of Scottland (SAUO)
GLS.............. Great Lakes Screw
GLS.............. Greene Line Steamers (SAUO)

GLS .... Green LASER System
GLS .... Ground Launch Sequence [*or Sequencer*] (NASA)
GLS .... Gypsy Lore Society (SAUO)
GLS .... Gypsy Lore Society, North American Chapter (EA)
GLS .... Gyro-stabilized Landing System (SAUS)
GLS .... Schuller Corp. [*NYSE symbol*] [*Formerly, Manville Corp.*] (SG)
GLSA .... General Ledger Subsidiary Account (AFM)
GLSA .... General Livestock Agent
GLSA .... Government Large Structures Assembly (SSD)
GLSA .... Gray Line Sightseeing Association [*Commercial firm*] (EA)
GLSA .... Great Lakes Seaplane Association [*Defunct*] (EA)
GLSBG .... Great Lakes Sugar Beet Growers (EA)
GLS(C) .... Government Launch Service (Cryogenic) (SSD)
GLSDB .... Global Lake Status Data Base (SAUO)
G L S E .... Generalized Least Squares Estimation (SAUS)
GLSE .... Generalized Weighted Least Squares Estimates [*Statistics*]
GLSECT .... Ground Liaison Section [*Military*] [*British*]
GLSEN .... Gay, Lesbian and Straight Educational Network
GLSEN .... Gay, Lesbian, and Straight Education Network
GLSFC .... Great Lakes Sport Fishing Council (EA)
GLSG .... Great Lakes Study Group (SAUO)
GLSGW .... Glasgow [*Scotland*]
GLSJ .... Global Legal Studies Journal (SAUO)
GLSK .... Sanniquellie [*Liberia*] [*ICAO location identifier*] (ICLI)
GLS Lamp ... General Lighting Service Lamp (SAUS)
GLSLB .... Great Lakes-St. Lawrence Basin (QUAC)
GLSLB .... Great Lakes-St. Lawrence Basin project (SAUO)
GLSM .... Gold Life Saving Medal [*Military decoration*]
GLSMT .... German Logistic Support Management Team (SAUO)
glsn .... Glassine (VRA)
GLSO .... Group Legal Services Organization
GLSOA .... Great Lakes Ship Owners Association (EA)
GLSP .... Good Large Scale Practice
GLSPI .... Great Lakes Spill Protection Institute
GLSR .... Gloster Southern Railroad [*Federal Railroad Administration identification code*]
GLSS .... Great Lakes Seaway System (SAUO)
GLSS .... Ground-Launch Support System (MCD)
Glss Ind .... Glass Industry (journ.) (SAUS)
GLST .... Sasstown [*Liberia*] [*ICAO location identifier*] (ICLI)
GLSTM .... Graduate of the London School of Tropical Medicine (DAS)
Glstnbry .... Glastonbury Bank & Trust Co. [*Associated Press*] (SAG)
GLSX .... Glacier State Distribution Services [*Private rail car owner code*]
GLSZ .... Global Stone [*Federal Railroad Administration identification code*]
GLT .... Gas LASER Tube
GLT .... Gauss-Languerre Technique (SAUS)
GLT .... General Corporation for Light Air Transport & Technical Sevices [*Libya*] [*ICAO designator*] (FAAC)
GLT .... General Labor and Trades
glt .... Gilding (VRA)
GLT .... Gilt [*Bookbinding*] (ROG)
glt .... Gilt (VRA)
GLT .... Gladstone [*Australia*] [*Airport symbol*] (OAG)
GLT .... Glass Lined Tubing
GLT .... Glatfelter [*P. H.*] Co. [*AMEX symbol*] (SPSG)
GLT .... Gloss Low Tack [*Ink*] (DGA)
GLT .... Golden Lion Tamarin [*South American monkey*]
GLT .... Greeting Letter Telegram (ADA)
GLT .... Gridded Line of Thrust (MCD)
GLT .... Ground-LASER Tracking
GLT .... Guide Light (AAG)
GL(T) .... Gun-Laying (Turret) (DEN)
GLTB .... Goleta National Bank [*NASDAQ symbol*] (SAG)
GLTB .... Greater London Training Board [*British*] (AIE)
GLTM .... Goddard Laser Tracking Network (SAUO)
GLTMC .... Golden Lion Tamarin Management Committee (EA)
GITN .... Glomerulo-Tubulo-Nephritis [*Medicine*]
GLTN .... Guillotine (MSA)
GLTN .... Tchien [*Liberia*] [*ICAO location identifier*] (ICLI)
GLTR .... Ground Launched Tacit Rainbow (SAUS)
GltS .... Glutamate Synthetase (SAUS)
GLTS .... Gun-Launch to Space
GLTT .... Glucose-Lactase Tolerance Test [*Medicine*] (MELL)
GL Tube .... Glass-type Loctal Tube (SAUS)
GLTX .... Geldtex, Inc. (SAUS)
GLTX .... Goldtex, Inc. (SAUO)
GLU .... Gambia Labour Union
GLU .... General Logic Unit [*Computer chip*]
GLU .... Global Land Use [*NASA*]
GLU .... Glucose [*Organic chemistry*] (DAVI)
GLU .... Glucuronidase (DB)
GLU .... Gluing (VLIE)
glu .... Glutamate [*An amino acid*] (DOG)
glu .... Glutamic Acid [*An amino acid*] (DOG)
Glu .... Glutamic Acid [*Also, E, GA*] [*An amino acid*]
Glu .... Glutamine [*An amino acid*] (DAVI)
Glu .... Glutamyl (SAUS)
GLU .... GL Utility Library (SAUS)
GLU .... GPS Landing Unit (SAUO)
GLU .... Great Lakes United (EA)
GLU .... Green Lake Resources Ltd. [*Vancouver Stock Exchange symbol*]
GLU .... Green Lay-Up (VLIE)
GLU .... Ground Laser Unit (SAUS)
GLU .... Gruene Liste Umweltschutz [*Green List Ecology*] [*Germany*] (PPE)
GLU .... Guyana Labour Union (SAUO)
GLU-5 .... Five-Hour Glucose Tolerance Test [*Medicine*] (DMAA)
GLUC .... Gluconate (SAUS)
GLUC .... Glucose [*Also, G, Glc*] [*A sugar*]
GLUC .... Glucosidase (DMAA)
GLUC .... Green Lay-Up Composites (VLIE)
GLUCEPTATE... Glucoheptonate [*USAN*] [*Organic chemistry*]
GLUC-S .... Urin Glucose Spot [*Test*] [*Endocrinology*] (DAVI)
Glucur .... Glucuronide [*Biochemistry*] (AAMN)
GluDG .... Glutamate Dehydrogenase
GLUE .... Global User Environment (SAUO)
GLUK .... GlasNet-Ukraine (SAUS)
GLULAM .... Glued Laminated Wood (PDAA)
GluN .... Glutamine [*An amino acid*] (BARN)
Glu(NH_2) .... Glutamine [*or Gln*] [*Also, Q*] [*An amino acid*]
glu ox .... Glucose Oxidase [*Also, GO, GOD*] [*An enzyme*] (AAMN)
GluR .... Glutamate Receptor [*Biochemistry*]
GLUT .... Glucose Transporter [*Biochemistry*]
GLUT .... GL Utility library Toolkit (SAUS)
GLUTAM .... Glutamine [*An amino acid*] (DAVI)
glutes .... Gluteus Muscles (ADWA)
GLUX .... Great Lakes Aviation [*NASDAQ symbol*] (TTSB)
GLUX .... Great Lakes Aviation Ltd. [*NASDAQ symbol*] (SAG)
GLV .... Gemini Launch Vehicle [*NASA*]
GLV .... Gibbon Ape Leukemia Virus (DMAA)
glv .... Globe Value (SAUS)
GLV .... Globe Valve (AAG)
GLV .... Glove
GLV .... Gloves (SAUS)
GLV .... Glove Valve (SAUS)
GLV .... Golden Vale Explorations Corp. [*Vancouver Stock Exchange symbol*]
GLV .... Golovin [*Alaska*] [*Airport symbol*] (OAG)
GLV .... Gould League of Victoria [*Australia*]
GLV .... Gross Leukemia Virus
GLVA .... Voinjama [*Liberia*] [*ICAO location identifier*] (ICLI)
GLVBF .... Galveston Resources Ltd. (Class B) [*NASDAQ symbol*] (COMM)
GLVC .... Great Lakes Valley Conference (PSS)
GLVNZNG .... Galvanizing
GLVS .... Galveston Resources Ltd. (SAUO)
GLVS .... Galveston Resourcss Ltd. (SAUO)
GLW .... Corning Delaware LP [*NYSE symbol*] (SAG)
GLW .... Corning Glass Works (SAUO)
GLW .... Corning, Inc. [*Wall Street slang name: "Glow Worm"*] [*NYSE symbol*] (SPSG)
GLW .... Glasgow (SAUS)
GLW .... Glasgow, KY [*Location identifier*] [*FAA*] (FAAL)
GLW .... Gross Laden Weight (HEAS)
GLW .... Gunnery Lieutenant's Writer [*British military*] (DMA)
GLWB .... Glazed Wallboard [*Technical drawings*]
GLWCAP .... Great Lakes Wetlands Conservation Action Plan [*Canada*]
GLWDA .... Great Lakes Waterways Development Association (EA)
GLWDS .... Glenwood Junction, MN [*American Association of Railroads railroad junction routing code*]
GLWPrM .... Corning Del L.P. 6% 'MIPS' [*NYSE symbol*] (TTSB)
GLWQA .... Great Lakes Water Quality Agreement [*Environmental Protection Agency*]
GLWQB .... Great Lakes Water Quality Board (SAUO)
GLWR .... Glassware
GLX .... Galela [*Indonesia*] [*Airport symbol*] (OAG)
Glx .... Giutamic Acid (SAUS)
GLX .... Glaxo Holdings PLC (SAUS)
GLX .... Glaxo Ltd. ADR [*Formerly, Glaxo Holdilngs Ltd. ADR*] [*NYSE symbol*] (SPSG)
GLX .... Glaxo Wellcome plc ADR [*NYSE symbol*] (TTSB)
Glx .... Glutamic Acid [*or Glutamine*] [*Also, Z*] [*An amino acid*]
Glx .... Glutamine (SAUS)
GLX .... Goldex Mines Ltd. [*Toronto Stock Exchange symbol*]
GLX .... McGill University (SAUO)
GLX .... McGill University RECON [*UTLAS symbol*]
GLXI .... Glenex Industries, Inc. (SAUO)
GLXIF .... Glenex Industries, Inc. [*NASDAQ symbol*] (COMM)
GLXW .... GalaxiWorld.com [*NASDAQ symbol*] (SG)
GLXW .... GLC, Ltd. [*NASDAQ symbol*] (NASQ)
GlxyFd .... Galaxy Foods Co. [*Associated Press*] (SAG)
GLY .... Clinton, MO [*Location identifier*] [*FAA*] (FAAL)
GLY .... Galaxy Minerals, Inc. [*Toronto Stock Exchange symbol*]
GLY .... Glossary (SAUS)
GLY .... Glycerite (STED)
Gly .... Glycerol [*Organic chemistry*] (DAVI)
GLY .... Glycerol (STED)
GLY .... Glycin (SAUS)
gly .... Glycinate [*Organic chemistry*]
gly .... Glycine [*An amino acid*] (DOG)
Gly .... Glycine [*Also, G*] [*An amino acid*]
GLY .... Glycocoll (DB)
GLY .... Glycogen (SAUS)
GLY .... Glycol (KSC)
GLY .... Glycyl (STED)
gly .... Glyph (VRA)
GLY .... Glysin (SAUS)
Gly .... Gulley (SAUS)
GLY .... Gully (ADA)
GLY .... Water-Glycol Mixture (SAUS)
glyc .... Glyceritum [*Glycerite*] (MAE)
GLYC .... Glycomed, Inc. (SAUO)
GLYCEROPH... Glycerophophas [*Pharmacy*] (ROG)

Glyc in W .... Glycerin in Water [*Medicine*] (DHSM)
GLYCN .... Glycerine
GLYCOS Hb... Glycosylated Hemoglobin (STED)
GLYC-POS .... Glycerine Suppositories (SAUS)
GLYCYRRH... Glycyrrhiza [*Licorice*] [*Pharmacology*] (ROG)
Gly-IPC .... Glycinergic Interplexiform Cell [*Physiology*]
GLYME......... Ethylene Glycol Dimethyl Ether [*Also, DME,EGDE*] [*Organic chemistry*]
Glyn & J...... Glyn and Jameson's English Bankruptcy Reports [*1821-28*] [*A publication*] (DLA)
Glyn & Jam... Glyn and Jameson's English Bankruptcy Reports [*1821-28*] [*A publication*] (DLA)
Glyn & J (Eng)... Glyn and Jameson's English Bankruptcy Reports [*1821-28*] [*A publication*] (DLA)
Glynn Wat Pow... Glynn on Water Powers [*A publication*] (DLA)
GLYP .... Glyphography (SAUS)
GLYP .... Glyptics (SAUS)
GLYP .... Glyptography (SAUS)
Glyph Jon H... Glyph. Johns Hopkins Textual Studies (journ.) (SAUS)
glypto .... Glypototheca (VRA)
GlyR............. Glycine Receptor [*Organic chemistry*]
GLYRRH ...... Glycyrrhiza (SAUS)
GLYT............ Genlyte Group, Inc. [*NASDAQ symbol*] (NQ)
GLZ.............. General Bronze Corporation (SAUS)
GLZ.............. Glaze (MSA)
glz............... Glaze (VRA)
glz............... Glazed (VRA)
GLZ.............. Great Lakes Group, Inc. [*Toronto Stock Exchange symbol*]
GLZ.............. Window Glazing
GLZD .... Glazed
GM............... Air America [*ICAO designator*] (AD)
GM............... Gabexate Mesilate [*A proteolytic enzyme inhibitor*]
GM............... Gainesville Midland Railroad Co. [*AAR code*]
G/M.............. Gallons per Minute
GM............... Galvanometer (SAUS)
GM............... Gambia [*ANSI two-letter standard code*] (CNC)
gm .... Gambia [*MARC country of publication code*] [*Library of Congress*] (LCCP)
GM............... Game Master (SAUS)
GM............... Gamma [*Third letter of the Greek alphabet*] (DAVI)
gm .... Gamma [*Medicine*] (EDAA)
Gm............... Gamma [*Subgroup of IgG*] [*Immunology*]
GM............... Gamma-Metrics (SAUO)
GM............... Gaseous Mixture (MSA)
GM............... Gas Meter
GM............... Gastric Mucosa [*Medicine*]
GM............... Gated Memory (IAA)
GM............... Gay Male [*Classified advertising*]
GM............... Gay Mate (SAUS)
GM............... Geiger-Meuller (SAUS)
G-M .... Geiger-Mueller [*Radiation counter*]
GM............... Generalized Myotonia [*Medicine*]
GM............... General Macroassembly (SAUS)
GM............... General Maintenance [*Army*]
GM............... General Maintenance Aptitude Area [*Military*] (AFIT)
GM............... General Manager
GM............... General Medical (MAE)
GM............... General Medicine
GM............... General Meetings [*Quakers*]
GM............... General Memorandum (FOTI)
GM............... General Memory (SAUS)
GM............... General Merchandise
GM............... General Merit [*Military*]
GM............... General Message (SAUS)
GM............... General MIDI [*Musical Instrument Digital Interface*] (CDE)
GM............... General Mortgage [*Bond*]
GM............... General Motors (SAUS)
GM............... General Motors Corp. [*NYSE symbol*] [*Toronto Stock Exchange symbol*] (SPSG)
GM............... Genetically Modified [*Medicine*] (WDAA)
GM............... Genetic Manipulation [*Medicine*] (DB)
GM............... Genl Motors [*NYSE symbol*] (TTSB)
GM............... Gentamicin [*Antibacterial compound*]
GM............... Gentil Membre [*Guest of Club Mediterranee, a vacation cooperative*]
GM............... Geographical Mazine (journ.) (SAUS)
GM............... Geography and Map (SAUO)
GM............... Geological Magazine (SAUO)
GM............... Geological Museum of Great Britain (SAUO)
GM............... Geologic Map (SAUO)
GM............... Geomagnetic (SAUS)
GM............... Geometric Mean
GM............... Geometric Scan (SAUS)
GM............... Geomorphology (SAUS)
GM............... George Medal [*British*]
GM............... Geriatric Medicine (MELL)
GM............... German Measles (MELL)
GM............... Giant Melanoma [*Oncology*]
GM............... Giant Melanosome (STED)
gm .... Gigameter
GM............... Gilford-Hutchinson [*Disease*] [*Medicine*] (DB)
GM............... Gill-Morrell [*Valve oscillator*] (DEN)
GM............... glaciomarine (SAUS)
GM............... Glass Mat [*Composites*]
GM............... Glass Metal (IAA)
GM............... Global Directmail Corp. [*NYSE symbol*] (SAG)
GM............... Global Marketplace
GM............... Global Memory (SAUS)
GM............... Global Mode (ACAE)
GM............... Global Model (SAUS)
GM............... Gluteus Medius [*Anatomy*]
GM............... Gold Medal
GM............... Gold Medallist (DAS)
GM............... Golf Course Operations and Management Programs [*Association of Independent Colleges and Schools specialization code*]
GM............... Good Mason [*Freemasonry*] (ROG)
GM............... Good Middling (SAUS)
GM............... Good Morning [*Amateur radio*]
GM............... Gopher Music Notes (journ.) (SAUS)
GM............... Grade Marked [*Construction term*] (MIST)
GM............... Gradient Mixer [*Chromatography*]
GM............... Grail Movement (EA)
Gm............... Gram (AMHC)
gm .... Gram (IDOE)
GM............... Gram
g-m.............. Gram-Meter (MAE)
GM............... Gramophone Motor (DEN)
Gm% .... Gram Percent [*Grams per deciliter*] [*Measurement*] (DAVI)
GM............... Grand Mal [*Epilepsy*]
GM............... Grand Marshal [*Freemasonry*] (ROG)
GM............... Grand Marshall (SAUO)
GM............... Grand Master [*Freemasonry*]
GM............... Grand Master Education (SAUS)
GM............... Grand Medal [*Ghana*]
GM............... Grand Minister [*Freemasonry*] (ROG)
gm .... Grandmother (GEAB)
GM............... Grandmother
GM............... Grand Multiparity [*Obstetrics*]
GM............... Grant Maintained (WDAA)
gm .... Grant Metre (SAUS)
GM............... Granulocyte-Macrophage (STED)
G/M.............. Granulocyte/Macrophage [*Ratio*] [*Hematology*]
GM............... Granulocyte Monocyte (STED)
GM............... Graphic Machine (ELAL)
GM............... Graphics Module (SAUS)
GM............... Grateful Med (SAUO)
GM............... Gravimetry (SAUS)
GM............... Gravitational Mass
GM............... Gravity Meter (SAUS)
GM............... Greater Manchester [*County in England*]
GM............... Great Musicians [*A publication*]
GM............... Great Musicians (journ.) (SAUS)
GM............... Greenland Environment Research Institute (SAUO)
GM............... Greenwich Meridian
GM............... Grid Modulation
G-M .... Grid-to-Magnetic Angle [*Navigation*] (INF)
GM............... Grog Money [*British military*] (DMA)
GM............... Gross Margin (SAUS)
GM............... Gross Motor
GM............... Ground Malfunction
GM............... Ground Mapping (ACAE)
GM............... Groundmass (SAUS)
GM............... Ground Mode
GM............... Group Management (TIMI)
GM............... Group Mark [*Computer science*]
GM............... Groupmark (SAUS)
GM............... Group Member (SAUO)
GM............... Group Mobile (CINC)
GM............... Group MODEM (MCD)
GM............... Group Multiplication (SAUO)
GM............... Group per Message (IAA)
GM............... Grouting Mortar (SAUS)
GM............... Growth Management (PA)
GM............... Growth Medium [*Medicine*] (STED)
GM............... Guam [*IYRU nationality code*] (IYR)
GM............... Guard Mail
GM............... Guessed Mean [*Psychology*] (BARN)
GM............... Guidance Memoranda (HEAS)
GM............... Guided Missile
GM............... Guided Munitions (SEWL)
GM............... Gun-Laying Mark I [*RADAR*]
GM............... GunMar Music [*Publisher*]
GM............... Gunmetal
G/M.............. Gun/Missile selector (SAUS)
GM............... Gun Mode (ACAE)
GM............... Gun Mount [*Military*] (CAAL)
GM............... Gunner's Mate [*Navy rating*]
GM............... Gypsy Moths [*An association*] (EA)
GM............... Metacentric Height [*Naval architecture*]
GM............... Monosialoganglioside [*Chemistry*]
Gm............... Mutual Conductance
GM............... Washington Memorial Library, Middle Georgia Regional Library, Macon, GA [*Library symbol*] [*Library of Congress*] (LCLS)
GM1.............. Gunner's Mate, First Class [*Navy rating*]
GM².............. Grams per Square Meter (WDAA)
GM2.............. Gunner's Mate, Second Class [*Navy rating*]
GM3.............. Gunner's Mate, Third Class [*Navy rating*]
GM100.......... Groupement Mobile 100 [*Elite French armed forces stationed in Vietnam*] (VNW)
GMA............. Clyidyl Methacrylate (SAUS)
GMA............. Gallery of Modern Art (SAUO)

GMA............ Gama Aviation Ltd. [*British*] [*ICAO designator*] (FAAC)
GMA............ Game Manufacturers Association (EA)
GMA............ Gardner, Mason, and Associates, Inc. (EFIS)
GMA............ Garment Manufacturers' Association [*Australia*]
G M A........... Gas Metal-Arc (SAUS)
GMA............ Gated Mode Acquisition [*Telecommunications*] (LAIN)
GMA............ Gemena [*Zaire*] [*Airport symbol*] (OAG)
GMA............ Genel Mental Ability (SAUS)
GMA............ General Maintenance Aptitude [*Military*] (MCD)
GMA............ General Marketing Application
GMA............ General Medical Assistance (TAD)
GMA............ General Mental Ability
GMA............ Gen State Airlines (SAUS)
GMA............ Geomechanics Abstracts [*Rock Mechanics Information Service*] [*Bibliographic database*] [*British*]
GMA............ Georgia Marble [*Federal Railroad Administration identification code*]
GMA............ Germin-3-Monoacetat (SAUS)
GMA............ Giant Molecular Association [*Galactic science*]
GMA............ Giant Molular Association (SAUS)
GMA............ Gilt Market Analysis [*MMS International*] [*Information service or system*] (CRD)
GMA............ Glasgow Mathematical Association (SAUO)
GMA............ Glass Manufacturers Association (SAUO)
GMA............ Glyceryl Methacrylate [*Organic chemistry*] (DAVI)
GMA............ Glycol Methacrylate [*Organic chemistry*]
GMA............ Good Morning America [*Television program*]
GMA............ Gospel Music Association (EA)
GMA............ Government Modification Authorization (AAG)
GMA............ Grail Movement of Australia
GMA............ Grand Rapids Furniture Market Association (SAUO)
GMA............ Granite Mountain [*Alaska*] [*Seismograph station code, US Geological Survey*] (SEIS)
GMA............ Grizzle Methacrylate (EDCT)
GMA............ Grocery Manufacturers Association (COE)
GMA............ Grocery Manufacturers of America (EA)
GMA............ Grocery Manufacturers of Australia (EERA)
GMA............ Gross Motor Activities (HGAA)
GM/A........... Ground Meat/Analyzer [*USDA*]
GMA............ Growth and Maturation Activity [*Biochemistry*]
GMA............ Growth Management Act
GMA............ Guided Missile Ammunition (AABC)
GMA............ Gunners Mate, Armorer (SAUS)
GMA............ Gunner's Mate (Armorers) [*U.S. Navy enlisted rating*] (AUER)
GM(A).......... Gunner's Mate (Aviation) [*U.S. Navy enlisted rating*] (AUER)
GMA............ Washington Growth Management Act (SAUS)
GMA............ Whitefield, NH [*Location identifier*] [*FAA*] (FAAL)
GMAA........... Agadir/Inezgane [*Morocco*] [*ICAO location identifier*] (ICLI)
GMAA........... Gold Mining Association of America
GMAA........... Graduate Management Association of Australia
GMAB........... Guided Missile Assembly Building (SAA)
GMAC........... Gaining Motor Air Command (MCD)
GMAC........... Gas Metal Arc Cutting [*Welding*]
GMAC........... General Motors Acceptance Corp.
GMAC........... Genetic Manipulation Advisory Committee (EERA)
GMAC........... Graduate Management Admission Council [*Los Angeles, CA*] (EA)
GMACC.......... Ground Mobile Alternate Command Center (ACAE)
GMAD........... General Motors Allison Division
GMAD........... General Motors Assembly Division
GMAG........... Genetic Manipulation Advisory Group [*British*]
GMAG........... Geophysics Magnetometer (SAUS)
GMagic......... General Magic, Inc. [*Associated Press*] (SAG)
GMAI........... Greg Manning Auctions [*NASDAQ symbol*] (TTSB)
GMAI........... Greg Manning Auctions, Inc. [*NASDAQ symbol*] (SAG)
GMAI........... Manning [*Greg*] Auctions, Inc. [*NASDAQ symbol*] (SAG)
GMAIC.......... Guided Missile and Aerospace Intelligence Committee (AFM)
GMAIW.......... Greg Manning Auctions Wrrt [*NASDAQ symbol*] (TTSB)
GMAJCOM........ Gaining Major Command [*Military*] (AFM)
GMAK........... Ground Mounted Adaption Kit (SAUS)
GMAL........... General Electric Macro Assembly Language (NASA)
GMAL........... Graves Medical Audiovisual Library (SAUS)
GMAN........... General Maneuver (ADWA)
G-Man.......... Government Man (SAUS)
GM&A........... General Management and Administration (SAUO)
GM & N......... Gulf Mobile & Northern Railroad
GM & O......... Gulf, Mobile & Ohio Railroad [*Later, Illinois Central Gulf Railroad*]
GM&S........... General (SAUS)
gm&s........... general medical and surgical (SAUS)
GM & S......... General Medicine and Surgery
Gmand Water Heat Pump J... Ground Water Heat Pump Journal (journ.) (SAUS)
GMann.......... Greg Manning Auctions, Inc. [*Associated Press*] (SAG)
GMann.......... Manning [*Greg*] Auctions, Inc. [*Associated Press*] (SAG)
GManning....... Greg Manning Auctions, Inc. [*Associated Press*] (SAG)
GManning....... Manning [*Greg*] Auctions, Inc. [*Associated Press*] (SAG)
GMAP........... Generalized Macroprocessor
GMAP........... General Macro Assembler Processor (SAUS)
GMAP........... General Macroassembly Program [*Honeywell, Inc.*]
GMAP........... General Marco Assembler Processor (SAUS)
GMAP........... General Micro Assembler Processor (SAUO)
GMAP........... Geometric Modeling Application Program (SAUS)
GMAP........... Geometric Modeling Applications Project (SAUO)
GMAP........... Global Master of Arts Program
GMAPS.......... General Map Analysis Planning System (SAUO)
GMARA.......... Geomagnetism and Aernnomy (SAUS)
GMARA.......... Geomagnetism and Aeronomy (journ.) (SAUS)
GMarC.......... Cobb County-Marietta Public Library (SAUS)
GMarC.......... Cobb County-Marietta Public Library, Marietta, GA [*Library symbol*] [*Library of Congress*] (LCLS)
GMarK.......... Kennesaw College, Marietta, GA [*Library symbol*] [*Library of Congress*] (LCLS)
GMarLC......... Life College, Marietta, GA [*Library symbol*] [*Library of Congress*] (LCLS)
GMarLG......... Lockheed-Georgia Co., Scientific and Technical Information Department (SAUO)
GMarLG......... Lockheed-Georgia Co., Scientific and Technical Information Department, Marietta,GA [*Library symbol*] [*Library of Congress*] (LCLS)
GMarRR......... Reid-Rowell, Marietta, GA [*Library symbol*] [*Library of Congress*] (LCLS)
GMarS.......... Southern Technical Institute, Marietta (SAUS)
GMarS.......... Southern Technical Institute, Marietta, GA [*Library symbol*] [*Library of Congress*] (LCLS)
GMAS........... General Management Assessment System (SAUO)
GMAS........... Glovers' Mutual Aid Society [*A union*] [*British*]
GMAS........... Ground Munitions Analysis Study (AABC)
GMasec......... Grupo Industrial Maseca SA de CV [*Associated Press*] (SAG)
GMaseca........ Grupo Industrial Maseca SA de CV [*Associated Press*] (SAG)
GMASI.......... Graduate Member of the Ambulance Service Institute [*British*] (DBQ)
GMason......... George Mason Bankshares [*Commercial firm*] [*Associated Press*] (SAG)
GMAT........... General Management Administration Test (WDAA)
GMAT........... General Mathematical Aptitude Test (BARN)
GMAT........... Graduate Management Admission Test
GMAT........... Graduate Management Aptitude Test (SAUS)
GMAT........... Greenwich Mean Astronomical Time
GMAT........... Tan-Tan/Plage Blanche [*Morocco*] [*ICAO location identifier*] (ICLI)
GMATS.......... General Motors Air Transport Section (SAUO)
GMATS.......... General Motors Air Transport System
GMATS.......... Government Metropolitan Area Telephone Service (SAUO)
GMAW........... Gas Metal-Arc Welder (SAUS)
GMAW........... Gas Metal Arc Welding
G M A W........ Gas Metal-Arc Welding (SAUS)
GMAWA.......... Glass Merchants' Association of Western Australia
GMAW-EG........ Gas Metal-Arc Welding (SAUS)
GMAW-EG........ Gas Metal-Arc Welding, Electrogas (SAUS)
GMAW-P......... Gas Metal Arc Welding - Pulsed Arc
GMAW-P......... Pulsed Gas Metal-Arc Welding (SAUS)
GMAW-S......... Gas Metal Arc Welding - Short Circuiting Arc
GMAW-S......... Short Circuiting Gas Metal-Arc Welding (SAUS)
GMAX........... Graphics Multi-Axis Module [*McDonnell-Douglas Automation Co.*]
GMAZ........... General Motors-Auto Terminal [*Federal Railroad Administration identification code*]
GMAZ........... Zagora [*Morocco*] [*ICAO location identifier*] (ICLI)
GMB............ Gambela [*Ethiopia*] [*Airport symbol*] (OAG)
GMB............ Gambia [*ANSI three-letter standard code*] (CNC)
GMB............ Gastric Mucosal Barrier (DB)
GMB............ General Mortgage Bond
GMB............ General, Municipal Boilermakers (WDAA)
GMB............ General Municipal Boilermakers and Allied Trades Union (WA)
GMB............ Glass Microballoon (MCD)
GMB............ Global Management Bureau
GMB............ Good Merchandise (or Merchantable) Brand (SAUS)
Gmb............ Good Merchantable Brand (MARI)
GMB............ Good Merchantable Brand [*Business term*]
GMB............ Good Morning Britain [*Early morning television program*] [*ITV*] [*British*]
GMB............ Grand Master Bowman (SAUS)
GMB............ Grand Master of the Bath [*British*]
GMB............ Granulomembranous Body [*Medicine*] (EDAA)
GMB............ Green Mountain Boy [*Pseudonym used by Henry Stevens*]
GMB............ Ground Maneuver Box (SAUS)
GMB............ Guided Missile Brigade [*Army*]
GMBA........... Global Mountain Biodiversity Assessment (SAUO)
GMBATU......... General Municipal Boilermakers' and Allied Trades Union [*British*]
GMBE........... Grand Master of the Order of the British Empire (EY)
GMBF........... Gastric Mucosa1 Blood Flow (SAUS)
GMBF........... Gastric Mucosal Blood Flow [*Medicine*]
GmbH........... Gesellschaft mit Beschraenkter Haftung [*Limited Liability Company*] [*German*]
GmbH & CoKG.... Gesellschaft mit Beschraenkter Haftung und Kommanditgesellschaft [*Combined Limited Partnership and Limited Liability Company*] [*German*]
GmbHG.......... Gesetz Betreffend der Gesellschaft mit Beschraenkter Haftung [*Law Governing Limited Liability Company*] [*German*] (ILCA)
GMBI........... Ground-based Midcourse Ballistic Interceptor (SAUS)
GMBIM.......... Genetics and Molecular Biology of Industrial Microorganisms [*Conference*]
GMBK........... Gigawatt Multiple Beam Klystron (SEWL)
GMBL........... Gimbal (AAG)
GMBM........... General Manager Business Management (SAUS)
GMBS........... Gamma-Maleimidobutyryloxysuccinimide (SAUS)
GMBS........... George Mason Bankshares [*NASDAQ symbol*] (SAG)
GMBS........... Glenn Miller Birthplace Society (EA)
GMC............ Ganglion Mother Cell [*Cytology*]
GMC............ Gem and Mineral Collection (SAUO)
GMC............ General Management Committee (WDAA)
GMC............ General Medical Clinic [*Medicine*] (EDAA)
GMC............ General Medical Council [*British*]
GmC............ General Microfilm Co. (SAUO)
GmC............ General Microfilm Co., Cambridge, MA [*Library symbol*] [*Library of Congress*] (LCLS)

GMC............ General Military Course (AFM)
GMC............ General Military Court (SAUO)
GMC............ General Monte Carlo Code [*Computer science*]
GMC............ General Motors Corp. [*ICAO designator*] (FAAC)
GMC............ General Motors Corporation (SAUO)
GMC............ General Musketry Course (SAUS)
GMC............ Geological Museum of China [*China*]
GMC............ George Mason College (SAUO)
GMC............ Georgia Military College [*Milledgeville*]
GMC............ Geostar Mining Corp. [*Vancouver Stock Exchange symbol*]
Gmc............ Germanic (BEE)
GMC............ Germanic [*Language, etc.*]
GMC............ Giant Molecular Cloud [*Cosmology*]
GMC............ Global Management Committee (SAUO)
GMC............ Global Marine Corporation (SAUO)
GMC............ Gold Master Candidate [*Compact-disc manufacturing*]
GMC............ Good Moral Character (SAUS)
GMC............ Gordon Military College [*Georgia*]
GMC............ Great Midwestern Conference [*College reports*]
GMC............ Grivet Monkey Cell Line
GMC............ Gross Maximum Capacity [*Electronics*] (IEEE)
GMC............ Gross Motor Coordination (IDYL)
GMC............ Ground Mobile Cenetheodolite
GMC............ Ground Movement Controller
GMC............ Groundwater Management Caucus (EA)
GMC............ Gruen Marketing Corporation (SAUO)
GMC............ Guaranteed Mortgage Certificate [*Federal Home Loan Mortgage Corp.*]
GMC............ Guard-Cell Mother Cell [*Botany*]
GMC............ Guggenheim Memorial Concerts (SAUS)
GMC............ Guided Missile Chart (SAUS)
GMC............ Guided Missile Command (SAUO)
GMC............ Guided Missile Committee [*Army*]
GMC............ Guided Missile Control (AAG)
GMC............ Guided Missile Council (SAUO)
GMC............ Guild of Memorial Craftsmen [*British*] (BI)
GMC............ Gulf Maritime Co. (SAUS)
GMC............ Gulf Maritime Company (SAUO)
GMC............ Gun Motor Carriage
GMC............ Gunner's Mate, Chief [*Navy rating*]
GMC............ Middle Georgia College, Cochran, GA [*OCLC symbol*] (OCLC)
gm-cal......... Gram Calorie (IDOE)
GMCB.......... Gunner's Mate, Construction Battalion [*Navy rating*]
GMCBA........ Gunner's Mate, Construction Battalion, Armorer [*Navy rating*]
GM(CBG)..... Gunner's Mate (Construction Battalion) (Armorer) [*U.S. Navy enlisted rating*] (AUER)
GMCBP........ Gunner's Mate, Construction Battalion, Powderman [*Navy rating*]
GMCC.......... General Magnaplate Corp. [*NASDAQ symbol*] (NQ)
GMCC.......... General Motors Ceramic Committee (SAUS)
GMCC.......... General NAS Maintenance Control Center [*FAA*] (TAG)
GMCC.......... Genl Magnaplate [*NASDAQ symbol*] (TTSB)
GMCC.......... Geophysical Monitoring for Climate Change (EERA)
GMCC.......... Geophysical Monitoring for Climatic Change [*National Oceanic and Atmospheric Administration*]
GMCC.......... Global Monitoring for Climatic Change [*Environmental science*] (COE)
GMCC.......... Global Warning for Climatic Change (SAUO)
gm/cc.......... Grams per Cubic Centimeter [*Medicine*] (EDAA)
GMCC.......... Ground Mobile Command Capability (CCCA)
GMCC.......... Ground Mobile Command Center
GMC Code... General Monte Carlo Code (SAUS)
GMCD.......... Grand Mal Convulsive Disorder [*Medicine*] (MELL)
GMCF.......... Goddard Mission Control Facility [*NASA*] (KSC)
GMCF.......... Guided Missile Control Facility (AAG)
GM-CFU....... Granulocyte-Macrophage Colony Forming Unit [*Medicine*] (EDAA)
GMCI........... Giftware Manufacturers' Credit Interchange (EA)
GMCL.......... Ground Measurements Command List (MCD)
gm-cm......... Gram-Centimeter (IDOE)
GMCM......... Guided Missile Countermeasure [*NATO*]
GMCM......... Guided Missile Countermeasures Master (SAUS)
GMCM......... Gunner's Mate, Master Chief [*Navy rating*]
gm/cm3....... Gramme per Cubic Centimetre (SAUS)
GMCO.......... General Mathematics Computing Option (SAUS)
GMCO.......... Guided Missile Control Officer (AAG)
GMCP.......... General Manager Conservation Policy (SAUS)
GMCP.......... Ground Mobile Command Post (SAUO)
GMCP.......... Guided Missile Control Party (IAA)
GMCPC........ General Motors Chevrolet Pontiac Canada (ACAE)
GMCR.......... General Monitor Checking Routine (SAUS)
GMCR.......... Genetic Mutant Cell Repository [*Medicine*] (EDAA)
GMCR.......... Globe Mackay Cable and Radio Corp. [*Philippines*] [*Telecommunications*]
GMCR.......... Green Mountain Coffee [*Commercial firm*] [*NASDAQ symbol*] (SAG)
GMCRF........ General Motors Cancer Research Foundation (HGEN)
GMCS.......... Group Medicare Cooperative Society (SAUO)
GMCS.......... Guided Missile Control System (SAUS)
GMCS.......... Gunner's Mate, Senior Chief [*Navy rating*]
GM-CSA....... Granulocyte-Macrophage Colony-Stimulating Activity [*Hematology*]
GMCSF........ Granulocyte-Macrophage Colony-Stimulating Factor (ADWA)
GM/CSO...... German Minesweeping Central Supply Office (SAUO)
GMCSS........ Global Multi-region Cloud System Study (SAUS)
GMCT.......... Giftware Manufacturers Credit Interchange (EA)
GMCY.......... Grant-Makers for Children and Youth (EA)
GMD........... Forschungszentrum Informationstechnik GmbH [*National research center for informatics, communication, and media*] [*Germany*] (DDC)
GMD........... Generalized Mutual Dependency (SAUS)
GMD........... General Management Directive
GMD........... General Marine Distress
GMD........... General Material Designation
GMD........... General Motors Defense Operations group (SAUO)
GMD........... General Motors Diesel [*Indian Railway*] [*Canada*] (TIR)
GMD........... Genomic Map Design (HGEN)
GMD........... Geometric Mean Distance
GMD........... Geometrodynamics
GMD........... Gesellschaft fuer Mathematik und Datenverarbeitung [*Society for Mathematics and Data Processing*] [*Germany*] [*Information service or system*] (IID)
GMD........... Global Missile Defense (SAUS)
GMD........... Glossary of Mental Disorders [*Medicine*] (EDAA)
GMD........... Glutamate Dehydrogenase [*Medicine*] (MELL)
GMD........... Glycopeptide Moiety Modified Derivative (DB)
GMD........... Gould Medical Dictionary (SAUS)
GMD........... Government Maintenance Depot (MCD)
GMD........... Gower's Muscular Dystrophy [*Medicine*] (MELL)
GMD........... Green-Monkey Disease (SAUS)
GMD........... Ground Meteorological Detector [*or Device*]
GMD........... Ground Meteorological Device (SAUS)
GMD........... Ground Meteorological Site (SAUS)
GMD........... Groundwater Modelling Department (SAUO)
GMD........... Groupo Mexicano Desarrollo [*NYSE symbol*] (SPSG)
GMD........... Grupo Mex de Desarrollo 'L'ADS [*NYSE symbol*] (TTSB)
GMD........... Grupo Mexicano Desarrollo [*NYSE symbol*] (SAG)
GMD........... Guided Missile Destroyers (SAUS)
GMD........... Guided Missiles Division (SAUS)
GMDA.......... Golf Manufacturers and Distributors Association (EA)
GMDA.......... Groundwater Management Districts Association (EA)
GMDA.......... Group Method of Determining Arguments [*Equation*]
GMDC.......... General Merchandise Distributors Council [*Colorado Springs, CO*] (EA)
GMDCB4...... Goegraphia Medica (journ.) (SAUS)
GMDD.......... Gaided Missile Development Division (SAUS)
GMDD.......... Generalized Multiple Disjoint Decomposition (ACAE)
GMDD.......... Guided Missile Development Division [*NASA*] (KSC)
GMDEP........ Guided Missile Data Exchange Program [*Navy*]
GMDES........ Gridded Meteorological Data Extraction System (SAUO)
GMDesB....... Grupo Mexicano Desarrollo [*Associated Press*] (SAG)
GMDH.......... Group Method of Data Handling [*Mathematical technique*]
GMDI........... Geophysical Models for Data Interpretation (SAUO)
GMDIL......... General Motors Distribution Ireland Ltd. [*Dublin, Ireland*]
GMD-IZ........ GMD-Informationszentrum fuer Informationswissenschaft und -Praxis [*GMD Information Center for Information Science and Information Work*] [*Information service or system*] (IID)
GMDL.......... GEC-Marconi Dynamics Limited (SAUO)
GMDL.......... Guided Missile Destroyer Leader (ACAE)
GMDP.......... Guaranteed Minimum Delivery Price (ADA)
GMDRL........ General Motors Defense Research Laboratories (SAUS)
GM/DRL....... General Motors Defense Research Laboratories, Santa Barbara, California (SAUO)
GMDRL........ General Motors Defense Research Laboratory (MCD)
GMDS.......... German Military Documents Section [*of AGO, Army*] [*World War II*]
GMDS.......... Global Managed Data Services (SAUO)
GMDSS........ Global Maritime Distress and Safety System (DA)
GM Dud....... Dudley's Georgia Reports [*A publication*] (DLA)
GM Dudl...... Dudley's Georgia Reports [*A publication*] (DLA)
GME........... Gelantine Manufacturers in Europe (SAUO)
GME........... Gelatine Manufacturers of Europe (EAIO)
GME........... Gelatin Manufacturers of Europe (SAUS)
GME........... Generalized Machine Equation (SAUS)
GME........... General Microelectronics
GME........... General Motors Corp. [*NYSE symbol*] (SAG)
GME........... General Motors Europe
GME........... Generic Macro Expander [*Telecommunications*] (TEL)
GME........... Genl Motors Cl'E' [*NYSE symbol*] (TTSB)
GME........... Geohydrologic Map Editor (SAUO)
GME........... Geometric Mean Error (SAUS)
GME........... German Minimum Economy [*Allied German Occupation Forces*]
GME........... Gilt Marbled Edges [*Bookbinding*]
GME........... Gimbal Module Electronics (SAUS)
GME........... Gimbal Mounted Electronics (KSC)
GME........... Glimmer Resources, Inc. [*Vancouver Stock Exchange symbol*]
GME........... Globe Microphone Evaluation
GME........... Globex Mining Enterprises (SAUO)
GME........... Gmelinite [*A zeolite*]
GME........... Gradient Maximum Entropy (SAUS)
GME........... Graduate Medical Education [*Program*] [*Army*]
GME........... Granulomatous Meningoencephalomyelitis (SAUS)
GME........... Greater Middle East
GME........... Great Meteor East [*Nuclear energy*] (NUCP)
GME........... Green, M. E., Jefferson City MO [*STAC*]
GME........... Group Modulating (or Modulation) Equipment (SAUO)
GME........... Guided Missile Evaluator
GMEA.......... Georgia Music Education Association (SAUO)
GMEA.......... Georgia Music Educators Association (SAUO)
GMECH........ General Mechanic (SAUO)
GMED.......... GeneMedicine, Inc. [*NASDAQ symbol*] (SAG)
GMED.......... GMI Group, Inc. (SAUO)
GM/EDS....... General Motors Electronic Data Systems (NITA)

GMEFC......... Golden Memories of Elvis Fan Club (EA)
GMEI........... Gulf of Mexico Estuarine Inventory (PDAA)
GMEL........... Groupement des Mathematiciens d'Expression Latine [*Group of Mathematicians of Romance Languages - GMRL*] (EAIO)
G Mem........ Gated Memory (SAUS)
G-MEM........ General Memory (NAKS)
GMEM.......... GPC [*General Purpose Computer*] Memory (NASA)
GME Method... Gradient Maximum Entropy Method (SAUS)
GMENAC...... Graduate Medical Education National Advisory Committee [*Department of Health and Human Services*]
GMEO.......... Grolier Multimedia Encyclopedia Online
GMEO.......... Ground Maintenance and Equipment Operations (SAUS)
GME Paper... Gilt Marbled Edges Paper (SAUS)
GME-PC....... General Motors Europe - Passenger Cars [*Switzerland*]
GMER.......... General Manager External Relations (SAUS)
GMERD......... Government Minimum Essential Requirements Document
GMET.......... General Metal & Abrasives Co. (SAUO)
GMET.......... Graphical Munitions Effects Tables (MCD)
GMET.......... Gun Metal
GMetO......... Group Meteorological Officer [*British military*] (DMA)
GMEV.......... General Motors Electric Vehicle [*General Motors Corp*]
GMEVALU.... Guided Missile Evaluation Unit (MUGU)
GMEVALU.... Guide Missile Evaluation Unit (SAUS)
GMexDes..... Grupo Mexicano Desarollo [*Associated Press*] (SAG)
GMF............ Galactic Magnetic Field
GMF............ Generalized Mainline Framework [*Computer science*]
GMF............ General Mail Facility
GMF............ General Motors Corp. and Fanuc Ltd. [*In company name GMF Robotics Corp.*]
GMF............ Generated Message Format (SAUS)
GMF............ Glass Manufactrs Federation (SAUO)
GMF............ Glass Manufacturers Federation
GMF............ Glass Microfilter
GMF............ Glial Maturation Factor [*Biochemistry*]
GMF............ Global Matching Figures Test [*Education*] (EDAC)
GMF............ Ground Mobile Force [*Military*] (SEWL)
GMF............ Ground Mobile Forces [*Military*] (RDA)
GMF............ Ground Monitor Facility (MCD)
GMF............ Guided Missile Facilities (NG)
GMF............ Milwaukee, WI [*Location identifier*] [*FAA*] (FAAL)
GMFA.......... Ouezzane [*Morocco*] [*ICAO location identifier*] (ICLI)
GMFB.......... Gang Mill Fixture Base (SAUS)
GMFC.......... Gary Morris Fan Club (EA)
GMFC.......... Gem and Mineral Federation of Canada (SAUO)
GMFC.......... General Mining and Finance Corporation (SAUO)
GMFC.......... Guided Missile Fire Control
GMFCS........ Guided Missile Fire Control System (NG)
G/MFCS....... Gun/Missele Fire Control System (SAUO)
GMFD.......... Germania Bank F.S.B. (Illinois) [*NASDAQ symbol*] (COMM)
GMFF.......... Fes/Saiss [*Morocco*] [*ICAO location identifier*] (ICLI)
GMFI........... Ifrane [*Morocco*] [*ICAO location identifier*] (ICLI)
GMFJ.......... Ghana Movement of Freedom and Justice [*Political party*]
GMFK.......... Er-Rachidia [*Morocco*] [*ICAO location identifier*] (ICLI)
GMFM......... Meknes/Bassatine [*Morocco*] [*ICAO location identifier*] (ICLI)
GMFMC....... Gulf of Mexico Fishery Management Council (MSC)
GMFN.......... Nador/Taouima [*Morocco*] [*ICAO location identifier*] (ICLI)
GMFO.......... Oujda/Angads [*Morocco*] [*ICAO location identifier*] (ICLI)
GMFP.......... Geometrical Mean Free Path (SAUS)
GMFP.......... Global Military Force Policy (SEWL)
GMFP.......... Guided Missile Firing Panel
GMFS.......... Geologic Mapping and Framework Studies (SAUO)
GMFSC........ Ground Mobile Forces Satellite Communications (MCD)
GMFSG........ Geologic Mapping and Framework Studies Group (SAUO)
GMFT.......... Touahar [*Morocco*] [*ICAO location identifier*] (ICLI)
GMF/TACSAT... Ground Mobile Forces/Tactical Satellite Communications (MCD)
GMFU.......... Fes/Sefrou [*Morocco*] [*ICAO location identifier*] (ICLI)
GMFZ.......... General Motors Corporation-Fisher Body Division [*Federal Railroad Administration identification code*]
GMFZ.......... Taza [*Morocco*] [*ICAO location identifier*] (ICLI)
GMG........... Gott Mein Gut [*God Is My Good*] [*Motto of Karl, Margrave of Baden-Durlach (1529-77); Ernst Friedrich, (1560-1604)*] [*German*]
GMG........... Grand Metropolitan and Guinness [*Proposed company*]
GMG........... Grenade-Launching Machine Gun (SAUS)
GMG........... Grenade Machine Gun [*Military*]
GMG........... Gross Maximum Generation [*Electronics*] (IEEE)
GMG........... Guided Missile Group (SAUO)
GMG........... Gunner's Mate (Guns) [*U.S. Navy enlisted rating*] (AUER)
GMG........... IUGS Commission for Marine Geology (SAUO)
GMG1......... Gunner's Mate, Guns, First Class [*Navy rating*] (DNAB)
GMG2......... Gunner's Mate, Guns, Second Class [*Navy rating*] (DNAB)
GMG3......... Gunner's Mate, Guns, Third Class [*Navy rating*] (DNAB)
GMGB.......... Guards Machine Gun Battalion [*British military*] (DMA)
GMGC.......... General Magic, Inc. [*NASDAQ symbol*] (SAG)
GMGC.......... Gunner's Mate, Guns, Chief [*Navy rating*] (DNAB)
GMGN.......... Guided Missile Group Netherlands (SAUO)
GMGO.......... German Military Geographical Office (SAUO)
GMGO.......... German Military Geophysical Office (SAUO)
GMGR.......... Guards Machine Gun Regiment [*British military*] (DMA)
GMGRU....... Guided Missile Group (MUGU)
GMGS.......... Guided Missile General Support (MCD)
GMGSA........ Gunner's Mate, Guns, Seaman Apprentice [*Navy rating*] (DNAB)
GMGSN........ Gunner's Mate, Guns, Seaman [*Navy rating*] (DNAB)
GMGW......... Geraghty & Miller, Inc. (SAUO)
GMH........... Chief of Military History (SAUS)
GMH........... Combined Military Hospital (SAUS)
GMH........... General Military Hospital (SAUO)
GMH........... General Motors Corp. [*NYSE symbol*] (SAG)
GM-H.......... General Motors-Holden (SAUS)
GMH........... General Motors-Holden's Ltd. [*Australia*] (ADA)
GMH........... Georgia Mental Health Institute, Atlanta (SAUS)
GMH........... Georgia Mental Health Institute, Atlanta, GA [*OCLC symbol*] (OCLC)
gmh............ German (SAUS)
gmh............ German, Middle High [*MARC language code*] [*Library of Congress*] (LCCP)
GMH........... Germinal Matrix Hemorrhage [*Medicine*] (DMAA)
GMH........... Greenville, KY [*Location identifier*] [*FAA*] (FAAL)
GMH........... Hughes Aircraft Co. (Aeronautical Operations) [*ICAO designator*] (FAAC)
GMHB.......... Growth Management Hearings Boards (SAUO)
GMHC.......... Gay Men's Health Crisis (EA)
GMHC.......... Grease Monkey Hldg [*NASDAQ symbol*] (TTSB)
GMHC.......... Grease Monkey Holding Corp. [*NASDAQ symbol*] (NQ)
GMHC.......... Great Monkey Holding Corp. (SAUO)
GMHE.......... General Motors Hughes Electronics Corporation (SAUS)
GMHE.......... GM Hughes Electronics Corp. (SAUS)
GMHRO........ General Manager Human Resources & Organisation (SAUS)
GMHS.......... Global Message Handling Service (SAUS)
GMHS.......... Global Message Handling System (SAUO)
GMHS.......... Government Message Handling Service (FOTI)
GMI............ Galtaco, Inc. [*Toronto Stock Exchange symbol*]
GMI............ Garnes Mountain [*Idaho*] [*Seismograph station code, US Geological Survey*] (SEIS)
GMI............ Gasmata [*Papua New Guinea*] [*Airport symbol*] (OAG)
GMI............ Gelatin Manufacturers Institute (SAUS)
GMI............ Gelatin Manufacturers Institute of America (EA)
GMI............ Gemini Fund, Inc. [*NYSE symbol*] (SPSG)
GMI............ Gemini II [*NYSE symbol*] (TTSB)
GMI............ General Media International
GMI............ General Medical Intelligence (MCD)
GMI............ General Memory Interface (SAUS)
GMI............ General Memory Interference (SAUO)
GMI............ General Military Intelligence (SAUO)
GMI............ General Mills (SAUS)
GMI............ General Mills, Incorporated, Minneapolis, MN [*OCLC symbol*] (OCLC)
GMI............ General Motors Institute
GMI............ Generic Management Information (SAUS)
GMI............ Geologic Map Index (SAUO)
GMI............ Germania Fluggesellschaft Koln [*Germany*] [*ICAO designator*] (FAAC)
GMI............ German Military Intelligence (SAUO)
GMI............ Gibson Music International (SAUO)
GMI............ Global Marine, Inc. (NOAA)
GMI............ Goddard Management Instruction [*NASA*]
g/mi........... Gram per Mile [*Automotive engineering*]
G/MI........... Grams per Mile (EEVL)
GMI............ Gray-McCrary Index (SAUO)
GMI............ Ground Moving Indication (ACAE)
GMI............ Guaranteed Minimum Income (ADA)
GMI............ Guarantee Material Inspection (MCD)
GMIA.......... Gelatin Manufacturers Institute of America (EA)
GMIA.......... Guided Missile Intercept Aerial (SAUS)
GMIC.......... General Microelectronics Corporation (SAUO)
GMIC.......... General Microwave Corporation (SAUO)
GMIC.......... Glass Microwave Integrated Circuit (SEWL)
GMIC.......... Graphic Memory Interface Controller [*Computer chip*]
GMIC.......... Guided Missile Intelligence Committee (CARL)
gmidg.......... garnish moulding (SAUS)
GMIE........... Grand Master of the Order of the Indian Empire [*British*]
GMI-EMI...... General Motors Institute - Engineering and Management Institute [*Flint, MI*]
GMIF........... Gandhi Memorial International Foundation (EA)
GMIFC......... George Michael International Fan Club (EA)
GMII........... Gigabit Media Independent Interface (SAUS)
GMII........... Ground Moving Target Indication (SAUS)
GMII........... Guaranteed Market Index Investment [*Canada*]
GMIL........... Spaceflight Tracking and Data Network Station (SAUS)
GMiM.......... Georgia Military College, Milledgeville (SAUS)
GMiM.......... Georgia Military College, Milledgeville, GA [*Library symbol*] [*Library of Congress*] (LCLS)
GMI Mech E... Graduate Member of the Institution of Mechanical Engineers [*British*]
GMI Model... General Memory Interface Model (SAUS)
GMIO.......... General Motors Internal Operations
GMIP.......... General Motors Improvement Project [*Investigating team sponsored by consumer-advocate Ralph Nader*]
GMIPr......... Gemini II cm Income Shrs [*NYSE symbol*] (TTSB)
GMIS.......... Generalized Management Information System
GMIS.......... GMIS, Inc. [*NASDAQ symbol*] (SPSG)
GMIS.......... Government Management Information Sciences (EA)
GMIS.......... Government Management Information System (SAUS)
GMIS.......... Grants Management Information System [*Department of Health and Human Services*] (GFGA)
GMISCA....... General Motors Information System and Communications Activity (HGAA)
GMI Short Pap Oreg Dep Geol Miner Ind... GMI Short Paper. Oregon Department of Geology and Mineral Industries (journ.) (SAUS)
GMITPM...... Gorgas Memorial Institute of Tropical and Preventive Medicine (SAUO)
GMiW.......... Georgia College, Milledgeville, GA [*Library symbol*] [*Library of Congress*] (LCLS)

GMIZ.......... Gooch Milling [*Federal Railroad Administration identification code*]
GMJ.......... Geological Map of Japan (SAUO)
GMJ.......... Macon Junior College, Macon, GA [*Library symbol*] [*Library of Congress*] (LCLS)
GMJC.......... Green Mountain Junior College [*Vermont*]
GMJD.......... Generic Master Job Definition (TIMI)
GMJSU.......... Gems (SAUS)
GMJSU.......... Gems, Minerals, and Jewelry Study Unit (EA)
GMK.......... Gold Mark Minerals [*Vancouver Stock Exchange symbol*]
GMK.......... Grand Master Key [*Locks*] (ADA)
GMK.......... Green Monkey Kidney (SAUS)
GMK.......... Green Monkey Kidney Cell
GMK.......... Gruma S.A. ADS [*NYSE symbol*] (SG)
GMK.......... Gyromagnetic Kompass
GMK Cell.......... Green Monkey Kidney Cell (SAUS)
GMKP.......... Grand Master of the Knights of St. Patrick
GMKT.......... Global Market Information, Inc. [*NASDAQ symbol*] (SAG)
GML.......... Galvanometer-Mirror Lightbeam
GML.......... Garrett Manufacturing Limited (SAUO)
GML.......... Gemial [*Slovakia*] [*ICAO designator*] (FAAC)
GML.......... Generalized Markup Language [*Computer science*]
GML.......... General Markup Language (SAUS)
GML.......... General Material List (ACAE)
GML.......... General Measurement Loop (MCD)
GML.......... General Mining Law (SAUO)
GML.......... Generic Markup Language (NITA)
GML.......... Geographic Macro Language (SAUO)
GML.......... George Moody Ltd. (SAUO)
GML.......... Global DirectMail [*NYSE symbol*] (TTSB)
GML.......... Glycerol Monolaurate [*Food-grade lipid*] [*Pharmacology*]
GML.......... Gold Maple Leaf [*Canadian coin*]
GML.......... Gold-Medal Resources Ltd. [*Vancouver Stock Exchange symbol*]
GML.......... Gold Mining Lease (SAUS)
GML.......... Gorgas Memorial Laboratory [*Panama*] [*Research center*] (RCD)
GML.......... Government Metallurgical Laboratory (SAUO)
g/ml.......... Gramme per Millilitre (SAUS)
gm/l.......... Grams per Liter (MAE)
g/ml.......... Grams per Milliliter (SAUS)
GML.......... Grand Master's Lodge [*Freemasonry*] (ROG)
GML.......... Graphic Machine Language
GML.......... Guided Missile Laboratory (ACAE)
GML.......... Guided Missile Launcher (NG)
GML.......... Mercer University, Law Library, Macon, GA [*OCLC symbol*] (OCLC)
G MLC.......... Gaussian Maximum Likelihood Classifier (SAUS)
GMLDG.......... Garnish Molding [*Mechanical engineering*]
GMLNO.......... Guided Missile Liaison Officer (SAUO)
GMLOF.......... Guided Missile Line of Flight (SAUS)
GMLR.......... German Military Logistic Representative (SAUO)
GMLR.......... Guided Missile and Large Rocket
GMLS.......... Guided Missile Launching System
GMLSC.......... Guided Missile Launching System Control (DWSG)
GMLSS.......... Guided Missile Launcher Sub System (ACAE)
GMM.......... Galvanomagnetic Method (IAA)
GMM.......... Gamboma [*Congo*] [*Airport symbol*] (AD)
GMM.......... Generalized Mixed Models
GMM.......... General Matrix Manipulator (OA)
GMM.......... General Methods of Moments [*Statistics*]
GMM.......... Geometric Math Model (SSD)
GMM.......... Glass-Metal Module (SAUS)
GMM.......... Glucose Monomycolate [*Biochemistry*]
GMM.......... Gluteus Maximus Muscle (MELL)
GMM.......... Goldberg-Maxwell-Morris [*Syndrome*] [*Medicine*] (DB)
GMM.......... Goldsmith Minerals [*Vancouver Stock Exchange symbol*]
gm-m.......... Gram Meter
gm-m.......... gram-meter (SAUS)
GMM.......... Granada Men and Motors (SAUO)
GMM.......... Graphical Multi-Meter
GMM.......... Graphics Mill Module [*McDonnell-Douglas Corp.*]
GMM.......... Guild of Master Mariners (SAUO)
GMM.......... Gunner's Mate, Missile [*Navy rating*]
GMM.......... Gunners Mate, Mounts (SAUS)
GMM.......... Mercer University, Macon, GA [*Library symbol*] [*Library of Congress*] (LCLS)
GMM.......... Mercer University, School of Medicine, Macon, GA [*OCLC symbol*] (OCLC)
GMM1.......... Gunner's Mate, Missile, First Class [*Navy rating*] (DNAB)
GMM2.......... Gunner's Mate, Missile, Second Class [*Navy rating*] (DNAB)
GMM3.......... Gunner's Mate, Missile, Third Class [*Navy rating*] (DNAB)
GMMA.......... Gas Meter Makers' Association [*A union*] [*British*]
GMMA.......... Gloucester Master Mariners Association (EA)
GMMA.......... Golda Meir Memorial Association (EA)
GMMB.......... Ben Slimane [*Morocco*] [*ICAO location identifier*] (ICLI)
GMMC.......... Casablanca/ANFA [*Morocco*] [*ICAO location identifier*] (ICLI)
GMMC.......... Geotechnical Micromorphology and Microanalysis Centre (SAUO)
GMMC.......... Godden Memorial Medical Centre (SAUO)
GMMC.......... Ground Master Measurements List (SAUS)
GMMC.......... Gunner's Mate, Missile, Chief [*Navy rating*] (DNAB)
GMMD.......... Beni-Mellal [*Morocco*] [*ICAO location identifier*] (ICLI)
GMME.......... Rabat/Sale [*Morocco*] [*ICAO location identifier*] (ICLI)
GMMF.......... Sidi Ifni [*Morocco*] [*ICAO location identifier*] (ICLI)
GMMG.......... Grand Master of the Order of St. Michael and St. George [*British*]
GMMI.......... Essaouira [*Morocco*] [*ICAO location identifier*] (ICLI)
GMMIS.......... GLCM Maintenance Management Information System (SAUO)
GMMJ.......... El Jadida [*Morocco*] [*ICAO location identifier*] (ICLI)
GMMK.......... Khouribga [*Morocco*] [*ICAO location identifier*] (ICLI)
GMML.......... Ground Master Measurements List
GMM-L.......... Mercer University, School of Law, Macon, GA [*Library symbol*] [*Library of Congress*] (LCLS)
GMMLU.......... Greneda Manual and Mental Labourer's Union [*Political party*] (PSAP)
GMMM.......... Casablanca [*Morocco*] [*ICAO location identifier*] (ICLI)
GMMMU.......... Ground Mounted Manned Maneuvering Unit (SAUS)
GMMN.......... Casablanca/Mohamed V [*Morocco*] [*ICAO location identifier*] (ICLI)
GMMO.......... Taroudant [*Morocco*] [*ICAO location identifier*] (ICLI)
GM MOL.......... Gram-Molecule (WDAA)
GMMR.......... General Mobilization Material Readiness [*DoD*]
GMMRI.......... Georgia Mining and Mineral Research Institute [*Georgia Institute of Technology*] [*Research center*] (RCD)
GMM RIT.......... GlasMetal Module Relase Interface Tape (SAUS)
GMMRIT.......... Glass-Metal Module Release Interface Tape (SAUS)
GMMS.......... Safi [*Morocco*] [*ICAO location identifier*] (ICLI)
GMMSA.......... Gunner's Mate, Missile, Seaman Apprentice [*Navy rating*] (DNAB)
GMMSN.......... Gunner's Mate, Missile, Seaman [*Navy rating*] (DNAB)
GMMT.......... Casablanca/Tit-Mellil [*Morocco*] [*ICAO location identifier*] (ICLI)
GMMTTR.......... Geometric Mean Time to Repair (SAUS)
GM-MVO.......... General Motors - Military Vehicles Operation (SAUS)
GMMX.......... Marrakech/Menara [*Morocco*] [*ICAO location identifier*] (ICLI)
GMMY.......... Kenitra/Tourisme [*Morocco*] [*ICAO location identifier*] (ICLI)
GMMZ.......... Quarzazate [*Morocco*] [*ICAO location identifier*] (ICLI)
GMN.......... Gorman [*TACAN station*] (MCD)
GMN.......... Gorman, CA [*Location identifier*] [*FAA*] (FAAL)
GMN.......... Gradient Moment Nulling [*Medicine*] (RAWO)
GMN.......... Greenman Brothers, Inc. [*AMEX symbol*] (SPSG)
GMN.......... Greenwich Mean Noon (ROG)
GMN.......... Ground Mapping Narrow (SAUS)
GMNA.......... Glutamyl(methoxy)naphthylamide [*Biochemistry*]
GMNA.......... Glutamynaphthylamide (SAUS)
GMNA.......... Guided Missile Nitric Acid (SAUS)
GMNC.......... GWEN Maintenance Notification Center (SAUO)
GmNE.......... Graphic Microfilm of New England, Waltham, MA [*Library symbol*] [*Library of Congress*] (LCLS)
gm neg.......... gram negative (SAUS)
GMNNR.......... Glasson Moss National Nature Reserve (SAUO)
GMNP.......... Guadalupe Mountains National Park (SAUS)
GMNP.......... Guadelupe Mountains National Park (SAUO)
Gmnp Psychother Psychodrama Sociometry... Group Psychotherapy, Psychodrama and Sociometry (journ.) (SAUS)
GmNY.......... Graphic Microfilm Corp., Valley Stream, NY [*Library symbol*] [*Library of Congress*] (LCLS)
GMNZ.......... General Motors New Zealand (SAUO)
GMO.......... Gadolinium Molybdate
GMO.......... General Medical Officer [*Navy*] (DNAB)
GMO.......... Genetically-Manipulated Organism [*Biochemistry*]
GMO.......... Genetically Modified Organism [*Biochemistry*]
GMO.......... Gill-Morrell Oscillator
GMO.......... Glyceryl Monooleate [*Organic chemistry*]
GMO.......... Glycol Monoacetate (SAUS)
GMO.......... Grants Management Officer (SAUS)
GMO.......... Groupe de Travail Charge de la Mise en Oeuvre de l'Information et de la Statistique Juridique [*Implementation Work Group on Justice Information and Statistics - IWG*] [*Canada*]
GMO.......... Guided Missile Officer
GMO.......... Gulf, Mobile & Ohio Railroad [*Later, Illinois Central Gulf Railroad*] [*AAR code*]
GMOBE.......... Grand Master of the Most Excellent Order of the British Empire (SAUO)
GMoC.......... Colquitt-Thomas Regional Library, Moultrie, GA [*Library symbol*] [*Library of Congress*] (LCLS)
GMOC.......... General Motors Corp. (EFIS)
GMOCU.......... Guided Missile Operation and Control Unit
GMOD.......... German Ministry of Defense (SAUO)
GMODC.......... General Motors Overseas Distribution Corporation (SAUO)
GMO Diode... Germanium Microwave Oscillating Diode (SAUS)
g/mol.......... Gramme per Mole (SAUS)
GMOL.......... Gram Molecule [*or Molecular*] [*Chemistry*] (IAA)
g-mol.......... Gram-Molecule (STED)
GMOP.......... General Management Operating Policy (FOTI)
GMorC.......... Clayton Junior College, Morrow, GA [*Library symbol*] [*Library of Congress*] (LCLS)
GMorGE.......... Genealogical Enterprises, Morrow, GA [*Library symbol*] [*Library of Congress*] (LCLS)
GMortGE.......... Genealogical Enterprises (SAUS)
GMOS.......... Generic Message Orientation System (SSD)
GMOs.......... Genetically Manipulated Organisms (EERA)
GMOs.......... Genetically Modified Organisms (SAUS)
GM Oscillation... Gill-Morell Oscillation (SAUS)
GMot.......... General Motors Corp. [*Associated Press*] (SAG)
GMOTS.......... Gun Maintenance & Operational Training System (SAUS)
GMOV.......... Glycine Mottle Virus [*Plant pathology*]
GMP.......... Gap Media Project [*An association*] (EA)
GMP.......... Garrison Military Police [*British*]
GMP.......... Gay Men's Press [*GMP is now the name of the company*]
GMP.......... Gemini Management Panel [*NASA*] (KSC)
GMP.......... General Management Plan [*National Park Service*]
GMP.......... General Matrix Program
GMP.......... General Medical Practice (WDAA)
GMP.......... General Medical Problem
GMP.......... Genetically Modified Plant (CARB)
GMP.......... Geometric Modelling Project [*Software*] [*British*] (NITA)
GMP.......... Georgia Milk Producers (SRA)

GMP .... German Military Police (SAUS)
GMP .... Glass, Molders, Pottery, Plastics, and Allied Workers International Union (NTPA)
GMP .... Global Mobile Phone (SAUS)
GMP .... Global Mobile Professional (SAUO)
GMP .... Glucose Monophosphate [*Medicine*] (MELL)
GMP .... Glycomacropeptide [*Biochemistry*]
G-MP .... G-Myeloma Protein [*Biochemistry*] (MAH)
G-MP .... G-Myeloma Proteins [*Biochemistry*] (DAVI)
GMP .... Good Management Practice
GMP .... Good Mining Practice (SAUO)
GMP .... Gordon Moore Park (SAUO)
GMP .... Grand Master of the Order of St. Patrick
GMP .... Granule Membrane Protein
GMP .... Grass-Model Polygraph
GMP .... Green Mansion Properties (SAUS)
GMP .... Green Mountain Power Corp. [*NYSE symbol*] (SPSG)
GMP .... Green Mountain Pwr [*NYSE symbol*] (TTSB)
GMP .... Gross Material Product (SAUS)
GMP .... Ground Map Pencil (DNAB)
GMP .... Ground Movement Planner [*Aviation*] (OA)
GMP .... Ground Movement Radar (SAUO)
GMP .... Groundwater Modeling Program [*US Army Engineer Waterways Experiment Station*] (RDA)
GMP .... Ground Water Monitoring Plan (SAUS)
GMP .... Guanine Monophosphate (SAUS)
GMP .... Guanosine Monophosphate [*Biochemistry*]
GMP .... Guanylic Acid (STED)
GMP .... Guaranteed Minimum Pension [*British*]
GMP .... Guaranteed Minimum Price
GMP .... Guild of Metal Perforators [*British*] (DBA)
GMP .... Gun Mount Processor (SAUS)
GMP .... Gurkha Military Police [*British military*] (DMA)
GMPA .... Game Meat Processors of Australia
G M P A ...... Gas-Metal-Plasma-Arc (SAUS)
GMPA .... General Material and Petroleum Activity [*NCAD*] [*Army*] (MCD)
GMPC .... Green Mountain Power Corp. (NRCH)
GMPCS .... Global Mobile Personal Communications System [*International Telecommunications Union*] [*Geneva, Switzerland*] (ECON)
GMPCS .... Global Mobile Personal Communications Systems (SAUO)
GMPG .... General Motors Proving Grounds [*Automotive engineering*]
GMPG .... Ground nautical Miles Per Gallon (SAUS)
GMPI .... Guilford-Martin Personnel Inventory [*Psychology*]
GMPL .... Grand Master of the Primrose League (SAUO)
GMPMA .... General Material and Petroleum Management Agency (MCD)
GMPPAW ..... Glass (SAUS)
GMPPAW ..... Glass, Molders, Pottery, Plastics, and Allied Workers International Union (EA)
GMPPI .... Ground Map Plan Position Indicator (SAUS)
GMPR .... General Maximum Price Regulation [*World War II*]
GMPR .... Geostationary Microwave Precipitation Radiometer (SAUS)
GMPrD .... General Motors 7.92% Dep Pfd [*NYSE symbol*] (TTSB)
GMPrG .... General Motors 9.12% Dep Pfd [*NYSE symbol*] (TTSB)
GMPrQ .... General Motors 9.125% Dep Pfd [*NYSE symbol*] (TTSB)
GMPS .... Great Masters in Painting and Sculpture [*A publication*]
GMP Standard... Global Mobile Phone Standard (SAUS)
GMPT .... Gum Print [*Gum bichromates*] (VRA)
GMQ .... Geomaque Explorations Ltd. [*Toronto Stock Exchange symbol*]
GMQ .... Good Marketable Quality [*Business term*]
GMQ .... Good Merchantable Ouality (SAUS)
Gmq .... Good Merchantable Quality (MARI)
GMQZ .... Granite Mountain Quarries [*Federal Railroad Administration identification code*]
GMR .... Gallops, Murmurs, or Rubs [*Medicine*] (STED)
GMR .... Gambier Island [*French Polynesia*] [*Airport symbol*] (OAG)
GMR .... General Mobilization Reserves [*DoD*]
GMR .... General Modular Redundancy
GMR .... General Motors Research
GMR .... Geometric Mean Radii
GMR .... Geometric Mean Radius (SAUS)
GMR .... German Military Representative (SAUO)
GMR .... Giant Magnetoresistance [*Materials science*]
GMR .... Giant Magneto Resistive (SAUS)
GMR .... Giant Magnetoresistive (CDE)
GMR .... Giant Magnetoresistive Element
GMR .... Giant Monopole Resonance (SAUS)
GMR .... GOES-Meteosat Relay (SAUS)
GMR .... Government Micro Resources Inc. (SAUO)
GMR .... Gradient Moment Reduction [*Medicine*] (RAWO)
GMR .... Graduated Mobilization Response (DOMA)
GMR .... Grain/Micrite Ratio (SAUS)
GMR .... Grampian Helicopter Charter Ltd. [*British*] [*ICAO designator*] (FAAC)
GMR .... Graphics Metafile Resources [*Computer science*]
GMR .... Greater Manchester Radio [*England*] (WDAA)
GMR .... Greatest Meridional Radius (SAUS)
GMR .... Gromer Aviation (SAUS)
GMR .... Ground Mapping RADAR
GMR .... Ground Mobile RADAR
GMR .... Ground Movement RADAR [*Military*]
GMR .... Group Medical Report
GMR .... Grupo Marxista Revolucionario [*Marxist Revolutionary Group*] [*Portuguese*] [*Political party*] (PPE)
GMR .... Gulf Mortgage & Realty Investments (SAUO)
GMRA .... Government Management Reform Act (SAUS)
GMRAO .... General Mobilization Reserve Acquisition Objective [*DoD*]
GMRC .... General Motors Research Center (SAUS)
GMRC .... Green Mountain Railroad Corp. [*AAR code*]
GMRD .... Guards Motorized Rifle Division (MCD)
GMRD .... Guided Missile Range Division [*NASA*] (KSC)
GMRD .... Guided Missile Research and Development (SAUO)
GMRD .... Guided Missile Research Division (SAUO)
GMRD .... Guided Missiles Range Division (SAUS)
GMRE .... General Motors Rotary Engine [*Automotive engineering*]
GMRK .... Gulfmark International [*NASDAQ symbol*] (SPSG)
GMRL .... General Motors Corp. Research Laboratories [*Warren, MI*]
GMRL .... General Motors Research Laboratries (SAUS)
GMRL .... Grain Marketing Research Laboratory [*Manhattan, KS*] [*Department of Agriculture*] (GRD)
GMRL .... Group of Mathematicians of Romance Languages [*See also GMEL*] [*Coimbra, Portugal*] (EAIO)
GMR Library... General Motors Research Laboratories Library (SAUO)
GMRMLN ..... Greater Midwest Regional Medical Library Network [*Illinois, Kentucky, Michigan, Ohio, S. Dakota*] (NITA)
GMRMO .... General Mobilization Reserve Materiel Objective [*DoD*]
GMRMR .... General Mobilization Reserve Materiel Requirement [*DoD*]
GMROI .... Gross Margin Return on Investment [*Air carrier designation symbol*]
GMRP .... GARP Multicast Registration Protocol (SAUS)
GMRS .... General Mobile Radio Service [*Telecommunications*] (TSSD)
GMRS .... General Mobilization Reserve Stock [*DoD*]
GMRS .... Ground Marker Release System [*Army*] (INF)
GMRSO .... General Mobilization Reserve Stockage Objective [*DoD*]
GMRT .... Gates MacGinitie Reading Test [*Educational test*]
GMRT .... Giant Meterwave Radio Telescope [*India*]
GMRT .... Ground-Mapping Radar Training (SAUS)
GMRWG .... Guided Missile Relay Working Group [*Navy*]
GMRX .... Great Miami Railroad [*Federal Railroad Administration identification code*]
GMRY .... Great Miami & Scioto Railway [*Federal Railroad Administration identification code*]
GMS .... Gabriel Marcel Society (EA)
GMS .... Galvanized Mild Steel (EDCT)
GMS .... Gas Mass Spectrometry (SAUS)
GMS .... Gas Measurement System
GMS .... GEC-Marconi Systems Pty Ltd. (SAUS)
GMS .... Gelatin Matrix System
GMS .... Gemini Mission Simulation (SAUO)
GMS .... Gemini Mission Simulator [*NASA*]
GMS .... Generalized Main Scheduling (SAUS)
GMS .... General Mail System
GMS .... General Maintenance System [*Computer science*] (BUR)
GMS .... General Material Services
GMS .... General Medical Services [*British*]
GM+S .... General Medicine and Surgery (SAUS)
GMS .... General Micro Systems Ltd. (NITA)
GMS .... General Military Science
GMS .... General Milk Sales [*Inactive*] [*An association*] (EA)
GMS .... Generation Management Station
GMS .... Genomic Mismatch Scanning [*Genetic technique*]
GMS .... Geographic Measurement Systems (SAUO)
GMS .... Geometric Modeling System (SAUS)
GMS .... Geometry (SAUS)
GMS .... Geophysical Monitoring Satellite [*DoD, NOAA*]
GMS .... George MacDonald Society [*Lincoln, England*] (EAIO)
GMS .... Geostationary Meteorological Satellite [*Japan*]
GMS .... Geriatric Mental State [*Medicine*] (DMAA)
GMS .... Giant Motor Synapse [*Anatomy*]
GMS .... Giant Motor Synchron (SAUS)
GMS .... Gichner Mobile Shelters (MCD)
GMS .... Gilbert-Meulengracht Syndrome [*Medicine*] (DMAA)
GMS .... Gilbert M. Smith Herbarium [*Stanford University*] [*Pacific Grove, CA*]
GMS .... Glen Miller Society (EAIO)
GMS .... Global Management System (SAUO)
GMS .... Global Messaging Service (SAUO)
GMS .... Global Mining Supply (SAUO)
GMS .... Glyceryl Monostearate [*Organic chemistry*]
GMS .... Gomori Methenamine Silver Stain [*Medicine*] (DMAA)
GMS .... Gomori's Methenamine Silver [*A biological stain*]
GMS .... Goniodysgenesis-Mental Retardation-Short Stature Syndrome [*Medicine*] (DMAA)
GMS .... Gospel Missionary Society (SAUO)
GMS .... Grant Maintained Schools [*British*] (DET)
GMS .... Grant-Maintained Status (ODBW)
GMS .... Grants Management Specialist (SAUS)
G/MS .... Graphics and/or Media Specialist
GMS .... Gravitational Mass Sensor
GMS .... Gravity Measuring System
GMS .... Greater Mekong Sub-Region [*East Asian development zone*]
GMS .... Ground Maintenance Support
GMS .... Ground Mapping [*or Marking*] System
GMS .... Ground Map Spoiled (SAUS)
GMS .... Groundwater Modeling System
GMS .... Group for Material Standardization (SAUO)
GMS .... Group Manufacturing Services (TIMI)
GMS .... Group Membership Scores [*Psychometrics*]
GMS .... Guardian-Morton Shulman Precious Metals, Inc. [*Toronto Stock Exchange symbol*] [*Vancouver Stock Exchange symbol*]
GMS .... Guidance Monitor Set [*Aerospace*] (AAG)
GMS .... Guided Missile (SAUS)
GMS .... Guided Missile School [*Dam Neck, VA*]
GMS .... Guided Missile Screen (SAUO)

GMS Guided Missile Simulator [*Military*] (CAAL)
GMS Guided Missile System
GMS Guide to Minerals Schools (SAUO)
GMS Gun Management System (SAUS)
GMS Master Construction Specification [*Canada*]
GMS Morehouse College, School of Medicine, Atlanta, GA [*OCLC symbol*] (OCLC)
GMSA General Motors South African
GMSA German Minesweeping Administration [*Allied German Occupation Forces*]
GMSA Global Multivariate Statistical Analysis (SAUS)
GMSA Seaman Apprentice, Gunner's Mate, Striker [*Navy rating*]
GMSB Guided Missile System Branch (SAUO)
GMSC Gateway Mobile Switching Center (SAUS)
GMSC General Medical Services Committee (SAUO)
GMSC General Medical Services Council [*British*] (BI)
GMSC Geologic Map Standards Committee (SAUO)
GMSC Guangdong Manpower Service Corp. (SAUS)
GMSC Guangdong Manpower Service Corporation (SAUO)
GMSD German Minsweeping Division (SAUO)
GM Search General Moto (SAUS)
GMSEP Georgia Media Specialist Evaluation Program (SAUO)
GMSER Guided Missile Service Report (NG)
GMSF German Minesweeper Flotilla (SAUO)
GMSF Goddard Manned Space Flight (SAUS)
GMSF Growth and Morphology of Supercritical Fluids (SAUS)
GMSFC George Marshall Space Flight Center [*Huntsville, AL*] (IEEE)
GMSFC George Marshall Spaceflight Center Consulting (SAUS)
GMSFN Global Manned Space Flight Network (SAA)
GMSI Gandalf Mobile Systems Incorporated (SAUS)
GMSI Gateway Medical Systems, Incorporated (SAUO)
GMSI GMSI Inc. (SAUO)
GMSI Grand Master of the Order of the Star of India [*British*]
GMSI Ground Modeling Systems Inc. (SAUO)
GMSI Ground Modeling Systems Incorporated (SAUO)
GMSIA Guided Missile System, Intercept-Aerial (MCD)
GMSK Gaussian Filtered Minimum Shift Keying (MCD)
GMSK Gaussian Mean Shift Keying (SAUS)
GMSK Gaussian Minimum Shift Keying (SAUS)
GMSK Global Method Shift Keying (SAUS)
GMSL Group Management Service Limited (SAUO)
G/MSL Guided Missile
GMSL Sidi Slimane [*Morocco*] [*ICAO location identifier*] (ICLI)
GMSLL Georgetown University. Monograph Series on Languages (SAUO)
GMSLL Georgetown University.Monograph Series on Languages (SAUS)
GMSN Seaman, Gunner's Mate, Striker [*Navy rating*]
GMSO German Mine Supplies Organization [*Allied German Occupation Forces*]
G M Soc Am Univ Y Bk Geological and Mining Society (SAUS)
GMSP Global Multi-Mission Service Platform (SEWL)
GMSQUAD Guided Missile Squadron (MUGU)
GMSR Gold Mining Stock Report (SAUO)
GMSR Guided Missile Service Record
GMSR Guided Missile Service Report (MCD)
GMSR Gulf & Mississippi Corp. (SAUO)
GMSR Gulf & Mississippi Railroad [*Federal Railroad Administration identification code*]
GMSR Gunner's Mate, Ship Repair [*Navy rating*] [*Obsolete*]
GMSRON Guided Missile Record (SAUS)
GMSRON Guided Missile Service Squadron (MUGU)
GMSRP Gunner's Mate, Ship Repair, Powderman [*Navy rating*] [*Obsolete*]
GMSS Geostationary Meteorological Satellite System (SAUO)
GMSS Global Meteorological Satellite System Program (SAUO)
GMSS Graphical Modeling and Simulation System
GMST Gemstar Intl. Group [*NASDAQ symbol*] (SG)
GMST General Military Subjects Instructor (SAUS)
GMST General Military Subjects Test
GMST Glossary of Merchant Ship Types (MCD)
GMST Greenwich Mean Sidereal Time (WGA)
GMSTE Gemstar Intl. [*NASDAQ symbol*] (TTSB)
GMSTF Gemstar International Group Ltd. [*NASDAQ symbol*] (SAG)
GMSTIS General Manager, Science, Technology and Information System (SAUO)
GMSTS Guided Missiles Service Test Station (SAUS)
GMSTS Guided Missile System Test Set (NATG)
GMSU General Maritime Stevedores' Union [*Philippines*]
GMSU Guided Missile Service Unit [*Air Force*]
GMSW Gross Maximum Shipping Weight
GMSW Gross Measures Weight (SAUS)
GMSY Generalized Multigroup System (SAUO)
GMT Garment
GMT Gas Missile Tube
GMT GATX Corp. [*Formerly, General American Transportation Corp.*] [*NYSE symbol*] (SPSG)
GMT Geiger-Mueller Tube
GMT Geimarine Technology (SAUS)
GMT Gemini Technology, Inc. [*Toronto Stock Exchange symbol*] [*Vancouver Stock Exchange symbol*]
GMT General American Transportation (SAUS)
GMT Generalized Machine Theory (SAUS)
GMT Generalized Multitasking
GMT General Machine Test [*Computer science*] (BUR)
GMT General Managers Team (SAUS)
GMT General Manufacturing Training (SAUS)
GMT General Mapping Tool (SAUO)
GMT General Military (SAUS)
GMT General Military Training (AFM)
GMT Generic Mapping Tools [*Marine science*] (OSRA)
GMT Geo Marine Technology (SAUS)
GMT Geomarine Technology
GMT Geometric Mean [*Antibody titers*] (STED)
GMT Geometric Mean Titer [*Analytical chemistry*]
G M T Geometric Mean Titre (SAUS)
GMT Geriatric Medicine Today (SAUS)
GMT Gingival Margin Trimmer [*Medicine*] (DMAA)
GMT Glass-Mat Reinforced Thermoplastic [*Automotive engineering*]
GMT Glass-Mat Thermoplastic
GMT Global Money Transfer (SAUS)
gmt Gourmet (ADWA)
GMT Government Maturity Test (MCD)
GMT Governor Macquarie Tower [*Sydney, New South Wales, Australia*]
GMT Graphics Mouse Technology [*Computer science*] (CIST)
GMT Greenwich Mean [*or Meridian*] Time
GMT Grimston Machine Tools Ltd. (SAUO)
GMT Group Method Techniques (FOTI)
GMT Grupoaereo Monterrey, SA de CV [*Mexico*] [*FAA designator*] (FAAC)
GMT Guided Missile Target (NG)
GMT Guided Missile Trainer
GMT Guided Missile Transporter (SAUS)
GMT Gunner's Mate, Technician [*Navy rating*]
GM(T) Gunner's Mate (Torpedo) [*U.S. Navy enlisted rating*] (AUER)
GMT Gunner's Mate (Turrets) [*U.S. Navy enlisted rating*] (AUER)
GMT Gunnery Maintenance Trainer [*Army*]
GMT1 Gunner's Mate, Technician, First Class [*Navy rating*] (DNAB)
GMT2 Gunner's Mate, Technician, Second Class [*Navy rating*] (DNAB)
GMT3 Gunner's Mate, Technician, Third Class [*Navy rating*] (DNAB)
GMTA Al Hoceima/Cote Du Rif [*Morocco*] [*ICAO location identifier*] (ICLI)
GMTA General Motors Task Authorization (ACAE)
GMTA Great Minds Think Alike [*Internet language*] (PCM)
GMTB General Motors Truck and Body (ACAE)
GMtbC Berry College (SAUS)
GMtbC Berry College, Mount Berry, GA [*Library symbol*] [*Library of Congress*] (LCLS)
GMTC Chief Gunner's Mate, Technician [*Navy rating*]
GMTC Game Tech International, Inc. [*NASDAQ symbol*] (NASQ)
GMTC General Motors Technical Center (SAUO)
GMTC Geometric Mean Titer of Controls (MELL)
GMTC Gland Manufacturers' Technical Committee (HEAS)
GMTC Glutamate Manufacturers Technical Committee (EA)
GMTCM Master Chief Gunner's Mate, Technician [*Navy rating*]
GMTCS Senior Chief Gunner's Mate, Technician [*Navy rating*]
GMTD Guided Missile Training Device (ACAE)
GMTestUNOTS Guided Missile Test Unit; Naval Ordnance Test Station (SAUS)
GMTF Gay Media Task Force (EA)
GMTF Geometric Modulation Transfer Function (MCD)
GMTI Gemini Technology (SAUS)
GMTI Greenman Technologies [*NASDAQ symbol*] (TTSB)
GMTI Greenman Technologies, Inc. [*NASDAQ symbol*] (SAG)
GMTI Ground Moving Target Indicator
GMTIF Gemini Technology, Inc. [*NASDAQ symbol*] (COMM)
GMTI/L Ground Moving Target Indication/Location (ACAE)
GMTIW Greenman Technologies Wrrt [*NASDAQ symbol*] (TTSB)
GMTL Goudy Memorial Typographic Laboratory (SAUO)
GMTN Tetouan/Sania R'Mel [*Morocco*] [*ICAO location identifier*] (ICLI)
GMTO General Military Training Office
GMTOA Green Mountain Textile Overseers Association (EA)
GMT(P) glass mat reinforced thermoplastics (SAUS)
GMTPr GATX Corp. $2.50 Cv Pfd [*NYSE symbol*] (TTSB)
GMTPrA GATX Corp. $3.875 cm Cv Pfd [*NYSE symbol*] (TTSB)
GMTR Giant Meterwave Radio Telescope (SAUS)
GMTR Guided Missile Test Round [*Military*] (CAAL)
GMTRB General Military Training Review Board (AFM)
GMTRY General Military Training Review Board (SAUS)
GMTRY Geometry (MSA)
GMTS Guided Missile Test Set (AFM)
GMTSA Gunner's Mate, Technician, Seaman Apprentice [*Navy rating*]
GMTSN Gunner's Mate, Technician, Seaman [*Navy rating*]
GMTT Ground Moving Target Tracker (ACAE)
GMTT Tanger/Boukhalf [*Morocco*] [*ICAO location identifier*] (ICLI)
GMTTR Geometric Mean Time to Repair [*Military*] (CAAL)
GMTU Guided Missile Test Unit (IAA)
GMTU Guided Missile Training Unit [*Navy*]
GM Tube Glass Metal Tube (SAUS)
GMtvB Brewton-Parker College, Mount Vernon, GA [*Library symbol*] [*Library of Congress*] (LCLS)
GMTX Gate Matrix to XY-data (SAUS)
GMU Gadjah Mada University [*Indonesia*]
GMU George Mason University [*Virginia*]
GMU Geotechnical mapping unit (SAUS)
GMU Gigabyte Memory Unit (SEWL)
GMU Goose Management Unit
GMU Gospel Missionary Union (EA)
GMU Granite Mountain [*Utah*] [*Seismograph station code, US Geological Survey*] (SEIS)
GMU Greenville, SC [*Location identifier*] [*FAA*] (FAAL)
GMU Groundwater Management Units (AUSE)
GMU Guided Missile Unit
GMU Gyro Mechanical Unit (ADWA)
GMU Mercer University, Macon, GA [*OCLC symbol*] (OCLC)
GMU L Rev George Masou University Law Review (SAUS)

GMUS .... Guildhall Museum [*London*]
GMusRNCM(Hons)... Graduate in Music of the Royal Northern College of Music [*British*] (DBQ)
GMUTS .... General Motors Uniform Test Standards [*Automotive engineering*]
GMUTU .... General Motors Uniform Test Standards (SAUS)
GMV .... Galinsoga Mosaic Virus
GMV .... Generalized Minimum Variance [*Control technology*]
GMV .... Glycine Mosaic Virus [*Plant pathology*]
GMV .... Golden Mosaic Virus (SAUS)
GMV .... Government Motor Vehicle (DNAB)
GMV .... Government Motor Vessel (SAUS)
GMV .... Gramme Molecular Volume (SAUS)
gmv .... Gram Molecular Volume (ABAC)
GMV .... Gram Molecular Volume [*Chemistry*]
GMV .... Grand Master of the Vails [*Freemasonry*]
GMV .... Guaranteed Maximum Value (SAUS)
GMV .... Guaranteed Minimum Value
GMV .... Guranteed Minimum Value (SAUS)
GMVDC .... Gay Men's VD Clinic (EA)
GMVIO .... Geomaque Explorations Ltd. (SAUO)
GMVIXC ...... GMX Communications, Inc. (SAUO)
GMVLS .... Guided Missile Vertical Launch System [*Canadian Navy*]
GMVX .... Genessee & Mohawk Valley Railroad [*Federal Railroad Administration identification code*]
GMW .... General Microwave Corp. [*AMEX symbol*] (SPSG)
GMW .... Generic Maintenance Workstation (SSD)
GMW .... Genl Microwave [*AMEX symbol*] (TTSB)
GMW .... Give me More Windows (SAUS)
GMW .... Gold Mountain [*Washington*] [*Seismograph station code, US Geological Survey*] (SEIS)
GMW .... Gramme Molecular Weight (SAUS)
GMW .... Gram Molecular Weight [*Chemistry*]
GMW .... Groundwater Monitoring Wells (SAUO)
GMW .... Guevara-McInteer-Wageman
GMW .... Guevara-Molecular Weight (SAUS)
GMW .... Wesleyan College, Macon, GA [*Library symbol*] [*Library of Congress*] (LCLS)
GMWA .... Gospel Music Workshop of America (EA)
GMWC .... Graphite Moderated, Water Cooled (PDAA)
GMWL .... Global Mean Water Line (QUAC)
GMWM .... Group Mark with Word Mark (VLIE)
GM/WM ...... Group Mark/Word Mark [*Computer science*] (OA)
GMWS .... Guided Missile Weapon System [*Military*] (CAAL)
GMWU .... General and Municipal Workers' Union [*British*]
GMWU .... General Municipal Workers Union (SAUS)
GMX .... Gasket Material Expert [*Automotive engineering*]
GMX .... Generalized Monitor Experimental (VLIE)
GMX .... Generealized Monitor Experimental (SAUS)
GMX .... Global Message Exchange (SAUO)
GMXC .... GMX Communications, Inc. (SAUS)
g/my .... gram per square meter (SAUS)
gmy .... Grams per Square Metre (SAUS)
GMZ .... Bowie, TX [*Location identifier*] [*FAA*] (FAAL)
GMZ .... General Mills [*Federal Railroad Administration identification code*]
GMZFO .... Gouvernement Militaire de la Zone Francaise d'Occupation [*Military Government of the French Zone of Occupation*] [*of Germany*]
GN .... Air Gabon [*ICAO designator*] (AD)
GN .... Buick Grand National (SAUS)
GN .... G1ucose Nitrogen (SAUS)
GN .... Gain (NASA)
GN .... Gandy-Nanta [*Disease*] [*Medicine*] (DB)
GN .... ganglioneuroma (SAUS)
GN .... Ganglion Nodosum [*Neurology*]
GN .... Gaseous Nitrogen (SAUS)
GN .... Gastroenterology Nursing (SAUO)
GN .... Gathering of Nations (EA)
GN .... Gaussian Noise (IAA)
GN .... Gaylactic Network [*An association*] (EA)
gn .... General (ADWA)
GN .... General (WGA)
GN .... Generalized Network (SAUO)
GN .... General Navigation (ACAE)
GN .... General Network (VLIE)
GN .... General Note (MSA)
GN .... General Notes (SAUS)
GN .... Generator (IAA)
Gn .... Genesis [*Old Testament book*]
GN .... Georgia Music (SAUS)
GN .... Georgian
GN .... [*The*] Georgia Northern Railway Co. (IIA)
GN .... German
GN .... German Navy (SAUO)
GN .... Get Next (VLIE)
gn .... Gilbert and Ellice Islands [*Tuvalu*] [*gb (Gilbert Islands) or tu (Tuvalu) used in records cataloged after October 1978*] [*MARC country of publication code*] [*Library of Congress*] (LCCP)
GN .... Girls Nation (EA)
GN .... Given Name (VLIE)
GN .... Gleyniedermoor (SAUS)
GN .... Glomerular Nephritis [*Medicine*]
G:N .... Glucose:Nitrogen [*Ratio*]
Gn .... Gnathion [*Medicine*] (EDAA)
GN .... Gnotobiote [*Medicine*] (DMAA)
GN .... Godfrey-Nash [*Forerunner of British HRG and Frazer-Nash automobiles*]
GN .... Golden Nematode [*A worm*]
GN .... Golden Nugget, Inc. (EFIS)
GN .... Golden Number [*Number used to fix the date of Easter*]
GN .... Golden Titan Resources [*Vancouver Stock Exchange symbol*]
GN .... Goldneck Summer Squash
Gn .... Gonadotropin [*Endocrinology*]
GN .... Gonococcus [*Medicine*] (MEDA)
GN .... Good Night [*Amateur radio*]
GN .... Gouty Nephropathy [*Medicine*] (MELL)
GN .... Gouty Node [*Medicine*] (MELL)
GN .... Government Notice (SAUS)
Gn .... Gradational (SAUS)
Gn .... Gradational, Non-Calcareous [*Soil*]
GN .... Graduate Nurse
GN .... Grain (MCD)
GN .... Gram-Negative [*Also, GRN*] [*Microbiology*]
GN .... Grand National [*Automobile racing*]
GN .... Grand Nehemiah [*Freemasonry*] (ROG)
GN .... Grandnephew (ADA)
GN .... Grandniece (ADA)
GN .... Grant Number (NITA)
GN .... Great Northern Railway (MHDW)
GN .... Great Northern Railway Co. (SAUO)
GN .... Great Novel (SAUS)
GN .... Green [*Maps and charts*]
GN .... Grid Neutralization (SAUS)
GN .... Grid North [*Army*] (ADDR)
GN .... Ground Nester [*Ornithology*]
GN .... Ground Network [*Remote sensing*] (EERA)
GN .... Ground Noise (ELAL)
GN .... Groundnut Meal (PDAA)
GN .... Group Number [*Dialog*] [*Searchable fields*] [*Information service or system*] (NITA)
GN .... Guanine Nucleotide [*Biochemistry*]
GN .... Guidance Note (HEAS)
GN .... Guide-Number [*Photography*]
GN .... Guinea [*ANSI two-letter standard code*] (CNC)
GN .... Gun [*s*] [*Freight*]
GN .... National Guard (Nicaragua) [*Political party*] (PSAP)
GN_2 .... Gaseous Nitrogen [*NASA*]
GNA .... Gaino, Inc. (SAUO)
GNA .... Gainsco (SAUS)
GNA .... Gainsco, Inc. [*AMEX symbol*] (SPSG)
GNA .... Galanthus Nivalis Agglutinin
GNA .... Gay Nurses' Alliance (EA)
GNA .... General Nursing Assistance (DMAA)
GNA .... Georgia Nurses Association (SRA)
GNA .... German Navy Association (SAUO)
GNA .... Ghana News Agency
GNA .... Global Network Academy [*On-line education*] [*Information retrieval*]
GNA .... Globewide Network Academy
GNA .... Gnangara [*Australia*] [*Geomagnetic observatory code*]
GNA .... Granada Exploration Corp. [*Vancouver Stock Exchange symbol*]
GNA .... Grand National Assembly (SAUO)
GNA .... Grants Pass, OR [*Location identifier*] [*FAA*] (FAAL)
GNA .... Graphics Navigation Aid (SAUS)
GNA .... Graphics Network Architecture
GNA .... Graysonia, Nashville & Ashdown Railroad Co. [*AAR code*]
GNA .... Great Northern Airlines, Inc. (SAUS)
GNA .... Great Northern Insured Annuity Corp. (SAUO)
GNA .... Greek National Army
GNA .... Servicios Àereos Gana SA de CV [*Mexico*] [*FAA designator*] (FAAC)
GNAA .... German Naval Air Arm (SAUS)
GNAA .... German Navy Air Arm (SAUO)
GNAACBJA... Greater North American Aviculturist and Color Bred Judges Association (SAUO)
GNAB .... Guide to New Australian Books [*A publication*]
GNAC .... Great Northeast Athletic Conference (PSS)
GNAC .... Guidance, Navigation and Control [*Military*] (IAA)
GNACBJA ..... Greater North American Color-Bred Judge Association [*Later, GNAACBJA*] (EA)
GnAcpt .... General Acceptance Corp. [*Associated Press*] (SAG)
GNACU .... Guidance & Navigation Avionics Control Unit (SAUS)
GNADS .... Gimbaled Night and Day Sight
GNAF .... Generalized Nonadjacent Form (SAUS)
GNAGS .... Ground Adjutant General Section [*World War II*]
GNAIW .... Glacial North Atlantic Intermediate Water
GNAL .... Georgia Nuclear Aircraft Laboratory (SAA)
GN & C .... Guidance, Navigation, and Control (MCD)
GN and C ...... Guidance, Navigation, and Control (SAUS)
GNAS .... General NAS [*FAA*] (TAG)
GNAS .... Grand National Archery Society [*British*]
G Nas .... Guillelmus Naso [*Flourished, 1220-34*] [*Authority cited in pre-1607 legal work*] (DSA)
GNAT .... General Numerical Analysis of Transport [*Computer program*]
GNAT .... Global Network of Astronomical Telescopes [*Proposed network*]
gnat .... Global Network of Automatic Telescopes (SAUS)
GNAT .... GNU Ada Translator (SAUS)
GNAT .... Grade-Nine Achievement Test (SAUS)
GNAT Program... General Numerical Analysis of Transport Program (SAUS)
GNATS .... Generalized Numerical Analysis of Thermal System (SAUS)
G N A T S.... Generalized Numerical Analysis of Thermal Systems (SAUS)
GNATS .... General Noise and Tonal System (NVT)
GNATS .... General Nonlinear Analysis of Two-Dimensional Structures [*Computer program*]

GNATS .... Graphic Navlink Aircraft Tracking System (SAUS)
GNATS .... Guidance and Navigational Tracking Satellite (SAUO)
GnAuto .... General Automation, Inc. [*Associated Press*] (SAG)
GNaV .... Graphic Area Navigation (SAUS)
GNavO .... Group Navigation Officer [*British military*] (DMA)
GNB .... ganglioneuroblastoma (SAUS)
GNB .... Global Air Link [*Nigeria*] [*ICAO designator*] (FAAC)
GNB .... Good News Bible [*Today's English Version*] [*A publication*] (BJA)
GNB .... Gould National Batteries, Inc. (SAUO)
GNB .... Gram-Negative Bacillus [*Microbiology*]
GNB .... Granby, CO [*Location identifier*] [*FAA*] (FAAL)
GNB .... Granby Resources Ltd. [*Vancouver Stock Exchange symbol*]
GNB .... Grenoble [*France*] [*Airport symbol*] (OAG)
GNB .... Guinea-Bissau [*ANSI three-letter standard code*] (CNC)
GNBC .... Glendale Bancorporation (SAUO)
GNBC .... Grainbelt [*Federal Railroad Administration identification code*]
GNBM .... Gram-Negative Bacillary Meningitis [*Medicine*]
GnBnd .... General Binding Corp. [*Associated Press*] (SAG)
GNC .... General Nautical Chart [*Navy*]
GNC .... General Navigation Computer (SAUS)
gnc .... general nuclear war (SAUS)
GNC .... General Nursing Care [*Medicine*]
GNC .... General Nursing Council
GNC .... General Nursing Council for England and Wales (SAUO)
GNC .... General Nutrition (SAUS)
GNC .... General Nutrition Center (SAUS)
GNC .... General Nutrition, Inc. [*NYSE symbol*] (COMM)
GNC .... Geologic Names Committee [*US Geological Survey*]
GNC .... Geriatric Nurse Clinician (DMAA)
GNC .... Global (SAUS)
GNC .... Global Navigation Chart [*Military*]
GNC .... Goddard Network Control [*NASA*] (MCD)
GNC .... Gram Negative Cocci [*Medicine*] (MELL)
GNC .... Grand National Championship [*Motorcycle racing*]
GNC .... Graphical Numerical Control (SAUO)
GNC .... Graphic Numerical Control [*Deltacam Systems Ltd.*] [*Software package*] [*British*] (MCD)
GNC .... Great National Coal (EFIS)
GNC .... Great Northwest Conference (PSS)
GNC .... Grid North Correction
GNC .... Gross Neutron Counter (PDAA)
GNC .... Ground Nutation Control (SAUS)
GNC .... Guaranty National [*NYSE symbol*] (TTSB)
GNC .... Guaranty National Corp. [*NYSE symbol*] (SPSG)
GNC .... Guidance (SAUS)
GNC .... Guidance and Navigation Computer [*NASA*] (KSC)
GNC .... Guidance, Navigation, and Control (NASA)
GNC .... Guidance Navigation Control (SAUS)
GNC .... Seminole, TX [*Location identifier*] [*FAA*] (FAAL)
GnCable .... General Cable PLC [*Associated Press*] (SAG)
GNCAM .... Glia-Neuron Cell Adhesion Molecule [*Cytology*]
GNCCA .... Grand National Curling Club of America
GNCD .... General Notice to Defence Contractors (SAUS)
GNCEW .... General Nursing Council for England and Wales
GNCI .... General Nutrition Co. [*NASDAQ symbol*] (SAG)
GNCI .... General Nutrition Companies, Inc. [*NASDAQ symbol*] (NASQ)
GNCI .... Genl Nutrition [*NASDAQ symbol*] (TTSB)
GNCIS .... Guidance, Navigation, and Control Integration Simulator (NASA)
GNCM .... General Communication, Inc. [*NASDAQ symbol*] (NQ)
GNCMA .... Genl Communication'A' [*NASDAQ symbol*] (TTSB)
GNCN .... Goran Capital, Inc. [*NASDAQ symbol*] (SAG)
GNCNF .... Goran Capital [*NASDAQ symbol*] (TTSB)
GnCom .... General Communications, Inc. [*Associated Press*] (SAG)
Gn Cpl .... Gun Corporal (SAUS)
GNCR .... Gencare Health System (SAUS)
GNCS .... Guidance, Navigation, and Control System (MCD)
GNCSA .... Good Neighbour Council of South Australia
GNCT .... Good Neighbour Council of Tasmania [*Australia*]
GNCTS .... GN & C [*Guidance, Navigation, and Control*] Test Station (MCD)
GNCTU .... Grand National Consolidated Trade-Union (SAUO)
GND .... Gallium-arsenide Negative-resistance Diode (SAUS)
GND .... Glutamate Neuronal Degeneration [*Found in Alzheimer's Disease*] [*Medicine*] (EDAA)
GND .... Gram-Negative Diplococci [*Medicine*] (MEDA)
GND .... Grand Airways, Inc. [*FAA designator*] (FAAC)
GND .... Grand Casinos [*NYSE symbol*] (TTSB)
GND .... Grand Casinos, Inc. [*NYSE symbol*] (SAG)
GND .... Grandview Resources, Inc. [*Toronto Stock Exchange symbol*] [*Vancouver Stock Exchange symbol*]
GND .... Grenada [*Windward Islands*] [*Airport symbol*] (OAG)
GND .... Gross National Demand (SAUS)
GND .... Ground (AAG)
Gnd .... Ground [*Medicine*] (EDAA)
gnd .... Ground (IDOE)
GND .... Ground-Detonated Flares [*Military*] (INF)
GND .... Grounded [*Electricity*] [*Electronics*]
GND .... North Georgia College, Stewart Library, Dahlonega, GA [*OCLC symbol*] (OCLC)
Gnd A .... Ground Angle (SAUS)
GNDACF .... Ground Alternate Command Facility (SAUO)
GnData .... General DataComm Industries, Inc. [*Associated Press*] (SAG)
GNDC .... Gram-Negative Diplococci [*Medicine*] (MELL)
GNDCG .... Ground Forces Commanding General [*World War II*]
GNDCK .... Ground Check [*Aviation*]
GND C/O .... Ground Checkout [*NASA*] (NASA)
GNDCON .... Ground Control
GNDCP .... Ground Command Post [*Army*]
GNDFG .... Ground Fog (SAUS)
GND HT XGR .... Ground Heat Exchanger (SAUS)
GNDI .... Gross National Disposable Income [*Economics*]
Gn Disp .... Gun Displacement (SAUS)
GNDR .... Gander Mountain [*NASDAQ symbol*] (TTSB)
GNDR .... Gander Mountain, Inc. [*NASDAQ symbol*] (NQ)
GNDRAD .... Groundward Looking Radiometer Stand (SAUS)
GNDVW .... Grandview, WA [*American Association of Railroads railroad junction routing code*]
GNDW .... Grandview Resources, Inc. (SAUO)
GnDyn .... General Dynamics Corp. [*Associated Press*] (SAG)
GNE .... Gane Energy Corp. Ltd. [*Toronto Stock Exchange symbol*]
GNE .... Genentech, Inc. [*NYSE symbol*] (SPSG)
GNE .... Generalized Nash-Equilibrium [*Game*]
GNE .... General Nuclear Engineering Company (SAUO)
GNE .... Government Nomenclature Equipment (DNAB)
GNE .... Gross National Affluent (SAUS)
GNE .... Gross National Effluent
GNE .... Gross National Expenditure
GNE .... Guidance and Navigation Electronics (KSC)
GNE .... Guidance and Navigation Equipment
GNEC .... General Nuclear Engineering Corp. (MCD)
GNEHAU .... Great Britain. Ministry of Agriculture Fisheries (SAUS)
GNEHAU .... Great Britain. Ministry of Agriculture, Fisheries and Food. National Agricultural Advisory Service. Experimental Husbandry Farms and Experimental Hort (SAUS)
GNEM .... Global Network for Environmental Monitoring [*Defunct*] (EA)
GNEMP .... General Employment Enterprises (SAUS)
GnEmp .... General Employment Enterprises, Inc. [*Associated Press*] (SAG)
GNEP .... Gross Nuclear Electricity Production (SAUO)
GNERD .... Gross National Expenditure on Research and Development (SAUO)
GNESIT .... Greater New England Society of Inhalation Therapists
GNET .... g02net, Inc. [*NASDAQ symbol*] (SG)
GNET .... Games Network, Inc. (SAUO)
GNET .... General Information Network (SAUS)
GNEX .... Genex Corp. (SAUO)
GNF .... Gannett Newspaper Foundation
GNF .... German Nuclear Forum (SAUS)
GNF .... Granada Foods (SAUS)
GNF .... Greibach Normal Form (SAUO)
GNF .... Guns Now Firing (SAUS)
GNFA .... Ghana National Farmers Council (SAUO)
GNFC .... Graceland News Fan Club [*Defunct*] (EA)
GNFCC .... German Nuclear Fuel Cycle Center (SAUO)
GNFMS .... Gaseous Nitrogen Flow Measuring System
GNG .... Gaussian Noise Generator [*Electronics*]
GNG .... Generation Gather Group [*Computer science*]
GNG .... Golden Nugget, Inc. [*NYSE symbol*] (COMM)
GNG .... Go No-Go (ACAE)
GNG .... Gooding (SAUS)
GNG .... Gooding, ID [*Location identifier*] [*FAA*] (FAAL)
GNG .... Granger Resources Corp. [*Vancouver Stock Exchange symbol*]
GNG .... Greenhouse Gas (SAUS)
GNGC .... Guide Network Group Connector (SAUO)
GNGCS .... Ground Forces Chief of Staff [*World War II*]
GNGDC .... Ground Forces Deputy Chief of Staff [*World War II*]
GNGPS .... Ground Forces Plans Section [*World War II*]
GNGRBRD .... Gingerbread
GnGrth .... General Growth Properties [*Associated Press*] (SAG)
GNGS .... Genoa Nuclear Generating Station (NRCH)
GNGSE .... Ground Forces Secretariat [*World War II*]
GNGX .... Boothe Leasing [*Private rail car owner code*]
GNH .... Grand National Hunt [*British*]
GNH .... Gross Night Hour [*Advertising*] (WDMC)
GnHost .... General Host Corp. [*Associated Press*] (SAG)
GnHous .... General Housewares Corp. [*Associated Press*] (SAG)
GNI .... GayNet International (SAUO)
GNI .... Genco Industry, Inc. [*Vancouver Stock Exchange symbol*]
GNI .... Generation of New Ideas (MHDB)
GNI .... Glat Northern Iron Ore Properties (SAUS)
GNI .... [*The*] GNI Group, Inc. [*Associated Press*] (SAG)
GNI .... Gram-Negative Infection [*Medicine*] (MELL)
GNI .... Grand Isle, LA [*Location identifier*] [*FAA*] (FAAL)
GNI .... Great Northern Iron Ore Properties [*NYSE symbol*] (SPSG)
GNI .... Grenoble Network Initiative (SAUO)
GNI .... Grid Node Interface (PDAA)
GNI .... Gross National Income [*Economics*]
GNI .... Gross National Investment (EERA)
GNIB .... German Newspaper Information Bureau (SAUO)
GNIB .... Guatemala News and Information Bureau (EA)
GNIC .... Gay News Information and Communication Network [*Information service or system*] (IID)
GNIC .... Guaranty National Corporation (SAUO)
GNID .... Gram-Negative Intracellular Diplococci [*Microbiology*]
GNIE .... Global Network Information Enterprise (SEWL)
GNIIS .... Geographic Names Information System (SAUS)
GNIM .... Generic Network Information Model (SAUS)
GNIN .... General Inquiry (VLIE)
GNIP .... Global Network for Isotopes in Precipitation (SAUO)
GNIP .... Global Network of Isotopes in Precipitation (SAUS)
GNIron .... Great Northern Iron Ore Properties [*Associated Press*] (SAG)
GNIS .... Geographic Names Information Service (SAUO)

GNIS .... Geographic Names Information System [*US Geological Survey*] [*Information service or system*]
GNIS .... Global Names Information System [*Computer science*]
GNJ .... Lexington, KY [*Location identifier*] [*FAA*] (FAAL)
GNK .... General Kinetics, Inc. (SAUO)
GNK .... Globalink, Inc. [*AMEX symbol*] (SAG)
GNKNT .... General Kinetia (SAUS)
GNKSA .... Good Net-Keeping Seal of Approval (SAUS)
GNL .... Galey & Lord, Inc. [*NYSE symbol*] (SAG)
GNL .... Gemco National, Inc. (SAUO)
GNL .... General
GNL .... General Aviation (SAUS)
GNL .... Georgia Nuclear Laboratories (SAUS)
GNL .... Georgia Nuclear Laboratory [*AEC*]
GNL .... Grade of Non-Linearity (SAUS)
GNL .... Great National Land [*Vancouver Stock Exchange symbol*]
GNL .... Greenwood [*Mississippi*] [*Airport symbol*] (AD)
GNLB .... Genelabs Technologies [*NASDAQ symbol*] (SPSG)
GNLT .... Greater Necklaced Laughing-Thrush [*North American bird banding code*] (BIBA)
GNLTD .... Granulated (MSA)
GNM .... Genetron Marine, Inc. [*Vancouver Stock Exchange symbol*]
GNM .... Ghana National Museum (SAUO)
GNM .... Global Network Mission (ACAE)
GNM .... Golden [*New Mexico*] [*Seismograph station code, US Geological Survey*] (SEIS)
GNM .... Good News Mission (EA)
GNM .... Guanambi [*Brazil*] [*Airport symbol*] (OAG)
GNMA .... Government National Mortgage Administration (AAGC)
GNMA .... Government National Mortgage Association [*Nickname: Ginnie Mae*]
GnMag .... General Magnaplate Corp. [*Associated Press*] (SAG)
GNMDF .... Global Network Meta-Data File (SAUS)
GnMicr .... General Microwave Corp. [*Associated Press*] (SAG)
GnMill .... General Mills, Inc. [*Associated Press*] (SAG)
GnMotr .... General Motors Corp. [*Associated Press*] (SAG)
GNMP .... Gettysburg National Military Park (SAUS)
GNMP .... Government Network Management Profile [*National Institute of Standards and Technology*]
GNMR .... Genmar Industries (SAUS)
GNMR .... Genmar Industries, Inc. (SAUO)
GNMS .... Gaseous Nitrogen Measuring System
GNMS .... Ground Network Management System [*Aviation*] (DA)
GNN .... Ghinnir [*Ethiopia*] [*Airport symbol*] (AD)
GNN .... Giant North Resources Ltd. [*Vancouver Stock Exchange symbol*]
GNN .... Ginn & Company (SAUO)
GNN .... Global Environmental Network (SAUO)
GNN .... Global Network Navigator [*An on-line publication and Internet reference guide*] (ECON)
GNN .... Gotham News Network (SAUO)
GNN .... Great Northern Nekoosa Corp. (SAUO)
GNN .... Gunnerudssatern [*Sweden*] [*Seismograph station code, US Geological Survey*] (SEIS)
GNNE .... Granite Co-Operative Bank (SAUS)
GNNED .... General Newsletter. National Research Council Divisionof Mechanical Engineering (SAUO)
GNO .... Gallium Neutrino Observatory (SAUS)
GNO .... Golden North Resource Corp. [*Toronto Stock Exchange symbol*] [*Vancouver Stock Exchange symbol*]
GNO .... Gross Product Originating (SAUO)
GNO .... Group Navigation Officer (SAUO)
GNOC .... Graphic Network Operator Console [*Hughes Network Systems, Inc.*]
GN of I .... Great Northern of Ireland [*Railway*] (ROG)
GNOM .... Genomica Corp. [*NASDAQ symbol*]
Gnom .... Gnomon [*Munich*] [*A publication*] (BJA)
GNOM .... Graphic and Numeric Operation Method (SAUS)
GNOMAC .... Greater New Orleans Microform Cooperative [*Library network*]
GNOME .... GNU Network Object Model Environment (SAUO)
G-NORM .... Grounded - Not Operationally Ready Maintenance (MCD)
G-NORS .... Grounded - Not Operationally Ready Supply (MCD)
GNOS .... Gallium Nitride-on-Sapphire (AAEL)
GNOS .... Global Network Operations Security (SEWL)
GNOS .... Goddard Network Operations Support [*NASA*] (KSC)
GNOX .... Golden North Resource Corp. (SAUO)
GNOXF .... Golden North Resources Corp. [*NASDAQ symbol*] (COMM)
GNOZ .... Grease Nozzle
G-NP .... Chemical Agent, Nonpersistent (SAUS)
GNP .... Gambia National Party (SAUO)
GNP .... Gas Naming Protocol [*Automotive emissions*]
GNP .... Gas, Nonpersistent
GNP .... Geriatric Nurse Practitioner (DMAA)
GNP .... Gerontological Nurse Practitioner
GNP .... Get Next within Parent (SAUS)
GNP .... Glacier National Park (SAUO)
GNP .... Global Nutritional Products (SAUO)
GNP .... Gombe National Park (SAUO)
GNP .... Good Neighbour Program [*Australia*]
GNP .... Gorongoza National Park (SAUO)
GNP .... Government Procurement (SAUO)
GNP .... Graphics Nesting Processor (MCD)
GNP .... Graphics Nesting Program (MCD)
GNP .... Grenada National Party [*Political party*] (PPW)
GNP .... Gross National Product [*Economics*]
GNP .... Tulsa, OK [*Location identifier*] [*FAA*] (FAAL)
GNP&BL .... Great Northern Pacific & Burlington Lines (SAUO)
GNP & BR .... Great Northern Piccadilly & Brompton Railway [*British*] (ROG)
GnPara .... General Parametrics Corp. [*Associated Press*] (SAG)
GNPC .... Ghana National Petroleum Corporation (SAUO)
GNPC .... Global Navigation and Planning Chart [*Military*]
GNPC .... Great Northern Paper Company (SAUO)
GnPhys .... General Physics Corp. [*Associated Press*] (SAG)
GNpN .... Norman Junior College, Norman Park, GA [*Library symbol*] [*Library of Congress*] (LCLS)
GNPP .... Ginna Nuclear Power Plant (NRCH)
GNPP .... Great Nigeria People's Party [*Political party*] (PPW)
GnPrcl .... General Parcel Service, Inc. [*Associated Press*] (SAG)
GNPRy .... Great Northern Pacific Railway (SAUO)
GNPT .... GP Financial Corp. [*NASDAQ symbol*] (SAG)
GNQ .... Equatorial Guinea [*ANSI three-letter standard code*] (CNC)
GNR .... Gaseous Nuclear Rocket
gnr .... General (SAUS)
GNR .... General Nuclear Reaction (SAUS)
GNR .... General Nuclear Response (SAUS)
GNR .... General Roca [*Argentina*] [*Airport symbol*] (OAG)
GNR .... Geographical Names Register [*New South Wales*] [*State*] (EERA)
GNR .... Global Natural Res [*NYSE symbol*] (TTSB)
GNR .... Global Natural Resources, Inc. [*NYSE symbol*] (SPSG)
G/N R .... Glucose to Nitrogen Ratio [*Medicine*] (AAMN)
GNR .... Goods Not Received (SAUS)
GNR .... Gram-Negative Rods (DMAA)
GNR .... Great Northern Railway
GNR .... Guest Name Record (IAA)
GNR .... Gunner (AFM)
gnr .... Gunner (WDAA)
G n R .... Guns n' Roses [*Rock recording group*]
GNRA .... Gateway National Recreation Area [*New York*] [*Department of the Interior*]
GNRA .... Government Management Reform Act (SAUO)
GNRA .... Government National Railway Association [*Proposed*] [*Nickname: Ginnie Rae*]
GNRA .... Grand National Racing Association (EA)
GnRad .... GenRad, Inc. [*Associated Press*] (SAG)
G/N Ratio .... Glucose Nitrogen Ratio (SAUS)
GNRB .... Grid Navigational Reference Beacon [*Navy*] (CAAL)
Gnr-Drv .... Gunner-Driver (SAUS)
GNRE .... Gross National Recreation Experience [*Refers to cost of recreation in relation to gross national product*]
GnRF .... Gonadotropin-Releasing Factor [*Also, GnRH, LH-RF, LH-RH, LH-RH/FSH-RH, LRF, LRH*] [*Endocrinology*]
GnRH .... Gonadotropin-Releasing Hormone [*Also, GnRF, LH-RF, LH-RH, LH-RH/FSH-RH, LRF, LRH*] [*Endocrinology*]
GnRHA .... Gonadotropin-Releasing Hormone Agonist [*Endocrinology*]
gnrl .... general (SAUS)
GNRP .... General Neighborhood Renewal Plan
GNRP .... Global Natural Resources Properties Ltd. (SAUO)
GNRP .... Guanine Nucleotide Release Protein [*Biochemistry*]
GNRR .... Georgia Northeastern Railroad [*Federal Railroad Administration identification code*]
GNRR .... Great Northern Railroad Company (SAUO)
GNRS .... Great Northern Railway Society [*British*] (DBA)
GNRTN .... Generation
GNRTNG .... Generating
GNRTR .... Generator
GNRY .... Great Northern Railway
GNRy .... Great Northern Railway Co. (SAUO)
GNRY .... Gunnery (AFM)
GNS .... Eastern Executive Air Charter Ltd. [*British*] [*FAA designator*] (FAAC)
GNS .... Gannett News Service
GNS .... Gasette Numismatique Suiss (SAUS)
GNS .... General Naval Staff [*NATO*] (NATG)
GNS .... Geonet Names Server (SAUS)
GNS .... German News Service (SAUO)
GNS .... German North Sea (RIMS)
GNS .... Get Nearest Server [*Computer science*] (DINT)
GNS .... Global Navigation System (HLLA)
GN's .... Global Negotiations
GNS .... Global Network Service [*British*] (TELE)
G/NS .... Glucose in Normal Saline [*Medicine*]
GNS .... Glutamine Synthetase [*Also, GS*] [*An enzyme*]
GNS .... GOMR Nadir Sounder (SAUS)
GNS .... Goose NORAD [*North American Air Defense*] Sector (IAA)
GNS .... Grain Neutral Spirits [*Alcohol*]
GNS .... Gram-Negative Sensitivity [*to antibiotics*]
GNS .... Gram-Negative Sepsis [*Medicine*] (MELL)
GNS .... Grand National Sportsman [*Car racing division*]
GNS .... Great North of Scotland Railway (ROG)
GNS .... Griffin's Nautical Series [*A publication*]
GNS .... Group of Negotiations on Services [*European Community*]
GNS .... Guidance and Navigation System
GNS .... Guineas [*Monetary unit*] [*Obsolete*] [*British*]
GNS .... Guns (SAUS)
GNS .... Gyrocompass Navigation System (SAUS)
GNSA .... Gensia Inc. [*NASDAQ symbol*] (TTSB)
GNSA .... Gensia Pharmaceuticals, Inc. [*NASDAQ symbol*] (SAG)
GNSA .... Gensia Sicor, Inc. [*NASDAQ symbol*] (NASQ)
GNSAW .... Gensia Pharmaceuticals Wrrt [*NASDAQ symbol*] (TTSB)
GNSH .... Grey Nuns of the Sacred Heart [*Roman Catholic religious order*]
GNSI .... Guild of Natural Science Illustrators (EA)
GNSM .... Gensym Corp. [*NASDAQ symbol*] (TTSB)
GNSM .... Graduate of the Northern School of Music [*Obsolete*] [*British*] (DBQ)
GNSMTH .... Gunsmith

GNSO .... Goddard Network Support Operations [*King's College*] [*Wilkes-Barre, PA*] [*NASA*] (KSC)
GNSP .... German North Sea Port (SAUS)
GNSP .... Gross National Sports Product [*Economics*]
GNSR .... Great North of Scotland Railway
GNSRA .... Great North of Scotland Railway Association (SAUO)
GNSS .... Genesis
GNSS .... Genesis Microchip [*NASDAQ symbol*] (SG)
GNSS .... Global Navigation Satellite System
GNsS .... Grammatik der Neusyrischen Sprache [*A publication*] (BJA)
GNSS .... Ground Network Scheduling System (SAUS)
GNSSA .... German North Sea Sub-Area (SAUO)
GNSSU .... Global Navigation Satellite Sensor Unit (HLLA)
GNST .... Glossary of Naval Ship Types (MCD)
GNSVL .... Gainesville, GA [*American Association of Railroads railroad junction routing code*]
GNSW .... Governor of New South Wales [*Australia*]
GNSWBR .... Great New South Wales Bike Ride [*Australia*]
GNT .... Business Air Ltd. [*British*] [*ICAO designator*] (FAAC)
GNT .... General Naval Training [*British military*] (DMA)
GNT .... Genstar Therapeutics [*AMEX symbol*] (SG)
GNT .... Giant
GNT .... Grant Exploration [*Vancouver Stock Exchange symbol*]
GNT .... Grants (SAUS)
GNT .... Grants, NM [*Location identifier*] [*FAA*] (FAAL)
GNT .... Great Northern Telegraph Co. [*Denmark*] [*Telecommunications*] (TEL)
GNT .... Great Northern Telegraph Co. Ltd. (SAUO)
GNT .... Green Tree Acceptance, Inc. (SAUO)
GNT .... Green Tree Financial, Inc. [*NYSE symbol*] (SPSG)
GNT .... Green Tree Finl [*NYSE symbol*] (TTSB)
GNT .... Ground Test [*NASA*] (KSC)
GNTA .... Genta, Inc. [*NASDAQ symbol*] (SPSG)
GNTC .... Girls' Naval Training Corps [*British*]
GNTE .... Granite Co-Operative Bank [*NASDAQ symbol*] (COMM)
GnthrInt .... Gunther International Ltd. [*Associated Press*] (SAG)
GNTI .... Gentia Software plc [*NASDAQ symbol*] (NASQ)
GNTLMN .... Gentlemen
GNTLY .... Gentilly, LA [*American Association of Railroads railroad junction routing code*]
GNTO .... Greek National Tourist Organization (EA)
GNTP .... Georgia Narcotics Treatment Project (SAUO)
GNTP .... Graduate Nurse Transition Program
GNTR .... Generator (FAAC)
GNTS .... Great Northern Transportation System [*Federal Railroad Administration identification code*]
GNTX .... Gentex Corp. [*NASDAQ symbol*] (NQ)
GNTY .... Guaranty Bancshares, Inc. [*NASDAQ symbol*] (NASQ)
GNTYL .... Giant Yellowknife Mines Ltd. (SAUO)
GNU .... Geologic Names Unit (SAUS)
GNU .... Golden Rule Resources Ltd. [*Toronto Stock Exchange symbol*]
GNU .... Goodnews Bay [*Alaska*] [*Airport symbol*] (OAG)
GNU .... South African Government of National Unity (SAUO)
GNUC .... [*The*] GNI Group, Inc. [*NASDAQ symbol*] (NQ)
GNULEX .... Geologic Names Unit Lexicon (SAUS)
GNV .... Gainesville [*Florida*] [*Airport symbol*]
GNV .... Geneva Steel Class A (SAUS)
GNV .... Geneva Steel Co. [*NYSE symbol*] (SPSG)
GNV .... Geneva Steel Co.'A' [*NYSE symbol*] (TTSB)
GNV .... Genoveva Resources, Inc. [*Vancouver Stock Exchange symbol*]
GNV .... Glycinenaphthol Violet [*An indicator*] [*Chemistry*]
GNV .... Grand Airways, Inc. [*ICAO designator*] (FAAC)
GNVA .... Genova (SAUS)
GNVA .... Genova, Inc. (SAUO)
GNVLF .... Greenville, FL [*American Association of Railroads railroad junction routing code*]
GNVLL .... Greenville Piers, NJ [*American Association of Railroads railroad junction routing code*]
GNVLM .... Greenville, MI [*American Association of Railroads railroad junction routing code*]
GNVLN .... Greenville, NC [*American Association of Railroads railroad junction routing code*]
GNVLT .... Greenville, TX [*American Association of Railroads railroad junction routing code*]
GNVN .... Government of North Vietnam
GNVQ .... General National Vocational Qualification [*British*] (ODBW)
GnvStl .... Geneva Steel [*Associated Press*] (SAG)
GNW .... General Nuclear War (SAUO)
GNW .... Greenwell Resources Corp. [*Vancouver Stock Exchange symbol*]
GNWF .... GNW Financial Corp. (SAUO)
GNWP .... Gross National Waste Product Forum [*Defunct*] (EA)
GNWR .... Gene & Wyoming Railroad Co. (SAUS)
GNWR .... Genesee & Wyoming, Inc. [*NASDAQ symbol*] (NASQ)
GNWR .... Genessee & Wyoming Railroad Co. [*AAR code*]
GNX .... Genex Resources [*Vancouver Stock Exchange symbol*]
GNX .... GlobalNetXchange
GNX .... Grand National X (SAUS)
GNY .... Fort Jay (SAUS)
GNY .... Fort Jay, NY [*Location identifier*] [*FAA*] (FAAL)
GNY .... German Navy [*ICAO designator*] (FAAC)
GNYADA .... Greater New York Automobile Dealers Association (SRA)
GNYCFS .... Greater New York Council for Foreign Students [*Later, English in Action*]
GNYF .... Greater New York Fund (SAUO)
GNYO .... Guild of New York Opera [*Record label*]
Gny Sgt .... Gunnery Sergeant (SAUO)
GNZ .... Ghanzi [*Botswana*] [*Airport symbol*] (AD)
GNZ .... Gisborne [*New Zealand*] [*Seismograph station code, US Geological Survey*] (SEIS)
GNZ .... Government of New Zealand
GO .... Canada - Transport Canada [*Canada*] [*ICAO designator*] (ICDA)
GO .... Collins Industries, Inc. (SAUO)
go .... Gabon [*MARC country of publication code*] [*Library of Congress*] (LCCP)
Go .... gadolinium (SAUS)
GO .... Galactose Oxidase [*An enzyme*]
GO .... Gambia Air Shuttle [*ICAO designator*] (AD)
GO .... Garrison Orders [*British military*] (DMA)
GO .... Gaseous Oxygen (SAUS)
GO .... Gas Officer (SAUS)
GO .... Gasoffizier [*Gas Officer*] [*German military - World War II*]
GO .... Gas Oil [*Also, G*] [*Petroleum technology*]
G-O .... Gas-Oil (SAUS)
G/O .... Gas/Oil Ratio (SAUS)
GO .... Gas Operated (ADA)
GO .... Gastro-Oesophageal [*Medicine*] (EDAA)
GO .... Gatactose Oxidase (SAUS)
GO .... Gaussian Orbitals [*Atomic physics*]
g/o .... gear box oil (SAUS)
GO .... Gearhart-Owen Industries, Inc. (EFIS)
go .... gear oil (SAUS)
GO .... Geek of Other (SAUO)
GO .... Generale Occidentale [*Commercial firm*]
GO .... Generalized Operations (MCD)
GO .... Generaloberst [*Full General*] [*German military - World War II*]
GO .... General Obligation [*Bond*] [*Business term*]
GO .... General Office [*or Officer*] [*Military*]
GO .... General Operations (ELAL)
GO .... General Order [*Military*] (ODA)
GO .... General Order [*Large numbers issued by commanders of both sides*] [*Civil War term*]
GO .... General Organization [*Identification card used at Madison Square Garden*]
GO .... General Output (SAUS)
GO .... Generated Output
GO .... Genius Operator Advertising Data Bank [*Gert Richter*] [*Germany*] [*Information service or system*] (CRD)
GO .... Geometric Operations (SAUO)
GO .... Geometric Optics (SAUS)
GO .... Geometric Optimization (SAUS)
GO .... Geometry-Optimized [*Calculations*]
GO .... Give Once (ACAE)
GO .... Global Options (EA)
GO .... Global Outreach [*An association*] (EA)
GO .... Glucose Oxidase [*Also, glu ox, GOD*] [*An enzyme*]
GO .... Glycerin Oleate (SAUS)
GO .... Goal Orientation (DIPS)
Go .... Godecke AG [*Germany*] [*Research code symbol*]
Go .... Goebel's Probate Court Cases [*Ohio*] [*A publication*] (DLA)
GO .... Goethite [*A mineral*]
Go .... Gofredus de Trano [*Deceased, 1245*] [*Authority cited in pre-1607 legal work*] (DSA)
go .... Gold (VRA)
GO .... Goniometer [*JETDS nomenclature*] [*Military*] (CET)
Go .... Gonion (DMAA)
GO .... Good Ordinary (SAUS)
GO .... Gordan-Overstreet [*Syndrome*] [*Medicine*] (DB)
GO .... Gothic [*Language, etc.*] (ROG)
GO .... Government Obligation [*Economics*]
GO .... Government Obligation Bond (EBF)
GO .... Government Operations Committee [*US Senate*]
GO .... Government Owned
GO .... Graduate Opportunities [*British*]
GO .... Grand Officer (SAUS)
GO .... Grand Orator [*Freemasonry*]
GO .... Grand Organist [*Freemasonry*] (ROG)
GO .... Grand Orient [*Freemasonry*] (ROG)
GO .... Graphic Output (SAUS)
GO .... Graphitic Oxide
GO .... Grasp Objects [*Psychometric test*]
GO .... Great Organ [*Music*]
GO .... Ground Out [*Baseball*]
GO .... Group Officer [*British military*] (DMA)
GO .... Group Owner (SAUO)
GO .... Growth Opportunities (SAUS)
G-O .... Grumman Olson [*Grumman Corp.*]
GO .... Guardian Office (SAUO)
GO .... Guest Observer
GO .... Guest Option [*Hotel plan, Hilton hotels*]
GO .... Gulf Oil Corp. (SAUO)
GO .... Gummed Only [*Envelopes*]
GO .... Gunnery Officer [*Navy*] [*British*]
GO .... Gunn Oscillator
GO .... Gurkha Officer [*British military*] (DMA)
GO .... Gym Officer (WDAA)
GO .... Institute for the Study of Labor and Economic Crisis (SAUO)
GO2 .... Gaseous Oxygen (MCD)
GO3OS .... Global Ozone Observing System (USDC)
GOA .... Alberta Government [*Canada*] [*ICAO designator*] (FAAC)
GOA .... Gardeners of America (EA)

GOA .... Generalized Osteoarthritis [*Medicine*]
GOA .... General Operating Agency
GOA .... Genoa [*Italy*] [*Airport symbol*] (OAG)
GOA .... Georgia Oilmen's Association (SRA)
GOA .... Georgia Optometric Association (SRA)
GOA .... Glacier-Ocean-Atmosphere [*Global system used for modelling*]
GOA .... Goa [*Panjim*] [*India*] [*Seismograph station code, US Geological Survey*] (SEIS)
GOA .... Golden Seal Resources Ltd. [*Vancouver Stock Exchange symbol*]
GOA .... Gone on Arrival [*Police terminology*] (IIA)
GOA .... Government of Argentina
GOA .... Government-Owned Aircraft
GOA .... Group, Operations Analysis [*Air Force*] (MCD)
GOA .... Gulf of Alaska (SAUS)
GOA .... Gun Owners of America (EA)
GOA .... Gyro Optics Assy (SAUS)
GOA .... Gyro Output Amplifier
GOA .... Gyroscope Output Amplifier (SAUS)
GOAC .... Geographic OPAREA [*Operating Area*] Coordinates (DNAB)
GOAC .... Gun Owners Action Committee (EA)
GOAD .... Good Order & Discipline (WDAA)
GOAD .... Group of Ancient Drama
GOAIS .... Generalized Officer Assignment On-Line System (SAUS)
GOAL .... Ascent Entertainment Group, Inc. [*NASDAQ symbol*] (SAG)
GOAL .... Ascent Entertainment Grp [*NASDAQ symbol*] (TTSB)
GOAL .... A Third World development agency (SAUO)
GOAL .... Game Oriented Activities for Learning (AIE)
GOAL .... Gay Officers' Action League (EA)
GOAL .... Gay Organized Alliance for Liberation (SAUO)
GOAL .... General Organization Analysis Language (IAA)
GOAL .... General Organization of the Alexandria Library
GOAL .... Generator for Optimized Application Language (IAA)
GOAL .... Generator for Optimized Application Languages (SAUS)
GOAL .... Georgia Occupational Award of Leadership (SAUO)
GOAL .... Global Command and Control System (SAUS)
GOAL .... Goal Systems International, Inc. (SAUO)
GOAL .... Ground Operations Aerospace Language [*Computer science*] [*NASA*]
GOAL .... Ground Operations Assembly Language [*Computer science*]
GOAL .... Gun Owners Action League (SAUS)
GOALI .... Grant Opportunities for Academic Liaison with Industry [*National Science Foundation*]
GOALS .... Generalized Officer Assignment On-Line System [*Navy*] (NVT)
GOALS .... General Operations and Logistics Simulation [*Boeing*]
GOALS .... General Optronics Line of Sight Atmospheric Lightwave Communication System [*General Optronics Corp.*] [*Edison, NJ*] [*Telecommunications service*] (TSSD)
GOALS .... Geometrical Optical Analysis of Lens Systems (PDAA)
GOALS .... Global Ocean and Land Surface (SAUS)
GOALS .... Global Ocean-Atmosphere-Land-Surface Interactions (EERA)
GOALS .... Global Ocean-Atmosphere-Land System [*Program*] [*Marine science*] (OSRA)
GOALS .... Goal-Oriented Approach to Life Cycle Software
GOALS .... Greater Orlando Area Legal Services [*Florida*]
GOAM .... GoAmerica, Inc. [*NASDAQ symbol*] (SG)
GOAM .... Government-Owned and Maintained [*Telecommunications*] (TEL)
GO&P .... General Operations and Plans (SAUO)
GO&P .... Griffith Observatory and Planetarium (SAUO)
GOAP .... Geosat Oceans Applications Program (SAUO)
GOAR .... Ground Observer Aircraft Recognition [*Army*]
GOAS .... Guidance Optical Alignment Shelter (KSC)
GOase .... Galactose Oxidase [*An enzyme*]
GOASEX .... Gulf of Alaska SEASAT Experiment [*National Oceanic and Atmospheric Administration*]
GOAT .... Galveston Orientation and Amnesia Test [*Medicine*] (DMAA)
GOAT .... Gerber Oscillogram Amplitude Translator
GOAT .... Give Our Animals Time (SAUO)
GOAT .... Glass Oceanographic Buoy (SAUS)
GOAT .... Goes Over All Terrain [*Vehicle*]
GOAT .... Goings On About Town [*The New Yorker magazine*] (WDMC)
GOAT .... Goose Operators Advanced Training (SAUO)
GOAT .... Grouped Optimal Aggregation Technique (MCD)
GOATS .... Group Operational Access Tester System [*AT & T*]
GOB .... General Obligation Bonds [*Finance*]
GOB .... General Officers Branch [*Air Force*]
GOB .... General Order of Battle
GOB .... General, Organic, and Biochemistry
GOB .... Glass Oceanographic Buoy
GOB .... Goba [*Ehtiopia*] [*Airport symbol*] (AD)
GOB .... Gobble (DSUE)
GOB .... Goldbrae Development Ltd. [*Vancouver Stock Exchange symbol*]
gob .... Good Ordinary Brand [*Business term*] (ODBW)
GOB .... Good Ordinary Brand [*Business term*]
GOB .... Government of Bangladesh
GOB .... Government of Brazil
GOB .... Government of Burma (CINC)
GOB .... Grants Operations Balance [*Environmental Protection Agency*] (ERG)
GOB .... Grants Operations Branch (SAUO)
GOB .... Ground Order of Battle (AFM)
GOBAB .... Gamma-Hydroxy-beta-aminobutyric Acid [*Pharmacology*]
GOBAC .... Gold-Plating Bath Analyzer and Controller (PDAA)
GOBEP .... Generalized One-Boson Exchange Potential
GOBI .... Golden Bishop [*North American bird banding code*] (BIBA)
GOBI .... Growth Monitoring, Oral Rehydration, Breastfeeding, and Immunization [*Program*] [*UNICEF plan to reduce child mortality in Third World countries*]
GOBILS .... Government Bill of Lading System
GO Bond .... General Obligation Bond (SAUO)
GOBR .... Group of Officials on Biotechnology Regulation (EERA)
GOBS .... Guardians of Better Speech (SAUS)
GOBU .... Government Operations Business Unit (SAUS)
GOC .... Gas-Oil Contact
goc .... gas-oil content (SAUS)
GOC .... Gas-Operated Core
GOC .... Gas-Orated Core (SAUS)
GOC .... General Occupational Classification
GOC .... General Officer Commanding [*Navy*]
GOC .... General Officer Commanding-in-Chief (SAUS)
GOC .... General Operating Committee
GOC .... General Operating Costs (SAUO)
GOC .... General Operator Console (SAUS)
GOC .... General Operators Certificate (SAUS)
GOC .... General Optical Council [*British*]
GOC .... German Oil Company (SAUO)
GOC .... Glass Owners Club (SAUO)
GOC .... Global Ocean Color (SAUO)
GOC .... Glycidoxycoumarin [*Biochemistry*]
GOC .... Gora [*Papua New Guinea*] [*Airport symbol*] (OAG)
GOC .... Government of Canada (FOTI)
GOC .... Government of Cuba
GOC .... Government Operations Committee
GOC .... Graphic Option Controller (NITA)
GOC .... Greatest Overall Coefficient (TEL)
GOC .... Greek Orthodox Church (BARN)
GOC .... Griffith Observatory [*California*] [*Seismograph station code, US Geological Survey*] (SEIS)
GOC .... Ground Observer Center (SAUO)
GOC .... Ground Operations Center (SAUS)
GOC .... Ground Operations Coordinator [*NASA*] (NASA)
GOC .... Group Operations Center (NATG)
GOC .... Guaranteed One Coat [*Brand of house paint*]
GOC .... Gulf Canada Corporation (SAUO)
GOC .... Gulf Oil Co. (SAUS)
GOC .... Gulf Oil Company (SAUO)
GOC .... Gunnery Officer's Console [*Army*] (AABC)
GOCA .... Graphics Object Content Architecture (CDE)
GOCA .... Ground Operations Control Area [*NASA*] (NASA)
GOCAP .... GARP Operational Control Center (SAUS)
GOCAP .... Graphic Output Circuit Analysis Program
GOCC .... GARP Operational Control Center [*Marine science*] (MSC)
GOCC .... GARP Operations Control Center (SAUS)
GOCC .... GATE Operational Contol Center (SAUS)
GOCC .... GATE [*GARP Atlantic Tropical Experiment*] Operational Control Centre [*Marine science*] (MSC)
GOCC .... General Order of the Commander-in-Chief [*British military*] (DMA)
GOCC .... Geodetic Operations Control Center [*NASA*]
GOCDB .... Global Ocean Climate Data Base (FOTI)
GOCE .... Gravity Field and Steady State Ocean Circulation Explorer
GOCESS .... Government-Operated Civil Engineering Supply Store
GOCHEM .... Gulf Oil Chemicals Co.
GOCI .... General Operator-Computer Interaction (IEEE)
GOCI .... Graham Owners Club International (EA)
GOC-in-C .... General Officer Commanding-in-Chief [*British*]
GOCL-II .... Gordon Occupational Check List II [*A checklist of 240 descriptions of activities related to occupations that do not require a college degree, developed by L.V. Gordon*] (DIPS)
GOCM .... Goals, Objectives, Commitments, and Measures [*Environmental science*] (COE)
GOCMV .... Greek Orthodox Community of Melbourne and Victoria [*Australia*]
GOCO .... Golden Oil Co. [*NASDAQ symbol*] (NQ)
GOCO .... Government-Owned/Commercial-Operated [*Facility*] (AFIT)
GOCO .... Government-Owned/Company-Operated (SAUO)
GOCO .... Government Owned, Contractor Operated (SEWL)
GO/CO .... Government-Owned/Contractor-Operated [*Facility*] (NG)
GOCO .... Government-Owned Corporation-Operated (SAUO)
GOCOM .... General Officer Command [*US Army Reserve*] (AABC)
GOCOSAT .... Government Communication Satellite (ACAE)
GOCP .... Government Outbound Calling Plan [*Communications term*] (DCT)
GOCR .... Gated-Off Controlled Rectifier
GOCRM .... General Officer Commanding Royal Marines [*British*]
GOCX .... Chevron Chemical [*Private rail car owner code*]
GOD .... Generation of Diversity [*Immunology*]
GOD .... Global Outdial (SAUS)
GOD .... Glucose Oxidase [*Also, glu ox, GO*] [*An enzyme*]
God .... Gofredus de Trano [*Deceased, 1245*] [*Authority cited in pre-1607 legal work*] (DSA)
GOD .... Golden Sceptre Resources [*Toronto Stock Exchange symbol*] [*Vancouver Stock Exchange symbol*]
GOD .... Good Old Days (SAUS)
GOD .... Government-Owned Depot
GOD .... Grasped Objects Discrimination [*Psychometric test*]
GOD .... Guaranteed Overnight Delivery
GOD .... Guidance and Orbit Determination [*NASA*] (PDAA)
GODA .... Guild of Drama Adjudicators [*British*] (BI)
GODAE .... Global Ocean Data Assimilation Experiment (SAUO)
GODAR .... Global Oceanographic Data Archaeology and Rescue (SAUO)
GODAR .... Global Oceanographic Data Archeology and Rescue (SAUS)

GODAS......... Graphically Oriented Design and Analysis System [*Computer science*]
GODB.......... Gal Oya Development Board [*Sri Lanka*] (BUAC)
GODB96....... Global Ocean Database 1996 (SAUS)
Godb (Eng)... Godbolt's English King's Bench Reports [*78 English Reprint*] [*A publication*] (DLA)
GODCO........ Gulf Oman Oilfelds Development Company (SAUO)
GODCO........ Gulf Oman Oilfields Development Co. (SAUS)
GODD.......... Goddard Industries, Inc. (SAUO)
Goddard....... Goddard on Easements [*A publication*] (DLA)
Goddard C... Goddard College (GAGS)
Godd Ease... Goddard on Easements [*A publication*] (DLA)
Godd Easem... Goddard on Easements [*A publication*] (DLA)
GODE.......... Gulf Organization for Development in Egypt
Godef & Sh RC... Godefroi and Shortt on Railway Companies [*A publication*] (DLA)
Godefroi...... Godefroi's Law of Trusts and Trustees [*A publication*] (DLA)
Godef Trust... Godefroi's Law of Trusts and Trustees [*A publication*] (DLA)
GODER......... Goderich, ON [*American Association of Railroads railroad junction routing code*]
godf............ Godfather (GEAB)
godm........... Godmother (GEAB)
Godo........... Godolphin on Admiralty Jurisdiction [*A publication*] (DLA)
Godo........... Godolphin's Abridgment of Ecclesiastical Law [*A publication*] (DLA)
Godo........... Godolphin's Orphan's Legacy [*A publication*] (DLA)
Godo........... Godolphin's Repertorium Canonicum [*A publication*] (DLA)
Godol.......... Godolphin's Orphan's Legacy [*A publication*] (DLA)
Godolph Adm Jur... Godolphin on Admiralty Jurisdiction [*2nd ed.*] [*1685*] [*A publication*] (DLA)
Godolph Ecc Law... Godolphin's Ecclesiastical Law [*A publication*] (DLA)
Godolph Leg... Godolphin's Orphan's Legacy [*A publication*] (DLA)
Godolph Orph Leg... Godolphin's Orphan's Legacy [*A publication*] (DLA)
Godolph Rep Can... Godolphin's Repertorium Canonicum [*A publication*] (DLA)
GODORT...... Government Documents Round Table [*American Library Association*]
GODORT ETF... GODORT [*Government Documents Round Table*] Education Task Force
GODORT FDTF... GODORT [*Government Documents Round Table*] Federal Documents Task Force
GODORT IDTF... GODORT [*Government Documents Round Table*] International Documents Task Force
GODORT MRGITF... GODORT [*Government Documents Round Table*] Machine-Readable Government Information Task Force
GODORT SLDTF... GODORT [*Government Documents Round Table*] State and Local Documents Task Force
GOD/POD..... Glucose Oxidase-Perioxidase Method (STED)
GOD-POD..... Glucose Oxidase-Peroxidase [*Also, PGO*] [*Enzyme mixture*]
GODS.......... Geniuses of Distinction Society [*Later, SGD*] (EA)
GODS.......... Global Orbiting Defence System (SAUS)
GODSEP....... Guidance and Orbit Determination for Solar Electric Propulsion [*NASA*]
Godson........ Godson's Mining Commissioner's Cases [*Ontario*] [*A publication*] (DLA)
Gods Pat...... Godson on Patents [*2nd ed.*] [*1840*] [*A publication*] (DLA)
GOE............ Gas, Oxygen, Ether [*Anesthesiology*]
GOe............ Gauss Oersted (SAUS)
GOE............ General Office Expenses (MHCS)
GOE............ General Operating Expenses (MCD)
GOE............ General Ordination Examination
GOE............ General OVERHAUSER Effect (SAUS)
GOE............ Geodome Resources Ltd. [*Toronto Stock Exchange symbol*] [*Vancouver Stock Exchange symbol*]
GOE............ Gonalia [*Papua New Guinea*] [*Airport symbol*] (OAG)
GOE............ Gore [*New Zealand*] [*Airport symbol*] (AD)
GO-E........... Go To Executive (SAUS)
GOE............ Government-Owned Equipment (MCD)
GOE............ Ground Operating Equipment [*Aerospace*] (NAKS)
GOE............ Ground Operating (or Operational) Equipment (SAUO)
GOE............ Ground Operational Equipment [*NASA*]
GOE............ Group Operations Entity (TIMI)
GOE............ Guide for Occupational Exploration [*A publication*] (DHP)
GOEA.......... Golden Eagle [*North American bird banding code*] (BIBA)
Goeb........... Goebel's Probate Court Cases [*Ohio*] [*A publication*] (DLA)
Goebel......... Goebel's Probate Reports [*Ohio*] [*A publication*] (DLA)
Goebel (Ohio)... Goebel's Probate Court Cases [*Ohio*] [*A publication*] (DLA)
Goebel's Rep... Goebel's Probate Reports [*Ohio*] [*A publication*] (DLA)
GOED.......... Geodome Resources Ltd. (SAUO)
GOED.......... Global Oceans Ecosystems Dynamics (SAUO)
GOEDEB....... General Organisation for the Exploitation and Development of the Euphrates Basin [*Syria*] (BUAC)
GOE for OAO... Ground Operational Equipment for the Orbiting Astronomical Obrvatory (SAUS)
GOE for OAO... Ground Operational Equipment for the Orbiting Astronomical Observatory [*NASA*] (MUGU)
GOE Mixture... Gas, Oxygen, and Ether Mixture (SAUS)
GOER.......... Governors Office of Employee Relations (SAUS)
GOE/RPIE..... Ground Operational Equipment/Real Property Installed Equipment [*NASA*] (AFM)
GOES.......... Gemini Order Entry System (SAUS)
GOES.......... Generation Outages and Equipment Status (SAUO)
GOES.......... Geostationary Environmental Satellite System (SAUS)
GOES.......... Geostationary Observatory Earth Satellite (CCCA)
GOES.......... Geo-Stationary Operational and Environmental Satellite (SAUS)
GOES.......... Geostationary Operational Environmental Satellite [*National Oceanic and Atmospheric Administration*]
GOES.......... Geostationary Orbital Earth Satellite (MCD)
GOES.......... Geostationary Orbiting Enviromental Satellite (ADWA)
GOES.......... Geostationary Orbiting Environmental Satellite
GOES.......... Geosynchronous Operational Environmental Satellite [*NASA*] (NASA)
GOES.......... Geosynchronous Orbital Environmental Satellite (SAUS)
GOES.......... Geosynchronous Orbiting Earth Satellite
GOES.......... Global Oceans Ecosystems Dynamics (SAUO)
GOES.......... Global Omnibus Environmental Survey (EERA)
GOES-8/9..... Geostationary Operational Environmental Satellite-8/9 (SAUS)
GOES-A........ Geostationary Operational Environmental Satellite - A (SAUO)
GOES/DCP... Geostationary Operational Environmental Satellite Data Collection Platform (MSC)
GOESECS..... Geochemical Ocean Section Study [*International Decade of Ocean Exploration*] (USDC)
GOES-M....... Geostationary Operational Environmental Satellite M [*NASA*]
GOES-N........ Geostationary Operational Environmental Satellite N [*NASA*]
GOES-Next... Next-Generation GOES [*Geostationary Operational Environmental Satellite*] (USDC)
GOES-O........ Geostationary Operational Environmental Satellite O [*NASA launch date proposed for April 2004*]
GOESs......... Geostationary Operational Environmental Satellites (SAUO)
GOETO........ Grand Order of European Tour Operators (BUAC)
GOETO........ Grand Order of European Tour Organizers (SAUO)
GOETO........ Grand Order of European Travel Organizers (SAUO)
GOETS......... Ground Operations Estimating Techniques System (ACAE)
GOEZS......... Global Ocean Euphotic Zone Study [*Marine science*] (OSRA)
GoF............ Gang of Five (SAUS)
GOF............ Glass Optical Fiber [*Materials science*]
GOF............ Global Ocean Flux (CARB)
Gof............. Gofredus de Trano [*Deceased, 1245*] [*Authority cited in pre-1607 legal work*] (DSA)
GOF............ Golden Fleece (journ.) (SAUS)
GOF............ Goodness of Fit (MCD)
GOF............ Good Old Friday [*Slang*]
GOF............ Government of France
GOF............ Government-Owned Facility
GOF............ Group of Forces (SAUO)
GOF............ Group of Frames (SAUS)
GOF............ San Angelo, TX [*Location identifier*] [*FAA*] (FAAL)
Gof&Sh RC... Godefroi and Shortt on Railway Companies (SAUO)
Gof&Sh RC... Godefroi and Shortt on Railway Companies (journ.) (SAUS)
GOFAR......... Global Ocean Floor Analysis and Research [*Navy*]
GOFC.......... Global Observations of Forest Cover (SAUO)
GOFC.......... Great Oaks Financial Corp. (SAUO)
GOF E......... Goffered Edges [*Bookbinding*] (DGA)
GOFI........... General Organization for Industrialization (SAUO)
G of I.......... Government of India (SAUO)
GOFLAS....... Ground Fuel Logistical Summary (SAUO)
GOFS.......... Geostationary Orbital Earth Satellite (SAUS)
GOFS.......... Global Ocean Flux Study [*Federal government*]
GOFS/DCP... Geostationary Operational Environmental Satellite (SAUS)
GOFTA......... Golf Facilities Trades Association (BUAC)
GOG............ GEOSECS Operations Group [*Marine science*] (MSC)
GOG............ Gerrity Oil & Gas [*NYSE symbol*] (SPSG)
GOG............ Golden Tag Resources [*Vancouver Stock Exchange symbol*]
GOG............ Government of Ghana
GOG............ Gynecologic Oncology Group (EA)
GOGAT......... Glutamate Synthase (BARN)
GOGECA....... Comite Generale de la Cooperation Agricole de la CEE [*General Committee of Agricultural Cooperation of the European Economic Community*] (PDAA)
GOGG.......... Ziguinchor [*Senegal*] [*ICAO location identifier*] (ICLI)
GOGK.......... Kolda [*Senegal*] [*ICAO location identifier*] (ICLI)
GOGO.......... Global One Distribution & Merchandising, Inc. [*NASDAQ symbol*] (SAG)
GOGO.......... Government-Owned/Government-Operated (EEVL)
GOGO.......... Nutri-Products, Inc. (SAUO)
Gog Or......... Goguet's Origin of Laws [*A publication*] (DLA)
Gog Or......... Goguets Origin of Laws (journ.) (SAUS)
GOGPr......... Gerrity O&G Cv Dep Pfd [*NYSE symbol*] (TTSB)
GOGS.......... Cap Skirring [*Senegal*] [*ICAO location identifier*] (ICLI)
GOGS.......... Glasgow Obstetrical and Gynaecological Society (SAUO)
Gogs........... Goggles (SAUS)
GOH............ Garments on Hangers [*Shipping*]
goh............. German (SAUS)
goh............. German, Old High [*MARC language code*] [*Library of Congress*] (LCCP)
GOH............ German Order of Harugari
GOH............ Geroderma Osteodysplastica Hereditaria [*Medicine*] (DMAA)
GOH............ Godthaab [*Denmark*] [*Airport symbol*]
GOH............ Goliath Gold Mines Ltd. [*Toronto Stock Exchange symbol*] [*Vancouver Stock Exchange symbol*]
GOH............ Goods on Hand (DS)
GOH............ Government of Honduras
GOH............ Guest of Honour (SAUO)
GOH............ Nuuk [*Greenland*] [*Airport symbol*] (OAG)
GOHBPR....... General Organization for Housing, Building, and Planning Research [*Egypt*] (BUAC)
GOHREM....... Geosynchronous Orbit High Resolution Earth Monitoring (SAUO)
GOHREM....... Geosynchronous Orbit High Resolution Earth Monitoring Satellite (SAUS)
GOHS.......... Gauceng Oral Health Services (SAUO)
GOI............. Fort Knox, KY [*Location identifier*] [*FAA*] (FAAL)
GOI............. GaAs on insulator (SAUS)
GOI............. Gallium Arsene on Insulator (SAUS)
GOI............. Gallium Arsenide on Insulator (AAEL)
GOI............. Gallup Organization Incorporated (SAUO)

GOI .... Gate Oxide Integrity (AAEL)
GOI .... Gearhart Industries, Incorporated (SAUO)
GOI .... General Oriental Investments Ltd. [*Vancouver Stock Exchange symbol*]
GOI .... Geostationary Operational Imager (SAUS)
GOI .... Goa [*India*] [*Airport symbol*] (OAG)
GO-I .... Go To Instruction (SAUS)
GOI .... Government of India (CARB)
GOI .... Government of Indonesia
GOI .... Government of Iran
GOI .... Government of Israel (MCD)
GOI .... Government of Italy
GOI .... Government-Owned Installation
GOI .... Gross Operating Income (SAUS)
GOI .... Ground Objectives Identification (SAUS)
GOI .... Group Operations Instruction [*British military*] (DMA)
GOI .... Gun Owners (SAUS)
GOI .... Gun Owners, Incorporated (SAUO)
GOIC .... Gulf Organization for Industrial Consulting [*Doha, Qatar*] (EAIO)
GOIE .... Government-Owned Industrial Equipment (SAA)
GOIFE .... Government of Israel Furnished Equipment (MCD)
GOIN .... Global Observation Information Network (CARB)
GOIN .... State Oceanographic Institute, State Committee on Hydrometeorology (SAUO)
Goir Fr Co ... Goirand's French Code of Commerce [*A publication*] (DLA)
GOIT .... Goyer Organization of Ideas Test (EDAC)
GOJ .... Blytheville, AR [*Location identifier*] [*FAA*] (FAAL)
GOJ .... Eurojet Aviation Ltd. [*British*] [*ICAO designator*] (FAAC)
GOJ .... Government of Japan (CINC)
GOK .... God Only Knows [*Facetious diagnosis for a puzzling medical case*]
GoK .... Government of Kenya
GOK .... Government of Korea
GOK .... Guthrie, OK [*Location identifier*] [*FAA*] (FAAL)
GOL .... General Operating Language [*Computer science*] (IEEE)
GOL .... Glabello-Opisthion Line (STED)
GOL .... Goal-Oriented Language
GOL .... Gold Beach, OR [*Location identifier*] [*FAA*] (FAAL)
GOL .... Golden [*Bergen Park*] [*Colorado*] [*Seismograph station code, US Geological Survey*] (SEIS)
GOL .... Golden Gate University. Law Review (journ.) (SAUS)
GOL .... Goldlund Mines Ltd. [*Toronto Stock Exchange symbol*]
GO-L .... Go To Logic (SAUS)
GOL .... Grain-Oilseeds-Livestock Model (SAUO)
GOL .... Graphic On-Line Language (SAUS)
GOL .... Guinness Overseas Ltd. [*British*]
GOLC .... Growth Opportunity License Charge (GART)
GOLD .... Gate-Drain Overlapped Device (MCD)
GOLD .... Generalized Organization of Large Databases (PDAA)
GOLD .... General On-Line Diagnostic (SAUS)
gold .... geometric on-line defilnition (SAUS)
GOLD .... Geometric On-Line Definition [*Computer science*] (PDAA)
GOLD .... Georgia Online Database (SAUO)
GOLD .... Global On-Line Data (ACAE)
Gold .... Goldesborough's [*or Gouldsborough's*] English King's Bench Reports [*A publication*] (DLA)
GOLD .... Gospel of Life Disciples [*An association*] (EA)
GOLD .... Graphic Online Language [*Computer science*] (IEEE)
GOLD .... Great Eastern Mines Ltd. (SAUO)
GOLD .... Guild of Lady Drivers [*British*] (BI)
Gold & G ..... Goldsmith and Guthrie's Appeals Reports [*Missouri*] [*A publication*] (DLA)
GOLD BDE ... Gold Bevelled Deckle Edges [*Printing*] (DGA)
GOLD BE ...... Gold Bevelled Edges [*Printing*] (DGA)
GOLDBERG ... Generally Operational Linear Digit-Controlled Biphase Electrical Retardance Gate [*IBM Corp.*]
GoldBks .... Golden Books Family Entertainment, Inc. [*Associated Press*] (SAG)
GoldBnc .... Gold Banc Corp., Inc. [*Associated Press*] (SAG)
Gold Bull ..... Gold Bulletin (journ.) (SAUS)
Gold Coast ... Judgments of the Full Court, Privy Council, and Divisional Courts, Gold Coast [*A publication*] (DLA)
Gold Coast ... Judgments of the Full Court, Privy Council and Divisional Courts, Gold Coast (journ.) (SAUS)
Gold Coast Geol Surv Bull ... Gold Coast Geological Survey. Bulletin (journ.) (SAUS)
Goldcp .... Goldcorp, Inc. [*Associated Press*] (SAG)
GoldcpA .... Goldcorp [*Associated Press*] (SAG)
GoldcpB .... Goldcorp [*Associated Press*] (SAG)
GOLD E .... Gold Edges [*Printing*] (DGA)
GoldEn .... Golden Enterprises, Inc. [*Associated Press*] (SAG)
Golden Bk .... Golden Book Magazine (journ.) (SAUS)
Golden Gate U ... Golden Gate University (GAGS)
Golden Gte UL Rev ... Golden Gate University. Law Review (journ.) (SAUS)
GOLDER .... Golder Associates, Inc. (SAUO)
Goldes .... Goldesborough's [*or Gouldsborough's*] English King's Bench Reports [*A publication*] (DLA)
GOLDF .... Silverado Mines [*NASDAQ symbol*] (TTSB)
GoldFd .... Gold Fields of South Africa Ltd. [*Associated Press*] (SAG)
GOLDFISH ... Generation of Little Descriptions for Improving and Sustaining Health (ADWA)
GOLDIS .... GCOS On-Line Data Information System (SAUS)
GoldIsl .... Golden Isles Financial Holdings, Inc. [*Associated Press*] (SAG)
Gold K .... Goldene Key (SAUS)
GoldnOil .... Golden Oil Co. [*Associated Press*] (SAG)
Gold Placer Deposits Foot East Cordillera Bolivia ... Gold Placer Deposits at the Foot of the Eastern Cordillera of Bolivia (journ.) (SAUS)
GOLD Project ... Glasgow On-Line Desk Project (SAUS)
GoldRs .... Gold Reserve Corp. [*Associated Press*] (SAG)
GOLDS .... General On-Line Display System (SAUO)
Golds Eq ...... Goldsmith's Doctrine and Practice of Equity [*6th ed.*] [*1871*] [*A publication*] (DLA)
Golds Eq ...... Goldsmiths Doctrine and Practice of Equity (journ.) (SAUS)
Goldsmitbs J Gemm ... Goldsmiths Journal and Gemmologist (journ.) (SAUS)
GOLD STAR ... Generalized Organization of Large Databases / Set-Theoretic Approach to Relations
GoldTri .... Golden Triangle Industries, Inc. [*Associated Press*] (SAG)
GoldTri .... Golden Triangle Royalty & Oil, Inc. [*Associated Press*] (SAG)
GOLE .... GICS On-Line Data Entry System (SAUO)
GoletaN .... Goleta National Bank [*Associated Press*] (SAG)
GOLF .... Global Oscillations at Low Frequency [*Aerospace*]
go lf .... Gold Leaf (VRA)
Golf .... Olfactory G Protein [*Physiology*]
GOLF .... S 2 Golf [*NASDAQ symbol*] (TTSB)
GOLF .... STwo Golf, Inc. [*NASDAQ symbol*] (SAG)
Golf Ent .... Golf Enterprises, Inc. [*Associated Press*] (SAG)
GolfTech ...... Golf Technology Holding, Inc. [*Associated Press*] (SAG)
GolfTS .... Golf Training Systems, Inc. [*Associated Press*] (SAG)
GolfTSy .... Golf Training Systems, Inc. [*Associated Press*] (SAG)
GOLIATH ...... Giant On-Line Instrument for the Acquisition and Total Handling of Data (SAUS)
GOLIP .... Ground Operations and Logistics Integration Panel [*NASA*] (SPST)
GOLKAR .... Sekber Golongan Karya [*Joint Secretariat of Functional Groups*] [*Indonesia*] [*Political party*] (PPW)
GOLPH .... Giannetti On-Line Psychosocial History [*Personality development test*] [*Psychology*]
GOLPS .... Greek Orthodox Ladies Philoptochos Society (EA)
GOLS .... General Online Stack System (IAA)
GOLS .... German Oceanic Lidar System (SAUO)
GOLS System ... General On-Line Stack System (SAUS)
GOLW .... Golden-Crowned Warbler [*North American bird banding code*] (BIBA)
GOM .... Gate-Oxide Monitor (SAUS)
GOM .... Geostatistical Orebody Modelling (SAUO)
GOM .... Global Observations and Modeling Project (SAUS)
GOM .... Global Ocean Monitoring (SAUO)
GOM .... God's Own Medicine [*Also, God's Medicine*] [*Morphine*] [*Slang*]
GOM .... Goma [*Zaire*] [*Airport symbol*] (OAG)
GOM .... Government of Malaysia (CINC)
GOM .... Government-Owned Material
GOM .... Grain and Oil Seeds Marketing Incentives Program (SAUS)
GOM .... Grand Old Man [*A venerated man, especially in a specific field*] [*Political slang*] [*See also HOM*]
GOM .... Ground Operations Manager [*Aerospace*] (NAKS)
GOM .... Group Occupancy Meter [*Telecommunications*] (NITA)
GOM .... Gulf of Mexico [*Also, GLFMEX*]
GOM .... Macon Junior College, Macon, GA [*OCLC symbol*] (OCLC)
GOM .... or WSMR [*Hugh L. Dryden Flight Research Center*] [*White Sands Missile Range*] (NASA)
GOMA .... General Officer Money Allowance [*Military*] (AABC)
GOMA .... Good Outdoor Manners Association (EA)
GOMAC .... Government Microcircuit Applications Conference
GOMAC .... Groupement des Opticiens du Marche Commun [*Common Market Opticians' Group*] [*Paris, France*]
GOMALCO .... Gobel O'Malley Co. [*Entertainer George Gobel's firm; O'Malley is business ma nager*]
Gomal Univ J Res ... Gomal University. Journal of Research (journ.) (SAUS)
GoMB .... Gulf of Mexico Basin (SAUS)
GOME .... Global Ozone Mapping Experiment (SAUS)
GOME .... Global Ozone Monitoring Experiment [*Marine science*] (OSRA)
GOMEET ...... Goals, Objectives, Means, Ends, Effects, and Timing [*Environmental science*] (COE)
Gomer .... Get Out of My Emergency Room [*Medical slang describing a patient who cannot describe his/her symptoms*]
GOMI .... Global Ozone Monitoring Instrument (CARB)
GOMMS .... Ground Operations and Material Management System (MCD)
GOMOS .... Global Ozone Monitoring by Occultation of Stars [*Marine science*] (OSRA)
GOMOT .... Global Observations, Modeling and Optical Techniques Section (SAUS)
GOMP .... Geophysical Observatories and Mapping Program (SAUO)
GOMPS .... Global Ocean Monitoring Payload Studies (SAUO)
GOMR .... Global Ozone Monitoring Radiometer
GOMR & R ... Government-Owned Material Repair and Reimbursement (MCD)
GOMS .... Geostationary Operational Meteorological Satellite [*Marine science*] (OSRA)
GOMS .... geostationary operational meterological satellite (SAUS)
GOMS .... Global Ocean Monitoring Satellite (SAUO)
GOMS .... Global Ozone Monitoring System (SAUO)
GOMS .... Goals, Operators, Methods, and Selection Rules (LDOE)
GOMS .... Grants Obligations Management System (SAUO)
GOMS .... Ground Operations Management System [*NASA*] (NASA)
GOMZ .... Gooch Mill [*Federal Railroad Administration identification code*]
GON .... Geon Co. [*NYSE symbol*] (SPSG)
gon .... Gondi [*MARC language code*] [*Library of Congress*] (LCCP)
GON .... Gonni Air Services Ltd. [*Suriname*] [*ICAO designator*] (FAAC)
GON .... Gonocal Ophthalmia Neonatorum (SAUS)
GON .... Gonococcal Ophthalmia Neonatorum [*Medicine*]
GON .... New London [*Connecticut*] [*Airport symbol*] (OAG)
GONAAR ...... Forest Science (journ.) (SAUS)
GOND .... Glaucomatous Optic Nerve Damage [*Medicine*] (DMAA)
GOND .... Gondola
GONE .... Plastigone Technologies, Inc. (SAUO)

GONG.......... Global Oscillations Network Group [*National Science Foundation*]
GONGO........ Government and NGO Organisation (SAUO)
GONGOs...... Governmental and Non-governmental Organizations (SAUO)
GONIO......... Goniometer [*RADAR instrument*] (DSUE)
Gonio.......... Gonioscopy (STED)
Gon lR......... Gonzaga Law Review (journ.) (SAUS)
GONP.......... Gal Oya National Pa (SAUS)
GONP.......... Gal Oya National Park (SAUO)
GONS.......... Gun Orientation Navigation System (SAUS)
GONS.......... Gun Oriented and Navigation System (SAUS)
GONT.......... Government on Taiwan
GON Timber... Gondsoroi Timber (SAUS)
Gonzaga U... Gonzaga University (GAGS)
Gonz Pub Lab L Rep... Gonzaga Special Report. Public Sector (SAUS)
Gonz Pub Lab L Rep... Gonzaga Special Report. Public Sector Labor Law [*A publication*] (DLA)
Gonz Univ.... Gonzaga University (SAUO)
GOO............ Gastric Outlet Obstruction [*Gastroenterology*] (DAVI)
GOO............ Generalized Overhauser Orbitals [*Atomic physics*]
GOO............ General Overhauser Orbitals (SAUS)
GOO............ Get Oil Out (EA)
GOO............ Goldsil Resources Ltd. [*Toronto Stock Exchange symbol*] [*Vancouver Stock Exchange symbol*]
GOO............ Goondiwindi [*Australia*] [*Airport symbol*] (OAG)
GOO............ Goosecreekite [*A zeolite*]
GOO............ Ground Observer Organization (NATG)
GOO............ Ground Operation Order (NATG)
GOO............ Group Operations Order [*British military*] (DMA)
GOOBS......... Going Out of Business Sale
GOOD.......... Diourbel [*Senegal*] [*ICAO location identifier*] (ICLI)
GOOD.......... Globally Only Open-access Data (SAUO)
GOOD.......... Goody Products (SAUS)
Good&Wood... Full Bench Rulings (SAUS)
Good & Wood... Full Bench Rulings, Edited by Goodeve and Woodman [*Bengal*] [*A publication*] (DLA)
GOOD-B'YE... God Be with You (ROG)
GOOD EGGS... Geriatric Order of Old Dolls Who Encourage the Generation Gap Singlemindedly [*Tongue-in-cheek teachers' organization*]
Good Ev....... Goodeve's Law of Evidence [*India*] [*A publication*] (DLA)
Good Ev....... Goodeves Law of Evidence (journ.) (SAUS)
Goodeve....... Goodeve on Real Property [*1883-1906*] [*A publication*] (DLA)
Good Govt.... Good Government [*A publication*]
GoodGy........ [*The*] Good Guys, Inc. [*Associated Press*] (SAG)
GOODL......... Goodland, KS [*American Association of Railroads railroad junction routing code*]
Goodmrk...... Goodmark Foods, Inc. [*Associated Press*] (SAG)
Good Pat..... Goodeve's Abstract of Patent Cases [*1785-1883*] [*England*] [*A publication*] (DLA)
Good Pat..... Goodeves Abstract of Patent Cases (journ.) (SAUS)
Good Pr....... Goodwin's Probate Practice [*A publication*] (DLA)
Goodrch....... Goodrich, BF, Co. [*Associated Press*] (SAG)
Goodrich...... BF Goodrich Co. Economic and Business Facts and Forecasts (journ.) (SAUS)
Goodrich-Amram... Goodrich-Amram Procedural Rules Service [*A publication*] (DLA)
GoodrP........ Goodrich Petroleum [*Associated Press*] (SAG)
GoodrPet...... Goodrich Petroleum [*Associated Press*] (SAG)
Good Ry C... Goodeve on Railway Companies and Passengers [*A publication*] (DLA)
Good Ry C... Goodeve on Railway Companies and Passengers (journ.) (SAUS)
Good Shepherd Sisters of Quebec... Servants of the Immaculate Heart of Mary (SAUO)
GoodT.......... Good Times Restaurants, Inc. [*Associated Press*] (SAG)
GoodTm....... Good Times Restaurants, Inc. [*Associated Press*] (SAG)
Goodyear..... [*The*] Goodyear Tire & Rubber Co. [*Associated Press*] (SAG)
goof............ general on-line orient function (SAUS)
GOOFC......... Grand Ole Opry Fan Club (EA)
GOOG.......... Linguere [*Senegal*] [*ICAO location identifier*] (ICLI)
GOOK.......... Kaolack [*Senegal*] [*ICAO location identifier*] (ICLI)
GOOMBY...... Get Out of My Backyard [*Slang*]
GOONQ........ Grand Officier de l'Ordre National du Quebec [*Canada*] (DD)
GOONS........ Guild of One Name Studies [*Organization to link people with a common surname for the study of family history*] [*British*]
GOOO........... Dakar [*Senegal*] [*ICAO location identifier*] (ICLI)
GOOS........... Global Ocean Observation System (ECON)
GOOS........... Global Ozone Observing System [*Marine science*] (OSRA)
GOOS........... Gunnery Officers Ordnance School
GOOSE......... Waysgoose [*Country fair*] (ROG)
GOOSES....... Goose Operational and Strategie Effectiveness Study (SAUO)
GOOS/SO..... GOOS Support Office (SAUS)
GOOV.......... Dakar [*Senegal*] [*ICAO location identifier*] (ICLI)
GOOY........... Dakar/Yoff [*Senegal*] [*ICAO location identifier*] (ICLI)
GOP............ General Defence Plan (SAUS)
GOP............ General Operating Procedures (SAUO)
GOP............ General Operational Plot
GOP............ General Operations Plot (SAUO)
GOP............ General Outpost [*Army*] (AABC)
GOP............ Generated Options Plans (SAUO)
GOP............ Geographical Observatories Programme (SAUO)
GOP............ Gold Point Resources [*Vancouver Stock Exchange symbol*]
GOP............ Gorakhpur [*India*] [*Airport symbol*] (OAG)
GOP............ Government of Pakistan (ECON)
GOP............ Government of the Philippines (CINC)
GOP............ Government-Owned Property
GOP............ Graham-McCormick Oil & Gas Partnership (SAUS)
GOP............ Grand Old Party [*The Republican Party*]
GOP............ Grille Opening Panel [*Automotive engineering*]
GOP............ Ground Observation Post (SAUS)
GOP............ Ground Observer Post
GOP............ Ground Operations Panel [*NASA*] (NASA)
GOP............ Group of Paths (SAA)
GOP............ Group of Pictures [*Computer science*]
GOP............ Group Operations Plan (SAUO)
GOP............ Gulf Oil-Pennsylvania [*Federal Railroad Administration identification code*]
Gopa........... Government Oil and Pipeline Agency (SAUS)
GOPAC........ GOP Action Committee
GOPAL......... GOP [*Grand Old Party*] Women's Political Action League (EA)
GOPAL......... GOP Womens Political Action Legal (SAUS)
GOPARS...... Government-Operated Parts Store
GOPARS...... Government Operated Part Stock (SAUS)
GOPB.......... Go Pushbutton (SAUS)
GOPDC........ Ghana Oil Palm Development Corporation (SAUO)
GOPE.......... Government-Owned Plant Equipment
GOPG.......... Ground Operations Planning Group [*NASA*] (NASA)
GOPIRB........ General Officer Product Improvement Review Board
GOPITS........ Grand Offertory Procession in the Sky [*Corporate sobriquet used by novelist William X. Kienzle*]
GOPL........... General Outpost Line [*Army*]
GOPO.......... Government-Owned/Privately-Operated (GFGA)
GOPP.......... Government-Owned Personal Property (SAUS)
GOPR.......... General Officers' Protocol Roster
GOPRINT..... Government Printer [*Queensland, Australia*]
GOPS.......... Giga Operations Per Second (NITA)
GOPs........... Video film is divided into Groups of Pictures (SAUO)
GOQ............ Genuine Occupational Qualification (DI)
GOQ............ Glucose Oxidation Quotient (STED)
GOQ............ Golmud [*China*] [*Airport symbol*] (OAG)
GOQS.......... General On-Line Query System (MCD)
GOR............ Collins Industries, Inc. (SAUS)
GOR............ Gained Output Ratio (IEEE)
GOR............ Gas-Oil Ratio (IEEE)
GOR............ Gastroesophageal Reflux [*Medicine*] (STED)
GOR............ General Ocean Research [*Navy ship symbol*]
GOR............ General Officer Review (MCD)
GOR............ General Operating Room
GOR............ General Operational Requirement
GOR............ General Overruling Regulation [*Office of Price Stabilization*] (DLA)
GOR............ Golden Range Resources, Inc. [*Toronto Stock Exchange symbol*]
GOR............ Goldstack Resources [*Vancouver Stock Exchange symbol*]
GOR............ Gordon Jewelry Corp. (SAUO)
GOR............ Gore [*Ethiopia*] [*Airport symbol*] (OAG)
GOR............ Gori [*Former USSR*] [*Seismograph station code, US Geological Survey*] (SEIS)
GOR............ Gradual-Onset-Rate [*Air Force*] (DOMA)
GOR............ Grille Opening Reinforcement [*Automotive engineering*]
GOR............ Gross Overriding Royalty (SAUS)
GOR............ Ground Operations Review (MCD)
GOR............ Group Operations Room (SAUO)
GOR............ Gun Operations Room [*British military*] (DMA)
GOR............ Gurkha Other Rank [*Military*] [*British*]
GORA.......... Government Oil Refineries Administration (SAUO)
GoranC........ Goran Capital, Inc. [*Associated Press*] (SAG)
GORC.......... Global Ocean Carbon Research Program (SAUO)
GORD.......... Gastro-Oesophageal Reflux Disease [*Medicine*] (WDAA)
Gord Dec..... Gordon on the Law of Decedents in Pennsylvania [*A publication*] (DLA)
Gord Dec..... Gordon on the Law of Decendents in Pennsylvania (journ.) (SAUS)
Gord Dig...... Gordon's Digest of United States Laws [*A publication*] (DLA)
Gord Dig...... Gordons Digest of United States Laws (journ.) (SAUS)
GORD HIGHRS... Gordon Highlanders [*Military*] [*British*] (ROG)
Gordon......... Gordon's Reports [*24-26 Colorado and 10-13 Colorado Appeals*] [*A publication*] (DLA)
Gord Tr........ Gordon's Treason Trials [*A publication*] (DLA)
Gore-B Comp... Gore-Brown on Companies [*43rd ed.*] [*1977*] [*A publication*] (DLA)
GOREDCO.... Gulf Oil Real Estate Development Co.
GOREDDCO... Gulf Oil Real Estate Development Company (SAUS)
GOREL......... Goreville, IL [*American Association of Railroads railroad junction routing code*]
GORF........... Goddard Optical Research Facility [*Goddard Space Flight Center*] [*NASA*]
GORF........... Goddards Optical Research Facility (SAUS)
G or G......... Gdynia or Gdansk (SAUS)
GORG.......... General Officers Review Group [*Air Force*]
Gorg............ Gorgias [*483-376BC*] [*Classical studies*] (OCD)
G Org.......... Grand-Orgue [*Great Organ*] [*Music*]
G ORG......... Great Organ [*Music*]
GORI........... Gross Overriding Royalty Interest (SAUS)
GORID......... Ground Optical Recorder for Intercept Determination
GORJE......... Generic Ordnance Ramjet Engine (MCD)
GORK.......... God Only Really Knows [*Facetious diagnosis for a puzzling medical case*]
GORK/DDC... Gorkha District Development Committee (SAUS)
GORMP........ Global Ozone Research And Monitoring Programme (SAUO)
GormRup...... Gorman-Rupp Co. [*Associated Press*] (SAG)
Gorn Mash Avtom... Gornye Mashiny i Avtomatika (journ.) (SAUS)
GORP.......... Goal-Oriented Replanner (SAUS)
GORP.......... Great Outdoor Recreation Pages (SAUO)
GORP.......... Ground Operational [*or Operations*] Requirements Plan [*NASA*]
GORP.......... Ground Operations Requirements Plan (SAUS)

GORP .... Ground-Operations Requirements Plan (SAUO)
GORP .... Ground Operations Review Panel [*NASA*] (NASA)
GORRUP ...... Gorman-Rupp Co. (SAUO)
GORS .... General Online Retrieval System (SAUS)
GORS .... General Organization of Remote Sensing (SAUO)
GORS .... Grant of Resident Status
GORS .... Ground Observation Reporting System
GORS .... Ground Observer RF [*Radio Frequency*] System [*NASA*] (NASA)
GORS .... Ground Operation Reporting System (SAUO)
GORSP .... Government Officials Responsible for Standardization Policies [*Economic Commission for Europe*] [*United Nations*] (PDAA)
GORT .... Gilmore Oral Reading Test [*Psychology*] (DAVI)
GORT .... Gray Oral Reading Tests
GORTA .... Third World development agency focusing on rural development (SAUO)
GORT-R .... Gray Oral Reading Tests - Revised [*Educational test*]
GORU .... Gun Order Responder Unit (SAUS)
GORX .... Graphite Oxidation from Reactor Excursion [*Engineering computer code*]
GORX .... Gulf & Ohio Railways [*Federal Railroad Administration identification code*]
GOS .... Gate Operating System [*Aviation*] (DA)
GOS .... General Operating Specification [*Air Materiel Command*] (AAG)
GOS .... General Operator Station (SAUS)
GOS .... General Overhaul Specification
GOS .... General-purpose Operator Station (SAUS)
GOS .... Geochemical Ocean Studies (SAUO)
GOS .... Geodetic Optical System
GOS .... Geomagnetic Observing System (EOSA)
GOS .... George Orwell Society (SAUO)
GOS .... Geostationary Operational Sounder (SAUS)
GOS .... Glasgow Outcome Score [*Medicine*] (DMAA)
GOS .... Global Observation Station (SAUO)
GOS .... Global Observation Study (FOTI)
GOS .... Global Observation System (SAUO)
GOS .... Global Observing System (EERA)
GOS .... Global Observing Systems [*Weather*]
GOS .... Global Operating System (IAA)
GOS .... Global Ozone Sensor (SAUS)
GOS .... Golden State Resources [*Vancouver Stock Exchange symbol*]
GOS .... Goldfields Air Services [*Australia*] [*ICAO designator*] (FAAC)
GOS .... Gosford [*Australia*] [*Airport symbol*] [*Obsolete*] (OAG)
GOS .... Gossip (DSUE)
GOS .... Government of Singapore (CINC)
GOS .... Government of Spain
GOS .... Government of Sweden (MCD)
GOS .... Government of Switzerland (SAUO)
GoS .... Grade of Service (CGWS)
GOS .... Grade of Service
GOS .... Grand Outside Sentinel [*Freemasonry*] (ROG)
GOS .... Graphical Output Scheme (PDAA)
GOS .... Graphic Operating System (SAUS)
GOS .... Graphics Operating System [*Tektronix*]
GOS .... Gross Operating Surplus [*Economics*]
GOS .... Ground Operations System (MCD)
GOS .... Ground Optical Station (SAUO)
GOS .... Group and Organization Studies (journ.) (SAUS)
GOS .... Group Operating Services (NRCH)
GOS .... Guidance Offset Bits (SAUS)
GOS .... Guild of Surveyors (BUAC)
GOS .... Lakeview, OR [*Location identifier*] [*FAA*] (FAAL)
Gos Alb .... Gossamer Albatross (SAUS)
GOSAMR ...... Gelation of Soils (SAUS)
GOSAMR ...... Gelation of Soils: Applied Microgravity Research (SAUS)
GosAtomNadzor ... Federal Supervisory Board for Nuclear and Radiation Safety (SAUO)
GOSB .... GSB Financial Corp. [*NASDAQ symbol*] (NASQ)
GOSC .... General (SAUS)
GOSC .... General Officer Steering Committee [*Military*] (MCD)
GosC .... General Osteopathic Council (SAUO)
GOSC .... Ground Operational Support Center (SAUO)
GOSC .... Group of Specialists on Cenozoic Paleoenvironments of the Southern High Latitudes (SAUO)
GosComStat ... State Committee for Statistics (SAUO)
GOSEAC ...... Group of Specialists on Antarctic Affairs and Conservation (SAUS)
GOSEAC ...... Group of Specialists on Environmental Affairs and Conservation (EERA)
Gos Eb .... Gospel of the Ebionites [*Biblical*] (RION)
Gosf .... Gosford's Manuscript Reports, Scotch Court of Session [*A publication*] (DLA)
GOSG .... General Officer Steering Group
GosGISCentre ... State Research and Innovation Centre of Geoinformation Systems and Technologies (SAUO)
GOSH .... Graphical Operating System Hack [*Computer science*]
GOSH .... Great Ormond Street Hospital (WDAA)
GOSH .... Grown Offspring, Still Home [*Lifestyle classification*]
GOSH .... Guild Software Houses (SAUS)
GOSH .... Oshkosh B Gosh, Inc. [*NASDAQ symbol*] (SAG)
GOSHA .... Oshkosh B'Gosh Cl'A' [*NASDAQ symbol*] (TTSB)
GOSHB .... Oshkosh B'Gosh Cl'B' [*NASDAQ symbol*] (TTSB)
GOSHN .... Goshen, IN [*American Association of Railroads railroad junction routing code*]
GOSI .... Generic Operating System Interface (AG)
GOSIC .... G3OS Information Center (SAUO)
GOSIP .... Government Open Systems Implementation Protocol [*Telecommunications*]
GOSIP .... Government Open Systems Interconnection Procurement (GART)
GOSIP .... Government Open Systems Interconnection Profile [*National Institute of Standards and Technology*] (GFGA)
GOSIP .... Government Open Systems Interconnection Profiles Computer science (EERA)
GOSIP .... Government Open Systems Interconnect Protocol [*Computer science*] (CIST)
GOSIP-UK .... Government Open Systems Interconnection Profile-United Kingdom (SAUS)
GOSIP-US .... Government Open Systems Interconnection Profile-United States (SAUS)
GOSL .... Government of Sri Lanka
GOSM .... Matam/Ouro Sogui [*Senegal*] [*ICAO location identifier*] (ICLI)
GOSN .... Goal Objective Strategy Need (VLIE)
GOSNIORKH ... State Institute of Lake and River Fisheries (SAUO)
GOSP .... Gas-Oil Separation Plant
GOSP .... Golden Spike National Historic Site
GOSP .... Gospel (ROG)
GOSP .... Government Open System Project (SAUS)
GOSP .... Podor [*Senegal*] [*ICAO location identifier*] (ICLI)
GOSPA .... Goals, Objectives, Strategies, Plans, Activities (BB)
GOSPLAN .... Gosudarstvennaja Planovaja Komissija [*Central Planning Commission*] [*Former USSR*]
GOSR .... Richard-Toll [*Senegal*] [*ICAO location identifier*] (ICLI)
GOSS .... General Overhaul Specifications (SAUS)
GOSS .... General Overhaul Specifications, Submarines (SAUO)
GOSS .... GOES Operational Support Systems (SAUO)
GOSS .... Gossamer Hat [*Tall hat*] (ROG)
GOSS .... Ground Operational [*or Operations*] Support System [*NASA*]
GOSS .... Saint Louis [*Senegal*] [*ICAO location identifier*] (ICLI)
GOSS .... Spot Station Operators Group (SAUS)
G O S S + D ... GEORGE Operating System Support and Development (SAUS)
GOSS-IMCC ... Ground Operational Support System-Intergrated Mission Control Center (SAUS)
G O S S I P ... Generalized Organizational System Summarizer and Information Processor (SAUS)
GOSSIP .... Generalized Organizational System Summatizer and Information Processor (SAUS)
GOSSIP .... Government Open Systems Interconnection Procurement Policy (SAUS)
GOSSOE .... SCAR Group of Specialists on Southern Ocean Ecology (SAUO)
GOSSP .... Global Observing Systems Space Panel (SAUO)
GOSS-SSIS ... Goal Oriented Social Services-Social Services Information System [*Medicine*] (EDAA)
GOSST .... Global Ocean Sea Surface Temperature (SAUS)
GOSSTANDART ... State Committee for Standardization, Metrology and Certification of the Russian Federation (SAUO)
GOSSTCOMP ... Global Ocean Sea Surface Temperature Computation (SAUS)
GOSSTCOMP ... Global Sea Surface Temperature Computation
GOSSTRAKH ... Gosudarstvennoe Strakhovanie [*State insurance*] [*Former USSR*]
GOST .... Committee of the Russian Federation for Standardisation, Metrology, and Certification (BUAC)
GOST .... Goddard Satellite Tracking [*NASA*] (MCD)
GOST .... Gossudarstvenny Obstschessojusny Standart [*All-Union State Standard*] [*Former USSR*]
GOST .... Government-Owned Special Tooling (SAUS)
GOST .... Guidance Optics and Sighting
GOSTA .... Global Ocean Surface Temperature Atlas (SAUS)
GOSUB .... Go To Subroutine (SAUS)
GOSY .... Graphic Output System (SAUS)
GOT .... Air Express in Norrkoping AB [*Sweden*] [*ICAO designator*] (FAAC)
GOT .... Aspartate Aminotransferase [*An enzyme*] (DAVI)
GOT .... Global Offset Table (SAUS)
GOT .... Glucose Oxidase Test [*Organic chemistry*] (DAVI)
GOT .... Glutamic-Oxaloacetic Transaminase [*Also, AAT, ASAT, AST*] [*An enzyme*]
GOT .... Goal of Treatment [*Medicine*] (MELL)
GOT .... Goldbelt Mines [*Vancouver Stock Exchange symbol*]
GOT .... Goteborg [*Sweden*] [*Seismograph station code, US Geological Survey*] [*Closed*] (SEIS)
GOT .... Gothenburg [*Sweden*] [*Airport symbol*] (OAG)
got .... Gothic [*MARC language code*] [*Library of Congress*] (LCCP)
GOT .... Gottschalks, Inc. [*NYSE symbol*] (SPSG)
GOT .... Government of Tunisia
GOT .... Government-Owned Terminal
GOT .... Gulf Oil-Texas [*Federal Railroad Administration identification code*]
GOTA .... Green Olive Trade Association (EA)
GOTB .... Bakel [*Senegal*] [*ICAO location identifier*] (ICLI)
G/OTBSR ..... Gas/Oil Tax Block Summary Record [*IRS*]
GOTCHA ...... Generalized Overall Toxics Control and Hazards Act (EEVL)
Gotchk .... Gottschalks, Inc. [*Associated Press*] (SAG)
GOTCO .... Gulf Oil Trading Co.
GOTCO .... Gulf Oil Trading Company (SAUO)
Goteb Ethnogr Mus ... Goteborgs Ethnographical Museum (journ.) (SAUS)
GOTFIA .... Groaning on the Floor in Agony (ADWA)
GOTG .... Government of the Gambia
Goth .... De Bello Gothico [*of Procopius*] [*Classical studies*] (OCD)
Goth .... Gothic (VRA)
GOTH .... Gothic [*Language, etc.*]
GOTH .... Gothic Energy [*NASDAQ symbol*] (TTSB)
GOTH .... Gothic Energy Corp. [*NASDAQ symbol*] (SAG)
GotHA .... Goteborgs Hogskolas Arsskrift [*Gothenburg*] [*A publication*] (BJA)
GothE .... Gothic Energy Corp. [*Associated Press*] (SAG)

Gothenburg Stud Phys... Gothenburg Studies in Physics (journ.) (SAUS)
Gothic.......... Gothic Energy Corp. [*Associated Press*] (SAG)
Gothic.......... Gothic Script (SAUS)
GothicEn...... Gothic Energy Corp. [*Associated Press*] (SAG)
Goth SE....... Gothenburg Studies in English (journ.) (SAUS)
GOTHW........ Gothic Energy Wrrt [*NASDAQ symbol*] (TTSB)
GOTHZ........ Gothic Energy Wrrt [*NASDAQ symbol*] (TTSB)
GOTK.......... Geotek Communications, Inc. [*NASDAQ symbol*] (NQ)
GOTK.......... Geotek Industries, Inc. (SAUO)
GOTK.......... Kedougou [*Senegal*] [*ICAO location identifier*] (ICLI)
GOTL.......... Gotaas-Larsen Shipping Corp. (SAUO)
GOTLF......... Gotaas-Larsen Shipping Corp. (MHDW)
GOTM.......... Glutamic Oxalacetic Transaminase, Mitochondrial [*Medicine*] (EDAA)
GOTN.......... Niokolo Koba [*Senegal*] [*ICAO location identifier*] (ICLI)
GOTO.......... GoTo.com, Inc. [*NASDAQ symbol*] (SG)
Go to E........ Go To Executive (SAUS)
GOTOH......... Go to Heaven [*Name of missionary, "Professor Gotoh," for Worldwide Church of God*]
Go to I......... Go To Instruction (SAUS)
Go to L......... Go To Logic (SAUS)
G/OTPSR...... Gas/Oil Tax Program Summary Record [*IRS*]
GOTR.......... Greek Orthodox Theological Review [*A publication*] (BJA)
GOTRAN...... Load and Go FORTRAN [*Computer science*]
GO Transit... Government of Ontario Transit System (SAUS)
GOTS.......... GALE Oceanographic Temperature Studies (SAUS)
GOTS.......... Government Off- The Shelf (DOMA)
GOTS.......... Government-off-the-Shelf (SAUS)
GOTS.......... Graphic-Oriented Timesharing System [*Computer science*] (IAA)
GOTS.......... Gravity-Oriented Test Satellite [*NASA*]
GOTS.......... Simenti [*Senegal*] [*ICAO location identifier*] (ICLI)
GOTT.......... Gott Corp. (SAUO)
GOTT.......... Tambacounda [*Senegal*] [*ICAO location identifier*] (ICLI)
Gott Anz...... Goettingischer Gelehrte Anzeigen [*A publication*] (OCD)
GOTTEX...... Gottlieb Textiles
Gott Nachr... Nachrichten von der Gesellschaft der Wissenschaften zu Goettingen [*A publication*] (OCD)
Gottschall.... Gottschall's Dayton Superior Court Reports [*Ohio*] [*A publication*] (DLA)
GOTU.......... Glider Operational Training Unit [*British military*] (DMA)
GOTV.......... Get Out the Vote (GNE)
GOU........... Garoua [*Cameroon*] [*Airport symbol*] (OAG)
GOU........... General Outdoor Advertising Co., Inc. (SAUO)
gou............ Gouache (VRA)
GOU........... Government of Uganda (ECON)
GOU........... Ground or Open Unbalanced (SAUS)
GOU........... Grupo de Oficiales Unidos [*Group of United Officers*] [*Argentina*]
GOU........... Gulf Canada Resources [*NYSE symbol*] (TTSB)
GOU........... Gulf Canada Resources Ltd. [*AMEX symbol*] [*Toronto Stock Exchange symbol*]
GOU........... Oglethorpe University, Atlanta, GA [*OCLC symbol*] (OCLC)
Gouc Col Se... Goucher College Series (journ.) (SAUS)
Goucher C... Goucher College (GAGS)
Goud Pand... Goudsmit's Pandects [*Roman law*] [*A publication*] (DLA)
Goud Pand... Goudsmit's Pandects (SAUS)
Goulcae J Educ... Goulcae Journal of Education (journ.) (SAUS)
GOULD........ Gould, OH [*American Association of Railroads railroad junction routing code*]
Gould.......... Gouldsborough's English King's Bench Reports [*A publication*] (DLA)
Gould & T.... Gould and Tucker's Notes on Revised Statutes of United States [*A publication*] (DLA)
GouldP......... Goulds Pumps, Inc. [*Associated Press*] (SAG)
Gould Pl...... Gould on the Principles of Pleading in Civil Actions [*A publication*] (DLA)
Gouldsb....... Gouldsborough's English King's Bench Reports [*A publication*] (DLA)
Gouldsb (Eng)... Gouldsborough's English King's Bench Reports [*A publication*] (DLA)
Gould's Dig... Gould's Arkansas Digest of Laws [*A publication*] (DLA)
Goulds Dig... Goulds Arkansas Digest of Laws (journ.) (SAUS)
Gould Sten Rep... Gould's Stenographic Reporter [*Monographic Series*] [*Albany, NY*] [*A publication*] (DLA)
Gould Wat... Gould on Waters [*A publication*] (DLA)
GOUMS........ Group Operational Units, Marines (SAUO)
GOUPrA....... Gulf Can ResAdjcm Ser 1 Pref [*NYSE symbol*] (TTSB)
Gour............ Gourick's Patent Digest [*1889-91*] [*A publication*] (DLA)
Gour............ Gouricks Patent Digest (journ.) (SAUS)
gour............ Gourmet (ADWA)
Gourl Gen Av... Gourlie on General Average [*A publication*] (DLA)
GOV............ Generator Output Voltage
GOV............ Global Government Plus Fund, Inc. [*NYSE symbol*] (SPSG)
GOV............ Golden Dividend Resources [*Vancouver Stock Exchange symbol*]
GOV............ Gouverneur Bancorp [*AMEX symbol*] (SG)
GOV............ Govalkot [*India*] [*Seismograph station code, US Geological Survey*] [*Closed*] (SEIS)
GOV............ Gove [*Australia*] [*Airport symbol*] (OAG)
GOV............ Govern (ROG)
Gov............. Governing (TBD)
gov............. Government (VRA)
GOV............ Government
GOV............ Government-Owned Vehicle [*GSA*] (TAG)
GOV............ Governor (AFM)
gov............. Governor (DD)
Gov............. Governor (TBD)
GOV............ Gunn Oscillator; Voltage-tunable (SAUS)
GOVA.......... Guide to Opportunities in Volunteer Archaeology (SAUS)
Gov Agric Res Cent Ghent Act Rep... Government Agricultural Research Centre. Ghent. Activity Report (journ.) (SAUS)
GOVAIR........ Government Aircraft (DNAB)
GOVAIRAUTHOUT... Travel via Government Aircraft Authorized Outside CONUS [*Military*]
GOVAIRAUTHVATL... Travel via Government Aircraft Authorized Outside CONUS Where Available [*Military*]
GOVAIRDIR... Travel via Government Aircraft Is Directed Where Necessary [*Military*]
GOVAIRDIROUT... Travel via Government Aircraft Is Directed Outside CONUS [*Military*]
GOVAIRDIRVAIL... Travel via Government Aircraft Is Directed Outside CONUS Where Available [*Military*]
GOVAIRPRI... Travel via Government Aircraft Outside CONUS Class-Priority Certified (SAUS)
GOVCOMLAIRAUTH... Travel via Government and/or Commercial Aircraft Authorized Where Necessary to Expedite Completion of Duty [*Military*]
GOVCOMLTRANSAUTH... Government and/or Commercial US Registry Transportation Authorized Outside (SAUS)
GOVCOMLTRANSAUTH... Travel via Government and/or Commercial US Registry Transportation Authorized Outside CONUS (SAUS)
GOVD.......... Governed (ROG)
GoVd........... Go-Video, Inc. [*Associated Press*] (SAG)
GOVECLOP... Government Closest to the People (SAUS)
Governmental Fin... Governmental Finance (journ.) (SAUS)
Govett......... Govett & Co. Ltd. [*Associated Press*] (SAG)
GOVG.......... Governing (MSA)
GOVIDE........ Go-Video, Inc. (SAUO)
GoVideo....... Go-Video, Inc. [*Associated Press*] (SAG)
Gov Inf Q...... Government Information Quarterly (journ.) (SAUS)
GOV IS........ Governor's Island [*Massachusetts*] (WDAA)
GOVMAR...... Governor, Marshall Islands
GOVMERAIR... Government or Commercial Aircraft (DNAB)
GOVMERAIRAUTH... Government and/or Commercial Aircraft Is Authorized Where Necessary (SAUS)
Gov Metall Lab Repub S Afr Rep... Government Metallurgical Laboratory. Republic of South Africa. Report (journ.) (SAUS)
GOVN.......... Govern (ROG)
GOVNMT...... Government [*United States Postal Service last word addressing abbreviation*]
GOVO.......... Go-Video, Inc. (SAUO)
Gov Ops....... Government Operations Committee [*House and Senate*] (AAGC)
Gov Pest Infest Lab Annu Rep... Government Pest Infestation Laboratory. Annual Report (journ.) (SAUS)
GOVPP......... Global Ocean Velocity Pilot Project (SAUS)
GovPrOff...... Government Printing Office (SAUO)
GovPtg Off... Government Printing Office (SAUO)
Gov Publ...... Government Publications (journ.) (SAUS)
Govr............ Governor
Gov Relat Note... Government Relations Note (journ.) (SAUS)
GOVS.......... Governments Division [*Census*] (OICC)
GOV STD..... Government Standards
Gov St U...... Governors State University (GAGS)
GOVT.......... Government (AFM)
govt........... Government (DD)
Govt........... Government [*Business term*] (EBF)
GOVT.......... Government Service [*Communications term*] (DCT)
GOVT.......... Govett & Co. Ltd. [*NASDAQ symbol*] (SAG)
govtalk........ Government Talk (SAUS)
Govt&Oppos... Government and Opposition (SAUS)
Govt Col Econ J... Government College Economic Journal (journ.) (SAUS)
Gov't Cont Rep... Government Contracts Reporter [*Commerce Clearing House*] [*A publication*] (DLA)
GOVTEL....... Government Telegram (IAA)
Govt Empl Rel Rep... Government Employee Relations Report (journ.) (SAUS)
Govt Empl Rel Rep BNA... Government Employee Relations Report. Bureau of National Affairs (journ.) (SAUS)
Govt Fin....... Governmental Finance (journ.) (SAUS)
Govt Fin R... Government Finance Review (journ.) (SAUS)
Govt Gaz W Aust... Government Gazette (SAUS)
GOVTHO....... Government House [*Canada*] (DNAB)
GOVTL......... Governmental
GOVTLAIRNOREUR... Commander, Allied Air Forces, Northern Europe
Govt Print.... Government Printer (SAUO)
GOVTRANSDIROUT... Travel via Government Transportation Directed Outside CONUS [*Military*]
GOVTRANSDIRVAIL... Travel via Government Transportation Directed Outside CONUS Where Available [*Military*]
Govt Stand... Government Standard (journ.) (SAUS)
GOW........... Georgia Power Co. (SAUO)
GOW........... Gowganda Resources, Inc. [*Toronto Stock Exchange symbol*] [*Vancouver Stock Exchange symbol*]
Gow............ Gow's English Nisi Prius Cases [*171 English Reprint*] [*A publication*] (DLA)
GOW........... Grand Old Woman [*England's Queen Victoria*]
GOW........... Gunnery Officer's Writer [*Navy*] [*British*]
GOWE.......... Golden White-Eye [*North American bird banding code*] (BIBA)
Gower B....... Gower Birds (journ.) (SAUS)
GOWEX........ Geometry of the Wake Experiment [*Military*] (MCD)
GOWG......... General Officer Working Group (SAUO)
GOWG......... Ground Operations Working Group (MCD)
GOWGF....... Gowganda Resources, Inc. (SAUO)
GOWI.......... Get on with it (SAUS)
GOWMA....... Gulf Oil Wholesale Marketers Association (EA)

Gow NP .... Gow's English Nisi Prius Cases [*171 English Reprint*] [*A publication*] (DLA)
Gow NP (Eng)... Gow's English Nisi Prius Cases [*171 English Reprint*] [*A publication*] (DLA)
GOWON .... Gulf Offshore Weather Observing Network [*Marine science*] (OSRA)
Gow Part ..... Gow on Partnerships [*A publication*] (DLA)
GOWR .... Grand Order of Water Rats [*British*] (BI)
GOX .... Galaxy Oil Co. (SAUO)
GOX .... Gaseous Oxygen
G O X .... Gas Oxygen (SAUS)
GOx .... Glucose Oxidase (SAUS)
GOX .... Greenville, SC [*Location identifier*] [*FAA*] (FAAL)
GOY .... Gal Oya [*Ceylon*] [*Airport symbol*] (AD)
GOY .... Gorny [*Former USSR*] [*Seismograph station code, US Geological Survey*] [*Closed*] (SEIS)
GOY .... GWE [*Global Weather Experiment*] Operational Year [*Marine science*] (MSC)
GOYA .... Get Off Your After-End [*Slang*] [*Bowdlerized version*]
GOYA .... Greek Organisation of Young Australians
GOYA .... Greek Orthodox Youth of America [*Later, GOYAL*] (EA)
GOYAL .... Greek Orthodox Young Adult League (EA)
GOZ .... Gorna Orjachovica [*Bulgaria*] [*Airport symbol*] (OAG)
GP .... a-Glycerol Phosphate (SAUS)
GP .... Albania [*License plate code assigned to foreign diplomats in the US*]
G-P .... Chemical Agent, Persistent (SAUS)
GP .... Ciba-Geigy AG [*Switzerland*] [*Research code symbol*]
GP .... Du Pont Code for Experimental Substances [*Medicine*] (EDAA)
GP .... Du Pont [*E. I.*] De Nemours & Co., Inc. [*Research code symbol*]
GP .... Gage Pressure (SAUS)
GP .... Galactic Plane [*Astronomy*]
GP .... Galactic Probe
GP .... Gallbladder Patient
GP .... Galley Proof (ADA)
gp .... galley proofs (SAUS)
GP .... Gallup Poll
GP .... Gallup Proof (SAUS)
GP .... Galvanized Pipe [*Technical drawings*]
GP .... Galvanized Plain [*Metal industry*]
GP .... Games Played [*Sports statistics*]
GP .... Gangliocytic Paraganglioma [*Medicine*] (MELL)
GP .... Gang Punch [*Computer science*]
GP .... Gaseous Propellant (SAUS)
GP .... Gas-Permeable (SAUS)
GP .... Gas, Persistent
GP .... Gas-Persistent Chemical Agent Gas (SAUS)
GP .... Gaspesian Park (SAUS)
GP .... Gas-Plasma [*Computer display panel*]
GP .... Gas Plasma General Purpose (SAUS)
GP .... Gas Pressure (MUGU)
GP .... Gas Producer
GP .... Gas Projectile (MCD)
GP .... Gastric Polyp [*Medicine*] (MELL)
GP .... Gastric Pressure [*Physiology*]
GP .... Gastroplasty [*Medicine*]
GP .... Gauge Pressure (IAA)
GP .... Gemini Airlines Ltd. (SAUO)
gp .... Gene Product [*Medicine*] (EDAA)
gp .... Gene Product (QSUL)
GP .... General Flactitioner (SAUS)
GP .... Generalized Programming [*Computer science*]
GP .... General Paralysis [*or Paresis*] [*Medicine*]
GP .... General Paresis (DB)
GP .... General Parsis (SAUS)
GP .... General Pause [*Music*]
GP .... General Physician (MELL)
GP .... General Plant Telephone [*Nuclear energy*] (NRCH)
GP .... General Poll (SAUS)
GP .... General Practice [*Medical specialty*] (DAVI)
GP .... General Practitioner [*of medicine*]
GP .... general practitioner or general practice (SAUS)
GP .... General Preferential Tariff (SAUS)
GP .... General Preferred Tariff [*Canada*]
GP .... General Principles [*FBI standardized term*]
GP .... General Processing (SAUS)
GP .... General Processor
GP .... General Product (BUR)
GP .... General Protection [*Computer science*] (BYTE)
GP .... General Provision
GP .... General Psychiatrist [*Medicine*] (EDAA)
GP .... General Public [*Merchandising slang*]
GP .... General Publication (KSC)
GP .... General Purpose
GP .... General Purpose Computer (ODA)
GP .... General Purpose, Gas Plasma (SAUS)
GP .... General with Parents' Consent [*Motion picture rating*] (BARN)
GP .... Generator Potential (SAUS)
GP .... Genesis Project (EA)
GP .... Genetic Prediabetes [*Endocrinology*]
GP .... Genetic Programming (SAUS)
GP .... Geographical Pole
GP .... Geographical Position
GP .... Geographic Point
gp .... geographic position (SAUS)
GP .... Geography Program (SAUS)
GP .... Geograpical Pole (SAUS)
GP .... Geological Prospecting (SAUS)
gp .... geometrical progression (SAUS)
GP .... Geometric Phase [*Mathematics*]
GP .... Geometric Progression
GP .... Geophysics (SAUS)
GP .... Georgia-Pacific [*NYSE symbol*] (TTSB)
GP .... Georgia-Pacific Corp. [*NYSE symbol*] (SPSG)
G-P .... Georgia-Pacific Plywood Co. (SAUO)
GP .... Georgia Power Company (SAUO)
GP .... Geraminable Propagule (SAUS)
GP .... German Patent (IAA)
GP .... Germinable Propagule [*Botany*]
GP .... Giant Pulse
GP .... Gimbal Package
GP .... Gimbal Platform (AAG)
GP .... Gimbal Point
GP .... Girard-Perregaux
GP .... Girard-Point [*Virus*]
GP .... Girls' PROUT [*Progressive Utilization Theory*] (EA)
GP .... Glia Precursor [*Biochemistry*]
GP .... Glide Path [*Aviation*]
GP .... Glider Pilot (SAUS)
GP .... Gliomatosis Peritonei [*Oncology*]
GP .... Globus Pallidus [*Brain anatomy*]
GP .... Gloria Patri [*Glory to the Father*] [*Latin*]
GP .... Glucose Phosphate [*Biochemistry*]
GP .... Glutamyl-Phenylalanine (SAUS)
GP .... Glutathione Peroxidase [*An enzyme*] (MAE)
GP .... Glycerophosphate [*Biochemistry*]
GP .... Glycogen Phosphorylase [*An enzyme*]
GP .... Glycolyl Phthalate [*Organic chemistry*]
GP .... Glycopeptide (DB)
GP .... Glycophorins (MELL)
gp .... Glycoprotein [*Medicine*] (EDAA)
GP .... Glycoprotein
GP .... Goal Post
GP .... Goal Programming
GP .... Going Public [*Investment term*]
GP .... Golbal Planning (SAUS)
GP .... Gold Point (SAUS)
GP .... Gold Points [*Investment term*]
GP .... Goodpasture [*Syndrome*] [*Medicine*] (DAVI)
GP .... Good Practice
GP .... Gopher-Protection (SAUS)
GP .... Government Property
GP .... Government Publications [*Northern Territory, Australia*]
GP .... Gozo Party [*Malta*] [*Political party*] (PPE)
GP .... Grace Period [*Business term*]
GP .... Graded Program
G-P .... Graduated Payment (SAUS)
GP .... Graduated Pension (WDAA)
GP .... Graduate in Pharmacy [*British*] (ROG)
GP .... Gram-Positive [*Also, GRP*] [*Microbiology*]
GP .... Grandmothers for Peace (EA)
GP .... Grand Passion
GP .... Grand Patron [*Freemasonry*]
GP .... Grand Prelate [*Freemasonry*]
GP .... Grand Prix
GP .... Grand Pursuivant [*Freemasonry*] (ROG)
GP .... Graphic Panel (COE)
GP .... Graphic Point (SAUS)
GP .... Graphic Processor (SAUS)
GP .... Graphic Production (SAUS)
GP .... Graphics Package [*Computer science*] (MHDI)
GP .... Graphics Processor
G/P .... Graphite Polyester
GP .... Graph Plotter (SAUS)
GP .... Grass Pollen [*Immunology*]
GP .... Grateful Patient (SAUS)
GP .... Gratitude Patient [*A nonpaying patient*] [*Medical slang*]
G/P .... Gravida Para [*Gynecology and obstetrics*] (DAVI)
GP .... Gravitational Redshift Space Probe [*Also, GRAVR*]
GP .... Gravity Probe (ACAE)
GP .... Gray Panthers (EA)
GP .... Great Peoples [*A publication*]
GP .... Great Portland Street [*London*] (DSUE)
GP .... Great Primer
GP .... Greenhouse Perennial [*Horticulture*] (ROG)
GP .... Green Party [*Germany*] (BUAC)
GP .... Greenpeace
GP .... Green Petal (SAUS)
G/P .... Green Phone [*NASA*] (KSC)
GP .... Grid Pulse (IAA)
GP .... Gripper (SAUS)
GP .... Gross Premium [*Insurance*] (AIA)
GP .... Gross Profit [*Business term*]
gp .... groundplane (SAUS)
GP .... Ground Plate (SAUS)
GP .... Ground Pneumatic (AAG)
GP .... Ground Post (IAA)
GP .... Ground Protection (SAUS)
GP .... Ground-Protective [*Relay*]
GP .... Ground Rods [*JETDS nomenclature*] [*Military*] (CET)
GP .... Group (AFM)
gp .... Group (VRA)

Gp Group (DB)
GP Groupe de Paris [*France*] (EAIO)
GP Group Printing (SAUO)
GP Group Processor (VLIE)
GP Growth in Total Profit (MHDB)
GP Growth Plate (MELL)
GP Guadalcanal Province (SAUS)
GP Guadeloupe [*ANSI two-letter standard code*] (CNC)
gp Guadeloupe [*MARC country of publication code*] [*Library of Congress*] (LCCP)
GP Guanosine Phosphate (SAUS)
GP Guaranteed Performance (SAUS)
GP Guidance Package
GP Guided Projectile [*Military*] (CAAL)
GP Guinea Pig
GP Gulf Province (SAUS)
GP Gun Pointer [*Naval gunnery*]
GP Gun Position (SAUS)
GP Gun Powder (SAUS)
GP Gun Program [*Military*] (MCD)
GP Gutta-Percha [*Dentistry*] (MAE)
GP Gutter Pair [*Philately*]
GP GWEN [*Ground Wave Emergency Network*] Project (EA)
GP Gypsum Plaster (SAUS)
GP Gyro Package
GP Hadag Air Seebaederflug [*ICAO designator*] (AD)
GP Parental Guidance Suggested [*Later, PG*] [*Movie rating*]
GPA Ciba-Geigy Corp. [*Research code symbol*]
GPA Garden Products Association (BUAC)
GPA Garlic Processors Association (BUAC)
GPA Gas Path Analysis (SAUS)
GPA Gas Pressure Activator (MCD)
GPA Gas Processors Association (EA)
GPA Gate Pulse Amplifier [*Computer science*] (IAA)
GPA Gay Press Association [*Later, GLPA*] (EA)
GPA General Passenger Agent
GPA General Peace Agreement (Mozambique) [*Political party*] (PSAP)
GPA General Procurement Agreements (VLIE)
GPA General Public Accounting (SAUS)
GPA General Public Assistance [*A form of public charity*]
GPA General Purchasing Agency [*Allied German Occupation Forces*]
GPA General-Purpose Amphibian [*Military vehicle*]
GPA General-Purpose Amplifier
GPA General-Purpose Analysis (IEEE)
GPA General-Purpose Array
GPA Geographic Phase-In Area [*Automotive emissions*]
GPA Georgians for Preservation Action [*An association*]
GPA Georgia Port Authority [*Federal Railroad Administration identification code*]
GPA Geschichte der Perser und Araber zur Zeit der Sasaniden [*A publication*] (BJA)
GPA Ghana Ports Authority (SAUS)
GPA GIDEP Problem Advisory (SAUS)
GPa Gigapascal [*SI unit of pressure*]
GPA Global Plan of Action (SAUO)
GPA Global Programme of Action for the Protection of the Marine Environment from Land-based Activities (SAUO)
GPA Global Programme on AIDS (SAUO)
GPA Global Program on AIDS [*Acquired Immune Deficiency Syndrome*] [*WHO*]
GPA Glycerine Producers Association (EA)
GPA Glycophorin A [*Biochemistry*]
GPA Goat Producers Association [*British*] (DBA)
GPA Gold Producers' Association [*Australia*]
GPA Golpazari [*Turkey*] [*Also, GLP*] [*Seismograph station code, US Geological Survey*] (SEIS)
GPA Goodpasture Antigen [*Medicine*] (EDAA)
GPA Governmental and Public Affairs (SAUS)
GPA Government Procurement Agreement (WDAA)
GPA Government Property Administration (MCD)
GPA Grade-Point Average [*Education*]
GPA Graduation Pledge Alliance [*An association*] (EA)
GPA Grandparents Anonymous (EA)
GPA Grandparents Anonymous Control Block (SAUS)
GPA Grapbical PERT Analog (SAUS)
GPA Graphia Philately Association (SAUS)
GPA Graphical PERT [*Program Evaluation and Review Technique*] Analog [*Computer science*] (IEEE)
GPA Graphics Philately Association (EA)
GPA Graphics Preparatory Association (EA)
GPA Green Party of Australia [*Political party*]
GPA Greenpeace Australia
GPA Green Peach Aphid [*Entomology*]
GPA Green Point Average [*Knowledge of the environment*] (WPI)
GPA Grounded Plate Amplifier
GPA Ground Plane Aerial (or Antenna) (SAUS)
GPA Ground Plane Antenna
GPA Group Practice Association [*Medicine*]
GPA Group Provisional Acceptance (SAUO)
GpA Guanylyladenosine (SAUS)
GPA Guidance Platform Assembly [*Military*] (AABC)
GPA Guidance Positioning Assembly
GPA Guide to the Performing Arts (journ.) (SAUS)
GPA Guinea Pig Albumin
GPA Guinness Peat Aviation [*Commercial firm*] [*British*]
GPA Gulfcoast Pulpwood Association (EA)
GPA Kingman Aviation, Inc. [*ICAO designator*] (FAAC)
GPA United States Government Printing Office - Serials, Alexandria, VA [*OCLC symbol*] (OCLC)
GPA WHO Global Programme on AIDS SP (SAUS)
GPA General Practitioners' Association (ODA)
GPAA Gold Prospectors Association of America (EA)
g-p-ab Gravida, Para, and Abortus [*Gynecology and obstetrics*] (DAVI)
GPABP Guinea Pig Anti-Bovine Protection (OA)
GPAC General-Purpose Analog Computer (DEN)
GPAC Grade Point Average Category (SAUS)
GPAC Graphics Package [*Computer science*] (MHDI)
GPAC Great Plains Agricultural Council (EA)
GPAC Great Plains Asbestos Control, Inc. (EFIS)
GPAC Ground Positioning Attitude Control (ACAE)
GPACK General Utility Package (MHDB)
GPAD Gallons per Acre per Day [*Irrigation*]
GPAD Graphics Program for Aircraft Design
GPADS General Purpose Airborne Data System (ACAE)
GPADS Guided Parafoil Aerial Delivery System
GPADS-L Delivery System-Light [*Army*] (INF)
gpae general-purpose aerospace equipment (SAUS)
GPAEVD Greater Philadelphia Alliance for the Eradication of Venereal Disease (SAUO)
GPAFX Guardian Park Ave. Cl.A [*Mutual fund ticker symbol*] (SG)
GPAI Genealogical Periodical Annual Index (GEAB)
GPAIS Guinea Pig Anti-Insulin Serum [*Immunochemistry*] (MAE)
GPAK Graphic Packaging Corp. (SAUO)
GPAL Gold Producers Association Limited (SAUO)
GPAL Gold Producers Association Ltd. (SAUS)
GPA-LBA Global Programme of Action for the Protection of the Marine Environment from Land-based Activities (SAUS)
GPALS Global Protection against Limited Strike [*Military*]
GPAM General-Purpose Armor Machine Gun
GPAM Graduated-Payment Adjustable Mortgage
GPAMS Ground Processing Automated Maintenance System (SAUO)
GP&RP Government Production and Research Property (ACAE)
GPAP General Purpose Associative Processor (PDAA)
GPAP General Purpose Avionic Processor (SAUS)
GPAR Generalized Performance Analysis Reporting (VLIE)
GPAR General Parametrics Corp. [*NASDAQ symbol*] (NQ)
GPARAFN Green Party Anti-Racist and Anti-Fascist Network (BUAC)
GPARM Graduated-Payment Adjustable-Rate Mortgage (WDAA)
GPARN Graduated Payment Adjustable Rate Mortgage (EBF)
GPARS Generic Phased Array Radar Simulator (CCCA)
GPAS General Performance Appraisals System
GPAS General Product Acceptance Standard [*Automotive engineering*]
GPAS General-Purpose Airborne Simulator
GPAT General-Purpose Automatic Test [*Air Force*]
GPAT Georgia Project for Assistive Technology (SAUO)
gpate general-purpose autnmatic test equipment (SAUS)
GPATE General-Purpose Automatic Test Equipment [*Army*] (MSA)
GPATS General-Purpose Automatic Test Set [*Air Force*] (IAA)
GPATS General-Purpose Automatic Test Station
GPATS General-Purpose Automatic Test System [*Air Force*]
GPAVTS Great Planes Area Vocational Technical School [*Oklahoma*]
GPAX General Purpose Automation Executive [*IBM*] (NITA)
GPAX General-Purpose Automation Executive (SAUS)
GPAX Grow Ventures Corp. (SAUS)
GPAY General Payments System
GPB General Purchasing Board
GPB General Purpose Basic [*Programming language*] (NITA)
GPB General Purpose Bomb (SEWL)
GPB General-Purpose Bomb (SAUS)
GPB General-Purpose Buffer
GPB Geon Process Butadiene
GPB Glossopharyngeal Breathing
GPB Glucose Phosphorylase B [*An enzyme*]
GPB Glycoprotein B [*Biochemistry*]
GPB Government Patents Board [*Functions transferred to Secretary of Commerce, 1961*]
GPB Gram-Positive Bacilli (MELL)
GPB Gram-Positive Bacteria (MELL)
GPB Gravity Probe B
GP-B Gravity Probe-B [*Experiment to test Einstein's Theory of General Relativity*]
GPB Greater Pacific Basin (SAUS)
GPB Ground Power Breaker [*Electronics*] (OA)
GPB Ground Power Breeder (SAUS)
GPB Pittsburgh, PA [*Location identifier*] [*FAA*] (FAAL)
GPBA General Produce Brokers Association (BUAC)
GPBEST General Purpose Boundary Element Software Technology (VLIE)
GPBIM General-Purpose Buffer Interface Module [*Computer science*] (MCD)
GPBP Guinea Pig Myelin Basic Protein [*Immunochemistry*]
GPBS Gas Pressure Bending System
G P B T O General Purpose Barbed Tape Obstacle (SAUS)
GPBTO General-Purpose Barbed Tape Obstacle [*Army*] (RDA)
GPBX Georgia-Pacific [*Private rail car owner code*]
GPC Gallons per Capita
gpc game play counselors (SAUS)
GPC Gandhi Peace Center (EA)
GPC Gas-Permeation Chromatography (QSUL)
GPC Gas-Phase Chromatography (SAUS)
GPC Gas-Pressure Cable (SAUS)
GPC Gas-to-Particle Conversion [*Atmospheric science*]

GPC .... Gastric Parietal Cell [*Cytology*] (AAMN)
GPC .... Gastrointestinal Pathology Club [*Later, GPS*] (EA)
GPC .... Gatineau Power Company (SAUO)
GPC .... Gauge Pressure Control
GPC .... Gay People at Columbia [*Later, CGLA*] (EA)
GPC .... Gel Permeation Chromatography
GPC .... Generalized Peripheral Controller (SAUS)
GPC .... General People's Congress [*Yemen*] [*Political party*] (EY)
GPC .... General People's Congress [*or Committee*] [*Libya*] [*Political party*] (PPW)
GPC .... General Periperal Controller (SAUS)
GPC .... General Peripheral (SAUS)
GPC .... General Peripheral Controller
GPC .... General Petroleum Co. [*Egypt*] (BUAC)
GPC .... General Physical Condition [*Medicine*]
GPC .... General Precision Connector (IAA)
GPC .... General Procurement Conditions (SAUS)
GPC .... General Purpose Carrier (SAUS)
GPC .... General-Purpose Carrier [*Military*]
GPC .... General-Purpose Computation (SAUS)
GPC .... General Purpose Computer (SAUS)
GPC .... General-Purpose Computer
GPC .... General Purpose Controller (SAUS)
GPC .... General Purposes Committee [*British*] (DCTA)
GPC .... Genuine Parts [*NYSE symbol*] (TTSB)
GPC .... Genuine Parts Co. [*NYSE symbol*] (SPSG)
GPC .... Geocentric Pendulum Control
GPC .... Georgia-Pacific [*Federal Railroad Administration identification code*]
GPC .... Georgia Peanut Commission (EA)
GPC .... Georgia Power Company (SAUO)
gpc............ Germanium Point-Contact (IDOE)
GPC .... Ghana Publishing Co.
GPC .... Ghana Publishing Company (SAUO)
GPC .... Giant Papillary Conjunctivitis [*Ophthalmology*]
GPC .... Giant Piston Core [*Geology*]
GPC .... Giant Pyramidal Cell (MELL)
GPC .... Glass-Polymer Composite (PDAA)
GPC .... Global and Planetary Change (SAUO)
GPC .... Global Petroleum Centre (SAUO)
GPC .... Global Plotting Chart [*Air Force*]
GPC .... Global Processing Center (EERA)
GPC .... Glycerophosphocholine (SAUS)
GPC .... Glycerylphosphorylcholine [*Biochemistry*]
GPC .... GNU Pascal Compiler (SAUS)
GPC .... Golay Pneumatic Cell
GPC .... Government Publications Center (SAA)
GPC .... Government Purpose Classification
GPC .... Gram-Positive Cocci [*Immunology*] (DAVI)
GPC .... Grande Prairie Regional College Library [*UTLAS symbol*]
GPC .... Granular Progenitor Cell [*Medicine*] (DMAA)
GPC .... Graphical Picture Drawing Language [*Computer science*] (PDAA)
GPC .... Graphic Performance Council (SAUO)
GPC .... Graphics Performance Characterization (AGLO)
GPC .... Grass Pollen Count [*Immunology*]
GPC .... Great Plains Coliseum [*Lawton, OK*]
GPC .... Greek Productivity Centre (BUAC)
GPC .... Greengate Polymer Coatings Ltd. (SAUO)
GPC .... Gross Profit Contribution
GPC .... Ground Power Contactor
GpC .... Group Captain (SAUO)
GpC .... Guanylylcytidine (SAUS)
GPC .... Guanylyl Phosphate Cytidine [*Medicine*] (EDAA)
GPC .... Guinea Pig Club (SAUO)
GPC .... Guinea Pig Complement [*Immunochemistry*]
GPC .... Gulf Park College (SAUO)
GPC .... Gulf Publishing Co.
GPC .... Gypsum-Plaster Ceiling [*Technical drawings*]
GPCA .... General-Purpose Communications Adapter
GPCA .... Golf Products and Components Association [*Defunct*] (EA)
GPCA .... Great Pyrenees Club of America (EA)
GP Cable ..... Gopher-Protected Cable (SAUS)
Gp Capt .... Group Captain [*British military*] (DMA)
GPCB .... General-Purpose Communications Base (MHDB)
GPCB .... GOAL [*Ground Operations Aerospace Language*] Program Control Block (MCD)
GPCC .... General Purpose Communication Channel (SAUS)
GPCC .... Global Precipitation Climatology Center [*Marine science*] (OSRA)
GPCC .... Global Precipitation Climatology Centre (EERA)
GPCC .... Grand Prix Contact Club [*British*] (DBA)
GPCD .... Gallons per Capita per Day
GPCE .... General Practice and Exhibition (SAUO)
GPCE .... Groupement Pharmaceutique de la CE [*Pharmaceutical Group of the EC*] (ECED)
GPC-ERR ..... General Passenger Committee - Eastern Railroads [*Defunct*] (EA)
GPCF .... General-Purpose Computing Facility (MHDB)
G Pch.......... Gang Punch (SAUS)
GPCI .... General Purpose Channel Interface
GPCI .... Geographic Practice Cost Index [*Medicare*]
GPCI .... Graphics Processor Command Interface
GPCK .... Guardian Packaging Corp. (SAUO)
GPCL .... General-Purpose Closed Loop [*Nuclear energy*] (NRCH)
GP CMDR .... Group Commander [*Military*] (WDAA)
GPCO .... Global Perspective Country Outlooks [*Global Perspective, Inc.*] [*Information service or system*] (CRD)
GPCOC .... General-Purpose Central Office Concentrator [*Telecommunications*]
Gp Comdr .... Group Commander (SAUS)
GPCP .... Genealized Process Control Programming (SAUS)
GPCP .... Generalized Process Control Programming [*Computer science*] (IEEE)
GPCP .... General-Purpose Contouring Program
GPC/P .... General Purpose Controller / Processor (SAUS)
GPCP .... General-Purpose Controller Processor (IAA)
GPCP .... Global Precipitation Chemistry Project [*Study of rain properties*]
GPCP .... Global Precipitation Climatology Program (SAUS)
GPCP .... Global Precipitation Climatology Project [*Marine science*] (OSRA)
GPCP .... Great Plains Conservation Program
GPCP-AIP .... Global Precipitation Climatology Project-Algorithm Intercomparison Project (SAUO)
GPCR .... Gas-to-Particle Conversion Rate [*Physics*]
GPCR .... G-Protein-Coupled Receptor [*Biochemistry*]
GPCR .... Great Proletarian Cultural Revolution [*People's Republic of China*]
GPcRE .... Great Pacific Real Estate Investment Trust, Inc. [*Associated Press*] (SAG)
GPCS .... General-Purpose Control System (IAA)
GPCS .... Guinea Pig Control Serum (OA)
GPCSA .... General Practice Computer Suppliers Association (BUAC)
GPCSC .... General Purpose Computer Support Center (SAUO)
GPCT .... George Peabody College for Teachers [*Later, George Peabody College for Teachers of Vanderbilt University*] [*Tennessee*]
GPC/TP .... Glycerophosphorylcholine to Total Phosphate Ratio (STED)
GPCU .... Ground Power Control Unit (SAUS)
GPCX .... Georgia-Pacific [*Private rail car owner code*]
GPCZ .... Governor of Panama Canal Zone (SAUO)
GPD .... Gallium-Phosphor-Diode (SAUS)
gpd .... Gallons per Day (COE)
GPD .... Gallons per Day
GPD .... Generalized Pair Decomposition (SAUS)
GPD .... General Pair Decomposition (IAA)
GPD .... General Passenger Department
GPD .... General Police Duties [*British military*] (DMA)
GPD .... General Political Department [*China*] [*Military*]
GPD .... General Protocol Driver (NITA)
GPD .... General Purpose Data (SAUS)
GPD .... General-Purpose Data
GPD .... General-Purpose Discipline [*IBM Corp.*]
GPD .... general purpose disziplin (SAUS)
GPD .... Generals for Peace and Disarmament [*Ittervoort, Netherlands*] (EAIO)
GPD .... Gimbal Position Display (KSC)
GPD .... Gimbal Position Indicator (SAUS)
GPD .... Glass Plasma Display [*Electronics*] (BARN)
GPD .... Glucose-6-phosphate Dehydrogenase [*Also, G6PD, G6PDH*] [*An enzyme*]
GPD .... Glycerophosphate Dehydrogenase
GPD .... Government Products Division (SAUO)
GPD .... Graduate Performance Diploma (PGP)
GPD .... Grams per Day (SAUS)
GPD .... Grams per Denier
GPD .... Graphics Products Division (SAUO)
GPD .... Greenpond [*New Jersey*] [*Seismograph station code, US Geological Survey*] (SEIS)
GPD .... Guinea Pig Dander (STED)
GPDA .... Grand Prix Drivers' Association
GPDA .... Gypsum Plasterboard Development Association [*British*] (BI)
GPDA .... Gypsum Products Development Association [*British*] (DBA)
GPDC .... Generalized Pressure Drop Correlation [*Chemical engineering*]
GPDC .... General Purpose Device Controller (SAUS)
GPDC .... General-Purpose Digital Computer
GPDF .... Gurage People's Democratic Front [*Ethiopia*]
GPDH .... Glucose-Phosphate Dehydrogenase (SAUS)
GPDH .... Glycerolphosphate Dehydrogenase [*An enzyme*]
GPDL .... Graphical Picture Drawing Language (SAUO)
GPDM .... Geopotential Decameter [*Telecommunications*] (TEL)
GPDM .... Gurage Peoples Democratic Movement (SAUO)
GPDO .... Gedeo Peoples Democratic Organization (SAUS)
GPDO .... General Permitted Development Order (WDAA)
GPDS .... General Purpose Digital Simulator (SAUO)
GPDS .... General-Purpose Discrete Simulator (MHDI)
GPDS .... General-Purpose Display System
GPDSC .... Girl's Public Day School Co. [*British*] (ROG)
GPDST .... Girls' Public Day School Trust [*British*]
GPDU .... Groupe de Planification des Derives Urbaines [*Canada*]
GPDUP .... Gambela Peoples Democratic Unity Party (SAUO)
GPDW .... Glacial Pacific Deep Water
GPDW .... Gypsum Dry Wall [*Technical drawings*]
GPDX .... General American Marks [*Private rail car owner code*]
GPE .... American Forum: Education in a Global Age (SAUO)
GPE .... Gas Phase Etching
GPE .... Gas Power Exchange
GPE .... General Precision Equipment (IAA)
GPE .... General-Purpose English (ADA)
GPE .... General-Purpose Equipment
GPE .... General-Purpose Evaporator [*Nuclear energy*] (NRCH)
GPE .... General Purpose Event (MWOL)
GPE .... Geometric Position Error (MCD)
Gp E .... Geophysical Engineer
GPE .... Georgia Power Capital LP [*NYSE symbol*] (SAG)
GPE .... Georgia Power Capital Trust I [*NYSE symbol*] (SAG)
GPE .... Georgia Power Co. [*NYSE symbol*] (SPSG)
GPE .... Global Perspectives in Education (EA)

GPE Glycerylphosphorylethanolamine [*Biochemistry*] (MAE)
GPE Golden Pheasant [*Vancouver Stock Exchange symbol*]
GPE Good Phonetic Equivalents (SAUS)
GPE Government Preliminary Evaluation (MCD)
GPE GP Express Airlines, Inc. [*ICAO designator*] (FAAC)
GPE Graduate Program in Ecology (SAUO)
GPE Grammaire du Palmyrenien Epigraphique [*A publication*] (BJA)
GPE Granulocyte Colony-Stimulating Factor Promoter Element (DMAA)
GPE Graphic Picture Enhancement
GPE Gravitational Potential Energy [*Geophysics*]
GPE Ground Processing Equipment (ACAE)
GPE Guided Projectile Establishment (BUAC)
GPE Guinea Pig Embryo [*Medicine*] (DMAA)
GPE Los Angeles, CA [*Location identifier*] [*FAA*] (FAAL)
GPED Gas Phase Electron Diffraction (SAUS)
GPEE General Purpose Encryption Equipment (SAUO)
GPEE Georgia Partnership for Excellence in Education (SAUO)
Gp En Geophysical Engineer (SAUS)
GPEN Ground Penetrating (SEWL)
Gp Eng Geophysical Engineer (SAUS)
Gp Engr Geophysical Engineer
GPEOD General Purpose Electro-Optical Director (SAUS)
GPEP Genel Professional Education of the Physician (SAUS)
GPEP General Professional Education of the Physician [*Panel report*] [*Association of American Medical Colleges*]
GPEPr Georgia Pwr $7.72Pfd [*NYSE symbol*] (TTSB)
GPEPrB Georgia Pwr $7.80 Pfd [*NYSE symbol*] (TTSB)
GPEPrP Georgia Pwr $1.90'A'Pfd [*NYSE symbol*] (TTSB)
GPEPrQ Georgia Pwr $1.9875 'A' Pfd [*NYSE symbol*] (TTSB)
GPEPrR Georgia Pwr $1.9375'A'Pfd [*NYSE symbol*] (TTSB)
GPEPrS Georgia Pwr $1.925'A'Pfd [*NYSE symbol*] (TTSB)
GPER Gas Projectile (SAUS)
GPER Gas Projectile, Extended Range (MCD)
GPER General Plant Equipment Requirements
GPERF Ground Passive Electronic Reconnaissance Facility
GPerfArts Guide to the Performing Arts (journ.) (SAUS)
GPES Ground Parachute Extraction System (ACAE)
GPES Ground Proximity Extraction System
G Pet Gospel of Peter [*Apocryphal work*]
GPET Graphic Plan Evaluation Tool (DMAA)
GPETE General-Purpose Electronic Test Equipment (NVT)
GPEXS General Parts Explosion System (IAA)
gpf Gallons per Flush (MIST)
GPF Gallons per Flush [*Plumbing*]
GPF Gandhi Peace Foundation [*India*] (EAIO)
GPF Gas Processing Facility (SAUS)
GPF Gas Production by Field (SAUO)
GPF Gas Proof (AABC)
GPF Gay Professional Female (ADWA)
GPF Generalized Production Function [*Industrial economics*]
GPF General Planning Forecast (SAUS)
GPF General Protection Failure (SAUS)
GPF General Protection Fault [*Computer programming*] (BYTE)
GPF General purpose facility (SAUS)
GPF General-Purpose Forces
GPF General Purpose Frigate (SAUS)
GPF General Purpose Furnace (SAUS)
GPF General-Purpose Furnace Black (SAUS)
GPF General Purpose Rocket (SAUS)
GPF Generic Packaging Facility (SAUS)
GPF Geospatial Prototype Facility (SAUS)
GPF Gibraltar Police Force (SAUO)
GPF Glomerular Plasma Flow [*Medicine*] (DMAA)
GPF Grain per Foot (SAUS)
GPF Grains per Foot
GPF Gram Parsons Foundation (EA)
GPF Grande Puissance Filloux [*World War II*]
GPF Granulocytosis-Promoting Factor [*Hematology*]
GPF Greater Palatine Foramen (MELL)
GPF Groove between Parallel Folds
GPF Ground Processing Facility (SAUS)
GPF Group Patching Frame (SAUO)
GPF Grout Processing Facility (SAUS)
GPF Guardian Pacific Rim Corp. [*Toronto Stock Exchange symbol*]
GPF Guinea Pig Fibrinogen
GPF GUI [*Graphical User Interface*] Programming Facility [*Computer science*]
Gpf GUI Programming Facility (HODG)
Gp Fl Group Flashing Light [*Nautical term*] (NTA)
GPF black General Purpose Furnace Black (EDCT)
GPFC Galaxy Patrol Fan Club (EA)
GPFC Gene Pitney Fan Club (EA)
GPFC General Practice Finance Corp. (BUAC)
GPFC General-Purpose Function Code (NVT)
GPFCS General Purpose Fire Control System (SAUS)
GP/F-HVP Guided Penetration/Fragmentation Hypervelocity Projectile (SAUS)
GPFI Grand Premier Financial, Inc. [*NASDAQ symbol*] (SAG)
GPFL Group Flashing [*Navigation signal lights*]
GPFLL Group Flashing Light [*Navigation*] (IAA)
GPFS General-Purpose Financial Statement (WDAA)
GPFS Greater Pacific Financial Services [*Australia*]
GPFU Gas Particulate Filter Unit (MCD)
GPG Gasification Power Generation (SAUO)
GPG Gas Plasma Gun (SAUS)
GPG Gate Pulse Generator (IAA)
GPG Generalized Projective Geometries (SAUS)
GPG General Physics Corp. (SAUS)
GPG General Planning Group
GPG GNU Privacy Guard (SAUS)
GPG Grains per Gallon [*Unit of measure for water hardness*]
GPG Grams per Gallon (GNE)
GPG Grande Portage [*Vancouver Stock Exchange symbol*]
GPG Graphic Product Generation (SAUO)
GPG Ground Power Generator (DWSG)
GPG Growth-Promoting Genes [*Medicine*] (DB)
GpG Guanylylguanosine (SAUS)
GPg Guinea Pig [*Medicine*] (EDAA)
GPG Guinness Peat Group [*British*]
GPGA Georgia Pecan Growers Association (SRA)
GPGA Georgia Propane Gas Association (SRA)
GPGAP Great Plains Gasification Associates Project (SAUS)
GP (Gas) Persistent Chemical Agent Gas
GPGE General Purpose Ground Equipment (SAUS)
GPGEA General Purpose Ground Equipment Avionics (SAUS)
GPGG Guinea Pig Gamma Globulin [*Immunochemistry*]
GPGL General-Purpose Graphic Language [*Computer science*] (IEEE)
GPGM General Purpose Ground Mines (SAUS)
GPGM Genung Pongkor Gold Mine (SAUO)
GPGS General Purpose Graphics System (SAUO)
GPGS Government Purchases of Goods and Services [*BTS*] (TAG)
GPGS Ground Power Generator System (DWSG)
GPGSN Great Plains Genetic Services Network (SAUO)
GPGZ Great Plains Gas [*Federal Railroad Administration identification code*]
gph Gallons per Hour (ADWA)
GPH Gallons per Hour
GPH Game Packing House (SAUO)
GPH General Physics Corp. [*NYSE symbol*] (SPSG)
GPH Genl Physics [*NYSE symbol*] (TTSB)
GPH Geological Publishing House (SAUS)
GPH Geophysics (SAUS)
G Ph Graduate in Pharmacy
GPH Grams per Hour (SAUS)
GPH Grand Pacific Hotel (SAUO)
GPH Graphite (MSA)
GPH Great Plains Historical Association (SAUO)
GPH Green Party of Hungary [*Political party*] (EAIO)
GPH Grenzpolizeihelfer [*Border Police Aide*] [*German*]
GPHA Georgia Public Health Association (SAUO)
GPHA Great Plains Historical Association [*Later, IGP*] (EA)
GpHd Group Head (SAUO)
GPHF General Pulaski Heritage Foundation (EA)
GPHF German Pharma Health Fund e.V. (SAUO)
GPHI Guild of Public Health Inspectors (SAUO)
GPHLV Guinea Pig Herpes-Like Virus [*Medicine*] (DMAA)
GPHMG General-Purpose Heavy Machine Gun (MCD)
GPHMO Group Practice Health Maintenance Organization [*Insurance*] (WYGK)
GPHN Giant Pigmented Hairy Nevus (DMAA)
GPHP Geomagnetism and Paleomagnetism Home Page (SAUO)
GPHP Give Peace Holiday Project (EA)
Gp HQ Group Headquarters (SAUO)
GPHS General-Purpose Heat Source [*Nuclear energy*]
GPHSC Group Project for Holocaust Survivors and Their Children (EA)
GPHTAR Geophytology (journ.) (SAUS)
GPHV Guinea Pig Herpes Virus (DMAA)
GPHW Gay Public Health Workers Caucus [*Later, LGCPHW*] (EA)
GPHY General Physics Corp. (SAUO)
GPI General Frinting Ink (SAUS)
GPI Generalized Packaging Interface (SAUS)
GPI Generalized Packing Interface (SAUS)
GPI General Paralysis of the Insane [*Literal translation, but also medical slang for eccentricity*]
GPI General Paralysis/Paresis of Insane [*Medicine*] (STED)
GPI General Patents Index [*A publication*]
GPI General Periodicals Index [*Information Access Co.*] [*Information service or system*] (CRD)
GPI General Precision, Inc.
GPI General Precision, Incorporated (SAUO)
GPI General Price Index (WDAA)
GPI General Printing Ink (DGA)
GPI General Process Interface (SAUS)
GPI General Purpose Inverter (SAUS)
GPI General-Purpose Inverter (KSC)
GPI Genetics and Public Issues Program (SAUS)
GPI Gibson Production International (SAUO)
GPI Gimbal Position Indicator (KSC)
GPI Gingival-Periodontal Index [*Dentistry*]
GPI Glass Packaging Institute (EA)
GPI Glide Path Indicator [*Aviation*] (NATG)
GPI Global Precipitation Index (SAUS)
GPI Global Progress Index
GPI Glucophosphate Isomerase [*An enzyme*]
GPI Glycerophosphoinositol (SAUS)
GPI Glycoprotein I (DMAA)
GPI Glycosyl-Phosphatidylinositol [*Biochemistry*]
GPI GOES [*Geostationary Operational Environmental Satellite*] Precipitation Index [*Marine science*] (OSRA)
GPI Gordon Personal Inventory [*Psychology*]
GPI Government Preliminary Inspection (MCD)
GPI Government Property Inventory (SAUS)

GPI.............. Grain Products Irradiator [*Nuclear energy*]
GPI.............. Grandmothers for Peace International [*An association*] (EA)
GPI.............. Graphics Programming Interface [*IBM Corp.*] (PCM)
GPI.............. Great Pacific Industries, Inc. [*Toronto Stock Exchange symbol*] [*Vancouver Stock Exchange symbol*]
GPI.............. Greenpeace International [*Netherlands*] (EAIO)
GPI.............. Grocery Prices Index [*British*]
GPI.............. Ground Point of Impact
GPI.............. Ground Point of Intercept (AFM)
GPI.............. Ground Point of Interception (PIPO)
GPI.............. Ground Position Indicator [*Dead-reckoning computer*]
GPI.............. Group 1 Automotive [*NYSE symbol*] (SG)
GPI.............. Growth Plate Injury (MELL)
GPI.............. Guapi [*Colombia*] [*Airport symbol*] (OAG)
GPI.............. Guardsman Products, Inc. [*NYSE symbol*] (SPSG)
GPI.............. Guinea Pig Ileum (DMAA)
GPI.............. Guinea Pig Ilium (SAUS)
GPIA........... General-Purpose Interface Adapter (IEEE)
GPIA........... General Purpose Interface Adaptor (NITA)
GPIA........... General Purpose Interface Assembly (SAUS)
GPIA........... Generic Pharmaceutical Industry Association (NTPA)
GPIB........... General-Purpose Analysis (SAUS)
GPIB........... General-Purpose Array (SAUS)
GPIB........... General Purpose Information/Interface Bus (SAUS)
GPIB........... General-Purpose Instrumentation Bus (SAUS)
GPIB........... General-Purpose Instrument Bus (IAA)
GPIB........... General Purpose Interface Board (SAUS)
GPIB........... Glycerophosphoric Acid (SAUS)
Gplb........... Glycoprotein Ib [*Medicine*] (EDAA)
GPIBA......... General Purpose Interface Bus Adapter [*Computer science*] (VLIE)
GPIBA......... General Purpose Interface Bus Array (SAUS)
GPIB/IEEE.... General-Purpose Interface Bus/Insitute of Electrical and Electronics Engineers (SAUS)
GPIB/IEEE.... General-Purpose Interface Bus/Institute of Electrical and Electonics Engineers (SAUS)
GPIC........... General-Purpose Intelligent Cable (MHDB)
GPIC........... General-Purpose Intercomputer [*Test*] (NVT)
GPIC........... Gulf Petrochemical Industries Co. [*Bahrain*] (BUAC)
GPID........... Guidance Package Installation Dolly [*Polaris missile*]
GPID........... Project on Goals, Processes and Indicators of Development (SAUO)
GPIEM......... International Marine Environment Award [*Marine science*] (OSRA)
GPIF........... General Purpose Interface [*Computer science*] (VLIE)
GPIFC......... Gene Pitney International Fan Club (EA)
GPII........... Geist Picture Interest Inventory [*Psychology*] (AEBS)
GPIMH......... Guinea Pig Intestinal Mucosal Homogenate (MAE)
GPIN........... Group Practice Improvement Network (ADWA)
Gp Int Qk Fl Lt... Group Interrupted Quick Flashing Light (SAUS)
GPIO........... General-Purpose Input/Output [*Computer science*]
GPIOP......... General Purpose Input Output Processor (SAUS)
GPIP........... General Plan and Implementation Programme (SAUS)
GPIP........... General Purpose Image Processor (SAUS)
GPIP........... Glide Path Intercept Point [*Aviation*]
GPIPID........ Guinea Pig Intraperitoneal Infectious Dose [*Clinical chemistry*] (MAE)
GPIR........... Ground Penetrating Imaging RADAR (SEWL)
GPIRS......... Global Positioning/Inertial Reference System (HLLA)
GPIS........... Gemini Problem Investigation Status [*NASA*] (IEEE)
GPIs........... General Purpose Interfaces (SAUO)
GPIS........... Giant Pulse Laser System (SAUS)
GPIS........... Groundwater Pumping Incentives Scheme [*Victoria*] (EERA)
GPISW......... General Purpose Infantry Support Weapon (SAUO)
GPIX........... Globus Growth Group, Inc. (SAUO)
GPIX........... Sunbelt Cement [*Private rail car owner code*]
GPIY........... Gross Profit this Year (SAUS)
GPJ............. Great Peace Journey [*Sweden*] (EAIO)
GP J Am Acad Gen Pract... GP. Journal of the American Academy of General Practice (journ.) (SAUS)
GPK........... Gentleman's Pocket Knife
GPK........... Goldpac Investments Ltd. [*Vancouver Stock Exchange symbol*]
GPK........... Guinea Pig Kidney Absorption (SAUS)
GPK........... Guinea Pig Kidney Antigen [*Immunochemistry*] (MAE)
GPKA......... Guinea Pig Kidney Absorption (Test) [*Clinical chemistry*]
GpKCD........ General-Purpose Keyboard and Display Control (SAUS)
GPKD......... General-Purpose Keyboard and Display Control [*Computer science*] (MDG)
GPKT......... Grand Priory of the Knights of the Temple [*Freemasonry*]
GPL............ Gallahad Petroleum [*Vancouver Stock Exchange symbol*]
GPL............ Gap Length (VLIE)
GPL............ Gastrophrenic Ligament (MELL)
GPL............ Gathering point low (SAUS)
GPL............ Gemini Programming Language (SAUO)
GPL............ Generalize (SAUS)
GPL............ Generalized Parameter List (VLIE)
GPL............ Generalized Programming Language [*Computer science*]
GPL............ General Precision Laboratory
GPL............ General Price Level (ADA)
GPL............ General Products Laboratory (SAUS)
GPL............ General Public License (NHD)
GPL............ General-Purpose Language [*Computer science*] (CSR)
GPL............ General Purpose Loader (NITA)
GPL............ General-Purpose Loop [*Nuclear energy*] (NRCH)
GPL............ General Purpose Programming Language (SAUS)
GPL............ Geographic Position Locator [*Navigation*]
GPL............ Giant Pulse LASER
GPL............ Gimbal Pickoff Loop
GPL............ Glide Path Landing (SAUS)
GPL............ GNU General Public License (SAUS)
GPL............ GNU Public License (SAUS)
GPL............ GOAL [*Ground Operations Aerospace Language*] Processing Language (MCD)
gpl............. Grams per Liter (SAUS)
GPL............ Graphical Programming Language (SAUS)
GPL............ Graphic Programming Language (SAUS)
GPL............ Graphics Programming Language [*Computer science*] (VLIE)
GPL............ Gravatom Projects Ltd. [*British*] (IRUK)
GPL............ Group Processing Logic (TEL)
GPL............ Guapiles [*Costa Rica*] [*Airport symbol*] (OAG)
GPL............ Guymon Public Library, Guymon, OK [*OCLC symbol*] (OCLC)
GPL............ Gypsum Lathe [*Technical drawings*]
GPL/1......... Graph Programming Language One (SAUS)
GPLA.......... General Price Level Accounting (ADA)
GPLA.......... General Price-Level Adjusted [*Finance*] (PDAA)
GPLA.......... General Purpose Line Adapter (SAUO)
GPLAD........ German Plastics (journ.) (SAUS)
GPLAN........ Generalized Database Planning System
GPLAN........ Generalized Plan (VLIE)
GPLAN........ Generalized Planning (SAUS)
GPLB.......... Grand Prix Association of Long Beach [*NASDAQ symbol*] (SAG)
GPLC.......... Guild of Professional Launderers and Cleaners [*British*] (BI)
GPLD.......... Government Property Lost or Damaged [*or Destroyed*]
GpLdr......... Group Leader (SAUO)
GPLE.......... Global Program Line Editor [*Beagle Bros.*]
GPLE.......... Global Programme Editor (SAUS)
GPLF.......... Gurage Peoples Liberation Front (SAUS)
GPLI........... General Purpose LAN Interface (SAUS)
GPL/I.......... Graphical Programming Language One (SAUS)
GPLI........... Group-Page-Line-Inserts (MCD)
GPLM.......... Gambela Peoples Liberation Movement (SAUO)
GPLP.......... General-Purpose Linear Programming [*Computer science*] (IEEE)
GPLR.......... Government-Purpose License Rights (AAGC)
GPLRG........ Gay Parents Legal and Research Group [*Defunct*] (EA)
GPLRG........ Gay Parents Research Group (SAUS)
GPLS.......... General Purpose Logic Simmulator (SAUS)
G P L S....... General Purpose Logic Simulator (SAUS)
GPLS.......... Giant Pulse LASER System
GPLS.......... Glide Path Landing System [*Aviation*] (IAA)
GPLS Scheme... Globally; Parallel; Locally Sequential Scheme (SAUS)
GPLUS........ Goal Programming for Land Use Planning System (SAUO)
GPLY.......... Gingivoplasty [*Dentistry*]
GPLZ.......... Good Pasture Lead [*Federal Railroad Administration identification code*]
GPM........... Gallons per Mile
gpm............ Gallons per Minute (ADWA)
GPM........... Gallons per Minute
Gpm............ Gallons per Minute
GPM........... Gas-Permeable Membrane
GPM........... Gas Plasma Monitor
GPM........... Gay Professional Male (ADWA)
GPM........... Generalized Perturbation Method (SAUS)
GPM........... Generalized Phrase Marker (SAUS)
GPM........... General Preventive Medicine
GPM........... General Purpose Macrogenerator (SAUS)
GPM........... General-Purpose Macrogenerator [*Computer science*] (IEEE)
GPM........... General-Purpose Maneuver
GPM........... General-Purpose Missile
GPM........... General Purpose Module (SAUS)
GPM........... General-Purpose Module (MHDB)
GPM........... Geometric Product Modelling (VLIE)
GPM........... Geopotential Meter
GPM........... Georgia Southern College, Statesboro (SAUS)
GPM........... Georgia Southern College, Statesboro, GA [*OCLC symbol*] (OCLC)
GPM........... Gepanzerte Pioniermaschine [*Armored Engineer Vehicle*] [*General Electric Co.*] [*German*] (MCD)
GPM........... Gestalt Photomapper (SAUS)
GPM........... Getty Petroleum Mktg. [*NYSE symbol*] (SG)
GPM........... Giant Pigmented Melanosome [*Medicine*] (DMAA)
GPM........... Goettinger Predigt-Meditationen [*A publication*] (BJA)
GPM........... Government Payment Bond (EBF)
GPM........... Gradient Pump Module
GPM........... Graduated Payment Mortgage [*Sometimes referred to as "Jeep"*]
GPM........... Grams per Mile
GPM........... Grams per Minute (SAUS)
GPM........... Grand Past Master [*Freemasonry*]
GPM........... Grand Prairie, TX [*Location identifier*] [*FAA*] (FAAL)
GPM........... Graphics Postprocessor Module [*McDonnell-Douglas Corp.*]
GPM........... Gravity Permanent Mold [*Casting*]
GPM........... Greater Pectoral Muscle (MELL)
GPM........... Grey Power Movement [*Australia*]
GPM........... Gross Processing Margin (MHDB)
GPM........... Gross Product Margin (SAUS)
GPM........... Gross Profit Margin (WDAA)
GPM........... Ground Potential Model [*Physics*]
GPM........... Ground Propulsion Mobility (SEWL)
GPM........... Groups per Message (SAUS)
GPM........... Groups [*of code transmitted*] per Minute [*or Message*] [*Telecommunications*]
GPM........... Gunnery Prize Money [*British military*] (DMA)
GPMA......... Gasoline Pump Manufacturers Association (EA)
GPMA......... Grocery Products Manufacturers Association [*Canada*] (BUAC)
GPMAL....... Gravida, Para, Multiple Births, Abortions, Live Births [*Obstetrics*]
GPMAS....... Gas-Phase Molecular Absorption Spectroscopy (SAUS)

GPMC .... Geoprocessing Map Call (SAUS)
GPMC .... Global Patient Movement Center (SAUO)
GPMC .... Green Paper on Mobile Communications (SAUS)
GPMC .... Grocery Products Manufacturers of Canada [*See also FCPA*]
GPMC .... Group and Pension Marketing Conference [*LIMRA*]
GPMCD .... Geoprocessing Map Call Deamon program (SAUS)
GPME .... Gas-Porous Membrane Electrode [*Electrochemistry*]
GPME .... General-Purpose Mission Equipment (NASA)
GPMF .... Gram Parsons Memorial Foundation (EA)
GPMFGND ... Great Peace March for Global Nuclear Disarmament [*Defunct*] (EA)
G P M G ...... General Purpose Machine Gun (SAUS)
GPMG .... General-Purpose Machine Gun [*Military*]
GPMGAD ...... Geophysical Mongraph (journ.) (SAUS)
GPMG(SF) ... General Purpose Machine Gun (Sustained Fire) (SAUS)
GPMG(T) ..... General-Purpose Machine Gun (Turret) (SAUS)
GPMH .... Good Practices in Mental Health (PDAA)
GPMMA .... Grain Processing Machinery Manufacturers Association (EA)
GPMP .... General Purpose Multiprocessing (SAUS)
GPMP .... Groundwater Protection Management Program (SAUS)
GPMP .... Group on Parts (SAUO)
GPMR .... Gallons Per Mile Ratio [*DOE*] (TAG)
GPMR .... Government PMR (SAUO)
GPMRC .... Global Patient Movement Requirements Center (SAUO)
GPM Routine... General Past Mortem Routine (SAUS)
GPMS .... Galileo Probe Mass Spectrometer
GPMS .... General Purpose Microprogram Simulator (SAUS)
GPMS .... General-Purpose Microprogram Simulator [*Computer science*] (IEEE)
GPMS .... General Purpose Microspogram Simulator (SAUS)
GPMS .... General Purpose Multiplex System (SAUS)
GPMS .... General-Purpose Multiplex System [*Aviation*]
GPMS .... Gross Performance Measuring System [*Air Force*]
GPMSP .... Good Postmarketing Surveillance Practice (DB)
Gpmt CP ...... Groupment Command Post (SAUO)
Gpmt OP ...... Groupment Observation Post (SAUO)
GPMU .... Graphical, Paper and Media Union [*British*]
GPMU .... Graphical, Print & Media Union (WDAA)
GPMX .... Gas Properties Management [*Private rail car owner code*]
GPN .... Garden Point [*Australia*] [*Airport symbol*] (OAG)
GPN .... General Performance Number
GPN .... Georgia Psychoeducational Network (SAUO)
GPN .... Glass Plate Negative
GPN .... Gold-Pan Resources, Inc. [*Vancouver Stock Exchange symbol*]
GPN .... Government Packet Network [*Canada*]
GPN .... Graduated Payment Mortgage (EBF)
GPN .... Graduate Practical Nurse
GPN .... Great Pacific Navigation Co. Ltd. (SAUO)
GPN .... Great Plains National Instructional Television Library (SAUS)
GPN .... Grey Power News [*Australia*] [*A publication*]
GPN .... Groupe des Plans Nucleaires (SAUS)
GPNA .... Glutamyl-P-Nitroanilide (SAUS)
GPNCO .... Great Pacifc Navigation Co. Ltd. (SAUO)
GPNDS .... Global Positioning and Nuclear Detection System (ACAE)
GPNITL .... Great Plains National Instructional Television Library
GPNNC .... General Purpose Non-Numerical Computer (ELAL)
GPNNC .... General Purpose Numeric Computer (SAUS)
GPNVG .... General Purpose Night Vision Goggles (SAUS)
GPO .... Gemini Program [*or Project*] Office [*NASA*] (KSC)
GPO .... Gemini Project Office (SAUS)
GPO .... General Periodicals Ondisc [*Database*]
GPO .... General Pico [*Argentina*] [*Airport symbol*] (OAG)
GPO .... General Post Office [*British*] [*Defunct*]
GPO .... General Practitioner Obstetrician
GPO .... General-Purpose Oscilloscope
GPO .... General-Purpose Outlet (ADA)
GPO .... General-Purpose Output [*Space Flight Operations Facility, NASA*]
GPO .... Genprobe Tech [*Vancouver Stock Exchange symbol*]
GPO .... Georgia Pacific-Oregon [*Federal Railroad Administration identification code*]
GPO .... GIANT Group [*NYSE symbol*] (TTSB)
GPO .... Giant Group Ltd. [*NYSE symbol*] (SPSG)
GPO .... Giant Portland Cement Co. (SAUO)
GPO .... Glycerin-1-Phosphate-Oxydase (SAUS)
GPO .... GOOS Programme Office (SAUS)
GPO .... GOOS Project Office (SAUO)
GPO .... Government Printing Office [*Environment term*] (EGA)
GPO .... Granulopoietin [*Hypothetical substance*] [*Hematology*]
GPO .... Great Plains Organization (SAUS)
GPO .... Gross Product Originating [*Department of Transportation*]
GPO .... Group Purchasing Organization [*Health insurance*]
GPO .... Guaranteed Purchase Option [*Insurance*]
GPO .... Guidance-Pilotage Orbital (SAUS)
GPO .... Gunner's Primary Optics (MCD)
GPO .... Gun Position Officer (NATG)
GPO .... Library of Congress, Government Printing Office [*Source file*] [*UTLAS symbol*]
GPO .... Portland, OR [*Location identifier*] [*FAA*] (FAAL)
GPO .... United States Government Printing Office, Alexandria, VA [*OCLC symbol*] (OCLC)
GPO .... US Government Printing Office (SAUS)
GPOA .... Guild of Prescription Opticians of America [*Later, OAA*] (EA)
GPOA .... Gun Position Officer's Assistant [*British military*] (DMA)
GPOB .... Government Printing Office Bookstore (OICC)
GPOCC .... Group Occulting (SAUO)
GPOCC .... Group Occulting Lights [*Navigation signal*]
Gp Occ Lt .... Group Occulting Light (SAUO)
Gp Occu ...... Group Occulting (SAUO)
Gp Offr .... Group Officer [*British military*] (DMA)
GPOI .... General Public Organization for Industrialization [*Libya*] (BUAC)
Gpolmsa ...... Groupo Imsa Sa de CV [*Associated Press*] (SAG)
GPO-PIA ...... Government Printing Office and Printing Industry of America (SAUO)
GpoRadio .... Grupo Radio Centro [*Associated Press*] (SAG)
GPOS .... General-Purpose Operating System
GPOS .... Government Printing Office Style Manual (SAUO)
gpp .... galley page proofs (SAUS)
GPP .... Gambia Peoples Party (SAUO)
GPP .... Generalized Post-Processor
GPP .... General Plant Project
GPP .... General Print and Punch (NITA)
GPP .... General Purchasing Power [*Accounting*]
GPP .... General purpose plant (SAUS)
GPP .... General Purpose Processor (MHDI)
GPP .... General-Purpose Programming [*Computer science*]
GPP .... Generative Production Process (VLIE)
GPP .... Generic Packetized Protocol (SAUS)
GPP .... Geophysical Prospecting (SAUS)
GPP .... Giant Pacific Petroleums, Inc. [*Vancouver Stock Exchange symbol*]
GPP .... Gimbal Position Potentiometer (SAUS)
GPP .... Glycosylated Plasma Protein [*Clinical chemistry*]
GPP .... Goal Programming Problem
GPP .... Gordon Personal Profile [*Psychology*]
GPP .... Grand Prix Points
GPP .... Graphic Part Programmer (PDAA)
GPP .... Greater Northern Paper Co. (SAUO)
GPP .... Gross Primary Production (SAUO)
GPP .... Gross Primary Productivity
GPP .... Gross Provincial Product (SAUS)
GPP .... Ground Power Panel
GPP .... Guarapuava [*Brazil*] [*Airport symbol*] (AD)
GPP .... Guild of Pastoral Psychology [*British*] (DBA)
GPP .... Guild of Public Pharmacists [*British*] (BI)
GPP .... Gyro Pitch Position
GPPA .... Gaelic Pre-School Playgroups Association (BUAC)
GPPA .... Georgia Peanut Producers Association (SRA)
GPPA .... Georgia Pork Producers Association (SRA)
GPPA .... Georgia Psychiatric Physicians Association (SRA)
GPPA .... Government Patent Policy Act [*1981*]
GPPA .... Grenada Planned Parenthood Association (BUAC)
GPPAW .... Glass (SAUS)
GPPAW .... Glass, Pottery, Plastics, and Allied Workers International Union (EA)
GPPB .... Gemini Program Planning Board [*NASA*] (KSC)
GPPB .... Government Procurement Practices Board [*Proposed*]
GPPC .... General Purpose Portable Communicator (EURO)
GPPC .... General Purpose Power Controller (SAUS)
GPPDI .... Global Primary Production Data Initiative (SAUS)
GPPDI .... Global Primary Productivity Data Initiative (SAUO)
GPPEDP ...... Genetics, Principles and Perpectives (journ.) (SAUS)
GPPEDP ...... Genetics, Principles and Perspectives (SAUS)
GPPF .... Gravitational Plant Physiology Facility (SAUS)
GPP-I .... Gordon Personal Profile and Inventory [*Personality development test*] [*Psychology*]
GPPIPCEE .... Groupement Professionel des Pharmaciens de l'Industrie Pharmaceutique de la CEE [*Professional Grouping of Pharmacists of the Pharmaceuticals Industry of the EEC*] (ECED)
GPPL .... Gypsum Plaster [*Technical drawings*]
GPPM .... Graphics Pages per Minute (ADWA)
gppm .... Graphics Pages per Minute [*Printer technology*] (PCM)
GPPQ .... General-Purpose Psychiatric Questionnaire
GPPS .... General Provisions Policy Statement (MCD)
GPPS .... General Purpose Polystyrene (SAUS)
GPPT .... Gel Precipitate (SAUS)
GPPT .... Group Personality Projective Test [*Psychology*]
GPPU .... Graphic Polygon Processing Utilities (SAUS)
GPPV .... Graff Pay per View [*NASDAQ symbol*] (SAG)
GPPX .... Georgia-Pacific [*Private rail car owner code*]
GPPX .... Giant Pacific Petroleum, Inc. (SAUO)
GPPXF .... Giant Bay Resources Ltd. [*NASDAQ symbol*] (COMM)
GPQ .... Carrollton, GA [*Location identifier*] [*FAA*] (FAAL)
GPQ .... Great Plains Quarterly (journ.) (SAUS)
GPQA .... Government Procurement Quality Assurance (SAUO)
GPR .... Gas Production Rate (SAUS)
GPR .... General Purpose Processor (SAUS)
GPR .... General Purpose Radar (SAUS)
GPR .... General-Purpose RADAR (MCD)
GPR .... General-Purpose Radiometer
GPR .... General-Purpose Receiver
GPR .... General Purpose Register (SAUO)
GPR .... General-Purpose Register [*Computer science*] (MDG)
GPR .... General-Purpose Relay
GPR .... General-Purpose Representative
GPR .... General Purpose Rubber (SAUS)
GPR .... Genio Populi Romani [*To the Genius of the Roman People*] [*Latin*]
GPR .... Glider Pilot Regiment [*Military unit*] [*British*]
GPR .... Golden Pyramid Resources, Inc. [*Vancouver Stock Exchange symbol*]
GPR .... Good Partial Remission [*Medicine*]
GPR .... Government Plant Representative
GPR .... Government Property Register [*of New South Wales*] [*State*] (EERA)
GPR .... Government Purpose Rights (AAGC)
GPR .... Grade Point Ratio (DHP)
GPR .... Grain-Burning Pattern Regulation (MCD)

GPR .... Gran Premio Romeo [*Alfa Romeo race car*] [*Italian*]
GPR .... Graphic Problem Representation (SAUS)
GPR .... Great Pacific Real Estate Investment Trust, Inc. [*AMEX symbol*] (SAG)
GPR .... Great Plains Railroad [*Federal Railroad Administration identification code*]
GPR .... Ground-Penetrating RADAR
GPR .... Ground-Probing Radar (SAUS)
GPR .... Group Practice (ACAE)
GPRA .... General Practice Reform Association [*Medicine*] (DAVI)
GPRA .... Gouvernement Provisoire de la Republique Algerienne [*Provisional Government of the Algerian Republic*]
GPRA .... Government Performance and Results Act [*1993*] (RDA)
GPRA .... Government Performance Review Act (SAUO)
GPRA .... Government Public Relations Association [*Defunct*]
GPRB .... Government of the Peoples Republic of Benin (SAUS)
GPRBC .... Guinea-Pig Red Blood Cell (DB)
GPRC .... Geophysical and Polar Research Center [*University of Wisconsin*]
GPRC .... Glass Passivated Rectifier Chip (SAUS)
GPrcl .... General Parcel Service, Inc. [*Associated Press*] (SAG)
GPRD .... Government Procurement Relation Department (SAUO)
GPRDM .... Gedeo Peoples Revolutionary Democratic Movement (SAUO)
GPRE .... Government Program Review and Evaluation
GP Relay ..... Ground-Protective Relay (SAUS)
GPRF .... General-Purpose Rocket Furnace (SAUS)
GPRF-G .... General-Purpose Rocket Furnace - Gradient
GPRF-I .... General-Purpose Rocket Furnace - Isothermal
GPRG .... Gadsden Purchase Refund Group [*Formerly, PRI*] [*Defunct*] (EA)
GPRG .... General Practice Research Group [*Medicine*] (EDAA)
GPRIP .... General Practice Rural Incentives Program (SAUS)
GPRL .... Giant Pulse Ruby LASER (IAA)
GPRL .... Gulf Puerto Rico Lines [*Steamship*] (MHDB)
GPRMC .... General purpose remote machining center (SAUS)
GPRMC .... Groupement des Plastiques Renforces et Materiaux Composites [*Organization of Reinforced Plastics and Composite Materials*] (EAIO)
GPRN .... GOAL [*Ground Operations Aerospace Language*] Test Procedure Release Notice [*NASA*] (NASA)
GPRO .... Gen-Probe (SAUS)
GPRO .... Gen-Probe, Inc. (SAUS)
GPRO .... Gen-Probe Industries, Inc. (SAUO)
GPRP .... Government Production and Research Property (SSD)
GPRR .... General-Purpose Radio Receiver
GPRS .... General Packet Radio Service
GPRS .... General Packet Radio System
GPRS .... General Parent Ring System [*Proposed chemical classification*]
GPRS .... General Plumbing & Roofing Services [*Commercial firm*] [*British*]
GPRS .... General Purpose Radar Simulator (ACAE)
GPRs .... General Purpose Registers (SAUS)
GPRS .... Global Personnel Recovery System [*Military*]
G P R S S ... General Purpose Remote Sensor System (SAUS)
GPRSS .... General-Purpose Remote Sensor System (PDAA)
GPRT .... General-Purpose Radio Transmitter
GPRT .... Guanine Phosphoribosyltransferase [*An enzyme*]
gps .... gage pressure switch (SAUS)
GPS .... Galapagos Islands [*Ecuador*] [*Airport symbol*] (OAG)
gps .... Gallons per Second (ADWA)
GPS .... Gallons per Second
GPS .... Gap (SAUS)
GPS .... Gap, Inc. [*Formerly, Gap Stores, Inc.*] [*NYSE symbol*] (SPSG)
GPS .... Gas-Presssure Sintering (SAUS)
GPS .... Gas-Pressure Sintering System (SAUS)
GPS .... Gastrointestinal Pathology Society (EA)
GPS .... Gauge Pressure Switch
GPS .... Generality and Problem Solving
GPS .... Generalized Preference Scheme [*Tariff policy*]
Gps .... general-parents motion pictures (SAUS)
GPS .... General Pavement Studies [*FHWA*] (TAG)
GPS .... General Practitioners Society (SAUO)
GPS .... General Precision Systems (SAUS)
GPS .... General Precision Systems, Incorporated (SAUS)
GPS .... General Problem Solver [*Computer science*]
GPS .... General Problem Solving (IDAI)
GPS .... General Problem Storage [*Computer science*] (ELAL)
GPS .... General Processing Subsystem (MCD)
GPS .... General Processing System (SAUS)
GPS .... General Process Simulator
GPS .... General Product Specification (SAUO)
GPS .... General Programming Subsystem (SAUS)
GPS .... General Purpose Satellite (ACAE)
GPS .... General-Purpose Shelter
GPS .... General-Purpose Simulation [*Formerly, Systems Simulator*] [*IBM Corp.*] [*Computer science*] (IAA)
GPS .... General Purpose Simulator (SAUS)
gps .... general-purpose solver (SAUS)
GPS .... General Purpose System (SAUS)
GPS .... Generic Processing System [*Computer science*] (TEL)
GPS .... Geographic Processor System (SAUS)
GPS .... Geological and Planetary Sciences (SAUO)
GPS .... Geophysical Processor System (SAUO)
GPS .... Geophysical Products System (SAUS)
GPS .... German Pacific Society (BUAC)
GPS .... German Philatelic Society (SAUO)
GPS .... Germany Philatelic Society (EA)
GPS .... Gibbs-Poole-Stockmeyer (SAUS)
GPS .... Gibraltar Philatelic Society (BUAC)
GPS .... GigaBIT [*Binary Digits*] per Second [*Transmission rate*] [*Computer science*]
GPS .... Global Pizza Service (SAUO)
GPS .... Global Planning System (SAUS)
GPS .... Global Positioning Satellite
GPS .... Global Positioning Satellite System [*Nautical term*] (NTA)
GPS .... Global Positioning Services (SAUS)
GPS .... Global Positioning System [*Formerly, NAVSTAR*] [*Air Force*]
GPS .... Global Position System [*Instrument*] (EERA)
GPS .... Global Precision System
GPS .... Global Product Specification (SAUS)
GPS .... Global Protection System (SAUS)
GPS .... Glycerophosphoserine (SAUS)
GPS .... Goodpasture's Syndrome [*Medicine*] (DAVI)
GPS .... Goodpasture Syndrome [*Medicine*] (EDAA)
GPS .... Good Practices Standard (ABAC)
GPS .... Government Paper Specification Standards
GPS .... Government Payroll System (SAUO)
GPS .... Government Procurement Service
GPS .... Graduate Division of Public Service (SAUO)
GPS .... Graduated Pension Scheme [*British*] (BARN)
GPS .... Grams per Second
GPS .... Grand Past Sojourner [*Freemasonry*] (ROG)
GPS .... Grand Principal Sojourner [*Freemasonry*]
GPS .... Grants Program Section (SAUS)
GPS .... Graphic Programming Services [*Computer science*] (IBMDP)
GPS .... Gray Platelet Syndrome [*Medicine*] (DMAA)
GPS .... Greater Public Schools (SAUO)
GPs .... Great Performances (SAUS)
GPS .... Great Persons Society (SAUO)
GPS .... Great Public Schools [*Australia*] (WDAA)
GPS .... Green Party of Switzerland [*Political party*] (PSAP)
GPS .... Ground Plane Simulator
GPS .... Ground Playback Station (SAUS)
GPS .... Ground Power Supply [*NASA*] (NASA)
GPS .... Ground Processing Simulation (MCD)
GPS .... Ground Processing System [*Aviation*]
GPS .... Ground Proximity Sensor
GPS .... Ground Water Protection Strategy [*Environmental Protection Agency*] (GFGA)
GPS .... Groups of Pulses per Second (DEN)
GPS .... Guidance Power Supply
GPS .... Guinea Pig Serum
GPS .... Guinea Pig Spleen
GPS .... Gunner's Primary Sight (MCD)
GPS .... Gyroscope Parameter Shift
GPSA .... Gas Processors Suppliers Association (EA)
GPSA .... General Practitioners Society of Australia (SAUO)
GPSA .... Global Positioning System-Active
GPSA .... Global Position Satellite (SAUS)
GPSC .... Gas Proportional Scintillation Counters [*Spectroscopy*]
GPSC .... General Purposes Sub-Committee (SAUO)
GPSC .... General Purpose Synchronous Communications board (SAUO)
GPSC .... Ghana Peace and Solidarity Council (SAUO)
GPSC .... Guinea Pig Spinal Cord
GPSCO .... Global Position System Consortium (EERA)
GPS CORS ... Global Positioning System Continuously Operating Reference Stations (SAUS)
GPSCS .... General-Purpose Satellite Communication System (MCD)
G P S D I C ... General Purpose Scientific Document Image Code (SAUS)
GPSDIC .... General-Purpose Scientific Document Image Code [*System*] [*National Institute of Standards and Technology*]
GPSDR .... Global Positioning System Demonstration Receiver (EOSA)
GPSDW .... General-Purpose Scientifc Document Writer (SAUS)
GPSDW .... General Purpose Scientific Document Writer (SAUS)
GPSDW .... General-Purpose Scientific Document Writer [*National Institute of Standards and Technology*]
G P S D W ... General Purpose Scientific Document Writer Glutamic-Pyruvic Transaminase (SAUS)
gpsdw .... general-purpose scientific doeument writer (SAUS)
GPSE .... General-Purpose Simulation Environment [*Computer science*]
GPSE .... Gunner's Primary Sight Extension
GPSG .... Generalized Phrase Structure Grammar [*Artificial intelligence*]
GPSI .... General Purpose Simulation (SAUS)
GPSI .... General Purpose Systems, Incorporated (SAUO)
GPSI .... Graphics Processor Software Interface (SAUS)
GPSI .... Great Plains Software [*NYSE symbol*] (SG)
GPSIC .... Global Positioning System Information Center (SAUO)
GPSIC .... GPS Industry Council (SAUO)
GPS/INS .... Global Positioning System/Inertial Navigation System [*Air Force*]
GPS-IPW .... Global Positioning System-Integrated Precipitable Water (SAUS)
GPSL .... General-Purpose Simulation Language [*Computer science*] (IAA)
GPS/MET ...... Global Positioning System/Meteorological (GOBB)
GPS/MET ...... GPS/Meteorological Satellite (SAUS)
GPSN .... General-Purpose Packet Satellite Network (MHDI)
GPS NCC ...... Global Positioning System Network Control Center [*Air Force*] (MCD)
GPSP .... General-Purpose Signal Processor
GPSP .... General Purpose Simulation Program [*Computer science*] (ITCA)
GPSP .... General-Purpose Software Program [*Computer science*]
GPSP .... General-Purpose String Processor (IAA)
GPSP .... Global Positioning System-Passive
GPS PC .... Global Positioning System Program Contractor [*Air Force*] (MCD)
GPSR .... Generic Pulsed Surface RADAR
GPSR .... Global Positioning Satellite Receiver (TIMI)

GPSS .... General [*or Generic*] Problem Statement Simulator
GPSS .... General Process Simulation Studies
GPSS .... General Purpose Satellite System (CCCA)
GPSS .... General-Purpose Simulation System [*formerly, Systems Simulator*] [*IBM Corp.*] [*1961*] [*Computer science*]
GPSS .... General-Purpose System Simulation (SAUS)
GPSS .... General Purpose System Simulator (NITA)
GPSS .... General-Purppose Simulation System (SAUS)
GPSS .... Generic Problem Statement Simulator (SAUS)
GPSS .... Global Positioning Satellite System
GPSSM .... General-Purpose Surface-to-Surface Missile [*Army*]
GPSSN .... Gas Presaure Sintered Silicon Nitride (SAUS)
GPSSN .... Gas Pressure Sintered Silicon Nitride (SAUS)
GPSSU .... Global Positioning System Sensor Unit (HLLA)
GPST .... Global Positioning System Time (SAUO)
GPST .... GPS Tester (SAUS)
GPST .... Group Seat Request [*Travel industry*] (TRID)
GPSU .... Ground Power Supply Unit [*NASA*] (AAG)
GPSX .... General Parcel Service, Inc. [*NASDAQ symbol*] (NQ)
GPSX .... Genl Parcel Service [*NASDAQ symbol*] (TTSB)
GPSX .... Gettysburg Passenger Service [*Federal Railroad Administration identification code*]
GPSXW .... General Parcel Svc Wrrt [*NASDAQ symbol*] (TTSB)
GPT .... Gallons per Ton
GPT .... Gas Phase Titration
GPT .... Gas Power Transfer (IEEE)
GPT .... GEC Plessey Telecommunications [*British*] (ECON)
GPT .... Gemini Pad Test [*NASA*] (KSC)
GPT .... Generalized Path Information Unit Trace [*Communications term*] (DCT)
GPt .... General Peripheral Controller (SAUS)
GPT .... General Perturbation Theory [*Nuclear science*]
GPT .... General Plant Telephone [*Nuclear energy*] (GFGA)
GPT .... General Portland Cement Co (SAUO)
GPT .... General Preferential Tariff (SAUS)
GPT .... General Preferred Tariff [*Canada*]
GPT .... General Purpose Terminal (SAUS)
GPT .... General-Purpose Terminal (IAA)
GPT .... General-Purpose Thermoplastic [*Insulation*]
GPT .... General Purpose Timer (SAUS)
GPT .... General-Purpose Tool
GPT .... General-Purpose Transport [*British military*] (DMA)
GPT .... Generic Principle Trainer (ACAE)
GPT .... Geometric and Positional Tolerance [*Drafting symbol*]
GPT .... Glass Precision Tubing
GPT .... Glass Probe Thermistor
GPT .... Glutamic-Pyruvic Transaminase [*Also, AAT, ALAT, ALT*] [*An enzyme*]
GPT .... Goldpost Resources, Inc. [*Toronto Stock Exchange symbol*]
GPT .... Governor Phillip Tower [*Sydney, New South Wales, Australia*]
GPT .... Graded Pattern Televiscope (SAUS)
GPT .... Grayson Perceptualization Test [*Psychology*]
GPT .... Greenpoint Financial Corp. [*NYSE symbol*] (SAG)
GPT .... Greenpoint Finl [*NYSE symbol*] (TTSB)
GPT .... Grid Pool Tank
GPT .... Gross Provisions Tester (ACAE)
GPT .... Group Projective Test [*Psychology*] (BARN)
GPT .... Guidance Position Tracking [*Aerospace*] (AAG)
GPT .... Guild of Professional Translators (SAUO)
GPT .... Guinea-Pig Trachea (SAUS)
GPT .... Gulfport/Biloxi [*Mississippi*] [*Airport symbol*] (OAG)
GPT .... Gypsum Tile [*Technical drawings*]
GPT .... Guild of Professional Toastmasters (ODA)
GPTA .... Gupta Corp. [*NASDAQ symbol*] (SAG)
GPTAE .... Gupta Corp. [*NASDAQ symbol*] (TTSB)
GP-TAP .... General Purpose-Trunk Access Port
GPTB .... Gunpell Target Board (SAUS)
GPTC .... Gambia Public Transport Corp. (BUAC)
GPTC .... Gas Piping Technology Committee
GPT-C .... Glutamic-Pyruvic Transaminase-C [*An enzyme*] (OA)
GPTE .... General-Purpose Test Equipment (MCD)
GPTEA .... General Purpose Test Equipment Avionics (SAUS)
GpTh .... Group Therapy
GPTI .... General Purpose Terminal Interchange (SAUS)
GPTI .... General-Purpose Terminal Interchanges [*Airline communication system*] [*Raytheon Co.*]
GPTI .... General Purpose Terminal Interface (SAUS)
GPTI .... Guangdong Posts & Telecommunications Institute [*China*] (BUAC)
GPTIRF .... General Purpose Thermal Imager Repair Facility (SAUS)
GPTJC .... Gosport Junction, IN [*American Association of Railroads railroad junction routing code*]
GPTM .... General Purpose Tracker Module (SAUS)
GPTM .... Gross Profit this Month (SAUS)
GPTR .... General-Purpose Tape Routine [*Computer science*] (PCM)
GPTR .... Geographical Problem Type Reports (SAUO)
GPTR .... Guidance Power Temperature Regulator
GPTS .... Geomagnetic Polarity Timescale
GPTTS .... Gunner's Primary Tank Thermal Sight [*Military*]
GPTU .... General Purpose Transport Unit (SAUS)
GPTU .... Glass Painters' Trade Union [*British*]
GPTV .... General-Purpose Test Vehicle (SAUS)
GPTX .... Global Payment Technologies, Inc. [*NASDAQ symbol*] (NASQ)
GPU .... Gas Power Unit (MUGU)
GPU .... Gas Pressurized Unit (ACAE)
GPU .... Gas Pumping Unit (SAUS)
GPU .... Gas Pump Unit
GPU .... General Postal Union [*Later, UPU*]
GPU .... General Processing Unit (SAUS)
GPU .... General Processor Unit
GPU .... General Public Utilities Corp. [*NYSE symbol*] (SPSG)
GPU .... General Public Utilities Corporation (SAUS)
GPU .... Generating Power Unit
GPU .... Genl Public Util [*NYSE symbol*] (TTSB)
GPU .... Geopotential Unit (IAA)
GPU .... Gosudarstvennoe Politicheskoe Upravlenie [*Government Political Administration*] [*Soviet secret service organization, also known as OGPU*] [*Later, KGB*]
GPU .... GPU, Inc. [*NYSE symbol*] [*Formerly, General Public Utility*] (SG)
GPU .... Graphics Processing Unit
GPU .... Graphics Processor Unit (SAUS)
GPU .... Grapper Pick Up (COE)
GPU .... Green Party of Ukraine (BUAC)
GPU .... Ground Power Unit
GPU .... Group Personnel Unit (HEAS)
GpU .... Guanylyluridine (SAUS)
GPU .... Guidance Power Unit (ACAE)
GPU .... Guinea Pig Unit [*Endocrinology*]
GPU .... Gun Pod Unit [*Military*] (MUSM)
GPUA&T .... G.B. Pant University of Agriculture and Technology (SAUO)
GPUN .... General Public Utilities Nuclear Corp. (NRCH)
GpUpG .... Guanylyluridylylguanosine (SAUS)
GPUR .... GOAL [*Ground Operations Aerospace Language*] Test Procedure Update Request (MCD)
GPUSA .... Greenpeace USA (EA)
GPUT .... Galactose Phosphate Uridyl Transferase [*An enzyme*] (MAE)
GPV .... General Public Service Corp. (SAUO)
GPV .... General Public Virus [*Computer science*] (NHD)
GPV .... General Purpose Vehicle (SAUO)
GPV .... General-Purpose Vehicle
GPV .... General-Purpose Vessel
GPV .... Gereformeerd Politiek Verbond [*Reformed Political League*] [*Netherlands*] [*Political party*] (PPE)
GPV .... Graphics Processing Unit (SAUS)
GPV .... Gun Powder Van (SAUS)
GPV .... Gyroscope Pickoff Voltage
GPVB .... General-Purpose Video Buffer
GPVCC .... General-Purpose Vehicle Coordinating Committee (SAUO)
GPVEC .... Great Plains Veterinary Educational Center [*University of Nebraska*] (GVA)
GPVEH .... General-Purpose Vehicle
GPVI .... Graphics Processor Video Interface (SAUS)
GPW .... Geneva Convention Relative to Treatment of Prisoners of War, 12 August 1949 [*Army*] (AABC)
GPW .... Georgia Power Co. (SAUO)
GPW .... Global Point Warning [*Military*]
GPW .... Gold Power Resources Corp. [*Vancouver Stock Exchange symbol*]
GPW .... Great Plains Wheat, Inc. (EA)
GPW .... Green Mountain Power Corp. (SAUO)
GPW .... Green Pulse Width [*Instrumentation*]
GPW .... Gross Plated Weight (SAUS)
GPW .... Gypsum-Plaster Wall [*Technical drawings*]
GPW 1929 .... Geneva Convention Relative to Treatment of Prisoners of War, 27 July 1929 [*Army*]
GPWA .... General Practitioners Writers Association (BUAC)
GPWA .... Grain Pool of Western Australia
GPWC .... Great Pines Water [*NASDAQ symbol*] (TTSB)
GPWC .... Great Pines Water Co. [*NASDAQ symbol*] (SAG)
GPWD .... General Political Warfare Department [*Military*]
GPWM .... Guild for the Promotion of Welsh Music (EAIO)
GPWS .... General-Purpose Workstation (SSD)
GPWS .... General Purpose Work System (SAUO)
GPWS .... Ground Proximity Warning System [*FAA*]
GPWU .... Granite Polishers' and Workers' Union [*British*]
GPWW .... Group Practice without Walls [*Medicine*] (AMHC)
GPWX .... Georgia-Pacific [*Private rail car owner code*]
gpx .... generalized programm extended (SAUS)
GPX .... Generalized Programming Extended [*Livermore Atomic Research Computer*] [*Sperry UNIVAC*]
GPx .... Glutathione Peroxidase [*An enzyme*]
GPx .... Glutathion-Peroxidase (SAUS)
GPX .... GP Strategies [*NYSE symbol*] [*Formerly, National Patent Development*]
GPX .... Greyhound Package Express
GPX .... Guided Projectile Experimental (ACAE)
GPY .... General Plywood Corp. (SAUO)
GPY .... Government Property Yard
GPY .... Gypsy Resources Ltd. [*Vancouver Stock Exchange symbol*]
G P Y S .... General Purpose Yard Simulator (SAUS)
GPYS .... General-Purpose Yard Simulator (PDAA)
GPYSA .... Geophysics (journ.) (SAUS)
GPZ .... Gazpromavia [*Former USSR*] [*FAA designator*] (FAAC)
GPZ .... Gebbies Pass [*New Zealand*] [*Seismograph station code, US Geological Survey*] (SEIS)
GPZ .... Grand Rapids [*Minnesota*] [*Airport symbol*] (OAG)
GPZ .... Guinier-Preston Zone (SAUS)
GP/ZD .... Group Propagate/Zero Detect (SAUO)
GPZOA .... GPz Owners of America [*Defunct*] (EA)
GQ .... Big Sky Airlines [*ICAO designator*] (AD)
GQ .... Double Geared (SAUS)
GQ .... Druk Air (SAUS)

GQ .... Equatorial Guinea [*ANSI two-letter standard code*] (CNC)
GQ .... General Quarters [*General Alert*] [*Navy*]
GQ .... Gentlemen's Quarterly [*A publication*] (WDAA)
GQ .... Golden West Airlines (MHDW)
GQ .... Governor of Queensland [*Australia*]
GQ .... Great Quotations [*A publication*]
GQ .... Group Quarters (SAUO)
GQ .... Grumman Corp. (SAUO)
GQ .... North Korea [*License plate code assigned to foreign diplomats in the US*]
GQA .... Get Quick Answer [*Communications*]
GQA .... Give Quick Answer [*Communications*]
GQA .... Government Quality Assurance (NATG)
GQA .... Grain Quality Analyzer (SAUS)
GQAA .... Government Quality Assurance Authority (SAUS)
GQ & A .... General's Branch, Quarter Master's Branch, and Adjutant's Branch [*Main divisions of Staff Duties*] [*Military*] [*British*]
GQAP .... General Question-Asking Program (STED)
GQAS .... Government Quality Assurance Service (SAUS)
GQDS .... Graphical Query and Design System
GQE .... Generalized Queue Entry [*Computer science*]
GQE .... Gilmore, AR [*Location identifier*] [*FAA*] (FAAL)
GQG .... Gallaudet College, Washington, DC [*OCLC symbol*] (OCLC)
GQG .... Grand Quartier-General [*French GHQ*]
GQI .... Geometric Quality Index
GQK .... Gallaudet College, Kendall Demonstration School, Washington, DC [*OCLC symbol*] (OCLC)
GQL .... Geographic Query Language (SAUO)
GQL .... Graphical Query Language (SAUS)
GQM .... Gallaudet College, Montessori School, Washington, DC [*OCLC symbol*] (OCLC)
GQM .... Geologic Quadrangle Maps (SAUO)
GQM .... Goal, Question, Metric (SAUS)
GQM .... Golden Queen Mining [*Vancouver Stock Exchange symbol*]
GQMS .... Garrison Quartermaster-Sergeant [*British military*] (DMA)
GQN .... U.S. Air Force Reserve (440th Airlift Wing) [*FAA designator*] (FAAC)
GQNA .... Aioun El Atrouss [*Mauritania*] [*ICAO location identifier*] (ICLI)
GQNB .... Boutilimit [*Mauritania*] [*ICAO location identifier*] (ICLI)
GQNC .... Tichitt [*Mauritania*] [*ICAO location identifier*] (ICLI)
GQND .... Tidjikja [*Mauritania*] [*ICAO location identifier*] (ICLI)
GQNE .... Bogue [*Mauritania*] [*ICAO location identifier*] (ICLI)
GQNF .... Kiffa [*Mauritania*] [*ICAO location identifier*] (ICLI)
GQNH .... Timbedra [*Mauritania*] [*ICAO location identifier*] (ICLI)
GQNI .... Nema [*Mauritania*] [*ICAO location identifier*] (ICLI)
GQNJ .... Akjoujt [*Mauritania*] [*ICAO location identifier*] (ICLI)
GQNK .... Kaedi [*Mauritania*] [*ICAO location identifier*] (ICLI)
GQNL .... Moudjeria/Letfotar [*Mauritania*] [*ICAO location identifier*] (ICLI)
GQNM .... Gran Quivira National Monument (SAUO)
GQNM .... Timbedra/Dahara [*Mauritania*] [*ICAO location identifier*] (ICLI)
GQNN .... Nouakchott [*Mauritania*] [*ICAO location identifier*] (ICLI)
GQNR .... Rosso [*Mauritania*] [*ICAO location identifier*] (ICLI)
GQNS .... Selibabi [*Mauritania*] [*ICAO location identifier*] (ICLI)
GQNT .... Tamchakett [*Mauritania*] [*ICAO location identifier*] (ICLI)
GQNU .... M'Bout [*Mauritania*] [*ICAO location identifier*] (ICLI)
GQNV .... Nouakchott [*Mauritania*] [*ICAO location identifier*] (ICLI)
GQP .... Gas Quenching Process
GQPA .... Atar [*Mauritania*] [*ICAO location identifier*] (ICLI)
GQPF .... F'Derick [*Mauritania*] [*ICAO location identifier*] (ICLI)
GQPP .... Nouadhibou [*Mauritania*] [*ICAO location identifier*] (ICLI)
GQPT .... Bir Moghrein [*Mauritania*] [*ICAO location identifier*] (ICLI)
GQPZ .... Zouerate [*Mauritania*] [*ICAO location identifier*] (ICLI)
GQQ .... Galion [*Ohio*] [*Airport symbol*] (OAG)
GQR .... Gauss Quadrature Rule
GQR .... Giant Quadrupole Resonance (SAUS)
GQR .... Golden Quail Resources Ltd. [*Vancouver Stock Exchange symbol*]
GQRV .... Golden Quail Resources Ltd. [*NASDAQ symbol*] (NQ)
GQRVF .... Golden Quail Res Ltd [*NASDAQ symbol*] (TTSB)
GQS .... General Quarter Session (SAUS)
GQS .... General Quarter Sessions (SAUO)
GQW .... Denver, CO [*Location identifier*] [*FAA*] (FAAL)
GQX .... Goldquest Exploration, Inc. [*Toronto Stock Exchange symbol*]
GR .... Aurigny Air Services [*ICAO designator*] (AD)
GR .... Beginn der Gelbreife (SAUS)
GR .... B.F. Goodrich Co. (SAUO)
GR .... Carnegie Library, Rome, GA [*Library symbol*] [*Library of Congress*] (LCLS)
GR .... Gag Reflex [*Medicine*] (EDAA)
GR .... Gambia Regiment [*British military*] (DMA)
GR .... Game Reserve [*State*] (EERA)
GR .... Gamma Radiation (SAUS)
GR .... Gamma Ray [*or Roentgen*]
GR .... Gamma Roentgen (STED)
gr .... Gamma Roentgen (STED)
GR .... G and Rome (journ.) (SAUS)
gr .... Garnet (SAUS)
GR .... Gas Ratio
GR .... Gas release (SAUS)
GR .... Gastric Resection [*Medicine*]
GR .... Gastric resection, great, greater, gross, grossly, group (SAUS)
GR .... Gastrin Receptor [*Medicine*] (EDAA)
GR .... Geared Radial [*Aircraft engine*]
GR .... Gender Role (DIPS)
GR .... Generalized Rash [*Medicine*] (STED)
GR .... General Purpose Register (NITA)
GR .... General Radio
GR .... General Radio Co. (SAUO)
GR .... General Reader
GR .... General Reconnaissance [*Marine Corps*]
GR .... General Reconnaissant (SAUS)
GR .... General Records (ELAL)
GR .... General Referee (SAUS)
GR .... General Refractories Ltd. (SAUO)
GR .... General Register [*Computer science*]
GR .... General Regulator (SAUS)
GR .... General Relativity [*Physics*]
GR .... General Relief [*Medicine*] (STED)
GR .... General Research
GR .... General Reserve
GR .... General Revenue (SAUO)
GR .... General Routine (SAUS)
GR .... General Rules (SAUO)
GR .... Generating Routine (SAUS)
G-R .... Generation-Recombination (SAUS)
GR .... Generator Run (IAA)
GR .... Generator Running (SAUS)
GR .... Genesis Rabbah (BJA)
GR .... Genetic Recombination [*Medicine*] (MELL)
GR .... Genetic Resources (SAUS)
GR .... Gentleman Rider [*Horsemanship*]
GR .... Georgia Review [*A publication*] (ANEX)
GR .... Georgist Registry [*An association*] (EA)
GR .... Georgius Rex [*King George*]
GR .... Germanic Review (journ.) (SAUS)
GR .... Germanium Rectifier
GR .... German Reports (MCD)
GR .... German Review (journ.) (SAUS)
GR .... German Roach [*Immunology*]
GR .... Germ Ring [*Embryology*]
GR .... Gisement Reperage (SAUS)
GR .... Glass-Reinforced
GR .... Glaxo Laboratories Ltd. [*Great Britain*] [*Research code symbol*]
GR .... Global Residual (SAUS)
GR .... Globorotaliid (SAUS)
GR .... Gloucestershire Regiment [*Military unit*] [*British*]
GR .... Glucocorticoid Receptor [*Endocrinology*]
GR .... Glucose Response [*Medicine*] (STED)
GR .... Glutathione Reductase [*An enzyme*]
G-R .... Gnome-Rhone [*Aircraft engine*]
G-R .... Goldbarg-Rutenberg [*Enzyme unit*]
GR .... Golden Rule [*Freemasonry*] (ROG)
GR .... Gold Reserve
GR .... Good Recovery (STED)
GR .... [*The*] Goodrich [*B. F.*] Co. [*NYSE symbol*] (SPSG)
GR .... Gospel Recordings (EA)
GR .... Government Regulation (AAG)
GR .... Government Reserve [*British*] (ADA)
GR .... Government Responsibility (MCD)
gr .... Government Revenue (MENA)
GR .... Government Rubber [*Synthetic rubber*] (IIA)
GR .... Grab Radon Sampling (SAUS)
GR .... Grab Rod (AAG)
Gr .... Grade (AL)
GR .... Grade (KSC)
gr .... Grade (WDMC)
GR .... Grade Resistance [*Hydraulics*]
GR .... Gradual-Release [*Pharmacy*]
gr .... Graduate (GEAB)
GR .... Graduate
GR .... Graduation Requirement (MCD)
G-R .... Graeco-Roman (SAUS)
gr .... Graft [*Medicine*] (EDAA)
Gr .... Grain (AMHC)
GR .... Grain (KSC)
gr .... Grain (WDMC)
gr .... Grains (ODBW)
GR .... Gram (KSC)
GR .... Grammar
gr- .... Gram-Negative [*Bacteria*] (DAVI)
G-R .... Gram-Negative Rods [*Biochemistry*] (DAVI)
GR .... Gramophone (journ.) (SAUS)
gr+ .... Gram-Positive [*Bacteria*] (DAVI)
G+R .... Gram-Positive Rods [*Biochemistry*] (DAVI)
GR .... Gram Roentgen (SAUS)
GR .... Grand [*Title*]
GR .... Grand Rapids Eastern Railroad [*Federal Railroad Administration identification code*]
GR .... Grand Rapids, Michigan
GR .... Grand Recorder [*Freemasonry*]
GR .... Grand Registrar [*Freemasonry*] (ROG)
GR .... Grange [*or Manor, a religious residence*]
GR .... Gran Rabinato (BJA)
GR .... Grant
GR .... Grant Recipient [*Job Training and Partnership Act*] (OICC)
Gr .... Grant's Jamaica Reports [*A publication*] (DLA)
Gr .... Grant's Pennsylvania Cases [*A publication*] (DLA)
Gr .... Grant's Upper Canada Chancery Reports [*A publication*] (DLA)
GR .... Granular Snow [*Skiing condition*]
GR .... Granulocyte (STED)
GR .... Granum [*Grain*] [*Latin*]
GR .... Graphical Representation (SAUS)

GR .... Graphic Reproduction [*A publication*] (DGA)
gr .... Graphite [*Medicine*] (EDAA)
Gr .... Graphite
GR .... Graph Reader (SAUS)
Gr .... Grashof Number [*IUPAC*]
Gr .... Grasp
GR .... Grass (ROG)
GR .... Grasse River (SAUS)
GR .... Grasse River Railroad Corp. (SAUO)
GR .... Grasse River R. R. Corp. [*AAR code*]
GR .... Grass Extract [*Immunology*]
GR .... Grass Runway (SAUS)
GR .... Grave Record [*Genealogy*]
GR .... Graves Registration [*Military*]
GR .... Graves Registration Service (SAUO)
GR .... Gravid (STED)
gr .... Gravid (STED)
Gr .... Gravida [*Obstetrics*] (DAVI)
GR .... Gravitational Radiation (SAUS)
gr .... Gravity (STED)
GR .... Gravity
GR .... Gravity Reference (ACAE)
gr .... Gray [*Unit*] [*Radiation therapy*] (DAVI)
GR .... Gray [*Thoroughbred racing*]
GR .... Great (MCD)
gr .... Great (NTIO)
GR .... Great Roll [*of the Pipe*] [*British*]
GR .... Grecian (ROG)
G-R .... Greco-Roman (SAUS)
GR .... Greece [*ANSI two-letter standard code*] (CNC)
Gr .... Greece (MILB)
gr .... Greece [*IYRU nationality code*] [*MARC country of publication code*] [*Library of Congress*] (LCCP)
gr .... Greek (ELAL)
Gr .... Greek (SHCU)
GR .... Greek
Gr .... Greenleaf's Reports [*1-9 Maine*] [*A publication*] (DLA)
GR .... Green Realignment [*An association*] (BUAC)
Gr .... Green's Reports [*A publication*] (DLA)
gr .... grey (SAUS)
GR .... Grid Reference (SAUS)
GR .... Grid Resistor
GR .... Grid Return
GR .... Grind (ADA)
GR .... Grinder (SAUS)
GR .... Grooved Roofing [*Lumber*]
gr .... Gross (ODBW)
GR .... Gross
GR .... Grossly (SAUS)
GR .... Gross Rate [*Insurance*] (AIA)
GR .... Gross Receipts [*Business term*]
GR .... Gross Requirement (AABC)
GR .... Gross Revenue [*Business term*]
Gr .... Ground
GR .... Ground attack, Reconnaissance (SAUO)
GR .... Ground Range
GR .... Ground Relay (ELAL)
GR .... Ground Rent (ROG)
GR .... Ground Round, Inc. (EFIS)
GR .... Ground Rule (MCD)
gr .... Group (WDMC)
GR .... Group
GR .... Group Replacement (SAUO)
GR .... Group Report
GR .... Grove (ADA)
GR .... Grown Rate (SAUS)
GR .... Growth (SSD)
GR .... Growth Rate [*Biology*]
GR .... Guanidine Rhodanate (SAUS)
GR .... Guaranty Resources (SAUO)
GR .... Guardrail
GR .... Guard Ring (BARN)
GR .... Gulf Rijad Bank [*Bahrain*]
GR .... Gulielmus Rex [*King William*]
GR .... Gun Control RADAR [*Military*] (CAAL)
GR .... Gunner
GR .... Gunnery Range
GR .... Gun Ready (SAUS)
GR .... Gurkha Rifles [*British military*] (DMA)
GR .... Gypsum Requirement (OA)
GR .... Hail [*ICAO*] (FAAC)
GRA .... Fayetteville, NC [*Location identifier*] [*FAA*] (FAAL)
GRA .... Game Research Association (SAUO)
GRA .... Gamma-Ray Absorption (SAUS)
GRA .... Gamma Ray Amplification
GRA .... Garda Representative Association [*Ireland*] (BUAC)
GRA .... Garmisch Recreation Area (SAUO)
GRA .... Gated Radionuclide Angiography [*Medicine*] (DMAA)
GRA .... General Research Agency (SAUO)
GRA .... Geologist Registration Act (SAUO)
GRA .... Geriatric Resource Assembly (ADWA)
GRA .... German Research Association (EA)
GRA .... Girls Rodeo Association [*Later, WPRA*] (EA)
GRA .... Glucocorticoid-Remediable Aldosteronism [*Medicine*]
Gra .... Glyceraldehyde [*Biochemistry*]
GRA .... Glycyrrhizic Acid [*Biochemistry*] (DB)
GRA .... Gombarts Reducing Agent [*Medicine*] (AAMN)
GRA .... Gonadotropin-Releasing Agent [*Endocrinology*] (MAE)
GRA .... Governmental Research Association (EA)
GRA .... Government Report Abstracts (SAUO)
GRA .... Government Reports Announcements [*Department of Commerce*] [*Database producer*]
GRA .... Government Research Announcements (SAUS)
GRA .... Government Responsibility Action
GRA .... Government Responsibility Authorized (MCD)
GR-A .... Government Rubber-Acrylonitrile [*Synthetic rubber*]
GRA .... Governments Reports Announcements (SAUS)
GRA .... Grace [*W. R.*] & Co. [*NYSE symbol*] (SPSG)
GRA .... Grace (W.R.) [*NYSE symbol*] (TTSB)
GRA .... Graduate Research Assistant
Gra .... Graham's Reports [*98-107 Georgia*] [*A publication*] (DLA)
Gra .... Grant [*Legal term*] (DLA)
GRA .... Grant Aid [*Military*] (AABC)
GRA .... Granule (SAUS)
Gra .... Granulocyte (SAUS)
GRA .... Graphic Recording Ammeter (IAA)
gra .... Graphics (VRA)
GRA .... Grass Roots Association (EA)
Gra .... Gratianus [*Flourished, 1151-59*] [*Authority cited in pre-1607 legal work*] (DSA)
GRA .... Gray (MSA)
GRA .... Graz [*Steiermark*] [*Austria*] [*Seismograph station code, US Geological Survey*] [*Closed*] (SEIS)
GRA .... Great American Airways [*ICAO designator*] (FAAC)
GrA .... Groningen University (SAUO)
GRA .... Group Random Access (SAUO)
GRA .... Growth Rate Adjustment [*Business term*]
GRA .... Guild for Religious Architecture [*Later, IFRAA*]
GRA .... Gyro Reference Assembly
GRA .... Greyhound Racing Association (ODA)
GRAAL .... Graph Algorithm (SAUS)
GRAAL .... Graph Algorithmic Language [*Computer science*]
GRA&I .... Government Reports Announcements & Index (SAUO)
Gra & Wat NT ... Graham and Waterman on New Trials [*A publication*] (DLA)
GRAB .... Galactic Radiation and Background (MCD)
GRAB .... Galatic Radiation and Background
GRAB .... Grade Ability (SAUS)
GRAB .... Group Room Availability Bank [*Sheraton Corp.*]
GraBAdHarv ... Graduate School of Busyness Administration, Harvard University (SAUO)
GRABS .... Giant Reusable Air Blast Simulator [*Air Force*]
GRABS .... Gradually Restrict Acceleration Braking and Steering (SAUO)
GRAC .... Grand Royal Arch Captain [*Freemasonry*]
GRAC .... Grand Royal Arch Chapter [*Freemasonry*] (ROG)
GRAC .... Great Rivers Athletic Conference (PSS)
GRAC .... Groupe de Recherche sur les Attitudes Envers la Criminalite [*Canada*]
GRACE .... Grace Agencies (SAUS)
Grace .... Grace [*W.R.*] & Co. [*Associated Press*] (SAG)
GRACE .... Grace Chemicals (SAUS)
GRACE .... Grace Line (SAUS)
GRACE .... Graphic Arts Composing Equipment
GRACE .... Grass Roots Art and Community Effort [*Vermont*]
GRACE .... Gravity Recovery and Climate Experiment [*NASA proposed mission, 2001*]
GRACE .... Group Routing and Charging Equipment [*British*]
GRACE .... Group Routing and Exchange Equipment (SAUO)
GRACE .... Mrs. Gould's Residential Advisory Centre for the Elderly [*British*] (CB)
GRACE .... WR Grace and Company (SAUO)
Grace Hosp Bull ... Grace Hospital. Bulletin (journ.) (SAUS)
Grace Th J ... Grace Theological Journal (journ.) (SAUS)
GRACF .... Graceville, FL [*American Association of Railroads railroad junction routing code*]
Graco .... Graco, Inc. [*Associated Press*] (SAG)
GRACO .... Gray Co., Inc.
GRACO .... Gray Company, Incorporated (SAUO)
GRACY .... Gracey, KY [*American Association of Railroads railroad junction routing code*]
grad .... By Degrees [*Therapy term*] (CTAA)
GRAD .... Gamma Ray Advanced Detector (SAUS)
GRAD .... Generalized Remote Access Database
GRAD .... General Recursive Algebra and Differentiation (IEEE)
GRAD .... Gradatim [*Gradually*] [*Pharmacy*]
GRAD .... Gradient (AFM)
GRAD .... Grading (WDAA)
grad .... Gradual (WDAA)
GRAD .... Gradual
Grad .... Graduate (AL)
grad .... Graduate (WDAA)
GRAD .... Graduate
GRAD .... Graduate Accumulation and Resume Distribution (SAUO)
grad .... Graduated (SHCU)
GRAD .... Graduate Resume Accumulation and Distribution [*Computer science*]
Grad .... Graduation (SAUS)
GradAIP .... Graduate of the Australien Institute of Physics (SAUS)
GRADB .... Generalized Remote Access Database (IEEE)
GRADB .... General Remote Access Data Bass (SAUS)
GradBHI .... Graduate of the British Horological Institute (DBQ)
GradCert .... Graduate Certificate

GradCertBus... Graduate Certificate in Business [*Australia*]
GradCertCommunic... Graduate Certificate in Communication [*Australia*]
GradCertFin... Graduate Certificate in Finance [*Australia*]
GradCertHelpSkills... Graduate Certificate in Helping Skills [*Australia*]
GradCertHRD... Graduate Certificate in Human Resource Development [*Australia*]
GradCertIndRels... Graduate Certificate in Industrial Relations [*Australia*]
GradCertLitEd... Graduate Certificate in Literacy Education [*Australia*]
GradCertMarkt... Graduate Certificate in Marketing [*Australia*]
GradCertMngt... Graduate Certificate in Management [*Australia*]
GradCertTESOL... Graduate Certificate in Teaching of English to Speakers of Other Languages [*Australia*]
Gradco......... Gradco Systems, Inc. [*Associated Press*] (SAG)
GRADCURR... Graduate Education in Classics (SAUS)
GRADD .... Graduate (journ.) (SAUS)
GRADD .... Graphics Adapter Device Driver (SAUS)
GradDIndDes... Graduate Diploma in Industrial Design [*Australia*]
GradDip....... Graduation Diploma (SAUS)
GradDipA..... Graduate Diploma of Arts [*Australia*]
GradDipAblsEd... Graduate Diploma in Aboriginal and Islander Education [*Australia*]
GradDipAcc... Graduate Diploma in Accounting [*Australia*]
GradDipAccom... Graduate Diploma in Accompaniment [*Australia*]
GradDipAcct... Graduate Diploma in Accounting
GradDipActng... Graduate Diploma in Accounting
GradDipAdmin... Graduate Diploma in Administration
GradDipAdultEd & Train... Graduate Diploma in Adult Education and Training [*Australia*]
GradDipAdvAcctg... Graduate Diploma in Advanced Accounting
GradDipAltDispRes... Graduate Diploma in Alternative Dispute Resolution [*Australia*]
GradDipAnalytChem... Graduate Diploma in Analytical Chemistry
GradDipAppCommunications... Graduate Diploma in Applied Communications
GradDipAppEc... Graduate Diploma in Applied Economics [*Australia*]
GradDipAppHist... Graduate Diploma in Applied History
GradDipAppLing... Graduate Diploma in Applied Linguistics
GradDipAppSc... Graduate Diploma in Applied Science [*Australia*]
GradDipAppScGenStud... Graduate Diploma in Applied Science, General Studies [*Australia*]
GradDipAppStats... Graduate Diploma in Applied Statistics
GradDipArts(ChLit)... Graduate Diploma in Arts (Children's Literature) [*Australia*]
GradDipArts(WelfAdmin)... Graduate Diploma in Arts (Welfare Administration) [*Australia*]
GradDipAsianLaw... Graduate Diploma in Asian Law [*Australia*]
GradDipAsianStudies... Graduate Diploma in Asian Studies
GradDipASOS... Graduate Diploma in Antarctic and Southern Ocean Studies [*Australia*]
GradDipAud... Graduate Diploma in Audiology [*Australia*]
GradDipAud... Graduate Diploma in Internal Auditing
GradDipBldgProjMgt... Graduate Diploma in Building Project Management
GradDipBldgProjMgt... Graduate Diploma in Building Projet (SAUS)
GradDipBus... Graduate Diploma in Business [*Australia*]
GradDipBusAdmin... Graduate Diploma in Business Administration
GradDipBusComp... Graduate Diploma in Business Computing
GradDipCCC... Graduate Diploma of Computer Control and Communications [*Australia*]
GradDipChildLit... Graduate Diploma in Children's Literature
GradDipClinBiochem... Graduate Diploma in Clinical Biochemistry
GradDipClinDent... Graduate Diploma in Clinical Dentistry [*Australia*]
GradDipCmlComptg... Graduate Diploma in Commercial Computing
GradDipComEd... Graduate Diploma in Commercial Education [*Australia*]
GradDipComLaw... Graduate Diploma of Commercial Law [*Australia*]
GradDipCommDataProc... Graduate Diploma in Commercial Data Processing
GradDipCommn... Graduate Diploma in Communication
GradDipCommunicationMgt... Graduate Diploma in Communication Management
GradDipComMus... Graduate Diploma of Community Music [*Australia*]
GradDipComMusMgmt... Graduate Diploma of Community Museum Management [*Australia*]
GradDipCompContSys... Graduate Diploma in Computer Controlled Systems
GradDipCompEd... Graduate Diploma in Computers in Education [*Australia*]
GradDipCompEng... Graduate Diploma in Digital Computer Engineering
GradDipCompSc... Graduate Diploma of Computer Science [*Australia*]
GradDipCompStud... Graduate Diploma in Computer Studies
GradDipComptgSc... Graduate Diploma in Computing Science
GradDipConfRes... Graduate Diploma in Conflict Resolution [*Australia*]
GradDipCouns... Graduate Diploma in Counselling
GradDipCPPhty... Graduate Diploma in Cardio Pulmonary Physiotherapy
GradDipCurric... Graduate Diploma in Curriculum [*Australia*]
GradDipDatAnal... Graduate Diploma in Data Analysis
GradDipDemog... Graduate Diploma in Demography
GradDipDesStud... Graduate Diploma in Design Studies
GradDipDiplSt... Graduate Diploma in Diplomatic Studies [*Australia*]
GradDipDP... Graduate Diploma in Data Processing
GradDipDramaEd... Graduate Diploma in Drama in Education [*Australia*]
GradDipE..... Graduate Diploma in Engineering [*Australia*]
GradDipEarlyChildSt... Graduate Diploma in Early Childhood Studies [*Australia*]
GradDipEc ... Graduate Diploma in Economics
GradDipEcDev... Graduate Diploma in Economics of Development
GradDipEcHist... Graduate Diploma in Economic History
GradDipEcmetrics... Graduate Diploma in Econometrics
GradDipEconDev... Graduate Diploma in Economic Development [*Australia*]
GradDipEconGeol... Graduate Diploma in Economic Geology [*Australia*]
GradDipEconHist... Graduate Diploma in Economic History [*Australia*]
GradDipEconmetrics... Graduate Diploma in Econometrics (SAUS)
GradDipEconom... Graduate Diploma in Econometrics [*Australia*]
GradDipEd ... Graduate Diploma in Education
GradDipEdAdmin... Graduate Diploma in Educational Administration [*Australia*]
GradDipEdCouns... Graduate Diploma in Educational Counseling [*Australia*]
GradDipEdCouns... Graduate Diploma in Educational Counselling (ADA)
GradDipEd(IndArts)... Graduate Diploma in Education (Industrial Arts)
GradDipEdStSptTchg... Graduate Diploma in Educational Studies Support Teaching [*Australia*]
GradDipEdStudies... Graduate Diploma in Educational Studies
GradDipEd(TAFE)... Graduate Diploma in Education (Technical and Further Education)
GradDipEdTrain... Graduate Diploma in Education and Training [*Australia*]
GradDipEmpRels... Graduate Diploma in Employment Relations
GradDipEng... Graduate Diploma in Engineering [*Australia*]
GradDipEng-PlantMgnt... Graduate Diploma in Engineering - Plant Management
GradDipEng-PlantMgnt... Graduate Diploma in Engineering-Plant Management (SAUS)
GradDipEnv & MunEng... Graduate Diploma in Environmental and Municipal Engineering
GradDipEnvSt... Graduate Diploma in Environmental Studies [*Australia*]
GradDipEpi... Graduate Diploma in Epidemiology [*Australia*]
GradDipExerSportSc... Graduate Diploma in Exercise and Sport Sciences
GradDipFA... Graduate Diploma of Fine Arts [*Australia*]
GradDipFamLaw... Graduate Diploma of Family Law [*Australia*]
GradDipFilm & Tele in Ed... Graduate Diploma in Film and Television in Education
GradDipFin... Graduate Diploma in Finance
GradDipFineArt... Graduate Diploma in Fine Art
GradDipForOdont... Graduate Diploma in Forensic Odontology [*Australia*]
GradDipGalSt... Graduate Diploma in Gallery Studies [*Australia*]
GradDipGeol... Graduate Diploma for Science Teachers (Geology)
GradDipGeront... Graduate Diploma in Gerontology
GradDipGraphCommEd... Graduate Diploma in Graphic Communication Education [*Australia*]
GradDipHealthServMgmt... Graduate Diploma in Health Services Management
GradDipHIM... Graduate Diploma in Health Information Management
GradDipHumanPhysiol & Pharmacol... Graduate Diploma in Human Physiology and Pharmacology [*Australia*]
GradDipImmunolMicrobiol... Graduate Diploma in Immunology and Microbiology [*Australia*]
GradDipIndDes... Graduate Diploma in Industrial Design
GradDipInfoMgt... Graduate Diploma in Information Management [*Australia*]
GradDipInfServ... Graduate Diploma in Information Services
GradDipInfStudies... Graduate Diploma in Information Studies
GradDipInfTech... Graduate Diploma in Information Technology [*Australia*]
GradDipIntComLaw... Graduate Diploma in International and Commercial Law [*Australia*]
GradDipIntLaw... Graduate Diploma in International Law
GradDipIntPropLaw... Graduate Diploma in Intellectual Property Law [*Australia*]
GradDipKnowlBasSys... Graduate Diploma in Knowledge Based (SAUS)
GradDipKnowlBasSys... Graduate Diploma in Knowledge Based Systems
GradDipLabRelLaw... Graduate Diploma in Labour Relations Law [*Australia*]
GradDipLandArch... Graduate Diploma in Landscape Architecture
GradDipLandDatMan... Graduate Diploma in Land Data Management
GradDipLangTchg... Graduate Diploma in Language Teaching [*Australia*]
GradDipLD... Graduate Diploma in Landscape Design
GradDipLegalPrac... Graduate Diploma in Legal Practice
GradDipLegSt... Graduate Diploma of Legal Studies [*Australia*]
GradDipLeisureStud... Graduate Diploma in Leisure Studies
GradDipLibInfStud... Graduate Diploma in Librarianship and Information Studies
GradDipLibSc... Graduate Diploma in Library Science (ADA)
GradDipLocalGovtEng... Graduate Diploma in Local Government Engineering
GradDipLoc & AppHist... Graduate Diploma in Local and Applied History
GradDipManipTh... Graduate Diploma in Manipulative Therapy
GradDipMatAnth... Graduate Diploma of Material Anthropology [*Australia*]
GradDipMatEng... Graduate Diploma in Materials Engineering [*Australia*]
GradDipMathMethods... Graduate Diploma in Mathematical Methods
GradDipMathSc... Graduate Diploma in Mathematics Science [*Australia*]
GradDipMathsEd... Graduate Diploma in Mathematics Education [*Australia*]
GradDipMediaComm & TechLaw... Graduate Diploma in Media Communications and Technology Law [*Australia*]
GradDipMelSt... Graduate Diploma of Melanesian Studies [*Australia*]
GradDipMentHlthSc... Graduate Diploma in Mental Health Science [*Australia*]
GradDipMgmt... Graduate Diploma in Management
GradDipMidwif... Graduate Diploma in Midwifery [*Australia*]
GradDipMinRes... Graduate Diploma in Mineral Resources
GradDipMktg... Graduate Diploma in Marketing
GradDipMolBiol... Graduate Diploma in Molecular Biology [*Australia*]
GradDipMovement & Dance... Graduate Diploma in Movement and Dance [*Australia*]
GradDipMultiStudies... Graduate Diploma in Multicultural Studies [*Australia*]
GradDipMunEng... Graduate Diploma in Municipal Engineering [*Australia*]
GradDipMus... Graduate Diploma in Music [*Australia*]
GradDipMusCur... Graduate Diploma of Museum Curatorship [*Australia*]
GradDipMusMgmt... Graduate Diploma in Museum Management [*Australia*]
GradDipMus(Op)... Graduate Diploma in Music (Opera) [*Australia*]
GradDipMus(Perf)... Graduate Diploma in Music (Performance) [*Australia*]
GradDipMus(Rep)... Graduate Diploma in Music (Repetiteur) [*Australia*]
GradDipNatResourcesLaw... Graduate Diploma in Natural Resources Law [*Australia*]
GradDipNurs... Graduate Diploma in Nursing
GradDipNursStudies... Graduate Diploma in Nursing Studies
GradDipNutr & Diet... Graduate Diploma in Nutrition and Dietetics
GradDipOffshEng... Graduate Diploma in Offshore Engineering [*Australia*]
GradDipOH & S... Graduate Diploma in Occupational Health and Safety
GradDipOR... Graduate Diploma in Operations Research
GradDipOrgDev... Graduate Diploma in Organisation Development
GradDipPaedPhty... Graduate Diploma in Paediatric Physiotherapy

GradDipPPT... Graduate Diploma in Pulp and Paper Technology [*Australia*]
GradDipProjMgt... Graduate Diploma in Project Management [*Australia*]
GradDipProp... Graduate Diploma in Property
GradDipPSM... Graduate Diploma in Public Sector Management
GradDipPsych... Graduate Diploma of Psychology [*Australia*]
GradDipPubEcPol... Graduate Diploma in Public Economic Policy
GradDipPubLaw... Graduate Diploma in Public Law
GradDipPubPol... Graduate Diploma in Public Policy
GradDipQlty... Graduate Diploma in Quality
GradDipQualTech... Graduate Diploma in Quality Technology
GradDipRc... Graduate Diploma in Rehabilitation Counselling
GradDipSc... Graduate Diploma in Science
GradDipScSoc... Graduate Diploma of Science and Society [*Australia*]
GradDipSEAsianStud... Graduate Diploma in Southeast Asian Studies
GradDipSecStud... Graduate Diploma in Secretarial Studies
GradDipSocAdmin... Graduate Diploma in Social Administration [*Australia*]
GradDipSocEcol... Graduate Diploma in Social Ecology [*Australia*]
GradDipSpecEd... Graduate Diploma in Special Education [*Australia*]
GradDipStats... Graduate Diploma in Statistics
GradDipStratSt... Graduate Diploma in Strategic Studies [*Australia*]
GradDipStrucEng... Graduate Diploma in Structural Engineering [*Australia*]
GradDipStudWel... Graduate Diploma in Student Welfare [*Australia*]
GradDipSurFin... Graduate Diploma in Metal Finishing and Surface Protection
GradDipSurvPrac... Graduate Diploma in Surveying Practice
GradDipT... Graduate Diploma in Teaching (ADA)
GradDipTax... Graduate Diploma in Taxation
GradDipTchrLib... Graduate Diploma in Teacher Librarianship (ADA)
GradDipTeach... Graduate Diploma in Teaching [*Australia*]
GradDipTeachLib... Graduate Diploma in Teacher Librarianship
GradDipTourism... Graduate Diploma of Tourism [*Australia*]
GradDipTrans & Dist... Graduate Diploma in Transport and Distribution
GradDipUEM... Graduate Diploma in Urban Estate Management
GradDipUltr... Graduate Diploma in Ultrasonography
GradDipUrb & RegPlan... Graduate Diploma in Urban and Regional Planning
GradDipURP... Graduate Diploma in Urban and Regional Planning
GradDip(VisArts)... Graduate Diploma in Visual Arts
GradDipWaterEng... Graduate Diploma in Water Engineering [*Australia*]
GradDipWeldTech... Graduate Diploma in Welding Technology
GradDipWelfAdmin... Graduate Diploma in Welfare Administration [*Australia*]
GradDipWomen'sStudies... Graduate Diploma in Women's Studies [*Australia*]
GradDipWomHlth... Graduate Diploma in Women's Health [*Australia*]
GRADE... Gestalt Recognition by Asymptotic Differential Equations
GRADE... Graphical Airspace Design Environment [*FAA*] (TAG)
GRADE... Ground Radar Detector Evaluation (SAUO)
Gradell... Gradell Industries, Inc. [*Associated Press*] (SAG)
GradeTeach... Grade Teacher (journ.) (SAUS)
GRADEX... Graded Exercise (NVT)
Grad Fac Phil J... Graduate Faculty Philosophy Journal (journ.) (SAUS)
Grad Fix... Grady on Fixtures [*A publication*] (DLA)
Grad Fix... Grady on Fixtures (journ.) (SAUS)
Grad Hind Inh... Grady's Hindoo Law of Inheritance [*A publication*] (DLA)
Grad Hind L... Grady's Manual of Hindoo Law [*A publication*] (DLA)
Grad Hind L... Gradys Manual of Hindoo Law (journ.) (SAUS)
GradIAE... Graduate of the Institution of Automobile Engineers [*British*]
GradIElecIE... Graduate of the Institution of Electrical and Electronics Incorporated Engineers [*British*] (DBQ)
Grad IERE... Graduate of the Institution of Electronic and Radio Engineers [*British*]
GradIISec... Graduate of the Institute of Industrial Security [*British*] (DBQ)
Grad IM... Graduate of the Institute of Metallurgists (BARN)
GradIM... Graduate of the Institute of Metals (SAUS)
Grad IM... Graduate of the Institution of Metallurgists (SAUO)
GradIMA... Graduate Member of the Institute of Mathematics and Its Applications [*British*] (DBQ)
GradIManf... Graduate Member of the Institute of Manufacturing [*British*] (DBQ)
Grad I Mech E... Graduate of the Institution of Mechanical Engineers [*British*]
GradIMF... Graduate of the Institute of Metal Finishing [*British*] (DBQ)
GradIMS... Graduate of the Institute of Management Specialists [*British*] (DBQ)
Grad Ind Co... Grady's Indian Codes [*A publication*] (DLA)
Grad Inst BE... Graduate Member of the Institute of British Engineers
GradInstBTM... Graduate of the Institute of Business and Technical Management [*British*] (DBQ)
GradInstNDT... Graduate of the British Institute of Non-Destructive Testing (DBQ)
Grad Inst P... Graduate Member of the Institute of Physics and the Physical Society [*British*]
GradInstPS... Graduate of the Institute of Purchasing and Supply [*British*] (DBQ)
GradIOP... Graduate of the Institute of Printing [*British*] (DBQ)
GradIPE... Graduate of the Institution of Production Engineers (SAUO)
GradIPM... Graduate of the Institute of Personnel Management [*British*] (DBQ)
GraDipUltr... Graduate Diploma in Ultrasonography (SAUS)
GradIS... Graduate Member of the Institute of Statisticians [*British*] (DBQ)
GradISM... Graduate of the Institute of Supervisory Management [*British*] (DBQ)
Grad MNDTS... Graduate Member of the Non-Destructive Testing Society of Great Britain
GradNIH... Graduate of the National Institute of Hardware [*British*] (DBQ)
GRADO... CNES Gravity Satellite (SAUO)
GradPRI... Graduate of the Plastics and Rubber Institute [*British*] (DBQ)
Grad Res Ed... Graduate Research in Education and Related Disciplines (journ.) (SAUS)
Grad RIC... Graduate Member of the Royal Institute of Chemistry [*British*]
Grad RIC... Graduate of the Royal Institute of Chemistry (SAUO)
GRADS... Generalized Remote Access Database System (IEEE)
GRADS... Great Falls Air Defense Sector (SAUS)
GRADS... Ground RADAR Aerial Delivery System (MCD)
GRADS... Ground Radar Air Delivery System (SAUO)
GRADSCOPE... Graduate Search by Computer after Personal Evaluation (AIE)
GradSCP... Graduate of the Society of Certified Professionals [*British*] (DBQ)
Grad SE... Graduate of the Society of Engineers (SAUO)
GradSemJ... Graduate Seminar Journal (journ.) (SAUS)
GradSLAET... Graduate of the Society of Licensed Aircraft Engineers and Technologists [*British*] (DBQ)
Grad Soc Eng... Graduate of the Society of Engineers (SAUO)
GRADU... Gradual
gradu... graduating (SAUS)
Graduate IElecIE... Graduate of the Institution of Electrical and Electronics Incorporated Engineers [*British*] (DBQ)
GradWeldI... Graduate of the Welding Institute [*British*] (DBQ)
GradWoman... Graduate Woman (journ.) (SAUS)
GRAE... Generally Regarded [*or Recognized*] as Effective [*Medicine*]
GRAE... Gouvernement de la Republique de l'Angola en Exile [*Government of the Republic of Angola in Exile*]
GRAE... Gouvernement de la Republique de l'Angola en Exile (SAUS)
GRAE... Governo Revolucionario de Angola no Exilio [*Revolutionary Angolan Government-in-Exile*] [*Portuguese*] (PD)
GRAEL... Green-Alternative European Link (SAUO)
GR Aero S... Graduate of the Royal Aeronautical Society [*British*]
GRAF... Graffiti [*Slang*] [*British*]
GRAF... Graphic Addition to FORTRAN [*Computer science*]
GRAF... Graphical Application Facility (TIMI)
GRAF... Gridded Representation of Analyses and Forecasts (SAUS)
GRAF... Ground Replay and Analysis Facility (GAVI)
GRAFCET... Graphe de Commande Etape-Transition [*State transition command graph*] [*Computer language*] (CDE)
GRAFEM... Graphic Finite Element Modeling [*Software*] [*Automotive engineering*]
GraffPay... Graff Pay per View [*Associated Press*] (SAG)
GRAFLAN... Graphic Language (SAUS)
GRAFMA... Grand Rapids Area Furniture Manufacturers Association (EA)
GRAFTABL... Load Graphics Table [*Computer science*]
Grafton... Smith's New Hampshire Reports [*A publication*] (DLA)
Graham... Graham Corp. [*Associated Press*] (SAG)
Grahamstown Hist Soc Ann... Grahamstown Historical Society. Annals (journ.) (SAUS)
Grah & W New Trials... Graham and Waterman on New Trials [*A publication*] (DLA)
GRAI... Government Reports Announcements and Index [*Department of Commerce*] [*A publication*]
GRAID... Graphical Aid [*Computer science*]
GRAIL... garnet-rutile-alumino-silicate-ilmenite (SAUS)
GRAIL... Gene Recognition and Analysis Internet Link (HGEN)
GRAIL... Graphical Input Language (SAUO)
GRAIL... Graphic Input Language [*Computer science*] (PDAA)
GRAIL... Gravity Radiation Antenna in Leyden (SAUS)
GRAIN... Bank of Granite Corp. (North Carolina) [*NASDAQ symbol*] (COMM)
GRAIN... Genetic Resources Action International [*Spain*]
GRAIN... Graphics-Oriented Relational Algebraic Interpreter
GRAINCORP... New South Wales Grain Corp. [*Australia*] [*Commercial firm*]
Grain Feed J Consol... Grain and Feed Journals Consolidated (journ.) (SAUS)
Grain Feed Rev... Grain and Feed Review (journ.) (SAUS)
Graingr... Grainger [*W.W.*], Inc. [*Associated Press*] (SAG)
Grain Prod News... Grain Producer News (journ.) (SAUS)
GRAJ... Gray Jay [*North American bird banding code*] (BIBA)
GRAK... Gray Kingbird [*North American bird banding code*] (BIBA)
GRAL... General (ROG)
Gram... De Grammaticis [*of Suetonius*] [*Classical studies*] (OCD)
GRAM... Generic Radar Analysis Model (ACAE)
GRAM... Global Reference Atmosphere Model (SSD)
GRAM... Globus Resource Allocation Manager
Gram... Gramaphone (SAUS)
gram... Grammar [*Copyediting*] (WDMC)
GRAM... Grammar [*or Grammatical*]
Gram... Grammatical (SAUO)
Gram... Gramophone [*Division of Record Corp. of America*] [*Record label*]
GRAM... Granulocyte Activating Mediator [*Immunochemistry*]
GRAM... Graphics Random Access Memory (TIMI)
GRAMA-COP... Grain Marketing Cooperative of the Philippines (BUAC)
GRAMC... Gramercy, LA [*American Association of Railroads railroad junction routing code*]
GRAMCO... Great American Management & Research Company International (SAUO)
GRAMICID... Gramicidin (SAUS)
Gramm... Grammatici scriptores (SAUS)
Gramm Lat... Grammatici Latini [*A publication*] (OCD)
Gramm Rom Frag... Grammaticae Romana Fragmenta [*A publication*] (OCD)
gram-neg... Gram-Negative [*Biochemistry*] (DAVI)
Gramo... Gramola [*Record label*] [*Belgium*]
GRAMP... Generalized Reliability and Maintainability Program [*Military*]
GRAMPA... General Analytical Model for Process Analysis (IEEE)
GRAMPA... Ground Resonance Automatic Multipoint Apparatus (SAUS)
GRAMPIES... Growing Retired Active Monied Person in Excellent State [*Lifestyle classification*]
gram-pos... Gram-Positive [*Biochemistry*] (DAVI)
GRAMPS... Graphic Map Production System (SAUO)
GRAMPS... Graphics for the Multipicture System [*Computer graphics*]
GRAMS... Generalized Reliability and Maintainability Simulator (MCD)
GRAMS... Gramophone Records [*Music or sound effects*]
GRAMS... Ground-based Radiometer Autonomous Measurement System (SAUS)
GRAMS... Ground Radiation Measurement System (SAUO)
GRAMS... Ground Recovery and Monitoring System (SAUS)
GRAN... Bank of Granite [*NASDAQ symbol*] (SAG)
GRAN... Global Rescue Alarm Network [*Program*] [*Navy*]

GRAN.......... Gombarts Reducing Agent - Negative [*Medicine*] (AAMN)
GRAN.......... Grain
GRAN.......... Grandmother (DSUE)
GRAN.......... Granite (MSA)
gran.......... Granite (VRA)
GRAN.......... Granodize
GRAN.......... Granular (WDAA)
Gran.......... Granulator (SAUS)
GRAN.......... Granulatus [*Granulated*] [*Pharmacy*]
GRANAS...... Global Radio Navigation System [*Aviation*] (DA)
GRANAT...... Great Annihilator [*Commonwealth - French satellite*] (ECON)
GranBd........ Granite Broadcasting Corp. [*Associated Press*] (SAG)
GranCr........ GranCare, Inc. [*Associated Press*] (SAG)
Grand.......... Grand Gaming Corp. [*Associated Press*] (SAG)
GRAND AM... Grand Marnier and Amaretto
GR&C.......... Gulf Resources & Chemical Corporation (SAUO)
Grand Canyon Nat History Assoc Bull... Grand Canyon Natural History Association. Bulletin (journ.) (SAUS)
GRANDE...... Gamma Ray and Neutrino Detector Experiment [*Proposed*] [*University of California, Irvine*]
GRANDE...... Ground Active Nutation Damping Electronics (ACAE)
GrandG........ Grand Gaming Corp. [*Associated Press*] (SAG)
GRANDO...... Grandioso [*Majestic*] [*Music*]
GR & P........ Grand Rapids & Petoskey Railway
GR&R.......... Gage Repeatablity and Reproducibility (SAUS)
GR&R.......... Gage Reproducibility and Reliability (SAUS)
GR & R........ Gauge Repeatability and Reproducibility [*Materials testing*]
GrandTel...... GrandeTel Technologies, Inc. [*Associated Press*] (SAG)
GRANEDA.... Graphische Netzplan-Darstellung (SAUS)
GRANFD...... Granada Foods (SAUS)
Grang.......... Granges, Inc. [*Associated Press*] (SAG)
Granger....... Granger's State Reports [*22-23 Ohio*] [*A publication*] (DLA)
GRANIS........ Graphical Natural Interference System (SAUS)
GRANITE...... Gamma Ray Astrophysics New Imaging Telescope
GranitFn...... Granite Financial, Inc. [*Associated Press*] (SAG)
GRANL......... Granulated
GRANO......... Granolithic
Grant.......... Grant of Elchies' Scotch Session Cases [*A publication*] (DLA)
Grant.......... Grant's Chancery Chamber Reports [*1850-65*] [*Upper Canada*] [*A publication*] (DLA)
Grant.......... Grant's Jamaica Reports [*A publication*] (DLA)
Grant.......... Grant's Pennsylvania Cases [*A publication*] (DLA)
Grant.......... Grant's Upper Canada Chancery Reports [*A publication*] (DLA)
Grant Bank... Grant on Banking [*A publication*] (DLA)
Grant Cas.... Grant's Pennsylvania Cases [*A publication*] (DLA)
Grant Cas (PA)... Grant's Pennsylvania Cases [*A publication*] (DLA)
Grant Ch...... Grant's Upper Canada Chancery Reports [*A publication*] (DLA)
Grant Ch (Can)... Grant's Upper Canada Chancery Reports [*A publication*] (DLA)
Grant Corp... Grant on Corporations [*A publication*] (DLA)
GRANT CPW... Grant County Public Works (SAUS)
Grant E & A... Grant's Error and Appeal Reports [*A publication*] (DLA)
Grant Err & App... Grant's Error and Appeal Reports [*A publication*] (DLA)
Grant Jamaica... Grant's Jamaica Reports [*A publication*] (DLA)
Grant PA...... Grant's Pennsylvania Cases [*A publication*] (DLA)
Gra N Tr....... Graham on New Trials [*A publication*] (DLA)
Grantsmanship Cent News... Grantsmanship Center. News (journ.) (SAUS)
Grant's R...... Grant's Jamaica Reports [*A publication*] (DLA)
GrantSt........ Granite State Bankshares, Inc. [*Associated Press*] (SAG)
Grant UC...... Grant's Upper Canada Chancery Reports [*A publication*] (DLA)
granulo........ Granulocyte [*Hematology*] (DAVI)
GRANV........ Granville, WI [*American Association of Railroads railroad junction routing code*]
GRAO.......... Gamma Ray Astronomy Observatory
GRAP.......... Greatest Response Amplitude Probability
GRAPD......... Greatest Response Amplitude Probability Data
GRAPD......... Guard Ring Avalanche Photodiode (IAA)
GRAPDEN.... Graphic Data Entry Unit [*Computer science*]
GRAPE......... gamma-ray attenuation porosity estimator (SAUS)
GRAPE......... Gamma Ray Attenuation Porosity Evaluator
GRAPE......... Graphical Analysis of Program Execution [*Computer science*]
GRAPE......... Grass Airborne Pollen Experiment (SAUO)
GRAPE......... Gravity Pipe [*A specialized computer*]
GRAPE......... Ground Receiving and Ranging Equipment (SAUS)
GRAPE-4...... GRAvity PipE no. 4 [*Computer science*]
Graph.......... Graphic (DIAR)
GRAPH......... Graphic
GRAPH......... Graphical Repair Discard Analysis Procedure Handbook
GRAPH......... Graphics (SAUS)
GRAPH......... Graphology (WDAA)
GRAPHAGE... Graphic Output Package (SAUS)
GRAPHDEN... Graphical Data Entry [*Computer science*] (MUGU)
Graphic Arts Bull... Graphic Arts Bulletin (journ.) (SAUS)
Graphic Arts Lit Abstr... Graphic Arts Literature Abstracts (journ.) (SAUS)
Graphic Arts Prog... Graphic Arts Progress (journ.) (SAUS)
Graphic As M... Graphic Arts Monthly (journ.) (SAUS)
Graphic Commun World... Graphic Communications World (journ.) (SAUS)
Graphic Comm Wk... Graphic Communications Weekly (journ.) (SAUS)
Graphic Sci... Graphic Science (journ.) (SAUS)
GRAPHIDI.... Graphical Interpretive Display System (SAUS)
Graphite....... Carbon (SAUS)
Graphs Comb... Graphs and Combinatorics (journ.) (SAUS)
Graph Scr.... Graphis Scripta (SAUS)
GRAPHSSY... Graphics Software System (SAUS)
GRAPHSYS... Graphic Software System (SAUS)
GRAPHSYS... Graphics Software System (SAUS)
GraphxZn..... Graphix Zone, Inc. [*Associated Press*] (SAG)
Grap Just..... Grapel's Translation of the Institutes of Justinian [*A publication*] (DLA)
Grap Just..... Grapels Translation of the Institutes of Justinian (journ.) (SAUS)
GRAPL......... Graphic Application Programming Language (SAUS)
GRAPO......... First of October Anti-Fascist Resistance Group (SAUS)
GRAPO......... Grupos de Resistencia Anti-Fascista Primero de Octubre [*October First Antifascist Resistance Groups*] [*Spain*] [*Political party*] (PPE)
Gra Pr.......... Graham's Practice of the New York Supreme Court [*A publication*] (DLA)
Grap Rom Law... Grapel's Sources of the Roman Civil Law [*A publication*] (DLA)
Grap Rom Law... Grapels Sources of the Roman Civil Law (journ.) (SAUS)
GRAR.......... Generally Recognized as Reasonable [*Medicine*] (DB)
GRAR.......... Government Report Authorization and Record (AAG)
GRAR.......... Great American Recreation, Inc. (SAUO)
GRAR.......... Grinding Arbor
GRARD........ Girard, KS [*American Association of Railroads railroad junction routing code*]
GRARD........ Goddard Range and Range Data [*NASA*] (KSC)
GRARE........ Ground-Receiving and Analog Ranging Equipment [*AFSCF*] (MCD)
GRARR........ Goddard Range and Range Rate [*Tracking system*] [*NASA*]
GRARR Tracking System... Goddard Range and Range Rate Tracking System (SAUS)
GRAS.......... generally recognised as safe (SAUS)
GRAS.......... Generally Recognized [*or Regarded*] as Safe [*FDA term*]
GRAS.......... Generally Regarded as Safe (NTIO)
GRAS.......... Ground Return Area Suppression (NATG)
Gras............ Group for Research in Administration and Sociology (SAUO)
GRASE........ Generally Recognized as Safe and Effective [*Medicine*] (DB)
GRASER...... Gamma Ray Amplification by Stimulated Emission of Radiation
GRASER...... Gamma Ray LASER (MCD)
GRASP........ Gamma Ray Astronomy with Spectroscopy and Positioning
GRASP........ GAO [*General Accounting Office*] Review and Approval of Accounting Systems Project (GFGA)
GRASP........ Gas Reservoir Area Simulation Programme (SAUO)
GRASP........ Generalised Remote Acquisition and Sensor Processing (SAUS)
GRASP........ Generalized Reentry Application Simulation Program [*NASA*] (KSC)
GRASP........ Generalized Remote Acquisition and Sensor Processing
GRASP........ Generalized Retrieval and Storage Program [*Computer science*]
GRASP........ Generally Recognized as Safe Petition [*FDA*]
GRASP........ General Read And Simulate Program (SAUS)
GRASP........ General Reduction and Analysis Support Package [*Military*] (CAAL)
GRASP........ General Resource Allocation and Selection Program [*NASA*] (KSC)
GRASP........ General Risk Analysis Simulation Program (SAUS)
G R A S P.... General Risk Analysis Simulation Programme (SAUS)
GRASP........ Generation of Random Access Sites Plans (SAUO)
GRASP........ Generic RADAR Analysis and Synthesis Program
GRASP........ Generic Retrieve/Archive Services Protocol (SAUO)
GRASP........ Geographical Resource Analysis Software Package (SAUS)
GRASP........ Global Retrieval Access and Information System for Property (EURO)
GRASP........ Gradient-Accelerated Spectroscopy (SAUS)
GRASP........ Graphia-Augmented Structural Post-Processing (SAUS)
GRASP........ Graphical Robot Applications Stimulation Package (SAUS)
GRasp.......... Graphic Animation System for Professionals [*Software package*] [*Paul Mace Software*] (PCM)
GRASP........ Graphics-Augmented Structural Post-Processing [*Module*]
GRASP........ Graphic Service Program (IEEE)
GRASP Lab... General Robotics and Active Sensory Processing Laboratory [*University of Pennsylvania*] [*Research center*] (RCD)
GRASP Lab... General Robotics and Actives Sensory ProcesingLaboratory (SAUS)
GRASP/OP... Generalized Retrieval and Sort Processor/Output (SAUO)
GRASR........ General Railroad and Airline Stabilization Regulations [*A publication*] (DLA)
GRASS........ Gamma Ray Ablation Sensing System (SAA)
GRASS........ Gas Release and Swelling Subroutine (PDAA)
GRASS........ Generalized Reactor Analysis Subsystem
GRASS........ Generalized Research Analysis Statistical System (SAUO)
GRASS........ General Random Audit Sample Selection Technique [*Military*] (AFIT)
GRASS........ General Retrieval and Storage System (SAUS)
GRASS........ Geographical Resources Analysis Support System [*Software*] [*Computer science*] (EERA)
GRASS........ Geographic Resources Analysis Support System [*Army*] (RDA)
GRASS........ Germinating Ray Acoustics Simulation System (MCD)
GRASS........ Gradient-Recalled Acquisition in a Steady State [*Medicine*] (RAWO)
GRASS........ Grassland Research and Serengeti Systems [*Model for simulation*]
GRASS........ Great Revolutionary American Standard System [*Book title*]
GRASS........ Ground-to-Air Scanner Surveillance
Grass Forage Sci... Grass and Forage Science (journ.) (SAUS)
Grassl.......... Grassland (SAUS)
Grass R........ Grass Roots [*A publication*]
Grasuate IElecIE... Graduate of the Institution of Electricaland Electronics Incorporated Engineers (SAUO)
grat............. Graticule (SAUS)
GRAT........... Gratis [*Free*] [*Latin*] (ROG)
Grat............ Grattan's Virginia Reports [*A publication*] (DLA)
GRAT........... Gratuity (AABC)
GRAT........... Gray-Backed Tern [*North American bird banding code*] (BIBA)
Grat Act....... Gratiarum Actio [*of Ausonius*] [*Classical studies*] (OCD)
GRATE......... Growth Rate [*Botany*]
GRATIS........ Generation (SAUS)
GRATIS........ Generation, Reduction, and Training Input System (IEEE)
Gratt........... Grattan's Virginia Supreme Court Reports [*1844-80*] [*A publication*] (DLA)
Gratt (VA).... Grattan's Virginia Reports [*A publication*] (DLA)

GRAUL......... Graduate Program in Applied Urban Linguistics (SAUO)
GRAUL......... Grand Rapids Area Union List of Serials [*Library network*]
Grav............. Gravel (SAUS)
Grav............. Graviation (SAUS)
GRAV........... Gravid [*Pregnant*] [*Medicine*]
Grav............. Gravimeter (SAUS)
Grav............. Gravimetric (SAUS)
Grav............. Gravitation (SAUS)
GRAV........... Gravitational
grav............. Gravity (CPH)
Grav De Jur Nat Gent... Gravina's De Jure Naturale Gentium, Etc. [*A publication*] (DLA)
Graver Water Cond Co Tech Repr... Graver Water Conditioning Company. Technical Reprint (journ.) (SAUS)
Graves......... Proceedings in English King's Council [*1392-93*] [*A publication*] (DLA)
GRAVR......... Gravitational Redshift Space Probe [*Also, GP*]
Grav Russ.... Greaves Edition of Russell on Crimes (SAUS)
GRAW........... Gray Wagtail [*North American bird banding code*] (BIBA)
GRAY........... Grayhound Electronics, Inc. (SAUO)
Gray............. Gray's Massachusetts Supreme Judicial Court Reports [*67-82 Massachusetts*] [*1854-60*] [*A publication*] (DLA)
Gray............. Grays Massachusetts Supreme Judicial Court Reports (journ.) (SAUS)
Gray............. Gray's Reports [*112-22 North Carolina*] [*A publication*] (DLA)
Gray Att Pr... Gray's Country Attorney's Practice [*9th ed.*] [*1869*] [*A publication*] (DLA)
Gray Att Pr... Grays Country Attorneys Practice (journ.) (SAUS)
GrayC........... Gray Communications Systems [*Associated Press*] (SAG)
GrayCom...... Gray Communications Systems [*Associated Press*] (SAG)
Gray Forms... Graydon's Forms of Conveyance [*A publication*] (DLA)
Gray Forms... Graydons Forms of Conveyance (journ.) (SAUS)
Graylands Ed News... Graylands Education News (journ.) (SAUS)
Gray (Mass)... Gray's Massachusetts Reports [*A publication*] (DLA)
Gray Perpetuities... Gray's Rule Against Perpetuities [*A publication*] (DLA)
Gray Perpetuities... Grays Rule Against Perpetuities (journ.) (SAUS)
GRAZ........... Grazioso [*Gracefully*] [*Music*]
GRAZO......... Grazioso [*Gracefully*] [*Music*]
GRB............. Gamma Ray Burst
GRB............. Gamma-Ray Bursters
GRB............. Garbo Industries [*Vancouver Stock Exchange symbol*]
GRB............. Gas Research Board (BUAC)
GRB............. Geophysical Research Board (SAUO)
GRB............. Geophysics Research Board
GRB............. Gerber Scientific [*NYSE symbol*] (TTSB)
GRB............. Gerber Scientific, Inc. [*NYSE symbol*] (SPSG)
GRB............. Gerber Sentific, Inc. (SAUO)
GRB............. Government Reservation Bureau
GRB............. Granatbuechse [*Antitank Grenade Rifle*] [*German*]
GRB............. Granolithic Base
GRB............. Green Bay [*Wisconsin*] [*Airport symbol*] (OAG)
GRB............. Group Psychotherapy (SAUO)
GRB............. Group Psychotherapy (journ.) (SAUS)
GRB............. Growth factor Receptor-Bound (SAUS)
GRB............. Guide to Reference Books (SAUS)
GRBAY......... Green Bay, WI [*American Association of Railroads railroad junction routing code*]
GRBC........... Goose Red Blood Cell
GRBC........... Great Banc (SAUS)
GRBC........... Great Southern Federal Savings Bank [*NASDAQ symbol*] (COMM)
GRBDS......... Gyroscopes-Rate Bomb-Direction System (AAG)
GRBF........... Generalized Radial Basis Function [*Mathematics*]
GRBL........... Garble (FAAC)
grbld........... Garbled (SAUS)
GRBM........... Global Range Ballistic Missile [*Air Force*]
GRBM........... Greek, Roman and Byzantine Monographs (journ.) (SAUS)
GRBM........... Ground Regional Battle Manager (ACAE)
GRBNKS...... Grand Banks (FAAC)
GRBR........... Gerber Energy International (SAUS)
GRBR........... Gerber Energy International, Inc. (SAUO)
Gr Br........... Great Britain (WGA)
Gr Brice....... Green's Edition of Brice's Ultra Vires [*A publication*] (DLA)
Gr Brit......... Great Britain
GRBS........... Gardeners' Royal Benevolent Society (BUAC)
GRBS........... Grating Rhomb Beam Sampler (ACAE)
GRBS........... Greek, Roman and Byzantine Studies (SAUO)
GRBSA......... Greek, Roman and Byzantine Scholarly Aids (journ.) (SAUS)
GRBU........... Gray Bunting [*North American bird banding code*] (BIBA)
GRBX........... Gearbox
GRC............. Gale Research Co. [*Later, GRI*]
GRC............. Gale Research Company (SAUO)
GRC............. gamma-ray counts (SAUS)
GRC............. Garchy [*France*] [*Seismograph station code, US Geological Survey*] (SEIS)
GRC............. Gearcase (MSA)
GRC............. Gendarmerie Royale du Canada [*Royal Canadian Mounted Police - RCMP*]
GRC............. General Railway Classification [*British*]
GRC............. General Reinsurance Corp. (EFIS)
GRC............. General Research and Development Policy Committee (SAUO)
GRC............. General Research Corp. [*Information service or system*] (IID)
GRC............. Generation of Reproducible Copy (SAUS)
GRC............. Generation Review Committee [*Nuclear Regulatory Commission*] (NRCH)
GRC............. Generic Reference Configuration (SAUS)
GRC............. Genetic Resources Center (SAUO)
GRC............. Geographic Resources Center [*University of Missouri - Columbia*] [*Research center*] (RCD)
GRC............. Geoscience Research Corp. (SAUO)
GRC............. Geotechnical Research Centre [*McGill University*] [*Canada*] [*Research center*] (RCD)
GRC............. Gerontology Research Center [*Department of Health and Human Services*] [*Research center*]
GRC............. Gerontotogy Research Center (SAUS)
GRC............. Glasgow Railway [*Federal Railroad Administration identification code*]
GRC............. Glass-fiber Reinforced Cement (SAUS)
GRC............. Glass-Fiber Reinforced Concrete
G R C........... Glass-fibre Reinforced Concrete (SAUS)
G R C........... Glass-Reinforced Cement (SAUS)
GRC............. Glass Reinforced Composite (SAUS)
GRC............. Glass-Reinforced Composite
GRC............. Glenmary Research Center (EA)
GRC............. Glenn Research Center [*NASA*] [*Astronomy term*]
GRC............. Global Reference Code [*Developed by Smithsonian Institution*]
GRC............. Gordon Research Conferences
GRC............. Gorman-Rupp [*AMEX symbol*] (TTSB)
GRC............. Gorman-Rupp Co. [*AMEX symbol*] (SPSG)
GRC............. Government of the Republic of China
GRC............. Government Relations Committee (ADWA)
GRC............. Government Research Centers Directory [*Later, GRD*] [*A publication*]
GRC............. Government Research Corp. [*Information service or system*] (IID)
GRC............. Government Research Corporation (SAUO)
GRC............. Grace
GRC............. Graduate Research Center (SAUO)
GRC............. Graduate Research Center of the Southwest [*Later, University of Texas at Dallas*]
GRC............. Grafted Rubber Concentrate [*Organic chemistry*]
GRC............. Grain Research Committee of WA (SAUO)
GRC............. Grand Cess [*Liberia*] [*Airport symbol*] (OAG)
GRC............. Graphite Reinforced Composite (SAUS)
GRC............. Greece [*ANSI three-letter standard code*] (CNC)
grc............. Greek, Ancient [*MARC language code*] [*Library of Congress*] (LCCP)
GRC............. Greek Red Cross (SAUO)
GRC............. Greene County District Library, Xenia, OH [*OCLC symbol*] (OCLC)
GRC............. Greenlandair Charter AS [*Denmark*] [*ICAO designator*] (FAAC)
GRC............. Grenn Rectifier Corporation (SAUO)
GRC............. Greyhound Racing Club (SAUO)
GRC............. Gross Replacement Cost (ADA)
GRC............. Ground Resolution Cell (SAUS)
GRC............. Group Repeat Count (SAUO)
GRC............. Growth and Change (journ.) (SAUS)
GRC............. Guard Ring Capacitor
GRC............. Gulf Reconstruction Center (JAGO)
GRC............. Gulf Research Corporation (SAUO)
GRCA........... German Representative Central Area (SAUO)
GRCA........... Glassfibre Reinforced Cement Association [*British*]
GRCA........... Golden Retriever Club of America (EA)
GRCA........... Grand Canyon National Park
Gr Ca........... Grant's Cases [*A publication*] (DLA)
GRCA........... Gray Catbird [*North American bird banding code*] (BIBA)
GRCA........... Ground Reference Coverage Area (DOMA)
Gr Cal........... Group Calculate (SAUO)
Gr Capt......... Group Captain [*British military*] (DMA)
GRCD........... German Rhine Coordination Directorate [*Allied German Occupation Forces*]
GRCDA......... Governmental Refuse Collection and Disposal Association (EA)
GRCESD....... Guizhou Provincial Research Centre of Economic & Social Development [*China*] (BUAC)
GRC Genet Resour Commun... GRC. Genetic Resources Communication (journ.) (SAUS)
GR CHAP...... Grand Chapter [*Freemasonry*] (ROG)
GRCHRSCHR... Die Griechische Christliche Schriftsteller der Ersten Drei Jahrhunderten (BJA)
GRCI........... German Radio Club International (SAUO)
GR/CIDS...... Genetic Resources/Communication, Information and Documentation System [*Databank*] (NITA)
GRC Int........ GRC International [*Associated Press*] (SAG)
Gr Cl........... Ground Cloth (SAUS)
GR/CL.......... Group and Class (SAUO)
GRCM........... Graduate of the Royal College of Music [*British*]
GRCO........... General radiochemical operator (SAUS)
GRCO........... General radius-chemical operator (SAUS)
GRCO........... Gradco Systems [*NASDAQ symbol*] (TTSB)
GRCO........... Gradco Systems, Inc. [*NASDAQ symbol*] (NQ)
GRCOL......... Ground Color (SAUS)
GR COUP...... Grosses Coupures (SAUS)
GRCOVSPR... Green Cove Springs, Florida (SAUO)
GR/CP.......... Group Registration for Contributions to Periodicals [*US Copyright Office form*]
Gr Cpt.......... Group Captain (SAUO)
GRCQ........... Grenfell Clinical Quarterly (journ.) (SAUS)
GrCr............. Grande Croix (EY)
GRCs........... Group Representation Constituencies (Singapore) [*Political party*] (PSAP)
GRCS........... Guard Rail Common Sensor [*Army*] (DOMA)
GR/CS.......... Guardrail/Common Sensor System [*Military*]
GRCS........... Gun Rocket Control System (SAUS)
GRCSCC....... Golden Ring Council of Senior Citizens Clubs [*Defunct*] (EA)
GRCSCTT...... Guardrail Common Sensor Commanders Tactical Terminal (SAUS)
GRCS GPF.... Guardrail Common Sensor Ground Processing Facility (SAUO)

GRCSW........ Graduate Research Center of the Southwest [*Formerly, Southwest Center for AdvancedStudies; later, University of Texas at Dallas*]
Gr Ctrl......... Group Control (SAUO)
Gr Ctrl Ent... Group Control Entry (SAUO)
Gr Ctrl Ex..... Group Control Exit (SAUO)
GRCTS......... Ground Combat Training Squadron
GRCTY......... Granite City, IL [*American Association of Railroads railroad junction routing code*]
GRCU........... Gun Rocket Control Unit (SAUS)
GrCu........... University of Crete, Crete, Greece [*Library symbol*] [*Library of Congress*] (LCLS)
GRCV........... Ground Cover [*Ecology*]
GRCV........... Guard Receiver (MCD)
GRCWA........ Grain Research Committee of Western Australia
GRCZ........... Granite City Steel [*Federal Railroad Administration identification code*]
GRD............ Gamma-Ray Detector (SAUS)
GRD............ Gastroesophageal Reflux Disease [*Gastroenterology*] (DAVI)
GRD............ Gateringdiode (SAUS)
GRD............ General Radio Discriminator (IAA)
GRD............ General Requirements Document (SAUS)
GRD............ Geographic Research Division (SAUO)
GRD............ Geophysics Research Directorate [*US*]
GRD............ Goldrich Resources, Inc. [*Vancouver Stock Exchange symbol*]
GRD............ Government Research Directory [*A publication*]
Grd............ Grade
GRD............ Grading
GRD............ Gradual, Reciprocated Defensification (SAUS)
GRD............ Gramicidin [*Antimicrobial compound*]
G-RD........... Gram-Rad (SAUS)
GR D........... Grand Duchess [*or Duke*] (ROG)
Gr D............ Grand Duchy (SAUO)
GRD............ Greatest Response Data
GRD............ Greenwood [*South Carolina*] [*Airport symbol*] (OAG)
GRD............ Grenada [*ANSI three-letter standard code*] (CNC)
GRD............ Grind (MSA)
grd............ Ground (VRA)
GRD............ Ground
GRD............ Ground Detector
GRD............ Ground Resolved Distance [*Satellite camera*]
GRD............ Ground Rule Double [*Baseball*]
Grd............ Ground Shells [*Quality of the bottom*] [*Nautical charts*]
GRD............ Guaranteed
GRD............ Guard
GRD............ Guardian Industries (SAUO)
GRD............ National Grid Co. [*British*] [*ICAO designator*] (FAAC)
GRDA........... Gin Rectifiers and Distillers Association [*British*] (DBA)
GRDAU......... Granddaughter (ROG)
GRDB........... Geoscientific Resource Data Base [*Queensland*] [*State*] (EERA)
GRDC........... Geological Research and Development Centre [*Indonesia*] (BUAC)
GRDC........... Global Runoff Data Center (SAUS)
GRDC........... Grains Research and Development Corporation [*Commonwealth*] [*State*] (EERA)
GRDC........... Gulf Research and Development Company (SAUO)
GrdCasn....... Grand Casinos, Inc. [*Associated Press*] (SAG)
GRDCUS....... Gulf Range Drone Control Upgrade System
GRDE........... Grade
GRDEI.......... Georgia RESA Director Evaluation Instrument (SAUO)
GrDelV......... Greater Delaware Valley Savings Bank [*Associated Press*] (SAG)
GRDEN......... Garden [*Commonly used*] (OPSA)
GRDF........... Gulf Rapid Deployment Force (SAUS)
GRDF........... Gypsum Roof Deck Foundation [*Later, NRDCA*] (EA)
GRDG........... Garden Ridge [*NASDAQ symbol*] (TTSB)
GRDG........... Garden Ridge Corp. [*NASDAQ symbol*] (SAG)
GrdIS........... Graduate Member of the Institute of Statisticians (SAUS)
Gr Div Ry...... Grand Division Railway (SAUO)
GRDL........... Geodetic Research and Development Laboratory [*Rockville, MD*] [*Department of Commerce*] (MSC)
GRDL........... Gradell Industries, Inc. [*NASDAQ symbol*] (SAG)
GRDL........... Gradual [*NWS*] (FAAC)
grdl............ gradually (SAUS)
GRDL........... Griddle (MSA)
GRDN........... Garden (ADA)
grdn............ Garden (ADWA)
GRDN........... Garden State Bancshares [*NASDAQ symbol*] (SAG)
GRDN........... Guardian
GRDN........... Guardian Technologies International, Inc. [*NASDAQ symbol*] (SAG)
GrdnB.......... Guardian Bancorp [*Associated Press*] (SAG)
GRDNR......... Gardener
GRDNS......... Gardens [*Commonly used*] (OPSA)
GRDNU......... Guardian Tech Intl Unit [*NASDAQ symbol*] (TTSB)
GR/D/O......... Granddaughter Of [*Genealogy*]
Grd Op......... Ground Operation (SAUS)
Grd Ops....... Ground Operations (SAUS)
GRDP........... Graphic Data Processing (IAA)
GrdPrd......... Guardsman Products, Inc. [*Associated Press*] (SAG)
GRDPRO....... Grid Procedure (SAA)
GrdPrx......... Grand Prix Association of Long Beach [*Associated Press*] (SAG)
GRDQ........... Groupe de Recherche sur la Demographie Quebecoise [*Research Group on Quebec Demography*] [*Canada*] (IRC)
GrdRnd........ Ground Round Restaurants, Inc. [*Associated Press*] (SAG)
GRDRS......... Geographically Referenced Data Storage and Retrieval System (SAUS)
GRDSR......... Geographically Referenced Data Storage and Retrieval System [*Canada*]
GRDSR......... Geographical Referenced Data Storage and Retrieval (SAUS)
GrdTch......... Guardian Technologies International, Inc. [*Associated Press*] (SAG)
GRDTN......... Graduation (MSA)
GRDTOT....... Grand Total (SAUS)
Grdwtr......... Groundwater Technology, Inc. [*Associated Press*] (SAG)
GRE............ Gamma Ray Experiment
GRE............ Gamma Ray Explorer (NASA)
GRE............ Gas Release Event (ABAC)
GRE............ GAUSSian Resolution Enhancemant (SAUS)
GRE............ General Real Estate Corp., Ltd. (SAUO)
GRE............ General Research Equipment (ABAC)
GRE............ Generated Repeatable Exams [*Education*]
GRE............ Generic Routing Encapsulation [*Computer science*]
GRE............ Glucocorticoid Responsive Element [*Endocrinology*]
GRE............ Going Rate Estimates (SAUS)
GRE............ Government Research Establishment
GRE............ Gradient-Recalled Echo [*Physics*]
GRE............ Graduate Record Exam (GAGS)
GRE............ Graduate Record Examination [*Higher education*]
GRE............ Graduate Record Examinations Board (EA)
GRE............ Graduate Reliability Engineering
GRE............ Grant-Related Expenditure [*British*]
GRE............ Graphics Engine (SAUS)
GRE............ Graphite-Reinforced Epoxy
GRE............ Gravitational Redshift Experiment (SSD)
Gre............. Greece (VRA)
GRE............ Greece (WDAA)
gre............. Greek, Modern [*MARC language code*] [*Library of Congress*] (LCCP)
GRE............ [*The*] Greens [*Australia*] [*Political party*]
GRE............ Greenstone Resources Ltd. [*Toronto Stock Exchange symbol*]
GRE............ Greenville, IL [*Location identifier*] [*FAA*] (FAAL)
GRE............ Grenada [*Seismograph station code, US Geological Survey*] (SEIS)
GRE............ Ground RADAR Equipment (IAA)
GRE............ Ground Read-Out Equipment (SAUS)
GRE............ Ground Reconnaissance Equipment
GRE............ Ground Reconstruction Electronics [*Used in photographing moon*] [*NASA*]
GRE............ Ground Reconstruction Equipment
GRE............ Ground Relay Equipment (SAUS)
GRE............ Ground Resolution Element (SAUS)
GRE............ Ground Run-Up Enclosure [*Aviation*] (DA)
GRE............ Grove Real Estate Asset Trust [*AMEX symbol*] (SAG)
GRE............ Guardian Royal Exchange [*Great Britain*]
GRE............ Guardian Royal Exchange Assurance [*British*]
GRE............ Gulf Resources & Chemical Corp. (SAUO)
Gre............. National Library of Greenland [*Nunatta Atuagaategarfi*], Nuuk, Greenland [*Library symbol*] [*Library of Congress*] (LCLS)
GRE............ SEEA-Southeast European Airlines [*Greece*] [*ICAO designator*] (FAAC)
GRE-A......... Graduate Record Examination-Analytical (ADWA)
GREA........... Grant-Related Expenditure Assessments [*British*]
GREACAM.... Guardian Royal Exchange Assurance Cameroun (BUAC)
GRE & E Div... Graves Registration and Effects Division [*Military*]
GREAT......... Gang Resistance, Education and Training (GOBB)
GREAT......... General Record of Enforcement Actions Tracked (SAUO)
GREAT......... Geriatric Education and Training Act [*1985*]
GREAT......... Gifted Resources Education Action Team Project (EDAC)
GREAT......... Gorda Ridge Eruption Assessment Team [*Marine science*] (OSRA)
GREAT......... Graduate Research, Engineering, and Technology Scholarships (FOTI)
GREAT......... Graduate Research in Engineering and Technology (SAUS)
GREAT......... Grampian Region Early Anistreplase Trial [*Cardiology study*]
GREAT......... Graphical Environment And Desktop (SAUS)
GREAT......... Graphics Research with Ellerbe Architects Technology (SAUO)
Greater Milw Dent Bull... Greater Milwaukee Dental Bulletin (journ.) (SAUS)
Greater St Louis Dent Soc Bull... Greater St. Louis Dental Society. Bulletin (journ.) (SAUS)
Great Lakes... Great Lakes Review (journ.) (SAUS)
Great Lakes Entomol... Great Lakes Entomologist (journ.) (SAUS)
Great Lakes Fish Comm Annu Rep... Great Lakes Fishery Commission. Annual Report (journ.) (SAUS)
Great Lakes Fish Comm Tech Rep... Great Lakes Fishery Commission. Technical Report (journ.) (SAUS)
Great Lakes Res Dir Univ Mich Publ... Great Lakes Research Division. University of Michigan. Publication (journ.) (SAUS)
Great Lakes Res Div Univ Mich... Great Lakes Research Division. University of Michigan. Publication (SAUO)
Great Lakes Res Rev... Great Lakes Research Review [*A publication*] (PABS)
Great Lon.... Greater London (SAUS)
Great Plains Agric Counc Publ... Great Plains Agricultural Council. Publication (journ.) (SAUS)
Great Red Spot... Anticyclone on Jupiter (SAUS)
Great Synag Cong J... Great Synagogue Congregational Journal (journ.) (SAUS)
Greav Cr L.... Greaves. Criminal Consolidation [*2nd ed.*] [*1862*] [*A publication*] (DLA)
Greaves....... Judgments of the Windward Islands Court of Appeal [*1866-1904*] [*A publication*] (DLA)
Greav Russ.... Greaves' Edition of Russell on Crimes [*A publication*] (DLA)
GREB........... Galactic Radiation Experiment Background (SAUO)
GREB........... Galactic Radiation Experiment Background Satellite [*Navy transit satellite*]
GREB........... General Reciprocating Engine Bulletin [*A publication*] (DNAB)
GREB........... Graduate Records Examination Board (WDAA)
GRE BOARD... Graduate Record Examinations Board (SAUO)
GREB Satellite... Galactic Radiation Experiment Background Satellite (SAUS)

GREC .... Geriatric Research, Education and Clinical Center (SAUS)
GRECA .... Group of Experts on Accident Consequences (SAUO)
GRECC .... Geriatric Research, Education, and Clinical Center [*Veterans Administration*]
GRED .... Generalized Random Extract Device [*Computer science*]
GRED .... Graph Editor for Signal Processing Programs (SAUS)
GREDI .... Groupe d'Etudes en Developpement International [*International Development Studies Group*] [*Canada*]
GREE .... General Requests for Ground-Based Electronics Equipment [*NASA*]
Greece&Rome New Surv Class... Greece and Rome. New Surveys in the Classics (journ.) (SAUS)
Greeen Cr .... Greens Criminal Law (journ.) (SAUS)
Greek Econ Rev... Greek Economic Review [*A publication*] (JLIT)
GREEMAIN... Agreement to Remain on Active Duty Until Date (SAUS)
GREEMAIN... Agreement to Remain on Active Duty Until Date Specified (DNAB)
GREEN .... General Research in the Environment for Eastern European Nations (SAUO)
GREEN .... Green [*Commonly used*] (OPSA)
Green .... Green College (SAUS)
Green .... Greenland (SAUS)
Green .... Greenlandic (DIAR)
Green .... Green's Reports [*A publication*] (DLA)
GREEN .... Guild to Revive Exhausted Nurses
Green & H Conv... Greenwood and Horwood's Conveyancing [*A publication*] (DLA)
GreenAP ...... Green [*A. P.*] Industries, Inc. [*Associated Press*] (SAG)
green Bag .... express go-ahead (SAUS)
Green Bag .... Green Bag; A Legal Journal [*Boston*] [*A publication*] (DLA)
Green BL ..... Green's Bankrupt Law [*A publication*] (DLA)
Green BL ..... Greens Bankrupt Law (journ.) (SAUS)
Greenbr .... [*The*] Greenbrier Companies, Inc. [*Associated Press*] (SAG)
Greenbri ...... Greenbriar Corp. [*Associated Press*] (SAG)
Green Bri ...... Green's Edition of Brice's Ultra Vires [*A publication*] (DLA)
Green Bull ... Green Bulletin (journ.) (SAUS)
Green Conv... Greenwood's Manual of Conveyancing [*9th ed.*] [*1897*] [*A publication*] (DLA)
Green Cr ...... Green's Criminal Law [*England*] [*A publication*] (DLA)
Green Cr Cas... Green's Criminal Cases [*A publication*] (DLA)
Green Crim Reports... Criminal Law Reports, by Green [*United States*] [*A publication*] (DLA)
Green Cr Law R... Green's Criminal Law Reports [*A publication*] (DLA)
Green Cr L Rep... Green's Criminal Law Reports [*A publication*] (DLA)
Green Cr Rep... Criminal Law Reports, by Green [*United States*] [*A publication*] (DLA)
Green Cruise... Greenleaf's Edition of Cruise's Digest of Real Property [*A publication*] (DLA)
Green Cts .... Greenwood on Courts [*A publication*] (DLA)
Greene .... Greene's Reports [*7 New York Annotated Cases*] [*A publication*] (DLA)
Green Ev ...... Greenleaf on Evidence [*A publication*] (DLA)
Green Forms... Greenings Forms of Declarations (journ.) (SAUS)
Green Forms... Greening's Forms of Declarations, Pleadings, Etc. [*A publication*] (DLA)
Greenh Pub Pol... Greenhood's Doctrine of Public Policy in the Law of Contracts [*A publication*] (DLA)
Greenh Pub Pol... Greenhoods Doctrine of Public Policy in the Law of Contracts (journ.) (SAUS)
Greenh Sh ... Greenhow's Shipping Law Manual [*A publication*] (DLA)
Greenh Sh ... Greenhows Shipping Law Manual (journ.) (SAUS)
Greenl .... Greenland (BARN)
Greenl .... Greenleaf's Reports [*1-9 Maine*] [*A publication*] (DLA)
Green L .... Greens Law Reports (journ.) (SAUS)
Greenl Cr ..... Greenleaf's Edition of Cruise's Digest of Real Property [*A publication*] (DLA)
Greenl Cruise... Greenleaf's Edition of Cruise's Digest of Real Property [*A publication*] (DLA)
Greenl Cruise Real Prop... Greenleaf's Edition of Cruise's Digest of Real Property [*A publication*] (DLA)
Greenl Cruise Real Prop... Greenleafs Edition of Cruises Digest of Real Property (journ.) (SAUS)
Greenl Ev .... Greenleaf on Evidence [*A publication*] (DLA)
Greenl Geosci... Greenland Geoscience (journ.) (SAUS)
Greenl Ov Cas... Greenleaf's Over-Ruled Cases [*A publication*] (DLA)
Greenl Test Ev... Greenleaf on the Testimony of the Evangelists [*A publication*] (DLA)
Greenman .... Greenman Technologies, Inc. [*Associated Press*] (SAG)
GreenNet ..... Global Computer Network for Environment, Peace and Human Rights (SAUO)
Green (NJ)... Green's New Jersey Law or Equity [*A publication*] (DLA)
Green Or Csa... Greenleafs Over-Ruled Cases (journ.) (SAUS)
Green Ov Cas... Greenleaf's Over-Ruled Cases [*A publication*] (DLA)
Green (RI) ... Green's Reports [*Rhode Island*] [*A publication*] (DLA)
Green Rom Law... Green's Outlines of Roman Law [*A publication*] (DLA)
Green Rom Law... Greens Outlines of Roman Law (journ.) (SAUS)
GREENS .... Global Redevelopment with Energy Environment Sustainability (SAUO)
GREENS .... Greens [*Commonly used*] (OPSA)
GreenS .... GreenStone Industries, Inc. [*Associated Press*] (SAG)
Green Sc Cr Cas... Green's Criminal Cases [*A publication*] (DLA)
Green Sc Tr... Green's Scottish Trials for Treason [*A publication*] (DLA)
Green Ship... Greenhow's Law of Shipowners [*A publication*] (DLA)
Green Ship... Greenhows Law of Shipowners (journ.) (SAUS)
GreenSt .... Green Street Financial Corp. [*Associated Press*] (SAG)
GreenStn ..... GreenStone Industries, Inc. [*Associated Press*] (SAG)
GREENTIE .... Global Remedy for the Environment and Energy Use-Technology Information Exchange
GREENTIE .... Greenhouse Gas Technology Information Exchange (SAUO)
GreenTR ...... GreenTree Financial Corp. [*Associated Press*] (SAG)
Greenw & M Mag Pol... Greenwood and Martin's Magistrates' Police Guide [*A publication*] (DLA)
Greenw Conv... Greenwood's Manual of Conveyancing [*9th ed.*] [*1897*] [*A publication*] (DLA)
Greenw Cts... Greenwood on Courts [*A publication*] (DLA)
Greenwich Time Rep... Greenwich Time Report (journ.) (SAUS)
GreenwSt ..... Greenwich Street Municipal Fund, Inc. [*Associated Press*] (SAG)
greeny .... environmentalist (SAUS)
GREER .... Greer, SC [*American Association of Railroads railroad junction routing code*]
Greer .... Greers Irish Land Acts (journ.) (SAUS)
Greer .... Greer's Irish Land Acts, Leading Cases [*1872-1903*] [*A publication*] (DLA)
GREF .... General Reserve Engineer Force [*British military*] (DMA)
Grefco .... General Refractories (SAUS)
GREFICOR ... Groupe de Recherche sur l'Efficacite Organisationnelle [*University of Quebec at Hull*] [*Research center*] (RCD)
G/REG .... Generator-Regulator [*Automotive engineering*]
G REG .... Grand Registrar [*Freemasonry*] (ROG)
GREG .... Gregorian (ROG)
Greg .... Gregorowski's Reports of the High Court [*A publication*] (DLA)
GREGG .... Gregg, OH [*American Association of Railroads railroad junction routing code*]
GregLA .... Pontificiae Universitatis Gregorianae Liber Annuus [*Rome*] [*A publication*] (BJA)
GRegO .... Group Regiment Officer [*British military*] (DMA)
Gregorowski... High Court Reports, Orange Free State [*A publication*] (DLA)
GREI .... Groupe de Recherche en Enseignement Individualise [*Canada*]
GreifBrA ...... Greif Brothers Corp. [*Associated Press*] (SAG)
GreifBrB ...... Greif Brothers Corp. [*Associated Press*] (SAG)
Greiner .... Greiner Engineering, Inc. [*Associated Press*] (SAG)
GREINER ...... Griner Engineering, Inc. (SAUO)
Grein Pr ...... Greiner's Louisiana Practice [*A publication*] (DLA)
GR EL .... Greatest Elongation (SAUS)
G Rel Per .... Guide to Religious Periodicals (journ.) (SAUS)
GRELY .... Greeley, CO [*American Association of Railroads railroad junction routing code*]
GREM .... Geopotential Research Explorer Mission (MCD)
GREM .... Gremlin [*Refers to a person unskilled in skateboarding*] [*Slang*] [*British*] (DSUE)
GREMAS ...... Genealogical Retrieval by Magnetic-tape Storage (SAUS)
GREMAS ...... Genealogische Recherche mit Magnetband-Speicherung [*Organic chemistry coding system*]
GREMAS ...... Generic Retrieval by Magnetic-Tape Storage [*Computer science*] (PDAA)
GREMEX ...... Goddard Research and Engineering Management Exercise [*NASA*]
GREMF .... Groupe de Recherche et d'Echange Multidisciplinaires Feministes [*Universite Laval, Quebec*] [*Canada*]
GREMLIN ..... Greater Manchester Local Government Information Network (SAUO)
GREMPA ...... Mediterranean Cooperative Research and Study Group on the Almond Tree (SAUO)
GREN .... Great Eastern Energy & Development Corp. (SAUO)
GREN .... Grenade (AABC)
Gren .... Grenier's Ceylon Reports [*A publication*] (DLA)
Grenada Agric Dep Rep... Grenada Agricultural Department. Report (journ.) (SAUS)
GRENAP ...... Greenlease Kidnapping
GRENDR ...... Grenadier (AABC)
Grenfld .... Greenfield Industries, Inc. [*Associated Press*] (SAG)
GREN GDS... Grenadier Guards (SAUO)
Grenier .... Grenier's Ceylon Reports [*A publication*] (DLA)
Grenm .... Greenman Brothers, Inc. [*Associated Press*] (SAG)
GRENV .... Greenville, SC [*American Association of Railroads railroad junction routing code*]
GRENW .... Greenwood, SC [*American Association of Railroads railroad junction routing code*]
GREP .... Generalized REgular Expression Parser (SAUS)
grep .... gets repeating patterns (SAUS)
grep .... Global Regular Expression and Print [*Computer science*] (CDE)
GREP .... Global Regular Expression Print (SAUS)
GREP .... Global Regular-Expression Purser [*Computer science*]
GREP .... Graphite Epoxy (ACAE)
GREP .... Graphite Epoxy Composite (SAUS)
GREPAT ...... Greenland Patrol [*Navy*]
GREPCO ...... Greenland Petroleum Consortium (SAUS)
GRE-Q .... Graduate Record Examination-Quantitative (ADWA)
GrEq .... Gresley's Equity Evidence [*A publication*] (DLA)
GRER .... Greenstone Resources Ltd. [*NASDAQ symbol*] (NQ)
GRERF .... Greenstone Res Ltd [*NASDAQ symbol*] (TTSB)
Gre Rom Law... Greene's Outlines of Roman Law [*A publication*] (DLA)
Gre Rom Law... Greenes Outlines of Roman Law (journ.) (SAUS)
GRES .... Global Renewable Energy Services [*Swinden, England*] [*Commercial firm*]
GRES .... Greatest Amount of Resources
Gres EqEv .... Gresley's Equity Evidence [*A publication*] (DLA)
GRESLET ..... Groupe de Recherche en Semantique, Lexicologie, et Terminologie [*Universite de Montreal, Quebec*] [*Canada*]
GRESP .... Green Spring, WV [*American Association of Railroads railroad junction routing code*]
GRETA .... Gamma-Ray Energy Tracking Array (SAUS)
GRETA .... Ground RADAR Emitter for Training Aviators [*Army*] (RDA)
GR et I .... Georgius Rex et Imperator [*George, King and Emperor*]
Gretton .... Oxford Quarter Sessions Records [*Oxford Record Society, No. 16*] [*A publication*] (DLA)

GRE-V .... Graduate Record Examination-Verbal (ADWA)
GrEv .... Greenleaf on Evidence [*A publication*] (DLA)
GREXIT .... Greatest Extreme in an Interval of Time (SAUS)
GREY .... Grey Advertising [*NASDAQ symbol*] (TTSB)
GreyAd .... Grey Advertising, inc. [*Associated Press*] (SAG)
Grey Deb .... Grey's House of Commons Debates [*A publication*] (DLA)
GreyhndL .... Greyhound Lines [*Associated Press*] (SAG)
GREYLN .... Greyhound Lines Inc. (SAUO)
GreyLne .... Greyhound Lines, Inc. [*Associated Press*] (SAG)
GRF .... Garbell Research Foundation (MCD)
GRF .... Gastrin-Releasing Factor [*Medicine*] (MELL)
GRF .... Gelatin, Resorcinol, and Formaldehyde
GRF .... Genetically-Related Factor [*Immunology*]
GRF .... Geographic Reference File [*Bureau of the Census*] (GFGA)
GRF .... Gerald Rudolf Ford [*US president, 1913-*]
GRF .... Gesneriad Research Foundation (EA)
GRF .... Glaucoma Research Foundation (SAUS)
GRF .... Golden Rule Foundation (EA)
GRF .... Gonadotropin-Releasing Factor [*Also, GnRF, GnRH, LH-RF, LH-RH/ FSH-RH, LRF, LRH*] [*Endocrinology*]
GRF .... Graefenberg Array [*Erlangen*] [*Federal Republic of Germany*] [*Seismograph station code, US Geological Survey*] (SEIS)
GRF .... Grain Research Foundation [*Australia*]
grf .... Grandfather (GEAB)
GRF .... Grandfather
GRF .... Graph (SAUS)
GRF .... Graphic Reproduction Federation (DGA)
GRF .... Grass Firm (SAUS)
GRF .... Grassland Research Foundation (EA)
GRF .... Gravity Research Foundation (EA)
Gr F .... Grazing Fire (SAUS)
GRF .... Greek Road Federation (BUAC)
GRF .... Grey Filly (SAUS)
GRF .... Ground Reaction Force [*Army*] (INF)
GRF .... Ground Repetition Frequency (SAUS)
GRF .... Group Repetition Frequency
GRF .... Growth Hormone Releasing Factor [*Somatoliberin*] [*Also, GH-RF, GH-RH*] [*Endocrinology*]
GRF .... Guanine-Nucleotide Release Factor [*Biochemistry*] (QSUL)
GRF .... Guaranty Reserve Fund
GRF .... Guild Resource File [*Guild Products, Inc.*] [*Computer science*] (PCM)
GRF .... Tacoma/Fort Lewis, WA [*Location identifier*] [*FAA*] (FAAL)
GRFC .... Growth Financial Corp. [*NASDAQ symbol*] (SAG)
GRFCE .... General Requirements For Coal Exploration (SAUO)
GR-FeSV .... Gardner-Rasheed Feline Sarcoma Virus
GRFF .... General Radio Frequency Fitting (IAA)
G/Rfg .... Grooved Roofing [*Lumber*] (DAC)
GRFIA .... Grinding and Finishing (journ.) (SAUS)
GRFL .... Gerald R. Ford Library
grfl .... Ground Floor [*Construction term*] (MIST)
GRFL .... Groundwater Remediation Field Laboratory [*Environmental science*] (BCP)
grflar .... Ground Floor Area [*Construction term*] (MIST)
GRFM .... General Radio Frequency Meter (IAA)
G R F M .... General Radio-Frequency Meter (SAUS)
GRFMA .... Grand Rapids Furniture Market Association [*Inactive*] (EA)
GRF-N .... Geographic Reference File-Names (SAUS)
GRFO .... Gun Range-Finder Operator
GR FOOD .... GR Foods, Inc. (SAUO)
GRFP .... Graphite Reinforced Fiber Plastic (ACAE)
GrFRP .... Graphite-Fiber-Reinforced Plastic [*Also, GFRP*]
GRFS .... Greencastle Federal Savings Bank (SAUS)
GRFTN .... Grafton, OH [*American Association of Railroads railroad junction routing code*]
GRFX .... Grinding Fixture
GRFZ .... Grand Fork Milling [*Federal Railroad Administration identification code*]
GRG .... Gastroenterology Research Group [*Defunct*] (EA)
GRG .... Gearing (MSA)
G R G .... Generalised Reduced Gradient (SAUS)
GRG .... Generalized Reduced Gradient
GRG .... General Recurrent Grant
GRG .... Geologic Review Group (SAUO)
GRG .... Georgetown [*Guyana*] [*Airport symbol*] (AD)
GRG .... Glass-Fiber Reinforced Gypsum [*Substitute wood*]
GRG .... Glycine-Rich Glycoprotein (DMAA)
GRG .... Gordetsky [*G.R.*] Telecommunications and General Management Consulting [*San Diego, CA*] [*Telecommunications*] (TSSD)
Grg .... Gorgias [*of Plato*] [*Classical studies*] (OCD)
GRG .... Grading (SAUS)
GRG .... Grandparents Raising Grandchildren (EA)
GRG .... Graphical Rewriting Grammar
GRG .... Greenery Rehabilitation Group, Inc. (SAUO)
GRG .... Gross Reserve Generation [*Electronics*] (IEEE)
GRG .... International Committee on General Relativity and Gravitation (SAUO)
GRGC .... Great Falls Gas Co. [*NASDAQ symbol*] (COMM)
GRGDB .... Gryehound Racing Grounds Development Board [*Victoria, Australia*]
GRGE .... Garage [*Classified Advertising*] (ADA)
GRGE .... Gorge [*Board on Geographic Names*]
Gr Gesch .... Griechische Geschichte [*A publication*] (OCD)
GRGI .... Greenery Rehabilitation Group, Inc. (MHDW)
GRGL .... Groundwater Residue Guidance Level [*Environmental Protection Agency*]
GRGS .... Grand Ridge Grade School (SAUO)
GRGS .... Ground Roll Guidance System (MCD)
GRGT .... Guam Remote Ground Terminal (SAUS)
GRGTN .... Georgetown, TX [*American Association of Railroads railroad junction routing code*]
GRGVL .... Greigsville, NY [*American Association of Railroads railroad junction routing code*]
GRGZ .... Grand Grit [*Federal Railroad Administration identification code*]
GRH .... Garuahi [*Papua New Guinea*] [*Airport symbol*] (OAG)
GRH .... Gas Recycle Hydrogenation [*Petroleum engineering*]
GRH .... Gentlemen's Right Handed [*Golf club*]
GRH .... Gonadotropin-Releasing Hormone (ADWA)
GRH .... Grahamstown [*South Africa*] [*Seismograph station code, US Geological Survey*] [*Closed*] (SEIS)
GRH .... Gramm-Rudman-Hollings [*Law*]
GRH .... Gramm-Rudman-Hollings Budget Deficit Control Act (AAGC)
GRH .... GRC International [*NYSE symbol*] (SPSG)
GRH .... Green Hills Aviation Ltd. (SAUO)
GRH .... Greer Hydraulics, Inc. (SAUO)
GRH .... Growth Hormone Releasing Hormone [*Somatoliberin*] [*Also, GH-RF, GRF*] [*Endocrinology*] (MAE)
GRHA .... Ground Handling (SAUS)
GRHA S/C .... Ground Handling Subcommittee (SAUS)
GrhmFL .... Graham-Field Health Products, Inc. [*Associated Press*] (SAG)
GRHQU .... Gruppen-Hauptquartier [*Group Headquarters*] [*German military - World War II*]
GRHS .... Germans-from-Russia Heritage Society (EA)
GRHX .... Gulf Railcar [*Private rail car owner code*]
GRI .... Gabriel Richard Institute (EA)
GRI .... Gale Research, Inc.
GRI .... Gallaudet Research Institute [*Gallaudet College*] [*Research center*] (RCD)
GRI .... Gamma Ray Imaging Telescope System (SAUS)
GRI .... Gamma Ray Inspection
GRI .... Gas Research Institute (EA)
GRI .... General Religions International (SAUS)
GRI .... General rules of interpretation (SAUS)
GRI .... Generic Run-Time [*Computer science*]
GRI .... Geographical Review of India (journ.) (SAUS)
GRI .... Geophysical Research Institute [*University of New England, Australia*]
GRI .... Geoscience Research Institute
GRI .... Geothermal Resources International (SAUO)
GRI .... Gidley Research Institute [*Research center*] (RCD)
GRI .... Ginseng Research Institute (EA)
GRI .... Glasgow Royal Infantry (SAUO)
GRI .... Glasshouse Research Institute (SAUO)
GRI .... Glider Developments, Inc. [*Vancouver Stock Exchange symbol*]
GRI .... Global Readiness Index
Gri .... Glyceric Acid [*Biochemistry*]
GRI .... Goodwin Railroad [*Federal Railroad Administration identification code*]
GRI .... Gospel Recordings, Inc.
GRI .... Government of the Ryukyu Islands
GRI .... Government Reports Index [*Formerly, USGRDR-I*] [*Department of Commerce*]
GRI .... Government Research Index (MCD)
GR-I .... Government Rubber-Isobutylene [*Synthetic rubber*]
GRI .... Graduate Realtors Institute
GRI .... Grand Island [*Nebraska*] [*Airport symbol*] (OAG)
GRI .... Graphical Interactive Display (SAUS)
GRI .... Grassland Research Institute [*Research center*] [*British*] (IRC)
GRI .... Grassroots International (EA)
GRI .... Gravure Research Institute [*Later, GAA*] (EA)
GRI .... Gristede's Sloan's [*AMEX symbol*] [*Formerly, Sloan's Supermarkets*] (SG)
GRI .... Groupe de Recherche et d'Intervention en Ideologie [*Universite du Quebec a Montreal*] [*Canada*]
GRI .... Group Repetition Interval (IEEE)
GRI .... Guaranteed Retirement Income
GRIB .... Gridded Binary [*Data Format*] [*Marine science*] (OSRA)
GRIB .... Gridded Binary Form [*Computer science*]
GRIBAT .... Graphics Interface Basic Acceptance Test (MCD)
GRIC .... Global Reach Internet Connection [*Computer science*]
GRIC .... Global Roaming Internet Connection [*Computer science*]
GRIC .... Graduate Member of the Royal Institute of Chemistry [*British*] (DBQ)
GRICAAS .... Grassland Research Institute, Chinese Academy of Agricultural Sciences (BUAC)
GRID .... Gas Research Institute Digest [*Acronym is used as title of publication*] [*A publication*]
GRID .... Gay-Related Immune Deficiency (DIPS)
GRID .... Gay-Related Immune Disease [*Medicine*] (WDAA)
GRID .... Gay-Related Immunodeficiency Disease [*Medicine*] (GOBB)
GRID .... Gec Rectangular Image and Data (SAUS)
GRID .... GEC [*General Electric Company*] Rectangular Image Data Processor (NITA)
GRID .... Global Resource Information Database [*NASA*]
GRID .... Gradient Imaging Display Software (SAUS)
GRID .... Graphical Interactive Display (SAUS)
GRID .... Graphical Intermediate Data Format (SAUS)
GRID .... Graphic Interactive Display (IEEE)
GRID .... Graphic Remote Integrated Display (SAUS)
GRID .... Graphic Remote Interface Display (SAUS)
GRID .... Graphic Reproduction by Integrated Design
GRID .... Graphic Retrieval and Information Display (NASA)
grid .... Gridiron [*Typography*] [*Theater*] (WDMC)
GRID .... Ground Radio Interface Devices (ACAE)

GRIDEQ........ Groupe de Recherche en Developpement de l'Est du Quebec [*Canada*]
grid OD........ Grid Organizational Development (DIPS)
GRIDS.......... Geographic Resources Information Data System [*Environmental Protection Agency*] (AEPA)
GRIDS.......... Geophysical Range Input Detection System
GRIDS.......... Gridded Resource Inventory Data System-Washington State (SAUS)
GRIDS.......... Grid Referenced Information Display System (SAUO)
GRIDS.......... Guidelines for Review and Internal Development in Schools (AIE)
GRIER.......... Ground Rescue, Infiltrate, Exfiltrate, Resupply (SAUS)
GRIF........... Government Research Institute of Formosa
GRIF........... Graduate Research, Internship, and Fellowshhip
GRIF........... Griffin Land & Nurseries, Inc. [*NASDAQ symbol*] (NASQ)
GRIF........... Griffin Technology, Inc. [*NASDAQ symbol*] (NQ)
GRIF........... Growth Hormone Release Inhibiting Factor [*Also, GH-RIF, GH-RIH, SRIF, SS*] [*Endocrinology*]
Grif Cr......... Griffith on Arrangements with Creditors [*A publication*] (DLA)
Grif Ct Mar... Griffith on Military Law and Courts-Martial [*A publication*] (DLA)
Grif Eq......... Griffith's Institutes of Equity [*A publication*] (DLA)
GRIFF.......... Griffith, IN [*American Association of Railroads railroad junction routing code*]
GRIFF.......... Groupe de Recherches Interdisciplinaires des Fertilisation des Forets [*Joint federal-provincial project*] [*Canada*]
Griffin Pat Cas... Griffin's Patent Cases [*1866-87*] [*A publication*] (DLA)
Griffin Pat Cs... Griffins Patent Cases (journ.) (SAUS)
Griffin PC..... Griffin's Abstract of Patent Cases [*England*] [*A publication*] (DLA)
Griffin PC..... Griffins Abstract of Patent Cases (journ.) (SAUS)
Griffith......... Griffith's Reports [*1-5 Indiana Appeals and 117-132 Indiana*] [*A publication*] (DLA)
Griffns Statist Monograph Ser... Griffins Statistical Monograph Series (journ.) (SAUS)
Griffon......... Griffon Corp. [*Associated Press*] (SAG)
Griff Pat Cas... Griffin's Patent Cases [*1866-87*] [*A publication*] (DLA)
GrifGam....... Griffin Gaming & Entertainment [*Associated Press*] (SAG)
Grif Inst....... Griffith's Institutes of Equity [*A publication*] (DLA)
Grif Jud Acts... Griffith on the Judicature Acts [*A publication*] (DLA)
Grif L Reg... Griffith's Law Register [*Burlington, NJ*] [*A publication*] (DLA)
Grif Mar Wom... Griffith's Married Women's Property Act [*A publication*] (DLA)
Grif Mil Law... Griffith on Military Law and Courts-Martial [*A publication*] (DLA)
Grif Pat C.... Griffin's Patent Cases [*1866-87*] [*A publication*] (DLA)
Grif PC......... Griffin's Patent Cases [*1866-87*] [*A publication*] (DLA)
Grif PLC........ Griffin's London Poor Law Cases [*1821-31*] [*A publication*] (DLA)
Grif PL Cas... Griffith's London Poor Law Cases [*1821-31*] [*A publication*] (DLA)
Grif Pr......... Griffith's Practice [*A publication*] (DLA)
Grif PRC....... Griffith's Poor Rate Cases [*A publication*] (DLA)
Grif PR Cas... Griffith's English Poor Rate Cases [*A publication*] (DLA)
Grif St.......... Griffith's Stamp Duties [*A publication*] (DLA)
GrifTch......... Griffin Technology, Inc. [*Associated Press*] (SAG)
GR-IH........... Growth Release-Inhibiting [*Medicine*] (EDAA)
GRIL............ Gale Research International Ltd.
GRIL............ Grill Concepts [*NASDAQ symbol*] (TTSB)
GRIL............ Grill Concepts, Inc. [*NASDAQ symbol*] (SAG)
GrillCon....... Grill Concepts, Inc. [*Associated Press*] (SAG)
GRILLE......... Grille Spectrometer (SAUS)
Grim Bank... Grimsey's Proceedings in Bankruptcy [*A publication*] (DLA)
GRIMCO....... CGBAPS Computing System (SAUO)
Grimke Ex..... Grimke on Executors and Administrators [*A publication*] (DLA)
Grimke Jus... Grimke's Justice [*A publication*] (DLA)
Grimke PL... Grimke's Public Laws of South Carolina [*A publication*] (DLA)
GRIN............ Geographic Reference Identification Number (SAUS)
GRIN............ Germplasm Resources Information Network [*Department of Agriculture*] [*Beltsville, MD*]
GRIN............ Glasgow Reference and Information Network (SAUS)
GRIN............ Graded Index (SAUS)
GRIN............ Graded-Index Fiber (ACRL)
GRIN............ Graded Refractive-Index [*Optics*]
GRIN............ Gradient of Refractive Index [*Optics*]
GRIN............ Grands Toys Intl [*NASDAQ symbol*] (TTSB)
GRIN............ Grand Toys International [*NASDAQ symbol*] (SAG)
GRIN............ Graphical Input [*Language*] [*Computer science*]
GRIN............ Graphical Interaction (SAUS)
GRIN............ Great Plains [*AAR code*]
GRIN-2......... Graphical Interaction [*Language*] [*Computer science*]
GRIN-A......... Geographical Review of (SAUS)
GRIND......... Graphical Interpretive Display (SAUS)
GRIND......... Grinding
GRIND......... Group Index (MCD)
Gr Ind Elim... Group Indication Elimination (SAUO)
GRINDER..... Graphical Interactive Network Designer
GRINL.......... Grinnell, IA [*American Association of Railroads railroad junction routing code*]
GRIN Language... Graphical Input Language (SAUO)
GRIN Language... Graphical Interaction Language (SAUO)
GRINM......... General Research Institute for Non-Ferrous Metals [*China*] (BUAC)
GRINS.......... General Retrieval Inquiry Negotiation Structure
GRINS.......... Graphical Input of SMILES [*Simplified Molecular Line Editor System*] Input
GRINSCH..... Graded Index Separate Confinement Heterostructure (AAEL)
GR Insights... Gas Research Insights (journ.) (SAUS)
GRINW......... Grand Toys Intl Wrrt [*NASDAQ symbol*] (TTSB)
gr/iny........... Grain per Square Inch (SAUS)
GRINZ.......... Genealogical Research Institute of New Zealand (SAUO)
GRIP............ Gay Rights in Prison [*An association*] (BUAC)
GRIP............ Gemini Reentry Integration Program [*NASA*]
GRIP............ General Retrieval of Information Program [*Hoechst Pharmaceutical Research Laboratories*] [*Personal indexing system*] [*British*] (NITA)
GRIP............ General Revenue Insurance Plan (SAUO)
GRIP............ Gerontological Information Program (SAUS)
GRIP............ Glucocorticoid Receptor-Interacting Protein [*Biology*]
GRIP............ Glutamate Receptor Interacting Protein [*Neurochemistry*]
GRIP............ Grandmet Information Processing [*British*]
GRIP............ Graphics Interaction with Proteins [*Computer graphics*]
GRIP............ Graphics Interactive Program (NITA)
GRIP............ Graphics Interactive Programming
GRIP............ Graphics Interactive Programming Language [*McDonnell-Douglas Corp.*]
GRIP............ Graphies Interactive Programming (SAUS)
GRIP............ Grass Roots Improvement Program (SAUO)
GRIP............ Greater Roxbury Incorporation Project (SAUO)
GRIP............ Greenland Icecore Project [*Europe*] [*Marine science*] (OSRA)
GRIP............ Greenland Icesheet Program [*Europe*] [*Marine science*] (OSRA)
GRIP............ Gross Revenue Insurance Program (FOTI)
GRIP............ Groupe de Recherche sur les Insectes Piqueurs [*University of Quebec at Trois-Rivieres*] [*Canada*] [*Research center*] (RCD)
GRIP............ Guaranteed Recovery of Investment Principal [*Economics*]
GRIP............ Guaranteed, Reliable, Interoperable, Processing [*Computer science*] (HODG)
GRIP............ International Grouping of Pharmaceuticals Distributors in the EEC (ECED)
GRIP............ Royal Grip [*NASDAQ symbol*] (TTSB)
GRIP............ Royal Grip, Inc. [*NASDAQ symbol*] (SAG)
GRIPHOS..... General Retrieval and Information Processing for Humanities-Oriented Studies (SAUS)
GRIPHOS..... General Retrieval and Information Processor for Humanities Oriented Studies
griphos........ general retrieval and information processor humanities-oriented studies (SAUS)
GRIPHOS..... General Retrieval and Infornmation Processing for Generating Station Humanities-Oriented Studies (SAUS)
GRIPP.......... Global Review and Inventory of Population Policies (FOTI)
GRIPS.......... Gaming, Random Interfacing, and Problem Structuring (PDAA)
G R I P S..... Garning Random Interfacing and Problem Structuring (SAUS)
GRIPS.......... GCM-Reality Intercomparison Project for SPARC (SAUS)
GRIPS.......... General Relation-Based Information Processing System - a retrieval language (SAUS)
GRIPS.......... Gift Reporting and Information Processing System (SAUO)
GRIPS.......... Government Raster Image Processing Software (SAUS)
GRIPS.......... Graphic Image Pagination System [*Penta Systems International*]
GRIPS.......... Ground Reconnaissance Information Processing System (DNAB)
GRIPS89...... Government Raster Image Processing Software and Data (SAUS)
GRIR............ Groupe de Recherche et d'Intervention Regionales [*Universite du Quebec a Chicoutimi*] [*Canada*]
GRIS............ Gamma-Ray Imaging Spectrometer
GRIS............ Global Resources Information System
gris............. Grisaille (VRA)
GRIS............ Grisons [*Canton in Switzerland*] (ROG)
GRIS............ Groupe de Recherche Interdisciplinaire en Sante [*Interdisciplinary Health Research Group - IHRG*] [*Universite de Montreal*] [*Canada*] [*Research center*]
GRISAH........ Groupe de Recherche et d'Intervention sur les Systemes d'Activities Humaines [*University of Quebec at Rimouski*] [*Research center*] (RCD)
GRISL.......... Grand Island, NE [*American Association of Railroads railroad junction routing code*]
GRISS.......... Golombok Rust Inventory of Sexual Satisfaction [*Test*] [*Psychology*]
GRIST.......... Gas Reactor in-pile Safety Test loop (SAUO)
GRIST.......... Grazing-Incidence Solar Telescope
GristMil....... Grist Mill Co. [*Associated Press*] (SAG)
GRISUR........ Grupo de Informacion y Solidaridad Uruguay [*Switzerland*]
Grisw........... Griswold's Reports [*14-19 Ohio*] [*A publication*] (DLA)
Griswold...... Griswold's Reports [*14-19 Ohio*] [*A publication*] (DLA)
Grisw Und... Griswold's Fire Underwriter's Text-Book [*A publication*] (DLA)
GRIT............ Gradual Reduction in Temperature (SAUS)
GRIT............ Gradual Reduction Tensions (SAUS)
GRIT............ Graduated and Reciprocated Initiatives in Tension Reduction [*C. Osgood*] (DIPS)
GRIT............ Graduated Reduction in Tensions [*Cold War term*]
GRIT............ Grantor-Retained Income Trust [*Estate planning*]
GRIT............ Grapple Removal Installation Tool (SAUS)
GRIT............ Greater Regional Industrial Technology (SAUS)
GRIT............ Grubb & Ellis Realty Income Trust (SAUO)
Grits............ Boiled Grits (SAUS)
GRITS.......... Gamma-Ray Imaging Telescope Study (SAUS)
GRITS.......... Gamma Ray Imaging Telescope System
GRITS.......... Geothermal Resource Interactive Temporal Simulation (PDAA)
GRITS.......... Goddard Range [*and Range Rate*] Instrumentation Tracking System [*NASA*] (AAG)
GRIV............ Gauley River Railroad [*Federal Railroad Administration identification code*]
GRIV............ Great River Junction, MS [*American Association of Railroads railroad junction routing code*]
GRIX............ Gulf Railcar [*Private rail car owner code*]
Griz............. Grizzly (SAUS)
Grizz............ Grizzly Bear (SAUS)
GRJ............. George [*South Africa*] [*Airport symbol*] (OAG)
GRJ............. Gorje [*Yugoslavia*] [*Seismograph station code, US Geological Survey*] [*Closed*] (SEIS)
GRJC........... Grand Rapids Junior College [*Michigan*]

GRJCT .... Grand Junction, TN [*American Association of Railroads railroad junction routing code*]

GRK .... Gear Rack

GRK .... Golden Rock Resources Ltd. [*Vancouver Stock Exchange symbol*]

GRK .... Goroka [*Papua New Guinea*] [*Seismograph station code, US Geological Survey*] [*Closed*] (SEIS)

GRK .... G Protein Receptor Kinase [*An enzyme*]

GRK .... Greek [*Language, etc.*]

GRK .... Killeen, TX [*Location identifier*] [*FAA*] (FAAL)

GRKA .... Greka Energy [*NASDAQ symbol*]

GRL .... Gamma Ray Laboratory (SAUS)

GRL .... General

GRL .... General Instrument Corp. (SAUO)

GRL .... Geophysical Research Letters [*A publication*]

GRL .... Gerontology Research Center, Baltimore, MD [*OCLC symbol*] (OCLC)

GRL .... Goldenrod Resources & Technology, Inc. [*Vancouver Stock Exchange symbol*]

GRL .... Government Research Laboratories

GRL .... Government Rubber L (SAUS)

Gr-L .... Graeco-Latin (SAUS)

GRL .... Grain Research Laboratory [*Canadian Grain Commission*] [*Research center*] (RCD)

GRL .... Greenland [*ANSI three-letter standard code*] (CNC)

GRL .... Grill

GRL .... Grille

GRL .... Gronlandsfly Ltd. [*Denmark*] [*ICAO designator*] (FAAC)

GRL .... Gross Reference List (DNAB)

GRL .... Gross Regional Loss (SAUS)

GRL .... Gross Requirements List (ACAE)

GRL .... Grundrichtungslinie [*Base line, a gunnery term*] [*German military - World War II*]

GRL .... Gulf Indonesia Resources [*NYSE symbol*] (SG)

GRLD .... Graphic Remote Interface Display (SAUO)

Grld .... Greenland (VRA)

GRLH .... Garland Reference Library of the Humanities (journ.) (SAUS)

GrLJ .... Georgetown Law Journal (journ.) (SAUS)

GRLL .... Roadhouse Grill, Inc. [*NASDAQ symbol*] (SAG)

GRLP .... Ground Lamp (IAA)

GrLR .... Great Lakes Review. A Journal of Midwest Culture (journ.) (SAUS)

GRLS .... Great River Library System [*Library network*]

Gr Lt .... Gunner Lieutenant (SAUO)

GRLZ .... Grain Land Co-Operative [*Federal Railroad Administration identification code*]

grm .... gaseous radiation monitor (SAUS)

grm .... gaseous radikation moniker (SAUS)

GRM .... Generalized Reed-Muller [*Codes*] (IEEE)

GRM .... Generalized Report Module Program [*Computer science*]

GRM .... Geographic Reference Manual (SAUS)

GRM .... Geophysical Research Mission [*Marine science*] (OSRA)

GRM .... Geopotential Research Mission [*NASA*]

GRM .... Germ [*or Germination*] (WGA)

GRM .... Germination (SAUS)

GRM .... Global Range Missile [*Air Force*]

GRM .... Golden Reward Mine (SAUO)

GRM .... Government Request Military (SAUO)

GR-M .... Government Rubber-Monovinylacetylene (SAUS)

GRM .... Grahamstown [*South Africa*] [*Seismograph station code, US Geological Survey*] (SEIS)

GRM .... Gram (ADA)

GRM .... Gramme [*Gram*] [*French*] (ROG)

GRM .... Grand Marais, MN [*Location identifier*] [*FAA*] (FAAL)

GRM .... Grand Metropolitan ADS [*NYSE symbol*] (SPSG)

GRM .... Grandmother

GRM .... Grand Reef Mine (SAUO)

GRM .... Graziano, R. M., Washington DC [*STAC*]

GRM .... Great Renunciation Movement (EA)

GRM .... Grenade carrier for Mortars (SAUS)

grm .... Grooming (IDYL)

grm .... Gross Rent (SAUS)

GRM .... Gross Rent Multiplier [*Business term*] (EMRF)

GRM .... Gruppe Revolutionaerer Marxisten [*Group of Revolutionary Marxists*] [*Austria*] [*Political party*] (PPE)

GRM .... Guarded Relay Multiplexer

GRM .... Guidance Rate Measurement

GRM .... Guidance Rate Measuring (SAUO)

GRM .... NASA Gravity Satellite (SAUO)

gr/m3 .... Grammes per Cubic Metre (SAUS)

GRMBL .... Grumble [*Computer hacker terminology*]

GRM Code .... Generalized Reed-Muller Code (SAUS)

GRMDA .... Gerrnan Medicine (journ.) (SAUS)

GRMI .... GRM Industries, Inc. (SAUO)

GRMMA .... German Medical Monthly (journ.) (SAUS)

GRMN .... Garment Graphics [*NASDAQ symbol*] (TTSB)

GRMN .... Garment Graphics, Inc. [*NASDAQ symbol*] (SAG)

GRMN .... Garmin Ltd. [*NASDAQ symbol*]

GRMNW .... Garment Graphics Wrrt'A' [*NASDAQ symbol*] (TTSB)

GRMNZ .... Garment Graphics Wrrt'B' [*NASDAQ symbol*] (TTSB)

grmo .... Grandmother (GEAB)

GrMonk .... Grease Monkey Holding Corp. [*Associated Press*] (SAG)

grmp .... generalized report module program (SAUS)

gr m p .... Grosso Modo Pulverisatum [*Ground in a Coarse Way*] [*Latin*] (STED)

GRMP .... Gurkha Royal Military Police (SAUO)

GRMPrA .... Grand Met Del L.P. 9.42% Pfd [*NYSE symbol*] (TTSB)

GRMRA .... Gift Retailers, Manufacturers, and Reps Association (EA)

GRMS .... Gravities Route Mean Square (SAUS)

grmt .... Garment (VRA)

GRMT .... Garment

GRMT .... Government Request Military Tarif (SAUS)

GRMT .... Grommet [*Automotive engineering*]

GRMV .... Green Ring Mottle Virus (SAUS)

GRMX .... Gopher State Railway Museum [*Private rail car owner code*]

GRMX .... Great Miami & Western Railway [*Federal Railroad Administration identification code*]

GrN .... C-14 dates by the Isotope laboratory of Groningen University (SAUS)

GRN .... Generalized Regulation Net (SAUS)

GRN .... General Re Corp. [*NYSE symbol*] (SPSG)

GRN .... Global Recycling Network (SAUO)

Grn .... Glycerone [*Biochemistry*]

GRN .... Goods Received Note (SAUS)

GRN .... Gordon, NE [*Location identifier*] [*FAA*] (FAAL)

GRN .... Government Rubber Nitrile (SAUO)

Gr N .... Graduate Nurse

GrN .... Gram-Negative (STED)

GRN .... Gram-Negative [*Also, GN*] [*Microbiology*]

GRN .... Granite [*Technical drawings*]

GRN .... Granule [*Medicine*]

GRN .... Granulin (DMAA)

GRN .... Green (KSC)

Grn .... Green (STED)

grn .... Green (VRA)

GRN .... Greenair Hava Tasimaciligi AS [*Turkey*] [*ICAO designator*] (FAAC)

GRN .... Greens [*Political party*] [*Australia*]

GRN .... Greenville & Northern Railway Co. [*AAR code*]

GRN .... Greenwich Library, Greenwich, CT [*OCLC symbol*] (OCLC)

GRN .... Grenoble [*France*] [*Seismograph station code, US Geological Survey*] (SEIS)

GRN .... Grenoble Energy [*Vancouver Stock Exchange symbol*]

GrN .... Groningen University (SAUO)

GRNA .... German Representative Northern Area (SAUO)

gRNA .... Guide Ribonucleic Acid [*Genetics*]

GRNBIO .... Granada Bio Sciences (SAUS)

GRNC .... GranCare, Inc. (SAUO)

GRNC .... Group Not Counted (SAUS)

GRNC .... Group Number No Count [*Military communication*]

GRNC .... Groups Not Counted (SAUS)

GRNCA .... Greencastle, IN [*American Association of Railroads railroad junction routing code*]

GRNCM .... Graduate of the Royal Northern College of Music [*British*] (DBQ)

GRND .... Grand

GRND .... Ground (ADA)

grnd .... Ground (ADWA)

grnd .... Ground (MIST)

GrnDan .... Green [*Daniel*] Co. [*Associated Press*] (SAG)

GrndM .... Grand Metropolitan Delaware Ltd. [*Associated Press*] (SAG)

GRNDMA .... Grandma

GrndMet .... Grand Metropolitan Ltd. [*Associated Press*] (SAG)

GRNDPA .... Grandpa

GrndPr .... Grand Premier Financial, Inc. [*Associated Press*] (SAG)

GRNDR .... Grinder [*s*] [*Freight*]

Grnds .... Grounds (DD)

GrndToy .... Grand Toys International [*Associated Press*] (SAG)

GrndUn .... Grand Union Co. [*Associated Press*] (SAG)

Grnet .... Greek Research and Technology Network (SAUO)

GRNHS .... Greenhouse

GRNL .... Gay Rights National Lobby (EA)

GRNL .... Greenland Newsletter. Greenland Home Rule Information Service (journ.) (SAUS)

Grnld .... Greenland (SAUS)

grnln .... Granulation (VRA)

Grnmn .... Greenman Technologies, Inc. [*Associated Press*] (SAG)

GrnMtn .... Green Mountain Coffee [*Associated Press*] (SAG)

GRNN .... General Regression Neural Network (IDAI)

G-R Noise .... Generation-Recombination Noise (SAUS)

GRNP .... General Remote Network Processor (SAUO)

GRNP .... Grant Geophysical, Inc. [*NASDAQ symbol*] (SAG)

GrnPtFin .... Greenpoint Financial Corp. [*Associated Press*] (SAG)

GRNR .... [*The*] Grand River Railway Co. [*AAR code*]

GRNS .... Greens [*Postal Service standard*] (OPSA)

GRNSD .... Global Research Network on Sustainable Development (SAUO)

grnsh .... Greenish [*Philately*]

GrnStCA .... Greenwich Street California Municipal Fund, Inc. [*Associated Press*] (SAG)

GrnstR .... Greenstone Roberts Advertising, Inc. [*Associated Press*] (SAG)

GrnstRs .... Greenstone Resources Ltd. [*Associated Press*] (SAG)

GRNT .... Granite

GRNT .... Grant Geophysical [*NASDAQ symbol*] (TTSB)

GRNT .... Grant Geophysical, Inc. [*NASDAQ symbol*] (SPSG)

GRNT .... Grant Tensor Geophysical (SAUS)

GRNT .... Guarantee (SAUS)

GRNTA .... Gerontologist (journ.) (SAUS)

GRNTD .... Guaranteed

GrnteC .... Granite Construction, Inc. [*Associated Press*] (SAG)

GrntG .... Grant Geophysical, Inc. [*Associated Press*] (SAG)

GrntGeo .... Grant Geophysical, Inc. [*Associated Press*] (SAG)

GRNTP .... Grant Geophysical $2.4375 Cv Pfd [*NASDAQ symbol*] (TTSB)

GrntrSft .... Greentree Software, Inc. [*Associated Press*] (SAG)

GrntT .... Grant Tensor Geophysical Corp. [*Associated Press*] (SAG)

GRNVL .... Greenville, MS [*American Association of Railroads railroad junction routing code*]

GrnwAir .... Greenwich Air Services, Inc. [*Associated Press*] (SAG)
GRNWD .... Greenwood, MS [*American Association of Railroads railroad junction routing code*]
GRNWJ .... Greenwich Junction, NY [*American Association of Railroads railroad junction routing code*]
GRO .... Gamma Ray Observatory [*NASA*] (EGAO)
GRO .... Gasoline Range Organic [*Chemistry*]
GRO .... General Register Office [*British*]
GRO .... General Routine Order
GRO .... Gerona [*Spain*] [*Airport symbol*] (OAG)
GRO .... Global and Remote Observations Section (SAUS)
Gro .... Glycerol [*Biochemistry*]
GRO .... Government Reform and Oversight Committee [*House of Representatives*] (AAGC)
GRO .... Grandparents Rights Organization (EA)
GRO .... Graphics Reporting Option [*Computer science*] (CIST)
GRO .... Graves Registration Officer [*Military*]
GRO .... Greenwich Royal Observatory [*British*] (BARN)
GRO .... Gross (MSA)
Gro .... Gross' Select Cases Concerning the Law Merchant [*Selden Society*] [*A publication*] (DLA)
Gro .... Grotius' Rights of War and Peace [*Many eds.*] [*1625-1901*] [*A publication*] (DLA)
GRO .... Ground Risks Only [*Insurance*] (AIA)
GRO .... Group (WGA)
GRO .... Group Reference Point (SAUO)
GRO .... Grove
GRO .... Grow Group, Inc. (SAUO)
GRO .... Growth Investment Corp. [*Toronto Stock Exchange symbol*]
GRO .... Growth-Related Protein (DMAA)
GRO .... Grozny [*Former USSR*] [*Seismograph station code, US Geological Survey*] (SEIS)
GRO .... Lineas Aereas Allegro SA de CV [*Mexico*] [*ICAO designator*] (FAAC)
GRO .... Mississippi Chemical [*NYSE symbol*]
GRO .... Rota Island, TT [*Location identifier*] [*FAA*] (FAAL)
GROA .... Geologic repository operations area (SAUS)
GROAT .... Graphical Output Package for Atlas Computer Laboratories (SAUS)
GROBAT .... Ground Order of Battle (SAUS)
GROBDM .... General Register Office for Births, Deaths, and Marriages [*A publication*] (DLA)
GROBDM .... General Register Office of Births, Deaths, and Marriages (SAUS)
GROC .... Grocery (WDAA)
GROCAP .... Gross Capability Estimator [*Air Force*]
GROD .... Government of the Republic of Djibouti (SAUS)
GROF .... Groff Industries, Inc. (SAUO)
GRO FCTR W/T ... Ground Course Flight Crew Working Team (SAUS)
GROFIS .... Ground Forces Intelligence Study (MCD)
GROIN .... Garbage Removal Or Income Now (SAUS)
GROJ .... Get Rid of Junk [*Garage sale sign*]
GROLD .... Groveland, NY [*American Association of Railroads railroad junction routing code*]
Grolier .... Grolier Society (SAUO)
GROLIES .... Guardian Reader of Limited Intelligence, Ethnic Skirt (BB)
GROM .... Graphic Read-Only Memory [*Computer science*] (IAA)
GROM .... Groman Corp. (SAUO)
GROM .... Grommet (KSC)
GROMI .... Grosvenor, MI [*American Association of Railroads railroad junction routing code*]
Gron .... Gronningen. Siglum for Tablets [*Leiden*] [*A publication*] (BJA)
Gronnd Water Monit Rev ... Ground Water Monitoring Review (journ.) (SAUS)
GROOM .... Grooming
GROOVE .... Generated Real-Time Output Operations on Voltage-Controlled Equipment [*Computer science*]
GROPAC .... Group Pacific
GROPE .... Graphical Representation of Protocols in Estelle (SAUS)
GROS .... Goods Receiving Online System (SAUS)
GROS .... Graphics Reconnaissance Operations System (SAUO)
GROS .... Grossman's, Inc. [*NASDAQ symbol*] (NQ)
gros .... Grossus [*Coarse*] [*Latin*] (MAE)
Grosmn .... Grossman's, Inc. [*Associated Press*] (SAG)
Gross St .... Gross' Illinois Compiled Statutes [*A publication*] (DLA)
gro t .... Gross Tons (ODBW)
GROT .... Grote [*or Grotius*] [*Literature*] (ROG)
GROT .... Grotesque (ADA)
GROT .... Grotto (ROG)
Grot De JB ... Grotius. De Jure Belli et Pacis [*A publication*] (DLA)
Grot De JrB ... Grotius. De Jure Belli et Pacis [*A publication*] (DLA)
Grotius .... Grotius. Latin Law [*A publication*] (DLA)
Grotius De Jure Belli ... Grotius. De Jure Belli et Pacis [*A publication*] (DLA)
Grot Soc'y ... Transactions. Grotius Society [*England*] [*A publication*] (DLA)
Ground Oper ... Ground Operations Review Panel (NAKS)
Ground Wat ... Ground Water Age (journ.) (SAUS)
Group Adv Psychiatry Rep ... Group for the Advancement of Psychiatry. Report (journ.) (SAUS)
Groupe .... Groupe AB SA [*Associated Press*] (SAG)
Group Fam Ther ... Group and Family Therapy (journ.) (SAUS)
Group Health J ... Group Health Journal (journ.) (SAUS)
Groupl .... Group 1 Software, Inc. [*Associated Press*] (SAG)
Group Legal Rev ... Group Legal Review [*A publication*] (DLA)
Group Organ Stud ... Group and Organization Studies (journ.) (SAUS)
Group Psych ... Group Psychotherapy and Psychodrama (SAUO)
Group Psych ... Group Psychotherapy and Psychodrama (journ.) (SAUS)
GROUPS .... Group Movement System (SAUO)
GROUT .... Graphical Output (SAUS)
GROV .... Grove [*Commonly used*] (OPSA)
GROV .... Grove Bank for Savings [*NASDAQ symbol*] (NQ)
GROV .... Grove Bank (MA) [*NASDAQ symbol*] (TTSB)
GROVE .... Grove [*Commonly used*] (OPSA)
Grove .... Groves Dictionary of Music and Musicians (journ.) (SAUS)
GROVE .... Groveton, NH [*American Association of Railroads railroad junction routing code*]
GroveB .... Grove Bank for Savings [*Associated Press*] (SAG)
Grove Chron Mus Hist ... Grove Chronology of Music History (journ.) (SAUS)
GroveR .... Grove Real Estate Asset Trust [*Associated Press*] (SAG)
GROVES .... Groves [*Commonly used*] (OPSA)
GROW .... Gay Rights for Older Women (SAUO)
GROW .... Goals, Reality, Options, Will (BB)
GROW .... Greater Opportunities through Work [*Proposed federal program*]
GROW .... Group Relations Ongoing Workshops
GROW .... Growing (SAUS)
Grow .... Growth [*A publication*]
GROW .... US Global Investors, Inc. [*NASDAQ symbol*] (SAG)
GrowBiz .... Grow Biz International, Inc. [*Associated Press*] (SAG)
GROWBY .... Green, Red, Orange, White, Blue, Yellow [*Military system of indicating what day of the week food products were made through colored packaging*]
GROWN .... Get-Rid-of-Westmoreland-Now [*Secret society whose members were junior Pentagon officers*] (VNW)
Gro-Wt .... Gross Weight (SAUS)
GROWTH .... Get Rid of Waste through Team Harmony
Growth Dev Aging ... Growth, Development and Aging (journ.) (SAUS)
GROX .... First Union Rail [*Private rail car owner code*]
GRP .... Gamma Ray Projector
GRP .... Gastrin-Releasing Peptide [*Endocrinology*]
GRP .... Gaussian Random Process [*Mathematics*]
GRP .... Gelatin Rigidized Panel
GRP .... General Receptor for Phosphoinositide [*Biochemistry*]
GRP .... Geographical Reference Points (GAVI)
GRP .... Geophysical Research program (SAUS)
GRP .... German Railway Police (SAUO)
GRP .... Giant Reef Petroleums [*Vancouver Stock Exchange symbol*]
GRP .... Glass Fibre Reinforced Plastic (SAUS)
GRP .... Glass-fibre Reinforced Plastic (SAUS)
G R P .... Glass-fibre Reinforced Polyester (SAUS)
GRP .... Glass Reinforced Plastic (SAUO)
GRP .... Glass-Reinforced Plastic [*or Polyester*]
GRP .... Glass Reinforced Polyester (SAUS)
GRP .... Glucocorticoid Receptor Protein [*Biochemistry*]
GRP .... Glucose Regulated Protein [*Biochemistry*]
GRP .... Government Railway Police [*Indian Railway*] (TIR)
GR-P .... Government Rubber-Polysulfide (SAUS)
GrP .... Gram-Positive (STED)
GRP .... Gram-Positive [*Also, GP*] [*Microbiology*]
GRP .... Granite Point, AK [*Location identifier*] [*FAA*] (FAAL)
GRP .... Grant Prideco [*NYSE symbol*] (SG)
GRP .... Grant-Related Poundage [*British*]
GRP .... Graphical Rational Patterns (SAUS)
GRP .... Graphite Reinforced Plastic (SAUS)
GRP .... Greater Response Probability (SAUO)
GRP .... Greater Romania Party [*Political party*] (BUAC)
GRP .... Greatest Response Probability
GrP .... Greenwood Publishing Corp., Westport, CT [*Library symbol*] [*Library of Congress*] (LCLS)
GRP .... Gross Rating Point [*Television*]
GRP .... Gross Regional Product
GRP .... Ground Relay Package (SAUO)
GRP .... Ground Relay Panel [*Aerospace*] (AAG)
GRP .... Groundwater Resource Protection (SAUS)
GRP .... Groundwater Resources and Protection (SAUO)
grp .... Group (DD)
GRP .... Group (KSC)
Grp .... Group (TBD)
GRP .... Group Reference Pilot [*Telecommunications*] (TEL)
GRP .... Group Repetition Interval [*Nautical term*] (NTA)
GRP .... Group Repetition Period (SAUO)
GRP .... Grundrichtungspunkt [*Base point, a gunnery term*] [*German military - World War II*]
GRP .... Guardia Republicana [*Peru*]
GRP .... Guidance Replacement Program (SAUS)
GRP .... Guyana Republican Party [*Political party*] (EA)
GRPA .... Genesee River Protection Act of 1989 (COE)
GRPA .... Guyana Responsible Parenthood Association (BUAC)
GRPA .... Guyana Rice Producers Association (BUAC)
GrPAB .... Gravida, Para, and Abortus [*Gynecology and obstetrics*] (DAVI)
GrPAB .... Pregnancy, Birth, Abortion [*Medicine*] (STED)
GRPC .... Gulf Regional Planning Commission
Grp Capt .... Group Captain [*British military*] (DMA)
GRPCO .... Greek Recovery Program Coordinating Office (SAUO)
Grp Comm O ... Group Communication Officer (SAUO)
GRPD .... GraphiCommunicator (journ.) (SAUS)
GRPH .... Graphic (MSA)
GRPH .... Graphic Industries [*NASDAQ symbol*] (TTSB)
GRPH .... Graphic Industries, Inc. [*NASDAQ symbol*] (NQ)
grph .... Graphite (VRA)
GRPH .... Region 4 Graphics System (SAUS)
GRPHA .... Graphics (journ.) (SAUS)
GRPHC .... Graphic
Grphln .... Graphic Industries, Inc. [*Associated Press*] (SAG)
GRPI .... Greenwich Pharmaceuticals, Inc. (SAUS)
GRPI .... Greenwich Pharmaceuticals, Incorporated (SAUO)

GRPJ .... Glass Reinforced Plastic Joint (SAUS)
GRPL .... Grand Rapids Public Library [*Michigan*]
G R P P .... Glass Reinforced Polypropylene (SAUS)
GRPP .... Glass-Reinforced Polypropylene (PDAA)
GRPRC .... Groundwater Resource Protection Regulatory Compliance (SAUS)
GRPS .... Glucose Ringer-Phosphate Solution (SAUS)
GRPS .... Groups (TVEL)
GrpTech .... Group Technologies Corp. [*Associated Press*] (SAG)
GRPZ .... Great Lakes Carbon Plant [*Federal Railroad Administration identification code*]
GRQ .... Goldrite Mining [*Vancouver Stock Exchange symbol*]
GRQ .... Groningen [*Netherlands*] [*Airport symbol*] (OAG)
GRQ .... Gross Requirements Queue (TIMI)
GRQ Message ... General Request Message (SAUS)
GRQU .... Gran Quivira National Monument
GRR .... Asia Tigers Fund [*NYSE symbol*] (SPSG)
GRR .... Gastric Reservoir Reduction [*Morbid obesity surgical treatment*]
GRR .... Gear Reduction Ratio [*Military*] (CAAL)
GRR .... General Radio Regulations (SAUO)
GRR .... Geneva Radio Regulations
GRR .... Genotypic Relative Risk [*Genetics*]
GRR .... Georgetown Railroad Co. [*AAR code*]
GRR .... Golden Rim Resources, Inc. [*Vancouver Stock Exchange symbol*]
GRR .... Gorron [*France*] [*Seismograph station code, US Geological Survey*] (SEIS)
GRR .... Government Research and Development Reports
GRR .... Grand Rapids [*Michigan*] [*Airport symbol*] (OAG)
GRR .... Granule for Reconstitution (SAUS)
GRR .... Graphic Reproduction Request (SAUS)
GRR .... Greek Research Reactor
GRR .... Gross Reproduction Rate (FOTI)
GRR .... Ground Radio Receiver (SAUO)
grr .... growler (SAUS)
GRR .... Guidance Reference Release (KSC)
GRR .... Kent County International Airport [*FAA*] (TAG)
GRRA .... Gramophone Record Retailers Association [*British*] (BI)
GRRA .... Guidance Reference Release Alert (SAUS)
GRRC .... Giant Resource Recovery Co. (EFIS)
GRRC .... Gurkha Rifles Regimental Centre [*British military*] (DMA)
GRREG .... Graves Registration [*Military*]
GRRF .... Genetic Resources Recognition Fund (SAUS)
GRRI .... Greenstone Rabasca Roberts, Inc. (SAUO)
GRRI .... Greenstone Roberts Adv [*NASDAQ symbol*] (TTSB)
GRRI .... Greenstone Roberts Advertising, Inc. [*NASDAQ symbol*] (SAG)
GRRL .... Greenwood Holdings, Inc. (SAUO)
Gr Rom Byz St ... Greek, Roman and Byzantine Studies (journ.) (SAUS)
G R R P .... Glass-fibre Reinforced Thermoplastics (SAUS)
GRRR .... Goddard Range and Range Rate (SAUO)
GRRRS .... Goddard Range and Range Rate System [*NASA*] (IAA)
GRRY .... Greenbriar River Railway [*Federal Railroad Administration identification code*]
GRRZ .... Geneva Railroad [*Federal Railroad Administration identification code*]
GRS .... Beta-Glucuronidase [*Organic chemistry*] (DAVI)
GRS .... Galvanized rigid steel (SAUS)
GRS .... Gamma Radiation Source
GRS .... Gamma Radiation Spectrometer
GRS .... Gamma Ray Spectrometer
GRS .... Gamma Ray Spectrometry (SAUS)
GRS .... Gamma-Ray Spectroscopy (SAUS)
GRS .... Gamma Ray Spectrum
GRS .... Gamma-ray subtraction (SAUS)
GRS .... Gaseous RADWASTE System [*Nuclear energy*] (NRCH)
GRS .... Gears (SAUS)
GRS .... General and Recursive Structuring (SAUS)
GRS .... General Begister Stack (SAUS)
GRS .... Generalized Retrieval System [*Computer science*]
GR-S .... General-Purpose Synthetic Rubber (SAUS)
GRS .... General Radio Service [*Canada*]
GRS .... General Railway Signal (SAUS)
GRS .... General Reconnaissance School [*British military*] (DMA)
GRS .... General Records Schedule (SAUO)
GRS .... General Records Schedules [*Military*] (AABC)
GRS .... General Reference Service (SAUS)
GRS .... General Register Set/Stack [*Computer science*]
GRS .... General Reporting System
GRS .... General Revenue Sharing [*Office of Revenue Sharing*]
GRS .... Generic Record Syntax (SAUS)
GRS .... Geocentric Reference System (SAUS)
GRS .... Geodetic Reference System (SAUO)
GRS .... Geriatric Rating Scale [*Medicine*] (DB)
GRS .... Geriatrics Review Syllabus (SAUO)
GRS .... German Dermatological Society (EAIO)
GRS .... German Research Satellite [*NASA*]
GRS .... Ghost Research Society (EA)
GRS .... Global Reference System (SAUO)
GRS .... Global Resource Serialization (SAUS)
GRS .... Golabi-Rosen Syndrome [*Medicine*] (DMAA)
GRS .... Golden Rule Society (EA)
GRS .... Goris [*Former USSR*] [*Seismograph station code, US Geological Survey*] (SEIS)
GR-S .... Government Rubber-Styrene [*Also, SBR*] [*Synthetic rubber*]
GRS .... Graduate Rabbinical School (BJA)
GRS .... Grand Recording Scribe [*Freemasonry*] (ROG)
grs .... Grandson (GEAB)
GRS .... Grandson (ROG)
GRs .... Granitic Regions (SAUS)
GRS .... Grass [*Maps and charts*]
GRS .... Grass Soft (SAUS)
GRS .... Gratiam Resources [*Vancouver Stock Exchange symbol*]
GRS .... Graves Registration Service [*Military*]
GRS .... Gravity Reference Signal [*or System*]
GRS .... Gravity Reference System (SAUO)
GRS .... Grease (MSA)
GRS .... Great Red Spot [*on planet Jupiter*]
grs .... greens (SAUS)
GRS .... Grid Reference Ship [*Navy*] (NVT)
GRS .... Grid Reference System (SAUO)
GRS .... Grigori Rasputin Society (EA)
GRS .... Gross (SAUS)
GRS .... Grosseto [*Italy*] [*Airport symbol*] (AD)
GRS .... Ground Radar Set (SAUS)
GRS .... Ground Receiving Station (SAUO)
GRS .... Ground Surveillance System (SAUS)
GRS .... Groupe Revolutionnaire Socialiste [*Socialist Revolution Group*] [*Martinique*] [*Political party*] (PPW)
GRS .... Groupe Revolutionnaire Socialiste [*Socialist Revolution Group*] [*France*] [*Political party*]
GRS .... Group Reset Message (SAUO)
GRS .... Guilford Railroad System [*Federal Railroad Administration identification code*]
GRS .... Gurkha Royal Signals (SAUO)
GRS .... Gyro Reference System (AAG)
GRS .... Shorter College, Rome, GA [*Library symbol*] [*Library of Congress*] (LCLS)
GRSA .... Germersheim Reserve Storage Activity (MCD)
GRSA .... Great Sand Dunes National Monument
GRS & MIC ... Gross and Microscopic [*Medicine*] (MEDA)
GRSC .... Graduate of the Royal Society of Chemistry [*British*] (DBQ)
GRSC .... Ground Radio Servicing Centre (SAUS)
GRSCSW .... Graduate Research Center of the Southwest (SAUO)
GRSDDB .... Ground, Remotely-Sensed and Documentary Data Bank (SAUO)
GRSE .... Gamma Ray Spectrometric Equipment
GRSE .... Garden Reach Shipbuilders and Engineers Ltd. (SAUO)
GRSE .... Guild of Radio Service Engineers (BARN)
GRSF .... Ground Radio Servicing Flight (SAUS)
GRSFE .... Geologic Remote Sensing Field Experiment (SAUO)
GRSHFT .... Gearshaft (MSA)
GrSimec .... Grupo Simec [*Commercial firm*] [*Associated Press*] (SAG)
GRSL .... Geologic Records and Samples Library (SAUO)
GRSL .... Great Salt Lake Basins (SAUS)
GRSL .... Guam Reference Standards Laboratory (DNAB)
GRSLND .... Grassland (RDA)
Gr S-Lt .... Gunner Sub-Lieutenant (SAUO)
GRSM .... Graduate of the Royal Schools of Music [*British*]
GRSM .... Great Smoky Mountains National Park [*Also, GSMNP*]
GRSM .... Group for Regional Studies in Museums (SAUO)
GR/S/O .... Grandson Of [*Genealogy*]
GRSP .... General Range Safety Plan [*NASA*]
GRSP .... General Revenue Sharing Program (SAUS)
GRSP .... Glass-Reinforced Structural Plastic
gr/sq in .... Grain per Square Inch (SAUS)
GRSs .... General Railway Signals (SAUS)
GRSS .... Geoscience and Remote Sensing Soc. (SAUS)
GRST .... General Recreation Screening Tool (IDYL)
GRST .... Grist Mill [*NASDAQ symbol*] (TTSB)
GRST .... Grist Mill Co. [*NASDAQ symbol*] (NQ)
GR ST .... Groom of the Stole [*British*]
Grs T .... Gross Ton (EBF)
GRST .... Gross Tons
GrStCA .... Greenwich Street California Municipal Fund, Inc. [*Associated Press*] (SAG)
GrStR .... Grundsteuer-Richtlinien (SAUS)
GRSU .... Geography Remote Sensing Unit [*University of California, Santa Barbara*]
GRS Waveband ... General Radio Service Waveband (SAUS)
GRSX .... Garland Railroad Spur Track [*Federal Railroad Administration identification code*]
GRSZ .... Greater Southwest [*Federal Railroad Administration identification code*]
GRT .... Gabon-Air-Transport [*ICAO designator*] (FAAC)
GRT .... Gamma Ray Telescope
GRT .... Gamma Ray Tube
GRT .... Gas Recombinant Technology [*Battery engineering*]
GRT .... General Reactor Technology (NRCH)
GRT .... General Recomplement Trigger (SAUS)
GRT .... General Recorded Tape (SAUS)
GRT .... General Recorded Tape Corp. (SAUO)
GRT .... General Relation Treaty (SAUO)
GRT .... General Relativity Theory (SAUS)
GRT .... Geodesy Research Group (SAUO)
GRT .... Geriatric Rehabilitation Team [*Australia*]
GRT .... Germanium Resistance Thermometer (ACAE)
GRT .... Glimcher Realty Trust [*NYSE symbol*] (SPSG)
GRT .... Government Rate Tender
GRT .... Graduate Respiratory Therapist
Grt .... Grant's Pennsylvania Cases [*A publication*] (DLA)
grt .... Graphic Technician [*MARC relator code*] [*Library of Congress*] (LCCP)
GRT .... Graphic Technology, Inc. (SAUS)

GRT .... Gratio [*Tennessee*] [*Seismograph station code, US Geological Survey*] (SEIS)
GRT .... Great (ROG)
GRT .... Gross Registered Tons [*Navigation*]
GRT .... Gross Requirements Tapes (ACAE)
GRT .... Ground Radio Telescope (SAUS)
GRT .... Ground-Readiness Test (SAUS)
GRT .... Ground-Received Times [*Solar wind measurements*]
GRT .... Ground Resistance Tester
GRT .... Group Rapid Transit [*TRB*] (TAG)
GRT .... GTC Transcontinental Group Ltd. [*Toronto Stock Exchange symbol*]
GRT .... Gujrat [*Pakistan*] [*Airport symbol*] (AD)
Gr(T) .... Gunner (Torpedo) [*British military*] (DMA)
GRT .... Gun Reference Time (SAUS)
GRT .... Tri-County Regional Library, Rome, GA [*Library symbol*] [*Library of Congress*] (LCLS)
GRTA .... Georgia Regional Transportation Authority
GRTA .... Government Reports and Topical Announcements [*Later, WGA*] [*National Technical Information Service*]
GRTA .... Group Relations Training Association (AIE)
Grt Barrier Reef Comm Pap... Great Barrier Reef Committee. Heron Island Research Station. Papers (journ.) (SAUS)
GrtBay .... Great Bay Power Corp. [*Associated Press*] (SAG)
GrtBayPw..... Great Bay Power Corp. [*Associated Press*] (SAG)
GRTC .... Green River Test Complex
GRTC .... Groupe de Recherches pour les Transports au Canada [*Canadian Transportation Research Forum*]
GrtCtrl............ Great Central Mines [*Associated Press*] (SAG)
GRTE .... Grand Teton National Park
GrteBayC ..... Greate Bay Casino [*Associated Press*] (SAG)
GrtFncl............ Great Financial Corp. [*Associated Press*] (SAG)
GRTG .... Granting
GRTG .... Grating (MSA)
GRTG .... Greeting
GRTH .... Growth
gr t/in .... Troy Grain per Inch (SAUS)
GRTIS .... Glide Return to Landing Site (SAUS)
GRTIS .... Glide Return to Launch Site (SAUS)
GRTK .... Group Technologies [*NASDAQ symbol*] (TTSB)
GRTK .... Group Technologies Corp. [*NASDAQ symbol*] (SAG)
GRTL .... Gulf Radiation Technology Laboratories (SAUO)
GRTLKS .... Great Lakes (FAAC)
GRTLS .... Glide Return to Landing Site (NASA)
GRTLS .... Glide Return to Launch Site (MCD)
GRTM .... Geared Roller Test Machine
GRTM .... Gross Ton-Mile (ADA)
GRTN .... Grid Return (MSA)
GrToy .... Grand Toys International [*Associated Press*] (SAG)
GRTP .... Gamma-Ray Transition Probability (SAUS)
GRTP .... Glass-Fiber Reinforced Thermoplastics (PDAA)
GRTP .... Glass Reinforced Thermoplastic
GRTPEP .... Australia.Commonwealth Scientific and Industrial Research Organisation. Groundwater Research. Technical Paper (journ.) (SAUS)
GrtPines .... Great Pines Water Co. [*Associated Press*] (SAG)
GrTr .... Graphite Treatment (SAUS)
GRTR .... Grater (MSA)
GRTR .... Greater [*Freight*]
GRTR .... [*The*] Greater New York Savings Bank [*NASDAQ symbol*] (NQ)
GRTR .... Greater N.Y. Svgs Bk [*NASDAQ symbol*] (TTSB)
GRTS .... Gart Sports Co. [*NASDAQ symbol*] (NASQ)
GRTS .... General Electric Remote Terminal Supervisor [*Honeywell*] (NITA)
GRTS .... General Electric Remote Terminal System (SAUS)
GRTS .... General Remote Terminal Supervisor
GRTS .... General Remote Terminal System (SAUO)
GRTS .... Geomagnetic Reversal Time Scale
GRTS .... Goddard Real Time System [*NASA*] (IAA)
GRTS .... Ground Tracking System (MCD)
GRTSFC .... Ginger Rogers: The Star Fan Club (EA)
GrtSoB .... Great Southern Bancorp, Inc. [*Associated Press*] (SAG)
GrtSoBcp ..... Great Southern Bancorp, Inc. [*Associated Press*] (SAG)
GRTSW .... Great Southwest, TX [*American Association of Railroads railroad junction routing code*]
GRTT .... Graduate Respiratory Therapist Technician [*Medicine*] (EDAA)
GRTU .... General Retailers and Traders Union [*Malta*] (BUAC)
Grtv ADR .... Grootvlei Proprietary Mines Ltd. [*Associated Press*] (SAG)
GrtWall .... Great Wall Electronic Internationl Ltd. [*Associated Press*] (SAG)
GRU .... General Register Unit (SAUS)
GRU .... Genetic Resources Unit (GNE)
GRU .... Geological Records Unit (SAUO)
GRU .... Geology at Radford University (SAUO)
GRU .... Geomorphic Response Unit (QUAC)
GRU .... Glavnoe Razvedivatelnoe Upravlenie [*Chief Administration for Intelligence*] [*Division of the General Staff of the Soviet Army*] [*Former USSR*]
GRU .... Gold Ridge Resources [*Vancouver Stock Exchange symbol*]
GRU .... Grajau [*Brazil*] [*Airport symbol*] (AD)
GRU .... Grid Reference Unit [*Military*] (CAAL)
GRU .... Group
Gru .... Grus [*Constellation*]
GRU .... Guidance Regulator Unit
GRU .... Gurkha Reserve Unit (SAUS)
GRU .... Gyro Reference Unit (SAUS)
GRU .... Gyroscope Reference Unit (MCD)
GRUB .... Grand Unified Bootloader (SAUS)
GRUB .... Grocery Update and Billing
GrubbEL .... Grubb & Ellis Co. [*Associated Press*] (SAG)
GRUCOM ..... Group Commander
Grudman .... Gramm-Rudman-Hollings Bill [*Proposed deficit-reducing bill, 1985-1986*]
GrUff .... Grand Ufficiale [*Grand Officer*] (EY)
GRUIT .... Get Real you Impudent Thing (SAUS)
GRULAC .... Group of Latin American Countries (SAUO)
GRUMB .... Grumbalds [*England*]
Grumpie ..... Grim Ruthless Upwardly Mobile Professional [*Lifestyle classification*]
Grumpie ..... Grown-Up Mature Person [*Lifestyle classification*]
GRUN .... Gruene, Inc. (SAUO)
GRUNCH .... Gross Universal Cash Heist [*Techno-economic term coined by Buckminster Fuller*]
GRUR .... Gewerblicher Rechtsschutz und Urheberrecht [*A publication*] (ILCA)
GRUR Int ..... Gewerblicher Rechtsschutz und Urheberrecht, Internationaler Teil [*A publication*] (ILCA)
GRUSL .... Group Sail [*Navy*] (NVT)
GRUSZAG ..... Georgian Telegraphic Agency, Tbilisi (BUAC)
GRUVAL .... Group Values (SAUO)
GRV .... General Rapier Vehicles (SAUS)
GRV .... Grantsville, MD [*Location identifier*] [*FAA*] (FAAL)
GRV .... Granville Island Brewing Co. Ltd. [*Vancouver Stock Exchange symbol*]
GRV .... Graphic Recording Voltmeter (IAA)
GRV .... Graphite Rod Vaporization
grv .... Gravure (VRA)
GRV .... Greenville [*Lake Wappapelo*] [*Missouri*] [*Seismograph station code, US Geological Survey*] [*Closed*] (SEIS)
GRV .... Groove (KSC)
GRV .... Grosvenor Aviation Services [*British*] [*ICAO designator*] (FAAC)
GRV .... Ground Reaction Vector (DMAA)
GRV .... Grove
GRVA .... Graphic Varmeter
GRVCIC .... Graphic Reproductions Visual Communications Industries Council (SAUS)
GRVD .... Grooved
GRVG .... Grooving
GR VJ POND... Grana Sex Pondere [*Six Grains by Weight*] [*Pharmacy*] (ROG)
GRVL .... Gravel
grvl .... gravelly (SAUS)
GRVR .... German Road Vehicle Regulation (SAUS)
GRVR .... Groover
GRVS .... Advanced Gravis ComputerTechnology Ltd. (SAUO)
GRVS .... Groves [*Postal Service standard*] (OPSA)
GRVXF .... Grove Explorations Ltd. (SAUO)
GRW .... Galactic Radio Wave
GRW .... General Railway Warrants [*US Military Government, Germany*]
GRW .... Giant Ragweed [*Medicine*] (EDAA)
GRW .... Giant Ragweed Test [*Medicine*] (DMAA)
GRW .... Goodyear-Reston-Winthrop [*Publishing group*]
GRW .... Graciosa Island [*Azores*] [*Airport symbol*] (OAG)
GRW .... Graphic Recording Wattmeter (IAA)
GRW .... Greater Washington Investors, Inc. (SAUO)
GRW .... Greenwich [*United Kingdom*] [*Later, HAD*] [*Geomagnetic observatory code*]
GRW .... Greenwich Resources Ltd. [*Toronto Stock Exchange symbol*] [*Vancouver Stock Exchange symbol*]
GRW .... Greenwood, MS [*Location identifier*] [*FAA*] (FAAL)
GRW .... Ground Wet (SAUS)
GRWA .... Grace's Warbler [*North American bird banding code*] (BIBA)
GRWAVE ..... Ground Wave (SAUS)
Grwd .... Grunewald (SAUS)
GRWG .... Geo Requirements Working Group (SAUS)
Gr Wght .... Gross Weight (SAUS)
GRWR .... Geologically-Related Web Resources (SAUO)
GRWR .... Great Walton Railroad [*Federal Railroad Administration identification code*]
GRWS .... Gimbaled Reaction Wheel Scanner
GRWSIM ..... Ground Warfare Simulation [*Military*]
GRWT .... Gradient Index Gross Weight (SAUS)
GR WT .... Grain Weight (SAUS)
gr wt .... Gross Weight (WDAA)
GRWT .... Gross Weight
GRX .... General Refractories Co. (SAUO)
GRX .... Granada [*Spain*] [*Airport symbol*] (OAG)
GRXR .... Ground Round Rest [*NASDAQ symbol*] (TTSB)
GRXR .... Ground Round Restauraunts, Inc. [*NASDAQ symbol*] (SAG)
GR/XRS .... Gamma-Ray/X-Ray Spectrometers (ACAE)
GRY .... Gary [*Diocesan abbreviation*] [*Indiana*] (TOCD)
GRY .... Gray (ADA)
GRY .... Gray Drug Stores, Inc. (SAUO)
GRY .... Greyhound Racing
GRY .... Greymouth [*New Zealand*] [*Seismograph station code, US Geological Survey*] [*Closed*] (SEIS)
GRY .... Grey Power [*Political party*] [*Australia*]
GRY .... Greystoke Exploration [*Vancouver Stock Exchange symbol*]
GRY .... Grimsey [*Iceland*] [*Airport symbol*] (OAG)
gry .... Gross Redemption Yield (BARN)
GRy .... Gross Redemption Yield (SAUS)
gry .... square grade (SAUS)
GryCm .... Gray Communications Systems [*Associated Press*] (SAG)
GRYE .... Greater Yellowlegs [*North American bird banding code*] (BIBA)
GRYP .... Gryphon Holdings [*NASDAQ symbol*] (SAG)
Gryphon .... Gryphon Holdings [*Associated Press*] (SAG)

grysh .... Grayish [*Philately*]
GRYX .... John H Grace [*Private rail car owner code*]
GRZ .... Galapagos Rift Zone [*Marine science*] (MSC)
GRZ .... Granophyric Roof Zone [*Geology*]
GRZ .... Graz [*Austria*] [*Airport symbol*] (OAG)
GS .... BAS Airlines [*ICAO designator*] (AD)
GS .... Defense General Supply Center (SAUO)
Gs .... force of gravity (SAUS)
G-S .... Gallard-Schlesinger [*Chemical manufacturing corporation*]
GS .... Gallard Schlessinger (SAUS)
gs .... Gallons (SAUS)
G/S .... Gallons per Second
GS .... Gallstone [*Medicine*] (DB)
GS .... Galpin Society (EA)
GS .... Galvanized Steel [*Telecommunications*]
GS .... Games Started [*Baseball*]
GS .... Gamma Scan [*Medicine*] (EDAA)
GS .... Gap Separation
GS .... Gap Shortened (SAUS)
GS .... Gardner Syndrome [*Medicine*]
GS .... Gasoline Supply
GS .... Gas scrubber (SAUS)
GS .... Gas Servicer (MCD)
GS .... Gas Signal (SAUS)
GS .... Gas Sulfide [*Process for obtaining heavy water*]
GS .... Gastric Shield [*Medicine*]
GS .... Gas turbine Systems technician (SAUO)
GS .... Gaudium et Spes [*Pastoral Constitution on the Church in the Modern World*] [*Vatican II document*]
GS .... Gauss [*Unit of magnetic flux density*] [*Preferred unit is T, Telsa*]
Gs .... Gauss
GS .... Geek of Science (SAUO)
GS .... Geneal Storage (SAUS)
GS .... General and Aviation Service Ltd (SAUS)
G/S .... General and Standard (ACAE)
GS .... Generalized Sign (SAUS)
Gs .... general motion pictures (SAUS)
GS .... General Schedule [*Federal employee job classification GS-1 to GS-18*]
GS .... General Search (IAA)
GS .... General Secretariat
GS .... General Secretary
GS .... General Semantics
GS .... General Service [*Literal translation, but used in sense of "excessively keen," or "overly acute"*] [*Army*] [*British*]
GS .... General Services Department (SAUS)
GS .... General Sessions
GS .... General Signal Corp. (EFIS)
GS .... General Solution (OA)
GS .... General Specials
GS .... General Specification (ACAE)
GS .... General Speed [*Military*]
GS .... General Staff [*Military*]
GS .... General Staff Officer (SAUO)
GS .... General Standard (SAUO)
GS .... General Statement (SAUS)
GS .... General Statistics
GS .... General Storage (IAA)
GS .... General Store (SAUS)
GS .... General Strike
GS .... General Subjects (MCD)
GS .... General Superintendent
GS .... General Support [*Military*]
GS .... General Support level of Maintenance (SAUS)
GS .... General Surgery
GS .... Generate Statement (SAUS)
GS .... Generating Station (SAUO)
GS .... Generating System (SAUO)
GS .... Genetical Society (BUAC)
GS .... Genetic Screening (MELL)
GS .... Geochemical Society (EA)
GS .... Geodetic Satellite (SAUS)
GS .... Geodetic Survey Satellite (SAUO)
GS .... Geographical Society (SAUO)
GS .... Geological Service (SAUO)
GS .... Geological Society [*British*] (EAIO)
GS .... Geological Survey [*Department of the Interior*]
GS .... Geophysical Signal (SAUS)
GS .... Georgia State College for Women (SAUO)
GS .... Geosynthesis (SAUS)
GS .... Geosynthetics (SAUS)
GS .... Geotechnical Services (SAUO)
GS .... German Ship (SAUS)
GS .... German Silver
GS .... Gerontological Society [*Later, GSA*] (EA)
GS .... Gesetzsammlung [*Collection of Statutes, Gazette*] [*German*] (ILCA)
GS .... Gestational Sac [*Medicine*] (RAWO)
GS .... Ghost Surgery (MELL)
GS .... Giant Slalom
GS .... Giemsa Stain (SAUS)
GS .... Gilbert's Syndrome [*Medicine*]
GS .... Gillette Co. (SAUO)
GS .... Gimbal, Stabilized (ACAE)
GS .... Girl Scouts of the United States of America (SAUO)
GS .... Girls' School (ADA)
GS .... Glaciological Society (SAUO)
GS .... Glamour Stock [*Investment term*]
GS .... Gland Seal [*System*] [*Nuclear energy*] (NRCH)
GS .... Gland Steam (SAUS)
gs .... glandular segment (SAUS)
GS .... Glanzmann-Saland [*Syndrome*] [*Medicine*] (DB)
GS .... Glass Show
GS .... Glazounov Society (EA)
GS .... Gleason's Score
GS .... Glide Slope [*Aviation*]
GS .... Gliding School [*British military*] (DMA)
GS .... Glomerular Sclerosis [*Medicine*]
GS .... Glow Start (SAUS)
GS .... Glucagonoma Syndrome [*Medicine*] (MELL)
G/S .... Glucose and Saline [*Medicine*] (EDAA)
GS .... Glucose and Saline [*Medicine*]
GS .... Glutamine Synthetase [*Also, GNS*] [*An enzyme*]
GS .... Glycogen Synthesis [*Medicine*] (MELL)
GS .... Glycolytic Substrate
GS .... Goal Shooter [*Netball*]
GS .... Goat Serum (DB)
GS .... Goldenhar Syndrome [*Medicine*] (DMAA)
GS .... Golden Shamrock Resources Corp. [*Vancouver Stock Exchange symbol*]
GS .... Goldman Sachs Group [*NYSE symbol*] (SG)
GS .... Gold Smoke [*Dispersion of ultrafine metal particles*]
GS .... Gold Standards
GS .... Golfing Society (SAUO)
GS .... Good Safety (SAUS)
GS .... Goudy Society (EA)
GS .... Gougerot-Sjoegren (DB)
GS .... Government Sale (SAUO)
GS .... Government Security [*Business term*]
GS .... Government Servant (SAUO)
GS .... Government Service
GS .... Government Staffs [*British*]
GS .... Government Stock (FOTI)
GS .... Grab Sample [*Analytical technique*]
G/S .... Grade-Stamped [*Construction term*] (MIST)
GS .... Grade System (AAG)
GS .... Gradual Student (SAUS)
GS .... Graduate School (SAUS)
GS .... Grain Size (SAUS)
GS .... Grain Size Metal (IAA)
GS .... Grammar School
GS .... Gram Stain [*Medicine*] (MELL)
GS .... Grand Scribe [*Freemasonry*]
GS .... Grand Secretary [*Freemasonry*]
GS .... Grand Sentinel [*Freemasonry*]
GS .... Grand Sentry [*Freemasonry*]
GS .... Grand Slalom (SAUS)
GS .... Grand Slam [*Baseball term*] (NDBD)
GS .... Grandson
GS .... Grand Speed (BARN)
GS .... Grand Steward [*Freemasonry*]
GS .... Gran Sport [*Automobile model designation*]
GS .... Granulocytic Sarcoma [*Medicine*] (MELL)
GS .... Graphics and Sound [*in Apple IIGS*] [*Apple Computer, Inc.*]
GS .... Graphics System (ELAL)
GS .... Grate Surface (SAUS)
G/S .... Gravity per Second (KSC)
GS .... Gray Scale (SAUS)
GS .... Great Gross (SAUS)
GS .... Great Seal [*British*]
GS .... Grebe Syndrome [*Medicine*] (MELL)
GS .... Greenhouse Shrub [*Horticulture*] (ROG)
GS .... Grip Strength
GS .... Grocery Store
GS .... Groenblad-Strandberg [*Syndrome*] [*Medicine*] (DB)
GS .... Gross Sales [*Business term*]
GS .... Gross Spread [*Business term*]
GS .... Grotius Society (SAUO)
GS .... Ground Segment (ACAE)
GS .... Ground Sensor
GS .... Ground Speed [*Aviation*]
G/S .... Groundspeed [*Aviation*] (PIAV)
GS .... Ground Stabilized (MUGU)
GS .... Ground Staff (SAUO)
GS .... Ground State (SAUS)
GS .... Ground Station [*Aerospace*] (AAG)
GS .... Ground Stopper (SAUS)
GS .... Ground Substance [*Medicine*] (MELL)
GS .... Ground Support (SAUS)
GS .... Ground Surface (IAA)
GS .... Ground Switch (SAUS)
GS .... Ground System (MCD)
G/S .... Ground to Slant (MCD)
GS .... Group Selector [*Telecommunications*] (TEL)
GS .... Group Separation (SAUO)
GS .... Group Separator [*Computer science*]
gs .... Group Specific [*Antigen*] [*Immunology*]
GS .... Group Structured [*Counseling group*]
GS .... Group Switch (SAUO)
GS .... Growth Stage
GS .... Growth Stock [*Investment term*]

G/S Grub-Screw (SAUS)
GS Grupo Socialista [*Socialist Group*] [*Portugal*] [*Political party*] (PPE)
GS G. Schirmer, Inc. [*Publisher*]
GS Guardship
GS Guard Society (EA)
GS Guard Squadron
GS Guerin-Stern [*Syndrome*] [*Medicine*] (DB)
GS Guidance Section (SAUS)
GS Guidance Simulator
GS Guidance Station [*Aerospace*] (AAG)
GS Guidance System [*Aerospace*] (AAG)
G/S Guided Steering [*Aerospace*] (NAKS)
GS Guide Slope (MUGU)
GS Guide Star (SAUS)
GS Guild of Surveyors [*Middlesex, England*] (EAIO)
GS Gulf Shelf [*Marine science*] (OSRA)
GS Gulf Stream (SAUS)
GS Gum Skips [*Philately*]
GS Gungywamp Society (EA)
GS Gunnery and Searchlight [*Control*] [*British*] [*World War II*]
GS Gunnery School [*Air Force*]
GS Gunnery Sergeant
GS Gunnery Support
GS Gun Sight (SAUS)
GS Guteral Steel (SAUS)
GS Gyroscope (IAA)
GS Gyrostabilizer
GS Pfizer Ltd. [*Great Britain*] [*Research code symbol*]
GS Savannah Public and Chatham-Effingham-Liberty Regional Library, Savannah, GA [*Library symbol*] [*Library of Congress*] (LCLS)
GS S. Georgia and S. Sandwich Island [*Internet country code*]
GS Snow Pellets [*ICAO*] (FAAC)
GS1 Gas turbine Systems technician first class (SAUO)
GS3 Gas turbine Systems technician third class (SAUO)
GSA Armstrong State College, Savannah, GA [*Library symbol*] [*Library of Congress*] (LCLS)
GSA Games and Sports in the Army (SAUO)
GSA Gardenia Society of America (EA)
GSA Garden Seed Association
GSA Garden State Airlines, Inc. [*ICAO designator*] (FAAC)
GSA Gas Service Agents (SAUS)
GSA Gas Supply Assembly (SAUS)
GSA Gastroenterological Society of Australia
GSA Geinsheim Staging Activity
GSA General Sales Agent [*Indian Railway*] (TIR)
GSA General Security Agency (SAUO)
GSA General Services Administration (POLM)
GSA General Services Administration, Washington, DC [*OCLC symbol*] (OCLC)
GSA General Services Agencies (SAUS)
GSA General Services Area (SAUS)
GSA General Somatic Afferent [*Nerve*] [*Anatomy*]
GSA General Storage Assignment (SAUS)
GSA General Studies Association [*British*]
GSA General Support Agreement (SAUS)
GSA General Support Announcement [*Public television*]
GSA General Syntax Analyzer [*Sperry UNIVAC*]
GSA Genetics Societies (or Society) of America (SAUO)
GSA Geographical Service Area (CGWS)
GSA Geographical Society of America (SAUO)
GSA Geographic Systems Analysis [*Information service or system*] (IID)
GSA Geological Society of Africa (BUAC)
GSA Geological Society of America (EA)
GSA Geological Society of Australia (EERA)
GSA Geological Survey of Alabama (SAUS)
GSA Geologicargia Speakers Association (SAUO)
GSA Geologic Spatial Analysis (SAUO)
GSA Geophysical Signal Analysis (SAUS)
GSA Geospatial analysis. (SAUS)
GSA Geothermal Steam Act of 1970 (COE)
GSA Germanistic Society of America (EA)
GSA German Studies Association (SAUO)
GSA Gerontological Society of America (EA)
GSA Girl Scouts of America
GSA Girl Scouts of the United States of America (SAUO)
GSA Girls' Schools Association [*British*]
GSA Glasgow School of Art [*Scotland*]
GSA Glass-Steagal Act [*1933*]
GSA Glide Slope Antenna [*Aviation*]
GSA Global Security Architecture (SAUO)
GSA Glutamatesemialdehyde [*Organic chemistry*]
GSA Goldfish Society of America (EA)
GSA Gourd Society of America [*Superseded by AGS*] (EA)
GSA Government in the Sunshine Act (COE)
GSA Government Servants Association (SAUO)
GSA Government Services Administration (SAUS)
GSA Governor of South Australia
GSA Graduate Student Association (SAUO)
GSA Great Salinity Anomaly [*Marine science*] (OSRA)
GSA Great Sand Dunes National Monument (SAUO)
GSA Greenhouse Suppliers Association (EA)
GSA [*The*] Green Party South Australia [*Political party*]
GSA Greenwich Sidereal Angle (SAUO)
GSA Gross Sarcoma Virus Antigen [*Immunology*] (MAE)
GSA Gross Soluble Antigen
GSA Ground based Surface-to-Air (SAUS)
GSA Ground-Based Surface-to-Air (MCD)
GSA Ground Safety Approval (MUGU)
GSA Groundstar Resources Ltd. [*Vancouver Stock Exchange symbol*]
GSA Ground Support Agency (SAUO)
GSA Group-Specific Antigen [*Immunology*]
GSA GS Financial Products [*NYSE symbol*] (SAG)
GSA GSM System Area (SAUO)
GSA Guanidinosuccinic Acid (MAE)
GSA Guaranteed Savings Account (SAUS)
GSA Guard Society of America (SAUO)
GSA Guidance System Analyst [*Aerospace*] (IAA)
GSA Guildford School of Acting (SAUO)
GSA Guild of Saint Alban
GSA Gulf & South American Steamship Co. (MHDB)
GSA Gunsight Surface Air (SAUS)
GSA Gun System Automation (SAUS)
GSA Gusau [*Nigeria*] [*Airport symbol*] (AD)
GSA Gustav-Sievert-Akademie (SAUS)
GSA/ADTS General Services Administration/Automated Data and Telecommunications Services (SAUO)
GSA-AT Glutamate Semialdehyde Aminotransferase [*An enzyme*]
GSAB General Surveys and Analysis Branch [*Department of Education*] (GFGA)
GSABC General Services Administration Board of Contracting (SAUO)
GSA-BCA General Services Administration - Board of Contract Appeals
GSAC Genome Sequencing and Analysis Conference
GSAC Golden State Athletic Conference (PSS)
GSACD Georgia Association for Supervision and Curriculum Development (SAUO)
GSA-CPO General Services Administration - Civilian Personnel Office
GSA-CPO General Services Administration-Cvilian Personnel Olffice (SAUS)
GSACR GSA Communications Representative (SAUO)
GSAD General safety assessment document (SAUS)
GSA DPA GSA Delegation of Procurement Authority (AAGC)
GSAFD Guidelines on Subject Access to Individual Works of Fiction [*American Library Association*]
GSA/FPRS General Services Administration/Federal Property Resources Services (OICC)
GSA-FSS General Services Administration-Federal Supply Service (SAUO)
GSA/FSS General Services Administration/Federal Supply Services (OICC)
GSAGR General Short Arc Geodetic Reduction (PDAA)
GSAI El Aaiun [*Western Sahara*] [*ICAO location identifier*] (ICLI)
GSAI General Services Administration Institute (SAUO)
GSAI Geological Society of America Inc. (SAUO)
GSAL Grupo de Solidariedade com America Latina [*Portugal*]
GSAM Generalized Sequential Access Method [*Computer science*]
GSAM Generalized Standard Addition Method [*Mathematics*]
GSAM Guangdong Society of Agri-Machinery [*China*] (BUAC)
GSAMAQ Geological Society of America. Memoir (journ.) (SAUS)
GSAMS Georgia Satellite Academic and Medical System (SAUO)
GSA/NARS General Services Administration/National Archives and Records Services [*Franklin D. Roosevelt Library*] [*Hyde Park, NY*] (OICC)
GS & F Georgia Southern & Florida Railway Co.
GS&LA Guam Savings and Loan Association (SAUO)
GSA/OFR General Services Administration/Office of the Federal Register (OICC)
GSA-OP General Services Administration - Office of Preparedness
GSA-P General Services Administration-Public Building Service (SAUS)
GSAP General Supported Accommodation Program [*New South Wales, Australia*]
GSAP Gun Sight Aiming Point
GSA-PBS General Services Administration - Public Building Service
GSAR Generalized SAR Processor (SAUS)
GSAR General Services Acquisition Regulation
GSAR General Services Administration Acquisition Regulations [*A publication*] (AAGC)
GSARRTS Generator, Starter, Alternator, Regulator and Rectifier Test Stand (SAUS)
GSAT General Satellite (NASA)
GSAT General telephone and electronics Satellite Corp. (SAUO)
GSAT Gesammelte Studien zum Alten Testament [*A publication*] (BJA)
GSAT Global Satellite Data Acquisition Team [*Marine science*] (OSRA)
GSAT Globesat Holding Corp. (SAUO)
GS/ATE General Support/Automatic Test Equipment (MCD)
GS/ATSS General Support/Automatic Test Support System (MCD)
GSB Gastric Stress Bleeding [*Medicine*]
GSB General Schools Budget [*British*] (DET)
GSB General Semantics Bulletin (journ.) (SAUS)
GSB General Services Building [*Nuclear energy*] (NRCH)
GSB General Stud Book [*Horses*]
GSB Ghana Standards Board (BUAC)
GSB Golden State Bancorp [*NYSE symbol*] (SG)
GSB Goldsboro, NC [*Location identifier*] [*FAA*] (FAAL)
GSB Gold Surface Barrier
GSB Go Subroutine (SAUS)
GSB Government Savings Bank [*Australia*]
GSB Graduate School of Business [*University of Chicago*] (ECON)
GSB Grand Standard Bearer [*Freemasonry*] (ROG)
GSB Grand Sword-Bearer [*Freemasonry*]
GSB Graphic Standards Board (SAUS)
GSB Gypsum Sheathing Board [*Technical drawings*]
GSBA Georgia School Boards Association (SAUO)
GSBAA General Service Board of Alcoholics Anonymous (SAUO)
GSBC Great Southern Bancorp [*NASDAQ symbol*] (TTSB)

GSBC .... Great Southern Bancorp, Inc. [*NASDAQ symbol*] (NQ)
GSBCA .... General Service Administration Board of Contract Appeals (SAUS)
GSBCA .... General Services Board of Contract Appeals
GSBG .... Gonadal Steroid-Binding Globulin [*Medicine*]
GSBI .... Gabungan Serikat Buruh Indonesia [*Federation of Indonesian Trade Unions*]
GSBI .... Granite State Bancshares [*NASDAQ symbol*] (TTSB)
GSBI .... Granite State Bankshares, Inc. [*NASDAQ symbol*] (NQ)
GSBK .... Germantown Savings Bank (SAUS)
GSBN .... Golden State Bancorp, Inc. [*NASDAQ symbol*] (NASQ)
GSBot .... Glass-Stoppered Bottle (SAUS)
GSBP .... Glycosylation Site Binding Protein [*Biochemistry*]
GSBPS .... Global Space-Based Positioning and Navigation System
GSBR .... Geosynchronous Space Based Radar (CCCA)
GSBR .... Gravel-Surface Built-Up Roof [*Technical drawings*]
GSBS .... Graduate School of Biomedical Sciences (SAUS)
GSC .... Galapagos Spreading Center [*Oceanography*]
GSC .... Gascoyne Junction [*Australia*] [*Airport symbol*] [*Obsolete*] (OAG)
GSC .... Gas Solid Chromatogram (SAUS)
GSC .... Gas Solid Chromatography (SAUS)
GSC .... Gelman Sciences [*AMEX symbol*] (TTSB)
GSC .... Gelman Sciences, Inc. [*AMEX symbol*] (SPSG)
GSC .... Gelman Sciens, Inc. (SAUO)
GSC .... General Service Cargo (SAUS)
GSC .... General Service Cargo Land Rover variant (SAUS)
GSC .... General Service Corps [*Military unit*] [*British*]
GSC .... General Staff College (SAUS)
GSC .... General Staff Corps [*Military*]
GSC .... General Staff Council [*Military*] (AABC)
GSC .... General Support Company [*Army*] (VNW)
GSC .... Genetically Significant Concentration [*Mutagenesis*]
GSC .... Genetically Significant Dose (SAUO)
GSC .... Genetics Society of Canada (SAUO)
GSC .... Genetics Society of China (BUAC)
GSC .... Genome Sequence Centre
GSC .... Geodetic Space Craft (SAUO)
GSC .... Geodetic Spacecraft (AAG)
GSC .... Geodetic Survey of Canada (SAUO)
GSC .... Geographical Society of Chicago (SAUO)
GSC .... Geographical Society of China (BUAC)
GSC .... Geographic Systems Corp. (SAUS)
GSC .... Geographic Systems Corporation (SAUO)
GSC .... Geological Society of Chicago (SAUO)
GSC .... Geological Society of China (BUAC)
GSC .... Geological Survey of Canada [*Marine science*] (MSC)
GSC .... Georgia Southwestern College (SAUO)
GSC .... GeoScience Centre (SAUO)
GSC .... Geotronics Service Center (SAUS)
GSC .... Gerontological Society of China (BUAC)
GSC .... Giant Serotonin-Containing [*Neuron*]
GSC .... Girls' School Company Ltd. [*British*] (BI)
GSC .... Gland Seal Condenser [*Nuclear energy*] (NRCH)
GSC .... Gland Steam Condenser [*Nuclear energy*] (NRCH)
GSC .... Glasgow [*Coma*] Scale [*Neurology*] (DAVI)
GSC .... Glenville State College [*West Virginia*]
GSC .... Global Standards Collaboration (SAUS)
GSC .... Golay Sequential Coding (CGWS)
GSC .... Golden Star Resources Ltd. [*Toronto Stock Exchange symbol*]
GSC .... Golden State Airlines, Inc. (SAUO)
GSC .... Gold Star Cable (SAUO)
GSC .... Goldstone [*California*] [*Seismograph station code, US Geological Survey*] (SEIS)
GSC .... Good Samaritan Coalition [*Defunct*] (EA)
GSC .... GOOS Steering Committee (SAUO)
GSC .... Grant Selection Committee (SAUS)
GSC .... Graphics Compatibility Standard (SAUS)
GSC .... Gravity Settling Culture
GSC .... Greater Sulphur Crested Cockatoo [*Bird*]
GSC .... Great Southwest Corp.
GSC .... Green Star; Cluster (SAUS)
GSC .... Grid Spot Converter (NVT)
GSC .... Ground Services Card (SAUS)
GSC .... Ground Services Cart
GSC .... Ground Speed Continue (or Continuing) (SAUS)
GSC .... Ground-Speed Continuing [*Aviation*]
GSC .... Ground Station Control (SSD)
GSC .... Ground Support Configuration (SAUS)
GSC .... Group Study Course
GSC .... Group Switching Center [*British*] [*Telecommunications*] (TEL)
GSC .... GSA [*General Services Administration*] Stock Catalog
GSC .... Guaranteed Savings Certificate (SAUS)
GSC .... Guardianship for Senior Citizens
GSC .... Guiana Space Center (MCD)
GSC .... Guidance Shipping Container
GSC .... Guidance System Console [*Aerospace*] (AAG)
GSC .... Guide Star Catalog
GSC .... Gulf South Conference (PSS)
GSC .... Gulf State Conference (SAUS)
GSC .... Gunnery Staff Course (SAUS)
GSCA .... General and Speciality Contractors Association (SAUO)
GSCA .... Georgia School Counselors Association (SAUO)
GSCA .... Giant Schnauzer Club of America (EA)
GSCA .... Gordon Setter Club of America (EA)
G/SCA .... Gunite/Shotcrete Contractors Association (NTPA)
GSCARNGARP ... General Staff Committees on Army National Guard and Army Reserve Policy (SAUO)
GSCAX .... Alliance Global: Small Cap.Cl.A [*Mutual fund ticker symbol*] (SG)
G Sc B .... Geological and Scientific Bulletin (journ.) (SAUS)
GSCBA .... Georgia State College of Business Administration (SAUO)
GSCC .... General Steel Casting Corp.
GSCC .... Global Simulation Control Center
GSCC .... Government Securities Clearing Corporation (AGLO)
GSCC .... Graphic Scanning Corp. (SAUS)
GSCC .... Greater Siamese Cat Club (EA)
GSCCMF .... Gujarat State Co-Operative Cotton Marketing Federation [*India*] (BUAC)
GSCD .... Ground Systems Control Document (SAUS)
GSCE .... Gas Source Control Equipment [*Electronics*] (AAEL)
GSCEP .... Georgia School Counselor Evaluation Program (SAUO)
GSCF .... Geriatric Sentence Completion Form [*Personality development test*] [*Psychology*]
GSC/Fd .... Gunnery Staff Course-Field (SAUO)
GSCG .... Ground Systems Coordination Group
GSCGX .... Goldman Sachs Capital Growth Cl.A [*Mutual fund ticker symbol*] (SG)
GSCH .... Gesell Developmental Schedules [*Clinical method for the study of sensorimotor growth of preschool children*] (DIPS)
GSCI .... GeoScience Corp. [*NASDAQ symbol*] (TTSB)
GSCI .... Goldman Sachs Commodity Index [*Finance*]
GSCI .... Ground Sound Control, Inc.
GSC/Loc .... Gunnery Staff Course-Locating (SAUO)
GSCM .... Gas Turbine Systems Technician, Master Chief [*Navy rating*] (DNAB)
GSCM .... Geological Survey of Canada. Memoir (journ.) (SAUS)
GSCM .... Global Supply Chain Model (GART)
GSCN .... General Scannning, Inc. [*NASDAQ symbol*] (SAG)
GSCN .... Genl Scanning [*NASDAQ symbol*] (TTSB)
GSCN .... Giant Serotonin-Containing Neuron (BABM)
GSCN .... Grantsmanship Center. News (journ.) (SAUS)
GSCNY .... German Society of the City of New York (EA)
GSCO .... Guidance Sustainer Cutoff [*Aerospace*] (AAG)
GSCP .... Generic Site Characterization Plan (SAUS)
GSCP .... Geological Survey of Canada. Paper (journ.) (SAUS)
GSCR .... Group-Specific Community Rating (ADWA)
GSCS .... Gas Turbine Systems Technician, Senior Chief [*Navy rating*] (DNAB)
GSCS .... Graphite and Shield Cooling System (SAUS)
GSCs .... Group Switching Centres (SAUO)
GSCS .... Senior Chief Gas Turbine Systems Technician (SAUS)
GSCSCERS .... Geographical Society of China Sub-Commission on Environmental Remote Sensing (BUAC)
GSCT .... Goldstein-Scheerer Cube Test [*Psychology*]
GSCT .... Government Security Certification Test (SAUO)
GSCT .... Guild of Sorting Clerks and Telegraphists [*A union*] [*British*]
GSCU .... Ground Service [*or Support*] Cooling Unit (KSC)
GSCW .... General Society of Colonial Wars (EA)
GSCW .... Georgia State College for Women [*Later, Women's College of Georgia*] (AEBS)
GSCWPPC .... Guam Stamp Club and Western Pacific Philatelic Collectors (EA)
GSCX .... General Sciences Corp. [*NASDAQ symbol*] (COMM)
GSCX .... Greelease [*Private rail car owner code*]
GSCZ .... Guernsey Stone [*Federal Railroad Administration identification code*]
GSD .... Gamma Sigma Delta (EA)
GSD .... Gate Stealer Display (MCD)
GSD .... General Services Department (SAUS)
GSD .... General Services Division (SAUO)
GSD .... General Sewing Data
GSD .... General Situation Display (SAUS)
GSD .... General Staff Department (SAUS)
GSD .... General Supply Depot
GSD .... General Support Detachment (SAUO)
GSD .... General Support Division [*Air Force*]
GSD .... General System Description [*Military*] (AABC)
GSD .... General System Development [*or Design*] (IAA)
GSD .... General Systems Development Corp. (SAUO)
GSD .... General Systems Development Corporation (SAUS)
GSD .... General Systems Division [*IBM Corp.*]
GSD .... Generating Significant Dose [*Nuclear energy*] (NRCH)
GSD .... Generator Starter Drive
GSD .... Generic Structure Diagram [*Telecommunications*] (TEL)
GSD .... Genetically Significant Dosage [*X-Ray*]
GSD .... Genetic Sex Determination [*Biology*]
GSD .... Genotypic Sex Determination [*Embryology*]
GSD .... Geodetic Survey Division (SAUS)
GSD .... Geographical Data of Sweden [*Sweden*] (EERA)
GSD .... Geographical Situation Display (SAUS)
GSD .... Geographical Survey Department (SAUO)
GSD .... Geographic survey data (SAUS)
GSD .... Geological Survey Department (SAUS)
GSD .... Geometric Standard Deviation [*Statistics*]
GSD .... Georgia School for the Deaf (SAUO)
GSD .... German Shepherd Dog (SPVS)
GSD .... Gerstmann-Straussler Disease [*Medicine*] (EDAA)
GSD .... Gesco Industries, Inc. [*Toronto Stock Exchange symbol*]
GSD .... Glycogen Storage Disease [*Medicine*]
GSD .... Glycogen Synthetase Deficiency [*Medicine*] (MELL)
GSD .... Goodman-Stannaforth Division [*Federal Railroad Administration identification code*]
GSD .... Government Support Date (MCD)
GSD .... Government Systems Division (SAUO)
GSD .... Grand Senior Deacon [*Freemasonry*]

GSD .... Grid Sphere Drag [*DoD satellite*]
GSD .... Ground Sample Distance (ACAE)
GSD .... Ground Station Data
GSD .... Guild of Softward Distributors (BUAC)
GSD .... Gunstock Deformity [*Medicine*] (MELL)
GSD .... Greenwich Sidereal Gate (ODA)
GSDA .... Great Southern Development Authority [*Western Australia*]
GSDA .... Grid Spaced Driver Assembly (SAUS)
GSDA .... Grounded Surface Distribution Apparatus (IAA)
GSDA .... Ground-Speed Drift Angle [*Aviation*] (NG)
GSDB .... Geonome Sequence Database (COE)
GSDB .... Geophysics and Space Data Bulletin [*A publication*] [*Air Force*]
GS-DBR .... Groung-Segment Development Baselinne Review (SAUS)
GSDC .... Geodetic Satellites Data Center (SAUS)
GSDC .... Get Set Day Care Program [*Later, CDCP*] (EA)
GSDCA .... German Shepherd Dog Club of America (EA)
GSDCB .... Geoscience Documentation (journ.) (SAUS)
GSDC Program... Get Set Day Care Program (SAUS)
GSDD .... General System Design Document (SAUO)
GSDE .... Ground System Development Environment (SAUO)
GSDF .... Global Sustainable Development Facility
GSDF .... Ground Self-Defense Force [*Japan*]
GSDFJ .... Ground Self-Defense Force Japan
GSDI .... Global Spatial Data Infrastructure (SAUO)
GSDL .... Ground Software Development Laboratory [*NASA*] (NASA)
GSDM .... Global Spatial Data Model (SAUO)
GSDN .... Garden Supply Dealers National (EA)
GSDN .... Global Software Defined Network [*Communications term*] (DCT)
GSDNM .... Great Sand Dunes National Monument (SAUO)
GSDO .... General [*Aviation*] Safety District Office
GSDP .... Geophysical Survey Data Processing System (SAUO)
GSDS .... Genealogy Software Distribution System (SAUS)
GSDS .... General Status Display System [*Graphics system*] (NITA)
GS/DS .... General Support/Direct Support
GSDS .... Geodetic Satellites Data service (SAUS)
GSDS .... Global Spatial Data System (SAUO)
GSDS .... Goldstone Duplicate Standard [*Deep Space Instrumentation Facility*] [*NASA*]
GSDSM .... Global Circulation Dust and Smoke Model (SAUO)
GSDSP .... Generalized Statistical Document Search Pattern (SAUO)
G S D T ...... Generalized Syntax Directed Translation (SAUS)
GSDT .... Generalized Syntax-Directed Translation (PDAA)
GSE .... Gas Turbine Systems Technician, Electrical [*Military*] (POLM)
GSE .... General Somatic Efferent [*Nerve*] [*Anatomy*]
GSE .... General Supply Equipment (SAUS)
GSE .... General Support Equipment [*Military*] (MUGU)
GSE .... Genital Self-Examination [*Medicine*] (EDAA)
GSE .... Geocentric Solar Ecliptic [*System*] [*NASA*]
GSE .... Geological Survey of Estonia (SAUO)
GSE .... Geometric Standard Error (PDAA)
GSE .... Global Security Environment (SAUS)
GSE .... Glutagen Sensitive Enteropathy [*Medicine*]
GSE .... Gluten-Sensitive Enteropathy [*Medicine*]
GSE .... Government Specified Equipment (SAUS)
GSE .... Government-Specified Equipment [*Military*] (DNAB)
GSE .... Government Sponsored Enterprise [*FNMA*] (EMRF)
GSE .... Government-Supplied Equipment (SAUS)
GSE .... Graduate School of Education (SAUO)
GSE .... Graduate Student of English (journ.) (SAUS)
GSE .... Graphical Service Extention (SAUS)
GSE .... Graphic Screen Editor (SAUS)
GSE .... Graphics Screen Editor (NITA)
GSE .... Grip Strong and Equal [*Neurology*] (DAVI)
GSE .... Gross Subsidy Equivalent [*Tariffs*] [*Australia*]
GSE .... Ground Service Equipment [*Air Force*]
GSE .... Ground Servicing Equipment (SAUS)
GSE .... Ground Support Equipment [*Aerospace*] (NAKS)
GSE .... Group of Scientific Experts
GSE .... Group Support Equipment
GSE .... Guias y Scouts de Europa [*Spain*] (EAIO)
GSE .... Gundle/SLT Environmental [*NYSE symbol*] (SG)
GSE1 .... Gas Turbine Systems Technician, Electrical, First Class [*Navy rating*] (DNAB)
GSE2 .... Gas Turbine Systems Technician, Electrical, Second Class [*Navy rating*] (DNAB)
GSE3 .... Gas Turbine Systems Technician, Electrical, Third Class [*Navy rating*] (DNAB)
GSE&I .... General Systems Engineering and Integration (ACAE)
GSE-BI .... Ground Support Equipment-Base Installation [*Aviation*] (SAA)
GSEC .... Gas Turbine Systems Technician, Electrical, Chief [*Navy rating*] (DNAB)
G SEC .... Grand Secretary [*Freemasonry*] (ROG)
GSECP .... Ground Support Engineering Change Proposal [*Aerospace*] (AAG)
GSED .... Ground Support Equipment Division [*Naval Air Engineering Center*]
GSEE .... Geniki Synomospondia Ergaton Hellados [*General Confederation of Greek Labor*]
GSEEI .... Ground Support Equipment End Item [*Military*]
GSEF .... Ground Subsystem Evaluation Facility [*Army*] (RDA)
GSEFA .... Gas Turbine Systems Technician, Electrical, Fireman Apprentice [*Navy rating*] (DNAB)
GSEFN .... Gas Turbine Systems Technician, Electrical, Fireman [*Navy rating*] (DNAB)
GSEI .... Georgia Superintendent Evaluation Instrument (SAUO)
GSEI .... Ground Support Equipment Illustration [*Military*] (MCD)
GSEID .... Ground Support Equipment Illustration Data [*Military*] (MCD)
GSEK .... Graphics Support Processor/Tektronix (SAUS)
GSEL .... Government Specified Equipment List [*Military*] (CAAL)
GSEL .... Ground Support Equipment Laboratory (SAUO)
GSEL .... Ground Support Equipment List [*NASA*] (NASA)
GSEL .... Guidance System Evaluation Laboratory [*Military*] (CAAL)
GSE-M .... Ground Support Equipment-Mechanical [*Aviation*] (SAA)
GSE-ME .... Ground Support Equipment-Maintenance Equipment [*Aviation*] (SAA)
GSE-MF .... Ground Support Equipment-Maintenance Facility [*Aviation*] (SAA)
GSERD .... Ground Support Equipment Recommendation Data [*Military*] (MCD)
GSERD .... Ground Support Equipment Requirement Data (SAUS)
GSEREWORKFAC... Ground Support Equipment Rework Facility (SAUS)
GSERS .... Ground Support Equipment Requirement Sheets (ACAE)
GSES .... Geocentric Solar Ecliptic System (SAUS)
GSES .... Government-Sponsored Enterprises [*Federal National Mortgage Association, Student Loan Marketing Association, etc.*]
GSES .... Ground Support Equipment Section (SAUO)
GSE-S .... Ground Support Equipment-Structure [*Aviation*] (SAA)
GSES .... GSE Systems [*NASDAQ symbol*] (TTSB)
GSES .... GSE Systems, Inc. [*NASDAQ symbol*] (SAG)
GSESD .... Ground Support Equipment Statistical Data (ACAE)
GSESD .... Ground Support Equipment Statistical Display (DNAB)
GSE-SE .... Group Support Equipment-Support Equipment [*Aviation*] (SAA)
GSE-SS .... Ground Support Equipment-Strategic System [*Aviation*] (SAA)
GSE-SS .... Ground Support Equipment-System and Service [*Aviation*] (SAA)
GSE-SS .... Ground Support Equipment-Systems Specification (IAA)
GSESS .... Ground Support Equipment Systems Specifications (SAUO)
GSE Sy .... GSE Systems, Inc. [*Associated Press*] (SAG)
GSE-T & H... Ground Support Equipment-Transportation and Handling [*Aviation*] (SAA)
GSETD .... General Systems Engineering and Technical Direction
GSE/TD .... General Systems Engineering/Technical Director (ACAE)
GSE-TS .... Ground Support Equipment-Test Stand [*Aviation*] (SAA)
GSEU .... Graduate Student Employees Union (SAUO)
GSEVDB .... Genetique, Selection, Evolution (journ.) (SAUS)
GSE-WSR ...... Ground Support Equipment-Weapon System Requirement [*Aviation*] (SAA)
GSF .... ACM Government Securities [*NYSE symbol*] (SPSG)
GSF .... ACM Gvt Securities [*NYSE symbol*] (TTSB)
GSF .... Galactosemic Fibroblasts [*Medicine*]
GSF .... Galaxy Science Fiction (journ.) (SAUS)
GSF .... General Semantics Foundation (EA)
GSF .... General Source File (SAUS)
GSF .... General Supply Fund
GSF .... General Support Force [*Air Force*]
GSF .... Genital Skin Fibroblast [*Medicine*] (DMAA)
GSF .... Georgia Southern & Florida Railway Co. [*AAR code*]
GSF .... Ghostscript Font (SAUO)
GSF .... Glial Stimulating Factor (QSUL)
GSF .... Global Strategy Fund [*British*]
GSF .... Government Superannuation Fund (SAUO)
GSF .... Greater Sciatic Foramen [*Medicine*] (MELL)
GSF .... Greenstick Fracture [*Medicine*] (MELL)
GSF .... Grenade Safety Fuze
GSF .... Gross Square Feet
GSF .... Ground Support Facilities [*Later, MGE*] [*Aerospace*] (AAG)
GSF .... Ground Support Fighter (MCD)
GSF .... Group of Soviet Forces
GSF .... Group of Soviet Forces in Germany (MCD)
GSF .... Gulf Sea Frontier
GSF .... Gunshot Fracture [*Medicine*] (MELL)
GSFA .... Gas Turbine Systems Technician Fireman Apprentice (SAUO)
GSFA .... Genealogical Society of Flemish Americans (EA)
GSFA .... Geological Society of Flemish Americans (SAUO)
GSFA .... Georgia State Florists Association (SAUO)
GSFB .... Geological Survey of Inland. Bulletin (journ.) (SAUS)
GSFC .... George Strait Fan Club (EA)
GSFC .... Goddard Space Flight Center [*Greenbelt, MD*] [*NASA*]
GSFC .... Green Street Financial [*NASDAQ symbol*] (TTSB)
GSFC .... Green Street Financial Corp. [*NASDAQ symbol*] (SAG)
GSFC .... Gujarat State Fertilizers Co. [*India*] (BUAC)
GSFC .... Gujarat State Financial Co. [*India*] (BUAC)
GSFC .... Gujarat State Financial Corporation (SAUO)
GSFG .... Group of Soviet Forces in Germany (NATG)
GSFIC .... Georgia State Financing and Investment Commission (SAUO)
GS Fin .... GS Financial Products [*Associated Press*] (SAG)
GSFL .... Gray-Spotted Flycatcher [*North American bird banding code*] (BIBA)
GSFLT .... Graduate School Foreign Language Test
GSFN .... Galaxy Science Fiction Novels (journ.) (SAUS)
GSFN .... Gas turbine Systems Technician Firemen (SAUO)
GSFNAK .... Geological Survey of Finland. Bulletin (journ.) (SAUS)
GSFP .... Group Soviet Forces Germany (CCCA)
GSFR .... Granulocyte Colony-Stimulating Factor Receptor (DMAA)
GSFS .... General Specifications for Ships (DNAB)
GSFS .... Great Science Fiction Stories (journ.) (SAUS)
GSFSA .... Georgia School Food Service Association (SAUO)
GSFSR .... Ground Safety and Flight Safety Requirements (AAG)
GSFU .... Glazed Structural Facing Units [*Technical drawings*]
GSFZ .... GW Seventy-Five [*Federal Railroad Administration identification code*]
GSG .... Galactosaemia Support Group (NRGU)
GSG .... Galvanized Sheet Gauge (SAUS)
GSG .... Garment Salesmen's Guild of New York [*Later, AG*] (EA)
GSG .... Garn-St. Germain Depository Institutions Act (EBF)
GSG .... General Support Group [*Army*] (AABC)
GSG .... Genetically Significant Dose (SAUS)

GSG .... Geological Society of Glasgow (SAUO)
GSG .... Glasgow, MT [*Location identifier*] [*FAA*] (FAAL)
GSG .... Glass-Silicone-Glass [*Electronics*] (DEN)
GSG .... Glass-Silicon-Glass (SAUS)
GSG .... Global Small Capital Fund [*AMEX symbol*] (SPSG)
GSG .... Grammar School for Girls (ADA)
GSG .... Grenzschutzgruppe [*Border Protection Group*] [*German*]
GSG .... Ground Studies Group [*Military*] (VNW)
GSG .... Ground Systems Group [*Hughes Aircraft Co.*]
GSG .... Guided Shape Granate (SAUS)
GSG .... Guild of St. Gabriel (BUAC)
GSG .... IUGS Global Sedimentary Geology Program (SAUO)
GSGA .... Geode Specialty Growers Association (EA)
GSGB .... Geological Survey and Museum of Practical Geology of Great Britain and Northern Ireland (SAUO)
GSGB .... Golf Society [*British*] (DBA)
GSGB .... Golf Society of Great Britain (BUAC)
GSGG .... Gadolinium, Scandium, Gallium, Garnet (MCD)
GSGM .... GeoStat Groundwater Modelling (SAUO)
GSGMEQ ...... Genetic, Social and General Psychology Monographs (journ.) (SAUS)
GSGO .... Greater Snow Goose [*North American bird banding code*] (BIBA)
GSGP .... Global Sedimentary Geology Program (SAUO)
GSGRX .... Goldman Sachs Growth & Income Cl.A [*Mutual fund ticker symbol*] (SG)
GSGs .... General Support Groups (SAUO)
GSGS .... Geodetic Service General Survey (SAUO)
GSGS .... Geographical Section General Staff [*British*]
GSGS .... Geological Sciences Gopher Server (SAUO)
GSGS maps... General Staff Geographical Section maps covering Africa, Asia, the East Indies and Europe (SAUS)
GSGT .... Gunnery Sergeant (DNAB)
GSH .... Gambia Air Shuttle Ltd. [*ICAO designator*] (FAAC)
GSH .... Gas Space Heater
GSH .... Gas Surge Header [*Nuclear energy*] (NRCH)
GSH .... Generalized Spin Hamilton (SAUO)
GSH .... Generalized Spin Hamiltonian (SAUS)
GSH .... General supplies history (SAUS)
GSH .... Global Schoolhouse [*Computer science*] [*Telecommunications*]
GSH .... Glomerular-Stimulating Hormone [*Endocrinology*] (MAE)
GSH .... Glutathione [*Biochemistry*]
GSH .... Glutathione-SH [*Reduced glutathione*] [*Biochemistry*]
GSH .... Golden Syrian Hamster (DB)
GSH .... Good Study Habits (SAUS)
GSH .... Goshen, IN [*Location identifier*] [*FAA*] (FAAL)
GSH .... Great Space Handshake (SAUS)
GSH .... Growth-Stimulating Hormone [*Endocrinology*] (DAVI)
GSH .... Guangshen Railway ADS [*NYSE symbol*] (TTSB)
GSH .... Reduced Gluthathione [*Biochemistry*] (DAVI)
GSHAP .... Global Seismic Hazard Assessment Program (SAUO)
GS-HG .... Geological Society-Hydrogeology Group (BUAC)
GSHL .... General Shale Products Corp. (SAUO)
GSHMSU ...... General Support and Heavy Maintenance Supply Unit (SAUO)
GSHMU .... General Support HAWK Maintenance Unit (SAUO)
GSHMU .... General Support Heavy Maintenance Unit (SAUO)
G Shot .... Gunshot (SAUS)
GSHP .... German Short-Haired Pointer (SPVS)
GSHP .... Ground-Source Heat Pump (SAUS)
GSHP .... Reduced Glutathione Peroxidase (STED)
GSHPx .... Gluthathione Peroxidase (SAUS)
GSHR .... Gandhi Society for Human Rights (EA)
GSHR .... Grand Slam Home Runs [*Baseball*]
GSHV .... Globe Stop Hose Valve (SAUO)
GSHV .... Ground Squirrel Hepatitis Virus
gsi .... gas installed (SAUS)
GSI .... Gencom Systems (SAUS)
GSI .... Generalized Scale Invariance (SAUS)
GSI .... General Safety Inspection (SAUS)
GSI .... General Safety Inspector [*Aviation*]
GSI .... General Science Index
GSI .... General Semiconductor Incorporated (SAUO)
GSI .... General Server Interface (SAUS)
GSI .... General Service Infantry [*Army*]
GSI .... General Steel Industries (SAUO)
GSI .... Generic Safety Issue (NRCH)
GSI .... Genetic Stock Identification [*Pisciculture*]
GSI .... Genuine Stress Incontinence [*Urology*] (DAVI)
GSI .... Geodetic Survey Institute (SAUS)
GSI .... Geographical Society of Ireland (BUAC)
GSI .... Geographical Survey Institute (EERA)
GSI .... Geographic Survey Institute (SAUO)
GSI .... Geographic Systems, Inc. [*Information service or system*] (IID)
GSI .... Geographic Systems, Incorpotated (SAUS)
GSI .... Geolical Survey Institute (SAUS)
GSI .... Geological Society of Israel (BUAC)
GSI .... Geological Survey Institute (SAUS)
GSI .... Geological Survey of India (SAUO)
GSI .... Geological Survey of Iran (SAUS)
GSI .... Geological Survey of Israel (SAUO)
GSI .... Geophysical Service International (SAUS)
GSI .... Gesneriad Society International (EA)
GSI .... Gestational Stress Incontinence [*Medicine*] (MELL)
GSI .... Giant Scale Integration (IAA)
GSI .... Gigantic Scale Integration (SAUS)
GSI .... Gigascale Integration [*Electronics*]
GSI .... Glide Slope Indicator [*Aviation*]
GSI .... Glide Speed Indicator
GSI .... Global Severity Index [*Medicine*] (DMAA)
GSI .... Gold and Silver Institute (SAUS)
GSI .... Gonosomatic Indices
GSI .... Gordon Diagnostic System [*Attention deficit disorder test*]
GSI .... Government Source Inspection
GSI .... Graduate Student Instructor
GSI .... Grand Scale Integration (BUR)
GSI .... Graphic Structure Input
GSI .... Graphic Systems International (SAUS)
GSI .... Greenwich Street Municipal Fund, Inc. [*NYSE symbol*] (SAG)
GSI .... Gross Scheduled Income (SAUS)
GSI .... Ground-Speed Indicator [*Aviation*] (MCD)
GSI .... Guild of Saint Ives (EA)
GSI .... Gunite/Shotcrete Association (SAUO)
GSIA .... Graduate School of Industrial Administration [*Carnegie Mellon University*]
GSIBAX .... Geological Society of India.Bulletin (journ.) (SAUS)
GSIC .... Great Southwest Industries Corporation (SAUO)
GSIC .... Gujarat Small Industries Corp. [*India*] (BUAC)
GSICO .... Glaucoma Society of the International Congress of Ophthalmology (EA)
GSID .... Global Server Identifier (SAUO)
GSID .... Ground-Emplaced Seismic Intrusion Detector (NVT)
GSID .... Ground Seismic Intrusion Detector (SAUO)
GSID .... Ground Seismic Intrusion Device (SAUO)
G/SIDBAD ..... General Staff Identification Badge [*Military decoration*] (GFGA)
GSIDC .... Arab Gulf States Information Documentation Center [*Information service or system*] (IID)
GSidekB .... Grupo Sidek SA de CV [*Associated Press*] (SAG)
GSIdentBad... General Staff Identification Badge [*Military decoration*] (AABC)
GSIFC .... Gene Summers International Fan Club (EA)
GSIFC .... Georgia Satellites International Fan Club (EA)
GSIFX .... Goldman Sachs Intl. Equity Cl.A [*Mutual fund ticker symbol*] (SG)
GSigsO .... Group Signals Officer [*British military*] (DMA)
GSIHS .... Group for the Study of Irish Historic Settlement [*British*]
GSII .... General Surgical Innovations, Inc. [*NASDAQ symbol*] (SAG)
GSII .... Genl Surgical Innovations [*NASDAQ symbol*] (TTSB)
GSIL .... German Silver
GSIL .... Goldsil Mining & Milling, Inc. (SAUO)
GSIM .... Graduate School of Integrative Medicine (SAUO)
GSIN .... Goods and Services Identification Number (SAUS)
GSIO .... General Staff Interpreter Officer [*Military*] [*British*]
GSIR .... Great Southern of India Railway [*Indian Railway*] (TIR)
GSIS .... Geographic Snow Information System (SAUO)
GSIS .... GeoSim Information Server (SAUO)
GSIS .... Graduate School of International Studies (SAUS)
GSIS .... Ground Safety Information System (SAUO)
GSIS .... Group for the Standardization of Information Services (NITA)
GSIS .... Group Scientific Information Service (SAUO)
GSISEA .... Government Service Insurance System Employees' Association [*Philippines*]
GSIT .... Group Shorr Imagery Test [*Personality development test*] [*Psychology*]
GSIU .... Ground Standard Interface Unit (MCD)
GSJ .... Geological Survey of Japan (SAUS)
GSJ .... Gold Spring Resources [*Vancouver Stock Exchange symbol*]
GSJBS .... Goldsmiths', Silversmiths', and Jewellers' Benevolent Society [*British*]
GSJV .... Green Street Joint Venture (EERA)
GSK .... Gamble-Skogmo, Inc. (SAUO)
GSK .... General Storekeeper [*Navy*]
GSK .... Geological Survey of Kenya (SAUS)
GSK .... George Simon Kaufman [*American playwright, 1889-1961*]
GSK .... Glycogen Synthase Kinase [*An enzyme*]
GSK .... Gold Seeker Resources Ltd. [*Vancouver Stock Exchange symbol*]
GSKT .... Gasket (KSC)
GSL .... Generalized Simulation Language [*Computer science*] (MDG)
GSL .... General Sales Licence (WDAA)
GSL .... General Sales List (DB)
GSL .... General Service Launch [*British military*] (DMA)
GSL .... Generation Strategy Language [*Computer science*] (IEEE)
GSL .... Geographic Air Surveys Ltd. [*Canada*] [*ICAO designator*] (FAAC)
GSL .... Geographic Sciences Laboratory [*Fort Belvoir, VA*] [*United States Army Engineer Topographic Laboratories*] (GRD)
GSL .... Geographic Systems Laboratory [*US Army Engineer Topographic Laboratories*]
GSL .... Geological Society of London (BARN)
GSL .... Geophysical Sciences Laboratory [*New York University*]
GSL .... Georgia Department of Education, Atlanta, GA [*OCLC symbol*] (OCLC)
GSL .... GeoStatistical Library (SAUO)
GSL .... Geotechnical Science Laboratories (SAUS)
GSL .... German Studies Library Group (SAUO)
GSL .... Girls' Service League [*Later, YCL*] (EA)
GSL .... Glycosphingolipid [*Biochemistry*]
GSL .... Gold Cup Resources [*Vancouver Stock Exchange symbol*]
GSL .... Gorilla Sign Language (BYTE)
GSL .... Graduate Student Loan
GSL .... Graphics Software Laboratories (SAUS)
GSL .... Graphics Subroutine Library (SAUS)
GSL .... Greater Somalia League (SAUO)
GSL .... Great Salt Lake [*Utah*]
GSL .... Great Salt Lake Minerals & Chemicals Corp. (SAUO)
GSL .... Great Slave Lake Railway (SAUS)
GSL .... Great Somalia League

GSL............. Ground Systems Laboratory
GSL............. Group Scout Leader (SAUO)
GSL............. Guaranteed Student League (SAUO)
GSL............. Guaranteed Student Loan [*later, Stafford Loan*] [*Department of Education*]
GSL............. Gulf Stream Locale (CARB)
GSL............. Gyro-Stabilized Laser (SAUS)
GSLA........... GS Financial Corp. [*NASDAQ symbol*] (NASQ)
GSLABHF..... Greater St. Louis Amateur Baseball Hall of Fame (EA)
GSLB........... Gold Star Lapel Button [*Military decoration*] (AABC)
GSLC........... Guaranty Financial [*NASDAQ symbol*] (TTSB)
GSLC........... Guaranty Financial Corp. [*NASDAQ symbol*] (SAG)
GSLC........... Guaranty Savings & Loan FA [*NASDAQ symbol*] (SAG)
GSLCV......... Globe Stop Lift Check Valve (SAUO)
GSLD........... Group Selector Long Distance [*Telecommunications*] (IAA)
GS-LD......... Group Selector-Long Distance (SAUO)
GSLG........... German Studies Library Group (EAIO)
GSLI............. General Services Life Insurance Company (SAUO)
GSLI............. GSI Lumonics, Inc. [*NASDAQ symbol*] (NASQ)
GSLIS.......... Graduate School of Library and Information Science (SAUS)
GSLL........... General Stores Load List (SAUO)
GSLMP........ Global Sea Level Monitoring Programme (SAUO)
GSLO........... Gland Seal Leak Off [*Nuclear energy*] (NRCH)
GSLP........... Gibraltar Socialist Labour Party [*Political party*] (PPW)
GSLP........... Global Sequential Local Par (SAUS)
GSLP........... Guaranteed Student Loan Program
GSLPEP....... Georgia Speech and Language Pathology Evaluation Program (SAUO)
GSLTA......... Girls' Schools Lawn Tennis Association [*British*] (BI)
GSLV........... Geostationary Launch Vehicle [*Indian Space Research Organization*]
GSLV........... Geostationary Satellite Launch Vehicle
GSLV........... Geosynchronous Launch Vehicle (SAUS)
GSLV........... Geosynchronous Satellite Launch Vehicle (SAUS)
GSM............. City of Savannah, Municipal Research Library, Savannah, GA [*Library symbol*] [*Library of Congress*] (LCLS)
GSM............. Garrison Sergeant-Major [*British*]
GSM............. Gas Turbine Systems Technician, Mechanical [*Military*] (POLM)
GSM............. Generalized Sequential Machine [*Computer science*]
GSM............. Generalized Sort/Merge [*Computer science*]
GSM............. General Sales Manager
GSM............. General Service Manager [*Automotive retailing*]
GSM............. General Service Medal [*British*]
GSM............. General Situation Map [*Military*] (NATG)
GSM............. General Stores Material [*Navy*]
GSM............. General Support Maintenance (MCD)
GSM............. General Synod Measures (ILCA)
GSM............. General Syntactic Processor (SAUS)
GSM............. General System Mobile [*Telephone*]
GSM............. General System Model [*Computer science*] (EERA)
GSM............. General Systems Model (SAUO)
GSM............. Geocentric Solar Magnetospheric [*System*] [*NASA*]
GSM............. Geological Society of Malaysia (EAIO)
GSM............. Geological Survey of Great Britain and Museum of Practical Geology (BI)
GSM............. Geologic Surface Model (SAUO)
GSM............. Gibson Spiral Maze [*Psychology*]
GSM............. Global Shared Memory (SAUO)
GSM............. Global System for Mobile Communication [*Computer science*]
GSM............. Global System for Mobiles [*European mobile-phone network*] (ECON)
GSM............. Gold Star Mothers
GSM............. Goldstream Resources Ltd. [*Vancouver Stock Exchange symbol*]
GSM............. Good Sound Marketable (SAUS)
GSM............. Good Sound Merchantable
GSM............. Gradient Solidification Method [*Optics*]
GSM............. Gram per Square Metre (SAUS)
GSM............. Grams per Square Meter
gsm.............. Grams per Square Metre (WDAA)
GSM............. Granite State Manufacturing (SAUS)
GSM............. Graphic Size Modification (SAUS)
GSM............. Graphics Schematics Module [*McDonnell-Douglas Corp.*]
GSM............. Graphics System Module
GSM............. Graphic Standard Metafile (SAUS)
GSM............. Grass Mountain [*Washington*] [*Seismograph station code, US Geological Survey*] (SEIS)
GSM............. Great Smokey Mountains Railway [*Federal Railroad Administration identification code*]
GSM............. Greek Society for Microbiology (BUAC)
GSM............. Greenough Stereomicroscope (SAUS)
GSM............. Gross Sales Monthly (SAUS)
GSM............. Gross Square Meters (SAUS)
GSM............. Ground Safety Monitor (ACAE)
GSM............. Ground Segment Manager (ACAE)
GSM............. Ground Signal Mixer
GSM............. Ground Station Module (ACAE)
GSM............. Ground Station Modules [*Communications*] [*Army*]
GSM............. Ground Supplied Material (SAUS)
GSM............. Ground Support Maintenance (MCD)
GSM............. Groupe Speciale Mobile [*European digital cellular radio standard*]
GSM............. Group Scout Master [*Scouting*]
GSM............. Guildhall School of Music [*London*]
GSM............. Guildhall School of Music and Drama (SAUO)
GSM............. Guild of Saint Matthew
GSM1........... Gas Turbine Systems Technician, Mechanical, First Class [*Navy rating*] (DNAB)
GSM2........... Gas Turbine Systems Technician, Mechanical, Second Class [*Navy rating*] (DNAB)
GSM3........... Gas Turbine Systems Technician, Mechanical, Third Class [*Navy rating*] (DNAB)
GSMA........... Global Scheduling Multiple Access (SAUO)
GSMA........... Goldstone-SFOF [*Space Flight Operations Facility*] Microwave Assembly [*NASA*]
GSMASK...... GN Geodesics and Mask (SAUS)
GSMB........... Grain Sorghum Marketing Board [*New South Wales, Australia*]
GSMB........... Graphic Standards Management Board
GSMBBK...... Geological Society of Malaysia. Bulletin (journ.) (SAUS)
GSMBE......... Gas-Source Molecular Beam Epitaxy [*Coating technology*]
GSMBYP...... Great Smoky Mountains National Park (SAUS)
GSMC........... Gas Turbine Systems Technician, Mechanical, Chief [*Navy rating*] (DNAB)
GSMC........... Greater Stuttgart Military Community (SAUO)
GSMD........... General Society of Mayflower Descendants (EA)
GSMD........... Geological Survey and Mines Department (SAUS)
GSMD........... Guildhall School of Music and Drama [*London*] (DI)
GSME........... Ground Support Maintenance Equipment [*Aerospace*]
GSMFA......... Gas Turbine Systems Technician, Mechanical, Fireman Apprentice [*Navy rating*] (DNAB)
GSMFC......... Gulf States Marine Fisheries Commission
GSMFC......... Gulf States Marine Fisheries Compact (COE)
GSMFN......... Gas Turbine Systems Technician, Mechanical, Fireman [*Navy rating*] (DNAB)
GSMI............ Global Spill Management, Inc. [*NASDAQ symbol*] (SAG)
GSML........... Generalized Standard Markup Language [*Also, SGML*]
GSML........... General Stores Material List
GSMMBJ...... Geological Survey of Malaysia. District Memoir (journ.) (SAUS)
GSMNBM...... Geological Society of Malaysia Newsletter (journ.) (SAUS)
GSMNP........ Great Smoky Mountains National Park [*Also, GRSM*]
GSMOL........ Golden State Mobilehome Owners League (SAUO)
GSMP........... General Switch Management Protocol (SAUS)
GSMP........... Generic Switch Management Protocol (SAUS)
GSMP........... German Society of Medical Physics [*Medicine*] (EDAA)
GSMP........... Global Services Management Platform [*Newbridge Network*]
GSMPAR...... Geological Survey of Malaysia. Geological Papers (journ.) (SAUS)
GSMR........... Gulf & Mississippi Railroad [*Federal Railroad Administration identification code*]
GSMS........... Geocentric Solar Magnetospheric System (SAUS)
GSMS........... Government Securities Management System [*The Bond Buyer, Inc.*] [*Information service or system*] (IID)
GSMS........... Government Services Marketing Services (SAUS)
GSMS........... Graduate Student of the Management Society (SAUO)
GSMS........... Growth of Strategic Materials in Space (MCD)
GSMS........... Gulf South Medical Supply [*NASDAQ symbol*] (TTSB)
GSMST......... Ground System Mission Simulation Tester (SAUS)
GSMT........... General Service Mechanical Transport (SAUO)
GSMT........... General Society of Mechanics and Tradesmen (EA)
GSN............. GCOS Surface Network (SAUO)
GSN............. General Steam Navigation (SAUO)
GSN............. Geological Society Newsletter (SAUO)
GSN............. Geological Survey of Namibia (SAUS)
GSN............. Gesneriad Saintpaulia News [*A publication*]
GSN............. Giant Serotonin-Containing Neuron [*Medicine*] (DMAA)
GSN............. Gifted with Special Needs
GSN............. Global Seismic Network (CARB)
GSN............. Global Seismographic Network (SAUO)
GSN............. Global Shopping Network (SAUO)
GSN............. Graph Support Node (SAUS)
GSN............. Greater Sciatic Notch [*Medicine*] (MELL)
GSN............. Green Student Network (BUAC)
GSN............. Greenwich Sideral Noon (SAUS)
GSN............. Greenwich Sidereal Noon (ROG)
GSN............. Group Selection Network (SAUO)
GSN............. Group Switching Network (SAUO)
GSN............. Mount Gunson [*Australia*] [*Airport symbol*] (OAG)
GSN............. Saipan International Airport [*FAA*] (TAG)
GSNA........... Goethe Society of North America (EA)
GSNB........... Grant Street National Park (SAUS)
GSNC........... General Steam Navigation Co. [*British*]
GSNCO......... General Steam Navigation Co. [*Shipping*] [*British*]
GS News Tech Rep... GS News Technical Report (journ.) (SAUS)
GSNF........... Global SchoolNet Foundation (SAUO)
GSNI............ Geological Survey of Northern Ireland (SAUS)
GSNI............ Grandparent Strengths and Needs Inventory [*Test*] (TMMY)
GSNS........... Global Satellite Navigation System (SAUS)
GSNS........... Guidance Control and Navigation Subsystem
GSNSW........ Geographical Society of New South Wales [*Australia*]
GSNT........... Genealogical Society of the Northern Territory [*Australia*]
GSNW........... Gateway Service for NetWare (SAUS)
GSNW........... Gateway Services for Netware (SAUO)
GSNWR........ Great Swamp National Wildlife Refuge (SAUO)
GSNX........... GaSonics International [*NASDAQ symbol*] (TTSB)
GSNX........... Gasonics International Corp. [*NASDAQ symbol*] (SAG)
GSO............. General Salary Order [*United States*] (DLA)
GSO............. General Services Officer
GSO............. General Spin Orbitals [*Atomic physics*]
GSO............. General Staff Officer [*Military*]
GSO............. General Stores Officer
GSO............. General Submarine Officer (DOMA)
GSO............. General Supply Office
GSO............. General Support Office
GSO............. Genus Equity Corp. (SAUO)

GSO .... Geo. S. Olive & Co. [*Telecommunications service*] (TSSD)
GSO .... Geostationary Earth Orbit (ISAK)
GSO .... Geostationary Orbit (MCD)
GSO .... Geostationary Satellite Orbit (SAUS)
GSO .... Geosynchronous Orbit
GSO .... German Service Organization (SAUO)
GSO .... Girls Service Organization (SAUO)
GSO .... Government Services Organization (DOMA)
GSO .... Government Solicitor's Office [*Australian Capital Territory*]
GSO .... Government Statistician's Office [*Queensland, Australia*]
GSO .... Government Superannuation Office [*Queensland, Australia*]
GSO .... Graduate School of Oceanography [*University of Rhode Island*]
GSO .... Graduate Service Overseas of the National Union of Students [*British*] (AEBS)
GSO .... Greensboro/High Point/Winston Salem [*North Carolina*] [*Airport symbol*]
GSO .... Ground Safety Office [*or Officer*] [*Air Force*]
GSO .... Ground Safety Officers Course (SAUO)
GSO .... Ground Speed Oscillator (SAUS)
GSO .... Ground-Speed Oscillator [*Aviation*]
GSO .... Ground Speed Outbound (SAUS)
GSO .... Ground Staff Office (ACAE)
GSO .... Ground Support Office [*or Officer*] [*Military*] (AFIT)
GSO .... Ground Support Officer (SAUO)
GSO .... Ground Support Operations [*Aerospace*] (MCD)
GSO .... Ground Systems Operations (MCD)
GSO .... Growth Stock Outlook Trust, Inc. (MHDW)
GSO .... GSFC Security Office (SAUS)
GSO .... GSR Goldsearch Resources [*Vancouver Stock Exchange symbol*]
GSO .... Gun Safety Officer
GSO .... Gyro Storage Oven
GSO .... Olive [*Geo S.*] & Co. [*Indianapolis, IN*] (TSSD)
GSO .... Piedmont Triad International Airport [*FAA*] (TAG)
GSO1 .... General Staff Officer 1st grade (SAUO)
GSO-1 .... General Staff Officer, grade 1 (SAUS)
GSO2 .... General Staff Officer 2nd grade (SAUO)
GSO-2 .... General Staff Officer, grade 2 (SAUS)
GSO3 .... General Staff Officer 3rd grade (SAUO)
GSO-3 .... General Staff Officer, grade 3 (SAUS)
GSoA .... Gerontological Society of America (DAVI)
GSOC .... German Science Operations Center (SAUS)
GSOC .... German Space Operation Center (or Centre) (SAUO)
GSOC .... German Space Operations Centre (SAUS)
GSOC .... Gold Star Owners Club (EA)
G Soc Am B... Geological Society of America. Bulletin (journ.) (SAUS)
G Soc Dublin J... Geological Society of Dublin. Journal (journ.) (SAUS)
G Soc Glas Tr... Geological Society of Glasgow. Transactions (journ.) (SAUS)
G Soc London Tr Pr Q J... Geolagical Society of London. Transactions. Proceedings. Quarterly Journal (journ.) (SAUS)
G Soc PA Tr... Geological Society of Pennsylvania. Transactions (journ.) (SAUS)
G Soc Tokyo J... Geological Society of Tokyo. Journal (journ.) (SAUS)
GSOF .... Group 1 Software [*NASDAQ symbol*] (TTSB)
GSOF .... Group 1 Software, Inc. [*NASDAQ symbol*] (NQ)
GS of W....... Grand Superintendent of Works [*Freemasonry*]
GSOH .... Good Sense of Humor (ODA)
GSO-I .... General Staff Officer-Intelligence (SAUO)
GSOIA .... General Security of Information Agreement
GSOL .... Global Sources [*NASDAQ symbol*] (SG)
GSOMIA .... General Security of Military Information Agreement (SAUS)
GSO-Ops ...... General Staff Officer-Operations (SAUO)
GSOP .... General Stock Ownership Plan
GSOP .... Ground Systems Operations (SAUS)
GSOP .... Guidance Systems Operation Plan [*NASA*] (KSC)
GSOPS .... Guide Star Production Operations Environment (SAUS)
GSOR .... General Staff Operational Requirements [*Army*] (AABC)
GSOR .... General Staff Operational Research (SAUO)
GSORD .... Geological Survey Open-File Report (journ.) (SAUS)
GS Ord Dep... General Stores Ordnance Depot (SAUO)
GSORTS .... GCCS Status of Resources and Training System (SAUO)
GSOS .... GPS Surface Observing System (SAUS)
GS/OS .... GS Operating System (SAUS)
GSOST .... Goldstein-Scheerer Object Sorting Test [*Psychology*]
GSOSTATS... Geosynchronous Satellite Orbital Statistics [*NASA*] (ACAE)
GSOTD .... Geek Site Of The Day (SAUS)
GSOWM .... Global Spectral Ocean Wave Model
GSP .... Galvanic Skin Potential [*Physiology*]
GSP .... Gang Summary Punch (SAUS)
gsp .... gas paid for (SAUS)
gsp .... gas planned (SAUS)
GSP .... Gel Supported Precipitation [*Method*] [*Chemistry*]
GSP .... Genealogical Society of Pennsylvania (EA)
GSP .... Generalised System of Preferences (ECON)
G S P .... Generalised System of Tariff Preferences (SAUS)
GSP .... Generalized Sequential Machine (SAUS)
GSP .... Generalized System of Preferences (SAUS)
GSP .... Generalized System of Tariff Preferences [*US Customs Service*]
GSP .... Generalized System Preferences (SAUS)
GSP .... General Safety Plan (SAUS)
GSP .... General Sea Harvest [*Vancouver Stock Exchange symbol*]
GSP .... General Semantic Problem (AAG)
GSP .... General Simulation Program [*Programming language*] (IEEE)
GSP .... General Space Planner (SAUO)
GSP .... General Strike for Peace
GSP .... General Strike Plan (NATG)
GSP .... General Strike Program (SAUO)
GSP .... General Survey Panel (STED)
GSP .... General Syntactic Processor
GSP .... General System of Preference (SAUS)
GSP .... Generic Server Passer (SAUS)
GSP .... Geodetic Satellite Program
GSP .... Geographical Society of Philadelphia (BUAC)
GSP .... Geographical Statistics Program (SAUO)
GSP .... Geological Survey of Pakistan (SAUS)
GSP .... Geologic Section Program (SAUO)
GSP .... Geophysical Statistics Project (SAUS)
GSP .... Georgia Scholar Program (SAUO)
GSP .... Georgia State Patrol (SAUO)
GSP .... German Short-haired Pointer (SPVS)
GSP .... German Society of Pennsylvania (EA)
GSP .... Girl Scouts of the Philippines
GSP .... Gladstone Stream [*New Zealand*] [*Seismograph station code, US Geological Survey*] (SEIS)
GSP .... Glassfibre-Strengthlened Polyester (SAUS)
GSP .... Global Service Provider (SAUO)
GSP .... Global Studies Program (SAUS)
GSP .... Glycogen Synthetase Phosphatase (STED)
GSP .... Glycosylated Serum Protein
GSP .... Good-Service Pension [*Navy*] [*British*]
GSP .... Government Security Policy (FOTI)
GSP .... Government Selected Price
GSP .... Government Sponsored Promotion (ADA)
GSP .... Government Standard Parts
GSP .... Graphics System Processor [*Texas Instruments, Inc.*] [*Computer hardware*]
GSP .... Graphic Subroutine Package [*Computer science*]
GSP .... Greenland Sea Project (SAUO)
GSP .... Green Star; Parachute (SAUS)
GSP .... Greenville/Spartanburg [*South Carolina*] [*Airport symbol*]
GSP .... Greer, SC [*Location identifier*] [*FAA*] (FAAL)
GSP .... Gross Social Product [*Economics*]
GSP .... Gross State Product (OICC)
GSP .... Ground Safety Plan (MUGU)
GSP .... Ground Support Personnel (SAUS)
GSP .... Ground Support Position (SAUS)
GSP .... Group Select Panel (ECII)
GSP .... Group Step Pulse (SAUO)
GSP .... Growth Fund of Spain [*NYSE symbol*] (SPSG)
GSP .... Guidance Signal Processor (KSC)
GSP .... Gulf States Power [*Federal Railroad Administration identification code*]
GSP .... M & M Aviation, Inc. [*ICAO designator*] (FAAC)
GSP .... Royal Geographical Society. Proceedings [*A publication*]
GSPA .... Gold Star Parents for Amnesty [*Defunct*] (EA)
GSPA .... Grain Sorghum Producers Association (EA)
GSPA .... Gulfport State Port Authority (SAUO)
GSPAN .... Graphic S Plane Analysis (SAUS)
GSPB .... Geodetic Satellite Policy Board (SAUO)
GSPC .... Gas Scintillation Proportional Chamber (SAUS)
GSPC .... Gas Scintillation Proportional Counter [*Instrumentation*]
GSPC .... Graphic Standards Planning Committee (NITA)
GSPC .... The Salafist Group for Call and Combat [*Government term*] (GA)
GSPCA .... German Shorthaired Pointer Club of America (EA)
GSPDC .... Geostationary Satellite Precipitation Data Centre (CARB)
GSPE .... Georgia Society of Professional Engineers (SRA)
GSPE .... Groupe Socialiste du Parlement Europeen [*Socialist Group in the European Parliament - SGEP*] (EAIO)
GSPECT .... Gated Single-Photon Emission Computed Tomography [*Medicine*] (RAWO)
GSPEP .... Georgia School Psychologist Evaluation Program (SAUO)
GSPG .... Graphics System Program Group (SAUO)
GSPGR .... Global System on Plant Genetic Resources (SAUO)
GSPHCT ...... Group Simplified Perturbed Hard Chain Theory [*Equation of state*]
GSPIA .... Graduate School of Public and International Affairs (SAUO)
GSPID .... Gain-Scheduled Proportional Integro-Differential (AAEL)
GSpl .... Gibbon Spleen [*Medicine*] (EDAA)
GSPL .... Gospel
GSPMR .... General Services Administration Property Management Regulation [*A publication*] (AAGC)
GSPN .... Greater Superficial Petrosal Nerve [*Medicine*] (EDAA)
GSPN .... Greater Superficial Petrosal Neurectomy [*Neurosurgery*] (DAVI)
GSPNG .... Geological Survey Papua New Guinea (SAUS)
GSPO .... Gemini Spacecraft Project Office [*NASA*] (MCD)
GSPO .... Global Studies Program Office (SAUO)
GSPO .... Ground Systems Project Officer (SAUS)
GSPOT .... Geometric Spot Analysis System (SAUS)
G (Spot) .... Graefenberg Spot [*Gynecology*]
G-spot .... Grafenberg spot (SAUS)
GSPP .... Gel-Supported Precipitation Process (SAUO)
GSPP .... Global Shared Productivity Program (WDAA)
GSPR .... General Session of Peace Roll [*British*] [*Legal term*] (ROG)
GSPR .... GSA [*General Services Administration*] Procurement Regulations
GSP-R .... Guidance Signal Processor-Repeater (KSC)
GSPRA .... Georgia School Public Relations Association (SAUO)
GSPRT .... Generalized Sequential Probability Ratio Test (PDAA)
GSPS .... Gamma-Ray Spectrometer Penetrator System (ACAE)
GSPS .... Generating Station Protection System [*Nuclear energy*] (NRCH)
GSPS .... Guarded Straddle Packer System (SAUS)
GSPS .... Guidance Spare Power Supply
GSPT .... Global Sports, Inc. [*NASDAQ symbol*] (NASQ)
GSPTEK .... Graphics Support Processor/Tektronix

GSPW .... Garden State Parkway (SAUS)
GSPWA .... Georgia Southern Peanut Warehousemen's Association (SRA)
GSPZ .... Gulf States Paper [*Federal Railroad Administration identification code*]
GSQ .... Generalized Sinusoidal Quantity
GSQ .... General Staff Quarters (SAUO)
GSQ .... Genus Equity Corp. [*Toronto Stock Exchange symbol*]
GSQ .... Geological Survey of Queensland [*Australia*]
GSQA .... Government Source Quality Assurance (SAUS)
GSQC .... Ground Surveillance Qualification Course [*Army*]
GSQNA .... Geological Society of South Africa. Quarterly News Bulletin (journ.) (SAUS)
GSQT .... Gun Ship Qualification Trials (MCD)
GSR .... Galvanic Skin Reflex (SAUS)
GSR .... Galvanic Skin Resistance [*Physiology*] (DAVI)
GSR .... Galvanic Skin Response [*or Reflex*] [*Physiology*]
GSR .... Galvanic Stimulation Rate [*Physiology*]
GSR .... Gap Spacing Routine (SAUS)
GSR .... Gardo [*Somalia*] [*Airport symbol*] (OAG)
GSR .... Gas Storage Reservoirs (SAUO)
GSR .... Generalized Schartzman Reaction [*Medicine*]
GSR .... General Service Recruit [*Navy*]
GSR .... General Service Request (ACAE)
GSR .... General Staff Requirement [*British*] (RDA)
GSR .... General Study References (SAUO)
GSR .... General Support Reinforcing [*Army*] (AABC)
GSR .... General Systems Research Ltd. [*Vancouver Stock Exchange symbol*]
gsr .... gene service reinforcement (SAUS)
GSR .... Geological Survey, Reston [*Virginia*] [*Seismograph station code, US Geological Survey*] (SEIS)
gsr .... Georgian Soviet Socialist Republic [*MARC country of publication code*] [*Library of Congress*] (LCCP)
GSR .... Germanium Stack Rectifier
GSR .... German Sanchez Ruiperez [*Founder and chairman of Anaya, a Spanish publishing enterprise*]
GSR .... Gigabit Speed Router (GART)
GSR .... Gigabit Switching Router (SAUS)
GSR .... Gland Steam Regulator [*Nuclear energy*] (NRCH)
GSR .... Glide Slope Receiver [*Aviation*]
GSR .... Global Shared Resources [*Computer science*] (IBMDP)
GSR .... Global-Support Software (SAUS)
GSR .... Glutathione Reductase [*Medicine*] (MELL)
GSR .... Golden Star Resources [*AMEX symbol*] (TTSB)
GSR .... Golden Star Resources Ltd. [*AMEX symbol*] (SPSG)
GSR .... Gondal State Railway [*Indian Railway*] (TIR)
GSR .... Gongwer's State Reports [*Ohio*] [*A publication*] (DLA)
GSR .... Government Spares Release (MCD)
GSR .... Government Synthetic Rubber (SAUO)
GSR .... Graphic Service Routines [*Computer science*] (MCD)
GSR .... Gray Scale Recording (SAUS)
GSR .... Great Southern Railway (SAUO)
GSR .... Great Swamp Research (SAUS)
GSR .... Green Shoe Manufacturing Co. (SAUO)
GSR .... Grid Space Relay
GSR .... Ground Sensor Relay (IAA)
GSR .... Ground Service Relay (MCD)
GSR .... Ground-Speed Returning [*Aviation*]
GSR .... Ground Surveillance RADAR
GSR .... Ground Surveillance Radio (SAUS)
GSR .... Group Sales Representative [*Health insurance*] (GHCT)
GSR .... Group Selective Register
GSR .... Group Surveillance Radar (SAUS)
GSR .... Gunshot Residue [*Forensics*]
GSR .... Gun Sound Ranging [*An acoustic device*]
GSRA .... Graduate Student Research Assistant
GSRB .... Glide Slope Reference Bar [*Aviation*]
GSRC .... Geological Survey Research Committee (SAUS)
GSRED .... Gas Supply Review (journ.) (SAUS)
GSRI .... Global Solar Radiation Index (PDAA)
GSRI .... Great Swamp Research Institute (EA)
GSRI .... Gulf South Research Institute
GSRIF .... Goldenhar Syndrome Research and Information Fund (ADWA)
GSRN .... Global Surface Radiation Network (CARB)
GSRP .... Gambian Socialist Revolutionary Party [*Political party*] (PD)
GSRP .... Graduate Student Researchers Program (SAUS)
GSRPS .... Group for the Study of Rocket Propulsion Systems (ACAE)
GSRS .... General Support Rocket System
GSRS .... Ground Support Rocket System (DWSG)
GSRS .... Ground Surveillance RADAR System
GSRT .... Gesell School Rediness Test (EDAC)
GSRTST ...... German Society for Rocket Technology and Space Travel (SAUO)
GSRV .... Globe Stop Radiator Valve (SAUO)
GSRVC .... Good Sam Recreational Vehicle Club (EA)
GSRX .... Gettysburg Scenic Rail Tour [*Federal Railroad Administration identification code*]
GSS .... Chieftain International Fund [*AMEX symbol*] (SPSG)
GSS .... Galvanized Steel Sheet [*Technical drawings*]
GSS .... Galvanized Steel Strand [*Telecommunications*] (TEL)
GSS .... Gamete Shedding Substance [*Endocrinology*]
GSS .... Gamma Scintillation System (MSA)
GSS .... Gamma Sigma Sigma (EA)
GSS .... Gatineau Satellite Station (SAUO)
GSS .... Geese Security Squad (SAUO)
GSS .... Generalised Stimulation system (SAUS)
GSS .... General Security Service (SAUS)
GSS .... General Service School [*Army*]
GSS .... General Simulation System [*Army*]
GSS .... General Social Services (SAUO)
GSS .... General Social Survey [*National Opinion Research Center*]
GSS .... General Specifications for Ships (SAUO)
GSS .... General Staff Support (IAA)
GSS .... General Supply Schedule
GSS .... General Support System
GSS .... General Switching System (SAUO)
GSS .... Generic Security Service (SAUS)
GSS .... Generic Service State (DINT)
GSS .... Genesis Airways Ltd. [*British*] [*FAA designator*] (FAAC)
GSS .... Geodetic Stationary Satellite
GSS .... Geodetic Survey Squadron (SAUO)
GSS .... Geographic Support System (SAUO)
GSS .... George Sand Studies (EA)
GSS .... Geospace Swing Station (SAUO)
GSS .... Geostationary Satellite (PDAA)
GSS .... Gerontology Special Interest Section [*American Occupational Therapy Association*]
GSS .... Gerstmann-Staussler Syndrome [*Medicine*]
GSS .... Gerstmann-Straeussler-Scheinker [*Disease*]
GSS .... Gertsmann-Staussler-Scheinker syndrome (SAUS)
GSS .... Ghost Story Society [*British*] (DBA)
GSS .... Gilbert and Sullivan Society (EA)
GSS .... Global Satellite System (SAUO)
GSS .... Global Security Service [*Computer science*] (DCDG)
GSS .... Global Space Station [*Proposed by NASA and ESA*]
GSS .... Global Subsurface System (DWSG)
GSS .... Global Surveillance Station (IAA)
GSS .... Global Surveillance System [*Air Force*]
GSS .... Gonad-Stimulating Substance [*Endocrinology*]
GSS .... Good Shepherd Sisters [*Australia*]
GSS .... Gossan Resources [*Vancouver Stock Exchange symbol*]
GSS .... Government Statistical Service [*British*]
GSS .... Government Supervisory Services (SAUO)
GSS .... Graduate Student Society (SAUO)
GSS .... Graphic Service System (SAUS)
GSS .... Graphic Software Systems Inc. (NITA)
GSS .... Graphic Support Software
GSS .... Gravity Sensors System [*Navigation*]
GSS .... Gray-Scale Sonography [*Medicine*]
GSS .... Grid Sheet Survey (SAUO)
GSS .... Ground Segment Subsystem (ACAE)
GSS .... Ground Support Software [*NASA*] (NASA)
GSS .... Ground Support System [*Aerospace*] (AAG)
GSS .... Group of Specialists on Seals (SAUO)
GSS .... Group Switching Subsystem (ACRL)
GSS .... Growth Space Station (KSC)
GSS .... Grumman Standard Specification (SAUS)
GSS .... Guidance System Simulator
GSS .... Gust Suppression System (SAUS)
GSS .... Gynecologic Surgery Society (NTPA)
GSS .... Rome, NY [*Location identifier*] [*FAA*] (FAAL)
GSSA .... General Support Service Area (MCD)
GSSA .... General Support Supply Activity (MCD)
GSSA .... Geological Survey South Africa (SAUS)
GSSA .... Georgia School Superintendents Association (SAUO)
GSSA .... Graduate Student Staff Assistant
GSSA .... Grassland Society of Southern Africa [*See also WVSA*] (EAIO)
GSSA .... Ground Support Systems Activation [*NASA*] (NASA)
GSSAPI .... Generic Security Service Application Program Interface
GSSC .... General Support Services Contractor (ABAC)
GSSC .... Georgia Schoolhouse Systems Council (SAUO)
GSSC .... Greater Super Six Club [*Defunct*] (EA)
GSSC .... Grenada Sunburst Systems Corporation (SAUO)
GSSC .... Ground Support Simulation Computer [*Aerospace*] (KSC)
GSSC .... Ground Support Systems Contractor [*NASA*] (NASA)
GSSC .... Savannah State College, Savannah, GA [*Library symbol*] [*Library of Congress*] (LCLS)
GSSD .... Gerstmann-Straeussler-Scheinker Disease [*Medicine*] (DMAA)
GSSDA .... Georgia State Skin Diving Association (SAUO)
GSSDAF ...... Gatineau Satellite Station Data Acquisition Facility (SAUS)
GSSE .... Association of General States of Students from Europe (SAUO)
GSSEL .... General and Standard Support Equipment List (ACAE)
GSSF .... General Supply Stock Fund [*Air Force*] (AFM)
GSSF .... Government Satellite Services Facility (SSD)
GSSF .... Ground Special Security Forces
GSSG .... Glutathione Disulfide (ADWA)
GSSG-R .... Glutathione Reductase [*An enzyme*] (DAVI)
GSSH .... Grand Street Settlement House (SAUO)
GSSI .... Government and Social Science Information (SAUS)
GSSI .... Ground Support System Integration (MCD)
GSSI .... Ground Support System Interaction (SAUS)
GSsiHi .... Coastal Georgia Historical Society, St. Simons Island, GA [*Library symbol*] [*Library of Congress*] (LCLS)
GSsiM .... [*The*] Methodist Museum, St. Simons Island, GA [*Library symbol*] [*Library of Congress*] (LCLS)
GSS/L .... General Staff Support / Large (SAUS)
GSSL .... General Staff Support Large (IAA)
GSS/L .... General Staff Support/Large (SAUO)
GSSL .... Genoa, Savona, Spezia, or Leghorn [*Italian ports*] (DS)
GS/SLD .... Ground Selector of Secondary Long-Distance (SAUO)
GSSLD .... Group Selector of Secondary Long Distance [*Telecommunications*] (IAA)

GSSLNCV ..... Genoa, Savona, Spezia, Leghorn, Naples, or Civita Vecchia [*Italian ports*] (DS)
GSS/M .... General Staff Support / Medium (SAUS)
GSSM .... General Staff Support Medium (IAA)
GSS/M .... General Staff Support/Medium (SAUO)
GSS/N .... Government Surplus Stores, New (SAUO)
GSSO .... General Stores Supply Office
GSSP .... Generally Accepted System Security Principles [*Computer science*] (ITCA)
GSSP .... Global Stratotype Section and Point [*Paleontology*]
GSSPr .... Chieftain Intl Fd $1.8125 Cv Pfd [*AMEX symbol*] (TTSB)
GSSPS .... Gravitationally Stabilized Solar Power System
GSSq .... Geodetic Survey Squadron [*Air Force*] (AFM)
GSSQX .... Goldman Sachs Core U.S. Equity Cl.A [*Mutual fund ticker symbol*] (SG)
GSSR .... Generalized Sanarelli-Shwartzman Reaction [*Medicine*] (MAE)
GSSR .... General Salary Stabilization Regulations [*United States*] (DLA)
GSS/R .... Government Surplus Stores, Reconditioned (SAUO)
GSSR .... Ground Support System Review [*Aerospace*] (AAG)
GSSR .... Ground System Support Requirements (ACAE)
Gss Rase ..... Glutathione Reductase [*Medicine*] (EDAA)
GSSRPL .... Guide to Social Science and Religion in Periodical Literature (journ.) (SAUS)
GSSS .... General Support Shot Set (SAUO)
GSSS .... Global Services Space Systems (SAUO)
GSSs .... Government Supply Sources (SAUS)
GSSS .... Ground Support System Specification [*Aerospace*] (AAG)
GSSS .... Guide Star Selection System (SAUS)
GSSS .... Gyro-Stabilised Sighting System (SAUS)
GSSSP .... Graduate Science Student Support Postdoctorals Survey [*National Science Foundation*] (GFGA)
GSST .... Gatherer, Stitcher, Side Sewer, and Trimmer [*Publishing*]
GSST .... Goldstein-Scheerer Stick Test [*Psychology*]
GSSTFR .... Gas-Solid-Solid Trickle Flow Reactor [*Chemical engineering*]
GSS/U .... Government Surplus Stores, Unreconditioned (SAUO)
GSSW .... Gas-Shielded Stud Weld (SAUS)
GSSW .... Gas-Shielded Stud Welding (PDAA)
GSSWEP ...... Georgia School Social Worker Evaluation Program (SAUO)
GSSZ .... Gulf State Steel [*Federal Railroad Administration identification code*]
GST .... Flying Boat [*Russian aircraft symbol*]
GST .... gamma-ray spectroscopy logging tool (SAUS)
GST .... Garter Stitch [*Knitting*] (ADA)
g-st .... garter-stitch (SAUS)
GST .... Gaseous Storage Toroidal (SAUS)
GST .... Gas Surge Tank [*Nuclear energy*] (NRCH)
GST .... Gate Sensitive Thyristor (IAA)
GST .... Gemini System Trainer [*NASA*] (IAA)
GST .... Genealogical Society of Tasmania [*Australia*]
GST .... General Sales Tax (GOBB)
GST .... General Scholarship Test for High School Seniors [*Education*] (AEBS)
GST .... General Screening Test
GST .... General Service Test (NATG)
GST .... General Service Truck [*British*]
GST .... General Staff Target (NATG)
GST .... General Staff with Troops [*Army*]
GST .... General Systems Theory
GST .... Generation-Skipping Transfer Tax
GST .... Generic Scan Tool [*Automobile service*]
GST .... Genetic Screening Test (MELL)
GST .... Genstar, Ltd. (SAUO)
GST .... Geographical Specialist Team [*Army*] (AABC)
GST .... Georgia School of Technology (SAUO)
GST .... German Summer Time (SAUO)
GST .... Gesammelte Studien zum Alten Testament [*A publication*] (BJA)
GST .... Glazed Structural Tile [*Technical drawings*]
GST .... Global Space Transport (IAA)
GST .... Global Storage Table (SAUS)
GST .... Global Symbol Table [*Computer science*] (CIST)
GST .... Glutathione S-Transferase [*An enzyme*]
GST .... Glutathione-S-Transferase [*Medicine*] (EDAA)
GST .... Gold Salt Therapy [*Medicine*] (DMAA)
GST .... Gold Sodium Thiomalate [*Organic chemistry*] (DAVI)
GST .... Gold Steel Titanium
GST .... Goods and Services Tax [*Canadian*] (ODBW)
GST .... Government Securities Trading [*Computer*]
GST .... Government Steam Train [*British*]
GST .... GPS Science and Technology Program (SAUS)
GST .... Graphic Stress Telethermometry [*Medicine*]
GST .... Gravity Stress Test (MELL)
GST .... Greenwich Sidereal [*or Standard*] Time
GST .... Ground Sensor Terminal (AABC)
GST .... Ground Special Tools (SAUS)
GST .... Ground Station Terminal (SAUS)
GST .... Ground Surface Temperature
GST .... Ground System Test [*NASA*] (NASA)
GST .... Group Striction [*Medicine*] (EDAA)
GST .... GST Telecommunications [*AMEX symbol*] (TTSB)
GST .... GST Telecommunications, Inc. [*AMEX symbol*] (SAG)
GST .... Guam Standard Time (SAUS)
GST .... Guidance Section Tester (ACAE)
GST .... Gunner Skills Test [*Army*] (INF)
GST .... Gust (SAUS)
GST .... Gustavus [*Alaska*] [*Airport symbol*] (OAG)
GSTA .... Ground Surveillance and Target Acquisition [*Military*] (MCD)
GSTAMIDS ... Ground Standoff Minefield Detection System [*Military*] (RDA)
GSTANSW .... General Studies Teachers' Association of New South Wales [*Australia*]
G ST B .... Grand Standard Bearer [*Freemasonry*] (ROG)
GSTC .... Goods and Services Tax Credit (FOTI)
GSTC .... Gorham State Teachers College [*Merged with University of Maine*]
GSTD .... Gold Standard [*NASDAQ symbol*] (TTSB)
GSTD .... Gold Standard, Inc. [*NASDAQ symbol*] (NQ)
G STD B ...... Grand Standard Bearer [*Freemasonry*]
GSTDN .... Ground Satellite Tracking Data Network (SAUO)
GSTDN .... Ground Spacecraft Tracking and Data Network [*Computer science*] (MHDI)
GSTDN .... Ground Space Flight Tracking and Data Network (NAKS)
GSTDN .... Ground Spaceflight Tracking and Data Network (SAUO)
GSTDN .... Ground Station Tracking Data Network (SAUO)
GSTE .... Guidance System Test Equipment
GSTE .... Gunnery Standard Training Exercise (SAUS)
GSTF .... Ground Systems Test Flow [*NASA*] (NASA)
GStG .... Georgia Southern College, Statesboro, GA [*Library symbol*] [*Library of Congress*] (LCLS)
GSTG .... Group Soviet Troops Germany (SAUO)
GSTH .... Ground Surface Temperature Histories (QUAC)
GSTHs .... Ground Surface Temperature Histories (SAUS)
GSTI .... Gerber Systems Technology, Incorporated (SAUO)
GSTK .... Good Stuff to Know
GS/TK .... Ground Speed/True Course (SAUS)
GSTM .... Gold Sodium Thiomalate [*Organic chemistry*] (DAVI)
GSTN .... General Switched Telephone Nertwork [*Telecommunications*] (OSI)
GSTN .... General Switching Telephone Network (SAUS)
GSTN .... Global Switched Telephone Network (SAUO)
GSTN .... Government Service Telephone Network (SAUS)
GSTOS .... General Specifications for Training Operations and Manuals (SAUO)
GSTP .... Agreement on a global system of trade preferences among developing countries (SAUO)
G S T P .... Generalised System of Tariff Preferences (SAUS)
GSTP .... Generalized System of Tariff Preferences [*US Customs Service*] (MHDW)
GSTP .... Generalized System of Trade Preferences (SAUO)
GSTP .... General System of Tariff Preferences (SAUS)
GSTP .... Global System of Trade Preferences [*United Nations Conference on Trade and Development*] [*Proposed*]
GSTP .... Ground Systems Test Plan (ACAE)
GSTP .... Ground System Test Procedure (IAA)
GSTR .... Geological Survey Triga Reactor (SAUO)
GSTR .... Globalstar Telecommunications, Ltd. [*NASDAQ symbol*] (NASQ)
GSTRB .... Ground Station Test Review Board (ACAE)
GSTRF .... Globalstar Telecommunications Ltd. [*NASDAQ symbol*] (SAG)
GSTRF .... Golbalstar Telecommunications [*NASDAQ symbol*] (TTSB)
G-string .... Capital-G-shaped string (SAUS)
GSTS .... German Student Travel Service
GSTS .... Ground-Based Surveillance and Tracking System (MCD)
GSTS .... Guidance System Test Set
GSTS .... Gusts [*NWS*] (FAAC)
GSTT .... Generation-Skipping Transfer Tax
GST Tele ..... GST Telecommunications, Inc. [*Associated Press*] (SAG)
GSTU .... Guidance System Test Unit
GSTV .... Digestive
GStX .... General Sciences Corp. (SAUO)
GSTX .... GST Telecommunications [*NASDAQ symbol*] (SG)
GSTY .... Gusty [*NWS*] (FAAC)
GSU .... Entergy Gulf States [*NYSE symbol*] (SAG)
GSU .... Gas Servicer Unit (MCD)
GSU .... Gedaref [*Sudan*] [*Airport symbol*] (AD)
GSU .... General Service Unit [*Marine Corps*]
GSU .... General Support Unit [*Army*] (AABC)
GSU .... Generator Step-Up Transformer [*Nuclear energy*] (NRCH)
GSU .... Geographically Separated Units [*Military*] (AFM)
GSU .... Georgia State University, Atlanta, GA [*OCLC symbol*] (OCLC)
GSU .... German Support Unit (SAUO)
GSU .... Glazed Structural Unit [*Technical drawings*]
GSU .... Golden Seven Industry [*Vancouver Stock Exchange symbol*]
GSU .... Governors State University [*Illinois*]
GSU .... Graduate Student Union (SAUO)
GSU .... Grain Services Union
GSU .... Ground Support Unit (ACAE)
GSU .... Group Switch Unit (SAUO)
GSU .... Guaranteed Supply Unit [*Telecommunications*] (OA)
GSU .... Guidance Switching Unit [*Aviation*]
GSU .... Gulf States Utilities Co. [*NYSE symbol*] (SPSG)
GSU .... Gunners Sight Unit (SAUS)
GSU .... United Nations General Service Union (SAUO)
GSUB .... Glazed Structural Unit Base [*Technical drawings*]
GSUC .... Ground Stub-Up Connection [*Aerospace*] (AAG)
GSUEG .... Governors State University Energy Group (EA)
GSUG .... Gross Seasonal Unavailable Generation [*Electronics*] (IEEE)
G (Suit) .... Antigravity Suit [*Air Force clothing for supersonic flight*]
G-suit .... Gravity Suit (ADWA)
GSUPr .... Entergy Gulf States $1.75 Pref [*NYSE symbol*] (TTSB)
GSUPrB .... Entergy Gulf States $4.40 Pfd [*NYSE symbol*] (TTSB)
GSUPrD .... Entergy Gulf States Dep Adj B Pfd [*NYSE symbol*] (TTSB)
GSUPrE .... Entergy Gulf States $5.08 Pfd [*NYSE symbol*] (TTSB)
GSUPrG .... Entergy Gulf States $4.52 Pfd [*NYSE symbol*] (TTSB)
GSUPrK .... Entergy Gulf States $8.80 Pfd [*NYSE symbol*] (TTSB)
G SUPT .... Grand Superintendent [*Freemasonry*]
GSUs .... Glazed Structural Units (SAUO)

GSUSA Gallipoli Society in the United States of America (EA)
GSUSA General Staff, United States Army
GSUSA Girl Scouts of the United States of America (SAUO)
GSUZ Gulf State Utilities [*Federal Railroad Administration identification code*]
GSV Gas Sampling Valve
GSV Gas Sampling Yalve (SAUS)
GSV Gas Service Co. (SAUO)
GSV Genealogical Society of Victoria [*Australia*]
GSV Geological Survey of Victoria (SAUO)
GSV Globe Stop Valve
GSV Golden Seville Resources Ltd. [*Vancouver Stock Exchange symbol*]
GSV Governor Steam Valve (IEEE)
GSV Grassland Society of Victoria (SAUO)
GSV Ground-to-Surface Vessel [*RADAR*] (NATG)
GSV Grumman Submersible Vehicle
GSV Guided Space Vehicle [*Air Force*]
GSV Savannah Area Vocational/Technical School, Savannah, GA [*Library symbol*] [*Library of Congress*] (LCLS)
GSVAD General Service Volunteer Aid Detachment [*British military*] (DMA)
GSVC Generalized Supervisor Calls [*Computer science*] (IBMDP)
GSVC Trace Generalized Supervisor Call Trace (SAUS)
GSVO Villa Cisneros [*Western Sahara*] [*ICAO location identifier*] (ICLI)
GSVP Ground Support Verification Plan [*NASA*] (NASA)
GSVR Ground-to-Surface Vessel Radar (SAUS)
GSVT Ground System Validation Test (MCD)
GSVZ Great Shenandoah Valley Development [*Federal Railroad Administration identification code*]
GSW Galvanized Steel Wire (IAA)
GSW General Service Wagon [*British military*] (DMA)
GSW Geological Survey of Wyoming (SAUS)
GSW Glazed Stone Ware (SAUS)
GSW Gold Star Wives of America (EA)
GSW Grand Senior Warden [*Freemasonry*] (ROG)
GSW Greater Southwest [*Ft. Worth and Dallas, Texas*] [*Airport symbol*] (AD)
GSW Great Southwest Railroad, Inc. [*AAR code*]
GSW Ground Saucer Watch (EA)
GSW GSW, Inc. [*Toronto Stock Exchange symbol*]
GSW Gunshot Wound [*Medicine*]
GSW 1812 General Society of the War of 1812 (EA)
GSWA Geological Survey of Western Australia (SAUO)
GSWA Gold Star Wives of America [*Later, GSW*] (EA)
GSWA Gunshot Wound to the Abdomen
GSWA International PEN - Centre of German-Speaking Writers Abroad (EAIO)
G SWD B Grand Sword Bearer [*Freemasonry*]
GSwE Emanuel County Junior College, Swainsboro, GA [*Library symbol*] [*Library of Congress*] (LCLS)
GSWH Gunshot Wound to Head [*Medicine*] (RAWO)
GSWM Global Scale Wave Model (SAUS)
GSWP Global Soil Wetness Project (SAUS)
GSWP Graduate School of World Problems (SAUO)
GSWR Galvanized Steel Wire Rope
GSWR Georgia Southwestern Railroad [*Federal Railroad Administration identification code*]
GSWR Glasgow and South Western Railway Co. (SAUO)
GSWR Global State of the World Report (SAUO)
GS-WRD Geological Survey - Water Resources Division
GSW Rope Galvanized Steel Wire Rope (SAUS)
GSWT General Staff with Troops [*Army*]
GSX Gaphics Systems Extension (SAUS)
GSX General Signal Corp. [*NYSE symbol*] (SPSG)
GSX Genl Signal [*NYSE symbol*] (TTSB)
GSX Gold & Stock Telegraph Co. (SAUO)
GSY Global Strategy Corp. [*Vancouver Stock Exchange symbol*]
GSY Guest Supply [*NYSE symbol*] (SG)
GSY Gulf Science Year [*1970*]
GSYB [*The*] Girls' School Year Book [*A publication*] (ROG)
GSZ Geological Survey of Zambia (SAUS)
GSZ Glazier Salvage [*Federal Railroad Administration identification code*]
GSZ Golden Sitka Resources [*Vancouver Stock Exchange symbol*]
GSZ Guernsey, WY [*Location identifier*] [*FAA*] (FAAL)
GT Gabbart [*Ship's rigging*] (ROG)
GT Gage Template (SAUS)
G/T Gain over noise-Temperature (SAUS)
G/T Gain/Temperature (SAUS)
G/T Gain to System Noise Temperature (CCCA)
G/T Gain to Temperature (ACAE)
G/T Gain to Thermal noise (SAUS)
GT Gait [*Medicine*] (EDAA)
GT Gait Training [*Orthopedics*] (DAVI)
GT Galactosyltransferase [*An enzyme*]
GT Galilean Telescope (SAUS)
GT Gamekeeper Thumb (MELL)
GT Game Theory
GT Gamma-Glutamyltransferase [*Also, GGT, GGTP*] [*An enzyme*]
GT Gamne Theory (SAUS)
GT Gamow-Teller [*Transition*] [*Nuclear physics*]
GT Gap Time (SAUS)
GT Garbage Truck
GT Gas Technologist (SAUS)
GT Gas Technology (SAUS)
GT Gas Thread (SAUS)
GT Gas Tight
GT Gastric Tonometry [*Medicine*] (MELL)
GT Gastrin [*Biochemistry*]
GT Gastrostomy [*Gastroenterology*] (DAVI)
GT Gastrostomy Tube [*Gastroenterology*] (DAVI)
GT Gastrotomy Tube [*Gastroenterology*] (DAVI)
GT Gas Tube (IAA)
GT Gas Turbine
GT Gas Turbine Engine (SAUS)
GT Gate-Triggered (SAUS)
GT Gate Tube (IAA)
GT Gauge Template (SAUS)
GT Gauge Theory (SAUS)
GT GB Airways Ltd. (SAUO)
GT Geared Turbine (SAUS)
GT Gee-Thaysen [*Disease*] [*Medicine*] (DB)
GT Gelling Temperature [*Analytical biochemistry*]
GT Gel Tube [*Electrophoresis*]
GT Gemini-Titan [*NASA*]
GT General Tariff (ADA)
GT General Technical Aptitude Area
GT General/Technical Score [*Standardized test*] [*Military*] (INF)
GT General Terms (FOTI)
GT General Test
GT General Time Corp. (SAUO)
GT General Tool
GT General Transport [*Military*]
GT Generation Time [*Microbiology*]
GT Generator Transmission (ACAE)
GT Gene Therapy (MELL)
GT Genetic Therapy
GT Genetic Transduction (MELL)
GT Genomic Tested [*Genetics*]
GT Gentleman Traveller
GT Geographic Tongue [*Medicine*] (MELL)
GT Geologian Tutkimuskeskus (SAUS)
GT Geometry and Topology (SAUO)
GT Georgia Institute of Technology
GT Geotectonics (SAUS)
GT German Title (NITA)
GT German Translation (MCD)
GT Gibraltar Airways Ltd. [*British*] [*ICAO designator*] (ICDA)
GT Gifted and Talented [*Education*]
GT Gift Tax (DLA)
GT Gigaton
Gt gigatonne [*One billion tonnes*] (EERA)
Gt Gigatonnes (SAUS)
GT Gilt
gt Gilt Top [*Bookbinding*] (WDMC)
GT Gilt Top [*Bookbinding*]
GT Gingiva Treatment [*Dentistry*] (MAE)
GT Give Tokens (SAUS)
GT Glacial Till Soil [*Agronomy*]
GT Glanzmann Thrombasthenia [*Medicine*] (DMAA)
GT Glass Transition (SAUS)
GT Glass Tube (DEN)
GT Global Teach (SAUO)
GT Global Telecommunications (SAUS)
GT Globe Thermometer
GT Glover Tower (SAUS)
GT Glow Tube (IAA)
GT Glucagon Test [*Medicine*] (EDAA)
GT Glucose Therapy [*Medicine*] (DMAA)
GT Glucose Tolerance [*Medicine*]
GT Glucose Transporter [*Biochemistry*]
GT Glucose Turnover [*Physiology*]
GT Glucuronosyltransferase [*An enzyme*]
GT Glumitocin [*Endocrinology*]
GT Glutamyl Transferase [*Liver-function test*] (CPH)
GT Glutamyl Transpeptidase [*An enzyme*]
GT Glyceryl Trinitrate [*Medicine*] (MELL)
GT Glycotyrosine [*Biochemistry*]
GT Gnomonic Tracking Chart [*Air Force*]
GT Goat (SAUS)
GT Good Templar
GT Good Tidings (EA)
GT Goodyear Canada, Inc. [*Toronto Stock Exchange symbol*]
GT [*The*] Goodyear Tire & Rubber Co. [*NYSE symbol*] (SPSG)
G/T Gooseneck Tunnel (SAUS)
GT Gopher Tape (SAUS)
GT Gopher Tape Armor [*Telecommunications*] (TEL)
GT Governor of Tasmania [*Australia*]
G/T Gradient-to-Cooling ratio (SAUS)
g/t Grams per Ton
GT Grand Theft
GT Grand Tiler [*Freemasonry*]
GT Grand Total (SAUS)
GT Grand Totalizer
GT Grand Touring [*Automobile model designation*]
GT Grand Treasurer [*Freemasonry*]
GT Grand Trunk (SAUS)
GT Grant [*Legal shorthand*] (LWAP)
GT Gran Turismo [*Grand Touring*] [*Automotive term*]
G/T Granulation Time
G/T Granulation Tissue
GT Graphics Terminal

GT............... Graph Theory (SAUS)
GT............... Gravitational Theory (SAUS)
GT............... Grease Trap (AAG)
gt............... Great (SHCU)
GT............... Great
GT............... Greater Than [*FORTRAN*]
GT............... Greater Trochanter [*Anatomy*]
Gt............... Great Organ [*Music*]
GT............... Great Thoughts [*A publication*] (ROG)
GT............... Great Toe [*Medicine*] (DMAA)
GT............... Green Thumb (EA)
GT............... Green Thumbs [*National Weather Service and Department of Agriculture Extension Service telecommunication system*]
GT............... Greenwich Time
GT............... Greetings Telegram (IAA)
GT............... Grid Track (SAUS)
GT............... Gross Terms (SAUS)
GT............... Gross Ton [*or Tonnage*]
GT............... Ground Team (MCD)
GT............... Ground Terminal (ACAE)
GT............... Ground Test [*NASA*] (NASA)
GT............... Ground Track
GT............... Groundtrack (SAUS)
GT............... Ground Transmit (AFM)
GT............... Ground-Tree Foraging [*Ecology*]
GT............... Groupe de Travail (SAUS)
GT............... Groupes Transport (SAUO)
GT............... Group Technology
GT............... Group Tensions [*Medicine*] (DMAA)
GT............... Group Theory (SAUO)
GT............... Group Therapy
GT............... GroupTherapy (SAUO)
GT............... Group Transformation
GT............... Grout [*Technical drawings*]
GT............... Guanidiniumisothiocyanat (SAUS)
GT............... Guard of Tent [*Oddfellows*] (ROG)
GT............... Guatemala [*ANSI two-letter standard code*] (CNC)
gt............... Guatemala [*MARC country of publication code*] [*Library of Congress*] (LCCP)
GT............... Guidance Transmitter (NVT)
GT............... Gun Tank (SAUS)
GT............... Gun Target (NVT)
GT............... Gun to Target
GT............... Gun Tractor [*British*]
GT............... Gun Turret
GT............... Gutta [*Drop of Liquid*] [*Pharmacy*]
GT............... Gut Tripe (SAUS)
GT............... Gyro Torque (MCD)
GT............... Journal of Geotechnical Engineering (journ.) (SAUS)
GT............... Triganglioside [*Chemistry*]
GT1............... Glycogenosis Type 1 [*Medicine*]
GTA............... Gallotannic Acid (SAUS)
GTA............... Gas Toxicity Analysis
GTA............... Gas Tungsten Arc
GTA............... Gas Turbine Association (NTPA)
GTA............... Gatt Textiles Arrangement (SAUS)
GTA............... Gay Theatre Alliance [*Defunct*] (EA)
GTA............... Gear Train Analyzer
GTA............... Gemini-Titan-Agena [*NASA*] (KSC)
GTA............... General Terms Agreement (MCD)
GTA............... General Threat Assessment (SAUS)
GTA............... General Training Assistance (ADA)
GTA............... Genetic Toxicology Association (EA)
GTA............... Gene Transfer Agent [*Genetics*]
GTA............... Gentra Inc. [*TS, exchange symbol*] (TTSB)
GTA............... Geography Teachers Association (SAUO)
GTA............... German Teachers' Association [*British*]
GTA............... Gimbaled Telescope Assembly (MCD)
GTA............... Gimbal Telescope Assembly (SAUS)
GTA............... Gitanair [*Italy*] [*ICAO designator*] (FAAC)
GTA............... Give Tokens Acknowledgement (SAUS)
GTA............... Glanzmann's Thrombasthenia [*Medicine*] (EDAA)
GTA............... Glass Tempering Association (EA)
GTA............... Global Transport Aircraft
GTA............... Glycerol Triacetate [*Known as Triacetin*] [*Organic chemistry*]
GTA............... Golf Trust of America [*AMEX symbol*] (SG)
GTA............... Gospel Truth Association (EA)
GTA............... Government Telecommunications Agency [*Canada*]
GTA............... Grading Terminal Assembly (SAUO)
GTA............... Graduate Teachers' Association [*A union*] [*British*]
GTA............... Graduate Teaching Assistant
GTA............... Grain Transportation Agency [*Winnipeg, MB*]
GTA............... Grand Theft Auto (WGA)
GTA............... Gran Turisimo Americano [*In automobile name Pontiac Firebird GTA*]
GTA............... Gran Turismo Automatico [*Automobile model designation*]
GTA............... Graphic Training Aid
GTA............... Graph Theoretic Algorithm (SAUS)
GTA............... Gravure Technical Association [*Later, GAA*] (EA)
GTA............... Great American First Savings Bank [*NYSE symbol*] (COMM)
GTA............... Ground Test Accelerator (SAUS)
GTA............... Ground Test Access (MCD)
GTA............... Ground Test Article [*NASA*] (NASA)
GTA............... Ground Torquing Assembly (MCD)
GTA............... Ground Training Aid [*Aerospace*] (AAG)
GTA............... Groupement Technique de Assureurs du Canada [*Government Telecommunications Agency*] [*Canada*]
GTA............... Group Training Association [*British*] (DCTA)
GTA............... GT Aviation [*British*] [*FAA designator*] (FAAC)
GTA............... Guam Telephone Authority (SAUS)
GTA............... Guards Tank Army (SAUS)
GTA............... Guide Tube Assembly (NRCH)
GTA............... Gun Trade Association (SAUO)
GTA............... Gun Trade Association Ltd. [*British*] (BI)
GTA............... Gutta [*Drop of Liquid*] [*Pharmacy*] (ROG)
GTAA............... Groupe de Travail Inter Agences sur l'Afrique Australe [*Inter-Agency Working Group on Southern Africa - IAWGSA*] [*Canadian Council for International Cooperation*]
GTAC............... Gas Tungsten Arc Cutting [*Welding*]
GTAC............... General Technical Advisory Committee [*for fossil energy*] [*Energy Research and Development Administration*]
GTAC............... Gene Therapy Advisory Committee (GVA)
GTAC............... Ground Tactical Air Controller (SAUS)
GTAC............... Ground-to-Air Cycle
GTACS............... Ground Target Attack Control System (SAUS)
GTACS............... Ground Theater Air Control System [*Military*]
GTAE............... General Telephone and Electronics (SAUS)
GTAG............... German Training Assistance Group (SAUO)
GTAM............... Graphic Terminal Access Method (SAUS)
GTAM............... Great Amerian Corp. (SAUO)
GTAM............... Ground-to-Air Missile (RDA)
GtAMg............... Great American Management & Investment, Inc. [*Associated Press*] (SAG)
GTAMS............... Ground to Air Measurements Systems (ACAE)
GT&............... General Telphone & Electronics (SAUS)
GT & A............... Ground Test and Acceptance [*NASA*] (NASA)
GT & C............... General Terms and Conditions
GT & E............... General Telephone & Electronics (NITA)
GTandE............... General Telephone and Electronics corporation (SAUO)
GT&EA............... Georgia Teachers and Education Association (SAUO)
GT&EI............... General Telephone & Electronics International (SAUO)
GT&EL............... General Telephone and Electronics Laboratories (SAUO)
GT & TM............... General Traffic and Transportation Manager
GTAO............... Graphic Training Aids Officer [*Army*]
GTAP............... General Technical Assistance Program (SAUS)
GTAPEG............... Groupe de Travail des APE Genevoises (SAUO)
GTAR............... GEG-Thomson Airborne Radar (SAUS)
GT armour............... Gopher Tape armour (SAUO)
GTAS............... Generic Testing and Analysis System (ADWA)
GTAS............... Generic Trending and Analysis System (SAUS)
GTASA............... Geography Teachers' Association of South Australia
GTASFA............... Grand Traverse Area Sportfishing Association [*Michigan*]
GTA Statement............... Go To Assignment Statement (SAUS)
GtAtPc............... Great Atlantic & Pacific Tea Co., Inc. [*Associated Press*] (SAG)
GTAV............... General Transport Administrative Vehicle
GTAW............... Gas Tungsten Arc Weld [*or Welding*]
G T A W............... Gas Tungsten-Arc Welding (SAUS)
GTAW............... Inert-Gas Tungsten-Arc Welding (SAUS)
GTAW-P............... Gas Tungsten Arc Welding - Pulsed Arc
GTAW-P............... Pulsed Gas Tungsten-Arc Welding (SAUS)
GTAX............... Gilman & Ciocia, Inc. [*NASDAQ symbol*] (SAG)
GTAXW............... Gilman & Ciocia Wrrt [*NASDAQ symbol*] (TTSB)
GTB............... Fort Drum, NY [*Location identifier*] [*FAA*] (FAAL)
GTB............... Gastrointestinal Tract Bleeding [*Medicine*] (DMAA)
GTB............... General Tariff Bureau Inc. Lansing MI [*STAC*]
GTB............... General Trade Books [*Publishing*]
GTB............... Glycinethymol Blue [*An indicator*] [*Chemistry*]
GTB............... Government Tourist Bureau (SAUO)
GTB............... Grand Traverse Bay, Michigan
GTB............... Gran Turismo Berlinetta [*Automobile model designation*]
GTB............... Green Tiger Beetles (SAUO)
GTB............... Guild of Traditional Butlers
GTBA............... Gasoline Grade Tertiary Butylacetate (SAUS)
GTBA............... Gasoline-Grade Tertiary-Butyl Alcohol [*Organic chemistry*]
GTBA............... Grade Tertiary Butyl Alcohol
Gt Basin Nat............... Great Basin Naturalist (SAUS)
GTBC............... Guild of Teachers of Backward Children [*British*] (BI)
GTBicyc............... GT Bicycles, Inc. [*Associated Press*] (SAG)
GTBOA............... Glad To Be Of Assistance (SAUS)
GTBOS............... Glad To Be Of Service (SAUS)
GT BR............... Great Britain (ROG)
Gt Brit............... Great Britain (WGA)
GTBWI............... Grand Traverse Bay Watershed Initiative
GTBX............... GT Bicycles [*NASDAQ symbol*] (TTSB)
GTBX............... GT Bicycles, Inc. [*NASDAQ symbol*] (SAG)
GTC............... Gain Time Constant (MCD)
GTC............... Gain Time Control
GTC............... Gas Turbine Compressor
GTC............... Gateway to Care
GTC............... Generalized Tonic-Clonic [*Seizure*] [*Medicine*] (DB)
GTC............... Generalized Tonic Convulsion [*Medicine*] (EDAA)
GTC............... General Teaching Council [*British*]
GTC............... General Telephone Company (SAUO)
GTC............... General Tool Contract (MCD)
GTC............... General Trading Companies (SAUO)
GTC............... General Trading Company (SAUO)
GTC............... General Transformation Corporation (SAUO)
GTC............... General Transistor Corp. (AAG)
GTC............... Genetic Thermal Cycler (SAUS)
GTC............... Genome Therapeutics Corp.

GTC ..... Geological Testing Consultant (SAUS)
GTC ..... Georgia Teachers College [*Later, Georgia Southern College*] (AEBS)
GTC ..... Geotechnical consultant (SAUS)
GTC ..... German Territorial Command (SAUS)
GTC ..... Gestational Trophoblastic Carcinoma [*Medicine*] (MELL)
GTC ..... Ghana Tobacco Company (SAUO)
GTC ..... Giant Cell Thyroiditis [*Medicine*] (DMAA)
GTC ..... Girls' Training Corps [*British*] (DAS)
GTC ..... Give Tokens Confirm (SAUS)
GTC ..... Global Tomorrow Coalition (EA)
GTC ..... Glycol Trim Console (MCD)
GTC ..... Golder, Thoma & Cressey [*Chicago, IL*] [*Telecommunications service*] (TSSD)
GTC ..... Good Till Canceled [*as in a brokerage order*]
GTC ..... Good Till Countermanded (SAUS)
GTC ..... Government Telegraph Code [*British*] [*World War II*]
GTC ..... Government Trade Commissioner (SAUO)
GTC ..... Government Training Centre [*British*]
GTC ..... Government Transport Corporation (SAUO)
GTC ..... Government Travel Center (SAUO)
GTC ..... Grand Touring Coupe [*In automobile name Lincoln Mark VII GTC*]
GTC ..... Grand Trunk Corp. (EFIS)
GTC ..... Gran Turismo Cabriolet [*Automobile model designation*]
GTC ..... Greater Toy Center (EA)
GTC ..... Greene, Tweed & Co. Ltd (SAUO)
GTC ..... Ground Test Conductor (MCD)
GTC ..... Group for Technical Coordination [*Marine science*] (MSC)
GTC ..... Group Training Command [*Air Force*] [*British*]
GTC ..... Group Training Company
GTC ..... Guam Territorial College (SAUO)
GTC ..... Guanidinium Thiocyanate [*Biochemistry*]
GTC ..... Guidance Transfer Container
GTC ..... Guild of Television Cameramen [*British*] (EA)
GTC ..... Gulf Transport [*AAR code*]
GTC ..... Gulf Transport Company (SAUO)
GTC ..... Man, WV [*Location identifier*] [*FAA*] (FAAL)
GTC3 ..... Greater than Category 3 (SAUS)
GTCA ..... Great-Tailed Grackle [*North American bird banding code*] (BIBA)
GTCA ..... Green-Throated Carib [*North American bird banding code*] (BIBA)
GTCC ..... Gas Turbine Combined Cycle [*Energy technology*]
GTCC ..... Generalized Tonic-Clonic [*Medicine*] (EDAA)
GTCC ..... German Touring Car Championship
GTCC ..... Government's Total Contract Cost (AAGC)
GTCC ..... Greater-than-Class-C [*Radioactive waste level definition*]
GTCC ..... Group Technology Characterization Code (IAA)
GTC-CVD ..... Gas-Temperature-Controlled Chemical Vapor Deposition (SAUS)
GTCE ..... Global Tropospheric Chemistry Experiment (EOSA)
GTCH ..... GTECH Corp. [*NASDAQ symbol*] (COMM)
GtChina ..... [*The*] Greater China Fund [*Associated Press*] (SAG)
GTCL ..... Graduate of Trinity College of Music, London
GTCM ..... Great Central Mines [*NASDAQ symbol*] (SAG)
GTCMY ..... Great Central Mines NL ADS [*NASDAQ symbol*] (TTSB)
GTCNA ..... German Territorial Command Northern Area (SAUO)
GT coy ..... General Transport company (SAUO)
GTCP ..... Gas Turbine Compressor and Power Plant (SAUS)
GTCP ..... Gas Turbine Compressor and Power Unit (NG)
GTCP ..... General Telephone Call Processing
GTCP ..... Global Tropospheric Chemistry Program [*Federal government*]
GTCR ..... Gate-Turnoff Controlled Rectifier [*Electronics*] (IAA)
GTCS ..... Generalized Tonic-Clonic Seizure [*Medicine*] (MELL)
GTCS ..... General Teaching Council for School [*British*]
GTCS ..... Gun Test & Control System (SAUS)
GTCSA ..... German Territorial Command Southern Area (SAUO)
GTCSM ..... Global Tropospheric Chemistry Systems Model (SAUS)
GTCU ..... Gas Turbine Control Unit (SAUS)
GTCU ..... Ground Thermal Conditioning Unit [*NASA*] (NASA)
GTCUs ..... Gas Turbine Change Units (SAUS)
GTCX ..... Ghost Town & Calico [*Federal Railroad Administration identification code*]
Gt^{D} ..... Duarte Variant Allele [*Genetics*] (DAVI)
GTD ..... Gas Turbine Division (SAUS)
GTD ..... Gear Test Data
GTD ..... General Technology Division (SAUS)
GTD ..... General Traffic Department
GTD ..... Geometrical Theory of Diffraction
GTD ..... Geometric and Technical Draughting [*British Olivetti Ltd.*] [*Software package*] (NCC)
GTD ..... Geometric Theory of Diffraction (SAUS)
GTD ..... Georgetown [*Delaware*] [*Seismograph station code, US Geological Survey*] (SEIS)
GTD ..... Gestational Trophoblastic Disease [*Medicine*] (MAE)
GTD ..... Glider Training Detachment (SAUO)
GTD ..... Graphic Tablet Display [*Computer science*] (IEEE)
GTD ..... Ground Target Detection
GTD ..... Group Delay Time (SAUO)
GTD ..... GT Global Developing Market Fund [*NYSE symbol*] (SPSG)
GTD ..... G.T. Global Dvlp Mkt Fund [*NYSE symbol*] (TTSB)
Gtd ..... Guaranteed (EBF)
gtd ..... Guaranteed (WDAA)
GTD ..... Guaranteed
GTD ..... Guaranteed Bond (EBF)
GTD ..... Guards Tank Division (MCD)
GTD ..... Guard Tank Division (SAUS)
GTD ..... Gun Turret Drive (SAUS)
GTD ..... Gun Turret Driver (SAUS)
GTDB ..... Generic Transformed Database
GTDC ..... Ghana Tourist Development Company (SAUO)
GTDHD ..... Give the Devil His Due [*Slang*]
GTDI ..... Guidelines for Trade Data Interchange (SAUS)
GTDI ..... Guideline Transportation Data Interchange (SAUS)
GTDM ..... Group Time Division Multiplexing (SAUS)
GTDMIS ..... GTD Bioassay System (SAUO)
GTDPL ..... Generalized Top-Down Parsing Language
GTDR ..... General Technical Data Restricted
GTDRI ..... Georgia Teacher Duties and Responsibilities Instrument (SAUO)
GTDS ..... Goddard Trajectory Determination System [*NASA*]
GTDvMk ..... GT Global Developing Market Facts [*Associated Press*] (SAG)
GTDX ..... Grand Traverse Dinner Train [*Federal Railroad Administration identification code*]
GTE ..... Gas Turbine Engine
gt-e ..... gas turbo-electric (SAUS)
GTE ..... Generalized Trace Facility (SAUS)
GTE ..... General-Purpose Thermoplastic Elastomer [*Insulation*]
GTE ..... General Telephone & Electric Company (CCCA)
GTE ..... General Telephone and Electronics [*Telecommunications company*] [*Stamford, CT*] (WDMC)
GTE ..... General Telephone Electric (SAUS)
GTE ..... General Telephone Electronics (SAUS)
GTE ..... General Telephone Equipment (MCD)
GTE ..... General Television and Electronics (SAUS)
gte ..... general total energy (SAUS)
GTE ..... Geometry Transfer Engine (SAUS)
GTE ..... Geotechnical Engineer (SAUS)
GTE ..... Geotechnical Engineering (SAUO)
GTE ..... Geothermal Energy
GTE ..... Gilt Top Edge [*Bookbinding*]
GTE ..... Global Tropospheric Experiment [*National Oceanic and Atmospheric Administration*]
GTE ..... Gothenburg, NE [*Location identifier*] [*FAA*] (FAAL)
GTE ..... Gran Turismo Europa [*Automobile model designation*]
GTE ..... Greater Than or Equal (SAUO)
GTE ..... Groote Island [*Australia*] [*Airport symbol*] (OAG)
GTE ..... Ground Telecommunication Equipment
GTE ..... Ground Test Equipment
GTE ..... Ground Training Engine [*Military*] (AFIT)
GTE ..... Ground Transport Equipment (KSC)
GTE ..... Group Translating Equipment
GTE ..... Group Translation Equipment (SAUO)
GTE ..... GTE Corp. [*Formerly, General Telephone & Electronics Corp.*] [*NYSE symbol*] (SPSG)
GTE ..... GTE Delaware LP [*NYSE symbol*] (SAG)
GTE ..... Guidance Test Equipment
GTE ..... Gunner Tracking Evaluator (PDAA)
GTE ..... Scientific Society of Mechanical Engineers (SAUO)
GTEA ..... Group Test Equipment Assembly
GTEC ..... Georgia Institute of Technology (SAUO)
GTEC ..... GTE California, Inc. [*Associated Press*] (SAG)
GTECC ..... GTE Communications Corp. (SAUO)
Gtech ..... GTECH Holdings Corp. [*Associated Press*] (SAG)
GTED ..... Gas Turbine Engine-Driven [*Generator*] (RDA)
GTEDE ..... GTE Delaware Ltd. [*Associated Press*] (SAG)
GTEDS ..... General Telephone and Electronics Data Services (SAUS)
GTEE ..... Grantee [*Legal shorthand*] (LWAP)
GTEE ..... Guarantee
GTEE OD ..... Guaranteed Overdraft (SAUS)
GTEF ..... GTE Florida, Inc. [*Associated Press*] (SAG)
G-T effect ..... Gibbs-Thompson Effect (SAUS)
GTEG ..... GeoTechnical Engineering Group (SAUO)
GTEI ..... General Telephone & Electronics (SAUS)
GTEI ..... Group Terminal Endpoint Identifier (SAUO)
GTEIS ..... General Telephone and Electronic Information Systems (SAUS)
GTEIS ..... General Telephone and Electronic Information Systems Inc. (SAUO)
GTEIS ..... General Telephone and Electronics Information System (SAUS)
GTEISC ..... GTE International Systems Co. (SAUO)
GTEL ..... Groundwater Technology, Inc. (EFIS)
GTEL ..... GTE California, Inc. [*NASDAQ symbol*] (NQ)
GTelevsa ..... Grupo Televisa [*Associated Press*] (SAG)
GTELN ..... GTE Calif 5% cm Pfd [*NASDAQ symbol*] (TTSB)
GTELO ..... GTE Calif 4.50% cm Pfd [*NASDAQ symbol*] (TTSB)
GTELP ..... GTE Calif 4.50% cm Pfd [*NASDAQ symbol*] (TTSB)
GTEM ..... Gigahertz Transverse Electromagnetic Mode (SAUS)
GTEM Cell ..... Gigahertz Transversal Electro-Magnetic Cell (SAUS)
GT-ENDOR ..... General Triple-Electron Nuclear Double Resonance [*Spectroscopy*]
GTEP ..... General Telephone and Electronics Practice [*Telecommunications*] (TEL)
GTEP ..... Georgia Teacher Evaluation Program (SAUO)
GTEP ..... Guaranteed Training Equipment Program (SAUS)
GTEPS ..... General Telephone and Electronics Data Services (SAUS)
GTETDS ..... Gas Turbine and Engine Type Designation System
GTE TMD ..... Guillotine Trimmed [*Bookbinding*] (DGA)
GTE/TRACE ..... Global Tropospheric Experiment/Transport and Atmospheric Chemistry near the Equator (SAUS)
GT Euro ..... GT Greater Europe Fund [*Associated Press*] (SAG)
gtev ..... gas-turbine electric vessel (SAUS)
GtewayD ..... Gateway Data Sciences Corp. [*Associated Press*] (SAG)
GTF ..... Gang Task Force (SAUO)
GTF ..... Gastrostomy Tube Feeding [*Medicine*] (EDAA)
GTF ..... Gaussian-Type Function (SAUS)
GTF ..... Generalized Test Function (SAUO)
GTF ..... Generalized Timing Format (SAUS)

GTF .... Generalized Trace Facility [*Computer science*] (ITCA)
GTF .... Generalized Transformation Function
GT/F .... General Telephone Company of Florida (NITA)
GTF .... General Timing Format (SAUS)
GTF .... General Trace Facility [*Computer science*] (ELAL)
GTF .... General Transcription Factor [*Genetics*]
GTF .... General Trust Fund (SAUO)
GTF .... Geothermal Test Facility (SAUO)
GTF .... German Territorial Forces (MCD)
GTF .... Global Telecommunications Fund (SAUS)
GTF .... Glucose Tolerance Factor [*Medicine*] (DMAA)
GTF .... Glucosyltransferase (DMAA)
GTF .... go-General Trace Facility (SAUS)
GTF .... Granite Test Facility (SAUO)
GTF .... Gravity Tube Feeder (SAUS)
GTF .... Greater Than Flag (MHDB)
GTF .... Great Falls [*Montana*] [*Airport symbol*] (OAG)
GTF .... Green Tree Frogs (SAUO)
GTF .... Ground Test Facility (ACAE)
GTF .... Grout Treatment Facility [*Environmental science*] (COE)
GTF .... G.T. Greater Europe Fd [*NYSE symbol*] (TTSB)
GTF .... GT Greater Europe Fund [*NYSE symbol*] (SPSG)
GTF .... Guidance Test Fixture
GTF .... Guilt Free Goodies [*Vancouver Stock Exchange symbol*]
GTFM .... Generalized Table File Maintenance (SAUO)
GTFN .... Great Financial [*NASDAQ symbol*] (TTSB)
GTFN .... Great Financial Corp. [*NASDAQ symbol*] (SAG)
GTFPARS .... Generalized Performance Analysis Reporting (HODG)
GTFT .... Generous Tit for Tat [*Game strategy*]
Gt^G .... Galactosemic Allele [*Genetics*] (DAVI)
GTG .... Game-Tying Goals [*Hockey*]
GTG .... GARP Task Group (SAUO)
gtg .... gas to gasoline (SAUS)
GTG .... Gas Turbine Generator
GTG .... Gating (SAUS)
GTG .... Glycerol Tolerant Gel [*Medicine*] (MELL)
GTG .... Golden Trend Energy [*Vancouver Stock Exchange symbol*]
GTG .... Gold Thioglucose
GTG .... Got To Go (SAUS)
GTG .... Grand Technologies Group (SAUO)
GTG .... Grantsburg, WI [*Location identifier*] [*FAA*] (FAAL)
GTG .... Ground Timing Generator (IAA)
GTG .... Ground-to-Ground [*Communications, weapons, etc.*]
GTGEEEPS ... Groupe de Travail sur la Gestion de l'Energie dans les Etablissements d'Enseignement Post-Secondaire [*Postsecondary Education Task Force on Energy Management PETFEM*] [*Canada*]
GTGL .... Give the Gift of Literacy Foundation [*Duxbury, MA*]
GTGS .... Gas Turbine Generator Set (AABC)
GTGT .... Gun Target (AABC)
GTGU .... Ground Test Guidance Unit (ACAE)
GTH .... Gas Tight High Pressure (IEEE)
GTH .... Genomic Thymus [*Genetics*]
GTH .... Gonadotropic Hormone [*Endocrinology*]
GTH .... Grand Touring High-Speed [*Tire design*]
GTH .... Graton Minerals Ltd. (SAUO)
GTH .... Groton Minerals Ltd. [*Vancouver Stock Exchange symbol*]
GTH .... Guthrie, TX [*Location identifier*] [*FAA*] (FAAL)
GthEnvr .... Growth Environmental, Inc. [*Associated Press*] (SAG)
GthFn .... Growth Financial Corp. [*Associated Press*] (SAG)
G Thom .... Gospel of Thomas [*Apocryphal work*]
GTHR .... Generalized Thyroid Hormone Resistance [*Medicine*] (MELL)
GTHRNG .... Gathering
GTHS .... German-Texan Heritage Society (EA)
GthSpn .... Growth Fund of Spain [*Associated Press*] (SAG)
G T - H T G R ... Gas Turbine High Temperature Gas-cooled Reactor (SAUS)
GT-HTGR .... Gas Turbine High-Temperature Gas-Cooled Reactor [*Nuclear energy*] (NRCH)
GTI .... Atlas Air, Inc. [*ICAO designator*] (FAAC)
GTi .... Coastal Plains Regional Library, Tifton, GA [*Library symbol*] [*Library of Congress*] (LCLS)
GTI .... Gasoline Turbo Injection (SAUS)
GTI .... Gas Turbine Institute (SAUO)
GTI .... General Telephone Company of Illinois (SAUO)
GTI .... General Transportation Importance
GTI .... Genital Tract Infection [*Medicine*] (CPH)
GTI .... Geopower Technologies Incorporated (SAUO)
GTI .... Georgia Institute of Technology (SAUS)
GTI .... Georgia Tech Research Institute (SAUS)
GTI .... German Tank Improvement (SAUS)
GTI .... GIS Technology Inc. (SAUO)
GTI .... Glass Technical Institute [*Commercial firm*] (EA)
GTI .... Glass-Tite Industries Inc. (SAUO)
GTI .... Glass Transition Temperature (SAUS)
GTI .... Glentech International Ltd. [*British*]
GTI .... Grand Turk Island
GTI .... Gran Turismo Injection (SAUS)
GTI .... Ground Test Instrumentation (MCD)
GTI .... Ground Transportable Interrogator (SAUS)
GTI .... GTI Corp. [*Associated Press*] (SAG)
GTI .... Guidance Technology, Incorporated (SAUO)
GTiA .... Abraham Baldwin Agricultural College, Tifton, GA [*Library symbol*] [*Library of Congress*] (LCLS)
GTIA .... Golf and Travel Industry Association (TRID)
GTICES .... Georgia Institute of Technology Integrated Civil Engineering System (SAUS)
GTiE .... Coastal Plains Experiment Station, Tifton, GA [*Library symbol*] [*Library of Congress*] (LCLS)
GTIG .... Gamma Thermometer Interest Group [*Nuclear energy*] (NRCH)
GT II .... Galactosyltransferase Isoenzyme II [*An enzyme*] (DAVI)
GTII .... Genetic Therapy (SAUS)
GTII .... Golden Triangle Ind [*NASDAQ symbol*] (TTSB)
GTII .... Golden Triangle Industries, Inc. [*NASDAQ symbol*] (SAG)
GTII .... Golden Triangle Industry [*NASDAQ symbol*] [*Formerly, Golden Triangle Roy & Oil*] (SG)
GTIL .... Government Technical Institute Library (SAUO)
GTIM .... Good Times Restaurants [*NASDAQ symbol*] (TTSB)
GTIM .... Good Times Restaurants, Inc. [*NASDAQ symbol*] (SAG)
GTIMW .... Good Times Restaurants Wrrt [*NASDAQ symbol*] (TTSB)
GTIMZ .... Good Times Restaurants Wrrt'B' [*NASDAQ symbol*] (TTSB)
GTIN .... Global Trade Item Number
G-TiN .... Gold Tin (SAUS)
Gt I-O .... Gate Input-Output (SAUS)
GTIO .... German Tourist Information Office (SAUO)
Gt I-O&Sec Adr ... Gate Input-Output and Secondary Address (SAUS)
GTIP .... Ground Test Integration Panel (SAUS)
GTIP .... Ground Tilt Isolation Platform
GTIS .... Gloucestershire Technical Information Service (NITA)
GTIS .... Great Ground-Based Traffic Information System (SAUS)
GTIS .... Ground-Based Traffic Information System [*Aviation*] (DA)
GTIS .... GT Interactive Software [*NASDAQ symbol*] (TTSB)
GTJ .... Gold Torch Resources [*Vancouver Stock Exchange symbol*]
GTJ .... Grace Theological Journal (journ.) (SAUS)
GTJ .... Gran Turismo Junior [*Automobile model designation*]
GTJ .... Guarantee Trust of Jersey Ltd. (SAUO)
GTJC .... Government Trade Joint Council (SAUO)
GTk .... Gasoline Tank (SAUS)
GTK .... Geological Survey of Finland (SAUS)
GTK .... Gimp Tool Kit (HODG)
GTK .... Grand Turk [*British West Indies*]
GTK .... Grosser Touren Kombiwagen [*Grand Touring Station Wagon*] [*German*]
GTK .... Gross Tonne Kilometre (EERA)
GTK .... GTECH Holdings [*NYSE symbol*] (TTSB)
GTK .... GTECH Holdings Corp. [*NYSE symbol*] (SPSG)
GTK .... GUI ToolKit (SAUS)
GTKM .... Gross Tonne KM [*Indian Railway*] (TIR)
GTL .... Gaseous Tritium Light [*Device*] [*Nuclear energy*] (NRCH)
GTL .... Gas-to-Liquid [*Vehicle power systems*]
GTL .... Gas Transport LASER
GTL .... Gas Turbine Laboratory [*MIT*] (MCD)
GTL .... Geomagnetic Tail Laboratory (MCD)
GTL .... Geometrical and Technological Language (SAUS)
GTL .... Geometrical Technological (SAUS)
GTL .... Geometrical Technological Language (SAUS)
GTL .... Geometric and Technical Language [*British Olivetti Ltd.*] [*Software package*] (NCC)
GTL .... Georgia Tech Language [*Computer science*] (CSR)
GTL .... Glass Technology Laboratories (SAUO)
GTL .... Glass Training Ltd. (AIE)
GTL .... Global Title Translation
GTL .... Gold Transistor Logic (SAUS)
GTL .... Government Test Laboratory (MSA)
GTL .... Great Lakes Nickel Ltd. [*Toronto Stock Exchange symbol*]
GTL .... Gunning Transceiver Logic (AEBE)
GTL .... Gun/Target Line [*Navy*] (NVT)
Gt Lakes .... Great Lakes (SAUS)
Gt Lakes Ent ... Great Lakes Entomologist (journ.) (SAUS)
GTLD .... Gaseous Tritium Light Device (SAUS)
GTLD .... Generic Top Level Domain (SAUS)
gTLD .... Generic Top-Level Domain [*Computer science*] (IGQR)
GTLD .... Gerneric Top Level DOMAIN (SAUS)
GT/LD .... Gifted & Learning Disabled
gTLD-MoU ... Generic Top Level Domain Memorandum of Understanding (TELE)
Gt Ldn .... Greater London (SAUO)
GtLkCh .... Great Lakes Chemical Corp. [*Associated Press*] (SAG)
GtLkeAv .... Great Lakes Aviation Ltd. [*Associated Press*] (SAG)
GTLL .... Golden Triangle Ind. [*NASDAQ symbol*] (SG)
GTLS .... Gaseous Tritium Light Source [*Nuclear energy*] (MCD)
GTLs .... Gas Transport Lasers (SAUS)
GTM .... Abraham Baldwin Agricultural College, Tifton, GA [*OCLC symbol*] (OCLC)
GTM .... Gang Temperature Monitor [*Environmental science*] (COE)
GTM .... Gas to Methanol [*Process developed by ICI*]
GTM .... Gas Turbine Model (SAUS)
GTM .... Generalized Tendomyopathy [*Medicine*] (EDAA)
GTM .... General Traffic Manager
GTM .... Geometry Technology Module [*NASA*]
GTM .... Getting the Message [*A reading program*]
GTM .... Global Traffic Meeting (SAUS)
GTM .... Global Travel Marketplace (SAUO)
GTM .... Good This Month [*Business term*]
GTM .... Grand Total Memory (SAUS)
GTM .... Ground Team Manager (MCD)
GTM .... Ground Test Missile
GTM .... Ground Test Motor (MCD)
GTM .... Group Talk Microphone
GTM .... Guatemala [*ANSI three-letter standard code*] (CNC)
GTM .... Guidance Test Missile (SAUS)

GTM .... Guidance Training Missile (ACAE)
GTM .... Guild of Temple Musicians (EA)
GTM .... Gyratory Testing Machine (SAUS)
GTMA .... Galvanised Tank Manufacturers' Association [*British*] (BI)
GTMA .... Gauge and Toolmakers Association [*British*] (DS)
GTMA .... Georgia Textile Manufacturers Association (SAUO)
Gt Man .... Greater Manchester (SAUO)
GTMB .... Guernsey Tomato Marketing Board (SAUO)
GTMBAQ ...... Georgetown Medical Bulletin (journ.) (SAUS)
GTMCA .... Geothermics (journ.). (SAUS)
GTMHR .... Gas Turbine Modular Helium Reactor [*Nuclear reactor*]
GTMIE .... Global Telemedia Intl [*NASDAQ symbol*] (TTSB)
GTMMM .... Det Gamle Testament [*S. Michelet, S.Mowinckel, og N. Mersel*] [*Oslo*] [*A publication*] (BJA)
GTMO .... Guantanamo Bay, Cuba
GTMOSI .... General Telecommunications Manager for Open Systems Interconnection (SAUS)
GTMS .... Global Thermospheric Mapping Study (SAUS)
GTMS .... Graphic Text Management System [*Computer science*] (DGA)
GTMS .... Ground Target Marking System
GTMTC .... Galvothermomagnetic Transport Coefficient (SAUS)
GTMV .... Gasoline-Tolerant Methanol Vehicle [*Chrysler Corp.*] [*Automotive engineering*]
GTN .... GeneticTechnology News (journ.) (SAUS)
GTN .... Germantown (SAUS)
GTN .... Gestational Trophoblastic Neoplasia [*Medicine*] (STED)
GTN .... Global Transportation Network (DOMA)
GTN .... Global Transportation System (SAUO)
GTN .... Global Trend Network (GNE)
GTN .... Global Trends Network [*USA*] (EERA)
GTN .... Glomerulotubulonephritis [*Medicine*] (STED)
GTN .... Glyceryl Trinitrate [*Also, NG, NTG*] [*Explosive, vasodilator*]
GTN .... Gotenba [*Japan*] [*Seismograph station code, US Geological Survey*] [*Closed*] (SEIS)
GTN .... Government Telecommunications Network [*British*] (EECA)
GTN .... Government Training News (SAUS)
GTN .... Great Eastern Line [*Vancouver Stock Exchange symbol*]
GTN .... Washington, DC [*Location identifier*] [*FAA*] (FAAL)
GTNC .... German Territorial Northern Command (SAUS)
GTNEEA .... Genetic Technology News (journ.) (SAUS)
GTNP .... Grand Teton National Park (SAUO)
GTNQA .... Geotechnique (journ.) (SAUS)
GT-NR .... Gas Turbine-Non Regenerative
GTNR .... Gentner Communications [*NASDAQ symbol*] (TTSB)
GTNR .... Gentner Communications Corp. [*NASDAQ symbol*] (NQ)
GTNRW .... Gentner Communications Wrrt [*NASDAQ symbol*] (TTSB)
GTNW .... General Telephone Co. of the Northwest
GtNYSv .... [*The*] Greater New York Savings Bank [*Associated Press*] (SAG)
GTO .... Gate-Triggered Oscillator (SAUS)
GTO .... Gate Turn Off [*Computer science*]
GTO .... Gate Turn Off - Thyristor (SAUS)
GTO .... Gaussian-Type Orbitals [*Atomic physics*]
GTO .... General Telecommunications Organization [*Oman*] [*Telecommunications service*]
GTO .... Geostationary Transfer Orbit [*Space technology*]
GTO .... Geosynchronous Transfer Orbit (SAUS)
GTO .... GEO Transfer Orbit (SAUS)
GTO .... Gigaton
GTO .... Global Trust Organization (HODG)
GTO .... Golgi Tendon Organ [*Anatomy*]
GTO .... Gorontalo [*Indonesia*] [*Airport symbol*] (OAG)
GTO .... Go to (SAUS)
GTO .... Government Team of Officials (SAUO)
GTO .... Government Telecommunications Organization (SAUS)
GTO .... Grand Touring Over 3.0 Liters [*Class of racing cars*]
GTO .... Gran Turismo Omologato [*Grand Touring, Homologated*] [*Automotive engineering*] [*Italian*]
GTO .... Graphics Text Organizer [*Computer science*]
GTO .... Graph-To-Occam (SAUS)
GTO .... Grenada Tourist Office (EA)
GTO .... Guaranteed Time Observer [*For telescope viewing*]
GTO .... Guide to Operations (SAUO)
GTOAA .... GTO Association of America (EA)
G-to-AGM .... Ground-to-Air Guided Missile (SAUS)
G-to-G .... Grid-to-Grid (SAUS)
GTOI .... Georgia Teacher Observation Instrument (SAUO)
GTOL .... Graphic Take-Off Language [*Computer science*] (PDAA)
GTOL .... Ground Takeoff and Landing (AAG)
GTOR .... Grantor [*Legal shorthand*] (LWAP)
GT ORM H ... Great Ormond Street Hospital for Children [*British*] (ROG)
GTOS .... Gantos, Inc. [*NASDAQ symbol*] (SAG)
GTO's .... Girls Together Outrageously [*or Organically*] [*Rock music group*]
GTOS .... Global Terrestrial Observing System [*Marine science*] (OSRA)
GTOS .... Ground Terminal Operations Support (SSD)
GTOSCR .... Gate Turnoff Silicon-Controlled Rectifier [*Electronics*] (IAA)
GTOSS .... Generalized Tethered Object System Simulation (SSD)
GTO Switch ... Gate Turn-off Switch (SAUS)
GTOT .... Gate Turn Off Thyristor (NITA)
GTO-Thyristor ... gate turn off thyrister (SAUS)
GTO Thyristor ... Gate Turn-off Thyristor (SAUS)
G to VG .... Good to Very Good (SAUS)
GTOW .... Gross Takeoff Weight [*of an aircraft*] [*Also, GTW*]
GTOWFC .... George Takei's Official Worldwide Fan Club [*British*] (EAIO)
GTP .... Gap Time Pulse (SAUS)
GTP .... General Telemetry Processor [*Telecommunications*] (ITD)
GTP .... General Test Plan (AAG)
GTP .... General Third Party [*Insurance*] (MARI)
GTP .... General Training Program
GTP .... General Transport Platoon (SAUO)
GTP .... Generate Target Position [*Military*] (CAAL)
GTP .... Generic Test Purpose (SAUS)
GTP .... Geometry Theorem Prover (SAUS)
GTP .... Geotechnical Project (SAUS)
GTP .... Global Technology Partners
GTP .... Global Time and Position [*Navigation systems*]
GTP .... Glutamyl Transpeptidase [*An enzyme*]
GTP .... Golay Transform Processor (IAA)
GTP .... Gone To Pee (SAUS)
GTP .... Government Technology Productivity
GTP .... GPRS Tunnel Protocol (SAUS)
GTP .... Grand Touring Prototype [*Race car designation*]
GTP .... Grand-Trunk Pacific (SAUO)
GTP .... Grand Trunk Pacific Railway
GTP .... Graphic Transform Package (MHDI)
GTP .... Great Northern Petroleums [*Vancouver Stock Exchange symbol*]
GTP .... Great Trunk Pacific Railway [*British*] (ROG)
GTP .... Green Tea Polyphenol [*Biochemistry*]
GTP .... Ground Testing Plotter (SAUS)
GTP .... Ground Test Plan (MCD)
GTP .... Ground Test Procedure (SAUS)
GTP .... Ground Test Programme (SAUS)
GTP .... Ground Track Plotter
GTP .... Group Transfer Polymerization (SAUS)
GTP .... Group-Transfer Polymerization [*Du Pont process*] [*1983*]
GTP .... Guanosine Triphosphate [*Biochemistry*]
GTPase .... Guanosine Triphosphatase [*An enzyme*]
GTP BP .... Guanosine Triphosphate Binding Protein (SAUS)
GTPD .... Geotechnical Project Design (SAUS)
GTPD .... Guild of Television Producers and Directors (SAUS)
GTPE .... Gun Time Per Engagement (SAUS)
GTPI .... Grupo de Trabajo para los Pueblos Indigenas [*Indigenous Peoples Working Group*] [*Netherlands*] (EAIO)
GTPNet .... Global Trade Point Network (SAUS)
GTPR .... Grand Trunk Pacific Railway
GTPS .... Gas Turbine Power System
GTPS .... Great American Bancorp [*NASDAQ symbol*] (TTSB)
GTPS .... Great American Bancorp, Inc. [*NASDAQ symbol*] (SAG)
GTPSS .... Ground Test Plan Summary Sheets (MCD)
GTPT .... Geometrical and True Positioning (SAUO)
GTPT .... Geometrical and True Positioning Tolerance
GTPU .... Gas Turbine Power Unit (MCD)
GTP Unit ...... Gas Turbine Power Unit (SAUS)
GTR .... Columbus [*Mississippi*] [*Airport symbol*] (OAG)
GTR .... Galvanic Tetanus Ratio [*Medicine*] (STED)
GTR .... Gantry Test Rack [*Aerospace*] (AAG)
GTR .... Garter (MSA)
GTR .... Gas Transmission Rate (SAUS)
GT-R .... Gas Turbine-Regenerative
GTR .... Generalized Time Reflex (STED)
GTR .... General Theory of Relativity
GTR .... Generic Threat Radar (SAUS)
GTR .... Geoid-to-Topography Ratio [*Planetary science*]
GTR .... Golden Terrace Resource Corp. [*Toronto Stock Exchange symbol*]
GTR .... [*The*] Goodyear Tire & Rubber Co.
GTR .... Government Technical Report
GTR .... Government Technical Representative
GTR .... Government Transportation [*or Travel*] Request
GTR .... Government Travel Regulation (SAUS)
GTR .... Grand Touring-Racing (SAUS)
GTR .... Grand Trunk Railway
GTR .... Grantex Aviation [*British*] [*FAA designator*] (FAAC)
GTR .... Granulocyte Turnover Rate [*Hematology*]
GTR .... Great Barrier Island [*New Zealand*] [*Airport symbol*] (AD)
Gtr .... Greater (BARN)
GTR .... Great River Railroad [*Federal Railroad Administration identification code*]
GTR .... Ground Testing Reactor (SAUS)
GTR .... Ground Test Reactor [*Air Force*]
GTR .... Ground Test Report (SAUS)
GTR .... Ground Truth Radiometer (SAUS)
GTR .... Grupo Tribasa S.A. ADS [*NYSE symbol*] (TTSB)
GTR .... Grupo Tribasa SA de CV [*NYSE symbol*] (SPSG)
GT/R .... Guard Transmit/Receive (MCD)
gtr .... Guitar (WDAA)
GTR .... Guitar [*Music*]
GTR .... Gurkha Transport Regiment [*Military unit*] [*British*]
GTRA .... Golden Triangle Railroad [*Federal Railroad Administration identification code*]
Gtr Ant .... Greater Antilles (SAUO)
GTRB .... Gas Turbine
GTRC .... Guitar Center [*NASDAQ symbol*] (SG)
GTRD .... Global Tape Recording Exchange (SAUS)
GTRD .... Greatest Total Resource Demand
G T R E .... Gas Turbine Research Establishment (SAUS)
GTRE .... Global Tape Recording Exchange (EA)
GTRE .... GranTree Corp. (SAUO)
G TREAS ...... Grand Treasurer [*Freemasonry*] (ROG)
G Trg .... General Staff, Training (SAUO)
G Trg .... General Training (SAUS)

GTRI .... Georgia Tech Research Institute [*Georgia Institute of Technology*] [*Research center*] (RCD)
GTribasa ...... Grupo Tribasa SA de Cv [*Associated Press*] (SAG)
GTRL .... Generic Tire-Roll [*Automotive emissions*]
GTRN .... Great Train Store [*NASDAQ symbol*] (TTSB)
GTRN .... Great Train Stores Co. [*NASDAQ symbol*] (SAG)
GTRNW .... Great Train Store Wrrt [*NASDAQ symbol*] (TTSB)
GTRO .... Glyceryl Triricinoleate [*Organic chemistry*]
GTRO .... Golden Triangle Royalty & Oil, Inc. [*NASDAQ symbol*] (NQ)
GTRP .... General Transpose [*Computer science*]
GTRR .... Georgia Institute of Technology Research Reactor
GTRR .... Georgia Technical Research Reactor (SAUO)
GTRR .... Grand Trunk Railroad [*British*] (ROG)
GTRR .... Grand Trunk Western Railroad (SAUO)
GTRY .... Grand Trunk Railway
GTS .... Gas Turbine Ship (IIA)
g/t/s .... gas-turbine ship (SAUS)
GTS .... Gas Turbine Starter (MCD)
GTS .... Gas Turbine Vessel (SAUS)
GTS .... Gated Transport Spectroscopy
Gts .... Gateshead (SAUS)
GTS .... GEM Test System (SAUS)
GTS .... Generalized Tonic Seizure [*Medicine*] (EDAA)
GTS .... Generalized Transition State [*Physical chemistry*]
GTS .... General Tabulation System
GTS .... General Technical Services, Inc. (MCD)
GTS .... General Telephone System (IAA)
GTS .... General Test Support (MCD)
GTS .... General Theological Seminary [*New York, NY*]
GTS .... General Troubleshooting
GTS .... Generic Equipment Model Test System (AAEL)
GTS .... GEODSS Test Site (SAUO)
GTS .... geological time scale (SAUS)
GTS .... Geostationary Technology Satellite
GTS .... Geostationary Test Satellite (SAUO)
GTS .... GeoTechnical Services (SAUO)
GTS .... German Telecommand Station (SAUO)
GTS .... Getting to Sleep [*Medicine*] (EDAA)
GTS .... Gettysburg Theological Studies (journ.) (SAUS)
GTS .... Gilles de la Tourette Syndrome [*Medicine*] (DMAA)
GTS .... Gimbal Trim System
GTS .... Girls' Technical School (ADA)
GTS .... Glider Training School [*British military*] (DMA)
GTS .... Global Telecommunications Service (ADWA)
GTS .... Global Telecommunication System [*World Meteorological Organization*] (IID)
GTS .... Global Tele-Systems Group (SAUO)
GTS .... Global Time Server (SAUO)
GTS .... Global Time Service (SAUO)
GTS .... Global Tracking Systems
GTS .... Global Treasury Services [*Barclays Bank*] [*British*]
GT's .... Globetrotters' Club (EAIO)
GTS .... Glucose Transport System [*Medicine*] (STED)
GTS .... GN & C [*Guidance, Navigation and Control*] Test Station [*NASA*] (NASA)
GTS .... GNS Test Station (SAUS)
GTS .... Golden Tech Resources Ltd. [*Vancouver Stock Exchange symbol*]
GTS .... Golden Treasury Series [*A publication*]
GTS .... Goldstone Tracking Station [*NASA*]
GTS .... Go To Statement (SAUS)
GTS .... Government Transport Service (SAUS)
GTS .... GPS Timing Simulator (SAUS)
GTS .... Grand Touring All-Season [*Tire design*]
GTS .... Grand Touring Supreme [*Auto racing*]
GTS .... Gran Turismo Spider [*Automobile model designation*]
GTS .... Graphics Terminal Scheduler (MCD)
GTS .... Graphics Terminal Services
GTS .... Graphics Terminal System
GTS .... Great Trigonometrical Survey of India (SAUO)
GTS .... Green Tobacco Sickness [*Illness resulting from exposure to dissolved nicotine*]
GTS .... Greenwich Time Signal (DEN)
GTS .... Ground Telemetry Subsystem
GTS .... Ground Terminal System
GTS .... Ground Test Station
GTS .... Ground Test Subsystem (SAUS)
GTS .... Ground Tracking Station (ACAE)
GTS .... Ground Tracking System (MCD)
GTS .... Ground Training System (MCD)
GTS .... Ground Transportation Services [*MTMC*] (TAG)
GTS .... Ground Transport System (SAUS)
GTS .... Group Technology System (MCD)
GTS .... Group Teleconferencing System [*Telecommunications*]
GTs .... Grupos Tacticos (SAUS)
GTS .... Guadalcanal Travel Service (SAUS)
GTS .... Guam Tracking Station [*NASA*] (MCD)
GTS .... Guidance Testing Set (SAUS)
GTS .... Guidance Test Set (AAG)
GTS .... Guinean Trawling Society (SAUO)
GTS .... Guinean Trawling Survey [*United Nations*]
GTS .... Gunners Thermal Sight (SAUS)
GTS .... Gunner Training System (SAUS)
GTS .... Gunnery Training School [*British military*] (DMA)
gts .... Guttae [*Drops*] [*Pharmacy*] (DAVI)
GTS .... Gyro Tilt Signal
GTS .... WMO Global Telecommunication System (SAUS)
GTSB .... Glyphosate-Tolerant Soya Beans
GTSB .... Glyphosate-Tolerant Soybeans
GTSC .... German Territorial Southern Command [*NATO*] (NATG)
GTSC .... Ground Testing and Simulation Committee (SAUO)
GTSC .... GTS Corp. [*NASDAQ symbol*] (COMM)
GTS Drtk ...... GTS Duratek [*Associated Press*] (SAG)
GTSF .... Gifted and Talented Screening Form [*Educational test*]
GTSF .... Guidance Test and Simulation Facility
GTSF .... Guidance Test Simulation Facility (SAUO)
GTSG .... Global TeleSystems Grp. [*NASDAQ symbol*] (SG)
GTSI .... Government Technology Services [*NASDAQ symbol*] (SPSG)
GTSI .... Government Technology Svcs [*NASDAQ symbol*] (TTSB)
GTSL .... Geotechnical Science Laboratories (SAUS)
GTSN .... Global Telemetered Seismograph Network (SAUO)
GTSP .... Global Temperature and Salinity Project (SAUS)
GTSP .... Global Tracer Scientific Panel (SAUO)
GTSPP .... Global Temperature and Salinity Pilot Program (SAUO)
GTSPP .... Global Temperature and Salinity Pilot Project (EERA)
GTSPP .... Global Temperature Salinity Profile Programme (SAUS)
GTS-R .... Grand Touring Sport-Race [*Automobile model designation*]
GTSS .... Gas Turbine Self-contained Starter (SAUO)
gtss .... gas turbine self contained starter (SAUS)
GTSS .... Gas Turbine Starting System (NG)
GTSS .... General Time Sharing System [*Computer science*]
GTST .... Gas tag sample trap (SAUS)
GTST .... Global Telecomm Solutions [*NASDAQ symbol*] (TTSB)
GTST .... Global Telecommunications Solutions, Inc. [*NASDAQ symbol*] (SAG)
GTST .... Greatest (ABBR)
GTSTD .... Grid Test of Schizophrenic Thought Disorder [*Psychology*]
GTSTW .... Global Tele Solutions Wrrt [*NASDAQ symbol*] (TTSB)
GTSW .... Greentree Software, Inc. [*NASDAQ symbol*] (NQ)
GTSWC .... Greentree Software [*NASDAQ symbol*] (TTSB)
GTSX .... Golf Training Systems [*NASDAQ symbol*] (TTSB)
GTSX .... Golf Training Systems, Inc. [*NASDAQ symbol*] (SAG)
GTSXU .... Golf Training Systems Unit [*NASDAQ symbol*] (TTSB)
GTSXW .... Golf Training Sys Wrrt [*NASDAQ symbol*] (TTSB)
Gtt .... Drops [*Therapy term*] (CTAA)
gtt .... Drops [*Therapy term*] (CTAA)
gtt .... Drops [*Medicine*] (MTAA)
GTT .... Gate Terminal (SAUS)
GTT .... Gelatin-Tellurite-Taurocholate [*Agar*] [*Medicine*] (MEDA)
GTT .... Gelatin-Tellurite-Taurocholate Agar [*Biochemistry*] (DAVI)
GTT .... General Agreement on Tariffs and Trades (SAUS)
GTT .... General Theory of Terminology (SAUO)
GTT .... Generated Target Tracking
GTT .... Geographical and Topographical Texts of the Old Testament [*A publication*] (BJA)
GTT .... Georgetown [*Australia*] [*Airport symbol*] (OAG)
GTT .... Gestational Trophoblastic Tumor [*Medicine*] (MELL)
gtt .... glass transition temperature (SAUS)
GTT .... Global Title Translation (SAUS)
GTT .... Global Title Transmission (SAUO)
GTT .... Glucose Tolerance Test [*Medicine*]
GTT .... Goettingen [*Federal Republic of Germany*] [*Geomagnetic observatory code*]
GTT .... Gone to Texas [*Sign on doors of New Englanders who had gone West, nineteenth century*]
GTT .... Gottingen [*Federal Republic of Germany*] [*Seismograph station code, US Geological Survey*] (SEIS)
GTT .... Government Technical Testing (SAUS)
GTT .... Grand Teton Industries, Inc. [*Vancouver Stock Exchange symbol*]
GTT .... Group Time (or Timing) Technique (SAUS)
GTT .... Group Timing Technique [*Industrial engineering*]
GTT .... Guttae [*Drops of Liquid*] [*Pharmacy*]
GTTACC .... Gas Turbine Technical Advisory and Co-ordinating Committee (SAUO)
GTTC .... Goodfellow Technical Training Center [*Military*]
GTTC .... Ground Tactical Training Centre (SAUS)
GTTC .... Gulf Transportation Terminal Command
G/T Temp ..... Gain-to-Noise Temperature (SAUS)
GTTF .... Gas Turbine Test Facility
GTTI .... Geophysics Technology Transfer Initiative (SAUS)
GTTIF .... Grande Tel Technologies [*NASDAQ symbol*] (TTSB)
GTTIF .... GrandeTel Technologies, Inc. [*NASDAQ symbol*] (SAG)
GTTLB .... GT Group Telecom 'B' [*NASDAQ symbol*] (SG)
GTTO .... Green-Tailed Towhee [*North American bird banding code*] (BIBA)
GTT QUIBUSD ... Guttis Quibusdam [*With Some Drops*] [*Pharmacy*] (ROG)
GtTrain .... Great Train Stores Co. [*Associated Press*] (SAG)
GtTrn .... Great Train Stores Co. [*Associated Press*] (SAG)
Gtts .... Drops per minute (SAUS)
GTTS .... Grants Treasury Tape System (SAUO)
GTTS .... Gyro Transfer Table System
GTU .... Gamma Theta Upsilon (EA)
GTU .... Garrison Transport Unit (SAUO)
GTU .... Gas Turbine Unit (SAUS)
GTU .... Gatelink Transceiver Unit [*Aviation*]
GTU .... General Terminal Unit (SAUS)
GTU .... Georgetown University, Medical Center Library, Washington, DC [*OCLC symbol*] (OCLC)
GTU .... Glycol Trim Unit (MCD)
GTU .... Graduate Theological Union (SAUO)
GTU .... Graduate Theological Union, University of Saskatchewan [*UTLAS symbol*]
GTU .... Grand Touring Under 3.0 Liters [*Class of racing cars*]

GTU ... Ground Terminal Unit (SAUS)
GTU ... Ground Test Unit
GTU ... Group Terminal Unit (SAUO)
GTU ... Guidance Test Unit
GTU ... Gulf States Utilities Co. (SAUO)
GTUB ... Geographic Tabulation Unit Base (SAUS)
GTUC ... Ghana Trades Union Congress
GTUSIdentBad ... Guard, Tomb of the Unknown Soldier Identification Badge [*Military decoration*] (AABC)
GTV ... Empresa de Aviacion Aerogaviota, SA [*Cuba*] [*FAA designator*] (FAAC)
GTV ... Galaxy Cablevision L.P. [*AMEX symbol*] (TTSB)
GTV ... Galaxy Cablevision Ltd. [*AMEX symbol*] (SPSG)
GTV ... Gas Toggle Valve
GTV ... Gas Tole Valve (SAUS)
GTV ... Gas Turbine Vessel (SAUS)
GTV ... Gate Trigger Valve (SAUS)
GTV ... Gate Valve (AAG)
GTV ... Glide Test Vehicle (SAUS)
GTV ... Granada Television (SAUO)
GTV ... Gran Turismo Veloce [*Automobile model designation*]
GTV ... Gross Tumor Volume [*Medicine*] (RAWO)
GTV ... Ground Test Vehicle (KSC)
GTV ... Ground Test Verification (SAUS)
GTV ... Ground Transport Vehicle
GTV ... Growth Test Vehicle (MCD)
GTV ... Guidance [*or Guided*] Test Vehicle
GTV ... Guided Tactical Vehicle [*Army*]
GTV ... Guided Test Vehicle
GTW ... Gateway Aviation [*Zambia*] [*FAA designator*] (FAAC)
GTW ... Gateway, Inc. [*NYSE symbol*] (SG)
GTW ... Global Technology Watch [*Information service or system*] (IID)
GTW ... Global Trading Web (HODG)
GTW ... Good This Week [*Business term*]
GTW ... Gottwaldov [*Former Czechoslovakia*] [*Airport symbol*] (OAG)
GTW ... Grand Trunk Western Railroad Co. [*AAR code*]
GTW ... Gross Takeoff Weight [*of an aircraft*] [*Also, GTOW*]
GTW ... Gross Tonnage Weight (SAUS)
GTW ... Gross Ton Weight (SAUS)
GTW ... Gross Total Weight (SAUS)
GTW ... Gross Train Weight (DCTA)
GTW ... Guild of Travel Writers [*British*]
GTWAPS ... Global Theater Weather Analysis and Prediction System (SAUO)
GTWAY ... Gateway [*Commonly used*] (OPSA)
GtWF ... Great Western Financial [*Associated Press*] (SAG)
GtWF ... Great Western Financial Corp. [*Associated Press*] (SAG)
GtWFn ... Great Western Financial Corp. [*Associated Press*] (SAG)
GTWG ... Ground Training Working Group (SAUO)
GTWOD ... Gas Turbine World (journ.) (SAUS)
GTWR ... Gross Train Weight Rating
GTWT ... Gridded Traveling-Wave Tube (MCD)
GTW Trains ... Grand Trunk Western Trains (SAUS)
GTWY ... Gateway (MCD)
gtwy ... Gateway (VRA)
GTWY ... Gateway Bank (Connecticut) [*NASDAQ symbol*] (COMM)
GtwyKY ... Gateway Bancorp, Inc. (Kentucky) [*Associated Press*] (SAG)
GTX ... Alma, MI [*Location identifier*] [*FAA*] (FAAL)
GTX ... General Test, Experimental (SAUS)
GTX ... General Tool Experimental (MCD)
GTX ... Gold Texas Resources Ltd. [*Vancouver Stock Exchange symbol*]
GTX ... Grant Industries (SAUS)
GTX ... Gran Turismo Experimental [*Grand Touring, Experimental*] [*Automotive term*]
GTX ... Graphics within Texts (NITA)
GTX ... Grayanotoxin [*Toxicology*] (LDT)
GTX ... Ground Transport Express [*Airport baggage computer*]
GTXT ... Generate Character Text [*Computer science*] (IAA)
GTXT ... Generate Text (SAUS)
GTY ... Getty Petroleum [*NYSE symbol*] (TTSB)
GTY ... Getty Petroleum Corp. [*NYSE symbol*] (SPSG)
GTY ... Getty Realty [*NYSE symbol*] (SG)
GTY ... Greatly (ABBR)
gty ... Gritty [*Quality of the bottom*] [*Nautical charts*]
Gty ... Guaranty (DLA)
GTY ... Guaranty Trustco Ltd. [*Toronto Stock Exchange symbol*]
GTY ... National Aviation Co. [*Egypt*] [*ICAO designator*] (FAAC)
GTY ... W.T. Grant Co. (SAUO)
GtyNtl ... Guaranty National Corp. [*Associated Press*] (SAG)
G Type ... General Type (SAUS)
GTZ ... Agency for Technical Cooperation (SAUS)
Gtz ... Galatz (SAUS)
GTZ ... Gateway Coal [*Federal Railroad Administration identification code*]
GTZ ... GERMAN AGENCY FOR TECHNICAL COOPERATION (SAUS)
GTZ ... German Development Agency (SAUO)
GTZ ... German Organization for Technical Assistance (SAUO)
GTZ ... German Technical Assistance Agency (SAUS)
GTZ ... Gran Turismo Zagato [*Automobile model designation*]
GTZ ... Guatemala Trade Zone (SAUO)
GU ... Aviateca [*ICAO designator*] (AD)
GU ... Gasschutzunteroffizier [*Gas Noncommissioned Officer*] [*German military - World War II*]
GU ... Gastric Ulcer [*Medicine*]
GU ... Gear Up [*Aviation*]
GU ... Geek Undecided (SAUO)
GU ... General Reserve Unit (SAUO)
GU ... Generations United (EA)
GU ... Generic (SAUS)
GU ... Generic Unit (TEL)
GU ... Genitourinary [*Medicine*]
GU ... Geographically Undesirable [*Slang*]
gu ... geographically unsuitable (SAUS)
GU ... Georgetown University [*Washington, DC*]
GU ... Get Unique (SAUS)
GU ... Giant Urticaria [*Medicine*] (MELL)
GU ... Gifu University (SAUO)
GU ... Glasgow University (SAUO)
GU ... Glucose Uptake [*Medicine*] (MELL)
GU ... Glucuronidase (SAUS)
GU ... Glycogenic Unit [*Medicine*]
GU ... Gonococcal Urethritis [*Medicine*]
GU ... Gonzaga University (SAUO)
GU ... Government Unit (SAUO)
GU ... Grafton & Upton Railroad Co. [*AAR code*]
GU ... Gramophone Unit (SAUS)
GU ... Grand United Friendly Society [*Australia*]
GU ... Gravitational Ulcer [*Medicine*]
GU ... Greater Union Organisation [*Australia*]
GU ... Group Unit (SAUO)
gu ... Guam [*MARC country of publication code*] [*Library of Congress*] (LCCP)
GU ... Guam [*Postal code*] [*ANSI two-letter standard code*] (CNC)
GU ... Guanase [*An enzyme*]
GU ... Guanethidine [*Medicine*] (EDAA)
GU ... Guarantee
GU ... Guatemala [*IYRU nationality code*] (IYR)
GU ... Guidance Unit
Gu ... Guillelmus de Tocco [*Authority cited in pre-1607 legal work*] (DSA)
GU ... Guinea
GU ... Gules [*Heraldry*]
GU ... Gunner (ADA)
GU ... Gutman Unit [*Medicine*] (EDAA)
GU ... University of Georgia (SAUO)
GU ... University of Georgia, Athens, GA [*Library symbol*] [*Library of Congress*] (LCLS)
GUA ... Aerotaxis de Aguascalientes SA de CV [*Mexico*] [*ICAO designator*] (FAAC)
GUA ... Group of Units of Analysis [*Medicine*] (DMAA)
GUA ... Guam [*Mariana Islands*] [*Seismograph station code, US Geological Survey*]
Gua ... Guanine [*Also, G*] [*Biochemistry*]
GUA ... Guanine Uracil Adenine [*A triplet of bases coding for the amino acid, valine*] (EES)
gua ... Guarani [*MARC language code*] [*Library of Congress*] (LCCP)
Gua ... Guatemala (MILB)
GUA ... Guatemala City [*Guatemala*] [*Airport symbol*] (OAG)
GUA ... Guidance Unit Assembly
GUA ... Guinea [*Monetary unit*] [*Obsolete*] [*British*] (ROG)
GUA ... International Guards Union of America
GUA ... University of Georgia, Athens, GA [*OCLC symbol*] (OCLC)
GuaAF ... Nieves M. Flores Memorial Library, Agana, Guam [*Library symbol*] [*Library of Congress*] (LCLS)
GUAD ... Guadeloupe (ROG)
Guad ... Guadelupe (SHCU)
GUADA ... Guadalupe, CA [*American Association of Railroads railroad junction routing code*]
Gual ... Gualcosius [*Flourished, 11th-12th century*] [*Authority cited in pre-1607 legal work*] (DSA)
Gualc ... Gualcosius [*Flourished, 11th-12th century*] [*Authority cited in pre-1607 legal work*] (DSA)
GUALO ... General Union of Associations of Loom Overlookers [*British*] (DCTA)
Guam Admin R ... Administrative Rules and Regulations of the Government of Guam [*A publication*] (DLA)
Guam Ag Exp ... Guam Agricultural Experiment Station. Publications (journ.) (SAUS)
Guam Civ Code ... Guam Civil Code [*A publication*] (DLA)
Guam Code Civ Pro ... Guam Code of Civil Procedure [*A publication*] (DLA)
Guam Gov't Code ... Guam Government Code [*A publication*] (DLA)
Guam Prob Code ... Guam Probate Code [*A publication*] (DLA)
Guam ST ... Guam Standard Time (SAUS)
GUAN ... GCOS Upper-air Network (SAUO)
GUAP ... Chief Directorate of the Aviation Industry (SAUO)
GUAR ... Guarantee (MSA)
guar ... Guarantee (SHCU)
Guar ... Guarantee [*Banking*] (TBD)
Guar ... Guaranteed (EBF)
guar ... Guaranteed (SHCU)
GUAR ... Guarantee Life Companies, Inc. [*NASDAQ symbol*] (SAG)
GUAR ... Guarantee Life Cos [*NASDAQ symbol*] (TTSB)
Guar ... Guarnerius [*Irnerius*] [*Flourished, 1113-18*] [*Authority cited in pre-1607 legal work*] (DSA)
GUARD ... Emergency Radio Channel (SAUO)
GUARD ... Government Employees United Against Discrimination [*An association*]
GUARD ... Guaranteed Assignment Retention Detailing [*Navy*] (NVT)
GUARD FIST ... Guard Unit Armor Device Full-Crew Interaction Simulation Trainer
GUARD II ... Expanded Guaranteed Assignment Retention Detailing (SAUS)
GUARDRAIL ... Airborne COMINT DF System (SAUO)
GUARDRAIL V ... Airborne HF/VHF/UHF Intercept And Location System (SAUO)
GUARDS ... Generalized Unified Ammunition Reporting Data System (MCD)
GUARDS ... General Unified Ammunition Reporting Data System (SAUO)
GUARDSMAN ... Guidelines and Rules for Data Systems Management (TEL)

GuardTc....... Guardian Technologies International, Inc. [*Associated Press*] (SAG)
GUAREE....... Guarantee (ROG)
GuarFin........ Guaranty Financial Corp. [*Associated Press*] (SAG)
GuarFS........ Guaranty Federal Savings Bank [*Associated Press*] (SAG)
GUARG........ Guaranteeing (SAUS)
GuarLife...... Guarantee Life Companies, Inc. [*Associated Press*] (SAG)
GUARNG....... Guam Army National Guard
GUAROR...... Guarantor [*Legal term*] (ROG)
GUARS......... Generalized Unified Ammunition Reporting data System (SAUS)
GuarSL........ Guaranty Savings & Loan FA [*Associated Press*] (SAG)
GUART......... Guaranty (ABBR)
GUARTE....... Guarantee (ABBR)
GUARTED.... Guaranteed (ABBR)
GUARTEG.... Guaranteeing (ABBR)
GUARTR...... Guarantor (ABBR)
GUASO........ Guatemalan Solidarity Committee (EA)
GUAT........... Guatemala
GuaU........... University of Guam, Agana, GU [*Library symbol*] [*Library of Congress*] (LCLS)
G U B.......... Generalized Upper Boundary (SAUS)
GUB............ Generalized Upper Bounding [*Computer science*]
GUB............ Government Union of Burma
GUB............ Greatest Upper Bound [*Computer science*]
GUB............ Guerrero Negro [*Mexico*] [*Airport symbol*]
GuB............ Guinea-Bissau (MILB)
GUB............ Law School Library, University of Georgia, Athens, GA [*OCLC symbol*] (OCLC)
GUBA.......... Growing Up Born Again [*Pronounced "goobah"*] [*Book published by Fleming H. Revell Co.*]
GUBC.......... Guyana United Broadcasting Co. (SAUS)
GUBC.......... Guyana United Broadcasting Company (SAUO)
GUBER......... Gubernatorial (ABBR)
GUBGF........ General Union of Bellhangers and Gas Fitters [*British*]
GUBI........... Gemeinschaft Unabhangiger Beratender Ingenieurbueros [*Association of German Consulting Engineers*]
GUBL........... Beyla [*Guinea*] [*ICAO location identifier*] (ICLI)
GUBR........... Gentleman Usher of the Black Rod [*British*] (ROG)
GUBSMW..... General Union of Braziers and Sheet Metal Workers [*British*]
GUBTW........ General Union of Bedding Trade Workers [*British*]
GUBU........... Grotesque, Unbelievable, Bizarre, Unprecedented [*Term coined by an Irish politician to describe certain incidents in Irish politics*]
GUC............ Good-until-Canceled Order [*Business term*]
GUC............ Great Unity Club (SAUS)
GUC............ Groupe d'Union Camerounaise [*Group for Cameroonian Union*]
GUC............ Guanine Uracil Cytosine [*A triplet of bases coding for the amino acid, valine*] (EES)
GUC............ Gucci Group NV [*NYSE symbol*] (SAG)
GUC............ Gunnison [*Colorado*] [*Airport symbol*] (OAG)
GUC............ Union Catalog of the Atlanta-Athens Area, Atlanta, GA [*OCLC symbol*] (OCLC)
GUCA.......... Ground Umbilical Carrier Assembly (SAUS)
Gucci........... Gucci Group NV [*Associated Press*] (SAG)
GUCCIAAC... General Union of Chamber of Commerce, Industry and Agriculture for Arab Countries [*Lebanon*] (EAIO)
GUCCO......... Guidance Computer Control Subsystem
GUCJ........... General Union of Carpenters and Joiners [*British*]
GUCL........... General-Use Consumable List [*Military*]
GUCO.......... Grand Union [*NASDAQ symbol*] (TTSB)
GUCO.......... Grand Union Co. [*NASDAQ symbol*] (SAG)
GUCO.......... Guilford Courthouse National Military Park
GUCOTROIS... Great, Unopposable Commandant of the Realm of Inextinguishable Sagacity [*Rank in Junior Woodchucks organization mentioned in Donald Duck comic by Carl Barks*]
GUCOW........ Grand Un Wrrt Ser 1 [*NASDAQ symbol*] (TTSB)
GUCOZ......... Grand Un Wrrt Ser 2 [*NASDAQ symbol*] (TTSB)
GUCP........... Ground Umbilical Carrier Plate (MCD)
GUCY........... Conakry/Gbessia [*Guinea*] [*ICAO location identifier*] (ICLI)
GUD............ Good [*Amateur radio shorthand*] (WDAA)
GUD............ Goundam [*Mali*] [*Airport symbol*] (OAG)
GUD............ Grand Unified Debugger (SAUS)
GUD............ Guardian Resources Corp. [*Vancouver Stock Exchange symbol*]
GUD............ Guide (ABBR)
GUDBK........ Guidebook (ABBR)
GUDD.......... Didi [*Guinea*] [*ICAO location identifier*] (ICLI)
GUDD.......... Guided (ABBR)
GU-De......... University of Georgia, DeRenne Georgia Library, Athens, GA [*Library symbol*] [*Library of Congress*] (LCLS)
Gude Pr....... Gude. Practice of the Crown Side of the Court of King's Bench [*1828*] [*A publication*] (DLA)
GUDG.......... Guiding (ABBR)
GUDNC........ Guidance (ABBR)
GUDPST....... Guidepost (ABBR)
GUDSPA...... General Union Democratic Students and Patriotic Afghan (EA)
GUE............ Generating Unit Electrical (SAUS)
GUE............ Georgians United for Education (SAUO)
GUE............ Graphical User Environment [*Computer science*]
GUE............ Group for the European Unitarian Left [*EC*] (ECED)
GUE............ University of Guelph [*UTLAS symbol*]
GUER.......... Guerilla
GUERAP....... General Unwanted Energy Rejection Analysis Program [*Air Force*]
G U E R A P... General Unwanted Energy Rejection Analysis Programme (SAUS)
GUERL......... Guerilla (ABBR)
GUERN......... Guernsey, WY [*American Association of Railroads railroad junction routing code*]
Guern Eq Jur... Guernsey's Key to Equity Jurisprudence [*A publication*] (DLA)
Guern Ins..... Guernsey on Questions of Insanity [*A publication*] (DLA)
Guern Mech L... Guernsey's Mechanics' Lien Laws of New York [*A publication*] (DLA)
GUESS......... General Purpose Expert System Shell [*Virginia Polytechnic Institute*] [*General framework for expert systems*] (NITA)
GUESS......... General Uncertainty Economic Simulation System (SAUO)
GUESS......... Geo-Urban-Eco-System-Simulation (SAUO)
GuestS......... Guest Supply, Inc. [*Associated Press*] (SAG)
GUEVERA...... Guerrilla Warfare Model (SAUO)
GUF............ French Guiana [*ANSI three-letter standard code*] (CNC)
GUF............ General University Funds (EERA)
GUF............ Global University Funding
GUF............ Government University Fund (SAUO)
GUF............ Grand Unified Force
GUFA.......... Fria [*Guinea*] [*ICAO location identifier*] (ICLI)
GUFEX......... Gulf Underwater Flare Experiment [*Marine science*] (MSC)
GUFFAW...... Government Undertaking for Finding Another Way [*Parliamentary slang*] [*British*] (DI)
GUFH.......... Faranah/Badala [*Guinea*] [*ICAO location identifier*] (ICLI)
GUFMEX...... Gulf of Mexico [*Project*] [*Marine science*] (OSRA)
GUFMEX...... Gulf of Mexico Experiment (SAUO)
GUFS........... Grand United Friendly Society [*Australia*]
GUFSA......... Griffith University Faculty Staff Association [*Australia*]
GUG............ Empresa Guatemalteca de Aviacion [*Guatemala*] [*ICAO designator*] (FAAC)
GUG............ Guanine Uracil Guanine [*A triplet of bases coding for the amino acid, valine*] (EES)
GUG............ Guari [*Papua New Guinea*] [*Airport symbol*] (OAG)
GUG............ N'Guigmi [*Niger*] [*Airport symbol*] (AD)
GUGA.......... Grounded Unity Gain Amplifier (IAA)
GuGIC......... Instituto de Nutricion de Centro America y Panama, Guatemala City, Guatemala [*Library symbol*] [*Library of Congress*] (LCLS)
GuGIN......... Instituto Centro Americano de Investigacion y Tecnologia Industrial, Guatemala City, Guatemala [*Library symbol*] [*Library of Congress*] (LCLS)
GUGL........... Gaoual [*Guinea*] [*ICAO location identifier*] (ICLI)
Gug Mus...... Guggenheim Museum (SAUO)
GUGO.......... Banankoro/Gbenko [*Guinea*] [*ICAO location identifier*] (ICLI)
GUGR.......... Gentleman Usher of the Green Rod [*British*] (ROG)
GuGS........... Universidad de San Carlos de Guatemala, Ciudad Universitaria, Guatemala City, Guatemala [*Library symbol*] [*Library of Congress*] (LCLS)
GUH............ Gunnedah [*Australia*] [*Airport symbol*] (OAG)
GUHA.......... General Unary Hypothesis Automation (IEEE)
GUI............ Gay Union International [*Paris, France*] (EAIO)
GUI............ Genitourinary Infection [*Medicine*] (PDAA)
GUI............ Golfing Union of Ireland (EAIO)
GUI............ Graphical User Interface [*Computer science*] (EERA)
GUI............ Graphics-based User Interface (SAUS)
GUI............ Graphic User Interface (SAUS)
GUI............ Guiana (ROG)
Gui............. Guido de Cumis [*Flourished, 13th century*] [*Authority cited in pre-1607 legal work*] (DSA)
Gui............. Guido de Suzaria [*Deceased, 1293*] [*Authority cited in pre-1607 legal work*] (DSA)
Gui............. Guillelmus de Accursio [*Deceased, 1314*] [*Authority cited in pre-1607 legal work*] (DSA)
Gui............. Guillelmus de Tocco [*Authority cited in pre-1607 legal work*] (DSA)
Gui............. Guinea (MILB)
GUI............ Guiria [*Venezuela*] [*Airport symbol*] (OAG)
gui............. Guitar (GROV)
GUI............ Guitar [*Music*]
GUIAC......... Guaiacum [*Lignum Vitae*] [*Pharmacy*] (ROG)
GUIB........... Graphical User Interface for Blind People
Gui-Bis........ Guinea-Bissau (SAUO)
Gui Cur........ Guinea Current (SAUS)
GUID.......... Globally Unique Identifiers [*Microsoft Corp.*] [*Computer science*] (PCM)
GUID.......... Global Universal Identification (SAUO)
GUID.......... Global Universal Identifier (SAUS)
GUID.......... Guidance (AAG)
Guid........... Guidance [*Medicine*] (EDAA)
GUID.......... Guide
GUID.......... Guidon Oil & Gas Co. (SAUO)
GUID.......... Kindia [*Guinea*] [*ICAO location identifier*] (ICLI)
Guidant....... Guidant Corp. [*Associated Press*] (SAG)
GUIDAR....... Guided Intrusion Detection and Ranging (PDAA)
GUIDE......... General Usage Inventory Director (MCD)
GUIDE......... General User Interface-system with Dialogue Entrance (SAUS)
GUIDE......... Graphical User Interface Design Editor (SAUS)
GUIDE......... Graphics User Interface Development Environment (SAUS)
Guideb........ Guidebook (SAUS)
Guideb Anna Field Conf Mont Geol Soc... Guidebook. Annual Field Conference. Montana Geological Society (journ.) (SAUS)
Guideb Geol Utah... Guidebook to the Geology of Utah (journ.) (SAUS)
Gui de Cu.... Guillelmus de Cuneo [*Deceased, 1335*] [*Authority cited in pre-1607 legal work*] (DSA)
Guidel Med... Guidelines in Medicine (journ.) (SAUS)
Guide Relig Per... Guide to Religious Periodicals (journ.) (SAUS)
Guide Relig Semi Rel Period... Guide to Religious and Semi-Religious Periodicals (journ.) (SAUS)
Guide Soc Sci Relig Period Lit... Guide to Social Science and Religion in Periodical Literature (journ.) (SAUS)
Gui de Su.... Guido de Suzaria [*Deceased, 1293*] [*Authority cited in pre-1607 legal work*] (DSA)

Gui de Suz... Guido de Suzaria [*Deceased, 1293*] [*Authority cited in pre-1607 legal work*] (DSA)
Gui de Suza... Guido de Suzaria [*Deceased, 1293*] [*Authority cited in pre-1607 legal work*] (DSA)
Guidhall Stud London Hist... Guildhall Studies in London History (journ.) (SAUS)
GUIDN .... Guidance (AABC)
GUIDNC .... Guidance
GUIDO .... Guidance and Navigation Officer [*NASA*]
GUIDO .... Guidance Officer [*Aerospace*] (NAKS)
GUIDON .... Graphical User Interface Developed by OCLC (SAUS)
Guid Pancir... Guido Pancirolus [*Deceased, 1599*] [*Authority cited in pre-1607 legal work*] (DSA)
Guid Pancirol... Guido Pancirolus [*Deceased, 1599*] [*Authority cited in pre-1607 legal work*] (DSA)
Guid Pap ..... Guido Papa [*Deceased, 1487*] [*Authority cited in pre-1607 legal work*] (DSA)
Guid Spec Educ Bull... Guidance and Special Education Bulletin (journ.) (SAUS)
GUII .... Guilford Transportation Industries [*Federal Railroad Administration identification code*]
GUIL .... Guilder (ABBR)
Guil Bene .... Guillelmus de Benedictis [*Flourished, 16th century*] [*Authority cited in pre-1607 legal work*] (DSA)
GUILD .... Government, University, Industry, Laboratory Development [*Microelectronics*]
GUILDF .... Guildford [*City in England*] (ROG)
Guildhall Lib... Guildhall Library (SAUS)
GUILDHL ...... Guildhall (ABBR)
Guild Law .... Guild Lawyer [*National Lawyers' Guild*] [*New York Chapter*] [*A publication*] (DLA)
Guild Prof Trans... Guild of Professional Translators (SAUO)
Guild Q .... National Lawyers Guild Quarterly [*A publication*] (DLA)
GUILFL .... Guileful (ABBR)
Guilford .... Guilford Mills, Inc. [*Associated Press*] (SAG)
Guilford Law Behav Ser... Guilford Law and Behavior Series (journ.) (SAUS)
GuilfrdP .... Guilford Pharmaceuticals, Inc. [*Associated Press*] (SAG)
GUILFY .... Guilefully (ABBR)
Guill .... Guillelmus Durandi [*Deceased, 1296*] [*Authority cited in pre-1607 legal work*] (DSA)
Guill de Montelaud... Guillelmus de Monte Lauduno [*Deceased, 1343*] [*Authority cited in pre-1607 legal work*] (DSA)
Guillel Bened... Guillelmus de Benedictis [*Flourished, 16th century*] [*Authority cited in pre-1607 legal work*] (DSA)
Guil Na .... Guillelmus Naso [*Flourished, 1220-34*] [*Authority cited in pre-1607 legal work*] (DSA)
GUILS .... Guileless (ABBR)
GUILSY .... Guilelessly (ABBR)
GUIMARC .... Guidelines Marketing Corp.
GUIN .... Guinea [*Monetary unit*] [*Obsolete*] [*British*] (ROG)
Guin .... Guinea (VRA)
GUIP .... Graphical User Interface for blind People (SAUS)
GUIRR .... Government-University-Industry Research Roundtable [*Academy of Sciences*]
GUISE .... Guidance System Evaluation [*Military*] (IAA)
Guit .... Guitar [*Music*]
Guiz .... Guizzardinus [*Deceased, 1222*] [*Authority cited in pre-1607 legal work*] (DSA)
GUIZ .... Gunderson Industries [*Federal Railroad Administration identification code*]
Guizot Rep Govt... Guizot's History of Representative Government [*A publication*] (DLA)
GUJ .... Guaratingueta [*Brazil*] [*Airport symbol*] (OAG)
guj .... Gujarati [*MARC language code*] [*Library of Congress*] (LCCP)
Gujar .... Gujarat University (SAUO)
Gujarat Agric Univ Res J... Gujarat Agricultural University. Research Journal (journ.) (SAUS)
Gujarat Statist Rev... Gujarat Statistical Review (journ.) (SAUS)
Guj Ind .... Gujarat, India (ILCA)
Guj L Rep ..... Guarat Law Reporter (journ.) (SAUS)
Guj L Rep ..... Gujarat Law Reporter [*A publication*] (ILCA)
Guj LT .... Gujarat Law Times (journ.) (SAUS)
GUJRD .... Gomal University. Journal of Research (journ.) (SAUS)
GUK .... Guanylate Kinase [*An enzyme*]
GUKE .... Kerouane [*Guinea*] [*ICAO location identifier*] (ICLI)
GUKR .... Glavnoe Upravlenie Kontrrazvedkoi [*Chief Administration for Counter-intelligence*] [*of the Ministry of War*] [*Former USSR*] [*World War II*]
GUKR .... Kamsar/Kawass [*Guinea*] [*ICAO location identifier*] (ICLI)
GUKU .... Kissidougou [*Guinea*] [*ICAO location identifier*] (ICLI)
GUL .... Georgetown University, Law Library, Washington, DC [*OCLC symbol*] (OCLC)
GUL .... Glasgow University Language Centre (SAUO)
GUL .... GSE [*Ground Support Equipment*] Utilization List [*NASA*] (NASA)
Gul .... Guillelmus de Cuneo [*Deceased, 1335*] [*Authority cited in pre-1607 legal work*] (DSA)
GUL .... Gull Air [*ICAO designator*] (FAAC)
GUL .... Gull Laboratories [*AMEX symbol*] (TTSB)
GUL .... Gull Laboratories, Inc. [*AMEX symbol*] (SPSG)
GUL .... Gully (ABBR)
GUL .... Gulmarg [*India*] [*Geomagnetic observatory code*]
GUL .... Gulton Industries, Inc. (SAUO)
GU-L .... University of Georgia, Law Library, Athens, GA [*Library symbol*] [*Library of Congress*] (LCLS)
GULAG .... Glavnoe Upravlenie Ispravitel'no-Trudovykh Lagerei [*Main Administration of Corrective Labor Camps*] [*Former USSR*]
GULB .... Gullible (ABBR)
GULB .... Labe/Tata [*Guinea*] [*ICAO location identifier*] (ICLI)
GULBLY .... Gullibly (ABBR)
GULBT .... Gullibility (ABBR)
GULC .... Georgetown University Law Center (AAGC)
GULC .... Glasgow University Language Centre [*University of Glasgow*] [*British*] (CB)
GULD .... Goulds Pumps [*NASDAQ symbol*] (TTSB)
GULD .... Goulds Pumps, Inc. [*NASDAQ symbol*] (NQ)
GULF .... Gays United for Liberty and Freedom (SAUO)
Gulf .... Gulf Oil Corporation (SAUO)
GULF .... Gulfwest Oil [*NASDAQ symbol*] (TTSB)
Gulf Caribb Fish Inst Univ Miami Proc... Gulf and Caribbean Fisheries Institute. University of Miami. Proceedings (journ.) (SAUS)
GULFCO .... Gulf United Corp. (EFIS)
Gulf Coast... Florida (SAUS)
Gulf Coast Assoc Geol Socs Trans... Gulf Coast Association of Geological Societies. Transactions (journ.) (SAUS)
GULFCOBASERVUNIT... Gulf Coast Base Service Unit (SAUO)
GULFCOBASESERVUNIT... Gulf Coast Base Service Unit
GULFCOBASFSERVUNIT... Gulf Coast Base Service Unit (SAUS)
GULFCON ..... Gulf Control
GULFGRU .... Gulf Group (SAUO)
Gulf Islands... Florida and Mississippi (SAUS)
Gulf Mex Sci... Gulf of Mexico Science [*A publication*] (PABS)
GULFNAVFACENGCOM... Gulf Division Naval Facilities Engineering Command
GULFP .... Gulfport, MS [*American Association of Railroads railroad junction routing code*]
Gulf Res Rep... Gulf Research Reports (journ.) (SAUS)
GULFSEAFRON... Gulf Sea Frontier
GulfSou .... Gulf South Medical Supply [*Associated Press*] (SAG)
GulfSou .... Sulf South Medical Supply [*Associated Press*] (SAG)
Gulf States... Florida (SAUS)
Gulfwest ...... Gulfwest Oil Co. [*Associated Press*] (SAG)
GULHEMP .... General Physique, Upper Extremity, Lower Extremity, Hearing, Eyesight, Mentality, and Personality [*Medicine*] (DMAA)
GULL .... Guillotine [*Bookbinding*] (DGA)
GULL .... Gull Laboratories, Inc. [*NASDAQ symbol*] (COMM)
GullLb .... Gull Laboratories, Inc. [*Associated Press*] (SAG)
GULO .... General Union of Loom Overlookers (WDAA)
GULP .... General Upgrade LAN [*Limited Access Network*] Program [*Computer science*] (PCM)
GULP .... General Utility Language Processor (SAUO)
GULP .... General Utility Language Program (SAUS)
GULP .... General Utility Library Program [*Computer science*]
GULP .... Graph Unification Logic Programming (SAUS)
GULP .... Grenada United Labor Party (SAUO)
GULP .... Grenada United Labour Party [*Political party*] (PPW)
GULP .... Group Universal Life Policy [*Insurance*] (DFIT)
GULP .... Group Universal Life Program
GULPH .... Guelph, ON [*American Association of Railroads railroad junction routing code*]
GULS .... General Use Laser System (ACAE)
GULT .... Gullet (ABBR)
GULTN .... Guillotine (ABBR)
GULTND .... Guillotined (ABBR)
GULTNG .... Guillotining (ABBR)
GULYG .... Gullying (ABBR)
GUM .... General Utility Mechanic
GUM .... Genito-Urinary Malignancy (SAUS)
GUM .... Genito-Urinary Medicine (SAUS)
GUM .... Glavnoye Upravleniye Militsii [*Main Administration of Militia*] [*Former USSR*] (LAIN)
GUM .... Glavny Universalny Magazin [*Department store in USSR*]
GUM .... Gosudarstvennyi Universal'nyi Magazin [*Government Department Store*] [*Moscow*]
GUM .... Grand Unified Monopoles [*Cosmology*]
GUM .... Guadalajara [*Mexico*] [*Seismograph station code, US Geological Survey*] (SEIS)
GUM .... Guam [*Marianas*] [*Airport symbol*] (AD)
GUM .... Guam [*ANSI three-letter standard code*] (CNC)
GUM .... Guide on the Expression of Uncertainty in Measurement (SAUS)
GUM .... Gulderand Mining [*Vancouver Stock Exchange symbol*]
GUMA .... Macenta [*Guinea*] [*ICAO location identifier*] (ICLI)
GUMBI .... Graphic User Microprogrammable Bit-slice Interpreter (SAUS)
GUMM .... GumTech International, Inc. [*NASDAQ symbol*] (SAG)
GUMM .... GumTech Intl [*NASDAQ symbol*] (TTSB)
GUMM .... Gurus of UNIX Meeting of Minds (SAUO)
GUMMW .... GumTech Intl Wrrt [*NASDAQ symbol*] (TTSB)
GUMNS .... Gumminess (ABBR)
GUMO .... Guam [*Mariana Islands*] [*Seismograph station code, US Geological Survey*] (SEIS)
GUMP .... Gas, Undercarriage, Mixture, and Prop [*Checkout procedure*]
GUMP .... Gas, Undercarriage, Mixture, Propellers (SAUS)
GUMSL .... Georgetown Univerity. Monaph Series on Languages and Linguistics (journ.) (SAUS)
GumT .... GumTech International, Inc. [*Associated Press*] (SAG)
GumTch .... GumTech International, Inc. [*Associated Press*] (SAG)
GUMZ .... Glavnoye Upravleniye Mestami Zaklyucheniya [*Main Administration of Places of Detention*] [*Former USSR*] (LAIN)
GUN .... General usage network (SAUS)
GUN .... Generic Unit Name (SAUS)
GUN .... Grantor Underwritten Note [*Banking*]
GUN .... Guaranteed Underwriting Facilities (TDOB)
GUN .... Guaranteed Underwritten Note (EBF)
GUN .... Gunboat (SAUS)

GUN .... Guncotton (ABBR)
GUN .... Guncrete (ABBR)
GUN .... Gundle Environmental Systems, Inc. [*AMEX symbol*] (SPSG)
GUN .... Gundle/SLT Environmental [*AMEX symbol*] (TTSB)
GUN .... Gunnery (MSA)
GUN .... Gunny (ABBR)
GUN .... Gunpowder (ABBR)
GUN .... Gunsteel Resources, Inc. [*Vancouver Stock Exchange symbol*]
GUN .... Montgomery, AL [*Location identifier*] [*FAA*] (FAAL)
GUNBT .... Gunboat (ABBR)
Gunby .... Gunby's District Court Reports [*1885*] [*Louisiana*] [*A publication*] (DLA)
Gunby (LA)... Gunby's District Court Reports [*1885*] [*Louisiana*] [*A publication*] (DLA)
Gunby's Dec... Gunby's District Court Reports [*1805*] [*Louisiana*] [*A publication*] (DLA)
GUND .... Gunned (ABBR)
Gun Dip .... Gunboat Diplomacy (SAUS)
GUNDLE .... Gundle Environmental Systems, Inc. (SAUO)
Gundle .... Gundle-SLT Environmental Systems, Inc. [*Associated Press*] (SAG)
Gundry .... Gundry. Manuscripts in Lincoln's Inn Library [*A publication*] (DLA)
GUNEG .... Gun Engagement Cycle Analysis (SAUS)
GUNEX .... Gunnery Exercise [*Navy*] (NVT)
GUNF .... Gulf United Nuclear Fuels Corp. (SAUO)
GUNFCO .... Gulf United Nuclear Fuels Corp. (SAUS)
GUNFCO .... Gulf United Nuclear Fuels Corporation (SAUO)
GUNFIT .... Gunfight (ABBR)
GUNFITR .... Gunfighter (ABBR)
GUNFO .... Gulf United Nuclear Fuels Corporation (SAUO)
GUNFR .... Gunfire (ABBR)
GUNG .... Gunning (ABBR)
GUNIO .... Russian Navy, Department of Navigation and Oceanography (SAUO)
GUNMA .... Gunman (ABBR)
Gunma J Libr Arts Sci... Gunma Journal of Liberal Arts and Science (journ.) (SAUS)
Gunma J Med Sci... Gunma Journal of Medical Sciences (journ.) (SAUS)
Gunma J Med Sci Suppl... Gunma Journal of Medical Sciences. Supplementum (journ.) (SAUS)
Gunma Rep Med Sci... Gunma Reports of Medical Sciences (journ.) (SAUS)
Gunma Symp Endocrinol... Gunma Symposia on Endocrinology (journ.) (SAUS)
GUN MOLL... Gonif's Molly [*Thief's Girl*] [*Yiddish*]
Gunn Tolls... Gunning on Tolls [*A publication*] (DLA)
GUNPWDR... Gunpowder (ABBR)
GUNR .... Gunnar Gold Mining, Inc. (SAUO)
GUNR .... Gunner (ABBR)
GUNRY .... Gunnery (ABBR)
GUNSGT .... Gunnery Sergeant
GUNSH .... Gunshot (ABBR)
GUNSM .... Gunsmith (ABBR)
GUNSS .... Gunnery Schoolship [*Navy*] (NVT)
GUNST .... Gunstock (ABBR)
GUNWHL .... Gunwhale (ABBR)
GUNYBG .... Gunnybag (ABBR)
GUNZ .... N,Zerekore/Konia [*Guinea*] [*ICAO location identifier*] (ICLI)
GUO .... Georgetown, TX [*Location identifier*] [*FAA*] (FAAL)
GUO .... Government Use Only (WDAA)
GUO .... Greater Union Organization (SAUO)
Guo .... Guanosine [*Also, G*] [*A nucleoside*]
GUOK .... Boke/Baralande [*Guinea*] [*ICAO location identifier*] (ICLI)
GUOO .... Grand United Order of Oddfellows [*Australia*]
GUOOF .... Grand United Order of Odd Fellows (EA)
GUP .... Gallup [*New Mexico*] [*Airport symbol*] (OAG)
GUP .... Gas Under Pressure
GUP .... Generic Ultimate Protocol (SAUS)
GUP .... Glass-Fiber-Reinforced Unsaturated Polyester [*Organic chemistry*]
gup .... Grading under Pavement [*Construction term*] (MIST)
GU-P .... Grifora Umbellata Polysaccharide [*Antineoplastic drug*]
GUP .... Guppy (ABBR)
GU-P .... University of Georgia, School of Pharmacy, Athens, GA [*Library symbol*] [*Library of Congress*] (LCLS)
GUPAC .... Gulf Permanent Assistance Committee [*Persian Gulf*]
GUPB .... GFS Bancorp [*NASDAQ symbol*] (TTSB)
GUPB .... GFSB Bancorp, Inc. [*NASDAQ symbol*] (SAG)
GUPCO .... Gulf Petroleum Corp. (SAUS)
GUPH .... Group for the Use of Psychology in History (EA)
Guppie .... Gay Urban Professional [*Lifestyle classification*]
GUPPY .... Greater Underwater Propulsive Power [*Type of submarine*]
GUPS .... Grand Unified Problem Solver
Gupta .... Gupta Corp. [*Associated Press*] (SAG)
GUQ .... Guanare [*Venezuela*] [*Airport symbol*] (OAG)
GUR .... Alotau [*Papua New Guinea*] [*Airport symbol*] (OAG)
GUR .... Global Utility Rate [*Medicine*] (EDAA)
GUR .... Glucose Utilization Rate (SAUS)
GUR .... Ground under Repair
GUR .... Gulfstream Resources Canada Ltd. [*Toronto Stock Exchange symbol*]
GUR .... Gurgu (ABBR)
GURC .... Gulf Universities Research Consortium (EA)
GURC .... Gulf Universities Research Corp.
GURF .... Generating utility references file (SAUS)
GURGLD .... Gurgled (ABBR)
GURGLG .... Gurgling (ABBR)
GURN .... Government of National Unity and Reconciliation (SAUO)
GURNT .... Guarantee (ABBR)
GURNTD .... Guaranteed (ABBR)
GURNTG .... Guarantying (ABBR)
GURNTR .... Guarantor (ABBR)
GURNTY .... Guaranty (ABBR)
GURR .... Gentleman Usher of the Red Rod [*British*] (ROG)
GURS .... General Update and Retrieval System (SAUS)
GURS .... Kouroussa [*Guinea*] [*ICAO location identifier*] (ICLI)
GURT .... Georgetown University. Round Table on Languages and Linguistics (journ.) (SAUS)
GURTG .... Guaranteeing (ABBR)
Gus .... Conductance of Upstream Segment [*Physics*] (DAVI)
GUS .... General User System (SAUS)
GUS .... Generic Update System [*Computer science*]
GUS .... Generic User System [*Computer science*]
GUS .... Genitourinary Sphincter [*Medicine*] (EDAA)
GUS .... Genitourinary System [*Medicine*]
GUS .... Geographic Underwriting System (SAUO)
GUS .... Geographic Update System (SAUS)
GUS .... Give Up Smoking [*Health Education Council campaign*] [*British*]
GUS .... Globe Universal Services (SAUO)
GUS .... Glucuronidase [*An enzyme*]
GUS .... Goldsboro Union Station [*Federal Railroad Administration identification code*]
GUS .... Graduate Institute of International Studies (SAUS)
GUS .... Greater User Service (TIMI)
GUS .... Great Universal Stores [*Mail-order firm*] [*British*]
GUS .... Grocers United Stores (SAUO)
GUS .... Group Unit Simulator (MCD)
GUS .... Guidance Unit Support (SAUS)
GUS .... Guidance Update System (ACAE)
GUS .... Guide to the Use of Standards (SAUO)
GUS .... Gunflint Resources Ltd. [*Vancouver Stock Exchange symbol*]
GUs .... Guns Unlimited (SAUS)
GUS .... Gusset (MSA)
GUS .... Peru, IN [*Location identifier*] [*FAA*] (FAAL)
GUSA .... Sangaredi [*Guinea*] [*ICAO location identifier*] (ICLI)
GUSB .... Guided Unified S-Band (MCD)
GUSB .... Sambailo [*Guinea*] [*ICAO location identifier*] (ICLI)
GUSCO .... Gulu Support for Children Organisation (SAUO)
GUSER .... GCOS Security Module
GUSF .... Government Uncovers Local Fences (SAUO)
GUSH .... Fountain Oil [*NASDAQ symbol*] (TTSB)
GUSH .... Fountain Oil, Inc. [*NASDAQ symbol*] (SAG)
GUSHD .... CanArgo Energy [*NASDAQ symbol*] [*Formerly, Fountain Oil*]
GUSHG .... Gushing (ABBR)
GUSHNS .... Gushiness (ABBR)
GUSHR .... Gushier (ABBR)
GUSHST .... Gushiest (ABBR)
GUSI .... Siguiri [*Guinea*] [*ICAO location identifier*] (ICLI)
GUSIT .... General Usage Shorts and Impedance Tests (SAUS)
GUSS .... Guided Social Simulation
GUSSIES .... Great Universal Stores [*Mail-order firm*] [*British*]
GUST .... Global User Service Task (SAUS)
GUST .... Gusset (ABBR)
gust .... gustation (SAUS)
gust .... gustatorily (SAUS)
gust .... gustatory (SAUS)
gust .... gustily (SAUS)
gust .... gustiness (SAUS)
gust .... gusto (SAUS)
GUST .... Gusty (SAUS)
GUSTNS .... Gustiness (ABBR)
GUSTO .... Global Utilization of Streptokinase and Tissue Plasminogen Activator for Occluded Coronary Arteries [*Cardiology study*]
GUSTO .... Global Utilization of Streptokinase and TPA [*Tissue Plasminogen Activator*]for Occluded Arteries [*Comparative study*]
GUSTO .... Guidance Using Stable Tuning Oscillations
GUSTR .... Gustier (ABBR)
GUSTST .... Gustiest (ABBR)
GUSTY .... Gustily (ABBR)
GUSYA .... Gunma Symposia on Endocrinology (journ.) (SAUS)
GUT .... Gand Unified Theory (SAUS)
GUT .... Genitourinary Tract [*Medicine*] (MELL)
GUT .... Grand Unified Theory [*Cosmology*]
GUT .... Gulf Titanium Ltd. [*Vancouver Stock Exchange symbol*]
GUT .... Gutter (MSA)
GUT .... Pittsburgh, PA [*Location identifier*] [*FAA*] (FAAL)
Gut Brac .... Guterbock's Bracton [*A publication*] (DLA)
GUTD .... Gutted (ABBR)
Gutenberg Society... International Association for Past and present History of the Art of Printing (SAUO)
GUTG .... Gutting (ABBR)
Guth L & T... Guthrie's Landlord and Tenant [*A publication*] (DLA)
Guth Pr .... Guthrie's Principles of the Laws of England [*1843*] [*A publication*] (DLA)
Guth Pr .... Guthries Principles of the Laws of England (journ.) (SAUS)
Guthrie .... Guthrie's Reports [*33-83 Missouri Appeals*] [*A publication*] (DLA)
Guthrie .... Guthrie's Sheriff Court Cases [*1861-92*] [*Scotland*] [*A publication*] (DLA)
Guth Sh Cas... Guthrie's Sheriff Court Cases [*1861-92*] [*Scotland*] [*A publication*] (DLA)
Guth Sher Cas... Guthrie's Sheriff Court Cases [*1861-92*] [*Scotland*] [*A publication*] (DLA)
Guth Tr Un... Guthrie on Trade Unions [*A publication*] (DLA)
GUTR .... Gutter (ABBR)
GUTRL .... Gutteral (ABBR)

GUTRY........ Gutterally (ABBR)
GUTS.......... Game on Urban Transport System [*Kins Developments Ltd.*] [*Software package*] (NCC)
GUTS.......... Georgians Unwilling to Surrender [*Organization founded by former governor, Lester Maddox*]
GUTS.......... Gothenburg University Terminal System [*IBM Corp.*] (EECA)
GUTS.......... Ground Up-to-Space (MCD)
GUTS.......... Guaranteed Ultimate Tensile Strength (SAUS)
GUTS.......... Guerilla Urban Traffic System [*Refers to driving in Boston*]
GUTS.......... Guidance Unit Test Station (ACAE)
gutt............ Goutte [*Drop*] [*Pharmacy*]
GUTT.......... Grand Unified Theory of the Tire
GUTT.......... Guttae [*Drops of Liquid*] [*Pharmacy*]
GUTT.......... Gutturi [*To the Throat*] [*Pharmacy*]
GUTTAT....... Guttatim [*Drop by Drop*] [*Pharmacy*] (GPO)
GUTT QUIBUSD... Guttis Quibusdam [*With a Few Drops*] [*Pharmacy*]
GUU............ Grundarfjordur [*Iceland*] [*Airport symbol*] (OAG)
GUU............ Guanine Uracil Uracil [*A triplet of bases coding for the amino acid, valine*] (EES)
GUU............ Gulu [*Uganda*] [*Airport symbol*] (AD)
GUUAM........ Georgia, Ukraine, Uzbekistan, Azerbaijan and Moldova
GUUG.......... Galactic Unix User Group (SAUO)
GUUG.......... German Unix User Group (SAUS)
GUUG.......... Gross Unit Unavailable Generation [*Electronics*] (IEEE)
GUV............ Gerecht und Volkommen [*Correct and Complete*] [*German*]
GUV............ Guri [*Venezuela*] [*Seismograph station code, US Geological Survey*] (SEIS)
GUVMA........ Glasgow University Veterinary Medical Association (GVA)
GUVZS......... Glasgow University Veterinary Zoological Society (GVA)
GU/WQ......... Washington Quarterly. Georgetown University Center for Strategic and International Studies (SAUS)
GUX............ Grand Union Co. (SAUO)
GUX............ Gunderson [*Federal Railroad Administration identification code*]
GUXD.......... Kankan/Diankana [*Guinea*] [*ICAO location identifier*] (ICLI)
GUY............ Air Guyane [*France*] [*ICAO designator*] (FAAC)
GUY............ French Guiana Space Center
GUY............ General Public Utilities Corp. (SAUO)
GUY............ Guyana [*ANSI three-letter standard code*] (CNC)
GUY............ Guyana Space Center (SAUS)
GUY............ Guymon, OK [*Location identifier*] [*FAA*] (FAAL)
GUY............ Guy, TX [*American Association of Railroads railroad junction routing code*]
Guyana Geol Surv Dep Rep... Guyana.Geological Survey Department. Report (journ.) (SAUS)
Guyana J Sci... Guyana Journal of Science (journ.) (SAUS)
Guyana Minist Agric Nat Resour Agric Land Dev Ann Rep... Guyana. Ministry of Agriculture and Natural Resources. Agriculture and Land Development Departments. Annual Report (journ.) (SAUS)
Guyana Minist Agric Nat Resour Geol Surv Dep Rep... Guyana. Ministry of Agriculture and Natural Resources. Geological Survey Department.Report (journ.) (SAUS)
Guyana Sugar Exp Stat Bull... Guyana Sugar Experiment Stations Bulletin. (journ.) (SAUS)
Guybau........ Guyana Bauxite (SAUS)
Guy For Med... Guy's Forensic Medicine [*7th ed.*] [*1895*] [*A publication*] (DLA)
Guy For Med... Guys Forensic Medicine (journ.) (SAUS)
Guy Med Jur... Guy's Medical Jurisprudence [*A publication*] (DLA)
Guy Med Jur... Guys Medical Jurisprudence (journ.) (SAUS)
Guyot Inst Feod... Guyot's Instituts Feodales [*A publication*] (DLA)
Guy Rep...... Guy's Repertoire de la Jurisprudence [*A publication*] (DLA)
Guys Hosp Gaz... Guys Hospital Gazette (journ.) (SAUS)
Guys Hosp Rep... Guys Hospital Reports (journ.) (SAUS)
GUZ............ Guiratinga [*Brazil*] [*Airport symbol*] (AD)
GUZL.......... Guzzle (ABBR)
GUZLD......... Guzzled (ABBR)
GUZLG......... Guzzling (ABBR)
GUZLR......... Guzzler (ABBR)
GV............... Galvanized [*Technical drawings*]
GV............... Gastric Volume [*Medicine*] (DMAA)
GV............... Gas Valve (SAUS)
GV............... Gas Ventilation [*Medicine*] (DMAA)
GV............... Gate Valve (DAC)
GV............... Genital Vein
GV............... Gentian Violet [*Also, MRC*] [*A dye*]
GV............... Genu Valgum (MELL)
GV............... Genu Varum (MELL)
GV............... Germinal Vesicle (PDAA)
GV............... Giant Viper (SAUS)
GV............... Gigavolt
GV............... Gingivectomy [*Medicine*] (MELL)
GV............... Girls Volunteers [*Australia*]
GV............... Give (ABBR)
GV............... Goerz-Visier [*Bomb sight manufactured by Goerz Co.*] [*German military - World War II*]
GV............... Goldfield Corp. [*AMEX symbol*] (SPSG)
GV............... Gomphrena Virus [*Plant pathology*]
GV............... Gonorrheal Vaginitis [*Medicine*] (MELL)
GV............... Government Valuation (SAUS)
GV............... Governor (DSUE)
GV............... Governor of Victoria [*Australia*]
GV............... Governor Valve (SAUO)
GV............... Granulosis Virus
GV............... Graphic Violence (SAUS)
GV............... Graphic Voltmeter (SAUS)
GV............... Gravimetric Volume
G-V............. Gravity-Velocity (MCD)
GV............... Great Value [*In automobile name Yugo GV*]
GV............... Green Valley [*Plant pathology*]
GV............... Grid Variation [*Navigation*]
GV............... Griseoviridin (SAUS)
GV............... Gross Valuation (SAUS)
GV............... Gross Virus [*Leukemogenesis*] [*Immunochemistry*]
GV............... Ground Visibility
GV............... Groundwater Vistas [*Computer science*]
GV............... Group Velocity [*Physics*] (IAA)
GV............... Growth Vessel
GV............... Grow Victoria [*Mental health organisation*] [*Australia*]
GV............... Guard Vessel [*Nuclear energy*] (NRCH)
GV............... Guidance Verification (SAUS)
gv................ Guinea [*MARC country of publication code*] [*Library of Congress*] (LCCP)
G V............. Gulfstream V
GV............... Gulp Valve [*Automotive engineering*]
GV............... Talair [*ICAO designator*] (AD)
GV............... Talair Pty.Ltd. (SAUO)
GVA............ Gamewardens of Vietnam Association (EA)
GVA............ Gay Veterans Association (EA)
GVA............ General Visceral Afferent [*Neurology*]
GVA............ Geneva [*Switzerland*] [*Airport symbol*] (OAG)
GVA............ Georgia Vocational Association (SAUO)
GVA............ Geschichte Vorderasien bis zum Hellenismus [*A publication*] (BJA)
GVA............ Giga-Voltampere (SAUS)
GVA............ Golden Nevada [*Vancouver Stock Exchange symbol*]
GVA............ Golden Nevada Resources, Inc. [*Toronto Stock Exchange symbol*]
GVA............ Goulburn Valley Airlines [*Australia*]
GVA............ GOX [*Gaseous Oxygen*] Vent Arm (NASA)
GVA............ Granite Construction [*NYSE symbol*] (SG)
GVA............ Grapevine Virus A [*Plant pathology*]
GVA............ Graphic Kilovolt-Ampere [*Meter*] (MSA)
GVA............ Graphic Volt-Amperemeter (SAUS)
GVA............ Gross Value Added (EURO)
GVA............ Gyroscope Vibration Absorber
GVA............ Henderson, KY [*Location identifier*] [*FAA*] (FAAL)
GVAC.......... Amilcar Cabral International/Sal Island [*Cape Verde*] [*ICAO location identifier*] (ICLI)
GVAC.......... Graphic Video Attributes Controller [*Computer chip*]
GVAL.......... Global Vaccine Awareness League (EA)
GVAO.......... Gross Value of Agricultural Output
GVaP.......... GEWEX [*Global Energy and Water Cycle Experiment*] Water Vapor Project [*Marine science*] (OSRA)
GVAP.......... Gross Value of Agricultural Production (SAUO)
GVAR.......... GOES I-M Variable (SAUS)
GVAR.......... GOES I-M Variable Data Format (SAUS)
GVaS.......... Valdosta State College, Valdosta, GA [*Library symbol*] [*Library of Congress*] (LCLS)
GVAWY........ Giveaway (ABBR)
GVAY.......... Galway (SAUS)
GVB............ Gelatine Veronal Buffer (PDAA)
GVB............ Generalized Valence Bond [*Physics*]
GVB............ Grapevine Virus B [*Plant pathology*]
GVB............ Guam Visitors Bureau (SAUO)
GVB............ Guaranteed Voltage Breakdown
GVBA.......... Boavista, Boavista Island [*Cape Verde*] [*ICAO location identifier*] (ICLI)
GVBA.......... Global Village Business Association (SAUO)
GVBD.......... Germinal Vesicle Breakdown [*Cytology*]
GVC............ General Videotex Corp.
GVC............ Girls' Venture Corps [*British*] (BI)
GVC............ Glazed Vitrified Clay
GVC............ Gold-Veneer Crown (MELL)
GVC............ Grand View College [*Iowa*]
GVC............ Graphics Vendor Control
GVC............ Guild Vector Colorimeter
GVCAC........ Girls' Venture Corps Air Cadets [*British*] (DBA)
GVCO.......... Grants to Voluntary Conservation Organisations (EERA)
GVD............ Generalverkehrsdirektion (SAUS)
GVD............ Global Vegetation Data (SAUO)
GVD............ Gravdal [*Norway*] [*Airport symbol*] (AD)
GVD............ Group View Display (MCD)
GVD............ Guns and Vehicles Division (SAUS)
GVDMS........ Ground Vehicle Dispensed Mine System (SAUO)
GVDSB......... Government Data Systems (journ.) (SAUS)
GVDSN......... Gott Verlaeszt die Seinen Nicht [*God Forsakes Not His Own*] [*Motto of Dorothee, Duchess of Braunschweig-Wolfenbuttel (1607-34)*] [*German*]
GVE............ Gasversicherung Euskirchen GmbH (SAUO)
GVE............ General Visceral Efferent [*Neurology*]
GVE............ Gordonsville, VA [*Location identifier*] [*FAA*] (FAAL)
GVE............ Group Value Engineering
GVE............ Grove (ADA)
GVE............ Grove Property Trust [*NYSE symbol*] (SG)
GVEN.......... Growth Ventures, Inc. (SAUO)
GVF............ Garnisonsverwendungsfaehig Feld [*Fit for Garrison Duty in the Field*] [*German military - World War II*]
GVF............ Golden Valley Microwave Foods, Inc. (SAUO)
GVF............ Goodness of Variance Fit (SAUS)
GVF............ Good Visual Field [*Ophthalmology*] (DAVI)
GVF............ Grazhdanskii Vozdushnyi Flot [*Civil Air Fleet*] [*Former USSR*]
GVFF.......... General Valence Force Field (SAUO)

GVFM .... Francisco Mendes, Santiago Island [*Cape Verde*] [*ICAO location identifier*] (ICLI)
GVG .... Flygaktiebolaget Gota Vingar [*Sweden*] [*FAA designator*] (FAAC)
GVG .... Gamma-Vinyl-GABA [*Biochemistry*]
GVG .... Giving (FAAC)
GVG .... Global Vacation Grp. [*NYSE symbol*] (SG)
GVG .... Greater-Vestibular Gland (MELL)
GVG .... Grundriss der Vergleichenden Grammatik der Semitischen Sprachen [*A publication*] (BJA)
GVGC .... Grand Valley Gas Co. (SAUO)
GVGI .... General Visual Slope Indicator [*FAA*] (TAG)
GVGSS .... Grundriss der Vergleichenden Grammatik der Semitischen Sprachen [*A publication*] (BJA)
GVH .... Garnisonsverwendungsfaehig Heimat [*Fit for Garrison Duty in Zone of Interior*] [*German military - World War II*]
GVH .... Goose Viral Hepatitis (SAUS)
GVH .... Government Vehicle (FAAC)
GVH .... Graft Versus Host [*Immunology*]
GVHBCIFC .... Gene Vincent and His Blue Caps International Fan Club (EAIO)
GVHD .... Graft-Versus Host Disease [*Medicine*]
GvHD .... Graft-Versus Host Disease [*Immunology*]
GVHR .... Graft-Versus-Host Reaction [*Immunology*]
GVHR .... Grant-Versus-Host Reaction [*Immunology*] (QSUL)
GVHRR .... Geostationary Very High Resolution Radiometer (SAUS)
GVHRR .... Geosynchronous Very-High-Resolution Radiometer
GVI .... Gas Vent Institute [*Defunct*] (EA)
GVI .... Global Vegetation Index (MCD)
GVI .... Global Village Idiot [*Astronomy term*]
GVI .... Green River [*Papua New Guinea*] [*Airport symbol*] (OAG)
GVI .... Green Vegetation Index (SAUO)
GVIAO .... Gross Value of Industrial and Agricultural Output
GVidO .... Ohoopee Regional Library, Vidalia, GA [*Library symbol*] [*Library of Congress*] (LCLS)
GVIL .... Global Village Commun [*NASDAQ symbol*] (TTSB)
GVIL .... Global Village Communications, Inc. [*NASDAQ symbol*] (SAG)
GVIO .... Gross Value of Industrial Output
GVIS .... Geographic Visualization (SAUS)
GVL .... Gainesville, GA [*Location identifier*] [*FAA*] (FAAL)
GVL .... Gero Vita Laboratories
GVL .... Global Van Lines (SAUO)
GVL .... Gold Vapor LASER [*Physics*]
GVL .... Gold Ventures Ltd. [*Vancouver Stock Exchange symbol*]
GvL .... Graft-Versus-Leukemia [*Medicine*]
GVL .... Graniteville Co. (SAUO)
GVL .... Gravel (KSC)
GVL .... Great Valley Laboratories (SAUO)
GVL .... Great Valley Labs (SAUS)
GVLD .... Guard Vessel Leak Detector (SAUS)
G/VLLD .... Ground/Vehicle Laser Locator Designation [*Homing device*] (NITA)
G/VLL-D .... Ground Vehicular LASER Locator Designator [*Military*]
G/VLLD .... Ground/Vehicular Laser Locator Designator (SAUS)
GVLS .... Global Vehicle Lighting System
GVM .... Generating Volt Meter (PDAA)
GVM .... Gross Vehicle Mass (SAUS)
GVM .... Gross Vehicle Weight (SAUO)
GVMA .... Maio, Maio Island [*Cape Verde*] [*ICAO location identifier*] (ICLI)
GVMDS .... Ground Vehicle Mine Dispensing System [*Military*]
GVMF .... Golden Valley Microwave Foods, Inc. (SAUO)
GVMI .... GV Medical, Inc. [*NASDAQ symbol*] (COMM)
GVMR .... Gross Vehicle Mass Rating [*Load that a vehicle can carry*]
GVMT .... Mosteiros, Fogo Island [*Cape Verde*] [*ICAO location identifier*] (ICLI)
GvN .... Georg-von-Neumayer-Station, Antarktis (SAUS)
GVN .... Given (ABBR)
GVN .... Global Volcanism Network (SAUO)
GVN .... Goodyear Video Network [*Training and motivational program*]
GVN .... Government of Vietnam
GVO .... Gaviota, CA [*Location identifier*] [*FAA*] (FAAL)
GVO .... Graeber-Verwaltungsoffizier [*Graves Registration Officer*] [*German military - World War II*]
GVO .... Gross Value of Output (MHDW)
GVOBI .... Gesetz- und Verordnungsblatt (SAUO)
GVP .... Gasoline Vapor Pressure (GNE)
GVP .... Gas Vesicle Protein (SAUS)
GVP .... General Vice President (WDAA)
GVP .... Gesamtdeutsche Volkspartei [*All-German People's Party*] [*Germany*] [*Political party*] (PPE)
GVP .... Government Vehicle Pool [*Victoria, Australia*]
GVP .... Gravis Computer Peripherals, Inc. [*Vancouver Stock Exchange symbol*]
GVP .... Greater Victoria Public Library [*UTLAS symbol*]
GVP .... Gross Value of Production
GVP .... Gross Vendor Product (GART)
GVP .... Group Visionary Productions, Inc. [*Studio City, CA*] [*Telecommunications*] (TSSD)
GVP .... GSE Systems [*AMEX symbol*] (SG)
GVPF .... Guinea Pig Vascular Permeability Factor [*Biochemistry*]
GVPM .... Grootvlei Proprietary Mines Ltd. [*NASDAQ symbol*] (SAG)
GVPN .... Global Unified Theory (SAUS)
GVPN .... Global Virtual Private Network [*Computer science*] (CDE)
GVPR .... Praia/Praia, Santiago Island [*Cape Verde*] [*ICAO location identifier*] (ICLI)
GVQ .... Batavia, NY [*Location identifier*] [*FAA*] (FAAL)
GVR .... Garden Valley Resources (SAUO)
GVR .... Gas Volume Ratio (COE)
GVR .... Geocentric Vertical Reference (SAUS)
GVR .... Glyn Valley Railway [*Formerly, E & GVR*] [*Wales*]
GVR .... Governador Valadares [*Brazil*] [*Airport symbol*] (OAG)
GVR .... Granville Resources, Inc. [*Vancouver Stock Exchange symbol*]
GVR .... Gray-Votaw-Rogers [*Psychology*] (AEBS)
GVR .... Green Valley Road [*California*] [*Seismograph station code, US Geological Survey*] (SEIS)
GVRD .... Greater Vancouver Regional District (SAUO)
GVRNMTL .... Governmental
GVRR .... Greenfield Village Railroad [*Federal Railroad Administration identification code*]
GVRT .... General Vehicular Research Tool (SAUS)
GVRX .... Genessee Valley Railway [*Federal Railroad Administration identification code*]
GVS .... Gastric Vertical Stapling [*Medicine*] (MELL)
GVS .... Generalized Value System (SAUS)
GVS .... Global Videophone Standard [*Telecommunications*] (CDE)
GVS .... Glove Vane System (ACAE)
GVS .... Goat Veterinary Society (GVA)
GVS .... Government Vehicle Service [*Postal Service*]
GVS .... Graniteville [*South Carolina*] [*Seismograph station code, US Geological Survey*] [*Closed*] (SEIS)
GVS .... Ground Vibration Survey [*Aerospace*]
GVS .... Gypsy Verification Environment (ACAE)
GVSC .... Generic VHSIC Spaceborne Computer (SAUS)
GVSC .... Sal Oceanic Area Control Center [*Cape Verde*] [*ICAO location identifier*] (ICLI)
GVSD .... Global Vegetation and Soil Data (SAUO)
GVSDC .... Georgia Vocational Staff Development Consortium (SAUO)
GVSF .... Sao Felipe, Fogo Island [*Cape Verde*] [*ICAO location identifier*] (ICLI)
GVSL .... GeoVision Systems Limited (SAUO)
GVSN .... Sao Nicolau, Sao Nicolau Island [*Cape Verde*] [*ICAO location identifier*] (ICLI)
GV-SOLAS ... Gesellschaft fuer Versuchstierkunde - Society of Labortory Animal Science [*Switzerland*] (EAIO)
GVSR .... Galveston Railroad [*Federal Railroad Administration identification code*]
G vs T .... Deceleration Units of Gravity versus Time (KSC)
GVSU .... Grand Valley State University [*Michigan*]
G vs V .... Deceleration Units of Gravity Versus Velocity (KSC)
GVSV .... Sao Vicente, Sao Vicente Island [*Cape Verde*] [*ICAO location identifier*] (ICLI)
GVT .... Dean Witter Government Income Trust SBI [*NYSE symbol*] (SPSG)
GVT .... Dean Witter Gvt Income SBI [*NYSE symbol*] (TTSB)
GVT .... Gain Variable dans le Temps (SAUS)
GVT .... Gated Video Tracker
GVT .... Glenvet Resources Ltd. [*Vancouver Stock Exchange symbol*]
GVT .... Global Virtual Time (SAUO)
GVT .... Government (WDAA)
GVT .... Gravity Vacuum Transit (SAUO)
GVT .... Gravity-Vacuum-Transporter (SAUO)
GVT .... Gravity Vacuum Tube (SAUS)
GVT .... Gravity Vacuum Tube System [*High-speed ground transportation*]
GVT .... Greenville, TX [*Location identifier*] [*FAA*] (FAAL)
GVT .... Ground Vibration Test [*Aerospace*] (MCD)
GVTA .... Ground Vibration Test Article [*Aerospace*] (NASA)
GVT-System ... Gravity-Vacuum-Transit-System (SAUO)
GVT System ... Gravity Vacuum Tube System (SAUS)
GvtTch .... Government Technology Services [*Associated Press*] (SAG)
GVTW .... Gross Vehicle Test Weight [*Automotive engineering*]
GVTY .... Gingivectomy [*Dentistry*]
GVU .... Graphic, Visualization, and Usability Center [*Georgia Institute of Technology*]
GVUGA .... Grounded Voltage Unity-Gain Amplifier (PDAA)
GVV .... GeoVision Vision (SAUO)
GVV .... German Volunteer Votetakers (SAUS)
GVV .... Gooseberry Vein-binding Virus (SAUS)
GVV .... Grangeville, ID [*Location identifier*] [*FAA*] (FAAL)
GVVA .... Goulburn Valley Viticultural Association [*Australia*]
GVW .... Grandview, MO [*Location identifier*] [*FAA*] (FAAL)
GVW .... Gross Vehicle Weight (MCD)
GVW .... Gross Vehicular Weight (WPI)
GVWG .... Global VLBI Working Group (SAUO)
GVWR .... Gross Vehicle Weight Rating
GVX .... Extra-Great Value [*In automobile name Yugo GVX*]
GVX .... Gavle [*Sweden*] [*Airport symbol*] (OAG)
GVX .... Geevax Ltd. [*British*] [*ICAO designator*] (FAAC)
GVX .... Grove Explorations Ltd. [*Vancouver Stock Exchange symbol*]
GVX .... Gruver, TX [*Location identifier*] [*FAA*] (FAAL)
GVY .... Glen Valley Mine (SAUS)
GVY .... Green Valley Mine [*Vancouver Stock Exchange symbol*]
GW .... Air Force Guide for Writing
GW .... Cases in the Griqualand West Local Division of the Supreme Court [*1910-46*] [*South Africa*] [*A publication*] (DLA)
GW .... Gambia Airways (SAUS)
GW .... Game Winning [*Baseball*]
GW .... Gamma World (SAUS)
GW .... Gastric Wrap [*Morbid obesity surgical treatment*]
GW .... Gas Welding (SAUS)
GW .... Gas well (SAUS)
GW .... Gate Way (ACAE)
GW .... Gateway, Gleichwelle, Grenzwelle (SAUS)
GW .... Gather Write (SAUS)
GW .... General Warning
GW .... General Will [*Collectivist theory of government*]

GW.............. Genital Warts (MELL)
GW.............. George Washington [*US general and president, 1732-1799*]
GW.............. George Washington Law Review (journ.) (SAUS)
GW.............. George Washington University [*Washington, DC*]
gw.............. Germany, West [*MARC country of publication code*] [*Library of Congress*] (LCCP)
GW.............. Germ Warfare
GW.............. Gigawatt
GW.............. Glasgow (SAUS)
GW.............. Glass Wool (SAUS)
GW.............. Glauben und Wissen (BJA)
GW.............. Glaxo Wellcome
GW.............. Glazed Weatherproof [*Tile*] (DICI)
GW.............. Gleichwelle (SAUS)
GW.............. Global Warming (QUAC)
GW.............. Global Water (EA)
GW.............. Global West (SAUS)
G-W.............. Globe-Wernicke (SAUS)
G/W.............. Glucose in Water [*Medicine*]
GW.............. Glycerine in Water [*Medicine*]
GW.............. Golden West Airlines [*ICAO designator*] (AD)
GW.............. Good Words [*A publication*] (ROG)
GW.............. Grab Working-Level Sampling (EEVL)
GW.............. Gradual Withdrawal [*Medicine*] (DMAA)
GW.............. Grand Warder [*Freemasonry*]
GW.............. Graphic Wattmeter (SAUS)
GW.............. Gravity Wave (SAUS)
GW.............. Gray-Wheelwright (STED)
GW.............. Great Writers [*A publication*]
GW.............. Green Weight (WDAA)
GW.............. Grenzwache [*Frontier Guard*] [*German military - World War II*]
GW.............. Grey Wolf [*AMEX symbol*] [*Formerly, DI Industries*] (SG)
GW.............. Gross Weight (NG)
GW.............. Groundwater (EPA)
GW.............. Groundwork for a Just World (EA)
GW.............. Group Work (MAE)
GW.............. Growth [*Business term*]
GW.............. Guardian Weekly [*A publication*] (BRI)
GW.............. Guard Wire (SAUS)
GW.............. Guerrilla Warfare (AABC)
GW.............. Guided Weapon [*Air Force*]
GW.............. Guided Wire [*British military*] (DMA)
GW.............. Guinea-Bissau [*ANSI two-letter standard code*] (CNC)
GW.............. Gulf & Western, Inc. (SAUO)
GW.............. Gymnast's Wrist (MELL)
GWA.............. General Work Area [*NASA*] (NASA)
GWA.............. German Wine Academy (SAUO)
GWA.............. Girl Watchers of America (SAUO)
GWA.............. Golden West Airlines (SAUO)
GWA.............. Goodes World Atlas (SAUS)
GWA.............. Governor of Western Australia
GWA.............. Grams of Water in Air (SAUS)
GWA.............. Grand Worthy Associate [*Freemasonry*] (ROG)
GWA.............. Greater Washington Investors, Inc. (SAUO)
GWA.............. Great Wall Airlines [*China*] [*ICAO designator*] (FAAC)
GWA.............. Great Westrn Air, Inc. [*FAA designator*] (FAAC)
GWA.............. [*The*] Greens (Western Australia) Inc.
GWA.............. Guards of Wales (SAUO)
GWA.............. Gunshot Wound of the Abdomen [*Emergency medicine*] (DAVI)
GWA.............. International PEN - Guatemalan Writers Abroad (EA)
GWAA.............. Garden Writers Association of America (EA)
GWAA.............. Golf Writers Association of America (EA)
GWAC.............. Governmentwide Agency Contract (GART)
GWAD.............. Great Warbirds Air Display [*British*]
GWAH.............. Global Women of African Heritage (EA)
GWAI.............. German Workshop on Artificial Intelligence [*A publication*]
GWAL.............. Great Wall Electronic International Ltd. [*NASDAQ symbol*] (SAG)
GWALY.............. Great Wall Electr Int. ADS [*NASDAQ symbol*] (TTSB)
GWAM.............. Get Well Analysis Module (SAUO)
GW & MRJS... Great Western & Midland Railway Joint Stock [*British*] (ROG)
GW&MRJS... Oreat Western & Midland Railway Joint Stock (SAUS)
GWAR.............. Generic waste acceptance report (SAUS)
GWasB.............. Bartram Trail Regional Library, Washington, GA [*Library symbol*] [*Library of Congress*] (LCLS)
GWAY.............. Galway [*County in Ireland*] (ROG)
GWAY.............. Gateway Communications, Inc. (SAUO)
GWayC.............. Waycross Junior College, Waycross, GA [*Library symbol*] [*Library of Congress*] (LCLS)
GWAZB.............. Gott Wende Alles zum Besten [*May God Turn Everything to the Best*] [*Motto of Amoene Amalie, Princess of Anhalt (d. 1626)*] [*German*]
GWB.............. General Well-Being [*Medicine*] (DMAA)
GWB.............. George Walker Bush [*U.S. president*]
GWB.............. George Washington Bridge (SAUO)
GWB.............. Gesetz Gegen Wettbewerbsbeschrankungen [*German Law Against Restraint of Competition*] (DLA)
GWB.............. Glycosylated Whole Blood [*Clinical chemistry*]
GWB.............. Gypsum Wallboard [*Technical drawings*]
GW-BASIC.............. Gee Whiz BASIC [*Computer science*]
GWBC.............. Gateway Bancorp, Inc. Kentucky [*NASDAQ symbol*] (SAG)
GWBC.............. Gateway Bancorp(Ky) [*NASDAQ symbol*] (TTSB)
GWBC.............. Governor William Bradford Compact [*An association*] (EA)
GWBM.............. Government War Book Measures (SAUS)
GWBOT.............. Greater Washington Board of Trade (SRA)
GWBS.............. Global Ward Behavior Scale (DB)
GWBS.............. Gun Work Breakdown Schedule (SAUS)
GWC.............. Gardner-Webb College [*Boiling Springs, NC*]
gwc.............. gas-water contact (SAUS)
GWC.............. General Watch Co.
GWC.............. George Washington Carver (SAUS)
GWC.............. George Williams College [*Downer's Grove, IL*]
GWC.............. Gippsland Waters Coalition (EERA)
GWC.............. Global Weather Center (SAUS)
GWC.............. Global Weather Central
GWC.............. Golden West Conventions (SAUS)
GWC.............. Grand Worthy Chief [*Templars*] [*Freemasonry*] (ROG)
GWC.............. Great Whale River [*Quebec*] [*Seismograph station code, US Geological Survey*] [*Closed*] (SEIS)
GWC.............. Greek War Cross (SAUO)
GWC.............. Green Widget Company
GWC.............. Gross Weight Category (DNAB)
GWC.............. Ground Water Council [*Defunct*]
GWC.............. Guard Well Capacitor
GWC.............. Omaha, NE [*Location identifier*] [*FAA*] (FAAL)
GWC.............. West Georgia College, Carrollton, GA [*OCLC symbol*] (OCLC)
GWCA.............. George Washington Carver National Monument
GWCC.............. Georgia World Congress Center
GWCC.............. GWC Corp. [*NASDAQ symbol*] (COMM)
GWCG.............. General Wiring Cables Group [*British*] (DBA)
GW CHAP.... Grand Worthy Chaplain [*Templars*] [*Freemasonry*] (ROG)
GWCHS.............. George Washington Carver High School (SAUO)
GWCI.............. Giftware Manufacturers' Credit Interchange [*Buffalo, NY*] (EA)
GWCLIBAF.... GWC Library (SAUO)
GWCM.............. George Washington Carver Museum (SAUO)
GWCMI.............. George Washington Carver Memorial Institute (SAUO)
GWCS.............. General Wireless Communications Service [*Telecommunications*] (OTD)
GWCS.............. Gunnery Weapon Control System (SAUO)
GWCSA.............. Greater World Christian Spiritualist Association (EA)
GWCSWBD.... Gunnery Weapon Control Switchboard
GWCT.............. Grand Worthy Chief Templar [*Templars*] [*Freemasonry*] (ROG)
GWCX.............. Great Western Chemical [*Private rail car owner code*]
GWD.............. Gaseous Waste Disposal [*System*] [*Nuclear energy*] (NRCH)
GWd.............. Gigawatt-days
GWD.............. Grinding Wheel Dresser
GWD.............. Gwadar [*Pakistan*] [*Airport symbol*] (OAG)
GWD.............. South African Law Reports, Griqualand West Local Division [*A publication*] (DLA)
GWDB.............. Groundwater Database
GWDB.............. Groundwater Development Bureau (SAUS)
GWDI.............. Global Weather Dynamics Inc. (SAUO)
GWDM.............. Grand Worthy Deputy Marshal [*Templars*] [*Freemasonry*] (ROG)
GWDP.............. Grouted Waste Disposal Program (SAUS)
GWDR.............. Ground Water Disinfection Rule (SAUS)
GWDR.............. Ground Water Disinfedtion Rule (SAUO)
GWDRS.............. Ground Winds Data Reduction System [*NASA*]
GWDS.............. Generalized Work Distress Scale (MELL)
GWDS.............. Government Wool Disinfecting Station (SAUO)
GWDS.............. Graphic Weather Display System [*FAA*] (TAG)
GWDU.............. Ground Window Display Utility [*NASA*] (SPST)
GWE.............. German Water Engineering GmbH (SAUS)
GWE.............. Gigawatt-Electric [*DOE*] (TAG)
GWe.............. Gigawatt Electrical
gwe.............. gigawatts electrical (SAUS)
GWE.............. Global Weather Experiment [*Marine science*] (MSC)
GWE.............. Glycerin and Water Enema [*Medicine*]
GWE.............. Gwelo [*Zimbabwe*] [*Airport symbol*] (OAG)
GWEF.............. Guided Weapons Evaluation Facility (MCD)
GWEN.............. Ground Wave Emergency Network
GWEN.............. Ground Wave Energy Network (SAUS)
GWeP.............. West Point-Pepperell, Inc. (SAUO)
GWeP.............. West Point-Pepperell, Inc., West Point, GA [*Library symbol*] [*Library of Congress*] (LCLS)
GWETA.............. Greater Washington Educational Television Association (SAUO)
GWEX.............. Global Ecology and Water Cycle Experiment (SAUO)
GWF.............. Galveston Wharves [*AAR code*]
GWF.............. Gating Waveform
GWF.............. Gay White Female [*Classified advertising*] (CDAI)
GWF.............. Global-Warming Factor [*Meteorology*]
GWF.............. Great Western Financial Corp. [*NYSE symbol*] (SPSG)
GWF.............. Great Westn Finl [*NYSE symbol*] (TTSB)
GWF.............. Groundwater Flow (SAUS)
GWF.............. Grouted Waste Facility (SAUS)
GWF.............. Lancaster, CA [*Location identifier*] [*FAA*] (FAAL)
GWFMS.............. Global Wind Field Monitoring System (SAUO)
GWFN.............. Global Weather Facsimile Network (MCD)
GWFPr.............. Great Westn Finl CvDep Pfd [*NYSE symbol*] (TTSB)
GWFPrA.............. Great Westn Finl 8.30% Dep Pfd [*NYSE symbol*] (TTSB)
GWFPrT.............. Great Westn Fin I 8.25% 'TOPrS' [*NYSE symbol*] (TTSB)
GWG.............. Game-Winning Goals [*Hockey*]
GWG.............. Gaussian Wave Group [*Physics*]
GWG.............. Generalized Wegener Granulomatosis [*Medicine*] (DMAA)
GWG.............. Gottes Wille Geschehe [*God's Will Be Done*] [*Motto of Juliane Ursula, Margravine of Baden (d. 1614)*] [*German*]
GWG.............. Groundwater Working Group [*Australia*]
GWG.............. Gullwing Group (EA)
GWGI.............. Gullwing Group International (EA)
GWGR.............. Great Western Railway of Iowa [*Federal Railroad Administration identification code*]
GWH.............. Gigawatt Hour [*DOE*] (TAG)

GWH .... Great Water Holt (EA)
GWH .... Guided Warheads
gwh/day .... gigawatt hours per day (SAUS)
GWHF .... George Williams Hooper Foundation [*Research center*] (RCD)
GWHIS .... Global-Wide Help and Information Systems [*On-line help system for Mosaic developers*]
GWHJD .... Ground Water Heat Pump Journal (journ.) (SAUS)
GWHNWR .... Great White Heron National Wildlife Refuge (SAUO)
GWHS .... George Washington High School (SAUO)
GWHS .... George Westinghouse High School (SAUO)
GWI .... Galvanized Wrought Iron (ADA)
GWI .... General Wage Increase (MCD)
GWI .... Global-Warming Index [*Meteorology*]
GWI .... Government-Wide Index [*Later, USGRDR*]
GWI .... Great Washington Investors, Inc. [*AMEX symbol*] (COMM)
GWI .... Greenhouse Warming Index [*Marine science*] (OSRA)
GWI .... Grinding Wheel Institute (EA)
GWI .... Ground-Water Information (SAUO)
GWI .... Ground Water Institute [*Defunct*] (EA)
GWI .... Guide to Western Illinois (SAUO)
GWI .... Gulf War Illness [*Medicine*]
GWIBIT .... Guild of Washington Incompetent Bureaucratic Idea Throatcutters [*An organizati on rumored to have been active in World War II*]
GWIC .... Geothermal World Info Center [*Later, REIC*] (EA)
GWIC .... Global Warming International Center [*An association*] (EA)
GWIG .... Grand Worthy Inside Guard [*Templars*] [*Freemasonry*] (ROG)
GWIGWO ...... Good Will In, Good Will Out [*Computer science*]
Gwil .... Gwillim's Tithe Cases [*England*] [*1224-1824*] [*A publication*] (DLA)
Gwill .... Gwillim's Tithe Cases [*England*] [*A publication*] (DLA)
Gwill Bac Abr ... Gwillim's Tithe Cases [*England*] [*A publication*] (DLA)
Gwill T Cas ... Gwillim's Tithe Cases [*England*] [*A publication*] (DLA)
Gwill Ti Cas ... Gwillim's Tithe Cases [*England*] [*A publication*] (DLA)
Gwil Ti Cas ... Gwillim's Tithe Cases [*England*] [*A publication*] (DLA)
GWIM .... Global Warming Impact Model (AAEL)
GWIN .... Goodwin Railroad, Inc. [*AAR code*]
GWIN .... Government Wide Intelligent Network [*Communications term*] (DCT)
GWIP .... Global Weather Intercept Position (SAUO)
GWIRD .... Government-Wide Index to Research and Development
GWJ .... Chicopee Falls, MA [*Location identifier*] [*FAA*] (FAAL)
GWJ .... Glue Weld Joint
GWJC .... Gardner-Webb Junior College [*Later, Gardner-Webb College*] [*North Carolina*]
GWKB .... Generalized Wentzel-Kramer-Brillouin (SAUS)
GWL .... Gateway Link (SAUS)
GWL .... George Washington University, Law Library, Washington, DC [*OCLC symbol*] (OCLC)
GWL .... Great-West Life Assurance Co. [*Toronto Stock Exchange symbol*]
GWL .... Grosswetterlage [*Meteorology*]
GWL .... Groundwater Level [*Hydrology*] (IAA)
GWL .... Gwalior [*India*] [*Airport symbol*] (OAG)
GWL .... Reports of Cases Decided in the Supreme Court of South Africa (Griqualand West Local Division), by Kitchin [*A publication*] (DLA)
GWLD .... Gaming World International, Inc. [*NASDAQ symbol*] (SAG)
GWLD .... Gaming World Intl. [*NASDAQ symbol*] (TTSB)
GWLD .... South Africa Law Reports, Griqualand West Local Division [*A publication*] (DLA)
GWLDW .... Gaming World Intl. Wrrt'A' [*NASDAQ symbol*] (TTSB)
GWLL .... Great Western Lacrosse League (PSS)
GWM .... Gay White Male [*Classified advertising*]
GWM .... Generic Window Manager (SAUS)
GWM .... George Washington University, Medical Library, Washington, DC [*OCLC symbol*] (OCLC)
GWM .... Global Wind Measurements (SAUO)
GWM .... Grand Worthy Marshal [*Templars*] [*Freemasonry*] (ROG)
GWM .... Graphics Window Manager (SAUS)
GWM .... Ground Water Monitor [*A publication*]
GWM .... Ground Water Monitoring
GWM .... Guam Tracking Station [*NASA*] (KSC)
GWM .... Guaranteed Weekly Minimum
GWMC .... Galvanized Ware Manufacturers Council (EA)
GWMD .... Ground Water Management District
GWMNP .... George Washington Memorial National Parkway (SAUO)
GWMR .... Ground Water Monitoring Review [*A publication*]
GWMS .... Gaseous Waste Management System [*Nuclear energy*] (NRCH)
GWMS .... Gas-Water Module Storage [*Nuclear energy*] (NRCH)
GWMU .... Government Workforce Management Unit [*Victoria, Australia*]
GWN .... Golden West Network [*Australia*]
GWN .... Goldwinn Resources Ltd. [*Vancouver Stock Exchange symbol*]
GWND .... Gowned (ABBR)
GWNRF .... Goldwinn Resources Ltd. (SAUO)
GWO .... General Wage Order (SAUS)
GWO .... General Watch Officer [*Army*] (AABC)
GWO .... General Work Order (TIMI)
GWO .... Great-West Lifeco, Inc. [*Toronto Stock Exchange symbol*]
GWO .... Greenwood [*Mississippi*] [*Airport symbol*] (OAG)
GWOA .... Guerrilla Warfare Operational Area [*Army*]
GWO & HP ... Gas Wall Oven and Hot Plate [*Classified advertising*] (ADA)
GWOB .... Guerrilla Warfare Operating Base (SAUO)
GWOG .... Grand Worthy Outside Guard [*Templars*] [*Freemasonry*] (ROG)
GWOTH .... Ground Wave Over-the-Horizon RADAR (DNAB)
GW OU .... Groundwater OU [*Operable Unit*] [*Environemental science*] (BCP)
GWOX .... Goodheart-Wilcox Co., Inc. (SAUO)
GWP .... Gateway Processor (SAUS)
GWP .... Gesellschaft fuer Wirtschaftspublizistik GmbH [*Society for Public Economics*] [*Germany*] (IID)
g-w-p .... Gift With Purchase [*Retail*] (WDMC)
GWP .... Gift with Purchase
GWP .... Global-Warming Potential [*Meteorology*]
GWP .... Government White Paper
GWP .... Government Working Group (FOTI)
GWP .... Grand Worthy Patriarch [*Freemasonry*] (ROG)
GWP .... Great Western Petroleum Corp. [*Vancouver Stock Exchange symbol*]
GWP .... Greenhouse Warming Potential (EERA)
GWP .... Gross World Product
GWP .... Gross Written Premiums [*Insurance*] (MARI)
GWP .... Guelph-Waterloo Program (SAUS)
GWP .... Guided Writing Procedure [*Reading improvement method*]
GWPA .... Ground Water Protection Act (SAUS)
GWPAS .... General Work Force Performance Appraisal System [*Marine science*] (OSRA)
GWPC .... Ground Water Protection Council (NTPA)
GWPCA .... German Wirehaired Pointer Club of America (EA)
GWPM .... Gross Words per Minute [*Computer science*] (IAA)
GWPMS .... Ground Water Policy and Management Staff [*Environmental Protection Agency*] (GFGA)
GWPS .... Gaseous Waste Processing System [*Nuclear energy*] (NRCH)
GWPS .... General Word Processor Support (SAUS)
GWPS .... Ground Water Protection Standard [*Environmental Protection Agency*] (GFGA)
GWPS .... Groundwater Protection Strategy [*Environmental science*] (EPAT)
GWpSO .... Group Weapons Staff Officer [*British military*] (DMA)
GWPU .... General Workers Professional Unions [*Bulgaria*]
GWQ .... GWR Resources [*Vancouver Stock Exchange symbol*]
GWQ .... San Francisco, CA [*Location identifier*] [*FAA*] (FAAL)
GWQAP .... Government-Wide Quality Assurance Program
GWQE .... General Water-Quality Engineering [*Survey*] [*Army*] (RDA)
GWR .... Generalized Wear Rating (SAUO)
GWR .... General War Reserves [*Army*] (AABC)
GWR .... Gill Withdrawal Reflex
GWR .... Great Western Railway (SAUO)
GWR .... [*The*] Great Western Railway Co. [*Prior to nationalization*] [*AAR code*]
GWR .... Great Western Railway of Colorado [*Federal Railroad Administration identification code*]
GWR .... Great Western Resources (SAUO)
GWR .... Great World Resources [*Vancouver Stock Exchange symbol*]
GWR .... Griqualand High Court Reports [*A publication*] (DLA)
GWR .... Ground Wave Radar (SAUS)
GWR .... Gwinner, ND [*Location identifier*] [*FAA*] (FAAL)
GWRAC .... General World Radio Administrative Conference (CCCA)
GWRBI .... Game-Winning Run Batted In [*Baseball term*] (NDBD)
GWRC .... Georgia Woodlands Railroad [*Federal Railroad Administration identification code*]
GWRDC .... Grape and Wine Research and Development Corporation (EERA)
GWRDC .... Grape and Wine Research and Development Council [*Australia*]
GWRI .... Ground Water Resources Institute [*Later, Ground Water Council*]
GWRL .... Geographic Web Resource Locator (SAUO)
GWRRA .... Gold Wing Road Riders Association (EA)
GWRX .... Geoworks [*NASDAQ symbol*] (TTSB)
GWRX .... Geoworks Corp. [*NASDAQ symbol*] (NASQ)
GW Ry of Can ... Great Western Railway of Canada (SAUO)
GWS .... Gar Wood Society (EA)
GWS .... Gaseous Waste System [*Nuclear energy*] (NRCH)
GWS .... Gateway Service (SAUS)
GWS .... Gatling Weapon System (SAUS)
GWS .... GEEIA [*Ground Electronics Engineering Installation Agency*] Workload Schedule (AFM)
GWS .... General War Subsystem (MCD)
GWS .... General War System (SAUO)
GWS .... Geneva Convention for the Amelioration of the Condition of the Wounded and Sick in Armed Forces in the Field, 12 August 1949 [*Army*] (AABC)
GWS .... George Washington School (SAUO)
GWS .... German Wine Society [*Canada*] (EAIO)
GWS .... Gir Wildlife Sanctuary (SAUO)
GWS .... Glashow-Weinberg-Salam Theories [*Physics*]
GWS .... Glenwood Springs, CO [*Location identifier*] [*FAA*] (FAAL)
GWS .... Global Wulfsberg Systems (SAUS)
GWS .... Grand Worthy Scribe [*Templars*] [*Freemasonry*] (ROG)
GWS .... Graphics Workshop (SAUO)
GWS .... Graphics Work Station (SAUO)
GWS .... Great Western Airlines, Inc. (SAUO)
GWS .... Great Western Society (EA)
GWS .... Great West Steel Industries Ltd. [*Toronto Stock Exchange symbol*] [*Vancouver Stock Exchange symbol*]
GWS .... Great White Spot [*Planetary science*]
GWS .... Grid Wire Sensor (SAUS)
GWS .... Groundwater Surveillance (ABAC)
GWS .... Guided Weapon Station (IAA)
GWS .... Guided Weapon System (SAUS)
GWS .... Gulf War Syndrome [*Medicine*]
GWS .... Gun Weapon System [*Military*] (CAAL)
GWS .... Gwil Industries, Inc. [*Toronto Stock Exchange symbol*] [*Vancouver Stock Exchange symbol*]
GWS 1929 ... Geneva Convention for the Amelioration of the Condition of the Wounded and Sick of Armies in the Field, 27 July 1929 (SAUO)
GWS-A & L ... Girl Watchers Society - Ankle and Leg Division
GWSAE .... Greater Washington Society of Association Executives (SRA)
GWSB .... Great Western Savings Bank (SAUO)
GWSC .... Ghana Water and Sewerage Corp.

GWSC .... Greater World Spiritual Centre [*British*] (EAIO)
GWSD .... Guild of Weavers, Spinner & Dyers (WDAA)
GWSF .... Georgia Warm Springs Foundation [*Later, RWSF*] (EA)
GWSH .... George Washington Corp. [*NASDAQ symbol*] (COMM)
Gw Sh .... Gwynne on Sheriffs [*A publication*] (DLA)
GW ship ...... Guided Weapon ship (SAUO)
GW Ship ...... Guided Weapons Ship (SAUS)
GWSI .... Great Western Systems, Incorporated (SAUO)
GWSI .... Groundwater Site Inventory (SAUS)
GWSIP .... Gun Weapon System Improvement Program [*Military*] (CAAL)
GWSIR .... Groundwater Modelling Software Internet Resources (SAUO)
GWSMN .... GeoWorks Snail Mail Network (SAUO)
GWSR .... General Wage Stabilization Regulations [*United States*] (DLA)
GWSRP .... Gun Weapon System Replacement Program (NVT)
GWSS .... Groundwater Supply Survey (GNE)
GWS Sea ..... Geneva Convention for the Amelioration of the Condition of the Wounded, Sick and Shipwrecked Members of the Armed Forces at Sea (SAUO)
GWS Sea ..... Geneva Convention for the Amelioration of the Condition of the Wounded, Sick, and Shipwrecked Members of the Armed Forces at Sea, 12 August 1949 [*Army*] (AABC)
GWSTN .... Ground Wireless Station (IAA)
GWSTV .... Golden West Subscription Television [*Cable TV programming service*]
GWSW .... GWI Switching Services [*Federal Railroad Administration identification code*]
GWSZ .... Great Western Sugar [*Federal Railroad Administration identification code*]
GWT .... Chicopee Falls, MA [*Location identifier*] [*FAA*] (FAAL)
GWT .... Gardner-Wells Tongs (MELL)
GWt .... Gigawatt Thermal
GWT .... Glazed Wall Tile [*Technical drawings*]
gwt .... Gramme Weight (SAUS)
GWT .... Grand Worthy Templar [*Templars*] [*Freemasonry*] (ROG)
GWT .... Gross Weight
GWT .... Gross Weight Ton (SAUS)
GWT .... Ground Water Table (SAUS)
GWT .... Ground Winds Tower [*NASA*] (NASA)
GWT .... Gunshot Wound of the Throat [*Emergency medicine*] (DAVI)
GWT .... GW Utilities Ltd. [*AMEX symbol*] (COMM)
GWT .... Westerland [*Germany*] [*Airport symbol*] (OAG)
GWTA .... Gift Wrappings and Tyings Association [*Defunct*] (EA)
GWTB .... Glazed Wall Tile Base [*Technical drawings*]
GWTD .... Ground Water Technology Division (SAUS)
GWTF .... Ground Water Task Force [*Office of Solid Waste and Emergency Response*] (COE)
GWth .... Gigawatt thermal (SAUS)
GWTI .... Groundwater Technology, Inc. [*NASDAQ symbol*] (NQ)
GWTP .... Groundwater Treatment Plant [*Environmental science*] (BCP)
GWTR .... Ground Water Treatment Rule [*Environment term*] (EGA)
GW TREAS ... Grand Worthy Treasurer [*Templars*] [*Freemasonry*] (ROG)
GWTSA .... Gamma-Weighted Two-Stream Approximation (ARMP)
GWTUF .... Government Workers' Trade Union Federation [*Ceylon*]
GWTW .... Gone with the Wind [*A novel by Margaret Mitchell; also, a motion picture*]
GWU .... Gambia Workers Union (SAUO)
GWU .... General Workers Union (SAUO)
GWU .... George Washington University [*Washington, DC*]
GWU .... Granite Workers' Union [*British*]
GWU .... Great Western United Corp. (SAUO)
GWU .... International Glove Workers' Union of America [*Later, ACTWU*]
GWUI .... Ground Water Under the Influence [*of surface water*] [*Environment term*] (EGA)
GW Univ ...... George Washington University (SAUO)
GWUSA .... General Workers Union of South Africa (SAUO)
GWV .... Glendale, WV [*Location identifier*] [*FAA*] (FAAL)
GWVA .... Great War Veterans' Association [*Canada*]
GWVI .... Gulf War Veteran's Illnesses (ADWA)
GWVSS .... Ground Wind Vortex Sensing System [*Aviation*] (DA)
GWVT .... Grand Worthy Vice Templar [*Templars*] [*Freemasonry*] (ROG)
GWW .... Goldsboro, NC [*Location identifier*] [*FAA*] (FAAL)
GWW .... Grainger, [*W. W.*] Inc. [*NYSE symbol*] (SPSG)
GWW .... Grainger (W.W.) [*NYSE symbol*] (TTSB)
GWW .... Ground Water for Windows [*Computer program*]
GWW .... Guaranteed Weekly Wage
GWW .... W.W. Grainger Co. (SAUO)
GWWD .... Greater Winnipeg Water District (SAUO)
GWWE .... Gateway Eastern Railroad [*Federal Railroad Administration identification code*]
GWWR .... Gateway Western Railway Co.
GWWS .... Gott Wirds Wohl Schaffen [*God Will Arrange*] [*Motto of Dorothee Auguste, Duchess of Braunschweig (1577-1625)*] [*German*]
GWY .... Galway [*Ireland*] [*Airport symbol*]
GWY .... Gateway Aviation Ltd. (SAUO)
GWY .... Goldways Resources [*Vancouver Stock Exchange symbol*]
GWY .... Gwynedd-Mercy College, Gwynedd, PA [*OCLC symbol*] (OCLC)
GWYN .... Gwynedd [*County in Wales*] (WGA)
GX .... Gencor Indus [*AMEX symbol*] (TTSB)
GX .... Gencor Industries [*AMEX symbol*] (SAG)
GX .... General Executive (FOTI)
GX .... Geochron Laboratories Inc. (SAUO)
GX .... GEO International Corp. [*NYSE symbol*] (COMM)
GX .... Global International Airways (SAUS)
GX .... Glycinxylidide [*Biochemistry*]
Gx .... Graded Exercise
GX .... Great Lakes Airlines [*ICAO designator*] (AD)
GXA .... CountryBaskets [*NYSE symbol*] (SAG)
GXA .... Countrybkts Australia Index Fd [*NYSE symbol*] (TTSB)
GXA .... Gunn-Diode X-Band Amplifier
GXC .... Global Exchange Carrier Corp. (SAUO)
GXD .... General X-Ray Diagnosis [*Medicine*]
GXD .... Graded [*Medicine*] (DAVI)
GXD EKG ..... Graded Exercixe Electrocardiogram [*Cardiology*] (DAVI)
GXF .... CountryBaskets [*NYSE symbol*] (SAG)
GXF .... Countrybkts France Index Fd [*NYSE symbol*] (TTSB)
GXG .... CountryBaskets [*NYSE symbol*] (SAG)
GXG .... Countrybkts Germany Index Fd [*NYSE symbol*] (TTSB)
GXG .... Negage [*Angola*] [*Airport symbol*] (OAG)
GXH .... CountryBaskets [*NYSE symbol*] (SAG)
GXH .... Countrybkts Hong Kong Index Fd [*NYSE symbol*] (TTSB)
GXI .... CountryBaskets [*NYSE symbol*] (SAG)
GXI .... Countrybkts Italy Index Fd [*NYSE symbol*] (TTSB)
GXI .... Glenex Industries, Inc. [*Vancouver Stock Exchange symbol*]
GXI .... Global Exchange, Inc.
GXJ .... CountryBaskets [*NYSE symbol*] (SAG)
GXJ .... Countrybkts Japan Index Fd [*NYSE symbol*] (TTSB)
GXK .... CountryBaskets [*NYSE symbol*] (SAG)
GXK .... Countrybkts UK Index Fd [*NYSE symbol*] (TTSB)
GXL .... General-Purpose Crosslinked Polyethylene [*Insulation*]
GXL .... Granges, Inc. [*AMEX symbol*] [*Toronto Stock Exchange symbol*] (SPSG)
GXL .... Grinnell, IA [*Location identifier*] [*FAA*] (FAAL)
GXM .... Gordex Minerals Ltd. [*Toronto Stock Exchange symbol*]
GXM .... Medical College of Georgia, Augusta, GA [*OCLC symbol*] (OCLC)
GXMN .... Gordex Minerals Ltd. (SAUO)
GXMNF .... Gordex Minerals Ltd. [*NASDAQ symbol*] (COMM)
G/XMTR .... Guidance Transmitter (AAG)
GXO .... Butler, PA [*Location identifier*] [*FAA*] (FAAL)
GXP .... Georgia-Pacific Plywood Co. (SAUO)
GXQ .... Coyhaique [*Chile*] [*Airport symbol*] (AD)
GXR .... CountryBaskets [*NYSE symbol*] (SAG)
GXR .... Countrybkts S.Africa Index Fd [*NYSE symbol*] (TTSB)
GXRZ .... Golden Spike Railroad Services [*Federal Railroad Administration identification code*]
GXS .... Goldex Resources [*Vancouver Stock Exchange symbol*]
GXSP .... Guierrezia Xylem Sap Potential [*Botany*]
GXSP .... Guiersia Xylem Sap Potential (SAUS)
GXT .... Graded Exercise Testing
GXT .... Grad Exercise Testing (SAUS)
GXU .... CountryBaskets [*NYSE symbol*] (SAG)
GXU .... Countrybkts US Index Fd [*NYSE symbol*] (TTSB)
GXU .... Wrightstown, NJ [*Location identifier*] [*FAA*] (FAAL)
GXV .... Golden Exodus [*Vancouver Stock Exchange symbol*]
GXY .... Galaxy Airways Ltd. [*Nigeria*] [*ICAO designator*] (FAAC)
GXY .... Galaxy Carpet Mills, Inc. (SAUO)
GXY .... Galaxy Industry Ltd. [*Vancouver Stock Exchange symbol*]
GXY .... Greeley, CO [*Location identifier*] [*FAA*] (FAAL)
GY .... Gaily (ABBR)
GY .... Galley
GY .... Galley-Yarn [*Crooked*] [*Slang*] [*British*] (DSUE)
GY .... Gardan [*France*] [*ICAO aircraft manufacturer identifier*] (ICAO)
GY .... GenCorp [*NYSE symbol*] (TTSB)
GY .... GenCorp, Inc. [*NYSE symbol*] (SPSG)
GY .... General Tire & Rubber Co. (SAUO)
GY .... Germany
GY .... Glamorgan Yeomanry (SAUO)
GY .... Goodyear [*Tire casing code*]
GY .... Gray
Gy .... Gray [*Symbol*] [*SI unit for absorbed dose acceleration*]
GY .... Greenish Yellow
GY .... Grey [*Unit of inpingent energy*]
GY .... Guaranty Trust Co. of Canada [*Toronto Stock Exchange symbol*]
GY .... Guidance Year [*DoD*]
GY .... Gunnery (ABBR)
GY .... Guy (SAUS)
GY .... Guyana [*ANSI two-letter standard code*] (CNC)
gy .... Guyana [*MARC country of publication code*] [*Library of Congress*] (LCCP)
GY .... Guyana Airways [*ICAO designator*] (AD)
GY .... Gyro (ABBR)
GY .... Gyrocar (ABBR)
GY .... Gyrocompass (ABBR)
GY .... Gyrodyne (ABBR)
GY .... Gyroscope
Gy .... Gyrus [*Brain anatomy*]
GYA .... German Youth Activities (SAUO)
GYA .... German Youth Assistance (SAUO)
GYA .... Got Ya Again [*Initialism used as name of second successful phony event staged by Washington, DC, law enforcement agents posing as fences*] [*See PFF Inc*]
GYA .... Guayaramerin [*Bolivia*] [*Airport symbol*] (OAG)
GYA .... Guyana Airways Corp. [*ICAO designator*] (FAAC)
GyAR .... Rhein-Westfalische Technische Hochschule, Aachen, Germany [*Library symbol*] [*Library of Congress*] (LCLS)
GyAsH .... Hofbibliothek, Aschaffenburg, Germany [*Library symbol*] [*Library of Congress*] (LCLS)
GYB .... Giddings, TX [*Location identifier*] [*FAA*] (FAAL)
GyBaA .... Archiv des Kreises Asch, Fernleihe, Bayern, Federal Republic of Germany [*Library symbol*] [*Library of Congress*] (LCLS)

GyBFU......... Freie Universitaet (Berlin), Garystrasse, Berlin, Germany [*Library symbol*] [*Library of Congress*] (LCLS)
GyBFU-P...... Freie Universitaet (Berlin), Fachbereich Politische Wissenschaft, Bibliothek, Berlin, Germany [*Library symbol*] [*Library of Congress*] (LCLS)
GyBIAI......... Ibero-Amerikanisches Institu Preussicher Kulturbesitz, Berlin, Germany [*Library symbol*] [*Library of Congress*] (LCLS)
GyBiU......... Universitat Bielfeld, Kurt Schumacher, Bielfeld, Germany [*Library symbol*] [*Library of Congress*] (LCLS)
GyBochU...... Ruhr-Universitat Bochum, Bochum, Germany [*Library symbol*] [*Library of Congress*] (LCLS)
GyBoDB....... Deutscher Bundestag, Abteilung Wissenschaftliche Dokumentation, Bonn, Germany [*Library symbol*] [*Library of Congress*] (LCLS)
GyBoFE........ Friedrich-Ebert-Stiftung, Archiv der Sozialen Demokratie, Bonn, Germany [*Library symbol*] [*Library of Congress*] (LCLS)
GyBoFN........ Friedrich-Naumann-Stiftung, Bonn, Germany [*Library symbol*] [*Library of Congress*] (LCLS)
GyBoGI......... Gesamtdeutsches Institut, Bonn, Germany [*Library symbol*] [*Library of Congress*] (LCLS)
GyBraTU...... Technische Universitat Carolo Wilhelmina zu Braunschweig, Braunschweig, Federal Republic of Germany [*Library symbol*] [*Library of Congress*] (LCLS)
GyBrSU........ Staatsbibliothek und Universitatsbibliothek, Breitenweg, Bremen, Germany [*Library symbol*] [*Library of Congress*] (LCLS)
GyBrU.......... Universitaet Bremen, Bremen, Germany [*Library symbol*] [*Library of Congress*] (LCLS)
GyBTU......... Technische Universitat Berlin, Berlin, Germany [*Library symbol*] [*Library of Congress*] (LCLS)
GYC............. German Youth Center (SAUO)
GYC............. Gibraltar Yacht Club (SAUO)
GYC............. Glasgow Yeomanry Cavalry [*British military*] (DMA)
GYC............. Global Energy Ltd. [*Vancouver Stock Exchange symbol*]
GYC............. Greater Yellowstone Coalition (EA)
GYC............. Young Harris College, Young Harris, GA [*Library symbol*] [*Library of Congress*] (LCLS)
GyDaD......... Deutsches Kunststoff-Institut, Darmstadt, Germany [*Library symbol*] [*Library of Congress*] (LCLS)
GyDaH......... Hessische Landes- und Hochschulbibliothek, Darmstadt (Schloss), Germany [*Library symbol*] [*Library of Congress*] (LCLS)
GyDaM......... E. Merck AG, Darmstadt, Germany [*Library symbol*] [*Library of Congress*] (LCLS)
GyDIZ.......... Institut fur Zeitungsforschung, Dortmund, Germany [*Library symbol*] [*Library of Congress*] (LCLS)
GyDMA........ Mikrofilmarchiv der Deutschsparchigen Presse e.V., Dortmund, Germany [*Library symbol*] [*Library of Congress*] (LCLS)
GyDuiH........ Gesamthochschulbibliothek Duisburg, Duisburg, Germany [*Library symbol*] [*Library of Congress*] (LCLS)
GyDuU......... Universitat Dusseldorf, Grabbeplatz, Dusseldorf, Germany [*Library symbol*] [*Library of Congress*] (LCLS)
GYE.............. Glory Explorations [*Vancouver Stock Exchange symbol*]
GYE.............. Guayaquil [*Ecuador*] [*Airport symbol*] (OAG)
GYE.............. Guinnes Yeast Extract (SAUS)
GyEU........... Friedrich-Alexander-Universitat zu Erlangen-Nurnberg, Erlangen, Germany [*Library symbol*] [*Library of Congress*] (LCLS)
GYFM........... General Yielding Fracture Mechanics (OA)
GyFmB......... Beilstein-Institut, Frankfurt/Main, Germany [*Library symbol*] [*Library of Congress*] (LCLS)
GyFmDB...... Deutsche Bibliothek, Zeppelinallee, Frankfurt am Main, Germany [*Library symbol*] [*Library of Congress*] (LCLS)
GyFmSU...... Stadt u Universitatsbibliothek, Senckenbergische Bibliothek Fernleihe, Frankfurt/Main, Federal Republic of Germany [*Library symbol*] [*Library of Congress*] (LCLS)
GYG............. Grayling, MI [*Location identifier*] [*FAA*] (FAAL)
GYG............. Valdosta State College, Valdosta, GA [*OCLC symbol*] (OCLC)
GyGiU.......... Justus Liebig Universitatsbibliothek Giessen, Giessen/Lahn, Federal Republic of Germany [*Library symbol*] [*Library of Congress*] (LCLS)
GyGoN......... Niedersachsische Staats- und Universitatsbibliothek, Gottingen, Germany [*Library symbol*] [*Library of Congress*] (LCLS)
GYH............. Greenville, SC [*Location identifier*] [*FAA*] (FAAL)
GyHanM....... Medizinische Hochschule, Karl Wiechert, Hannover-Kleefeld, Germany [*Library symbol*] [*Library of Congress*] (LCLS)
GyHaS......... Staats- und Universitatsbibliothek Hamburg, Hamburg, Germany [*Library symbol*] [*Library of Congress*] (LCLS)
GyHeM......... Max-Planck-Institut fuer Medizinisch Forschung, Heidelberg, Germany [*Library symbol*] [*Library of Congress*] (LCLS)
GyHeU-SS.... Universitat Heidelberg Sinologisches Seminar de Universitat Heidelberg, Heidelberg, Germany [*Library symbol*] [*Library of Congress*] (LCLS)
GyHGU......... University of Gottingen, Hannover, Germany [*Library symbol*] [*Library of Congress*] (LCLS)
GyHoU......... Universitat Hohenheim (Landwirtschaftliche Hochschule), Stuttgart-Hohenheim, Germany [*Library symbol*] [*Library of Congress*] (LCLS)
GyHTIB........ Universitaetsbibliothek der Technischen Universitaet Hannover und Technische Informationsbibliothek, Hannover, Federal Republic of Germany [*Library symbol*] [*Library of Congress*] (LCLS)
GYIL............ German Yearbook of International Law [*A publication*] (DLA)
GyJuK.......... Kernforschungsanlage Julich, Julich, Germany [*Library symbol*] [*Library of Congress*] (LCLS)
GYK............. Giant Yellowknife Mines Ltd. (SAUO)
GyKaU......... Universitat Trier-Kaiserslautern, Kaiserslautern, Germany [*Library symbol*] [*Library of Congress*] (LCLS)
GyKG.......... Gesellschaft fuer Kernforschung mbH, Karlsruhe, Germany [*Library symbol*] [*Library of Congress*] (LCLS)
GyKiU.......... Christian-Albrechts-Universitat Kiel, Kiel, Germany [*Library symbol*] [*Library of Congress*] (LCLS)
GyKoB.......... Bundesanzeiger Verlagsgesellschaft, mbH, Koln, Germany [*Library symbol*] [*Library of Congress*] (LCLS)
GYM............ General Yardmaster [*Railroading*]
GYM............ Guaymas [*Mexico*] [*Airport symbol*] (OAG)
GYM............ Guaymas [*Mexico*] [*Seismograph station code, US Geological Survey*] (SEIS)
GYM............ Guaymas, Mexico [*Remote site*] [*NASA*] (NASA)
Gym............. Gymnasium (DIAR)
gym............. Gymnasium (VRA)
GYM............ Gymnasium
GYM............ Gymnastic
GYM............ Gymnastics (ADA)
GYM............ Sport Supply Group [*AMEX symbol*] (SAG)
GYM.WS..... Sport Supply Grp Wrrt [*AMEX symbol*] (TTSB)
GyMB........... Boehringer Mannheim GmbH, Mannheim, Germany [*Library symbol*] [*Library of Congress*] (LCLS)
GYMB.......... [*The*] Gymboree Corp. [*NASDAQ symbol*] (SAG)
Gymbree...... [*The*] Gymboree Corp. [*Associated Press*] (SAG)
GYMES........ Great Yarmouth Mediterranean Herring Exporters Association (SAUO)
GyMIZ.......... Institut fur Zeitgeschichte [*Institute of Modern History*], Munchen, Federal Republic of Germany [*Library symbol*] [*Library of Congress*] (LCLS)
GyMLM........ Ludwig Maxmilians Universitatsbibliothek Munchen, Munich, Federal Republic of Germany [*Library symbol*] [*Library of Congress*] (LCLS)
GYMM......... HealthTech Intl [*NASDAQ symbol*] (TTSB)
GYMMW...... HealthTech Intl Wrrt'A' [*NASDAQ symbol*] (TTSB)
GYMN.......... Gymnasium (ABBR)
GYMNST...... Gymnast (ABBR)
GYMPI......... Gyromagnetic Polarizing Interferometer (SAUS)
GYMS.......... Concept 90 Marketing, Inc. (SAUO)
GYMST........ Gymnast (ABBR)
GYMSTC...... Gymnastic (ABBR)
GYMSTCY.... Gymnastically (ABBR)
GYMSTIC..... Gymnastic [*Freight*]
GyMuW........ Westfalische Wilhelms-Universitat Munster, Munster, Germany [*Library symbol*] [*Library of Congress*] (LCLS)
GYMZ.......... Gay Mine [*Federal Railroad Administration identification code*]
GYN............ Goiania [*Brazil*] [*Airport symbol*] (OAG)
gyn.............. Gynecologist (SHCU)
GYN............ Gynecologist
Gyn............. Gynecology [*Medicine*] (AMHC)
gyn.............. Gynecology (SHCU)
GYN............ Gynecology
GYNAE........ Gynaecology [*British*]
GYNAEC...... Gynaecologist [*or Gynaecology*] [*British*] (ADA)
GYNAECOL... Gynaecology [*British*]
Gynaecol Endocr... Journal of Gynaecological Endocrinology (journ.) (SAUS)
GYNC.......... Gynecologic (ABBR)
GYNCL........ Gynecological (ABBR)
GYNCLGY.... Gynecology
Gyn Dyn....... General Dynamics (SAUS)
GYNE.......... Gynecare [*NASDAQ symbol*] (SAG)
GYNE.......... Gynecare Inc. [*NASDAQ symbol*] (TTSB)
gyne............ Gynecology [*Medicine*] (DAVI)
GyNeA......... Augustana Hochschule Bibliothek, Neuendettelsau, Federal Republic of Germany [*Library symbol*] [*Library of Congress*] (LCLS)
Gynecol....... Gynecology
Gynecol Obstet Invest... Gynecologic and Obstetric Investigation (journ.) (SAUS)
Gynecol Oncol... Gynecologic Oncology (journ.) (SAUS)
Gynecre....... Gynecare, Inc. [*Associated Press*] (SAG)
GYNOA........ Gynecologic Oncology (journ.) (SAUS)
GYNST........ Gynecologist (ABBR)
GyNU.......... Friedrich-Alexander-Universitat zu Erlangen-Nurnberg, Abteilung fur Wirtschafts-und Socialwissenschaften, Nurnberg, Germany [*Library symbol*] [*Library of Congress*] (LCLS)
GYNX.......... Gynex, Inc. (SAUO)
GYP............ CGC, Inc. [*Toronto Stock Exchange symbol*]
GYP............ Eagle Aviation [*British*] [*FAA designator*] (FAAC)
GYP............ Guild of Young Printers (DGA)
GYP............ Gympie [*Australia*] [*Airport symbol*]
GYP............ Gypsum (KSC)
GYP............ Gypsy (ABBR)
GYP............ Gyro Yaw Position
GYPB.......... Glycogen Phosphorylase (SAUS)
Gyp Bd........ Gypsum Board (SAUS)
GYPD.......... Gypped (ABBR)
GYPG.......... Gypping (ABBR)
GYPS.......... Gypsum
GYPSIOL..... Gypsiologic (ABBR)
gypsiol........ gypsiology (SAUS)
GYPSM........ Gypsum, IA [*American Association of Railroads railroad junction routing code*]
GYPSU........ Gypsum, KS [*American Association of Railroads railroad junction routing code*]
Gypsum....... Calcium Sulfate (SAUS)
Gypsum Lime... Gypsum and Lime (journ.) (SAUS)
GYPSY........ General Image Processing System
GYR............ Gigayear [*A billion years*]
GYR............ Goodyear (SAUS)
GYR............ Goodyear, AZ [*Location identifier*] [*FAA*] (FAAL)
GYR............ Gyrafrance [*France*] [*ICAO designator*] (FAAC)

GYR .... Gyration (ABBR)
GYR .... Gyratory (SAUS)
GYR .... Gyrus (ABBR)
GYRA .... Gyrate (ABBR)
GYRAD .... Gyrated (ABBR)
GYRAG .... Gyrating (ABBR)
GYRAN .... Gyration (ABBR)
GYRAR .... Gyrator (ABBR)
GYRARY .... Gyratory (ABBR)
GYRCMPS .... Gyrocompass (ABBR)
GYRMTR .... Gyrometer (ABBR)
GYRO .... Gyrocompass (ABBR)
GYRO .... Gyrodyne [*NASDAQ symbol*] (SAG)
GYRO .... Gyrodyne Co. Amer [*NASDAQ symbol*] (TTSB)
GYRO .... Gyroplane (ABBR)
GYRO .... Gyroscope (AAG)
GYROA .... Gyro A (NAKS)
GYROCOMP .... Gyrocompassing (NAKS)
GYROCOMP .... Gyroscope Compassing
GYROCOP .... Gyrocopter (ABBR)
Gyrocopter .... Autogyro Helicopter (SAUS)
Gyrody .... Gyrodyne Company of America, Inc. [*Associated Press*] (SAG)
GYRODYN .... Gyrodynamic (ABBR)
gyrodyn .... gyrodynamicist (SAUS)
Gyrodyn .... Gyrodynamics (SAUS)
GYROLITE .... Gyro Satellite (SAUS)
GYRPLN .... Gyroplane (ABBR)
GYRSCP .... Gyroscope (ABBR)
GYRSTBR .... Gyrostabilizer (ABBR)
GYRTD .... Gyrated (ABBR)
GyRU .... Universitat Regensburg, Regensburg, Germany [*Library symbol*] [*Library of Congress*] (LCLS)
Gy/s .... Gray je Sekunde (SAUS)
GySalS .... Stadtbucherei Salzgitter, Joachim Campe, Salzgitter, Germany [*Library symbol*] [*Library of Congress*] (LCLS)
GySaU .... Universitat des Saarlandes, Saarbrucken, Germany [*Library symbol*] [*Library of Congress*] (LCLS)
GYSCO .... Great Yarmouth Shipping Co. (MHDW)
GYS Co .... Great Yarmouth Shipping Company (SAUO)
GySgt .... Gunnery Sergeant [*Military*] (POLM)
GYSGT .... Gunnery Sergeant
GySIA .... Institut fuer Auslandsbeziehungen, Stuttgart, Germany [*Library symbol*] [*Library of Congress*] (LCLS)
GYSR .... Geyser (ABBR)
GYSTC .... Georgia Youth Science and Technology Centers (SAUO)
GySU .... Universitat Stuttgart, Stuttgart, Germany [*Library symbol*] [*Library of Congress*] (LCLS)
GySW .... Wuerttembergische Landesbibliothek, Konrad Adenauer, Stuttgart, Germany [*Library symbol*] [*Library of Congress*] (LCLS)
GyTrU .... Universitat Trier-Kaiserslautern, Schneidershof, Trier, Germany [*Library symbol*] [*Library of Congress*] (LCLS)
GYW .... International Finance Corp. [*AMEX symbol*] (SAG)
GyWitS .... Stadtbucherei Witten, Witten, Germany [*Library symbol*] [*Library of Congress*] (LCLS)
GyWK .... Kalle Aktiengesellschaft, Litteraturabteilung, Wiesbaden-Biebrich, Germany [*Library symbol*] [*Library of Congress*] (LCLS)
GyWoS .... Niedersachsische Staatsarchiv, Wolfenbuttel, Germany [*Library symbol*] [*Library of Congress*] (LCLS)
GYY .... Gary, IN [*Location identifier*] [*FAA*] (FAAL)
GZ .... Air Rarotonga [*ICAO designator*] (AD)
GZ .... Ganzfeld [*Whole Field*] [*ESP test*] [*German*]
gz .... Gaza Strip [*MARC country of publication code*] [*Library of Congress*] (LCCP)
GZ .... Geneva Elevator [*Federal Railroad Administration identification code*]
GZ .... Gigahertz [*1,000 megahertz*] [*Preferred form is GHz*] (MCD)
Gz .... Graetz Number [*Physics*]
gz .... grid zone (SAUS)
GZ .... Ground Zero [*An association*] (EA)
GZ .... Ground Zero [*Atomic detonation*]
GZ .... Guilford-Zimmerman Personality Test [*Psychology*] (MAE)
Gz .... Guizzardinus [*Deceased, 1222*] [*Authority cited in pre-1607 legal work*] (DSA)
G-Z .... Giacobini-Zinner (a Comet) [*Astronomy*] (ODA)
GZA .... Alverno College, Milwaukee, WI [*OCLC symbol*] (OCLC)
GZA .... GZA GeoEnvironmental Technologies, Inc. [*Associated Press*] (SAG)
GZAS .... Guilford-Zimmerman Aptitude Survey [*Test*]
GZAS:GR .... Guilford-Zimmerman Aptitude Survey: General Reasoning [*Test*]
GZAS:NO .... Guilford-Zimmerman Aptitude Survey: Numerical Operations [*Test*]
GZAS:PS .... Guilford-Zimmerman Aptitude Survey: Perceptual Speed [*Test*]
GZAS:SO .... Guilford-Zimmerman Aptitude Survey: Spatial Orientation [*Test*]
GZAS:SV .... Guilford-Zimmerman Aptitude Survey: Spatial Visualization [*Test*]
GZAS:VC .... Guilford-Zimmerman Aptitude Survey: Verbal Comprehension [*Test*]
GZB .... Carroll College, Waukesha, WI [*OCLC symbol*] (OCLC)
GZC .... Carthage College, Kenosha, WI [*OCLC symbol*] (OCLC)
G Z C .... Gas-size Exclusion Chromatography (SAUS)
GZD .... Glazed (DGA)
GZD .... Milwaukee Public Library, Milwaukee, WI [*OCLC symbol*] (OCLC)
GZE .... University of Wisconsin-Eau Claire, Eau Claire, WI [*OCLC symbol*] (OCLC)
GZEA .... GZA GeoEnvironmental Technologies [*NASDAQ symbol*] (SAG)
GZEA .... GZA GeoEnvironmental Technologies, Inc. (NQ)
GZF .... Eau Claire Public Library, Eau Claire, WI [*OCLC symbol*] (OCLC)
GZG .... Blackford, VA [*Location identifier*] [*FAA*] (FAAL)
GZG .... Brown County Library, Green Bay, WI [*OCLC symbol*] (OCLC)
GZG .... Gonzales Gold Mines Ltd. [*Vancouver Stock Exchange symbol*]
GZH .... University of Wisconsin-Madison, Health Sciences, Madison, WI [*OCLC symbol*] (OCLC)
GZI .... Globin Zine Insulin [*Medicine*] (EDAA)
GZI .... University of Wisconsin-Madison, Instructional Materials Center, Madison, WI [*OCLC symbol*] (OCLC)
GZII .... Guilford-Zimmerman Interest Inventory [*Vocational guidance test*]
GZIP .... GNU Zip (SAUS)
GZJ .... University of Wisconsin-Milwaukee, School of Library Science, Milwaukee, WI [*OCLC symbol*] (OCLC)
GZK .... Oshkosh Public Library, Oshkosh, WI [*OCLC symbol*] (OCLC)
GZL .... Gazelle Resources Ltd. [*Vancouver Stock Exchange symbol*]
GZL .... Guzzle (ABBR)
GZL .... University of Wisconsin-Madison, Law Library, Madison, WI [*OCLC symbol*] (OCLC)
GZLD .... Guzzled (ABBR)
GZLG .... Guzzling (ABBR)
GZLR .... Guzzler (ABBR)
GZM .... Gaz Metropolitain, Inc. [*Toronto Stock Exchange symbol*]
GZM .... University of Wisconsin-Madison, Madison, WI [*OCLC symbol*] (OCLC)
GZMG .... Gradient Zone Melting (IAA)
GZMO .... Genzyme Molecular Oncology Division [*NASDAQ symbol*] (NASQ)
GZMO .... German Zonal Meteorological Organization (SAUO)
GZN .... Grid Azimuth (SAUS)
GZN .... Ground Zero [*Nevada*] [*Seismograph station code, US Geological Survey*] [*Closed*] (SEIS)
GZN .... University of Wisconsin-Milwaukee, Milwaukee, WI [*OCLC symbol*] (OCLC)
GZNG .... Grazing (SAUS)
GZO .... Gizo [*Solomon Islands*] [*Airport symbol*] (OAG)
GZO .... University of Wisconsin-Oshkosh, Oshkosh, WI [*OCLC symbol*] (OCLC)
GZOB .... Glowna Zydowska Organizacja Bojowa [*A publication*] (BJA)
GZON .... Graphix Zone [*NASDAQ symbol*] (TTSB)
GZON .... Graphix Zone, Inc. [*NASDAQ symbol*] (SAG)
GZP .... University of Wisconsin-Parkside, Kenosha, WI [*OCLC symbol*] (OCLC)
GZPP .... Ground Zero Pairing Project (EA)
GZQ .... Marquette University, Milwaukee, WI [*OCLC symbol*] (OCLC)
GZR .... Golden Zone Resources [*Vancouver Stock Exchange symbol*]
GZR .... Wisconsin Department of Public Instruction, Reference and Loan Library, Madison,WI [*OCLC symbol*] (OCLC)
GZRC .... Ground Zero Rescue Center (SAUS)
GZRC .... Ground Zero Resource Center [*Defunct*] (EA)
GZS .... Gesellschaft fuer Zahlungssysteme [*International banking*] [*Germany*]
GZS .... Gozaisho [*Japan*] [*Seismograph station code, US Geological Survey*] [*Closed*] (SEIS)
GZS .... Pulaski, TN [*Location identifier*] [*FAA*] (FAAL)
GZS .... University of Wisconsin-Stout, Menomonie, WI [*OCLC symbol*] (OCLC)
GZSRAA .... Gezira Research Station and Substations. Annual Report (journ.) (SAUS)
GZT .... Gaziantep [*Turkey*] [*Airport symbol*] (OAG)
GZT .... Greenwich Zone Time
GZT .... University of Wisconsin-Whitewater, Whitewater, WI [*OCLC symbol*] (OCLC)
GZTC .... Genzyme Transgenics [*NASDAQ symbol*] (TTSB)
GZTC .... Genzyme Transgenics Corp. [*NASDAQ symbol*] (SAG)
GZTPRD .... Ground Zero Tape Read (IAA)
GZTS .... Guilford-Zimmerman Temperament Survey [*Psychology*]
GZU .... University of Wisconsin-La Crosse, La Crosse, WI [*OCLC symbol*] (OCLC)
GZV .... University of Wisconsin-Platteville, Platteville, WI [*OCLC symbol*] (OCLC)
GZW .... University of Wisconsin-Green Bay, Green Bay, WI [*OCLC symbol*] (OCLC)
GZX .... La Crosse Public Library, La Crosse, WI [*OCLC symbol*] (OCLC)
GZX .... Peoria, IL [*Location identifier*] [*FAA*] (FAAL)
GZY .... Wisconsin Interlibrary Loan Service, Madison, WI [*OCLC symbol*] (OCLC)

H
By Acronym

H................. Air Force Training Category
H................. Altitude
H................. Altitude Rate [*Symbol*] (NASA)
H................. Angular impulse (SAUS)
H................. Atmospheric Head (AAG)
H................. Blister Chemical Agent (SAUS)
H................. Boltzmann Function [*Physics*] (BARN)
H................. Bracco Industria Chimica [*Italy*] [*Research code symbol*]
h................. Coefficient of Heat Transfer [*Symbol*] [*Thermodynamics*]
H................. Declared or Paid after Stock Dividend or Split-Up [*Investment term*] (DFIT)
h................. Dihydro [*As substituent on nucleoside*] [*Biochemistry*]
H................. Dose equivalent (SAUS)
H................. Electronic Countermeasures Evaluator (SAUS)
H................. Enthalpy [*Symbol*] [*IUPAC*] (DEN)
H................. Exposure [*Symbol*] [*IUPAC*]
h----............. French Union [*MARC geographic area code*] [*Library of Congress*] (LCCP)
h................. Hacia [*Around*] [*Spanish*]
H................. Haemaphysalis [*A genus of tick*] [*Entomology*] (DAVI)
H................. Haftarah (BJA)
H................. Hagelkorn [*Hailstone*] [*Bomb*] [*German military - World War II*]
H................. Haggai [*Freemasonry*]
H................. Hail [*Meteorology*]
H................. Hair (MELL)
H................. Haler [*Monetary unit*] [*Former Czechoslovakia*]
H................. Half
H................. Half-Word Designator [*Computer science*]
H................. Hall
H................. Hallucis (MELL)
H................. HALON [*Halogenated Hydrocarbon*] (NFPA)
H................. Halothane [*Also, HAL*] [*An anesthetic*]
H................. Halt [*Computer science*] (MDG)
H................. Ham (SAUS)
H................. Hamiltonian (ADWA)
H................. Hamiltonian Function [*Mathematics*]
H................. Hamlet
H................. Hamlyn Publishing [*British*]
H................. Hand [*Music*]
H................. Handage (MELL)
H................. Handbook (SAA)
H................. Handicapped (GOBB)
H................. Handily [*Horse racing*]
h................. Hand-Rearing [*of experimental animals*] (DMAA)
H................. Handy's Ohio Reports [*12 Ohio Decisions*] [*A publication*] (DLA)
h................. Harbor (MIST)
H................. Harbor [*Maps and charts*]
H................. Harcourt General, Inc. [*Formerly, General Cinema Corp.*] [*NYSE symbol*] (SPSG)
H................. Hard [*or Hardness*] [*Pencil leads*]
H................. Hardness [*Of precious stones*]
H................. Hardware [*Computer science*] (MDG)
H................. Hardy [*Horticulture*]
H................. Hare's English Chancery Reports [*A publication*] (DLA)
H................. Harmonic (IDOE)
H................. Harmonic Mean [*Psychology*]
h................. Harmonized [*Apparent inconsistency explained and shown not to exist*] [*Used in Shepard's Citations*] [*Legal term*] (DLA)
H................. Harn (SAUS)
h................. Harpsichord
H................. Harrier (ROG)
H................. Harry [*Phonetic alphabet*] [*Royal Navy*] [*World War I*] [*Pre-World War II*] (DSUE)
H................. Has
H................. Hashish [*Medicine*] (EDAA)
H................. Hassle [*Sweden*] [*Research code symbol*]
H................. Hatch [*Technical drawings*]
H................. Hauch [*Antigen*] [*Immunology*]
H................. Haustus [*A Drink*] [*Pharmacy*]
H................. Have (ROG)
H................. Haven (ADA)
H................. Hawaii Reports [*A publication*] (DLA)
(H)............... Hazardous [*Task classification*] [*NASA*] (NASA)
H................. Hazardous Cargo [*Shipping*]
H................. Hazards (PIPO)
H................. Haze [*Weather reports*]
H................. Hazor (BJA)
H................. Hazy (ABBR)
H................. H-Beam [*Architecture*]
H................. Head [*Anatomy*] (DAVI)
H................. Head [*Horse racing*]
H................. Head [*Linguistics*]
H................. Header (NFPA)
H................. Head, Hand, and Chest Sets [*JETDS nomenclature*] [*Military*] (CET)
H................. Headlines (ABBR)
H................. Headquarters (ABBR)
H................. Healthy
H................. Hearing [*Motor vehicle violation code used in state of Maryland*] (MVRD)
H................. Hearing Power (ROG)
H................. Heart [*Freemasonry*] (ROG)
H................. Hearts (ADA)
H................. Heart Trouble [*Classification system used by doctors on Ellis Island to detain, re-examine, and possibly deny entry to certain immigrants*]
H................. Heartwood [*Forestry*]
H................. Heat [*or Heater*]
H................. Heater (ABBR)
H................. Heaton Mint [*British*]
H................. Heavy [*Medicine*] (EDAA)
H................. Heavy Lift Cargo Airlines Ltd. [*British*]
H................. Heavy Sea [*Navigation*]
H................. Hebrew (BJA)
h................. Hecto [*A prefix meaning multiplied by* 10^2] [*SI symbol*]
H................. Heel [*Music*]
H................. Heelstick [*Medicine*] (DAVI)
H................. Heft [*Part*] [*German*]
H................. Height
h................. Height [*Symbol*] [*IUPAC*]
H................. Heir
h................. Heiress (GEAB)
H................. Helicopter [*When the second letter or only letter*] [*Designation for all US military aircraft*]
H................. Helicopteros do Brasil SA [*Brazil*] [*ICAO aircraft manufacturer identifier*] (ICAO)
H................. Helium [*Chemical symbol is He*] (AAG)
H................. Helix
H................. Hell (GOBB)
H................. Hemagglutinating [*Virology*]
H................. Hematite [*A mineral*]
H................. Hemic Subgroup [*Magnetite, chromite, hematite*] [*CIPW classification*] [*Geology*]
H................. Hemin [*Hematology*]
H................. Hemisphere [*Anatomy*] (DAVI)
H................. Hemolysis [*Medicine*] (EDAA)
H................. Hemophilus [*Microbiology*] (MAE)
H................. Hemorrhoid (MELL)
H................. Hence
H................. Henry (DCOM)
H................. Henry [*Symbol*] [*SI unit of inductance*]
H................. Henry (King of England) (DLA)
H................. Henry's Law Constant
H................. Heparin [*Pharmacology*] (DAVI)
h................. Heplode [*Electronics*] (OA)
H................. Herb [*Botany*]
H................. Herbivore
H................. Heres [*Heir*] [*Legal term*] [*Latin*]
H................. Hermit
H................. Hernia [*Gastroenterology*] (DAVI)
H................. Heroin [*Slang*]
H................. Hertzog's High Court Reports [*South Africa*] [*A publication*] (DLA)
H................. Heterophyes [*A genus of trematode worms*] [*Gastroenterology*] (DAVI)
H................. Heterozygosity [*Cytology*]
H................. Hettangian [*Geology*]
H................. Hexadecimal (BUR)
H................. Hexapole (OA)
H................. Hexode [*Electronics*] (OA)
H................. Hic [*Here*] [*Latin*]
H................. Hieroglyphics [*Freemasonry*] (ROG)
H................. High [*Engineering*]
H................. Highest [*Price Quoted of a Stock*] [*Finance*] (BARN)

H High Season [*Airline fare code*]
H High Strength Bar Joist [*Construction term*] (MIST)
H High-Viscosity Fuel
H Hilary Term [*England*] [*Legal term*] (DLA)
H Hilkoth (BJA)
H Hill (ROG)
H Hill's New York Reports [*A publication*] (DLA)
H Hindu (ABBR)
H Hinged [*Philately*]
H Hippelates [*A genus of insects*] [*Entomology*] (DAVI)
H His [*Medicine*] (EDAA)
H Hispanic
H Histamine [*Anesthesiology*]
H Histidine [*One-letter symbol*]
H Histidinemethemoglobin [*Medicine*] (MELL)
H Histoplasma [*Biochemistry*] (DAVI)
H Histoplasmosis [*Medicine*] (EDAA)
H Historiae [*of Sallust*] [*Classical studies*] (OCD)
H Historical Re-Issue [*Record cataloging*]
H+ History (SPVS)
H History [*Secondary school course*] [*British*]
H Hits [*Baseball*]
H Hoffmann [*Reflex*] [*Neurology*]
H Hold [*Baseball term*] (NDBD)
H Holding [*Electronics*]
H Holiness (BJA)
H Holland [*IYRU nationality code*] (IYR)
H Holy
H Holzknecht [*Unit*]
H Home
H Homobonus de Cremona [*Deceased, 1272*] [*Authority cited in pre-1607 legal work*] (DSA)
H Homosexual
H Honor
H Honorary [*Academic degree*]
H Hooker
H Hope [*Freemasonry*] (ROG)
H Hopper-Tainer [*A form of container*] [*British*] (DCTA)
h Hora [*Hour*] [*Latin*]
H Horizon (ABBR)
h Horizontal (WDMC)
H Horizontal
H Horizontal Force of the Earth's Magnetism [*Amplitude of a tide*]
H Hormone [*Endocrinology*]
H Horn
H Horrific [*Film certificate*] [*British*]
H Horror [*Literary genre*] (WDAA)
H Horse [*Thoroughbred racing*]
H Hose (NFPA)
H Hospice (MELL)
H Hospital [*Traffic sign*] [*British*]
H Hospital Plane [*When suffixed to Navy plane designation*]
H Host [*Freemasonry*] (ROG)
H Hostiensis [*Deceased, 1271*] [*Authority cited in pre-1607 legal work*] (DSA)
H Hostile [*Military*]
H Hot
H Hotel
H Hounsfield Unit [*Medicine*] (MAE)
h Hour (ADWA)
H House
H House Bill [*Legal term*] (DLA)
H House of Representatives
H How [*Phonetic alphabet*] [*World War II*] (DSUE)
H Howard's United States Supreme Court Reports [*42-65 United States*] [*A publication*] (DLA)
H Hoy [*Ship's rigging*] (ROG)
H Hoyre [*Conservative Party*] [*Norway*] [*Political party*] (PPE)
h HTML [*Hypertext Markup Language*] [*Computer science*] [*Telecommunications*]
H Hue (VLIE)
H Hue slider (SAUS)
H Hugolinus de Presbyteris [*Flourished, 1197-1238*] [*Authority cited in pre-1607 legal work*] (DSA)
H Huguccio [*Deceased, 1210*] [*Authority cited in pre-1607 legal work*] (DSA)
H Hull (ADA)
H Humalog (MELL)
h Human (DB)
H Human
H Human Being [*Rorschach*] [*Psychology*]
H Human Figure (DIPS)
H [*The*] Humanitarian [*A publication*] (ROG)
H Humidifier (EEVL)
H Humidity
h Hundred (WDMC)
H Hundred
H Hungary
H Hun-Stoffe [*Mustard gas*] [*Formerly, HS*] [*Also, HD, HT, M*]
H Hupp Corp. (SAUO)
H Husband
H Hussars [*Military unit*] [*British*]
H Hyaluronidase [*Medicine*] (EDAA)
h Hybrid
H Hydrant
H Hydraulics (ADA)
H Hydrodynamic Head
H Hydrogen [*Chemical*] (EERA)
H Hydrographer to the navy (SAUS)
H Hydrographic Survey [*Navy*] [*British*]
H Hydrolysis
H Hydroxydaunomycin [*See also ADR, Adriamycin*] [*Antineoplastic drug*]
H Hygiene [*Preventive and Industrial Medicine*] [*Medical Officer designation*] [*British*]
H Hymenolepis [*A genus of tapeworm*] [*Gastroenterology*] (DAVI)
H Hyoscine [*Organic chemistry*]
H Hypermetropia [*Ophthalmology*]
H Hyperopia [*Ophthalmology*] (ROG)
H Hyperphoria [*Ophthalmology*] (DAVI)
H Hyperplasia [*Medicine*]
H Hypertension (MELL)
h Hypodermic (DMAA)
H Hypodermic
H Hypothalamus [*Medicine*] (DB)
H Hypothesis
H Instructor [*Army skill qualification identifier*] (INF)
H Magnetic Field Strength [*Symbol*]
H Magnetizing Force [*Symbol*] (DEN)
H Momentum [*Measurement*]
H Mustard (SAUS)
H Mustard Gas [*Also, HD, HS, HT, M*] [*Poison Gas*] [*US Chemical Corps symbol*]
H Nondirectional Radio Homing Beacon [*Navigation charts*]
H Oersted [*Unit of magnetizing force*] [*Physics*] (DMAA)
h Planck Constant [*Symbol*] [*IUPAC*]
h Precision of Process (DIPS)
H Recording [*Communications term*] (DCT)
H Regarding [*JETDS nomenclature*]
H Restaurants, Cafes, and Hotel Lounges [*Public-performance tariff class*] [*British*]
H Search/Rescue [*When the first letter of a pair*] [*Designation for all US military aircraft*]
H Silo Stored [*Missile launch environment symbol*]
H St Louis [*Branch in the Federal Reserve regional banking system*] (BARN)
H Total Energy (ROG)
H Turkiye Halk Bankasi [*Bank*] [*Turkey*]
H Vectorcardiogram Electrode [*Cardiology*] (DAVI)
H Halfpage [*Advertising*] (ODA)
h Heat Transfer [*Physics*] (ODA)
H Heavy [*Immunology*] (ODA)
h Hip (ODA)
H_0 Hubble's Constant [*Astronomy*]
H_1 Alternative Hypothesis (DAVI)
H1 Haploid Cell Line 1
H-1 Iroquois Transport [*Military*] (POLM)
H^1 Protium [*or Light hydrogen*] [*Chemical element*] (DAVI)
H^2 Deuterium [*Also, D*] [*Radioisotope of hydrogen*]
H-2 Diethylaminoethanol [*Medicine*] (EDAA)
H2 Hawaii (Kauai) [*Spaceflight Tracking and Data Network*] [*NASA*]
H^2 Hot and Heavy [*In reference to a romance*]
H2 How To (SAUS)
H2 Hydrogen
H2A Happy to Accommodate
H2B Husband-to-Be
H_2BT Hydrogen Breath Test
H2CUS Hope to See You Soon
H2GN Have to Go Now
H2H Human-to-Human
H2O Water [*Compound*] (RDA)
H_2O_2 Hydrogen Peroxide [*Pharmacology*] (DAVI)
H_2S Hydrogen Sulfide (GNE)
H_2SO_4 Sulfuric Acid [*Chemistry*] (DAVI)
H_2Urd Dihydrouridine [*Also, D, hU*] [*A nucleoside*]
H 0/3 Head 0 or 3 (SAUS)
H_3 Tritium [*Also, T*] [*Radioisotope of hydrogen*]
H_3BO_3 Boric Acid [*Pharmacology*] (DAVI)
H4 Solomon Islands [*Aircraft nationality and registration mark*] (FAAC)
H_4 Tetrahydro [*Biochemistry*]
H_4folate Tetrahydrofolate [*Biochemistry*]
H_4furan Tetrahydrofuran [*Organic chemistry*]
H4P High Performance Parallel Processing Project (SAUS)
H_4pyran Tetrahydropyranyl [*Organic chemistry*]
H5 Henry V [*Shakespearean work*]
H6PD Hexose-6-Phosphate Dehydrogenase (SAUS)
H8 Henry VIII [*Shakespearean work*]
H1/2 Half-Hardened (SAUS)
H1/4 Hindquarters (SPVS)
H24 Operating 24 hours (SAUO)
H24 Twenty-Four Hour [*Continuous*] Operation [*Aviation*]
H 2/5 Head 2 or 5 (SAUS)
H-1211 Halon 1211 (SAUS)
H-1301 Halon 1301 (SAUS)
HA Apogee Altitude (NASA)
HA CASA [*Construcciones Aeronauticas Sociedad Anonima*] [*Spain*] [*ICAO aircraft manufacturer identifier*] (ICAO)
HA Chem. Werke Albert [*Germany*] [*Research code symbol*]
HA Habitual Abortion [*Medicine*]
HA Haemagglutination (SAUS)

HA.... Haemagglutinin (SAUS)
Ha.... Hahnium [Proposed name for chemical element 105]
HA.... Haiti [or Haitian] (WDAA)
Ha.... Hakim-Adams [Medicine] (EDAA)
HA.... Half Action (ACAE)
HA.... Half Adder [Circuitry] (MSA)
HA.... Half Adding (SAUS)
HA.... Half Adjust (SAUS)
HA.... HAL, Inc. [AMEX symbol] (COMM)
Ha.... Hallah (BJA)
HA.... Hallux Abductus [Orthopedics] (DAVI)
HA.... Halothane Anesthia [Medicine] (MELL)
HA.... Hamburg-Antwerp (SAUS)
HA.... Hamilton Aerospace (SAUS)
HA.... Hand Actuated (IAA)
HA.... Hand-Actuated (SAUS)
HA.... Hand Applanation (SAUS)
H/A.... Hand/Automatic [Nuclear energy] (NRCH)
HA.... Handelsakademie (SAUS)
HA.... Hanford Operations Office (SAUS)
HA.... H Antigen (DB)
HA.... Hard Aggregate (SAUS)
HA.... Hard Axis (SAUS)
HA.... Hardboard Association (SAUO)
Ha.... Hardened in Air (SAUS)
HA.... Hardness Assurance (MSA)
HA.... Hardware [Computer science] (IAA)
HA.... Hardware Age (SAUS)
HA.... Hardy Annual [Horticulture] (ROG)
Ha.... Hare's English Vice-Chancellors' Reports [66-68 English Reprint] [1841-53] [A publication] (DLA)
HA.... Harmonic Analysis (SAUS)
HA.... Harmonic Approximation (SAUS)
HA.... Harmonic Average (SAUS)
HA.... Harmonie Associates (EA)
HA.... Harness Assembly
Ha.... Hartmann Number [IUPAC]
HA.... Hatch (RIMS)
HA.... Hatch Act [1887]
HA.... Hatchway (DS)
Ha.... Hawaii (SHCU)
HA.... Hawaii [or Hawaiian] (WDAA)
HA.... Hawaiian Air (SAUS)
HA.... Hawaiian Air Lines (SAUO)
HA.... Hawaiian Airlines 'A' [AMEX symbol] (TTSB)
HA.... Hawaiian Airlines, Inc. [ICAO designator] (ICDA)
HA.... Hawaiian Airlines, Inc. [AMEX symbol] (SAG)
HA.... Hazard Analysis (NASA)
HA.... Hazard Assessment [Environmental science] (COE)
HA.... Hazardous Area
HA.... Hazards Assessment (SAUS)
HA.... Headache
HA.... Head Address (SAUS)
HA.... Head Aim (ACAE)
HA.... Head Amplifier (SAUS)
HA.... Header Authentication (VLIE)
HA.... Headmasters [or Headmistresses] Association (EA)
HA.... Headquarters Administration (SAUO)
HA.... Headquarters Administration Division [Coast Guard]
H/A.... Head to Abdomen (DMAA)
HA.... Health Academy [An association] (EA)
HA.... Health Act (OICC)
HA.... Health Advisory (GNE)
HA.... Health Affairs [Army] (DOMA)
HA.... Health Alliance [Consumer representation] (ECON)
HA.... Health Alliances (SAUS)
HA.... Health and Affairs (ACAE)
HA.... Health Assessment (BCP)
HA.... Health Authority (SAUS)
HA.... Healthy America [An association] [Defunct] (EA)
HA.... Hearing Aid
HA.... Heated Aerosol (IDYL)
HA.... Heavy Armor (SAUS)
HA.... Heavy Artillery
HA.... Heavy Atoms
HA.... Hectare (AAG)
ha.... Hectare (DMAA)
HA.... Hectocotylized Arm
HA.... Heeres-Atmer [Service Oxygen Breathing Apparatus] [German military - World War II]
HA.... Hefte von Auschwitz (BJA)
HA.... Height Age [Medicine] (EDAA)
HA.... Height of Apogee
HA.... Heir Apparent
HA.... Helicopter Attack (SAUS)
HA.... Hellenic Army (MCD)
HA.... Hemadsorbent (MELL)
HA.... Hemadsorption [Hematology]
HA.... Hemagglutinating Activity [Hematology] (DAVI)
HA.... Hemagglutinating Antibody [Hematology] (DAVI)
HA.... Hemagglutinating Antigen [Hematology] (DAVI)
HA.... Hemagglutination [Hematology]
HA.... Hemagglutinin (SAUS)
HA.... Hemolytic Anemia [Hematology]
HA.... Hemophiliac with Adenopathy [Medicine] (EDAA)
HA.... Henry Adams, Inc. [Baltimore, MD] (TSSD)
HA.... Henson Associates [Television production company]
HA.... Hepatic Agenesis (MELL)
HA.... Hepatic Artery [Anatomy] (MAE)
HA.... Hepatitis A (SAUS)
HA.... Hepatitis Associated [Virus]
HA.... Heptaldehyde-Aniline (EDCT)
HA.... Heptaldehyde-Aniline Condensate (EDCT)
HA.... Heptoic Aldehyde (SAUS)
HA.... Herpes Association [British] (DBA)
HA.... Heterophile Antibody [Immunochemistry]
HA.... Heyden Antibiotic [Pharmacology]
HA.... High Altitude
HA.... High Amplitude (IAA)
HA.... High Angle
HA.... High Anxiety (MAE)
HA.... High Aperture (SAUS)
HA.... High Authority of the ECSC [European Coal and Steel Community] (ILCA)
HA.... High Availability (SAUS)
HA.... Higher Authority
HA.... Highway Act (SAUS)
HA.... Highways Act [British] (ILCA)
HA.... Hindustan Aircraft Ltd., Bangalore (SAUO)
HA.... Hippuric Acid (MELL)
HA.... Hiram Abiff [Freemasonry] (ROG)
HA.... Histamine [Medicine] (DB)
HA.... Histocompatibility Antigen (DB)
HA.... Historia Animalium [of Aristotle] [Classical studies] (OCD)
HA.... Historical Association [British] (EAIO)
HA.... History Abstracts [Database] (NITA)
HA.... Hoc Anno [This Year] [Latin]
HA.... Hockey Association [British]
HA.... Hoe Automation (SAUS)
H/A.... Holding Activity
HA.... Holic Angle (SAUS)
HA.... Holiness Army (ROG)
HA.... Homatropina (SAUS)
HA.... Home Address
HA.... Home Automation (SAUS)
HA.... Homesteaders Association [Defunct] (EA)
HA.... Horse Artillery
HA.... Horticultural Abstracts
HA.... Horticultural Abstracts (journ.) (SAUS)
HA.... Horton's Arteritis [Medicine] (EDAA)
HA.... Hosanna Army (ROG)
HA.... Hospice Association (EA)
HA.... Hospital Academy (EA)
HA.... Hospital Admission
HA.... Hospital Apprentice [Navy rating]
HA.... Hospital Association (SAUO)
HA.... Hospitalman Apprentice (SAUO)
HA.... Host Agent (SAUS)
HA.... Hostile Aeroplane [British military] (DMA)
HA.... Hostile Aircraft (SAUS)
HA.... Hot Air
HA.... Hounsfield Unit [On computerized tomography] [Radiology] (DAVI)
HA.... Hour Angle [Navigation]
HA.... Hour Aspect (SAUS)
HA.... House Account [Business term]
HA.... House Administration (DLA)
HA.... House of Assembly (SAUO)
HA.... Housewives Association [Australia]
HA.... Housing Allowance [Military]
HA.... Housing Assistance [HUD]
HA.... Housing Assistant (SAUO)
HA.... Housing Authority
HA.... Hoverclub of America (EA)
H-A.... Howson-Algraphy (DGA)
HA.... Huius Anni [This Year's] [Latin]
HA.... Human Adaptability
HA.... Human Albumin (MELL)
HA.... Humanalbumin (SAUS)
HA.... Human Argininosuccinate Lyase [An enzyme]
HA.... Humanitarian Assistance [Environmental science] (COE)
HA.... Humic Acid [Organic chemistry]
HA.... Humor Association (EA)
HA.... Humorolics Anonymous (EA)
HA.... Hungaria (SAUS)
HA.... Hungarian Association [Australia]
HA.... Hungary (SAUS)
HA.... Hyaluronic Acid [Biochemistry]
HA.... Hydraulic Actuator (SAUS)
HA.... Hydraulic Association of Great Britain (BI)
HA.... Hydraulics Association (SAUS)
HA.... Hydrocephalus Association (EA)
HA.... Hydrologic Atlas (SAUO)
HA.... Hydrophone Allowance [British military] (DMA)
HA.... Hydrotechnique Association (SAUO)
HA.... Hydroxyapatite [Also, HAP] [A mineral]
HA.... Hydroxylapatite [Inorganic chemistry]
HA.... Hyperalimentation [Intravenous feeding] (DAVI)
HA.... Hyperandrogenism [Medicine] (EDAA)
HA.... Hypermetropia, Absolute [Ophthalmology]
HA.... Hypersensitivity Alveolitis [Medicine] (DB)

HA .... Hypertensive Angiopathy (SAUS)
HA .... Hypoglycemic Association [*Australia*]
HA .... Hypothalmic Amenorrhea [*Medicine*] (DAVI)
HA .... Netherlands [*IYRU nationality code*] (IYR)
HA .... P-Hydroxyanisole (SAUS)
HA1 .... Hemadsorption [*Virus*], Type 1 [*Hematology*] (DAVI)
HA2 .... Hemadsorption Type 2 [*Virus*] [*Medicine*] (DB)
HAA .... Haflinger Association of America (EA)
HAA .... Haitian-American Association [*Defunct*]
HAA .... Haloacetic Acids [*Environmental chemistry*]
HAA .... Handbooks of Archaeology and Antiquities [*A publication*]
HAA .... Handicapped Artists of America (EA)
HAA .... Hands Across America [*Defunct*] (EA)
HAA .... Harrison Air [*Canada*] [*ICAO designator*] (FAAC)
HAA .... Hasvik [*Norway*] [*Airport symbol*] (OAG)
HAA .... Head Access Area [*Nuclear energy*] (NRCH)
HAA .... Hearing Aid Amplifier
HAA .... Heater Amplifier Assembly
HAA .... Heavy Antiaircraft (SAUS)
HAA .... Heavy Antiaircraft Artillery
HAA .... Height Above Aerodrome (SAUS)
HAA .... Height Above Airport (SAUS)
HAA .... Helicopter Administrative Area (SAUS)
HAA .... Helicopter Airline Association (EA)
HAA .... Helicopter Association of America [*Later, HAI*] (EA)
HAA .... Helicopter Association of Australia
HAA .... Helix Aspersa Agglutinin (SAUS)
HAA .... Hemolytic Anemia Antigen [*Immunochemistry*]
HAA .... Hepatitis Associated Antibodies (SAUS)
HAA .... Hepatitis Associated Antigen [*Clinical chemistry*]
HAA .... Heptaminol Adenosinemonophosphate Amidate [*Biochemistry*]
HAA .... Herpetological Association of Africa (SAUO)
HAA .... Heterocyclic Aromatic Amines
HAA .... High-Altitude Abort [*NASA*] (KSC)
HAA .... High-Altitude Application
HAA .... Hispanic American Almanac [*A publication*]
HAA .... Historic Aircraft Association [*British*]
HAA .... Home Automation Association (EA)
HAA .... Honduran-American Association (EA)
HAA .... Horticulture Awareness Association (EA)
HAA .... Hospice Association of America (NTPA)
HAA .... Hospital Activity Analysis [*British*]
HAA .... Hotel Accountants Association (SAUS)
HAA .... Hotel Accountants Association of New York City (EA)
HAA .... Houseboat Association of America (EA)
HAA .... Housing Action Area (SAUO)
HAA .... Housing Assistance Administration [*HUD*]
HAA .... Human Action Analysis (VLIE)
HAA .... Human Asset Accounting (ADA)
HAA .... Humanist Association of America (SAUO)
HAAA .... Addis Ababa [*Ethiopia*] [*ICAO location identifier*] (ICLI)
HAAB .... Addis Ababa/Bole International [*Ethiopia*] [*ICAO location identifier*] (ICLI)
HAAC .... Harper Adams Agricultural College (SAUO)
HAAC .... Heart of America Athletic Conference (PSS)
HAAC .... Heavy Attack Air Commander (SAUO)
HAAC .... Heavy Attack Aircraft Commander (DNAB)
HAAC .... Helicopter Air-to-Air Combat (SAUO)
HAAC .... Housing Aid & Advice Centre [*England*]
HAAC .... Hydraulic Actuator Assembly Container
HAACT .... Heavy Attack Air Commander Training (SAUO)
HAACT .... Heavy Attack Aircraft Commander Training (DNAB)
HAAD .... Adaba [*Ethiopia*] [*ICAO location identifier*] (ICLI)
HAAD .... High-Altitude Aircraft Detection
HAADA .... Horatio Alger Association of Distinguished Americans (EA)
HAADF .... High-Angle Annular Dark-Field [*Microscopy*]
HAADS .... High Altitude Altitude Determination System (ACAE)
HAAF .... Hunter Army Airfield (SAUS)
HAAFCE .... Headquarters, Allied Air Force, Central Europe [*NATO*]
HAAFCE .... Headquarters Allied Air Forces Central Europe (SAUO)
HAAFE .... Hawaiian Army and Air Force Exchange [*Military*]
HAAFSE .... Headquarters Allied Air Forces Southern Europe (SAUO)
HAAG .... Agordat [*Ethiopia*] [*ICAO location identifier*] (ICLI)
HAAg .... Hepatitis A Antigen [*Immunology*] (DAVI)
HAAI .... Handicapped Artists of America, Incorporated (SAUO)
HAAL .... Addis Ababa/Liddetta [*Ethiopia*] [*ICAO location identifier*] (ICLI)
HAALS .... High Accuracy Airborne Location System (SAUO)
HAALS .... High-Accuracy Airborne Location System (MCD)
HAAM .... Arba Minch [*Ethiopia*] [*ICAO location identifier*] (ICLI)
HAAMS .... High-Altitude Airdrop Mission Support (SAUS)
HA and D .... Havre, Antwerp and Dunkirk (SAUS)
Ha & Tw .... Hall and Twell's English Chancery Reports [*1849-50*] [*A publication*] (DLA)
HAAO .... High-Altitude Airborne Observation
HAAP .... Hawthorne Army Ammunition Plant (MCD)
HAAP .... Heavy Anti-Armor Projectile (SAUS)
HAAP .... High Air Pollution Potential
HAAP .... High-Altitude Aerial Photograph (CARB)
HAAP .... High-Altitude Air Pollution Program [*FAA*] (MCD)
HAAP .... Holston Army Ammunition Plant
HAAP .... Homebase and Advanced Assignment Program (SAUO)
HAAP .... Home-Based Advanced Assignment Program [*Military*]
hAAP .... Human Amyloid-Precursor Protein [*Neurobiology*]
HA-AP .... Human Authentication Application Programming Interface (GART)
Ha App .... Appendix to Volume 10 of Hare's Vice-Chancellor's Reports [*England*] [*A publication*] (DLA)
HAA Regt .... Heavy Anti-Aircraft Regiment (SAUO)
HAARP .... High-Altitude Auroral Research Project [*Jointly operated by the Department of Defense and the Geophysical Institute at the University of Alaska*]
HAARP .... High-Frequency Active Auroral Research Program
HAARS .... High-Altitude Airdrop Resupply System
HAARS .... High Altitude Airdrop System (SAUO)
HAARS .... High Altitude Altitude Reference System (ACAE)
HAARS .... Hourly Attendance and Absence Reporting System [*Military*] (MCD)
HAART .... Highly Active Antiretroviral Therapy [*Medicine*]
HAAS .... Asmara App [*Ethiopia*] [*ICAO location identifier*] (ICLI)
HAAS .... Honeywell Automotive Accounting System (IAA)
HAAs .... Housing Action Areas (SAUO)
HAASDO .... Honorary Adviser on Army Stores Depots Organization (SAUO)
HAA/SS .... High Altitude Active/Semiactive Seeker (ACAE)
HAAT .... Head Above Average Terrain (SAUS)
HAAT .... Height above Average Terrain
HAAT .... Height of Antenna Above Average Terrain [*Broadcasting*] (WDMC)
HAAT .... High Above Average Terrain (SAUS)
HAATC .... Heavy Antiaircraft Artillery Tactical Control (SAUO)
HAATC .... High Altitude Air Traffic Control (SAUO)
HAATC .... High-Altitude Air Traffic Control
HAAW .... Awash [*Ethiopia*] [*ICAO location identifier*] (ICLI)
HAAW .... Heavy Antitank/Assault Weapon [*Army*]
HAAX .... Axum [*Ethiopia*] [*ICAO location identifier*] (ICLI)
HAAY .... Asmara/Yohannes IV [*Ethiopia*] [*ICAO location identifier*] (ICLI)
HAB .... Habacuc [*Old Testament book*] [*Douay version*]
Hab .... Habakkuk [*Old Testament book*]
HAB .... Habitability (ACAE)
HAB .... Habitat [*Dwelling*] (ROG)
HAB .... Habitation
HAB .... Habitual [*FBI standardized term*]
HAB .... Haboro [*Japan*] [*Seismograph station code, US Geological Survey*] [*Closed*] (SEIS)
HAB .... Hamburg Africa Bank (SAUS)
HAB .... Hamilton, AL [*Location identifier*] [*FAA*] (FAAL)
HAB .... Hanford Advisory Board (SAUS)
HAB .... Harmful Algal Blooms (SAUS)
HAB .... Hazards Analysis Board [*Air Force*]
HAB .... Hear a Book (SAUS)
HAB .... Hearing Aid Battery
HAb .... Heart Antibody [*Medicine*] (CPH)
HAB .... Heavy Assault Bridge
HAB .... Hemangioblastoma [*Medicine*] (EDAA)
HAB .... Hepatitis B [*Virus*] [*Infectious diseases*] (DAVI)
HAB .... High Altitude Base (SAUS)
HAB .... High-Altitude Bombing [*Military*]
HAB .... High Altitude Burst (ACAE)
HAB .... High-Alumina Basalt [*Geology*]
HAB .... Hiram Abiff [*Freemasonry*] (ROG)
HAB .... Historic American Buildings [*Survey*] [*Library of Congress*]
HAB .... Home Address Back (VLIE)
HAB .... Home Address Block
HAB .... Horizontal Assembly Building [*NASA*] (KSC)
HAB .... Horizontal Axis Bearing
HAB .... Hot Air Balloon
HAB .... Humanities Association Bulletin (SAUO)
HAB .... Humanities Association Bulletin (journ.) (SAUS)
HAB .... Hybrid Antibody [*Immunology*]
HAB .... Hydraulics Appeals Board (SAUO)
HAB .... United States Habitation Module (SAUS)
HABA .... Hardwood Agents and Brokers Association (SAUS)
HABA .... Health and Beauty Aids [*Retailing*] (AABC)
haba .... Health and Beauty Aids [*Advertising*] (WDMC)
HABA .... (Hydroxyazobenzene)benzoic Acid [*Also, HBABA*] [*Organic chemistry*]
HABA .... Hydroxyphenylazobenzoic Acid (SAUS)
HaBaD .... Hokhmah, Bimah, Daat [*Germinal, Developmental, and Conclusive Knowledge*] [*Hebrew*]
HABAT .... Hambro American Bank and Trust Company (SAUO)
HABB .... Bunno Bedele [*Ethiopia*] [*ICAO location identifier*] (ICLI)
HABBA .... (Hydroxyazobenzene)benzoic Acid [*Organic chemistry*]
HABC .... Baco [*Ethiopia*] [*ICAO location identifier*] (ICLI)
HABC .... Habersham Bancorp [*NASDAQ symbol*] (SAG)
HAB CORP .... Habeas Corpus [*You Have the Body*] [*Legal*] [*Latin*] (ROG)
hab corp .... Habeas Corpus (SHCU)
HABD .... Bahar Dar [*Ethiopia*] [*ICAO location identifier*] (ICLI)
HABD .... Hydrazobenzene Derivative [*Organic chemistry*]
HABDIR .... Harmful Algae Bloom Directory (SAUS)
HABE .... Beica [*Ethiopia*] [*ICAO location identifier*] (ICLI)
HABE .... Haber, Inc. [*NASDAQ symbol*] (COMM)
HABE .... High-Altitude Balloon Experiment
Habersh .... Habersham Bancorp [*Associated Press*] (SAG)
HABF .... Hepatic Artery Blood Flow
HAB FAC POSS ... Habere Facias Possessionem [*A writ to put the plaintiff in possession*] [*Latin*] [*Legal term*] (ROG)
Hab Fa Poss ... Habere Facias Possessionem [*A writ to put the plaintiff in possession*] [*Legal term*] [*Latin*]
HAB FA SEIS ... Habere Facias Seisenam [*A writ to put the plaintiff in actual possession*] [*Latin*] [*Legal term*] (ROG)
HAB FA SEIS ... Habere Facias Seisinam [*That You Cause to Have Seisin*] [*Latin*] [*Legal term*] (DLA)
HABGT .... Hutt Adaptation of the Bender-Gestalt Test

habit .... Habitat (BARN)
HABIT .... Health and Behavior Information Transfer (SAUO)
Habitat .... Commission on Human Settlements (SAUO)
HABITAT .... Homeless Americans and Individuals Taking Action Together (SAUS)
HABITAT .... United Nations Center (or Centre) for/on Human Settlements (SAUO)
HABITAT .... United Nations World Conference on Human Settlements (SAUO)
HABP .... Harmful Algal Blooms Programme (SAUS)
HABP .... Hypersonic Arbitrary Body Program [*NASA*]
HABPS .... Hardened Array Solar Power System (SAUS)
HABS .... High-Altitude Bombing System (SAUS)
HABS .... High-Altitude Bombsight (NATG)
HABS .... Historic American Buildings Survey [*Library of Congress*]
HABS .... Human relations area files Automated Bibliographic System (SAUS)
HABT .... Habeat [*Let Him Have*] [*Pharmacy*]
HABT .... Habitability Technology (SSD)
HABTA .... Habituate (ABBR)
HABTAD .... Habituated (ABBR)
HABTAG .... Habituating (ABBR)
HABTAN .... Habitation (ABBR)
HABTAN .... Habituation (ABBR)
HABTB .... Habitable (ABBR)
HABTL .... Habitual (ABBR)
HABTLNS .... Habitualness (ABBR)
HABTU .... Habitue (ABBR)
HABTY .... Habitually (ABBR)
HABU .... Bulchi [*Ethiopia*] [*ICAO location identifier*] (ICLI)
HABY .... Haberdashery (DSUE)
HAc .... Acetic Acid (SAUS)
HAC .... Hachijojima Island [*Japan*] [*Airport symbol*] (OAG)
HAC .... Hachinohe [*Japan*] [*Seismograph station code, US Geological Survey*] (SEIS)
HAC .... Hague Arbitration Convention (SAUO)
HAC .... Haitian Air Corps
HAC .... Handicapped Action Committee
HAC .... Hanging Arm Cast (MELL)
HAC .... Harbor and Approach Chart (SAUO)
HAC .... Hawaii Aeronautics Commission (SAUO)
HAC .... Hazards Assessment Center [*Environmental science*] (COE)
HAC .... Heading Alignment Center (SAUS)
HAC .... Heading Alignment Circle [*NASA*] (NASA)
HAC .... Heading Alignment Cone [*NASA*] (NASA)
HAC .... Heading Alignment Cylinder (MCD)
HAC .... Headquarters Advisory Committee (SAUO)
HAC .... Headquarters Area Command [*Military*]
HAC .... Heads and Chairs (SAUS)
HAC .... Health Advisory Council [*Generic term*] (DHSM)
HAC .... Health Advisory Council [*New South Wales, Australia*]
HAC .... Health of America Conference (SAUS)
HAC .... Health Policy Advisory Center (SAUO)
HAC .... Hearing Aid with Compression
HAC .... Heating and Air Conditioning (EEVL)
HAC .... Heavy-Aggregate Concrete (DEN)
HAC .... Heavy Antitank Convoy
HAC .... Heavy Attack Aircraft Commander
HAC .... Helicopter Air Control [*Military*] (CAAL)
HAC .... Helicopter Aircraft Command (SAUO)
HAC .... Helicopter Aircraft Commander (NVT)
HAC .... Helicoptere Anti-Charanti-tank helicopter (SAUO)
HAC .... Hellenic Advancement Council [*Australia*]
HAc .... Hemagglutin Activity on Chick [*Medicine*] (EDAA)
HAC .... Henebury Aviation Co. [*Australia*] [*ICAO designator*] (FAAC)
HAC .... Herbicide Assessment Commission
HAC .... Herbicide Assessment Committee (SAUO)
HAC .... Hexamethylmelamine [*Altretamine*], Adriamycin, Cyclophosphamide [*Antineoplastic drug regimen*]
HAC .... Hierarchical Abstract Computer (MHDI)
HAC .... Hierarchical Arc Consistency (SAUS)
HAC .... High Acceleration Cockpit (SAUS)
HAC .... High-Acceleration Cockpit [*Air Force*]
HAC .... High-Altitude Compensation [*Automotive engineering*]
HAC .... High Alumina Cement (SAUS)
HAC .... High-Aluminous Concrete
HAC .... Higher Authority Communications (SAUS)
HAC .... Highway Action Coalition
HAC .... Hines Administrative Center [*Veterans Administration*]
HAC .... Historians of American Communism (EA)
HAC .... Historical Artillery Corps [*British*] [*An association*] (DBA)
HAC .... Historical Atlas of Canada [*Project*]
HAC .... Holland America Cruises [*Formerly, Holland-America Line*]
HAC .... Holland Australia Club [*Australia*]
HAC .... Honourable Armery Co. (SAUS)
HAC .... Honourable Artillery Co. [*Military unit*] [*British*]
HAC .... Honourable Artillery Company (SAUO)
HAC .... Honourable Artillery Corps (SAUO)
HAC .... Horticultural Advisory Council (SAUS)
HAC .... Horticultural Advisory Council for England and Wales (BI)
HAC .... Hospitals Accreditation Committee [*Australia*]
HAC .... Hot and Cold (IAA)
HAC .... House Application Committee (SAUS)
HAC .... House Appropriations Committee [*US Congress*] (AAG)
HAC .... Housing Advisory Committee (SAUO)
HAC .... Housing Advisory Council [*South Australia*]
HAC .... Housing Assistance Council (EA)
HAC .... Hover and Approach Coupler (MCD)
HAC .... Hughes Aircraft Company (SAUO)
HAC .... Human Artificial Chromosome [*Genetics*]
HAC .... Humanities Association of Canada [*See also ACH*]
HAC .... Hydraulic Analog Computer (VLIE)
HAC .... Hydrogen-Assisted Cracking (SAUS)
HAC .... Hydrogenated Amorphous Carbon [*Inorganic chemistry*]
HAC .... Hydroxyapatite Crystal (SAUS)
HAC .... Hyperactive Child (MELL)
HAC .... Hyperadrenocorticism [*Medicine*] (MELL)
HACA .... Hammered Aluminum Collectors Association (EA)
HACC .... Harrisburg Area Community College (SAUO)
HACC .... Hellenic-American Chamber of Commerce (NTPA)
HACC .... Help and Action Coordinating Committee [*Defunct*] [*France*] (EAIO)
HACC .... High Alumina Cement Concrete (SAUS)
HACC .... Holland-American Chamber of Commerce (SAUO)
HACC .... Home and Community Services (SAUO)
HAcc .... Horizontal advective Acceleration (SAUS)
HACC .... Human-Assisted Computer Control (SAUS)
HACCP .... Hazard Analysis and Critical Control Point System (SAUO)
HACCP .... Hazard Analysis Critical Control Point [*Quality control*]
HACCP .... Hazard Analysis Critical Control Points
HACD .... Home Area Customer Dialing (VLIE)
HACE .... High-Altitude Cerebral Edema [*Medicine*]
HACE .... High-Order Automatic Cross-Connect Equipment (VLIE)
HACEK .... Hemophilus, Actinobacillus, Cardiobacterium, Eikenella, and Kingella [*Gram-negative bacilli*]
HA Cell .... High Amperage Cell (SAUS)
HACES .... Helicopter Air Combat Engagement Simulation (SAUS)
HACH .... Hach Co. [*NASDAQ symbol*] (NQ)
HACHD .... Hatched (ABBR)
HACHG .... Hatching (ABBR)
HAChT .... High-Affinity Choline Transport
HACHWY .... Hatchway (ABBR)
HACHY .... Hatchery (ABBR)
HACI .... Hughes Aircraft Company, International Division (SAUO)
HACJ .... Helicopter-Applique Communications Jammer (SAUS)
hack .... hacking (SAUS)
HACK .... Hackney [*Borough of London*]
Hack Gen Aw ... Hackett on the Geneva Award Acts [*A publication*] (DLA)
Hackworth ... Hackworths Digest of International Law (SAUS)
HACL .... Harvard Air Cleaning Laboratory (NRCH)
HACL .... Host Access Class Library (SAUS)
HACL .... Hostility Adjective Check List [*Psychology*]
HACLA .... Housing Authority of the City of Los Angeles
HACLCS .... Harpoon Aircraft Command and Launch Control Set [*Missiles*] (NVT)
HACLCS .... Harpoon Aircraft Command Launch Control System (SAUO)
HACLS .... Harpoon Aircraft and Launch System (SAUS)
HACLS .... Harpoon Aircraft Command and Launch Subsystem [*Missiles*] (MCD)
HACLS .... Harpoon-type Aircraft Command and Launch Subsystem Missile (SAUS)
HACMP .... High Availability Cluster Management Protocol (SAUS)
HACMP .... High Availability Cluster Multi-Processing [*IBM Corp.*]
HACN .... Hacienda (ABBR)
HAC NOCT ... Hac Nocte [*Tonight*] [*Pharmacy*]
HACOM .... Headquarters Area Command [*Military*]
HACP .... Heavy Artillery Command Post (SAUS)
HACR .... Heating, Air Conditioning & Refrigeration (SAUS)
HACR .... Helicopter Active Control Rotor (SAUS)
HACR .... Hereditary Adenomatosis of the Colon and Rectum [*Medicine*] (DMAA)
HACS .... Hazard Assessment Computer System [*Coast Guard*]
HACS .... Hazards Assessment Computer System (SAUO)
HACS .... Helicopter Armoured Crashworthy Seat (SAUS)
HACS .... High-Angle Control Section (SAUS)
HACS .... High-Angle Control System [*British military*] (DMA)
HACS .... Homeostatic Adaptive Control System
HACS .... Hyperactive Child Syndrome
HACSG .... Hyper Active Children's Support Group [*British*]
HACSS .... Hibernian Australian Catholic Benefit Society (SAUO)
HACT .... High-Affinity Choline Transport
HACTL .... Home Air Command Technical Leaflets (SAUO)
HACTL .... Hong Kong Air Cargo Terminal Limited (SAUO)
HACTU .... Human Action Counselling and Training Unit [*British*] (DI)
HACU .... Handling and Conditioning Unit (VLIE)
HACU .... Hispanic Association of Colleges and Universities
HACV .... Heavy Armament Combat Vehicle (SAUS)
HACV .... Heavy Armored Combat Vehicle (MILB)
HACWO .... Home Air Command Weekly Orders (SAUO)
HAD .... Casper, WY [*Location identifier*] [*FAA*] (FAAL)
HAD .... Hadassah (BJA)
Had .... Haddington's Manuscript Reports, Scotch Court of Session [*A publication*] (DLA)
Had .... Hadley's Reports [*45-48 New Hampshire*] [*A publication*] (DLA)
HAD .... Hadson Corp. [*NYSE symbol*] (COMM)
HAD .... Haemadsorption (SAUS)
HAD .... Half Amplitude Duration [*Telecommunications*] (TEL)
HAD .... Half-Anplitude Duration (SAUS)
HAD .... Halmstad [*Sweden*] [*Airport symbol*] (OAG)
HAD .... Handicappers for Accountable Democracy (EA)
HAD .... Hardness Assurance Document
HAD .... Hartland [*United Kingdom*] [*Geomagnetic observatory code*]
HAD .... Hassan Addakhil Dam [*Morocco*] [*Seismograph station code, US Geological Survey*] (SEIS)
HAD .... Hawaii Air Defense
HAD .... Hawaiian Air Depot (SAUO)
HAD .... Head Acceleration Device (PDAA)

HAD............ Health Assessment Document [*Environmental Protection Agency*] (GFGA)
HAD............ Health Assessment Documents [*Environment term*] (EGA)
HAD............ Health Care Alternatives Development (HCT)
HAD............ Hearing Aid Dispenser [*Otorhinolaryngology*] (DAVI)
HAD............ Heat-Activated Device (NRCH)
HAD............ Helicopter Approach/Departure [*Military*] (CAAL)
HAD............ Helicopteros Andes [*Chile*] [*ICAO designator*] (FAAC)
HAD............ Helium Abundance Detector [*Instrumentation*]
HAD............ Hemadsorption [*Hematology*]
HAD............ Herein After Described [*Legal*] [*British*] (MHDI)
HAD............ Herein Afterr Described (SAUS)
HAD............ Heterologous Antibody Disease [*Medicine*] (MELL)
HAD............ Hexamethylmelamine, Adriamycin, Diamminedichloroplatinum [*Cisplatin*] [*Antineoplastic drug regimen*]
HAD............ High Accuracy Data (SAUS)
HAD............ High-Accuracy Data [*System*] (MUGU)
HAD............ High Alcohol Drinking [*Rat strain*]
HAD............ High-Altitude Density [*Sounding rocket*]
HAD............ High-Altitude Diagnostic [*Unit*] [*Rocket launcher*]
HAD............ High-Aluminum Defect (SAUS)
HAD............ HIV-Associated Dementia (SAUS)
HAD............ Hole-Accumulated Diode [*Sony Corp.*]
HAD............ Hole Accumulation Diode (SAUS)
HAD............ Home Address Data (SAUS)
HAD............ Home Air Depot (SAUO)
HAD............ Honeywell Aeronautical Division (SAUO)
HAD............ Horizontal Array of Dipoles
HAD............ Horizontal Diffusion (SAUS)
HAD............ Hospital Administration [*or Administrator*]
HAD............ Hospital Administrator (SAUO)
HAD............ Hypersonic Aerothermal Dynamics (SAA)
HAD............ Hypophysectomized Alloxandiabetic (SAUS)
HADA.......... Hawaiian Air Defense Area (SAUO)
HADA.......... Hawaiian Defense Area
HADA.......... High Availability Disk Array [*Computer science*] (AGLO)
HADAPS....... Hydrographic Automated Data Acquisitioning and Processing System (MCD)
HADARS...... Hydrographic Automated Data Acquisitioning and Processing System (SAUO)
HADAS......... Helmet Airborne Display and Sight (MCD)
HADB.......... Dagabour [*Ethiopia*] [*ICAO location identifier*] (ICLI)
HADB.......... Hazardous Substances Data Bank [*National Library of Medicine*] [*Information service or system*]
HADB.......... High-Altitude Dive Bomb [*Military*]
HADC.......... Dessie/Combolcha [*Ethiopia*] [*ICAO location identifier*] (ICLI)
HADC.......... HIV [*Human Immunodeficiency Virus*] -Associated Dementia Complex [*Medicine*]
HADC.......... Holloman Air Development Center [*Air Force*]
Had Chy Jur... Haddan's Administrative Jurisdiction of the Court of Chancery [*A publication*] (DLA)
Hadco.......... Hadco Corp. [*Associated Press*] (SAG)
HADD.......... Dembidollo [*Ethiopia*] [*ICAO location identifier*] (ICLI)
Hadd........... Haddington's Manuscript Reports, Scotch Court of Session [*A publication*] (DLA)
HADD.......... Harmful Alteration, Disruption or Destruction of Fish Habitat Permit (FOTI)
HADD.......... Hawaiian Air Defense Division
HADD.......... Hydroxyapatite Deposition Disease [*Medicine*] (DAVI)
Haddington... Haddington's Manuscript Reports, Scotch Court of Session [*A publication*] (DLA)
HADE.......... Hadson Europe, Inc. (SAUO)
HA-DEC....... Hour Angle-Declination [*Type of antenna mounting*]
HADES........ Helicopter Acoustic Detection System (ACAE)
HADES........ Hughes Analog Design Expert System (ACAE)
HADES........ Hunting Area-Denial System (SAUS)
HADES........ Hypersonic Air Data Entry System
HAd-I.......... Hemadsorption Inhibition (STED)
HADIL.......... Halifax-Dartmouth Industries Ltd. (SAUO)
HADIOS........ Honeywell Analog-Digital Input-Output Subsystem (IAA)
HADIS.......... Hadamard Imaging Spectrometer (PDAA)
HADIS.......... High-speed Avionics Data Instrumentation System (SAUS)
HADIS.......... Huddersfield and District Information Service [*British*] (NITA)
HADIZ.......... Hawaiian Air Defense Identification Zone
HADL.......... Dallol [*Ethiopia*] [*ICAO location identifier*] (ICLI)
Hadl........... Hadley's Reports [*45-48 New Hampshire*] [*A publication*] (DLA)
HADLAPS..... Hydrographic Automated Logging And Processing Systems (SAUS)
Hadley......... Hadley's Reports [*45-48 New Hampshire*] [*A publication*] (DLA)
HAD Loan.... Housing Assistance Division Loan (SAUO)
Hadl Rom Law... Hadley's Introduction to the Roman Law [*A publication*] (DLA)
HADM.......... Debre Marcos [*Ethiopia*] [*ICAO location identifier*] (ICLI)
HADM.......... Heavy Atomic Demolition Munition [*Military*] (AABC)
HADN.......... Danguilla [*Ethiopia*] [*ICAO location identifier*] (ICLI)
HAD-N......... Haemadsorption-Neutralization (SAUS)
HAD(N)........ Head of Aircraft Department (Naval) [*British*]
Hadng.......... Hardinge, Inc. [*Associated Press*] (SAG)
HADO.......... Dodola [*Ethiopia*] [*ICAO location identifier*] (ICLI)
HADOPAD.... High-Altitude Delayed Opening Parachute Actuation Device (MCD)
HADOSS...... HWWA-Dossiers [*Society for Business Information*] [*Information service or system*] (IID)
HADR.......... Dire Dawa/Aba Tenna Dejazmatch Yilma [*Ethiopia*] [*ICAO location identifier*] (ICLI)
Hadr........... Hadrian [*of Scriptores Historiae Augustae*] [*Classical studies*] (OCD)
HADR.......... Halsey Drug Co., Inc. (SAUO)
HADR.......... Hughes Air Defence (or Defense) Radar (SAUS)
HADR.......... Hughes Air Defense RADAR [*Military*]
HAD Rocket... High-Altitude Density Rocket (SAUS)
Hadronic J... Hadronic Journal (journ.) (SAUS)
Hadronic J Suppl... Hadronic Journal Supplement (journ.) (SAUS)
HADS.......... Hadson Corp. (SAUO)
HADS.......... Hawaii Air Defense System
HADS.......... Hawaiian Air Defense System (SAUO)
HADS.......... Helicopter Air Data System (SAUO)
HADS.......... Hierarchical Applications Data Structure (SAUS)
HADS.......... High Accuracy Digital Sensor (SAUS)
HADS.......... High Altitude Defense System (ACAE)
HADS.......... High-Altitude Dive Bomb (SAUS)
HADS.......... Hospital Anxiety and Depression Scale [*Medicine*] (DMAA)
HADS.......... Hughes Advanced Development System (ACAE)
HADS.......... Hydrometeorological Automated Data System (SAUS)
HADS.......... Hypersonic Air Data Sensor (IEEE)
HADS.......... Hypersonic Air Data System (SAUS)
HADT.......... Debre Tabor [*Ethiopia*] [*ICAO location identifier*] (ICLI)
HADTS........ High-Accuracy Data Transmission System (MUGU)
HADZ.......... Hawthorne Army Ammunition Depot [*Federal Railroad Administration identification code*]
HAE............ Haemonetics Corp. [*NYSE symbol*] (SPSG)
HAE............ Hannibal, MO [*Location identifier*] [*FAA*] (FAAL)
HAE............ Hatia [*Bangladesh*] [*Airport symbol*] (AD)
HAE............ Havasupai [*Arizona*] [*Airport symbol*] (OAG)
HAE............ Health Appraisal Examination (DMAA)
HAE............ Hearing Aid Evaluation [*Otorhinolayrngology*] (DAVI)
HAE............ Height Above Ellipsoid (SAUS)
HAE............ Hepatic Artery Embolization [*Medicine*] (DAVI)
HAE............ Hereditary Angioedema [*Medicine*] (STED)
HAE............ Hereditary Angioneurotic Edema [*Medicine*]
HAE............ High Altitude Endurance
HAE............ Honorary Academician Extraordinary of the Royal Academy-Sir Winston Churchill, K.G. (SAUO)
HAE............ Hot-Air Engine (SAUS)
HAEA.......... Hungarian Atomic Energy Agency (SAUO)
HAEB.......... Header Analysis Error Byte (SAUS)
HAEC.......... High Altitude Economic Carrier (PDAA)
HAEC.......... High Altuide Economic Center (SAUS)
HAEC.......... House of Representatives Armed Services Committee (SAUS)
HAEC.......... Human Aortic Endothelial Cell
HAEC.......... Human Artificial Episomal Chromosome (HGEN)
Haeck.......... Haeckelian (SAUS)
Haeck.......... Haeckelism (SAUS)
HAECO........ Hong Kong Aircraft Engineering Company Ltd. (SAUO)
HAECO........ Hong Kong Aircraft Engineering Co. (SAUS)
HAEE.......... Harwell Atomic Energy Establishment
HAEH.......... Horizontal Axis Electrical Hairspring
HAEM.......... Haemolysis [*British*]
HAEMAT...... Haematocrit [*British*]
HAEMATOL... Haematology [*British*]
Haemon....... Haemonetics Corp. [*Associated Press*] (SAG)
HAEMORRH... Haemorrhage [*British*]
HAEMP........ High-Altitude Electromagnetic Pulse
HAER.......... Historic American Engineering Record [*Department of the Interior*]
HAES.......... Haitian Association of Engineers and Scientists (SAUO)
HAES.......... Hawaii Agricultural Experiment Station [*Honolulu*]
HAES.......... High Altitude Effects Simulation (SAUO)
HAES.......... High-Altitude Effects Simulation [*Defense Nuclear Agency*]
HAES.......... High Altuide Effects Simulation (SAUS)
HaF............ Hageman Factor (STED)
HAF............ Haifa [*Israel*] [*Seismograph station code, US Geological Survey*] [*Closed*] (SEIS)
HAF............ Half Moon Bay, CA [*Location identifier*] [*FAA*] (FAAL)
HAF............ Hallmark Financial Services [*AMEX symbol*] (SAG)
HAF............ Halogen Acid Furnace (EEVL)
HAF............ Head Administration and Finance (SAUS)
HAF............ Headquarters, Air Force (AFM)
HAF............ Headquarters, Allied Forces
HAF............ Heavy Aircraft Fuel (MSA)
HAF............ Hebrew Arts Foundation (EA)
HAF............ Helicopter Assault Force (NVT)
HAF............ Helicopter Association of Florida (SAUO)
HAF............ Hellenic Air Force [*Greece*] [*ICAO designator*] (FAAC)
HAF............ Hellenic Armed Forces (NATG)
HAF............ Helms Athletic Foundation [*Later, Citizens Savings Athletic Foundation*] (EA)
HAF............ Helvetia-America Federation (SAUO)
HAF............ Hepatic Arterial Flow [*Medicine*] (STED)
HAF............ High Abrasion Furnace (SAUS)
HAF............ High-Abrasion Furnace (IEEE)
HAF............ High-Altitude Fluorescence (IEEE)
HAF............ High-Altitude Fuze [*To activate weapons*]
HAF............ High Angle Firing (SAUS)
HAF............ Home Air Force (SAUO)
HAF............ Honduran Air Force (SAUS)
HAF............ Hospital Affiliates International, Inc. (SAUO)
HAF............ Human Antitumor Factor [*Biochemistry*]
HAF............ Hypersonic Aerothermaldynamic Facility
HAFB.......... Heavy Assault Floating Bridge [*British military*] (DMA)
HAFB.......... Hill Air Force Base (SAA)
HAFB.......... Hillfield Airbase [*Federal Railroad Administration identification code*]
HAFB.......... Holloman Air Force Base [*New Mexico*]
HAFB.......... Hollowan Air Force Base (SAUS)
HAFB.......... Homestead Air Force Base (SAUO)

HAF Black.... High Abrasion (or Abrasive) Furnace Black (SAUS)
HAFBLCK..... High-Abrasion Furnace Black (IAA)
HAFC........... High-Altitude Forecast Center
HAFC........... Horizontal Automatic Frequency Control [*Computer science*] (AGLO)
HAFC........... Hoyt Axton Fan Club (EA)
HAFCE......... Headquarters Allied Forces Central Europe (SAUO)
HAFCS......... Howitzer Advanced Fire Control System (SAUS)
HAFE........... Harpers Ferry National Historical Park
Haff............. Myoglobinuria [*Medicine*] (EDAA)
HAFID.......... Hydrogen Atmosphere Flame Ionization Detector
HAFM.......... Helium Accumulation Fluence Monitor (SAUS)
HAFMED....... Headquarters, Allied Forces, Mediterranean
HAFN........... Fincha [*Ethiopia*] [*ICAO location identifier*] (ICLI)
HAFNE......... Headquarters Allied Forces Northern Europe (SAUO)
HAFO........... Home Accounting and Finance Office
HAFOE......... High Air Flow with Oxygen Enrichment (PDAA)
HAFOP......... Health Advocates for Older People (ADWA)
HAFP........... Hawaii Academy of Family Physicians (SRA)
HAFP........... Human Alpha-Fetoprotein [*Medicine*] (EDAA)
HAFRA......... Hat and Allied Feltmakers Research Association (SAUO)
HAFS........... Heilongjiang Academy of Forestry Sciences (SAUO)
HAFS........... Homosexuals Anonymous Fellowship Services (EA)
HAFSE......... Headquarters Allied Forces Southern Europe (SAUO)
HAFSE......... Headquarters, Armed Forces, Southern Europe (SAUS)
Hafslnd........ Hafslund Nycomed AS [*Associated Press*] (SAG)
Hafslnd........ Hafslund Nycomed AS [*Associated Press*] (SAG)
HAFTB......... Holloman Air Force Test Base [*New Mexico*] (AAG)
Hag............. Hagan's Reports [*Utah*] [*A publication*] (DLA)
Hag............. Hagan's Reports [*West Virginia*] [*A publication*] (DLA)
Hag............. Haggai [*Old Testament book*]
Hag............. Haggard's English Admiralty Reports [*A publication*] (DLA)
Hag............. Hagigah (BJA)
HAG............ [*The*] Hague [*Netherlands*] [*Airport symbol*] (AD)
HAG............ Hardware Analysis Group (SAUO)
HAG............ Harvest Aviation Ltd. [*British*] [*ICAO designator*] (FAAC)
HAG............ Heat-Aggregated Globulin (DB)
HAG............ Heavy Artillery Group (SAUO)
HAG............ Helicopter Action Group (NVT)
HAG............ High Explosive Anti-Armor Grenade (SAUS)
HAG............ Hold for Arrival of Goods
HAG............ Home Address Gap [*Computer science*] (MHDB)
HAG............ Housing Association Grant [*British*]
HAG............ Human Antihemophilic Globulin [*Medicine*] (EDAA)
HAG............ Humanitarian Assistance Group [*Iraq*]
HAG............ Hydrothermally-Altered Granite [*Geology*]
HAG............ Hydroxyaminoguanidine [*Biochemistry*]
Hag Adm..... Haggard's English Admiralty Reports [*A publication*] (DLA)
Hagan.......... Hagan's Reports [*Utah*] [*A publication*] (DLA)
HAGB.......... Goba [*Ethiopia*] [*ICAO location identifier*] (ICLI)
HAG COM.... Haga Comitum [*The Hague*] [*Imprint*] (ROG)
Hag Con...... Haggard's English Consistory Reports [*161 English Reprint*] [*A publication*] (DLA)
HAGE.......... Human Activity and Global Environment (SAUO)
Hag Ecc....... Haggard's English Ecclesiastical Reports [*162 English Reprint*] [*A publication*] (DLA)
HAGER......... Hagersville, ON [*American Association of Railroads railroad junction routing code*]
HAGG.......... Heat-Aggregated Gamma Globulin [*Clinical chemistry*]
HAGG.......... Hyperimmune Antivariola Gamma Globulin
Hagg Adm... Haggard's English Admiralty Reports [*A publication*] (DLA)
Hagg Adm (Eng)... Haggard's English Admiralty Reports [*161 English Reprint*] [*A publication*] (DLA)
Haggar......... Haggar Corp. [*Associated Press*] (SAG)
Hagg Con..... Haggard's English Consistory Reports [*161 English Reprint*] [*A publication*] (DLA)
Hagg Cons... Haggard's English Consistory Reports [*161 English Reprint*] [*A publication*] (DLA)
Hagg Consist... Haggard's English Consistory Reports [*161 English Reprint*] [*A publication*] (DLA)
Hagg Consist (Eng)... Haggard's English Consistory Reports [*161 English Reprint*] [*A publication*] (DLA)
Hagg Ecc..... Haggard's English Ecclesiastical Reports [*162 English Reprint*] [*A publication*] (DLA)
Hagg Eccl.... Haggard's English Ecclesiastical Reports [*162 English Reprint*] [*1827-33*] [*A publication*] (DLA)
Hagg Eccl (Eng)... Haggard's English Ecclesiastical Reports [*162 English Reprint*] [*A publication*] (DLA)
HAGH.......... Ghinnir [*Ethiopia*] [*ICAO location identifier*] (ICLI)
HAGH.......... Hydroxyacyl-Glutathione Hydrolase (DMAA)
hagio........... hagiogracies (SAUS)
hagio........... hagiogracy (SAUS)
hagio........... hagiographer (SAUS)
hagio........... hagiographist (SAUS)
hagio........... hagiography (SAUS)
hagio........... hagiol (SAUS)
hagio........... hagiolater (SAUS)
hagio........... hagiolatrous (SAUS)
hagio........... hagiologies (SAUS)
hagio........... hagiolotry (SAUS)
hagio........... hagioscope (SAUS)
hagio........... hagioscopic (SAUS)
HAGIOL....... Hagiology (ABBR)
HAGL........... Galadi [*Ethiopia*] [*ICAO location identifier*] (ICLI)
HAGL........... Haggle (ABBR)
HAGL........... Hand-Held Grenade Launcher (SAUO)
HAGLD......... Haggled (ABBR)
HAGLG......... Haggling (ABBR)
HAGLR......... Haggler (ABBR)
HAGLST....... Hagiologist (ABBR)
HAGM.......... Gambella [*Ethiopia*] [*ICAO location identifier*] (ICLI)
HAGN.......... Gondar [*Ethiopia*] [*ICAO location identifier*] (ICLI)
Hagn & M.... Hagner and Miller's Reports [*2 Maryland Chancery*] [*A publication*] (DLA)
Hagn & Mill... Hagner and Miller's Reports [*2 Maryland Chancery*] [*A publication*] (DLA)
HAGO........... Gode [*Ethiopia*] [*ICAO location identifier*] (ICLI)
HAGO........... Heavy Atmospheric Gas Oil [*Petroleum product*]
HAGR........... Gore [*Ethiopia*] [*ICAO location identifier*] (ICLI)
HAGR........... Hamilton Grange National Memorial
HAGS........... Hispanic American Geriatrics Society (EA)
HAGTN......... Hagerstown, MD [*American Association of Railroads railroad junction routing code*]
HAGTNS....... Haughtiness (ABBR)
HAGTR......... Haughtier (ABBR)
HAGTST....... Haughtiest (ABBR)
HAGTY......... Haughtily (ABBR)
HAGU........... Gura [*Ethiopia*] [*ICAO location identifier*] (ICLI)
Hague Ct Rep... Hague Court Reports [*A publication*] (DLA)
HAH............ Healthcare Association of Hawaii (SRA)
HAH............ Jacksonville, NC [*Location identifier*] [*FAA*] (FAAL)
HAH............ Moroni [*Comoro Islands*] Hahaia Airport [*Airport symbol*] (OAG)
HAHA.......... Hartmann-Hahn Condition or Match (SAUS)
HA-HA-SO.... Help, Assert, Humor, Avoid, Self-Talk, and Own It [*Assertive strategy*]
HAHI........... Help At Home [*NASDAQ symbol*] (TTSB)
HAHI........... Help At Home, Inc. [*NASDAQ symbol*] (SAG)
HAHIW......... Help At Home Wrrt [*NASDAQ symbol*] (TTSB)
HAHM.......... Debre Zeit/Harar Meda [*Ethiopia*] [*ICAO location identifier*] (ICLI)
HAHN.......... Hahn Automotive Warehouse [*NASDAQ symbol*] (TTSB)
HAHN.......... Hahn Automotive Warehouse, Inc. [*NASDAQ symbol*] (SAG)
HahnAut....... Hahn Automotive Warehouse, Inc. [*Associated Press*] (SAG)
Hahnemann U... Hahnemann University (GAGS)
HAHO.......... Harmony Holdings [*NASDAQ symbol*] (TTSB)
HAHO.......... Harmony Holdings, Inc. [*NASDAQ symbol*] (SAG)
HAHO.......... High Altitude High Opening (SAUO)
HAHO.......... High Altitude/High Opening [*Army*] (ADDR)
HAHO.......... High-Altitude High Opening (SAUS)
HAHP.......... Heat Activated Heat Pump (SAUS)
HAHR.......... Hispanic American Historical Review [*A publication*] (BRI)
HAHS.......... Hooved Animal Humane Society (EA)
HA(HS)........ Hospital Apprentice, High School
HAHS.......... Hossana [*Ethiopia*] [*ICAO location identifier*] (ICLI)
HAHST......... High-Altitude High Speed Target (SAUS)
HAHT.......... Hypersonic Arc-Heated Tunnel [*Langley Research Center*] [*NASA*]
HAHTG......... Horse Anti-Human Thymus Globulin [*Immunology*] (MAE)
HAHTsite..... HAHTsite Integrated Internet Development System (HODG)
HAHU.......... Humera [*Ethiopia*] [*ICAO location identifier*] (ICLI)
HAI............. Century Aviation International Ltd. [*Canada*] [*FAA designator*] (FAAC)
hai............. Haida [*MARC language code*] [*Library of Congress*] (LCCP)
HAI............. Haiti (ABBR)
HAI............. Haiwee [*California*] [*Seismograph station code, US Geological Survey*] [*Closed*] (SEIS)
HAI............. Hampton Indus [*AMEX symbol*] (TTSB)
HAI............. Hampton Industries, Inc. [*AMEX symbol*] (SPSG)
HAI............. Handbook of Artillery Instruments (SAUS)
HAI............. Handwriting Analysts, Incorporated (SAUO)
HAI............. Handwriting Analysts, International (EA)
HAI............. Hawaiian Airlines, Inc. (EFIS)
HAI............. Health Action International (EA)
HAI............. Helicopter Altitude Indicator (SAUO)
HAI............. Helicopter Association International (EA)
HAI............. Helicopter Attitude Indicator
HAI............. Hellenic Aerospace Industries (SAUO)
HAI............. Hellenic Aerospace Industry [*Greek*]
HAI............. Hellenic Aerospace Industry Ltd. (SAUO)
HAI............. Hellenic Arms Industry [*Greek*]
HAI............. Hemagglutination Inhibition [*Immunochemistry*]
HAI............. Hemagglutination Inhibition Assay (SAUS)
HAI............. Hemagglutinin Inhibition (STED)
HAI............. Hepatic Arterial Infusion (STED)
HAI............. Hepatic Artery Infusion [*Chemotherapy*]
HAI............. High-Altitude Interceptor (SAUS)
HAI............. Historically Advantaged Institute (SAUS)
HAI............. Holland Automation International [*Software retailer*] (NITA)
HAI............. Holocaust Awareness Institute (SAUS)
HAI............. Hospital-Acquired Infection [*Medicine*]
HAI............. Hospital Audiences (EA)
HAI............. Hospital Audiences Inc. (SAUS)
HAI............. Hot Air Intake [*Automotive engineering*]
HAI............. Human Awareness Institute (SAUS)
HAI............. Hydroscience Associates, Inc., Emerson (SAUS)
HAI............. Hypoglycemia Association, Inc. (NRGU)
HAI............. Three Rivers, MI [*Location identifier*] [*FAA*] (FAAL)
HAIA........... Hearing Aid Industry Association [*British*] (DBA)
HAIA........... Home Arts and Industries Association (SAUO)
HAIA........... Honorary Member, American Institute of Architects (DAC)
HAIC........... Harwyn Industries Corporation (SAUO)
HAIC........... Hearing Aid Industry Conference [*Later, HIA*] (EA)
HAIC........... Hermetic Aircraft International Corporation (SAUO)
HAIC........... Hetero-Atom in Context (SAUS)

HAIC Indexing... Hetero-Atom-in-Context Indexing (SAUS)
HAID .... Hand Acoustic Intrusion Detector (SAUO)
HAID .... Hand-Emplaced Acoustic Intrusion Detector (NVT)
HAID .... Hispanic Americans Information Directory [*A publication*]
HAIDE .... Hostile Aircraft Identification Equipment (DWSG)
HAIDEX .... Hughes Artificial Intelligence Diagnostic Expert [*Hughes Aircraft Co.*] [*Army*]
HAIDEX .... Hughes Artificial Intelligence Expert (ACAE)
HAIG .... Helsinki Agreements Implementation Group (SAUO)
HAII .... Human Analysis & Interpretation of Intelligency (SAUO)
HAIIS .... Headquarters Administration Issuance Index System (SAUO)
HAIIS .... Headquarters Administrative Issuance Index System [*Military*] (DNAB)
HAIKU .... Heat Advection Investigation in the East Kuroshio (SAUS)
HAIL............ High-Altitude Inversion Layer (SAUS)
HAIL............ Holographic Array for Ionospheric Lightning [*Astrophysics*]
Hailes.......... Dalrymple (Lord Hailes). Decisions of the Scotch Court of Session [*1776-91*] [*A publication*] (DLA)
Hailes Ann... Hailes' Annals of Scotland [*A publication*] (DLA)
Hailes Dec... Hailes' Decisions, Scotch Court of Sessions [*A publication*] (DLA)
HAILSWATH... South Dakota Hail Studies (SAUS)
HAIN .... Hain Food Group [*Toronto Stock Exchange symbol*] (SG)
HAIN .... Health Action Information Network (ADWA)
HainFood....... Hain Food Group, Inc. [*Associated Press*] (SAG)
Hain JP........ Haine's Illinois Justice of the Peace [*A publication*] (DLA)
HAINS........... High Accuracy Inertial Navigation System (SAUO)
HAIR .... Help Alopecia International Research [*Defunct*] (EA)
HAIR .... High Accuracy Instrumentation Radar (SAUO)
HAIR .... High-Accuracy Instrumentation RADAR (DNAB)
HAIR .... High Altitude IR (SAUS)
HAIR-AN ...... Hyperandrogenism, Insulin Resistance, and Acanthosis Nigricans Syndrome [*Medicine*] (DMAA)
HAIRCTTNG... Haircutting
HAIRDS........ High-Altitude Infrared Detecting Set (MCD)
HAIRS.......... High-Altitude Infrared Source (SAUS)
HAIRS.......... High-Altitude Test and Evaluation of Infrared Sources (MCD)
HAIS .... Hawaiian Air Intelligence System (SAUO)
HAIS .... Hydroacoustic Information System (SAUS)
HAISAM .... Hashed Index Sequential Access Method (PDAA)
HAISC .... Hughes Aircraft International Service Company (ACAE)
HAISCO .... Hughes Aircraft International Service Co. (SAUO)
HAISS .... High-Altitude Infrared Sensor System
HAIST .... Human Abilities In Software Technology (SAUS)
HAIT............ Haiti
Hait............. Haitian (DIAR)
HAIT............ Hash Algorithm Information Table
HAIT............ Hemagglutination Inhibition Test [*Medicine*] (EDAA)
HAIZ............ Halbuck Industries [*Federal Railroad Administration identification code*]
HAJ............. Hajvairy Airlines [*Pakistan*] [*ICAO designator*] (FAAC)
HAJ............. Hanover [*Germany*] [*Airport symbol*] (OAG)
HAJC........... Hawaiian Area Joint Committee [*Military*] (CINC)
HAJJ .... Jijiga [*Ethiopia*] [*ICAO location identifier*] (ICLI)
HAJM........... Jimma [*Ethiopia*] [*ICAO location identifier*] (ICLI)
HAK .... Adelanto, CA [*Location identifier*] [*FAA*] (FAAL)
HAK .... Haikou [*China*] [*Airport symbol*] (OAG)
HAK .... Hakodate [*Japan*] [*Seismograph station code, US Geological Survey*] (SEIS)
Hak.............. Hamster Kidney [*Medicine*] (EDAA)
HAK .... Harka Air Services [*Nigeria*] [*FAA designator*] (FAAC)
HAK .... Hawkish (ABBR)
HAK .... Horizontal Access Kit (NASA)
HAKASH....... Hayl Kashish [*Elderly Army*] [*Israel*]
HAKD .... Kabre Dare [*Ethiopia*] [*ICAO location identifier*] (ICLI)
HAKL .... Kelafo [*Ethiopia*] [*ICAO location identifier*] (ICLI)
HAKO........... Hako Minuteman, Inc. (SAUO)
HakSoc........ Hakluyt Society (SAUO)
Hal.............. Halakha (BJA)
Hal.............. Halex (SAUS)
Hal.............. Halieuticon Liber [*of Ovid*] [*Classical studies*] (OCD)
HAL............. Halifax [*Nova Scotia*] [*Seismograph station code, US Geological Survey*] (SEIS)
Hal.............. Hallah (BJA)
HAL............. Halliburton Co. [*NYSE symbol*] [*Toronto Stock Exchange symbol*] (SPSG)
Hal.............. Halogen [*Medicine*] (EDAA)
hal.............. Halogen (IDOE)
HAL............. Halogen (WDAA)
hal.............. halogenic (SAUS)
HAL............. Haloperidol [*A tranquilizer*]
Hal.............. Halothane [*Medicine*] (EDAA)
HAL............. Halothane [*Also, H*] [*An anesthetic*]
HAL............. Hamburg-America Line (SAUS)
HAL............. Hamburg-Amerika Linie [*Hamburg-America Steamship Co.*]
HAL............. Hamburg-Atlantic Line (SAUO)
HAL............. Handicapped Assistance Loan
HAL............. Hard Array Logic (SAUS)
HAL............. Hardboards Australia Ltd. (SAUS)
HAL............. Hardware Abstraction Layer [*Computer science*] (PCM)
HAL............. Harwell Automated Library (SAUS)
HAL............. Harwell Automated Loans [*Library circulation system*]
HAL............. Hash Algorithm Library
HAL............. Hawaiian Airlines, Inc. [*ICAO designator*] (FAAC)
HAL............. Hawaiian Airlines, Limited (SAUO)
HAL............. Hazards Assessment Laboratory [*Colorado State University*] [*Research center*] (RCD)
H-A-L.......... Head-Arm-Leg [*Medicine*]
HAL............. Heads-Up Audio-Vision Logistics [*NASA*]
HAL............. Health Affairs Library (SAUO)
HAL............. Height Above Landing (SAUS)
HAL............. Height above Landing Area (SAUO)
HA(L).......... Helicopter Attack Squadron (Light) (CINC)
HAL............. Hemispheric Activation Level [*Computer science*] (BYTE)
HAL............. Hepatic Artery Ligation [*Medicine*]
HAL............. Hetra Assembler Language (SAUS)
HAL............. Heuristically-Programmed Algorithmic [*Name of computer in film, "2001: A Space Odyssey." Acronym is also considered to have been formed by combining the letters before IBM in the alphabet*]
HAL............. High Activity Locations (SAUS)
HAL............. Highly Active Liquid [*Nuclear energy*] (NUCP)
HAL............. Highly Automated Logic [*Computer science*]
HAL............. High-Order Algorithmic Language (SSD)
HAL............. High Order Articulated Language (SAUS)
HAL............. High-Order Articulated Language [*Computer science*] (MCD)
HAL............. High Order Assembly Language (SAUS)
HAL............. High-Order Assembly Language [*Computer science*] (NASA)
HAL............. High Temperature Acoustic Levitator (SAUS)
HAL............. Hindustan Aeronautics Limited (SAUO)
HAL............. Hindustan Aircraft Limited (SAUO)
HAL............. Hoechst Australia Ltd. [*Commercial firm*]
HAL............. Holding and Approach-to-Land [*Procedure*] [*Aviation*]
HAL............. Holland America Line (SAUS)
HAL............. Holland-America Line [*Later, Holland America Cruises*]
HAL............. Home Automated Living
HAL............. Honeywell Author Language (SAUS)
HAL............. Hot Air Levelling (SAUS)
HAL............. House Programmed Array Logic (SAUS)
HAL............. Houston Aerospace Language [*NASA*] (NASA)
HAL............. Houston Area League
HAL............. Human Access Language [*Computer science*]
HAL............. Hyperalimentation [*Intravenous feeding*] (DAVI)
HAL............. Hypogastric Artery Ligation [*Medicine*]
HAL............. Hypoplastic Acute Leukemia [*Medicine*] (MELL)
HALA .... Awash [*Ethiopia*] [*ICAO location identifier*] (ICLI)
HALA .... Height Above Landing Area (SAUS)
HALAMINE... Halogenated Amine (ACAE)
Hal Anal ...... Hale's Analysis of the Law [*A publication*] (DLA)
Hal & Tw..... Hall and Twell's English Chancery Reports [*47 English Reprint*] [*A publication*] (DLA)
HALAP .... Hughes Associative Linear Array Processor (ACAE)
HALAT .... Hebraeisches und Aramaeisches Lexikon zum Alten Testament [*Leiden*] (BJA)
HALB .... Halberton [*England*]
Halbtn.......... Halliburton Co. [*Associated Press*] (SAG)
Halc............ Halcomb's Mining Cases [*England*] [*A publication*] (DLA)
HALC .... High Affinity-Low Capacity (DMAA)
HALCA .... Highly Advanced Laboratory for Communications and Astronomy [*Japanese satellite*]
Hal Civ Law... Hallifax's Analysis of the Civil Law [*A publication*] (DLA)
Halc Min Cas... Halcomb's Mining Cases [*England*] [*A publication*] (DLA)
HALCON....... High-Altitude Long-Focus Convergent Mapping System
HALCON Mapping System... High-Altitude Long-focus Convergent Mapping System (SAUS)
Hal Const Hist... Hallam's Constitutional History of England [*A publication*] (DLA)
HALDIGS...... Howard and Lajes Digital Graphic System (SAUO)
HALDIS........ Halifax and District Information Service [*British*] (NITA)
HALE........... Haleakala National Park
Hale............ Hale's English Common Law [*A publication*] (DLA)
Hale............ Hale's Reports [*33-37 California*] [*A publication*] (DLA)
HALE........... High-Altitude, Long-Endurance [*Proposed unmanned reconnaissance drone*] [*Military*]
HALE........... High Altitude Long Endurance study (SAUO)
HALE........... Hilevel Assembly Language Environment [*Hilever Technology Inc.*] [*Operating systems assembler*] (NITA)
Hale Anal .... Hale's Analysis of the Law [*A publication*] (DLA)
Hale C L...... Hale's History of the Common Law [*A publication*] (DLA)
Hale Com Law... Hale's History of the Common Law [*A publication*] (DLA)
Hale Cr Prec... Hale's Precedents in (Ecclesiastical) Criminal Cases [*1475-1640*] [*A publication*] (DLA)
Hale De Jure Mar... Hale's De Jure Maris, Appendix to Hall on the Sea Shore [*A publication*] (DLA)
Hale De Port Mar... Hale's De Portibus Maris [*A publication*] (DLA)
Hale Ecc...... Hale's English Ecclesiastical Reports [*1583-1736*] [*A publication*] (DLA)
Hale Hist Eng Law... Hale's History of the English Law [*A publication*] (DLA)
Hale Jur HL... Hale's Jurisdiction of the House of Lords [*1796*] [*A publication*] (DLA)
HalEP........... Hallwood Energy Partners Ltd. [*Associated Press*] (SAG)
Hale Parl..... Hale's History of Parliament [*2nd ed.*] [*1745*] [*A publication*] (DLA)
Hale PC....... Hale's Pleas of the Crown [*England*] [*A publication*] (DLA)
Hale PC (Eng)... Hale's Pleas of the Crown [*England*] [*A publication*] (DLA)
Hale Prec .... Hale's Precedents in (Ecclesiastical) Criminal Cases [*1475-1640*] [*A publication*] (DLA)
Hale's.......... Hale's Precedents in (Ecclesiastical) Criminal Cases [*1475-1640*] [*A publication*] (DLA)
Hale Sug CM... Hale's Suggestion on Courts-Martial [*A publication*] (DLA)
Hale Sum .... Hale's Summary of the Pleas of the Crown [*England*] [*A publication*] (DLA)
Hal Ev.......... Halsted's Digest of the Law of Evidence [*A publication*] (DLA)

HALEX .... Halogen Lamp Experiment (SAUS)
HALF .... Half-plate (VRA)
Half Adj .... Half Adjust (SAUS)
HALFCE .... Headquarters Allied Land Forces Central Europe (SAUO)
HALFSE .... Headquarters Allied Land Forces Southern Europe (SAUS)
HALFSE .... Headquarters Land Forces Southern Europe (SAUO)
HALFSEE .... Headquarters Allied Land Forces Southeastern Europe (SAUO)
halftmb .... Half-timber (VRA)
Halh Gent L... Halhed's Code of Gentoo Laws [*A publication*] (DLA)
HALIF .... Halifax, NS [*American Association of Railroads railroad junction routing code*]
Halifax .... Halifax Corp. [*Associated Press*] (SAG)
Halifax .... Sisters of Charity of St. Vicent-de-Paul (SAUO)
Halifax Anal... Halifax' Analysis of the Roman Civil Law [*A publication*] (DLA)
Hal Int Law... Halleck's International Law [*A publication*] (DLA)
Halk .... Halkerston's Compendium of Scotch Faculty Decisions [*A publication*] (DLA)
Halk .... Halkerston's Digest of the Scotch Marriage Law [*A publication*] (DLA)
Halk .... Halkerston's Latin Maxims [*A publication*] (DLA)
Halk Comp... Halkerston's Compendium of Scotch Faculty Decisions [*A publication*] (DLA)
Halk Dig ...... Halkerston's Digest of the Scotch Marriage Law [*A publication*] (DLA)
Halk Lat Max... Halkerston's Latin Maxims [*A publication*] (DLA)
Halk Max ..... Halkerston's Latin Maxims [*A publication*] (DLA)
Halk Tech Terms... Halkerston's Technical Terms of the Law [*A publication*] (DLA)
Hall .... Decisions of the Water Courts [*1913-36*] [*South Africa*] [*A publication*] (DLA)
Hall .... Hallett's Reports [*1, 2 Colorado*] [*A publication*] (DLA)
HALL .... Hall Financial Group, Inc. [*NASDAQ symbol*] (COMM)
Hall .... Hallmark [*Record label*] [*Canada*]
HALL .... Hallmark Capital [*NASDAQ symbol*] (TTSB)
HALL .... Hallmark Capital Corp. [*NASDAQ symbol*] (SAG)
HALL .... Hall Occupational Orientation Inventory [*Hall and Tarrier*] (TES)
Hall .... Hall's New York Superior Court Reports [*A publication*] (DLA)
Hall .... Hall's Reports [*56, 57 New Hampshire*] [*A publication*] (DLA)
HALL .... Lalibela [*Ethiopia*] [*ICAO location identifier*] (ICLI)
Hall Adm ..... Hall's Admiralty Practice and Jurisdiction [*A publication*] (DLA)
Hall ALJ ..... Hall's American Law Journal [*A publication*] (DLA)
Hallam .... Hallam's Constitutional History of England [*A publication*] (DLA)
Hall Am LJ... Hall's American Law Journal [*A publication*] (DLA)
Hall & T .... Hall and Twell's English Chancery Reports [*47 English Reprint*] [*A publication*] (DLA)
Hall & Tw.... Hall and Twell's English Chancery Reports [*47 English Reprint*] [*A publication*] (DLA)
Hall & Tw (Eng)... Hall and Twell's English Chancery Reports [*47 English Reprint*] [*A publication*] (DLA)
Hal Law .... Halsted's New Jersey Law Reports [*6-12 New Jersey*] [*A publication*] (DLA)
HALLC .... Harpoon Aircraft Command and Launch Control (SAUS)
Hall Ch Pr ... Halliday's Elementary View of Chancery Proceedings [*A publication*] (DLA)
Hall Civ Law... Hallifax's Analysis of the Civil Law [*A publication*] (DLA)
Hall (Col)..... Hallett's Reports [*1, 2 Colorado*] [*A publication*] (DLA)
Hall Const Hist... Hallam's Constitutional History of England [*A publication*] (DLA)
Hall Const L... Hall's Tracts on Constitutional Law [*A publication*] (DLA)
Halleck Int Law... Halleck's International Law [*A publication*] (DLA)
HALL ED ...... High-Attitude Large Optics (SAUS)
HALL ED ...... Hindered Amines Liquid Stabilizer (SAUS)
Hall Emerig Mar Loans... Hall's Essay on Maritime Loans from the French of Emerigon [*A publication*] (DLA)
Hallett .... Hallett's Reports [*1, 2 Colorado*] [*A publication*] (DLA)
Hall Hist ..... Hallam's Constitutional History of England [*A publication*] (DLA)
Hallifax Anal (of Civil Law)... Hallifax's Analysis of the Civil Law [*A publication*] (DLA)
Hallif CL ...... Hallifax's Analysis of the Civil Law [*A publication*] (DLA)
Hall Int Law... Halleck's International Law [*A publication*] (DLA)
Hall Int Law... Hall on International Law [*A publication*] (DLA)
Hall Jour Jur... Journal of Jurisprudence (Hall's) [*A publication*] (DLA)
Hall Law of W... Halleck's Law of War [*A publication*] (DLA)
Hall LJ .... Hall's American Law Journal [*A publication*] (DLA)
Hall Marit Loans... Hall's Essay on Maritime Loans from the French of Emerigon [*A publication*] (DLA)
Hall Mex Law... Hall's Laws of Mexico Relating to Real Property, Etc. [*A publication*] (DLA)
HallmF .... Halmark Financial Services [*Associated Press*] (SAG)
HallmkCa ..... Hallmark Capital Corp. [*Associated Press*] (SAG)
Hall Neut ..... Hall's Rights and Duties of Neutrals [*1874*] [*A publication*] (DLA)
Hall NH .... Hall's Reports [*56, 57 New Hampshire*] [*A publication*] (DLA)
Hall (NY) ..... Hall's New York Superior Court Reports [*A publication*] (DLA)
HALLO .... Hang Alle Laffe Landverraders Op [*Hang All Cowardly Traitors to Their Country*] [*Greeting for Dutch Nazis allegedly coined by the Netherlands people during World War II*]
HALLO .... Hang Alle Landverraders Op [*Hang all traitors*] [*Dutch*] [*WWII phrase*]
HALLPASS... Hadamard Transform Laser Long-Path Absorption Spectrometer System (SAUO)
Hall Profits a Prendre... Hall's Treatise on the Law Relating to Profits a Prendre, Etc. [*A publication*] (DLA)
HallRlty .... Hallwood Realty Partners [*Associated Press*] (SAG)
HallRty .... Hallwood Realty Partners Ltd. [*Associated Press*] (SAG)
Hall's Am LJ... Hall's American Law Journal [*A publication*] (DLA)
Hall Shores... Hall's Rights in the Sea Shores [*A publication*] (DLA)
Hall's J Jur... Journal of Jurisprudence (Hall's) [*A publication*] (DLA)
hallu .... hallucinant (SAUS)
hallu .... hallucinate (SAUS)
HALLUC .... Hallucination
Hallwd .... Hallwood Group, Inc. [*Associated Press*] (SAG)
HallwdCon... Hallwood Consolidated Resources [*Associated Press*] (SAG)
Hal Min Law... Halleck's Mining Laws of Spain and Mexico [*A publication*] (DLA)
HALO .... HA-LO [*NASDAQ symbol*] (SAG)
HALO .... HA-LO Industries [*NASDAQ symbol*] (TTSB)
HA-LO .... HA-LO Industries, Inc. [*Associated Press*] (SAG)
HALO .... Handling of Alarms with Logic [*Nuclear reactors*]
HALO .... High-Altitude Large Optics [*Air Force*] (MCD)
HALO .... High Altitude Learjet Observatory (ACAE)
HALO .... High-Altitude Learjet Observatory (SAUS)
HALO .... High Altitude Long Operation [*Airplane*]
HALO .... High Altitude Low Observable (SAUS)
HALO .... High Altitude/Low Opening
HALO .... High-Altitude, Low-Opening Parachute Jump
HALO .... High Altituds (SAUS)
HALO .... High Arcal Learning Objectives (AIE)
HALO .... Hongkong Automated Library Operations (SAUS)
HALO .... Hughes Automated Lunar Observer [*NASA*]
HALOE .... Halogen Occultation Experiment (SAUO)
HALON .... Halogenated Hydrocarbon
HALO Parachute... High-Altitude Low Opening Parachute (SAUS)
HALP .... HAWK [*Homing All the Way Killer*] Equipment Logistics Program [*Army*]
HALP .... Husbands of Airline Pilots
HAL-PC .... Houston Area League of PC [*Personal Computer*] Users
HALPRO ...... Halverson Project [*World War II plan to bomb Japan from China*]
Hals .... Halsted's New Jersey Law Reports [*6-12 New Jersey*] [*A publication*] (DLA)
HALS .... Harwell Automated Loans System (SAUS)
HALS .... Hawaii Association of Land Surveyors (SAUO)
HAL/S .... High-Order Assembly Language for Shuttle Flight Computer (MCD)
HAL/S .... High-Order Assembly Language for Spacelab Usage [*NASA*] (NASA)
HAL/S .... High-Order Assembly Language/ Shuttle (NAKS)
HAL/S .... High Order Programming Language for Spacelab Usage (NAKS)
HALS .... Hindered Amine Light Stabilizer (SAUS)
HALS .... Hindered Amine Light Stabilizers [*for plastics*]
HALS .... Houston Area Library System [*Library network*]
HALS .... Hydrographic Airborne Laser Sounder (SAUS)
Halsbury ...... Halsbury's Statutes of England [*A publication*] (DLA)
Halsbury's S Is... Halsbury's Statutory Instruments [*A publication*] (DLA)
Halsbury's Statutes... Halsbury's Statutes of England [*A publication*] (DLA)
Hals Ch .... Halsted's New Jersey Equity Reports [*A publication*] (DLA)
Hals Eq .... Halsted's New Jersey Equity Reports [*A publication*] (DLA)
Halsey .... Halsey Drug Co. [*Associated Press*] (SAG)
HALSIM .... Hardware Logic Simulator [*Computer science*] (IEEE)
HALSOL .... High-Altitude Solar Energy (PS)
HALSS .... High-Altitude Lidar Sensing Station (CARB)
HALST .... Halstead [*Urban district in England*]
Halst .... Halsted's New Jersey Equity Reports [*A publication*] (DLA)
Halst .... Halsted's New Jersey Law Reports [*6-12 New Jersey*] [*A publication*] (DLA)
Halst Ch ...... Halsted's New Jersey Chancery Reports [*A publication*] (DLA)
HalstdE .... Halstead Energy Corp. [*Associated Press*] (SAG)
HalstdEn ..... Halstead Energy Corp. [*Associated Press*] (SAG)
Halsted (NJ)... Halsted's New Jersey Chancery Reports [*A publication*] (DLA)
Halst Ev ...... Halsted's Digest of the Law of Evidence [*A publication*] (DLA)
HALT .... Help Abolish Legal Tyranny [*In organization name HALT-ALR*] (EA)
HALT .... High Accuracy Line Track (SAUS)
HALT .... High-Altitude Laser Targeting (SAUS)
HALT .... High-Altitude LASER Transmittance (MCD)
HALT .... Highley Accelerated Life Testing (SAUO)
HALT .... Highly Accelerated Lift Test (SAUS)
HALT .... Holdup Alert - Local Transmission [*Bank robbery alarm system*]
HALT .... Houston Anti-Litter Team (SAUO)
HALT .... Hungry Angry Lonely Tired [*Slogan used by Alcoholics Anonymous members to determine whether their emotions are so out of control that they may be tempted to take a drink*]
HALT .... Hydrate Addition at Low Temperatures (SAUS)
HALT-ALR .... HALT - An Organization of Americans for Legal Reform (EA)
Halterm .... Halifax Container Terminal (SAUS)
HalterM .... Halter Marine Group, Inc. [*Associated Press*] (SAG)
HaLV .... Hamster Leukemia Virus
HalwdCn ...... Hallwood Consolidated Resources Corp. [*Associated Press*] (SAG)
HALWR .... High-Accuracy LASER Warning Receiver
HALX .... Holland American Line-Westours [*Private rail car owner code*]
HALZ .... Halstead Elevator [*Federal Railroad Administration identification code*]
HAM .... Amateur Radio Operator (SAUS)
HAM .... Hairy Anatomy Marine [*See also BAM*] [*Slang term for male marines*] [*Bowdlerized version*]
HAM .... Hamarfly, AS [*Norway*] [*FAA designator*] (FAAC)
HAM .... Hamburg [*Germany*] [*Airport symbol*] (OAG)
HAM .... Hamburg [*Germany*] [*Seismograph station code, US Geological Survey*] (SEIS)
HAM .... Hamilton Aviation, Inc. (SAUO)
Ham .... (Hamilton of) Haddington's Manuscript Cases, Scotch Court of Session [*A publication*] (DLA)
Ham .... Hamitic (SAUS)
Ham .... Hamlet [*Shakespearean work*]
ham .... Hammered (VRA)
HAM .... Hammer Throw (SAUS)
Ham .... Hammond's India and Burma Election Cases [*A publication*] (DLA)
Ham .... Hammond's Reports [*1-9 Ohio*] [*A publication*] (DLA)
HAM .... Hampshire College, Amherst, MA [*OCLC symbol*] (OCLC)

Ham........ Hampshire Regiment (SAUO)
HAM........ Hand Adding Machine (SAUS)
HAM........ Hand Addressing Machine (SAUS)
HAM........ Hand Held Monitor (HEAS)
HAM........ Hardware Associated (or Associative) Memory (SAUS)
HAM........ Hardware Associative Memory [*Computer science*] (DIT)
HAM........ Harry Armenius Miller [*Automotive engineer*]
HAM........ Hearing Aide of Minnesota (SRA)
HAM........ Hearing Aid Microphone
HAM........ Heart of Africa Mission (SAUO)
HAM........ Heat-of-Absorption Measurement (SAUS)
HAM........ Heat-of-Adsorption Measurement (SAUS)
HAM........ Heavy Atom Method
HAM........ Heavy Automotive Maintenance
HAM........ Height Adjustment Maneuver (MCD)
HAM........ Hexamethylmelamine, Adriamycin, L-Phenylalanine Mustard [*Antineoplastic drug regimen*] (DAVI)
HAM........ Hexamethylmelamine, Adriamycin, Melphalan [*Antineoplastic drug regimen*]
HAM........ Hexamethylmelamine, Adriamycin, Methotrexate [*Antineoplastic drug regimen*]
HAM........ Hierarchical Access Method
HAM........ High-Activity Mode (IAA)
HAM........ High-Altitude Missile (MCD)
HAM........ High-Availability Manager (IAA)
HAM........ High-Speed Automatic Monitor
HAM........ Histocompatibility Antigen Modifier [*Genetics*]
HAM........ Historical Anthology of Music (SAUO)
HAM........ Hold and Modify [*Computer display mode*]
HAM........ Home Access Mortgage
HAM........ Home Amateur [*Radio*]
HAM........ Home Amature Mechanic (SAUS)
HAM........ Home Apnea Monitoring [*Medicine*] (MELL)
HAM........ Honda of America Manufacturing
HAM........ Hospital-Acquired Meningitis (MELL)
HAM........ HTLV-I Associated Myelopathy (SAUS)
HAM........ Human Albumin Microsphere [*Clinical anesthesiology*]
HAM........ Human Alveolar Macrophage [*Immunology*]
HAm........ Human Amnion (DMAA)
HAM........ Human Associative Memory
HAM........ Hybrid Access Method (SAUS)
HAM........ Hydrogenic Atoms in Molecules (SAUS)
HAM........ Hymns Ancient and Modern
HAM........ Hypertext Abstract Machine (SAUS)
HAM........ Hypoparathyreoid-Addison-Moniliasis (SAUS)
HAM........ Hypoparathyroidism, Addison's Disease, and Musculocutaneous Candidiasis [*Medicine*]
HAMA........ Hamilton Anxiety Scale [*Psychiatry*] (DMAA)
HAM-A........ Hamilton Rating Scale for Anxiety (SAUS)
HAMA........ Human Anti-Mouse Antibody [*Medicine*]
HAMA........ Human Anti-Murine Antibody [*Medicine*] (DMAA)
Ham A & O... Hamerton, Allen, and Otter's English Magistrates' Cases [*3 New Sessions Cases*] [*A publication*] (DLA)
Ham & J........ Hammond and Jackson's Reports [*45 Georgia*] [*A publication*] (DLA)
HAMAS........ Movement for an Islamic Society (Algeria) [*Political party*] (PSAP)
HAMB........ Hambledon [*England*]
HAMB........ Hamburg [*West Germany*] (ROG)
HAMB........ Hamburger Hamlet Restaurants [*NASDAQ symbol*] (SPSG)
HAMBGR........ Hamburger
HAMBN........ Hambone, CA [*American Association of Railroads railroad junction routing code*]
HAMC........ Harbin Aircraft Manufacturing Co. (SAUO)
HAMC........ Harbin Aircraft Manufacturing Company (SAUO)
HAMCHAM... Haitian-American Chamber of Commerce and Industry (EA)
HAMCHAM... Honduran-American Chamber of Commerce [*See also CCHA*] (EA)
HAMCO........ HAWK [*Homing All the Way Killer*] Assembly and Missile Checkout (AAG)
Ham Cont.... Hammon on Contracts [*A publication*] (DLA)
Ham Cust..... Hamel's Laws of the Customs [*A publication*] (DLA)
HAMD........ Hamilton Depression [*Scale*] [*Psychology*] (DB)
HAM-D........ Hamilton Psychiatric Rating Scale for Depression
HAM-D........ Hamilton Rating Scale for Depression (SAUS)
HAMD........ Helicopter Ambulance Medical Detachment
HAME........ Mieso [*Ethiopia*] [*ICAO location identifier*] (ICLI)
Hamel Cust... Hamel's Laws of the Customs [*A publication*] (DLA)
Ham Fed...... Hamilton's Federalist [*A publication*] (DLA)
H-AMI........ Host-Automated Message Interface (SAUS)
HAMIL........ Hamilton, OH [*American Association of Railroads railroad junction routing code*]
Hamilton...... (Hamilton of) Haddington's Manuscript Cases, Scotch Court of Session [*A publication*] (DLA)
Hamilton...... Hamilton on Company Law [*3 eds.*] [*1891-1910*] [*A publication*] (DLA)
Hamilton...... Hamilton's American Negligence Cases [*A publication*] (DLA)
HAMIM........ Hizbul Muslimin [*Islamic Front*] [*Malaysia*] [*Political party*] (FEA)
Ham Ins....... Hammond on Fire Insurance [*A publication*] (DLA)
Ham Ins....... Hammond on Insanity [*A publication*] (DLA)
Ham Int....... Hamel's International Law [*A publication*] (DLA)
HAMIS........ Hanford Nuclear Inventory System (SAUS)
HAMJ........ Maji [*Ethiopia*] [*ICAO location identifier*] (ICLI)
HAMK........ Makale [*Ethiopia*] [*ICAO location identifier*] (ICLI)
HAML........ Hamilton Oil Corp. [*NASDAQ symbol*] (COMM)
Haml........ Hamlet [*Shakespearean work*] (BARN)
HAML........ Masslo [*Ethiopia*] [*ICAO location identifier*] (ICLI)
HamlFn........ Hamilton Financial Services Corp. [*Associated Press*] (SAG)
Hamlin........ Hamlin's Reports [*81-93 Maine*] [*A publication*] (DLA)
Hamline U... Hamline University (GAGS)
HAMLR........ Hamler, OH [*American Association of Railroads railroad junction routing code*]
HAMM........ Metema [*Ethiopia*] [*ICAO location identifier*] (ICLI)
Ham Mar Laws... Hammick's Marriage Laws [*2nd ed.*] [*1887*] [*A publication*] (DLA)
HAMMARR... Hazardous Materials Management and Resource Recovery [*University of Alabama*] [*Research center*] (RCD)
HAMMER..... Hanfords Hazardous Materials Management of Emergency Resources (SAUS)
HAMMER..... Hazardous Materials Management and Emergency Response (SAUS)
HAMMER..... Hughes Advanced Multi-Mission Radar (ACAE)
Hammersleys... Hammersley Mountains of Australia (SAUS)
HAMMO........ Hammond, IN [*American Association of Railroads railroad junction routing code*]
Hammond.... Hammond's Reports [*36-45 Georgia*] [*A publication*] (DLA)
Hammond.... Hammond's Reports [*1-9 Ohio*] [*A publication*] (DLA)
Hammond & Jackson... Hammond and Jackson's Reports [*45 Georgia*] [*A publication*] (DLA)
HAMN........ Mendi [*Ethiopia*] [*ICAO location identifier*] (ICLI)
Ham NP........ Hammond's Nisi Prius [*A publication*] (DLA)
HAMO........ Motta [*Ethiopia*] [*ICAO location identifier*] (ICLI)
HAMOCC...... Hamburg Ocean Carbon Cycle
HAMOR........ Hardware Area VS Machine Operations Reference (SAUS)
HAMOS........ High-Altitude Synoptic Meteorological Observation (SAA)
HAMOTS...... High-Altitude Multiple Object Tracking System [*Air Force*]
HAMP........ Hampshire Group Ltd [*NASDAQ symbol*] (TTSB)
Hamp........ Hampshire Regiment (SAUO)
HAMP........ Hampstead [*Region of London*]
HAMP........ Hampton National Historic Site
Hamp........ Hampton Roads (SAUS)
HAMP........ Hexamethylmelamine, Adriamycin, Methotrexate, Cisplatin [*Antineoplastic drug regimen*] (DAVI)
HAMP........ High-Altitude Measurement Probe
HAMP........ Hop and Stamp [*Dance terminology*]
HAMP........ Horizontal Amplifier (SAUS)
Ham Part..... Hammond on Parties to Action [*A publication*] (DLA)
Ham Parties... Hammond on Parties to Action [*A publication*] (DLA)
HampGp...... Hampshire Group Ltd. [*Associated Press*] (SAG)
Ham Pl........ Hammond's Principles of Pleading [*1819*] [*A publication*] (DLA)
HAMPS........ Hampshire [*County in England*]
Hamps........ Hampshire Regiment (SAUO)
HAMPS........ Heavy Airborne Multipurpose System (MCD)
HAMPS........ Host AUTODIN Message Processing System (SAUO)
Hamps Co Cas... Hampshire County Court Reports [*England*] [*A publication*] (DLA)
HAMPS R..... Hampshire Regiment [*Military unit*] [*British*] (ROG)
Hamptl........ Hampton Industries, Inc. [*Associated Press*] (SAG)
Hamptons.... East Hampton (SAUS)
Hamptons.... Hampton Heath (SAUS)
Hampton U... [*The*] Hampton University (GAGS)
Hamp Tr...... Hampson. Trustees [*2nd ed.*] [*1830*] [*A publication*] (DLA)
HAMR........ Mui River [*Ethiopia*] [*ICAO location identifier*] (ICLI)
HAMRC........ Hammers Plastic Recycling [*NASDAQ symbol*] (TTSB)
HAMS........ Hardness Assurance, Maintenance and Surveillance (SAUO)
HAMS........ Hardness Assurance Monitoring System (MCD)
HAMS........ Headquarters and Maintenance Squad
HAMS........ Headquarters and Maintenance Squadron (SAUS)
HAMS........ High Altitude Mapping System (ACAE)
HAMS........ Hour Angle of the Mean Sun [*Navigation*]
HAMS........ Massawa [*Ethiopia*] [*ICAO location identifier*] (ICLI)
HAMS........ Smithfield Companies [*NASDAQ symbol*] (SAG)
HAMSA........ Hearing Aid Manufacturers and Suppliers Association (SAUO)
HAMSCAT.... Hazardous Material Shipping Computer-Assisted Training (SAUS)
HAMSDET.... Headquarters and Maintenance Squadron Detachment [*Marine Corps*] (DNAB)
HAMSTERS... Haemophilia: A Mutation, Structure, Test, and Resource Site (ADWA)
HaMSV........ Harvey Murine Sarcoma Virus [*Medicine*] (MEDA)
HAMT........ Heavy Artillery Mechanical Transport (SAUO)
HAMT........ Human-Aided Machine Translation
HAMT........ Human-Assisted Machine Translation (SAUO)
HAMT........ Mizan Teferi [*Ethiopia*] [*ICAO location identifier*] (ICLI)
HAMTC........ Hanford [*Washington*] Atomic Metal Trades Council
HAMTF........ Hispanic American Ministries Task Force (SAUO)
HAMTF........ Hispanic American Ministries Task Force of JSAC [*Joint Strategy and Action Committee*] [*Defunct*] (EA)
HAM-TMC.... Houston Academy of Medicine-Texas Medical Center Library (SAUS)
HaMuSV...... Harvey Murine Sarcoma Virus
HAN........ Chandler, AZ [*Location identifier*] [*FAA*] (FAAL)
HAN........ Hambro Resources, Inc. [*Vancouver Stock Exchange symbol*]
Han........ Handel Society (SAUS)
Han........ Handy's Ohio Reports [*12 Ohio Decisions*] [*A publication*] (DLA)
HAN........ Hanford [*Washington*] [*Seismograph station code, US Geological Survey*] (SEIS)
HAN........ Hanford Area Network (SAUS)
HAN........ Hanford Complex (SAUS)
HAN........ Hanford Test Reactor (SAUO)
Han........ Hannay's New Brunswick Reports [*12, 13 New Brunswick*] [*A publication*] (DLA)
HAN........ Hanoi [*Vietnam*] [*Airport symbol*] (OAG)
HAN........ Hanover [*Former state in Germany*]
Han........ Hansard's Book of Entries [*1685*] [*A publication*] (DLA)
HAN........ Hanson Ltd. [*AMEX symbol*] (SAG)
Han........ Hanson PLC [*Associated Press*] (SAG)
HAN........ Hanson plc ADR [*NYSE symbol*] (TTSB)
Han........ Hanson's Bankruptcy Reports [*1915-17*] [*A publication*] (DLA)

HAN .... Hanson Trust Ltd. [*NYSE symbol*] (SPSG)
HAN .... Harmful Algae News (SAUS)
HAN .... Hawaii Association of Nurserymen (SRA)
HAN .... Health Activation Network [*Later, WHAN*] (EA)
HAN .... Heroin-Associated Nephropathy [*Medicine*] (DAVI)
HAN .... Hex Aluminum Nut
HAN .... Highly Advanced National Projects (SAUO)
HAN .... Hydroxylamine Nitrate [*Organic chemistry*] (NUCP)
HAN .... Hydroxyl Ammonium Nitrate (SAUS)
HAN .... Hydroxylammonium Nitrate [*Component of liquid propellants*] [*Inorganic chemistry*]
HAN .... Hyperplastic Alveolar Nodules [*Precancerous lesions in mice*]
HANA .... Halibut Association of North America (EA)
HANA .... Hana Biologics, Inc. [*NASDAQ symbol*] (COMM)
HANA .... Hanaro Telecom ADS [*NASDAQ symbol*] (SG)
HANA .... Helvetia Association of North America [*Defunct*] (EA)
HANA2000 ... Hanford Area Network Architecture 2000 (SAUS)
HANBA .... Hollow Anistropic Beam Analysis (PDAA)
Hanb Pat ..... Hanbury's Judicial Error in the Law of Patents [*A publication*] (DLA)
Hanb Us ...... Hanbury-Jones on Uses [*A publication*] (DLA)
HancBT .... Hancock [*John*] Bank & Thrift Opportunity Fund [*Associated Press*] (SAG)
Hanc Conv ... Hancock's System of Conveyancing [*Canada*] [*A publication*] (DLA)
HANCF .... Hanford Critical Facilities (SAUS)
HancFab ...... Hancock Fabrics, Inc. [*Associated Press*] (SAG)
HancHd .... Hancock Holding Co. [*Associated Press*] (SAG)
HAND .... Handex Corp. [*NASDAQ symbol*] (TTSB)
HAND .... Handex Environmental Recovery, Inc. [*NASDAQ symbol*] (NQ)
hand .... Handling (ELAL)
HAND .... Handspring, Inc. [*NASDAQ symbol*]
Hand .... Hand's Reports [*40-45 New York*] [*A publication*] (DLA)
Hand .... Handy's Ohio Reports [*12 Ohio Decisions*] [*A publication*] (DLA)
HAND .... Have a Nice Day
HAND .... Hawaii Association for National Defence (SAUO)
H & A .... Health and Accident [*Insurance*]
H&A .... Honours and Awards (ACII)
H&A Ins .... Health and Accidence Insurance (SAUS)
H & A Ins .... Health and Accident Insurance (DAVI)
HandAms ..... Handes Amsorya [*Vienna*] (BJA)
H & ASHD ... Hypertension and Arteriosclerotic Heart Disease [*Medicine*]
HANDB .... Handbook
H and B .... Hard and Black (SAUS)
H & B .... Holland & Barrett [*Grocery and health food shop chain*] [*British*]
H & B .... Hudson and Brooke's Irish King's Bench Reports [*1827-31*] [*A publication*] (DLA)
Handb Gk Myth... Handbook of Greek Mythology [*A publication*] (OCD)
Handb Mag... Handbook for Magistrates [*1853-55*] [*A publication*] (DLA)
H & BR .... Hull & Barnsley Railway [*British*] (ROG)
H & BT .... Huntingdon & Broad Top Railroad
H & BTM ..... Huntingdon & Broad Top Mountain Railroad & Coal Co. (IIA)
H & BTM ..... Huntington & Broad Top Mountain Railroad & Coal Co. (MHDB)
H&BV .... Houston and Brazos Valley Railway Company (SAUO)
Handb Veg Sci... Handbook of Vegetation Science (SAUS)
H & C .... Head and Cover (MSA)
H & C .... Hepatitis and Cirrhosis (MELL)
H&C .... Heroin & Cocaine (WDAA)
H and C .... Heroin and Cocaine (DSUE)
H & C .... Hoffmann & Campe [*Publisher*] [*Germany*]
H&C .... Hot and Cold (DMAA)
H & C .... Hurlstone and Coltman's English Exchequer Reports [*A publication*] (DLA)
H & C .... Hypoventilation and Cyanosis [*Medicine*] (MELL)
Hand Ch P... Hand's Chancery Practice [*A publication*] (DLA)
H & Cie .... Hentsch & Compagnie [*Bank*] [*Switzerland*]
H&CP .... Hospital and Community Psychiatry (DMAA)
H&CP .... Hospital and Community Psychiatry (journ.) (SAUS)
H & CR .... Handling and Checkout Requirements
Hand Cr Pr... Hand's Crown Practice [*A publication*] (DLA)
H&CS .... Home and Colonial Stores (SAUO)
H&C Water... Hot and Cold Water (SAUS)
H & D .... Hardened and Dispersed (AFM)
H&D .... Hunter and Driffield [*Curve*] (STED)
H & D .... Hurter and Driffield [*Chemists for whom H & D Curve and H & D Speed System are named*] (DEN)
H & D .... Lalor's Supplement to Hill and Denio's New York Reports [*A publication*] (DLA)
H & D Pr ..... Holmes and Disbrow's Practice [*A publication*] (DLA)
H&E .... Haemorrhage and Exudate (SAUS)
H&E .... Haemotoxylin and Eosin (SAUS)
H&E .... Haemotoxylin and Exudate (SAUS)
H & E .... Hematoxylin and Eosin [*Biological stain*]
H & E .... Hemorrhage and Exudate [*Medicine*]
H & E .... Heredity and Environment
H & E .... History and Examination
HANDE .... Hydrofoil Analysis and Design [*Computer science*]
Han Deb ...... Hansard's Parliamentary Debates [*A publication*] (DLA)
Handex .... Handex Environmental Recovery, Inc. [*Associated Press*] (SAG)
H and F .... Horizontal and Flat (SAUS)
Hand Fines... Hand on Fines and Recoveries [*A publication*] (DLA)
H&F Pool ..... Heated and Filtered Pool (SAUS)
H & G .... Harden and Grind [*Technical drawings*]
H & G .... Harris and Gill's Maryland Court of Appeals Reports [*1826-29*] [*A publication*] (DLA)
H & G .... Headed and Gutted [*Fish processing*]
H & G .... Hicks & Greist [*Advertising agency*]
H & G .... Home and Garden Bulletins [*A publication*]
H&G .... Home and Garden (journ.) (SAUS)
H & G .... Hurlstone and Gordon's English Exchequer Reports [*A publication*] (DLA)
H&GCF .... Hebrew and Gentile Christian Fellowship (SAUO)
HandH .... Handy & Harman [*Associated Press*] (SAG)
H & H .... Harrison and Hodgin's Upper Canada Municipal Reports [*1845-51*] [*A publication*] (DLA)
H & H .... Hemoglobin and Hematocrit [*Clinical chemistry*]
H & H .... Holland & Holland [*Custom gun maker*]
H&H .... Horn & Hardart Co. (EFIS)
H & H .... Horn and Hurlstone's English Exchequer Reports [*1838-39*] [*A publication*] (DLA)
H&HN .... Hospitals & Health Networks (SAUO)
H & HQ .... Headquarters and Headquarters Company [*Army*]
H&HRR .... Harlem and Hudson River Railroad (SAUS)
H & HS .... Headquarters and Headquarters Squadron [*Marine Corps*]
H & I .... Harassing and Interdiction
H&I .... Harassing and Interdictory (SAUS)
H and I .... Harassment and Interdiction Fires [*Military*]
H&I .... Harrassing and Interdiction (SAUS)
Handicap ..... Handicapped (SAUS)
HANDICP ..... Handicap
HANDITAL.... Association of Italian Families and Friends of Handicapped Children [*Australia*]
H & J .... Harris and Johnson's Maryland Court of Appeals Reports [*1800-26*] [*A publication*] (DLA)
H & J .... Hayes and Jones' Irish Exchequer Reports [*1832-34*] [*A publication*] (DLA)
H & J .... Hyphenation and Justification [*Typography*]
H & J Forms... Hayes and Jarman's Concise Forms of Wills [*18th ed.*] [*1952*] [*A publication*] (DLA)
H & J Ir .... Hayes and Jones' Irish Exchequer Reports [*1832-34*] [*A publication*] (DLA)
H & John ..... Harris and Johnson's Maryland Reports [*A publication*] (DLA)
H&K .... Heckler & Koch
H & K .... Hill & Knowlton, Inc. [*Public relations firm*]
H & K .... Holbrook & Kellogg [*Publisher*] (AAGC)
H&K .... Homing and Kill [*Military*] (ACAE)
H&L .... Harbour and Light Department (SAUO)
H&L .... Hargour and Light Department (SAUS)
H & L .... Heart and Lungs [*Medicine*]
Handlm .... Handleman Co. [*Associated Press*] (SAG)
H & M .... Hay and Marriott's English Admiralty Reports [*A publication*] (DLA)
H & M .... Hemming and Miller's English Vice-Chancellors' Reports [*A publication*] (DLA)
H & M .... Hening and Munford's Reports [*11-14 Virginia*] [*A publication*] (DLA)
H & M .... Hit and Miss (WDAA)
H and M ...... Hull and Machinery (SAUS)
H and M ...... Hull and Materials (SAUS)
H&MA .... Hotel and Motel Association (SAUO)
Handmaids of Mary... Sisters Servants of Mary (SAUO)
H & McH ..... Harris and McHenry's Maryland Court of Appeals Reports [*1785-99*] [*A publication*] (DLA)
H & M Ch.... Hemming and Miller's English Vice-Chancellors' Reports [*A publication*] (DLA)
H & McHenry... Harris and McHenry's Maryland Reports [*A publication*] (DLA)
handmd .... Handmade (VRA)
H&MID .... Health and Medical Informatics Digest (SAUS)
H&M RR ...... Hudson & Manhattan Railroad (SAUS)
H & MS .... Headquarters and Maintenance Squadron [*Marine Corps*]
H & M (VA)... Hening and Munford's Reports [*11-14 Virginia*] [*A publication*] (DLA)
H & N .... Head and Neck [*Medicine*]
H & N .... Holmes and Narver, Inc. (NRCH)
H & N .... Hum and Noise (DEN)
H & N .... Hurlstone and Norman's English Exchequer Reports [*156, 158 English Reprint*] [*A publication*] (DLA)
H & NH .... Hartford & New Haven Railroad
H&N mot ..... Head and Neck Motion (STED)
H&O .... Hook and Oil (SAUS)
H&O Damage... Hook and Oil Damage (SAUS)
H and O Damage... Hooks and Oil Damage (SAUS)
H&P .... History and Physical [*Medicine*] (AMHC)
H & P .... History and Physical [*Examination*] [*Medicine*]
H&P .... Hodgen and Pearson [*Suspension traction*] (STED)
H & P .... Hopwood and Philbrick's English Election Cases [*1863-67*] [*A publication*] (DLA)
H&P .... Hopwood and Philbricks English Election Cases (journ.) (SAUS)
H&P .... Hydraulic and Pneumatic (SAUS)
Hand Pat ..... Hand on Patents [*A publication*] (DLA)
H&P Examination... History and Physical Examination (SAUS)
H & Q .... Hambrecht & Quist [*Investment banking firm*]
H & Q Hlt .... H & Q Healthcare Fund [*Associated Press*] (SAG)
H & Q Lfe .... H & Q Life Sciences Investors [*Associated Press*] (SAG)
H & R .... Harper & Row Publishers, Inc.
H&R .... Harrison and Rutherfords English Common Pleas Reports (journ.) (SAUS)
H & R .... Harrison and Rutherfurd's English Common Pleas Reports [*1865-66*] [*A publication*] (DLA)
H&R .... Hoisting and Rigging (SAUS)
H&R .... Holding and Reconsignment (SAUS)
H & R .... Holding and Reconsignment [*Military*]
H & R .... Hysterectomy and Radiation [*Medicine*]
H & R .... Hysteria and Repression (MELL)
H & R Bank... Hazlitt and Roche's Bankruptcy Reports [*A publication*] (DLA)

H&R Inc .... Harrington & Richardson, Inc. (SAUO)
H & RPO ...... Holding and Reconsignment Point [*Military*]
H&RWC .... Hazardous and Radiological Waste Control (SAUS)
H & S .... Harris and Simrall's Reports [*49-52 Mississippi*] [*A publication*] (DLA)
H & S .... Head and Shoulders [*Photography*]
H & S .... Headquarters and Service [*Battery*] [*Army*]
H & S .... Headquarters and Supply Company [*Marine Corps*] (VNW)
H&S .... Health and Safety (journ.) (SAUS)
H&S .... Health and Status (ACAE)
H&S .... Health and Strength (journ.) (SAUS)
H & S .... Hearing and Speech (MELL)
H&S .... Hemorrhage and Shock [*Medicine*] (STED)
HANDS .... High-Altitude Nuclear Detection Studies [*National Institute of Standards and Technology*]
H&S .... Home & School (SAUS)
H&S .... Humphries & Smith [*Authors of Music Publishing in the British Isles*]
H & S .... Hypocalcemia and Seizures (MELL)
H&S .... Hysterotomy and Sterilization (SAUS)
H&SCO .... Headquarters and Service Company (SAUO)
handscr .... Handscroll (VRA)
H&SCTB .... Heavy & Specialized Carners Tariff Bureau (SAUS)
H & SCTB .... Heavy & Specialized Carriers Tariff Bureau
H&SE .... Health & Safety Executive (WDAA)
H&SF .... Heart and Stroke Foundation (SAUO)
HANDSID ..... Hand Emplaced Seismic Intrusion Detection (SAUO)
H&SM .... Health and Safety Manual [*A publication*] [*Department of Energy*] (COE)
H&S Mgmt ... Handling and Shipping Management (journ.) (SAUS)
H & STR ...... Headquarters and Service Troop [*Army*]
H & T .... Hall and Twell's English Chancery Reports [*1849-50*] [*A publication*] (DLA)
H & T .... Handling and Transportation (KSC)
H & T .... Hardened and Tempered [*Steel*]
H&T .... History and Theory (journ.) (SAUS)
H & T .... Hospitalization and Treatment
H&T .... Hospitalize and Treat (SAUS)
H&T Self Def ... Harrigan and Thomons Cases on the Law of Self-Defense (journ.) (SAUS)
H & T Self-Def ... Harrigan and Thompson's Cases on the Law of Self-Defense [*A publication*] (DLA)
H & Tw .... Hall and Twell's English Chancery Reports [*1849-50*] [*A publication*] (DLA)
H&V .... Hardening and Vulnerability (ACAE)
H and V .... Heating and Ventilating (SAUS)
H and V .... Heating and Ventilation (NATG)
H&V .... Hemigastectomy and Vagotomy (SAUS)
H & V .... Hemigastrectomy and Vagotomy [*Medicine*]
H&V .... Horizontal and Vertical (WDMC)
H&V Eng ...... H&V Engineer (SAUS)
H&W .... Harland and Wolff Ltd. (SAUO)
H & W .... Harrison and Wollaston's English King's Bench Reports [*A publication*] (DLA)
H & W .... Hazzard and Warburton's Prince Edward Island Reports [*A publication*] (DLA)
H&W .... Hazzard and Warburtons Prince Edward Island Reports (journ.) (SAUS)
H&W .... Health & Welfare (SAUO)
H & W .... Holm & Wonsild [*Steamship*] (MHDB)
H & W .... Hurlstone and Walmsley's English Exchequer Reports [*1840-41*] [*A publication*] (DLA)
Handy .... Handy's Ohio Reports [*12 Ohio Decisions*] [*A publication*] (DLA)
Handy (Ohio) ... Handy's Ohio Reports [*12 Ohio Decisions*] [*A publication*] (DLA)
Handy R ...... Handy's Cincinnati Superior Court Reports [*Ohio*] [*A publication*] (DLA)
HANE .... Hereditary Angioneurotic Edema [*Medicine*]
HANE .... High-Altitude Nuclear Effects [*Study*]
HANE .... High-Altitude Nuclear Explosion
Hane Cr Dig ... Hanes' United States Digest of Criminal Cases [*A publication*] (DLA)
Han Ent .... Hansard's Book of Entries [*1685*] [*A publication*] (DLA)
Hanes .... Hanes' English Chancery [*A publication*] (DLA)
HANES .... Health and Nutrition Examination Survey [*Public Health Service*]
Hanf .... Hanford's Entries [*1685*] [*A publication*] (DLA)
HANFA .... Hanley Falls, MN [*American Association of Railroads railroad junction routing code*]
HANFO .... Heavy Ammonium Nitrate and Fuel Oil (SAUS)
HANFORD .... Hanford Site [*Department of Energy*] [*Richland, WA*] (GAAI)
Hanford Reach ... Hanford Reach of the Columbia River (SAUS)
Hanfrd .... Hannaford Brothers, Inc. [*Associated Press*] (SAG)
H-A-N-G .... Hamburg-American North-German (SAUS)
HANG .... Hawaii Air National Guard (SAUS)
HANG .... Hawaiian Air National Guard (FAAC)
HANG .... Hawal Air National Guard (SAUS)
HANG .... Neghelle [*Ethiopia*] [*ICAO location identifier*] (ICLI)
HANGB .... Headquarters Air National Guard Bureau (MUSM)
HangOr .... Hanger Orthopedic Group, Inc. [*Associated Press*] (SAG)
HANGUL ...... Korean/U.S. Bilingual Teletype (SAUO)
HANHADES ... Hawk & Nike-Hercules Air Defense Effectiveness & Survivability Study (SAUO)
Hanh Mar Wom ... Hanhart on the Laws Relating to Married Women [*A publication*] (DLA)
Han Hor .... Hanover on the Law of Horses [*A publication*] (DLA)
HANJ .... Nejjo [*Ethiopia*] [*ICAO location identifier*] (ICLI)
HanJI .... Hancock, John, Investors Trust [*Associated Press*] (SAG)
HanJI .... John Hancock Investors Trust [*Associated Press*] (SAG)
HanJS .... Hancock, John, Income Securities Trust [*Associated Press*] (SAG)
HanJS .... John Hancock Income Securities Trust [*Associated Press*] (SAG)
HANK .... Hanks Seafood Company, Inc. (SAUO)
HANK .... Nekemte [*Ethiopia*] [*ICAO location identifier*] (ICLI)
HAN/LCD ..... Hybrid Assigned Nematic/Liquid Crystal Display (TEL)
Hanm .... Lord Kenyon's English King's Bench Reports, Notes, Edited by Hanmer [*A publication*] (ILCA)
Han Mar Wom ... Hanhart on the Laws Relating to Married Women [*A publication*] (DLA)
Hanmer .... Lord Kenyon's English King's Bench Reports, Notes, Edited by Hanmer [*A publication*] (DLA)
Hann .... Hannay's New Brunswick Reports [*12, 13 New Brunswick*] [*A publication*] (DLA)
HANN .... Hannibal, MO [*American Association of Railroads railroad junction routing code*]
Hanna .... Hanna [*M. A.*] Co. [*Associated Press*] (SAG)
Han (NB) ..... Hannay's New Brunswick Reports [*12, 13 New Brunswick*] [*A publication*] (DLA)
HANOV .... Hanover, PA [*American Association of Railroads railroad junction routing code*]
HanovGld ...... Hanover Gold Company, Inc. [*Associated Press*] (SAG)
HANP .... Homeopathic Academy of Naturopathic Physicians (ADWA)
hANP .... Human Atrial Natriuretic Peptide [*Biochemistry*]
HANP .... Human Atrium Natriuretic Peptide (DB)
Han Prob ..... Hanson on the Probate and Legacy Acts [*A publication*] (DLA)
HanPtDiv ..... Hancock [*John*] Patriot Premium Dividend Fund I [*Associated Press*] (SAG)
HanPtDv2 ..... Hancock [*John*] Patriot Premium Dividend Fund II [*Associated Press*] (SAG)
HanPtGlb ..... Hancock [*John*] Patriot Global Dividend Fund [*Associated Press*] (SAG)
HanPtPfd ..... Hancock, John, Patriot Preferred Dividend Fund [*Associated Press*] (SAG)
HanPtPfd ..... Hancock [*John*] Patriot Prferred Dividend Fund [*Associated Press*] (SAG)
HanPtSel ..... Hancock [*John*] Patriot Select Dividend Trust [*Associated Press*] (SAG)
HANS .... Hansen Nat [*NASDAQ symbol*] (TTSB)
HANS .... Hansen Natural Corp. [*NASDAQ symbol*] (SAG)
HANS .... Head and Neck Support (LDOE)
HANS .... Health Action Network Society (ADWA)
HANS .... High-Altitude Navigation System
HANSA .... Hanscom Satellite Analysis (ACAE)
HANSA .... Healthcare Advanced Networked System Architecture (EURO)
Hans Al .... Hansard on Aliens [*A publication*] (DLA)
Hansb .... Hansbrough's Reports [*76-90 Virginia*] [*A publication*] (DLA)
Hans Deb ..... Hansard's Parliamentary Debates [*A publication*] (DLA)
Hansen .... Hansen Natural Corp. [*Associated Press*] (SAG)
Hans Ent ...... Hansard's Book of Entries [*1685*] [*A publication*] (DLA)
Hanson .... Hanson Trust Ltd. [*Associated Press*] (SAG)
Hans Parl Deb ... Hansard's Parliamentary Debates [*A publication*] (DLA)
Hans Pr .... Hanson on Probate Acts [*A publication*] (DLA)
HANTAG .... Hanford Area Network Technical Advisory Group (SAUO)
HANTAG .... Hanford Technical Advisory Group (SAUS)
HANTRB .... Hanford Technical Review Board (SAUS)
Hants .... Hampshire (DIAR)
HANTS .... Hampshire [*County in England*]
HanvDir .... Hanover Direct, Inc. [*Associated Press*] (SAG)
HANX .... Hansen's Forwarding [*Private rail car owner code*]
HANYS .... Healthcare Association of New York State (SRA)
HANZ .... Hotel Association of New Zealand (SAUO)
HAO .... Hamilton, OH [*Location identifier*] [*FAA*] (FAAL)
HAO .... Hardware Action Officer [*Military*] (AABC)
HAO .... Health Action Overseas (ADWA)
HAO .... Hearing Aid Follow-Up and Orientation [*Otorhinolaryngology*] (DAVI)
HAO .... High Activity Oxide (SAUS)
HAO .... High-Altitude Observatory [*Boulder, CO*] [*National Center for Atmospheric Research*]
HAO .... Hip Osteoarthritis [*Medicine*] (MELL)
HAO .... Home Address Operation (SAUS)
HAO .... Horticultural Advisory Officer (SAUO)
HAO .... Hospitals, Administration, and Organizations [*British*]
HAO .... Hughes Aeronautical Operations (ACAE)
HAO .... Hydrated Aluminium Oxide (SAUS)
HAO .... Hydrogenated Anthracene Oil (SAUS)
HAOA .... High Angle of Attack [*Combat aircraft*] [*Navy*]
HAOA .... Hight Angle of Attack (SAUS)
HAOB .... Headquarters Accounting Operations Branch (SAUO)
HAOC .... Haynes-Apperson Owners Club (EA)
HAOC .... Hexaazaoctadecahydrocoronene [*Organic chemistry*]
HAOG .... Handbuch der Altorientalischen Geisteskultur [*A publication*] (BJA)
H/A or D ..... Havre-Antwerp or Dieppe (SAUS)
HA or D .... Havre, Antwerp, or Dunkirk [*Business term*]
HAOS .... Houston Area Oxidant Study [*Environmental Protection Agency*] (GFGA)
HAOS .... Hydroxylamine-ortho-sulfonic Acid [*Organic chemistry*]
HAOSS .... High-Altitude Orbital Space Station (IEEE)
HAP .... Hafnium Column Product [*Nuclear energy*] (NRCH)
HAP .... Hampshire Aircraft Parks [*British military*] (DMA)
HAP .... Handicapped Aid Program (DAVI)
HAP .... Happy
HAP .... Happy Bay [*Australia*] [*Airport symbol*] (OAG)
HAP .... Hardware Allocation Panel
HAP .... Harwood Academic Publishers [*British*]
HAP .... Hazard Abatement Program (SAUO)

HAP .... Hazardous Air Pollutant
HAP .... Heading Axis Perturbation
HAP .... Health Access Project (SAUS)
HAP .... Health Alliance Plan
HAP .... Heat Shock Activator Protein [*Biochemistry*]
HAP .... Height Above Plate [*Roofing*]
HAP .... Held After Positioning (STED)
HAP .... Helicopter Assault Primary (SAUS)
HAP .... Heredopathia Atactica Polyneuritiformis [*Medicine*]
HAP .... High-Acid Column Product (NRCH)
HAP .... High-Altitude Platform
HAP .... High-Altitude Probe (AAG)
HAP .... High-Amplitude Peristalsis (STED)
HAP .... High Average Power (SAUS)
HAP .... Hilson Adolescent Profile [*Psychology*] (DHP)
HAP .... Histamine Acid Phosphate (STED)
HAP .... Histamine Phosphate Acid [*Biochemistry*] (DAVI)
HAP .... Home Attendant Program (SAUS)
HAP .... Home Owners Assistance Program [*Military*] (AABC)
HAP .... Honeycomb Aluminum Panel
HAP .... Honeywell Array Processor (SAUS)
HAP .... Hook-Associated Protein [*Genetics*]
HAP .... Horizontal Axis Pivot
HAP .... Hospital Acquired Pneumonia [*Medicine*] (STED)
HAP .... Host Access Protocol (ACAE)
HAP .... Host-Associated Population [*Ecology*]
HAP .... Housing Assistance Payment (SAUO)
HAP .... Housing Assistance Program
HAP .... Human Activity Profile (IDYL)
HAP .... Humoral Antibody Production [*Medicine*] (DMAA)
HAP .... Huntingtin-Associated Protein [*Biochemistry*]
HAP .... Hutch Apparel Ltd. [*Vancouver Stock Exchange symbol*]
HAP .... Hydrated Antimony Pentaoxide [*Inorganic chemistry*]
HAP .... Hydraulic Actuator Package (ACAE)
HAP .... Hydrogen Ammonium Percolate, fuel (SAUS)
HAP .... Hydrolyzed Animal Protein [*Food technology*]
HAP .... Hydroxyacetophenone [*Organic chemistry*]
HAP .... Hydroxyapatite [*Also, HA*] [*A mineral*]
HAP .... Hydroxylamine Perchlorate [*Organic chemistry*]
HAP .... Hydroxylammonium Perchlorate (SAUS)
HAP .... Hydroxylated Ammonium Perchlorate (ACAE)
HAP .... Hyperboloid Approximation Procedure
HAP .... Hyperpolarizing Afterpotential [*Electrophysiology*]
HAP .... Whitsunday Resort (Long Island) [*Australia*] [*Airport symbol*]
HAPA .... Haitian-American Psychiatric Association (ADWA)
HAPA .... Handicapped Adventure Playground Association [*British*] (DBA)
HAPA .... Hemagglutinating Anti-Penicillin Antibody [*Virology*] (MAE)
HAPAB .... Health Aspects of Pesticides Abstract Bulletin [*Environmental Protection Agency*]
HAPAG .... Hamburg-American Line (SAUS)
HAPC .... Hospital-Acquired Penetration Contact [*Medicine*] (MAE)
HAPCWS ...... Holt-Atherton Pacific Center for Western Studies [*University of the Pacific*] [*Research center*] (RCD)
hapd .... happened (SAUS)
HAPD .... Home-Automated Peritoneal Dialysis [*Medicine*] (MELL)
HAPDAR ...... Hard Point Demonstration Array RADAR
HAPDEC ...... Hard Point Decoys (MCD)
HAPDONG .... Association Agency of Korean Newspapers (SAUO)
HAP Dosemeter... Haloid Azo-dye Paraffin Dosemeter (SAUS)
HAPE .... High-Altitude Particle Experiment (SAUO)
HAPE .... High-Altitude Pulmonary Edema
HA-PE .... Hydroxylapatite-Polyethylene (SAUS)
HAPEMS ...... Hazardous Air Pollutants Enforcement Management System [*Environmental Protection Agency*] (GFGA)
HAP/ESP ...... Hughes Aerobot Program/Elevated Sensor Program (ACAE)
HAPEX .... Hydrological Atmospheric Pilot Experiment [*Marine science*] (OSRA)
HAPEX .... Hydrological Atmospheric Pilot Experiments (EERA)
HAPEX .... Hydrologic Atmospheric Pilot Experiment (SAUS)
HAPEX-MOBILHY... Hydrologic-Atmospheric Pilot Experiment-Modelisation du Bilan Hydrique (SAUO)
HAPEX-Sahel... Hydrological and Atmospheric Pilot Experiment in the Sahel (SAUS)
HAPEX-Sahel... Hydrological Atmospheric Pilot Experiment (SAUO)
HAPFACT ..... Hazardous Air Pollutant Health Effects Fact (ADWA)
HAPFACT ..... Hazardous Air Pollutant Health Effects Fact Sheets (SAUO)
HAPFF-EUR... HAWK [*Homing All the Way Killer*] Project Field Facility - Europe (MCD)
HAPI .... Harrier Approach Path Indicator (SAUO)
HAPI .... Harris API [*Application Programming Interface*] [*Computer science*]
HaPI .... Health and Psychosocial Instruments (ADWA)
HAPI .... Helicopter Approach Path Indicator (MCD)
HAPI .... Helicopter Approach Plate Indicator System (SAUS)
HAPI .... High Altitude Plasma Instrument (ADWA)
HAPI .... High-Altitude Plasma Instrument (SAUS)
HAPI .... Hispanic American Periodicals Index
HAPI .... Holding as Previously Instructed [*Aviation*] (FAAC)
HAPI .... Host Application Programming Interface
HA-PLA .... Hydroxylapatite-Polylactic Acid (SAUS)
HAPLR .... Hennen's American Public Library Rating [*Index*]
HAP-NICA .... Humanitarian Assistance Project for Independent Agricultural Development in Nicaragua [*Defunct*] (EA)
HAPO .... Hanford Atomic Products Operations [*General Electric Co.*]
HAPO .... High-Altitude Pulmonary Oedema [*Medicine*] (DMAA)
HAPORTH .... Halfpennyworth [*British*] (ROG)
Happ .... Happening (SAUS)
H App .... Heir Apparent (DAS)
HAPP .... High Air Pollution Potential
HAPP .... High Altitude Pollution Program (SAUO)
HAPP .... High-Altitude Pollution Project [*FAA*]
HAPP .... High-Altitude Powered Platforms (MCD)
HAPP .... House Assessment Prescription Program (SAUS)
HAPP .... Hughes Aircraft Post Processor (ACAE)
HAPPE .... High-Altitude Particle Experiment (SAUS)
HAPPE .... High-Altitude Particle Program Experiment [*NASA*]
HAPPE .... Honeywell Associative Parallel Processing Ensemble
HAPPI .... Height and Plan Position Indicator (PDAA)
HAPPI .... Household and Personal Products Industry [*A publication*]
Happiness ... Happiness Express, Inc. [*Associated Press*] (SAG)
HAPPS .... Hazardous Air Pollutant Prioritization System [*Environmental Protection Agency*] (GFGA)
HAPS .... Hazardous Air Pollutants
HAPS .... Health Aspects of Pesticides
HAPS .... Helicopter Acoustic Processing System (SAUS)
HAPS .... Helicopter Airfield Performance Simulator (SAUS)
HAPS .... Hepatic Arterial Perfusion Scintigraphy [*Cardiology*] (DAVI)
HAPS .... Historic Aircraft Preservation Society Ltd. [*British*] (BI)
HAPS .... Housing Assistance Payments (SAUS)
HAPS .... Houston Automatic Priority Spooling [*Computer science*] (NRCH)
HAPS .... Houston Automatic Priority System (SAUS)
HAPS .... Hunter Area Pathology Service (SAUO)
HAPS .... Hydrazine Auxillary Propulsion System (IGSL)
HAPS .... Hydroxyalkylpropyl Sephadex [*Analytical biochemistry*]
HAPSA .... High Altitude Probe Satellite (ACAE)
HAPSE .... Harris Ada Programming Support Environment (HODG)
HAPT .... Haptoglobin [*Hematology*] (DAVI)
HAPT .... Hitachi Automatically Programmed Tools (SAUS)
HAPTO .... Haptoglobin (STED)
HAPTONG .... Haptong Tongsin [*Press agency*] [*South Korea*]
HAPUB .... High-Speed Arithmetic Processing Unit Board
HAPUG Modulation... Harbich, Pungs, Gerth Modulation (SAUS)
HAP-USA ..... Handicapped Aid Program - USA [*Defunct*] (EA)
HaPV .... Hamsterpolyomavirus (SAUS)
HAPY .... Happiness Express [*NASDAQ symbol*] (TTSB)
HAPY .... Happiness Express, Inc. [*NASDAQ symbol*] (SAG)
HAQ .... Headache Assessment Questionnaire [*Neurology*] (DAVI)
HAQ .... Health Assessment Questionnaire (DMAA)
HAQO .... Hydroxyalninoquinoline Oxide (SAUS)
HAQO .... Hydroxyaminoquinoline Oxide [*Organic chemistry*]
HAR .... Atomic Energy Research Establishment (SAUO)
Har .... Harari (BJA)
HAR .... Harbor (AFM)
HAR .... Harbor Advisory Radar (SAUS)
HAR .... Harbor Airlines, Inc. [*ICAO designator*] (FAAC)
HAR .... Hardness Assessment Report
HAR .... Hardware Affiliated Representatives [*Defunct*] (EA)
HAR .... Harford Community College, Bel Air, MD [*OCLC symbol*] (OCLC)
HAR .... Harman International Industries, Inc. [*NYSE symbol*] (SPSG)
HAR .... Harmonic
HAR .... Harmonisation Agreement for Labelling Cables and Wires (SAUS)
Har .... Harradine Group [*Australia*] [*Political party*]
Har .... Harrington's Delaware Reports [*A publication*] (DLA)
Har .... Harrington's Michigan Chancery Reports [*A publication*] (DLA)
HAR .... Harrisburg-New Cumberland [*Pennsylvania*] [*Airport symbol*] (AD)
HAR .... Harrisburg, PA [*Location identifier*] [*FAA*] (FAAL)
Har .... Harrison's Condensed Louisiana Reports [*A publication*] (DLA)
Har .... Harrison's Michigan Chancery Reports [*A publication*] (DLA)
Har .... Harrison's Reports [*15-17, 23-29 Indiana*] [*A publication*] (DLA)
HAR .... Hartford [*Connecticut*] [*Seismograph station code, US Geological Survey*] [*Closed*] (SEIS)
HAR .... Harum [*Of These*] [*Pharmacy*] (ROG)
HAR .... Harvey Aluminum, Inc. (SAUO)
HAR .... Hazard Action Report (MCD)
HAR .... Heinemann, A. R., East Saint Louis IL [*STAC*]
HAR .... Helicopter, search-and-Rescue (SAUS)
HAR .... High-Altitude Radar Altimeter (SAUS)
HAR .... High-Altitude Recombination (SAUS)
HAR .... High-Altitude Recombination Energy (IAA)
HAR .... High Altitude Research Program (SAUO)
HAR .... High-Altitude Retinopathy [*Medicine*] (STED)
HAR .... Highway Advisory Radio [*Vehicle communications*]
HAR .... Home Address Record (SAUS)
HAR .... Home Address Register
HAR .... Homogeneous Aqueous Reactor [*Nuclear energy*] (NUCP)
HAR .... Honorary Air Reserve [*Air Force*]
HAR .... Horse of the Americas Registry (EA)
HAR .... Hospital Accounts Receivable (SAUS)
HAR .... Hover Agility Rotor (RDA)
HAR .... Humanities Association Review [*A publication*] (ANEX)
HAR .... Hydrogen Absorption Reaction (SAUS)
HAR .... Hyperacute Rejection [*Medicine*]
H-Ar .... Public Archives, Honolulu, HI [*Library symbol*] [*Library of Congress*] (LCLS)
HAR03 .... Region 2 Water Quality Models (SAUO)
HARA .... Hanau Auto Racing Association (SAUO)
HARA .... Harassment (SAUS)
HARA .... High-Altitude RADAR Altimeter [*NASA*]
HARA .... High-Altitude Resonance Absorption (SAUS)
HARA .... High-Assault Risk Area [*DoD*]
HARA .... Hughes Aircraft Retirees' Association (ACAE)
HARA Antenna... High-Altitude Radar Altimeter Antenna (SAUS)

HARAC......... High-Altitude Resonance Absorption Calculation (IEEE)
Har & G....... Harris and Gill's Maryland Reports [*A publication*] (DLA)
Har & Gil..... Harris and Gill's Maryland Reports [*A publication*] (DLA)
Har & Gill.... Harris and Gill's Maryland Reports [*A publication*] (DLA)
Har & G Rep... Harris and Gill's Maryland Reports [*A publication*] (DLA)
Har & J....... Harris and Johnson's Maryland Reports [*A publication*] (DLA)
Har & J (MD)... Harris and Johnson's Maryland Reports [*A publication*] (DLA)
Har & John... Harris and Johnson's Maryland Court of Appeals Reports [*1800-26*] [*A publication*] (DLA)
Har & Johns MD Rep... Harris and Johnson's Maryland Reports [*A publication*] (DLA)
Har & McH... Harris and McHenry's Maryland Reports [*A publication*] (DLA)
Har and M'Hen... Harris and McHenry's Maryland Reports [*A publication*] (DLA)
Har & Ruth... Harrison and Rutherford's English Common Pleas Reports [*1865-66*] [*A publication*] (DLA)
Har & W...... Harrison and Wollaston's English King's Bench Reports [*A publication*] (DLA)
Har & Woll... Harrison and Wollaston's English King's Bench Reports [*A publication*] (DLA)
HA Range.... Hamburg-Antwerp Range (SAUS)
HARAO......... Hartford Aircraft Reactor Area Office (SAUS)
HARAO......... Hartford Aircraft Reactors Area Office (SAUO)
Har App....... Hare's English Chancery Reports, Appendix to Vol. X [*A publication*] (DLA)
HARAS......... Hughes Active RADAR Augmentation System
HARB........... Harbor [*Maps and charts*] (ROG)
HARB........... Harbor Federal Savings Bank [*NASDAQ symbol*] (SAG)
HARB........... Historic Architectural Review Board (SAUS)
HARB........... Homestead Air Reserve Base (DEMM)
Harb & Nav C... Harbors and Navigation Code [*A publication*] (DLA)
HarbFed....... Harbor Federal Bancorp [*Associated Press*] (SAG)
Harbngr....... Harbinger Corp. [*Associated Press*] (SAG)
HARBOR...... Harbor [*Commonly used*] (OPSA)
HarborH....... Harborside Healthcare Corp. [*Associated Press*] (SAG)
HARBORS...... Harbors [*Commonly used*] (OPSA)
HarbourF..... Harbourton Financial Services LP [*Associated Press*] (SAG)
HARBR......... Harbor [*Commonly used*] (OPSA)
HarbrFd....... Harbor Federal Savings Bank [*Associated Press*] (SAG)
Harbrgr....... Harbinger Corp. [*Associated Press*] (SAG)
Har Bus R.... Harvard Business Review [*A publication*] (BRI)
HARC........... Halon Alternatives Research Corporation (NTPA)
HARC........... Hanford Academic Research Committee (SAUS)
Harc............ Harcarse's Decisions, Scotch Court of Session [*1681-91*] [*A publication*] (DLA)
HARC........... HarCor Energy Co. [*NASDAQ symbol*] (NQ)
HARC........... Helical Axial Rate Control (MCD)
HARC........... Heritage Arms Rescue Committee (WDAA)
HARC........... Hester Adrian Research Centre [*University of Manchester*] [*British*] (CB)
HARC........... High-Altitude RADAR Controller
HARC........... High-Altitude Reconnaissance (SAUS)
HARC........... Houston Advanced Research Center
HARC........... Houston Area Research Center (SAUS)
HARC........... Hudson Amateur Radio Council (SAUO)
HARC........... Human Affairs Research Center (SAUO)
HARC-C........ Houston Advanced Research Center-C [*Video compression algorithm based on wavelet theory and programmed in C*] (DCDG)
HARCFT....... Harbor Craft
HARCFT....... Harbour Craft (SAUS)
Har Cft Co... Harbor Craft Company (SAUO)
HarcG.......... Harcourt General, Inc. [*Associated Press*] (SAG)
HarcGn........ Harcourt General, Inc. [*Associated Press*] (SAG)
Har Ch........ Harrington's Michigan Chancery Reports [*A publication*] (DLA)
Har Ch Pr..... Harrison's Chancery Practice [*A publication*] (DLA)
Har Chy....... Harrington's Michigan Chancery Reports [*A publication*] (DLA)
HARCO......... Hyperbolic Area Control (IAA)
HARCO......... Hyperbolic Area Coverage [*Navigation*]
Har Col Jur... Hargrave's Collectanea Juridica [*1791-92*] [*A publication*] (DLA)
Har Com...... Harrison's Compilation of the Laws of New Jersey [*A publication*] (DLA)
Har Com Proc... Harrison's Common Law Procedure Act [*Canada*] [*A publication*] (DLA)
HarcorE........ HarCor Energy Co. [*Associated Press*] (SAG)
Har Ct Mar... Harwood's Practice of United States Naval Courts-Martial [*A publication*] (DLA)
HARCVS....... Honorary Associate of the Royal College of Veterinary Surgeons [*British*]
HARD........... Handling and Reloading Device (SAUS)
Hard............ Harden (SAUS)
HARD........... Hardin, MO [*American Association of Railroads railroad junction routing code*]
Hard............ Hardin's Kentucky Reports [*A publication*] (DLA)
Hard............ Hardres' English Exchequer Reports [*145 English Reprint*] [*A publication*] (DLA)
HARD........... Hardware (WDAA)
HARD........... Hardware Resources for Development (SAUO)
HARD........... Helicopter and Airplane RADAR Detection
HARD........... Helicopter & Airplane Radio Detection (SAUS)
HARD........... High Performance Artillery Rocket (SAUS)
HARD........... Horizontal Acoustic Range Depiction (NVT)
hardbd......... Hardboard (VRA)
Hard Eccl L... Harding on Ecclesiastical Law [*A publication*] (DLA)
Har Del........ Harrington's Delaware Reports [*1-5 Delaware*] [*A publication*] (DLA)
Hard El Pet... Hardcastle on Election Petitions [*A publication*] (DLA)
Hardes......... Hardesty's Delaware Term Reports [*A publication*] (DLA)
HARDEX....... Harbor Defense Exercise [*Navy*] (NG)
HARDEX....... Harbour Defence Exercise (SAUS)
HARDIE........ Harmonisation of Roadside and Driver Information in Europe (EURO)
Har Dig........ Harris' Georgia Digest [*A publication*] (DLA)
Har Dig........ Harrison's Digest of English Common Law Reports [*A publication*] (DLA)
Hardin......... Hardin Bancorp, Inc. [*Associated Press*] (SAG)
Hardin......... Hardin's Kentucky Reports [*A publication*] (DLA)
Harding U.... Harding University (GAGS)
Hardin (KY)... Hardin's Kentucky Reports [*A publication*] (DLA)
Hardin-Simmons U... Hardin-Simmons University (GAGS)
HARDIS........ Hotel and Restaurant Design and Interiors Exhibition [*British*] (ITD)
HARDMAN... Hardware-Manpower Program [*Navy*]
HARDMAN... Military Manpower/Hardware Integration Program (SAUO)
HARDMAN II... Marine Corps Military Manpower/Hardware Integration System II (SAUO)
HARDMON... Hardware Monitor [*Computer science*] (MHDI)
Hardr.......... Hardres' English Exchequer Reports [*145 English Reprint*] [*1655-69*] [*A publication*] (DLA)
Hardr (Eng)... Hardres' English Exchequer Reports [*145 English Reprint*] [*A publication*] (DLA)
Hardres........ Hardres' English Exchequer Reports [*145 English Reprint*] [*A publication*] (DLA)
HARDS......... High-Altitude Radiation Detection System (MCD)
Hard Soft..... Hard and Soft (journ.) (SAUS)
Hard St L..... Hardcastle on Statutory Law [*A publication*] (DLA)
Hard Tr M.... Hardingham on Trade Marks [*A publication*] (DLA)
HARDTS....... High-Accuracy RADAR Data Transmission System (MUGU)
Hardw.......... Cases Tempore Hardwicke, by Lee [*England*] [*A publication*] (DLA)
Hardw.......... Cases Tempore Hardwicke, by Ridgeway [*England*] [*A publication*] (DLA)
Hardw Cas Temp... Cases Tempore Hardwicke, by Lee and Hardwicke [*A publication*] (DLA)
Hardw (Eng)... Cases Tempore Hardwicke, by Lee [*England*] [*A publication*] (DLA)
Hardw (Eng)... Cases Tempore Hardwicke, by Ridgeway [*England*] [*A publication*] (DLA)
Hardw NB.... Hardwicke's Note Books [*A publication*] (DLA)
HARDWR..... Hardware [*Computer science*]
HARE........... Handy and Accurate Reflection Model for Crop Experiment (SAUO)
Hare............ Hare's English Vice-Chancellors' Reports [*66-68 English Reprint*] [*1841-53*] [*A publication*] (DLA)
HARE........... Harrier, Inc. (SAUO)
HARE........... Hazard Avoidance Reconnaissance Extender
HARE........... High-Altitude Ramjet Engine
HARE........... High-Altitude Recombination Energy (SAUS)
HARE........... High-Altitude Recombination-Energy Propulsion (AAG)
HARE........... High-Altitude Reconnaissance ELINT (SAUS)
HARE........... Humans Against Rabbit Exploitation (EA)
HARE........... Hydrazine Auxiliary Rocket Engine
Hare & W.... Hare and Wallace's American Leading Cases [*A publication*] (DLA)
Hare & Wallace Amer Leading Cases... American Leading Cases, Edited by Hare and Wallace [*A publication*] (DLA)
Hare & Wallace Lead Cases (Am)... American Leading Cases, Edited by Hare and Wallace [*A publication*] (DLA)
Hare & Wal LC... American Leading Cases, Edited by Hare and Wallace [*A publication*] (DLA)
Hare App..... Hare's English Chancery Reports, Appendix to Vol. X [*A publication*] (DLA)
HAREC......... Harmonized Amateur Radio Examination Certificate (SAUO)
Hare Const Law... Hare's American Constitutional Law [*A publication*] (DLA)
Hare Disc.... Hare on Discovery of Evidence [*A publication*] (DLA)
Hare Elec..... Hare on Elections [*A publication*] (DLA)
Hare (Eng)... Hare's English Vice-Chancellors' Reports [*66-68 English Reprint*] [*1841-53*] [*A publication*] (DLA)
Hare Ev........ Hare on Discovery of Evidence [*A publication*] (DLA)
HAREM........ Halieutic Radar Experiment Mediterranean Sea (SAUO)
HAREM........ Heparin Assay Rapid Easy Method [*Medicine*] (DMAA)
HAREP......... Harbour Repairs (SAUS)
HARE Propulsion... High-Altitude Recombination Energy Propulsion (SAUS)
HARES......... High Altitude Radiation Environment Study [*FAA*] (PDAA)
HARF........... Holland Australia Retirement Foundation of Victoria [*Australia*]
Harg............ Hargrave's State Trials [*A publication*] (DLA)
Harg............ Hargrove's Reports [*68-75 North Carolina*] [*A publication*] (DLA)
HARG........... Harper Group [*NASDAQ symbol*] (TTSB)
HARG........... Harper Group, Inc. [*NASDAQ symbol*] (NQ)
HARG........... High-Speed Autoradiography
Harg & B Co Litt... Hargrave and Butler's Edition on Coke upon Littleton [*A publication*] (DLA)
Harg Co Litt... Hargrave's Notes to Coke on Littleton [*A publication*] (DLA)
Harg Coll Jur... Hargrave's Collectanea Juridica [*1791-92*] [*A publication*] (DLA)
HARGE......... Harger, MI [*American Association of Railroads railroad junction routing code*]
Harg Exer.... Hargrave's Jurisconsult Exercitations [*A publication*] (DLA)
Harg Jur Arg... Hargrave's Juridical Arguments and Collections [*A publication*] (DLA)
Harg Law Tracts... Hargrave's Law Tracts [*A publication*] (DLA)
Harg LT....... Hargrave's Law Tracts [*A publication*] (DLA)
Hargrave & Butlers Notes on Co Litt... Hargrave and Butler's Notes on Coke upon Littleton [*A publication*] (DLA)
Hargr Co Litt... Hargrave's Notes to Coke on Littleton [*A publication*] (DLA)
Hargrove...... Hargrove's Reports [*68-75 North Carolina*] [*A publication*] (DLA)
Harg State Tr... Hargrave's State Trials [*A publication*] (DLA)
Harg St Tr... Hargrave's State Trials [*A publication*] (DLA)
Harg Th....... Hargrave on the Thellusson Act [*A publication*] (DLA)
HARH........... High-Altitude Retinal Hemorrhage [*Medicine*]

HARH.......... High Area Rate Hunter (SAUS)
HARI.......... High-Altitude Regime Interceptor (SAUS)
HARI.......... Hospital-Acquired Respiratory Infection (MELL)
Hari Rao...... Indian Income Tax Decisions [*A publication*] (DLA)
HARIS.......... High Altitude Radiation Instrument System (SAUO)
HARIS.......... High-Altitude Radiological Instrumentation System
HarisHa.......... Harris & Harris Group [*Associated Press*] (SAG)
HarisSvg...... Harris Savings Bank [*Associated Press*] (SAG)
Haristn......... Hariston Corp. [*Associated Press*] (SAG)
Har Just....... Harris' Justinian [*A publication*] (DLA)
HARK.......... Hardened Reentry Kill [*Air Force*]
Harken......... Harken Energy Corp. [*Associated Press*] (SAG)
HARL.......... Harleysville Savings Association [*NASDAQ symbol*] (NQ)
HARL.......... Harleysville Savings Bank [*NASDAQ symbol*] (TTSB)
HARL.......... Human Attention Research Laboratory (SAUS)
Harland......... Manchester Court Leet Records [*A publication*] (DLA)
HARL CBM... Harleian Collection, British Museum (DLA)
HarleyD........ Harley Davidson, Inc. [*Associated Press*] (SAG)
Harleys......... Harleysville Group, Inc. [*Associated Press*] (SAG)
HARLG......... High Accuracy Ring Laser Gyro (ACAE)
HARLI.......... Harlingen, TX [*American Association of Railroads railroad junction routing code*]
HARLID......... High Angular Resolution Laser-Irradiation Detector (SAUS)
HARL MISC... Harleian Miscellany [*British*] (ROG)
HARL MSS... Harleian Manuscripts [*British*] (ROG)
Harlnd.......... Harland [*John H.*] Co. [*Associated Press*] (SAG)
HARLOT....... Height [*Depth*] of Burst, Altitude of Targets, Resources, Location, Objectives, and Time [*Nuclear war games*]
HARLS.......... Horse Antiserum to Rabbit Lymphocytes [*Immunology*]
Harlyn.......... Harlyn Products, Inc. [*Associated Press*] (SAG)
HarlyNat....... Harleysville National Corp. [*Associated Press*] (SAG)
HarlySV........ Harleysville Savings Association [*Associated Press*] (SAG)
HARM.......... Harmonic (WDAA)
Harm........... Harmonica [*of Ptolemy*] [*Classical studies*] (OCD)
Harm........... Harmon's Reports [*13-15 California*] [*A publication*] (DLA)
Harm........... Harmon's Upper Canada Common Pleas Reports [*A publication*] (DLA)
HARM.......... Harmony
HARM.......... Harwell Acid Rain Model
HARM.......... Hazard Assessment Rating Methodology (SAUS)
HARM.......... Hazardous Atmospheric Release Model [*Marine science*] (OSRA)
HARM.......... Heparin Assay Rapid Method (DMAA)
HARM.......... High-Acceleration Rocket-Missile
HARM.......... High Availability, Reliability and Maintainability (SAUS)
HARM.......... Highspeed Advanced Radiation Missile (SAUS)
HARM.......... High-Speed Anti-RADAR Missile
HARM.......... High-speed Anti-Radiation (SAUS)
HARM.......... High-Speed Anti-Radiation Missile (COE)
HARM.......... Humans Against Rape and Molestation (SAUO)
HARM.......... Hypertension, Anemia, Renal, Malabsorption [*Medicine*] (MELL)
Harma.......... Harmannus [*Authority cited in pre-1607 legal work*] (DSA)
harma.......... harmattan (SAUS)
Har Mag...... Harvard Magazine (journ.) (SAUS)
Harman........ Harman International Industries, Inc. [*Associated Press*] (SAG)
HarmBrk....... Harmony Brook, Inc. [*Associated Press*] (SAG)
HarmLgt....... Harmonic Lightwaves, Inc. [*Associated Press*] (SAG)
HarmLt......... Harmonic Lghtwaves, Inc. [*Associated Press*] (SAG)
HARMN........ Harriman, TN [*American Association of Railroads railroad junction routing code*]
Harmon........ Harmon Industries, Inc. [*Associated Press*] (SAG)
Harmon........ Harmon's Upper Canada Common Pleas Reports [*A publication*] (DLA)
HARMONICA... Harmonised Access and Retrieval for Music-Oriented Networked Information-Concerted Action (SAUS)
HarmPd........ Harmony Products, Inc. [*Associated Press*] (SAG)
Harm Pens... Harmon's Manual of United States Pension Laws [*A publication*] (DLA)
HARN.......... Harness (MSA)
HARN.......... High Accuracy Reference Network [*Mathematics*]
HARNET....... [*The*] Hong Kong Academic and Research Network [*Computer science*] (TNIG)
HARNG........ Hawaii Army National Guard (CINC)
Harnish........ Harnischfeger Industries, Inc. [*Associated Press*] (SAG)
HARN LTHR... Harness Leather (SAUS)
Harold.......... Harold's Stores, Inc. [*Associated Press*] (SAG)
HAROTS....... High-Accuracy RADAR Data Transmission System
HARP.......... Halpern's AntiRADAR Point
Harp............ Harper's South Carolina Equity Reports [*A publication*] (DLA)
Harp............ Harper's South Carolina Law Reports [*1823-30*] [*A publication*] (DLA)
Harp............ Harpocration [*Classical studies*] (OCD)
HARP.......... Harpoon (WDAA)
HARP.......... Harpsichord (WDAA)
Harp............ Harpsichordist (SAUS)
HaRP........... Harrier Review Panel [*Military*]
HaRP........... Hawaiian Rainband Project (SAUS)
HARP.......... Hazard Assessment of Rocket Propellants
HARP.......... Health Activities Recommendation Panel (SAUS)
HARP.......... Health Administration Responsibility Project (ADWA)
HARP.......... Health and Air Research Program (SAUO)
HARP.......... Heater Above Reheat Point (SAUO)
HARP.......... Heating, Air Conditioning, Refrigeration, Plumbing (ADA)
HARP.......... Heimlich-Armstrong-Rieveschl-Patrick [*Heart pump for aerospace use*]
HARP.......... Helicopter Advanced Rotor Program (SAUS)
HARP.......... High-Altitude Reconnaissance Platform
HARP.......... High Altitude Reconnaissance Project (ACAE)
HARP.......... High-Altitude Relay Point
HARP.......... High Altitude Release Point (SAUO)
HARP.......... High-Altitude Release Point (SAUS)
HARP.......... High-Altitude Research Probe (IAA)
HARP.......... High Altitude Research Problem (SAUO)
HARP.......... High Altitude Research Program (SAUO)
HARP.......... High-Altitude Research Program [*or Project*] [*Military*]
HARP.......... High Altitude Research Programme (SAUS)
HARP.......... High-Altitude Research Project (SAUS)
HARP.......... High-Altitude Research Projectile (SAUS)
HARP.......... High-Altitude Rocket Probe [*Army*]
HARP.......... High Angle Attack Research Program (SAUS)
HARP.......... Hitachi Arithmetic Processor [*Computer science*] (IEEE)
HARP.......... Holding and Reconsignment Point (IAA)
HARP.......... Homeless and At-Risk Population (DMAA)
HARP.......... Honeywell Acoustic Research Program (SAUO)
HARP.......... Honeywell Acoustic Research Project (SAUO)
HARP.......... Hughes Advanced Rotor Program (SAUS)
HARP.......... Hybrid Automated Reliability Predictor
HARP.......... Hyperbolic Analyzer Retarding Potential (SAUS)
Harp Baz...... Harpers Bazaar (SAUS)
Harp Con Cas... Harper's Conspiracy Cases [*Maryland*] [*A publication*] (DLA)
Har Pen Man... Harmon's Manual of United States Pension Laws [*A publication*] (DLA)
Harp Eq........ Harper's South Carolina Equity Reports [*A publication*] (DLA)
Harp Eq (SC)... Harper's South Carolina Equity Reports [*A publication*] (DLA)
Harper.......... Harper's Conspiracy Cases [*Maryland*] [*A publication*] (DLA)
Harper.......... Harper's South Carolina Equity Reports [*A publication*] (DLA)
Harper.......... Harper's South Carolina Law Reports [*1823-30*] [*A publication*] (DLA)
HarpGp......... Harper Group, Inc. [*Associated Press*] (SAG)
HARPI.......... Hardpoint Interceptor
HARPI.......... Height Azimuth Range Position Indicator (SAUS)
Harp L.......... Harper's South Carolina Law Reports [*1823-30*] [*A publication*] (DLA)
Harp L (SC)... Harper's South Carolina Law Reports [*1823-30*] [*A publication*] (DLA)
HARPPS....... Heat, Absence of Use, Redness, Pain, Pus, Swelling [*Medicine*] (MEDA)
Har Prob...... Harrison on Probate and Divorce [*A publication*] (DLA)
HAR-Program... High-Altitude Research Program (SAUS)
HARPS......... Heathrow Airport Radar Processing System (SAUS)
HARPS......... Hybrid AUTODIN Red Patch Service (SAUO)
HARPS......... Hybrid AUTODIN Red Patch System (MCD)
HARPSS........ High Altitude Remote Platform Surveillance System (ACAE)
HARP-TAP... High Altitude Remotely Piloted-Target Acquisition Platform (ACAE)
HARPY......... Hydrofoil Advanced Research Study Program [*Navy*]
Harr............. Harrington's Delaware Reports [*1-5 Delaware*] [*A publication*] (DLA)
Harr............. Harrington's Michigan Chancery Reports [*A publication*] (DLA)
Harr............. Harrison's Law Reports [*16-19 New Jersey*] [*A publication*] (DLA)
Harr............. Harrison's Reports [*15-17, 23-29 Indiana*] [*A publication*] (DLA)
Harr............. Harris' Reports [*A publication*] (DLA)
Harr Adv...... Harris' Hints on Advocacy [*18th ed.*] [*1943*] [*A publication*] (DLA)
HarrahE........ Harrahs Entertainment, Inc. [*Associated Press*] (SAG)
Harr & Cl Conv... Harris and Clarkson on Conveyancing, Etc. [*A publication*] (DLA)
Harr & G...... Harris and Gill's Maryland Reports [*A publication*] (DLA)
Harr & H...... Harrison and Hodgin's Upper Canada Municipal Reports [*1845-51*] [*A publication*] (DLA)
Harr & Hodg... Harrison and Hodgin's Upper Canada Municipal Reports [*1845-51*] [*A publication*] (DLA)
Harr & J...... Harris and Johnson's Maryland Reports [*A publication*] (DLA)
Harr & J (MD)... Harris and Johnson's Maryland Reports [*A publication*] (DLA)
Harr & M..... Harris and McHenry's Maryland Reports [*A publication*] (DLA)
Harr & McH... Harris and McHenry's Maryland Reports [*A publication*] (DLA)
Harr & McHen... Harris and McHenry's Maryland Reports [*A publication*] (DLA)
Harr & McH (MD)... Harris and McHenry's Maryland Reports [*A publication*] (DLA)
Harr & M'H... Harris and McHenry's Maryland Reports [*A publication*] (DLA)
Harr & R...... Harrison and Rutherford's English Common Pleas Reports [*1865-66*] [*A publication*] (DLA)
Harr & Ruth... Harrison and Rutherford's English Common Pleas Reports [*1865-66*] [*A publication*] (DLA)
Harr & Sim... Harris and Simrall's Reports [*49-52 Mississippi*] [*A publication*] (DLA)
Harr & W..... Harrison and Wollaston's English King's Bench Reports [*A publication*] (DLA)
Harr & W (Eng)... Harrison and Wollaston's English King's Bench Reports [*A publication*] (DLA)
Harr & Woll... Harrison and Wollaston's English King's Bench Reports [*A publication*] (DLA)
Harr Ch........ Harrington's Michigan Chancery Reports [*A publication*] (DLA)
Harr Ch (Mich)... Harrington's Michigan Chancery Reports [*A publication*] (DLA)
Harr Ch R..... Harrington's Michigan Chancery Reports [*A publication*] (DLA)
Harr Con LA R... Harrison's Condensed Louisiana Reports [*A publication*] (DLA)
Harr Cr L..... Harris' Principles of the Criminal Law [*22nd ed.*] [*1973*] [*A publication*] (DLA)
Harr (Del).... Harrington's Delaware Reports [*1-5 Delaware*] [*A publication*] (DLA)
Harr Dig...... Harrison's Digest of English Common Law Reports [*A publication*] (DLA)
Har Resp..... De Haruspicum Responso [*of Cicero*] [*Classical studies*] (OCD)
Harr (GA)..... Harris' Georgia Digest [*A publication*] (DLA)
Harr Hints.... Harris' Hints on Advocacy [*18th ed.*] [*1943*] [*A publication*] (DLA)
Harring........ Harrington's Delaware Reports [*1-5 Delaware*] [*A publication*] (DLA)
Harring........ Harrington's Michigan Chancery Reports [*A publication*] (DLA)
Harring Ch (Mich)... Harrington's Michigan Chancery Reports [*A publication*] (DLA)
Harrington... Harrington's Delaware Supreme Court Reports [*1832-55*] [*A publication*] (DLA)

Harrington... Harrington's Michigan Chancery Reports [*A publication*] (DLA)
Harris.......... Harris Corp. [*Associated Press*] (SAG)
Harris.......... Harris' Reports [*A publication*] (DLA)
Harris & G... Harris and Gill's Maryland Reports [*A publication*] (DLA)
Harris & Gill's MD R... Harris and Gill's Maryland Reports [*A publication*] (DLA)
Harris & J... Harris and Johnson's Maryland Reports [*A publication*] (DLA)
Harris & S... Harris and Simrall's Reports [*49-52 Mississippi*] [*A publication*] (DLA)
Harris & Sim... Harris and Simrall's Reports [*49-52 Mississippi*] [*A publication*] (DLA)
Harris & Simrall... Harris and Simrall's Reports [*49-52 Mississippi*] [*A publication*] (DLA)
HarrisCS...... Harris Computer Systems Corp. [*Associated Press*] (SAG)
Harris Dig.... Harris' Georgia Digest [*A publication*] (DLA)
Harrison...... Harrison's Law Reports [*16-19 New Jersey*] [*A publication*] (DLA)
Harrison...... Harrison's Reports [*15-17, 23-29 Indiana*] [*A publication*] (DLA)
Harrison Ch... Harrison's Chancery Practice [*A publication*] (DLA)
Harrison Dig... Harrison's Digest of English Common Law Reports [*A publication*] (DLA)
Harr Just..... Harris' Translation of the Institute of Justinian [*A publication*] (DLA)
Harr (Mich)... Harrington's Michigan Chancery Reports [*A publication*] (DLA)
Harr Min...... Harris on Titles to Mines [*A publication*] (DLA)
Harr Mun Law... Harrison's Municipal Law of Ontario [*A publication*] (DLA)
Harr NJ........ Harrison's Law Reports [*16-19 New Jersey*] [*A publication*] (DLA)
Harrod......... Harrodsburg First Financial Bancorp, Inc. [*Associated Press*] (SAG)
HARRPA....... Hydrocarbon and Rosin Resins Producers Association (SAUO)
Harr Prin..... Harris' Principiae Primae Legum [*A publication*] (DLA)
Harr Proc..... Harrison's Common Law Procedure Act [*Canada*] [*A publication*] (DLA)
Harr Rom Law... Harris' Elements of Roman Law [*A publication*] (DLA)
HARRS......... High-Altitude Radio Relay System (DNAB)
Harr St......... Harvard Studies in Classical Philology (journ.) (SAUS)
HARRTF....... Hurricane Andrew Recovery and Reconstruction Trust Fund (DEMM)
HARS........... Harris Financial, Inc. [*NASDAQ symbol*] (NASQ)
HARS........... Harris Savings Bank [*NASDAQ symbol*] (SAG)
HARS........... Hazardous Area Reporting Service [*Aviation*] (FAAC)
HARS........... Heading and Attitude Reference System (SAUS)
HARS........... Heading Attitude Reference Set (SAUO)
HARS........... Heading Attitude Reference System (MCD)
HARS........... Heavy Assault Rocket System (MCD)
HARS........... Helicopter Attitude Reference System (MCD)
HARS........... High-Altitude Route Structure workstation (SAUS)
HARS........... High Altitude Route System [*FAA*] (TAG)
HARS........... Historic Aircraft Restoration Society [*Australia*]
HARSAP....... Harbor Survey Assistance Program [*Naval Oceanographic Office*]
Harsco......... Harsco Corp. [*Associated Press*] (SAG)
Hars Pr........ Harston's California Practice and Pleading [*A publication*] (DLA)
Har St Tr..... Hargrave's State Trials [*A publication*] (DLA)
HART........... Cardiopulmonary Technologies (SAUS)
HART........... Halt All Racist Tours [*British*] (DI)
HART........... Hardened Amplifier for Radiation Transients
Hart............ Hartley's Digest of Texas Laws [*A publication*] (DLA)
Hart............ Hartley's Reports [*4-10 Texas*] [*A publication*] (DLA)
HART........... Hayden Analysis and Reporting Tool [*Computer science*]
HART........... Heartland Wireless Communications, Inc. [*NASDAQ symbol*] (SAG)
HART........... Height-Area Rain Threshold (SAUS)
HART........... Heparin-Aspirin Reinfarction Trial [*Medicine*] (DMAA)
HART........... Heparin-Aspirin Reperfusion Trial [*Cardiology*]
HART........... Heuristic Algorithmic Resource Timer (SAUO)
HART........... High Acceleration Rocket (SAUS)
HART........... High-Acceleration Rocket, Tactical (DNAB)
HART........... High Altitude Reconnaissance Technology (ACAE)
HART........... Highway Advisory Radio Tactical (SAUO)
HART........... Highway Aid by Radio Truck (IAA)
HART........... Honolulu Area Rapid Transit (SAUO)
HART........... Hospital Access and Response Terminal [*Health insurance*] (GHCT)
HART........... Hypervelocity Aircraft Rocket, Tactical
Hart & H...... Hartley and Hartley's Reports [*11-21 Texas*] [*A publication*] (DLA)
Hart Bank.... Hart's Bankrupt Law and Practice [*A publication*] (DLA)
HartC........... Hartford Capital I [*Associated Press*] (SAG)
HartC........... Hartford Capital II [*Associated Press*] (SAG)
Hart Dig....... Hartley's Digest of Texas Laws [*A publication*] (DLA)
Hartfd Cou... Hartford Courant (journ.) (SAUS)
HartfSemRec... Hartford Seminary Record (SAUO)
HartfSemRec... Hartford Seminary Record (journ.) (SAUS)
Hart Hartm... Hartmannus Hartmanni [*Deceased, 1586*] [*Authority cited in pre-1607 legal work*] (DSA)
HartHnk....... Harte Hanks Communications [*Associated Press*] (SAG)
Hartley......... Hartley's Reports [*4-10 Texas*] [*A publication*] (DLA)
Hartley & Hartley... Hartley and Hartley's Reports [*11-21 Texas*] [*A publication*] (DLA)
Hartley & Hartley Rep... Hartley and Hartley's Reports [*11-21 Texas*] [*A publication*] (DLA)
Hartman Pist... Hartmannus Pistoris [*Deceased, 1601*] [*Authority cited in pre-1607 legal work*] (DSA)
Hartm Pistor... Hartmannus Pistoris [*Deceased, 1601*] [*Authority cited in pre-1607 legal work*] (DSA)
Hartmx......... Hartmarx Corp. [*Associated Press*] (SAG)
Hart Pist...... Hartmannus Pistoris [*Deceased, 1601*] [*Authority cited in pre-1607 legal work*] (DSA)
Hartran........ Haltwell Atlas Fortran (SAUS)
HARTRAN.... Hardwell FORTRAN [*Computer science*] (IEEE)
HARTRAN.... Heading Altitude System (SAUS)
HARTRAN.... Helicopter Avionics System (SAUS)
HARTRAN.... High-Angle Scattering (SAUS)
HARTRAN.... Hungarian Academy of Sciences (SAUS)
HARTS......... Hardening Technology Studies Program (MCD)
HARTS......... Hydrometeorological Automatic Recording and Telemetering System (SAUO)
HARU........... Handbuch fuer Rundfunk und Fernsehen [*Handbook for Radio and Television*] [*NOMOS Datapool*] [*Database*]
HARU........... Heading & Attitude Reference Unit (SAUS)
HARV........... Harassment Vehicle (MCD)
Harv............ Harvard (SAUS)
Harv............ Harvard University (SAUS)
HARV........... Harvard University [*Massachusetts*]
Harv............ Harvard Vocarium [*Record label*]
HARV........... Harvest
HARV........... Harvey Universal, Inc. [*NASDAQ symbol*] (SAG)
HARV........... High-Alpha Research Vehicle (SAUS)
HARV........... High Altitude Reconnaissance Vehicle (ACAE)
HARV........... High Altitude Research Vehicle (SAUO)
HARV........... High-Altitude Research Vehicle (SAUS)
HARV........... High Angle-of-attack Research Vehicle (SAUS)
HARVAN...... Harriman and Vance [*Code name for 1968 Paris peace talks on Vietnam, derived from the surnames of US negotiators W. Averell Harriman and Cyrus R. Vance*]
HARV and MARV... Harvey Ratner and Marvin Wolfenson [*Proprietors of Target Centre basketball arena*] (ECON)
Harvard........ Harvard/Smithsonian Center for Astrophysics (SAUS)
Harvard BsnsR... Harvard Business Review (SAUO)
Harvard BsnsR... Harvard Business Review (journ.) (SAUS)
Harvard Bus Rev... Harvard Business Review [*A publication*] (JLIT)
Harvard LR... Harvard Law Review [*A publication*] (SAFN)
Harvard Stud in Class Philol... Harvard Studies in Classical Philology (journ.) (SAUS)
Harvard U.... Harvard University (GAGS)
Harv Bus World... Harvard Business World (DLA)
HarvCas....... Harveys Casinos Resorts [*Associated Press*] (SAG)
Harv CR CL Law Rev... Harvard Civil Rights - Civil Liberties Law Review [*A publication*] (ILCA)
Harv Ed Rev... Harvard Educational Review [*A publication*] (DLA)
Harv Env L Rev... Harvard Environmental Law Review [*A publication*] (DLA)
HARVEST..... Highly Active Residues Vitrification and Engineered Storage [*Nuclear energy*] [*British*] (NUCP)
HARVEST..... Highly Active Residues Vitrification Engineering Studies [*Nuclear energy*] [*British*] (NUCP)
HarvestH...... Harvest Home Financial Corp. [*Associated Press*] (SAG)
HarveyE....... Harvey Entertainment Co. [*Associated Press*] (SAG)
HarveyU....... Harvey Universal, Inc. [*Associated Press*] (SAG)
HarvGradM... Harvard Graduates Magazine (journ.) (SAUS)
HarvI........... Harvard Industries, Inc. [*Associated Press*] (SAG)
HarvInd........ Harvard Industries, Inc. [*Associated Press*] (SAG)
Harv Int'l L Club Bull... Harvard International Law Club. Bulletin [*A publication*] (DLA)
Harv Int'l L Club J... Harvard International Law Club. Journal [*A publication*] (DLA)
HarvJAsiatic Stud... Harvard Journal of Asiatic Studies (SAUO)
HarvJAsiatic Stud... Harvard Journal of Asiatic Studies (journ.) (SAUS)
HarvLaw R... Harvard Law Review (SAUO)
HarvLaw R... Harvard Law Review (journ.) (SAUS)
HarvLibBull... Harvard Library Bulletin (SAUO)
HarvLibBull... Harvard Library Bulletin (journ.) (SAUS)
Harv L Lib Inf Bull... Harvard Law Library. Information Bulletin [*A publication*] (DLA)
HarvLRev..... Harvard Law Review (SAUO)
Harv LS Rec... Harvard Law School. Record [*A publication*] (DLA)
HarvMo........ Harvard Monthly (SAUO)
HarvMo........ Harvard Monthly (journ.) (SAUS)
HarvstFn...... Harvest Financial Corp. [*Associated Press*] (SAG)
Harv Stud..... Harvard Studies in Classical Philology [*A publication*] (OCD)
HarvTheolR... Harvard Theological Review (SAUO)
HarvTheolR... Harvard Theological Review (journ.) (SAUS)
Harv Univ.... Harvard University (SAUO)
Harv Women's LJ... Harvard Women's Law Journal [*A publication*] (DLA)
Harv W Tax Ser... Harvard World Tax Series [*A publication*] (DLA)
HARVY......... Harvard Securities Group PLC (MHDW)
HARVY......... Harvey, IL [*American Association of Railroads railroad junction routing code*]
HARW.......... Harwich [*Municipal borough in England*]
HARWAS...... Horizontal-Axis Rotating-Wing Aeronautical System (PDAA)
HARX........... Hawaii Railway [*Federal Railroad Administration identification code*]
HARY........... Harry's Farmers Market [*NASDAQ symbol*] (TTSB)
HARY........... Harry's Farmers Markets [*NASDAQ symbol*] (SAG)
HaryFar........ Harry's Farmers Markets [*Associated Press*] (SAG)
HARYOU...... Harlem Youth Opportunities Unlimited (SAUO)
HARYOU-ACT... Harlem Youth Opportunities Unlimited - Associated Community Teams [*A kind of Peace Corps for Harlem area of New York City*]
HARZ........... Harrison Radiator [*Federal Railroad Administration identification code*]
HAS............. Hail [*Saudi Arabia*] [*Airport symbol*] (OAG)
HAS............. Hamburg Airlines, GmbH [*Germany*] [*ICAO designator*] (FAAC)
HAS............. Hamilton Anxiety Scale [*Psychology*] (DB)
HAS............. Hanford Analytical Services (SAUS)
HAS............. Harassment Vehicle [*Military*]
HAS............. Hardened Aircraft Shelter [*British military*] (DMA)
HAS............. Hasbro, Inc. [*AMEX symbol*] (SPSG)
HAS............. Hastings [*New Zealand*] [*Seismograph station code, US Geological Survey*] [*Closed*] (SEIS)
HAS............. Hawaiian Academy of Science (SAUO)
HAS............. Hawick Archaeological Society (SAUO)

HAS .... Head Address Set (SAUS)
HAS .... Heading Altitude Sensor (IAA)
HAS .... Heading Altitude System
HAS .... Heading and Attitude Sensor (SAUS)
HAS .... Heading and Attitude System (SAUS)
HAS .... Headmaster Association of Scotland (SAUO)
HAS .... Headmasters Association of Scotland (SAUS)
HAS .... Health Advisory Service (SAUS)
HAS .... Health Advocacy Services [*AARP*]
HAS .... Health Application Systems [*Medicine*] (EDAA)
HAS .... Health Assessment Summary (EEVL)
HAS .... Helical Aerial System (SAUS)
HAS .... Helical Antenna System
HAS .... Helicopter Air Service (SAUO)
HAS .... Helicopter Anti-Submarine
HAS .... Helicopter Approach System (SAUS)
HAS .... Helicopter Assault Secondary (SAUS)
HAS .... Helicopter Aviation Sales (SAUO)
HAS .... Helicopter Avionics System [*Air Force*]
HAS .... Helium Atom-Beam Scattering [*Materials science*]
HAS .... Helium Atom Scattering (SAUS)
HAS .... Hellenic Affilliation Scale (SAUS)
HAS .... Hellenic Astronautical Society (SAUO)
HAS .... Hepatic Angiosarcoma [*Medicine*] (MELL)
HAS .... High Altitude Sampler (SAUO)
HAS .... High-Altitude Sampler
HAS .... High Altitude Search (ACAE)
HAS .... High-Altitude Sensor (SAUS)
HAS .... High Altitude Syncope [*Medicine*] (MELL)
HAS .... High-Angle Strafe
HAS .... High Apgar Score [*Medicine*] (MELL)
HAS .... High Availability Subsystem (SAUS)
HAs .... Highest Asymptomatic [*Medicine*] (EDAA)
HAS .... Highest Asymptomatic [*Dose*] [*Medicine*]
HAS .... Highest Average Salary
HAS .... Hindered Amine Stabilizers (SAUS)
HAS .... Holddown Alignment Support (NASA)
HAS .... Holmes-Adie Syndrome [*Medicine*] (MELL)
HAS .... Holograph Assessment System
HAS .... Hood, Aircrew Survival (SAUS)
HAS .... Horatio Alger Society (EA)
HAS .... Horizontal Air Shower (SAUS)
HAS .... Hospital Accounting System (SAUS)
HAS .... Hospital Adjustment Scale [*Psychology*]
HAS .... Hospital Administrative Services
HAS .... Hospital Advisory Service [*British*]
HAS .... Hospital Advisory Service for England and Wales (SAUS)
HAS .... Hospital Albert Schweitzer [*Medicine*] (EDAA)
Has .... Hospitality (journ.) (SAUS)
HAS .... Housing Assistance Section (SAUO)
HAs .... Housing Assistants (SAUS)
HAS .... Hover Augmentation System
HAS .... Hubbard Association of Scientologists (or Scientology) (SAUO)
HAS .... Human Adult Serum [*Medicine*] (EDAA)
HAS .... Human Albumin Solution [*Clinical chemistry*]
HAS .... Humanities and Area Studies (SAUS)
HAS .... Hungarian Academy of Sciences (SAUO)
HAS .... Hyaluronic Acid Synthase [*An enzyme*]
HAS .... Hydraulic Actuation System (MCD)
HAS .... Hydraulic Adjustable Speed
HAS .... Hydrogen-Active Species (SAUS)
HAS .... Hydrogen Actuation System (NASA)
HAS .... Hydroxy-Aluminosilicate [*Inorganic chemistry*]
HAS .... Hydroxylamine Acid Sulfate [*Inorganic chemistry*]
HAS .... Hydroxylammonium Sulfate [*Inorganic chemistry*]
HAS .... Hygiene Assessment System [*British*] (GVA)
HAS .... Hyperalimentation Solution [*Pharmacology*] (DAVI)
HAS .... Hypertensive Arteriosclerotic [*Cardiology*]
HAS .... Hypoxanthine and Azaserine [*Medium*]
HASA .... Hypersonic Aerospace Sizing Analysis (SAUS)
HASAC .... Health and Safety Advice Centre (HEAS)
HASAM .... Hardened Aircraft Shelter Attack Munition (SAUS)
HASAWA .... Health and Safety at Work Act [*1974*] [*British*] (NUCP)
HASB .... Assab [*Ethiopia*] [*ICAO location identifier*] (ICLI)
Hasb .... Hasbrouck's Reports [*Idaho*] [*A publication*] (DLA)
Hasbro .... Hasbro, Inc. [*Associated Press*] (SAG)
HASC .... Hanford Analytical Service Council (SAUO)
HASC .... Headquarters, Air Service Command [*Air Force*]
HASC .... Hellenic Air Support Command (SAUS)
HASC .... Historical Automobile Society of Canada
HASC .... Hospitality Association of South Carolina (SRA)
HASC .... House Armed Services Committee [*US Congress*] (AABC)
HASC .... House Armed Services Subcommittee on Military Personnel and Compensation (SAUO)
HASC .... Hughes Aircraft South Carolina (ACAE)
HASC .... Hyderabad Army Service Corps [*British military*] (DMA)
HASCI .... Human Applications Standard Computer Interface [*Keyboard*] (MCD)
HASCO .... Haitian-American Sugar Company (SAUO)
HASCO .... HAWK [*Homing All the Way Killer*] Assembly System Checkout (SAA)
HASCO .... Helicopter and Airplane Services Corporation (SAUO)
HASCOG .... Health and Safety Co-Ordinating Group (HEAS)
HASCVD .... Hypertensive Arteriosclerotic Cardiovascular Disease [*Cardiology*] (MAE)
HASD .... Hanford Self Assessment Database (SAUS)
HASD .... Highest Asymptomatic Dose [*Medicine*] (EDAA)
HASD .... Humanist Association of San Diego (SAUO)
HASD .... Sodo [*Ethiopia*] [*ICAO location identifier*] (ICLI)
HASDA .... High-Accuracy Strapdown Accelerometer (SAUS)
HAS Dose .... Highest Asymptomatic Dose (SAUS)
HASE .... Head Angulation Sighting Equipment [*British military*] (DMA)
HASE .... Hydrophobic Alkali Soluble Emulsion [*Paint technology*]
HASELL .... Height/Airframe/Safety/Engine/Location/Lookout (SAUS)
HASG .... Helicopter Airworthiness Study Group (SAUO)
Hash .... Hashish [*Medicine*] (EDAA)
HASH .... Hashish (GOBB)
haSH .... Human Achaete-Scute Homologue [*Genetics*]
HASH .... Sheik Hussein [*Ethiopia*] [*ICAO location identifier*] (ICLI)
HASHD .... Hypertensive Arteriosclerotic Heart Disease (MELL)
HASI .... Hubbard Association of Scientologists (or Scientology) International (SAUO)
HASI .... Hughes Aircraft Systems International (ACAE)
HASINS .... High Accuracy Submersible Inertial Navigation System (PDAA)
HASIS .... House Armed Services Investigation Subcommittee [*US Congress*]
HASJPL .... H. Allen Smith Jet Propulsion Laboratory [*Former name, JPL, continues to be used as official name*] [*Name adopted in 1973 to honor retiring congressman*]
Hask .... Haskell's Reports for United States Courts in Maine (Fox's Decisions) [*A publication*] (DLA)
Haskel .... Haskel International, Inc. [*Associated Press*] (SAG)
HASL .... Hawaii Association of School Librarians
HASL .... Health and Safety Laboratory [*ERDA*]
HASL .... Hertfordshire Association of Special Libraries [*British*] (NITA)
HASL .... Hot-Air Solder Leveling [*Materials science*]
Hasler Rev ... Hasler Review (journ.) (SAUS)
Hasl Med Jur ... Haslam's Medical Jurisprudence [*A publication*] (DLA)
HASM .... Hanford Analytical Services Management (SAUS)
HASM .... Hanford Analytical Services Program (SAUS)
HASM .... Hanford Analytic Sample Management (SAUS)
HASM .... Hardened Aircraft Shelter Munition (SAUS)
HASM .... Historic American Sheet Music
HASO .... Assosa [*Ethiopia*] [*ICAO location identifier*] (ICLI)
HASP .... Hanford Analytical Services Program (SAUO)
HASP .... Hardware Assisted Software Polling (SAUO)
HASP .... Hawaiian Armed Services Police (SAUO)
HASP .... Health & Safety Plan (SAUO)
HASP .... Health and Safety Program (SAUO)
HAsP .... Health Aspects of Pesticides [*Medicine*] (DMAA)
HASP .... Heuristic Adaptive Surveillance Project (ACAE)
HASP .... High Accuracy Satellite Position (ACAE)
HASP .... High Altitude Sampling Plane
HASP .... High-Altitude Sampling Plane (SAUO)
HASP .... High-Altitude Sampling Program [*Air Force*]
HASP .... High-Altitude Sounding Program (IAA)
Hasp .... High altitude sounding projectile (SAUO)
HASP .... High-Altitude Sounding Projectile
HASP .... High Altitude Space Platform (SAUO)
HASP .... High-Altitude Space Platform
HASP .... High-Altitude Space Probe (IAA)
HASP .... High Altitude Surveillance Platform (ACAE)
HASP .... High-Level Automatic Scheduling Program (BUR)
HASP .... Hollog-Nosed Active Seeker Program (ACAE)
HASP .... Horn of Africa Support Project (SAUO)
HASP .... Hospital Admission and Surveillance Program (MEDA)
HASP .... Housten Automatic Spooling Priority system (SAUS)
HASP .... Houston Atomic Spooling Priority (SAUS)
HASP .... Houston Attached Support Processor (SAUS)
HASP .... Houston Automated Spooling Program (SAUS)
HASP .... Houston Automatic Simulator of Peripherals (SAUS)
HASP .... Houston Automatic Spooling and Printing (SAUS)
HASP .... Houston Automatic Spooling Priority (SAUS)
HASP .... Houston Automatic Spooling Priority System [*Computer science*]
HASP .... Houston Automatic Spooling Procedure (SAUS)
HASP .... Houston Automatic Spooling Processor [*IBM equipment operating system*] (NITA)
HASP .... Houston Automatic Spooling Program [*Computer science*] (ITCA)
HASP .... Houston Automatic Spool Process (SAUS)
HASPA .... High-Altitude Superpressure Powered Aerostat [*Navy*]
HASPE .... Harris ADA Programming Support Environment (SAUS)
HASPID .... House Armed Services Permanent Investigations Subcommittee [*US Congress*] (AAG)
HASP/MLI .... Houston Automatic Spooling Program/Multi-Leaving Interface [*Communications term*] (DCT)
HASP/RJE .... Houston Automatic Spooling Priority with Remote Job Entry (SAUO)
HASPS .... Hardened Array Solar Power System [*Military*]
HASPS .... Hardened Solar Panel System (SAUS)
HASP System ... Houston Automatic Spooling and Printing System (SAUS)
HASQ .... Hardware-Assisted Software Queue
HASQAP .... Hanford Analytic Services Quality Assurance Plan (SAUS)
HASR .... Hauserman, Inc. [*NASDAQ symbol*] (COMM)
HASR .... High-Altitude Sounding Rocket
HASRD .... Health and Safety Research Division [*Oak Ridge National Laboratory*]
HASS .... Hardware and Services Schedule (ACAE)
HASs .... High Altitude Samplers (SAUO)
HASS .... High-Altitude Seeker System (SAUS)
HASS .... High Availability Subsystem (SAUS)
HASS .... Highland and Agricultural Society of Scotland (SAUO)
HASS .... Highly Accelerated Stress Screening [*Vibration testing*]
HASSS .... High-Accuracy Spacecraft Separation System (IAA)

HAST .... Harrier Avionics Systems Trainer (SAUO)
HAST .... Hastings Entertainment, Inc. [*NASDAQ symbol*] (NASQ)
Hast .... Hastings' Reports [*69, 70 Maine*] [*A publication*] (DLA)
HASt .... Hauptannahmestelle (SAUS)
HAST .... Hausa Speaking Test [*Center for Applied Linguistics*] (TES)
HAST .... Health Systems Trust (SAUS)
HAST .... High-Altitude Selection Test [*British military*] (DMA)
HAST .... High-Altitude Supersonic Target [*Later, HAHST*] (MCD)
HAST .... Highly Accelerated Stress Testing (AAEL)
HAST .... Humanitarian Assistance Survey Team
HASTAM ...... Health and Safety Technology Management (AIE)
Hast Cen R... Hastings Center Report [*A publication*] (BRI)
HASTE .... Have Auger Sensor Test and Evaluation (SAUS)
HASTE .... Hazard Assessment System for Toxic Emissions [*Computer-based emergency management system*] [*Environmental Research & Technology*]
HASTE .... Helicopter Ambulance Service to Emergencies (SAUO)
HASTE .... Helicopter Assault Survivability in a Threat Environment (MCD)
HASTI .... Hastings, NE [*American Association of Railroads railroad junction routing code*]
HASTI .... High-Altitude Strike Indicator
Hasting .... Hastings Manufacturing Co. [*Associated Press*] (SAG)
Hastings Cent Rep... Hastings Center. Report (journ.) (SAUS)
Hastings C Law... University of California Hastings College of Law (GAGS)
Hast Int & Comp L Rev... Hastings' International and Comparative Law Review [*A publication*] (DLA)
HASTs .... High-Altitude Supersonic Targets (SAUO)
Hast Tr .... Trial of Warren Hastings [*A publication*] (DLA)
HASVR .... High-Altitude Space Velocity RADAR (AAG)
HASW .... High-Activity Solid Waste (SAUS)
HASWA .... Health and Safety at Work Act [*British*]
HASY .... Handling Systems (SAUS)
HASZ .... Harvest State Co-Operative [*Federal Railroad Administration identification code*]
HAT .... Halsted Aphasia Test [*Medicine*] (EDAA)
HAT .... Handbuch zum Alten Testament [*A publication*] (BJA)
HAT .... Handover Transmitter (IAA)
HAT .... Harbour Acceptance Testing (SAUS)
HAT .... Harbour Acceptance Trials [*Missile*] [*British*]
HAT .... Hardened and Tempered (IAA)
HAT .... Hardened Antenna Technology (SAUO)
HAT .... Hardness Assurance Test
HAT .... Hardware Acceptance Team (SAUS)
HAT .... Harmonic Attenuation Table [*or Test*] (DAVI)
HAT .... Hashed Address Table (SAUS)
HAT .... Hat Corporation of America (SAUO)
Hat .... Hatran (BJA)
HAT .... Hatteras Income Sec [*NYSE symbol*] (TTSB)
HAT .... Hatteras Income Securities, Inc. [*NYSE symbol*] (SPSG)
HAT .... Hatteras, NC [*Location identifier*] [*FAA*] (FAAL)
HAT .... Hawaiian Archives for Tsunamis
HAT .... Head Address Transfer (SAUS)
HAT .... Head, Arms, and Trunk [*Anatomy*] (DAVI)
HAT .... Heathlands [*Australia*] [*Airport symbol*] [*Obsolete*] (OAG)
HAT .... Heavy Artillery Tractor [*British military*] (DMA)
HAT .... Height above Runway Touchdown Zone Elevation [*Aviation*]
HAT .... Height above Terrain
HAT .... Height Above Touchdown (PDAA)
HAT .... Helicopter Acquisition Test (MCD)
HAT .... Helicopter Automatic Track (SAUO)
HAT .... Heterophil Antibody Titer (DB)
HAT .... High-Altitude Target
HAT .... High Altitude Temperature (PDAA)
HAT .... High-Altitude Temperature Rocket
HAT .... High-Altitude Testing [*Sounding rocket*]
HAT .... High-Altitude Transmitter
HAT .... High-Angle Threat
HAT .... Highest Astronomical Angle [*Nautical term*] (NTA)
HAT .... Highest Astronomical Tide
HAT .... Highly Aphid Transmissible [*Plant pathology*]
HAT .... Histone Acetyltransferase [*An enzyme*]
HAT .... History Advertising Trust [*British*] (DBA)
HAT .... Home Area Toll [*Telecommunications*] (TEL)
HAT .... Horizontal Alidade Tie
HAT .... Horizontal Axis Turbine (SAUS)
HAT .... Hospital Alliance of Tennessee (SRA)
HAT .... Hospital Arrival Time (MELL)
HAT .... Housing Action Trust [*British*] (ECON)
HAT .... Housing Association Trust (SAUO)
HAT .... Hug-a-Tree and Survive (EA)
HAT .... Hypervelocity Ammunition Technology (SAUS)
HAT .... Hypoxanthine-Aminopterin-Thymidine [*Medium*] [*Biochemistry*]
HATA .... Hong Kong Association of Travel Agents (SAUO)
HATACS .... Helicopter Air-to-Air Combat Simulation (MCD)
HATAPH .... Hexaalkyltriamidophosphazohydride (SAUS)
HATBG .... Hattiesburg, MS [*American Association of Railroads railroad junction routing code*]
HATCA .... Hungarian Air Traffic Controllers Association (SAUO)
HATCDS .... High-Altitude Terrain Contour Data Sensor (MSA)
Hatcher's Kan Dig... Hatcher's Kansas Digest [*A publication*] (DLA)
HATF .... Hydraulic Actuator Test Fixture
HATFPEV ..... Hatfield Peverel [*England*]
HATG .... Horse Anti-Human Thymocyte Globulin [*Immunology*] (AAMN)
HATH .... Hathaway Corp. [*NASDAQ symbol*] (NQ)
HATH .... Heterosexual Attitudes toward Homosexuality [*Scale*]
Hathwy .... Hathaway Corp. [*Associated Press*] (SAG)
HATIS .... Helmet Acquisition and Target Indication System (SAUS)
HATIS .... Helmet Acquisition & Tracking Indication System (SAUS)
HAT/LANT.... Habitability Assistance Team/Atlantic (DNAB)
HATLS .... Hostile Artillery Positions (RDA)
HATLS .... Hostile Artillery Target Locating System (SAUO)
HATMD .... High Altitude Theater Missile Defense (SAUS)
HATO .... Handling Tool (AAG)
HATO .... Tendaho [*Ethiopia*] [*ICAO location identifier*] (ICLI)
HATOFF .... Highest Astronomical Tide of the Foreseeable Future (PDAA)
HATOL .... Horizontal Altitude Take-Off and Landing (PDAA)
HATOM .... Highest Astronomical Tide of the Month (PDAA)
HATOY .... Highest Astronomical Tide of the Year (PDAA)
HATP .... Tippi [*Ethiopia*] [*ICAO location identifier*] (ICLI)
HAT/PAC...... Habitability Assistance Team/Pacific (DNAB)
HATR .... Hazardous Air Traffic Report
HATR .... Headquarters Area Technical Representative (SAUO)
HATR .... High-temperature Attenuated Total Reflectance (SAUS)
HATR .... Horizontal Attenuated Total Reflection [*Spectroscopy*]
HATRA .... Hosiery and Allied Trades Research Association [*British*] (BI)
HATRAC....... Handover Transfer and Receiver Accept Change [*SAGE*]
HATRACK..... Hurricane and Typhoon Tracking (SAUO)
HATREMS.... Hazardous and Trace Emissions Monitoring System [*Environmental science*] (COE)
HATREMS.... Hazardous and Trace Emissions System [*Environmental Protection Agency*]
HATRIC .... Harbor Traffic Ranging Identification and Communication (SAUO)
HATRICS ...... Hampshire Technical Research Industrial and Commercial Service [*British*] (NITA)
HAT Rocket... High-Altitude Testing Rocket (SAUS)
HATRON ...... Heavy Attack Squadron (MUGU)
HATRS .... High-Altitude Transmit/Receive Satellite (SAUS)
HATS .... Hardened Tactical Shelters
HATS .... Harmonization of Advanced Telecommunications Systems (SAUS)
Hats .... Hatsell's Parliamentary Precedents [*1290-1818*] [*A publication*] (DLA)
HATS .... HAWK Advanced Training Simulator (SAUS)
HATS .... Hazard Abatement Tracking System [*Environmental science*] (COE)
HATS .... Head and Torso Simulator [*A dummy developed by British Telecommunications Ltd.*]
HATS .... Heading, Altitude, True Airspeed [*Aviation*] (CAAL)
HATS .... Helicopter Advanced Tactical System (MCD)
HATS .... Helicopter Antitank Target System (SAUO)
HATS .... Helicopter Attack System
HATS .... Helicopter Automatic Targeting System (SAUS)
HATS .... Helmet Attitude Tracking System (SAUO)
HATS .... Heuristic Automated transportation Mode System (SAUO)
HATS .... Heuristic Automated Transportation System (MCD)
HATS .... High-Accuracy Targeting Subsystem
HATS .... High-Altitude Target-Skylite (SAUS)
HATS .... High Altitude Terrain Contour Data Sensor (SAUO)
HATS .... High-Altitude Terrain Contour Data Sensor
HATS .... High-Altitude Terrain Sensor (SAUS)
HATS .... High Altitude Test Stand (SAUO)
HATS .... High-Altitude Test Stand
HATS .... Holden's Air Transport Services [*Australia*]
HATS .... Hour Angle of the True Sun [*Navigation*]
HATS .... Huntsville Association of Technical Societies
HATS .... Hybrid Automatic Test System (SAUO)
HATS .... Tessenei [*Ethiopia*] [*ICAO location identifier*] (ICLI)
Hats Pr .... Hatsell's Parliamentary Precedents [*1290-1818*] [*A publication*] (DLA)
Hats Prec..... Hatsell's Parliamentary Precedents [*1290-1818*] [*A publication*] (DLA)
Hatt .... Hattusilis (BJA)
HATT .... Heparin-Associated Thrombocytopenia and Thrombosis [*Medicine*] (DMAA)
HATT .... High-Speed Aeronautical Technologies Testbed (SAUS)
HATTS .... Hemagglutination Treponemal Test for Syphilis [*Medicine*] (DMAA)
HattSe .... Hatteras Income Securities, Inc. [*Associated Press*] (SAG)
HATT-X .... High-Speed Aeronautical Technologies Testbed-Experimental (SAUS)
HATU .... Heavy Air Training Unit
HATU .... Heavy Attack Training Unit
HATV .... High-Altitude Test Vehicle
HATV .... Hydrofoil Amphibious Tracked Vehicle (SAUO)
HATW .... Heavy Attack Training Wing (SAUO)
HATWG .... Heavy Attack Training Wing (SAUS)
HATWING .... Heavy Attack Wing
HATWINGLANT... Heavy Attack Wing, Atlantic Fleet
HATWINGPAC... Heavy Attack Wing, Pacific Fleet
HATZ .... Hallett [*Federal Railroad Administration identification code*]
HAU .... Haudompre [*France*] [*Seismograph station code, US Geological Survey*] (SEIS)
HAU .... Haugesund [*Norway*] [*Airport symbol*] (OAG)
HAU .... Haultain Resources Ltd. [*Vancouver Stock Exchange symbol*]
hau .... Hausa [*MARC language code*] [*Library of Congress*] (LCCP)
HAU .... Hebrew Actors Union (EA)
HAU .... Helena, MT [*Location identifier*] [*FAA*] (FAAL)
HAU .... Hemagglutination Unit [*Hematology*]
HAU .... Horizontal Arithmetic Unit
HAU .... Hybrid Arithmetic Unit
HAUAV .... High-Altitude Unpiloted Aerial Vehicles (SAUS)
HAUL .... Allied Holdings [*NASDAQ symbol*] (TTSB)
HAUL .... Allied Holdings, Inc. [*NASDAQ symbol*] (SAG)
HAUP .... Hauppauge Digital [*NASDAQ symbol*] (TTSB)
HAUP .... Hauppauge Digital, Inc. [*NASDAQ symbol*] (SAG)
HaupD .... Hauppauge Digital, Inc. [*Associated Press*] (SAG)
HaupgD .... Hauppauge Digital, Inc. [*Associated Press*] (SAG)

HAUPTW...... Hauptwerk [*Masterpiece*] [*German*]
HAUPW...... Hauppague Digital Wrrt'A' [*NASDAQ symbol*] (TTSB)
HAURIEND.... Hauriendus [*To Be Drunk*] [*Pharmacy*] (ROG)
HAUS.......... Hauser Chemical Research [*NASDAQ symbol*] (TTSB)
HAUS.......... Hauser Chemical Research, Inc. [*NASDAQ symbol*] (SAG)
HAUS.......... Hauser, Inc. [*NASDAQ symbol*] (SAG)
HausCh........ Hauser Chemical Research, Inc. [*Associated Press*] (SAG)
Hauser......... Hauser, Inc. [*Associated Press*] (SAG)
haust.......... Haustus [*Drink*] [*Latin*] (STED)
HAUST......... Haustus [*A Drink*] [*Pharmacy*]
HAUST PURG... Haustus Purgans [*Purging Draught*] [*Pharmacy*] (ROG)
HAUT.......... Hautboy [*Oboe*]
Haut........... Heautontimorumenos [*of Terence*] [*Classical studies*] (OCD)
HAV............ Hallux Abducto Valgus [*Orthopedics*] (DAVI)
HAV............ Havana [*Cuba*] [*Airport symbol*] (OAG)
HAV............ Havering [*Borough in England*]
HAV............ Haversine [*Mathematics*]
HAV............ Havilah [*California*] [*Seismograph station code, US Geological Survey*] [*Closed*] (SEIS)
Hav............ Haviland's Prince Edward Island Chancery Reports, by Peters [*1850-72*] [*Canada*] [*A publication*] (DLA)
Hav............ Havildar [*British military*] (DMA)
HAV............ Heating and Ventilation (SAUS)
HAV............ Heavily Armed Vehicle (SAUO)
HAV............ Heavily Armed Vessel (SAUS)
HAV............ Heavily Armed Vessels
HAV............ Hemadsorption Virus [*Medicine*] (DB)
HAV............ Hepatitis A Virus
HAV............ High-Accuracy Voltmeter
HAV............ High-Activity Variant [*Cells*] (DB)
HAV............ High Asset Value (SAUS)
HAV............ Hilprecht Anniversary Volume. Studies in Assyriology and Archaeology Dedicated to Hermann V. Hilprecht [*Leipzig*] [*A publication*] (BJA)
HAV............ Hot Air Vulcanization
HAV............ Hypovirulence-Associated Virus
HAVA.......... Harvard Industries [*NASDAQ symbol*] (TTSB)
HAVA.......... Harvard Industries, Inc. [*NASDAQ symbol*] (NQ)
HAVAB......... Hepatitis A Virus Antibody [*Medicine*] (STED)
HAVAg......... Hepatitis A Virus Antigen [*Immunochemistry*]
HAVAGO...... Horizontal And Vertical Adjustment of Geodetic Observations (SAUO)
HAVC.......... Health Audiovisual On-Line Catalog [*Northeastern Ohio Universities*] [*Information service or system*] [*Defunct*]
HAVCAP....... High Asset Value Combat Air Patrol (SAUS)
Hav Ch Rep... Haviland's Prince Edward Island Chancery Reports [*1850-72*] [*A publication*] (DLA)
HAVCO......... Have Complied
HAVE.......... Heating and Ventilation Estimating [*Tipdata Ltd.*] [*Software package*] (NCC)
HAVE.......... Height Average (IAA)
HAVE.......... Homemaking and Volunteer Experience (DICI)
HAVEN......... Haven [*Commonly used*] (OPSA)
HAVEN......... Help Addicts Voluntarily End Narcotics
HavenB........ Haven Bancorp [*Associated Press*] (SAG)
Haverty........ Haverty Furniture Companies, Inc. [*Associated Press*] (SAG)
HAVi........... Home Audio Video Interoperability
Havil........... Haviland's Prince Edward Island Reports [*A publication*] (DLA)
HA Virus...... Haemadsorption Virus (SAUS)
HA Virus...... Hemadsorption Virus (SAUS)
Hav-Maj....... Havildar-Major [*British military*] (DMA)
HAVN.......... Haven [*Commonly used*] (OPSA)
HAVN.......... Haven Bancorp [*NASDAQ symbol*] (SAG)
HAVO.......... Hawaii Volcanoes National Park
HAVOC........ Heritage and Videotex over the Country (SAUS)
HAVOC........ Histogram Average Ogive Calculator
Hav PEI........ Haviland's Prince Edward Island Reports [*A publication*] (DLA)
HAVREP....... Abridged Arrival Report [*Navy*] (NVT)
HAVREP....... Have Report [*Navy*] (ANA)
Havrfld......... Haverfield Corp. [*Associated Press*] (SAG)
Havrty.......... Haverty Furniture Companies, Inc. [*Associated Press*] (SAG)
HAVS.......... Hand Arm Vibration Syndrome (LDOE)
HAVS.......... Harpoon Asset Visibility System (MCD)
HAVT.......... Hardness Assurance Verification Testing (MCD)
HAVT.......... Haverty Furniture [*NASDAQ symbol*] (TTSB)
HAVT.......... Haverty Furniture Companies, Inc. [*NASDAQ symbol*] (NQ)
HAVTA......... Haverty Furniture'A' [*NASDAQ symbol*] (TTSB)
HAW............ Fargo, ND [*Location identifier*] [*FAA*] (FAAL)
HAW............ Hafnium Column Waste [*Nuclear energy*] (NRCH)
Haw............ Hawaii (BEE)
HAW............ Hawaii (KSC)
haw............ Hawaiian [*MARC language code*] [*Library of Congress*] (LCCP)
HAW............ Hawaiian Ammunition Depot (SAUO)
HAW............ Hawaii-Continental United States Submarine Cable (SAUS)
Haw............ Hawaii Supreme Court Reports [*A publication*] (DLA)
Haw............ Hawarde's Star Chamber Cases [*A publication*] (DLA)
Haw............ Hawkins' Annual Reports [*19-24 Louisiana*] [*A publication*] (DLA)
Haw............ Hawkins' Pleas of the Crown [*England*] [*A publication*] (DLA)
HAW............ Hawksbill Resources, Inc. [*Vancouver Stock Exchange symbol*]
Haw............ Hawley's Reports [*10-20 Nevada*] [*A publication*] (DLA)
HAW............ Heavy Antiarmor Weapon
HAW............ Heavy Anti-Tank Assault Weapon (SAUO)
HAW............ Heavy Antitank Weapon (INF)
HAW............ Heavy Assault Weapon
HAW............ Helicopter Assault Wave
HAW............ High-Acid Waste [*Nuclear energy*] (NRCH)
HAW............ High Active Waste [*Nuclear energy*]
HAW............ High-Activity Waste (SAUS)
HAW............ Highly Active Waste
HAW............ Holidays and Anniversaries of the World [*A publication*]
HAW............ Home All the Way [*Military*] (CAAL)
HAW............ Hour Angle West (SAUS)
HAW............ Hypersonic Aerodynamic Weapon (DOMA)
HAWA.......... Hammond Ambassador World Atlas (SAUS)
HAWA.......... Hawaii
HAWADS....... High-Altitude Weather Aircraft Data System (SAUS)
Hawaii......... Hawaii Reports [*A publication*] (DLA)
Hawaiian Rep... Hawaii Reports [*A publication*] (DLA)
HAWAIIANSEAFRON... Hawaiian Sea Frontier [*Nautical term*] (NTA)
Hawaii BN... Hawaii Bar News [*A publication*] (DLA)
Hawaii Dist... United States District Court, District of Hawaii (DLA)
Hawaii Med J... Hawaii Medical Journal (journ.) (SAUS)
Hawaii PUC Dec... Hawaii Public Utilities Commission Decisions [*A publication*] (DLA)
Hawaii Rep... Hawaii Reports [*A publication*] (DLA)
Hawaii Rev Stat... Hawaii Revised Statutes [*A publication*] (DLA)
Hawaii Rules & Reg... Hawaii Rules and Regulations [*A publication*] (DLA)
Hawaii Sess Laws... Session Laws of Hawaii [*A publication*] (DLA)
HawAir......... Hawaiian Airlines, Inc. [*Associated Press*] (SAG)
Hawarde....... Hawarde's Star Chamber Cases [*A publication*] (DLA)
Hawarde St Ch... Hawarde's Star Chamber Cases [*A publication*] (DLA)
Haw Ass....... Hawes on Assignments [*A publication*] (DLA)
HAWB.......... House Air Waybill [*Shipping*] (DS)
HAWC.......... Help for Abused Women and Children (SAUS)
HAWC.......... High Active Waste Concentrate (SAUO)
HAWC.......... Homing and Warning Computer (MCD)
HAWC.......... Wacca [*Ethiopia*] [*ICAO location identifier*] (ICLI)
Haw Cr Rep... Hawley's American Criminal Reports [*A publication*] (DLA)
HAWCS........ Hughes Aircraft Wireless Control Society (ACAE)
HAWDC........ Hotel Association of Washington, D.C. (SRA)
HAWDF........ Honorary Adviser to the War Department Fleet (SAUO)
Haw Div....... Hawaiian Division (SAUO)
HAWE.......... Hamburg-Wechsler Intelligence Test [*Psychology*]
HAWE.......... Honorary Association for Women in Education (SAUO)
HawEl.......... Hawaiian Electric Industries, Inc. [*Associated Press*] (SAG)
Hawes Jur.... Hawes on Jurisdiction of Courts [*A publication*] (DLA)
HAWFCAR.... Helicopter Adverse Weather Fire Control/Acquisition Radar (SAUS)
Haw Fed....... Hawaii Federal [*Legal term*] (DLA)
HAWHA........ Heart of America Walking Horse Association (EA)
HAWIC......... Hamburg-Wechsler Intelligence Test for Children (STED)
HAWIK......... Hamburg-Wechsler-Intelligenztest fuer Kinder [*Hamburg-Wechsler Intelligence Test for Children*] [*Psychology*]
Haw Isls...... Hawaiian Islands (SAUS)
HAWK.......... Have Alimony, Will Keep
HAWK.......... Hawkesbury [*England*]
Hawk........... Hawkins' Pleas of the Crown [*England*] [*A publication*] (DLA)
HAWK.......... Hawks Industries [*NASDAQ symbol*] (TTSB)
HAWK.......... Hawks Industries, Inc. [*NASDAQ symbol*] (NQ)
HAWK.......... Homing All the Way Killer [*Small missile*]
HAWK.......... Hunting and Angling With Kids
Hawk Abr..... Hawkins' Abridgment of Coke upon Littleton [*A publication*] (DLA)
HawkB.......... Hawkeye Bancorp [*Associated Press*] (SAG)
HawkC.......... Hawkins Chemical, Inc. [*Associated Press*] (SAG)
Hawk Coke Abr... Hawkins' Abridgment of Coke upon Littleton [*A publication*] (DLA)
Hawk Co Litt... Hawkins' Coke upon Littleton [*A publication*] (DLA)
HAWK/HIP... HAWK Improvement Program (SAUS)
Hawkins....... Hawkins' Annual Reports [*19-24 Louisiana*] [*A publication*] (DLA)
HAWKITS..... Hazards Awareness Kits (SAUS)
Hawk PC...... Hawkins' Pleas of the Crown [*England*] [*A publication*] (DLA)
HAWK-PIP... HAWK Product Improvement Program (SAUS)
Hawk Pl Cr... Hawkins' Pleas of the Crown [*England*] [*A publication*] (DLA)
Hawks.......... Hawks Industries, Inc. [*Associated Press*] (SAG)
Hawks.......... Hawks' North Carolina Reports [*A publication*] (DLA)
HAWKS........ HITRAN Atmospheric Workstation (SAUO)
Hawks (NC)... Hawks' North Carolina Reports [*A publication*] (DLA)
Hawk Wills... Hawkins' Construction of Wills [*A publication*] (DLA)
Hawl........... Hawley's Reports [*10-20 Nevada*] [*A publication*] (DLA)
Hawl Cr R.... Hawley's American Criminal Reports [*A publication*] (DLA)
Hawley........ Hawley's American Criminal Reports [*A publication*] (DLA)
Hawley........ Hawley's Reports [*10-20 Nevada*] [*A publication*] (DLA)
Hawley's Crim Rep... Hawley's American Criminal Reports [*A publication*] (DLA)
Hawn........... Hawaii Reports [*A publication*] (DLA)
HAWNA........ Hawaiiana (SAUS)
HAWNA........ Hawaiian Studies
Hawn Isl...... Hawaiian Islands (SAUO)
HAWP.......... Homing and Warning Programmer (MCD)
HAWR.......... Helicopter Attack Warning RADAR (NVT)
Haw Rep...... Hawaii Reports [*A publication*] (DLA)
Haw Rev Stat... Hawaii Revised Statutes [*A publication*] (DLA)
Haw Rev Stat Ann... Hawaii Revised Statutes Annotated [*A publication*] (AAGC)
HAWS.......... Hawaiian Area Wideband System (SAUO)
HAWS.......... Heavy Anti-Armor Weapon System (SAUS)
HAWS.......... High Arctic Weather Station (FOTI)
HAWS.......... Homing and Warning Computer (SAUS)
HAWSEAFRON... Hawaiian Sea Frontier
Haw Sess Laws... Session Laws of Hawaii [*A publication*] (DLA)
HAWT.......... Horizontal Axis Wind Turbine [*Generator*] [*Also, HAWTG*] (MCD)
HAWTADS.... Helicopter Adverse Weather Target Acquisition and Destruction System (SAUO)

HAWTADS.... Helicopter Adverse Weather Target Acquisition and Detection System (ACAE)
HAWTADS.... Helicopter All-Weather Target Acquisition and Designation System
HAWTADS.... HELLFIRE [*Heliborne LASER Fire and Forget*] All-Weather Target Acquisition and Destruction System (MCD)
HAWTADS.... HELLFIRE all weather target acquisition and destruction system (SAUO)
Haw Tel....... Hawaii Telephone Co. (SAUO)
HawtFn........ Hawthorne Financial Corp. [*Associated Press*] (SAG)
HAWTG........ Horizontal Axis Wind Turbine Generator [*Also, HAWT*]
HAWTH........ Hawthorne, IL [*American Association of Railroads railroad junction routing code*]
Hawthorn..... Hawthorne Books (SAUS)
Haw WC...... Hawes' Will Case [*A publication*] (DLA)
HAX............ Hafnium Column Extractant [*Nuclear energy*] (NRCH)
HAX............ Hangar 5 Air Services Norway [*FAA designator*] (FAAC)
HAX............ Helicopter Armored Experiment
HAX............ Muskogee, OK [*Location identifier*] [*FAA*] (FAAL)
HAY............ Haycock, AK [*Location identifier*] [*FAA*] (FAAL)
HAY............ Hayes Albion Corp. (SAUO)
HAY............ Hayes-Dana, Inc. [*Toronto Stock Exchange symbol*]
Hay............ Hayes' Irish Exchequer Reports [*1830-32*] [*A publication*] (DLA)
Hay............ Hayes' Reports [*Calcutta*] [*A publication*] (DLA)
HAY............ Hayes Wheels International [*NYSE symbol*] (SPSG)
HAY............ Hayfield [*California*] [*Seismograph station code, US Geological Survey*] (SEIS)
Hay............ Hay's High Court Appeals Reports [*1862-63*] [*Bengal, India*] [*A publication*] (DLA)
Hay............ Hay's Poor Law Decisions [*1711-1859*] [*Scotland*] [*A publication*] (DLA)
Hay............ Hay's Scotch Decisions [*A publication*] (DLA)
Hay............ Haywood's North Carolina Reports [*A publication*] (DLA)
Hay............ Haywood's Tennessee Reports [*A publication*] (DLA)
Hay Acc....... Hay's Decisions on Accidents and Negligence [*1860*] [*Scotland*] [*A publication*] (DLA)
Hay & H...... Hayward and Hazelton's United States Circuit Court Reports [*District of Columbia*] [*A publication*] (DLA)
Hay & Haz... Hayward and Hazelton's United States Circuit Court Reports [*District of Columbia*] [*A publication*] (DLA)
Hay & J....... Hayes and Jones' Irish Exchequer Reports [*A publication*] (DLA)
Hay & Jo..... Hayes and Jones' Irish Exchequer Reports [*1832-34*] [*A publication*] (DLA)
Hay & M...... Hay and Marriott's English Admiralty Reports [*A publication*] (DLA)
Hay & Mar... Hay and Marriott's English Admiralty Reports [*A publication*] (DLA)
Hay & Marr... Hay and Marriott's English Admiralty Reports [*A publication*] (DLA)
Hay & M (Eng)... Hay and Marriott's English Admiralty Reports [*A publication*] (DLA)
Hay (Calc)... Hay's Reports [*Calcutta*] [*A publication*] (DLA)
Hay Dec....... Hay's Decisions on Accidents and Negligence [*1860*] [*Scotland*] [*A publication*] (DLA)
HAYDN......... Hayden, AZ [*American Association of Railroads railroad junction routing code*]
Hay Eq......... Haynes' Outlines of Equity [*5th ed.*] [*1880*] [*A publication*] (DLA)
Hayes.......... Hayes' Irish Exchequer Reports [*1830-32*] [*A publication*] (DLA)
Hayes.......... Hayes Wheels International [*Associated Press*] (SAG)
Hayes & J... Hayes and Jones' Irish Exchequer Reports [*1832-34*] [*A publication*] (DLA)
Hayes & J (Ir)... Hayes and Jones' Irish Exchequer Reports [*1832-34*] [*A publication*] (DLA)
Hayes & Jo... Hayes and Jones' Irish Exchequer Reports [*1832-34*] [*A publication*] (DLA)
Hayes & Jon... Hayes and Jones' Irish Exchequer Reports [*1832-34*] [*A publication*] (DLA)
Hayes & J Wills... Hayes and Jarman's Concise Forms of Wills [*18th ed.*] [*1952*] [*A publication*] (DLA)
Hayes Con Conv... Hayes' Concise Conveyancer [*A publication*] (DLA)
Hayes Conv... Hayes on Conveyancing [*A publication*] (DLA)
Hayes Cr & P... Hayes on Crimes and Punishments [*A publication*] (DLA)
Hayes Exch... Hayes' Irish Exchequer Reports [*1830-32*] [*A publication*] (DLA)
Hayes Exch (Ir)... Hayes' Irish Exchequer Reports [*1830-32*] [*A publication*] (DLA)
Hayes Heirs... Hayes' Dispositions to Heirs in Tail, Etc. [*A publication*] (DLA)
Hayes Intr.... Hayes' Introduction to Conveyancing [*A publication*] (DLA)
Hayes Lim... Hayes on Limitations as to Heirs of the Body, Etc. [*A publication*] (DLA)
Hayes R Est... Hayes' Real Estate [*A publication*] (DLA)
Hayes UD & T... Hayes' Law of Uses, Devises, and Trust [*A publication*] (DLA)
Hay Exch..... Hayes' Irish Exchequer Reports [*1830-32*] [*A publication*] (DLA)
Hay Exp....... Hay on Expatriation [*A publication*] (DLA)
Hayford........ Gold Coast Native Institutions [*A publication*] (DLA)
Hayn Ch Pr... Haynes' Chancery Practice [*1879*] [*A publication*] (DLA)
Hayn Eq....... Haynes' Outlines of Equity [*5th ed.*] [*1880*] [*A publication*] (DLA)
Haynes Alloy Dig... Haynes Alloys Digest (journ.) (SAUS)
Haynes Dig... Haynes Digest (journ.) (SAUS)
Haynes Eq... Haynes' Outlines of Equity [*5th ed.*] [*1880*] [*A publication*] (DLA)
Hayn Lead Cas... Haynes' Students' Leading Cases [*A publication*] (DLA)
HAYP.......... Hire-A-Youth Program (SAUS)
Hay PL......... Hay's Poor Law Decisions [*1711-1859*] [*Scotland*] [*A publication*] (DLA)
HAYR.......... Hayridge [*England*]
HAYSP......... Hays, PA [*American Association of Railroads railroad junction routing code*]
HAYSTAQ..... Have You Stored Answers to Questions [*Computer science*]
Hayw.......... Haywood's North Carolina Reports [*A publication*] (DLA)
Hayw.......... Haywood's Tennessee Reports [*A publication*] (DLA)
Hayw & H.... Hayward and Hazelton's United States Circuit Court Reports [*District of Columbia*] [*A publication*] (DLA)
Hayw & HDC... Hayward and Hazelton's United States Circuit Court Reports [*District of Columbia*] [*A publication*] (DLA)
HaywdB....... Haywood Bancshares, Inc. [*Associated Press*] (SAG)
Hayw LR...... Hayward's Law Register [*Boston*] [*A publication*] (DLA)
Hayw Man... Haywood's Manual of the Statute Laws of North Carolina [*A publication*] (DLA)
Hayw NC...... Haywood's North Carolina Reports [*A publication*] (DLA)
Haywood Tenn Rep... Haywood's Tennessee Reports [*A publication*] (DLA)
Hayw Tenn... Haywood's Tennessee Reports [*A publication*] (DLA)
HAZ............. Hayes Lemmerz International [*NYSE symbol*] [*Formerly, Hayes Wheels International*] (SG)
HAZ............. Hazard [*or Hazardous*] (KSC)
HAZ............. Hazardous (SAUS)
HAZ............. Hazardous Cargo [*Environmental science*] (COE)
HAZ............. Heat-Affected Zone
HAZ............. Heat-Annealed Zone [*Metallurgy*]
HAZAL......... Hahameinu Zikhronam Livrakha [*Our Sages of Blessed Memory*] [*Hebrew*]
HAZAN......... Hazard Analysis
Haz & R M War... Hazlitt and Roche on Maritime Warfare [*A publication*] (DLA)
HAZARD....... Hazardous Waste Data Base (SAUO)
Hazard Waste Cousult... Hazardous Waste Consultant [*A publication*] (PABS)
HAZCARGO... Hazardous Cargo [*National Highway Traffic Safety Administration Fatal Accident Recording System code*]
HAZCHEM.... Hazardous Chemical
HAZCHEM.... Hazardous Material Identification System (SAUS)
HazChem Code... Hazardous Chemicals Code (SAUO)
Haz Com...... Hazard Communication (AMHC)
HazCom....... Hazard Communication (SARE)
HAZCOM...... Hazardous Communication Standards [*Occupational Safety and Health Administration*] (RDA)
haz con........ Hazard Control (SAUS)
HAZCON....... Hazardous Condition (NVT)
HAZDAT....... Hazardous Substance Data Management System (SAUS)
HazDat........ Hazardous Substance Release/Health Effects Database (SAUO)
HAZE............ Homogeneous Assembly Zero Energy (SAUS)
HAZEL.......... Homogeneous Assembly Zero Energy Laboratory (SAUS)
HAZEL.......... Homogeneous Assembly Zero Energy Level [*AERE*]
HAZFILE....... Hazards File [*National Chemical Emergency Centre*] [*British*] (NITA)
HAZINF........ Hazardous Chemicals Information and Disposal [*University of Alberta*] [*Canada*] [*Information service or system*] (CRD)
HAZMACON... West Coast Hazardous Materials Management Conference (TSPED)
HazMat........ Hazardous Material [*Environmental science*] (COE)
HAZMAT...... Hazardous Material
HAZMAT...... Hazardous Material Response and Assessment Division [*Marine science*] (OSRA)
HAZMAT...... Hazardous Materials Response and Assessment Division [*National Oceanic and Atmospheric Administration*] (USDC)
HAZMIN....... Hazardous Waste Minimization
HAZMIT........ Hazard Mitigation (DEMM)
HAZ/MZ........ Heat-Affected Zone/Melted Zone (SAUS)
HAZOP......... Hazard and Operability [*Chemical engineering*]
HAZOP......... Hazard and Operability Study (EEVL)
HAZOP......... Hazard Operational analysis (SAUS)
Haz PA Reg... Hazard's Pennsylvania Register [*A publication*] (DLA)
Haz PA Reg (PA)... Hazard's Pennsylvania Register [*A publication*] (DLA)
Haz P Reg... Hazard's Pennsylvania Register [*A publication*] (ILCA)
HAZRAP....... Hazardous Waste Remedial Actions Program [*Environmental science*] (COE)
Haz Reg....... Hazard's Pennsylvania Register [*A publication*] (DLA)
HAZs........... Heat-Affected Zones (SAUO)
Haz US Reg... Hazard's United States Register [*A publication*] (DLA)
HAZW.......... Hazardous Waste Collection Database [*Environment term*] (EGA)
HAZWMP..... Hazardous Waste Management Plan (SAUS)
HAZWOP...... Hazardous Waste Operations (SAUS)
HazWOPER... Hazardous Waste Operations and Emergency Response (SAUS)
HAZWOPER... Hazardous Waste Operations and Emergency Response Regulations (SAUS)
HAZWRAP.... Hazardous Waste Remedial Action Program [*Oak Ridge National Laboratory*]
HB............... Air Melanesiae [*ICAO designator*] (AD)
HB............... Bell Helicopter Co., Brantly Helicopter Corp., Brditschka [*Heinrich Brditschka Flugzeugbau*] [*ICAO aircraft manufacturer identifier*] (ICAO)
HB............... Brinell Hardness (SAUS)
HB............... Brinell Hardness Number [*Also, BH, BHN, BHNo*]
H_B............... Deuterium [*Radioisotope of hydrogen*] (DAVI)
HB............... Farbwerke Hoechst AG [*Germany*] [*Research code symbol*]
Hb............... Habakkuk [*Old Testament book*]
Hb............... Haemoglobin [*Medicine*] (WDAA)
hb............... Halfback (ADWA)
HB............... Halfback [*Football*]
HB............... Half Bound [*Bibliography*]
HB............... Half Bow [*Music*] (ROG)
HB............... Half Breadth (AAG)
HB............... Half Brick (SAUS)
HB............... Halk Bankasi [*Peoples Bank of Turkey*] [*See also THB*]
HB............... Hallelujah Band
HB............... Halogen Bulb
HB............... Hampton & Branchville Railroad Co. [*AAR code*]
Hb............... Handbook (DIAR)
hb............... Handbook (ELAL)
HB............... Handbook (NASA)

HB............... Handlebar (ROG)
HB............... Hard Black [*Pencil leads*]
HB............... Hardboard (ADA)
HB............... Hard-Boiled [*Egg*]
HB............... Hardy Biennial [*Horticulture*] (ROG)
HB............... Harvard Bulletin (journ.) (SAUS)
HB............... Hatchback [*Automotive advertising*]
HB............... Hawkes Bay (SAUS)
HB............... Hawthorne Books (SAUS)
HB............... Head Backward (STED)
HB............... Headband (IAA)
HB............... Health Benefit
HB............... Health Benefits (SAUO)
HB............... Health Board [*Ireland*]
HB............... Heart Block [*Medicine*]
HB............... Heartburn (MELL)
HB............... Heat Budget Instrument (SAUS)
HB............... Heat to Boiling Point [*Calorimetry*]
HB............... Heavy Barrel [*Rifles*]
HB............... Heavy Battery (SAUS)
HB............... Heavy Bombardment [*or Bomber*]
HB............... Heavy Bomber (SAUS)
HB............... Heavy Bombing (SAUS)
Hb............... Hebrew (BJA)
HB............... Heel to Buttock (DMAA)
HB............... Held Back (DMAA)
HB............... Held Backward (STED)
HB............... Hemoglobin [*Medicine*] (DMAA)
Hb............... Hemoglobin [*Biochemistry, medicine*]
HB............... Hemolysis Blocking [*Medicine*] (STED)
HB............... Henricus Boich [*Flourished, 1320-30*] [*Authority cited in pre-1607 legal work*] (DSA)
HB............... Hepatitis B [*Medicine*]
HB............... Herba [*Herb*] [*Pharmacology*] (ROG)
HB............... Herders Bibelkommentar [*A publication*] (BJA)
HB............... Herri Batazuna [*Union of the People*] [*Spain*] [*Political party*] (PPE)
H-B............... Hexadecimal-to-Binary [*Computer science*] (IEEE)
HB............... High Band (AAG)
HB............... High Bay (KSC)
HB............... High Boilers
HB............... High Bridge (SAUS)
HB............... Highways and Byways [*A publication*]
HB............... Hill-Burton [*Federal grant and loan program for construction and modernization of medical facilities*]
HB............... Hillenbrand Industries, Inc. [*NYSE symbol*] (SPSG)
HB............... Hinged Block [*British military*] (DMA)
HB............... His Beatitude [*or His Blessedness*]
HB............... His Blessedness (SAUO)
HB............... His Bundle [*Cardiology*]
HB............... Historical Branch [*Army*]
HB............... Historical Bulletin (journ.) (SAUS)
HB............... Hit by Ball [*or Hit Batsman*] [*Baseball*]
HB............... Hold Breakfast [*Medicine*]
HB............... Holiness Band
HB............... Hollowback (DAC)
HB............... Hollow Bark (MIST)
HB............... Hollow Base (SAUS)
HB............... Home Banking (SAUO)
HB............... Home Base (ACAE)
HB............... Home Bus (SAUS)
HB............... Homing Beacon [*Aviation*]
HB............... Honey Bee
HB............... Honeywell-Bull
HB............... Horizontal Baffle (NRCH)
HB............... Horizontal Bands [*Navigation markers*]
HB............... Horizontal Beacon (SAUS)
HB............... Horizontal Bomber
HB............... Horizontal Branch (SAUO)
HB............... Horizontal-Branch [*Astronomy*]
HB............... Horizontal Bridgman [*Crystal growing technique*]
HB............... Horizontal Buoy (SAUS)
HB............... Hormone Binding [*Endocrinology*]
HB............... Horn Book Magazine [*A publication*] (BRI)
HB............... Horse Battery (SAUS)
HB............... Hose Bib (AAG)
HB............... Hospital Bed (DAVI)
HB............... Hot Boning [*Meat processing*]
HB............... House Bill [*In state legislatures*]
HB............... Housebound (MAE)
HB............... Housebreaking
HB............... Household Bank (SAUS)
HB............... Household Battalion [*British military*] (DMA)
HB............... Household Goods/Baggage
HB............... House of Bishops (SAUS)
HB............... Housing Benefit [*British*]
HB............... Howitzer Battery (SAUS)
HB............... Human Behavior [*National Science Foundation project*]
HB............... Human Being [*Slang*]
HB............... Hunchback (MELL)
HB............... Huntington Beach [*California*]
HB............... Hutchinson-Boeck [*Disease*] [*Medicine*] (DB)
HB............... Hybridoma [*Cytology*]
HB............... Hybridoma Bank (DMAA)
HB............... Hydroxybenzene (SAUS)
HB............... Hyoid Body (DMAA)
HB............... Hyoid Bone (MELL)
HB............... Hyperion Bay [*Television program title*]
HB-............... Swiss nationality marks for aircraft registration (SAUO)
HB............... United People (Spain) [*Political party*] (PSAP)
HB-8............... Hexagonal Bipyramidal (DB)
HB-9............... Heptagonal Bipyramidal (DB)
HB10............... Home Base (SAUS)
HbA............... Adult Haemoglobin (SAUS)
HBA............... Bible Atlas [*Hurlbut*] [*A publication*] (BJA)
HBA............... General Hotel, Boarding House, and Apartments [*British*]
HBA............... Halley Bay [*Antarctica*] [*Seismograph station code, US Geological Survey*] [*Closed*] (SEIS)
HBA............... Handbook Art
HBA............... Handicapped Boaters Association [*Defunct*] (EA)
HBA............... Harrison Bay, AK [*Location identifier*] [*FAA*] (FAAL)
HBA............... Health and Beauty Aid [*Retailing*]
HBA............... Health Benefit Advisor [*CHAMPUS*]
HBA............... Helium Breeder Associates (SAUO)
HbA............... Hemoglobin, Adult [*Medicine*]
HBA............... Herring Buyers Association [*British*] (DBA)
HBA............... Hispanic Bankers Association (SAUO)
HBA............... Hispanic Bar Association (EA)
HBA............... Hobart [*Tasmania*] [*Airport symbol*] (OAG)
HBA............... Hoist Builders Association (SAUO)
HBA............... Hollywood Bowl Association (SAUO)
HBA............... Home Baking Association (EA)
HBA............... Home Base [*Military*] (NVT)
HBA............... Home Builders Account (SAUS)
HBA............... Home Builders Association (SAUO)
HBA............... Honest Ballot Association (EA)
HBA............... Honours Bachelor of Arts (SAUS)
HBA............... Honours Bachelor of Arts in Business Administration (DD)
HBA............... Horizontal Baffle Assembly [*Nuclear energy*] (NRCH)
HBA............... Hospital Benefit Association (SAUO)
HBA............... Host Bus Adapter [*Computer science*]
HBA............... Housing Builders Association (SAUO)
HBA............... Human Biology Association (NTPA)
HBA............... Hydraulic and Boatyard Association [*A union*] [*British*]
HBA............... Hydraulic Brake Assist [*Automotive engineering*]
HBA............... Hydrazinobenzoic Acid [*Organic chemistry*]
HBA............... Hydrobenzoate [*Organic chemistry*]
HBA............... Hydrogen-Bond Acceptor [*Chemistry*]
HBA............... Hydroxybenzoic Acid (SAUS)
HBA............... Hydroxybutyrate (SAUS)
HBA............... Trail Lake Flying Service, Inc. [*ICAO designator*] (FAAC)
HBAA............... Human Betterment Association of America (SAUO)
HBAb............... Hepatitis B Antibody [*Immunology*]
Hbaba............... Hydroxybenzene-Azobenzoic [*Medicine*] (EDAA)
HBABA............... Hydroxybenzeneazobenzoic Acid (SAUS)
HBAC............... Hypodynamic Beta-Adrenergic Circulatory [*Medicine*] (EDAA)
h/back............... hardback (SAUS)
HBAG............... Handbag
HBAg............... Hepatitis B Antigen [*Immunology*]
HBAH............... Hydroxybenzoic Acid Hydrazide [*Reagent*]
HbAlc............... Glycosolated hemoglobin (SAUS)
HBAM............... Historic Buildings and Ancient Monuments Act [*Town planning*] [*British*]
HBAM............... Home Builders Association of Maryland (SRA)
HBAM............... Home Builders Association of Massachusetts (SRA)
HBAN............... Huntington Bancshares [*NASDAQ symbol*] (TTSB)
HBAN............... Huntington Bancshares, Inc. [*NASDAQ symbol*] (NQ)
HB & T............... Houston Belt & Terminal Railway Co.
HB&T............... Huntingdon & Broad Top Railroad (SAUO)
HBAO............... High Boiling Aromatic Oils (LDOE)
H-bar............... Capital-H-shaped bar (SAUS)
HBAR............... Head Bar Address Register [*Computer science*] (MHDB)
H-BAR............... Heavy Barrel [*Rifles*]
HBAR............... Heavy-Barrel Automatic Rifle (SAUS)
H Bar............... Horizontal Bar (SAUS)
HBARO............... Barometric Altitude (GAVI)
HBART............... Hobart, IN [*American Association of Railroads railroad junction routing code*]
HbAS............... Hemoglobin A and Hemoglobin S [*Medicine*] (MEDA)
HBAT............... Having Been Assigned to This Organization [*or Headquarters*]
HBAVS............... Human Betterment Association for Voluntary Sterilization [*Later, AVS*] (EA)
HBB............... Hemoglobin Beta-Chain [*Medicine*] (EDAA)
HbB............... Hemoglobin in the Blood [*Medicine*] (DB)
HBB............... Historic Buildings Bureau [*British*]
HBB............... Hit by Bullet (SPVS)
HBB............... Hobbs, NM [*Location identifier*] [*FAA*] (FAAL)
HBB............... Hollow-Bored Bar (SAUS)
HBB............... Hook-Basal Body [*Genetics*]
HBB............... Hoover Ball & Bearing Co. (SAUO)
HBB............... Hospital Blood Bank
HBB............... Human Beta-Globin [*Genetics*]
Hbb............... Hydroxybenzyl Benzimidazole [*Medicine*] (EDAA)
HBB............... Hydroxybenzyl Benzimidazole [*Clinical chemistry*] (MAE)
HBBA............... Bujumbura [*Burundi*] [*ICAO location identifier*] (ICLI)
HbBC............... Hemoglobin-Binding Capacity [*Medicine*] (DB)
HBBD............... Hydroxybenzylbutanediol [*Clinical chemistry*]
HBBE............... Gitega [*Burundi*] [*ICAO location identifier*] (ICLI)
HBBI............... Home Building Bancorp [*NASDAQ symbol*] (SAG)
HBBK............... Kiofi-Mosso [*Burundi*] [*ICAO location identifier*] (ICLI)
HBBL............... Hydroxybenzylbutyrolactone [*Clinical chemistry*]

HBBL .... Nyanza-Lac [*Burundi*] [*ICAO location identifier*] (ICLI)
HBBM .... Mugera [*Burundi*] [*ICAO location identifier*] (ICLI)
HBBN .... Nyakagunda [*Burundi*] [*ICAO location identifier*] (ICLI)
HBBW .... Hold Breakfast for Blood Work [*Medicine*]
HBC .... Haitian Aviation Line SA [*ICAO designator*] (FAAC)
HBC .... Hajji Baba Club (EA)
HBC .... Handbooks for Bible Classes [*A publication*]
HBC .... Handlebar Control [*Early automobiles*] (ROG)
HBC .... Health Benefit Card (ADA)
HBC .... Health Benefits Counselor (SAUS)
HBC .... Heavy Bar Chair (SAUS)
Hb C .... Hemoglobin C [*An abnormal hemoglobin*] [*Hematology*] (DAVI)
HBC .... Hepatitis B Core [*Medicine*] (EDAA)
HBc .... Hepatitis B Core [*Immunology*] (MAE)
HBC .... Highamerica Balloon Club (EA)
HBC .... High Blood Cholesterol
HBC .... High Breaking Capacity (IAA)
HBC .... Higher Binding-Energy Component (SAUS)
HBC .... Historic Buildings Council [*British*]
HBC .... [*The*] History Book Club
HBC .... Hit By Car (SAUS)
HBC .... Hobart Brothers Co. (EFIS)
HBC .... Hokkaido Broadcasting Company (SAUO)
HBC .... Home Banking Computer (SAUS)
HBC .... Homogeneous Boundary Condition
HBC .... Honeywell Business Computer [*or Compiler*]
HBC .... Hong Kong Bank of Canada (ECON)
HBC .... Horseshoe Bay [*British Columbia*] [*Seismograph station code, US Geological Survey*] [*Closed*] (SEIS)
HBC .... Hostage Bracelet Committee (EA)
HBC .... House Budget Committee
HBC .... HSBC Holdings ADS [*NYSE symbol*] (SG)
HBC .... Hudson's Bay Company [*Facetious translations include "Here before Christ," "Here before Columbus," and "Hungry Belly Co.."*]
HBC .... Human Biology Council (EA)
HBC .... Human Body Counter (IAA)
HBC .... Hydrogen Bubble Chamber
HBC .... Hyperbaric Chamber (SSD)
HBC .... Theodore Hamm Brewing [*Federal Railroad Administration identification code*]
HBCA .... Hudson's Bay Company Archives [*Canada*] (QUAC)
HBcAb .... Hepatitis B Core Antibody [*Immunology*] (MAE)
HBcAb .... Hepatitis B core antigen Antibody (SAUS)
HBCAG .... Hepatitis B Core Antigen [*Medicine*] (DB)
HBCAg .... Hepatitis B Core Antigen [*Immunology*]
HBCC .... Heftel Broadcasting Corp. [*NASDAQ symbol*] (NASQ)
HbCC .... Homozygous Hemoglobin C Disease [*Medicine*] (EDAA)
HBCC .... Hosted Bus Controller Chip [*Electronics*]
HBCC .... Hosted Bus Controller Circuit [*Electronics*]
HBCC .... House Banking and Currency Committee (SAUO)
HBCCA .... Heftel Broadcasting'A' [*NASDAQ symbol*] (TTSB)
HBCCA .... Heftel Broadcasting Corp. [*NASDAQ symbol*] (SAG)
HBCD .... Hexabromocyclododecane [*Flame retardant*] [*Organic chemistry*]
HBCF .... Hydrobromofluorocarbons [*Organic chemistry*]
HBC-Fuse .... High-Breaking Capacity Fuse (SAUS)
HBCG .... Heat-Aggregated Calmette-Guerin [*Medicine*] (EDAA)
HBCI .... Heritage Bancorp, Inc. [*NASDAQ symbol*] (SAG)
HBCI .... Home Banking Computer Interface (SAUS)
HBCM .... High Bay Ceramic Melter (SAUS)
HBCN .... Hazard Beacon (MSA)
HbCO .... Carbon Monoxide Hemoglobin [*Medicine*] (MELL)
HbCO .... Carboxyhemoglobin [*Medicine*] (MELL)
HhCO .... Hemoglobin, Carboxy [*Biochemistry, medicine*]
HBCO .... Hungarian Broadcasting Corp. [*NASDAQ symbol*] (SAG)
HBComm ..... Honours Bachelor of Commerce (SAUS)
HBCOW .... Hungarian Broadcasting Wrrt [*NASDAQ symbol*] (TTSB)
Hb CS .... Hemoglobin Constant Spring [*An abnormal hemoglobin*] [*Hematology*] (DAVI)
HBCU .... Historically Black Colleges and Universities
HBCU/MI ...... Historically Black Colleges and Universities/Minority Institute (SAUO)
HBD .... Half Byte Decimal (SAUS)
HBD .... Hardboard [*Technical drawings*]
HBD .... Has Been Drinking [*Medical notation*]
HBD .... Headboard (SAUS)
Hb D .... Hemoglobin D [*An abnormal hemoglobin*] [*Hematology*] (DAVI)
HBD .... Hepatobiliary Dysfunction [*Medicine*]
HBD .... Herein Before Described (SAUS)
HBD .... Horizontal to Base Down (SAUS)
HBD .... Hormone Binding Domain [*Endocrinology*]
HBD .... Hubbard, OH [*Location identifier*] [*FAA*] (FAAL)
HBD .... Hydrogen Bond Donor [*Solvent*]
HBD .... Hydroxybutyrate Dehydrogenase [*Also, HBDH*] [*An enzyme*]
HBD .... Hydroxybutyric Dehydrogenase (SAUS)
HBDC .... Home Base Development Committee [*Navy*]
HBDE .... Huntington Beach Development Engineering [*McDonnell Douglas Aircraft Corp.*]
HBDH .... Hydroxybutyrate Dehydrogenase [*Also, HBD*] [*An enzyme*]
HB Diode ..... High-Barrier Diode (SAUS)
HBDIX .... SMBS Investment Grade Bond Cl.B [*Mutual fund ticker symbol*] (SG)
HBDL .... Hot-Bus, Dead-Line (SAUS)
HBDLER Act ... Harbour Boards Dry Land Endowment Revesting Act (SAUO)
HBDMA .... Hat Block and Die Makers Association (EA)
HBDMI .... Historical Biographical Dictionaries Master Index [*A publication*]
HBDR .... Helicopter Battle Damage Repair (RDA)
HBDS .... Hypergraph-Based Data Structures
HBDT .... High BIT [*Binary Digit*] Density Tape [*Skylab*] [*NASA*]
HBDT .... Human Basophil Degranulation Test [*Medicine*] (DMAA)
HBE .... Hamilton Board of Education Schools [*UTLAS symbol*]
HbE .... Hemoglobin E [*Medicine*] (STED)
HBe .... Hepatitis B Early [*Antibody or antigen*] [*Immunology*] (DAVI)
HBe .... Hepatitis B envelope (SAUS)
HBE .... High Bay Extension (SAUS)
HBE .... His Bundle Electrogram [*Cardiology*]
HBE .... Honeybee, Inc. (SAUO)
HBEA .... Hawaii Business Education Association (EDAC)
HBeAb .... Hepatitis B e antigen Antibody (SAUS)
HB$_e$Ab .... Hepatitis B Early Anitibody [*Immunology*] (DAVI)
HBeAb .... Hepatitis B Early Antibody [*Medicine*] (STED)
HBEAG .... Hepatitis B Early Antigen [*Medicine*] (STED)
HBeAg .... Hepatitis B, Early Antigen [*or Antibody*] [*Immunology*]
H-beam .... Capital H-shaped beam (SAUS)
HBEC .... Hanford Business Exchange Conference (SAUS)
HBED .... Bis(hydroxybenzyl)ethylenediaminediacetic Acid [*Organic chemistry*]
HBEF .... Health and Beauty Employers Federation [*British*] (DBA)
HBEF .... Hubbard Brook Experimental Forest
HBEI .... Home Bancorp of Elgin, Inc. [*NASDAQ symbol*] (SAG)
HBEN .... High Byte Enable
HBEN .... Home Beneficial Corp. [*NASDAQ symbol*] (NQ)
HBENB .... Home BeneficialCl'B' [*NASDAQ symbol*] (TTSB)
HBEP .... Hispanic and Black Employment Programs (COE)
HBES .... Home and Building Electronic Systems (SAUO)
HBES .... Human Behavior and Evolution Society [*An association*]
HBF .... Fetal Hemoglobin [*Medicine*] (STED)
HbF .... Haemoglobin, Foetal (SAUS)
HBF .... Hamilton Board of Education [*UTLAS symbol*]
HBF .... Hand Blood Flow [*Cardiology*] (DAVI)
HBF .... Harmless Bulk Fertilizer (RIMS)
HBF .... Harts Bluff [*South Carolina*] [*Seismograph station code, US Geological Survey*] (SEIS)
HBF .... Hauptbahnhof [*Main Railroad Station*] [*German*]
HBF .... Hemispheric Blood Flow [*Medicine*] (DMAA)
HbF .... Hemoglobin F [*Medicine*] (STED)
HbF .... Hemoglobin, Fetal [*Also, HgF*] [*Medicine*]
HBF .... Hemoglobinuric Bilious Fever [*Medicine*] (DB)
HBF .... Hepatic Blood Flow
HBF .... High Bleeding Frequency [*Medicine*]
HBF .... Hospital Benefit Fund (SAUO)
HBF .... House-Builders Federation [*British*] (DBA)
HBF .... Hypothalamic Blood FLow [*Medicine*] (DMAA)
HBFC .... hydrobromofluorocarbon (SAUS)
HBFG .... Host Behavior Functional Group
HBFP .... Hematoxylin Basic Fuchsin Pecric (SAUS)
HBFTB .... Hair, Bass and Fibre Trade Board (SAUO)
HBFW .... Home Bancorp [*NASDAQ symbol*] (SAG)
HBG .... Half Bridge/Gateway (ACAE)
HBG .... Harrisburg [*Diocesan abbreviation*] [*Pennsylvania*] (TOCD)
HBG .... Hattiesburg [*Mississippi*] [*Airport symbol*] (AD)
HBG .... Hattiesburg, MS [*Location identifier*] [*FAA*] (FAAL)
HBG .... Health Benefit Groups (SAUO)
HBG .... Hongkong Bank Group (SAUO)
HBG .... Hope Brook Gold, Inc. [*Toronto Stock Exchange symbol*]
HBG .... Huntington Botanical Gardens (SAUO)
HBG .... Hydroxybenzoylglycine [*Biochemistry*]
HBG .... (Hydroxybutyl)guanine [*Biochemistry*]
Hbg-A .... Adult Hemoglobin [*Medicine*] (EDAA)
HBGF .... Heparin-Binding Growth Factor [*Biochemistry*]
HBGI .... Holson Burnes Group, Inc. [*NASDAQ symbol*] (SAG)
HBGM .... Home Blood Glucose Monitoring [*Medicine*]
HBGM .... Hypersonic Boost-Glide Missile
HBGMA .... Hughes Basic Gross Motor Assessment [*Jeanne E. Hughes*] (TES)
HBGS .... Human Blood Group Substance [*Medicine*] (DB)
HB Guide ..... Horn Book Guide [*A publication*] (BRI)
Hb H .... Hemoglobin H [*An abnormal hemoglobin*] [*Hematology*] (DAVI)
HBH .... Hertford British Hospital, F-92000 Levallois (SAUO)
HBH .... History Behind the Headlines [*A publication*]
HBH .... Hobart Bay [*Alaska*] [*Airport symbol*] (OAG)
HBH .... Hydraulic Brake Hose [*Automotive engineering*]
HBHC .... Hancock Holding [*NASDAQ symbol*] (TTSB)
HBHC .... Hancock Holding Co. [*NASDAQ symbol*] (SAG)
HBHC .... Hospital-Based Home Care
HBI .... Hemibody Irradiation [*Oncology*]
HbI .... Hemoglobin I [*Biochemistry, medicine*]
HBI .... High Serum-Bound Iron [*Biochemistry*] (MAE)
HBI .... Hindustan Bible Institute (EA)
HBI .... HomeBase, Inc. [*NYSE symbol*] (SG)
HBI .... Horizontal Blanking Interval (DOM)
HBI .... Hospital Bureau, Inc. [*Formerly, HBSS*] (EA)
HBI .... Hot Biquetted Iron
HBI .... House-Breaking Implements [*British police term*]
HBI .... Houston Biotechnology, Inc. [*AMEX symbol*] (SPSG)
HBIA .... Hairdressing and Beauty Industry Association [*Australia*]
HBID .... Hereditary B9 Intraepithelial Dyskeratosis (SAUS)
HBIG .... Hepatitis B Immune Globulin [*Immunology*]
HBIg .... Hepatitis B Immuniglobulin [*Medicine*] (EDAA)
HBIG .... Hepatitis B Immunoglobulin (HEAS)
HBII .... Houston Biomedical, Inc. (SAUO)
HBIX .... Hagler Bailly [*NASDAQ symbol*] (SG)
HBIZ .... Harvest Brand [*Federal Railroad Administration identification code*]
HBJ .... Harcourt Brace & Jovanovich (EFIS)
HBJ .... Harcourt, Brace, Jovanovich, Inc. (SAUO)

HBJ High-Band Jammer (MCD)
HBJCT H & B Junction, SC [*American Association of Railroads railroad junction routing code*]
HBJ Publications Harcourt Brace Jovanovich Publications (SAUS)
HBK Habekacin [*Antibacterial*]
HBK Handbook
HBK Hardback [*Book cover*] (NTCM)
HBK Hardwood Bleached Kraft [*Pulp and paper technology*]
HBK Hartebeesthoek [*South Africa*] [*Geomagnetic observatory code*]
HBK Hatchback
HBk Herders Bibelkommentar [*A publication*] (BJA)
HBK Hinchinbrook, AK [*Location identifier*] [*FAA*] (FAAL)
HBK Hollow Back [*Of lumber*] (BARN)
hbk hollowback (SAUS)
HBL Habib Bank Limited [*Pakistan*]
Hbl Haemoglobin (SAUS)
HBL Harbor Belt Line Railroad
HBL Heeresbetriebsstofflager [*Army Gasoline-Supply Depot*] [*German military - World War II*]
HBL Hepatoblastoma (DB)
HBL Heublein, Inc. (SAUO)
HBL Hudson Bay Lowland (SAUO)
HBL Huntington Beach Public Library, Huntington Beach, CA [*OCLC symbol*] (OCLC)
HBL Hydrostatic Balanced Loading (SAUS)
HBLA Human B-Lymphocyte Antigen (DB)
HBLB Horserace Betting Levy Board [*British*]
HBLC Host Based Library Catalogue [*Computer science*]
HBLLSB Heard Best at Left Lower Sternal Border [*Cardiology*] (DAVI)
HBLO Home Base Ledger Office (SAUO)
HBLR Hidden Broad-Line Region [*Spectra*]
HBLRR Harbor Belt Line Railroad (MHDB)
HBLUSB Heard Best at Left Upper Sternal Border [*Cardiology*] (DAVI)
HBLV Human B-Lymphotropic Virus
HBM Half Bridge Monorail [*Mobot Corp.*] [*Gantry robot*] (NITA)
HBM Health Belief Model (DMAA)
HBM Heavy Ballistic Missile
HBM Held by Manufacturer
HBM Helicoidal Bianisotropic Medium (SAUS)
HbM Hemoglobin M [*Biochemistry*] (MAH)
HBM High-Beta Model (MCD)
HBM Hobart Mills [*California*] [*Seismograph station code, US Geological Survey*] (SEIS)
HBM Homing Ballistic Missile (ACAE)
HBM Horizontal Boring Mill
HBM Hudson Bay Mining & Smelting Co. Ltd. [*Toronto Stock Exchange symbol*]
HBM Human Body Model (SAUS)
HBM Hydraulic Bore-Hole Mining [*Coal*]
HBM Hydrologic Bench Mark (SAUO)
HBM Hypertonic Buffered Medium (DMAA)
HBM Mali-Tinbouctou Air Service [*ICAO designator*] (FAAC)
HBMA Home-Based Maintenance Allowance
HBMC Homebush Bay Ministerial Council [*New South Wales, Australia*]
HBMC Hydroxybutylmethylcellulose (SAUS)
HBMCIT Haagen and Black Multiple Choice Intelligibility Test [*Medicine*] (EDAA)
HBMN Hydrologic Bench Mark Network (SAUO)
HBMPI High Burst/Mean Point of Impact (SAUO)
HBMS His [*or Her*] Britannic Majesty's Service
HBMT Haploidentical Bone Marrow Transplantation [*Medicine*] (MELL)
HBN Hazard Beacon
HBN Health-Based Number [*Environmental science*]
HB(N) Heavy Bomber (Night) [*British military*] (DMA)
HBN Heterobuccal Nerve (SAUS)
HBN Hexagonal Boron Nitride (SAUS)
HBNK Highland Federal Bank [*NASDAQ symbol*] (SAG)
HBNNR Hickling Broad National Nature Reserve (SAUO)
HBNR Hydrogen-Bond Network Rearrangement [*Physical chemistry*]
HBNWR Holla Bend National Wildlife Refuge (SAUO)
HBO HBO & Co. [*Associated Press*] (SAG)
HBO Health Benefits Organization [*Insurance*]
HBO Heavy Batch Oven (SAUS)
H Bo Henricus Boich [*Flourished, 1320-30*] [*Authority cited in pre-1607 legal work*] (DSA)
HBO Home Box Office [*Cable-television system*]
HBO Horizontal-Branch Oscillation [*Astronomy*]
HBO Host Byte Order (SAUS)
HBO Humboldt, NE [*Location identifier*] [*FAA*] (FAAL)
HBO Hyperbaric Oxygen [*Also, HPO, OHP*] [*Medicine*]
HBO Hyperbaric Oxygenation (DMAA)
HbO_2 Hemoglobin, Oxy [*Biochemistry, medicine*]
h/board hardboard (SAUS)
H/BOARD Headboard (SAUS)
HBOC HBO & Co. [*NASDAQ symbol*] (COMM)
HBOC Hereditary Breast Ovarian Cancer (MELL)
HBOC Hyperbaric Oxygen Chamber (SAUS)
H Body Hookean Body (SAUS)
HBOG Hudsons Bay Oil and Gas (SAUS)
HBOI Harbor Branch Oceanographic Institution [*Fort Pierce, FL*]
HBOL Hartford Steam Boiler Inspection & Insurance Co. [*NASDAQ symbol*] (COMM)
H-BOMB Hydrogen Bomb (GOBB)
H-bomb Hydrogen Bomb (WDAA)
H/Bone Herring-Bone (SAUS)
HbOr Handbuch der Orientalistik [*Leiden*] [*A publication*] (BJA)
HBOs Health Benefit Organizations (SAUS)
HBO S Oxyhemoglobin (SAUS)
HBOT Hyperbaric Oxygen Therapy [*Medicine*] (DAVI)
HBP Committee of Housing, Building and Planning (SAUO)
HBP Dauphin County Library System, Harrisburg, PA [*OCLC symbol*] (OCLC)
HbP Haemoglobin, Primitive (SAUS)
HBP Hamilton Board of Education, Education Centre Library [*UTLAS symbol*]
HBP Handbook Production
HBP Handlebar Palsy [*Medicine*] (MELL)
HBP Harvard Botany Page (SAUO)
HBP Health Benefits Program (SAUS)
HBP Heartbeat Period [*Medicine*] (DMAA)
HBP Held for Blueprint (MCD)
HBP Helicobacter Pylori [*Medicine*] (MELL)
HBP Hepatic Binding Protein [*Biochemistry*]
HBP High Band Processor (TIMI)
HBP High Blood Pressure [*Medicine*]
HBP Highway Bridge Parapet (PDAA)
HbP Hilfsbuch des Pehlevi [*A publication*] (BJA)
HBP Hit by Pitcher [*Baseball*]
HBP Hospital-Based Practice (DMAA)
HBP Hospital Benefits Payment
HBP Hydraulic Bench Press
HBP Hydrocortisone(butyrate)propionate [*Endocrinology*]
HBP People's Unity Party (Uzbekistan) [*Political party*] (PSAP)
HbP Primitive [*Fetal*] Hemoglobin
HBPA Horsemen's Benevolent and Protective Association (EA)
HBPA Hydrogenated Bisphenol A [*Organic chemistry*]
HBPE Health Based Physical Education
HB Pencil Hard Black Pencil (SAUS)
H-BPH Hawaii Regional Library for the Blind and Physically Handicapped, Honolulu, HI [*Library symbol*] [*Library of Congress*] (LCLS)
HBPIC High Blood Pressure Information Center [*Public Health Service*] (IID)
HBPIO Health Benefits Program Information Officer (SAUO)
HBPM Home Blood Pressure Monitoring [*Medicine*]
HBPP Humboldt Bay Power Plant (NRCH)
HBPR High Bypass Ratio (SAUS)
HBPS Home Building Plan Service (SAUO)
HBPSA Hydroxybutylidene-p-aminobenzenesulfonic [*Organic chemistry*]
HBP/SEM Committee of Housing, Building and Planning Seminar (SAUO)
HBPT Heterojunction Bipolar PhotoTransistor (SAUS)
HBP/WP Committee of Housing, Building and Planning Working Party (SAUO)
HBR Haibara [*Japan*] [*Seismograph station code, US Geological Survey*] (SEIS)
HBR Ham Band Receiver (IAA)
HBR Hansell's Bankruptcy Reports [*1915-17*] [*A publication*] (DLA)
HBR Harbor [*Maps and charts*]
HBR Harborside Healthcare Corp. [*NYSE symbol*] (SAG)
HBr Hardness, Brinell (SAUS)
HBR Harvard Business Review (journ.) (SAUS)
HBR Has Been Reviewed (AAG)
HBR High BIT [*Binary Digit*] Rate (KSC)
HBR High Burst Rate (PDAA)
HBR Highway Bunched-signalling Receiver (SAUS)
HBR Hobart, OK [*Location identifier*] [*FAA*] (FAAL)
HBR Hudson Bay Railway (SAUO)
HBR Hull & Barnsley Railway Co. (SAUO)
HBr Hydrobromic Acid (MAE)
HBR Hydrobromide (SAUS)
HBr Hydrogen Bromide (LDT)
HbR Methemoglobin Reductase (STED)
HBRA Howitzer Battery, Royal Artillery (SAUO)
HBRACW Has Been Reviewed and Concurred With (AAG)
HBRDC Honey Bee Research and Development Council [*Australia*]
HBRF Hercules-Baachus Resin Formulation
HBRGA Howitzer Battery, Royal Garrison Artillery (SAUO)
HBRI Hospital Bureau Research Institute [*Defunct*] (EA)
H/BRK Hand Brake [*Automotive engineering*]
HBRK Harmony Brook [*NASDAQ symbol*] (TTSB)
HBRK Harmony Brook, Inc. [*NASDAQ symbol*] (SAG)
Hbr Mr Harbor Master
HBR-online Harvard Business Review-Online [*John Wiley & Son*] (NITA)
HBRRP Highway Bridge Replacement and Rehabilitation Program [*Department of Transportation*]
HBRS Harbors [*Postal Service standard*] (OPSA)
HBRY Hudson Bay Railroad [*Federal Railroad Administration identification code*]
HbS Haemoglobin, Sickle-cell (SAUS)
HBS Half Bar Symbology
HBS Halifax Building Society (SAUO)
HBS Hanks Balanced Salt [*Solution*] [*Cell incubation medium*]
HBS Harbor Boat Service [*Military*]
HBS Hardware Breakdown Structure (ACAE)
HBS Harvard Business School
HBS Havergal Brian Society (EAIO)
HBS Haywood Bancshares, Inc. [*AMEX symbol*] (SAG)
HBS Health Behavior Scale [*Psychiatry*] (DAVI)
HBS Heavy Bomber Support
HBS Helicopter Blade Slap
HbS Hemoglobin, Sickle [*Medicine*]
HBS Henry Bradshaw Society [*British*]
HBS Hepatitis B Surface [*Medicine*] (STED)

HBS .... Hermanas Contemplativas del Buen Pastor (TOCD)
HBS .... Herringbone Strutting [*Construction*]
HBS .... Hexbase Script (SAUS)
HBS .... High Beta Stellator Experiment (SAUO)
HBS .... High Byte Strobe [*Computer science*] (MHDI)
HBS .... Highway Bunched-signalling Sender (SAUS)
HBS .... Hoboken Shore Railroad [*AAR code*]
HBS .... Hole-Burning Spectroscopy
HBS .... Home Bus System (SAUS)
HBS .... Honey Bee Spiroplasma [*Bacteriology*]
HBS .... Hope Botanic Gardens (SAUO)
HBS .... Horizontal Bracing Systems [*Environmental science*] (COE)
HBS .... Hot Bench System (ACAE)
HBS .... Hot Blade Stripper
HBS .... Household Budgets Survey (EURO)
HBS .... Hulking Building Syndrome (SAUS)
HBS .... Hyperkinetic Behavior Syndrome [*Medicine*]
HbS .... Sickle-Cell Hemoglobin [*Medicine*] (STED)
HbS .... Sulfhemoglobin [*Medicine*] (STED)
HBSA .... Harvard Business School Association (COBU)
HBSA .... Historical Breechloading Smallarms Association [*British*] (DBA)
HBSA .... Hungarian Boy Scout Association (EA)
HBSAA .... Hack and Band Saw Manufacturers Association of America (SAUO)
HBSAB .... Hepatitis B Surface Antibody [*Immunology*] (PDAA)
HBsAB .... Hepatitis B Surface Antibody [*Medicine*] (STED)
HBsAb .... Hepatitis B surface antigen Antibody (SAUS)
HB_sAg .... Hepatitis B Surface Antigen [*Immunology*] (DAVI)
HBSAG .... Hepatitis B Surface Antigen [*Medicine*] (DB)
HBsAg/adr ... Hepatitis B Surface Antigen Manifesting Group-Specific Determinant A and Subtype-Specific Determinants D and R [*Medicine*] (STED)
HBSANSW ... Health and Building Surveyors' Association of New South Wales [*Australia*]
HBSC .... Health Behaviors in School-Aged Children (SAUO)
HBSC .... Hematopoietic Blood Stem Cell [*Medicine*] (DMAA)
HbSC .... Hemoglobin C Sickle Cell Disease [*Medicine*]
HBSC .... Heritage Bancorp, Inc. [*NASDAQ symbol*] (NASQ)
HBScF .... Honours Bachelor of Science in Forestry (SAUS)
HbSD .... Hemoglobin Disease [*Medicine*] (EDAA)
HBSG .... Home Birth Support Group [*Australia*]
HBSI .... Hamptons Bancshares, Incorporated (SAUO)
HBSMA .... Hack and Band Saw Manufacturers Association of America
HBSMAA ...... Hack and Band Saw Manufacturers Association of America (EA)
HBSS .... Hanks Balanced Salt Solution [*Cell incubation medium*]
HBSS .... Hanks Basic Salt Solution (SAUS)
HBSS .... Hanks Buffered Salt Solution (SAUS)
HbSS .... Hemoglobin SS [*Medicine*] (EDAA)
HBSS .... Hospital Bureau of Standards and Supplies [*Later, HBI*]
HBT .... Habeat [*Let Him Have*] [*Pharmacy*] (ROG)
HBT .... Harbor Bay Telecommunications [*Alameda, CA*] (TSSD)
HBT .... Harbourton Financial Services LP [*NYSE symbol*] (SAG)
HBT .... Heflex Bioengineering Test [*NASA*]
HBT .... Herringbone Twill
HBT .... Heterojunction Bipolar Transistor [*Electronics*]
HBT .... Heterostructure Bipolar Transistor (MED)
HBT .... Hetrojunction Bipolar Mobility Transistor (NITA)
HBT .... Historically Black Technikon (SAUS)
HBT .... Hit by Truck (SPVS)
HBT .... Hobart Mills [*California*] [*Seismograph station code, US Geological Survey*] (SEIS)
HBT .... Homologous Blood Transfusion (MELL)
HBT .... Houston Belt & Terminal Railway Co. [*AAR code*]
HBT .... Human Brain Thromboplastin [*Clinical chemistry*]
HBT .... Human Breast Tumor [*Type of cell line*]
HBT .... Hydrogen Breath Test (MELL)
HBT .... Hydroxybenzotriazole [*Organic chemistry*]
HBT .... Sand Point, AK [*Location identifier*] [*FAA*] (FAAL)
HBTA .... HB [*Homeward Bound Ministries*] Tract Association (EA)
HBTA .... Hutchinson Board of Trade Association (EA)
HBTC .... Hierarchical Block Truncation Coding (SAUS)
HBTI .... Harcourt Butler Technological Institute (SAUO)
HBTX .... High Beta Toroidal Experiment (PDAA)
HBU .... Aurora, OR [*Location identifier*] [*FAA*] (FAAL)
HBU .... Historically Black University (SAUO)
HBU .... Hollandsche Bank-Unie [*Netherlands*]
HBU .... Houston Baptist University [*Texas*]
HBU .... Hub Bearing Unit
HBUA .... Hungarian Baptist Union of America (EA)
HBUF .... Homestyle Buffet, Inc. (SAUO)
Hb Unit .... Haemoglobin Unit (SAUS)
HBV .... Harrisonburg [*Virginia*] [*Seismograph station code, US Geological Survey*] (SEIS)
HBV .... Hebbronville, TX [*Location identifier*] [*FAA*] (FAAL)
HBV .... Hepatitis B Vaccine
HBV .... Hepatitis B Virus
HBV .... Honey Bee Venom [*Immunology*]
HBVP .... Hepatitis B Virus Polymerase [*An enzyme*]
HBVS .... Hepatitis B Virus Integration Site [*Medicine*] (DMAA)
HBW .... Half Bandwidth [*Electronics*]
HBW .... Harcourt, Brace & World, Inc. (SAUO)
HBW .... High Birth Weight [*Medicine*] (MAE)
HBW .... High-Speed Black and White [*Photography*]
HBW .... Hillsboro, WI [*Location identifier*] [*FAA*] (FAAL)
HBw .... Historische Burowelt [*A publication*]
HBW .... Hot Bridge Wire (SAUS)
HBW .... Wolf [*Howard B.*], Inc. [*AMEX symbol*] (SPSG)
HBWA .... High-Band Warning Antenna (MCD)
HB Wall .... Half Brick Wall (SAUS)
HBWMA .... Home Brewing and Winemaking Manufacturers Association [*British*] (DBA)
HBWR .... Halden Boiling Heavy Water Reactor (SAUO)
HBWR .... Halden Boiling Water Reactor [*Norway*] [*Nuclear energy*]
HBWR .... Heavy Boiling Water Reactor (SAUO)
HBWR .... High-Band Warning Receiver (MCD)
HBWTA .... Home Brewing and Winemaking Trade Association [*British*] (DBA)
HBWX .... Georgia Power [*Private rail car owner code*]
HBX .... Explosive (SAUS)
HBX .... Hobo Railroad Express [*Federal Railroad Administration identification code*]
HBY .... Hereby (ROG)
HBZ .... Heber Springs, AR [*Location identifier*] [*FAA*] (FAAL)
HbZ .... Hemoglobin Zuerich (DB)
Hc .... Altitude at Chosen Position [*Nautical term*] (NTA)
HC .... Command Chaplain [*AFSC*]
HC .... Critical Height [*Aviation*] (DA)
HC .... Cross of Honour [*British military*] (DMA)
HC .... Crystal Holder [*JETDS nomenclature*] [*Military*] (CET)
HC .... Ecuador [*International civil aircraft marking*] (ODBW)
HC .... Habeas Corpus [*You Have the Body*] [*Legal term*] [*Latin*] (DLA)
HC .... Habitual Criminal
HC .... Hadley Centre for climate prediction and research (SAUS)
HC .... Hagerstown College (SAUO)
HC .... Hague Convention
HC .... Hair Cell [*Otology*]
HC .... Hairdressing Council (BUAC)
HC .... Haiti Air International [*ICAO designator*] (AD)
HC .... Halcyon Club (SAUO)
HC .... Half Calf
HC .... Half-Caste (ADA)
HC .... Half Cell (SAUS)
HC .... Half-Changes [*Statistics*]
HC .... Half Chest
HC .... Half Covered [*Marine insurance*] (ROG)
HC .... Half Cycle (SAUS)
HC .... Halochromism (SAUS)
HC .... Halochromy (SAUS)
HC .... Halt Command (SAUS)
HC .... Hamilton Circuit (SAUS)
HC .... Hamline College (SAUO)
HC .... Hammingcode (SAUS)
HC .... Handbooks for the Clergy [*A publication*]
HC .... Hand Carry
HC .... Hand-Colored [*Photography*]
HC .... Hand Compute (SAUS)
HC .... Hand Control [*Technical drawings*]
HC .... Hand Controlled (SAUS)
HC .... Hand Controller [*Aerospace*] (NAKS)
HC .... Hand Crank
HC .... Hand Cut [*Envelopes*]
HC .... Hand-Held Unit Chromatography
HC .... Handicapped [*Medicine*]
HC .... Handling Capacity (DEN)
HC .... Hanging Cast (MELL)
HC .... Hanging Ceiling (OA)
HC .... Hannibal Connecting Railroad Co. (SAUO)
HC .... Hannibal Connecting R. R. [*AAR code*]
HC .... Hanover College (SAUO)
HC .... Hanover Compressor [*NYSE symbol*] (SG)
H-C .... Harbison-Carborundum (SAUS)
HC .... Hard Cancer (MELL)
HC .... Hard Case [*Gunnery*]
HC .... Hard Copy [*Computer science*]
HC .... Hardcore
HC .... Hard Cover (ADWA)
H/C .... Hard Covered (SAUS)
HC .... Hard Cradle Balancer (SAUS)
HC .... Hardened Concrete (SAUS)
HC .... Harding College (SAUO)
HC .... Hardware Capability (NITA)
HC .... Hardware Check (SAUS)
HC .... Hardware Command (SAUO)
HC .... Harmless Cloud (SAUS)
HC .... Harpur College (SAUO)
HC .... Hartford College (SAUO)
HC .... Hartford Courant (SAUS)
HC .... Hartnell College (SAUO)
HC .... Hartwick College (SAUO)
HC .... Harvard Circular (journ.) (SAUS)
HC .... Harvard College (SAUO)
HC .... Hastings Center (EA)
HC .... Hastings College (SAUO)
HC .... Hatz Club (EA)
HC .... Hauling Class
HC .... Hauling Code
HC .... Haute-Contre [*Alto*] [*Music*]
HC .... Haverford College (SAUO)
HC .... Hazardous Cargo (SAUS)
HC .... Hazardous Constitutients (GNE)
HC .... Head Card (SAUS)
HC .... Head Circumference [*Medicine*]
HC .... Head Compression (AAMN)

HC .... Head Constrictor [*Medicine*] (EDAA)
HC .... Head Control (SAUS)
HC .... Headcount
HC .... Header Card (SAUS)
HC .... Header Check (SAUS)
HC .... Heading Card (SAUS)
HC .... Headmaster Commander [*Navy*] [*British*]
HC .... Headmasters Conference (BUAC)
HC .... Headquarters City [*Dialog*] [*Searchable field*] [*Information service or system*] (NITA)
HC .... Headquarters Command [*Military*]
HC .... Headquarters Commission (SAUO)
HC .... Headteachers Conference (SAUS)
HC .... Health Canada (SAUO)
HC .... Health Category (SAUO)
HC .... Health Certificate [*British*] (ADA)
HC .... Health Circular (HEAS)
HC .... Heal the Children (EA)
HC .... Healthy Control [*Medicine*] (DMAA)
HC .... Heart Catheterization (MELL)
HC .... Heart Cycle [*Cardiology*] (MAE)
HC .... Heat Capacity [*Electronics*] (EECA)
HC .... Heat-Cleaned (SAUS)
HC .... Heat Coil (SAUS)
HC .... Heat Conduction (SAUS)
HC .... Heat Conservation [*Medicine*] (EDAA)
HC .... Heat Control (IAA)
HC .... Heat Controlled (SAUS)
HC .... Heat Count (SAUS)
HC .... Heated Coil (NITA)
HC .... Heater Coil (SAUS)
HC .... Heater Cord
HC .... Heating Cabinet (AAG)
HC .... Heating Coil (AAG)
HC .... Heat of Combustion (ROG)
HC .... Heavy Chain [*Immunoglobulin*]
HC .... Heavy Clouds (SAUS)
HC .... Heavy Concrete (SAUS)
HC .... Heavy Current [*Electronics*] (IAA)
HC .... Heel Cords [*Medicine*] (EDAA)
HC .... Heidelberg College (SAUO)
HC .... Held Code (SAUS)
HC .... Held Covered [*Insurance*]
HC .... Helene Curtis Industries, Inc. [*NYSE symbol*] (SPSG)
H/C .... Helicopter (NATG)
HC .... Helicopter, Cargo (SAUS)
HC .... Helicopter Combat (NVT)
HC .... Helicopter Combat Support Squadron [*Navy*] (DNAB)
HC .... Helicopter Command (NVT)
HC .... Helicopter Controler (SAUS)
HC .... Helicopter Coordinator [*Military*] (CAAL)
HC .... Helicopter Council
HC .... Helium Circulation [*System*]
HC .... Helminthosporium carbonum [*A toxin-producing fungus*]
HC .... Helper Component [*Biology*]
HC .... Hematopoietic Cell [*Hematology*]
HC .... Hemoglobin Concentration [*Medicine*] (HGAA)
HC .... Hendrix College (SAUO)
HC .... Heparin Cofactor [*Medicine*] (MELL)
HC .... Hepatic Candidiasis [*Medicine*] (MELL)
HC .... Hepatic Catalase [*An enzyme*] (MAE)
HC .... Hepatic Coma [*Medicine*]
HC .... Hepatitis C (SAUS)
HC .... Heptachlor (ABAC)
HC .... Heralds College (SAUS)
HC .... Herding Certified [*Purebred canine award*]
HC .... Hereditary Coproporphyria (DB)
HC .... Heritage Committee [*Australian Capital Territory*]
Hc .... Hermitian conjugate (SAUS)
HC .... Hershey College (SAUO)
HC .... Hertford College (SAUO)
HC .... Herzberg Continuum [*Spectral region*]
HC .... Hesston College (SAUO)
HC .... Heterogeneous Catalysis (SAUS)
HC .... Heuristic Concepts (IEEE)
HC .... Hexachlorethane (SAUS)
HC .... Hexachlorethane-Zinc (SAUS)
HC .... Hexachloroethane [*Organic chemistry*]
HC .... Hexadecimal Code (SAUS)
HC .... Hickman Catheter [*Medicine*] (DAVI)
HC .... High Calorie (AAMN)
HC .... High Capacitance (SAUS)
HC .... High Capacity (SAUS)
HC .... High-Capacity
HC .... High Carbon [*Steel*]
HC .... High Chair (SAUS)
HC .... High Church
HC .... High Churchman [*British*] (ROG)
HC .... High Color (CDE)
HC .... High commissioner(er) (ODA)
HC .... High Conditioners [*Psychology*]
HC .... High Conductivity [*Copper*]
HC .... High Conversion (SAUS)
HC .... High Cost of Living
HC .... High Court
HC .... High Court of Justice (SAUO)
HC .... High Current
HC .... Higher Certificate [*Academic degree*] (AIE)
HC .... Highest Commendation (SAUS)
HC .... Highland Cyclists [*British military*] (DMA)
HC .... Highly Commended (SAUS)
HC .... High-Speed CMOS [*Computing*] (ODA)
HC .... Highway Code [*A publication*] (DLA)
HC .... Highway Contract (TBD)
HC .... Hillsdale College (SAUO)
HC .... Hippocampal
HC .... Hiram College (SAUO)
HC .... Hire Car (ADA)
HC .... Histamine Challenge [*Medicine*] (MELL)
HC .... Histamine Club [*Later, HRSNA*] (EA)
HC .... Histoplasma Capsulatum (SAUS)
HC .... Historical Commission
HC .... Historical Cost (ADA)
HC .... Hockey Club
HC .... Hoist Crane (SAUS)
HC .... Hold Cargo (SAUS)
HC .... Hold Covered (SAUS)
HC .... Holder Crystal (SAUS)
HC .... Holding Coil (MSA)
HC .... Holding Company [*Business term*]
HC .... Holiday Camps [*Public-performance tariff class*] [*British*]
HC .... Hollerith Card (SAUS)
HC .... Hollerith Code (SAUS)
HC .... Hollins Critic [*A publication*] (ANEX)
HC .... Hollow Cathode (SAUS)
HC .... Hollow Charge (SAUS)
HC .... Hollow Core [*Technical drawings*]
HC .... Holy Communion
HC .... Holy Cross
HC .... Home Care
HC .... Home Computer (IAA)
HC .... Home Consumption (SAUS)
HC .... Home Counties (SAUS)
HC .... Homogeneous Catalysis (SAUS)
HC .... Honor Contracts [*Insurance*]
HC .... Honoris Causa [*For the Sake of Honor, Honorary*] [*Latin*]
HC .... Hood College (SAUO)
HC .... Hope College (SAUO)
HC .... Horizontal Cell [*Eye anatomy*]
HC .... Horizontal Check (IAA)
HC .... Horizontal Cross-Connect (SAUS)
Hc .... Hornyhead Chub [*Ichthyology*]
HC .... Hors Concours [*Not Competing*] [*French*]
HC .... Hose Cabinet [*or Connection*] [*NFPA pre-fire planning symbol*] (NFPA)
HC .... Hose Cart [*Early fire engines*] (ROG)
HC .... Hose Clamp (MSA)
HC .... Hose Connector (SAUS)
HC .... Hospital Company (SAUO)
HC .... Hospital Corps [*or Corpsman*] [*Navy*]
HC .... Hospital Course (DAVI)
HC .... Host Cell [*Parasitology*]
HC .... Host Computer
HC .... Host Country (NATG)
HC .... Hostel Care
HC .... Hot and Cold
HC .... Hot Carrier (SAUS)
HC .... Hot Cathode (SAUS)
HC .... Hot Compress (MELL)
HC .... Hour Circle
HC .... House Cable [*Telecommunications*] (TEL)
HC .... House Call [*Medicine*]
HC .... House Committee (SAUO)
HC .... Household Cavalry [*British*]
HC .... House of Clergy (SAUS)
HC .... House of Commons [*British*]
HC .... House of Correction
HC .... Housing Census
HC .... Housing Commission [*Australia*]
HC .... Housing Committee (SAUO)
HC .... Howard College (SAUO)
HC .... Hroswitha Club (EA)
HC .... Hug Club (EA)
HC .... Humid Crepidations [*Medicine*] (ROG)
HC .... Humidity Control
HC .... Humphreys College (SAUO)
HC .... Hungarian Congress (EA)
HC .... Hunter College (SAUO)
HC .... Hunterian Club (SAUO)
HC .... Hunting-Clan Air Transport (SAUO)
HC .... Huntington College (SAUS)
HC .... Huntington's Chorea [*Medicine*]
HC .... Hupmobile Club (EA)
HC .... Huron College (SAUO)
HC .... Hussan College (SAUO)
HC .... Hutchinson College (SAUO)
HC .... Hyaline Casts [*Clinical chemistry*]
HC .... Hybrid Circuit [*Electronics*] (IAA)
HC .... Hybrid Coil (SAUS)

HC .... Hybrid Computer [*for processing both analog and digital data*] (NASA)
HC .... Hydatid Cyst (MELL)
HC .... Hyderabad Contingent [*British military*] (DMA)
HC .... Hydranencephaly [*Medicine*] (AAMN)
HC .... Hydraulic Circuit (SAUS)
HC .... Hydraulic Clean (MSA)
HC .... Hydraulic Components (SAUS)
HC .... Hydraulic Concussion (DB)
HC .... Hydraulic Conductivity (ABAC)
HC .... Hydraulic Controller (SAUS)
HC .... Hydraulic Coupling (DCTA)
HC .... Hydraulic Cylinder
HC .... Hydrocarbon [*Organic chemistry*]
HC .... Hydrocodone [*Medicine*] (MEDA)
Hc .... Hydrocolloid (DMAA)
HC .... Hydrocortisone [*Endocrinology*]
HC .... Hydrocracking
HC .... Hydrogen Chemisorption (SAUS)
HC .... Hydrogen Chloride (AABC)
HC .... Hydrogen Control (SAUS)
H/C .... Hydrogen to Carbon Atomic Ratio (EG)
HC .... Hydrographic Center [*Defense Mapping Agency*]
HC .... Hydrophobic Cellulose (DB)
HC .... Hyoid Cornu [*Medicine*] (EDAA)
HC .... Hypatia Cluster [*Defunct*] (EA)
HC .... Hypothetical Construct (DIPS)
HC .... Hysteresis Comparator
HC .... Hysterical Convulsions (MELL)
HC .... Pechiney-Progil [*France*] [*Research code symbol*]
HC .... Reports of the High Court of Griqualand West [*South Africa*] [*A publication*] (DLA)
HC .... Screening Smoke [*Mixture*]
HC-3 .... Hemicholinium-3 (LDT)
HC3 .... Hemicholinium No. 3 (SAUS)
HC4 .... Helicopterborne Command and Control Communications Central
HC-54 .... Douglas C-54 modified (SAUS)
HC-130H .... Hercules Search-and-Rescue Aircraft [*Air Force*] (POLM)
HCA .... Absent by Reason of Being Held by Civil Authorities [*Military*]
HCA .... Big Spring [*Texas*] [*Airport symbol*] (AD)
HCA .... Habitat Conservation Area
HCA .... Haitian Coalition on AIDS (EA)
HCA .... Half-Cone Angle (SAUO)
HCA .... Hand Copy Adapter (SAUS)
HCA .... Hanford Contractors Association (SAUO)
hca .... Harmonica
HCA .... Harness and Cable Assembly
HCA .... Hazardous Communications Act (COE)
HCA .... Heading Crossing Angle (SAUO)
HCA .... Head of Contracting Activity [*Military*] (AABC)
HCA .... Head of Contracting Agency (DOMA)
HCA .... Headquarters Commitment Authorization [*Military*] (DNAB)
HCA .... Health Care Administration
HCA .... Health Care Aide (DAVI)
HCA .... Health Care Analysis (SAUO)
HCA .... Health Care Assistant (MEDA)
HCA .... Heartbeat Collision Avoidance (SAUS)
HCA .... Heart Cell Aggregate [*Cytology*]
HCA .... Heisey Collectors of America (EA)
HCA .... Held by Civil Authorities
HCA .... Helicopter Club of America (EA)
HC(A) .... Helicopter Coordinator (Airborne) (NVT)
HCA .... Helicopter Council of America (SAUO)
HCA .... Hemispherical Coverage Antenna (TIMI)
HCA .... Hepatocellular Adenoma [*Medicine*]
HCA .... Heptine Carbonic Acid (SAUS)
HCA .... Hermes Carrier Aircraft (SAUS)
HCA .... Heterocyclicamine
HCA .... Heterocyclic Amines (ADWA)
HCA .... Heterocyclic Antidepressant [*Psychopharmaceutical*]
HCA .... Hexachloroacetone [*Organic chemistry*]
HCA .... High conductivity Copper Association (SAUO)
HCA .... High Contamination Area (SAUS)
HCA .... High Court of Admiralty (SAUO)
HCA .... High Courts of Admiralty [*British*]
HCA .... Hispanic Computing Association (EA)
HCA .... Historic Cost Accounts [*London Stock Exchange*]
HCA .... Hobby Clubs of America (EA)
HCA .... Hobie Class Association (EA)
HCA .... Hollow Cylinder Apparatus [*Nuclear energy*] (NUCP)
HCA .... Holy Childhood Association (EA)
HCA .... Home Care Aide [*Medicine*] (DMAA)
HCA .... Homocysteate [*Biochemistry*]
HCA .... Horder Centre for Arthritics (SAUO)
HCA .... Horizon Crossing Ascending
HCA .... Hospital Care Corporation of America [*NYSE symbol*] (COMM)
HCA .... Hospital Caterers Association [*British*]
HCA .... Hospital Corporation of America (SAUO)
HCA .... Hot Cranking Amperes [*Battery*] [*Automotive engineering*]
HCA .... Hoverclub of America (EA)
HCA .... Human Component Analysis
HCA .... Humanitarian and Civic Assistance (DOMA)
HCA .... Humanitarian Civic Action
HCA .... Hunter Club of America (EA)
HCA .... Hunting-Clan Air Transport Ltd.
HCA .... Hyderabad Contingent Artillery [*British military*] (DMA)
HCA .... Hydrochloric Acid (SAUS)
HCA .... Hydrocortisonacetat (SAUS)
HCA .... Hydrocortisone Acetate [*Pharmacology*]
HCA .... Hydrogen Chloride Absorber (EEVL)
HCA .... Hydroxylcarbonate Apatite (SAUS)
HCA .... Hypertrophic Cardiomyopathy Association (BUAC)
HCA .... Lake Havasu Air Service [*ICAO designator*] (FAAC)
HCA .... State Health Care Authority (SAUO)
HCAA .... Hebrew Christian Alliance of America [*Later, MJAA*]
HCAA .... Hellenic Civil Aviation Authority (SAUS)
HCAA .... National CPA Health Care Advisors Association (SAUO)
HCAAO .... Hawaii Council of Associations of Apartment Owners (SRA)
HCAAS .... Homeless Childrens Aid and Adoption Society (SAUS)
HCAB .... Health Care Advisory Board (SAUO)
HCAB .... Higher Committee for Agrarian Reform (SAUS)
HCAC .... Hazardous Chemicals Advisory Committee [*New South Wales, Australia*]
HC ACE .... Hydrocortisone Acetate (SAUS)
HCAM .... Health Care Association of Michigan (SRA)
HC & C .... Harvard Capital & Consulting [*An investment fund*] [*Czechoslovakia*] (ECON)
HC&ES .... Hull Chemical and Engineering Society (SAUO)
HC&H .... Hovering Craft and Hydrofoil (journ.) (SAUS)
HC&S .... Hawaiian Commercial and Sugar Co. (SAUO)
HCAP .... Handicapped
H-CAP .... Hexamethylmelamine, Cyclophosphamide, Adriamycin, Platinol [*Cisplatin*] [*Antineoplastic drug regimen*]
H-Caps .... Heroin Capsules (SAUS)
HCAR .... Higher Committee for Agrarian Reform [*Egypt*] (BUAC)
HCAR .... Historic Commands of the American Revolution (EA)
HCAS .... Highway Cost Allocation Study [*Also, FHCAS*]
HCAV .... Hunt Clubs Association of Victoria [*Australia*]
HCAV .... Hyperactive Children's Association of Victoria [*Australia*]
HCAW .... Home Care Association of Washington (SRA)
HCAX .... Hennepin County Regional Rail [*Federal Railroad Administration identification code*]
HCB .... H&CB ADS [*NYSE symbol*]
HCB .... Hard Convex Body [*Equation of state*]
HCB .... Hard Core Base (SAUS)
HCB .... Hard-Covered Book (WDAA)
HCB .... Heating and Cooling of Buildings (SAUS)
HCB .... Heaviside-Campbell Bridge [*Electronics*]
HCB .... Hemisphere Cylinder Body
HCB .... Hexachlorbenzol (SAUS)
HCB .... Hexachlorobenzene [*Organic chemistry*]
HCB .... Hexachlorobutadeine (ABAC)
HCB .... High Capability Buoy [*Marine science*] (MSC)
HCB .... High-Capacity Bomb
HCB .... Highland Cyclist Battalion [*British military*] (DMA)
HCB .... Hollow Concrete Block
HCB .... Hollow-Cone Beam (SAUS)
HCB .... Hoopes Conductivity Bridge [*Electronics*]
HCB .... House of Commons Bill [*British*]
HCB .... Hungarian Credit Bank
HCB .... Hydrocortisone Butyrate [*Glucocorticoid*]
HCBA .... Hotel and Catering Benevolent Association (ODA)
HCB-CBED .... Hollow-Cone Beam/Convergent-Beam Electron Diffraction (SAUS)
HCBD .... Hexachlorobutadiene [*Organic chemistry*]
HCBI .... Health Conference for Business and Industry [*Defunct*]
HCBK .... Hudson Chartered Bancorp [*NASDAQ symbol*] (TTSB)
HCBK .... Hudson Chartered Bancorp, Inc. [*NASDAQ symbol*] (SAG)
HCBP .... Hexachlorobiphenyl [*Organic chemistry*]
HCBS .... Home and Community-Based Services [*Department of Health and Human Services*] (GFGA)
HCBS .... Host Computer Basic Software (IAA)
HCBS .... Hot Cross Bun Skull (MELL)
HC BUT .... Hydrocortisone Butyrate (SAUS)
HCBWAG .... Home and Community-Based Waiver for Aged [*Department of Health and Human Services*] (GFGA)
HCBWAGD .... Home and Community-Based Waiver for Aged and Physically and Developmentally Disabled [*Department of Health and Human Services*] (GFGA)
HCBWAGPD .... Home and Community-Based Waiver for Aged and Physically Disabled [*Department of Health and Human Services*] (GFGA)
HCBWMI .... Home and Community-Based Waiver for Mentally Ill [*Department of Health and Human Services*] (GFGA)
HCBWMRDD .... Home and Community-Based Waiver for Mentally Retarded and Developmentally Disabled [*Department of Health and Human Services*] (GFGA)
HCBWPDS .... Home and Community-Based Waiver for Physically Disabled [*Department of Health and Human Services*] (GFGA)
HCC .... Hand Control Clutch (DNAB)
HCC .... Hardware Capability Code [*Dialog*] [*Searchable field*] [*Information service or system*] (NITA)
HCC .... Harlem Cultural Council (EA)
HCC .... Harshaw Chemical Company (SAUO)
HCC .... Hawaii Control Center [*Missiles*] (MUGU)
HCC .... HCC Insurance Holdings [*NYSE symbol*] (SAG)
HCC .... Health Care Card (ADA)
HCC .... Health Care Center (WDAA)
HCC .... Health Care Corporation (SAUO)
HCC .... Health Coordinating Council
HCC .... Heat Capacity Mapping Mission (SAUO)
HCC .... Heat Conservation Center (STED)

HCC .... Hebrew Culture Council (SAUO)
HCC .... Heliax Coaxial Cable
HCC .... Helicopter Control Center (NVT)
HCC .... Helicopter Coordination Center
HCC .... Helicopter Crash Crane (DNAB)
HCC .... Hemispherical Combustion Chamber (GOBB)
HCC .... Hepatitis Contagiosa Canis [*Virus*]
HCC .... Hepatocellular Carcinoma [*Oncology*]
HCC .... Hepatoma Carcinoma Cell [*Medicine*] (DB)
HCC .... Hereditary Colon Cancer
HCC .... Hermetic Chip Carrier
HCC .... Hexachlorocyclohexane (STED)
HCC .... Hibbing Community College, Hibbing, MN [*OCLC symbol*] (OCLC)
HCC .... High Carbon Coke (SAUS)
HCC .... Himalayan Climate Centre (QUAC)
HCC .... Hindustan Construction Company (SAUO)
HCC .... History of Chief Complaint [*Medicine*]
HCC .... Hobart Chamber of Commerce [*Australia*]
HCC .... Hoist Crane Control (SAUS)
HCC .... Hole Count Check (SAUS)
HCC .... Hollow Copper Conductor
HCC .... Hollywood Comedy Club (EA)
HCC .... Holy Cross [*California*] [*Seismograph station code, US Geological Survey*] (SEIS)
HCC .... Holyoke Community College [*Massachusetts*]
HCC .... Home Care Coordinator [*Medicine*]
HCC .... Honda Car Club [*Defunct*] (EA)
HCC .... Honda Civic Club [*Later, H-I*] (EA)
HCC .... Honeycomb Corrugated Construction
HCC .... Horizontal Continuous Casting (SAUS)
HCC .... Horticultural Co-ordination Committee (SAUO)
HCC .... Hospital Chaplaincies Council (BUAC)
HCC .... Hospital Conveyance Corps [*British military*] (DMA)
HCC .... Host Country Contributions [*Peace Corps*]
HCC .... Housing Consultative Council for England (BUAC)
HCC .... Hovermail Collectors' Club (BUAC)
HCC .... Hubcap Collector's Club (EA)
HCC .... Hull Construction Certificate
HCC .... Hummel Collectors Club (EA)
HCC .... Humor Correspondence Club (EA)
HCC .... Hurthle Cell Cancer (MELL)
HCC .... Husband-Coached Childbirth (MELL)
HCC .... Hyderabad Contingent Cavalry [*British military*] (DMA)
HCC .... Hydraulic Cement Concrete
HCC .... Hydrocarbon Concentration [*Automotive engineering*]
HCC .... Hydroxycholecalciferol [*Biochemistry*]
HCCA .... Heavy Construction Contractors Association
HCCA .... Hellenic Chamber of Commerce in Australia
HCCA .... Horseless Carriage Club of America (EA)
HCCAACT ..... Health Care Consumers' Association of the Australian Capital Territory
HCCAPS .... Helmet Compatible Communications/Aural Protection System
HCCAS .... Hardware Configuration Statistical Accounting System (SAUO)
HCCBE .... Hungarian Central Committee for Books and Education (EA)
HCCC .... Computer Center [*Haverford College*] [*Research center*] (RCD)
HCCC .... Health Care Compare Corp. (SAUO)
HCCC .... HealthCare COMPARE Corp. [*NASDAQ symbol*] (NQ)
HCCC .... Health Care Complaints Commission [*Australia*]
HCCC .... Helix Countercurrent Chromatography
HCCC .... Hyalinizing Clear Cell Carcinoma [*Medicine*] (PALA)
HCCC .... Hyderabad Co-Operative Commercial Corp. [*India*] (BUAC)
HCCC .... Hyderabad Co-operative Commercial Corporation (SAUO)
HCCD .... Historical Canadian Climate Database (CARB)
HCCD .... Historical Canadian Climate Dataset (QUAC)
HCCG .... Discharge [*from Military Service*] under Honorable Conditions, Convenience of Government
HCCG .... Honorable Condition Convenience of the Government (SAUS)
HCCH .... Hexachlorocyclohexane [*Organic chemistry*]
HCCI .... HCC Industries, Inc. [*NASDAQ symbol*] (COMM)
HCCI .... Health Care Coordination Initiative [*Federal Government of Canada, Veterans Affairs*]
HCCI .... Homogeneous-Charge, Compression-Ignition [*Automotive engines*]
HCC Ins .... HCC Insurance Holdings [*Associated Press*] (SAG)
HCCJ........... Harvard Center for Criminal Justice (SAUO)
HCCM .... Discharge [*from Military Service*] under Honorable Conditions, Convenience of Man
HCCM .... Hadley Centre Climate Model
HCCM .... Hardware Command and Control Manager (ACAE)
HCCM .... Heat Capacity Mapping Mission (SAUS)
HCCM .... High-Performance Common Channel Module [*Telecommunications*]
HCCM .... Honorable Condition Convenience of the Man (SAUS)
HCCO .... Hector Communications [*NASDAQ symbol*] (TTSB)
HCCO .... Hector Communications Corp. [*NASDAQ symbol*] (SAG)
HCCP .... Hexachlorocyclopentadiene [*Also, HCP, HEX*] [*Organic chemistry*]
HCCP .... Honorary Certified Claims Professional
HCCPD......... Hexachlorocyclopentadiene (COE)
HC/CPP....... Historical Cost/Current Purchasing Power
HCC Virus.... Hepatitis Contagiosa Canis Virus (SAUS)
HCCX........... Hercules Cement [*Private rail car owner code*]
HC CYP .... Hydrocortisone Cypionate (SAUS)
HCCZ .... Harrison Cement [*Federal Railroad Administration identification code*]
HCD .... College of the Holy Cross, Worcester, MA [*OCLC symbol*] (OCLC)
HCd............. Hair Cadmium Level [*Medicine*]
HCD .... Handcarried (AABC)
HCD .... Hard-Copy Device [*Computer science*] (ECII)
HCD .... Hardware Configuration Definition (SAUS)
HCD .... Headquarters Camp Davis (SAUO)
HCD .... Heavy Chain Deposition [*Medicine*] (MELL)
HCD .... Heavy Chain Disease [*Protein*]
HCD .... Helath Care Delivery (STED)
HCD .... Herniated Cervical Disk [*Medicine*] (MELL)
HCD .... High Caloric Density (STED)
HCD .... High-Calorie Diet (MELL)
HCD .... High Capacity Disk (SAUS)
HCD .... High Carbohydrate Diet [*Medicine*] (DMAA)
HCD .... High Current Density (SAUS)
HCD .... High-Current Density
HCD .... High Current Diode (SAUS)
HCD .... High-Current Diode
HCD .... Highest Common Denominator
HCD .... Hoffman Core Driver
HCD .... Hollow Cathode Discharge [*Spectrometry*]
HCD .... Homologous Canine Distemper [*Antiserum*]
HCD .... Horizon Crossing Descending
HCD .... Horizontal Correlation Distance
HCD .... Hot-Carrier Diode (IEEE)
HCD .... Housing and Community Development (SAUO)
HCD .... Hughes Communications Division (SAA)
HCD .... Human Capacity Development (SAUO)
HCD .... Hutchinson, MN [*Location identifier*] [*FAA*] (FAAL)
HCD .... Hydrocarbons-Dilution [*Automotive emissions*]
HCD .... Hydrocolloid Dressing [*Dermatology*]
HCD .... Hyundai California Design [*Concept car*]
HCDA .... Hipyothetical Core-Disruptive Accident (SAUS)
HCDA .... Housing and Community Development Act (GFGA)
HCDA .... Hydrodynamic Core Disruptive Accident [*Nuclear energy*] (NRCH)
HCDA .... Hypothetical Core Disruptive Accident [*Nuclear energy*]
HCD Antiserum... Homologous Canine Distemper Antiserum (SAUS)
HCDB .... Historical Cost Database
HCDC .... Heritage Climate Data Collection (SAUS)
HCDC .... House of Commons Defence Committee (SAUO)
HCDCS .... Harmonized Commodity Description and Coding System (SAUS)
HCDD .... Hexachlorodibenzodioxin [*Organic chemistry*]
HCDE .... Homothetic-Constant Differences of Elasticities of Substitution [*Statistics*]
HCDE .... Human-Centered Design Environment
HCDJ .... Hyperostosis Corticalis Deformans Invenilis [*Medicine*] (MELL)
HCDM .... Hungarian Christian Democratic Movement [*Slovakia*] (BUAC)
HCDN .... Hydroclimate Data Network (SAUO)
HCDN .... Hydro-Climatic Data Network (SAUO)
HCDP .... Discharge [*from Military Service*] under Honorable Conditions, Dependency Existing Prior to Enlistment
HCDP .... Health Care Demand Plan (SAUO)
HCDP .... Honorable Condition Dependency Existing Prior to Enlistment (SAUS)
HCD Plan..... Consolidated Housing & Community Development Plan (SAUO)
HCDR .... Hardware Critical Design Review (MCD)
HCDR .... Hours and Cost Detail Report
HCDS .... Health Care Delivery System (SAUS)
HCDT .... Hollow-Cathode Discharge Tube (SAUS)
HCDV .... Hilcoast Development [*NASDAQ symbol*] (TTSB)
HCDV .... Hilcoast Development Corp. [*NASDAQ symbol*] (SAG)
HCDWP........ Hazardous Chemical Defense Waste Management Program (SAUS)
HCE.............. Hard Coal Equivalent [*Unit of energy used in Euratom*] [*Medicine*] (EDAA)
hce............... Hard-Coal Equivalents (BARN)
HCE.............. Haveth Childer Everywhere [*Key phrase in "Finnegan's Wake"*]
HCE.............. Health Care Education
HCE.............. Heater Control Electronics (ACAE)
HCE.............. Heptachlor Epoxide (ABAC)
HCE.............. Here Comes Everybody [*Key phrase in "Finnegan's Wake"*]
HCE.............. Hic Conditus Est [*Here Lies Buried*] [*Latin*]
HCE.............. High Commissioner for Eire (SAUO)
HCE.............. Highly Compensated Employee [*Human resources*] (WYGK)
HCE.............. Hollow-Cathode Effect (IEEE)
HCE.............. Human Capital Exchange
HCE.............. Human-Caused Error
HCE.............. Humphrey Chimpden Earwicker [*Hero of "Finnegan's Wake"*]
HCE.............. Hydrocarbons-Exhaust [*Automotive emissions*]
HCEA .... Hairdressers and Cosmetologists Employers' Association [*Australia*]
HCEA .... Healthcare Convention & Exhibitors Association (NTPA)
HCEA .... Health Care Exhibitors Association (EA)
HCEA .... Holland Cheese Exporters Association [*Later, DDB*] (EA)
HCEBT .... Houston Cotton Exchange and Board of Trade [*Defunct*] (EA)
HCEC .... Hospital Care Evaluation Committee (MEDA)
HCEC .... Hospital Committee of the European Community (BUAC)
HCED .... Hand Controller Engage Driver (NASA)
HCEE............ Discharge [*from Military Service*] under Honorable Conditions, Expiration of Enlistment
HCEE............ Honorable Condition Expiration of Enlistment (SAUS)
HCEEP .... Handicapped Children's Early Education Programs
HCEI............. Hydrocarbon Emission Index [*Automotive engineering*]
HCER .... High Capacity Extended Range (SAUS)
HCES .... Honam Crop Experiment Station (SAUO)
HCES .... Hull Chemical and Engineering Society (SAUO)
HCEX .... High-Speed Color Exterior
HCEX .... Hypercharge Exchange (SAUS)
HCEZ............ Hawley Co-Operative Elevator [*Federal Railroad Administration identification code*]
HCF.............. Fluorocarbon without Chlorine (ECON)
HCF.............. Haemolytic Complement Fixation (SAUS)

HCF .... Hagerstown CATI [*Computer-Assisted Telephone Interviewing*] Facility [*Bureau of the Census*] (GFGA)
HCF .... Halt and Catch Fire [*Computer hacker terminology*] (NHD)
HCF .... Hardened Compact Fiber
HCF .... Health Care Facility [*Medicine*] (EDAA)
HCF .... Health Care Financing (SAUO)
HCF .... Health Care Finder
HCF .... [*The*] Healthcare Forum (EA)
HCF .... Heat Control Filter
HCF .... Hebrew Christian Fellowship (EA)
HCF .... Hebrew Culture Foundation (EA)
HCF .... Height Correction Factor
HCF .... Hepatitis C Foundation (ADWA)
HCF .... Hereditary Capillary Fragility [*Medicine*] (DMAA)
HCF .... High-Calorific Fuel (SAUS)
HCF .... High Capacity File (SAUS)
HCF .... High Carbohydrate, High Fiber [*Nutrition*]
HCF .... High-Carbon Ferrochrome [*Metallurgy*]
HCF .... High Circle Fatique
HCF .... High Coefficient of Friction [*Engineering*]
HCF .... High-Cost Fund (GART)
HCF .... High-Cycle Fatigue [*Rocket engine*]
HCF .... Highest Common Factor [*Mathematics*]
HCF .... HIM [*Hardware Interface Module*] Configuration File [*NASA*] (NASA)
HCF .... Honeycomb Foundation (IIA)
HCF .... Honorary Chaplain to the Forces [*British*]
HCF .... Hood College, Frederick, MD [*OCLC symbol*] (OCLC)
HCF .... Host Command Facility
HCF .... Hot Channel Factor [*Environmental science*] (COE)
HCF .... Hulls Compaction Facility (SAUO)
HCF .... Hundred Cubic Feet (SAUS)
HCF .... Hungarian Cultural Foundation (EA)
HCF .... Hypocaloric Carbohydrate Feeding (DB)
HCFA .... Health Care Finance Administration (SAUO)
HCFA .... Health Care Financing Administration [*HHS*]
HCFAR .... Health Care Financing Administration Rulings [*A publication*] (DLA)
HCFC .... Halogenated Chloro Fluorocarbon (SAUS)
HCFC .... Helen Cornelius Fan Club (EA)
HCFC .... Hydrochlorofluorocarbon [*Organic chemistry*]
HCFC-22 ...... Hydrochlorofluorocarbon-22 (SAUS)
HCFC-141b... Hydrochlorofluorocarbon-141b (SAUS)
HCFC-142b... Hydrochlorofluorocarbon-142b (SAUS)
HCFD .... Hydrochemical Form Die [*Tool*] (AAG)
HCFF .... High-Capacity Fog Foam [*Navy*] (NVT)
HCFF/AFFF... High-Capacity Fog Foam/Aqueous Film-Forming Foam (DNAB)
HCFI .... Health Concepts IV, Inc. (SAUO)
HCFMS .... Holy Cross Foreign Mission Society (EA)
HCFP .... HealthCare Financial Partners, Inc. [*NASDAQ symbol*] (SAG)
HCFR .... Health Care Financing Review [*A publication*] (DLA)
HCF Rev ...... Health Care Financing Review [*A publication*] (DLA)
HCFSG .... Health Care Financing Study Group (EA)
hCFSH .... Human Chorionic Follicle-Stimulating [*Medicine*] (EDAA)
HCFTA .... Home and Contract Furnishing Textiles Association [*British*] (DBA)
hCFTR .... Human Cystic Fibrosis Transmembrane Conductance Regulator [*Genetics*]
hCFU .... Human Colony-Forming Unit [*Genetics*]
HCG .... Griqualand High Court Reports [*A publication*] (DLA)
HCG .... Hardware Character Generator
HCG .... Hermanas Catequistas Guadalupanas [*Sister Catechists of Guadeloupe*] [*Roman Catholic women's religious order*]
HCG .... Hexagonal Coupling (SAUS)
HCG .... Home Capital Group, Inc. [*Toronto Stock Exchange symbol*]
HCG .... Horizontal Location of Center of Gravity
hcg .... horizontal location of centre of gravity (SAUO)
HCG .... Hughes Communications Galaxy, Incorporated (ACAE)
hCG .... Human Chorionic Gonadotropin [*A hormone*] (PAZ)
HCG .... National Humanitarian Coordination Group (SAUO)
HCGB .... Helicopter Club of Great Britain (BUAC)
HCGB .... Hover Club of Great Britain (SAUO)
HCGF .... Haematopoietic Cell Growth Factor [*Biochemistry*]
HCGN .... Hypocomplementemic Glomerulonephritis [*Nephrology*] (DAVI)
HCGO .... Heavy Coker Gas Oil [*Petroleum technology*]
HCGPF .... Hematopoietic Cell Growth Potentiating Factor (DB)
HCGR .... Heavy Chain Gene Rearrangement [*Medicine*] (MELL)
hCGRP .... Human Calcitonin Gene-Related Peptide [*Biochemistry*]
HCGS .... Hope Creek Generating Station (NRCH)
HCH .... Crossville, TN [*Location identifier*] [*FAA*] (FAAL)
HCH .... Halogenated Cyclic Hydrocarbons (SAUS)
H-CH .... Handy-Cap Horizons [*Defunct*] (EA)
HCH .... Health Care for the Homeless (DMAA)
HCH .... Health-Chem Corp. [*AMEX symbol*] (SPSG)
HCH .... Herbert Clark Hoover [*US president, 1874-1964*]
HCH .... Herding Champion [*Prefix*]
HCH .... Hexachlorocyclohexane [*Also, BHC, GBH*] [*Insecticide*]
HCH .... National Health Care for the Homeless Council (SAUO)
HCHASC .... House of Commons Home Affairs Select Committee [*British*] (WDAA)
HCHB .... Herbert C. Hoover Building (SAUS)
HCHBK .... Hatchback [*Automotive advertising*]
HCHC .... High Carbon, High Chrome
HChD .... Diploma in Higher Chiropodial Theory of the Institute of Chiropodists [*British*] (DBQ)
HCHD .... Harris County Hospital District (SAUO)
HCHE .... High Capacity High Explosive (SAUS)
HCHF .... High Carbohydrate, High Fiber [*Nutrition*]
Hchg .... Hechinger Co. [*Associated Press*] (SAG)
HCHGC .... Hollingworth Center for Highly Gifted Children (EA)
HCHI .... Hand Chain Hoist Institute (SAUO)
HCHM .... Highway Controller/Health Monitor (SAUS)
HCHO .... Aldehydes [*Organic chemistry*]
HCHO .... Formaldehyde [*Organic chemistry*] (DAVI)
HCHP .... Harvard Community Health Plan (DMAA)
HCHP .... Health Care for the Homeless Program [*Defunct*] (EA)
HCHP .... High-Capacity Heat Pipe (SSD)
HCHS .... Handicapped Children's Home Service [*Later, Easter Seal Home Service*] (EA)
HCHS .... Hydrocortisone Hemisuccinate [*Medicine*] (MELL)
HCHWA .... Hereditary Cerebral Hemorrhage with Amyloidosis [*Medicine*] (EDAA)
HCHWA-D ..... Hereditary Cerebral Hemorrhage with Amyloidosis of the Dutch Type [*Medicine*]
HCI .... Handgun Control, Inc. (EA)
HCI .... Hardness-Critical Item (MSA)
HCI .... Hawthorne Communications, Inc.
HCI .... HCI Holdings Ltd. [*Toronto Stock Exchange symbol*]
HCI .... Health Care International [*British*]
HCI .... Health Care on the Internet (SAUO)
HCI .... Health Commons Institute
HCI .... Heritage Communications, Incorporated (SAUO)
HCI .... Hierarchically Classified Index
HCI .... High-Current Inductor
HCI .... Highes Communications, Inc. (SAUS)
HCI .... Home Center Institute (EA)
HCI .... Horizon Crossing Indicator (ACAE)
HCI .... Host Computer Interface
HCI .... Hot Carrier Injection (AAEL)
HCI .... Hotel and Catering Institute (SAUO)
HCI .... Hughes Communications, Inc. [*Hughes Aircraft Co.*] [*Los Angeles, CA*]
HCI .... Hughes Communications International (SAUO)
HCI .... Human Computer Interaction (SAUS)
HCI .... Human-Computer Interaction [*Computer science*]
HCI .... Human-Computer Interface (RDA)
HCI .... Hybrid Computer Interface (MHDB)
HCI .... Hyderabad Contingent Infantry [*India*] [*Army*]
HCI .... Hydrochloric Acid (MELL)
HCI .... Hydrochloride (CPH)
HCI .... Hydrogen Chloride (ABAC)
HCI .... Order of the Hashimite Chain of Iraq (SAUO)
HCIA .... HCIA, Inc. [*NASDAQ symbol*] (SAG)
HCIA .... Highlander Class International Association (EA)
HCIB .... Health Computer Information Bureau (SAUS)
HCID .... Health Cost Index Database (SAUO)
HCIED .... High Commissioner for India Education Department (SAUO)
HCIG .... Health Care Industry Group (SAUO)
HCIH .... Hubei Cancer Institute and Hospital [*China*] (BUAC)
HCIL .... Hague Conference on International Law (SAUO)
HCIL .... Herbert Controls & Instrument, Letchworth (SAUO)
HCIL .... Human-Computer Interaction Laboratory [*University of Maryland*] (PCM)
HCIm .... HealthCare Imaging Services, Inc. [*Associated Press*] (SAG)
HCIMA .... Hotel Catering and Institutional Management Association (SAUO)
HcIMP .... Hydrocolloid Impression [*Dentistry*]
HCIN .... Hydrocarbon-Induced Neoplasm [*Medicine*] (MELL)
HCIR .... Health Cost Index Report (SAUO)
HCIS .... Health Care Information System (DMAA)
HCIS .... Hospital Communication and Information System [*McDonnell Douglas Automation Co.*]
HCIS .... House Committee on Internal Security [*Formerly, HUAC*] [*Dissolved, 1975*] [*US Congress*]
HCIS .... House Committee on International Security (SAUO)
HCIS-10 ...... Hot-Carriers In Semiconductors, Tenth conference (SAUS)
HCITB .... Hotel and Catering Industry Training Board [*British*] (BI)
HCITE .... Horizontal Cargo Integration Test Equipment (MCD)
H-CITE .... Horizontal-Cargo Integration Test Equipment (SAUS)
HCJ .... High Court of Justice
HCJ .... Holy Child Jesus (SAUS)
HCJ .... Honeywell Computer Journal (SAUO)
HCJA .... High Court Journalists' Association (BUAC)
HCJB .... High Court Junior Beadle [*Ancient Order of Foresters*]
HCJC .... Henderson County Junior College [*Texas*]
HCJC .... Howard County Junior College [*Texas*]
HCJFC .... Harry Connick, Jr., Fan Club (EA)
HC Jour .... House of Commons Journals [*England*] [*A publication*] (DLA)
HCJW .... High Court Junior Woodward [*Ancient Order of Foresters*]
HCK .... Hematopoietic Cell Kinase (DMAA)
HCK .... Holtzer-Cabot Corp. (EFIS)
HCK .... Human Cervical Keratinocyte [*Cytology*]
HCKRY .... Hickory
HCL .... Central Hispano Capital Ltd. [*NYSE symbol*] (SAG)
HCL .... Hairy Cell Leukemia [*Medicine*]
HCL .... Hamburg-Chicago Line [*Steamship*] (MHDB)
HCL .... Hanging Closet (SAUS)
HCL .... Hard Contact Lens [*Ophthalmology*]
HCL .... Hardware Compatibility [*Computer science*]
HCL .... Hardware Compatibility List [*Microsoft Corp.*]
HCL .... Hardware Configuration List (SAUO)
HCL .... Harold Cohen Library [*University of Liverpool*] [*British*] (NITA)
HCL .... Harpoon Check List [*Missiles*] (MCD)
HCL .... Harvard College Library (SAUO)
HCL .... Helenair Corp [*Saint Lucia*] [*FAA designator*] (FAAC)
HCL .... Helicopter Combat Leger (SAUS)

HCL............ Helium Cadmium LASER
HCL............ High, Common, Low [*Relay*] (IEEE)
HCL............ High Cost of Living
HCL............ Hilar Cell Tumor [*Medicine*] (MELL)
HCL............ Hindustan Copper Limited (SAUO)
HCL............ Hod Carriers, Building and Common Laborers (SAUS)
HCL............ Hollow Cathode Lamp
HCL............ Homing Control Logic (SAUS)
HCL............ Hopper Card Lever (SAUS)
HCL............ Horizontal Center Line
HCL............ Host Control Links (SAUS)
HCL............ Hue, Chroma and Luminance (SAUS)
HCL............ Human Cultured Lymphoblastoid [*Cells*]
HCL............ Human Cultured Lymphoblasts [*Medicine*] (DMAA)
HCL............ Huron College [*UTLAS symbol*]
HCL............ Husson College, Bangor, ME [*OCLC symbol*] (OCLC)
HCL............ Hycel, Inc. (SAUO)
HCL............ Hyderabad Contingent Lancers [*British military*] (DMA)
HCl............ Hydrochloric Acid
HCL............ Hydrochloride (SAUS)
HCl............ Hydrogen Chloride (LDT)
HCL............ International Hod Carriers', Building and Common Laborers' Union of America [*Later, Laborers' International Union of North America*]
HCLA.......... Health Care Liability Alliance (ADWA)
HCLA.......... Hungarian Catholic League of America (EA)
HCLC.......... Holding Company Liquidating Commission (SAUO)
HCLD.......... Housing Construction and Land Development
HCLE.......... Humanities Center for Liberal Education
HCLE.......... International Hod Carriers, Building and Common Laborers Union of America (SAUO)
HCLF.......... Health Care Libraries Forum [*Association of Specialized and Cooperative Library Agencies*]
HCLF.......... High Carbohydrate, Low Fiber [*Nutrition*]
HCLF.......... Horizontal Cask Lifting Fixture [*Nuclear energy*] (NRCH)
HCLIP......... Harvard Computer-Aided Legal Instruction Project (DLA)
HCLIP......... Home Care Live-In Plan (SAUS)
HCLL.......... Homecall, Inc. (SAUO)
HcllMed...... Housecall Medical Resources, Inc. [*Associated Press*] (SAG)
HCLM.......... Health Care Labor Manual [*A publication*] (DLA)
HC-LN......... High Control/Low Nurturance [*Psychology*]
HCLP.......... Hierarchical Constraint Logic Programming (SAUS)
HCLP.......... Home Conversion Loan Program [*Canada*]
HCLP.......... Hungarian-English Contrastive Project (SAUO)
HCLPr........ Centl Hispano Cap 10.50% Pref [*NYSE symbol*] (TTSB)
HCLPrB....... Central Hispano Cap 9.43% Pref [*NYSE symbol*] (TTSB)
HCLs.......... Hard Contact Lenses [*Medicine*] (EDAA)
HCM............ Haitian Campaign Medal
HCM............ Half-Cycle Magnetizer (IDOE)
HCM............ Halifax Conservatory of Music
HCM............ Hanover Capital Mtg. [*AMEX symbol*] (SG)
HCM............ Harcum, VA [*Location identifier*] [*FAA*] (FAAL)
HCM............ Hard Copy Module (NASA)
HCM............ Hard Core Monitor [*Computer science*] (IAA)
HCM............ HARDMAN [*Hardware-Manpower Program*] Comparability Methodology [*Army*]
HCM............ Harshaw Chemical Company (SAUO)
HCM............ Hawaiian Campaign Medal (SAUO)
HCM............ Health Care Maintenance (DAVI)
HCM............ Health Care Management (SAUO)
HCM............ Heat Capacity Mapper (SAUS)
HCM............ Heat Cure Melt
HCM............ High Capacity Multiplexing [*Telecommunications*] (ACRL)
HCM............ Highway Capacity Manual [*FHWA*] (TAG)
HCM............ Hispanic Christian Male (ADWA)
HCM............ History of Coal Mining (SAUO)
HCM............ Hostile Cervical Mucus [*Medicine*] (MELL)
HCM............ Hughes Computer Model (ACAE)
HCM............ Human Capital Management [*Human resources*] (GART)
HCM............ Hundred Club of Massachusetts (EA)
HCM............ Hydraulic Core Mock-Up [*Nuclear energy*] (NRCH)
HCM............ Hydrocarbon Mass [*Automotive engineering*]
HCM............ Hypercalcemia of Malignancy [*Medicine*]
HCM............ Hypersonic Cruise Missile
HCM............ Hypertrophic Cardiomyopathy [*Cardiology*]
HCM............ Hyundai Color Monitor (SAUS)
HCMA.......... Alula [*Somalia*] [*ICAO location identifier*] (ICLI)
HCMA.......... Hotel Credit Managers Association [*Defunct*] (EA)
HCMA.......... Hypertrophic Cardiomyopathy Association of America (NRGU)
HCMB.......... Baidoa [*Somalia*] [*ICAO location identifier*] (ICLI)
HCMC.......... Candala [*Somalia*] [*ICAO location identifier*] (ICLI)
HCMC.......... Ho Chi Minh City [*Vietnam*]
HCMD.......... Bardera [*Somalia*] [*ICAO location identifier*] (ICLI)
HCME.......... Eil [*Somalia*] [*ICAO location identifier*] (ICLI)
HCME.......... United Hatters, Cap, and Millinery (BUAC)
HCMF.......... Bosaso [*Somalia*] [*ICAO location identifier*] (ICLI)
HCMF.......... Henry Clay Memorial Foundation (EA)
HCMG.......... Gardo [*Somalia*] [*ICAO location identifier*] (ICLI)
HCMH.......... Hargeisa [*Somalia*] [*ICAO location identifier*] (ICLI)
HCMI........... Berbera [*Somalia*] [*ICAO location identifier*] (ICLI)
HCMI........... Homeless Chronically Mentally Ill [*Medicine*]
HCMJ.......... Lugh Ferrandi [*Somalia*] [*ICAO location identifier*] (ICLI)
HCMK.......... Kisimayu [*Somalia*] [*ICAO location identifier*] (ICLI)
HCML.......... El Bur [*Somalia*] [*ICAO location identifier*] (ICLI)
HCMM......... Heat Capacity Map Mission [*NASA*]
HCMM......... Heat Capacity Mapping Mission [*Satellite*] (EERA)
HCMM......... Heat Capricity Mapping Mission (SAUS)
HCMM......... Heavy Capability Mapping Mission [*Satellite*]
HCMM......... Hereditary Cutaneous Malignant Melanoma [*Medicine*] (DMAA)
HCMM......... Highly Conductive Mold Media (SAUS)
HCMM......... Mogadishu [*Somalia*] [*ICAO location identifier*] (ICLI)
HCMM/AEM-1... Heat Capacity Mapping Mission/Applications Explorer Mission-1 (EOSA)
HCMMS....... Health Care Material Management Society (EA)
HCMN.......... Belet Uen [*Somalia*] [*ICAO location identifier*] (ICLI)
HCMO.......... Obbia [*Somalia*] [*ICAO location identifier*] (ICLI)
HCMOC........ High-performance Complemantary Metal Oxide Semiconductor (SAUS)
HCMOS........ High Density Complementary Metal Oxide on Silicone (SAUS)
HCMOS........ High-Density Complementary Metal-Oxide Semiconductor (AAEL)
HCMOS........ High-Speed Complementary Metal-Oxide Semiconductor (MCD)
HCMP.......... Hazardous Chemical Management Program (SAUS)
HCMP.......... Las Anod [*Somalia*] [*ICAO location identifier*] (ICLI)
HCMPA........ Home Counties Master Printers Alliance (SAUS)
HCMR.......... Galcaio [*Somalia*] [*ICAO location identifier*] (ICLI)
HCMR.......... Heat Capacity Mapping Radiometer [*NASA*]
HCMS.......... Discharge [*from Military Service*] under Honorable Conditions, Medical Survey
HCMS.......... Hardware Configuration Management System (SAUS)
HCMS.......... Harlequin Color Management System (SAUS)
HCMS.......... Scusciuban [*Somalia*] [*ICAO location identifier*] (ICLI)
HCMT.......... Ho Chi Minh Trail (SAUO)
HCMTB........ Hat, Cap and Millinery Trade Board (SAUO)
HCMTS........ High-Capacity Mobile Telecommunications System (TEL)
HCMTS........ High Capacity Mobile Telephone System (SAUS)
HCMU.......... Discharge [*from Military Service*] under Honorable Conditions, under Age ofAuthorized Enlistment
HCMU.......... Erigavo [*Somalia*] [*ICAO location identifier*] (ICLI)
HCMU.......... Hebrew Cabinet Makers' Union [*British*]
HCMV.......... Burao [*Somalia*] [*ICAO location identifier*] (ICLI)
HCMV.......... Human Cytomegalovirus
HCMW......... Discharge [*from Military Service*] under Honorable Conditions, Minor Enlisted Without Consent, under Eighteen at Time of Discharge
HCMW......... United Hatters, Cap, and Millinery Workers International Union (EA)
HCN............ Hardware Change Notification (TIMI)
HCN............ Health Care REIT [*NYSE symbol*] (SAG)
HCN............ Health Communications Network [*Medical University of South Carolina*] [*Charleston*] [*Telecommunications*] (TSSD)
HCN............ Hereditary Chronic Nephritis [*Medicine*] (MELL)
HCN............ Hilton Communications Network [*Hilton Hotels Corp.*] [*Beverly Hills, CA*] [*Telecommunications service*] (TSSD)
HCN............ Historical Climate Network
HCN............ Historical Climatology Network (SAUO)
HCN............ Home Counties Newspapers [*British*] (DGA)
HCN............ House Committee on Narcotics (SAUO)
HCN............ Hydrocyanic Acid [*Inorganic chemistry*]
HCN............ Hydrogen Cyanide [*Also, AC*] [*Inorganic chemistry*]
HCN............ Hygienic Community Network (EA)
HCN............ Hypercalcemic Nephropathy [*Medicine*] (MELL)
HCNC.......... Highly Conjugated Noncentrosymmetric (SAUS)
HCND.......... Historical Climatology Network-Daily (SAUO)
HCNM.......... High Commissioner on National Minorities (BUAC)
HCNSW........ Heritage Council of New South Wales [*Australia*]
HCNZ.......... Housing Corporation of New Zealand (SAUO)
HCO............ Hackney Carriage Office [*British*] (WDAA)
HCO............ Hangar Control Officer [*Navy*]
HCO............ Harco Air Services [*Nigeria*] [*ICAO designator*] (FAAC)
HCO............ Hard Copy Output (SAUS)
HCO............ Harvard College Observatory
HCO............ Head of Contracting Office [*Marine science*] (OSRA)
HCO............ Headquarters Catalog Office
HCO............ Health Care Officer (WDAA)
HCO............ Health Care Online (IDYL)
HCO............ Health Care Organization (HCT)
HCO............ Hearing Carry-Over [*Hearing-impaired technology*]
HCO............ Heavy Cycle Oil [*Petroleum technology*]
HCO............ Helicopter Control Officer [*British military*] (DMA)
HCO............ Higher Clerical Officer [*Civil Service*] [*British*]
HCO............ Highly-Chlorinated Oil (IAA)
HCO............ Horizontal Control Operator [*Military*]
HCO............ Howe Coal-Oklahoma [*Federal Railroad Administration identification code*]
HCO............ Huntco, Inc. [*NYSE symbol*] (SAG)
HCO............ Hydrogenated Coconut Oil (PDAA)
HCO_3............ Bicarbonate [*Pharmacology*] (DAVI)
HcoA............ Health Care of Australia (SAUS)
HCOA.......... Home Centers of America (SAUO)
HCOC.......... Honorary Colonel of the Corps [*Army*]
HCOF.......... High Command of Forces (SAUS)
HCOHSA...... Health Care Occupational Health and Safety Association (SAUO)
HCom.......... High Commissioner (SAUO)
HCOM.......... Hughes Cost of Ownership Model (ACAE)
H/comb........ Honeycomb (SAUS)
H Conf Rept... House of Representatives Conference Report (BARN)
HCONN........ Hose Connector
HConRes...... House Concurrent Resolution (WPI)
H Con Res.... House of Representatives Concurrent Resolution (DLA)
HCOP.......... Health Care Opportunities Program [*Department of Health and Human Services*]
HCOPIL........ Hague Conference on Private International Law (BUAC)
HCOPL......... Hubbard Communication Office Policy Letter (SAUS)

HCOR.......... HealthCor Holdings, Inc. [*NASDAQ symbol*] (SAG)
HCOR.......... Honorary Colonel of the Regiment
HCOW.......... Horizon Organic Holding Corp. [*NASDAQ symbol*] (NASQ)
HCP.......... Habitat Conservation Plan [*Ecology*]
HCP.......... Halon Control Panel (SAUS)
HCP.......... Hamiltonian Cycle Problem [*Computer science*]
HCP.......... Handicap
HCP.......... Handicapped (SAUO)
HCP.......... Handicap Race [*Horse racing*]
HCP.......... Hangar Control Position [*Navy*]
HCP.......... Harbor Control Post
HCP.......... Hard Copy Printer [*Computer science*]
HCP.......... Hardness-Critical Process (MSA)
HCP.......... Harpoon Control Panel (ACAE)
HCP.......... Health Care Practitioner (ADWA)
HCP.......... Health Care Products, Inc. [*Toronto Stock Exchange symbol*]
HCP.......... Health Care Property Investors, Inc. [*NYSE symbol*] (SPSG)
HCP.......... Healthy Cities Project (BUAC)
HCP.......... Hearing Conservation Program (LDOE)
HCp.......... Heat of Combustion (of an Element under Constant Pressure) (ROG)
HCP.......... Hemispherical Candlepower [*Optics*] (IAA)
HCP.......... Hepatocatalase Peroxidase [*An enzyme*] (MAE)
HCP.......... Hereditary Coproporphyria [*Medicine*] (MAE)
HCP.......... Hexachlorocyclopentadiene [*Also, HCCP, HEX*] [*Organic chemistry*]
HCP.......... Hexachlorophene [*Germicide*]
HCP.......... Hexagonal Close Packed (SAUS)
HCP.......... Hexagonal Close-Packed [*Crystallography*]
HCP.......... Hexagonal Closest Packing (SAUS)
HCP.......... High-Calcium Pyroxene [*Mineralogy*]
HCP.......... High Card Point (SAUS)
HCP.......... High Cell Passage (DB)
HCP.......... High Chair with Plate (SAUS)
HCP.......... High Commissioner for the Philippines (SAUO)
HCP.......... High speed Channel Processor (SAUS)
HCP.......... Holiday Caravan Parks [*Public-performance tariff class*] [*British*]
HCP.......... Home Consumption Price
HCP.......... Honors Cooperative Program (SAUS)
HCP.......... Horizontal Candlepower
HCP.......... Host Command Processor [*Computer science*] (ELAL)
HCP.......... Host Communications Processor
HCP.......... Host Configuration Processor (SAUS)
HCP.......... House of Commons Paper (SAUO)
HCP.......... House of Commons Proceedings (SAUS)
HCP.......... Hungarian Civic Party [*Slovakia*] (BUAC)
HCP.......... Hybrid Combustion Process (RDA)
HCP.......... Hydorthermal Coal Process [*Environmental science*] (COE)
HCP.......... Hydrazine Catalytic Plenum
HCP.......... Hydrothermal Coal Process (SAUS)
HCP.......... Hydroxycalcium Phenoxide [*Organic chemistry*]
HCP.......... Hydroxycyclopentenone
HCP.......... Hydroxyproline-Containing Protein
HCP.......... Hypervelocity Countermeasures Program
HCP.......... Hypothermal Coal Process (GNE)
HCPA.......... Health-Care Power of Attorney [*Medicine*] (MELL)
HCPA.......... HIMAD Command Post Automation (SAUS)
HCPAA.......... Hungarian Catholic Priests' Association in America (EA)
HCPB.......... Hanford Corporate Planning Board (SAUS)
HCPC.......... Harris County Psychiatric Center (SAUS)
HCPC.......... Health Care Compliance Packaging Council (EA)
HCP Crystal... Hexagonal Close-Packed Crystal (SAUS)
HCPCS.......... HCFA [*Health Care Financing Administration*] Common Procedures Coding System [*Department of Health and Human Services*] (GFGA)
HCPCS.......... HCFAs Common Procedure Coding System (SAUS)
HCPDG.......... Health Care Professionals Discussion Group [*American Occupational Therapy Association*]
HCPE.......... Hybrid Collective Protection Equipment (ACAE)
HCPNI.......... Hardware Cloth and Poultry Netting Institute (SAUO)
HCPNY.......... Harbor Carriers of the Port of New York (EA)
HCPO.......... Hopi Cultural Preservation Office (SAUS)
HCPOTP.......... Health Care Practitioner Other Than Physician (MEDA)
HCPOTP.......... Health Care Professionals other than Physicians (HCT)
HCPP.......... Handbook of Consumer Protection Program (SAUS)
HCPP.......... Hanford Chemical Processing Plant (SAUS)
HCPP.......... Health Care Prepayment Plan
HCPP.......... Sanitation Handbook of Consumer Protection Programs (SAUO)
HCPRU.......... Hot Climate Physiological Research Unit [*Nigeria*] (BUAC)
HCPS.......... Hemispherical Candlepower Second [*Optics*] (IAA)
HCPS.......... Horizontal Candlepower Seconds
HCP-SAD.......... High Cell Passage Street-Alabama-Dufferin [*Strain*] [*Medicine*] (DB)
HCPT.......... Handicapped Childrens Pilgrimage Trust (BUAC)
HCPT.......... Historic Churches Preservation Trust [*British*] (BI)
HCPT.......... Hydroxycamptothecin [*Antineoplastic drug*]
HCPTP.......... Hanford Chemical Processing Technology Plan (SAUS)
HCPTR.......... Helicopter (CINC)
HCPU.......... High Capacity Pick-Up (SAUS)
HCPV.......... Hydrocarbon Pore Volume [*Petroleum technology*]
HCPWT.......... House Committee on Public Works and Transportation (COE)
H/CQ.......... Habitability/Crew Quarters (KSC)
HCQ.......... Halls Creek [*Australia*] [*Airport symbol*] [*Obsolete*] (OAG)
HCQ.......... Harbours Corp. of Queensland [*Australia*]
HCQ.......... Hot Carrier Quad
HCQ.......... Hydroxychloroquine [*Disease modifying antirheumatic drug*]
HCQIA.......... Health Care Quality Improvement Act [*1986*] (HCT)
HCQIP.......... Health Care Quality Improvement Program (ADWA)
HCR.......... Gas-Cooled Reactor (SAUS)
HCR.......... Hard Copy Response (SAA)
HCR.......... Hardware Check Routine
HCR.......... Hardware Correction Report
HCR.......... Haut Commissariat des Nations Unies pour les Refugies [*United Nations High Commission for Refugees - UNHCR*] [*Switzerland*]
HCR.......... HCR Manor Care [*NYSE symbol*] (SG)
HCR.......... Health Care & Retirement Corp. [*NYSE symbol*] (SPSG)
HCR.......... Heat-Curable Rubber (SAUS)
HCR.......... Heat-Cured Rubber (SAUS)
HCR.......... HEIS Change Request form (SAUS)
HCR.......... Heme-Controlled Repressor (DB)
HCR.......... Hemin Controlled Repressor [*Biochemistry*]
HCr.......... Hemoglobin Content of Reticulocytes [*Medicine*] (PALA)
HCR.......... High Charge Retention (PDAA)
HCR.......... High Chief Ranger [*Ancient Order of Foresters*]
HCR.......... High Commissioner for Refugees (SAUO)
HCR.......... High Commission for Refugees (SAUS)
HCR.......... High Consistency Refining (SAUS)
HCR.......... High Council of the Republic (Togo) [*Political party*] (PSAP)
HCR.......... High Court Reports, India [*A publication*] (DLA)
HCR.......... High Cross Range
HCR.......... Highway Contract Route
HCR.......... Hodge Computer Research, Inc. (SAUO)
HCR.......... Holy Cross [*Alaska*] [*Airport symbol*] (OAG)
HCR.......... Horizontal Control Rod (SAUS)
HCR.......... Host Cell Reactivation [*Medicine*] (MELL)
HCR.......... House Concurrent Resolution [*US Congress*]
HCR.......... Household Cavalry Regiment [*British military*] (DMA)
HCr.......... Houston's Delaware Criminal Cases [*A publication*] (DLA)
HCR.......... Human Computing Resources (SAUS)
HCR.......... Human-Controlled Repressor [*Genetics*] (DAVI)
HCR.......... Hurricane Rescue Craft, Inc. [*Vancouver Stock Exchange symbol*]
HCR.......... HWVP Comment Record (SAUS)
HCR.......... Hydrochloric Acid [*Organic chemistry*] (DAVI)
HCR.......... Hysterical Conversion Reaction [*Psychiatry*] (DAVI)
HCRAO.......... Hat Creek Radio Astronomy Observatory (SAUS)
HCRAO.......... Hot Creek Radio Astronomy Observatory (SAUO)
HCRC.......... Hallwood Consolidated Resources Corp. [*NASDAQ symbol*] (SAG)
HCRC.......... Hillsdale County Railroad Co., Inc. [*AAR code*]
HCRC.......... Holland College Royalty Center (SAUS)
HCRC.......... Honeywell Corporation Research Center (SAUO)
HCRC.......... Hotel and Catering Research Centre [*British*] (IRUK)
HCRC.......... Human Communication Research Centre (BUAC)
HCRD.......... Health Care Research Division [*Brooke Army Medical Center*]
HCRE.......... Homeopathic Council for Research and Education (EA)
HCREF.......... Health Care Research and Educational Foundation [*Later, AAMAREF*] (EA)
HC-REMA.......... Health Care Resource Management (EURO)
HC Res.......... House of Representatives Concurrent Resolution [*Legal term*] (DLA)
HCRF.......... Health Care Research Foundation [*Australia*]
HCRF.......... Hydrographic Chart Raster Format (SAUS)
HCRF.......... Hypercarbic Respiratory Failure (MELL)
HCRG.......... High Country Review Group (SAUO)
HCRI.......... Healthcare Recoveries [*NASDAQ symbol*] (SG)
HCRI.......... Health Care Research Institution [*Australia*]
HCRIS.......... Hospital Cost Report Information System (MEDA)
H'crit.......... Hematocrit (STED)
H'CRIT.......... Hematocrit [*Medicine*]
HCRL.......... Hanford Cultural Resources Laboratory (SAUS)
HCRM.......... Holocaust Curriculum Resources Material (BJA)
HCRMS.......... Health Care Resource Management Society (ADWA)
HCRNWF.......... High Court Reports, North West Frontier [*A publication*] (DLA)
HCRNWP.......... High Court Reports, Northwest Provinces [*India*] [*A publication*] (DLA)
HCRO.......... High Cross-Range Orbiter (KSC)
HCRON.......... Helicopter Combat Support Squadron [*Navy*] (DNAB)
HCRP.......... Hominid Corridor Research Project [*Palaeontology*]
HCR-PT.......... High Council of the Republic-Transitional Parliament (D. Rep. Congo) [*Political party*] (PSAP)
HCRR.......... High Current Reference Resistor (SAUS)
HCRR.......... Home Counties Reserve Regiment [*British military*] (DMA)
HCRR.......... Honey Creek Railroad [*Federal Railroad Administration identification code*]
HCRS.......... Heritage Conservation Recreation Service [*Abolished, 1981, functions transferred to National Park Service*] [*Department of the Interior*]
HCRS.......... Horizontal Control Rod System (SAUS)
HCRST.......... Hardware Clipping (SAUS)
HCRST.......... Hardware Clipping, Rotation, Scaling, and Translation (MHDI)
HCRSV.......... Hibiscus Chlorotic Ringspot Virus [*Plant pathology*]
HCRW.......... Hot and Cold Running Water
HCRX.......... Heber Creeper Railway [*Federal Railroad Administration identification code*]
HCRY.......... Huron Central Railway [*Federal Railroad Administration identification code*]
HCS.......... Combat Search and Rescue Special Warfare Support Helicopter (SAUS)
HCS.......... Hajdu-Cheney Syndrome [*Medicine*] (DMAA)
HCS.......... Hammered Chainmakers' Society [*A union*] [*British*]
HCS.......... Handicapped Children's Services
HCS.......... Hanford Computer Store (SAUS)
HCS.......... Hard-Clad Silica [*Materials science*]
HCS.......... Hard Copy System [*Computer science*] (MHDI)
HCS.......... Hardware Certification Sheet (SAUS)
HCS.......... Harris Consultive Services, Inc. [*Information service or system*] (IID)

HCS .... Harry C. Stutz [*Designer of early automobile*]
HCS .... Harvard Chinese Students (SAUO)
HCS .... Harvey Cushing Society [*Later, AANS*] (EA)
HCS .... Hazard Communication Standard [*OSHA*]
HCS .... Hazardous Chemicals Secretariat [*Victoria, Australia*]
HCS .... Hazardous Communications Standards (SAUO)
HCS .... Header Check Sequence [*Computer science*]
HCS .... Headlamp Cleaning System [*Automotive engineering*]
HCS .... Health Care Support [*System*] [*IBM Corp.*]
HCS .... Health Care System (SAUS)
HCS .... Health Computing Services [*Australia*]
HCS .... Healthy Cities Secretariat [*Australia*]
HCS .... Hebei Crop Society (BUAC)
HCs .... Hebrews converted to Roman Catholicism (SAUS)
HCS .... Heliborne Common Sensor (SAUO)
HCS .... Helicopter Combat Search (SAUS)
HCS .... Helicopter Combat Search and Rescue/Special Warfare Support Squadron [*Military*] (POLM)
HCS .... Helicopter Combat Support (SAUO)
HCS .... Helicopter Computer System (SAUO)
HCS .... Helicopter Control Ship [*Navy*] (NVT)
HCS .... Helicopter Coordination Section (COE)
HCS .... Helium Circulator Seal (IEEE)
HCS .... Hellenic Chamber of Shipping (BUAC)
HCS .... High-Carbon Steel
HCS .... High Cetene Standard (SAUS)
HCS .... High Clad Silica (PDAA)
HCS .... High-Compression Swirl [*Automotive engineering*]
HCS .... High Court Secretary [*Ancient Order of Foresters*]
HCS .... Histochemical Society (EA)
HCS .... Holy Crown Society [*Hungary*] (BUAC)
HCS .... Home Civil Servant [*British*]
HCS .... Home Civil Service [*British*]
HCS .... Home Cure Service (SAUO)
HCS .... Home Run Control System [*Computer science*]
HCS .... Homogeneous Computer System
HCS .... Hospital Car Service
HCS .... Host Composition System [*Infograph Ltd.*] (NITA)
HCS .... Host Computer System (ADWA)
HCS .... Hot Carrier Suppressed (SAUS)
HCS .... Hot-Carrier Suppressed (AAEL)
HCS .... Hot Cell Services (SAUO)
HCS .... Hourglass Contraction of Stomach [*Gastroenterology*] (DAVI)
HCS .... House Committee Substitute [*US Congress*]
HCS .... Hover Coupler System (DWSG)
HCS .... HUD [*Housing and Urban Development*] Clearinghouse Service
HCS .... Hughes Communications Services, Incorporated (ACAE)
HCS .... Human Chorionic Somatomammotrophin [*Also, CGP, hcs, HPL*] [*Endocrinology*]
hCS .... Human Chorionic Somatomammotropin [*Human Placental Lactogen*] [*Medicine*] (STED)
hCS .... Human Choriosomatotropin (EDCT)
HCS .... Human Cord Serum
HCS .... Humidity Control System (SAUS)
HCS .... Hummocky Cross-Stratification [*Sedimentology*]
HCS .... Hundred Call Seconds [*Telecommunications*]
HCS .... Hungarian Castle Series (SAUO)
HCS .... Hybrid Computation and Simulation (SSD)
HCS .... Hydrogen Chloride Scrubber (EEVL)
HCS .... Hydrogen Control System (NRCH)
HCS .... Hydrological Communications Satellite (SAUS)
HCS .... Hydromechanical Control System (KSC)
HCS .... Hydroxycorticosteroids [*Pharmacology*] (DAVI)
HCS .... Membership Section for Health Care Systems [*An association*] (EA)
HCS4 .... Helicopter Combat Support Special Squadron (SAUS)
HCSA .... Halogenated Cleaning Solvent Association (EA)
HCSA .... Hate Crimes Statistics Act
HCSA .... Hexylcarbonate of Salicylic Acid [*Analgesic*]
HCSA .... Hospital Consultants' and Specialists' Association [*British*] (DCTA)
HCSA .... Hospitals Consultants and Specialists Association (SAUO)
HCSA .... House Committee on Space and Astronautics [*US Congress*] (AAG)
HCSAS .... Hardware Configuration Status Accounting System (SAUO)
HCSB .... High Court Senior Beadle [*Ancient Order of Foresters*]
HCSB .... Home & City Savings Bank (SAUO)
HCSBC .... Historical Commission, Southern Baptist Convention (EA)
HCSC .... Health Care Service Contractor (AMHC)
HCSC .... Higher Command and Staff Course (SAUS)
HCSCIA .... Health Care Studies and Clinical Investigation Activity [*Fort Sam Houston, TX*] [*Army*]
HCSD .... Health Care Studies Division [*Academy of Health Sciences*] [*Army*]
HCSDS .... High-Capacity Satellite Digital Service [*AT & T*] (TSSD)
HCSF .... Hanford Calibration and Standards Facility (SAUS)
HCSF .... Hard Clad Silicia Fibre (SAUS)
HCSF .... Histamine-Producing Cell-Stimulating Factor [*Biochemistry*]
HCSF .... Hydrocarbons Scale Factor [*Automotive emissions*]
HCSG .... Health Care Services Group [*NASDAQ symbol*] (SAG)
HCSG .... Healthcare Services Group, Inc. [*NASDAQ symbol*] (NQ)
HCSG .... Healthcare Svcs Group [*NASDAQ symbol*] (TTSB)
HCSG .... Hyperactive Children's Support Group [*England*]
HCSHT .... High-Carbon Steel, Heat-Treated
HCSI .... Health Correspondence Schools International (SAUO)
HCSI .... Hughes Communications Services, Inc. (NASA)
HCSL .... Hybrid Computational Science Laboratory
HCSL .... Hybrid Computation and Simulation Laboratory
HCSLP .... Hungarian Committee of Socialist Labor Party [*Defunct*] (EA)
HCSM .... Human Chorionic Somatomammotropin [*Endocrinology*]
HCSM .... Mogadishu [*Somalia*] [*ICAO location identifier*] (ICLI)
HCS/MRR .... Helicopter Combat Support/Medium Range Recovery (ACAE)
HCSN .... High-Capacity Satellite Network (SAUS)
HCSNSW .... Home Care Service of New South Wales [*Australia*]
HCSP .... Health Care Service for Prisoners (WDAA)
HCSP .... High-Capacity Signal Processor
HCSPR .... Hundred Call Seconds Per Hour [*Telecommunications*] (ACRL)
HCSR .... E. O. Hulburt Center for Space Research (MCD)
HCSR .... Higher Council for Scientific Research (SAUO)
HCSRDG .... Health and Community Services Research and Development Grants [*Australia*]
HCSS .... Head Compartment Support Structure [*Nuclear energy*] (NRCH)
HCSS .... High-Capacity Storage System [*Novell, Inc.*] [*Computer science*] (PCM)
HCSS .... Home and Colonial School Society [*British*]
HCSS .... Hospital Computer Sharing System (IEEE)
HCSS .... Hypersensitive Carotid Sinus Syndrome (MELL)
HCSS&T .... House Committee on Science, Space and Technology (SAUS)
HCST .... Hydrothermal Cyclis Shear Test (SAUS)
HCSTR .... Homogeneous Continuous Stirred Tank Reactor [*Chemical engineering*]
HCSW .... High Court Senior Woodward [*Ancient Order of Foresters*]
HCT .... Haematocrit (SAUS)
HCT .... Halftone Calibration Technology (SAUS)
HCT .... Hamburger ComputerTage (SAUS)
HCT .... Hard Copy Task [*Computer science*] (ELAL)
HCT .... Hardware Compatibility Test [*Microsoft Corp.*] (PCM)
HCT .... Hayes Center, NE [*Location identifier*] [*FAA*] (FAAL)
HCT .... Health Care Technology (SAUS)
HCT .... Health Check Test (DMAA)
HCT .... Heart-Circulation-Training [*Physical fitness*]
HCT .... Heat Coagulation Test (MELL)
HCT .... Heater Center Tap [*Electronics*] (ECII)
HCT .... Heater Center Top
HCT .... Heavy Crawler Tractor (SAUS)
HCT .... Hector Communications [*AMEX symbol*] (SG)
HCT .... Helicopter Control Trainer (SAUS)
Hct .... Hematocrit (ADWA)
hct .... hematocrit [*Therapy term*] (CTAA)
HCT .... Hematocrit [*Medicine*]
HCT .... Hematopoietic Cell Transplantation [*Medicine*] (MELL)
HCT .... Herpetological Conservation Trust (BUAC)
HCT .... Hieracium Control Trust (SAUO)
HCT .... High Commission Territories (SAUO)
HCT .... High Commission Territories Corps [*Military unit*] [*British*]
H Ct .... High Court
HCT .... High Court Treasurer [*Ancient Order of Foresters*]
HCT .... High-speed CMOS logic with TTL-compatible logic levels (SAUS)
HCT .... High-Speed Complementary Metal-Oxide Semiconductor Transistor-Transistor Logic Compatible (AAEL)
HCT .... Histamine Challenge Test [*Biochemistry*] (DAVI)
HCT .... Historic Control Trial [*Medicine*] (DMAA)
HCT .... Hollow Cathode Tube
HCT .... Home Communication Terminal (SAUS)
HCT .... Homocytotropic [*Medicine*] (MAE)
HCT .... Honey Culture Test (SAUO)
HCT .... Hook Control Table (VLIE)
HCT .... Hot Cathode Tube
HCT .... Hot Compact Turret (SAUS)
HCT .... Howitzer Crew Trainer [*Military*]
HCT .... Huddersfield College of Technology (SAUO)
HCT .... Hull Collector Tank
hCt .... Human Calcitonin [*Endocrinology*]
HCT .... Human Chorionic Thyrotrophin [*Endocrinology*]
HCT .... Hybrid Computer Technique (SAUS)
HCT .... Hydraulic Components Test
HCT .... Hydrochlorothiazide [*Drug*] [*Also, HCTZ, HCZ*] [*Organic chemistry*]
HCT .... Hydrocortisone [*Endocrinology*]
HCTA .... Health Careers Tutors' Association (BUAC)
HCTB .... Hotel and Catering Training Board [*British*]
HCTBA .... Hotel and Catering Trades Benevolent Association [*British*] (BI)
HCTC .... Health Care Technology Center [*Medicine*] (EDAA)
HCTC .... Hotel and Catering Training Co. (AIE)
HCTD .... Hepatic Computed Tomography Density [*Medicine*] (EDAA)
HCTDS .... High-Capacity Terrestrial Digital Service [*AT & T*] (TSSD)
HCTEE .... Hematology and Cell Therapy. Electronic Edition (SAUO)
HCTF .... Helium Component Test Facility [*Nuclear energy*] (NUCP)
HCTF .... Hot Cell Training Facility (SAUS)
HCTL .... Healthcare Technologies Ltd. [*NASDAQ symbol*] (NQ)
HCTL .... Hunting Communication Technology (SAUS)
HCTLDC .... Hungarian Central Technical Library and Documentation Centre (SAUS)
HCTLF .... Healthcare Technologies Ltd [*NASDAQ symbol*] (TTSB)
HCTLR .... High Commission Territories Reports [*Basutoland, Bechuanaland, and Swaziland*] [*A publication*] (DLA)
HCTLS .... High-speed Complimentary Transistor Low-Power Schottky (SAUS)
HCTR .... High Capacity Trunk Radio (SAUS)
HCTR .... High-Capacity Trunk Radio
HCTS .... High Cholesterol and Tocopherol Supplement [*Medicine*] (EDAA)
HCTS .... House Call Tax Service
HCTSS .... Health Care Technology Study Section [*HEW*] (EGAO)
HCTU .... Home Cervical Traction Unit [*Medicine*] (DAVI)
Hctz .... Hydrochlorothiazide [*Medicine*] (AMHC)
HCTZ .... Hydrochlorothiazide [*Drug*] [*Also, HCT, HCZ*] [*Organic chemistry*]

HCU .... Handheld Computer Unit
HCU .... Harbor Clearance Unit [*Navy*] (NVT)
HCU .... Harbor Control Unit
HCU .... Hard Copy Unit
HCU .... Health Care Unit [*DoD*] (GFGA)
HCU .... Heavy Conversion Unit [*British military*] (DMA)
HCU .... Helicopter Control Unit (NVT)
HCU .... Helium Charging Unit (AAG)
HCU .... Hoist Control Unit (SAUS)
HCU .... Home Computer User (VLIE)
HCU .... Homing Comparator Unit (AAG)
HCU .... Homocystinuria [*Medicine*]
HCU .... Horse Canyon [*Utah*] [*Seismograph station code, US Geological Survey*] (SEIS)
HCU .... Humanitarian Coordination Unit (SAUO)
HCU .... Hydraulic Charging Unit (NASA)
HCU .... Hydraulic Control Unit [*Nuclear energy*] (NRCH)
HCU .... Hydraulic Coupling Unit [*Automotive engineering*]
HCU .... Hydraulic Cycling Unit (AFM)
HCU .... Hyperplasia Cystica Uteri [*Medicine*] (DMAA)
HCU .... Hypertape Control Unit (SAUS)
HCUA .... Honeywell Computer Users Association (HGAA)
HCUA .... House Committee on Unamerican Activities (CARL)
HCUAA .... House Committee on Un-American Activities (SAUS)
HCUDET ...... Harbor Clearance Unit Detachment [*Navy*] (DNAB)
HCUND .... Hospitality Committee for United Nations Delegations (EA)
HCUP .... Hospital Cost and Utilization Project [*Department of Health and Human Services*] (GFGA)
HCUP-3 .... Healthcare Cost and Utilization Project (SAUO)
HCUS .... Discharge [*from Military Service*] under Honorable Conditions, Unsuitable
HCUSA .... High Commissioner for the Union of South Africa (SAUO)
HCUT .... Homfray Carpets Unit Trust [*Commercial firm*] [*British*]
HCV .... Hand Control Valve (NRCH)
HCv .... Heat of Combustion (of an Element under Constant Volume) (ROG)
HCV .... Heavy Commercial Vehicle
HCV .... Hepatitis C Virus
HCV .... Hercules Ventures [*Vancouver Stock Exchange symbol*]
HCV .... High Calorific Value [*of a fuel*]
HCV .... High Capacity Voice (ACRL)
HCV .... Hog Cholera Virus (DMAA)
HCV .... Housing Commission of Victoria (SAUO)
HCV .... Hull Check Valve
HCV .... Hutchinson Cablevision [*British*]
HCV .... Hydraulic Check Valve (GFGA)
HCV .... Hydraulic Control Valve
HCV .... Hydrogen Check Valve (SAUS)
HCVA .... High-Contrast Visual Acuity [*Medicine*] (EDAA)
HCVA .... Historic Commercial Vehicle Association (SAUO)
HC Valve ..... Hand Control Valve (SAUS)
HCVC .... Historic Commercial Vehicle Club [*British*] (DCTA)
HCVC .... Historic Commercial Vehicle Society (BUAC)
HCVCS .... Historic Commercial Vehicle Cooperative Society [*Australia*]
HCVD .... Hypertensive Cardiovascular Disease [*Medicine*]
HCVF .... Hot Cell Verification Facility (SAUS)
HCVIS .... High Clouds Visible [*NWS*] (FAAC)
HCVRCS .... Hill Counselor Verbal Response Category System (EDAC)
HCW .... Health Care Worker (MELL)
HCW .... Home Computing Weekly (journ.) (SAUS)
HCW .... Hoosier Conference for Women (PSS)
HCW .... Paine Webber Group [*AMEX symbol*] (SAG)
HCWI .... High-Chromium White Iron
HC Wkly Inf Bull... House of Commons Weekly Information Bulletin [*A publication*] (DLA)
HCWP .... Hospital Council of Western Pennsylvania (SAUO)
HCWU .... Hotel and Catering Workers Union (BUAC)
HCY .... Cowley/Lovell/Byron, WY [*Location identifier*] [*FAA*] (FAAL)
HCy .... Haemocyanin (SAUS)
Hcy .... Homocysteine [*An amino acid*]
HCYR .... Horry Country Railway [*Federal Railroad Administration identification code*]
HCZ .... Hercules [*Federal Railroad Administration identification code*]
HCZ .... Hydrochlorothiazide [*Drug*] [*Also, HCT, HCTZ*] [*Organic chemistry*]
HCZ .... Hydrogen Convection Zone
HD .... Air-Conditioning Apparatus [*JETDS nomenclature*] [*Military*] (CET)
HD .... Air-Cushion Vehicle built by Hovercraft Development [*England*] [*Usually used in combination with numerals*]
HD .... Distilled Mustard (SAUS)
HD .... Grand National Party (South Korea) [*Political party*] (PSAP)
HD .... Haab-Dimmer [*Syndrome*] [*Medicine*] (DB)
HD .... Haglund Deformity [*Medicine*] (MELL)
HD .... Hajna-Damon Broth [*Medicine*] (DMAA)
HD .... Half Day (SAUS)
HD .... Half Duplex (ACAE)
HD .... Half-Duplex [*Telecommunications*] (DCDG)
HD .... Half Duplex Transmission [*Data communication*] (CET)
HD .... Hamming-Distance (SAUS)
HD .... Hand (ROG)
HD .... Hand-Drawn
HD .... Handover (SAUS)
HD .... Hanford Decommissioning (SAUS)
HD .... Hank's Dilator [*Medicine*] (MELL)
HD .... Hanmonic Distortion (SAUS)
HD .... Hansen's Disease [*Leprosy*] [*Medicine*]
HD .... Harassment Drone (SAUS)
HD .... Harbor Defense [*Military*]
HD .... Harbor Drive (SAUS)
HD .... Harbour Defence (SAUS)
HD .... Hard (MSA)
HD .... Hard Disk [*Computer science*]
HD .... Hard Disk High Density (SAUS)
HD .... Hard Drawn (SAUS)
HD .... Hard-Drawn [*Metallurgy*]
HD .... Hard Drive (GOBB)
HD .... Hardware Design
HD .... Hardwood (ADWA)
H-D .... Harley-Davidson
HD .... Harmonic Definition (SAUS)
HD .... Harmonic Distortion
HD .... Harmonic Distortion Head (SAUS)
HD .... Harmonisation Document (SAUS)
HD .... Harmonized Document (JAGO)
HD .... Hartnup Disease [*Medicine*] (MELL)
H/D .... Havre-Dunkirk (SAUS)
HD .... Hawaiian Department [*Army*] [*World War II*]
HD .... Head (AAG)
Hd .... Head (TBD)
hd .... Head (WDMC)
HD .... Head Diameter
H/D .... Head/Disk [*Computer science*] (VLIE)
HD .... Head Driver (IAA)
HD .... Headed (SAUS)
HD .... Heading
HD .... Heading to Detail (VLIE)
Hd .... Headland [*Maps and charts*]
HD .... Headquarters [*United States Postal Service last word addressing abbreviation*]
HD .... Headquarters Department (SAUO)
HD .... Headquarters Detachment (SAUO)
HD .... Heard (ROG)
HD .... Hearding Distance (SAUS)
HD .... Hearing Distance [*Medicine*]
HD .... Heart Disease [*Medicine*]
H-D .... Heat-Damaged (SAUS)
HD .... Heat Detector [*NFPA pre-fire planning symbol*] (NFPA)
HD .... Heat Dissipation (DNAB)
HD .... Heaven Dust [*Medicine*] (EDAA)
HD .... Heavy Decoys (SAUS)
HD .... Heavy Distillate [*Fuel technology*]
HD .... Heavy Draft (SAUS)
HD .... Heavy Drop (SAUO)
HD .... Heavy-Duty
HD .... Height Displacement (SAUS)
HD .... Helicopter Delivered
HD .... Helicopter Direction (DNAB)
HD .... Helicopter Director [*Military*] (CAAL)
HD .... Heloma Durum [*A hard corn*] [*Orthopedics*] (DAVI)
HD .... Hematologic Disorder [*Medicine*] (MELL)
HD .... Hemidesmosome [*Cytology*]
HD .... Hemidiaphragm [*Medicine*] (EDAA)
HD .... Hemodialysis [*Nephrology*]
HD .... Hemodilution
HD .... Hemolytic Disease [*Medicine*] (MELL)
HD .... Hemolyzing Dose [*Medicine*]
HD .... Henry Draper [*Astronomy term*] [*Catalog entry*]
HD .... Henry Draper Catalogue [*Astronomy*]
HD .... Hepatic Disease [*Medicine*] (MELL)
HD .... Hepatosis Diaetetica [*Veterinary science*] (OA)
HD .... Herniated Disc [*Medicine*]
HD .... Hexadecimal Code [*Computer science*] (IAA)
H-D .... Hexadecimal-to-Decimal [*Computer science*] (IEEE)
HD .... Hexagonal Domain Structure
HD .... Hexanedione [*Organic chemistry*]
HD .... Hierarchical Dependency (SAUS)
HD .... Hierarchical Diagnosis (SAUS)
HD .... Hierarchical Direct
HD .... High Day [*Communications term*] (DCT)
HD .... High-Definition
HD .... High Demand
HD .... High Density
HD .... High Detergent (WGA)
HD .... High Dose [*Medicine*]
HD .... High Drag [*Navy*] (NVT)
HD .... High Dust
HD .... High Duty (SAUS)
HD .... High Dynamic
HD .... Highland Division [*British military*] (DMA)
HD .... Highly Desirable (KSC)
HD .... Hilda Doolittle [*Initials used as pen name of American poet, 1886-1961*]
HD .... Hip Disarticulation [*Medicine*]
HD .... Hip Dislocation (MELL)
HD .... Hip Dysplasia (SAUS)
HD .... Hirschsprung's Disease [*Medicine*] (DMAA)
HD .... Histone Deacetylase [*An enzyme*]
HD .... Historical Department (SAUO)
HD .... Historical Development
HD .... Historical Division [*Air Force*]
HD .... Historic Deerfield (EA)
HD .... Historic District (SAUS)

HD Hitachi chip ID code (SAUS)

HD Hodgkin's Disease [*Medicine*]

HD Hogshead

HD Holddown

HD Home Defence [*British*] [*World War II*]

HD [*The*] Home Depot, Inc. [*NYSE symbol*] (SPSG)

HD Home Dog

HD Homoeodomain [*Genetics*]

HD Homoserine Dehydrogenase [*An enzyme*]

HD Honorable Discharge [*Military*]

HD Honorary Degree [*Freemasonry*] (ROG)

HD Hoover Dam (SAUS)

hd Hora Decubitus [*At Bedtime*] [*Latin*] (STED)

HD Hora Decubitus [*At Bedtime*] [*Pharmacy*]

HD Horizontal Distance [*Photography*] (OA)

HD Horizontal Drain

HD Horizontal Drive

HD Hormone-Dependent [*Medicine*] (DB)

HD Horse-Drawn

HD Hospital Day (DAVI)

HD Host-Dependent (SAUS)

HD Hot Drawing (SAUS)

HD Hot Drive [*Automotive testing*]

HD Hourly Difference [*Navigation*]

HD House Doctor (SAUS)

HD House Document

HD House Dust (DMAA)

HD House of Delegates (SAFN)

HD Housing Debtline [*Telephone service*] [*British*]

HD Housing Density

HD Hub Diameter (SAUS)

HD Huddersfield [*Postcode*] (ODBW)

HD Human Development

HD Human Dialogue Service (VLIE)

HD Human Diploid [*Medicine*] (EDAA)

HD Humanitarian Deferment [*Military*]

HD Humanitarian Demining [*Military*]

HD Humper Dears (EA)

HD Hundred

HD Hunter and Driffield [*System to indicate film emulsion speed*] (BARN)

HD Huntington's Disease [*Medicine*]

HD Hurel Dubois [*Societe de Construction des Avions Hurel Dubois*] [*France*] [*ICAO aircraft manufacturer identifier*] (ICAO)

HD Hurricane Deck

HD Hydatid Disease [*Medicine*] (MAE)

HD Hydralazine [*Antihypertensive drug*]

HD Hydrodynamics (SAUS)

HD Hydrogendeuterium (SAUS)

HD Hydrogen Drain (MCD)

HD Hydrographic Department (SAUO)

HD Hydroxydopamine (DB)

H-D Hypothetico-Deductive

HD Hypotonic Duodenogram [*Medicine*]

HD Mustard Gas [*Also, H, HS, HT, M*] [*Poison gas*] [*US Chemical Corps symbol*]

HD New York Helicopter [*ICAO designator*] (AD)

HDA Hail Detection Algorithm [*Marine science*] (OSRA)

HDA Halopredone Diacetate [*Endocrinology*]

HdA Handwoerterbuch des Deutschen Aberglaubens [*A publication*] (BJA)

HDA Hard Disk Assembly [*Computer science*] (AGLO)

HDA Harding Lake [*Alaska*] [*Seismograph station code, US Geological Survey*] (SEIS)

HDA Hardwood Distributors Association (EA)

HDA Harris Daishowa Australia Ltd. [*Commercial*] (EERA)

HDA Hawaii Dental Association (SAUO)

HDA Head Disk Assembly

HDA Headquarters, Department of the Army

HDA Heaviest Duty Available [*Motor vehicle specifications*]

HDA Heavy-Duty Amplifier

HDA Held for Detail Available (MCD)

HDA Hemispherical Deflection Analyser (SAUS)

HDA Heteroduplex Analysis (DMAA)

HDA Heteroduplex gel shift Analysis (SAUS)

HDA Hexadecenyl Acetate [*Pheromone*] [*Organic chemistry*]

HDA Hexanediamine [*or Hexamethylenediamine*] [*Organic chemistry*]

HDA High Density Acid (SAUS)

HDA High-Density Acid

HDA High-Density Amorph [*Materials science*]

HDA High Duty Alloys Ltd.

HDA Higher Duties Allowance (ADA)

HDA Highway-to-group Demultiplexer Address-generator (SAUS)

HDA Hispanic Dental Association (NTPA)

HDA Hodgkin's Disease Association [*British*] (DBA)

HDA Holddown Arm (KSC)

HDA Holistic Dental Association (EA)

HDA Honda [*Colombia*] [*Airport symbol*] (AD)

HDA Hong Kong Dragon Airlines Ltd. [*ICAO designator*] (FAAC)

HDA Horizontal Danger Angle [*Navigation*]

HDA Horticultural Dealers Association (EA)

HDA Hospital Doctors Association [*British*] (DBA)

HDA Housekeeping Data Acquisition (MCD)

HDA Housing and Development Administration [*New York City*]

HDA Housing Developers Association Ltd. [*British*] (BI)

HDA Huldra Silver [*Vancouver Stock Exchange symbol*]

HDA Huntington's Disease Association [*Australia*]

HDA Hybrid Detective Assembly (ACAE)

HDA Hydrodealkylation (EDCT)

HDA Hydrogen Diffusion Anode [*Electrochemistry*]

HDA Hydroxycitronellal Diethyl Acetal (SAUS)

HDA Hydroxydopamine [*Also, HDM, OHDA*] [*Biochemistry*]

HDAC Dictionary of the Apostolic Church [*James Hasting*] [*A publication*] (BJA)

HDAC Headache (KSC)

HDAC Heavy-Duty Air Cylinder

HDAC High-Dose Cytarabine (STED)

HDAC Histone Deacetylase [*An enzyme*]

HDAD High Density Array Development (ACAE)

HD-Additive Heavy Duty Additive (SAUS)

HDAF Home Defence Air Force (SAUO)

HDAg Hepatitis Delta Antigen [*Immunology*]

HDAI Huntington's Disease Association of Ireland (BUAC)

HDAL Hexadecenal [*Pheromone*] [*Organic chemistry*]

HDALE Hopedale, OH [*American Association of Railroads railroad junction routing code*]

HDAM Hierarchical Direct Access Method [*Computer science*] (MCD)

HD&R Human Development and Relationships (SAUS)

HDAOS Hydroxysulfopropyldimethooxyaniline (SAUS)

HDAP Heavy-Duty Automatic Press

HDARAC High Dose Cytarabine [*Medicine*] (DMAA)

HDAS Hardened Digital Data Acquisition System [*US Army Waterways Experiment Station*] (RDA)

HDAS Historical Dictionary of American Slang [*Random House*]

HDAS Home Deposit Assistance Scheme [*Australia*]

HDAS House Defense Appropriations Subcommittee [*US Congress*] (AAG)

HDAS Hybrid Data Acquisition System

HDAS Hydrographic Data Acquisition System

HDASHY Haberdashery

HDAT Handheld Data Acquisition Terminal (SAUS)

HDATA Hydrogene Data [*National College of Chemistry of Paris*] [*France*] [*Information service or system*] (IID)

HDATZ High-Density Air Traffic Zone

HdAW Handbuch der Altertumswissenschaft [*A publication*] (BJA)

HDB [*A*] Dictionary of the Bible [*James Hasting*] [*A publication*] (BJA)

HDB Hamper, Deritend, Birmingham [*Pseudonym used by William Hamper*]

HDB Health Database Plus [*Information Access Co.*] [*Information service or system*] (PCM)

HDB Herpes-Dissociated Buffer [*Medicine*]

HDB High-Density Binary (TEL)

HDB High Density Bipolar (NITA)

HDB High-Density Bipolar Code [*Telecommunications*] (TEL)

HDB High Density Bombing (SAUS)

HDB High Density Buffer (SAUS)

HDB Higher Data Byte (SAUS)

HDB Home Defence Brigade (SAUS)

HDB Horizontal Dynamic Balancing

HDB Hunter Development Board [*Australia*]

HDB3 High-Density Binary Three Level Signal (TEL)

HDB3 High Density Bipolar 3 (SAUS)

HDB-3 High-Density Bipolar-3 (IDOE)

HDB3 High Density Bipolar Code of Order 3 (SAUS)

HDB3 Code High Density Bipolar 3 Code (SAUS)

HDBA Horizontal Dynamic Balancing Adjustment

HdBAA Handbook of the British Astronomical Association (SAUO)

HDBC High Density Bipolar Coding (VLIE)

HDBD Hydroxybutyric Dehydrogenase [*An enzyme*] (DAVI)

HDBF Heavy Duty Business Forum (EA)

HDBH High Day Busy Hour (SAUS)

HDBH Hydroxybutyric Dehydrogenase [*Clinical chemistry*] (CPH)

HDBK Handbook (AFM)

hdbk Handbook (WDMC)

HDBMS Hierarchical Database Management System

HDBV Host Data Base View [*Computer science*] (VLIE)

HDC Claremont Men's College, Claremont, CA [*OCLC symbol*] (OCLC)

HDC Half Double Crochet

HDC Half Duplex Circuit (SAUS)

HDC Hand-Drawn Check (SAUS)

HDC Hangar Deck Control (SAUS)

HDC Harbor Defense Command [*Army*]

HDC Hard Disk Controller

HDC Harry Diamond Center [*Army*]

HDC Hasselblad Data Camera (MCD)

HDC Hawaiian Defense Command

HDC Head of Civil Defense (SAUO)

HDC Heavy Double Cotton (SAUS)

HDC Heavy Duty Clamp (SAUS)

HDC Heavy-Duty Contractor (MCD)

HDC Heavy Duty Cooling (HAWK)

HDC Helicopter Direction Center

HDC Helium Direct-Current (SAUS)

HDC Hemoglobin Dissociation Curve [*Medicine*] (MELL)

HDC Henry Draper Catalogue (SAUS)

HDC Hierarchical Distributed Control [*Computer science*]

HDC High Density Center (SAUS)

HDC High Density CMOS (SAUS)

HDC High Density Cotton (SAUS)

HDC High Dirt Capacity [*A type of filter*] [*Pall Trinity Micro Corp.*]

HDC High-Dose Chemotherapy [*Medicine*] (MELL)

HDC High Duty Cycle (IAA)

HDC High-Speed Data Channel (VLIE)

HDC............ Hill Descent Control [*Automotive engineering*]
HDC............ Histidine Decarboxylase [*An enzyme*]
HDC............ Historical Data Center (SAUS)
HDC............ Holder in Due Course [*Owner or holder of a negotiable instrument at some future time*]
HDC............ Holston Defense Corp. (MCD)
HDC............ Home Data Channel (SAUS)
HDC............ Horticultural Development Council (SAUO)
HDC............ Hospital Data Center [*American Hospital Association*] [*Information service or system*] (IID)
HDC............ Hough Development Corp. [*Cleveland*]
HDC............ Housing Department and Construction Ltd. (SAUO)
HDC............ Housing Development and Construction Ltd. (SAUO)
HDC............ Housing Development Corp. (EA)
HDC............ Human Diploid Cell [*Cytology*] (DAVI)
HDC............ Hungarian Data Center [*Defunct*] (EA)
HDC............ Hybrid Device Controller (NASA)
HDC............ Hydrodynamic Chromatography
HDC............ Hydrogen Depolarized Carbon Dioxide Concentrator (OA)
HDC............ Hypodermoclysis (STED)
HDCC........... High Density Ceramic Card (ACAE)
HDCCAMS.... High-Dose Cyclophosphamide and Adriamycin [*Antineoplastic drug regimen*] (DAVI)
HDCD........... Head Card (SAUS)
HD-CD......... High Definition Compact Disc (SAUS)
HDCD........... High Definition Compatible Digital [*Compact-disc technology*] (PS)
HDCD........... High Density CD (SAUS)
HDCES......... Hot/Dry Clothing and Equipment System [*Army*] (INF)
HDCG........... Dictionary of Christ and the Gospels [*James Hasting*] [*A publication*] (BJA)
HDCG........... Honorable Discharge, Convenience of Government [*Military*]
HDCH........... Headache
HDCM........... Honorable Discharge, Convenience of Man [*Military*]
HDCO........... Hadco Corp. [*NASDAQ symbol*] (NQ)
HDCOL......... Hand Colored (VRA)
HDCP........... Harbour Defence Command Post (SAUS)
HDCR........... Hard Chromium
HDCR........... Higher Diploma of the College of Radiographers (SAUS)
HDCR........... Hillsdale County Railway [*Federal Railroad Administration identification code*]
HDCR(R) or (T)... Higher Award in Radiodiagnosis or Radiotherapy, College of Radiographers [*British*] (DBQ)
HDCS........... Hughes Developmental Correlation Sensor (ACAE)
HDCS........... Human Diploid Cell Strains [*Immunology*]
HDCS........... Human Diploid Cell System (STED)
HDCSV......... Human Diploid Cell Strain Vaccine [*Medicine*] (DB)
HDCV........... Human Diploid Cell Vaccine [*For rabies*]
HDD............ Halogenated Dibenzodioxin [*Organic chemistry*]
HDD............ Hard Disk Drive [*Computer science*]
HDD............ Head-Down Display [*Aviation*]
HDD............ Headsdown Display
HDD............ Heating Degree Days [*Agriculture*]
HDD............ Heavy-Duty Detergent
HDD............ Heavy-Duty Diesel [*Vehicle*]
HDD............ Heavy Duty Distribution [*A publication*]
HDD............ High Definition Display (SAUS)
HDD............ High-Density Data (KSC)
HDD............ High-Density Disk [*Computer science*] (ITCA)
HDD............ High-Dosage Depth [*Medicine*] (DMAA)
HDD............ Higher Dental Diploma [*British*]
HDD............ Homopolar Disk Dynamo
HDD............ Housing Development Directorate (SAUS)
HDD............ Human Disorientation Device
HDD............ Hyderabad [*Pakistan*] [*Airport symbol*] (OAG)
HDD............ Hydrogen Donor Diluents [*Petroleum chemistry*]
HDDA........... Hexacadienacetate (SAUS)
HDDA........... Hexadecadienyl Acetate [*Pheromone*] [*Organic chemistry*]
HDDA........... Hexanediol Diacrylate [*Also, HDODA*] [*Organic chemistry*]
HDDA........... Hiexadecadienylacetate (SAUS)
HDDB........... High Dummy Discriptor Block (SAUS)
HDDD........... High-Density Disk Drive (SAUS)
HDDE........... Heavy-Duty Diesel Engine [*Motor vehicle specifications*]
HD-DI.......... Heavy-Duty Direct Injection [*Diesel engines*]
HDDI........... Host-Displaywriter Document Interchange [*Communications term*] (DCT)
HDDP........... Honorable Discharge, Dependency Existing Prior to Enlistment [*Military*]
HDDP........... Hospital Discharge Demonstration Project (EDAC)
HDDR........... HD Digital Recording (SAUS)
HDDR........... Head-Down Display Radar (SAUS)
HDDR........... Head Down Display Recorder (SAUS)
HDDR........... High Density Digital magnetic Recording (SAUS)
HDDR........... High Density Digital Recorder (SAUS)
HDDR........... High-Density Digital Recording
HDDR........... High Density Digital Tape Recorder (SAUS)
HDDR........... High Digital Density Recording (SAUS)
HD DRN....... Hard Drawn (SAUS)
HDDS........... High-Density Data System [*Computer science*]
HDDS........... Honorable Discharge, Dependency Arising Since Enlistment [*Military*]
HDDT........... Heavy-Duty Diesel Transient [*Automotive emissions*]
HDDT........... Heavy-Duty Diesel Truck (EPAT)
HDDT........... High-Density Digital Tape
HDDU........... Head Down Display Unit (SAUS)
HDDV........... Heavy-Duty Diesel Vehicle
HDE............ Hauptgemeinschaft Deutscher Einzelhandel (SAUS)
HDE............ HDE [*Federal Railroad Administration identification code*]
HDE............ Heavy Duty Engine [*Automotive engineering*]
HDE............ Henry Draper Extension (SAUS)
HDE............ High-Dose Epinephrine [*Medicine*]
HDE............ Higher Diploma in Education (SAUS)
HDE............ Highly Distributed Environment (SAUO)
HDE............ Holdrege, NE [*Location identifier*] [*FAA*] (FAAL)
HDE............ Homogeneous Differential Equation
HDEC........... Highly Integrated Digital Electronic Control (ACAE)
HDEC........... Holocaust Documentation and Education Center (EA)
HDEC........... Hughes-Developed Electronic Countermeasures (ACAE)
HDECERT..... Heavy-Duty Engine Certification Data (SAUS)
HDED........... Hard Decision Error Detector (SAUS)
HDED........... Heavy-Duty Enzyme Detergent
HDEE........... Honorable Discharge, Expiration of Enlistment [*Military*]
HDEG........... Union List of Higher Degree Theses in Australian Libraries [*University of Tasmania Library*] [*Australia*] [*Information service or system*] (CRD)
HDeH........... Hawker De Havilland [*Australia*]
HDEHP......... diethylhexylphosphoric acid (SAUS)
HDEP........... High Definition Electronic Production (NTCM)
HDEP........... High-Density Electronic Packaging
HDEPS......... Harvard Department of Earth and Planetary Science (SAUO)
HDERU......... Heavy Duty Ejector Release Unit (SAUS)
HDES........... Head of Defence Services (SAUS)
HDES........... Hydrodynamic Equilibrium System [*For chromatography*]
HDEU........... Heating and Domestic Engineers' Union [*British*]
HDF............ Haitian Development Fund [*Later, MH*] (EA)
HDF............ Halogenated Dibenzofuran [*Organic chemistry*]
HDF............ Handle Door Fastener
HDF............ Hartmann Dispersion Formula
HDF............ HDSL Dual Framer (SAUS)
HDF............ Hereditary Disease Foundation (EA)
HDF............ Hierarchical Data Format [*Computer science*]
HDF............ High-Density Flexible
HDF............ High-Desirable Facility (SAUS)
HDF............ High-Frequency Direction Finding [*Electronics*]
HDF............ Highly Dispersive Filter (SAUS)
HDF............ Home Defence Force (SAUO)
HDF............ Horizontal Data Flow (SAUS)
HDF............ Horizontal Distributing Frame
HDF............ Horyal Democratic Front (SAUS)
HDF............ Host Data Facility (SAUS)
HDF............ Host Defensive Factor [*Immunology*] (AAMN)
HDF............ Hubble Deep Field [*Astronomy*]
HDF............ Human Diploid Fibroblasts [*Cytology*]
H/DF........... Human/Dolphin Foundation (EA)
HDF............ Human Factor Division of Air Research and Development. (SAUS)
HDF............ Hungarian Democratic Forum [*Political party*] (EY)
HDFD........... High Density Floppy Disk (SAUS)
HDFI........... Host Digital Facilities Interface [*Communications term*] (DCT)
HDFLINT...... Heading Flash Intensity (SAUS)
HDFP........... Hypertension Detection and Follow-Up Program [*NHLBI*]
HDFPA......... High Density Focal Plane Array (SAUS)
HDFPT......... High Density Focal Plane Technology (ACAE)
HDFRZ......... Hard Freeze [*NWS*] (FAAC)
HDFS System... High Definition Film and Sound System (SAUS)
HDG............ Halsey Drug Co. [*AMEX symbol*] (CTT)
HDG............ Heading (AFM)
Hdg............ Heading (PIAV)
HDG............ Heavy-Duty Gasoline-Powered Vehicle (EEVL)
HDG............ High Density Graphite (SAUS)
HDG............ High-Dose Group [*Medicine*] (DMAA)
HDG............ Holographic Diffraction Grating (SAUS)
HDG............ Horizontal Drugs Group (EURO)
HDG............ Hot Dip Galvanization
HDGA........... Hot Dip Galvanizers Association [*British*] (BI)
HDGAF......... Hot Dip Galvanizing After Fabrication [*Metallurgy*]
HDGCP......... Human Dimensions of Global Change Program (SAUO)
HDG-DTL..... Heading to Detail (SAUS)
HDGEC......... Human Dimensions of Global Environmental Change (EERA)
HDGECP....... Human Dimensions of Global Environmental Change Program [*Marine science*] (OSRA)
HDGH........... Hodgson Houses, Inc. (SAUO)
HDG-HDG..... Heading to Heading (SAUS)
HDGP........... High-Drag General-Purpose [*Navy*] (DNAB)
hdgs............ Headings (SAFN)
HDG/S......... Heading Selected (SAUS)
HDGS........... High Dollar Group Sort (EBF)
HDG SEL...... Heading Select (GAVI)
HDGT........... Heavy-Duty Gasoline Truck (EPAT)
HDGV........... Heavy Duty Gasoline-Powered Vehicle (COE)
HDH............ Hauptverband der Deutschen Holz und Kunststoffe Verarbeitenden Industrie und Verwandter Industriezweige eV [*Germany*] (EY)
HDH............ Hawker De Havilland Australia PTY. Ltd. (SAUO)
HDH............ HDLC Distant Host (SAUO)
HDH............ Heart Disease History [*Medicine*] (MAE)
HDH............ Hemihydrate-Dihydrate [*Chemical technology*]
HDH............ High level Data link control distant Host (SAUS)
HDH............ Histidinol Dehydrogenase [*An enzyme*]
HDH............ Howden [*D. H.*] & Co. Ltd. [*Toronto Stock Exchange symbol*]
HDH............ Hydrocracking-Distillation-Hydrotreatment (ECON)
HDH............ Hydrogen Dehydrogenase [*An enzyme*]
HDH............ Mokuleia, HI [*Location identifier*] [*FAA*] (FAAL)
HDHD........... Hawaiian District Harbors Division (SAUO)

HDHD.......... Hilf Du Heilige Dreifaltigkeit [*Help Thou Holy Trinity*] [*Motto of Johann Georg I, Prince of Anhalt-Dessau (1567-1618)*] [*German*]
HD/HE.......... Hospital Design/Hospital Equipment [*British*]
HDHL.......... High-Density Helicopter Landing [*Army*]
HDHNH.......... Hydrodenitrogenation (SAUS)
HDHP.......... Huntington District Home Page (SAUO)
HDHQ.......... Hostility and Direction of Hostility Questionnaire [*Psychology*]
HDHS.......... Haul Down and Handling System [*Canadian Navy*]
HD-HT.......... Hemodilution Combined with Hypotension
HDHVPS.......... High-Density/High-Voltage Power Supply (DNAB)
HDI.......... Cleveland, TN [*Location identifier*] [*FAA*] (FAAL)
HDI.......... Haftpflichtverband der Deutschen Industrie (SAUS)
HDI.......... Hamilton Depression Inventory [*Test*] (TMMY)
HDI.......... Hard Drives International (PCM)
HDI.......... Harley-Davidson, Inc. [*NYSE symbol*] (SPSG)
HDI.......... Hawaiian Development Irradiator [*AEC*]
HDI.......... Head-Disc Interference [*Head crash*] (NITA)
HDI.......... Head Disk Interface (SAUS)
HDI.......... Headquarters Operating Instruction
HDI.......... Heavy Defence Industries (SAUS)
HDI.......... Heavy-Duty Industrial [*Internal combustion engines*]
HDI.......... Heidi Device Interface
HDI.......... Helicopter Direction Inbound [*Military*] (CAAL)
HDI.......... Hemorrhagic Disease of Infants [*Medicine*] (DMAA)
HDI.......... Henry Dunant Institute [*Switzerland*] (BUAC)
HDI.......... Hexamethylen-1,6-Diisocyanat (SAUS)
HDI.......... Hexamethylene Diisocyanate [*Organic chemistry*]
HDI.......... High Definition Imaging
HDI.......... High Density Interconnect (SAUS)
HDI.......... High-Density Interconnect
HDI.......... High Dose Implantation (SAUS)
HDI.......... Historically Disadvantaged Institute (SAUS)
HDI.......... Hoops Device Interface (SAUS)
HDI.......... Horizon Direction Indicator (SAUS)
HDI.......... Horizontal Data Indicator (ACAE)
HDI.......... Horizontal Display Indicator (NG)
HDI.......... Hoteles Dinamicos SA de CV [*Mexico*] [*ICAO designator*] (FAAC)
HDI.......... House Dress Institute (EA)
HDI.......... Household Disposable Income
HDI.......... Human Development Index [*Human Development Report*] [*United Nations Development Program*]
HDI.......... Human Development Institute
HDIC.......... High Density Integrated Circuit (ACAE)
HDIC.......... High Density Interconnect Circuit (SAUS)
HDIC.......... High Digital Integrated Circuit (SAUS)
HDIE.......... Healthdyne Info Enterprises [*NASDAQ symbol*] (TTSB)
HDIE.......... HIE, Inc. [*NASDAQ symbol*] (NASQ)
HDIF.......... Heavy-Duty Industrial Filter
HDIL.......... Health and Drug Information Library
HD Instruction... Halt Device Instruction (SAUS)
HDIP.......... Hazardous Duty Incentive Pay [*Air Force*] (AFM)
HDIP.......... High Density Integrated Processor
HDIP.......... High-Dose Immunological Paralysis [*Medicine*]
H Dip E.......... Higher Diploma in Education [*British*]
HDipEd.......... Higher Diploma in Education [*Academic degree*] (AIE)
HDipT.......... Higher Diploma of Teaching
HDIR.......... Heavy-Duty Industrial Relay
H disease.... Harts disease (SAUS)
H Dist Ct...... United States District Court, District of Hawaii (DLA)
HDIT.......... Hereditament [*Legal shorthand*] (LWAP)
HDIT.......... Home Drug Infusion Therapy [*Medicine*]
HDiv.......... Horizontal Divergence (SAUS)
HDIV.......... Hughes Dynamic Imagery Viewer
HDJ.......... Hydrographic Department of Japan (SAUO)
HDK.......... Hidaka [*Japan*] [*Seismograph station code, US Geological Survey*] (SEIS)
HDK.......... Husband Doesn't Know (IIA)
hdkf.......... Handkerchief (ADWA)
HDKF.......... Handkerchief
HDL.......... Handel Society [*Record label*]
HDL.......... Handle (KSC)
HDL.......... Handleman Co. [*NYSE symbol*] (SPSG)
HDL.......... Hardware Definition Language (SAUS)
HDL.......... Hardware Description Language [*Computer science*]
HDL.......... Hardware Design Language (SAUS)
HDL.......... Harly Diamond Laboratories (SAUS)
HDL.......... Harry Diamond Laboratories [*Formerly, DOFL*] [*Adelphi, MD*] [*Army*]
HDL.......... Headline (WGA)
HDL.......... Hidalgo County Library System, McAllen, TX [*OCLC symbol*] (OCLC)
HDL.......... High-Density Cholesterol (SAUS)
HDL.......... High Density Lipoprotein (SAUS)
HDL.......... High-Density Lipoprotein [*Biochemistry*]
HDL.......... High-level Data Labotatory (SAUS)
HDL.......... High Level Data Link (SAUS)
HDL.......... High-Level Design Language (AEBE)
HDL.......... Holdenville, OK [*Location identifier*] [*FAA*] (FAAL)
HDL.......... Hovercraft Development Limited (SAUO)
HDL.......... Hydrologic Data Laboratory [*Agricultural Research Service*] (PDAA)
HDLA.......... High-Level Data Link Control Adapter [*Data communication*] (MHDI)
HDLC.......... Hierarchical Data Link [*Computer science*] (CIST)
HDL-C.......... High-Density Lipoprotein - Cell Surface Receptor [*Biochemistry*]
HDL-C.......... High Density Lipoprotein-Cholesterol (SAUS)
HDLC.......... High-Density Lipoprotein Cholesterol [*Physiology*]
HDL-C.......... High Density Lipoprotein Fraction [*Biochemistry*] (DAVI)
HDLC.......... High Level Data Link Communications (SAUS)
HDLC.......... High Level Data Link Control (SAUS)
HDLC.......... High-Level Data Link Control [*International Standards Organization*] [*Data communication*]
HDLC.......... High-level Data Link Controller (SAUS)
HDLCM.......... High Density Line Conditioning Module
HDL Control... High Level Data Link Control (SAUS)
HDLD.......... Headland (SAUS)
HDLD.......... Heavy-Duty Liquid Detergent
HDLE.......... Hartsdale, IN [*American Association of Railroads railroad junction routing code*]
HDLE.......... Horse Racing Hurdle (SAUS)
HDLE.......... Hurdle
HDLG.......... Handling (AABC)
HDLI.......... Housing & Development Law Institute (SAUO)
HDLM.......... High-Level Data Linkage Module [*Data communication*] (MHDB)
HDLNR.......... Headliner
HDLP.......... High-Density Lipoprotein [*Biochemistry*] (AAMN)
HDLP.......... Holdup [*FBI standardized term*]
HDLR.......... Handler (AABC)
HDLR.......... Hexadecimal Symbolic Loader [*Computer science*] (MHDI)
HDLS.......... Hardware Description Language System (IAA)
HDLS.......... Headless (KSC)
HDLTSBENDS... Half Despatch Lay Time Saved Both Ends (RIMS)
HDLW.......... Distance at Which a Watch Is Heard with Left Ear [*Medicine*]
HDM.......... Haddam [*Connecticut*] [*Seismograph station code, US Geological Survey*] (SEIS)
HDM.......... Hamadan [*Iran*] [*Airport symbol*] (AD)
HDM.......... Hand-Deboned Meat
HDM.......... Hardware Device Module [*Computer science*] (VLIE)
HDM.......... Harmonic Distortion Meter (DEN)
HDM.......... Hexadimethrine (STED)
HDM.......... Hierarchical Desgin Method (SAUS)
HDM.......... Hierarchical Development Method [*Computer science*]
HDM.......... Hierarchical Development Methodology (VLIE)
HDM.......... High Data Mode (SAUS)
HDM.......... High Density Magnum (SAUS)
HDM.......... High-Density Microsome [*Cytology*]
HDM.......... High Density Modem [*Computer science*] (VLIE)
HDM.......... High-Density Module (GART)
HDM.......... High Dry Matter (SAUS)
HDM.......... High Duty Metal (SAUS)
HDM.......... High-Power Deformable Mirror (ACAE)
HDM.......... Hizbia Dighill e Mirifle [*Somali political party*]
HDM.......... Host Defense Mechanism [*Medicine*] (MELL)
HDM.......... Hot Dark Matter [*Astronomy*]
HDM.......... House Dust Mite
HDM.......... Hudson & Manhattan [*AAR code*]
HDM.......... Humic Degradation Matter (DICI)
HDM.......... Hydrodemetalation [*Petroleum refining*]
HDM.......... Hydrodensimeter (SAUS)
HDM.......... Hydrodynamic Machining [*Manufacturing term*]
HDM.......... Hydrodynamic Modulation
HDM.......... Hydroxydopamine [*Also, HDA, OHDA*] [*Biochemistry*]
HDMA.......... Hardwood Dimension Manufacturers Association [*Later, NDMA*] (EA)
HDMA.......... Heavy Duty Manufacturers' Association
HDMC.......... Helicopter Depot Maintenance Center (MCD)
HDMCC.......... Howdy Doody Memorabilia Collectors Club (EA)
HDME.......... Hanging Drop Mercury Electrode (SAUS)
HDMF.......... Hybrid D-Median Filter (SAUS)
HDMI.......... High-Density Multichip Interconnect [*Semiconductor packaging*]
HDMIC.......... High Density Microwave Integrated Circuit (ACAE)
HDML.......... Handheld Device Markup Language [*Computer science*] (PCM)
HDML.......... Harbor Defense Motor Launch [*NATO*] (NATG)
HDMO.......... Heavy-Duty Motor Oil
HDMP.......... High-Dose Methylprednisolone (STED)
HDMP.......... Horizon Definition Measurement Program (DNAB)
HDMR.......... High-Density Moderated Reactor (IEEE)
HDMR.......... High Density Multitrack Recording (SAUS)
HDMR.......... High-Density Multitrack Recording (MCD)
HDMS.......... High Density Memory Set (SAUO)
HDMS.......... High-Density Memory System
HDMS.......... High-Density MODEM System [*Microcom*] [*Norwood, MA*] [*Computer science*]
HDMS.......... Hizb Dastur Mustaghil Somalia [*Somali Independent Constitution Party*]
HDMS.......... Honeywell Distributed Manufacturing System (NITA)
HDMS.......... Honorable Discharge, Medical Survey [*Military*]
HDMSW.......... High-Density Mach Shock Wave
HDMT.......... High-Density Multi-Track
HD-MTD.......... High Density Magnetic Tape Drive (SAUS)
HDMTX.......... High Dose Methotrexate [*Antineoplastic drug regimen*]
HDMTX-CF... High-Dose Methotrexate-Citrovorum Factor [*Antineoplastic drug regimen*]
HDMTX-LV... High-Dose Methotrexate, Leucovorin [*Antineoplastic drug regimen*]
HDMU.......... Honorable Discharge, under Age of Authorized Consent [*Military*]
HDMW.......... Honorable Discharge, Minors Enlisted without Consent, under Eighteen at Discharge [*Military*]
HDN.......... Harden (KSC)
HDN.......... Hayden, CO [*Location identifier*] [*FAA*] (FAAL)
HDN.......... Hemolytic Disease of the Newborn [*Medicine*]
Hdn.......... Herodianus [*Greek scholar, c. 200AD*] [*Classical studies*] (OCD)
HDN.......... Heyden Chemical Corp. (SAUO)
HDN.......... High-Density Nebulizer [*Medicine*] (MAE)
HDN.......... High-Density Network [*Indian Railway*] (TIR)
HDN.......... Hildon Mining [*Vancouver Stock Exchange symbol*]

HDN .... Hydrodenitrogenation [*of chemical compounds*]
HDN .... Steamboat Springs [*Colorado*] [*Airport symbol*] [*Obsolete*] (OAG)
hDNA .... Deoxyribonucleic Acid, heteroduplex [*Biochemistry, genetics*]
hDNA .... Deoxyribonucleic Acid, Histone [*Biochemistry, genetics*]
HDNA .... Habonim Dror North America (EA)
HDNA .... Hinged Deoxyribonucleic Acid [*Biochemistry, genetics*]
HDNDS .... Humboldt Del Norte Dental Society (SAUO)
HDNG .... Hardinge, Inc. [*NASDAQ symbol*] (SAG)
HDNG .... Heading (VLIE)
HDNP .... High Density Nickel Powder (SAUS)
HDNPRSGR... Headquarters Squadron Personnel Group
HDNS .... Hardness (MSA)
HDNSW .... High-Density Nuclear Shock Wave
HDNT .... Headnote
HdO .... Handbuch der Orientalistik [*Leiden*] [*A publication*] (BJA)
HDO .... Harbor Defence Only [*Military*] (WDAA)
HDO .... Helicopter Direction Outbound [*Military*] (CAAL)
HDO .... Help Desk Outsourcing (GART)
HDO .... High Density Overlay (SAUS)
HDO .... Home Dish Only (SAUS)
HDO .... Hondo, TX [*Location identifier*] [*FAA*] (FAAL)
HDO .... Horizontal Parallax Only (SAUS)
HDOC .... Handy Dandy Orbital Computer (IEEE)
HDOC .... House Document
HDOCP .... Heavy-Duty Oil Classification Panel [*Automotive engineering*]
HDODA .... Hexanediol Diacrylate [*Also, HDDA*] [*Organic chemistry*]
HD Oil .... Heavy Duty Oil (SAUS)
HDOL .... Hexadecenol [*Pheromone*] [*Organic chemistry*]
HDOP .... Hanford Dose Overview Panel (SAUS)
HDOP .... Harbour Defence Observation Post (SAUS)
HDOP .... Horizontal Dilution of Precision
HDOS .... Hard Disk Operating System
HDOS .... Heath Disk Operating System (SAUS)
HDOS .... Hughes-Danbury Optical Systems, Inc. (SAUO)
HDOT .... Inertial Vertical Speed (GAVI)
HDOV .... Hardover
HDP .... Halftone Digital Proof (SAUS)
HDP .... Hankyore Demokrat Party [*South Korea*] [*Political party*] (EY)
HDP .... Harpoon Data Processor [*Missiles*] (MCD)
HDP .... Hearing Dog Project [*Later, HDRC*] (EA)
HDP .... Heavy-Duty Petrol (SAUS)
HDP .... Hell Data Processing (SAUS)
HDP .... Hexose Diphosphate [*Biochemistry*]
HDP .... Hiburd Properties [*Vancouver Stock Exchange symbol*]
HDP .... High Definition Progressive (VLIE)
HDP .... High Delta Pressure (COE)
HDP .... High Density Plasma (SAUS)
HDP .... High-Density Plasma (SAA)
HDP .... High-Density Polyethylene (STED)
HDP .... High-Desirable Performance (SAUS)
HDP .... High Detonation Pressure
HDP .... High Discharge Pressure (SAUS)
HDP .... High-Discharge Pressure (IEEE)
HDP .... Holddown Post (NASA)
HDP .... Horizontal Data Processing
HDP .... Housing Development Program
HDP .... Huer Demokrat Parti [*Free Democrat Party*] [*Turkish Cyprus*] [*Political party*] (EY)
HDP .... Human Dimension of Global Environmental Change Programme [*The International Social Science Council*] (ECON)
HDP .... Human Dimensions Program (SAUS)
HDP .... Humpty Dumpty Physics (SAUS)
HDP .... Huntington's Disease Protein [*Biochemistry*]
HDP .... Hydrazine Diperchlorate (SAUS)
HDP .... Hydrostatic Deformation Potential (SAUS)
HDP .... Hydroxydimethylpyrimidine [*Organic chemistry*]
HDP .... Hydroxymethyline Diphosphonate [*Medicine*] (EDAA)
HDP .... People's Democratic Party (Uzbekistan) [*Political party*] (PSAP)
HDPA .... Hydroxydiphenylamine (SAUS)
HDPAA .... Heparin-Dependent Platelet-Associated Antibody [*Medicine*] (DMAA)
HDPC .... Harbour Defence Patrol Craft (SAUS)
HDPC .... Health Data Policy Committee [*Department of Health and Human Services*] (GFGA)
HDPCM .... Hybrid Differential Pulse Code Modulation (SAUS)
HDP-DIS ...... Human Dimensions of Global Environmental Change Programme Data and Information System (SAUS)
HDPE .... High-Density Polyethylene [*Plastics*]
HDPF .... Holographic Data Processing Facility (SAUS)
HDPF .... Hughes Data Processing Facility (ACAE)
HDPG .... Half Deck Plate Girder (SAUS)
HDPI .... Hyundai Precision Industry (SAUS)
HDPLD .... High Density Programmable Logic Device (SAUS)
HDPPA .... Housing Development and Public Participation Administration [*Turkey*] (ECON)
HDPS .... High-Density Power Supply
HDQ .... Headquarters [*Colorado*] [*Seismograph station code, US Geological Survey*] [*Closed*] (SEIS)
HDQ .... High Definition Quincunx (VLIE)
HDQAMC ...... Headquarters Air Materiel Command (SAUO)
HDQR .... Headquarters
hdqrs .... Headquarters (NTIO)
HDQRS .... Headquarters
H'd-Qrts ...... Headquarters [*Civil War term*]
HDQTRS ...... Headquarters (NASA)
HDR .... Hair's Daily Requirement [*Brand of shampoo*]
HDR .... Hand Rail
HD-R .... Harddisk Recording (SAUS)
HDR .... Hardening Design Responses
HDR .... Hardware Design Review (SAUS)
HDR .... HDSL Dual Regenerator (SAUS)
hdr .... Header (ELAL)
Hdr .... Header [*Construction term*] (MIST)
HDR .... Header [*Automotive engineering*]
HDR .... Header High Dynamic Range (SAUS)
HDR .... [*File*] Header Label [*Computer science*] (ECII)
HDR .... Head of Data Record (SAUS)
HDR .... Head Record (SAUS)
HDR .... Health Data Recorder [*Computer science*] (PDAA)
HDR .... Heart Disease Resources [*Medicine*] (EDAA)
HDR .... Heavy-Duty Rescue [*Emergency vehicles*]
HDR .... Heldor Industries, Inc. [*AMEX symbol*] (COMM)
HDR .... High availability Data Replication (SAUS)
HDR .... High Data Rate
HDR .... High Data Register
HDR .... High Definition RADAR
HDR .... High-Density Recorder [*Deep Space Instrumentation Facility, NASA*]
HDR .... High Density Recording (NITA)
HDR .... High-Density Route [*Indian Railway*] (TIR)
HDR .... High Dose Rate [*Medicine*] (DMAA)
HDR .... High Dynamic Range (SAUS)
HDR .... High-Level Design Review (SAUS)
HDR .... Hold Down and Release (SAUS)
HDR .... Home Dockyard Regulations [*Navy*] (MCD)
H-Dr .... Horse-Drawn [*Obsolete*] [*Army*]
HDR .... Hot Dry Rock [*Geothermal science*]
HDR .... Housing & Development Reporter (SAUO)
HDR .... HPSC, Inc. [*AMEX symbol*]
HDR .... Humanitarian Daily Ration [*Army*] (INF)
HDRA .... Heavy Duty Representatives Association (EA)
HDRA .... Henry Doubleday Research Association [*Coventry, England*] (EAIO)
HDRA .... High-Data-Rate Assembly (MCD)
HDRA .... High Desert Racing Association
HDRAA .... Henry Doubleday Research Association of Australia
HDRANCE .... Hindrance (ROG)
H-D RBC ...... Heat-Damaged Red Blood Cell (SAUS)
HDRC .... Hearing Dog Resource Center (EA)
HDRC .... High Dynamic Range Camera [*Electronics*]
HDR/ELF ...... High Data Rate Extremely Low Frequency (SAUS)
HDRF .... Heart Disease Research Foundation (EA)
HDRI .... Hannah Dairy Research Institute [*British*] (BI)
HDRIV .... Hood River, OR [*American Association of Railroads railroad junction routing code*]
HDRL .... High-Data-Rate LASER (MCD)
HDRL .... High-Dose Reference Laboratory (CARB)
HDRM .... High-Data-Rate Multiplexer (MCD)
HDRN .... Hadron, Inc. [*NASDAQ symbol*] (COMM)
HDRO .... House Democratic Research Organization [*Defunct*] (EA)
HD-ROM ...... High Density-Read-Only Memory [*Computer science*]
HDRP .... HDR Power Systems, Inc. [*NASDAQ symbol*] (COMM)
HDRR .... High-Data Rate Recorder
HDRR .... Holloman Development Research Report [*Air Force*] (MCD)
HDRS .... Hamilton Depression Rating Scale (SAUS)
HDRS .... High-Data Rate Switch (MCD)
HDRS .... High Density Recording System (SAUS)
HDRS .... Home Defence Radio System (SAUS)
HDRSS .... High-Data-Rate Storage System [*or Subsystem*] [*NASA*] (MCD)
HDRT .... High Density Recording Tape (SAUS)
HDRV .... Heavy Duty Recovery Vehicle (SAUS)
HDRV .... Human Diploid-Cell Rabies Vaccine
HDRW .... Distance at Which a Watch Is Heard with Right Ear [*Medicine*]
HDS .... Half Duplex System (SAUS)
HDS .... Hamilton Depression Scale (SAUS)
HDS .... Handicapped Driving Systems [*Burnsville, MN*]
HDS .... Hardware Description Sheet (NASA)
HDS .... Hardware Design System
HDS .... Hardware Development System (SAUS)
HDS .... Harlequin Dispersed Screening (SAUS)
HDS .... HDS Network Systems, Inc. [*Associated Press*] (SAG)
HDS .... Head of Defence Sales [*British*] (RDA)
HDS .... Headquarters Distribution System (SAUS)
HDS .... Heads [*Automotive engineering*]
HDS .... Head Set [*Telecommunications*] (TEL)
H/DS .... Head-to-Disk Separation (SAUS)
H/DS .... Head-to-Drum Separation (SAUS)
HDS .... Health and Diet Survey [*Department of Health and Human Services*] (GFGA)
HDS .... Helicopter Delivery Service (SAUS)
HDS .... Help Desk Services
HDS .... Herbicide Delivery Systems [*Aquatic Plant Control Research Program*] [*Army Corps of Engineers*]
HDS .... Herdis International Canada, Inc. [*Vancouver Stock Exchange symbol*]
HDS .... Hermes Data System [*Hermes Precisa International*] (NITA)
HDS .... Herniated Disc Syndrome [*Medicine*]
HDS .... Hierarchical Distributed System (VLIE)
HDS .... High Definition Systems (SAUS)
HDS .... High Density Satellite (SAUS)
HDS .... High Density Sludge (SAUS)
HDS .... High-resolution Data Service (SAUS)
HDS .... Hills Department Stores, Inc. [*NYSE symbol*] (SPSG)

HDS .... Historical Data Server [*Computer science*] (DINT)
HDS .... Historical Data System [*Air Force*] (MCD)
HDS .... Historical Diving Society (BUAC)
HDS .... History of Dermatology Society (EA)
HDS .... Holland Drink Service (SAUO)
HDS .... Holographic Diffractive Structure [*Advanced Environmental Research Group*]
HDS .... Holy Days of Obligation [*Roman Catholicism*] (ROG)
HDS .... Homogeneous Distinguishing Sequence (SAUS)
HDS .... Hopsital Discharge Survey (SAUO)
HDS .... Horizontal Display System (ACAE)
HDS .... Hospital Discharge Survey [*Public Health Service*]
HDS .... Household Delivery Service [*British Post Office facility*] (DCTA)
HDS .... Hrvatski Demokratski Stranka [*Croatian Democratic Party*] [*Political party*] (EY)
HDS .... Huang Diffuse Scattering (SAUS)
HDS .... Hughes Driving Simulator (ACAE)
HDS .... Human Development Services (SAUO)
HDS .... Humungous Development Syndrome (EERA)
HDS .... Hundreds (SAUS)
HDS .... Hybrid Development System
HDS .... Hydrodesulfurization
HDS .... Hydrogen Detection System
HDS .... Office of Human Development Services [*Department of Health and Human Services*]
HDSA .... Huntington's Disease Society of America (EA)
HDSB .... Heavy Dry Support Bridge [*Army*] (RDA)
HDSC .... Harpoon Data System Cabinet [*Missiles*] (MCD)
HDSC .... Harris Data Services Corp (SAUS)
HDSC .... High Density Signal Carrier (VLIE)
Hd Schm .... Head Schoolmaster (SAUS)
HdSchm .... Head Schoolmaster [*Navy*] [*British*]
HDSCS .... Hospital Disaster Support Communications System
HD/SCSI .... Hard Disk/Small Computer System Interface (SAUS)
Hd Sd .... Hard Sand (SAUS)
HDSD .... Hydrogen Defect Shallow Donors (AAEL)
HDSE .... Hawker Siddeley Dynamics Engineering (SAUS)
HD(S)E .... Home Defence Security Executive [*British*] [*World War II*]
HDSHK .... Handshake [*Computers*] (MSA)
HDSI .... High-Rate Digital Subscriber Line [*Communications term*] (DCT)
HDSL .... High Bit/Data Rate/Speed Digital Subscriber Line (SAUS)
HDSL .... High Bit/Data Rate/Speed Digital Subscriber Link (SAUS)
HDSL .... High Bit Rate Digital Subscriber Line [*Computer science*] (CDE)
HDSL .... High Bit-rate Digital Subscriber Link (SAUS)
HDSL .... High-bit-rate Digital Subscriber Loop (SAUS)
HDSL .... High Bit-speed Digital Subscriber Line (SAUS)
HDSL .... High Bit-speed Digital Subscriber Link (SAUS)
HDSL .... High-Data-Rate Digital Subscriber Line [*Telecommunications*] (DOM)
HDSL .... High Data rate digital Subscriber Link (SAUS)
HDSL .... High Data speed digital Subscriber Line (SAUS)
HDSL .... High Data speed Digital Subscriber Link (SAUS)
HDSL .... High Density Subscriber Loop (CGWS)
HDSL .... High-level Data Specification Language (SAUS)
HDSL .... High-rate Digital Subscriber Link (SAUS)
HDSL .... High-speed Digital Subscriber Line (SAUS)
HDSL .... High-Speed Digital Subscriber Loop [*Computer science*]
HDSM .... High-Density Surface Mount (TIMI)
HDSN .... Hudson River Basin (SAUS)
HDSN .... Hudson Technology, Inc. [*NASDAQ symbol*] (SAG)
HDS-NA .... High Definition System for North America
HDS Nt .... HDS Network Systems, Inc. [*Associated Press*] (SAG)
HDSP .... Hardship (AABC)
HDSPr .... Hills Stores Sr'A' Cv Pfd [*NYSE symbol*] (TTSB)
HDS Process ... Hydrodesulphurization Process (SAUS)
HDSR .... Historical Data Storage and Retrieval
HDSRIM .... High-Density, Structural Reaction Injection Molding [*Plastics*]
HDSS .... Hardpoint Defense System Study (ACAE)
HDSS .... Hierarchical Data Storage System (SAUS)
HDSS .... Holographic Data Storage System
HDSS .... Hospital Decision Support System (SAUS)
HDST .... Hawaiian Daylight Saving Time (SAUO)
HDST .... Headset (MCD)
HDST .... High-Density Shock Tube (IEEE)
HDSVLY .... Hudson Valley (FAAC)
HDSW .... Handwoerterbuch der Sozialwissenschaft [*Dictionary of the Social Sciences*] [*A publication*]
HDSX .... HDS Network Systems [*NASDAQ symbol*] (TTSB)
HDSX .... HDS Network Systems, Inc. [*NASDAQ symbol*] (SAG)
HDSX .... Rail America Equipment [*Private rail car owner code*]
HDSXW .... HDS Network Sys Wrrt [*NASDAQ symbol*] (TTSB)
HDT .... Half Disappearance Time (MELL)
HDT .... Half Duplex Teletype (KSC)
HDT .... Hard Disk ToolKIT [*Computer science*]
HDT .... Hardtop (GOBB)
HDT .... Hardware Demonstration Test (SAUO)
HDT .... Heat Deflection Temperature [*of plastics*]
HDT .... Heat Deflection Test (SAUS)
HDT .... Heat Distortion Temperature
HDT .... Heavy-Duty Thermoplastic Insulation [*Automotive engineering*]
HDT .... Heavy Duty Truck [*Environmental Protection Agency*]
Hdt .... Herodotus [*Greek historian, c. 484BC*] [*Classical studies*] (OCD)
HDT .... Hexadecanethiol [*Organic chemistry*]
HDT .... Hexamethylene Diisocyanate (EDCT)
HDT .... High Density Tape (ACAE)
HDT .... Highest Dose Tested (EEVL)
HDT .... Hi-Pot Dwell Time
HDT .... Horse-Drawn Transport (SAUS)
HDT .... Host Digital Terminal [*Telecommunications*] (ACRL)
HDT .... Humboldt, TN [*Location identifier*] [*FAA*] (FAAL)
HDT .... Hydrodynamic Technology (SAUS)
HDT .... Hydrotreating [*or Hydrotreated*] [*Petroleum technology*]
HDT-A .... High Density Tape (SAUS)
HDTA .... High-Density Traffic Airport
HDTC .... Healthdyne Technologies [*NASDAQ symbol*] (SAG)
HDTC .... Heavy Duty Transient Cycle
HDTCS .... Hexadecyltrichlorosilane [*Organic chemistry*]
HDTI .... High Definition Thermal Imager (SAUS)
HDTI .... Human Development Training Institute (SAUO)
HDTL .... Harlequin Display List Technology (SAUS)
HDTM .... Half-Duplex Transmission Module [*Telecommunications*] (ACRL)
HDTMA .... Heavy-Duty Truck Manufacturers Association (EA)
HDTMA .... Hexadecyltrimethylammonium
HDTP .... Handheld Device Transport Protocol (SAUS)
HDTP .... Hardtop
HDTR .... High Density Tape Recorder (ACAE)
HDTS .... Harbor Drive Test Site (SAUS)
HDTS .... High Density Tape Transcription System (SAUO)
HDTUL .... Heat-Deflection Temperature under Load (SAUS)
HDTV .... High Definition Television (SAUS)
HDTV .... High-Definition Television [*Offers wider-screen pictures with high resolution that improves their depth, clarity, and detail*]
HDTV .... High Density Television (SAUS)
HDTV .... High Dissolving Television (SAUS)
HD Type .... High Dielectric Type (SAUS)
HDU .... Haemodialysis Unit (SAUS)
HDU .... Hard Disc Unit (NITA)
HDU .... Head-Drop Unit (SAUS)
HDU .... Heads-Up Display Unit [*Aviation*] (RDA)
HDU .... Heat-Dissipation Unit (ABAC)
HDU .... Helmet Display Unit (SAUS)
HDU .... Hemodialysis Unit [*Medicine*]
HDU .... High Dependency Unit [*Medicine*] (DMAA)
HDU .... Home Defence Unit [*British military*] (DMA)
HDU .... Hose Down Unit (DOMA)
HDU .... Hosedrogue Unit (SAUS)
HDU .... Hose Drum Unit (SAUO)
HDU .... Hyde Park [*Utah*] [*Seismograph station code, US Geological Survey*] (SEIS)
HDUE .... High Dynamic User Equipment
HDUP .... Half Duplex (SAUS)
HDUR .... Hungarian Democratic Union of Romania [*Political party*] (BUAC)
H/DUTY .... Heavy Duty (SAUS)
HDV .... Halt Device (IAA)
HDV .... Heavy Duty Vehicle [*Environmental Protection Agency*]
HDV .... Hepatitis Delta Virus
HDV .... Hepatitis D Virus [*Medicine*] (DMAA)
HDV .... Hepatocyte-Directed Vesicle (DB)
HDV .... High-Definition Video
HDV .... High Density-Version (SAUS)
HDV .... High-Dollar Value
HDV .... Horse-Drawn Vehicle
HDV .... Human Delta Virus (SAUS)
HDV .... Hydrodevanadization [*Petroleum technology*]
HDV .... Hydrodynamic Voltammogram [*Electrochemistry*]
HDV .... Hydrodynamic Volume [*Physical chemistry*]
HDVD .... High Definition Video-Disk (SAUS)
HDVD .... High Definition Volumetric Display (SAUS)
HD Vest .... H. D. Vest, Inc. [*Associated Press*] (SAG)
HDVIP .... Heavy-Duty Vehicle Inspection Program
HDVP .... High Dynamics Vehicles Project (SAUS)
HDVS .... H.D.Vest [*NASDAQ symbol*] (TTSB)
HDVS .... High Definition Video System
HDVS .... Vest [*H.D.*], Inc. [*NASDAQ symbol*] (SPSG)
HDW .... Hanford Defense Waste (SAUS)
HDW .... Hard Drawn Wire (SAUS)
HDW .... Hardware [*Computer science*] (KSC)
HDW .... Hearing Distance with Watch [*Medicine*]
HDW .... High-Pressure Demineralized Water (NRCH)
HDWA .... Hardware [*Computer science*] (IAA)
HDWA .... Health Department of Western Australia
HDWC .... Hardware Cloth
HDWC .... Hawaii Deep Water Cable (SAUS)
hdwd .... Hardwood (ADWA)
HDWD .... Hardwood
HDWD .... Headword (SAUS)
HDWDM .... High Density Wavelength-Division Multiplexing (SAUO)
hdwe .... Hardware (VRA)
HDWE .... Hardware
HDW-EIS .... Hanford Defense Waste Environmental Impact Statement (SAUS)
HDWHL .... Hand Wheel (SAUS)
HDWND .... Headwind (FAAC)
HDWRE .... Hardware (WGA)
HDWS .... How Do We Stand
Hdwt .... Hundredweight
HDWTS .... Half Demurrage Weather Timed Saved (RIMS)
HDWY .... Headway Corporate Resources
HDWY .... Headway Corporate Resources, Inc. [*NASDAQ symbol*] (SAG)
HDWY .... Hideaway
HDX .... Half Duplex [*Telecommunications*] (NITA)
HDX .... Half Duplex Transmission [*Data communication*]

HDX .... Hand-Held Dental X-Ray (RDA)
HDX .... Hitachi Data and Telex Exchange (SAUS)
HDX .... Home Defence Exercise (SAUS)
HDX Circuit... Half Duplex Circuit (SAUS)
HDY .... Haadyai [*Thailand*] [*Airport symbol*] (OAG)
HDY .... Heavy-Duty
HDYN .... Healthdyne, Inc. [*NASDAQ symbol*] (COMM)
HDZ .... Croatian Democratic Union [*Political party*] (BUAC)
HDZ .... Hrvatska Demokratska Zajednica [*Croatian Democratic Union*] [*Political party*] (EY)
HDZ .... Hydralazine [*Medicine*] (EDAA)
HDZNV .... De Handschriften van de Dode Zee in Nederlandse Vertaling [*Amsterdam*] [*A publication*] (BJA)
HE............... Altitude Error (GAVI)
He............... Book of Helaman (SAUS)
HE............... Green Bay Aviation [*ICAO designator*] (AD)
HE............... Hall Effect [*Electromagnetism*] (OA)
HE............... Hammerless Ejector (SAUS)
HE............... Handling Duplex (SAUS)
HE............... Handling Engineer (SAUS)
HE............... Handling Equipment
HE............... Hanford Environmental Health Foundation (SAUO)
HE............... Hard Exudate [*Ophthalmology*] (DAVI)
HE............... Hardware Evaluator [*NASA*]
HE............... Hardware Executive
HE............... Harmful Environment (SAUS)
HE............... Hawaiian Electric Industries, Inc. [*NYSE symbol*] (SPSG)
he............... Head [*Anatomy*] (DAVI)
HE............... Head End
HE............... Header Extension [*Telecommunications*] (ACRL)
HE............... Heading Error (SAUS)
HE............... Health Economics (SAUO)
HE............... Hearing Examiner [*Also, ALJ*]
HE............... Hearsay Evidence [*Legal shorthand*] (LWAP)
He............... Heart (DMAA)
HE............... Heat Engine
HE............... Heat Exchange [*or Exchanger*]
HE............... Heat Exhaustion (MELL)
HE............... Heating Element (SAUS)
HE............... Heavy Enamel (AAG)
HE............... Heavy Equipment (AFM)
HE............... [*The*] Hebrew [*A publication*] (BJA)
HE............... Hebrews [*Old Testament book*]
He............... Hedstrom Number [*Chemistry*] (DAVI)
HE............... Height of Eye [*Navigation*]
HE............... Heinkel [*German aircraft type*] [*World War II*]
HE............... Hektoen Enteric Agar [*Medicine*] (DMAA)
HE............... Helio Aircraft Co. [*ICAO aircraft manufacturer identifier*] (ICAO)
He............... Helium [*Chemical element*]
HE............... Helium Embrittlement (SAUS)
HE............... Hemagglutinating Encephalomyelitis [*Neurology*] (DAVI)
HE............... Hematoxylin and Eosin [*Biological stain*]
HE............... Hemicylindrical [*Leaf characteristic*] [*Botany*]
HE............... Hemoglobin Electrophoresis [*Medicine*] (AAMN)
HE............... Hepatic Encephalography [*Medicine*]
HE............... Hepatic Encephalopathy [*Medicine*]
HE............... Hepatic Extraction [*Endocrinology*]
HE............... Hepatoma (DB)
HE............... Heptachlorine Epoxide (SAUS)
HE............... Hereditary Elliptocytosis [*Medicine*]
HE............... Her Eminence (SHCU)
HE............... Her Excellency (SAUS)
HE............... Hermes Electronics (SAUO)
HE............... Hernia Equivalent [*Medicine*] (EDAA)
HE............... Herpes Encephalitis [*Medicine*] (EDAA)
He............... Hertz (SAUS)
HE............... Heterologous (MELL)
HE............... Hexane-Extractable Compound
HE............... Hic Est [*Here Is, That is, or This is*] [*Latin*]
HE............... High Efficiency
HE............... High Elongation (SAUS)
HE............... High Energy (MCD)
HE............... High Energy Astrophysics (SAUS)
HE............... High-Energy Astrophysics (NASA)
HE............... Higher Education [*Educational Resources Information Center (ERIC) Clearinghouse*] [*George Washington University*] (PAZ)
HE............... Higher Elongation (MCD)
HE............... Highest Electroendosmosis [*Analytical biochemistry*]
HE............... High Explosive (AAG)
HE............... High Explosive Anti-Armour (SAUS)
HE............... High Exposure [*Medicine*] (EDAA)
HE............... Highly Elliptic (ACAE)
HE............... His Eminence
HE............... His [*or Her*] Excellency
HE............... Historia Ecclesiastica [*of Eusebius*] [*Classical studies*]
HE............... Historical Period Ending Date [*Dialog*] [*Searchable field*] [*Information service or system*] (NITA)
HE............... Hoc Est [*That Is or This Is*] [*Latin*]
HE............... Hollis & Eastern Railroad Co. [*AAR code*]
HE............... Hollow Enzyme [*Medicine*] (DMAA)
HE............... Holographic Element (ACAE)
HE............... Holy Empire [*Freemasonry*]
HE............... Holy Eucharist
HE............... Home Economics [*Secondary school course*] [*British*]
HE............... Honda Engineering
HE............... Horizontal Equivalent
HE............... Horticultural Enterprise [*A publication*]
HE............... Hot Electron (SAUS)
HE............... House Error [*Publishing*] (WDMC)
HE............... Housekeeping Element (TEL)
HE............... Hub End (BARN)
HE............... Human Engineering
HE............... Human Enolase [*An enzyme*]
HE............... Human Enteric [*Virology*]
HE............... Human Error [*Environmental science*] (COE)
HE............... Human Events [*A publication*] (BRI)
HE............... Human Exposure Dose [*Medicine*]
HE............... Hydraulics Engineer
HE............... Hydro-Electric (SAUS)
HE............... Hydrogen Electrode (SAUS)
HE............... Hydrogen Embrittlement
HE............... Hydrogen Evolution (SAUS)
HE............... Hydromagnetic Emission (IAA)
HE............... Hydrophone Effect [*Navy*] (NVT)
HE............... Hydrostatic Equilibrium (ACAE)
HE............... Hydroxyecdysone [*Endocrinology*]
HE............... Hygienic Effect
HE............... Hygienic Electrician [*British*] (ROG)
HE............... Hyperextension [*Medicine*] (EDAA)
HE............... Hypo Eliminator [*Photography*] (DGA)
HE............... Hypogonadotrophic Eunuchoidism [*Medicine*]
HE............... Hypophysectomy [*Medicine*] (DAVI)
HE............... International Institute for Hydraulic and Environmental Engineering (SAUO)
HE .... Home Establishment (ODA)
HEA............. Centre des Hautes Etudes Americaines [*Paris*]
HEA............. Hairdressing Employers Association (BUAC)
HEA............. Handkerchief and Embroidery Association (SAUO)
HEA............. Health Education Authority [*British*]
HEA............. Health Effects Assessment [*Environmental Protection Agency*] (AEPA)
HEA............. Heating Engineering Association (BUAC)
HEA............. Helena Esperanto-Asocio (SAUO)
HEA............. Heliavia-Transporte Aereo Lda. [*Portugal*] [*ICAO designator*] (FAAC)
HEA............. Hemorrhagic Arteries [*Veterinary medicine*]
He-a............. Hepatoma (SAUS)
HEA............. Herat [*Afghanistan*] [*Airport symbol*] [*Obsolete*] (OAG)
HEA............. Hexone-Extracted Acetone [*Chemistry*] (DAVI)
HEA............. High-Efficiency Antireflection [*Optics*]
HEA............. Higher Education Act [*1965*]
HEA............. Higher Education Authority [*Ireland*] (AIE)
HEA............. Higher Education Awards (ACII)
HEA............. Hockey East Association (PSS)
HEA............. Home Economics Association (SAUO)
HEA............. Horticultural Education Association [*British*]
HEA............. Horticulture Exhibitors Association [*British*] (DBA)
HEA............. Hot Electron Amplifier
HEA............. Hughes Employees' Association (ACAE)
HEA............. Human Erythrocyte Antigen [*Hematology*] (DAVI)
HEA............. Hunter Education Association (EA)
HEA............. Hydrogen Engineering Applications Ltd. (SAUO)
HEA............. Hydroxyethyl Acrylate [*Organic chemistry*]
HEA............. Hydroxyethylamine (SAUS)
HEA............. Hyundai Electronics of America (SAUO)
HEAA .... Higher Education Act Amendment [*1992*]
HEAA .... High Explosive Anti-Aircraft (SAUS)
HEAA .... High Explosive, Anti-Armour (SAUS)
HEAA .... Home Economics Association for Australia (BUAC)
HEAA .... Home Economics Association of Africa (BUAC)
HEAA Shell... High Explosive Anti-Aircraft Shell (SAUS)
HEAB .... High Energy Astrophysics Branch [*NASA*]
HEAC .... Higher Education Accommodation Consortium [*British*] (DBA)
HEA Coating... High Efficiency Antireflection Coating (SAUS)
HEAD .... Hand-Held Encryption and Authentication Device (RDA)
Head .... Head's Tennessee Supreme Court Reports [*1858-59*] [*A publication*] (DLA)
HEAD .... Health Emergency and Dispensary, Inc. (SAUO)
HEAD .... Helium-Atom Diffraction (PDAA)
HEAD .... High Efficiency Amplifier embodying Dohertz principles (SAUS)
HEAD .... Higher Education Affairs Directorate
HEAD .... High Explosive, Air Defence (SAUS)
HEADCOM.... Headquarters Command [*Military*]
HEADE .... High Erucic Acid Development Effort
Head Neck... Head and Neck (SAUS)
HEADS .... Hanford Emergency Alarm Dispatch System (SAUS)
HEADS .... Hughes Enhanced Anti Jam Data Link (ACAE)
HEADSS........ Helicopter Escort, Air Defense Suppression System
HEADS-UP ... Health Care Delivery Simulator for Urban Population (SAUO)
Head (Tenn)... Head's Tennessee Reports [*38-40 Tennessee*] [*A publication*] (DLA)
Headway...... Headway Corporate Resources, Inc. [*Associated Press*] (SAG)
HEAE .... Hyperacute Experimental Autoimmune Encephalomyelitis [*Medicine*] (PDAA)
HEAF............ Heavy End Aviation Fuel
HEAF............ High Energy Aircraft Fuel (SAUS)
HEAF............ High-Energy Air Filter (SAUS)
HEAF............ Higher Education Assistance Foundation
HEAF............ High Explosives Application Facility
HEAF............ Human Error Analysis Record (SAUS)
HEAFS .... High-Explosive Anti-Tank Fin-Stabilized [*Military*] (PDAA)

HEAI............ Historical Equipment Association [*Federal Railroad Administration identification code*]
HEAL............ Hanford Education Action League (SAUS)
HEAL............ Health Economics Analysis Letters (SAUO)
HEAL............ Health Education and Adult Literacy
HEAL............ Health Education Assistance Loan [*Bureau of Health Professions*]
HEAL............ Healthwatch, Inc. [*NASDAQ symbol*] (NQ)
HEAL............ Home Environment Aid for Living (SAUS)
HEAL............ Human Ecology Action League (EA)
HEAL............ Human Exposure Assessment Location [*Environmental Protection Agency*] (GFGA)
HEALD........ Healthwatch Inc. [*NASDAQ symbol*] (TTSB)
Heal JS Comp... Healy on Joint Stock Companies [*A publication*] (DLA)
HEALNet...... Health Evidence Application and Linkage Network (SAUO)
Heal Pews... Heale's Law of Church Pews [*A publication*] (DLA)
HEALS......... Honeywell Error Analysis and Logging System
HealSB........ Health Standards Board
HEALT.......... Helicopter Employment and Assault Landing Table (NVT)
HEALTH....... Happiness, Energy, and Longevity through Health [*Title of 1979 film directed by Robert Altman*]
Health & SC... Health and Safety Code [*A publication*] (DLA)
HEALTHBENCH... Health Information and Decision Support Workbench (SAUO)
Healthcare... Healthcare Marketing Report (journ.) (SAUS)
Health Care Manage Rev... Health Care Management Review (journ.) (SAUS)
Healthc Comput Commun... Healthcare Computing and Communications (journ.) (SAUS)
Health Econ... Health Economics [*A publication*] (JLIT)
Health Educ Q... Health Education Quarterly (journ.) (SAUS)
Health Educ Q Suppl... Health Education Quarterly. Supplement (journ.) (SAUS)
Health Environ Dig... Health & Environment Digest [*A publication*] (PABS)
Health LabSci... Health Laboratory Science (SAUO)
Health Lab Sci... Health Laboratory Science (journ.) (SAUS)
HEALTHLINE... Health Planning and Administration [*National Library of Medicine*] [*Database*]
Health Manage Q... Health Management Quarterly (journ.) (SAUS)
Health Marketing Quart... Health Marketing Quarterly [*A publication*] (JLIT)
Health Phys... Health Physics (SAUO)
Health Phys... Health Physics (journ.) (SAUS)
Health Psychol... Health Psychology (journ.) (SAUS)
Health Safety Work... Health and Safety at Work (journ.) (SAUS)
Health Saf Ind Commer... Health and Safety in Industry and Commerce (journ.) (SAUS)
Health Services Res... Health Services Research [*A publication*] (JLIT)
HealthSTAR... Health Services, Technology, Administration, and Research (ADWA)
HEAMF......... Hydroxyethylated Acid Modified Flour (OA)
HE Ammunition... High Explosive Ammunition (SAUS)
HE&W.......... Health, Environment & Work (SAUO)
HEANET....... Higher Education Authority Network [*Irish*] [*Computer science*] (TNIG)
HEAO........... High Energy Astronomical Observatory (SAUS)
HEAO........... High-Energy Astronomy Observatory [*Pronounced "hee-oh"*] [*NASA*]
HEAO........... High Energy Astrophysical Observatory (SAUS)
HEAO 1........ High Energy Astronomy Observatory 1 (SAUO)
HEAP........... Helicopter Extended Area Platform
HEAP........... High Energy Aim Point (SAUS)
HEAP........... High-Energy Aim Point [*Weaponry*] (MCD)
HEAP........... High Explosive Anti-Personnel (SAUS)
HEAP........... High-Explosive Armor-Piercing [*Weaponry*]
HEAP........... Home Energy Assistance Program (SAUS)
HEAP........... Hydrogen Electric Arc Pyrolysis (EDCT)
HE-APERS-FRAG... High Explosive, Anti-Personnel, Fragmentation (SAUS)
HEAP Rocket... High Explosive Anti-Personal Rocket (SAUS)
HEAPS......... Hawaiian Environmental Analysis and Prediction System (MUGU)
HEAPS......... Health Education and Promotion System (ADWA)
HEAPS......... High Energy Alpha-Proton Spectrometer (PDAA)
HEAP-T........ High Explosive, Anti-Personnel, Tracer (SAUS)
HEAR........... El Arish/El Arish [*Egypt*] [*ICAO location identifier*] (ICLI)
HEAR........... Health Associated Representatives [*Later, HIRA*] (EA)
HEAR........... Hear Center (EA)
HEAR........... Hearing
HEAR........... Hearing Education and Awareness for Rockers [*An association*]
HEAR........... Hearing Education through Auditory Research [*In association name, HEAR Center*] (EA)
HEAR........... Hereafter (ROG)
HEAR........... High Erucic Acid Rapeseed [*Agricultural chemistry*]
HEAR........... High Explosive Anti-Armor (SAUS)
HEAR........... Hospital Emergency Administrative Radio (SAUS)
HEAR........... Hospital Emergency Ambulance Radio (LAIN)
HEAR........... Hospital Emergency Area Radio (SAUS)
HEAR........... Human Error Action Report [*NASA*] (KSC)
Heard Civ Pl... Heard's Civil Pleading [*A publication*] (DLA)
Heard Cr Pl... Heard's Criminal Pleading [*A publication*] (DLA)
Heard Cur Rep... Heard's Curiosities of the Law Reporters [*A publication*] (DLA)
Heard Eq Pl... Heard's Equity Pleading [*A publication*] (DLA)
Heard Lib & Sl... Heard on Libel and Slander [*A publication*] (DLA)
Heard's Shortt Extr Rem... Heard's Edition of Shortt on Extraordinary Legal Remedies [*A publication*] (DLA)
Hear Exam... Hearing Examiner [*Legal term*] (DLA)
HEAR-FOUND... Hearing, Educational Aid and Research Foundation [*Defunct*] (EA)
HEARN......... Hearne, TX [*American Association of Railroads railroad junction routing code*]
Hearnshaw... Southampton Court Leet Records [*A publication*] (DLA)
Hear Res..... Hearing Research (journ.) (SAUS)
HEARS......... Higher Education Administration Referral Service [*Defunct*] (EA)
HEART......... Hardened Electronic and Radiation Technology
HEART......... Health Equity and Access Reform Today [*Plan*]
HEART......... Health Evaluation and Risk Tabulation (MCD)
HEART......... Higher Education Action Research Team (AIE)
HEART......... Horizontal European Activities in Rehabilitation Technology (SAUO)
HEART......... Household Employment Association for Reevaluation and Training [*Later, Personnel Resources*]
HEART......... Hughes Employees' Association Running and Track Club (ACAE)
HEART......... Human Engineering Analysis and Requirements Tool (SAUS)
HEART......... Hydrometer Erosion and Recession Test (MCD)
HEARTHFIRE... High-Energy Accelerator Reactor for Thermonuclear Fusion with Ion Beam of Relativistic Energy (GOBB)
HeartInd...... Heartland Partners Ltd. [*Associated Press*] (SAG)
Heart Lung... Heart and Lung. Journal of Critical Care (journ.) (SAUS)
Heartprt....... Heartport, Inc. [*Associated Press*] (SAG)
Heartsong R... Heartsong Review [*A publication*] (BRI)
Heartst......... Heartstream, Inc. [*Associated Press*] (SAG)
HEART System... Hawaii Environmental Area Rapid Transport System (SAUS)
HeartTc........ Heart Technology, Inc. [*Associated Press*] (SAG)
Heart Vessels... Heart and Vessels (journ.) (SAUS)
Heart Vessels Suppl... Heart and Vessels. Supplement (journ.) (SAUS)
HEARU......... Higher Education Advisory and Research Unit (SAUS)
Hearx........... Hearx Ltd. [*Associated Press*] (SAG)
HEAS........... Health Effects Assessment (AUEG)
HEAS........... Home Energy Advisory Service [*Victoria, Australia*]
HEASARC..... High Energy Astrophysics Science Archive Research Center (SAUO)
HEASDA....... Home Economics Association of Seventh-Day Adventists (EA)
HEAST......... Health Effects Assessment Summary Tables
HEAT............ Asyut [*Egypt*] [*ICAO location identifier*] (ICLI)
HEAT............ Heater (SAUS)
HEAT............ Heat Escape Lessening Posture (SAUS)
HEAT............ Heating (SAUS)
HEAT............ Helicopter External Air Transport (MCD)
HEAT............ Helpdesk Expert Automation Tool [*Bendata Management Systems, Inc.*]
HEAT............ Help Eliminate Auto Thefts (GOBB)
HEAT............ High Energy Antimatter Telescope
HEAT............ High-Enthalpy Ablation Test
HEAT............ High Enthalpy Arc Tunnel [*NASA*]
HEAT............ High-Explosive, Antitank [*Weaponry*]
HEAT............ Highly Expendable Aerial Target (SAUS)
HEAT............ Hostile Expendable Aerial Target (SAUS)
HEAT............ Human Equality Action Team (SAUO)
HEAT............ Human Erythrocyte Agglutination Test [*Hematology*]
HEAT............ Hydroxyphenyl Ethyl Aminoethyl Tetralone (SAUS)
HEAT............ Petroleum Heat & Pwr'A' [*NASDAQ symbol*] (TTSB)
Heat Air Cond J... Heating and Air Conditioning Journal (journ.) (SAUS)
Heat/Combust Equip News... Heating/Combustion Equipment News (journ.) (SAUS)
HEAT-FS....... High Explosive Anti-Tank Fin Stabilised (SAUS)
HEATFS-T.... High Explosive Anti-Tank Fire-Stabilized-Tracer (SAUS)
HEATH......... Heath, OH [*American Association of Railroads railroad junction routing code*]
Heath........... Heath's Reports [*36-40 Maine*] [*A publication*] (DLA)
HEATH......... Heavy Water Deuterium Oxide (SAUS)
HEATH......... Higher Education and the Handicapped [*An association*] (EA)
Heath Max... Heath's Maxims [*A publication*] (DLA)
HEAT-MP..... High Explosive, Anti-Tank, Multi-Purpose (SAUS)
HEAT-MP-T... High Explosive Anti-Tank, Multi-Purpose, Tracer (SAUS)
HEAT Projectile... High Explosive Anti-Tank Projectile (SAUS)
Heat Recovery Syst CHP... Heat Recovery Systems and CHP (journ.) (SAUS)
HEAT Shell... High Explosive Anti-Tank Shell (SAUS)
HEAT-T........ High Explosive, Anti-Tank, Tracer (SAUS)
Heat Technol... Heat and Technology (journ.) (SAUS)
Heat Technol... Heat Technology (journ.) (SAUS)
HEAT-T-HVY... High Explosive, Anti-Tank, Tracer, Heavy (SAUS)
HEAT-T-MP... High Explosive, Anti-Tank, Tracer, Multi-Purpose (SAUS)
HEAT-TP...... High-Explosive Antitank, Training Projectile [*Weaponry*] (MCD)
HEAT-TP-T... High Explosive, Anti-Tank, Target Practice, Tracer (SAUS)
Heat Transf Eng... Heat Transfer Engineering (journ.) (SAUS)
Heat Transf Jpn Res... Heat Transfer. Japanese Research (journ.) (SAUS)
Heat Transf Sov Res... Heat Transfer-Soviet Research (journ.) (SAUS)
Heat Treat... Heat Treating (journ.) (SAUS)
Heaven B..... Heaven Bone
HEAVN......... Heavener, OK [*American Association of Railroads railroad junction routing code*]
HEAVY GOLD... War Consumables Computation (SAUS)
HEAVYPHOTORON... Heavy Photographic Squadron
Heavy Veh Syst... Heavy Vehicle Systems [*A publication*] (CABS)
HEAX........... Alexandria [*Egypt*] [*ICAO location identifier*] (ICLI)
Heb............. Epistle of Paul the Apostle to the Hebrews (SAUS)
HEB............. Handheld Electronic Book (TELE)
HEB............. Hanford Environmental Baseline (SAUS)
HEB............. Hebraic [*Language, etc.*] (ROG)
heb.............. Hebrew [*MARC language code*] [*Library of Congress*] (LCCP)
HEB............. Hebrew
Heb............. Hebrews [*New Testament book*]
HEB............. Heinemann Educational Books [*London, England*]
HEB............. Hematoencephalitic Barrier (SAUS)
HEB............. Hemispherx BioPharma [*AMEX symbol*] (SG)
HEB............. Hepar Embryonis Bovis [*Embryonic bovine liver cells used in tissue culture studies of viruses*] [*Medicine*]
HEB............. High Efficiency Binding (SAUS)
HEB............. High Energy Beam (ACAE)
HEB............. Hollow Electron Beam
HEBA........... Home Extension Building Association (BUAC)
HEBAH......... Heat Engine/Battery Hybrid (PDAA)

HEBBLE........ High-Energy Benthic Boundary Layer Experiment [*Oceanography*]
HEBC.......... Heavy Enamel Bonded Cotton [*Wire insulation*]
HEBD.......... Hebdomada [*A Week*] [*Pharmacy*] (ROG)
hebd.......... hebdomadal (SAUS)
HEBDC......... Heavy Enamel Bonded Double Cotton [*Wire insulation*] (AAG)
HebdC......... Hebdomadal Council (SAUO)
hebdo......... hebdomadaries (SAUS)
hebdo......... hebdomadary (SAUS)
hebdom........ Hebdomada [*First Week of Life*] [*Latin*] (STED)
HEBDOM........ Hebdomada [*A Week*] [*Pharmacy*]
hebdomag...... hebdomadal magazine (SAUS)
HEBDP......... Heavy Enamel Bonded Double Paper [*Wire insulation*] (AAG)
HEBDS......... Heavy Enamel Bonded Double Silk [*Wire insulation*] (AAG)
HEBE.......... Higher Education Business Enterprises Ltd. (AIE)
HEBF.......... High Explosive Blast Fragmentation (SAUS)
HEBL.......... Abu Simbel [*Egypt*] [*ICAO location identifier*] (ICLI)
HEBO.......... Heavy Enamel single Paper Bonded (SAUS)
HEBP.......... Heavy Enamel Bonded Paper [*Wire insulation*]
Hebr.......... Hebraic (BJA)
Hebr.......... Hebrew (ADWA)
HEBR.......... Hebrew
Hebrew C...... Hebrew College (GAGS)
HebrUCA....... Hebrew Union College Annual (SAUO)
HEBS.......... Health Education Board for Scotland (BUAC)
HEBS.......... Heavy Enamel Bonded Silk [*Wire insulation*]
HEBS.......... High-Energy Battery System
HEBT.......... High-Energy Beam Transport [*For protons*]
HEC........... Ecole des Hautes Etudes Commerciales, Bibliotheque [*UTLAS symbol*]
HEC........... Hamster Embryonic Cell
HEC........... Hardened Electronic Component
HEC........... Harken Energy Co. [*AMEX symbol*] (SPSG)
HEC........... Hartford Engineers Club (SAUS)
HEC........... Hasselblad Electric Camera
HEC........... Hastings Environment Council (EERA)
HEC........... Hautes Etudes Commerciales (DD)
HEC........... Hawaii Electric Company (SAUO)
HEC........... Hazeltime Electronics Corp. (SAUS)
HEC........... Header Error Check (MLOA)
HEC........... Header Error Checksum (RALS)
HEC........... Header Error Control [*Telecommunications*] (ACRL)
HEC........... Health Education Council [*British*] (DAVI)
HEC........... Health Evaluation Center (DAVI)
HEC........... Heard European Countries (SAUO)
HEC........... Heavy Enamel Single Cellophane [*Wire insulation*] (IAA)
HEC........... Heavy Enamel Single Cotton [*Wire insulation*] (AAG)
HEC........... Heavy Engineering Corp. (SAUS)
Hec........... Hecate [*A publication*]
HEC........... Hector, CA [*Location identifier*] [*FAA*] (FAAL)
HEC........... Hector Resources, Inc. [*Vancouver Stock Exchange symbol*]
Hec........... Hecuba [*of Euripides*] [*Classical studies*] (OCD)
HEC........... Helicopter Element Coordinator [*Navy*] (ANA)
HEC........... Heliservicio Campeche SA de CV [*Mexico*] [*ICAO designator*] (FAAC)
HEC........... Hella Electronics Corp. [*Automotive industry supplier*]
HEC........... Hepatoma Cells [*Oncology*]
HEC........... High Emission Cathode
HEC........... High Endurance Cutter (SAUS)
HEC........... High-Energy Chemistry
HEC........... High Energy Corona (ABAC)
HEC........... Higher Education (ECON)
HEC........... Higher Education Corporanon (SAUS)
HEC........... Hodgin's Election Cases [*Ontario*] [*A publication*] (DLA)
HEC........... Hoffman Electronics Corp. (SAUS)
HEC........... Hollerith Electronic Computer
HEC........... Home Equity Conversion
HEC........... Hooker Electrochemical Company (SAUO)
HEC........... Horowitz-Eastman-Crane Method (SAUS)
HEC........... Human Economy Center (EA)
HEC........... Human Endometrial Cancer [*Oncology*]
HEC........... Human Endothelial Cell [*Cytology*]
HEC........... Human Enteric Coronavirus
HEC........... Human Environment Center (EA)
HEC........... Human Epithelial Cell [*Cytology*]
HEC........... Human Equivalent Concentration (EEVL)
HEC........... Hybrid Electronic Center [*Automotive electronics*]
HEC........... Hydro-Electric Commission, Tasmania (SAUS)
HEC........... Hydrogen Embrittlement Cracking (PDAA)
HEC........... Hydrologic Engineering Center [*Davis, CA*] [*Army*] (GRD)
HEC........... Hydroxyergocalciferol [*Organic chemistry*] (MAE)
HEC........... (Hydroxyethyl)cellulose [*Organic chemistry*]
HEC........... Hydroxyethyl Cellulose (SAUS)
HEC........... Hydroxyethylcysteine [*Organic chemistry*]
HEC........... United States Department of Health and Human Services, Health Care Financial Administration, Baltimore, MD [*OCLC symbol*] (OCLC)
HECA.......... Cairo/International [*Egypt*] [*ICAO location identifier*] (ICLI)
HECA.......... Harpoon Environmental Correction Aid [*Navy*] (ANA)
HECA.......... High Efficiency Charcoal Adsorber (SAUS)
HECA.......... Higher Education Consultants Association (SAUO)
HECA.......... Hyperbaric Environmental Control Assembly (SAUO)
HECAD......... Human Engineering Computer-Aided Design [*Air Force*]
HECATE........ Heat Exchanger Computerized Aid for Technical Engineering (IAA)
HECB.......... Higher Education Coordinating Board
HECB.......... Highways Engineering Computing Branch (SAUO)
HECC.......... Cairo [*Egypt*] [*ICAO location identifier*] (ICLI)
HECC.......... Higher Education Coordinating Council of Metropolitan St. Louis [*Library network*]
HECC.......... Hooker Electro-Chemical Co.
HECC.......... House Energy and Commerce Committee (GFGA)
HECD.......... Hall Electrolytic Conductivity Detector [*Analytical instrumentation*]
HECD.......... Helium Cadmium [*LASER*] (DGA)
HeCd.......... Helium-Cadmium (SAUS)
HEC-EA........ Hanford Environmental Compliance-Environmental Assessment (SAUS)
HECG.......... Higher Education Centre Germany (SAUO)
HECGUP........ Hybrid Electric Vehicle Ground-Up Competition
HECH.......... Hechinger Co. [*NASDAQ symbol*] (NQ)
HECHA......... Hechinger Co. Cl'A' [*NASDAQ symbol*] (TTSB)
HECHB......... Hechinger Co. Cl'B' Cv [*NASDAQ symbol*] (TTSB)
HECI.......... Hawkins Energy [*NASDAQ symbol*] (TTSB)
HECI.......... Hawkins Energy Corp. [*NASDAQ symbol*] (SAG)
HECI.......... Human-Interface Equipment Catalog Item (TEL)
heck.......... Heckelphone
Heck Cas...... Hecker's Cases on Warranty [*A publication*] (DLA)
HECKS......... Helicopter Close and Kill System [*Military*] (ACAE)
HeclaM........ Hecla Mining Co. [*Associated Press*] (SAG)
HECLI......... Hanford Environmental Compliance Line Item (SAUS)
HECLINET...... Health Care Literature Information Network [*Institut fuer Krankenhausbau*] [*Germany*] [*Information service or system*] (IID)
HeclM......... Hecla Mining Co. [*Associated Press*] (SAG)
HE CLS B...... Heating Coils in Bunker (SAUS)
HE Cls B...... Heating Coils in Bunkers [*on a ship*] (DS)
HE Cls C...... Heating Coils in Cargo Tanks [*on a ship*] (DS)
HE CLS CT...... Heating Coils in Cargo Tanks (SAUS)
HECM.......... Home Equity Conversion Mortgage [*Federal Housing Authority*]
HECM.......... Hughes Electronic Counter Measures (ACAE)
HECMAR........ Human Engineering Criteria for Maintenance and Repair [*GE, NASA*]
HECO.......... Hawaiian Electric Co. (SAUS)
HECO.......... Hawaiian Electric Company (SAUO)
HECO.......... Heckethorn Manufacturing & Supply Company (SAUO)
HECO.......... Heckethorn Manufacturing Co. (SAUS)
HECO.......... Hydro-Electric Commission of Ontario (SAUO)
HE COMP....... Helium Compressor (SAUS)
HECP.......... Hanford Environmental Compliance Plan (SAUS)
HECP.......... Harbor Entrance Control Post [*Nautical charts*]
HECP.......... Herbaceous Energy Crops Program (SAUO)
HECPOST....... Harbor Entrance Control Post (SAUO)
HECR.......... Hanford Environmental Compliance Report (SAUS)
HECR.......... High Explosive Continuous Rod (SAUS)
HECRE......... High-Energy Cosmic Ray Experiment [*Balloon flight*] [*NASA*]
HECSA......... Humphreys Engineering Center Support Activity (AAGC)
HECSAGON...... Horowitz-Eastman-Crane Symbol Array Governed by Orthodox Notation (NITA)
HECSE......... Higher Education Consortium on Special Education (EDAC)
HECSU......... Higher Education Careers Service Unit (AIE)
HECT.......... Head Equivalent Computed Tomography (DB)
HECT.......... Hectare (WDAA)
HECT.......... Hydro-Electricity Commission of Tasmania (SAUO)
HectCm........ Hector Communications Corp. [*Associated Press*] (SAG)
HECTO......... Hectograph
HECTOG........ Hectogram
HECTOL........ Hectoliter
HECTOM........ Hectometer [*100 meters*]
hectom........ hectometre (SAUS)
HECTOR........ Heated Experimental Carbon Thermal Oscillator Reactor [*British*]
HECTOR........ Heterogeneous Computer Together (SAUS)
HECTOR........ Hot Enriched Carbon-moderated Thermal Oscillator Reactor (SAUO)
HECTR......... Hydrogen Event-Containment Transient Response (SAUS)
HECUA......... Higher Education Consortium for Urban Affairs (EA)
HECV.......... Heavy Enamel Cotton Varnish [*Wire insulation*]
HECV.......... Helium Check Valve (MCD)
HECV.......... Human Enteric Coronavirus
HECVES........ Harbor Entrance Control Vessel
He-cy......... Hepatocyte (SAUS)
HED........... Hall Effect Device
HED........... Haut-Einheits-Dosis [*Unit Skin Dose*] [*Radiation therapy*]
HED........... Haut-Erythem-Dosis [*Skin erythema dose*] [*Radiation therapy*] (DAVI)
HED........... Hazard Evaluation Division [*Environmental Protection Agency*]
HED........... Hazeltime Electronics Division (SAUO)
HED........... Headline [*Advertising*] (DOAD)
hed........... Headline (WDMC)
HED........... Head, N.V. [*NYSE symbol*]
HED........... Headquarters (CINC)
HED........... Hedley Pacific Mining [*Vancouver Stock Exchange symbol*]
HeD........... Helper Determinant (STED)
HED........... Herendeen Bay, AK [*Location identifier*] [*FAA*] (FAAL)
HED........... Hidrotic Ectodermal Dysplasia [*Dermatology*]
HED........... High-Energy Detector [*NASA*]
HED........... Higher Education Diploma (SAUO)
HED........... High-Explosive Delay [*Weaponry*] (MCD)
HED........... Historical Earthquake Data (NRCH)
HED........... Historical English Dictionary [*A publication*]
HED........... Horizontal Electrical Dipole (IEEE)
HED........... Hot Electron Diode (SAUS)
HED........... Howardite, Eucrite, Diogenite [*Meteorite composition*]
HED........... Human Engineering Data
HED........... Human Engineering Deficiency [*Medicine*] (GOBB)
HED........... Human Engineering Discrepancy [*Nuclear energy*] (NRCH)

HED .... Hydraulically Extendable Dipperstick [*for tractors*]
HED .... Hydrotropic Electron-Donor [*Medicine*] (DMAA)
HED .... Hymnal-Epic Dialect (BJA)
HED .... Hypohidrotic Ectodermal Dysplasia [*Medicine*]
HEDA .... High Explosive Delayed Action (SAUS)
HEDAD .... Human Engineering Design Approach Document (ACAE)
HEDAD-O .... Human Engineering Design Approach Document-Operator (SAUO)
HEDB .... High Energy Density Battery (ACAE)
HEDC .... Hasselblad Electric Data Camera
HEDC .... Heavy Enamel Double Cotton [*Wire insulation*]
HEDC .... High Explosive Depth Charge (SAUS)
HEDC .... Houston Economic Development Council (SAUO)
HEDCC .... Human Error Data Control Center [*NASA*] (KSC)
HEDCO .... Hawaii Economic Development Corporation (SAUO)
HEDCO .... Higher Education for Development Cooperation [*Eire*] (BUAC)
HEDCOM .... Headquarters Command [*Military*]
HED Comdt .... Headquarters Commandant (SAUO)
HEDCV .... Heavy Enanmel Double Cotton Varnish (SAUS)
HEDDS .... Hawaii Educational Dissemination Diffusion System [*Hawaii State Department of Education*] [*Honolulu*] [*Information service or system*] (IID)
HEDF .... High Energy Density Facility [*Proposed site for testing nuclear bombs*]
HEDF .... High-Speed Electro-Drive Fan [*Automotive engineering*]
HEDF .... Hundred-percent Edited Detail File (SAUS)
HEDGE .... Human Factor Evaluation Data for General Equipment
HEDGE .... Human Factors Engineering Data Guide for Evaluation
Hedges .... Hedges' Reports [*2-6 Montana*] [*A publication*] (DLA)
HEDH .... Heat Exchanger Design Handbook (SAUO)
HEDH .... Hypohidrotic Ectodermal Dysplasia-Hypothyroidism [*Syndrome*] [*Medicine*] (DMAA)
HEDI .... High Endoatmospheric Defense Interceptor [*Military*] (RDA)
HEDING .... Hedingham [*England*]
HEDIS .... Health Plan Employer Data and Information Set
HEDL .... Hanford Engineering and Development Laboratory [*Richland, WA*] [*Department of Energy*]
HEDL .... Hanford Environmental Health Development Laboratory (SAUS)
HEDM .... High-Energy-Density Materials (SAUS)
HEDM .... High Energy Density Matter (ADWA)
HEDM .... High Explosive Dual Mode (SAUS)
HEDNA .... Hotel Electronic Distribution Network Association (TVEL)
HEDOP .... Hanford Environmental Dose Overview Panel (SAUS)
HEDP .... Hearing Ear Dog Program (EA)
HEDP .... High Explosive Double Purpose (SAUS)
HEDP .... High-Explosive Dual-Purpose [*Cartridge*] (RDA)
HEDP .... (Hydroxyethylidene)diphosphonic Acid [*Also, EHDP*] [*Organic chemistry*]
HE/DPSD .... High Explosive, Dual Purpose, Self-Destruction (SAUS)
HEDR .... Hanford Environmental Dose Reconstruction [*Radiobiology*]
HEDRON .... Headquarters Squadron [*Obsolete*]
HEDRONFAIRWING ... Headquarters Squadron Fleet Air Wing
HEDS .... Hall-Effect Distribution System (SAUS)
HEDS .... Hanford Environmental Data System (SAUS)
HEDS .... Heavy Enamel Double Silk [*Wire insulation*]
HEDS .... Herpetic Eye Disease Study
HEDS .... High Elliptical Orbiting Scientific (SAUS)
HEDS .... High Endoatmospheric Defense System
HEDS .... High Endo Designation Sensor (ACAE)
HEDS .... High Energy Dislocation Structure (SAUS)
HEDS .... Higher Education Data Sharing (EDAC)
HEDS .... High-Explosive, Discarding Sabot [*Weaponry*] (AAG)
HEDS .... Hydraulic End Design System [*Computer-aided design*]
HED SCHED ... Headline Schedule (SAUS)
HEDSET .... Harmonic Electronic Data Set (SAUS)
HEDSET .... Harmonised Electronic Data Set (HEAS)
HEDS Program ... High Elliptical Orbiting Scientific Program (SAUO)
HEDSUPPACT ... Headquarters Support Activity
HEDSV .... Heavy Enamel Double Silk Varnish [*Wire insulation*] (AAG)
HEDT .... Health Edutech, Inc. (SAUO)
HEDTA .... Hydroxyethylene Diaminetetraacetic Acid (SAUS)
HEDUSAFE ... Headquarters United States Air Force Europe (SAUS)
HEDUSAFE ... Headquarters, United States Air Force in Europe (SAUO)
HEE .... Heerlen [*Netherlands*] [*Seismograph station code, US Geological Survey*] (SEIS)
HEE .... Helena/West Helena, AR [*Location identifier*] [*FAA*] (FAAL)
HEE .... Heli Europe [*Belgium*] [*ICAO designator*] (FAAC)
HEE .... Hemiconvulsion, Hemiplegia, and Epilepsy Syndrome [*Neurology*] (DAVI)
HEE .... High Express Emotion (SAUS)
HEE .... Household Earnings and Expenditure
HEE .... Hydrogen Environment Embrittlement (SAUS)
HEEA .... Home Economics Education Association (EA)
HEEB .... High-Energy Electrolyte Battery
HEED .... Health and Education Department (SAUS)
HEED .... Health and Environmental Effects Document [*Environmental Protection Agency*] (AEPA)
HEED .... Health and Environmental Effects Documents [*Environment term*] (EGA)
HEED .... Helicopter Emergency Egress Device (SAUS)
HEED .... High-Energy Electron Diffraction
HEEDA .... Health and Environmental Effects Data Analysis (SAUS)
HEEDTA .... (Hydroxyethyl)ethylenediaminetetracetate [*or -tetracetic*] Acid [*Organic chemistry*]
HEEEL .... High-Energy Electronically Excited LASER
HEEI .... (Hydroxyethyl)ethyleneimine [*Organic chemistry*]
HEEM .... Embaba [*Egypt*] [*ICAO location identifier*] (ICLI)
HEEM .... Hardsite Engagement Effectiveness Model (PDAA)
HEENT .... Head, Ears, Eyes, Nose, Throat
HEEO .... High Electroendosmosis [*Analytical biochemistry*]
HEEP .... Health and Environmental Effects Documents [*Environment term*] (EGA)
HEEP .... Health and Environmental Effects Profile [*Environmental Protection Agency*] (AEPA)
HEEP .... Health Effects of Environmental Pollutants [*A publication*]
HEEP .... Health Effects of Environmental Pollution [*Database*] (NITA)
HEEP .... Highway Engineering Exchange Program (EA)
HEEP .... Highway Engineers Exchange Program (SAUS)
HE/ER .... High Effect Extended Range (SAUS)
HEER .... High Explosive Extended Ranage (SAUS)
HEERA .... Higher Education Employer-Employee Relations Act (SAUO)
HEERA .... Higher Education External Relations Association (AIE)
HEERFB .... High Explosive, Extended Range, Full Bore (SAUS)
HE/EXJAM ... Hand Emplaced Expendable Jammer (SAUO)
HEF .... Haemagglutintin-Esterase-Fusion [*Protein*]
HEF .... Hamster Embryo Fibroblast [*Medicine*] (DMAA)
HEF .... Health Education Foundation (EA)
HEF .... Hearth Electric Furnace
HEF .... Heat-Curing Epoxy Film
HEF .... Heated Effluents [*Cornell University*] [*Database*] (NITA)
HEF .... Heavy Element Facility [*Nuclear energy*] (NUCP)
hef .... heifer (SAUS)
HEF .... High Efficiency (ACAE)
HEF .... High Elevation Fire (SAUS)
HEF .... High-Elongation Furnace Black (SAUS)
HEF .... High Energy Forging (SAUS)
HEF .... High Energy Forming
HEF .... High-Energy Fuel [*Air Force*]
HEF .... High Energy Fuels Division (SAUO)
HEF .... High-Expansion Foam
HEF .... Hispana Esperanto-Federacio (SAUO)
HEF .... Hispanic Energy Forum [*Defunct*] (EA)
HEF .... Hospital Employees Federation (SAUS)
HEF .... Houston Environmental Foresight (SAUO)
HEF .... Human Ecology Fund (EA)
HEF .... Human Embryo Fibroblast [*A cell line*]
HEF .... Hydroxyethylflurazepam [*Sedative*]
HEF .... Manassas, VA [*Location identifier*] [*FAA*] (FAAL)
HEFA .... Higher Education Facilities Act of 1963
HEFA .... Higher Education Funding Act [*Australia*]
HEFA .... Highly Enriched Fuel Assembly (SAUS)
HEFA .... Hospital Employees' Federation of Australia (BUAC)
HEFA .... Human Embryo and Fertilisation Authority (BUAC)
HEFC .... Higher Education Facilities Commission
HEFC .... Higher Education Funding Council (WDAA)
HEFCAD .... High Energy Friction Characteristics and Durability [*Automotive transmissions*]
HEFCE .... Higher Education Funding Council for England
HEFCW .... Higher Education Funding Council for Wales (GVA)
HEFG .... Hall Effect Function Generator
HEFOE .... Hydraulic Electrical Fuel Oxygen Engine (COE)
HEFOE .... Hydraulic, Engine, Fuel, Oxygen, Electrical (DNAB)
HEFR .... Human Engineering Final Report (ACAE)
HEFRAG .... High-Explosive, Fragmentation [*Artillery*] (INF)
HE-FRAG-FS ... High Explosive, Fragmentation, Fin-Stabilised (SAUS)
HEFS .... Helicopter Emergency Flotation System (SAUS)
HE-FS .... High Explosive, Fin-Stabilised (SAUS)
HEFS-FRAG ... High Explosive Fin Stabilized-Fragmentation (SAUS)
HEFT .... Heavy-Element Fission Tracer
HEFT .... High Explosive, Follow Through (SAUS)
Heftel .... Heftel Broadcasting Corp. [*Associated Press*] (SAG)
HEFTH .... Henceforth (ROG)
HEFU .... High-Energy Firing Unit [*Army*] (AABC)
HEG .... Haftentschaedigunsgesetz [*A publication*] (BJA)
HEG .... Hall Effect Generator
HEG .... Heavy Enamel Glass (SAUS)
HEG .... Helium Gauge (MCD)
HEG .... Hemgold Resources Ltd. [*Vancouver Stock Exchange symbol*]
HEG .... Hemorrhagic Erosive Gastritis [*Gastroenterology*] (DAVI)
HEG .... Hexaethylene Glycol [*Organic chemistry*]
HEG .... Histioeosinophilic Granuloma [*Medicine*]
HEG .... Homogeneous Exposure Group [*Concept for acessing cancer risk*]
HEG .... Jacksonville, FL [*Location identifier*] [*FAA*] (FAAL)
HEGA .... High Efficiency Gas Absorber (SAUS)
HEGEL .... Hegeler, IL [*American Association of Railroads railroad junction routing code*]
HEGF .... High-Energy Gas Fracturing [*For freeing natural gas from rock*]
HEGF .... Human Epidermal Growth Factor [*Biochemistry*]
HEG-FIO .... Human Engineering Laboratory Field Office (SAUS)
HEGIS .... Higher Education General Information Survey [*Office of Education*]
HEGIS .... Higher Education General Information System (SAUS)
HEGL .... High Energy Gas Laser (SAUS)
HEGN .... Hurghada [*Egypt*] [*ICAO location identifier*] (ICLI)
HEGO .... Heated Exhaust Gas Oxygen [*Automotive engineering*]
HEGOG .... Heated Exhaust Gas Oxygen Ground [*Automotive engineering*]
HEGP .... Gases and Particles (SAUS)
HEGR .... El-Gora [*Egypt*] [*ICAO location identifier*] (ICLI)
HEGR .... High-Energy Gamma Ray
HEGRA .... High-Energy Gamma Ray Array [*Canary Islands*]
HEGRA .... High Energy Gamma Ray Astronomy
HEGS .... Helicopter External Gondola System

HEGV .... Helium Gauge Valve (MCD)
HEH .... Heho [*Myanmar*] [*Airport symbol*] (OAG)
HEH .... High Explosive, Heavy (SAUS)
HEH .... His [*or Her*] Exalted Highness [*Term applied only to personages of British India*]
HEH .... (Hydroxyethyl)hydrazine [*Organic chemistry*]
HEH .... Hyperkinetic Heart (SAUS)
HEH .... Newark, OH [*Location identifier*] [*FAA*] (FAAL)
HEHB .... High Enrichment-High Burnup (SAUS)
HEHC .... Hydroxyethylhomocysteine [*Organic chemistry*]
HEHF .... Hanford Environmental Health Foundation [*Nuclear energy*]
HEHL .... Henry E. Huntington Library (SAUO)
HEHO .... Head End Hop Off (SAUS)
HEHO .... Herbert Hoover National Historic Site
HEHO .... High End Hop Off (SAUS)
HEHP .... Hazardous Pollutants Research (SAUO)
HEHP .... Heavy Equipment Handling Package
HEHR .... Highest Equivalent Heart Rate [*Cardiology*] (DAVI)
HEHS .... Health, Education, and Human Services Division [*GAO*] (AAGC)
HEI .... Hall-Effect Imaging [*Medical imaging*]
HEI .... Halographic Exposure Index (SAUS)
HEI .... Hangar Engineering Item
HEI .... Health and Energy Institute (EA)
HEI .... Health Effects Institute [*Research center*] (RCD)
HEI .... Heat Exchange Institute (EA)
HEI .... Heico Corp. [*AMEX symbol*] (SPSG)
HEI .... Heidelberg [*Konigstuhl*] [*Federal Republic of Germany*] [*Seismograph station code, US Geological Survey*] (SEIS)
HEI .... Heidelberg College, Tiffin, OH [*OCLC symbol*] (OCLC)
HEI .... Held for Engineering Investigation (SAUS)
HEI .... Hettinger, ND [*Location identifier*] [*FAA*] (FAAL)
HEI .... HIF Eimiskipafelag Islands (SAUS)
HEI .... High-Energy Ignition (KSC)
HEI .... High-Energy Intermediate [*Medicine*] (DAVI)
HEI .... Higher Education Institute [*Australia*]
HEI .... Higher Education Institution
HEI .... Higher Education International (BUAC)
HEI .... High-Explosive, Incendiary [*Weaponry*]
HEI .... Holographic Exposure Index (PDAA)
HEI .... Homogeneous Enzyme Immunoassy [*Biochemistry*] (DAVI)
HEI .... Hospice Education Institute (EA)
HEI .... Hotel Enterprises Inc. (SAUS)
HEI .... Hourly Earnings Index (OICC)
HEI .... House Ear Institute (EA)
HEI .... Human Embryonic Intestine Cells [*Medicine*] (DMAA)
HEI .... Human Engineering Institute
HEI .... Human Exploration Initiative (SAUS)
HEI .... Humidity-Electronic Indicator
HEI .... Humiliation Elimination Incorporation (SAUO)
HEIA .... High Explosive Immediate Action (SAUS)
HEIA .... Hydrogen Energy Industry Association (BUAC)
HEIAC .... Hydraulic Engineering Information Analysis Center [*Army Corps of Engineers*] (IID)
HEI-AR .... Health Effects Institute-Asbestos Research
HEIAS .... Human Engineering Information and Analysis Service [*Tufts University*]
HEIB .... Home Economists In Business (SAUS)
HEIBS .... High Energy Ion Bombardment Simulation Facility (SAUO)
HEIC .... Honourable East India Co. [*British*]
HE-ICM .... High Explosive - Improved Conventional Ammunition
HEICN .... Honourable East India Co. Navy [*British military*] (DMA)
Heico .... Heico Corp. [*Associated Press*] (SAG)
HEICS .... Honourable East India Company Service (SAUO)
HEID .... Heidemij NV [*NASDAQ symbol*] (SAG)
HEIDA .... (Hydroxyethyl)iminodiacetic Acid [*Organic chemistry*]
HEIDELB .... Heidelberg [*City in Germany*] (ROG)
Heidemj .... Heidemij NV [*Associated Press*] (SAG)
HEIDF .... Heidemij N.V. [*NASDAQ symbol*] (TTSB)
HEIDI .... Higher Education Data Base [*Information service or system*] (IID)
HEIE .... High-Energy Isotope Experiment (SSD)
HEIFE .... Heihe Basin Field Experiment
HEIFE .... Heihe River Field Experiment (SAUO)
HEIFER .... High Frequency Relay (NVT)
HEIGHT .... Heights [*Commonly used*] (OPSA)
HEIGHTS .... Heights [*Commonly used*] (OPSA)
HEII .... HEI, Inc. [*NASDAQ symbol*] (NQ)
Heilig .... Heilig-Meyers Co. [*Associated Press*] (SAG)
HEIM .... Heroin Economic Interdiction Model (ACAE)
HEI Mn .... HEI, Inc. [*Associated Press*] (SAG)
Hein .... William S. Hein and Co., Inc. [*Publisher*] (DLA)
HE inj .... Hyperextension Injury [*Orthopedics*] (DAVI)
HEINS .... Hannover Environmental Information System (SAUO)
HeinWr .... Hein-Werner Corp. [*Associated Press*] (SAG)
Heinz .... Heinz [*H.J.*] Co. [*Associated Press*] (SAG)
HEIP .... High Explosive Incendiary Plug (SAUS)
HEIR .... Health Effects of Ionizing Radiation [*Medicine*] (DAVI)
HEIR .... High-Energy Ionizing Radiation [*Radiation therapy*] (DAVI)
HE/IR .... High Explosive Infra-Red (SAUS)
Heir App .... Heir Apparent (SAUS)
Heir Pres .... Heir Presumptive (SAUS)
HEIRS .... Health Education Information Retrieval System (SAUS)
HEIS .... Hanford Environmental Information System (SAUS)
HEIS .... High-Energy Ion Scattering Spectroscopy
HEIS .... Higher Education Information Service (AIE)
HEIS .... Host/EMSP Interface Software (SAUS)
HEISAP .... High Explosive Incendiary Semi-Armour Piercing (SAUS)
HEISD .... High Explosive Incendiary Self-Destroying (SAUS)
Heisk .... Heiskell's Tennessee Supreme Court Reports [*1870-74*] [*A publication*] (DLA)
Heisk (Tenn) .... Heiskell's Tennessee Reports [*48-59 Tennessee*] [*A publication*] (DLA)
HEIST .... High-Energy Isotope Spectrometer Telescope (MCD)
HEIST .... Higher Education Information Services Trust (BUAC)
HeistC .... Heist [*C. H.*] Corp. [*Associated Press*] (SAG)
HEIT .... High-Explosive, Incendiary [*Shell*] Traced [*i.e., fitted with tracer*] [*Weaponry*]
HEIT .... High-Explosive Incendiary Tracing (SAUS)
HEITDISD .... High Explosive Incendiary Tracer Dark Ignition Self-Destroying (SAUS)
HEITSD .... High Explosive Incendiary Tracer Self-Destroying (SAUS)
HEITV .... Higher Education Instructional Television [*West Virginia*] (EDAC)
HEIX .... Home Economics Information Exchange (BUAC)
HEIZ .... Heinz [*Federal Railroad Administration identification code*]
HEK .... Heavy Enamel Single Cellophane [*Wire insulation*] (AAG)
HEK .... Hemingway, SC [*Location identifier*] [*FAA*] (FAAL)
HEK .... Heptachlor Epoxide Ketone (SAUS)
HEK .... Human Embryo Kinase [*Medicine*] (DMAA)
HEK .... Human Embryonic Kidney [*Type of cell line*]
HEKB .... El Nakab/El Nakab [*Egypt*] [*ICAO location identifier*] (ICLI)
HEKN .... Heekin Can, Inc. [*NASDAQ symbol*] (COMM)
HEL .... Handbooks of English Literature [*A publication*]
HEL .... Hardware Emulation [*Computer science*]
HEL .... Hardware Emulation Layer [*Computer science*]
HEL .... Hartford Electric Light Co. (SAUO)
HEL .... Hazard Evaluation Laboratory Limited [*Herts, England*]
HEL .... Header Extension Length [*Telecommunications*] (ACRL)
HEL .... Helena [*Diocesan abbreviation*] [*Montana*] (TOCD)
HEL .... Helicol Helicopteros Nacionales de Colombia [*ICAO designator*] (FAAC)
HEL .... Helicopter (AABC)
hel .... Helicopter (MILB)
Hel .... Heliodor [*Record label*] [*Great Britain*]
hel .... Heliotrope [*Philately*]
HEL .... Hellenic Resources [*Vancouver Stock Exchange symbol*]
Hel .... Hellenistic [*Period*]
HEL .... Helsingfors [*Helsinki*] [*Finland*] [*Seismograph station code, US Geological Survey*] (SEIS)
HEL .... Helsinki [*Finland*] [*Airport symbol*] (OAG)
HEL .... Helvetia [*Switzerland*] (ROG)
HEL .... Hen-Egg White Lysozyme [*Also, HEWL*] [*An enzyme*]
HEL .... High-Energy LASER
HEL .... High Explosive, Light (SAUS)
HEL .... History of English Law, Edited by W. Holdsworth [*A publication*] (DLA)
HEL .... Home-Equity Line (SAUS)
HEL .... Home Equity Loan
HEL .... Hugoniot Elastic Limit [*Thermodynamics*]
HEL .... Human Embryonic Lung [*Type of cell line*]
HEL .... Human Engineering Laboratories (or Laboratory) (SAUO)
HEL .... Human Engineering Laboratory [*Aberdeen Proving Ground, MD*] [*Army*]
HEL .... Human Erythroleukemia [*Type of cell line*]
HEL .... Hunting Engineering Ltd.
HEL .... Hydraulic Engineering Laboratory [*University of California at Berkeley*]
HeLa .... Helen Lake [*Tumour cells*] [*Medicine*] (BABM)
HeLa .... Henrietta Lacks [*Pseudonym, Helen Lake*] [*Line of tumor cells*]
HELAB .... High-Energy LASER Assessment Board (MCD)
HELAC .... Helix Linear Accelerator (PDAA)
HELAIRDET .... Helicopter Air Detachment [*Canadian Navy*]
HELANTISUBRON .... Helicopter Antisubmarine Squadron [*Navy*]
HELANTISUBRONDET .... Helicopter Antisubmarine Squadron Detachment [*Navy*] (DNAB)
HELAPS .... High Efficiency Linear Amplification by Parametic Synthesis (PDAA)
HELASRON .... Helicopter Antisubmarine Squadron [*Navy*]
HELAST .... Human Engineering Laboratory Armor Systems Test [*Army*] (RDA)
HELATKRON .... Helicopter Attack Squadron [*Navy*] (DNAB)
HELA Tumor Cell .... Helen Lake Tumor Cell (SAUS)
HELB .... High-Energy LASER Beam
HELB .... High-Energy Line Break [*Nuclear energy*] (NRCH)
HELBAT .... Human Engineering Laboratories Battalion Artillery Test [*Army*]
HELC .... Hastings English Language Centre (SAUO)
HELCAP .... Human Engineering Laboratory Counterair Program [*Army*] (RDA)
HELCAR .... Helicopter Collision Avoidance RADAR (NG)
HELCIS .... Helicopter Command Instrumentation System (MCD)
HELCM .... High-Energy LASER Countermeasures (MCD)
HELCO .... Hartford Electric Light Co.
HELCO .... Hilo Electric Co. (SAUS)
HELCOM .... Baltic Marine Environment Protection Commission - Helsinki Commission (EAIO)
HELCOM .... Helsinki Commission for the Protection of the Baltic Marine Environment (SAUS)
HELCOMBSUPPRON .... Helicopter Combat Support Squadron [*Navy*] (DNAB)
HELCOM/MORS .... Helsinki Commission/ Monitoring of Radioactive Substances in the Baltic Sea (SAUO)
HELCOS .... High-Energy LASER Component Servicing (MCD)
HELD .... Helicopter Laser Designator (SAUS)
HELDAF .... High Energy Laser Device and Facilities (ACAE)
HELDK .... Helicopter Deck (RIMS)
HELDREF .... Helen Dwight Reid Educational Foundation

HELE........... Helen of Troy Corp. [*NASDAQ symbol*] (NQ)
HELE........... Helen of Troy Ltd [*NASDAQ symbol*] (TTSB)
H Electrode... Head Electrode (SAUS)
HELEN......... Greek transliteration project (SAUS)
HELEN......... Helena, GA [*American Association of Railroads railroad junction routing code*]
HELEN......... Hydrogenous Exponential Liquid Experiment [*British*]
HeleneC....... Helene Curtis Industries, Inc. [*Associated Press*] (SAG)
HelenTr........ Helen of Troy Corp. [*Associated Press*] (SAG)
HELETS........ High Energy Laser Experimental Test System (ACAE)
HELEX.......... Helium Extraction
HELEX.......... High Energy Laser Experimental (SAUS)
HELEX.......... Hydrogenous Exponential Liquid Experiment (SAUS)
HELF............ Human Embryonic Lung Fibroblasts [*Biochemistry*]
HELFAST...... Human Engineering Laboratory Forward Ammo Supply and Transfer (SAUO)
HELFAST...... Human Engineering Laboratory Forward Area Supply and Transfer [*Army*] (RDA)
HEL-FI......... Human Engineering Laboratory Field Office [*Charlottesville, VA*] [*Military*]
HEL-FIO....... Human Engineering Laboratory Field Office [*Charlottesville, VA*] [*Military*]
HELHAT....... Human Engineering Laboratory Helicopter Armament Test [*Army*] (RDA)
HELI............ Helicopter (AFM)
HELI............ Heliport [*ICAO designator*] (FAAC)
HELI............ Helisys Inc. [*NASDAQ symbol*] (TTSB)
Helian.......... Helian Health Group, Inc. [*Associated Press*] (SAG)
HELICAR...... Helicopter Radar (ACAE)
Heli Intnl..... Helicopter International (journ.) (SAUS)
HELIK.......... Helicopter Killer (SAUS)
HELILEX....... Helicopter Landing Exercise [*Amphibious*] [*Navy*] (NVT)
helio............ heliochrome (SAUS)
helio............ heliodon (SAUS)
helio............ heliodor (SAUS)
helio............ helioelectric (SAUS)
helio............ helioengraving (SAUS)
Helio............ Heliogram (SAUS)
helio............ heliograph (SAUS)
helio............ heliogravure (SAUS)
helio............ heliology (SAUS)
helio............ heliostat (SAUS)
helio............ heliotherapy (SAUS)
helio............ heliotrope (SAUS)
helio............ heliotype (SAUS)
HELIOD........ Heliodorus [*Greek writer, c. 200AD*] (ROG)
Heliogab...... Heliogabalus [*of Scriptores Historiae Augustae*] [*Classical studies*] (OCD)
Heliont........ Helionetics, Inc. [*Associated Press*] (SAG)
HELIOPS...... Helicopter Operations Panel (SAUS)
HELIOS........ Handicapped People in Europe Living Independently in Open Society (BUAC)
HELIOS........ Helicopter Instrument & Operational Procedures Simulator (SAUS)
Helios.......... Helios - Joies de la Musique [*Record label*] [*France*]
HELIOS........ Heteropowered Earth-Launched Inter-Orbital Spacecraft (KSC)
HELIP........... HAWK [*Homing All the Way Killer*] European Limited Improvement Program [*NATO*]
HELIPAD...... Helicopter Landing Pad (SAUS)
HELIPATH.... Helicopter Position and Terrain Height
HELIST......... Human Engineering Laboratory Infantry System Test [*Army*] (RDA)
Helisys........ Helisys, Inc. [*Associated Press*] (SAG)
HELITEAM.... Helicopter Team
HELITECH.... International Helicopter Technology and Operations Conference and Exhibition [*British*] (ITD)
HELITOW..... Helicopter TOW (SAUS)
HELIVALS.... Helicopter In-flight Validation System (PDAA)
HELIX........... Harwell Electrochemical Ion Exchange Process [*British*] (NUCP)
HelixTch...... Helix Technologies [*Associated Press*] (SAG)
HELK............ High Energy Laser Kill (SAUS)
Hell.............. Hellenica [*of Xenophon*] [*Classical studies*] (OCD)
HELL............ Higher Education Learning Laboratory (EA)
HELLASLAB... Hellenic Association of Laboratories (SAUO)
Hell Dicht.... Hellenistische Dichtung in der Zeit des Kallimachos [*A publication*] (OCD)
Hellen.......... Hellenic [*Classical studies*] (BARN)
Hellen.......... Hellenism (SAUS)
Hellen.......... Hellenistic (SAUS)
HELLFIRE.... Heliborne LASER Fire and Forget [*Missile system*] [*Army*] (RDA)
HELLFIRE.... Helicopter-Launched Fire-and-Forget Missile (SAUS)
HELLFIRE/GLD... HELLFIRE [*Heliborne LASER Fire and Forget*]/Ground LASER Designator [*Army*] (RDA)
HELLFIRRE/GLD... Hellfire Ground Laser Designator (SAUS)
HELLIS......... Health, Literature, Library and Information Services [*Medicine*] (EDAA)
HELLO......... Helping Educators Link Learners Online
HelloD......... Hello Direct, Inc. [*Associated Press*] (SAG)
HELLOG....... Human Engineering Laboratory Logistics [*Systems concept study*] (MCD)
Hell Oxy...... Hellenica Oxyrhynchia [*Classical studies*] (OCD)
HELLP.......... Hemolysis, Elevated Liver Enzymes, and Low Platelet Count [*Clinical chemistry*]
HELM........... Health and Environment Library Modules (ADWA)
HELM........... Helmet Cells [*Cytology*] (DAVI)
Helm............ Helm's Reports [*2-9 Nevada*] [*A publication*] (DLA)
HELMAP...... high Energy Laser Mission Applications Project (ACAE)
HELMEPA.... Hellenic Marine Environmental Protection Association (EERA)
HELMEPA.... Hellenic Marine Environment Protection Association
HELMET....... High Energy Laser Metereological System (SAUS)
HELMID....... Helmet Mounted Infantry Display (ACAE)
HELMINERON... Helicopter Mine Countermeasures Squadron [*Military*] (MUSM)
HELMINERONDET... Helicopter Mine Countermeasures Squadron Detachment (SAUS)
helminthol... helminthology (SAUS)
HELMIS........ Helicopter Mission Model (SAUS)
HELMOT...... Helicopter Military Operations Technology (SAUS)
HelmP.......... Helmerich & Payne, Inc. [*Associated Press*] (SAG)
HelmRes...... Helm Resources, Inc. [*Associated Press*] (SAG)
HELMS......... Helicopter Lift Margin System (MCD)
HELMS......... Helicopter Malfunction System (SAUS)
HELMS......... Helicopter Multifunction System
Helmstr....... Helmstar Group [*Associated Press*] (SAG)
HELNAVS..... Helicopter Navigation System (RDA)
HELO........... Heavy Lift Operability (PDAA)
helo............ Helicopter (ADWA)
HELO........... Helicopter (NG)
HELO........... Heliport (SAUS)
HELO........... Hello Direct, Inc. [*NASDAQ symbol*] (SAG)
HELO........... High-Energy Liquid Oxidizer
HELO........... Hispanic Elected Local Officials (EA)
HELOA......... Higher Education Liaison Officers Association (BUAC)
HELOC......... Home Equity Line of Credit (EBF)
HELOLEX..... Helicopter Landing Exercise (SAUO)
HELOPS....... Helicopter Operations (DNAB)
HELOPSUPPFAC... Helicopter Operational Support Facility (DNAB)
HELOQUALS... Helicopter Qualifications [*Navy*] (NVT)
HELORADE... Helicopter Operations in Selected RADAR Environment (MCD)
HELORS....... Hellenic Operational Research Society [*Greece*] (BUAC)
HELOS......... Harwell Electro Osmosis Process [*British*] (NUCP)
HELOS......... Highly Eccentric Lunar Occultation Satellite
HELOSCAT... Helicopter Scatterometer (SAUS)
HELOSID..... Helicopter-Delivered Seismic Intrusion Detector (NVT)
HELOTING... Helicopter Training (SAUS)
HELOTNG.... Helicopter Training (NVT)
HELP........... Harlem Eastside Lifesaving Program [*Television program*]
HELP........... Harris Enhanced Language for Programmable Logic (NITA)
HELP........... Haulage Emergency Link Protection (SAUS)
HELP........... Hawaii Early Learning Profile [*Child development test*] [*Psychology*]
HELP........... HAWK [*Homing All-the-Way Killer*] Equipment Logistics Program [*Military*] (GFGA)
HELP........... Hazard Elimination is Loss Prevention (ACAE)
HELP........... Hazardous Emergency Leaks Procedure (SAUS)
HELP........... Header List Printing (SAUS)
HELP........... Health and Energy Learning Project (EA)
HELP........... Health, Education, Labor, and Pensions
HELP........... Health Education Library for People (ADWA)
HELP........... Health Education Library Program [*Library network*]
HELP........... Health Emergency Loan Program [*Planned parenthood*] (DAVI)
HELP........... Health Evaluation and Learning Program
HELP........... Health Evaluation through Logical Processing [*Computer science*] (DAVI)
HELP........... Heat Escape Lessening Posture [*First aid technique*]
HELP........... Heavy Vehicle Electronic License Plate
HELP........... Heckman Electronic Library Program (SAUO)
HELP........... Helicopter Electronic Landing Path [*Army*]
HELP........... Helicopter Emergency Life-Saving Program (SAUS)
HELP........... Helium Liquid Program [*NASA*]
HELP........... Help Elderly Locate Positions (SAUS)
HELP........... Help End Lead in Petrol [*An association*] (BUAC)
Help............ Helper Average (MIST)
HELP........... Help Establish Lasting Peace
HELP........... Help-Institute for Body Chemistry (EA)
HELP........... HELP, International [*Defunct*] (EA)
HELP........... Helpmate Robotics, Inc. [*NASDAQ symbol*] (SAG)
HELP........... Heroin Emergency Life Project
HELP........... Herpetics Engaged in Living Productively [*Later, Herpes Research Center*] (EA)
HELP........... Heuristic Etching-pattern Layout Program (SAUO)
HELP........... High Energy Landing Problem (SAUS)
HELP........... High Energy Laser Program (ACAE)
HELP........... High Energy Leadless Package (SAUS)
HELP........... High Energy-Level Pneumatic automobile bumpers (SAUS)
HELP........... High Energy Lightweight Propellant (SAUS)
HELP........... High-Energy Lightweight Propellant
HELP........... Highly Extendable Language Processor [*Computer science*]
HELP........... High School Education Law Project (SAUS)
HELP........... Highway Emergency Locating Plan
HELP........... Hitachi Effective Library for Programming (SAUO)
HELP........... Holiday Endeavour for Lone Patients [*An association*] (BUAC)
HELP........... Home Education Livelihood Program [*New Mexico*]
HELP........... Home Emergency Ladies' Pal [*Book title*]
HELP........... Home Energy Loan Program (SAUO)
HELP........... Home Environment and Living Program (SAUS)
HELP........... Home Equity Living Plan (SAUS)
HELP........... Homophile Effort for Legal Protection [*An association*] [*Defunct*] (EA)
HELP........... Honeywell Equipment Lease (or Leasing) Plan (SAUO)
HELP........... Honeywell Equipment Lease Plan
HELP........... Honeywell Equipment Leasing Plan (SAUO)
HELP........... Hospital Employees Labor Program [*Medicine*] (EDAA)
HELP........... Hospital Equipment Loan Project
HELP........... Housewives Elect Lower Prices [*New York women's lobby group*]

HELP.......... Howitzer Extended Life Program
HELP.......... How to Enjoy Living in this Place (SAUO)
HELP.......... Hughes Emergency Locator Pack
HELP.......... Hydrologic Evaluation of Landfill Performance [*Environmental Protection Agency*]
HELPEN....... High Energy laser Penetration (ACAE)
HELPIS....... Higher Education Learning Programmes Information Service [*British Universities Film & Video Council*] [*Database*]
HELP MOD... EL Hydrologic Evaluation of Landfill Performance Model (SAUS)
HELP MODEL... Hydrologic Evaluation of Landfill Performance Model (SAUO)
Helpmte....... Helpmate Robotics, Inc. [*Associated Press*] (SAG)
HELPR......... Handbook of Electronic Parts Reliability
HELPS......... Handicapped Education Learner's Planning System [*Battelle Memorial Institute*] [*Information service or system*] (IID)
HELPS......... Health Environment Long-Range Planning Support [*A computer model*]
HELPS......... Heavy Equipment Lift Pre-Positioning Ship (MUSM)
HELPS......... Helicopter Protection and Support (SAUS)
HELPS......... Helmet-Position Sensing System
HELPS......... Highway Emergency Locating Paging Service [*For motorist assistance*]
HELPU......... Helpmate Robotics Unit [*NASDAQ symbol*] (TTSB)
HELPW......... Helpmate Robotics Wrrt [*NASDAQ symbol*] (TTSB)
HELRAPS...... Heliborne Long-Range Acoustic Path Sonar (SAUS)
HELRAS....... Helicopter Long-Range Acoustic Sensor [*Military*] (CAAL)
HELRAS....... Helicopter Long Range Active Sensor (SAUS)
HELRAS....... Helicopter Long Range Active Sonar (SAUS)
HELRATS..... High-Energy LASER RADAR Acquisition and Tracking System (MCD)
HELREC....... Health Record
HelrFn......... Heller Financial [*Associated Press*] (SAG)
HELRG......... High-Energy LASER Review Group [*Terminated, 1977*] [*DoD*]
HELS........... High-Energy LASER System
HELSA......... High Energy laser System Analysis (ACAE)
Helsinki Convention... Convention on the protection of the marine environment of the Baltic Sea area (SAUO)
Helsinki Univ Technol Lab Phys... Helsinki University of Technology. Laboratory (journ.) (SAUS)
Helsinki Univ Technol Lab Phys... Helsinki University of Technology. Laboratory Physics (SAUO)
Helsinki Univ Technol Res Pap... Helsinki University of Technology. Research Papers (journ.) (SAUS)
HELSP......... Hanford Electrical Load Shedding Plan (SAUS)
HELSRD....... Health Effects and Life Science Research Division (HGEN)
HELST......... Helston [*Municipal borough in England*]
Helstar......... Heliborne Loitering System with Thermal imaging and Radar (SAUS)
HELSTF........ High-Energy LASER System Test Facility [*Army*] (DOMA)
HELSUPPRON... Helicopter Combat Support Squadron [*Navy*]
HELSUPPRONDET... Helicopter Combat Support Squadron Detachment [*Navy*] (DNAB)
HELT........... Hedonism Limitation Talks [*British*] (DI)
HELTA.......... High Endurance Lighter-Than-Air Project (SAUO)
HELTA.......... High Energy Laser Technology Assessment (SAUS)
HELTA.......... High-Energy Laser Technology Assessment (SAUO)
HELTAD....... Helicopter Tank Destroyer [*Military*]
HELTADS..... High-Energy LASER Tactical Air Defense System
HELTAS........ Helicopter Towed Array Support (SAUS)
HELTAS........ High Energy Laser Target Acquisition System (ACAE)
HELTAS........ High-Energy LASER Technology Applications Study (MCD)
HELTRARON... Helicopter Training Squadron [*Navy*]
Helv............. Ad Helviam [*of Seneca the Younger*] [*Classical studies*] (OCD)
HELV............ Helvetica [*Typography*] (WDAA)
HELVBES..... High Energy Laser Vacuum Beam Entry System (ACAE)
Helv Chim Acta... Helvetica Chimica Acta (MEC)
HELWEPS.... High-Energy LASER Weapon System [*Navy*] (MED)
HELWS........ High-Energy LASER Weapon System (MCD)
HELWS/TAS... High Energy Laser Weapon System/Target Acquisition System (ACAE)
HELX........... Helix Technology [*NASDAQ symbol*] (TTSB)
HELX........... Helix Technology Corp. [*NASDAQ symbol*] (NQ)
HELX........... Luxor [*Egypt*] [*ICAO location identifier*] (ICLI)
HEM............ Hall Effect Multiplier
HEM............ Handbook of Emergency procedures (SAUO)
HEM............ Handbook on Emergency Measures (NATG)
HEM............ Harmonisation of Environmental Measurement (EERA)
HEM............ Hatchlike Experiment Module [*NASA*] (NASA)
HEM............ Hazardous Environment Machine (SAUS)
HEM............ Heat Exchanger Method (RDA)
HEM............ Heavy Equipment Maintenance
HEM............ Helicopter-Borne Electromagnetics (SAUS)
HEM............ Hematite [*A mineral*]
HEM............ Hematology [*Medicine*] (DHSM)
hem............ Hematuria [*Urology*] (DAVI)
HEM............ Hemisphere
HEM............ Hemisphere Fund, Inc. (SAUO)
hem............ Hemlock (MIST)
HEM............ Hemlo Gold Mines, Inc. [*Toronto Stock Exchange symbol*] [*AMEX symbol*]
HEM............ Hemmeter Aviation, Inc. [*ICAO designator*] (FAAC)
HEM............ Hemoglobin [*Medicine*] (WDAA)
HEM............ Hemolysis [*Medicine*]
Hem............ Hemolytic [*Hematology*] (DAVI)
HEM............ Hemorrhage [*Medicine*] (WDAA)
hem............ Hemorrhoid [*Gastroenterology*] (DAVI)
HEM............ High Energy Microwave (TIMI)
HEM............ High level Entity Management (SAUS)
HEM............ Hitchhike Experiment Module (MCD)
HEM............ Homogeneous Equilibrium Model (NRCH)
HEM............ Horizontal Eye Movement (SAUO)
HEM............ Hostile Environment Machine (SAUS)
HEM............ Human Exposure Model [*Environmental science*] (COE)
HEM............ Human Exposure Modeling (GFGA)
HEM............ Hybrid Electro-Magnetic (SAUS)
HEM............ Hybrid Electromagnetic Mode (SAUS)
HEM............ Hydraulic Equipment Manufacturers (SAUO)
HEM............ Hydrogenic Effective Mass (AAEL)
HEM............ Hydroxyethylmorpholine [*Organic chemistry*]
HEM............ Sparta, TN [*Location identifier*] [*FAA*] (FAAL)
HEMA.......... Health Education Media Association [*Defunct*] (EA)
HEMA.......... Heavy Engineering Manufacturers Association (SAUO)
HEMA.......... HemaCare Corp. [*NASDAQ symbol*] (NQ)
HEMA.......... Hematology Profile [*Medicine*] (DAVI)
HEMA.......... Hot Melt Equipment Manufacturers Association (EA)
HEMA.......... Hydroxyethyl Methacrylate [*Organic chemistry*]
HemaC......... HemaCare Corp. [*Associated Press*] (SAG)
HEMAC........ Hybrid Electro-Magnetic Antenna Coupler (SAUS)
Hemagn....... Hemagen Diagnostics [*Associated Press*] (SAG)
Hem & M..... Hemming and Miller's English Vice-Chancellors' Reports [*A publication*] (DLA)
Hem & M (Eng)... Hemming and Miller's English Vice-Chancellors' Reports [*A publication*] (DLA)
Hem & Mill... Hemming and Miller's English Vice-Chancellors' Reports [*A publication*] (DLA)
HEMAR........ Human Engineering Criteria for Maintenance and Repair [*GE, NASA*]
Hemasure.... Hemasure, Inc. [*Associated Press*] (SAG)
HEMAT........ Heavy Expanded Mobility Ammunition Trailer [*Military*]
hemat.......... Hematocrit [*Medicine*] (DAVI)
Hemat.......... Hematocrit [*Medicine*] (EDAA)
HEMAT........ Hematology [*Medicine*]
hemat ab..... Hematologic Abnormality [*Medicine*]
hematem..... Hematemesis [*Gastroenterology*] (DAVI)
HEMATL....... Hematologist
HEMATLGY... Hematology
hematol....... hematologist (SAUS)
Hematol....... Hematology [*or Hematologist*] [*Medicine*]
hematol....... hematolymphangioma (SAUS)
hematol....... hematolysis (SAUS)
hematol....... hematolytic (SAUS)
HEMC........... Hanford Electrical Management Committee (SAUS)
HEMC........... Hanford Energy Management Committee (SAUS)
HEMC........... High Explosive Medium Capacity (SAUS)
HEMDE........ Hemdale Communications [*NASDAQ symbol*] (TTSB)
HEME........... High Efficiency Mist Eliminator (SAUS)
HEME........... Hostile Electromagnetic Emission (MCD)
HEME........... Hydroxyethyl Methyl (Cellulose) [*Organic chemistry*]
HEMEL......... Hexamethylmelamine (SAUS)
HEMF........... Handling Equipment Maintenance Facility [*Charleston Naval Shipyard*]
HEMF........... High-Efficiency Metal Fiber (ABAC)
HEMF........... High Efficiency Metal Filter (SAUS)
HEMF........... Hydroxy (Ethyl) Methyl Furanone [*Organic chemistry*]
HEM FIR...... Hemlock Fir (SAUS)
Hemgn......... Hemagen Diagnostics [*Associated Press*] (SAG)
hemi............ Hemiparalysis [*Medicine*] (EDAA)
HEMI............ Hemiparalysis [*Medicine*]
hemi............ Hemiparesis [*Medicine*] (EDAA)
hemi............ Hemiplegia [*Medicine*] (EDAA)
HEMI............ Hemiplegia [*Medicine*]
hemi............ Hemiplegia/paresis [*Therapy term*] (CTAA)
Hemi............ Hemisphere [*Neurology*] (DAVI)
HEMI............ Hemispherical [*S-band antenna*]
HEMiBioR.... Harmonization Ecological Electromagnetic Monitoring in Biosphere (SAUS)
HEMID.......... Hand-Emplaced Electromagnetic Intrusion Detector (SAUO)
HEMI Engine... Hemispherical Combustion Chamber Engine (SAUS)
Heming........ Hemingway's Mississippi Reports [*A publication*] (DLA)
Heming (Miss)... Hemingway's Mississippi Reports [*A publication*] (DLA)
HEMIS......... Harmonization of Environmental Measurements Information System (SAUS)
HEMIS......... Health Education Materials Information Service (SAUO)
HEMIS......... Hemisphere (AFM)
Hemis.......... Hemispherx BioPharma, Inc. [*Associated Press*] (SAG)
HEMISEARCH... Hemispherical Search [*First frequency-scanning RADAR*] (MCD)
Hemispx....... Hemispherx BioPharma, Inc. [*Associated Press*] (SAG)
HE Missile... High Energy Missile (SAUS)
HEMIT.......... High Electron Mobile Transistor (SAUS)
HEML........... High-Energy Microwave Laboratory [*Kirtland AFB*] [*Air Force*] (DOMA)
HEMLAW..... Helicopter Mounted LASER Weapon (MCD)
Hemlo.......... Hemlo Gold Mines, Inc. [*Associated Press*] (SAG)
HEMLOC...... Heliborne Emitter Location/Countermeasures
HEMM.......... Heavy Earth-Moving Machinery (SAUS)
HEMM.......... Mersa-Matruh [*Egypt*] [*ICAO location identifier*] (ICLI)
Hemmant..... Hemmant's Select Cases in Exchequer Chamber [*Selden Society Publications, Vol. 51*] [*1377-1460*] [*A publication*] (DLA)
HEMMS........ Hand-Emplaced Minefield Marking Set
HEMMS........ Hand-Emplaced Minefield Marking System (MCD)
HEMO.......... Hemodialysis Study (SAUS)
hemo........... Hemoglobin [*Medicine*] (DAVI)
HEMO.......... Hemolysis [*or Hemolyze*] [*Medicine*] (DAVI)
hemo........... Hemophilia [*Medicine*] (DAVI)
Hemo........... Hemostat (SAUS)

HEMO .... HemoTec, Inc. [*NASDAQ symbol*] (COMM)
hemocyt .... Hemocytometer (MAE)
hemolysis .... hemocytolysis (SAUS)
HEMOR .... Hemorrhage [*Medicine*]
hemorr .... Hemorrhage [*Medicine*] (DAVI)
HEMOSID ..... Hemosiderin (STED)
HEMP .... Hanford Electrical Management Plan (SAUS)
HEMP .... Hanford Environmental Management Plan (SAUS)
HEMP .... Hanford Environmental Management Program (SAUS)
HEMP .... Hardware Engineering Management Planning (SAUS)
HEMP .... Help End Marijuana Prohibition [*An association*]
Hemp .... Hempstead's Arkansas Reports [*A publication*] (DLA)
Hemp .... Hempstead's United States Circuit Court Reports [*A publication*] (DLA)
HEMP .... High-Altitude Electromagnetic Pulse (MCD)
HEMP .... High Explosive Multi-Purpose (SAUS)
HEMP .... High-level Entity Management Protocol (SAUS)
HEMPA .... Hexamethylphosphoric Triamide [*Also, HMP, HMPA, HMPT, HPT*] [*Organic chemistry*] (MCD)
HEMPAS ...... Hereditary Erythrocytic Multinuclearity with Positive Acidified Serum [*Medicine*] (PALA)
HEMPE .... Henry, Edward, Mary, Philip, Elizabeth [*Bacon's prophecy*]
HEMPP .... Hanford Environmental Manager Program Plan (SAUS)
HEMP-PM .... Hanford Environmental Manager Program-Program Manager (SAUS)
Hempst .... Hempstead's Arkansas Reports [*A publication*] (DLA)
Hempst .... Hempstead's United States Circuit Court Reports [*A publication*] (DLA)
HEMR .... Hybrid Electromechanical Relay (SAUS)
HEMRI .... Hereditary Multifocal Relapsing Inflammation [*Medicine*] (DMAA)
HEMS .... Helicopter Electromagnetic Survey (SAUS)
HEMS .... Helicopter Emergency Medical Services (STED)
HEMS .... Helicopter Multifunction System (SAUO)
HEMS .... High-level Entity Management System (SAUS)
HEMSiD .... Hemosiderin [*Hematology*] (DAVI)
Hem Soc ...... Hemlock Society (SAUO)
HEMT .... HF Bancorp, Inc. [*NASDAQ symbol*] (SAG)
HEMT .... High Electron Mobility Transfer (SAUS)
HEMT .... High Electron Mobility Transistor [*Computer science*]
HEMT .... High Electron Mobility Transition (SAUO)
HEMT .... High Electron Movement Transistor (SAUO)
HEMT .... Hydrodynamic Elastic Magnets Plastic
HEMT FET .... High Electron Mobility Transistor FET [*Field Effect Transistor*] [*Honeywell*] (NITA)
HEMTT .... Heavy Expanded Mobility Tactical Truck [*Army*] (RDA)
HEMT/UMHE ... Higher Education Ministries Team/United Ministries in Higher Education (EA)
HEMV .... Helium Manual Valve (MCD)
HEMW .... Hybrid Electromagnetic Wave (MSA)
HEM Wave ... Hybrid Electro-Magnetic Wave (SAUS)
HEMX .... Hemispherx BioPharma, Inc. [*NASDAQ symbol*] (SAG)
HEMXU .... Hemispherx BioPharma Unit [*NASDAQ symbol*] (TTSB)
HEN .... Cape Henry (GAAI)
HEN .... Harris Electronic News [*Service suspended*] [*Information service or system*] (IID)
HEN .... Health Education Network (SAUS)
HEN .... Heat-Exchanger Network [*Chemical engineering*]
HEN .... Hemorrhages, Exudates, and/or Nicking [*Ophthalmology*] (DAVI)
HEN .... Hengchun [*Republic of China*] [*Seismograph station code, US Geological Survey*] (SEIS)
HEN .... Henley International, Inc. [*Later, MAXXIM Medical*] [*AMEX symbol*] (SPSG)
Hen .... Henricus Boich [*Flourished, 1320-30*] [*Authority cited in pre-1607 legal work*] (DSA)
Hen .... Henry (King of England) (DLA)
HEN .... Holistic Education Network (EDAC)
HEN .... Home Enteral Nutrition [*Medicine*] (DMAA)
HEN .... Home Entertainment Network [*Cable-television system*]
HEN .... Hotel, Echo, November [*Russian submarine*]
HENA .... Hemeroteca Nacional [*Database*] [*Ministerio de Cultura*] [*Spanish*] [*Information service or system*] (CRD)
HENA .... Home Economics and Needlework Association (SAUO)
Hen Am Pl ... Hening's American Pleader [*A publication*] (DLA)
Hen & M ...... Hening and Munford's Virginia Supreme Court Reports [*1806-10*] [*A publication*] (DLA)
Hen & Mun ... Hening and Munford's Reports [*11-14 Virginia*] [*A publication*] (DLA)
Hen Bo .... Henricus Boich [*Flourished, 1320-30*] [*Authority cited in pre-1607 legal work*] (DSA)
HENDEL .... Helium Engineering Demonstration Loop [*Nuclear energy*] (NUCP)
Henderson St U ... Henderson State University (GAGS)
HENDN .... Henderson, NC [*American Association of Railroads railroad junction routing code*]
HENE .... Helium Neon [*LASER*] (DGA)
HeNe .... Helium-Neon (SAUS)
HENEC .... High Endoatmospheric Nuclear Effects Code (ACAE)
Hen For L .... Henry on Foreign Law [*A publication*] (DLA)
Hen Forms ... Hennell's Forms [*A publication*] (DLA)
HENILAS ...... Helicopter Night-Landing System
Hen JP .... Hening's Virginia Justice of the Peace [*A publication*] (DLA)
Hen LA Dig ... Hennen's Louisiana Digest [*A publication*] (DLA)
Hen Law ...... Hennepin Lawyer [*A publication*] (DLA)
Hen Man Cas ... Henry's Manumission Cases [*A publication*] (DLA)
Hen Max ...... Hening's Maxims [*A publication*] (DLA)
HENNA .... Home Executives National Networking Association
HENP .... High Energy and Nuclear Physics Program [*Department of Energy*]
HENR .... Higher Energy Nuclear Reaction (SAUS)
HENR .... Human Equivalent Noise Ratio (SAUS)
HENRE .... High-Energy Neutron Reactions Experiment [*Nuclear energy*]
Henric .... Henricus Boich [*Flourished, 1320-30*] [*Authority cited in pre-1607 legal work*] (DSA)
Henry .... Henry Ford Commercial College (SAUS)
Henry .... Patrick Henry Commercial College (SAUS)
HenryJk .... Henry [*Jack*] & Associates, Inc. [*Associated Press*] (SAG)
Henry Judg ... Henry's Judgment in Ordwin V. Forbes [*A publication*] (DLA)
HENSA .... Higher Education National Software Archive for Microcomputers (SAUS)
HENSA .... Higher Education National Software Archives (SAUS)
Hen St .... Hening's Statutes [*Virginia*] [*A publication*] (DLA)
HENT .... Head, Eyes, Ears, Nose, and Throat [*Medicine*] (HGAA)
Hent Forms ... Hent's Forms and Use of Blanks in California [*A publication*] (DLA)
HENV .... New Valley [*Egypt*] [*ICAO location identifier*] (ICLI)
HEO .... Hanford Environmental Oversight (SAUS)
HEO .... High Earth Orbit (IEEE)
HEO .... High Elliptical Orbit Satellite
HEO .... High-Energy Orbit [*NASA*] (NASA)
HEO .... Higher Executive Officer [*Civil service*] [*British*]
HEO .... Higher Executive Order
HEO .... Highest Elected Official (SAUS)
HEO .... High Farth Orbit (SAUS)
HEO .... Highly Eccentric Orbit (ACAE)
HEO .... Highly Elliptical Orbit (SAUS)
HEO(A) .... Higher Executive Officer (Administration) [*Civil service*] [*British*]
HEOB .... High-Energy Organic Battery
HEOB .... Hostile Electronic Order of Battle (SAUS)
HEOC .... Higher Echelon Operational Concept (SAUO)
HEOC .... Higher Education Opportunities Committee (EA)
HEOC .... Honeywell Electro-Optics Center (SAUO)
HEOD .... Harbor Explosive Ordnance Disposal Team [*Navy*] (VNW)
HEOD .... Hexachloro Epoxy Octahydroendohexa Dimethanonaphthalene (SAUS)
HEOEA .... Hughes Electro Optical Employees' Association (ACAE)
HEOEBS .... High-Energy Organic Electrolyte Battery System
HEOI .... Higher Education Orientation Inventory (DHP)
HE-OM .... High Explosive OTO Munition (SAUS)
HEOP .... Hanford Environmental Oversight Program (SAUS)
HEOP .... Higher Education Opportunity Program (SAUS)
HEOP .... Higher Equal Opportunity Program [*Education*]
HEOS .... HAWK Electro-Optical Sensor (SAUS)
HEOS .... High Eccentric Orbiting Satellite (SAUS)
HEOS .... High-Elliptic-inclined Orbit Satellite (SAUS)
HEOS .... Highly Eccentric [*or Elliptical*] Orbit Satellite
HEOY .... Handicapped Employee of the Year [*Award given to federal employees*] (RDA)
HEP .... Habitat Evaluation Procedure [*Fishery science*]
HEP .... Halkin Emek Partisi [*People's Labor Party*] [*Turkey*] [*Political party*] (EY)
HEP .... Hall Effect Probe
HEP .... Hallwood Energy Partners Ltd. [*AMEX symbol*] (SPSG)
HEP .... Hardsite Engagement Program
HEP .... Harvard Evolution Page (SAUO)
HEP .... Head-End Power [*Indian Railway*] (TIR)
HEP .... Hemolysis End Point [*Medicine*] (STED)
HEP .... Heparin [*Medicine*] (STED)
HEP .... Hepatic [*Pertaining to the liver*] [*Pharmacy*] (ROG)
Hep .... Hepatitis (ADWA)
hep .... Hepatitis [*Gastroenterology*] (DAVI)
HEP .... Hepatoerythropoietic Porphyria [*Medicine*]
HEP .... Hepatology [*Gastroenterology*] (DAVI)
HEP .... Heterogeneous Element Processor [*Computer science*] (RDA)
HEP .... High Egg Passage [*Rabies vaccine*]
HEP .... High Energy Particle (SAUS)
HEP .... High-Energy Particle
HEP .... High Energy Phosphate (SAUS)
HEP .... High-Energy Phosphate [*Biochemistry*]
HEP .... High Energy Physics (SAUS)
HEP .... High-Energy Physics
HEP .... High-Energy Pulse
HEP .... Higher Education Panel (EA)
HEP .... High Explosive Penetrating (SAUS)
HEP .... High Explosive Plastic (SAUS)
HEP .... High-Explosive Plastic [*Weaponry*]
HEP .... High-Explosive Plastic Projectile (SAUS)
HEP .... High Explosive Plugged (SAUS)
HEP .... High-Explosive Plugged [*Weaponry*]
HEP .... High School Equivalency Program
HEP .... High-School Equivalency Program (SAUO)
HEP .... Hi-Peg Resources Ltd. [*Vancouver Stock Exchange symbol*]
HEP .... Hispanic Employment Program [*DoD*] (MCD)
HEP .... Histamine Equivalent Prick Unit [*Immunology*]
HEP .... Hole-Electron Pair
HEP .... Home Exercise Program (SAUS)
HEP .... Homogeneous Element Processor (SAUS)
HEP .... Horizontal Enterprise Portal (GART)
HEP .... Host-End Processor (SAUS)
HEP .... Household Evaluation Program (SAUO)
hEP .... Human Endorphin [*Medicine*] (STED)
HEP .... Human Engineering Plan
HEp .... Human Epithelial [*Cells*]
HEP .... Human Epithelial Cell [*Medicine*] (EDAA)
HEP .... Human Error Probability (IEEE)
HEP .... Humboldt Egg Parasite (SAUS)

HEP .... Hydrazine Electrolysis Plenum
HEP .... Hydroelectric Plant
HEP .... Hydroelectric Power
HEP .... Hydrogen Embrittlement Proof
HEP.C .... Hallwood Energy Ptnrs L.P.'C' [*AMEX symbol*] (TTSB)
HEp-1 .... Human Cervical Carcinoma Cells [*Medicine*] (STED)
HEp-2 .... Human Laryngeal Tumor Cells [*Medicine*] (STED)
HEPA .... Hamster Egg Penetration Assay
HEPA .... High-Efficiency Particle Accumulator (NASA)
HEPA .... High Efficiency Particle Air (SAUS)
HEPA .... High Efficiency Particle Arrest (SAUS)
HEPA .... High Efficiency Particulate Absolute (SAUS)
HEPA .... High Efficiency Particulate Air (SAUS)
HEPA .... High-Efficiency Particulate Air [*Filter*]
HEPA .... High Efficiency Particulate Arresting (SAUS)
HEPA .... Hydroxyethyl Phosphonic Acid [*Organic chemistry*]
HEP-AC .... Hepatitis Battery-Acute [*Gastroenterology*] (DAVI)
HEPAC .... High Energy Physics Advisory Council (SAUS)
HEPAC .... High-Energy Physics Advisory Council (SAUO)
HEPAD .... High-Energy Proton and Alpha Detector
HEPAF .... High-Efficiency Particle Air Filter
HEPALIS .... Higher Education Policy and Administration Library and Information Service (SAUO)
HEPAP .... High Energy Physics Advisory Panel (SAUS)
HEPAP .... High-Energy Physics Advisory Panel [*Department of Energy*] [*Washington, DC*] (EGAO)
HEPAT .... High Explosive Plastic-Anti-Tank (SAUS)
Hepb .... Hepburn's Reports [*Pennsylvania*] [*A publication*] (DLA)
Hepb .... Hepburn's Reports [*California*] [*A publication*] (DLA)
HEPB .... High-Energy Pipe Break [*Nuclear energy*] (NRCH)
HEPB .... Higher Education Personnel Board (SAUO)
HEPC .... Handloom Export Promotion Council [*India*] (BUAC)
Hep-C .... Hepatitis C Virus
HEPC .... High Energy Proportional Counter on Spectrum-X-Gamma (SAUS)
HEPC .... Hydro-Electric Power Commission [*Canada*] (PDAA)
HEPCA .... Heavy Engineering Projects Corporation of Australia (SAUO)
HEPCA .... House Employees Position Classification Act [*1964*]
HEPC App .... Hydro-Electric Power Commission Approved (SAUO)
HEPCAT .... Helicopter Pilot Control and Training
HEPCC .... Heavy Electrical Plant Consultative Council (BUAC)
HEp Cell .... Human Epithelial Cell (SAUS)
HEPCO .... Hydro-Electric Power Commission of Ontario (SAUO)
HEPD .... Heat Engine Propulsion Division (SAUS)
HEPD .... High Explosive Point Detonating (SAUS)
HE-PD .... High-Explosive - Point Detonating [*Weaponry*] (MCD)
HEPDEX .... High-Energy Proton Detection Experiment
HEPDEX .... High-Energy Proton-Detection Experiment (SAUO)
HEPDI .... High Explosive Plugged Dark Ignition (SAUS)
HEPDNP .... High Explosive Point Detonating Nose Plug (SAUS)
HE/PDSD .... High Explosive, Point Detonating, Self-Destruction (SAUS)
HEPES .... Hydroxyethylpiperazineethanesulfonic Acid [*A buffer*]
HEPES Acid .... Hydroxyethylpiperazineethanesulfonic Acid (SAUS)
HEPF .... High Exposure Plutonium Facility (SAUS)
HEPG .... High Energy Physics Group (SAUS)
HEPG .... High-Energy Physics Group (SAUO)
HEPI .... Haute Ecole Populaire Internationale [*Denmark*] (BUAC)
HEPI .... HEP [*High Energy Physics*] Index (NITA)
HEPI .... Higher Education Price Index (EDAC)
HEPI .... High Explosive, armour Piercing & Incendiary (SAUS)
HEPI .... High Explosive Perforating Incendiary (SAUS)
HEPI .... High resolution Earth Processes Imager (SAUS)
HEPIC .... High Energy Physics Information Center (SAUS)
HEPL .... High-Energy Physics Laboratory [*Stanford University*] (MCD)
HEPL .... High-Energy-Pulse LASER (PDAA)
HEPL .... Hydro-Electric Physics Laboratory (SAUS)
hep lock .... Heparin Lock (IDYL)
HEPM .... Hispanic Employment Program Manager [*DoD*]
HEPM .... Human Embryonic Palatal Mesenchymal [*Type of cell line*]
HepNet .... Hepatitis Information Network (ADWA)
HEPNET .... High Energy Physics Network (ACAE)
HEPnet .... High Energy Physics Network [*Computer science*] (TNIG)
HEPO .... Hydro-Electric Power Commission of Ontario (SAUO)
HEPOD .... Hereditary Expansile Polyostotic Dysplasia [*Medicine*] (DMAA)
HEPODRUG .... Health Post and Drug Retailers (SAUS)
HEPP .... Hardware Engineering Production Plan (SAUS)
HEPP .... High-Energy Particle Physics Group [*Florida State University*] [*Research center*] (RCD)
HEPP .... High Exposure Plutonium Process (SAUS)
HEPP .... High Exposure Plutonium Program (SAUS)
HEPP .... Hoffman Evaluation Program and Procedure (SAUO)
HEPP .... Human Engineering Program Plan
HEPP .... Hydroelectric Power Plant (SAUS)
HEPP .... Northwest Association of Horticulturists, Entomologists, and Plant Pathologists [*Defunct*] (EA)
HEPPF .... High Explosive Pulsed Power Facility (SAUS)
HEPPS .... Hydroxyethylpiperazinepropanesulfonic Acid [*A buffer*]
HEPR .... Hard grade Ethylene Propylene Rubber (SAUS)
HEPR .... Health Education Professional Resources (SAUO)
HE/PR .... High Explosive, Practice (SAUS)
HEPRA .... Hellenic Public Relations Association (BUAC)
HEPS .... Helicopter Personnel Escape, Protection, and Survival (DNAB)
HEPS .... High Energy Particle Spectrometer (SAUS)
HEPS .... High-Energy Particle Spectrometer (MCD)
HEPS .... High Energy Prespark [*Analytical chemistry*]
HEPS .... High-Energy Propellant Safety (MCD)
HEPS .... High Energy Proton Spectrometer (SAUS)
HEPS .... Hydraulic Electric Power Steering
HEPS .... Hydroelectric Power Station (SAUS)
HEPS .... Pesticides Research (SAUS)
HEPS .... Port Said [*Egypt*] [*ICAO location identifier*] (ICLI)
HEPSS .... Helicopter Escape and Personnel Survival System (MCD)
HEP-T .... High Explosive Plastic Tracer (SAUS)
HEP-T .... High-Explosive Plastic Tracer [*Weaponry*] (AABC)
HEP-UP .... High School Education Program at University of Pennsylvania
HEP Virus .... High Egg Passage Virus (SAUS)
HE-PX .... High-Explosive Proximity Fuse [*Weaponry*] (MCD)
HEPX .... Hydro-Electric Power Commission of Ontario [*Private rail car owner code*]
HEQ .... Health Education Quarterly (SAUO)
HEQ .... Holyoke, CO [*Location identifier*] [*FAA*] (FAAL)
HEQC .... Higher Education Quality Control [*British*] (DET)
HEQC .... Higher Education Quality Council (BUAC)
HER .... Harsh Environmental Recorder (SAUS)
HER .... Harvard Educational Review [*A publication*] (BRI)
HER .... Health and Education Resources (EA)
HER .... Hearsay Evidence Rule [*Legal shorthand*] (LWAP)
HER .... Helena Rubinstein, Inc. (SAUO)
HER .... Hellenic Electric Railway (SAUS)
HER .... Hemorrhagic Encephalopathy of Rats (DMAA)
HER .... Heraklion [*Greece*] [*Airport symbol*] (OAG)
Her .... Herald [*Record label*] [*Great Britain*]
HER .... Heraldic (SAUS)
her .... Heraldry (VRA)
HER .... Heraldry
Her .... Hercules [*Constellation*]
Her .... Herefordshire Regiment (SAUO)
her .... Herero [*MARC language code*] [*Library of Congress*] (LCCP)
HER .... Heres [*Heir*] [*Legal term*] [*Latin*]
Her .... Heritage (DIAR)
HER .... Heritage Petróleum [*Vancouver Stock Exchange symbol*]
Her .... Hermannus [*Authority cited in pre-1607 legal work*] (DSA)
HER .... Hermanus [*South Africa*] [*Seismograph station code, US Geological Survey*] (SEIS)
Her .... Herne's Law of Charitable Uses [*A publication*] (DLA)
Her .... Herodian [*Period*]
Her .... Heroides [*of Ovid*] [*Classical studies*] (OCD)
HER .... Hershey Foods Corp., Hershey, PA [*OCLC symbol*] (OCLC)
HER .... Hex'air [*France*] [*ICAO designator*] (FAAC)
HER .... High-Efficiency Radiator [*General Motors Corp.*] [*Automotive engineering*]
HER .... High-Energy Ray
HER .... High-Energy Rotor [*Helicopter*] [*Army*]
HER .... Higher Education Resources (SAUO)
HER .... High Evaporation Rate (SAUS)
HER .... HIM [*Hardware Interface Module*] Equipment Rack [*NASA*] (NASA)
HER .... Home Energy Rebate (SAUO)
HER .... Horizontal Earth Rate
HER .... Human EGF [*Epidermal Growth Factor*] Receptor [*Biochemistry*]
HER .... Human Embryonic Retinoblast
HER .... Human Error Rate
HER .... Human Estrogen Receptor [*Endocrinology*]
HER .... Hydrogen Evolution Reaction [*Metallurgy*]
HER .... Hyperenvironmental RADAR
Her .... Quis Rerum Divinarum Heres [*Philo*] (BJA)
HER2 .... Human Epidermal Growth Factor Receptor2 [*Medicine*]
HERA .... Hadron-Electron Ring Accelerator
HERA .... Hadron-Elektron-Ring Anlage [*Hadron-Electron Ring Accelerator*] [*Germany*]
HERA .... Heavy Engineering Research Association (SAUO)
HERA .... Helicopter Radar (SAUS)
HERA .... Heritage Australia Information System [*Computer science*] (EERA)
HeRA .... Hermes Robotic Arm
HERA .... High Energy Reaction Analysis Group [*Switzerland*] (BUAC)
HERA .... High-Explosive Rocket Assisted [*Weaponry*]
HERA .... Homemakers Equal Rights Association [*Defunct*] (EA)
HERAC .... Health and Environmental Research Advisory Committee [*Department of Energy*] [*Washington, DC*] (EGAO)
Heracl .... Heraclidae [*of Euripides*] [*Classical studies*] (OCD)
Heraclid Pont .... Heraclides Ponticus [*Fourth century BC*] [*Classical studies*] (OCD)
Her Aconza .... Henricus Acconzaioco [*Flourished, 1374-82*] [*Authority cited in pre-1607 legal work*] (DSA)
HERALD .... Harbor Echo Ranging and Listening Device
HERALD .... Helicopter Equipment for Radar And Laser Detection (SAUS)
Herald .... Heraldic (DIAR)
HERALD .... Heterogeneous Experimental Reactor Aldermaston (SAUO)
HERALD .... Heterogenous Experimental Reactor, Aldermaston (SAUS)
HERALD .... Highly Enriched Reactor, Aldermaston [*British*] (DEN)
HERAP .... Health and Environmental Risk Analysis Program [*Department of Energy*]
HERAP .... Human Error Research and Analysis Program (MCD)
HERAS .... Hellenic Kadar System (SAUS)
HERATES .... Hourly Earnings Rate
HERB .... Herbaceous (WDAA)
HERB .... Herbalife International, Inc. [*NASDAQ symbol*] (NQ)
HERB .... Herbalist (ROG)
HERB .... Herbarium (WDAA)
HERBA .... Herbalife Intl'A' [*NASDAQ symbol*] (SG)
Herb Ant .... Herbert's Antiquities of the Inns of Court, Etc. [*A publication*] (DLA)
HERBB .... Hanscom Electronic Request [*for Proposals*] Bulletin Board [*Air Force*]

HERBIC........ Herbicide
Herblfe........ Herbalife International, Inc. [*Associated Press*] (SAG)
HERB RECENT... Herbarium Recentium [*Of Fresh Herbs*] [*Pharmacy*]
HERBRECS... Queensland Herbarium Plant Specimen Data Base [*State*] [*Computer science*] (EERA)
HERC.......... Hadson Energy Resources (EFIS)
HERC.......... Health Economics Research Center [*University of Wisconsin - Madison*] [*Research center*] (RCD)
HERC.......... HERC Products [*NASDAQ symbol*] (SAG)
Herc.......... Hercules [*Constellation*]
HERC.......... Home Education Resource Center [*Defunct*] (EA)
HERC.......... Humber Estuarial Research Committee (SAUO)
Her Char U... Herne's Law of Charitable Uses [*A publication*] (DLA)
Her Chat...... Herman on Chattel Mortgages [*A publication*] (DLA)
HERCULE..... Heritage and Culture through Libraries in Europe (TELE)
HERCULES... Heavy Equipment Recovery Combat Utility Lift and Evacuation System [*Military*]
HERCULES... Helicopter Remote Classification and Localization System (PDAA)
HERCULES... Hierarchical Editor and Router for Chips Using Logic Entry and Simulation (ACAE)
HERCULES... High-Energy Radiation Camera Using Light-Emitting Showers
Herculs........ Hercules, Inc. [*Formerly, Hercules Power Co.*] [*Associated Press*] (SAG)
HERD.......... Health and Environmental Review Division [*Environmental Protection Agency*] (GFGA)
HERD.......... Health Effects Research Division (SAUS)
HERD.......... High-Explosives Research and Development (MCD)
HerdCor........ Herder Correspondence [*London/New York*] [*A publication*] (BJA)
HERDESNAVAV... Hereby Designated as a Student Naval Aviator (DNAB)
HERDET....... Hereby Detached from Duty Assigned [*Military*]
HerdKor....... Herder-Korrespondenz [*Freiburg Im Breisgau*] [*A publication*] (BJA)
HERDSA....... Higher Education Research and Development Society of Australasia Inc. (SAUO)
HERDUFLY... Hereby Detailed to Duty Involving Flying (DNAB)
HERE.......... Hastings' Encyclopaedia of Religion and Ethics [*A publication*] (BJA)
HERE.......... Herefordshire [*County in England*]
HERE.......... Home Economics Resources in Education [*British*] (DBA)
HERE.......... Hotel Employees and Restaurant Employees International Union (EA)
HERE.......... Human Endurance Range Extender (SAUS)
hered.......... Hereditary (DMAA)
HERED......... Heredity
HEREDET..... Hereby Detached from Duty Assigned [*Military*] (DNAB)
HEREDITS.... Hereditaments (ROG)
HEREF......... Herefordshire [*County in England*]
Hereford...... Herefordshire [*County in England*] (BARN)
Hereford & Worcs... Hereford & Worcester (DIAR)
HEREFORD LI... Herefordshire Light Infantry, Territorial Army (SAUO)
HEREFORDS... Herefordshire [*County in England*]
HEREFS........ Herefordshire [*County in England*]
Heref/Worcs... Hereford and Worcester [*County in Wales*] (WGA)
HEREIU........ Hotel Employees and Restaurant Employees International Union (NTPA)
Herenn Modest... Herennius Modestinus [*Flourished, 3rd century*] [*Authority cited in pre-1607 legal work*] (DSA)
Her Est........ Herman's Law of Estoppel [*A publication*] (DLA)
Her Ex......... Herman's Law of Executors [*A publication*] (DLA)
HERF.......... Hazards of Electromagnetic Radiation to Fuel (TEL)
HERF.......... High Energy Radiated Electromagnetic Felds (SAUS)
HERF.......... High Energy Radiation Field (ACAE)
HERF.......... High Energy Radiation to Fuel
HERF.......... High Energy Radio Frequency (SAUS)
HERF.......... High-Energy Radio Frequency
HERF.......... High-Energy Rate Forging [*Metalworking*]
HERF.......... High-Energy Rate Forming
HERFS......... High Energy Rate Forging Systems (SAUS)
HERI.......... Heavy Oil/Enhanced Recovery Index [*Alberta Oil Sands Technology and Research Authority*] [*Information service or system*]
HERI.......... Henan Energy Research Institute (BUAC)
HERI.......... Higher Education Research Institute [*University of California, Los Angeles*] [*Research center*]
HERI.......... Home Economics Research Institute [*Iowa State University*] [*Research center*] (RCD)
HERID......... High Energy Railgun Integration Demonstration (SAUS)
HeritPpn....... Heritage Propane Partners LP [*Associated Press*] (SAG)
HeritUS........ Heritage US Government [*Associated Press*] (SAG)
HERJ.......... High-Explosive Ramjet [*Weaponry*]
Her Jur........ Heron's Jurisprudence [*1860*] [*A publication*] (DLA)
HERL.......... Health Effects Research Laboratory [*Research Triangle Park, NC*] [*Environmental Protection Agency*] (GRD)
Herley.......... Herley Industries, Inc. [*Associated Press*] (SAG)
HerLibrSci... Herald of Library Science (SAUO)
HerLibrSci... Herald of Library Science (journ.) (SAUS)
HERLIS........ Helicopter Extended Range Laser Illuminating System (SAUS)
HERL/MIS.... Health Effects Research Laboratory Management Information System [*Environment term*] (EGA)
Herm.......... Hermand's Consistorial Decisions [*Scotland*] [*A publication*] (DLA)
Herm.......... Hermas [*Biblical*] (RION)
Herm.......... Hermetic (SAUS)
Herm.......... Hermogenianus [*Flourished, 4th century*] [*Authority cited in pre-1607 legal work*] (DSA)
Hermand...... Hermand's Consistorial Decisions [*Scotland*] [*A publication*] (DLA)
Herm Chat Mortg... Herman on Chattel Mortgages [*A publication*] (DLA)
Her (Mel)..... Herald (Melbourne) [*A publication*]
HERMES...... Hand Emplaced Remote Monitoring Electronic Surveillance System (SAUS)
HERMES...... Handling through European Railways Message Electronic System (SAUS)
HERMES...... Harmonised European Research on Models of Energy Systems (EURO)
HERMES...... Head End Research facility on Mockup Engineering Scale (SAUO)
HERMES...... Heavy Element and Radioactive Material Electromagnetic Separator [*British*]
HERMES...... Helicopter Energy and Rotor Management System (SAUO)
HERMES...... Heuristic Emergency Response Management Expert System (SAUS)
HERMES...... Heuristic Mechanized Documentation Information Service (SAUS)
HERMES...... High Resolution Evaluation of Radiances from Meteorological Satellites (SAUS)
Herm Estop... Herman's Law of Estoppel [*A publication*] (DLA)
Herm Ex'ns... Herman's Law of Executions [*A publication*] (DLA)
HERMIES..... Hostile Environment Robotic Machine Intelligence Experiment Series [*Oak Ridge National Laboratory*]
Hermo......... Hermogenianus [*Flourished, 4th century*] [*Authority cited in pre-1607 legal work*] (DSA)
Her Mort...... Herman on Mortgages of Real Estate [*A publication*] (DLA)
Hermot........ Hermotimus [*of Lucian*] [*Classical studies*] (OCD)
Herm Schil... Hermannus Schildis [*Deceased, 1357*] [*Authority cited in pre-1607 legal work*] (DSA)
HERMT........ Hermitage, AR [*American Association of Railroads railroad junction routing code*]
HERN.......... Hernia [*or Herniated*] [*Medicine*]
HERN.......... High Explosive, Rocket-Assisted
HERN.......... Ras-Nasrani [*Egypt*] [*ICAO location identifier*] (ICLI)
HERO.......... Hazard of Electromagnetic Radiation of Ordnance (SAUS)
HERO.......... Hazardous Emanations of Radiation to Ordnance (SAUS)
HERO.......... Health Education Resource Organization (EA)
HERO.......... Heath Educational Robot [*Heath Co.*]
HERO.......... Heath Robot (SAUS)
HERO.......... Heritage Education and Review Organization [*Defunct*] (EA)
He-Ro.......... He-Ro Group [*Associated Press*] (SAG)
Hero.......... Heroin (SAUS)
HERO.......... High-Energy Radiation to Ordnance [*Army*]
HERO.......... Historical Evaluation and Research Organization (AEBS)
HERO.......... Home Economics Related Occupations
HERO.......... Home Economics Research Organization (SAUO)
HERO.......... Hydrothermal Environment Research Observatory [*US-French Marine collaboration*]
Herod.......... Herodas [*Third century BC*] [*Classical studies*] (OCD)
HEROD......... Herodotus [*Greek historian, c. 484BC*] [*Classical studies*] (ROG)
HERODE....... Handling the Electronic Representation of mixed text-image Office Documents based on ECMA standard 101 (SAUS)
HERODIAN... Herodianus [*Greek scholar, c. 200AD*] [*Classical studies*] (ROG)
HEROS......... German Command and Control System (SAUO)
HERP.......... Bulletin of the New York Herpetological Society (SAUO)
HERP.......... Hazards of Electromagnetic Radiation to Personnel (TEL)
HERP.......... Herpetology [*or Herpetologist*]
HERP.......... High-Energy Radiation to Personnel
HERP.......... Human Exposure Rodent Potency (SAUS)
HERP.......... Hydrological Emscher Radar Project (SAUO)
HERPES....... High-Energy Recovery Pressure and Enthalpy Sensor (IAA)
HERPET....... Herpetology (ADA)
HERPG......... Hanford Emergency Response Planning Guideline (SAUS)
HERPOCO.... Hercules Powder Co. (SAUS)
HERPOCO.... Hercules Powder Company (SAUO)
Her Prec...... Herne's Precedents [*A publication*] (DLA)
Herps.......... Herpetological Books, Papers, Specimens (SAUS)
herps.......... herpetologists (SAUS)
HERR.......... Home Economics Research Reports
HERS.......... Hardware Error Recovery System [*Sperry UNIVAC*]
HERS.......... Health Education Research Service [*Department of Health and Human Services*]
HERS.......... Health Evaluation and Referral Service
HERS.......... Heart and Estrogen/Progestin Replacement Study [*Medicine*]
HERS.......... Hemorrhagic Fever with Renal Syndrome [*Medicine*] (EDAA)
HERS.......... Heritage Financial Services, Inc. [*NASDAQ symbol*] (NQ)
HERS.......... Herself
HERS.......... High-Energy-Range Spectrometer [*Instrumentation*]
HERS.......... Higher Education Resource Services (EA)
HERS.......... Highway Economic Requirements System [*FHWA*] (TAG)
HERS.......... Home Economics Reading Service [*Recipe clipping service*]
HERS.......... Home Educational and Recreational System (SAUS)
HERS.......... Home Emergency Response System
HERS.......... Home Energy Rating System [*Thermal technology*] (PS)
HERS.......... Human Ecology Research Service (SAUS)
HERS.......... Hyperion Energy Recovery System (GNE)
HERS.......... Hysterectomy Educational Resources and Services Foundation (EA)
HERS.......... National Heart Education Research Society (EA)
Hersch......... Herschel (SAUS)
HERSCP....... Hazardous Exposure Reduction and Safety Criteria Plan [*NASA*] (NASA)
HERST......... Hearst, ON [*American Association of Railroads railroad junction routing code*]
HERT.......... Headquarters Emergency Relocation Team (SAUO)
HERT.......... HERT Emergency Response Team (SAUS)
Hert........... Hertford College, Oxford (SAUS)
HERTF......... Hertford [*City in England*] (ROG)
Hertf.......... Hertford College (SAUO)
HERTF......... High-Energy Radiation Test Facility [*Military*]
HERTF......... High Energy Research & Technology Facility (SAUS)

HertgBc .... Heritage Bancorp, Inc. [*Associated Press*] (SAG)
HertgFS .... Heritage Financial Services [*Associated Press*] (SAG)
HERTIS .... Hertfordshire County Council Technical Information Service (SAUS)
HERTIS .... Hertfordshire Technical Information Service (SAUO)
HERTIS .... Hertfordshire Technical Library and Information Service [*British*] (NITA)
HERTIS .... High-Energy Real-Time Inspections System (PDAA)
Hert M & Serv... Hertslet on Master and Servant [*A publication*] (DLA)
Hert Map Eur... Hertslet's Map of Europe [*A publication*] (DLA)
HERTS .... Hertfordshire [*County in England*] (EY)
Herts .... Hertfordshire [*County in England*] (ODBW)
HERTS .... Hertfordshire Regiment, Territorial Army (SAUO)
Hert Treat.... Hertslet's Treaties [*A publication*] (DLA)
Hertzog .... Hertzog's Reports of Transvaal High Court [*A publication*] (DLA)
HertzT .... Hrtz Technology Group [*Associated Press*] (SAG)
HertzTc .... Hertz Technology Group [*Associated Press*] (SAG)
HERU .... Health Economics Research Unit [*University of Aberdeen*] [*Scotland*] (IRC)
HERU .... Higher Education Research Unit (SAUO)
HERV .... Hostile Environment Recovery Vehicle
HERV .... Human Endogenous Retrovirus
HervTS .... Hervormde Teologiese Studies [*Pretoria, South Africa*] [*A publication*] (BJA)
HervTST .... Hervormde Teologiese Studies [*Pretoria, South Africa*] [*A publication*] (BJA)
Her X-1 .... Hercules X-1 (SAUS)
HERZ .... Hertz Technology Group [*NASDAQ symbol*] (SAG)
HerzfldC .... Herzfeld Caribbean Basin Fund [*Associated Press*] (SAG)
HES .... Hamlet Evaluation Survey [*South Vietnam*]
HES .... Hamlet Evaluation System (SAUS)
HES .... Handendstelle (SAUS)
HES .... Hanford Engineering Service [*Nuclear energy*] (NRCH)
HES .... Hardcopy Exploitation Segment (SAUS)
HES .... Harvard Expedition to Samaria (BJA)
HES .... Haskell Education Services
HES .... Hawaiian Entomological Society (BUAC)
HES .... Head End Steering
HES .... Healthcare Evaluation System [*National Planning Data Corp.*] [*Information service or system*] (CRD)
HES .... Health Economic Service (SAUO)
HES .... Health Education Service [*Publication*] [*Medicine*] (EDAA)
HES .... Health Examination Survey [*NCHS*]
HES .... Heavy Enamel Single Silk [*Wire insulation*] (AAG)
HES .... Heli Services [*France*] [*ICAO designator*] (FAAC)
HES .... Helium Emergency Supply
HES .... Hematoxylin-Eosin Stain [*Medicine*] (EDAA)
Hes .... Hesba (SAUS)
HES .... Hesiod [*Greek poet, c. 800BC*] [*Classical studies*] (ROG)
Hes .... Hesione (SAUS)
Hes .... Hesketh (SAUS)
Hes .... Hespendes (SAUS)
Hes .... Hesperus (SAUS)
Hes .... Hessels (SAUS)
HES .... Hess Environmental Services, Inc. (EFIS)
HES .... Hess Oil & Chemical Corporation (SAUO)
HES .... Hetastarch [*Biochemistry*]
HES .... Hic Est Sepultus [*Here Is Buried*] [*Latin*] (ROG)
HES .... High Energy Scattering (SAUS)
HES .... High Energy Scrubber (EEVL)
HES .... Higher Elementary School (ADA)
HES .... High Explosive Shell (SAUS)
HES .... High Explosive Spotter (SAUO)
HES .... High-Explosive Spotting [*Weaponry*]
HES .... High Explosive Substitute (SAUS)
HES .... History of Economics Society (EA)
HES .... History of Education Society (EA)
HES .... Home Electronic Systems (HEAS)
HES .... Home Entertainment Service [*Cable-television system*] (IAA)
HES .... Home Entertainment System
HES .... Homeowners Emergency Services, Inc.
HES .... House Exchange System [*Telecommunications*] (NITA)
HES .... Hughes Earth Station [*Aerospace*]
HES .... Humane Education Society (SAUO)
HES .... Human Embryonic Skin [*or Spleen*] [*Medicine*] (DMAA)
HES .... Human Environmental Services (SAUO)
HES .... Hurricane Evacuation Study (SAUO)
HES .... Hydro-Electric Securities Corporation (SAUO)
HES .... Hydroxyethyl Starch [*Plasma volume expander*]
HES .... Hypereosinophilic Syndrome [*Medicine*]
HES .... Hyperprostaglandin E Syndrome [*Medicine*] (EDAA)
HES .... Hypertext Editing System [*Computer science*]
HES .... Hyphen Editorial System (SAUS)
HES .... Lonely, AK [*Location identifier*] [*FAA*] (FAAL)
HESA .... Higher Education Statistics Agency (SAUO)
HESAP .... Health and Environmental Study Audit Program (SAUO)
HESB .... Hahnemann Elementary School Behavior Rating Scale [*Test*]
HESB .... Hessische Bibliographie [*Database*] [*Arbeitsgemeinschaft Hessische Bibliographie*] [*German*] [*Information service or system*] (CRD)
HESC .... Human Environment Scientists Committee (SAUS)
HESC .... International Congress of Scientists on the Human Environment (BUAC)
HESC .... St. Catherine/St. Catherine [*Egypt*] [*ICAO location identifier*] (ICLI)
HeSCA .... Health Science Communications Association (SAUS)
HESCA .... Health Sciences Communications Association (EA)
HES Corporation... Hydro-Electric Securities Corp. (SAUS)
HES Corporation... Hydro-Electric Securities Corporation (SAUO)
HESD .... Harris Electronics Systems Division (ACAE)
HESD .... High Explosive Self-Destroying (SAUS)
HESD .... Hospital Equipment and Supplies Directory [*A publication*]
HESDC .... Higher Education Student Data Collection [*Australia*]
HESDEP .... Helicopter Sensor Development Program
HESE .... Helium Selenium [*LASER*] (DGA)
HESEA .... Hughes El Segundo Employees' Association (ACAE)
HESEC .... Hanford Environmental Science and Engineering Consortium (SAUS)
HESES .... Higher Education Students Early Statistics (AIE)
HESF .... High-Energy Symmetric Fission
HESH .... High-Explosive, Squash Head [*Weaponry*] (NATG)
HESH Shell... High Explosive Squash Head Shell (SAUS)
HESH-T .... High Explosive Squashed (SAUS)
HESH-T .... High Explosive, Squash Head, Tracer (SAUS)
HESI .... Hunter Environmental Services, Incorporated (SAUO)
HESID .... Hand-Emplaced Seismic Intrusion Device (SAUO)
HESI-M .... Hudson Education Skills Inventory-Mathematics (TES)
HESIS .... Hazard Evaluation System and Information Service (SAUO)
HESI-W .... Hudson Education Skills Inventory-Writing (TES)
HESM .... Hospital Electrical Safety Meter [*Medicine*] (EDAA)
HESN .... Aswan [*Egypt*] [*ICAO location identifier*] (ICLI)
HESO .... High-Energy Solid Oxidizer
HESO .... Hospital Educational Services Officer [*Navy*]
HESODAC .... Helicopter SONAR Data Collection
HESP .... Health and Environmental Studies Program [*Department of Energy*] (IID)
HESP .... High-Efficiency Solar Panel
HESP .... High Energy Solar Panel (ACAE)
HESP .... High Energy Solar Physics (SAUS)
HESPA .... High Efficiency Submicron Particulate Air (SAUS)
HESP&E .... Higher Echelon Spare Parts and Equipment (SAUO)
Hesperia .... Hesperia. The Journal of the American School of Classical Studies at Athens [*A publication*] (ABAR)
HESR .... Huron & Eastern Railway [*Federal Railroad Administration identification code*]
HESRE .... Hamlet Evaluation System Monthly Report (MCD)
HESS .... Health, Environment, Safety, and Security
HESS .... High-Energy Squib Simulator [*NASA*] (NASA)
HESS .... High Energy Stereoscopic System (SAUS)
HESS .... High Latitude Ecosystems as Sources and Sinks of Trace Gases (SAUO)
HESS .... History of Earth Sciences Society (EA)
HESS .... Houston Engineering and Scientific Society (SAUO)
HESS .... Human Engineering Systems Simulator [*Air Force*]
HESSAD .... Household Expenditure Survey - Small Area Data [*Australian Bureau of Statistics*]
HESSES .... High-Energy Squib Simulators [*NASA*] (KSC)
HESSI .... High Energy Solar Spectroscopic Imager [*NASA*]
HEST .... Heavy-end aviation fuel Emergency Service Tanks (SAUS)
HEST .... Herbrew Speaking Test [*Center for Applied Linguistics*] (TES)
HEST .... High Energy Shock Tunnel (IAA)
HEST .... High-Energy Shock Tunnel (SAUO)
HEST .... High Explosion Simulation Technique (SAUS)
HEST .... High Explosive Simulation Test (SAUS)
HEST .... High Explosives Simulation Technique
HEST .... High Explosives Simulation Test (SAUS)
HESTOR .... Helium Storage (SAUS)
HESV .... Heavy Enamel Single-silk Varnish (SAUS)
HESZ .... Heskett #1 [*Federal Railroad Administration identification code*]
HET .... Haldane Educational Trust (BUAC)
HET .... Hall Effect Thruster [*Electric thruster type*]
HET .... Hall Effect Transducer
HET .... Harrah's Entertainment [*NYSE symbol*] (TTSB)
HET .... Harrahs Entertainment, Inc. [*NYSE symbol*] (SAG)
HET .... Harris Environmental Technologies, Inc. (EFIS)
HET .... Health Education Technologies [*New York, NY*] (TSSD)
HET .... Health-Education Telecommunications [*HEW*]
HET .... Heat isolatic pressing (SAUS)
HET .... Heavy Equipment Transporter
HET .... Helium Equilibration Time (MAE)
HET .... Henryetta, OK [*Location identifier*] [*FAA*] (FAAL)
HET .... Heritage Education Trust (BUAC)
HET .... Herschel Emulsifier Tester [*Lubricants*]
HET .... Heterodyne (DEN)
Het .... Heterophil [*Medicine*] (EDAA)
HET .... Heterozygosity [*Cytology*]
het .... Heterozygous [*Medicine*] (EDAA)
Het .... Hetley's English Common Pleas Reports [*124 English Reprint*] [*A publication*] (DLA)
HET .... High Education Test (SAUS)
HET .... High Energy Telescope (SAUS)
HET .... High-Energy Telescope [*Geophysics*]
HET .... Higher Educational Test [*British military*] (DMA)
HET .... High-Explosive [*Shell*] Traced [*i.e., fitted with tracer*] [*Weaponry*]
HET .... HITIL [*Hardware in-the-Loop*] Encapsulation Methodology
HET .... Hobby Eberly Telescope [*Texas*]
HET .... Hohhot [*China*] [*Airport symbol*] (OAG)
HET .... Horizontal Electrical Tunnel (NRCH)
HET .... Hot Electron Transistor (SAUS)
HET .... Houston - ET [*Texas*] [*Seismograph station code, US Geological Survey*] [*Closed*] (SEIS)
HET .... Hydroxyethyl Terephthalate [*Organic chemistry*]
HET .... TAF Helicopters SA [*Spain*] [*ICAO designator*] (FAAC)
HETA .... Harpoon Engagement Training Aid (SAUS)

HETA........... Hazard Evaluation and Technical Assistance [*National Institute for Occupational Safety and Health*]
HETAC......... Heavy Transport Aircraft [*Military*]
HETB........... Heart of England Tourist Board (DCTA)
HET-BE........ Heterophile Beef [*Immunology*] (DAVI)
HETC........... Heat Engine Trials Committee (SAUO)
HETC........... Heavy Equipment Test Chamber (MCD)
HETC........... Higher Education Telecommunications Consortium (SAUS)
HETC........... Toxic Substances Research (SAUS)
HETCOR....... Heteronuclear Correlation (SAUS)
Het CP......... Hetley's English Common Pleas Reports [*124 English Reprint*] [*A publication*] (DLA)
HETDI.......... High Explosive Tracer Dark Ignition (SAUS)
HETE........... High Energy Transient Experiment [*NASA*]
HETE........... High Energy Transient Explorer
HETE........... Higher Education Teachers of English (AIE)
HETE........... Hydroxyarachidonic Acid (MELL)
HETE........... Hydroxyeicosatetraenoic Acid [*Biochemistry*]
Het (Eng)..... Hetley's English Common Pleas Reports [*124 English Reprint*] [*A publication*] (DLA)
HETERO........ Heterosexual (DSUE)
heterocl....... heteroclite (SAUS)
HETEROG..... Heterogeneous (ROG)
HET-ESF...... Headquarters Emergency Tansportation-Emergency Support Function (SAUO)
hetetosex..... heterosexuality (SAUS)
HETF........... Hill Engineering Test Facility [*Air Force*]
HET-GP....... Heterophile Guinea Pig [*Immunology*] (DAVI)
HETGS......... High Energy Transmission Grating Spectrometer (SAUS)
Hetl............. Hetley's English Common Pleas Reports [*124 English Reprint*] [*A publication*] (DLA)
HETM........... High Explosive Time Mechanical (SAUS)
HETM........... Hybrid Engineering Test Model (NASA)
HETMA......... Heavy Edge Tool Manufacturers' Association [*British*] (BI)
HETMAC....... (Hydroxyethyl)trimethylammonium Chloride [*Organic chemistry*]
HETOC......... Hudson-Essex-Terraplane Owners Club (EA)
HETP........... Head End Treatment Plant [*Nuclear energy*] [*British*]
HETP........... Height Equivalent to a Theoretical Plate [*Chemical engineering*]
HETP........... Hexaethyl Tetraphosphate [*Organic chemistry*]
HETP........... High Equivalent to a Theoretical Plate (SAUS)
HETP........... Human Engineering Test Plan
HET-PF........ High Explosive, Tracer, Percussion Fuze (SAUS)
HET-PR........ Heterophile Presumptive [*Immunology*] (DAVI)
HETR........... El-Tor [*Egypt*] [*ICAO location identifier*] (ICLI)
HETRS......... Hanford Electronic Time Reporting System (SAUS)
HETS........... Heavy Equipment Transporter System [*Army*] (RDA)
HETS........... Heavy Equipment Transport System (SAUS)
HETS........... Height Equivalent to a Theoretical Stage [*Chemical engineering*] (NRCH)
HETS........... High-Efficiency Transfer Solution [*CINNA/BIOTECX International, Inc.*] [*Analytical biochemistry*]
HETS........... High Energy Telescope System (SAUS)
HETS........... High-Energy Telescope System [*Geophysics*]
HETS........... High Energy Transfer Stage (SAUS)
HETS........... High-Energy Transfer Stage
HETS........... Hyper-Environmental Test Station (SAUS)
HETSD......... High Explosive, Tracer, Self-Destroying [*Weaponry*] (SAA)
HE-T SD...... High Explosive, Tracer, Self-Destruct (SAUS)
HET-WG....... Heavy Equipment Transporter - Working Group (SAUO)
HEU............. Heulandite [*A zeolite*]
HEU............. High Estimate Unconstrained
HEU............. Highly Enriched Uranium [*Nuclear reactor technology*]
HEU............. HUD Electronics Unit (SAUS)
HEU............. Hull Electronics Unit [*Military*] (RDA)
HEU............. Humanist and Ethical Union (SAUO)
HEU............. Hydroelectric Unit
HEU............. Schenectady, NY [*Location identifier*] [*FAA*] (FAAL)
HEU EIS....... Disposition of Surplus Highly Enriched Uranium Environmental Impact Statement
HEUI............ Hydraulic Electronic Unit Injector [*Fuel system*] [*Automotive engineering*]
HEUNI.......... Helsinki Institute for Crime Prevention and Control affiliated with the United Nations (SAUO)
heur............. heuristic (SAUS)
HEUR........... Hydrophobic Ethoxylated Urethane Resin [*Paint technology*]
HEURAS....... Secretariat of the European Associations in Higher Education (BUAC)
HEUS........... High-Energy Upper Stage [*NASA*]
HEU/Th........ Highly Entiched Uranium/Thorium Fuel (SAUS)
HEV............. Health and Environment (AABC)
HEV............. Hemagglutinating Encephalomyelitis Virus [*Medicine*] (DMAA)
HEV............. Hepatitis E Virus (MELL)
HEV............. Hepatoencephalomyelitis Virus [*Medicine*] (DB)
HEV............. High Endothelial Venule [*Cytology*]
HEV............. High-Walled Endothelial Venule [*Anatomy*]
HEV............. Human Enteric Virus
HEV............. Hybrid-Electric Vehicle
Hev.............. Nahal Hever Caves (BJA)
HEVA........... Hydrolyzed Ethylene-Vinyl Acetate [*Plastics technology*]
HEVAC......... Heating, Ventilating, and Air-Conditioning Association [*Federation of Environmental Trade Associations*] [*British*]
HEVAC......... Heating, Ventilating and Air Conditioning Exhibition (SAUS)
HEVAC......... Heating, Ventilating, and Air Conditioning Manufacturers Association Ltd. [*British*] (BI)
HE Virus...... Human Enteric Virus (SAUS)
HEVLE.......... Hermansville, MI [*American Association of Railroads railroad junction routing code*]
HEVN........... HE Ventures, Inc. [*NASDAQ symbol*] (COMM)
HEVR........... Heavier (WDAA)
HEVRA......... Heads of European Veterinary Regulatory Agencies (GVA)
HEVS........... Helenium Virus S [*Plant pathology*]
HEW............. Department for Health, Education and Welfare (SAUS)
HEW............. Department of Health, Education, and Welfare [*Sometimes facetiously translated "Halls of Eternal Warfare"*] [*Later, HHS*]
HEW............. Department of Health, Education, and Welfare, Washington, DC [*OCLC symbol*] (OCLC)
HEW............. Half Energy Width
HEW............. Hanford Engineering Works [*Nuclear energy*]
HEW............. Hanford Engineer Works (SAUS)
HEW............. Health Education and Welfare [*Marine science*] (OSRA)
HEW............. Hewitt-Robins, Inc. (SAUO)
HEW............. Housing, Education and Welfare (SAUS)
HEW............. Houston, TX [*Location identifier*] [*FAA*] (FAAL)
HEW............. US Department of Health, Education and Welfare (SAUS)
HE-WAM...... Hand Emplaced WAM (SAUS)
HEWC........... Highly Enriched Waste Concentrate (PDAA)
HEWGAR...... Department of Health, Education and Welfare Grant Appeals Board (AAGC)
HEWH........... High-Explosive Warhead [*Weaponry*]
HEWL........... Hen Egg White Lysozyme [*Also, HEL*] [*An enzyme*]
Hewlett-Packard J... Hewlett-Packard Journal (journ.) (SAUS)
HewlPk......... Hewlett-Packard Co. [*Associated Press*] (SAG)
HEW-na....... National Library of Medicine (SAUO)
HEW-nih...... National Institutes of Health (SAUO)
HEWPR........ Department of Health, Education, and Welfare [*Later, HHS*] Procurement Regulations
HEWPR........ Health, Education and Welfare Procurement Regulations (SAUS)
HEWS.......... Humanitarian Early Warning System (SAUO)
HEW-ssa...... Social Security Administration (SAUO)
HEW-sz....... Saint Elizabeths Hospital (SAUO)
HEX............. Handicapped Education Exchange [*Amateur Radio Research and Development Corp.*] [*Information service or system*] (IID)
HEx............. Hard Exudate (STED)
HEX............. Hatfield Executive Aviation Ltd. [*British*] [*ICAO designator*] (FAAC)
HEX............. Heat Exchanger (KSC)
HEX............. Heck's, Inc. [*NYSE symbol*] (COMM)
HEX............. Helsinki Exchanges Group Ltd Oy
HEX............. Hemlo Explorations [*Vancouver Stock Exchange symbol*]
HEX............. Hexachlorocyclopentadiene [*Also, HCCP, HCP*] [*Organic chemistry*]
HEX............. Hexachord [*Music*] (ADA)
hex.............. Hexadecimal (AEBE)
HEX............. Hexadecimal [*System*]
hex.............. Hexagon (SHCU)
HEX............. Hexagon [*or Hexagonal*]
Hex.............. Hexamethylmelamine (STED)
HEX............. Hexamethylmelamine [*Altretamine*] [*Also, HMM, HXM*] [*Antineoplastic drug*]
HEX............. Hexateuch (ROG)
hex.............. Hexatic (MEC)
HEX............. Hexosaminidase (DB)
HEX............. High Explosive (DNAB)
HEX............. Hydraulics, External (DNAB)
HEX............. Santo Domingo [*Dominican Republic*] [*Airport symbol*] (OAG)
HEXA........... Hexamethylene Tetramine [*Organic chemistry*] (WDAA)
HEX A.......... Hexosaminidase A (STED)
HEX-A.......... Hexosaminidase-A
Hexa-CAF.... Hexamethylmelamine, Cyclophosphamide, Amethopterin [*Methotrexate*], Fluorouracil [*Antineoplastic drug regimen*]
Hexal........... Hexogen/aluminium powder (SAUS)
HEX B.......... Hesosaminidase B (STED)
HEX-B.......... Hexosominidase-B
HEX-BCH...... Hexachloronorbornadiene [*Organic chemistry*] (EPA)
HEXCALC..... Hexadecimal Calculator [*Computer science*] (MHDI)
Hexcel......... Hexcel Corp. [*Associated Press*] (SAG)
HEXE........... High Energy X-Ray Experiment
HEXFET........ Hexagonal Metal-Oxide Field-Effect Transistor (SAUS)
HEXHD......... Hexagonal Head
HEXIT.......... Hexadecimal Digit [*Computer science*] (NHD)
HEXL........... Methohexital [*A barbiturate*] [*Pharmacology*] (DAVI)
HEXOS......... Humidity Exchange Over the Sea (SAUO)
HEX SOC...... Hexagonal Socket (SAUS)
HEX SOCH... Hexagonal Socket Head (SAUS)
HEXTE......... High Energy X-Ray Timing Experiment (SAUS)
HEY............. Ozark/Fort Rucker, AL [*Location identifier*] [*FAA*] (FAAL)
Heyl Imp D... Heyl's United States Import Duties [*A publication*] (DLA)
HEYM........... Herrold's Egg Yolk Medium [*For growing microorganisms*]
Heyw Ca...... Heywood's Table of Cases [*Georgia*] [*A publication*] (DLA)
Heyw Co Ct... Heywood's County Courts Practice [*4th ed.*] [*1876*] [*A publication*] (DLA)
Heyw Elec... Heywood on Elections [*A publication*] (DLA)
Heywood & Massey... Heywood and Massey's Court of Protection Practice [*9th ed.*] [*1971*] [*A publication*] (DLA)
Hez.............. Hezekiah (SAUS)
HEZ............. Holdregg Elevator [*Federal Railroad Administration identification code*]
HEZ............. Natchez [*Mississippi*] [*Airport symbol*] (OAG)
HEZOBOLLAH... Hezb Allah [*Party of God*] [*Arabic*] [*An Iranianian terrorist organization*]
Hez-PBAN.... Heliothis Zea Pheromone Biosynthesis Activating Neuropeptide
HF............... Dorsey Laboratories [*Research code symbol*]

HF First Air [*ICAO designator*] (AD)
HF Frequency (SAUS)
HF Haemorrhagic Factor (SAUS)
Hf Hafnium [*Chemical element*]
HF Hageman Factor [*Factor XII*] [*Hematology*]
HF Hagen Factor (DB)
HF Hair Follicle (MELL)
HF Hale Foundation (EA)
HF Half (AAG)
hf Half (WDMC)
HF Half Forward (ADA)
HF Hammer Form (MCD)
H/F Handling Fee [*Coupon redemption*]
HF Handling Fixture (MCD)
HF Handwriting Foundation
HF Hangman's Fracture [*Medicine*] (MELL)
HF Hankes Foundation (EA)
HF Hanuman Foundation (EA)
HF Haplotype Frequency (STED)
HF Harassing Fire [*Military*] (AABC)
HF Hardenability Factor (SAUS)
HF Hard Faced (SAUS)
HF Hard Facing (SAUS)
HF Hard Failure
HF Hard Feces (STED)
HF Hard Filled [*Capsules*] [*Pharmacy*]
HF Hard Firm [*Pencil leads*]
HF Harmonic Filter (ACAE)
HF Harmonic Function (SAUS)
HF Harry Franco [*Pseudonym used by Charles F. Briggs*]
HF Hartree-Fock [*Orbitals*] [*Atomic structure*]
HF Harvest Fluid (DB)
HF Hawthorne Farms (SAUS)
HF Hayden Foundation (SAUO)
HF Hay Fever [*Medicine*]
HF Haynes Foundation (SAUO)
HF Hazard Free (SAUS)
HF Hazard Function
HF Haze Filter [*Photography*]
HF Hazelden Foundation (EA)
HF Head Forward (STED)
HF Head of Fetus (STED)
HF Heart Failure [*Medicine*]
HF Heat Flow [*Physiology*]
Hf Heat of Combustion of Fuel [*Aviation*] (DA)
HF Heavy Fuel [*Engine technology*]
HF Heckscher Foundation (SAUO)
HF Heeresfahrzeug [*Army Vehicle*] [*German military - World War II*]
HF Height Finder [*or Finding*] [*RADAR*]
H/F HeLa [*Helen Lake*]/Fibroblast [*Hybrid*] [*Cytology*] (DAVI)
H/F Held For [*Investment term*] (DFIT)
HF Heller Financial 'A' [*NYSE symbol*] (SG)
HF Helper Factor [*Immunology*]
HF Hemochromatosis Foundation (EA)
HF Hemofiltration (MELL)
HF Hemorrhagic Factor [*Medicine*]
HF Hemorrhagic Fever [*Medicine*] (DAVI)
HF HEPA Filter (SAUS)
HF Hepatic Fat
HF Hepatic Fibrosis [*Medicine*] (MELL)
HF Hepatocyte Function (STED)
HF Heptaline Formate (SAUS)
HF Hercules Furens [*of Euripides*] [*Classical studies*] (OCD)
HF Heritage Foundation [*Washington, DC*] (EA)
HF Hertfordshire Regiment (SAUO)
HF Hertz Frequency (STED)
HF Hesperian Foundation (EA)
HF High Fantasy (SAUS)
HF High Fat [*Type of diet*]
HF High Field (IAA)
HF High Flow (MAE)
HF High Flux (IAA)
HF High Foliage Forager [*Ecology*]
HF High Food Density [*Ecology*]
hf High Frequency (WDMC)
HF High Frequency [*Electronics*]
HF High Frontier (EA)
HF High Functionality (SAUS)
HF High Rate Forward
HF Hind Foot (SAUS)
HF Hip Fracture (MELL)
HF Hippocampal Fissure [*Neuroanatomy*]
HF History File (SAUS)
HF Hold Fire [*Military*]
HF Holding Fixture (MSA)
HF Hollow Fiber
HF Hollow Filter [*Dialyzer*] (STED)
H-F Holstein-Friesian [*Cattle breed*]
HF Holyearth Foundation (EA)
HF Holy Family Fraternity (SAUO)
HF Holy Father (ROG)
HF Home Favorite
HF Home Fleet [*Obsolete*] [*British*]
HF Home Forces [*Military*] [*British*]
HF Home Freezer (SAUS)
HF Home Freight (SAUS)
HF Home Front
HF Homeopathic Foundation [*Later, FHR*] (EA)
HF Homogeneous Flow (SAUS)
HF Hook Fast (SAUS)
HF Horizontal Flight (NASA)
HF Horse and Foot (SAUS)
HF Hot Finished [*Drawing*] (DAC)
HF Hot Firing (MCD)
HF Hot Flashes (MELL)
HF Hot Fomentation (STED)
HF House File (OICC)
HF House Formula [*An in-house formula found in a particular hospital or clinic*] (DAVI)
HF House of Fabrics, Inc. [*NYSE symbol*] (SPSG)
HF Hull Filter
HF Human Factors
HF Human Fibroblast [*Medicine*] (DMAA)
HF Human Foreskin [*Anatomy*]
HF Huna Forschunggesellschaft [*Huna Research Association - HRA*] [*Switzerland*] (EAIO)
HF Hundred Feet
HF Hyden Foundation (SAUO)
HF Hydraulic Fluid (SAUS)
HF Hydrofluoric Acid (LDT)
HF Hydrogen Fill (MCD)
HF Hydrogen Fluoride [*Inorganic chemistry*] (AFM)
HF Hyper Filtration (SAUS)
HF Hyperfine (SAUS)
HF Hyperfocal (SAUS)
HF Messerschmitt-Boelkow-Blohm [*Germany*] [*ICAO aircraft manufacturer identifier*] (ICAO)
HF Wander AG [*Switzerland*] [*Research code symbol*]
HFA Haemophilia Foundation of Australia
HFA Haifa [*Israel*] [*Airport symbol*] (OAG)
HFA Hardened Flexible Array
HFA Hard Factory Automation (SAUS)
HFA Hard Fiber Association (SAUS)
HFA Hard Fibres Association (EA)
HFA Hardware Federation of Australia
HFA Harmelink Family Association (EA)
HFA [*The*] Harry Fox Agency
HFA Hartshorn Family Association (EA)
HFA Hawaii Flooring Association (SRA)
HFA Headquarters Field Army (NATG)
HFA Hearing-Failed to Appear [*Motor vehicle violation code used in state of Maryland*] (MVRD)
HFA Heat and Flame Resistant, Armored (IAA)
HFA Heavy Field Artillery
HFA Hexafluoroacetone [*Organic chemistry*]
HFA Hexafluoroaceytlacetone [*Organic chemistry*]
HFA Higdon Family Association (EA)
HFA High-Fidelity Actuator [*Electronics*]
HFA High Flow Alarm (IEEE)
HFA High Force Actuator [*Engineering*]
HFA High-Frequency Accelerometer (NASA)
HFA High Frequency Aerial (SAUS)
HFA High Frequency Amplifier (SAUS)
HFA High-Frequency Amplifier [*Electronics*] (IAA)
HFA High Frequency Antenna (SAUS)
HFA High-Frequency Antenna (KSC)
HFA High Functioning Autism
HFA Hinman Family Association (EA)
HFA Hired Fishermen's Association [*A union*] [*British*]
HFA Historical Farm Association (EA)
HFA Hitchhikers for America (EA)
HFA Holiday Fun Association (SAUO)
HFA Hollywood Film Archive (SAUS)
HFA Homofolic Acid [*Biochemistry*]
HFA Hospital Finance Authority (GHCT)
HFA Hourly Faculty Association (SAUO)
HFA Housing Finance Agency [*Eire*] (BUAC)
HFA Humane Farming Association (EA)
HFA Hydrofluoroalkane [*Organic chemistry*]
HFA Hydrogen-Fueled Aircraft
HFA Hydrologic Field Assistant (SAUO)
HFAA Hardanger Fiddle Association of America (EA)
HFAA High-Frequency Airborne Antenna
HFAA Holstein-Friesian Association of America (EA)
HFAARS High Frequency Adaptive Antenna Receiving System
HFAB House of Fabrics, Inc. [*NASDAQ symbol*] (SAG)
HFAC Hardened Flush Aircraft (SAUS)
HFAC Human Factors Association of Canada
HFAF Hawaiian Foundation for American Freedoms (SAUO)
HFAF Hawaii Foundation for American Freedoms (EA)
HFAJ High Frequency Anti-Jam (SAUO)
HFAJ/LEIP High Frequency Anti-Jam/Link Eleven Improvement Program (SAUS)
HFAK Hollow Fiber Artificial Kidney [*Medicine*] (AAMN)
HFAM Helicopter Familiarization (MCD)
HF & OR Human Factors and Operations Research [*Army*] (MCD)
HFAR Honduran Foundation for Agricultural Research (SAUO)
HFARA Honorary Foreign Associate of Royal Academy [*British*]
HFAS High Frequency Acoustic Sounder (SAUS)
HFAS High Frequency Aerial System (SAUS)
HFAS High-Frequency Antenna System (KSC)

HFAS .... Honeywell File Access System
HFB .... Hand Form Block (MSA)
HFB .... Helium Filled Bubble [*For study of air flow*]
HFB .... Heptafluorobutyrate [*or Heptafluorobutyric*] [*Organic chemistry*]
HFB .... Hopper-Feeder-Bolter (SAUS)
HFB .... Horizontal Flow Barrier [*Computer science*]
HFB .... Hughes Flying Boat (ACAE)
HFBA .... Hebrew Free Burial Association (EA)
HFBA .... Heptafluorobutyric Acid [*Organic chemistry*]
HFBC .... High Field Bubble Chamber, Didcot (SAUO)
HFBC .... High Frequency Broadcasting (SAUS)
HFBC .... High Frequency Broadcasting Schedule [*Databank*] (NITA)
HFBcp .... HF Bancorp, Inc. [*Associated Press*] (SAG)
HF BD .... Half-Bound [*or Binding*] (WDAA)
Hf-Bd .... High-Frequency Band [*Electricity*]
HFBF .... Home Federal Bank of Florida (SAUO)
HFBI .... Heptafluorobutyrylimidazole [*Organic chemistry*]
HFBLB .... Hokkaido Farmland Bride Liaison Bureau (SAUO)
HFB Method... Hartree-Fock-Bogoliubov Method (SAUS)
HFBR .... High-Flux Beam Reactor (GAAI)
HFBR .... High Flux Beam Research Reactor [*Nuclear energy*]
HFBR .... Hollow-Fiber Bioreactor [*Chemical engineering*]
HFBS .... High Frequency Broadcasting Schedule (SAUS)
HFBUP .... High-Frequency Backup Program [*Military*] (CAAL)
HfC .... Hafnium Carbide (SAUS)
HFC .... Hand-Filled Capsules [*Pharmacy*] (DAVI)
HFC .... Hanford Facilities Core (SAUS)
HFC .... Hanna Furnace [*Federal Railroad Administration identification code*]
HFC .... Hard Faced Composite (SAUS)
HFC .... Hard-Filled Capsules [*Pharmacy*] (DAVI)
HFC .... Harpers Ferry Center [*National Park Service*] (GRD)
HFC .... Heart Fan Club (EA)
HFC .... Heat Flow and Convection (NASA)
HFC .... Hierarchical File System [*Computer science*] (DDC)
HFC .... High-Energy LASER Fire Control
HFC .... Higher Fire Control [*British military*] (DMA)
HFC .... High Fan Control (HAWK)
HFC .... High-Frequency Choke
HFC .... High-Frequency Correction
HFC .... High-Frequency Current
HFC .... Histamine-Forming Capacity (DB)
HFC .... Historians Film Committee (NTPA)
HFC .... Holy Family College [*California, Pennsylvania, Wisconsin*]
HFC .... Home Finance Contract
HFC .... Hope Foundation Communicators [*Australia*]
HFC .... Hospital Financial Control [*McDonnell Douglas Automation Co.*]
HFC .... Household Financing Corp. (CDAI)
HFC .... Household Food Consumption
HFC .... Human Factors Checklists [*Navy*]
HFC .... Human Factors Council
HFC .... Human Freedom Center (SAUO)
HFC .... Hybrid Fiber-Coax [*Telecommunications*]
HFC .... Hybrid Fiber Coaxial
HFC .... Hybrid Fiber-Coaxial Cable (GART)
HFC .... Hydraulic Flight Control (NASA)
HFC .... Hydrofluorocarbon [*Organic chemistry*]
HFC .... Hydrogen Fuel Cell [*Automotive engineering*]
HFC .... Hyperfine Coupling [*Spectroscopy*]
HFCA .... Holy Family Christian Association [*In 1983 movie "Zelig"*]
HFCAA .... Hatters' Fur Cutters Association of America [*Formerly, HFCAUS*] (EA)
HFCAS .... Hampshire Field Club and Archaeological Society (SAUO)
HFCAUS .... Hatters' Fur Cutters Association of the United States [*Later, HFCAA*]
HFCC .... Henry Ford Community College [*Dearborn, MI*]
HFCC .... Howitzer Fire-Control Computer (SAUS)
HFCD .... High Frequency Communications Division (SAUS)
HFCD .... Hino Fuel Economy Clean Air High-Durability [*Hino diesel engines*]
HFCE .... HFIR [*High-Flux Isotope Reactor*] Critical Experiment [*Nuclear energy*] (NRCH)
HF-CF .... Half-Calf [*Bookbinding*] (DGA)
HFC/ISR .... High Frequency Communications/Intelligence System-Rear (SAUS)
HF-CL .... Half-Cloth [*Bookbinding*] (DGA)
HF-COL .... Half Column [*Advertisement*] (DGA)
HFCRSP .... High-Frequency Communications Replacement System Program (LAIN)
HFCS .... Harpoon Fire Control System [*Missiles*] (MCD)
HFCS .... Helicopter Fire Control System (SAUS)
HFCS .... High-Fructose Corn Sweetener [*or Syrup*]
HFCS .... Honeywell Financial and Corporate Planning System (HGAA)
HFCS .... Household Food Consumption Survey (SAUO)
HFCT .... Hawaii Federation of College Teachers (SAUO)
HFCT .... Hydraulic Flight Control Test (NASA)
HFCU .... Hydromechanical Fuel Control Unit (SAUS)
HFCUR .... High-Frequency Current
HFCV .... Helium Flow Control Valve (KSC)
HFCVD .... Hot Filament Chemical Vapor Deposition [*Coating technology*]
HFCVSTP .... Hydrogen Fuel Cell Vehicle Study and Test Program [*Environmental science*] (COE)
HFCWD .... Holidays, Festivals, and Celebrations of the World Dictionary [*A publication*]
HFD .... Halifax Developments Ltd. [*Toronto Stock Exchange symbol*]
HFD .... Hanford Fire Department (SAUS)
HFD .... Hartford, CT [*Location identifier*] [*FAA*] (FAAL)
HFD .... Hatfield BAE [*British*] [*ICAO designator*] (FAAC)
HFd .... Heavy Field (SAUS)
HFD .... Held for Detail
HFD .... Helicopter Flight Director (SAUS)
HFD .... Helium Fill to Distribution Unit [*Aerospace*] (AAG)
HFD .... Hemorrhagic Fever of Deer [*Medicine*] (DMAA)
HFD .... Hereford [*British depot code*]
HFD .... Herefordshire [*County in England*] (ROG)
HFD .... High-Fiber Diet (DMAA)
HFD .... High Field Domain (SAUS)
HFD .... High Forceps Delivery [*Obstetrics*] (DAVI)
HFD .... HomeFed Corp. (EFIS)
HFD .... Home Federal S&L Assn. (California) [*NYSE symbol*] (COMM)
HFD .... Home Furnishings Daily [*A publication*] [*Formerly HFD-Weekly Home Furnishings*] (WDMC)
HFD .... Horizon Flight Director [*Aircraft*]
HFD .... Horizontal Right Datum (SAUS)
HFD .... Hospital Field Director [*Red Cross*]
HFD .... Host Funding 'A' [*AMEX symbol*] (TTSB)
HFD .... Host Funding, Inc. [*AMEX symbol*] (SAG)
HFD .... Hot Form Die
HFD .... Human Factor Division [*Air Research and Development Command*] [*Air Force*] (AAG)
HFD .... Human Factors Design (DMAA)
HFD .... Human Figures Drawing Test [*Education*] (EDAC)
HFD .... Hydro-Form Die
HFDA .... High Fidelity Dealers Association (BUAC)
HFDA .... High Film Density Area (DMAA)
HFDA .... Hospital Food Directors Association
HFdeSJ .... Franciscan Sisters of St. Joseph (Mexico City) (TOCD)
HFDF .... High Frequency Detecting and Finding (SAUS)
HFDF .... High-Frequency Direction Finding [*Pronounced "huff duff"*] [*Electronics*]
HFDF .... High Frequency Distributing Frame (SAUS)
HFDF .... High-Frequency Distribution Frame (IEEE)
HF/DF .... Hydrogen Fluoride/Deuterium Fluoride (MCD)
HFDF Station... High Frequency Direction Finding Station (SAUS)
HFDK .... Human Fetal Diploid Kidney [*Type of cell line*]
HFDL .... High Frequency Data Link (HLLA)
HFDL .... Host Forms Description Language [*Xerox software*] (NITA)
HFDL .... Human Fetal Diploid Lung [*Type of cell line*]
HFDM .... High-Frequency Digital MODEM (LAIN)
HFDS .... High Functionally Distributed System (SAUS)
HFDS .... Hydrogen Fluid Distribution System (MCD)
HFdSvF .... Home Federal Financial Corp. [*Associated Press*] (SAG)
HFDT .... Human Figures Drawing Test [*Psychology*] (DHP)
HFD Unit .... Helium Fill to Distribution Unit (SAUS)
HFE .... Hardware Forwarding Engine [*Computer science*] (DINT)
HFE .... Health Facility for the Elderly
HFE .... Heat-Flow Electronics
HFE .... Heat-Flow Experiment
HFE .... Hefei [*China*] [*Airport symbol*] (OAG)
HFE .... Helmholtz Free Energy
HFE .... Hexafluorodiethyl Ether [*Convulsant*]
HFE .... High Frequency Executive (NASA)
HFE .... Hillside Energy [*Vancouver Stock Exchange symbol*]
HFE .... Human Factors Engineering (AABC)
HF/E .... Human Factors/Engineering (SAUO)
HFE .... Human Factors Evaluation (MCD)
HFE .... Human Factors in Electronics (MCD)
HFE .... Human Factors in Electronics (journ.) (SAUS)
HFE .... Hydrofluorether
HFE .... Pittsburgh, PA [*Location identifier*] [*FAA*] (FAAL)
HFEA .... Hughes Fullerton Employees' Association (ACAE)
HFEA .... Human Factors Engineering Analysis [*or Assessment*] [*Army*] (RDA)
HFEA .... Human Fertilization and Embryology Authority [*British*]
HFEA .... Human Fertilization Embryo Authority [*Great Britain*]
HFEAA .... Historic Fire Engine Association of Australia
HFEC .... Human Foreskin Epithelial Cell [*Medicine*] (DMAA)
HFED .... Heart Federal Savings & Loan Association (SAUO)
HFEF .... High Flux Experimental Facility [*Nuclear energy*]
HFEF .... Hot Fuel Examination Facility [*Nuclear energy*]
HFEFN .... Hot Fuel Examination Facility North (SAUO)
HFEF-N .... Hot Fuel Examination Facility-North (SAUS)
HFEFS .... Hot Fuel Examination Facility South (SAUO)
HFEF-S .... Hot Fuel Examination Facility-South (SAUS)
HFEP .... Host Front End Processor (SAUO)
HFEP .... Host Front End Protocol (ACAE)
HFES .... Human Factors and Ergonomics Society (NTPA)
HFET .... Hellmann-Feynmann Electrostatic Theorem [*Physics*]
HFET .... Heterojunction Field Effect Transistor (AAEL)
HFET .... Highway Fuel Economy Test [*Environmental Protection Agency*]
HFET .... Home Federal S&L Assn. of Upper East Tennessee [*NASDAQ symbol*] (COMM)
HFET .... Human Factors Engineering Testing (MCD)
HFeU .... Hepatic Iron (Ferrum) Uptake [*Physiology*]
HFF .... Hartree-Fock Field (SAUS)
HFF .... Heavy Freight Flight [*British military*] (DMA)
HFF .... High Flight Foundation (EA)
HFF .... High Frequency Filter (SAUS)
HFF .... High-Frequency Furnace
HFF .... Hoffman, NC [*Location identifier*] [*FAA*] (FAAL)
HFF .... Horizontal Falling Film (PDAA)
hFF .... Human Follicular Fluid [*Physiology*]
HFF .... Human Foreskin Fibroblast [*A cell line*]
HFF .... Hydraulic Fluid Filter
HFF .... Hypervelocity Flow Field

HFF .... Hypervelocity Free Flight Facility (SAUS)
HFFACO .... Hanford Federal Facility Agreement and Consent Order (SAUS)
HFFB .... Harrodsburg First Financial Bancorp, Inc. [*NASDAQ symbol*] (SAG)
HFFB .... Harrodsburg First Finl Bancorp [*NASDAQ symbol*] (TTSB)
HFFC .... Hart Family Fan Club (EA)
HFFC .... Helen Forrest Fan Club (EA)
HFFC .... HF Financial [*NASDAQ symbol*] (TTSB)
HFFC .... HF Financial Corp. [*NASDAQ symbol*] (SAG)
HFFF .... Djibouti/Ambouli [*Djibouti*] [*ICAO location identifier*] (ICLI)
HFFF .... Hungarian Freedom Fighters Federation USA (EA)
HFFF .... Hypervelocity Free Flight Facility
HF Fnc .... HF Financial Corp. [*Associated Press*] (SAG)
HFFS .... HELLFIRE Fire and Forget Seeker [*Missile*]
HFG .... Harmonic Frequency Generator
HFG .... Heavy Free Gas (IEEE)
HFG .... High Frequency Gas (WDAA)
HFG .... Human Factors Group
HFGA .... Hall of Fame for Great Americans (EA)
HFGI .... Harrington Financial Group, Inc. [*NASDAQ symbol*] (SAG)
HFGI .... Harrington Fin'l Grp [*NASDAQ symbol*] (TTSB)
HFGO .... Home Fleet General Order (SAUS)
HfH .... Habitats for Humanity (SAUS)
HFH .... Harnischfeger Industries [*NYSE symbol*] (SAG)
HFH .... Henry Ford Hospital (SAUO)
HFH .... Home from Hospital (BUAC)
HFHC .... Heritage Financial Corp. [*NASDAQ symbol*] (COMM)
HFHI .... Habitat for Humanity International (EA)
HFHL .... High-Frequency Hearing Loss [*Otorhinolaryngology*] (DAVI)
HFH Steel .... Half-Hard Steel (SAUS)
HFHT .... Handling Fixture - Hoist Tool (MCD)
HFHTB .... Human Factors Howitzer Test Bed (SAUS)
HFI .... Health Facilities Information File [*Australia*]
HFI .... Health First International (EA)
HFI .... Height Finding Instrument (SAUS)
HFI .... Helicopter Foundation International (EA)
HFI .... Hepatitis Foundation International
HFI .... Hereditary Fructose Intolerance [*Medicine*]
HFI .... High Fidelity Institute
HFI .... High Frequency Inductance (SAUS)
HFI .... High-Frequency Input (IAA)
HFI .... Hjukrunarfelag Islands (BUAC)
HFI .... Hocker Federation International (EA)
HFI .... Home for Incurables [*Australia*]
HFI .... Horizontal Flight Testing (SAUS)
HFI .... Hubei Fisheries Science Research Institute [*China*] (BUAC)
HFI .... Hudson Foods, Inc., Class A [*NYSE symbol*] (SPSG)
HFI .... Human Fibroblast Interferon [*Medicine*] (DMAA)
HFI .... Hunt Foods and Industries, Incorporated (SAUO)
HFI .... Hydraulic Fluid Index (PDAA)
HFI .... Hydrogen Flame Ionization (SAUS)
HFI .... Hyperfine Interaction
HFI .... Hyperostosis Frontalis Interna [*Medicine*] (MELL)
HFIA .... Heat and Frost Insulators and Asbestos Workers (MHDB)
HFIA .... Home Furnishings International Association (EA)
HFIAW .... Heat and Frost Insulators and Asbestos Workers (SAUS)
HFIAW .... International Association of Heat and Frost Insulators and Asbestos Workers (EA)
HFIB .... Hexafluoroisobutylene [*Organic chemistry*]
HFIC .... Harpoon Firing Interlock Closed [*Missiles*] (MCD)
HFIC .... HF Intra-task force Communications (SAUS)
HFIC .... High-Frequency Intra-Task Force Communications (LAIN)
HFIC .... Home Furnishings Industry Committee [*Defunct*] (EA)
HFIC .... Human Factors Information Center (SAA)
HFID .... Heated Flame Ionization Detection [*Analytical chemistry*]
HFID .... Heated Flame Ionization Detector (EEVL)
HF-ID .... High Frequency Identification (SAUS)
HFID .... Hydrogen Flame Ionization Detection (or Detector) (SAUS)
HFIF .... Human Fibroblast Interferon [*Cytology*]
HFIH .... High-Frequency Induction Heating (PDAA)
HFIIC .... Hearth Furniture Interim Industrial Council (SAUO)
HFIM .... High-Frequency Instruments and Measurements (IEEE)
HFIN .... Horizon Financial Services, Inc. [*NASDAQ symbol*] (COMM)
HFIP .... Hexafluoroisopropanol [*or Hexafluoroisopropyl*] [*Organic chemistry*]
HFIP .... High-Frequency Improvement Program (LAIN)
HFIR .... High Flux Intensity Reactor (SAUS)
HFIR .... High Flux Isotope Reactor
HFIR .... Oak Ridge High Flux Isotope Reactor (SAUS)
HFITR .... High-Field Ignition Test Reactor [*Nuclear energy*] (MCD)
HFIW .... High-Frequency Induction Welding [*Manufacturing term*]
HFIX .... Hunt Foods and Industries [*Private rail car owner code*]
HFJ .... High-Frequency Jammer
HFJV .... High-Frequency Jet Ventilation [*Pulmonary ventilation*]
HFK .... Human Foreskin Keratinocyte [*Cytology*]
HFL .... Heliflyg AG [*Sweden*] [*ICAO designator*] (FAAC)
HFL .... Heliport Right Laboratory (SAUS)
HFL .... Helium Fill Line
HFL .... Hesperia Fine Sandy Loam [*A soil type*]
HFL .... High Free Lift (SAUS)
HFL .... Highly Flammable Liquid (HEAS)
HFL .... Homestead Financial (EFIS)
HFL .... Human Factors Laboratory [*University of South Dakota*] [*National Institute of Standards and Technology*] [*Research center*]
HFL .... Human Fetal Lung
HFL .... Hydrogen Fluoride Laser (ACAE)
HFLA .... Handling Fixture - Line Accessory (MCD)
HFLD .... Handling Fixture - Line Dolly (MCD)
HFLM .... Hydro Flame Corp. (SAUO)
HFLRI .... High Frequency Limited Range Intercept
HFLS .... Hanford Fire Logistics System (SAUS)
H flu .... Hemophilus Influenzae [*Bacteriology*] (DAVI)
HFM .... Hachette Filipacchi Magazines [*A publication*]
HFM .... Hand and Foot Monitor (SAUS)
HFM .... Hand, Foot, and Mouth [*Disease*]
HFM .... Hazardous Fluids Module (SAUS)
HFM .... Health and Fault Management (SAUS)
HFM .... Health Facilities Management (SAUO)
HFM .... Heat Flow Meter (SAUS)
HFM .... Heavy Force Modernization [*Army*]
HFM .... Heavy Forces Modernization (SAUS)
HFM .... Held for Manufacturing
HFM .... Held for Material
HFM .... Hemifacial Microsomia [*Medicine*] (DMAA)
HFM .... Hemophilia Foundation of Michigan (SAUO)
HFM .... Henry Ford Museum (SAUO)
HFM .... High Fidelity Magic (SAUS)
HFM .... High Field Magnetism (SAUS)
HFM .... High-Field Magnetometer [*Instrumentation*]
HFM .... High Frequency Microphone (SAUS)
HFM .... High-Frequency Mode (IAA)
HFM .... Hold for Money [*Business term*]
HFM .... Hollow Fiber Membrane (NASA)
HFM .... Horizonatal Flexible Mandrel (PDAA)
HFM .... Hot Film Meter [*Automotive engines*]
HFM .... Hot Forming (SAUS)
HFM .... National Society for Healthcare Foodservice Management (NTPA)
HFMA .... Hardwood Flooring Manufacturers' Association (BUAC)
HFMA .... Hardwood Plywood Manufacturers Association (SAUO)
HFMA .... Healthcare Financial Management Association (EA)
HFMA .... Health Food Manufacturers Association [*British*] (DBA)
HFMA .... Hospital Financial Management Association [*Later, Healthcare Financial Management Association*] (EA)
HFMB .... Hollow-Fiber Membrane Bioreactor (DB)
HFMD .... Hand-Foot-and-Mouth Disease (PDAA)
HFMD .... Home Federal Corp. [*NASDAQ symbol*] (NQ)
HFMD .... Home Federal (MD) [*NASDAQ symbol*] (TTSB)
HF Method .... Hartree-Fock Method (SAUS)
HFMF .... Home-Finish Monolithic Floor (SAUS)
HFMF .... Home-Furnish Monolithic Floor (SAUS)
HFMI .... Highly Filled Materials Institute [*Stevens Institute of Technology*]
HFMO .... Highest Filled Molecular Orbital (SAUS)
HF-MOR .... Half-Morocco [*Bookbinding*] (DGA)
HFMP .... Heavy Force Modernization Plan (SAUS)
HFM Press .... Hot Forming Press (SAUS)
HFMR .... HF [*High Frequency*] Modem Replacement (DOMA)
HFMR .... High-Fat Milk Replacer (SAUS)
HFMRA .... Honorary Foreign Member of the Royal Academy
HFMS .... High Frequency Monitoring System (SAUS)
HFMS .... Highway Fleet Management System (MCD)
HFMS .... Hospital Finance Management System (SAUS)
HFMS .... Hospital Formulary Management System (SAUO)
HFMS .... Human Factors Measurement System
HFMSS .... Heavy Force Modernization Survivability System
HFMSSP .... Heavy Force Modernization System Safety Plan [*Army*]
HFMU .... High-Fidelity Mock-Up [*NASA*] (NASA)
HFN .... High Flash Naphta (SAUS)
HFN .... Hofn [*Iceland*] [*Airport symbol*] (OAG)
HFN .... Human Fibronectin [*Cytochemistry*]
HFNC .... HFNC Financial [*NASDAQ symbol*] (TTSB)
HFNC .... HFNC Financial Corp. [*NASDAQ symbol*] (SAG)
HFNCFn .... HFNC Financial Corp. [*Associated Press*] (SAG)
HFNS .... High Flux Neutron Source (SAUS)
HFO .... Half Fare Order (SAUS)
HFO .... Heavy Fuel Oil
HFO .... Height Finder Operator (MUGU)
HFO .... Heterodyne-Frequency Oscillator (SAUS)
HFO .... High-Frequency Oscillator
HFO .... Hole Full of Oil (SAUS)
HFO .... Honolulu, HI [*Location identifier*] [*FAA*] (FAAL)
HFO .... Hydrogenated Fish Oil (SAUS)
HFOD .... Heptafluorodimethyloctanedione (SAUS)
HFO-HOM .... High Frequency Oscillator-High-Order Multiplier (SAUS)
HFORL .... Human Factors Operation Research Laboratory [*Air Force*]
HFOS .... HERL-RTP Forced Oscillation System (SAUS)
HFOSL .... Human Factors and Organizational Systems Laboratory [*Navy Personnel Research and Development Center*] [*San Diego, CA*]
HFOV .... High-Frequency Oscillatory Ventilation [*Medicine*] (DAVI)
HFOX .... Home Federal Savings Bank (Ohio) [*NASDAQ symbol*] (COMM)
HFP .... Hamdard Foundation Pakistan (EAIO)
HFP .... Hand Feed Punch (SAUS)
HFP .... Heat-Flow Probe (ACAE)
HFP .... Held for Planning (MCD)
HFP .... Helical Flight Path
HFP .... Helium Fuel-Tank Pressurization (AAG)
HFP .... Hexafluoropropylene [*Organic chemistry*]
HFP .... Highfield Property Investments Ltd. [*Toronto Stock Exchange symbol*]
HFP .... High Fragmentation Projectile (SAUS)
HFP .... High Fuel Pump (HAWK)
HFP .... Hostile Fire Pay [*Special pay for hazardous duty*] [*Military*] (AABC)
HFP .... Host-to-Front End Protocol (SAUS)
HFP .... Hot Full Power [*Nuclear energy*] (NRCH)

HFP............ Huron Forest Products Joint Venture [*Commercial*] (EERA)
HFP............ Hybrid Fabrication Procedure (MCD)
HFP............ Hypofibrinogenic Plasma
HFPA.......... Hollywood Foreign Press Association (EA)
HFPA.......... Home Fashions Products Association (EA)
HFPA.......... Hydroxyfarnesylphosphonic Acid [*Organic chemistry*]
HFPAC........ High Frequency Powder Air Conveyor (PDAA)
HFPCS........ Health Facilities Planning and Construction Service
HFPER........ Human Factors Program Final Report (SAUS)
HFPFR........ Human Factors Program Final Report (SAUO)
HFPO.......... Hexafluoropropylene Epoxide (EDCT)
HFPO.......... Hexafluoropropylene Oxide [*Organic chemistry*]
HFP/PFH..... Humanist Feminist Party (Belgium) [*Political party*] (PSAP)
HFPPV........ High-Frequency Positive Pressure Ventilation [*Medicine*]
HFPR.......... Handling Fixture - Production (MCD)
HFPR.......... Human Factors and Personnel Resources (DNAB)
HFPRI......... Hokkaido Forest Products Research Institute (SAUS)
HFPS.......... Hay Fever Prevention Society
HFPS.......... High-Frequency Phase Shifter [*Telecommunications*]
HFPS.......... Home Fallout Protection Survey [*Formerly, EFPH*] [*Civil Defense*]
HFPSI......... Human Factors Personnel Selection Inventory [*Interpersonal skills and attitudes test*]
HFPT........... Health Fitness Physical Therapy [*NASDAQ symbol*] (SAG)
HFPT........... Held for Perishable Tools
HFPT........... Hlth Fitness Physl Therapy [*NASDAQ symbol*] (TTSB)
HFR............ Hallstsom Faunal Reserve (SAUS)
Hfr............. Heart Frequency [*Medicine*] (EDAA)
HFR............ Heart Frequency (SAUS)
hfr.............. heifer (SAUS)
HFR............ Height Finder RADAR (CET)
HFR............ Held for Release (SAUS)
HFR............ Heli France [*ICAO designator*] (FAAC)
HFR............ H Frame (SAUS)
HFR............ High Fill Rate [*Valve*] [*Automotive engineering*]
HFR............ High Flux Reactor [*Netherlands*] [*Nuclear energy*]
Hfr............. High Frequency (STED)
HFR............ High Frequency of Recombination [*Medicine*]
HFR............ High Frequency Range (SAUS)
HFR............ High Frequency Recombinants (or Recombination) (SAUS)
HFR............ High-Frequency Resistor
HFR............ Hold for Release [*Advertising*] (BARN)
HFR............ Human Factors Research
HFRA.......... High-Frequency Recovery Antenna (KSC)
HFRA.......... Honorary Fellow of the Royal Academy [*British*]
HFRA.......... Honorary Foreign Member of the Royal Academy (SAUS)
H-F Radar.... Height Finder Radar (SAUS)
HF Radios... High Frequency Radios (SAUS)
HFRB.......... Hawaii Fire Rating Bureau (SAUO)
HFRB.......... High Frequency Radio Broadcast (SAUS)
HFRB.......... High Frequency Regional Broadcast (SAUO)
HFRDF........ High-Frequency Radio Direction Finding (IAA)
HFRDF........ High-Frequency Repeater Distribution Frame (DEN)
HFRE.......... Hydraulic Fluid Replenishment Equipment
HFRF.......... Help for Russia Fund (SAUO)
HFRG.......... High-Frequency Radio Group [*Military*] (CAAL)
Hfr mutant... High-Frequency Recombination Mutant (STED)
HFRO.......... Hill Farming Research Organization (SAUO)
HFRP.......... Harvard Family Research Project (STAH)
HFR Press... H Frame Press (SAUS)
HFRR.......... Hydrofluoric Acid Reprocessor Return [*System*] (AAEL)
HFRS.......... Hemorrhagic Fever with Renal Stones [*Medicine*] (MELL)
HFRS.......... Hemorrhagic Fever with Renal Syndrome [*Medicine*]
HFRSc........ Forged Roll Scleroscope Hardness Number, Model c (SAUS)
HFRSd........ Forged Roll Scleroscope Hardness Number, Model d (SAUS)
HFRT.......... High-Frequency Radio Transmitter
HFRT.......... High Frequency Resonance Technique (SAUS)
HFRW......... High-Frequency Resistance Welding [*Manufacturing term*]
HFRZ.......... Halbfranzband [*Half-Calf Binding*] [*Publishing*] [*German*]
HFS............ Australian Department of Health and Family Services (SAUO)
HFS............ French Frigate Shoals, HI [*Location identifier*] [*FAA*] (FAAL)
HFS............ Hagfors [*Sweden*] [*Seismograph station code, US Geological Survey*] (SEIS)
HFS............ Hands-Free System [*Automotive engineering*]
HFS............ Hardware Failure Summary (SAUS)
HFS............ Harrison Fisher Society (EA)
HFS............ Health and Family Services (SAUS)
HFS............ Heat Flow Sensor (SAUS)
HFS............ Heat Flux Sensor
HFS............ Heavy Flushing Spray
HFS............ Height Finder Supervisor (SAUS)
HFS............ Hemifacial Spasm [*Medicine*]
HFS............ HFS, Inc. [*Associated Press*] (SAG)
HFS............ Hierarchical File Storage (ACRL)
HFS............ Hierarchical File System [*Computer science*]
HFS............ High-Field Superconductor (SAUS)
HFS............ High-Frequency Stimulation [*Physiology*]
HFS............ High Frequency Switching (SAUS)
HFS............ High-Fructose Syrup (EDCT)
HFS............ Holstein Friesian Society of Great Britain and Ireland (DBA)
HFS............ Holy Family Seminary [*Connecticut*]
HFS............ Horizontal Flight Simulator (MCD)
HFS............ Hospital Financial Support (DMAA)
HFS............ Hospitality Franchise Systems [*NYSE symbol*] (SPSG)
HFS............ Hostile Fire Simulator [*Military*] (MCD)
HFS............ Hot Finished Seamless (SAUS)
HFS............ Household Financial Services [*Australia*]
HFS............ Household Food Security (FOTI)
HFS............ Human Factors Society (EA)
HFS............ Human Factors Study
HFS............ Human Factor System (SAUO)
HFS............ Hydrogen Forward-scattering Spectrometry (SAUS)
HFS............ HyperFine Shift (AAEL)
hfs............. Hyperfine Structure (STED)
HFS............ Hyperfine Structure
HFS............ Hypothetical Future Samples [*Statistics*]
HFSA.......... Hardin Bancorp [*NASDAQ symbol*] (TTSB)
HFSA.......... Home Federal Savings Bank (N. Carolina) [*NASDAQ symbol*] (COMM)
HFSA.......... Human Factors Society of America (SAUO)
HFSA.......... Hydrofluorsilicic Acid [*Inorganic chemistry*]
HF/SB......... High Frequency Sideband (SAUS)
HFSB.......... Home Federal Savings Bank (S. Carolina) [*NASDAQ symbol*] (COMM)
HFSC.......... Hamilton Financial Services Corp. [*NASDAQ symbol*] (SAG)
HFSC.......... Human Fetal Spinal Cord
HFSC.......... Hyperfine Splitting Constant [*Spectroscopy*]
HF-SCF....... Hartee-Fock Self-Consistent Field (MEC)
HFSD.......... Heating and Fueling Systems Division (SAUS)
HFSE.......... High-Field-Strength Elements [*Geochemistry*]
HFSE.......... Human Factors and Safety Engineering (DNAB)
HFSF.......... High Flux Solar Furnace (SAUS)
HFSF.......... Home Federal Financial Corp. [*NASDAQ symbol*] (SAG)
HFSF.......... Home Federal S&L Assn. of San Francisco [*NASDAQ symbol*] (COMM)
HFSF.......... Hot Fuel Storage Facility (SAUS)
HFSG.......... Healthcare Financing Study Group (EA)
HFSH.......... Human Follicle Stimulating Hormone [*Endocrinology*]
hFSH.......... Human Follicle-Stimulating Hormone [*Medicine*] (STED)
HFSIW........ Hospitality Franchise Sys Wrrt [*NASDAQ symbol*] (TTSB)
HFSL.......... Home Owners Federal Savings and Loan Association (SAUO)
HFSM.......... High Fidelity Simulation Model (SPST)
HFSNAP...... High Frequency Steerable Null Antenna Processor (ACAE)
HF Solvent... High Flash Solvent (SAUS)
HFSP.......... Hanukah Factor Serine Protease (DMAA)
HFSP.......... Human Frontier Science Program [*An international effort, proposed by Japan in 1987*]
HFSS.......... High Frequency Search System (SAUS)
HFSS.......... High-Frequency Sounder System (SSD)
HFSS.......... Hyperfine Structure Spectrum (SAUS)
HF/SSB....... High Frequency/Single Sideband (SAUO)
HFSSB........ High-Frequency Single Sideband [*Telecommunications*]
HFSSC........ High-Frequency Swept Spectrum Communications
HFST.......... Hearing-for-Speech Test
HFST.......... High-Flux Scram Trip [*Nuclear energy*] (IEEE)
HFSU.......... Heat Flux Sensing Unit
HFSV.......... High Flow Shutoff Valve
HFSWR....... High-Frequency Surface Wave RADAR
HFSZ.......... Hoxie Farm Supply [*Federal Railroad Administration identification code*]
HFT............ Hachette-Filipacchi Telematique [*Information service or system*] (IID)
HFT............ Hammerfest [*Norway*] [*Airport symbol*] (OAG)
HFT............ Hartree-Fock Theory (SAUS)
HFT............ Hawaii Federation of Teachers (SAUO)
HFT............ Heat Flux Transducer (SAUS)
HFT............ Heavy Fire Team [*Military*]
HFT............ Heft (ROG)
HFT............ Height Finder Technican (SAUS)
HFT............ Heiney Family Tree (EA)
HFT............ Held for Tooling
HFT............ Hepatic Function Test [*Medicine*] (EDAA)
HFT............ Hidden Figures Test [*Medicine*] (EDAA)
HFT............ Hidden Frames Test [*Education*] (EDAC)
HFT............ Higher Formation Trainer (SAUS)
HFT............ High-Flux Telescope
HFT............ High-Frequency of Transduction [*Virology*]
HFT............ High Frequency Transceiver (SAUS)
HFT............ High Frequency Transducing (SAUS)
HFT............ High-Frequency Transduction (STED)
HFT............ High-Frequency Transfer (DB)
HFT............ High Function Terminal (SAUS)
HFT............ Hollyfordair Travel Ltd. [*New Zealand*] [*ICAO designator*] (FAAC)
HFT............ Home Farm Trust (BUAC)
HFT............ Horizontal Flight Test (NAKS)
HFT............ Horizontal Flight Testing [*NASA*] (KSC)
HFT............ Hot Functional Testing [*Nuclear energy*] (NRCH)
HFT............ Human Factors Team (SAUO)
HFT............ International Symposium on Human Factors in Telecommunications (BUAC)
HFT............ Itraoperative Intra-Arterial Fibrinolytic Therapy [*Medicine*] (EDAA)
HFTA.......... Hexafluorothioacetone [*Organic chemistry*]
HFTA.......... High Frequency Towed Array
HFT&E........ Human Factors Test and Evaluation (SAUO)
HFTB.......... Handling Fixture - Tow Bar (MCD)
HFTC.......... High-Frequency Track Circuit [*Indian Railway*] (TIR)
HFTE.......... Hemispheric Free Trade Expansion (SAUO)
HFTE.......... Human Factors Test and Evaluation [*Military*] (MCD)
HFTF.......... Horizontal Flight Test Facility [*NASA*] (NASA)
HFTL.......... Held for Tool Liaison
HFTS.......... Horizontal Flight Test Simulator [*NASA*] (NASA)
HFT/S......... How to Flight/How to Support (SAUS)

HFTS .... Human Factors Trade Studies [*Navy*]
HFTUAAM .... High Frequency Tuning Unit Antenna Automatic Matching (SAUS)
HFTX .... High Frequency Transmitter (SAUS)
HFU .... Hand-Foot-Uterus Syndrome [*Medicine*] (DMAA)
HFU .... Heat-Flow [*or Flux*] Unit [*Nuclear energy*]
HFU .... Heeres-Funkstelle [*Army Radio Station*] [*German military - World War II*]
HFUEA .... Hughes Fullerton Employees' Association (ACAE)
H Function ... Hamiltonian Function (SAUS)
HFUPR .... Hourly Fetal Urine Production Rate [*Medicine*] (AAMN)
HFUS .... Historic Festivals of the United States [*A publication*]
HFV .... High-Frequency Ventilation [*Medicine*]
HFV .... Horizontal Flight Vector
HFV .... Human Foamy Virus
HF-VEL .... Half-Vellum [*Bookbinding*] (DGA)
HFVOA .... Hull Fishing Vessel Owners' Association (BUAC)
HFW .... Hanford Facility Waste (SAUS)
HFW .... Haverfordwest [*Wales*] [*Airport symbol*] (AD)
HFW .... High Frequency Wave (SAUS)
HFW .... Hole Full of Water [*Drilling*] (DICI)
HFW .... Horizontal Full Width (SAUS)
HFW .... Housing for Women (BUAC)
HFWA .... Heritage Financial Corp. [*NASDAQ symbol*] (NASQ)
HFWA .... High-Frequency Wave Analyzer
HFWB .... High Freqency Wire Broadcasting (PDAA)
HFWE .... Having Fun with Elvis [*Fan club*] (EA)
HFWF .... Hired Farm Working Force
HFX .... Halifax City Regional Library [*UTLAS symbol*]
HFX .... High-Frequency Transceiver [*or Transducer*]
HG .... Centreline Air Services Ltd. [*British*] [*ICAO designator*] (ICDA)
HG .... Die Hethitischen Gesetze. Documenta et Monumenta Orientis Antiqui 7 [*Leiden*] [*A publication*] (BJA)
Hg .... Haggai [*Old Testament book*]
HG .... Half Gross (DNAB)
HG .... Hammurabi's Gesetz (BJA)
HG .... Hand Generator
HG .... Hand Ginned (SAUS)
HG .... Hand Grip (DMAA)
HG .... Handgrip Exercise (DB)
HG .... Harbor Airlines [*ICAO designator*] (AD)
HG .... Hard Gelatin [*Pharmacy*]
HG .... Hard Gypsum (SAUS)
HG .... Harmonic Generator
HG .... Harrogate [*Postcode*] (ODBW)
HG .... Having (ROG)
HG .... Head Gasket [*Automotive engineering*]
HG .... Head Gear (SAUS)
HG .... Headgear [*Mining engineering*] (IAA)
HG .... Head Group (SAUO)
HG .... Heavy Grain (SAUS)
hg .... Hectogram (ADWA)
hg .... Hectogram (MIST)
HG .... Hectogram
HG .... Height Gauge (SAUS)
HG .... Helical Gear (SAUS)
HG .... Heliogram
Hg .... Hemoglobin [*Medicine*] (GOBB)
HG .... Hemoglobin [*Biochemistry, medicine*]
HG .... Heptadecapeptide Gastrin [*Endocrinology*]
HG .... Heritage Group (SAUO)
HG .... Herpes Genitalis [*Infectious disease*] (DAVI)
HG .... Herpes Gestationis [*Medicine*]
HG .... Herter-Gee [*Syndrome*] [*Medicine*] (DB)
HG .... Heschl's Gyrus [*Brain anatomy*]
Hg .... Heterodera glycenes [*A nematode*]
HG .... Hexylene Glycol [*Organic chemistry*]
HG .... Higher Grade
HG .... High Gain [*Medicine*] (EDAA)
HG .... High German [*Language, etc.*]
HG .... High Glucose [*Clinical chemistry*]
HG .... High Grade (SAUS)
HG .... High Grain (NASA)
HG .... His [*or Her*] Grace
HG .... Hitchhiker Goddard mission (SAUS)
HG .... Holy Ghost
HG .... Holy Grail (ADWA)
HG .... Home Guard [*British*]
HG .... Homing Guidance (AAG)
HG .... Horizon Grow [*Astronomy*] (OA)
HG .... Horse Guards [*British*]
HG .... Hotchkiss Gunner [*British military*] (DMA)
HG .... House & Garden (SAUS)
HG .... Housing Guaranty
HG .... Hull Gage (SAUS)
HG .... Hull Gauge
HG .... Human Gastrin (SAUS)
HG .... Human Genetics (journ.) (SAUS)
HG .... Human Genome [*Medicine*] (MELL)
HG .... Human Gonadotrophin [*Endocrinology*]
HG .... Human Growth [*Factor*] [*Endocrinology*] (DAVI)
HG .... Hutchinson-Gilford [*Disease*] [*Medicine*] (DB)
Hg .... Hydrargyrum [*Mercury*] [*Chemical element*]
HG .... Hydraulic Gate (SAUS)
HG .... Hydrogen Gas [*System*] [*Nuclear energy*] (NRCH)
HG .... Hydrogen Generator
HG .... Hydrogeology (SAUS)
HG .... Hydrophilic Group [*Surfactant technology*]
HG .... Hydrostatic Gage (SAUS)
HG .... Hyperglycemic-Glycogenolytic [*Factor*] [*Endocrinology*]
HG .... Hypertensive Group [*Cardiology*]
HG .... Hypobranchial Gland
HG .... Hypoglycemia [*Medicine*] (DMAA)
Hg .... Mercury [*Chemical*] (EERA)
HG .... Office of Hearings and Appeals (SAUO)
HG .... Workout Handily from Gate [*Horse racing*]
HGA .... Hammel Green and Abrahamson, Inc. [*A national leader in innovative design*]
HGA .... Handweavers Guild of America (EA)
HGA .... Hang Glider Association (EA)
HGA .... Hardware Graphics Accelerator [*Computer science*]
HGA .... Hargeisa [*Somalia*] [*Airport symbol*] (OAG)
HGA .... Harvey Gray & Associates
HGA .... Head Gimbal Assembly (SAUS)
HGA .... Heated Graphite Atomizer (SAUS)
HGA .... Heat Generator Assembly (KSC)
HGA .... Heptagonal Games Association (EA)
HGA .... Hercules Graphics Adapter (PCM)
HGA .... Hereditary Grand Almoner [*Freemasonry*]
HGA .... Heritage U.S. Government Income Fund [*NYSE symbol*] (SPSG)
HGA .... High Gain Aerial (or Antenna) (SAUS)
HGA .... Hobby Greenhouse Association (EA)
HGA .... Hobby Greenhouse Owners Association of America [*Defunct*] (EA)
HGA .... Hobby Guild of America (EA)
HGA .... Hogan Air [*ICAO designator*] (FAAC)
HGA .... Holographic Grating Axicon (ACAE)
HGA .... Holological Guild of Australia (SAUO)
HGA .... Homogentisate [*Biochemistry*]
HGA .... Homogentisic Acid [*Biochemistry*] (MAE)
HGA .... Hop Growers Association (SAUO)
HGA .... Hop Growers of America (EA)
HGA .... Hotel Greeters of America [*Later, HMGI*]
HGA .... Hungarian Gypsy Association (SAUO)
HGAA .... Hydride Generation Atomic Absorption [*Analytical chemistry*]
HGAC .... High Gain Aerial (or Antenna) Controller (SAUS)
HGAC .... Human Genetics Advisory Commission [*British*]
HGAC .... Human Genetics Advisory Committee (WDAA)
H G & L Rev ... Harvard Gay & Lesbian Review [*A publication*] (BRI)
HGAS .... HERL-RTP Gas/Aerosol System (SAUS)
HGAS .... High Gain Aerial (or Antenna) System (SAUS)
HGB .... Handelsgesetzbuch [*Commercial Code*] [*German*] [*Legal term*] (DLA)
HGB .... Hanford Gable Butte [*Washington*] [*Seismograph station code, US Geological Survey*] (SEIS)
hgb .... Hemoglobin [*Therapy term*] (CTAA)
Hgb .... Hemoglobin [*Medicine*] (DB)
HGB .... Hemoglobin [*Biochemistry, medicine*]
HGB .... Hot Gas Bonder
HGB .... Household Goods Carriers' Bureau Agent, Arlington VA [*STAC*]
Hgb & Hct ... Hemoglobin and Hematocrit [*Hematology*] (DAVI)
Hgb-CO .... Carboxyhemoglobin [*Medicine*] (EDAA)
Hgb-CO .... Hemoglobin-Carbon Monoxide Saturation [*Medicine*] (EDAA)
HGB EL .... Hemoglobin Electrophoresis [*Hematology*] (DAVI)
HGB Elect ..... Hemoglobin Electrophoresis [*Hematology*] (DAVI)
Hgb F .... Hemoglobin Fetal [*Also, HbF, HgF*] [*Medicine*] (DAVI)
HGB Message ... Hardware failure-oriented Group Blocking Message (SAUO)
HGBN .... Herringbone [*Electronics, engineering*]
HGB-PL .... Hemoglobin Plasma [*Hematology*] (DAVI)
HGBS .... Methemoglobin-Sulfhemoglobin [*Hematology*] (DAVI)
HGC .... Hartford Graduate Center (SAUS)
HGC .... Hercules Graphics [*Computer science*] (CDE)
HGC .... Hercules Graphics Controller (SAUS)
HGC .... High resolution Graphies Control (SAUS)
HGC .... Hudson General Corp. [*AMEX symbol*] (SPSG)
HGC .... Human Genome Center (SAUS)
HGC .... Hypergolic Clean
HGCA .... Hebrew and Gentile Christian Association (SAUO)
HGCA .... Home Grown Cereals Authority (PDAA)
HGCA .... Home-Grown Cereals Authority (SAUO)
HGCB .... Household Goods Carriers' Bureau (EA)
HGCC .... Hot Gas Clean Up (SAUS)
HGCC .... Human Genome Coordinating Committee (HGEN)
HGCCSO .... Higher Grades Conference of Civil Service Organizations (SAUO)
HgCdTe .... Mercury-Cadmium-Telluride (SAUS)
HGCP .... Hercules Graphics Card Plus (SAUS)
HGCS .... Human Granulocyte Colony Stimulating (SAUS)
HGCSD .... Harris-Galveston Coastal Subsidence District (SAUO)
HGCSD .... Harris Government Communication System Division (ACAE)
HG-CSF .... Human Granulocyte, Colony Stimulation Factor [*Hematology*]
HGCU .... Heavy Glider Conversion Unit [*British military*] (DMA)
HGD .... Hangard Aviation Ltd. [*Mongolia*] [*ICAO designator*] (FAAC)
HGD .... Hawthorne Gold [*Vancouver Stock Exchange symbol*]
HGD .... High Grade Dysplasia [*Medicine*]
HGD .... Highway-to-Group Demultiplexer (SAUO)
HGD .... Hob Generating Diameter (SAUS)
HGD .... Hogshead
HGD .... Hour-Glass Device (SAUS)
HGD .... Hughenden [*Australia*] [*Airport symbol*] (OAG)
HGD .... Hypersensitivity Glomerular Disease [*Medicine*] (MELL)
HGD .... Hysterical Gait Disorder [*Medicine*] (MELL)
hg den .... Hearing Denied [*Legal term*] (HGAA)
HGDFS .... High Gain Direction Finding System (PDAA)

HGDH.......... His [*or Her*] Grand Ducal Highness
HGDP.......... Human Genome Diversity Project [*Genetics*]
HGDS.......... Hazardous Gas Detection Systems (KSC)
HGDS.......... High Gradient Directional Solidification (SAUS)
HGE.......... Handling Ground Equipment
HGE.......... Harmonisation Group on ECDIS (SAUO)
HGE.......... Heavy Gold Electroplate (SAUS)
HGE.......... Hemorrhage [*Medicine*] (ROG)
HGE.......... Hemorrhagic Gastroenteritis (SAUS)
HGE.......... Het Gilgamesj-Epos [*A publication*] (BJA)
HGE.......... Hinge [*Automotive engineering*]
HGE.......... Human Granulocytic Ehrlichiosis [*Medicine*]
HGE.......... Hybrid Geotempered Envelope [*Architecture*]
HGE.......... Hydraulic Grade Elevations (NRCH)
HGEA.......... Hawaii Government Employees Association (SAUO)
HGEC.......... Hindustan General Electrical Corp. (SAUS)
HGEC.......... Hindustan General Electrical Corporation (SAUO)
HGED.......... High-Gain Emissive Display [*Technology*]
HGEEA.......... Huntsville General Electric Engineers Association (SAUO)
HGET.......... Hanford General Employee Training (SAUS)
HGF.......... Heliglobe Industries [*France*] [*FAA designator*] (FAAC)
HGF.......... Helmholtz-Gemeinschaft Deutscher Forschungs-zentren [*Helmholtz association of German research centres*]
HGF.......... Hematopoietic Growth Factor [*Biochemistry Medicine*]
HgF.......... Hemoglobin, Fetal [*Also, HbF*] [*Medicine*]
Hg-F.......... Hemoglobin-Fetal (SAUS)
HGF.......... Hemopoietic Growth Factor [*Hematology*]
HGF.......... Hepatocyte Growth Factor [*Biochemistry*]
HGF.......... Home-Grown Fruits Ltd. (SAUO)
HGF.......... Horizontal Gradient Freeze (AAEL)
HGF.......... Hot Gas Facility (SAUS)
HGF.......... Household Goods Forwarders Tariff Bureau, Washington DC [*STAC*]
HGF.......... Human Growth Foundation (EA)
HGF.......... Hyperglycemic-Glycogenolytic Factor [*Later, Glucagon*] [*Endocrinology*]
HGFA.......... Henry George Foundation of America (EA)
HGFA.......... Household Goods Forwarders Association of America [*Washington, DC*]
HGFGB.......... Henry George Foundation of Great Britain (SAUO)
HGFN.......... HomeGold Financial [*NASDAQ symbol*] [*Formerly, Emergent Group*]
HGG.......... Herpetic Geniculate Ganglionitis [*Medicine*] (DB)
HGG.......... Hot Gas Generator
HGG.......... Human Gamma-Globulin [*Endocrinology*]
HGG.......... Human Gas Generator (SAUS)
HGG.......... Hypogammaglobulinaemia (SAUS)
HG GA.......... Height Gage (SAUS)
HGGM.......... Human Gastric Gel Mucin [*Medicine*] (EDAA)
HGGR.......... Haggar Corp. [*NASDAQ symbol*] (SAG)
HGH.......... Hangzhou [*China*] [*Airport symbol*] (OAG)
HGH.......... Historische Grammatik der Hebraeischen Sprache [*H. Bauer and P. Leander*] [*A publication*] (BJA)
HGH.......... Hughes & Hatcher, Inc. (SAUO)
hGH.......... Human Growth Hormone (DOG)
HGH.......... Human Growth Hormone [*Also, hGH*] [*Endocrinology*]
HGHF/SF.......... Hepatocyte Growth Factor/Scatter Factor (ADWA)
HGHGHG.......... Hilf Gott, Hilf Gott, Hilf Gott [*God Help, God Help, God Help*] [*Motto of Sophie Elisabeth, Countess of Schwarzenburg (1565-1621)*]
Hghland.......... Highland Federal Bank [*Associated Press*] (SAG)
Hghlds.......... Highlands (DD)
HGHR.......... Higher
hGHR.......... Human Growth Hormone Receptor [*Genetics*] (DOG)
HGHSC.......... Home Grown Herbage Seeds Committee (BUAC)
Hght.......... Height (SAUS)
HghwyH.......... Highway Holdings Ltd. [*Associated Press*] (SAG)
HGI.......... Hardgrove Grindability Index
HGI.......... Henry George Institute (EA)
HGI.......... HGI Realty [*NYSE symbol*] (TTSB)
HGI.......... Horizon Group [*NYSE symbol*] [*Formerly, HGI Realty*] (SG)
HGI.......... Horizon Group, Inc. [*NYSE symbol*] (SAG)
HGI.......... Horizon Outlet Centers [*NYSE symbol*] (SPSG)
HGI.......... Hostility-Guilt Inventory (DB)
HGIC.......... Harleysville Group, Inc. [*NASDAQ symbol*] (NQ)
HGI Rlty.......... HGI Realty, Inc. [*Associated Press*] (SAG)
HGIS.......... Hanford Geographic Information System (SAUS)
HGIS.......... Hypermedia Geographical Information Systems (SAUO)
HGJ.......... Hongo [*Japan*] [*Seismograph station code, US Geological Survey*] (SEIS)
HGL.......... Hamilton Group Ltd. [*Toronto Stock Exchange symbol*]
HGL.......... Helgoland [*Germany*] [*Airport symbol*] (OAG)
HGL.......... Hemoglobin Gene Loci [*Medicine*] (MELL)
HGL.......... Heregulin (DMAA)
HGL.......... Hewlett-Packard Graphics Language [*Image Format*] (AAEL)
HGL.......... Hierarchical Graph Language (SAUS)
HGL.......... High Gain Link
HGL.......... High Go Low Test
HGL.......... Homach Gap Lathe
HGL.......... Human Genome Laboratory (SAUS)
HGL.......... Hydraulic Grade Line (ADWA)
HGL.......... Hyperbolic Type Gas Lens (IAA)
HG Language.......... High German Language (SAUS)
HGLDS.......... Highlands (MCD)
HGLF.......... High-Grain/Low-Fiber [*Cereal*] (OA)
HGLND.......... Highland
HGL Test.......... High Go Low Test (SAUS)
HGM.......... Harmonic Gradient Method (SAUS)
HGM.......... Heavy Guided Missile (SAUS)
HGM.......... Hectogram (ROG)
HGM.......... Hemlo Gold Mines (SAUO)
HGM.......... Hepatogastric Ligament [*Medicine*] (MELL)
HGM.......... Hereditary Grand Master [*Freemasonry*] (ROG)
HGM.......... Hits per Gun per Minute (SAUS)
HGM.......... Home Guard Medal (SAUO)
HGM.......... Homestake Gold Mine (SAUO)
HGM.......... Horizontal Galvanometer Mirror (SAUS)
HGM.......... Hot Gas Manifold (NASA)
HGM.......... Human Gene-Mapping
HGM.......... Human Genome Meeting (HGEN)
HGM.......... Human Glucose Monitoring [*Medicine*] (MELL)
HGM.......... Hyoglossus Muscle [*Medicine*] (MELL)
HGMAA.......... Hang Glider Manufacturers Association of America [*Defunct*] (EA)
HGMC.......... Harmony Gold Mining Co. Ltd. [*NASDAQ symbol*] (SAG)
HGMCR.......... Human Genetic Mutant Cell Repository
HGMD.......... Human Gene Mutation Database (ADWA)
HG/MD.......... Hybrid Gun/Missile Demonstration (ACAE)
HGMF.......... High-Gradient Magnetic Filter (SAUS)
HGMF.......... High-Gradient Magnetic Filtration
HGMGR.......... Household Goods Military and Government Rate Tariff
HGMIS.......... Human Genome Management Information System (HGEN)
HGML.......... Human Gene-Mapping Library [*Database*]
HGML.......... Hypertext General Markup Language [*Computer science*] (VLIE)
HGMM.......... Hereditary Grand Master Mason [*Freemasonry*]
HGMN.......... Hair Growing Marketing Network (SAUS)
HGMN.......... Herb Growing and Marketing Network (EA)
HGMP.......... Human Genome Mapping Project (SAUO)
HGMP-RC.......... Human Genome Mapping Project Resource Centre (SAUO)
HGMS.......... Helicopter Gravity-Measuring System [*Naval Oceanographic Office*]
HGMS.......... High-Gradient Magnetic Separation (EDCT)
HGMS.......... High-Gradient Magnetic Separator (NRCH)
HGMU.......... Heavy Glider Maintenance Unit [*British military*] (DMA)
HGMUS.......... Horizontal Generator Mock-Up System [*NASA*]
HGN.......... Horizontal Gaze Nystagmus Test
HGN.......... Human Genome News [*A publication*] (HGEN)
HGN.......... Hypocomplementemic Glomerulonephritis [*Medicine*] (EDAA)
HGN.......... Hypogastric Nerve [*Anatomy*]
HGN.......... Hypoglossal Nerve [*Medicine*] (MELL)
HGN.......... Mae Hong Son [*Thailand*] [*Airport symbol*] (OAG)
HG/NG.......... Hydrogen Gas/Nitrogen Gas (NRCH)
HGO.......... Halsgerichtsordnung [*German*]
HGO.......... Heavy Gas Oils [*Petroleum product*]
HGO.......... Hepatic Glucose Output [*Physiology*]
HGO.......... Hermes Global Orbiter [*NASA, proposed*]
HGO.......... Hip Guidance Orthosis [*Medicine*] (EDAA)
HGO.......... Houston Grand Opera (SAUO)
HGO.......... Hugo, CO [*Location identifier*] [*FAA*] (FAAL)
HGO.......... Human Glucose Output [*Hematology*] (DMAA)
HGO.......... Korhogo [*Ivory Coast*] [*Airport symbol*] (OAG)
HgO.......... Mecuric Oxide [*Medicine*] (EDAA)
HGOA.......... Houston Grand Opera Association (SAUO)
HGOAA.......... Hobby Greenhouse Owners Association of America (SAUO)
HGOR.......... High Gas-Oil Ratio (SAUS)
HGP.......... Handset, General Purpose (SAUS)
HGP.......... Hanford Generating Plant (SAUO)
HGP.......... Hanford Generating Project (SAUO)
HGP.......... Hard Gas-Permeable [*Contact lenses*]
HGP.......... Hard Gypsum Plaster (SAUS)
HGP.......... Hepatic Glucose Production [*Hematology*] (DMAA)
HGP.......... Horizontal Ground Plane [*Automotive engineering*]
HGP.......... Hormonal Growth Promotant
HGP.......... Human Genome Program [*Genetics*]
HGP.......... Human Genome Project (HGEN)
HGP.......... Humbug Gulch Press (SAUO)
HGP.......... Hungarian Green Party [*Political party*] (BUAC)
HGP.......... Hungarian Gypsy Party [*Political party*] (BUAC)
HGP.......... Hyperglobulinemic Purpura [*Medicine*] (DMAA)
HGP-OIMLA.......... Hindustani Ghadar Party-Organization of Indian Marxist-Leninists Abroad (SAUO)
HGPRT.......... Hypoxanthine-Guanine Phosphoribosyltransferase [*AO HPRT*] [*An enzyme*]
HG-PRTase.......... Hypoxanthine-Guanine Phosphoribosyltransferase [*Also, HGPRT, HPRT*] [*An enzyme*] (DAVI)
HGPRT LOCUS.......... Hypoxanthine Guanine Phosphoribosyl Transferase Locus (LDT)
HGPS.......... High-Grade Plow Steel
HGPS.......... Hutchinson-Gilford Progeria Syndrome [*Medicine*] (DMAA)
HGPT.......... Hard Gloss Paint (SAUS)
HGPX.......... Harrison Gypsum [*Private rail car owner code*]
HGR.......... Hagerstown [*Maryland*] [*Airport symbol*] (OAG)
HGR.......... Hangar (KSC)
HGR.......... Hanger
HGR.......... Hanger Orthopedic Group, Inc. [*AMEX symbol*] (SPSG)
HGR.......... Haubitzgranate [*Howitzer Shell*] [*German military - World War II*]
HGR.......... Headgear Receiver [*Mining engineering*] (IAA)
HGR.......... Helium Graphite Reactor (SAUS)
HGR.......... High Group Receiving
HGR.......... High River Resources Ltd. [*Vancouver Stock Exchange symbol*]
HGR.......... Histoire Generale des Religions [*A publication*] (BJA)
HGR.......... Hluhluwe Game Reserve (SAUO)
HGR.......... Hot Gas Reinjection (PDAA)
HGR.......... Human Glucocorticoid Receptor [*Endocrinology*]
HGR.......... Hypervelocity Guided Rocket (SAUS)
HGR & SPTFAC.......... Hangar and Support Facility [*NASA*] (NASA)

HGRF .... Hot Gas Radiating Facility
HGRF .... Human Growth-Hormone Releasing Factor [*Biochemistry*]
hGRH .... Human Growth Hormone-Releasing Hormone [*Medicine*] (EDAA)
HGRM .... Hemogram [*Hematology*] (DAVI)
HGR Unit ..... High Group Receiving Unit (SAUO)
HGS .... Congregation de Hermanas Guadalupanas de la Salle (TOCD)
HGS .... Freetown [*Sierra Leone*] Hastings Airport [*Airport symbol*] (OAG)
HGS .... Hagensborg Resources Ltd. [*Vancouver Stock Exchange symbol*]
HGS .... Halliburton Geophysical Services, Inc. (TIMI)
HGS .... Harness Goat Society (BUAC)
HGS .... Harvard Germanic Studies (journ.) (SAUS)
HGS .... Head-Up Guidance System [*Aviation*]
HGS .... Heeresgasschutzschule (SAUS)
HGS .... Holographic Ground System (SAUO)
HGS .... Holographic Guidance System (SAUS)
HGS .... Hot Gas System
HGS .... Human Genome Sciences [*Commercial firm*]
H-GS .... Hurdy-Gurdy Society [*British*] (DBA)
HGS .... Hutsonville Grade School (SAUO)
HGS .... Hydrogen Gas Saver (MCD)
HGS .... Hydrogenous Gas Delivery System (SAUS)
HGS .... Hydrological Growing Season (SAUS)
HGS .... Hydrologic Growing Season (SAUS)
HGS .... Hyperbolic Grid System
HGSC .... Hoare Govett Small Companies Index [*British*]
HGSD .... Heavy Gauge Solid Drawn [*Conduit*]
HGSDP .... Hungarian Gypsy Social Democratic Party [*Political party*] (BUAC)
HGSE .... Harvard Graduate School of Education
HGSE .... Hot Gas Soldering Equipment
HGSEI .... Home and Garden Show Executives International [*Defunct*] (EA)
HGSHS .... Harvard Group Scale of Hypnotic Susceptibility [*Psychology*]
HGSI .... Human Genome Sciences [*NASDAQ symbol*] (TTSB)
HGSI .... Human Genome Sciences, Inc. [*NASDAQ symbol*] (SAG)
HGSIL .... High-Grade Squamous Intraepithelial Lesion [*Medicine*] (MELL)
HGSIL .... High-Grade Squamous Intraepithelial Lesions [*Medicine*]
HGSITVC .... Hot Gas Secondary Injection Thrust Vector Control (PDAA)
HGSL .... Hanford Geotechnical Sample Library (SAUS)
HGSP .... Home Guard Sector Point (SAUO)
HGSS .... Hellfire Ground Support Simulator (SAUS)
HGSSS .... Henry George School of Social Science (SAUO)
HGSW .... Heavy Gauge Screwed Welded [*Conduit*]
HGSW .... Horn Gap Switch
HGT .... Fort Hunter-Liggett (Jolon), CA [*Location identifier*] [*FAA*] (FAAL)
HGT .... Height (KSC)
hgt .... Height (SHCU)
HGT .... High Gelling Temperature [*Analytical biochemistry*]
HGT .... High Group Transmitting
hgt .... hogget (SAUS)
HGT .... Household Goods Transportation Association, Washington DC [*STAC*]
HGT .... Hugoton Royalty Trust [*NYSE symbol*] (SG)
HGT .... Hydrostatic-Gauging Technology [*Engineering*]
HGT .... Hypergeometric Group Testing [*Computer science*] (OA)
HGTA .... Honours Graduate Teachers' Association [*British*]
HGTAC .... Home Grown Timber Advisory Committee (BUAC)
HGTB .... Haiti Government Tourist Bureau (SAUO)
HGTMA .... Home-Grown Timber Marketing Association (SAUO)
HGTMC .... Home Grown Timber Marketing Corp. Ltd. [*British*] (BI)
HGTP .... Hanford Grout Technology Program (SAUS)
HGTPJC .... Home-Grown Threshed Peas Joint Committee (SAUO)
HGTS .... Heights [*Commonly used*] (OPSA)
hgts .... hoggets (SAUS)
HGTT .... Home-Grown Timber Trade (SAUO)
HGTV .... Home & Garden Television
HGTV .... Home and Garden Television Network
HGTVC .... Hot Gas Thrust Vector Control
HGU .... Horizon Gyroscope Unit [*Aviation*] (AIA)
HGU .... Mount Hagen [*Papua New Guinea*] [*Airport symbol*] (OAG)
HGUC .... Helsinki Guarantees for Ukraine Committee [*Defunct*] (EA)
HGV .... Heavy Goods Vehicle (SAUO)
HGV .... Heavy Goods Vehicles
HGV .... Hepatitis G Virus
HGV .... Highgrade Ventures [*Vancouver Stock Exchange symbol*]
HGV .... Hydrogen Gas Valve (MCD)
HGV .... Hypersonic Glide Vehicle (ACAE)
HGVSX .... SMBS Govt. Securities Cl.B [*Mutual fund ticker symbol*] (SG)
HGVT .... Horizontal Ground Vibration Test [*NASA*] (NASA)
HGW .... Heat-Generaring Waste (SAUS)
HGW .... Heat-Generative Radioactive Wastes [*Nuclear energy*]
HGW .... Hyper-Quenched Glassy Water [*Material science*]
HGWA .... Household Goods for Warders Association (SAUO)
HGWP .... Halocarbon Global-Warming Potential [*Meteorology*]
HGWS .... H. G. Wells Society (EA)
HGWY .... Highway (WGA)
HgwyH .... Highway Holdings Ltd. [*Associated Press*] (SAG)
HGX .... Lawrence, MA [*Location identifier*] [*FAA*] (FAAL)
HGZG .... Hilf Gott zu Glueck [*May God Help Us to Fortune*] [*Motto of Magdalene, Princess of Anhalt (1585-1657)*] [*German*]
HH .... Double Hard [*Pencil leads*]
HH .... Extra Hard [*Pencil leads*]
HH .... Fairchild/Republic [*ICAO aircraft manufacturer identifier*] (ICAO)
HH .... Habitat for Humanity (EA)
HH .... Haiti (SAUS)
HH .... Half Hard [*Metallurgy*]
HH .... Half Hardy [*Horticulture*]
H/H .... Half Height [*of an International Standards Organization container*] (DCTA)
HH .... Halogenated hydrocarbons (SAUS)
HH .... Halothane Hepatitis [*Medicine*] (DMAA)
HH .... Halothane Hypoxia [*Medicine*]
HH .... Hamish Hamilton [*Publisher*] [*British*]
HH .... Hamizrah Hehadash [*Jerusalem*] [*A publication*] (BJA)
HH .... Hampshire Hunt [*British*]
HH .... Handhole (AAG)
HH .... Hands [*Units of measure, especially for the height of horses*]
Hh .... Hands High [*Equine term*] (TED)
hh .... Hands High [*Equine term*] (TED)
HH .... Hanging Handset [*Telecommunications*] (TEL)
HH .... Happy Humpers (EA)
HH .... Harbridge House Europe (SAUO)
HH .... Hard of Hearing
HH .... Hargraves-Haserick (SAUO)
HH .... Harvest Help [*An association*] [*British*] (EAIO)
HH .... Hashomer Hatzair (EA)
H/H .... Hatch/Hold (SAUS)
HH .... Haunt Hunters (EA)
H/H .... Havre to Hamburg [*Shipping*]
HH .... Hawaii State Library System, Honolulu, HI [*Library symbol*] [*Library of Congress*] (LCLS)
HH .... Hayward and Hazelton's United States Circuit Court Reports [*District of Columbia*] [*A publication*] (DLA)
HH .... Hazardous Hydrocarbons (SAUS)
HH .... Head, Head [*Coin-tossing possibility*]
HH .... Head-Holmes [*Syndrome*] [*Medicine*] (DB)
HH .... Heading to Heading (VLIE)
HH .... Headlamp Housing [*Automotive engineering*]
HH .... Head-to-Head [*Polymer structure*]
HH .... Healthy [*Medicine*] (EDAA)
HH .... Healthy Hemophiliac [*Medicine*] (DMAA)
HH .... Heard of Hearing (SAUS)
HH .... Heavily Hinged (SAUS)
HH .... Heavy Hail (SAUS)
HH .... Heavy Helicopter [*Military*] (VNW)
HH .... Heavy Hinged [*Philately*]
HH .... Heavy Hole (SAUS)
HH .... Heavy Hydrogen
HH .... Heil Hitler [*Political organization*] [*British*]
HH .... Helen Hunt Jackson [*American novelist, 1830-1885*] [*Initials used as pseudonym*]
H-H .... Heli-Home [*Recreational vehicle*]
HH .... Hemmets Haerold [*Record label*] [*Sweden*]
H/H .... Hemoglobin and Hematocrit [*Medicine*] (STED)
Hh .... Hemopoietic Histocompatibility (STED)
HH .... Henderson and Haggard [*Inhaler*] [*Medicine*] (DAVI)
HH .... Hepatic Hydatidosis [*Medicine*] (MELL)
HH .... Herbig-Haro [*Astronomy*]
HH .... Hereditary Haemochromatosis [*Medicine*]
HH .... Here's Health [*Exhibition*] [*British*]
HH .... Herfindahl-Hirschman [*Economic indicator*]
HH .... Herman Hospital [*Houston, TX*]
HH .... Hermann Hospital (SAUS)
HH .... Her (or His) Honour (SAUO)
HH .... Hertfordshire Hunt [*British*] (ROG)
HH .... Hesketh Hubbard Art Society (SAUO)
HH .... Hetch Hetchy Railroad (IIA)
Hh .... Heterozygous [*Medicine*] (EDAA)
HH .... Hiatal Hernia [*Medicine*]
HH .... High Heels [*Doll collecting*]
HH .... High-Powered, Nondirectional Radio Homing Beacon [*Navigation*]
HH .... Himmelberger-Harrison Manufacturing [*Federal Railroad Administration identification code*]
HH .... His [*or Her*] Highness
HH .... His Holiness
HH .... His Honour [*British*] (ADA)
HH .... Historical Handbook
HH .... Hitchhiker (SAUS)
HH .... Hodgson's Horse [*British military*] (DMA)
HH .... Hogarth [*H.*] and Sons [*Steamship line*] (MHDW)
HH .... Hogshead (DNAB)
HH .... Hold Harmless (OICC)
H/H .... Hold/Hatch (SAUS)
HH .... Holding Hands (SAUS)
HH .... Holidays for Humanity [*An association*] (EA)
HH .... Holistic Health [*Medicine*] (DAVI)
HH .... Home Health [*Medicine*] (DAVI)
HH .... Home Help [*Medicine*]
HH .... Hommel AG [*Switzerland*] [*Research code symbol*]
HH .... Homonymous Hemianopsia [*Ophthalmology*]
HH .... Homozygous [*Medicine*] (EDAA)
HH .... Hooper Holmes, Inc. [*AMEX symbol*] (SPSG)
HH .... Horizontal-Horizontal (ACAE)
H/H .... Hospital/Homebound (SAUO)
H/H .... Host to Host (VLIE)
HH .... Hour (SAUS)
HH .... Hour Hand [*Clocks*] (ROG)
HH .... Household
H/H .... House to House (ADA)
HH .... Hughes Helicopters (MCD)
HH .... Human Hair [*Doll collecting*]
HH .... Humbert Humbert [*Character in Vladimir Nabokov's "Lolita"*]

HH .... Hunter-Hurler [*Syndrome*] [*Medicine*] (DB)
HH .... Hydroxyhexamide [*Organic chemistry*] (MAE)
HH .... Hydroxyhexenal [*Organic chemistry*]
HH .... Hyperactive Help [*Australia*]
HH .... Hypergastrinemic Hyperchlorhydria [*Medicine*] (DB)
HH .... Hypnogogic Hallucinations [*Medicine*]
HH .... Hypogonadism [*Endocrinology*] (DAVI)
HH .... Hypogonadotrophic [*Endocrinology*] (DAVI)
HH .... Hyporeninemic Hypoaldosteronism [*Endocrinology*]
H-H .... Hypoxia-Hypercapnia (SAUS)
HH .... Les Hieroglyphes Hittites [*A publication*] (BJA)
HH .... Rotary-Wing Air-Sea-Rescue Aircraft [*Navy symbol*] (MUGU)
HH .... Somali Airlines [*ICAO designator*] (AD)
HH-65 .... Dolphin [*Search-and-rescue helicopter*] [*Coast Guard*] (POLM)
HHA .... Anderson [*H. H.*] Line [*Steamship*] (MHDB)
HHA .... Half-Hardy Annual [*Horticulture*] (ROG)
H(Ha) .... Hare Tempore Wigram, Etc. [*1841-53*] [*A publication*] (DLA)
HHA .... Hatton Heritage Association (EA)
HHA .... Health Hazard Appraisal (STED)
HHA .... Health Hazard Assessment [*Army*]
HHA .... Hereditary Hemolytic Anemia [*Medicine*]
HHA .... Hexahydric Alcohol (SAUS)
HHA .... Hickory Handle Association (EA)
HHA .... High Hardness Armor [*Military*]
HHA .... High High Alarm (ECII)
HHA .... Historic House Association [*British*]
HHA .... Home Health Agency
HHA .... Home Health Aid (DAVI)
HHA .... Hungarian Horse Association (EA)
HHA .... Hydro Home Appliances Ltd. [*Formerly, Hemgold Resources Ltd.*] [*Vancouver Stock Exchange symbol*]
HHA .... Hypothalamo-Hypophyseal-Adrenal [*Endocrinology*]
HHAA .... Historic House Association of America (EA)
HHAA .... Hypothalamo-Hypophyseal-Adrenal Axis (STED)
HHAB .... Hig-Hinge Abduction Brace [*Medicine*] (MELL)
HHAG .... Human Health Assessment Group [*Environmental Protection Agency*]
HHALSA .... Heritage Hills Area Library Services Authority [*Library network*]
HH&E .... Human Health and the Environment (SARE)
HHANES .... Hispanic Health and Nutrition Examination Survey [*Department of Health and Human Services*] (GFGA)
HHAR .... Health Hazard Assessment Report [*Army*]
HHB .... Bernice Pauahi Bishop Museum, Honolulu, HI [*Library symbol*] [*Library of Congress*] (LCLS)
HHB .... Half-Hardy Biennial [*Horticulture*] (ROG)
HHB .... Happy Hours Brotherhood (EA)
HHB .... Hattiesburg, MS [*Location identifier*] [*FAA*] (FAAL)
HHB .... Headquarters and Headquarters Battery [*Army*]
HHb .... Hemoglobin, Reduced [*Biochemistry, medicine*]
HHb .... Hemoglobin Un-Ionized [*Hematology*] (DAVI)
HHB .... Hexahydroxybenzene (SAUS)
HHB .... HQ Battery (SAUS)
HHB .... Hypochemoglobinemia [*Medicine*] (STED)
HHb .... Hypohebmoglobinemia [*Medicine*] (EDAA)
HHBLG .... Hobby Horse Brigade of the Legion of Guardsmen (EA)
HHBS .... Hereford Herd Book Society (SAUO)
HHBX .... HHB Systems, Inc. (SAUO)
HHC .... Chatham College, Pittsburgh, PA [*OCLC symbol*] (OCLC)
HHC .... Hammer Head Crane (NASA)
HHC .... Handheld Computer
HHC .... Hand-Held Controller (SAUS)
HHC .... Harlem Hospital Center [*Medicine*] (EDAA)
HHC .... Harley Hummer Club (EA)
HHC .... Harte-Hanks Communications, Inc. (EFIS)
HHC .... Headquarters and Headquarters Company [*Army*]
HHC .... Heavy Helicopter Company [*Military*] (VNW)
HHC .... Help Holland Council (SAUO)
HHC .... Hemoglobin-Haptoglobin Complex (DB)
HHC .... Hepatic Hydatid Cyst [*Medicine*] (MELL)
HHC .... Higher Harmonic Control (MCD)
HHC .... Highland Crow Resources Ltd. [*Toronto Stock Exchange symbol*] [*Vancouver Stock Exchange symbol*]
HHC .... Highly Hazardous Chemical (LDOE)
HHC .... Home Health Care [*Medicine*] (DAVI)
HHC .... Honolulu Community College, Honolulu, HI [*Library symbol*] [*Library of Congress*] (LCLS)
HHC .... Hoover Historical Center (EA)
HHC .... Horizon CMS Healthcare Corp. [*NYSE symbol*] (SAG)
HHC .... Houdini Historical Center (EA)
HHC .... Hovercraft-Helicopter Carrier
HHC .... HQ Company US (SAUO)
HHC .... Hughes Harmonic Control (SAUS)
HHC .... Hughes Helicopter Company (SAUO)
HHC .... Human Health Criteria (EEVL)
HHC .... New York City Health and Hospitals Corp. (EA)
HHCA .... Home Health Care of America (SAUO)
HHCA .... Home Health Corp. of America, Inc. [*NASDAQ symbol*] (SAG)
HHCC .... Higher Harmonic Circulation Control [*Rotor*] [*Navy*]
HHCC .... Home Health Care Classification (SAUO)
hHCF .... Human Humoral Hypercalcemic Factor [*Oncology*]
HHCL .... Hale's History of the Common Law [*A publication*] (DLA)
HHCL .... H-Hour Coordinating Line [*Army*] (AABC)
HHCL .... Howell Henry Chaldecott Lury [*Advertising agency*] [*British*]
HHCRU .... Hearing Health Care Research Unit (SAUO)
HHCS .... High Altitude Hypertrophic Cardiomyopathy Syndrome [*Medicine*] (MELL)
HHCs .... Human Health Costs (SAUS)
HHCU .... Hand-Held Control Unit (SAUS)
HHCX .... Champlin Petroleum [*Private rail car owner code*]
HHD .... Doctor of Honorary Humanities
HHD .... Doctor of Humanities
HHD .... Headquarters and Headquarters Detachment [*Army*] (AABC)
HHD .... High Heparin Dose [*Medicine*] (DMAA)
HHD .... High Holy Days (BJA)
hhd .... Hogshead (ADWA)
Hhd .... Hogshead (SAUS)
HHD .... Hogshead
HHD .... Home Dialysis [*Medicine*] (DMAA)
HHD .... Home Hemodialysis [*Medicine*] (STED)
HHD .... Honorary Humanities Doctor (SAUS)
HHD .... Hypertensive Heart Disease [*Medicine*]
HHDDE .... Heavy Heavy-Duty Diesel Engine [*Motor vehicle specifications*]
HHDDV .... Heavy Heavy-Dity Diesel Vehicle (SAUS)
HHDE .... Hydro-Hypodynamic Environment [*Medicine*] (EDAA)
HHDN .... Hexachlorohexahydrodimethanonaphthalene [*Insecticide, commonly called Aldrin*]
HHDS .... Herd Health Declaration Scheme (SAUO)
HHDW .... Handy, Heavy Deadweight (SAUS)
HHDW .... Heavy Handy Deadweight [*Scrap*] [*Shipping*]
HHDWS .... Heavy Handy Deadweight Scrap (SAUO)
HHDWS .... Heavy Handy Deadweight Scrap Iron [*Shipping*] (DS)
HHE .... Hand-Held Equipment (DWSG)
HHE .... Health Hazard Evaluation (ADWA)
HHE .... Health Hazard Evaluation Program (SAUO)
HHE .... Heli-Holland BV [*Netherlands*] [*ICAO designator*] (FAAC)
HHE .... Helium to Heat Exchanger (AAG)
HHE .... Hemiconvulsions, Hemiplegia, Epilepsy [*Medicine*]
HHE .... Herringer-Hulster Effect
HHE .... Household Economics Research Division [*of ARS, Department of Agriculture*]
HHE .... Household Effects [*Insurance*]
HHE .... Human Health and the Environment (GNE)
HHEC .... Hispanic Higher Education Coalition [*Defunct*] (EA)
HHEFG .... Hughes Hall Effect Function Generator
HHEG .... Hughes Hall Effect Generator
HHELS .... Hybrid High Energy LASER System
HHE-P .... East-West Center, Population Institute, Honolulu, HI [*Library symbol*] [*Library of Congress*] (LCLS)
HHES .... Hex Head Electrical Squib
HHES .... Housing and Household Economic Statistics [*US Census Bureau*]
HHESD .... Population Division and Housing and Household Economics Statistics Division [*Bureau of the Census*] [*Also, an information service or system*] (IID)
HHF .... Canadian, TX [*Location identifier*] [*FAA*] (FAAL)
HHF .... Friends of the Library of Hawaii, Honolulu, HI [*Library symbol*] [*Library of Congress*] (LCLS)
HHF .... Health for Haiti Foundation (EA)
HHF .... High-Heat Flux (SAUS)
HHF .... Household Furniture [*Insurance*]
HHF .... Hyper-High-Frequency (DEN)
HHFA .... Housing and Home Finance Agency [*Terminated 1965, functions taken over by HUD*]
HHFC .... Harvest Home Financial Corp. [*NASDAQ symbol*] (SAG)
HHFC .... Harvest Home Finl [*NASDAQ symbol*] (TTSB)
HHFC .... H. H. Franklin Club (EA)
HHFM .... High-Humidity Face Mask [*Medicine*] (MEDA)
HHFS .... Hilar High-Frequency Stimulation [*Neurophysiology*]
HHFT .... Heavy Helicopter Fire Team (DNAB)
HHFT .... Heavy Helo Fire Team [*Military*] (VNW)
HHG .... High-Harmonic Generation [*Physics*]
HH-G .... Hitchhiker (Goddard Space Flight Center) [*NASA*]
HHG .... Household Goods [*Insurance*]
HHG .... Human Hypophysary Gonadotropin (SAUS)
HHG .... Hypertrophic Hypersecretory Gastropathy [*Medicine*] (DMAA)
HHG .... Hypogonadotropic Hypogonadism [*Medicine*]
HHGCB .... Household Goods Carriers Bureau
HHGFAA .... Household Goods Forwarders Association of America (EA)
HHGI .... Hospital Newspapers Group, Inc. (SAUO)
HHGP .... Harris & Harris Group [*NASDAQ symbol*] (TTSB)
HHGP .... Harris & Harris Group, Inc. [*NASDAQ symbol*] (NQ)
HHGR .... Helian Health Group, Inc. [*NASDAQ symbol*] (NQ)
HHGTTG .... Hitch-Hikers Guide to the Galaxy (SAUS)
HHH .... Devine, TX [*Location identifier*] [*FAA*] (FAAL)
HHH .... Harder than Half Hard (SAUS)
HHH .... Harrison Horncastle Holdings [*Investment firm*] [*British*]
HHH .... Hash House Harriers International (BUAC)
HHH .... Hawaii Medical Library, Inc., Honolulu, HI [*Library symbol*] [*Library of Congress*] (LCLS)
HHH .... Helicsa [*Spain*] [*FAA designator*] (FAAC)
HHH .... Helm Capital [*AMEX symbol*] [*Formerly, Helm Resources*] (SG)
HHH .... Helm Resources, Inc [*AMEX symbol*] (SAG)
HHH .... Heritage Entertainment, Inc. [*AMEX symbol*] (COMM)
HHH .... High-High-High (SAUS)
HHH .... High, Hot, and a Helluva lot [*Enema*] [*Medicine*] (EDAA)
HHH .... Hilton Head Island [*South Carolina*] [*Airport symbol*] (OAG)
HHH .... Hincherton Hayfever Helmet [*Clear plastic head-enclosing device that allegedly relieves hayfever symptoms*]
HHH .... Holistic Health Havens (EA)
HHH .... Hubert Horatio Humphrey [*American politician, 1911-1978*]
HHH .... Hyperornithinemia, Hyperammonemia, Homocitrillinuria Syndrome [*Medicine*] (DMAA)

HHH .... Triple Hard [*Pencil leads*]
HHHA .... Homemaker Home Health Aide (OICC)
HHHC .... Hunt the Hunters Hunt Club (SAUO)
HHH-CRC ..... Hubert H. Humphrey Cancer Research Center [*Boston University*] [*Research center*] (RCD)
HHHH .... FourHealth, Inc. [*NASDAQ symbol*] (SAG)
HHHHH .... Hilf, Himmlischer Herr, Hoechster Hort [*Help, Heavenly Father, Highest Treasure*] [*Motto of Elisabeth, Duchess of Saxony-Coburg (1540-94)*] [*German*]
HHHIPA .... Hubert H. Humphrey Institute of Public Affairs (SAUS)
HHHMU .... Hydrazine Hand-Held Maneuvering Unit (MCD)
HHHO .... Hypotonia-Hypomentia-Hypogonadism-Obesity [*Medicine*]
HHHS .... Halogenated Hydrocarbon Hepatitis Syndrome [*Medicine*] (EDAA)
HHHS .... Hincherton Hayfever Helmets (SAUS)
HHI .... Ha-Hevra ha-Historit ha-Israelit [*Historical Society of Israel*] (EAIO)
HHI .... Hampton Healthcare, Inc. [*AMEX symbol*] (COMM)
HHI .... Hand-Held Imager (SAUS)
HHI .... Harmony Heights [*Idaho*] [*Seismograph station code, US Geological Survey*] [*Closed*] (SEIS)
HHI .... Harness Horsemen International (EA)
HHi .... Hawaiian Historical Society, Honolulu, HI [*Library symbol*] [*Library of Congress*] (LCLS)
HHI .... Hawaii County Library, Hilo, HI [*Library symbol*] [*Library of Congress*] (LCLS)
HHI .... Head-of-Household Income (WDMC)
HHI .... Hellenic Hydrobiological Institute (SAUO)
HHI .... Herfindahl-Hirschmann Index [*Economics*]
HHI .... Histologic HCM [*Hypertrophic Cardiomyopathy*] Index
HHI .... Home Holdings [*NYSE symbol*] (SPSG)
HHI .... Homer Hoyt Institute
HHI .... Horton Hydrocarbons, Inc. [*Vancouver Stock Exchange symbol*]
HHI .... Hughes Helicopter, Inc.
HHI .... Hyundai Heavy Industries (SAUS)
HHI .... Wahiawa, HI [*Location identifier*] [*FAA*] (FAAL)
HHIA .... Headway Head Injuries Association (BUAC)
HHIC .... Hilo College, Hilo, HI [*Library symbol*] [*Library of Congress*] (LCLS)
HHIE .... Hearing Handicap Inventory for the Elderly [*Medicine*] (EDAA)
HHIE-S .... Hearing Handicap Inventory for the Elderly-Screening Version [*Medicine*] (EDAA)
HHIN .... Hanford Health Information Network (SAUS)
H-hinge .... Capital-H-shaped hinge (SAUS)
HHIP .... Hand-Held Information Processor
HHIRF .... Holifield Heavy Ion Research Facility [*Department of Energy*]
HHIS .... Home-Health Information System (GART)
HHJ .... Harold Hunt, Jr. (SAUO)
HHJ .... Hunt, Harold, Jr., Bala-Cynwyd PA [*STAC*]
HHK .... Honor Hong Kong (SAUS)
HHK .... Kapiolani Community College, Honolulu, HI [*Library symbol*] [*Library of Congress*] (LCLS)
HHL .... Court of Session Cases, House of Lords [*Scotland*] [*A publication*] (DLA)
HHL .... Haddon Hall Library [*A publication*]
HHL .... Helicopter Hire Ltd. [*British*] [*ICAO designator*] (FAAC)
HHL .... High Hazard Laboratory (SAUS)
HHL .... Hollywood Hotline [*Information service or system*] (IID)
HHLA .... Handkerchief and Household Linens Association (BUAC)
HHLA .... Huricane Hydrocarbons, Ltd. [*NASDAQ symbol*] (NASQ)
HHLD .... Hand-Held Laser Designator (ACAE)
HHLD .... Household [*Marketing*]
HHLGCS .... [*Department of*] Health, Housing, Local Government and Community Services (EERA)
HHLH .... Heaviest Heavy Lift Helicopter (MCD)
HHLL .... Hand-Held Laser Locator (SAUS)
HHLL .... Histocytoid Hemangioma-Like Lesion [*Medicine*] (PALA)
HHLR .... Hand-Held LASER Range-Finder [*Military*] (RDA)
HHLR .... Horace Hardy Lestor Reactor
HHLRF .... Hand-Held LASER Range-Finder [*Military*] [*British*] (INF)
HHLT .... Hand-Held Logic Tool (SAUS)
HHIU-W .... University of Hawaii at Hilo, West Hawaii Library, Kealakekua, HI [*Library symbol*] [*Library of Congress*] (LCLS)
H + Hm .... Compound Hypermetropic Astigmatism [*Ophthalmology*]
HHM .... Haemohydrometry (SAUS)
HHM .... Hand-Held Map (SAUS)
HHM .... Hawkes Hospital of Mount Carmel, Mount Carmel Medical Center Library, Columbus, OH [*OCLC symbol*] (OCLC)
HHM .... Health and Healing Ministries (EA)
HH-M .... Hitchhiker (Marshall Space Flight Center) [*NASA*]
HHM .... Humoral Hypercalcemia of Malignancy [*Medicine*]
HHM .... Hungry Horse [*Montana*] [*Seismograph station code, US Geological Survey*] (SEIS)
HHM .... Kotzebue, AK [*Location identifier*] [*FAA*] (FAAL)
HHM .... Sisters of the Holy Humility of Mary [*Roman Catholic religious order*]
HHMC .... Hawaiian Mission Children's Society, Honolulu, HI [*Library symbol*] [*Library of Congress*] (LCLS)
HHMHDB ..... Hispanic Health and Mental Health Data Base [*National Institute of Mental Health*] [*Information service or system*] (CRD)
HHMI .... Howard Hughes Medical Institute
hh/mm .... Hours/Minutes (HGAA)
HHMMWV .... Heavy Highly Mobile Multiple Wheeled Vehicle (SAUS)
HHMS .... Hydrostatic Head Monitoring Station (SAUO)
HHMT .... Helene Harris Memorial Trust (BUAC)
HHMU .... Handheld Maneuvering Unit [*NASA*]
HHN .... Hahnemann Medical College and Hospital, Philadelphia, PA [*OCLC symbol*] (OCLC)
HHN .... Hand-Held Nebulizer [*Pharmacology*] (DAVI)
HHN .... Harte-Hanks Newspapers (SAUO)
HHN .... Hot Hydrogen Nozzle
HHNA .... Home Healthcare Nurses Association (NTPA)
HHNC .... His Highness the Nizam's Cavalry [*British military*] (DMA)
HHNC .... Hyperglycemic Hyperosmolar Nonketotic Coma [*Endocrinology*] (CPH)
HHNK .... Hyperosmolar Hyperglycemic Nonketotic (Coma) [*Also, NKHHC*] [*Medicine*]
HHNS .... Hyperglycemic Hyperosmolar Nonketotic Syndrome [*Medicine*] (EDAA)
HHNS .... Hyperosmolar Hyperglycemic Nonketotic Syndrome [*Medicine*] (MTAA)
HHNSR .... Hudson Highlands National Scenic Riverway (SAUS)
HHO .... Helping Hand Organization (SAUO)
HHO .... Houston Helicopters, Inc. [*ICAO designator*] (FAAC)
HHOC .... Headquarters, Headquarter and Operations Company (SAUO)
HHOC .... Holistic Health Organizing Committee (EA)
HHOCC .... Holiday Happenings Ornament Collectors Club (EA)
HHOJ .... Ha Ha Only Joking [*Computer hacker terminology*] (NHD)
HHOK .... Ha Ha Only Kidding
HHOS .... Ha Ha Only Serious
HHOT .... H&H Oil Tool Company, Inc. [*NASDAQ symbol*] (COMM)
H-hour .... Hostile operations commencement hour (SAUS)
H-Hour .... Hour Hour (SAUS)
HHP .... Half-Hardy Perennial [*Horticulture*] (ROG)
HHP .... Handheld Processor
HHP .... Head of Household Program [*IRS*]
HHP .... High Holding Power (SAUS)
HHP .... Hospital Health Plan
HHP .... Household Pet (WGA)
HHP .... Hydraulic Hand Pump
HHP .... Hydraulic Horse Power
HHP .... Pineapple Research Institute, Honolulu, HI [*Library symbol*] [*Library of Congress*] (LCLS)
HHPA .... Hexahydrophthalic Anhydride [*Organic chemistry*]
HHPC .... Hale's History of the Pleas of the Crown [*A publication*] (DLA)
HHPC .... Hand-Held Programmable Calculator (MCD)
HHPC .... High Harmonic Pitch Control (PDAA)
HHPCL .... Himal Hydropower & Construction Pr. Lmt. Com. (SAUS)
HHPDMU ..... High-Horsepower Diesel Electric Multiple Unit [*Indian Railway*] (TIR)
HHPL .... Herbert Hoover Presidential Library (SAUO)
HHPLA .... Herbert Hoover Presidential Library Association (EA)
HHPP .... Hydro-Hydrogen Pilot Project
HHPRT .... Human Hypoxanthine Phosphoribosyltransferase [*An enzyme*]
HHPS .... Hot High Pressure Separator [*Chemical engineering*]
HHQ .... Headquarters and Headquarters Company (SAUO)
HHQ .... Higher Headquarters (ACAE)
HHR .... Hand Held Radar (SAUS)
HHR .... Hawthorne, CA [*Location identifier*] [*FAA*] (FAAL)
HHR .... Health and Human Resources (SAUS)
HHR .... High Reserve Resources [*Vancouver Stock Exchange symbol*]
HHR .... Hydralazine, Hydrochlorothiazide, and Reserpine (DMAA)
HHRA .... Heartland Human Relations Association (SAUO)
HHRA .... Holographic Helmet Reticle Assembly (ACAE)
HHRB .... Hand-Held Rationing Radiometer (SAUS)
HHRC .... Health and Human Resource Center (SAUO)
HHRD .... Horsehead Resource Dvlp [*NASDAQ symbol*] (TTSB)
HHREA .... Health and Human Relations Education Association [*Australia*]
HHRF .... Hand Heid Rangefinder (SAUS)
HHRH .... Hereditary Hypophosphatemic Rickets with Hypercalciuria [*Medicine*] (DMAA)
HHRH .... Hypothalamic Hypophysiotropic Releasing Hormone (DB)
HHRM .... Hanford Hoisting and Rigging Manual (SAUS)
HHRSD .... Helicopter Hauldown and Rapid Securing Device [*Military*] (CAAL)
HHS .... Department of Health and Human Services [*Formerly, HEW*]
HHS .... Haaren High School (SAUO)
HHS .... Hackney Horse Society (SAUO)
HHS .... Hand-Held Scanner (CIST)
HHS .... Harris Hematoxylin Solution (SAUS)
HHS .... Harte-Hanks, Inc. [*NYSE symbol*] [*Formerly, Harte-Hanks Communications*]
HHS .... Hawaiian Historical Society (BUAC)
HHS .... Hawaiian Humane Society (SAUO)
HHS .... Hawaiian Sugar Planters' Association, Experiment Station, Honolulu, HI [*Library symbol*] [*Library of Congress*] (LCLS)
HHS .... Headquarters and Headquarters Squadron (SAUO)
HHS .... Headquarters, Headquarters and Service Battery (SAUO)
HHS .... Health and Human Services (DICI)
HHS .... Hearing Handicap Scale [*Medicine*] (EDAA)
HHS .... HEHF information and scheduling system (SAUS)
HHS .... Helicopter Handling System (SAUS)
HHS .... Helpers of the Holy Souls [*France*] (BUAC)
HHS .... Hereditary Hemolytic Syndrome [*Medicine*] (MELL)
HHS .... Hex Head Squib
HHS .... Hex Head Steel (IAA)
HHS .... High High Star (ACAE)
HHS .... High Strength Steel (EDCT)
HHS .... Historical Harp Society (BUAC)
HHS .... Historic Heritage Strategy (SAUO)
HHS .... Home Health Services (MELL)
HHS .... Horse Hemolyzate Supernatant
HHS .... Hospital and Health Services (SAUO)
HHS .... Huguenot Historical Society (EA)
HHS .... Human Head Simulator (SAUS)
HHS .... Hungarian Historical Society [*Australia*]

HHS .... Hunter High School (SAUO)
HHS .... Hypothenar Hammer Syndrome [*Medicine*]
HHS .... Office of Health and Human Services (SAUS)
HHS .... Society of Helpers (TOCD)
HHS .... Society of Helpers of the Holy Souls [*Roman Catholic women's religious order*]
HHS .... US Department of Health and Human Services (GNE)
HHSA .... Home Health Services Association [*Later, HHSSA*] (EA)
HHSA .... Honolulu Star-Bulletin and Advertiser, Honolulu, HI [*Library symbol*] [*Library of Congress*] (LCLS)
HHSAR .... Department of Health and Human Services Acquisition Regulations (GFGA)
HHSAR .... Health and Human Services Acquisition Regulation (AAGC)
HHSB .... Hahnemann High School Behavior Rating Scale [*Psychology*]
HHS/BMS ..... High High Star/Background Mapping by Satellite/Sensor (ACAE)
HHSD .... Holographic Horizontal Situation Display
HHSF .... Habitat and Human Settlements Foundation [*United Nations*] (EY)
HHSG .... Herpes Help Support Group [*Australia*]
HHSGAB ...... Department of Health and Human Services Grant Appeals Board (AAGC)
HHSI .... High-Head Safety Injection [*Nuclear energy*] (NRCH)
HHSMU .... Hand-Held Self-Maneuvering Unit (SAA)
HHSP .... Highland Hammock State Park (SAUO)
HHSPR .... Health and Human Services Procurement Regulations (AAGC)
HHSRA .... Holographic Helmet Sight Reticle Assembly (ACAE)
HHSSA .... Home Health Services and Staffing Association (EA)
HHSZYM ...... Hashomer Hatzair Socialist Zionist Youth Movement (EA)
HHT .... Hand-Held Tester [*Automotive engineering*]
HHT .... Head Balter Traction (MELL)
HHT .... Headquarters and Headquarters Troop [*Army*] (AABC)
HHT .... Hereditary Hemorrhagic Telangiectasia [*Medicine*]
HHT .... Heredity Haemorrhagic Telangiectasia (SAUS)
HHT .... Higher High Tensile (SAUS)
HHT .... High-Temperature Helium Turbine (PDAA)
HHT .... Holland Historical Trust (EA)
HHT .... Homoharringtonine [*Antineoplastic drug*]
HHT .... Horn-Hellersberg Test [*Psychology*]
HHT .... Hurricane Hollow [*Tennessee*] [*Seismograph station code, US Geological Survey*] [*Closed*] (SEIS)
HHT .... Hush House Tiedown
HHT .... Hydroxyheptadecatrienoic Acid [*Organic chemistry*]
HHT .... Hypothalamic Hypophysical Thyroid (SAUS)
HHT .... Hypothalamo-Hypophyseal Tract [*Medicine*] (MELL)
HHTA .... Hypothalamohypophyseothyroidal Axis (STED)
HHTG .... House Heating [*Freight*]
HHTG .... Household Heating (SAUS)
HHTI .... Hand-Held Thermal Imager [*Navy*] [*British*]
HHTK .... Hand-Held Test Kit (SAUS)
HHTM .... United States Army, Tripler Army Medical Center, Honolulu, HI [*Library symbol*] [*Library of Congress*] (LCLS)
HHTNSW ..... Historic Houses Trust of New South Wales [*Australia*]
HHTR .... Hand-Held Tactical RADAR (DNAB)
HHTs .... Hand-Held Terminals (SAUO)
HHTT .... Hexahexylthiotriphenylene [*Organic chemistry*]
HHTTFS ...... Huddersfield Healders and Twisters Trade and Friendly Society [*A union*] [*British*] (DCTA)
HHTU .... Hand-Held Teaching Unit (SAUS)
HHTV .... Hand-Held Thermal Viewer (SAUS)
HHTx .... Head Halter Traction (STED)
HHTYAY ...... Happy Holidays to You and Yours (ADWA)
HHUD .... Holographic Head-Up Display (ACAE)
HHUMC .... Hadassah-Hebrew University Medical Center (SAUO)
HHV .... Hand-Held Viewer (SAUS)
HHV .... Heavy-High-mobility [*Multipurpose Wheeled*] Vehicle [*See also HMMWV*] (DOMA)
HHV .... Heavy HMMWV Variant (SAUS)
HHV .... Help Hospitalized Veterans (EA)
HHV .... Higher Heating Value (EEVL)
HHV .... High Heating Value Hydrocyclone (EDCT)
HHV .... High Heat [*or Heating*] Value
HHV .... Human Herpes Virus
HHV-6 .... Human Herpes Virus-6 [*Medicine*] (TAD)
HHVC .... Higher Harmony Vibration Control (SAUS)
HHVT .... High frame (or resolution) Rate Video Technology (SAUS)
HHW .... Higher High Water [*Tides and currents*]
HHW .... High-Heat Waste (NRCH)
HHW .... Household Hazardous Waste
HHWI .... Higher High-Water Interval
HHWP .... Household Hazardous Waste Project (EA)
HHX .... Heavy-Lift Helicopter, Experimental (SAA)
HHY .... Savannah, TN [*Location identifier*] [*FAA*] (FAAL)
HHYF .... Harness Horse Youth Foundation (EA)
HHZYM .... Hashomer Hatzair Zionist Youth Movement (EA)
HI .... Habitability Improvement [*Navy*] (NVT)
HI .... Haemagglutinin Inhibition (SAUS)
HI .... Hair International (NTPA)
HI .... Halt Instruction (SAUS)
HI .... Hammersley Iron (SAUS)
HI .... Hampton Institute (SAUO)
HI .... Handicap International [*Belgium*] (BUAC)
HI .... Handicap Introductions (EA)
HI .... Handling Instructions (MCD)
HI .... Handwriting Institute (SAUO)
HI .... Hanford Information (SAUS)
HI .... Harcost Industries
HI .... Hardware Indicator (SAUS)
HI .... Hardware Interrupt
HI .... Harold Institute [*Defunct*] (EA)
HI .... Harris Intertype (SAUS)
HI .... Harris-Intertype Corp. (SAUO)
HI .... Harvest Index [*Agronomy*]
HI .... Hat Institute (EA)
HI .... Hawaii [*Postal code*]
HI .... Hawaiian Islands
HI .... Hawaii Reports [*A publication*] (DLA)
HI .... Hazard Index (GNE)
HI .... Hazard Installation (HEAS)
HI .... Head Injury [*Neurology*] (DAVI)
HI .... Healthcare Infomediary (GART)
HI .... Health Inspector [*British military*] (DMA)
HI .... Health Instrument Division (SAUO)
HI .... Health Insurance
HI .... Heard Island [*Region*] (EERA)
HI .... Hearing Impaired (OICC)
HI .... Heart Infusion (STED)
HI .... Heartland Institute [*Research center*] (RCD)
HI .... Heat Inactivated (STED)
HI .... Heat Index
HI .... Heat Input (STED)
HI .... Heat Insulation (SAUS)
HI .... Heavily Included [*Colored gemstone grade*]
HI .... Heavy Environment (SAUS)
HI .... Heavy Ion (SAUS)
HI .... Heavy Iron (SAUS)
HI .... Height Indicator (NVT)
HI .... Height of Instrument (SAUS)
HI .... Hemagglutination Inhibition [*Immunochemistry*]
HI .... Hepatic Insufficiency (STED)
HI .... Hepatobiliary Imaging [*Medicine*] (BABM)
HI .... Hercules Incorporated (SAUO)
HI .... Herder-Institut e.V. (SAUS)
Hi .... Hering illusion (SAUS)
Hi .... Hiburnium [*Supposed chemical element, discovered 1922*]
HI .... Hic Iacet [*Here Lies*] [*Latin*]
HI .... Hideaways International [*Commercial firm*] (EA)
HI .... High [*Computer science*] (AAG)
hi .... High (ADWA)
HI .... High Impact
HI .... High Impulsiveness (MAE)
HI .... High Intensity
HI .... High-Intensity Lights (PIPO)
HI .... High Signal (SAUS)
HI .... Hindi (WDAA)
HI .... Hirth KG [*Germany*] [*ICAO aircraft manufacturer identifier*] (ICAO)
HI .... Hispanic Institute (EA)
HI .... Histadruth Ivrith of America
Hi .... Histidine [*An amino acid*] (MAE)
HI .... Histidine (STED)
HI .... Histone (SAUS)
HI .... Hofmann Industries, Inc. (EFIS)
HI .... Holding Instruction (SAUS)
HI .... Holiday Inns, Inc. (EFIS)
HI .... Holton Inter-Union Railway Co. (SAUO)
HI .... Holton Inter-Urban Railway Co. [*AAR code*]
HI .... Homicidal Ideation [*Psychiatry*] (DAVI)
H-I .... Hondacar International (EA)
HI .... Honeywell, Inc. (NASA)
HI .... Hoover Institution (SAUS)
HI .... Horizontal Interval
HI .... Hormone Dependent [*Medicine*] (STED)
HI .... Hormone-Independent [*Medicine*] (DB)
HI .... Hormone Insensitive [*Medicine*] (STED)
HI .... Hospital Induced (STED)
HI .... Hospital Insurance
HI .... Host Interface (SAUS)
HI .... Hot Issue [*Investment term*]
HI .... Hotline International (BUAC)
HI .... Household Capital Trust II [*NYSE symbol*] (SAG)
HI .... Household International, Inc. [*NYSE symbol*] (SPSG)
HI .... Housekeeping Instruction (SAUS)
HI .... Housing Improvement
HI .... Houston Instrument, Inc. (SAUO)
HI .... Howell Instruments, Inc. (SAUO)
HI .... Hudson Institute (EA)
HI .... Human Interaction
HI .... Human Interest
HI .... Human Interface [*Computer science*] (EERA)
HI .... Humanity International [*An association*] (EA)
HI .... Humidity Index
HI .... Humoral Immunity (DB)
HI .... Huna International (SAUO)
HI .... Hybrid Index [*Botany*]
HI .... Hydraulic Institute (EA)
HI .... Hydraulic Intensifier (SAUS)
HI .... Hydraulics Institute (SAUS)
HI .... Hydriodic Acid [*Inorganic chemistry*]
HI .... Hydrodynamic Interaction [*Chemistry*]
HI .... Hydrogen Injection (SAUS)
HI .... Hydrogen Iodide [*Inorganic chemistry*]
HI .... Hydronics Institute (EA)

HI .... Hydroxyindole [*Biochemistry*] (DAVI)
HI .... Hyperglycemic Index [*Medicine*] (STED)
HI .... Hypomelanosis of Ito [*Medicine*] (DMAA)
HI .... Hypothermic Ischemia (DB)
Hi .... Methemoglobin [*Symbol*] [*Medicine*]
HI .... Papillon Airways [*ICAO designator*] (AD)
HI-12 .... High Twelve International (EA)
HIA .... Canadian Eagle Aviation Ltd. [*ICAO designator*] (FAAC)
HIA .... Handkerchief Industry Association [*Defunct*] (EA)
HIA .... Harrisburg International Airport (MCD)
HIA .... Hawaiian Irrigation Authority (BUAC)
HIA .... Hazard Integration Analysis (SAUS)
HIA .... Headwear Institute of America (EA)
HIA .... Health Industries Association [*Later, HIMA*]
HIA .... Hearing Industries Association (EA)
HIA .... Heart Infusion Agar [*Medicine*]
HIA .... Heat Infusion Agar [*Microbiology*] (DAVI)
HIA .... Held [*or Hold*] in Abeyance [*Military*] (AFM)
HIA .... Hemagglutination Inhibition Antibody [*Immunochemistry*]
HIA .... Herring Industry Act (SAUO)
HIA .... Herzberg Institute of Astrophysics (SAUS)
HIA .... Histadruth Ivrith of America (EA)
HIA .... Hold in Abeyance [*Military*]
HIA .... Holiday Corp. [*NYSE symbol*] (COMM)
HIA .... Holiday Inns, Inc. (SAUO)
HIA .... Holographic Imaging Apparatus (SAUS)
HIA .... Home Improvement Association (SAUO)
HIA .... Homeopathic Institute of Australia (SAUO)
HIA .... Homopolar Inductor Alternator (PDAA)
HIA .... Horological Institute of America [*Later, AWI*]
HIA .... Hospital Industries Association (SAUO)
HIA .... Housing Industry Association
HIA .... Human Interface Architecture (SAUS)
HIA .... Hungarian Imperial Association (SAUO)
HIA .... Hydrologic Investigations Atlas (SAUO)
HIA .... Hydroxyndole Acetic Acid (SAUS)
HIA .... Whitehall, MT [*Location identifier*] [*FAA*] (FAAL)
HIA .... Housing Improvement Association (ODA)
HIAA .... Health Insurance Association of America [*Washington, DC*] (EA)
HIAA .... Health Insurance Association of Australia (SAUO)
HIAA .... Hobby Industry Association of America (EA)
HIAC .... Health Industry Advisory Committee [*Terminated, 1974*] (EGAO)
HIAC .... Health Insurance Advisory Committee [*Australia*]
HIAC .... Herring Industry Advisory Council (SAUO)
HIAC .... High Accuracy [*RADAR*]
HIAC .... High-Altitude Camera (SAUS)
HI Acid .... Hydriodic Acid (SAUS)
HIAD .... Handbook of Instructions for Aircraft Designers
HIAD .... Handbook of Instructions for Airplane Designers (SAUO)
HIAD .... High Altitude Defense (ACAE)
HIADS .... Hawaiian Integrated Air Defense System
HIAFSB .... Handbook of Instructions for Air Force Subsystem Designers
HIAFSD .... Handbook of Instructions for Air Force Subsystem Designers (SAUS)
HIAG .... Healthcare International Audit Group (EA)
HIAGSE .... Handbook of Instructions for Aircraft Ground Support Equipment Designers
HIAGSED .... Handbook of Instructions for Aircraft Ground Support Equipment Designers (SAUO)
HIA Journal ... Horological Institute of America Journal (journ.) (SAUS)
HIAK .... Harpoon Interface Adapter Kit (DWSG)
HIAL .... Hawaii Intercollegiate Athletic League (PSS)
HIAL .... High Intensity Approach Lighting [*Aviation*] (PIAV)
HIALS .... High-Intensity Approach Lighting System [*Airport runways*]
HIALT .... High Altitude (MCD)
HI/AMBBA .... Hair International/Associated Master Barbers and Beauticians of America (EA)
HIAN .... Head Injury Association of Niagara (SAUO)
HI&E .... Hazard Identification and Evaluation (SAUS)
HI and RH ... Her (or His) Imperial and Royal Highness (SAUO)
HI and RH ... His [*or Her*] Imperial and Royal Highness
HIANG .... Hawaii Air National Guard (MUSM)
HIANSW .... Health Informatics Australia-NSW (SAUO)
HIAP .... Health Insurance Advocacy Program (SAUS)
HIAP .... Hobbs Industrial Air Park (SAUO)
HIAP .... Human Intracisternal A-Type Particle [*Cytology*]
HIAPER .... High-Altitude Integrated Airborne Platform for Environmental Research
HIAPER .... High-Performance Instrumented Airborne Platform for Environmental Research (SAUS)
HIAPSD .... Handbook of Instructions for Aerospace Personnel Subsystem Designers (SAUO)
HIARA .... Hail Insurance Adjustment and Research Association [*Later, NCIA*] (EA)
HIAS .... High Incidence Auto-Stabilizer (PDAA)
HIAS .... Human Intellect Augmentation System (SAUS)
HIASD .... Handbook of Instructions for Aerospace Systems Design
HIAVA .... High Availability (VLIE)
HIAVA System ... High Availability System (SAUS)
HIAVED .... Handbook of Instructions for Aerospace Vehicle Equipment Design
HIAWA .... Hiawatha, KS [*American Association of Railroads railroad junction routing code*]
HI-AYH .... Hostelling International-American Youth Hostels [*An association*] (EA)
Hib .... Haemophilus Influenzae Type B (PAZ)
HIB .... Haemophilus Influenzae, Type B
HIB .... Hawaiian Freight Tariff Bureau Inc., Maywood CA [*STAC*]
HIB .... Health Insurance Benefit (SAUO)
HIB .... Heart Infusion Broth [*Medicine*] (DMAA)
HIB .... Heavy-Ion Beam (SAUS)
HIB .... Hemolytic Immune Body (DB)
HIB .... Hemophilus Influenzae Type B [*Medicine*]
HiB .... Hemophilus Influzena Type B (SAUS)
HIB .... Hibbing [*Minnesota*] [*Airport symbol*] (OAG)
Hib .... Hibernia (DIAR)
HIB .... Hibernia [*Ancient name for Ireland*] (ROG)
HIB .... Hibernia Corp. Class A [*NYSE symbol*] (SPSG)
Hib .... Hibernian (SAUS)
HIB .... Hibiscus Air Services Ltd. [*New Zealand*] [*ICAO designator*] (FAAC)
HIB .... High-Impedance Bridge
HIB .... High Iron Briquetting (DICI)
HIB .... Hoop-Iron Bond [*Construction*]
Hi-B.A. .... High School Evangelism Fellowship (EA)
HIBA .... Hawaiian International Billfish Association (EA)
HIBA .... Hydroxyisobutyrate (SAUS)
HIBA .... Hydroxyisobutyric Acid [*Organic chemistry*]
HIBAC .... Health Insurance Benefits Advisory Council [*Department of Health and Human Services*] [*Inactive*]
HIBAL .... High-Altitude Balloon
HIBAT .... Helicopter Identification By Acoustic Techniques (SAUS)
Hibb .... Hibbard's Reports [*New Hampshire*] [*A publication*] (DLA)
HIBB .... Hibbett Sporting Goods, Inc. [*NASDAQ symbol*] (SAG)
Hibbett .... Hibbett Sporting Goods, Inc. [*Associated Press*] (SAG)
HIBBI .... Hibbing, MN [*American Association of Railroads railroad junction routing code*]
HIBC .... Health Industry Bar Code (VLIE)
HIBC .... Hibernia Corporation (SAUO)
HIBC .... Horizontal Integration of Battle Command (SAUS)
HIBC .... Hydrogen-Induced Blister Cracking [*Metallurgy*]
HIBCC .... Health Industry Bar Code Council (SAUO)
HIBCC .... Health Industry Business Communications Council (EA)
Hibern .... Hibernia Corp. [*Associated Press*] (SAG)
Hibern .... Hibernia Corp, Class A [*Associated Press*] (SAG)
Hibernat .... Hibernation (SAUS)
HiberSv .... Hibernia Savings Bank [*Associated Press*] (SAG)
HIBEX .... High Acceleration Experimental (SAUS)
HIBEX .... High Boost Experiment (ACAE)
HIBEX .... High-Impulse Booster Experiments [*DARPA/Army*]
HIBEX/HAPDAR ... High Impulse Booster Experiment / Hardpoint Demonstration Array RADAR (SAA)
Hi-Bi .... High Birefringence (SAUS)
HiBiCMOS .... Hitachi Bipolar CMOS [*Complementary Metal Oxide Semiconductor*] (NITA)
Hibid .... Hong Kong Interbank Bid Rate (NUMA)
HIBIRD .... Helicopter Identification By Infra-Red Detection (SAUS)
HIBN .... Hibernia Foods Ltd. [*NASDAQ symbol*] (SAG)
HIBNY .... Hibernia Foods plc ADS [*NASDAQ symbol*] (TTSB)
HIBOR .... Hong Kong Interbank Offered Rate (DFIT)
HIBR .... Huxley Institute for Biosocial Research (EA)
HIBRAD .... Helicopter Identification By Radar Detection (SAUS)
HIBREL .... High-Brightness Relay [*Military*] (SDI)
HIBRI .... High Brightness (SAUS)
HibrnFd .... Hibernia Foods Ltd. [*Associated Press*] (SAG)
HIBS .... Health Information Base System (VLIE)
HIBS .... Heavy Ion Backscattering Spectrometry (AAEL)
HIBT .... High-Interest Books for Teens [*A publication*]
HIBT .... Howard Ink Blot Test [*Psychology*]
HIBU .... Hydrological Institute and Belgrade University [*Marine science*] [*Yugoslavia*] (OSRA)
HIBUF .... Hibernia Foods PLC [*NASDAQ symbol*] (SAG)
HIBUF .... Hibernia Foods Unit [*NASDAQ symbol*] (TTSB)
HIBW .... Hibernia Foods PLC [*NASDAQ symbol*] (SAG)
HIBWF .... Hibernia Foods Wrrt'C' [*NASDAQ symbol*] (TTSB)
HIBZ .... Hibernia Foods PLC [*NASDAQ symbol*] (SAG)
HIBZF .... Hibernia Foods Wrrt'D' [*NASDAQ symbol*] (TTSB)
HIC .... Habitat International Coalition (BUAC)
HIC .... Habitat International Council [*The Hague, Netherlands*] (EAIO)
HIC .... Hand Indicator Controller (NRCH)
HIC .... Happy Irish Celebration
HIC .... Hardware Indenture Code (KSC)
HIC .... Hayes International Corp.
HIC .... Headend Interface Converter (SAUS)
HIC .... Head Injury Criteria [*Medicine*]
HIC .... Head Injury Criterion (SAUO)
HIC .... Health Information Center (SAUO)
HIC .... Health Information Council [*An association*] (EA)
HIC .... Health Insurance Claim Number [*Medicare*] (DHSM)
HIC .... Health Insurance Council [*Later, Consumer and Professional Relations Division of HIAA*] (EA)
HIC .... Hearing-Impaired Children (SAUS)
HIC .... Heart Information Center
HIC .... Heavy Ion Cloud [*Astrophysics*]
HIC .... Heavy Ion Counter (SAUS)
HIC .... Height Input Converter (ACAE)
HIC .... Hemispheric Insurance Conference
HIC .... Herring Industry Committee (SAUO)
HIC .... Hickam Air Force Base, Hawaii [*NASA*] (NASA)
HIC .... Hierarchical Information Control (SAUS)
HI-C .... High-Conversion Critical Experiment (IEEE)
HIC .... High Dielectric Constant (IAA)
HIC .... Highest Incoming Channel [*Telecommunications*] (CIST)

HIC.............. High Information Content (TIMI)
HIC.............. High Integrated Circuit (SAUS)
HIC.............. High-Integrity Containers (GAAI)
HIC.............. High-Intensity Conflict [*Military*]
HIC.............. Highlands Insurance Group [*NYSE symbol*] (TTSB)
HIC.............. Highly Indebted Country
HIC.............. Highly Ionized Cloud [*Galactic science*]
HIC.............. Historical Intelligence Collection [*CIA*]
HIC.............. Hole-in-Corner [*Paper*] (DSUE)
HIC.............. Home Improvement Council (SAUO)
HIC.............. Homing Indicator and Control (SAUS)
HIC.............. Homosexual Information Center (EA)
HIC.............. Honduras Information Center (EA)
HIC.............. Host Interface Computer (SAUS)
HIC.............. Hot Idle Compensation [*Automotive engineering*]
HIC.............. Hot Isostatic Compaction
HIC.............. Household and Industrial Chemical
HIC.............. Human Interaction Component (VLIE)
HIC.............. Humidity Indicator Controller [*Aerospace*]
HIC.............. Hybrid Integrated Circuit
HIC.............. Hydraulic Integrated Circuit
HIC.............. Hydrogen-Induced Cracking [*Metallurgy*]
HIC.............. Hydrogen Ion Concentration [*Medicine*] (MELL)
HIC.............. Hydrographic Information Committee [*NATO*] (NATG)
HIC.............. Hydrologist In Charge (SAUS)
HIC.............. Hydrophobic Interaction Chromatography
HIC.............. White Cloud, MI [*Location identifier*] [*FAA*] (FAAL)
HICA........... Honey Industry Council of America [*Defunct*] (EA)
HICA........... Hydroxyisocaproic Acid (DMAA)
HICADIP...... Hitachi Computer-Aided Drafting of Isometric Piping (SAUS)
Hi Cal......... High Calorie (AMHC)
hi-cal.......... High Calorie [*or Caloric*] [*Type of diet*] (DAVI)
HICA/MYDP... Hazard Identification Capability Assessment and Multi-Year Development Plan [*Federal Emergency Management Agency*] (GFGA)
HICAP.......... Health Insurance Counseling and Advocacy Program (SAUS)
HICAP.......... Hierarchical Interactive Computer-Aided Placement (VLIE)
HICAP.......... High-Capacity (IAA)
HICAP.......... High Capacity Artillery Projectile [*Military*]
Hicap........... High-Capacity Digital Transport Service [*Pacific Bell*]
HICAP.......... High-Capacity Firefighting Foam Station [*Environmental science*] (COE)
HICAP.......... High-Capacity Projectile (NVT)
HICAP.......... High [*Altitude*] Combat Air Patrol (NVT)
HICAP.......... Histogram Cluster Analysis Program (SAUO)
HICAPCOM... High-Capacity Communication System
HICAPCOM System... High Capacity Communication System (SAUS)
HICAS.......... High-Capacity Active Control Suspension [*Automotive engineering*]
HICAT.......... High-Altitude Clear Air Turbulence [*Aviation*]
HI-CC........... High-Conversion Critical Experiment [*Nuclear energy*] (GFGA)
Hi-C Cell...... High Capacity Cell (SAUS)
HICCS.......... Hardware Inventory Configuration Contrtol System (SAUO)
HICCUP........ Hearing Impaired Consultants Creating Unique Partnerships [*An association*]
HICD........... Habitat International Coalition (SAUO)
H-ICDA......... International Classification of Diseases - Adopted Code for Hospitals
HICEB.......... Hanford Inter-Contractors Electrical Board (SAUS)
HICEM.......... HIAS-JCA Emigration Association (SAUO)
HICF............ Health Insurance Claim Form
HICH............ Hypertensive Intracranial Hemorrhage [*Medicine*] (MELL)
Hi CHO........ High Carbohydrate (AMHC)
HICHS.......... Helicopter Internal Cargo Handling System
HICIP........... Hybrid Image Classification Instruction Package (SAUS)
HICK........... Hickok Electrical Instrument Co. [*NASDAQ symbol*] (SAG)
HICK........... Hickok, Inc. [*NASDAQ symbol*] (SAG)
hick............ Hickory (VRA)
HICKA.......... Hickok Inc. 'A' [*NASDAQ symbol*] (TTSB)
Hick Ct Mar... Hickman on Naval Courts-Martial [*A publication*] (DLA)
Hickok......... Hickok, Inc. [*Associated Press*] (SAG)
Hickory........ Hickory Tech Corp. [*Associated Press*] (SAG)
Hicks Ethics... Hicks' Organization and Ethics of Bench and Bar [*A publication*] (DLA)
Hicks Leg Research... Hicks on Materials and Methods of Legal Research [*A publication*] (DLA)
Hicks Men & Books... Hicks on Men and Books Famous in the Law [*A publication*] (DLA)
HICLASS...... Hierarchical Classification [*Indexing*]
HI CLASS..... Hughes Integrated Classification System [*Hughes Aircraft Co.*] (NITA)
HiCN............ Cyanmethemoglobin [*Immunology*] (DAVI)
HICO........... Hastings Instrument Co. (SAUS)
HICO........... Hastings Instrument Company (SAUO)
HICOA.......... Head Injury Council of Australia
HICOCOM.... Allied High Control Commission for Germany (SAUO)
HICOG.......... High Commissioner for Germany
HICOM.......... Heavy Industries Corp. of Malaysia (ECON)
HiCom.......... High Command (SAUS)
HICOM.......... High Command
HICOM.......... High Command Communications System (SAUS)
HICOM.......... High Commission [*or Commissioner*]
HICOM.......... High Technology Communication (SAUO)
Hi Com Ind... High Commissioner in India (SAUO)
HICOMRY.... High Commissioner of Ryukyu Islands
HICOMSEVONET... High Command Secure Voice Network [*Navy*] (NVT)
HICOMTERPACIS... High Commissioner Trust Territory, Pacific Islands
hi-con.......... High Contrast [*Cinematography*]
HICON.......... Higher Echelons Concept Study (SAUO)
HICPAC........ Hospital Infection Control Practices Advisory Committee (ADWA)
HICRV.......... Human Intracisternal Retrovirus [*Medicine*]
HICS............ Hardened Intersite Cable System (CET)
HICS............ Hierarchical Information Control System [*Japanese*]
HICS............ Holt International Children's Services (EA)
HI-CSFN...... Huxley Institute - Canadian [*Medicine*] (EDAA)
HICSS.......... Hawaii International Conference on System Sciences (BUAC)
HICX............ Huntsville International Intermodal Center [*Federal Railroad Administration identification code*]
HID.............. Hallucinations, Illusions and Delusions (SAUS)
HID.............. Hamer Butte [*Idaho*] [*Seismograph station code, US Geological Survey*] (SEIS)
HID.............. Handbook on Injectable Drugs (SAUO)
HID.............. Hardware Installation Data (CAAL)
HID.............. Hardware Interface Device (NASA)
HID.............. Headache, Insomnia, Depression [*Syndrome*]
HID.............. Head-In Display (SAUS)
HID.............. Helium Ionization Detector [*Instrumentation*]
HID.............. Herniated Intervertebral Disc [*Medicine*] (DMAA)
HID.............. Hierarchical Identification
HID.............. High Density (IAA)
HID.............. High-Impact Design (NRCH)
HID.............. High-Intensity Discharge [*Vapor lamp*]
HID.............. High-Interstitial Defect (SAUS)
HID.............. High-Iron Diamine
HID.............. HIM [*Hardware Interface Module*] Interface Distributor (NASA)
HID.............. Housing Industry Dynamics [*Originator and databank*] (NITA)
HID.............. Human Immune Deficiency [*Immunology*]
HID.............. Human Infectious Dose [*Medicine*] (DMAA)
HID.............. Human Interface Device (SAUS)
HID.............. Hyperkinetic Impulse Disorder [*Medicine*]
HIDA............ Health Industry Distributors Association (EA)
HIDA............ Hepatoiminodiacetic Acid [*Scan*] [*Radiology*] (DAVI)
HIDA............ Home Improvement Dealers Association of America (EA)
HID-AB........ High-Iron Diamine-Alcian Blue [*A biological stain*]
HIDACZ........ High-Density Airspace Control Zone (MCD)
HIDAD.......... Helicopter Insecticide Dispersal Apparatus, Dry (NG)
HIDAD.......... High Density Array Development programme (SAUS)
HIDAF.......... Helicopter Insecticide Dispersal Apparatus, Fog (NG)
HIDAL.......... Helicopter Insecticide Dispersal Apparatus, Liquid (NG)
HIDAM.......... Hierarchical Indexed Direct Access Method [*Computer science*] (BUR)
HIDAN.......... High-Density Air Navigation
HIDAS.......... Helicopter Integrated Defensive Aids System (SAUS)
HIDB............ Highlands and Islands Development Board [*Scotland*] (ECON)
HIDC............ Hexamethylindodicarbocyanine (SAUS)
HIDC............ Housing Industry Development Council [*Australia*]
HIDC............ Hydrogen-Induced Delayed Cracking (SAUS)
HIDE............ Heavy-Duty Engine (SAUS)
HIDE............ Helicopter Integrated Direction Equipment
HIDE............ Hide project (SAUS)
HIDE............ High-Absorption Integrated Defense Electromagnetic Warfare System
HIDE............ Human Insulin-Degrading Enzyme [*An enzyme*]
HIDE............ Hydrogen-Induced Deformation Experiment (SAUS)
HIDEA.......... High Desert Engineering Association (SAUO)
HIDEC.......... Highly Integrated Digital Electronic Control (SAUO)
HIDEC.......... Highly Integrated Digital Engine Control (MCD)
HIDECS........ Hierarchical Decomposition of Systems (SAUS)
HIDES.......... Hardware Implant Detection Study (ACAE)
HIDES.......... High-Absorption Integrated Defense Electromagnetic System (SAUS)
HIDES.......... Highway Design System (SAUS)
HIDE Warfare System... High-absorption Integrated Defense Electromagnetic Warfare System (SAUS)
HIDF............ Horizontal Intermediate Distribution Frame (SAUS)
HIDF............ Horizontal Side of an Intermediate Distribution Frame [*Telecommunications*] (TEL)
HIDI............. Health-Care Instruments and Devices Institute [*State University of New York at Buffalo*] [*Research center*] (RCD)
HIDIS........... Highland District (SAUS)
HID Lamp.... High Intensity Discharge Lamp (SAUS)
HiD/LoD...... High-Density/Low-Density Tariff
HIDM........... High Information Delta Modulation [*Computer science*] (BUR)
HIDOC.......... Hierarchical Documentation (SAUS)
HIDOC Writer... Hierarchical Documentation Writer (SAUS)
HIDRESS...... High Data Rate Storage Subsystem (SAUS)
HIDS............ Headquarters Information Distribution System (SAUS)
HIDSS.......... Helmet Integrated Display Sighting System (SAUO)
HIDSS.......... Helmet Integrated Display Sight System (ACAE)
HID Syndrome... Headache-Insomnia-Depression Syndrome (SAUS)
HIDTA.......... High Intensity Drug Trafficking Area
Hi-D Tariff... High Density Tariff (SAUS)
HIDTC.......... Hangar and Industrial Door Technical Council [*Defunct*] (MSA)
HIDVL.......... High Intensity-Discharge Vapor Lamp (SAUS)
HIE.............. Health Informatics Europe (SAUO)
HIE.............. Heat Input Equivalent (PDAA)
HIE.............. Height Integration Equipment
HIE.............. Helicopter Installed Equipment (SAUS)
HIE.............. Help in Emergency (ADA)
HIE.............. Hibernation Information Exchange [*Later, IHS*]
HI-E............. High Efficiency (SAUS)
HIE.............. Histrionic Instruction Education (SAUS)
HIE.............. Homelessness Information Exchange (EA)
HIE.............. Human Intestinal Epithelium [*Medicine*] (DMAA)
HIE.............. Hypoxi-Ischemic Encephalopathy [*Neurology*] (DAVI)

HIE............ Whitefield, NH [*Location identifier*] [*FAA*] (FAAL)
HIEAT........... Highest Temperature Equaled for All Time [*NWS*] (FAAC)
HIEC............ Hanford Instrument Evaluation Committee (SAUS)
HIEDIC......... Health Industry EDI Corporation (AG)
HiEF............ High-Efficiency Particulate Filter [*Industrial hygiene term*] (OHS)
HIEFM.......... Highest Temperature Equaled for the Month [*NWS*] (FAAC)
HIEFSS........ Hospital, Institution, and Educational Food Service Society [*Later, Dietary Managers Association - DMA*] (EA)
HIEME......... Higher Institute of Electrical and Mechanical Engineering (SAUS)
HIER........... Hieroglyphics (WDAA)
Hier........... Hieronymus [*Jerome*] [*348-420AD*] (BJA)
HIER........... Hierusolymo [*Jerusalem*] (ROG)
HIER........... Hungarian Institute for Educational Research (BUAC)
Hier Gabr..... Hieronymus Gabrielius [*Deceased, 1587*] [*Authority cited in pre-1607 legal work*] (DSA)
hiergl.......... Hieroglyph (VRA)
Hiero........... Hieroglyphics
Hiero Cag.... Hieronymus Cagnolus [*Deceased, 1551*] [*Authority cited in pre-1607 legal work*] (DSA)
Hiero Cagno... Hieronymus Cagnolus [*Deceased, 1551*] [*Authority cited in pre-1607 legal work*] (DSA)
Hieron......... Hieronymus [*Jerome*] [*348-420AD*] (OCD)
Hieron Cagno... Hieronymus Cagnolus [*Deceased, 1551*] [*Authority cited in pre-1607 legal work*] (DSA)
Hieron Gabriel... Hieronymus Gabrielius [*Deceased, 1587*] [*Authority cited in pre-1607 legal work*] (DSA)
Hieron Grat... Hieronymus Gratus [*Deceased, 1544*] [*Authority cited in pre-1607 legal work*] (DSA)
Hier Schurf... Hieronymus Schurff [*Deceased, 1554*] [*Authority cited in pre-1607 legal work*] (DSA)
Hier Torniel... Hieronymus Torniellus [*Deceased, 1575*] [*Authority cited in pre-1607 legal work*] (DSA)
HIES............ Hadassah Israel Education Services [*Jerusalem*]
HIES............ Health Insurance/Employer Survey [*Department of Health and Human Services*] (GFGA)
HIES............ Hydrographic Image Exploitation System (SAUO)
HIESE.......... Highest Temperature Equaled so Early [*NWS*] (FAAC)
HIESL.......... Highest Temperature Equaled so Late [*NWS*] (FAAC)
HIEST.......... Highlight Image Enhancement Screen Technology (SAUS)
HIF.............. Hardware Interchange Format (RALS)
HIF.............. Health Information Foundation
HIF.............. Heavy Ion Fusion (PDAA)
HIF.............. Higher Integrative Functions [*Neurology*]
HIF.............. Higher Intellectual Function (SAUS)
HIF.............. High-Impedance Follower
HIF.............. Hocker International Federation (EA)
HIF.............. Hokkaido International Foundation (SAUO)
HIF.............. Horizontal Integral Float [*Automotive engineering*]
HIF.............. Hot Isostatic Forging (SAUS)
HIF.............. Hot Isothermal Forging (SAUS)
HIF.............. Housing Insurance Fund [*New Deal*]
HIF.............. Human-Initiated Failure
HIF.............. Hydrologic Instrumentation Facility (SAUO)
HIF.............. Hyper-G Interchange Format (SAUS)
HIF.............. Hypoxia-Inducible Factor [*Physiology*]
HIF.............. International Helsinki Federation for Human Rights [*Austria*] (EAIO)
HIF.............. Ogden, UT [*Location identifier*] [*FAA*] (FAAL)
HIF.............. Salomon Brothers High Income Fund [*NYSE symbol*] (SPSG)
HIFA............ Home Insurance Federation of America
HIFAM.......... High-Fidelity Amplitude Modulation (DEN)
HIFAR.......... High Flux Australian Reactor (SAUS)
HIFAR.......... High Flux Australian Research Reactor (SAUO)
HIFAR.......... High-Frequency Fixed Array RADAR
HIFAX-NET... Hitachi Facsimile-Network (SAUS)
HIFBS.......... Heat-Inactivated Fetal Bovine Serum [*Immunology*]
HIFC............ Hog Intrinsic Factor Concentrate
HIFCS.......... Heat-Inactivated Fetal Calf Serum (DB)
HIFD............ High capacity Floppy Disk (SAUS)
HIFD............ High Density Floppy Disk (SAUS)
HIFE............ Household Income, Facilities, and Equipment (FOTI)
HIFET.......... Heterointerface Field-Effect Transistor (SAUS)
HIFI............. Cambridge Soundworks, Inc. [*NASDAQ symbol*] (SAG)
HIFI............. Hawaii Imaging Fabry-Perot Interferometer
HIFI............. Height Interpolation by Finite Elements (SAUS)
HIFI............. HFIR [*High-Flux Isotope Reactor*] Irradiation Facility Improvement [*Nuclear energy*]
HIFI............. High Fibre Biscuits [*British*]
hi-fi............. High-Fidelity [*Printing*] (WDMC)
HI-FI............ High-Fidelity [*Usually, in reference to home sound-reproducing equipment*]
Hi Fi............. High Fidelity and Musical America (SAUS)
Hi Fi............. High Fidelity (journ.) (SAUS)
HIFI............. High Fidelity Records [*Record label*]
HIFI............. High-Intensity Food Irradiator
HIFI............. Hypertext Interface For Information (SAUS)
Hi-Fi News... High-Fidelity News (journ.) (SAUS)
HIFIVE......... High Fidelity Interactive Visual Environment (SAUS)
HI-FIX.......... High-accuracy-position Fixing (SAUS)
HIFLEX......... High Flexibility (SAUS)
HIFN............ Hi/fn, Inc. [*NASDAQ symbol*] (NASQ)
HIFN............ Human Interferon (DB)
hIFNa.......... Human Interferon Type Alpha (DB)
HIFNY.......... Hospitality Industry Foundation of New York (SAUO)
HIFO............ Highest In, First Out [*Accounting*]
HIFO............ Highest-In-First-Out
Hifo............. Highest-In-First-Out (SAUS)
HIFO............ High Input, First Output [*Computer science*] (ECII)
HIFOR.......... High-Level Forecast [*Meteorology*]
HIFPA.......... Hispanic Institute for the Performing Arts [*Defunct*] (EA)
HIFR............ Helicopter In-Flight Refueling (NVT)
HIFR............ Hover-In-Flight Air Data System (SAUS)
HIFR............ Hover In-Flight Refuelling (SAUO)
HIFRAG........ High Fragmentation (MCD)
HIFRENSA.... Sociedad Hispano-Francesa de Energia Nuclear SA [*Nuclear energy*] [*Spanish*] (NRCH)
HIFS............ Hingham Institution for Savings [*NASDAQ symbol*] (CTT)
HIFT............ Hardware Implemented Fault Tolerance
HIFT............ Heard Island Feasibility Test [*Marine science*] (OSRA)
HIFTO.......... How I Feel Toward Others [*Psychology*] (EDAC)
HIFU............ High-Intensity Focused Ultrasound
HIFV............ Heavy Infantry Fighting Vehicle (SAUS)
HIFX............ High Intensity Flash X-Ray (ACAE)
HIG.............. Hartford Capital I [*NYSE symbol*] (SAG)
HIG.............. Hartford Capital II [*NYSE symbol*] (SAG)
HIG.............. Hartford Finl Svcs Gp. [*NYSE symbol*] (SG)
HIG.............. Hartford Insurance Group (SAUO)
HIG.............. Hawaii Institute of Geophysics [*University of Hawaii*] [*Seismograph station code, US Geological Survey*] [*Research center*] (SEIS)
HIG.............. Hazardous Installation Group (HEAS)
HIG.............. Heli-Inter Guyane [*France*] [*FAA designator*] (FAAC)
HIG.............. Hermetically Sealed, Integrating Gyroscope
HIG.............. Higginsville, MO [*Location identifier*] [*FAA*] (FAAL)
HIG.............. High Input Grant [*Real estate*] [*Canada*]
HIG.............. High-Integrating Gyroscope (KSC)
HIG.............. Honeywell Integrating Gyro
HIg.............. Human Immunoglobulin [*Biochemistry*] (MAE)
HIG.............. Hypervelocity Intercept Guidance
HIG.............. ITT Hartford Group [*NYSE symbol*] (TTSB)
HIGAD.......... High-Impulse Gun Airborne Demonstrator (MCD)
HIGE............ Hovering in Ground Effect [*Army*]
HIGED.......... Handbook of Instructions for Ground Equipment Designers (MCD)
HIGFET......... Heterostructure Insulated Gate Field Effect Transistor (NITA)
HIGFETS....... Heterostructure Isolated Gate Field Effect Transistor (ACAE)
HIGGENS...... Human Interface Graphical Generation System (SAUS)
Higgins......... Higgins' Tennessee Court of Civil Appeals Reports [*A publication*] (DLA)
HIGH............ High Core Threshold (SAUS)
HIGH............ Highland Railway [*British*] (ROG)
HIGH............ Highland Superstores, Inc. [*NASDAQ symbol*] (COMM)
HIGHB.......... Highbury College of Divinity [*British*] (ROG)
High Bail..... Highmore on Bail [*A publication*] (DLA)
HIGH-COM... High Fidelity Compander System (SAUS)
High Ct........ High Court Reports, Northwest Provinces [*India*] [*A publication*] (DLA)
High Educ R&D... Higher Education Research and Development (journ.) (SAUS)
High Energy Phys Nucl Phys... High Energy Physics and Nuclear Physics (journ.) (SAUS)
High Ex Rem... High on Extraordinary Legal Remedies [*A publication*] (DLA)
High Extr Leg Rem... High on Extraordinary Legal Remedies [*A publication*] (DLA)
HIGH GASSER... High Geographic Aerospace Search RADAR
High Inj....... High on Injunctions [*A publication*] (DLA)
Highl........... Highland (SAUS)
HighldInc..... Highlander Income Fund, Inc. [*Associated Press*] (SAG)
HIGH LI....... Highland Light Infantry [*Military*] [*British*] (ROG)
High Lun...... Highmore on Lunacy [*A publication*] (DLA)
High Mort.... Highmore on Mortmain [*A publication*] (DLA)
High-Perform Ceram... High Performance Ceramics (journ.) (SAUS)
High Perform Plast... High Performance Plastics (journ.) (SAUS)
High Perform Polym... High Performance Polymers (journ.) (SAUS)
High Perform Syst... High Performance Systems (journ.) (SAUS)
High Pressu... High Pressure (NAKS)
HIGHPRO..... High Protein (SAUS)
High Purity Subst... High Purity Substances (journ.) (SAUS)
High Rec..... High on the Law of Receivers [*A publication*] (DLA)
HIGHRS....... Highlanders [*British*]
High-Speed Surf Craft... High-Speed Surface Craft (journ.) (SAUS)
Hight........... Hight's Reports [*57-58 Iowa*] [*A publication*] (DLA)
High Technol... High Technology (journ.) (SAUS)
High Temp-High Press... High Temperatures-High Pressures (journ.) (SAUS)
High Temp Mater Process... High Temperature Materials and Processes (journ.) (SAUS)
High Temp Sci... High Temperature Science (SAUO)
High Temp Sci... High Temperature Science (journ.) (SAUS)
High Temp Technol... High Temperature Technology (journ.) (SAUS)
HIGHVISION... High Definition Television (SAUS)
Highvld........ Highveld Steel & Vanadium Corporation Ltd. [*Associated Press*] (SAG)
HIGHWAY.... Highway [*Commonly used*] (OPSA)
Highway Engr... Highway Engineer (journ.) (SAUS)
Highwd........ Highwood Resources Ltd. [*Associated Press*] (SAG)
Highwd........ Highwoods Properties, Inc. [*Associated Press*] (SAG)
Highw Res Board Proc Annu Meet... Highway Research Board. Proceedings of the Annual Meeting (journ.) (SAUS)
HighwResRec... Highway Research Record (SAUO)
Highw Res Rec... Highway Research Record (journ.) (SAUS)
HIGHWY...... Highway [*Commonly used*] (OPSA)
Highwy........ HighwayMaster Communications, Inc. [*Associated Press*] (SAG)
Highwym..... HighwayMaster Communications, Inc. [*Associated Press*] (SAG)
HIGNFY....... Have I Got News for You (WDAA)
Hig Pat Dig... Higgins' Digest of Patent Cases [*1890*] [*A publication*] (DLA)

HIGPrQ........ Hartford Cap I 7.70% 'QUIPS' [*NYSE symbol*] (TTSB)
HIGS............ Hypervelocity Interceptor Guidance Simulation
HIGSED........ Handbook of Instructions for Aircraft Ground Support Equipment Designers (SAUO)
HIGSS............ Hypervelocity Intercept Guidance Simulator Study
Hig Waterc... Higgins' Pollution and Obstruction of Watercourses [*1877*] [*A publication*] (DLA)
HIH............ Greensboro, NC [*Location identifier*] [*FAA*] (FAAL)
HIH............ His [*or Her*] Imperial Highness
HIH............ Hypertensive Intracerebral Hemorrhage [*Medicine*] (DMAA)
HIHA............ High Impulsiveness, High Anxiety [*Psychology*] (DAVI)
HIHAT............ High-Resolution Hemispherical Reflector Antenna Technique
HIHATIg....... Hyperimmune Human Anti-Tetanus [*Medicine*] (EDAA)
HiHb............ Hemiglogin [*Medicine*] (EDAA)
HIHE............ Hunter Institute of Higher Education [*Australia*]
HIHED.......... Handbook of Instructions for Ground Equipment Designers (SAUO)
HI-HICAT..... High High-Altitude Clear Air Turbulence [*Aviation*]
HIHO............ High Insertion, High Opening (SAUS)
HIHO............ Highway Holdings Ltd. [*NASDAQ symbol*] (SAG)
HIHOE.......... Hydrogen, Ions, Helium, Oxygen in the Exosphere (MUGU)
HIHRC.......... Humanitas International Human Rights Committee (EA)
HI HUM........ High Humidity (SAUS)
HIHW............ Highway Holdings Ltd. [*NASDAQ symbol*] (SAG)
HIH-WFJD.... Hearts in Harmony - World Family of John Denver [*An association*] (EA)
HII............ Haemagglutination Inhibition Immunoassay (SAUS)
HII............ Healthcare Integrated Svcs. [*AMEX symbol*] (SG)
HII............ Healthcare International, Incorporated (SAUO)
HII............ Health Images, Inc. [*NYSE symbol*] (SPSG)
HII............ Health Industries Institute (EA)
HII............ Health Information Infrastructure (SAUO)
HII............ Health Insurance Institute (EA)
HII............ Heard Island [*Seismograph station code, US Geological Survey*] [*Closed*] (SEIS)
HII............ Hemagglutination-Inhibition Immunoassay [*Immunochemistry*] (DAVI)
HII............ Heritage Interpretation International
HII............ High Input Impedance
HII............ Host International, Incorporated (SAUO)
HII............ Housing Institute of Ireland (BUAC)
HIID............ Harvard Institute for International Development [*Harvard University*] [*Research center*] (RCD)
HIID............ Heavy Ion-Induced Desorption [*Analytical chemistry*]
HIII............ Harmann International Industries, Incorporated (SAUO)
HIIMP.......... High Impedance (SAUS)
HiIncо.......... High Income Advantage Trust [*Associated Press*] (SAG)
HiIncoOp..... High Income Opportunity Fund [*Associated Press*] (SAG)
HiInIII.......... High Income Advantage Trust III [*Associated Press*] (SAG)
HIIP............ High Impact Incarceration Program [*60-day paramilitary regimen for prisoners*]
HIIPS.......... HUD [*Department of Housing and Urban Development*] Integrated Information Processing Service (GFGA)
HIIR............ Halogenated Isobutene-Isoprene Rubber (SAUS)
HIIS............ Honeywell Institute for Information Science (IEEE)
HIiS............ Schistocytes [*Hematology*] (DAVI)
HIIYSP........ Himalayan International Institute of Yoga Science and Philosophy (SAUO)
HIJ............ Hiroshima [*Japan*] [*Airport symbol*] (OAG)
HIJ............ Horological Institute of Japan (SAUS)
HIJ............ Sisters of the Holy Infant Jesus [*Roman Catholic religious order*]
HIJMS.......... His Imperial Japanese Majesty's Ship
HIK............ High Permittivity (DEN)
Hik............ Hiker (SAUS)
Hik............ Hiking (SAUS)
HIK............ Hikone [*Japan*] [*Seismograph station code, US Geological Survey*] (SEIS)
HIK............ Hikurangi Airlines [*New Zealand*] [*FAA designator*] (FAAC)
HIK............ Honolulu, HI [*Location identifier*] [*FAA*] (FAAL)
HIK............ Hook Interface Kit (SAUS)
HIL............ Great Bend, KS [*Location identifier*] [*FAA*] (FAAL)
HIL............ Hardware-in-the-Loop
HIL............ Hazardous Immiscible Liquid (SAUS)
HIL............ Hazardous Industrial Liquid (SAUS)
HIL............ Hees International Bancorp, Inc. [*Toronto Stock Exchange symbol*]
HIL............ Helium Impurities Loop [*Nuclear energy*] (NRCH)
HIL............ High-Intensity Light
HIL............ High Intensity Lighting (SAUS)
Hil............ Hilary Term [*England*] [*Legal term*] (DLA)
HIL............ Hilo [*Hawaii*] [*Seismograph station code, US Geological Survey*] (SEIS)
HIL............ Human Interface Link (SAUS)
HIL............ Hypoxic-Ischemic Lesion [*Medicine*] (DAVI)
HILA............ Health Insurance Logistics Automated (SAUS)
HILA............ High Impulsiveness, Low Anxiety (MAE)
HILAB.......... Heavy Ion Laboratory (PDAA)
Hil Abr........ Hilliard's American Law [*A publication*] (DLA)
HILAC.......... Heavy-Ion Linear Accelerator [*Nuclear energy*]
HILAN.......... High Level Language (SAUS)
HILAP.......... High Latitude Particle (PDAA)
HILASD........ Hard Link Arm Safe Device (MCD)
HILAST........ High-Altitude Large Area Surveillance Tactic [*Military*] (CAAL)
HILAT.......... High Latitude (SAUS)
HILAT.......... High-Latitude Research Satellite [*Defense Nuclear Agency*]
HILBIO........ Effects of Human Activity on High Altitude Biodiversity (SAUS)
HilbRog........ Hilb, Rogal & Hamilton Co. [*Associated Press*] (SAG)
HILC............ Hampshire Inter-Library Center [*Library network*]
HILC............ High-Intermediate Level Cell [*Nuclear energy*] (NRCH)
HILCADS...... High Level Container Airdrop System (SAUS)
HilcstDv....... Hilcoast Development Corp. [*Associated Press*] (SAG)
HILDA.......... High Latitude Diffusive-Advective model (SAUS)
HILDCAA...... High Intensity, Long-Duration, Continuous Aurora Event, Activity (SAUS)
HILDCAA...... High-Intensity, Long-Duration, Continuous Aurora Event, Activity [*Astrophysics*]
Hild Ins........ Hildyard on Insurance [*A publication*] (DLA)
Hild Mar Ins... Hildyard's Marine Insurance [*A publication*] (DLA)
Hil Elem Law... Hilliard's Elements of Law [*A publication*] (DLA)
HILEX.......... High-Level Exercise [*NATO*] (MUSM)
Hilgardia Calif Agric Exp Stn... Hilgardia. California Agricultural Experiment Station (journ.) (SAUS)
HILI............ Heavy Ion, Light Ion
HILI............ Higher Layers and Internetworking [*Computer science*] (ACRL)
HILI............ High Level Interface (SAUS)
HILI............ Hilite Industries, Inc. [*NASDAQ symbol*] (SAG)
HILIS.......... High Light Intensity System (PDAA)
Hilite.......... Hilite Industries, Inc. [*Associated Press*] (SAG)
HILJ............ Harvard International Law Journal [*A publication*]
HILL............ Hill [*Commonly used*] (OPSA)
Hill............ Hill's New York Supreme Court Reports [*1841-44*] [*A publication*] (DLA)
Hill............ Hill's South Carolina Law Reports [*A publication*] (DLA)
HILLA.......... High-Input Low Labor Agriculture (SAUS)
Hill Abr........ Hilliard's Abridgment of Real Property Law [*A publication*] (DLA)
Hill Am Jur... Hilliard's American Jurisprudence [*A publication*] (DLA)
Hill Am Law... Hilliard's American Law [*A publication*] (DLA)
Hill & D...... Lalor's Supplement to Hill and Denio's New York Reports [*A publication*] (DLA)
Hill & Den... Lalor's Supplement to Hill and Denio's New York Reports [*A publication*] (DLA)
Hill & Den Supp... Lalor's Supplement to Hill and Denio's New York Reports [*A publication*] (DLA)
Hill & D Supp... Hill and Denio's Lalor's Supplement [*New York*] [*A publication*] (DLA)
Hill & Redman... Hill and Redman's Law of Landlord and Tenant [*16th ed.*] [*1976*] [*A publication*] (DLA)
Hill B & I...... Hilliard on Bankruptcy and Insolvency [*A publication*] (DLA)
Hill Bank..... Hilliard on Bankruptcy and Insolvency [*A publication*] (DLA)
HillBd.......... Hillside Bedding Corp. [*Associated Press*] (SAG)
Hill Ch......... Hill's Equity South Carolina Reports [*1833-37*] [*A publication*] (DLA)
Hill Ch Pr.... Hill's Chancery Practice [*A publication*] (DLA)
Hill Cont...... Hilliard on Contracts [*A publication*] (DLA)
HILLD.......... Hillsdale, IN [*American Association of Railroads railroad junction routing code*]
Hill Elem Law... Hilliard's Elements of Law [*A publication*] (DLA)
Hillenbd....... Hillenbrand Industries, Inc. [*Associated Press*] (SAG)
Hill Eq......... Hill's Equity South Carolina Reports [*1833-37*] [*A publication*] (DLA)
Hill Eq (SC)... Hill's Equity South Carolina Reports [*1833-37*] [*A publication*] (DLA)
Hill Fixt....... Hill's Law of Fixtures [*A publication*] (DLA)
Hilliard RP... Hilliard on Real Property [*A publication*] (DLA)
Hill Ill Chy... Hill's Illinois Chancery Practice [*A publication*] (DLA)
Hill Ill Com Law... Hill's Illinois Common Law Jurisdiction and Practice [*A publication*] (DLA)
Hill Inj......... Hilliard on the Law of Injunctions [*A publication*] (DLA)
Hill Lib & Law... Hill's Liberty and Law [*A publication*] (DLA)
Hill Mor....... Hilliard's Law of Mortgages [*A publication*] (DLA)
Hill Mortg.... Hilliard's Law of Mortgages [*A publication*] (DLA)
Hill New Trials... Hilliard on New Trials [*A publication*] (DLA)
Hill N Tr...... Hilliard on New Trials [*A publication*] (DLA)
Hill NY........ Hill's New York Reports [*A publication*] (DLA)
Hill NYR...... Hill's New York Reports [*A publication*] (DLA)
Hill Prob...... Hill's Illinois Probate Jurisdiction and Practice [*A publication*] (DLA)
Hill Real Prop... Hilliard on Real Property [*A publication*] (DLA)
Hill Rem....... Hilliard on Remedies for Torts [*A publication*] (DLA)
HILLS.......... Hills [*Commonly used*] (OPSA)
Hill Sales.... Hilliard on Sales of Personal Property [*A publication*] (DLA)
Hill's Ann Codes & Laws... Hill's Annotated Codes and General Laws [*Oregon*] [*A publication*] (DLA)
Hill's Ann St & Codes... Hill's Annotated General Statutes and Codes [*Washington*] [*A publication*] (DLA)
HillsBd......... Hillside Bedding Corp. [*Associated Press*] (SAG)
Hill SC......... Hill's Equity South Carolina Reports [*1833-37*] [*A publication*] (DLA)
Hill SC......... Hill's South Carolina Law Reports [*A publication*] (DLA)
Hill's Code... Hill's Annotated Codes and General Laws [*Oregon*] [*A publication*] (DLA)
Hill's Code... Hill's Annotated General Statutes and Codes [*Washington*] [*A publication*] (DLA)
HillsStrs...... Hills Stores Co. [*Associated Press*] (SAG)
HillStr......... Hills Stores Co. [*Associated Press*] (SAG)
Hill Tax........ Hilliard on the Law of Taxation [*A publication*] (DLA)
Hill Torts..... Hilliard on the Law of Torts [*A publication*] (DLA)
Hill Tr.......... Hill on Trustees [*A publication*] (DLA)
Hill Vend..... Hilliard on the Law of Vendors [*A publication*] (DLA)
Hillyer.......... Hillyer's Reports [*20-22 California*] [*A publication*] (DLA)
HILNNEP...... Health Information Library Network of Northeastern Pennsylvania [*Library network*]
HILO............ High Insertion, Low Opening (SAUO)
HiLo............ Hi-Lo Automotive, Inc. [*Associated Press*] (SAG)
HILOW.......... Health Information Libraries of Westchester [*Library network*]
HILP............ Health Information Library Program [*Library network*]
HILS............ Halogen Interchangeable Light Source
HILS............ High-Intensity Learning Systems

HILS............ High Intensity Lightweight Searchlight (PDAA)
HILT............ High Impetus, Low Flame Temperature (MCD)
HILT............ High-Intensity Language Training (AEBS)
Hil T............ Hilary Term [*England*] [*Legal term*] (DLA)
Hilt............ Hilton's New York Common Pleas Reports [*A publication*] (DLA)
Hil Term 4 Will IV... Hilary Term 4, William IV [*A publication*] (DLA)
HILTN............ Hilton, GA [*American Association of Railroads railroad junction routing code*]
Hilt (NY)...... Hilton's New York Common Pleas Reports [*A publication*] (DLA)
Hilton............ Hilton Hotels Corp. [*Associated Press*] (SAG)
Hil Torts...... Hilliard on the Law of Torts [*A publication*] (DLA)
HIL VAC....... Hilary Vacation [*British*] [*Legal term*] (DLA)
HILY SITTGS... Hilary Sittings [*British*] [*Legal term*] (ROG)
HIM............ Hardware Interface Module [*NASA*] (NASA)
HIM............ Hardware Interface Module Hierarchy of Interpretive Modules (MHDI)
HIM............ Hazardous Industrial Material (SAUS)
HIM............ Health Information Management (SAUO)
HIM............ Health Insurance Manual
HIM............ Heavy Interdiction Missile
HIM............ Heliocentric Information Map (SAUO)
HIM............ Helps International Ministries (EA)
HIM............ Hemopoietic Inductive Microenvironment (STED)
HIM............ Hepatitis-Infectious Mononucleosis [*Medicine*] (DB)
HIM............ Herald International Mailings Ltd. [*British*]
Him............ Heroin [*Medicine*] (EDAA)
HIM............ Hexosephosphate Isomerase (STED)
HIM............ Hierarchy of Interpretive Modules (SAUS)
HIM............ High Impact
HIM............ High Inclination Mission (SAUS)
HIM............ High-Intensity Microphone
HIM............ Hill Interaction Matrix [*Psychology*]
him............ Himachali [*MARC language code*] [*Library of Congress*] (LCCP)
HIM............ Himac Resources Ltd. [*Vancouver Stock Exchange symbol*]
HIM............ Himeji [*Japan*] [*Seismograph station code, US Geological Survey*] (SEIS)
HIM............ Horizontal Impulse
HIM............ Host Interface Manager (NITA)
HIM............ Host Interface Module [*Communications term*] (DCT)
HIM............ Hotel Institute Montreux [*Switzerland*] (ECON)
HIM............ Hot Ionized Medium [*Astrophysics*]
HIM............ Human Individual Metamorphosis [*Flying saucer cult*]
HIM............ Human Integrated Manufacturing
HIM............ Hyperimmunoglobulin M Syndrome [*Medicine*]
HIM............ Hyper Immunoglobulin Syndrome [*Medicine*]
HIMA............ Health Industry Manufacturers Association (EA)
HIM-A............ Hill Interaction Matrix-A [*Personality development test*] [*Psychology*]
HIMAA............ Health Information Management Association of Australia (SAUO)
HIMAAWS...... High Mobility Armored Assault Weapons System (SAUO)
HIMAC............ Heavy-Ion Medical Accelerator in Chiba [*Japan*]
HIMAC............ Highly Integrated Multiplexer (or Multiplexor) Channel (SAUS)
HIMACS......... Hanford Information Management and Control System (SAUS)
HIMAD............ High and Medium Air Defense (SAUS)
HIMAD............ High and Medium Altitude Air Defense (SAUO)
HIMAD............ High-Medium Air Defense (SAUS)
HIMAD............ High-to-Medium-Altitude Air Defense (AABC)
HIMAD............ High to Medium Range Air Defense (SAUO)
HIMADS......... High-to-Medium-Altitude Air Defense System (SAUS)
Hi mag............ High Manification [*Medicine*] (EDAA)
HIMAG............ High-Mobility-Agility [*Test for combat vehicles*] (RDA)
HIMAIL............ Hitachi Integrated Message and Information Library (SAUS)
Himal............ Himalaya (SAUS)
HIM&CC....... Healthcare Information Management & Communication Canada (SAUO)
HIMARS......... High Mobility Artillery Rocket System [*Army*] (DOMA)
HIMARS......... History Management and Retrieval System (SAUO)
HIMAT............ Highly Maneuverable Aircraft Technology Testbed [*Rockwell International Corp.*] (MCD)
HiMAT............ Highly Manoeuvrable Aircraft Technology (SAUO)
HIMAT............ High Maneuverable Advanced-fighter Technology (SAUS)
HiMaTE......... High Mach Turbine Engine (ADWA)
HIMB............ Hawaii Institute of Marine Biology [*University of Hawaii*] [*Research center*] (RCD)
HIMC............ Hepatic Intramitochondrial Crystalloid [*Medicine*] (DMAA)
HIMD............ Handbook of Instructions for Missile Designers
HIMEM......... High Memory (SAUS)
HIMES............ Highly-Maneuverable Experimental Spacecraft (SAUS)
HIMES............ Highly Maneuverable Experimental Space Vehicle (SAUS)
HIMES............ History Management and Retrieval System (SAUO)
HIMEZ............ High-altitude Missile Engagement Zone (SAUO)
HIMEZ............ High Missile Engagement Zone (SAUS)
HIMG............ Health Images, Inc. [*NASDAQ symbol*] (COMM)
HIMI............ Heilongjiang Institute of Medical Information [*China*] (BUAC)
HI MI............ High Mileage (WDAA)
HIMIC............ Highly-Indebted Middle-Income Country
HIMM............ Hallberg Index of Male Menopause (SAUS)
HIMMC............ HQ and Maintenance Management Co. (SAUS)
HIMMC............ HQ and Maintenance Management Company (SAUO)
HIMO............ High Mobility [*Vehicle analysis*] (MCD)
HIMOCS......... High Mobility Cannon System (SAUS)
HIMOS............ High-Injection Metal-Oxide Semiconductor (CIST)
HIMOWC....... High-Mobility Weapons Carrier [*Army*] (MCD)
HIMP............ High-Dose Intravenous Methylprednisolone [*Medicine*] (DMAA)
HIMP............ High Impact
HIMPOS......... Hierarchical Multiprocessor Operating System (SAUS)
Him Pra......... All India Reporter, Himachal Pradesh [*A publication*] (DLA)
HIMR............ Handbook of Inspection Maintenance Requirements [*Navy*] (MCD)
HIMR............ Hearing-Impaired Mentally Retarded
HIMS............ Hanford Issues Management System (SAUS)
HIMS............ Harrier Information Management System (SAUS)
HIMS............ Heavy Interdiction Missile System (MCD)
HIMS............ Helicopter Independent Manoeuvring Systems (SAUS)
HIMS............ Helicopter In-Flight Monitoring System [*Army*] (RDA)
HIMS............ High Resolution Image Information Management System (SAUO)
HIMS............ Himself
HIMS............ HMMWV [*High-Mobility Multipurpose Wheeled Vehicle*] Interchange Mount System [*Military*] (INF)
HIMS............ Housing Information Management System
HIMS............ Human Intervention and Motivation Study (ACAE)
HIMS............ HUMINT [*Human Intelligence*] Information Management System
HIMSD............ Handbook of Instructions for Missiles and Space Vehicles (SAUS)
HIMSEUR...... HAWK [*Homing All the Way Killer*] Intensified Management System Europe Program [*Military*]
HIMSS............ Healthcare Information and Management Systems Society (EA)
HIMSS............ High-Resolution Microwave Spectrometer Sounder (EOSA)
HIMT............ Hemagglutination Inhibition Morphine Test [*Immunochemistry*] (DMAA)
HI MU............ High Mu-factor (SAUS)
HIMV............ Hippeastrum Mosaic Virus [*Plant pathology*]
HIMZ............ Hannibal Iron & Metal [*Federal Railroad Administration identification code*]
HIN............ Chadron, NE [*Location identifier*] [*FAA*] (FAAL)
HIN............ Health Identification Number
HIN............ Health-Info-Net (SAUS)
HIN............ Health Information Network (ADWA)
HIN............ Health Insurance Network Hinck Hinckley (SAUS)
HIN............ Heli Inter [*France*] [*ICAO designator*] (FAAC)
HIN............ Heterotrophic Intestinal Nitrification [*Metabolism*]
HIN............ Hidden Lake Gold Mines [*Vancouver Stock Exchange symbol*]
HIN............ High Intensity
HIN............ High-Intensity Noise
HIN............ Hinchinbrook Island [*Alaska*] [*Seismograph station code, US Geological Survey*] (SEIS)
hin............ Hindi [*MARC language code*] [*Library of Congress*] (LCCP)
HIN............ Holocaust Information Network (EA)
HIN............ Honeywell Information Network (SAUS)
HIN............ Hull Identification Number [*USCG*] (TAG)
HIN............ Hybrid Integrated Network [*Bell System*] [*Telecommunications*]
HIN............ Hybrid Untegrated Network (SAUS)
HIN............ Hydrocarbon-Induced Nephropathy [*Medicine*]
HINAS............ Historic Naval Ships Association of North America (EA)
HINASW......... Historic Naval Ships of the World [*Later, HINAS*] (EA)
HIncII............ High Income Advantage Trust II [*Associated Press*] (SAG)
Hincmar Epist... Hincmari Epistolae [*A publication*] (DLA)
HINCS............ Heat-Inactivated Newborn Calf Serum (DB)
HIND............ Health Care Item Name Directory [*A publication*]
Hind............ Hindi (SHCU)
HIND............ Hindi (WDAA)
HIND............ Hindu (WDAA)
HIND............ Hindustan (SAUS)
Hind............ Hindustan
Hind............ Hindustani (BEE)
HIND............ Hindustani [*Language, etc.*]
HinD............ Housewives in Dialogue [*An association*] (BUAC)
HINDALCO... Hindustan Aluminium Corp. [*India*] (BUAC)
H in DC......... Holder in Due Course [*Owner or holder of a negotiable instrument at some future time*]
Hinde Ch Pr... Hinde's Modern Practice of the High Court of Chancery [*A publication*] (DLA)
HINDEX......... HANES [*Health and Nutrition Examination Survey*] Data Index [*Department of Health and Human Services*] (GFGA)
Hind LJ......... Hindu Law Journal [*A publication*] (DLA)
Hind LQ......... Hindu Law Quarterly [*A publication*] (DLA)
Hind Pat...... Hindmarch on Patents [*A publication*] (DLA)
Hind Pr......... Hind's Practice [*A publication*] (DLA)
HINDU............ Histogram Inspired Neighbourhood Discerning Unsupervised (SAUO)
Hindustan Antibiot Bull... Hindustan Antibiotics Bulletin (journ.) (SAUS)
HINE............ Edward Hines Lumber Co. [*NASDAQ symbol*] (COMM)
Hine & N Ass... Hine and Nicholas on Assignment of Life Policies [*A publication*] (DLA)
Hine & N Dig... Hine and Nicholas. Insurance Digest [*A publication*] (DLA)
HINEKF......... Hinekford [*England*]
Hines............ Hines' Reports [*83-96 Kentucky*] [*A publication*] (DLA)
H Inf............ Hypodermoclysis Infusion (STED)
HINF............ Hypodermoclysis Infusion [*Medicine*]
HINFO............ Host Information (SAUS)
HING............ High-Intensity Noise Generator
Hinglish......... Hindi and English (SAUS)
HingmS......... Hingham Institution for Savings [*Associated Press*] (SAG)
HINIL............ High-Noise-Immunity Logic (MCD)
HINLHBS....... Hunting Improvement and National Light Horse Breeding Society (SAUO)
HINOP............ Health Information Network of the Pacific (SAUS)
HINP............ Hundred Islands National Park (SAUO)
HINPADS....... Helicopter Integrated Processing And Display System (SAUS)
HINS............ Hanover Insurance (EFIS)
HINS............ Health Information Network Services [*Database search service*] (OLDSS)
HINS............ Helicopter Integrated Navigation System [*Canadian Navy*]
Hinsdle......... Hinsdale Financial Corp. [*Associated Press*] (SAG)
HINT............ Happy Idiot News Talk

HINT .... Happy Idiot News Team [*Also, Happy Idiot News Talk*] [*Broadcasting*] (WDMC)
HINT .... Hierarchical Integration (SAUS)
HINT .... High Intensity
Hint............ Hinton [*Flocculation test for syphilis*] [*Medicine*] (STED)
HINT .... Hinton [*Test*] [*Medicine*]
HINT .... Hinton Test (SAUS)
HINT .... Housewares Industry News and Topics [*A publication*] (EAAP)
HINTN......... Hinton, IA [*American Association of Railroads railroad junction routing code*]
HINWR......... Hawaiian Islands National Wildlife Refuge (SAUO)
HINX .... Heritage Inks International [*Private rail car owner code*]
HIO .... Halt Input/Output (SAUS)
HIO .... Health Insuring Organization (DMAA)
HIO .... High Income Opportunity Fund [*NYSE symbol*] (SAG)
HIO .... High Input/Output (SAUS)
HIO .... High Interest Object
HIO .... Hillsboro, OR [*Location identifier*] [*FAA*] (FAAL)
HIO .... Hours of Operation (SAUS)
HIO .... Hypoiodism [*Medicine*]
HIO .... Hypoiodite [*Salt of hypoiodous acid*] (STED)
HIO .... Smith Barney High Income Opportunity Fund [*NYSE symbol*] (SPSG)
HIOMT .... Hydroxyindole O-Methyltransferase [*Also, HOMT*] [*An enzyme*]
HIOOS.......... Headquaters Integrated Office System (SAUS)
HIOS .... Headquarters Integrated Office System [*Military*] (GFGA)
HIOS .... Heath/Zenith Instrument Operating (SAUS)
HIOS .... High Index of Suspicion [*Medicine*] (DMAA)
HiOS .... High Island Offshore System (SAUS)
HI-OVIS........ Highly Interactive Optical Video Information System (SAUS)
HIP.............. Habitability Improvement Plan [*Navy*]
HIP.............. Hanford Integrated Planning (SAUS)
HIP.............. Hanford Inventory Program (SAUS)
HIP.............. Hanford Isotope Production (SAUS)
HIP.............. Hanford Isotopes Plant [*Nuclear energy*]
HIP.............. Hardware Interface Program (NASA)
HIP.............. Harpoon Indicator Panel [*Missiles*] (MCD)
HIP.............. HAWK [*Homing All the Way Killer*] Improvement Program
HIP.............. Hazard Input Program (SAA)
HIP.............. Health Illness Profile (DMAA)
HIP.............. Health Insurance Plan
HIP.............. Hearing Impaired Peer
HIP.............. Help for Incontinent People (EA)
HIP.............. Hex Inline Package (SAUS)
HIP.............. Hierarchical Information Processor (SAUS)
HIP.............. Higher Intermediate Point [*Travel industry*] (TVEL)
HIP.............. High-Impact Pressure
HIP.............. High-Intent Priority [*In the record business, a heavily promoted disk*]
HIP.............. High Internal Phase [*Emulsion chemistry*]
HIP.............. High Involvement Product (BB)
HIP.............. Highly Ionized Plasma
HIP.............. High-Potential Iron Protein
HIP.............. Hipotronics, Inc. [*AMEX symbol*] (COMM)
hip .... Hipped Roof [*Construction term*] (MIST)
Hip............... Hippocampus (DB)
HIP.............. Historically-Informed Performance (SAUS)
HIP.............. Homeless Information Project (BUAC)
HIP.............. Homograft Incus Prosthesis [*Medicine*] (DMAA)
HIP.............. Honduran Independence Party (SAUO)
HIP.............. Hoover Institution Press (DGA)
HIP.............. Horizontal Injection Press
HIP.............. Hospital Improvement Project
HIP.............. Hospital Infections Program (SAUO)
HIP.............. Hospital Insurance Program
HIP.............. Host-IMP Protocol (SAUS)
HIP.............. Host Information Processor (NITA)
HIP.............. Host Interface Port [*Computer science*]
HIP.............. Host Interface Processor [*Computer science*] (PDAA)
HIP.............. Host-IPLI Protocol (SAUS)
HIP.............. Hot Isostatically Pressed [*Materials processing*]
HIP.............. Hot Isostatic Pressing (or Pressure) (SAUS)
HIP.............. Hot Isostatic Processing (SAUS)
HIP.............. Hot Metal Intranet Publisher (SAUS)
HIP.............. Housing Improvement Program [*Federal government*]
HIP.............. Howitzer Improvement Program
HIP.............. Humanizing, Individualizing and Personalizing (SAUS)
HIP.............. Hydrostatic Indifference Point
HIP.............. Hyperbolic Integer Programming [*Computer science*] (PDAA)
HIP.............. Hypnotic Induction Profile
HIP .... Human Information Processing [*Accounting*] (ODA)
HIPA .... Health Insurance Persistency Award [*Later, HIQA*] [*LIMRA*]
HIPA .... Heparin-Induced Platelet Activation [*Medicine*] (DMAA)
HIPA .... High Performance Amplifier (ACAE)
HIPA .... Home Improvement Products Association [*Defunct*] (EA)
HIPA .... Honey Importers and Packers Association (BUAC)
HIPAA......... Health Insurance Portability & Accountability Act
HIPAA......... Health Insurance Portability and Accountability Act of 1996
HIPAA......... Health Insurance Portability and Accountability Act of 1997 (SEAT)
HIPAAS....... High-Performance Advanced Attack Systems (MCD)
HIPAAS....... High-Performance Attack Aircraft System (MCD)
HIPAC .... Heavy-Ion Plasma Accelerator (IAA)
HIPAC .... High-Performance Aircraft Cannon (MCD)
HIPAC .... Hitachi Parametron Automatic Computer
HIPACS....... Hospital Picture Archiving and Communication System. (SAUO)
HIPACT....... High Power Acoustic Coaxial Transducer (SAUS)
HIPA-NET..... Hitachi Packet-switching-Network (SAUS)
HIPAR.......... High Intensity Pulse Acquisition Radar (SAUS)
HIPAR.......... High-Performance Precision Approach Control RADAR (MCD)
HIPAR.......... High-Power Acquisition RADAR (AAG)
HIPAR.......... High Power Illumination Radar (SAUO)
HIPAS.......... Height Performance Attack System (ACAE)
HIPAS.......... High Performance Active Sonar (SAUS)
HIPAS.......... High Performance Armament System (SAUS)
HIPAS.......... High Performance Sonar (SAUS)
HIPAS.......... Hunting Image Processing And Analysing System (SAUO)
HIPASS........ High Pass (SAUS)
HIP/ATBM.... HAWK [*Homing All the Way Killer*] Improvement Program / Anti-Tactical Ballistic Missle (SAA)
HIPBBSN...... Hot-Isostatic Pressed Reaction-Bonded Silicon Nitride (SAUS)
HIPC .... Health Information Policy Council [*Department of Health and Human Services*] (GFGA)
HIPC .... Health Insurance Plan of California
HIPC .... Health Insurance Purchasing Collective (DMAA)
HIPC .... Health Insurance Purchasing Cooperative (ECON)
HIPC .... Heavily Indebted Poor Country
HIPC .... High Chamber Pressure (NAKS)
HIPC .... High Plains Corp. [*NASDAQ symbol*] (NQ)
HIPC .... High Pressure Chamber
HIPCO.......... Hunt International Petroleum Co. (SAUS)
HIPCO.......... Hunt International Petroleum Company (SAUO)
HIPCOR........ High-Power Coherent Radar (SAUS)
HIPCORE...... High Power Coherent Radar (SAUS)
HIPD .... High Intensity Powder Diffractometer (SAUS)
HIPDA.......... Hydroxyisophthalyl Dihydroxarnic Acid (SAUS)
HIPDB.......... Healthcare Integrity and Protection Data Bank (MHCS)
HIPE............ Hospital In-Patient Enquiry [*British*]
HIPED .... Heterogeneous Intelligent Processing for Engineering Design (SAUS)
HIPEG .... High Performance Experimental Gun (SAUS)
HIPEG .... High-Performance External Gun
HIPEG .... High Performance Gun (ACAE)
HIPEHT........ High-Performance Electrothermal Hydrazine Thruster (MCD)
HIPER .... High Performance European Radio (SAUS)
HIPERARC ... High-Performance Archiheater (MCD)
HI-PERF....... High Performance [*Automotive engineering*]
HiPerf.......... High Performance
HIPERFLIR.... High Performance Forward Looking Infra-Red (SAUS)
HIPERLAN.... High Performance Radio Local Area Network (SAUO)
HIPERNAS ... High-Performance Navigation System
Hiperspace... High-Performance Space (GART)
HIPERTHINO... High-Performance Throttleable Injector (KSC)
HIPEX .... Harmonic Identification Pitch Extraction (PDAA)
HIPFERRITE... Hot Isolation Pressed Ferrite (SAUS)
HIPG .... Human Information Processing Group [*Princeton University*]
HIPH .... High Institute of Public Health Alexandria University [*Egypt*] (BUAC)
HIPHAS........ High Power Phased Array Experiment (ACAE)
HiPHIVE....... Hawaii Public Health Internet Virtual Emporium (SAUO)
HI-PI .... High-Performance Intercept
HIPIC .... High-Pressure Impregnation Carbonization (MCD)
HIPIP .... High Potential Iron Protein [*Biochemistry*]
HIPIR .... High Powered Illuminating Radar (SAUS)
HIPIR .... High-Power Illuminator RADAR [*Army*] (AABC)
HIPL............ High Pulse Repetition Laser (SAUS)
HiPlains....... High Plains Corp. [*Associated Press*] (SAG)
HIPLEX .... High Plains Experiment (SAUO)
HIPNT .... High Point, NC [*American Association of Railroads railroad junction routing code*]
HIPO .... Hemihypertrophy, Intestinal Web, Preauricular Skin Tag, and Congenital Corneal Opacity Syndrome [*Medicine*] (DMAA)
HIPO .... Hierarchical Input Process Output [*Diagram used in software assessment*] (NITA)
HIPO .... Hierarchy plus Input-Process-Output [*Computer science*]
Hipo .... High-Potential Employee
HIPO .... High Potential Incident [*Environmental science*] (COE)
HIPO .... High Power (ACAE)
HIPO .... Highway Post Office [*Bus or truck equipped with mail distribution facilities*]
HIPO .... Hilfspolizei [*Auxiliary Police*] [*German*]
Hipo............. Hippolytus Marsilius [*Deceased, 1529*] [*Authority cited in pre-1607 legal work*] (DSA)
HIPO .... Hospital Indicator for Physicians' Orders
HIPOD.......... High Performance Portable Discoid (ACAE)
HIPOE .... High Pressure Oceanographic Equipment (SAUS)
hipot .... High Potential (IDOE)
HIPOT .... High Potential (KSC)
HIPOTT .... High-Potential Test (IEEE)
HIPOW......... Hot Isostatic Pressing of Waste [*Nuclear energy*] (NUCP)
HIPOX.......... High-Pressure Oxygen (AAEL)
HIPP .... Handbook of Institutional Pharmacy Practice (SAUO)
HIPP .... Hanford Integrated Planning Process (SAUS)
HIPP .... High-Energy Impulse Pumpable Propellant (MCD)
HIPP .... Himalayan Interdisciplinary Paleoclimate Project (QUAC)
HIPP .... Hippocrates [*Greek physician, 460 -377 BC*]
Hipp............. Hippolytus [*of Euripides*] [*Classical studies*] (OCD)
HiPPAG........ High Pressure Pure-Air Generator (SAUS)
Hipparch...... Hipparchus [*of Plato*] [*Classical studies*] (OCD)
Hipparcos.... High-Precision Parallax Collecting Satellite [*European Space Agency*]
HIPPARCOS... High Precision Parallax Collection Satellite (SAUS)
Hipp Bonacoss... Hippolytus Bonacossa [*Deceased, 1591*] [*Authority cited in pre-1607 legal work*] (DSA)
HIPPI .... High Performance Parallel Interface [*Computer science*]
HIPPI .... High Performance Peripheral Interface (SAUS)

HIPPI-FP...... High Performance Parallel Interface-Framing Protocol (SAUS)
HIPPI-IPI-3... High Performance Parallel Interface-Intelligent Peripheral Interface (SAUS)
HIPPI-LE...... High Performance Parallel Interface-Link Encapsulation (SAUS)
HIPPI-PH...... High Performance Parallel Interface-Physical layer (SAUS)
HIPPI-SC...... High Performance Parallel Interface-Switch Control (SAUS)
HIPPO.......... Habitat Destruction, Introduced Species, Pollution, Population Growth, Overexploitation
HIPPO.......... High Internal Pressure Producing Orifice (MCD)
HIPPO.......... Hippodrome [*London*] (DSUE)
hippo.......... Hippopotamus (ADWA)
HIPPO.......... Hippopotamus (DSUE)
Hippoc.......... Hippocrates [*Greek physician, 460 -377 BC*] [*Classical studies*] (OCD)
HIPPY.......... High Performance Parallel Interface (SAUS)
HIPPY.......... Home Instruction Program for Preschool Youngsters [*Israel*]
HIPR.......... High Internal Phase Ratio
HIPR.......... High Pressure (KSC)
HIPRA.......... High Speed Digital Processor Architecture (ADWA)
HIPRES.......... High Pressure
HIPRI.......... High Priority (NG)
Hip Riminal... Hippolytus Riminaldus [*Deceased, 1589*] [*Authority cited in pre-1607 legal work*] (DSA)
HIPrJ.......... Houshld 7.35% cm Dep Pfd [*NYSE symbol*] (TTSB)
HIPro.......... High-Protein (MEDA)
HIPrT.......... Household Cap Tr 8.25% 'TOPrS' [*NYSE symbol*] (TTSB)
HIPrX.......... Househld 9.50%'91 cm Dep Pfd [*NYSE symbol*] (TTSB)
HIPrZ.......... Household 8.25% cm Dep Pfd [*NYSE symbol*] (TTSB)
HIPS.......... Harwell Image Processing System (SAUO)
HIPS.......... Health Insurance Plans Survey [*Department of Health and Human Services*] (GFGA)
HIPS.......... Helmet Initiated Pointing System (MCD)
HIPS.......... High-Impact Polystyrene [*Plastics technology*]
HIPS.......... Hyperintense Proximal Scanning
HIPSA.......... Hallicrafters Incremental Power Spectrum Analyzer
HIPSAF.......... High Performance Space Feed (ACAE)
HIPSF.......... High-Performance Space Feed
HIPSN.......... Hot Isostatically Pressed Silicon Nitride (SAUS)
HIPS-PE.......... High-Impact Polystyrene-Polyethylene (SAUS)
HIPS-PVDC... High-Impact Polystyrene-Polyvinylidene Chloride (SAUS)
HIPS-PVDGPE... High-Impact Polystyrene-Polyvinylidene Chloride-Polyethylene (SAUS)
HIPS-PVDOPP... High-Impact Polystyrene-Polyvinylidene Chloride-Polypropylene (SAUS)
HIPT.......... Hi-Port Industries, Inc. [*NASDAQ symbol*] (COMM)
HIPTOC.......... High Power Testing of Optical Components (SAUS)
HIPU.......... Hazardous Installation Policy Unit (HEAS)
HIPX.......... Houston Industries [*Private rail car owner code*]
HIQ.......... High Intelligence Quotient (SAUO)
HI-Q.......... High IQ (SAUS)
HIQ.......... High Quality [*Home video system*] (IAA)
HIQ.......... Housing Intelligence Quotient
HIQ.......... New York, NY [*Location identifier*] [*FAA*] (FAAL)
HIQA.......... Health Insurance Quality Award [*Formerly, HIPA*] [*LIMRA*]
HIQSA.......... Horizontal Impulse Reaction (SAUS)
HIQSA.......... Hydroxyiodoquinolinesulfonic Acid (SAUS)
HIR.......... Diversified Corp. Resources [*AMEX symbol*] (SG)
HIR.......... Halogen Infrared [*Lighting*]
HIR.......... Hamersley Iron Railway (SAUO)
HIR.......... Hammersley Iron Proprietary Ltd. Railway [*Australia*] (DCTA)
HIR.......... Handbook of Inspection Regulations (SAUO)
HIR.......... Handbook of Inspection Requirements [*Navy*] (MCD)
HIR.......... Harbour Improvement Rate (SAUS)
HIR.......... Harmful Interference to Radio (SAUS)
HIR.......... Harvard International Review [*A publication*]
HIR.......... Hazardous Incident Report (MCD)
HIR.......... Head Injury Routine [*Medicine*] (DMAA)
HIR.......... Health Insurance Regulation
HIR.......... Helicopter Instrument Rules
HIR.......... HELWS-Integrated RADAR
HIR.......... Heron Island Resort (SAUO)
hir.......... Hierarchy (ELAL)
HIR.......... Hierarchy [*Computer science*]
HI-R.......... High Intensity Survey Meter (SAUS)
HIR.......... Hilton Resource Corp. [*Vancouver Stock Exchange symbol*]
HIR.......... Hiram College, Hiram, OH [*OCLC symbol*] (OCLC)
HIR.......... Hiram Walker-Gooderham & Worts, Ltd. (SAUO)
HIR.......... Hiring (ROG)
HIR.......... Hiroshima [*Japan*] [*Seismograph station code, US Geological Survey*] (SEIS)
HIR.......... Holton Inter-Urban Railway [*Federal Railroad Administration identification code*]
HIR.......... Honiara [*Guadalcanal*] [*Airport symbol*] (OAG)
HIR.......... Horizontal Impulse Reaction (MSA)
HIR.......... Household Issuance Record [*Food Stamp Program*] (GFGA)
HIR.......... Human Insulin Receptor [*Biochemistry*]
HIR.......... Hydrospace Information Report (MCD)
HIR.......... Hydrostatic Impact Rocket (NATG)
HIRA.......... Handheld Infrared Alarm (PDAA)
HIRA.......... Health Industry Representatives Association (EA)
HIRAB.......... High Resolution Atomic Beam (SAUS)
HIRAC.......... High Random Access
HIRAD.......... Hitachi Re-Adhesion Device (SAUS)
HIRAM.......... Highest position Random-Acess Memory (SAUS)
HIRAM.......... High Resolution Aerial Mapping (ACAE)
HIRAM.......... HYCOR Infrared Anti-Missile (SAUS)
HIRAN.......... High Intensity Radar Aids to Navigator (SAUS)
HIRAN.......... High Precision Short Range Navigation (ACAE)
HIRAN.......... High Range Navigation (SAUO)
HIRAP.......... High Capacity Rocket Assisted Projectile (SAUO)
HIRAP.......... High-Resolution Accelerometer Package (MCD)
HiRAP.......... High-Resolution Accelerometer Package (NAKS)
HIRAS.......... High Resolution Array Scanner (SAUS)
HIRB.......... Health Insurance Registration Board (SAUO)
HIRC.......... Head Injuries Rehabilitation Centre [*British*] (CB)
HIRC.......... Health Information Resource Center (EA)
HIRC.......... Holy Innocents Reparation Committee (EA)
HIRC.......... Housing Industry Research Committee (SAUO)
HIRCIS.......... High-Resolution Capacitive Imaging Sensor [*Instrumentation*]
HIRCK.......... High Rock, NC [*American Association of Railroads railroad junction routing code*]
HIR CLDS VBS... Higher Clouds Visible (SAUS)
HIRD.......... High Information Rate Display (SAUS)
HIRD.......... High Information Rate Display for Aircraft Cockpits (SAUO)
HIRD.......... High-Intensity Radiation Device
HIRD.......... HURD of Interface Representing Depth (SAUS)
HIRDL.......... High-Intensity Radiation Development Laboratory [*Brookhaven National Laboratory*] [*Department of Energy*]
HIRDLS.......... High-Resolution Dynamics Limb Sounder (EOSA)
HIRE.......... Help through Industry Retraining and Employment [*Program*] [*Department of Labor*]
HIRE.......... Hooking Is Real Employment (SAUS)
HIRE.......... Hughes Infra Red Equipment (ACAE)
HIREL.......... High Reliability (IAA)
HI-REL.......... High-Reliability Program (SAUO)
HirelHld.......... Hirel Holdings, Inc. [*Associated Press*] (SAG)
HIRENS.......... High Resolution Narrow Swath (SAUS)
HI Rep.......... Hawaiian Islands Reports [*A publication*] (DLA)
HI-RES.......... Highly Integrated Raster Based Exploration System (SAUO)
hi-res.......... High Resolution (ADWA)
HI-RES.......... High Resolution [*Computer science*]
HIRES.......... High-Resolution Echelle Spectrograph
HIRES.......... HI RESolution (SAUS)
HIRES.......... Hypersonic In-Flight Refueling System
HIREWIMP... High Resolution Wind Measurement Program (SAUO)
HI-REZ.......... High Resolution (GOBB)
HIRF.......... Handbook of Infantry Range Finder (SAUS)
HIRF.......... High-Intensity Radiated Field [*Aviation*]
HIRF.......... High Intensity Radiation Field (ADWA)
HIRF.......... High Intensity Reciprocity Failure (SAUS)
HIRF.......... High-Intensity Reciprocity Failure
HIRI.......... Hawaiian Independent Refinery Inc. (SAUS)
HIRI.......... Hi Rise Recycling Systems [*NASDAQ symbol*] (SAG)
HIRI.......... Home Improvement Research Institute (EA)
HIRIS.......... High Resolution Image Spectrometer (SAUS)
HIRIS.......... High-Resolution Imaging Spectrometer
HIRIS.......... High Resolution Infra-Red System (SAUS)
HIRIS.......... High Resolution Interferometer Spectrometer (ACAE)
HiRise.......... Hi Rise Recycling Systems [*Associated Press*] (SAG)
HIRIV.......... How Will Arrival Report Be Filed Concerning [*Aviation*] (FAAC)
HIRL.......... High Intensity Runway Edge Lights (PIPO)
HIRL.......... High-Intensity Runway Lights [*Aviation*]
HIRL.......... Hirel Holdings, Inc. [*NASDAQ symbol*] (SAG)
HIRL.......... Hypervelocity Impact Research Facility (SAUO)
HIRLAM.......... High-Resolution Limited Area Model (ARMP)
HIRM.......... High-Incidence Research Model (MCD)
HIRNS.......... Helicopter Infrared Navigation System (SAUS)
HIRO.......... Health Insurance Regional Office
HIROCC.......... Hawaiian Region Operations Control Center (ACAE)
HIROCC.......... Hawaii Region Operations Control Center (SAUO)
HIROP.......... Hand-Held Infrared Controller Overpopulation [*Computer science*]
Hiroshima J Med Sci... Hiroshima Journal of Medical Sciences (journ.) (SAUS)
HIRPI.......... High Resolution Pointable Images (ACAE)
HIRR.......... High Infra-Red Reflectance (SAUS)
HIRRLS.......... High Resolution Research Limb Sounder (ACAE)
HIRS.......... Harker's Information Retrieval Systems [*Harker's Specialist Book Importers*] [*Information service or system*] (IID)
HIRS.......... Health Information Resources and Services (ADWA)
HIRS.......... Health Information Resources Service
HIRS.......... Heath Information Resources and Services (SAUS)
HIRS.......... Helicopter Infra-Red System (SAUS)
HIRS.......... High Impulse Retrorocket System (SAUS)
HIRS.......... High-Impulse Retrorocket System
HIRS.......... High Infrared Radiometer Sounder (SAUS)
HIRS.......... High-Resolution Infrared Radiation Sounder
HIRS.......... High Resolution Sciences, Inc. (SAUO)
HIRS.......... Holographic Information Retrieval System (SAUO)
HIRSADAP... High Resolution Real Time Synthetic Array Processor (ACAE)
HIRSADAP... High Resolution Synthetic Apperture Data Processor (ACAE)
Hirsch.......... Hirsch International Corp. [*Associated Press*] (SAG)
HIRSI.......... High Resolution Spectral Infrared (SAUS)
HIRSO.......... High-Resolution Solar Optical Telescope
HIRSP.......... Wisconsin Health Insurance Risk Sharing Plan (SAUO)
HIRSS.......... Hover Infra-Red Suppressor System (SAUS)
HIRS/SMRD... High-Impulse Retrorocket System/Spin-Motor Rotation Detector (SAUS)
HIRT.......... High Reynolds Number Tunnel
HIRTA.......... High Intensity Radio Transmission Area [*Army*] (DOMA)
HIRU.......... Health Information Research Unit (ADWA)
HIRUD.......... Hirudo [*A Leech*] [*Pharmacy*] (ROG)

HIRUM......... Hughes Inertial Reference Unit (ACAE)
HIRUP......... High Intensity Radiation Utilization Project (SAUO)
HIRZB......... Horizon Bank (SAUS)
HIS.............. CIGNA High Income Shares [*NYSE symbol*] (SPSG)
HIS.............. Haptic Intelligence Scale [*Psychology*] (AEBS)
HIS.............. Hardware Information System (MCD)
HIS.............. Hardware Interrupt System (IAA)
HIS.............. Hayman Island [*Australia*] [*Airport symbol*] (OAG)
HIS.............. Headquarters Information System (SAUS)
HIS.............. Health Information Series [*Federal government*]
HIS.............. Health Information Services [*Department of Health and Human Services*]
HIS.............. Health Information Services [*Australia*]
HIS.............. Health Information System (DMAA)
HIS.............. Health Interview Survey [*National Institutes of Health*]
HIS.............. Heavily Instrumented (SAUS)
HIS.............. Heavy-Ion Source
HIS.............. Heiss Island [*Former USSR*] [*Geomagnetic observatory code*]
HIS.............. Heliborne Illumination System (CINC)
HIS.............. Helicopter Illumination System (SAUO)
HIS.............. Helicopter Integrated System (ACAE)
HIS.............. Helicopter Interservice (SAUS)
his............... Henry I. Siegel Co. Inc. (SAUO)
HIS.............. Hic Iacet Sepultus [*Here Lies Buried*] [*Latin*]
HIS.............. Hierarchical Intensive Search [*of the literature*]
HIS.............. High Integrity Systems [*Computer company*] [*British*] (NITA)
HIS.............. High-Intensity Spectrometer
HIS.............. High-Interest Shipping (MCD)
HIS.............. High-resolution Infrared Sounder (SAUS)
HIS.............. High Resolution Interferometer Sounder (EOSA)
HIS.............. High Resolution Interferometer Spectrometer (SAUS)
HIS.............. High-Resolution Interferometer Spectrometer
HIS.............. High-spectral resolution Interferometer Sounder (SAUS)
HIS.............. Hispaniola Airways [*Dominican Republic*] [*ICAO designator*] (FAAC)
HIS.............. Histatin (DMAA)
HIS.............. Histidine (DB)
his............... Histidine [*An amino acid*] (DOG)
His............... Histidine [*An amino acid*]
His............... Histidyl (SAUS)
HIS.............. Histogram Scanning
HIS.............. Historian [*or History*] (EY)
HIS.............. Historical Division (SAUO)
HIS.............. Hit Indicator System
HIS.............. Holographic Illumination System (SAUS)
HIS.............. Holt Information System (SAUS)
HIS.............. Home Incapacity Scale (MELL)
HIS.............. Home Information Systems (TIMI)
HIS.............. Home Interactive System (SAUS)
HIS.............. Homogeneous Information Sets
HIS.............. Honeywell Information Systems, Inc. (IEEE)
HIS.............. Hood Inflation System (DNAB)
HIS.............. Horizontal Impact Sensor [*Automotive safety systems*]
HIS.............. Horticultural Improvement Scheme (SAUS)
HIS.............. Horwitz Information Services [*Information service or system*] (IID)
HIS.............. Hospital Infection Society [*British*] (DBA)
HIS.............. Hospital Information System [*Computer science*]
HIS.............. Hospitality and Information Service (EA)
HIS.............. Hostile Intelligence Service (SAUS)
HIS.............. House Information Systems [*House of Representatives*] [*Washington, DC*]
HIS.............. Hue, Intensity, Saturation (SAUS)
HIS.............. Human Intrusion Studies (SAUS)
HIS.............. Hungarian Intelligence Service (SAUO)
HIS.............. Hunters' Improvement and National Light Horse Breeding Society (BUAC)
HIS.............. Hunters' Improvement Society [*British*] (BI)
HIS.............. Hybrid Infrared Source
HIS.............. Hydrologic Information System (SAUO)
HIS.............. Hyperimmune Serum [*Medicine*] (DMAA)
HIS.............. Hypermedia Indexing Schema (SAUS)
HISA........... Hawaii International Services Agency
HISA........... Headquarters and Installation Support Activity [*Army*] (AABC)
HISA........... Health Informatics Society Australia (SAUO)
HISA........... Human Implications of Scientific Advancement (FOTI)
HISAC......... High-Speed Airdrop Container [*Military*] (RDA)
HISAM......... Hardware Initiated Standalone Memory (NASA)
HISAM......... Hierarchical Indexed Sequential Access Method [*Computer science*] (BUR)
HISAM......... Surface-to-Air Missile High (SAUS)
HISAR......... Hughes Integrated Synthetic Aperture Radar [*Hughes Electronics*]
HISARS........ Hydrological Information Storage and Retrieval System (SAUS)
HISARS........ Hydrological Storage and Retrieval Information System (SAUS)
HISARS........ Hydrologic Information Storage and Retrieval System [*North Carolina State University*] [*Raleigh, NC*]
HISB........... Health Insurance Standards Board
HISC........... House Internal Security Committee
HI-SCALE..... Heliospheric Instrument for Spectra, Composition, and Anisotropy at Low Energies [*Astronomy*]
HISCC......... Healthcare Informatics Standards Coordinating Committee (AG)
HISDAM....... Hierarchical Indexed Sequential Direct Access Method [*Computer science*]
HISE........... High Interference Signaling Environment
HiSEA......... Hawaii Society of Enrolled Agents (SAUO)
HISEACOTS... High Sea State Container Transfer System [*Army*] (RDA)
HISG........... Human Immune Serum Globulin [*Immunochemistry*]
HISGS......... Human Insulin Solicitors Group Scotland (BUAC)
HISHA......... Highlands and Islands Sheep Health Association (BUAC)
HiShear....... Hi-Shear Industries, Inc. [*Associated Press*] (SAG)
HiShearT..... Hi Shear Technology Corp. [*Associated Press*] (SAG)
HiShearTc.... Hi Shear Technology Corp. [*Associated Press*] (SAG)
HISI........... Health Information Systems Incorporated (SAUO)
HISI........... Honeywell Information Systems, Inc.
HisJ........... Hispanic Journal (journ.) (SAUS)
HISKEW....... Health Insurance Skeleton Eligibility Write-off File [*Department of Health and Human Services*] (GFGA)
HISL........... High Intensity Strobe Light [*Aviation*] (PIAV)
HISLIB......... Effluent Guidelines GC/MS Screening Analysis Data Base (SAUS)
HISM........... How I See Myself Scale [*Psychology*] (EDAC)
HISMO......... Historical Monograph (SAUO)
HISOS......... Helicopter Integrated Sonar System (SAUS)
HISP........... Health Information Sharing Project (SAUS)
HISP........... Heat-Inactivated Serum Pool [*Clinical chemistry*]
HISP........... High Speed channel connector (SAUS)
Hisp........... Hispania [*A publication*] (BRI)
Hisp........... Hispanic (DIAR)
Hisp........... Hispaniola (SAUS)
HISP........... Historic Independent Smallholders' Party [*Hungary*] [*Political party*] (BUAC)
Hispa.......... Hispavox [*Record label*] [*Spain*]
HISPA......... International Association for the History of Physical Education and Sport [*Belgium*]
Hispan........ Hispanic (SAUS)
HISPEED...... High-Speed Encryption Equipment Digital (SAUS)
HISPID........ Herbarium Information Standards and Protocols for Interchange of Data [*Australia*]
HI-SPOT....... High Altitude Surveillance Platform for Over-the-horizon Targeting (SAUS)
HISPOT........ High-Altitude Surveillance Platform for Over-the-Horizon Targeting (MCD)
HISPP......... Healthcare Informatics Standards Planning Panel (AG)
HISPP......... Healthcare Information Standards Planning Panel (IDYL)
HISRAN........ High-Precision SHORAN [*Short-Range Navigation*]
HISRE......... Historical Reference Request (SAUO)
HISS........... Hanford Inactive Site Surveillance (SAUS)
HISS........... Hanford Inactive Site Survey (SAUS)
HISS........... Healthcare Imaging Services [*NASDAQ symbol*] (TTSB)
HISS........... Helicopter Icing Spray System (RDA)
HISS........... Helicopter Inflight Spray System (MCD)
HISS........... Heritage Information Statistical System (SAUO)
HISS........... Herpetological Information Search Systems
HISS........... Hierarchical Interactive Schematic System (ACAE)
HISS........... High-Intensity Sound Simulator
HISS........... High-Intensity Sound System
HISS........... Holographic Ice Surveying System (PDAA)
HISS........... Horizon IR Surveillance Sensor (SAUS)
HISS........... Hospital Information Support System (WDAA)
HISS........... Hover Infrared Suppressor System (SAUS)
HISSG......... Healthcare Information Systems Sharing Group (EA)
HISSG......... Hospital Information Systems Sharing Group (SAUO)
HISSS......... High Speed Strike System [*Military*]
HISSZ......... Healthcare Imaging Sv Wrrt'B' [*NASDAQ symbol*] (TTSB)
HIST........... Gallery of History, Inc. [*NASDAQ symbol*] (SAG)
HIST........... Heavy Isotope Spectrometer Telescope (ACAE)
HIST........... High Input Shock Test
Hist........... Histamine [*Medicine*] (DB)
Hist........... Histidinemia [*Medicine*] (AAMN)
HIST........... Histoire [*History*] [*French*] (ROG)
HIST........... Histology (ADA)
Hist........... Historia [*A publication*] (OCD)
Hist........... Historiae [*of Tacitus*] [*Classical studies*] (OCD)
HIST........... Historian [*or History*] (AFM)
hist............ Historian (GEAB)
Hist........... Historical (AL)
hist............ Historical (SHCU)
HIST........... Historical [*Linguistics*]
Hist........... Historically (SAUS)
Hist........... History (AL)
hist............ History (VRA)
HIST........... Hospital In-Service Training
HIST........... Hyderabad Imperial Service Troops [*British military*] (DMA)
HI-STAB....... High Stability (SAUS)
HistAb......... Historical Abstracts
Hist Abs....... Historical Abstracts (journ.) (SAUS)
Hist Abstr.... Historical Abstracts [*A publication*] (JLIT)
Hist An........ Historia Animalium [*of Aristotle*] [*Classical studies*] (OCD)
Hist Anc Geog... [*A*] History of Ancient Geography [*A publication*] (OCD)
Hist&PolSc... History & Political Science (DD)
Hist & T....... History and Theory [*A publication*] (BRI)
HI-STAR....... High Speed Towed Array Research (ACAE)
Hist Athen Const... [*A*] History of the Athenian Constitution [*A publication*] (OCD)
Hist Aug....... Historia Augusta [*A publication*] (OCD)
HistBull....... Historical Bulletin (journ.) (SAUS)
Hist Conscr... Quomodo Historia Conscribenda Sit [*of Lucian*] [*Classical studies*] (OCD)
Hist Dist...... Historic District (SAUS)
Hist Eccl...... Historia Ecclesiastica [*of Eusebius*] [*Classical studies*] (OCD)
Hist Econ Ideas... History of Economic Ideas [*A publication*] (JLIT)
Hist Econ Rev... History of Economics Review [*A publication*] (JLIT)
Hist Ed R..... History of Education Review [*A publication*]

HISTEP .... High-Speed Integrated Space Transportation Evaluation Program (IAA)
Hist G .... History of Greece [*A publication*] (OCD)
Hist Gk Phil... History of Greek Philosophy [*A publication*] (OCD)
HistJ .... Historical Journal (SAUO)
Hist J .... Historisches Jahrbuch [*A publication*] (ODCC)
HISTL........... Historical
Hist Learn Sci Finland... History of Learning and Science in Finland (journ.) (SAUS)
HISTLINE..... History of Medicine On-Line [*National Library of Medicine*] [*Bibliographic database*] (IID)
HistM........... Historical Magazine (SAUO)
HistM........... Historical Magazine (journ.) (SAUS)
Hist Mag PE Ch... Historical Magazine of the Protestant Episcopal Church (journ.) (SAUS)
HistMSSCom... Historical Manuscripts Commission (SAUO)
HISTN .... Historian (AABC)
Hist Num ..... Historia Numorum [*A publication*] (OCD)
HISTO .... Histogram (SAUS)
histo .... Histology [*Medicine*] (DAVI)
histo .... Histoplasma [*Medicine*] (DAVI)
histo .... Histoplasmin [*Skin test*] [*Medicine*] (DAVI)
histo .... Histoplasmosis [*Medicine*] (DAVI)
Histochem Cell Biol... Histochemistry and Cell Biology (journ.) (SAUS)
Histochem J... Histochemical Journal (journ.) (SAUS)
Hist of Greek Maths... History of Greek Mathematics [*A publication*] (OCD)
Histol........... Histological (SAUO)
HISTOL........ Histology
Histol Histopathol... Histology and Histopathology (journ.) (SAUS)
HISTORIA.... Heraldic Images Storing Applications (TELE)
HISTORIC.... Hursley Information System Terminal Oriented Retrieval Information Center (VLIE)
HISTORIC.... Hursley Information System Terminal-Oriented Retrieval Information Center (SAUS)
HISTORIC.... Hursley Information System Terminal Originated Reference and Information Control (SAUS)
HistOutl .... Historical Outlook (journ.) (SAUS)
HISTOX........ Historical Toxicology Information Data System (SAUS)
Hist Pl .... Historia Plantarum [*of Theophrastus*] [*Classical studies*] (OCD)
Hist Polit Economy... History of Political Economy [*A publication*] (JLIT)
HISTRAP....... Heavy Ion Storage Ring for Atomic Physics
HISTRCL...... Historical
HISTRF........ High Sensitivity Track FLIR (SAUS)
Hist Rom Rel... Roemische Religions-Geschichte [*A publication*] (OCD)
HISTRU........ Hydraulic System Test and Repair Unit [*Army*] (MCD)
HISU............ Hoover Institution on War, Revolution and Peace (SAUS)
HISWA.......... Herd Improvement Service of Western Australia [*Animal husbandry*]
HISXE.......... Heavy Ion-Induced Satellite X-Ray Emission [*Analytical chemistry*]
HIT.............. Haemagglutination Inhibition Test (SAUS)
HIT.............. Harbin Institute of Technology (SAUS)
HIT.............. Hawk Instrumentation Team (ACAE)
HIT.............. Hawthorn Institute of Technology [*Australia*]
HIT.............. Hazard Information Transmission [*Chemical Manufacturers Association*] (FFDE)
HIT.............. Headline International Talent [*Commercial firm*]
HIT.............. Health Inca Tea (SAUS)
HIT.............. Health Indication Test [*Engine system*]
HIT.............. Health Insurance Tax [*Social Security Administration*] (GFGA)
HIT.............. Heavy Industrial Turbines (EFIS)
HIT.............. HELWS-Integrated Tracker
HIT.............. Hemagglutination Inhibition Test [*for pregnancy*] [*Medicine*]
HIT.............. Heparin Induced Thrombocytopenia [*Hematology*] (DAVI)
HIT.............. Heterojunction Interface Trap (ACAE)
HIT.............. Heuristic Ideation Technique [*A procedure for generating ideas or solutions to a problem by analyzing a series of generalizations*] (WDMC)
HIT.............. Hibernation Induction Trigger [*Biochemistry*]
HIT.............. High Incidence Target [*Crime computer*]
HIT.............. High Information Transformer (SAUS)
HIT.............. High Intensity Tutoring (EDAC)
HIT.............. High-Interest Tracker (MCD)
HIT.............. High Interest Tracks
HIT.............. High Isolation Transformer (SAUS)
HIT.............. High-Isolation Transformer (IEEE)
HIT.............. High Italian Technology [*Automotive engineering*]
HIT.............. High-Level Interprocessor Transfer (DGA)
HIT.............. High Torque [*Engineering*] (IAA)
HIT.............. Himeji Institute of Technology (SAUS)
HIT.............. Hiroshima Institute of Technology (SAUS)
HIT.............. Histamine Inhalation Test [*Immunology*]
HIT.............. Histamine Ion Transfer (STED)
HIT.............. Histidine Triad [*Biochemistry*]
HIT.............. Hitachi Innovative Technology (SAUS)
HIT.............. Hitachi Ltd. [*NYSE symbol*] (SPSG)
Hit............... Hittite (BJA)
HIT.............. Hokkaido Institute of Technology (SAUS)
HIT.............. Holtzman Inkblot Technique (STED)
HIT.............. Holtzman Inkblot Test [*Psychology*]
HIT.............. Home Infusion Therapy (MELL)
HIT.............. Home Intravenous Therapy (MELL)
HIT.............. Homing Interceptor Technology [*Navigation*] (IEEE)
HIT.............. Hong Kong International Terminals (SAUO)
HIT.............. Horizons Technology Inc. (SAUO)
HIT.............. Housing Investment Trust [*AFL-CIO*]
HIT.............. Houston International Teleport [*Houston, TX*] [*Telecommunications*] (TSSD)
HIT.............. Huazhong Institute of Technology (SAUS)
HIT.............. Hughes Improved Terminal [*Aviation*] (MCD)
HIT.............. Hughes, Induced Turbulence
HIT.............. Human Interface Technology (VLIE)
HIT.............. Hunter Institute of Technology [*Australia*]
HIT.............. Hypersonic Interference Technique
HIT.............. Hypertrophic Infiltrative Tendinitis [*Medicine*] (MAE)
HIT.............. Hypertrophied Inferior Turbinate (STED)
HIT.............. Hypervelocity Impulse Tuned (SAUS)
HIT.............. Hypervelocity Impulse Tunnel (MCD)
HITA............ Hamper Industry Trade Association [*British*] (DBA)
HITAB.......... High-Altitude Target and Background [*Program*] (MUGU)
HITAC.......... Hitachi Computer (DIT)
HITAC.......... Hitachi Computer Services (NITA)
Hitachi......... Hitachi Ltd. [*Associated Press*] (SAG)
Hitachi Rev... Hitachi Review (journ.) (SAUS)
HITADS........ Helmet Integrated Tracking and Display System (MCD)
HITAHR........ Hawaii Institute of Tropical Agriculture and Human Resources [*University of Hawaii*] [*Research center*] (RCD)
HIT and MISS... Hitler and Mussolini [*Slang*] (DSUE)
HITAS.......... Heuristic Intelligent Threat Assessment System (SAUS)
HITB............ Haemophilus Influenzae Type B [*Meningitis*] [*Medicine*] (STED)
HI/TC........... Half Inch Tape Cartridge [*Pressure group*] (NITA)
HITC............ Hexamethylindotricarbocyanine (SAUS)
Hitch Pr & Proc... Hitch's Practice and Procedure in the Probate Court of Massachusetts [*A publication*] (DLA)
HIT Computer... High Incidence Target Computer (SAUS)
HiTcPhr........ Hi Tech Pharmacal Co. [*Associated Press*] (SAG)
HIT-D........... Hand-held Inertial Target-Designator (SAUS)
HITEC.......... Health Information Technologies and Education Center [*University of Texas Health Science Center*] [*Houston, TX*] [*Computer science*]
HITEC.......... High Temperature Emission Control System (SAUS)
HITEC.......... Highway Innovation Technology
HITECC........ Higher Introductory Technology and Engineering Conversion Courses [*Education*] [*British*]
HI TECH....... High Technology (WDAA)
HITEE.......... Hungarian Institute for Testing Electrical Equipment (SAUS)
HITEE.......... Hungarian Institute for Testing Electrical Equipment, Budapest (SAUO)
HI-TEMP...... High Temperature (WDAA)
HITEMP........ High Temperature Engine Materials Program (SAUS)
HITEMP........ High Temperature Turbine Engine Program (SAUS)
Hi Ten.......... High Tensile
HIT ERIN...... Heritage Information Team (SAUO)
HITES.......... Hydrocortisone, Insulin, Transferrin, Estradiol, and Selenium (STED)
HI Test......... Hemagglutination Inhibition Test (SAUS)
HITEX.......... High Temperature Experiment (SAUS)
HITEX.......... High Temperature Isotope Exchange (SAUS)
HITF............ Health Insurance Trust Fund
HitFd........... Hibernia Foods PLC [*Associated Press*] (SAG)
HITFSM........ Highway Users Federation for Safety and Mobility (SAUO)
HITH............ Hospital in the Home (ADWA)
HITHA.......... Historic Irish Tourist Houses and Gardens Association (BUAC)
HITI............. High Integrity Trip Initiator (PDAA)
HITK............ Hi Tech Pharmacal Co. [*NASDAQ symbol*] (SAG)
HITK............ HITK Corp. (SAUO)
HITL............ Hardware-in-the-Loop
HITL............ Human-in-the-Loop (SAUS)
HITLS.......... Hardware in the Loop Simulation [*Computer science*] (MCD)
HITM........... Hole In The Mirror (SAUS)
HITMORE..... Helicopter Installed Television Monitor and Recorder (MCD)
HITMP.......... Highest Temperature [*NWS*] (FAAC)
Hitox........... Hitox Corporation of America [*Associated Press*] (SAG)
HITP............ High-Ignition-Temperature Propellant
Hit Pom....... Hither Pomerania (SAUS)
HITPRO........ Hit Probability [*Military*] (MCD)
HITP-SEAP... High-Ignition-Temperature Propellants Self-Extinguishing at Atmospheric Pressure [*Cartridge*] (RDA)
HITRAC........ High Technology Training Access (SAUS)
HITRAN........ High-Resolution Transmission (ARMP)
HITRAN........ High Resolution Transmission Molecular Absorption Database (CARB)
HITRESS...... High Test Recorder and Simulator System (SAUS)
HITRUN........ Hit and Run [*National Highway Traffic Safety Administration Fatal Accident Recording System code*]
HITS............ Handbook of Information Technology Standards [*A publication*]
HITS............ Hargave Information Technology Service (SAUS)
HITS............ Hargrave Information Technology Services (SAUS)
HITS............ HAWK [*Homing All the Way Killer*] Institutional Training System [*Military*] (RDA)
HITS............ Headquarters Invoice Tracking System (SAUO)
HITS............ Hercules Integrated Telecommunications System [*Telecommunications*]
HITS............ Hierarchical Integrated Test Simulator (SAUO)
HITS............ Hierarchical Intended Thesaurus System (SAUS)
HITS............ High-definition Indoor Trainer for Small-arms (SAUS)
HITS............ High Income Trust Securities [*Drexel Burnham Lambert, Inc.*]
HITS............ High-Rate Multiplexer Input/Output Test System (NASA)
HITS............ High-Speed Integrated Test System
HITS............ Hobbyist's Interchange Tape Standard [*Data recording*]
HITS............ Holloman Infrared Target Simulator (OA)
HITS............ Home Information Technology Study [*Department of Education*] (GFGA)

HITS............ Homicide Investigation Tracking System (SAUS)
HITS............ Honeywell Independent Thermal Sight (SAUS)
HITS............ Hostile Identification/Targeting System (SAUS)
HITS............ Hughes Integrated Tank Sight (SAUS)
HITS............ Human Intelligence Tasking System (ACAE)
HITS............ Hydroacoustic Impact Timing System (SAUS)
HITS............ Hyperlink Induced Topic Research (VLIE)
HITT............ Heparin-Induced Thrombocytopenia and Thrombosis [*Medicine*] (EDAA)
HITT............ Hittite
Hitt Cod....... Hittel's California Codes [*A publication*] (DLA)
Hittell's Laws... Hittel's California General Laws [*A publication*] (DLA)
HITTS.......... Harpoon Interactive Tactical Training System (SAUS)
HITTS.......... Heparin-Induced Thrombosis-Thrombocytopenia Syndrome [*Medicine*] (DMAA)
HITWG......... Hole In The Wall Gang [*A sleep-away camp for kids with life-threatening illnesses*] (PCM)
hiu.............. Hawaii [*MARC country of publication code*] [*Library of Congress*] (LCCP)
HIU.............. Heading Indicator Unit (SAUS)
HIU.............. Head Injury Unit (MELL)
HIU.............. Headseat Interface Unit (MCD)
HIU.............. Headset Interface Unit (NAKS)
HIU.............. High Interest Unit [*Navy*] (ANA)
Hi-U............ High-Usage [*Telecommunications*]
HIU.............. Higuerote [*Venezuela*] [*Airport symbol*] (AD)
HIU.............. Homing Instrumentation Unit (MCD)
HIU.............. Host Interface Unit
HIU.............. Hydrologic Information Unit (SAUO)
HIU.............. Hydrostatic Interface Unit (SAUS)
HIU.............. Hyperplasia Interstitialis Uteri [*Medicine*] (DMAA)
HIU.............. Hypnosis Investigation Unit (SAUO)
HIUS............ Hispanic Institute in/of the United States (SAUO)
HIUS............ Hispanic Institute in the United States [*Later, HI*] (EA)
HIUS............ Hispanic Institute of the United States (SAUS)
HIUV............ Historical Institute of the University of Vienna (SAUO)
HI-UX........... Hitachis UNIX (SAUS)
HIV.............. CEL-SCI Corp. [*AMEX symbol*] (NASQ)
HIV.............. Helium Isolation Valve [*NASA*] (NASA)
HIV.............. History Institute Victoria [*Australia*]
HIV.............. Human Immunodeficiency Virus
HIV-1 PR..... Human Immunodeficiency Virus-1 Protease [*An enzyme*]
HIV-Ab......... Human Immunodeficiency Virus Antibody [*Medicine*] (TAD)
HIVAC.......... High-Value Accounting Control
HIVAC.......... High-Value Asset Control
HIVAC.......... Human Immunodeficiency Virus Vaccine [*Medicine*]
HIV Ag......... Human Immunodeficiency Virus Antigen [*Medicine*] (EDAA)
HIVAL.......... High Velocity Automatic Launch (SAUS)
HI-VALU....... High-Priority Air Force Contract [*Generally in missile field*] (AAGC)
HIVAN.......... Human Immunodeficiency Virus-Associated Nephropathy [*Medicine*] (DMAA)
HIVAP.......... High Velocity Armor-Piercing Projectile (SAA)
HIVAT.......... Home Intravenous Antibiotic Therapy (MELL)
HIVATIS....... HIV/AIDS Treatment Information Service (SAUO)
HIVD............ Herniated Intervertebral Disc [*Medicine*] (DAVI)
HIVE............ High Integrity Voting Equipment (PDAA)
HIVemir....... HIV: An Electronic Media Information Review (SAUO)
HIVemir....... HIV. An Electronic Media Information Review (journ.) (SAUS)
HIVES.......... High-Volume Electrostatic Sampler (MCD)
HIV-G.......... Human Immunodefiency Virus-Association Gingivitis [*Medicine*] (EDAA)
HIVI............ Husband Is Village Idiot (BB)
HIVIES........ Human Immunodeficiency Virus Information Exchange and Support Group (EA)
HIVIG.......... Human Immunodeficiency Virus Immunoglobulin [*Medicine*]
HIVIP.......... Hitachi Visual Image Processing (SAUS)
HIVIP.......... Hitachi Visual Image Processing Robot (SAUS)
HIVIP Robot... Hitachi Visual Image Processing Robot (SAUS)
HiVit............ High Vitamin [*Pharmacology*] (DAVI)
HIVNET........ HIV Vaccine Prevention Trials Network (SAUS)
hi-vol........... High-Volume Air Sampler [*Environmental science*] (FFDE)
HI-VOL......... High-Volume Sampler (COE)
HIVORS........ Hitachi Voice Response System (SAUS)
HIVOS.......... High Vacuum Orbital Simulation (SAUO)
HIVOS.......... High-Vacuum Orbital Simulator
HIVOS.......... Humanistic Institute for Co-operation with Developing Countries (SAUO)
HIVOS.......... Humanistisch Institut voor Ontwikkelings Samenwerking [*Humanistic Institute for Co-Operation with Developing Countries*] [*Hague, Netherlands*] (EAIO)
HIVOS Foundation... Humanistic Institute for Cooperation with Developing Countries (SAUO)
HIVR............ Host Interactive Voice Response [*Telecommunications*] (ITD)
HIV-SF......... HIV-Suppressive Factors [*Medicine*]
HIVSS.......... Highlands and Islands Veterinary Services Scheme (GVA)
HIVT............ Health Insurance of Vermont, Inc. (SAUO)
HIW.............. Hazardous Industrial Waste (SAUS)
HIW.............. Highwoods Properties, Inc. [*NYSE symbol*] (SAG)
Hiwa............ Highway (SAUS)
HIWAS......... Hazardous Inflight Weather Advisory Service [*Aviation*] (FAAC)
HI WAT........ High Water (SAUS)
HIWAY......... Highway [*Commonly used*] (OPSA)
HIWAY......... Line Source Model for Gaseous Pollutants (SAUO)
HIWD........... Highwood Resources Ltd. [*NASDAQ symbol*] (NQ)
HIWDF......... Highwood Res Ltd [*NASDAQ symbol*] (TTSB)
HIWDU......... Hanford Inactive Waste Disposal Unit (SAUS)
HIWRP......... Hoover Institution on War, Revolution, and Peace (EA)
HIWS........... High-Level Waste and Standards [*Environmental science*] (COE)
HIWSC......... Health Industry Wage and Salary Committee [*Terminated, 1974*] (EGAO)
HIWSD......... Handbook of Instructions for Weapon Systems Designers
HIWSE......... Hanford Inactive Waste Site Evaluation Program (SAUS)
HIWY........... Highway [*Commonly used*] (OPSA)
HIX.............. Heat-Inactivated Muscle Extract
HIX.............. Helix Systems Ltd. [*Vancouver Stock Exchange symbol*]
HIX.............. Hopkinsville, KY [*Location identifier*] [*FAA*] (FAAL)
HIXAT.......... Highest Temperature Exceeded for All Time [*NWS*] (FAAC)
HIXE............ Heavy Ion Induced X-ray Emission (SAUS)
HIXFM.......... Highest Temperature Exceeded for the Month [*NWS*] (FAAC)
HIXSE.......... Heavy-Ion-induced X-ray Satellite Emission (SAUS)
HIXSE.......... Highest Temperature Exceeded so Early [*NWS*] (FAAC)
HIXSL.......... Highest Temperature Exceeded so Late [*NWS*] (FAAC)
HIY.............. Hampshire Imperial Yeomanry [*British military*] (DMA)
HIY.............. Hertfordshire Imperial Yeomanry [*British military*] (DMA)
HIY.............. Holiday Institute of Yonkers (EA)
HiYdPl......... High Yield Plus Fund [*Associated Press*] (SAG)
HiYld........... High Yield Income Fund [*Associated Press*] (SAG)
HIZ.............. Harlem Industries [*Federal Railroad Administration identification code*]
HIZA............ Informationsdienst-AUSTAUSCH [*Information Service-EXCHANGE*] [*NOMOS Datapool*] [*Database*] (IID)
HJ................ Air-Cushion Vehicle built by Hoverjet [*Usually used in combination with n umerals*] [*Canada*]
HJ................ Halt and Jump [*Computer science*] (BUR)
HJ................ Headphone Jack (SAUS)
HJ................ Hebra-Jadassohn [*Disease*] [*Medicine*] (DB)
HJ................ Heilige Johannes [*Saint John*] [*Freemasonry*] [*German*]
HJ................ Hepatojugular [*Reflex*] [*Medicine*]
HJ................ Hermanas Josefinas (TOCD)
HJ................ Hetero Junction (SAUS)
HJ................ Hic Jacet [*Here Lies*] [*Latin*]
HJ................ High Jump
HJ................ Hinge Jaw (MSA)
HJ................ Holt-Jackson [*Commercial firm*] [*British*]
HJ................ Honest John [*A type of short range, unguided Army rocket*]
HJ................ Hose Jacket (KSC)
HJ................ Hot Junction (SAUS)
HJ................ Howell-Jolly [*Bodies*] [*Hematology*]
HJ................ Hybrid Junction (SAUS)
HJ................ Operating hours during daylight (SAUS)
HJ................ Station Open from Sunrise to Sunset [*ITU designation*] (CET)
HJ................ Sunrise to Sunset [*ICAO*] (FAAC)
HJA.............. Air Haiti [*ICAO designator*] (FAAC)
HJAS............ Harry James Appreciation Society (EAIO)
HJAS............ Harvard Journal of Asiatic Studies [*A publication*] (BRI)
HJB.............. Howell-Jolly Bodies [*Hematology*] (DAVI)
HJB.............. Hydrodynamic Journal Bearing
HJBS............ Hashemite Jordan Broadcasting Service (SAUO)
HJBT............ Heterojunction Bipolar Transistor (MCD)
HJC.............. Hagerstown Junior College [*Maryland*]
HJC.............. Hansoms of John Clayton [*An association*] (EA)
HJC.............. Harcum Junior College [*Pennsylvania*]
HJC.............. Heathrow Jet Charter Ltd. [*British*] [*ICAO designator*] (FAAC)
HJC.............. Henderson-Jones Chondromatosis [*Medicine*] (MELL)
HJC.............. Hershey Junior College (SAUO)
HJC.............. Hibbing Junior College [*Later, Hibbing Community College*] [*Minnesota*]
HJC.............. Highland Junior College [*Kansas*]
HJC.............. Hinds Junior College [*Raymond, MS*]
HJC.............. Holmes Junior College [*Goodman, MS*]
HJC.............. Holyoke Junior College [*Later, Holyoke Community College*] [*Massachusetts*]
HJC.............. Hutchinson Junior College [*Kansas*]
HJCB............ Heralding Jesus Christ Broadcasting (SAUS)
HJCC............ Honolulu Japanese Chamber of Commerce (EA)
HJCF............ Hungarian Jewish Cultural Federation (BUAC)
HJD.............. Heliocentric Julian Date (SAUS)
HJD.............. Heliocentric Julian Day [*Astronomy*]
HJD.............. Heterojunction Device
HJD.............. Hospital for Joint Diseases (SAUS)
HJD.............. Las Hermanas de Juan Diego (TOCD)
HJD.............. Los Hermanos de Juan Diego (TOCD)
HJDMC......... Hospital for Joint Diseases and Medical Center [*Medicine*] (EDAA)
HJE.............. Hot Jet Exhaust
HJED............ Heliocentric Julian Ephemeris Date (SAUS)
H-J Equations... Harkins-Jura Equations (SAUS)
HJFET.......... Hetero-Junction-gate Field Effect Transistor (SAUS)
HJH.............. Hebron, NE [*Location identifier*] [*FAA*] (FAAL)
HJI............... Hachtmann, J. I., Newark NJ [*STAC*]
HJJ.............. Hachijojima [*Japan*] [*Seismograph station code, US Geological Survey*] (SEIS)
HJL.............. Hamlin Jet Ltd. [*British*] [*ICAO designator*] (FAAC)
HJL.............. Honest John Launcher [*See also HJ*] [*Army*]
HJLP............ Hungarian Justice and Life Party [*Political party*] (BUAC)
HJM.............. Akron-Canton, OH [*Location identifier*] [*FAA*] (FAAL)
HJM.............. H. J. Mulliner [*British coachbuilder*]
HJM.............. Hot Jet Model
HJMX............ Sterling Fuels [*Private rail car owner code*]
H Joint Res... House Joint Resolution (AAGC)
HJP.............. Hand Jewel Pusher

HJP Heat Jacketed Pump
HJP Hydraulic Jet Propulsion (SAUS)
HJPA Holmes Junge Protected Area (SAUO)
HJPP Heat Jacketed Proportioning Pump
HJR Henry James Review [*A publication*] (ANEX)
HJR Hepatojugular Reflex [*Medicine*]
HJR Honest John Rocket [*See also HJ*] [*Army*]
HJR House Joint Resolution
HJR Khajuraho [*India*] [*Airport symbol*] (OAG)
HJRes House Joint Resolution (WPI)
HJ Res House Joint Resolution
HJS Hebrew Jewellers' Society [*A union*] [*British*]
HJS Helijet [*Spain*] [*ICAO designator*] (FAAC)
HJS Helsingen Juutalainen Seurakunta [*Finland*] [*A publication*] (BJA)
HJS Hic Jacet Sepultus [*Here Lies Buried*] [*Latin*]
HJSA Hamburger Jute und Sisal Association (BUAC)
HJSC Hospital Junior Staff Committee [*British*] (DI)
HJT Head Joint [*Technical drawings*]
HJW Hammon, Jensen, Wallen & Associates (SAUO)
HK Handelskammer [*Chamber of Commerce*] [*German*]
HK Hand Knob (SAUS)
HK Handkommentar zum Alten Testament [*Goettingen*] [*A publication*] (BJA)
H-K Hands to Knee [*Medicine*]
HK Hand-to-Knee [*Medicine*] (EDAA)
h-k hand to knee (SAUS)
HK Hank [*Cotton*] (ROG)
HK Hauptwerk [*Masterpiece*] [*German*]
HK Hawker De Havilland Australia Pty. Ltd., Kaman Aircraft Corp. [*ICAO aircraft manufacturer identifier*] (ICAO)
HK Heater Kit
HK Heat Killed [*Medicine*] (MAE)
HK Heckler and Koch [*Machine gun*] (MCD)
HK Heel-to-Knee (DMAA)
HK Hevra Kaddisha (BJA)
HK Hexagonal Keratotomy [*Medicine*] (EDAA)
HK Hexakinase (SAUS)
HK Hexokinase [*An enzyme*]
HK High Key (SAUS)
HK High-Priority Key [*IRS*]
HK Hoeheres Kommando [*Higher Command*] [*German military - World War II*]
HK Hoffa-Kastert [*Syndrome*] [*Medicine*] (DB)
HK Hold Confirmed [*Travel industry*] (TVEL)
HK Homoserine Kinase [*An enzyme*]
HK Hong Kong [*ANSI two-letter standard code*] (CNC)
hk Hong Kong [*MARC country of publication code*] [*Library of Congress*] (LCCP)
HK Hook
HK Host Key (SAUS)
HK Hotkey [*Computer science*] (PCM)
HK Housekeeping
HK House of Keys [*Isle Of Man*]
Hk Hulk [*Nautical charts*]
HK Human Kidney
H-K Hunter-Killer [*Missile*] (MUGU)
HK Hyperkeratosis [*Medicine*] (MELL)
H-K Hypoascorbemia-Kwashiorkor [*Orthomolecular medicine*]
HK Hypokalemia [*Medicine*] (MELL)
HK Knoop Hardness Number
HK People's Liberation [*Revolutionary group*] [*Turkey*]
HK South Pacific Island Airways [*ICAO designator*] (AD)
HK Housekeeper Allowance [*Taxation*] (ODA)
HKA Blytheville, AR [*Location identifier*] [*FAA*] (FAAL)
HKA Hand Knitting Association (EA)
HKA Ho-Kashyap Algorithm (SAUS)
HKA Hong Kong Airways Ltd.
HKA Hypokalemic Alkalosis [*Medicine*] (MELL)
HKA Superior Aviation, Inc. [*ICAO designator*] (FAAC)
HKAB Hong Kong Association of Banks (ECON)
HKACL Hong Kong Association of Certification Laboratories (SAUO)
HKAFO Hip-Knee-Ankle-Foot Orthosis [*Medicine*]
HKAM Amboseli [*Kenya*] [*ICAO location identifier*] (ICLI)
HKamCF Canada-France-Hawaii Telescope Corp. Kamuela, HI [*Library symbol*] [*Library of Congress*] (LCLS)
HK&S Hong Kong and Shanghai Bank (SAUO)
HKAO Hip-Knee-Ankle Orthosis [*Medicine*]
HKAS Hong Kong Accreditation Service (SAUS)
HkAT Handkommentar zum Alten Testament [*Goettingen*] [*A publication*] (BJA)
HKB Hard Kernel Bunch (IAA)
HKB Hepatitis Knowledge Base (NITA)
HKBA Busia [*Kenya*] [*ICAO location identifier*] (ICLI)
HKBA Hong Kong Bank Australia
HKBC Hong Kong Bank of Canada
HKBR Bura [*Kenya*] [*ICAO location identifier*] (ICLI)
HKBU Bungoma [*Kenya*] [*ICAO location identifier*] (ICLI)
HKC Henkel Corp., Minneapolis, MN [*OCLC symbol*] (OCLC)
HKC Hong Kong [*Seismograph station code, US Geological Survey*] (SEIS)
HKC Human Kidney Cell [*Medicine*] (DMAA)
HKC Shirley, NY [*Location identifier*] [*FAA*] (FAAL)
HKCAS Hong Kong Certification Body Accreditation Scheme (SAUS)
HKCC Hong Kong Cable Communications
HKCE Hong Kong Commodities Exchange
HKCEC Hong Kong Catholic Education Council (BUAC)
HK Cells Human Kidney Cells (SAUS)
HKCL Hong Kong Container Line (SAUO)
HKCPEC Hong Kong Committee for Pacific Economic Cooperation
HKCS Hong Kong Chemical Society
HKCS Hong Kong Computer Society (DDC)
HKCW Hong Kong Council of Women (BUAC)
HKD Hakodate [*Japan*] [*Airport symbol*] (OAG)
HKDF Hong Kong Defence Force (SAUO)
HKDGP Hornsby Ku-ring-gai Division of General Practice (SAUO)
HKDR Hong Kong Depository Receipt (SAUS)
HKDS Croatian Christian Democratic Party [*Political party*]
HKECIC Hong Kong Export Credit Insurance Corp. (SAUS)
HKECIC Hong Kong Export Credit Insurance Corporation (SAUO)
HKEL Eldoret [*Kenya*] [*ICAO location identifier*] (ICLI)
HKEL Hong Kong Export Lines (SAUO)
HKEM Embu [*Kenya*] [*ICAO location identifier*] (ICLI)
HKES Eliye Springs [*Kenya*] [*ICAO location identifier*] (ICLI)
HKF Halbkettenfahrzeug [*Half-Track Vehicle*] [*German military - World War II*]
HKF Hancock Fabrics [*NYSE symbol*] (TTSB)
HKF Hancock Fabrics, Inc. [*NYSE symbol*] (SPSG)
HKF Handkerchief
HKF Middletown, OH [*Location identifier*] [*FAA*] (FAAL)
HKFE Hong Kong Futures Exchange
HKFG Kalokol [*Kenya*] [*ICAO location identifier*] (ICLI)
H Kg Hong Kong (SAUO)
HKG Housekeeping (SSD)
HKGA Garissa [*Kenya*] [*ICAO location identifier*] (ICLI)
HKGA Hong Kong Geographical Association. (SAUO)
HKGCC Hong Kong General Chamber of Commerce (SAUS)
HKGMA Hosiery and Knit Goods Manufacturers Association (SAUO)
HKGS Church of Jesus Christ of Latter-Day Saints, Genealogical Society Library, Kaneohe Stake Branch, Kaneohe, HI [*Library symbol*] [*Library of Congress*] (LCLS)
HKGT Garba Tula [*Kenya*] [*ICAO location identifier*] (ICLI)
HKH Chicago, IL [*Location identifier*] [*FAA*] (FAAL)
HKHB Homa Bay [*Kenya*] [*ICAO location identifier*] (ICLI)
HKHO Hola [*Kenya*] [*ICAO location identifier*] (ICLI)
HKI Helen Keller International (EA)
HKI Hong Kong Influenza (MELL)
HKI Husiki [*Japan*] [*Seismograph station code, US Geological Survey*] (SEIS)
HKIA Hong Kong Institute of Architects (BUAC)
HKIAS Hong Kong Inspection Bodies Accreditation Scheme (SAUS)
HKIBOR Hong Kong Inter-Bank Offered Rate (MHDW)
HKIL Hong Kong Islands Line (SAUO)
HKIPD Hanford Key Individual Phone Directory (SAUS)
HKIS Isiolo [*Kenya*] [*ICAO location identifier*] (ICLI)
HKJ Hashemite Kingdom of Jordan (BARN)
HKJSMA Hong Kong Jade and Stone Manufacturers Association (BUAC)
HKK Hokitika [*New Zealand*] [*Airport symbol*] (OAG)
HKKA Kabarak [*Kenya*] [*ICAO location identifier*] (ICLI)
HKKE Keekorok [*Kenya*] [*ICAO location identifier*] (ICLI)
HKKG Kakamega [*Kenya*] [*ICAO location identifier*] (ICLI)
HKKI Kisumu [*Kenya*] [*ICAO location identifier*] (ICLI)
HKKK Helsingin Kauppakorkeakoulun Kirjasto [*Helsinki School of Economics Library*] [*Finland*] [*Information service or system*] (IID)
HKKL Kilaguni [*Kenya*] [*ICAO location identifier*] (ICLI)
HKKR Kericho [*Kenya*] [*ICAO location identifier*] (ICLI)
HKKS Kisii [*Kenya*] [*ICAO location identifier*] (ICLI)
HKKT Kitale [*Kenya*] [*ICAO location identifier*] (ICLI)
HKL Haleakala [*Hawaii*] [*Seismograph station code, US Geological Survey*] (SEIS)
HKL Hoyrekvinners Landsforbund [*Women's Organization of the Conservative Party*] [*Norway*] [*Political party*] (EAIO)
HKLA Hong Kong Library Association (BUAC)
HKLG Lokitaung [*Kenya*] [*ICAO location identifier*] (ICLI)
HKLJ Hong Kong Law Journal [*A publication*] (DLA)
HKLK Lokichoggio [*Kenya*] [*ICAO location identifier*] (ICLI)
HKLM Heat-Killed Listeria Monocytogene [*Medicine*] (MAE)
HKLO Lodwar [*Kenya*] [*ICAO location identifier*] (ICLI)
HKLR Hong Kong Law Reports [*A publication*] (DLA)
HKLT Loitokitok [*Kenya*] [*ICAO location identifier*] (ICLI)
HKLU Lamu [*Kenya*] [*ICAO location identifier*] (ICLI)
HKLY Loyengalani [*Kenya*] [*ICAO location identifier*] (ICLI)
HKM High-velocity Kill Mechanism (SAUS)
H-K M Hunter-Killer Missile (SAUS)
HKM Hypermetropic Keratomileusis [*Ophthalmology*]
HKM Hyperopic Keratomileusis (SAUS)
HKM Hypervelocity Kill Mechanism [*Air Force*]
HKM Morgan Stanley Group, Inc. [*AMEX symbol*] (SAG)
HKMA Hawick Knitwear Manufacturers Association [*British*] (DBA)
HKMA Hong Kong Management Association (BUAC)
HKMA Hong Kong Monetary Authority [*Banking*]
HKMA Mandera [*Kenya*] [*ICAO location identifier*] (ICLI)
HKMB Marsabit [*Kenya*] [*ICAO location identifier*] (ICLI)
HKME Keith Group of Companies, Inc. (SAUO)
HKMG Magadi [*Kenya*] [*ICAO location identifier*] (ICLI)
HKMI Maralal [*Kenya*] [*ICAO location identifier*] (ICLI)
HKMK Mulika [*Kenya*] [*ICAO location identifier*] (ICLI)
HKML Malindi [*Kenya*] [*ICAO location identifier*] (ICLI)
HKMO Mombasa/Moi International [*Kenya*] [*ICAO location identifier*] (ICLI)
HKMR Mackinnon Road [*Kenya*] [*ICAO location identifier*] (ICLI)

HKMS .... Hong Kong Mathematical Society (BUAC)
HKMSC .... Hong Kong Military Service Corps [*British military*] (DMA)
HKMU .... Makindu [*Kenya*] [*ICAO location identifier*] (ICLI)
HKMY .... Moyale [*Kenya*] [*ICAO location identifier*] (ICLI)
HKN .... Harken Technologies, Inc. [*Vancouver Stock Exchange symbol*]
HKN .... Health Knowledge Network
HKN .... Hoskins [*Papua New Guinea*] [*Airport symbol*] (OAG)
HKN .... Jim Hankins Air Service, Inc. [*FAA designator*] (FAAC)
HKNA .... Nairobi/Jomo Kenyatta International [*Kenya*] [*ICAO location identifier*] (ICLI)
HKNC .... Helen Keller National Center for Deaf-Blind Youths and Adults (EA)
HKNC .... Nairobi [*Kenya*] [*ICAO location identifier*] (ICLI)
HKNCDBYA... Helen Keller National Center for Deaf-Blind Youths and Adults (EA)
HKNF .... Hong Kong Naval Force (SAUO)
HKNI .... Nyeri [*Kenya*] [*ICAO location identifier*] (ICLI)
HKNK .... Nakuru [*Kenya*] [*ICAO location identifier*] (ICLI)
HKNMA .... Hong Kong National Musicology Association (BUAC)
HKNMRS ...... Hong Kong National Music Research Society (BUAC)
HKNO .... Narok [*Kenya*] [*ICAO location identifier*] (ICLI)
HKNT .... Handkommentar zum Neuen Testament [*A publication*] (BJA)
HKNV .... Naivasha [*Kenya*] [*ICAO location identifier*] (ICLI)
HKNW .... Nairobi/Wilson [*Kenya*] [*ICAO location identifier*] (ICLI)
HKNY .... Nanyuki [*Kenya*] [*ICAO location identifier*] (ICLI)
HKO .... Hip-Knee Orthosis [*Medicine*]
HKP .... Hidden Lake [*Pennsylvania*] [*Seismograph station code, US Geological Survey*] [*Closed*] (SEIS)
HKP .... Hong Kong Polytechnic (BUAC)
HKP .... Hookup (MSA)
HKP .... Kaanapali [*Hawaii*] [*Airport symbol*] (OAG)
HKPC .... Hong Kong Productivity Council and Centre (BUAC)
HKPO .... Hong Kong Philharmonic Orchestra (SAUO)
HKR .... Hallmark Resources [*Vancouver Stock Exchange symbol*]
HKR .... Hong Kong Regiment [*British military*] (DMA)
HKR .... Hooker [*Ship's rigging*] (ROG)
HKR .... Hydrolytic Kinetic Resolution
HKRE .... Nairobi/Eastleigh [*Kenya*] [*ICAO location identifier*] (ICLI)
HKRP .... Hinged Knee Replacement Prosthesis (MELL)
HKS .... Heel, Knee, and Skin [*Medicine*] (EDAA)
HKS .... Heel-Knee-Shin [*Test*] [*Neurology*] (DAVI)
HKS .... Helikopter Service AS [*Norway*] [*ICAO designator*] (FAAC)
HKS .... Hyperkinesis Syndrome [*Medicine*] (DMAA)
HKS .... Jackson, MS [*Location identifier*] [*FAA*] (FAAL)
HKSA .... East African School of Aviation [*Kenya*] [*ICAO location identifier*] (ICLI)
HKSB .... Samburu [*Kenya*] [*ICAO location identifier*] (ICLI)
HKSC .... Hong Kong Study Circle (EA)
HKSE .... Hong Kong Stock Exchange (SAUS)
HKSM .... Henry Krumb School of Mines (SAUO)
HKSRA .... Hong Kong and Singapore Royal Artillery [*British military*] (DMA)
HKSRGA ...... Hong Kong and Singapore Royal Garrison Artillery [*British military*] (DMA)
HKSU .... Hong Kong Seamen's Union
HKT .... Cable & Wireless HKT ADR [*NYSE symbol*] (SG)
HKT .... Heterotopic Kidney Transplant (MELL)
HKT .... Hiram, King of Tyre [*Freemasonry*]
HKT .... Hockley [*Texas*] [*Seismograph station code, US Geological Survey*] (SEIS)
HKT .... Hollow Kathode Tube
HKT .... Hong Kong Telecom ADR [*NYSE symbol*] (TTSB)
HKT .... Hong Kong Telecommunications Ltd. [*NYSE symbol*] (CTT)
HKT .... Hot Kathode Tube
HKT .... Phuket [*Thailand*] [*Airport symbol*] (OAG)
HKTA .... Hong Kong Tourist Association (SAUO)
HKTAG .... Hong Kong Trade Advisory Group [*British Overseas Trade Board*] (DS)
HKTC .... Hongkong Telephone Co. (SAUS)
HKTC .... Hongkong Telephone Company (SAUO)
HKTC .... Hong Kong Training Council (SAUO)
HKTDC .... Hong Kong Trade Development Council (BUAC)
HK Tel .... Hong Kong Telecommunications Ltd. [*Associated Press*] (SAG)
HKTV .... Hong Kong Television (SAUS)
HKU .... Hong Kong University
HkU .... University of Hong Kong, Hong Kong, Hong Kong [*UK*] [*Library symbol*] [*Library of Congress*] (LCLS)
HKUST .... Hong Kong University of Science and Technology (ECON)
HKV .... Homing Kill Vehicle [*Military*] (ACAE)
HKVC .... Hong Kong Volunteer Corps [*British military*] (DMA)
HK virus ...... Hong-Kong type of influenza virus (SAUS)
HKVO .... Hong Kong Volunteer Corps (SAUS)
HKVO .... Voi [*Kenya*] [*ICAO location identifier*] (ICLI)
HKWJ .... Wajir [*Kenya*] [*ICAO location identifier*] (ICLI)
HKX .... Ellington Air Force Base, TX [*Location identifier*] [*FAA*] (FAAL)
HKX .... Hong Kong Express (SAUO)
HKY .... Canstar Sports, Inc. [*Toronto Stock Exchange symbol*]
HKY .... Hickory [*North Carolina*] [*Airport symbol*] (OAG)
HKYNA .... Hydroxykynurenic Acid [*Organic chemistry*]
HKZ .... Minneapolis, MN [*Location identifier*] [*FAA*] (FAAL)
HL .... Das Heilige Land (BJA)
HL .... Hairline (DAVI)
HL .... Hairy Leukemia (MELL)
HL .... Half-Leather (SAUS)
HL .... Half Length [*Photography*] (DGA)
HL .... Half-Life [*of radioactive elements*]
HL .... Half Line [*Illustration*] (DGA)
hl .... Halite [*CIPW classification*] [*Geology*]
HL .... Hallux Limitus [*Podiatry*] (DAVI)
HL .... HALON [*Halogenated Hydrocarbon*] System [*NFPA pre-fire planning symbol*] (NFPA)
HL .... Haloperidol (DAVI)
HL .... Haltlepool (SAUS)
HL .... Handelslehranstalt (SAUS)
HL .... Hand Lantern (AAG)
HL .... Hard Labor
HL .... Hardline (MCD)
HL .... Harelip
HL .... Hariana Lancers [*British military*] (DMA)
HL .... Harwell Laboratory (SAUS)
HL .... Haul (MSA)
HL .... Hawser Laid
HL .... Hawthorn-Leslie [*Indian Railway*] [*Newcastle-upon-Tyne*] [*UK*] (TIR)
HL .... Hazardous Liquid (SAUS)
HL .... Header Label [*Computer science*] (IAA)
H/L .... Heading Line (SAUS)
HL .... Headlamp [*Automotive engineering*]
HL .... Headlight (SAUS)
HL .... Head Linesman [*Football*]
HL .... Headmaster-Lieutenant [*Navy*] [*British*]
HL .... Heap Leaching (SAUS)
HL .... Hearing Level
HL .... Hearing Loss
HL .... Heart and Lungs (SAUS)
HL .... Heavily Loaded (SAUS)
HL .... Heavy Lift
HL .... Heavy Loaded (SAUS)
HL .... Heavy Loading (IAA)
HL .... Hebrew Leader (BJA)
HL .... Hebrew Letters (BJA)
HL .... Hebrew Literature (BJA)
HL .... Hecla Mining Co. [*NYSE symbol*] (SPSG)
hl .... Hectoliter (ADWA)
HL .... Hectoliter (GPO)
hL .... Hectoliter (STED)
HL .... Heel Line (MSA)
HL .... Height-Length
HL .... Height Loss [*Aviation*] (DA)
HL .... Heilig [*Holy, Saint*] [*German*]
HL .... Heir-at-Law
HL .... Helium Level
HL .... Heparin Lock [*Pharmacology*] (DAVI)
HL .... Heptagonal League (PSS)
HL .... Herpetologists' League (EA)
HL .... Hickman Line [*Cardiology*] (DAVI)
H-L .... Highest and Lowest (SAUS)
HL .... Highland Light Infantry (SAUO)
HL .... High Latitude (ARMP)
HL .... High Level
H/L .... Highlight (DGA)
H/L .... Highlights (SAUS)
HL .... Highline (MSA)
H/L .... High or Low
HL .... Highway Luxury [*Tire design*]
HL .... Hill
HL .... Hinge Line [*Technical drawings*]
HL .... Histiocytic Lymphoma [*Oncology*]
HL .... Histocompatibility Locus [*Immunology*]
HL .... Hittite Laws (BJA)
HL .... Hoc Loco [*In This Place*] [*Latin*]
HL .... Hodges-Lehmann Estimator [*Statistics*]
HL .... Hodgkin's Lymphoma [*Medicine*]
HL .... Holds List [*Travel industry*] (TVEL)
Hl .... Hole (SAUS)
HL .... Holiday Airlines (MHDW)
HL .... Home Lines [*Steamship*] (MHDW)
HL .... Home Loss
HL .... Homestead Lease (SAUS)
HL .... Honors List (ADA)
HL .... Hop Level (SAUS)
HL .... Horizontal Landing (KSC)
HL .... Horizontal Length (SAUS)
HL .... Horizontal Line
HL .... Hose-Layer (WDAA)
HL .... Host Language
HL .... Hot Line [*Alert system*] (AAG)
HL .... House of Laity (SAUS)
HL .... House of Lords [*British*]
HL .... House of Lords Cases (Clark) [*England*] [*A publication*] (DLA)
HL .... Howard League [*An association*] (EAIO)
HL .... Huius Loci [*Of This Place*] [*Latin*]
HL .... Human Leukocyte [*Medicine*] (EDAA)
HL .... Human Lymphoid [*Immunology*]
HL .... Hyborean Legion (EA)
HL .... Hydraulic Lime (SAUS)
HL .... Hydraulics Laboratory [*Army*]
HL .... Hydrodynamics Laboratory [*MIT*] (MCD)
HL .... Hydrogen Line (MCD)
HL .... Hydrology Laboratory [*Department of Agriculture*] [*Information service or system*] (IID)
H/L .... Hydrophile/Lipophile [*Followed by a number*]
HL .... Hygienic Laboratory [*US*]
HL .... Hyperlipemia [*Medicine*] (MELL)

HI .... Hypermetropia, Latent [*Medicine*] (DMAA)
HL .... Hypermetropia, Latent [*Ophthalmology*]
HI .... Hyperopia Latent [*Ophthalmology*] (DAVI)
HL .... Hypertrichosis Lanuginosa [*Medicine*]
HL .... Law Reports, House of Lords, English and Irish Appeals [*1866-75*] [*A publication*] (DLA)
HL .... Mustard/Lewisite Mix [*Poisonous gas*] [*Army*]
HL .... VEB Deutsche Hydrierwerk, Rodleben [*East Germany*] [*Research code symbol*]
HL7 .... Health Level Seven (SAUO)
HLA .... Halifax Library Association (SAUO)
HLA .... Hall's Lagoon [*Australia*] [*Seismograph station code, US Geological Survey*] [*Closed*] (SEIS)
HLA .... Hat Leather Association (EA)
HLA .... Hawaii Library Association (BUAC)
HLA .... Heart, Lungs, Abdomen (SAUS)
HLA .... Heavy-Lift Airship (MCD)
HLA .... Heavylift Cargo Airlines Ltd. [*British*] [*ICAO designator*] (FAAC)
HLA .... Helicopter Landing Area (SAUO)
HLA .... Helicopter Loggers Association (EA)
HLA .... Highlander Income Fund, Inc. [*AMEX symbol*] (SAG)
HLA .... High-Level Analog (MCD)
HLA .... High Level Architecture [*Department of Defense*]
HLA .... High Level Assembler (VLIE)
HLA .... High Low Alarm [*Electronics*] (ECII)
HLA .... High-Speed Line Adapter (MHDI)
HLA .... Histo-compatibility Antigens (SAUS)
HLA .... Histocompatibility Leukocyte Antigen (DB)
HLA .... Histocompatibility Locus Antigens [*System*] [*Immunology*]
HLA .... Historical Labor Applications [*Military*] (AFIT)
HLA .... Homologous Leucocytic Antibodies
HLA .... Homologous Leukocyte Antibody (STED)
HLA .... Horizontal Line Array (MCD)
HLA .... Human Leucocyte Antigen [*Immunology*]
HLA .... Human Leucocytic Antigen (SAUS)
HL-A .... Human Leukocyte- [*or Lymphocyte-*] Antigen [*System for recognizing foreign tissue*] [*Immunology*]
HLA .... Human Life Amendment
HLA .... Human Lymphocyte Antibody (STED)
HLA .... Human Lymphocyte Antigen (STED)
HLA .... Hungarian Logistics Association (BUAC)
HLA .... Hydraulic Lash Adjuster [*Automotive engine design*]
HLA .... Hypoplastic Left Atrium [*Cardiology*] (DAVI)
HLA-A .... Human Leucocyte Antigen A [*Medicine*] (EDAA)
HLAA .... Human Leucocyte Antigen A [*Medicine*] (EDAA)
HLA Antigen ... Human Leucocyte Allo Antigen (SAUS)
HLaB .... Brigham Young University, Hawaii Campus, Laie, HI [*Library symbol*] [*Library of Congress*] (LCLS)
HLA-B .... Human Jeukocyte Antigen B [*Medicine*] (MTAA)
HLA-B .... Human Leucocyte Antigen B [*Medicine*] (EDAA)
HLAB .... Human Leucocyte Antigen B [*Medicine*] (EDAA)
HLABC .... Health Libraries Association of British Columbia (SAUO)
HLAC .... Host Link Adapter Card [*Ideacomm Gateway*]
HLA-C .... Human Leucocyte Antigen C [*Medicine*] (EDAA)
HLAC .... Human Leucocyte Antigen C [*Medicine*] (EDAA)
HLAD .... Hearing-Lookout Assist Device [*Navigation*] (OA)
HLAD .... High-Level Air Defence [*Military*] [*British*]
HLAD .... Horse-Liver Alcohol Dehydrogenase [*Also, HLADH, HLALD*] [*An enzyme*]
HLA-D .... Human Jeukocyte Antigen D [*Medicine*] (MTAA)
HLADH .... Horse-Liver Alcohol Dehydrogenase [*Also, HLAD, HLALD*] [*An enzyme*]
HLA/DZ .... Helicopter Landing Area/Drop Zone [*Military*] (MCD)
HLA/DZA .... Helicopter Landing Area/Drop Zone Study (SAUS)
HLA/DZS .... Helicopter Landing Area/Drop Zone Study [*Military*] (MCD)
HLAF .... High-Level Arithmetic Function
HLaGS .... Church of Jesus Christ of Latter-Day Saints, Genealogical Society Library, Laie Branch, Laie, HI [*Library symbol*] [*Library of Congress*] (LCLS)
HLAH .... Hanks Lactalbuminhydrolysate (SAUS)
HLAHWG .... High Level Ad Hoc Working Group [*NATO*] (NATG)
HLAIS .... High-Level Analog Input Subsystem [*Computer science*] (MHDI)
HLAIS .... High Level Analog Input System (NITA)
HLAL .... High Level Assembler Language (NAKS)
HLAL .... High-Level Assembly Language (MCD)
HLA-L .... Human Leukocyte Antigen L [*Medicine*] (MTAA)
HLALD .... Horse-Liver Alcohol Dehydrogenase [*Also, HLAD, HLADH*] [*An enzyme*]
HLA-LD .... Human Lymphocyte Antigen-Lymphocyte Defined (STED)
HL-A LD .... Human Lymphocyte-Antigen Lymphocyte Defined [*Immunology*]
HLAN .... Hanford Local Area Network (SAUS)
HLAN .... Huge Local Area Network (VLIE)
H-LAND .... Headland (ADA)
HL&AG .... Henry E. Huntington Library and Art Gallery (SAUO)
HL&PCO .... Houston Lighting and Power Co. (SAUS)
HL&PCO .... Houston Lighting and Power Company (SAUO)
HL & T .... Hunter's Landlord and Tenant [*Scotland*] [*A publication*] (DLA)
HLA neg .... Heart, Lung, and Abdomen Negative [*Medicine*] (EDAA)
HLA negative ... Heart, Lungs, and Abdomen Negative [*Medicine*] (STED)
HLAP .... High Level-alarm Probe (SAUS)
HLAPCO .... Houston Lighting and Power Co. (SAUS)
HLAPCO .... Houston Lighting and Power Company (SAUO)
HLAPI .... High Level Application Programming Interface (VLIE)
HLAS .... Handbook of Latin American Studies
HLAS .... Hot Line Alert System
HLASD .... Hand-Link Arm Safe Device
HLA-SD .... Human Lymphocyte Antigen-Serologically Defined (STED)
HL-A SD .... Human Lymphocyte-Antigen Serologically Defined [*Immunology*]
HLAV .... Horseradish Latent Virus [*Plant pathology*]
HLB .... Batesville, IN [*Location identifier*] [*FAA*] (FAAL)
HLB .... Federal Home Loan Bank Board, Accounts Payable, Washington, DC [*OCLC symbol*] (OCLC)
HLB .... Harvard Library Bulletin (journ.) (SAUS)
HLB .... High-Line Airways, Inc. [*Canada*] [*ICAO designator*] (FAAC)
HLB .... Hotel Licensing Board (SAUO)
HLB .... Hydrophile-Lipophile Balance [*Surfactant technology*]
HLB .... Hydrophilic Lipophilic Balance (SAUS)
HLB .... Hypotonic Lysis Buffer [*Analytical biochemistry*]
HLBA .... High Level Bus Analyzer (SAUS)
HLBB .... Home Loan Bank Board [*Federal agency*] (GPO)
HLBC .... Heavy Liquid Bubble Chamber (SAUS)
HLBI .... Human Lymphoblastoid Interferon [*Antineoplastic drug*]
HLBR .... Heel Breaster
HLBRD .... Halberd
HLBTJ .... Hilbert Junction, WI [*American Association of Railroads railroad junction routing code*]
HLC .... Hapag-Lloyd Container (SAUS)
HLC .... HAWK [*Homing All the Way Killer*] Logistics Complex (MCD)
HLC .... Hazleton Laboratories Corporation (SAUO)
HLC .... Header Label Check (SAUS)
HLC .... Headmaster Lieutenant-Commander [*Navy*] [*British*]
HLC .... Health Locus of Control (SAUS)
HLC .... Heat Loss Center (DMAA)
HLC .... Heavy Lift Capability (ADWA)
HLC .... Heavy/Light Corps (MCD)
HLC .... Helicap [*France*] [*ICAO designator*] (FAAC)
HLC .... High Level Caves (COE)
HLC .... High-Level Cell [*Nuclear energy*] (NRCH)
HLC .... High-Level Center (IAA)
HLC .... High Level Committee (SAUS)
HLC .... High-Level Compiler (IAA)
HLC .... Hill City, KS [*Location identifier*] [*FAA*] (FAAL)
HLC .... Hispanic Literature Criticism [*A publication*]
HLC .... Homeowner's Land Corp. [*Federal agency formed in 1932*] [*Investment term*]
HLC .... Homogenized Leaf Curing [*Tobacco industry*]
HLC .... Hospital Library Council (SAUO)
HLC .... House of Lords Cases (SAUO)
HLC .... House of Lords Cases (Clark) [*England*] [*A publication*] (DLA)
HLC .... Human Lactation Center (EA)
HLC .... Human Life Center (EA)
HLCA .... Hill Livestock Compensatory Allowances [*British*] (WDAA)
HLCADS .... High-Level Container Airdrop System [*Army*] (RDA)
HL Cas .... House of Lords Cases (Clark) [*England*] [*A publication*] (DLA)
HL Cas (Eng) ... House of Lords Cases [*A publication*] (DLA)
HLC-ATC .... Heavy-Lift Helicopter Advanced Technology Component [*Program*] [*Army*] (RDA)
HLCC .... Home-Laundering Care Code [*British*] (DI)
HLCC .... Home-Laundering Consultative Council [*British*] (DI)
HLCF .... Hardened Launch Control Facility (MUGU)
HLCF .... Heat-Labile Citrororum Factor [*Biochemistry*]
HLCF .... Holy Land Conservation Fund (EA)
HLCL .... Helical
HLCL .... Human Lymphoblastoid Cell Line (DB)
HLCM .... Holy Land Christian Mission (EA)
HLCMI .... Holy Land Christian Mission International [*Later, HLCM*] (EA)
HLCO .... Healthco International Inc. [*NASDAQ symbol*] (COMM)
HLCO .... High Low Close Open (SAUS)
HLCPS .... Helical Compression
HLCPTR .... Helicopter (MSA)
HLCS .... Harm Low Cost Seeker (SAUS)
HLCS .... Heat Limiter Control Switch
HLCS .... High-Level Compaction Station [*Nuclear energy*] (NRCH)
HLCS .... High-Level Control Station [*Hazardous materials control*]
HLC Tyre .... High Load Capacity Tyre (SAUS)
HLCU .... Hapag-Lloyd Container Unit (SAUS)
HLCU .... High Lift Control Unit (SAUS)
HLCV .... Hot Leg Check Valve [*Nuclear energy*] (NRCH)
HLCZ .... Harvestland Co-Operative [*Federal Railroad Administration identification code*]
HLD .... Doctor of Humane Letters
HLD .... Hailar [*China*] [*Airport symbol*] (OAG)
HL-D .... Haloperidol Decanoate [*Pharmacology*] (DAVI)
HLD .... Hardened Laser Designator (ACAE)
HLD .... Hardware Logic Diagram (VLIE)
HLD .... Harold's Stores, Inc. [*AMEX symbol*] (SPSG)
HLD .... Head Level Display (SAUS)
hld .... held (SAUS)
HLD .... Helium Leak Detector
HLD .... Herniated Lumbar Disc [*Medicine*]
HLD .... High-Level Designator (DINT)
HLD .... Hit and Locating Device (SAUO)
hld .... Hold (WDMC)
HLD .... Hold
HLD .... Holdings [*Online database field identifier*]
HLD .... Holiday Airlines Havacilik Ve Turizm Sanayi Ve Ticaret, AG [*Turkey*] [*FAA designator*] (FAAC)
HLD .... Hollywood Investments [*Vancouver Stock Exchange symbol*]
HLD .... Home Laundry Detergent
HLD .... Hypersensitivity Lung Disease [*Medicine*]

HLDA .... High-Level Design Automation
HLDA .... Hold Acknowledge [*Computer science*]
HLDB .... Hot-Line, Dead-Bus (SAUS)
HLDBU .... Homeland Defense Business Unit
HLDC .... High-Level Data Link Control (MCD)
HLDDN .... Holddown
HLDG .... High Level Defense Group (SAUO)
HLDG .... Holding (MSA)
HLDH .... Heat-Stable Lactic Dehydrogenase [*Clinical chemistry*]
HLDI .... Highway Loss Data Institute (EA)
HLDI .... Hole Die (SAUS)
HLDLC .... High-Level Data Link Control [*Computer science*] (DOM)
HLDN .... Holddown (MSA)
HLDNG .... Holding
HLDNV .... Holdenville, OK [*American Association of Railroads railroad junction routing code*]
HLDP .... High Lift Diesel Pump (SAUS)
HLDR .... Holder
Hldr of Proc .... Holder of Procuration [*Banking*] (TBD)
HLDS .... Hydrogen Leak Detection System (NASA)
HLDS .... Vermont-New Hampshire-New York Hospital Libraries [*Library network*]
HLDTL .... High Level Data Transistor Logic (NITA)
HLDTL .... High-Level Diode Transistor Logic [*Computer science*] (MHDI)
HLDV .... Heavy Light-Duty Vehicle [*Automotive emissions*]
HLDW .... High-Level Defense Waste (ABAC)
HLDY .... Holiday
HldyRV .... Holiday RV Superstores, Inc. [*Associated Press*] (SAG)
HLE .... First Air [*British*] [*ICAO designator*] (FAAC)
HLE .... Hailey, ID [*Location identifier*] [*FAA*] (FAAL)
HLE .... Hale Resources Ltd. [*Toronto Stock Exchange symbol*]
HLE .... Halle [*German Democratic Republic*] [*Seismograph station code, US Geological Survey*] (SEIS)
HLE .... Hazleton Laboratories Europe Ltd. [*British*] (IRUK)
HLE .... Heat-Labile Enterotoxin [*Medicine*] (MELL)
HLE .... High Level Exposure (SAUS)
HLE .... High-Low-Junction Emitter (PDAA)
HLE .... Horse Liver Esterase
HLE .... Human Leucocyte Elastase [*An enzyme*]
HLE .... Human Liver Esterase (SAUS)
HLE .... Hydrogen Line Emission
HLED .... Home Leave Eligibility Date (WDAA)
HLEG .... Hydrolysate Lactalbumin Earle's Glucose [*Medicine*] (DMAA)
HLEM .... Horizontal-Loop Electromagnetic Method (SAUS)
HLENA .... Helena, AR [*American Association of Railroads railroad junction routing code*]
HLEPG .... High Level Exercise Planning Group (SAUO)
HLES .... Haute Limite Elastique Sondable (SAUS)
HLEXT .... Helical Extension
HLF .... Hallicrafters Company (SAUO)
HLF .... Hall's Legal Forms [*A publication*] (DLA)
HLF .... Hapag Lloyd Fluggesellschaft GmbH [*Germany*] [*ICAO designator*] (FAAC)
HLF .... Heart and Lung Foundation [*Defunct*] (EA)
HLF .... Heat-Labile Factor
HLF .... Heat Loss Factor (SAUS)
HLF .... Heller Financial [*NYSE symbol*] (SPSG)
HLF .... Hepatic Leukaemia Factor [*Medicine*]
HLF .... Hidden Lake Formation [*Geology*]
HLF .... High-Level Formating (SAUS)
HLF .... High-Level Function [*Communications term*] (DCT)
HLF .... High Loss Ferrite
HLF .... Holistic Life Foundation [*Later, Feathered Pipe Foundation*] (EA)
HLF .... Horizontal Laminar Flow (AAEL)
HLF .... Horizontal Line Frequency
HLF .... House Leadership Fund (EA)
HLF .... Hultsfred [*Sweden*] [*Airport symbol*] (OAG)
HLF .... Human Lactoferrin [*Biochemistry*]
HLF .... Human Life Foundation (EA)
HLF .... Human Lung Fluid [*Medicine*]
HLF .... Hyperbolic LOFAR Fix [*Military*] (CAAL)
HLF .... Hyper Low Frequency (SAUS)
HLFL .... Buattifel [*Libya*] [*ICAO location identifier*] (ICLI)
HLFM .... Half-Moon
HLFM .... High-Level Flux Monitor
HLFPrA .... Heller Finl 8.125% Sr'A' Pfd [*NYSE symbol*] (TTSB)
HLFQ .... Harrington Lesbian Fiction Quarterly [*A publication*]
HLFT .... Holographic Lensless Fourier Transform (PDAA)
HLFTN .... Halftone (VRA)
HLG .... Dr. John W. Tintera Memorial Hypoglycemia Lay Group (EA)
Hlg .... Halogen (SAUS)
HLG .... Hauling
HLG .... HAWK [*Homing All the Way Killer*] Logistics Group (AABC)
HLG .... Heligoland [*Federal Republic of Germany*] [*Seismograph station code, US Geological Survey*] (SEIS)
HLG .... High-Level Group [*NATO*]
HLG .... Historic Landscapes Group [*British*] (DBA)
HLG .... Hollinger, Inc. [*Toronto Stock Exchange symbol*] [*Vancouver Stock Exchange symbol*]
HLG .... Homing Level Gauge
HLG .... Hot Leg [*Nuclear energy*]
HLG .... Housing and Local Government [*A publication*] (DLA)
HLG .... Hybrid Lens Guide (PDAA)
HLG .... Ministry of Housing and Local Government (SAUO)
HLG .... Wheeling [*West Virginia*] [*Airport symbol*] (AD)
HLG .... Wheeling, WV [*Location identifier*] [*FAA*] (FAAL)
HLGC .... Hannibal-La Grange College [*Missouri*]
HLGL .... Giallo/Warehouse 59 E [*Libya*] [*ICAO location identifier*] (ICLI)
HLGP .... Heavy Lift General Purpose (SAUS)
HLGRF .... Hollinger Inc. [*NASDAQ symbol*] (TTSB)
HLGS .... Hot Line Gunsight System
HLGT .... Ghat [*Libya*] [*ICAO location identifier*] (ICLI)
HLH .... Haroldson Lafayette Hunt (SAUS)
HLH .... Heavy-Lift Helicopter
HLH .... Helix-Loop-Helix [*Genetics*]
HLH .... Hertfordshire Light Horse [*British military*] (DMA)
HLH .... High-Level Heating [*Nuclear science*] (OA)
HLH .... High-Low-High (SAUS)
HLH .... Human Luteinizing Hormone [*Endocrinology*]
HLH .... Hypoplastic Left Heart [*Cardiology*]
HLH .... Ulanhot [*China*] [*Airport symbol*] (OAG)
HLHC .... Hertfordshire Local History Council (SAUO)
h/l HL .... Hind Legs (SPVS)
HLHS .... Heavy-Lift Helicopter System
HLHS .... Hidden Line Hidden Surface (SAUS)
HLHS .... Hypoplastic Left-Heart Syndrome [*Medicine*]
HLHSR .... Hidden Line & Hidden Surface Removal (SAUS)
HLHSR .... Hidden Line Hidden Surface Removal (SAUS)
HLI .... Hard Limited Integrator (SAUS)
HLI .... Hartford Life 'A' [*NYSE symbol*] (SG)
HLI .... Hemolysis Inhibition [*Medicine*] (AAMN)
HLI .... Highland Light Infantry [*Military unit*] [*British*]
HLI .... Holly Springs, MS [*Location identifier*] [*FAA*] (FAAL)
HLI .... Holmium LASER Illuminator
HLI .... Host Language Interface
HLI .... Human Leukocyte Interferon [*Medicine*] (DMAA)
HLI .... Human Life International (EA)
HLIA .... Historic Landmarks of Irish America [*A publication*]
HLIC .... Highland Light Infantry of Canada [*Military unit*]
HLIC .... Housing Loans Insurance Corporation (SAUO)
H/Lift .... Heavy Lift (SAUS)
H/LIN .... Head Lining [*Automotive engineering*]
HLIPS .... High Level Image Processing System (SAUS)
HLIS .... Hill Land Improvement Scheme (SAUO)
HLISRDI .... Hubei Light Industrial Scientific Research Design Institute [*China*] (BUAC)
HLIT .... Harmonic, Inc. [*NASDAQ symbol*] (NASQ)
HLIT .... Harmonic Lightwaves [*NASDAQ symbol*] (TTSB)
HLIT .... Harmonic Lightwaves, Inc. [*NASDAQ symbol*] (SAG)
HLIV .... High-Level Input Voltage
HLIV .... Hot Leg Isolation Valve [*Nuclear energy*] (NRCH)
HLJ .... Hindu Law Journal [*A publication*] (DLA)
HL Jour .... House of Lords Journals [*England*] [*A publication*] (DLA)
HLK .... Haleakala [*Hawaii*] [*Seismograph station code, US Geological Survey*] (SEIS)
HLK .... Heart, Liver, Kidney [*Medicine*] (MAE)
HLK .... Heli-Link [*Switzerland*] [*ICAO designator*] (FAAC)
HLK .... Kauai Public Library Association, Linhue, HI [*Library symbol*] [*Library of Congress*] (LCLS)
HLK .... Salomon, Inc. [*AMEX symbol*] (SAG)
HLK .... Salomon Inc. 5.25% HP'ELKS' [*AMEX symbol*] (TTSB)
HLKF .... Kufra [*Libya*] [*ICAO location identifier*] (ICLI)
HLL .... Half-Loop Loss (SAUS)
HLL .... Hallett [*Antarctica*] [*Seismograph station code, US Geological Survey*] [*Closed*] (SEIS)
HLL .... Halley Resources Ltd. [*Vancouver Stock Exchange symbol*]
HLL .... Hard Lunar Landing [*Aerospace engineering*] (IAA)
HLL .... Havelet Leasing Ltd. [*British*] [*ICAO designator*] (FAAC)
HLL .... Hebrew Language and Literature (BJA)
HLL .... Hellenic Lines Ltd. (SAUS)
HLL .... Higher Level Language (SAUS)
HLL .... High-Level Language [*Computer science*]
HLL .... High-Level Logic (IAA)
HLL .... High Liquid Level [*Engineering*]
HLL .... Highspeed Low-Power Low-Voltage (SAUS)
HLL .... Hill [*Board on Geographic Names*]
HLL .... Hill Corp. (SAUO)
HLL .... Hypoplastic Left Lung [*Medicine*] (DMAA)
HLLAPI .... High-Level Application Program Interface [*Computer science*] (PCM)
HLLAPI .... High Level Language Application Program Interface (NITA)
HLLAPI .... HLL Application Program Interface (SAUS)
HLLB .... Benghazi/Benina [*Libya*] [*ICAO location identifier*] (ICLI)
HLLC .... High Level Language Computer (SAUS)
HLLCS .... High Level Language Computer System (SAUS)
HLLL .... Tripoli [*Libya*] [*ICAO location identifier*] (ICLI)
HLLM .... High Level Language Machine (SAUS)
HLLMRK .... Hallmark
HLLO .... Metega [*Libya*] [*ICAO location identifier*] (ICLI)
HLLQ .... El Beida/Labraq [*Libya*] [*ICAO location identifier*] (ICLI)
HLLS .... Sebha [*Libya*] [*ICAO location identifier*] (ICLI)
HLLT .... Tripoli/International [*Libya*] [*ICAO location identifier*] (ICLI)
HLLV .... Heavy-Lift Launch Vehicle [*Rocketry*] (MCD)
HLLW .... High-Level Liquid Waste [*Nuclear energy*]
HLLW .... Hollow [*Commonly used*] (OPSA)
HLLWT .... High-Level Liquid Waste Tank [*Nuclear energy*] (NRCH)
HL LX .... High Level Language X (SAUS)
HllywP .... Hollywood Productions, Inc. [*Associated Press*] (SAG)
HLM .... Hampshire Local Militia [*British military*] (DMA)
HLM .... Harpoon Logic Module [*Missiles*] (MCD)
HLM .... Helmstar Group [*AMEX symbol*] (SPSG)

HLM .... Helmville [*Montana*] [*Seismograph station code, US Geological Survey*] [*Closed*] (SEIS)
HLM .... Henry Louis Mencken [*American author/critic*]
HLM .... Heterogeneous LAN [*Local Area Network*] Manager (ACRL)
HLM .... Hierarchical Linear Modeling
HLM .... High-Latitude Mode
HLM .... High-Level Meeting (DCTA)
HLM .... High-Level Mixer
HLM .... Holland, MI [*Location identifier*] [*FAA*] (FAAL)
HLM .... Hypothesized Local Maximum (SAUS)
HLMB .... Marsa Brega [*Libya*] [*ICAO location identifier*] (ICLI)
HLME .... D.H. Holmes Company Ltd. [*NASDAQ symbol*] (COMM)
HLMI .... High-Load Melt Index [*Plastics*] [*Automotive engineering*]
HLML .... High-Level Microprogramming Language
HLMR .... Hunter-Leggitt Military Reservation (AABC)
HLMS .... High Latitude Monitoring Station [*Marine science*] (OSRA)
HLMS .... Holmes Protection Group [*NASDAQ symbol*] (TTSB)
HLMS .... Holmes Protection Group, Inc. [*NASDAQ symbol*] (SAG)
HLMT .... Helmet (NASA)
HLMX .... HL Mills [*Private rail car owner code*]
HLN .... Halton Reinsurance Co. Ltd. [*Toronto Stock Exchange symbol*]
HLN .... Helena [*Montana*] [*Airport symbol*] (OAG)
HLN .... Hellenic Air SA [*Greece*] [*ICAO designator*] (FAAC)
HLN .... Hexagonal Long Nipple (SAUS)
HLN .... Holland Furnace Company (SAUO)
HLN .... Hualilan [*Argentina*] [*Seismograph station code, US Geological Survey*] (SEIS)
HLN .... Human Lesch-Nyhan [*Cell*] (DB)
HLN .... Hyperplastic Liver Nodules [*Medicine*]
HLNCC .... High-Level Neutron Coincidence Counter [*Nuclear energy*] (NRCH)
HLND .... Highlands [*Board on Geographic Names*]
HLND .... Homeland Bankshares [*NASDAQ symbol*] (TTSB)
HLND .... Homeland Bankshares Corp. [*NASDAQ symbol*] (SAG)
HLNE .... Hillsboro & North Eastern Railway Co. [*AAR code*]
HLNF .... Ras Lanouf V 40 [*Libya*] [*ICAO location identifier*] (ICLI)
HLNFPF .... Human Life and Natural Family Planning Foundation [*Defunct*] (EA)
HLNG .... Headlining
HLNL .... Hydroxylysinonorleucine [*Biochemistry*]
HLNP .... Hattah Lake National Park (SAUO)
HLNP .... Hattatt Lakes National Park (SAUS)
HLNR .... Health Lawyers News Report [*A publication*] (DLA)
HLNSS .... Holiness
HLNW .... High-Level Nuclear Waste (BARN)
HLNWR .... Havasu Lake National Wildlife Refuge (SAUO)
HLNWR .... Hutton Lake National Wildlife Refuge (SAUO)
HLO .... High-Latitude Operation
HLO .... High-Level Override [*Nuclear energy*] (NRCH)
HLO .... Hi-Lo Automotive [*NYSE symbol*] (SPSG)
HLO .... Holly Oil Company (SAUO)
HLO .... Horizontal Lockout
HLO .... Samaritan Air Service Ltd. [*Canada*] [*ICAO designator*] (FAAC)
HLOA .... Heart Labs of America, Inc. [*NASDAQ symbol*] (SAG)
HLOAE .... Heart Labs Amer [*NASDAQ symbol*] (TTSB)
HLON .... Hon [*Libya*] [*ICAO location identifier*] (ICLI)
HLOS .... Hardware Limited Operating Strategy (HAWK)
HLOS .... High Level Languages Operations per Second (CCCA)
HLOS .... Horizontal Line-Of-Sight (SAUS)
HLOUK .... Headquarters and Liaison Officer in the United Kingdom (SAUO)
HLOV .... High-Level Output Voltage
HLOWE .... Heart Labs Amer Wrrt [*NASDAQ symbol*] (TTSB)
H/LP .... Headlamp [*Automotive engineering*]
HLP .... Heavy-Lift Pontoon
HLP .... Heavy-Lift Preposition [*Ship*] (DOMA)
HLP .... Hel [*Poland*] [*Geomagnetic observatory code*]
HLP .... Helicopter Landing Platform (SAUS)
HLP .... Help (SAUS)
HLP .... Helper
HLP .... Help File [*Computer science*]
HLP .... Hepatic Lipoperoxidation (DB)
HLP .... High Level Programming (SAUS)
HLP .... Hilina Pali [*Hawaii*] [*Seismograph station code, US Geological Survey*] (SEIS)
HLP .... Hind-Leg Paralysis [*Veterinary Science*] (DB)
HLP .... Holophane Corp. [*NYSE symbol*]
HLP .... Home and Law Publishers [*British*]
HLP .... Houston Lighting & Power (SAUO)
HLP .... Hyperlipidemia (SAUS)
HLP .... Hyperlipoproteinemia [*Medicine*]
HLP .... Hypersonic Local Pressure
HLP .... Jakarta [*Indonesia*] [*Airport symbol*] (OAG)
HLPH .... Holophane Corp. [*NASDAQ symbol*] (SAG)
HlpHm .... Help At Home, Inc. [*Associated Press*] (SAG)
HlpHme .... Help At Home, Inc. [*Associated Press*] (SAG)
HLPI .... Higher Layer Protocol Identifier [*Telecommunications*] (ACRL)
HLPI .... High-Level Programming Interface
HLPIU .... High Level Process Interface Unit (SAUS)
HLPL .... Howard League for Penal Reform [*An association*] [*British*] (EAIO)
Hlpmte .... Helpmate Robotics, Inc. [*Associated Press*] (SAG)
Hlpr .... Helper (BARN)
HLPR .... Helper
HLPR .... Howard League for Penal Reform (SAUO)
HLPrB .... Hecla Mining Sr'B'Cv Pfd [*NYSE symbol*] (TTSB)
HLPS .... Heavy Lift Prepositioning Ship [*Navy*]
HLPS .... Hot Liquid Process Simulation (ADWA)
HLPS .... Human Life Protection Society [*Australia*]
HLPSA .... Hazardous Liquid Pipeline Safety Act (GFGA)
HLPX .... Houston Lighting and Power [*Private rail car owner code*]
HLPZ .... Houston Light & Power [*Federal Railroad Administration identification code*]
HLQ .... High Level Qualifier (SAUS)
HLQ .... High-Level Question (DMAA)
HLQ .... Highly Luminous QUASAR [*Astronomy*]
HLQ .... Holocellulose/Lignocellulose Quotient (SAUS)
HLQ .... Huntington Library Quarterly (SAUO)
HLQC .... Hora Locoque Consuetis [*At the Usual Time and Place*] [*Latin*]
HLQL .... High-Level Query Language
HLQN .... Harlequin (WGA)
HLQS .... Hora Locoque Solitis [*At the Usual Time and Place*] [*Latin*]
HLR .... Hand-Held LASER Range-Finder
HLR .... Harvard Law Review [*A publication*] (BRI)
HLR .... Heart-Lung Resuscitation [*or Resuscitator*] [*Medicine*]
HLR .... Heli Air Services [*Bulgaria*] [*ICAO designator*] (FAAC)
HLR .... Helicopter LASER Range-Finder
HLR .... Highland Ranch [*Colorado*] [*Seismograph station code, US Geological Survey*] [*Closed*] (SEIS)
HLR .... High Level Radiation (SAUS)
HLR .... High Level Radioactivity (SAUS)
HLR .... High-Level Representation
HLR .... High Level Resources Ltd. [*Vancouver Stock Exchange symbol*]
HLR .... Holder (KSC)
HLR .... Hollinger International, Inc. [*NYSE symbol*] (SAG)
HLR .... Home Location Register (ACRL)
HLR .... Home Location Registry (SAUS)
HLR .... Horizontal Long Range (SAUS)
HLR .... Housing Law Reports [*A publication*]
HLR .... Houston Law Review [*A publication*] (ILCA)
HLR .... Killeen, TX [*Location identifier*] [*FAA*] (FAAL)
HLR .... Walter E. Heller International Corp. (SAUO)
HLRA .... Dahra/Warehouse 32 [*Libya*] [*ICAO location identifier*] (ICLI)
HLRA .... Handbag Liners and Repairers Association (BUAC)
HLRA .... Health Labour Relations Association [*Canada*]
HLRC .... High Latitude Rocket Campaign [*A cooperative study by 7 laboratories in the UK*] (PDAA)
HLRC .... High Level Radiochemistry Facility (SAUS)
HL Rep .... English House of Lords Reports [*A publication*] (DLA)
HLRF .... Jaref/Sirte [*ICAO location identifier*] (ICLI)
HLRM .... High-Level Radio Modulator
HLRO .... House of Lords Record Office [*British*] (DLA)
HL Rope .... Hawser Laid Rope (SAUS)
HLRS .... Highway Location Reference Standard (SAUO)
HLRS .... Homosexual Law Reform Society [*British*] (BI)
HLRSC .... Holland Lop Rabbit Specialty Club (EA)
HLRT .... HealthRite, Inc. [*NASDAQ symbol*] (SAG)
HLRV .... Heavy Lift Research Vehicle [*Military*]
HLRV .... Hibiscus Latent Ringspot Virus [*Plant pathology*]
HLRW .... High-Level Radioactive Waste (GNE)
HLRZ .... Holroyd [*Federal Railroad Administration identification code*]
HLS .... Haiti Air Freight [*ICAO designator*] (FAAC)
HLS .... Halt Line State (SAUS)
HLS .... Harmonic Light Scattering [*Physics*]
HLS .... Harvard Law School [*Massachusetts*]
HLS .... Harvard University, Cambridge, MA [*OCLC symbol*] (OCLC)
HLS .... Health Learning Systems
HLS .... Heavy Lift Ship [*Army ship designation*] (POLM)
HLS .... Heavy Lift System (SAUS)
HLS .... Heavy-Lift System
HLS .... Heavy Liquid Separation (SAUS)
HLS .... Heavy Logistics System
HLS .... Heavy Logistic Support (SAUS)
HLS .... Helicopter Landing Site [*Military*] (INF)
HLS .... Helicopter Landing System
HLS .... High Level Scheduler (NITA)
HLS .... High-Level Service [*Computer science*]
HLS .... Hills (MCD)
HLS .... Hinge Moment Load Simulator (SAUS)
HLS .... Hippel-Lindau Syndrome [*Medicine*] (DMAA)
HLS .... Hoc Loco Situs [*Laid in This Place*] [*Latin*]
HLS .... Holes (ADA)
HLS .... Holograph Letter Signed
HLS .... Horizontal Liquid Spring
HLS .... Hue, Luminance, and Saturation [*Computer science*] (DCDG)
HLS .... Hue, Luminance, Saturation (SAUS)
HLS .... Huntingdon Life Sciences [*British*]
HLS .... Hurricane Local Statement (SAUO)
HLS .... Hurricane Statement [*Telecommunications*] (OTD)
HLS .... Hurst Lodge School (SAUO)
HLS .... Hyperbaric Lighting Set [*NASA*] (SPST)
HLS .... St. Helens [*Tasmania*] [*Airport symbol*] (AD)
HLSA .... Hole Saw (SAUS)
HLSC .... Hampton Railway [*Federal Railroad Administration identification code*]
HLSC .... Helicopter Logistic Support Center (NVT)
HLSC .... High Level Service Circuit (SAUS)
HLSC .... Human Life Cycle Safe Concentration (LDOE)
HL Sc App Cas ... English Law Reports, House of Lords, Scotch and Divorce Appeal Cases [*1866-75*] [*A publication*] (DLA)
HLSD .... Essider [*Libya*] [*ICAO location identifier*] (ICLI)
HLSD .... Heel Sanding
HLSDE .... Hillside (TVEL)
HLSE .... High-Level, Single-Ended

HLSI............ Hybrid Large Scale Integrated (PDAA)
HL Signal.... High Low Signal (SAUS)
HLSL............ Harward Law School Library (SAUS)
HLSM............ Homopolar Linear Synchronous Motor (SAUS)
HLSP............ Heitler-London-Slater-Pauling [*Method*] [*Physics*]
HLSP............ Horseshoe Lake State Park (SAUO)
HLSP............ Hospital Library Service Program (SAUS)
HLSRS.......... High Level Sisal Research Station (SAUO)
HLSS............ Harry Lundeberg School of Seamanship (SAUO)
HLSTO.......... Hailstones [*NWS*] (FAAC)
HLSUA.......... Honeywell Large Systems Users Association (EA)
HLSV............ Helium Latching Solenoid Valve
HLSW............ High-Level Solidified Waste [*Nuclear energy*] (NRCH)
HLSX............ Hillsdale Railroad [*Federal Railroad Administration identification code*]
HLT............. Halt [*Computer science*] (MDG)
HLT............. Halt Operation (SAUS)
HLT............. Hamilton [*Australia*] [*Airport symbol*] (OAG)
HLT............. Heart-Lung Transplantation [*Medicine*] (DMAA)
HLT............. Heli Transport [*France*] [*ICAO designator*] (FAAC)
HLT............. Heterodyne Look-Thru [*Telecommunications*] (TEL)
HLT............. Hierarchial Lapped Transform [*Telecommunications*]
HLT............. High-Level Tactical
HLT............. High-Level Terminal (CAAL)
HLT............. High Level Test (SAUS)
HLT............. Highly Leveraged Transaction [*Banking*]
HLT............. Hilton Hotels Corp. [*NYSE symbol*] (SPSG)
HLT............. Holborn Law Tutors (SAUO)
HLT............. Human Lipotropin [*Medicine*] (DMAA)
hLT............. Human Lymphocyte Transformation [*Immunology*] (MAE)
HLT............. Hurrricane Liaison Team (SAUO)
HLTA............ Halt Acknowledge [*Computer science*]
HltCmp........ HealthCare COMPARE Corp. [*Associated Press*] (SAG)
HltCrIm........ HealthCare Imaging Services, Inc. [*Associated Press*] (SAG)
HltcrRty....... Healthcare Realty Trust [*Associated Press*] (SAG)
HltcrTc......... Healthcare Technologies Ltd. [*Associated Press*] (SAG)
HLTD............ Ghadames [*Libya*] [*ICAO location identifier*] (ICLI)
HLTF............ High-Level Task Force (DOMA)
hlth............. Health (STED)
HLTH............ Health
HLTH............ Healtheon Corporation [*NASDAQ symbol*] (NASQ)
HlthCFP........ HealthCare Financial Partners, Inc. [*Associated Press*] (SAG)
HlthCh.......... Health-Chem Corp. [*Associated Press*] (SAG)
HlthCor......... HealthCor Holdings, Inc. [*Associated Press*] (SAG)
HlthCP.......... Health Care Property Investors, Inc. [*Associated Press*] (SAG)
HlthCr........... Health Care REIT [*Associated Press*] (SAG)
HlthCSv........ Health Care Services Group [*Associated Press*] (SAG)
Hlthdyn......... Healthdyne, Inc. [*Associated Press*] (SAG)
HlthdynT....... Healthdyne Technologies [*Associated Press*] (SAG)
HlthdyT......... Healthdyne Technologies [*Associated Press*] (SAG)
HlthFit.......... Health Fitness Physical Therapy [*Associated Press*] (SAG)
HlthMSys...... Health Management Systems, Inc. [*Associated Press*] (SAG)
Hlthpln......... Healthplan Services Corp. [*Associated Press*] (SAG)
HlthplnSv...... Healthplan Services Corp. [*Associated Press*] (SAG)
HlthPro......... Health Professionals [*Associated Press*] (SAG)
Hlth Prof...... Health Professions (SAUS)
HlthPwr........ Health Power [*Associated Press*] (SAG)
HlthRite........ HealthRite, Inc. [*Associated Press*] (SAG)
HlthRsk........ Health Risk Management, Inc. [*Associated Press*] (SAG)
Hlthsrc......... Healthsource, Inc. [*Associated Press*] (SAG)
Hlthsrce....... Healthsource, Inc. [*Associated Press*] (SAG)
Hlthsth......... Healthsouth Corp. [*Associated Press*] (SAG)
HlthSys........ Health Systems Design Corp. [*Associated Press*] (SAG)
HlthSys........ Health Systems International [*Associated Press*] (SAG)
HlthTc.......... HealthTech International, Inc. [*Associated Press*] (SAG)
HlthTch........ HealthTech International, Inc. [*Associated Press*] (SAG)
HlthTech....... HealthTech International, Inc. [*Associated Press*] (SAG)
Hlthwtch....... Healthwatch, Inc. [*Associated Press*] (SAG)
HltImg.......... Health Images, Inc. [*Associated Press*] (SAG)
HLTL............ High-Level Test Language
HLTL............ High Level Transistor Logic (SAUS)
HLTL............ High-Level Transistor Logic
HltMetr........ Health O Meter Products [*Associated Press*] (SAG)
HltMgt.......... Health Management Associates, Inc. [*Associated Press*] (SAG)
HltMInc........ Health Management, Inc. [*Associated Press*] (SAG)
HltMSys....... Health Management Systems, Inc. [*Associated Press*] (SAG)
HLTP............ Hilltop
HltPlanet...... Healthy Planet Products, Inc. [*Associated Press*] (SAG)
Hltplx........... Healthplex, Inc. [*Associated Press*] (SAG)
HltRet.......... Health & Retirement Property Trust [*Associated Press*] (SAG)
HLTRF.......... Hospitality Lodging and Travel Research Foundation [*Also known as Research Foundation*] (EA)
HLTTL.......... High-Level Transistor Translator Logic
HLT/TSC...... High-Level Terminal/Tactical Support Center (SAUO)
HLTU............ Hierarchical Threshold Logic Unit (VLIE)
HLTV............ High-Loan-to-Value [*Business term*]
HltwAm........ Healthwise of America, Inc. [*Associated Press*] (SAG)
HLTyL........... High Level Transistor Transistor Logic (SAUS)
HLTZ............ Holliday Tyler [*Federal Railroad Administration identification code*]
HLU............. Heli Union Heli Prestations [*France*] [*ICAO designator*] (FAAC)
HLU............. High Level User (VLIE)
Hlu.............. Honolulu (SAUS)
HLU............. Houailou [*New Caledonia*] [*Airport symbol*] (OAG)
HLU............. House Logic Unit
HLV............. Hallsville, MO [*Location identifier*] [*FAA*] (FAAL)
HLV............. Heavy Launch Vehicle (SAUS)
HLV............. Heavy-Lift Vehicle
HLV............. Heliserv SA de CV [*Mexico*] [*ICAO designator*] (FAAC)
HLV............. Heracleum Latent Virus [*Plant pathology*]
HLV............. Herpes-Like Virus
HLV............. Hypoplastic Left Ventricle [*Cardiology*] (DAVI)
HLVA............ Hospital Lady Visitors Association (SAUO)
HLVG............ Das Heilige Land in Vergangenheit und Gegenwart [*A publication*] (BJA)
HLVW........... Heavy Logistic Vehicle Wheeled (SAUS)
HLW............. Halbleinwand [*Half-Bound Cloth*] [*Bookbinding, publishing*] [*German*]
HLW............. Handbuch der Literaturwissenschaft [*Potsdam*] [*A publication*] (BJA)
HLW............. Hattiesburg, Camp Shelby, MS [*Location identifier*] [*FAA*] (FAAL)
HLW............. Helwan [*Egypt*] [*Seismograph station code, US Geological Survey*] (SEIS)
HLW............. Higher Low Water
HLW............. High-Level Radioactive Waste (LDT)
HLW............. High-Level Waste [*Nuclear energy*]
HLWC........... High-Level Waste Calcination [*Nuclear energy*] (NRCH)
HLWC........... High-Level Waste Concentrate [*Nuclear energy*] (NRCH)
HLWD........... High-Level Waste Concentrator Distillate [*Nuclear energy*] (NRCH)
HlwdE........... Hallwood Energy Corp. [*Associated Press*] (SAG)
HlwdP........... Hollywood Park, Inc. [*Associated Press*] (SAG)
HlwdPk......... Hollywood Park, Inc. [*Associated Press*] (SAG)
HLWE........... Helicopter Laser Warning Equipment (SAUS)
HLWF........... High-Level Waste Concentrator Feed [*Nuclear energy*] (NRCH)
HLWF........... High Level Waste Forms (SAUS)
HLWI............ Higher Low-Water Interval
HLW-ICB...... High Level Waste-Interface Control Board (SAUO)
HL WIO C..... Hard Labor without Confinement (SAUS)
HLWIP.......... High Level Waste Immobilisation Program [*Nuclear energy*] (NUCP)
HL Wkly Inf Bull... House of Lords Weekly Information Bulletin [*A publication*] (DLA)
HLWN........... Highest Low-Water Neap Tide (WDAA)
HLW/OC....... Hard Labor without Confinement
HLWOG......... High-Level Liquid Waste Off-Gas [*Nuclear energy*] (NRCH)
HLWRP......... Hoover Library on War, Revolution and Peace (SAUO)
HLWS........... High-Level Waste Solidification (ABAC)
HLWS........... High-Level Waste Surge [*Nuclear energy*] (NRCH)
HLX............. Galax/Hillsville, VA [*Location identifier*] [*FAA*] (FAAL)
HLX............. Halter Marine Group, Inc. [*AMEX symbol*] (SAG)
HLX............. Helix
HLX............. Helix Circuits, Inc. [*Toronto Stock Exchange symbol*]
HLX............. Helix-Turn-Helix (QSUL)
HLXA............ Helix Angle
HLY............. Haley Industries Ltd. [*Toronto Stock Exchange symbol*]
HLY............. Halley Bay [*United Kingdom*] [*Geomagnetic observatory code*]
HLY............. Heavily (SAUS)
HLY............. Holly Sugar Corporation (SAUO)
HLY............. Valparaiso, FL [*Location identifier*] [*FAA*] (FAAL)
HlyPd........... Holly Products [*Associated Press*] (SAG)
HLYR............ Haze Layer Aloft (SAUS)
HLYSP.......... Holly Springs, MS [*American Association of Railroads railroad junction routing code*]
HLYVL.......... Haleyville, AL [*American Association of Railroads railroad junction routing code*]
HLYW........... Hollywood Entertainment [*NASDAQ symbol*] (SG)
HLYW........... Hollywood Entertainment Corp. [*NASDAQ symbol*] (SAG)
HlywdCa....... Hollywood Casino Corp. [*Associated Press*] (SAG)
HlywdE......... Hollywood Entertainment Corp. [*Associated Press*] (SAG)
HLYX............ Holly Sugar [*Private rail car owner code*]
HLZ............. Hamilton [*New Zealand*] [*Airport symbol*] (OAG)
HLZ............. Helicopter Landing Zone
HLZA............ Zella 74 [*Libya*] [*ICAO location identifier*] (ICLI)
HLZBL.......... Holzblaeser [*Woodwind Instrument*] [*Music*]
HLZL............ Helicopter Landing Zone Locator
HM............... Air-Cushion Vehicle Built by Hovermarine [*Usually used in combination with numerals*]
HM............... Air Mahe [*ICAO designator*] (AD)
HM............... Habitation Module (SSD)
HM............... Haematite (SAUS)
HM............... Hahns Macaw [*Bird*]
HM............... Half Morocco
HM............... Hallmark
HM............... Hamarein Air [*United Arab Emirates*] [*ICAO designator*] (ICDA)
HM............... Hampshire Regiment (SAUO)
HM............... Handelsministerium (SAUO)
HM............... Hand-Made (SAUS)
HM............... Hand Motion [*Vision*] [*Neurology*] (DAVI)
HM............... Hand Movement
HM............... Hands of Mercy [*An association*] (EA)
HM............... Harbor Master
HM............... Hard Magnetic (SAUS)
HM............... Hardness Maintenance (MSA)
HM............... Hardware Malfunction (SAUS)
HM............... Hardware Monitoring (SAUS)
HM............... Hardware Multiple
HM............... Harmonic Mean [*Music*]
HM............... Harmonic Motion (SAUS)
HM............... Harper's Magazine [*A publication*] (BRI)
Hm............... Haymarket (SAUS)
HM............... Hazardous Material (DNAB)
HM............... Head Master (SAUO)
HM............... Head Mistress (SAUO)
HM............... Head Motion [*Gravity*]

HM .... Head Movement (SAUO)
HM .... Health Maintenance (DB)
HM .... Health Ministries (EA)
HM .... Health Monitoring [*Environmental science*] (COE)
HM .... Healthy Male (ROG)
HM .... Heard and McDonald Islands [*ANSI two-letter standard code*] (CNC)
hm .... Heard and McDonald Islands [*MARC country of publication code*] [*Library of Congress*] (LCCP)
HM .... Heart Murmur [*Cardiology*] (MAE)
HM .... Heated Mirrors [*Automotive engineering*]
HM .... Heater Middle (IAA)
HM .... Heater Mid-tap (SAUS)
HM .... Heavily Muscled (STED)
HM .... Heavy Maintenance [*Ordnance*]
h-m .... Heavy-Media (SAUS)
HM .... Heavy Metal [*Rock music type*]
HM .... Heavy Metal [*Inorganic chemistry*]
HM .... Heavy Mobile
hm .... Hectometer (ADWA)
HM .... Hectometer [*100 meters*]
hm .... hectometre (SAUS)
hm .... hectometric (SAUS)
HM .... Heimlich Maneuver [*Medicine*] (MELL)
HM .... Heine-Medin [*Disease*] [*Medicine*] (DB)
HM .... Helicopter Mine Countermeasure Squadron [*Military*] (POLM)
HM .... Heloma Molle [*Medicine*] (MELL)
hm .... Hematite [*CIPW classification*] [*Geology*]
HM .... Hemifacial Microsomia [*Medicine*] (MELL)
H/m .... Henry per Meter
HM .... Hepatic Metabolism (STED)
HM .... Hepatic Microcirculation [*Physiology*]
HM .... Heritage Manor (BJA)
HM .... Hermeter Master [*Freemasonry*] (ROG)
hM .... Herrschende Meinung [*Prevailing Opinion*] [*German*] (ILCA)
HM .... Hexamethylmelamine (STED)
HM .... Hidden Memory (SAUS)
HM .... High Magnification (SAUS)
HM .... High-Meaningfulness [*Psychology*]
HM .... High Melting (OA)
HM .... High-Melting (SAUS)
HM .... High-Modulus (SAUS)
HM .... High Molecular [*Weight*] [*Also, HMW*] [*Organic chemistry*]
HM .... High-Resolution Monochrome (VLIE)
HM .... Hinge Mount (MCD)
HM .... His [*or Her*] Majesty
HM .... Hispanic Male (MELL)
HM .... Historia Mathematica [*A publication*]
HM .... History of Medicine (SAUO)
HM .... Hoc Mense [*In This Month*] [*Latin*]
HM .... Hoist Motor (SAUS)
HM .... Hold Mode (SAUS)
HM .... Hollerith Machine (SAUS)
HM .... Hollow Metal [*Technical drawings*]
HM .... Hologram Memory (SAUS)
HM .... Holosystolic Murmur [*Medicine*] (MELL)
HM .... Holter Monitor (STED)
HM .... Home (ROG)
HM .... Home Mission
HM .... Homestake Mining Co. [*NYSE symbol*] (SPSG)
HM .... Home Zone (JAGO)
HM .... Homogenization Medium
HM .... Honorary Member [*Freemasonry*] (ROG)
HM .... Honourable Mention (SAUS)
HM .... Horizontal Marriage
HM .... Horizontal Meridian [*Optics, eye anatomy*]
HM .... Horniman Museum [*London*]
HM .... Hoshen Mishpat, Shulhan 'Arukh (BJA)
HM .... Hospital Corpsman [*Navy rating*]
HM .... Hospital Management (STED)
HM .... Hot Mix (SAUS)
HM .... Houghton Mifflin Co. [*Publisher*]
HM .... Hours, Minutes (ROG)
HM .... House Magazine [*Australia*] [*A publication*]
HM .... Housing Management [*HUD*]
HM .... Huius Mensis [*This Month's*] [*Latin*]
HM .... Human Milk [*Biochemistry*] (MAE)
HM .... Humidity Mask (MELL)
HM .... Huntingdon Militia [*British military*] (DMA)
HM .... Hybrid Modulation (SAUS)
HM .... Hydatidiform Mole [*Gynecology*]
HM .... Hydra Medium [*Culture medium*]
HM .... Hydraulic Modelling (SAUS)
HM .... Hydrogen MASER
HM .... Hydromagnetic (SAUS)
HM .... Hydromechanical (SAUS)
HM .... Hydrometallurgy (SAUS)
HM .... Hydrometeorological
hm .... Hydroxymethyl [*As substituent on nucleoside*] [*Biochemistry*]
HM .... Hyperimmune Mice
HM .... Hypermedia (SAUS)
Hm .... Hyperopia Manifest [*Ophthalmology*] (DAVI)
HM .... Hypothetical Machine (MHDB)
HM .... Hypoxic-Metabolic (STED)
HM .... Hysteresis Motor [*Electronics*] (IAA)
Hm .... Manifest Hypermetropia [*Medicine*]
Hm .... Manifest Hyperopia [*Medicine*] (PALA)
HM .... Marine Helicopter Squadron
HM .... Master of Humanities
HM .... Sandoz [*Italy*] [*Research code symbol*]
HM .... Sisters of the Humility of Mary [*Roman Catholic religious order*]
HM1 .... Hospital Corpsman, First Class [*Navy rating*]
HM2 .... Hospital Corpsman, Second Class [*Navy rating*]
HM^2 .... Square Hectometer
HM^3 .... Cubic Hectometer (WDAA)
HM3 .... Hospital Corpsman, Third Class [*Navy rating*]
HMA .... Haemorrhages and Microaneurysms [*Medicine*] (EDAA)
HMA .... Hapten-Modified Agent (DB)
HMA .... Hard Magnetic Alloy (SAUS)
HMA .... Hardware Manufacturers' Association [*British*] (BI)
HMA .... Hardwood Manufacturers Association (EA)
Hma .... Harmona [*Record label*] [*Austria*]
HMA .... Hawaii Medical Association (BUAC)
HMA .... Head Masters Association (SAUO)
HMA .... Head Mirror Assembly (SAUS)
HMA .... Health Management Associates, Inc. [*NYSE symbol*] (SPSG)
HMA .... Helicopter Attack Squadron [*Military*] (POLM)
HMA .... Hellenic Marketing Association (BUAC)
H/Ma .... Hemorrhages (SAUS)
HMA .... Heteroduplex Mobility Analysis [*Genetics*]
HMA .... High Memory Area [*Computer science*] (PCM)
HMA .... Highway Memory Address (SAUS)
HMA .... Hoist Manufacturers Association [*Later, HMI*] (EA)
HMA .... Home Manufacturers Association [*Later, HMC*] (EA)
HMA .... Home Medical Advisor [*Schueler Corp.*]
HMA .... Home Mission Association [*Episcopalian*]
HMA .... Hondo, TX [*Location identifier*] [*FAA*] (FAAL)
HMA .... Hop Merchants Association [*British*] (BI)
HMA .... Host-Mediated Assay (SAUS)
HMA .... Hot Melt Adhesive
HMA .... Hot Melt Applicator
HMA .... Hot Mix Asphalt (SAUS)
HMA .... Hub Management Architecture (SAUS)
HMA .... Hybrid Microcircuit Assembly (ACAE)
HMA .... Hydroxymethyladenine [*Biochemistry*]
HMA .... Hypergol Maintenance Area (MCD)
HMA .... Hyundai Motor America, Inc.
HMA .... Marine Attack Helicopter Squadron (VNW)
HMA .... Marine Helicopter Squadron Attack (NVT)
HMAA .... Haitian Medical Association Abroad [*Later, AMHE*] (EA)
HMAA .... Horse and Mule Association of America (SAUO)
HMAC .... Hash-Based Message Authentication Code [*Computer science*] (DINT)
HMAC .... Hashing for Message Authentication (SAUS)
HMAC .... Hazardous Materials Advisory Committee (SAUO)
HMAC .... Hazardous Materials Advisory Council (EA)
HMAC .... Health Manpower Advisory Council
HMAC .... High-Performance Memory Array Controller (CIST)
HMAC .... Horticultural Market Access Committee [*Australia*]
HMAC .... Hot Mix Asphaltic Concrete (ABAC)
HMAC .... House Military Affairs Commission (SAUO)
HMAC .... Hugo Marom Aviation Consultants Ltd. (SAUO)
HMACI .... His [*or Her*] Majesty's Alkali and Clean Air Inspectorate [*British*] (DCTA)
HMACI .... Hugo Marom Aviation Consultants International Inc. (SAUO)
HMAF .... His [*or Her*] Majesty's Armed Forces
HMAI .... Handbook of Middle-American Indians (SAUS)
HMAI .... Her Majesty's Agricultural Inspectorate (HEAS)
H MAJ:T .... Hans Majestaet [*His Majesty*] [*Swedish*]
HMA/L .... Helicopter Attack/Light Squadron [*Military*] (POLM)
HMANA .... Hawk Migration Association of North America (EA)
HM&E .... Hull Machinery and Electrical (SAUS)
HM & LP .... Hand Motion and Light Perception [*Medicine*] (DAVI)
HM & M .... Home Maintenance and Modification Program [*Australia*]
HM & SG .... Hirshhorn Museum and Sculpture Garden [*Smithsonian Institution*]
HMAR .... Hvide Marine Inc. [*NASDAQ symbol*] (SAG)
HMARC .... Houston Metropolitan Archives and Research Center (SAUO)
HMAS .... History of Medicine and Allied Sciences, Inc. [*Medicine*] (EDAA)
HMAS .... Hyperimmune Mouse Ascite [*Medicine*] (DMAA)
HmaScn .... HumaScan, Inc. [*Associated Press*] (SAG)
HMAT .... High Mobility Avionics Tester (ACAE)
HMAV .... His [*or Her*] Majesty's Army Vessel [*British military*] (DMA)
HMAX .... Huntsman [*Private rail car owner code*]
HMB .... Garden City, KS [*Location identifier*] [*FAA*] (FAAL)
HMB .... Haemophilus Maintenance Broth [*Microbiology*]
HMB .... Hamburg [*New York*] [*Seismograph station code, US Geological Survey*] [*Closed*] (SEIS)
HMB .... Handbook on Military Bicycles (SAUO)
HMB .... Hazara Mountain Battery [*British military*] (DMA)
HMB .... Health Management Board (SAUS)
HMB .... Hexamethylbenzene [*Organic chemistry*]
HMB .... Holderbank Management und Beratung AG [*Switzerland*]
HMB .... Homatropine Methobromide [*Medicine*] (EDAA)
HMB .... Homatropine Methylbromide [*Anticholinergic*]
HMB .... Home Mission Board (SAUO)
HMB .... Hops Marketing Board [*British*]
HMB .... Horton-Magath-Brown [*Syndrome*] [*Medicine*] (DB)
HMB .... Houston Main Building (SAUS)
HMB .... Hudson Message Base (SAUS)
HMB .... Hughes Mining Barge [*Support vessel for Glomar Explorer*]

HMB............ Hukbong Mapagpalaya ng Batan [*People's Liberation Army*] [*Philippines*]
HMB............ Hydroxy(methoxy)benzaldehyde [*Organic chemistry*]
HMB............ Hydroxymethoxybenzophenone [*Organic chemistry*]
HMBA.......... Hebrew Master Bakers Association [*Defunct*] (EA)
HMBA.......... Hexamethylene Bis(Acetamide) [*Organic chemistry*]
HMBA.......... Hotel and Motel Brokers of America (EA)
HMBA.......... Hydroxymercurbenzoate (SAUS)
HMBA.......... Hydroxymethyl(methyl)benzanthracene [*Organic chemistry*]
HmBBc......... Home Building Bancorp [*Associated Press*] (SAG)
HMBC.......... Heteronuclear Multiple-Bond Connectivities (SAUS)
HMBC.......... Heteronuclear Multiple-Bond Correlation [*Physics*]
HMBCEE...... Horace Mann Bond Center for Equal Education [*Defunct*] (EA)
HMBCP........ Heat and Material Balance Computer Program (SAUS)
HMBDV........ His [*or Her*] Majesty's Boom Defence Vessel
HmBElg........ Home Bancorp of Elgin, Inc. [*Associated Press*] (SAG)
HmbHm........ Hamburger Hamlet Restaurants, Inc. [*Associated Press*] (SAG)
HMBP.......... Hazardous Materials Business Plans (SARE)
HMBP.......... Heavy Machine Building Plant (SAUO)
H-MBP-H..... Human-Mannose Binding Protein-H
HMBS.......... His [*or Her*] Majesty's British Ship
HMBT.......... Hardware Master Bit Table (SAUS)
HMBT.......... Hydrazino(methyl)Benzothiazole [*Organic chemistry*]
HMBZ.......... Heileman's Brewing [*Federal Railroad Administration identification code*]
HMC............ Chief Hospital Corpsman (SAUS)
HMC............ Halley Multicolor Camera [*Instrumentation*]
HMC............ Hammerson Canada, Inc. [*Toronto Stock Exchange symbol*]
HMC............ Hand-Mirror Cell [*Oncology*]
HMC............ Hard Minerals Committee (SAUO)
HMC............ Harvey Mudd College (SAUO)
HMC............ Hastings Manufacturing Co. (EFIS)
HMC............ Heading Marker Correction (SAA)
HMC............ Head Masters' Conference [*British*]
HMC............ Healing Ministry Centre [*Australia*]
HMC............ Health Ministers Council (EERA)
HMC............ Health Monitor Computer (SAUS)
HMC............ Heavy Mechanical Complex (SAUS)
HMC............ Heavy Media Cyclone (SAUS)
HMC............ Heavy Mortar Company (SAUO)
HMC............ Hermits of Mount Carmel (TOCD)
HMC............ Heroin, Morphine, and Cocaine [*Mixture*] [*Slang*]
HMC............ High Moisture Shelled Corn (OA)
HMC............ High speed Measure Centre (SAUS)
HMC............ Highspeed Memory Controller (SAUS)
HMC............ High-Strength Molding Compound (SAUS)
HMC............ High-Strength Sheet Molding Compound
HMC............ His [*or Her*] Majesty's Council (ROG)
HMC............ His [*or Her*] Majesty's Customs
HMC............ Histocompatibility Complex, Major [*Medicine*] (EDAA)
HmC............ Historian's Microfilm Co., Cazenovia, NY [*Library symbol*] [*Library of Congress*] (LCLS)
HMC............ Historical Manuscripts Commission [*British*]
HMC............ Holland Mills [*Quebec*] [*Seismograph station code, US Geological Survey*] [*Closed*] (SEIS)
HMC............ Home Manufacturers Councils of NAHB [*National Association of Home Builders of the US*] (EA)
HMC............ Home Medical Care [*Medicine*] (EDAA)
HMC............ Homestake Mining Company (SAUO)
HMC............ Honda Motor Co. Ltd. [*NYSE symbol*] (SPSG)
HMC............ Horizontal Microcode (SAUS)
HMC............ Horizontal Motion Carriage [*Engineering*] (OA)
HMC............ Horticultural Marketing Council [*British*] (BI)
HMC............ Hospital Corpsman, Chief [*Navy rating*]
HMC............ Houghton Mifflin Co., Boston, MA [*OCLC symbol*] (OCLC)
HMC............ Household Mortgage Corp. (ODBW)
HMC............ Houston Medical Center Building (SAUS)
HMC............ Howard Mold Count [*Food quality measure*]
HMC............ Howitzer Motor Carriage
HMC............ Hughes Management Club (ACAE)
HMC............ Human Metaphase Chromosome [*Medicine*] (EDAA)
HMC............ Hundred Million Club (EA)
HMC............ Hybrid Microcircuit (NASA)
HMC............ (Hydroxymethyl)carboline [*Biochemistry*]
HMC............ Hydroxymethylcystosine [*Organic chemistry*]
HMC............ Hydroxymethyl Cytosine [*Biochemistry*] (DAVI)
HMC............ Hydroxypropyl(methyl)cellulose [*Synthetic food gum*] [*Organic chemistry*]
HMC............ Hyoscine, Morphine, and Cactine [*Tablets*] [*Medicine*]
HMC............ Hypergolic Maintenance and Checkout (NASA)
HMC............ Hypertelorismus, Mikrotie, Clefting (SAUS)
HMC .... Hospital Management Committee (ODA)
HMCA.......... Hospital and Medial Care Association [*British*] (DBA)
HMC & E..... His [*or Her*] Majesty's Customs and Excise [*British*] (DCTA)
HMC&H........ Hahnemann Medical College and Hospital (SAUO)
HMCC.......... Hazardous Materials Control Committee [*General Motors Corp.*]
HMCC.......... Housewife/Mother Career Concept (EDAC)
HMCC.......... Houston Mission Control Center [*NASA*] (KSC)
HMCC.......... Hypergolic Maintenance and Checkout Cell (NASA)
HMCCMP..... Human Mammary Carcinoma Cell Membrane Proteinase [*Medicine*] (DMAA)
HMC Council... Healthcare Marketing & Communications Council (NTPA)
HMCES........ Hydrogen Mitigation Controlled Exhaust System (SAUS)
HMCF.......... Hypergolic Maintenance and Checkout Facility [*NASA*] (NASA)
HMCI.......... Her Majesty's Chief Inspector of Schools [*British*] (BUAC)
HMCI.......... Homecorp, Inc. [*NASDAQ symbol*] (SAG)
HMCII.......... Higher Military Command, Interior and Islands (MCD)
HMCIP........ His/Her Majesty's Chief Inspector of Prisons [*British*] (WDAA)
HMCIS........ His (or Her) Majestys Chief Inspector of Schools (SAUS)
HMCK.......... Hummock (SAUS)
HMCL.......... Hand-Mirror Cell Leukemia [*Oncology*]
HMCM.......... Hospital Corpsman, Master Chief [*Navy rating*]
HMCN.......... His [*or Her*] Majesty's Canadian Navy
HMCNA........ Home Missions Council of North America (SAUO)
HMCO.......... Henley Manufacturing Corp. (SAUO)
HM Comm... Historical Manuscripts Commission (SAUO)
HMCR.......... Huntsville & Madison County Railroad [*Federal Railroad Administration identification code*]
HMCRI........ Hazardous Materials Control Research Institute (EA)
HMCS.......... His [*or Her*] Majesty's Canadian Ship
HMCS.......... His [*or Her*] Majesty's Civil Service
HMCS.......... His [*or Her*] Majesty's Colonial Steamer [*In use in 19th century*]
HMCS.......... Hoffman Modulation Contrast System
HMCS.......... Hospital Corpsman, Senior Chief [*Navy rating*]
HMCS.......... Senior Chief Hospital Corpsman (SAUS)
HMCT.......... Highway Movements Control Team (SAUO)
HMCV.......... Human Cytomegalovirus
HMCX.......... Holtrachem Manufacturing [*Private rail car owner code*]
HMCyS........ His (or Her) Majestys Ceylonese Ship (SAUS)
HMD............ Charlie Hammonds Flying Service, Inc. [*FAA designator*] (FAAC)
HMD............ Hamada [*Japan*] [*Seismograph station code, US Geological Survey*] (SEIS)
HMD............ Hammond Corp. (SAUO)
HMD............ Head/Helmet Mounted Display (SAUS)
HMD............ Head-Mounted Display [*Virtual reality technology*] (PS)
HMD............ Heard Island and McDonald Islands [*ANSI three-letter standard code*] (CNC)
HMD............ Helicopter Mine Dispenser (SAUS)
HMD............ Helmet-Mounted Display
HMD............ Hemmed (SAUS)
HMD............ Heterodyne Matrix Detector
HMD............ High-Mobility Demonstrator [*Military vehicles*]
HMD............ His [*or Her*] Majesty's Destroyer [*British military*] (DMA)
HMD............ His [*or Her*] Majesty's Dockyard [*Navy*] [*British*]
HMD............ His [*or Her*] Majesty's Drifter
HMD............ History of Medicine Division (SAUO)
HMD............ HLM Design [*AMEX symbol*] (SG)
HMD............ Hollow-Metal Door (DAC)
HMD............ Homeopathic Doctor of Medicine (SAUO)
HMD............ Homeopathic Medical Doctor [*Medicine*]
HMD............ Hot Metal Detector [*Electronics*] (IAA)
HMD............ Hot-Mix Design (SAUS)
HMD............ Hughes Maintenance Depot (ACAE)
HMD............ Hughes Microprogrammable Display (ACAE)
HMD............ Humid (MSA)
HMD............ Humidity (SAUS)
HMD............ Hyaline Membrane Disease [*Later, RDS*] [*Medicine*]
HMD............ Hydraulic Mean Depth
HMD............ HydrazinomethylDOPA [*Biochemistry*]
HMD............ Hydrostatic Motor-Driven
HMDA.......... Hexamethylenediamine [*Organic chemistry*]
HMDA.......... Home Mortgage Disclosure Act
HMDAA........ Hydroxymethyl Diacetone Acrylamide [*Organic chemistry*]
HMDBA........ Hollow Metal Door and Buck Association (EA)
HMDBA........ Hydrogen-Mitigation Design-Basis Accident (SAUS)
HMDC.......... Hanford Materials Durability & Conservation Program (SAUS)
HMDD.......... Helmet-Mounted Display Device [*Military*]
HMDE.......... Hanging Mercury Drop Electrode [*Electrochemistry*]
HMDE/ASV... Hanging Mercury Drop Electrode/Anodic Stripping Voltage (SAUS)
HMDE/DPCSV.... Hanging Mercury Drop Electrode/ Differential-Pulse Continuous Stripping Voltage (SAUS)
HMDEs......... Hanging Mercury Drop Electrodes (SAUS)
HMDF.......... Hollow Metal Door and Frame [*Technical drawings*]
HMDF.......... Horizontal Side of Main Distribution Frame (TEL)
hMDH.......... Halophilic Malate Dehydrogenase [*An enzyme*]
HMDI.......... Diisocyanato dicyclohexylmethane (SAUS)
HMDI.......... Hexamethylene Diisocyanate [*Organic chemistry*]
HMDP.......... Homology Database (HGEN)
HMDP.......... Hydroxymethylenediphosphonate [*Organic chemistry*]
HMDS.......... Her Majesty's Diplomatic Service [*British*] (BUAC)
HMDS.......... Hexamethyldisilazane [*Organic chemistry*]
HMDS.......... Hexamethyldisiloxane [*Organic chemistry*]
HMDS.......... Hospital Morbidity Data System
HMDSO........ Hexamethyldisiloxane [*Organic chemistry*]
HMDT.......... Hanford Multipurpose Thermoluminescent Dosimeter (SAUS)
HMDTA........ Hexamethylenediamine Tetraacetic Acid (SAUS)
HMDV.......... Hoof-and-Mouth Disease Virus (SAUS)
HMDY.......... Hemodynamics, Inc. [*NASDAQ symbol*] (COMM)
HMDZ.......... Hexamethyldisilazane [*Organic chemistry*]
HME............ Hassi Messaoud [*Algeria*] [*Airport symbol*] (OAG)
HME............ Health Media Education (EA)
HME............ Heat and Moisture Exchanger (MAE)
HME............ Heat, Massage, Exercise [*Medicine*]
HME............ Hierarchical Mixtures of Experts (IDAI)
HME............ Hierarchical Modelling Environment (VLIE)
HME............ High Mobility Entrencher (SAUS)
HME............ High Vinyl-Modified Epoxy (MCD)
HME............ Home Medical Equipment
HME............ Home Properties of New York [*NYSE symbol*] (SAG)
HME............ Hull, Mechanical, Electrical [*Ship equipment*] [*Navy*]

HME Human Macrophage Metalloelastase (SAUS)
HMEA Hatters Machinery and Equipment Association [*Defunct*] (EA)
HMEA Hazard Mode and Effects Analysis (SAUS)
HME&O Hull, Mechanical, Electrical and Ordnance (SAUO)
HmeBc Home Bancorp [*Associated Press*] (SAG)
HMEC Human Mammary Epithelial Cell [*Cytology*]
Hmecrp Homecorp, Inc. [*Associated Press*] (SAG)
HMED Heavy Military Electronics Department (SAA)
HmeDep [*The*] Home Depot, Inc. [*Associated Press*] (SAG)
HMEED Heavy Military Electronic Equipment Division [*General Electric Co.*] (AAG)
HMEG Homogeneous Multipolar Equivalent Generator (SAUS)
HmeHlth Home Health Corporation of America, Inc. [*Associated Press*] (SAG)
HMEI Her Majesty's Explosives Inspectorate (HEAS)
HMEI Hughes Missile Electronics, Incorporated (ACAE)
HMEIA Health Manpower Education Initiative Award
HmeOil Home Oil Co. Ltd. [*Associated Press*] (SAG)
HMEP Hazardous Materials Emergency Preparedness (DEMM)
HMEP Helmet-Mounted Equipment Platform (SAUS)
Hmeplx Homeplex Mortgage Investments [*Associated Press*] (SAG)
HmePrp Home Properties of New York [*Associated Press*] (SAG)
HMES Heavy Military Electronic System [*General Electric Co.*] (IAA)
HMEs Hough Mode Extensions (SAUS)
HmeStat Home State Holdings, Inc. [*Associated Press*] (SAG)
HMF 5-Hydroxymethylfurfural
HMF Handbook of Military Forces (MCD)
HMF Harbor Maintenance Fee [*Import/Export fee*]
HMF Haslemere Music Festival (SAUO)
HMF Hastings Manufacturing Co. [*AMEX symbol*] (SPSG)
HMF Health Maintenance Facility (MCD)
HMF Heavy-Metal Fluoride (SAUS)
HMF Heliospheric Magnetic Field [*Solar physics*]
HMF High Mach Flow
HMF High Magnetic Field
HMF High Modulus Furnace (SAUS)
HMF His [*or Her*] Majesty's Forces
HMF Hollow Metal Frame (SAUS)
HMF Horizontal Mating Facility [*NASA*] (KSC)
HMF Hum Modulation Factor (DEN)
HMF Hydroxymethylfuraldehyde [*Organic chemistry*]
HMF Hydroxymethylfurfural [*Organic chemistry*] (DAVI)
HMF Hypergol Maintenance Facility [*NASA*] (NASA)
HMFblack High Modulus Furnace Black (EDCT)
HMFD Home Federal Corp. (SAUO)
HmFedIN Home Federal Bancorp [*Associated Press*] (SAG)
HMFF Hoc Monumentum Fieri Fecit [*Caused This Monument to Be Made*] [*Latin*]
HMFG Heavy Metal Fluoride Glass
HMFI His [*or Her*] Majesty's Factory Inspectorate [*Department of Employment*] [*British*]
HMFIC Head Military Figure in Charge
HMFIHQ His [*or Her*] Majesty's Factory Inspectorate Headquarters [*Department of Employment*] [*British*]
HmFnFL Home Financial Corp. Florida [*Associated Press*] (SAG)
HMfW Help Model for Windows
HMG Hardware Message Generator [*Telecommunications*] (TEL)
HMG Harvard University, Gutman Library, Cambridge, MA [*OCLC symbol*] (OCLC)
HMG Heavy Machine Gun
HMG Higher Middle German (SAUS)
HMG High Mobility Group [*of nonhistone proteins*] [*Biochemistry*]
HMG High Modulus Graphite [*Epoxy composite*] (MCD)
HMG His [*or Her*] Majesty's Government
HMG Historical Metallurgy Group (SAUO)
HMG HMG/Courtland Prop [*AMEX symbol*] (TTSB)
HMG HMG Property Investors, Inc. [*Formerly, Hospital Mortgage Group*] [*AMEX symbol*] (SPSG)
HMG Human Menopausal Gonadotrophin [*Endocrinology*]
hMG Human Menopausal Gonadotropin [*Medicine*] (DMAA)
HMG Hydroxymethylglutaryl [*Biochemistry*]
HMGB His [*or Her*] Majesty's Gunboat
HMGC HMG Worldwide [*NASDAQ symbol*] (TTSB)
HMGC HMG Worldwide Corp. [*NASDAQ symbol*] (SAG)
HMGCC Her Majesty's Government Communications Centre [*British*] (PDAA)
HMGCO Hydroxymethylglutarylcoenzyme [*Organic chemistry*]
HMG CoA Hepatic Hydroxymethylglutaryl Coenzyme A [*Organic chemistry*] (DAVI)
HMG-CoA Hydroxy-Methylglutaryl-Coenzyme A Reductase [*Medicine*] (MEDA)
HMGF High Modulus Glass Fiber
HMGI Hotel-Motel Greeters International (EA)
HMGN Hemagen Diagnostics [*NASDAQ symbol*] (SAG)
HMGP Hazard Mitigation Grant Program (DEMM)
HMGT Homegate Hospitality, Inc. [*NASDAQ symbol*] (SAG)
HMG Wd HMG Worldwide Corp. [*Associated Press*] (SAG)
HMH Heintz, M. H., Chicago IL [*STAC*]
HMH Helicopter Light Squadron [*Military*] (POLM)
HMH Helmet-Mounted Head-Up-Display (SAUS)
HMH His [*or Her*] Majesty's Household
HMH Hispanic Marketing Handbook [*A publication*]
HMH Home Hill [*Australia*] [*Airport symbol*]
HMH Horizon Mental Health Management [*AMEX symbol*] (SAG)
HMH Marine Helicopter Squadron Heavy
HMHB Healthy Mothers, Healthy Babies (EA)
HMHB Healthy Mothers, Healthy Babies National Coalition (PAZ)
HMHCEA Hazardous Materials Hazard Cause and Effect Analysis (SAUO)
HMHCY Hexamethyl Hexacyclen [*Organic chemistry*]
HMHD High Molecular Weight, High Density
HMHDPE High Molecular High Density Polyethyene (SAUS)
HMHEC Hydrophobically-Modified Hydroxyethylcellulose [*Organic chemistry*]
HMHF Hydrophobic Microporous Hollow Fiber [*Membranes for chemical reactions*]
HMHM Horizon Mental Health Management [*NASDAQ symbol*] (SAG)
HMHM Horizon Mental Health Mgmt [*NASDAQ symbol*] (TTSB)
HMHP Hospital Management, Hospital Problems [*British*]
HMHS Hereditary Master of the Household of Scotland (SAUO)
HMHS His [*or Her*] Majesty's Hospital Ship
HMHS Horace Mann High School (SAUO)
HMHUD Helmet-Mounted Head-Up Display (SAUS)
HM/HW Hazardous Materials/Hazardous Waste (SAUS)
HMHX Marine Heavy Helicopter, Experimental (SAUS)
HMHX Tank Car Company of America [*Private rail car owner code*]
HMI Hahn-Meitner Institute [*Germany*]
HMI Hall-Moody Institute (SAUO)
HMI Halogen Metallide Iodide (SAUS)
HMI Handbook of Maintenance Instructions
HMI Hardware Monitor Interface
HMI Hardwood Manufacturers Institute (SAUS)
HMI Hazardous Material Incident [*Nuclear energy*]
HMI Healed Myocardial Infarction [*Cardiology*] (AAMN)
HMI Health-Mor, Incorporated (SAUO)
HMI Heavy Maintenance Interval (SAUS)
HMI Held Multiplant produced Items (SAUS)
HMI Hexamethyleneimine [*Trademark*] [*Celanese Corp.*]
HMI Highland Home Industries (SAUS)
HMI Hoisting Machinery Institute (SAUS)
HMI Hoist Manufacturers Institute (EA)
HMI Horizontal Motion Index [*Printer technology*]
HMI Horticultural Marketing Inspectorate [*Ministry of Agriculture, Fisheries, and Food*] [*British*]
HMI Host Message Interface (SAUS)
HMI Host Micro Interface [*CompuServe, Inc.*] [*Computer science*] (PCM)
HMI House Magazine Institute [*Later, NY/IABC*]
HMI Hub Management Interface [*Novell, Inc.*] (PCM)
HMI Hughes Medical Institute (SAUO)
HMI Hull Measuring Instrument [*Nautical term*] (NTA)
HMI Human Machine Interface
HMI Hydragyrum Mercury Medium Arc Length and Iodide [*An arc lamp*] (WDMC)
HMI Hypomelanosis of Ito [*Medicine*] (DMAA)
HMI Her (or His) Majesty's Inspector (of Schools) (ODA)
HMIA Haitian Migrant Interdiction Operation (SAUS)
HMIC Heinkel-Messerschmitt-Isetta Club [*Defunct*] (EA)
HMIC Hybrid Microwave Integrated Circuit (ACAE)
HMID Hazardous Material Inventory Database (SAUS)
HMIDPC Hazardous Material Inventory Database Personal Computer (SAUS)
HMIED Honorary Member of the Institute of Engineering Designers (SAUS)
HMIF His [*or Her*] Majesty's Inspector of Factories (ROG)
HMIG Hazardous Materials Indentification Guide (SARE)
HMII Health Mor, Inc. [*NASDAQ symbol*] (SAG)
HMII HMI Industries [*NASDAQ symbol*] (SAG)
HMI Ind HMI Industries [*Associated Press*] (SAG)
HMIM Her Majesty's Inspectorate of Mines (HEAS)
HMIME Honorary Member of the Institution of Mining Engineers (SAUO)
HMIMF His [*or Her*] Majesty's Indian Military Forces
HMI Min E Honorary Member of the Institution of Mining Engineers (SAUO)
HMIN His [*or Her*] Majesty's Indian Navy
HMINET HMI-Network (SAUS)
HMINET I, II Hahn-Meitner Institut Network [*Communications term*] (DCT)
HMINF His (or Her) Majestys Indian Military Forces (SAUS)
HMIO Haitian Migrant Interdiction Operation [*Haitian-US agreement, allowing US Coast Guard to board Haitian vessels on high seas*]
HMIP His [*or Her*] Majesty's Inspectorate of Pollution [*British*]
hMIP Human Macrophage Inflammatory Protein [*Immunochemistry*]
HMIPI His [*or Her*] Majesty's Industrial Pollution Inspectorate for Scotland (DCTA)
HMIPIS Her Majesty's Industrial Pollution Inspectorate for Scotland (HEAS)
HMIRA Hazardous Materials Information Review Act (FOTI)
HMIRS Hazardous Materials Incident Report System (LDOE)
HMIS Hazardous Materials Identification System [*National Paint and Coating Association*]
HMIS Hazardous Materials Information Section (SAUS)
HMIS Hazardous Materials Information System (MCD)
HMIS Hazardous Materials Inventory Statement (AAEL)
HMIS Headquarters Manufacturing Information System (VLIE)
HMIS Health Management Information System (SAUS)
HMIS Health Monitoring Information System (TIMI)
HMIS HERL-RTP Management Information System (SAUO)
HMIS His [*or Her*] Majesty's Indian Ship [*British military*] (DMA)
HMIS His [*or Her*] Majesty's Inspector of Schools (ROG)
HMIS Hospital Management Information System
HMIS Hospital Medical Information System [*Medicine*] (DMAA)
Hmisph Hemispherx BioPharma, Inc. [*Associated Press*] (SAG)
HMIT Her [*or His*] Majesty's Inspector of Taxes [*British*] (ODBW)
HMIX Hazardous Material Information Exchange (SAUS)
HMJ Homer, IL [*Location identifier*] [*FAA*] (FAAL)
HMK HA-LO Industries [*NYSE symbol*] (SG)
HMK Heart Muscle Kinase [*An enzyme*]
HMK Highmark Resources [*Vancouver Stock Exchange symbol*]
HMK His (or Her) Majesty the King (SAUS)
HMK Housemaid's Knee (MELL)

HML............ Hamilton [*Ontario*] [*Seismograph station code, US Geological Survey*] [*Closed*] (SEIS)
HML............ Hammermill Paper Company (SAUO)
HML............ Hammond Metallurgical Laboratory [*Yale*] (MCD)
HML............ Harbor Motor Launch
HML............ Hard Mobile Launcher [*Boeing Aerospace-Loral Defense Systems*]
HML............ Hardware Modelling Library [*Mentor Graphics*] (NITA)
HML............ Harper Memorial Library (SAUO)
HML............ Harvest Maintenance Language (SAUS)
HML............ Hawaii Medical Library, Inc., Honolulu, HI [*OCLC symbol*] (OCLC)
HML............ Heeresmunitionslager [*Army Ammunition Depot*] [*German military - World War II*]
HML............ Hellenic Mediterranean Lines (SAUO)
HML............ Her (or His) Majesty's Lieutenant (ODA)
HML............ His [*or Her*] Majesty's Lieutenant
HML............ Horace Mann League of the USA (EA)
HML............ Horace Mann-Lincoln Institute (SAUS)
HML............ Houston Metals Corp. [*Vancouver Stock Exchange symbol*]
HML............ Hughes Microelectronics, Limited (ACAE)
HML............ Human-Machine Language (VLIE)
HML............ Human Milk Lysozyme [*An enzyme*]
HML............ Huntsman Marine Laboratory [*Canada*] (MSC)
HML............ Marine Helicopter Squadron Light
HMLC.......... High-Mobility Load Carrier [*British military*] (DMA)
HMLC.......... High-Speed Multi-Line Controller (VLIE)
HMLD.......... Handmade Loft-Dried Paper (DGA)
HMLI.......... High Memory Load Indicator (SAUS)
HMLI.......... Horace Mann-Lincoln Institute of School Experimentation [*Columbia University*] (AEBS)
HMLK.......... Hammer Lock (VLIE)
HMLK.......... Hemlock Federal Financial Corp. [*NASDAQ symbol*] (NASQ)
HmlnBk........ Homeland Bankshares Corp. [*Associated Press*] (SAG)
Hm Lock...... Hammer Lock (SAUS)
HMLR.......... His [*or Her*] Majesty's Land Registry
HMLT.......... Hamlet
HMLTN........ Hamilton, OH [*American Association of Railroads railroad junction routing code*]
HMLUIC....... Hunt MLU Integration Contractor (SAUS)
HMM............ Hamamatsu [*Japan*] [*Seismograph station code, US Geological Survey*] (SEIS)
HMM............ Hamilton, MT [*Location identifier*] [*FAA*] (FAAL)
HMM............ Hammond Manufacturing Co. Ltd. [*Toronto Stock Exchange symbol*]
HMM............ Hard Magnetic Material (SAUS)
HMM............ Hardware Multiply Module
HMM............ Heavy Meromyosin [*Biochemistry*]
HMM............ Helicopter Medium Squadron [*Military*] (POLM)
HMM............ Hexamethoxy(methyl)melamine
HMM............ Hexamethylmelamine [*Altretamine*] [*Also, HEX, HXM*] [*Antineoplastic drug*]
HMM............ Hidden Markov Modeling [*Computer science*]
HMM............ His (or Her) Majestys Minister (SAUS)
HMM............ Horizon Mission Methodology [*NASA*]
HMM............ Hyundai Merchant Marine (SAUS)
HMM............ Marine Helicopter Squadron Medium
HMMA.......... 4-Hydroxy-3-Methoxymandelic Acid (STED)
HMMA.......... Hexamethoxymethyl Melamine
HMMA.......... Hydroxymethoxymandelic Acid [*Also, VMA*] [*Biochemistry*]
HMMFC........ House Merchant Marine and Fisheries Committee
HMMH.......... High Mobility Material Handler (SAUS)
HMMHE........ High Mobility Material Handling Equipment (SAUS)
HMML.......... Hill Monastic Manuscript Library [*Saint John's University, Collegeville, MN*]
HMML.......... His [*or Her*] Majesty's Motor Launch
HMMMS........ His [*or Her*] Majesty's Motor Mine Sweeper
HMMP.......... Hazardous Materials Management Plan (AAEL)
HMMP.......... HyperMedia Management Protocol [*Computer science*]
HMMR.......... High-Resolution Multifrequency Microwave Radiometer (MCD)
HMMS.......... Hanford Materials Management System (SAUS)
HMMS.......... HELLFIRE Modular Missile System
HMMS.......... Helmet-Mounted Mobility Sensor [*Military*]
HMMS.......... Highway Maintenance Management System (SAUS)
HMMS.......... Hino Micro Mixing System [*Diesel engines*]
HMMS.......... Hyper-Media Management Schema [*Computer science*]
HMMU.......... Hazardous Materials Management Unit (SAUS)
HMMWV....... High-Mobility Multipurpose Wheeled Vehicle [*Nicknamed "hummer"*] [*Army*] (RDA)
HMMWV-L... High-Mobility Multipurpose Wheeled Vehicle - Lightweight
HMMX.......... Marine Medium Helicopter, Experimental (SAUS)
HMN............ Alamogordo, NM [*Location identifier*] [*FAA*] (FAAL)
hmn............ Harmonium (GROV)
HMN............ Hemmings Motor News [*A publication*]
HMN............ Heptamethylnonane [*Fuel*]
HMN............ Horace Mann Educators Corp. [*NYSE symbol*] (SPSG)
HMN............ Hospitality Motor Inns, Inc. (SAUO)
Hmn............ Human (TBD)
HMN............ Human
HMNAR........ Hart Mountain National Antelope Refuge (SAUO)
HMNC.......... Harmonic (MSA)
HMNF.......... HMN Financial [*NASDAQ symbol*] (TTSB)
HMNF.......... HMN Financial, Inc. [*NASDAQ symbol*] (SAG)
HMNFE........ Her Majesty's Norfolk Flax Establishment [*British*] (BUAC)
HMN Fn........ HMN Financial, Inc. [*Associated Press*] (SAG)
HMN Fuel..... Heptamethylnonane Fuel (SAUS)
HMNII.......... Her Majesty's Nuclear Installations Inspectorate (HEAS)
HMNIP.......... Hydrophobically-Modified Nonionic Polymers [*Organic chemistry*]
Hmn Res...... Human Resources (TBD)
HMNZS........ His [*or Her*] Majesty's New Zealand Ship
HMO............ Habitability Module Outfitting (SSD)
HMO............ Hardware Microcode Optimizer
HMO............ Hazard Mitigation Officer [*Department of Emergency Management*] (DEMM)
HMO............ Health Maintenance Organization
HMO............ Heart Minute Output [*Cardiology*]
HMO............ Hermosillo [*Mexico*] [*Airport symbol*] (OAG)
HMO............ H. Mason [*Oregon*] [*Seismograph station code, US Geological Survey*] (SEIS)
HMO............ Honolulu Magnetic Observatory (CINC)
HMO............ Housing Market Outlook (FOTI)
HMO............ Hueckel Approximation for Molecular Orbitals (SAUS)
HMO............ Hueckel Molecular Orbital [*Atomic physics*]
HMO............ Hypothethical Mean Organism (SAUS)
HMOA.......... Health Maintenance Organization Acts of 1973 and 1988 (WYGK)
HMOA.......... HMO American, Inc. [*NASDAQ symbol*] (COMM)
HMOC.......... Hybrid Method of Characteristics [*Environmental Protection Agency*] (AEPA)
HMOCS........ His [*or Her*] Majesty's Overseas Civil Service
HMOM.......... HyperMedia Object Manager [*Computer science*]
HMO Method... Huckel Molecular Orbital Method (SAUS)
HMOR.......... High Modulus of Rupture (SAUS)
HMOS.......... Habitability Module Outfitting System (SSD)
HMOS.......... Health Maintenance Organization Service [*Public Health Service*]
HMOS.......... High-Density Metal-Oxide Semiconductor (AAEL)
HMOS.......... High-Performance Metal-Oxide Semiconductor (AAEL)
HMOS.......... High resolution Metal Oxide Semiconductor (SAUS)
HMOS.......... High-Speed Metal-Oxide Semiconductor [*ROM*]
HMOS-E....... HMOS [*High Speed Metal Oxide Semiconductor*] Erasable (NITA)
HMOSFET..... Heterostructure MOSFET (SAUS)
HMOW.......... His [*or Her*] Majesty's Office of Works (ROG)
HmowG........ Homeowners Group, Inc. [*Associated Press*] (SAG)
HMOX.......... Heme Oxygenase (DMAA)
HMP............ Habitat Management Plan
HMP............ Handmade Paper
HMP............ Hanford Mission Plan (SAUS)
HMP............ Harper's Magazine Press
HMP............ Health Maintenance Program (MELL)
HMP............ Health Management Plan (SAUS)
HMP............ Heavy Machine-Gun Pod [*Military*] (MUSM)
HMP............ Heavy MAG Pod (SAUS)
HMP............ Heavy Metal Poisoning (MELL)
HMP............ Heidelberg Military Post (SAUO)
HMP............ Heineke-Mikulicz Pyloroplasty [*Medicine*] (MELL)
HMP............ Helmet-Mounted Pick-Offs (MCD)
HMP............ Her [*or His*] Majesty's Prison [*British*] (BARN)
HMP............ Heterogeneous Multi-Processing (SAUS)
HMP............ Hexametaphosphate (SAUS)
HMP............ Hexamethylphosphoramide [*or Hexamethylphosphoric Triamide*] [*Also, HEMPA, HMPA, HMPT, HPT*] [*Organic chemistry*]
HMP............ Hexasodium Metaphosphate [*Inorganic chemistry*]
HMP............ Hexosemonophosphat (SAUS)
HMP............ Hexose Monophosphate Pathway [*Biochemistry*] (DAVI)
HMP............ Hierarchical Multiprocessing (GART)
HMP............ High Melting Point
HMP............ High-Methoxy Pectin [*Food technology*]
HMP............ His/Her Majesty's Prison [*British*] (WDAA)
HMP............ Hoc Monumentum Posuit [*He, or She, Erected This Monument*] [*Latin*]
HMP............ Honda-Mrkos-Pajdusakova [*Comet*]
HMP............ Host Monitoring Protocol (SAUS)
HMP............ Hot Moist Packs [*Medicine*]
HMP............ Hughes Multiprocessor (ACAE)
HMP............ Human Menopausal [*Medicine*] (STED)
HMP............ Humidity Monitoring Panel
HMP............ Hybrid Memory Products Ltd. (SAUO)
HMP............ Hydraulic Maintenance Panel (AAG)
HMP............ Hydromotive Pressure (STED)
HMP............ Hydroxymethyl Hydroperoxide [*Organic chemistry*]
HMP............ Hydroxymethyl(methyl)propanediol [*Organic chemistry*]
HMP............ Hydrozene Monopropellant (MCD)
HMP............ Hypermedia Presentation (SAUS)
HMP............ Papair Terminal SA [*Haiti*] [*ICAO designator*] (FAAC)
HMPA.......... Hawaii Macadamia Producers Association (BUAC)
HMPA.......... Hexamethylphosphoramide [*or Hexamethylphosphoric Triamide*] [*Also, HEMPA, HMP, HMPT, HPT*] [*Organic chemistry*]
HMPA.......... Hydroxymethyl Phosphonic Acid [*Organic chemistry*]
HMPAA........ Hydrophobically-Modified Polyacrylamide [*Organic chemistry*]
HMPAO........ Hexamethylpropylenamine Oxime [*Organic chemistry*]
HMPD.......... Hazardous Materials Packaging Directory (SAUS)
HMPD.......... Hoffman Military Products Division
HMPDH........ 2-Hydroxy-4-Methylpentanoic Acid Dehydrogenase (DB)
HMPEC........ Historical Magazine of the Protestant Episcopal Church (journ.) (SAUS)
HMPG.......... Hydroxy(methoxy)phenylglycol [*Biochemistry*] (AAMN)
HMPGTS...... His [*or Her*] Majesty's Procurator General and Treasury Solicitor
HMPI............ His [*or Her*] Majesty's Pollution Inspectorate [*British*] (DCTA)
HMPIPI........ Her Majesty's Industrial Pollution Inspectorate (EERA)
HMPMA........ Historical Motion Picture Milestones Association
HMPP.......... Hexose Monophosphate Pathway [*Biochemistry*]
HmPrt.......... Home Port Bancorp, Inc. [*Associated Press*] (SAG)
HMPS.......... Hexose Monophosphate Shunt [*Biochemistry*]
HMPS.......... Hitachi Mathematical Programming System (SAUS)

HMPS .... Horizon Medical Products, Inc. [*NASDAQ symbol*] (NASQ)
HMPSA .... Hot Melt Pressure Sensitive Adhesive
HMPT .... Hexamethylphosphoric Triamide [*Also, HEMPA, HMP, HMPA, HPT*] [*Organic chemistry*]
HMPT .... Human Factors, Manpower, Personnel, and Training [*Military*] (RDA)
HMPT .... Hydro Mechanical Power Train (SAUO)
HMPT .... Hydro-Mechanical Power Transmission (SAUS)
HMPTN .... Hampton, FL [*American Association of Railroads railroad junction routing code*]
HmpU .... Hampton Utilities Trust [*Associated Press*] (SAG)
HMPX .... Halstead Metal Products [*Private rail car owner code*]
HMPY .... Hardware Multiplier (SAUS)
HMQ .... Health Management Quarterly (journ.) (SAUS)
HMQ .... Her Majesty the Queen (SAUO)
HMQ .... Homer, LA [*Location identifier*] [*FAA*] (FAAL)
HMQC .... Heteronuclear Multiple-Quantum Coherence [*Physics*]
HMQC .... Heteronuclear Multiple-Quantum Correlation (SAUS)
HMR .... Hamilton Ranch [*California*] [*Seismograph station code, US Geological Survey*] (SEIS)
HMR .... Hammer (MSA)
HMR .... Hazardous Materials Regulation [*Department of Transportation*]
HMR .... Headquarters/House Modification Request (SAUO)
HMR .... Health Management Resources [*Diet program*]
HMR .... High Moisture Resistant
HMR .... Histocytic Medullary Reticulosis [*Oncology*]
HMR .... HMR World Enterprise [*Vancouver Stock Exchange symbol*]
HMR .... Hoboken Manufacturers [*AAR code*]
HMR .... Hoechst Marion Roussel
HMR .... Home Meal Replacement
Hmr .... Homer (DA)
HMR .... Hotel, Motel, Resort Database [*American Database Corp.*] [*Santa Barbara, CA*] [*Information service or system*] (IID)
HMR .... Human Milk Ribonuclease [*An enzyme*]
hMR .... Human Mineralocorticoid Receptor [*Endocrinology*]
HMR .... Humidity-Mixing Ratio (SAUS)
HMR .... Hungry Mind Review [*A publication*] (BRI)
HMR .... Hybrid Modular Redundancy
HMRA .... Hadassah Medical Relief Association (EA)
HMRB .... Hazardous Materials Regulation Board
HMRC .... Heineman Medical Research Center (SAUO)
HMRCS .... His (or Her) Majestys Royal Canadian Ship (SAUS)
HMRF .... Huber-Markov Random Field (SAUS)
HMRI .... Honorary Member of the Royal Institution of Great Britain (SAUO)
HMRI .... Hospital Medical Records Institute (ADWA)
HMRI .... Hubei Mechanical Research Institute [*China*] (BUAC)
HMRI .... Huntington Medical Research Institutes [*Huntington Memorial Hospital*] [*Research center*] (RCD)
HMRL .... Harvard Materials Research Laboratory (SAUS)
HMRL .... His [*or Her*] Majesty's Royal Licence (ROG)
HMRN .... Hull Moulding Release Note
H-mRNA ..... Ribonucleic Acid, H-Chain Messenger [*Biochemistry, genetics*]
HMRP .... Hurricane Microseismic Research Problem [*Aerology*]
HMRR .... His [*or Her*] Majesty's Reserve Regiment [*British military*] (DMA)
HMRRP .... Hazardous Materials Release Response Policy [*Stanford University*]
HMRS .... Historical Model Railway Society [*British*] (BI)
HMRT .... Heavy Material Recovery Team (SAUS)
HMRT .... Heavy Mobile Repair Team (SAUS)
HMRT .... His (or Her) Majestys Rescue Tug (SAUS)
HMRTE .... Human Milk Reverse Transcriptase Enzyme [*Medicine*] (DMAA)
HMS .... Hammer Makers' Society [*A union*] [*British*]
HMS .... Hanford Medical Scheduling (SAUS)
HMS .... Hanford Meteorological Station (SAUS)
HMS .... Hanford Meteorological System (SAUS)
HMS .... Hanford Meteorology Surveys [*Nuclear energy*] (NRCH)
HMS .... Hardened Memory System
HMS .... Harmonic Multiplier Source
HMS .... Harvard Medical School
HMS .... Harvard University Medical School, Countway Library of Medicine, Boston, MA [*OCLC symbol*] (OCLC)
HMS .... Hazardous Materials Safety [*RSPA*] (TAG)
HMS .... Hazardous Materials System (SAUS)
HMS .... Hazardous Materials Systems [*A publication*] (EAAP)
HMS .... Hazards Monitoring System [*NASA*] (KSC)
HMS .... Health Mobilization Series
HMS .... Heavy Materiel Supply Units [*Military*]
HMS .... Heavy-Media Separation [*Mining engineering*] (IAA)
HMS .... Heavy Metal Scraps (RIMS)
HMS .... Helmet-Mounted Sight [*Aviation*]
HMS .... Helmet Mounted Sonar (SAUS)
HMS .... Hemin Storage
HMS .... Hemus Air [*Bulgaria*] [*ICAO designator*] (FAAC)
HMS .... Hestair Management Services Ltd. (SAUO)
HMS .... Heterodyne Millimeter-Wave Spectrometer (SAUS)
HMS .... Hexagonal Mesoporous Silica [*Inorganic chemistry*]
HMS .... Hexose Monophospate Shunt (PDAA)
HMS .... Hierarchical Memory Storage [*Computer science*]
HMS .... High-altitude Multispectral Sounder (SAUS)
HMS .... High Melt Strength [*Plastic moldings*]
HMS .... High Performance Management System (SAUS)
HMS .... Highway Mobile Source [*Environmental Protection Agency*] (GFGA)
HMS .... His [*or Her*] Majesty's Service
HMS .... His [*or Her*] Majesty's Ship
HMS .... His [*or Her*] Majesty's Steamer
HMS .... Historical Metallurgy Society [*British*] (EAIO)
HMS .... History Memory System (MCD)
HMS .... History of Mine Safety (SAUO)
HMS .... Home Marketing Services (SAUS)
HMS .... Home Mission Society (SAUO)
HMS .... Home Missions Society (SAUO)
HMS .... Honeywell's Manufacturing System [*Honeywell Information Systems Ltd.*] [*Software package*] (NCC)
HMS .... Hospital Management System (SAUS)
HMS .... Hospital Marketing Services, Inc. [*Commercial firm*] (DAVI)
HMS .... Host Marriott Services Corp. [*NYSE symbol*] (SAG)
HMS .... Hours, Minutes, Seconds
HMS .... Hughes Materials Specification (ACAE)
HMS .... Hull Monitoring System (PDAA)
HMS .... Hull-Mounted Set (SAUS)
HMS .... Humility of Mary Service (EA)
HMS .... Hungarian Meteorological Service (SAUS)
HMS .... Hydrogen Mitigation System (SAUS)
HMS .... Hypothetical Mean Strain (SAUS)
HMSA .... Hardware Manufacturers Statistical Association [*Later, BHMA*]
HMSA .... Hawaii Medical Service Association (SAUO)
HMSA .... Hawk Mountain Sanctuary Association (EA)
HMSA .... Head-Mounted Sonic Aid (SAUS)
HMSA .... Health Manpower Shortage Area
HMSA .... Historic Motor Sports Association (EA)
HMSA .... Hydroxymethanesulfonate [*Organic chemistry*]
HMSAS .... His [*or Her*] Majesty's South African Ship (DAS)
HMSAS .... Hypertrophic Muscular Subaortic Stenosis [*Cardiology*] (MAE)
HMS(BOE) ... Hazardous Materials Systems (Bureau of Explosives) (EA)
HMSC .... Hatfield Marine Science Center [*Marine science*] (OSRA)
hMSC .... Human Mesenchymal Stem Cells
HMSC .... HumaScan, Inc. [*NASDAQ symbol*] (SAG)
HMSC .... Huntsman Marine Science Center (SAUS)
HMS/D .... Helmet Mounted Sight/Display (SAUS)
HMSD .... Homestead Savings Association (SAUO)
HMSDC .... Hybrid Multiplexed Synchro Digital Converter (SAUS)
HMS Display... Helmet Mounted Symbolic Display (SAUS)
HMSF .... Hexanmethylenetetraselenafulvalene (SAUS)
HMSG .... Hirshhorn Museum and Sculpture Garden (SAUO)
HMSH .... Hanford Museums of Science and History (SAUS)
HMSI .... Hebei Machinery Science Institute [*China*] (BUAC)
HMSL .... Hemerdon Mining & Smelting Limited (SAUO)
HMSLD .... Helium Mass Spectrometer Leak Detector (SAUS)
HMSM .... Heavy Mortar, Smart Munition
HMS/M .... His [*or Her*] Majesty's Submarine
HMSN .... Hereditary Motor and Sensory Neuropathy [*Medicine*] (MELL)
HMSO .... His [*or Her*] Majesty's Stationery Office
HMSO .... Honolulu Magnetic and Seismological Observatory
HMSR .... Hazardous Material Shipment Record (SAUS)
HMSR .... HemaSure Inc. [*NASDAQ symbol*] (TTSB)
HMSRR .... Harpoon Missile Select Relay Rack [*Missiles*] (MCD)
HMSS .... Helmet-Mounted Sight Set
HMSS .... Helmet Mounted Sight System [*Military*] (ACAE)
HMSS .... HMSS, Inc. (SAUO)
HMSS .... Hospital Management Systems Society [*Later, HIMSS*] (EA)
HMSS .... Religious Sisters of the Apostolate of the Blessed Sacrament (TOCD)
HMSS .... Sisters of Mercy of the Blessed Sacrament (TOCD)
HMSST .... Hydrogen Mitigation System Source Term (SAUS)
HMSTD .... Homestead
Hmstke .... Homestake Mining Co. [*Associated Press*] (SAG)
HMSU .... High-Resolution Microwave Sounding Unit (CARB)
HMSY .... Health Management Systems [*NASDAQ symbol*] (TTSB)
HMSY .... Health Management Systems, Inc. [*NASDAQ symbol*] (SAG)
HMT .... Air Nova [*British*] [*ICAO designator*] (FAAC)
HMT .... Hand Microtelephone (IAA)
HMT .... Hardware Measurement Tool (SAUS)
HMT .... Hazardous Materials Table [*Environmental science*] (COE)
HMT .... Health Management Teams (SAUS)
HmT .... Helminthosporium maydis race T [*A toxin-producing fungus*]
HMT .... Hematocrit [*Medicine*] (EDAA)
HMT .... Hemet, CA [*Location identifier*] [*FAA*] (FAAL)
HMT .... Hexamethoxytriphenylene [*Organic chemistry*]
HMT .... Hexamethylenetetramine [*Also, HMTA*] [*Organic chemistry*]
HMT .... Hexamethylenetetranmine (SAUS)
HMT .... Hexamethylentetraamin (SAUS)
HMT .... Hexamethylentetramin (SAUS)
HMT .... High Mobility Trailer
HMT .... High Mobility Trainer (SAUS)
HMT .... Hindustan Machine Tools Ltd. (SAUO)
HMT .... His [*or Her*] Majesty's Transport
HMT .... His [*or Her*] Majesty's Trawler
HMT .... His [*or Her*] Majesty's Troopship [*British military*] (DMA)
HMT .... His [*or Her*] Majesty's Tug [*British military*] (DMA)
HMT .... Histamine Methyltransferase [*An enzyme*]
HMT .... Hospital Management Team [*Medicine*] (EDAA)
HMT .... Host Marriot [*Formerly, Marriott Corp.*] [*NYSE symbol*] (SPSG)
HMT .... Human Metallothioneine [*Biochemistry*]
hMT .... Human Molar Thyrotropin (MAE)
HMT .... Hydrazine Monopropellant Thruster
hMT .... Hydroxymethyl Uracil [*Organic chemistry*] (DAVI)
HMT .... Hypoxanthine/Methotrexate/Thymidine Medium (SAUS)
HMTA .... Hazardous Materials Transportation Act [*1975*]
HMTA .... Hexamethylenetetramine [*Also, HMT*] [*Organic chemistry*]
HMTA .... Hotel-Motel Association (SAUO)
HMTAX .... Local Hotel/Motel Excise Tax (SAUO)
HMTC .... Hazardous Materials Technical Center [*Rockville, MD*] [*DoD*] (GRD)
HMTC .... Hexamethylenetetramine Camphorate (SAUS)

HMTF.......... Hydrodynamic Modulation Transfer Function (SAUS)
HMTPSD...... HAWK [*Homing All the Way Killer*] Missile Test Program System Device (DWSG)
HMTR.......... Hazardous Materials Transportation Regulations [*Environmental science*] (COE)
HMTR.......... Highly Mobile Tactical Radar (SAUS)
HMTS.......... Health Message Testing Services [*Department of Health and Human Services*] (GFGA)
HMTS.......... His [*or Her*] Majesty's Telegraph Ship
HMTSeF....... Hexamethylenetetraselenafulvalene (SAUS)
HMTSF......... Hexamethylenetetraselenafulvalenium [*Organic chemistry*]
HMTSF......... Hexamethylentetraselenofulvalin (SAUS)
HMTSF-TCNQ... Hexamethylentetraselenofulvalintetracyanochinodimethan (SAUS)
HMTT.......... Hexamethyl Trithiane (SAUS)
HMTT.......... Hexamethyltrithiane [*Organic chemistry*]
HMTT.......... High-Mobility Tactical Trucks (MCD)
HMTT.......... HMT Technology Corp. [*NASDAQ symbol*] (SAG)
HMTTch....... HMT Technology Corp. [*Associated Press*] (SAG)
HMTTeF....... Hexamethylenetetratellurafulvalene (SAUS)
HMTTF......... Hexamethylenetetrathiofulvalene (SAUS)
HMTUSA...... Hazardous Materials Transportation and Uniform Safety Act
HMTUSA...... Hazardous Materials Uniform Safety Act (SAUO)
HmtwBc....... Hometown Bancorp, Inc. [*Associated Press*] (SAG)
HMU............ Hammond, LA [*Location identifier*] [*FAA*] (FAAL)
HMU............ Hardware Mockup (NASA)
HMU............ Hazardous Material Unit (SAUS)
HMU............ Health Monitoring Unit (SAUS)
HMU............ Helmet Mounted Unit (SAUS)
HMU............ Hot Mock-Up (SAUS)
HMU............ Hydraulic Management Unit
HMU............ Hydraulic Mock-Up
HMU............ Hydromechanical Unit
HMU............ Hydroxymethyl Uracil (SAUS)
HMU............ Hydroxymethyluracil [*Organic chemistry*]
HMUT.......... High-Modulus Undertread [*Tire design*]
HMUX.......... Hybrid Multiplexer [*Telecommunications*]
HMV............ Henbane Mosaic Virus [*Plant pathology*]
HMV............ High Magnification Viewer
HMV............ High Mass Vehicle
HMV............ High Velocity Missile (SAUS)
HMV............ His Master's Voice [*Phonograph records*]
HMV............ Holston Mountain, TN [*Location identifier*] [*FAA*] (FAAL)
HMV............ Hydrodynamically Modulated Voltammetry [*Analytical chemistry*]
HMV............ Hydrogen Manual Valve (MCD)
HMVEC........ Human Dermal Microvascular Endothelial Cell [*Biochemistry*]
HMVMA........ High Mach Vehicle Mission Applications (ACAE)
HMVS.......... Hyper Velocity Medium Support Weapon System (SAUS)
HMW........... Dutch Society of Sciences (SAUO)
HMW........... Hamilton Watch Co. (SAUO)
HMW........... Health, Morale, and Welfare (COE)
HMW........... Hectometric Wave (SAUS)
HMW........... Height of Maxwind (SAUS)
HMW........... High Molecular Weight [*Also, HM*] [*Organic chemistry*]
HMW........... How to Market to Women [*A publication*]
HMW........... Hypervelocity Missile Weapon (SAUS)
HMWA......... Hairdressing Manufacturers' and Wholesalers' Association [*British*] (BI)
HMWC......... Health of Munition Workers Committee [*World War I*] [*British*]
HMWC......... Heigh Molecular Weight Component (SAUS)
HMWC......... High-Mobility Weapons Carrier [*Army*]
HMWC......... High Molecular Weight Component (MELL)
HMWC/CSV... High-Mobility Weapons Carrier/Combat Support Vehicle [*Army*] (MCD)
HMWFC....... High-Molecular-Weight Fibrin Complex [*Medicine*] (EDAA)
HMWG......... Huma Multipurpose Women's Group [*Kenya*] (BUAC)
HMWGP....... High Molecular Weight Glycoprotein [*Medicine*] (DMAA)
HMW HDPE... High Molecular Weight High-Density Polyethylene (SAUS)
HMWK......... Advanced Voice Technologies [*NASDAQ symbol*] (TTSB)
HMWK......... Advanced Voice Technologies, Inc. [*NASDAQ symbol*] (SAG)
HMWK......... High Molecular Weight Kininogen [*Biochemistry*]
HMWKa....... High Molecular Weight Kallikrein [*Biochemistry*]
HMWKU....... Advanced Voice Tehcnol's 'Unit' [*NASDAQ symbol*] (TTSB)
HMWKW...... Advanced Voice Technol Wrrt [*NASDAQ symbol*] (TTSB)
HMWP......... High-Molecular-Weight Protein [*or Polypeptide*] [*Biochemistry*]
HMWPE....... High-Molecular-Weight Polyethylene (MCD)
HMWRK....... Homework
HMWS......... Hypervelocity Missile Weapon System (SAUS)
HMX........... Advanced Marine Helicopter Squadron (SAUS)
HMX........... Cyclotetramethylene Tetranitramine (SAUS)
HMX........... Denver, CO [*Location identifier*] [*FAA*] (FAAL)
HMX........... Hartmarx Corp. [*NYSE symbol*] (SPSG)
HMX........... Heat, Massage, Exercise [*Medicine*]
HMX........... Helicopter Squadron [*Military*] (POLM)
HMX........... High-Melting Explosive [*Proprietary name for cyclotetramethylene tetramintriamine*]
HMX........... Marine Helicopter Experimental Squadron
HMX........... Phlegmatised octol (SAUS)
HMX-1........ Marine Helicopter Experimental Squadron One [*Organized in 1947 for the development and study of helicopter tactics*]
HMXB......... High-Mass X-Ray Binary [*Star system*]
HMY........... Heilig-Meyers Co. [*NYSE symbol*] (SPSG)
HMY........... High Modulus Yarn
HMY........... His [*or Her*] Majesty's Yacht [*Navy*] [*British*]
HMY........... Hundred Million Years (SAUO)
HMY........... Lexington, OK [*Location identifier*] [*FAA*] (FAAL)
hmy............ square hectometer (SAUS)
HMyP.......... Hierarchical Multimicroprocessor (SAUS)
HMZ........... Nigerian International Air Services Ltd. [*ICAO designator*] (FAAC)
hn.............. Hac Nocte [*This Night*] [*Latin*] (WDAA)
HN.............. Haematemesis Neonatorum (DB)
HN.............. Hafslund Nycomed ADS [*NYSE symbol*] (SPSG)
HN.............. Handling-Normal (SAUS)
HN.............. Hardware Capability Name (NITA)
Hn.............. Haven [*Maps and charts*]
HN.............. Haygarth's Node [*Medicine*] (MELL)
HN.............. Head and Neck (DMAA)
HN.............. Headline News [*Cable television channel*]
HN.............. Head Nurse
HN.............. Headquarters Name [*Dialog*] [*Searchable field*] [*Information service or system*] (NITA)
HN.............. Health Notice (HEAS)
HN.............. Hear Now [*An association*] (EA)
HN.............. Helium Neon [*LASER*] (DGA)
HN.............. Heller-Nelson [*Syndrome*] [*Medicine*] (DB)
HN.............. Hemagglutinin-Neuraminidase [*An enzyme*]
HN.............. Hematemesis Neonatorum [*Medicine*] (DMAA)
HN.............. Hemorrhage of Newborn [*Medicine*] (DMAA)
hn.............. Henna [*Philately*]
Hn.............. Henricus de Baila [*Flourished, 1169-70*] [*Authority cited in pre-1607 legal work*] (DSA)
HN.............. Hensen's Node [*Medicine*] (MELL)
HN.............. Hereditary Nephritis [*Medicine*] (MAE)
HN.............. Heroes of the Nations [*A publication*]
HN.............. Herpes Network [*Defunct*] (EA)
hn.............. Heterogeneous Nuclear [*Biochemistry*]
HN.............. Hexagonal Nipple (SAUS)
HN.............. Hexagonal Nut
HN.............. Hexagon Nut (SAUS)
HN.............. High Foliage Nester [*Ecology*]
HN.............. High Necrosis [*Medicine*] (DMAA)
HN.............. High Nitrogen [*Clinical chemistry*]
HN.............. High Nutrition
HN.............. Hilar Node [*Medicine*] (MAE)
HN.............. Hindustan-Aeronautics Ltd. [*India*] [*ICAO aircraft manufacturer identifier*] (ICAO)
HN.............. Histamine-Containing Neuron (DB)
HN.............. Hoc Nocte [*Tonight*] [*Pharmacy*]
HN.............. Holds Need [*Travel industry*] (TVEL)
HN.............. Home Nursing
HN.............. Honda [*Society of Automotive Engineers auto manufacturer code for service information interchange*]
HN.............. Honduras [*ANSI two-letter standard code*] (CNC)
hn.............. Horn (WDAA)
HN.............. Horn
HN.............. Hospitalman [*Nonrated enlisted man*] [*Navy*]
HN.............. Host Nation (AABC)
HN.............. Host to Network [*Computer science*]
HN.............. House Nigger [*Derogatory nickname for an obsequious black person*]
HN.............. Human Nutrition [*Dietetics*] (DAVI)
HN.............. Human Nutrition Research Division [*of ARS, Department of Agriculture*]
HN.............. [*The*] Hutchinson & Northern Railway Co. [*AAR code*]
HN.............. Hydronephrosis [*Medicine*] (MELL)
HN.............. Hypertrophic Neuropathy [*Medicine*] (DMAA)
HN.............. Naturalis Historia [*of Pliny the Elder*] [*Classical studies*] (OCD)
HN.............. Nitrogen Mustard [*Also, M, MBA, NM*] [*Antineoplastic drug, war-gas base*] [*Army symbol used with numerals, as HN1*]
HN.............. NLM-Dutch Airlines [*ICAO designator*] (AD)
HN.............. Sunset to Sunrise [*ICAO*] (FAAC)
HN_2............. Mechlorethamine [*Nitrogen mustard*] (MEDA)
HN_2............. Nitrogen Mustard [*Antineoplastic drug*] (DAVI)
HN3............ Nitrogen mustard gas (SAUS)
HNA............ Chicago, IL [*Location identifier*] [*FAA*] (FAAL)
HNA............ Hanamaki [*Japan*] [*Airport symbol*] [*Obsolete*] (OAG)
HNA............ Harrison Narcotic Act
HNA............ Henson Aviation, Inc. (SAUO)
HNA............ Heparin Neutralizing Activity [*Medicine*]
HNA............ Hierarchical Network Architecture
HNA............ Higher National Authority (SAUS)
HNA............ High Nickel Alloy
HNA............ Hitachi Network Architecture
HNA............ Hockey North America (EA)
HNA............ Hospice and Palliative Nurses Association (SAUO)
HNA............ Hospice Nurses Association (EA)
HNA............ Host Nation Approval (SAUO)
HNA............ Host Nation Assistance (SAUS)
HNA............ Hsinhua News Agency (SAUO)
HNA............ Hungarian National Alliance (BUAC)
HNA............ Hydraulic Network Analysis (SAUS)
HNA............ Hydroxynaphthoic Acid (SAUS)
HNAA.......... Holistic Nurses Association of Australia
HNAB.......... Hexanitroazobenzene [*Organic chemistry*]
HNAD.......... Hyperosmolar Nonacidotic Diabetes [*Medicine*] (MELL)
HNADC........ Honorary Naval Aide-de-Camp [*British*]
HNAL.......... Hitachi Numerical Analysis (SAUS)
HNANB........ Hepatitis nonA nonB (SAUS)
HNARMENTD... Hereinafter Mentioned [*Legal*] [*British*] (ROG)
HNAT.......... Hartford National Corp. (SAUO)
HNB............ Hexanitrobiphenyl (SAUS)
HNB............ Hexnitrobenzene (ACAE)

HNB .... Hrvatska Narodna Banka [*Croatian National Bank*]
HNB .... Human Neuroblastoma (DB)
HNB .... Huntingburg, IN [*Location identifier*] [*FAA*] (FAAL)
HNB .... Hydroxynitrobenzyl [*Organic chemistry*]
HNB .... Hydroxynitrobenzylbromide [*Organic chemistry*] (MAE)
HNB .... New Britain General Hospital, Health Sciences Library, New Britain, CT [*OCLC symbol*] (OCLC)
HNBA .... Hispanic National Bar Association (EA)
HNBC .... Harleysville National Corp. [*NASDAQ symbol*] (SAG)
HNBC .... Harleysville Natl [*NASDAQ symbol*] (TTSB)
HNBEFMENTD... Hereinbefore Mentioned [*Legal*] [*British*] (ROG)
HNBI .... Hellenic National Broadcasting Institute (SAUO)
HNBK .... Handbook (WDAA)
H-NBR .... Hydrogenated Nitrile Butadiene Rubber (SAUS)
HNC .... Center for Disease Control, Atlanta, GA [*OCLC symbol*] (OCLC)
HNC .... Hand Numerical Control (IAA)
HNC .... Harbors and Navigation Code (SAUS)
HNC .... Hartford National Corp. (EFIS)
HNC .... Heavy Nuclei Collector (SAUS)
HNC .... Higher National Certificate [*British*]
HNC .... High National Council
HNC .... Holistic Nurse Certified (NUJO)
HNC .... Human Nature Cooperative (SAUO)
HNC .... Human Nature Council (SAUO)
HNC .... Human Nutrition Center [*Oklahoma State University*] [*Research center*] (RCD)
HNC .... Human Nutrition Council (SAUO)
HNC .... Hypernephroma Cell (DB)
HNC .... Hypothalamic-Neurohygophysical Complex (SAUS)
HNC .... Hypothalamo-Neurohypophyseal Complex [*Endocrinology*]
HNC/D .... Higher National Certificate/Diploma (ACII)
HNCF .... Hospice of North Central Florida (NRGU)
HNCIAWPRC... Hungarian National Committee of the International Association on Water Pollution Research and Control (SAUO)
HNCIMU .... Hungarian National Committee for the International Mathematical Union (SAUO)
HNCIP .... Housewifes Non-Contributory Invalidity Pension (SAUS)
HNCMT .... Hawkesbury Nepean Catchment Management Trust [*Resource management*] [*Australia*]
HN-CMT .... Hypertrophic Neuropathy of the Charcot-Marie-Tooth [*Medicine*] (EDAA)
HNCO .... Henley Manufacturing Corp. [*NASDAQ symbol*] (COMM)
HNCS .... HNC Software [*NASDAQ symbol*] (TTSB)
HNCS .... HNC Software, Inc. [*NASDAQ symbol*] (SAG)
HNCS .... Homogenous Numerically Calculated Surface [*Automotive lighting*]
HNC Sft .... HNC Software, Inc. [*Associated Press*] (SAG)
HND .... Croatian Numismatic Society (SAUO)
HND .... Hand (WGA)
HND .... Higher National Degree (SAUS)
HND .... Higher National Diploma [*British*]
HND .... Highways for National Defense [*MTMC*] (TAG)
HND .... Hinderliter Industries, Inc. [*AMEX symbol*] (COMM)
HND .... Honduras [*ANSI three-letter standard code*] (CNC)
HND .... Huntsville Nuclear Division [*Army Corps of Engineers*] (RDA)
HND .... State Historical Society of North Dakota, Bismarck, ND [*OCLC symbol*] (OCLC)
HND .... Tokyo [*Japan*] Haneda Airport [*Airport symbol*] (OAG)
HNDBK .... Handbook
HNDC .... Hittman Nuclear & Development Company (SAUO)
HND CONT ... Hand Control (SAUS)
HNDCPD ...... Handicapped
HNDCRFT .... Handicraft
HNDDIPRT ... Hand-Discharge Printed (SAUS)
HND GEN ..... Hand Generator (SAUS)
HNDI .... Hinderliter Industries, Inc. (SAUO)
HNDICS .... Hellenic National Defence Integrated Communication System (SAUO)
HNDLER ...... Handler (NASA)
Hndlg/Shpng... Handling & Shipping Charges (SAUS)
HNDLR .... Handler
HNDM .... Hareri National Democratic Movement (SAUO)
HNDO .... Hadiya Nationality Democratic Organization (SAUS)
HNDP .... Handicap
HNDPRNT .... Handprint
HNDR .... Heteronuclear Double Resonance (IAA)
HNDRL .... Hand Rail
HND RST .... Hand Reset (SAUS)
HNDSN .... Henderson, KY [*American Association of Railroads railroad junction routing code*]
HNDST .... Handset
HNDT .... Holographic Nondestructive Testing
HNDT .... Holography and Nondestructive Testing (SAUS)
HNDWL ...... Handwheel
HNDY .... Handy
HNDYMN .... Handyman
HNE .... Harriman & Northeastern R. R. [*AAR code*]
HNE .... Hexanitroethane (SAUS)
HNE .... HN Engineering, Inc. [*Burnaby, BC*] [*Telecommunications*] (TSSD)
HNE .... Human Neutrophil Elastase [*An enzyme*]
HNE .... Hydronuclear Experiments [*Nuclear physics*]
HNE .... Hydroxynonenal [*Biochemistry*]
HNE .... National Institute of Environmental Health Sciences, Research Triangle Park, NC [*OCLC symbol*] (OCLC)
HNE .... Tahneta Pass Lodge, AK [*Location identifier*] [*FAA*] (FAAL)
HNEA .... Hughes Newport Employees' Association (ACAE)
HNED .... Horizontal Null External Distance (OA)
HNEI .... Hawaii Natural Energy Institute [*University of Hawaii at Manoa*] [*Research center*] (RCD)
HNEPI .... Hunan Environmental Protection Institute [*China*] (BUAC)
HNEQ .... Method of Homogeneous Nonequilibrium (SAUO)
HNET .... Houston Network (SAUS)
HNET .... Houston Network Controller [*NASA*] (KSC)
HNET .... Road Net File (SAUO)
HNF .... Hepatocyte Nuclear Factor [*Biochemistry*]
HNF .... Hereditary Nephritis Foundation (SAUO)
HNF .... HIPPI Networking Forum (SAUS)
HNF .... Home Nursing Foundation (SAUO)
HNF .... Hungarian National Front [*Political party*] (BUAC)
HNF .... Hydrazine Nitroform (SAUS)
HNF1 .... Hepatocyte Nuclear Factor 1 [*Genetics*]
HNFBR .... Horn Fiber
HNFC .... Hinsdale Financial [*NASDAQ symbol*] (TTSB)
HNFC .... Hinsdale Financial Corp. [*NASDAQ symbol*] (SAG)
HNG .... Hanging (MSA)
hng .... Hanging (VRA)
HNG .... Hawaiian National Guard (SAUO)
HNG .... Hawaii National Guard (SAUS)
HNG .... Heavy Narrow Gap [*Nuclear energy*] (NUCP)
HNG .... Hienghene [*New Caledonia*] [*Airport symbol*] [*Obsolete*] (OAG)
HNG .... Hilfsfonds fuer die Opfer der Nuernberger Gesetze [*A publication*] (BJA)
HNG .... Hinge (MSA)
HNG .... Hongo [*Japan*] [*Seismograph station code, US Geological Survey*] [*Closed*] (SEIS)
HNG .... Houston Natural Gas Corporation (SAUO)
Hng .... Hungarian Patent Document (journ.) (SAUS)
HNGL .... Helium Neon Gas LASER
HNGNA .... Hellenic National Graduate Nurses Association [*Greece*] (BUAC)
HNGR .... Hangar (KSC)
HNGRY .... Hungry
HNGS .... Hamilton National Genealogical Society (EA)
HNGS .... Hellenic Naval General Staff (SAUS)
hngscr .... Hanging Scroll (VRA)
HNH .... Handy & Harman [*NYSE symbol*] (SPSG)
HNH .... Hanover [*New Hampshire*] [*Seismograph station code, US Geological Survey*] (SEIS)
HNH .... Hoonah [*Alaska*] [*Airport symbol*] (OAG)
HNHE .... Human Nutrition and Home Economics Bureau (SAUO)
HNHIA .... Headway National Head Injuries Association (BUAC)
HNHIC .... Hepatic Nonheme Iron Content [*Physiology*]
HNI .... Health News Institute [*Defunct*]
HNI .... Holmes & Narver, Inc. (MCD)
HNI .... Holmes and Narver, Incorporated (SAUO)
HNI .... HON Industries [*NYSE symbol*]
HNI .... Hospitalization not Indicated (MELL)
HNI .... National Institutes of Health, Bethesda, MD [*OCLC symbol*] (OCLC)
HNIC .... Head Nigger in Charge [*Slang*]
HNIC .... Hockey Night in Canada [*Television program*]
HNickJS .... Hicksville Junior High School, Hicksville, NY [*Library symbol*] [*Library of Congress*] (LCLS)
HNIG .... Human Normal Immunoglobulin [*Medicine*] (PDAA)
HNIL .... High-Noise-Immunity Logic
HNIS .... Heritage Bancorp, Inc. (Massachusetts) [*NASDAQ symbol*] (COMM)
HNIS .... Human Nutrition Information Service [*Hyattsville, MD*] [*Department of Agriculture*]
HNIW .... Hexanitrohexazaisowurtzitane [*An explosive*]
HNJ .... Hyphenation and Justification (SAUS)
HN(JC) .... Hospitalman (Junior College) [*Navy*] (DNAB)
HNK .... Hancock, NY [*Location identifier*] [*FAA*] (FAAL)
HNK .... Hinchinbrook Island [*Australia*] [*Airport symbol*]
HNKC .... Hyperosmolar Nonketotic Coma [*Medicine*] (MELL)
HNKDC .... Hyperosmolar Nonketotic Diabetic Coma [*Medicine*] (STED)
HNKDS .... Hyperosmolar Nonketotic Diabetic State [*Medicine*] (STED)
HNL .... Hareri National League (SAUS)
HNL .... Helium Neon LASER
HNL .... Histiocytic Necrotizing Lymphadenitis [*Medicine*] (MELL)
HNL .... Holifield National Laboratory [*Later, Oak Ridge National Laboratory*]
HNL .... Honduran Lempira (SAUS)
Hnl .... Honolulu (SAUS)
HNL .... Hourly Noise Level
HNLC .... High Nutrient, Low Chlorophyll [*Biological oceanography*]
HNLG .... Handling
HNLM .... High Noise-Level Margin
HNLN .... Hospitalization No Longer Necessary (STED)
HNM .... Hana [*Hawaii*] [*Airport symbol*] (OAG)
HNM .... Hanna Mining Corp. (SAUO)
HNM .... Helicopter Noise Model [*OST*] (TAG)
HNM .... Hertzberg-New Method [*Standard periodical binding*]
HNM .... Hexanitromannite [*Organic chemistry*]
HNM .... High Neonatal Morality (MELL)
HNM .... M.A. Hanna Co. [*NYSE symbol*] (COMM)
HNMATA ...... Hosiery Needle Makers and Allied Trades Association (SAUO)
HNMC .... Honda New Model Center
HNML .... Hindu Meal [*Airline notation*]
HNMP .... Hypertext Network Management Platform [*Communications term*] (DCT)
HNMR .... High-Resolution Nuclear Magnetic Resonance
HNMS .... High NATO Military Structure (NATG)
HNMZ .... Hobelt #7 Mine [*Federal Railroad Administration identification code*]
HNN .... Henderson, WV [*Location identifier*] [*FAA*] (FAAL)
HNN .... Hydrocephalus News & Notes (SAUO)

HNNNR .... Henna Ness National Nature Reserve (SAUS)
HNNNR .... Herma Ness National Nature Reserve (SAUO)
HNNS .... Hughes Night Navigation System (ACAE)
HNO .... Hals-Nasen-Ohrenklinik und Poliklinik (SAUS)
HNO .... Henderson, TX [*Location identifier*] [*FAA*] (FAAL)
HNO .... Hercegnovi [*Yugoslavia*] [*Airport symbol*] (AD)
HNO .... Honcho Gold Mines, Inc. [*Vancouver Stock Exchange symbol*]
HNO .... Hrvatski Narodni Odbor [*Croatian National Resistance*] [*Former Yugoslavia*] (PD)
HNO_3 .... Nitric Acid [*Chemistry*] (DAVI)
HNODC .... Hellenic National Oceanographic Data Centre (SAUS)
HNOE .... Heteronuclear Overhauser Effect (SAUS)
HNOSB .... Hardened Nuclear Optical Sensor Bed (ACAE)
HNOy .... Nitrous acid (SAUS)
HNP .... Haddam Neck Plant [*Nuclear energy*] (NRCH)
HNP .... Haleakala National Park (SAUO)
HNP .... Hartsville Nuclear Plant (NRCH)
HNP .... Harvard Negotiation Project
HNP .... Hereditary Nephritic Protein (STED)
HNP .... Herniated Nucleus Pulposus [*Medicine*]
HNP .... Herstigte Nasionale Party [*Reconstituted National Party*] [*South Africa*] [*Political party*] (PPW)
HNP .... High Needle Position [*on dial*]
HNP .... High Nitrile Polymer (SAUS)
HNP .... Huaneng Power International, Inc. [*NYSE symbol*] (SAG)
HNP .... Human Neurophysin [*Medicine*] (MELL)
HNP .... Hungarian National Party [*Political party*] (BUAC)
HNP .... Minneapolis, MN [*Location identifier*] [*FAA*] (FAAL)
HNP .... Parklawn Health Library, Rockville, MD [*OCLC symbol*] (OCLC)
HNPA .... Home Numbering Plan Area [*AT & T*]
HNPCC .... Hereditary Nonpolyposis Colon Cancer [*Medicine*]
HNPCC .... Hereditary Nonpolyposis Colorectal Cancer [*Medicine*] (HGEN)
HNPF .... Hallam Nuclear Power Facility [*Decommissioned*] [*AEC*]
HNPL .... High-Level Network Processing Language [*Computer science*] (MHDI)
HNPO .... Host Nation Procurement Office (SAUS)
HNPP .... Hereditary Neuropathy with Liability to Pressure Palsies
HNPSA .... Homeland Non-Party Serbian Association (BUAC)
HNQ .... Hydroxynaphthoquinone [*Organic chemistry*]
HNR .... Haiti National Airlines [*ICAO designator*] (FAAC)
HNR .... Handwritten Numeral Recognition (IAA)
HNR .... Harlan, IA [*Location identifier*] [*FAA*] (FAAL)
HNR .... Heaston Resources Ltd. [*Vancouver Stock Exchange symbol*]
HNR .... Hiss Noise Reduction (SAUS)
HNR .... Honiara [*Solomon Islands*] [*Seismograph station code, US Geological Survey*] (SEIS)
hnr .... Honoree [*MARC relator code*] [*Library of Congress*] (LCCP)
HNR .... Nordic Council of Organisations for the Disabled (BUAC)
HNRC .... HOMS National Reference Centre (SAUO)
HNRC .... Human Nutrition Research Center (SAUS)
HNRC .... USDA [*United States Department of Agriculture*] Human Nutrition Research Center on Aging at Tufts [*Tufts University*] [*Research center*] (RCD)
HNRIM .... Human Nutrition Research and Information Management System [*National Institute of Health*]
HNRIMS ...... Human Nutrition Research Information Management System (SAUS)
HnRNA .... Heterogeneous nuclear Ribonucleic Acid (SAUS)
hnRNA .... Ribonucleic Acid, Heterogeneous Nuclear [*Biochemistry, genetics*]
hnRNP .... Heterogeneous nuclear Ribonucleoprotein (SAUS)
hnRNP .... Ribonucleoprotein, Heterogeneous [*Biochemistry*]
HNRS .... Honors (ADA)
HNRTA .... Henrietta, MO [*American Association of Railroads railroad junction routing code*]
HNRYA .... Henryetta, OK [*American Association of Railroads railroad junction routing code*]
HNS .... Croatian People's Party [*Political party*] (PSAP)
HNS .... Draft International Convention on Liability and Compensation for Damage in Connection with the Carriage of Hazardous and Noxious Substances by Sea (SAUO)
HNS .... Haines [*Alaska*] [*Airport symbol*] (OAG)
HNS .... Hamilton Normal School
HNS .... Hanes Corporation (SAUO)
HNS .... Haveeru News Service [*Maldives*] (EY)
HNS .... Hazardous and Noxious Substance
HNS .... Hazardous Substances by Sea (SAUS)
HNS .... Hazleton Nuclear Science Corp. (SAUO)
HNS .... Head and Neck Surgery [*Medical specialty*] (DHSM)
HNS .... Head, Neck, and Shaft [*of a bone*] [*Osteology*]
HNS .... Helgeson Nuclear Services, Inc. (SAUO)
HNS .... Hellenic Naval Ship (SAUS)
HNS .... Hellenic News Service (SAUO)
HNS .... Hexanitrostilbene [*High explosive*]
HNS .... High Nitrogen Solubility (SAUS)
HNS .... Holy Name Society [*Defunct*] (EA)
HNS .... Home Nursing Supervisor [*Red Cross*]
HNS .... Hospitality Network Service (SAUS)
HNS .... Host Nation Support [*Military*]
HNS .... Hrvatska Narodna Stranka [*Croatian People's Party*] [*Political party*]
HNS .... Hughes Network Systems
HNS .... Hyperbolic Navigation System (SAUO)
HNS .... Hypernasal Speech (MELL)
HNSA .... Host Nation Support Agreement [*Navy*] (ANA)
HNSC .... House National Security Committee (SAUS)
HNSD .... Hansard (DCTA)
HNSF .... Hungarian National Sports Federation (EA)
HNSHA .... Hereditary Nonspherocytic Hemolytic Anemia [*Medicine*]
HNSHA .... Hereditary Nonspherocytic Hemolytic Leukemia [*Medicine*] (STED)
HNSI .... Home Nutritional Services (EFIS)
HNSMS .... Host Nation Support Management System (SAUO)
HN-SN .... House Number/Street Name (SAUS)
HNSR .... Hand Shears (SAUS)
HNST .... Hexanitrostilbene [*High explosive*] (MCD)
HNSX .... Honeywell-NEC Supercomputers, Inc.
HNT .... Habit of Nervous Tension [*Medicine*] (EDAA)
HNT .... Handbuch zum Neuen Testament [*A publication*] (BJA)
HNT .... Helicopteros Internacionales, SA de CV [*Mexico*] [*FAA designator*] (FAAC)
HNT .... Hostage Negotiating Team (LAIN)
HNT .... National Center for Toxicological Research, Jefferson, AR [*OCLC symbol*] (OCLC)
HNTB .... Halstead Neuropsychological Test Battery (EDAC)
HNTD .... Highest Non-Toxic Dose (OA)
HNTG .... Hunting (MSA)
HntgIn .... Huntingdon International Holdings Ltd. [*Associated Press*] (SAG)
H-NTLA .... Hiskey-Nebraska Test of Learning Aptitude (EDAC)
HNTR .... Hunter
HNU .... Hainan University (BUAC)
HNU .... Henan University (BUAC)
HNUA .... Heptylnonylundecyladipat (SAUS)
HNUP .... Heptylnonylundecylphthalat (SAUS)
HNV .... Hanover Direct [*Formerly, Horn & Hardart Co.*] [*AMEX symbol*] (SPSG)
HNV .... Has Not Voided [*Urology*]
HNV .... Hoover Planning Co., Inc. (SAUO)
HNV-IRD ...... Helicopter Night Vision Infrared Detector (ACAE)
HNVS .... Helicopter Night Vision System (PDAA)
HNVS .... Hughes Night Vision System [*Aviation*]
HNW .... Head, Nut, and Washer [*Construction*]
HNW .... Heeresnachrichtenwesen [*Army Communications System*] [*German military - World War II*]
HNW .... Hein-Werner Corp. [*AMEX symbol*] (SPSG)
HNW .... Human Noise and Wildlife (SAUO)
HNW .... Placerville, CA [*Location identifier*] [*FAA*] (FAAL)
HNWI .... High Net Worth Individual
HNWR .... Hagerman National Wildlife Refuge (SAUO)
HNWR .... Honcon National Wildlife Refuge (SAUS)
HNWR .... Horicon National Wildlife Refuge (SAUO)
HNY .... Hamilton [*New York*] [*Seismograph station code, US Geological Survey*] (SEIS)
HNY .... Happy New Year
HNY .... Hennessy Resource Corp. [*Vancouver Stock Exchange symbol*]
HNY .... Honey (WGA)
HNYB .... Honeybee
HNYCMB ...... Honeycomb
HNZ .... Havelock North [*New Zealand*] [*Seismograph station code, US Geological Survey*] [*Closed*] (SEIS)
HNZ .... Heinz [*H. J.*] Co. [*NYSE symbol*] (SPSG)
HNZ .... H.J. Heinz Company (SAUO)
HNZPr .... Heinz $1.70 cm Cv Pfd [*NYSE symbol*] (TTSB)
HO .... Airways International [*ICAO designator*] (AD)
HO .... Charterair [*ICAO designator*] (AD)
HO .... Habitual Offender (SAUS)
HO .... Haem Oxygenase [*An enzyme*]
HO .... Hale Observatories [*Formerly, Mount Palomar and Mount Wilson Observatories*]
H-O .... Half of 'O' Gauge [*Model railroading*]
HO .... Halogenated Organic Carbons (GNE)
H/O .... Hand-Off (ACAE)
HO .... Hand-Operated (SAUS)
HO .... Hand Orthosis [*Medicine*]
HO .... Handout (FOTI)
HO .... Hand Over (MCD)
H/O .... Handover (NAKS)
HO .... Hang Over (ACAE)
HO .... Hardened in Oil (SAUS)
H/O .... Hard Over (KSC)
HO .... Hard Overhung Balancer (SAUS)
HO .... Hardware Operation (SAUS)
HO .... Harmonic Oscillator
HO .... Hazardous Organics [*Environmental science*]
HO .... Head Office
HO .... Headquarters Offices (EEVL)
HO .... Health Occupations (SAUO)
HO .... Hearing Office (SAUS)
HO .... Hearing Officers (SAUO)
HO .... Heel Off Ground [*Medicine*]
ho .... held over (SAUS)
H/O .... Hematology and Oncology (DAVI)
HO .... Heme Oxygenase (SAUS)
HO .... Herbarium of the Tasmanian Museum and Art Gallery (SAUO)
HO .... Hertzian Oscillator (SAUS)
ho .... heterothallic (SAUS)
HO .... Heterotopic Ossification [*Osteology*]
HO .... High Oblique [*Aerospace*]
HO .... High Order [*Computer science*] (OA)
HO .... High Output [*Automotive engineering*]
HO .... High Oxygen (MAE)
HO .... Hip Orthosis [*Medicine*]
HO .... Hippocratic Oath (MELL)
H/O .... History Of [*Medicine*]

HO .... History Office (MCD)
HO .... Hoist
HO .... Hold [*Shipping*] (DS)
HO .... Holding Out [*Cashier fraud*]
HO .... Hold Over (SAUS)
HO .... Holdover [*Theater*]
Ho .... Holmium [*Chemical element*]
HO .... Holt-Oram [*Syndrome*] [*Medicine*] (DB)
HO .... Holy Day of Obligation [*Roman Catholicism*]
HO .... Holy Orders (ROG)
HO .... Home Office [*British*]
HO .... Home Only [*British military*] (DMA)
HO .... Homeowners' [*Insurance*]
HO .... Homestead
Ho .... Homobonus de Cremona [*Deceased, 1272*] [*Authority cited in pre-1607 legal work*] (DSA)
HO .... Homologous (MELL)
ho .... homothallism (SAUS)
ho .... Honduras [*MARC country of publication code*] [*Library of Congress*] (LCCP)
ho .... Honeycomb Lung [*Medicine*] (EDAA)
HO .... Hook Opening (SAUS)
HO .... Horizontally Opposed [*Automotive engineering*]
HO .... Horizontal Output (IAA)
Ho .... Horse (DMAA)
Ho .... Hosea [*Old Testament book*] (BJA)
Ho .... Hostiensis [*Deceased, 1271*] [*Authority cited in pre-1607 legal work*] (DSA)
HO .... Hostilities Only [*Applied to men who joined for duration of war only*] [*Navy*] [*British*] [*World War II*]
HO .... Hotel (ROG)
HO .... Hours of Operation
HO .... House
HO .... Housekeeping Operation (SAUS)
HO .... House Officer
HO .... Housing Operations (SAUO)
HO .... Houston Oil Trust [*AMEX symbol*] (COMM)
HO .... Human Operator (IAA)
HO .... Hunting Oscillator (IAA)
h/o .... husband of (SAUS)
HO .... Hybrid Orbital (SAUS)
HO .... Hydraulic Operator (NRCH)
HO .... Hydrogen-Oxygen [*NASA*] (NASA)
HO .... Hydrographic Office [*Terminated, 1963; later, NOO*] [*Navy*]
ho .... Hydroxy [*As substituent on nucleoside*] [*Also, oh*] [*Biochemistry*]
HO .... Hyperbaric Oxygen [*Medicine*]
HO .... Hyperostosis [*Medicine*] (MELL)
HO .... Observation Helicopter
Ho .... Observed Altitude
HO .... Observed Height (SAUS)
HO .... Service Available to Meet Operational Requirements [*ICAO*] (FAAC)
HOA .... Hands Off - Automatic (AAG)
HOA .... Heavy Observation Aircraft
HOA .... Hechalutz Organization of America [*Defunct*] (EA)
HOA .... High Oxygen Affinity (MELL)
HOA .... Hip Osteoarthritis [*Medicine*] (DMAA)
HOA .... Homeowners Assistance Fund, Defense [*DoD*]
HOA .... House of Assembly [*South Australia*]
HOA .... (Hydroxyethyl)oxamic Acid [*Organic chemistry*]
HOA .... Hypertrophic Osteoarthropathy [*Medicine*] (DMAA)
HOAA .... Home Office Association of America (NTPA)
HOAB .... Heptyloxyazoxybenzene [*Organic chemistry*]
HOACGA .... Heart of America Carnival Glass Association (EA)
Ho A Cs .... Howards New York Appeal Cases (journ.) (SAUS)
HOAF .... Home Owners Assistance Fund program (SAUO)
HoaFIMechE .... Honorary Fellow of the Institution of Mechanical Engineers (SAUS)
HOAI .... Home Office Addicts' Index (WDAA)
HOAI .... Human Outreach and Advancement Institute
HOAL .... Homes on Aboriginal Land [*Australia*]
HOALM .... Holographic Optic Addressed Light Modulation (IAA)
HOALM .... Holographic Optically Addressed Light Modulation (SAUS)
HOAM .... Hand Operated Adding Machine (SAUS)
HOAM .... Healthwise of America, Inc. [*NASDAQ symbol*] (SAG)
Ho&ForR .... Home and Foreign Review (journ.) (SAUS)
HO&FWD .... Hook, Oil and Fresh Water Damage (SAUS)
HO&GCM .... Heavy Oil and Gascut Mud (SAUS)
HO & RC .... Humble Oil & Refining Co. (MHDW)
HO&RC .... Humble Oil and Refining Company (SAUO)
HOANSW .... Hospital Officers' Association of New South Wales [*Australia*]
HOAP .... Home Owners Assistance Program (SAUO)
HOAP .... Home Ownership Assistance Program [*Farmers Home Administration*]
HOAP .... Housing Opportunity Allowance Program (SAUO)
HOAP .... Housing Opportunity Assistance Program [*Federal Home Loan Bank Board*]
HOAP .... Hydroxydaunomycin [*Adriamycin*], Cytosine Arabinoside, Vincristine, Prednisone [*Antineoplastic drug regimen*] (DAVI)
HOAP-BLEO .... , ara-C , Prednisone, Bleomycin [*Vincristine*] [*Cytarabine*] [*Antineoplastic drug regimen*]
HOAP-BLEO .... Hydroxydaunomycin, Oncovin, ara-C, Prednisone, Bleomycin (SAUS)
HoaRhLG .... Horse Anti-Rhesus Lymphocyte Globulin [*Immunology*]
HOARS .... Hands-On Annotated Recorded Search (NITA)
HOAs .... Heavy Observation Aircrafts (SAUS)
HOATS .... Human Ovarian Antitumor Serum [*Antineoplastic compound*]
HoaTTG .... Horse Anti-Tetanus Toxoid Globulin [*Immunology*]
HOB .... H2O Reactor (SAUS)
HOB .... Half-Octave Bandwidth
HOB .... Head of Bed [*Medicine*] (EDAA)
HoB .... Head of Bed [*Medicine*] (EDAA)
HOB .... Head of Bus (ACRL)
HOB .... Heater Outlet Box (SAUS)
HOB .... Height [*Depth*] of Burst
HOB .... Highest Order Bit (SAUS)
HOB .... High of Burst (SAUS)
HOB .... High Order Bit (SAUS)
HOB .... Hobarth Corporation (SAUO)
Hob .... Hobart's English King's Bench Reports [*80 English Reprint*] [*A publication*] (DLA)
HOB .... Hobbs [*New Mexico*] [*Airport symbol*] (OAG)
HOB .... Hobbs Public Library, Hobbs, NM [*OCLC symbol*] (OCLC)
HOB .... Hobby
HOB .... Home-on-Burn
HOB .... Homing on Offset Beacon
HOB .... Horizontal Oscillating Barrel (PDAA)
HOB .... Hot Ore Briquetting (DICI)
HOB .... House Office Building [*US Congress*]
HOB .... Hyperbaric [*Medicine*] (EDAA)
HOBA .... [*A*] History of the Book in Australia [*Project*]
Hobart .... Hobart's English King's Bench Reports [*80 English Reprint*] [*A publication*] (DLA)
Hobart (Eng) .... Hobart's English King's Bench Reports [*80 English Reprint*] [*A publication*] (DLA)
HOBC .... High-Output Ballast Cleaner [*Indian Railway*] (TIR)
HOBC .... Holographic Bubble Chamber (SAUS)
HOBC .... Howard Bancorp [*NASDAQ symbol*] (COMM)
HOBDH .... Hydroxybutyrate Dehydrogenase (DB)
HOBE .... Honeycomb Before Expansion (SAUS)
HOBE .... Horseshoe Bend National Military Park
HOBGI .... Honorable Order of the Blue Goose, International [*West Bend, WI*] (EA)
HOBIC .... Hotel Billing Information Center (VLIE)
HOBIS .... Home Ownership Building Industry Scheme [*Australia*]
HOBIS .... Hotel Billing Information System [*Telecommunications*] (TEL)
HOBITS .... Haifa On-line Bibliographic Text System [*University of Haifa Library*] [*Information service or system*] (IID)
HOBN .... Home Office Business Network [*Information service or system*] (IID)
HOBO .... Homing Bomb (SAUS)
HOBO .... Homing Optical Bomb (MCD)
Hobonus .... Homobonus de Cremona [*Deceased, 1272*] [*Authority cited in pre-1607 legal work*] (DSA)
HOBOS .... Homing Bomb System [*Air Force*]
HOBOT .... House-cleaning Robot (SAUS)
HOBP .... Hydroxy(octylidene)bis(phosphonic Acid) [*Organic chemistry*]
Hob R .... Hobart's English Common Pleas Reports [*80 English Reprint*] [*1613-25*] [*A publication*] (DLA)
Hob R .... Hobart's English King's Bench Reports [*80 English Reprint*] [*A publication*] (DLA)
HOBS .... High-Orbital Bombardment System (KSC)
HOBS .... Home and Office Banking Service [*Bank of Scotland*] (ECON)
HOBS .... Homing Bomb System [*Air Force*]
HOBT .... Hydroxybenzotriazole
HOBUPSOB .... Head of Bed Up for Shortness of Breath [*Medicine*] (DAVI)
HOBY .... Hugh O'Brian Youth Foundation (EA)
HOBYAA .... Hugh O'Brian Youth Foundation Alumni Association (EA)
HOC .... Halogenated Organic Carbons (EEVL)
HOC .... Halogenated Organic Compound [*Organic chemistry*] (FFDE)
HOC .... Handover Coordinator (SAA)
HOC .... Hands-On Component
HOC .... Hazardous Organic Constituents (SAUS)
HOC .... Health Officer Certificate (DAVI)
HOC .... Heat of Combustion
HOC .... Heavy Oil Cracking [*Process*] [*Petroleum industry*]
HOC .... Height Overlap Coverage [*RADAR*]
HOC .... Held on Charge (SAUS)
HOC .... Heterodyne Optical Correlation (IAA)
HOC .... Highest Outgoing Channel [*Telecommunications*] (CIST)
HOC .... High Output Current
HOC .... Hillman Owners Club [*Lancing, Sussex, England*] (EAIO)
HOC .... Hillsboro, OH [*Location identifier*] [*FAA*] (FAAL)
HOC .... Hindustan Organic Chemicals (SAUO)
HOC .... History of Coverage (MCD)
HOC .... Hokushin Computer (SAUS)
HOC .... Holland Organizing Centre (SAUO)
HOC .... Holly Corp. [*AMEX symbol*] (SPSG)
HOC .... Hollywood Overseas Committee (IIA)
HOC .... House of Charity (SAUO)
HOC .... House of Commons [*British*]
HoC .... Hoven & Co., Bakersfield, CA [*Library symbol*] [*Library of Congress*] (LCLS)
HOC .... Hughes Operations Center (ACAE)
HOC .... Hughes Operations Chief (ACAE)
HOC .... Human Ovarian Cancer [*Cytology*]
HOC .... Hurricane Operations Center (AFM)
HOC .... Hydraulic Overspeed Control [*Mechanical power transmission*]
HOC .... Hydrofoil Ocean Combatant
HOC .... Hydrology Overview Committee (SAUO)
HOC .... Hydrophobic Organic Chemical [*Physical chemistry*]
HOC .... Hydrophobic Organic Compound [*Marine science*] (OSRA)
HOC .... Hydrophobic Organic Contaminant [*Environmental science*]

HOC .... Hydroxycorticoid (MELL)
HOC .... Hydroxycorticosteroid [*Endocrinology*]
HOC .... Hyperosmolar Coma (MELL)
HOCA .... High Osmolar Contrast Agent [*Medicine*]
HOCA .... Hurst/Olds Club of America (EA)
HOCarm .... Hermits of Our Lady of Mt. Carmel (TOCD)
HOCAS .... Hands On Collective And Stick (SAUS)
HOCCU .... Heavy Oil Catalytic Cracking Unit [*Petroleum refining*]
HOCEM .... Hierarchically Organized Cybernetic Electric Machine (SAUS)
HOCI .... Hypochlorous Acid (SAUS)
HOCM .... High Osmolar Contrast Medium (DB)
HOCM .... Hypertrophic Obstructive Cardiomyopathy [*Cardiology*]
HOCO .... Ad Hoc Conference (SAUS)
HOCOLEA ..... Heads of Commonwealth Operational Law Enforcement Agencies [*Australia*]
HOC Process... Heavy Oil Cracking Process (SAUS)
HOCPRU ...... Hot Climate Physiological Research Unit (SAUO)
HOCRE .... Home Office Central Research Establishment (BUAC)
HOCS .... Home Office Communication System (VLIE)
HoCT .... Household Capital Trust [*Associated Press*] (SAG)
HoCT .... Household Capital Trust II [*Associated Press*] (SAG)
HOCUS .... Hand or Computer Universal Simulation [*PE Computer Services Ltd.*] [*Software package*] [*British*]
HOCUS .... Hand or Computer Universal Simulation (or Simulator) (SAUS)
HOC VESP ... Hoc Vespere [*Tonight*] [*Pharmacy*]
hoc vesp ...... This evening [*Or tonight*] [*Medicine*] (EDAA)
HOCX .... Head-On Collision Line [*Private rail car owner code*]
HoD .... Head of Department [*British*] (DET)
HOD .... Head of Department
HOD .... Head Out Display (SAUS)
HOD .... Heat of Detonation
HOD .... Hebrew Order of David
HOD .... Higher Order Differentiation (SAUS)
HOD .... Higher Order Digit (SAUS)
HOD .... Highway Overlay District (PA)
HOD .... Historic Overlay District (PA)
HOD .... Hodeidah [*Yemen Arab Republic*] [*Airport symbol*] (OAG)
Hod .... Hodges' English Common Pleas Reports [*1835-37*] [*A publication*] (DLA)
HoD .... Hodgkin's Disease [*Oncology*] (DAVI)
HOD .... Hoffer-Osmond Diagnostic Test [*Psychology*]
HOD .... Home on Decoy [*Military*] (CAAL)
HOD .... Home on Military (SAUS)
HOD .... Host-on-Demand [*Computer science*] (ITCA)
HOD .... Hurt on Duty
HOD .... Hyperbaric Oxygen Drenching
HOD .... Test Hoffer, Osmond and Desmond Test (SAUS)
HODA .... Hawkfarm One Design Association (EA)
HODAG .... Housing Development Action Grant [*HUD*]
HODCRA ...... Hampton One-Design Class Racing Association (EA)
Hodg .... Hodges' English Common Pleas Reports [*1835-37*] [*A publication*] (DLA)
Hodg .... Hodgin's Election Cases [*Ontario*] [*A publication*] (DLA)
Hodg Can Elec Cas... Hodgin's Canada Election Cases [*A publication*] (DLA)
HODGE .... Hodge, LA [*American Association of Railroads railroad junction routing code*]
Hodg El .... Hodgins' Upper Canada Election Cases [*A publication*] (DLA)
Hodg El Cas... Hodgin's Election Cases [*Ontario*] [*A publication*] (DLA)
Hodg El Cas (Ont)... Hodgin's Election Cases [*Ontario*] [*A publication*] (DLA)
Hodge Presb Law... Hodge on Presbyterian Law [*A publication*] (DLA)
Hodges .... Hodges' English Common Pleas Reports [*1835-37*] [*A publication*] (DLA)
Hodges (Eng)... Hodges' English Common Pleas Reports [*1835-37*] [*A publication*] (DLA)
HODGJ .... Hodge Junction, TX [*American Association of Railroads railroad junction routing code*]
Hodg Ont Elect... Hodgin's Election Cases [*Ontario*] [*A publication*] (DLA)
Hodg Ry ...... Hodges' Law of Railways [*A publication*] (DLA)
HODI .... Homozygous Diabetes Insipidus [*A genetic variety of rat*]
HODIDS .... Home/Office Data/Information Delivery Sytem (SAUS)
HODOS .... Hole Drilling Operating System (SAUS)
HODRAL ...... Hokushin Data Reduction Algorithm Language (SAUO)
HODS .... Hydrographic Oceanographic Data Sheets (NG)
HO-DSP .... Higher Order Domain Specific Part (VLIE)
HOD Test ..... Hoffer, Osmond and Desmond Test (SAUS)
HOE .... Head of Epididymis [*Medicine*] (MELL)
HOE .... Height of Eye [*Navigation*]
HOE .... Hoechst-Roussel Pharmaceuticals, Inc. [*Research code symbol*]
HOE .... Holographic Optical Element
HOE .... Holographic Optical Equipment (SAUS)
HOE .... Homerville, GA [*Location identifier*] [*FAA*] (FAAL)
HOE .... Homing Overlay Equipment (MCD)
HOE .... Homing Overlay Experiment [*Ballistic missile defense*] (RDA)
HOE .... Human and Organizational Errors [*Engineering*]
HOE .... Hydraulically Operated Equipment
HOEI .... Hover-One-Engine-Inoperative (PDAA)
HOEN .... Hoenig Group [*NASDAQ symbol*] (TTSB)
HOEN .... Hoenig Group, Inc. [*NASDAQ symbol*] (SPSG)
Hoenig .... Hoenig Group, Inc. [*Associated Press*] (SAG)
HOESY .... Heteronuclear Overhauser Enhancement Spectroscopy (SAUS)
HOET .... Heavy Oil Engine Tractor [*British*]
HOF .... Hafuf [*Saudi Arabia*] [*Airport symbol*] (OAG)
HOF .... Hall of Fame
HOF .... Head of Faculty [*Education*] (AIE)
HoF .... Head of Faculty [*British*] (DET)
HOF .... Head of Form (IAA)
HOF .... Heat of Formation
HoF .... Height of Fundus [*Obstetrics*]
HOF .... Hepatic Outflow [*Medicine*] (DMAA)
HOF .... High-Octane Fuel (SAUS)
HOF .... High Output Failure [*Medicine*] (MELL)
HOF .... Hof [*Federal Republic of Germany*] [*Seismograph station code, US Geological Survey*] (SEIS)
HOF .... Hofmann Industries, Inc. [*AMEX symbol*] (COMM)
HOF .... Home Office Facility
HOF .... Home Ownership Fund (SAUO)
HOF .... Homing Fixture (MCD)
HOF .... Horizons of Friendship [*Canada*] (BUAC)
HOF .... House of Fraser [*Department store conglomerate*] [*British*]
HOF .... St. Paul, MN [*Location identifier*] [*FAA*] (FAAL)
HOFC .... Hall and Oates Fan Club (EA)
HofC .... House of Commons [*British*] (WDAA)
H of C .... House of Commons [*British*]
H of C .... House of Correction (SAUO)
HOFCO .... Horizontal Function Checkout (KSC)
HOFD .... Heterogeneous Opposed Flow Diffusion
HOFD .... Home Office Factory Department (SAUO)
H of F .... Hall of Fame (WDAA)
HofF .... Height of Fundus [*Obstetrics*] (DAVI)
H of F .... Height of Fundus [*Obstetrics*]
HOFF .... Hoffmann [*Reflex*] [*Medicine*]
Hoff .... Hoffman's Land Cases, United States District Court [*A publication*] (DLA)
Hoff .... Hoffman's New York Chancery Reports [*A publication*] (DLA)
HOFF .... Horizon Offshore, Inc. [*NASDAQ symbol*] (NASQ)
H of F .... Hour of Fuel (SAUS)
Hoff Ch .... Hoffman's New York Chancery Reports [*A publication*] (DLA)
Hoff CR .... Hoffman's New York Chancery Reports [*A publication*] (DLA)
Hoff Dec ...... Hoffman's Decisions [*A publication*] (DLA)
Hoff Ecc L.... Hoffman's Ecclesiastical Law [*A publication*] (DLA)
Hoff Land..... Hoffman's Land Cases, United States District Court [*A publication*] (DLA)
Hoff Land Cas... Hoffman's Land Cases, United States District Court [*A publication*] (DLA)
Hoff LC .... Hoffman's Land Cases, United States District Court [*A publication*] (DLA)
Hoff L Cas ... Hoffman's Land Cases, United States District Court [*A publication*] (DLA)
Hoff Lead Cas... Hoffman's Leading Cases [*A publication*] (DLA)
Hoff Leg St... Hoffman's Course of Legal Study [*A publication*] (DLA)
HOFFM .... Hereditary Order of the First Families of Massachusetts (EA)
Hoffm .... Hoffman's Land Cases, United States District Court [*A publication*] (DLA)
Hoffm .... Hoffman's New York Chancery Reports [*A publication*] (DLA)
Hoffman Ch R... Hoffman's New York Chancery Reports [*A publication*] (DLA)
Hoffman's Ch R... Hoffman's New York Chancery Reports [*A publication*] (DLA)
Hoff Mast..... Hoffman's Master in Chancery [*A publication*] (DLA)
Hoff Mast Ch... Hoffman's Master in Chancery [*A publication*] (DLA)
Hoffm Ch ..... Hoffman's Land Cases, United States District Court [*A publication*] (DLA)
Hoffm Ch ..... Hoffman's New York Chancery Reports [*A publication*] (DLA)
Hoffm Ch (NY)... Hoffman's New York Chancery Reports [*A publication*] (DLA)
Hoffm Dec (F)... Hoffman's Decisions, United States District Court [*A publication*] (DLA)
Hoffm Land Cas (F)... Hoffman's Land Cases, United States District Court [*A publication*] (DLA)
Hoffm Ops (F)... Hoffman's Opinions, United States District Court [*A publication*] (DLA)
Hoffm Rep Land Cases... Hoffman's Land Cases, United States District Court [*A publication*] (DLA)
Hoff NY .... Hoffman's New York Chancery Reports [*A publication*] (DLA)
Hoff Op .... Hoffman's Opinions [*A publication*] (DLA)
Hoff Out ...... Hoffman's Legal Outlines [*A publication*] (DLA)
Hoff Pr Rem... Hoffman's Provisional Remainders [*A publication*] (DLA)
Hoff Pub P... Hoffman's Public Papers [*New York*] [*A publication*] (DLA)
Hoff Ref ...... Hoffman on Referees [*A publication*] (DLA)
H of H .... Holy of Holies [*Freemasonry*] (ROG)
H of IF .... House of Ill Fame
HOFIN .... Hostile Fire Indicator (SAUS)
H of J .... Hospitallers of Jerusalem [*Freemasonry*] (ROG)
H of K .... House of Keys (SAUO)
H of L .... Height of Lift (SAUS)
HOFL .... Home Financial [*NASDAQ symbol*] (TTSB)
HOFL .... Home Financial Corporation of Florida [*NASDAQ symbol*] (SAG)
H of L .... House of Lords (SAUO)
Hof LR .... Hofstra Law Review (journ.) (SAUS)
H of N .... Hydrographer of the Navy [*British*]
HoFor .... Home Forces (SAUO)
HOFR .... Heat resisting, Oil resisting and Flame Retardant (SAUS)
HOFR .... Home of Franklin D. Roosevelt and Vanderbilt Mansion National Historic Sites
H of R .... House of Representatives (SAUO)
H of S .... House of Solomon [*Freemasonry*] (ROG)
HOFS .... Hybrid Optical Fire Sets (SAUS)
HOFS .... Hydrogen-Oxygen Fuel System [*NASA*]
HOFSL .... Home Office Forensic Science Laboratory [*British*]
HofSp .... Hybrid of Species (SAUS)
Hofstra Lab LF... Hofstra Labor Law Forum [*A publication*] (DLA)
Hofstra Lab LJ... Hofstra Labor Law Journal [*A publication*] (DLA)
Hofstra U ..... Hofstra University (GAGS)

HOFTU .... Hunter Operational Fighter Training Unit [*India*] [*Air Force*]
HOG .... Halothane, Oxygen, and Gas [*Nitrous oxide*] [*Anesthesiology*] (DAVI)
HOG .... Harley-Davidson Owners Group (BUAC)
HOG .... Harley Owners' Group (EA)
HOG .... Head End Off-Gas [*Nuclear energy*] (NRCH)
HOG .... Head of Government (ADA)
HOG .... Head-On Generator [*Indian Railway*] (TIR)
HOG .... Heavy Ordnance Gunship (NVT)
HOG .... Hepatic Output of Glucose [*Medicine*] (EDAA)
HOG .... High Old Genius [*Slang*] [*British*]
Hog .... (Hogan of) Harcarse's Scotch Session Cases [*A publication*] (DLA)
Hog .... Hogan's Irish Rolls Court Reports [*A publication*] (DLA)
HOG .... Holguin [*Cuba*] [*Airport symbol*] (OAG)
HOG .... Homing Optical Guidance
HOG .... Hondo Oil & Gas Co. [*AMEX symbol*] (SPSG)
HOGA .... Hyperornithinemia with Gyrate Atrophy [*Medicine*] (DMAA)
Hogan .... (Hogan of) Harcarse's Scotch Session Cases [*A publication*] (DLA)
Hogan .... Hogan's Irish Rolls Court Reports [*A publication*] (DLA)
Hogan .... Hogan Systems, Inc. [*Associated Press*] (SAG)
Hogan (Ir) .... Hogan's Irish Rolls Court Reports [*A publication*] (DLA)
HOGC .... Handbook of Occupational Groups and Series of Classes
HOGE .... Hover Out of Ground Effect (SAUS)
HOGE .... Hover-Out-of-Ground Environment
HOGEN .... Hold Off Generator (MSA)
HOGHPOWS ... Highpower Outgoing Wavefront for Sampling (SAUS)
HOGHPOWS ... Holographic Gratings for High Power Outgoing Wavefront Samplings (ACAE)
HOGI .... Harken Oil & Gas, Inc. [*NASDAQ symbol*] (COMM)
HOGN .... Hogan Systems, Inc. [*NASDAQ symbol*] (NQ)
HOGS .... Homing Optical Guidance System
Hog St Tr .... Hogan's Pennsylvania State Trials [*A publication*] (DLA)
Hogue .... Hogue's Reports [*1-4 Florida*] [*A publication*] (DLA)
HOH .... Hard of Hearing (MAE)
HOH .... HDSL Overhead Bit Handling (SAUS)
HOH .... Head of Household [*IRS*]
HOH .... Heard on the Hill [*US Congress*]
HOH .... Help Our Headaches Group [*Australia*]
HOH .... Hereford Otter Hounds
HOH .... High-Degree Helioseismometer
HOH .... Hohenheim [*Federal Republic of Germany*] [*Seismograph station code, US Geological Survey*] [*Closed*] (SEIS)
HOH .... Hydrogen-Oxygen-Hydrogen [*Water*] (HGAA)
Ho/Ha .... Hold/Hatch (SAUS)
HOHAHA .... Homonuclear Hartmann-Hahn Spectroscopy (SAUS)
HOHI .... Handbook of Overhaul Instructions [*Navy*]
HOHI .... HOH Water Technology Corp. (SAUO)
HOHI .... Home Ownership and Home Improvement (SAUS)
HOH of J .... Holy Order of the Hospital of Jerusalem [*Freemasonry*] (ROG)
HOHP .... Holocaust Oral History Project [*An association*] (EA)
HOI .... Handbook of Operating Instructions [*Navy*]
HOI .... Handbook of Overhaul Instructions [*Navy*] (MCD)
HOI .... Hao Island [*French Polynesia*] [*Airport symbol*] (OAG)
HOI .... Headquarters Office Instruction
HOI .... Headquarters Operating Instructions [*Air Force*] (AFM)
HOI .... Health Optimizing Institute (EA)
HOI .... Health Outcomes Institute (ADWA)
HOI .... Hear O Israel (EA)
HOI .... Hospital Onset of Infection [*Medicine*] (DMAA)
HOI .... House of Issue [*Banking*]
HOI .... Hypoiodous Acid (STED)
HOI .... Hytran Operations Interpreter (SAUO)
Holg .... Horse Immunoglobulin [*Immunology*]
HOIL .... Hand Operated Impact Loader (SAUS)
Holnt .... Household International, Inc. [*Associated Press*] (SAG)
HOIP .... Home Office Inspector of Prisons (SAUO)
HOIS .... Hostile Intelligence Service [*Military*] (MCD)
HOIS .... House Office Information System (SAUS)
HOIT .... Hostile Intelligence Threat (SAUS)
HOJ .... Home-On-Jam (SAUO)
HOJ .... Home on Jamming
HOJ .... Hope [*Jamaica*] [*Seismograph station code, US Geological Survey*] (SEIS)
HOJITOJ .... Home on Jam/Track on Jam (SAUS)
HOJO .... Howard Johnson [*Restaurant chain*] [*Slang*]
HOK .... Hellmuth, Obata & Kassabaum [*Architectural firm*]
HOK .... Hilum of Kidney (MELL)
HOK .... Hohkeppel [*Federal Republic of Germany*] [*Seismograph station code, US Geological Survey*] (SEIS)
HOK .... Hoko Exploration [*Vancouver Stock Exchange symbol*]
HOK .... Hooker Creek [*Airport symbol*]
HOK .... House of Keys [*Isle Of Man*]
hoke .... hokum (SAUS)
HOKEYS .... Home Owners' Loan Corporation Bonds (MHDB)
HOKLAS .... Hong Kong Laboratory Accreditation Scheme (SAUS)
HOK X .... Hooker Electrochemical Co. (SAUS)
HOK X .... Hooker Electrochemical Company (SAUO)
HOL .... Head of Line (SAUS)
HOL .... Higher Order Logic [*Computer science*]
HOL .... High- [*or Higher-*] Order Language [*Computer science*]
HOL .... Holco Mortgage Acceptance Corp. [*AMEX symbol*] (SPSG)
hol .... Holiday (ADWA)
HOL .... Holiday (AFM)
HOL .... Holiday Airlines, Inc. [*ICAO designator*] (FAAC)
HOL .... Holiday and Leave [*Military*] (NVT)
HOL .... Hollinger Argus Ltd. [*Toronto Stock Exchange symbol*]
HOL .... Hollow (MSA)
Hol .... Holocene (SAUS)
HOL .... House of Lords [*British*]
HOL .... Humanization of Labor (IID)
HOLA .... Hispanic Organization of Latin Actors (EA)
HOLA .... Home Owners' Loan Act of 1933
HOLAB .... Holographic Alignment Brassboard (ACAE)
Holarct Ecol ... Holarctic Ecology (SAUS)
HOLBK .... Holbrook, AZ [*American Association of Railroads railroad junction routing code*]
HOLC .... High-Order Language Computer (NASA)
HOLC .... Home Owners' Loan Corp. [*Terminated, 1942*]
Ho L Cas .... Clark's House of Lords Cases [*1847-66*] [*England*] [*A publication*] (DLA)
Holc Debt & Cr ... Holcombe's Law of Debtor and Creditor [*A publication*] (DLA)
Holc Eq Jur ... Holcombe's Equity Jurisdiction [*A publication*] (DLA)
Holc L Cas ... Holcombe's Leading Cases of Commercial Law [*A publication*] (DLA)
Holco .... Holco Mortgage Acceptance Corp. [*Associated Press*] (SAG)
HOLD .... American Holdings, Inc. [*NASDAQ symbol*] (SAG)
HOLD .... Call Hold [*Telecommunications*] (DOM)
HOLD .... Hemostatic Occlusive Leverage Device [*Cardiology*] (DAVI)
HOLDCP .... Hold, Computed (SAUS)
HOLDET .... Higher Order Language Development and Evaluation Tool [*Computer science*] (MHDB)
Hold LR .... Holdsworth Law Review [*A publication*] (SAFN)
HOLDPB .... Hold Pushbutton (SAUS)
HOLD-UP .... Hook Loads During Launch Program (ACAE)
HOLEBC .... Holographic Lexan Bubble Chamber (SAUS)
HOLF .... Helicopter Outlying Field
Holg .... Horse Immunoglobulin [*Immunology*] (DAVI)
holgr .... Hologram (VRA)
HOLI .... Hollinger International, Inc. [*NASDAQ symbol*] (SAG)
Holinger .... Hollinger, Inc. [*Associated Press*] (SAG)
Holl .... Holland (VRA)
HOLL .... Holland
Holl .... Hollinshead's Reports [*1 Minnesota*] [*A publication*] (DLA)
HOLLAND .... Here Our Love Lives and Never Dies [*Correspondence*] (DSUE)
Holl Comp Deeds ... Holland on Composition Deeds [*A publication*] (DLA)
Holl El Jur ... Holland's Elements of Jurisprudence [*A publication*] (DLA)
Hollinger .... Hollinger International, Inc. [*Associated Press*] (SAG)
Hollins C .... Hollins College (GAGS)
Hollinshead ... Hollinshead's Reports [*1 Minnesota*] [*A publication*] (DLA)
Holl Jur .... Holland's Elements of Jurisprudence [*A publication*] (DLA)
Holl Just .... Holland's Institutes of Justinian [*A publication*] (DLA)
Hollng .... Hollinger International, Inc. [*Associated Press*] (SAG)
HOLLOW .... Hollow [*Commonly used*] (OPSA)
HOLLOWS .... Hollow [*Commonly used*] (OPSA)
Hollow Sect ... Hollow Section (journ.) (SAUS)
HOLLY .... Holly, MI [*American Association of Railroads railroad junction routing code*]
HollyCp .... Holly Corp. [*Associated Press*] (SAG)
HollyH .... Holly Holdings, Inc. [*Associated Press*] (SAG)
HollyHld .... Holly Holdings, Inc. [*Associated Press*] (SAG)
HollyP .... Holly Holdings, Inc. [*Associated Press*] (SAG)
HollyPd .... Holly Products [*Associated Press*] (SAG)
HOLM .... Higher-Order Language Machine [*Computer science*] (KSC)
Holm .... Holmes' Reports [*15-17 Oregon*] [*A publication*] (DLA)
Holm .... Holmes' United States Circuit Court Reports [*A publication*] (DLA)
Holm Com Law ... Holmes on the Common Law [*A publication*] (DLA)
Holmes .... Holmes' United States Circuit Court Reports [*A publication*] (DLA)
HOLMES .... Home Office Large Major Enquiry System [*Computer system*] [*British*]
HolmPr .... Holmes Protection Group, Inc. [*Associated Press*] (SAG)
Holm Statesman ... Holmes' Statesman [*A publication*] (DLA)
HOLN .... Health Organization of the League of Nations (SAUO)
Holo .... Holocaust (SAUS)
HOLO .... Holograph (WDAA)
HOLO .... HoloPak Technologies [*NASDAQ symbol*] (SPSG)
HOLO .... Holotype
Holocamera ... Holographic Camera (SAUS)
Holocene .... Holocene, The (SAUS)
Holog .... Hologram (SAUS)
Hologic .... Hologic, Inc. [*Associated Press*] (SAG)
HoLoPak .... HoloPak Technologies [*Associated Press*] (SAG)
Holophne .... Holophane Corp. [*Associated Press*] (SAG)
Ho Lords C ... Clark's House of Lords Cases [*1847-66*] [*England*] [*A publication*] (DLA)
Ho Lords Cas ... Clark's House of Lords Cases [*1847-66*] [*England*] [*A publication*] (DLA)
HOLP .... Hydraulic Overload Protection
HOLS .... Home Opportunity Loans Scheme [*Australia*]
HOLSA .... Health-Oriented Libraries of San Antonio [*Library network*]
HolsnB .... Holson Burnes Group, Inc. [*Associated Press*] (SAG)
HOLSW .... Holsworthy [*England*]
Holt .... Holt's English Equity Reports [*1845*] [*A publication*] (DLA)
Holt .... Holt's English King's Bench Reports [*A publication*] (DLA)
Holt .... Holt's English Nisi Prius Reports [*A publication*] (DLA)
Holt Adm .... Holt's English Admiralty Cases (Rule of the Road) [*1863-67*] [*A publication*] (DLA)
Holt Adm Ca ... Holt's English Admiralty Cases (Rule of the Road) [*1863-67*] [*A publication*] (DLA)
Holt Adm Cas ... Holt's English Admiralty Cases (Rule of the Road) [*1863-67*] [*A publication*] (DLA)
Holt Eq .... Holt's English Equity Reports [*1845*] [*A publication*] (DLA)
Holthouse .... Holthouse's Law Dictionary [*A publication*] (DLA)

HOLTJ.......... Holt Junction, AL [*American Association of Railroads railroad junction routing code*]
Holt KB........ Holt's English King's Bench Reports [*A publication*] (DLA)
Holt L Dic.... Holthouse's Law Dictionary [*A publication*] (DLA)
Holt Lib....... Holt on Libels [*A publication*] (DLA)
Holt Nav....... Holt on Navigation [*A publication*] (DLA)
Holt NP....... Holt's English Nisi Prius Reports [*A publication*] (DLA)
Holt Reg...... Holt on Registration of Title [*A publication*] (DLA)
Holt R of R... Holt's English Admiralty Cases (Rule of the Road) [*A publication*] (DLA)
Holt Sh........ Holt on Shipping [*A publication*] (DLA)
Holt Shipp... Holt on Shipping [*A publication*] (DLA)
HOLUA......... Home Office Life Underwriters Association [*St. Louis, MO*] (EA)
HOLUG......... Houston On Line Users Group (NITA)
HOLUPK....... Holiday, Upkeep [*Military*] (NVT)
HOLV........... Hop Latent Virus [*Plant pathology*]
HOLW........... Hollow
HOLWG........ High- [*or Higher-*] Order Language Working Group [*Computer science*] (RDA)
HOLWS........ Hollow [*Commonly used*] (OPSA)
HOLX........... Holiday Airlines, Inc. [*Air carrier designation symbol*]
HOLX........... Hologic Inc. [*NASDAQ symbol*] (TTSB)
HOLYK......... Holyoke, MA [*American Association of Railroads railroad junction routing code*]
Holy Names C... Holy Names College (GAGS)
HOLZ........... Higher Order Laue Zone [*Crystal diffraction lines*]
HOLZ........... Holman Cement [*Federal Railroad Administration identification code*]
HOM............ Hanford Occupational Medical system (SAUS)
HOM............ Heartless Old Man [*Alternative sobriquet for William Gladstone, 1809-98, British statesman and prime minister, who was known to admirers as GOM, which see*]
HOM............ Hectometric Emissions [*Radio astronomy*]
HOM............ Hexamethylmelamine, Oncovin [*Vincristine*], Methotrexate [*Antineoplastic drug regimen*] (DAVI)
HOM............ Higher Order Mismatch (SAUS)
HOM............ Higher Order Mode (SAUS)
HOM............ High-Order Multiplier (IAA)
HOM............ High Osmolar Medium (STED)
HOM............ Homer [*Alaska*] [*Airport symbol*] (OAG)
HOM............ Homer [*Alaska*] [*Seismograph station code, US Geological Survey*] (SEIS)
HOM............ Homer [*Greek poet, c. 800BC*] [*Classical studies*] (ROG)
Hom............ Homerton College (SAUO)
Hom............ Homiletics (journ.) (SAUS)
HOM............ Homily (ROG)
HOM............ Homing
hom............ hominy (SAUS)
Hom............ Homobonus de Cremona [*Deceased, 1272*] [*Authority cited in pre-1607 legal work*] (DSA)
hom............ homonym (SAUS)
Hom............ Homoptera [*Entomology*]
HOM............ Hoskins Manufacturing Co. (SAUO)
HOM............ Hotine Oblique Mercator (SAUS)
HoM............ Howell Microfilms Co., College, MD [*Library symbol*] [*Library of Congress*] (LCLS)
HOMA.......... Heads of Marine Agencies [*Commonwealth*] [*State*] (EERA)
HOMA.......... Home Federal Savings & Loan of Atlanta (SAUS)
HOMA.......... Houston Oil and Minerals (SAUO)
HOMAC........ Home Mortgage Access Corp. (EMRF)
HomBen....... Home Beneficial Corp. [*Associated Press*] (SAG)
HomBib........ Homiletica en Biblica [*The Hague*] [*A publication*] (BJA)
HOMC.......... Hamac, Inc. (SAUO)
HOMCO........ Houston Oil Field Materials Company (SAUO)
HOMCOR..... Homonuclear Correlation (SAUS)
HOME.......... Highly Optimized Microscope Environment (SAUO)
HOME.......... History of Middle Earth (SAUO)
HOME.......... Holy Order of Mother Earth (SAUO)
HOME.......... Home Centers (DIY) Ltd. [*NASDAQ symbol*] (SAG)
HOME.......... Homedco Group (SAUO)
HOME.......... Homemakers Organized for More Employment (SAUS)
HOME.......... Home Observation for Measurement of the Environment [*Child development test*] [*Psychology*]
HOME.......... Home Oncology Medical Extension [*A home treatment program*]
HOME.......... Home Oppoltunities Made Equal (SAUS)
HOME.......... Home Oriented Maternity Experience [*Defunct*] (EA)
HOME.......... Home Ownership Made Easy Association [*Defunct*] (EA)
HOME.......... Home Ownership Made Easy Plan (SAUO)
Home.......... Home's Manuscript Decisions, Scotch Court of Session [*A publication*] (DLA)
HOME.......... Homestead National Monument
HOME.......... Homeworkers Organized for More Employment (EA)
HOME.......... Horned Order's Magickal Existence [*An association*] (EA)
HOME.......... International American Homes, Inc. (SAUO)
Home Auto... Home and Auto Buyer Guide (journ.) (SAUS)
Home (Cl).... Clerk Home's Decisions, Scotch Court of Session [*1735-44*] [*A publication*] (DLA)
Home (Clk)... Home's Manuscript Decisions, Scotch Court of Session [*A publication*] (DLA)
HomeCnt...... Home Centers (DIY) Ltd. [*Associated Press*] (SAG)
Home Com N... Home Computer News (journ.) (SAUS)
Home Ct of Sess... Home's Manuscript Decisions, Scotch Court of Session [*A publication*] (DLA)
HOME EC..... Home Economics (SAUS)
Home Ec Bul... Home Economics Bulletin (journ.) (SAUS)
Home Econ News... Home Eonomics News (journ.) (SAUS)
Home Econ Newsl... Home Economics Newsletter (journ.) (SAUS)
Home Econ Res J... Home Economics Research Journal (journ.) (SAUS)
Home Energy Dig Wood Burn Q... Home Energy Digest and Wood Burning Quarterly (journ.) (SAUS)
HOMEF........ Home Centers [*NASDAQ symbol*] (TTSB)
Home Gard... Home Garden (journ.) (SAUS)
HomeGdn Bull... Home and Garden Bulletins (journ.) (SAUS)
Home GeogMo... Home Geographic Monthly (SAUO)
Home Geog Mo... Home Geographic Monthly (journ.) (SAUS)
Homegte...... Homegate Hospitality, Inc. [*Associated Press*] (SAG)
Home H Dec... Home's Manuscript Decisions, Scotch Court of Session [*A publication*] (DLA)
Home Health Care Serr Q... Home Health Care Services Quarterly (journ.) (SAUS)
Home Health J... Home Health Journal (journ.) (SAUS)
Home Health Nurse... Home Health Nurse (journ.) (SAUS)
Home Health Rev... Home Health Review (journ.) (SAUS)
HomeHld..... Home Holdings [*Associated Press*] (SAG)
Home Impmrements Jnl... Home Improvements Journal (journ.) (SAUS)
HOMEJ......... Home Junction, OK [*American Association of Railroads railroad junction routing code*]
HOMEO........ Homeopathy (ADA)
Homeo......... Homeopathy (STED)
Home Off Lib Bull... Home Office Library Bulletin (journ.) (SAUS)
Home Off Res Bull... Home Office Research Bulletin (journ.) (SAUS)
Homeop........ Homeopathy [*Medicine*] (EDAA)
HOMEOP...... Homeopathy [*Medicine*]
HomePNA.... Home Phoneline Networking Alliance [*Telecommunications*]
HomePNA.... Home Phone Networking Alliance
HOMER........ Hazardous Organic Mass Emission Rate (AAEL)
HOMER........ High-Altitude Ozone Measuring and Educational Rocket [*NASA*]
Homer......... Homeric (SAUS)
HOMES........ Homeowner-Mortgage Eurosecurities [*Salomon Brothers*] [*Real estate*]
HOMES........ Housing Operations Management System [*DoD*]
HOMES........ Huron, Ontario, Michigan, Erie, Superior [*Great Lakes*]
Home Sci..... Home Science (journ.) (SAUS)
HomeSh........ Home Shopping Network, Inc. [*Associated Press*] (SAG)
HOMES lakes... Huron, Ontario, Michigan, Erie, Superior lakes (SAUO)
HOMESWEST... Western Australian State Housing Commission
HomeTB....... Hometown Buffet, Inc. [*Associated Press*] (SAG)
Home Tech... Home Techniques (journ.) (SAUS)
HomeV......... Homestead Village, Inc. [*Associated Press*] (SAG)
Home Video... Home Video Publisher (journ.) (SAUS)
HomeVil...... Homestead Village, Inc. [*Associated Press*] (SAG)
HOMF.......... Home Fed Bancorp [*NASDAQ symbol*] (TTSB)
HOMG.......... Home Grocer.com, Inc. [*NASDAQ symbol*] (SG)
HOMG.......... Homeowners Group [*NASDAQ symbol*] (TTSB)
HOMG.......... Homeowners Group, Inc. [*NASDAQ symbol*] (NQ)
HOMHS........ Home Office and Ministry of Home Security (SAUO)
HOMI........... Homicide (DLA)
HOMIC......... Homicide [*Legal shorthand*] (LWAP)
Hominoid..... Hominoidea (SAUS)
HOMO.......... Highest Occupied Molecular Orbital [*Atomic physics*]
HOMO.......... Homeopath [*or Homeopathic*] (WDAA)
HOMO.......... Homogenous
homo........... Homosexual (STED)
HOMO.......... Homosexual
Homob......... Homobonus de Cremona [*Deceased, 1272*] [*Authority cited in pre-1607 legal work*] (DSA)
HOMOCO..... Homemakers & Mothers Cooperatives, Inc.
HomoD......... Homo Dei. Przeglad Ascetyczno-Duszpasterski [*Warsaw/Wroclaw*] [*A publication*] (BJA)
HOMOEO...... Homoeopathy [*Medicine*]
Homoeop Q... Homoeopathic Quarterly (journ.) (SAUS)
Homoepath... Homoeopathic Digest (journ.) (SAUS)
Homogeneou Catal Org Inorg Chem... Homogeneous Catalysis in Organic and Inorganic Chemistry (journ.) (SAUS)
homolat....... Homolateral (STED)
HOMOLAT.... Homolateral [*Medicine*]
HOMO/LUMO gap... Energy difference between the Highest Occupied Molecular Orbital and the Lowest Unoccupied Molecular Orbital (SAUS)
Homomilk.... Homogenized Milk (SAUS)
homop.......... homophobia (SAUS)
HOMOs........ Highest Occupied Molecular Orbitals (SAUO)
HOMOtO...... Homemakers & Mothers Cooperatives, Inc. (SAUO)
HOMP.......... Halifax Ocean Meeting Point
HOMPR........ Hang On, Mobile Phones Ringing. (SAUS)
Hom Pst Rev... Homiletic and Pastoral Review (journ.) (SAUS)
Hom R.......... Homiletic Review (journ.) (SAUS)
HOMR.......... Human Oriented Mishap Reduction (ACAE)
HOMREP....... Homicide Report (SAUS)
HOMS.......... Harbor Operations and Maintenance Support [*Navy*] (VNW)
HOMS.......... Hellfire Optimized Missile System [*Army*] (DOMA)
HOMS.......... Home State Holdings, Inc. [*NASDAQ symbol*] (SAG)
HOMS.......... Homing Optical Missile System (SAUS)
HOMS.......... Homing Overlay Missile Simulation (ACAE)
HOMS.......... Homme et Societe (journ.) (SAUS)
HOMS.......... Hubble Optical Mechanical Simulator (SAUS)
HOMS.......... Hydrological Operational Multipurpose Subprogramme [*World Meteorological Organization*] [*Information service or system*] (IID)
HOMS.......... Hydrological Operational Multipurpose System (SAUS)
hom sap...... Homo Sapiens (BARN)
HOMSTD...... Homestead (DLA)
HOMT.......... Hydroxyindole O-Methyltransferase [*Also, HIOMT*] [*An enzyme*]
HOMV.......... Hop Mosaic Virus [*Plant pathology*]

Hom Wld..... Human World (journ.) (SAUS)
HOMX......... PLM Transportation Equipment [*Private rail car owner code*]
HON............ Handbook of the Nations [*A publication*]
HON............ Handover Number (SAUS)
HON............ Hazardous Organic NESHAP [*National Emission Standards for Hazardous Air Polluta nts*] (GNE)
HON............ Health On the Net Foundation (SAUO)
HON............ Helicopter Operations Net (SAUO)
HON............ Hold Off Normal
HON............ Hold of Normal (SAUS)
Hon............ Honduras (SHCU)
HON............ Honduras
hon............ Honey (ADWA)
HON............ Honey (DSUE)
Hon............ Honeybees
HON............ Honeywell Electro-Optics Center Library, Lexington, MA [*OCLC symbol*] (OCLC)
HON............ Honeywell, Inc. [*Formerly, MH, M-H*] [*NYSE symbol*] (SPSG)
HON............ Honington FTU [*British*] [*ICAO designator*] (FAAC)
HON............ Honiton [*Municipal borough in England*]
HON............ Honolulu [*Hawaii*] [*Seismograph station code, US Geological Survey*] (SEIS)
hon............ honor (SAUS)
hon............ Honorable (GEAB)
Hon............ Honorable (TBD)
HON............ Honorable
hon............ honorarium (SAUS)
HON............ Honorary (MSA)
Hon............ Honorary (WDAA)
hon............ honored (SAUS)
Hon............ Honorius de Kent [*Flourished, 1185-1208*] [*Authority cited in pre-1607 legal work*] (DSA)
Hon............ Honour (SAUO)
Hon............ Honourable (WDAA)
hon............ Honourably (SAUS)
HON............ Huron [*South Dakota*] [*Airport symbol*] (OAG)
HON............ Hydroxyoxo-L-norvaline [*Antibiotic*]
HONA.......... Health of Naval Aviation (DOMA)
HON AF........ Honorary Admiral of the Fleet [*Navy*] [*British*] (ROG)
Hon ARAM... Honorary Associate of the Royal Academy of Music [*British*]
HonARCM.... Honorary Associate of the Royal College of Music [*British*] (DI)
HonASTA...... Honorary Associate of the Swimming Teachers' Association [*British*] (DBQ)
HONBLE....... Honorable
HONCAUS.... Honoris Causa [*For the Sake of Honor, Honorary*] [*Latin*] (ADA)
Hond........... Honduras (VRA)
HOND.......... Honduras
HOND.......... Honoured (ROG)
Honda.......... Honda Motors Co. Ltd. [*Associated Press*] (SAG)
Honda Meml Ser Mater Sci... Honda Memorial Series on Materials Science (journ.) (SAUS)
HonDis......... Honourable Discharge (SAUS)
HonDLitt...... Honorary Doctor of Letters
Hondo.......... Hondo Oil & Gas Co. [*Associated Press*] (SAG)
hondreng..... honorary doctor of engineering (SAUO)
HonDrRCA... Honorary Doctorate of the Royal College of Art [*British*] (DBQ)
HonDSc......... Honorary Doctor of Science
HONE........... Hands On Network Environment (SAUS)
HONEA......... Honea Path, SC [*American Association of Railroads railroad junction routing code*]
HONER......... Hemispherical Optimized Net Radiometer (SAUS)
HONEST....... Helicopter Operations in a Night Environment Against a Simulated Target [*Military*] (MCD)
Honeywell Comput J... Honeywell Computer Journal (journ.) (SAUS)
HonFBID...... Honorary Fellow of the British Institute of Interior Design (DBQ)
HonFBID...... Honorary Fellow of the British Institute of Interior (SAUS)
Hon FEIS...... Honorary Fellow of the Educational Institute of Scotland
HonFHCIMA... Honorary Fellow of the Hotel, Catering, and Institutional Management Association [*British*] (DBQ)
HonFHQMA... Honorary Fellow of the Hotel, Catering and Institutional Management Association (SAUS)
HonFHQMA... Honorry Fellow of the Hotel, Catering and Institutional Management Association (SAUO)
HonFIGasE... Honorary Fellow of the Institution of Gas Engineers [*British*] (DBQ)
HonFIIM....... Honorary Fellow of the Institution of Industrial Managers [*British*] (DBQ)
HonFIMarE... Honorary Fellow of the Institute of Marine Engineers [*British*] (DBQ)
HonFIMechE... Honorary Fellow of the Institution of Mechanical Engineers [*British*] (DBQ)
HonFIMM..... Honorary Fellow of the Institution of Mining and Metallurgy [*British*] (DBQ)
HonFInstE.... Honorary Fellow of the Institute of Energy [*British*] (DBQ)
HonFInstMC... Honorary Fellow of the Institute of Measurement [*British*] (DBQ)
HonFInstNDT... Honorary Fellow of the British Institute of Non-Destructive Testing (DBQ)
HonFIOP...... Honorary Fellow of the Institute of Printing [*British*] (DI)
HonFIPlant E... Honorary Fellow of the Institution of Plant Engineers (SAUO)
HonFIQA...... Honorary Fellow of the Institute of Quality Assurance [*British*] (DBQ)
HonFIRSE.... Honorary Fellow of the Institution of Railway Signal Engineers [*British*] (DBQ)
HonFISP...... Honorary Fellow of the Institute of Sewage Purification (SAUO)
HonFITD...... Honorary Fellow of the Institute of Training and Development [*British*] (DI)
HonFIWHTE... Honorary Fellow of the Institution of Works and Highways Technician Engineers [*British*] (DBQ)
HonFIGsE..... Honorary Fellow of the Institution of Gas Engineers (SAUS)
Hon FNDTS... Honorary Fellow of the Non-Destructive Testing Society of Great Britain
HonFPRI...... Honorary Life Member of the Plastics and Rubber Institute [*British*] (DBQ)
HonFPRI...... Honorary Life Member of the Plastics and Rubber Institute (SAUS)
Hon FRAM... Honorary Fellow of the Royal Academy of Music [*British*]
Hon FRCM... Honorary Fellow of the Royal College of Music [*British*] (WDAA)
HonFRINA.... Honorary Fellow of the Royal Institution of Naval Architects (SAUO)
Hon FRPS.... Honorary Fellow of the Royal Photographic Society [*British*]
Hon FS......... Honora Fellow of the Educational Institute of Scotland (SAUS)
HonFSCP..... Honorary Fellow of the Society of Certified Professionals [*British*] (DBQ)
HonFSE........ Honorary Fellow of the Society of Engineers, Inc. [*British*] (DBQ)
HonFSGT..... Honorary Fellow of the Society of Glass Technology [*British*] (DBQ)
HonFSLAET... Honorary Fellow of the Society of Licensed Aircraft Engineers and Technologists [*British*] (DBQ)
HonFTCL...... Honorary Fellow of the Society of Glass Technology (SAUO)
Hon FTCL..... Honorary Fellow of Trinity College of Music, London [*British*] (WDAA)
Hon FTSC.... Honorary Fellow of the Tonic Sol-fa College (WDAA)
HonFWeldI... Honorary Fellow of the Welding Institute [*British*] (DBQ)
HonFWeldI... Honorary Fellow of the Welding Institute (SAUS)
Hongik Univ J... Hongik University. Journal (journ.) (SAUS)
Hong Kong LJ... Hong Kong Law Journal [*A publication*] (DLA)
Hong Kong LR... Hong Kong Law Reports [*A publication*] (DLA)
Hong Kong LR... Hong Kong Law Reports (journ.) (SAUS)
Hong Kong Nurs J... Hong Kong Nursing Journal (journ.) (SAUS)
Hong Kong UL Jo... Hong Kong University. Law Journal [*A publication*] (DLA)
Hong Kong UL Jo... Hong Kong University. Law Journal (journ.) (SAUS)
Hong Kong Univ Fish J... Hong Kong University. Fisheries Journal (journ.) (SAUS)
HONGR........ Honegger, IL [*American Association of Railroads railroad junction routing code*]
HonGSM...... Honorary Member of the Guildhall School of Music and Drama [*British*] (DBQ)
HONI........... HON Indus [*NASDAQ symbol*] (TTSB)
HONI........... Hon Industries, Inc. [*NASDAQ symbol*] (NQ)
HonInd.......... Hon Industries, Inc. [*Associated Press*] (SAG)
HONKAY...... Hokkaido National Agricultural Experiment Station. Soil Survey Report (journ.) (SAUS)
HON L.......... Honorary Lieutenant [*Navy*] [*British*] (ROG)
HONLEA....... Heads of National Drug Law Enforcement Agencies (SAUS)
HonLife MInstGas E... Honorary Life Member of the Institute of Gas Engineers (SAUO)
HON M......... Honorary Member (ROG)
HonMGSM... Honorary Member of the Guildhall School of Music (SAUO)
HonMIAE...... Honorary Member of the Institution of Automobile Engineers (SAUO)
HonMIEI....... Honorary Member of the Institution of Engineering Inspection (SAUO)
HonMInstGas E... Honorary Member of the Institute of Gas Engineers (SAUO)
HonMInst NDT... Honorary Member of the British Institute of Non-Destructive Testing (DBQ)
HonMIPlant E... Honorary Member of the Institution of Plant Engineers (SAUO)
Hon MNDTS... Honorary Member of the Non-Destructive Testing Society of Great Britain
HonMRAM... Honorary Member of the Royal Academy of Music (SAUO)
HonMRCM... Honorary Member of the Royal College of Music (SAUO)
HonMRDI..... Honorary Member of Royal Designers for Industry (SAUO)
HonMRIN..... Honorary Member of the Royal Institute of Navigation [*British*] (DBQ)
Hon Mst........ Honorary Magistrate (SAUS)
HonMTCM.... Honorary Member of the Trinity College of Music (SAUO)
HonMWES... Honorary Member of the Women's Engineering Society [*British*] (DBQ)
HONO.......... Honolulu [*Hawaii*] (CINC)
Honolulu Ad... Honolulu Advertiser (journ.) (SAUS)
HONOR........ An Automated Bank Teller Network in the State of Florida [*Communications term*] (DCT)
honor.......... Honorably (GEAB)
honor.......... Honorary (GEAB)
Hon RAM...... Honorary Member of the Royal Academy of Music [*British*]
HonRCM....... Honorary Member of the Royal College of Music [*British*] (DBQ)
HonRM......... Honorary Member of the Royal School of Church Music (SAUS)
HonRNCM.... Honorary Member of the Royal Northern College of Music [*British*] (DBQ)
Hon RSCM... Honorary Member of the Royal School of Church Music [*British*]
honry.......... Honorary (DD)
Hons........... Honors (DD)
HONS.......... Honors
HON SCH MOD LANG... Honour School of Modern Languages [*British*] (ROG)
HON SEC..... Honorary Secretary (ROG)
Honse Mag... House Mazine (journ.) (SAUS)
HONSTIC...... Hong Kong Scientific and Technical Information Centre (SAUS)
HON SURG LIEUT COL... Honorary Surgeon Lieutenant-Colonel [*Military*] [*British*] (ROG)
HONTAI-2.... The Name of Fiber Optic Cable Route Connecting Hong Kong to Taiwan [*Communications term*] (DCT)
Hon TCL...... Honorary Member of Trinity College of Music, London [*British*] (WDAA)
Ho Number... Hodgsons Number (SAUS)
HON VA....... Honorary Vice-Admiral [*Navy*] [*British*] (ROG)
HONX.......... Harvest States Co-Operatives [*Private rail car owner code*]
HONY.......... Honorary (WGA)
Honywel...... Honeywell, Inc. [*Associated Press*] (SAG)
HOO............ Avila College, Kansas City, MO [*OCLC symbol*] (OCLC)
HOO............ Glacier Water Services, Inc. [*AMEX symbol*] (SAG)
HOO............ Hanford Operations Office [*Nuclear energy*] (MCD)

HOO .... Hiroo [*Japan*] [*Seismograph station code, US Geological Survey*] (SEIS)
HOO .... House Officer Observer (SAUS)
HOO .... Quang Duc [*South Vietnam*] [*Airport symbol*] (AD)
HOOC .... Hooker Chemical [*Federal Railroad Administration identification code*]
HOOCCOOH... Oxalic Acid [*Medicine*] (EDAA)
HOOD .... Hereditary Osteo-Onychodysplasia [*Medicine*]
HOOD .... Hierarchical Object-Oriented Design [*Computer science*] (ODBW)
Hood .... Neighborhood [*Slang*]
Hood C .... Hood College (GAGS)
Hood Ex .... Hood on Executors [*A publication*] (DLA)
HoodEx .... Hood on Executors (journ.) (SAUS)
HOODS .... Hereditary Onycho-Osteodysplasia Syndrome [*Medicine*] (STED)
Ho of Reps... House of Representatives (SAUO)
HOOI .... Hall Occupational Orientation Inventory (STED)
HOOK .... Handbook of Occupational Keywords [*For use in employment services*] [*Department of Labor*]
HOOK .... Hook Drugs, Inc. (SAUO)
Hook .... Hooker's Reports [*25-62 Connecticut*] [*A publication*] (DLA)
HOOK .... Redhook Ale Brewery, Inc. [*NASDAQ symbol*] (SAG)
Hooker .... Hooker's Reports [*25-62 Connecticut*] [*A publication*] (DLA)
Hoon .... Hoonahan's Sind Reports [*India*] [*A publication*] (DLA)
Hoonahan .... Hoonahan's Sind Reports [*India*] [*A publication*] (DLA)
HOOP .... GSC Panel for the Health of the Ocean Module (SAUS)
HOOP .... Handbook of Operating Procedures
HOOP .... Health of Ocean Module (SAUS)
HOOP .... Helicopter Of Opportunity (SAUS)
HOOP .... Sure Shot International, Inc. [*NASDAQ symbol*] (SAG)
HoopHl .... Hooper Holmes, Inc. [*Associated Press*] (SAG)
HOOPS .... Hierarchical Object-Oriented Picture System [*Computer science*]
HOOPW .... Hooper Holmes, Inc. (SAUO)
HOOPW .... Sure Shot Intl Wrrt [*NASDAQ symbol*] (TTSB)
Hoosier Dome... Hoosier Dome Stadium (SAUS)
Hoosier Sch Lib... Hoosier School Libraries (journ.) (SAUS)
HOOT .... Heating-Oil-Operability Test (SAUO)
HOOV .... Hoover's Inc. [*NASDAQ symbol*] (SG)
HOP .... Handoff Point [*Aviation*] (FAAC)
HOP .... HEDL [*Hanford Engineering Development Laboratory*] Overpower [*Nuclear energy*] (NRCH)
HOP .... Helicopter Operations (FAAC)
HOP .... Helium Oxidizer-Tank Pressure (AAG)
HOP .... Help Other People [*Scout motto*]
HOP .... Heritage of Pride [*An association*] (EA)
HOP .... High Order Position (SAUS)
HOP .... High-Order Position (AFIT)
HOP .... High Oxygen Pressure
HOP .... Holding Procedures (SAA)
HOP .... Holidays One-Parents [*An association*] (BUAC)
HOP .... Homecast Open Protocol (SAUS)
HOP .... Home Opportunity Program (SAUO)
HOP .... Hong Kong Outline Plan (SAUS)
HOP .... Hope [*Jamaica*] [*Seismograph station code, US Geological Survey*] [*Closed*] (SEIS)
HOP .... Hopkinsville, KY [*Location identifier*] [*FAA*] (FAAL)
HOP .... Hostile Observation Post (SAUS)
HOP .... House Operating Tape [*Telecommunications*] (TEL)
HOP .... Hybrid Operating Program [*Computer science*] (IEEE)
HOP .... Hydrogen Overpotential (SAUS)
HOP .... Hydrographic Office Publications [*Obsolete*] [*Navy*]
HOP .... Hydroxydaunomycin [*Adriamycin*], Oncovin , Prednisone [*Vincristine*] [*Antineoplastic drug regimen*]
HOP .... Hydroxyproline [*Medicine*] (EDAA)
HOPA .... Hopantenate Calcium [*Cerebral activator*]
HOPA .... Hospital-Based Organ Procurement Agency (MELL)
Hop & C ...... Hopwood and Coltman's English Registration Appeal Cases [*A publication*] (DLA)
Hop & Colt... Hopwood and Coltman's English Registration Appeal Cases [*A publication*] (DLA)
Hop & Ph..... Hopwood and Philbrick's English Registration Appeal Cases [*A publication*] (DLA)
Hop & Phil... Hopwood and Philbrick's English Registration Appeal Cases [*A publication*] (DLA)
HOPBEG ...... British Hotel and Public Building Equipment Group (SAUO)
HOPC .... Home Office Prison Commission (SAUO)
HOPC .... Hydro Optics, Inc. (SAUO)
HOPD .... Hospital Out-Patient Department (MEDA)
HOPE .... Hackers on Planet Earth [*An association*]
HOPE .... Halley Optical Probe Experiment
HOPE .... Harbingers of Productive English (SAUS)
HOPE .... Healthcare Opposed to Euthanasia [*An association*] (BUAC)
HOPE .... Health Omnibus Programs Extension Legislation (SAUS)
HOPE .... Health Opportunities for People Everywhere (SAUO)
HOPE .... Health Organization to Preserve the Environment
HOPE .... Health-Oriented Physician Education
HOPE .... Hellenic Organisation for the Promotion of Exports (BUAC)
HOPE .... Helping Outstanding Pupils Educationally (SAUO)
HOPE .... Help Obese People Everywhere
HOPE .... Help Organise Peaceful Energy [*An association*] (BUAC)
HOPE .... Help Organize Peace Everywhere (SAUO)
HOPE .... Help Our Public Education (SAUO)
HOPE .... Highlights of Personal Experience in Agriculture Department
HOPE .... Highly Instrumented Orbiting Primate Experiment
HOPE .... Hispanic Organization of Professionals and Executives [*Silver Spring, MD*] (EA)
HOPE .... Holistic Orthogonal Parameter Estimation [*Medicine*] (DMAA)
HOPE .... Home Ownership and Opportunity for People Everywhere [*Program*] [*HUD*]
HOPE .... Homes of Private Enterprise (EA)
HOPE .... Hope, AR [*American Association of Railroads railroad junction routing code*]
Hope .... Hope (of Kerse). Manuscript Decisions, Scotch Court of Session [*A publication*] (DLA)
HOPE .... Hospital-Oriented Programmed Environment
HOPE .... Housing Opportunities for People Everywhere (SAUO)
HOPE .... Housing Opportunity and Equality (SAUO)
HOPE .... Housing Our People Economically
HOPE .... Humanistic Organization for Personal Expansion
HOPE .... Hydrogen-Oxygen Primary Extraterrestrial [*Fuel cell*] [*NASA*]
HOPE .... People-to-People Health Foundation (EA)
HOPEC .... Hand-Operated Positive Energy Control
HOPEC .... Hydrogen Organization for Progress, Education, and Cooperation [*Defunct*] (EA)
HOPECO...... Hormoz Petroleum Co. [*Iran*] (BUAC)
Hope Com Law... Hope's Compendium of the Commercial Law of the Pacific [*A publication*] (DLA)
Hope Com Law... Hopes Compendium of the Commercial Law of the Pacific (journ.) (SAUS)
Hope Dec..... Hope (of Kerse). Manuscript Decisions, Scotch Court of Session [*A publication*] (DLA)
HOPE Fuel Cell... Hydrogen-Oxygen Primary Extraterrestrial Fuel Cell (SAUS)
HOPE Fuel Cell Program... Hydrogen-Oxygen Primary Extraterrestrial Fuel Cell Program (SAUS)
HOPEG .... Hotel and Public Building Equipment Group (SAUO)
Hope Maj Pr... Hope's Major Practicks [*Scotland*] [*A publication*] (DLA)
Hope Min Pr... Hope's Minor Practicks [*Scotland*] [*A publication*] (DLA)
HOPES .... High Oxygen-Pulping Enclosed System (PDAA)
HOPG .... Highly Oriented Pyrolytic Graphite [*Engineering*]
HOPG .... Honeywell Proving Ground (SAUS)
HOPH .... Home of Peace Hospitals [*Australia*]
HOPI .... Handbook of Operating Instructions [*Navy*] (MCD)
HOPI .... History of Present Illness [*Medicine*] (HGAA)
HOPI .... Hughes Optical Products, Incorporated (ACAE)
HOPING .... Helping Other Parents in Normal Grieving (EA)
Hopk .... Hopkins' New York Chancery Reports [*A publication*] (DLA)
Hopk Adm.... Hopkinson's Pennsylvania Admiralty Judgments [*A publication*] (DLA)
Hopk Adm.... Hopkinsons Pennsylvania Admiralty Judgments (journ.) (SAUS)
Hopk Adm Dec... Admiralty Decisions of Hopkinson in Gilpin's Reports [*A publication*] (DLA)
Hopk Av....... Hopkins' Average [*4th ed.*] [*1884*] [*A publication*] (DLA)
Hopk Av....... Hopkins Average (journ.) (SAUS)
Hopk CC ...... Hopkins' New York Chancery Reports [*A publication*] (DLA)
Hopk Ch....... Hopkins' New York Chancery Reports [*A publication*] (DLA)
Hopk Chanc Rep... Hopkins' New York Chancery Reports [*A publication*] (DLA)
Hopk Judg... Hopkinson's Pennsylvania Admiralty Judgments [*A publication*] (DLA)
Hopk Judg... Hopkinsons Pennsylvania Admiralty Judgments (journ.) (SAUS)
Hopk Mar Ins... Hopkins on Marine Insurance [*A publication*] (DLA)
Hopk Mtr Ins... Hopkins on Marine Insurance (journ.) (SAUS)
HOPKN .... Hopkins, MN [*American Association of Railroads railroad junction routing code*]
Hopk Rep..... Hopkins' New York Chancery Reports [*A publication*] (DLA)
Hopk Rep..... Hopkins New York Chancery Reports (journ.) (SAUS)
Hopk W....... Hopkinson's Works [*Pennsylvania*] [*A publication*] (DLA)
Hopk Wks..... Hopkinson's Works [*Pennsylvania*] [*A publication*] (DLA)
Hopk Works (PA)... Hopkinson's Works [*Pennsylvania*] [*A publication*] (DLA)
HOPL .... History of Programming Languages
HOPM .... Hydraulic Oil Power Module (DNAB)
Hop Min ...... Hope's Minor Practicks [*Scotland*] [*A publication*] (DLA)
HOPO .... Holders of Public Office
HOPP .... Half-Object Plus Protocol (RALS)
HOPR .... Holly Holdings, Inc. [*NASDAQ symbol*] (SAG)
HOPR .... Holly Products [*NASDAQ symbol*] (SAG)
HOPRD .... Holly Products 10% Cv'D'Pfd [*NASDAQ symbol*] (TTSB)
HOPRW .... Holly Products Wrrt [*NASDAQ symbol*] (TTSB)
HOPS .... Hart Brewing [*NASDAQ symbol*] (TTSB)
HOPS .... Harvest Operating System (SAUS)
HOPS .... Heads of Public Services (SAUS)
HOPS .... Heineken Operations Planning System [*Heineken USA*]
HOPS .... Helmet-Mounted Optical Projection System
HOPS .... Helmet Optical Position Sensor (SAUS)
HOPS .... Heterodyne Optical Optimization Communication System with Stops [*NASA*]
HOPS .... Highway Optimization Programme System (SAUO)
HOPS .... HOst Proximity Service [*Computer science*]
HOPSTOP .... Hopper Stop (SAUS)
HOPT .... Handbook of Powder Technology (journ.) (SAUS)
HOPT .... Hypoparathyroidism [*Endocrinology*]
HOPTE .... High Order Path Terminating Equipment (SAUS)
HOPTN .... Hoppeston, IL [*American Association of Railroads railroad junction routing code*]
HO Publ .... Hydrographic Office. Publication (journ.) (SAUS)
HO Purdue Univ Coop Ext Serv... HO-Purdue University. Cooperative Extension Service (journ.) (SAUS)
HOPW .... Handbook of Public Works (SAUO)
HOPWA .... Housing Opportunities for Persons with AIDS (SAUO)
Hopw & C.... Hopwood and Coltman's English Registration Appeal Cases [*A publication*] (DLA)
Hopw & Colt... Hopwood and Coltman's English Registration Appeal Cases [*A publication*] (DLA)
Hopw & P.... Hopwood and Philbrick's English Registration Appeal Cases [*A publication*] (DLA)

Hopw & Phil... Hopwood and Philbrick's English Registration Appeal Cases [*A publication*] (DLA)
HOPZ... Hormel Plant Properties [*Federal Railroad Administration identification code*]
HOQ... Hansard Oral Questions [*Database*] [*House of Commons*] [*Canada*] [*Information service or system*] (CRD)
HOQ... High Order Quotient (SAUS)
HOQ... Hof [*Germany*] [*Airport symbol*] (OAG)
HOQ... Home Office Quote (NITA)
HOQ... Hysteroid-Obsessoid Questionnaire [*Psychology*]
HOQNO... Heptyl(hydroxy)quinoline N-Oxide [*Organic chemistry*]
HOQUI... Hoquiam, WA [*American Association of Railroads railroad junction routing code*]
HOR... Heliocentric Orbit Rendezvous (MCD)
HOR... Hoger Onderwijs Reactor
HOR... Holder of Record [*Investment term*]
HOR... Home of Record
HOR... Home on Record (SAUS)
HOR... Hoover-Owens-Rentschler [*Engines*]
HOR... Horace [*Roman poet, 65-8BC*] [*Classical studies*] (ROG)
Hor... Horayoth (BJA)
HOR... Horizon (KSC)
HOR... Horizon Air-Taxi Ltd. [*Switzerland*] [*ICAO designator*] (FAAC)
Hor... Horizon (journ.) (SAUS)
hor... Horizontal (WDMC)
HOR... Horizontal
Hor... Horizontal Lights [*Navigation signal*]
HOR... Horn & Hardart Co. [*Later, Hanover Direct*] [*AMEX symbol*] (SPSG)
Hor... Horolium (SAUS)
Hor... Horologium [*Constellation*]
HOR... Horology
HOR... Hot Resources Ltd. [*Vancouver Stock Exchange symbol*]
HoR... House of Representatives (SAUS)
HOR... Hydrogen-Oxygen Reaction (SAA)
HOR... University of Minnesota, the Hormel Institute, Austin, MN [*OCLC symbol*] (OCLC)
HORA... High Out of Range Alarm [*Electronics*] (ECII)
Hora Bk... Horn Book Mazine (journ.) (SAUS)
HORAD... Horizontal RADAR Display
Hor & Th Cas... Horrigan and Thompson's Cases on Self-Defense [*A publication*] (DLA)
Hor&Th Cas... Horrigan and Thompsons Cases on Self Defense (journ.) (SAUS)
HORA SOM... Hora Somni [*At Bedtime*] [*Latin*] (WDAA)
HORATIO... Human Operator Response Analyser and Timer for Infrequent Occurrences (PDAA)
Horat Mand... Horatius Mandosius [*Deceased, 1594*] [*Authority cited in pre-1607 legal work*] (DSA)
HORC... Horizon Health Corp. (SAUS)
HORC... Horizon Health Corporation (SAUO)
HOR CL... Horizontal Clearance [*Nautical charts*]
HORD... Hordeum [*Barley*] [*Pharmacy*] (ROG)
HORD... Hydrogen-Oxygen Recombination Device (SAUS)
HOR DECU... Hora Decubitus [*At Bedtime*] [*Pharmacy*]
HOR DECUB... Hora Decubitus [*At Bedtime*] [*Pharmacy*] (ROG)
hor decub... Hora Decubitus [*At Bedtime*] [*Latin*] (WDAA)
HO-RE-CA... Federation Internationale des Organisations d'Hoteliers, Restaurateurs, et Cafetiers [*International Organization of Hotel and Restaurant Associations*] (EAIO)
HORECA... International Union of National Associations of Hotel, Restaurant and Cafe Keepers (SAUO)
HORECOM... International Exhibition for the Hotel and Restaurant Trades Communities
HOREN... Horizontal Enlarger [*Photography*]
HOREP... Hot Photographic Report
HOREP... Hot Report
HORF... High Output Renal Failure [*Medicine*] (MELL)
Hor Fr... Hovenden on Frauds (journ.) (SAUS)
Horg... Hammond Organ
HORIN... Horine, MO [*American Association of Railroads railroad junction routing code*]
HOR INTERM... Horis Intermediis [*In the Intermediate Hours*] [*Pharmacy*]
Horitz... Horizontal (NITA)
Horiz... Horizon (DIAR)
HORIZ... Horizon (MSA)
HORIZ... Horizontal (AABC)
Horiz... Horizontal (AMHC)
horiz... Horizontal (IDOE)
HORIZ... Horizontal Polarization
Horiz Biochem Biophys... Horizons in Biochemistry and Biophysics (journ.) (SAUS)
HorizFS... Horizon Financial Services Corp. [*Associated Press*] (SAG)
HorizMH... Horizon Mental Health Management [*Associated Press*] (SAG)
HoriznGp... Horizon Group, Inc. [*Associated Press*] (SAG)
Horizons Bib Th... Horizons in Biblical Theology (journ.) (SAUS)
HORIZ SENS BAL... Horizontal Sensitivity Balance (SAUS)
HORL... Home Office Reference Laboratory, Inc. (SAUO)
H or M... Hit or Miss (MIST)
Horm... Hormone (SAUS)
HORM... Hybrid Orbital Rehybridization Method [*Atomic physics*]
Horm Behav... Hormones and Behavior (journ.) (SAUS)
Horm Cancer Sel Pap Discuss Clin Cancer Semin... Hormones and Cancer. Select Papers and Discussion from the Clinical Cancer Seminar (journ.) (SAUS)
Horm Cell Regul... Hormones and Cell Regulation (journ.) (SAUS)
Hormel... Hormel [*George*] & Co. [*Associated Press*] (SAG)
Hormel Inst Univ Minn Annu Rep... Hormel Institute. University of Minnesota. Annual Report (journ.) (SAUS)
Horm Metab Res... Hormone and Metabolic Research (journ.) (SAUS)
Horm Metab Res Suppl... Hormone and Metabolic Research Supplement (journ.) (SAUS)
Horm Metab Res Suppl Ser... Hormone and Metabolic Research. Supplement Series (journ.) (SAUS)
HorMn... Horace Mann Educators Corp. [*Associated Press*] (SAG)
Hormone Beh... Hormones and Behavior (journ.) (SAUS)
Hormone Met... Hormone and Metabolic Research (journ.) (SAUS)
Horm Steroids Proc Int Con... Hormonal Steroids. Proceedings of the International Conference on Hormonal Steroids (journ.) (SAUS)
HORMV... Hordeum Mosaic Virus [*Plant pathology*]
Horn Afr... Horn of Africa (journ.) (SAUS)
Horn & H... Horn and Hurlstone's English Exchequer Reports [*1838-39*] [*A publication*] (DLA)
Horn&H... Horn and Hurlstones English Exchequer Reports (journ.) (SAUS)
Hornbk... Hornbeck Offshore Services, Inc. [*Associated Press*] (SAG)
Horne Dip... Horne on Diplomacy [*A publication*] (DLA)
Horne Mir... Horne's Mirror of Justice [*A publication*] (DLA)
Horne MJ... Horne's Mirror of Justice [*A publication*] (DLA)
Horner... Horner's Reports [*11-23 South Dakota*] [*A publication*] (DLA)
Horner's Ann St... Horner's Annotated Revised Statutes [*Indiana*] [*A publication*] (DLA)
Horner's Rev St... Horner's Annotated Revised Statutes [*Indiana*] [*A publication*] (DLA)
HORN GN... Homblende Gneisses (SAUS)
HORN GN... Hornblende Gneisses [*Geology*]
Horo... Horologium [*Constellation*]
Horo... Horoscope (SAUS)
Horol... Horological (SAUS)
horol... Horology (ADWA)
HOROL... Horology
Horol Inst Am J... Horological Institute of America Journal (journ.) (SAUS)
Hor Osc... Horizontal Oscillator (SAUS)
HORP... Height Of Ray Path (SAUS)
Horr & B Mun Ord... Horr and Bemis' Treatise on Municipal Police Ordinances [*A publication*] (DLA)
Horr & T Cas Self-Def... Horrigan and Thompson's Cases on Self-Defense [*A publication*] (DLA)
Horr & Th... Horrigan and Thompson's Cases on Self-Defense [*A publication*] (DLA)
Horrn Immun Proc Int Conf... Hormones and Immunity. Proceedings of the International Conference on Hormones and Immunity (journ.) (SAUS)
HORS... Kentucky Hors Center, Inc. (SAUO)
HORSA... Hut Operation Raising School-leaving Age (SAUS)
HorsAb... Horsemans Abstracts (journ.) (SAUS)
HORSCERA... House of Representatives Standing Committee on the Environment (EERA)
HORSC-ERA... House of Representatives Standing Committee on the Environment Recreation, and the Arts [*Australia*] (BUAC)
HORSE... Heavy Operational Repair Squadron Engineer [*Air Force*] (AFM)
HORSE... Hydrofoil-Operated Rocket Submarine (NATG)
HORSEC... House of Representatives Standing Committee on Environment and Conservation [*Australia*] (BUAC)
Horsh... Horsham Corp. [*Associated Press*] (SAG)
Horshd... Horsehead Resource Development Company, Inc. [*Associated Press*] (SAG)
HOR SOM... Hora Somni [*At Bedtime*] [*Pharmacy*]
HORT... Hines Horticulture [*NASDAQ symbol*] (SG)
hort... Hortensis [*Of a Garden*] [*Latin*]
hort... Horticultural (SHCU)
hort... Horticulture (SHCU)
HORT... Horticulture
Hort... Horticulture (journ.) (SAUS)
Hort... Horticulture News (journ.) (SAUS)
HORTI... Horticulture [*Freight*]
HORTIC... Horticulture
Hortic Bull... Horticultural Bulletin (journ.) (SAUS)
Hortic Cent Loughgall Annu Rep... Horticultural Centre Loughgall. Annual Report (journ.) (SAUS)
Hortic Dig Univ Hawaii Coop Ext Serv... Horticulture Digest. University of Hawaii. Cooperative Extension Service (journ.) (SAUS)
Hortic Div Tokai Kinki Agric Exp Stn Rep... Horticultural Division of Tokai Kinki Agricultural Experiment Station. Reports (journ.) (SAUS)
Hortic Educ Assoc Yearb... Horticultural Education Association. Yearbook (journ.) (SAUS)
Hortic News NJ State Hortic Soc... Horticultural News. New Jersey State Horticultural Society (journ.) (SAUS)
Hortic NZ... Horticulture in New Zealand (journ.) (SAUS)
Hortic Res... Horticultural Research (journ.) (SAUS)
Hortic Res Inst Ont Rep... Horticultural Research Institute of Ontario. Report (journ.) (SAUS)
Hortic Rev... Horticultural Reviews (journ.) (SAUS)
HORTL... Horticultural
Hort Mach Leafl... Horticultural Machinery Leaflet (journ.) (SAUS)
Hort N... Horticultural News (journ.) (SAUS)
Hort Pl Breed... Horticultul Plan Breeding (journ.) (SAUS)
Hort Res... Horticultural Research (journ.) (SAUS)
Hort Res Rec... Holticultural Research Record. New South Wales Department of Agriculture. Division of Horticulture (journ.) (SAUS)
HortSci... HortScience (journ.) (SAUS)
HORU... Home Office Research Unit (BUAC)
HOR UN SPAT... Horae Unius Spatio [*At the End of an Hour*] [*Pharmacy*]

HOR UN SPATIO... Horae Unius Spatio [*At the End of an Hour*] [*Pharmacy*] (ROG)
HORUS........ Hypersonic Orbital Research and Utilization System (SAUS)
HORUS........ Hypersonic Orbital Upper Stage (SAUS)
HORV........... Hydraulic and Optical Repair Vehicle (PDAA)
Horw YB...... Horwood's Year Books of Edward I [*A publication*] (DLA)
Horw YB...... Horwoods Year Books of Edward I (journ.) (SAUS)
HorzBcTx..... Horizon Bancorp, Inc. (TX) [*Associated Press*] (SAG)
HorznFin...... Horizon Financial Corp. [*Associated Press*] (SAG)
HOS............ Croatian Defense Association [*Political party*]
HOS............ Hardware Operating System (SAUO)
HOS............ Hardwired Operating System (SAUS)
HOS............ Hardwire Operating System (IAA)
HOS............ Hawaiian Orchid Society (SAUO)
HOS............ Heads of Systems (SAUS)
HOS............ Health Online Service [*Computer science*] [*Medicine*]
HOS............ Health Opinion Survey (SAUS)
HOS............ Heated Oxygen Sensor [*Automotive engineering*]
HOS............ Heat of Solution
HOS............ Heckscher-Ohlin-Samuelson [*Theorem*]
HOS............ Helicopter Operations from Ships other than aircraft carriers (SAUS)
HOS............ Helicopter Oxygen System (SAUS)
HOS............ HELIOS Observation System (SAUS)
HOS............ Higher Order Software, Inc.
HOS............ Higher Order Statistics (SAUS)
HOS............ High-Order Software [*Computer science*] (NASA)
HOS............ History of Science (SAUS)
H-o-S.......... Holland-on-Sea (SAUS)
HOS............ Holland Shipbuilding (journ.) (SAUS)
HOS............ Home Orchard Society (EA)
HOS............ Hooker Air Services Ltd. (SAUO)
HOS............ Hoosier Southern Railroad [*Federal Railroad Administration identification code*]
HOS............ Horizontal Obstacle SONAR (IAA)
HoS............ Horse Serum [*Immunology*]
HOS............ Hosana [*Ethiopia*] [*Airport symbol*] (AD)
Hos............ Hosea [*Old Testament book*]
Hos............ Hosea Book of (SAUS)
HOS............ Hosebe, SIC [*Ukraine*] [*FAA designator*] (FAAC)
Hos............ Hostiensis [*Deceased, 1271*] [*Authority cited in pre-1607 legal work*] (DSA)
HOS............ Hostile
HOS............ Human Operator Simulator (MCD)
HOS............ Human Osteosarcoma [*Medicine*]
HOS............ Hungarian Office for Standardization (SAUO)
HOS............ Hydrocarbon Oxidation Studies (SAUS)
HOS............ Hydrographic Office Scale [*Obsolete*]
HOSA.......... Health Occupations Students of America (EA)
HOSA.......... Hearing Office Systems Administrator [*Computer science*]
HOSA.......... Home Owner Services Administration (SAUS)
HOSA.......... Hydroxylamine-O-Sulfonic Acid (SAUS)
HOSAT......... Hands-On Stick and Throttle (ACAE)
HOSC.......... Hardened Operational Site Concept (AAG)
HOSC.......... History of Science Cases
HOSC.......... Huntsville Operations Support Center [*NASA*] (KSC)
HOSCOM...... Hospital Comparisons (SAUO)
HOSCORP.... New York City Health and Hospitals Corp. (EA)
hose............ hosiery (SAUS)
Hosea.......... Hosea's Reports [*Ohio*] [*A publication*] (DLA)
Hosea's Rep... Cincinnati Superior Court Decisions [*Ohio*] [*A publication*] (DLA)
HOSG........... Helicopter Operations Study Group (SAUO)
HOSI........... Handbook of Service Instructions
HOSIA.......... Hospitals (journ.) (SAUS)
Hosiery St... Hosiery Statistics (journ.) (SAUS)
HOSJ........... Sovereign Hospitaller Order of Saint John (EA)
Hoskins........ Hoskins' Reports [*2 North Dakota*] [*A publication*] (DLA)
HOSM.......... Host Operations Systems Monitor (SAUO)
HOSP........... High Order Storage Position (SAUS)
HOSP........... Hospice (GOBB)
Hosp........... Hospital (AL)
hosp........... Hospital (VRA)
HOSP........... Hospital
HOSP........... Hospital Aircraft [*ICAO designator*] (FAAC)
Hosp........... Hospitalia (journ.) (SAUS)
Hosp........... Hospitalisation (SAUS)
Hosp........... Hospitalis (journ.) (SAUS)
Hosp........... Hospitality (journ.) (SAUS)
Hosp........... Hospital (journ.) (SAUS)
HOSP........... Hosposable Products, Inc. [*NASDAQ symbol*] (NQ)
HOSP........... Hot Springs National Park
HospAb........ Hospital Abstracts (journ.) (SAUS)
Hosp Abstr Serv... Hospital Abstract Service (journ.) (SAUS)
HOSPACT..... Hospital Patient Accounting (PDAA)
Hosp Adm Can... Hospital Administration in Canada (journ.) (SAUS)
Hosp Admin... Hospital Administration [*A publication*]
Hosp Admin Cur... Hospital Administration Currents (journ.) (SAUS)
Hosp Admitting Mon... Hospital Admitting Monthly (journ.) (SAUS)
Hosp and Health... Hospital and Health Services Administration (journ.) (SAUS)
Hosp Assoc J... Hospitals Association. Journal (journ.) (SAUS)
Hosp Bond Rev... Hospital Bond Review (journ.) (SAUS)
Hosp Build Bull... Hospital Building Bulletin (journ.) (SAUS)
Hosp Buyer... Hospital Buyer (journ.) (SAUS)
Hosp Byers Guide... Hospital Buyers Guide (journ.) (SAUS)
Hosp C.......... Hospital Corps (SAUO)
Hosp Care... Hospital Care (journ.) (SAUS)
HOSPCO...... Hospital Co. [*Marine Corps*]
Hosp Employ Health... Hospital Employee Health (journ.) (SAUS)
Hosp Eng..... Hospital Engineering (journ.) (SAUS)
Hosp Equip Supplies... Hospital Equipment and Supplies (journ.) (SAUS)
Hosp Fin Mgt... Hospital Financial Management (journ.) (SAUS)
Hosp Food Nutr Focus... Hospital Food and Nutrition Focus (journ.) (SAUS)
Hosp Formul... Hospital Formulary (journ.) (SAUS)
Hosp Formul Manage... Hospital Formulary Management (journ.) (SAUS)
Hosp Forum... Hospital Forum (journ.) (SAUS)
Hosp Gift Shop Manage... Hospital Gift Shop Management (journ.) (SAUS)
Hosp Health Care Newsl... Hospital Health Care Newsletter (journ.) (SAUS)
Hosp Health Serv Rev... Hospital and Health Services Review (journ.) (SAUS)
Hosp Hlt Care... Hospital and Health Care (journ.) (SAUS)
Hosp Hlth Care... Hospital and Health Care [*A publication*]
Hosp Hlt Man... Hospital and Health Management (journ.) (SAUS)
Hospice J.... Hospice Journal (journ.) (SAUS)
Hosp Infect Control... Hospital Infection Control (journ.) (SAUS)
Hosp Ins...... Hospital Insurance (DAVI)
Hosp Int....... Hospital International (journ.) (SAUS)
Hospit Abstr... Hospital Abstracts (journ.) (SAUS)
Hospitality Educ... Hospitality Educator (journ.) (SAUS)
Hospital Mag... Hospital Mazine (journ.) (SAUS)
Hospital Mus News... Hospital Music Newsletter (journ.) (SAUS)
Hospit Mge Rev... Hospital Management Review (journ.) (SAUS)
Hosp J......... Hospital Journal [*A publication*]
Hosp JA....... Hospital Journal of Australia (journ.) (SAUS)
Hosp J Aust... Hospital Journal of Australia [*A publication*]
Hosp Jt Dis Bull... Hospital for Joint Diseas. Bulletin (journ.) (SAUS)
Hosp Law Newsletter... Hospital Law Newsletter (journ.) (SAUS)
Hosp Libr..... Hospital Libraries (journ.) (SAUS)
Hosp Manag... Hospital Management (journ.) (SAUS)
Hosp Manage Commun... Hospital Management Communications (journ.) (SAUS)
Hosp Manage Q... Hospital Management Quarterly (journ.) (SAUS)
Hosp Manager... Hospital Manager (journ.) (SAUS)
Hosp Mater Manage... Hospital Materials Management (journ.) (SAUS)
Hosp Mater Manage Q... Hospital Materiel Management Quarterly (journ.) (SAUS)
Hosp Med.... Hospital Medicine (journ.) (SAUS)
Hosp Med Staff Advocate... Hospital Medical Staff Advocate (journ.) (SAUS)
Hosp Med Statf... Hospital Medical Staff (journ.) (SAUS)
Hospos........ Hosposable Products, Inc. [*Associated Press*] (SAG)
Hosp Peer Rev... Hospital Peer Review (journ.) (SAUS)
Hosp Pharm... Hospital Pharmacist (journ.) (SAUS)
Hosp Pharm... Hospital Pharmacy (journ.) (SAUS)
Hosp Physician... Hospital Physician (journ.) (SAUS)
HospPT........ Hospitality Properties Trust [*Associated Press*] (SAG)
Hosp Purch Manage... Hospital Purchasing Management (journ.) (SAUS)
HOSPRAT..... Hospital Ration (SAUS)
HOSPRATS... Hospital Rations [*Navy*]
Hosp Risk Manage... Hospital Risk Management (journ.) (SAUS)
Hosp Secur Saf Manage... Hospital Security and Safety Management (journ.) (SAUS)
Hosp Sgt...... Hospital Sergeant (GFGA)
HospSt......... Hospital Staffing Services, Inc. [*Associated Press*] (SAG)
Hosp Superv... Hospital Supervision (journ.) (SAUS)
Hosp Superv Bull... Hospital Supervisors Bulletin (journ.) (SAUS)
Hosp Technol Ser... Hospital Technology Series (journ.) (SAUS)
Hosp Tn....... Hospital Train (SAUS)
Hosp Top..... Hospital Topics (journ.) (SAUS)
Hosp Trib..... Hospital Tribune (journ.) (SAUS)
Hosp Trustee... Hospital Trustee (journ.) (SAUS)
HOSPTY....... Hospitality
Hosp Week... Hospital Week (journ.) (SAUS)
HospWwde... Hospitality Worldwide Services, Inc. [*Associated Press*] (SAG)
HOSS.......... Halo Orbit Space Station [*NASA*]
HOSS.......... Hand Order Transmeter
HOSS.......... Homing Optical System Study
HOSS.......... Homing System Survey (MCD)
HOSS.......... Hornbeck Offshore Services, Inc. [*NASDAQ symbol*] (NQ)
HOSS.......... Housing Sales Survey (SAUS)
HOSS.......... Hydrogen/Oxygen Second Stage (MCD)
HOS-STPL.... Hospital Operating System - Structured Programming Language [*Computer science*] (CSR)
HOST........... America Pop, Inc. (SAUO)
HOST........... Amerihost Properties [*NASDAQ symbol*] (TTSB)
HOST........... Amerihost Properties, Inc. [*NASDAQ symbol*] (NQ)
HOST........... Hardened Optical Sensor Testbed (ACAE)
HOST........... Harmonically Optimized Stabilization Technique (SAUS)
HOST........... Harmonic Optimized Stabilization Technique (IAA)
HOST........... Hawaii Ocean Science and Technology Park [*Research center*] (RCD)
HOST........... Headquarters On-Line System for Transportation (SAUO)
HOST........... Healthcare Open Systems and Trials (ADWA)
Host............ Hostiensis [*Deceased, 1271*] [*Authority cited in pre-1607 legal work*] (DSA)
HOST........... Hostile
HOST........... Hosting for Overseas Students [*An association*] (BUAC)
HOST........... Hot Section Technology (SAUS)
HOST........... Hot Spot Tracking (DNAB)
HOST........... Hypo-Osmotic Shock Treatment [*Analytical biochemistry*]
HOSTA......... Home Station (SAUO)
HOSTAC....... Helicopter Operations from Ships other than Aircraft Carriers [*Supplement*] (DOMA)
Host Def...... Host Defense (journ.) (SAUS)
HOSTEX....... Home Study Exchange (EA)
HOSTF......... Host Ventures Ltd. (SAUO)
HostFdg....... Host Funding, Inc. [*Associated Press*] (SAG)

Hosti........... Hostiensis [*Deceased, 1271*] [*Authority cited in pre-1607 legal work*] (DSA)
HOSTID......... Host Identifier (ACRL)
HostM......... Host Marriott Corp. [*Associated Press*] (SAG)
HostMar....... Host Marriott Corp. [*Associated Press*] (SAG)
HostMS........ Host Marriott Services Corp. [*Associated Press*] (SAG)
HOSTS......... Hostess (ROG)
HOSTWOY... Home of Selection and Completion of Travel within One Year Is Authorized [*Military*]
HOT............ Baltic Airlines Ltd. [*ICAO designator*] (FAAC)
HOT............ Birmingham Aerocentre, Ltd. [*British*] [*FAA designator*] (FAAC)
HOT............ Hand Over Transmitter
HOT............ Hands-on-Training
HOT............ Harpoon On-board Trainer (SAUS)
HOT............ HAT [*Hypoxanthine-Aminopterin-Thymidine*] with Ouabain [*Growth medium*] [*Biochemistry*]
HOT............ Hawaiian Ocean Time Series (USDC)
HOT............ Hawaii Ocean Time (SAUO)
HOT............ Hawk and Owl Trust (BUAC)
HOT............ Helicopter Operational Trainer (SAUS)
HOT............ Higher Order Term (SAUS)
HOT............ High-Occupancy Toll Lane
HOT............ High Operating Temperature (SAUS)
HOT............ High Output Turbo [*Automotive engineering*]
HOT............ High-Subsonic Optically Teleguided [*Antitank system*] (INF)
HOT............ Holographic One-Tube [*Goggles*] (MCD)
HOT............ Holographic-One-Two (PDAA)
HOT............ Home on Target [*Military*] (CAAL)
HOT............ Homing Optics Technology (ACAE)
HOT............ Horizontal Output Transformer
HOT............ Horizontal Output Tube
HOT............ Hotel Investors Trust/Corporation [*NYSE symbol*] (COMM)
HOT............ Hot Springs [*Arkansas*] [*Airport symbol*] (OAG)
HOT............ Human Old Tuberculin
HOT............ Hyperbaric Oxygen Therapy [*Medicine*] (DAVI)
HOT............ Hypertension Optimal Treatment [*Antihypertensive medicine*]
Hot............ Hypotropia [*Medicine*] (MELL)
HOT............ Starwood Hotels & Resorts [*NYSE symbol*] [*Formerly, HSN, Inc.*] (SG)
HOT............ Starwood Lodging Trust [*NYSE symbol*] (SAG)
HOTAC......... Helicopter Optical Tracking and Control
HOTAC......... Hotel Accommodation Service [*British*]
HOTAC......... Hotel Ammodation Service (SAUS)
HOTAS......... Hands on Throttle and Stick [*Aviation*] (MCD)
HOTASA....... Hands On Throttle and Stick Aid (SAUS)
HOTASTA..... Hands On Throttle And Sticking Training Aid (SAUS)
HOTBUN...... Have Not Yet Begun to Fight [*Simulated war game*]
HOTC.......... Heart of Texas Conference (PSS)
HOTCE........ Hot Critical Experiments [*Nuclear energy*]
HOTCOG...... Heart of Texas Council of Governments
HOT-DAM.... Higher Order Tree Dual Approximation Method (SAUS)
HOTDAM...... High Order Tree Dual Approximation Method (SAUS)
HOTEF......... Helicopter Operational Test & Evaluation Facility (SAUS)
HOTEF......... Helicopter Operational Test and Evaluation Flight [*Canadian Navy*]
Hot Lab Equip Conf Proc... Hot Laboratories and Equipment Conference. Proceedings (journ.) (SAUS)
HOTLIPS...... Home and Office Techniques for a Local Image Processing Station (SAUO)
HOTLIPS...... Honorary Order of Trumpeters Living in Possible Sin
HOTO.......... Health of the Oceans [*Marine science*] (OSRA)
HOTOA........ Hospital Topics (journ.) (SAUS)
HOTOL......... Horizontal Takeoff and Landing [*Name of proposed aircraft under development by the British government*]
HOTPHOTOREP... Hot Photographic Report (MCD)
HOTPHOTOREP... Hot Photo Interpretation Report (SAUO)
HOTRAN...... Hover and Transition [*Simulator*]
HOTREC....... Confederation of the National Hotel and Restaurant Associations in the EC (ECED)
HOTS.......... Hands-On Training Simulator [*Vehicle*]
HOTS.......... Hawaii Ocean Time-Series (SAUO)
HOTS.......... Heads of Technical Services (SAUS)
HOTS.......... Hearing Office Tracking System [*Computer science*]
HOTS.......... Higher Order Thinking Skills [*Education*]
HOTS.......... Holiday and Overtime Tracking System (SAUS)
HOT-SHOT... Hydrogen-Oxygen Turbine: Super-High Operating Temperatures [*Hydrogen utilization technology*]
HOTSIT........ Hot Situation (MCD)
HOTT.......... Hands On Technology Transfer [*Computer science*] (GART)
HOTT.......... Hands-on Turret Trainer [*Military*]
HOTT.......... Hot Off The Tree (SAUS)
HOTT.......... Hot Topic, Inc. [*NASDAQ symbol*] (SAG)
HotTopic...... Hot Topic, Inc. [*Associated Press*] (SAG)
HOTTS......... Harpoon Operator/Team Training System (SAUS)
Hot Work Technol... Hot Working Technology (journ.) (SAUS)
HOTX.......... Hands-On Training Exercise [*Military*] (ADDR)
HOTZ.......... House Track [*Federal Railroad Administration identification code*]
HOU........... [*William P.*] Hobby Airport [*FAA*] (TAG)
HOU........... Houston [*Texas*] [*Seismograph station code, US Geological Survey*] (SEIS)
HOU........... Houston [*Texas*] [*Airport symbol*]
HOU........... Houston Indus [*NYSE symbol*] (TTSB)
HOU........... Houston Industries, Inc. [*NYSE symbol*] (SPSG)
Hou........... Houston Oilers [*National Football League*] [*1960-96*] (NFLA)
Hou........... Houston's Delaware Reports [*A publication*] (DLA)
HOU........... United States Department of Housing and Urban Development, Washington, DC [*OCLC symbol*] (OCLC)
Hou Ang Sax Law... Houard's Anglo-Saxon Laws, Etc. [*A publication*] (DLA)
Houard Ang Sax Laws... Houard's Anglo-Saxon Laws [*A publication*] (DLA)
HouB........... Houston Biotechnology, Inc. [*Associated Press*] (SAG)
Houck Mech Lien... Houck on Mechanics' Lien Law [*A publication*] (DLA)
Houck Mech Lien... Houck on Mechanics Lien Law (journ.) (SAUS)
Houck Riv.... Houck on the Law of Navigable Rivers [*A publication*] (DLA)
Houck Riv.... Houck on the Law of Navigable Rivers (journ.) (SAUS)
Hou Dict...... Houard's Dictionary of the Customs of Normandy [*A publication*] (DLA)
Hough Am Cons... Hough's American Constitutions [*A publication*] (DLA)
Hough Am Cons... Houghs American Constitutions (journ.) (SAUS)
Hough CM... Hough's Military Law and Courts-Martial [*A publication*] (DLA)
Hough C-M Cas... Hough's Court-Martial Case Book [*1821*] [*London*] [*A publication*] (DLA)
Houghtn....... Houghton Pharmaceuticals, Inc. [*Associated Press*] (SAG)
Houghton..... Houghton's Reports [*97 Alabama*] [*A publication*] (DLA)
Hough V-Adm... Reports of Cases in Vice-Admiralty of Province of New York [*1715-88*] [*1925 Reprint*] [*A publication*] (DLA)
HougM......... Houghton Mifflin Co. [*Associated Press*] (SAG)
HouInd......... Houston Industries, Inc. [*Associated Press*] (SAG)
HOUND......... Humble, Old, Unattractive, Nonverbal, and Dumb (DIPS)
HO Univ KY Coll Agr Coop Ext Serv... HO-University of Kentucky. College of Agriculture. Cooperative Extension Service (journ.) (SAUS)
HOUS........... Housing
HOUS........... Housing Division [*Census*] (OICC)
Hous........... Houston's Delaware Reports [*A publication*] (DLA)
Hous & Dev Rep... Housing and Development Reporter [*Bureau of National Affairs*] [*A publication*] (DLA)
Hous&Dev Rep BNA... Housing and Development Reporter. Bureau of National Affairs (journ.) (SAUS)
HousBio....... Houston Biotechnology, Inc. [*Associated Press*] (SAG)
Hous Build Pl... Housing, Building and Planning (journ.) (SAUS)
House.......... House of Representatives in the United States (SAUS)
House.......... Oxford Universitys Christ College (SAUO)
House&Gd... House and Garden (journ.) (SAUS)
House B....... House Beautiful (journ.) (SAUS)
House Bldr... House Builder (journ.) (SAUS)
Housebold... Household and Personal Products Industry (journ.) (SAUS)
House Garden Build Guide... House and Garden Building Guide (journ.) (SAUS)
househ......... household (SAUO)
HOUSE-INFO... Homeowners Using Savings and Energy Information to Negotiate Fair Offers [*Student legal action organization*] (EA)
housek......... housekeeping (SAUO)
House Mag... House Magazine [*A publication*]
House of L... House of Lords Cases [*A publication*] (DLA)
House Words... Household Words (journ.) (SAUS)
HOUSG......... Housing
HOUSHD...... Household [*Marketing*] (ROG)
HoushInt...... Household International, Inc. [*Associated Press*] (SAG)
Housig Fin R... Housing Finance Review (journ.) (SAUS)
Housing 80... Housing Industry, 1980-2000 (journ.) (SAUS)
Housing Abs... Housing Abstracts (journ.) (SAUS)
Housing&Constr Tech Bull... Housing and Construction Technical Bulletin (journ.) (SAUS)
Housing & Devel Rep... Housing and Development Reporter [*Bureau of National Affairs*] [*A publication*] (DLA)
Housing Aust... Housing Australia [*A publication*]
Housing Aust... Housing Australia (journ.) (SAUS)
Housing Eur... Housing Europe (journ.) (SAUS)
Housing Finance Rev... Housing Finance Review [*A publication*] (JLIT)
Housing Mag... Housing Magazine (journ.) (SAUS)
Housing Mo... Housing Monthly (journ.) (SAUS)
Housing Plann Rev... Housing and Planning Review (journ.) (SAUS)
Housing Rer... Housing Review (journ.) (SAUS)
Housing Stud... Housing Studies [*A publication*] (JLIT)
Housing Vic... Housing Victoria [*A publication*]
Housing Vic... Housing Victoria (journ.) (SAUS)
Housing W Aust... Housing Western Australia [*A publication*]
Housing W Aust... Housing Western Australia (journ.) (SAUS)
Hous Law..... Houston Lawyer [*A publication*] (DLA)
Hous Life Ass... Houseman's Life Assurance [*9th ed.*] [*1977*] [*A publication*] (DLA)
HousP......... Housing and Planning References (journ.) (SAUS)
Hous Pr....... Housman's Precedents in Conveyancing [*1861*] [*A publication*] (DLA)
Hous Res Pap... Housing Research Papers (journ.) (SAUS)
Houst.......... Houston's Delaware Reports [*A publication*] (DLA)
Houst Cr...... Houston's Delaware Criminal Cases [*A publication*] (DLA)
Houst Cr Cas... Houston's Delaware Criminal Cases [*A publication*] (DLA)
Houst Crim Cas... Delaware Criminal Cases [*A publication*] (DLA)
Houst Crim Cases... Delaware Criminal Cases [*A publication*] (DLA)
Houst Crim (Del)... Houston's Delaware Criminal Cases [*A publication*] (DLA)
Houst Crim Rep... Delaware Criminal Cases [*A publication*] (DLA)
Houst Cr Rep... Delaware Criminal Cases [*A publication*] (DLA)
HoustEx....... Houston Exploration Co. (The) [*Associated Press*] (SAG)
HoustInd...... Houston Industries, Inc. [*Associated Press*] (SAG)
Houston....... Houston's Delaware Supreme Court Reports [*1855-93*] [*A publication*] (DLA)
Houston BJ... Houston Business Journal (journ.) (SAUS)
Houston Geol Soc Bull... Houston Geological Society. Bulletin (journ.) (SAUS)
Houston Law... Houston Law Review (journ.) (SAUS)
Houston Law... Houston Lawyer [*A publication*] (DLA)
Houston Sym... Houston Symphony. Program Notes (journ.) (SAUS)
Houst St Tr... Houston's Law of Stoppage in Transitu [*A publication*] (DLA)
Hou Sym Orch... Houston Symphony Orchestra (SAUO)

HOV .... Heat of Vaporization
HOV .... High Occupancy Vehicle [*Commuter routes*] [*Acronym usually followed by a number indicating the minimum number of people per vehicle*]
HOV .... High-Occupancy Vehicle (SAUS)
HOV .... Homogeneity of Variance [*Statistics*]
Hov .... Hovenden on Frauds [*A publication*] (DLA)
Hov .... Hovenden's Supplement to Vesey, Jr.'s, English Chancery Reports [*1789-1817*] [*A publication*] (DLA)
HOV .... Hovercraft [*Military*] [*British*]
HOV .... Hovering (SAUS)
HOV .... Hovnanian Enterprises, Inc. [*AMEX symbol*] (SPSG)
HOV .... Orsta/Volda [*Norway*] [*Airport symbol*] (OAG)
HOV .... United States Department of Housing and Urban Development, Region I, Boston, MA [*OCLC symbol*] (OCLC)
HOV .... Wichita, KS [*Location identifier*] [*FAA*] (FAAL)
Hov Ann....... Hoveden's Annals [*A publication*] (DLA)
Hov Craft Hydrof... Hovering Craft and Hydrofoil (journ.) (SAUS)
HOVE .... Hovenweep National Monument
Hoved .... Hoveden's Chronica [*A publication*] (DLA)
Hovercr Wld... Hovercraft World (journ.) (SAUS)
HOVEROC .... Hover Rocket (SAUS)
Hov Fr .... Hovenden on Frauds [*A publication*] (DLA)
HOVI .... Handbook of Overhaul Instructions [*Navy*]
HOVI .... Hopewell Village National Historic Site
Hovis .... Hominis Vis [*The Strength of Man*] [*Latin*]
HOV Lane .... High-Occupancy Vehicle Lane (SAUS)
HOVNEIV...... Hovnanian Enterprises, Inc. (SAUO)
HovnEn .... Hovnanian Enterprises, Inc. [*Associated Press*] (SAG)
HOVO........... High Oleic Vegetable Oil
HO Voice ..... Hartfords Other Voice (journ.) (SAUS)
Hov Sup....... Hovenden's Supplement to Vesey, Jr.'s, English Chancery Reports [*1789-1817*] [*A publication*] (DLA)
Hov Supp..... Hovenden's Supplement to Vesey, Jr.'s, English Chancery Reports [*1789-1817*] [*A publication*] (DLA)
HOVVAC....... Hovering Vehicle Versatile Automatic Control
HOW .... Handicapped Organized Women [*In association name, HOW, Inc.*] (EA)
HOW .... Hand over Word
HOW .... Hands Off Our Water [*An association*] (BUAC)
HOW .... Happiness of Womanhood [*Also known as LOH*] [*Defunct*]
HOW .... Healing Our World [*An association*]
HOW .... Help Our World
HOW .... Hercules on Water [*Aircraft*] (MCD)
HOW .... High-Order Word (SSD)
HOW .... Home Owners Warranty [*National Association of Home Builders*]
How .... Howard's New York Practice Reports [*A publication*] (DLA)
How .... Howard's Reports [*2-8 Mississippi*] [*A publication*] (DLA)
How .... Howard's United States Supreme Court Reports [*42-65 United States*] [*A publication*] (DLA)
HOW .... Howell Industries, Inc. [*AMEX symbol*] (SPSG)
How .... Howell's Reports [*22-26 Nevada*] [*A publication*] (DLA)
HOW .... Howitzer (KSC)
how............. Howitzer (MILB)
HOW .... Howrah [*India*] [*Seismograph station code, US Geological Survey*] (SEIS)
HO-W........... Hydrographic Office-Washington, DC [*Terminated, 1963; later, NOO*] [*Navy*] (MCD)
How A Cas... Howard's New York Appeal Cases [*A publication*] (DLA)
How & Beat... Howell and Beatty's Reports [*22 Nevada*] [*A publication*] (DLA)
How & H St... Howard and Hutchinson's Mississippi Statutes [*A publication*] (DLA)
How&H St.... Howard and Hutchinsons Mississippi Statutes (journ.) (SAUS)
How & N...... Howell and Norcross' Reports [*23, 24 Nevada*] [*A publication*] (DLA)
How & Nor... Howell and Norcross' Reports [*23, 24 Nevada*] [*A publication*] (DLA)
How Ann St... Howell's Annotated Statutes [*Michigan*] [*A publication*] (DLA)
How App...... Howard's New York Appeal Cases [*A publication*] (DLA)
How App...... Howards New York Appeal Cases (journ.) (SAUS)
How App Cas... Howard's New York Court of Appeals Cases [*A publication*] (DLA)
How App Cases... Howard's New York Court of Appeals Cases [*A publication*] (DLA)
HOWAQ........ Hot Water Quenching (SAUS)
Howard........ Howard's Mississippi Supreme Court Reports [*1834-43*] [*A publication*] (DLA)
Howard Pr ... Howard's New York Practice Reports [*A publication*] (DLA)
Howard Pr Rep... Howard's New York Practice Reports [*A publication*] (DLA)
Howard Rep... Howard's United States Supreme Court Reports [*A publication*] (DLA)
Howard Rep... Howards United States Supreme Court Reports (journ.) (SAUS)
Howard SC... United States Reports [*Vols. 42-65*] [*A publication*] (DLA)
Howard's Prac Reports... Howard's New York Practice Reports [*A publication*] (DLA)
Howard's Practice... Howard's New York Practice Reports [*A publication*] (DLA)
Howard's Spec Term Rep... Howard's New York Practice Reports [*A publication*] (DLA)
Howard U .... Howard University (GAGS)
Howard Univ Rev Sci... Howard University Reviews of Science (journ.) (SAUS)
Howard U Pr... Howard University Press (journ.) (SAUS)
HOWBTRY ... Howitzer Battery (DNAB)
How C.......... Howard's Irish Chancery Practice [*A publication*] (DLA)
How Cas ...... Howard's New York Court of Appeals Cases [*A publication*] (DLA)
How Cas ...... Howards New York Court of Appeals Cases (journ.) (SAUS)
How Cas ...... Howard's Property Cases [*A publication*] (DLA)
How Cas ...... Howards Property Cases (journ.) (SAUS)
How Ch........ Howard's Irish Chancery Practice [*A publication*] (DLA)
How Ch P .... Howard's Irish Chancery Practice [*A publication*] (DLA)
How Ch Pr... Howard's Irish Chancery Practice [*A publication*] (DLA)
How Cr Tr.... Howison's Virginia Criminal Trials [*A publication*] (DLA)
How Cr Tr.... Howisons Virginia Criminal Trials (journ.) (SAUS)
How Ct App Cas... Howard's New York Court of Appeals Cases [*A publication*] (DLA)
How Ct App Cs... Howards New York Court of Appeals Cases (journ.) (SAUS)
HOWD.......... Helicopter Obstacle Warning Device (SAUS)
How EE........ Howard's Irish Equity Exchequer Reports [*A publication*] (DLA)
Howell NP ... Howell's Nisi Prius Reports [*Michigan*] [*A publication*] (DLA)
Howell St Tr... Howell's English State Trials [*1163-1820*] [*A publication*] (DLA)
Howe Pr ...... Howe's Practice [*Massachusetts*] [*A publication*] (DLA)
Howe Pr ...... Howes Practice (journ.) (SAUS)
How Eq Exch... Howard's Irish Equity Exchequer Reports [*A publication*] (DLA)
How Eval Health Programs... How to Evaluate Health Programs (journ.) (SAUS)
How J .... Howard Journal [*A publication*] (DLA)
HOWL.......... Hands Off Wildlife [*British*] (DI)
HOWL.......... Help Our Wolves Live
HowlC.......... Howell Corp. [*Associated Press*] (SAG)
HowlCp........ Howell Corp. [*Associated Press*] (SAG)
Howl In........ Howell Industries, Inc. [*Associated Press*] (SAG)
How L Rev... Howard Law Review [*A publication*] (DLA)
How L Rev... Howard Law Review (journ.) (SAUS)
HOWLS........ Hostile Weapons Locator Study [*DARPA/Army*] (MCD)
How NP (Mich)... Howell's Nisi Prius Reports [*Michigan*] [*A publication*] (DLA)
How NS .... Howard's New York Practice Reports, New Series [*A publication*] (DLA)
How (NY)..... Howard's New York Practice Reports [*A publication*] (DLA)
How Pat....... Howson on Patents [*A publication*] (DLA)
How Po Ca... Howard's Property Cases [*A publication*] (DLA)
How Po Cas... Howard's Irish Property Cases [*1720-73*] [*A publication*] (DLA)
How Po Css... Howards Irish Property Cases (journ.) (SAUS)
How Pr .... Howard's New York Practice Reports [*A publication*] (DLA)
How Prac..... Howard's New York Practice Reports [*A publication*] (DLA)
How Prac NS... Howard's New York Practice Reports, New Series [*A publication*] (DLA)
How Prac (NY)... Howard's New York Practice Reports [*A publication*] (DLA)
How Prac Rep... Howard's New York Practice Reports [*A publication*] (DLA)
How Pr NS... Howard's New York Practice Reports, New Series [*A publication*] (DLA)
How Prob Pr... Howell's Probate Practice [*Ontario, Canada*] [*A publication*] (DLA)
How Pr Rep... Howard's New York Practice Reports [*A publication*] (DLA)
How Pr Sup C... Howard's New York Practice Reports [*A publication*] (DLA)
HOWR.......... However
Howr............ Howitzer [*British military*] (DMA)
How SC........ Howard's United States Supreme Court Reports [*A publication*] (DLA)
Hows Pat..... Howson on Patents [*A publication*] (DLA)
HOWSR........ Howsoever (ROG)
Hows Reis Pat... Howson on Reissued Patents [*A publication*] (DLA)
Hows Reis Pat... Howson on Reissued Patents (journ.) (SAUS)
How St......... Howell's Annotated Statutes [*Michigan*] [*A publication*] (DLA)
How St......... Howells Annotated Statutes (journ.) (SAUS)
How State Tr... Howell's English State Trials [*1163-1820*] [*A publication*] (DLA)
How St Tr .... Howell's English State Trials [*1163-1820*] [*A publication*] (DLA)
HOWT.......... Howard Terminal [*Later, HT*] [*AAR code*]
HOWT.......... Howtek Inc. [*NASDAQ symbol*] (TTSB)
Howtar......... Howitzer-Mortar (SAUS)
Howtek .... Howtek, Inc. [*Associated Press*] (SAG)
HOW-TO ...... Housing Operation with Training Opportunity [*Office of Economic Opportunity*]
How US .... Howard's United States Supreme Court Reports [*A publication*] (DLA)
HOX .... Homeobox [*Genetics*]
HOX .... New Orleans, LA [*Location identifier*] [*FAA*] (FAAL)
HOx............. Odd Hydrogen (SAUS)
HOXIE .... Hoxie, AR [*American Association of Railroads railroad junction routing code*]
HOY .... Holland Schweiz (journ.) (SAUS)
HOY .... Hoy Island [*Scotland*] [*Airport symbol*] [*Obsolete*] (OAG)
Hoyt Comp L... Hoyt's Compiled Laws of Arizona [*A publication*] (DLA)
Hoyt Comp L... Hoyts Compiled Laws of Arizona (journ.) (SAUS)
HOY Timber... Holygent Timber (SAUS)
HOYU........... Hospitality Yukon. Yukon Visitors Association (journ.) (SAUS)
HOZ .... Highway Oil [*Federal Railroad Administration identification code*]
HOZ .... Horizontal
HP................ Air Hawaii [*ICAO designator*] (AD)
HP................ ALAS, SA [*Uruguay*] [*ICAO designator*] (ICDA)
HP................ All India Reporter, Himachal Pradesh [*A publication*] (DLA)
HP................ America West Airlines [*ICAO designator*] (AD)
HP................ Haemophilus Pleuropneumoniae (DB)
HP................ Half Pay
HP................ Half Plate [*Photography*]
HP................ Half Price (ROG)
HP................ Halogen Phosphorus [*Medicine*] (EDAA)
HP................ Hand-Held Photo
HP................ Handicapped Person
H-P............... Handley-Page Ltd.
HP................ Handling and Propulsion (AAG)
HP................ Handling Procedure (MCD)
HP................ Handmade Paper
HP................ Handpainted (WGA)
HP................ Hand Pump (SAUS)
HP................ Hannah's Prayer [*Christian infertility/pregnancy loss group*]
Hp................ Haptoglobin [*Hematology*]
HP................ Hard Palate [*Medicine*] (MELL)

HP .... Hard Pipe (SAUS)
HP .... Hard Plastic [*Doll collecting*]
HP .... Hard Point
HP .... Hardy Perennial [*Horticulture*] (ROG)
HP .... Harmonic Progression
hp .... Harp (GROV)
Hp .... Harp [*Music*]
HP .... Harvard Photometry (SAUS)
HP .... Harvard Pulsar (SAUS)
HP .... Harvard Pump [*Medicine*] (MELL)
HP .... Hauptpunkte [*Crystallography*]
HP .... Haustus Purgans [*Purging Draught*] [*Pharmacy*] (ROG)
HP .... Haut Parleur [*Loudspeaker*] [*French*]
HP .... Hawker Siddeley Aviation Ltd. [*British*] [*ICAO aircraft manufacturer identifier*] (ICAO)
HP .... Hay-Pasturage [*Agriculture*]
HP .... Hazard Prevention [*A publication*] (EAAP)
HP .... Head Postmaster [*British*] (DCTA)
HP .... Headquarters Pamphlet [*Military*] (MCD)
HP .... Healthcare Product
HP .... Health Physicist (SAUS)
HP .... Health Physics [*Nuclear energy*] (NRCH)
HP .... Health Plan (AMHC)
hp .... Heaping (STED)
HP .... Heatable Plastic (SAUS)
HP .... Heating Plant (NATG)
HP .... Heat Pipe (SAUS)
HP .... Heat Production [*Medicine*] (EDAA)
HP .... Heat Pump (SAUS)
hp .... Hectopig (SAUS)
HP .... Heenan Petroleum Ltd. [*Toronto Stock Exchange symbol*]
HP .... Height of Perigee
HP .... Heir Presumptive
HP .... Helicobacter Pylori (SAUS)
HP .... Helicopter (NATG)
HP .... Heliodor [*Record label*] [*Great Britain*]
HP .... Hellas Planitia [*A filamentary mark on Mars*]
HP .... Helmerich & Payne, Inc. [*NYSE symbol*] (SPSG)
Hp .... Hematoporphyrin (STED)
HP .... Hemel Hempstead [*Postcode*] (ODBW)
HP .... Hemiparkinsonism [*Medicine*] (EDAA)
H/P .... Hemipelvectomy [*Medicine*]
Hp .... Hemiplegia [*Medicine*]
HP .... Hemoperfusion [*Medicine*] (EDAA)
HP .... Hemophilus Pleuropneumoniae [*Medicine*] (EDAA)
HP .... Henderson & Pollard Ltd. [*New Zealand*]
HP .... Heparin [*Medicine*] (EDAA)
HP .... Heptode [*Electronics*] (IAA)
Hp .... Heptyl [*Biochemistry*]
HP .... Hesperian Foundation (EA)
HP .... Heterophase Polymerization (SAUS)
HP .... Hewlett-Packard Co.
HP .... Hexamethylmelamine and Cisplatin [*Cisplatinum*] [*Antineoplastic drug*] (DAVI)
HP .... Hiding Power [*Paint technology*]
HP .... Higher Power (SAUS)
HP .... Highest Possible (ROG)
HP .... Highly Purified
HP .... High Pass [*Electronics*]
HP .... High Performance
HP .... High Polymer (SAUS)
H/P .... High Position (MDG)
HP .... High Positive (SAUS)
HP .... High-Positive (MDG)
HP .... High-Potency [*Pharmacy*]
HP .... High Potential (SAUS)
HP .... High Power
HP .... High Pressure
h-p .... High-Pressure (IDOE)
HP .... High-Pressure Cylinder [*Especially, a locomotive cylinder*]
HP .... High Priest
HP .... High Priority
HP .... High Productivity
HP .... High Protein [*Nutrition*]
HP .... High Purity (AAEL)
HP .... Highway Patrol (GOBB)
HP .... Himachal Pradesh [*Indian Railway*] (TIR)
HP .... Hippocampal Pyramidal Cell [*Neuroanatomy*]
HP .... Hip Prosthesis (MELL)
HP .... Hire Purchase
HP .... Historical Period [*Dialog*] [*Searchable field*] [*Information service or system*] (NITA)
HP .... Historic Park (SAUS)
HP .... Hit by Pitcher [*Baseball*]
HP .... Hit Points (SAUS)
HP .... Holding Pattern [*Aviation*]
HP .... Holding Pipette
HP .... Holding Potential [*Neurophysiology*]
HP .... Holiday Pay [*Army*] (AABC)
HP .... Holiday Project (EA)
HP .... Hollow Point [*Gunnery*]
hp .... hollowpoint (SAUS)
HP .... Hollow Point Bullet
HP .... Homeland Party [*Afghanistan*] [*Political party*] (BUAC)
HP .... Homeopathic Pharmacopoeia
HP .... Home Page (SAUS)
HP .... Horizontally Pivoted (SAUS)
hp .... Horizontally Polarized (SAUS)
HP .... Horizontal Parallax [*Navigation*]
HP .... Horizontal Plane (MELL)
HP .... Horizontal Polarization
HP .... Horse Power (SAUS)
hp .... Horsepower (IDOE)
HP .... Hospital (SAUS)
HP .... Hospital Participation [*Blood program*] [*Red Cross*]
HP .... Hospital Pharmacist [*Medicine*] (EDAA)
HP .... Host Processor
HP .... Hot Pack [*or Pad*] [*Physical therapy*]
HP .... Hot Pad (SAUS)
HP .... Hot Pilot [*An egotistic flying cadet*] [*Slang*] [*Air Force*]
HP .... Hot Plate (SAUS)
HP .... Hot-Pressed [*Paper*]
HP .... Hot Pressing (SAUS)
HP .... House Painter (ROG)
HP .... House Physician
HP .... Houses of Parliament [*British*]
H/P .... House-to-Pier (SAUS)
HP .... Hughes Policy (ACAE)
HP .... Hughes Procedure (ACAE)
HP .... Hughes Process (ACAE)
HP .... Humanist Party [*Australia*] [*Political party*]
HP .... Human Pituitary [*Endocrinology*] (MAE)
HP .... Human Plasma [*Hematology*]
HP .... Human Potential (DHP)
HP .... Humeral Plate [*Entomology*]
HP .... Humeroscapular Periarthritis [*Medicine*] (MELL)
HP .... Hundred Pounds
HP .... Hunger Project (EA)
HP .... Hurricane Program (SAUO)
HP .... Hybrid Perpetual (SAUS)
HP .... Hydranth Pulse (SAUS)
HP .... Hydraulic Platform (WDAA)
HP .... Hydraulic Power (SAUS)
HP .... Hydrazine Perchlorate (SAUS)
HP .... Hydrocollator Pack [*Physical therapy*] (DAVI)
HP .... Hydrogen Peroxide (MELL)
HP .... Hydrogen Purge (MCD)
HP .... Hydrogen Purifier (SAUS)
HP .... Hydrophilic Petrolatum [*Pharmacology*] (DAVI)
HP .... Hydrostatic Pressure
HP .... Hydroxyproline [*An amino acid*]
HP .... Hydroxypyruvate [*Medicine*] (EDAA)
HP .... Hyertension + Proteinuria (SAUS)
HP .... Hygroscopicity Potential (PDAA)
hp .... hyperbolic (SAUS)
HP .... Hyperbolic Paraboloid (SAUS)
HP .... Hyperparathyroidism [*or Hyperthyroidism*] [*Endocrinology*]
HP .... Hyperperistalsis [*Medicine*] (MELL)
HP .... Hyperphoria
HP .... Hyperplasia [*Medicine*] (MELL)
HP .... Hyperpolarization
HP .... Hypersensitivity Pneumonitis [*Medicine*]
HP .... Hypertension and Proteinuria [*Medicine*]
HP .... Hypertransfused Polycythemic [*Medicine*]
HP .... Hypophoria [*Medicine*] (EDAA)
HP .... Hypophsrynx [*Qtorhinolaryngology*] (DAVI)
HP .... Hysterical Personality
HP .... Members of HM armed forces on half-pay (SAUO)
HP .... Perigee Altitude (NASA)
HP .... Smith & Nephew Pharmaceuticals Ltd. [*Great Britain*] [*Research code symbol*]
HP 08 B .... Hundreds Position...8 Bit (SAUS)
HPA .... Hamburg Port Authority (SAUO)
HPA .... Handley Page Association [*British*] (DBA)
HPA .... Handling and Positioning Aid (ACAE)
HPA .... Hazardous Products Act (FOTI)
HPA .... Head of a Procuring Activity [*Army*] (AABC)
HPA .... Head Post Assembly
HPA .... Head Postmen's Association [*A union*] [*British*]
HPA .... Heads of Procuring Activities (MCD)
HPA .... Health Policy Agenda for the American People (HCT)
HPA .... Health Projects Abroad [*An association*] (BUAC)
HPA .... Hearth Products Association (NTPA)
HPA .... Hectopascal [*ICAO designator*] (FAAC)
hPa .... Hectopascals (WEAT)
hPa .... Hekto Pascal (SAUS)
HPA .... Helix Pomatia Agglutinin (SAUS)
HPA .... Hemagglutinating Penicillin Antibody [*Medicine*] (DB)
HPA .... Hen Packers Association [*British*] (DBA)
HPA .... Heritage Preservation Association (WDAA)
HPA .... Heteropoly Acid [*Inorganic chemistry*]
HPA .... Heteropolyanion (DB)
HPA .... Heuristic Path Algorithm
HPA .... Hewlett-Packard Associates (SAUS)
HPA .... High Performance Absorber (SAUS)
HPA .... High Performance Alloy (SAUS)
HPA .... High Power Amplifier (SAUO)
HPA .... High-Power Amplifier
HPA .... High Power Array (SAUS)
HPA .... High Pressure Air (SAUS)

HPA .... High-Pressure Air
HPA .... High-vision Promotion Association (SAUO)
HPA .... Historical Preservation of America [*Publisher*] (EA)
HPA .... Historic Preservation Agency (SAUO)
HPA .... History, Physical, Admit (SAUS)
HPA .... Holding and Positioning Aid (IEEE)
HPA .... Horizontal Planar Array (CAAL)
HPA .... Horn Parabola Aerial (or Antenna) (SAUS)
HPA .... Hornparabola Antenna (SAUS)
HPA .... Hospital Physicians Association [*British*]
HPA .... Hospital Physics Association (SAUO)
HPA .... Hospital Presidents Association (NTPA)
HPA .... Host Processor Adapter (IAA)
HPA .... House Plants Australia
HPA .... Human Papillomavirus [*or Parvovirus*] (MAE)
HPA .... Hurlingham Polo Association [*Midhurst, Sussex, England*] (EAIO)
HPA .... Hybridization Protection Assay [*Analytical biochemistry*]
HPA .... Hydraulic Pneumatic Area (AAG)
HPA .... Hydraulic Project Approval (SAUS)
HPA .... Hydroxyphenylacetic Acid [*Biochemistry*] (DB)
HPA .... Hydroxypropyl Acrylate [*Organic chemistry*]
HPA .... Hypophyseal-Pituitary Axis (SAUS)
HPA .... Hypothalamic-Pituitary-Adrenal [*Axis*] [*Endocrinology*] (DAVI)
HPA .... Hypothalamic-Pituitary-Adrenocortical [*Endocrinology*]
HPA .... Lifuka [*Tonga Islands*] [*Airport symbol*] (OAG)
HPA .... Pearl Airways Compagne Haitienne [*Haiti*] [*ICAO designator*] (FAAC)
HPAA .... High Performance Aerial Assembly (SAUS)
HPAA .... High-Performance Antenna Assembly (MHDI)
HPAA .... High-Pressure Air Accumulator
HPAA .... Hispanic Public Affairs Association (EA)
HPAA .... Housing Pressure Altitude Advance [*Automotive engineering*]
HPAA .... Hydroperoxyarachidonic Acid (STED)
HPAA .... Hydroxyphenylacetic Acid [*Biochemistry*] (MAE)
HPAA .... Hyoothalamo-Pituitary-Adrenal Axis (STED)
HPAAS .... High-Performance Aerial Attack System (MCD)
HPAC .... Hawaii Performing Arts Co. (SAUS)
HPAC .... Hawker Pacific Aerospace [*NASDAQ symbol*] (NASQ)
HPAC .... Health Policy Advisory Center (EA)
HPAC .... Heating, Piping and Air Conditioning (journ.) (SAUS)
HPAC .... High-Performance Affinity Chromatography
HPAC .... High-Pressure Air Compressor (NVT)
HP/A/C .... Home Port/Area/City [*Code*] [*Navy*] (DNAB)
H-PAC .... Human-Piloted Alien (SAUS)
H-PAC .... Human-Piloted Alien Craft [*Flying saucer*]
HPAC .... Hydro-Press Accessory (SAUS)
HPAC .... Hypothalamo-Pituitary-Adreno-Cortical [*Medicine*] (DMAA)
HP Act .... Historic Places Act (SAUO)
HPAD .... Host Packet Assembler/Disassembler (ACRL)
HPAD .... Host PAD (SAUS)
HPAE .... High-pH Anion-Exchange [*Analytical chemistry*]
HPAEC .... High pH Anion Exchange Chromatography
HPAF .... Hydraulic Performance Analysis Facility (MCD)
HPAG .... High-Performance Air-to-Ground
HPAG .... High Performance Application Gateway (SAUS)
HPAG .... High Power Amplifier Group (SAUO)
HPAG Rocket... High Performance Air-to-Ground Rocket (SAUS)
HPAH .... Hydroxy Polycyclic Aromatic Hydrocarbon [*Environmental chemistry*]
HPAL .... High Plains Agriculture Laboratory [*University of Nebraska - Lincoln*] [*Research center*] (RCD)
HPAL .... Holland Pan-American Line (SAUO)
HPA Line .... High Pressure Air Line (SAUS)
HP & A .... Hull Propulsion and Auxiliaries [*Navy*] (DNAB)
HP&R .... Highway Planning and Research [*MTMC*] (TAG)
HPANH .... Hydroxy Polycyclic Aromatic Nitrogen Heterocycle [*Environmental chemistry*]
HPAOA .... High Performance Army Observation Aircraft (SAUS)
HPAP .... Human Placental Alkaline Phosphatase [*An enzyme*]
HPAR .... Air-Resistance Horsepower [*Automotive engineering*]
HPAS .... High-Performance Adhesive System
HPAS .... High-Pressure Air System
HPASH .... Hydroxy Polycyclic Aromatic Sulfur Heterocycle [*Environmental chemistry*]
HP-ATLAS .... Hewlett-Packard-Abbreviated Test Language for Avionic Systems (SAUS)
HPB .... Handmaids of the Precious Blood [*Roman Catholic religious order*]
HPB .... Hand-Printed Books
HPB .... Harbor Patrol Boat
HPB .... Health Canada, Health Protection Branch (SAUO)
HPB .... Health Protection Branch (SAUS)
HPB .... Helena Petrovna Blavatsky [*Famous 19th-century occultist*]
HPB .... Hepatobiliary [*Medicine*] (DMAA)
HPB .... Hermann Professional Building (SAUS)
HPB .... High Police Band (SAUS)
HPB .... High-Probability Behavior
HPB .... Hinged Plotting Board
HPB .... Hooper Bay [*Alaska*] [*Airport symbol*] (OAG)
HPBC .... Home Port Bancorp, Inc. [*NASDAQ symbol*] (CTT)
HPBC .... Homopolar Pulse Billet Heating (SAUS)
HPBC .... Hyperpolarizing Bipolar Cell [*In the retina*]
HPBDA .... High Performance Bi-Polar Device Array (ACAE)
HPBF .... Hepatotrophic Portal Blood Factor [*Medicine*] (DMAA)
HPBID .... Host Processor/Bus Interface Dedicated (SPST)
HPBIDS .... Hewlett Packard Broadband Internet Delivery System (SAUS)
HPBL .... Hoechst Pharmaceutical Research Laboratories (SAUS)
HPBL .... Human Peripheral Blood Leukocyte
HPBN .... Hot-Pressed Boron Nitride [*Materials science and technology*]
HPBS .... High Performance Bus System (SAUS)
HPBs .... Hinged Plotting Boards (SAUS)
HPBVWA .... High-Power Broadband Vehicular Whip Antenna [*Army*]
HPBW .... Half-Power Beamwidth [*or Bandwidth*] (IEEE)
HPC .... Hale's Pleas of the Crown [*England*] [*A publication*] (DLA)
HPC .... Handheld PC [*Personal Computer*]
HPC .... Hand Punched Card (SAUS)
HPC .... Hanford People Core (SAUS)
HPC .... Hard Processing Channel (IAA)
HPC .... Hawkins' Pleas of the Crown [*England*] [*A publication*] (DLA)
HPC .... Health Physics Center [*Nuclear energy*] (NRCH)
HPC .... Health Policy Council [*Defunct*] (EA)
HPC .... Health Promotion Council of Southeastern Pennsylvania (SAUO)
HPC .... Helicopter Performance Computer (NG)
HPC .... Helicopter Plane Commander
HPC .... Hemangiopericytoma (STED)
HPC .... Hematopoietic Progenitor Cell [*Hematology*]
HPC .... Hemipalmitoylcarnitinium [*Biochemistry*]
HPC .... Hemisphere Publishing Co.
HPC .... Hendon Police College (SAUO)
HPC .... Hercules, Inc. [*Formerly, Hercules Powder Co.*] [*NYSE symbol*] (SPSG)
HPC .... Hercules Powder Co. (SAUS)
HPC .... Hereditary Prostate Cancer [*Medicine*]
HPC .... Heticopter Performance Computer (SAUS)
HPC .... Highland Park College (SAUO)
HPC .... High-level of Plasma Corticosterone (SAUS)
HPC .... High Performance Computer
HPC .... High Performance Computing (EGAO)
HPC .... High-Performance Concrete (FOTI)
HPC .... High Pin Count (SAUS)
HPC .... High Point College [*North Carolina*]
HPC .... High Power Characterization (SAUS)
HPC .... High Power Converter (ACAE)
HPC .... High-Pressure Compressor (MCD)
HPC .... High-Pressure Constant (DNAB)
HPC .... Hindustan Paper Corp. [*India*] (BUAC)
HPC .... Hippocampal Pyramidal Cell [*Neuroanatomy*]
HPC .... Hippocampus [*Brain anatomy*]
HPC .... History of Present Complaint [*Medicine*] (STED)
HPC .... History of Present Condition (SAUS)
HPC .... Hobart Peace Centre [*Australia*]
HPC .... Hollerith Punched Card (SAUS)
HPC .... Home Policy Committee of War Cabinet [*British*] [*World War II*]
HPC .... Hope, AR [*Location identifier*] [*FAA*] (FAAL)
HPC .... Horizonted Parity Check (SAUS)
HPC .... Horticultural Policy Council (EERA)
HPC .... Hot Pipe Chase [*Nuclear energy*] (NRCH)
HPC .... Hours per Calculator (TIMI)
HPC .... House Production Council (SAUO)
HPC .... Howard Payne College [*Texas*]
HPC .... Hydraulic Package Container
HPC .... Hydraulic Piston Corer
HPC .... Hydrological Processes and Climate (SAUS)
HPC .... Hydrometeorological Prediction Center (SAUO)
HPC .... Hydrophobic Chromatography [*Medicine*] (EDAA)
HPC .... Hydrothermal Power Co. (SAUS)
HPC .... Hydroxpropylcellulose (SAUS)
HPC .... Hydroxyphenylcinchoninic Acid [*Pharmacology*]
HPC .... Hydroxypropylcellulose [*Organic chemistry*]
HPC-1 .... Hereditary Prostate Cancer 1-Gene [*Medicine*] (EDAA)
HPCA .... High Performance Computing Act (TNIG)
HPCA .... Hiroshima Peace Center Associates [*Defunct*] (EA)
HPCA .... Hiroshima Peace Center Association (SAUO)
HPCA .... Housing Pressure Cold Advance [*Automotive engineering*]
HPCA .... Human Progenitor Cell Antigen [*Medicine*] (EDAA)
HPC Acid .... Hydroxyphenyl-Cinchoninic Acid (SAUS)
HPCB .... Hundreds Position C Bit (SAUS)
HPCblack .... Hard Processing Channel Black (EDCT)
HPC Black ...... Hard-Processing Channel Black (SAUS)
HPCBR .... High-Pressure Chamber
HPCC .... High Performance Computing and Communication [*Computer science*]
HPCC .... High-Performance Computing and Communications Program [*Department of Energy*]
HPCC .... High-Performance Control Center [*Aerospace*] (AAG)
HPCC .... High Power Core Characterizer (SAUS)
HPCC .... High-Precision Contour Control
HPCCEY .... Handbook of Plant Cell Culture (journ.) (SAUS)
HPCCIT .... High Performance Computing, Communications and Information Technology Subcommittee (SAUS)
HPCE .... High-Performance Capillary Electrophoresis [*Analytical biochemistry*]
HPCEC .... Hanford Protective Clothing and Equipment Committee (SAUS)
HPCF .... High-Performance Carbon Fiber [*Materials science*]
HPCG .... Hand-Held Protein Crystal Growth (SAUS)
HPCGS .... Household Purchasing Characteristics Generating System (SAUS)
HPCHA .... High Red Cell Phosphatidylcholine Anemia [*Medicine*] (MELL)
HPCHD .... Harpsichord [*Music*]
Hpchdst .... Harpsichordist (SAUS)
HPCI .... High Performance Computing Initiative (SAUS)
HPCI .... High Power Coolant Injection (SAUS)
HPCI .... High-Pressure Coolant Injection [*Nuclear energy*] (NRCH)
HPCI Pump... High Pressure Coolant Injection Pump (SAUS)
HPCIS .... High-Pressure Coolant Injection System [*Nuclear energy*] (NRCH)

HPCI Turbine... High Power Coolant Injection Turbine (SAUS)
HPCL.......... Hewlett-Packard Control Language [*Computer science*] (DDC)
HPCL.......... Hindustan Petroleum Corp. Ltd. [*India*] (BUAC)
HPcL.......... Leeward Community College, Pearl City, HI [*Library symbol*] [*Library of Congress*] (LCLS)
HPCM.......... High-Power Countermeasures
HPCM.......... High-speed Pulse Code Modulation (SAUS)
HPCM.......... Human Placenta Conditioned Medium
HPCM.......... Hybrid Pulse Code Modulation (PDAA)
HPCN.......... High Performance Computing and Networking (SAUS)
HPCO.......... High-Pressure Cut-Off [*Air conditioning systems*] [*Automotive engineering*]
HPCPC.......... High-Performance Centrifugal Partition Chromatography
HPCQA.......... Human Pathology (journ.) (SAUS)
HPCRB.......... Hydraulic Power Control Relay Box
HPCRC.......... High-Performance Computer and Research Center [*Department of Energy*]
HPCS.......... Health Protection Computer System (SAUS)
HPCS.......... High Performance Communication Server (SAUO)
HPCS.......... High Performance Computing Section (SAUS)
HPCS.......... High Performance Computing System
HPCS.......... High Performance Computing Systems (SAUS)
HPCS.......... High Performance Control Storage (SAUS)
HPCS.......... High Pressure Combustion Sintering (SAUS)
HPCS.......... High-Pressure Core Spray [*Nuclear energy*] (NRCH)
HPCS.......... High Pressure Core Spraying System (SAUS)
HPCS System... High Pressure Core Spray System (SAUS)
HPCU.......... Hard-Programmable Control Unit (SAUS)
HPCUS.......... Homeopathic Pharmacopoeia Convention of the United States
HPCX.......... Hercules Powder [*Private rail car owner code*]
HP CYL.......... High-Pressure Cylinder (WDAA)
HPCZ.......... Holland Paving [*Federal Railroad Administration identification code*]
HPD.......... Dialysate of Hydropenic Plasma [*Hematology*] (DAVI)
HPD.......... Haloperidol [*Tranquilizer*]
HPD.......... Hammerson Properties Investment & Development Corp. Ltd. [*Toronto Stock Exchange symbol*]
HPD.......... Hand-Point Defense [*Military*] (IIA)
HPD.......... Harbor Police Department (SAUS)
HPD.......... Hard Point Defense
hpd.......... Harpsichord (WDAA)
HPD.......... Harpsichord (journ.) (SAUS)
HPD.......... Haut Pouvoir de Destruction (SAUS)
HPD.......... Hawaii Police Department (SAUO)
HPD.......... Hazelcrest Park District (SAUO)
HPD.......... Health Policy Division (HEAS)
HPD.......... Hearing Protection Device
HPD.......... Hearing Protective Device (SAUS)
HPD.......... Hematoporphyrin Derivative [*Antineoplastic compound*]
HPD.......... Hertford Production Design Ltd. (SAUO)
HPD.......... Heure Probable de Depart (SAUS)
HPD.......... Highest Posterior Density (SAUS)
HPD.......... Highly Probable Drunk (SAUS)
HPD.......... Highly Probably Drink [*Chemical depedency*] (DAVI)
HPD.......... High Performance Diesel (SAUS)
HPD.......... High Performance Division (SAUS)
HPD.......... High Performance Drone (SAUS)
HPD.......... High-Performance Drone
HPD.......... High-Power Density
HPD.......... High Power Destruction (SAUS)
HPD.......... High-Power-Discriminator
HPD.......... High Power Drive (SAUS)
HPD.......... High Power Driver [*Computer science*] (VLIE)
HP-D.......... High Pressure Drain (SAUS)
HPD.......... High-Pressure Drain (DNAB)
HPD.......... High Progressivity/Density (SAUS)
HPD.......... High-Protein Diet
HPD.......... Histrionic Personality Disorder [*Medicine*] (MELL)
HPD.......... Home Peritoneal Dialysis [*Nephrology*] (DAVI)
HPD.......... Horizontal Polar Diagram
H-PD.......... Hough-Powell Digitizer
HPD.......... Hourly Precipitation Data [*A publication*]
HPD.......... Housing Preservation and Development (SAUO)
HPD.......... Hybrid Power Divider (SAUS)
HPD.......... Hydraulic Pump Discharge (AAG)
HPD.......... Hydraulic Pump Drive [*Mechanical engineering*]
HPD.......... Hydrometeorological Processes Division (SAUO)
HPD.......... Hypothalamic-Pituitary Dsyfunction [*Medicine*] (MELL)
HPDC.......... High Performance Distributed Computing (VLIE)
HPDC.......... High Pressure Data Center [*National Institute of Standards and Technology*] [*Information service or system*] (IID)
HPDC.......... High-Pressure Die Casting
HPDF.......... High-Performance Demonstration Facility
HPDF.......... Horizontal Payloads Processing Facility
HPDGF.......... Human Platelet-Derived Growth Factor [*Biochemistry*]
HP-DHA.......... High-Purity Dual Hardness Armor (KSC)
HPDI.......... Hard Point Defense Interceptor
HPDI.......... High-Pressure Direct-Injection [*Automotive engines*]
HPDIM.......... Hard Point Defense Intercept Missile (MCD)
HPDJ.......... Hewlett-Packard Desk Jet (VLIE)
HPDL.......... High-Power Diode LASER (VLIE)
HPDLRL.......... High-Power Diffraction Limited Raman LASER
HPDM.......... High-Performance Demonstration Motor (MCD)
HPDM.......... High Power Destruction Mine (SAUS)
HPDMU.......... High-Powered Diesel Multiple Unit [*Indian Railway*] (TIR)
HPDO.......... Hadia People's Democratic Organisation [*Ethiopia*]
HPDO.......... High Performance Diesel Oil (PDAA)
HPDP.......... Hispanic Policy Development Project (EA)
HPDPI.......... Health Promotion and Disease Prevention Initiative [*Pronounced "hippy dippy"*] [*Department of Health and Human Services*]
HPDPS.......... Hewlett-Packard Distributed Print System (SAUS)
HpD-PT.......... Hepatoporphyrin Derivative-Phototherapy [*Medicine*]
HPDR.......... High Performance Doppler RADAR (VLIE)
HPDS.......... Hard Point Defense System
HPDSC.......... High-Pressure Differential Scanning Calorimetry [*Lubricants*]
HPDT.......... Handicapped Persons Discrimination Board (SAUS)
HPDT.......... High Performance Designer Terminal (TIMI)
HPDU.......... Heat Power Distribution Unit (ACAE)
HPE.......... Harbor Patrol Element [*Navy*] (VNW)
HPE.......... Heat-Producing Element
HPE.......... Heptasaccharide Phytoalexin Elicitor [*Organic chemistry*]
HPE.......... High Performance Estate Wagon (SAUS)
HPE.......... High-Performance Estate Wagon [*Automobile model designation*]
HPE.......... High-Power Effects [*Radio interference*]
HPE.......... High Pressure Electrolyser (SAUS)
HPE.......... High Pressure Equipment (SAUS)
HPE.......... History and Physical Examination [*Medicine*]
HPE.......... Holoprosencephaly [*Medicine*]
HPE.......... Hope [*Amateur radio shorthand*] (WDAA)
HPE.......... Human Proenkephalin [*Biochemistry*]
HPE.......... Hydrogenous Polyethylene
HPE.......... Hydrostatic Permeability Edema [*Medicine*] (MELL)
HPE.......... Inomeni Parataksis Ethnikofronon [*United Front of Nationalists*] [*Political party*] (PPE)
HPEA.......... Health Programs Extension Act [*Medicine*] (EDAA)
HPEAA.......... Health Professions Educational Assistance Act [*Medicine*] (EDAA)
HPEC.......... Handicraft Promotion and Export Centre [*Afghanistan*] (BUAC)
HPEC.......... High-Productivity Energy Crop
HPEC.......... Hydroxpropylethylcellulose (DB)
HP EGS.......... Hewlett Packard Engineering Graphics System (NITA)
HPEK.......... Paul B. Elder Co. [*Research code symbol*]
HPEL.......... Horn Point Environmental Laboratories [*University of Maryland*] (PDAA)
HPEM.......... Hybrid Plasma Equipment Model (AAEL)
HPEO.......... Protonous Poly(ethylene oxide) [*Organic chemistry*]
HPEP.......... High Performance Electrophoresis (SAUS)
HPER.......... Hastings and Prince Edward Regiment [*British military*] (DMA)
HPER.......... Health, Physical Education, and Recreation
HPERB.......... Hawaii Public Employment Relations Board (SAUO)
HPERD.......... Health, Physical Education, Recreation, and Dance (AEE)
HPES.......... Human Performance Enhancement System [*Engineering*]
HPES.......... Human Performance Evaluation System (SAUS)
HP-ESSQ.......... High Pass Error Spectrum Shaping Quantizer (SAUS)
HPETE.......... Hydroxypemxyeicosatetraenoic Acid (SAUS)
HPETE.......... Hydroxyperoxyeicosatetraenoic Acid [*Biochemistry*]
HPEW.......... High-Powered Early Warning (NATG)
HPEWL.......... Hopewell, VA [*American Association of Railroads railroad junction routing code*]
HPEX.......... High Priority Exit (SAUS)
HPEZ.......... House Public Elevator [*Federal Railroad Administration identification code*]
HPF.......... Hammond, LA [*Location identifier*] [*FAA*] (FAAL)
HPF.......... Harbor Patrol Fleet
HPF.......... Hazardous Processing Facility (SSD)
HPF.......... Heat Pipe Furnace
HPF.......... Heparin-Precipitable Fraction (MAE)
HPF.......... Hepatic Plasma Flow [*Medicine*] (DMAA)
HPF.......... Highest Possible [*or Probable*] Frequency [*Electronics*]
hpf.......... Highest Possible Frequency (WDMC)
HPF.......... Highest Priority First (SAUS)
HPF.......... Highest Probable Frequency (SAUS)
HPF.......... Highly Possible Frequency (SAUS)
HPF.......... High Pass Filter
HPF.......... High Performance File (SAUS)
HPF.......... High Performance FORTRAN [*Computer language*]
HPF.......... High Performance, Fragmentation (SAUS)
HPF.......... High Possible Frequency (VLIE)
HPF.......... High Powered Field (SAUS)
HPF.......... High Power Factor [*Construction term*] (MIST)
hpf.......... High-Power Field [*Medicine*] (EDAA)
HPF.......... High-Power Field [*Microscopy*]
HPF.......... High-Protein Fraction [*Food technology*]
HPF.......... Hispanic Professional Female (ADWA)
HPF.......... Historic Preservation Fund [*National Trust for Historic Preservation*]
HPF.......... Historic Pullman Foundation (EA)
HPF.......... Horace Plunkett Foundation (SAUO)
HPF.......... Horace Plunkett Foundation for Cooperative Studies (BUAC)
HPF.......... Horizontal Position Finder (IAA)
HPF.......... Horizontal Processing Facility [*Operation and Checkout*] [*NASA*] (NASA)
HPF.......... Host Preparation Facility (MHDI)
HPF.......... Hot-Pressed Ferrite (IAA)
HPF.......... Human Powered Flight (DICI)
HPF.......... Hypocaloric Protein Feeding (DB)
HPF.......... Palpebral Fissure Width (SAUS)
HPF Ballast... High Power Factor Ballast (SAUS)
HPFC.......... High-Performance Fuel Cell
HPFCR.......... Health Physics Field Change Request (SAUS)
HPFD.......... High Pressure Fuel Duct (SAUS)
HPFD.......... Hughes Process Flow Diagram (ACAE)
HPFD.......... Hybrid Personal Floating Device (SAUS)

HPFF........... High Pressure Fluid-Filled
HPFH........... Heredita Persistence of Fetal Hemoglobin (SAUS)
HPFH........... Hereditary Persistence of Fetal Hemoglobin [*Hematology*]
HP-FL........... Hewlett-Packard Fiber Optic Link (SAUS)
HPFL........... Highpass Filter (MSA)
HPFL........... High-Performance Fuels Laboratory
HPFL........... Holly Park Field Laboratory [*University of Nevada - Reno*] [*Research center*] (RCD)
HPFM........... Hydropress Form [*Tool*] (AAG)
HPFN........... High-Pass Filtered Noise [*Medicine*] (EDAA)
HPFP........... High Performance Fragmentation Projectile (SAUS)
HPFP........... High-Pressure Fire Protection (NRCH)
HPFP........... High-Pressure Fuel Pump (KSC)
HPFRS........... High-Profile Frequency Reference Standard
HPFS........... High-Performance File System [*Computer science*]
HPFS........... High Pressure Fire Service (SAUS)
hPFSH........... Human Pituitary Follicle-Stimulating Hormone [*Endocrinology*] (MAE)
HPFSH........... Human Pituitary Follicle-Stimulating Hormone [*Medicine*] (STED)
HPFSH........... Human Pituitary Gonadotropin (DB)
HPFT........... High-Pressure Fuel Turbopump [*Aerospace*] (NAKS)
HPFTP........... High-Pressure Fuel Turbopump (NASA)
HPFW........... High Pressure Filtered Water (SAUS)
HPG........... Hard Page (SAUS)
HPG........... Harvard Presentation Graphics [*Software Publishing Corp.*] [*Computer software*]
HPG........... Helicobacter Pylori-Associated Gastritis [*Medicine*] (EDAA)
HPG........... Heritage Propane Partners LP [*NYSE symbol*] (SAG)
HPG........... High Performance Generator (SAUS)
HPG........... High Performance Graphics (SAUS)
HPG........... High-Power Generator
HPG........... High-Power Ground (IAA)
HPG........... High-Power Group
HPG........... High-Pressure Gas (KSC)
HPG........... High-Pressure Gelatine (IAA)
HPG........... High Pressure Gun (SAUS)
HPG........... Homopolar Generator [*To power high-technology experiments*]
HPG........... Horticultural Postharvest Group [*Queensland, Australia*]
HPG........... Human Pituitary Gonadotrophin [*Endocrinology*]
hPG........... Human Pituitary Gonadotropin [*Medicine*] (STED)
HPG........... Hydroxypropyl Guar [*Organic chemistry*]
HPG........... Hyper-Pure Germanium (SAUS)
HPG........... Hypothalamic, Pituitary, Gonadal [*Endocrinology*]
HPG........... p-Hydroxyphenylglycine (DB)
HPGA........... Hawaii Personnel and Guidance Association (SAUO)
HPGA........... High Pressure Gas Atomization (SAUS)
HPGC........... Heading per Gyro Compass [*Navigation*]
HPGC........... Hypopressure Gas Chromatography
HPGC........... Hypopure Gas Chromatography (SAUS)
HPGe........... High Purity Germanium (STED)
HpGe........... Hyperpure Germanium [*Also, HPG*] [*Chemistry*]
HPGF........... Hybridoma/Plasmacytoma Growth Factor [*Biochemistry*]
HPGIDB........... Health Physics Great Ideas Database (SAUS)
HPGL........... Gross Load Horsepower [*Automotive engineering*]
HPGL........... Hewlett Packard General Language (AGLO)
HPGL........... Hewlett-Packard Graphics Language
HPGMI........... Hunter Post Graduate Medical Institute (SAUO)
HPGN........... High-Precision Geodetic Network (SAUO)
HPGPM........... Hits per Gun per Minute (NVT)
HPG Radar... High Power Ground Radar (SAUS)
hpGRF........... Human Pancreas Growth Hormone-Releasing Factor [*Immunochemistry*]
HPGS........... High-Performance Graphics System [*Computer science*] (MHDB)
HPGS........... High-Pressure Gas System (NASA)
HPH........... Halothane-Percent-Hour (STED)
HPH........... Harnischfeger Industries [*NYSE symbol*] (SAG)
HPH........... High-Performance Hoist (MCD)
HPH........... High-Pressure Hose
HP/h........... Horse Power/hour (SAUS)
HPH........... Horsepower-Hour
HPHBA........... Havard Public Health Alumni Bulletin (journ.) (SAUS)
HPHC........... Harvard Pilgrim Health Care
HPHD........... High-Pressure High-Density
HPHF........... Hereditary Persistence of Hemoglobin F [*Genetics*] (DOG)
HP/HIP........... Hot Pressing followed by Hot Isostatic Pressing (SAUS)
HPHP........... Hydroxypivalyl Hydroxypivalate [*Organic chemistry*]
HP-HR........... Horsepower-Hour
HPHT........... High Pressure High Temperature [*Engineering*]
HPHW........... High Pressure Hot Water (SAUS)
HPI........... Cleveland, OH [*Location identifier*] [*FAA*] (FAAL)
HPI........... Handicap Problems Inventory [*Psychology*]
HPI........... Hardwood Plywood Institute [*Later, HPMA*] (EA)
HPI........... Health Practices Inventory (EDAC)
HPI........... Health Professionals, Inc. [*AMEX symbol*] (SPSG)
HPI........... Health Promotion Institute (EA)
HPI........... Heavy Positive Ion
HPI........... Heifer Project, Incorporated (SAUO)
HPI........... Heifer Project International (EA)
HPI........... Height-Position Indicator (DEN)
HPI........... Hellenic Purchasing Institute (BUAC)
HPI........... Helme Products, Incorporated (SAUO)
HPI........... Helpful Programs, Inc. [*Computer science*]
HPI........... Hepatic Perfusion Index [*Medicine*] (DMAA)
HPI........... Heston Personality Inventory [*Test*] (STED)
HPI........... Hewlett-Packard Interface (SAUS)
HPI........... High Performance Imagery (SAUS)
HPI........... High-Performance Insulation (MCD)
HPI........... High Performance Interceptor (ACAE)
HPI........... High Performance Isolation (AAEL)
HPI........... High Position Indicator (SAUS)
HPI........... High-Power Illuminator (NATG)
HPI........... High-Pressure Injection [*Nuclear energy*] (NRCH)
HPI........... High Pressure Isolation (SAUS)
HPI........... High-Pressure Isolation
HPI........... High Probability of Intercept (SAUS)
HPI........... High Probability-of-Intercept
HPI........... History of Present Illness
HPI........... Hogan Personality Inventory [*Test*] (TMMY)
HPI........... Holland in South East Asia (journ.) (SAUS)
HPI........... Homing Position Indicator (NATG)
HPI........... Host Port Interface (SAUS)
HPI........... Host Processor Interface (SAUS)
HPI........... Hours Post Inoculation
HPI........... Howe Peak [*Idaho*] [*Seismograph station code, US Geological Survey*] (SEIS)
HPI........... Hull Product Improvement [*Navy*] (CAAL)
HPI........... Human Productivity Institute (EA)
HPI........... Human Proinsulin (DB)
HPI........... Human Protein Index (DB)
HPI........... Hydraulic Pressure Indicator
HPI........... Hydrocarbon Processing Industry
HPIA........... (Hydroxyphenylisopropyl)adenosine
HPIB........... Hanford Permanent Isolation Barrier (SAUS)
HPIB........... Hewlett-Package Interface Bus (SAUS)
HPIB........... Hewlett-Packard Interface Bus (ADWA)
HP-IB........... Hewlett-Packard Interface Bus [*Instrumentation*]
HPIC........... Health Physics Information Center (SAUO)
HPIC........... Health Promotion Information Centre (BUAC)
HPIC........... Hearing Performance Inventory for Children
HPIC........... High-Performance Immunoaffinity Chromatography
HPIC........... High Performance Immunocinity Chromatoaphy (SAUS)
HPIC........... High Power IC (SAUS)
HPICS........... Heat Pipe Instrument Control System (SAUS)
HPIEC........... High-Performance Ion Exchange Chromatography
HPIEC........... High-Pressure Ion Exchange Chromatography
HP IL........... Hewlett Packard Interface Loop (NITA)
HPIL........... Hewlett-Packard Interface Loop (SAUS)
HPI Lamp.... High Pressure Iodide Lamp (SAUS)
HPIM........... High Performance Image Analysis (SAUS)
HPIM........... High-Pressure Injection Molding (EDCT)
HPI-MSRG... Human Performance International, Motor Sport Research Group [*Research center*] (RCD)
HPIP........... High-Pressure Intensifier Pump
HPIP........... Houghton Pharmaceuticals, Inc. [*NASDAQ symbol*] (SAG)
HPIR........... Heat Pipe Radiator (SAUS)
HPIR........... High-Power Illuminator RADAR [*Army*] (AABC)
HPIR........... High-Probability-of-Intercept Receiver [*Telecommunications*] (IEEE)
HPIS........... High-Performance Insulation System
HPIS........... High-Pressure Injection System [*Nuclear energy*] (NRCH)
HPIS........... Hospital Plan Insurance Services (SAUO)
HPISS........... High-Power Illuminator Signal Source (MCD)
HPIT........... High-Performance Infiltrating Technique [*Materials science*]
HPIX........... Montell USA [*Private rail car owner code*]
HPJ........... Help Project [*Computer science*] (PCM)
HPJ........... High Power Jammer (SAUS)
HPJ........... High-Power Jammer
HPJ........... High-Pressure Jet
HPJC........... Highland Park Junior College [*Later, Highland Park College*] [*Michigan*]
HP Journal... Hewlett-Packard Journal (journ.) (SAUS)
HPK........... High-Power Klystron
HPK........... Histidine Protein Kinase [*An enzyme*]
HPK........... Hollywood Park [*NYSE symbol*] (SG)
HPK........... Honorary Physician to the King [*British*]
HPKA........... High-Power Klystron Amplifier
HPKMB........... Hieratische Papyrus aus den Koeniglichen Museen zu Berlin [*A publication*] (BJA)
HPKO........... Hardened Palm Kernel Oil (SAUS)
HPL........... Halifax Public Library (SAUO)
HPL........... Hamilton Public Library [*UTLAS symbol*]
HPL........... Hartford Public Library, Hartford, CT [*OCLC symbol*] (OCLC)
HPL........... Haut Pouvoir Lethal (SAUS)
HPL........... Headquarters Pay List (SAUO)
HPL........... Heliportugal-Trabalhos e Transporte Aereo, Representacoes, Importacao e Exportacao Lda. [*Portugal*] [*ICAO designator*] (FAAC)
HPL........... Helix Pomatia Lektin (SAUS)
HPL........... Herts Pharmaceuticals Limited (SAUO)
HPL........... Hewlett-Packard Language (SAUO)
HPL........... Highest Point Level (SAUS)
HPL........... High Level Programming Language (SAUS)
HPL........... High Performance Logic (AAEL)
HPL........... High Polar Latitude [*Geophysics*]
HPL........... High-Power LASER
HPL........... High-Pressure Laminate [*Plastics*]
HPL........... High Pressure Liquid (HAWK)
HPL........... Himal Power Ltd. (SAUO)
HPL........... Home Product Link (SAUS)
HPL........... Horn Point Environmental Laboratories (SAUS)
Hpl........... Hospital (SAUS)
HPL........... Hotel Properties Ltd. [*Singapore*] (ECON)

HPL.......... Houston Pipe Line (SAUS)
HPL.......... Houston Public Library (SAUO)
HPL.......... Human Pamtid Lysozyme (SAUS)
HPL.......... Human Pancreatic Lipase [*An enzyme*]
HPL.......... Human Parotid Lysozyme [*An enzyme*]
HPL.......... Human Performance Laboratory [*Ball State University*] [*Research center*] (RCD)
HPL.......... Human Peripheral Lymphocyte
hPL.......... Human Placental Lactogen (STED)
HPL.......... Human Placental Lactogen [*Also, CGP, HCS*] [*Endocrinology*]
hPL.......... Human Platelet Lactogen [*Medicine*] (EDAA)
HPL.......... Hutton Procedural Language (SAUS)
HPL.......... Hybrid Programming Language [*Computer science*]
HPL.......... Hyperplexia (STED)
HPL.......... Nucla, CO [*Location identifier*] [*FAA*] (FAAL)
HPLA.......... Hoover Presidential Library Association (SAUO)
HPLA.......... Hydroxyphenyllactic Acid [*Pharmacology*] (MAE)
HPLAC.......... High-Performance Liquid Affinity Chromatography
HPLAC.......... High-Pressure Liquid-Affinity Chromatography (DMAA)
HPLAP.......... Human Placental Alkaline Phosphatase [*An enzyme*]
HPLB.......... High Power Laser Blinding (SAUS)
HPLC.......... Herbage Plant Liaison Committee (SAUO)
HPLC.......... High-Performance [*or High-Pressure*] Liquid Chromatography
HPLC.......... High-Precision Liquid Chromatography (CARB)
HPLC.......... High-Pressure Liquid Chromatography [*Medicine*] (PALA)
HPLE.......... Hereditary Polymorphic Light Eruption [*Medicine*] (EDAA)
HP-LEC.......... High Pressure Liquid Encapsulated Czochralski (SAUS)
HPLF.......... High-Pressure Low-Flow
HPLF.......... Hydrolyzed Polar Lipid Fraction [*Biochemistry*]
HPLJ.......... Hewlett-Packard Laser Jet (SAUS)
HPLJ.......... High-Pressure Liquid Jet
HPLL.......... High Pressure Life Laboratory (PDAA)
HPLL.......... Hybrid Phase-Locked Loop (PDAA)
HPLMN.......... Home Public Land Mobile Network (SAUS)
HPLO.......... High-Performance, Low-Observable
HPLO.......... High Power Laser Optics (ACAE)
HP/LP.......... High-Power/Low-Power
HPLPC.......... High-Performance Low-Pressure Chromatography
HPLPLC.......... High Performance Low-Pressure Liquid Chromatography (SAUS)
HPLR.......... Hinge Pillar [*Technical drawings*]
HPLRP.......... Health Professionals Loan Repayment Program [*Military*]
HPLS.......... Hanford Patrol Logistics System (SAUS)
hpls.......... hopeless (SAUS)
HPLSDO.......... History and Philosophy of the Life Sciences. Pubblicazioni della Stazione Zoologica di Napoli. Section II (journ.) (SAUS)
HPL/T.......... High-Productivity Languages/Tools (SAUS)
HPLV.......... High-Pressure Low-Volume [*Automotive painting*]
HPLX.......... Exxon USA [*Private rail car owner code*]
HPLX.......... Healthplex, Inc. [*NASDAQ symbol*] (NQ)
HPLX.......... HERL-RTP Plexiglas System (SAUS)
HPM.......... Haing-Pay Melanoma (SAUS)
HPM.......... Harding-Passey Melanoma [*Oncology*] (AAMN)
HPM.......... Hard-Part Machining (SAUS)
HPM.......... Hartig Plastics Machinery (SAUO)
HPM.......... Hazardous Production Material [*Forest industry*] (WPI)
HPM.......... Head Positioning Mechanism
HPM.......... Head Position Monitor
HPM.......... Head Postmaster's Manual [*British*] (DCTA)
HPM.......... Headquarters of Provost Marshal (SAUO)
HPM.......... Health Physics and Medical Division (SAUO)
HPM.......... Hemiplegic Migraine [*Neurology*] (DAVI)
HPM.......... High-Performance Membrane [*Medicine*] (DMAA)
HPM.......... High Performance Motor (SAUS)
HPM.......... High-Pitched Murmur [*Medicine*] (MELL)
HPM.......... High-Polymer Molecular [*Film*]
HPM.......... High-Power Microwave
HPM.......... High-Power Multiplier (DNAB)
HPM.......... High-Priority Mail (TSSD)
HPM.......... High Purity Metal (AAEL)
HPM.......... Hispanic Professional Male (ADWA)
HPM.......... Historical Photographs of Mining (SAUO)
HPM.......... Honeycomb Propellant Matrix (SAA)
HPM.......... Horizontal Panel Mount
HPM.......... Hot Press Molding
HPM.......... How Products are Made [*A publication*]
HPM.......... Human Performance Model [*Human Engineering Laboratory*] [*Aberdeen Proving Ground, MD*] (RDA)
HPM.......... Human Peritoneal Macrophage [*Immunology*]
HPM.......... Human Potential Movement [*Psychotherapy*]
HPM.......... Hybrid Phase Modulation (SAUS)
HPM.......... Hydraulic Press Manufacturers (SAUO)
HPM.......... Hydraulic Pump Motor
HPM.......... Hydraulic Punching Machine
HPM.......... Hyper-Page-Mode [*Computer science*] (PCM)
HPMA.......... Hardwood Plywood Manufacturers Association [*Reston, VA*] (EA)
HPMA.......... Heat Pump Manufacturers' Association [*British*]
HPMA.......... High-Power Microwave Assembly (AAG)
HPMA.......... Hydroxypropyl Methacrylate [*Organic chemistry*]
HPMAA.......... Honey Packers and Marketers' Association of Australia
HPMC.......... High-Performance Membrane Chromatography
HPMC.......... Housing Production and Management Credit [*HUD*]
HPMC.......... Hydroxypropyl(methyl)cellulose [*Synthetic food gum*] [*Organic chemistry*]
HPMCF.......... High Purity Milled Carbon Fiber
HP Metric.......... Horse Power, Metric (SAUS)
HPMG.......... Human Postmenopausal Gonadotropin (SAUS)
Hp Mi.......... Hippias Minor [*of Plato*] [*Classical studies*] (OCD)
HPMIDC.......... Himachul Pradesh Mineral and Industrial Development Corp. [*India*] (BUAC)
HPMIS.......... Health Programs Management Information System (SAUS)
HPML.......... High Pressure Mercury Lamp (SAUS)
HPMM.......... Horizontal Planar Motion Mechanism (PDAA)
HPMNJ.......... High-Power Microelectronic Noise Jammer
HPMP.......... Hanford Performance Measurement Program (SAUS)
HPMS.......... High-Performance Main Storage (IAA)
HPMS.......... Highway Performance-Monitoring System [*Department of Transportation*] (GFGA)
HPMS Acid.......... Hydroxy-2-Pyridine-Methane-Sulphonic Acid (SAUS)
HPMSK.......... High-Priority Mission Support Kit [*Military*] (AFIT)
HPMV.......... High-Pressure Mercury Vapor
HPMWA.......... High Power Microwave Amplifier (SAUS)
HPN.......... Central Hispano International, Inc. [*NYSE symbol*] (SAG)
HPN.......... Harrison, Purchase, and North Castle [*Airport*]
HPN.......... Haustus Purgans Noster [*Purging Draught from the Doctor's Own Prescription*] [*Pharmacy*] (ROG)
HPN.......... Health Physics Network [*Nuclear energy*] (NRCH)
HPN.......... Heavy Primary Nuclei
HPN.......... Hepsin (DMAA)
HPN.......... High Pass Network
HPN.......... High Pass Notch (IAA)
HPN.......... Home Numbering Plan (SAUS)
HPN.......... Home Parenteral Nutrition
HPN.......... Horsepower Nominal
HPN.......... Hosp Parch News (SAUS)
HPN.......... Hydrogenation of Pyrolysis Naphtha [*Petroleum refining*]
H Pn.......... Hydropneumatic (SAUS)
HPN.......... Hydroxypropyl Nitrate [*Organic chemistry*]
HPN.......... Hypertension [*Medicine*]
HPN.......... White Plains [*New York*] [*Airport symbol*] (OAG)
HPNA.......... Home Phoneline Networking Alliance
HPNA.......... Home Phone Networking Architecture (AGLO)
HPNA.......... Hospice and Palliative Nurses Association (SAUO)
HPND.......... Human Pronatriodilatin [*Endocrinology*]
HPNET.......... High-Energy Physics Networks (AGLO)
HPNJ.......... High-Power Noise Jammer
HPNO.......... Home Public Network Operator (SAUS)
HPnP.......... Home Plug and Play [*Technology*]
HPNPr.......... Centl Hispano Intl9.875% 'MIPS' [*NYSE symbol*] (TTSB)
HPNS.......... High-Pressure Nervous Syndrome [*Deep-sea diving*]
HPNS.......... Hunters Point Naval Shipyard
HPO.......... Hamilton Philharmonic Orchestra (SAUO)
HPO.......... Head Post Office
HPO.......... Health Care Purchasing Organization [*Insurance*] (WYGK)
HPO.......... High Performance Option (SAUS)
HPO.......... High-Performance Option (MCD)
HPO.......... High Power Oscillator (SAUS)
HPO.......... High Preferred Orientation (SAUS)
HPO.......... High-Pressure Oxygen [*Also, HBO, OHP*]
HPO.......... High-volume Page Output Controller (SAUS)
HPO.......... Highway Post Office [*Bus or truck equipped with mail distribution facilities*]
HPO.......... Hippo Valley [*Zimbabwe*] [*Airport symbol*] (AD)
HPO.......... Historic Preservation Office (SAUS)
HPO.......... Home Port [*Navy*] (NVT)
HPO.......... Hourly Postflight (MCD)
HPO.......... Hourly Postflight Overhaul (SAUS)
HPO.......... Hydrogenated Palm Oil
HPO.......... Hydroperoxide (DMAA)
HPO.......... Hydrophilic Ointment [*Pharmacy*] (DAVI)
HPO.......... Hydroxylamine Phosphate Oxime [*Organic chemistry*]
HPO.......... Hypertrophic Pulmonary Osteoarthropathy [*Medicine*] (DAVI)
HPOA.......... Hypothalamic-Pituitary-Ovarian Axis [*Medicine*] (EDAA)
HPOC.......... High Plains Oil Corp. (SAUS)
HPOC.......... High Plains Oil Corporation (SAUO)
HPOD.......... Hydroperoxyoctadecadienoic Acid [*Organic chemistry*]
HPOF.......... High-Pressure Oil-Filled [*Cable*]
HPOF Cable.......... High Pressure Oil Filled Cable (SAUS)
HPOFS.......... High Performance Optical File System (SAUS)
H Points.......... High Points (journ.) (SAUS)
HPOL.......... Health Manpower Shortage Area Placement Opportunity List [*Department of Health and Human Services*] (GFGA)
HPOL.......... High Power Optical Laboratory (SAUS)
HPOL.......... History and Politics Out Loud
HPOM.......... Home Page Objects Model (SAUS)
HPOP.......... High-Pressure Oxidizer Pump (NASA)
HPOQ.......... Health Policy Quarterly (journ.) (SAUS)
HPOS.......... Hardware Performance Optimization System (ACAE)
HPOT.......... Helipotentiometer
HPOT.......... High Potential (IAA)
HPOT.......... High-Pressure Oxidizer Turbopump [*Aerospace*] (NAKS)
HPOT.......... Hydroperoxyoctadecatrienoic Acid [*Organic chemistry*]
HPOTP.......... High-Pressure Oxidizer Turbopump
HP-OV.......... Hewlett Packard Open View (SAUS)
HPOX.......... High-Pressure Oxygen (AFM)
HPP.......... Half Page Printer
HPP.......... Half Power Point [*LASER technology*]
HPP.......... Hamiltonian Path Problem [*Mathematics*]
HPP.......... Harvard Project Physics
HPP.......... Harward Project Physics (SAUS)
HPP.......... Hawker Pacific Proprietary (SAUO)

HPP .... Health Physics Program (NRCH)
HPP .... Health Promotion Pilot
HPP .... Health Promotion Practice (SAUO)
HPP .... Healthy Planet Products, Inc. [*AMEX symbol*] (SAG)
HPP .... Hepp [*Alaska*] [*Seismograph station code, US Geological Survey*] (SEIS)
HPP .... Hereditary Pyropoikilocytosis [*Medicine*]
HPP .... Hernieuwde Progressieve Partij [*Renewed Progressive Party*] [*Surinam*] [*Political party*] (PPW)
HPP .... Hewlett-Packard Printer (SAUS)
HPP .... High-Performance Plastic
HPP .... High Performance Polymer (SAUS)
HPP .... High Performance Processor (SAUS)
HPP .... High Power Pistol (SAUS)
HPP .... High Precision Photogrammetry (SAUS)
HPP .... High Pressure Physics (SAUS)
HPP .... High Pressure Polyethylene (SAUS)
HPP .... High Pressure Pump (SAUS)
HPP .... Hinged Penile Prosthesis [*Medicine*] (MELL)
HPP .... Holding under Promise of Payment
HPP .... Homogeneous Poisson Process (SAUS)
HPP .... Hot Pilot Plant fuel reprocessing (SAUS)
HPP .... Hot Processing Plant [*Nuclear energy*]
HPP .... Human Pancreatic Polypeptide [*Endocrinology*]
HPP .... Hungarian People's Party [*Croatia*] [*Political party*] (BUAC)
HPP .... Hydraulic Pneumatic Panel (AAG)
HPP .... Hydrolyzed Plant Protein (SAUS)
HPP .... Hydroxyphenyl Pyruvate [*Organic chemistry*]
HPP .... Hydroxypyrazolopyrimidine (SAUS)
HPP .... Hyperplastic Polyps [*Medicine*] (MELL)
HPP .... Hypokalemic Periodic Paralysis [*Medicine*] (MELL)
HPPA .... Hewlett-Packard Precision Architecture (SAUS)
HPPA .... High Performance Pipe Association (BUAC)
HPPA .... High-Performance Precision Architecture (RALS)
HPPA .... Horses' and Ponies' Protection Association [*British*] (DI)
HPPA .... Hospital Purchaser-Provider Agreement (ADWA)
HPPA .... Hydroxyphenylpyruvic Acid [*Organic chemistry*]
HP Paper .... Hot Pressed Paper (SAUS)
HPPB .... Historic Pensacola Preservation Board (SAUO)
HPPC .... Health Plan Purchasing Cooperatives
HPPC .... Herbal Production and Processing Company Ltd. (SAUO)
HPPC .... High Performance Computing and Communications (TNIG)
HP PCIB .... Hewlett Packard Personal Computer Instruments Bus (NITA)
HPPCL .... Hewlett-Packard Printer Control Language
HP/PCS .... Hewlett Packard/Process Computer Systems (SAUO)
HP/PCS .... Hewlett-Packard/Process Computer Systems (SAUS)
HPPD .... Hours per Patient Day [*Medicine*] (DMAA)
HPPF .... Horizontal Payloads Processing Facility (MCD)
HPPF .... Human Plasma Protein Fraction [*Medicine*] (EDAA)
HPPH .... (Hydroxyphenyl)phenylhydantoin [*Biochemistry*] (AAMN)
HPPI .... High-Performance Parallel Interface [*Computer science*]
HPPIDE .... Health and Population Perspectives and Issues (journ.) (SAUS)
H-P Plan ...... Hire Purchase Plan (SAUS)
HPPLC .... High-Performance Preparative Liquid Chromatography
HPPM .... High-Performance Propulsion Module (MCD)
HPPO .... High Pressure Partial Oxidation (PDAA)
HPPO .... Hydroxyphenyl Pyruvate Oxidase [*Medicine*] (EDAA)
HPPP .... High-Pressure Pump Pad (COE)
HPPP .... High-Priority Production Program [*NATO*] (NATG)
HPPR .... Hydroxypyrazolopyrimidine Ribonucleoside [*Biochemistry*]
HPPRA .... Hydrocarbon Processing and Petroleum Refiner (journ.) (SAUS)
HPPS .... Harper & Row Publisbers, Inc. (SAUO)
HPPS .... Hewlett-Packard Payment Scheme (SAUS)
HPPS .... Hewlett-Packard Printer Submodule (IAA)
HPPS .... High-Performance Paper Society (SAUO)
HPPS .... High Pressure Pump Station (SAUS)
HPPS .... House of Pacific Relations (SAUO)
HPPS .... Housing and Planning References (SAUO)
HPPS .... Hughes Photoelectric Reader (SAUO)
HPPS .... Hughes Post Processor, Surveyor
HPPT .... High Power Physics Testing (SAUS)
HPPT .... Hypertext Text Transfer Protocol [*Computer science*] (TNIG)
HPPTS .... Hydraulic Package Pressure Test Set
HPPX .... Huntsman Polypropylene [*Private rail car owner code*]
HPPZ .... Haywood Power Plant [*Federal Railroad Administration identification code*]
HPQ .... Highly Polarized Quasar [*Galactic science*]
HPQC .... High-Pressure Quick-Connect
HPQS .... Highly Parallel Query System [*Computer science*] (HODG)
HPQSTDB .... Health Physics Quality Safety Tracking Database (SAUS)
HPQY .... High Purity Quartz Yarn [*Materials science*]
HPR .... Halden Reactor Project [*Norway*]
HPR .... Halt and Proceed [*Computer science*] (SAA)
HPR .... Hardware Problem Report (MCD)
HPR .... Heart Profile Recorder [*Medicine*]
HPR .... Heat Pipe Reactor
HPr .... Heat-Stable Protein [*Medicine*] (EDAA)
HPR .... Heure Probable de Retour (SAUS)
HPR .... Hic Pace Requiescat [*May He Here Rest in Peace*] [*Latin*] (ROG)
HPR .... Highly Protected Risk [*Insurance*]
HPR .... High Penetration Resistant (PDAA)
HPR .... High Performance Radar (SAUS)
HPR .... High Performance Routing (SAUS)
HPR .... High-Performance Routing [*Computer science*] (CDE)
HPR .... High-Polymer Rheology
HPR .... High-Powered RADAR (NATG)
HPR .... High Priority Request (SAUS)
HPR .... Holding Period Return (PDAA)
HPR .... Homiletic and Pastoral Review (journ.) (SAUS)
HPR .... Hopper [*Freight*]
hpr .... Hopper hot Particle Rolling (SAUS)
HPR .... Horsepower
HPR .... Hosptial Peer Review (MEDA)
HPR .... Host-Plant Resistance [*Entomology, phytochemistry*]
HPR .... Hot Particle Rolling (PDAA)
HPR .... Housing and Planning References [*A publication*]
HPR .... Howard's New York Practice Reports [*A publication*] (DLA)
HPr .... Howard's New York Practice Reports, New Series [*A publication*] (DLA)
HPR .... Howards New York Practice Reports, New Series (journ.) (SAUS)
HPR .... HPR, Inc. [*Associated Press*] (SAG)
HPR .... Hughes Photoelectric Reader
HPR .... Hughes Processes Requirement (ACAE)
HPR .... Human Performance Reliability
HPR .... Human Progesterone Receptor [*Endocrinology*]
HPr .... Human Prolactin [*Medicine*] (EDAA)
HPR .... Human Prolactin [*Endocrinology*]
HPR .... Hungarian Peoples Republic (SAUS)
HPR .... Hydrogen Pressure Regulator (MCD)
HPR .... Hydroxyphenylretinamide [*Biochemistry*]
HPR .... Hyperion Resources [*Vancouver Stock Exchange symbol*]
HPR .... Hypophosphatemic Rickets [*Medicine*] (MELL)
HPR .... Rick Lucus Helicopters Ltd. [*New Zealand*] [*FAA designator*] (FAAC)
HPrA .... Harcourt Genl'A'cm CvStk [*NYSE symbol*] (TTSB)
HPRA .... Health Physics Research Abstracts (SAUS)
HPRA .... Heat Pipe Radiator Assembly (SAUS)
HPRA .... Hungarian Public Relations Association (BUAC)
HPRAC .... Health Professions Regulatory Advisory Council (SAUO)
HPRASA ...... High Plains Regional Aquifer System (SAUO)
HPRC .... Hereditary Papillary Renal Cancer [*Medicine*]
HPRC .... Houston Petroleum Research Center (SAUS)
HPRCC .... High Plains Regional Climate Center [*NCPO*]
HPRE .... Homogeneous Power Reactor Experiment (SAUO)
HPRES .... Pressure Altitude (GAVI)
HPRF .... High Pulse Recurrence Frequency (MCD)
HPRF .... High Pulse Repetition Frequency (SAUS)
HPRF .... Hypersonic Propulsion Research Facility
HPRFICW ..... High Pulse Repetition Frequency Interrupted Continuous Wave (ACAE)
HPRI .... HPR Inc. [*NASDAQ symbol*] (SAG)
HPRILIM ...... Hangzhou Project and Research Institute of Light Industry Machinery [*China*] (BUAC)
HPRIN .... Health Promotion Research Internet Network (SAUO)
HPRK .... Hollywood Park [*NASDAQ symbol*] (TTSB)
HPRK .... Hollywood Park, Inc. [*NASDAQ symbol*] (SAG)
HPRKZ .... Hollywood Park $0.70 Dep Cv Pfd [*NASDAQ symbol*] (TTSB)
HPRL .... Human Performance Research Laboratory [*University of Utah*] [*Research center*] (RCD)
HPRL .... Human Prolactin [*Endocrinology*]
HPRLG .... High-Precision Ring Laser Gyro (SAUS)
HPRM .... Health Promotion Monographs (journ.) (SAUS)
Hpro .... Hydroxyproline [*Medicine*] (EDAA)
HPROM .... Harris Programmable Read-Only Memory (SAUS)
HPRP .... High Performance Reporting Post (SAUO)
HPRP .... High-Performance Reporting Post (NATG)
HPRP .... High-Powered RADAR Post (NATG)
HPRP .... Homes Per Rating Point [*Advertising*] (DOAD)
HPRP .... Human Platelet-Rich Plasma [*Medicine*] (DMAA)
HPRP .... Human Potential Research Project [*University of Surrey*] [*British*] (AIE)
HPRPC .... High-Performance Reversed Phase Chromatography
HPRR .... Health Physics Research Reactor [*Oak Ridge, TN*] [*Oak Ridge National Laboratory*] [*Department of Energy*]
HPRR .... High-Performance Research Reactor (SAUO)
HPRS .... Health Physics Records Storage (SAUS)
HPRS .... Hellenic Public Relations Society [*Greece*] (BUAC)
HPRS .... High-Pressure Recirculation System [*Nuclear energy*] (NRCH)
HPRS .... Hopkins Psychiatric Rating Scale [*Personality development test*] [*Psychology*]
HPRS .... Houghton Poultry Research Station [*British*] (ARC)
HPR Screen ... High Penetration Resistant Screen (SAUS)
HPRT .... HCI Preview Response Time (SAUS)
HPRT .... Heartport Inc. [*NASDAQ symbol*] (TTSB)
HPRT .... High Power Recovery Turbine (SAUS)
HPRT .... Hypoxanthine-Guanine-Phosphoribosyl Transferase (DOG)
HPRT .... Hypoxanthine Phosphoribosyltransferase [*Also, HGPRT*] [*An enzyme*]
HPRU .... Handicapped Persons Research Unit (NITA)
HPRV .... High-Pressure Relief Valve (KSC)
HPRV .... Hydrogen Pressure Relief Valve (SAUS)
HPRW .... High Pressure Raw Water (SAUS)
HPRWP .... Health Physics Radiation Work Permit Database (SAUS)
HPS .... Antisubmarine Helicopter (NATG)
HPS .... Crown Aviation, Inc. (SAUO)
HPS .... Haitian Philatelic Society (EA)
HPS .... Hamburger Philologische Studien (journ.) (SAUS)
HPS .... Handbook of Paper Science (journ.) (SAUS)
HPS .... Hanford Plant Standard [*Formerly, HWS*] [*Nuclear energy*] (NRCH)
HPS .... Hanna Pacific [*Vancouver Stock Exchange symbol*]
HPS .... Hantavirus Pulmonary Syndrome [*Medicine*]

HPS .... Hardened Power System
HPS .... Hardy Plant Society (EAIO)
HPS .... Harlem Preparatory School (SAUO)
Hps .... Harpsichord (SAUS)
HPS .... Harpsicord [*Music*] (WGA)
HPS .... Hazardous Polluting Substances [*Shipping*] (DCTA)
HPS .... Head Position Sensing (SAUS)
HPS .... Head Protection System [*Automotive safety*]
HPS .... Health Physics Society (EA)
HPS .... Health Physics Society Standards Committee
HPS .... Health Physics Station [*Nuclear energy*] (NRCH)
HPS .... Health Physics Surveillance (SAUS)
HPS .... Health Physics Systems, Inc. (SAUO)
HPS .... Healthplan Services Corp. [*NYSE symbol*] (SAG)
HPS .... Heat Protection System
HPS .... Heel Pain Syndrome (MELL)
HPS .... Helium Pressure Switch (MCD)
HPS .... Hellenic Philatelic Society (BUAC)
HPS .... Hellenic Physical Society (BUAC)
HPS .... Helmet Pointing Sight (SAUS)
HPS .... Helmet Pointing System (SAUS)
HPS .... Hematoxylin-Phloxine-Saffron [*Biochemistry*] (MAE)
HPS .... Hepatoportal Sclerosis [*Medicine*] (MELL)
HPS .... Hermansky-Pudlak Syndrome [*Medicine*]
HPS .... Hermetic Pivoting Seal
HPS .... Hexbase Publishing System (SAUS)
HPS .... Hidden Predictive Saccades [*Ophthalmology*]
HPS .... Highest Points Scored (ROG)
HPS .... Highest Possible Score (SAUS)
HPS .... Highland Pony Society (BUAC)
HPS .... Highly Parallel Systems [*Computer science*] (GART)
HPS .... High-Performance Paper Society (SAUO)
HPS .... High Performance System (HAWK)
HPS .... High Power Switching (SAUS)
HPS .... High Pressure Separator (SAUS)
HPS .... High-Pressure Separator [*Chemical engineering*]
HPS .... High Pressure Sintering (SAUS)
HPS .... High-Pressure Sintering [*Ceramic technology*]
HPS .... High Pressure Sodium (SAUS)
HPS .... High-Pressure Sodium
HPS .... High Pressure Steam (SAUS)
HPS .... High-Pressure Steam [*Technical drawings*]
HPS .... High Primary Sequence (IAA)
HPS .... High-Protein Supplement [*Nutrition*]
HPS .... High Protestant Society (SAUO)
HPS .... His-Purkinje System (DB)
HPS .... History and Philosophy of Science (SAUS)
HPS .... Hops per Second (CCCA)
HPS .... Horizontal Pull Slipmeter (SAUS)
HPS .... Hospitalization Proneness Scale [*Psychometrics*]
HPS .... Hot Pressed Sheet (SAUS)
HPS .... HP Pealth Physics Station (SAUS)
HPS .... Hull Pressure Switch
HPS .... Human Placental Somatomammotropin (DB)
HPS .... Human Platelet Suspension [*Medicine*] (MELL)
HPS .... Hybrid Propulsion System
HPS .... Hydraulic Power Section [*Later, HPU*] (AAG)
HPS .... Hydraulic Power Supply
HPS .... Hydraulic Power System (KSC)
HPS .... Hydro-Pneumatic Suspension
HPS .... Hydroxypropyl Starch [*Organic chemistry*]
HPS .... Hypertrophic Pyloric Stenosis [*Medicine*]
HPSA .... Health Professional Shortage Area (DMAA)
HPSA .... Hellenic Philatelic Society of America (EA)
HPSA .... Honors Program Student Association of the American Sociological Association (EA)
HPSA .... Hydraulic Package Servovalve Actuator
HPSB .... High Performance Serial Bus (SAUS)
HPSC .... HC, Inc. (SAUO)
HPSC .... Heading per Standard Compass [*Navigation*]
HPSC .... Health Programs Systems Center
HPSC .... High Pressure Self-Combustion Sintering (SAUS)
HPSC .... Hot Pressed Silicon Carbide (SAUS)
HPSC .... HPSC, Inc. [*NASDAQ symbol*] (NQ)
HPSC .... Hydraulic Package Storage Container
HPSCI .... House Permanent Select Committee on Intelligence (MCD)
HPSCU .... High Performance Signal Conditioning Unit (SAUS)
HPSD .... High-Power Switching Device
HPSEB .... Himachal Pradash State Electricity Board [*India*] (BUAC)
HPSEC .... High Performance Size Exclusion Chromatography (SAUS)
HPSEC .... High-Performance Size Exclusion Chromatography
HPSEC .... High-Pressure Size Exclusion Chromatography
HPSF .... High-Pressure Stopped Flow [*Spectrometry*]
HPSG .... Head Driven Phrase Structure Grammar [*Artificial intelligence*]
HPSI .... Harpsichord [*Music*]
HPSI .... Health Professions Stress Inventory [*Medicine*]
HPSI .... High Pressure Safety Ignition (SAUS)
HPSI .... High-Pressure Safety Injection (NRCH)
HPSI .... High-Pressure Spray Post-Accident Injection [*Environmental science*] (COE)
HPSIP .... High-Pressure Safety Injection Pump (NRCH)
HPSIS .... High-Pressure Safety Injection System (IEEE)
HPSK .... Hydraulic Power Supply Kit
HPSL .... Health Professions Student Loans
HPSL .... Hewlett-Packard Support Line (SAUO)
HPSL .... High Pressure Sodium Lamp (SAUS)
HPSLT .... High Power Semiconductor Laser Technology (ADWA)
HPSM .... High Performance Stand-Off-Motor (SAUS)
HPSN .... High Performance Scalable Networking (SAUO)
HPSN .... Hot-Pressed Silicon Nitride (RDA)
HPSO .... Historical and Philosophical Society of Ohio (SAUO)
HPSO .... Historical and Philosophical Society of Ohio. Bulletin (journ.) (SAUS)
HPSOM .... High-Performance Stand-Off Motor (MCD)
HPSP .... Health Professions Scholarship Program [*Army*]
HPSP .... Heat Pipe Sandwich Panel (ACAE)
HPSP .... High Precision Scan Platform (ACAE)
HPSPLE .... High Performance Signal Processing for Laboratory Environments (SAUS)
HPSR .... High-Pressure Spray Post-Accident Recirculation [*Environmental science*] (COE)
HPSRM .... High Performance Solid Rocket Motor (SAUS)
HPSS .... High Pressure Single Spool (SAUS)
HPSS .... Hogan Personnel Selection Series (DHP)
HPSS .... Hrvatska Pucka Seljacka Stranka [*Croatian People's Peasant Party*] [*Former Yugoslavia*] [*Political party*] (PPE)
HPSSC .... Health Physics Society Standards Committee (SAUO)
HPSSNJ .... High-Power Self-Screening Noise Jammer [*Military*] (CAAL)
HPST .... Harpist (SAUS)
HPST .... High Portable Satellite Terminal (SAUS)
HPSTC .... Highest Point of Single Tooth Contact (SAUS)
HPSTGC .... Heading per Steering Compass [*Navigation*]
HPSTI .... Human Pancreatic Secretory Trypsin Inhibitor (DB)
HPSV .... High-Pressure Solenoid Valve
HPSW .... High-Pressure Service Water [*Nuclear energy*] (NRCH)
HPSW .... Horizontally Polarized Shear Wave [*Physics*]
HPSWS .... High-Pressure Service Water System [*Nuclear energy*] (NRCH)
HPSY .... Health Psychology (journ.) (SAUS)
HP System ... Hydranth Pulse System (SAUS)
HPT .... American Home Products Corp. (SAUO)
HPT .... Habitat Partioning by Therevids (SAUO)
HPT .... Hampton, IA [*Location identifier*] [*FAA*] (FAAL)
Hpt .... Haptoglobin (STED)
HPT .... Head per Track (BUR)
HPT .... Health Physics Technician (ABAC)
HPT .... Height-Pressure Test (SAUS)
HPT .... Hexamethylphosphoric Triamide [*Also, HEMPA, HMP, HMPA, HMPT*] [*Organic chemistry*]
HPT .... High Payoff Target (SAUS)
HPT .... High-Payoff Target [*Military*] (INF)
HPT .... High Performance Train (SAUS)
HPT .... High-Performance Train (ADA)
HPT .... High Point
HPT .... High-Potential Test [*or Tester*]
HPT .... High Pot Tester (SAUS)
HPT .... High Power Transmission set (SAUS)
HPT .... High-Power Transmitter Memory (DWSG)
HPT .... High Precision Thermostat (SAUS)
HPT .... High-Pressure Tap
HPT .... High-Pressure Test
HPT .... High-Pressure Tin (SAUS)
HPT .... High Pressure Top (SAUS)
HPT .... High-Pressure Turbine (NRCH)
HPT .... High Profile Terminal (IAA)
HPT .... Histamine Provocation Test (STED)
HPT .... Home Port [*Navy*] (NVT)
HPT .... Home Pregnancy Test (ADWA)
HPT .... Homonuclear Polarization Transfer [*Physics*]
HPT .... Horizontal Plot Table
HPT .... Hormone Pregnancy Test
HPT .... Horsepower Tonnage (DOMA)
HPT .... Hospitality Properties Trust [*NYSE symbol*] (SAG)
HPT .... Hot Plate Test (STED)
HPT .... Human Performance Technology [*Training term*] (LPT)
hPT .... Human Placental Thyrotropin (STED)
HPT .... Human Placenta Thyrotrophin [*Endocrinology*]
HPT .... Hydrocylic Pressure Testing
HPT .... Hydropneumatic Trailer (MCD)
HPT .... Hydroxypyrenetrisulfonate (SAUS)
HPT .... Hygromycin Phosphotransferase
HPT .... Hyperparathyroidism [*or Hyperthyroidism*] [*Endocrinology*]
HPT .... Hypothalmic-Pituitary-Thyroid (STED)
HPTA .... High-Power Test Area (SAUO)
HPTA .... High Pressure Technology Association [*British*]
HPTA .... Hinckley Pilot 35 Association (EA)
HPTA .... Hire Purchase Trade Association [*British*] (BI)
HPTB .... High-Pressure Turbine [*on a ship*] (DS)
HPTC .... Hydrostatic Pressure Test Certification (SAUS)
HPTD .... High Point, Thomasville & Denton Railroad Co. [*AAR code*]
HPTDC .... Himachal Pradesh Tourist Development Corp. [*India*]
HPTE .... Bis(hydroxyphenyl)trichloroethane [*Organic chemistry*]
HPTE .... Heptachlor Epoxide
HPTE .... High-Performance Turbine Engine [*Air Force*]
HPTE .... High Precision Tracking Experiment (SAUS)
HPTET .... High Performance Turbine Engine Technologies (or Technology) (SAUS)
HPTF .... Hydraulic Power Transmission Fluid (MCD)
HPTH .... Hyperparathyroid Hormone (DB)
HPTH .... Hyperparathyroidism [*Medicine*] (MEDA)
HPTI .... High Performance Terminal Interceptor (ACAE)
HPTIN .... Human Pancreatic Trypsin Inhibitor [*Medicine*] (STED)

HP Tire........ High Pressure Tire (SAUS)
HPTL........... High-Payoff Target List [*Military*] (INF)
HPT-LAK Disks... Head per Track-Look-Alike Disks (SAUS)
HPTLC......... High-Performance Thin-Layer Chromatography
HPTLC......... High Power Thin Layer Chromatography (SAUS)
HPTM.......... Home Prothrombin Time Monitoring [*Medicine*] (MELL)
HPTON......... Hampton, SC [*American Association of Railroads railroad junction routing code*]
HPTP.......... Hydraulic Power Transfer Panel
HPTR.......... High Power Tank Reactor (SAUS)
HPTS.......... Health Policy Tracking Service (SAUO)
HPTS.......... High Performance Third Stage (SAUS)
HPTS.......... High-Performance Third Stage [*Rocket*] [*Army*] (AABC)
HPTS.......... High Performance Transaction Systems (SAUS)
HPTS.......... High-Powered Transmit Set (DWSG)
HPTS.......... High Power Transmission System (ACAE)
HPTS.......... High Power Transmit Sets (SAUS)
HPTS.......... Hydroxypyrenetrisulfonic Acid [*Organic chemistry*]
HP Turbine... High Pressure Turbine (SAUS)
HPTW.......... Hauptwerk [*Masterpiece*] [*German*]
HPU........... Hale Pohaku [*Hawaii*] [*Seismograph station code, US Geological Survey*] (SEIS)
HPU........... Hand Portable Unit (CGWS)
HPU........... Hansard's Publishing Union (ROG)
HPU........... Heater Probe Unit (DMAA)
HPU........... High-Pressure Unit
HPU........... Hot Plate Unit (SAUS)
HPU........... Hours per Unit (TIMI)
HPU........... Hydraulic Power Unit (MCD)
HPU........... Hydraulic Pumping Unit (AABC)
HP(UK)........ Hunter Personnel (United Kingdom) Ltd.
HPUS.......... Homeopathic Pharmacopoeia of the United States
HP-UX......... Hewlett-Packards UNIX implementation (SAUS)
HP-UX......... Hewlett Packard Unix Operating System (SAUS)
HP/UX......... HPs Version of UNIX Operating System (SAUS)
HPUZ.......... Houston Public Elevator [*Federal Railroad Administration identification code*]
HPV........... Haemophilus Pertussis Vaccine [*Medicine*] (STED)
HPV........... Helium Precharge Valve (SAUS)
HPV........... Helium Pressure Vessel
HPV........... Hemophilus Pertussis Vaccine [*Medicine*] (MAE)
HPV........... Hepatic Portal Vein [*Medicine*] (DB)
HPV........... High-Passage Virus
HPV........... High-Powered Vehicle
HPV........... High-Power Veractor
HPV........... High-Pressure Valve
HPV........... High Pressure Vapour (HAWK)
HPV........... High-Pressure Vent (AAEL)
HPV........... High-Priority Violator (GNE)
HPV........... High Production Volume [*Manufacturing*]
HPV........... Human Papilloma Virus (SAUS)
HPV........... Human Parvovirus [*Medicine*] (DB)
HPV........... Human-Powered Vehicle
HPV........... Hypoxic Pulmonary Vasoconstriction [*Medicine*]
HPV........... Parvovirus (SAUS)
HPV........... Princeville [*Hawaii*] [*Airport symbol*] (OAG)
HPVA.......... Hardwood, Plywood, and Veneer Association (NTPA)
HPVA.......... Human-Powered Vehicle Association (SAUO)
HPVC.......... Hypoxic Pulmonary Vasoconstriction [*Medicine*] (MELL)
HPVD.......... Hypertensive Pulmonary Vascular Disease [*Medicine*]
HPVDC......... High-Pressure Vacuum Die Casting
HPV-DE........ High-Passage Virus [*Grown in*] Duck Embryo [*Cells*]
HPV-DK........ High-Passage Virus [*Grown in*] Dog Kidney [*Cells*]
HPVEE......... Hewlett-Packard Visual Engineering Environment (SAUS)
HPVG.......... Hepatic Portal Venous Gas (MAE)
HPVI.......... Human Papillomavirus [*Medicine*] (MELL)
HPVLE......... Hopkinsville, KY [*American Association of Railroads railroad junction routing code*]
HPVR.......... Hypoxic Pulmonary Vascular Response [*Anesthesiology*]
HPV Reg....... High Power Voltage Regulator (SAUS)
HPVS.......... Hydropneumatic Vehicle Suspension [*Automotive engineering*]
HP VUE........ Hewlett-Packard Visual User Environment [*Computer science*]
HPW........... Half-Peak Width (SAUS)
HP/W.......... Health Promotion/Wellness Program [*Medicine*] (DMAA)
HPW........... High Performance Workstation (SAUS)
HPW........... High Power Window (SAUS)
HPW........... High-Purity Water
HPW........... Homopolar Pulse Welding (SAUS)
HPW........... Hopewell, VA [*Location identifier*] [*FAA*] (FAAL)
HPW........... Hot Pressure Welding
HPW........... Hours per Week
HPW........... Paine Webber Group [*AMEX symbol*] (SAG)
HPWG.......... Handling and Performance Working Group (SAUO)
HP-WGT........ Horsepower-to-Weight (TIMI)
HPWO.......... High Performance Work Organization
HPWR.......... Health Power [*NASDAQ symbol*] (SAG)
HPWSol........ High-Protein Wash Solution [*Clinical chemistry*]
Hpx........... Hemopexin [*Medicine*] (MELL)
HPX........... Homeplex Mortgage Investments [*NYSE symbol*] (SPSG)
HPX........... Homeplex Mtge Invmts [*NYSE symbol*] (TTSB)
HPX........... Hydrogen Peroxide (ACAE)
HPX........... (Hydroxypropyl)xylan [*Organic chemistry*]
HPX........... Partial Hepatectomy (DB)
HPY........... Baytown, TX [*Location identifier*] [*FAA*] (FAAL)
HPY........... HPY Industry Ltd. [*Vancouver Stock Exchange symbol*]
HPZ........... Helicopter Protected Zone [*Military*] (DA)
HPZ........... High Potential Zones (SAUO)
HPZ........... High-Pressure Zone
HPZ........... Hydridopolysilylazane (SAUS)
HPZE.......... High-Performance Zone Electrophoresis
HPz Rak....... Hohl-Panzerrakete (SAUS)
HQ............ British Aerospace PLC (SAUS)
HQ............ Business Express [*ICAO designator*] (AD)
HQ............ Hambrecht & Quist Group [*NYSE symbol*] (SG)
H-Q........... Hamstring-Quadriceps [*Anatomy*]
HQ............ Harmful Quantity (SAUS)
HQ............ Hawker Siddeley Aviation Ltd. [*British*] [*ICAO designator*] (ICDA)
HQ............ Hazard Quotient [*Toxicology*]
HQ............ Headquarter (SAUS)
Hq............ Headquarters (AL)
HQ............ Headquarters Companies [*San Francisco, CA*] (TSSD)
HQ............ Health Systems International [*NYSE symbol*] (SAG)
HQ............ Heussler Air Service [*ICAO designator*] (AD)
HQ............ Highly Qualified (AFM)
HQ............ High Quality [*Home video systems*]
HQ............ Hind Quarters (SPVS)
HQ............ Historical Quotes [*Information retrieval*]
HQ............ Hoc Quaere [*Look For This or See This*] [*Latin*]
HQ............ Hollywood Quarterly (SAUO)
HQ............ Home Quarters Warehouse, Inc.
HQ............ Hong Qi [*Red Flag*] [*China*]
HQ............ Hoop Quotient [*Basketball*]
HQ............ HQ Minerals Ltd. [*Vancouver Stock Exchange symbol*]
HQ............ Hydro-Quebec [*Institut de Recherche d'Hydro-Quebec*] [*Canada*]
HQ............ Hydroquinone [*Organic chemistry*]
HQ............ Hydroxyquinoline [*Organic chemistry*]
HQ............ New York Helicopter [*ICAO designator*] (AD)
HQA........... Handbook of Quality Assurance (SAUS)
HQA........... Hardware Quality Assurance (SAUS)
HQA........... Hardware Quality Audit (ACAE)
HQ(A)......... Headquarters Administration Office [*British police*]
HQA........... Middletown, PA [*Location identifier*] [*FAA*] (FAAL)
HQAAFCE....... Headquarters Allied Air Forces Central Europe (SAUS)
HQAAFV........ Headquarters, Australian Army Forces, Vietnam (SAUO)
HQ AFCC....... Headquarters Air Force Communications Command (SAUO)
HQ AFLC....... Headquarters Air Force Logistics Command (SAUO)
HQ AFROTC... Headquarters Air Force Reserve Officers (SAUO)
HQAMC......... Headquarters Air Mobility Command (SAUO)
HQ AMF........ Headquarters ACE Mobile Force (SAUS)
HQ AMF........ Headquarters Allied Command Europe Mobile Force (SAUO)
HQ&HQ Co... Headquarters and Headquarters Company (SAUO)
HQ & SERV... Headquarters and Service [*Marine Corps*]
Hq & Serv Co... Headquarters and Service Company (SAUO)
HQAP.......... Hardware Quality Assurance Plan (ACAE)
HQASC......... Headquarters, Air Support Command [*NATO*] (NATG)
HQ ATC........ Headquarters Air Training Command (SAUO)
HQB........... Headquarters Building Frankurt/Main (SAUO)
HQB........... Los Angeles, CA [*Location identifier*] [*FAA*] (FAAL)
HQBA.......... Headquarters Base Area
HQBC.......... Headquarters, Bomber Command [*Later, HQSTC*] [*British*] (NATG)
HQBN.......... Headquarters Battalion (DNAB)
HQBP.......... High Quality Bonus Point [*Advancement system*] [*Navy*] (NVT)
HQBTRY........ Headquarters Battery [*Military*] (DNAB)
HQC........... Handling Quality Criteria
HQC........... Headquarters Command [*Air Force*]
HQC........... Headquarters Company (SAUO)
HQC........... Hydraulic Quick Coupler
HQC........... Hydroquinone Cream [*Pharmacy*] (DAVI)
HQC........... Hydroxyquinoline Citrate [*Antiseptic*]
HQC........... Hyperquasicenter
HQ-CAP........ Headquarters, Civil Air Patrol
HQCB.......... Healthcare Quality Certification Board (SAUO)
HQCC.......... Headquarters, Coastal Command [*British*] (NATG)
HQCDO......... Headquarters Case Development Officer [*Environmental Protection Agency*] (GFGA)
HQCG.......... Headquarters, Coast Guard (SAUO)
HQCMD......... Headquarters Command [*Military*]
HQCO.......... Headquarters Company [*Military*] (DNAB)
HQCOM......... Headquarters Command [*Military*] (KSC)
HQCOMD........ Headquarters Command [*Air Force*]
HQCOMDT... Headquarters Commandant (NATG)
Hq Comdt & PM... Headquarters Commandant and Provost Marshal (SAUO)
HQCOMDUSAF... Headquarters Command, United States Air Force
Hq CONARC... Headquarters, Continental Army Command (SAUO)
HQCS.......... Heraldic Quality Control System (AABC)
HQ CST........ Headquarters Command & Staff Training (SAUS)
HQDA.......... Headquarters, Department of the Army
Hq Det........ Headquarters Detachment (SAUO)
HQDM.......... Headquarters Data Manager (KSC)
HQDP.......... Headquarters, Department of the Pacific [*Marine Corps*]
HQ DSA........ Headquarters, Defense Supply Agency
HQDT.......... Handling Qualities During Tracking (SAUS)
HQDTMS........ Headquarters, Defense Traffic Management Service
HQE........... Hansard Questions Ecrites [*Hansard Written Question - HWQ*] [*Database*] [*House of Commons*] [*French*] [*Information service or system*] (CRD)
HQE........... Hardware Quality Engineer (MCD)
HQE........... High Quality Environment (SAUS)
HQE........... Hydroquinone Electrode (SAUS)
HQEARC........ Headquarters, Equipment Authorization Review Center [*Army*]

HQES .... High-Quality Epitaxial Silicon
HQF .... High Quality Facsimile (DGA)
HQFC .... Headquarters, Fighter Command [*NATO*] (NATG)
Hq FE .... Headquarters, Far East (SAUO)
HQG .... Hugoton, KS [*Location identifier*] [*FAA*] (FAAL)
HQGRO .... Headquarters Graves Registration Office (SAUO)
HQH .... H&Q Healthcare Inv [*NYSE symbol*] (TTSB)
HQH .... H & Q Healthcare Investors [*NYSE symbol*] (SPSG)
HQHRA .... Half-Quarter Horse Registry of America (EA)
HQI .... Hydro-Quebec International (SAUS)
HQIADS .... Headquarters, Integrated Air Defense System [*Air Force*]
HQIR .... Hydro-Quebec Institute of Research (SAUO)
HQJTF .... Headquarters, Joint Task Force (MCD)
HQK .... Gulf of Mexico, LA [*Location identifier*] [*FAA*] (FAAL)
HQL .... Cullowhee, NC [*Location identifier*] [*FAA*] (FAAL)
HQL .... H&Q Life Sciences Investors [*NYSE symbol*] (TTSB)
HQL .... High-Quality Life
HQ L of CR Sigs ... Headquarters, Lines of Communication Royal Signals (SAUO)
HQM .... Highland Queen Mines Ltd. [*Vancouver Stock Exchange symbol*]
HQM .... High-Quality Matrix [*Electronics*]
HQM .... Hoquiam, WA [*Location identifier*] [*FAA*] (FAAL)
HQM .... Hydro-Quebec, Bibliotheque [*UTLAS symbol*]
HQ MAC .... Headquarters Military Airlift Command (SAUO)
HQMC .... Headquarters, Marine Corps
Hq MC .... Headquarters Motor Command (SAUO)
HQMD .... Headquarters Management Directive [*NASA*]
Hq ME .... Headquarters, Middle East (SAUO)
HQMME .... Hydroquinone Monomethyl Ether [*Organic chemistry*]
HQMSS .... Headquarters Mission Support System (SAUS)
HQMTMTS .... Headquarters, Military Traffic Management Terminal Service (DNAB)
HQMTS .... Headquarters, Military Trafic Management Terminal Service (SAUS)
HQN .... Haplequin Lake [*Alaska*] [*Seismograph station code, US Geological Survey*] (SEIS)
HQNAVMARCOPMATA ... Headquarters, Navy-Marine Corps Military Affiliate Radio System Station (SAUS)
HQNAVMARCORMARSTA ... Headquarters, Navy-Marine Corps Military Affiliate Radio System Station (DNAB)
HQNAVMATCOM ... Headquarters, Naval Material Command
HQ NI Ops ... Headquarters Northern Ireland Operations (SAUO)
HQNMC .... Headquarters, Naval Material Command (AFIT)
HQNO .... Heptyl(hydroxy)quinoline N-Oxide [*Organic chemistry*]
HQO .... Hansard Questions Orale [*Hansard Oral Questions - HOQ*] [*Database*] [*House of Commons*] [*French*] [*Information service or system*] (CRD)
HQO .... Hydroxyquinoline Oxide (SAUS)
HQOC .... Headquarters Operational Command [*Australia*]
HQOI .... HQ Office International, Inc. (SAUO)
Hq Op Gr RE ... Headquarters Railway Operating Group, Royal Engineers (SAUO)
HQOS .... HQ Office Supplies Walhouse, Inc. (SAUO)
HQ PACAF ... Headquarters Paccific Air Force (SAUO)
HQPM .... Hughes Quality Practice Manual (ACAE)
HQR .... Handling Qualities Rating [*Cooper-Harper*]
HQRS .... Handling Qualities Rating Scale (MCD)
HQS .... Headquarters
HQS .... Headquarters Staff [*British military*] (DMA)
HQS .... High Quality Screening (SAUS)
HQS .... High-Quality Silicon
HQS .... High-Quality Sound [*Home video system*] (IAA)
HQS .... Housing Quality Standards (SAUO)
HQSA .... Hydroxyquinolinesulfonic Acid [*Organic chemistry*]
HQ SAC .... Headquarters Strategic Air Command (SAUO)
HQ SACLANT ... Headquarters of the Supreme Allied Commander, Atlantic (SAUS)
HQSB .... Headquarters Special Branch (SAUO)
HQSC .... Headquarters, Signals Command [*British*] (NATG)
HQSF .... High-Quality Surface Finish
HQSQ .... Headquarters Squadron
HQSQDN .... Headquarters, Support Squadron [*Military*] (DNAB)
HQSQN .... Headquarters Squadron [*Marine Corps*]
HQSRN .... Headquarters Staff of the Royal Navy [*British*]
HQSTC .... Headquarters RAF Strike Command (SAUS)
HQSTC .... Headquarters, Strike Command [*Formerly, HQBC*] [*British*] (NATG)
HQSVCBN .... Headquarters, Service Battalion [*Military*] (DNAB)
HQSVCCO .... Headquarters, Service Company [*Military*] (DNAB)
HQT .... Coats (SAUS)
HQT .... Coats, NC [*Location identifier*] [*FAA*] (FAAL)
HQT .... Halogen Quenched Tube
HQ TAC .... Headquarters Tactical Air Command (SAUO)
HQTC .... Headquarters, Transport Command [*British*] (NATG)
HQTC .... High "Q" Tuned Circuit
HQTR .... Headquarters (KSC)
Hqtrs .... Headquarters (SAUO)
HQTV .... High-Quality Television [*Home video system*] (IAA)
HQU .... Headquarters Unit (SAUS)
HQUNTAC .... Armed Forces Headquarters (SAUS)
HQUSACE .... Headquarters, U.S. Army Corps of Engineers
HQ USAF .... Headquarters, United States Air Force (AFM)
HQVM .... High Quality Video Mode (SAUS)
HQW .... Helical Quantum Wire (SAUS)
HQX .... Bin-Hexed File (SAUS)
HR .... Air Bremen [*ICAO designator*] (AD)
HR .... Croatia [*Internet country code*]
HR .... Hague Resolutions
HR .... Hail and Rain [*Meteorology*] (BARN)
hr .... Hair (VRA)
hr .... Hairless Mouse [*Endocrinology*] (DMAA)
hr .... Hairspace [*Printing*] (WDMC)
HR .... Hair Space between Letters [*Proofreader's mark*]
HR .... Half-Reversal [*Psychometrics*]
HR .... Half-Yearly Review
HR .... Hallux Rigidus [*Orthopedics*] (DAVI)
HR .... Hall Wardrobes [*Classified advertising*] (ADA)
HR .... Halorhodopsin [*Biochemistry*]
HR .... Halstead-Reitan [*Neuropsychological battery*] (DAVI)
HR .... Halton Rifles [*British military*] (DMA)
HR .... Hamman-Rich [*Syndrome*] [*Medicine*] (DB)
HR .... Handling Room
HR .... Handling Routine (SAUS)
HR .... Hand RADAR (IAA)
HR .... Hand Reach [*Automotive engineering*]
HR .... Hand Receipt (AABC)
HR .... Hand Reset
Hr .... Harbor [*Nautical term*] (HRNC)
HR .... Hard-Pock Mining (SAUS)
HR .... Hard Rolled
HR .... Hardware Reliability (MCD)
HR .... Hardware Representation (SAUS)
HR .... Harrington Rod [*Orthopedics*] (DAVI)
H-R .... Haut-Rhin (SAUS)
HR .... Hazard Ratio [*Industrial hygiene term*] (OHS)
HR .... Hazard Report (MCD)
HR .... Hazards Research (SAUS)
HR .... Hazards Review (SAUS)
HR .... Heading Record (SAUS)
HR .... Healthcare Realty Trust [*NYSE symbol*] (SPSG)
HR .... Hear [*Amateur radio shorthand*] (WDAA)
HR .... Heart Rate [*Medicine*]
HR .... Heart Resistant (SAUS)
HR .... Heart Rhythm [*Cardiology*]
HR .... Heater (IAA)
HR .... Heating Rate (ARMP)
HR .... Heating Resistor (SAUS)
HR .... Heat Rash (MELL)
HR .... Heat Reflector
HR .... Heat Regenerator (SAUS)
HR .... Heat Resistance (SAUS)
HR .... Heat Resistant (SAUS)
HR .... Heat Resisting [*Technical drawings*]
HR .... Heavy-Duty Relay (IAA)
HR .... Height Range [*RADAR*]
HR .... Height, Room (SAUS)
HR .... Heir (ROG)
HR .... Helicopter Request [*Military*] (NVT)
HR .... Helicopter, Rescue (SAUS)
HR .... Helium Rebottled [*System*]
HR .... Helium, Refrigerated (AAG)
HR .... Hellenic Register [*Greek ship classification society*] (DS)
HR .... Hemirectococcygeus (DB)
HR .... Hemophilia Research [*An association*] [*Defunct*] (EA)
HR .... Hemorrhagic Retinopathy [*Ophthalmology*]
Hr .... Henricus de Baila [*Flourished, 1169-70*] [*Authority cited in pre-1607 legal work*] (DSA)
HR .... Henry Russell [*Astronomy*]
HR .... Here [*Amateur radio shorthand*] (WDAA)
HR .... Hermetic Rite [*Freemasonry*] (ROG)
HR .... Heroes of the Reformation [*A publication*]
HR .... Herr [*Sir, Mr.*] [*German*]
H-R .... Hertzsprung-Russell [*Diagram*] [*Astronomy*]
HR .... Hessischer Rundfunk [*Hessian Radio Network*] [*Germany*]
HR .... Heterogeneous Reactor (SAUS)
HR .... Heterosexual Relations [*Scale*]
H-R .... Hewitt-Robins (SAUO)
HR .... Hexazopararosaniline (SAUS)
HR .... Hierarchical Review (SAUO)
HR .... Higher (ROG)
HR .... Higher Rate
HR .... Highhams Railway [*Wales*]
HR .... Highland Railway [*Scotland*]
HR .... Highland Regiment [*British military*] (DMA)
HR .... Highly Reinforcing (SAUS)
HR .... Highly Resistive (SAUS)
HR .... High-Range [*RADAR*] (DEN)
HR .... High Rate (ACAE)
HR .... Highrate (SAUS)
HR .... High-Rate Reverse [*Ecology*]
HR .... High Reduction [*Microforms*] (NITA)
HR .... High Reflectance (SAUS)
HR .... High Reflection (SAUS)
HR .... High Reflector (IAA)
HR .... High Resilience [*Plastics*]
HR .... High Resilient (SAUS)
HR .... High Resistance
HR .... High Resistor (SAUS)
HR .... High Resolution (MCD)
HR .... High Resolving (SAUS)
HR .... High Resonance-Damping (SAUS)
HR .... High Rise
HR .... High Risk
HR .... High Run
HR .... High-Speed Radial [*Automotive tires*]
HR .... High-S Radial (SAUS)

HR .... Hillside Review (SAUS)
hr .... Hinge Remnant [*Philately*]
HR .... Hispanic Review (journ.) (SAUS)
HR .... Histamine Release [*Immunology*]
HR .... Historical Record (NASA)
HR .... Historical Reports (SAUO)
HR .... Historical Research (FOTI)
HR .... History Report (MCD)
HR .... Histrical Record (SAUS)
HR .... Hit Rate (MUGU)
HR .... Hit Ratio
HR .... Hoechst-Roussel Pharmaceuticals, Inc. [*Research code symbol*]
HR .... Hoerner [*Horns*] [*Music*]
HR .... Hoge Raad [*Dutch Supreme Court*] (DLA)
HR .... Hoist Ring (SAUS)
HR .... Hojesteret [*Supreme Court*] [*Netherlands*] (ILCA)
HR .... Holding Register
HR .... Holiday Route (CDAI)
HR .... Holmes Ribgrass (SAUS)
HR .... Homeostatic Regulators [*British*]
H/R .... Home-Road ratio (SAUS)
HR .... Home Room (SAUS)
HR .... Home Rule
HR .... Home Rules (SAUS)
HR .... Home Run [*Baseball*]
HR .... Homing Relay (SAUS)
HR .... Homoreactant [*Medicine*]
Hr .... Honduras (MILB)
HR .... Hook Rail (MSA)
HR .... Horizon Sensor (SAUS)
HR .... Horizontally-pivoted Reversible (SAUS)
HR .... Horizontal Resistance [*Plant pathology*]
HR .... Horizontal Retort
HR .... Horizontal Rule (SAUS)
HR .... Hormonal Response [*Medicine*] (DMAA)
HR .... Hormone Receptor (MELL)
HR .... Hormone Receptor Complex [*Endocrinology*]
HR .... Hormone-Responsive (DB)
HR .... Horology Program [*Association of Independent Colleges and Schools specialization code*]
HR .... Hose Rack (AAG)
HR .... Hospitalman Recruit
HR .... Hospital Record
HR .... Hospital Recruit
HR .... Hospital Report (MAE)
HR .... Hotel Rates
HR .... Hot Rolled (MSA)
HR .... Hot Rolling (SAUS)
HR .... Hour (AAG)
Hr .... Hour (AMHC)
hr .... Hour
HR .... Hourly Report (DNAB)
HR .... House of Representatives
HR .... House of Representatives Bill [*with Number*]
HR .... House of Representatives Recedes (SAUO)
HR .... House of Ruth (EA)
HR .... House Recedes
HR .... House Record (SAUS)
HR .... House Report
HR .... House Resolution
HR .... House Roll [*Legal term*] (DLA)
HR .... Housing and Rent Act (SAUO)
HR .... Howship-Romberg [*Syndrome*] [*Medicine*] (DB)
HR .... Hudson Review [*A publication*] (BRI)
HR .... Humanitarian Reassignment [*Military*] (AFM)
HR .... Human Reliability
HR .... Human Resources
HR .... Human Rights Convention [*Council of Europe*] (DLA)
HR .... Humber Register [*St. Albans, Hertfordshire, England*] (EAIO)
HR .... Humidity, Relative
Hr .... Hussar [*British military*] (DMA)
HR .... Hydraulic Research (SAUS)
HR .... Hydraulics Research Ltd. [*British*] (IRUK)
HR .... Hydrogen Recombiner (NRCH)
HR .... Hydrogen Relief (NASA)
HR .... Hypersensitive Response [*Biology*]
HR .... Hypophosphatemic Rickets [*Medicine*] (DMAA)
HR .... International Harvester Co. (SAUO)
HR .... Relative Humidity (SAUS)
HR .... Robin Avions [*Pierre Robin*] [*France*] [*ICAO aircraft manufacturer identifier*] (ICAO)
HR .... Rockwell Hardness (SAUS)
HR .... Shore
HR2D .... High-Resolution, Two-Dimensional [*Electrophoresis*]
HR 10 .... Keogh Plan (EBF)
HRA .... Hanford Remedial Action (SAUS)
HRA .... Harbin Railway Administration [*China*] (BUAC)
HRA .... Hard Replacement Assembly (MCD)
HRA .... Hardware Retailers Association (SAUO)
HRA .... Harness Release Actuator (DNAB)
HRA .... Harvey Group, Inc. (SAUS)
HRA .... Haura [*South Arabia (Yemen)*] [*Airport symbol*] (AD)
HRA .... Health Resources Administration [*Abolished, 1982, functions transferred to Health Resources and Services Administration*] [*HEW*]
HRA .... Health Risk Appraisal [*or Assessment*] [*Medicine*]
HRA .... Health Risk Assessment (SAUS)
HRA .... Heart Rate Acceleration
HRA .... Heart Rate Audiometry
HRA .... Heavy Replaceable Assembly (SAUS)
HRA .... Heavy Replacement Assembly (SAUS)
HRA .... Heli-Iberica [*Spain*] [*ICAO designator*] (FAAC)
HRA .... Hemispherical Reflective Aerial (SAUS)
HRA .... Hemispherical Reflective Antenna
HRA .... HF [*High-Frequency*] Recovery Antenna
HRA .... Highest Rank Aboard (SAUS)
HRA .... Highlands Restricted Area (PIAV)
HRA .... High Radiation Area (SAUS)
HRA .... High-Radiation Area (DNAB)
HRA .... High Resolution Array
HRA .... High Right Atrial (SAUS)
HRA .... High Right Atrium [*Anatomy*]
HRA .... High-Speed Research Aircraft (PDAA)
HRA .... Histamine Releasing Activity [*Medicine*] (DAVI)
HRA .... Historical Records of Australia (SAUO)
HRA .... Historical Records of Australia (journ.) (SAUS)
HRA .... Honorary Royal Academician [*British*]
HRA .... Horse Rangers' Association (BUAC)
HRA .... Horticultural Research Association (BUAC)
HRA .... Hotels and Restaurants Association (SAUO)
HRA .... Hot-Rolled and Annealed (SAUS)
HRA .... Hourly Rolling Average (EEVL)
HRA .... Hour of Revival Association [*British*]
HRA .... Housing Revenue Account [*British*]
HRA .... Housing Review Account (SAUS)
HRA .... Humanitarian and Refugee Affairs [*Department of Defense*]
HRA .... Human Reliability Analysis [*Engineering*]
HRA .... Human Resource Accounting (ADA)
HRA .... Human Resources Abstracts (journ.) (SAUS)
HRA .... Human Resources Administration (journ.) (SAUS)
HRA .... Human Resources Advisor (SAUO)
HRA .... Human Rights Advocates (EA)
HRA .... Huna Research Associates (SAUO)
HRA .... Huna Research Association [*See also HF*] [*Switzerland*] (EAIO)
HRA .... Hunters Rights Association (SAUS)
HRA .... Hydraulic Rotary Actuator
HRA .... Hypersonic Research Airplane [*NASA*]
HRA .... Hypnotic Research Association (SAUO)
HRAA .... High-Rate Acquisition Assembly (MCD)
HRAA .... Hire and Rental Association of Australia
HRAA .... Hypnotic Research Association of Australia (SAUO)
HRAC .... Hypersonic Research Aircraft (SAUS)
HRAD .... Human Resource Acquisition Department (SAUO)
HRAD .... Hunger Relief and Development [*An association*] (EA)
HRAE .... High Right Atrial/Atrium Electrogram [*Medicine*] (EDAA)
HRA EIS .... Hanford Remedial Action Environmental Impact Statement
HRA-EIS .... Hanford Remedial Action Environmental Impact Statement and Comprehensive Land Use Plan (SAUS)
HRAES .... High Resolution Auger Electron (SAUS)
HRAF .... Human Relations Area Files (EA)
HRAF .... Human Relations Areas Files [*Yale University*]
HRAG .... Helena Rubinstein Art Gallery (SAUO)
HRAG .... International Human Rights Advisory Group [*Switzerland*]
HRAI .... Heating, Refrigerating, and Air Conditioning Institute of Canada
HRAI .... Human Rights Advocates International (EA)
HRAM .... Hazard Ranking and Allocation Methodology (MCD)
HRAM .... Hierarchical Random Access Memory [*Computer science*]
HR&ED .... Human Research & Engineering Directorate (SAUS)
HR&IH .... His (or Her) Royal and Imperial Highness (SAUS)
HR & IH .... His [*or Her*] Royal and Imperial Highness (ROG)
HR&T .... Heat Resolution and Transport (SAUS)
HRANSW .... Harness Racing Authority of New South Wales [*Australia*]
HRAP .... Heat Rejection Augmentation Package (SAUS)
HRAP .... High Resolution Accelerometer Package (SAUS)
HRAP .... Housing Relocation Assistance Program [*US Army Corps of Engineers*]
HRAP .... Hydrologic Rainfall Analysis Project (SAUO)
HRAR .... Hereafter
HRART .... Hampton Roads Army Terminal
HRAS .... High-Rate Activated Sludge [*Waste treatment*]
HRAT .... Hampton Roads Army Terminal
HRAT .... Hereat [*Legal*] [*British*] (ROG)
HRAT .... Human Resources Applicant Tracking (SAUS)
HRAV .... High Resolution Airborne Video (SAUS)
HRAV .... Human Resources Availability (NVT)
HRB .... Block [*H. & R.*], Inc. [*NYSE symbol*] (SPSG)
HRB .... Croatian Revolutionary Brotherhood [*Former Yugoslavia*] (PD)
HRB .... H & R Block (EFIS)
HRB .... Harbin [*Manchuria*] [*Airport symbol*] (OAG)
HRB .... Hardship Relief Board [*Victoria, Australia*]
HRB .... Hazard Review Board
HRB .... High Rate Bioreactor [*Chemical Engineering*]
HRB .... High-Resolution Bathymetry [*Instrumentation*]
HRB .... Highway Research Board [*Later, TRB*] (EA)
HRB .... Highway Research Bureau (SAUO)
HRB .... Hinged Rotor Blade
HRB .... Hockey Rules Board [*Walton-On-Thames, Surrey, England*] (EAIO)
HRB .... Hopkins Research Bulletin (journ.) (SAUS)
HRB .... House of Representatives Bill
HRB .... Housing and Redevelopment Board (SAUO)

HRB Human Resources Branch (SAUO)
HRB Hurbanovo [*Czechoslovakia*] [*Seismograph station code, US Geological Survey*] (SEIS)
HRBA Havana Rabbit Breeders Association (EA)
HRBA Hoist Rotation Beam Assembly [*Military*] (CAAL)
HRBC Harbinger Corp. [*NASDAQ symbol*] (SAG)
HRBC High Rate Battery Charge (ACAE)
HRBC Historical Review of Berks County (journ.) (SAUS)
HRBC Horse Red Blood Cells [*Also, HRC*]
HRBF Harbor Federal Bancorp [*NASDAQ symbol*] (SAG)
HRBI Hotot Rabbit Breeders International (EA)
HRBOR Harbor [*Commonly used*] (OPSA)
HRBR VU Harbor View (SAUS)
HRBS High Rate Bit Synchronizer (ACAE)
HRBT Hudson River Bancorp [*NASDAQ symbol*] (SG)
HRC Hairdressers' Registration Council [*British*] (BI)
HRC Haitian Refugee Center (EA)
HRC Half Rate Channel (SAUS)
HRC Hardness Rockwell C [*Materials testing*]
HRC Hardwood Research Council (EA)
HRC Harmonically Related Carrier Frequency (SAUS)
HRC Harmonic Response Characteristic (SAUS)
HRC Harris Ranch [*California*] [*Seismograph station code, US Geological Survey*] [*Closed*] (SEIS)
HRC Hasselblad Reflex Camera (MCD)
HRC HEALTHSOUTH Rehabilitation Corp. [*NYSE symbol*] (SPSG)
HRC HEATH [*Higher Education and the Handicapped*] Resource Center (EA)
HRC Helium Research Center
HRC Herpes Resource Center (EA)
HRC Herpes Resource Center American Social Health Association (EA)
HRC Highland Regional Council [*Scotland*]
HRC Highly Reflective Clouds (SAUS)
HRC High Redundant Code (SAUS)
HRC High Reinforcement Content [*Plastics*]
HRC High Resolution Camera
HRC High Resolution CCD Camera (SAUS)
HRC High Resolution Chromatography (SAUS)
HRC High-Resolution Chromatography (DB)
HRC High Risk Characteristics (SAUS)
HRC High-Rupturing Capacity
HRC Holiday Rambler Corp.
HRC Hollycroft Resource Corp. [*Vancouver Stock Exchange symbol*]
HRC Holocaust Resource Center (EA)
HRC Holy Roman Church (WDAA)
HRC Holy Rosary Confraternity (SAUO)
HRC Honda Racing Corp.
HRC Honey Research Council [*Australia*]
HRC Honeywell Radiation Center (SAUS)
HRC Horizontal Redundancy Check (IEEE)
HRC Horse Racing Commission (SAUS)
HRC Horse Red Blood Cells [*Also, HRBC*]
HRC Horticultural Research Center [*Southern Illinois University at Carbondale*] (RCD)
HRC Horticultural Research Center [*University of Massachusetts*] (RCD)
HRC House Rules Committee (SAUO)
HRC Howard Research Corp.
HRC Humacao Regional College (SAUO)
HRC Humanities Research Council (SAUO)
HRC Human Relations Commission (SAUO)
HRC Human Relations Committee [*Military*] (VNW)
HRC Human Renal Carcinoma [*Medicine*] (DB)
HRC Human Resource Circular (SAUO)
HRC Human Resources Center (EA)
HRC Human Resources Committee
HRC Human Resources Conference (SAUO)
HRC Human Resources Council (GNE)
HRC Human Rights Campaign (EA)
HRC Human Rights Commission
HRC Human Rights Committee
HRC Huntingdon Research Centre Ltd. [*British*] (IRUK)
HRC Hunting Retriever Club (EA)
HRC Hybrid Receiver Circuit
HRC Hybrid Ring Control [*Computer science*] (TNIG)
HRC Hybrid River Circuit (SAUS)
HRC Hydraulics-Resonance Changer (DNAB)
HRC Hydrosphere Resource Consultants (SAUO)
HRC Hypertension Research Center [*Indiana University*] [*Research center*] (RCD)
HRC Hypothetical Reference Circuit [*Telecommunications*] (TEL)
HRC Hypothetical Reference Connection (SAUS)
HRC Rockwell Hardness (C Scale)
HRCA Honorary Member of the Royal Cambrian Academy of Art (SAUO)
HRCA Honorary Royal Cambrian Academician [*British*]
HRCB Hammer Circuit Breaker (VLIE)
HRCC High-Ratio Compact Chamber [*Automotive engineering*]
HRCC Humanities Research Council of Canada [*See also CCRH*] [*Later, SSHRCC*]
HRC/CCPR Human Rights Committee (EA)
HRCD Hohokam Resource Conservation and Development (SAUO)
HRCF Human Rights Campaign Fund (EA)
HRCFFD Human Rights Campaign Fund's Field Division (EA)
HRC-Fuse High-Rupturing Capacity Fuse (SAUS)
HRCG Hexagonal Reducing Coupling (SAUS)
HRCI Human Resource Certification Institute (SAUS)
HRCJ High Resolut Chromatogr... HRG Journal of High Resolution Chromatography (journ.) (SAUS)
HRCLY Huntingdon International Holdings plc [*NASDAQ symbol*] (COMM)
HR Con Res... House of Representatives Concurrent Resolution [*Legal term*] (DLA)
HRCP High Range Cutie Pie (SAUS)
HRCPX Heritage Capital Apprec. Trust Cl.A [*Mutual fund ticker symbol*] (SG)
HRCQ Highway-Route-Controlled Quantities [*Environmental Protection Agency*]
HRCQ Highway Route Controlled Quantity (SAUS)
HRCS Hazard Response Computer System (SAUO)
HRCS Horizontal Rod Cooling System (SAUS)
HRCT High-Resolution Computed Tomography (STED)
HRCVX Heritage Income-Growth Trust Cl.A [*Mutual fund ticker symbol*] (SG)
HRD Conference on Current Theory and Practice in Human Resource Development (SAUO)
HRD Hamburger Romanistische Dissertationen (journ.) (SAUS)
HRD Hanford Reach Database (SAUS)
HRD Hannaford Brothers, Inc. [*NYSE symbol*] (SPSG)
HRD Hard (VLIE)
hrd Hard [*Quality of the bottom*] [*Nautical charts*]
HRD Harding Carpets Ltd. [*Toronto Stock Exchange symbol*]
HRD Hard Top [*Automotive advertising*]
HRD Hardware requirements document (SAUS)
HRD Harstad [*Norway*] [*Airport symbol*] (AD)
HRD Heard [*Amateur radio shorthand*] (WDAA)
HRD Heroin-Related Death [*Epidemiology*]
HRD Hertzsprung-Russell Diagram [*Astronomy*]
HRD High Rate Demodulator (ACAE)
HRD High-Rate Demultiplexer (SSD)
HRD High-Rate Discharge (MCD)
HRD High-Rate Dosimeter (MCD)
HRD High-Resolution Data (SAUO)
HRD High Resolution Diagnostic diskette (SAUS)
HRD High Resolution Display (SAUS)
HRD High-Resolution Display
HRD High Roughage Diet (PDAA)
HRD Hoff Research and Development Laboratories, Inc. (SAUO)
HRD Holocaust Remembrance Day (BJA)
HRD Human Related Deaths
HRD Human Resource Development (EERA)
HRD Human Resources Data
HRD Human Resources Department (SAUS)
HRD Human Resources Development
HRD Human Resources Director (ADWA)
HRD Human Resources Division [*GAO*] (AAGC)
HRD Hum Related Deaths (SAUS)
HRD Hurricane Research Division [*Miami, FL*] [*National Oceanic and Atmospheric Administration*] (GRD)
HRD Hydraulic Rate Damper
HRD Hydrometeorology Research Division (SAUS)
HRD Kountze/Silsbee, TX [*Location identifier*] [*FAA*] (FAAL)
HRDA High-Rate Data Assembly (MCD)
HRDA High-Rate Deposit Account (WDAA)
HRDA Human Resources Development Agency (SAUO)
HRDB High-Resolution Data Base (SAUO)
HRDB Human Resources Data Base (TIMI)
HRDB Human Resources Development Branch [*Environmental Protection Agency*] (EPA)
HRDC Honeybee Research and Development Committee [*Australia*]
HRDC Human Resources Development Center (SAUO)
HRDC Human Resources Development Command [*Military*] (DNAB)
HRDC Human Resources Development Council (SAUO)
HRDD Human Resources Development Division (SAUO)
HRDF Human Resource Development Foundation (SAUS)
HRDG Harding Associates, Inc. (SAUO)
HRDG Harding Lawson Associates Group, Inc. [*NASDAQ symbol*] (SAG)
HRDG High Resolution Digital Generator (SAUS)
HRDG Human Resources Development Group [*British*]
HRDGG Human Rights, Democracy, Good Governance (FOTI)
HrdgLaw Harding Lawson Associates Group, Inc. [*Associated Press*] (SAG)
HRDI High-Rate Demultiplexer Instrument (SSD)
HRDI High-Resolution Doppler Imager (MCD)
HRDI High Resolution Doppler Interferometer (SAUS)
HRDI High Resolution Dynamic Imaging (SAUS)
HRDI High-Resolution Dynamic Imaging [*Electrophoresis*]
HRDI Hospital Reserve Disaster Inventory (SAUS)
HRDI Human Resources Development Institute (EA)
HRDITS Hereditaments [*Legal*] [*British*] (ROG)
HRDL High Rate Data Link (SAUS)
HRDL High Resolution Doppler Lidar (SAUS)
HRDL Hudson River Day Line [*AAR code*]
HRDL Hypothetical Reference Digital Link (SAUS)
hrdly hardly (SAUS)
HRDM High-Rate Demultiplexer (MCD)
HR Doc House of Representatives Document (DLA)
HRDP Human Resources [*Research*] and Development Program
HRDP Hypothetical Reference Digital Path [*Meteorology*]
HRDPO Human Resources Development Project Office [*Military*] (DNAB)
HRDR High-Rate Digital Recorder (MCD)
HRDRSSR Hairdresser
HRDS Handbook on Repairs to Dial Sight (SAUO)
HRDS High-Rate Data Section (NASA)
HRDS High Rate Data Station (SAUS)
HRDS High-Rate Data System (SAUS)
HRDS Human Resource Development Staff

HRDS .... Hypothetical Reference Digital Section (SAUS)
HRDT .... High Resolution Daylight Telescope (SAUS)
HRDTM .... High Resolution Digital Terrain Model (SAUO)
HRDTY .... Heredity
hrdwd .... Hardwood (REAL)
hrdwd flrs .... Hardwood Floors (REAL)
HRDWRE .... Hardware (WGA)
HRE .... Aerosucre SA [*Colombia*] [*ICAO designator*] (FAAC)
HRE .... Harare [*Zimbabwe*] [*Airport symbol*] (OAG)
HRE .... Hazards Research Equipment (SAUS)
HRE .... Hepatic Reticuloendothelial [*Medicine*] (MELL)
HRE .... Highbridge Exploration Ltd. (SAUO)
HRE .... High-Resolution Electrocardiography
HRE .... High Resolution Electrophoresis (SAUS)
HRE .... High-Resolution Electrophoresis [*Analytical biochemistry*]
HRE .... Highridge Exploration Ltd. [*Toronto Stock Exchange symbol*]
HRE .... Holy Roman Emperor [*or Empire*]
HRE .... Homogeneous Reactor Experiments (NRCH)
HRE .... Hormone Receptor Enzyme [*Endocrinology*] (DMAA)
HRE .... Hormone Regulatory Element [*Endocrinology*]
HRE .... Hormone-Responsive Element [*Endocrinology*]
HRE .... Hovering Rocket Engine (MCD)
HRE .... HRE Properties [*Formerly, Hubbard Real Estate Investments*] [*Associated Press*] (SAG)
HRE .... Hubbard Real Estate Investments (SAUO)
HRE .... Human Relations Education (MCD)
HRE .... Human Research and Engineering Directorate [*Army*] (RDA)
HRE .... Human Resources Effectiveness (TIMI)
HRE .... Human Response Element of DNA [*Endocrinology*]
HRE .... Hydrazine Rocket Engine
HRE .... Hydro Reconnaissance Experimental [*British military*] (DMA)
HRE .... Hypersonic Ramjet Engine
HRE .... Hypersonic Research Engine [*NASA*]
HRE .... Hypoxia-Responsive Element [*Molecular medicine*]
HREAA .... Health and Research Employees' Association of Australia
HREBIU .... Hotel and Restaurant Employees and Bartenders International Union [*Later, HERE*] (EA)
HREBU .... Hotel and Restaurant Employees and Bartenders Union (SAUO)
HREC .... Health Record
HREC .... Hepatic Reticuloendothelial Cell (STED)
Hrec and stud .... Historical Record and Studies (SAUO)
H Rec A Sc .... Historical Records of Australian Science [*A publication*]
H Rect A Sc .... Historical Records of Australian Science (journ.) (SAUS)
HREE .... Heavy Rare-Earth Elements
HREELS .... High Resolution Electron Energy Loss Spectroscopy (SAUS)
HREELS .... High-Resolution Electron Energy Loss Spectroscopy
HREELS .... High Resolution Electron Energy Loss Spectrum (SAUS)
HREF .... Horticulture Research Experimental Farm (SAUS)
HREF .... Hypertext Reference [*Computer science*] (CDE)
H reflex .... Hoffman reflex (SAUS)
H Regt RA .... Heavy Regiment, Royal Artillery (SAUO)
HREH .... High Renin Essential Hypertension [*Medicine*] (DB)
HRELES .... High-Resolution Energy-Loss Electron Spectroscopy
HRELS .... High-Resolution Energy-Loss Spectroscopy (MCD)
HREM .... High Resolution Electron Microscope (SAUS)
HREM .... High-Resolution Electron Microscopy
HREOC .... Human Rights and Equal Opportunity Commission (EERA)
H Rep .... House of Representatives Report (AAGC)
HRept .... House of Representatives (SAUO)
HRept .... House of Representatives Reports [*A publication*] (DLA)
HREQ .... Hold Request (VLIE)
HRES .... High-Resolution Electronic System
HRES .... High Resolution Electron Spectroscopy (SAUS)
HRES .... Horizons Research, Inc. (SAUO)
HRes .... House Resolution (WPI)
H Res .... House Resolution, United States House of Representatives
HRET .... Health Related Fitness Test (EDAC)
HRET .... Hospital Research and Educational Trust (EA)
HREU .... Hotel and Restaurant Employees and Bartenders International Union [*Later, HERE*]
HREU .... Hotels and Restaurants Employees Union (SAUS)
HREX .... Heavy Railroad Excavations [*Private rail car owner code*]
HREX .... Human Radiation Experiments (ADWA)
HREX .... Human Radiation Experiments Information Management System (SAUO)
HRF .... Hardware Routing Engine [*Computer science*] (GART)
HRF .... Harris Return Flow (STED)
HRF .... Hat Research Foundation (SAUO)
HRF .... Health-Related Facility (SAUS)
HRF .... Heavy Rebuild Factories (SAUS)
HRF .... Height Range Finder (SAUS)
HRF .... Height-Ranger Finder
HRF .... Hemochromatosis Research Foundation (EA)
HRF .... Herb Research Foundation (EA)
HRF .... High Rate of Fire (NATG)
HRF .... High Reliability Fighter (ACAE)
HRF .... High-Resolution Facsimile [*Telecommunications*]
HRF .... Histamine Releasing Factor [*Immunology*]
HRF .... History Record Folder (MCD)
HRF .... Home-Run Factor (SAUS)
HRF .... Homologous Restriction Factor [*Medicine*] (MELL)
HRF .... Human Research Facility (SSD)
HRF .... Human Resource Facility (SAUO)
HRF .... Human Resources Function (VLIE)
HRF .... Hussmann Refrigerator Co. (SAUO)
HRF .... Hypersonic Rarefield Flow (SAUS)
HRF .... Hypothalamic Releasing Factor [*Medicine*] (MELL)
HRF .... Sisters of the Holy Rosary of Fatima (Mexico) (TOCD)
HRFA .... High-Resolution Frequency Analysis [*of periodic phenomena*]
HRFA .... Hungarian Reformed Federation of America (EA)
HRFA .... Huron River Fishing Association [*Michigan*]
HRFADM .... Annual Research Reviews. Hypothalamic Releasing Factors (journ.) (SAUS)
HRFAX .... High-Resolution Facsimile [*Telecommunications*] (TEL)
HRFBS .... Hill Radnor Flock Book Society [*British*] (DBA)
HRFC .... Hierarchical Routing and Flow Control (SAUS)
HR-FESEM .... High Resolution Field Emission Scanning Electron Microscopy (SAUS)
HRFIMS .... High-Resolution Field-Ionization Mass Spectrometry (ABAC)
HRFPA .... High Rate Focal Plane Assembly (ACAE)
HRFRS .... High-resolution Film Recorder Subsystem (SAUS)
HRG .... Halford-Robins-Godfrey [*British sports car maker*]
HRG .... Harrington Public Library, Harrington, DE [*OCLC symbol*] (OCLC)
HRG .... Healthcare Resource Groups (SAUO)
HRG .... Health Research Group
HRG .... Hearing (ROG)
HRG .... Hemispherical Resonating Gyro (PDAA)
HRG .... Heritage Roses Group (EA)
HRG .... He-Ro Group [*NYSE symbol*] (SPSG)
HRG .... High Resolution Graphics (VLIE)
HRG .... High River Gold [*Vancouver Stock Exchange symbol*]
HRG .... High River Gold Mines Ltd. [*Toronto Stock Exchange symbol*]
HRG .... Histidine-Rich Glycoprotein [*Biochemistry*]
HRG .... Horizontal Ribbon Growth (SAUS)
HRG .... Human Rights Group [*Edinburgh, Scotland*] [*Defunct*] (EAIO)
HRG .... Hurghada [*Egypt*] [*Airport symbol*] (OAG)
HRG .... Hydrocarbon Research Group (SAUO)
HRGA .... High Rate Geographical Areas (SAUO)
HRGC .... High-Resolution Gas Chromatography
HRGC .... Human Response to Global Change (SAUS)
HRGI .... Honorary Member of the Royal Glasgow Institute of the Fine Arts (SAUS)
HRGM .... High-Resolution Ground Map
HRGM .... Hogg Robinson & Gardner Mountain [*Insurance broker*] [*British*]
HRGM/TD .... High Resolution Ground Map/Target Designation (ACAE)
HRGP .... Hydroxyproline-Rich Glycoprotein [*Biochemistry*]
HRGs .... Health Research Groups (SAUO)
HRGS .... High Resolution Gamma Spectrometry (SAUS)
HRGTN .... Herington, KS [*American Association of Railroads railroad junction routing code*]
HRH .... Hand Receipt Holder (MCD)
HRH .... High-Rate Heat
HRH .... High Resistance Hold (SAUS)
HRH .... Hilb, Rogal & Hamilton [*NYSE symbol*] (TTSB)
HRH .... His [*or Her*] Royal Highness
HRH .... Home of Rest for Horses (SAUO)
HRH .... Howard Robard Hughes [*1905-1976*] [*American businessman*]
HRH .... Hypoplastic Right Heart [*Cardiology*]
HRH .... Hypothalamic-Releasing Hormone (DB)
HRH .... Royal Tongan Airlines [*Tonga*] [*ICAO designator*] (FAAC)
HRHA .... Honorary Member of the Royal Hibernian Academy [*British*]
HRHA .... Honorary Member of the Royal Hibernian Academy of Arts (SAUO)
HRHA .... Hydronic Radiant Heating Association (EA)
HRHC .... Hilb, Rogal & Hamilton Co. (SAUO)
HRHE .... Hanford Region Historic Earthquake (SAUS)
HR/HI .... High Risk/High Impact (SAUS)
HRHR .... High-Risk Hearing Register
HRH Relay .... High Resistance Hold Relay (SAUS)
HR(HS) .... Hospital Recruit (High School) [*Navy*] (DNAB)
HRI .... Hannah Research Institute [*British*] (ARC)
HRI .... Hard Rock International [*Restaurant chain*]
HRI .... Harrington Rod Instrumentation [*Orthopedics*] (DAVI)
HRI .... Hayes Resources, Inc. [*Toronto Stock Exchange symbol*]
HRI .... Hazard Risk Index (LDOE)
HRI .... Health Research, Inc. [*New York State Department of Health*] [*Research center*] (RCD)
HRI .... Health Research International
HRI .... Heart Research Institute [*Australia*]
HRI .... Height-Range Indicator [*Electronics*]
HRI .... Hierarchical Richness Index [*Biodiversity*] (EERA)
HRI .... High-Resolution Image [*or Imager*] [*Astronomy*]
HRI .... High Resolution Interferometer (ACAE)
HRI .... Hilton Reservations International (TVEL)
HrI .... Holbrook Research Institute, Oxford, MA [*Library symbol*] [*Library of Congress*] (LCLS)
HRI .... Holcomb Research Institute [*Butler University*]
HRI .... Honorary Member of the Royal Institute of Painters in Water Colours [*British*]
HRI .... Honorary Member of the Royal Institute of Painters in Water-Colours (SAUO)
HRI .... Horizon Reference Indicator [*Aerospace*] (AAG)
HRI .... Horticultural Research Institute (EA)
HRI .... Horticultural Research International (SAUS)
HRI .... Hotel Reservations International (SAUO)
HRI .... Hotel, Restaurant, and Institutional [*Business*]
HRI .... Howe Research Institute (SAUS)
HRI .... Human Relations Inventory [*Psychology*]
HRI .... Human Resources Institute [*State University of New York at Buffalo*] [*Research center*] (RCD)
HRI .... Human Rights International (EA)

HRI .... Human Rights Internet (EA)
HRI .... Internet: International Human Rights Documentation Network (EA)
HRIA .... High Resolution Imager Assembly (SAUS)
HRIAF .... HRS Industries (SAUS)
HRIC .... Hacienda Resorts, Inc. (SAUS)
HRIC .... Hacienda Resorts, Incorporated (SAUO)
HR-ICP-AES ... High Resolution Inductively Coupled Plasma-Atomic Emission Spectrophotometry (SAUS)
HRIF .... Histamine-Release Inhibitory Factor [*Antiinflammatory*]
HRIG .... Human Rabies Immune Globulin [*Immunology*]
HRIg .... Human Rabies Immunoglobulin [*Medicine*] (EDAA)
HRIG .... Human Rabies Immunoglobulin [*Medicine*] (STED)
HRIGV .... HRI Group, Inc. [*NASDAQ symbol*] (COMM)
HRII .... High Resolution Imaging Interferometer (SAUS)
HRIM .... High Resolution Infrared Measurement (VLIE)
HRIN .... Herein [*Legal*] [*British*] (ROG)
HRIN .... Human Resource Information Network [*Executive Telecom System, Inc.*] [*Information service or system*] (IID)
HRINAR .... Hereinafter [*Legal*] [*British*] (ROG)
HRINBEFE .... Hereinbefore [*Legal*] [*British*] (ROG)
HRINBFR ..... Hereinbefore [*Legal*] [*British*] (ROG)
HRIO .... Height-Range Indicator Operator [*Electronics*]
HRIO .... Horticultural Research Institute of Ontario [*Canada*] [*Research center*] (RCD)
HRIP .... Hic Requiescit in Pace [*Here Rests in Peace*] [*Latin*]
HRIP .... Highway Research in Progress [*British*]
HRIR .... High Resolution Infra-Red (SAUS)
HRIR .... High Resolution Infrared Radiation (SAUS)
HRIR .... High-Resolution Infrared Radiometer
HRIR .... High Resolution Infrared Receiver (IAA)
HRIR .... High Resolution Infrared Reception (SAUS)
HRIR Data ... High Resolution Infra-Red Data (SAUS)
HRIRS .... High-Resolution Infrared Radiation Sounder
HRIRS .... High Resolution Infra-Red Spectroscopy
HRIS .... High-Repetition Illuminator System
HRIS .... High Resolution Imaging Spectrometer [*Instrument*] (EERA)
HRIS .... High-Resolution Infrared Radiation Sounder
HRIS .... High Resolution Infrared Sounder (ACAE)
HRIS .... Highway Research Information Service [*National Academy of Sciences*] [*Washington, DC*]
HRIS .... House of Representatives Information System
HRIS .... Human Resources Information System (WYGK)
HRISAK .... Food and Nutrition (journ.) (SAUS)
HRISI .... High Resolution Imaging Spectrometer Industrial (SAUS)
HRISM .... Human Resources for Information Systems Management
HRIZ .... Horizon Gold Corp. (SAUO)
HRJ .... High-Range Juno [*Survey meter for radiation*]
HRJ .... Human Rights Journal (journ.) (SAUS)
HRJ Res ..... House of Representatives Joint Resolution [*Legal term*] (DLA)
HRK .... Hardrock Extension, Inc. [*Toronto Stock Exchange symbol*]
HRK .... Hard Rock International ADS (SAUS)
HRK .... Kharkov [*Former USSR*] [*Airport symbol*] (OAG)
HRK .... Racine, WI [*Location identifier*] [*FAA*] (FAAL)
HR-KMAG .... Historical Report - Korea Military Advisory Group
HR-KMG ..... Historical Report-Korea Military Advisory Group (SAUO)
HRL .... Hardware Requirements List
HRL .... Harlingen [*Texas*] [*Airport symbol*] (OAG)
HRL .... Harlin Resources [*Vancouver Stock Exchange symbol*]
HRL .... Head Rotated Left [*Medicine*]
HRL .... Heat Rejection Loop
HRL .... High Refraction Layer
HRL .... High-Repetition LASER
HRL .... High-Resolution LOFAR [*Military*] (CAAL)
HRL .... Historical Record Log (SAA)
HRL .... Horizontal Reference Line [*Technical drawings*]
HRL .... Hormel Foods [*NYSE symbol*] (TTSB)
HRL .... Horn Rapids Landfill (SAUS)
HRL .... Hughes Research Laboratories [*Hughes Aircraft Co.*]
HRL .... Human Resources Laboratory [*Air Force*] (MCD)
HRL .... Hydraulics Research Laboratory [*British*]
HRL .... Hydrogeology Research Laboratory (SAUO)
HRL .... Hydrological Research Laboratory [*Silver Spring, MD*] [*National Weather Service*] (GRD)
HRLA .... Human Reovirus-Like Agent [*Medicine*] (DMAA)
HRLC .... High-Resolution Liquid Chromatography
HRLD .... Harolds Stores, Inc. (SAUS)
HRLDD .... Human Resources, Learning and Development Director
HR-LED .... High Radiance Light Emitting Device (SAUS)
HR-LED .... High Radiance Light Emitting Diode (SAUS)
HR-LED .... High Radiation Light Emitting Device (SAUS)
HR-LED .... High Radiation Light Emitting Diode (SAUS)
HRLEELS ..... High Resolution Low-Energy Electron Loss Spectroscopy (SAUS)
HRLEL .... High Radiation Level Examination Laboratory (SAUS)
HRLEL .... High-Radiation-Level Examination Laboratory (SAUO)
HRLF .... Holographic Reciprocity Law Failure (SAUS)
HRLI .... High-Repetition LASER Illuminator
HRLIS .... High-Repetition LASER Illuminating System
HRLJ .... Human Rights Law Journal [*A publication*]
HRLM .... High-Resolution Light Microscopy
HRLN .... Harlyn Products, Inc. [*NASDAQ symbol*] (COMM)
HRLR .... High Repitition Laser Rangefinder (SAUS)
HRLS .... High-Repetition LASER System
HRLSD .... Health and Rehabilitative Library Services Division [*Later, ASCLA*] [*American Library Association*]
HRLV .... Hungarian Raps Leaf Virus (SAUS)
HRLY .... Herley Industries [*NASDAQ symbol*] (TTSB)
HRLY .... Herley Industries, Inc. [*NASDAQ symbol*] (NQ)
HRLY .... Herley Microwave Systems, Inc. [*NASDAQ symbol*] (COMM)
HRM .... Hard-Rock Mining (SAUS)
HRM .... Hardware Read-In Mode
HRM .... Hermes Ventures [*Vancouver Stock Exchange symbol*]
HRM .... High-Rate Multiplexer (MCD)
HRM .... High-Ratio Multiplier (NASA)
HRM .... High-Reliability Module (IAA)
HRM .... High Resolution Map (SAUS)
HRM .... High Resolution Mapping (ACAE)
HRM .... High-Resolution Monitor (MCD)
HRM .... His [*or Her*] Royal Majesty [*British*]
HRM .... Hoisting and Rigging Manual (COE)
HRM .... Holistic Resource Management (ECON)
HRM .... HOMS Reference Manual (SAUS)
HRM .... Hopwise Reliable Multicast (SAUS)
HRM .... Hot Rod Magazine [*A publication*]
HRM .... Hot Rod Magazine (journ.) (SAUS)
HRM .... Human Reproductive Medicine (journ.) (SAUS)
HRM .... Human Resource Management (journ.) (SAUS)
HRM .... Human Resources Management
HRM .... Human Resources Manager (SAUS)
HRM .... Human Rights Monitor [*A publication*]
HRM .... Hydrocarbon Reservoir Management (SAUO)
HRM .... University of Hartford, West Hartford, CT [*OCLC symbol*] (OCLC)
HRMA .... Hampton Roads Maritime Association (SAUO)
HRMA .... High Resolution Mirror Assembly
HRMA .... [*British Columbia*] Human Resources Management Association (AC)
Hrm ADR ..... Harmony Gold Mining Co. Ltd. [*Associated Press*] (SAG)
HR Mag ...... HR Magazine [*A publication*] (BRI)
HRMC .... Harts Range Meta-igneous Complex [*Geology*]
HRMC .... Human Resources Management Center [*Navy*]
HRMC/D ...... Human Resources Management Center/Detachment [*Navy*] (DNAB)
HRMD .... Human Resource Managment Division (SAUO)
HRMD .... Human Resources Management Detachment [*Navy*] (DNAB)
HRMDDHG .... Herr, Regiere Mich durch Deinen Heiligen Geist [*Lord, Rule Me through Thy Holy Spirit*] [*Motto for a number of 16th and 17th century German and Bavarian rulers*]
HrmHld .... Harmony Holdings, Inc. [*Associated Press*] (SAG)
HRMI .... Health Risk Management, Inc. [*NASDAQ symbol*] (SAG)
HRMI .... High Resolution Microwave Imager (SAUS)
HRMI .... Human Resources Management Instructor [*Navy*] (DNAB)
HRMIS .... Human Resources Management Information System (SAUS)
HRMMR .... High Resolution Multifrequency Microwave Radiometer (SAUS)
HRMN .... Harmon Indus [*NASDAQ symbol*] (TTSB)
HRMN .... Harmon Industries, Inc. [*NASDAQ symbol*] (NQ)
HRMOB .... Association of Human Resources Management and Organizational Behavior [*Later, AM*] (EA)
HRMP .... Harvard Radio Meteor Project
Hr Mr .... Harbor Master [*Nautical term*] (HRNC)
Hr Mr .... Harbour Master [*Nautical term*] (NTA)
Hr Mr .... Harbourmaster [*Nautical term*] (NTA)
HR/MR .... Human Readable/Machine Readable System (SAUS)
HRMR .... Human Read/Machine Read [*Microfilm memory system*]
HRMR .... Hunter Melnor, Inc. (SAUO)
HRMS .... Health Risk Management Service [*Australian Capital Territory*]
HRMS .... Height Root Mean Square (IAA)
HRMS .... High-Resolution Mass Spectrometry
HRMS .... High Resolution Microwave Survey [*Astronomy*]
HRMS .... High Resolution Multispectral Scanner (SAUS)
HRMS .... Human Resource Management Services, Inc. [*Database producer*] (IID)
HRMS .... Human Resource Management System
HRMS .... Human Resources Management School [*Navy*] (DNAB)
HRMS .... Human Resources Management Specialist [*Navy*] (NVT)
HRMSI .... High Resolution Multispectral Stereo Imager (SAUS)
HRMSS .... Human Resources Management Support System [*Navy*] (NVT)
HRMST .... Human Resources Management Support Team [*Navy*] (DNAB)
HRMTG .... Hermitage
HR/MTI .... High-Resolution/Moving Target Indicator (DNAB)
HRMTI .... High Resolution Multispectral Thermal Imager (SAUS)
HRMVS .... High Resolution Multispectral Video System (SAUO)
HRMY .... Harmony Products, Inc. [*NASDAQ symbol*] (SAG)
HRN .... Airwork Ltd. [*British*] [*ICAO designator*] (FAAC)
HRN .... Harlyn Products, Inc. [*AMEX symbol*] (SPSG)
HRN .... Harness
HRN .... Harwin Exploration & Development, Inc. [*Vancouver Stock Exchange symbol*]
HRN .... Herrn [*Sirs, Gentlemen*] [*German*] (ROG)
HRN .... Hexagonal Reducing Nipple (SAUS)
HRN .... Highest Response-Ratio Next (VLIE)
HRN .... High Resolution Navigation mode (SAUS)
HRN .... Hoerner [*Horns*] [*Music*]
HRN .... Human Research Need (RDA)
HRN .... Human Resources Need (MCD)
HRN .... Human Resources Network [*Information service or system*] (EA)
HRN .... Human Rights Network [*British*]
HRNA .... Haflinger Registry of North America (EA)
HRNA .... Heterogeneous Ribonucleic Acid (SAUS)
hRNA .... Ribonucleic Acid, Heterogeneous [*Biochemistry, genetics*]
HRNAR .... Hereinafter
HRNB .... Halstead-Reitan Neuropsychological Battery [*Medicine*] (EDAA)
HRNB .... History: Reviews of New Books [*A publication*] (BRI)
HRNES .... Host Remote Node Entry System

HRNG.......... Hearing
HRNHAR...... Horn & Hardart Co. (SAUO)
HRNS.......... Homatropine Retinoscopy (SAUS)
HRNSW........ Historical Records of New South Wales (journ.) (SAUS)
HRNTB......... Halstead-Reitan Neuropsychological Test Battery [*Intended to measure brain functioning*] (DIPS)
HRNTWT...... High Reynolds Number Transonic Wind Tunnel
HRO............ Harrison [*Arkansas*] [*Airport symbol*] (OAG)
HRO............ Hermiston [*Oregon*] [*Seismograph station code, US Geological Survey*] (SEIS)
HRO............ HERO Industries Ltd. [*Toronto Stock Exchange symbol*] [*Vancouver Stock Exchange symbol*]
HRO............ Homes Registration Office
HRO............ House of Ronnie, Inc. (SAUO)
HRO............ Housing Referral Office [*Military*]
HRO............ Human Resource Office (SAUO)
HRO............ Human Resources Office
HROAN........ Hardware Realization of Adaptive Networks (ACAE)
HROB.......... Hi-Tech Robotics Ltd. (SAUO)
HROI.......... High Resolution Optical Imager (SAUS)
HROI.......... High Resolution Optical Instrument (EOSA)
HROI.......... Honorary Member of the Royal Institute of Oil Painters [*British*]
HROK.......... Home Federal Savings & Loan Association of the Rockies (SAUO)
HROM.......... High Resolution Ozone Mapping (SAUO)
HRON.......... Hereon [*Legal*] [*British*] (ROG)
HROS.......... High Resolution Objective Spectrometer (SAUS)
HRP............ Haitian Refugee Project [*Defunct*] (EA)
HRP............ Halden Reactor Project (SAUO)
HRP............ Hampton Roads Ports (SAUO)
HRP............ Hand Retractable Plunger (SAUS)
HRP............ Harper & Row Publishers, Inc. (SAUO)
HRP............ Harvard Revised Photometry (SAUS)
HRP............ Health & Rehabilitation Properties Trust (SAUS)
HRP............ Health & Retirement Properties Trust [*Formerly, Health/Rehabilitation Property*] [*NYSE symbol*] (SPSG)
HRP............ Heat-Resistant Phenolic
HRP............ Heat-Resisting Plastic
HRP............ Helicopter Reference Point (SAUS)
HRP............ High-Risk Patient [*Medicine*] (DMAA)
HRP............ High Risk Personnel (SAUS)
HRP............ High-Risk Pregnancy (MELL)
HRP............ Highway Regulating Point (AABC)
HRP............ Histidine-Rich Protein [*Biochemistry, immunochemistry*]
HRP............ Historical Review Press [*British*]
HRP............ Holding and Reconsignment Point [*Military*] (AABC)
HRP............ Horizontal Radiation Pattern [*Electronics*] (DEN)
HRP............ Horseradish Peroxidase [*An enzyme*]
HRP............ Hovering Recoverable Probe (ACAE)
HRP............ HRPT Properties Tr. [*NYSE symbol*] [*Formerly, Health & Retirement Properties Tr.*]
HRP............ Human Reliability Program (AFM)
HRP............ Human Remains Pouch (SAUS)
HRP............ Human Resource Planning (journ.) (SAUS)
HRP............ Human Resources Planning (SAUS)
HRP............ Human Rights Party [*Ann Arbor, MI*]
HRP............ Human Rights Program [*Harvard University*] [*Research center*] (RCD)
HRP............ Huntsville Research Park (SAUO)
HRP............ Hypergroup Reference Pilot [*Telecommunications*] (NITA)
HRP............ Home Responsibilities Protection (ODA)
HRPA.......... Hebrew Religious Protection Association of Greater New York (EA)
HRPA.......... Higher Random-Phase Approximation (SAUS)
HRPA.......... Hudson River Pilots Association (SAUO)
HRPAC........ Human Rights Political Action Committee (EA)
HRP and L... Hot Rolled, Picled and Limed (SAUS)
HRPAO........ Human Resources Professionals Association of Ontario [*Canada*]
HRPC.......... High-Range Pressure Control
HRP Compound... Heat-Resistant Phenolic Compound (SAUS)
HRPD.......... Hamburg Rating Scale for Psychiatric Disorders [*Medicine*] (DMAA)
HRPD.......... High Repetition-Rate Pulsed Doppler (ACAE)
HRPD.......... High-Resolution Powder Diffractometer [*Crystallographic instrument*]
HRPD.......... High Resolution Pulse Doppler Radar (ACAE)
HRPD.......... Human Resources Planning and Development (SAUO)
HRPE.......... Hampton Roads Port of Embarkation (SAUO)
HRPF.......... Hexadecimal Reference Publication Format (VLIE)
HRPI.......... High-Resolution Pointable Imager
HRPI.......... High-Risk Premature Infant (MELL)
HRPL.......... Hot-Rolled, Pickled and Limed (SAUS)
HRPM.......... High-Resolution Permanent Magnet (MHDI)
HRPM.......... Human Resources Program Manager (SAUS)
HRPO.......... Horseradish Peroxidase [*Also, HRP*] [*An enzyme*]
HRPO.......... Hot Rolled, Pickled, and Oiled (MSA)
HRPP.......... Health Resources Planning Program [*Medicine*] (EDAA)
hr pp........... Hours Postprandial [*Usually preceded by a numeral*] [*Pharmacology*] (DAVI)
HRPP.......... Human Rights Protection Party [*Western Samoa*] [*Political party*] (PPW)
HRPRAS...... High-Risk, People-Related Accident Syndrome (DICI)
HRPS.......... Hazard Reduction Precedence Sequence (NASA)
HRPS.......... High Risk Point Sources [*Environmental science*] (COE)
HRPS.......... Human Resource Payroll Salary (SAUS)
HRPS.......... Human Resource Planning Society [*New York, NY*] (EA)
HRPS.......... Hydrogen Recombination and Purge System [*Nuclear energy*] (NRCH)
HRPT.......... High-Resolution Picture Transmission [*Service*]
HRPT.......... High Resolution Pressure Transducer (ACAE)
HRPT.......... Highway Regulating Point Team [*MTMC*] (TAG)
HRPT.......... Hyperparathyroidism [*Medicine*] (DMAA)
HRPVD........ High-Rate Physical Vapor Deposition [*Metal*]
HRQ............ Hold Request (IAA)
HRQC.......... Highway Route Controlled Quality (SAUS)
HRQL.......... Health-Related Quality-of-Life [*Medicine*]
HRQOL........ Health Related Quality of Life
HRR............ Handipped Rights and Regulations (journ.) (SAUS)
HRR............ Hardy-Rand-Rittler [*Test for color blindness*] (DIPS)
HRR............ Head Rotated Right [*Medicine*]
HRR............ Health Risk Review (HEAS)
HRR............ Healy, AK [*Location identifier*] [*FAA*] (FAAL)
HRR............ Heart Rate Range [*Medicine*]
HRR............ Heart Rate Reserve (SAUS)
HRR............ Heat Rating Reserve
HRR............ Heat Rejection Radiator
HRR............ Heat Release Rate [*Engineering*]
HRR............ Heiliges Roemisches Reich [*Holy Roman Empire*] [*German*] (ROG)
HRR............ Heron Resources Ltd. [*Vancouver Stock Exchange symbol*]
HRR............ Higher Reduced Rate (SAUS)
HRR............ High Range Resolution
HRR............ High-Range-Resolution (SAUS)
HRR............ High-Reliability Relay
HRR............ High-Resolution RADAR
HRR............ Highway Research Record (SAUO)
HRR............ Hot Repair Room (SAUS)
HRR............ Huckleberry Railroad [*Federal Railroad Administration identification code*]
HRR............ Human Resource Representative (SAUO)
HRRA.......... Human Resources Research Association (SAUO)
HRRC.......... Hearing Rehabilitation Research Center [*Walt Disney*] (BABM)
HRRC.......... Home Recording Rights Coalition (EA)
HRRC.......... Housatonic Railroad [*Federal Railroad Administration identification code*]
HRRC.......... Human Resources Research Center
HRRC.......... Human Rights Resource Center (EAIO)
HRRC.......... Walt Disney Hearing Rehabilitation Research Center [*Ear Research Institute*]
HRRD.......... Human Resources Research Development Program
HR Rel......... Historicorum Romanorum Reliquiae [*A publication*] (OCD)
HR Rep........ House of Representatives Reports [*A publication*] (DLA)
HR Rept....... House of Representatives Reports [*A publication*] (DLA)
HR Rev........ Human Rights Review [*A publication*] (SAFN)
HRRI........... Heart Rate Retardation Index [*Medicine*] (DMAA)
HRRI........... Human Resources Research Institute
Hrringtn....... Harrington Financial Group, Inc. [*Associated Press*] (SAG)
HRRL.......... High Repetition Rate Laser (ACAE)
HRRL.......... Human Resources Research Laboratory [*Air Force*] (MCD)
HRRM.......... High Range-Resolution Monopulse (PDAA)
hrRNA......... Ribonucleic Acid, Heavy Ribosomal [*Biochemistry, genetics*]
HRRO.......... Human Resources Research Office [*NASA*] (AAG)
HRRP.......... Hanford Radiological Records Program (SAUS)
HRRP.......... Human Resources Research Program (SAUO)
HRRR.......... Heart Regular Rate and Rhythm (SAUS)
HRRS.......... Houghton Poultry Research Station (SAUS)
HRRTC........ High Resolution Real Time Clock (SAUS)
HRRTS........ High Resolution Remote Tracking Sonar (SAUS)
HRRVC........ Holiday Rambler Recreational Vehicle Club (EA)
HRRWC........ Hudson River Region Wine Council (EA)
HRRX.......... On-Track Railcar Services [*Private rail car owner code*]
HRS............ Hair Replacement System
HRS............ Hal Roach Studios, Inc.
HRS............ Hamilton Rating Scale (MAE)
HRS............ Hamman-Rich Syndrome [*Medicine*] (MELL)
HRS............ Hard Red Spring [*Wheat*]
HRS............ Hardware Requirements Specification (SAUS)
HRS............ Harp Renaissance Society [*Defunct*] (EA)
HRS............ Harris Corp. [*NYSE symbol*] (SPSG)
HRS............ Harris, GA [*Location identifier*] [*FAA*] (FAAL)
HRS............ Hawaii Revised Statutes [*A publication*]
HRS............ Hazardous Ranking System (SAUO)
HRS............ Hazard Ranking System [*Environmental Protection Agency*]
HRS............ Heading Reference System (AAG)
HRS............ Health and Rehabilitation Services (SAUS)
HRS............ Health Resources Statistics (SAUS)
HRS............ Heat Rejection System
HRS............ Heavy Repair Shop (SAUO)
HRS............ Hellenic Register of Shipping (SAUS)
HRS............ Hepatorenal Syndrome [*Medicine*]
HRS............ High-Rate Station
HRS............ High-Resolution data Service (SAUS)
HRS............ High Resolution Sensing (SAUS)
HRS............ High-Resolution Spectrograph [*Hubble Space Telescope*] [*NASA*]
HRS............ High Resolution Spectrometry (SAUS)
HRS............ High Rise Syndrome [*Animal fell off balcony/windowsill*] (SPVS)
HRS............ Historical Records and Studies (journ.) (SAUS)
HRS............ Historical Records Survey (journ.) (SAUS)
HRS............ Historic Record Society [*Record label*]
HRS............ Hollidaysburg & Roaring Spring Railroad [*Federal Railroad Administration identification code*]
HRS............ Holographic Readout System (AAEL)
HRS............ Holographic Reflex Sight (SAUS)
HRS............ Home Reunion Society [*British*]
HRS............ Honorary Reserve Section

HRS .... Honorary Reserve Station (SAUO)
HRS .... Hop Research Station (SAUO)
HRS .... Horizon Reference Set (MCD)
HRS .... Horizontal Recovery System
HRS .... Hormone Receptor Site [*Endocrinology*]
HRS .... Hospital Reading Society [*Defunct*] (EA)
HRS .... Host Residence System (SAUS)
HRS .... Host Resident Software
HRS .... Hotel Reservation Service (SAUO)
HRS .... Hot Record Society (SAUO)
HRS .... Hot Rolled Steel
HRS .... Hours (NATG)
hrs .... Hours (ODBW)
HRS .... Housing Referral Service [*Military*] (AABC)
HRS .... Hovering Rocket System [*Army*]
HRS .... H. Royer Smith Co. (SAUO)
HRS .... Human Resources System (MHDB)
HRS .... Human Resource System (SAUS)
HRS .... Hunza Research Society [*Defunct*] (EA)
HRS .... Hurricane Research Service [*Information service or system*] (IID)
HRS .... Hussars [*Military unit*] [*British*]
HRS .... Hydrant Refuelling System (IAA)
HRS .... Hydraulics Research Station [*Research center*] [*British*]
HRS .... Hydro Research System (SAUS)
HRS .... Hydrostatic Research System (SAUS)
HRs .... Hydroxethylrutosides [*Medicine*] (EDAA)
HRS .... Hyper-Rayleigh Scattering [*Physics*]
HRS .... Missionary Sisters of Our Lady of the Holy Rosary [*Roman Catholic religious order*]
HRSA .... Health Resources and Services Administration [*Department of Health and Human Services*]
HRSA .... Historical Radio Society of Australia
HRSA .... Honorary Member of the Royal Scottish Academy
HRSA .... Hotel & Restaurant Suppliers Association Inc. (AC)
HRSA .... Human Resources Services Administration (HVTR)
HRSBM .... Heated Raw Soybean Meal (SAUS)
HRSC .... High Resolution Stereo Camera (SAUS)
HRSC .... Hudson River Sloop Clearwater (EA)
HRSC .... Human Sciences Research Council (SAUO)
HRSCMR .... High-Resolution Surface-Composition Mapping Radiometer (PDAA)
HRSCO .... Housing Referral Service Coordination Office (SAUO)
HRSCX .... Heritage Small Cap Stock Cl.A [*Mutual fund ticker symbol*] (SG)
HRS-D .... Hamilton Rating Scale for Deafness
HRS-D .... Hamilton Rating Scale for Depression [*Medicine*] (DMAA)
HRSD .... Hard Rock Silo Development
HRSD .... Hazardous Response Support Division [*Environmental Protection Agency*]
HRSEM .... High-Resolution Scanning Electron Microscopy (OA)
HRSG .... Heat Recovery Steam Generator [*Industrial engineering*]
hrsg .... Herausgegeben [*Edited, Published*] [*German*]
HRSH .... Hirsch International Corp. [*NASDAQ symbol*] (SAG)
HRSH .... Hirsch Intl. Corp'A' [*NASDAQ symbol*] (TTSB)
Hrshey .... Hershey Foods Corp. [*Associated Press*] (SAG)
HRSI .... Hal Roach Studios, Incorporated (SAUO)
HRSI .... High-Temperature Reusable Surface Insulation [*Space shuttle*] [*NASA*]
HRSIM .... High Resolution Selected Ion Monitoring (SAUS)
HRSMR .... High Resolution Soil Moisture Radiometer (SAUS)
HRSN .... Hariston Corp. [*NASDAQ symbol*] (SAG)
HRSNA .... Histamine Club (SAUO)
HRSNA .... Histamine Research Society of North America (EA)
HRSNF .... Hariston Corp. [*NASDAQ symbol*] (TTSB)
HRSNV .... Harrisonville, MO [*American Association of Railroads railroad junction routing code*]
HRSO .... High Resolution Solar Observatory (SAUO)
HRSP .... Association of Human Resource Systems Professionals (EA)
HRSP .... Human Resource Systems Professionals (SAUS)
HRSR .... Heat Recovery/Seed Recovery [*System*]
HRSR .... High Resolution Scanning Radiometer [*Instrument*] (EERA)
HRSRASC .... Heavy Repair Shop, Royal Army Service Corps (SAUO)
HRSRS .... Hartbeestehoek Radio Space Research Station (SAUO)
HRSS .... High Resolution Surveillance System (CCCA)
HRSS .... Host Residence Software System (SAUS)
HRSS .... Host Resident Software System
HRSS .... Hrvatska Republikanska Seljacka Stranka [*Croatian Republican Peasant Party*] [*Former Yugoslavia*] [*Political party*] (PPE)
HRSSCC .... High-Resolution Spin Scan Cloud Camera (NOAA)
HRST .... High Resolution Sensing Technology (SAUS)
HRSTYLNG .... Hairstyling
HRSTYLST .... Hairstylist
HRSV .... Hydrangea Ringspot Virus [*Plant pathology*]
HRSW .... Honorary Member of the Royal Scottish Society of Painters in Water Colours (SAUO)
HRSW .... Honorary Member of the Royal Scottish Water Colour Society
HRSX .... Hawaiian Railway Society [*Federal Railroad Administration identification code*]
HRT .... Arrhythmia Research Technology [*AMEX symbol*] (SPSG)
HRT .... Hard Return (SAUS)
HRt .... Hard-Return (ADWA)
HRT .... Hartford [*Diocesan abbreviation*] [*Connecticut*] (TOCD)
HRT .... Hartwell Railway Co. [*AAR code*]
Hrt .... Heart (WPI)
HRT .... Heart
HRT .... Heart Rate [*Cardiology*] (DAVI)
HRT .... Heat Rejection and Transport (SSD)
HRT .... Heavy Rail Transit (PDAA)
HRT .... Helmholtz Reciprocal Theorem [*Physics*]
Hrt .... Hertfordshire [*County in England*] (WGA)
HRT .... High Rate Tape (SAUS)
HRT .... High-Rate Telemetry [*NASA*]
HRT .... High Resolution Timer (SAUS)
HRT .... High-Resolution Tracker
HRT .... Highway Regulation Team (SAUO)
HRT .... Hillcrest Resources Ltd. [*Toronto Stock Exchange symbol*]
HRT .... Hiring, Retention, and Tenure [*of college professors*]
HRT .... Home Record Tape (SAUS)
HRT .... Homogeneous Reactor Test
HRT .... Honolulu Rapid Transit (SAUO)
HRT .... Horizontal Return Tubular Burner (EDCT)
HRT .... Hormone Replacement Therapy [*Medicine*]
HRT .... Hospitals Remuneration Tribunal [*Australia*]
HRT .... Hostage Rescue Team [*Pronounced "hurt"*] [*FBI standardized term*]
HRT .... Human Resources Training
HRT .... Hydraulic Retention Time
HRT .... Mary Esther, FL [*Location identifier*] [*FAA*] (FAAL)
HRT .... Transporte Aereo Rioplatense [*Argentina*] [*ICAO designator*] (FAAC)
HRTB .... Heritage Bancorp of California (SAUO)
HRTC .... Historic Rehabilitation Tax Credit
HrtCC .... Heart Cubic Content (DAC)
HRTD .... High-Rising Terminal Declarative [*Linguistics*]
HRTE .... Human Reverse-Transcriptase Enzyme (DB)
HRTEM .... High-Resolution Transmission Electron Microscope [*or Microscopy*]
HRTF .... Head-Related Transfer Functions
HRTF .... High-Resolution Tangential Flow Filtration
HrtFa .... Heart Facial Area (DAC)
HRTFD .... Hartford, CT [*American Association of Railroads railroad junction routing code*]
HrtfdSt .... Hartford Steam Boiler & Inspection [*Associated Press*] (SAG)
HrtG .... Heart Girth (DAC)
HRTG .... Heritage
HRTG .... Heritage. Alberta Department of Culture, Youth and Recreation (journ.) (SAUS)
HRTG .... Heritage Bancorporatian (SAUS)
HrtgMd .... Heritage Media Corp. [*Associated Press*] (SAG)
HrtgMda .... Heritage Media [*Associated Press*] (SAG)
HRTI .... Hart Industries, Inc. (SAUO)
HRTI .... High Resolution Thermal Imager (SAUS)
HRTI .... Hospital Research and Testing Institute [*Medicine*] (EDAA)
HRTIR .... High Resolution Thermal Infrared Radiometer (SAUS)
HrtLabs .... Heart Labs of America [*Associated Press*] (SAG)
HrtLb .... Heart Labs of America [*Associated Press*] (SAG)
HRTLND .... Heartland Partners Ltd. (SAUO)
HrtlndE .... Heartland Express, Inc. [*Associated Press*] (SAG)
HRTM .... Hardware Real-Time Monitor (SAUS)
HRTOF .... High-n Rydberg Time-Of-Flight (SAUS)
HRTS .... High-Rate Telemetry System [*NASA*]
HRTS .... High Resolution Target Sonar (SAUS)
HRTS .... High-Resolution Telescope and Spectrograph
HRTS .... High-Risk Test Site [*Later, Research Test Site*]
HRTS .... Hollywood Radio and Television Society (EA)
HRTS .... Hydroelectric Research and Technical Services (SAUO)
HRTS .... Hyper-Real-Time Simulation
HRTSG .... Hydroelectric Research and Technical Services Group (SAUO)
HRTT .... Heart Technology, Inc. [*NASDAQ symbol*] (SAG)
HRTVX .... Heartland Value Fund [*Mutual fund ticker symbol*] (SG)
HRTWD .... Heartwood [*Forestry*] (WGA)
Hrtwd .... Heartwood (WPI)
HrtWire .... Heartland Wireless Communications, Inc. [*Associated Press*] (SAG)
HRTWN .... Hawaii Regional Tsunami Warning Network [*Marine science*] (OSRA)
HR Type .... Heat Resistant Type (SAUS)
HRU .... Hardcopy Reconstruction Unit (SAUS)
HRU .... Harrisburg-Dayton [*Vancouver Stock Exchange symbol*]
HRU .... Heading Reference Unit
HRU .... Herrington, KS [*Location identifier*] [*FAA*] (FAAL)
HRU .... High Risk Units (SAUO)
HRU .... Hostage Rescue Unit (LAIN)
HRU .... Human Research Unit (SAUO)
HRU .... Human Resources Unit (HEAS)
HRU .... Hydrologic Research Unit (SAUO)
HRU .... Hydrostatic Release Unit (TRID)
HRUM .... Health Revolutionary Unity [*Medicine*] (EDAA)
HRUP .... High-Risk Urban Problem [*Environmental Protection Agency*] (GFGA)
HRV .... Harvard - Oak Ridge [*Massachusetts*] [*Seismograph station code, US Geological Survey*] (SEIS)
HRV .... Heat Rate Variability
HRV .... Heat Recovery Ventilator
HRV .... Heavy Recovery Vehicle [*Marine Corps*] (VNW)
HRV .... High Resolution Video (EOSA)
HRV .... High Resolution Visible [*Imager*]
HRV .... Historical Records of Victoria [*A publication*]
HRV .... Human Reovirus [*Medicine*] (DMAA)
HRV .... Human Rhinovirus [*Medicine*]
HRV .... Hydraulic Relief Valve
HRV .... Hyperbaric Rescue Vessel (SAUS)
HRV .... Hypersonic Research Vehicle
HRV .... New Orleans, LA [*Location identifier*] [*FAA*] (FAAL)
HRVC .... Hudson River Valley Commission (SAUO)
HRVIR .... High Resolution Visible Infrared (SAUS)
HRVIS .... High Resolution Visible Imager (SAUS)

HRVL .... Human Resources, Veterans, and Labor [*Office of Management and Budget*]
HRVLA .... Human Reovirus-Like Agent (CPH)
HRVS .... High Resolution Visible Sensor (SAUS)
HRVY .... Harvey Entertainment [*NASDAQ symbol*] (TTSB)
HRVY .... Harvey Entertainment Co. [*NASDAQ symbol*] (SAG)
HRW .... Hard Red Winter [*Wheat*]
HRW .... Heated Rear Window [*Automotive accessory*]
HRW .... Holt, Rinehart & Winston, Inc. (SAUO)
HRW .... Human Rights for Women (EA)
HRW .... Human Rights Watch (EA)
HRWA .... Human Rights Watch/Africa [*New York*] (EA)
HRWH .... Human Rights Watch - Helsinki [*An association*] (EA)
HRWMC .... House of Representatives Ways and Means Committee (WDAA)
HRWNIC .... House of Representatives Ways and Means Committee (SAUS)
HRWS .... Helicopter Remote Wind Sensor
HRWW .... Hard Red Winter Wheat (FOTI)
HRW Wheat... Hard Red Winter Wheat (SAUS)
HRX .... Hereford, TX [*Location identifier*] [*FAA*] (FAAL)
HRX .... Hypothetical Reference Connection [*Meteorology*]
HRXRD .... High Resolution X-Ray Diffraction (SAUS)
HRXRD .... High Resolution X-Ray Diffractometry (SAUS)
HRXRD .... High Resolution X-Ray Diffractrometry (SAUS)
HRXRS .... High-Resolution X-Ray Spectroscopy
HRY .... Hallwood Realty Partners Ltd. [*AMEX symbol*] (SPSG)
HRY .... Hallwood Rlty Ptnrs L.P. (New) [*AMEX symbol*] (TTSB)
HRY .... Head Rice Yield
HRYC .... Halifax River Yacht Club (SAUO)
HRYC .... Hampton Roads Yacht Club (SAUO)
HRYG .... Gisenyi [*Rwanda*] [*ICAO location identifier*] (ICLI)
HRYI .... Butare [*Rwanda*] [*ICAO location identifier*] (ICLI)
HRYO .... Gabiro [*Rwanda*] [*ICAO location identifier*] (ICLI)
HRYR .... Kigali [*Rwanda*] [*ICAO location identifier*] (ICLI)
HRYU .... Ruhengeri [*Rwanda*] [*ICAO location identifier*] (ICLI)
HRZ .... Hertz Corp'A' [*NYSE symbol*] (SG)
HRZ .... High Rainfall Zone
Hrz .... Horizontal (SAUS)
HRZA .... Kamembe [*Rwanda*] [*ICAO location identifier*] (ICLI)
HRZB .... Horizon Bank [*NASDAQ symbol*] (NQ)
HRZB .... Horizon Financial [*NASDAQ symbol*] (TTSB)
HRZB .... Horizon Financial Corp. [*NASDAQ symbol*] (SAG)
HrzBcWV .... Horizon Bancorp (West Virginia) [*Associated Press*] (SAG)
HrzBTX .... Horizon Bancorp, Inc. (Texas) [*Associated Press*] (SAG)
HrzHlt .... Horizon CMS Healthcare Corp. [*Associated Press*] (SAG)
HrzHlt .... Horizon Healthcare Corp. [*Associated Press*] (SAG)
HrzMH .... Horizon Mental Health Management [*Associated Press*] (SAG)
hrzn .... Horizon (ADWA)
HRZN .... Horizon Industries, Inc. (SAUO)
HRZ Press ... Horizontal Press (SAUS)
HS .... Aeronoleggi e Lavoro Aereo (AERAL) [*Italy*] [*ICAO designator*] (ICDA)
HS .... Air-Cushion Vehicle built by Hoversport [*US*] [*Usually used in combination with numerals*]
HS .... CHS Electronics [*NYSE symbol*]
Hs .... Deuterium (SAUS)
HS .... Die Heilige Schrift des Alten Testaments [*Bonn*] [*A publication*] (BJA)
HS .... Habitability System [*NASA*] (KSC)
HS .... Habituation Stimulus [*to light*]
hs .... hail and snow (SAUS)
HS .... Hair Space [*Publishing*] (DGA)
HS .... Hakluyt Society (EA)
HS .... Halfsheet [*Publishing*] (DGA)
HS .... Half Strength
HS .... Half Subtractor [*Circuitry*]
HS .... Halleworden-Spatz [*Syndrome*] [*Medicine*] (DB)
H-S .... Hamilton Standard (SAA)
HS .... Hamstring (MELL)
HS .... Handbook of Statistics (journ.) (SAUS)
HS .... Handset
HS .... H & S Railroad [*Federal Railroad Administration identification code*]
HS .... Hand-Starter
HS .... Hand Surgery [*Medical specialty*] (DHSM)
HS .... Hand Switch [*Nuclear energy*] (NRCH)
HS .... Hanford Specifications (SAUS)
HS .... Hanford Square (SAUS)
HS .... Hansard Society [*British*] (ILCA)
HS .... Harbor Service (SAUO)
HS .... Harbour Service (SAUS)
HS .... Hardened Site
HS .... Hardness Surveillance (MSA)
HS .... Hard Sized (SAUS)
HS .... Hard Sized Paper (DGA)
H/S .... Hard/Soft [*Two tops for convertible automobile*]
HS .... Hard/Soft Ratio (SAUS)
HS .... Hard Solder (SAUS)
HS .... Hard Sphere Model (SAUS)
HS .... Hardstand
HS .... Hard Standing (SAUO)
HS .... Hard Stripping [*Agriculture*] (OA)
HS .... Harleian Society (SAUO)
HS .... Harmonised System [*Customs commodity coding and description*] [*British*]
HS .... Harness or Saddlery
HS .... Hartford & Slocomb Railroad Co. [*AAR code*]
HS .... Hartman's Solution [*Dentistry*]
HS .... Hartman Systems (SAUS)
HS .... Harvard Speciality Company, Inc. (SAUO)
HS .... Harveian Society of London (SAUO)
HS .... Harvey Society (EA)
Hs .... Hassium [*Proposed name and symbol for recently-discovered element*]
HS .... Hauptsatz [*Leading Theme*] [*Music*]
HS .... Have Sold [*Travel industry*] (TVEL)
HS .... Hawker Siddeley (SAUO)
HS .... Hawker Siddeley Aviation Ltd. [*British*] [*ICAO aircraft manufacturer identifier*] (ICAO)
HS .... Haydn Society [*Record label*]
HS .... Hazardous Substance (MELL)
HS .... Header Statement (SAUS)
HS .... Heading Statement (SAUS)
HS .... Headquarters State (NITA)
HS .... Head Set [*Telecommunications*] (IAA)
HS .... Head Sling
HS .... Headspace [*Above liquids*]
HS .... Headspace Sampler [*Instrumentation*]
HS .... Heads Sampler (SAUS)
HS .... Head Start (SAUS)
HS .... Head Suppression (AAG)
HS .... Health Services Technician [*Military*] (POLM)
HS .... Healthsource, Inc. [*NYSE symbol*] (SPSG)
HS .... Health Study (SAUS)
HS .... Heard Sounds (SAUS)
HS .... Heart Sounds [*Medicine*]
HS .... Heated Seats
HS .... Heater Shield (SAUS)
HS .... Heather Society (EA)
HS .... Heating Surface
HS .... Heating System
HS .... Heat Shield [*Aerospace*] (AAG)
HS .... Heat-Shrinkable (SAUS)
HS .... Heat Sink (SAUS)
HS .... Heat Stable
HS .... Heat Switch (SAUS)
HS .... Heaviside [*Ionosphere*] (AAG)
HS .... Heavy-duty Synthetic (SAUS)
HS .... Heel Spur [*Orthopedics*] (DAVI)
HS .... Heel Stick [*For blood samples*] [*Medicine*] (DAVI)
HS .... Heel Strike [*Medicine*]
H-S .... Heel-to-Shin [*Test*] [*Neurology*] (DAVI)
HS .... Height above Spherical Earth
HS .... Height of Site (SAUS)
Hs .... Height, Storey (SAUS)
HS .... Helical Spring
HS .... Helicopter Antisubmarine Squadron (SAUS)
HS .... Helicopter Squadron
HS .... Helicopter Squadron, Antisubmarine (MCD)
HS .... Helicopter System
HS .... Helios Semiconductor (IAA)
HS .... Helmet Shield
HS .... Helminthosporium sacchari [*A toxin-producing fungus*]
H/S .... Helper/Suppressor [*Cell ratio*]
HS .... Heme Synthetase [*An enzyme*] (AAMN)
HS .... Hemingway Society (EA)
Hs .... Hemisphere (journ.) (SAUS)
HS .... Hemisuccinyl (SAUS)
HS .... Hemlock Society (EA)
HS .... Hemorrhagic Septicemia (SAUS)
HS .... Hemorrhagic Shock [*Medicine*]
HS .... Hemstitched
HS .... Henoch-Schoenlein Syndrome [*Medicine*]
HS .... Heparin Sulfate [*Biochemistry*]
HS .... Hepatic Scintigraphy [*Medicine*]
HS .... Hepatosplenic Schistosomiasis [*Medicine*]
HS .... Heraldisk Selskab [*Denmark*] [*An association*] (EAIO)
HS .... Heraldry Society (EA)
HS .... Hereditary Spherocytosis [*Medicine*]
HS .... Hermetically Sealed (IAA)
HS .... Herpes Simplex
HS .... Heuristic Search (SAUS)
HS .... Hic Sepultus [*Here Is Buried*] [*Latin*]
HS .... Hic Situs [*Here Lies*] [*Latin*] (GPO)
HS .... Hide Substance (SAUS)
HS .... Hidradenitis Suppurative [*Medicine*]
HS .... Hierarchically Structured [*Indexing language*] (NITA)
HS .... Hierarchical Sequential [*Computer science*] (ELAL)
HS .... Hierarchical Sequential Organization [*Computer science*] (ITCA)
HS .... Highest Score (ADA)
HS .... Highly Sensitive System (MCD)
HS .... High School
HS .... High Sensitivity
HS .... High Shear (SAUS)
HS .... High Shock Resistant (IAA)
HS .... High Similarity (SAUS)
HS .... High-Similarity [*Psychology*]
HS .... High Speed
HS .... High-Speed Adapter (IAA)
HS .... High-Speed Arithmetic (IAA)
HS .... High Spin (EDCT)
HS .... High Spontaneous Activity
HS .... High Stability (SAUS)

HS .... High Stage (MCD)
HS .... High Strength [*Steel*] [*Automotive engineering*]
HS .... High Structure (SAUS)
HS .... High Survivability (SAUS)
HS .... Highway Safety
HS .... Hindenberg Society (EA)
HS .... Hinged Seat (AAG)
HS .... Hinge Side
HS .... Histamine Sensitive [*Immunology*]
HS .... Histiocyte Society (SAUO)
HS .... Historical Period Starting Date [*Dialog*] [*Searchable field*] [*Information service or system*] (NITA)
HS .... Historical Studies (journ.) (SAUS)
HS .... Historical Survey
HS .... Historic Site (SAUS)
hs .... History [*Medicine*] (DMAA)
HS .... History Section [*Reference and Adult Services Division*] [*American Library Association*]
HS .... Hoc Sensu [*In This Sense*] [*Latin*] (GPO)
HS .... Hohenzollern Society (EA)
HS .... Hollaender-Simons [*Disease*] [*Medicine*] (DB)
HS .... Hollerith System (SAUS)
HS .... Hollow Spindle (SAUS)
HS .... Holographic Stereogram (OA)
HS .... Holy Sea (SAUS)
HS .... [*The*] Holy See
HS .... Home Secretary [*British*]
HS .... Home Service [*British*] (MILB)
HS .... Home Station [*DoD*]
HS .... Homestead (ADA)
HS .... Home Surgeon [*Medicine*] [*British*]
HS .... Homing Sequence (IAA)
HS .... Homologous Serum
HS .... Honorary Secretary
HS .... Hopper Soliday Corp. (SAUO)
HS .... Horae Soederblomianae (BJA)
hs .... Hora Somni [*Hour of Sleep*] [*Latin*] (STED)
HS .... Hora Somni [*At Bedtime*] [*Pharmacy*]
HS .... Horizon Scanner
HS .... Horizon Search (SAUS)
HS .... Horizon Sensor
HS .... Horizontally Selective [*Medicine*] (DMAA)
HS .... Horizontally Sliding (SAUS)
HS .... Horizontal Shear
HS .... Horizontal Stripes [*On buoys, beacons*]
HS .... Horizontal Synchronizing (SAUS)
HS .... Horizontal Synchronous [*Computer science*]
HS .... Horizontal System [*Government arrangement*] (OICC)
HS .... Hormones [*Medicine*] (EDAA)
HS .... Horner Syndrome [*Medicine*] (DMAA)
HS .... Horse Serum [*Immunology*]
HS .... Horticultural Society (SAUO)
HS .... Hospital Services (FOTI)
HS .... Hospital Ship
HS .... Hospitals Staff (SAUO)
HS .... Hospital Staff
HS .... Hospital Surgeon [*British military*] (DMA)
HS .... Host Software Testing Section (SAUS)
HS .... Hot Shop [*Nuclear energy*] (NRCH)
HS .... Hot Soak [*Automotive engineering*]
HS .... Hot Spraying
HS .... Hot Stage (SAUS)
HS .... Hot Stuff [*Slang*] [*Bowdlerized version*]
hs .... Hour of Sleep [*At bedtime*] [*Therapy term*] (CTAA)
HS .... Hours of Scheduled Operations (SAUS)
HS .... Hours of Sleep [*Medicine*]
hs .... House (VRA)
HS .... House Supervisor
HS .... House Surgeon
HS .... Housing Scheme [*British*]
HS .... Housing Statistics
HS .... Housman Society (EA)
HS .... Hughes Space (ACAE)
HS .... Hughes Standard (ACAE)
HS .... Humane Society (ROG)
HS .... Humanities in the South (journ.) (SAUS)
HS .... Human Source (FOTI)
HS .... Hume Society (EA)
HS .... Humic Substances [*Biology*]
HS .... Hundred Square Feet (DNAB)
HS .... Hun-Stoffe [*US Chemical Corp. symbol for mustard gas*] [*Also, HD, HT, M*] [*Later, H*]
HS .... Hurler's Syndrome [*Medicine*]
HS .... Hybrid Switching [*Telecommunications*]
HS .... Hydraulic Supply
HS .... Hydraulic System
HS .... Hydrazine Sulfate [*Toxic substance*] [*Inorganic chemistry*]
HS .... Hydrofoil Ship
HS .... Hydrogen Sulfide (GNE)
HS .... Hydrogen Swelling [*Chemistry*]
HS .... Hydrographic Society (SAUO)
HS .... Hydrostatic (SAUS)
HS .... Hydroxylamine Sulfate (EDCT)
HS .... Hypersensitization (SAUS)
HS .... Hypersonic
Hs .... Hypochondriasis [*Psychology*]
HS .... Hypothetical Syllogism [*Rule of inference*] [*Logic*]
HS .... International Journal of Health Services (journ.) (SAUS)
HS .... Marshall's Air [*ICAO designator*] (AD)
HS .... Sandoz Pharmaceuticals [*Research code symbol*]
HS .... Service Available During Scheduled Operations [*ICAO*] (FAAC)
HS .... Siglum for Tablets in the Frau Professor Hilprecht Collection of Babylonian Antiquities [*Jena*] (BJA)
HS .... Thailand [*International civil aircraft marking*] (ODBW)
HSA .... CHS Aviation Ltd. [*Kenya*] [*ICAO designator*] (FAAC)
HSA .... Haiku Society of America (EA)
HSA .... Handicapped SCUBA Association (EA)
HSA .... Hanford Strategic Analysis (SAUS)
HSA .... Harvard Student Agencies [*Inc.*]
HSA .... Hawaii Surfing Association (EA)
HSA .... Hawker Siddeley Aviation Ltd. [*British*]
HSA .... Hawley-Smoot Act [*1930*]
HSA .... Hazardous Substance Analysis (SAUS)
HSA .... Hazardous Substances Act (DMAA)
HSA .... Headquarters Support Activity
HSA .... Head Side Airbag [*Automotive safety systems*]
HSA .... Health and Safety Assurance (SAUS)
HSA .... Health Schools Australia (SAUS)
HSA .... Health Scientist Administrator (MELL)
HSA .... Health Security Act (MELL)
HSA .... Health Service Academy [*Pakistan*]
HSA .... Health Service Action [*Later, CNHS*] [*An association*] (EA)
HSA .... Health Service Agreement
HSA .... Health Service Area [*Military*] (AABC)
HSA .... Health Services Administration [*Abolished, 1982, functions transferred to Health Resources and Services Administration*]
HSA .... Health Services Administration. Publications (journ.) (SAUS)
HSA .... Health Systems Agency [*New York, NY*]
HSA .... Heat Shield Abort [*Aerospace*] (IAA)
HSA .... Heat-Stable Antigen [*Immunochemistry*]
HSA .... Hegel Society of America (EA)
HSA .... Hemispherical Analyzer (SAUS)
HSA .... Hepatic Stimulating Activity [*Physiology*]
HSA .... Heraldry Society of Australia
HSA .... Herb Society of America (EA)
HSA .... Hereditary Sideroblastic Anemia [*Medicine*] (DMAA)
HSA .... Hidden Surface Algorithm (SAUS)
HSA .... Hierarchical Sequential Access (SAUS)
HSA .... High Specific Activity [*Radioisotope*]
HSA .... High Speed Access (SAUS)
HSA .... High-Speed Adapter (SAUS)
HSA .... High-Speed Adder (SAUS)
HSA .... High-Speed Arithmetic (SAUS)
HSA .... High Strength Adhesive (SAUS)
HSA .... High-Strength Adhesive
HSA .... Highway Safety Act [*1970*]
HSA .... Highway Switch Address (SAUS)
HSA .... Hill Start Assist [*Transmission and braking systems*] [*Automotive engineering*]
HSA .... Hispanic Society of America (EA)
HSA .... Hispanic Surname American
HSA .... Historic Sites Act of 1935 (COE)
HSA .... Hollandse Signaalapparaten [*Dutch*]
HSA .... Holly Society of America (EA)
HSA .... Holocaust Survivors of Auschwitz (EA)
HSA .... Home Servicemens Association (SAUO)
HSA .... Homo Sapiens [*Human species*]
HSA .... Horizon Sensor Assembly
HSA .... Horsemanship Safety Association (EA)
HSA .... Horse Serum Albumin [*Immunology*]
HSA .... Horseshoe Abscess [*Medicine*] (MELL)
HSA .... Hospital Savings Association (DAVI)
HSA .... Housing Subsidies Act (SAUO)
HSA .... Humane Society of Australia
HSA .... Human Serum Albumin
HSA .... Hungarian Scouts Association (EA)
HSA .... Hunt Saboteurs Association (EAIO)
HSA .... Hydrologic Study Area (SAUO)
HSA .... Hydroponic Society of America (EA)
HSA .... Hymn Society of America [*Later, HSUSC*] (EA)
HSA .... Hypersomnia-Sleep Apnea Syndrome [*Medicine*] (MAE)
HSA .... Hypersonic Aircraft (SAUS)
HSA .... New Hampshire State Library, Processing Center, Concord, NH [*OCLC symbol*] (OCLC)
HSAA .... Health Sciences Advancement Award [*National Institutes of Health*]
HSA&D .... High School of Art and Design (SAUO)
HSAAP .... Holston Army Ammunition Plant (AABC)
HSAB .... Hard and Soft Acids and Bases [*Chemistry*]
HSAB .... Heavy Stores Adapter Beam (SAUS)
HSAB .... Hydroxy(succinimidyl)azidobenzoate [*Organic chemistry*]
HSAC .... Health Safety and Analysis Center (SAUS)
HSAC .... Health Security Action Council (EA)
HSAC .... Helicopter Safety Advisory Conference (EA)
HSAC .... High Speed Access [*NASDAQ symbol*] (SG)
HSAC .... High-Speed Analog Computer (DEN)
HSAC .... Historic Shipwrecks Advisory Committee [*Victoria, Australia*]
HSAC .... House Science and Astronautics Committee [*US Congress*] (AAG)
HSAD .... Hypoactive Sexual Arousal Disorder (SEAT)
HSAFOKF .... Help Save America for Our Kids' Future (EA)
HSAG .... HEPES-Saline-Albumin-Gelatin [*Medium*] [*Microbiology*]

HSAI .... Healthcare Services of America, Incorporated (SAUO)
HSAK .... Akobo [*Sudan*] [*ICAO location identifier*] (ICLI)
HSAL .... High Speed Algebraic Logic (ADWA)
HSAL .... High-Speed Arithmetic Logic (SAUS)
HSAL .... Hispanic Society of America Library (SAUO)
HSALU .... High-Speed Arithmetic and Logic Unit (IAA)
HSAM .... Helicopter Survivability Assessment Model (MCD)
HSAM .... Hierarchical Sequential Access Method [*Computer science*]
HSAM .... High-Speed Accounting Machine (IAA)
HSAN .... Hereditary, Sensory, and Autonomic Neuopathy [*Medicine*] (MELL)
HS&E .... Health, Safety and Environment (SAUS)
HS&F .... Huntin', Shootin' & Fishin' [*Antiquarian book category*] (WDAA)
HS & O .... Heads of Services and Offices [*Red Cross*]
HS & SS .... Headquarters and Service Squadron
HSANSW .... Health Services Association of New South Wales [*Australia*]
HSAP .... Heat-Stable Alkaline Phosphatase [*An enzyme*]
HSAP .... Honeycomb Sandwich Aluminum Panel
HSAPrA .... HSBC AmericasAdj Rt cm A Pfd [*NYSE symbol*] (TTSB)
HSAR .... High School Airman Apprentice (SAUS)
HSAR .... Holographic Synthetic Aperture Radar (SAUS)
HSArg .... High-Speed Autoradiography [*Medicine*] (EDAA)
HSARG .... High-Speed Scintillation Autoradiography
HSAS .... Hard Stability Augmentation System
HSAS .... Headquarters Support Activity - Saigon [*Obsolete*] [*Military*] (CINC)
HSAS .... Houldsworth School of Applied Science (SAUS)
HSAS .... Hypertrophic Subaortic Stenosis [*Cardiology*]
HSAT .... Atbara [*Sudan*] [*ICAO location identifier*] (ICLI)
HSAT .... Die Heilige Schrift des Alten Testaments [*Bonner Bibel*] [*A publication*] (BJA)
H-SAT .... Heavy Communications Satellite (SAUS)
H-SAT .... Heavy Satellite (PDAA)
HSATes .... Die Heilige Schrift des Alten Testaments [*Bonner Bibel*] [*A publication*] (BJA)
HSA-UWC .... Holy Spirit Association for the Unification of World Christianity
HSAW .... Aweil [*Sudan*] [*ICAO location identifier*] (ICLI)
HSAW .... Humane Society And Welfare Ring (SAUO)
HSB .... Harrisburg, IL [*Location identifier*] [*FAA*] (FAAL)
HSB .... Hartford Steam Boiler Inspection & Insurance Co. [*NYSE symbol*] (SPSG)
HSB .... Hartford Stm Boiler Ins [*NYSE symbol*] (TTSB)
HSB .... Heat-Shield Boost [*Aerospace*]
Hsb .... Hefner-Stilb (SAUS)
HSB .... Helmet Stowage Bag [*NASA*] (KSC)
HSB .... Hermetically Sealed Bushing
HSB .... High School and Beyond Survey [*Department of Education*] (GFGA)
HSB .... High Speed Boat (DOMA)
HSB .... High-Speed Buffer
HSB .... High-Speed Bus [*Computer science*]
HSB .... Hobbyists Sourcebook [*A publication*]
HSB .... Home Defense Brigades (SAUS)
HSB .... Horizontal Sounding Balloon (IAA)
HSB .... Hospitals Superannuation Board [*Victoria, Australia*]
HSB .... HSB Group [*NYSE symbol*] (SG)
HSB .... Hue/Saturation/Brightness [*Color model*] [*Printer technology*] (PCM)
HSB .... Human Sexual Behavior (SAUS)
HSB .... Humidity Sounder for Brazil
HSB .... Hunter-Schreger Bands [*Tooth structure*]
HSB .... Hutterian Brethren [*Hutterian Society of Brothers*] [*Acronym is based on former name,*] (EA)
HSBA .... Herdwick Sheep Breeders Association [*British*] (DBA)
HSBA .... High Speed Bus Adaptor (NITA)
HSBA .... High Speed Rail Association (SAUO)
HSBA .... Historic Statistics of Black America [*A publication*]
HSBA .... Horizontal Static Balancing Adjustment
H-SB-BL .... Hydrogenated Styrene Butadiene Block Copolymer (SAUS)
HSBC .... Hongkong and Shanghai Banking Corp.
HSBEA .... Hughes Santa Barbara Employees' Association (ACAE)
HSBG .... Heel Stick Blood Gas [*Medicine*] (DAVI)
HSBI .... Hyde Stud Bloodstock Investments Ltd. [*British*]
HSBK .... Hibernia Savings Bank [*NASDAQ symbol*] (NQ)
HSBK .... Hibernia Savings Bk [*NASDAQ symbol*] (TTSB)
HSBP .... High-Speed Bench Press
HSBR .... Bor [*Sudan*] [*ICAO location identifier*] (ICLI)
HSBR .... High-Speed Bombing RADAR
HSBRAM .... Hanford Site Baseline Risk Assessment (SAUS)
HSBT .... Bentu [*Sudan*] [*ICAO location identifier*] (ICLI)
HSBT .... High-Speed Bipolar Technologie (SAUS)
HSC .... Haemopoieric Stem Cell (SAUS)
HS+C .... Half Sample plus Complement (SAUS)
HS + C .... Half-Sample plus Complement [*Statistics*]
HSC .... Half Select Current (SAUS)
HS-C .... Hamilton Standard Carbon Dioxide Absorbent Material (NASA)
HSC .... Hampden-Sydney College [*Virginia*]
HSC .... Hand and Shoe Contamination (SAUS)
HSC .... Hand-Schueller-Christian [*Disease*] [*Medicine*]
HSC .... Hardware-Software Configuration [*Computer science*]
HSC .... Hardware/Software Coordination (NASA)
HSC .... Harmonized System Code [*File indexing*]
HSC .... Harsco Corp. [*NYSE symbol*] (SPSG)
HSC .... Hawker Siddeley Canada, Inc. [*Toronto Stock Exchange symbol*] [*Vancouver Stock Exchange symbol*]
HSC .... Hazardous Materials Spill Center [*Department of Energy*]
HSC .... Health and Safety Code (SAUS)
HSC .... Health and Safety Commission [*Department of Employment*] [*British*]
HSC .... Health Sciences Consortium (EA)
HSC .... Health Service Command (SAUS)
HSC .... Health Services Centre [*Institute of Organisation and Social Studies, Brunel University*] [*British*] (CB)
HSC .... Health Services Command [*Army*]
HSC .... Heat Seal Cable (SAUS)
HSC .... Heat Seal Connection (SAUS)
HSC .... Heat-Shock Cognate [*Biochemistry*]
HSC .... Heat Sterilization Compound
HSC .... Heavy & Specialized Carriers Tariff Bureau, Washington DC [*STAC*]
HSC .... Heavy Stores Carrier (SAUS)
HSC .... Helicopter Service Center (SAUS)
HSC .... Hematopoietic Stem Cell [*Hematology*]
HSC .... Henderson State College [*Later, Henderson State University*] [*Arkansas*]
HSC .... Heraldry Society of Canada (EAIO)
HSC .... Hermetically Sealed Container (SAUS)
HSC .... Hermetic-Sealed Container (MSA)
HSC .... Hierarchical Storage Controller (ACRL)
HSC .... Higher School Certificate [*British*]
HSC .... Higher State of Consciouness (SAUO)
HSC .... High School Completion (OICC)
HSC .... High School of Commerce (SAUO)
HSC .... High Short-Circuit (MIST)
HSC .... High-Speed Card (SAUS)
HSC .... High-Speed Carry
HSC .... High-Speed Channel [*Computer science*]
HSC .... High Speed Club (SAUO)
HSC .... High-Speed Computer (SAUS)
HSC .... High-Speed Computing (SAUS)
HSC .... High-Speed Concentrator
HSC .... High Speed Connect (SAUS)
HSC .... High-Speed Counter (SAUS)
HSC .... High-Speed Craft (SAUS)
HSC .... High Sulphur Content (PDAA)
HSC .... High-Swirl Combustion [*Engine*]
HSC .... Hiydrogen Stress Cracking (SAUS)
HSC .... Holly Sugar Corp. (EFIS)
HSC .... Home Products Safety Council (EA)
HSC .... Home Security Circulat (SAUO)
HSC .... Home Service Corps (SAUO)
HSC .... Home Shopping Club [*of the Home Shopping Network*]
HSC .... Honourable Society of Cymmrodorion (SAUO)
HSC .... Horizon Scanner (MSA)
HSC .... Horizontal Sweep Circuit (SAUS)
HSC .... Hospital for Sick Children [*Toronto, ON*] [*Canada*]
HSC .... Hot Stove Club (EA)
HSC .... House Space Committee [*US Congress*] (AAG)
HS/C .... House Spacecraft (KSC)
HSC .... Human Skin Collagen
HSC .... Human Systems Center (SAUS)
HSC .... Humboldt State College [*Later, Humboldt State University*] [*California*]
HSC .... Humor Stamp Club (EA)
HSC .... Hunting Surveys & Consultants [*Commercial firm*] [*British*]
HSC .... Huntington Society of Canada
HSC .... Hydrocarbon Subcommittee (SAUS)
HSC .... Hydrogen Stress Cracking (PDAA)
HSC .... International Code of Safety for High-Speed Craft (SAUO)
HSc .... Scleroscope Hardness Number Model c (SAUS)
HSC .... United States Army Health Services Command (SAUO)
HSCA .... Health Sciences Communications Association (DAVI)
HSCA .... Horizontal Sweep Circuit Analyzer
H Scan .... H Scanner (SAUS)
HSCB .... High Sensitivity Circuit Breaker (SAUS)
HSCB .... High-Speed Circuit Breaker [*Indian Railway*] (TIR)
HSCC .... Heavy Specialized Carriers Conference [*Later, SC & RA*]
HSCC .... High-Level Serial Communication Controller (AGLO)
HSCC .... High-Speed Combat Craft (SAUS)
HSCC .... Historical Society of Southern California (SAUO)
HSCC .... Hollywood Studio Collectors Club (EA)
HSCD .... Hand-Schueller-Christian Disease (MEDA)
HSCD .... Hazardous Site Control Division [*Environmental Protection Agency*] (GFGA)
HSCD .... Headquarter Hazardous Site Control Division (SAUS)
HSCDS .... High-Sensitivity Collision Detection System [*Automotive safety*]
HSCDS .... High-Speed Cable Data Service (SAUS)
HSCE .... Higher School Certificate Examination (ADA)
HSC Engine ... High-Swirl Combustion Engine (SAUS)
HSCF .... Health Sciences Computing Facility [*UCLA*]
HSCF .... High-Speed Card Feed (SAUS)
HSCG .... Erkowit/Carthago [*Sudan*] [*ICAO location identifier*] (ICLI)
H Sch .... High School (journ.) (SAUS)
HSchein .... Henry Schein, Inc. [*Associated Press*] (SAG)
H Sch M .... High School Magazine [*A publication*] (BRI)
HSchQ .... High School Quarterly (SAUO)
HSchQ .... High School Quarterly (journ.) (SAUS)
H Sch Tech ... High School Teacher (journ.) (SAUS)
HSCI .... High School Characteristics Index [*Research test*] [*Psychology*]
HSCI .... High-Speed Communications Interface (SAUS)
HSCL .... Harvard Studies in Comparative Literature (journ.) (SAUS)
HSCL .... High-Speed Command Link
HSCL .... Hindustan Steel Construction Ltd. (SAUS)
HSCL .... Hopkins Symptom Checklist [*Psychology*] (DHP)
HSCL .... Housecall Medical Resources, Inc. [*NASDAQ symbol*] (SAG)

HSCLCS .... Harpoon Shipboard Command and Launch Control Set [*Missiles*] (NVT)
HSCLS .... Harpoon Shipboard Command and Launch Subsystem [*Missiles*] (MCD)
HSCM .... High-Speed Computing Machine (SAUS)
HSCO .... Hungarian Shipping Co. Ltd. (SAUO)
HS-CoA .... Reduced Coenzyme A [*Biochemistry*] (DAVI)
HSCOCS .... House Select Committee on the Outer Continental Shelf [*US Congress*] [*Marine science*] (MSC)
HSCOR .... House Staff Check on Rounds [*Medicine*]
HSCP .... Harvard Studies in Classical Philology (journ.) (SAUS)
HSCP .... Health Science Cluster Program [*University of Connecticut*] [*Research center*] (RCD)
HSCP .... Heat-Shock Cognate Protein [*Biochemistry*]
HSCP .... High School Completion Program (SAUO)
HSCP .... High-Speed Card Perforator (SAUS)
HSCP .... High-Speed Card Punch [*Computer science*] (AABC)
HSCP .... Historical Sources Collection Program
HSCPA .... Hospital and Community Psychiatry (journ.) (SAUS)
HSCR .... High-Speed Card Reader [*Computer science*] (AABC)
HSCR .... High-Strength Cold-Rolled (PDAA)
HSCR .... High Sub-Chief Ranger [*Ancient Order of Foresters*]
HSCRA .... Hastings Center. Report (journ.) (SAUS)
HSCRC .... Health Services Cost Review [*Medicine*] (EDAA)
HSCRG .... Historic Stock Car Racing Group
HSCS .... Helicopter Subcontrol Ship [*Navy*] (NVT)
HSCS .... High Speed Communications Subsystem (ACAE)
HSCS .... High-Speed Contact Sense (VLIE)
HSCS .... High-Speed Core Storage (VLIE)
HSCSBW ...... History of Science Series (journ.) (SAUS)
HSCSC .... Hodgkin Self-Concept Scale for Children [*Psychology*] (DHP)
HSCSD .... High-Speed Circuit-Switched Data (VLIE)
HSCT .... High-Speed Civil Transport [*Supersonic plane*]
HSCT .... High Speed Commercial Transport [*MTMC*] (TAG)
HSCT .... High-Speed Compound Terminal [*Computer science*] (MCD)
HSCT .... High-Speed Computer Terminal (SAUS)
HSCT .... Hughes Satellite Communications Terminal
HSCT .... Hypersonic Civil Transport (SAUS)
HSCT .... Hypersonic Commercial Transport [*Airplane*]
HSCTB .... Heavy and Specialized Carriers Tariff Bureau (SAUS)
HSCTT .... High-Speed Card Teletypewriter Terminal [*Computer science*] (CET)
HSCU .... Helicopter Subcontrol Unit (NVT)
HSCU .... Hydraulic Supply and Checkout Unit (NASA)
HS/CV .... Home Shopper/Cable Value [*Cable television channel*]
HSCW .... Helicopter Sea Control Wing (NVT)
HSCX .... Horry County Railroad-South Carolina [*Federal Railroad Administration identification code*]
HSCZ .... Highline Seven Elevator [*Federal Railroad Administration identification code*]
HSD .... Doctor of Health and Safety (PGP)
HSD .... Hamilton Standard Division (NASA)
HSD .... Hard Site Defense (SAUS)
HSD .... Hardsite Defense [*Army*] (AABC)
HSD .... Hard/Soft Display (NITA)
HSD .... Harnosand [*Sweden*] [*Airport symbol*] (AD)
HSD .... Hawker-Siddeley Dynamics
HSD .... Health and Safety Department (SAUO)
HSD .... Health and Safety Directive (SAUS)
HSD .... Health Services Department (SAUS)
HSD .... Heat-Sensing Device (DNAB)
HSD .... Heat-Storage Device (SAUS)
HSD .... Height Sensing Device
HSD .... Hemisphere Development Corp. [*Vancouver Stock Exchange symbol*]
HSD .... Hierarchically Structured Data (SAUS)
HSD .... Hierarchical Structured Data Set (IAA)
HSD .... Higher Anti-Submarine Detector [*British military*] (DMA)
HSD .... Highest Significant Difference (SAUS)
HSD .... High-Speed Data
HSD .... High-Speed Diesel (SAUS)
HSD .... High-Speed Displacement (IEEE)
HSD .... High-Speed Draft [*Print quality*]
HSD .... High-Sulfur Diesel Fuel [*Petroleum marketing*]
HSD .... HIMACS Systems Development (SAUS)
HSD .... Hit Scoring Device
HSD .... Hollow Spherical Dipole (SAUS)
H(SD) .... Holtzman Sprague-Dawley Rat [*Medicine*] (DMAA)
HSD .... Homer Semana Dia (BJA)
HSD .... Home Satellite Dish (NTCM)
HSD .... Homestead Village, Inc. [*AMEX symbol*] (SAG)
HSD .... Honestly Significant Difference
HSD .... Horizontal Situation Display
HSD .... Hot Sensor Download (SAUS)
HSD .... Hot Shut Down (SAUS)
HSD .... Hot Side
HSD .... Hughes Standard Design (ACAE)
HSD .... Human Services Division [*Air Force*]
HSD .... Human Systems Division [*Brooks Air Force Base, TX*] [*United States Air Force Systems Command*] (GRD)
HSD .... Hydraulic Steering and Diving [*System*] (DNAB)
HSD .... Hydropneumatic Suspension Device
HSD .... Hydroxysteroid Dehydrogenase [*An enzyme*]
HSD .... Hypertonic Saline Dextran [*Medicine*]
HSd .... Scleroscope Hardness Number Model d (SAUS)
HSDA .... Heat Strain Decision [*Army*] (RDA)
HSDA .... High-Speed Data Acquisition [*Computer science*]
HSDA .... High-Speed Data Assembly [*Ground Communications Facility, NASA*]
HSDA .... Homomorphic Statistical Deconvolution Algorithm (SAUS)
HS-DARS ..... High-Speed Data Acquisition and Reduction System
HS-DARS ..... High-Speed-Data Acquisition and Reduction System (SAUS)
HSDAS .... High-Speed Data Acquisition System (VLIE)
HSDB .... Debba [*Sudan*] [*ICAO location identifier*] (ICLI)
HSDB .... Hastings' Shorter Dictionary of the Bible [*A publication*] (BJA)
HSDB .... Hazardous Substance Data Base (SAUO)
HSDB .... Hazardous Substances Data Bank [*National Library of Medicine*] [*Information service or system*] (IID)
HSDB .... High-Speed Data Buffer
HSDB .... High Speed Data Bus [*Computer science*] (DOMA)
HSDC .... Hawaii State Data Center [*Hawaii State Department of Planning and Economic Development*] [*Information service or system*] (IID)
HSDC .... Health Systems Design [*NASDAQ symbol*] (TTSB)
HSDC .... Health Systems Design Corp. [*NASDAQ symbol*] (SAG)
HSDC .... High-Speed Data Card (VLIE)
HSDC .... High-Speed Data Channel (IAA)
HSDC .... Hybrid Synchro-to-Digital Converter (SAUS)
HSDCA .... High-Speed Data Channel Adapter (VLIE)
HSDD .... Half Second Delay Detonator (SAUS)
HSDE .... Hawker Siddeley Dynamics Engineering Ltd. (SAUO)
HSDE .... High School Driver Education [*Department of Transportation*]
HSDF .... High-Speed Digital Filter
HSDG .... Hamburg-Sudamerikanische Dampschiffarts-Gesellschaft [*Hamburg-South American Steamship Co.*] [*Shipping*] (ROG)
HSDG .... High School Diploma Graduate [*Military*]
HSDH .... Homoserine Dehydrogenase (SAUS)
HSDH .... Hydroxysteroid Dehydrogenase
HSDI .... Health Self Determination Index (MEDA)
HSDI .... High-Speed Data Interface
HSDI .... High-Speed Digital Interface (SAUS)
HSDI .... High-Speed Direct Injection [*Diesel engines*]
HSDI .... Hughes Space Defense, Incorporated (ACAE)
HS Dir .... Director of Health and Safety (PGP)
HSDL .... Dilling [*Sudan*] [*ICAO location identifier*] (ICLI)
HSDL .... Hierarchical Scan Description Language [*Computer science*] (TIMI)
HSDL .... High-bit-rate Digital Subscriber Line (SAUS)
HSDL .... High-Speed Data Line [*or Link*]
HSDL .... High Speed Data Link (SAUO)
HSDL .... High-Speed Data Link (SAUS)
HSDL .... High-Speed Digital Line (SAUS)
HSDL .... High-Speed Digital Subscriber Line [*Telecommunications*] (ITD)
HSDLA .... Home School Legal Defense Association (PAZ)
HSDM .... Harvard School of Dental Medicine (SAUO)
HSDM .... Hemisphere Development Corp. (SAUO)
HSDM .... High-Speed Die Mounter
HSDMF .... Hemisphere Development Ltd. [*NASDAQ symbol*] (COMM)
HSDMS .... Highly Secure Database Management System [*Computer science*] (MHDI)
HSDN .... Dongola [*Sudan*] [*ICAO location identifier*] (ICLI)
HSD Oil .... High-Speed Diesel Oil (SAUS)
HSDP .... Hanford site Development Plan (SAUS)
HSDP .... Hardsite Data Processor [*Army*] (AABC)
HSDP .... High-Speed Data Processor (SAUS)
HSDP .... High-Speed Digital Processor (SAUS)
HSDP .... High-Speed Display Processor [*Computer science*] (TIMI)
HSDP .... Hungarian Social Democratic Party [*Political party*] (EY)
HSDR .... High-Speed Data Regeneration (SAUS)
HSDR .... High-Speed Digital Recording (SAUS)
HSDRA .... High-Speed Data Regeneration Assembly (SAUS)
HSDRS .... High-Speed Digital Recording System (SAUS)
HSDS .... Hellfire Shore Defence System (SAUS)
HSDS .... High-Speed Drum System (SAUS)
HSDS .... Horizontal Situation Display System
HSDS .... Hot Spot Detection System (SAUS)
HSD Set .... Hierarchically Structured Data Set (SAUS)
HSD-SMS .... Movement for Autonomous Democracy of Moravia and Silesia (Czech Rep.) [*Political party*] (PSAP)
HSDT .... High-Speed Data Transmission (SAUS)
HSDT .... High-Speed Data Transport (SAUS)
HSDT .... High-Speed Diesel Train (SAUS)
HSDT .... High-Speed Distributor Transmitter
HSDT .... Hopper Side Tanks [*on a ship*] (DS)
HSDT .... Hypersonic Small Disturbance Theory (SAUS)
HSDU .... Hospital Sterilization and Disinfection Unit (SAUS)
HSDZ .... Damazin [*Sudan*] [*ICAO location identifier*] (ICLI)
HSE .... Compania Helicopteros del Sureste SA [*Spain*] [*ICAO designator*] (FAAC)
HsE .... Hawker-Siddeley Electronics Ltd., Microform Division, Fairfield, V, Australia [*Library symbol*] [*Library of Congress*] (LCLS)
HSE .... Headquarters Support Element (SAUO)
HSE .... Health and Safety Executive [*Department of Employment*] [*Sheffield, England*]
HSE .... Health & Safety in Employment (SAUO)
HSE .... Health Safety and Environmental (SAUO)
HSE .... Heat Shield Entry [*Aerospace*] (IAA)
HSE .... Heat-Shock Element [*Genetics*]
HSE .... Heat-Stable Esterase (PDAA)
HSE .... Helsinki Stock Exchange [*Finland*]
HSE .... Hemorrhagic Shock and Encephalopathy [*Medicine*] (DMAA)
HSE .... Herpes Simplex Encephalitis [*Medicine*]
HSE .... Hic Sepultus Est [*Here Lies Buried*] [*Latin*]
HSE .... Highly Siderophile Element [*Biology*]
HSE .... High School Equivalency (OICC)

HSE............. High-Speed Encoder (IAA)
HSE............. High-Speed Enrichment [*Automotive fuel systems*]
HSE............. High-Speed Exchange (VLIE)
HSE............. High-Speed Signal Control Equipment [*Data communication*] (MHDI)
HSE............. Hinton School of English (SAUO)
HSE............. Historically Socialist Economy (ECON)
HSE............. Hitachi Software Engineering (SAUS)
HSE............. Hole Storage Effect (SAUS)
HSE............. Home Sports Entertainment [*Cable-television system*]
HSE............. Honolulu Stock Exchange [*Hawaii*]
Hse............. House
HSE............. HS Resources, Inc. [*NYSE symbol*] (SAG)
HSE............. Hungarian Studies in English (journ.) (SAUS)
HSE............. Hydrostatic Equilibrium (SAUS)
HSE............. Hydrostatic Extrusion (SAUS)
HSEAD......... Historical Society of Early American Decoration [*Defunct*] (EA)
HSEB........... Haryana State Electricity Board (SAUO)
Hse Builder... House Builder (journ.) (SAUS)
HSEC........... Historical Society of the Episcopal Church (EA)
HSECC......... Hanford Site Entry Control Center (SAUS)
HSED........... Hazardous Site Evaluation Division [*Office of Solid Waste and Emergency Response*] (COE)
HSEF........... High School Evangelism Fellowship (EA)
HseFbr......... House of Fabrics, Inc. [*Associated Press*] (SAG)
HseFbrc....... House of Fabrics, Inc. [*Associated Press*] (SAG)
HSEHLD....... Household
HSEHOLD.... Household
HSEKPR....... Housekeeper (ROG)
HSEL........... High-Speed Selector Channel
HSELAN....... High-Speed ELAN (SAUS)
HSELINE...... Health and Safety Executive Online [*Health and Safety Executive*] [*Bibliographic database*] [*British*]
HSELL.......... Hiroshima Studies in English Language and Literature (journ.) (SAUS)
HSEN........... Home Sports Entertainment Network [*Cable TV programming service*]
Hse of Lords Select Commit Eur Commun Rep... House of Lords. Select Committee on the European Communities. Report (journ.) (SAUS)
HSEP........... Heart Synchronized Evoked Potential [*Medicine*] (DMAA)
HSEP........... High-Speed Electrostatic Printer
HSEP........... Hospital Surgical Expansion Package [*Air Force*] (DOMA)
HSERC......... Historical Society of the Evangelical and Reformed Church [*Later, ERHS-UCC*] (EA)
H/serf.......... High-Scope Educational Research Foundation (EA)
HSERF......... High-Score Educational Research Foundation (SAUO)
HSES........... Hanford Science and Engineering Supercomputer (SAUS)
HSES........... Hanford Scientific and Engineering System (SAUS)
HSES........... Helper Self-Exploration Scale [*Psychology*] (DHP)
HSES........... Hemorrhagic Shock-Encephalopathy Syndrome [*Medicine*] (DMAA)
HSES........... Hughes Satellite Earth Station
HSES........... Hydrostatic Equilibrium System [*For chromatography*]
HSE Syndrome... Hemorrhagic Shock and Encephalopathy Syndrome (SAUS)
HSET........... Hino Super Flow Turbine [*Diesel engine*]
HSETC......... Health Sciences Education and Training Command [*Navy*] (DNAB)
HSEUBC....... Historical Society of the Evangelical United Brethren Church [*Later, General Commission on Archives and History of the United Methodist Church*] (EA)
HSEZ........... Harvest State Elevator [*Federal Railroad Administration identification code*]
HSF............. Harness and Saddling Factory (SAUO)
HSF............. Hartford Seminary Foundation [*Connecticut*]
HSF............. Hawaiian Sea Frontier
HSF............. Health, Safety and Fire (SAUS)
HSF............. Heart and Stroke Foundation of Canada (SAUO)
HSF............. Heart Surgery Forum (SAUO)
HSF............. Heat-Shock Transcription Factor [*Genetics*]
HSF............. Heat-Stable Fraction
HSF............. Heat Stimulated Flow (PDAA)
HSF............. Hepatocyte Stimulating Factor [*Endocrinology*]
HSF............. High Seas Fleet [*British military*] (DMA)
HSF............. High-Speed Feed (SAUS)
HSF............. High-Speed Flight (SAUS)
HSF............. High-Speed Flow (SAUS)
HSF............. High-Starch Fraction [*Food technology*]
HSF............. Histamine-Induced Suppressor Factor [*Immunology*]
HSF............. Histamine-Sensitizing Factor [*Immunology*]
HSF............. Home Service Force [*British*] (BARN)
HSF............. Hospital Saturday Fund (SAUO)
HSF............. Hotel Sundry Fund [*Air Force*]
HSF............. Household Sample File (SAUS)
HSF............. Human Services Forum [*Defunct*] (EA)
HSF............. Hybrid Simulation Facility (SAUS)
HSF............. Hyderabad State Force [*British military*] (DMA)
HSF............. Hypathalamic Secretory Factor (SAUS)
HSF............. Hypergol Servicing Facility [*NASA*] (NASA)
HSF............. Hypersonic Flow
HSF............. Hypothalamic Secretory Factor [*Endocrinology*]
HSF/ACTH.... Hypothalamic Secretory Factor / Adreno-Corticotropic Hormone (SAUS)
HSF-ACTH.... Hypothalmic Secretory Factor for Adreno-Corticotropic Hormone (PDAA)
HSFAE......... High-Speed Fuel Air Explosive
HSFB........... High Speed Fleet Broadcast (DOMA)
HSFC........... Hank Snow Fan Club [*Defunct*] (EA)
HSFC........... Heart and Stroke Foundation of Canada (NRGU)
HSFD........... Hanford Site Forms Database (SAUS)
HSFD........... Hanford Surplus Facilities Decommissioning (SAUS)
HSFF........... High-Speed Force Feed
HSFG........... High Strength Friction Grip (PDAA)
HSFI............ Hanford Strategic Facilities Initiative (SAUS)
HSFI............ High School of Fashion Industries (SAUO)
HSFMC........ Huguenot Society of the Founders of Manakin in the Colony of Virginia (SAUO)
HSFMCV...... Huguenot Society of the Founders of Manakin in the Colony of Virginia (EA)
HSFO........... High Sulphur Fuel Oil
HSFOVR...... Hemispherical Field of View (SAUS)
HSFP........... Hanford Surplus Facilities Program (SAUS)
HSFP........... Hanford Surplus Facility Program (SAUS)
HSFPJ......... Holocaust Survivors and Friends in Pursuit of Justice (EA)
HSFS........... El Fasher [*Sudan*] [*ICAO location identifier*] (ICLI)
HSFS........... High Sierra File System (SAUS)
HSFS........... High-Speed Flight Station [*NASA*]
HSFS........... Hydrostatic Equilibrium System (SAUS)
HSFV........... High Speed Freight Vehicle (PDAA)
HSG............. Harris Steel Group, Inc. [*Toronto Stock Exchange symbol*]
HSG............. Hawker Siddeley Group Ltd. (SAUO)
HSG............. Headquarters, Support Group [*Military*]
HSG............. Health and Safety Guide [*Toxicology*]
HSG............. Herpes Simplex Genitalis
HSG............. High School for Girls (ADA)
HSG............. High School Graduate [*Classified advertising*]
HSG............. High Sierra Group [*Nevada-based group proposing CD-ROM standards*]
HSG............. High Speed Gas (SAUO)
HSG............. High Speed Generation [*Hybrid vehicles*] [*Automotive engineering*]
HSG............. High-Speed Grinding (PDAA)
HSG............. High Sustained G2 Acceleration [*NASA*] (NASA)
HSG............. Historical Society of Ghana (SAUO)
HSG............. Holy Shroud Guild (EA)
HSG............. Home-Station Gunnery [*Military*] (INF)
HSG............. Horizontal Sweep Generator [*Telecommunications*] (OA)
HSG............. Housing (AABC)
HSG............. Human Standard Globulin [*Medicine*]
HSG............. Hydrocephalus Support Group, Inc. (NRGU)
HSG............. Hydro-Shift Gun (SAUS)
HSG............. Hysterectomy Support Group [*British*] (DBA)
HSG............. Hysterosalpingogram [*Gynecology*]
HSG............. Hysterosalpingography [*Medicine*] (DMAA)
HSG............. Hysterosalpinogram (SAUS)
HSGB........... Haflinger Society [*British*] (DBA)
HSGB........... Hysterosalpingography [*Gynecology*] (DAVI)
HSGBI......... Huguenot Society of Great Britain and Ireland (EAIO)
HS-GC......... Headspace Sampling-Gas Chromatography
HS-GC......... Heads Sampling-Gas Chromatography (SAUS)
HSGF........... Gedaref/Azaza [*Sudan*] [*ICAO location identifier*] (ICLI)
HSGF........... Hematopoietic Stem-Cell Growth Factor (DB)
hSGF........... Human Skeletal Growth Factor [*Medicine*] (EDAA)
HSGF........... Human Skeletal Growth Factor
HSGG........... Dinder/Galegu [*Sudan*] [*ICAO location identifier*] (ICLI)
HSGM.......... Hierarchical Symbolic Grouping for Multi-Spectral Data (SAUO)
HSGM.......... Honorary Sergeant Major of the Regiment
HSGMOC..... Honorary Sergeant Major of the Corps [*Marine Corps*]
HSGMOR..... Honorary Sergeant Major of the Regiment [*Army*]
HSGN........... Geneina [*Sudan*] [*ICAO location identifier*] (ICLI)
HSGO........... Gogerial [*Sudan*] [*ICAO location identifier*] (ICLI)
HSGP........... High School Geography Project [*Defunct*]
HSGP........... Human Sialoglycoprotein [*Biochemistry*] (DB)
HSGPA......... High School Grade Point Average (DHP)
HSGPC......... High-Speed Gel Permeation Chromatography
HSGR........... High-Speed General Register (SAUS)
HSGR........... High-Speed Ground Transported Reactor (SAUS)
HSGREFSVCSYS... Housing Referral Service Record System [*Military*] (DNAB)
HSGT........... High School Graduation Test (SAUO)
HSGT........... High Speed Ground Transit (ADWA)
HSGT........... High-Speed Ground Transportation
HSGT........... High-Speed Ground Transporter (SAUS)
HSGT........... Hitachi Software Global Technology, Ltd. (SAUO)
HSGTC......... High-Speed Ground Test Center [*Later, TTC*] [*Pueblo, CO*]
HSGTJ......... High-Speed Ground Transportation Journal (journ.) (SAUS)
HSGT System... High-Speed Ground Transportation System (SAUS)
HSGZ........... Harvest States Grain [*Federal Railroad Administration identification code*]
HSGZA4....... Hokkaido Journal of Orthopedic and Traumatic Surgery (journ.) (SAUS)
HSH............. Handmaids of the Sacred Heart of Pohang (TOCD)
HSH............. Hanford Services Handbook (SAUS)
HSH............. Hebrew School Headache (BJA)
HSH............. Heinemann's Scientific Handbooks [*A publication*]
HSH............. Helix-Span-Helix [*Protein structure*]
HSH............. His [*or Her*] Serene Highness [*Used for certain Continental European princes or princesses*]
HSH............. Horseshoe (ROG)
HSH............. Hydrogenated Starch Hydrolysates [*Medicine*] (MELL)
HSHC........... Hemisuccinate of Hydrocortisone (STED)
HSHH........... Hill Staffers for the Hungry and Homeless (EA)
HSHKA......... Bulletin. Korean Fisheries Society (journ.) (SAUS)
H/SHLD........ Heat Shield [*Automotive engineering*]
HSHLD......... Household (MSA)

Hshld .... Household Bank (SAUS)
HS/HM .... High-Strength/High-Modulus (SAUS)
HSHP .... High School for Health Professions
HSHRSSS .... High-Speed/High-Resolution Side Scan Sonar System [*National Oceanic and Atmospheric Administration*]
HS/HT .... Harmonised System/Harmonised Tariff [*British*] (WDAA)
HSHTDS .... Handbook of Shock Trauma (journ.) (SAUS)
HSI .... Habitat Suitability Index (SAUS)
HSI .... Handbook of Service Instructions (MCD)
HSI .... Hang Seng Index [*Hong Kong Futures Exchange Index*]
HSI .... Hardware Software Integration (ACAE)
HSI .... Hardware/Software Interface (IAA)
HSI .... Harpoon Standard Initiator (MCD)
HSI .... Hastings [*Nebraska*] [*Airport symbol*] (OAG)
HSI .... Hayes Synchronous Interface (SAUS)
HSI .... Heading Select Indicator (ACAE)
HSI .... Headquarters Staff Instruction
HSI .... Headquarters Staff Instructor (AAGC)
HSI .... Health Development Services, Inc. [*Toronto Stock Exchange symbol*]
HSI .... Health Services (SAUS)
HSI .... Health Services Incorporated (SAUO)
HSI .... Health Services International (SAUO)
HSI .... Heat Stress Index
HSI .... Heaviest Single Item (SAUS)
HSI .... Heraldry Society of Ireland (EA)
HSI .... Herpes Simplex I [*Titer and virus*] [*Medicine*] (DAVI)
HSI .... HERTIS [*Hertfordshire Technical Library and Information Service*] Subj ect Index (NITA)
HSI .... High School Equivalency Index
HSI .... High Solar Intensity
HSI .... High Speed Impact (SAA)
HSI .... High-Speed Interface (SAUS)
HSI .... High-Speed Interferometer [*Measures chemical components of smog*] (KSC)
HSI .... High Strand Intensity
HSI .... Hi-Shear Industries, Inc. [*NYSE symbol*] (SPSG)
HSI .... Hispanic Serving Institution
HSI .... Historical Society of Israel (SAUO)
HSI .... Home and School Institute (EA)
HSI .... Home Security Intl. [*AMEX symbol*] (SG)
HSI .... Horizontal Situation Indicator [*Aviation*]
HSI .... Host Speed Interface (SAUS)
HSI .... Hot Section Inspection [*Aviation*] (PIPO)
HSI .... Hoya Society International (EA)
HSI .... Hsinkong [*Republic of China*] [*Also, SGK*] [*Seismograph station code, US Geological Survey*] (SEIS)
HSI .... Hue-Saturation-Intensity [*Video monitor*] (BYTE)
HSI .... Humane Society International (SAUO)
HSI .... Humanist Science Incorporated (SAUO)
HSI .... Human Seminal Plasma Inhibitor [*Medicine*] (DMAA)
HSI .... Human Suffering Index (SAUS)
HSI .... Human-System Interaction (SAUS)
HSI .... Human-System Interface (SAUS)
HSI .... Human Systems Integration
HSI .... Hungarian Scientific Instruments (journ.) (SAUS)
HSIA .... Halogenated Solvents Industry Alliance (EA)
HSIC .... Henry Schein, Inc. [*NASDAQ symbol*] (SAG)
HSIC .... High-Speed Integrated Circuit (SAUS)
HSIC .... High-Speed Interface Controller (SAUS)
HSIC .... Schein [*Henry*], Inc. [*NASDAQ symbol*] (SAG)
HSI/CDI .... Horizontal Situation Indicator / Course Deviation Indicator [*Aviation*] (PDAA)
HSI-CDI .... Horizontal Situation Indicator-Course Deviation Indicator (SAUS)
HSICNI .... Honourable Society of the Inns of Court of Northern Ireland
HSIF .... Hardware/Software Integration Facility (SSD)
HSI Hung Sci Instrum ... HSI. Hungarian Scientific Instruments (journ.) (SAUS)
HSII .... Heidrick & Struggles International, Inc. [*NASDAQ symbol*] (NASQ)
HSIIL .... High-Speed Integrated Injection Logic (IAA)
HSIK .... How Should I Know (ADWA)
HSIL .... High-Grade Squamous Intraepithelial Lesions [*OCLC symbol*]
HSIM .... High-Speed Interface Message (SAUS)
HSIM .... High Speed Interface Module (SAUS)
HSIM .... Hill Samuel Investment Management [*British*]
HSIMI .... Hill Samuel Investment Management International Ltd. (SAUO)
HSIMP .... High-Speed Interface Message Processor (IAA)
HSIN .... Health Sciences Information Network (SAUS)
HSINFET .... Hybrid Schottky Injection Field-Effect Transistor (SAUS)
Hsinhua .... New China News Agency (SAUO)
HSIP .... Hsinchu Science-Based Industrial Park [*Taiwan*] (ECON)
HSIQ .... High School Interest Questionnaire [*Vocational guidance test*]
H/SIR .... Hardware/Software Integration Review (MCD)
HSIR .... High-Speed Information Retrieval (SAUS)
HSIRMC .... Hazardous Substance Incident Response Management Course [*Navy*]
HSIRS .... Health and Safety Inspection Report System (SAUO)
HSIS .... Health Sciences Information Service (SAUS)
HSIS .... High Speed Interface/SNA (SAUS)
HSIS .... Highway Safety Information Service [*National Highway Safety Administration*] (IID)
HSIS .... Highway Safety Information System (SAUS)
HSIS .... Human Services Information System (SAUO)
HSIS .... Human Settlements Infornmation System (SAUS)
HSIT .... Hypersonic Strong Interaction Theory (SAUS)
HSIU .... Haile Selassie I University Library (SAUO)
HSIX .... Housing Starts [*Private rail car owner code*]
HSIZ .... Holly Sugar Industries [*Federal Railroad Administration identification code*]
HSJ .... Health Service Journal (SAUO)
HSJ .... Heat Shield Jettison [*Aerospace*] (IAA)
HSJ .... Homologous Serum Jaundice [*Medicine*] (EDAA)
HSJ .... Honeycombed Sandwich Joint
HSJ .... Hoshina [*Japan*] [*Seismograph station code, US Geological Survey*] (SEIS)
HS/JR .... High School/Junior College (SAUO)
HSJUMC .... Historical Society of the United Methodist Church (SAUO)
HSK .... Hackensack, MN [*Location identifier*] [*FAA*] (FAAL)
HSK .... Heat Sink Kit
HSK .... Herpes Simplex Keratitis [*Medicine*] (DMAA)
HSK .... Herpes Stromal Keratitis [*Medicine*]
HSK .... Homoserine Kinase (SAUS)
HSK .... Honeysuckle Creek Tracking Station [*NASA*] (KSC)
HSK .... Honorary Surgeon of the King [*British*]
HSK .... Horizontal Sling Kit [*NASA*] (NASA)
HSK .... Horseshoe Kidney [*Medicine*] (MELL)
HSK .... Hsinking [*Sirkyo, Chang Chun*] [*Republic of China*] [*Seismograph station code, US Geological Survey*] (SEIS)
HSK .... HSK Minerals Ltd. [*Toronto Stock Exchange symbol*]
HSKA .... Heska Corp. [*NASDAQ symbol*] (NASQ)
HSKA .... Kassala [*Sudan*] [*ICAO location identifier*] (ICLI)
HSKG .... Khashm El Girba [*Sudan*] [*ICAO location identifier*] (ICLI)
HSKI .... Kosti/Rabak [*Sudan*] [*ICAO location identifier*] (ICLI)
HSKJ .... Kago Kaju [*Sudan*] [*ICAO location identifier*] (ICLI)
HSKL .... Haskel International, Inc. [*NASDAQ symbol*] (SAG)
HSKL .... Haskel Intl 'A' [*NASDAQ symbol*] (TTSB)
HSKP .... Kapoeta [*Sudan*] [*ICAO location identifier*] (ICLI)
HSKPG .... Housekeeping (AFM)
hskpr .... Housekeeper (BARN)
HSL .... Hardware Simulation Laboratory (NASA)
HSL .... Harlequin Screening Library (SAUS)
HSL .... Hartford Studies in Literature (journ.) (SAUS)
HSL .... Hawaii State Library (SAUO)
HSL .... Hazardous Substance List [*Code of Federal Regulations*] (FFDE)
HSL .... Health and Safety Laboratory
HSL .... Health Sciences Library (SAUS)
HSL .... Health Service Laboratory [*Army*] (AABC)
HSL .... Heat-Stabilized Lubricated [*Plastics*]
HSL .... Heenan Senlac Resources Ltd. [*Toronto Stock Exchange symbol*]
HSL .... Helicopter Antisubmarine Squadron Light (NVT)
HSL .... Herpes Simplex Labialis
HSL .... High-Speed Launch [*Navy*]
HSL .... High-Speed Line (SAUS)
HSL .... High-Speed Logic
HSL .... Highway Safety Literature [*Database*] (NITA)
HSL .... Highway Safety Literature Service [*National Academy of Science*] [*Washington, DC*]
HSL .... Hispania Lineas Aereas SL [*Spain*] [*ICAO designator*] (FAAC)
HSL .... History of Science Library (SAUO)
HSL .... Home-School Liaison (AIE)
Hsl .... Homoserine Lactone [*An amino acid*]
HSL .... Hormone-Sensitive Lipase [*An enzyme*]
HSL .... Hue, Saturation, Lightness [*Color model*] (PCM)
HSL .... Hue Saturation Luminance Monitor (SAUS)
HSL .... Huslia [*Alaska*] [*Airport symbol*] (OAG)
HSL .... Hypertonic Saline (SAUS)
HSL .... Hytran Simulation Language [*Computer science*] (PDAA)
HSLA .... High Speed Line Adaptor (NITA)
HSLA .... High-Strength Light-Alloy (SAUS)
HSLA .... High-Strength Low-Alloy [*or Light-Alloy*] [*Steel*]
HSLA .... Home and School Library Association (SAUO)
HS Lab .... Health Service Laboratory (SAUO)
HSLAN .... High Speed Local Area Network [*Telecommunications*] (ACRL)
HSLA Steel ... High-Strength Low-Alloy Steel (SAUS)
HSLC .... Health Sciences Libraries Consortium (ADWA)
HSLC .... High-Speed Line Card (SAUS)
HSLC .... High-Speed Liquid Chromatography
HSLC .... High-Speed Single Line Controller (MHDB)
HSLC .... Historic Society of Lancashire and Cheshire (SAUO)
HSLCG .... Health Science Libraries of Central Georgia [*Library network*]
HSLCM .... High Speed Line Control Module (SAUO)
HSLCM .... High-Speed Line Control Module (SAUS)
HSLDA .... Home School Legal Defense Association (EA)
HSLI .... Health Sciences Librarians of Illinois (SAUO)
HSLI .... Kadugli [*Sudan*] [*ICAO location identifier*] (ICLI)
HSLIC .... Health Science Libraries Information Cooperative [*Library network*]
HSLKFIN .... High Silky Finish (SAUS)
HSLLADS .... High-Speed Low-Level Aerial Delivery System (SAUS)
HSLLADS .... High-Speed, Low-Level Airdrop System [*Military*] (INF)
HSLLC .... High-Speed Liquid-Liquid Chromatography
HSLM .... Health Sciences Libraries of Minnesota (SAUO)
HSLM .... High-Speed Line Manager (SAUS)
HSLMIP .... Health Sciences Library Management Internal Program (SAUS)
HSLN .... High-Speed Local Network [*Telecommunications*] (OSI)
HSLP .... Haydn Society [*Record label*]
HSLP .... High-Speed Line Printer (SAUS)
HSLR .... Lirangu [*Sudan*] [*ICAO location identifier*] (ICLI)
HSLS .... Croatian Social Liberal Party [*Political party*] (PSAP)
HSL'S .... Hlinkova Slovenska l'Udova Strana [*Hlinka's Slovak People's Party*] [*Also, SL'S*] [*Political party*] (PPE)
HSLSS .... Health Service Logistics Support System (SAUS)
HSLW .... Helical Spring Lock Washer (SAUS)

HSLWI .... Helical Spring Lock Washer Institute
HSM .... Hand and Shoe Monitor [*Radiation detection*]
HSM .... Handbook of Soil Mechanics (journ.) (SAUS)
HSM .... Handing and Shipping Management (journ.) (SAUS)
HSM .... Hardened Silo Missile
HSM .... Hard Structure Module
HSM .... Hard Structure Munition
HSM .... Hardware-Specific Module (SAUS)
HSM .... Harmonic Subcarrier Method (MCD)
HSM .... Hart, Schaffner & Marx (SAUO)
HSM .... Harvard Semitic Museum (BJA)
HSM .... Health Services and Mental Health Administration [*Later, ADAMHA*] [*Abolished, 1973*] [*HEW*]
HSM .... Hepatosplenomegaly [*Gastroenterology*] (DAVI)
HSM .... Hermit Sisters of Mary (TOCD)
HSM .... Herschel Stirring Method [*Lubricants*]
HSM .... Heterosexual Male (MELL)
HSM .... Hierarchical Storage Management [*Computer science*]
HSM .... Hierarchic Sequential Access Method [*Computer science*] (ITCA)
HSM .... High-Speed Machining (MCD)
HSM .... High-Speed Measurement (IAA)
HSM .... High-Speed Mechanics (SAUS)
HSM .... High-Speed Memory [*Computer science*]
HSM .... High-Speed Modular (SAUS)
HSM .... High-Speed Motor [*Electrical engineering*]
HSM .... High-Speed Multiplication (SAUS)
HSM .... His [*or Her*] Serene Majesty
HSM .... Historical Society of Montana (SAUO)
HSM .... Hollow-Spindle hydraulic Motor (SAUS)
HSM .... Holosystolic Murmur [*Cardiology*] (DAVI)
HSM .... Horsham Corp. [*Toronto Stock Exchange symbol*] [*NYSE symbol*]
HSM .... HOSC Shuttle Manager (SAUS)
HSM .... Hospital - Surgical - Medical
HSM .... Host Security Module (SAUS)
HSM .... Host Switching Module [*Communications term*] (DCT)
HSM .... Humanitarian Service Medal (MCD)
HSM .... Human Systems Management (journ.) (SAUS)
HSM .... Hussmann Intl. [*NYSE symbol*] (SG)
HSM .... Hydraulic System Module (MCD)
HSM .... Hydro-Shock Munition (SAUS)
HSMA .... Hotel Sales Management Association [*Later, HSMAI*] (EA)
HSMAI .... Hospitality Sales and Marketing Association International (NTPA)
HSMAI .... Hotel Sales and Marketing Association International (EA)
HSMAI-EO .... Hotel Sales and Marketing Association International - European Office [*Utrecht, Netherlands*] (EAIO)
HSMB .... High-Speed Memory Block (SAUS)
HSMB .... Hybrid Superconducting Magnetic Bearing
HSMB .... Hydronautics Ship Model Basin (SAUS)
HSMC .... Health Services Management Centre (SAUO)
HSMCDR .... High-Speed Multichannel Data Recorder [*Instrumentation*]
HSMD .... High Speed Mobile Data (SAUS)
HSMD .... Maridi [*Sudan*] [*ICAO location identifier*] (ICLI)
HSMET .... Health Systems and Medical [*Medicine*] (EDAA)
HSMF .... Holocaust Survivors Memorial Foundation (EA)
HSMGC .... Heavy Section Machine Gun Corps [*British military*] (DMA)
HSMHA .... Health Services and Mental Health Administration [*Later, ADAMHA*] [*Abolished, 1973*] [*HEW*]
HSMI .... Health Services Management Inspection (ACAE)
HSMIMP .... High-Speed Modular Interface Message Processor
HSMK .... Rumbek [*Sudan*] [*ICAO location identifier*] (ICLI)
HSML .... High-Speed Modular Logic (SAUS)
HSMO .... High-Speed Membrane Osmometry (MCD)
HSMO .... Hospital Senior Medical Officer [*Australia*]
HSMO .... Hydraulic System Mineral Oil [*Mechanical engineering*]
HSMPE .... Harmonic Structure Matching Pitch Estimation (SAUS)
HSMPE8 .... Herbs, Spices and Medicinal Plants (journ.) (SAUS)
HSMR .... Merowe [*Sudan*] [*ICAO location identifier*] (ICLI)
HSMS .... Hazardous Substance Management System (BCP)
HSMS .... High Speed Message Services (AAEL)
HSMS .... High-Speed Microwave Switch
HSMSR .... Hardsite Missile Site RADAR [*Army*] (AABC)
HSM Station ... High-Speed Measurement Station (SAUS)
HSMT .... Helical Scan Magnetic Tape (SAUS)
HSM-WA .... Hard Structure Munition Weaponization Analysis (MCD)
HSMX .... Hessen Steam Museum [*Federal Railroad Administration identification code*]
HSN .... Haglund Industry International [*Vancouver Stock Exchange symbol*]
HSN .... Hanson-Street Nail (MEDA)
HSN .... Hawthorne Society. Newsletter (journ.) (SAUS)
HSN .... Heart Sounds Normal [*Medicine*] (MELL)
HSN .... HEIS Sample Number (SAUS)
HSN .... Hereditary Sensory Neuropathies (SAUS)
HSN .... Hereditary Sensory Neuropathy [*Neurology*]
HSN .... Hermaphrodite-Specific Neuron [*Cytology*]
HSN .... Herpes Simplex Neonatorum (STED)
HSN .... Highly Saturated Nitrile Rubber (SAUS)
HSN .... High Speed Network
HSN .... Home Shopping Network, Inc. [*NYSE symbol*] (SPSG)
HSN .... Hospital Satellite Network [*Los Angeles, CA*] [*Cable-television system*]
HSN .... Hsinchu [*Republic of China*] [*Seismograph station code, US Geological Survey*] (SEIS)
HSN .... Hughes Sports Network [*Formerly, SNI*]
HSN .... Southern Air Ltd. [*British*] [*ICAO designator*] (FAAC)
HSNA .... Hsinhua News Agency (SAUO)
HSNA .... Nasir [*Sudan*] [*ICAO location identifier*] (ICLI)
HSNBG .... Harrisonburg, VA [*American Association of Railroads railroad junction routing code*]
HSND .... Shendi [*Sudan*] [*ICAO location identifier*] (ICLI)
HSNG .... Housing
HSNH .... Nahud [*Sudan*] [*ICAO location identifier*] (ICLI)
H/SNK .... Heat Sink [*Automotive engineering*]
HSNL .... HEIS Sample Number Library (SAUS)
HSNL .... Nyala [*Sudan*] [*ICAO location identifier*] (ICLI)
HSNM .... Nimule/Nimule [*Sudan*] [*ICAO location identifier*] (ICLI)
HSNP .... Hawker-Siddeley Nuclear Power Co. Ltd. [*British*]
HSNP .... High-Speed Nonimpact Printer [*Acronym pronounced "hisnip"*] [*Computer science*]
HSNP .... Hot Springs National Park (SAUO)
HSNPC .... Hawker-Siddeley Nuclear Power Company (SAUO)
HSNPL .... Harvard Studies and Notes in Philology and Literature (journ.) (SAUS)
HSNPP .... Hlinka Slovak National People's Party [*Political party*]
HSNR .... Halstead Energy Corp. [*NASDAQ symbol*] (SAG)
HSNR .... Huleh Swamp Nature Reserve (SAUO)
HSNR .... Sennar [*Sudan*] [*ICAO location identifier*] (ICLI)
HSNS .... High School News Service [*Fleet Hometown News Center*] (DNAB)
HSNSW .... Haemophilia Society of New South Wales [*Australia*]
HSNT .... Historical Society of the Northern Territory [*Australia*]
HSNTA .... New Testament Apocrypha [*E. Henneke and W. Schneemelcher*] [*A publication*] (BJA)
HSNW .... New Halfa [*Sudan*] [*ICAO location identifier*] (ICLI)
HSNY .... Handel Society of New York (SAUO)
HSNY .... Holland Society of New York (EA)
HSNY .... Horticultural Society of New York Inc. (SAUO)
HSO .... Compania Helicopteros de Transporte SA [*Spain*] [*ICAO designator*] (FAAC)
HSO .... Habitation/Station Operations (SSD)
HSO .... Haifa Symphony Orchestra (BJA)
HSO .... Hamburg Symphony Orchestra (SAUO)
HSO .... Headquarters Signal Officer (NATG)
HSO .... Head Selection Operation (SAUS)
HSO .... Health & Safety Officer (SARE)
HSO .... Health Services Officer (SAUS)
HSO .... Hershey Oil Corp. (SAUO)
HSO .... Higher Scientific Officer [*British*]
HSO .... High Specific Outlet (SAUS)
HSO .... High Specific Output [*Automotive engineering*]
HSO .... High-Speed Operation (SAUS)
HSO .... High Speed Optimized [*General Tire Co.*] [*Automobile tires*]
HSO .... High Sulphur Content (SAUS)
HSO .... Human Services Officer (SAUO)
HSO .... Hydrogen Seal Oil [*System*] (NRCH)
HSO .... Hydrogen Sulphate (SAUS)
HSOB .... El Obeid [*Sudan*] [*ICAO location identifier*] (ICLI)
hSOD .... Human Superoxide Dismutase [*Medicine*] (EDAA)
HSOD .... Human Superoxide Dismutase [*An enzyme*]
HSODTN .... High-Speed Optical Data Transfer Network (SAUS)
HSOM .... Habitation/Station Operations Module (SSD)
h som .... Hora Somni [*Hour of Sleep*] [*Latin*] (STED)
H SOM .... Hora Somni [*At Bedtime*] [*Pharmacy*]
HSOR .... Hydroxysteroid Oxidoreductase [*Medicine*] (MELL)
HSORS .... High Seas Oil Recovery System
HSOS .... Helicopter Stabilized Optronic Sight (SAUS)
HSOT .... Howitzer Strap-On Trainer [*Military*] (RDA)
HSP .... Croatian Party of Rights [*Political party*] (PSAP)
HSP .... Half-Shade Plate
HSP .... Hanford Site Practices (SAUS)
HSP .... Hanford Strategic Plan (SAUS)
HSP .... Hardwire Safing Panel
HSP .... Haute Societe Protestante [*Protestant High Society*] (IIA)
HSP .... Head Start Program [*Education*]
HSP .... Health and Safety Plan (BCP)
HSP .... Health and Safety Practices (COE)
HSP .... Health Service Plan
HSP .... Health Stabilization Program [*NASA*] (NASA)
HSP .... Health Systems Plan [*HEW*]
hsp .... Heat Shock Protein [*Gene*] (DMAA)
HSP .... Heat Shock Protein [*Physiology*]
Hsp .... Heat-Shock-Protein (QSUL)
HSP .... Heavy, Stressed Platform
HSP .... Hemostatic Screening Profile [*Medicine*] (DMAA)
HSP .... Henoch-Schoenlein Purpura [*Medicine*] (AAMN)
HSP .... Heparin Sulfate Proteoglycan [*Biochemistry*]
HSP .... Hereditary Spastic Paraplegia [*Medicine*]
HSP .... Highly Sensitive Person
HSP .... High Softening Point (SAUS)
HSP .... High Speed Peering (SAUS)
HSP .... High-Speed Photography (SAUS)
HSP .... High Speed Photometer
HSP .... High-Speed Photometer (SAUS)
HSP .... High-Speed Plating (SAUS)
HSP .... High Speed Printer (SAUO)
HSP .... High-Speed Printer [*Computer science*]
HSP .... High-Speed Printing (SAUS)
HSP .... High-Speed Processor (SAUS)
HSP .... High-Speed Publishing (SAUS)
HSP .... High-Speed Pulse
HSP .... High-Speed Punch (IAA)
HSP .... Hispanic Broadcasting 'A' [*NYSE symbol*]

HSP .... Historical Society of Pennsylvania
HSP .... Historic State Park (SAUS)
HSP .... Hollow Soft Point [*Bullet*] (DICI)
HSP .... Home Services Program [*Australia*]
HSP .... Hospital Corporation of America (SAUO)
HSP .... Hospital Service Plan [*British*]
HSP .... Hospital Surgical Plan (SAUS)
HSP .... Hot Springs, VA [*Location identifier*] [*FAA*] (FAAL)
HSP .... Hot Stamping Press
HSP .... Hrvatska Stranka Prava [*Croatian Party of Rights*] [*Former Yugoslavia*] [*Political party*] (PPE)
HSP .... Hughes Spare Part (ACAE)
HSP .... Human Sciences Program (SAUO)
HSP .... Human Sciences Project [*National Science Foundation*]
HSP .... Human Serum Prealbumin
HSP .... Human Serum Protein (DB)
HSP .... Hungarian Socialist Party [*Political party*] (EY)
HSP .... Hydrocarbon Solids Process [*Tosco Corp.*] [*Oil shale pyrolysis*]
HSP .... Hysterosalpingography (STED)
HSPA .... Hanford Site Performance Assessment (SAUS)
HSPA .... Hawaiian Sugar Planters' Association (EA)
HSPA .... High School of the Performing Arts (SAUS)
HSPA .... High School Proficiency Assessment
HSPA .... High-Speed Parallel Adder
HSPA .... Home Savings Association of Pennsylvania (SAUO)
HSPA .... Human Service Personnel Association [*Defunct*] (EA)
HSPA .... Pachella [*Sudan*] [*ICAO location identifier*] (ICLI)
HSPC .... Hanford Strategic Planning Council (SAUO)
HSPC .... Health and Science Policy Committee (ADWA)
HSPC .... Heat Sterilizable Potting Compound
HSPC .... High-Speed Printer Control (SAUS)
HSPC .... Hospice
HSPDEXCH... High-Speed Exchange (SAUS)
HSPDP .... Hill State People's Democratic Party [*India*] [*Political party*] (PPW)
HSPE .... High Strength Polyethylene [*Organic chemistry*]
HSPEX .... SMBS Special Equities Cl.B [*Mutual fund ticker symbol*] (SG)
HSPF .... Heating Seasonal Performance Factor
HSPF .... Hydrological Simulation Program [*Environment term*] (EGA)
HSPF .... Hydrological Simulation Program FORTRAN (SAUS)
HSPF .... Hydrologic Simulation Program Fortran
HSPG .... Hansard Society of Parliamentary Government (SAUO)
HSPG .... Heparan Sulfate Proteoglycan [*Biochemistry*]
HSPH .... Harvard School of Public Health (MELL)
HSPh .... Harvard Studies in Classical Philology (journ.) (SAUS)
HSPh .... Studies in Classical Philology (SAUS)
HSPhS .... Historical Studies in the Physical Sciences (journ.) (SAUS)
HSPI .... Health and Safety Policy Liaison (HEAS)
HSPI .... High-Speed Printer Interface (MCD)
HSPI .... Pibor [*Sudan*] [*ICAO location identifier*] (ICLI)
HSPL .... Harvard Studies and Notes in Philology and Literature [*Publication*] (SAUS)
HSPL .... High-Speed Perceptual Learning (SAUS)
HSPL .... Holyhead Steam Packet Line (SAUO)
HSPL .... Hull Steam Packet Line (SAUO)
HSPLS .... Hawaii State Public Library System [*Hawaii State Department of Education*] [*Information service or system*] (IID)
HSPM .... High-Speed Print Mechanism (SAUS)
HSPN .... Henoch-Schonlein Purpura Nephritis [*Medicine*] (MELL)
HSPN .... High-Speed Packet Network (SAUS)
HSPP .... Hawker Siddeley Power Plant Ltd. (SAUO)
HSPP .... High-Speed Pattern Processing (SAUS)
HSP Pitch .... High Softening Point Pitch (SAUS)
HSP Press ... High-Speed Press (SAUS)
HSPPS .... Hanford Site Past Practices Strategy (SAUS)
HSPQ .... High School Personality Questionnaire [*Psychology*]
HSPR .... High School Percentile Rank
HSpS .... Daughters of the Holy Spirit Nazareth of the Good Shepherd (TOCD)
HSPS .... Heat Shock Protein Synthesis
HSPS .... Henoch-Schoelein Purpura Syndrome [*Medicine*] (WDAA)
HSPS .... High-Speed Peripheral Shelf (SAUS)
HSPS .... Highway Safety Program Services (SAUO)
HSPS .... Highway Safety Program Standard [*Department of Transportation*]
HSPS .... Hydrographic Survey Platform System (MCD)
HSPSCB .... High Security Psychiatric Services Commissioning Board (SAUO)
HSPSD .... High-Speed Packet Switched Data [*Computer science*] (ACRL)
HSPT .... High School Placement Test
HSPT .... High School Proficiency Test
HSPT .... High-Speed Paper Tape (SAUS)
HSPTAL .... High-Speed Paper Tape Absolute Loader [*Computer science*] (MDG)
HSPTP .... High-Speed Paper Tape Punch [*Computer science*] (AABC)
HSPTR .... High-Speed Paper Tape Reader [*Computer science*] (CET)
HSPU .... Householders for Safe Pesticide Use [*Australia*]
HSQ .... Health Status Questionnaire (SAUO)
HSQ .... Heat-Shield Qualification [*NASA*] (KSC)
HSQ .... Helping Smokers Quit [*American Cancer Society*] (EA)
HSQ .... Home Screening Questionnaire [*Test*] [*Psychology*]
HSQ .... Honorary Surgeon to the Queen (SAUS)
HSQ .... Houston, TX [*Location identifier*] [*FAA*] (FAAL)
HSQB .... Health Standards and Quality Bureau [*HEW*]
HSQC .... Heteronuclear Single Quantum Coherence [*Spectrum*]
HSQC .... Heteronuclear Single Quantum Correlation [*Spectrum*]
HSQR .... High-Strength Quick Release (MCD)
HSR .... Hampshire Swine Registry (EA)
HSR .... Handbook of Structural Repair (MCD)
HSR .... Harbor Surveillance RADAR [*Navigation*] (IAA)
HSR .... Hardware Specification Review (SAUS)
HSR .... Hardware Status Register (MCD)
HSR .... Hardware Support Resources (ACAE)
HSR .... Harleco Synthetic Resin (MAE)
HSR .... Hart-Scott-Rodino Antitrust Improvements Act [*1976*]
HSR .... Harvard Standard Regions (SAUS)
HSR .... Hazard Summary Report (SAUO)
HSR .... Health Service Region [*Army*] (AABC)
HSR .... Health Systems Research (SAUS)
HSR .... Heated Serum Reagin [*Immunochemistry*] (DAVI)
HSR .... Heat Shield Recovery [*Aerospace*] (IAA)
HSR .... Helicopter Search and Rescue (SAUO)
HSR .... High School Percentile Rank
HSR .... High-Speed RADAR (MCD)
HSR .... High-Speed Rail
HSR .... High-Speed Railway (SAUS)
HSR .... High-Speed Reader [*Computer science*]
HSR .... High-Speed Relay
HSR .... High Speed Research (SAUS)
HSR .... High Stocking Rate [*Agriculture*] (OA)
HSR .... High-Strength Resin (SAUS)
HSR .... High-substance Speed Rewind (SAUS)
HSR .... Hi Shear Technology Corp. [*AMEX symbol*] (SAG)
HSR .... Hoboken Shore Railroad (SAUO)
HSR .... Holographic Spectrum Reconstruction (SAUS)
HSR .... Homestead Resources, Inc. [*Vancouver Stock Exchange symbol*]
HSR .... Homogeneously Staining Region [*Cytology*]
HSR .... Horizontal Size Ratio [*Ophthalmology*]
HSR .... Hot Springs, SD [*Location identifier*] [*FAA*] (FAAL)
HSR .... Hull & Selby Railway Co. (SAUO)
HSR .... Human Science Research [*Concept car*] [*Automotive engineering*]
HSR .... Hungarian Studies Review (journ.) (SAUS)
HSR .... Hybrid Statistical Receiver (SAUS)
HSRA .... Half Saddlebred Registry of America (EA)
HSRA .... Harvard-Smithsonian Reference Atmosphere
HSRA .... Health Services and Resources Administration (DAVI)
HSRA .... High-Speed Data Regeneration Assembly [*Ground Communications Facility, NASA*]
HSRA .... High Speed Rail Association (EA)
HSRA .... High-Speed Rail Association (SAUS)
HSRA .... Hollow Shaft Rotary Actuator
HSRAM .... Hanford Site Risk Assessment Methodology (SAUS)
HSR & D ...... Health Services Research and Development Service [*Washington, DC*] [*Veterans Administration*] (GRD)
HSRC .... Hazardous Substance Research Center (SAUO)
HSRC .... Health Services Research Center [*Georgia Institute of Technology*] [*Research center*] (RCD)
HSRC .... HEALTHSOUTH Rehabilitation Corp. [*NASDAQ symbol*] (COMM)
HSRC .... High School Red Cross
HSRC .... High-Speed Rail Concept (SAUS)
HSRC .... Highway Safety Research Center [*University of North Carolina, Chapel Hill*] [*Research center*] (RCD)
HSRC .... Human Sciences Research Council [*South Africa*]
HSRC .... Human-Subjects Review Committee [*Medicine*] (BABM)
HSRC .... Hypothetical Signalling Reference Connection (SAUS)
HSRCM .... Hanford Site Radiological Control Manual (SAUS)
HSRD .... Health Services Research and Development [*Series*] [*A publication*]
HSRD .... Hypertension Secondary to Renal Disease [*Medicine*]
HSRD .... National Center for Health Services Research and Development (SAUO)
HSrep .... Health & Safety Representative (WDAA)
HSRFO .... High-Sulfur Residual Fuel Oil [*Petroleum technology*]
HSRI .... Health Services Readiness Inspection (ACAE)
HSRI .... Health Systems Research Institute
HSRI .... Highly Sensitive Refractive Index
HSRI .... Highway Safety Research Center (SAUS)
HSRI .... Highway Safety Research Institute [*University of Michigan*]
HSRIOP .... High Speed RAD [*Rapid Access Data Dram*] Input/Output Processor [*Xerox*] (NITA)
HSRJ .... Raga [*Sudan*] [*ICAO location identifier*] (ICLI)
HSRJE .... High-Speed Remote Job Entry (SAUS)
HSRL .... Harvard Studies in Romance Languages (journ.) (SAUS)
HSRL .... High Spectral Resolution Lidar (SAUS)
HSR/MLA .... High Speed Rail/Maglev Association
HSRMWR .... High Spatial Resolution Millimeter Wave Radiometer (SAUS)
HSRN .... Heavy Straight Run Naphtha [*Petroleum chemistry*]
HSRN .... Homogeneous Suspension Reactor Netherland (SAUO)
HSRN .... Renk [*Sudan*] [*ICAO location identifier*] (ICLI)
HSRO .... High-Speed Repetitive Operation
HSRP .... Headquarters Systems Replacement Program [*Military*] (GFGA)
HSRP .... High Speed Research Program [*NASA*] [*Marine science*] (OSRA)
HSRP .... High-Speed Rotary Prism
HSRP .... Hot Standby Router Protocol (SAUS)
HSRPA .... Health Services Report (journ.) (SAUS)
HSRPROJ .... Health Services Research Projects in Progress (SAUO)
HSRR .... Hardin Southern Railroad [*Federal Railroad Administration identification code*]
HSRRB .... Human Subjects Research Review Board [*Army*] (RDA)
HSRS .... Health-Sickness Rating Scale (DMAA)
HSRS .... High Spectral Resolution Sounder (SAUS)
HSRS .... High-Speed Resetting Switches (SAUS)
HSRS .... Hurricane Supersonic Research Site
HS Rsc .... HS Resources, Inc. [*Associated Press*] (SAG)
HSRT .... Heat Shield Recovery Time (SAUS)
HSRT .... Hydraulic System Response Test (ACAE)

HSRTC......... Health and Safety Research and Test Center [*Bureau of Mines*]
HSRTM........ High-Speed Resin Transfer Molding [*Automotive engineering*]
HSRTM........ Holding High-Strength Resin Transfer Molding (SAUS)
HSRTP......... Health Services Research and Training Program [*Purdue University*] [*Research center*] (RCD)
HSRU.......... Health Services Research Unit (SAUO)
HSRV.......... Human Spumaretrovirus
HSS............ British Library Catalog: Humanities and Social Sciences [*Information service or system*] (CRD)
HSS............ Croatian Peasant Party [*Political party*] (PSAP)
HSS............ Fellow of the Historical Society (SAUO)
HSS............ Habitability Support System (MCD)
HSS............ Hallervorden-Spatz Syndrome [*Medicine*] (AAMN)
HSS............ Hardware Specification Sheet (IAA)
HSS............ Hars Systems, Inc. [*Vancouver Stock Exchange symbol*]
HSS............ Harvard Semitic Series (journ.) (SAUS)
HSS............ Health and Social Services (SAUO)
HSS............ Health Service Support [*Army*] (DOMA)
HSS............ Health Surveillance System [*Shell Oil Co.*]
HSS............ Heavy Service-Steer [*Tire engineering*]
HSS............ Heeres-Sauerstoffschutzgeraet [*Service Oxygen Breathing Apparatus*] [*German military - World War II*]
HSS............ Heidke Skill Score (SAUS)
HSS............ Helicopter Support Ship (SAUO)
HSS............ Helmet Sight Subsystem (RDA)
HSS............ Hepatic Stimulator Substance
HSS............ Heraldry Society of Scotland [*Edinburgh*] (EAIO)
HSS............ Hermanas del Servico Social (TOCD)
HSS............ Hierarchical Service System (SAUS)
HSS............ Hierarchy Service System [*Toshiba Corp.*]
HSS............ High School Size
HSS............ High Speed Reader (NAKS)
HSS............ High-Speed Simultaneous [*Electric trip mechanism*]
HSS............ High-Speed Skip (SAUS)
HSS............ High-Speed Steel (SAUS)
HSS............ High-Speed Stop (SAUS)
HSS............ High-Speed Storage [*Computer science*] (IEEE)
HSS............ High-Speed Supernatant [*Medicine*] (DAVI)
HSS............ High-Speed System [*Ground Communications Facility, NASA*]
HSS............ High Spread Shears
HSS............ High-Strength Stainless Steel (PDAA)
HSS............ High-Strength, Steel
HSS............ High-Stress Strain (MCD)
HSS............ Hispano-Suiza Society (EA)
HSS............ Historiae Societatis Socius [*Fellow of the Historical Society*] [*Latin*]
HSS............ History of Science Society (EA)
HSS............ Hokkaido University [*Japan*] [*Seismograph station code, US Geological Survey*] (SEIS)
HSS............ Hollow Structural Section (SAUS)
HSS............ Home Sea Service (SAUO)
HSS............ Homogeneity Spoil Spectroscopy (SAUS)
HSS............ Honeycomb-Supported Screen
HSS............ Hospital and Specialist Services [*British*]
HSS............ Hospital Shared Services (ADWA)
HSS............ Hospital Staffing Services, Inc. [*NYSE symbol*] (SPSG)
HSS............ Hot Springs, NC [*Location identifier*] [*FAA*] (FAAL)
HSS............ Hrvatska Seljacka Stranka [*Croatian Peasant Party*] [*Former Yugoslavia*] [*Political party*] (PPE)
HSS............ Hull Seal Section
HSS............ Hungarian State Symphony (SAUO)
HSS............ Hunter Sensor Suite [*Military*]
HSS............ Hybrid Simulation System
HSS............ Hydraulic Subsystem Simulator (NASA)
HSS............ Hydraulic System Simulator (MCD)
HSS............ Hydrological Sensing Satellite (SAUS)
HSS............ Hydrologic Sensing Satellite (DNAB)
HSS............ Hydropneumatic Suspension System (MCD)
HSS............ HyperSonic Sound
HSS............ Hypertonic Saline Solution
HSS............ Hypertrophic Subaortic Stenosis [*Cardiology*]
hss............ To be Taken at Bedtime [*Latin*] [*Hora Somnisumendum*] [*Medicine*] (EDAA)
HSSA.......... Handbag Supply Salesmen's Association (EA)
HSSA.......... Health and Safety Science Abstracts [*Cambridge Scientific Abstracts*] [*Information service or system*] (CRD)
HSSA.......... Helmet Sight Sensor Assembly (ACAE)
HSSA.......... High Speed Steel Association [*British*] (BI)
HSSA.......... History of Science Society of America (SAUO)
HSSA.......... Hydrographic Society of South Africa (SAUO)
HSSALB....... Health Service Support Air Land Battle
HSSC.......... Harmonised System of Survey and Certification (SAUO)
HSSC.......... Heavy SEAL [*Sea-Air-Land*] Support Craft (NVT)
HSSC.......... High-Speed Surface Craft, Incorporating Hovering Craft and Hydrofoil (journ.) (SAUS)
HSSC.......... Historical Society of Southern California (SAUO)
HSSCC........ Hereditary Site-Specific Colon Cancer [*Medicine*] (EDAA)
HSSCC........ Hot-Salt-Induced Stress-Corrosion Cracking (SAUS)
HSSCQ........ Historical Society of Southern California Quarterly (SAUO)
HSSCT........ High-Speed Shorts and Continuity Tester (SAUS)
HSSD.......... High-Speed Serial Data [*Automotive electronics*]
HSSD.......... High-Speed Switched Digital (SAUS)
HSSD.......... Hospital Sterile Supply Department (DMAA)
HSSDB........ High-Speed Serial Data Buffer (MCD)
HSSDB........ High Speed Serial Data Bus
HSSDC........ High-Speed Serial Data Connection (or Connector) (SAUS)
HSSDS........ High-Speed Switched Digital Service [*AT & T*] (TSSD)
HSSE.......... High Soap Suds Enema [*Gastroenterology*] (DAVI)
HSSFC........ Humanities and Social Sciences Federation of Canada (SAUO)
HSSFP........ Hanford Site Strategic Facilities Plan (SAUS)
HSSG.......... Heeres-Sauerstoffschutzgeraet [*Service Oxygen Breathing Apparatus*] [*German military - World War II*]
HSSG.......... High Speed Study Group (SAUO)
HSSG.......... High-Speed Symbol Generator
HSSG.......... Holograph Stress Strain Gauge
HSSGT........ High-Speed Guided Ground Transportation [*TXDOT*] (TAG)
HSSH.......... Hanford Site Services Handbook (SAUS)
HSSHMTS.... High-Speed Servo-Hydraulic Material Testing System
HSSI........... High-Speed Serial Interface [*Telecommunications*]
HSSI........... High-Speed Synchronous Interface [*Computer science*]
HSSI........... Highway Safety Statistical Indicator
HSSI........... Hospital Staffing Services, Incorporated (SAUO)
HSSI........... Hughes Simulations Systems, Incorporated (ACAE)
HSSJ.......... Juba [*Sudan*] [*ICAO location identifier*] (ICLI)
HSSJB........ Health and Social Services Journal (journ.) (SAUS)
HSSL.......... Helicopter Self Screening Launcher (SAUS)
HSSL.......... Historical Society of Sierra Leone (SAUO)
HSSM.......... Malakal [*Sudan*] [*ICAO location identifier*] (ICLI)
HSSN.......... High-Speed Switching Network (SAUS)
HSSO.......... Health Services Support Officer (SAUS)
HSSO.......... Hungarian State Symphony Orchestra (SAUO)
HSSP.......... Port Sudan [*Sudan*] [*ICAO location identifier*] (ICLI)
HSSPF........ Hoehere SS und Polizeifuehrer (BJA)
HSSPLAN.... Health Service Support Plan [*Army*]
HSSR.......... Hermit Sisters of Romuald (TOCD)
HSSR.......... High School Seaman Recruit (SAUS)
HSSR.......... High-Speed Sequential Retrieval [*Computer science*] (TIMI)
HSSR.......... High-Speed Solid State Recorder
HSSR.......... Hybrid Solid State Relay (SAUS)
HSSR.......... Hydrogeochemical and Stream Sediment Reconnaissance (PDAA)
HSSS.......... Helicopter Secure Speech System (SAUS)
HSSS.......... High-Speed Stainless Steel (SAUS)
HSSS.......... Hydraulic System Service Set (ACAE)
HSSS.......... Khartoum [*Sudan*] [*ICAO location identifier*] (ICLI)
HSSSM........ Highly Sensitive Ship Synthesis Model (DNAB)
HSSSR........ High School Students for Social Responsibility (EA)
HSSSTP...... Hanford Site-Specific Science and Technology Plan (SAUS)
HSST.......... Heavy Section Steel Technology [*Nuclear Regulatory Commission*]
HSST.......... High-Speed Service Tool (SAUS)
HSST.......... High-Speed Surface Transport (MCD)
HSSTD........ Historical Sea Surface Temperature Data Project [*WMO*] (MSC)
HSSTD........ Historical Sea Surface Temperature Dataset [*Marine science*] (OSRA)
HSSTR........ High-Speed Synchronous Transmitter/Receiver (VLIE)
HSSTS........ High-Speed Surface Transport System (SAUS)
HSSU.......... Hospital Sterile Supply Unit (DMAA)
HSSU.......... Sterile Supply Unit (SAUS)
HSSV.......... High-Speed Surface Vessel (SAUS)
HSSW.......... High Salinity Shelf Water [*Oceanography*]
HSSW.......... Wadi Halfa/Nuba Lake [*Sudan*] [*ICAO location identifier*] (ICLI)
HST............ Hanford Safety Team (SAUS)
HST............ Harmonic and Spurious Totalizer
HST............ Harmonized Sales Tax (FOTI)
HST............ Harry S Truman [*US president, 1884-1972*]
HST............ Harvard Step Test [*Physical tolerance test*]
HSt............ Harvard Studies in classical philology (SAUO)
HST............ Hauldown, Securing, and Training (ACAE)
HST............ Hawaiian-Aleutian Standard Time
HST............ Hawaiian Standard Time
HST............ Hawaiian Sugar Technologists (SAUO)
HST............ Hawaii Standard Time (SAUS)
H ST........... Head Steward [*Navy*] [*British*] (ROG)
HST............ Health and Safety Training (SAUS)
HST............ Health Screening Test (DAVI)
HST............ Health Systems Trust (SAUO)
HST............ Heat Shrinkable Tubing
HST............ Hebrew Speaking Test (TMMY)
HST............ Heist [*C.H.*] Corp. [*AMEX symbol*] (SPSG)
HST............ Helicopter Support Team [*Navy*] (NVT)
HST............ Hemoccult Slide Test (DB)
HST............ Hermetic Seal Transformer Co. (SAUO)
HST............ Hexobarbital Sleeping Time [*In experimental animals*]
HST............ Highest Spring Tide (SAUS)
HST............ High Soft Tech (SAUO)
HST............ High-Speed Tape (SAUS)
HST............ High Speed Taxi-Way Turn Off [*Aviation*] (DA)
HST............ High-Speed Technology [*Computer science*] (BYTE)
HST............ High-Speed Telegraphy (SAUS)
HST............ High-Speed Telemetry
HST............ High-Speed Teleprinting (SAUS)
HST............ High-Speed Terminal (SAUS)
HST............ High-Speed Test (SAUS)
HST............ High-Speed Text (SAUS)
HST............ High-Speed Tractor (SAUS)
HST............ High-Speed Train [*British*]
HST............ High-Speed Tunnel [*NASA*]
HST............ High-Speed Typewriter (SAUS)
Hst............ History (SAUS)
HST............ History of Science and Technology (SAUS)
HST............ Hoist (MSA)

HST Hollands Export Magarine. Holland Shipping and Trading (journ.) (SAUS)
HST Homestead [*Florida*] [*Airport symbol*] (OAG)
HST Homestead, FL [*Location identifier*] [*FAA*] (FAAL)
HST Homogenate Survival Time
HST Horizontal Seismic Trigger (IEEE)
HST Host (SAUS)
HST Hot Shot Tunnel
HST Housing Study Tours [*British*]
HST Hoyer-Schlesinger-Turner, Inc. (EFIS)
HST Hubble Space Telescope [*Great Observatory Program*] [*NASA*]
HST Hunter Stockton Thompson
HSt Hydro-Space Technology, Inc. (SAUO)
HST Hydrostatic Transmission [*Automotive engineering*]
HST Hyper-Sonic Transport (SAUS)
HST Hypervelocity Shock Tunnel (OA)
HSTA Hawaii State Teachers Association (SAUO)
HSTA Honda Sport Touring Association (EA)
HSTAMIDS Handheld Standoff Minefield Detection System [*Military*] (RDA)
HST&M History of Science, Technology, and Medicine (ADWA)
HSTAR Health Services/Technology Assessment Research (ADWA)
HSTAR Helicopter Surveillance and Target Acquisition RADAR
HSTAT Health Services/Technology Assessment Text [*National Library of Medicine*] [*Information service or system*]
H State High State (SAUS)
HSTC Heidelberg Sports Touring Club (SAUO)
HSTC Henderson State Teachers College [*Later, HSC*] [*Arkansas*]
HSTC House Science and Technology Committee [*Medicine*] (EDAA)
HSTCO High-Stability Temperature-Compensated Crystal Oscillator [*Electronics*] (OA)
HSTCXO High-Stability Temperature-Compensated Crystal Oscillator
HSTEC Health Sciences Training and Education Command (SAUO)
H STEPH Henricus Stephanus [*Imprint*] [*Latin*] (ROG)
HSTF Heat-Shock Transcription Factor [*Genetics*]
HSTF Hexone Storage & Treatment Facility (SAUS)
HSTF Human Serum Thymus Factor [*Immunochemistry*] (DAVI)
HSTH Hose Thread
HSTI Hartford State Technical Institute (SAUO)
HSTK Herpes Simplex Thymidine Kinase [*An enzyme*]
HSTL Harry S Truman Library
HSTL High-Speed Telemetry Link
HSTO Hard Stop (SAUS)
HSTO Tong [*Sudan*] [*ICAO location identifier*] (ICLI)
HSTP Hard Stop (MCD)
HSTP Hardware and Software Turnover Plan (SAUO)
HSTP Heat Sterilization Test Program
HSTP High-Speed Transport Protocol (SAUS)
HSTR Amer Homestar [*NASDAQ symbol*] (TTSB)
HSTR American Homestar Corp. [*NASDAQ symbol*] (SAG)
HSTR High-Speed Token Ring (SAUS)
H Str Hudson Strait (SAUO)
HSTR Torit [*Sudan*] [*ICAO location identifier*] (ICLI)
HSTRA High-Speed Token Ring Alliance (GART)
HSTRA High-Strength Thermal-Resistant Alloy
HSTRU Hydraulic System Test and Repair Unit [*Army*] (RDA)
HSTS High Pressure Side Temperature Sensor (SAUS)
HSTS High-Pressure Side Temperature Sensor [*Air conditioning systems*] [*Automotive engineering*]
HSTS High Speed Text Search System (ACAE)
HSTS High-Speed Text System (SAUS)
HSTS Horizontal Stabilizer Trim Setting
HSTS Hostess (SAUO)
HSTS Host Software Testing Section [*Social Security Administration*]
HSTS House Subcommittee on Traffic Safety (SAUO)
HSTS Hydraulic Subsystems Test Station (MCD)
HSTSF Harry S Truman Scholarship Foundation (EA)
HSTSP Hardware and Software Turnover Support Plan (SAUO)
HSTT High-Speed Tape Transmitter (SAUS)
HSTT High-Speed Test Track
HSTTL High-Speed Transistor-Transistor Logic
HSTTY High Speed Teletypewriter (SAUO)
HSTTY High-Speed Teletypewriter (SAUS)
HSTU Human Science and Technology University (SAUO)
HSTU Tumbura [*Sudan*] [*ICAO location identifier*] (ICLI)
HSTV High-Speed Test Vehicle (SAUS)
HSTV High-Survivability Test Vehicle (MCD)
HSTV-L High-Speed Test Vehicle-Light (SAUS)
HSTVL High Survivability Test Vehicle, Lightweight [*Military*]
HSTVX Heritage Value Equity Cl.A [*Mutual fund ticker symbol*] (SG)
HSTW High School That Work (SAUO)
HSTW Humane Society of Tinplate Workers [*A union*] [*British*]
HSTyL High-Speed Transistor-Transistor Logic (SAUS)
HS Type High Shock-resistant Type (SAUS)
HSTZ Herzog Stone [*Federal Railroad Administration identification code*]
HSU Hardin-Simmons University [*Texas*]
HSU Hartridge Smoke Unit [*Automotive engineering*]
HSU Helium Service Unit (MCD)
HSU Helium Speech Unscrambler [*Deep sea diving*]
HSU Henderson State University [*Arkadelphia, AR*]
HSU Hero of the Soviet Union [*Award*] (DOMA)
HSU High-Speed Unit (SAUS)
HSU High Speed Utility (SAUS)
HSU Highway Speed Uniformity [*Automotive tire testing*]
HSU Humboldt State University [*Los Angeles, CA*]
HSU Hydraulic Supply Unit
HSUA Health Services Union of Australia
H-substance Histamine-like substance (SAUS)
HSUG Housing Statistics Users Group (EA)
HSUL Haile Selassie University Libraries (SAUO)
HS/UMC Historical Society of the United Methodist Church (EA)
HSUNA Humanist Student Union of North America
HSUR Half Symmetric Unstable Resonator (PDAA)
HSURC Health Services Utilization and Research Commission (SAUO)
HSURIA Half Symmetric Unstable Resonator with Intracavity Axicon (PDAA)
HSUS Humane Society of the United States
HSUSA Hemlock Society U.S.A. (EA)
HSUSA Heraldry Society of the United States of America (EA)
HSUSC Hymn Society in the United States and Canada (EA)
HSV Haemophilia society of Victoria [*Australia*]
HSV Head Small Veins [*Anatomy*]
HSV Head Suppression Valve (AAG)
HSV Heliservico-Sociedade Portuguesa de Exploracao de Meios Aeros Lda. [*Portugal*] [*ICAO designator*] (FAAC)
HSV Herpes Simplex Virus
HSV Highly Selective Vagotomy [*Medicine*]
HSV High-Speed Video [*Instrumentation*]
HSV High-Stage Valve (MCD)
HSV Hop Stunt Viroid [*Medicine*] (DMAA)
HSV Hue, Saturation, and Value [*Color model*] (BYTE)
HSV Hull Solenoid Valve
HSV Huntsville [*Alabama*] [*Airport symbol*]
HSV Hydraulic Selector Valve
HSV Hydrogen Saturated Vacancy [*Photovoltaic energy systems*]
HSV Hydroxyinterlayered Smectite or Vermiculite
HSV Hyperviscosity Syndrome [*Medicine*] (DB)
HSV-1 Herpes Simplex [*Medicine*] (TAD)
HSV1 Herpes Simplex, Type 1 [*Medicine*]
HSV-2 Herpes Simplex II [*Medicine*] (TAD)
HSV2 Herpes Simplex, Type 2 [*Medicine*]
HSV2 Herpes Simplex Virus Type 2
HSVA Health Systems Vendors Association [*San Francisco, CA*] (EA)
HSVB High-Speed Video Bus (SAUS)
HSVD Hankels Singular Value Decomposition (SAUS)
HSVD Horizontal Situation Video Display (SAUS)
HSVE Herpes Simplex Virus Encephalitis [*Medicine*]
HSVgD Herpes Simplex Virus Glycoprotein D [*Biochemistry*]
HSVI Herpes Simplex Virus type 1 (SAUS)
HSVL Highveld Steel & Vanadium Corp. Ltd. [*NASDAQ symbol*] (NQ)
HSVLY Highveld Steel & VanadiumADR [*NASDAQ symbol*] (TTSB)
HSVMA High-Speed Video Motion Analyzer (VLIE)
HSVP High Speed Vector Processor (ACAE)
HSVPS High-Speed Vector Processor System (SAUS)
HSVtk Herpes Simplex Virus Thymidine Kinase [*Medicine*] (DMAA)
HSW Aerocombi SA [*Spain*] [*ICAO designator*] (FAAC)
HSW Headquarters Support Wing (SAUO)
HSW Heat-Sensitive Wire (SAUS)
HSW Heat Sink Welding [*Nuclear energy*] (NRCH)
HSW Helena Southwestern Railroad Co. [*AAR code*]
HSW High Salt Waste (SAUS)
HSW Hot Spot [*Washington*] [*Seismograph station code, US Geological Survey*] [*Closed*] (SEIS)
HSWA Hazardous and Solid Waste Act (SAUS)
HSWA Hazardous and Solid Waste Amendments [*1984 amendments to RCRA*]
HSWA Health and Safety at Work Act (SAUO)
HSWDC Historical Society of Washington, DC (EA)
HSWF Strontium Hot Semiworks Facility (SAUS)
HSWG High-Speed Wire Guidance
HSWH High-Solid Waste Header [*Nuclear energy*] (NRCH)
HSWJC HSW Junction, AR [*American Association of Railroads railroad junction routing code*]
HSWMUR Hanford Site Waste Management Units Report (SAUS)
HSWO Hierarchical Step-Wise Optimization (SAUS)
HSWP Hungarian Socialist Workers' Party [*Political party*] (PPW)
HSWRS Housewares
HSWS High Speed Waveform Sampler (ACAE)
HSWT High-Speed Wind Tunnel (SAUS)
HSWW Wau [*Sudan*] [*ICAO location identifier*] (ICLI)
HSX Hollywood Stock Exchange
HSXP High-Speed Xerographic Printer (SAUS)
HSY Hard-Sphere-Yukawa Model (SAUS)
HSY Health and Society (journ.) (SAUS)
HSY Hershey Foods Corp. [*NYSE symbol*] (SPSG)
HSY Hosiery
HSYA Yambio [*Sudan*] [*ICAO location identifier*] (ICLI)
HSYE Yei [*Sudan*] [*ICAO location identifier*] (ICLI)
HSYL Yirol [*Sudan*] [*ICAO location identifier*] (ICLI)
HSyn Heme Synthase (DB)
HSYN Horizontal Synchronization (SAUS)
HSYNC Horizontal Synchronous [*Computer science*]
HSYS Hale Systems, Inc. (SAUO)
HSZA Zalingei [*Sudan*] [*ICAO location identifier*] (ICLI)
HSZD Hermetically Sealed Zener Diode
HT Air Tchad [*ICAO designator*] (AD)
HT Haavara-Transfer (BJA)
HT Hadamard-Transform [*Mathematics*]
HT Haiti [*ANSI two-letter standard code*] (CNC)
ht Haiti [*MARC country of publication code*] [*Library of Congress*] (LCCP)
HT Half-Thickness [*Medicine*] (EDAA)

HT .... Half-Tilt Containers (DCTA)
HT .... Half Timbered (SAUS)
HT .... Half-Time [*Survey*] [*Shipping*]
HT .... Half-Title [*Publishing*]
HT .... Half Tone [*Printing*] (NITA)
ht .... Halftone [*Photography*] [*Art*] (WDMC)
HT .... Half-Tracked [*Vehicle*] (NATG)
H-T .... Half-Truck [*British*]
HT .... Halo Test [*Medicine*] (MELL)
HT .... Halt and Transfer
HT .... Hammer Toe [*Orthopedics*] (DAVI)
HT .... Hand-Held Terminal [*Computer science*] (MHDB)
HT .... Handling Time
HT .... Handmaids of the Most Holy Trinity (TOCD)
HT .... Hand Test [*Psychology*]
HT .... Hand Transceiver
HT .... Hand Translation (MCD)
HT .... Hand Tremor [*Medicine*] (EDAA)
HT .... Handy Talky [*Radio*]
HT .... Hardness Testing (SAUS)
HT .... Hard Tool (SAUS)
HT .... Hard Top [*Automobile advertising*]
HT .... Hardware Test (VLIE)
HT .... Hashimoto's Thyroiditis [*Medicine*] (DMAA)
HT .... Haustus [*A Drink*] [*Pharmacy*]
HT .... Hawaiian Telephone (SAUO)
HT .... Hawaiian Territory [*Prior to statehood*]
HT .... Hawaiian Theater [*Military*]
HT .... Hawaiian Time
HT .... Hawaii Time (SAUS)
HT .... Headed Type
H/T .... Head per Track (VLIE)
HT .... Head, Tail [*Coin-tossing probability*]
HT .... Head Thickness (SAUS)
HT .... Head-to-Tail [*Polymer structure*]
HT .... Head Turn [*Industrial engineering*]
HT .... Hearing Test (CPH)
ht .... Heart [*Medicine*] (EDAA)
HT .... Heart
ht .... Heart Tones [*Medicine*] (EDAA)
HT .... Heart Tones [*Medicine*]
HT .... Heart Transplantation
HT .... Heat (AAG)
HT .... Heater Tap (SAUS)
Ht .... Heating (MIST)
HT .... Heat Therapy (MELL)
HT .... Heat Transfer (NASA)
HT .... Heat Treat
HT .... Heat Treated (SAUS)
HT .... Heat Treatment (SAUS)
HT .... Heavy Tank
HT .... Heavy Terminal [*AFSCF*] (MCD)
HT .... Heavy Thermoplastic (IAA)
HT .... Heavy Traffic (SAUS)
HT .... Heavy Truck (SAUS)
HT .... Hebrew Text (BJA)
HT .... Height (AAG)
Ht .... Height (AMHC)
ht .... Height [*Also, h*] (WDMC)
Ht .... Height of Heart (STED)
HT .... Height of Target
HT .... Heights [*Commonly used*] (OPSA)
HT .... Height Technician [*Air Force*]
HT .... Height Telling [*RADAR*]
HT .... Helen Thomas [*British author*]
HT .... Helicopter Training Squadron [*Navy symbol*] (NVT)
HT .... Heliotropin (SAUS)
HT .... Hemagglutination Titer [*Medicine*] (MAE)
HT .... Hematologic Toxin [*Medicine*] (MELL)
HT .... Hematoxylin (SAUS)
HT .... Hemothorax [*Medicine*] (MELL)
HT .... Herald Tribune [*A publication*]
HT .... Herd Test
HT .... Hersha Hospitality Trust [*AMEX symbol*] (SG)
H-T .... Hesperis-Tamuda (journ.) (SAUS)
Ht .... Heterozygote [*Medicine*] (DMAA)
HT .... Hibernation Trigger (BARN)
HT .... High-held Terminal (SAUS)
HT .... High Technology (MCD)
HT .... High Temperature
HT .... High Tenacity (SAUS)
Ht .... High Tension (STED)
HT .... High Tension
HT .... High Threshold (SAUS)
HT .... High Tide
HT .... High Times (journ.) (SAUS)
HT .... High Torque [*Engineering*] (IAA)
HT .... High Tracheostomy [*Medicine*] (MELL)
HT .... High Transform [*Computer science*]
HT .... High Treason
HT .... Hilbert Transform (SAUS)
HT .... Hilly Terrain (CGWS)
HT .... Hired Transport (SAUS)
HT .... Histologic Technician [*or Technologist*] (MAE)
HT .... Histologic Transformation [*Medicine*]
HT .... Historic Towns [*A publication*]
HT .... History Today [*A publication*] (BRI)
HT .... Hittite Texts in the Cuneiform Character from Tablets in the British Museum [*London*] (BJA)
HT .... Hoc Tempore [*At This Time*] [*Latin*]
HT .... Hoc Titulo [*In, or Under, This Title*] [*Latin*]
HT .... Hoisting Tool (MCD)
HT .... Holding Time [*Telecommunications*] (TEL)
HT .... Hollow Tile [*Technical drawings*]
HT .... Holy Trinity
HT .... Home Terminal (VLIE)
HT .... Home Trade (SAUS)
HT .... Home Treatment [*Medicine*]
HT .... Homing Terrier [*Missile*]
HT .... Homing Transponder (SAUS)
HT .... Homing Transponders
HT .... Homing Type (NATG)
HT .... Horizontal Tab [*Computer science*] (DOM)
HT .... Horizontal Tabulate (NITA)
HT .... Horizontal Tabulation [*Computer science*]
HT .... Horizontal Tabulator (SAUS)
HT .... Horological Times [*A publication*] (EAAP)
HT .... Horsed Transport [*Military*]
HT .... Horserace Totalisator [*Set up in 1926 to provide alternative form of betting and to generate income from improvement of racing*] [*British*]
HT .... Hospital Train
HT .... Hospital Treatment (SAUS)
HT .... Hot Report (NATG)
HT .... Hot Tin (MSA)
HT .... Hot Topics
HT .... Hot Transient Exhaust Emissions [*Automotive engineering*]
HT .... Houma-Thibodaux [*Diocesan abbreviation*] [*Louisiana*] (TOCD)
HT .... House Trailer (AFM)
HT .... Howard Terminal [*AAR code*]
HT .... Hubbard Tank [*Medicine*]
HT .... Hughes Tool Co. (SAUO)
HT .... Huhner Test [*Gynecology*]
HT .... Hull Maintenance Technician [*U.S. Navy enlisted rating*] (AUER)
HT .... Hull Technician [*Navy*]
HT .... Human Teratocarcinoma [*A cell line*]
HT .... Human Thrombin [*Cytochemistry*]
HT .... Human Toxicology (journ.) (SAUS)
HT .... Human Tumor [*Oncology*]
HT .... Hunter Transport [*Commercial firm*] [*British*]
HT .... Hunting Time (SAUS)
HT .... Hybrid Tea [*Roses*] (ROG)
HT .... Hybrid Transformer (SAUS)
HT .... Hydraulic Turbine (SAUS)
HT .... Hydrocortisone Test [*Medicine*] (DB)
HT .... Hydrolyzable Tannin Level
HT .... Hydrophobic Tail [*Surfactant technology*]
HT .... Hydrotalcite [*Mineralogy*]
HT .... Hydrotherapy [*Medicine*]
HT .... Hydrothermally Treated [*Environmental science*] (COE)
HT .... Hydrotreating [*Also, HDT*] [*Petroleum technology*]
HT .... Hydroxyl Terminated (MCD)
HT .... Hydroxytryptamine [*Biochemistry*]
HT .... Hydroxytyplamine (SAUS)
HT .... Hypermetropia (SAUS)
Ht .... Hypermetropia, Total [*Ophthalmology*]
Ht .... Hyperopia, Total [*Ophthalmology*] (AAMN)
Ht .... Hypertension (ADWA)
HT .... Hypertension [*Cardiology*] (DAVI)
HT .... Hyperthyroidism [*Endocrinology*] (MAE)
HT .... Hypertransfusion (DB)
HT .... Hypertriglyceridemia [*Medicine*]
HT .... Hypertropia [*Medicine*]
HT .... Hypodermic Tablet [*Medicine*]
HT .... Hypotension [*Medicine*]
Ht .... Hypothalamus (STED)
HT .... Hypothalamus [*Neurology*]
HT .... Hypothermally Treated (GNE)
HT .... Hypoxanthine/Thymidine Medium (SAUS)
H(T) .... Intermittent Hypertropia (STED)
HT .... Mustard Gas [*Also, H, HD, HS, M*] [*Poison gas*] [*US Chemical Corps symbol*]
HT .... Mustard-T mixture (SAUS)
Ht .... total Hypermetropia (SAUS)
Ht .... total Hyperopia (SAUS)
HT .... Tritiated Hydrogen (SAUS)
HT1 .... Hull Maintenance Technician, First Class [*Navy*] (DNAB)
HT2 .... Hull Maintenance Technician, Second Class [*Navy*] (DNAB)
HT3 .... Hull Maintenance Technician, Third Class [*Navy*] (DNAB)
HTA .... Handbooks of Theology [*A publication*]
HTA .... Hardcourt Tennis Association (SAUO)
HTA .... Harness Tracks of America (EA)
HTA .... Harris Tweed Association [*British*] (DBA)
HTA .... Health Technology Assessment (ADWA)
HTA .... Heavier than Air
HTA .... Hedge-to-Arrive [*Business term*]
HTA .... Help the Aged [*AAIA*] [*Superseded by*] (EA)
HTA .... Herb Trade Association (EA)
HTA .... Hermes Training Aircraft (SAUS)
HTA .... Heteroduplex Tracking Analysis [*Genetics*]

HTA.......... Heterogeneity Arrangement (SAUS)
HT-A.......... Heterophile Transplantation Antigen (SAUS)
HTA.......... Heterophil Transplantation Antigen [*Medicine*] (DMAA)
HTA.......... High Temperature Accelerant (SAUS)
HTA.......... High-Temperature Adhesive
HTA.......... High Temperature Alarm [*Environmental science*] (COE)
HTA.......... High-Temperature Alloy
HTA.......... High Temperature Amorphous (SAUS)
HTA.......... High Temperature Ashing (SAUS)
HTA.......... High-Temperature Ashing [*Analytical chemistry*]
HTA.......... Highway Traffic Act
HTA.......... Hohenfels Training Area [*NATO*]
HTA.......... Horizontal Test Assembly (SAUS)
HTA.......... Horticultural Trades Association [*British*] (BI)
HTA.......... Household Textiles Association [*British*] (BI)
HTA.......... Humanist Teachers' Association [*British*]
HTA.......... Human Thymocyte Antigen (STED)
HTA.......... Hydro ThermAblator
HTA.......... Hydroxytryptamine [*Biochemistry*] (MAE)
HTA.......... Hyperion 1997 Term Trust [*NYSE symbol*] (SPSG)
HTA.......... Hypophysiotropic Area [*of hypothalamus*] [*Endocrinology*]
HTA.......... Hypothetical Task Assignment (SAUS)
HTAB.......... Hexadecyltrimethylammonium Bromide [*Organic chemistry*]
HTAC.......... Hanford Training Assessment Center (SAUS)
HTAC.......... Hard Target Attack Capability (ACAE)
HTAC.......... Hexadecyltrimethylammonium Chloride [*Organic chemistry*]
HTAC.......... High-Tension Alternating Current (IAA)
HTACC.......... Hardened Tactical Air Control Centers (ACAE)
HTACS.......... Human Thyroid Adenyl Cyclase Stimulator [*Endocrinology*]
HTAD.......... High Temperature Aerosol Decomposition [*Chemistry*]
HTADS.......... Helmet Target Acquisition & Designation System (SAUS)
ht aer.......... Heated Aerosol [*Pharmacology*] (DAVI)
HTAF.......... Hellenic Tactical Air Force (SAUO)
HTAH.......... High-Temperature Air Heat [*for magnetohydrodynamic power plants*] (MCD)
HT & C.......... Heat Transfer and Cryogenics
HT&W.......... Hoosac Tunnel & Wilmington (SAUO)
HTANSW.......... History Teachers' Association of New South Wales [*Australia*]
HTAR.......... Arusha [*Tanzania*] [*ICAO location identifier*] (ICLI)
HTARS.......... HEMTT Tanker, Aviation, Refuelling System (SAUS)
HTAS.......... Hug-a-Tree and Survive (EA)
HT(ASCP).......... Histologic Technician (American Society of Clinical Pathologists) (DMAA)
HTAT.......... Human Tetanus Antitoxin [*Medicine*] (CPH)
HTB.......... Hairdressing Training Board (AIE)
HTB.......... Hair Tuning Bar
htb.......... hautboy (SAUS)
HTB.......... Heat Treat Block (MCD)
HTB.......... Heavens To Betsy (SAUS)
HTB.......... Hexadecimal-to-Binary [*Computer science*]
HTB.......... Hexagonal Tungsten Bronze (SAUS)
HTB.......... High-Tech Ceramics (SAUS)
HTB.......... High Technology Brigade (ACAE)
HTB.......... High Temperature Corrosion (SAUS)
H-TB.......... High-Tension Battery
HTB.......... High-Tension Braided Sheath [*Automotive engineering*]
HTB.......... Highway Tariff Bureau [*Later, AMCTB*]
HTB.......... Hollow-ware Trade Board (SAUO)
HTB.......... Horizontal Toggle Clamp (SAUS)
HTB.......... Horserace Totalisator Board (SAUO)
HTB.......... Hot Tub Bath [*Medicine*]
HTB.......... Howitzer Test Bed (RDA)
HTB.......... Human Tumor Bank [*Medicine*] (DMAA)
HTB.......... Hungarian Tourist Board (EAIO)
HTB.......... Hypergolic Test Building (KSC)
HTB.......... Hyperion 2002 Term Trust [*NYSE symbol*] (SPSG)
HTBA.......... Hood's Texas Brigade Association (EA)
HTBB.......... HomeTown Buffet [*NASDAQ symbol*] (TTSB)
HTBB.......... Hometown Buffet, Inc. [*NASDAQ symbol*] (SAG)
HTBDR.......... High-Temperature Burner-Duct Recuperator System
Htbk.......... Hatchback (BARN)
HTBK.......... Hatchback
HTBK.......... Heritage Bank (SAUS)
HTBK.......... Heritage Commerce Corp. [*NASDAQ symbol*] (NASQ)
HTBU.......... Bukoba [*Tanzania*] [*ICAO location identifier*] (ICLI)
HTBW.......... Helicopter Targets in Bad Weather (SAUS)
HTC.......... Chief Hull Maintenance Technician (SAUS)
HTC.......... Hagerstown Telephone Center (SAUS)
HTC.......... Haiti Trans Air SA [*ICAO designator*] (FAAC)
HTC.......... Handicapped Travel Club (EA)
HTC.......... Hand Tool Carrier [*NASA*] (KSC)
HTC.......... Hanford Training Center (SAUS)
HTC.......... Hard Target Capability (SAUS)
HTC.......... Harris Teachers College [*Missouri*]
HTC.......... Harris Transducer Corp. (MCD)
HTC.......... Hartco Enterprises, Inc. [*Toronto Stock Exchange symbol*]
HTC.......... Heading to Come (SAUS)
HTC.......... Headline to Come (SAUS)
HTC.......... Head to Come [*Publishing*]
HTC.......... Healing the Children [*An association*] (EA)
HTC.......... Health Care Telecommunications Corp. [*Camp Hill, PA*] (TSSD)
HTC.......... Heat Transfer Coefficient (SAUS)
HTC.......... Heavy Teflon Coating
HTC.......... Heavy Terminal Complex (MCD)
HTC.......... Heavy Triple Coil (SAUS)
HTC.......... Hebrew Teachers College [*Massachusetts*]
HTC.......... Hebrew Theological College [*Skokie, IL*] (BJA)
HTC.......... Height-to-Time Converter
HTC.......... Height Tracking Console (MCD)
HTC.......... Helicopter Transit Controller (MCD)
HTC.......... Helsinki Telephone Company [*Communications term*] (DCT)
HTC.......... Hepatoma Cells [*Cytology*] (DAVI)
HTC.......... Hepatoma Tissue Culture [*Medicine*]
HTC.......... Higher Technician Certificate (SAUS)
HTC.......... High-Tar Content [*of cigarettes*]
HTC.......... High-Temperature Carbonization
HTC.......... High-Temperature Catalyst
HTC.......... High-Temperature Coil
HTC.......... High-Temperature Conditioning
HTC.......... High Temperature Contact (SAUS)
HTC.......... High Temperature Crystallizable (or Crystallization) (SAUS)
HTC.......... Hight to Time Converter (SAUS)
HTC.......... Highway Traffic Control
HTC.......... Homozygous Typing Cells [*Immunochemistry*]
HTC.......... Horizontal Tabulation Character [*Computer science*] (ELAL)
HTC.......... Horizontal Transfer Corridor (SAUS)
HTC.......... House Transportation Committee (SAUO)
HTC.......... Hughes Tool Co.
HTC.......... Hull Maintenance Technician, Chief [*Navy*] (DNAB)
HTC.......... Humidity Test Control (SAUS)
HTC.......... Hungarian Telephone and Cable Corp. [*AMEX symbol*] (SAG)
HTC.......... Huston-Tillotson College, Austin, TX [*OCLC symbol*] (OCLC)
HTC.......... Hybrid Tape Circuit (SAUS)
HTC.......... Hybrid Technology Computer
HTC.......... Hydraulic Temperature Control (AAG)
HTC.......... Hydraulic Test Chamber (AAG)
HTC.......... Hydrofoil Test Craft
HTC.......... Hydrogen Transfer Catalysis [*Chemistry*]
HTC.......... Hydrographic Topographic Center (SAUO)
HTC.......... Hypertensive Crisis [*Cardiology*] (DAVI)
HTC.......... Hypertrophic Cicatrix [*Medicine*] (MELL)
HTCA.......... Human Tumor Clonogenic Assay [*In-vitro testing system*]
HTCC.......... High-Temperature Co-Fired Ceramic
HTCC.......... Hungarian Telephone & Cable Corp. [*NASDAQ symbol*] (SAG)
HTCD.......... High-Temperature Catalytic Oxidation [*Chemistry*]
HTCE.......... Historical Tank Content Estimate (ABAC)
HTCH.......... Chunya [*Tanzania*] [*ICAO location identifier*] (ICLI)
HTCH.......... Hutchinson Technology [*NASDAQ symbol*] (TTSB)
HTCH.......... Hutchinson Technology, Inc. [*NASDAQ symbol*] (NQ)
HTCHNG.......... Hitching
HTCHY.......... Hatchery
HTCI.......... High-Tensile Cast Iron
HTCID.......... High-Tolerance Current-Injection-Logic Device (SAUS)
HTCM.......... Master Chief Hull Maintenance Technician [*Formerly, SFCM*] [*Navy rating*]
HTCO.......... Hickory Tech [*NASDAQ symbol*] (TTSB)
HTCO.......... Hickory Tech Corp. [*NASDAQ symbol*] (SAG)
HTCO.......... High-Temperature Catalytic Oxidation [*Chemistry*]
HTCS.......... Head Temperature Control System (SAUS)
HTCS.......... High Critical Temperature Superconductor (AAEL)
HTCS.......... High Tc Superconductors (SAUS)
HTCS.......... Senior Chief Hull Maintenance Technician [*Formerly, SFCS*] [*Navy rating*]
HTCT.......... High Temperature Chemical Technology (SAUS)
HTCV.......... Hop Trefoil Cryptic Virus [*Plant pathology*]
HT-CVD.......... High Temperature-Chemical Vapor Deposition (SAUS)
HTCVD.......... High Temperature CVD (SAUS)
HTCVD.......... Hypertensive Cardiovascular Disease (MELL)
HTCW.......... Helicopter Targets in Clear Weather (SAUS)
HTCX.......... Harbor Tank Line [*Private rail car owner code*]
HTCZ.......... Hibbing Taconite [*Federal Railroad Administration identification code*]
HTD.......... Hand Target Designator
HTD.......... Hand-Tool Dexterity [*Motor performance test*]
HTD.......... Heated (MSA)
HTD.......... Heat Transfer Division
HTD.......... Heterojunction Tunneling Diode (SAUS)
HTD.......... Higher Technician Diploma (SAUS)
HTD.......... Higher Telegraphist Detector [*British military*] (DMA)
HTD.......... High Temperature Deformation (SAUS)
HTD.......... High-Temperature Deposits [*Lubricants*]
HTD.......... High-Temperature Distillation
HTD.......... High-Torque Drive [*Engineering*]
HTD.......... Highway Traffic Director (SAUS)
HTD.......... Horizontal Tactical Display (NG)
HTD.......... Hospital for Tropical Diseases (SAUO)
HTD.......... Human Therapeutic Dose
HTD.......... Huntingdon International Holdings Ltd. [*NYSE symbol*] (CTT)
HTDA.......... Dar Es-Salaam/Dar Es-Salaam [*Tanzania*] [*ICAO location identifier*] (ICLI)
HTDA.......... High Temperature Dilute Acid (SAUS)
HTDC.......... Dar Es-Salaam [*Tanzania*] [*ICAO location identifier*] (ICLI)
HTDC.......... High-Tension Direct Current (IAA)
HTDE.......... Half Time Digit Emitter (SAUS)
HTDE.......... High-Technology Demonstrator Engine (MCD)
HTDL.......... High-Temperature Detection Lens
HTDM.......... Helicopter Team Defense Missile
HTDM.......... Hybrid Time Division Multiplexing (SAUS)
HTDO.......... Dodoma [*Tanzania*] [*ICAO location identifier*] (ICLI)
HTDP.......... Horizontal Time-Dependent Positioning (SAUS)
HTDPL.......... Heated Pool (SAUS)

HTDQ.......... Dar Es-Salaam [*Tanzania*] [*ICAO location identifier*] (ICLI)
HTD RM....... Heated Room (SAUS)
HTDS.......... Hanford Thyroid Disease Study (SAUS)
HTDS.......... High Temperature Drawing Salt (SAUS)
HTDS.......... Host Target Development System (SAUO)
HTDS.......... Host Terminal Data Server
HTDS.......... Hydrofoil Tactical Data System
HTDT.......... Heavy Truck Driver Trainer [*Army*]
HTDU.......... High Temperature Demonstration Unit (SAUS)
HTDU.......... High Temperature Demonstrator Unit (SAUS)
HTDU.......... Horizontal Tactical Display Unit
HTDW.......... Heterosexual Development of Women [*Medicine*] (EDAA)
HTE.......... England (SAUS)
HTE.......... England AFB (Alexandria), LA [*Location identifier*] [*FAA*] (FAAL)
HTE.......... Half Time Emitter (SAUS)
HTE.......... Hard-to-Enumerate (SAUS)
HTE.......... Heat Treating Exposition (SAUS)
HTE.......... Heavy-Duty Thermoplastic Elastomer Insulation [*Automotive engineering*]
HTE.......... High-Temperature Electrolysis (MCD)
HTE.......... High Temperature Electronics (AAEL)
HTE.......... High Temperature Elongation
HTE.......... Holyrood Amenity Trust, Edinburgh (SAUO)
HTE.......... Hornet Test Equipment (SAUS)
HTE.......... Hydraulic Test Equipment
HTE.......... Hypergroup Translating Equipment (NITA)
HTE.......... Hypertensive Encephalopathy [*Medicine*] (CPH)
HTE.......... Hypothenar Eminence [*Medicine*] (MELL)
HTEA.......... Hughes Torrance Employees' Association (ACAE)
HTEC.......... High Technology
HTEC.......... Hydrogen Technology Evaluation Center [*Upton, NY*] [*Brookhaven National Laboratory*] [*Department of Energy*] (GRD)
HTEC.......... Hydron Technologies [*NASDAQ symbol*] (TTSB)
HTEC.......... Hydron Technologies, Inc. [*NASDAQ symbol*] (SPSG)
HTEF.......... Heat Transfer Efficiency Factor [*Engineering*]
HTEK.......... Hytek Microsystems, Inc. (SAUO)
HTEL.......... Hungarian Teleconstruct [*NASDAQ symbol*] (SAG)
HTEM.......... Human Thymic Epithelial Medium [*Endocrinology*]
HTENY.......... Hartogen Energy Canada (SAUS)
HTES.......... High-Technology Ejection Seat
HTES.......... High-Technology Escape System (MCD)
HTESP.......... High-Temperature Electrostatic Precipitator [*Anti-smoke pollution device*]
H/TEU.......... Hull/Turret Electronics Unit (SAUS)
H/TEU.......... Hull/Turret Electronic Unit (TIMI)
HTEXCH....... Heat Exchanger (MCD)
HTF.......... Hard to Find
HTF.......... Heat Transfer Fluid
HTF.......... Heat Treat Fixture (MCD)
HTF.......... Height Finding (MSA)
HTF.......... Heritage Trails Fund (EA)
Htf.......... Hertfordshire Regiment (SAUO)
HTF.......... Heterothyrotropic Factor [*Medicine*] (MAE)
HTF.......... High Temperature Fatigue (SAUS)
HTF.......... High-Temperature Foam [*Lubricants*]
HTF.......... Highway Trust Fund
HTF.......... Horizontal Tube Feeder (SAUS)
HTF.......... House Tube Feeding [*Medicine*] (DMAA)
HTF.......... Housing Trust Fund (PA)
HTF.......... How-to-Fight [*Manuals*] [*Military*]
HTF.......... Hydromechanical test facility (SAUS)
HTF.......... Hyper-g Text Format (SAUS)
HTF.......... Hypersonic Tunnel Facility [*NASA*]
HTF.......... Societe Helitrans France [*ICAO designator*] (FAAC)
HTFA.......... Hull Maintenance Technician, Fireman Apprentice [*Navy*] (DNAB)
HTFC.......... High-Temperature Fuel Cell
HTFDC.......... Hartford City, IN [*American Association of Railroads railroad junction routing code*]
HTFFA.......... Heat and Fluid Flow (journ.) (SAUS)
HTFFR.......... High-Temperature Fast-Flow Reactor [*See also HTFS*]
HTFFS.......... Heat Transfer and Fluid Flow Service [*British*]
HTFFT.......... Heat Transfer Fluid Flow Thermodynamics (NRCH)
HTFI.......... Fort Ikoma [*Tanzania*] [*ICAO location identifier*] (ICLI)
HTFIP.......... Humid Tropical Forest Inventory Project (SAUO)
HTFM.......... How to Fight Manual [*Military*] (MCD)
HTFMI.......... Heat Transfer and Fluid Mechanics Institute (MCD)
HTFN.......... Hull Maintenance Technician, Fireman [*Navy*] (DNAB)
HTFORE....... Heretofore (ROG)
HTFRI.......... High-Tactile Fidelity Rim Interface [*Tire design*]
HTFS.......... Heat Transfer and Fluid Flow Service [*Also, HTFFS*] [*British*]
HTF/S.......... How to Fight/How to Support [*Military*] (MCD)
HTFT.......... High Temperature Furnace Technology (SAUS)
HTFW.......... High-Temperature Fluid-Wall [*Incineration process*]
HTFX.......... Heat Treat Fixture
HTG.......... Handbuch Theologischer Grundbegriffe [*Munich*] [*A publication*] (BJA)
HTG.......... Heating (KSC)
HTG.......... Heritage Media Corp. [*AMEX symbol*] (CTT)
HTG.......... High-Temperature Gas [*Reactor*]
HTG.......... Hobart Town Gazette [*A publication*]
HTG.......... Honest-to-God Cash Flow Yields [*Finance*] (EMRF)
HTG.......... Hydrostatic Tank Gauging (SAUS)
HTG.......... Hypertriglyceridemia [*Medicine*]
Htg&Vent..... Heating and Ventilating (SAUS)
HTGBG.......... Huntingburg, IN [*American Association of Railroads railroad junction routing code*]
HTGC.......... High-Temperature Gas-Cooled Reactor (BARN)
HTGCR.......... High-Temperature Gas-Cooled Reactor
HTGF.......... Human Transforming Growth Factor [*Biochemistry*]
HTGL.......... Hepatic Triglyceride Lipase [*An enzyme*]
HTGL.......... High Temperature Gasdynamics Laboratory [*Stanford University*] [*Research center*] (RCD)
HTGMD.......... Heritage Media Corp. (SAUO)
HTGPF.......... High-Temperature General-Purpose Furnace
HTGR.......... High-Temperature Gas-Cooled Reactor
HTGR.......... High Temperature Gas Reactor (EERA)
HTGR-CX..... High-Temperature Gas-Cooled-Reactor Critical Experiment
HTGRE.......... High-Temperature Gas-Cooled-Reactor Experiment
HTGR SC/C... HTGR Steam Cycle Cogeneration (SAUS)
HTGTN.......... Huntington, WV [*American Association of Railroads railroad junction routing code*]
HTH.......... Hawthorne [*Nevada*] [*Airport symbol*] [*Obsolete*] (OAG)
HTH.......... Head-to-Head (AAEL)
HTH.......... Heart to Heart Foundation (EA)
HTH.......... Helix-Turn-Helix [*Protein structure*]
HTH.......... Hexagon Tungsten Honeycomb
HTH.......... High-Temperature Heater
HTh.......... High Tension [*Medicine*] (EDAA)
HTH.......... High-Test Hypochlorite (WGA)
HTH.......... Homeostatic Thymus Hormone [*Immunology*]
HTH.......... Home Town Honey [*Slang*]
HTH.......... Hope this Helps [*Astronomy term*]
HtH.......... Human-to-Human [*Medicine*] (EDAA)
HTH.......... Hypothalamus [*Medicine*] (DMAA)
HTHA.......... Hearing and Tinnitus Help Association [*Later, AEAR*] (EA)
HtHaN.......... Northern Montana College, Havre, MT [*Library symbol*] [*Library of Congress*] (LCLS)
HTHD.......... Hypertensive Heart Disease [*Medicine*] (MAE)
HTHE.......... High Temperature Heat Exchanger (EEVL)
HTHL.......... Horizontal Takeoff Horizontal Landing
HTHM.......... High Toxic Hazard Material
HTHP.......... High Temperature/High Pressure (SAUS)
HTHP.......... Hugh-Temperature/High Pressure (SAUS)
HTHPA.......... High Temperatures-High Pressures (journ.) (SAUS)
HTHR.......... Hawthorne Financial Corp. [*NASDAQ symbol*] (NQ)
HTHR.......... Hawthorne Finl [*NASDAQ symbol*] (TTSB)
HTHR.......... High-Tension/High-Resistance [*Automotive engineering*]
HT-HS.......... High-Temperature, High-Shear Viscometer
HTHSR.......... High-Temperature, High-Shear-Rate [*Viscosity measurement*]
HThSt.......... Harvard Theological Studies (journ.) (SAUS)
HTI.......... Haiti [*ANSI three-letter standard code*] (CNC)
HTI.......... Haiti International Air SA [*ICAO designator*] (FAAC)
HTI.......... Hamilton Island [*Australia*] [*Airport symbol*] (OAG)
HTI.......... Hamilton Technology, Inc.
HTI.......... Hand Tools Institute (EA)
HTI.......... Headquarters Top Inputs (SAUS)
HTI.......... Healthtrust-Hospital Co. (SAUO)
HTI.......... Heartland Technology, Inc. [*AMEX symbol*] (NASQ)
HTI.......... Heat Transfer Instrument System [*Nuclear energy*] (NUCP)
HTI.......... Heavy Tip-In [*Automotive testing*]
HTI.......... Hemispheric Thrombotic Infarction [*Medicine*] (DMAA)
HTI.......... Hemorrhagic Toxin Inhibitor [*Hematology*]
HTI.......... High-Technology Intensive (SAUS)
HTI.......... High Temperature Impact (SAUS)
HTI.......... High Temperature Incineration (or Incinerator) (SAUS)
HTI.......... High-Temperature Incinerator
HTI.......... High Temperature Insulation (SAUS)
HTI.......... High Temperature Isotope (SAUS)
HTI.......... High-Temperature Isotropic
HTI.......... High Twelve International (SAUO)
HTI.......... Hindu Test Information (journ.) (SAUS)
HTI.......... Home Testing Institute, Inc. (NTCM)
HTI.......... Horizons Technology, Inc.
HTI.......... Horizontal Tactics Indicator
HTI.......... Horizontal Technology Insertion
HTI.......... Horizontal Technology Integration [*Business term*] (INF)
HTI.......... Hughes Training Inc. (SAUS)
HTI.......... Hughes Training Incorporated (SAUO)
HTI.......... Humanities Text Initiative (SAUS)
HTI.......... Hymn Tune Index [*A publication*]
HTIG.......... Homologous Tetanus Immune Globulin [*Medicine*] (DMAA)
hTIg.......... Human Tetanus Immunoglobulin [*Medicine*] (STED)
HTIG.......... Hungry Tiger, Incorporated (SAUO)
HT Insulation... Heavy Thermoplastic Insulation (SAUS)
HTIP.......... Hanford Technology Integrated Program (SAUS)
HTIP.......... Horizontal Technology Integration Plan (SAUS)
HTIP.......... Housing Technology Incentives Program (SAUS)
HT-IR.......... Hadamard Transform-Infrared Spectroscopy (SAUS)
HTIR.......... Iringa [*Tanzania*] [*ICAO location identifier*] (ICLI)
HTIS.......... Hadamard Transform Imaging Spectroscopy (SAUS)
HTIS.......... Heat Transfer Instrument System (NRCH)
HT/IT.......... Homing Terrier/Improved Tartar [*Missile*] (MCD)
HTJ.......... Hardware Trade Journal (journ.) (SAUS)
HTJ.......... H-Plane Tee Junction
HTJPA.......... Heat Transfer. Japanese Research (journ.) (SAUS)
HTK.......... Hard-Target Kill [*Military*] (GFGA)
HTK.......... Head to Come [*A notation on copy that the headline will be written and set later*] (WDMC)
HTK.......... Head to Kum [*Come*] [*Publishing*]

HTK.......... Heel to Knee (DMAA)
HTK.......... Hit to Kill [*Military*] (ACAE)
HTK.......... Howtek, Inc. (SAUO)
HTKA.......... Kigoma [*Tanzania*] [*ICAO location identifier*] (ICLI)
HTKI.......... Kilwa Masoko [*Tanzania*] [*ICAO location identifier*] (ICLI)
HTKJ.......... Kilimanjaro [*Tanzania*] [*ICAO location identifier*] (ICLI)
HTKNT.......... Herders Theologischer Kommentar zum Neuen Testament [*Freiburg*] [*A publication*] (BJA)
HTKO.......... Kongwa [*Tanzania*] [*ICAO location identifier*] (ICLI)
HTKP.......... Hard-Target Kill Potential [*Military*] (MCD)
HTKP.......... Hard Target Kill Probability (SAUS)
HTKT.......... Kilimatinde [*Tanzania*] [*ICAO location identifier*] (ICLI)
HTL.......... Hamster Tumor Line (DB)
HTL.......... Hanford Technical Library (SAUS)
HTL.......... Hearing Threshold Level
HTL.......... Heartland Partners Ltd. Class A [*AMEX symbol*] (SPSG)
HTL.......... Heat Transfer Laboratory [*MIT*] (MCD)
HTL.......... Heat Transfer Loop (NRCH)
HTL.......... Heavy-Traffic Licence (SAUS)
HTL.......... Helicopter Transportable Launcher (MUGU)
HTL.......... Helper T-Lymphocyte [*Immunology*]
HTL.......... High-Level Transistor Logic
HTL.......... High-noise Threshold Logic (SAUS)
HTL.......... High Temperature Lacquer (SAUS)
HTL.......... High-Temperature Lacquer
HTL.......... High Threshold Logic
HTL.......... High Tide Level (SAUS)
HTL.......... High Turbulence Level
HTL.......... High voltage Transistor Logic (SAUS)
HTL.......... Histologic Technologist [*Medicine*] (MEDA)
HTL.......... Histotechnologist [*Medicine*] (STED)
HTL.......... Hotel (WDAA)
HTL.......... Hotel Call, Time, and Charges Mandatory [*Telecommunications*] (TEL)
HTL.......... Hot Tub Lung (MELL)
HTL.......... Houghton Lake, MI [*Location identifier*] [*FAA*] (FAAL)
HTL.......... Human T-Cell Leukemia [*Medicine*] (STED)
HTL.......... Human T-Cell Lymphoma [*Medicine*] (STED)
HTL.......... Human Thymic Leukemia [*Medicine*] (STED)
HTL.......... Hydroxyl Terminated Liquid (SAUS)
HTLA.......... High Temperature Low-Activity (SAUS)
HTLA.......... High-Titer, Low-Acidity [*Hematology*]
HTLA.......... Human T-Lymphocyte Antigen (DMAA)
HTL(ASCP)... Histotechnologist (American Society of Clinical Pathologists) (DMAA)
HTLB.......... High-Technology Light Brigade [*Army*] (INF)
HTLD.......... Heartland Express, Inc. [*NASDAQ symbol*] (NQ)
HTLD.......... High-Technology Light Division [*DoD*]
HTLD.......... Houston Test for Language Development [*Education*]
HTLDC.......... Hsinchu Tidal Land Development Planning Commission (SAUS)
HTLI.......... Lindi [*Tanzania*] [*ICAO location identifier*] (ICLI)
HTLL.......... High Test Level Language (NASA)
HTLM.......... Lake Manyara [*Tanzania*] [*ICAO location identifier*] (ICLI)
HTLO.......... Lobo Wildlife Lodge [*Tanzania*] [*ICAO location identifier*] (ICLI)
HTLR.......... High-Tension/Low-Resistance [*Automotive engineering*]
HTLR.......... High Torque, Low Rev
HTLS.......... Higher Torque/Low-Speed (DNAB)
HTLS.......... High Thoracic Left Sympathectomy [*Medicine*] (EDAA)
HTLT.......... HTL Telemanagement Ltd. [*Burtonsville, MD*] (TSSD)
HTLT.......... Hughes Transportable Link Terminal
HTLTR.......... High-Temperature Lattice Test Reactor
HTLU.......... Hierarchized Threshold Logic Unit (SAUS)
HTLV.......... Human T-Cell Leukemia Virus (NTIO)
HTLV.......... Human T-Cell Lymphotropic [*formerly, Leukemia*] Virus
HTLV-1.......... Human T-Cell Lymphotropic Virus 1 [*medicine*] (MEC)
HTLV-I.......... Human T Cell Lymphotropic Virus I [*Medicine*] (TAD)
HTLV-II.......... Human T Cell Lymphotropic Virus II [*Medicine*] (TAD)
HTLV-III.......... Human T-Cell Lymphotrophic Virus-Type Three
HTLV-III/LAV... Human T-Cell Lymphotropic Virus Type Three/Lymphadenopathy-Associated Virus
HTLV-MA.......... Human T-Cell Leukemia Virus-Associated Membrane Antigen [*Medicine*] (STED)
HTLVR.......... Human T-Cell Leukemia Virus Receptor [*Medicine*] (DMAA)
HTM.......... Haemophilus Test Medium [*Medicine*] (EDAA)
HTM.......... Hardened Target Munitions (SAUS)
HTM.......... Hard Target Munition (SAUS)
HTM.......... Hard Tube Modulator [*Electronics*]
HTM.......... Hard Tube Monitor [*Electronics*] (IAA)
HTM.......... Harpoon Trainer Module [*Missiles*] (MCD)
HTM.......... Heat Transfer Medium [*Engineering*]
HTM.......... Heat Transfer Meter
HTM.......... Heat Transfer Model (SAUS)
HTM.......... Heat Transfer Module [*Furnace*]
HTM.......... Held to Maturity
HTM.......... High Tempature Melter (ABAC)
HTM.......... High Temperature (IEEE)
HTM.......... High-Temperature Materials
HTM.......... High Temperature Measuring (SAUS)
HTM.......... High Temperature Metallography (SAUS)
HTM.......... High-Temperature Metallography
HTM.......... High Throughput Mission (SSD)
HTM.......... High-Trajectory Missiles (NRCH)
HTM.......... Hole-Transport Material [*Materials science*]
HTM.......... Hydrologic Transport Model (SAUS)
HTM.......... Hypothesis Testing Model (IEEE)
HTM.......... Whitman, MA [*Location identifier*] [*FAA*] (FAAL)
HTMA.......... Hawaii Territorial Medical Association (SAUO)
HTMA.......... Hydraulic Tool Manufacturers Association [*Milwaukee, WI*] (EA)
HTMA.......... Mafia [*Tanzania*] [*ICAO location identifier*] (ICLI)
HTMAEW.......... Home Timber Merchants' Association of England and Wales (BI)
HTMB.......... Heat Titment of Metals (journ.) (SAUS)
HTMB.......... Mbeya [*Tanzania*] [*ICAO location identifier*] (ICLI)
HTMC.......... High Temperature Materials Corp. (SAUS)
HTMC.......... High Temperature Materials Corporation (SAUO)
HTMD.......... High-Technology Motorized Division
HTMD.......... Hold Time Management Display [*NASA*]
HTMD.......... Mwadui [*Tanzania*] [*ICAO location identifier*] (ICLI)
HTM-DB.......... High Temperature Materials Data Bank [*Commission of the European Communities*] [*Information service or system*] (IID)
HTMG.......... Morgororo [*Tanzania*] [*ICAO location identifier*] (ICLI)
HTMI.......... Masasi [*Tanzania*] [*ICAO location identifier*] (ICLI)
HTMIAC.......... High Temperature Materials Information Analysis Center Information Analysis Center [*Formerly, TEPIAC*] [*West Lafayette, IN*] [*DoD*] (GRD)
HTMK.......... Mikumi [*Tanzania*] [*ICAO location identifier*] (ICLI)
HTML.......... High Temperature Materials Laboratory [*Oak Ridge, TN*] [*Oak Ridge National Laboratory*] [*Department of Energy*] (GRD)
HTML.......... Hypertext Markup Language [*Telecommunication*]
html.......... Hypertext Markup Language [*Computer science*]
HTMMC.......... High Temperature Metal Matrix Composite (SAUS)
HTMMP.......... Helo Transportable Mulit-Mission Platform [*Experimental military vehicle*]
HTMO.......... Mombo [*Tanzania*] [*ICAO location identifier*] (ICLI)
HTMOS.......... High-Temperature Metal Oxide Semiçonductor
HTMP.......... High-Temperature Thermomechanical Processing [*Alloy heat resistance*]
HTMP.......... High-Temperature Thermomechanical Pulp [*Pulp and paper technology*]
HTMP.......... Hydrooxytetramethylpiperidine (SAUS)
HTMP.......... Hydroxy(tetramethyl)piperidineoxyl [*Organic chemistry*]
HTMP.......... Mpanda [*Tanzania*] [*ICAO location identifier*] (ICLI)
HTMR.......... High Temperature Metals Recovery [*For hazardous waste treatment*]
HTMR.......... High Threshold Mechanoreceptor [*Neurophysiology*]
HTMR.......... Msembe-Ruaha National Park [*Tanzania*] [*ICAO location identifier*] (ICLI)
HTMS.......... High-Temperature Mass Spectrometry
H-TMS.......... Honeywell Test Management System (SAUS)
HTMS.......... Moshi [*Tanzania*] [*ICAO location identifier*] (ICLI)
HTMT.......... Mtwara [*Tanzania*] [*ICAO location identifier*] (ICLI)
HTMU.......... Musoma [*Tanzania*] [*ICAO location identifier*] (ICLI)
HTMW.......... Mwanza [*Tanzania*] [*ICAO location identifier*] (ICLI)
HTMX.......... Mpwapwa [*Tanzania*] [*ICAO location identifier*] (ICLI)
HTN.......... Haiti North Airline [*ICAO designator*] (FAAC)
HTN.......... Hantaan [*Virus*]
HTN.......... HazTECH News [*A publication*]
HTN.......... Heat Treatable Nodular (SAUS)
HTN.......... Heterodyne (FAAC)
HTN.......... Hocking Technical College, Nelsonville, OH [*OCLC symbol*] (OCLC)
HTN.......... Home Theatre Network [*In network name "HTN Plus"*] [*Cable-television system*]
HTN.......... Hotan [*China*] [*Airport symbol*] (OAG)
HTN.......... Houghton Mifflin Co. [*NYSE symbol*] (SPSG)
HTN.......... HUD [*Department of Housing and Urban Development*] Teleprocessing Network
HTN.......... Hughes Television Network [*New York, NY*] [*Cable-television system*]
HTN.......... Hypertension [*Medicine*]
HTN.......... Hypertensive Nephropathy [*Medicine*] (STED)
HTN.......... Miles City, MT [*Location identifier*] [*FAA*] (FAAL)
HTNA.......... Nachingwea [*Tanzania*] [*ICAO location identifier*] (ICLI)
htnd.......... Heightened (VRA)
HTNG.......... Ngerengere [*Tanzania*] [*ICAO location identifier*] (ICLI)
HTNJ.......... Njombe [*Tanzania*] [*ICAO location identifier*] (ICLI)
HTNR.......... High-Temperature Nitric Oxide Reduction [*Combustion technology*]
HTNS.......... Helicopter Tactical Navigation System (SAUS)
HTNSL.......... Hierarchical Type Neural Simulation Language (SAUS)
HTNSL.......... High Tensile [*Mechanics*]
HTNT.......... High Technology National Training (AIE)
HTO.......... East Hampton [*New York*] [*Airport symbol*] (OAG)
HTO.......... Hazardous Tritium Oxides [*Environmental science*] (COE)
HTO.......... Hereto (ROG)
HTO.......... Heterotopic Ossification [*Orthopedics*] (DAVI)
HTO.......... High-Temperature Oxidation (IEEE)
HTO.......... High Throughput Screening [*Chemistry*]
HTO.......... High Tibial Osteotomy [*Orthopedics*] (DAVI)
HTO.......... Highway Transportation Officer [*Army*]
HTO.......... Horizontal Take-Off (SAUS)
HTO.......... Hospital Transfer Order
HTO.......... Hydrous Titanium Oxide (PDAA)
HTO.......... Hyperion 2005 Investment Grade Opportunity Term Trust [*NYSE symbol*] (SPSG)
HTO.......... Tritiated Hydrogen Oxide (SAUS)
HTO.......... Tritiated Water (SAUS)
HTO.......... Tritium Oxide (SAUS)
HTOFORE.......... Heretofore
H to H.......... Heel to Heel
H to H.......... Heel-to-Heel (SAUS)
HTOH.......... Hydroxytryptophol [*Laboratory*] (DAVI)
HTOHL.......... Horizontal Take-Off, Horizontal Landing (SAUS)
HTOL.......... Horizontal Takeoff and Landing [*Proposed aircraft under development by the British government*] (IAA)
h-top.......... hardtop (SAUS)

HTOP1 .... Human Topoisomerase 1 (SAUS)
HTOR .... 5-Hydroxytryptamine Oxygenase Regulator [*Medicine*] (EDAA)
HTOS .... High Throughput Organic Synthesis [*Chemistry*]
HTOT .... High-Temperature Operating Test (MCD)
HTOVL .... Horizontal Take-Off Vertical Landing [*Aviation*] (PDAA)
H-T P .... Half Title Page (SAUS)
HTP............. Hardness Test Army (SAUS)
HTP............. Hardness Test Plan [*Army*] (AABC)
HTP............. Harris-Teeter Property (SAUS)
HTP............. Heat Transfer Printing [*Textile technology*]
HTP............. High Temperature and Pressure (GNE)
HTP............. High Temperature Performance (SAUS)
HTP............. High Temperature Phase (SAUS)
HTP............. High-Temperature Photochemistry [*Aerochem Research Laboratories, Inc.*] [*Analytical chemistry*]
HTP............. High-Temperature Photolysis [*Physics*]
HTP............. High Temperature Physics (SAUS)
HTP............. High Temperature Plastic (SAUS)
HTP............. High Temperature Polymerization (SAUS)
HTP............. High Temperature Pretreatment (SAUS)
HTP............. High Temperature Pyrolysis (SAUS)
HTP............. High-Test Hydrogen-Peroxide
HTP............. High Test Peroxide (SAUS)
HTP............. High Thermal Performance (SAUS)
HTP............. Highway Traffic Point [*MTMC*] (TAG)
HTP............. Historical Trend Processor (SAUS)
H-T-P .... [*A*] House, a Tree, a Person [*Psychological drawing test*]
HTP............. House-Tree-Person (DIPS)
HTP............. Humidity Test Procedure
HTP............. Humor Test of Personality [*Psychology*]
HTP............. Hydraulically Tuned Pulsed (SAUS)
HTP............. Hydrogen Peroxide (SAUS)
HTP............. Hydrostatic Transmission Pump [*Hydraulics*]
HTP............. Hydrothermal Processing (SAUS)
HTP............. Hydroxytryptophan [*Biochemistry*]
HTP............. Hydroxytyptophane (SAUS)
HTP............. Hypothromboplastinemia [*Medicine*] (DB)
HTPB .... Hydroxyl-Terminated Polybutadiene [*Organic chemistry*]
HTPB .... Hydroxyl-Terminated Polybutylene [*Organic chemistry*] (NASA)
HTPB .... Hydroxy-Terminated Polybutadiene [*Organic chemistry*]
H-T-P/D-A-P... House-Tree-Person and Draw-a-Person as Measures of Abuse in Children: A Quantitative Scoring System [*Test*] (TMMY)
HTPE........... Pemba [*Tanzania*] [*ICAO location identifier*] (ICLI)
HTPF........... Hard Target Programmable Fuze (SAUS)
HTPFP .... High Technology Professionals for Peace [*Defunct*] (EA)
HTPHA......... Huguenot-Thomas Paine Historical Association (EA)
HTPIB .... Hydroxy Terminated Polyisobutylene (SAUS)
HTPLT......... High Temperature Power Life Tester (SAUS)
HTPM.......... Harvard Total Project Manager [*Computer software*]
HTPN .... Home Total Parenteral Nutrition [*Medicine*]
HTPO .... Hanford Transition Program Office (SAUS)
HTPO .... Human Thyroid Peroxidase [*An enzyme*]
HTPP .... Hardness Test Program Plan
HTPS .... High Tension Power Supply (SAUS)
HTPS .... Hull-Turret Position Sensor [*Military*] (RDA)
HTP Test...... House-Tree-Person Test (SAUS)
HTPV .... High-Temperature Power and Voltage (IAA)
HTR .... Halt and Transfer
HTR .... Hanford Test Reactor (NRCH)
HTR .... Hard Tissue Replacement [*Dentistry*]
HTR .... Hard-to-Reach [*Communications term*] (DCT)
HTR .... Harvard Theological Review [*A publication*] (ODCC)
HTR .... Hateruma [*Japan*] [*Airport symbol*] (OAG)
HTR .... Heated-Tube Reactor [*Chemical engineering*]
HTR .... Heater (AAG)
HTR .... Heavy and Tactical Rescue (SAUO)
HTR .... Hemolytic Transfusion Reaction [*Medicine*]
HTR .... High-Temperature Reactor
HTR .... High-Temperature Resistor
HTR .... High Thermal Regime (ACAE)
HTR .... Highway Traffic Regulation (AABC)
HTR .... Hitachi Training Reactor [*Japan*]
HTR .... Holstenair Lubeck, Luftverkehrsservice GmbH [*Germany*] [*ICAO designator*] (FAAC)
HTR .... Homing Terrier Retrofit [*Missile*] (MCD)
HTR .... Homogeneous Thorium Reactor
HTR .... Hours to Run (ADA)
HTR .... Household Tracking Report [*Television ratings*] (NTCM)
HTR .... HTR Industries, Inc. [*Vancouver Stock Exchange symbol*]
HTR .... Human Transferrin Receptor [*Biochemistry*]
HTR .... Hydrothermal Reaction (SAUS)
HTR .... Hydroxyl Terminated Polybutyiene (NAKS)
HTR .... Hyperion Total Return Fund [*NYSE symbol*] (SPSG)
HTR .... Hypermetropia, Right [*Ophthalmology*] (DAVI)
HTRA .... Height Reply Analysis (SAUS)
HTRAC .... Half-Track [*A type of military vehicle*] (AABC)
HTRAM .... Hazmat Transportation Risk Assessment Model (SAUS)
HTRAP......... Height Reply Analysis Processor (SAA)
HTRB .... High-Temperature Reverse Bias [*Electronics*] (IAA)
HTRB Test ... High Temperature Reverse Bias Test (SAUS)
HTRD .... Heat Transfer Rotating Disc [*Engineering*]
HTRDA......... High-Temperature Reactor Development Associates
HTRE .... Heat Transfer Reactor Experiment
HTRE .... High-Temperature Reactor Experiment [*Department of Energy*] (GAAI)
HTRES .... Heat Resistant (SAUS)
HT RES........ Heat Resisting (SAUS)
HTRF .... Hollywood Park Enterprises, Inc. (SAUO)
HTRF .... Homogeneous Time Resolved Fluorescence [*Analytical Chemistry*]
HTRF .... Human Telomeric Repeat-Binding Factor [*Genetics*]
HTRFZ .... Hollywood Park Realty Enterprises, Inc. [*NASDAQ symbol*] (COMM)
HTRI .... Heat Transfer Research Institute (NRCH)
HTRI .... High Technology Recruitment Index [*A publication*]
HTRIN.......... Holy Trinity
HTRK .... Half-Track [*A type of military vehicle*]
HTRN .... HERL-RTP Training System (SAUS)
HTROL......... Help To Run Our-Lines [*Military*]
H TRON .... Home TRON [*The Real-Time Operating System Nucleus*] (NITA)
HTRR .... Harpoon Transfer Relay Rack [*Missiles*] (MCD)
Htrs............. Heaters (MIST)
HTRS .... High-Temperature Reflectance Spectroscopy (DB)
HTRW .... Hazardous, Toxic, and Radiological Waste [*US Army Corps of Engineers*]
HTS............. Hadamard Transform Spectrometer (SAUS)
HTS............. Half-Time Survey [*Shipping*]
HTS............. Hamden Testing Services, Inc.
HTS............. Hard Target Sensor (SAUS)
HTS............. Harmonized Tariff Schedule Nomenclature (JAGO)
HTS............. Harmonized Tariff System
HTS............. HARM Targeting System (SAUO)
HTS............. Harness Tracks Security [*Defunct*] (EA)
HTS............. Harris Typesetting System (SAUS)
HTS............. Harvard Theological Studies [*A publication*] (ODCC)
HTS............. Hawaiian Tracking Station
HTS............. Head, Track and Sector (SAUS)
HTS............. Head, Track, and Selector
HTS............. Head Traumatic Syndrome [*Medicine*] (DMAA)
HTS............. Heal-to-Shin [*Test*] [*Neurology*] (DAVI)
HTS............. Heat Transfer Salt (SAUS)
HTS............. Heat Transfer Section
HTS............. Heat Transfer System
HTS............. Heat Transport Section [*Apollo*] [*NASA*]
HTS............. Heat Transport System [*NASA*] (NASA)
HTS............. Heat-Treated Steel
HTS............. Heavy-Duty Thermoset Elastomer Insulation [*Automotive engineering*]
HTS............. Heel-to-Shin [*Medicine*] (EDAA)
HTS............. Heights (MCD)
Hts.............. Heights (TBD)
HTS............. Height-Telling Surveillance
HTS............. HeLa Tumor Suppression [*Medicine*] (DMAA)
HTS............. Helitrans Air Service, Inc. [*ICAO designator*] (FAAC)
HTS............. Hemangioma-Thrombocytopenia Syndrome [*Medicine*] (MEDA)
HTS............. High Technology Solution (DGA)
HTS............. High Temperature gas-cooled reactor System (SAUS)
HTS............. High Temperature Shift (SAUS)
HTS............. High Temperature Steam (SAUS)
HTS............. High-Temperature Steam
HTS............. High Temperature Storage (SAUS)
HTS............. High-Temperature Superconducting
HTS............. High-Temperature Superconductivity (ECON)
HTS............. High-Temperature Superconductor [*Materials science*]
HTS............. High-Temperature Switch [*Automotive electronics*]
HTS............. High Tensile Steel (SAUS)
HTS............. High-Tensile Steel
HTS............. High Tensile Strength [*Mechanics*]
HTS............. High-Tension Separation (IAA)
HTS............. High Tension Supply (SAUS)
HTS............. High-Tension Supply (IAA)
HTS............. High-Tension Synthetic Insulation [*Automotive engineering*]
HTS............. High Throughput Screening [*For drug screening*]
HTS............. High-Throughput Screening (SAUS)
HTS............. High Thrust Solenoid (SAUS)
HTS............. Hold Tag System (TIMI)
HTS............. Home Team Sports [*Cable-television system*]
HTS............. Host-to-Satellite
HTS............. House Territories Subcommittee (SAUO)
HTS............. How to Support [*Manuals*] [*Military*] (MCD)
HTS............. Hughes Text System (ACAE)
HTS............. Human Thyroid Stimulator [*Endocrinology*]
HTS............. Hunting Technical Services (SAUS)
HTS............. Huntington [*West Virginia*] [*Airport symbol*] (OAG)
HTS............. Hybrid Test Set
HTS............. Hydraulic Test Set [*or Station*]
HTS............. Hydraulic Test Station (SAUS)
HTS............. Hydrodynamic Test System
HTS............. Hyper-Thin Septum (SAUS)
HTSA .... Highway Traffic Safety Administration (COE)
HTSA .... History Trust of South Australia
HTSA .... Host-Tenant Support Agreement [*Military*]
HTSC .... High-Temperature Semiconductor [*Electronics*]
HTSC .... High-Temperature Superconductivity [*Materials science*]
HTSC .... High-Temperature Superconductor [*Materials science*]
HTSC .... Highway Traffic Safety Center [*Michigan State University*]
HTSC .... Hughes Technical Services Company (ACAE)
HTSCA .... Human Tumor Stem Cell Assay [*Oncology*]
HTS Company... Humble Time-Sharing Co. (SAUS)
HTS Company... Humble Time-Sharing Company (SAUO)
HTSD .... Singida [*Tanzania*] [*ICAO location identifier*] (ICLI)
HTSE........... Same [*Tanzania*] [*ICAO location identifier*] (ICLI)

HTSEC .... High-Temperature Size-Exclusion Chromatography
HTSF .... High-Temperature Sodium Facility [*Nuclear energy*] (NRCH)
HTSF .... Hydrated Textured Soy Flour
HTSH .... Human Thyroid Stimulating Hormone [*Also, htsh*] [*Endocrinology*]
HTSH .... Mafinga [*Tanzania*] [*ICAO location identifier*] (ICLI)
HTSHLD .... Heat Shield
HTSI .... Hughes Training Systems, Incorporated (ACAE)
HTSI .... Human Thyroid-Stimulating Immunoglobulin (PDAA)
HTSIM .... Height Stimulator (IAA)
HTSJ .... High Temperature-Society of Japan (SAUO)
HTSK .... Heat Sink (MSA)
HTSL .... Heat Transfer Simulation Loop (IEEE)
HTSL .... High Temperature Sodium Loop (PDAA)
HTSM .... High-Temperature Skim Milk (OA)
HTSN .... Seronera [*Tanzania*] [*ICAO location identifier*] (ICLI)
HTSO .... Songea [*Tanzania*] [*ICAO location identifier*] (ICLI)
HT/SPC .... Heat Treating/Statistical Process Control (SAUS)
HTSR .... High Temperature Steam Reformer (SAUS)
HTSR .... High-Temperature Strain Gauge
HTSS .... Hamilton Test Simulation System (SAUS)
HTSS .... Honeywell Time-Sharing System [*Computer science*] (IEEE)
HTSSE .... High-Temperature-Superconductivity Space Experiment [*Navy*]
HTST .... Heartstream Inc. [*NASDAQ symbol*] (TTSB)
HTSt .... Hervormde Teologiese Studies [*Pretoria, South Africa*] [*A publication*] (BJA)
HTST .... High-Temperature Short-Time [*Pasteurization*] [*Food processing*]
HTST Pasteurization ... High Temperature-Short Time Pasteurization (SAUS)
HTSU .... Sumbawanga [*Tanzania*] [*ICAO location identifier*] (ICLI)
HTSUP .... Height Supervisor [*RADAR*]
HTSUS .... Harmonized Tariff Schedule of the United States [*Formerly, TSUS*]
HTSY .... Shinyanga [*Tanzania*] [*ICAO location identifier*] (ICLI)
HT/SZ .... Height/Size (DNAB)
HTT .... Air Tchad, Societe de Transport Aeriens [*Chad*] [*ICAO designator*] (FAAC)
HTT .... Hallett [*Australia*] [*Seismograph station code, US Geological Survey*] (SEIS)
HTT .... Hand Thrust Test [*Medicine*] (EDAA)
HTT .... Hard Target Tracking (ACAE)
HTT .... Heat-Treatment Temperature
HTT .... Heavy Tactical Transport
HTT .... Heavy Tracked Tractor (SAUS)
HTT .... Helicoptere de Troupes (SAUS)
HTT .... High Technology Testbed (ACAE)
HTT .... High Technology Transfer Co. [*Czechoslovakia*] (ECON)
HTT .... High-Temperature Tetragonal [*Physics*]
HTT .... High-Temperature Thermomechanical Treatment [*Steel forging*]
HTT .... High Temperature Treatment [*Materials science*]
HTT .... High-Temperature Tunnel [*NASA*]
HTT .... High-Tension Thermoplastic Insulation [*Automotive engineering*]
HTT .... High-Tension Tunnel (SAUS)
HTT .... High Touch Therapy (MELL)
HTT .... Hook Tongue Terminal
HTT .... Hot Tube Test [*Lubricants*]
HTT .... Hydraulics, Turbine Throttle (DNAB)
HTT .... Hyperion 1999 Term Trust [*NYSE symbol*] (SPSG)
HTTA .... Highway and Traffic Technicians Association [*British*] (EAIO)
HTTB .... High-Technology Test Bed [*Army*]
HTTB .... Tabora [*Tanzania*] [*ICAO location identifier*] (ICLI)
HTTF .... High Temperature Test Facility (SAUS)
HTTG .... Tanga [*Tanzania*] [*ICAO location identifier*] (ICLI)
HTTL .... High-Speed Transistor-Transistor Logic (IAA)
HTTMT .... High-Temperature Thermomechanical Treatment [*Steel forging*]
HTTP .... Hypertext Markup Language (SAUS)
HTTP .... Hypertext Transfer (SAUS)
HTTP .... Hyper Text Transfer Protocol (SAUS)
http .... Hypertext Transfer Protocol (AAEL)
HTTP .... Hypertext Transmission Protocol (SAUS)
HTTP .... Hyper Text Transport Protocol (SAUS)
HTTP .... HyperText Transport Protocol [*Computer science*] (IGQR)
HTTPD .... Hypertext Transfer Protocol DAEMON (SAUS)
HTTP-NG .... HTTP Next Generation (SAUS)
HTTPNG .... Hypertext Transfer Protocol-Next Generation (SAUS)
HTTPS .... HyperText Transport Protocol Secure [*Computer science*] (IGQR)
HTTPS .... HyperText Transport Protocol Server [*Computer science*] (DDC)
HTTR .... Heat Treat
HTTR .... High Temperature Test Reactor (SAUS)
HTTR .... High Temperature Thorium Reactor (SAUS)
HTTS .... Hybrid Thermal Treatment System [*Incinerator*] [*IT Corp.*] (RDA)
HTTS .... Hydroquench Thrust Termination System [*NASA*] (KSC)
HTTT .... High-Temperature Turbine Technology [*Power generation*]
HTTU .... Tunduru [*Tanzania*] [*ICAO location identifier*] (ICLI)
HTTVMT .... High Temperature Thermovibrational (SAUS)
HTTVMT .... High Temperature Thermovibrational Mechanical Treatment (SAUS)
HTU .... Handheld Terminal Unit
HTU .... Handheld Thermal Unit
HTU .... Harbin Technical University (SAUO)
HTU .... HDSL Transmission Unit (SAUS)
HTU .... Head Trauma Unit [*Medicine*] (IDYL)
HTU .... Heat Transfer Unit
HTU .... Height of a Transfer Unit [*Distillation*]
HTU .... Helicopter Training Unit (SAUS)
HTU .... Horizontal Trail Unit (MCD)
HTU .... Hoyt Peak [*Utah*] [*Seismograph station code, US Geological Survey*] (SEIS)
HTUEA .... Hughes Tucson Employees' Association (ACAE)
HTUR .... Urambo [*Tanzania*] [*ICAO location identifier*] (ICLI)
HTV .... Half Thickness Value (NRCH)
HTV .... Harlech Television [*Wales*]
HTV .... Hearst-Argyle Television [*NYSE symbol*]
HTV .... Herpes-Type Virus
HTV .... High-Altitude Test Vehicle (MUGU)
HTV .... High Temperature and Velocity (SAUS)
HTV .... Hiroshima Television (SAUO)
HTV .... Hi Tech Ventures, Inc. [*Vancouver Stock Exchange symbol*]
HTV .... Home Video Tutorial
HTV .... Homing Test Vehicle (NG)
HTV .... Horlicks Television (SAUO)
HTV .... Hospital Patient Transport Vehicle
HTV .... Hull Test Vehicle [*for submarines*] (MCD)
HTV .... Hybrid Test Vehicle [*Gasoline and electric motor*]
HTV .... Hydrothermal Vent [*Geology*]
HTV .... Hypersonic Test Vehicle [*Air Force*]
HTVB .... High Temperature Vacuum Brazing (SAUS)
HTVD .... Hypertensive Vascular Disease [*Cardiology*] (DAVI)
HTVL .... Horizontal Takeoff Vertical Landing
HTVN .... Hispanic Television Network
HTW .... Chesapeake, OH/Huntington, WV [*Location identifier*] [*FAA*] (FAAL)
HTW .... Hard Target Weapon (ACAE)
HTW .... Haystack [*Washington*] [*Seismograph station code, US Geological Survey*] (SEIS)
HTW .... Hazardous and Toxic Waste
HTW .... Heel and Toe Wear [*Tire maintenance*]
HTW .... Helicopter Trap Weapon (SAA)
HTW .... High-Temperature Water
HTW .... High-Temperature Wire
HTW .... Hoosac Tunnel & Wilmington R. R. [*AAR code*]
HTWH .... Wazo Hill [*Tanzania*] [*ICAO location identifier*] (ICLI)
HTWI .... High Temperature Wire Insulation (ACAE)
HTWK .... Ngare Nairobi [*Tanzania*] [*ICAO location identifier*] (ICLI)
ht wkt .... Hit Wicket [*Cricket*] (BARN)
HTWN .... Hometown Bancorp, Inc. [*NASDAQ symbol*] (NQ)
HTWS .... Hawaii Tsunami Warning System [*Marine science*] (OSRA)
HTWS .... High Tension Wireless Station (SAUS)
HTWT .... Hexone Tank Waste Treatment (SAUS)
HTX .... Hemothorax [*Medicine*] (MELL)
HTX .... High Temperature Crystalline (SAUS)
HTX .... Histrionicotoxin (DB)
HTX .... HTML Extensions (SAUS)
HTXA .... Hitox Corp. of America [*NASDAQ symbol*] (CTT)
HTXGR .... Heat Exchanger (KSC)
HTXR .... High Temperature X-Ray Powder Diffraction (EDCT)
HTXRD .... High-Temperature X-Ray Diffraction
HTXS .... High Troughput X-ray Spectroscopy Mission (SAUS)
HTY .... Hatizyo [*Japan*] [*Geomagnetic observatory code*]
HTYP .... Heliotype [*Modified collotype*] (VRA)
HTZ .... Hato Corozal [*Colombia*] [*Airport symbol*] (OAG)
HTZA .... Zanzibar [*Tanzania*] [*ICAO location identifier*] (ICLI)
HU .... Central Airlines Ltd. [*Nigeria*] [*ICAO designator*] (ICDA)
hU .... Dihydrouridine [*Two-letter symbol; see H_2Urd*]
HU .... Habitat Unit (SAUS)
HU .... Haifa University (BJA)
HU .... Hamburger University [*McDonald's Corp.*]
HU .... Hampton Utilities Trust (SAUS)
HU .... Hangup [*Telecommunications*] (TEL)
HU .... Hanyang University (SAUO)
HU .... Harvard University [*Cambridge, MA*]
HU .... Health Unlimited (SAUO)
HU .... Heat Unit (MAE)
H/U .... Heatup [*Nuclear energy*] (NRCH)
HU .... Hebrew University [*Jerusalem*] (BJA)
HU .... Height Unit (SAUS)
HU .... Hemagglutinating Unit [*Immunochemistry*]
HU .... Hemoglobin Unit [*Of hydrolytic enzyme activity*]
HU .... Hemolytic Unit [*Hematology*]
HU .... High-Usage [*Telecommunications*] (TEL)
HU .... Hiroshima University (SAUO)
HU .... Hokkaido University (SAUO)
HU .... Hongshan University (SAUO)
HU .... Horizontal Arithmetic Unit [*Computer science*] (MHDI)
HU .... Hosei University (SAUO)
HU .... Hospital Unit (DOMA)
HU .... Host Unit [*Communications term*] (DCT)
HU .... Housing Unit [*Bureau of the Census*] (GFGA)
HU .... Hubbert Unit [*Petroleum technology*]
HU .... Hudson United Bancorp [*NYSE symbol*] (SG)
Hu .... Hughes' Kentucky Reports [*A publication*] (DLA)
HU .... Hughes Tool Co. [*Aircraft Division*] [*ICAO aircraft manufacturer identifier*] (ICAO)
Hu .... Hughes' United States Circuit Court Reports [*A publication*] (DLA)
Hu .... Hughes United States Circuit Court Reports (journ.) (SAUS)
Hu .... Hugo de Alberico [*Flourished, 1168-71*] [*Authority cited in pre-1607 legal work*] (DSA)
Hu .... Hugolinus de Presbyteris [*Flourished, 1197-1238*] [*Authority cited in pre-1607 legal work*] (DSA)
Hu .... Huguccio [*Deceased, 1210*] [*Authority cited in pre-1607 legal work*] (DSA)
HU .... Hull (DNAB)
Hu .... Human (DB)
HU .... Human Urine [*Medicine*] (DMAA)
HU .... Hungary [*ANSI two-letter standard code*] (CNC)

hu .... Hungary [*MARC country of publication code*] [*Library of Congress*] (LCCP)
Hu .... Hungary (MILB)
HU .... Hydroureter [*Medicine*] (MELL)
HU .... Hydroxyurea [*Also, HYD, HYDREA*] [*Antineoplastic drug*]
HU .... Hyperemia Unit
HU .... Trinidad and Tobago Air Services [*ICAO designator*] (AD)
HU .... University of Hawaii, Honolulu, HI [*Library symbol*] [*Library of Congress*] (LCLS)
HUA .... Heads Up, Ace (SAUS)
HUA .... Highway Users Association (SAUO)
HUA .... Hockey Umpires' Association [*British*]
HUA .... Housing and Urban Affairs (SAUO)
HUA .... Huancayo [*Peru*] [*Seismograph station code, US Geological Survey*] (SEIS)
HUA .... Human Urinary Albumin [*Clinical chemistry*]
HUA .... Humber Aviation Ltd. [*British*] [*ICAO designator*] (FAAC)
HUA .... Huntsville, AL [*Location identifier*] [*FAA*] (FAAL)
HUA .... Hurricane Watch [*Telecommunications*] (OTD)
HUA .... Hydrologic Unit Area (SAUO)
HUAA .... Home Uterine Activity Assessment [*Medicine*] (DMAA)
HUAC .... House Un-American Activities Committee [*Later, HCIS*] [*US Congress*]
HUAM .... Harvard University Art Museums (SAUO)
HUAM .... Home Uterine Activity Monitoring
HuanPw .... Huaneng Power International, Inc. [*Associated Press*] (SAG)
HUAR .... Arua [*Uganda*] [*ICAO location identifier*] (ICLI)
Hu-Ar .... Magyar Orszagos Leveltar, Budapest, Hungary [*Library symbol*] [*Library of Congress*] (LCLS)
HUB .... Handicapped United in Brotherhood
HUB .... Hanford Unit Billing (SAUS)
HUB .... Houston, TX [*Location identifier*] [*FAA*] (FAAL)
HUB .... Hub Airlines, Inc. [*FAA designator*] (FAAC)
HUB .... Hubbell [*Harvey*] [*NYSE symbol*] (SAG)
HUBA .... Hudson Bay [*AAR code*]
HU-Bau .... Haushaltsunterlage-Bau (SAUS)
Hubb .... Hubbard's Reports [*45-51 Maine*] [*A publication*] (DLA)
Hubbard .... Hubbard's Reports [*45-51 Maine*] [*A publication*] (DLA)
HubbelB .... Hubbell, Harvey [*Associated Press*] (SAG)
Hubb Succ .... Hubback's Evidence of Succession [*A publication*] (DLA)
HUBC .... HUBCO, Inc. [*NASDAQ symbol*] (SAG)
HUBCO .... HUBCO, Inc. [*Associated Press*] (SAG)
HubelA .... Hubbell [*Harvey*], Inc. [*Associated Press*] (SAG)
HubelB .... Hubbel [*Harvey*], Inc. [*Associated Press*] (SAG)
Hub Ev .... Hubback's Evidence of Succession [*A publication*] (DLA)
HUBEX .... Huaihe River Basin Experiment (SAUS)
HUBF .... Human Upstream Binding Factor [*Genetics*]
HuBG .... Allamin Gorkij Konyvtar, Budapest, Hungary [*Library symbol*] [*Library of Congress*] (LCLS)
HUBG .... Hub Group 'A' [*NASDAQ symbol*] (TTSB)
HUBG .... Hub Group, Inc. [*NASDAQ symbol*] (SAG)
HubGrp .... Hub Group, Inc. [*Associated Press*] (SAG)
HUBIA .... Human Biology (journ.) (SAUS)
HuBKPV .... Human BK Polyomavirus
Hub Leg Direc ... Hubbell's Legal Directory [*A publication*] (DLA)
Hub Leg Direc ... Hubbells Legal Directory (journ.) (SAUS)
HuBM .... Orszagos Muszaki Konyvtar es Dokumentacios Kozpont, Budapest, Hungary [*Library symbol*] [*Library of Congress*] (LCLS)
HUBNET .... Hospitals and University at Buffalo Library Resource Network (SAUO)
Hub Prael JC ... Huber's Praelectiones Juris Civilis [*A publication*] (DLA)
Hub Suc .... Hubback's Evidence of Succession [*A publication*] (DLA)
Hub Suc .... Hubbacks Eviden of Succession (journ.) (SAUS)
HUBZ .... Hubinger [*Federal Railroad Administration identification code*]
HUBZone .... Historically Underutilized Business Zone (AAGC)
HUC .... Handheld and Ubiquitous Computing (SAUS)
HUC .... Heat Unity Coating (SAUS)
HUC .... Hebrew Union College [*Later, HUC-JIR*]
HUC .... Hebrew Union College, Jewish Institute of Religion, Cincinnati, OH [*OCLC symbol*] (OCLC)
HUC .... High Usage Circuit (SAUS)
HUC .... Hook Up and Commissioning Conference [*Offshore Conference and Exhibitions Ltd.*] [*British*]
HUC .... Humacao [*Puerto Rico*] [*Airport symbol*] (OAG)
HUC .... Human Umbilical Cord [*Medicine*] (EDAA)
HUC .... Human Use Committee
HUC .... Hydrologic Unit Code (SAUO)
HUC .... Hypouricemia [*Medicine*]
HUCA .... Hebrew Union College Annual (SAUO)
HUCI .... Haitian Unity Council, Inc. [*Defunct*] (EA)
HUCIA .... Harvard University Center for International Affairs (SAUO)
HUC-JIR .... Hebrew Union College - Jewish Institute of Religion [*Formerly, HUC*] [*Cincinnati, OH*]
HUCJIR .... Hebrew Union College Jewish Institute of Religion (SAUO)
HUCJIR .... Hebrew Union College-Jewish Institute of Religion (SAUS)
HUCO .... Hughes NADGE [*NATO Air Defense Ground Environment*] Consortium
HUCR .... Harvard University Character Recognition (or Recognizer) (SAUO)
HUCR .... Highest Useful Compression Ratio [*Aerospace*]
HUCZ .... Huron Chemical [*Federal Railroad Administration identification code*]
HUD .... Department of Housing and Urban Development
HUD .... Handicapped Users' Database [*CompuServe Information Service*] [*Information service or system*] (CRD)
HUD .... Head-Up Display
HUD .... Hong Kong United Dockyard (SAUS)
HUD .... Horizons Unlimited [*FAA designator*] (FAAC)
HUD .... Horizontal Unit Displacement [*Military*] (INF)
HUD .... Housing and Urban Development [*Environment term*] (EGA)
HUD .... Hudson Resources Ltd. [*Vancouver Stock Exchange symbol*]
HUD .... Hungarian Digest (journ.) (SAUS)
HUD .... Hypertonic Uterine Dysfunction [*Medicine*] (MELL)
HUD .... Hypotonic Uterine Dysfunction [*Medicine*] (MELL)
HUDA .... Housing and Urban Development Act
HUDAC .... Housing and Urban Development Association of Canada
Hud & B .... Hudson and Brooke's Irish King's Bench Reports [*1827-31*] [*A publication*] (DLA)
Hud & Br .... Hudson and Brooke's Irish King's Bench Reports [*1827-31*] [*A publication*] (DLA)
Hud & Bro ... Hudson and Brooke's Irish King's Bench Reports [*1827-31*] [*A publication*] (DLA)
HUDAR .... Housing and Urban Development Acquisition Regulations [*A publication*] (AAGC)
HUD BCA .... Department of Housing and Urban Development Board of Contract Appeals (AAGC)
HUDC .... Head-Up Display Computer (SAUS)
HUDC .... Housing and Urban Development Corp. (SAUS)
HUDC .... Housing and Urban Development Corporation (SAUO)
HudCB .... Hudson Chartered Bancorp, Inc. [*Associated Press*] (SAG)
HUDCO .... Housing and Urban Development Corporation (SAUO)
HUDD .... Housing and Urban Development Department [*More commonly, HUD*] (KSC)
HUDDLE .... Hull Urban Design Development Laboratory Enterprises, Inc.
HUDE .... Head-Up Display Electronics (NASA)
HUDEA .... Human Development (journ.) (SAUS)
HuDeAgE .... Debreceni Agrartudomanyi Egyetem, Debrecen, Hungary [*Library symbol*] [*Library of Congress*] (LCLS)
HU/DEAP .... Harvard University Division of Engineering and Applied Physics [*Cambridge, MA*]
Hudeiba Res Stn Annu Rep ... Hudeiba Research Station. Annual Report (journ.) (SAUS)
HuDeK .... Debreceni Reformatus Kollegium Nagykonyvtara, Debrecen, Hungary [*Library symbol*] [*Library of Congress*] (LCLS)
HuDeOE .... Debreceni Orvostudomanyi Egyetem, Debrecen, Hungary [*Library symbol*] [*Library of Congress*] (LCLS)
HUD-EU .... Head-Up Display Electronic Unit (SAUS)
Hud Exec .... Hudson's Executor's Guide [*A publication*] (DLA)
HUD-FDA .... Housing and Urban Development-Federal Housing Administration (SAUS)
HUDG .... History at the Universities Defence Group (SAUO)
HudGn .... Hudson General Corp. [*Associated Press*] (SAG)
HUD-HPMC ... Department of Housing and Urban Development, Assistant Secretary for Housing Production and Mortage Credit (SAUO)
Hud Inst .... Hudson Institute (SAUO)
HUDMAP .... HUD [*Department of Housing and Urban Development*] Mortgage Accounting Project
HUDPR .... Housing and Urban Development [*Department*] Procurement Regulations
HUDS .... Hudson Hotels Corp. [*NASDAQ symbol*] (SAG)
HudsFd .... Hudson Foods, Inc. [*Associated Press*] (SAG)
HudsHotl .... Hudson Hotels Corp. [*Associated Press*] (SAG)
HudsnCB .... Hudson Chartered Bancorp, Inc. [*Associated Press*] (SAG)
Hudson .... Hudson on Building Contracts [*A publication*] (DLA)
Hudson Internat Legis ... Hudsons International Legislation (journ.) (SAUS)
HudsonTc .... Hudson Technology, Inc. [*Associated Press*] (SAG)
Hudson World Court ... Hudsons World Court Reports (journ.) (SAUS)
HUD System ... Head-Up Display System (SAUS)
HUDT .... Headquarters User Data Terminal (SAUS)
HUDU .... Heads-Up Display Unit [*Aviation*]
HUDWAC .... Heads-Up Display Weapons Aiming Computer (IEEE)
HUDWAS .... Heads-Up Display Weapons Aiming System [*Air Force*] (MCD)
HUDWASS ... Head-Up Display Weapon Aiming Sub-System (SAUO)
Hud Wills .... Hudson on Wills [*A publication*] (DLA)
HUDX .... Hudson Technologies [*Private rail car owner code*]
HUE .... Health Understanding and Education (SAUO)
HUE .... Humera [*Ethiopia*] [*Airport symbol*] (OAG)
HUEC .... Entebbe Area Control Center [*Uganda*] [*ICAO location identifier*] (ICLI)
HUEN .... Entebbe/International [*Uganda*] [*ICAO location identifier*] (ICLI)
HuEPO .... Human Erythropoietin [*Medicine*] (EDAA)
huEPO .... Human Erythropoietin [*Biochemistry*]
HUET .... Helicopter Underwater Escape Trainer (SAUS)
HUF .... Highway Users Federation (SAUO)
HUF .... Highway Users Federation for Safety and Mobility [*Later, ASF*] (EA)
HUF .... Horny Unattached Female (SAUS)
HUF .... Huffy Corp. [*NYSE symbol*] (SPSG)
HUF .... Hungarian Foreign Trade (journ.) (SAUS)
HUF .... Hungarian Forint (SAUS)
HUF .... Terre Haute [*Indiana*] [*Airport symbol*] (OAG)
HUFAA .... Human Factors (journ.) (SAUS)
HUFB .... Hungarofilm Bulletin (journ.) (SAUS)
Huffy .... Huffy Corp. [*Associated Press*] (SAG)
HUFIT .... Human Factor Laboratories in Information Technologies (SAUO)
HUFK .... Huffman Koos, Inc. (SAUO)
HUFP .... Fort Portal [*Uganda*] [*ICAO location identifier*] (ICLI)
HUFSAM .... Highway Users Federation for Safety and Mobility [*FHWA*] (TAG)
HU-FSH .... Human Urinary Follicle-Stimulating Hormone [*Medicine*] (DMAA)
HUFSM .... Highway Users Federation for Safety and Mobility
HUG .... Hastech Users Group (EA)
HUG .... Head of Units Group [*American Library Association*]
HUG .... Help Us Grow (SAUS)
HUG .... Hiram Ulysses Grant [*US general and president, 1822-1885*]

HUG .... Honeywell Users Group
HUG .... Hopitaux Universitaires de Geneve [*Switzerland*]
HUG .... Hughes Supply, Inc. [*NYSE symbol*] (SPSG)
HUG .... Hug-Laf-Luv (EA)
Hug .... Hugo de Alberico [*Flourished, 12th century*] [*Authority cited in pre-1607 legal work*] (DSA)
Hug .... Hugolinus de Presbyteris [*Flourished, 1197-1238*] [*Authority cited in pre-1607 legal work*] (DSA)
Hug .... Huguccio [*Deceased, 1210*] [*Authority cited in pre-1607 legal work*] (DSA)
HUG .... Hungarian Economy (journ.) (SAUS)
HUG .... Lonely, AK [*Location identifier*] [*FAA*] (FAAL)
HUGA .... Human Genome Analyzer [*System for analysis of DNA*] [*Institute of Physical and Chemical Research, Japan*] [*Genetics*]
HUGE .... Hewlett packard Unsupported Gnu Emacs (SAUS)
HUGE .... High-Field, Ultrathin Gel Electrophoresis [*Analytical biochemistry*]
HUGE .... Humagen, Inc. (SAUO)
Hugh .... Hughes' Circuit Court Reports [*A publication*] (DLA)
Hugh .... Hughes' Kentucky Reports [*A publication*] (DLA)
HUGH .... Human Growth Hormone (MELL)
Hugh Abr ..... Hughes' Abridgment [*1663-65*] [*England*] [*A publication*] (DLA)
Hugh Con ..... Hughes' Precedents in Conveyancing [*2nd ed.*] [*1855-57*] [*A publication*] (DLA)
Hugh Conv ... Hughes' Precedents in Conveyancing [*2nd ed.*] [*1855-57*] [*A publication*] (DLA)
Hugh Ent ..... Hughes' Entries [*1659*] [*A publication*] (DLA)
Hugh Eq D ... Hughes' Edition of Van Heythuysen's Equity Draftsman [*A publication*] (DLA)
HUGHES ...... Hughes Aircraft Company (SAUO)
Hughes .... Hughes Air West [*ICAO designator*] (AD)
Hughes .... Hughes' Kentucky Supreme Court Reports [*1785-1801*] [*A publication*] (DLA)
Hughes .... Hughes Resources, Inc. [*Associated Press*] (SAG)
Hughes .... Hughes' United States Circuit Court Reports [*A publication*] (DLA)
Hughes Fed Prac ... Hughes' Federal Practice [*A publication*] (DLA)
HUGHES-NEL ... Hughes Aircraft Company - Nuclear Electronics Laboratory (SAUO)
HUGHES-NEL ... Hughes Aircraft Company-Nuclear Electronics Laboratory (SAUS)
Hughes (US) ... Hughes' Circuit Court Reports [*United States*] [*A publication*] (DLA)
Hugh Ins ...... Hughes on Insurance [*A publication*] (DLA)
Hugh Prec ... Hughes' Precedents in Conveyancing [*2nd ed.*] [*1855-57*] [*A publication*] (DLA)
HughSp .... Hughes Supply, Inc. [*Associated Press*] (SAG)
Hugh Wills ... Hughes on Wills [*A publication*] (DLA)
Hugh Wr ...... Hughes on Writs [*A publication*] (DLA)
HUGO .... Helicopter Unit Ground Operations (SAUO)
HUGO .... Highly Unusual Geophysical Operation [*A meteorological research vehicle*]
HUGO .... Highly Usable Geophysical Observation (SAUO)
HUGO .... Holland User Group for OS/2 (SAUO)
Hugo .... Hugolinus [*Authority cited in pre-1607 legal work*] (DSA)
HUGO .... Hugoton Energy Corp. [*NASDAQ symbol*] (SAG)
HUGO .... Human Genome Organization [*Genetics*]
Hugo Hist Dr Rom ... Hugo's Histoire du Droit Romain [*A publication*] (DLA)
Hugo Hist du Droit Rom ... Hugo's Histoire du Droit Romain [*A publication*] (DLA)
Hugol .... Hugolinus de Presbyteris [*Flourished, 1197-1238*] [*Authority cited in pre-1607 legal work*] (DSA)
HugotEn .... Hugoton Energy Corp. [*Associated Press*] (SAG)
HUG's .... Home User Groups [*Computer science*]
HUG-SMS .... Honeywell Users Group - Small and Medium Systems [*Later, NAHU*]
HUGSMS ...... Honeywell Users Group-Small and Medium Systems (SAUO)
HUG-SS ...... Honeywell Users Group, Small and Medium Systems (SAUO)
HUGU .... Gulu [*Uganda*] [*ICAO location identifier*] (ICLI)
Hugu .... Huguccio [*Deceased, 1210*] [*Authority cited in pre-1607 legal work*] (DSA)
Huguenot Soc S Afr Bull ... Huguenot Society of South Africa. Bulletin (journ.) (SAUS)
HUH .... Huahine [*French Polynesia*] [*Airport symbol*] (OAG)
HUH .... Hualalai [*Hawaii*] [*Seismograph station code, US Geological Survey*] (SEIS)
HuH .... Hughes Hall (SAUS)
HUH .... University of Hawaii, Hamilton Library, Honolulu, HI [*OCLC symbol*] (OCLC)
HUHEA .... Human Heredity (journ.) (SAUS)
HUHO .... Hughes Homes, Inc. (SAUO)
HUI .... Headache Unit Index [*Medicine*] (DMAA)
HUI .... Hue [*South Vietnam*] [*Airport symbol*] (AD)
HUIFM .... Human Leukocyte Interferon Milieu [*Biochemistry*] (DAVI)
HuIFN .... Human Interferon [*Biochemistry*]
HUIS .... High-Dose Urea in Invert Sugar (AAMN)
HUJ .... Hebrew University [*Jerusalem*] (BJA)
HuJCPV .... Human JC Polyomavirus
HUJI .... Harakat ul-Jihad al-Islami [*Government term*] (GA)
HUJI .... Jinja [*Uganda*] [*ICAO location identifier*] (ICLI)
HUJI-B .... Harakat ul-Jihad-I-Islami/Bangladesh [*Government term*] (GA)
HUK .... Human Urinary Kallikrein [*Medicine*] (DMAA)
HUK .... Hungarian-Ukranian Heavy Lift Ltd. [*Hungary*] [*ICAO designator*] (FAAC)
HUK .... Hunter-Killer [*Operations against submarines*] [*Navy*]
HUKASWEX ... Hunter-Killer Antisubmarine Warfare Exercise [*Navy*] (NVT)
HUKB .... Hostile, Unknown, Faker, and Big Photo [*Used in Semi-Automatic Ground Environment to designate certain tracks and raids*] (SAA)
HUKB .... Kabale [*Uganda*] [*ICAO location identifier*] (ICLI)
HuKeAgE ...... Agrartudomanyi Egyetem, Keszthely, Hungary [*Library symbol*] [*Library of Congress*] (LCLS)
HUKF .... Kabalega Falls [*Uganda*] [*ICAO location identifier*] (ICLI)
HUKFOR ...... Hunter-Killer Forces [*Navy*]
HUKFORLANT ... Hunter-Killer Forces, Atlantic [*Navy*]
HUKFORPAC ... Hunter-Killer Forces, Pacific [*Navy*]
HUKP .... Hostile, Unknown, Faker, and Pending [*Used in SAGE to designate certain tracks and raids*]
HUKS .... Hostile, Unknown, Faker, Special Track Identities [*Used in SAGE to designate certain tracks and raids*] (SAA)
HUKS .... Hukbong Mapagpalaya ng Bayan [*People's Liberation Army, Philippines*] (CINC)
HUKS .... Hunter-Killer Submarine [*Navy*]
HUKS .... Kasese [*Uganda*] [*ICAO location identifier*] (ICLI)
HUL .... Hardware Utilization List (NASA)
HUL .... Harvard University, Cambridge, MA [*OCLC symbol*] (OCLC)
HUL .... Helsinki University Library (SAUO)
HUL .... High Usage Line (SAUS)
HUL .... Hoist Up Limit (SAUS)
HUL .... Hokkaido University Library (SAUO)
HUL .... Home University Library [*A publication*]
HUL .... Houlton, ME [*Location identifier*] [*FAA*] (FAAL)
HUL .... Houston Law Review (journ.) (SAUS)
Hul .... Hullin (BJA)
HUL .... Hull in England (SAUS)
HULA .... Highly-integrated Unit Logic Assembly (SAUS)
HULA .... Lake George [*Uganda*] [*ICAO location identifier*] (ICLI)
HULAX .... Hawaiian Tax Free Trust [*Mutual fund ticker symbol*] (SG)
HULDA .... Hull Design and Analysis (SAUO)
HULI .... Lira [*Uganda*] [*ICAO location identifier*] (ICLI)
HULL .... High-Usage Load List (DNAB)
Hull Cost ..... Hullock on Costs (journ.) (SAUS)
Hull Costs .... Hullock on Costs [*A publication*] (DLA)
Hull Univ Occas Pap Geogr ... Hull University. Occasional Papers in Geography (journ.) (SAUS)
Hult Conv .... Hulton's Convictions [*1835*] [*A publication*] (DLA)
Hult Conv .... Hultons Convictions (journ.) (SAUS)
HULTEC .... Hull-to-Emitter Correlation [*Navy*] (CAAL)
HULTIS .... Hull Technical Interloan Scheme [*British*] (NITA)
HULTIS .... Humberside Libraries Technical Interloan Scheme (SAUO)
HUM .... Harakat ul-Mujahidin [*Movement of Holy Warriors*] [*Government term*] (GA)
HUM .... Health and Usage Monitoring (DA)
HUM .... Heat or Hot Packs, Ultrasound, and Massage [*Medicine*] (STED)
HUM .... Hematourimetry (STED)
HUM .... Highly Unusual Methods (ECON)
HUM .... Horny Unattached Male (SAUS)
HUM .... Houma [*Louisiana*] [*Airport symbol*] (OAG)
HUM .... Humana, Inc. [*NYSE symbol*] (SPSG)
hum .... humane (SAUS)
hum .... humanism (SAUS)
Hum .... Humanist [*A publication*] (BRI)
HUM .... Humanitarian (ROG)
Hum .... Humanities (AL)
HUM .... Humanities
Hum .... Humanity (SAUS)
HUM .... Humble (ROG)
Hum .... Humerus [*Medicine*] (EDAA)
hum .... Humerus (STED)
HUM .... Humidity (NASA)
Hum .... Hummingbird
HUM .... Hummingbird Helicopters Maldives (Pvt) Ltd. [*ICAO designator*] (FAAC)
HUM .... Humorous (ADA)
Hum .... Humphrey's Tennessee Supreme Court Reports [*1839-51*] [*A publication*] (DLA)
HUM .... Hydrologic Unit Map (SAUO)
HU-M .... University of Hawaii, Leahi Hospital, Hastings H. Walker Medical Library, Honolulu, HI [*Library symbol*] [*Library of Congress*] (LCLS)
HUMA .... Mbarara/Obote [*Uganda*] [*ICAO location identifier*] (ICLI)
HUMAN .... Help Us Make a Nation (EA)
Human .... Humanism (DIAR)
Humana .... Humana, Inc. [*Associated Press*] (SAG)
Human Comm Res ... Human Communications Research (journ.) (SAUS)
Human Eng ... Human Engineering (SAUS)
Humane R ... Humane Review (journ.) (SAUS)
HuMaNet ...... Human-Machine Network (SAUS)
Human Life R ... Human Life Review (journ.) (SAUS)
Human Reprod Med ... Human Reproductive Medicine (journ.) (SAUS)
Human Resource Dev ... Human Resource Development (journ.) (SAUS)
Human Resource Devel Quart ... Human Resource Development Quarterly [*A publication*] (JLIT)
Human Rts J ... Human Rights Journal [*A publication*] (DLA)
Human Rts Rev ... Human Rights Review [*A publication*] (DLA)
Human S ..... Human Studies (journ.) (SAUS)
Hum Antibodies Hybridomas ... Human Antibodies and Hybridomas (journ.) (SAUS)
HUMARA ...... X-Linked Human Androgen Receptor [*Medicine*] (PALA)
Humaras ...... Human Rights Association of Swaziland (SAUO)
HUMARIS .... Human Materials Resources Information System (DIT)
Hum Assoc R ... Humanities Association. Review/Revue. Association des Humanites (journ.) (SAUS)
Humb .... Humble
Hum Behav ... Human Behavior (journ.) (SAUS)
Humber .... Humberside [*County in England*] (WGA)
Humber de Bou ... Humbertus de Bouen [*Authority cited in pre-1607 legal work*] (DSA)
HumBiol ...... Human Biology (SAUO)

Hum Biol Oceania... Human Biology in Oceania (journ.) (SAUS)
Humbird...... Hummingbird Communication Industries [*Associated Press*] (SAG)
HUMBLE...... Humble Oil Co. (SAUO)
HUMBRO...... Human Resources Research Office (SAUO)
HUMBT...... Humboldt, TN [*American Association of Railroads railroad junction routing code*]
HUMC...... Health & Usage Monitoring Computer (SAUS)
HUMC...... Hummingbird Communications [*NASDAQ symbol*] (SG)
Hum Cancer Immunol... Human Cancer Immunology (journ.) (SAUS)
HUMCAT...... Humanoid Catalog [*Mutual Unidentified Flying Object Network*]
HUMCF...... Hummingbird Communication Industries [*NASDAQ symbol*] (SAG)
HUMCF...... Hummingbird Communications [*NASDAQ symbol*] (TTSB)
Hum Chrom Newsl... Human Chromosome Newsletter (journ.) (SAUS)
Hum Commun... Human Communications (journ.) (SAUS)
Hum-Comput Interact... Human-Computer Interactions (journ.) (SAUS)
Hum Con...... Humanist Conference (SAUS)
HuMe...... Human Melanoma (SAUS)
Hume...... Hume's Court of Session Decisions [*1781-1822*] [*Scotland*] [*A publication*] (DLA)
Hum Ecol Forum... Human Ecology Forum (journ.) (SAUS)
Hum Ecol Risk Assess... Human and Ecological Risk Assessment [*A publication*] (PABS)
Hume Com... Hume's Commentaries on Crimes [*Scotland*] [*A publication*] (DLA)
Hume Hist Eng... Hume's History of England [*A publication*] (DLA)
Hume Hist Eng... Humes History of England (journ.) (SAUS)
Hum Environ Swed... Human Environment in Sweden (journ.) (SAUS)
Hume Stud... Hume Studies (journ.) (SAUS)
Hum Ev...... Human Events (journ.) (SAUS)
HUMEVAC...... Humanitarian Emergency Evacuation [*Military*] (NVT)
Hum Exp Toxicol... Human and Experimental Toxicology (journ.) (SAUS)
Hum Factors... Human Factors [*A publication*] (CABS)
Hum Fertl...... Human Fertility (journ.) (SAUS)
HumGen...... Human Genome Sciences, Inc. [*Associated Press*] (SAG)
Hum Genet... Human Genetics (journ.) (SAUS)
Hum Gene ther... Human Gene therapy (SAUS)
Hum Genet Suppl... Human Genetics. Supplement (journ.) (SAUS)
Hum Hair Symp Pap... Human Hair Symposium. Papers (journ.) (SAUS)
HumI...... Humanities Index
HUMI...... Masindi [*Uganda*] [*ICAO location identifier*] (ICLI)
HUMID...... Hughes Unit Malfunction Isolation Detector
Hum Immunol... Human Immunology (journ.) (SAUS)
HUMINS...... Hospital Unified Management Information System (SAUS)
HUMINT...... Human Intelligence [*Spies, double agents, etc.*] [*CIA*] (AFM)
HUMINT...... Human Resources Intelligence (SAUO)
HUMME...... Hummelstown, PA [*American Association of Railroads railroad junction routing code*]
Hum Mind Discuss Nobel Conf... Human Mind, a Discussion at the Nobel Conference (journ.) (SAUS)
Hum Nes...... Human Needs (journ.) (SAUS)
Hum Nutr Appl Nutr... Human Nutrition. Applied Nutrition (journ.) (SAUS)
Hum Nutr Compr Treatise... Human Nutrition. A Comprehensive Treatise (journ.) (SAUS)
Hum Nutr Food Sci Nutr... Human Nutrition. Food Sciences and Nutrition (journ.) (SAUS)
HUMO...... Highest Unoccupied Molecular Orbital (DB)
HUMO...... Hughes Homes, Inc. (SAUO)
HUMO...... Moroto [*Uganda*] [*ICAO location identifier*] (ICLI)
HUMP...... Howard University Mississippi [*Medicine*] (EDAA)
HUMP...... Humphrey Hospitality Tr Inc. [*NASDAQ symbol*] (TTSB)
HUMP...... Humphrey Hospitality Trust, Inc. [*NASDAQ symbol*] (SAG)
Humph...... Humphrey's Tennessee Reports [*20-30 Tennessee*] [*A publication*] (DLA)
Hum Pharmacol Drug Res... Human Pharmacology and Drug Research (journ.) (SAUS)
Humph Dist Reg... Humphreys. District Registry Practice and Procedure [*1977*] [*A publication*] (ILCA)
Humph Prec... Humphry's Common Precedents in Conveyancing [*2nd ed.*] [*1882*] [*A publication*] (DLA)
Humphry...... Humphrey Hospitality Trust, Inc. [*Associated Press*] (SAG)
Hum Physiol... Human Physiology (journ.) (SAUS)
Hum Potential... Human Potential (journ.) (SAUS)
Hum Reprod... Human Reproduction (journ.) (SAUS)
Hum Reprod Proc World Con... Human Reproduction. Proceedings of World Congress (journ.) (SAUS)
HUMRESMANCEN... Human Resources Management Center (SAUS)
HUMRESMANDET... Human Resources Management Detachment [*Navy*] (DNAB)
HUMRESMANSCOL... Human Resources Management School [*Navy*] (DNAB)
HUMRESMANSCOLDET... Human Resources Management School Detachment [*Navy*] (DNAB)
Hum Resour Forum... Human Resources Forum (journ.) (SAUS)
Hum Resour Manage... Human Resource Management (journ.) (SAUS)
Hum Resour Plann... Human Resource Planning (journ.) (SAUS)
Hum Rev...... Humanities Review (journ.) (SAUS)
Hum Righ...... Human Rights (journ.) (SAUS)
HumRRO...... Human Resources Research Office [*George Washington University*]
HumRRO...... Human Resources Research Organization (EA)
Hum Rts LJ... Human Rights Law Journal [*A publication*] (DLA)
Hum Rts Q... Human Rights Quarterly [*A publication*] (DLA)
Hum Rts USSR... Human Rights in the Union of Soviet Socialist Republics [*A publication*] (DLA)
Hum Rts USSR... Human Rights in the Union of Soviet Socialist Republics (journ.) (SAUS)
HUMS...... Health and Usage Monitoring System (SAUO)
HUMS...... Humanitarian Reasons
Hum Sci...... Human Science (journ.) (SAUS)
Hum Soc...... Humane Society (SAUO)
Hum Syst Manage... Human Systems Management (journ.) (SAUS)
Hum Toxicol... Human Toxicology (journ.) (SAUS)
HUMV...... Human light Vehicle (SAUS)
HUN...... Hualien [*Taiwan*] [*Airport symbol*] (OAG)
HUN...... Hundersingen [*Federal Republic of Germany*] [*Seismograph station code, US Geological Survey*] (SEIS)
HUN...... Hundred (MUGU)
hun...... Hungarian [*MARC language code*] [*Library of Congress*] (LCCP)
HUN...... Hungary [*ANSI three-letter standard code*] (CNC)
Hun...... Hun's New York Appellate Division Supreme Court Reports [*A publication*] (DLA)
Hun...... Huns NY Supreme Court Reports (journ.) (SAUS)
HUN...... Hunt Corp. [*NYSE symbol*] [*Formerly, Hunt Manufacturing*] (SG)
HUN...... Hunting Business Aviation [*British*] [*ICAO designator*] (FAAC)
HUN...... Huntington Resources, Inc. [*Vancouver Stock Exchange symbol*]
HUN...... Hunt Manufacturing Co. [*NYSE symbol*] (SPSG)
HUN...... Hyperuricemic Nephropathy [*Medicine*] (MELL)
Hun...... New York Supreme Court Reports [*A publication*] (DLA)
HUNA...... Huna Research [*An association*] (EA)
HUNA...... Namulonge Agrometeorology Station [*Uganda*] [*ICAO location identifier*] (ICLI)
HUND...... Highly Unusual Neutron Detector (SAUS)
hund...... Hundred (GEAB)
HUND...... Hundred
HUNDAS...... Hunting Digital Acquisition System (SAUO)
HUNDRED...... Hiroshima University New Document Retrieval and Dissemination (SAUO)
HUNDREDSB... Hundredsbarrow [*England*]
HUNEDR...... Human Neurobiology (journ.) (SAUS)
Hung...... Hungarian (DIAR)
Hung...... Hungarica (SAUS)
Hung...... Hungary (VRA)
HUNG...... Hungary
Hung Annu Meet Biochem Proc... Hungarian Annual Meeting for Biochemistry. Proceedings (journ.) (SAUS)
Hungarian J Indust Chem Vezprem... Hungarian Journal of Industrial Chemistry Vezprem (journ.) (SAUS)
HUNGARNET... Hungarian Academic and Research Network (TELE)
HUNGAROLAB... Hungarian Association of Testing Laboratories (SAUO)
HungB...... Hungarian Broadcasting Corp. [*Associated Press*] (SAG)
HungBd...... Hungarian Broadcasting Corp. [*Associated Press*] (SAG)
HungBrd...... Hungarian Broadcasting Corp. [*Associated Press*] (SAG)
Hung Build Bull... Hungarian Building Bulletin (journ.) (SAUS)
Hung Econ... Hungarian Economy (journ.) (SAUS)
HUNGF...... Hungerford [*England*]
Hung For Sci Rev... Hungarian Forest Scientifical Review (journ.) (SAUS)
Hung Heavy Ind... Hungarian Heavy Industries (journ.) (SAUS)
Hung J Chem... Hungarian Journal of Chemistry (journ.) (SAUS)
Hung J Ind Chem... Hungarian Journal of Industrial Chemistry (journ.) (SAUS)
Hung J Min Metall... Hungarian Journal of Mining and Metallurgy (journ.) (SAUS)
Hung L Rev... Hungarian Law Review (journ.) (SAUS)
Hung Mach... Hungarian Machinery (journ.) (SAUS)
Hung Med Arch... Hungarian Medical Archives (journ.) (SAUS)
Hung Med Biblio... Hungarian Medical Bibliography (journ.) (SAUS)
Hung Med J... Hungarian Medical Journal (journ.) (SAUS)
Hung Min J... Hungarian Mining Journal (journ.) (SAUS)
HUNGN...... Hungarian
Hung Notes World Hung Educ Serv... Hunger Notes. World Hunger Education Service (journ.) (SAUS)
Hung Pharmacol Soc Congr... Hungarian Pharmacological Society. Congress (journ.) (SAUS)
Hung R...... Hungarian Review (journ.) (SAUS)
Hung S...... Hungarian Survey (journ.) (SAUS)
Hung Sci Instrum... Hungarian Scientific Instruments (journ.) (SAUS)
Hung St Engl... Hungarian Studies in English (journ.) (SAUS)
Hung Tanner... Hungarian Tanner (journ.) (SAUS)
Hung Tech Abstr... Hungarian Technical Abstracts (journ.) (SAUS)
HungTel...... Hungarian Telephone and Cable Corp. [*Associated Press*] (SAG)
HungTelc...... Hungarian Teleconstruction & Cable Corp. [*Associated Press*] (SAG)
Hung Vet J... Hungarian Veterinary Journal (journ.) (SAUS)
H Unit...... Holzknecht Unit (SAUS)
HUNMARC... Hungarian MARC (SAUS)
HUNNE...... Huntsman, NE [*American Association of Railroads railroad junction routing code*]
HunQ...... Hungarian Quarterly (journ.) (SAUS)
HUNT...... Hunt [*Federal Railroad Administration identification code*]
HUNT...... Hunterdon Pharmaceuticals (SAUS)
Hunt...... Hunter's Torrens Cases [*Canada*] [*A publication*] (DLA)
Hunt...... Hunt's Annuity Cases [*England*] [*A publication*] (DLA)
Hunt Ann Cas... Hunt's Annuity Cases [*England*] [*A publication*] (DLA)
HuntBnk...... Huntington Bankshares [*Associated Press*] (SAG)
Hunt Bound... Hunt's Law of Boundaries and Fences [*A publication*] (DLA)
Hunt Bound... Hunts Law of Boundaries and Fences (journ.) (SAUS)
Hunt Cas...... Hunt's Annuity Cases [*England*] [*A publication*] (DLA)
Huntco...... Huntco, Inc. [*Associated Press*] (SAG)
Hunt Eq...... Hunt's Suit in Equity [*A publication*] (DLA)
Hunt Eq...... Hunts Suit in Equity (journ.) (SAUS)
Hunter C (CUNY)... Hunter College of The City University of New York (GAGS)
Hunter Nat Ht... Hunter Natural History (journ.) (SAUS)
Hunter Res Found J... Hunter Valley Research Foundation. Journal (journ.) (SAUS)
Hunter Rom Law... Hunter on Roman Law [*A publication*] (DLA)
Hunter Suit Eq... Hunter's Proceeding in a Suit in Equity [*A publication*] (DLA)
Hunter Valley Res Fdn Monograph... Hunter Valley Research Foundation. Monograph (journ.) (SAUS)

Hunter Valley Res Found Spec Rep... Hunter Valley Research Foundation. Special Report (journ.) (SAUS)
HUNTEST..... Hunting and Testing [*Apollo*] [*NASA*]
Hunt Fr Conv... Hunt's Fraudulent Conveyances [*2nd ed.*] [*1897*] [*A publication*] (DLA)
hunth.......... Hundred Thousand (BARN)
Huntington... Huntington Library, Art Gallery and Botanical Gardens (SAUS)
HuntJB......... Hunt [*J.B.*] Transport Services, Inc. [*Associated Press*] (SAG)
Hunt L & T... Hunter's Landlord and Tenant [*Scotland*] [*A publication*] (DLA)
Hunt Lib Bull... Huntington Library. Bulletin (journ.) (SAUS)
Hunt Mer Mag... Hunt's Merchants' Magazine [*A publication*] (DLA)
Hunt Mer Mag... Hunts Merchants Magazine (journ.) (SAUS)
HuntMf......... Hunt Manufacturing Co. [*Associated Press*] (SAG)
Hunt Rom L... Hunter on Roman Law [*A publication*] (DLA)
Hunts........... Huntingdonshire (DIAR)
HUNTS......... Huntingdonshire [*County in England*]
HUNTS......... Huntsville, AL [*American Association of Railroads railroad junction routing code*]
Hunt's AC.... Hunt's Annuity Cases [*England*] [*A publication*] (DLA)
Hunt Suit..... Hunter's Proceeding in a Suit in Equity [*A publication*] (DLA)
Hunt Torrens... Hunter's Torrens Cases [*Canada*] [*A publication*] (DLA)
Hunt Tr........ Huntingdon's Trial [*A publication*] (DLA)
Huntwy........ Huntway Partners Ltd. [*Associated Press*] (SAG)
HUO............ Huguenot, NY [*Location identifier*] [*FAA*] (FAAL)
HUORAY...... Human Organization (journ.) (SAUS)
HuOSzK........ Orszagos Szechenyi Konyvtar [*National Szechenyi Library*], Budapest, Hungary [*Library symbol*] [*Library of Congress*] (LCLS)
HUP............ Hangup
HUP............ Harvard University Press (DGA)
HUP............ Helicopter Utility (Piasecki)
HUP............ Homogenous Uniparental Embryo [*Embryology*]
HUP............ Horizon Ultraviolet Program
HUP............ Hospital of the University of Pennsylvania
HUP............ Hospital Utilization Project [*Western Pennsylvania*]
HUP............ Hot Uniaxially Pressing (SAUS)
HUP............ Hudspeth, TX [*Location identifier*] [*FAA*] (FAAL)
hup............ Hupa [*MARC language code*] [*Library of Congress*] (LCCP)
HUP............ Hydrogen Uranyl Phosphate [*Inorganic chemistry*]
HuPaB......... Pannonhalmi Szent Benedek Rend Kozponti Konyvtara, Pannonhalma, Hungary [*Library symbol*] [*Library of Congress*] (LCLS)
HUPAS......... Hofstra University Pro Arte Symphony (SAUS)
HUPATS....... Heuristic Paper Trimming System (BUR)
HUPCM........ Hybrid Unidigit Pulse Code Modulation (IAA)
HUPD.......... Harvard University Police Department (SAUO)
HuPE........... Pecsi Tudomanyegyetem, Pecs, Hungary [*Library symbol*] [*Library of Congress*] (LCLS)
HUPH.......... Humphrey, Inc. (SAUO)
HUPHD........ Human Physiology (journ.) (SAUS)
HUPL.......... Helicopter Utilities Proprietary Ltd. (SAUO)
HUPPAE....... Harvard University. Papers of the Peabody Museum of Archaeology and Ethnology (journ.) (SAUS)
HUPPIE........ Hispanic Urban Professional [*Lifestyle classification*]
HUPr........... Harvard University Press (SAUO)
HUPr........... Hydrogemuranylphosphate tetrahlydrate (SAUS)
HUPS.......... H6000 Utilization Project System (SAUS)
HUPW......... Hot Ultrapure Water (AAEL)
HUQ............ Houn [*Libya*] [*Airport symbol*] (OAG)
HUR............ Hardware Usage Report (MCD)
HUR............ Heat Up Rate (IEEE)
HUR............ Homes Using Radio [*Ratings*] (NTCM)
HUR............ Hurn [*England*] [*Airport symbol*] (AD)
HUR............ Huron District Office (SAUO)
HUR............ Hurricane [*Alaska*] [*Seismograph station code, US Geological Survey*] (SEIS)
HUR............ Hydroxyurea [*Antineoplastic drug*] (DAVI)
HUR............ Miami Air Charter [*ICAO designator*] (FAAC)
HURA.......... Health Underserved Rural Areas
HURC.......... Hurco Companies [*NASDAQ symbol*] (TTSB)
HURC.......... Hurco Companies, Inc. [*NASDAQ symbol*] (NQ)
HURCN........ Hurricane
Hurco.......... Hurco Companies, Inc. [*Associated Press*] (SAG)
HURD.......... HIRD of Unix-Replacing Daemons (SAUS)
HurD........... Hurricane Deck (SAUS)
Hurd F & B... Hurd on the Laws of Freedom and Bondage in the United States [*A publication*] (DLA)
Hurd F&B..... Hurd on the Laws of Freedom and Bondage in the United States (journ.) (SAUS)
Hurd Hab Cor... Hurd on the Write of Habeas Corpus (journ.) (SAUS)
Hurd Hab Cor... Hurd on the Writ of Habeas Corpus [*A publication*] (DLA)
Hurd Pers Lib... Hurd on Personal Liberty [*A publication*] (DLA)
Hurd's Rev St... Hurd's Illinois Revised Statutes [*A publication*] (DLA)
Hurd St........ Hurd's Illinois Statutes [*A publication*] (DLA)
Hurd St........ Hurds Illinois Statutes (journ.) (SAUS)
HUREP......... Hurricane Report
HUREVAC.... Hurricane Evacuation (NVT)
HURI........... Harvard Ukrainian Research Institute
HURI........... Hughes Resources, Inc. [*NASDAQ symbol*] (SAG)
HURIDOCS... Human Rights Information and Documentation System (EA)
HURIDOCS... Human Rights International Documentation System (EA)
HURL.......... Hawaii Undersea Research Laboratory [*University of Hawaii*] [*Research center*] (RCD)
HURL.......... Hawaii Underwater Research Laboratory (SAUO)
Hurl & C...... Hurlstone and Coltman's English Exchequer Reports [*A publication*] (DLA)
Hurl & Colt... Hurlstone and Coltman's English Exchequer Reports [*A publication*] (DLA)
Hurl & G...... Hurlstone and Gordon's English Exchequer Reports [*A publication*] (DLA)
Hurl & Gord... Hurlstone and Gordon's English Exchequer Reports [*A publication*] (DLA)
Hurl & N...... Hurlstone and Norman's English Exchequer Reports [*156, 158 English Reprint*] [*A publication*] (DLA)
Hurl & Nor... Hurlstone and Norman's English Exchequer Reports [*156, 158 English Reprint*] [*A publication*] (DLA)
Hurl & W..... Hurlstone and Walmsley's English Exchequer Reports [*1840-41*] [*A publication*] (DLA)
Hurl & Walm... Hurlstone and Walmsley's English Exchequer Reports [*1840-41*] [*A publication*] (DLA)
Hurl Bonds... Hurlstone on Bonds [*A publication*] (DLA)
Hurl Colt...... Hurlstone and Coltman's English Exchequer Reports [*A publication*] (DLA)
Hurls & W (Eng)... Hurlstone and Walmsley's English Exchequer Reports [*1840-41*] [*A publication*] (DLA)
Hurlst & C... Hurlstone and Coltman's English Exchequer Reports [*A publication*] (DLA)
Hurlst & C (Eng)... Hurlstone and Coltman's English Exchequer Reports [*A publication*] (DLA)
Hurlst & G... Hurlstone and Gordon's English Exchequer Reports [*A publication*] (DLA)
Hurlst & N (Eng)... Hurlstone and Norman's English Exchequer Reports [*156, 158 English Reprint*] [*A publication*] (DLA)
Hurlst & W... Hurlstone and Walmsley's English Exchequer Reports [*1840-41*] [*A publication*] (DLA)
HURMES...... Human Rights Media Service for Rapid Flow of Human Rights News (SAUO)
HURN.......... Huron, SD [*American Association of Railroads railroad junction routing code*]
HURON........ Huron, OH [*American Association of Railroads railroad junction routing code*]
Huron Hist N... Huron Historical Notes (journ.) (SAUS)
HURR.......... Housing and Urban-Rural Recovery Act (SAUS)
Hurr............ Hurrian (BJA)
HURRA........ Housing and Urban-Rural Recovery Act of 1983
HURRAH...... Help Us Reach and Rehabilitate America's Handicapped [*State-Federal rehabilitation program*]
HURRAN...... Hurricane Analog
HURRAO...... Human Use Review and Regulatory Affairs Office [*Army*] (RDA)
HURR-EVAC... Hurricane Evacuation (DNAB)
HURREVAC... Hurricane Evacuation program (SAUO)
HURT.......... HealthRite, Inc. [*NASDAQ symbol*] (SAG)
HURT.......... Hospital Utilization Review Team (STED)
HURTS........ Honeywell 6000 Reporting System (SAUO)
HUS............ Hardened Unique Storage [*Environmental science*] (COE)
HUS............ Harvard Ukrainian Studies (journ.) (SAUS)
HUS............ Helicopter Utility Squadron
HUS............ Hemolytic-Uremic Syndrome [*Nephrology*]
HUS............ Heussler Air Service Corp. [*ICAO designator*] (FAAC)
HUS............ Hughes [*Alaska*] [*Airport symbol*] (OAG)
hus............. Husband (GEAB)
HUS............ Husband [*Legal shorthand*] (LWAP)
HUS............ Hustings Court [*Court type found in state of Virginia*] (MVRD)
HUS............ Hyaluronidase Unit for Semen (MAE)
HUS............ Hypergolic Umbilical System (SAUS)
HuSA.......... Human Serum Albumin (DB)
HUSAFICPA... Headquarters, United States Army Forces, Central Pacific Area
HUSAFMIDPAC... Headquarters, United States Army Forces, Middle Pacific [*World War II*]
Husat.......... Human Science and Advanced Technology Research Institute (SAUS)
HUSAT........ Human Sciences Advanced Technology Unit [*Longborough University*] [*British*]
HUSAT........ Human Sciences and Advanced Technology Research Centre [*University of Technology*] [*British*] (CB)
HUSB.......... Home Unity Savings & Loan Association (SAUO)
husb........... Husband
HUSB.......... Husbandry
HUSB & W... Husband and Wife (DLA)
HUSBC........ Hungarian-United States Business Council (NTPA)
HUSBD........ Husband (ROG)
Husb For Med... Husband's Forensic Medicine [*A publication*] (DLA)
Husb Mar Wom... Husband on Married Women [*A publication*] (DLA)
HUSBN........ Husbandman
HUSFU........ Hard Summary Fault Unit (SAUO)
HUSIA......... Hungarian Scientific Instruments (journ.) (SAUS)
HUSICON..... Humanides, Science and Conservation (SAUS)
HUSITA....... Human Service Information Technology Applications (SAUO)
HUSL.......... Harvard Underwater Sound Laboratory (SAUO)
HUSL.......... Hebrew University. Studies in Literature (journ.) (SAUS)
HUSLONET... Hungarian-Slovak Network (TELE)
HUSO.......... Soroti [*Uganda*] [*ICAO location identifier*] (ICLI)
HuSpK......... Sarospataki Reformatus Kollegium Nagykonyvtara, Sarospatak, Hungary [*Library symbol*] [*Library of Congress*] (LCLS)
HUSS.......... Helicopter Underslung Spray System (SAUO)
HUSS.......... Hussars [*Military unit*] [*British*] (ROG)
HUST.......... Huazhong University of Science and Technology (SAUO)
Hust............ Hustings Court [*As in Virginia*] [*Legal term*] (DLA)
HUSTLE....... Helium Underwater Speech Translating Equipment
Hust L Tit.... Huston on Land Titles in Pennsylvania [*A publication*] (DLA)

HUSTN......... Houston, TX [*American Association of Railroads railroad junction routing code*]
HUSUSA...... Human Society of the United States of America (SAUO)
HUSZ.......... Hudson Seeders [*Federal Railroad Administration identification code*]
HuSzOE........ Szegedi Orvostudomanyi Egyetem, Szeged, Hungary [*Library symbol*] [*Library of Congress*] (LCLS)
HUT............ Hard Upper Torso (MCD)
HUT............ HEDL [*Hanford Engineering Development Laboratory*] Up Transient [*Nuclear energy*] (NRCH)
HUT............ Held-Up Transient (IAA)
HUT............ Helicopter Undergraduate Training (SAUO)
HUT............ Helsinki University of Technology
HUT............ High-Usage Intertoll Trunk [*Data communication*] (MHDI)
HUT............ Hold Up Tank (IEEE)
HUT............ Homes Using Television [*Television ratings*]
HUT............ Hopkins Ultraviolet Telescope
HUT............ Households Using Television [*Television ratings*]
HUT............ Humboldt Energy [*Vancouver Stock Exchange symbol*]
h ut............ Hustidine Utilization [*Medicine*] (EDAA)
HUT............ Hutchinson [*Kansas*] [*Airport symbol*] (OAG)
Hut............. Hutton's English Common Pleas Reports [*1612-39*] [*A publication*] (DLA)
HUTCH......... Humidity-Temperature Chart (PDAA)
Hutch.......... Hutcheson's Reports [*81-84 Alabama*] [*A publication*] (DLA)
HUTCH......... Hutchinson, KS [*American Association of Railroads railroad junction routing code*]
Hutch Car.... Hutchinson on Carriers [*A publication*] (DLA)
Hutch Carr... Hutchinson on Carriers [*A publication*] (DLA)
Hutch Code... Hutchinson's Code [*Mississippi*] [*A publication*] (DLA)
Hutch JP...... Hutcheson's Justice of the Peace [*A publication*] (DLA)
Hutch JP...... Hutchesons Justice of the Peace (journ.) (SAUS)
HutchT......... Hutchinson Technology, Inc. [*Associated Press*] (SAG)
Hut Ct Req... Hutton's Courts of Requests [*A publication*] (DLA)
HUTE.......... Hard User Terminal Element (SAUO)
HUTG.......... High Usage Trunk Group (SAUO)
HUTHAS....... Human Thymus Anti-Serum [*Medicine*] (MAE)
HUTI........... Human Urinary Trypsin Inhibitor (DB)
HUTO.......... Tororo [*Uganda*] [*ICAO location identifier*] (ICLI)
HUTR.......... Howard University Training Reactor (SAUO)
HUTR.......... Hubbell Trading Post National Historic Site
HUTRON...... Helicopter Utility Squadron
HUTSAT...... Helsinki University of Technology Satellite
HUTSCAT..... Helsinki University of Technology Scatterometer (SAUO)
HUTSLAR..... Helsinki University of Technology Side-Looking Airborne Radar (SAUO)
Hutt............ Hutton's English Common Pleas Reports [*1612-39*] [*A publication*] (DLA)
Hutt Ct Req... Hutton's Courts of Requests [*A publication*] (DLA)
Hutt Ct Req... Huttons Courts of Requests (journ.) (SAUS)
Hutton......... Hutton's English Common Pleas Reports [*1612-39*] [*A publication*] (DLA)
Hutton (Eng)... Hutton's English Common Pleas Reports [*1612-39*] [*A publication*] (DLA)
HUTTS......... Hayes Universal Tow Target System (SAUS)
HUTZ.......... Hunter Transport [*Federal Railroad Administration identification code*]
HUU............ Detroit, MI [*Location identifier*] [*FAA*] (FAAL)
HUU............ Huanuco [*Peru*] [*Airport symbol*] (OAG)
HUV............ Hudiksvall [*Sweden*] [*Airport symbol*] (OAG)
HUV............ Human Umbilical Vein [*Medicine*] (DMAA)
HUVE.......... Human Umbilical Vein Endothelial
HUVEC........ Human Umbilical Vein Endothelial Cell [*Cytology*]
HUW........... Hours Under Way (SAUS)
HUW........... Hurricane Warning [*Telecommunications*] (OTD)
HUX............ Harvard University [*Cambridge, MA*]
HUX............ Sacramento, CA [*Location identifier*] [*FAA*] (FAAL)
Hux Judg..... Huxley's Second Book of Judgments [*1675*] [*England*] [*A publication*] (DLA)
Hux Judg..... Huxleys Second Book of Judgments (journ.) (SAUS)
HUY............ Hull [*England*] [*Airport symbol*] (AD)
HUY............ Humberside [*England*] [*Airport symbol*] (OAG)
Huyck Felt Bull... Huyck Felt Bulletin (journ.) (SAUS)
HUZ............ Huaraz [*Peru*] [*Seismograph station code, US Geological Survey*] (SEIS)
HUZ............ Mesquite, TX [*Location identifier*] [*FAA*] (FAAL)
HUzT........... Hermeneutische Untersuchungen zur Theologie [*Tuebingen*] [*A publication*] (BJA)
HV.............. Air Central [*ICAO designator*] (AD)
HV.............. Air-Cushion Vehicle built by Hover Vehicles [*New Zealand*] [*Usually used in combination with numerals*]
HV.............. Boeing-Vertol Division [*The Boeing Co.*] [*ICAO aircraft manufacturer identifier*] (ICAO)
HV.............. Half Value (SAUS)
HV.............. Hallux Valgus [*Orthopedics*] (DAVI)
HV.............. Hand Valve [*Nuclear energy*] (NRCH)
h/v............. Harbour View
HV.............. Hardness according to Vickers (SAUS)
HV.............. Hardness Vickers (SAUS)
HV.............. Hard Valve (DEN)
HV.............. Hardware Virtualizer [*Computer science*] (IEEE)
HV.............. Haricots Verts [*Green Beans*] [*French*]
HV.............. Harvard College (SAUO)
HV.............. Harvard University (SAUO)
HV.............. Has Voided [*Medicine*] (DAVI)
HV.............. Have [*Amateur radio shorthand*] (WDAA)
HV.............. Health Visitor
HV.............. Heart Volume (SAUS)
HV.............. Heater Voltage
HV.............. Heating and Ventilation (AAG)
HV.............. Heating Value (SAUS)
HV.............. Heat of Vaporization (ROG)
HV.............. Heavy (AABC)
hv.............. Heavy (VRA)
H-V............. Height-Velocity
HV.............. Helminthosporium victoriae [*A toxin-producing fungus*]
HV.............. Hemovac [*Medicine*] (EDAA)
HV.............. Hepatic Vein [*Anatomy*]
HV.............. Herpesvirus
HV.............. Hic Verbis [*In These Words*] [*Latin*]
HV.............. Hidden Variable (SAUS)
HV.............. High in Volatiles [*Commercial grading*]
HV.............. Highly Variegated Maize
HV.............. High tension/Voltage (SAUS)
HV.............. High Vacuum (ADA)
HV.............. High Velocity
HV.............. High Viscosity (SAUS)
HV.............. High Visibility (DS)
hv.............. High Voltage (WDAA)
HV.............. High Voltage
HV.............. High Volume
HV.............. Hoc Verbum [*This Word*] [*Latin*]
HV.............. Home Video [*Television*]
HV.............. Home Visit (SAUS)
HV.............. Homing Vehicle (ACAE)
H/V............. Horizontal/Vertical (SAUS)
HV.............. Horizontal-Vertical Intersection [*Lighting*] [*Automotive engineering*]
HV.............. Hospital Visit (AAMN)
HV.............. Housatonic Valley Railroad [*Federal Railroad Administration identification code*]
HV.............. Hyaline-Vascular [*Oncology*]
HV.............. Hydration Value (SAUS)
HV.............. Hydraulic Valve (SAUS)
HV.............. Hydrogen Vent (MCD)
HV.............. Hydroxyl Value [*Analytical chemistry*]
HV.............. Hypervariable
HV.............. Hyper Velocity (SAUS)
HV.............. Hyperventilation
HV.............. Vatican [*International civil aircraft marking*] (ODBW)
HV.............. Vickers Hardness Number [*Also, VH, VHN*]
HV6............ Heracleum Virus 6 [*Plant pathology*]
HVA............ Analalava [*Madagascar*] [*Airport symbol*] (OAG)
HVA............ Health Visitors' Association [*A union*] [*British*] (DCTA)
HVA............ Heeresverwaltungsamt [*Army Administration Office*] [*German military - World War II*]
HVA............ Herpesvirus Ateles
HVA............ High Value Unit (SAUS)
HVA............ High-Velocity Anomaly [*Seismology*]
HVA............ High-Voltage-Activated [*Neurochemistry*]
HVA............ High Voltage Adapter (SAUS)
HVA............ High Voltage Apparatus (SAUS)
hva............. homovanillic (SAUS)
HVA............ Homo Vanillic Acid (SAUS)
HVA............ Homovanillic Acid [*Biochemistry*]
HVA............ Hypervitamintosis A [*Medicine*] (MELL)
HVA............ Methoxy-Hydroxyphenylacetic Acid [*Chemistry*] (DAVI)
HVA............ Newair, Inc. [*ICAO designator*] (FAAC)
HVA............ New Haven Airways, Inc. (SAUO)
HVAA.......... High-Value Airborne Assets (DOMA)
HVAB.......... High-Volatile A Bituminous (SAUS)
HVAC.......... Heating, Ventilating, and Air Conditioning
HVAC.......... Heating, Ventilation, and Air Conditioning
HVAC.......... High Vacuum (IEEE)
HVAC.......... High-Voltage Actuator [*Electronics*] (IEEE)
HVAC.......... High-Voltage Alternating Current
HVAC.......... House Veterans' Affairs Committee [*House of Representatives*]
HVACC........ High-Voltage Apparatus Coordinating Committee [*ANSI*]
HVAC System... Heating, Ventilating and Air Conditioning System (SAUS)
HV ADJ........ High Voltage Adjustment (SAUS)
HVAF.......... High-Velocity Air Filter (EG)
H vag.......... Hemophilus Vaginalis [*Gynecology*] (DAVI)
HVAGL........ High Velocity Automatic Grenade Launcher (SAUO)
HV & C........ Heating, Ventilating, and Cooling (AAG)
HVAO.......... Hybrid-Valence Atomic Orbital (MEC)
HVAP.......... High-Velocity, Armor-Piercing [*Projectile*]
HVAPDS....... High-Velocity, Armor-Piercing, Discarding Sabot [*Projectile*]
HVAPDSFS.... High-Velocity, Armor-Piercing, Discarding Sabot, Fin Stabilized [*Projectile*] (MCD)
HVAPDS-T.... High Velocity, Armour-Piercing, Discarding Sabot, Tracer (SAUS)
HVAPFSDS.... High-Velocity, Armor-Piercing, Fin Stabilized, Discarding Sabot [*Projectile*] (MCD)
HVAP-T........ Hypervelocity, Armor-Piercing - Tracer [*Projectile*] (AABC)
HVAR.......... High-Velocity Aircraft Rocket
HVAR(HE).... High-Velocity Aircraft Rocket (High Explosive) (DNAB)
HVARHE....... High-Velocity Aircraft Rocket-High Explosive (SAUS)
HVAS.......... Hydraulic Valve Adjuster System [*Automotive engineering*]
HVAST........ Hull Vibration and Strength Analysis (SAUS)
HVAT.......... High Velocity Anti-Tank (SAUS)
HVATKRON... Heavy Attack Squadron (DNAB)
HVB............ Hauptverbandplatz [*Clearing Station*] [*German military - World War II*]
HVB............ Hawaii Visitors Bureau (SAUS)

HVB .... Heptyl Viologen Bromide (SAUS)
HVB .... Hervey Bay [*Australia*] [*Airport symbol*] (OAG)
HVB .... High-Voltage Bias
HVBB .... High-Volatile B Bituminous (SAUS)
HVBF .... Hemangioma and Vascular Birthmarks Foundation (NRGU)
HVBI .... Hamburgisches Verordnungsblatt (journ.) (SAUS)
HVBO .... Heterojunction Valence-Band Offset (SAUS)
HVBP .... High Velocity Ballistic Protection (SAUS)
HVC .... Hardened Voice Channel [*NASA*] (KSC)
HVC .... Hardened Voice Circuit (CET)
HVC .... Haverford College, Haverford, PA [*OCLC symbol*] (OCLC)
HVC .... Hav-Info Computers, Inc. [*Vancouver Stock Exchange symbol*]
HVC .... Hayden's Viburnum Compound [*Medicine*]
HVC .... Health Visitor's Certificate [*British*]
HVC .... Helium Vacancy Cluster (SAUS)
HVC .... Hernandez Valley [*California*] [*Seismograph station code, US Geological Survey*] (SEIS)
HVC .... High-Velocity Cloud [*Astronomy*] (OA)
HVC .... High Vocal Center [*Songbird anatomy*]
HVC .... High Voltage Circuit (SAUS)
HVC .... High-Voltage Connector
HVC .... High-Voltage Control
HVC .... Hopkinsville, KY [*Location identifier*] [*FAA*] (FAAL)
HVC .... Horizontal-Vertical Control (SAUS)
HVC .... Hudson Valley Conference (PSS)
HVC .... Hue, Value, Chroma (SAUS)
HVC .... Hydrogen Check Valve (NAKS)
HVc .... Hyperstriatum Ventralis Pars Caudalis [*Bird brain anatomy*]
HVc .... Ventral Hyperstriatum Caudal Nucleus [*Neuroanatomy*]
HVCA .... Heating and Ventilating Contractors' Association [*British*]
HVCB .... Hawaii Visitors and Convention Bureau (ROAS)
HVCB .... High-Volatile C Bituminous (SAUS)
HVCC .... Hairy Vetch as a Cover Crop [*Agriculture*]
HVCC .... Hudson Valley Community College (SAUO)
HVCE .... High-Voltage Capillary Electrophoresis
HVCH .... Hardened Voice Channel (MSA)
HVCMOS .... High Voltage CMOS [*Complementary Metal Oxide Semiconductor*] (NITA)
HV-CMOS .... High Voltage Complementary Metal Oxide on Silicon (SAUS)
HVCS .... High-Vacuum Calibration System (PDAA)
HVCZ .... HVC Chemical [*Federal Railroad Administration identification code*]
HVD .... Half-Value Depth (IAA)
HVD .... Heaters, Vents, and Drains [*System*] [*Nuclear energy*] (NRCH)
HVD .... Height-Velocity Diagram
HVD .... Helmet Visor Display (ACAE)
HVD .... Hendrik Verwoerd Dam [*South Africa*] [*Seismograph station code, US Geological Survey*] (SEIS)
HVD .... High Velocity Detonation (SAUS)
HVD .... High-Velocity Detonation
HVD .... High-Viscosity Dispenser [*Packaging*]
HVD .... High Voltage Differential (SAUS)
HVD .... High Voltage Discharge (SAUS)
HVD .... Hydroviscous Drive (DNAB)
HVD .... Hypertensive Vascular Disease [*Medicine*]
HVDB .... Heptyl Viologen Dibromide (SAUS)
HVDC .... High Voltage Direct Converter (SAUS)
HVDC .... High-Voltage Direct Current
HVDCT .... High-Voltage Direct-Current Transmission [*Electronics*]
HVDF .... Direction Finder (SAUS)
HVDF .... High- and Very-High-Frequency Direction Finding
HVDK .... Havard Knitwear, Inc. (SAUO)
HVDP .... Heavy Drop [*Military*] (AABC)
HVDRR .... Hypocalcemic Vitamin D-Resistant Rickets [*Medicine*]
HVDS .... Hypergolic Vapor Detection System [*NASA*] (NASA)
HVE .... Hanksville, UT [*Location identifier*] [*FAA*] (FAAL)
HVE .... Hepatic Vascular Exclusion [*Medicine*] (MEDA)
HVE .... High-Vacuum Environment
HVE .... High-Vacuum Evaporator
HVE .... High Voltage Electron (SAUS)
HVE .... High-Voltage Electrophoresis (AAMN)
HVE .... High Voltage Engineering Corp. (SAUO)
HVE .... Home Video Entertainment (SAUS)
HVE .... Horizontal Vertex Error (OA)
HVEC .... High Voltage Engineering Corp.
HVEC .... Human Vascular Endothelial Cells
HVECA .... Heating and Ventating Engineer and Journal of Air Conditioning (journ.) (SAUS)
HVEF .... Harvest Financial Corp. [*NASDAQ symbol*] (SAG)
HVEL .... Hypervelocity
HVEM .... High Vacuum Electron Microscope (SAUS)
HVEM .... High Voltage Electron Microscope (SAUS)
HVEM .... High-Voltage Electron Microscopy
HVES .... High Vacuum Evaporation System (SAUO)
HVES .... High-Vacuum Evaporation System
HVES .... High Voltage Electrical Stimulation (SAUS)
HVES .... High-Voltage Electrical Stimulation [*Meat treatment*]
HVEZ .... Highview Elevator [*Federal Railroad Administration identification code*]
HVF .... Harmonically Varying Field
HVF .... Haverford College, Haverford, PA [*OCLC symbol*] (OCLC)
HVF .... High Velocity Forming (SAUS)
HVF .... High-Viscosity Fuel Oil (DCTA)
HVF .... Humphrey Visual Field (SAUS)
HVFB .... High-Velocity Fluidized Bed [*Chemical engineering*]
HVFD .... Haverfield Corp. [*NASDAQ symbol*] (NQ)
HVFL .... Heavy Fuel (RIMS)
HVFS .... High-Vacuum Flame Sterilization [*Food technology*]
HVG .... Haveg Industries, Inc. (SAUO)
HVG .... High Velocity Gun (SAUS)
HVG .... High-Voltage Generator
HVG .... High-Voltage Gradient
HVG .... Honningsvag [*Norway*] [*Airport symbol*] (OAG)
HVG .... Host Versus Graft [*Medicine*]
HVG .... Hypervelocity Gun [*Military*] (SDI)
HVGL .... High Velocity Grenade Launcher [*Projectile*] (PDAA)
HVGLS .... High-Velocity Grenade Launcher System [*Projectile*] (MCD)
HVGO .... Hanover Gold [*NASDAQ symbol*] (TTSB)
HVGO .... Hanover Gold Company, Inc. [*NASDAQ symbol*] (SAG)
HVGO .... Heavy Vacuum Gas Oil [*Petroleum product*]
HVGS .... High Velocity Gun System (SAUS)
HVH .... Herpes Virus Hominis (SAUS)
HVH .... Hydrogen Vent Header [*Nuclear energy*] (NRCH)
HVHA .... High-Velocity Hot-Air [*Oven*]
HVHAI .... High-Velocity Hot-Air Impingement [*Organic chemistry*]
HVHD .... High-Voltage-Hold-Down (PDAA)
HVHF .... High and Very-High Frequency (IAA)
HVHMA .... Herpesvirus Hominis Membrane Antigen [*Medicine*] (MEDA)
HVHMD .... Holographic Visor Helmet-Mounted Display [*Air Force*]
HVHW .... Health Values. Achieving High Level Wellness (journ.) (SAUS)
HVI .... Haltman Value Inventory (SAUS)
HVI .... Hartman Value Inventory [*Psychology*]
HVI .... Heart and Vascular Institute
HVI .... Hellenic Vehicle Industry (SAUS)
HVI .... Hepatic Volumetric Index
HVI .... High-Value Item (NATG)
HVI .... High Viscosity Index [*Lubricants*]
HVI .... High-Volume Impactor (SAUS)
HVI .... High-Volume Instrument [*Agricultural research*]
HVI .... Home Ventilating Institute [*Later, HVIDAMCA*] (EA)
HVI .... Horizon Village [*Vancouver Stock Exchange symbol*]
HVI .... Human Visual Inspection (SAUS)
HVI .... Hypervelocity Impact (SPST)
HVIC .... High-Voltage Integrated Circuit [*Computer science*]
HVIDAMCA .... Home Ventilating Institute Division of the Air Movement Control Association (EA)
HvideM .... Hvide Marine, Inc. [*Associated Press*] (SAG)
HV-IIL .... High Voltage Integrated Injection Logic (SAUS)
HVIO .... High-Volume Industrial Organics [*Environmental science*] (GFGA)
HVIRS .... Hull Vibration Information Retrieval System (PDAA)
HVIS .... Hypervelocity Impact Symposium (SAUS)
HVIS .... Hypervelocity Impact System (SAUS)
HVIT .... High-Volume Information Transfer
HVJ .... Hemagglutinating Virus of Japan [*Medicine*]
HVK .... Holmavik [*Iceland*] [*Airport symbol*] (OAG)
HVK .... Hovik Medical [*Vancouver Stock Exchange symbol*]
HVL .... Half-Value Layer [*Radiology*]
HVL .... Half-Wave Layer (SAUS)
HVL .... Hanseatic V Line (SAUS)
HVL .... Heeresverpflegungslager [*Army Ration Depot*] [*German military - World War II*]
HVL .... Highly Volatile Liquid (TAG)
HVL .... High Voltage Laboratory [*MIT*] (MCD)
HVL .... Hypervelocity Launcher [*Military*] (SDI)
HVLD .... HERL-RTP Validation System (SAUS)
HVLL .... Hudson Valley Lacrosse League (PSS)
HVLP .... High-Velocity, Low Penetration Paint
HVLP .... High-Volume Low-Pressure [*Spray-painting process*]
HVLS .... Huron Valley Library System [*Library network*]
HVLTDS .... Hypervelocity Launcher Terminal Defense (SAUS)
HV/LVPS .... High Voltage/Low Voltage Power Supply (SAUS)
HVM .... Heater Vent Module (HAWK)
HVM .... Heterodyne Vegetation Meter (IAA)
HVM .... High Velocity Metalworking (PDAA)
HVM .... High-Velocity Missile [*Military*] (DAVI)
HVM .... High-Voltage Mode
HVM .... High Voltage Module (SAUS)
HVM .... High Volume Modules (SAUS)
HVM .... Hydraulic Valve Motor
HVM .... Hyper-Velocity Missile (SAUO)
HVM .... Hypervelocity Munition
HVM .... Sisters, Home Visitors of Mary [*Roman Catholic religious order*]
HVMAC .... Hudson Valley Men's Athletic Conference (PSS)
HVMC .... Harbor View Medical Center (SAUS)
HVMC .... High-Variation Medical Condition
HVME .... Hull Vibration Monitoring Equipment (SAUS)
HVMF .... High Valency Metal Fluoride (SAUS)
HVML .... High Volume Minelayer (SAUS)
Hv MORS .... Heavy Mobile Ordnance Repair Shop (SAUO)
HVMOS .... High Voltage Metal-Oxide Semiconductor (SAUS)
HVMS .... High Velocity Medium Support (SAUS)
HVMS .... High Voltage Mass Separator (SAUS)
HVMS .... Hypervelocity Support Weapon (SAUS)
HVMVI .... High-Voltage Mercury-Vapor Isolator
HVN .... Hang Khong Viet Nam [*ICAO designator*] (FAAC)
HVN .... Havana [*Cuba*] [*Geomagnetic observatory code*]
HVN .... Haven (MCD)
HVN .... Home View Network [*Cable-television system*]
HVN .... New Haven [*Connecticut*] [*Airport symbol*] (OAG)
HVNP .... Hawaii Volcanoes National Park (SAUO)
HVO .... Croatian Defence Council (SAUO)

HVO .... Hallux Valgus Orthosis [*Medicine*] (MELL)
HVO .... Hawaiian Volcano Observatory [*Kilauea*] [*Hawaii*] [*Seismograph station code, US Geological Survey*] (SEIS)
HVO .... Health Volunteers Overseas (EA)
HVOC .... Halogenated Volatile Organic Compound
HVODS .... HOSC Voice Operational Data Switch (SAUS)
HVOF .... High-Velocity Oxygen/Fuel [*Coating technology*]
HVOSM .... Highway Vehicle Object Simulation Model [*Computer-aided design*] [*Automotive engineering*]
HVOT .... Hooper Visual Organization Test [*Psychology*]
HVP .... Half-Value Period
HVP .... Hardware Verification Program (CAAL)
HVP .... Hartman Value Profile [*Personality development test*] [*Psychology*]
HVP .... Hayes Verification Protocol [*Computer science*]
HVP .... Healthcare Vertical Portal (GART)
HVP .... Heart Valve Prostheses [*Medicine*]
HVP .... Herpes Virus Papio [*Medicine*] (DB)
HVP .... High-Vacuum Pump
hvp .... High-Value Package (SAUS)
HVP .... High-Value Product
HVP .... High Velocity Penetrator (SAUS)
HVP .... High Video Pass (NVT)
HVP .... High-Voltage Potential (IAA)
HVP .... High Voltage Power (SAUS)
HVP .... High-Volume Production (TIMI)
HVP .... Horizontal & Vertical Position (SAUS)
HVP .... Host Vehicle Pallet
HVP .... Hudson Vitamin Products (SAUO)
HVP .... Hydrolyzed Vegetable Protein [*Food additive*]
HVP .... Hypervelocity Projectile [*Military*] (MUSM)
HVPC .... High Voltage Power Corp. (SAUS)
HVPC .... High Voltage Power Corporation (SAUO)
HVPE .... High-Voltage Paper Electrophoresis
HVPE .... Hydride Vapor Phase Epitaxy [*Crystallography*]
HVPF .... Human Vascular Permeability Factor [*Biochemistry*]
HVPG .... Hepatic Venous Pressure Gradient [*Medicine*]
HVPHOTORON... Heavy Photographic Squadron (DNAB)
HVPI .... High-Voltage Plasma Interaction (SSD)
HVPI .... Holland Vocational Preference Inventory [*Psychology*]
HVPIC .... Hierarchical Visual Pattern Image Coding (SAUS)
HVPM .... High Vapor Pressure Metals (ABAC)
HVPO .... Hudson Valley Philharmonic Orchestra (SAUO)
HVPR .... High-Voltage Phase Retard
HVPS .... High-Voltage Power Supply
HVPS .... High-Volume Precipitation Spectrometer (SAUS)
HVPS .... High-Volume Printing System [*Computer science*]
HVPVE .... High-Voltage Photovoltaic Effect [*Physics*]
HVR .... Hard Vertical Rotating Balancer (SAUS)
HVR .... Hardware Vector to Raster
HVR .... Havre [*Montana*] [*Airport symbol*] (OAG)
HVR .... Helicopter Visual Rules
HVR .... Highland Valley Resources Ltd. [*Vancouver Stock Exchange symbol*]
HVR .... Highly Variable Regions [*Of chromosomes*] [*Genetics*]
HVR .... High Resolution Visible Range (SAUS)
HVR .... High-Resolution Visible Range
HVR .... High-Vacuum Rectifier
HVR .... High-Voltage Rectifier
HVR .... High-Voltage Regulator (MSA)
HVR .... High-Voltage Relay
HVR .... High-Voltage Resistor
HVR .... Home Video Recorder (NTCM)
HVR .... Hover (MCD)
HVR .... Hyderabad Volunteer Rifles [*British military*] (DMA)
HVR .... Hypervariable Region [*Genetics*]
HVR .... Hypoxic Ventilatory Response [*Medicine*]
HVRA .... Hawaiian Volcano Research Association (SAUO)
HVRA .... Heating and Ventilating Research Association [*British*]
HVRAP .... Hyper-Velocity Rocket-Assisted Projectile (PDAA)
HVREA .... Heating and Ventilating Review (journ.) (SAUS)
HVRL .... High Voltage Research Laboratory [*MIT*] (MCD)
HVRNG .... Hovering
HVRX .... Heber Valley Railroad [*Federal Railroad Administration identification code*]
HVS .... Hard Vertical Static Balancer (SAUS)
HVS .... Hardware Verification System (SAUS)
HVS .... Hartsville, SC [*Location identifier*] [*FAA*] (FAAL)
HVS .... Herpesvirus of Saimiri
HVS .... Herpes Virus Sensitivity [*Medicine*] (MELL)
HVS .... High Vacuum Seal (SAUS)
HVS .... High-Voltage Switch
HVS .... High-Volume Sampler (SAUS)
HVS .... Hirsutism-Virilizing Syndromes [*Medicine*] (MELL)
HVS .... Housing Vacancy Survey (SAUS)
HVS .... Hue, Value, Saturation [*Graphic arts*] (WDMC)
HVS .... Human Vaginal Swab [*Medicine*]
HVS .... Human Visual System
HVS .... Hypersonic Vehicle Shield
HVS .... Hypovolemic Shock [*Medicine*] (MELL)
HVSA .... High Voltage Slow Activity (SAUS)
HVSA .... High-Voltage Solar Array
H vs A .... Home Versus Advice [*Medicine*] (STED)
HVSC .... High Voltage Selenium Cartridge (SAUS)
HVSC .... High-Volume Squeeze Casting
HVSCR .... High-Voltage Selenium Cartridge Rectifier
HVSD .... High-Value Site Defense (SAUS)
HVSD .... Hydrogen-Detected Ventricular Septal Defect [*Medicine*] (MAE)
HVSD/ADAM... High Vale Site Defense/Air Defense Anti-Missile (SAUS)
HVSE .... High-Voltage Solar Experiment
HVSEM .... High Voltage Scanning Electron Microscopy (SAUS)
HVSF .... High Velocity Sheet Forming (PDAA)
HVSF .... Honeywell Verification Simulation Facility (NASA)
HVSL .... Holidays, Vacation, and Sick Leave (NASA)
hVSMC .... Human Vascular Smooth Muscle Cell [*Biology*]
HVSP .... High-Voltage Solar Panel
HVSR .... Hocking Valley Scenic Railway [*Federal Railroad Administration identification code*]
HVSS .... Horizontal Volute Spring Suspension [*Projectile*]
HVST .... High-Voltage Switching Transistor
HVSU .... Heating Ventilating Supply Unit (NRCH)
HVSV .... Human Vesicular Stomatitis Virus [*Medicine*] (EDAA)
HVSZ .... Harvest States [*Federal Railroad Administration identification code*]
HVT .... Half-Value Thickness
HVT .... Haverty Furniture [*NYSE symbol*]
HVT .... HealthVest [*AMEX symbol*] (COMM)
HVT .... Health Visitor Teacher (SAUS)
HVT .... Herpesvirus of Turkeys (STED)
HVT .... Hidden Variable Theory [*Physics*]
HVT .... High Vacuum Tube (SAUS)
HVT .... High-Value Target (NVT)
HVT .... High-Voltage Termination
HVT .... High-Voltage Tester
HVT .... High-Voltage Threshold (IAA)
HVT .... High-Voltage Transformer
HVT .... Hydraulic Variable Timing (SAUS)
HVT .... Hydraulic Variable-Valve Train [*Automotive engine design*]
HVT .... Hypersonic Velocity Technology (ACAE)
HVTA .... High Value Target Acquisition (SAUS)
HVTB .... High-Voltage Thermal Battery (DNAB)
HVTEM .... High-Voltage Transmission Electron Microscopy (DB)
HVTIP .... High Volume Transaction Interface Package (SAUO)
HVTIP .... High-Volume Transaction Interface Package (SAUS)
HVTL .... High Voltage Transmission Line (SAUS)
HVTP .... High-Velocity, Target-Practice [*Projectile*]
HVTP .... Hypervelocity, Target-Practice [*Projectile*]
HVTPDS .... High-Velocity, Target-Practice, Discarding Sabot [*Projectile*]
HVTP-T .... High Velocity, Target Practice-Tracer (SAUS)
HVTP-T .... Hypervelocity, Target-Practice - Tracer [*Projectile*] (AABC)
HVTR .... Home Videotape Recorder (IAA)
HVTR .... Home Video Tape Recorder (or Recording) (SAUO)
HVTS .... High Voltage Test System (SAUO)
HVTS .... High-Volume Time Sharing [*Computer science*]
HVTS .... Hypervelocity Techniques Symposium (SAUS)
HVTU .... High Voltage Transformer Unit (SAUS)
HVU .... Altus, OK [*Location identifier*] [*FAA*] (FAAL)
HVU .... Hansel Valley [*Utah*] [*Seismograph station code, US Geological Survey*] (SEIS)
HVU .... Heating Ventilation Unit (MCD)
HVU .... High-Value Unit [*Torpedo defense system*] (MCD)
HVUCAP .... High-Value Unit Combat Air Patrol [*Navy*] (DOMA)
HVUS .... Hypocomplementemic Vasculitis Urticaria Syndrome [*Medicine*] (STED)
HVV .... Helium Vent Valve (MCD)
HVV .... Hyperlink Vector Voting (SAUS)
HVV .... Hyper Velocity Vehicle (ACAE)
HVW .... High-Voltage Waveform
HVW .... High-Voltage Wire
HVWAC .... Hudson Valley Women's Athletic Conference (PSS)
HVWP .... Hospitalized Veterans Writing Project (EA)
HVWS .... Hebrew Veterans of the War with Spain (EA)
HVY .... Happy Valley, AK [*Location identifier*] [*FAA*] (FAAL)
HVY .... Harveys Casinos Resorts [*NYSE symbol*] (SAG)
HVY .... Heavy (AFM)
Hvy .... Heavy (MIST)
Hvy Mort ...... Heavy Mortar (SAUS)
Hvy Regt RA... Heavy Regiment, Royal Artillery (SAUO)
Hvy Veh .... Heavy Vehicle (SAUS)
Hvy Wkr .... Heavy Wrecker (SAUS)
HW .... Guernsey Airlines Ltd. (SAUO)
HW .... Half Wave
HW .... Half Width (SAUS)
HW .... Half Word (CET)
HW .... Hammer Welding (SAUS)
HW .... Handset, Wall (SAUS)
HW .... Handset, Wall Model (TEL)
HW .... Handwritten (BJA)
HW .... Hanford Works (SAUO)
H/W .... Hardware (ACAE)
hw .... Hardware (ELAL)
H/w .... Hardware (NAKS)
HW .... Hardware [*Computer science*] (NASA)
HW .... Hard Water (SAUS)
HW .... Hard Wired (NITA)
HW .... Hardwired (SAUS)
HW .... Hardwood
HW .... Hardy-Weinberg Equilibrium [*of genes*] [*Also, HWE*]
HW .... Hauptwachtmeister [*First Sergeant*] [*German military - World War II*]
HW .... Hauptwerk [*Masterpiece*] [*German*]
HW .... Havasu Airlines [*ICAO designator*] (AD)
HW .... Hawkinson [*Tire retread brand*]
HW .... Hayem-Widal [*Syndrome*] [*Medicine*] (DB)

HW Hayrem-Widal [*Syndrome*] (STED)
HW Hazardous Waste (GFGA)
HW Headwaiter
HW Head Wardmaster [*Navy*] [*British*] (ROG)
HW Head Wave (SAUS)
HW Head Width
HW Head Wind [*Navigation*]
HW Headwind (SAUS)
HW Healing Well (DMAA)
HW Hearing Waived [*Motor vehicle violation code used in state of Maryland*] (MVRD)
HW Heart Weight (STED)
HW Heavy Wall
HW Heavy Water
HW Heavy Weapons [*British military*] (DMA)
H/W Heavy Weathering
HW Heavy Weight (SAUS)
hW Hectowatt (SAUS)
HW Helsinki Watch (SAUS)
HW Hemisphere Width (STED)
HW Heparin Well [*Pharmacology*] (DAVI)
HW Herewith [*Enclosures*] [*Navy*]
HW Herpetic Whitlow [*Medicine*] (MELL)
HW Hertwig-Weyers [*Syndrome*] [*Medicine*] (DB)
HW Hertzian Wave (SAUS)
HW Hethitisches Woerterbuch [*Heidelberg*] [*A publication*] (BJA)
HW High Water [*Tides and currents*]
H/W Highway
HW High Wing [*Aviation*] (AIA)
HW Hispanic Writers [*A publication*]
HW Historical Wyoming (journ.) (SAUS)
HW His-Werner [*Disease*] [*Medicine*] (DB)
HW Hit Wicket
HW Hollow (SAUS)
HW Homework (SAUS)
HW Homing Weapons (NVT)
HW Hookworm (MELL)
HW Hot Water
HW Hotwell [*Nuclear energy*] (NRCH)
HW Hot Wheels [*Mattel*]
HW Hot Wire (KSC)
HW Housewife
HW How (WGA)
HW Howard Aero Manufacturing [*ICAO aircraft manufacturer identifier*] (ICAO)
HW Howler [*Communications; electronics*]
HW Howmet Corp. (SAUO)
HW Hunter-Wheel
HW North-Wright Air Ltd. [*ICAO designator*] (AD)
HW2000 Highway 2000 (SAUS)
HWA Hackensack Water Co. (SAUO)
HWA Hallman, W. A., St. Paul MN [*STAC*]
HWA Handwritten by Amanuensis (BJA)
HWA Hawa-Air [*Belgium*] [*ICAO designator*] (FAAC)
HWA Hemlock Woolly Adelgid
HWA High Wind Watch [*Telecommunications*] (OTD)
HWA Hill-Williford Aviation, Inc. (SAUO)
HWA Holloway White Allom [*Building contractor*] [*British*]
HWA Home Workers Association (NTPA)
HWA Hops Warehousing Association [*British*] (BI)
HWA Horror Writers of America [*An association*]
HWA Hot Wire Anemometer
HWA Hwalien [*Karenko*] [*Republic of China*] [*Seismograph station code, US Geological Survey*] (SEIS)
HWAA Heereswaffenamt [*Army Ordnance Office*] [*German military - World War II*]
HWAAP Hawthorne Army Ammunition Plant (AABC)
HWAC Hazardous Waste Action Coalition (SAUO)
HWAD Hawthorne Army Depot [*Umatilla, Oregon*]
HWADM Hypersonic Wide-Area Defense Missile (MCD)
HWAI Horseback Writers and Artists, International (EA)
HWAIFC Hank Williams Appreciation International Fan Club (EA)
HWAL Holland West-Afrika Line [*Steamship*] (MHDB)
HWAR Hazardous Waste Disposal Analysis Report (SAUS)
Hware Hardware Today (journ.) (SAUS)
HWAY Highway [*Commonly used*] (OPSA)
HWAY Humble Way (journ.) (SAUS)
HWB Half Word Boundary (SAUS)
HWB Handwoerterbuch [*Pocket Dictionary*] [*German*]
HWB Hot Water Boiler [*on a ship*] (DS)
HWB Hot Water Bottle (STED)
hwb Hot Water Bottle
HWB Hot Weather Boot [*Military*] (INF)
HWBC Hartford Whalers Booster Club (EA)
HWBDU Hot Weather Battle Dress Uniform [*Army*] (INF)
HWBDU Hot Weather Battle Fluid (SAUS)
HWBF High-Water-Based Fluid [*Hydraulic and cutting fluids*]
HWBI Handwoerterbuch des Islam [*Leiden*] [*A publication*] (BJA)
HWBL Home for Working Boys in London (SAUO)
HWBR Half-Wave Bridge Rectifier
HWBTA Home Wine and Beer Trade Association (EA)
HWC Half Wave Circuit (SAUS)
HWC Half Wave Current (SAUS)
HWC Half Word Constant (SAUS)
HWC Hazardous Waste Center (SAUO)
HWC Hazardous Waste Containment (SAUS)
HWC Hazardous Waste Coordinator (SAUS)
HWC Health and Welfare Canada
HWC Hein-Werner Corp. (EFIS)
HWC Heriot-Watt College (SAUO)
HWC Hoerner Waldorf Corporation (SAUO)
HWC Hot Water Circulating [*Technical drawings*]
HWC Hurricane Warning Center [*Marine science*] (OSRA)
HWCA Housing of Working Classes Act [*British*] (ROG)
HWCC Harpoon Weapon Control Console [*Missiles*] (MCD)
HWCC Hollywood Casino'A' [*NASDAQ symbol*] (TTSB)
HWCC Hollywood Casino Corp. [*NASDAQ symbol*] (SAG)
HWCD HWC Distribution Corp. (SAUO)
HWCF High Water Content Fluid [*Hydraulics*]
HWCI Hardware Configuration Item
HWCL Hazardous Waste Control Law [*California*] (SARE)
HWCP Hardware Code Page (SAUS)
HWCR Higher Worth Control Rod [*Nuclear energy*] (NUCP)
HWCS Helicopter Wire Cutter System (MCD)
HWCTR Heavy-Water Components Test Reactor [*Nuclear energy*]
HWCU Heated Window Control Unit
HWD Half-Wave Dipole (SAUS)
HWD Hardwood [*Technical drawings*]
HWD Hayward, CA [*Location identifier*] [*FAA*] (FAAL)
HWD Hazardous Waste Disposal
HWD Heartworm Disease (DMAA)
HWD Height, Width, Depth (SAUS)
HWD Highwood Resources Ltd. [*Toronto Stock Exchange symbol*]
HWD Hill/Wendover/Dugway [*Ranges*] [*Military*] (MCD)
HWD Hollywood Casino'A' [*AMEX symbol*] (SG)
HWD Horizontal Weather Depiction
HWD Hot Wire Detector [*Analytical instrumentation*]
HWD2 Region 2 RCRA Facilities Hazard Rating Model (SAUO)
HWDGR Hazardous Waste Disposal Guidelines and Regulations (EEVL)
HWDJC Howard Junction, PA [*American Association of Railroads railroad junction routing code*]
HWDMS Hadous Waste Disposal Management System (SAUS)
HWDMS Hazardous Waste Data [*or Disposal*] Management System [*Environmental Protection Agency*]
HWDYKY How Well Do You Know Yourself [*Psychological testing*]
HWE East West Center, Honolulu, HI [*OCLC symbol*] (OCLC)
HWE Hardy-Weinberg Equilibrium [*of genes*] [*Also, HW*]
HWE Hardy-Weinberg Expectation [*Genetics*]
HWE Healthy Worker Effect (DMAA)
HWE Home War Establishment (SAUO)
HWE Hot Wall Epitaxy (SAUS)
HWE Hot Water Extract (DMAA)
HWEC Hallwood Energy Corp. [*NASDAQ symbol*] (NQ)
HWED Hazardous Waste Enforcement Division [*Environmental Protection Agency*] (EPA)
HWEP Hot Wire Emissive Probe
HWERL Hazardous Waste Engineering Research Laboratory [*Cincinnati, OH*] [*Environmental Protection Agency*] (GRD)
HWESF Hanford Waste Encapsulation and Storage Facility (SAUO)
HWF Aberdeen/Amory, MS [*Location identifier*] [*FAA*] (FAAL)
HWF Hairdressing World Federation (SAUO)
HWF Hazardous Waste Federation (EA)
HWF & C High-Water Full and Change [*Tides and currents*]
HWFE Housewife [*Medicine*] (EDAA)
HWFET Highway Fuel Economy Test [*Environmental Protection Agency*]
HWFPB Half Word Fixed Point Binary (SAUS)
HW-FW Half Wave - Full Wave (EPA)
HWG Halifax Wire Gauge (SAUS)
HWG Hallwood Group, Inc. [*NYSE symbol*] (SPSG)
HWG House Wednesday Group (EA)
HWG HTML Writers Guild (SAUO)
HWGCR Heavy Water Gas-Cooled Reactor (SAUO)
HWGCR Heavy-Water Moderated Gas-Cooled Reactor [*Nuclear energy*]
HWGL Home for Working Girls in London (SAUO)
HWGTF Hazardous Waste Groundwater Task Force [*Environmental Protection Agency*] (GFGA)
HWGTF Hazardous Waste Groundwater Test Facility (EEVL)
HWGW Hiram Walker - Gooderham & Worts [*Canada*]
HWGWTF Hazardous Waste Groundwater Task Force (SAUO)
HWGWTF Hazardous Waste Groundwater Test Facility (SAUO)
HWH Hot Water Heater (MSA)
HWHF Hazardous Waste Handling Facility (SAUO)
HWHH Half-Width at Half-Height (PDAA)
HWHM Half Width at Half Maximum (AAEL)
HWI Hardware Interpreter
HWI Hardware Wholesalers, Inc.
HWI Hawk Inlet, AK [*Location identifier*] [*FAA*] (FAAL)
HWI Hawkwatch International (EA)
HWI Hazardous Waste Inspectorate (HEAS)
HWI Head Width Index
HWI Helical Washer Institute [*Defunct*] (EA)
HWI High-Water Interval
HWI Horsehair Worms in Illinois (SAUO)
HWI Howard Winters, Incorporated (SAUO)
HWID Hardware Identifier (SAUS)
HWIL Hardware-in-the-Loop
HWIM Hear What I Mean [*Speech recognition system*]
HWIN Hot Water-Insoluble Nitrogen [*Analytical chemistry*]
HWIQ High-Water Inequality (SAUS)

HWIR.......... Hazardous Waste Indentification Rule [*Environmental Protection Agency*]
HWIS.......... Hazardous Waste Information System (SARE)
HWITL.......... Hardware in the Loop
HWJFC.......... Hank Williams Jr. Fan Club (EA)
HWK.......... Harvey Woods Ltd. (SAUS)
HWK.......... Hawker [*Australia*] [*Airport symbol*] (OAG)
HWK.......... Hawkins Chemical, Inc. (SAUO)
HWK.......... Hawk Resources, Inc. [*Vancouver Stock Exchange symbol*]
HWK.......... Kaufman [*H. W.*] Financial Group, Inc. [*AMEX symbol*] (SPSG)
HWK.......... Swazi Air Charter (Pty) Ltd. [*Swaziland*] [*ICAO designator*] (FAAC)
HWKB.......... Hawkeye Bancorp [*NASDAQ symbol*] (NQ)
HWKC.......... Hawkeye Bancorporation (Class C) [*NASDAQ symbol*] (COMM)
HwkEn.......... Hawkins Energy Corp. [*Associated Press*] (SAG)
HWKN.......... Hawkins Chemical [*NASDAQ symbol*] (TTSB)
HWKN.......... Hawkins Chemical, Inc. [*NASDAQ symbol*] (NQ)
HWL.......... Hardy-Weinberg Law (SAUS)
HWL.......... Harvey Woods Ltd. [*Toronto Stock Exchange symbol*]
HWL.......... Hauptwiderstandslinie [*Main line of resistance in a delaying action*] [*German military - World War II*]
HWL.......... Henry Wadsworth Longfellow [*Initials used as pseudonym*]
HWL.......... High-Water Line [*Technical drawings*]
HWL.......... Historic World Leaders [*A publication*]
HWL.......... Hot Water Line (AAG)
HWL.......... Howell Corp. [*NYSE symbol*] (SPSG)
HWLB.......... High-Water London Bridge (SAUS)
HWLC.......... Harold Washington Library Center [*Chicago Public Library*]
HWLC.......... Hotwell Level Control [*System*] [*Nuclear energy*] (NRCH)
HWLD.......... Healthworld Corp. [*NASDAQ symbol*] (NASQ)
HWLI.......... High-Water Lunitidal Interval
HWLL.......... Howell Corp. [*NASDAQ symbol*] (SAG)
HWLLP.......... Howell Corp.$3.50 Cv'A'Pfd [*NASDAQ symbol*] (TTSB)
HWLM.......... High-Water Line Mark (SAUS)
HWLS.......... Hostile Weapons Locating System (MCD)
HWLT.......... Hazardous Waste Land Treatment (GNE)
HWLWR.......... Heavy-Water-Moderated, Boiling Light-Water-Cooled Reactor [*Nuclear energy*] (NRCH)
HWM.......... Half-Width Method (SAUS)
HWM.......... Hazardous Waste Management
HWM.......... Hazardous Waste Material [*Industrial hygiene term*] (OHS)
HWM.......... Hersham & Walton Motors [*British specialty car maker*]
HWM.......... High Molecular Weight
HWM.......... High-Water Mark [*Maps and charts*]
HWM.......... Highway Memory (SAUS)
HWM.......... High Wet Modulus [*Test for rayon*]
HWM.......... Hiram Walker Museum (SAUO)
HWM.......... Hot-Water-Cure Mortar (PDAA)
HWM.......... Howmet International [*NYSE symbol*] (SG)
HWM.......... Hypermedia World Map (SAUO)
HWM.......... Maui County Free Library, Wailuku, HI [*Library symbol*] [*Library of Congress*] (LCLS)
HWMA.......... Hazardous Waste Management Act (SAUO)
HWMA.......... Hazardous Waste Management Association
HWMC.......... House Ways and Means Committee
HWMD.......... Hazardous Waste Management Division [*Environmental Protection Agency*] (GFGA)
HWMF.......... Hazardous Waste Management Facility
HWMJA.......... Hawaii Medical Journal (journ.) (SAUS)
HWMNT.......... High-Water Mark Neap Tide (SAUS)
HWMONT.......... High-Water Mark Ordinary Neap Tide (SAUS)
HWMOST.......... High-Water Mark Ordinary Spring Tide (SAUS)
HWMP.......... Hanford Waste Management Plan (SAUS)
HWMP.......... Hazardous Waste Management Plan
HWMR.......... Heavy Water Moderated Reactor [*Nuclear energy*] (NUCP)
HWMS.......... Hazardous Waste Management System (SAUO)
HWMST.......... High-Water Mark Spring Tide (SAUS)
HWMTP.......... Hanford Waste Management Technology Plan (SAUS)
HWMU.......... Hazardous Waste Management Units (SARE)
HWN.......... Haldwani [*India*] [*Airport symbol*] (AD)
HWN.......... Hazard Warning Network
HWN.......... High-Water Neaps
HWN.......... Honolulu, HI [*Location identifier*] [*FAA*] (FAAL)
HWNA.......... Hosiery Wholesalers National Association (EA)
HWNC.......... Haywood Savings and Loan Association (SAUO)
HWNT.......... High-Water Neap Tide (SAUS)
HWO.......... Hazardous Waste Operations (SAUS)
HWO.......... Hollywood, FL [*Location identifier*] [*FAA*] (FAAL)
HWO.......... Homosexual World Organization
HWO.......... Hotel Waldorf Astoria (SAUO)
HWO.......... Hot Water Oxidizer (PDAA)
HWO.......... Hurricane Warning Office [*National Weather Service*]
HWOCR.......... Heavy-Water Moderated Organic-Cooled Reactor [*Nuclear energy*]
HWOK.......... Heel Walking Normal (STED)
HWOL.......... Healthworld Online (SAUO)
HWONT.......... High-Water of Ordinary Neap Tides (SAUS)
HWONT.......... High-Water, Ordinary Neap Tides (SAUS)
HWOP.......... Hazardous Waste Operating Permit (SAUS)
HWOP.......... Hazardous Waste Operations Permit (SAUS)
HWOP.......... Hazardous Waste Operations Plan (SAUS)
HWOS.......... High-Water Ordinary Springs (SAUS)
HWOST.......... High-Water Ordinary Spring Tides [*Maps and charts*]
HWP.......... Half-Wave Plate
HWP.......... Half Write Pulse (SAUS)
HWP.......... Hardware Work Package (MCD)
HWP.......... Hardwired Processor (SAUS)
HWP.......... Harmonic Wire Projector (IAA)
HWP.......... Hazardous Work Permit (SAUS)
HWP.......... Heavy-Water Plant [*Nuclear energy*]
HWP.......... Heavy Water Project (SAUO)
HWP.......... Height/Weight Proportional (ADWA)
HWP.......... Hepatic Wedge Pressure (STED)
HWP.......... Hermes Writing Process (SAUS)
HWP.......... Hewlett-Packard Co. [*NYSE symbol*] (SPSG)
HWP.......... Hot Wet Pack (STED)
HWP.......... Hours Waiting Parts (MCD)
HWP.......... Hungarian Workers' Party [*Political party*] (PPW)
HWP.......... Hutchinson-Weber-Pentz [*Syndrome*] (STED)
HWPB.......... Heavy Weather Patrol Boats (CINC)
HWPC.......... Hollywood Women's Political Committee (EA)
HWPF.......... Hazardous Waste Processing Facility (EEVL)
HWPX.......... Hiram Walker and Sons [*Private rail car owner code*]
HWQ.......... Hansard Written Questions [*Database*] [*House of Commons*] [*Canada*] [*Information service or system*] (CRD)
HWQ.......... Harlowton, MT [*Location identifier*] [*FAA*] (FAAL)
HWQ.......... High-Water Quadrature
HWQ.......... Tropic High-Water Inequality (SAUS)
HWR.......... Half-Wave Rectifier
HWR.......... Hazardous Waste Research (SAUO)
HWR.......... Heavy-Water Reactor [*Nuclear energy*]
HWR.......... Hot Water Return
HWR.......... Walker [*Hiram*] Resources Ltd. [*Toronto Stock Exchange symbol*] [*Vancouver Stock Exchange symbol*] (SPSG)
HWRC.......... Hazardous Waste Research Center [*Louisiana State University*] [*Research center*] (RCD)
HWRC.......... Hot-Water Recirculation (DAC)
HWRCB.......... Highways and Road Construction (journ.) (SAUS)
HWRF.......... Hazardous Waste Research Fund (SAUO)
HWRF.......... Heavy Water Reactor Facility (SAUS)
HWRFS.......... Heavy Height Reheat Fuel System (SAUS)
HWRTF.......... Hazardous Waste Restrictions Task Force (GNE)
HWRU.......... Hardware Roll-Up (SAUS)
HWS.......... Hanford Works Specification (SAUS)
HWS.......... Hanford Works Standard [*or Specification*] [*Later, HPS*] [*Nuclear energy*] (NRCH)
HWS.......... Harassment Weapon System (MCD)
HWS.......... Harpoon Weapons System (NVT)
HWS.......... Hazardous Waste Service (SAUO)
HWS.......... Heat Wedge Spectrometer (SAUS)
HWS.......... Helicopter Weapons System
HWS.......... High Water of Spring Tide
HWS.......... High-Water of Spring Tide (SAUS)
HWS.......... Highway Switch (SAUS)
HWS.......... Hospitality Worldwide Svcs. [*AMEX symbol*] (SG)
HWS.......... Hot Water Soluble
HWS.......... Hot Water Supply (SAUS)
HWS.......... Hot Water System (SAUS)
HWS.......... Hurricane Warning Service (SAUO)
HWS.......... Hurricane Warning System (WDAA)
HWSA.......... Hazardous Waste Services Association [*Defunct*] (EA)
HWSA.......... Hazardous Waste Staffing Area (SAUS)
HWSB.......... Heavy Wet Support Bridge (SAUS)
HWSD.......... Hazardous Waste Site Data Base (SAUO)
HWSFC.......... Hazardous Waste Superfund Collection [*Environmental Protection Agency*] (AEPA)
HWSFD.......... Hazardous Waste Superfund Database [*Environmental Protection Agency*] (AEPA)
HWSI.......... Health Ways Systems, Inc. (SAUS)
HWSI.......... Health Ways Systems, Incorporated (SAUO)
HWSMC.......... Hazardous Waste Site Management Contractor (SAUS)
HWSNAM.......... Hawaiian Shell News (journ.) (SAUS)
HWSS.......... Harassment Weapon System Sensor (ACAE)
HWSS.......... Hazardous Waste and Superfund Staff [*Environmental Protection Agency*] (GFGA)
HWSS.......... Hot Water Service System (SAUS)
HWSSG.......... Heavy Weapons Special Study Group [*Military*] (MCD)
HWST.......... High Water, Spring Tide (SAUO)
HWST.......... High-Water, Spring Tide (SAUS)
HWSTD.......... High Water Speed Technology Demonstrator [*Marine Corps*] (DOMA)
HWSU.......... Hospital and Welfare Services Union (SAUO)
HW/SW.......... Hardware/Software (MCD)
HWSX.......... Hiram Walker and Sons [*Private rail car owner code*]
HWT.......... Handbook of Weapon Training (SAUS)
HWT.......... Handbook on Weapon Training (SAUO)
HWT.......... Heavy-Weight Torpedo (DOMA)
HWT.......... Herald and Weekly Times Ltd. (SAUO)
hwt.......... Hot Water Tank (REAL)
HWT.......... Hot Water Temperature
HWT.......... Hundredweight (SAUS)
HWT.......... Hypersonic Wind Tunnel
HWTA.......... Houston World Trade Association (SAUO)
HWTC.......... Hazardous Waste Treatment Council (EA)
HWTC.......... Highway Traffic Control
HWTF.......... Hazardous Waste Treatment Facility (SAUO)
HWTH.......... Herewith (ROG)
HWTHN.......... Hawthorne, NJ [*American Association of Railroads railroad junction routing code*]
HWTR.......... Heavy Weapons Testing Range [*Military*] (MCD)
HWTS.......... Heavy Weapons Thermal Sight [*Military*]
HWTS.......... Humm-Wadsworth Temperament Scale [*Psychology*]
HWTS.......... Hypersonic Wing Test Structure (SAUS)

HWTU .... Hanford Waste Treatment Units (SAUS)
HWU .... Hazardous Waste Unit (SAUS)
H-W U .... Heriot-Watt University (SAUO)
HWU .... Historically White University (SAUO)
HWVD .... Hot-Wall Vapor Deposition (SAUS)
HWVE .... Hot-Wall Vacuum Evaporation [*Photovoltaic energy systems*]
HWVP .... Hanford Waste Vitrification Plant [*Department of Energy*] (GAAI)
HWVP .... Hanford Waste Vitrification Program (COE)
HWVR .... However (FAAC)
HWW .... Headlamp Wash and Wipe (ODA)
HWW .... High Wind Warning [*Telecommunications*] (OTD)
HWW .... Horan, Wall & Walker [*Publisher*] (ADA)
HWW .... Hot and Warm Working (SAUS)
HWW .... H. W. Wilson Co. [*Publisher*]
HWWB .... Hardwood Weather Board (ADA)
HWWC .... Hand Wash With Care (SAUS)
HWWS .... Hyperfiltration Wash Water Recovery System [*NASA*] (NASA)
hwy .... Highway (ADWA)
Hwy .... Highway (ASC)
HWY .... Highway
HWY .... Hundred Woman Years [*of exposure*] [*Radiation*]
HWY .... Huntway Partners LP [*NYSE symbol*] (CTT)
HWY .... Huntway Refining [*NYSE symbol*] [*Formerly, Huntway Partners LP*]
HWYM .... HighwayMaster Communic [*NASDAQ symbol*] (TTSB)
HWYM .... HighwayMaster Communications, Inc. [*NASDAQ symbol*] (SAG)
HWY MI .... Highway Miles
HWY of Exposure... Hundred Woman Years of Exposure (SAUS)
HwyResAb ... Highway Research Abstracts (journ.) (SAUS)
HWZ .... Hunt-Wesson [*Federal Railroad Administration identification code*]
HWZOA .... Hadassah, The Women's Zionist Organization of America (EA)
HX .... Half Duplex (IAA)
HX .... Halifax Corp. [*AMEX symbol*] (SPSG)
HX .... Halifax Engineering, Inc. [*AMEX symbol*] (COMM)
HX .... Hamburg Airlines [*ICAO designator*] (AD)
HX .... Have Cancelled [*Travel industry*] (TRID)
HX .... Headroom Extension (SAUS)
HX .... Heat Exchange (SAUS)
HX .... Heat Exchanger (MCD)
Hx .... Hemopexin [*Medicine*] (EDAA)
HX .... Hereodox [*Commercial firm*] [*British*]
HX .... Hexagonal [*Technical drawings*]
Hx .... Hexode (DEN)
Hx .... Hexyl [*Biochemistry*]
HX .... High Expansion Foam (WDAA)
HX .... High Index (SAUS)
HX .... Histiocytosis X [*or Histocytosis X*] [*Hematology*]
Hx .... History [*Medicine*]
Hx .... Hospitalization (DAVI)
HX .... Hydrogen Exchange (PDAA)
Hx .... Hypophysectomized [*Medicine*]
Hx .... Hypoxanthine [*Also, Hyp, HYPX*] [*Biochemistry*]
HX .... No Specific Working Hours [*ICAO*] (FAAC)
HX .... Operating hours on request (SAUO)
HX .... South Pacific Island Airways, Inc. (SAUO)
HXB .... Helix Biotech [*Vancouver Stock Exchange symbol*]
hXBP .... Human X Box Binding Protein [*Genetics*]
HXBT .... Helicopter Expendable Bathythermograph [*Naval Oceanographic Office*]
HXC .... Bear Stearns Companies, Inc. [*AMEX symbol*] (SAG)
HxCDD .... Hexachlorodibenzo-para-dioxin [*Organic chemistry*]
HXCL .... Hexcel
HXD .... Hard X-Ray Detector
HXDP .... Honeywell Experimental Distributed Processor (SAUS)
HXF .... Hartford, WI [*Location identifier*] [*FAA*] (FAAL)
HXIS .... Hard X-Ray Imaging Spectrometer
HXK .... Berlin, NH [*Location identifier*] [*FAA*] (FAAL)
HXL .... Hexcel Corp. [*NYSE symbol*] (SPSG)
HXM .... Hazleton, PA [*Location identifier*] [*FAA*] (FAAL)
HXM .... Helicopter Experimental, Medium (MCD)
HXM .... Hexamethylmelamine [*Altretamine*] [*Also, HEX, HMM*] [*Antineoplastic drug*]
HXO .... Oxford, NC [*Location identifier*] [*FAA*] (FAAL)
HXODA .... Hexyloctyldecyladipat (SAUS)
HXODP .... Hexyloctyldecylphthalat (SAUS)
HXP .... Bear Stearns Companies, Inc. [*AMEX symbol*] (SAG)
H-XPS .... High Power Crosspoint Switch (SAUS)
HXQ .... Hard X-Ray Quanta
HXR .... Hard X-Ray (SAUS)
HXr .... Head X-ray (SAUS)
HXR .... Hudson & Manhattan Corp. (SAUO)
HXR .... Hypoxanthine Riboside [*Medicine*] (EDAA)
HXRBS .... Hard X-Ray Burst Spectrometer
HXSA .... Hexenylsuccinic Anhydride (SAUS)
HXT .... Hard X-Ray Telescope
HXT .... Houston Industries 7 Percent,'ACES' [*NYSE symbol*] (SG)
HXV .... Herpes Simplex Virus [*Infectious disease*] (DAVI)
HXW .... Hopkinsville, KY [*Location identifier*] [*FAA*] (FAAL)
HXWXL .... Height by Width by Length (IEEE)
HXX .... Hay [*Australia*] [*Airport symbol*] (OAG)
HX-XO .... Hypoxanthine-Xanthine Oxidase (DB)
Hy .... All India Reporter, Hyderabad [*A publication*] (DLA)
H-Y .... Harvard-Yale (WDAA)
HY .... Hatha Yoga [*Medicine*] (EDAA)
hy .... Heavy (MILB)
HY .... Heavy [*Track condition*] [*Thoroughbred racing*]
H/Y .... Heavy Tarnish
HY .... Hebrew Year [*Freemasonry*] (ROG)
hy .... Henry [*Variation of the preferred H*] (IDOE)
HY .... Hertfordshire Yeomanry [*British military*] (DMA)
Hy .... Highway
HY .... High Yield [*Material Strength*] (DOMA)
H-Y .... Histocompatibility Y [*Immunology*]
Hy .... History [*Medicine*]
HY .... Hitler Youth (SAUO)
HY .... Hundred Yards
Hy .... Hyaluronic Acid [*Medicine*] (EDAA)
HY .... Hybrid (AAEL)
HY .... Hydrant (ADA)
HY .... Hydrocollator [*Hot*] Pack [*Medicine*]
HY .... Hydrography
Hy .... Hypermetropia [*Ophthalmology*]
Hy .... Hyperopia [*Ophthalmology*] (MAE)
hy .... Hypersthene [*CIPW classification*] [*Geology*]
HY .... Hypobranchial [*Gland*]
Hy .... Hypothenar [*Anatomy*]
hy .... Hysteria [*Psychiatry*] (DAVI)
HY .... Hyundai [*Society of Automotive Engineers auto manufacturer code for service information interchange*]
HY .... Liberian World Airlines, Inc. (SAUO)
HY .... Metro Airlines [*ICAO designator*] (AD)
HYA .... High Voltage-Activated (SAUS)
HYA .... Hyack Air Ltd. [*Canada*] [*ICAO designator*] (FAAC)
HYA .... Hyannis [*Massachusetts*] [*Airport symbol*] (OAG)
Hya .... Hydra [*Constellation*] (WDAA)
Hy A .... Hydro- og Aerodynamisk Laboratorium (SAUS)
Hya .... Hydrus [*Constellation*]
Hyacinth Control J... Hyacinth Control Journal (journ.) (SAUS)
HYACS .... Hybrid Analog-Switching Attitude Control System for Space Vehicles
Hyacs .... Hydrofoil Air Cushlon Ship
Hy AD Regt... Heavy Air Defence Regiment (SAUO)
HYAI .... Hear You Are, Inc. [*An association*] (PAZ)
HYAL .... Hyal Pharmaceutical Corp. [*NASDAQ symbol*] (SAG)
HYALF .... Hyal Pharmaceutical [*NASDAQ symbol*] (TTSB)
HyalPhr .... Hyal Pharmaceutical Corp. [*Associated Press*] (SAG)
HY & T .... Hooppole, Yorktown & Tampico Railroad (IIA)
HYAPP .... Hays Army Ammunition Plant
HYAS .... Hydrogasification [*Gas from coal fuel*]
Hyatts PC.... Hyatts PC News Report (journ.) (SAUS)
HYB .... Herzl Year Book (journ.) (SAUS)
HYB .... Hybrid (MSA)
HYB .... Hybrid Systems [*Telecommunications*] (NITA)
HYB .... Hyderabad [*India*] [*Seismograph station code, US Geological Survey*] (SEIS)
HYB .... New American High Income Fund [*NYSE symbol*] (SPSG)
HYBALL .... Hybrid Analog Logic Language (MCD)
HYBALL .... Hydraulic Ball (SAUS)
HYBD .... Hycor Biomedical [*NASDAQ symbol*] (TTSB)
HYBD .... Hycor Biomedical, Inc. [*NASDAQ symbol*] (NQ)
HYBDW .... Hycor Biomedical Wrrt [*NASDAQ symbol*] (TTSB)
HYBLOC .... Hybrid Computer Block Oriented Compiler (IAA)
HYBMED .... Hybrid Microelectronic Device (MSA)
HYBN .... Hybridon Inc. [*NASDAQ symbol*] (TTSB)
HYBR .... Hybritech, Inc. (SAUO)
Hybrid .... Hybridization (SAUS)
Hybrid Circuit Technol... Hybrid Circuit Technology (journ.) (SAUS)
Hybridon .... Hybridon, Inc. [*Associated Press*] (SAG)
HYBRT .... Hybart, AL [*American Association of Railroads railroad junction routing code*]
Hy Bty .... Heavy Battery (SAUS)
HYC .... Hampshire Yeomanry Cavalry [*British military*] (DMA)
HYC .... Haney [*British Columbia*] [*Seismograph station code, US Geological Survey*] (SEIS)
HYC .... Harlem Yacht Club (SAUO)
HYC .... Hartford Yacht Club (SAUO)
HYC .... Haverhill Yacht Club (SAUO)
HYC .... Hertfordshire Yeomanry Cavalry [*British military*] (DMA)
HYC .... Hydraulic Coupling [*of a ship*] (DS)
HYC .... Hypercom Corp. [*NYSE symbol*] (SG)
HYCANS .... Hydrofoil Collision Avoidance and Navigation System (ACAE)
HYCATS .... Hydrofoil Collision Avoidance and Tracking System [*Developed by Sperry*]
HYCO .... Hybrid Computer (SAUS)
HYCOL .... Hybrid Computer Link
HY-COM .... Highway Communications
HY-COM system... Highway Communications system (SAUO)
HYCON .... Hydraulic Control (SAUS)
Hycor .... Hycor Biomedical, Inc. [*Associated Press*] (SAG)
HYCOS .... Hydrological Cycle Observing System (SAUS)
HYCOTRAN... Hybrid Computer Translator
HYCOTRANS... Hybrid Composit Structures for Crashworthy Body Shells and Safe Transportation Structures
HYCPP .... High Yield Catalyst Polypropylene (PDAA)
Hyd .... All India Reporter, Hyderabad (journ.) (SAUS)
HYD .... Coeur D'Alene, ID [*Location identifier*] [*FAA*] (FAAL)
HYD .... High-Viscosity Dispenser (SAUS)
HYD .... Hyderabad [*India*] [*Airport symbol*] (OAG)
Hyd .... Hydralazine [*Medicine*] (EDAA)
HYD .... Hydrant (MSA)
HYD .... Hydrargyrum [*Mercury*] [*Pharmacy*]
HYD .... Hydrate (SAUS)

HYD .... Hydrated
HYD .... Hydration (MELL)
HYD .... Hydraulic (AAG)
Hyd .... Hydraulic (MIST)
hyd .... Hydraulic (MIST)
HYD .... Hydraulics (NAKS)
HYD .... Hydraulic Subsystem (NAKS)
HYD .... Hydroaphic (SAUS)
HYD .... Hydroelectric Power [*Type of water project*]
HYD .... Hydrogenation [*Chemistry*]
HYD .... Hydrographic
HYD .... Hydrographical (SAUS)
HYD .... Hydrometals, Ind. (SAUO)
HYD .... Hydrostatical (SAUS)
HYD .... Hydrostatics
HYD .... Hydrous
HYD .... Hydroxyurea [*Also, HU, HYDREA*] [*Antineoplastic drug*]
Hyd .... Hydrus [*Constellation*] (WDAA)
HYD .... International Hydron Corp. (SAUO)
HYDAC .... Hybrid Digital-Analog Computing [*System*] [*Satellite*]
HYDAP .... Hybrid Digital-Analog Pulse Time (MCD)
HYDAPT .... Hybrid Digital-Analog Pulse Time
HYDAS .... Hydrographic Data Acquisition System (PDAA)
HYDAT .... Hydrodynamic Analysis Tool (DNAB)
HYDATA .... Hydrological Database & Analysis
HYDCA .... Hydrocarbure (journ.) (SAUS)
HYDE .... Hyde Athletic Industries, Inc. [*NASDAQ symbol*] (NQ)
Hyde .... Hyde's Bengal Reports [*India*] [*A publication*] (DLA)
HYDEA .... Hyde Athletic Indus'A' [*NASDAQ symbol*] (TTSB)
HydeAt .... Hyde Athletic Industries, Inc. [*Associated Press*] (SAG)
HydeAth ...... Hyde Athletic Industries, Inc. [*Associated Press*] (SAG)
HYDEB .... Hyde Athletic Indus'B' [*NASDAQ symbol*] (TTSB)
HYDEL .... Hydroelectrical (SAUS)
Hyderabad ... Indian Law Reports, Hyderabad Series [*A publication*] (DLA)
HYDI .... Hydromer, Incorporated (SAUO)
Hydi .... Hydrus [*Constellation*]
HYDICE .... Hyper-spectral Digital Imagery Collection Experiment [*National Oceanic and Atmospheric Administration*]
HYDKAK .... Pings. Hoshi College of Pharmacy (SAUS)
HYDL .... Hydril Co. [*NASDAQ symbol*]
HYDLAPS ..... Hydrographic Data Logging and Plotting System (EERA)
HYDLAPS ..... Hydrographic Data Logging and Processing Systems (SAUS)
HYDM .... Hydrometer
HYDO .... Hydraulic Oil
HYD'PR .... Hydroxyproline [*An amino acid*] (DAVI)
HYD PRO UN ... Hydraulic Propulsion Units [*on a ship*] (DS)
HYDR .... Hydragogue [*Cathartic*] [*Pharmacy*] (ROG)
HYDR .... Hydraulic (MSA)
Hydr .... Hydrographer [*British military*] (DMA)
HYDR .... Hydrostatics (ROG)
HYDRA .... Hybrid Defense Radio (SAUS)
HYDRA .... Hydramatic [*Automotive engineering*]
HYDRA .... Hydraulic [*or Hydrologic*] Analysis
HYDRA .... Hydrographic Digital Positioning and Depth Recording [*System*] [*NOO*]
HYDRA .... Hydrolic Analysis (SAUS)
HYDRA .... Hydrologic Analysis (SAUS)
HYDRAPAD ... Hydraulic Positioning and Drilling (SAUS)
HYDRARG .... Hydrargyrum [*Mercury*] [*Pharmacy*]
HYDRAT .... Chloral Hydrate [*Pharmacology*] (DAVI)
HYDRAUL .... Hydraulics (ROG)
Hydraul&Air Engng ... Hydraulic and Air Engineering (journ.) (SAUS)
Hydraul Pneum Mech Power ... Hydraulic Pneumatic Mechanical Power (journ.) (SAUS)
HYDRAWELD ... Hydraulic-Drawn Welded (SAUS)
Hydrazine Water Treat Proc Int Conf ... Hydrazine and Water Treatment. Proceedings of the International Conference (journ.) (SAUS)
HYDREA .... Hydroxyurea [*Also, HU, HYD*] [*Antineoplastic drug*]
HYDRELC ..... Hydroelectric (MSA)
HYDRESS .... High Data Range Storage Subsystem (SAUO)
Hydride Symp ... Hydride Symposium (journ.) (SAUS)
HYDRLC .... Hydraulic
hydro .... Hydroelectric (ADWA)
HYDRO .... Hydroelectric (GOBB)
HYDRO .... Hydrographical Department (SAUO)
HYDRO .... Hydrographic Office [*Terminated, 1963; later, NOO*] [*Navy*]
HYDRO .... Hydrography
HYDRO .... Hydropathic (ADA)
HYDRO .... Hydrostatic (KSC)
HYDRO .... Hydrotherapy [*Medicine*]
Hydrobiol ..... Hydrobiologia (journ.) (SAUS)
Hydrobiol ..... Hydrobiology (SAUS)
Hydrobiol Bull ... Hydrobiological Bulletin (journ.) (SAUS)
HydrobiolJ ... Hydrobiological Journal (SAUO)
Hydrobiol J ... Hydrobiological Journal (journ.) (SAUS)
Hydrobiol Stud ... Hydrobiological Studies (journ.) (SAUS)
Hydrocarbon Process ... Hydrocarbon Processing (journ.) (SAUS)
Hydrocarbon Process Pet Refiner ... Hydrocarbon Processing and Petroleum Refiner (journ.) (SAUS)
Hydroc Proc ... Hydrocarbon Processing (journ.) (SAUS)
Hydrocyclones Pap Int Conf ... Hydrocyclones. Papers Presented at the International Conference (journ.) (SAUS)
HYDRODYN ... Hydrodynamics
HYDROELEC ... Hydroelectric
Hydroelec Engr ... Hydroelectric Engineer (SAUS)
Hydro Electr Power ... Hydro Electric Power (journ.) (SAUS)
HYDROG ...... Hydrogaphic (SAUS)
Hydrog .... Hydrogeography
Hydrog .... Hydrographer of the Navy [*British*]
HYDROG ...... Hydrographic
Hydrog Bull ... Hydrographic Bulletin (journ.) (SAUS)
Hydrogen Met ... Hydrogen in Metals (journ.) (SAUS)
Hydrogen Prog ... Hydrogen Progress (journ.) (SAUS)
Hydrogen Re ... Hydrogen Relief (NAKS)
Hydrogeol J ... Hydrogeology Journal [*A publication*] (PABS)
Hydrog Rev ... Hydrographic Review (journ.) (SAUS)
Hydrogr J ..... Hydrographic Journal [*A publication*] (PABS)
HYDROIND ... Hydrography of the Indian Ocean (SAUS)
Hydro Int ..... Hydro International [*A publication*] (PABS)
HYDROL ...... Hydrologic
Hydro Lab J ... Hydro-Lab Journal (journ.) (SAUS)
HYDROLANT ... Hydrographic Information for the Atlantic [*Navy*] (DNAB)
HYDROLANT ... Hydrographic Warning-Atlantic (SAUO)
HYDROLANT ... Hydrographic Warning-Atlantic Ocean (SAUS)
HYDROLANT ... Hydrography of the Atlantic Ocean (SAUS)
Hydrol J .... Hydrological Journal (journ.) (SAUS)
Hydrol Process ... Hydrological Processes (journ.) (SAUS)
Hydrol Sci Bull ... Hydrological Sciences Bulletin (journ.) (SAUS)
Hydrol Sci Bull Int Assoc Hydrol Sci ... Hydrological Sciences Bulletin. International Association of Hydrological Sciences (journ.) (SAUS)
Hydrol Sci Bull Sci Hydrol ... Hydrological Sciences. Bulletin des Sciences Hydrologiques (journ.) (SAUS)
Hydrol Sci J ... Hydrological Sciences Journal [*A publication*] (CABS)
Hydrol Symp ... Hydrology Symposium (journ.) (SAUS)
Hydrol Water Resor Ariz Southwest ... Hydrology and Water Resources in Arizona and the Southwest (journ.) (SAUS)
Hydrom .... Hydromechanics (SAUS)
Hydromag .... Hydromagnetics (SAUS)
HYDROMAN ... Hydraulic Manipulator (SAUS)
Hydromech&Hydraul Engng Abstr ... Hydromechanics and Hydraulic Engineering Abstracts (journ.) (SAUS)
HYDROPAC ... Hydrographic Information for the Pacific [*Navy*] (DNAB)
HYDROPAC ... Hydrographic Warning-Pacific Ocean (SAUS)
HYDROPAC ... Hydrography of the Pacific Ocean (SAUS)
HYDROPNEU ... Hydropneumatic [*Freight*]
hydros .... Hydrostatics (BARN)
Hydro-Sci Eng ... Hydro-Science and Engineering [*A publication*] (PABS)
Hydrosp .... Hydrospace (SAUS)
HYDROX ...... Hydrogen-Oxygen [*Fuel system*] (DNAB)
HYDROX ...... Hydroxyline (SAUS)
Hydr Pow Transm ... Hydraulic Power Transmission (journ.) (SAUS)
Hydr Res ...... Hydraulics Research (journ.) (SAUS)
HYDRSS ...... High Data Range Storage Subsystem (SAUO)
HYDRST ...... Hydrostatic (MSA)
HydrTch ...... Hydron Technologies, Inc. [*Associated Press*] (SAG)
HYDT .... Hydrant (ADA)
HYDTD .... Hydrated (MSA)
HYDX .... Hydroxide (IAA)
HYDZ .... Hydrazine (ACAE)
HYE .... Healthy Years Equivalent (DMAA)
HYE .... Hyeres Aero Service [*France*] [*ICAO designator*] (FAAC)
HYF .... Hayfields [*Papua New Guinea*] [*Airport symbol*] (OAG)
HYF .... Hong Kong and Yaumati Ferry (SAUS)
HYF .... Humbligny [*France*] [*Seismograph station code, US Geological Survey*] (SEIS)
HYF .... Hydrofoil (SAUS)
HyF .... Hytone Film Lab, Inc., Des Moines, IA [*Library symbol*] [*Library of Congress*] (LCLS)
HYFA .... Hydrometeor Free Atmosphere (SAUS)
HYFA .... Hypothetical Fund Allocation (SAUO)
HYFAC .... Hydrogenated Fatty Acid (SAUS)
HYFAC .... Hypersonic Research Facilities [*NASA*]
HYFES .... Hypersonic Flight Environmental Simulator
HYFIX .... Hyperbolic Fix
HYFLO .... Hydroformylated Linseed Oil (SAUS)
HYFLTE .... Hypersonic Flight-Test Experiment (SAUS)
HYFT .... High-Yield Fallout Trajectory (DNAB)
HYG .... Hydaburg [*Alaska*] [*Airport symbol*] (OAG)
hyg .... Hygiene (IDYL)
HYG .... Hygiene
HYG .... Hygroscopic
HYGA .... Hygeia Sciences, Inc. (SAUO)
HYGA .... Hygenia Sciences, Inc. (SAUS)
HYGAS .... Hydrogen Gasification
HYGL .... Hypergolic (KSC)
HY Gland ..... Hypobranchial Gland (SAUS)
HYGN .... Hygiene
HYGNST ...... Hygienist
HYGR .... Hygroscopical (SAUS)
hygrom .... hygrometer (SAUS)
hygrom .... hygrometist (SAUS)
HYGS .... Hydrogenics Corp. [*NASDAQ symbol*]
HygSanit ..... Hygiene and Sanitation (SAUO)
HYGST .... Hygienist (AABC)
HY/HS .... High Yield/High Stereospecificity Technology [*for polypropylene*] [*Himont Corp.*]
HYI .... High Yield Income Fd [*NYSE symbol*] (TTSB)
HYI .... High Yield Income Fund [*NYSE symbol*] (SPSG)
Hyi .... Hydrus [*Astronomy*] (ODA)
HYK .... Huyck Corporation (SAUO)

HYKOE3 .... Han Guk Journal of Genetic Engineering (journ.) (SAUS)
HYL .... Hollis, AK [*Location identifier*] [*FAA*] (FAAL)
HYL .... Hoyle Resources Ltd. [*Vancouver Stock Exchange symbol*]
HYL .... Hybrid Language Assembler (SAUS)
Hyl .... Hydroxylysine [*Also, Hylys*] [*An amino acid*]
HYLA .... Hybrid Language Assembler
HYLIFE .... High-Yield Lithium Injection Fusion Energy (MCD)
HYLO .... Hyaline [*Cytology*] (DAVI)
HYL Process... Hojalata y Lamina Process (SAUS)
Hylys .... Hydroxylysine [*or (OH)Lys*] [*Also, Hyl*] [*An amino acid*]
HYM .... Hyman, TX [*Location identifier*] [*FAA*] (FAAL)
Hym .... Hymenoptera [*Entomology*]
HYMA .... Hebrew Young Men's Association
HYMATIC ..... Hydraulic Multiplate Active Traction Intelligent Control [*Automotive engineering*]
HYMNB .... Hyomen (journ.) (SAUS)
Hymn Hom Ap... Hymnus Homericus ad Apollinem [*Classical studies*] (OCD)
Hymn Hom Bacch... Hymnus Homericus ad Bacchum [*Classical studies*] (OCD)
Hymn Hom Cer... Hymnus Homericus ad Cererem [*Classical studies*] (OCD)
Hymn Hom Mart... Hymnus Homericus ad Martem [*Classical studies*] (OCD)
Hymn Hom Merc... Hymnus Homericus ad Mercurium [*Classical studies*] (OCD)
Hymn Hom Pan... Hymnus Homericus ad Panem [*Classical studies*] (OCD)
Hymn Hom Ven... Hymnus Homericus ad Venerem [*Classical studies*] (OCD)
Hymnol .... Hymnologist (SAUS)
Hymnol .... Hymnology (SAUS)
HYMNS .... Hydrogen MASER for Navigation Satellite (MCD)
HYMOSS ...... Hybrid Mosaic on Stacked Silicon [*Materials science*]
HYMV .... Hypochoeris Mosaic Virus [*Plant pathology*]
HYN .... Halcyon Resources Ltd. [*Vancouver Stock Exchange symbol*]
HYNET .... Intercomparison of Operational Hydrological Network Design Techniques (SAUO)
HYO .... Husky Oil Ltd. (SAUO)
HYOCY .... Hyocyamine Sulfate (SAUS)
Hyogo Univ Tech Educ J Ser 3... Hyogo University of Teacher Education. Journal. Series 3. Natural Sciences, Practical Life Studies (journ.) (SAUS)
HYOSCYAM... Hyoscyamus [*Henbane*] [*Pharmacology*] (ROG)
HYP .... Harvard, Yale, and Princeton Universities
HYP .... High Yield Plus Fund [*NYSE symbol*] (SPSG)
HYP .... Hydrolysed Vegetable Protein (SAUS)
HYP .... Hydroxprolin (SAUS)
HYP .... Hydroxybenzylpindolol [*Neuropharmacology*]
Hyp .... Hydroxyproline [*Also, Hypro*] [*An amino acid*]
hyp .... Hypalgesia (STED)
HYP .... Hypergolic
HYP .... Hyperresonance
HYP .... Hypertrophy
hyp .... hyphenate (SAUS)
HYP .... Hyphen Character [*Computer science*]
HYP .... Hypnosis
HYP .... Hypodermic (ROG)
hyp .... Hypophysis (STED)
hyp .... Hypopnea [*Therapy term*] (CTAA)
hyp .... Hypotenuse (SHCU)
HYP .... Hypotenuse [*Mathematics*]
HYP .... Hypothalamus [*Neuroanatomy*]
hyp .... Hypothesis (MIST)
HYP .... Hypothesis
HYP .... Hypothetical (WDAA)
Hyp .... Hypoxanthine [*Also, Hx, HYPX*] [*Biochemistry*]
Hyp2005 ...... Hyperion 2005 Investment Grade Opportunity Term Trust [*Associated Press*] (SAG)
HYPACE .... Hybrid Programmable Attitude Control Electronics [*NASA*]
HYPAR .... Hysterectomy Produced and Artificially Reared (PDAA)
HYPARS .... Hyperbolic Paraboloid Surface (MCD)
HYPAS .... Hydraulic Power-Assisted Steering
HYPD .... Harvard, Yale, Princeton, Dartmouth Chess League (SAUO)
HYPECO .... Hybrid Poultry Breeding Corporation (SAUO)
HYPER .... Hydrographic Personnel [*Navy*]
HYPER .... Hyperactive (GOBB)
hyper .... hypercritical (SAUS)
HYPER .... Hyperhydrated, Hyperventilating with Hyperpyrexia, Hyperexcitability, and Hyperrigidity [*Characteristics of drowning*]
HYPER .... Hypertapes (SAUS)
hyper A .... Hyperactive (STED)
hyperal .... Hyperalimentation [*Intravenous feeding*] [*Medicine*] (DAVI)
HYPERB .... Hyperbola [*Mathematics*]
HYPERDIP ... Hyper Diploidy (SAUS)
HYPERDOP... Hyperbolic Doppler
Hyperfine Interact... Hyperfine Interactions (journ.) (SAUS)
hyper-IgE ..... Hyperimmunoglobulinemia E [*Medicine*] (STED)
HYPERIGN ... Hypergolic Ignition (KSC)
HYPER ISC... Hyperchannel Inter-Systems Communication (SAUS)
HYPERLIB .... Hypertext Interfaces to Library Information Systems (TELE)
HYPERNET... Hyper-Network (SAUS)
hyperpara ..... Hyperparathyroidism [*Endocrinology*] (DAVI)
HYPERT .... Hypertape (SAUS)
HyperT4 .... Hyperthyroidism (SPVS)
hyper T & A... Hypertrophy of Tonsils and Adenoids [*Medicine*] (MAE)
hyper T & A... Hypertropy of Tonsils and Adenoids [*Otorhinolaryngology*] (DAVI)
Hypertens Suppl... Hypertension Supplement (journ.) (SAUS)
hypes .... Hypesthesia (STED)
HYPH .... Hydrophone
HypmdCm ..... Hypermedia Communications, Inc. [*Associated Press*] (SAG)
hypn .... Hypertension (DMAA)
HYPN .... Hypertension
hypno .... Hypnosis (STED)
HYPNO .... Hypnosis
hypnot .... hypnotic (SAUS)
HYPNOT .... Hypnotism
Hypnot .... Hypnotist (SAUS)
HYPNS .... Hypnosis
HYPO .... High Power [*Water boiler atomic reactor*] [*Dismantled*]
HYPO .... High Power Output Reactor (SAUO)
HYPO .... High Power Water Boiler (SAUO)
HYPO .... High Power Water Boiler Reactor (SAUS)
HYPO .... Hypochondria (DSUE)
hypo .... hypochondriacal (SAUS)
hypo .... Hypochromaria (STED)
hypo .... Hypochromasia [*Hematology*]
Hypo .... Hypodermic (DMAA)
hypo .... Hypodermic (STED)
HYPO .... Hypodermic
hypo .... hypodermically (SAUS)
hypo .... Hypodermic Injection [*Medicine*] (IDYL)
hypo .... Hyposulfate [*Solium Thiosulphate*] [*A compound used in photography*] (WDMC)
HYPO .... Hyposulfite of Sodium [*Photography*] (ROG)
HYPOC .... Hypochromasia [*Hematology*] (DAVI)
HYPOCON .... Hypochondria (DSUE)
hypodip .... hypodiploidy (SAUS)
HYPOT .... Hypotenuse [*Mathematics*] (ROG)
HypoT4 .... Hypothyroidism (SPVS)
HYPOTH .... Hypothesis (ADA)
hypoth .... Hypothesis (ADWA)
HYPOTH .... Hypothetical (MSA)
HYPO Water Boiler... High Power Water Boiler (SAUS)
HYPOX .... Hypophysectomy [*Medicine*]
HYPP .... Hyperkalemic Periodic Paralysis [*Medicine*]
HYPP .... Hypersegmented Neutrophil [*Hematology*] (DAVI)
HYPR .... Hypermedia Communications [*NASDAQ symbol*] (SAG)
HYPREM ...... Hyper Response Electric Motor (SAUS)
HypRF .... Hypothalamic Releasing Factor (DB)
HyprnSft ...... Hyperion Software, Inc. [*Associated Press*] (SAG)
HyprnTR ...... Hyperion Total Return & Income Fund [*Associated Press*] (SAG)
Hypro .... Hydroxyproline [*or (OH)Pro*] [*Also, Hyp*] [*An amino acid*]
HyprSf .... Hyperion Software, Inc. [*Associated Press*] (SAG)
Hyps .... Hypsipyle [*of Euripides*] [*Classical studies*] (OCD)
HYPSES .... Hydrographic Precision Scanning Echo Sounder
hypst .... Hypostyle (VRA)
HYPT .... Hyperion Telecommunications'A' [*NASDAQ symbol*] (SG)
HYPT .... Hyperion Telecommunications, Inc. [*NASDAQ symbol*] (NASQ)
HypT02 .... Hyperion 2002 Term Trust [*Associated Press*] (SAG)
HypT97 .... Hyperion 1997 Term Trust [*Associated Press*] (SAG)
HypT99 .... Hyperion 1999 Term Trust [*Associated Press*] (SAG)
HYPTP .... Hypertape (SAUS)
HYPUB .... Hypanthium Pubescence [*Botany*]
HYPX .... Hypoxanthine [*Also, Hx, Hyp*] [*Biochemistry*]
HYPZ .... Hi-Yield Products [*Federal Railroad Administration identification code*]
HYR .... Hayward [*Wisconsin*] [*Airport symbol*] (OAG)
HYR .... Hycroft Resources & Development Corp. [*Vancouver Stock Exchange symbol*]
Hy RA .... Heavy Battery, Royal Artillery (SAUO)
Hy Regt .... Heavy Regiment (SAUO)
HYREX .... Hydrological Radar Experiment
HYRROM ..... Hydrological Rainfall Runoff Model
HYS .... Hays [*Kansas*] [*Airport symbol*] (OAG)
HYS .... Hysterectomy [*Medicine*] (AAMN)
Hys .... Hysterectomy [*Medicine*] (EDAA)
hys .... Hysterectomy [*Medicine*] (EDAA)
HYS .... Hysteria
hys .... hysterics (SAUS)
HYSAA .... Hygiene and Sanitation (journ.) (SAUS)
HYSAM .... Hypersonic Surface-to-Air Missile (MCD)
HYSAP .... Hydrographic Survey Assistance Program (SAUS)
HYSAS .... Hybrid Signal Analysis System (ACAE)
HYSAS .... Hydrofluidic Stability Augmentation System
HYSAT .... Hybrid Sensor Experiment Satellite Study (ACAE)
HYSCAN .... Hybrid Scanning (SAUS)
HYSCAN Radar System... Hybrid Scanning Radar System (SAUS)
HYSIM .... Highway Driving Simulator [*MM*] (TAG)
HYSL .... Hyperion Solutions [*Formerly, Arbor Software*] [*NASDAQ symbol*]
HY-SPLIT ..... Hybrid Single Particle Lagrangian Integrated Trajectories [*Model*] [*Marine science*] (OSRA)
HYSQ .... Hyseq, Inc. [*NASDAQ symbol*] (NASQ)
HYST .... Hyster Co. (SAUO)
Hyst .... Hysterectomy [*Medicine*] (AMHC)
hyst .... Hysterectomy [*Medicine*]
Hyst .... Hysteresis (SAUS)
HYSTAD .... Hydrofoil Stabilization Device
HYSTCK .... Haystack
hyster .... Hysterectomy [*Gynecology*] (DAVI)
hysterec .... hysterectomic (SAUS)
HYSTERO ..... Hysterosalpingogram [*Gynecology*] (DHSM)
HYSTERO ..... Hysterosalpinogram (SAUS)
HYSTOR ...... Hydrogen Storage (SAUS)
HySTP .... Hypervelocity System Technology Program (SAUO)
HYSTRU ...... Hydraulic System Test and Repair Unit [*Army*] (MCD)
HYSTU .... Hydrofoil Special Trials Unit (SAUO)
HYSUCAT ..... Hydrofoil Supported Catamaran (SAUS)
HYSURCH .... Hydrographic Surveying and Charting [*System*] [*NOO*]

HYSW .... Hyperion Software [*NASDAQ symbol*] (TTSB)
HYSW .... Hyperion Software, Inc. [*NASDAQ symbol*] (SAG)
Hyswas .... Hydrofoil Small Waterplane Area Ship
HYT .... High Year of Tenure
HYT .... High-Yield Tax-Exempt [*Finance*] (BARN)
HYT .... Humaita [*Brazil*] [*Airport symbol*] (AD)
HYTAC .... Hydraulic Tachometer
HYTAM .... Hypersonic Tactical Missile (MCD)
HYTD .... DECS Trust IV [*NASDAQ symbol*] (NASQ)
HYTEA .... Hypertext Authoring Environment (SAUS)
HYTEA .... Hypertext Environment for Authoring (SAUS)
HYTEC .... Hydrogen Thermal Electrochemical Converter
HYTELNET ... Hypertext browser for TELNET-accessible sites (SAUS)
HYTEMCO .... High Temperature Coefficient nickel-iron alloy (SAUS)
HYTIME .... Hypermedia/Time-based structuring language (SAUS)
HYTIWYG ..... How You Test is What You Get [*Education*] (AIE)
HyTk .... Heavy Tank (SAUS)
HYTK .... Hytek International Corp. (SAUO)
HYTOR .... High Touring (SAUS)
HYTRAN .... Hybrid Translator (IAA)
HYTREC .... Hydrospace Target Recognition, Evaluation, and Control
HYTRESS ..... High-Test Recorder and Simulator System (IEEE)
HYTRESS ..... Hyway Test Recorder and Simulator System (SAUO)
HYTROSS .... High-Test Recorder and Simulator System
HYU .... Chesterfield, VA [*Location identifier*] [*FAA*] (FAAL)
HYU .... Lilly Contingent Payment Units [*AMEX symbol*] (SPSG)
HYU .... Lilly CtgntPymt Units [*AMEX symbol*] (TTSB)
HYV .... High Yielding Variety [*Agriculture*]
HYVE .... Hydrogen Ventilated Enclosure (PDAA)
HYVIA .... Hyper-Velocity Interceptor Armament (SAUS)
HYW .... Conway, SC [*Location identifier*] [*FAA*] (FAAL)
HYWAYS ...... Hybrid with Advanced Yield for Surveillance [*Strategic Defense Initiative*]
HYWN .... Hypersonic Wedge Nozzle (MCD)
HYWV .... High-Yielding Wheat Variety (GNE)
HYX .... Hydra Explorations Ltd. [*Toronto Stock Exchange symbol*]
HYZ .... Thief River Falls, MN [*Location identifier*] [*FAA*] (FAAL)
HZ .... Dust Haze [*Aviation*]
HZ .... Farmer's Movement (Slovakia) [*Political party*] (PSAP)
HZ .... Habitable Zone [*Beyond the solar system*]
HZ .... Hazard Zone (SAUO)
HZ .... Haze (WDAA)
HZ .... Hazeltine Corporation (SAUO)
Hz .... Headquarters Zip Code [*Dialog*] [*Searchable field*] [*Information service or system*] (NITA)
HZ .... Henebery Aviation [*ICAO designator*] (AD)
HZ .... Heritability Zone (SAUS)
HZ .... Herpes Zoster [*Medicine*]
Hz .... Hertz [*Symbol*] [*SI unit of frequency*] (AABC)
hz .... Hertz (ELAL)
hz .... Hertz (MIST)
Hz .... Hertzian (SAUS)
HZ .... Historische Zeitschrift [*A publication*] (ODCC)
HZ .... Hydralazine [*Antihypertensive agent*]
HZ .... Saudi Arabia [*International civil aircraft marking*] (ODBW)
HZ .... Thurston Aviation Ltd. (SAUO)
HZA .... Hauptzollamt [*Chief Customs Office*] [*German*] (DLA)
HZA .... Herut Zionists of America (EA)
HZAN .... Herpes Zoster Acute Neuralgia [*Medicine*] (MELL)
HZBBA .... Horizons in Biochemistry and Biochemistry (journ.) (SAUS)
HZBL .... Holzblaeser [*Woodwind Instrument*] [*Music*]
HzBW .... Hertz Bandwidth (SAUS)
HZD .... Hydrated Zirconium Dioxide (SAUS)
HZDS .... Movement for a Democratic Slovakia [*Political party*] (PSAP)
HZE .... Highly Charged and Energetic Particles (SAUS)
HZE .... High Z and E [*Particles in outer space*]
Hzea .... Heliothis Zea [*Corn ear worm*]
HZFO .... Hamster Zona-Free Ovum [*Test*] [*Medicine*] (MEDA)
HZFS .... Horizon Financial Services Corp. [*NASDAQ symbol*] (SAG)
HZFS .... Horizon Financial Svcs [*NASDAQ symbol*] (TTSB)
HZG .... Hanzhong [*China*] [*Airport symbol*] (OAG)
HZGX .... Herzog Contracting [*Federal Railroad Administration identification code*]
HZI .... Hemizona Assay Index [*Medicine*] (MELL)
HZI .... Herpes Zoster Infection [*Medicine*] (MELL)
HZI .... Histamine Zinc Insulin [*Medicine*] (EDAA)
HZI .... Hy & Zel's, Inc. [*Toronto Stock Exchange symbol*]
HZIR .... Horizon Air Industries, Inc. (SAUO)
HZK .... Atlanta, GA [*Location identifier*] [*FAA*] (FAAL)
Hzk .... Hezekiah (SAUS)
HZK .... Husavik [*Iceland*] [*Airport symbol*] (OAG)
HZL .... Hazelton Airlines [*Australia*] [*ICAO designator*] (FAAC)
HZL .... Hazleton [*Pennsylvania*] [*Airport symbol*] [*Obsolete*] (OAG)
HZL .... Herpes Zoster Lesion [*Medicine*] (MELL)
HZL .... Hindustan Zink Limited (SAUO)
HZMP .... Horizontal Impulse (IEEE)
HZN .... Hazen (SAUS)
HZN .... Hazen, NV [*Location identifier*] [*FAA*] (FAAL)
HZN .... Horizon Airlines Ltd. [*Nigeria*] [*FAA designator*] (FAAC)
HzNPV .... Heliothis Zea Nuclear Polyhedrosis Virus
HZNT .... Handbuch zum Neuen Testament [*Lietzmann*] [*A publication*] (BJA)
HZO .... Herpes Zoster Ophthalmicus [*Ophthalmology*]
HZO .... Hydrated Zirconium Oxide (SAUS)
HZO .... Hydrous Zirconium Oxide [*Medicine*] (EDAA)
HZO .... MarineMax
HZOO .... Hunick Zoo. Monthly Publication of Tanana Chiefs Conference (journ.) (SAUS)
HZP .... Horizon Pharmacies [*!AMX*] (SG)
HZP .... Hot Zero Power [*Nuclear energy*] (NRCH)
HZP .... Hyperbolic Zone Plate (PDAA)
HZP .... Zionsville, IN [*Location identifier*] [*FAA*] (FAAL)
HZQC .... Homonuclear Proton Zero-Quantum Coherence (SAUS)
HZR .... New Roads, LA [*Location identifier*] [*FAA*] (FAAL)
HZRN .... Horizontal Reaction
HzSC .... Hazardous Substances Consent (HEAS)
HZTS .... Hybrid Thermal Treatment System (SAUS)
HZV .... Herpes Zoster Virus
HZW .... Wichita, KS [*Location identifier*] [*FAA*] (FAAL)
HZWV .... Horizon Bancorp West Virginia [*NASDAQ symbol*] (SAG)
HZWV .... Horizon Bancorp (WV) [*NASDAQ symbol*] (SAG)
HZY .... Hazy (WGA)
HZYC .... Hadassah Zionist Youth Commission (EA)
HZYO .... Hashomer Hatzair Zionist Youth Organization [*Later, HHSZYM*] (EA)

I

By Acronym

I.................... Airborne Intercept (SAUS)
I.................... Air Force Training Category [*No training*]
I.................... Angle of Incidence
I.................... Carlo Erba [*Italy*] [*Research code symbol*]
i.................... Class Interval [*Statistics*]
I.................... Current [*Communications term*] (DCT)
I.................... Electric Current [*Symbol*] [*IUPAC*]
I.................... Electric Flow in Amperes (NTIO)
I.................... Fighter [*Russian aircraft symbol*]
I.................... First Interstate Bancorp. [*NYSE symbol*] (SPSG)
I.................... I-Band (MELL)
I.................... I-Beam [*Structural metal shape*]
I.................... Ibuprofen [*A drug*]
I.................... Ice (ADWA)
I.................... Iconoscope (IAA)
I.................... Id [*That*] [*Latin*] (GPO)
I.................... Idaho
I.................... Identification
I.................... Idus [*The Ides*] [*Latin*]
I.................... Ihr [*Your*] [*German*]
I.................... Illinois State Library, Springfield, IL [*Library symbol*] [*Library of Congress*] (LCLS)
I.................... Illite [*A mineral*]
I.................... Illuminated (WDMC)
I.................... Illumination (IAA)
I.................... Illuminous Intensity (SAUS)
I.................... Image [*File*] [*Computer science*] [*Telecommunications*]
I.................... Imaginary (IAA)
I.................... Imaginary Number (NTIO)
i.................... Imaginary Number (SHCU)
i.................... Imaginary Unit (WGA)
i.................... Immortalis [*Immortal*] [*Latin*] (GPO)
I.................... Imperator [*or Imperatrix*] [*Emperor or Empress*] [*Latin*]
I.................... Imperial
I.................... Imperial Paper (DGA)
i.................... Imperial Savings (SAUS)
I.................... Implantation (MELL)
I.................... Implicit
I.................... Impression (DAVI)
i.................... Improbatur [*Latin*]
i.................... Impurity [*Medicine*] (EDAA)
I.................... Inactive (STED)
i.................... Inactive [*Chemistry*]
I.................... Inboard (DS)
I.................... Incendiary [*Bomb*]
I.................... Inch (ODA)
I.................... Incident Ray (IDOE)
I.................... Incisal [*Dentistry*] (DAVI)
I.................... Incision (MELL)
i.................... incisor (SAUS)
i.................... Incisor (Deciduous) [*Dentistry*]
I.................... Incisor (Permanent) [*Dentistry*]
I.................... Inclination
I.................... Income
I.................... Incompatible
I.................... Incomplete
I.................... Incontinent [*Medicine*]
I.................... Increased (STED)
I.................... Incumbent (ROG)
I.................... Independence (IDYL)
I.................... Independent
i.................... Independent Pump [*Liquid gas carriers*]
I.................... Independent School [*British*]
I.................... Index
I.................... Index Number (DIPS)
I.................... India [*Phonetic alphabet*] [*International*] (DSUE)
I.................... Indian (WGA)
I.................... India National Congress [*Political party*] (PSAP)
i----............... Indian Ocean [*MARC geographic area code*] [*Library of Congress*] (LCCP)
I.................... Indicated [*or Indicative*]
I.................... Indicated Horsepower
I.................... Indicated Main Engine
I.................... Indicator
I.................... Induction
I.................... Industrial
I.................... Industrial Premises [*Public-performance tariff*] [*British*]
I.................... Industrial Training School [*British*] (ROG)
I.................... Inertia (AAG)
I.................... Inertias (SAUS)
I.................... Infantry
I.................... Infield
I.................... Informal [*FCC special temporary authorization*] (NTCM)
I.................... Information [*Computer science*]
I.................... Infra (IAA)
I.................... Inhalation (DMAA)
I.................... Inhibition (STED)
I.................... Inhibitor (DMAA)
I.................... Inhibitory
I.................... Initial
I.................... Ink [*Phonetic alphabet*] [*Royal Navy*] [*World War I*] [*Pre-World War II*] (DSUE)
i.................... Ink (VRA)
I.................... Inlet [*Rotary piston meter*]
I.................... Inner
I.................... Inosine [*One-letter symbol; see Ino*]
I.................... Inphase (SAUS)
I.................... Input
I.................... Inside
I.................... Inside Edge [*Skating*]
I.................... Insoluble
I.................... Inspection (ACAE)
I.................... Inspector
I.................... Inspiration (STED)
I.................... Inspired [*Medicine*] (DAVI)
I.................... Instantaneous
I.................... Instantaneous Current (IDOE)
I.................... Instantaneous Value (IDOE)
I.................... Institute [*or Institution*]
I.................... Institutional (WDMC)
I.................... Instruction
I.................... Instructional Program (NTCM)
I.................... Instructor (WDAA)
I.................... Instrumental [*or Instrumentation*]
I.................... Instrument Correction
I.................... Insulated (DS)
I.................... Insulated Tank [*Liquid gas carriers*]
I.................... Insulin (MELL)
I.................... Intact (DAVI)
I.................... Intake (AAMN)
I.................... Integer (IAA)
I.................... Integral (IAA)
I.................... Intelligence
I.................... Intensity
I.................... Intensity of Magnetism (STED)
I.................... Interbank [*Credit cards*]
I.................... Intercalary (STED)
I.................... Intercept-Aerial [*Missile mission symbol*]
I.................... Interceptor
I.................... Interchangeability (AAG)
I.................... Intercooled [*Automotive engineering*]
i.................... Interest (SHCU)
I.................... Interest [*Economics*]
I.................... Interference [*Broadcasting*]
I.................... Interim [*FCC*] (NTCM)
I.................... Interlocked Metallic Armor [*Technical drawings*]
I.................... Intermediate [*Vessel load line mark*]
I.................... Intermediate Slope [*Skiing*]
I.................... Intermittent (DMAA)
I.................... Intermittent Operation during the Time Indicated [*Broadcasting*]
I.................... Intern
I.................... Internal
I.................... Internal Medicine (AAMN)
I.................... International
I.................... Internist [*Medicine*]
I.................... Interphone (IAA)
I.................... Interphone and PA [*Communications term*] (DCT)
I.................... Interpole (IAA)
I.................... Interpreter
I.................... Interrupt [*Computer science*] [*Telecommunications*]
I.................... Interstate [*Highways*]
I.................... Intestine

I ..... Intransitive
I ..... Intrapictures [*Electronics*] (ACRL)
I ..... Intrinsic Semiconductor (IDOE)
I ..... Intrinsic-Type, Semiconductor Material
I ..... Introduced [*Ecology*]
I ..... Introversion
I ..... Invasive
I ..... Inventory
I ..... Inverted Sentence [*Used in correcting manuscripts, etc.*]
I ..... Inverter
I ..... Investment
I ..... Iodine [*Chemical element*]
I ..... Ionic Strength
I ..... Ionization Potential (ODA)
i ..... I-Orbital (MEC)
I ..... Iota [*Ninth letter of the Greek alphabet*] (DAVI)
I ..... Iraqi
I ..... Ireland
I ..... Iris (MELL)
I ..... Irnerius [*Flourished, 1113-18*] [*Authority cited in pre-1607 legal work*] (DSA)
I ..... Iron [*Symbol is Fe*] [*Chemical element*] (ROG)
I ..... Irradiated (NASA)
I ..... Irregular (ROG)
I ..... Irrigation [*Medicine*]
I ..... Ischium (MELL)
I ..... Island [*Maps and charts*]
I ..... Isle
i ..... Isochromosome (MAE)
I ..... Isoflurane [*An anesthetic*]
I ..... Isoleucine [*One-letter symbol; see Ile*] [*An amino acid*]
I ..... Isometric [*Botany*]
i ..... Isopentenyl [*As substituent on nucleoside*] [*Biochemistry*]
I ..... Isopin (WDAA)
I ..... Isoproterenol [*An adrenergic*]
I ..... Isotope (DMAA)
I ..... Isotropic Phase (SAUS)
I ..... Israeli
I ..... Issue (ROG)
I ..... Italy [*IYRU nationality code*]
I ..... ITEL Corp. (SAUO)
I ..... Item [*Phonetic alphabet*] [*World War II*] (DSUE)
I ..... Luminous Intensity [*Symbol*] [*IUPAC*]
I ..... Minneapolis [*Branch in the Federal Reserve regional banking system*] (BARN)
I ..... Moment of Inertia [*Symbol*] [*IUPAC*]
I ..... One [*Roman numeral*]
I ..... Paid This Year, Dividend Omitted, Deferred, or No Action Taken at Last Dividend Meeting [*Investment term*] (DFIT)
I ..... Radiant Intensity [*Symbol*] [*IUPAC*]
I ..... Registro Italiano [*Shipping*] (ROG)
I ..... Requires a Doctor [*Search and rescue symbol that can be stamped in sand or snow*]
i ..... Tourist Information [*Traffic sign*] [*British*]
I ..... Unit Matrix (ODA)
I^0 ..... Primary (DAVI)
I2 ..... Image Intensification
I2 ..... Image Intensifier (SAUS)
I2 ..... International Interchangeability
I_2 ..... Iodine [*Chemical element*] (DAVI)
I^2C ..... Inter-Integrated Circuit [*Philips*] (NITA)
I2F ..... Intelligent Influence Fuze (SAUS)
I^2L ..... Integrated Injection Logic [*Microprocessing*]
I2L ..... Integrated Injector Logic (AAEL)
$I^{2L2}AS$ ..... Infantry Issues and Lessons Learned Analysis System [*Software*] (INF)
I^2R ..... Imaging Infrared [*Pronounced "eye-squared ar"*]
I2S ..... Infra-red Imaging System (SAUS)
I2S ..... Integrated Information System [*Marine Corps*]
I2S ..... International Imaging Systems Inc. (SAUO)
I2S2 ..... Intelligence Information Subsystem [*Military*]
I2S(FIN) ..... Integrated Information System (Financial) [*Marine Corps*]
I2S(LOG) ..... Integrated Information System (Logistics) [*Marine Corps*]
I2S(MPR) ..... Integrated Information System (Manpower) [*Marine Corps*]
I2S(MPR/MMS) ..... Integrated Information System (Manpower and Functional Area Manpower Management System) [*Marine Corps*]
I2S(OPS) ..... Integrated Information System (Operational) [*Marine Corps*]
I2T2 ..... Intelligence Interactive Test Terminal
I3 ..... Illinois Innovators and Inventors (SAUS)
I3 ..... IMA Interoperability Initiative (SAUO)
I^3L ..... Isoplanar Integrated Injection Logic
I3L-II ..... Isoplanar Integrated Injection Logic II 3-Micron (Second Generation) High Performance Bipolar Technology (SAUS)
I3WG ..... Inter-Service Interoperability Implementation Working Group (SAUO)
I4L ..... ISDN for Linux (SAUS)
I5DO ..... Institute for Systems Design and Optimization (SAUS)
I5FSC ..... International Society of Free Space Colonizers (SAUO)
I5/W ..... Invert Sugar [*5%*] in Water [*Medicine*]
I-10/S ..... Invert Sugar [*10%*] in Saline [*Medicine*]
I14Y ..... Interoperability [*The 14 replaces the fourteen letters between I and Y*] [*Computer hacker terminology*] (NHD)
I18N ..... Internationalization [*The 18 replaces the eighteen letters between I and N*] [*C omputer hacker terminology*] (NHD)
I-129 ..... Iodine-129
I300I ..... International 300mm Initiative (AAEL)
IA ..... Comando de Material - Fabrica Militar de Aviones [*Argentina*] [*ICAO aircraft manufacturer identifier*] (ICAO)
IA ..... IATA [*International Air Transport Association*] Containers [*Shipping*] (DCTA)
IA ..... Ibotenic Acid [*Organic acid*] (DMAA)
IA ..... Ice Age
IA ..... Identical Additional (SAUS)
IA ..... Identification and Authentication (SAUS)
IA ..... Ileostomy Association of Great Britain and Ireland
IA ..... Image Acquisition [*Computer graphics*]
IA ..... Image Amplification [*Radiology*] (DAVI)
IA ..... Image Amplifier (SAUS)
IA ..... Image Analysis (SAUS)
IA ..... Image Array (SAUS)
IA ..... Imagery Analyst (MCD)
IA ..... Im Auftrage [*By Order Of*] [*German*]
IA ..... Imitation Art Paper (DGA)
IA ..... Immediate Access (IAA)
IA ..... Immediate Action [*Military*]
IA ..... Immediate Annuity
IA ..... Immediately Available
IA ..... Immune Adherence [*Immunology*]
Ia ..... Immune Region Associated Antigen [*Immunology*]
Ia ..... Immune Response Gene-Associated Antigen [*Immunology*] (DAVI)
IA ..... Immunoadsorbent [*Medicine*] (MELL)
IA ..... Immunoassay (ABAC)
IA ..... Immunobiologic Activity [*Immunology*] (AAMN)
IA ..... Impedance Angle
IA ..... Imperial Airways (SAUO)
IA ..... Imperial Airways Ltd. [*British*] (ADA)
IA ..... Implementation Agency (SAUS)
IA ..... Implementation Agreement (VLIE)
IA ..... Implementation Arrangement (SAUS)
IA ..... Implementing Agency (KSC)
IA ..... Implied Association (SAUO)
IA ..... Import Administration
IA ..... Import Annual Data [*Department of Commerce*] (GFGA)
IA ..... Impotents Anonymous (EA)
IA ..... Improvement Assessment [*Recycling*]
IA ..... In Absentia [*In Absence*] [*Latin*]
IA ..... Inactive Account [*Banking*]
IA ..... Inactive Aerospace Vehicle [*or Aircraft*]
IA ..... Incentive Award [*Military*]
IA ..... Incident Actions [*Environmental science*] (COE)
IA ..... Incidental Appendectomy [*Medicine*]
IA ..... Income Averaging (MHDB)
IA ..... Incoming Access (SAUS)
IA ..... Incorporated Accountant
IA ..... Incremental Analysis [*Statistics*]
IA ..... Incurred Accidentally [*Medicine*] (MEDA)
IA ..... Independent Action (EA)
IA ..... Independent Americans (EA)
IA ..... Index Accumulator (SAUS)
IA ..... Index Analyzer (SAUS)
IA ..... Index Array (IAA)
IA ..... India Alert [*An association*] (EA)
IA ..... Indiana [*Obsolete*] (ROG)
IA ..... Indian Affairs (DLA)
IA ..... Indian Airlines (PDAA)
IA ..... Indian Army
IA ..... Indian Artillery [*British military*] (DMA)
IA ..... Indicated Altitude [*Navigation*]
IA ..... Indicator of Authoritativeness [*Library symbol*]
IA ..... Indirect Address (NITA)
IA ..... Indirect Addressing
IA ..... Individual Assistance (DEMM)
IA ..... Indo-Aryan [*Linguistics*]
IA ..... Indolaminergic-Accumulating [*Cytology*] (DAVI)
IA ..... Indolic Acid (MELL)
IA ..... Indulin Agar [*Microbiology*]
IA ..... Industrial Accounting (SAUS)
IA ..... Industrial Application (SAUS)
IA ..... Industrial Artists (SAUS)
IA ..... Industrial Arts (OICC)
IA ..... Industrial Arts Education (SAUO)
IA ..... Industry Application (IAA)
IA ..... Infantile Apnea [*Medicine*] (MELL)
IA ..... Infected Area
IA ..... Infectious Arthritis (MELL)
IA ..... Inferior Angle [*Anatomy*]
IA ..... Information Addressee (SAUS)
IA ..... Information Agency
IA ..... Information America [*Information service or system*] (IID)
IA ..... Information Anxiety (SAUS)
IA ..... Information Appliance (SAUO)
IA ..... Information Approximation (SAUS)
IA ..... Information Architecture (SAUO)
IA ..... Information Association (COE)
IA ..... Information Assurance
IA ..... Informations Acquisition (SAUS)
IA ..... Infra-Audible [*Sound*]
IA ..... Infrastructure Analyst (SAUS)
IA ..... Ingenious Addressing (SAUS)
IA ..... Inhalation Anesthesia (MELL)
IA ..... Inherent Address (SAUS)

IA................ Initial Allowance (SAUS)
IA................ Initial Appearance [*RADAR*]
IA................ Initial Assessment [*Environmental science*] (COE)
IA................ Initial Authorization
IA................ Initiative America (EA)
I/A................ Innovative/Alternative [*Recycling technologies*]
IA................ Input Acknowledge (MCD)
IA................ Input Axis (KSC)
IA................ Insertion Approval (NRCH)
IA................ Inspection Administration [*Navy*]
IA................ Inspection Authorization (GAVI)
IA................ Inspector of Armourers (SAUO)
IA................ Inspiratory Assistance (SAUS)
I/A................ Installment Agreement
IA................ Institut de l'Amiante [*Asbestos Institute - AI*] (EA)
I/A................ Institute of Accountants (SAUS)
I/A................ Institute of Acoustics (SAUS)
IA................ Institute of Actuaries [*British*]
IA................ Institute of Architects [*Australia*]
IA................ Instruction Address [*Computer science*]
IA................ Instructional Aide (SAUS)
IA................ Instructional Allowance [*British military*] (DMA)
IA................ Instruction Alignment (SAUS)
IA................ Instruction Area (SAUS)
IA................ Instruction Array (SAUS)
IA................ Instructions for Armourers (SAUO)
I/A................ Instructor of Artillery (SAUS)
IA................ Instrument Abstracts
IA................ Instrument Air [*System*] [*Nuclear energy*] (NRCH)
IA................ Instrumental Analysis (SAUS)
IA................ Instrumentation Amplifier (IEEE)
IA................ Insulin Antibody [*Immunology*]
IA................ Insurance Adjustment
I/A................ Insurance Auditor
IA................ Intangible Asset [*i.e., Patented rights*]
IA................ Integrated Adapter
IA................ Intel Architecture (SAUS)
IA................ Intelligence Analysis
IA................ Intelligence Annex (SAUS)
IA................ Intelligence Assessment (DOMA)
IA................ Intelligent Actuatot (ACII)
IA................ Intelligent Agent
IA................ Intelligent Assistant [*Computer science*]
IA................ Intelligenzalter [*Mental Age*] [*Psychology*]
IA................ Intemperate to Alcohol [*An alcoholic*] [*Slang*]
IA................ Inter-Action (MCD)
IA................ Interagency Agreement (GNE)
IA................ Inter Aide [*France*] (BUAC)
IA................ Inter Alia [*Among Other Things*] [*Latin*]
IA................ Intercept Arm (MUGU)
IA................ Interceptor Aviation (SAUS)
IA................ Intercessors for America (EA)
IA................ Interchangeable Alternate
IA................ Interchange Address (NITA)
IA................ Interciencia Association [*Caracas, Venezuela*] (EAIO)
IA................ Intercity Airways [*Australia*]
IA................ Intercoiffure America (EA)
IA................ Intercultural Awareness
IA................ Interface Accepted (SAUS)
I/A................ Interface Adapter (NASA)
IA................ Interface Amplifier
IA................ Interflora Australia
IA................ Interim Action [*Environment term*] (EGA)
IA................ Intermediate Air [*Combustion*]
IA................ Intermediate Amplifier
IA................ Intermediate Area (SAUS)
IA................ Internal Affairs (SAUS)
IA................ Internal Audit
IA................ Internal Auditory (Ear)
IA................ International Affairs. Moscow (journ.) (SAUS)
IA................ International Affiliation of Independent Accounting Firms [*Later, Independent Accountants International*] (EA)
IA................ International Alert (EA)
IA................ International Alliance of Theatrical Stage Employees (NTCM)
IA................ International Alliance of Theatrical Stage Employees and Motion Picture Machine Operators of the United States and Canada (SAUO)
IA................ International Alliance of Theatrical Stage Employees and Moving Picture Machine Operators of the United States and Canada
IA................ International Alphabet
IA................ International Angstrom
IA................ International Atlas (SAUS)
IA................ Interpretive Authority (SAUS)
IA................ Intersite Architecture (SAUS)
IA................ Interval Arithmetic (VLIE)
IA................ Interval Availability
IA................ Interworking Implemantation Agreement (SAUO)
IA................ Intra-Amniotic [*Medicine*] (AAMN)
IA................ Intra Aortic [*Cardiology*] (MAE)
IA................ Intra Arterial (SAUS)
IA................ Intra-Arterial [*Cardiology*]
ia................ Intraarterial [*Medicine*] (DB)
IA................ Intra-Articular [*Medicine*]
IA................ Intra-Atrial [*Cardiology*]
IA................ Intra-Auricular [*Cardiology*] (DAVI)
IA................ Invalid Address (SAUS)
IA................ Inventory Adjustment (SAUS)
IA................ Inverter Assembly
IA................ Iodine Absorber (ABAC)
IA................ Ion Accelerator (SAUS)
Ia................ Iowa (BEE)
IA................ Iowa [*Postal code*]
IA................ Iowa Reports [*A publication*] (DLA)
Ia................ Iowa State Library Commission, Des Moines, IA [*Library symbol*] [*Library of Congress*] (LCLS)
IA................ Iphigenia Aulidensis [*of Euripides*] [*Classical studies*] (OCD)
IA................ Iraqi Airways [*ICAO designator*]
IA................ Iron Age
IA................ Irrespirable Atmosphere (SAUS)
IA................ Irrigation Area (ADA)
IA................ Irrigation Association (EA)
I/A................ Isle Of Angelsey [*Wales*] (ROG)
IA................ Isle Of Aran
IA................ Isolation Amplifier
IA................ Isophthalic Acid [*Organic chemistry*]
IA................ Isotopic Analysis (SAUS)
IA................ Israel Atomic (SAUO)
IA................ Issuing Agency (AFM)
IA................ Issuing Authority (SAUS)
IA................ Italian Army (NATG)
I/A................ Item Accounting (MCD)
IA................ Iteration Algorithm (SAUS)
IA................ Law Reports, Privy Council, Indian Appeals [*India*] [*A publication*] (DLA)
IA................ Millenia, Inc. [*AMEX symbol*] (SAG)
IA................ Telegraph and Public Address [*JETDS nomenclature*]
IA................ Inter-American (ODA)
IA-1................ Image Array Processor (NITA)
IA-2................ International Alphabet-2 [*Standard telegraphy code*] (NITA)
IA-5................ International Alphabet 5 (NITA)
IA5................ International Alphabet Number 5 [*Communications term*] (DCT)
IA-64................ Intel Architecture 64-Bit Chip (HODG)
IA-64................ 64-Bit Intel Architecture [*Computer science*] (MWOL)
IaA................ Ames, Public Library, Ames IA [*Library symbol*] [*Library of Congress*] (LCLS)
IAA................ Chicago State University, Chicago, IL [*OCLC symbol*] (OCLC)
IAA................ Ibero-Armorican Arc [*A geological area of western Europe*]
IAA................ Iliac Artery Aneurysm [*Medicine*] (MELL)
IAA................ Illinois Agricultural Association (SRA)
IAA................ Imidazoleacetic Acid [*Also, I-AC, IMAA*] [*Biochemistry*]
IAA................ Immediate Action Authority (AAG)
IAA................ Inactive Aerospace (or Aircraft) vehicle Authorization (SAUS)
IAA................ In Amguel [*Issek Toufreg*] [*Algeria*] [*Seismograph station code, US Geological Survey*] [*Closed*] (SEIS)
IAA................ Incorporated Accountants and Auditors [*British*] (DAS)
IAA................ Incorporated Association of Architects and Surveyors (SAUO)
IAA................ Independent Administrators Association of California (SRA)
IAA................ Independent Airlines Association (EA)
IAA................ Indian Army Act [*British military*] (DMA)
IAA................ Indian Association of America (EA)
IAA................ Indoleacetic Acid [*Plant growth promoter*]
IAA................ Indolyl Acetic Acid (SAUS)
IAA................ Inex Adria Aviopromet [*Yugoslavia*] [*ICAO designator*] (FAAC)
IAA................ Infectious Agent Arthritis [*Medicine*] (DB)
IAA................ Infra-Abdominal Abscess [*Medicine*] (MELL)
IAA................ Initial Address Acknowledgment (SAUS)
IAA................ Inpatient Ambulatory Activity Questionnaire [*Medicine*]
IAA................ Inspector Army Aircraft (SAUO)
IAA................ Institute for Altemative Agriculture (SAUS)
IAA................ Institute for Arthritis and Autoimmunity [*Nile Research Center*] [*West Haven, CT*]
IAA................ Institute of Administrative Accountants [*Sevenoaks, Kent, England*] (EAIO)
IAA................ Institute of Administrative Accounting (SAUS)
IAA................ Institute of Administrative Accounting and Data Processing Limited [*British*] (NITA)
IAA................ Institute of African Alternatives (BUAC)
IAA................ Institute of Arbitrators Australia
IAA................ Institute of Archeology and Anthropology [*University of South Carolina at Columbia*] [*Research center*] (RCD)
IAA................ Institute of Automobile Assessors [*British*] (BI)
IAA................ Instrumental Activation Analysis
IAA................ Insulin Autoantibody [*Immunology*]
IAA................ Insurance Accountants Association [*Later, SIA*]
IAA................ Insurance Application Architecture (GART)
IAA................ Integrated Audit/Appraisal (SAUS)
IAA................ Intelligence Analysts Associates [*Air Force*]
IAA................ Interamerican Accounting Association [*Mexico City, Mexico*] (EA)
IAA................ Interim Access Authorization
IAA................ Interim ASOC Automation (SAUO)
IAA................ Intermediate Assembly Area (SAUO)
IAA................ Interment Association of America [*Later, PIAA*] (EA)
IAA................ Internal Accounting Association (SAUO)
IAA................ Internal Aids Approach (SAUS)
IAA................ International Academy of Architecture (BUAC)
IAA................ International Academy of Astronautics [*Paris, France*] (EA)
IAA................ International Acetylene Association [*Later, CGA*]
IAA................ International Actuarial Association (BUAC)
IAA................ International Advertising Association [*Later, AAF*] (EA)
IAA................ International Aerobus Association (SAUO)

IAA .... International Aerosol Association [*Zurich, Switzerland*] (EAIO)
IAA .... International Aerospace Abstracts [*American Institute of Aeronautics and Astronautics*] [*A publication*] (AEBS)
IAA .... International Allergy Association (SAUO)
IAA .... International Antituberculosis Association (DAVI)
IAA .... International Apple Association [*Later, IAI*] (EA)
IAA .... International Arthroscopy Association (EA)
IAA .... International Asphalt Association (SAUO)
IAA .... International Association for Aerobiology (BUAC)
IAA .... International Association of Agriculturists (BUAC)
IAA .... International Association of Allergology [*Later, IAACI*]
IAA .... International Association of Art [*See also AIAP*] (EA)
IAA .... International Association of Art-Painting, Sculpture, Graphic Art (SAUO)
IAA .... International Association of Art-Painting, Sculpture, Print-making (SAUO)
IAA .... International Association of Astacology (EA)
IAA .... International Association of Astrology (SAUS)
IAA .... International Astrological Association
IAA .... International Astronautical Academy (BUAC)
IAA .... International Aviation Affairs [*FAA*] (MCD)
IAA .... Interruption of the Aortic Arch [*Medicine*] (DMAA)
IAA .... Intimate Apparel Associates [*Defunct*] (EA)
IAA .... Inventors Association of America (EA)
IAA .... Inventors Association of Australia (SAUO)
IAA .... Investment Advisers Act [*1940*]
IAA .... Iodoacetamide [*Organic chemistry*]
IAA .... Iodoacetic Acid (SAUS)
IAA .... Iododacetic Acid [*Organic chemistry*]
IAA .... Iowa Auctioneers Association (SRA)
IAA .... Ireland-Australia Association (BUAC)
IAA .... Irish Aquaculture Association (BUAC)
IAA .... Irish Architectural Archive (BUAC)
IAA .... Irish Astronomical Association (EAIO)
IAA .... Islamic Army of Aden [*Government term*] (GA)
IAA .... Isoamyl Acetate (SAUS)
IAA .... Isoamyl Amine (SAUS)
IAA .... Israel Antiquities Authority
IAA .... Israel Archives Association (BUAC)
IAAA .... Illinois Agricultural Aviation Association (SRA)
IAAA .... Inflammatory Abdominal Aortic Aneurysm [*Medicine*] (DMAA)
IAAA .... Institute of Afro-American Affairs [*New York University*] [*Research center*] (RCD)
IAAA .... Institute of Air Age Activities (SAUO)
IAAA .... Integrated Advance Avionics for Aircraft
IAAA .... Inter-American Accounting Association
IAAA .... Inter-American Association of Broadcasters (SAUO)
IAAA .... Intermarket Association of Advertising Agencies [*Dayton, OH*] (EA)
IAAA .... International Academy of Aquatic Art (EA)
IAAA .... International Airforwarder and Agents Association (SAUO)
IAAA .... International American Albino Association (NTPA)
IAAA .... Irish Amateur Athletic Association (BUAC)
IAAA .... Irish Association of Advertising Agencies (BUAC)
IAAAA .... Intercollegiate Association of Amateur Athletes of America (EA)
IAAABBP .... International Association of African and American Black Business People (SAUO)
IAAAI .... International Archives of Allergy and Applied Immunology [*Medicine*] (EDAA)
IAAALD .... Inter-American Association of Agricultural Librarians and Documentalists [*Cost Rica*] (BUAC)
IAAAM .... International Association for Aquatic Animal Medicine (EA)
IAAAM .... International Association for/of Aquatic Animal Medicine (SAUO)
IaAAR .... United States Department of Agriculture, Agricultural Research Service, NationalAnimal Disease Laboratory, Ames, IA [*Library symbol*] [*Library of Congress*] (LCLS)
IAAATDC .... International Association for Advancement of Appropriate Technology for Developing Countries (EA)
IAAB .... Inter-American Association of Broadcasters [*Later, IAB-AIR*]
IAAB .... Inter-American Association of Broadcasting (SAUO)
IAAB .... Interim Aviation Airframe Bulletin (DNAB)
IAAB .... International Association of Broascasters (SAUS)
IAABA .... International Association of Aircraft Brokers and Agents (SAUO)
IAABB .... International Association of Amateur Boat Builders (EA)
IAABO .... International Association of Approved Basketball Officials (EA)
IaAc .... Ackley Public Library, Ackley, IA [*Library symbol*] [*Library of Congress*] (LCLS)
IAAC .... Income-Averaging Annuity Contract (FOTI)
IAAC .... Inter-Agency Advisory Committee for MEDPOL (SAUS)
IAAC .... Interagency Assessment Advisory Committee (GNE)
IAAC .... Inter-American Accounting Conference (SAUO)
IAAC .... Interamerican Accreditation Cooperation (or Corporation) (SAUS)
IAAC .... International African-American Corporation (SAUO)
IAAC .... International Agricultural Aviation Center (SAUS)
IAAC .... International Agricultural Aviation Centre [*Defunct*] (EA)
IAAC .... International Agriculture Aviation Center (SAUS)
IAAC .... International Air Cargo Consolidators (SAUS)
IAAC .... International Antarctic Analysis Center (or Centre) (SAUS)
IAAC .... International Antarctic Analysis Centre (BUAC)
IAAC .... International Assets Holding Corp. [*NASDAQ symbol*] (SAG)
IAAC .... International Association for Analog Computing (SAUS)
IAAC .... International Association of Art Critics [*Australia*]
IAAC .... Intl Asset Holding [*NASDAQ symbol*] (TTSB)
IAAC .... Israel Association for Automatic Control (SAUO)
IAACC .... Ibero-American Association of Chambers of Commerce [*See also AICO*] [*Bogota, Colombia*] (EAIO)
IAACC .... Inter-Allied Aeronautical Commission of Control
IAACC .... Inter-Allied Aeronautical Control Commission (SAUO)
IAACC .... International Association of Agricultural Economists (SAUO)
IAACI .... International Association of Allergology and Clinical Immunology (EA)
IAACN .... International and American Associations of Clinical Nutritionists (NTPA)
IAACW .... International Assets Hldg Wrrt [*NASDAQ symbol*] (TTSB)
IaAcW .... World Journal, Ackley, IA [*Library symbol*] [*Library of Congress*] (LCLS)
IaAdeCoC .... Dallas County Courthouse, Adel, IA [*Library symbol*] [*Library of Congress*] (LCLS)
IaAdeN .... Dallas County News, Adel, IA [*Library symbol*] [*Library of Congress*] (LCLS)
IAADF .... Inter-American Association for Democracy and Freedom (SAUO)
IAADFS .... International Association of Airport Duty-Free Stores (SAUS)
IaAdN .... Adair News, Adair, IA [*Library symbol*] [*Library of Congress*] (LCLS)
IAADP .... International Association of Assistance Dog Partners (SAUO)
IAADS .... Integrated Anti-Airborne Defense System (SAUS)
IAADS .... Interim Automated Air Defense System (ACAE)
IAAE .... Institute for Application of Atomic Energy [*China*] (BUAC)
IAAE .... Institute of Automotive and Aeronautical Engineers (WDAA)
IAAE .... Institution of Automotive and Aeronautical Engineers (SAUO)
IAAE .... International Association Autism-Europe (BUAC)
IAAE .... International Association of Agricultural Economists (EA)
IAAE .... Israel Association of Agricultural Engineering (BUAC)
IAAEE .... International Association for the Advancement of Ethnology and Eugenics (SAUO)
IAAEES .... International Association for the Advancement of Earth and Environmental Sciences (SAUO)
IAAE Journal .... Institution of Automotive and Aeronautical Engineers Journal (journ.) (SAUS)
IAAEM .... International Association of Aquaculture Economics and Management
IAAER .... International Association for the Advancement of Educational Research (SAUO)
IAAF .... International Agricultural Aviation Foundation (EA)
IAAF .... International Amateur Athletic Federation [*See also FIAA*] [*British*] (EAIO)
IAAF .... International Association of Art for the Future [*Indonesia*] (EAIO)
IAAFA .... Inter-American Air Force Academy [*Operated by US Air Force to provide training for Latin American countries*]
IAAFF .... Iona Appliances, Inc. [*NASDAQ symbol*] (SAG)
IaAfSE .... Afton Star-Enterprise, Afton, IA [*Library symbol*] [*Library of Congress*] (LCLS)
IAAG .... Inter-Agency Advisory Group on AIDS (SAUO)
IAAG .... Inter-American Association of Gastroenterology (EA)
IAAG .... International Association of Aeronomy and Geomagnetism (SAUO)
IAAGB .... Institute of Arctic and Alpine Geochronological Research (SAUS)
IAAH .... International Action Against Hunger (EAIO)
IAAH .... International Association for Adolescent Health (BUAC)
IAAHU .... International Association of Accident and Health Underwriters [*Later, NAHU*]
IAAI .... Innovative Applications of Artificial Intelligence (GART)
IAAI .... Insurance Auto Auctions [*NASDAQ symbol*] (SPSG)
IAAI .... International Airports Authority of India (BUAC)
IAAI .... International Association of Arson Investigators (EA)
IAAI .... Intra-Articular Anesthetic Injection [*Medicine*] (MELL)
IAAI .... Italian Association for Artificial Intelligence (BUAC)
IaAIBI .... IBIA News, Ames, IA [*Library symbol*] [*Library of Congress*] (LCLS)
IAAIP .... Inter-American Association of Industrial Property [*See also ASIPA*] [*Buenos Aires, Argentina*] (EAIO)
IAAIS .... International Association of Audio Information Services (SAUO)
IaAIS .... Iowa Starter, Iowa State University, Ames, IA [*Library symbol*] [*Library of Congress*] (LCLS)
IAAJ .... International Association of Agricultural Journalists (BUAC)
IaAkRT .... Akron Register-Tribune, Akron, IA [*Library symbol*] [*Library of Congress*] (LCLS)
IAAL .... International Association of Applied Linguistics (EA)
IAAL .... Israel Association for Applied Linguistics (SAUO)
IaAlb .... Albia Public Library, Albia, IA [*Library symbol*] [*Library of Congress*] (LCLS)
IaAlbMHi .... Monroe County Historical Society, Albia, IA [*Library symbol*] [*Library of Congress*] (LCLS)
IaAlbN .... Monroe County News, Albia, IA [*Library symbol*] [*Library of Congress*] (LCLS)
IaAlbUR .... Albia Union-Republican, Albia, IA [*Library symbol*] [*Library of Congress*] (LCLS)
IaAlcAM .... Appeal and Marathon Republic, Albert City, IA [*Library symbol*] [*Library of Congress*] (LCLS)
IaAld .... Alden Public Library, Alden, IA [*Library symbol*] [*Library of Congress*] (LCLS)
IAALD .... International Association of Agricultural Librarians and Documentalists (EA)
IaAlg .... Algona Public Library, Algona, IA [*Library symbol*] [*Library of Congress*] (LCLS)
IaAlgKA .... Kossuth County Advance, Algona, IA [*Library symbol*] [*Library of Congress*] (LCLS)
IaAlgUD .... Upper Des Moines, Algona, IA [*Library symbol*] [*Library of Congress*] (LCLS)
IaAll .... Allerton Public Library, Allerton, IA [*Library symbol*] [*Library of Congress*] (LCLS)
IaAlnBCo .... Butler County Courthouse, Allison, IA [*Library symbol*] [*Library of Congress*] (LCLS)
IaAlnTJ .... Butler County Tribune-Journal, Allison, IA [*Library symbol*] [*Library of Congress*] (LCLS)

IaAlta.......... Alta Public Library, Alta, IA [*Library symbol*] [*Library of Congress*] (LCLS)
IaAltaA.......... Alta Advertiser, Alta, IA [*Library symbol*] [*Library of Congress*] (LCLS)
IaAltn.......... Alton Public Library, Alton, IA [*Library symbol*] [*Library of Congress*] (LCLS)
IaAlto.......... Altoona Public Library, Altoona, IA [*Library symbol*] [*Library of Congress*] (LCLS)
IaAltoH.......... Herald-Mitchellville Index, Altoona, IA [*Library symbol*] [*Library of Congress*] (LCLS)
IAAM.......... Incorporated Association of Assistant Masters [*British*]
IAAM.......... Independent Accountants Association of Michigan (SRA)
IAAM.......... International Academy of Aerospace Medicine [*Medicine*] (EDAA)
IAAM.......... International Association of Agricultural Medicine [*Medicine*] (EDAA)
IAAM.......... International Association of Aircraft Manufacturers (SAUO)
IAAM.......... International Association of Assembly Managers (NTPA)
IAAM.......... International Association of Auditorium Managers (EA)
IAAM.......... International Association of Automotive Modelers [*Defunct*] (EA)
IAAM.......... International Association of Manufacturers of Aerospace Equipment (SAUO)
IAAM.......... Irish Anti-Apartheid Movement (EAIO)
IAAM.......... Islamic Alliance of Afghan Mujahedins (SAUO)
IAAMC.......... International Association of Association Management Companies (NTPA)
IAAMRH.......... International Association of Agricultural Medicine an Rural Health (SAUO)
IAAMSS.......... Incorporated Association of Assistant Masters in Secondary Schools (SAUO)
IAAN.......... International Association Ayurveda and Naturopathy (SAUO)
IaAna.......... Anamosa Public Library, Anamosa, IA [*Library symbol*] [*Library of Congress*] (LCLS)
IaAnaE.......... Anamosa Eureka, Anamosa, IA [*Library symbol*] [*Library of Congress*] (LCLS)
IaAnaJ.......... Anamosa Journal, Anamosa, IA [*Library symbol*] [*Library of Congress*] (LCLS)
IA&C.......... International Affairs and Communications (SAUO)
IA&ND.......... Indian Affairs and Northern Development (SAUO)
IA&RN.......... Inspection Advise & Release Nute (SAUS)
IA & T.......... Integration, Assembly, and Test
IAANG.......... Iowa Air National Guard (MUSM)
IaAniF.......... Fontanelle Observer, Anita, IA [*Library symbol*] [*Library of Congress*] (LCLS)
IaAniT.......... Anita Tribune, Anita, IA [*Library symbol*] [*Library of Congress*] (LCLS)
IaAnk.......... Kirkendall Public Library, Ankeny, IA [*Library symbol*] [*Library of Congress*] (LCLS)
IaAnkD.......... Des Moines Area Community College, Ankeny, IA [*Library symbol*] [*Library of Congress*] (LCLS)
IaAnkFB.......... Faith Baptist Bible College, Ankeny, IA [*Library symbol*] [*Library of Congress*] (LCLS)
IaAnkP.......... Ankeny Press-Citizen, Ankeny, IA [*Library symbol*] [*Library of Congress*] (LCLS)
IaAnt.......... Anthon Public Library, Anthon, IA [*Library symbol*] [*Library of Congress*] (LCLS)
IaAntH.......... Anthon Herald, Anthon, IA [*Library symbol*] [*Library of Congress*] (LCLS)
IAANZ.......... Institute of Actuaries of Australia and New Zealand (SAUO)
IAAO.......... Interlochen Arts Academy Orchestra (SAUO)
IAAO.......... International Association of Assessing Officers (EA)
IAAOC.......... International Association of Addiction and Offender Counselors (SEAT)
IAAOC.......... International Association of Addictions and Offender Counseling (EA)
IAAOPA.......... International Association of Aircraft Owners and Pilots Associations (SAUO)
IaAp.......... Aplington Legion Memorial Library, Aplington, IA [*Library symbol*] [*Library of Congress*] (LCLS)
IAAP.......... Illinois Association for Applied Psychology (SAUO)
IAAP.......... Intensive Agricultural Area Program (SAUO)
IAAP.......... International Association for Analytical Psychology (EA)
IAAP.......... International Association of Administrative Professionals
IAAP.......... International Association of African Palynology (QUAC)
IAAP.......... International Association of Amusement Parks [*Later, IAAPA*]
IAAP.......... International Association of Applied Psychology [*Nijmegen, Netherlands*] (EA)
IAAP.......... Iowa Army Ammunition Plant (AABC)
IAAPA.......... International Association of Amusement Parks and Attractions (EA)
IAAPEA.......... International Associations Against Painful Experiments on Animals (SAUS)
IAAPF.......... Iona Appliances [*NASDAQ symbol*] (TTSB)
IAAPG.......... Interagency Advanced Power Group (SAUO)
IAAPO.......... International Association of Amusement and Park Owners
IAAR.......... Imidazoleacetic Acid Ribonucleotide (DMAA)
IAAR.......... Independent Association of American Registrars (SAUO)
IAAR.......... Independent Associaton of Accredited Registrars [*For quality control*]
IAAR.......... United States Information Agency Acquisition Regulation [*A publication*] (AAGC)
IAARC.......... International Administrative Aeronautical Radio Conference [*Also known as WARC*]
IAARC.......... International Association for/of Automation and Robotics in Construction (SAUO)
IAARC.......... International Association of Agricultural Students (SAUO)
IAARC.......... International Association of Automation and Robotics in Construction (SAUS)
IAARD.......... Integrated Avionics Architecture, Requirements, and Design (SPST)
IaArl.......... Arlington Public Library, Arlington, IA [*Library symbol*] [*Library of Congress*] (LCLS)
IaArmJ.......... Armstrong Journal, Armstrong, IA [*Library symbol*] [*Library of Congress*] (LCLS)
IAAS.......... Immigrants Appeals Advisory Service (BUAC)
IAAS.......... Incorporated Association of Architects and Surveyors [*British*] (DBA)
IAAS.......... Institute of Acoustics, Academia Sinica (BUAC)
IAAS.......... Institute of Advanced Arab Studies (SAUO)
IAAS.......... Institute of Advanced Architectural Studies (SAUO)
IAAS.......... Institute of African Asian Studies (BUAC)
IAAS.......... Institute of Auctioneers and Appraisers in Scotland (EAIO)
IAAS.......... Institute of Auctioneers and Apprentices in Scotland (BUAC)
IAAS.......... International Association for Atmospheric Science (BUAC)
IAAS.......... International Association of Academies of Sciences (SAUO)
IAAS.......... International Association of Agricultural Students [*See also AIEA*] [*Uppsala, Sweden*] (EAIO)
IaAS.......... Iowa State University of Science and Technology, Ames, IA [*Library symbol*] [*Library of Congress*] (LCLS)
IAASA.......... Indian Australian Association of South Australia
IAASE.......... Independent Appeals Authority for School Examinations (AIE)
IAASE.......... Inter-American Association of Sanitary Engineering [*Later, Inter-American Association of Sanitary and Environmental Engineering*] (EA)
IAASEE.......... Inter-American Association of Sanitary and Environmental Engineering (SAUO)
IAASEES.......... Inter-American Association of Sanitary Engineering and Environmental Sciences (EAIO)
IAASM.......... International Academy of Aviation and Space Medicine (EAIO)
IAASP.......... International Association of Airport and Seaport Police [*Canada*] (EAIO)
IAASS.......... International Association of Applied Social Science (SAUO)
IAASS.......... International Association of Applied Social Scientists [*Later, CCI*]
IaAS-V.......... Iowa State University of Science and Technology, School of Veterinary Medicine, Ames, IA [*Library symbol*] [*Library of Congress*] (LCLS)
IaAT.......... Ames Daily Tribune, Ames, IA [*Library symbol*] [*Library of Congress*] (LCLS)
IaAt.......... Atlantic Public Library, Atlantic, IA [*Library symbol*] [*Library of Congress*] (LCLS)
IAAT.......... International Association Against Torture (EAIO)
IAATA.......... International Association of Antarctic Tour Operators (SAUO)
IAATI.......... International Association of Auto Theft Investigators (SAUO)
IaAtL.......... Atlantic Public Library, Atlantic, IA [*Library symbol*] [*Library of Congress*] (LCLS)
IAATM.......... International Association for Accident and Traffic Medicine (EA)
IaAtNT.......... Atlantic News-Telegraph, Atlantic, IA [*Library symbol*] [*Library of Congress*] (LCLS)
IaAu.......... Audubon Public Library, Audubon, IA [*Library symbol*] [*Library of Congress*] (LCLS)
IaAub.......... Auburn Public Library, Auburn, IA [*Library symbol*] [*Library of Congress*] (LCLS)
IaAubE.......... Auburn Enterprise, Auburn, IA [*Library symbol*] [*Library of Congress*] (LCLS)
IaAuCoC.......... Audubon County Courthouse, Audubon, IA [*Library symbol*] [*Library of Congress*] (LCLS)
IaAuNA.......... Audubon News-Advocate, Audubon, IA [*Library symbol*] [*Library of Congress*] (LCLS)
IaAur.......... Aurelia Public Library, Aurelia, IA [*Library symbol*] [*Library of Congress*] (LCLS)
IaAurS.......... Aurelia Sentinel, Aurelia, IA [*Library symbol*] [*Library of Congress*] (LCLS)
IAAV.......... Alliance of Atomic Veterans [*International Alliance of Atomic Vetrans*] [*Acronym is based on former name,*] (EA)
IaAv.......... Avoca Public Library, Avoca, IA [*Library symbol*] [*Library of Congress*] (LCLS)
IAAV.......... International Association of Airborne Veterans (EA)
IaAvJH.......... Avoca Journal-Herald, Avoca, IA [*Library symbol*] [*Library of Congress*] (LCLS)
IAAW.......... Interim Airfield Attack Weapon (SAUS)
IAAW.......... International Association of African Writers (SAUO)
IaAWD.......... Wildlife Disease Association, Ames, IA [*Library symbol*] [*Library of Congress*] (LCLS)
IAAWS.......... Infantry Antiarmor Weapon Systems [*Military*] (INF)
IaB.......... Burlington Free Public Library, Burlington, IA [*Library symbol*] [*Library of Congress*] (LCLS)
IAB.......... Identa-Band (DAVI)
IAB.......... Idle Air Bleed [*Fuel system*] [*Automotive engineering*]
IAB.......... Immigration Appeal Board [*Canada*]
IAB.......... Increasing Assurance Benefits (SAUS)
IAB.......... Indirect Address Buffer
IAB.......... Induced Abortion (MELL)
IAB.......... Industrial Accident Board
IAB.......... Industrial Advisers to the Blind Ltd. [*British*] (BI)
IAB.......... Industrial Advisory Board [*World War II*]
IAB.......... Industrial Arbitration Board [*British*]
IAB.......... Industry Advisory Board (SAUO)
IAB.......... Information Access Branch [*Environment term*] (EGA)
IAB.......... Initiation Area Discriminator (VLIE)
IAB.......... Institute of Animal Behavior [*Rutgers University*] [*Research center*] (RCD)
IAB.......... Institute of Arctic Biology [*Research center*] (RCD)
IAB.......... Institut fuer Arbeitsmarkt- und Berufsforschung [*Institute for Employment Research*] [*Federal Employment Institute*] [*Germany*] (IID)
IAB.......... Instrumentation Analysis Branch (SAA)

IAB.............. Interactive Application Builder (VLIE)
IAB.............. Interagency Board of Examiners [*Civil Service Commission*]
IAB.............. Inter-America Bank (WDAA)
IAB.............. Inter-American Bank (SAUO)
IAB.............. Interim Airframe Bulletin (MCD)
IAB.............. Interim Armament Bulletin (MCD)
IAB.............. Internal Auto Boresight (ACAE)
IAB.............. International Abstracting Board [*Also, ICSU AB*] [*International Council of Scientific Unions*]
IAB.............. International Academy of Broadcasting (SAUO)
IAB.............. International Air Bahama (SAUO)
IAB.............. International Antilles Bank (SAUO)
IAB.............. International Aquatic Board (BUAC)
IAB.............. International Association of Bibliophiles [*See also AIB*] [*Paris, France*] (EAIO)
IAB.............. International Association of Boards of Examiners in Optometry (EA)
IAB.............. International Association of Bookkeepers [*British*] (EAIO)
IAB.............. International Association of Broadcasting (NTCM)
IAB.............. International Association of Bureaucrats (SAUO)
IAB.............. International Association of Business (EA)
IAB.............. International Council of Scientific Unions Abstracting Board (SAUO)
IAB.............. Internationale Akademie fuer Bader-, Sport-, und Freizeitheitbau [*International Board for Aquatic, Sports, and Recreation Facilities*] [*Bad Neustadt/Saale, Federal Republic of Germany*] (EAIO)
IAB.............. Internet Activities Board (MLOA)
IAB.............. Internet Activity Board (RALS)
IAB.............. Internet Advertising Bureau
IAB.............. Internet Architecture Board
IAB.............. Interrupt Address to Bus [*Computer science*]
IAB.............. Intra-Abdominal [*Artery*]
IAB.............. Intraabdominally (SAUS)
IAB.............. Intra-Aortic Balloon [*Cardiology*]
IAB.............. Invalid Answerback (SAUS)
IAB.............. Iowa Administrative Bulletin [*A publication*] (AAGC)
IAB.............. Irish Association for the Blind (BI)
IAB.............. Island Arc Basalt [*Geology*]
IAB.............. Isoamyl Benzoate (SAUS)
IAB.............. Isoamyl Butyrate (SAUS)
IAB.............. Italian American Business [*American Chamber of Commerce in Italy*] [*A publication*]
IAB.............. IUS [*Interior Upper Stage*] Assembly Building [*NASA*] (MCD)
IAB.............. John Crerar Library, Chicago, IL [*OCLC symbol*] (OCLC)
IAB.............. Wichita, KS [*Location identifier*] [*FAA*] (FAAL)
IABA............ Inter-American Bar Association (EA)
IABA............ International Aerospace Business Advisors (SAUO)
IABA............ International Air Brokers Association (SAUO)
IABA............ International Aircraft Brockers Association (SAUO)
IABA............ International Amateur Boxing Association
IABA............ International Association of Aircraft Brokers and Agents [*Norway*] (EAIO)
IABA............ Intra-Aortic Balloon Assist [*Cardiology*]
IABA............ Irish Amateur Boxing Association (BI)
IaBag.......... Bagley Public Library, Bagley, IA [*Library symbol*] [*Library of Congress*] (LCLS)
IaBagG......... Bagley Gazette, Bagley, IA [*Library symbol*] [*Library of Congress*] (LCLS)
IAB-AIR........ International Association of Broadcasting-Asociaci"n Internacional de Radiodifusi"n (SAUO)
IAB-AIR........ International Association of Broadcasting - Asociacion Internacional de Radiodifusion [*Formerly, Inter-American Association of Broadcasters*] (EA)
IaBanR......... Bancroft Register, Bancroft, IA [*Library symbol*] [*Library of Congress*] (LCLS)
IA Bar Rev... Iowa Bar Review [*A publication*] (DLA)
IaBatB......... Batavia Beacon, Batavia, IA [*Library symbol*] [*Library of Congress*] (LCLS)
IaBaxNE....... Baxter New Era, Baxter, IA [*Library symbol*] [*Library of Congress*] (LCLS)
IaBaxWC...... Baxter Women's Club, Baxter, IA [*Library symbol*] [*Library of Congress*] (LCLS)
IaBay........... Bayard Public Library, Bayard, IA [*Library symbol*] [*Library of Congress*] (LCLS)
IaBayN......... Bayard News, Bayard, IA [*Library symbol*] [*Library of Congress*] (LCLS)
IABB............ Inter-American Bank Bond (MHDW)
IABBE.......... International Association for Better Basic Education (EA)
IABBE.......... International Association of Black Business Educators [*Defunct*] (EA)
IABBS.......... International Amateur Boat Building Association (SAUO)
IABBS.......... International Amateur Boat Building Society [*Defunct*]
IABC............ Idle Air Bypass Control [*Fuel system*] [*Automotive engineering*]
IABC............ Insulation Applicators Association of British Columbia (SAUO)
IABC............ International Association of Bookstall Contractors (SAUO)
IABC............ International Association of Building Companions [*See also IBO*] [*Marche-En-Famenne, Belgium*] (EAIO)
IABC............ International Association of Business Communicators (EA)
IABC............ Intra-Aortic Balloon Catheter [*Cardiology*] (DAVI)
IABC............ Intra-Aortic Balloon Counterpulsation [*Cardiology*]
IaBclHi......... Ida County Historical Society, Battle Creek, IA [*Library symbol*] [*Library of Congress*] (LCLS)
IABCP.......... Intra-Aortic Balloon Counterpulsation [*Medicine*] (EDAA)
IaBcT........... Battle Creek Times, Battle Creek, IA [*Library symbol*] [*Library of Congress*] (LCLS)
IABD............ Ischemic-Anoxic Brain Damage [*Medicine*] (MELL)
IaBDHi......... Des Moines County Historical Society, Burlington, IA [*Library symbol*] [*Library of Congress*] (LCLS)
IABE............ Ibero-American Bureau of Education [*See also OEI*] [*Madrid, Spain*] (EAIO)
IABE............ Internacia Asocio de Bankistoj Esperantistaj (SAUO)
IaBedTP....... Bedford Times-Press, Bedford, IA [*Library symbol*] [*Library of Congress*] (LCLS)
IaBelm......... Belmond Public Library, Belmond, IA [*Library symbol*] [*Library of Congress*] (LCLS)
IaBelmI........ Belmond Independent, Belmond, IA [*Library symbol*] [*Library of Congress*] (LCLS)
IABEM.......... International Association for Boundary Element Methods (BUAC)
IaBepU......... Belle Plaine Union, Belle Plaine, IA [*Library symbol*] [*Library of Congress*] (LCLS)
IaBetN......... Bettendorf News, Bettendorf, IA [*Library symbol*] [*Library of Congress*] (LCLS)
IaBev........... Bellevue Public Library, Bellevue, IA [*Library symbol*] [*Library of Congress*] (LCLS)
IaBevHL....... Bellevue Herald-Leader, Bellevue, IA [*Library symbol*] [*Library of Congress*] (LCLS)
IABF............ Inter-American Bar Foundation (EA)
IABF............ International Amateur Basketball Federation (SAUO)
IABF............ International Association of Business Forecasting (EA)
IABG............ International Association of Botanic Gardens [*Australia*] (EA)
IABG............ International Association of Buying Groups [*See also IVE*] (EAIO)
IABG............ International Association on Biomedical Gerontology (BUAC)
IABHC.......... Interagency Bird Hazard Committee (SAUO)
IABI............. Intel Application Binary Interface (SAUS)
IAB-ICSU...... International Abstracting Board-International Council of Scientific Unions (SAUO)
IABIN........... Inter-American Biodiversity Information Network (SAUO)
IABK............ International Association of Book-Keepers [*Sevenoaks, Kent, England*] (EA)
IaBl............. Bloomfield Public Library, Bloomfield, IA [*Library symbol*] [*Library of Congress*] (LCLS)
IABL............ Independent Association of Builders' Labourers [*A union*] [*British*]
IABLA.......... Inter-American Bank for Latin America (WDAA)
IaBlak.......... Blakesburg Public Library, Blakesburg, IA [*Library symbol*] [*Library of Congress*] (LCLS)
IaBlaSP........ South Benton Star Press, Blairstown, IA [*Library symbol*] [*Library of Congress*] (LCLS)
IaBlD........... Bloomfield Democrat, Bloomfield, IA [*Library symbol*] [*Library of Congress*] (LCLS)
IaBlDR......... Davis County Republican, Bloomfield, IA [*Library symbol*] [*Library of Congress*] (LCLS)
IaBlGen........ Davis County Genealogical Society, Bloomfield, IA [*Library symbol*] [*Library of Congress*] (LCLS)
IABM............ Idiopathic Aplastic Bone Marrow [*Medicine*] (MELL)
IABM............ International Academy of Biological Medicine [*Defunct*] (EA)
IABM............ International Association of Broadcasting Manufacturers [*Hayes, Middlesex, England*] (EAIO)
IABM............ International Association of Broadcast Monitors (EA)
IABMCP....... International Academy of Behavioral Medicine, Counseling and Psychotherapy (EA)
IABMS.......... International Association of Botanical and Mycological Societies (BUAC)
IaBo............. Ericson Public Library, Boone, IA [*Library symbol*] [*Library of Congress*] (LCLS)
IABO............ Internacia Asocio de Bibliistoj kaj Orientalistoj [*International Association of Biblicists and Orientalists - IABO*] (EA)
IABO............ International Association for Biological Oceanography [*Aberdeen, Scotland*] (EAIO)
IABO............ International Association for/of Biological Oceanography (SAUO)
IABO............ International Association of Biblicists and Orientalists (BUAC)
IABO............ International Association of Biological Oceanography (SAUS)
IaBoCoC....... Boone County Courthouse, Boone, IA [*Library symbol*] [*Library of Congress*] (LCLS)
IaBonR......... Bonaparte Record-Republican, Bonaparte, IA [*Library symbol*] [*Library of Congress*] (LCLS)
IaBoNR......... Boone News-Republican, Boone, IA [*Library symbol*] [*Library of Congress*] (LCLS)
IaBonRR....... Bonaparte Record-Republican, Bonaparte, IA [*Library symbol*] [*Library of Congress*] (LCLS)
IABP............ International Arctic Buoy Program [*Marine science*] (OSRA)
IABP............ International Association of Businessmen and Professionals (EA)
IABP............ Intra-Aortic Balloon Pump [*Cardiology*]
IABP............ Intra-Aortic Balloon Pumping (SAUS)
IABPA.......... Intra-Aortic Balloon Pumping Assistance [*Cardiology*] (AAMN)
IABPAI......... International Association of Blue Print and Allied Industries [*Later, IRGBA, IRA*] (EA)
IABPBD........ International Alliance of Bill Posters, Billers, and Distributors of US and Canada [*Defunct*]
I-ABPC......... Inter-Allied Bureau of Press Control (SAUO)
IABPC.......... International Association of Book Publishing Consultants [*Inactive*] (EA)
IABPC.......... Intraaortic Balloon Counterpulsation [*Medicine*] (DB)
IABPFF........ International Association of Black Professional Fire Fighters (EA)
IABR............ Index to Australian Book Reviews [*A publication*]
IaBrBEN....... Brighton Enterprise-News, Brighton, IA [*Library symbol*] [*Library of Congress*] (LCLS)
IaBreN......... Breda News, Breda, IA [*Library symbol*] [*Library of Congress*] (LCLS)
IaBrEN......... Brighton Enterprise-News, Brighton, IA [*Library symbol*] [*Library of Congress*] (LCLS)
IA B Rev...... Iowa Bar Review [*A publication*] (DLA)
IABRG.......... Institute of Applied Biology Research of Guinea (SAUS)
IaBriNT........ Britt News-Tribune, Britt, IA [*Library symbol*] [*Library of Congress*] (LCLS)

IABRM .... International Association for Bear Research and Management (EA)
IaBroC .... Brooklyn Chronicle, Brooklyn, IA [*Library symbol*] [*Library of Congress*] (LCLS)
IABS .... Installation Automated Budget System [*Army*]
IABS .... Institute for Applied Behavioral Science [*Medicine*] (EDAA)
IABS .... Integration of Algebraic Boolean Simulation (SAUS)
IABS .... International Absorbents [*NASDAQ symbol*] (SAG)
IABS .... International Advisory Committee for Biological Standardization (SAUO)
IABS .... International Alban Berg Society (EA)
IABS .... International Association for Biological Standardization (BUAC)
IABS .... International Association for Business and Society (BUAC)
IABS .... International Association for Byzantine Studies [*See also AIEB*] [*Thessaloniki, Greece*] (EAIO)
IABS .... International Association for/of Biological Standardization (SAUO)
IABS .... International Association of Biological Standardization [*See also AISB*] [*ICSU*] [*Geneva, Switzerland*] (EAIO)
IABS .... International Association of Buddhist Studies (EA)
IABS .... International Association of Byznatine Studies (BUAC)
IABSE .... International Association for Bridge and Structural Engineering [*ICSU*] [*Zurich, Switzerland*] [*Research center*] (EA)
IABSE .... International Association of Structural & Bridge Engineers (SAUO)
IABSF .... Internatoinal Amateur Boat Surfing Federation (BUAC)
IABSF .... Intl Absorbents [*NASDAQ symbol*] (TTSB)
IABSIW .... International Association of Bridge and Structural Iron Workers (SAUO)
IABSIW .... International Association of Bridge, Structural, and Ornamental Iron Workers (BARN)
IABSOIW .... International Association of Bridge, Structural and Ornamental Iron Workers (SAUO)
IABT .... Illinois Association of Biology Teachers (EDAC)
IABTI .... International Association of Bomb Technicians and Investigators (EA)
IaBucCT .... Buffalo Center Tribune, Buffalo Center, IA [*Library symbol*] [*Library of Congress*] (LCLS)
IABWMT .... International Association of Black and White Men Together [*Later, NABWMT*] (EA)
IAC .... ANSI International Advisory Council (AG)
IAC .... Chicago, IL [*Location identifier*] [*FAA*] (FAAL)
IAC .... De Paul University, Chicago, IL [*OCLC symbol*] (OCLC)
IAC .... Ibrahim Ali Commission (SAUO)
IAC .... Iceberg Athletic Club (EA)
IAC .... Identification Accuracy [*Rate*] (MCD)
IAC .... Idle Air Control [*Automotive engineering*]
IAC .... Image Analysis Computer (MELL)
I-Ac .... Imidazoleacetic Acid [*Biochemistry*] (AAMN)
IAC .... Immigration Appeal Cases [*Canada*] [*A publication*] (DLA)
IAC .... Immunization Action Coalition (EA)
IAC .... Immunologically Activated Cell (QSUL)
IAC .... Import Advisory Committee (SAUO)
IAC .... Improved Anode Catalyst
IAC .... In Any Case [*Computer hacker terminology*]
IAC .... Increment Accumulator (SAUS)
IAC .... Indiana Administrative Code [*A publication*] (AAGC)
IAC .... Indian Airlines Corp. [*ICAO designator*] (FAAC)
IAC .... Indian Airlines Corporation News (SAUO)
IAC .... Indian Army Circular [*British military*] (DMA)
IAC .... Indo-Asian Culture (journ.) (SAUS)
IAC .... Industrial Accident Commission Decisions [*A publication*] (DLA)
IAC .... Industrial Acoustics Company Ltd (SAUO)
IAC .... Industrial Acustics Co. (SAUS)
IAC .... Industrial Acustics Company (SAUO)
IAC .... Industrial Advisory Committee (SAUO)
IAC .... Industrial Advisory Council (SAUO)
IAC .... Industrial Applicatons Center (ACAE)
IAC .... Industrial Arbitration Court (SAUO)
IAC .... Industrial Area Committees (SAUS)
IAC .... Industrial Assurance Commissioner (SAUO)
IAC .... Industries Assistance Commission (EERA)
IAC .... Industry Advisory Commission (SAUO)
IAC .... Industry Advisory Committee [*World War II*]
IAC .... Industry Advisory Committee on Survey and Mapping [*Queensland*] [*State*] (EERA)
IAC .... Industry Advisory Conference [*Underwriters Laboratories*] [*Telecommunications*]
IAC .... Industry Advisory Council [*Formerly, DIAC*]
IAC .... Industry Assistance Commission (SAUS)
IAC .... Industry Assitance Commission (SAUO)
IAC .... Ineffective Airway Clearance [*Medicine*] (DMAA)
IAC .... Information Access Co. [*Information service or system*] (IID)
IAC .... Information Access Company (SAUO)
IAC .... Information Access Corporation (SAUO)
I/AC .... Information/Action Control (SAUS)
IAC .... Information Analysis Center [*DoD*]
IAC .... Information and Communication
IAC .... Inheritance of Acquired Characteristics
IAC .... Initial Alignment Control (SAUS)
IAC .... Initial Approach Course [*Aviation*]
IAC .... Inner Approach Channel
IAC .... Innovative Academic Courses (SAUS)
IAC .... Inpatient Acute Care (MELL)
IAC .... Installation-Alteration-Cancellation (SAUS)
IAC .... Installation and Checkout (IAA)
IAC .... Instantaneous Airborne Count (MCD)
IAC .... Institute for Advanced Concepts [*In 1980 film "Simon"*]
IAC .... Institute for Antiquity and Christianity [*Claremont University*] [*Research center*] (RCD)
IAC .... Institute of Administration and Commerce of South Africa (BUAC)
IAC .... Institute of Amateur Cinematographers [*British*] (BI)
IAC .... Institute of Applied Clicheology
IAC .... Institute of Astrophysics of the Canaries
IAC .... Institute of Company Accountants (SAUO)
IAC .... Instituto Colombiano de Codification y Automatizacion Comercial (AG)
IAC .... Instruction Address Change (SAUS)
IAC .... Instructor Aircraft Commander (ACAE)
IAC .... Instructor Aircraft Operator (SAUS)
IAC .... Instrument Approach Chart (AAG)
IAC .... Instrument Array Cable
IAC .... Instrumentation and Control (IAA)
IAC .... Instrument-on-a-Card (SAUS)
IAC .... Insurance Acts Committee (SAUO)
IAC .... Insurance Advertising Conference [*Later, IMCA*] (EA)
IAC .... Integrated Access Controller [*Communications term*] (DCT)
IAC .... Integrated Analyses Center (SAUO)
IAC .... Integrated Analysis Capability (SAUS)
IAC .... Integrated Avionics Computer (HLLA)
IAC .... Integrating Assembly Contractor
IAC .... Integrating Associate Contractor
IAC .... Integration, Assembly, and Checkout
IAC .... Intelligence Advisory Committee
IAC .... Intelligence Analysis Center [*Marine Corps*] (MCD)
IAC .... Intelligent Asynchronous Controller [*Computer terminal connector*] (NITA)
IAC .... Interactive Array Computer
IAC .... Inter-African Committee on Traditional Practices affecting the Health of Women and Children in Africa (SAUO)
IAC .... Inter Afrique Charters (BUAC)
IAC .... Interagency Commission for Outdoor Recreation (SAUO)
IAC .... Interagency Committee (SAUO)
IAC .... Interagency Committee for Outdoor Recreation [*Department of the Interior*]
IAC .... Interagency Conference (MCD)
IAC .... Inter-American Capital (SAUO)
IAC .... Inter-American Conference (SAUO)
IAC .... Inter-American Council
IAC .... Interapplication Communication [*Apple Computer, Inc.*]
IAC .... Inter-Applications Communication [*Computer science*] (EERA)
IAC .... Interarray Communications (NVT)
IAC .... Interdepartmental Advisory Committee [*World War II*]
IAC .... Interface Adapter Unit (SAUS)
IAC .... Interface Assurance Contractor
IAC .... Interference Absorption Circuit (SAUS)
IAC .... Intergrated Avionics Computer (DA)
IAC .... Interim Acceptance Criteria (NRCH)
IAC .... Interim Action Committee [*British*]
IAC .... Intermediate Air Command [*Air Force*] (AFM)
IAC .... Intermittent Abdominal Compression
IAC .... Internal Acoustic Canal (SAUS)
IAC .... Internal Auditory Canal [*Anatomy*]
IAC .... International Academic Center (or Centre) (SAUS)
IAC .... International Academy of Ceramics [*See also AIC*] [*Geneva, Switzerland*] (EAIO)
IAC .... International Academy of Cytology [*Quebec, PQ*] (EA)
IAC .... International Accounting Center (SAUO)
IAC .... International Activities Committee [*American Chemical Society*]
IAC .... International Advisory Committee [*ANSI*]
IAC .... International Advisory Committee on Research in the Natural Sciences (SAUS)
IAC .... International Advisory Council for Homosexual Men and Women in Alcoholics Anonymous (EA)
IAC .... International Aerobatic Club (EA)
IAC .... International Aerological Commission (SAUO)
IAC .... International Agricultural Center (or Centre) (SAUO)
IAC .... International Agricultural Centre (SAUO)
IAC .... International Agricultural Club (EA)
IAC .... International Air Commission (SAUO)
IAC .... International Air Convention
IAC .... International Algebraic Compiler
IAC .... International Alpine Conference (BUAC)
IAC .... International American Ceramics Inc. (SAUO)
IAC .... International Analysis Code [*Meteorology*]
IAC .... International Anesthesiology Clinics [*Medicine*] (EDAA)
IAC .... International Anti-Counterfeiting Coalition (EA)
IAC .... International ANTOR Committee (SAUO)
IAC .... International Apple Core (RALS)
IAC .... International Arms Corporation (SAUO)
IAC .... International Artists Cooperation (SAUO)
IAC .... International Association for Cybernetics [*See also AIC*] [*Namur, Belgium*] (EAIO)
IAC .... International Association of Charities [*See also AIC*] (EAIO)
IAC .... International Association of Cybernetics (SAUS)
IAC .... International Astronautical Congress
IAC .... International Athletes Club (BUAC)
IAC .... International Athletics Club (SAUO)
IAC .... International Aviation Corporation (SAUO)
IAC .... Internet Application Component (GART)
IAC .... Interposed Abdominal Compression [*Medicine*] (STED)
IAC .... Interposed Abdominal Counterpulsation [*Medicine*]
IAC .... Interpret as Command (SAUS)

IAC.............. Inter-Regional Athletic Conference (PSS)
IAC.............. Intertrust Accumulation Certificate (SAUO)
IAC.............. Interview after Combat (SAUS)
IAC.............. Intra-Arterial Catheter [*Medicine*] (MELL)
IAC.............. Intra-Arterial Chemotherapy [*Medicine*]
IAC.............. Inventory of Anger Communication [*Personality development test*] [*Psychology*]
IAC.............. Ion-Assisted Coating (SAUS)
IAC.............. Iowa Administrative Code [*A publication*] (AAGC)
IAC.............. Ipsilateral Associational-Commissural [*Anatomy*]
IAC.............. Iranian Airways Company (SAUO)
IAC.............. Iranian Airways Company, Teheran (SAUO)
IAC.............. Irish Air Corps (SAUO)
IAC.............. Irvine Apartment Communities [*NYSE symbol*] (SAG)
IAC.............. Isoamyl Caprate (SAUS)
IAC.............. Isolated Adrenal Cell [*Endocrinology*] (DAVI)
IAC.............. Israel Aliyah Center (EA)
IAC.............. Italian Aircraft Corporation (SAUO)
IAC.............. Iteractive Analog Computer (SAUS)
IaCa............ Duncan Memorial Library, Casey, IA [*Library symbol*] [*Library of Congress*] (LCLS)
IACA............ Independent Air Carriers Association [*Defunct*] (EA)
IACA............ Indian Air Corporations Act (SAUO)
IACA............ Indian Arts and Crafts Association (EA)
IACA............ Inter-American College Association (EA)
IACA............ Inter-American Cultural Association (EA)
IACA............ International Air Carrier Association [*Zaventhem, Belgium*] (EAIO)
IACA............ International Air Charter Association [*Switzerland*] (BUAC)
IACA............ International Arts and Culture Association
IACA............ International Association for Classical Archaeology [*See also AIAC*] [*Rome, Italy*] (EAIO)
IACA............ International Association of Consulting Actuaries (MHDB)
IACA............ Intra-Application Communication Area [*Computer science*] (PCM)
IACA............ Irish American Cultural Association (EA)
IACA............ Italian Association of Chartered Accountants (SAUO)
IACAAC........ International Artists' Cooperation Audio Art Center [*Defunct*] (EA)
IACAAN........ International Committee on Avian Anatomical Nomenclature (BUAC)
IACAC.......... Inter-American Commercial Arbitration Commission (BUAC)
IACAC.......... International Association of Civil Aviation Chaplains (EA)
IACACS........ Interdenominational Advisory Committee on Army Chaplaincy Services (SAUO)
IAC/ADP....... Interagency Committee on Automatic Data Processing [*Office of Management and Budget*]
IACAHP........ Inter-African Advisory Committee for Animal Health and Production (BUAC)
IACAPAP...... International Association for Child and Adolescent Psychiatry and Allied Professions [*Copenhagen, Denmark*] (EA)
IaCar........... Carroll Public Library, Carroll, IA [*Library symbol*] [*Library of Congress*] (LCLS)
IaCarCH....... Carroll County Historical Society Museum, Carroll, IA [*Library symbol*] [*Library of Congress*] (LCLS)
IaCarl.......... Carlisle Public Library, Carlisle, IA [*Library symbol*] [*Library of Congress*] (LCLS)
IaCarlC........ Carlisle Citizen, Carlisle, IA [*Library symbol*] [*Library of Congress*] (LCLS)
IaCarsT........ Carson Times, Carson, IA [*Library symbol*] [*Library of Congress*] (LCLS)
IaCarTH....... Daily Times-Herald, Carroll, IA [*Library symbol*] [*Library of Congress*] (LCLS)
IaCasPA....... Cascade Pioneer-Advertiser, Cascade, IA [*Library symbol*] [*Library of Congress*] (LCLS)
IaCb............ Council Bluffs Free Public Library, Council Bluffs, IA [*Library symbol*] [*Library of Congress*] (LCLS)
IACB............ Indian Arts and Crafts Board [*Department of the Interior*]
IACB............ Inter-Agency Consultative Board (EY)
IACB............ Inter-Agency Coordination Board (SAUO)
IACB............ Inter-American Coffee Board (SAUO)
IACB............ International Advisory Committee on Bibliography [*UNESCO*] (WDAA)
IACB............ International Association for Cryptologic Research (SAUO)
IACB............ International Association of Convention Bureaus [*Later, IACVB*] (EA)
IACB............ Intra-Aortic Counterpulsation Balloon [*Cardiology*] (DAVI)
IACBC.......... International Advisory Committee for Biological Control (SAUS)
IACBC.......... International Advisory Committee on Biological Control (BUAC)
IACBD.......... International Academy for Child Brain Development (EA)
IACBDT........ International Advisory Committee on Bibliography, Documentation and Terminology (SAUO)
IaCbN........... Nonpareil, Council Bluffs, IA [*Library symbol*] [*Library of Congress*] (LCLS)
IAC Bulletin... Institute of Amateur Cinematographers Bulletin (journ.) (SAUS)
IACC............ Icelandic American Chamber of Commerce (NTPA)
IACC............ IIM-ASM Cooperation Committee (SAUS)
IACC............ Improved Air crew Chemical warfare defense Coverall (SAUS)
IACC............ India-America Chamber of Commerce (EA)
IACC............ Indo-American Chamber of Commerce (PDAA)
IACC............ Industrial Analysis and Control Council
IACC............ Integrating Assembly and Checkout Contractor
IACC............ Inter-Agency Air Cartographic Committee
IACC............ Interamerican Confederation of Cattlemen (EA)
IACC............ Inter-American Cultural Council (EA)
IACC............ International Agricultural Coordination Commission (BUAC)
IACC............ International Air Cargo Corp. [*Egypt*] [*ICAO designator*] (FAAC)
IACC............ International Alliance of Catholic Churches (EA)
IACC............ International Americas Cup Class [*Yachting*]
IACC............ International Art Cinemas Confederation (EAIO)
IACC............ International Association for Cell Culture (BUAC)
IACC............ International Association for Cell Cultures (SAUS)
IACC............ International Association of Cereal Chemistry (SAUO)
IACC............ International Association of Colour Consultants (SAUO)
IACC............ International Association of Commercial Collectors (NTPA)
IACC............ International Association of Conference Centers (EA)
IACC............ International Association of Congress Centres (BUAC)
IACC............ Iran American Chamber of Commerce (EA)
IACC............ Island Arts and Crafts Club, Victoria [*1910, IACS from 1922*] (NGC)
IACC............ Israel-America Chamber of Commerce and Industry (EAIO)
IACC............ Italian-American Chamber of Commerce (EA)
IACC............ Italy-America Chamber of Commerce (EA)
IaCc............ John E. Clegg Library, Central City, IA [*Library symbol*] [*Library of Congress*] (LCLS)
IACCA.......... Inter-agency Committee on the Climate Agenda (SAUO)
IACCA.......... Irish Association of Company and Commercial Accountants (BUAC)
IACCB.......... Illinois Association of Community College Biologists (EDAC)
IACCC.......... Inter-Agency Climate Change Committee (SAUO)
IACCC.......... International Association for Cross-Cultural Communication (BUAC)
IACCD.......... Inter-American Confederation of Continental Defense (SAUO)
IACCE.......... Inter-American Confederation for Catholic Education [*Bogota, Colombia*] (EAIO)
IACChE........ Inter-American Confederation for Chemical Engineering (SAUO)
IACCHE........ Inter-American Confederation of Chemical Engineering (BUAC)
IACCI........... International Association of Computer Crime Investigators [*Defunct*] (EA)
IACCI........... International Association of Credit Card Investigators (EA)
IACCI........... International Association of Financial Crimes Investigators (NTPA)
IaCcL........... Linn News-Letter, Central City, IA [*Library symbol*] [*Library of Congress*] (LCLS)
IACCN.......... Inventory Accounting Cost Control Number System (MCD)
IACCP.......... Inter-American Council of Commerce and Production
IACCP.......... International Association for Cross-Cultural Psychology [*Canada*] (EA)
IACCP.......... International Association for/of Cross-Cultural Psychology (SAUO)
IAC-CPR....... Interposed Abdominal Compression - Cardiopulmonary Resuscitation
IACD............ Implantable Automatic Cardioverter-Defibrillator [*Medicine*] (MELL)
IACD............ International Agricultural College, Deventer (SAUO)
IACD............ International Association for Community Development (BUAC)
IACD............ International Association of Clothing Designers (EA)
IACD............ Intra-Atrial Conduction Defect (STED)
IACD............ Irish Association for Curriculum Development (AIE)
IACDB.......... International Action Committee for Democracy in Burma (BUAC)
IACDE.......... International Association of Clothing Designers and Executives (NTPA)
IAC Dec....... Decisions of the Industrial Accident Commission of California [*A publication*] (DLA)
IACDLA........ International Advisory Committee on Documentation, Libraries, and Archives [*UNESCO*] (DIT)
IACDOCTERPAS... International Advisory Committee on Documentation, Terminology in Pure and Applied Science (SAUO)
IACDT.......... International Advisory Committee for Documentation and Technology (SAUS)
IACDT.......... International Advisory Committee for Documentation and Terminology (BUAC)
IACDT.......... International Advisory Committee for Documentation and Terminology in Pure and Applied Science (SAUO)
IACDT.......... International Association of Certified Duncan Teachers (EA)
IACE............ Institute of Adult and Continuing Education (SAUO)
IACE............ Intergovernmental Advisory Council on Education (AEE)
IACE............ International Air Cadet Exchange
IACE............ International Association for Computing in Education [*Also, an information service or system*] (EA)
IACED.......... Inter-African Advisory Committee on Epizootic Diseases
IACED.......... Interagency Committee on Environment and Development (EERA)
IACEE.......... International Association for Continuing Engineering Education (BUAC)
IaCenv......... Drake Public Library, Centerville, IA [*Library symbol*] [*Library of Congress*] (LCLS)
IaCenvI........ Iowegian & Citizen, Centerville, IA [*Library symbol*] [*Library of Congress*] (LCLS)
IACES.......... International Air Cushion Engineering Society (BUAC)
IACESC........ Inter-American Council for Education, Science, and Culture
IACESR........ Irish Association for Cultural, Economic, and Social Relations (BUAC)
IACET.......... International Association for Continuing Education and Training (EA)
IaCf............. Cedar Falls Public Library, Cedar Falls, IA [*Library symbol*] [*Library of Congress*] (LCLS)
IACF............ Inter-American Cement Federation [*Colombia*] (EAIO)
IACF............ International Amateur Cycling Federation (EA)
IACF............ International Association for Cultural Freedom [*Defunct*] (EA)
IACFA.......... International Adult Cystic Fibrosis Association [*Netherlands*] (BUAC)
IaCfE........... Eastern Area Library Cooperative, Cedar Falls, IA [*Library symbol*] [*Library of Congress*] (LCLS)
IACFEC........ Inter-American Consultative, Financial and Economic Committee (SAUO)
IACFHG........ Inter Action Council of Former Heads of Government (EA)
IaCfHi.......... Cedar Falls Historical Society, Cedar Falls, IA [*Library symbol*] [*Library of Congress*] (LCLS)
IACFM.......... International Association of Concert and Festival Managers [*Later, ISPAA*] (EA)
IaCfNI.......... Northern Iowan, Cedar Falls, IA [*Library symbol*] [*Library of Congress*] (LCLS)
IaCfR........... Cedar Falls Record, Cedar Falls, IA [*Library symbol*] [*Library of Congress*] (LCLS)
IaCfT........... University of Northern Iowa, Cedar Falls, IA [*Library symbol*] [*Library of Congress*] (LCLS)

IACG .... Institute for American Church Growth (EA)
IACG .... Inter Agency Consultative Group (ACAE)
IACG .... Interagency Consultative Group (SAUS)
IACG .... Inter-Agency Consultative Group for Space Science (SAUS)
IACG .... Intermittent Angle-Closure Glaucoma (MELL)
IACGEC .... Inter-Agency Committee on Global Environmental Change (SAUO)
IaCh .... Free Public Library, Chariton, IA [*Library symbol*] [*Library of Congress*] (LCLS)
IACH .... Inter-Association Committee on Health
IACH .... International Association of Colour Healers (BUAC)
IACHA .... Iowa Automated Clearing House Association
IaChc .... Charles City Public Library, Charles City, IA [*Library symbol*] [*Library of Congress*] (LCLS)
IaChcP .... Charles City Press, Charles City, IA [*Library symbol*] [*Library of Congress*] (LCLS)
IaChe .... Cherokee Public Library, Cherokee, IA [*Library symbol*] [*Library of Congress*] (LCLS)
IACHE .... International Association of Cylindrical Hydraulic Engineers (EA)
IaCheCHi ..... Cherokee County Historical Society, Cherokee, IA [*Library symbol*] [*Library of Congress*] (LCLS)
IaCheCoC ..... Cherokee County Courthouse, Cherokee, IA [*Library symbol*] [*Library of Congress*] (LCLS)
IACHEI .... International Association of Consultants in Higher Education Institutions (BUAC)
IaChHP .... Chariton Herald-Patriot, Chariton, IA [*Library symbol*] [*Library of Congress*] (LCLS)
IaChL .... Chariton Leader, Chariton, IA [*Library symbol*] [*Library of Congress*] (LCLS)
IaChoT .... Charter Oak Times, Charter Oak, IA [*Library symbol*] [*Library of Congress*] (LCLS)
IACHR .... Inter-American Commission of/on Human Rights (SAUO)
IACHR .... Inter-American Commission on Human Rights (EA)
IACHT .... International Association Colon Hydro Therapy (NTPA)
IaChu .... Churdan City Library, Churdan, IA [*Library symbol*] [*Library of Congress*] (LCLS)
IACI .... Idiopathic Arterial Calcification of Infancy [*Medicine*] (DMAA)
IACI .... Industrial Acoustics Co., Inc. [*NASDAQ symbol*] (NQ)
IACI .... Inter-American Children's Institute [*Uruguay*] [*Research center*] (IRC)
IACI .... Inter-American Copyright Institute (BUAC)
IACI .... International Association of Conference Interpreters (BUAC)
IACI .... Intra-Arterial Contrast Injection [*Medicine*] (EDAA)
IACI .... Iran Aircraft Industries (MCD)
IACI .... Iran Aircraft Industry (SAUO)
IACI .... Irish American Cultural Institute (EA)
IACI .... Irish-American Cultural Institute (SAUO)
IACIA .... Incorporated Association of Cost and Industrial Accountants (SAUO)
IACIA .... Interagency Committee for International Athletics [*Defunct*]
IACID .... Inter-American Center for Integral Development [*OAS*]
IACIS .... International Association for Computer Information Systems (NTPA)
IACIS .... International Association of Colloid and Interface Scientists (BUAC)
IACITC .... International Advisory Committee of the International Teletraffic Congress (EAIO)
IACJ .... Inter-American Council of Jurists [*Organization of American States*] [*Washington, DC*]
IaCjGS .... Columbus Gazette & Columbus Safeguard, Columbus Junction, IA [*Library symbol*] [*Library of Congress*] (LCLS)
IACK .... Interrupt Acknowledge (SAUS)
IACKL .... Interrupt Acknowledgment Latency [*Computer science*]
IaCkvS .... Clarksville Star, Clarksville, IA [*Library symbol*] [*Library of Congress*] (LCLS)
IACL .... Internal Association of Criminal Law (BUAC)
IACL .... International Academy of Comparative Law (BUAC)
IACL .... International Aeradio Caribbean Limited (SAUO)
IACL .... International Association for/of Constitutional Law (SAUO)
IACL .... International Association of Constitutional Law [*See also AIDC*] [*Belgrade, Yugoslavia*] (EAIO)
IACL .... International Association of Criminal Law (SAUO)
IACL .... Interpersonal Adjective Checklist Leary [*Medicine*] (EDAA)
IaCla .... Clarion Public Library, Clarion, IA [*Library symbol*] [*Library of Congress*] (LCLS)
IACLA .... International Association of Clinical Laser Acupuncturists (EA)
IaClad .... Clarinda Public Library, Clarinda, IA [*Library symbol*] [*Library of Congress*] (LCLS)
IaCladHJ ..... Clarinda Herald-Journal, Clarinda, IA [*Library symbol*] [*Library of Congress*] (LCLS)
IaClaM .... Wright County Monitor, Clarion, IA [*Library symbol*] [*Library of Congress*] (LCLS)
IaClar .... Edna Zybell Memorial Library, Clarence, IA [*Library symbol*] [*Library of Congress*] (LCLS)
IaClarCHi ..... Cedar County Historical Society, Clarence, IA [*Library symbol*] [*Library of Congress*] (LCLS)
IACLE .... International Association of Contact Lens Educators
IACLEA .... International Association of Campus Law Enforcement Administrators (EA)
IaClfC .... Clearfield Chronicle, Clearfield, IA [*Library symbol*] [*Library of Congress*] (LCLS)
IaCli .... Clinton Public Library, Clinton, IA [*Library symbol*] [*Library of Congress*] (LCLS)
IaCliC .... Clinton Corn Processing Co., Clinton, IA [*Library symbol*] [*Library of Congress*] (LCLS)
IaCliCC .... Clinton Community College, Clinton, IA [*Library symbol*] [*Library of Congress*] (LCLS)
IaCliCHi ...... Clinton County Historical Society, Clinton, IA [*Library symbol*] [*Library of Congress*] (LCLS)
IaCliH .... Clinton Herald, Clinton, IA [*Library symbol*] [*Library of Congress*] (LCLS)
IaCliM .... Mount Saint Clare College, Clinton, IA [*Library symbol*] [*Library of Congress*] (LCLS)
IaCll .... Clear Lake Public Library, Clear Lake, IA [*Library symbol*] [*Library of Congress*] (LCLS)
IaClvS .... Clarksville Star, Clarksville, IA [*Library symbol*] [*Library of Congress*] (LCLS)
IACM .... Institute of Applied and Computational Mathematics [*Greece*] (BUAC)
IACM .... International Association for Computational Mechanics [*International Council of Scientific Unions*]
IACM .... International Association of Circulation Managers
IACM .... International Association of Color Manufacturers (NTPA)
IACM .... International Association of Concert Managers [*Later, ISPAA*] (EA)
IACM .... Intra-Arterial Contrast Medium [*Medicine*] (EDAA)
IACMAG .... International Association for Computer Methods and Advances in Geomechanics (BUAC)
IACME .... Inter-American Committee for Mathematical Education (SAUS)
IACME .... Inter-American Committee of Mathematical Education (BUAC)
IACME .... International Association of Coroners and Medical Examiners (EA)
IACME .... International Association of Crafts and Small- and Medium-Sized Enterprises [*Switzerland*] (EY)
IACMHA .... Illinois Association of Community Mental Health Agencies (SRA)
IACMP .... International Association of Career Management Professionals (NTPA)
IACMST .... Inter-Agency Committee on Marine Science and Technology (SAUS)
IACNET .... Inter-American Citrus Network [*Chile*] (BUAC)
IACNRE .... International Association for Conservation of Natural Resources and Energy
IACO .... Conservative Orthopedics International Association (EA)
IACO .... Illinois Association of County Officials (SRA)
IACO .... Information Advantage, Inc. [*NASDAQ symbol*] (NASQ)
IACO .... Integrated Assembly and Checkout (SSD)
IACO .... Inter-African Coffee Organization (EAIO)
IACO .... Inter-American Coffee Organisation (BUAC)
IACO .... International Activities Coordination Office (SAUS)
IACO .... International Association of Conference Centers (SAUO)
IACO .... International Association of Correctional Officers (EA)
IACOA .... Independent Armored Car Operators Association (EA)
IACOCCA ..... I Am Chairman of Chrysler Corp. of America [*Acronym formed from name of Chrysler chairman Lee Iacocca*]
IACOD .... International Advisory Committee on Documentation, Libraries and Archives (SAUO)
IACOD .... International Agency for Cooperation on Development (SAUO)
IACODLA ...... International Advisory Committee on Documentation, Libraries, and Archives [*UNESCO*] (BUAC)
IAC of Cal .... Decisions of the Industrial Accident Commission of California [*A publication*] (DLA)
IaCogM .... Coggan Monitor, Coggan, IA [*Library symbol*] [*Library of Congress*] (LCLS)
IaCol .... Colfax Free Public Library, Colfax, IA [*Library symbol*] [*Library of Congress*] (LCLS)
IaColJ .... Jasper County Tribune, Colfax, IA [*Library symbol*] [*Library of Congress*] (LCLS)
IaColn .... Collins Public Library, Collins, IA [*Library symbol*] [*Library of Congress*] (LCLS)
IACOMS .... International Advisory Committee on Marine Sciences [*UNESCO*] (ASF)
IaCon .... Conrad Public Library, Conrad, IA [*Library symbol*] [*Library of Congress*] (LCLS)
IaConR .... Conrad Record, Conrad, IA [*Library symbol*] [*Library of Congress*] (LCLS)
IaCoon .... Coon Rapids Enterprise, Coon Rapids, IA [*Library symbol*] [*Library of Congress*] (LCLS)
IACOP .... International Armaments Cooperative Opportunities Plan
IACORDS ..... International Association of Cold Region Development Studies (SAUO)
IaCorn .... Corning Free Public Library, Corning, IA [*Library symbol*] [*Library of Congress*] (LCLS)
IaCornFP ...... Adams County Free Press, Corning, IA [*Library symbol*] [*Library of Congress*] (LCLS)
IaCorrN .... Correctionville News, Correctionville, IA [*Library symbol*] [*Library of Congress*] (LCLS)
IaCorv .... Coralville Public Library, Coralville, IA [*Library symbol*] [*Library of Congress*] (LCLS)
IaCorvC .... Coralville Courier, Coralville, IA [*Library symbol*] [*Library of Congress*] (LCLS)
IaCorwH .... Corwith Herald, Corwith, IA [*Library symbol*] [*Library of Congress*] (LCLS)
IaCoryTR ...... Corydon Times-Republican, Corydon, IA [*Library symbol*] [*Library of Congress*] (LCLS)
IaCoryWC .... Wayne County Courthouse, Corydon, IA [*Library symbol*] [*Library of Congress*] (LCLS)
IaCoryWCoC ... Wayne County Courthouse, Corydon, IA [*Library symbol*] [*Library of Congress*] (LCLS)
IACOSPAR ... Inter-American Committee on Space Research (SAUS)
IACP .... Industrial Arts Curriculum Project [*Education*] (AEE)
IACP .... Integrated Air Cancer Project [*Environmental Protection Agency*]
IACP .... Inter-African Council for Philosophy (BUAC)
IACP .... International Academy of Compounding Pharmacists (GVA)
IACP .... International Association for Child Psychiatry and Allied Professions (SAUO)
IACP .... International Association of Chiefs of Police (EA)
IACP .... International Association of Cities and Ports (BUAC)
IACP .... International Association of Computer Programmers

IACP International Association of Cooking Professionals (EA)
IACP International Association of Culinary Professionals (NTPA)
IACP Intra-Aortic Counterpulsation [*Cardiology*] (DAVI)
IACP Investment Advisory Centre of Pakistan (BUAC)
IACPA Inter-American Council of Psychiatric Associations (DAVI)
IACPAP International Association for Child Psychiatry and Allied Professions [*Later, IACAPAP*]
IACPP International Association for Cross-Cultural Psychology (BUAC)
IACPP International Association of Crime Prevention Practitioners (EA)
IACPR Inter-American Committee of Presidential Representatives
IACPR International Association of Corporate and Professional Recruiters (SAUO)
IACPS Inter-American Committee on Peaceful Settlement [*Defunct*] [*Defunct*] (EA)
IACPS International Academy of Chest Physicians and Surgeons (EA)
IACPWR Inter-Allied Committee on Post-War Requirements [*World War II*]
IaCr Cedar Rapids Public Library, Cedar Rapids, IA [*Library symbol*] [*Library of Congress*] (LCLS)
IACR Institue of Arable Crop Research [*British*]
IACR Integrated Approach to Crop Research (SAUO)
IACR Inter-American College for Radiology (SAUS)
IACR Inter-American College of Radiology (SAUO)
IACR Inter-American Congress of Radiology
IACR Inter-American Congress on Radiology (SAUO)
IACR International Agreement Competitive Restrictions (AAGC)
IACR International Association for Cryptologic Research (EA)
IACR International Association of Cancer Registries [*Lyon, France*] (EAIO)
IACRAO Illinois Association of Collegiate Registrars and Admissions Officers (SRA)
IaCrC Coe College, Cedar Rapids, IA [*Library symbol*] [*Library of Congress*] (LCLS)
IACRD Inter-American Center for Regional Development (EAIO)
IACRDP International Association of Cross-Reference Directory Publishers (EA)
IACRDVT Inter-American Center for Research and Documentation on Vocational Training (SAUS)
IACRDVT Inter-American Centre for Research and Documentation on Vocational Training [*See also CINTERFOR*] [*Montevideo, Uruguay*] (EAIO)
IaCre Cresco Public Library, Cresco, IA [*Library symbol*] [*Library of Congress*] (LCLS)
IACREE International Association of Corporate Real Estate Executives (EA)
IaCreHC Howard County Courthouse, Cresco, IA [*Library symbol*] [*Library of Congress*] (LCLS)
IACREOT International Association of Clerks, Recorders, Election Officials, and Treasurers (SAUO)
IaCres Matilda J. Gibson Memorial Library, Creston, IA [*Library symbol*] [*Library of Congress*] (LCLS)
IaCresco Cresco Public Library, Cresco, IA [*Library symbol*] [*Library of Congress*] (LCLS)
IaCrescoCoC Howard County Courthouse, Cresco, IA [*Library symbol*] [*Library of Congress*] (LCLS)
IaCrescoTP Cresco Times-Plain Dealer, Cresco, IA [*Library symbol*] [*Library of Congress*] (LCLS)
IaCresNA Creston News-Advertiser, Creston, IA [*Library symbol*] [*Library of Congress*] (LCLS)
IaCreTP Cresco Times-Plain Dealer, Cresco, IA [*Library symbol*] [*Library of Congress*] (LCLS)
IaCrG Cedar Rapids Gazette, Cedar Rapids, IA [*Library symbol*] [*Library of Congress*] (LCLS)
IaCrK Kirkwood Community College, Cedar Rapids, IA [*Library symbol*] [*Library of Congress*] (LCLS)
IACRL Italian-American Civil Rights League
IaCrL Linn County Heritage Society, Cedar Rapids, IA [*Library symbol*] [*Library of Congress*] (LCLS)
IACRLRD International Association for Comparative Research on Leukemia and Related Diseases (SAUO)
IaCrM Iowa Masonic Library, Cedar Rapids, IA [*Library symbol*] [*Library of Congress*] (LCLS)
IaCrMM Mount Mercy College, Cedar Rapids, IA [*Library symbol*] [*Library of Congress*] (LCLS)
IaCrMT Micro-Technology, Inc., Cedar Rapids, IA [*Library symbol*] [*Library of Congress*] (LCLS)
IaCroyHi Wayne County Historical Society, Croydon, IA [*Library symbol*] [*Library of Congress*] (LCLS)
IACRP International Association for the Child's Right to Play (EAIO)
IACRS Inter-Agency Committee on Radiation Safety (SAUO)
IACRS International Association of Concrete Repair Specialists (EA)
IACS IAL Consultancy Services [*Southall, England*] [*Telecommunications*] (TSSD)
IACS Indian Association for the Cultivation of Science (BUAC)
IACS Inertial Attitude Control System [*Aerospace*]
IACs Information/data Analysis Centers (SAUS)
IACS Integrated Access and Crossconnect System (ACRL)
IACS Integrated Acoustic Communication System [*Military*] (NVT)
IACS Integrated Area Control System (SAUO)
IACS Integrated Armament Control System (MCD)
IACS Integrated Avionics Communications System (SAUO)
IACS Integrated Avionics Control System (RDA)
IACS Integrated Avionics Crew Station (ACAE)
IACS Integred Acoustic Communication System (SAUS)
IACS Interactive Computer System [*Information science*]
IACS Intermediate Altitude Communication Satellite (IAA)
IACS International Academy of Christian Sociologists (BUAC)
IACS International Academy of Cosmetic Surgery [*Rome, Italy*] (EA)
IACS International Alliance for Cooperation among Schools (SAUO)
IACS International Annealed Copper Standard
IACS International Arms-Control Symposium
IACS International Association of Classification Societies (EAIO)
IACS International Association of Cooking Schools (EA)
IACS International Association of Counseling Services (EA)
IACS Irish-Australian Cultural Society (SAUO)
IACS Island Arts and Crafts Society, Victoria [*1922, founded 1910 as IACC*] (NGC)
IACS Italian-American Cultural Society (EA)
IACSAC Inter-American Catholic Social Action Confederation (SAUO)
IACSC International Association of Cold Storage Contractors (NTPA)
IACSD Inter-Agency Committee on Sustainable Development (SAUS)
IACSE Integrated Advisory Committee on Security Equipment (SAUO)
IACSE Interagency Advisory Committee on Security Equipment
IACS-LDR Integrated Acoustic Communication System - Low Data Rate (MCD)
IACSM International Association of Computer Service Managers
IACSP International Association of Counterterrorism and Security Professionals
IACSS Inter-American Conference on Social Security [*See also CISS*] [*Mexico City, Mexico*] (EAIO)
IACSS International Association for Computer Systems Security (EA)
IACST Inter-American Committee for Science and Technology
IACST International Association for Commodity Science and Technology (EAIO)
IACSW Interstate Association of Commissions on the Status of Women
IACT Illinois Association of Classroom Teachers (SAUO)
IACT Indiana Association of Cities and Towns (SAUO)
IACT Inter-Association Commission on Tsunami [*Brussels, Belgium*] (EAIO)
IACT International Alliance for Compatible Technology (SAUO)
IACT International Association for Clear Thinking (EA)
IACT International Association of Colon Therapy (EA)
IACT International Association of Counselors and Therapists (EA)
IACT International Association to Combat Terrorism [*Defunct*] (EA)
IACTE Iowa Association of Colleges for Teacher Education (SAUO)
IACTP International Association of Correctional Training Personnel (NTPA)
IACUC Institutional Animal Care and Use Committee [*Department of Agriculture*]
IACUG International Association of Computer Users Groups (EA)
IACUSD International Association of College and University Security Directors (SAUO)
IACV Idle Air Control Valve [*Fuel system*] [*Automotive engineering*]
IACV International Association of Cancer Victims [*Medicine*] (EDAA)
IACVB International Association of Convention and Visitor Bureaus (EA)
IACVF International Association of Cancer Victims and Friends (SAUO)
IACVF International Association of Cancer Victors and Friends (EA)
I/ACVIA Interaction/American Council for Voluntary International Action (EA)
IACW Inter-American Commission of Women [*Organization of American States*] [*Washington, DC*]
IACW Inter-American Congress of Women (SAUO)
IACW International Association of Crime Writers (EAIO)
IACWC International Advisory Committee on Wireless Communication (SAUS)
IACWC International Advisory Committee on Wireless Communications (SAUO)
IACWD Interagency Advisory Committee on Water Data (SAUO)
IAD Eastern Illinois University, Charleston, IL [*OCLC symbol*] (OCLC)
IAD Herative Array Divider (SAUS)
IAD Immediate Action Directive
IAD Immediate Action Drill [*Military*] (LAIN)
IAD Inactivating Dose [*Medicine*] (DMAA)
IAD Index of Axis Deficiency [*Embryology*]
IAD Industrial Automation Division (TIMI)
IAD Inebriates Acts Department (SAUO)
IAD Inflammatory Airway Disease [*Equine term*] (TED)
IAD Information Acquisition and Dissemination (SAUS)
IAD Information and Documentation [*British Film Institute*]
IAD Inhibiting Antibiotic Dose [*Medicine*] (STED)
IAD Initial Address Designator [*Computer science*] (CIST)
IAD Initiation Area Discriminator [*RADAR*]
IAD Inland Steel Company (SAUO)
IAD Inland Steel Industries, Inc. [*NYSE symbol*] (SPSG)
IAD Installation, Assembly or Detail (SAUS)
IAD Institute for American Democracy (EA)
IAD Instructional Advance Directive
IAD Instructor in Air Duties (SAUO)
IAD Integrated Access Device [*BBN Communications Corp.*]
IAD Integrated Airbase Defense
IAD Integrated Antenna Detector (SAUS)
IAD Integrated Area Development (SAUS)
IAD Integrated Automated Documentation (SAUS)
IAD Integrated Automatic Documentation [*System*]
IAD Interactive Debugging [*Computer science*] (CIST)
IAD Inter-American Development Bank (SAUO)
I-AD Inter-American Dialogue (SAUS)
IAD Interest Adjustment Date (FOTI)
IAD Interface Agreement Document (KSC)
IAD Interface Analysis Document (KSC)
IAD Internal Absorbed Dose
IAD Internal Aerodynamics (SAUS)
IAD Internal Affairs Department (SAUO)
IAD Internal Affairs Division (SAUO)
IAD Internal Audit Division [*Environmental Protection Agency*] (GFGA)
IAD International Activities Division [*Central Intelligence Agency*] (CARL)

IAD.............. International Agricultural Distribution (SAUS)
IAD.............. International Association of Documentalists and Information Officers [*France*] (EY)
IAD.............. International Astrophysical Decade
IAD.............. International Automotive Design
IAD.............. Internationale Arbeitsgemeinschaft Donauforschung [*International Working Association for Danube Research*] (EAIO)
IAD.............. Internet Addiction Disorder (SAUS)
IAD.............. Internet Address Detector (SAUS)
IAD.............. Interrupt Analyzer/Distributor (SAUS)
IAD.............. Inventory Adjustment Document
IAD.............. Inventory Available Date (TEL)
IAD.............. Ion-Assisted Deposition [*Coating technology*]
IAD.............. Ion Beam Activated Deposition [*Coating technology*]
IAD.............. Irish Aircraft Distributors Ltd. (SAUO)
IAD.............. Irish Association for Documentation (SAUO)
IAD.............. Washington [*District of Columbia*] Dulles Airport [*Airport symbol*]
IaDa............. Davenport Public Library, Davenport, IA [*Library symbol*] [*Library of Congress*] (LCLS)
IADA............ Idaho Automobile Dealers Association (SRA)
IADA............ Illinois Automobile Dealer Association (SRA)
IADA............ Independent Aeronautical Dealers Association [*Defunct*] (EA)
IADA............ Independent Automotive Damage Appraisers Association [*Milwaukee, WI*] (EA)
IADA............ Inland Auto Dismantlers Association (SRA)
IADA............ International Association for Conservation of Books, Paper and Archival Material (SAUO)
IADA............ International Atomic-Development Authority [*Proposed by Bernard M. Baruch, 1946, but never created*]
IADA............ Internationale Arbeitsgemeinschaft der Archiv-, Bibliotheks-, und Graphikrestauratoren [*International Association for Conservation of Books, Paper, and Archival Material*] (EAIO)
IADA............ Interstate Agreement on Detainers Act [*1970*]
IADA............ Iowa Automobile Dealers Association (SRA)
IaDaCM........ Catholic Messenger, Davenport, IA [*Library symbol*] [*Library of Congress*] (LCLS)
IaDaCoC...... Scott County Courthouse, Davenport, IA [*Library symbol*] [*Library of Congress*] (LCLS)
IaDaGL........ Grant Law Library, Davenport, IA [*Library symbol*] [*Library of Congress*] (LCLS)
IaDaM.......... Davenport Public Museum, Davenport, IA [*Library symbol*] [*Library of Congress*] (LCLS)
IaDaMC........ Marycrest College, Davenport, IA [*Library symbol*] [*Library of Congress*] (LCLS)
IaDaP.......... Palmer College of Chiropractic, Davenport, IA [*Library symbol*] [*Library of Congress*] (LCLS)
IaDaPM........ Putnam Museum, Davenport, IA [*Library symbol*] [*Library of Congress*] (LCLS)
IaDaQT........ Quad City Times, Davenport, IA [*Library symbol*] [*Library of Congress*] (LCLS)
IaDaSA........ Saint Ambrose College, Davenport, IA [*Library symbol*] [*Library of Congress*] (LCLS)
IADA-UT....... Independent Auto Dealers Association - Utah (SRA)
IaDayR......... Dayton Review, Dayton, IA [*Library symbol*] [*Library of Congress*] (LCLS)
IADB............ Innovative/Alternative Pollution Control Technology Facility File Data Base (SAUS)
IADB............ Inter-American Defense Board (EA)
IADB............ Inter-American Development Bank [*Also, IDB*]
IADB-MED.... Inter-American Defense Board Medal [*Military decoration*]
IADBWA....... Inter-American Development Bank's Wives Association (EA)
IADC............ Andean Development Corporation (SAUO)
IaDc............. Dallas Center Public Library, Dallas Center, IA [*Library symbol*] [*Library of Congress*] (LCLS)
IADC............ Image Assisted Data Capture (SAUS)
IADC............ Inter-Agency Space Debris Coordination Committee (SAUS)
IADC............ Inter-American Defense College [*Washington, DC*]
IADC............ Inter-American Development Commission
IADC............ Inter-American Drug Commission (SAUS)
IADC............ Interdepartmental Advisory and Development Committee (EERA)
IADC............ International Alliance for Distribution by Cable [*Formerly, International Alliancefor Distribution by Wire*] (EA)
IADC............ International Association of Defense Counsel (EA)
IADC............ International Association of Dentistry for Children [*British*] (EAIO)
IADC............ International Association of Dredging Companies [*The Hague, Netherlands*] (EA)
IADC............ International Association of Drilling Contractors
IADC............ International Association of Insurance Counsel (SAUO)
IaDCC.......... College Chips, Luther College, Decorah, IA [*Library symbol*] [*Library of Congress*] (LCLS)
IADCCT........ International Association of Duncan Certified Ceramic Teachers (EA)
IADCJ.......... International Association of Dentistry for Children Journal [*Medicine*] (EDAA)
I/ADCSP....... Initial/Advanced Defense Communications Satellite Program (SAA)
I/ADCSP....... Interim/Advanced Defense Communications Satellite Program (DNAB)
IADD............ Index to American Doctoral Dissertations (journ.) (SAUS)
IADD............ International Association of Diecutting and Diemaking (NTPA)
IADE............ Integral Absolute Delay Error (SAUS)
IADE............ Integral of Absolute Delay Error (IAA)
IADE............ Interactive Data Enhancement (ACAE)
IAdEM.......... Internacia Asocio de Esperantistaj Matematikistoj [*International Association of Esperantist Mathematicians*] (EAIO)
IaDen........... Denison Carnegie Library, Denison, IA [*Library symbol*] [*Library of Congress*] (LCLS)
IaDenB......... Denison Bulletin, Denison, IA [*Library symbol*] [*Library of Congress*] (LCLS)
IaDenR......... Denison Review, Denison, IA [*Library symbol*] [*Library of Congress*] (LCLS)
IADES.......... Integrated Attitude Detection and Estimation System (SAUS)
IaDewO........ Observer, De Witt, IA [*Library symbol*] [*Library of Congress*] (LCLS)
IaDexM........ Dexter Museum, Dexter, IA [*Library symbol*] [*Library of Congress*] (LCLS)
IADF............ Icelandic Air Defence Force (SAUS)
IADF............ Inter-American Association for Democracy and Freedom (EA)
IADF............ Iraqi Air Defence Forces (SAUS)
IADF............ Irish American Defense Fund [*Defunct*] (EA)
IADFA.......... International Association of Dento-Facial Abnormalities [*Medicine*] (EDAA)
IADGES........ Indian Air Defence Ground Environment System (SAUS)
IADH............ Inappropriate Antidiuretic Hormone [*Endocrinology*] (MAE)
IADH............ International Association of Dentistry for the Handicapped [*Toronto, ON*] (EAIO)
IADHS.......... Inappropriate Antidiuretic Hormone Syndrome [*Endocrinology*]
IaDiaR......... Diagonal Reporter, Diagonal, IA [*Library symbol*] [*Library of Congress*] (LCLS)
IADIC........... Integration Analog-to-Digital Converter (IEEE)
IADIS........... Irish Association for Documentation and Information Science (SAUO)
IADIS........... Irish Association for Documentation and Information Services (NITA)
IADIS........... Irish Association of Documentation and Information Services (SAUS)
IADIWU........ International Association for the Development of International and World Universities [*See also AIDUIM*] [*Aulnay-Sous-Bois, France*] (EAIO)
IaDJ............. Decorah Journal, Decorah, IA [*Library symbol*] [*Library of Congress*] (LCLS)
IADL............ Instrumental Activities of Daily Living (SAUS)
IADL............ Instrumental Activities of Daily Living Survey [*Department of Health and Human Services*] (GFGA)
IADL............ International Association of Democratic Lawyers [*Brussels, Belgium*] (EA)
IADL............ Italian-American Defense League (SAUS)
IaDL............. Luther College, Decorah, IA [*Library symbol*] [*Library of Congress*] (LCLS)
IADLA.......... International Association for the Development of Documentation (SAUS)
IADLA.......... International Association for the Development of Documentation, Libraries and Archives in Africa (SAUO)
IaDm............ Des Moines Public Library, Des Moines, IA [*Library symbol*] [*Library of Congress*] (LCLS)
IADM........... Inverse Augmented Data Manipulator (SAUS)
IaDmB.......... Iowa Commission for the Blind, Des Moines, IA [*Library symbol*] [*Library of Congress*] (LCLS)
IaDmBR....... Business Record, Des Moines, IA [*Library symbol*] [*Library of Congress*] (LCLS)
IaDmC.......... Iowa State Commerce Commission, Records and Information Center, Des Moines, IA [*Library symbol*] [*Library of Congress*] (LCLS)
IaDmCI........ Central Iowa Regional Library System, Des Moines, IA [*Library symbol*] [*Library of Congress*] (LCLS)
IaDmD.......... Drake University, Des Moines, IA [*Library symbol*] [*Library of Congress*] (LCLS)
IaDmDC....... Dowling College, Des Moines, IA [*Library symbol*] [*Library of Congress*] (LCLS)
IaDmD-L...... Drake University, Law School, Des Moines, IA [*Library symbol*] [*Library of Congress*] (LCLS)
IaDmE.......... Iowa State Education Association, Des Moines, IA [*Library symbol*] [*Library of Congress*] (LCLS)
IAD-MEMA... International Aftermarket Division - Motor and Equipment Manufacturers Association (NTPA)
IADMFR....... International Association of Dento-Maxillo-Facial Radiology (EAIO)
IaDmG.......... Grand View College, Des Moines, IA [*Library symbol*] [*Library of Congress*] (LCLS)
IaDmHN....... Highland Park News, Des Moines, IA [*Library symbol*] [*Library of Congress*] (LCLS)
IaDmL.......... Iowa Legionnaire, Des Moines, IA [*Library symbol*] [*Library of Congress*] (LCLS)
IaDmLN....... Lee Town News, Des Moines, IA [*Library symbol*] [*Library of Congress*] (LCLS)
IaDmMet...... Des Moines Metropolitan Service Area Library Cooperative, Des Moines, IA [*Library symbol*] [*Library of Congress*] (LCLS)
IaDmOF....... Odd Fellows Temple, Des Moines, IA [*Library symbol*] [*Library of Congress*] (LCLS)
IaDmPH....... Pioneer Hi-Bred International, Inc., Des Moines, IA [*Library symbol*] [*Library of Congress*] (LCLS)
IaDmR.......... Daily Record, Des Moines, IA [*Library symbol*] [*Library of Congress*] (LCLS)
IaDmRT....... Des Moines Register-Tribune, Des Moines, IA [*Library symbol*] [*Library of Congress*] (LCLS)
IaDmS.......... College of Osteopathic Medicine and Surgery, Des Moines, IA [*Library symbol*] [*Library of Congress*] (LCLS)
IADMS......... International Association for Dance Medicine and Science
IaDmV.......... United States Veterans Administration Hospital, Des Moines, IA [*Library symbol*] [*Library of Congress*] (LCLS)
IADN............ Integrated Atmospheric Deposition Network [*Environmental Protection Agency*] (EPAT)
IaDN............. Norwegian-American Historical Museum and Library, Decorah, IA [*Library symbol*] [*Library of Congress*] (LCLS)
IaDo............. Dows Community Library, Dows, IA [*Library symbol*] [*Library of Congress*] (LCLS)
IADO............ Instituto Argentine de Oceanografia [*Marine science*] (OSRA)
IADO............ Iran Agriculture Development Organization (SAUO)

IADO .... Iranian Agriculture Development Organization (SAUS)
IaDon .... Donnellson Public Library, Donnellson, IA [*Library symbol*] [*Library of Congress*] (LCLS)
IaDonS .... Donnellson Star, Donnellson, IA [*Library symbol*] [*Library of Congress*] (LCLS)
IaDooP .... Press, Doon, IA [*Library symbol*] [*Library of Congress*] (LCLS)
IADP .... INTELSAT Assistance and Development Program
IADP .... Intensive Agricultural District Program (SAUS)
IADP .... Inter-American Driving Permit
IADP .... International Association of Dollbaby Parents [*Defunct*] (EA)
IADPC .... Inter-Agency Data Processing Center (SAUO)
IADPC .... Interagency Data Processing Committee
IADPG .... Intelligence Automatic Data Processing Group (CINC)
IaDPO .... Decorah Public Opinion, Decorah, IA [*Library symbol*] [*Library of Congress*] (LCLS)
IADPPNW .... International Architects (SAUS)
IADPPNW .... International Architects Designers Planners for the Prevention of Nuclear War (SAUO)
IaDQT .... Quad City Times, Davenport, IA [*Library symbol*] [*Library of Congress*] (LCLS)
IADR .... Institute for Animal Disease Research [*Research center*] [*British*] (IRC)
IAdr .... Instruction Address (SAUS)
IADR .... International and American Associations for Dental Research (SAUO)
IADR .... International Association for Dental Research (EA)
IADRS .... International Association of Dive Rescue Specialists (EA)
IADRWG ...... Interagency Alternative Dispute Resolution Working Group
IADS .... Iceland Air Defence System (SAUS)
IADS .... Immunoadsorbent (DB)
IAds .... Immunoadsorption [*Medicine*] (EDAA)
IADS .... Imperial Alliance for the Defence of Sunday (SAUO)
IADS .... Integrated Air Defense System (MCD)
IADS .... Intensive Area Development Scheme (SAUS)
IADS .... Interactive Authoring and Display System (SAUO)
IADS .... Interim Air Defense System (SAUO)
IADS .... International Agricultural Development Service [*Later, WIIAD*] [*Department of Agriculture*]
IADS .... International Air Defense System (SAUS)
IADS .... International Association of Dental Students [*British*]
IADS .... International Association of Department Stores [*See also AIGM*] (EAIO)
IA DSA .... Intra-Arterial Digital Subtraction Arteriography [*Cardiology*] (DAVI)
IADSA .... Intraaterial Digital Subtraction Angiography [*Medicine*]
IAD-System... Integrated-Automated-Documentation System (SAUS)
IADT .... Initial Active Duty for Training [*Military*] (AABC)
IADT .... Initial Active Duty Training (SAUO)
IADT .... Integrated Automatic Detection and Tracking [*Military*] (CAAL)
IADT .... Integrated Automatic Direction System (SAUS)
IaDu .... Carnegie-Stout Free Public Library, Dubuque, IA [*Library symbol*] [*Library of Congress*] (LCLS)
IaDuA .... Aquinas Institute, Dubuque, IA [*Library symbol*] [*Library of Congress*] (LCLS)
IaDuAn .... Antique Trade Weekly, Dubuque, IA [*Library symbol*] [*Library of Congress*] (LCLS)
IaDuCl .... Clarke College, Dubuque, IA [*Library symbol*] [*Library of Congress*] (LCLS)
IaDuCo .... Clarke Courier, Dubuque, IA [*Library symbol*] [*Library of Congress*] (LCLS)
IaDuL .... Loras College, Dubuque, IA [*Library symbol*] [*Library of Congress*] (LCLS)
IaDuLe .... Dubuque Leader, Dubuque, IA [*Library symbol*] [*Library of Congress*] (LCLS)
IaDuN .... New Melleray Abbey, Dubuque, IA [*Library symbol*] [*Library of Congress*] (LCLS)
IaDunR .... Dunlap Reporter, Dunlap, IA [*Library symbol*] [*Library of Congress*] (LCLS)
IaDuT .... Schools of Theology in Dubuque, Dubuque, IA [*Library symbol*] [*Library of Congress*] (LCLS)
IaDuU .... University of Dubuque, Dubuque, IA [*Library symbol*] [*Library of Congress*] (LCLS)
IaDuU-S ...... University of Dubuque, Theological Seminary, Dubuque, IA [*Library symbol*] [*Library of Congress*] (LCLS)
IaDuW .... Wartburg Theological Seminary, Dubuque, IA [*Library symbol*] [*Library of Congress*] (LCLS)
IaDuWi .... Dubuque Witness, Dubuque, IA [*Library symbol*] [*Library of Congress*] (LCLS)
IaDv .... Denver Public Library, Denver, IA [*Library symbol*] [*Library of Congress*] (LCLS)
IaDvF .... Forum, Denver, IA [*Library symbol*] [*Library of Congress*] (LCLS)
IADWS .... Interim Air Defense Weapon System [*Army*]
IaDy .... Matthias M. Hoffman Public Library, Dyersville, IA [*Library symbol*] [*Library of Congress*] (LCLS)
IaDyC .... Dyersville Commercial, Dyersville, IA [*Library symbol*] [*Library of Congress*] (LCLS)
IaDysR .... Dysart Reporter, Dysart, IA [*Library symbol*] [*Library of Congress*] (LCLS)
IADZ .... Inner Air Defense Zone (SAUO)
IaE .... Eagle Grove Public Library, Eagle Grove, IA [*Library symbol*] [*Library of Congress*] (LCLS)
IAE .... Felician College, Chicago, IL [*OCLC symbol*] (OCLC)
IAE .... In Any Event [*Internet language*] [*Computer science*]
IAE .... Information Analysis and Evaluation (SAUS)
IAE .... Information and Education (IAA)
IAE .... Infrared Auroral Emission
IAE .... Institut d'Administration des Entreprises [*Institute of Company Management*] [*Information service or system*] (IID)
IAE .... Institute for Agricultural Engineering (SAUO)
IAE .... Institute for Atomic Energy, Kjeller (SAUO)
IAE .... Institute for the Advancement of Engineering (EA)
IAE .... Institute of Aeronautical Engineers (SAUO)
IAE .... Institute of Army Education (SAUO)
IAE .... Institute of Atomic Energy [*Academy of Sciences, USSR*]
IAE .... Institute of Automobile Engineers
IAE .... Institution of Agricultural Engineers (SAUO)
IAE .... Institution of Automotive Engineers (SAUO)
IAE .... Instituto Asistencia Estadual (SAUO)
IAE .... Integral Absolute Error (SAUS)
IAE .... Integral of Absolute Error
IAE .... Integrated Absolute Error (SAUS)
IAE .... Integrated Applications Environment [*Computer science*] (GART)
IAE .... Integrated Architecture Experiment (ACAE)
IAE .... Inter-Asia Equities [*Vancouver Stock Exchange symbol*]
IAE .... Intergral Absolute Error (SAUS)
IAE .... International Aero Engines (ACAE)
IAE .... International Animal Exchange (SAUO)
IAE .... International Archives of Ethnography. Leiden (SAUS)
IAE .... International Association for Ecology (SAUO)
IAE .... International Association of Ethicists (EA)
IAE .... International Atomic Exposition (SAUS)
IAE .... Interstate Airlines Ltd. [*Nigeria*] [*ICAO designator*] (FAAC)
IAE .... Intra-Atrial Electrocardiogram [*Cardiology*] (MAE)
IAE .... Iscrizioni Antico-Ebraici Palestinesi (BJA)
IAE .... Iskra Associated Enterprise [*Yugoslavia*] [*Telecommunications*]
IAEA .... Institute of Asian Economic Affairs (SAUO)
IAEA .... Institute of Automotive Engineer Assessors [*British*] (EAIO)
IAEA .... Institute of Automotive Engineers of America (SAUO)
IAeA .... Institution of Aeronautical Engineers (SAUO)
IAEA .... Inter-American Education Association (EA)
IAEA .... International Advertising Executives' Association (NTCM)
IAEA .... International Agricultural Exchange Association [*British*] (EA)
IAEA .... International Association for Educational Assessment (EA)
IAEA .... International Association of Aeronomy and Geomagnetism (SAUS)
IAEA .... International Association of Empirical Aesthetics [*Paris, France*] (EAIO)
IAEA .... International Atomic Energy Accord (DOMA)
IAEA .... International Atomic Energy Agency [*Database originator and operator*] [*United Nations*] [*Austria*]
IAEA .... International Atomic Energy Authority (SAUS)
IAEA .... Iraqi Atomic Energy Authority (SAUO)
IAEAC .... International Association of Environmental Analytical Chemistry [*Therwil, Switzerland*] (EAIO)
IAEACPD ...... Inter-American Emergency Advisory Committee for Political Defense
IAEA-MEL .... IMEL and Monaco Laboratory (SAUS)
IAEA-MEL .... International Atomic Energy Agency Marine Environmental Laboratory [*Marine science*] (OSRA)
IaEarE .... Earlham Echo, Earlham, IA [*Library symbol*] [*Library of Congress*] (LCLS)
IaEarv .... Ruth Suckhow Memorial Library, Earlville, IA [*Library symbol*] [*Library of Congress*] (LCLS)
IaEaryN .... Early News, Early, IA [*Library symbol*] [*Library of Congress*] (LCLS)
IAEA Tech Rep Ser... International Atomic Energy Agency. Technical Report Series (journ.) (SAUS)
IAEC .... International Adult Education Circle (SAUO)
IAEC .... International Association of Electrical Contractors [*See also AIE*] (EAIO)
IAEC .... International Association of Environmental Coordinators [*Belgium*] (DCTA)
IAEC .... International Atomic Energy Committee
IAEC .... Israel Atomic Research Energy (SAUS)
IAECOSOC.... Inter-American Economic and Social Council [*United Nations*]
IAED .... International Association of Exchange Dealers [*British*] (EA)
IAEDB .... International Association for the Education of Deafblind (SAUO)
IaEdd .... Eddyville Public Library, Eddyville, IA [*Library symbol*] [*Library of Congress*] (LCLS)
IaEddT .... Eddyville Tribune, Eddyville, IA [*Library symbol*] [*Library of Congress*] (LCLS)
IaEdgR .... Edgewood Reminder, Edgewood, IA [*Library symbol*] [*Library of Congress*] (LCLS)
IAEDP .... International Association of Eating Disorders Professionals (EA)
IAEDT .... International Association of Equine Dental Technicians (EA)
IaEE .... Eagle, Eagle Grove, IA [*Library symbol*] [*Library of Congress*] (LCLS)
IAeE .... Institute of Aeronautical Engineers
IAeE .... Institution of Aeronautical Engineers (SAUO)
IAEE .... International Association for Earthquake Engineering [*ICSU*] [*Tokyo, Japan*] (EAIO)
IAEE .... International Association for Energy Economics (EERA)
IAEE .... International Association for/of Earthquake Engineering (SAUO)
IAEE .... International Association of Earthquake Engineering (or Engineers) (SAUS)
IAEE .... International Association of Earthquake Engineers (SAUO)
IAEE .... International Association of Energy Economists (EA)
IAEE .... International Automotive Engineering Exposition (SAUS)
IAEE .... Israel Association of Environmental Engineers (SAUO)
IAEEA .... International Association for the Evaluation of Educational Achievement (SAUO)
IAEF .... Internacia Asocio de la Esperantistaj Fervojistoj (SAUO)
IAEG .... International Association for Engineering Geology (SAUS)
IAEG .... International Association for/of Engineering Geology (SAUO)
IAEG .... International Association of Engineering Geologists (SAUO)

IAEG............ International Association of Engineering Geology [*International Union of Geological Sciences*] [*ICSU*] [*Paris, France*] (EA)
IAEGC.......... Inter-Agency Electronic Grants Committee
IAEI............ International Association of Electrical Inspectors (EA)
IAEJ............ Interfaith Action for Economic Justice (EA)
IAEKM.......... International Association of Electronic Keyboard Aeronomy Manufacturers (SAUO)
IAEKM.......... International Association of Electronic Keyboard Manufacturers (NTPA)
IAEL............ Inital Allowance Equipage List (SAUS)
IAEL............ Initial Allowance Equipage List [*Military*] (CAAL)
IAEL............ International Aero Engineers Ltd. (SAUO)
IAEL............ International Association for Esperanto in Libraries [*See also TEBA*] (EAIO)
IAEL............ International Association of Electrical Leagues [*Later, ILEA*] (EA)
IAEL............ International Association of Entertainment Lawyers [*Amsterdam, Netherlands*] (EAIO)
IaElbTHi....... Tama County Historical Society, Elberon, IA [*Library symbol*] [*Library of Congress*] (LCLS)
IaEld............ Eldon Carnegie Library, Eldon, IA [*Library symbol*] [*Library of Congress*] (LCLS)
IaEldF.......... Eldon Forum, Eldon, IA [*Library symbol*] [*Library of Congress*] (LCLS)
IaEldoHHi.... Hardin County Historical Society, Eldora, IA [*Library symbol*] [*Library of Congress*] (LCLS)
IaEldoHi....... Hardin County Historical Society, Eldora, IA [*Library symbol*] [*Library of Congress*] (LCLS)
IaEldoHL...... Herald-Ledger, Eldora, IA [*Library symbol*] [*Library of Congress*] (LCLS)
IaEldoI......... Hardin County Index, Eldora, IA [*Library symbol*] [*Library of Congress*] (LCLS)
IaEldr........... Scott County Library, Eldridge, IA [*Library symbol*] [*Library of Congress*] (LCLS)
IaEldrN........ North Scott Press, Eldridge, IA [*Library symbol*] [*Library of Congress*] (LCLS)
IaElgE.......... Elgin Echo, Elgin, IA [*Library symbol*] [*Library of Congress*] (LCLS)
IaElk............ Elkader Public Library, Elkader, IA [*Library symbol*] [*Library of Congress*] (LCLS)
IaElkCR........ Clayton County Register, Elkader, IA [*Library symbol*] [*Library of Congress*] (LCLS)
IaElkHi......... Elkader Historical Society, Elkader, IA [*Library symbol*] [*Library of Congress*] (LCLS)
IaElkhR........ Elk Horn-Kimballton Review, Elk Horn, IA [*Library symbol*] [*Library of Congress*] (LCLS)
IaEll............. Elliott Public Library, Elliott, IA [*Library symbol*] [*Library of Congress*] (LCLS)
IaElmR......... Elma Reminder, Elma, IA [*Library symbol*] [*Library of Congress*] (LCLS)
IaEls............ Ellsworth Public Library, Ellsworth, IA [*Library symbol*] [*Library of Congress*] (LCLS)
IaEm............ Emmetsburg Public Library, Emmetsburg, IA [*Library symbol*] [*Library of Congress*] (LCLS)
IAEM............ Institute of Higher Military Studies (SAUS)
IAEM............ International Association for Exposition Management (NTPA)
IAEM............ International Atomic Energy Agency (USDC)
IaEmD.......... Emmetsburg Democrat, Emmetsburg, IA [*Library symbol*] [*Library of Congress*] (LCLS)
IaEmR.......... Emmetsburg Reporter, Emmetsburg, IA [*Library symbol*] [*Library of Congress*] (LCLS)
IAEMS.......... International Association of Environmental Mutagen Societies [*Helsinki, Finland*] (EAIO)
IAEO............ International Atomic Energy Organization (SAUO)
IAEP............ International Academy of Eclectic Psychotherapists [*St. Ives, NSW, Australia*] (EAIO)
IAEP............ International Assessment for Educational Progress (SAUS)
IAEP............ International Association of Equine Practitioners (GVA)
IAEP............ International Atomic Energy Pool (SAUO)
IAEPC.......... Incorporated Association of Electric Power Companies (SAUO)
IaEpD.......... Divine Word College, Epworth, IA [*Library symbol*] [*Library of Congress*] (LCLS)
IAEPO.......... International Association of Educational Peace Officers (EA)
IAER............ Institute of Applied Economic Research [*Concordia University*] [*Canada*] [*Research center*] (RCD)
IAERU.......... Institute for Atomic Energy Rikkyo University (SAUO)
IaEs............ Estherville Public Library, Estherville, IA [*Library symbol*] [*Library of Congress*] (LCLS)
IAeS............ Institute of Aeronautical Sciences (SAUO)
IAeS............ Institute of Aeronautical Services (SAUO)
IAES............ Institute of Aerospace [*formerly, Aeronautical*] Sciences
IAeS............ Institute of Aerospace Sciences (SAUO)
IAES............ Intelligent Array Expansion System (SAUS)
IAES............ Interim Alternative Educational Setting
IAES............ Interim Aquanaut Equipment System (PDAA)
IAES............ International Academy for Environmental Safety
IAES............ International Academy of Environmental Safety (SAUO)
IAES............ International Association for the Exchange of Students (SAUO)
IAES............ International Association of Electrotypers and Stereotypers [*Later, Printing Platemakers Association*]
IAESC.......... Inter-American Economic and Social Council [*United Nations*]
IAESC.......... International Association of Evening Student Councils [*Later, USAES*] (EA)
IaEsN.......... Estherville Daily News, Estherville, IA [*Library symbol*] [*Library of Congress*] (LCLS)
IAESP.......... Indiana Association of Elementary School Principals (SAUO)
IAESP.......... Iowa Association of Elementary School Principals (SAUO)
IAESR.......... Institute of Applied Economic and Social Research (EERA)
IAE Standards... Institution of Automobile Engineers Standards (SAUS)
IAESTE......... International Association for the Exchange of Students for Technical Experience [*Lisbon, Portugal*] (EAIO)
IAESTE/US... International Association for the Exchange of Students for Technical Experience-United States (SAUO)
IaEsxFN....... First National Bank, Essex, IA [*Library symbol*] [*Library of Congress*] (LCLS)
IaEsxI.......... Essex Independent, Essex, IA [*Library symbol*] [*Library of Congress*] (LCLS)
IAET............ In-Flight Aeromedical Evacuation Team
IAET............ International Association for Enterostomal Therapy (EA)
IAETE.......... Institute for the Advancement of Emerging Technologies in Education
IAETF.......... International Anti-Euthanasia Task Force (EA)
IAETL.......... International Association of Environmental Testing Laboratories (or Laboratory) (SAUO)
IaEveN......... Everly News, Everly, IA [*Library symbol*] [*Library of Congress*] (LCLS)
IAEVG.......... International Association for Educational and Vocational Guidance [*See also AIOSP*] [*Belfast, Northern Ireland*] (EAIO)
IAEVI........... International Association for Educational and Vocational Information [*See also AIISUP*] [*Paris, France*] (EAIO)
IaEvS........... Black Hawk County Sun, Evansdale, IA [*Library symbol*] [*Library of Congress*] (LCLS)
IAEWP.......... International Association of Educators for World Peace (EA)
IaExJ........... Audubon County Journal, Exira, IA [*Library symbol*] [*Library of Congress*] (LCLS)
IAF.............. EPAG - Group Air France [*ICAO designator*] (FAAC)
IAF.............. First Australia Fund, Inc. [*AMEX symbol*] (SPSG)
IAF.............. Governors State University, Park Forest South, IL [*OCLC symbol*] (OCLC)
IAF.............. Idiopathic Alveolar Fibrosis [*Medicine*] (DMAA)
IAF.............. Image Analysis Facility [*Computer science*] (PDAA)
IAF.............. Immobilizing Accelerating Factor (PDAA)
IAF.............. Incentive Advance Funding (SAUO)
IAF.............. Independent Air Force [*British military*] (DMA)
IAF.............. Indian Air Force
IAF.............. Indian Airforce (SAUS)
IAF.............. Indian Armoured Formation (SAUO)
IAF.............. Indian Army Form [*British military*] (DMA)
IAF.............. Indian Auxiliary Force [*British*]
IAF.............. Indirect-Arc Furnace (SAUS)
IAF.............. Indium Arsenide Filter
IAF.............. Indonesian Air Force
IAF.............. Induced-Air Flotation [*Chemical engineering*]
IAF.............. Industrial Air Filtration
IAF.............. Industrial Areas Foundation (EA)
IAF.............. Information and Forwarding (MUGU)
IAF.............. Information of the Armed Forces (SAUS)
IAF.............. Inhibiting Activity Factor [*Medicine*] (MELL)
IAF.............. Initial Approach Fix [*Aviation*] (AFM)
IAF.............. Initiative America Foundation (EA)
IAF.............. Institut Armand-Frappier [*University of Quebec*] [*Formerly, Institute of Microbiology and Hygiene of Montreal*] [*Research center*] (RCD)
IAF.............. Institute for Alternative Futures [*Defunct*] (EA)
IAF.............. Institute on American Freedoms [*Defunct*]
IAF.............. Instrument Air Filter
IAF.............. Instrument Approach Fix
IAF.............. Interactive Applications Facility (SAUO)
IAF.............. Interactive Facility [*Control Data Corp.*]
IAF.............. Inter-African Force (SAUS)
IAF.............. Interallied Force [*NATO*] (NATG)
IAF.............. Inter-American Force (SAUO)
IAF.............. Inter-American Foundation (MCD)
IAF.............. International Abolitionist Federation [*India*]
IAF.............. International Accreditation Forum [*For quality control*]
IAF.............. International Activities Fund [*Canadian Labour Congress*] [*See also FAI*]
IAF.............. International Aeronautical Federation
IAF.............. International Aikido Federation [*Tokyo, Japan*] (EAIO)
IAF.............. International Apparel Federation [*Berlin, Federal Republic of Germany*] (EAIO)
IAF.............. International Aquaculture Foundation (EA)
IAF.............. International Arab Federation
IAF.............. International Archery Federation (EA)
IAF.............. International Association for Falconry and Conservation of Birds of Prey (EAIO)
IAF.............. International Association Futuribles (SAUO)
IAF.............. International Association of Firefighters (SAUO)
IAF.............. International Astronautical Federation [*ICSU*] [*Research center*] [*France*]
IAF.............. International Athletic Footwear and Apparel Manufacturers Association [*Zurich, Switzerland*] Defunct] (EAIO)
IAF.............. International Automobile Federation (SAUO)
IAF.............. International Autumn Fair [*British*] (ITD)
IAF.............. Internet Address Finder [*Computer science*]
IAF.............. Internet Administration Framework (GART)
IAF.............. Interview After Flight (SAUS)
IAF.............. Intra-Alaska Facsimile [*National Weather Service*]
IAF.............. (Iodoacetamido)fluorescein [*Biochemical label*]
IAF.............. Islamic Action Front [*Political party*] [*Jordan*]
IAF.............. Israeli Air-Force [*ICAO designator*] (FAAC)
IAF.............. Italian Air Force (NATG)
IAF.............. Italian American Forum [*Defunct*] (EA)
IAF.............. Office of Information for the Armed Forces (AABC)

IAFA Inter-American Foundation for the Arts [*Defunct*]
IAFA International Association for the Fantastic in the Arts (EA)
IAFA International Aviation Facilities Act [*1948*]
IAFA Internet Anonymous FTP Archive (SAUO)
IAFAC Inter-American Federation of Automobile-Clubs (SAUO)
IAFAE Inter-American Federation for Adult Education
IaFair Fairfield Public Library, Fairfield, IA [*Library symbol*] [*Library of Congress*] (LCLS)
IaFairL Fairfield Daily Ledger, Fairfield, IA [*Library symbol*] [*Library of Congress*] (LCLS)
IaFairM Maharishi International University, Fairfield, IA [*Library symbol*] [*Library of Congress*] (LCLS)
IaFarmL Van Buren County Leader, Farmington, IA [*Library symbol*] [*Library of Congress*] (LCLS)
IAFAW International Association of Friends of Angkor Wat (EAIO)
IaFay Fayette Community Library, Fayette, IA [*Library symbol*] [*Library of Congress*] (LCLS)
IaFayHHi Fayette County Helpers Club and Historical Society, Fayette, IA [*Library symbol*] [*Library of Congress*] (LCLS)
IaFayL Fayette Leader, Fayette, IA [*Library symbol*] [*Library of Congress*] (LCLS)
IaFayU Upper Iowa University, Fayette, IA [*Library symbol*] [*Library of Congress*] (LCLS)
IAFB Institute of Applied Forth Research (SAUS)
IAFB Interim Airframe Bulletin
IAFC Instantaneous Automatic Frequency Control
IAFC Inter-American Freight Conference (SAUO)
IAFC Inter-American Freight Conference - Section C (EA)
IAFC Interim Airframe Change (NG)
IAFC International Association of Financial Consultants (BARN)
IAFC International Association of Fire Chiefs (EA)
IAFC Irwin Allen Fan Club [*Defunct*] (EA)
IAFCF International Association of Fire Chiefs Foundation (EA)
IAFCI Inter-American Federation of the Construction Industry [*See also FIIC*] [*Mexico City, Mexico*] (EAIO)
IaFcS Forest City Summit, Forest City, IA [*Library symbol*] [*Library of Congress*] (LCLS)
IAFCT International Association of French-Speaking Congress Towns [*See also AIVFC*] [*France*] (EAIO)
IaFcW Waldorf College, Forest City, IA [*Library symbol*] [*Library of Congress*] (LCLS)
IaFd Fort Dodge Public Library, Fort Dodge, IA [*Library symbol*] [*Library of Congress*] (LCLS)
IAFD International Association of Food Distribution (SAUS)
IAFD International Association of/on Food Distribution (SAUO)
IAFD International Association on Food Distribution
IaFdIC Iowa Central Community College, Fort Dodge, IA [*Library symbol*] [*Library of Congress*] (LCLS)
IaFdM Fort Dodge Messenger, Fort Dodge, IA [*Library symbol*] [*Library of Congress*] (LCLS)
IAFE International Association of Fairs and Exhibitions (SAUS)
IAFE International Association of Fairs and Expositions (EA)
IAFE International Association of Fish Ethologists [*Normal, IL*] (ASF)
IAFEC International Association of Family Entertainment Center (NTPA)
IAFEREX International Agency for Earth Resources Experiments (SAUO)
IAFES International Association for the Economics of Self-Management [*Belgrade, Yugoslavia*] (EAIO)
IAFF Institute of Australian Flora and Fauna (SAUO)
IAFF International Air Freight Forwarder (AABC)
IAFF International Art Film Federation (SAUO)
IAFF International Association of Fire Fighters (EA)
IAFFT International Airforce Field Team (SAUS)
IAFI Infantile Amaurotic Family Idiocy [*Medicine*]
IAFIS Integrated Automated Fingerprint Identification System [*FBI standardized term*]
IAFLUP International Association of French-Language University Presses [*Defunct*] (EA)
IaFm Cattermole Memorial Library, Fort Madison, IA [*Library symbol*] [*Library of Congress*] (LCLS)
IAFM Integrated Air-Fuel Module
IAFM International Archives of Folk Music (SAUO)
IaFmD Fort Madison Democrat, Fort Madison, IA [*Library symbol*] [*Library of Congress*] (LCLS)
IaFmLHi North Lee County Historical Society, Fort Madison, IA [*Library symbol*] [*Library of Congress*] (LCLS)
IAFMM International Association of Fish Meal Manufacturers [*Potters Bar, Hertfordshire, England*] (EAIO)
IAFN International Association of Forensic Nurses (NTPA)
IAFN International Association of Forensic Nursing (EA)
IaFon Fonda Public Library, Fonda, IA [*Library symbol*] [*Library of Congress*] (LCLS)
IaFonT Fonda Times, Fonda, IA [*Library symbol*] [*Library of Congress*] (LCLS)
IaFontO Fontanelle Observer, Fontanelle, IA [*Library symbol*] [*Library of Congress*] (LCLS)
IAFP Inter-American Forces of Peace (SAUS)
IAFP Intergovernmental Affairs Fellowship Program (RDA)
IAFP International Alliance of Film Producers [*Later, IAIP*] (EA)
IAFP International Association for Financial Planning (EA)
IAFP International Association of Filipino Patriots (EA)
IAFP International Association of Financial Planners (SAUO)
IAFP International Association of Financial Planning (SAUO)
IAFPE Indian American Forum for Political Education (EA)
IAFraMCoS International Association of Fracture Mechanics of Concrete Structures (SAUO)
IaFre Upham Memorial Library, Fredericksburg, IA [*Library symbol*] [*Library of Congress*] (LCLS)
IaFremG Fremont Gazette, Fremont, IA [*Library symbol*] [*Library of Congress*] (LCLS)
IaFreN Fredericksburg News, Fredericksburg, IA [*Library symbol*] [*Library of Congress*] (LCLS)
IaFreR Fredericksburg Review, Fredericksburg, IA [*Library symbol*] [*Library of Congress*] (LCLS)
IAFS Industry Analysis & Forecast Service (SAUS)
IAFS Integrated Air-Fuel System [*Automotive engineering*]
IAFS International Animated Film Society (EA)
IAFS International Association for Fire Safety (SAUO)
IAFS International Association for Food Self-Sufficiency (EA)
IAFS International Association of Family Sociology (EA)
IAFS International Association of Forensic Sciences [*Defunct*] (EA)
IAFSA International Association of French-Speaking Aircrews (EAIO)
IAFSDEI International Association of French-Speaking Directors of Educational Institutions (EAIO)
IAFSS International Association for Fire Safety Science (NTPA)
IAFTA Integrated Avionics Fault Tree Analyzer (MCD)
IAFU Improve Assault Fire Unit (SAUS)
IAFU Improved Assault Fire Units [*Military*] (MCD)
IAFV Infantry Armed Fighting Vehicle (SAUS)
IAFV Infantry Armored Fighting Vehicle (NATG)
IAFV Infantry Armoured Fighting Vehicle (SAUS)
IAFVH Indian Advanced Field Veterinary Hospital [*British military*] (DMA)
IAFWA International Association of Fish and Wildlife Agencies (EA)
IAFWNO Inter-American Federation of Working Newspapermen's Organizations
IAG Epag-Group Air France [*FAA designator*] (FAAC)
IAG Greenville College, Greenville, IL [*OCLC symbol*] (OCLC)
IAG Implementation Advisory Group (SAUO)
IAG Industry Advisory Group [*Underwriters Laboratories*] [*Telecommunications*]
IAG Inertial Artillery Goniometer (SAUS)
IAG Institute for Australasian Geodynamics [*Flinders University*] [*Australia*]
IAG Institute of American Genealogy (SAUO)
IAG Institute of Animal Genetics (SAUO)
IAG Institute of Applied Geology (SAUO)
IAG Instruction Address Generation [*Computer science*]
IAG Instrumentation Advisory Group (SAUO)
IAG Intelligence Analysis Group [*Military*]
IAG Interactive Application Generation (SAUO)
IAG Interactive Application Generator (HGAA)
IAG Interagency Advisory Group [*Civil Service Commission*]
IAG Interagency Agreement
IAG Interagency Agreement Group (SAUS)
IAG Interagency Group (SAUS)
IAG Inter-Association Group
IAG Intergovernmental Agreement on the Environment [*Commonwealth*] [*State*] (EERA)
IAG Internal Audit Group [*British*] (GVA)
IAG International Academy of Gnathology - American Section (EA)
IAG International Administrative Data Processing Group (SAUO)
IAG International Advisory Group
IAG International Applications Group [*IFIP*]
IAG International Art Guild (EA)
IAG International Arts Guild (SAUS)
IAG International Association of Geodesy [*ICSU*] [*Paris, France*] (EAIO)
IAG International Association of Geologists (SAUO)
IAG International Association of Geophysical Contractors (SAUO)
IAG International Association of Gerontology (EA)
IAG International Auditing Guidelines (SAUO)
IAG Niagara Falls, NY [*Location identifier*] [*FAA*] (FAAL)
IaG Stewart Public Library, Grinnell, IA [*Library symbol*] [*Library of Congress*] (LCLS)
IAGA International Association of Geomagnetism and Aeronomy [*ICSU*] [*Scotland*] (ASF)
IAGA International Association of Geomagnetism and Agronomy (SAUO)
IAGA International Association of Golf Administrators (EA)
IAGA Irish Amateur Gymnastics Association (EAIO)
IAGAE International Association for Eutonie Gerda Alexander (SAUO)
IAGAE International Association for Gerda Alexander Eutony [*See also AIEGA*] [*Switzerland*] (EAIO)
IAGAL Industry Advisory Group for Air Logistics
IaGar Garner Public Library, Garner, IA [*Library symbol*] [*Library of Congress*] (LCLS)
IaGarL Garner Leader and Signal and Herald, Garner, IA [*Library symbol*] [*Library of Congress*] (LCLS)
IaGavoHi Garnavillo Historical Society, Garnavillo, IA [*Library symbol*] [*Library of Congress*] (LCLS)
IaGavoT Granavillo Tribune, Granavillo, IA [*Library symbol*] [*Library of Congress*] (LCLS)
IAGB&I Ileostomy Association of Great Britain and Ireland (SAUO)
IAGBN International Absolute Gravity Base Network (SAUS)
IaGc Gilmore City Public Library, Gilmore City, IA [*Library symbol*] [*Library of Congress*] (LCLS)
IAGC Instantaneous Automatic Gain Circuit (SAUS)
IAGC Instantaneous Automatic Gain Control [*or Circuit*] [*RADAR*]
IAGC International Association for Geochemistry and Cosmochemistry (SAUS)
IAGC International Association for/of Geochemistry and Cosmochemistry (SAUO)

IAGC .... International Association of Geochemistry and Cosmochemistry [*Edmonton, AB*] (EA)
IAGC .... International Association of Geomagnetism and Cosmochemistry (SAUO)
IAGC .... International Association of Geophysical Contractors (EA)
IAGCW .... International Association of Greeting Card Workers
IAGD .... Illinois Academy of General Dentistry (SAUO)
IAGD .... Iowa Academy of General Dentistry (SRA)
IAGEC .... Interagency Committee on Global Environmental Change (SAUO)
IaGen .... Iowa State Genealogical Society, Genealogical Library, Des Moines, IA [*Library symbol*] [*Library of Congress*] (LCLS)
IaGeoN .... Lyon County News, George, IA [*Library symbol*] [*Library of Congress*] (LCLS)
IaGeoR .... Lyon county Register, George, IA [*Library symbol*] [*Library of Congress*] (LCLS)
IAGFA .... International Association of Governmental Fair Agencies (EA)
IAGFCC .... International Association of Game, Fish and Conservation Commissioners (SAUO)
IaGG .... Grinnell College, Grinnell, IA [*Library symbol*] [*Library of Congress*] (LCLS)
IaGHR .... Herald-Register, Grinnell, IA [*Library symbol*] [*Library of Congress*] (LCLS)
IaGjG .... Globe Free Press, Grand Junction, IA [*Library symbol*] [*Library of Congress*] (LCLS)
IAGL .... Interactive Applicon Graphics Language [*Automotive engineering*]
IaGle .... Glenwood Public Library, Glenwood, IA [*Library symbol*] [*Library of Congress*] (LCLS)
IaGleOT .... Opinion-Tribune, Glenwood, IA [*Library symbol*] [*Library of Congress*] (LCLS)
IaGliG .... Glidden Graphic, Glidden, IA [*Library symbol*] [*Library of Congress*] (LCLS)
IAGLL .... International Association of Germanic Languages and Literatures [*See also IVG*] (EAIO)
IAGLO .... International Association of Governmental Labor Officials [*Later, NAGLO*] (EA)
IAGLP .... International Association of Great Lakes Ports (EA)
IAGLR .... International Association for Great Lakes Research (EA)
IAGM .... International Association of Garment Manufacturers [*Absorbed by NOSA*] (EA)
IAGMA .... Illuminating and Allied Glassware Manufacturers Association [*Defunct*] (EA)
IAGMA .... International Assembly of Grocery Manufacturers Associations (EAIO)
IAGOD .... International Association for/on the Genesis of Ore Deposits (SAUO)
IAGOD .... International Association for the Genesis of Ore Deposits (SAUS)
IAGOD .... International Association of the Genesis of Ore Deposits [*ICSU*] [*Prague, Czechoslovakia*] (EAIO)
IAGOD .... International Association on the Genesis of Ore Deposits (SAUS)
IaGow .... Gowrie News, Gowrie, IA [*Library symbol*] [*Library of Congress*] (LCLS)
IAGP .... Illinois Association of Groundwater Professionals (SRA)
IAGP .... International Antarctic Glaciological Project [*Defunct*] (EA)
IAGP .... International Association of Geographic Pathology (DAVI)
IAGP .... International Association of Group Psychotherapy (EA)
IaGra .... Graettinger Public Library, Graettinger, IA [*Library symbol*] [*Library of Congress*] (LCLS)
IaGraT .... Graettinger Times, Graettinger, IA [*Library symbol*] [*Library of Congress*] (LCLS)
IaGrc .... Grundy Center Public Library, Grundy Center, IA [*Library symbol*] [*Library of Congress*] (LCLS)
IaGrcI .... Iowa Farm Bureau Spokesman, Grundy Center, IA [*Library symbol*] [*Library of Congress*] (LCLS)
IaGrcR .... Grundy Center Register, Grundy Center, IA [*Library symbol*] [*Library of Congress*] (LCLS)
IaGre .... Greene Public Library, Greene, IA [*Library symbol*] [*Library of Congress*] (LCLS)
IAgrE .... Institution of Agricultural Engineers [*British*] (DBA)
IaGrefFP .... Adair County Free Press, Greenfield, IA [*Library symbol*] [*Library of Congress*] (LCLS)
IaGreR .... Greene Recorder, Greene, IA [*Library symbol*] [*Library of Congress*] (LCLS)
IaGrisA .... Griswold American, Griswold, IA [*Library symbol*] [*Library of Congress*] (LCLS)
IAgS .... Institute of Agricultural Secretaries (DBA)
IAGS .... Inter-American Geodetic Survey
IAGS .... International Association for Germanic Studies (EAIO)
IAGS .... International Association of Gandhian Studies (SAUO)
IAGS .... Irish Assessment & Guidance Service (ACII)
IAGT .... Indirect Antiglobulin Test [*Medicine*] (MELL)
IaGucG .... Guthrian, Guthrie Center, IA [*Library symbol*] [*Library of Congress*] (LCLS)
IaGucT .... Guthrie Center Times, Guthrie Center, IA [*Library symbol*] [*Library of Congress*] (LCLS)
IAGUS .... International Association of Genito-Urinary Surgeons (DAVI)
IaGut .... Guttenberg Public Library, Guttenberg, IA [*Library symbol*] [*Library of Congress*] (LCLS)
IaGutP .... Guttenberg Press, Guttenberg, IA [*Library symbol*] [*Library of Congress*] (LCLS)
IAGW .... International Acoustic Gravity Waves (SAUS)
IAH .... Houston [*Texas*] Intercontinental [*Airport symbol*] (OAG)
IAH .... Idiopathic Adrenal Hyperplasia [*Medicine*]
IAH .... Illinois Institute of Technology, Chicago, IL [*OCLC symbol*] (OCLC)
IAH .... Immune Adherence Haemagglutination [*Immunochemistry*] (PDAA)
IAH .... Implantable Artificial Heart
IAH .... Institute for Animal Health [*Agricultural and Food Research Council*] [*British*] (IRC)
IAH .... Institute for the Advancement of Health [*Defunct*] (EA)
IAH .... Inter-American Highway (SAUS)
IAH .... Interdivisional Administration Specification (SAUS)
IAH .... International Association for Hydrology (SAUS)
IAH .... International Association for/of Hydrology (SAUO)
IAH .... International Association of Hydrogeologists [*Arnhem, Netherlands*] (EA)
IAH .... International Association of Hydrologists (SAUO)
IAH .... International Association of Hydrology
IAH .... Internationales Arbeiter-Hilfswerk [*International Workers Aid*] [*Bonn, Federal Republic of Germany*] (EAIO)
IAH .... Internet Architect Holdrs. Tr. [*AMEX symbol*] (SG)
IAH .... Island Airlines Hawaii (SAUO)
IAH .... Isonicotinic Acid Hydrazide [*Medicine*] (MELL)
IAHA .... Immune Adherence Hemagglutination [*Immunochemistry*]
IAHA .... Indiana Association of Homes for the Aging (SRA)
IAHA .... Institute for the Advancement of Hawaiian Affairs
IAHA .... Inter-American Hospital Association [*Defunct*]
IAHA .... Inter-American Hotel Association
IAHA .... International Animal Husbandry Association (SAUO)
IAHA .... International Arabian Horse Association (EA)
IAHA .... International Association of Historians of Asia [*Quezon City, Philippines*] (EA)
IAHA .... International Association of Hospitality Accountants [*Austin, TX*] (EA)
IAHA .... Iowa Association of Homes for the Aging (SRA)
Ia-HA .... Iowa State Department of History and Archives, Des Moines, IA [*Library symbol*] [*Library of Congress*] (LCLS)
IAHAIO .... International Association of Human-Animal Interaction Organizations (EA)
IaHamb .... Hamburg Public Library, Hamburg, IA [*Library symbol*] [*Library of Congress*] (LCLS)
IaHambR .... Hamburg Reporter, Hamburg, IA [*Library symbol*] [*Library of Congress*] (LCLS)
IaHampC .... Hampton Chronicle, Hampton, IA [*Library symbol*] [*Library of Congress*] (LCLS)
IaHampCoC .... Franklin County Courthouse, Hampton, IA [*Library symbol*] [*Library of Congress*] (LCLS)
IaHampFC .... Franklin County Courthouse, Hampton, IA [*Library symbol*] [*Library of Congress*] (LCLS)
IaHampFN .... US Farm News, Hampton, IA [*Library symbol*] [*Library of Congress*] (LCLS)
IaHampHi .... Franklin County Historical Society, Hampton, IA [*Library symbol*] [*Library of Congress*] (LCLS)
IaHampJ .... Dumont Journal, Hampton, IA [*Library symbol*] [*Library of Congress*] (LCLS)
IaHampT .... Hampton Times, Hampton, IA [*Library symbol*] [*Library of Congress*] (LCLS)
IaHar .... Harlan Public Library, Harlan, IA [*Library symbol*] [*Library of Congress*] (LCLS)
IaHarNA .... Harlan News-Advertiser, Harlan, IA [*Library symbol*] [*Library of Congress*] (LCLS)
IaHarS .... Shelby County Museum, Harlan, IA [*Library symbol*] [*Library of Congress*] (LCLS)
IaHarT .... Harlan Tribune, Harlan, IA [*Library symbol*] [*Library of Congress*] (LCLS)
IaHart .... Hartley Public Library, Hartley, IA [*Library symbol*] [*Library of Congress*] (LCLS)
IaHartP .... Hartley Public Library, Hartley, IA [*Library symbol*] [*Library of Congress*] (LCLS)
IaHartS .... Hartley Sentinel, Hartley, IA [*Library symbol*] [*Library of Congress*] (LCLS)
IaHaw .... Hawarden Public Library, Hawarden, IA [*Library symbol*] [*Library of Congress*] (LCLS)
IAHB .... Institute for the Advancement of Human Behavior (EA)
IAHB .... International Association of Human Biologists [*ICSU*] [*Newcastle-Upon-Tyne, England*] (EAIO)
IAHC .... International Ad Hoc Committee (PCM)
IAHC .... Internet Ad Hoc Coalition [*Computer science*]
IAHC .... Internet Ad Hoc Committee
IAHC .... Internet International Ad Hoc Committee (SAUS)
IAHCP .... International Academy of Health Care Professionals (EA)
IAHCSM .... International Association of Healthcare Central Service Materials Management (EA)
IAHCSM .... International Association of Hospital Central Service Management (SAUO)
IAHCSMM .... International Association of Healthcare Central Service Material Management (NTPA)
IAHD .... Idiopathic Acquired Hemolytic Disease [*Medicine*] (MAE)
IAHD .... International Association of Hillel Directors (EA)
IAHE .... International Association for Hydrogen Energy (EA)
IAHEES .... Iowa Agriculture and Home Economics Experiment Station [*Iowa State University*] [*Research center*] (RCD)
IaHeJ .... Hedrick Journal, Hedrick, IA [*Library symbol*] [*Library of Congress*] (LCLS)
IAHES .... Implantable Artificial Heart Energy System
IAHF .... International Aerospace Hall of Fame (SAUO)
IAHFIAW .... International Association of Heat and Frost Insulators and Asbestos Workers (SAUO)
IAHHP .... International Association of Holistic Health Practitioners (EA)
IAHI .... International Archives of the Hystory of Ideas (journ.) (SAUS)
IAHI .... International Association of Hail Insurers (EA)
IAHI .... International Association of Holiday Inns (EA)
IaHi .... State Historical Society of Iowa, Iowa City, IA [*Library symbol*] [*Library of Congress*] (LCLS)

IAHIC .... International Association of Home Improvement Councils [*Defunct*] (EA)
IAHM .... Incorporated Association of Head Masters [*British*]
IAHM .... Incorporated Association of Headmasters (SAUS)
IAHM .... International Academy of the History of Medicine [*Defunct*] (EA)
IAHM .... International Association of Head Masters (SAUS)
IAHMS .... International Association of Hotel Management Schools (EA)
IaHoDHi .... Delaware County Historical Society, Hopkinton, IA [*Library symbol*] [*Library of Congress*] (LCLS)
IaHoDL .... Delaware County Leader, Hopkinton, IA [*Library symbol*] [*Library of Congress*] (LCLS)
IaHoL .... Lenox College, Hopkinton, IA [*Library symbol*] [*Library of Congress*] (LCLS)
IaHol .... Stubbs Public Library, Holstein, IA [*Library symbol*] [*Library of Congress*] (LCLS)
IaHolA .... Holstein Advance, Holstein, IA [*Library symbol*] [*Library of Congress*] (LCLS)
IAHP .... Institute for the Achievement of Human Potential (SAUO)
IAHP .... Institutes for the Achievement of Human Potential (EA)
IAHP .... International Academy of the History of Pharmacy (SAUO)
IAHP .... International Association of Health Policy (SAUO)
IAHP .... International Association of Heart Patients [*Formerly, IAPP*] (EA)
IAHP .... International Association of Horticultural Producers
IAHP .... International Association of Hygienic Physicians (NTPA)
IAHP .... International Society for the History of Psychoanalysis (SAUO)
IAHR .... International Association for Hydraulic Research [*ICSU*] [*Delft, Netherlands*] (EA)
IAHR .... International Association for/of Hydraulic Research (SAUO)
IAHR .... International Association for the History of Religions [*Marburg, Federal Republic of Germany*] (EAIO)
IAHR .... International Association of Hydraulic Research (SAUS)
IAHRC .... Inter-American Human Rights Commission
IAHR/N .... Numen. International review for the history of religions. International Association for the History of Religions (SAUO)
IAHR/N .... Numen. International review for the history of religions. International Association for the History of Religions. Leiden (SAUS)
IAHRONA .... International Arabian Horse Registry of North America (EA)
IAHS .... Infection-Associated Hemophagocytic Syndrome [*Medicine*] (MELL)
IAHS .... International Academy of the History of Science [*Paris, France*] (EA)
IAHS .... International Association for Hospital Security [*Later, IAHSS*] (EA)
IAHS .... International Association for Housing Science (EA)
IAHS .... International Association for Hydrological Sciences (SAUS)
IAHS .... International Association for/of Hospital Security (SAUO)
IAHS .... International Association for/of Housing Science (SAUO)
IAHS .... International Association for/of Hydrological Sciences (SAUO)
IAHS .... International Association of Housing Science (SAUS)
IAHS .... International Association of Hydrological Sciences
IAHS .... International Automotive Hall of Shame (EA)
IAHSS .... International Association for Healthcare Security and Safety (EA)
IAHSSP .... International Association of Home Safety and Security Professionals (EA)
IAHU .... International Association of Health Underwriters [*Later, NAHU*] (EA)
IaHubS .... South Hardin Signal-Review, Hubbard, IA [*Library symbol*] [*Library of Congress*] (LCLS)
IaHud .... Hudson Public Library, Hudson, IA [*Library symbol*] [*Library of Congress*] (LCLS)
IaHudH .... Hudson Herald, Hudson, IA [*Library symbol*] [*Library of Congress*] (LCLS)
IaHul .... Sioux County Index, Hull, IA [*Library symbol*] [*Library of Congress*] (LCLS)
IaHulR .... Sioux County Index-Reporter, Hull, IA [*Library symbol*] [*Library of Congress*] (LCLS)
IaHum .... Humbolt Public LIbrary, Humbolt, IA [*Library symbol*] [*Library of Congress*] (LCLS)
IaHume .... Humeston Public Library, Humeston, IA [*Library symbol*] [*Library of Congress*] (LCLS)
IaHumeN .... Humeston New Era, Humeston, IA [*Library symbol*] [*Library of Congress*] (LCLS)
IaHumHi .... Humbolt County Historical Association, Humbolt, IA [*Library symbol*] [*Library of Congress*] (LCLS)
IaHumI .... Humbolt Independent, Humbolt, IA [*Library symbol*] [*Library of Congress*] (LCLS)
IaHumR .... Humbolt Republican, Humbolt, IA [*Library symbol*] [*Library of Congress*] (LCLS)
IaHweye .... Hawkeye Public Library, Hawkeye, IA [*Library symbol*] [*Library of Congress*] (LCLS)
IAI .... Hayner Public Library, Alton, IL [*Library symbol*] [*Library of Congress*] (LCLS)
IAI .... Icelandic Airlines Incorporated (SAUO)
IAI .... Idiopathic Autonomic Insufficiency [*Medicine*] (MELL)
IAI .... Illinois State University, Normal, IL [*OCLC symbol*] (OCLC)
IAI .... Inactive Aerospace (or Aircraft) vehicle Inventory (SAUS)
IAI .... Inactive Aerospace Vehicle [*or Aircraft*] Inventory
IAI .... Inactive Aircraft Inventory (ACAE)
IAI .... Independent Accountants International (EAIO)
IAI .... Indo-Africa, Inc. (ECON)
IAI .... Infection and Immunity (SAUO)
IAI .... Infertility Associates International [*Commercial firm*] (EA)
IAI .... Informational Acquisition and Interpretation
IAI .... Information Associates of Ithaca [*Information service or system*] (IID)
IAI .... Initial Address Information [*Telecommunications*] (TEL)
IAI .... Institute for Atomic Information (SAUS)
IAI .... Institute for Atomic Information for the Lay Man (SAUO)
IAI .... Institute for International Collaboration in Agriculture and Forestry (SAUO)
IAI .... Institute of Arbitrators, Incorporated (SAUO)
IAI .... Integrated Aircraft Instrumentation
IAI .... Inter-African Institute (SAUO)
IAI .... Inter-American Institute (USDC)
IAI .... Inter-American Institute for Global Change Research [*Marine science*] (OSRA)
IAI .... International Acquisition and Interpretation (SAUS)
IAI .... International Affiliation of Independent Accounting Firms (NTPA)
IAI .... International African Institute [*British*]
IAI .... International Alliance for Interoperability (SAUO)
IAI .... International Anthropological Institute (SAUO)
IAI .... International Apple Institute (EA)
IAI .... International Association for Identitication (SAUO)
IAI .... International Association of Incubators (EA)
IAI .... International Automotive Institute (SAUO)
IAI .... Intra-Abdominal Infection [*Gastroenterology*] (DAVI)
IAI .... Ion Acoustic Instability (SAUS)
IAI .... Ion Acoustic Instability Enterprises (PDAA)
IAI .... Ion Atom Interaction
IAI .... Isethionyl Acetimidate [*Biochemistry*]
IAI .... Israel Aircraft Industries Ltd. [*ICAO designator*] (FAAC)
IAI .... Israel Aviation Industries (SAUO)
IAI .... Istituto Affairi Internazionali [*Institute for International Affairs*] [*Italy*]
IAIA .... Institute of American Indian and Alaska Native Culture and Arts Development (EA)
IAIA .... Institute of American Indian Arts (SAUO)
IAIA .... International Association for Impact Assessment (EA)
IaIa .... Iowa City Public Library, Iowa City, IA [*Library symbol*] [*Library of Congress*] (LCLS)
IAIAA .... International Association for Iranian Art and Archaeology (EA)
IAIABC .... International Association of Industrial Accident Boards and Commissions (SAUO)
IAIAD .... International Acronyms, Initialisms, and Abbreviations Dictionary [*A publication*]
IAIAF .... International Affiliation of Independent Accounting Firms (EA)
IaIaI .... Daily Iowan, Iowa City, IA [*Library symbol*] [*Library of Congress*] (LCLS)
IAIALAR .... Ibero-American Institute of Agrarian Law and Agrarian Reform [*See also IIDARA*] [*Mexida, Venezuela*] (EAIO)
IaIaP .... Iowa City Press-Citizen, Iowa City, IA [*Library symbol*] [*Library of Congress*] (LCLS)
IAIAS .... Inter-American Institute of Agricultural Sciences [*Later, IICA*] [*OAS*]
IaIaS .... Seven Rivers Library Cooperative, Iowa City, IA [*Library symbol*] [*Library of Congress*] (LCLS)
IAIB .... International Association of Islamic Banks
IAIBS .... Ion-Assisted Ion-Beam Sputtering (SAUS)
IAIC .... Information Analysis, Inc. [*NASDAQ symbol*] (NASQ)
IAIC .... International Academy of Indian Culture (EAIO)
IAIC .... International Association of Insurance Counsel [*Later, IADC*] (EA)
IAICM .... International Association of Ice Cream Manufacturers [*Later, IICA*] (EA)
IAICU .... International Association of Independent Colleges and Universities (EA)
IAICV .... International Association of Ice Cream Vendors (NTPA)
IAID .... Indium Arsenide Infrared Detector
IaIdgIHi .... Ida County Historical Society, Ida Grove, IA [*Library symbol*] [*Library of Congress*] (LCLS)
IaIdgPR .... Ida County Pioneer-Record, Ida Grove, IA [*Library symbol*] [*Library of Congress*] (LCLS)
IAIDPA .... International Association for Information and Documentation in Public Administration (EAIO)
IAIDPA .... International Association for/of Information and Documentation in Public Administration (SAUO)
IAIDPA .... International Association of Information and Documentation in Public Administration (SAUS)
IAIE .... Integral Absolute Ideal Error (SAUS)
IAIE .... Integral of Absolute Ideal Error (IAA)
IAIE .... Inter-American Institute of Ecology [*Ecological Society of America*]
IAIE .... International Association for Integrative Education [*Versoix, Switzerland*] (EAIO)
IAIES .... Institute for Advanced Interdisciplinary Engineering Studies [*Purdue University*] (MCD)
IAIES .... International Association of Intermodal Equipment Surveyors [*Defunct*] (EA)
IaIf .... Carnegie Ellsworth Public Library, Iowa Falls, IA [*Library symbol*] [*Library of Congress*] (LCLS)
IaIfC .... Iowa Falls Citizen, Iowa Falls, Iowa [*Library symbol*] [*Library of Congress*] (LCLS)
IaIfE .... Ellsworth Commumity College, Iowa Falls, IA [*Library symbol*] [*Library of Congress*] (LCLS)
IaIfT .... Hardin County Times, Iowa Falls, IA [*Library symbol*] [*Library of Congress*] (LCLS)
IAIG .... Industrial Analytical Instrumentation Group (ACII)
IAIH .... Intra-uterine Artificial Insemination Homologous (SAUS)
IAII .... Inter-American Indian Institute [*OAS*] [*Mexico City, Mexico*] (EA)
IAIIB .... International Association of Independent Information Brokers (SAUO)
IAIM .... International Association of Infant Massage (EA)
IAIMR/YB .... Yearbook. Tulane University. Inter-American Institute for Musical Research (SAUS)
IAIMS .... Integrated Academic Information Management System [*Georgetown University Medical Center*]
IAIN .... Inter-Anglican Information Network (SAUO)
IAIN .... International Association of Institutes of Navigation [*British*] (EAIO)
IaInd .... Indianola Public Library, Indianola, IA [*Library symbol*] [*Library of Congress*] (LCLS)

IaIndianR..... Record-Herald and Tribune, Indianola, IA [*Library symbol*] [*Library of Congress*] (LCLS)
IaIndianS..... Simpson College, Indianola, IA [*Library symbol*] [*Library of Congress*] (LCLS)
IaIndpB........ Independence Bulletin-Journal, Independence, IA [*Library symbol*] [*Library of Congress*] (LCLS)
IaIndpBC...... Buchanan County Courthouse, Independence, IA [*Library symbol*] [*Library of Congress*] (LCLS)
IaIndpC........ Independence Conservative, Independence, IA [*Library symbol*] [*Library of Congress*] (LCLS)
IaIndpCoC.... Buchanan County Courthouse, Independence, IA [*Library symbol*] [*Library of Congress*] (LCLS)
IaIndR.......... Record-Herald and Tribune, Indianola, IA [*Library symbol*] [*Library of Congress*] (LCLS)
IaIndS.......... Simpson College, Indianola, IA [*Library symbol*] [*Library of Congress*] (LCLS)
IA International... Independent Accountants International (BUAC)
IaInwH......... West Lyon Herald, Inwood, IA [*Library symbol*] [*Library of Congress*] (LCLS)
IaIonCHi...... Chickasaw County Historical Society, Ionia, IA [*Library symbol*] [*Library of Congress*] (LCLS)
IAIP............. Inorganic Ablative Insulative Plastic
IAIP............. International Association of Independent Producers (EA)
IAIP............. International Association of Individual Psychology (EA)
IAIPS........... Integrated Automated Intelligence (SAUS)
IAIPS........... Integrated Automated Intelligence Processing System (MCD)
IAIPS........... Intelligence Analyst Integrated Processing System (SAUO)
IAIR............. Independent Air Holdings, Inc. (SAUO)
IAIR............. International Academy for Intercultural Research (SEAT)
IAIR............. International Association of Industrial Radiation [*France*] (PDAA)
IAIR............. International Association of Insurance Receivers (NTPA)
IAIRI............ International Association of Insurance and Reinsurance Intermediaries [*See also BIPAR*] [*Paris, France*] (EAIO)
IAIRS........... Installation Aircraft Inventory Report (SAUS)
IAIRS........... Installation Aircraft Inventory Reporting System [*Army*]
IAIS............. Improved Avionics Intermediate Shop (SAUS)
IAIS............. Industrial Aerodynamics Information Service [*British*] (IID)
IAIS............. Insulin Autoimmune Syndrome [*Medicine*] (DMAA)
IAIS............. International Aircraft Investors [*NASDAQ symbol*] (NASQ)
IAIS............. International Association of Independent Scholars (EA)
IAIS............. International Association of Legal Science (SAUO)
IAIS............. Iowa Interstate Railroad [*Federal Railroad Administration identification code*]
IAIs............. Israeli Aircraft Industries (SAUO)
IAITO........... International Association of Independent Tanker Owners
IAIU............. Insurance Agents International Union
IAJ.............. Idle Air Jet [*Fuel system*] [*Automotive engineering*]
IAJ.............. Immoblization of Ankle Joint (MELL)
IAJ.............. Institute for Administrative Justice [*University of the Pacific*] [*Research center*] (RCD)
IAJ.............. International Association of Judges [*Rome, Italy*] (EAIO)
IaJ.............. Jefferson Public Library, Jefferson, IA [*Library symbol*] [*Library of Congress*] (LCLS)
IAJA............ International Association of Jazz Appreciation (EA)
IAJAM.......... Industrial Association of Juvenile Apparel Manufacturers (EA)
IAJAP........... International Association of Jai Alai Players (EA)
IaJB............. Jefferson Bee, Jefferson, IA [*Library symbol*] [*Library of Congress*] (LCLS)
IAJBBSC...... International Association of Jim Beam Bottle and Specialties Clubs (EA)
IAJC............ Inter-American Juridical Committee
IAJE............ Internacia Asocio de Juristoj-Esperantistoj (SAUO)
IAJE............ Internacia Socio de Juristoj-Esperantistoj [*International Association of Esperantist Lawyers*]
IAJE............ International Association of Jazz Educators (EA)
IaJesC......... Jesup Citizen Herald, Jesup, IA [*Library symbol*] [*Library of Congress*] (LCLS)
IaJew........... Montgomery Memorial Library, Jewell, IA [*Library symbol*] [*Library of Congress*] (LCLS)
IaJewR......... South Hamilton Record-News, Jewell, IA [*Library symbol*] [*Library of Congress*] (LCLS)
IAJFCM........ International Association of Juvenile and Family Court Magistrates [*Paris, France*] (EA)
IaJGCoC....... Greene County Courthouse, Jefferson IA [*Library symbol*] [*Library of Congress*] (LCLS)
IaJH............ Iowa Journal of History and Politics (SAUO)
IaJH............ Jefferson Herald, Jefferson, IA [*Library symbol*] [*Library of Congress*] (LCLS)
IaJoN........... Northern Polk County News, Johnston, IA [*Library symbol*] [*Library of Congress*] (LCLS)
IAJP............ Interamerican Journal of Psychology [*A publication*] (DHP)
IAJRC.......... International Association of Jazz Record Collectors (EA)
IAJS............ International Al Joison Society (SAUO)
IAJS............ International Al Jolson Society (EA)
IAJV............ International Association of Justice Volunteerism (EA)
IAJVS.......... International Association of Jewish Vocational Services (NTPA)
IAK............. International Air Cargo Corp. [*Egypt*] [*ICAO designator*] (FAAC)
IAK............. International Auschwitz Committee (SAUO)
IAK............. Internationales Auschwitz-Komitee [*International Auschwitz Committee*] [*Warsaw, Poland*] (EAIO)
IAK............. Internet Access Kit (SAUS)
IaK............. Keokuk Public Library, Keokuk, IA [*Library symbol*] [*Library of Congress*] (LCLS)
IAK............. Lake Forest College, Lake Forest, IL [*OCLC symbol*] (OCLC)
IaKaIN......... Kalona News, Kalona, IA [*Library symbol*] [*Library of Congress*] (LCLS)
IaKan........... Kanawha Public Library, Kanawha, IA [*Library symbol*] [*Library of Congress*] (LCLS)
IaKanR......... Kanawha Reporter, Kanawha, IA [*Library symbol*] [*Library of Congress*] (LCLS)
IaKanRL....... Rural Life, Kanawha, IA [*Library symbol*] [*Library of Congress*] (LCLS)
IAKE............ International Association of Knowledge Engineers (EA)
IaKe............ Keosauqua Public Library, Keosauqua, IA [*Library symbol*] [*Library of Congress*] (LCLS)
IaKen........... Kensett Public Library, Kensett, IA [*Library symbol*] [*Library of Congress*] (LCLS)
IaKeoE......... Keota Eagle, Keota, IA [*Library symbol*] [*Library of Congress*] (LCLS)
IaKeVR........ Van Buren County Register, Keosauqua, IA [*Library symbol*] [*Library of Congress*] (LCLS)
IaKey........... Keystone Public Library, Keystone, IA [*Library symbol*] [*Library of Congress*] (LCLS)
IAKF............ International Amateur Karate Federation (EA)
IaKG............ Keokuk Gate City, Keokuk, IA [*Library symbol*] [*Library of Congress*] (LCLS)
IaKiN........... Kingsley News-Tribune, Kingsley, IA [*Library symbol*] [*Library of Congress*] (LCLS)
IaKK............ Keosippi Library Cooperative, Keokuk, IA [*Library symbol*] [*Library of Congress*] (LCLS)
IaKn............ Knoxville Public Library, Knoxville, IA [*Library symbol*] [*Library of Congress*] (LCLS)
IaKnE.......... Knoxville Express, Knoxville, IA [*Library symbol*] [*Library of Congress*] (LCLS)
IaKnJ.......... Knoxville Journal, Knoxville, IA [*Library symbol*] [*Library of Congress*] (LCLS)
IaKnV.......... United States Veterans Administration Hospital, Knoxville, IA [*Library symbol*] [*Library of Congress*] (LCLS)
IAKS............ Internationaler Arbeitskreis Sport- und Freizeiteninrichtungen [*International Working Group for the Construction of Sports and Leisure Facilities*] (EAIO)
IaKS............ Keokuk Savings Bank and Trust Co., Keokuk, IA [*Library symbol*] [*Library of Congress*] (LCLS)
IAL.............. Icelandic Airlines (SAUO)
IAL.............. Icelandic Airlines-Loftfeider (SAUS)
IAL.............. Immediate Action Letter (NASA)
IAL.............. Imperial Airways Ltd. [*British*]
IAL.............. Imperial Art League [*British*] (BI)
IAL.............. Indian Airlines (PDAA)
IAL.............. Infrared Aiming Light [*Military*] (INF)
IAL.............. Initial (SAUS)
IAL.............. Inland Air Lines (SAUO)
IAL.............. Inland Airlines
IAL.............. Insertion Approval Letter (SAUS)
IAL.............. Installation and Logistics (IAA)
IAL.............. Instrumental Approach and Landing (SAUS)
IAL.............. Instrument Approach and Landing (SAUS)
IAL.............. Instrument Approach and Landing Chart [*Aviation*]
IAL.............. Intel Architecture Laboratories (SAUO)
IAL.............. Interdivisional Administration List (SAUS)
IAL.............. Interlaminar Adhesive Layer
IAL.............. Interlamnar Adhesive Layer (SAUS)
IAL.............. International Aeradio, Limited (SAUO)
IAL.............. International Aeradio PLC [*British*] [*ICAO designator*] (FAAC)
IAL.............. International Affairs (London) [*A publication*]
IAL.............. International Air Traffic League (SAUO)
IAL.............. International Algebraic Language [*Programming language*] [*Replaced by ALGOL*]
IAL.............. International Algorithmic Language [*Computer science*] (BUR)
IAL.............. International Aluminum Corp. [*NYSE symbol*] (SPSG)
IAL.............. International Aluminum-Lithium Conference (SAUS)
IAL.............. International Association of Laryngectomees (EA)
IAL.............. International Association of Lighthouse Authorities (SAUO)
IAL.............. International Association of Lighting Designers (SAUO)
IAL.............. International Association of Limnology (PDAA)
IAL.............. International Association of Linguistics (DIT)
IAL.............. International Association of theoretical and applied Limnologists (SAUO)
IAL.............. International Association of Theoretical and Applied Limnology [*ICSU*] (EA)
IAL.............. Intl Aluminum [*NYSE symbol*] (TTSB)
IAL.............. Investment Analysis Language [*Computer science*] (BUR)
Ia-L............. Iowa State Law Library, Des Moines, IA [*Library symbol*] [*Library of Congress*] (LCLS)
IAL.............. Irish Academy of Letters (BI)
IaL.............. Lamoni Public Library, Lamoni, IA [*Library symbol*] [*Library of Congress*] (LCLS)
IAL.............. Loyola University, Chicago, IL [*OCLC symbol*] (OCLC)
IALA............ International African Law Association
IALA............ International Association of Lighthouse Authorities [*Paris, France*] (EA)
IALA............ International Auxiliary Language Association [*Later, UMI*]
IALA............ Islamic Alliance for the Liberation of Afghanistan (PD)
IALACS........ International Association of Latin American and Caribbean Studies (EAIO)
IaLamtL....... Lamont Leader, Lamont, IA [*Library symbol*] [*Library of Congress*] (LCLS)
IaLanJ......... Allamakee Journal, Lansing, IA [*Library symbol*] [*Library of Congress*] (LCLS)

IaLau Laurens Public Library, Laurens, IA [*Library symbol*] [*Library of Congress*] (LCLS)

IaLauS Laurens Sun, Laurens, IA [*Library symbol*] [*Library of Congress*] (LCLS)

IAlb Albion Public Library, Albion, IL [*Library symbol*] [*Library of Congress*] (LCLS)

IALBA Inter-American Biographical and Library Association (SAUO)

IA L Bull Iowa Law Bulletin [*A publication*] (DLA)

IALC Instantaneous Automatic Level Control (IDOE)

IALC Institute of Allegheny Life and Culture (EA)

IALC Instrument Approach and Landing Chart [*Aviation*]

IALC International Arid Lands Consortium (EERA)

IALC International Association of Lions Clubs

IALC International Association of Lyceum Clubs

IALC Irish-American Labor Coalition [*Later, ALCHRNI*] (EA)

IALC Italian American Librarians Caucus (EA)

IaLC Lamoni Chronicle, Lamoni, IA [*Library symbol*] [*Library of Congress*] (LCLS)

IALCE International Air Lift Control Element (SAUS)

IALCE International Airlift Control Element (SAUO)

IaLcG Lake City Graphic, Lake City, IA [*Library symbol*] [*Library of Congress*] (LCLS)

IALCO International Aircraft Leasing Company (SAUO)

IALCRF International Association for Liberal Christianity and Religious Freedom (SAUO)

IAlCU Alton Community Unit 11, Alton, IL [*Library symbol*] [*Library of Congress*] (LCLS)

IALD International Association of Lighting Designers (EA)

IALDC Incorporated Association of London Dyers and Cleaners (SAUO)

IAlE East Alton Elementary 13, Alton, IL [*Library symbol*] [*Library of Congress*] (LCLS)

IALE Instrumented Architectural Level Emulation

IALE Integral Absolute Linear Error (SAUS)

IALE Integral of Absolute Linear Error (IAA)

IALE International Association for Landscape Ecology (SAUO)

IALEFI International Association of Law Enforcement Firearms Instructors (EA)

IALEIA International Association of Law Enforcement Intelligence Analysts (EA)

IaLelS Daily Sentinel, Lellars, IA [*Library symbol*] [*Library of Congress*] (LCLS)

IaLem Le Mars Public Library, Le Mars, IA [*Library symbol*] [*Library of Congress*] (LCLS)

IaLemS Daily Sentinel, Le Mars, IA [*Library symbol*] [*Library of Congress*] (LCLS)

IaLemW Westmar College, Le Mars, IA [*Library symbol*] [*Library of Congress*] (LCLS)

IaLeo Leon Public Library, Leon, IA [*Library symbol*] [*Library of Congress*] (LCLS)

IaLeoJR Leon Journal-Reporter, Leon, IA [*Library symbol*] [*Library of Congress*] (LCLS)

IaLew Lewis Public Library, Lewis, IA [*Library symbol*] [*Library of Congress*] (LCLS)

IALF Inter-American Literacy Foundation (EA)

IALF International Association of Law Firms [*Defunct*] (EA)

IaLG Graceland College, Lamoni, IA [*Library symbol*] [*Library of Congress*] (LCLS)

IALGPC International Association of Lesbian/Gay Pride Coordinators (EA)

IAlH Alton Memorial Hospital, Alton, IL [*Library symbol*] [*Library of Congress*] (LCLS)

IALHI International Association of Labour History Institutions [*Zurich, Switzerland*] (EAIO)

IALI International Association of Labour Inspection (SAUO)

IALL International Association for Labor Legislation (SAUO)

IALL International Association for Labour Legislation (SAUO)

IALL International Association for Learning Laboratories (EA)

IALL International Association of Law Libraries (EAIO)

IaLL Lamoni Public Library, Lamoni, IA [*Library symbol*] [*Library of Congress*] (LCLS)

IALL Bull Bulletin. International Association of Law Libraries [*A publication*] (DLA)

IALM Integrated Anchor Leg Mooring [*Naval engineering*]

IALM International Association of Lighting Maintenance (SAUO)

IALMC International Association of Lighting Maintenance Contractors [*Later, NALMCO*] (EA)

IaLmG Lake Mills Graphic, Lake Mills, IA [*Library symbol*] [*Library of Congress*] (LCLS)

IAlMH Alton Mental Health Center, Development and Training Center, Staff Library, Alton, IL [*Library symbol*] [*Library of Congress*] (LCLS)

IALMH International Academy of Law & Mental Health (AC)

IaLnP Lost Nation Press, Lost Nation, IA [*Library symbol*] [*Library of Congress*] (LCLS)

IaLoH Logan Herald-Observer, Logan, IA [*Library symbol*] [*Library of Congress*] (LCLS)

IaLoHi Harrison County Historical Society, Logan, IA [*Library symbol*] [*Library of Congress*] (LCLS)

IaLohr J. J. Hands Library, Lohrville, IA [*Library symbol*] [*Library of Congress*] (LCLS)

IaLowS Sun News, Lowden, IA [*Library symbol*] [*Library of Congress*] (LCLS)

IALP International Association of Logopedics and Phoniatrics [*Dublin, Republic of Ireland*] (EA)

IA/LP Ion Analyzer and Langmuir Probe (ACAE)

IaLpcPR La Porte City Progress-Review, La Porte City, IA [*Library symbol*] [*Library of Congress*] (LCLS)

IaLpN Lake Park News, Lake Park, IA [*Library symbol*] [*Library of Congress*] (LCLS)

IALR International Anthropological and Linguistic Review (journ.) (SAUS)

IALRW International Association of Liberal Religious Women (EA)

IALS Idaho Association of Land Surveyors (SAUO)

IALS Institute of Applied Language Studies [*Edith Cowan University*] [*Australia*]

IALS International Agency Liaison Service (SAUO)

IALS International Association of Legal Science [*See also AISJ*] [*Paris, France*] (EAIO)

IAlsA Alsip-Merrionette Park Library District, Alsip, IL [*Library symbol*] [*Library of Congress*] (LCLS)

IALSFAI International Association for Life-Saving and First Aid to the Injured (SAUO)

IaLsH Lime Springs Herald, Lime Springs, IA [*Library symbol*] [*Library of Congress*] (LCLS)

IALSSA International Air Line Stewards and Stewardesses Association

IAlStA Saint Anthony's Hospital, Medical Library, Alton, IL [*Library symbol*] [*Library of Congress*] (LCLS)

IAlStJ Saint Joseph's Hospital, Medical Information Services, Alton, IL [*Library symbol*] [*Library of Congress*] (LCLS)

IAlta Altamont Public Library, Altamont, IL [*Library symbol*] [*Library of Congress*] (LCLS)

IALtd Imperial Airways Limited (SAUO)

IaLtR Lone Tree Reporter, Lone Tree, IA [*Library symbol*] [*Library of Congress*] (LCLS)

IaLuHi Lucas County Historical Society, Lucas, IA [*Library symbol*] [*Library of Congress*] (LCLS)

IaLv Lake View Public Library, Lake View, IA [*Library symbol*] [*Library of Congress*] (LCLS)

IaLvR Lake View Resort, Lake View, IA [*Library symbol*] [*Library of Congress*] (LCLS)

IAM Altos Hornos de Mexico ADS [*NYSE symbol*] (SG)

IAM Altos Hornos de Mexico SA de CV [*NYSE symbol*] (SAG)

IAM Anderson Public Library, Anderson, IN [*OCLC symbol*] (OCLC)

IAM Ignition Ackowledge Module [*Diesel engine controls*] [*Automotive engineering*]

IAM ILA [*Instruction Look Ahead*] Associative Memory [*Computer science*]

IAM Image Analyzing Microscope (PDAA)

IAM Imagery Analysis Memorandum (MCD)

IAM Immediate Access Memory [*Computer science*] (VLIE)

IAM Immobilized Artificial Membranes [*Chemistry*]

IAM Immunization Action Month (SAUS)

IAM Improved Aimpoint Maintenance (ACAE)

IAM Impulse Amplitude Modulation (IAA)

IAM In Amenas [*Algeria*] [*Airport symbol*] (OAG)

IAM Incidental Amplitude Modulation

IAM Indefinite Admittance Matrix [*Network analysis*] (IEEE)

IAM Independent Aiming Mark (SAUS)

IAM Independent Atom Model (SAUS)

IAM Indexed Access Method [*Computer science*] (VLIE)

IAM Indian-Artifact Magazine (SAUS)

IAM Induced Athwartship Magnetism (SAUS)

IAM Inertially Aided Munition (ACAE)

IAM Information Asset Management (SSD)

IAM Initial Address Message (TEL)

IAM Initial Approach Mode (SAUS)

IAM Innovation Access Method [*Computer science*] (MHDI)

IAM Inscriptions Antiques du Maroc (BJA)

IAM Institute of Administrative Management [*British*] (DCTA)

IAM Institute of Advanced Motorists [*British*]

IAM Institute of Appliance Manufacturers [*Later, GAMA*] (EA)

IAM Institute of Applied Mathematics [*University of British Columbia*] [*Canada*] [*Research center*] (RCD)

IAM Institute of Aviation Medicine [*Royal Canadian Air Force*]

IAM Institute of the American Musical (EA)

IAM Intelligent Actuation & Measurement (ACII)

IAM Interactive Algebraic Manipulation [*Computer science*]

IAM Interactive Ancient Mediterranean (SAUS)

IAM Interaural Amplitude Modulation [*Audiology*]

IAM Intermediate Access Memory (NITA)

IAM Internal Acoustic Meatus [*Medicine*] (MAE)

IAM Internal Auditory Meatus [*Anatomy*]

IAM International Academy of Management [*Knoxville, TN*] (EA)

IAM International Academy of Medicine (SAUO)

IAM International Academy of Metabology (EA)

IAM International Academy of Myodontics (EA)

IAM International Academy of Myodontics, Oceanic Chapter [*Sydney, NSW, Australia*] (EAIO)

IAM International Afro-American Museum [*Later, AAM*] (EA)

IAM International Amco Corp. [*Toronto Stock Exchange symbol*]

IAM International Assistance Mission (SAUO)

IAM International Association of Machinists (SAUS)

IAM International Association of Machinists and Aerospace Workers (EA)

IAM International Association of Metaphysicians

IAM International Association of Meteorology (SAUS)

IAM International Association of Microbiologists (SAUO)

IAm Intraamniotic (SAUS)

IAM Inventory Accounting Monetary (SAUO)

Ia-M Iowa State Medical Library, Des Moines, IA [*Library symbol*] [*Library of Congress*] (LCLS)

IAMA Incorporated Advertising Managers Association (SAUS)

IAMA Independent Agricultural Merchants' Association [*Australia*]

IAMA Informed Americans Monitor (EA)

IAMA........... International Abstaining Motorists' Association [*Hagersten, Sweden*] (EAIO)
IAMA........... International Academy of Myodontics, Asian Chapter [*Tokyo, Japan*] (EAIO)
IAMA........... International Arts Medicine Association [*Philadelphia, PA*]
IAMA........... International Association of Machinists and Aerospace Workers (SAUO)
IAMA........... Intimate Apparel Manufacturers Association (EA)
IAMA........... Irish Association of Municipal Authorities (SAUO)
IaMa........... Marshalltown Public Library, Marshalltown, IA [*Library symbol*] [*Library of Congress*] (LCLS)
IAMACS....... International Association for Mathematics and Computers in Simulation (SAUO)
IAMAL......... Insects Affecting Man and Animals Laboratory (SAUO)
IaMall......... Mallard Public Library, Mallard, IA [*Library symbol*] [*Library of Congress*] (LCLS)
IaMalv......... Malvern Public Library, Malvern, IA [*Library symbol*] [*Library of Congress*] (LCLS)
IaMalvL....... Malvern Leader, Malvern, IA [*Library symbol*] [*Library of Congress*] (LCLS)
IAMAM......... International Association of Museums of Arms and Military History [*Ingolstadt, Federal Republic of Germany*] (EA)
IaMancP...... Manchester Press, Manchester, IA [*Library symbol*] [*Library of Congress*] (LCLS)
lam & fus.... Laminectomy and Fusion [*Medicine*] (STED)
IAMANEH..... International Association for Maternal and Neonatal Health [*Zurich, Switzerland*] (EAIO)
IaMannM..... Manning Monitor, Manning, IA [*Library symbol*] [*Library of Congress*] (LCLS)
IaManS........ Marion Sentinel, Marion, IA [*Library symbol*] [*Library of Congress*] (LCLS)
IaMansJ....... Manson Journal, Manson, IA [*Library symbol*] [*Library of Congress*] (LCLS)
IaManT........ Manilla Times, Manilla, IA [*Library symbol*] [*Library of Congress*] (LCLS)
IaManyS...... Manly Signal, Manly, IA [*Library symbol*] [*Library of Congress*] (LCLS)
IAMAP......... International Association for Meteorology and Atmospheric Physics (SAUS)
IAMAP......... International Association for/of Meteorology and Atmospheric Physics (SAUO)
IAMAP......... International Association of Meteorology and Atmospheric Physics (EA)
IaMap.......... Mapleton Public Library, Mapleton, IA [*Library symbol*] [*Library of Congress*] (LCLS)
IAMAP-IAHS... IAMAP-International Association of Hydrological Sciences (SAUO)
IaMapP........ Mapleton Press, Mapleton, IA [*Library symbol*] [*Library of Congress*] (LCLS)
IaMaq.......... Maquoketa Free Public Library, Maquoketa, IA [*Library symbol*] [*Library of Congress*] (LCLS)
IaMaqHi....... Jackson County Historical Society, Maquoketa, IA [*Library symbol*] [*Library of Congress*] (LCLS)
IaMaqP........ Maquoketa Community Press, Maquoketa, IA [*Library symbol*] [*Library of Congress*] (LCLS)
IaMaqS........ Jackson Sentinel, Maquoketa, IA [*Library symbol*] [*Library of Congress*] (LCLS)
IaMara......... Marathon Public Library, Marathon, IA [*Library symbol*] [*Library of Congress*] (LCLS)
IaMarc......... Marcus Public Library, Marcus, IA [*Library symbol*] [*Library of Congress*] (LCLS)
IaMare......... Marengo Public Library, Marengo, IA [*Library symbol*] [*Library of Congress*] (LCLS)
IaMarePR.... Marengo Pioneer-Republican, Marengo, IA [*Library symbol*] [*Library of Congress*] (LCLS)
IaMari.......... Marion Carnegie Library, Marion, IA [*Library symbol*] [*Library of Congress*] (LCLS)
IAMAS......... International Association of Meteorology and Atmospheric Sciences (EERA)
IAMAT.......... International Association for Medical Assistance to Travelers (SAUO)
IaMaTR........ Marshalltown Times-Republican, Marshalltown, IA [*Library symbol*] [*Library of Congress*] (LCLS)
IAMAW......... International Association of Machinists and Aerospace Workers (MCD)
IaMaxHi....... Community Historical Society, Maxwell, IA [*Library symbol*] [*Library of Congress*] (LCLS)
IaMay.......... Maynard Community Library, Maynard, IA [*Library symbol*] [*Library of Congress*] (LCLS)
IaMayr......... Mount Ayr Public Library, Mount Ayr, IA [*Library symbol*] [*Library of Congress*] (LCLS)
IaMayrHi...... Ringgold County Historical Society, Mount Ayr, IA [*Library symbol*] [*Library of Congress*] (LCLS)
IaMayrR....... Record-News, Mount Ayr, IA [*Library symbol*] [*Library of Congress*] (LCLS)
IAMB........... International Anti-Militarist Bureau against War and Reaction (SAUO)
IAMB........... International Association for the Protection of Monuments and Restoration of Buildings (EAIO)
IAMB........... International Association of Macrobiologists (SAUO)
IAMB........... Irish Association of Master Bakers (BI)
IAMBE......... International Association for Medicine and Biology of the Environment (SAUS)
IAMBE......... International Association of Medicine and Biology of Environment [*See also AIMBE*] [*Paris, France*] (EAIO)
IAMBI........... Iambic Verse (DSUE)
IaMbr.......... Marble Rock Public Library, Marble Rock, IA [*Library symbol*] [*Library of Congress*] (LCLS)
IAMC........... Indian Army Medical Corps
IAMC........... Institute for Advancement of Medical Communication [*Defunct*] (EA)
IAMC........... Institute of Association Management Companies (EA)
IAMC........... Inter-American Markets Corp. [*Latin America*]
IAMC........... Inter-American Markets Corporation (SAUO)
IAMC........... Inter-American Music Council (EAIO)
IAMC........... International Association for Mobilization of Creativity
IaMc........... Mason City Public Library, Mason City, IA [*Library symbol*] [*Library of Congress*] (LCLS)
IAMCA......... International Association of Milk Control Agencies (EA)
IAMCB......... International Association for Mass Communication Research (SAUO)
IaMcG.......... Mason City Globe-Gazette, Mason City, IA [*Library symbol*] [*Library of Congress*] (LCLS)
IaMcg.......... McGregor Public Library, McGregor, IA [*Library symbol*] [*Library of Congress*] (LCLS)
IaMcGG........ Mason City Globe-Gazette, Mason City, IA [*Library symbol*] [*Library of Congress*] (LCLS)
IaMcgHi....... McGregor Historical Society, McGregor, IA [*Library symbol*] [*Library of Congress*] (LCLS)
IaMcgN........ North Iowa Times, McGregor, IA [*Library symbol*] [*Library of Congress*] (LCLS)
IAMCL.......... International Association of Metropolitan City Libraries (SAUO)
IaMcN.......... North Iowa Cooperative Library Extension, Mason City, IA [*Library symbol*] [*Library of Congress*] (LCLS)
IaMcNC........ North Iowa Area Community College, Mason City, IA [*Library symbol*] [*Library of Congress*] (LCLS)
IAMCR......... International Association for Mass Communication Research [*British*]
IAMCS......... International Alliance of Messianic Congregations and Synagogues (EA)
IAMD........... International Association of Managing Directors (SAUO)
IAMDA......... International Alpha Micro Dealers Association (SAUO)
IAME........... Inter-American Musical Editions (SAUO)
IAME........... International Association for Modular Exhibitry (EA)
IAME........... International Association of Medical Esperantists (EA)
IAME........... Israel Association for Merchandise Economics (SAUO)
IAMEA......... Inter-American Economic Affairs. Editorial Office. Box 181, Washington (SAUS)
IaMedi......... Mediapolis Public Library, Mediapolis, IA [*Library symbol*] [*Library of Congress*] (LCLS)
IaMediN....... New Era, Mediapolis, IA [*Library symbol*] [*Library of Congress*] (LCLS)
IaMel........... Melvin Public Library, Melvin, IA [*Library symbol*] [*Library of Congress*] (LCLS)
IaMelbR....... Melbourne Record, Melbourne, IA [*Library symbol*] [*Library of Congress*] (LCLS)
IaMer........... Merrill Public Library, Merrill, IA [*Library symbol*] [*Library of Congress*] (LCLS)
IAMEX.......... Taiwan Area Mesoscale Experiment (SAUO)
IAMFC.......... International Association for Marriage and Family Counselors (EA)
IAMFE.......... International Association on Mechanization of Field Experiments [*Aas, Norway*] (EA)
IAMFES........ International Association of Milk (SAUS)
IAMFES........ International Association of Milk, Food, and Environmental Sanitarians (EA)
IAMFPA........ International Association of Mouth and Foot Painting Artists (EA)
IAMFS.......... International Association for Maxillo-Facial Surgery (EA)
IAMFS.......... International Association of Milk and Food Sanitarians (SAUO)
IAMG........... International Association for Mathematical Geology (EA)
IAMHIST...... International Association for Audio-Visual Media in Historical Research and Education (SAUS)
IAMHIST...... International Association of Audio-Visual Media in Historical Research and Education [*Bologna, Italy*] (EAIO)
IAMI............ Iron Age Metalworking International (SAUO)
IAMI............ Iron Age Metalworking International (journ.) (SAUS)
IAMIC.......... International Association of Music Information Centres (TELE)
IAMIC.......... International Association of Mutual Insurance Companies [*See also AISAM*] (EAIO)
IaMidaHA.... Amana Heritage Society, Middle Amana, IA [*Library symbol*] [*Library of Congress*] (LCLS)
IaMil........... Milo Public Library, Milo, IA [*Library symbol*] [*Library of Congress*] (LCLS)
IaMilf.......... Milford Memorial Library, Milford, IA [*Library symbol*] [*Library of Congress*] (LCLS)
IaMilfM........ Milford Mail, Milford, IA [*Library symbol*] [*Library of Congress*] (LCLS)
IaMilfN........ Milford News, Milford, IA [*Library symbol*] [*Library of Congress*] (LCLS)
IaMisv......... Missouri Valley Public Library, Missouri Valley, IA [*Library symbol*] [*Library of Congress*] (LCLS)
IaMisvTN..... Missouri Valley Times-News, Missouri Valley, IA [*Library symbol*] [*Library of Congress*] (LCLS)
IAML........... International Association of Music Librarians (SAUO)
IAML........... International Association of Music Libraries (NITA)
IAML........... International Association of Music Libraries, Archives and Documentation Centres (SAUO)
IAMLADP..... Inter-Agency Meeting on Language Arrangements, Documentation, and Publications [*United Nations*]
IAMLANZ..... International Association of Music Librarians, Australia/New Zealand Branch (SAUO)
IAMLO......... International African Migratory Locust Organization [*See also OICMA*] (EA)
IAMLT......... International Association of Medical Laboratory Technologists [*Bootle, Merseyside, England*] (EA)
IAML-US...... International Association of Music Libraries, United States Branch (NTPA)
IAMM.......... International Association of Master Mariners (SAUO)

IAMM International Association of Medical Museums [*Later, IAP*]
IAMMA Institute of Agricultural Market Management & Administration [*India*]
IAMM&D Institute for Advanced Materials (SAUS)
IAMM & D Institute for Advanced Materials, Mechanics, and Design [*Army Materiel Command*]
IAMMM International Association of Margaret Morris Method [*Glasgow, Scotland*] (EAIO)
IAMN Istanbul Asariatica Muzeleri Nesriyati (BJA)
i amniot Intra-Amniotic [*Medicine*] (AAMN)
IAMO Inter-African and Malgasy Organization (SAUO)
IAMO Inter-American Municipal Organization (SAUO)
IaMonM Monroe Mirror, Monroe, IA [*Library symbol*] [*Library of Congress*] (LCLS)
IaMono Murphy Memorial Library, Monona, IA [*Library symbol*] [*Library of Congress*] (LCLS)
IaMonoB Monona Billboard, Monona, IA [*Library symbol*] [*Library of Congress*] (LCLS)
IaMonoHi Monona Historical Society, Monona, IA [*Library symbol*] [*Library of Congress*] (LCLS)
IaMont Monticello Public Library, Monticello, IA [*Library symbol*] [*Library of Congress*] (LCLS)
IaMontE Monticello Express, Monticello, IA [*Library symbol*] [*Library of Congress*] (LCLS)
IaMonteR Montezuma Republican, Montezuma, IA [*Library symbol*] [*Library of Congress*] (LCLS)
IaMontHi Jones County Historical Society, Monticello, IA [*Library symbol*] [*Library of Congress*] (LCLS)
IaMontJHi Jones County Historical Society, Monticello, IA [*Library symbol*] [*Library of Congress*] (LCLS)
IaMoraU Moravia Union, Moravia, IA [*Library symbol*] [*Library of Congress*] (LCLS)
IaMorn Mellinger Memorial Library, Morning Sun, IA [*Library symbol*] [*Library of Congress*] (LCLS)
IaMornN Morning Sun News-Herald, Morning Sun, IA [*Library symbol*] [*Library of Congress*] (LCLS)
IaMou Garrett Memorial Library, Moulton, IA [*Library symbol*] [*Library of Congress*] (LCLS)
IaMouT Moulton Weekly Tribune, Moulton, IA [*Library symbol*] [*Library of Congress*] (LCLS)
IAMP Imagery Acquisition and Management Plan
IAMP Institute of Atomic and Molecular Physics (SAUS)
IAMP Inter-Agency Motor Pool (WDAA)
IAMP International Academy of Medicine and Psychology [*Australia*] (EA)
IAMP International Association of Mathematical Physics (EA)
IAMP International Association of Meat Processors (EA)
IaMp Mount Pleasant Public Library, Mount Pleasant, IA [*Library symbol*] [*Library of Congress*] (LCLS)
IaMpI Iowa Wesleyan College, Mount Pleasant, IA [*Library symbol*] [*Library of Congress*] (LCLS)
IaMpN Mount Pleasant News, Mount Pleasant, IA [*Library symbol*] [*Library of Congress*] (LCLS)
IAMPO International Association of Mechanical and Plumbing Officials (SAUO)
IAMPTH International Association of Master Penmen and Teachers of Handwriting (SAUS)
IAMQS International Academy of Molecular and Quantum Sciences (SAUS)
IAMR Institute of Applied Manpower Research (SAUO)
IAMR Institute of Arctic Mineral Resources [*University of Alaska*]
IAMR Inter-American Music Review (journ.) (SAUS)
IAMR International Association for Medical Research and Cultural Exchange
IAMRC International Antarctic Meteorological Research Center (PDAA)
IAMRC International Antarctic Meteorological Research Centre (PDAA)
IAMRI International Association of Marine Radio Interests (SAUO)
IAMS Individual Aerial Mobility System [*Military*] (MCD)
IAMS Individual Alert Measures (SAUO)
IAMS Initial Attack Management System [*Weather system*]
IAMS Instantaneous Audience Measurement System
IAMS Institute for Archaeo-Metallurgical Studies [*British*] (IRUK)
IAMS Institute of Advanced Manufacturing Sciences [*University of Cincinnati*]
IAMS Institute of Advanced Manufacturing Sciences, Inc. (SAUO)
IAMS Institute of Advanced Marketing Studies (SAUO)
IAMS Institute of Advanced Marketing Studies - American Marketing Association (EA)
IAMS Institute of Applied Mathematics and Statistics [*University of British Columbia*] [*Research center*] (RCD)
IAMS Integrated Academic Information Management System (SAUS)
IAMS Integrated Armament Management System (SAUS)
IAMS International Advanced Microlithography Society [*Defunct*] (EA)
IAMS International Association for Mission Studies [*Hamburg, Federal Republic of Germany*] (EAIO)
IAMS International Association of Microbiological Societies [*ICSU*] [*Later, IUMS*]
IAMS International Association of Mission Studies (SAUO)
IAMS International Association of Municipal Societies (SAUO)
IAMS International Association of Municipal Statisticians [*Later, IARUS*]
IAMSLIC International Association of Aquatic and Marine Science Libraries & Information Centers [*Marine science*] (OSRA)
IAMSLIC International Association of Aquatic and Marine Science Libraries and Information Centers (or Centres) (SAUS)
IAMSLIC International Association of Marine Science Libraries and Information Centers (or Centres) (SAUO)
IAMSO Inter-African and Malagasy States Organization (NATG)
IAMT Inter-Allied Military Tribunal (SAUO)
IAMT International Association for Machine Translation
IAMT International Aviation Management Training Institute (SAUO)
IAMTACT Institute of Advanced Machine Tool and Control Technology [*British*]
IAMTCT Institute of Advanced Machine Tool and Control Technology (MCD)
IAMTEC Institute of Advanced Machine Tool and Control Technology (SAUS)
IAMTF Inter-Agency Maritime Task Force (SAUO)
IAMTI International Aviation Management Training Institute (SAUO)
IAM/TMD Institute of Administrative Management / Telecommunications Managers Division (HGAA)
IAM/TMD Institute of Administrative Management/Telecommunications Managers Division (SAUO)
IAMTS International Association of Model and Talent Scouts (EAIO)
IaMu P. M. Musser Public Library, Muscatine, IA [*Library symbol*] [*Library of Congress*] (LCLS)
IaMuJ Muscatine Journal, Muscatine, IA [*Library symbol*] [*Library of Congress*] (LCLS)
IAMUS Installation Automated Manpower Utilization System [*Army*]
IaMvC Cornell College, Mount Vernon, IA [*Library symbol*] [*Library of Congress*] (LCLS)
IaMvCor Cornellian, Mount Vernon, IA [*Library symbol*] [*Library of Congress*] (LCLS)
IaMvH Hawkeye and Libson Herald, Mount Vernon, IA [*Library symbol*] [*Library of Congress*] (LCLS)
IaMvS Sun Hawkeye Record, Mount Vernon, IA [*Library symbol*] [*Library of Congress*] (LCLS)
IAMW Improved Antimateriel Warhead
IAMWF Inter-American Mine Workers Federation (SAUO)
IAMWH Improved Antimateriel Warhead
IAMWMW International Association of Ministers' Wives and Ministers' Widows (EAIO)
IAMY International Assembly of Muslim Youth (SAUO)
IAN Compania Internadia de Aviacion [*Colombia*] [*ICAO designator*] (FAAC)
IAN Idiopathic Aseptic Necrosis [*Medicine*] (DMAA)
IAN Illustrated Australian News [*A publication*]
IAN Imagery Analysis Notice (MCD)
IAN Indoleacetonitrile (LDT)
IAN Informatsionnoye Agentstvo Novosti [*Novosti Press Agency*] [*Russian Federation*]
IAN Integrated Access Node (SAUS)
IAN Integrated Acoustic Network (SAUS)
IAN Interim Admission Note [*Medical records*] (DAVI)
IAN Intern Admission Note [*Medical records*] (DAVI)
IAN International Area Network (SAUS)
IAN International Artist Network (EA)
IAN Internationale des Amis de la Nature [*International Federation of Friends of Nature*]
IAN Isoamyl Nitrate (SAUS)
IAN Kennedy-King College of the City College of Chicago, Chicago, IL [*OCLC symbol*] (OCLC)
IAN Kiana [*Alaska*] [*Airport symbol*] (OAG)
IANA Institute of Alaska Native Arts (SAUS)
IANA Intermodal Association of North America
IANA International Alliance of Nutrimedical Associations (EA)
IANA Internet Address Naming Authority [*Computer science*] (ACRL)
IANA Internet Assigned Numbers Authority
IANAD I Am Not a Doctor [*Internet*]
IANAL I Am Not a Lawyer [*Internet*]
IANAP Interagency Noise Abatement Program
IaNas Nashua Public Library, Nashua, IA [*Library symbol*] [*Library of Congress*] (LCLS)
IaNasCHi Chickasaw County Historical Society, Nashua, IA [*Library symbol*] [*Library of Congress*] (LCLS)
IaNasPN Plainfield News, Nashua, IA [*Library symbol*] [*Library of Congress*] (LCLS)
IaNasR Nashua Reporter, Nashua, IA [*Library symbol*] [*Library of Congress*] (LCLS)
IANC International Academy of Nutritional Consultants [*AANC*] [*Absorbed by*] (EA)
IANC International Airline Navigation Council (SAUO)
IANC International Airline Navigation (or Navigators) Council (SAUS)
IANC International Airline Navigators Council [*Defunct*]
IANC International Air Navigation Convention
IANC International Anatomical Nomenclature (SAUS)
IANC International Anatomical Nomenclature Committee [*British*] (EAIO)
IANC Invest-in-America National Council [*Later, RA*] (EA)
IANCA Interamerican Naval Coordinating Authority (CINC)
IAND International Association of Nitrox Divers
I&A Identification and Authentication (SAUS)
I & A Indexing and Abstracting (NITA)
IandA Indexing and Abstracting (SAUS)
I & A Information and Action (MUGU)
I & A Inspection and Acceptance
I&A Integration and Assembly (SAUS)
I & A Irrigation and Aspiration [*Ophthalmology*] (DAVI)
I & B Improvement and Betterments [*Real estate*]
I&B Improvements and Betterments (SAUS)
I & C Impact and Capabilities [*Study*] [*DoD*]
I & C Incision and Curettage [*Medicine*] (CPH)
I & C Information and Coordination (ADA)
I & C Inspected and Condemned [*Military*] (AAG)
I & C Installation and Calibration (SAA)
I&C Installation and Check (SAUS)
I&C Installation and Checkout (ACAE)
I & C Installation and Checkout [*Military*] (AFM)

IandC .... Installation and Construction (SAUS)
I & C .... Installation and Construction [*Military*]
IandC .... Instrument and Communication (SAUS)
I & C .... Instrument and Controls
I and C .... Instrumentation and Communication
I & C .... Instrumentation and Communications [*Cable system*] (KSC)
I & C .... Instrumentation and Control [*Aerospace*] (AAG)
I&C .... Instrumentation and Control (ABAC)
I&C .... Instrumentation and Controls Division (SAUO)
I & C .... Integration and Checkout (KSC)
I & C .... Issues and Criteria
I & C in Scot... Instrumentation and Control in Scotland [*A publication*]
I&CO .... Installation and Checkout (ACAE)
I & C/O .... Installation and Checkout (NASA)
I&CPS .... Industrial & Commercial Power Systems (SAUS)
I & CRB .... Investigation and Censure Review Branch [*BUPERS*]
I&C Room.... Instrumentation & Control Room (SAUS)
I&CS .... Information and Communications System (ACAE)
I & C(S) .... Instrumentation and Communication (System)
I&D .... Incision and Drainage [*Medicine*] (AMHC)
IandD .... Incision and Drainage (SAUS)
I & D .... Incision and Drainage [*Medicine*]
I and D .... Information and Documentation (NITA)
I & D .... Initiation and Development
I & D .... Install and Dismantle [*Expositions and exhibitions*]
I & D .... Integrate and Dump Detection [*Telecommunications*] (TEL)
I&D .... Integration and Development [*Training term*] (LPT)
I & D .... Irrigation and Debridement [*Surgery*] (DAVI)
I & D .... Irrigation and Drainage [*Surgery*] (DAVI)
IandE .... Identification and Exposition (SAUS)
i&e .... Identification and Exposition [*Also, ident-and-expo*] (WDMC)
I & E .... Industrial and Entertainment Funds [*Correctional institutions*]
I & E .... Information and Editorial [*Career program*]
I & E .... Information and Education [*Military*]
I & E .... Innovation and Entrepreneurship
I&E .... Inspection and Enforcement (SAUO)
I&E .... Inspection and Evaluation (SAUO)
I & E .... Inspiratory and Expiratory [*Medicine*] (MELL)
I&E .... Instruments and Electronics (SAUS)
I & E .... Intake and Exhaust [*Automotive engineering*]
I&E .... Internal and External (SAUS)
I & E .... Internally and Externally (NRCH)
I&E .... Investigations and Education Program (SAUO)
IandE .... Investment and Equipment (SAUS)
I&EC .... Industrial and Engineering Chemistry (SAUO)
I&EC .... Industrial and Engineering Chemistry (journ.) (SAUS)
I&ED .... Information and Education Department (SAUO)
I&ED .... Information and Education Division (SAUO)
I&EW .... Intelligence and Electronic Warfare (SAUO)
I & H .... Information and Historical [*Military*]
I&I .... Illness and Injuries (DMAA)
I & I .... Industrial and Institutional [*Business term*]
I & I .... Infiltration and Inflow [*Environmental science*] (FFDE)
I & I .... Insolence and Insubordination [*Military*] (MUSM)
I&I .... Insolence and Insubordination [*Military*] (MUSM)
I & I .... Inspector and Instructor [*For reserve units*] [*Marine Corps*] (DOMA)
I&I .... Instruction and Inspection (SAUO)
I & I .... Intelligence and Interdiction [*Military*] (VNW)
I & I .... Intoxication and Intercourse
I&I .... Introduce and Interview (SAUS)
IandI .... Inventory and Inspection (SAUS)
I & IA .... Interior and Insular Affairs
I&I Report ... Inventory and Inspection Report (SAUS)
I & KP .... Initial and Key Personnel
I&KP .... Instructor and Key Personnel (SAUS)
I&KPC .... Instructor & Key Personnel Course (SAUS)
I&L .... Installations and Logistics (ACAE)
I & L .... Installations and Logistics
I & M .... Improvement and Modernization (AABC)
I&M .... Industrial and Military (SAUS)
I&M .... Inspection and Maintenance [*Environmental science*] (COE)
I & M .... Inspection and Maintenance
IandM .... Installation and Maintenance (SAUS)
I & M .... Installation and Maintenance
I&M .... Inventory and Monitoring (SAUS)
I & MA .... Inventory and Management Analysis (AFM)
I&ME .... Indiana and Michigan Electric Co. (SAUO)
I & N .... Immigration and Nationality Laws Administrative Decisions [*Department of Justice*] [*A publication*] (DLA)
I & N .... Immigration and Naturalization [*Service*] [*Department of Justice*]
I & N Dec.... Immigration and Nationality Laws Administrative Decisions [*A publication*] (DLA)
I&N Reporter... Immigration and Naturalization Reporter (SAUS)
I&NS .... Immigration and Naturalization Service (SAUO)
I & O .... In and Out (MAE)
I&O .... Individual and Organization performance (SAUS)
I&O .... Industry and Occupation (SAUO)
I & O .... Inlet and Outlet (MSA)
I & O .... Intake and Output [*Medicine*]
I & O .... Issues & Observations [*A publication*] (EAAP)
I & OH .... Inlet and Outlet Head (MSA)
I & OM .... Intermediate and Organizational Maintenance (MCD)
I & OP .... In and Out Processing [*Computer science*] (AFM)
IandP .... Indexed and Paged (SAUS)
I & P .... Indexed and Paged
I & P .... Inerting and Preheating [*Nuclear energy*] (NRCH)
I&P .... Intelligence & Planning (SAUS)
I&P .... Island and Peninsular (SAUO)
I&PS .... Information and Publishing Systems, Inc. (SAUO)
I&PS .... Institutional and Program Support (SAUS)
I&PS .... Instrumentation and Protective Service (SAUO)
I & R .... Information and Referral [*Services*] [*Used to assist the handicapped*]
IandR .... Information and Retrieval (SAUS)
I & R .... Initiative and Referendum
I&R .... Insertion and Removal [*Medicine*] (STED)
I & R .... Instruction and Research [*Individually-guided education*] (AEE)
I&R .... Instrumentation and Range (SAUS)
I & R .... Integrity and Reliability [*Military*] (AFIT)
I & R .... Intelligence and Reconnaissance
I & R .... Interchangeability and Replaceability [*or Replacement*] (AAG)
I&R .... Interchangeability and Replacement (SAUS)
I&R Center... Information and Referral Center (SAUS)
I&R Mgmt.... Information and Records Management (journ.) (SAUS)
I&RS .... Information and Research Services (SAUO)
I&RS .... Instrument and Range Safety (SAUS)
I & RS .... Instrumentation and Range Safety [*NASA*] (KSC)
I&RTS .... Integration and Runtime Specification (SAUS)
I&RTS .... Integration and Run Time Specifications
I&S .... Board of Inspection and Survey (SAUO)
I&S .... DoD Interchangeable and Substitutability System (SAUS)
I&S .... Industries & Science Department (ACII)
IandS .... Inspection and Security (SAUS)
I & S .... Inspection and Security
I&S .... Installation and Service (SAUS)
I & S .... Installation and Services
I&S .... Instrumentation and Range Safety (SAUS)
I&S .... Intelligence & Surveillance (SAUS)
I & S .... Interchangeability and Substitutability (AFM)
I&S .... Interchangeability and Substitute (SAUS)
I&S .... Interchangeability and Substitution (SAUO)
IANDS .... International Association for Near-Death Studies [*See also AEEPM*] (EA)
I&S .... Interoperability and Standardization (SAUO)
I & S .... Investigation and Suspension
I & S .... Iron and Steel
I&S Bulletin... Industry and Supply Bulletin (SAUS)
I&SCD .... Indoctrination and Special Courses Department (SAUO)
I & SE .... Installation and Service Engineering (IEEE)
I&SI .... Information and Software Integration (SAUS)
I & SM .... Iron & Steelmaker [*A publication*] (EAAP)
I&SM .... Iron & Steelmaker (journ.) (SAUS)
I&SN .... Infrastructure and Switched Network (SAUS)
I&SR .... Institutional and Staff Relations (SAUS)
I&SSFR .... Investigation and Security Service Field and Representatives (SAUO)
I & SSFR ..... Investigation and Security Service Field Representative [*Veterans Administration*]
I & T .... Inspection and Test (NRCH)
I&T .... Inspection and Testing (SAUO)
I & T .... Installation and Test [*Army*] (AABC)
I&T .... Integration and Test (ACAE)
I & T .... Integration and Test
I&T .... Integration and Testing (SAUS)
I&T .... Integraton and Test (SAUS)
I&T .... Internal Thoracic Artery [*Medicine*] (DMAA)
I&T .... Intolerance and Toxicity [*Medicine*] (DMAA)
I & T(P) .... Inspection and Test (Planning) (MCD)
I&TS .... Information and Technology Services (SAUS)
I & TT .... Ike and Tina Turner [*Singers*]
I&V .... Infection and Vaccinology
I&W .... Indication and Warning [*Environmental science*] (COE)
I&W .... Indications and Warning [*Military*] (MUSM)
I&W .... Intelligence and Warning (SAUS)
I&WS .... Indications and Warning System (SAUS)
IANE .... Institute of Advanced Nursing Education (SAUS)
IANE .... Iowa Northern Railway [*Federal Railroad Administration identification code*]
IANEC .... Inter-American Nuclear Energy Commission [*Organization of American States*] (NRCH)
IANEC .... Inter-American Nuclear Energy Committee (SAUS)
IaNeoG .... Gazette Reporter and Minden-Shelby News, Neloa, IA [*Library symbol*] [*Library of Congress*] (LCLS)
IANET .... Integrated Access Network [*Computer science*] (MHDB)
IaNev .... Nevada Public Library, Nevada, IA [*Library symbol*] [*Library of Congress*] (LCLS)
IaNevJ .... Nevada Evening Journal, Nevada, IA [*Library symbol*] [*Library of Congress*] (LCLS)
IaNewM .... Newell Mirror, Newell, IA [*Library symbol*] [*Library of Congress*] (LCLS)
IaNewt .... Newton Public Library, Newton, IA [*Library symbol*] [*Library of Congress*] (LCLS)
IaNewtCoC... Jasper County Courthouse, Newton, IA [*Library symbol*] [*Library of Congress*] (LCLS)
IaNewtHi .... Newton Historical Society, Newton, IA [*Library symbol*] [*Library of Congress*] (LCLS)
IaNewtJC ...... Jasper County Courthouse, Newton, IA [*Library symbol*] [*Library of Congress*] (LCLS)
IaNewtN .... Newton Daily News, Newton, IA [*Library symbol*] [*Library of Congress*] (LCLS)
IANF .... Individual Account Number File [*IRS*]
IANF .... Inter-Allied Nuclear Force (AABC)

IaNhE New Hampton Economist, New Hampton, IA [*Library symbol*] [*Library of Congress*] (LCLS)
IaNhT New Hampton Tribune, New Hampton, IA [*Library symbol*] [*Library of Congress*] (LCLS)
IANI Intelligent Access to Nordic Information (TELE)
IANI Israel Agency for Nuclear Information (SAUS)
IaNl H. J. Nugen Public Library, New London, IA [*Library symbol*] [*Library of Congress*] (LCLS)
IaNlJ New London Journal, New London, IA [*Library symbol*] [*Library of Congress*] (LCLS)
IA/NLP International Association for Neuro-Linguistic Programming (EAIO)
IANLP International Association of Neuro-Linguistic Programming (EA)
IANLS International Association for Neo-Latin Studies [*St. Andrews, Scotland*] (EAIO)
IaNm New Market Public Library, New Market, IA [*Library symbol*] [*Library of Congress*] (LCLS)
IaNmM New Market Monitor, New Market, IA [*Library symbol*] [*Library of Congress*] (LCLS)
IaNoengR North English Record, North English, IA [*Library symbol*] [*Library of Congress*] (LCLS)
IANOS International Assembly of National Organisations of Sport (SAUO)
IaNosA Nora Springs Advertiser, Nora Springs, IA [*Library symbol*] [*Library of Congress*] (LCLS)
IaNowdA Northwood Anchor, Northwood, IA [*Library symbol*] [*Library of Congress*] (LCLS)
IaNowdCoC Worth County Courthouse, Northwood, IA [*Library symbol*] [*Library of Congress*] (LCLS)
IaNowdWC Worth County Courthouse, Northwood, IA [*Library symbol*] [*Library of Congress*] (LCLS)
IaNowkN North Warren Town and County News, Norwalk, IA [*Library symbol*] [*Library of Congress*] (LCLS)
IANPE Institute for the Advancement of Notary Public Education (EA)
IANPM International Academy of Nutrition and Preventive Medicine (EA)
IANR Institute of Agriculture & Natural Resources (SAUS)
IANRP International Association of Natural Resource Pilots (EA)
IANS Institute of Applied Natural Science (EA)
IaNsS New Sharon Star, New Sharon, IA [*Library symbol*] [*Library of Congress*] (LCLS)
IANSW Ileostomy Association of New South Wales [*Australia*]
IANSW Institute of Architects of New South Wales (SAUO)
IANTD International Association of Nitrox and Technical Divers
IANTN Inter-American Naval Telecommunications Network (MCD)
IANU Italo-American National Union (SAUO)
IaNv New Virginia Public Library, New Virginia, IA [*Library symbol*] [*Library of Congress*] (LCLS)
IANVB International Association for Non-Violent Sport (SAUO)
IaNvN New Virginian, New Virginia, IA [*Library symbol*] [*Library of Congress*] (LCLS)
IANVOCC International Association of Non-Vessel Operating Common Carriers (NTPA)
IANVS International Association for Non-Violent Sport [*See also AICVS*] [*Monte Carlo, Monaco*] (EAIO)
IANW International Academic Networkshops (SAUS)
IANYM In A New York Minute (SAUS)
IANZ Institute of Actuaries of New Zealand (SAUO)
IANZ International Accreditation New Zealand (SAUS)
IANZone International Antarctic Zone (SAUS)
IAnZone International Antarctic Zone Programme (SAUS)
IAO Immediately after Onset [*Medicine*]
IAO In and Out (SAUS)
IAO In and Out of Clouds [*ICAO*] (FAAC)
IAO Incorporated Association of Organists [*British*]
IAO Independent Air Operations (SAUS)
IAO Independent Aviation Operators
IAO Individual Assistance Officer [*Department of Emergency Management*] (DEMM)
IAO Information Activities Office [*or Officer*]
IAO Institute of Ambulance Officers [*Australia*]
IAO Institute of Apostolic Oblates (EA)
IAO Insurers Advisory Organization (SAUS)
IAO Insurers' Advisory Organization of Canada
IAO Inter-Agency Committee on Oceanography (SAUO)
IAO Intermittent Aortic Occlusion [*Cardiology*]
IAO Internal Automation Operation
IAO International Academy of Orthodontics (SAUO)
IAO International Association for/of Orthodontics (SAUO)
IAO International Association of Orthodontics (EA)
IAO International Automation Operation (SAUS)
IAO Internet Application Object (SAUS)
IAO Northeastern Illinois University, Chicago, IL [*OCLC symbol*] (OCLC)
IAOA Indicated Angle-of-Attack (GAVI)
IAOAD International Association of Original Art Diffusors (EAIO)
IaOak Eckels Memorial Library, Oakland, IA [*Library symbol*] [*Library of Congress*] (LCLS)
IaOakA Oakland Acorn, Oakland, IA [*Library symbol*] [*Library of Congress*] (LCLS)
IAOC Indian Army Ordnance Control [*British*]
IAOC Indian Army Ordnance Corps (SAUO)
IAOC Irish Amateur Open Championship [*Golf*] (ROG)
IaOcD Democrat, Orange City, IA [*Library symbol*] [*Library of Congress*] (LCLS)
IaOch Ocheyedan Public Library, Ocheyedan, IA [*Library symbol*] [*Library of Congress*] (LCLS)
IaOchMH Melvin News, Ocheyedan, IA [*Library symbol*] [*Library of Congress*] (LCLS)
IaOchMN Melvin News, Ocheyedan, IA [*Library symbol*] [*Library of Congress*] (LCLS)
IaOchP Ocheyedan Press, Ocheyedan, IA [*Library symbol*] [*Library of Congress*] (LCLS)
IaOcM Mid-America Reformed Seminary, Orange City, IA [*Library symbol*] [*Library of Congress*] (LCLS)
IaOcN Northwestern College, Orange City, IA [*Library symbol*] [*Library of Congress*] (LCLS)
IaOcSC Sioux County Capital, Orange City, IA [*Library symbol*] [*Library of Congress*] (LCLS)
IAOD In Addition to Other Duties [*Military*]
IAOD International Academy of Optimum Dentistry [*Defunct*] (EA)
IAOD International Association of Opera Directors (EAIO)
IaOdC Odebolt Chronicle, Odebolt, IA [*Library symbol*] [*Library of Congress*] (LCLS)
IAOE International Arctic Ocean Expedition (SAUO)
IAOE International Association of Optometric Executives (EA)
IaOe Oelwein Public Library, Oelwein, IA [*Library symbol*] [*Library of Congress*] (LCLS)
IaOeR Daily Register, Oelwein, IA [*Library symbol*] [*Library of Congress*] (LCLS)
IAOG International Administrative management domain Operators Group (SAUS)
IaOgd Ogden Public Library, Ogden, IA [*Library symbol*] [*Library of Congress*] (LCLS)
IaOgdR Ogden Reporter, Ogden, IA [*Library symbol*] [*Library of Congress*] (LCLS)
IAOH In Appreciation of the Hollies (EA)
IAOHRA International Association of Official Human Rights Agencies (EA)
IAOL International Association of Orientalist Librarians (EA)
IAOL International Association of Orientalist Libraries (SAUO)
IAOM International Association of Oral Myology (DMAA)
IAOMO International Association of Olympic Medical Officers [*Rugby, Warwickshire, England*] (EAIO)
IAOMS International Association of Oral and Maxillofacial Surgeons (EA)
IAOMT International Academy of Oral Medicine and Toxicology
IaOn Onawa Public Library, Onawa, IA [*Library symbol*] [*Library of Congress*] (LCLS)
IaOnCoC Monona County Courthouse, Onawa, IA [*Library symbol*] [*Library of Congress*] (LCLS)
IaOnD Onawa Democrat, Onawa, IA [*Library symbol*] [*Library of Congress*] (LCLS)
IaOnS Onawa Sentinel, Onawa IA [*Library symbol*] [*Library of Congress*] (LCLS)
IAOO Irish Agricultural Officers Organisation (BI)
IAOO Irish Agricultural Officers Organization (SAUO)
IAOP International Association of Oral Pathologists (EA)
IAOPA International Aircraft Owners and Pilots Association (SAUO)
IAOPA International Association of Owners and Pilots of Private Airplanes (SAUO)
IAOPA International Council of Aircraft Owner and Pilot Associations (EA)
IAOPA-EUR IAOPA European Region (SAUS)
IAOPS Indiana Association of Osteopathic Physicians and Surgeons (SRA)
IaOrM Mid-American Reformed Seminary, Orange City, IA [*Library symbol*] [*Library of Congress*] (LCLS)
IAOS Inspector of Army Ordnance Services (SAUO)
IAOS International Association for Official Statistics [*International Statistical Institute*] [*Voorburg, Netherlands*] (EAIO)
IAOS International Association of Ocular Surgeons (EA)
IAOS International Association of Official Statistics (SAUO)
IAOS International Association of Oral Surgeons (EAIO)
IAOS Irish Agricultural Organisation Society Ltd. (BI)
IaOsa Sage Library, Osage, IA [*Library symbol*] [*Library of Congress*] (LCLS)
IaOsaCoC Mitchell County Courthouse, Osage, IA [*Library symbol*] [*Library of Congress*] (LCLS)
IaOsaP Mitchell County Press-News, Osage, IA [*Library symbol*] [*Library of Congress*] (LCLS)
IaOsc Osceola Public Library, Osceola, IA [*Library symbol*] [*Library of Congress*] (LCLS)
IaOscCoC Clarke County Courthouse, Osceola, IA [*Library symbol*] [*Library of Congress*] (LCLS)
IaOscS Osceola Sentinel, Osceola, IA [*Library symbol*] [*Library of Congress*] (LCLS)
IaOsk Oskaloosa Public Library, Oskaloosa, IA [*Library symbol*] [*Library of Congress*] (LCLS)
IaOskH Oskaloosa Daily Herald, Oskaloosa, IA [*Library symbol*] [*Library of Congress*] (LCLS)
IaOskMHi Mahaska County Historical Society, Oskaloosa, IA [*Library symbol*] [*Library of Congress*] (LCLS)
IaOskW William Penn College, Oskaloosa, IA [*Library symbol*] [*Library of Congress*] (LCLS)
IaOss Ossian Public Library, Ossian, IA [*Library symbol*] [*Library of Congress*] (LCLS)
IaOssB Ossian Bee, Ossian, IA [*Library symbol*] [*Library of Congress*] (LCLS)
IAOT International Association for Oxygen Therapy
IAOT International Association of Organ Teachers (SAUO)
IAOT International Association of Organ Teachers USA [*Later, KTA*] (EA)
IAOT International Aviation Organization Training (SAUS)
IaOt Ottumwa Public Library, Ottumwa, IA [*Library symbol*] [*Library of Congress*] (LCLS)
IaOtC Ottumwa Heights College, Ottumwa, IA [*Library symbol*] [*Library of Congress*] (LCLS)

IaOtCo .... Ottumwa Courier, Ottumwa, IA [*Library symbol*] [*Library of Congress*] (LCLS)
IaOtS .... Southern Iowa Library Cooperative, Ottumwa, IA [*Library symbol*] [*Library of Congress*] (LCLS)
IAOUG.......... International Association of Underwater Games (SAUO)
IAOWS .... Inspector of Army Ordnance Workshop Services (SAUO)
IaOxj............ Wreigie Memorial Library, Oxford Junction, IA [*Library symbol*] [*Library of Congress*] (LCLS)
IAP.............. Image Analysis Processor (SAUS)
IAP.............. Image Analysis Processor Internet Access Provider (SAUO)
IAP.............. Image Array Processor
IAP.............. Imagery Architecture Plan (SAUS)
IAP.............. Imaging Atom Probe (AAEL)
IAP.............. Imitation Art Paper (DGA)
IAP.............. Immediate Access Processing (SAUS)
IAP.............. Immunosuppressive Acidic Protein [*Immunochemistry*] (DMAA)
IAP.............. Improved Accuracy Program (MCD)
IAP.............. Imsge Array Processor (SAUS)
IAP.............. Incentive Awards Program [*of the federal government, administered by CSC*]
IAP.............. Incentive Awards Program. Indoor Air Pollution (SAUO)
IAP.............. Incident Action Plan [*Department of Emergency Management*] (DEMM)
IAP.............. Independent Agrochemical Observer (SAUS)
IAP.............. Individual Annoyance Prediction (EEVL)
IAP.............. Individualized Accommodation Plan (SAUO)
IAP.............. Indoor Air Pollution
IAP.............. Industry Applications Programs [*Computer science*] (IBMDP)
IAP.............. Inerting and Preheating (IAA)
IAP.............. Inhibitor-of-Apoptosis
IAP.............. Inhibitor of Apoptosis Protein [*Cytology*]
IAP.............. Initial Aiming Point [*Gunnery*]
IAP.............. Initial Approach [*Aviation*]
IAP.............. Initial Approach Procedure (SAUS)
IAP.............. Initial Approved Program
IAP.............. Inlet Absolute Pressure
IAP.............. Inorganic Ablative Plastic
IAP.............. Inosinic Acid Pyrophosphorylase (DB)
IAP.............. Institute of Animal Physiology [*British*]
IAP.............. Institute of Arthropodology and Parasitology [*Georgia Southern University*] [*Research center*] (RCD)
IAP.............. Institute of Atmospheric Physics [*University of Arizona*] [*Research center*]
IAP.............. Institute of Australian Photography (SAUO)
IAP.............. Institutional Assistance Program (SAUS)
IAP.............. Institution of Analysis and Programmers (WDAA)
IAP.............. Institution of Analysts & Programmers (SAUO)
IAP.............. Instrument Approach Procedure [*Aviation*] (AFM)
IAP.............. Insurance Accounting Principles
IAP.............. Integrated Action Plan
IAP.............. Integrated Actuation Package (SAUS)
IAP.............. Integrated Aeronautic Program [*Military*] (AFIT)
IAP.............. Interactive Application Processor (SAUS)
IAP.............. Interactive Programming [*Computer science*]
IAP.............. Interarray Processor (NVT)
IAP.............. Interceptor Aim Points
IAP.............. Interdivisional Administration Practice (SAUS)
IAP.............. Interference Avoidance Processor (SAUS)
IAP.............. Intermittent Acute Porphyria [*Medicine*]
IAP.............. Internal Air Portability
IAP.............. Internal Array Processor [*Data General Corp.*]
IAP.............. International Academy of Pathology (EA)
IAP.............. International Academy of Poets (SAUO)
IAP.............. International Academy of Proctology [*Defunct*] (EA)
IAP.............. International Activities Program [*US Army Western Command*]
IAP.............. International Aero Press
IAP.............. International Affiliates Program (SAUS)
IAP.............. International Airport
IAP.............. International Association for Planetology (SAUO)
IAP.............. International Association of Parapsychologists (EA)
IAP.............. International Association of Photoplatemakers (EA)
IAP.............. International Association of Planetology [*Brussels, Belgium*] (EA)
IAP.............. International Association of Psychotechnics (SAUO)
IAP.............. International Association of Pteridologists (EERA)
IAP.............. International Atomic Energy Pool (SAUO)
IAP.............. International Atomic Pool (SAUS)
IAP.............. Internet Access Pack (SAUS)
IAP.............. Internet Access Provider [*Computer science*] (VLIE)
IAP.............. Intra-Abdominal Pressure
IAP.............. Intra-Arterial Pressure
IAP.............. Intracisternal A-Particle [*Biochemistry*]
IAP.............. Intrasystem Analysis Program (ACAE)
IAP.............. Inventors Assistance Program (SAUS)
IAP.............. Iodoantipyrine [*Biochemistry*]
IAP.............. Iona Appliances, Inc. [*Toronto Stock Exchange symbol*]
IAP.............. Iranian Aircraft Program [*Military*] (MCD)
IAP.............. ISDN Access Internetworking Profile (SAUS)
IAP.............. Islamic Association for Palestine
IAP.............. Islet-Activating Protein [*Biochemistry*]
IAP.............. Isopropylantipyrine [*Biochemistry*]
IAP.............. Oakton Community College, Morton Grove, IL [*OCLC symbol*] (OCLC)
IAP.............. Portland, OR [*Location identifier*] [*FAA*] (FAAL)
IAP2............. International Arctic Polynia Programme (SAUO)
IAPA............. Idaho Association of Public Accountants (SRA)
IAPA............. Illinois Academy of Physician Assistants (SRA)
IAPA............. Illinois Asphalt Pavement Association (SRA)
IAPA............. Industrial Accident Prevention Association [*Canada*] (HGAA)
IAPA............. Instrument Approach Procedures Automation [*FAA*] (TAG)
IAPA............. Inter-American Parliamentary Association (SAUO)
IAPA............. Inter-American Police Academy (AABC)
IAPA............. Inter-American Press Association (EA)
IAPA............. International Airline Passengers Association (EA)
IAPA............. International Association of Parametric Analysts (SAUO)
IAPA............. International Association of Physicians in Audiology (EAIO)
IAPA............. International Association of Plastic Arts (SAUO)
IAPA............. International Association of Police Artists (SAUO)
IAPA............. Irish Association of Professional Archaeologists (SAUO)
IAPAC .... Injection Assistee par Air Comprise [*Pneumatic Direct Fuel Injection*] [*French*]
IAPAC .... International Association of Physicians in AIDS Care (EA)
IaPal .... Palmer Public Library, Palmer, IA [*Library symbol*] [*Library of Congress*] (LCLS)
IaPanV.......... Guthrie County Vedette, Panora, IA [*Library symbol*] [*Library of Congress*] (LCLS)
IAPAP .... International Association of Pure and Applied Physics (SAUO)
IaParE........... Eclipse-News-Review, Parkersburg, IA [*Library symbol*] [*Library of Congress*] (LCLS)
IaParnHi ...... Iowa County Historical Society, Parnell, IA [*Library symbol*] [*Library of Congress*] (LCLS)
IAPAS .... Integrated Avionics Processing System (SAUS)
IAPA/SIP...... Inter American Press Association (NTPA)
IaPau .... Paullina Free Public Library, Paullina, IA [*Library symbol*] [*Library of Congress*] (LCLS)
IaPauT .... Paullina Times, Paullina, IA [*Library symbol*] [*Library of Congress*] (LCLS)
IAPB............. Inter-Allied Personnel Board [*World War II*]
IAPB............. International Agency for the Prevention of Blindness (EA)
IAPB............. International Association for the Prevention of Blindness [*Later, InternationalAgency for the Prevention of Blindness*] (EA)
IAPBPPV...... International Association of Plant Breeders for the Protection of Plant Varieties (EAIO)
IAPBT........... International Association of Piano Builders and Technicians (EA)
IAPC............. Institute for the Advancement of Philosophy for Children (EA)
IAPC............. Instrument Approach Procedure Chart [*Aviation*] (NOAA)
IA-PC .... Intel Architecture Personal Computer (MWOL)
IAPC............. Inter-American Peace Committee [*Later, Inter-American Committee on Peacef ul Settlement*] [*OAS*]
IAPC............. Interim Applications Program Committee (SAUO)
IAPC............. International Association for Pollution Control [*Defunct*] (EA)
IAPC............. International Association for Public Cleansing (SAUO)
IAPC............. International Association of Pet Cemeteries (EA)
IAPC............. International Association of Political Consultants (EA)
IAPC............. International Auditing Practices Committee
IaPcN........... Prairie City News, Prairie City, IA [*Library symbol*] [*Library of Congress*] (LCLS)
IAPCO .... International Association of Private Container Owners (SAUO)
IAPCO .... International Association of Professional Congress Organizers [*Brussels, Belgium*] (EAIO)
IAPCU .... Iowa Association of Private Colleges and Universities (SAUO)
IAPCW .... International Association for the Promotion of Child Welfare (SAUO)
IAPD .... International Association of Paediatric Dentistry [*British*] (EAIO)
IAPD .... International Association of Parents of the Deaf [*Later, ASDC*] (EA)
IAPD .... International Association of Plastics Distributors (NTPA)
IAPDOI......... Italian Association for the Production and Distribution of On-Line Information (SAUO)
IAPE............. Independent Association of Publishers' Employees (EA)
IaPe.............. Pella Public Library, Pella, IA [*Library symbol*] [*Library of Congress*] (LCLS)
IaPeC............ Central College, Pella, IA [*Library symbol*] [*Library of Congress*] (LCLS)
IAPEC........... International Agency for the Promotion for/of Ear Care (SAUO)
IaPeCh.......... Pella Chronicle, Pella, IA [*Library symbol*] [*Library of Congress*] (LCLS)
IaPeCR .... Central Ray, Pella, IA [*Library symbol*] [*Library of Congress*] (LCLS)
IaPerC .... Chief, Perry, IA [*Library symbol*] [*Library of Congress*] (LCLS)
IaPersHi ...... Harrison County Historical Society, Persia, IA [*Library symbol*] [*Library of Congress*] (LCLS)
IAPES........... International Association of Personnel in Employment Security (EA)
IAPESGW..... International Association of Physical Education and Sports for Girls and Women (SAUS)
IaPet............. Kirchner-French Memorial Library, Peterson, IA [*Library symbol*] [*Library of Congress*] (LCLS)
IaPetP........... Peterson Patriot, Peterson, IA [*Library symbol*] [*Library of Congress*] (LCLS)
IAPF............. Inter-American Peacekeeping Force
IAPFM........... Institute for Applied Public Financial Management (SAUO)
IAPG .... Iberian Atlantic Planning Guidance (NATG)
IAPG .... Interagency Advanced Power Group
IAPG .... Interagency Arctic Policy Group [*Marine science*] (OSRA)
IAPG .... Inter-American Parliamentary Group on Population and Development [*An association*] (EA)
IAPG .... Interatrial Pressure Gradient [*Medicine*] (EDAA)
IAPG .... International Association of Physical Geography (BARN)
IAPG .... International Association of Psychoanalytic Gerontology [*Paris, France*] (EAIO)
IAPG .... Item Analysis Program, General (PDAA)
IAPGPD........ Inter-American Parliamentary Group on Population and Development (EA)

IAPGR Institute of Animal Physiology and Genetics Research [*Research center*] [*British*] (IRC)

IAPGWB Incorporated Association for Promoting the General Welfare of the Blind (SAUO)

IAPH International Association of Paper Historians (DGA)

IAPH International Association of Ports and Harbors [*Japan*]

IAPHC International Association of Printing House Craftsmen (EA)

IA Phys Institute of Animal Physiology (SAUO)

IAPI Argentine Industrial Production Institute (SAUO)

IAPI Industrial Air Pollution Inspectorate (PDAA)

IAPI Institute of Advertising Practitioners in Ireland (BI)

IAPI Institute of American Poultry Industries [*Later, PEIA*] (EA)

IAP-IASA International Airport-Integrated System Architecture (SAUO)

IaPierP Pierson Press, Pierson, IA [*Library symbol*] [*Library of Congress*] (LCLS)

IAPIP International Association for the Protection of Industrial Property

IAPK Internacia Asocio de Postmarkkolektantoj (SAUO)

IAPL Initial Allowance Parts List [*Military*] (CAAL)

IAPL International Association for Penal Law (SAUO)

IAPL International Association for Philosophy and Literature (EA)

IAPL International Association of Penal Law [*Freiburg, Federal Republic of Germany*] (EAIO)

IaPlaBHi Bremer County Historical Society, Plainsfield, IA [*Library symbol*] [*Library of Congress*] (LCLS)

IaPleN Marion County News, Pleasantville, IA [*Library symbol*] [*Library of Congress*] (LCLS)

IAPIHC International Association of Printing House Craftsmen (SAUO)

IAPLIT Interamerican Program for Linguistics and Language Teaching (SAUS)

IAPLLT Interamerican Program for Linguistics and Language Teaching (EA)

IAPLSP International Association for Philosophy of Law and Social Philosophy [*See also AIPDPS*]

IAPM Institute of Applied Physiology and Medicine [*Formerly, Institute of Environmenta l Medicine and Physiology*] [*Research center*] (RCD)

IAPM International Academy of Preventive Medicine (EA)

IAPM International Association of Photoplate Makers (DGA)

IAPM International Association of Progressive Montessorians (SAUO)

IAPMA International Association of Hand Papermakers and Paper Artists (EAIO)

IAPMJ International Academy of Preventive Medicine Journal [*Medicine*] (EDAA)

IAPMO International Association of Plumbing and Mechanical Officials (EA)

IAPN International Association of Professional Numismatists [*See also AINP*] [*Zurich, Switzerland*] (EAIO)

IAPNH International Association of Professional Natural Hygienists (EA)

IAPO Industrial Accountable Property Officer [*Air Force*]

IAPO Interchangeable at Attachment Point Only (AAG)

IAPO International ACSYS Project Office (SAUO)

IAPO International Association for/of Physical Oceanogaphy (SAUO)

IAPO International Association for Physical Oceanography (SAUS)

IAPO International Association of Physical Oceanography [*Later, IAPSO*]

IAPO International Association of Printers' Overseers (DGA)

IaPocR Pocahontas Record Democrat, Pocahontas, IA [*Library symbol*] [*Library of Congress*] (LCLS)

IAPOI International Association of Public Opinion Institutes (SAUO)

IaPolc Polk City Community Library, Polk City, IA [*Library symbol*] [*Library of Congress*] (LCLS)

IaPolcN Big Creek News, Polk City, IA [*Library symbol*] [*Library of Congress*] (LCLS)

IaPom Pomeroy Public Library, Pomeroy, IA [*Library symbol*] [*Library of Congress*] (LCLS)

IaPomH Pomeroy Herald, Pomeroy, IA [*Library symbol*] [*Library of Congress*] (LCLS)

IaPos Postville Public Library, Postville, IA [*Library symbol*] [*Library of Congress*] (LCLS)

IaPosH Postville Herald, Postville, IA [*Library symbol*] [*Library of Congress*] (LCLS)

IAPP Insulinoma Amyloid Polypeptide (DB)

IAPP International Arctic Polynia Programme (SAUO)

IAPP International Arctic Polynya Programme (SAUS)

IAPP International Association for Plant Physiologists (SAUO)

IAPP International Association for Plant Physiology [*Australia*] (EAIO)

IAPP International Association for Preventive Pediatrics (DAVI)

IAPP International Association for the/of Plant Physiology (SAUO)

IAPP International Association for the Plant Physiology (SAUS)

IAPP International Association of Pacemaker Patients [*Later, IAHP*] (EA)

IAPP International Association of Plant Physiology (SAUS)

IAPP International Association of Police Professors [*Later, ACJS*]

IAPP International Association of Prevention Programs (SAUO)

IAPP Ion Acoustic Plasma Pulse

IAPP Islet Amyloid Polypeptide [*Biochemistry*]

IAPPHAP International Association for Past and Present History of the Art of Printing (EA)

IAPPI International Association of Public Pawnbroking Institutions [*Milan, Italy*] (EA)

IAPPP International Amateur-Professional Photoelectric Photometry [*An association*]

IAPPW International Association of Pupil Personnel Workers (EA)

IAPR Indian Air Patrol Reserve (SAUO)

IAPR Inflatable Air Portable Roadway (SAUS)

IAPR Institute of Advanced Philosophic Research (EA)

IAPR International Association for/on Pattern Recognition (SAUO)

IAPR International Association for Pattern Recognition [*British*] (EA)

IAPR International Association for Psychotronic Research [*Prague, Czechoslovakia*] (EA)

IAPR International Association on Pattern Recognition (SAUS)

IaPrcWHi Wayne County Historical Society, Promise City, IA [*Library symbol*] [*Library of Congress*] (LCLS)

IAPRD Israel Annals of Psychiatry and Related Disciplines [*Publication*] [*Medicine*] (EDAA)

IaPreT Preston Times, Preston, IA [*Library symbol*] [*Library of Congress*] (LCLS)

IaPreWHi Wayne County Historical Society, Promise City, IA [*Library symbol*] [*Library of Congress*] (LCLS)

IAPRI International Association for the Properties of Steam (SAUO)

IAPRI International Association of Packaging Research Institutes [*British*] (EAIO)

IaPri Primghar Public Library, Primghar, IA [*Library symbol*] [*Library of Congress*] (LCLS)

IaPriB O'Brien County Bell, Primghar, IA [*Library symbol*] [*Library of Congress*] (LCLS)

IAPRS International Association for Psychosocial Rehabilitation Systems (SEAT)

IAPS Incorporated Association of Preparatory Schools [*British*] (DCTA)

IAPS Independent Association of Preparatory Schools

IAPS Inductosyn Angle Position Simulator

IAPS Institute for Advanced Pastoral Studies (EA)

IAPS Interim Antenna Pointing Subsystem [*Deep Space Instrumentation Facility, NASA*]

IAPS International Academy of Political Science (SAUO)

IAPS International Affiliation of Planning Societies (SAUO)

IAPS International Association for the Production of Steam (SAUO)

IAPS International Association for the Properties of Steam [*Later, IAPWS*] (EA)

IAPS International Association for the Study of People and their Physical Surroundings (SAUO)

IAPS International Association of Pipe Smokers Clubs (SAUO)

IAPS International Association of Social Scientists, Architects and Planners (SAUO)

IAPS Ion Auxiliary Propulsion System (ACAE)

IAPSAC International Association of Parents and Professionals for Safe Alternatives in Childbirth (SAUO)

IAPSC Inter-African Phytosanitary Commission

IAPSC Inter-African Phyto-Sanitary Council (SAUO)

IAPSC International Association of Pipe Smokers Clubs (EA)

IAPSC International Association of Professional Security Consultants (EA)

IAPSO Inter-Agency Procurement Services Office (SAUO)

IAPSO International Association for Physical Sciences of the Ocean (SAUS)

IAPSO International Association for Plant Taxonomy (SAUO)

IAPSO International Association for the Physical Sciences of the Ocean (EA)

IAPSP Inter-American Program for Social Progress [*AID*]

IAPSRS International Association for/of Psychosocial Rehabilitation Services (SAUO)

IAPSRS International Association of Psycho-Social Rehabilitation Services (EA)

IAPSU Inter-Agency Procurement Services Unit (SAUO)

IAPSUN International Association of Political Scientists for the United Nations (SAUO)

IAPT International Association for Plant Taxonomy [*Utrecht, Netherlands*] (EA)

IAPT International Association of Plant Taxonomists (EERA)

IA/PT Item Acquisition/Production Trade-Off Model

IAPTA International Allied Printing Trades Association (EA)

IAPTE International Academy of Pediatric Transdisciplinary Education [*British*] (EAIO)

IAPUP International Association on the Political Use of Psychiatry [*Amsterdam, Netherlands*] (EAIO)

IAPV Institute Against Prejudice and Violence (EA)

IAPV Intermittent Abdominal Pressure Ventilation [*Medicine*] (DMAA)

IAPW International Association for/of Personnel Women (SAUO)

IAPW International Association for Personnel Women (EA)

IAPW International Association of Personnel Women (SAUS)

IAP-WASAD International Action Programme on Water and Sustainable Agricultural Development (SAUO)

IaPwdC Packwood Clarion, Packwood, IA [*Library symbol*] [*Library of Congress*] (LCLS)

IAPWG Interagency Arctic Policy Working Group (SAUO)

IAPWS International Association for the Properties of Water and Steam (EA)

IAQ Independent Activities Questionnaire [*Psychology*]

IAQ Indoor Air Quality

IAQ International Academy for Quality [*Grobenzell, Federal Republic of Germany*] (EAIO)

IAQ International Association for Quality (SAUO)

IAQ Parkland College, Champaign, IL [*OCLC symbol*] (OCLC)

IAQA/C Interstate Air Quality Agencies /Commissions [*Environmental Protection Agency*]

IAQC International Association for/of Quality Circles (SAUO)

IAQC International Association for Quality Circles (SAUS)

IAQC International Association of Quality Circles (EA)

IAQDE Independent Association of Questioned Document Examiners (EA)

IAQ INFO Indoor Air Quality Information Clearinghouse [*Environmental Protection Agency*] (AEPA)

IAQINFO Indoor Air Quality Information [*Clearinghouse*] [*Environment term*] (EGA)

IAQMS International Academy of Molecular Quantum Sciences (SAUO)

IAQR Indian Association for Quality and Reliability (SAUO)

IAQR International Association of/on Quaternary Research (SAUO)

IAQR International Association on Quaternary Research (SAUS)

IAR............ Iliamna Air Taxi, Inc. [*ICAO designator*] (FAAC)
I-Ar............ Illinois State Library, Archives Division, Springfield, IL [*Library symbol*] [*Library of Congress*] (LCLS)
IAR............ Imagery Analysis Report (MCD)
IAR............ Immediate Asthma Reaction (MELL)
IAR............ Inactive Air Reserve
IAR............ Indefinite Appointment Review (SAUS)
IAR............ Indirect Address Register
IAR............ Individual Action Report
IAR............ Industrial All Risks (MARI)
IAR............ Information Analysis and Retrieval [*Computer science*] (ECII)
IAR............ Initial Address Register [*Computer science*] (HGAA)
IAR............ Initial Address Reject (SAUS)
IAR............ Inspection Acceptance Record (SAA)
IAR............ Institute for Aerobics Research (EA)
IAR............ Institute for Agricultural Research (SAUS)
IAR............ Institute for Agricultural Research and Special Services (SAUO)
IAR............ Institute for Air Research (WDAA)
IAR............ Institute for American Relations (SAUO)
IAR............ Institute for Atmospheric Radioactivity [*Feiberg, Germany*] (CARB)
IAR............ Institute for Atomic Research (SAUO)
IAR............ Institute of Agricultural Research (SAUS)
IAR............ Institute of American Relations [*Defunct*] (EA)
IAR............ Institute of Andean Research (EA)
IAR............ Institute of Asian Research [*Canada*] (IRC)
IAR............ Institute of Atomic Research (SAUS)
IAR............ Instruction Address Register [*Computer science*] (MDG)
IAR............ Instruction Approval Release (SAUS)
IAR............ Instrument Accommodation Review (ACAE)
IAR............ Instrument Air Receiver (AAG)
IAR............ Integrated Alternator Regulator [*Automotive engineering*]
IAR............ Integrated Avionics Racks (SAUS)
IAR............ Integrity and Reliability [*Military*] (AFIT)
IAR............ Intelligence and Reconnaissance (IAA)
IAR............ Intelligence Automation Requirements (SAUO)
IAR............ Interagency Rate (AFM)
IAR............ Interavia Aerospace Review [*Interavia Publications*] [*Information service or system*] (CRD)
IAR............ Interment Is Authorized for the Remains Of [*Military*]
IAR............ Internal Academic Reviews (SAUS)
IAR............ Internal Assessment Review (SAUO)
IAR............ International Art Register
IAR............ International Association of Radiopharmacology (EA)
IAR............ International Audio Report (SAUS)
IAR............ International Authority for the Ruhr (SAUO)
IAR............ Interrupt Address Register
IAR............ Intersection of Air Routes [*Aviation*]
IAR............ Inventory Adjustment Rate
IAR............ Inventory Adjustment Report [*Military*]
IAR............ Inventory Adjustment Request (SAUS)
IAR............ Iodine-Azide Reaction (DB)
IAR............ Isobaric Analog Resonance [*Nuclear structure*]
IAR............ Roosevelt University, Chicago, IL [*OCLC symbol*] (OCLC)
IARA............ Industrial Arbitration Registrars' Association [*Australia*]
IARA............ Interadministrative Revenue Accounting (SAUS)
IARA............ Inter-Allied Reparations Agency [*Brussels*]
IARA............ International Aerosol Research Assembly (SAUO)
IARA............ International Animal Rights Alliance [*Defunct*] (EA)
IARA............ International Association of Rebekah Assemblies, IOOF [*Independent Order of Odd Fellows*] (EA)
IaRa............ Rake Public Library, Rake, IA [*Library symbol*] [*Library of Congress*] (LCLS)
IARAC............ International Association of Recognized Automobile Clubs (SAUO)
IA RAN............ Institute of Archaeology, Russian Academy of Sciences (BUAC)
IARASM............ Institute for Advanced Research in Asian Science and Medicine (EA)
IARB............ Indefinite Appointment Review Board (SAUS)
IARB............ Inspection Analysis Review Board (MCD)
IArb............ Institute of Arbitrators [*British*] (DI)
IARB............ Italian Aviation Research Branch of Air-Britain (SAUO)
IArc............ Arcola Public Library, Arcola, IL [*Library symbol*] [*Library of Congress*] (LCLS)
IARC............ Independent Assessment and Research Centre [*British*] (CB)
IARC............ Indian Agricultural Research Council (SAUO)
IARC............ Interagency Arctic Research Policy Committee (SAUO)
IARC............ International Action for the Rights of the Child [*See also AIDE*] [*Paris, France*] (EAIO)
IARC............ International Agency for Research of/on Cancer (SAUO)
IARC............ International Agency for Research on Cancer [*World Health Organization*] [*Lyon, France*] [*Research center*] (EAIO)
IARC............ International Agricultural Research Center
IARC............ International Agricultural Research Centre (EERA)
IARC............ International Amateur Radio Club (SAUO)
IARC............ International Amateur Recording Contest (SAUO)
IARC............ International Arctic Research Center (SAUO)
IAR/C............ Interviewing, Assessment, and Referral or Counseling (ADA)
IARCA............ International Association Residential and Community Alternatives (EAIO)
IARCA............ International Community Corrections Association (NTPA)
IaRcA............ Rockwell City Advocate, Rockwell City, IA [*Library symbol*] [*Library of Congress*] (LCLS)
IARCB............ International Asian Research Conference Board (SAUO)
IARCC............ Interagency Arctic Research Coordinating Committee [*Terminated, 1978*] [*National Science Foundation*]
IARCC............ Interagency Arctic Research Coordination Committee (SAUS)
IaRcCHi............ Calhoun County Historical Society, Rockwell City, IA [*Library symbol*] [*Library of Congress*] (LCLS)
IaRcfR............ Rockford Register, Rockford, IA [*Library symbol*] [*Library of Congress*] (LCLS)
IARCH............ Institute of Action Research for Community Health (ADWA)
IARC Monogr Eval Carcinog Risks Hum... IARC Monographs on the Evaluation of Carcinogenic Risks to Humans (journ.) (SAUS)
IARC Monogr Eval Carcinog Risks Hum Suppl... IARC Monographs on the Evaluation of Carcinogenic Risks to Humans. Supplement (journ.) (SAUS)
IARC Sci Publ... IARC Scientific Publications (journ.) (SAUS)
IArcSD............ Arcola Community Unit School District, Arcola, IL [*Library symbol*] [*Library of Congress*] (LCLS)
IARD............ Incorporated Association of Retail Distributors (SAUO)
IARD............ Information Analysis and Retrival Division (SAUS)
IARD............ International Association for Rural Development (AIE)
IARDP............ Incorporated Association for the Relief of Distressed Protestants (SAUO)
IARE............ Improved Amphibious Reconnaissance Equipment [*Military*] (MCD)
IARE............ Institute of Animal Resource Ecology [*University of British Columbia*] [*Research center*] (RCD)
IARE............ International Association of Railway Employees (EA)
IAREC............ Irrigated Agriculture Research and Extension Center [*Washington State University*] [*Research center*] (RCD)
IaRedf............ Redfield Public Library, Redfield, IA [*Library symbol*] [*Library of Congress*] (LCLS)
IaRedfRS............ Dexfield Review Sentinel, Redfield, IA [*Library symbol*] [*Library of Congress*] (LCLS)
IaRedo............ Red Oak Public Library, Red Oak, IA [*Library symbol*] [*Library of Congress*] (LCLS)
IaRedoE............ Red Oak Express, Red Oak, IA [*Library symbol*] [*Library of Congress*] (LCLS)
IaReiC............ Reinbeck Courier, Reinbeck, IA [*Library symbol*] [*Library of Congress*] (LCLS)
IaRemBE............ Remsen Bell-Enterprise, Remsen, IA [*Library symbol*] [*Library of Congress*] (LCLS)
IaRen............ Renwick Public Library, Renwick, IA [*Library symbol*] [*Library of Congress*] (LCLS)
IARF............ International Amateur Racquetball Federation (EA)
IARF............ International Association for Liberal Christianity and Religious Freedom (SAUS)
IARF............ International Association for Religious Freedom [*Germany*] (EY)
IARF............ International Association for Religious Freedom, United States Chapter (EA)
IARF............ Ischemic Acute Renal Failure [*Medicine*] (DB)
IARFA............ Independent Aluminum Residential Fabricators Association (EA)
IARFP............ International Association of Registered Financial Planners (EA)
IArg............ Argonne National Laboratory, Argonne, IL [*Library symbol*] [*Library of Congress*] (LCLS)
IArgoC............ CPC International, Inc., Argo, IL [*Library symbol*] [*Library of Congress*] (LCLS)
IARI............ Indian Agricultural Research Institute
IARI............ Industrial Advertising Research Institute [*Later, CMC*] (EA)
IaRicP............ Richland Plainsman, Richland, IA [*Library symbol*] [*Library of Congress*] (LCLS)
IARIGAI............ International Association of Research Institutes for the Graphic Arts Industry [*St. Gallen, Switzerland*]
IARIGAI............ PIRA, The Research Association for the Paper and Board, Printing and Packaging Industries (SAUO)
IARIL............ International Association of Rural and Isolated Libraries [*Australia*]
IaRinD............ Ringsted Dispatch, Ringsted, IA [*Library symbol*] [*Library of Congress*] (LCLS)
IaRiR............ Riceville Record, Riceville, IA [*Library symbol*] [*Library of Congress*] (LCLS)
IARIW............ International Association for Research in Income and Wealth (EA)
IARIW............ International Association for Research on Income and Wealth (EERA)
IARI-WTC............ Indian Agricultural Research International, Water Technology Center (SAUO)
IARL............ International Association for Liberal Christianity and Religious Liberty (SAUO)
IARLD............ International Association for Research in Learning Disabilities
IArlh............ Arlington Heights Public Library, Arlington Heights, IL [*Library symbol*] [*Library of Congress*] (LCLS)
IARM............ Inspectorate of Armaments (PDAA)
IARM............ Interim Antiradiation Missile (MCD)
IARM............ International Academy of Reproductive Medicine (SAUO)
IARM............ International Association of Ropeway Manufacturers (SAUO)
IARMCLRS... International Agreement Regarding the Maintenance of Certain Lights in the Red Sea (EA)
IARMI............ International Association of Rattan Manufacturers and Importers [*Defunct*] (EA)
IARMS............ Integrated Aircrew Resource Management System (SAUO)
IARN............ Immediate Air Request Net (SAUO)
IARN............ International Amateur Radio Network
IARO............ Indian Army Reserve of Officers
IaRol............ Rolfe Public Library, Rolfe, IA [*Library symbol*] [*Library of Congress*] (LCLS)
IaRolA............ Rolfe Arrow, Rolfe, IA [*Library symbol*] [*Library of Congress*] (LCLS)
IAROO............ International Association of Railway Operating Officers (EA)
IARP............ Indian Association for Radiation Protection (SAUO)
IARP............ Inflation Accounting Research Project (SAUS)
IARP............ International Advanced Robotic Program (SAUO)
IARP............ International Amateur Radio Permission (SAUO)
IARP............ International Antarctic Regime Project (SAUO)

IARP .... International Association for Religion and Parapsychology [*Tokyo, Japan*] (EA)
IARP .... International Association of Retired Persons [*Superseded by IFA*] (EA)
IARP .... International Atmospheric Research Program (SAUS)
IARPC .... Interagency Arctic Research Policy Committee (SAUO)
IARPCB .... International Association for Research on Plantain and other Cooking Bananas (SAUO)
IARQ .... Intellectual Achievement Responsibility Questionnaire [*Psychology*] (EDAC)
IARR .... Internal Average Relative Reflectance (SAUS)
IARR .... International Association for Radiation Research [*Rijswijk, Netherlands*] (EAIO)
IARRCIS .... Interim ARRC Information System (SAUS)
IaRrLCoC .... Lyon County Courthouse, Rock Rapids, IA [*Library symbol*] [*Library of Congress*] (LCLS)
IaRrLR .... Lyon County Reporter, Rock Rapids, IA [*Library symbol*] [*Library of Congress*] (LCLS)
IARS .... Improved Aerial Refueling System (SAUO)
IARS .... Improved Aerial Refueling System Program
IARS .... Independent Air Revitalization System (NASA)
IARS .... Institute for Advanced Russian Studies [*Smithsonian Institution*]
IARS .... Institute of African Research and Studies, University of Cairo (SAUO)
IARS .... Institute of Agricultural Research Statistics (SAUO)
IARS .... International Anesthesia Research Society (EA)
IARSA .... Idiopathic Acquired Refractory Sideroblastic Anemia [*Medicine*] (DMAA)
IARSB .... International Association of Rolling Stock Builders [*See also AICMR*] (EAIO)
IARSC .... International Association of Religious Science Churches [*Later, RSI*] (EA)
IARSL .... Institute of Agricultural Remote Sensing Laboratory (SAUO)
IARSL .... Institute of Agriculture Remote Sensing Laboratory [*University of Minnesota*]
IARSS .... Illinois Association of Regional Superintendents of Schools (SAUO)
IArt .... Arthur Public Library, Arthur, IL [*Library symbol*] [*Library of Congress*] (LCLS)
IART .... Incident/Accident Response Team (SAUS)
IART .... Integra Life Sciences [*NASDAQ symbol*] (TTSB)
IART .... Integra LifeSciences Corp. [*NASDAQ symbol*] (SAG)
i arter .... Intra-Arterial [*Cardiology*] (AAMN)
IArtSD .... Arthur Community School District, Arthur, IL [*Library symbol*] [*Library of Congress*] (LCLS)
IARU .... International Amateur Radio Union (EA)
IARU .... Irish Amateur Rowing Union [*British*] (EAIO)
IaRu .... Ruthven Public Library, Ruthven, IA [*Library symbol*] [*Library of Congress*] (LCLS)
IARUS .... International Association for Regional and Urban Statistics [*Voorburg, Netherlands*] (EA)
IaRuZ .... Ruthven Zipcode, Ruthven, IA [*Library symbol*] [*Library of Congress*] (LCLS)
IaRvB .... Rock Valley Bee, Rock Valley, IA [*Library symbol*] [*Library of Congress*] (LCLS)
IARVO .... Incorporated Association of Rating and Valuation Officers (SAUO)
IARW .... International Association of Refrigerated Warehouses (EA)
IAS .... Iasi [*Romania*] [*Airport symbol*] (OAG)
IAS .... Iasi [*Romania*] [*Seismograph station code, US Geological Survey*] (SEIS)
IAS .... Ideal Adsorbed Solution [*Physical chemistry*]
IAS .... Idiopathic Ankylosing Spondylitis [*Medicine*] (MELL)
IAS .... IEEE Industry Applications Society (EA)
IAS .... Illness Adaptation Scale (EDAC)
IAS .... Image Analysis System (SAUO)
IAS .... Immediate Access Storage (AFM)
IAS .... Immediate Access Store (SAUS)
IAS .... Immediate Air Support (SAUS)
IAS .... Immunisation Awareness Society (SAUO)
IAS .... Immunosuppressive Acidic Substance [*Biochemistry*] (DB)
IAS .... Impact Assessment Sheet (NASA)
IAS .... Impact Assessment Study
IAS .... Improved Armour System (SAUS)
IAS .... Incineration at Sea Site Monitoring and Permits File (SAUS)
IAS .... Incorporated Association of Architects and Surveyors (SAUO)
IAS .... Incorporated Association of Surveyors (SAUO)
IAS .... Independent Associated Spiritualists (SAUO)
IAS .... Index Amortizing Swap
IAS .... India-America Society
IAS .... Indiana Academy of Science (SAUO)
IAS .... Indian Administrative Service [*British*]
IAS .... Indian Astronautical Society
IAS .... Indicated Air Speed
IAS .... Individual Article Supply (TELE)
IAS .... Industrial Applications Society (SAUS)
IAS .... Industrial (or Industry) Applications Society (SAUO)
IAS .... Industry Applications Society (SAUS)
IAS .... Industry Applications Specialist (TIMI)
IAS .... Inelastic Atom Scattering (PDAA)
IAS .... Infant Appnea Syndrome [*Medicine*] (MELL)
IAS .... Infantile Arteriosclerosis [*Medicine*] (MELL)
IAS .... Information Access Service (SAUO)
IAS .... Information Acquisition System (MCD)
IAS .... Information Adaptive System (SAUS)
IAS .... Information Adoptive System (ACAE)
IAS .... Information and Advisory Services (HEAS)
IAS .... Infrared Absorbed Spectroscopy (SAUS)
IAS .... Initial Assessment Study (BCP)
IAS .... Insert a Segment [*Travel industry*] (TVEL)
IAS .... Inspector of Army Schools [*British military*] (DMA)
IAS .... Institute for Advanced Studies [*Army*]
IAS .... Institute for Advanced Study (SAUS)
IAS .... Institute for Aerospace Studies (SAUS)
IAS .... Institute for Airspace Science (SAUS)
IAS .... Institute for American Strategy [*Later, ASCF*]
IAS .... Institute for Atmospheric Sciences [*South Dakota School of Mines*] [*Research center*] [*Environmental Science Services Administration*]
IAS .... Institute for/of Advanced Studies (or Study) (SAUO)
IAS .... Institute for the Advancement of Sailing [*Commercial firm*] (EA)
IAS .... Institute of Accounting Staff (SAUO)
IAS .... Institute of Advanced Studies [*Australian National University*]
IAS .... Institute of Advanced Study (SAUS)
IAS .... Institute of Aerospace [*formerly, Aeronautical*] Sciences [*Later, AIAA*]
IAS .... Institute of Agricultural Sciences (SAUO)
IAS .... Institute of Alcohol Studies [*British*] (DBA)
IAS .... Institute of American Strategy (SAUS)
IAS .... Institute of American Studies (SAUO)
IAS .... Institute of Andean Studies (EA)
IAS .... Institute of Animal Sciences (ASF)
IAS .... Institute of Applied Physics [*Russia*]
IAS .... Institute of Asian Studies (EA)
IAS .... Institute of Aviation Studies [*University of Newcastle*] [*Australia*]
IAS .... Institute of the Aerospace Sciences (SAUS)
IAS .... Instructor Aid System (MCD)
IAS .... Instrument Air System [*Nuclear energy*] (NRCH)
IAS .... Instrument Approach System
IAS .... Instrumentation Acquisition System (ACAE)
IAS .... Insulin Autoimmune Syndrome [*Medicine*] (MELL)
IAS .... Integrated Acoustic Sensor (SAUS)
IAS .... Integrated Aerial System (SAUS)
IAS .... Integrated Air Surveillance (ACAE)
IAS .... Integrated Analytical System (IAA)
IAS .... Integrated Antenna System (SAUS)
IAS .... Integrated Assessment System [*Test*] (TMMY)
IAS .... Integrated AUTODIN [*Automatic Digital Information Network*] System [*DoD*]
IAS .... Integrated Automation Systems
IAS .... Integrated AUTOVON System (SAUS)
IAS .... Integrated Avionics Sub-System (SAUS)
IAS .... Integrated Avionics System (MCD)
IAS .... Intelligence Analysis Squadron
IAS .... Intelligence Analyst Station (SAUS)
IAS .... Intelligent Analyst System (ACAE)
IAS .... Intelligent Array Subsystem Core
IAS .... Intelligent Authoring Systems (EDAC)
IAS .... Intellisoft Accounting Series [*Computer science*] (PCM)
IAS .... Interactive Analysis System [*Computer science*] (PCM)
IAS .... Interactive Applications Supervisor
IAS .... Interactive Application System (IAA)
IAS .... Interagency Archaeological Services
IAS .... Inter-American System
IAS .... Interatrial Septum [*Cardiology*] (MAE)
IAS .... Interatrial Shunting [*Medicine*] (DMAA)
IAS .... Interdisciplinary American Studies
IAS .... Interest Assessment Scales
IAS .... Interface Applications Software (SAUS)
IAS .... Intermediate Access Store (SAUS)
IAS .... Internal Alignment Sensor (MCD)
IAS .... Internationa1 Association of Siderographists (SAUO)
IAS .... International Academy of Sciences (EAIO)
IAS .... International Accountants Society
IAS .... International Accounting Standards
IAS .... International AIDS Society (EAIO)
IAS .... International Aircraft Standards (SAUO)
IAS .... International Air Service Co. [*ICAO designator*] (FAAC)
IAS .... International Applied Systems (NITA)
IAS .... International Army Staff (MCD)
IAS .... International Aroid Society (EA)
IAS .... International Arthurian Society (SAUO)
IAS .... International Association of Sedimentologists [*Liege, Belgium*] (EA)
IAS .... International Association of Sedimentology (SAUO)
IAS .... International Association of Seismology (SAUS)
IAS .... International Association of Siderographers (EA)
IAS .... International Atherosclerosis Society (EA)
IAS .... International Audiovisual Society (EA)
IAS .... International Auditing Standards (SAUS)
IAS .... International Automobile Salon (SAUO)
IAS .... International Aviation Service [*FAA*]
IAS .... International Aviation Services [*Belgium*]
IAS .... Internet Access Server (SAUS)
IAS .... Interpretive Analytical Service (SAUO)
IAS .... Intra-American Seas (SAUS)
IAS .... Intra-Amniotic Saline [*Infusion*] [*Medicine*]
IAS .... Intra-Articular Steroid [*Physiology*]
IAS .... Intrument Approach System (SAUS)
IAS .... Intrusion Alarm System
IAS .... Invariant-Azimuth States (PDAA)
IAS .... Inventory of American Sculpture
IAS .... Investors Arbitration Service (SAUS)
IAS .... Inzhnerno-Aviatsionnaia Sluzhba (SAUS)
IAS .... Iowa Academy of Science (SAUO)

IAS .... Irish Archaeological Society (SAUO)
IAS .... Irish Archeological Society (SAUS)
IAS .... Irish Aviation Services (SAUO)
IAS .... Isobaric Analog State
IAS .... Isolated Aerial (or Antenna) System (SAUS)
IAS .... Israeli Air Services (MCD)
IAS .... Los Angeles, CA [*Location identifier*] [*FAA*] (FAAL)
IAS .... Sangamon State University, Springfield, IL [*OCLC symbol*] (OCLC)
IASA .... Idaho Association of School Administrators (SRA)
IASA .... Ileostomy Association of South Australia
IASA .... Illinois Association of School Administrators (SRA)
IASA .... Importers' Association of South Australia
IASA .... Independent Automotive Service Association (EA)
IASA .... Indo-American Sports Association [*Later, FIA-USC*]
IASA .... INSCOM [*Intelligence and Security Command*] Automated Systems Support Activity [*Army*] (MCD)
IASA .... Institute for Atomic Sciences in Agriculture
IASA .... Institute of Agricultural Secretaries of Australasia
IASA .... Insurance Accounting and Statistical Association [*Later, Insurance Accounting and Systems Association*] (EA)
IASA .... Insurance Accounting and Systems Association [*Durham, NC*] (EA)
IASA .... Integrated Assessment of Security Assistance [*Military*]
IASA .... Integrated AUTODIN [*Automatic Digital Information Network*] System Architecture (MCD)
IASA .... Interatrial Septal Aneurysm [*Medicine*] (DMAA)
IASA .... International Air Safety Association (EA)
IASA .... International Alliance for Sustainable Agriculture (EA)
IASA .... International Alliance of Sustainable Agriculture (SAUS)
IASA .... International Association for Statistical Computing (SAUO)
IASA .... International Association of Schools in Advertising
IASA .... International Association of Sound Archives [*Milton, Keynes, England*] (EAIO)
IASA .... Iowa Association of School Administrators (SAUO)
IASA .... Irish Amateur Swimming Association (EAIO)
IASAA .... International Agricultural Students Association of the Americas (EA)
IaSab .... Sabula Public Library, Sabula, IA [*Library symbol*] [*Library of Congress*] (LCLS)
IASAC .... International Association of Silver Art Collectors (EA)
IaSacLS .... Lytton Star, Sac City, IA [*Library symbol*] [*Library of Congress*] (LCLS)
IaSacS .... Sac Sun, Sac City, IA [*Library symbol*] [*Library of Congress*] (LCLS)
IASAI .... Image Analysis Systems and Artificial Intelligence (SAUS)
IASAIL .... International Association for the Study of Anglo-Irish Literature [*Maynooth, Republic of Ireland*] (EAIO)
IASAJ .... International Association of Supreme Administration Jurisdictions GG2 [*See also AIHJA*] (EAIO)
IaSal .... Crew Public Library, Salem, IA [*Library symbol*] [*Library of Congress*] (LCLS)
IaSan .... Sanborn Public Library, Sanborn, IA [*Library symbol*] [*Library of Congress*] (LCLS)
IaSanP .... Sanborn Pioneer, Sanborn, IA [*Library symbol*] [*Library of Congress*] (LCLS)
IASAP .... Intercollege Association for Study of the Alcohol Problem (SAUO)
IASAP .... Intercollegiate Association for Study of the Alcohol Problem (EA)
IASAP .... International Arctic Seas Assessment Project [*Marine science*] (OSRA)
IASB .... Illinois Association of School Boards (EDAC)
IASB .... Installation Aviation Standardization Board (MCD)
IASB .... Institute of Agronomic Sciences of Burundi (SAUS)
IASB .... International Academy at Santa Barbara (EA)
IASB .... International Accounting Standards Board
IASB .... International Aircraft Standards Bureau (SAUS)
IASB .... Iowa Association of School Boards (SRA)
IASBFLC .... Institute for the Advanced Study of Black Family Life and Culture (EA)
IASBO .... Indiana Association of School Business Officials (SAUO)
IASBO .... Iowa Association of School Business Officials (SAUO)
IASC .... Indexing and Abstracting Society of Canada [*Toronto, ON*]
IASC .... Indian Army Service Corps [*British military*] (DMA)
IASC .... Inter-Agency Standing Committee (SAUO)
IASC .... Inter-American Safety Council (EA)
IASC .... Inter-American Scout Committee [*See also CIE*] [*San Jose, Costa Rica*] (EAIO)
IASC .... Inter-American Society for Chemotherapy (ADWA)
IASC .... Inter-American Statistical Teaching Center
IASC .... International Accounting Standards Committee [*of the International Federation of Accountants*] [*British*] (EAIO)
IASC .... International Afroid Science Conference (MCD)
IASC .... International Aloe Science Council (EA)
IASC .... International Arctic Science Committee
IASC .... International Arctic Service Committee (SAUS)
IASC .... International Association for Statistical Computing (EA)
IASC .... International Association of Science Clubs (SAUO)
IASC .... International Association of Seed Crushers [*British*] (EAIO)
IASC .... International Association of Skal Clubs [*Spain*] (EAIO)
IASC .... International Association of Skateboard Companies (EA)
IASC .... Intimate Apparel Square Club (EA)
IASC .... Italian American Stamp Club (EA)
IaSc .... Sioux City Public Library, Sioux City, IA [*Library symbol*] [*Library of Congress*] (LCLS)
IASCA .... International Auto Sound Challenge Association (EA)
IaScB .... Briar Cliff College, Sioux City, IA [*Library symbol*] [*Library of Congress*] (LCLS)
IASCB .... Ibero-American Society for Cell Biology [*See also SIABC*] (EAIO)
IASCB .... International Association of Sand Castle Builders (EA)
IASCCA .... International Association for the Study of the Cultures of Central Asia (SAUO)
IASCD .... Idaho Association of Soil Conservation Districts (SRA)
IASCD .... Illinois Association for Supervision and Curriculum Development (SRA)
IASCE .... International Association for the Study of Cooperation in Education (SAUO)
IaSce .... Sioux Center Public Library, Sioux Center, IA [*Library symbol*] [*Library of Congress*] (LCLS)
IaSceD .... Dordt College, Sioux Center, IA [*Library symbol*] [*Library of Congress*] (LCLS)
IASC-GCPO ... IASC Global Change Programme Office (SAUO)
IASC-GCWG ... IASC Global Change Working Group (SAUO)
IASCH .... Institute for Advanced Studies in Contemporary History (SAUO)
IASCH .... Institute for the Advanced Studies in Contemporary History (SAUS)
IaSchH .... Schaller Herald, Schaller, IA [*Library symbol*] [*Library of Congress*] (LCLS)
IaSchIL .... Schleswig Leader, Schleswig, IA [*Library symbol*] [*Library of Congress*] (LCLS)
IaScM .... Morningside College, Sioux City, IA [*Library symbol*] [*Library of Congress*] (LCLS)
IaScNR .... Northwest Regional Library System, Sioux City, IA [*Library symbol*] [*Library of Congress*] (LCLS)
IASCO .... International Air Service Company (SAUO)
IASCO .... International Association of Service Companies [*NACSA*] [*Absorbed by*] (EA)
IASCP .... Institute for Advanced Study of the Communication Processes [*University of Florida*] [*Research center*] (RCD)
IASCP .... International Association for the Study of Common Property (EA)
IASCS .... International Association for Shopping Center Security (EA)
IaScS .... Siouxland Libraries Cooperative, Sioux City, IA [*Library symbol*] [*Library of Congress*] (LCLS)
IaScT .... Trinity College, Sioux City, IA [*Library symbol*] [*Library of Congress*] [*Obsolete*] (LCLS)
IaScWI .... West Iowa Technical Community College, Sioux City, IA [*Library symbol*] [*Library of Congress*] (LCLS)
IASD .... Industrial Automation Services Division (SAUS)
IASD .... Instant Ammunition Selection Device (SAUS)
IASD .... Inter Atrial Septal Defect (SAUS)
IASD .... Interatrial Septal Defect [*Cardiology*]
IASD .... Interauricular Septal Defect [*Medicine*] (DB)
IASDI .... Inter-American Social Development Institute [*Later, IAF*]
IASE .... Installation and Service Engineering (SAUS)
IASE .... Inter-American Association of Sanitary Engineering (SAUO)
IaSEA .... Iowa Society of Enrolled Agents (SAUO)
IASECS .... International Association of Students of Economics and Commercial Sciences (SAUO)
IASEES .... International Association of South-East European Studies [*See also AIESEE*] [*Bucharest, Romania*] (EAIO)
IaSeyH .... Seymour Herald, Seymour, IA [*Library symbol*] [*Library of Congress*] (LCLS)
IASF .... Instrumentation for Aerospace Simulation Facilities (SAUS)
IASF .... Instrumentation in Aerospace Simulation (SAUS)
IASF .... Instrumentation in Aerospace Simulation Facilities
IASF .... International Amateur Surfing Federation (EA)
IASF .... International Amateur Swimming Federation (EA)
IASF .... International Atlantic Salmon Foundation [*Canada*] (EA)
IASF .... Irish American Sports Foundation (EA)
IASFC .... Instrumentation for Aerospace Simulation Facilities Committee (SAUO)
IASG .... Inflation Accounting Steering Group (MHDB)
IASG .... International Airline Support Group (EFIS)
IASG .... International Automotive Sector Group (SAUO)
IASG .... Internet Addiction Support Group (SAUO)
IASG .... Internetwork Address Sub-Group
IASH .... International Association of Scientific Hydrology [*Later, International Association of Hydrological Sciences*] [*of International Union of Geodesy and Geophysics*]
IASH .... Isolated Asymmetric Septal Hypertrophy [*Medicine*] (DMAA)
IASH .... Israeli Academy of Sciences and Humanities
IaSh .... Shenandoah Public Library, Shenandoah, IA [*Library symbol*] [*Library of Congress*] (LCLS)
IaShe .... Sheldon Public Library, Sheldon, IA [*Library symbol*] [*Library of Congress*] (LCLS)
IaShefP .... Sheffield Press, Sheffield, IA [*Library symbol*] [*Library of Congress*] (LCLS)
IaSheHi .... Sheldon County Historical Society, Sheldon, IA [*Library symbol*] [*Library of Congress*] (LCLS)
IaSheM .... Sheldon Mail, Sheldon, IA [*Library symbol*] [*Library of Congress*] (LCLS)
IaSheS .... Sheldon Sun, Sheldon, IA [*Library symbol*] [*Library of Congress*] (LCLS)
IASHR .... International Association for the Study of History of Religions (SAUO)
IaShr .... Shell Rock Public Library, Shell Rock, IA [*Library symbol*] [*Library of Congress*] (LCLS)
IaShrN .... Shell Rock News, Shell Rock, IA [*Library symbol*] [*Library of Congress*] (LCLS)
IASHS .... Institute for Advanced Study in Human Sexuality (DAVI)
IASI .... Improved Atmospheric Sounding Interferometer (EOSA)
IASI .... Infrared Atmospheric Sounding Instrument (SAUS)
IASI .... Infrared Atmospheric Sounding Interferometer
IASI .... Inter-American Statistical Institute (EA)
IASI .... International Alliance Services, Inc. [*NASDAQ symbol*] (SAG)
IASI .... International Association for Sports Information [*The Hague, Netherlands*] (EA)

IASIA .... Institute for Advanced Studies in Immunology and Aging (ADWA)
IASIA .... International Association of Schools and Institutes Administration (BUAC)
IASIA .... International Association of Schools and Institutes of Administration (BUAC)
IaSibCoC...... Osceola County Courthouse, Sibley, IA [*Library symbol*] [*Library of Congress*] (LCLS)
IaSibG .... Sibley Gazette and Tribune, Sibley, IA [*Library symbol*] [*Library of Congress*] (LCLS)
IaSidAH .... Sidney Argus-Herald, Sidney, IA [*Library symbol*] [*Library of Congress*] (LCLS)
IaSidCoC...... Fremont County Courthouse, Sidney, IA [*Library symbol*] [*Library of Congress*] (LCLS)
IASIF............ International Association of Shareholders in IO-Funds (SAUO)
IaSigCoC...... Keokuk County Courthouse, Sigourney, IA [*Library symbol*] [*Library of Congress*] (LCLS)
IaSigNR .... Sigourney News-Review, Sigourney, IA [*Library symbol*] [*Library of Congress*] (LCLS)
IASILL.......... International Association for the Study of the Italian Language and Literature [*See also AISLLI*] [*Padua, Italy*] (EAIO)
IASIW .... Institute for the Advanced Study of Information Warfare (SAUO)
I-ASK .... Inter-Active Status Kiosk [*Indian Railway*] (TIR)
IASK............. International Association of Specialized Kinesiologists (SAUO)
IASL............. Illinois Association of School Librarians (SAUO)
IASL............. Integrated Aircraft Systems Laboratory (SAUS)
IASL............. Inter-American School of Librarianship [*Colombia*] (BUAC)
IASL............. International Association for the Study of the Liver [*Gottingen, Federal Republic of Germany*] (EAIO)
IASL............. International Association of/on School Librarianship (SAUO)
IASL............. International Association of School Librarians (SAUO)
IASL............. International Association of School Librarianship (PDAA)
IASL............. International Association of State Lotteries (BUAC)
IASL............. Irish Association of School Librarians (SAUO)
IaSl.............. Storm Lake Public Library, Storm Lake, IA [*Library symbol*] [*Library of Congress*] (LCLS)
IaSla............ Slater Public Library, Slater, IA [*Library symbol*] [*Library of Congress*] (LCLS)
IaSlaT.......... Tri County Times, Slater, IA [*Library symbol*] [*Library of Congress*] (LCLS)
IaSlB............ Buena Vista College, Storm Lake, IA [*Library symbol*] [*Library of Congress*] (LCLS)
IASLC........... International Association for the Study of Lung Cancer (EA)
IASLIC .... Indian Association for/of Special Libraries and Information Centers (or Centres) (SAUO)
IASLIC .... Indian Association for Special Libraries and Information Centers (SAUS)
IASLIC .... Indian Association for Special Libraries and Information Centres (NITA)
IASLIC Bull... Indian Association of Special Libraries & Information Centres Bulletin (journ.) (SAUS)
IASLM.......... Integrated Aerial System-Loitering Mode (SAUS)
IaSlPT.......... Storm Lake Pilot-Tribune, Storm Lake, IA [*Library symbol*] [*Library of Congress*] (LCLS)
IASM............ Independent Association of Stocking Manufacturers [*Defunct*]
IASM............ Institute of Aerospace Safety and Management [*University of Southern California*]
IASM............ International Association for Seminar Management (EA)
IASM............ International Association of Structural Movers (EA)
IASM............ Istituto per l'Assistenza allo Sviluppo del Mezzogiorno [*Italy*] (EY)
IASMABT ..... International Association of Structural Mechanics and Reactor Technology (SAUO)
IASMAL......... International Academy of Social and Moral Sciences, Arts and Letters (SAUO)
IASMHF .... International Association of Sports Museums and Halls of Fame (EA)
IASMIRT ...... International Association for Structural Mechanics in Reactor Technology (EAIO)
IASMW .... International Association of Sheet Metal Workers (BARN)
IASN .... Intelligence Analysis Support Network (SAUO)
IAS/NAB....... International Arthurian Society/North American Branch [*Canada*] (EAIO)
IASnet.......... [*The*] Institute for Automated Systems Network (TNIG)
IASO .... International Association for the Study of Obesity (SAUO)
IASOC .... International Association for the Study of Organized Crime (EA)
IaSolE.......... Solon Economist, Solon, IA [*Library symbol*] [*Library of Congress*] (LCLS)
IASOR.......... Ice and Snow on Runway [*Aviation*]
IASOS .... Institute for Antarctic and Southern Ocean Studies (SAUS)
IASOS .... Institute of Antarctic and Southern Ocean Studies (EERA)
IASP............. Integrated Attack Sensor Package
IASP............. Interactive Automatic System for Photointerpretation (SAUS)
IASP............. Inter-American Society of Psychology (BUAC)
IASP............. International Arts and Sciences Press
IASP............. International Association for Social Progress
IASP............. International Association for Suicide Prevention (EA)
IASP............. International Association for the Study of Pain (EA)
IASP............. International Association in Support of Perestroika (BUAC)
IASP............. International Association of Scholarly Publishers [*Norway*]
IASP............. International Association of Science Parks [*France*] (BUAC)
IASP............. International Association of Space Philatelists (EA)
IASP............. International Association of Sports Physicians [*Defunct*] (EA)
IASP............. International Association of Sublimation Printers (EA)
IASP............. International Atmospheric Surveillance Program (SAUS)
IASP............. Internet Access Service Provider (SAUO)
IASPA .... International Association for Semiotics of Performing Arts (SAUO)
IASPA .... International Auto Show Producers Association (EA)
IASPC .... International Association of Strategic Planning Consultants [*Defunct*] (EA)
IaSpeHi........ Parker Historical Society of Clay County, Spencer, IA [*Library symbol*] [*Library of Congress*] (LCLS)
IASPEI .... International Association of Seismology and Physics of the Earth's Interior [*ICSU*] [*Newbury, Berkshire, England*] (EAIO)
IASPG .... Integrated AUTODIN System Planning Group (SAUO)
IASPHA......... International American Saddlebred Pleasure Horse Association (EA)
IaSplB.......... Spirit Lake Beacon, Spirit Lake, IA [*Library symbol*] [*Library of Congress*] (LCLS)
IaSplCoC...... Dickinson County Courthouse, Spirit Lake, IA [*Library symbol*] [*Library of Congress*] (LCLS)
IASPM .... Infrared Atmospheric and Signature Prediction Model (SAUS)
IASPM .... Infrared Atmospheric Signature Prediction Model (ACAE)
IASPM .... International Association for the Study of Popular Music [*Berlin, German Democratic Republic*] (EAIO)
IASPM .... International Association of Scientific Paper Makers (SAUO)
IASPO .... International Association of Senior Police Officers (SAUO)
IA-SPOX....... Intel Architecture SPOX (HODG)
IASPPV .... International Association of Former Soviet Political Prisoners and Victims of Communist Regime
IaSpr........... Springville Public Library, Springville, IA [*Library symbol*] [*Library of Congress*] (LCLS)
IASPS .... International Association for Statistics in Physical Sciences
IASR .... Institute of Agronomic Sciences of Rwanda (SAUS)
IA/SR .... Intelligence Analysis/Storage and Retrieval (SAUO)
IASR .... Intermediate Altitude Sounding Rocket (MUGU)
IASR .... International Academy for Suicide Research (SEAT)
IASR .... Interruption Address Storage Register (NITA)
IASRA.......... International Arthur Schnitzler Research Association (EA)
IaSrBP .... Bulletin-Press, Sioux Rapids, IA [*Library symbol*] [*Library of Congress*] (LCLS)
IASRI .... Indian Agricultural Statistics Research Institute (BUAC)
IASRP .... Integrated AUTODIN System Requirements Panel (SAUO)
IASRR.......... Institute of African Studies. Research Review [*A publication*]
IASS............. Institute of Advanced Architectural Studies (BUAC)
IASS............. Insurance Accounting and Statistical Society
IASS............. Inter-American Schools Service (SAUO)
IASS............. International Air Safety Seminar
IAss .... International Assembly (SAUO)
IASS............. International Association for/of Semiotic Studies (SAUO)
IASS............. International Association for Scandinavian Studies [*Norwich, England*] (EAIO)
IASS............. International Association for Semiotic Studies (BUAC)
IASS............. International Association for Shell and Spatial Structures [*Madrid, Spain*] (EA)
IASS............. International Association for Shell Structures (SAUO)
IASS............. International Association of Sanskrit Studies (EA)
IASS............. International Association of Security Service (EA)
IASS............. International Association of Semiotic Studies [*Palermo, Italy*] (EA)
IASS............. International Association of Soil Science
IASS............. International Association of Survey Statisticians [*See also AISE*] [*France*] (EA)
IASS............. International Aviation Snow Symposium (SAUO)
IASS............. Internet Alphaserver System Software (SAUS)
IASS............. Inverter/ATCS [*Active Thermal Control Subsystem*] Support Structure (MCD)
IASSD .... International Association of School Security Directors [*Later, NASSD*] (EA)
IASSIST .... International Association for Social Science Information Service and Technology (EA)
IASSIST .... International Association for Social Science Information Service a Technology (SAUO)
IASSIST .... International Association for Social Science Information Services and Technology (NITA)
IASSMD .... International Association for the Scientific Study of Mental Deficiency [*Dublin, Republic of Ireland*] (EA)
IASSRF .... International Amateur Snowshoe Racing Federation (EA)
IASSS .... International Association for Shell and Spatial Structures (SAUO)
IASST........... International Association for Sea Survival Training (SAUO)
IASSW .... International Association of Schools of Social Work [*Austria*]
IAST............. Institute for Addictions Studies and Training (SAUS)
IAST............. Instrument for the Analysis of Science Teaching (EDAC)
IAST............. Integrated Avionic System Trainer [*Military*] (CAAL)
IAST............. International Association of Scuba Technicians
IAST............. International Association to Save Tyre (BUAC)
IAST............. Irish Association for Sail Training (BUAC)
IAST1........... Information Analysis Support Tool [*Computer science*] (HODG)
IASTA........... Institute for Advanced Studies in the Theatre Arts (EA)
IaStacM .... Monitor-Review, Stacyville, IA [*Library symbol*] [*Library of Congress*] (LCLS)
IaStaE.......... Saint Ansgar Enterprise, St. Ansgar, IA [*Library symbol*] [*Library of Congress*] (LCLS)
IaStan.......... Stanton Community Library, Stanton, IA [*Library symbol*] [*Library of Congress*] (LCLS)
IaStanV........ Stanton Viking, Stanton, IA [*Library symbol*] [*Library of Congress*] (LCLS)
IaStaw .... Stanwood Public Library, Stanwood, IA [*Library symbol*] [*Library of Congress*] (LCLS)
IaStc .... Gutenkunst Public Library, State Center, IA [*Library symbol*] [*Library of Congress*] (LCLS)
IaStcE .... State Center Enterprise, State Center, IA [*Library symbol*] [*Library of Congress*] (LCLS)
IASTE........... International Association for the Exchange of Students for Technical Experiments (SAUO)

IASTE........... International Association for the Study of Traditional Environments (BUAC)
IASTED........ International Association of Science and Technology for Development [*Calgary, AB*] (EAIO)
IASTG.......... International Association of Structural/Tectonic Geologists (BUAC)
IaStoc.......... Story City Public Library, Story City, IA [*Library symbol*] [*Library of Congress*] (LCLS)
IaStocH........ Story City Herald, Story City, IA [*Library symbol*] [*Library of Congress*] (LCLS)
IaStrp........... Strawberry Point Public Library, Strawberry Point, IA [*Library symbol*] [*Library of Congress*] (LCLS)
IaStrpP........ Strawberry Point Press-Journal, Strawberry Point, IA [*Library symbol*] [*Library of Congress*] (LCLS)
IaStuH......... Stuart Herald, Stuart, IA [*Library symbol*] [*Library of Congress*] (LCLS)
IASTWL........ International Association for Social Tourism and Workers' Leisure (EAIO)
IaSu............. General N. B. Baker Library, Sutherland, IA [*Library symbol*] [*Library of Congress*] (LCLS)
IASU............ International Association of Satellite Users [*Later, IASUS*] (EA)
IA Sup Vol... English Law Reports, Indian Appeals, Supplementary Volume [*A publication*] (DLA)
IASUS.......... International Association of Satellite Users and Suppliers (EA)
IASV............ Internationale Arbeitsgemeinschaft von Sortimentsbuchhaendler Vereinigungen [*International Community of Booksellers' Associations*]
IASW............ Irish Association of Social Workers [*Ireland*] (BUAC)
IaSwc........... Swea City Public Library, Swea City, IA [*Library symbol*] [*Library of Congress*] (LCLS)
IASWG......... Inter-Country Adoption Social Workers Group (BUAC)
IASWR......... Institute for Advanced Studies of World Religions (EA)
IASWS......... International Association for Sediment Water Science [*Switzerland*] (BUAC)
IASWS......... International Association of Severe Weather Specialists (NTPA)
IAsy............. Ashley Public Library, Ashley, IL [*Library symbol*] [*Library of Congress*] (LCLS)
IASY............. International Active Sun Years
IAsyCD........ Ashley Community Consolidated District 15, Ashley, IL [*Library symbol*] [*Library of Congress*] (LCLS)
IAT............... Image Annotation Tape (SAUS)
IAT............... Image Auto Tracker
IAT............... Immediate Attitude Trim (ACAE)
IAT............... Immunoaugmentative Therapy [*Oncology*]
IAT............... Import Address Table (SAUS)
IAT............... Income After Taxes (SAUS)
IAT............... Indexable Address Tag (SAUS)
IAT............... Indexible Address Tag (SAA)
IAT............... Indicated Air Temperature (AFM)
IAT............... Indirect Antiglobulin Test [*Clinical chemistry*]
IAT............... Indivdual Acceptance Test (SAUS)
IAT............... Individual Acceptance Tests
IAT............... Individual Aircraft Tracking Program (MCD)
IAT............... Induction Air Temperature (SAUS)
IAT............... Information Access Technology (SAUO)
IAT............... Information Assessment Team (NRCH)
IAT............... Innovative Advanced Technology (SAUS)
IAT............... Inside Air Temperature
IAT............... Inspection Apply Template (MCD)
IAT............... Instillation Abortion Time [*Medicine*] (STED)
IAT............... Institute for Advanced Technology [*Control Data Corp.*] [*Bloomington, MN*] [*Telecommunications*]
IAT............... Institute for Applied Technology [*Superseded by NEL*] [*National Institute of Standards and Technology*]
IAT............... Institute of Admiral Technology (SAUS)
IAT............... Institute of Advanced Technology (SAUS)
IAT............... Institute of Agricultural Technology [*Vietnam*] (BUAC)
IAT............... Institute of Air Transport (BUAC)
IAT............... Institute of Animal Technicians (SAUO)
IAT............... Institute of Animal Technology [*London*]
IAT............... Institute of Armament Technology (SAUS)
IAT............... Institute of Asphalt Technology [*British*]
IAT............... Institute of Atomic Physics (SAUO)
IAT............... Institute of Automatics and Telemechanics (SAUS)
IAT............... Intake Air Temperature [*Automotive engineering*]
IAT............... Integrated Access Terminal [*Communications term*] (DCT)
IAT............... Integrated Assembly Test (SAUS)
IAT............... Integrated Avionics Test (MCD)
IAT............... Integration Acceptance Test [*Military*] (CAAL)
IAT............... Intelligence Analysis Team (SAUO)
IAT............... Intelligent Actuators & Transmitters (ACII)
IAT............... Interactive Audio Teletraining System [*Valencia Community College*] [*Orlando, FL*] (TSSD)
IAT............... Interionic Attraction Theory
IAT............... Internal Air Transportability (MCD)
IAT............... Internal Average Temperature (SAUS)
IAT............... International Academy of Tourism (SAUO)
IAT............... International Aerospace Technologies Processing System (SAUS)
IAT............... International Air Transport Association [*ICAO designator*] (FAAC)
IAT............... International Air Travelling (SAUS)
IAT............... International Art Transport (SAUO)
IAT............... International Association for Time-Keeping (BUAC)
IAT............... International Association of Trichologists (EA)
IAT............... International Atomic Time
IAT............... International Automatic Time
IAT............... Interrupt Address Table (SAUS)
IAT............... Intraoperative Autologous Transfusion [*Medicine*]
IAT............... Invasive Activity Test [*Oncology*]
IAT............... Inventory of Affective Tolerance [*Psychology*]
IAT............... Iodine Azide Test [*Medicine*]
IAT............... Iowa Achievement Test [*Psychology*] (DAVI)
IAT............... Iowa Terminal Railroad Co. [*AAR code*]
IAT............... Island Air Transfer Ltd. (SAUO)
IAT............... Southern Illinois University, Edwardsville Campus, Edwardsville, IL [*OCLC symbol*] (OCLC)
IATA............. International Airline Telecommunications Association (SAUO)
IATA............. International Air Traffic Association (SAUO)
IATA............. International Air Transport [*formerly, Traffic*] Association [*Canada*]
IATA............. International Air Transport Authority (BUAC)
IATA............. International Air Transport Organisation (SAUS)
IATA............. International Amateur Theatre Association [*Denmark*]
IATA............. International Appropriate Technology Association [*Defunct*] (EA)
IATA............. International Association for Advancement of Appropriate Technology for Developing Countries (SAUO)
IATA............. International Association of Trade Associations (SAUO)
IATA............. International Reciprocal Trade Association (SAUO)
IATA............. Internatonal Air Transport Association (SAUO)
IATA............. Is Amended to Add
IATACS........ Improved Army Tactical Communications System (DOMA)
IATACS........ Integrated Acquisition Tracking and Aimpoint Control System (ACAE)
IATADS........ Initial Airborne Target Acquisition Designation System (MCD)
IATAE........... International Accounting and Traffic Analysis Equipment [*Telecommunications*] (NITA)
IATAFI.......... International Association for Technology Assessment and Forecasting (SAUO)
IATAL........... International Association of Theoretical and Applied Limnology [*See also SILTA*] (EA)
IATAN.......... International Airlines Travel Agency Network (TRID)
IATA-RAR.... International Air Transport Association Restricted Articles Regulations (SAUO)
IATAS........... Interim Airborne Target Acquisition System (CCCA)
IATB............. International Aviation Theft Bureau [*ACPI*] [*Superseded by*] (EA)
IATC............. India-America Trade Council (SAUO)
IATC............. Inlet Air Temperature Control (SAUS)
IATC............. Inter-American Telecommunications Commission
IATC............. Inter-American Travel Congresses
IATC............. International Air Traffic Communications
IATC............. International Air Transport Commission (SAUO)
IATC............. International Air Transport Conference (SAUO)
IATC............. International Air Transport Convention (SAUO)
IATC............. International Association of Theatre Critics (BUAC)
IATC............. International Association of Tool Craftsmen (EA)
IATC............. International Association of Torch Clubs (EA)
IATC............. International Association of Trauma Counseling (NTPA)
IATC............. International Association of Triathlon Clubs (EA)
IATCA........... International Air Transportation Competition Act of 1979
IATCA........... International Auditor Training and Certification Association (SAUO)
IATCB........... Interdepartmental Air Traffic Control Board
IATCL........... International Association for Textile Care Labelling (EA)
IATCR........... International Air Traffic Communications Receiver Station
IATCR Station... International Air Traffic Communications Receiving Station (SAUS)
IATCR station... International Air Traffic Communications Reciever station (SAUO)
IATCS........... International Air Traffic Communications Station
IATCS........... International Air Traffic Communications System (MCD)
IATCT........... International Air Traffic Communications Transmitter Station
IATCTS......... International Air Traffic Communications Transmitter Station (SAUO)
IATCT station... International Air Traffic Communications Transmitter station (SAUO)
IATCT Station... International Air Traffic Communications Transmitting Station (SAUS)
IATD............. Is Amended to Delete
IATDB........... Interim Air Toxics Database (SAUS)
IATDMCT..... International Association of Therapeutic Drug Monitoring and Clinical Toxicology (SAUO)
IATDP........... International Association of Textile Dyers and Printers [*See also AITIT*] (EAIO)
IATE............. Illinois Association of Teachers of English (SAUO)
IATE............. Intermediate Automatic Test Equipment
IATE............. Intermediate-Level Automatic Test Equipment (PDAA)
IATE............. International Accounting and Traffic Analysis Equipment [*Telecommunications*] (TEL)
IATE............. International Association for/of Television Editors (SAUO)
IATE............. International Association for Television Editors
IATE............. International Association for Temperance Education [*Later, IVES*] (EA)
IATE............. International Association of Trade Exchanges [*Later, IRTA*] (EA)
IATE............. International Association of Travel Exhibitors (EA)
IATEFL......... International Association of Teachers of English as a Foreign Language [*Whitstable, Kent, England*] (EAIO)
IATEL........... International Association of Testing and Environmental Laboratories (SAUO)
IATF............. Interagency Task Force [*for Indochina*] [*South Vietnam refugee relief*]
IATF............. Inter-Association Task Force on Campus Alcohol and Other Substance Abuse Issues [*An association*] (EA)
IATF............. International Airline Training Fund (BUAC)
IATFAI.......... Inter-Association Task Force on Alcohol Issues (EA)
IATFD........... Inter-Agency Task Force on Data (SAUS)
IATFIS.......... Inter-Agency Task-Force on Information Exchange and the Transfer of Technology (SAUS)

IATFIS.......... Inter-Agency Task Force on Information Exchange and Transfer of Technology (SAUO)
IATFIS.......... Inter-Agency Task Force on Information Systems (SAUO)
IATG............ International Association of Teachers of German [*See also IDV*] [*Copenhagen, Denmark*] (EAIO)
IATH............ Institute for Advanced Technology in the Humanities (BUAC)
IATI............ Inter-Alpha-Trypsin Inhibitor (DMAA)
IATI............ International Association of Teachers of Italian [*Belgium*] (EAIO)
IaTip........... Tipron Public Library, Tipron, IA [*Library symbol*] [*Library of Congress*] (LCLS)
IaTipCoC...... Cedar County Courthouse, Tipton, IA [*Library symbol*] [*Library of Congress*] (LCLS)
IaTit............ Titonka Public Library, Titonka, IA [*Library symbol*] [*Library of Congress*] (LCLS)
IATJ............ International Association of Travel Journalists (EA)
IATL............ International Academy of Trial Lawyers (EA)
IATL............ International Association of Theological Libraries
IATLIS.......... Indian Association of Teachers of Library Science (SAUO)
IATM............ Institute of Applied Tropical Medicine (SAUS)
IATM............ International Association for Testing Materials (IEEE)
IATM............ International Association of Tour Managers (DI)
IATM............ International Association of Transport Museums [*See also AIMT*] [*Berne, Switzerland*] (EAIO)
IATME.......... International Association of Terrestrial Magnetism and Electricity (SAUO)
IATM-NAR.... International Association of Tour Managers-North American Region (SAUO)
IATMO.......... International Academy of Tumor Marker Oncology (BUAC)
IATN............ International Association of Telecomputer Networks (EA)
IATO............ Independent Acceptance Test Organization (SAUS)
IATO............ International Air Transport Organization (BUAC)
IATO............ International Association of Theatre Audience Organizations (SAUO)
IaTo............ Toledo Public Library, Toledo, IA [*Library symbol*] [*Library of Congress*] (LCLS)
IaToC.......... Toledo Chronicle, Toledo, IA [*Library symbol*] [*Library of Congress*] (LCLS)
IATOD.......... In Addition to Other Duties [*Military*]
IATP............ Individual Aircraft Tracking Program (MCD)
IATP............ Institute for Agriculture and Trade Policy (EA)
IATP............ Institutional Admissions Testing Program
IATP............ International Agricultural Training Program (SAUS)
IATP............ International Agricultural Training Programme (BUAC)
IATP............ International Airlines Technical Pool (PDAA)
IATP............ International Association of Tungsten Producers
IATPA.......... IAT Patients Association (SAUS)
IATR............ International Association for Tamil Research [*Malaysia*] (BUAC)
IATR............ International Association of Teachers of Russian (BUAC)
IATR............ Iowa Traction Railroad [*Federal Railroad Administration identification code*]
IATR............ Is Amended to Read
IATRA.......... International Academy of Toxicological Risk Assessment (EA)
IaTraS.......... Traer Star-Clipper, Traer, IA [*Library symbol*] [*Library of Congress*] (LCLS)
IaTriL........... Tripoli Leader, Tripoli, IA [*Library symbol*] [*Library of Congress*] (LCLS)
IATROS........ Organisation Mondiale des Medicins Independants [*International Organization of Private and Independent Doctors*] (EAIO)
IatrosHlt....... Iatros Health Network, Inc. [*Associated Press*] (SAG)
IATS............ Individual Accession and Training Study (SAUO)
IATS............ Individual Accession and Training System (MCD)
IATS............ Institute for Advanced Talmudic Studies [*Beth Medrash Govoha*] [*Canada*] (IRC)
IATS............ Intake Air Temperature Sensor [*Automotive engineering*]
IATS............ Intermediate Automatic Test System (SAUS)
IATS............ International Association for Tibetan Studies (BUAC)
IATSC.......... International Aeronautical Telecommunications Switching Center
IATSE.......... International Alliance of Theatrical Stage Empioyees (SAUS)
IATSE.......... International Alliance of Theatrical Stage Employees and Moving Picture Machine Operators of the United States and Canada (SAUO)
IATSE&MPMO... International Alliance of Theatrical Stage Employees and Motion Picture Machine Operators of the United States and Canada (SAUO)
IATSIS.......... Institute of Aboriginal and Torres Strait Islander Studies [*Australia*]
IATSS.......... International Association of Traffic and Safety Sciences [*Tokyo, Japan*] (EAIO)
IATSS.......... International Association of Traffic Safety Sciences (SAUS)
IATSW.......... Indian Association of Trained Social Workers (BUAC)
IATT............ International Academy of Twirling Teachers (EA)
IATTC.......... Inter-American Tropical Tuna Commission (EA)
IATU............ Inter-American Telecommunications Union [*US*]
IATUL.......... International Association of Technical (or Technological) University Libraries (SAUO)
IATUL.......... International Association of Technical University Libraries (BUAC)
IATUL.......... International Association of Technological University Libraries [*Goteborg, Sweden*]
IATUL Newsletter... International Association of Technological University Libraries Newsletter (journ.) (SAUS)
IATUL Newsletter... International Association of Technological University Library Newsletter (SAUO)
IATUL Proc... International Association of Technological University Libraries Proceedings (SAUO)
IATUL Proc... International Association of Technological University Libraries Proceedings (journ.) (SAUS)
IATUL Q....... IATUL Quarterly (journ.) (SAUS)
IATV............ ACTV, Inc. [*NASDAQ symbol*] (SAG)
IATV............ Income Approach to Value (MHDB)
IATV............ Interactive Alphanumeric Television
IATVC.......... Integrated Aerofin/Thrust Vector Control (SAUS)
IATVPM........ International Association of Teachers of Veterinary Preventive Medicine (SAUO)
IAU.............. Austin College, Sherman, TX [*OCLC symbol*] (OCLC)
IAU.............. Index Arithmetic Unit (SAUS)
IAU.............. Industrial Applications Unit (SAUO)
IAU.............. Infrastructure Accounting Unit (SAUS)
IAU.............. Infrastructure Account Unit (NATG)
IAU.............. Initial Alignment Unit
IAU.............. Institute for American Universities (EA)
IAU.............. Interface Adapter (or Adaptor) Unit (SAUS)
IAU.............. Interface Adapter Unit [*Computer science*] (MCD)
IAU.............. International Academic Union (EA)
IAU.............. International Accunting Unit (SAUS)
IAU.............. International Association of Universities [*France*]
IAU.............. International Astronomical Society (SAUS)
IAU.............. International Astronomical Union [*ICSU*] [*Paris, France*] [*Research center*] (IRC)
IAU.............. Internationale Armbrustschutzen Union [*International Crossbow Shooting Union*] (EAIO)
IAU.............. Intrusion Alarm Unit (SAUS)
iau.............. Iowa [*MARC country of publication code*] [*Library of Congress*] (LCCP)
IAU.............. ISDN Access Unit (SAUS)
IAU.............. Italian Actors Union (EA)
IaU.............. University of Iowa, Iowa City, IA [*Library symbol*] [*Library of Congress*] (LCLS)
IAub............ Auburn Public Library, Auburn, IL [*Library symbol*] [*Library of Congress*] (LCLS)
IaU-B.......... University of Iowa, Botany-Chemistry Library, Iowa City, IA [*Library symbol*] [*Library of Congress*] (LCLS)
IAUC............ IAU Circular (SAUO)
IAUC............ IAU International Astronomical Union Circular [*Astronomy term*]
IAUC............ Irish-American Unity Conference (SAUO)
IAUD............ Internal Audit (SAUS)
IAUD............ International Association for a/the Union of Democracies (SAUO)
IAUD............ International Association for a Union of Democracies [*Defunct*] (EA)
IAUEC.......... International Association of Underwater Engineering Contractors (BUAC)
IAUF............ Interamerican Underwater Festival
IAug............ Tri-County Public Library District, Augusta, IL [*Library symbol*] [*Library of Congress*] (LCLS)
IAUL............ Inter-African Union of Lawyers (BUAC)
IaU-L.......... University of Iowa, College of Law, Iowa City, IA [*Library symbol*] [*Library of Congress*] (LCLS)
IaU-M.......... University of Iowa, Health Sciences Library, Iowa City, IA [*Library symbol*] [*Library of Congress*] (LCLS)
IAUMS.......... Installation, Administrative Use, and Command Design Motor Vehicle Management System [*Army*]
IAUP............ International Association of Universities (or University) Presidents (SAUO)
IAUP............ International Association of University Presidents
IAUP............ Internet User Account Provider (SAUO)
IAUPD.......... International Association for Urban Planning and Design (SAUO)
IAUPE.......... International Association of University Professors of English [*British*]
IAUPL.......... International Association of University Professors and Lecturers (EAIO)
IAUPPR........ Inter-American University Press of Puerto Rico (SAUO)
IAUPR.......... Inter-American University of Puerto Rico (SAUO)
IaUpV.......... Vennard College, University Park, IA [*Library symbol*] [*Library of Congress*] (LCLS)
IAur............ Aurora Public Library, Aurora, IL [*Library symbol*] [*Library of Congress*] (LCLS)
IAUR............ Institute for Art and Urban Resources (EA)
IAUR............ Institute of Art and Urban Resources (SAUS)
IaUr............ Urbandale Public Library, Urbandale, IA [*Library symbol*] [*Library of Congress*] (LCLS)
IAurC.......... Aurora College, Aurora, IL [*Library symbol*] [*Library of Congress*] (LCLS)
IAURIF........ Institut d'Amenagement et d'Urbanisme de la Region de l'Ile de France (NITA)
IaUrN.......... Urbandale News, Urbandale, IA [*Library symbol*] [*Library of Congress*] (LCLS)
IaUrP.......... Urbandale Public Library, Urbandale, IA [*Library symbol*] [*Library of Congress*] (LCLS)
IAURRE........ International Association for Urban and Regional Research and Education (SAUO)
IAUSD.......... Inter-American Union for Scientific Development (SAUO)
IaUte.......... Ute Public Library, Ute, IA [*Library symbol*] [*Library of Congress*] (LCLS)
IAUYMF........ International Association of Users of Yarn of Man-made Fibres (SAUO)
IAV.............. Airavia [*France*] [*ICAO designator*] (FAAC)
IAV.............. Identified Aerial Vehicle
IA(V).......... Ileostomy Association (Victoria) [*Australia*]
IAV.............. Inaccessible Valve [*Tire maintenance*]
IAV.............. Index of Adjustment and Values (AEBS)
IAV.............. Indium Antimode Varactor
IAV.............. Infantry Armored Vehicle [*Army*] (MUSM)
IAV.............. Initial Attack Vehicle [*Fire fighting*]
IAV.............. Innotech Aviation Enterprises Ltd. [*Toronto Stock Exchange symbol*]
IAV.............. Institute for American Values (EA)

IAV Interim Armored Vehicle
IAV Intermittent Assisted Ventilation [*Medicine*] (MEDA)
IA/V Internal Audio and Video (SAUS)
IAV International Association for/of Video-VIDION (SAUO)
IAV International Association for Video-VIDION (SAUS)
IAV International Association of Video (SAUS)
IAV International Association of Volcanology (SAUO)
IAV International Association of Volcanology (or Vulcanology) (SAUS)
IAV Intra-Arterial Vasopressin [*Cardiology*]
IAV Intransit Asset Visibility (MCD)
IAV Inventory Adjustment Voucher [*Military*] (AFM)
IAV Island-Arc Volcanic [*Geology*]
IAV Issue Authority Voucher
IAV Southern Illinois University, School of Medicine, Springfield, IL [*OCLC symbol*] (OCLC)
IAV VIDION/International Association of Video (EA)
IAVA Industrial Audio-Visual Association [*Later, AVMA*] (EA)
IAVA International AIDS Vaccine Initative
IaVaO Vail Observer, Vail, IA [*Library symbol*] [*Library of Congress*] (LCLS)
IAVB International Association for/of Visceral Biomechanics (SAUO)
IAVB International Association of Visceral Biomechanics (SAUS)
IAVC Indian Army Veterinary Corps [*British military*] (DMA)
IAVC Instantaneous Automatic (SAUS)
IAVC Instantaneous Automatic Video Control (IEEE)
IAVC Instantaneous Automatic Volume Control [*Electronics*]
IAVC International Audio-Visual Center (or Centre) (SAUS)
IAVC International Audio-Visual Centre (SAUO)
IAVCB International Association of Visitors and Convention Bureaus (SAUO)
IAVCM International Association of Visual Communications Management [*Formerly, SRE*]
IAVD Interactive Videodisc [*Army*] (INF)
IAVE Industrial Arts and Vocational Education (AEBS)
IAVE Interaction Analysis for Vocational Educators (SAUS)
IAVE International Association for Volunteer Education (EA)
IAVE International Association for Volunteer Effort (SAUO)
IAVE International Association of Volunteer Effort (EA)
IAveECI Institute of Automotive Engineers Council (SAUO)
IAVFH International Association of Veterinary Food Hygiene (SAUO)
IAVFH International Association of Veterinary Food Hygienists
IAVG International Association for Vocational Guidance
IAVGO Industrial Accident Victims Group of Ontario (SAUO)
IAVH International Association of Veterinary Homeopathy (SAUO)
IAVI International AIDS Vaccine Initiative
IAVI International Association of Voice Identification [*Later, IAI*] (EA)
IAVI Italian Academy of Veterinary Informatics (GVA)
IaVilR Villisca Review, Villisca, IA [*Library symbol*] [*Library of Congress*] (LCLS)
IaVin Vinton Public Library, Vinton, IA [*Library symbol*] [*Library of Congress*] (LCLS)
IaVinT Cedar Valley Times, Vinton, IA [*Library symbol*] [*Library of Congress*] (LCLS)
IAVM Intramedullary Arteriovenous Malformation [*Medicine*] (STED)
IAVMS Installation Automated Vehicle Management System (SAUO)
IaVol Volga Public Library, Volga, IA [*Library symbol*] [*Library of Congress*] (LCLS)
IAVP Intravenous Atypical Vascular Pathogenesis (SAUS)
IAVRT Independent Association of Victorian Registered Teachers [*Australia*]
IAVS International Association for Vegetation Science [*See also IVV*] [*Gottingen, Federal Republic of Germany*] (EAIO)
IAVSD International Association for Vehicle System Dynamics (SAUS)
IAVSD International Association for Vehicle Systems Dynamics [*ICSU*] [*Delft, Netherlands*] (EAIO)
IAVTC International Audio-Visual Technical Center (or Centre) (SAUS)
IAVTC International Audio-Visual Technical Centre [*Netherlands*]
IAW Image Analysis Workstation (SAUS)
IAW Imagery Analysis Workpoint (SAUS)
IAW Improved Antimateriel Warhead
IAW In Accordance With
IAW Indications and Warning (SAUS)
IAW Institute of the American West [*Later, INAW*] (EA)
IAW International Alliance of Women [*See also AIF*] [*Valetta, Malta*] (EAIO)
IAW International Association of Wholesalers [*Defunct*]
IAW Ion Acoustic Wave (SAUS)
IAW Iraqi Airways [*ICAO designator*] (FAAC)
IAW Isotopic Atomic Weight
IAW Triton College, River Grove, IL [*OCLC symbol*] (OCLC)
IaW Waterloo Public Library, Waterloo, IA [*Library symbol*] [*Library of Congress*] (LCLS)
IAWA Independent American Whiskey Association [*Later, ABAA*] (EA)
IAWA International Active Women Association (SAUO)
IAWA International Association of Wood Anatomists [*Utrecht, Netherlands*] (EA)
IAWA International Aviation Women Association (NTPA)
IAWA Irish Amateur Weightlifting Association (EAIO)
IAWA Irish Amateur Wrestling Association (EAIO)
IaWa Washington Public Library, Washington, IA [*Library symbol*] [*Library of Congress*] (LCLS)
IAW/AA Integrated Attack Warning/Attack Assessment (SAUO)
IaWaJ Washington Evening Journal, Washington, IA [*Library symbol*] [*Library of Congress*] (LCLS)
IaWal Walnut Public Library, Walnut, IA [*Library symbol*] [*Library of Congress*] (LCLS)
IaWall Wall Lake Public Library, Wall Lake, IA [*Library symbol*] [*Library of Congress*] (LCLS)
IaWap Wapello Public Library (Keck Memorial Library), Wapello, IA [*Library symbol*] [*Library of Congress*] (LCLS)
IaWapCoC Louisa County Courthouse, Wapello, IA [*Library symbol*] [*Library of Congress*] (LCLS)
IaWapR Wapello Republican, Wapello, IA [*Library symbol*] [*Library of Congress*] (LCLS)
IaWas Washta Library, Washta, IA [*Library symbol*] [*Library of Congress*] (LCLS)
IaWauE Jerico Community Echo, Waucoma, IA [*Library symbol*] [*Library of Congress*] (LCLS)
IaWaukAC Allamakee County Courthouse, Waukon, IA [*Library symbol*] [*Library of Congress*] (LCLS)
IaWaukCoC Allamakee County Courthouse, Waukon, IA [*Library symbol*] [*Library of Congress*] (LCLS)
IaWaukD Waukon Democrat, Waukon, IA [*Library symbol*] [*Library of Congress*] (LCLS)
IaWauke Waukee Public Library, Waukee, IA [*Library symbol*] [*Library of Congress*] (LCLS)
IaWaukR Waukon Republican-Standard, Waukon, IA [*Library symbol*] [*Library of Congress*] (LCLS)
IaWavBHi Bremer County Historical Society, Waverly, IA [*Library symbol*] [*Library of Congress*] (LCLS)
IaWavCoC Bremer County Courthouse, Waverly, IA [*Library symbol*] [*Library of Congress*] (LCLS)
IaWavD Waverly Democrat, Waverly, IA [*Library symbol*] [*Library of Congress*] (LCLS)
IaWavH Waverly House, Waverly, IA [*Library symbol*] [*Library of Congress*] (LCLS)
IaWavI Bremer County Independent, Waverly, IA [*Library symbol*] [*Library of Congress*] (LCLS)
IaWavW Wartburg College, Waverly, IA [*Library symbol*] [*Library of Congress*] (LCLS)
IaWayN Wayland News, Wayland, IA [*Library symbol*] [*Library of Congress*] (LCLS)
IaWb Enlow Public Library, West Branch, IA [*Library symbol*] [*Library of Congress*] (LCLS)
IaWbe West Bend Public Library, West Bend, IA [*Library symbol*] [*Library of Congress*] (LCLS)
IaWbeJ West Bend Journal, West Bend, IA [*Library symbol*] [*Library of Congress*] (LCLS)
IaWbH Herbert Hoover Presidential Library, West Branch, IA [*Library symbol*] [*Library of Congress*] (LCLS)
IaWbT West Branch Times, West Branch, IA [*Library symbol*] [*Library of Congress*] (LCLS)
IaWbuN Des Moines County News, West Burlington, IA [*Library symbol*] [*Library of Congress*] (LCLS)
IaWC Daily Courier, Waterloo, IA [*Library symbol*] [*Library of Congress*] (LCLS)
IAWC In Accordance with Contract
IAWC International Association of Whaling Corporations (SAUO)
IAWCC International Association of Wall and Ceiling Contractors [*Later, AWCI*] (EA)
IAWCC/GD International Association of Wall and Ceiling Contractors - Gypsum Drywall Contractors International [*Later, AWCI*] (EA)
IAWCM International Association of Wiping Cloth Manufacturers (EA)
IAWCR International Association of Women Chefs and Restaurateurs (NTPA)
IaWdmB New Iowa Bystander, West Des Moines, IA [*Library symbol*] [*Library of Congress*] (LCLS)
IaWdmGS Church of Jesus Christ of Latter-Day Saints, Genealogical Society Library, Des Moines Branch, West Des Moines, IA [*Library symbol*] [*Library of Congress*] (LCLS)
IaWdmNB New Iowa Bystander, West Des Moines, IA [*Library symbol*] [*Library of Congress*] (LCLS)
IAWE International Association for Wind Engineering [*Aachen, Federal Republic of Germany*] (EAIO)
IAWEC International Alliance of Women for Equal Citizenship (SAUO)
IaWec Kendall Young Library, Webster City, IA [*Library symbol*] [*Library of Congress*] (LCLS)
IaWecAJ Aberdeen-Angus Journal, Webster City, IA [*Library symbol*] [*Library of Congress*] (LCLS)
IaWecF Freeman-Journal, Webster City, IA [*Library symbol*] [*Library of Congress*] (LCLS)
IaWelmA Wellman Advance, Wellman, IA [*Library symbol*] [*Library of Congress*] (LCLS)
IaWels Wellsburg Public Library, Wellsburg, IA [*Library symbol*] [*Library of Congress*] (LCLS)
IAWF International Amateur Wrestling Federation (SAUO)
IAWF International Association of Wildland Fire (NTPA)
IaWG Henry W. Grout Museum of History and Science, Waterlook, IA [*Library symbol*] [*Library of Congress*] (LCLS)
IAWG Industrial Avionics Working Group (SAUO)
IAWG Interagency Working Group (MCD)
IAWG Inter-American War Game (MCD)
IAWGD Inter-Agency Group on Desertification (SAUS)
IAWGSA Inter-Agency Working Group on Southern Africa [*Canadian Council for International Cooperation*]
IaWH Hawkeye Institute of Technology, Area VII, Waterloo, IA [*Library symbol*] [*Library of Congress*] (LCLS)
IAWH Improved Antimateriel Warhead
IaWhaP What Cheer Patriot-Chronicle, What Cheer, IA [*Library symbol*] [*Library of Congress*] (LCLS)
IaWhHi Loess Hills Historical Society of Monona County, Whiting, IA [*Library symbol*] [*Library of Congress*] (LCLS)
IaWhitC Whittmore Champion, Whittmore, IA [*Library symbol*] [*Library of Congress*] (LCLS)

IAWHPJ........ International Association of Women and Home Page Journalists (EA)
IaWij........ Wilton Public Library, Wilton Junction, IA [*Library symbol*] [*Library of Congress*] (LCLS)
IaWijS........ S-R Advocate News, Wilton Junction, IA [*Library symbol*] [*Library of Congress*] (LCLS)
IaWinfB........ Beacon and Wayland News, Winfield, IA [*Library symbol*] [*Library of Congress*] (LCLS)
IaWinN........ Winthrop News, Winthrop, IA [*Library symbol*] [*Library of Congress*] (LCLS)
IaWint........ Winterset Public Library, Winterset, IA [*Library symbol*] [*Library of Congress*] (LCLS)
IaWintM........ Winterset Madisonian, Winterset, IA [*Library symbol*] [*Library of Congress*] (LCLS)
IAWISP........ International Accidental War Information Sharing Project [*Nuclear Age Peace Foundation*] (EA)
IaWl........ Free Public Library, West Liberty, IA [*Library symbol*] [*Library of Congress*] (LCLS)
IAWL........ International Association for/of Water Law (SAUO)
IAWL........ International Association for Water Law [*See also AIDA*] [*Rome, Italy*] (EAIO)
IAWL........ International Association of Water Law (SAUS)
IaWlI........ West Liberty Index, West Liberty, IA [*Library symbol*] [*Library of Congress*] (LCLS)
IAWM........ Industrial Association of Wales and Monmouthshire (SAUO)
IAWM........ International Alliance for Women in Music (NTPA)
IAWM........ International Association of Women Ministers (EA)
IaWmbgI........ Iowa County Farmer, Williamsburg, IA [*Library symbol*] [*Library of Congress*] (LCLS)
IaWmbgJT... Williamsburg Jounal-Tribune, Williamsburg, IA [*Library symbol*] [*Library of Congress*] (LCLS)
IAWMC........ International Association of Workers for Maladjusted Children (SAUO)
IAWMC........ International Association of Workers for Troubled Children and Youth [*See also AIEJI*] (EAIO)
IaWob........ Woodbine Public Library, Woodbine, IA [*Library symbol*] [*Library of Congress*] (LCLS)
IaWobT........ Woodbine Twiner, Woodbine, IA [*Library symbol*] [*Library of Congress*] (LCLS)
IaWow........ Woodward Public Library, Woodward, IA [*Library symbol*] [*Library of Congress*] (LCLS)
IaWowN........ Northeast Dallas County Record, Woodward, IA [*Library symbol*] [*Library of Congress*] (LCLS)
IAWP........ Inter-National Association for Widowed People (EA)
IAWP........ International Association of Women Philosophers [*Zurich, Switzerland*] (EAIO)
IAWP........ International Association of Women Police (EA)
IaWp........ West Point Public Library, West Point, IA [*Library symbol*] [*Library of Congress*] (LCLS)
IaWpB........ West Point Bee, West Point, IA [*Library symbol*] [*Library of Congress*] (LCLS)
IAWPC........ International Association on Water Pollution Research and Control (SAUO)
IAWPR........ International Association of/on Water Pollution Research (SAUO)
IAWPR........ International Association of Water Pollution Research (SAUS)
IAWPR........ International Association of Water Polo Referees (EA)
IAWPR........ International Association on Water Pollution Research [*Later, IAWPRC*]
IAWPRC........ Indian Association on Water Pollution Research and Control (SAUO)
IAWPRC........ International Association for/on Water Pollution Research and Control (SAUO)
IAWPRC........ International Association on Water Pollution Research and Control [*British*] (EA)
IAWQ........ International Association of/on Water Quality (SAUO)
IAWQ........ International Association on Water Quality (SAUS)
IAWR........ Institute for Air Weapons Research (SAUS)
IAWR........ Institute of Air Weapons (SAUS)
IAWR........ Institute of Air Weapons Research [*Air Force*]
IAWR........ Internationale Arbeitsgemeinschaft der Wasserwerke im Rheineinzugsgebiet [*International Association of Waterworks in the Rhine Basin Area - IAWRBA*] (EAIO)
IAWRBA........ International Association of Waterworks in the Rhine Basin Area (EAIO)
IAWRT........ International Association of Women in/on Radio and Television (SAUO)
IAWRT........ International Association of Women in Radio and Television (NTCM)
IAWS........ Intercollegiate Association for/of Women Students (SAUO)
IAWS........ Intercollegiate Association for Women Students (SAUS)
IAWS........ Intercollegiate Association of Women Students (AEBS)
IAWS........ International Academy of Wood Science (SAUO)
IAWS........ Irish Agricultural Wholesale Society (SAUO)
IAWS........ Irish Agricultural Wholesale Society Ltd. (BI)
IAWSP........ Intergrated Aviation Wind Shear Plan (SAUS)
IAWT........ International Association for World Tourism (TVEL)
IAWT........ International Association of World Tourism (TRID)
IAWTC........ Integrated Air Warfare Training Complex [*Military*] (CAAL)
IaWu........ Heiseman Memorial Library, West Union, IA [*Library symbol*] [*Library of Congress*] (LCLS)
IaWuCoC........ Fayette County Courthouse, West Union, IA [*Library symbol*] [*Library of Congress*] (LCLS)
IaWuU........ Fayette County Union, West Union, IA [*Library symbol*] [*Library of Congress*] (LCLS)
IAWWE........ International Association of Workshop Way Educators (EA)
IaWyo........ Roche Memorial Library, Wyoming, IA [*Library symbol*] [*Library of Congress*] (LCLS)
IAX........ Image Application Executor (SAUS)
IAX........ University of Illinois at the Medical Center, Chicago, IL [*OCLC symbol*] (OCLC)
IAY........ Island Canyon Mines, Inc. [*Vancouver Stock Exchange symbol*]
IAY........ University of Illinois at Chicago Circle, Chicago, IL [*OCLC symbol*] (OCLC)
IAYB........ Interim Accessory Bulletin (DNAB)
IAYC........ Interim Accessory Change (MCD)
IAYF........ Information at Your Fingertips
IAYM........ International Association of Youth Magistrates [*Later, IAJFCM*]
IAYMC........ International Association of Y's Men's Clubs [*Geneva, Switzerland*] (EA)
IAYP........ International Association of Young Philosophers (SAUO)
IAZ........ Industrie Air Charter [*France*] [*ICAO designator*] (FAAC)
IAZ........ Inner Artillery Zone
IAZ........ Western Illinois University, Macomb, IL [*OCLC symbol*] (OCLC)
IaZN........ Tri-County News, Zearing, IA [*Library symbol*] [*Library of Congress*] (LCLS)
IB........ I-Beam [*Lumber*] (DAC)
IB........ Iberia Air Lines of Spain [*ICAO designator*] (AD)
IB........ Iberia International Airlines of Spain (SAUS)
ib........ Ibidem [*Latin*] [*In the same place*] (WDMC)
IB........ Ibidem [*In the Same Place*] [*Latin*]
Ib........ Ibis [*of Ovid*] [*Classical studies*] (OCD)
IB........ Ibrahim-Beck [*Disease*] [*Medicine*] (DB)
IB........ Ice Box (SAUS)
IB........ Idaho Branch Office (SAUO)
IB........ Ideal Bypass [*Medicine*] (EDAA)
IB........ Identification Beacon [*Aviation*] (IAA)
IB........ Identification Block (SAUS)
IB........ Identifier Block
IB........ Illegal Behavior (SAUS)
IB........ Imbibition Printing [*Cinematography*] (WDMC)
IB........ Immigration Branch (SAUO)
IB........ Immune Body
IB........ Impact Bag (SAA)
IB........ Imperial Bank (SAUO)
IB........ Imperial Beach (SAUS)
IB........ In-Band (SAUS)
I/B........ In Board (SAUS)
IB........ Inboard (NASA)
IB........ In Bond [*Wines and Spirits*]
IB........ Inbound
IB........ In Britain (SAUO)
IB........ In Bulk (IAA)
IB........ Incendiary Bomb
IB........ Incentive Base (VLIE)
IB........ Incentive-Based Policy [*for environmental improvement*]
IB........ Inclusion Body [*Cytology*]
ib........ Indent Both (WDMC)
IB........ Index Bit (SAUS)
IB........ Index Block (SAUS)
IB........ Index Bureau (SAUO)
IB........ Index of Body Build [*Anatomy*]
IB........ India-Burma [*World War II*]
IB........ Indicator Board (SAUS)
IB........ Individual Bias
IB........ Induction Balance (ADA)
IB........ Induction Brazing
IB........ Industrial Benefit (SAUS)
IB........ Industrial Business [*Insurance term*] [*British*]
IB........ Industrialised Building (SAUS)
IB........ Industrialized Building (PDAA)
IB........ Inert Building [*NASA*] (KSC)
IB........ Infant Botulism [*Medicine*] (MELL)
IB........ Infantry Battalion [*Army*]
IB........ Infantry Brigade [*British military*] (DMA)
IB........ Infectious Bronchitis [*Medicine*]
IB........ Infinite Baffle (SAUS)
IB........ Information Bank (SAUS)
IB........ Information Bit (SAUS)
IB........ Information Bulletin
IB........ Information Bureau [*Telecommunications*] (TEL)
IB........ Information Bus (IAA)
IB........ Inner Bottom [*Technical drawings*]
IB........ Inner Bound (SAUS)
IB........ Input Block (SAUS)
IB........ Input Buffer [*Telecommunications*] (TEL)
IB........ Input Bus [*Computer science*]
IB........ Inquiry Branch (SAUO)
IB........ Insect Biochemistry [*Medicine*] (EDAA)
IB........ Inspection Bulletin
IB........ Institute of Bankers [*Later, CIB*] [*British*] (DI)
IB........ Institute of Biology [*British*]
IB........ Institute of Brewing [*Also, IOB*] [*British*]
IB........ Institute of Building [*British*]
IB........ Instructional Brochure (SAUS)
IB........ Instruction Bank [*Computer science*]
IB........ Instruction Block (SAUS)
IB........ Instruction Book
IB........ Instruction Brochure (SAUS)
IB........ Instruction Buffer (SAUS)
IB........ Instruction Bus [*Computer science*]
IB........ Instructor Bombardier (SAUS)
IB........ Insulation Board (SAUS)
IB........ Integration Broker (GART)

IB .... Intelligence Branch
IB .... Intelligent Backtracking (SAUS)
IB .... Interbank (EBF)
IB .... Interbedded (SAUS)
IB .... Interface Board (SAUS)
IB .... Interface Bus [*Computer science*]
IB .... Internal Bond [*Pulp and paper technology*]
IB .... Internal Browning [*of Fruits and Vegetables*] (BARN)
IB .... Internal Bus [*Computer science*]
IB .... International Baccalaureate
IB .... International Bank (EFIS)
IB .... International Bank for Reconstruction and Development [*Also known as World Bank*]
IB .... International Bibliography (journ.) (SAUS)
IB .... International Broadcasting
I B .... International Business (SAUS)
IB .... International Butec Industry [*Vancouver Stock Exchange symbol*]
IB .... International Rugby Football Board (SAUO)
IB .... Internet Bridge (ACAE)
IB .... Interposer Bail (SAUS)
IB .... Interpreter's Bible
IB .... Intra Bank S.A.L. (SAUO)
IB .... Introducing Broker (MHDB)
IB .... Invalid Behaviour (SAUS)
IB .... Investigation Branch [*British*] [*Australia*] (DCTA)
IB .... Invoice Book [*Business term*]
IB .... Invoice Booklet (SAUS)
IB .... Inward Bound (SAUS)
IB .... Ion Beam (SAUS)
IB .... Ion Bombardment (SAUS)
IB .... Irish Baron (ROG)
IB .... Iron Body (SAUS)
IB .... Iron Bolts
IB .... Ironing Board (MSA)
IB .... Is Between (MHDB)
IB .... Isobutylene (SAUS)
IB .... Isolation Bed [*Infectious disease*] (DAVI)
IB .... Issue Book [*DoD*]
IB .... Lineas Aereas du Espanalos [*Iberia*] [*Spain*] [*ICAO designator*]
IB .... RAB [*Radio Advertising Bureau*] Instant Background [*A publication*]
IB2 .... Interconnecting Box 2 radio (SAUS)
IB2CR .... Interconnecting Box 2 Crew and Remote (SAUS)
IB4J .... Instant BASIC for Java (SAUS)
IBa .... Barrington Area Library District, Barrington, IL [*Library symbol*] [*Library of Congress*] (LCLS)
IBA .... Bradley University, Peoria, IL [*OCLC symbol*] (OCLC)
IBA .... Ibadan [*Nigeria*] [*Airport symbol*] (OAG)
IBA .... Igniter Booster Assembly [*Aerospace*]
IBA .... Important Bird Area (SAUO)
IBA .... Independent Bakers Association (EA)
IBA .... Independent Banker (journ.) (SAUS)
IBA .... Independent Bankers Association (SAUO)
IBA .... Independent Bar Association (EA)
IBA .... Independent Board Authority [*Board granting franchises to new companies*] [*British*]
IBA .... Independent Broadcast Authority (ACAE)
IBA .... Independent Broadcasting Association (SAUO)
IBA .... Independent Broadcasting Authority [*Formerly, ITA*] [*British*]
IBA .... Indian Banks Association (PDAA)
IBA .... Indo-British Association (SAUO)
IBA .... Indolebutyric Acid [*Plant growth regulator*]
IBA .... Indonesian-British Association (DS)
IBA .... Industrial Bankers Association (SAUS)
IBA .... Industrial Biotechnology Association (EA)
IBA .... Inflatable Boat Association (EA)
IBA .... Information Block Address (SAUS)
IBA .... Inhomogeneously Broadened Absorber [*Optics*]
IBA .... Inner Blanket Assembly [*Nuclear energy*] (NRCH)
IBA .... Inspection by Attribute
IBA .... Institute for Bioenergetic Analysis [*Later, IIBA*] (EA)
IBA .... Institute for Briquetting and Agglomeration (EA)
IBA .... Institute of Bioenergetic Analysis (SAUS)
IBA .... Institute of British Architects
IBA .... Institute of Business Appraisers (EA)
IBA .... Institution of Business Agents [*British*]
IBA .... Interacting Boson Approximation (SAUS)
IBA .... Interceptor Body Armor [*Military*]
IBA .... International Backgammon Association (EA)
IBA .... International Backpackers Association [*Later, AHS*] (EA)
IBA .... International Balloon Association (EA)
IBA .... International Banana Association (EA)
IBA .... International Banker Association (EA)
IBA .... International Bankers Association (SAUO)
IBA .... International Banking Act [*1978*]
IBA .... International Bar Association [*British*] (EA)
IBA .... International Bartenders Association [*Paris, France*] (EAIO)
IBA .... International Baseball Association (EA)
IBA .... International Basketball Association [*Defunct*] (EA)
IBA .... International Bauxite Association [*Kingston, Jamaica*]
IBA .... International Biliary Association [*Later, IHBPA*] (EAIO)
IBA .... International Biographical Archive (SAUO)
IBA .... International Biographical Association (SAUO)
IBA .... International Biometric Association (EA)
IBA .... International Board of Auditors (NATG)
IBA .... International Bocce Association (EA)
IBA .... International Bodyguard Association (EA)
IBA .... International Bookstall Contractors Association (SAUO)
IBA .... International Border Area
IBA .... International Bowling Association (SAUO)
IBA .... International Boxing Association (SAUO)
IBA .... International Braford Association (EA)
IBA .... International Bridge Academy [*The Hague, Netherlands*] (EA)
IBA .... International Brigade Association (SAUO)
IBA .... International Briqueting Association (SAUO)
IBA .... International Briquetting Association (SAUO)
IBA .... International Broadcasting Authority (SAUS)
IBA .... International Bryozoology Association [*See also AIB*] [*Paris, France*] (EAIO)
IBA .... Investing Builders Association
IBA .... Investment Bankers Association (SAUS)
IBA .... Investment Bankers Association of America [*Later, SIA*] (EA)
IBA .... Invitation, Bid, Award (FOTI)
IBA .... Iodosobenzoic Acid [*Organic chemistry*] (RDA)
IBA .... Ion Backscattering Analysis (SAUS)
IBA .... Ion-Backscattering Analysis (IAA)
IBA .... Ion Beam Analysis
IBA .... Isobornyl Acetate (SAUS)
IBA .... Isobutyl Acetate (SAUS)
IBA .... Isobutyl Alcohol (SAUS)
IBA .... Isobutylamine [*Organic chemistry*]
IBA .... Lineas Aereas Iberoamericanas [*Chile*] [*FAA designator*] (FAAC)
IBAA .... Independent Bankers Association of America (EA)
IBAA .... International Bankers Association of America (SAUO)
IBAA .... International Business Aircraft Association (DA)
IBAA .... International Business Analysts Association (NTPA)
IBAA .... Investment Bankers Association of America (SAUO)
IBAA .... Italian Baptist Association of America [*Later, AEIM*] (EA)
IBAC .... Caligula [*the Poisoner*] [*the Hun*] [*the Emperor*] [*Initials that form the name of the villain in "Captain Marvel" comic strip and indicate the sources of his power*]
IBAC .... Identity Based Access Control (SAUS)
IBAC .... In-Band, Adjacent Channel (SAUS)
IBAC .... Information Bulletin of Australian Criminology [*A publication*]
IBAC .... Instantaneous Broadcast Audience Counting (IAA)
IBAC .... International Bullet and Ammunition Company (SAUO)
IBAC .... International Business Aviation Council (EA)
IBACOS .... Integrated Building and Construction Solutions
IBAD .... Ion-Beam-Assisted Deposition [*Organic chemistry*]
IBADIZ .... International Boundary Air Defense Identification Zone (SAUS)
IBAE .... Institute of British Agricultural Engineers (SAUO)
IBAE .... Ion Beam Assisted Etching (AAEL)
IBAF .... Interim Brigade Afloat Force [*Prepositioning force*] [*Army*] (DOMA)
IBAG .... Ich Bau auf Gott [*I Build on God*] [*Motto of Heinrich Posthumus, Count Reuss (1572-1635)*] [*German*]
IBAH .... IBAH, Inc. [*NASDAQ symbol*] (SAG)
IBAH .... Inter-African Bureau for Animal Health (SAUO)
IBAHP .... Inter-African Bureau for Animal Health and Production (SAUO)
IBAHP .... Inter-African Bureau for Animal Health and Protection
IBAHRS .... Inflatable Body and Head Restraint System [*Aviation*] (RDA)
IBAHRS .... Integrated Body and Head Restraint System (SAUS)
IBALS .... Interactive Balancing through Simulation (PDAA)
IBAM .... India Board of Alternative Medicine (SAUO)
IBAM .... Institute of Business Administration and Management (SAUO)
IBAMA .... Brazilian Environmental Agency (SAUO)
IBAMA .... National Environment and Renewable Natural Resources Institute (SAUO)
IBAN .... Imperial Bancorp [*NASDAQ symbol*] (NQ)
I (Bank) .... Instruction Bank [*Computer science*]
IBAP .... Intervention Board for Agricultural Produce (SAUO)
IBAP .... Intervention Board for Agricultural Products [*Government body*] [*British*]
IBAP .... Intervention Board of Agricultural Produce (SAUS)
IBAPT .... Incorporated British Association of Physical Training (SAUO)
I Bar .... I Baruch [*Apocrypha*] (BJA)
IBAR .... Inter-African Bureau for Animal Resources (SAUO)
IBAR .... Inter-African Bureau of Animal Resources [*Kenya*]
IBarA .... American Can Co., Barrington, IL [*Library symbol*] [*Library of Congress*] (LCLS)
IBarAS .... Allstate Insurance Co., Barrington, IL [*Library symbol*] [*Library of Congress*] (LCLS)
IBarQ .... Quaker Oats Co., Research Library, Barrington, IL [*Library symbol*] [*Library of Congress*] (LCLS)
IBart .... Alpha Park Public Library, Bartonville, IL [*Library symbol*] [*Library of Congress*] (LCLS)
IBartL .... Limestone Community High School, Bartonville, IL [*Library symbol*] [*Library of Congress*] (LCLS)
IBAS .... Improved Bradley Acquisition Subsystem [*Army*] (RDA)
IBAS .... Improved Bradley Acquisition System [*Army*] (INF)
IBAS .... Indonesian Business Association of Singapore (SAUO)
IBAS .... Informationssystem Beliebiger Andwendungssystem [*Germany*] (NITA)
IBAS .... Input Beam Alignment System (ACAE)
IBAS .... Instructional-Based Appraisal System [*Education*]
IBAS .... Intelligent Body Assembly System [*Robotics*] [*Nissan Motor Co. Ltd.*]
IBAS .... International Business Assistance Service (SAUO)
IBASA .... International Radio Air Safety Association (SAUO)
IBASES .... Intel Baseline AGP System Evaluation Suite (SAUS)
IBASF .... Intervals Between Aircraft in Stream Type Formation [*Aviation*] (FAAC)
IBASS .... Intelligent Business Applications Support System (SAUO)

IBAT............ Improved Brilliant Anti-Armor [*Army*] (RDA)
IBAT............ Independent Bankers Association of Texas (SRA)
IBAT............ Intravascular Bronchoalveolar Tumor [*Medicine*] (DMAA)
IBatF............ FERMILAB, Batavia, IL [*Library symbol*] [*Library of Congress*] (LCLS)
IBAU............ Institute of British- American Understanding (SAUO)
IBAU............ Institute of British-American Understanding (SAUS)
IBAW............ Independent Community Bankers Association of Wisconsin (TBD)
IBA West..... Insurance Brokers and Agents of the West
IBB.............. Binter Canarais [*Spain*] [*ICAO designator*] (FAAC)
IBB.............. Chicago Transit Authority, Chicago, IL [*OCLC symbol*] (OCLC)
IBB.............. Illinois Inspection Bureau (SAUO)
IBB.............. Initial Body Burden (SAUS)
IBB.............. Institute for British Business (COBU)
IBB.............. Institute of British Bakers (BI)
IBB.............. Institute of British Bankers (SAUO)
IBB.............. Intentional Bases on Balls [*Baseball*]
IBB.............. International Bank Bond (MHDB)
IBB.............. International Biodeterioration Bulletin (SAUO)
IBB.............. International Book Bank (EA)
IBB.............. International Bortherhood of Boilermakers, Iron Ship Builders, Blacksmiths, Forgers, and Helpers (NTPA)
IBB.............. International Bowling Board (EA)
IBB.............. International Brotherhood of Bookbinders [*Later, Graphic Arts International Union*]
IBB.............. Intestinal Brush Border [*Medicine*] (MAE)
IBB.............. Invest in Britain Bureau
IBB.............. Isobutylbenzene [*Organic chemistry*]
IBB.............. Isobutyl Benzoate (SAUS)
IBBA............ Inland Bird Banding Association (EA)
IBBA............ International Brangus Breeders Association (EA)
IBBA............ International Business Brokers Association [*Defunct*] (EA)
IBBA............ Irish Basketball Association (DBA)
IBBB............ Intra-Blood-Brain-Barrier [*Medicine*] (EDAA)
IBBBA.......... International Bundle Branch Block Association (EA)
IBBBB.......... Incomplete Bilateral Bundle Branch Block (SAUS)
IBBC............ International Business Communications Council [*Japan*] (ECON)
IBBCA.......... International Bathymetric Chart of the Caribbean Sea and Gulf of Mexico [*Marine science*] (OSRA)
IBBD............ Inner Balance Bead Design [*Tire design*]
IBBDFH........ International Brotherhood of Blacksmiths, Drop Forgers and Helpers (SAUO)
IBBEA.......... Interstate Banking and Branching Efficiency Act
IBBFIC......... International B & B [*Bed and Breakfast*] Fly-Inn Club (EA)
IBBH............ Internationaler Bund der Bau-Haolzarbeiter [*International Federation of Building and Woodworkers*]
IBBISBBFH... International Brotherhood of Boilermakers, Iron Ship Builders, Blacksmiths, Forgers and Helpers (SAUO)
IBBIT............ Internal Bean Bacterial Infusion Test [*Plant pathology*]
IBBL............ Islamic Bank of Bangladesh [*Commercial bank*] (EY)
IBBM............ Ion-Binding/Ion-Bouncing Model [*Physical chemistry*]
IBBM............ Iron Body Brass Mounted (SAUS)
IBBM............ Iron Body Bronze Mounted (SAUS)
IBBN............ Inhomogeneous Big Bang Nucleosynthesis [*Cosmology*]
IBBR............ Inter-Bank Bid Rate (SAUS)
IBBR............ International Beefalo Breeders' Registry (EA)
IBBRIS......... International Biodeterioration Bulletin. Reference Index [*A publication*]
IBBRIS......... International Biodeterioration Bulletin Reference Index Supplement (SAUO)
IBBRIX......... International Biodeterioration Bulletin Reference Index (journ.) (SAUS)
IBBT............ International Brotherhood of Bikers' Teardrops (EA)
IBBTPS........ Ivory and Bone Brushmakers' Trade Protection Society [*A union*] [*British*]
IBBY............ International Board on Books for Young People [*Basel, Switzerland*] (EA)
IBC.............. De Paul University, Law Library, Chicago, IL [*OCLC symbol*] (OCLC)
IBC.............. Groapackmittel, Gefahrgutumschlieaung mit einem Fassungsraum bis 3000 Liter (SAUS)
IBC.............. Iceland Base Command [*Army*] [*World War II*]
IBC.............. Idaho Bean Commission (SRA)
IBC.............. Ignore Block Character [*Computer science*] (VLIE)
IBC.............. Illegal Border Crosser (SAUO)
IBC.............. Illini-Badger Conference (PSS)
IBC.............. Illinois Benedictine College (SAUO)
IBC.............. Imperial Bushmen Contingent [*British military*] (DMA)
IBC.............. Impurity Band Conduction (ACAE)
IBC.............. Inadequate, But Cute (SAUS)
IBC.............. In-Band Control (DINT)
IBC.............. Independent Bakers' Cooperative [*W. E. Long Co.*] (EA)
IBC.............. Independent Bankers of Colorado (TBD)
IBC.............. Independent Breweries Company (SAUO)
IBC.............. Informatica Bulgarien Corp. [*Bulgaria*] [*ICAO designator*] (FAAC)
IBC.............. Information-Based Complexity [*Mathematics*]
IBC.............. Information Bit Content (SAUS)
IBC.............. Input Bias Current
IBC.............. Input Block Count (SAUS)
IBC.............. Insect Biotech Canada [*Queen's University*] [*Research center*] (RCD)
ibc............... Inside Back Cover [*Publishing*] (WDAA)
IBC.............. Inside Back Cover
IBC.............. Institute Builders Risk Clause (MARI)
IBC.............. Institute for Biomedical Communication [*South African Medical Research Council*] [*Information service or system*] (IID)
IBC.............. Institute of Buddhist Culture, World (SAUO)
IBC.............. Institute of Building Control [*British*] (DBA)
IBC.............. Institutional Biosafety Committee [*National Institutes of Health*]
IBC.............. Instrument Bus Computer
IBC.............. Insurance Bureau of Canada
IBC.............. Integral Business Computing (SAUO)
IBC.............. Integrated Block Channel (MHDB)
IBC.............. Integrated Block Controller (NITA)
IBC.............. Integrated Broadband Communications (MHDB)
IBC.............. Integrated Business Communications [*British*] (NITA)
IBC.............. Integrated Business Computers [*Manufacturer*] (NITA)
IBC.............. Intelligent Broadband Controller (NITA)
IBC.............. Intelligent Buildings Corp. [*Broomfield, CO*] [*Telecommunications service*] (TSSD)
IBC.............. Interboard Committee for Christian Work in Japan [*Later, JNAC*] (EA)
IBC.............. Interbuilding Coffin (SAUS)
IBC.............. Intercollegiate Broadcasting System (SAUS)
IBC.............. Interconnect Backplane Capability
IBC.............. Interdigitated Back Contact (SAUS)
IBC.............. Interface Buffer Controller (SAUS)
IBC.............. Inter-Island Broadcasting Corporation (SAUO)
IBC.............. Intermediate Bulk Carrier (SAUS)
IBC.............. Intermediate Bulk Container (SAUS)
IBC.............. Intermediate Bulk Containers [*Shipping*]
IBC.............. International Ballet Competition
IBC.............. International Ballet Council
IBC.............. International Banana Club (EA)
IBC.............. International Bancorp Ltd. (SAUO)
IBC.............. International Banking Center (SAUS)
IBC.............. International Banking Centre [*British*]
IBC.............. International Banking Corporation (SAUO)
IBC.............. International Bathymetric Chart [*Marine science*] (OSRA)
IBC.............. International Betta Congress (EA)
IBC.............. International Bibliographical Centre (SAUO)
IBC.............. International Biographical Center (or Centre) (SAUS)
IBC.............. International Biographical Centre [*British*] (CB)
IBC.............. International Biometric Conference (SAUS)
IBC.............. International Biophysical Center
IBC.............. International Biotoxicological Center [*World Life Research Institute*] [*US*] (ASF)
IBC.............. International Board of Cytopatholog (SAUS)
IBC.............. International Board of Cytopathology [*International Academy of Cytology*] [*Quebec, PQ*] (EAIO)
IBC.............. International Borzoi Council (EA)
IBC.............. International Botanical Congress (SAUO)
IBC.............. International Boundary and Water Commission (SAUO)
IBC.............. International Boxing Club (SAUO)
IBC.............. International BRCA [*Breast Cancer*] Consortium
IBC.............. International Brightness Coefficient
IBC.............. International Broadcasting Committee (CARL)
IBC.............. International Broadcasting Convention [*Legal term*] (DLA)
IBC.............. International Broadcasting Corp. [*Vancouver Stock Exchange symbol*]
IBC.............. International Bulk Chemical
IBC.............. International Bus Collectors Club (EA)
IBC.............. International Business Centre (SAUS)
IBC.............. International Business Communications [*Commercial firm*] [*British*]
IBC.............. International Business Company (SAUO)
IBC.............. International Business Consultants [*Commercial firm*]
IBC.............. International Business Consulting SA (SAUS)
IBC.............. International Business Contacts
IBC.............. International Business Corporation (SAUO)
IBC.............. International Business Council (EA)
IBC.............. International Federation of the Blue Cross [*Formerly, International Federation of the Temperance Blue Cross Societies*] (EA)
IBC.............. Internet Business Center [*Information service or system*] (IID)
IBC.............. Interstate Bakeries [*NYSE symbol*] (TTSB)
IBC.............. Interstate Bakeries Corp. [*NYSE symbol*] (SPSG)
IBC.............. Interstate Brands Corporation (SAUO)
IBC.............. Inuit Broadcasting Corporation (SAUO)
IBC.............. Inverted Bowl Centrifuge
IBC.............. Iodine Binding Capacity [*of starch*]
IBC.............. Ion Binding Capacity (SAUS)
IBC.............. Iowa Business Council (SRA)
IBC.............. Iron-Binding Capacity [*Clinical chemistry*]
IBC.............. Isobaric Cooling [*Geology*]
IBC.............. Isobutyl Carbinol (SAUS)
IBC.............. Iwate Broadcasting Company (SAUO)
IBC.............. World Institute of Buddhist Culture
IBCA............ Department of the Interior Board of Contract Appeals
IBCA............ Idaho Building Contractors Association (SRA)
IBCA............ Illinois Bulk Carriers Association (SRA)
IBCA............ Indiana Beef Cattle Association (SRA)
IBCA............ Industrial Bag and Covers Association (SAUO)
IBCA............ Industry Bar Code Alliance (EA)
IBCA............ Institute of Burial and Cremation Administration [*British*]
IBCA............ Interior Board of Contract Appeals (SAUO)
IBCA............ Interior Board of Contract Appeals (in United States Interior Decisions) [*A publication*] (DLA)
IBCA............ International Braille Chess Association [*Abcoude, Netherlands*] (EA)
IBCA............ International Brick Collectors' Association (EA)
IBCA............ International Broadcasting Corp. [*NASDAQ symbol*] (COMM)
IBCA............ International Bureau for Cultural (or Culture) Activities (SAUO)
IBCA............ Isobutyl Cyanoacrylate [*Organic chemistry*]
IBCAM.......... Institute of British Carriage and Automobile Manufacturers (BI)
IBCASA........ International Banking Campaign Against South Africa [*Later, ICABA*] (EAIO)

IBCC............ Integrated Battlefield Control Concept (SAUO)
IBCC............ Intelligent Business Communications Corporation (SAUO)
IBCC............ International Benchcraft Course (SAUS)
IBCC............ International Building Classification Committee [*Netherlands*]
IBCC............ International Business Communications Centers (SAUO)
IBCC............ International Business Communications Council (ECON)
IBCC............ International Business Contact Club
IBCC............ International Business Council of Canada (SAUO)
IBCC............ Intra-Bureau Change Committee
IBCCA.......... International Bathymetric Chart of the Caribbean Sea and the Gulf of Mexico (SAUS)
IBC Code..... International Code for the Construction and Equipment of Ships Carrying Dangerous Chemical in Bulk (SAUO)
IBC Code..... International Code for the Construction and Equipment of Ships carrying Dangerous Chemicals in Bulk (SAUS)
IBCCSE........ International Board of Computing in Civil and Structural Engineering (SAUO)
IBCE............ Indo-British Cultural Exchange
IBCE............ International Binding Center at Elat [*Israel*]
IBCE............ International Bureau for Cultural Exchange (SAUO)
IBCEA.......... International Bathymetric Chart of the Central Eastern Atlantic [*Marine science*] (OSRA)
IBCFA.......... Injected Beam Cross Field Amplifier (IAA)
IBCFP.......... International Board of Standards and Practices for Certified Financial Planners (SAUO)
IBCHMB....... International Research Center on Hydraulic Machinery Beijing (SAUS)
IBCI............ International Bank of Commerce and Industry (SAUS)
IBCL............ Instrument Bus Control Language [*National Instruments Corp.*] [*Austin, TX*]
IBCL............ Interface Bus Control Language [*Computer science*]
IBCM............ Integrated Battlefield Casualty Manikin [*Medical training*] [*Navy*]
IBCM............ International Bathymetric Chart of the Mediterranean and its Geological/Geophysical Series (SAUS)
IBCM............ International Business Council Midamerica (EA)
IBCN............ Integrated Broadband Communication Network [*Telecommunications*]
IBCO............ Institution of Building Control Officers (SAUO)
IBCOS.......... In-Built Check-Out System (SAUS)
IBCP............ Imperial British Conservative Party [*Political party*] (ADA)
IBCP............ Independent Bank Corp. [*NASDAQ symbol*] (NQ)
IBCP............ IRRI-Burma-CIDA Project (SAUO)
IBCRSGA...... International Bathymetric Chart of the Red Sea and Gulf of Aden [*Proposed*] [*Marine science*] (OSRA)
IBCS............ Inflight Blood Collection System [*On space flights*]
IBCS............ Integrated Battlefield Control System [*Army*]
IBCS............ Integrated Bridge Control System (SAUS)
IBCS............ Intel Binary Compatibility Specification (SAUS)
IBCS............ Intel Binary Compatibility Standard (SAUS)
IBCS............ Interlink Business and Communications Services [*British telecommunications service company*] (NITA)
IBCS............ International Bureau of Chambers of Commerce (SAUS)
IBCS............ International Bureau of Commercial Statistics (SAUO)
IBCS/TRICAP... Integrated Battlefield Communications Systems / Triple Capability-Armoured, Infantry and Air Cavalry [*Military*] (PDAA)
IBCS/TRICAP... Integrated Battlefield Communications Systems/Triple Capability - Armoured, Infantry and Air Cavalry (SAUO)
IBCSVP........ International Breeding Consortium for St. Vincent Parrot (EAIO)
IBCT............ Interim Brigade Combat Team [*Military*]
IBCTs.......... Interim Brigade Combat Teams
IBCUSCAN... International Boundary Commission, United States and Canada (SAUO)
IBCWIO........ International Bathymetric Chart of the Western Indian Ocean [*Marine science*] (OSRA)
IBCWP.......... International Bathymetric Chart of the Western Pacific [*Marine science*] (OSRA)
IBCX............ Indiana Boxcar [*Private rail car owner code*]
IBD.............. Baylor College of Dentistry, Dallas, TX [*OCLC symbol*] (OCLC)
IBD.............. Ibadan [*Nigeria*] [*Geomagnetic observatory code*]
IBD.............. Identical-By-Descent [*Genetics*]
IBD.............. Incomplete Block Design (MCD)
IBD.............. Incorporated Bureau of British Decorators and Interior Designers (SAUO)
IBD.............. Incorporated Institute of British Decorators and Interior Designers (SAUS)
IBD.............. Infectious Bursal Disease [*Avian pathology*]
IBD.............. Inflammatory Bowel Disease [*Medicine*]
IBD.............. Inhabited Building Distance [*Army*] (AABC)
IBD.............. Institute of British Decorators (SAUO)
IBD.............. Institute of Business Designers (EA)
IBD.............. Interest-Bearing Debentures (SAUS)
IBD.............. Interest Bearing Deposit [*Banking*] (ADA)
IBD.............. Interior Ballistic Division [*Ballistic Research Laboratory*] [*Army*] (RDA)
IBD.............. Intermediate Block Diagram (IAA)
IBD.............. International Baccalaureate Diploma (SAUS)
IBD.............. International Bank of Detroit (SAUO)
IBD.............. International Broadcasting Division (SAUO)
IBD.............. International Bureau for Declarations of Death (SAUO)
IBD.............. International Business Database [*Information service or system*] (IID)
IBD.............. International Business Development Program [*Northwestern University*] [*Research center*] (RCD)
IBD.............. International Business Drive (SAUO)
IBD.............. Internationale Bildungs- und Informations- Datenbank [*International Education and Information Data Bank*] [*Thiede & Thiede Mittelstandische Systemberatung GmbH*] [*Information service or system*] (IID)
IBD.............. Intrinsic Boundary Dislocation (SAUS)
IBD.............. Investor's Business Daily [*A publication*]
IBD.............. Ion Beam Deposition [*Coating technology*]
IBD.............. Irritable Bowel Disease [*Medicine*] (DMAA)
IBD.............. Ischemic Bowel Disease [*Medicine*] (DAVI)
IBD.............. Sandoz Pharmaceuticals [*Research code symbol*]
IBDA............ Indirect Bomb-Damage Assessment
IBDA............ International Balance Disorder Association [*Defunct*] (EA)
IBDA............ International Bird Dog Association (EA)
IBD-APM...... Identity-By-Descent Affected-Pedigree-Member [*Genetics*]
IBDB............ Internationaal Belasting Documentatie Bureau [*International Bureau of Fiscal Documentation*] (EAIO)
IBDB............ International Battery Data Base [*Robert Morey Associates*] [*Information service or system*] (IID)
IBDC............ Indian Business Development Center (SAUS)
IBDCC.......... International Barbie Doll Collectors Club (EA)
IBDEA.......... Inernational Beverage Dispensing Equipment Association (NTPA)
IBDH............ Inboard Chromatography Data Handler (SAUS)
IBDI............ International Bureau of Documentation and Information (SAUS)
IBDI............ International Bureau of Documentation and Information on Sport (NITA)
IBDL............ Intermediate Battery Data Link (SAUO)
IBDM............ Interim Bomber Defense Missile
IBDN............ Insulated Building Distribution Network [*Northern Telecom*]
IBDPW.......... International Brotherhood of Du Pont Workers (EA)
IBDS............ Improved Biological Detection System [*Military*] (MCD)
IBDS............ Integrated Board Design System (TIMI)
IBDT............ Insulation Breakdown Tester
IBDU............ Isobutylidene Diurea (SAUS)
IBDU............ Isobutylidenediurea [*Organic chemistry*]
IBDV............ Infectious Bursal Disease Virus
IBDVS.......... Indian Base Depot Veterinary Stores [*British military*] (DMA)
IBE.............. Ibague [*Colombia*] [*Airport symbol*] (OAG)
IBE.............. Iberia-Lineas Aereas de Espana SA [*Spain*] [*ICAO designator*] (FAAC)
IBE.............. Inert-Ion Beam Etching
IBE.............. Inner Back End (MSA)
IBE.............. Institute for Biological Engineering
IBE.............. Institute of Biological Engineering
IBE.............. Institute of British Engineers (DAS)
IBE.............. Institute of Broadcast Engineers [*Later, SBE*] (NTCM)
IBE.............. Institute of Building Estimators, Ltd. (SAUO)
IBE.............. Institution of Body Engineers [*British*] (BI)
IBE.............. Institution of British Engineers (SAUO)
IBE.............. Integrity Basis Earthquake (SAUS)
IBE.............. International Beverage Co. [*Vancouver Stock Exchange symbol*]
IBE.............. International Broadcast Engineer (SAUO)
IBE.............. International Broadcast Engineer (journ.) (SAUS)
IBE.............. International Bureau for Epilepsy [*Alderley Edge, Cheshire, England*] (EAIO)
IBE.............. International Bureau of Education [*See also BIE*] [*UNESCO*] (EAIO)
IBE.............. Interval Between Eruptions [*of Geyser*]
IBE.............. Inventory by Exception (MHDB)
IBE.............. Ion Beam Epiplantation (SAUS)
IBE.............. Ion Beam Etching (AAEL)
IBE.............. Isoelectronic Bound Exciton [*Electronics*] (AAEL)
IBE.............. Rosary College, River Forest, IL [*OCLC symbol*] (OCLC)
IBea............ Beardstown Public Library, Beardstown, IL [*Library symbol*] [*Library of Congress*] (LCLS)
IBEA............ Imperial British East Africa (SAUO)
IBEA............ Industrial Base Engineering Activity (RDA)
IBE(A).......... Institution of Biomedical Engineering (Australia)
IBEA............ International Biomedical Expedition to the Antarctic (SAUO)
IBEA............ Intervention Board Executive Agency (SAUO)
I-beam.......... Capital-I-shaped metal beam (SAUS)
IBEAR.......... International Business Education and Research Program [*University of Southern California*] [*Research center*] (RCD)
IBEC............ Indo-British Economic Committee (SAUO)
IBEC............ International Bank for Economic Cooperation [*Moscow, USSR*] (EY)
IBEC............ International Basic Economic Cooperation [*Investment term*] (DS)
IBEC............ International Basic Economic Corporation (SAUO)
IBEC............ International Basic Economy Corporation (SAUO)
IBEC............ International Book Exchange Centre (SAUO)
IBEC............ International Business Engineering Company (SAUO)
IBECO.......... Inboard Booster Engine Cutoff (MCD)
IBECS.......... Innovative Beam Control Study (ACAE)
IBED............ Inborn Error of Development (MELL)
IBED............ Inter-African Bureau for Epizootic Diseases [*Later, IBAR*]
IBED............ Inter-African Bureau of Epizootic Diseases (SAUO)
IBED............ Ion Beam Enhanced Deposition (SAUS)
IBEDIC System... International Bureau of Education, Documentation and Information System (SAUS)
IBEDOC........ International Bureau of Education Documentation and Information System (NITA)
IBEE............ International Builders Exchange Executives (EA)
IBEE............ Ion-Bombardment Enhanced Etching (SAUS)
IBEF............ International Bio-Environmental Foundation (EA)
IBEG............ International Book Export Group
IBel............ Belleville Public Library, Belleville, IL [*Library symbol*] [*Library of Congress*] (LCLS)
IBEL............ Interest-Bearing Eligible Liabilities
IBEL............ Interest-Bearing Eligible Liability (SAUS)
IBelC.......... Belleville Area College, Belleville, IL [*Library symbol*] [*Library of Congress*] (LCLS)

IBelHS........ Altoff High School, Belleville, IL [*Library symbol*] [*Library of Congress*] (LCLS)
IBelHSD....... Harmony-Emge-Ellis School District 175, Belleville, IL [*Library symbol*] [*Library of Congress*] (LCLS)
IBelS........... Saint Henry's Seminary, Belleville, IL [*Library symbol*] [*Library of Congress*] (LCLS)
IBelSCM...... Saint Clair County Mental Health Board, Belleville, IL [*Library symbol*] [*Library of Congress*] (LCLS)
IBelSD......... Belleville Public Schools District 118, Belleville, IL [*Library symbol*] [*Library of Congress*] (LCLS)
IBelSH......... Saint Elizabeth's Hospital, Belleville, IL [*Library symbol*] [*Library of Congress*] (LCLS)
IBelTSD....... Belleville Township High School District 201, Belleville, IL [*Library symbol*] [*Library of Congress*] (LCLS)
IBelv........... Ida Public Library, Belvidere, IL [*Library symbol*] [*Library of Congress*] (LCLS)
IBelVS......... Belle Valley School, Belleville, IL [*Library symbol*] [*Library of Congress*] (LCLS)
IBelw........... Bellwood Public Library, Bellwood, IL [*Library symbol*] [*Library of Congress*] (LCLS)
IBem........... Bement Township Library, Bement, IL [*Library symbol*] [*Library of Congress*] (LCLS)
IBEM........... Idiopathic Benign Familial Myoclonus [*Medicine*] (EDAA)
IBEM........... International Board of Environmental Medicine (EA)
IBemSD....... Bement Community Unit School District, Bement, IL [*Library symbol*] [*Library of Congress*] (LCLS)
IBEN........... Incendiary Bomb with Explosive Nose
IB-EP.......... Immunoreactive Beta-Endomorphin [*Immunochemistry*] (DMAA)
IBEP........... Integrated Border Environment Plan [*Mexico/US border policy*] (CROSS)
IBEP........... International Border Environmental Plan (SAUO)
IBer........... Berwyn Public Library, Berwyn, IL [*Library symbol*] [*Library of Congress*] (LCLS)
Iber........... Iberia Airlines of Spain (SAUS)
IBER........... Institute for Biomedical Engineering Research [*University of Akron*] [*Research center*] (RCD)
IBEREED...... International Bureau of Education Research in Education (SAUS)
IBerk........... Berkeley Public Library, Berkeley, IL [*Library symbol*] [*Library of Congress*] (LCLS)
IBERLANT.... Iberian Atlantic (SAUS)
IBERLANT.... Iberian Atlantic Area [*NATO*] (NATG)
IBERLANT.... Iberian Atlantic Area command (SAUS)
IBERMARC... Spanish MARC (SAUS)
IBerMH........ MacNeal Memorial Hospital, Berwyn, IL [*Library symbol*] [*Library of Congress*] (LCLS)
IBerO.......... Olympic Savings & Loan Association, Berwyn, IL [*Library symbol*] [*Library of Congress*] (LCLS)
Ibero-Am /Stockholm... Ibero-Americana. Nordic Journal of Latin American Studies. Institute of Latin American Studies, University of Stockholm (journ.) (SAUS)
IBERT.......... Institute for Better Education through Resource Technology
IBES........... Illinois Bureau of Employment Security (SAUO)
IBES........... Institutional Brokers Estimate System [*Lynch, Jones & Ryan*] [*Database*] [*New York, NY*] [*Information service or system*] (IID)
IBES........... Integrated Building and Equipment Scheduling (SAUO)
IBES........... Integration Building and Equipment Scheduling (PDAA)
IBES........... International Bronchoesophagological Society (EA)
IBES........... International Business Earth Stations [*Communications Satellite Corp.*]
IBET........... Trans World Gaming [*NASDAQ symbol*] (TTSB)
IBET........... Trans World Gaming Corp. [*NASDAQ symbol*] (SAG)
IBETA.......... Irish Business Equipment Trade Association (DBA)
IBeth.......... Bethalto Public Library, Bethalto, IL [*Library symbol*] [*Library of Congress*] (LCLS)
IBethCU....... Bethalto Community Unit 8, Bethalto, IL [*Library symbol*] [*Library of Congress*] (LCLS)
IBETW......... Trans World Gaming Wrrt [*NASDAQ symbol*] (TTSB)
IBEU........... Independent Bakery Employees Union (EA)
IBEW........... International Brotherhood of Electrical Workers (EA)
IBEWA......... International Brotherhood of Electrical Workers of America (SAUO)
IBEX........... International Biotechnology Exposition (SAUO)
IBEX........... International Building Exposition
IBEX........... International Business Exchange (SAUO)
IBF............. Chicago Municipal Reference Library, Chicago, IL [*OCLC symbol*] (OCLC)
IBF............. First Iberian Fund [*AMEX symbol*] (TTSB)
IBF............. First Iberian Fund, Inc. [*AMEX symbol*] (SPSG)
IBF............. Imaginary Basketball Federation (EA)
IBF............. Immature Brown-Fat [*Cells*]
IBF............. Immunoglobulin-Binding Factor [*Immunology*] (MAE)
IBF............. Incident Bright-Field (SAUS)
IBF............. Incomplete Beta Function (SAUS)
IBF............. Input Bridging Fault (SAUS)
IBF............. Input Buffer Full [*Computer science*] (MHDB)
IBF............. Institute of Banking and Finance (SAUO)
IBF............. Institute of British Foundrymen (EAIO)
IBF............. Interdepartmental Billing Form (SAUS)
IBF............. Internally Blown Flap [*Aviation*]
IBF............. Internally Blown Flop (SAUS)
IBF............. International Badminton Federation [*Cheltenham, Gloustershire, England*] (EAIO)
IBF............. International Balint Federation [*Brussels, Belgium*] (EAIO)
IBF............. International Balut Federation [*Bangkok, Thailand*] (EAIO)
IBF............. International Bandy Federation [*Lulea, Sweden*] (EAIO)
IBF............. International Banking Facility
IBF............. International Bar Flies (SAUO)
IBF............. International Bar Fly [*Sign in Harry's New York Bar, Paris*]
IBF............. International Baseball Federation (SAUO)
IBF............. International Bicycle Fund (EA)
IBF............. International Bobsled Federation
IBF............. International Bodyboarding Federation (SAUO)
IBF............. International Bodysurfing Federation (SAUO)
IBF............. International Bond Fund (SAUS)
IBF............. International Booksellers Federation [*Formerly, ICBA*] [*Austria*] (EA)
IBF............. International Boxing Federation (EA)
IBF............. International Business Forum (SAUS)
IBF............. Internationales Begegnungszentrum Friedenshaus [*Germany*] (EAIO)
IBFA........... Interacting Boson-Fermion Approximation (SAUS)
IBFAN......... International Baby Food Action Network (EA)
IBFC........... Iron Butterfly Fan Club [*Later, IBIN*] (EA)
IBFCC......... International Border Fancy Canary Club (EA)
IBF Cells...... Immature Brown Fat Cells (SAUS)
IBFD........... International Bureau of Fiscal Documentation (EAIO)
IBFEG......... Internationaler Bund Freier Evangelischer Gemeinden [*International Federation of Free Evangelical Churches - IFFEC*] (EA)
IBFF........... Impulse Base Flow Facility [*NASA*]
IBFG........... Internationaler Bund Freier Gewerkschaften [*International Confederation of Free Trade Unions*]
IBFI............ International Business Forms Industries (EA)
IBFI............ International Business Forms Industries (or Industry) (SAUS)
IBFM........... Institute of Broadcasting Financial Management [*Later, BCFMA*]
IBFM........... Interacting Bosonfermion Model (SAUS)
IBFMP......... International Bureau of the Federations of Master Printers
IBFN........... Integrated Broadband Fiber Optic Network [*Telecommunications*]
IBFO........... International Brotherhood of Firemen and Oilers (EA)
IBFRBTWB... International Book Fair of Radical Black and Third World Books
IBFS........... Interim Billing and Follow-Up System [*Social Security Administration*] (GFGA)
IBFS........... International Benjamin Franklin Society [*Defunct*] (EA)
IBG............. CNA Financial Corp., Library, Chicago, IL [*Inactive*] [*OCLC symbol*] (OCLC)
IBG............. Iliac Bone Graft [*Medicine*] (MELL)
IBG............. Incorporated Brewers Guild (SAUO)
IBG............. Insoluble Bone Gelatin [*Cardiology*] (DMAA)
IBG............. Institute for Behavioral Genetics [*University of Colorado - Boulder*] [*Research center*] (RCD)
IBG............. Institute of British Geographers (BI)
IBG............. Inter Block Gap
IBG............. Intermediate BTU [*British Thermal Unit*] Gas
IBG............. International Boxing Guild
IBG............. International Business Games (SAUO)
IBG............. Internationale Begegnung in Gemeinschaftsdiensten [*Germany*] (EAIO)
IBG............. Internationale Brecht Gesellschaft [*International Brecht Society*] (EAIO)
IBG............. Internationale Bruckner Gesellschaft [*Vienna, Austria*] (EAIO)
IBG............. Internationales Buro fuer Gebirgsmechanik [*International Bureau of Strato-Mechanics - IBSM*] (EAIO)
IBGF........... Interpolation Based Grid File (SAUS)
IBGI............ Independent Bank Group, Inc. [*NASDAQ symbol*] (COMM)
IBGIS.......... Image-Based Geographic Information System (SAUS)
IBGP........... International Biosphere-Geosphere Programme (SAUO)
IBGS........... Intravascular Blood Gas System [*Medicine*] (DB)
IBGTT.......... Interim Battle Group Tactical Trainer (SAUO)
IBH............. Inclusion Body Hepatitis (SAUS)
IBH............. Initial Beachhead [*Military*]
IBHA........... Insulation, Building and Hardboard Association (SAUO)
IBHA........... Insulation, Building, and Hard Board Association [*British*] (BI)
IBHA........... Insulation, Building and Hardwood Association (SAUO)
IBHA........... Interconnecting Box Harness adaptor (SAUS)
IBHA........... International Buckskin Horse Association (EA)
IBHC........... Inclusion Body Hepatitis of Chickens (SAUS)
IBHD........... Initial Beachhead [*Military*]
IBHE........... Illinois Board of Higher Education (SAUO)
IBHF........... International Boxing Hall of Fame (EA)
IBHFC......... Illini-Badger-Hawkeye Football Conference (PSS)
IBHFM......... International Boxing Hall of Fame (SAUO)
IBHFM......... International Boxing Hall of Fame Museum (EA)
IBHI............ Independent Bureau on Humanitarian Issues (SAUO)
IBHR........... International Bibliography of the History of Religions [*A publication*] (BJA)
IBHS........... International Bibliography of Historical Sciences (journ.) (SAUS)
IBHV........... International Briquettes Holding [*NASDAQ symbol*] (NASQ)
IBi............. Blue Island Public Library, Blue Island, IL [*Library symbol*] [*Library of Congress*] (LCLS)
i-bi-........... British Indian Ocean Territory [*MARC geographic area code*] [*Library of Congress*] (LCCP)
IBI............. College of Du Page, Glen Ellyn, IL [*OCLC symbol*] (OCLC)
IBI............. I Believe It (VLIE)
IBI............. Illinois Bureau of Investigation (SAUO)
IBI............. Independent Black Institution
IBI............. Independent Broadcast Institute [*British*]
IBI............. Indiana Bureau of Investigation (SAUO)
IBI............. Individualized Bilingual Instruction (EDAC)
IBI............. Information Builders, Inc. [*New York*] [*Commercial firm*] (CDE)
IBI............. Institute for Biotechnology Information (HGEN)
IBI............. Insulation Board Institute [*Later, ABPA*] (EA)
IBI............. Intelligent Buildings Institute (EA)
IBI............. Interburst Interval [*Electrophysiology*]
IBI............. Intergovernmental Bureau for Informatics [*Telecommunications*] (EA)

IBI .... Intergovernmental Bureau for/of Informatics (SAUO)
IBI .... Interim Ballistic Instrumentation
IBI .... Intermittent Bladder Irrigation [*Medicine*]
IBI .... International Bankers, Incorporated (SAUO)
IBI .... International Biomass Institute (EA)
IBI .... International Biotechnologies, Inc.
IBI .... International Brace Resources [*Vancouver Stock Exchange symbol*]
IBI .... International Broadcasting Institute (SAUS)
IBI .... International Broadcast Institute [*Later, IIC*]
IBI .... International Bureau for Informatics (CSR)
IBI .... International Business Information (SAUS)
IBI .... International Business Intelligence [*A publication*]
IBI .... International Business Intelligence (journ.) (SAUS)
IBI .... Internationales Burgen-Institut [*International Castles Institute*] [*Rozendaal, Netherlands*] (EA)
IBI .... Interpersonal Behavior Inventory [*Veterans Administration*]
IBI .... Interview-Oriented Background Investigation (MCD)
IBI .... Intimate Brands 'A' [*NYSE symbol*] (TTSB)
IBI .... Intimate Brands, Inc. [*NYSE symbol*] (SAG)
IBI .... Invoice Book Inbound (SAUS)
IBI .... Invoice Book Inward [*Business term*]
IBI .... Ischemic Brain Infarction [*Medicine*] (DMAA)
IBI .... Islamic Bank International
IBIA .... Institute of British Industrial Art
IBIA .... Interior Board of Indian Affairs (SAUO)
IBIA .... Interior Board of Indian Affairs (in United States Interior Decisions) [*A publication*] (DLA)
IBIA .... International Bunker Industry Association Ltd. (SAUO)
IB (I and II) ... Information Bank (I and II) (NITA)
IBIB .... Isobutyl Isobutyrate [*Organic chemistry*]
IBIC .... Interface Bus Interactive Control [*Computer science*]
IBICC .... Incorporated British Institute of Certified Carpenters (BI)
IBICT .... Instituto Brasileiro de Informacao em Ciencia e Tecnologia [*Brazilian Institute for Information in Science and Technology*] [*National Council of Scientific and Technological Development*] [*Information service or system*] (IID)
ibid .... Ibidem (ELAL)
IBID .... Ibidem [*In the Same Place*] [*Latin*]
IBID .... International Bibiliography, Information Documentation (SAUO)
IBID .... International Bibliographical Description
IBID .... International Bibliography, Information and Documentation (SAUS)
IBIDS .... International Bibliographic Information on Dietary Supplements (SAUO)
IBIE .... International Brewing Industries Exhibition (SAUO)
IBI-ICC .... IBI [*Intergovernmental Bureau for Informatics*] International Computat ion Centre (NITA)
IBI-ICC .... Intergovernmental Bureau for Informatics-International Computation Center (SAUS)
IBI-ICC .... Intergovernmental Bureau for Information-International Computation Centre (SAUO)
IBIL .... Intermediate Bilirubin (SAUS)
IBILI .... Indirect Bilirubin [*Medicine*] (EDAA)
IBIM .... Intelligence Bus Interface Module (SAUS)
IBIN .... Indigenous Peoples Biodiversity Information Network (SAUO)
IBIN .... Integrated Brands [*NASDAQ symbol*] (SAG)
IBIN .... Integrated Brands 'A' [*NASDAQ symbol*] (TTSB)
IBIN .... Iron Butterfly Information Network (EA)
IBIO .... International Biotechnologies, Inc. (SAUO)
IBiol .... Institute of Biology [*British*] (DI)
IBION .... Issue Based Indian Ocean Network (SAUO)
IBIP .... Information Based Indicia Program (SAUS)
IBIP .... International Books in Print [*A publication*]
IBIS .... Ibis Technology Corp. [*NASDAQ symbol*] (SAG)
IBIS .... ICAO [*International Civil Aviation Organization*] Bird Strike Information System [*Information service or system*] (IID)
IBIS .... Image-Based Information System (SAUO)
IBIS .... Imaging (SAUS)
IBIS .... Imaging Background Limited Infrared System (ACAE)
IBIS .... Indonesian Biodiversity Information System (SAUO)
IBIS .... Industrialk Base Information System (AAGC)
IBIS .... Infrared Background Imaging Seeker (MCD)
IBIS .... Infrared Background -limiting Imaging Seeker (SAUS)
IBiS .... Initiative in Biomolecular Structures [*University of New South Wales*] [*Australia*]
IBIS .... Input Output Buffer Information Specification (AEBE)
IBIS .... Inspectors Based in Schools [*British*] (AIE)
IBIS .... Integrated Bathy Information System (SAUS)
IBIS .... Integrated Bibliographic Information System (SAUS)
IBIS .... Integrated Blade Inspection System (ACAE)
IBIS .... Integrated Botanical Information System [*Computer database*]
IBIS .... Integrated Building Industry System (PDAA)
IBIS .... Intelligent Business Information System (NITA)
IBIS .... Intense Beam Ion Source (SAUS)
IBIS .... Intense Bounced Ion Source (SAUS)
IBIS .... Intense Bunched Ion Source (IEEE)
IBIS .... Intensive Biometric Intertidal Survey [*Botany*]
IBIS .... Interactive Body Mind Information System (ADWA)
IBIS .... International Bank Information System
IBIS .... International Book Information Service
IBIS .... International Book Information Services, Inc. (SAUO)
IBIS .... International Breast Cancer Intervention Study
IBIS .... International Bryological Information Service (SAUO)
IBIS .... Intranet Business Information System (PDAA)
IBIS .... Inventaire Bibliographique des Isiaca (BJA)
IBIS .... Irritable Bowel Information & Support Association of Australia, Inc. (NRGU)
IBIS .... Issue Based Documentation System (SAUS)
IBIS .... Issue-Based Information System [*Computer science*]
IBiS .... Saint Francis Hospital, Blue Island, IL [*Library symbol*] [*Library of Congress*] (LCLS)
IBISA .... IBI Security Service, Inc. (Class A) [*NASDAQ symbol*] (COMM)
IB Israel ...... Information Bulletin. Communist Party of Israel, Central Committee (SAUO)
IBisSD .... Bismarck-Henning Community Unit School District, Bismarck, IL [*Library symbol*] [*Library of Congress*] (LCLS)
IbisTc .... Ibis Technology Corp. [*Associated Press*] (SAG)
IbisTech .... Ibis Technology Corp. [*Associated Press*] (SAG)
IBIS-TV .... Integrated Booking and Information System (SAUS)
IBISW .... Ibis Technology Wrrt [*NASDAQ symbol*] (TTSB)
IBIT .... ICBM [*Intercontinental Ballistic Missile*] Blast Interference Test (MCD)
IBIT .... Initiated BIT (MCD)
IBIT .... Initisted Built-In Test (SAUS)
IBIT .... Intergovernmental Bureau for Information Technology (SAUS)
IBIT .... Interruptive BIT (SAUS)
IBIT .... Issue by Issue Tally
IBJ .... Industrial Bank of Japan
IBJ .... Instrument Bearing Jewel
IBJ .... Loop College, Chicago, IL [*OCLC symbol*] (OCLC)
IBJCA .... International Blue Jay Class Association (EA)
IBJ Data ...... Industrial Bank of Japan Database [*Originator and databank on trade and economics*] [*Japan*] (NITA)
IBJI .... Industrial Bank of Japan International Ltd. (ECON)
IBJM .... International Board of Jewish Missions (EA)
IBK .... Independent Bankshares [*AMEX symbol*] (TTSB)
IBK .... Independent Bankshares, Inc. [*AMEX symbol*] (SAG)
IBK .... [*The*] Industrial Bank of Kuwait
IBK .... Infectious Bovine Keratoconjunctivitis [*Veterinary medicine*]
IBK .... Innsbruck [*Austria*] [*Seismograph station code, US Geological Survey*] (SEIS)
IBK .... Institute of Bookkeepers [*British*] (DAS)
IBK .... International Banknote Company, Inc. [*AMEX symbol*] (COMM)
IBK .... Knox College, Galesburg, IL [*OCLC symbol*] (OCLC)
IBKA .... Ikatan Buruh Kereta Api [*Railroad Workers' Union*] [*Indonesia*]
IBKB .... Ikatan Buruh Kendaaran Bermotor [*Motor Transport Workers' Union*] [*Indonesia*]
IBKC .... Infectious Bovine Keratoconjunctivitis (PDAA)
I BKR .... Ice Breaker [*Freight*]
IBL .... Automated Dutch union catalogue for periodicals (SAUO)
IBL .... Boehringer Mannheim Corp., Indianapolis, IN [*OCLC symbol*] (OCLC)
IBL .... Immunoblastic Lymphadenopathy [*Medicine*] (CPH)
IBL .... Input Buffer Limit (SAUS)
IBL .... Inside of the Battery Limits [*Engineering Economics*]
IBL .... Intelligence Branch and Library (SAUO)
IBL .... Interest-Bearing Liability
IBL .... Interior Ballistics Laboratory [*Aberdeen, MD*] [*Army*]
IBL .... Intermediate Behavioral Language (SAA)
IBL .... International Brotherhood of Longshoremen
IBL .... International Business Lawyer (SAFN)
IBL .... Irish Biscuits Limited (SAUO)
IBL .... Iroquois Brands Ltd. [*AMEX symbol*] (COMM)
IBLA .... Inter-American Bibliographical and Library Association (EA)
IBLA .... Interior Board of Land Appeals [*Department of the Interior*]
IBLC .... International B-24 Liberator Club (EA)
IBLE .... International Brotherhood of Locomotive Engineers (EA)
IBLM .... International Bureau of Legal Metrology
IBlo .... Withers Public Library, Bloomington, IL [*Library symbol*] [*Library of Congress*] (LCLS)
IBloA .... Illinois Agricultural Association, Bloomington, IL [*Library symbol*] [*Library of Congress*] (LCLS)
IBloC .... Corn Belt Library System, Bloomington, IL [*Library symbol*] [*Library of Congress*] (LCLS)
IBloHi .... McLean County Historical Society, Bloomington, IL [*Library symbol*] [*Library of Congress*] (LCLS)
IBloMH .... Mennonite Hospital Association, Medical-Nursing Library, Bloomington, IL [*Library symbol*] [*Library of Congress*] (LCLS)
IBloSF .... State Farm Insurance Co., Bloomington, IL [*Library symbol*] [*Library of Congress*] (LCLS)
IBloStJ .... Saint Joseph's Hospital, Bloomington, IL [*Library symbol*] [*Library of Congress*] (LCLS)
IBloW .... Illinois Wesleyan University, Bloomington, IL [*Library symbol*] [*Library of Congress*] (LCLS)
IBLP .... Institute of Basic Life Principals (EA)
IBLS .... International Brotherhood of Live Steamers (EA)
IBLT .... Interacting Boundary-Layer Theory (SAUS)
IBM .... I Blame Microsoft (BB)
IBM .... Ice-Binding Motif [*Biochemistry*]
IBM .... Inadequate, but Marketable (SAUS)
IBM .... Inclusion Body Myositis
IBM .... Independent Community Bankers of Maine (TBD)
IBM .... Indian Bureau of Mines (SAUO)
IBM .... Individual-Based Model [*Marine science*] (OSRA)
IBM .... Induced Bowel Movement (SAUS)
IBM .... Industrial Business Machines (SAUS)
IBM .... Infinite Barrier Model (SAUS)
IBM .... Ingrained Batch Mentality (SAUS)
IBM .... Instant Big Mouth [*Martini*] [*Slang*]
IBM .... Institute for Burn Medicine (SAUO)
IBM .... Institute of Baths Management [*British*] (BI)
IBM .... Institute of Baths Management, Inc. (SAUO)

IBM .... Institute of Builders Merchants [*British*] (DBA)
IBM .... Instituto de Biologia Marina, San Antonia [*Argentina*] [*Marine science*] (OSRA)
IBM .... Integrated Background Monitoring (SAUS)
IBM .... Interacting Boson Model [*Of nuclear structure*]
IBM .... Intercontinental Ballistic Missile
IBM .... Intermediate Ballistic Missile (SAUO)
IBM .... International Biosciences Networks (SAUS)
IBM .... International Brotherhood of Magicians (EA)
IBM .... International Business Machines [*Associated Press*] (SAG)
IBM .... International Business Machines Corp. [*Facetious translations: I Buil t a Macintosh; I Buy Money; Inferior But Marketable; Insidious Black Magic; It'sBeen Malfunctioning; Incontinent Bowel Movement*] [*NYSE symbol*] [*Toronto Stock Exchange symbol*] (SPSG)
IBM .... International Business Machines, Inc. (SAUO)
IBM .... Intl Bus. Machines [*NYSE symbol*] (TTSB)
IBM .... Ion-Beam Modification (SAUS)
IBM .... Kimball, NE [*Location identifier*] [*FAA*] (FAAL)
IBM .... Kirkland & Ellis, Chicago, IL [*OCLC symbol*] (OCLC)
IBM .... Interacting Boson Model [*Physics*] (ODA)
IBMA .... Independent Battery Manufacturers Association (EA)
IBMA .... Independent Battery Manufacturers of America (SAUO)
IBMA .... Interior Board of Mine Operations Appeals (in United States Interior Decisions) [*A publication*] (DLA)
IBMA .... International Bar Managers Association (SAUO)
IBMA .... International Bluegrass Music Association (EA)
IBMA .... International Business Music Association (NTPA)
IBMA .... Isobutoxymethyl Acrylamide [*Organic chemistry*]
IBMARNR .... Brazilian Institute of Environment and Renewable Natural Resources (SAUO)
IBMBR .... Inter-Bank Market Bid Rate (SAUS)
IBMC .... International Brotherhood of Motorcycle Campers (EA)
IBMC .... International Buddhist Meditation Center (EA)
IBMCE .... IBM Customer Engineer (SAUO)
IBMCUA ...... IBM Computer Users' Association (NITA)
IBME .... Institute of Biomedical Engineering [*University of Toronto*] [*Research center*] (RCD)
IBMG .... Idaho Bureau of Mines and Geology (SAUS)
IBMI .... International Bureau of Mining Thermophysics (SAUO)
IBMIS .... Improved Ballistic Missile Target System (SAUO)
IBMK .... Isobutyl Methyl Ketone [*Organic chemistry*]
IBM/LPS ...... IBM Linear Programming System (SAUO)
IBMM .... Integrated Book Manufacturing Machine
IBMM .... International Bluegrass Music Museum
IBMM .... Ion Beam Modification of Materials (SAUS)
IBMNSW ...... Independent Bread Manufacturers of New South Wales [*Australia*]
IBMOC .... Intercontinental Ballistic Missile Operational Capability (AAG)
IB-MOS .... Ion Beam Metal-Oxide Semiconductor (SAUS)
IBMP .... International Board of Medicine and Psychology [*Later, IAMP*] (EA)
IBMP .... Isobutyl(methoxy)pyrazine [*Organic chemistry*]
IBM PC .... International Business Machines Personal Computer (DCDG)
IBM PC AT ... International Business Machine Personal Computer Advanced Technology (SAUS)
IBM PC ATE ... International Business Machine Personal Computer Advanced Technology Enhanced (SAUS)
IBM PC ATX ... International Business Machine Personal Computer Advanced Technology Expanded (SAUS)
IBM PC XT ... International Business Machine Personal Computer Expanded Technology (SAUS)
IBMPrA .... Intl Bus. Mach 7 1/2% Dep Pfd [*NYSE symbol*] (TTSB)
IBMR .... International Bureau for Mechanical Reproduction (SAUO)
IBMS .... Intelligent Battery Management System (SAUS)
IBMS .... International Bone and Mineral Society (SAUO)
IBMS .... Ion Beam Mass Spectrometer
IBMS .... Ion Beam-Modified Surface (SAUS)
IBMT .... Intensive Basic Military Training (SAUO)
IBMT .... International Bureau of Mining and Thermophysics (SAUS)
IBMTR .... International Bone Marrow Transplant Registry
IBM TSS ...... International Business Machine's Timesharing System (TEL)
IBM WU .... IBM Workers United (NITA)
IBMX .... Isobutylmethylxanthine [*Also, MIX*] [*Biochemistry*]
IBMZ .... International Business [*Federal Railroad Administration identification code*]
IBN .... Blackburn College, Carlinville, IL [*OCLC symbol*] (OCLC)
IBN .... ICICI Bank ADS [*NYSE symbol*] (SG)
IBN .... Identification Beacon
IBN .... Indexed by Name (IAA)
IBN .... Indigenous Biodiversity Network (SAUO)
IBN .... Institut Belge de Normalisation [*Belgian Institute for Standardization*] [*Information service or system*] (IID)
IBN .... Integrated Broadband Network (SAUS)
IBN .... Integrated Business Network (SAUO)
IBN .... Interest-Based Negotiations (FOTI)
IBN .... International Biosciences Network
IBN .... International Booking Network (SAUO)
IBND .... Independent Community Banks of North Dakota (TBD)
IBNJ .... Independence Bancorp, Inc. [*NASDAQ symbol*] (SAG)
IBNJ .... Independence Bancorp NJ [*NASDAQ symbol*] (TTSB)
IBNJP .... Independence Banc 9% Cv Pfd [*NASDAQ symbol*] (TTSB)
IBNM .... Independent Community Bankers of New Mexico (TBD)
IBNR .... Incurred but Not Reported [*Insurance*]
IBNR .... Incurred but Not Reported Losses [*Insurance*]
IBNRPR .... Incurred but Not Reported Properly [*Insurance*] (MARI)
IBNS .... Inter-Borough Nomination Scheme [*British*] (DI)
IBNS .... International Bank Note Society (EA)
IBNY .... Independent Bankers Association of New York State (TBD)
IBO .... Ibotenic Acid [*Organic acid*]
IBO .... Idabel, OK [*Location identifier*] [*FAA*] (FAAL)
IBO .... Independent Budget Office
IBO .... Instruction by Objective
IBO .... Inter-Base Object (SAUS)
IBO .... International Baccalaureate Office [*See also OBI*] [*Later, International Baccalaureate Organization*] [*Grand-Saconnex, Switzerland*] (EAIO)
IBO .... International Baccalaureate Organization (SAUO)
IBO .... International Bowhunting Organization
IBO .... International Broadcasting Organization
IBO .... Internationale Bouworde [*International Association of Building Companions - IABC*] [*Marche-En-Famenne, Belgium*] (EAIO)
IBO .... Invoice Book Outbound [*Business term*]
IBO .... Lutheran General Hospital, Park Ridge, IL [*OCLC symbol*] (OCLC)
IBOA .... Irish Bank Officials' Association [*Northern Ireland*]
IBOB .... International Brotherhood of Old Bastards (EA)
IBOC .... In-Band On-Channel
IBOC .... Internal Binary Operation Code (SAUS)
IBOC .... International Bancshares Corp. [*NASDAQ symbol*] (NASQ)
IBOC .... Iso and Bizzarrini Owners Club (EA)
IBOC .... Isobutoxycarbonylation [*Organic chemistry*]
IB of TCWHA ... International Brotherhood of Teamsters, Chauffeurs, Warehousemen and Helpers of America (SAUO)
IBOL .... Integrated Business-Oriented Language (SAUS)
IBOL .... Interactive Business-Oriented Language
IBOLS .... Integrated Business-Oriented Language Support (IAA)
IBOMA .... Inter-Bank Organisation and Methods Association (COBU)
IBOND .... IGOSS [*Integrated Global Ocean Station System*] Basic Observation Network Design [*Marine science*] (MSC)
IBOND .... Sub- group of Experts on IGOSS Basic Observations Network Design (SAUO)
IBOP .... Institute of British Oil Paintings
IBOP .... Interagency Business Opportunities Page
IBOP .... International Balance of Payments (AAGC)
IBOP .... International Balance of Payments Reporting System
IBOP .... International Brotherhood of Operative Potters [*Later, IBPAW*] (EA)
IBOP .... International Brotherhood of Operative Pottery and Allied Workers (SAUS)
IBOP .... International Business Opportunity Program (SAUS)
IBOP Reporting System ... International Balance of Payments Reporting System (SAUS)
IBOS .... International Business Opportunities Service [*World Bank*] [*United Nations*] (DUND)
IBOT .... In-Branch Operator Training [*British*] (DCTA)
IBOT .... Introduction to the Books of the Old Testament [*A publication*] (BJA)
IBoT .... Istanbul Arkeoloji Muzelerinde Bulunan Bogazkoy Tableteri I and II [*Istanbul*] [*A publication*] (BJA)
IBOW .... Intact Bag of Waters [*Medicine*] (STED)
IBOY .... International Biodiversity Observation Year 2001-2002 (SAUO)
IBP .... IBP, Inc. [*NYSE symbol*] (SPSG)
IBP .... Incremental Bar Printer (SAUS)
IBP .... Indicated Boiling Point [*Physics*]
IBP .... Industrial Base Program
IBP .... Informed Birth and Parenting [*Later, IH/IBP*] (EA)
IBP .... Initial Boiling Point (MCD)
IBP .... Initial Boiling Point Facilities (SAUS)
IBP .... Inner [*Edge of*] Basal Piece
IBP .... Institute for Better Packaging [*Later, PPC*] (EA)
IBP .... Institute for Business Planning
IBP .... Institute of British Photographers (DGA)
IBP .... Insulated Binding Post
IBP .... Integrated Basic Research [*of ASRA*] [*National Science Foundation*]
IBP .... International Baccalaureate Program (SAUO)
IBP .... International Balance of Payments (AFM)
IBP .... International Bar Price (TIMI)
IBP .... International Biological Program [*Concluded, 1974*] [*National Academy of Sciences*]
IBP .... International Biophysical Program (CARB)
IBP .... International Book Project (EA)
IBP .... Intra-Aortic Ballon Pumping [*Cardiology*] (DMAA)
IBP .... Intraspecific Brood Parasitism [*Biology*]
IBP .... Ion-Beam Processing (SAUS)
IBP .... Ion Beam Projector
IBP .... Iowa Beef Processors (SAUS)
IBP .... Iowa Beef Processors, Inc. (SAUO)
IBP .... Iron Binding Protein (SAUS)
IBP .... Principia College, Elsah, IL [*OCLC symbol*] (OCLC)
IBPA .... Illinois State Bowling Proprietors Association (SRA)
IBPA .... Iminobispropylamine [*Organic chemistry*]
IBPA .... Indiana Bowling Proprietors Association (SRA)
IBPA .... International Book Printers Association [*Later, NABM*] (EA)
IBPA .... International Bridge Press Association (EA)
IBPA .... International Business Press Associates (PDAA)
IBPA .... Israel Book Publishers Association (SAUO)
IBPAT .... International Brotherhood of Painters and Allied Trades (EA)
IBPAW .... International Brotherhood of Pottery and Allied Workers [*Formerly, IBOP*] (EA)
IBpB .... Bedford Park Public Library District, Bedford Park, IL [*Library symbol*] [*Library of Congress*] (LCLS)
IBPCA .... International Bureau of the Permanent Court of Arbitration (EAIO)
IBPCS .... International Bureau for Physico-Chemical Standards (SAUO)

IBP/CT........ International Biological Programme Conservation of Terrestrial Biological Communities (SAUO)
IBP/CT........ International Biological Programme/Conservation of Terrestrial Biological Communities [*London, England*]
IBPCT.......... International Bureau for the Publication of Customs Tariffs (SAUO)
IBPCT.......... International Customs Tariffs Bureau [*International Bureau for the Publi cation of Customs Tariffs*] [*Acronym is based on former name,*] (EA)
IBPDMS....... Improved Point Defense Missile System [*Sea Sparrow*] (DOMA)
IBPDSMS..... Improved Basic Point Defense Surface Missile System (DNAB)
IBPF............ International Black Peoples' Foundation [*Defunct*] (EA)
IBPFM.......... Independent Board for Presbyterian Foreign Missions (EA)
IBPG........... Icon-Based Program Generators [*Software*] [*Computer science*]
IBPGR......... International Board for Plant Genetic Resources [*FAO*] [*Italy*]
IBPI............. International Bureau for Protection and Investigation (SAUO)
IBPI............. IntraBiotics Pharmaceuticals [*NASDAQ symbol*] (SG)
IBPIO.......... International Buoy Programme for the Indian Ocean (SAUO)
IBPM........... International Brotherhood of Papermakers [*Later, United Paperworkers International Union*]
IBPMS......... Indirect Blood Pressure Measuring System
IBPO........... International Brotherhood of Police Officers (EA)
IBPOEW....... Improved Benevolent and Protective Order of Elks of the World (SAUS)
IBPOEW....... Improved Benevolent Protective Order of Elks of the World (EA)
IBP/PM........ International Biological Program/ Productivity-Marine Section (SAUO)
IBP Record... Institute of British Photographers Record (SAUS)
IBPS............ Integrated Bibliography Pilot Study (SAUO)
IBPS............ International Baltic Pollution Studies (SAUS)
IBPSA.......... International Bowling Pro Shop and Instructors Association (NTPA)
IBPSA.......... International Building Performance and Simulation Association (SAUO)
IBPSY.......... International Baltic Pollution Study Year (SAUO)
IBQ.............. Illness Behavior Questionnaire (MELL)
IBQ.............. Institutional Bond Quote Service [*Database*] [*Chase Econometrics Interactive Data*] [*Information service or system*] (CRD)
IBQ.............. International Baron Resources [*Vancouver Stock Exchange symbol*]
IBQ.............. Quincy College, Quincy, IL [*OCLC symbol*] (OCLC)
IBQA........... Institute of Building Quality Australia
IBR.............. Iberia Air Lines of Spain (MCD)
IBR.............. Inclusion Body Rhinitis (SAUS)
IBR.............. Incorporate-by-Reference (SAUS)
IBR.............. Incorporated by Reference (SARE)
IBR.............. Incorporation by Reference (COE)
IBR.............. Infectious Bovine Rhinitis (SAUS)
IBR.............. Infectious Bovine Rhinotracheitis [*Also, IBRV*] [*Virus*]
IBR.............. Information-Bearing Radiation (SAUS)
IBR.............. Infrablack Region
IBR.............. Institute for Basic Research [*National Institute of Standards and Technology*]
IBR.............. Institute for Behavioral Research [*York University*] [*Canada*] [*Research center*] (IID)
IBR.............. Institute for Biblical Research (EA)
IBR.............. Institute for Bioregional Research (SAUS)
IBR.............. Institute for Biotechnology Research [*University of Waterloo*] [*Research center*] (RCD)
IBR.............. Institute for/of Behavioral Research (SAUO)
IBR.............. Institute of Behavioral Research (SAUS)
IBR.............. Institute of Biosocial Research (SAUO)
IBR.............. Institute of Boiler and Radiator Manufacturers [*Later, Hydronics Institute*] (EA)
IBR.............. Institutes for Behavior Resources (EA)
IBR.............. Integral Boiling Reactor
IBR.............. Integrally Bladed Rotor (SAUS)
IBR.............. Integrated Bridge Rectifier (IEEE)
IBR.............. Interbuildings Record Association (SAUO)
IBR.............. Intermediate Bit Rate (SAUS)
IBR.............. International Bio-Research Inc. (SAUO)
IBR.............. International Boxing Ring (SAUO)
IBR.............. International Business Reply [*Post Office*] [*British*]
IBR.............. Intra-Base Radio (SAUS)
IBR.............. Irish Broadcasting Revenue
IBR.............. Issues in Bank Regulation [*Bank Administration Institute*] [*A publication*]
IBR.............. Rockford College, Rockford, IL [*OCLC symbol*] (OCLC)
IBra............. Bradford Public Library, Bradford, IL [*Library symbol*] [*Library of Congress*] (LCLS)
IBRA........... Interconnecting Box Radio Adaptor (SAUS)
IBRA........... Interim Biogeographical Regionalisation for Australia (SAUO)
IBRA........... International Bee Research Association [*Cardiff, Wales*] (EA)
IBRA........... International Bible Reading Association [*Redhill, Surrey, England*] (EAIO)
IBRA........... International Broadcasting Association (SAUS)
IBRA........... International Broadcasting Association AB (SAUO)
IBRAD......... International Bank for Reconstruction and Development (SAUO)
IBRAE......... Institute of Nuclear Safety of the Russian Academy of Sciences (SAUO)
IBRAM......... Intermediary Ballistic Range Missile (SAUO)
IBRAPE........ Industria Brasileira de Produtos Eletronicos e Electricos, SA
IBRC........... In-Band, Reserved Channel (SAUS)
IBRC........... Indiana Business Research Center [*Indiana University*] [*Bloomington, IN*] [*Information service or system*] (IID)
IBRC........... International Bird Rescue Center (SAUO)
IBRC........... International Business Relations Council (SAUO)
IBRD........... International Bank for Reconstruction and Development [*Also known as World Bank*]
IBre............. Breese Public Library, Breese, IL [*Library symbol*] [*Library of Congress*] (LCLS)
IBreD.......... Breese Elementary District 12, Breese, IL [*Library symbol*] [*Library of Congress*] (LCLS)
IBreMHS...... Mater Dei High School, Breese, IL [*Library symbol*] [*Library of Congress*] (LCLS)
IBreSJH....... Saint Joseph's Hospital, Breese, IL [*Library symbol*] [*Library of Congress*] (LCLS)
IBRFC.......... International Buddy Rich Fan Club (EA)
IBRG........... International Biodeterioration Research Group (EA)
IBri.............. Brighton Memorial Library, Brighton, IL [*Library symbol*] [*Library of Congress*] (LCLS)
IBRI............. Interdisciplinary Biblical Research Institute (EA)
IBRI............. International Building Research Institute (SAUO)
IBRIC.......... Institute for Behavioral Research in Creativity [*Research center*] (RCD)
IBritishE....... Institute of British Engineers
IBRL............ Initial Bomb Release Line
IBRM........... Institute of Baths and Recreation Management [*British*]
IBRM........... Institute of Boiler and Radiator Manufacturers [*Later, Hydronics Institute*]
IBRM........... International Basic Res [*NASDAQ symbol*] (TTSB)
IBRM........... International Basic Resources, Inc. [*NASDAQ symbol*] (NQ)
IBRMA......... Institute for Biophysical Research and Macromolecular Assemblies [*Johns Hopkins University*]
IBRMR......... Institute for Basic Research on Mental Retardation
IBro............. Brookfield Free Public Library, Brookfield, IL [*Library symbol*] [*Library of Congress*] (LCLS)
IBRO........... Inter-Bank Computer Bureau (ELAL)
IBRO........... Inter-Bank Research Organization (SAUO)
IBRO........... International Brain Research Organization [*Paris, France*] (EA)
IBRO........... International Brewers Research Organization (SAUS)
IBRON......... International Brain Research Organization News [*Medicine*] (EDAA)
IBrov........... Broadview Public Library, Broadview, IL [*Library symbol*] [*Library of Congress*] (LCLS)
IBrowSD...... Brownstown Community School District No. 201, Brownstown, IL [*Library symbol*] [*Library of Congress*] (LCLS)
IBRP........... Introduction to Biomedical Research Program (SAUS)
IBRRC......... International Bird Rescue Research Center (EA)
IBRRC......... International Bird Rescue Research Center (or Centre) (SAUO)
IBRS........... Index to Book Reviews in the Sciences [*A publication*]
IBRS........... Inpatient Behavioral Rating Scale [*Medicine*] (DB)
IBRS........... Inpatient Behavior Rating Scale (STED)
IBRS........... Intra-Base Radio System (SAUO)
IBrS............ Suburban Library System, Burr Ridge, IL [*Library symbol*] [*Library of Congress*] (LCLS)
IBrus........... South County Public Library District of Calhoun County, Brussels, IL [*Library symbol*] [*Library of Congress*] (LCLS)
IBrusRSD..... Brussels-Richwood Community Consolidated School District 41, Brussels, IL [*Library symbol*] [*Library of Congress*] (LCLS)
IBrusSD....... Brussels Community High School District 37, Brussels, IL [*Library symbol*] [*Library of Congress*] (LCLS)
IBrv............ Bridgeview Public Library, Bridgeview, IL [*Library symbol*] [*Library of Congress*] (LCLS)
IBRV........... Infectious Bovine Rhinotracheitis Virus [*Also, IBR*]
IBS............. Ball State University, Muncie, IN [*OCLC symbol*] (OCLC)
IBS............. Ibaraki Broadcasting System (SAUS)
IBS............. Ibis [*Belgium*] [*ICAO designator*] (FAAC)
IBS............. Ichthyosis Bullosa of Siemens [*Medicine*]
IBS............. Ichthyosis Bullosa Siemens (SAUS)
IBS............. Identical by State [*Genetics*]
IBS............. Imidazole Buffered Saline [*Clinical chemistry*]
IBS............. Immediate Business Systems [*Commercial firm*] [*British*]
IBS............. Immunoblastic Sarcoma [*Medicine*] (DMAA)
IBS............. Imo Broadcasting Service (SAUS)
IBS............. Impulse Balance System
IBS............. Incentive Bonus Scheme [*British*]
IBS............. Incorporated Bronte Society [*Keighley, West Yorkshire, England*] (EAIO)
IBS............. Indian Boy Scouts (SAUO)
IBS............. Inflatable Boat, Small (NVT)
IBS............. Informationsbankensystem (SAUS)
IBS............. Input Buffer Storage (SAUS)
IBS............. Input Buffer Store (SAUS)
IBS............. Inside Bathing Solution [*Medicine*] (STED)
IBS............. Institute for Basic Standards [*Later, NSL*] [*National Institute of Standards and Technology*]
IBS............. Institute for Biotechnological Studies [*University of Kent*] [*British*] (IRUK)
IBS............. Institute for Brew Studies (NTPA)
IBS............. Institute of Basic Standards (SAUO)
IBS............. Institute of Behavioral Science [*University of Colorado - Boulder*] [*Research center*] (RCD)
IBS............. Institute of Behavioural Studies [*University of Newcastle*] [*Australia*]
IBS............. Institute of Biblical Studies (SAUO)
IBS............. Institute of Black Studies [*Defunct*] (EA)
IBS............. Institute of Buddhist Studies (SAUS)
IBS............. Integrated Baseline System (ABAC)
IBS............. Integrated Booking System [*Army*] (RDA)
IBS............. Integrated Boresight Sensor (ACAE)
IBS............. Integrated Bridge System (MCD)
IBS............. Integrated Business Systems [*Trifid Software*] (NITA)
IBS............. Integriertes Banken-System (SAUO)
IBS............. INTELSAT Business Service [*MCI Communications Corp.*]
IBS............. Interactive Billing Service (AGLO)

IBS .... Interbed-Storage Package [*Geological program*]
IBS .... Interbomb Spacing (DNAB)
IBS .... Inter-Byte Separation [*Automotive engineering*] [*Electronics*]
IBS .... Inter-Byte Spacing [*Computer science*]
IBS .... Intercollegiate Broadcasting System (EA)
IBS .... Interference Blanker Set
IBS .... Interlibrary Borrowing Service (SAUS)
IBS .... International Bach Society [*Defunct*] (EA)
IBS .... International Bank for Settlements (MHDW)
IBS .... International Bank of Singapore (SAUO)
IBS .... International Belt Skimmer (SAUS)
IBS .... International Benchrest Shooters (EA)
IBS .... International Benevolent Society (EA)
IBS .... International Bentham Society (EAIO)
IBS .... International Bible Society (EA)
IBS .... International Bible Students (SAUO)
IBS .... International Bibliography of the Social Sciences, Economics, and Sociology [*International Committee for Social Science Information and Documentation*] [*Information service or system*] (CRD)
IBS .... International Biogenic Society (SAUO)
IBS .... International Biometric Society (NTPA)
IBS .... International Bookbinders Secretariat (DGA)
IBS .... International Book Committee (SAUO)
IBS .... International Book Service, Inc.
IBS .... International Boundary Study [*A publication*]
IBS .... International Brancost Society (SAUO)
IBS .... International Brancusi Society (EA)
IBS .... International Brecht Society [*See also IBG*] (EA)
IBS .... International Broadcasting Service (SAUO)
IBS .... International Bronchoesophagological Society (EA)
IBS .... International Bulb Society (EAIO)
IBS .... International Bureau of Scouting (SAUO)
IBS .... International Business Services [*Telecommunications*] (TSSD)
IBS .... International Business Show (SAUS)
IBS .... Internet Broadcasting Services (SAUS)
IBS .... Internet Broadcasting Systems
IBS .... Interpersonal Behavior Survey [*Psychology*]
IBS .... Intron Binding Site [*Genetics*]
IBS .... Ion Beam Scanning
IBS .... Ion Beam Splitter (SAUS)
IBS .... Ion Beam Sputtering
IBS .... Ion-Beam Synthesis [*Chemistry*] (ODA)
IBS .... Ionospheric Beacon Satellite (PDAA)
IBS .... Iota Beta Sigma [*An association*] (WDMC)
IBS .... Irritable Bowel Syndrome [*Medicine*]
IBS .... Island Base Section [*Navy*]
IBS .... ISNAR Biotechnology Service (SAUO)
IBS .... Isobaric Solution (DMAA)
IBS .... Israel Broadcasting Service (SAUO)
IBS .... Institute of Bankers in Scotland (ODA)
IBSA .... Immunoreactive Bovine Serum Albumin [*Immunochemistry*]
IBSA .... Inanimate Bird Shooting Association (SAUO)
IBSA .... Inanimate Bird-Shooting Association (SAUO)
IBSA .... International Barber Schools Association (EA)
IBSA .... International Bible Student Association (SAUO)
IBSA .... International Bible Students Association (EA)
IBSA .... International Biotechnology Suppliers Association (SAUO)
IBSA .... International Blind Sports Association [*See also AISA*] [*Farsta, Sweden*] (EAIO)
IBSA .... International Board Sailing Association (SAUO)
IBSA .... Iodinated Bovine Serum Albumin (DMAA)
IBSAC .... Industrialized Building Systems and Components (IEEE)
IBSAC .... Industrialized Building Systems and Components Exhibition (SAUO)
IBSAF .... International Bureau for Standardization of Artificial Fibres (SAUO)
IBS Asian Electron News ... IBS Asian Electronics News (journ.) (SAUS)
IBSAT .... Indexing by Statistical Analysis Techniques (PDAA)
IBSC .... Independent Banks of South Carolina (SRA)
IBSC .... International Bankcard Services Corp. (SAUO)
IBSC .... Iranian-British Shipping Company (SAUO)
IBSCA .... Ion Beam Spectrochemical Analysis (PDAA)
IB(Scot) .... Institute of Bankers in Scotland (ODBW)
IBSD .... Independent Community Bankers of South Dakota (TBD)
IBSD .... Information-Based School Development
IBSDF .... International Business Schools [*NASDAQ symbol*] (SAG)
IBSDF .... Intl Business Schs [*NASDAQ symbol*] (TTSB)
IBSE .... Initial Blood Storage Experiment (SAUS)
IBSE .... Ion Beam Sputter Etching (SAUS)
IBSEDEX .... International Building Services Abstracts Index (SAUS)
IBSEDEX .... International Building Services Index [*Database*] [*BSRIA*] [*Information service or system*] (CRD)
IBSF .... IBS Financial [*NASDAQ symbol*] (TTSB)
IBSF .... IBS Financial Corp. [*NASDAQ symbol*] (SAG)
IBSF .... International Boatsurfing Federation (SAUO)
ibsf .... Little Brothers of Saint Francis (TOCD)
IBSFC .... International Baltic Sea Fishery Commission [*Warsaw, Poland*] (ASF)
IBS Fncl .... IBS Financial Corp. [*Associated Press*] (SAG)
IBSG .... Internetwork Broadcast Sub-Group
IBSGR .... Isiolo Buffalo Spring Game Reserve (SAUO)
IBSH .... Institute of the Brothers of the Sacred Heart [*See also IFSC*] [*Rome, Italy*] (EAIO)
IBSHR .... Integral Boiling and Superheat Reactor
IBSI .... Independent Bankshares, Incorporated (SAUO)
IBSIN .... Innovations in Building Sustainable Industries (SAUS)
IBSM .... Institute of Building Site Management [*British*] (BI)
IBSM .... International Bureau of Strata Mechanics [*See also IBG*] (EAIO)
IBSMA .... Interior Board of Surface Mine Appeals (SAUO)
IBSMA .... Interior Board of Surface Mine Appeals (in United States Interior Decisions) [*A publication*] (DLA)
ibSN .... Ibero-American Society for Neurochemistry (SAUO)
IBSN .... Infantile Bilateral Striatal Necrosis [*Ophthalmology*]
IBSNAT .... International Benchmark Sites Network for Agrotechnology Transfers (SAUS)
IBSP .... Idaho Bureau of State Planning (SAUO)
IBSP .... Integrin-Binding Sialoprotein (DMAA)
IBSR .... Individual Base Stock Requirements (SAUS)
IBSR .... Individual Battle Shooting Range (PDAA)
IBSR .... Interactive Bibliographic Search and Retrieval (NITA)
IBSR .... Inverse Boresight Ranging (MCD)
IBSRAM .... International Board for Soil Research and Management [*Thailand*]
IBSRAM .... International Board of Soil Resources and Management (SAUO)
IBSS .... Infra-red Background Sensor Survey (SAUS)
IBSS .... Infrared Background Signature Survey [*Military*] (SDI)
IBSS .... Infrared Background Space Surveillance Experiment (SAUS)
IBSS .... Infrared Background Survey Satellite (SAUS)
IBSS .... Infrared Backscatter Signature Survey (SAUS)
IBSS .... Insect Balanced Salt Solution [*Cytology*]
IBSS .... Institute of Biology of the Southern Seas
IBSS .... International Banking Summer School (SAUO)
IBSS .... IR Background Signature Survey (SAUS)
IBS/SPS .... Inflatable Boat, Small/Silent Propulsion System (MCD)
IBSSU .... Internal Bearing Stabilized Sighting Unit (MCD)
IBSSU .... International Bearing Stabilized Sighting Unit (SAUO)
IBST .... Institute of British Surgical Technicians (BI)
IBST .... International Bureau of Social Tourism [*See also BITS*] [*Brussels, Belgium*] (EAIO)
IBST .... International Bureau of Software Test
IBSTF .... IBS Technologies Ltd. [*NASDAQ symbol*] (COMM)
IBSTP .... International Bureau for the Suppression of Traffic in Persons (DI)
IBSWU .... International Boot and Shoe Workers' Union
IBSYS .... Initial Basic System (SAUS)
IBSYS .... International Business Machines System
IBT .... Field Museum of Natural History, Chicago, IL [*OCLC symbol*] (OCLC)
IBT .... Ibertrans Aerea SL [*Spain*] [*FAA designator*] (FAAC)
IBT .... IBS Technologies Ltd. [*Vancouver Stock Exchange symbol*]
IBT .... Illinois Bell Telephone (ROAS)
IBT .... Illinois Bureau of Tourism (SAUS)
IBT .... Immunobead Binding Test [*Biochemistry*]
IBT .... Immunoblastic T-Cell [*Lymphadenopathy*]
IBT .... Implantable Beacon Transmitter [*Oceanography*]
IBT .... Inclined Bottom Tank [*Fermenter*]
IBT .... Income Before Taxes (AAGC)
IBT .... Incompatible Blood Transfusion (PDAA)
IBT .... Independent Bankers Division of Tennessee Bankers Association (TBD)
I-BT .... India-Burma Theater [*World War II*]
IBT .... Indianapolis Ballet Theatre
IBT .... Indirect Business Tax (SAUO)
IBT .... Industrial Bio-Test Laboratories, Inc.
IBT .... Industrial Biotest Laboratory (SAUO)
IBT .... Initial Boiling-Point Temperature
IBT .... Initial Brake Temperature [*Automotive engineering*]
IBT .... Ink Blot Test [*Rorschach test*] [*Psychology*] (DAVI)
IBT .... Institute of Banking Techniques (SAUS)
IBT .... Instructor Based Training (SAUS)
IBT .... Instrument Bend Test (SAUS)
IBT .... Instrumented Bend Test
IBT .... Insulation Breakdown Tester
IBT .... Integrated Bipolar Transistor (SAUS)
IBT .... Integrated Business Terminal [*Computer science*] (PDAA)
IBT .... International Bank & Trust Ltd. (SAUO)
IBT .... [*The*] International Bridge & Terminal Co. [*AAR code*]
IBT .... International Broadcasting Trust [*British*]
IBT .... International Brotherhood of Teamsters [*Union*]
IBT .... International Brotherhood of Teamsters, Chauffeurs, Warehouseman and Helpers of America (SAUO)
IBT .... International Brotherhood of Teamsters, Chauffeurs, Warehousemen, and Helpers ofAmerica (EA)
IBT .... Interrupt Bit Table (ELAL)
IBT .... Ion Beam Technology
IBT .... Ion-Compatiple Base Transistor Technology (SAUS)
IBT .... Ion-Implantation Base Transistor Technology (SAUS)
IBT .... Ion-Implanted Base Transistor
IBT .... Irrational Beliefs Test [*Psychology*]
IBT .... Isatin-Beta-Thiosemicarbasone (SAUS)
IBT .... Isatin-beta-thiosemicarbazone [*Organic chemistry*]
IBTA .... Individualized Behavior Therapy for Alcoholics (SAUS)
IBTA .... Interest-Bearing Transaction Account (DICI)
IBTA .... International Baton Twirlers Association (SAUO)
IBTA .... International Baton Twirling Association of America and Abroad [*Defunct*] (EA)
IBTA .... International Business Travel Association (SAUO)
IBTC .... International Brands and Their Companies [*Formerly, ITND*] [*A publication*]
IBTC .... International Business and Technical Consultants (SAUO)
IBTCWH .... International Brotherhood of Teamsters, Chauffeurs, Warehousemen and Helpers (SAUS)
IBTCWHA .... International Brotherhood of Teamsters, Chauffeurs, Warehousemen and Helpers of America (SAUS)
IBTE .... Imperial Board of Telecommunications (SAUO)
IBTE .... Interactive Bureau of Technical Education (SAUS)

IBTE .... International Bureau for Technical Education (SAUO)
IBTE .... International Bureau of Technical Education (SAUS)
IB Test .... Inkblot Test (SAUS)
IBTF .... Investment Bank for Trade and Finance [*United Arab Emirates*]
IBTI .... Intercontinental Bureau of Translators and Interpreters (SAUO)
IBTMA .... International Black Toy Manufacturers Association (EA)
IBTO .... International Broadcasting and Television Organization (NTCM)
IBTOM .... Iranian B'nei Torah Movement (EA)
IBTP .... Interceptor Blast Traversal Program (SAUS)
IBTR .... Ipsilateral Breast Tumor Recurrence [*Medicine*] (STED)
IBTS .... Insert Bit String [*Computer science*] (PCM)
IBTS .... International Beer Tasting Society (EA)
IBTS .... International Beer Testing Society (SAUO)
IBTS .... International Bicycle Touring Society (EA)
IBTS .... Italian Broadcasting and Telecommunication Show (SAUS)
IBTT .... Implantation Base Transistor Technology (SAUS)
IBTT .... International Bureau for Technical Training (SAUO)
IBTTA .... International Bridge, Tunnel, and Turnpike Association (EA)
IBTU .... Instructors Basic Training Unit
IBTU .... International Bureau of Transport Users (SAUS)
IBU .... Eureka College, Eureka, IL [*OCLC symbol*] (OCLC)
IBU .... Ibukiyama [*Ibukisan*] [*Japan*] [*Seismograph station code, US Geological Survey*] [*Closed*] (SEIS)
IBU .... Ibuprofen [*Medicine*] (STED)
IBU .... Ikatan Buruh Umum [*General Workers' Union*] [*Indonesia*]
IBU .... Imperial Bushel (WDAA)
IBU .... Independent Business Unit
IBU .... Inland Boatmen's Union of the Pacific
IBU .... Instruction Buffer Unit [*Computer science*] (IAA)
IBU .... Interference Blanking Unit
IBU .... International Banking Unit (SAUO)
IBU .... International Benzoate Unit [*Pharmacology*]
IBU .... International Box-Union (SAUO)
IBU .... International Broadcasting Union [*Defunct*] (NTCM)
IBU .... International Burgers Now Ltd. [*Vancouver Stock Exchange symbol*]
IBU .... International Business Unit [*British*] [*Information service or system*] (IID)
I-Bu .... Isobutyl [*Medicine*] (EDAA)
IBu .... Isobutyryl (SAUS)
IBU .... Itambacuri [*Brazil*] [*Airport symbol*] (AD)
IBucSD .... Buckley-Loda Community Unit School District, Buckley, IL [*Library symbol*] [*Library of Congress*] (LCLS)
IBud .... Mason Memorial Public Library, Buda, IL [*Library symbol*] [*Library of Congress*] (LCLS)
IBUFG .... Internetwork Broadcast/Unknown Functional Group
IBUMP .... I-Beam Bumper [*Automotive safety systems*]
IBun .... Bunker Hill Public Library, Bunker Hill, IL [*Library symbol*] [*Library of Congress*] (LCLS)
IBunMCD .... Macoupin Community District 8, Bunker Hill, IL [*Library symbol*] [*Library of Congress*] (LCLS)
IBUPL .... International Bureau for the Unification of Penal Law (SAUO)
ibuprofen .... Isobutylphenylpropionic Acid (BARN)
IBUPU .... International Bureau of the Universal Postal Union (SAUO)
IBur .... South Stickney District Library, Burbank, IL [*Library symbol*] [*Library of Congress*] (LCLS)
IBure .... Leepertown Township Library, Bureau, IL [*Library symbol*] [*Library of Congress*] (LCLS)
IBureLSD .... Leepertown Consolidated Community School District 175, Bureau, IL [*Library symbol*] [*Library of Congress*] (LCLS)
IBUS .... Input Bus (SAUS)
IBV .... Infectious Bronchitis Vaccine [*Pharmacology*] (DAVI)
IBV .... Infectious Bronchitis Virus [*Avian*]
IBV .... Inspection by Variables
IBV .... Intercontinental Ballistic Vehicle (SAUO)
IBV .... International Bellevue Ventures Ltd. [*Vancouver Stock Exchange symbol*]
IBV .... Internationale Buchhandler-Vereinigung [*International Booksellers Federation - IBF*] (EAIO)
IBV .... Newberry Library, Chicago, IL [*OCLC symbol*] (OCLC)
IBVA .... Interactive Brain Wave Analyzer [*IBVA Technology*] [*Computer science*] (PCM)
IBVE .... Isobutyl Vinyl Ether [*Organic chemistry*]
IBVEA .... International Bureau of Veterinary Educational Aids (SAUO)
IBVM .... Institute of the Blessed Virgin Mary [*Sisters of Loretto*] [*Roman Catholic religious order*]
IBVP .... Initial Boundary Value Problem (SAUS)
IBW .... Borg-Warner Corp., Des Plaines, IL [*OCLC symbol*] (OCLC)
IBW .... Ideal Body Weight [*Medicine*]
IBW .... Impulse Bandwidth (MCD)
IBW .... In Black and White [*A publication*]
IBW .... Infantry Brigade Workshop (SAUO)
IBW .... Information Bandwidth (SAUS)
IBW .... Institute of the Black World [*Defunct*] (EA)
IBW .... Intelligence Bandwidth
IBW .... Intelligence-Based Warfare
IBW .... Internal Bore Weld [*Nuclear energy*] (NUCP)
IBW .... Internal Bore Welding (SAUS)
IBW .... International Black Writers (EA)
IBW .... International Boiler Works (SAUO)
IBW .... International Business Week
IBW .... Ion Beam Weapon
IBW .... Irrotationally Bound Water [*Biophysics*]
IBW .... Israel Book World [*A publication*]
IBWA .... International Bank for West Africa Ltd.
IBWA .... International Black Writers and Artists (EA)
IBWA .... International Bottled Water Association (EA)
IBWA .... International Boxing Writers Association (EA)
IBWC .... International Black Women's Congress (EA)
IBWC .... International Black Writers Conference [*Later, IBW*] (EA)
IBWC .... International Boundary and Water Commission
IBWCA .... International Barbed Wire Collectors Association (EA)
IBWC-PRB .... International Boundary and Water Commission-Planning and Reports Branch (SAUO)
IBWC-PRB .... International Bourdary and Water Commission (SAUS)
IBWCUSMEX .... International Boundary and Water Commission, United States and Mexico (SAUO)
IBWDA .... Idaho Beer and Wine Distributors Association (SRA)
IBWM .... International Bureau of Weights and Measures
IBWN .... International Bureau of Weights and Measures (ECII)
IBWP .... Idaho National Engineering Laboratory Buried Waste Program (SAUO)
IBWS .... International Bureau of Whaling Statistics (SAUO)
IBWW .... International Federation of Building and Woodworkers (SAUO)
IBX .... Battelles Internal Telephone System (SAUS)
IBX .... Iberiotoxin [*Biochemistry*]
IBX .... Integrated Business Exchange (MCD)
IBX .... Intermediate Branch Exchange (SAUS)
IBX .... Schiff, Hardin & Waite, Chicago, IL [*OCLC symbol*] (OCLC)
IBY .... Intelligence Bay (SAUS)
IBY .... International Baltic Year (SAUO)
IBY .... International Bank of Yemen
IBY .... International Biological Year
IBY .... International Book Year [*1972*] [*UNESCO*]
IBY .... International Business Aircraft, Inc. [*FAA designator*] (FAAC)
IBYAN .... International Bean Yield and Adaptation Nursery (SAUO)
Ibyc .... Ibycus [*Sixth century BC*] [*Classical studies*] (OCD)
IBYC .... Institute in Basic Youth Conflicts (EA)
IBZ .... Columbia College, Chicago, IL [*Inactive*] [*OCLC symbol*] (OCLC)
IBZ .... Ibiza [*Spain*] [*Airport symbol*] (OAG)
IBZ .... Inner Border Zone
IBZ .... International Business Air [*Sweden*] [*ICAO designator*] (FAAC)
IC .... Chicago Public Library, Chicago, IL [*Library symbol*] [*Library of Congress*] (LCLS)
IC .... IC-card (SAUS)
IC .... Ice Chest
IC .... Ice Concentration (ACAE)
IC .... Ice Crystals
ic .... Iceland [*MARC country of publication code*] [*Library of Congress*] (LCCP)
IC .... Iceland [*NATO*]
IC .... Icing [*Aviation*] (FAAC)
IC .... Icon [*Plate engraving*]
IC .... Icteric [*Medicine*] (DAVI)
IC .... Idaho College (SAUO)
IC .... Identification Card (SAUS)
IC .... Identification Character (SAUS)
IC .... Identification Code
IC .... Identifying Code (SAUS)
IC .... Identity Card (BARN)
IC .... Identity Code (SAUS)
IC .... Idle Character (SAUS)
IC .... Idling Cycle (SAUS)
IC .... Iesus Christus [*Jesus Christ*] [*Latin*]
IC .... If Clause (SAUS)
IC .... Ignatius College (SAUS)
IC .... Ignition Control (HAWK)
IC .... Ignore Character (SAUS)
IC .... Ileocecal [*Gastroenterology*] (DAVI)
IC .... Iliac Chamber [*Anatomy*] (IAA)
IC .... Iliac Crest [*Medicine*] (MELL)
IC .... Iliococcygeal [*Muscle*] [*Anatomy*] (DAVI)
IC .... Iliocostal [*Muscle*] [*Anatomy*] (DAVI)
IC .... Illegal Character (SAUS)
IC .... Illinois Central [*Illinois Central Gulf Railroad Co.*] [*AAR code*]
IC .... Illinois Central Corp. [*NYSE symbol*] (SPSG)
IC .... Illinois Central Gulf Railroad Co. (SAUO)
IC .... Illinois College (SAUO)
IC .... Image Chamber (IAA)
IC .... Image Check (IAA)
IC .... Image Coding (SAUS)
IC .... Image Communications [*Computer graphics*]
IC .... Image Converter (SAUS)
IC .... Imagination, Cognition and Personality (journ.) (SAUS)
IC .... Immaculata College (SAUO)
IC .... Immediate Care [*Medicine*] (MELL)
IC .... Immediate Constituent
IC .... Immune Complex [*Immunology*]
IC .... Immune Cytotoxicity [*Immunochemistry*] (DAVI)
IC .... Immunochemistry (SAUS)
IC .... Immunocompromised [*Medicine*] (MELL)
IC .... Immunoconjugate [*Medicine*] (MELL)
IC .... Immunocytochemistry [*Immunochemstry*] (DAVI)
IC .... Imparity Check (SAUS)
IC .... Impedance Cardiogram/raphy [*Medicine*] (EDAA)
IC .... Imperial College [*London*] (WDAA)
IC .... Imperial College of Science and Technology (SAUO)
IC .... Imperial Conference (SAUO)
IC .... Impetigo Contagiosa [*Medicine*] (MELL)
IC .... Implementation and Conversion (MCD)
I/C .... Implementation/Conversion (SAUO)

IC .... Implementatioh of Change
IC .... Implied Consent [*Motor vehicle violation code used in state of Maryland*] (MVRD)
IC .... Import Certificate (SAUS)
IC .... Imported Content
IC .... Impoverished Conditions
IC .... Impregnated Cable (SAUS)
IC .... Impregnated Carbon (SAUS)
IC .... Impression Cylinder [*Typography*] (DGA)
IC .... Improved Capability [*for aircraft*] (MCD)
IC .... Improved Cylinder [*Gunnery*]
IC .... Impulse Conductor (MSA)
IC .... Inbound Collect (SAUS)
IC .... In Calf (SAUS)
IC .... Incarnational Consecration (TOCD)
ic .... In Casu [*In This Case*] [*Latin*]
IC .... Incense Cedar [*Botany*]
IC .... Incentive Compensation (MCD)
IC .... In Characters (SAUS)
i/c .... In Charge (WDAA)
IC .... In Charge Of
IC .... Incident Command (SARE)
IC .... Incident Commander [*Environmental science*] (COE)
IC .... Incident Control [*Environmental science*] (COE)
I/C .... Incoming [*Telecommunications*] (TEL)
IC .... In Command (ADA)
IC .... In Commission (SAUS)
IC .... In-Commission (MCD)
IC .... Incompetent Cervix [*Medicine*] (MELL)
IC .... Incomplete (DAVI)
IC .... In Compliance [*FDA*]
ic .... in conference (SAUS)
IC .... Increase (IAA)
IC .... Incremental Computer (SAUS)
IC .... Incremental Cost (KSC)
IC .... Incue [*News broadcasting*] (NTCM)
IC .... Incurved Cactus [*Horticulture*]
IC .... Indefinite Chill (SAUS)
IC .... Independent Carrier (SAUS)
IC .... Independent Contractor
IC .... Independent Telephone Co. [*Telecommunications*]
IC .... Independent Telephone Company (SAUO)
IC .... Index Catalogue
IC .... Index Chemicus [*See also ICRS*]
I/C .... Index Concordance [*International Serials Catalogue*] [*A publication*]
IC .... Index Correction [*on a sextant*] [*Navigation*]
IC .... Index of Coincidence (MHDB)
IC .... Indian Airlines [*ICAO designator*] (AD)
IC .... Indian Airlines Corporation (SAUO)
IC .... Indian Cases [*India*] [*A publication*] (DLA)
IC .... Indian Culture (journ.) (SAUS)
IC .... Indicating Controller (NRCH)
IC .... Indication Cycle (IAA)
IC .... Indicator and Control
IC .... Indicator Card (SAUS)
IC .... Indifference Curve [*Economics*]
IC .... Indirect Calorimetry [*Physiology*] (DAVI)
IC .... Indirect Correlation (SAUS)
IC .... Individual/Collective (MCD)
IC .... Individual Combatants (SAUS)
IC .... Individual Counsel (DNAB)
IC .... Individual Counseling [*Psychology*] (DAVI)
IC .... Individualism-Collectivism (SAUS)
IC .... Indochina
I-C .... Indo-Chinese (SAUS)
IC .... Inductance-Capacitance
IC .... Induction Coil (SAUS)
IC .... Inductive Capacitive (SAUS)
IC .... Inductive Coupling
IC .... Industrial Chemistry (SAUS)
IC .... Industrial Collaboration (SAUS)
I/C .... Industrial/Commercial
IC .... Industrial Concentration (MHDB)
IC .... Industrial Court (DLA)
IC .... Industrialized Country (SAUO)
IC .... Industry Commission (SAUO)
IC .... Industry Committee (SAUO)
IC .... Industry Competitive (AFIT)
IC .... Indy Car [*Motorsports*]
IC .... Inertial Component
IC .... Infection Control (HCT)
IC .... Inferior Colliculus [*Also, ICC*] [*Brain anatomy*]
IC .... Infinite Capitalism [*Book title*]
IC .... Informal Communication
IC .... Information Carrier (SAUS)
IC .... Information Center
IC .... Information Circular
IC .... Information Code (SAUS)
IC .... Information Codes (NITA)
IC .... Information Collection (SAUS)
IC .... Information Configuration (SAUS)
IC .... Information Content (DEN)
IC .... Infrared Cell (SAUS)
IC .... Infrastructure Committee (SAUS)
IC .... Infrastructure Committee of the North Atlantic Council [*NATO*]
IC .... Ingenieur Constructeur [*Academic degree*]
IC .... Inhibiting Circuit (SAUS)
IC .... Inhibition Concentration [*Biochemistry*]
IC .... Inhibitory Concentration [*Toxicology*]
IC .... Iniciativia per Catalunya [*Spain*] [*Political party*] (EY)
IC .... Initial Calibration
IC .... Initial Card (SAUS)
IC .... Initial Cell (SAUS)
IC .... Initial Command (SAUS)
IC .... Initial Conditions
IC .... Initial Course [*Navigation*]
IC .... Initiation of Contraction
IC .... Inland Container [*Shipping*] (DCTA)
IC .... Inlet Contact
IC .... Inner Cabin
IC .... Inner Canthal Distance [*Medicine*] (DMAA)
IC .... Inner Circle [*An association*] (EA)
IC .... Inner Circle [*Numismatics*]
IC .... Inner City (SAUS)
IC .... Inner Core [*Geology*]
IC .... Innocent Civilian [*Military*]
IC .... Inorganic Carbon
IC .... Input Card (SAUS)
IC .... Input Channel (SAUS)
IC .... Input Circuit
IC .... Input Code (IAA)
IC .... Input Controler (SAUS)
I/C .... Input Controller (MCD)
IC .... Input Current
IC .... Inquiry Control (SAUS)
IC .... Inscribed Circle (IAA)
IC .... Insert Character (SAUS)
IC .... Insert Cursor (SAUS)
IC .... Insertion Character (SAUS)
IC .... Inside Cloud Lightning [*Meteorology*]
IC .... Inspected and Condemend (SAUS)
IC .... Inspected and Condemned [*Military*]
IC .... Inspecting Commander [*Military*] [*British*] (ROG)
IC .... Inspection Card
IC .... Inspection Carriage [*Indian Railway*] (TIR)
IC .... Inspection Chamber
IC .... Inspection Committee
IC .... Inspiratory Capacity [*Physiology*]
IC .... Inspiratory Center [*Physiology*]
IC .... Inspiratory Center (or Centre) (SAUS)
IC .... Installation Contractor (SAUS)
IC .... Installed Capacity [*Electronics*] (IEEE)
IC .... Institute for Congress
IC .... Institute of Ceramics [*Stoke-On-Trent, Staffordshire, England*] (EAIO)
ic .... Institute of Charity (TOCD)
IC .... Institute of Charity [*Rosminians*] [*Roman Catholic religious order*]
IC .... Institute of Chemistry [*British*]
IC .... Institute of Chemists (SAUO)
IC .... Institutes and Centers (HVTR)
IC .... Institutional Care [*British*]
IC .... Institutional Characteristics [*of the Integrated Postsecondary Education Data System*] [*Department of Education*] (GFGA)
IC .... Institutional Co-Operation (FOTI)
IC .... Instruction Cache (SAUS)
IC .... Instruction Card (MSA)
IC .... Instruction Cell
IC .... Instruction Code (AAG)
IC .... Instruction Code (or Coding) (SAUS)
IC .... Instruction Complement (SAUS)
IC .... Instruction Counter [*Computer science*]
IC .... Instruction Cycle [*Computer science*] (IAA)
IC .... Instructor in Cookery [*Navy*] [*British*] (ROG)
I/C .... Instrumentation Control (SAUS)
IC .... Instrumentation Controller (KSC)
IC .... Instrument Cluster [*Automotive engineering*]
IC .... Instrument Correction
IC .... Instrument Correlation (WDAA)
IC .... Insulated Conductor (SAUS)
IC .... Insulated Conductors (MCD)
IC .... Insulating Compound (IAA)
IC .... Intake Closes [*Valve position*]
IC .... Integrated Chip (SAUS)
IC .... Integrated Chromatography
IC .... Integrated Circuit [*Electronics*]
IC .... Integrated Circuit graphics system (SAUS)
IC .... Integrated Communications (MCD)
IC .... Integrating Center
IC .... Integrating Contractor (AAG)
IC .... Integration Committee (SAUS)
IC .... Integration Contractor (SAUS)
IC .... Integration Control (MCD)
IC .... Integrator Card (IAA)
IC .... Intellectual Capital
IC .... Intelligence Center (CAAL)
IC .... Intelligence Collator [*British police term*]
IC .... Intelligence Collection [*Military*] (MCD)
IC .... Intelligence Committee [*NATO*] (NATG)
IC .... Intelligence Community [*Military*] (MCD)
IC .... Intelligence Corps [*Military unit*] [*British*]
IC .... Intelligence Correlation [*Training term*] (LPT)

IC................ Intelligence Cycle (LAIN)
IC................ Intelligencs Center (SAUS)
IC................ Intelligent Copier [*Electrophotography*] (DGA)
IC................ Intensive Care [*Medicine*]
IC................ Intensive Conservation Area Committees (SAUO)
IC................ Interaction Coefficient (SAUS)
IC................ Intercept Centre (SAUS)
IC................ Intercept Controller
IC................ Intercepting Chamber (SAUS)
IC................ Interceptor Command
IC................ Interceptor Computer (IAA)
I/C................ Interchange
IC................ Interchange Center
IC................ Interchemical Corporation (SAUO)
IC................ Inter Cibos [*Between Meals*] [*Pharmacy*]
IC................ Intercity (SAUS)
I/C................ Intercom (KSC)
i/c................ Intercom (PIAV)
I/C................ Intercommunication (SAUS)
IC................ Intercommunications
I/C................ Intercommunicator
IC................ Intercomputer (MCD)
IC................ Intercomputer Channel (KSC)
IC................ Intercomputer Communication (NAKS)
IC................ Interconnect Carrier [*Telecommunications*]
IC................ Interconnection (IAA)
IC................ Intercontrole Inc. (SAUO)
IC................ Intercostal [*Between the ribs*] [*Medicine*]
IC................ Intercrystalline Corrosion [*Metallurgy*]
IC................ Intercultural Communication (SAUS)
IC................ Interexchange Carrier [*Telecommunications*]
IC................ Interface Control [*or Controller*]
IC................ Interface Coordinator (MCD)
IC................ Interfacial Communications (MCD)
IC................ Interference Contrast (SAUS)
IC................ Interference Control (IAA)
IC................ Intergovernmental Council (SAUO)
IC................ Intergovernment Committee (SAUO)
IC................ Interim Change (AFM)
IC................ Interim Commission
IC................ Interim Committee
IC................ Interior Communication
IC................ Interior Communications (SAUO)
IC................ Interior Communications Electrician [*Navy rating*]
IC................ Inter LATA Carrier (SAUS)
IC................ Interlock Code (SAUS)
IC................ Intermediate Care [*Medicine*]
IC................ Intermediate Chain [*Biochemistry*]
IC................ Intermediate Circuit (IAA)
IC................ Intermediate Command
IC................ Intermediate Conversion (SAUS)
IC................ Intermediate Cross-connect (SAUS)
IC................ Intermittent Catheterization [*Urology*] (DAVI)
IC................ Intermittent Claudication [*Medicine*] (MAE)
IC................ Internal Capsule [*Neuroanatomy*]
IC................ Internal Carotid [*Artery*] [*Cardiology*] (DAVI)
IC................ Internal Cerebral [*Neurology*] (DAVI)
IC................ Internal Cholecystectomy [*Gastroenterology*] (DAVI)
IC................ Internal Circumference (SAUS)
IC................ Internal Classification (SAUS)
IC................ Internal Clock (SAUS)
IC................ Internal Code (SAUS)
IC................ Internal Combustion
IC................ Internal Communications (CAAL)
IC................ Internal Computer (SAUS)
IC................ Internal Conjugate [*Diameter*] [*Gynecology*] (DAVI)
IC................ Internal Connection [*Electronics*]
IC................ Internal Control [*Business term*] (EBF)
IC................ Internal Conversion [*Nuclear science*] (OA)
IC................ Internal Coupling (GART)
IC................ International Center (SAUS)
IC................ International Classification (DAVI)
IC................ International Code (SAUS)
IC................ International Colloquium (SAUS)
IC................ International Conference
IC................ International Control
IC................ International Cooperation
IC................ International Corp. [*Generic term*]
IC................ International Corporation (SAUO)
IC................ International Corps (SAUO)
IC................ International Council (SAUO)
IC................ International Court of Justice (SAUO)
IC................ International Curator Resources [*Vancouver Stock Exchange symbol*]
IC................ Internet Commerce
IC................ Internment Camp
IC................ Internuclear Company
IC................ Internuclear Company, Inc. (SAUO)
IC................ Interpretation Canada [*Federal agency*]
IC................ Interpreter Code (SAUS)
IC................ Interrogation Coding (SAUS)
IC................ Interrupt Controller (VLIE)
IC................ Interrupted Current (SAUS)
IC................ Interrupting Capacity (IAA)
IC................ Interruption Code (IAA)
IC................ Interspecies Communication [*An association*] (EA)
IC................ Interstate Club (EA)
IC................ Interstate Commerce Reports [*A publication*] (DLA)
IC................ Interstitial Cells [*Histology*]
IC................ Interstitial Cyst [*Pulmonary medicine*]
IC................ Interstitial Cystitis [*Nephrology*]
IC................ Intervalve Coupling (DEN)
IC................ Intracapsular (CPH)
IC................ Intracardiac [*Medicine*]
IC................ Intracarotid [*Medicine*] (MAE)
IC................ Intracavitary [*Medicine*]
IC................ Intracellular
IC................ Intracerebral [*Medicine*]
ic................ Intracerebroventricular [*Also, ICTV, ICV*] [*Brain anatomy*]
IC................ Intracisternal [*Neruology*] (DAVI)
IC................ Intracloud [*Climatology*]
IC................ Intracoronary [*Cardiology*]
IC................ Intracranial
ic................ intracutan (SAUS)
IC................ Intracutaneous [*Medicine*]
IC................ Intraductal Carcinoma [*Medicine*] (MEDA)
ic................ intrakutan (SAUS)
IC................ Intrapleural Catheter [*Medicine*] (DAVI)
IC................ Invalid Character (SAUS)
IC................ Invalid Code (SAUS)
IC................ Inventory Control (SAUS)
IC................ Inventory Count (SAUS)
IC................ Inverse Check
IC................ Inverse Conduction (SAUS)
IC................ Investement Council (AAEL)
IC................ Investment Casting (SAUS)
IC................ Investment Commission (SAUS)
IC................ Investment Committee (SAUS)
IC................ Investment Company
IC................ Investment Council (SAUO)
IC................ Investment Counselor (MHDB)
IC................ Investment Tax Credit
IC................ Investors Chronicle (SAUO)
IC................ Invited Contractor
IC................ Iola College (SAUO)
IC................ Iona College (SAUO)
IC................ Ion Chamber [*Nucleonics*]
IC................ Ion Chromatography
IC................ Ion Counter (SAUS)
IC................ Ionization Chamber
IC................ Iowa Conference (PSS)
I-C................ Iran-Contra scandal (SAUS)
IC................ Irish Constitution (ADA)
IC................ Iron City [*Pittsburgh, PA*]
IC................ Ironclad (MIST)
IC................ Iron Cokes (SAUS)
I-C................ Iron-Constantant (SAUS)
IC................ Iron Curtain (SAUS)
IC................ Irregular Cavalry [*British military*] (DMA)
IC................ Irrigation Consultant (SAUS)
IC................ Irritable Colon [*Medicine*]
IC................ Ischemic Cardiomyopathy [*Cardiology*]
IC................ Ischemic Contracture [*Hematology*]
IC................ I See [*Computer hacker terminology*]
IC................ Islamic Congress
IC................ Islamic Culture (journ.) (SAUS)
IC................ Islamic Investment Company (SAUO)
IC................ Island of Calleja [*Neuroanatomy*]
IC................ Islet Cells [*of the pancreas*] [*Endocrinology*]
IC................ Isolation Condenser (NRCH)
IC................ Isovolumic Contraction [*Medicine*] (DMAA)
IC................ Itaska College (SAUO)
IC................ Itawamba College (SAUO)
IC................ Item Code (SAUS)
IC................ Ithaca College (SAUO)
IC................ Izquierda Cristiana [*Christian Left*] [*Chile*] [*Political party*] (EY)
IC................ Jesus [*First and third letters of His name in Greek*]
IC................ Untermetallic Compound [*Chemistry*] (ODA)
IC................ Vietnamese Sisters Incarnational Consecration (TOCD)
IC................ Imum Coeli [*Lowest point on the ecliptic below the horizon*] [*Astrology*] (ODA)
IC1................ Interior Communications Electrician, First Class [*Navy rating*]
IC2................ Interior Communications Electrician, Second Class [*Navy rating*]
IC3................ Improved Closed-Cycle Cooler (SAUS)
IC3................ Integrated Combat Command and Control [*Army*]
IC3................ Intelligent Command, Control and Communications (SAUS)
IC3................ Interior Communications Electrician, Third Class [*Navy rating*]
IC3CP................ Intertheater C3 COMSEC Package (SAUO)
IC3I................ Improved Command, Control, Communications and Intelligence (SAUS)
IC3I................ Integrated C3I (SAUS)
IC4A................ Intercollegiate Association of Amateur Athletes of America [*Also, IAAAA, ICAAAA*]
IC50................ Inhibition of Protein Content, 50% [*Biochemistry*]
ICA................ Art Institute of Chicago, Chicago, IL [*Library symbol*] [*Library of Congress*] (LCLS)
ICA................ Aurora College, Aurora, IL [*OCLC symbol*] (OCLC)
ICa................ Cairo Public Library, Cairo, IL [*Library symbol*] [*Library of Congress*] (LCLS)
ICA................ Empresas ICA Sociedad ADS [*NYSE symbol*] (SPSG)
ICA................ Ica [*Peru*] [*Seismograph station code, US Geological Survey*] (SEIS)

ICA.............. Icabaru [*Venezuela*] [*Airport symbol*] (AD)
ICA.............. Icaro [*Italy*] [*FAA designator*] (FAAC)
ICA.............. Idaho Cattle Association (SRA)
ICA.............. Idaho Counseling Association (SEAT)
ICA.............. Ignition Control Additive (IAA)
ICA.............. Illinois Coal Association (SRA)
ICA.............. Illinois Correctional Association (SAUO)
ICA.............. Illinois Cosmetology Association (SRA)
ICA.............. Image Component Attribute (SAUS)
ICA.............. Immediate Constituent Analyzer [*Computer science*] (DIT)
ICA.............. Immunocytochemical Analysis
ICA.............. Immunological Chromatographic Analysis
ICA.............. Imperial Corporation of America (SAUO)
ICA.............. Imperial Savings Association (SAUO)
ICA.............. In-Circuit Analyzer (SAUS)
ICA.............. Inclinator Company of America (SAUO)
ICA.............. Independent Cattlemen's Association of Texas (SRA)
ICA.............. Independent Colleges of Arkansas (SRA)
ICA.............. Independent Column Approximation (ARMP)
ICA.............. Independent Computing Architecture
ICA.............. Independent Console Architecture (SAUS)
ICA.............. Independent Cost Analysis (AAGC)
ICA.............. Independent Cost Assessment (MCD)
ICA.............. Index of Competitive Ability (PDAA)
ICA.............. Indiana Correctional Association (SAUO)
ICA.............. Indian Community Action
ICA.............. Indigenous Communications Association (EA)
ICA.............. Individual Combat Actions [*Army*]
ICA.............. Indoor Cricket Association (SAUO)
ICA.............. Industrial Caterers Association (SAUS)
ICA.............. Industrial Catering Association [*British*]
ICA.............. Industrial Clean Air Corporation (SAUO)
ICA.............. Industrial Communications Agency (SAUS)
ICA.............. Industrial Communications Association (HGAA)
ICA.............. Industrial Conciliation Act (SAUO)
ICA.............. Industrial Cooperative Association (EA)
ICA.............. Industrial Coordination Act (SAUS)
ICA.............. Industrial Copartnership Association (SAUO)
ICA.............. Industry and Commerce Association of South Dakota (SRA)
ICA.............. Information Centre for Aeronautics (SAUO)
ICA.............. Information Company of America (SAUO)
ICA.............. Information Connection Architecture (SAUS)
ICA.............. Information Content Architecture (SAUS)
ICA.............. Initial Cruise Altitude
ICA.............. Injector Cam Actuation [*Diesel engines*]
ICA.............. Inner Circle of Advocates [*Tucson, AZ*] (EA)
ICA.............. Institut Canadien d'Acupuncture [*Canadian Acupuncture Institute*]
ICA.............. Institut Canadien des Actuaires [*Canadian Institute of Actuaries*]
ICA.............. Institut Culturel Africain [*African Cultural Institute*] (EAIO)
ICA.............. Institute for Cell Analysis [*University of Miami*] [*Research center*] (RCD)
ICA.............. Institute of Canadian Advertising (SAUS)
ICA.............. Institute of Chartered Accountants (SAUO)
ICA.............. Institute of Chartered Accountants in England and Wales (BI)
ICA.............. Institute of Clinical Analysis
ICA.............. Institute of Company Accountants [*British*] (DAS)
ICA.............. Institute of Consumer Advisers [*British*] (DBA)
ICA.............. Institute of Contemporary Art (SAUO)
ICA.............. Institute of Contemporary Arts [*British*]
ICA.............. Institute of Cost Analysis [*Later, SCEA*] (EA)
ICA.............. Institute of Criminal Anthropology (SAUO)
ICA.............. Institute of Cultural Affairs (EA)
ICA.............. Instruction Change Authorization (SAUS)
ICA.............. Instrumentation Control and Automation [*Water industry*] [*British*]
ICA.............. Instrument Compressed Air (AAG)
ICA.............. Instrument Control and Automation
ICA.............. Insurance Council of Australia (SAUO)
ICA.............. Integrated Chameleon Architecture (SAUS)
ICA.............. Integrated Circuit Amplifier (SAUS)
ICA.............. Integrated Circuit Array
ICA.............. Integrated Color Analysis (QUAC)
ICA.............. Integrated Colour Analysis (SAUS)
ICA.............. Integrated Communications Adapter (MCD)
ICA.............. Integrated Communications Architecture [*Navy*] (DOMA)
ICA.............. Integrated Conformal Array
ICA.............. Integrated Cost Accounting
ICA.............. Integration Change Allowance (MCD)
ICA.............. Intelligence Collection Area [*Military*] (NATG)
ICA.............. Intelligent Channels Architecture (SAUS)
ICA.............. Intelligent Communication Adapter (SAUS)
ICA.............. Intelligent Communications Adapter [*Computer hardware*] (PCM)
ICA.............. Intelligent Console Architecture (PCM)
ICA.............. Interapplication Communication Architecture [*Computer science*] (BTTJ)
ICA.............. Interbank Card Association [*Mastercard International*] (EA)
ICA.............. Inter City Airlines [*British*]
ICA.............. Intercity Airlines (SAUO)
ICA.............. Intercompany Agreement (IAA)
ICA.............. Intercomputer Adapter
ICA.............. Intercontinental Airways (SAUO)
ICA.............. Intercountry Adoption (STED)
ICA.............. Intercultural Association (SAUO)
ICA.............. Inter-Cultural Cooperation Association (SAUO)
ICA.............. Interface Connector Assembly (SAUS)
ICA.............. Interface Control Agreement
ICA.............. Intergovernmental Council for ADP [*Automatic Data Processing*]
ICA.............. Inter-governmental Council for Automatic data processing (SAUS)
ICA.............. Interlochen Center for the Arts (EA)
ICA.............. Intermediate Care Area (STED)
ICA.............. Intermountain College Association (AEBS)
ICA.............. Intermuseum Conservation Association (EA)
ICA.............. Internal Carotid Artery [*Anatomy*]
ICA.............. International Cancer Alliance (SAUS)
ICA.............. International Caribbean Airways (SAUO)
ICA.............. International Cartographic Assoc. (SAUS)
ICA.............. International Cartographic Association [*Australia*] (EA)
ICA.............. International Carwash Association (EA)
ICA.............. International Caterers Association [*Defunct*] (EA)
ICA.............. International Catholic Auxiliaries (EA)
ICA.............. International Center for Aquaculture [*Auburn University*] [*Research center*] (RCD)
ICA.............. International Central Archive (SAUS)
ICA.............. International Ceramic Association (EA)
ICA.............. International Chefs Association (SAUO)
ICA.............. International Chianina Association (EAIO)
ICA.............. International Chiropractors Association (EA)
ICA.............. International Christian Aid (SAUS)
ICA.............. International Civil Aircraft (SAUO)
ICA.............. International Claim Association [*Rock Island, IL*] (EA)
ICA.............. International Clarinet Association (NTPA)
ICA.............. International Classified Advertising (SAUO)
ICA.............. International Coffee Agreement [*Signed September, 1962*]
ICA.............. International College of Angiology (EA)
ICA.............. International Colonization Association (SAUO)
ICA.............. International Color Authority (SAUS)
ICA.............. International Commercial Arbitration (BARN)
ICA.............. International Commission on Acoustics [*Aachen, Federal Republic of Germany*] (EAIO)
ICA.............. International Committee of Aerospace Activities (SAUO)
ICA.............. International Commodities (or Commodity) Agreement (SAUO)
ICA.............. International Commodity Agreement
ICA.............. International Common Access (SAUS)
ICA.............. International Communication Agency [*Also, USICA*] [*Formerly called BECA and USIA, it later became known again as USIA*]
ICA.............. International Communication Association (EA)
ICA.............. International Communications Association (EA)
ICA.............. International Comodities Agreement (SAUS)
ICA.............. International Computer Association
ICA.............. International Confederation of Accordionists [*Vienna, Austria*] (EA)
ICA.............. International Confederation of Agriculture (SAUO)
ICA.............. International Confederation of Associations (SAUO)
ICA.............. International Conference of Administrators of Residential Centers for Youth [*Defunct*] (EA)
ICA.............. International Congress of Acarology
ICA.............. International Congress of Accountants
ICA.............. International Congress of Acoustics (SAUO)
ICA.............. International Congress of Africanists [*Lagos, Nigeria*] (EAIO)
ICA.............. International Congress of African Studies (EAIO)
ICA.............. International Congress of Americanists [*Manchester, England*] (EA)
ICA.............. International Congress of Archivists (SAUO)
ICA.............. International Congress on Acoustics (SAUS)
ICA.............. International Contractors Association (SAUO)
ICA.............. International Control Agency (SAUO)
ICA.............. International Co-op Alliance (SAUS)
ICA.............. International Cooperarive Alliance (SAUS)
ICA.............. International Cooperation Administration [*Later, Agency for International Development*]
ICA.............. International Cooperation Administration, Dept. of State (SAUS)
ICA.............. International Cooperative Administration (SAUO)
ICA.............. International Co-Operative Alliance [*Grand-Saconnex, Switzerland*] (EA)
ICA.............. International Cooperative Association (SAUO)
ICA.............. International Copper Association [*British*] (IRC)
ICA.............. International Council for Aquaculture (SAUO)
ICA.............. International Council on Archives [*UNESCO*] (EA)
ICA.............. International Court of Arbitration (SAUS)
ICA.............. International Credit Association [*St. Louis, MO*] (EA)
ICA.............. International Cultural Association (SAUO)
ICA.............. International Cyclist Association (SAUO)
ICA.............. Interrupt Communications Area (VLIE)
ICA.............. Interstate Commerce Act [*1887*]
ICA.............. Interstitial Cystitis Association of America (NRGU)
ICA.............. Intra-application Communications Area (SAUO)
ICA.............. Intracranial Anatomy [*Medicine*] (STED)
ICA.............. Intracranial Aneurysm [*Medicine*]
ICA.............. Invalid Care Allowance [*British*]
ICA.............. Inventors Club of America (SAUS)
ICA.............. Inventors Clubs of America (EA)
ICA.............. Inventory Control Area (SAUS)
ICA.............. Investigate and Corrective Action (SAUS)
ICA.............. Investigative and Corrective Action (KSC)
ICA.............. Investment Canada Act
ICA.............. Investment Company Act [*1940*]
ICA.............. Investment Company of America (SAUO)
iCa.............. Ionized Calcium (STED)
ICA.............. Ionized Calcium Analyzer
ICA.............. Iowa Cattlemen's Association (SRA)
ICA.............. Iowa Code, Annotated [*A publication*] (DLA)
ICA.............. Iowa Corrections Association (SAUO)
ICA.............. Irish Countrywomen's Association (BI)

ICA............. Iron Caulkers' Association [*A union*] [*British*]
ICA............. Islamic Cement Association (SAUO)
ICA............. Islet Cell Antibody [*Immunology*]
ICA............. Islet Cell Autoantibodies (SAUS)
ICA............. Isocyanic Acid (SAUS)
ICA............. Isolated Channel Architecture (SAUS)
ICA............. Isolated Code Announcement (SAUS)
ICA............. Isotropically Conductive Adhesive [*Electronics*] (AAEL)
ICA............. Italian Charities of America (EA)
ICA............. Item Change Analysis (KSC)
ICA............. Item Control Area (NRCH)
ICA............. Jewish Colonisation Association (SAUO)
ICAA............ Iceland Civial Aviation Agency (SAUS)
ICAA............ Indian Church Aid [*British*] (BI)
ICAA............ Information Centre for Aeronautics (SAUS)
ICAA............ Inspector under Cruelty to Animals Act (SAUO)
ICAA............ Institut Canadien des Affaires Africaines [*Canadian Institute of African Affairs*]
ICAA............ Institute of Chartered Accountants in/of Australia (SAUS)
ICAA............ Institute of Chartered Accountants of Alberta (SAUS)
ICAA............ Institute of Chartered Accountants of Australia (SAUO)
ICAA............ Insulation Contractors Association of America (EA)
ICAA............ Integrated Cost Accounting Application
ICAA............ Internal Carotid Artery Aneurysm [*Medicine*] (MELL)
ICAA............ International Call Areas Award (SAUS)
ICAA............ International Christian Accrediting Association (EA)
ICAA............ International Civil Airports Association [*Orly, France*] (EAIO)
ICAA............ International Civil Aviation Authority [*Database originator*] [*Canada*] (NITA)
ICAA............ International Committee for Museums of Applied Arts (SAUO)
ICAA............ International Committee of Aerospace Activities (SAUS)
ICAA............ International Committee on Aerospace Activities (SAUO)
ICAA............ International Committee on Arctic Arboviruses
ICAA............ International Council of Accrediting Agencies [*Australia*] (EAIO)
ICAA............ International Council on Alcohol and Addictions [*Switzerland*]
ICAA............ Invalid Children's Aid Association [*London*]
ICAA............ Investment Counsel Association of America (EA)
ICAAAA........ Intercollegiate Association of Amateur Athletes of America [*Also, IAAAA, IC4A*] (EA)
ICAAC.......... Interscience Conference on Antimicrobial Agents and Chemotherapy
ICAAE.......... International Center for Aquaculture and Aquatic Environments (GVA)
ICAA European Community Bureau... International Civil Airports Association European Community Bureau (SAUO)
ICAAP.......... International Consortium for the Advancement of Academic Publication
ICAAS.......... Integrated Control and Avionics for Air Superiority (MCD)
ICAAS.......... Integrated Controls/Avionics for Air Superiority (SAUO)
ICAAS.......... International Campaign Against Apartheid in Sports (SAUO)
ICAB............ International Cargo Advisory Bureau
ICAB............ International Council Against Bullfighting (EA)
ICAb............ Islet Cell Antibody (STED)
ICABA.......... International Campaign Against Banking on Apartheid (EAIO)
ICABF.......... American Bar Foundation, Chicago, IL [*Library symbol*] [*Library of Congress*] (LCLS)
ICAC............ American College of Surgeons, Chicago, IL [*Library symbol*] [*Library of Congress*] (LCLS)
ICAC............ Imperial Communications Advisory Committee (SAUO)
ICAC............ Improved Constant Altitude Control (SAUS)
ICAC............ Independent College Assistance Center (EA)
ICAC............ Independent Commission Against Corruption
ICAC............ Indiana Collegiate Athletic Conference (PSS)
ICAC............ Information Centre Advisory Committee (SAUS)
ICAC............ Institute for/of Chartered Accountants of the Caribbean (SAUO)
ICAC............ Institute of Clean Air Companies (NTPA)
ICAC............ Instrumentation Calibration and Checkout (IAA)
ICAC............ International Civil Aviation Committee (SAUO)
ICAC............ International Committee for Accounting Co-Operation
ICAC............ International Committee of Anti-Militarist Clergymen (SAUO)
ICAC............ International Conference on Analytical Chemistry (SAUS)
ICAC............ International Cotton Advisory Committee (EA)
ICAC............ Irish Continuity Army Council (SAUO)
ICACAC........ International Collegiate Automotive Clean Air Competition (SAUS)
ICACCP........ International Commission Against Concentration Camp Practices [*Brussels, Belgium*] [*Defunct*] (EAIO)
ICACE.......... Intelligence Center, Allied Command Europe (SAUS)
ICACET........ International Cartographic Association Committee on Training (SAUO)
ICACGP........ International Commission on Atmospheric Chemistry and Global Pollution (SAUO)
ICACM.......... Associated Colleges of the Midwest, Periodical Bank, Chicago, IL [*Library symbol*] [*Library of Congress*] (LCLS)
ICACM.......... International Conference on Advances in Composite Materials (SAUS)
ICACMu........ American Conservatory of Music, Chicago, IL [*Library symbol*] [*Library of Congress*] (LCLS)
ICAD............ Individual Chemical Agent Detector (ACAE)
ICAD............ Individual Concern and Deficiency [*Environmental science*] (COE)
ICAD............ Inhibitor of Caspase-Activated Deoxyribonuclease [*Biochemistry*]
ICAD............ Institute of Cultural Action for Development (SAUO)
ICAD............ Integrated Computer-Aided Design (SAUS)
ICAD............ Integrated Conservation and Development (SAUO)
ICAD............ Integrated Control and Display
ICAD............ Integrated Controls and Displays (SAUS)
ICAD............ Integrated Cover and Deception (SAUS)
ICAD............ Intelligent Computer-Aided Design
ICAD............ Interactive Computer Aided Design (ACAE)
ICAD............ International Committee for Automobile Documentation
ICAD............ International Committee on Automobile Documentation (SAUS)
ICAD............ International Council of Amateur Dancers (SAUO)
ICADA.......... American Dental Association, Chicago, IL [*Library symbol*] [*Library of Congress*] (LCLS)
ICADD.......... International Committee for Accessible Document Design (SAUO)
ICADE.......... Interactive Computer-Aided Design Evaluation
ICADEM........ Integrated Computer-Aided Design, Engineering and Manufacturing (SAUS)
ICADIS......... Instituto Centroamericano de Documentacion y Investigacion Social (EA)
ICADS.......... Integrated Control and Display System (SAUS)
ICADS.......... Integrated Correlation and Display System [*Air Force*] (DOMA)
ICADS.......... Integrated Cover and Deception Systems [*Military*] (MCD)
ICADS.......... Interdata Computer Aided Drafting System (SAUO)
ICADS.......... Interdata Computer-Aided Drafting System (SAUS)
ICADTS........ International Committee on Alcohol, Drugs, and Traffic Safety [*Linkoping, Sweden*] (EA)
ICADTS........ International Council on Alcohol, Drugs and Traffic Safety (SAUO)
ICAE............ Insurance Consumer Affairs Exchange (NTPA)
ICAE............ Integrated Communications Adapter Extended (BUR)
ICAE............ Integrated Communications Adapter Extension (SAUS)
ICAE............ International Centre for Art Education (EAIO)
ICAE............ International Commission of Agricultural Engineering
ICAE............ International Commission on Agricultural Engineering (SAUS)
ICAE............ International Commission on Atmospheric Electricity (EA)
ICAE............ International Conference of Agricultural Economists [*Later, IAAE*]
ICAE............ International Control of Atomic Energy (SAUO)
ICAE............ International Council for Adult Education [*Toronto, ON*] (EAIO)
ICAE............ United States Army, Corps of Engineers, Chicago, IL [*Library symbol*] [*Library of Congress*] (LCLS)
ICAEC.......... International Confederation of Associations of Experts and Consultants [*Paris, France*] (EA)
ICAED.......... Inter-African Advisory Committee on Epizootic Diseases (SAUO)
ICAEL.......... Intersocial Commission for the Accreditation of Echocardiography Laboratories (ADWA)
ICAEL.......... Intersocietal Commission for the Accreditation of Echocardiography Laboratories (SAUO)
ICAEO.......... International Center for Athletic and Educational Opportunities (EA)
ICAER.......... Individual Clothing and Equipment Record (SAUO)
ICAES.......... International Congress of Anthropological and Ethnological Sciences (SAUO)
ICAESD........ International Center for African Economic and Social Documentation (SAUO)
ICA European Community Bureau... International Civil Airports Association European Community Bureau (SAUO)
ICAEW.......... Institute of Chartered Accountants in England and Wales
ICAF............ Industrial College of the Armed Forces (ADWA)
ICAF............ Internal Carotid Artery Flow [*Medicine*] (STED)
ICAF............ International Clearinghouse on Adolescent Fertility (SAUO)
ICAF............ International Committee on Aeronautical Fatigue [*Delft University of Technology*] [*Netherlands*] (EAIO)
ICAF............ International Congress of African Studies (SAUO)
ICAF............ International Contemporary Art Fair [*London, England*]
ICAFFH........ International Commission for the Anthropology of Food and Food Habits (SAUO)
ICAFFH........ International Committee for the Anthropology of Food and Food Habits (SAUO)
ICAFI........... International Commission of Agriculture and Food Industries (SAUO)
ICAFI........... International Commission on Agriculture and Food Industries (SAUS)
ICAG............ Althemer & Gray, Chicago, IL [*Library symbol*] [*Library of Congress*] (LCLS)
ICAH............ American Hospital Association, Chicago, IL [*Library symbol*] [*Library of Congress*] (LCLS)
ICah............ Cahokia Public Library, Cahokia, IL [*Library symbol*] [*Library of Congress*] (LCLS)
ICAHM.......... International Committee on Archaeological Heritage Management (QUAC)
ICahP.......... Parks College of Saint Louis University, Cahokia, IL [*Library symbol*] [*Library of Congress*] (LCLS)
ICahSD........ Cahokia Community Unit School District 187, Cahokia, IL [*Library symbol*] [*Library of Congress*] (LCLS)
ICAI............. American Institute of Baking, Chicago, IL [*Library symbol*] [*Library of Congress*] (LCLS)
ICAI............. Image Classification Artificial Intelligence (SAUS)
ICAI............. Institut Canadien des Affaires Internationales [*Canadian Institute of International Affairs*]
ICAI............. Institute for Computer-Assisted Information (SAUS)
ICAI............. Institute for Computer-Assisted Instruction (SAUS)
ICAI............. Institute of Chartered Accountants in Ireland (EAIO)
ICAI............. Institute of Cultural Affairs International (EA)
ICAI............. Intelligent Computer-Aided Instruction (IDAI)
ICAI............. Intelligent Computer-Assisted Instruction
ICAI............. Intelligent Computer-Assisted Instructional System (SAUS)
ICAI............. International Commission for Agricultural and Food Industries (SAUO)
ICAI............. International Commission for Agricultural Industries
ICAI............. International Commission of Agricultural Industries (SAUO)
ICAI............. International Committee for Aid to Intellectuals (SAUO)
ICAI............. International Conference on Artificial Intelligence (SAUS)
ICAIE........... International Committee Against Involuntary Exile (EA)
ICAIF........... International Computer-Assisted Instruction Facility (AEBS)
ICAIR........... Interdisciplinary Planning and Information Research (SAUO)
ICAIT........... International Conference on Advanced Information Technology (SAUS)
ICAITI......... Central American Research Institute for Industrial Technology (SAUS)

ICAITI.......... Instituto Centroamericano de Investigacion y Tecnologia Industrial [*Central American Institute of Research and Industrial Technology*] [*Guatemala*] [*Research center*] (IRC)
ICAJ.......... Institut Canadien d'Administration de la Justice (AC)
ICAK.......... International College of Applied Kinesiology (EA)
ICaL.......... Cairo Public Library, Cairo, IL [*Library symbol*] [*Library of Congress*] (LCLS)
ICAL.......... Initiative on Communication Arts for Children (AIE)
ICAL.......... International Combustion Australia Limited (SAUO)
ICALA.......... American Library Association, Chicago, IL [*Library symbol*] [*Library of Congress*] (LCLS)
ICALEO.......... International Congress on Applications of Lasers and Electro-Optics [*Laser Institute of America*]
ICALP.......... International Colloquium on Automata (SAUS)
ICALP.......... International Colloquium on Automata, Languages and Programming (SAUO)
ICALPE.......... International Centre for Alpine Environments [*Chambery, France*] (CARB)
ICALU.......... International Confederation of Arab Labour Unions
ICAM.......... American Medical Association, Chicago, IL [*Library symbol*] [*Library of Congress*] (LCLS)
I-CAM.......... Improved Chemical Agent Monitor (SAUS)
ICAM.......... Improved Cobra Agility and Maneuverability [*Military*] (MCD)
ICAM.......... Institute of Corn and Agricultural Merchants (SAUS)
ICAM.......... Institute of Corn and Agricultural Merchants Ltd. [*British*] (BI)
ICAM.......... Integrated Coastal Area Management (SAUS)
ICAM.......... Integrated Communications Access Method [*Computer science*]
ICAM.......... Integrated Computer-Aided Manufacturing (IEEE)
ICAM.......... Integrated Computer-Aided Manufacturing Program (SAUO)
ICAM.......... Interactive Cartographic Automated Mapping (SAUS)
ICAM.......... Intercellular Adhesion Molecule [*Biochemistry*]
ICAM.......... International Center for the Advancement of Management Education (SAUS)
ICAM.......... International Civil Aircraft Markings (ACAE)
ICAM.......... International Confederation of Architectural Museums [*Montreal, PQ*] (EAIO)
ICAM.......... International Conference on Advanced Materials (SAUS)
ICAM.......... International Conference on Arctic Margins (SAUO)
ICAM.......... Iowa Collaborative Assessment Modules
ICAM-1.......... Intercellular Adhesion Molecule-1 (SAUS)
ICAMA.......... Interstate Compact on Adoption and Medical Assistance [*Public human service program*] (PHSD)
ICAMAS.......... International Center for Advanced Mediterranean Agronomic Studies [*FAO*]
ICAMAS.......... International Centre for Advanced Mediterranean Agronomic Studies (SAUO)
ICAMC.......... International Conference on Automatic Control of Mines and Collieries
ICAMC.......... International Conference on Automation of Mines and Collieries (SAUO)
ICAMCI.......... International Conference on the Application of Mini-and Micro-Computers in Information (SAUS)
ICAME.......... International Center for the Advancement of Management Education [*Stanford University*]
ICAME.......... International Commission on the Applications of the Mossbauer Effect (SAUO)
ICAME.......... International Committee on Application of Mossbauer Effect (SAUS)
ICAME.......... International Conference on the Applications of the Mossbauer Effect
ICAMI.......... International Committee Against Mental Illness (EA)
ICAMP.......... Integrated Computer Aided Manufacturing Program (ELAL)
ICAMP.......... Integrated Conventional Ammunition Maintenance Plan [*DoD*] (RDA)
ICAMPS.......... International Conference and Exhibition on Advances in Materials and Processes (SAUS)
ICAMQ.......... International Committee of Automation of Mines and Quarries [*Budapest, Hungary*] (EAIO)
ICAMQ.......... International Committee on Automation of Mines and Quarries (SAUS)
ICAMR.......... Interagency [*or Interdepartmental*] Committee for Applied Meteorological Research
ICAMR.......... Interdepartmental Committee for Applied Meteorological Research (USDC)
ICAMRS.......... International Civil Aviation Message Routing System
ICAMS.......... Industrial Central Atmosphere Monitoring System [*Perkin Elmer Corp.*] [*Computer controlled chemical detection system*] (NITA)
ICAMT.......... International Centre of Ancient and Modern Tapestry
ICAMT.......... International Committee for Architecture and Museum Techniques (SAUO)
ICAN.......... Individual Circuit Analysis [*Telecommunications*] (TEL)
ICAN.......... Individual Customer Access Network (SAUO)
ICAN.......... Iniciativa Canaria [*Spain*] [*Political party*] (EY)
ICAN.......... Institute of Chartered Accountants of Nigeria (SAUS)
ICAN.......... Insurance Consumer Action Network (SAUS)
ICAN.......... Inteactive Computer Aided of Norway (SAUS)
ICAN.......... Integrated Circuit Analysis [*Computer science*]
ICAN.......... Integrated Composite Analyzer [*Materials science*]
ICAN.......... Integrated Control of All Needs (SAUO)
I-CAN.......... Integrated Customer Access Network (SAUO)
ICAN.......... Interactive Computer Aids to Norway (SAUS)
ICAN.......... Interlibrary Cooperation & Networking [*Association of Specialized and Cooperative Library Agencies*] [*American Library Association*]
ICAN.......... Interlibrary Cooperation and Networking Section [*ASCLA*] (AL)
ICAN.......... International Cesarean Awareness Network [*Formerly Cesarean Prevention Movement (CPM)*] (PAZ)
ican.......... International Children's Anophthalmia Network (NRGU)
ICAN.......... International College of Applied Nutrition (EA)
ICAN.......... International Commission for Air Navigation
ICAN.......... International Committee of Air Navigation (SAUO)
ICAN.......... International Committee on Air Navigation (SAUS)
ICAN.......... International Convention for Air Navigation (SAUO)
ICAN.......... Invalid Children's Aid Nationwide [*British*] (EAIO)
ICAN.......... Iowa Computer-Assisted Network [*Iowa State Library*] [*Des Moines*] [*Information service or system*] (IID)
ICan.......... Parlin-Ingersoll Public Library, Canton, IL [*Library symbol*] [*Library of Congress*] (LCLS)
ICA/NCC.......... International Carwash Association/National Carwash Council [*Later, ICA*] (EA)
IC & C.......... Installation Calibration and Checkout (KSC)
IC & C.......... Instrumentation Calibration and Checkout (SAA)
IC & C.......... Invoice Cost and Charges [*Business term*]
IC and C.......... Invoice, Cost and Charges (SAUS)
IC & CY.......... Inns of Court and City Yeomanry [*Military unit*] [*British*]
IC&D.......... Installation, Checkout and Demonstration (ACAE)
IC&ER.......... Individual Clothing and Equipment Record (SAUO)
IC & FCD.......... Interior Communication and Fire Control Distribution (MSA)
IC & RFS.......... Indoor Citrus and Rare Fruit Society [*Defunct*] (EA)
IC&RR.......... Inventory Control and Requirements Review (SAUO)
IC & RR.......... Inventory Control and Requirements Review Board [*CNO*]
ICANN.......... Internet Corporation for Assigned Names and Numbers
ICANN.......... Internet Corporation of Assigned Names and Numbers
ICanS.......... Spoon River College, Canton, IL [*Library symbol*] [*Library of Congress*] (LCLS)
ICAO.......... American Osteopathic Association, Chicago, IL [*Library symbol*] [*Library of Congress*] (LCLS)
ICAO.......... Institute of Chartered Accountants of Ontario (SAUS)
ICAO.......... Internal Carotid Artery Occlusion [*Medicine*] (MAE)
ICAO.......... International Civil Aeronautics Organization (SAUS)
ICAO.......... International Civil Airlines Operation (SAUS)
ICAO.......... International Civil Aviation Organisation (or Organization) (SAUO)
ICAO.......... International Civil Aviation Organization [*Montreal, PQ*] [*United Nations*]
ICAOPA.......... International Council of Aircraft Owner and Pilot Associations (DI)
ICAP.......... Improved Capability [*for aircraft*] (MCD)
ICAP.......... Improved Cobra Armament Program [*Military*] (MCD)
ICAP.......... Increased Capability (SAUS)
ICAP.......... Independent Cinema Artists and Producers (EA)
ICAP.......... Indian Community Action Program (OICC)
ICAP.......... Inductively Coupled Argon Plasma [*Spectrometry*]
ICAP.......... Industrial Committee of Ammunition Producers (SAUS)
ICAP.......... Industrial Conversion Assistance Program (SAUS)
ICAP.......... Institute of Certified Ambulance Personnel [*British*] (BI)
ICAP.......... Instituto Centroamericano de Administracion Publica [*Central American Institute of Public Administration*] [*Costa Rica*]
ICAP.......... Integrated Circuit Application Program (ACAE)
ICAP.......... Integrated Computer-Aided Production (SAUS)
ICAP.......... Integrated Contractor Assessment Program (ACAE)
ICAP.......... Integrated Correction Action Plan [*Military*] (MCD)
ICAP.......... Integrated Criminal Apprehension Program
ICAP.......... Interactive Circuit Analysis Program (SAUS)
ICAP.......... Inter-American Committee for/of the Alliance for Progress (SAUS)
ICAP.......... Inter-American Committee for the Alliance for Progress [*Superseded by Permanent Executive Committee of the Inter-American Economic and Social Council*]
ICAP.......... Intermediate Communication Associative Processor [*Computer science*]
ICAP.......... Intermediate Course Applications Programming (SAUS)
ICAP.......... International Centre for the Application of Pesticides [*British*] (IRUK)
ICAP.......... International Circumpolar Arctic Ice Drilling Project (SAUO)
ICAP.......... International Civil Aviation Policy (SAUS)
ICAP.......... International Code Assessment and Applications Programme (HEAS)
ICAP.......... International Code of Advertising Practice (DI)
ICAP.......... International College Art Program [*Red Cross Youth*]
ICAP.......... International Committee of Architectural Photogrammetry
ICAP.......... International Conference on Antennas and Propagation (SAUO)
ICAP.......... International Conference on Atomic Physics (SAUS)
ICAP.......... International Congress of Applied Psychology (PDAA)
ICAP.......... International Flight Planning Procedures (SAUS)
ICAP.......... Internet Calendar Access Protocol (SAUS)
ICAP.......... Intracisternal A Particle (DB)
ICAP.......... Inventory for Client and Agency Planning (TES)
ICAPE.......... International Chemical and Petroleum Engineering Exhibition (SAUO)
ICAPES.......... Inductively Coupled Argon Plasma Emission Spectroscopy (MEC)
ICAPP.......... Ice core Circum-Arctic Paleoclimate Programme (SAUO)
ICAPP.......... Integrated Conventional Ammunition Procurement Plan
ICAPP.......... Intellectual Capital Partnership Program [*Georgia*]
ICAP Quarterly Review... Institute of Certified Ambulance Personnel Quarterly Review (journ.) (SAUS)
ICAPR.......... Interdepartmental Committee on Air Pollution Research [*British*]
ICAPR.......... International Communications Agency Procurement Regulation [*A publication*] (AAGC)
ICAPS.......... Integral Carrier ASW [*Antisubmarine Warfare*] Prediction System [*Marine science*] (MSC)
ICAPS.......... Integrated Carrier Acoustic Prediction System [*Navy*] (NVT)
ICAPS.......... Integrated Command Acoustic Prediction System (SAUO)
ICAPS.......... Integrated Command Anti-Submarine Warfare Precition System (SAUS)
ICAPS.......... Integrated Command ASW [*Antisubmarine Warfare*] Prediction System [*Navy*] (CAAL)
ICAPS.......... Intelligence Civic Actions Program [*Army*] (VNW)
ICAPS.......... Interactive California Agricultural Projection System (SAUO)
ICAPS.......... Internal Control Audit Planning Summary (AAGC)

ICAQUO........ Inventory of Contaminants in Aquatic Organisms [*Databank*] (NITA)
ICAR........ ICAR [*Interstate Cinderellans and Revenuers*] Educational Club (EA)
ICAR........ Indian Council for Agricultural Research
ICAR........ Indian Council for/of Agricultural Research (SAUO)
ICAR........ Indian Council of Agricultural Research (SAUS)
ICAR........ Inner Circle of American Revenuers (EA)
ICAR........ Institute for Conflict Analysis and Resolution [*George Mason University*] [*Research center*] (RCD)
ICAR........ Integrated Camera and Radiometer (SAUS)
ICAR........ Integrated Command Accounting and Reporting
ICAR........ Intercargo Corp. [*NASDAQ symbol*] (NQ)
ICAR........ Interface Control Action Request (NRCH)
I-CAR........ Inter-Industry Conference on Auto Collision Repair (EA)
ICAR........ Intermediate Car (TVEL)
ICAR........ Intermediate-Size Car (TRID)
ICAR........ International Cannabis Alliance for Reform (SAUO)
ICAR........ International Cannabis Alliance Reform (DI)
ICAR........ International Center for Action Research (SAUS)
ICAR........ International Centers for AIDS Research (SAUO)
ICAR........ International Collaboration in AIDS Research (SAUS)
ICAR........ International Committee Against Racism (SAUO)
ICAR........ International Conference on Advanced Robotics (SAUS)
ICAR........ International Congress on Animal Reproduction (GVA)
ICAR........ International Consultative Agency for Radiocommunications (SAUO)
ICAR........ International Cooperation in Aviation Research (SAUS)
ICAR........ Inventory of Canadian Agricultural Research (SAUS)
ICAR........ Inventory of Canadian Agri-Food Research [*Canandian Agricultural Research Council*] [*Information service or system*]
ICAR........ Investigation and Corrective Action Report (KSC)
ICAR........ Italian Car Registry (EA)
ICARA........ International Child Abduction Remedies Act [*1988*]
ICARA........ International Conference on Assistance for Refugees in Africa [*See also CIARA*] [*United Nations*] [*Geneva, Switzerland*] (EAIO)
ICARA........ International Conference on Assistance for/to Refugees in Africa (SAUO)
IC Arb Q........ Indian Council of Arbitration. Quarterly [*A publication*] (DLA)
ICarbS........ Southern Illinois University, Carbondale, IL [*Library symbol*] [*Library of Congress*] (LCLS)
i-card........ Intra-Cardiac/ial [*Medicine*] (EDAA)
ICARDA........ International Center for Agricultural Research in Dry Areas [*Syria*]
ICARDA........ International Centre for Agricultural Research in the Dry Areas (SAUS)
ICARDS........ Integrated Carrier [*or Command*] ASW Prediction System
ICARE........ Image Cartography Expert (SAUS)
ICARE........ International Center for the Advancement of Research and Education (SAUO)
ICARE........ International Center for the Advancement of Research Education (SAUS)
ICARE........ International Christian Aid Relief Enterprises [*Australia*]
ICARE........ International Council for Amateur Radio in Education (SAUO)
ICARES........ Institut International Catholique de Recherches Socio-Ecclesiales [*International Catholic Institute for Socio-Religious Research*] [*Later, FERES*]
ICARIS........ International Campaign Against Racism in Sport (SAUO)
ICarl........ Carlinville Public Library, Carlinville, IL [*Library symbol*] [*Library of Congress*] (LCLS)
ICarlB........ Blackburn College, Carlinville, IL [*Library symbol*] [*Library of Congress*] (LCLS)
ICarlMCD........ Macoupin Community District 1, Carlinville, IL [*Library symbol*] [*Library of Congress*] (LCLS)
ICarly........ Case-Halstead Library, Carlyle, IL [*Library symbol*] [*Library of Congress*] (LCLS)
ICarlyS........ Carlyle School, Carlyle, IL [*Library symbol*] [*Library of Congress*] (LCLS)
ICARMI........ International Council of the Architects of Historical Monuments (SAUO)
ICARMO........ International Council of the Architects of Historical Monuments
ICArmour........ Armour & Co., Chicago, IL [*Library symbol*] [*Library of Congress*] [*Obsolete*] (LCLS)
ICARP........ International Committee on Applied Research in Population (SAUO)
ICARP........ International Conference for Arctic Research Planning (SAUO)
ICarr........ Carrollton Public Library, Carrollton, IL [*Library symbol*] [*Library of Congress*] (LCLS)
ICarrCD........ Carrollton Community Unit, District 1, Carrollton, IL [*Library symbol*] [*Library of Congress*] (LCLS)
ICarSD........ Charleston Community Unit School District, Charleston, IL [*Library symbol*] [*Library of Congress*] (LCLS)
ICart........ Carthage Public Library, Carthage, IL [*Library symbol*] [*Library of Congress*] (LCLS)
ICARUS........ Image Correction and Registration Utility System (SAUS)
ICARUS........ Imaging Cosmic and Rare Underground Signal
ICARUS........ Index of Conservation and Analytical Records: Unified System [*Computer science*]
ICARUS........ Industrial Computer (SAUS)
ICARUS........ Industrial Computer Applications, Retrieval and Utility Systems Corp. (SAUO)
ICARUS........ Interagency Climate-Aerosol Radiative Uncertainties and Sensitivities (SAUS)
ICARUS........ Inter-Continental Aerospacecraft-Range Unlimited System
ICARUS........ Intercontinental Aerospacecraft-Range Unlimited System (SAUS)
Icarus........ International Journal of the Solar System (journ.) (SAUS)
ICARUS........ Inter-Urban Control and Roads Utilization Simulation (SAUO)
ICARVS........ Interplanetary Craft for Advanced Research in the Vicinity of the Sun (SAUS)
ICAS........ Acme Steel Co., Chicago, IL [*Library symbol*] [*Library of Congress*] (LCLS)
ICas........ Casey Township Library, Casey, IL [*Library symbol*] [*Library of Congress*] (LCLS)
ICAS........ Image Capture and Analysis System (SAUS)
ICAS........ Improved Cobra Armament System [*Military*] (MCD)
ICAS........ Independent Collision Avoidance System
ICAS........ Information Communication Assistance System (SAUO)
ICAS........ Instant Computer Arbitration Search [*Database*] [*Labor Relations Press*] [*Information service or system*] (CRD)
ICAS........ Institute for Central American Studies (SAUO)
ICAS........ Institute for Chartered Accountants in Scotland (SAUS)
ICAS........ Institute of Chartered Accountants in Scotland (SAUO)
ICAS........ Institute of Chartered Accountants of Saskatchewan (SAUS)
ICAS........ Institute of Chartered Accountants of Scotland (AIE)
ICAS........ Institute of Combined Arms and Support [*Fort Leavenworth, KS*] [*Army*]
ICAS........ Institute of Contemporary Asian Studies [*Monash University*] [*Australia*]
ICAS........ Integrated Circuit Applications Specifications (ADWA)
ICAS........ Integrated Component Assembly System (SAUS)
ICAS........ Integrated Condition Assessment System
ICAS........ Integrated Configuration Accounting System (SAUO)
ICAS........ Integrated Control and Avionics Air Superiority (SAUS)
ICAS........ Intel Communicating Applications Specifications (SAUO)
ICAS........ Intel Communications Amplifications Specification [*Interface*]
ICAS........ Interdepartmental Committee for Atmospheric Sciences [*Terminated, 1976*]
ICAS........ Interdepartmental Committee on Aerial Surveys (SAUS)
ICAS........ Interdepartmental Committee on Atmospheric Sciences (SAUS)
ICAS........ Interdepartmental Communication for Atmospheric Science (SAUS)
ICAS........ Interdepartment Council on Radio Propagation and Standards (NTCM)
ICAS........ Interface Control Action Sheet (DNAB)
ICAS........ Intermitted Commercial and Amateur Service (SAUS)
ICAS........ Intermittent Commercial and Amateur Service [*Radio*]
ICAS........ International Center for Asian Studies (SAUO)
ICAS........ International Computer Access System (SAUS)
ICAS........ International Conference on Atomic Spectroscopy (SAUO)
ICAS........ International Council of Aeronautical Sciences (SAUS)
ICAS........ International Council of Aerospace Sciences (SAUO)
ICAS........ International Council of Air Shows (EA)
ICAS........ International Council of Associations of Surfing (EA)
ICAS........ International Council of the Aeronautical Sciences
ICAS........ Interstate Council on the Problems of the Aral Sea (SAUO)
ICAS........ Inupiat Community of the Arctic Slope (SAUO)
ICAS........ Irish Cooperative Organisation Society (SAUO)
ICAS........ Isolated Children's Assistance Scheme
ICA-S........ School of the Art Institute of Chicago, Chicago, IL [*Library symbol*] [*Library of Congress*] (LCLS)
ICASA........ International Consortium for Application of Systems Approach to Agriculture (SAUO)
ICASALS........ International Center for Arid and Semi-Arid Land Studies [*Texas Technological University*]
ICASALS........ International Center (or Centre) for Arid and Semi-Arid Land Studies (SAUO)
ICASALS........ International Centre for Arid and Semi-Arid Land Studies (SAUS)
ICASB........ Iowa Council of Area School Bnards (SAUS)
ICASB........ Iowa Council of Area School Boards (SAUO)
ICASC........ Acme Steel Co., Chicago, IL [*Library symbol*] [*Library of Congress*] (LCLS)
ICASC........ International Contraception, Abortion, and Sterilization Campaign [*Later, WGNRR*] (EAIO)
ICASE........ Injection-Coupled Acoustic Stability Evaluation (MCD)
ICASE........ Institute for Computer Applications in Science and Engineering [*Universities Space Research Association*] [*Research center*] (RCD)
I-CASE........ Integrated Computer-Aided Software Engineering
ICASE........ International Council of Associations for Science Education [*See also FIAPS*] (EAIO)
ICASEL........ Institute for Commonwealth and American Studies and English Literature (SAUO)
ICASHS........ International Center for Advanced Study in the Health Sciences [*Medicine*] (EDAA)
ICASIS........ International Center for Arid and Semiarid Land Studies (SAUS)
ICASIS........ International Conference of African States on Insurance Supervision [*See also CICA*] [*Gabon*] (EAIO)
ICASO........ International Committee of Acquired Immunodeficiency Syndrome Service Organisations (DMAA)
ICASO........ International Council of AIDS Service Organizations (SAUO)
ICASS........ International Cooperative Administrative Support Services (SAUO)
ICasSD........ Casey Community Unit School District, Casey, IL [*Library symbol*] [*Library of Congress*] (LCLS)
ICASSI........ International Committee for Adlerian Summer Schools and Institutes (SAUO)
ICASSP........ International Conference on Acoustics, Speech and Signal Processing (SAUO)
ICAST........ International Center for Aerospace Science and Technology (SAUS)
ICAST........ International Conference on Amorphous Semiconductor Technology (SAUS)
ICasv........ Caseyville Public Library, Caseyville, IL [*Library symbol*] [*Library of Congress*] (LCLS)
ICASVR........ International Committee on Atmosphere-Soil-Vegetation Relations (CARB)

ICat .... Catlin Public Library, Catlin, IL [*Library symbol*] [*Library of Congress*] (LCLS)
ICAT .... In Commission, Active [*Vessel status*] [*Navy*] (DNAB)
ICAT .... Institute for Combat Arms and Tactics (SAUS)
I-CAT .... Intelligent Computer-Aided Troubleshooting
ICAT .... International Catastrophe Aversion Team (SAUS)
ICAT .... International Committee for the Coordination of Clinical Application and Teaching of Autogenic Therapy [*North Vancouver, BC*] (EAIO)
ICAT .... International Committee on Autogenic Therapy (SAUO)
ICAT .... International Convention of Amateurs in Television (SAUO)
ICATL .... International Council of Associations of Theological Libraries (EA)
ICATO .... Iran Civil Aviation Training Organization (SAUS)
ICATO .... Iranian Civil Aviation Training Organization (SAUO)
ICATS .... Intermediate Capacity Automated Telecommunications System [*Air Force*] (CET)
ICATS .... International Centre of Advanced Tourism Studies (SAUO)
ICATU .... International Confederation of Arab Trade Unions
ICATVT .... International Centre for Advanced Technical and Vocational Training [*British*]
ICA-USNC .... International Cartographic Association U.S. National Committee (SAUS)
ICA-USNC .... International Cartographic Association-U.S. National Committee (SAUO)
ICAV .... American Veterinary Medical Association, Chicago, IL [*Library symbol*] [*Library of Congress*] (LCLS)
ICAV .... Instantaneous Crankshaft Angular Velocity [*Engine engineering*]
I cav .... Intracavity [*Medicine*] (EDAA)
ICAV .... Intracavity [*or Intracavitary*] [*Medicine*]
ICAVE .... International Coalition Against Violent Entertainment (EA)
ICAVL .... Intersocietal Commission for the Accreditation Vascular Laboratories (ADWA)
ICAVS .... United States Army, Medical Department, Veterinary School, Chicago, IL [*Library symbol*] [*Library of Congress*] (LCLS)
ICAW .... International Conference on Automation in Warehousing (SAUO)
ICAWA .... Indo-Chinese Australian Women's Association [*Australia*]
ICAWS .... Improved Cannon Artillery Weapon System (ACAE)
ICB .... Barat College of the Sacred Heart, Lake Forest, IL [*OCLC symbol*] (OCLC)
ICB .... Icebird Airline Ltd. [*Iceland*] [*ICAO designator*] (FAAC)
ICB .... Image Capture Board [*Video monitor*] [*AT & T*] (BYTE)
ICB .... Incoming Call Barred [*Telecommunications*] (TEL)
ICB .... Indian Coffee Board (SAUO)
ICB .... Individual Case Basis (TEL)
ICB .... Industrial and Commercial Bank [*China*]
ICB .... Industrial Coordination Bureau (SAUO)
ICB .... Inertia Compensated Balance
ICB .... Information Collection Budget [*Office of Management and Budget*] (GFGA)
ICB .... Information Control Block (SAUS)
ICB .... Information Control Branch (SAUO)
ICB .... Initial Calibration Blank (SAUS)
ICB .... Inner-Core Boundary [*Geology*]
ICB .... Institute of Canadian Bankers (SAUS)
ICB .... Institute of Collective Bargaining (SAUS)
ICB .... Institute of Collective Bargaining and Group Relations (EA)
ICB .... Institute of Comparative Biology (BARN)
ICB .... Integrated Circuit Breadboard [*Electronics*] (IAA)
ICB .... Integrated Circuits Breadboard (SAUS)
ICB .... Integration Change Board [*NASA*]
ICB .... InterCapital Income Securities, Inc. [*NYSE symbol*] (SPSG)
ICB .... Intercostal Block [*Medicine*] (MELL)
ICB .... Interface Control Board (NRCH)
ICB .... Interference Calibration Blank (ABAC)
ICB .... Interim Change Bulletin (NASA)
ICB .... Interior Control Board
ICB .... Interlocking Concrete Block (SAUS)
ICB .... Intermediate Control Break (SAUS)
ICB .... Internal Common Bus [*Computer science*]
ICB .... Internal Coolant Bypass (SAUS)
ICB .... International Christian Broadcasters [*Defunct*] (EA)
ICB .... International City Bank (SAUO)
ICB .... International City Bank & Trust Co. (EFIS)
ICB .... International Commodity Bodies (JAGO)
ICB .... International Commodity Body (SAUO)
ICB .... International Competitive Bid (NATG)
ICB .... International Computer Bibliography [*A publication of National Computing Center*]
ICB .... International Conference of Benzol Producers (SAUO)
ICB .... International Congress of Biochemistry (SAUO)
ICB .... International Container Bureau [*Paris*]
ICB .... International Convention Bureau (SAUO)
ICB .... International Co-operative Bank (SAUO)
ICB .... International Co-operative Bulletin [*A publication*]
ICB .... International Credit Bank (SAUO)
ICB .... International Custom Brokers Ltd. (SAUO)
ICB .... Internet Citizens Band (SAUS)
ICB .... Interrupt Control Binary digit (SAUS)
ICB .... Interrupt Control Block (NASA)
ICB .... Interruption Control Block (SAUS)
ICB .... Interstate Computer Bank (SAUS)
ICB .... Intracerebral Bleeding [*Medicine*] (EDAA)
ICB .... Intracranial Bleeding [*Medicine*] (STED)
ICB .... Ionized Cluster Beam (SAUS)
ICB .... Isochromatid Breaks (SAUS)
ICB .... Ivory Coast Basin [*Geology*]
ICBA .... Independent Community Bankers of Alabama (TBD)
ICBA .... International Community of Booksellers' Associations [*Later, IBF*]
ICBA .... Israel Cattle Breeders Association (SAUO)
ICBAD .... Improved Chemical Biological Agent Decontaminant (ACAE)
ICBAH .... Booz, Allen & Hamilton, Inc., Chicago, IL [*Library symbol*] [*Library of Congress*] (LCLS)
ICBAM .... Interpersonal Communication Behavior Analysis Method (PDAA)
ICBAM .... Interpersonal Communication Behaviour Analysis Method (SAUS)
ICBB .... Ind Coope Burton Brewery [*British*]
ICBB .... International Commission for Bee Botany [*Later, ICPBR*] (EA)
ICBBA .... International Cornish Bantam Breeders' Association (EA)
ICBC .... Blue Cross Association, Chicago, IL [*Library symbol*] [*Library of Congress*] (LCLS)
ICBC .... IMAX Cargo Bay Camera (SAUS)
ICBC .... Inclined Cleated Belt Conveyor
ICBC .... Institute of Certified Business Counselors (EA)
ICBC .... Insurance Corporation of British Columbia
ICBC .... Interagency Committee an Black Contamination (SAUS)
ICBC .... Interagency Committee on Back Contamination [*Aerospace*]
ICBC .... International Cataloguing and Bibliographic Control [*Library science*] (TELE)
ICBC .... International Center for Biological Control [*University of California, Berkeley and Riverside*]
ICBC .... International Colorado Beetle Committee (SAUO)
ICBC .... International Commercial Bank of China [*Taiwan*]
ICBC .... International Committee for Biological Control (SAUS)
ICBCG .... Boston Consulting Group, Chicago, IL [*Library symbol*] [*Library of Congress*] (LCLS)
ICBCL .... Brook College, Chicago, IL [*Library symbol*] [*Library of Congress*] (LCLS)
ICBD .... Ice Core Data Bank (SAUO)
ICBD .... International Center for Brewing and Distilling (SAUS)
ICBD .... International Children's Book Day [*Australia*]
ICBD .... International Council of Ballroom Dancing [*British*] (EAIO)
ICBD .... Ionized Cluster Beam Deposition [*Coating technology*]
ICBE .... International Commission on Biological Effects (COE)
ICBEN .... International Commission on the Biological Effects of Noise (SAUO)
ICBF .... Beatrice Foods Co., Chicago, IL [*Library symbol*] [*Library of Congress*] (LCLS)
ICBF .... Inner Cortical Blood Flow [*Medicine*] (DMAA)
ICBG .... Idiopathic Calcification of Basal Ganglia [*Medicine*] (DMAA)
ICBG .... International Cooperative Biodiversity Groups (SAUS)
ICBI .... International Consumer Brands, Incorporated (SAUO)
ICBIF .... Inner City Business Improvement Forum
ICBK .... Intercontinental Bank [*NASDAQ symbol*] (SAG)
ICBK .... International Centrum voor Beurzen en Kongressen [*Belgium*] (EAIO)
ICBL .... Institute for Computer Based Learning (SAUS)
ICBL .... International Campus Book Link (SAUS)
ICBL .... International Conference on the Biology of Lipids (SAUO)
ICBLB .... International Committee for Breaking the Language Barrier
ICBM .... Bank Marketing Association, Chicago, IL [*Library symbol*] [*Library of Congress*] (LCLS)
ICBM .... Independent Community Bankers of Minnesota (TBD)
ICBM .... Institute for Chemistry and Biology of the Marine environment (SAUO)
ICBM .... Intercontinental Ballistic Missile
ICBM .... International Commission on the Biological Effects of Noise (SAUO)
ICBMS .... Intercontinental Ballistic Missile System
ICBMTMS .... Intercontinental Ballistic Missile Test Maintenance Squadron
ICBN .... International Code for Botanical Nomenclature (SAUS)
ICBN .... International Code for/of Botanical Nomenclature (SAUO)
ICBN .... International Code of Botanical Nomenclature
ICBN .... International Commission on the Biological Effects of Noise (GNE)
ICBN .... International Committee on Bacteriological Nomenclature (SAUO)
ICBo .... Bozzel & Jacobs Corp., Information Center, Chicago, IL [*Library symbol*] [*Library of Congress*] (LCLS)
ICBO .... International Conference of Building Officials (EA)
ICBO .... Interracial Council for Business Opportunities (SAUS)
ICBO .... Interracial Council for Business Opportunity [*New York, NY*] (EA)
ICBO ES .... International Conference of Building Officials Evaluation Services (SAUS)
ICBOSS .... Interactive Computer-Based Office Support System [*Military*] (MCD)
ICBP .... Intercompany Billing Price (SAUO)
ICBP .... International Committee for Bird Protection (SAUO)
ICBP .... International Conference of Benzol Producers (SAUO)
ICBP .... International Council for Bird Preservation [*Cambridge, England*] (EAIO)
icbp .... Intracellular Binding Proteins (SAUS)
ICBP .... Intracellular-Binding Proteins [*Medicine*]
ICBPA .... Insurance Company and Bank Purchasing Agents Association
ICBP(AS) .... International Council for Bird Protection (Australian Section)
IC-BPH .... Illinois Regional Library for the Blind and Physically Handicapped, Chicago Public Library, Chicago, IL [*Library symbol*] [*Library of Congress*] (LCLS)
ICBR .... Ice-Cuber
ICBR .... Increased Chromosomal Breakage Rate [*Medicine*] (DMAA)
ICBR .... Input Channel Buffer Register [*Computer science*] (IAA)
ICBR .... Institute for Child Behavior Research (IID)
ICBRSD .... International Council for Building Research, Studies and Documentation (SAUO)
ICBS .... Impulsive Classroom Behavior Scale (EDAC)
ICBS .... Incorporated Church Building Society [*British*]
ICBS .... Interconnected Business System
ICBS .... International Call-Boy Service (SAUO)

ICBS............ International Cigar Band Society [*Defunct*] (EA)
ICBS............ National Association of Blue Shield Plans [*Later, BSA*], Chicago, IL [*Library symbol*] [*Library of Congress*] (LCLS)
ICBT............ Intercontinental Ballistic Transport
ICBT............ Intercostobronchial Trunk [*Medicine*] (DAVI)
ICBT............ International Conference on Biodiversity and Tourism (SAUO)
ICBU............ Intensive Care Baby Unit (ROAS)
ICBU............ Irish Catholic Benevolent Union (SAUO)
ICBVI.......... Idaho Commission for the Blind and Visually Impaired (ROAS)
ICBW.......... I Could Be Wrong [*Online dialog*] (ROAS)
ICBWR........ Improved-Cycle Boiling-Water Reactor [*Nuclear energy*]
ICBY............ International Council on Books for Young People (SAUO)
ICC.............. Article 19 - International Centre on Censorship (EAIO)
ICC.............. Association Internationale de Chimie Cerealiere [*International Association for Cereal Chemistry*] [*Also, AICC*]
ICc.............. Calumet City Public Library, Calumet City, IL [*Library symbol*] [*Library of Congress*] (LCLS)
ICC.............. Calumet College, Whiting, IN [*OCLC symbol*] (OCLC)
ICC.............. Chief Interior Communications Electrician (SAUS)
ICC.............. Cook County Clerk's Office, Chicago, IL [*Library symbol*] [*Library of Congress*] (LCLS)
ICC.............. Ice Crystal Cloud
ICC.............. Ignition Control Compound (EDCT)
ICC.............. Illegal Code Combination (SAUS)
ICC.............. Illinois Cancer Council Comprehensive Cancer Center [*Research center*] (RCD)
ICC.............. Illinois Classical Conference (SAUS)
ICC.............. Image Converter Camera
ICC.............. Immunocompetent Cell [*Medicine*] (MAE)
ICC.............. Immunocytochemistry [*Immunology*]
ICC.............. Immunologically Competent Cell (QSUL)
ICC.............. Imperial Camel Corps [*British military*] (DMA)
ICC.............. Imperial Communication Committee (SAUO)
ICC.............. Imperial Communications [*World War II*]
ICC.............. Imperial Cricket Conference (SAUO)
ICC.............. Improved Command Center (SAUO)
ICC.............. Improved Contemporary Comparison (SAUS)
ICC.............. Inadequate Core Cooling [*Nuclear energy*] (NRCH)
ICC.............. Income Capital Certificate
ICC.............. Incoming Trunk Circuit (SAUS)
ICC.............. Independence Community College (SAUO)
ICC.............. Independent Channel Controller (SAUS)
ICC.............. Independent Communications Center (SAUO)
ICC.............. Independent Community Consultants (EA)
ICC.............. Index of Cranial Capacity [*Cladistics*]
ICC.............. Indiana Central College (SAUO)
ICC.............. Indiana Collegiate Conference (SAUS)
ICC.............. Indian Childhood Cirrhosis [*Medicine*] (MAE)
ICC.............. Indian Claims Commission [*Terminated, 1976*]
ICC.............. Indian Cryogenics Council (SAUO)
ICC.............. Indian Cultural Center [*Defunct*] (EA)
ICC.............. Individual Camouflage Cover (SAUS)
ICC.............. Individual Concealment Cover
ICC.............. Industrial and Commercial Company
ICC.............. Industrial Capacity Committee of the Production Council [*British*] [*World War II*]
ICC.............. Industrial Communication Council
ICC.............. Industrial Communications Council (SAUO)
ICC.............. Industrial Contract Cleaners (SAUO)
ICC.............. Industrial Control Center (NITA)
ICC.............. Infantry Combat Command (SAUS)
ICC.............. Inferior Colliculus [*Also, IC*] [*Brain anatomy*]
ICC.............. Infinity Color-Corrected System [*Optics*]
ICC.............. Information and Coordination Center (SAUO)
ICC.............. Information and Coordination Central
ICC.............. Information Center Complex [*ORNL*] (GRD)
ICC.............. Information Coding Classification (SAUS)
ICC.............. Information Commissioner of Canada (SAUS)
ICC.............. Information Control Center [*Military*] (IAA)
ICC.............. Information Control Center (or Centre) (SAUS)
ICC.............. Information Control Console (DNAB)
ICC.............. Information Coordination Center (SAUO)
ICC.............. Information Coordination Central (SAUO)
ICC.............. Information Co-ordination Centre (SAUS)
ICC.............. Information Coordination Control [*Computer*] (MCD)
ICC.............. Information Co-ordination Post (SAUS)
ICC.............. Initial Communications Connectivity [*DoD*]
ICC.............. Initial Connectivity Capability project (SAUS)
ICC.............. Initial Contingency Capability (MCD)
ICC.............. Iniut Circumpolar Conference (SAUO)
ICC.............. Injury Control Center [*An association*] (EA)
ICC.............. Inkatha Central Committee (SAUS)
ICC.............. Input Code Converter (SAUS)
ICC.............. Inspectorate Coordinating Committee (SAUO)
ICC.............. Installation Calibration and Checkout (KSC)
ICC.............. Institut Canadien de Conservation [*Canadian Conservation Institute - CCI*]
ICC.............. Institute Cargo Clauses (MARI)
ICC.............. Institute Circumpolaire Canadien [*Canadian Circumpolar Institute, University of Alberta*] (IRC)
ICC.............. Institute of Chinese Culture (EA)
ICC.............. [*Myasnikov*] Institute of Clinical Cardiology [*Russian*]
ICC.............. Instituto Cartografico de Cataluna [*Spain*] [*ICAO designator*] (FAAC)
ICC.............. Instrumentation Checkout Complex (MCD)
ICC.............. Instrumentation Classification Code (SAUS)
ICC.............. Instrumentation Control Center (AAG)
ICC.............. Instrument Center Correction (SAUS)
ICC.............. Instrument Control Center (KSC)
ICC.............. Instrument Control Computer
ICC.............. Integrated Chip Circuit
ICC.............. Integrated Circuit Computer (SAUS)
ICC.............. Integrated Cluster Controller
ICC.............. Integrated Command and Control
ICC.............. Integrated Communications Center (MCD)
ICC.............. Integrated Communications Control (MCD)
ICC.............. Integrated Composites Centre (SAUS)
ICC.............. Intelligent Channel Controller (SAUS)
ICC.............. Intelligent Communications Control (SAUS)
ICC.............. Intelligent Cruise Control [*Automotive engineering*]
ICC.............. Intensive Care Certificate [*Medicine*]
ICC.............. Intensive Coronary Care [*Medicine*]
ICC.............. Interagency Coordinating Committee (SAUO)
ICC.............. Interagency Coordinating Council (SAUO)
ICC.............. Inter-American Cultural Council
ICC.............. Inter-American Investment Corporation (SAUO)
ICC.............. Interceptor Control Concept (ACAE)
ICC.............. Interchangeable Cycle Check (MCD)
ICC.............. Interchannel Communicator (MCD)
ICC.............. Interchannel Comparators (SAUS)
ICC.............. Inter-Company Correspondence
ICC.............. Intercomputer Channel (NASA)
ICC.............. Intercomputer Communication (MCD)
ICC.............. Intercomputer Communications Corporation (SAUO)
ICC.............. Intercomputer Coupler (IAA)
ICC.............. Intercounty Championship (ODA)
ICC.............. Interdepartmental Intelligence Conference (SAUO)
ICC.............. Interface Control Chart (NASA)
ICC.............. Interface Control Check (SAUS)
ICC.............. Interface-Controlled Crystallization (SAUS)
ICC.............. Interface-Coordinating Committee (SAUO)
ICC.............. Intergovernmental Consultative Committee (SAUO)
ICC.............. Interim Consultative Committee (SAUO)
ICC.............. Interior Communications Electrician, Chief [*Navy rating*]
ICC.............. Intermarket Clearing Corporation (SAUO)
ICC.............. Intermediate Control Change (SAUS)
ICC.............. Intermediate Co-pilots Course (SAUO)
ICC.............. Intermediate Cryptanalysis Course [*Military*] (DNAB)
ICC.............. Intermode Communication Channel (SAUS)
ICC.............. Internal Conversion Coefficient [*Radiology*]
ICC.............. International Association Cereal Science and Tecnology (SAUS)
ICC.............. International Association for Cereal Chemistry (SAUO)
ICC.............. International Association for Cereal Science and Technology [*Formerly, International Association of Cereal Chemists*] [*Acronym represents association's former name*] [*Austria*]
ICC.............. International Cablecasting Technologies [*Vancouver Stock Exchange symbol*]
ICC.............. International Camaro Club (EA)
ICC.............. International Carboniferous Congress (SAUS)
ICC.............. International Catalog Card (SAUS)
ICC.............. International Cello Centre [*Duns, Scotland*] (EAIO)
ICC.............. International Chamber of Commerce [*See also CCI*] [*Paris, France*] (EAIO)
ICC.............. International Channel Controller (SAUS)
ICC.............. International Chessology Club (EA)
ICC.............. International Children's Centre [*Paris, France*]
ICC.............. International Christian Committee (SAUO)
ICC.............. International Clergy Council (EA)
ICC.............. International Climatological Commission (SAUO)
ICC.............. International College in Copenhagen [*Denmark*]
ICC.............. International College of Chiropractors (EA)
ICC.............. International Color Committee (SAUO)
ICC.............. International Color Consortium
ICC.............. International Commerce Consortium (SAUS)
ICC.............. International Commercial Center (SAUO)
ICC.............. International Committee for Conservation (SAUS)
ICC.............. International Committee of ICOM [*International Council of Museums*] for Conservation [*Later, ICOM-CC*] (EAIO)
ICC.............. International Communication Conference (SAUS)
ICC.............. International Communications Conference (CCCA)
ICC.............. International Communications Corp. [*Miami, FL*] (CSR)
ICC.............. International Communications Corporation (SAUO)
ICC.............. International Computaprint Corp. [*Fort Washington, PA*]
ICC.............. International Computaprint Corporation (SAUO)
ICC.............. International Computation Center [*Sponsored by UNESCO*] [*Rome, Italy*]
ICC.............. International Computation Center (or Centre) (SAUO)
ICC.............. International Computer Casting [*Information service or system*] (IID)
ICC.............. International Computer Center (HGAA)
ICC.............. International Computer Center (or Centre) (SAUS)
ICC.............. International Computer Conference (SAUS)
ICC.............. International Computing Center (SAUS)
ICC.............. International Computing Centre [*United Nations*] (ECON)
ICC.............. International Conference on Communications [*IEEE*]
ICC.............. International Conference on Continuous Casting (SAUS)
ICC.............. International Conference on Creep (SAUS)
ICC.............. International Congregational Council
ICC.............. International Congress of Catalysis (SAUO)
ICC.............. International Congress of Chemotherapy (SAUO)
ICC.............. International Congress on Catalysis (SAUS)
ICC.............. International Container Corporation (SAUO)

ICC.............. International Control Center (SAUS)
ICC.............. International Control Centre [*Telecommunications*] (NITA)
ICC.............. International Control Commission [*Representatives of Canada, India, and Poland charged with supervising thecease-fire in Laos established at Geneva Conference of 1962*]
ICC.............. International Controls Corporation (SAUO)
ICC.............. International Convention Center [*British*] (ECON)
ICC.............. International Convention Centre (SAUS)
ICC.............. International Cooperation Council [*Later, UDC*]
ICC.............. International Coordinating Committee (SAUS)
ICC.............. International Coordinating Committee for the Presentation of Science and the Development of Out-of-School Scientific Activities [*See also CIC*] (EAIO)
ICC.............. International Coordinating Committee for Welfare and Development (SAUO)
ICC.............. International Coordinating Committee of Financial Analysts Associations (SAUO)
ICC.............. International Coordinating Committee of World Sports Organizations for the Disabled (SAUO)
ICC.............. International Correspondence College (SAUO)
ICC.............. International Correspondence Colleges (SAUS)
ICC.............. International Corrosion Council [*Orsay, France*] (EAIO)
ICC.............. International Counseling Center (EA)
ICC.............. International Creative Center (or Centre) (SAUO)
ICC.............. International Cricket Conference (EA)
ICC.............. International Cricket Council (SAUO)
ICC.............. International Criminal Court (SAUS)
ICC.............. [*The*] International Critical Commentary on the Holy Scriptures of the Old and New Testament [*Edinburgh*] [*A publication*] (BJA)
ICC.............. International Cultural Council (SAUO)
ICC.............. International Standing Committee for the Study of Corrosion and Protection of Underground Pipelines (SAUO)
ICC.............. Internet Chess Club
ICC.............. Internet Content Coalition [*Computer science*]
ICC.............. Interprocessor Communication and Control Routine (MCD)
ICC.............. Interrupt Controller Circuit (SAUS)
ICC.............. Interstate Carriers Conference (EA)
ICC.............. Interstate Commerce Classification (SAUO)
ICC.............. Interstate Commerce Commission [*Independent government agency*]
ICC.............. Interventional Cardiac Catheterization [*Medicine*]
ICC.............. Intra-Class Correlation
ICC.............. Intra-Class Correlation Coefficient
ICC.............. Intracompany Correspondence (AAG)
ICC.............. Inuit Circumpolar Conference [*Godthaab, Greenland, Denmark*] (EAIO)
ICC.............. Invalid Character Check (SAUS)
ICC.............. Invasive Cancer of the Cervix [*Oncology*]
ICC.............. Inventory Control Center [*of Field Army Support Command*]
ICC.............. Inventory Control Company
ICC.............. Inverted Common Collector (SAUS)
ICC.............. Invitational Computer Conference
ICC.............. Irish Council of Churches
ICC.............. Island Coordinating Council (SAUS)
ICC.............. Islanders Coordinating Council (SAUS)
ICC.............. Issue Category Code (NITA)
ICC.............. Isthmian Canal Commission (SAUS)
ICC.............. Italian Chamber of Commerce (EA)
ICC.............. Italian Culture Council (EA)
ICC.............. Item Category Code
ICC.............. Item Characteristic Curve [*Statistics*]
ICCA............ Independent Computer Consultants Association (EA)
ICCA............ Infants' and Children's Coat Association [*Later, ICGSCA*] (EA)
ICCA............ Initial Cash Clothing Allowance [*Military*]
ICCA............ Institut Canadien de la Construction en Acier [*Canadian Institute of Steel Construction*]
ICCA............ Institut Canadien des Comptables Agrees [*Canadian Institute of Chartered Accountants*]
ICCA............ Interagency Coordinating Committee for Astronomy [*Federal Council for Science and Technology*] [*Terminated, 1976*]
ICCA............ InterAmericas Communications Corp. [*NASDAQ symbol*] (SAG)
ICCA............ Intercontinental Corrugated Case Association (SAUO)
ICCA............ International Cocoa Agreement (SAUO)
ICCA............ International Commission for Cellulose Analysis (SAUO)
ICCA............ International Commission on Commercial Activities (EAIO)
ICCA............ International Community Corrections Association (EA)
ICCA............ International Computer Chess Association
ICCA............ International Computer Conference on Computer Applications in Developing Countries (SAUS)
ICCA............ International Conference on Computer Applications [*in developing countries*] [*1977*]
ICCA............ International Congress and Convention Association [*Amsterdam, Netherlands*] (EA)
ICCA............ International Consumer Credit Association [*Later, ICA*] (EA)
ICCA............ International Conventions and Congresses Association [*Australia*]
ICCA............ International Correspondence of Corkscrew Addicts (EA)
ICCA............ International Corrugated Case Association [*Paris, France*] (EAIO)
ICCA............ International Council for Commercial Arbitration [*Vienna, Austria*] (EAIO)
ICCA............ International Council of Chemical Associations
ICCaC........... Carnow, Coninleas & Associates, Ltd., Chicago, IL [*Library symbol*] [*Library of Congress*] (LCLS)
ICCAC.......... Interagency Clean Car Advisory Committee [*HEW*] [*Terminated*] (EGAO)
ICCAD.......... International Center for Computer-Aided Design (MHDB)
ICCAD.......... International Centre for Computer Aided Design (PDAA)
ICCAD.......... International Conference on Computer Aided Design (SAUO)
ICCAIA......... International Coordinating Council of Aerospace Industries Associations (EA)
ICCAIA......... International Coordinating Council of Aerospace Industries (or Industry) Associations (SAUO)
ICCAM......... Integrated Climate Change Analysis Model (SAUS)
ICCAM......... International Committee of Children's and Adolescents' Movements
ICCAP.......... International Coordinating Committee for the Accountancy Profession (SAUS)
ICCAP.......... International Coordinating (or Coordination) Committee for the Accountancy Profession (SAUO)
ICCAP.......... International Co-ordination Committee for the Accountancy Profession (SAUS)
ICCAP.......... International Coordination Committee for the Accounting Profession
ICCARD........ International Commission for Central American Recovery and Development
ICCAS.......... Chicago Academy of Sciences, Matthew Laflin Memorial Library, Chicago, IL [*Library symbol*] [*Library of Congress*] (LCLS)
ICCAS.......... International Center for Communication Arts and Sciences
ICCAS.......... International Center for Communication of Arts and Sciences (SAUS)
ICCAS.......... International Conference on Computer Applications in the Automation of Shipyard (SAUS)
ICCAS.......... International Conference on Computer Applications in the Automation of Shipyard Operation and Ship Design (SAUO)
ICCAT.......... International Commission for the Conservation of Atlantic Tunas [*Spain*]
ICCATA........ International Coordinating Council of Aerospace Industries Assiciations (SAUO)
ICCATCI....... International Committee to Coordinate Activities of Technical Groups in CoatingsIndustry [*Paris, France*] (EAIO)
ICCATCI....... International Committee to Coordinate Activities of Technical Groups in the Coatings Industry (SAUS)
ICCB............ Illinois Community College Board (SAUO)
ICCB............ In-containment CAPS blower (SAUS)
ICCB............ Institute of Chemistry and Cell Biology [*Harvard Medical School*]
ICCB............ Insulated Case Circuit Breaker (DWSG)
ICCB............ Integrated Change Control Board [*NASA*] (NASA)
ICCB............ Intergovernmental Consultation and Coordination Board (SAUS)
ICCB............ Intergrated Change Control Board (SAUS)
ICCB............ Interim Configuration Control Board (ACAE)
ICCB............ Intermediate Change Control Board
ICCB............ Intermediate Configuration Control Board [*Western Electric*] (AABC)
ICCB............ Internal Configuration Control Board (SAUS)
ICCB............ International Catholic Child Bureau [*Geneva, Switzerland*]
ICCB............ International Center for Cooperation in BioInformatics [*UNESCO*]
ICCB............ Internet Control and Configuration Board [*Computer science*] (ACRL)
ICCBA.......... International Christian Classic Bikers Association (SAUO)
ICCBC.......... Intergovernmental Committee on the Convention of Biological Diversity (SAUO)
ICCBC.......... International Committee for Colorado Beetle Control (SAUO)
ICCBD.......... Intergovernmental Committee on the Convention of/on Biological Diversity (SAUS)
ICCBD.......... Intergovernmental Committee on the Convention on Biological Diversity (SAUO)
IC-CBPH....... Chicago Library Services for the Blind and Physically Handicapped (Subregional),Chicago Public Library, Chicago, IL [*Library symbol*] [*Library of Congress*] (LCLS)
ICC Bulletin... International Computation Center (or Centre) Bulletin (journ.) (SAUS)
ICCC............ Columbia College, Chicago, IL [*Library symbol*] [*Library of Congress*] (LCLS)
ICCC............ Ice Cream Connoisseurs Club [*Defunct*] (EA)
ICCC............ ImmuCell Corp. [*NASDAQ symbol*] (NQ)
ICCC............ Immucell Corporation (SAUO)
ICCC............ Imperial College Computing Center (PDAA)
ICCC............ Indian Central Coconut Committee (SAUO)
ICCC............ Industrial Closed-Circuit Cooler (SAUS)
ICCC............ Infantry Captains Career Course [*Military*]
ICCC............ Information and Computing Centers Corp. (SAUS)
ICCC............ Information and Computing Centers Corporation (SAUO)
ICCC............ Information Center on Children's Cultures [*Defunct*] (EA)
ICCC............ Inter-Client Communication Convention (SAUS)
ICCC............ Inter-Council Co-ordinating Committee (SAUO)
ICCC............ International Center (or Centre) for Comparative Criminology (SAUO)
ICCC............ International Centre for Clinical Criminology (SAUO)
ICCC............ International Christian Chamber of Commerce (COBU)
ICCC............ International Christian Cycling Club USA (EA)
ICCC............ International Classification of Childhood Cancer (SAUO)
ICCC............ International Color Computer Club (EA)
ICCC............ International Computer Communications Conference (CCCA)
ICCC............ International Concentration Camp Committee [*Vienna, Austria*] (EAIO)
ICCC............ International Concerns Committee for Children (EA)
ICCC............ International Concerns for Children [*An association*] (EA)
ICCC............ International Conference Centers (or Centres) Consultants (SAUO)
ICCC............ International Conference of Catholic Charities
ICCC............ International Conference of Coordination Chemistry
ICCC............ International Conference on Circuits and Computers (MCD)
ICCC............ International Conference on Computer Communication (SAUO)
ICCC............ International Conference on Computers in Cardiology (SAUS)
ICCC............ International Conference on Coordination in/of Chemistry (SAUS)
ICCC............ International Conferences on Coordination Chemistry (SAUO)
ICCC............ International Congress on Construction Communications (SAUO)
ICCC............ International Council for Computer Communication (EA)
ICCC............ International Council of Christian Churches (EA)
ICCC............ International Council of Community Churches (EA)

ICCC........ International Cybernetics Congress Committee (SAUO)
ICCCA........ International C Class Catamaran Association of America (EA)
ICC-CAPA........ Commission on Asian and Pacific Affairs of the International Chamber of Commerce (SAUO)
ICC-CAPA........ International Chamber of Commerce-Commission on Asian and Pacific Affairs (SAUS)
ICCCM........ Inter-Client Communications Conventions Management (SAUS)
ICCCM........ Inter-Client Communications Conventions Manual (RALS)
ICCCS........ Integrated Continuous Controlled Color System (DGA)
ICCCS........ International Contamination Control Conference and Symposium (SAUS)
ICCD........ Imaging Charge Coupled Devices (ACAE)
ICCD........ Improved Computer-Controlled Dwell [*Automotive engineering*]
ICCD........ Information Center on Crime and Delinquency [*National Council on Crime and Delinquency*] (IID)
ICCD........ Institute of Chocolate and Confectionery Distributors [*British*] (BI)
ICCD........ Intensified Charge-Coupled Device [*Electronics*]
ICCD........ Intergovernmental Commission for Chagas Disease (ECON)
ICCD........ Internal Coordination Control Drawing
ICCD........ International Committee for a Community of Democracies (SAUO)
ICCD........ International Convention to Combat Desertification (SAUS)
ICC Digest... International Chamber of Commerce Digest (journ.) (SAUS)
ICCDP........ Integrated Circuit Communications Data Processor (MHDI)
ICCE........ Iceland Command & Control Enhancement (SAUS)
ICCE........ Iceland Communications and Control Enhancement
ICCE........ International Centre for Conservation Education (SAUO)
ICCE........ International Commission of/on Continental Erosion (SAUO)
ICCE........ International Commission on Continental Erosion (CARB)
ICCE........ International Conference on Compound II-VI Semiconductors (SAUS)
ICCE........ International Congress on Combustion Engines
ICCE........ International Council for Computers in Education (EA)
ICCE........ International Council for Correspondence Education [*Later, ICDE*]
ICCE........ International Council of Commerce Employers
ICCE........ Intracapsular Cataract Extraction [*Ophthalmology*]
ICCEA........ International Committee for the Study and Conservation of Earthen Architecture (EAIO)
ICCEC........ India Chemists and Chemical Engineers Club (EA)
ICCEcPI........ Intracapsular Cataract Extraction with Peripheral Iridectomy [*Ophthalmology*]
ICCEE........ International Classification Commission for Electrical Engineering (SAUO)
ICCEE........ International Classification Commission for Electrical Engineering (or Engineers) (SAUS)
ICCEF........ International Conference on the Combined Effects of Environmental Factors (SAUO)
ICCERSP........ Interagency Coordinating Committee for Earth Resource Survey Programs (SAUO)
ICCERSP........ Interagency Coordinating Committee of the Earth Resources Survey Program (SAUS)
ICCET........ Imperial College of Science and Technology Centre for Environmental Technology [*British*] (IRUK)
ICCF........ Interaction Computing and Control Facility (NITA)
ICCF........ Interactive Computer Controlling Facility (SAUS)
ICCF........ Interactive Computing and Control Facility [*IBM Corp. program product*]
ICCF........ Interexchange Carrier and Carrier Forum [*Exchange Carriers Standards Association*] [*Telecommunications*]
ICCF........ International Computing and Control Facility (SAUS)
ICCF........ International Conference on Cold Fusion (SAUS)
ICCF........ International Correspondence Chess Federation
ICCF........ International Permanent Committee on Canned Foods (SAUO)
ICCFM........ International Confederation of Christian Family Movements (EAIO)
ICCFS........ Imperial College of Science and Technology Centre for Fusion Studies [*British*] (IRUK)
ICCFTI........ International Center for Companies of the Food Trade and Industry (EA)
ICCG........ Incomplete Conjugate Gradient (AAEL)
ICCG........ Intercommunication-Communication Control Group [*Navy*] (NVT)
ICCG........ International Catholic Conference of Guiding (EAIO)
ICCG........ International Conference on Crystal Growth (PDAA)
ICCGB........ Indian Chamber of Commerce in Great Britain (DS)
ICCGB........ Italian Chamber of Commerce in Great Britain (DS)
ICCGC........ International Computer Color Graphics Conference (SAUS)
ICCGR........ Intergranular Cyclic Crack Growth Rate [*Nuclear energy*] (NUCP)
ICCGR........ International Cyclic Crack Growth Rate (SAUS)
ICCH........ Cook County Hospital, Dr. Frederick Tice Memorial Library, Chicago, IL [*Library symbol*] [*Library of Congress*] (LCLS)
ICch........ Country Club Hills Public Library District, Country Club Hills, IL [*Library symbol*] [*Library of Congress*] (LCLS)
ICCH........ International Catholic Confederation of Hospitals [*Later, IHF*] (EA)
ICCH........ International Commodities Clearing House [*British*] [*Business term*]
ICCH........ International Commodity Clearing House Ltd. (SAUO)
ICCH........ International Conference and Computers and the Humanties (SAUS)
ICCH........ International Conference on Computers and the Humanities
ICC Handler... Inter-Computer Coupler Handler (SAUS)
ICChC........ Chapman & Cutter, Law Library, Chicago, IL [*Library symbol*] [*Library of Congress*] (LCLS)
ICChH........ Children's Memorial Hospital, Joseph Brennemann Medical Library, Chicago, IL [*Library symbol*] [*Library of Congress*] (LCLS)
ICCHHH........ International Club for Collectors of Hatpins and Hatpin Holders (ADWA)
ICchP........ Country Club Hills Public Library District, Country Club Hills, IL [*Library symbol*] [*Library of Congress*] (LCLS)
ICCHP........ International Conference on Computers for Handicapped Persons (SAUO)
ICCHRLA........ Inter-Church Committee on Human Rights in Latin America [*Canada*] (EAIO)
ICCHS........ Intercampus Committee for Handicapped Students (EA)
ICCHZ........ International Catholic Confederation of Hospitals (SAUO)
ICCI........ Insight Communications [*NASDAQ symbol*] (SG)
ICCI........ Inter-Church Commission on Immigration and Refugee Resettlement (SAUO)
ICCI........ Inter-Continental Computing Incorporated (SAUO)
ICCI........ International Christian Committee for Israel (SAUO)
ICCI........ International Conference on Composite Interfaces (SAUS)
ICCI........ International Conference on Computing and Information (SAUO)
ICCIA........ Interim Coordinating Committee for International Commodity Arrangements (SAUO)
ICCIA........ Italian Chamber of Commerce and Industry in Australia
ICC-IBI........ International Computation Center-Intergovernmental Bureau for Informatics (SAUO)
ICC-IBIT........ International Computation Center-Intergovernmental Bureau for Information Technology (SAUO)
ICCICA........ Interim Co-ordinating Committee for International Commodity Arrangements
ICCICA........ Interim Coordinating Coomittee on International Commodity Agreements (SAUS)
ICCICE........ Islamic Chamber of Commerce, Industry and Commodity Exchange [*See also CICIEM*] [*Karachi, Pakistan*] (EAIO)
ICCIDD........ International Consultative Council of/on Iodine Deficiency Disorders (SAUO)
ICCILMB........ Interim Committee for Coordination of Investigations of the Lower Mekong Basin (EA)
ICCIMA........ International Conference on Computational Intelligence and Multimedia Applications (SAUO)
ICCIR........ International Coordination Committee for Immunology of Reproduction [*Bulg aria*] [*Research center*] (IRC)
ICCJ........ International Committee for Cooperation of Journalists (SAUO)
ICCJ........ International Committee for the Cooperation of Journalists (NATG)
ICCJ........ International Council of Christians and Jews [*Heppenheim, Federal Republic of Germany*] (EAIO)
ICCK........ Chadwell, Kayser, Ruggles, McGee & Hasting, Chicago, IL [*Library symbol*] [*Library of Congress*] (LCLS)
iCCK........ Immunireactive Cholecystokinin [*Medicine*] (EDAA)
ICCK........ Immunoreactive Cholecystokinin [*Medicine*] (MELL)
ICCL........ Cook County Law Library, Chicago, IL [*Library symbol*] [*Library of Congress*] (LCLS)
ICCL........ Inhomogeneous Channel Current Limiter (SAUS)
ICCL........ Interface Control Configuration List
ICCL........ International Commission on Climate (SAUO)
ICCL........ International Committee for the Centennial of Light
ICCL........ International Committee of Comparative Law
ICCL........ International Committee on Computational Linguistics (SAUO)
ICCL........ International Council for Christian Leadership (SAUO)
ICCL........ International Council of Cruise Lines (NTPA)
ICCL........ Irish Council for Civil Liberties (EAIO)
ICCLA........ International Center for Coordination of Legal Assistance [*Switzerland*] (PDAA)
ICCLA........ International Centre for Coordination of Legal Assistance (SAUO)
ICCLA/CLC... International Committee on Christian Literature for Africa and Christian Literature Council (SAUO)
ICCLY........ International Council to Combat Lethal Yellowing
ICCM........ Idiopathic Congestive Cardiomyopathy [*Medicine*]
ICCM........ Inadequate Core Cooling Monitor [*Nuclear energy*] (NUCP)
ICCM........ Incoming Call Center Management [*Telecommunications*] (AGLO)
ICCM........ Institute for Computer Capacity Management (NTPA)
ICCM........ Institute of Critical Care Medicine [*University of Southern California*] [*Research center*] (RCD)
ICCM........ Intercontinental Cruise Missile (IAA)
ICCM........ International Christian Classic Motorcyclists (EA)
ICCM........ International Committee for the Conservation of Mosaics [*Hungerford, Berkshire, England*] (EAIO)
ICCM........ International Conference on Composite Materials (SAUO)
ICCM........ International Council of Catholic Men [*See also FIHC*] [*Vatican City, Vatican City State*] (EAIO)
ICCM........ Interstitial Cell-Conditioned Medium [*Clinical chemistry*]
ICCM........ Isoconcentration Contour Migration (SAUS)
ICCM........ Master Chief Interior Communications Electrician [*Navy rating*]
ICCM........ University of Health Sciences - Chicago Medical School, Chicago, IL [*Library symbol*] [*Library of Congress*] (LCLS)
ICCMB........ International Committee for the Conservation of Mud Brick (SAUS)
ICC/MC Functions... Integration of Communications Center and Message Center Functions (SAUO)
ICCME........ Intersociety Council on Continuing Medical Education (SAUO)
ICCMG........ Clausen, Miller, Gorman, Caffrey & Witous, Chicago, IL [*Library symbol*] [*Library of Congress*] (LCLS)
ICCMHC........ Idiana Council of Community Mental Health Centers (SRA)
ICCMO........ International College of Cranio-Mandibular Orthopedics (NTPA)
ICCMS........ International Committee on the Challenges of Modern Society (SAUO)
ICCMS........ International Conference on Composite Materials and Structures (SAUS)
ICCN........ Cook County School of Nursing, Chicago, IL [*Library symbol*] [*Library of Congress*] (LCLS)
ICCN........ International Committee of Catholic Nurses [*See also CICIAMS*] [*Vatican City, Vatican City State*] (EAIO)
ICCNA........ CNA Financial Corp., Chicago, IL [*Library symbol*] [*Library of Congress*] (LCLS)
ICCNA........ International Center for Control of Nutritional Anemia [*University of Kansas*] [*Research center*] (RCD)

ICCND......... International Conference on Children and National Development [*Medicine*] (EDAA)
ICCNL......... International Committee of Chairmen of National Libraries (WDAA)
ICCO......... Chicago College of Osteopathic Medicine, Chicago, IL [*Library symbol*] [*Library of Congress*] (LCLS)
ICCO......... Inter-Church Coordination Committee for Development Projects (SAUO)
ICCO......... International Carpet Classification Organization [*Brussels, Belgium*] (EAIO)
ICCO......... International Cocoa Organisation (SAUS)
ICCO......... International Cocoa Organization [*London, England*] (EAIO)
ICCO......... International Council of Containership Operators [*British*] (DCTA)
ICC of H & HH... International Club for Collectors of Hatpins and Hatpin Holders (EA)
ICComE......... Commonwealth Edison Co., Chicago, IL [*Library symbol*] [*Library of Congress*] (LCLS)
ICCon......... Continental Group Co., Inc., Chicago, IL [*Library symbol*] [*Library of Congress*] (LCLS)
ICConB......... Continental Illinois National Bank and Trust Co., Research and Information Services, Chicago, IL [*Library symbol*] [*Library of Congress*] (LCLS)
ICCOR......... Intercommand Coordination (SAUO)
ICcP......... Calument City Public Library, Calumet City, IL [*Library symbol*] [*Library of Congress*] (LCLS)
ICCP......... Idaho Chemical Processing Plant (SAUO)
ICCP......... Impressed Current Cathodic Protection (SAUS)
ICCP......... Impressed Current Corrosion Protection
ICCP......... Improved Computer Control Panel (SAUS)
ICCP......... Information, Computer and Communications Policy (MHDI)
ICCP......... Information, Computers and Communications Policy (SAUO)
ICCP......... Institute for Certification of Computer Professionals (EA)
ICCP......... Institute for the Certification of Computer Professionals (SAUS)
ICCP......... Institute for the Certification of Computing Professionals (SAUO)
ICCP......... Institute of Certification of Computer Professionals (SAUS)
ICCP......... Integrated Communication Control Panel (MCD)
ICCP......... Intelligence Civilian Career Program [*Army*] (AABC)
ICCP......... Interdepartmental Committee on Commercial Policy (SAUO)
ICCP......... Interface Control and Converter Processor (ACAE)
ICCP......... Interface Coordination and Control Procedure (NASA)
ICCP......... Intergovernmental Committee for the Cartagena Protocol (SAUO)
ICCP......... International Camp Counselor Program (EA)
ICCP......... International Climate Change Partnership (EPAT)
ICCP......... International Commission for Coal Petrology (SAUS)
ICCP......... International Commission on Cloud Physics (SAUO)
ICCP......... International Committee for Coal Petrology [*Liege, Belgium*] (EAIO)
ICCP......... International Conference on Cataloging Principles
ICCP......... International Conference on Cataloguing Principles (SAUS)
ICCP......... International Coordinating Committee for NGOs on the Question of Palestine (SAUO)
ICCP......... International Council for Children's Play [*Groningen, Netherlands*] (EAIO)
ICCPBS......... International Chemical Congress of Pacific Basin Societies (EA)
ICCPC......... International Computation Centers Preparatory Committee (SAUS)
ICCPC......... International Computing Centers Preparatory Committee (SAUS)
ICCP Plant... Internal Combustion Catapult Power Plant (SAUS)
ICCPPS......... International Conference on Ceramic Powder Processing Science (SAUS)
ICCPR......... International Covenant on Civil and Political Rights; Adopted 16 December 1966 by UN General Assembly (SAFN)
ICCPR66...... International Covenant on Civil and Political Rights of 16 December 1966 and Protocol Thereto (SAFN)
ICCR......... Indian Council for Cultural Relations (SAUO)
ICCR......... Instrument Calibration Control Record (SAUS)
ICCR......... Interactive Cash and Credit Register [*Datacap Systems, Inc.*]
ICCR......... Inter-Church Committee for Refugees (SAUO)
ICCR......... Interdisciplinary Centre for Comparative Research in the Social Sciences (SAUS)
ICCR......... Interfaith Center on Corporate Responsibility (EA)
ICCR......... International Charge Card Registry (SAUS)
ICCR......... International Committee for Coal Research [*Brussels, Belgium*] (EAIO)
ICCR......... International Committee for Contraceptive Research
ICCR......... International Consultative Committee for Radio Communication (SAUO)
ICCR......... International Consultative Committee for Radiocommunication (SAUS)
ICCR......... Interstate Commerce Commission Reports [*A publication*] (DLA)
ICCra......... Crane Co., Chicago, IL [*Library symbol*] [*Library of Congress*] (LCLS)
ICC Rep...... Interstate Commerce Commission Reports [*A publication*] (DLA)
ICCRI......... International Committee for Classification of Rubber Information (SAUS)
ICCROM...... International Centre for Conservation at Rome (SAUS)
ICCROM...... International Centre for the Study of the Preservation and the Restoration of Cultural Property [*Rome, Italy*] (EAIO)
ICCS......... Ice Center Communications System (SAUS)
ICCS......... Ice Centre Communications System (SAUS)
ICCS......... Improved Command & Control System (SAUS)
ICCS......... Improved UK air defence ground environment Command and Control System (SAUS)
ICCS......... Industrial Combustion Control System (SAUS)
ICCS......... Inner Canister Closure System (SAUS)
ICCS......... Institute of Computer & Communication Systems (SAUO)
ICCS......... Integrated Carrier Catapult Station (MCD)
ICCS......... Integrated Carrier Catapult System (DNAB)
ICCS......... Integrated Catapult Control Station (MCD)
ICCS......... Integrated Chassis Control System [*Automotive*]
ICCS......... Integrated Command & Control System (SAUS)
ICCS......... Integrated Communications Cabling System (SAUO)
ICCS......... Integrated Communications Collection System [*Military*] (MCD)
ICCS......... Intercomputer Communication System
ICCS......... Interdisciplinary Center for Creative Studies [*State University College at Buffalo*] [*Research center*] (RCD)
ICCS......... Inter-European Commission on Church and School (SAUO)
ICCS......... Interface Configuration Control System (DNAB)
ICCS......... Interim Command and Control System (MCD)
ICCS......... International Capital Consultant Services (SAUO)
ICCS......... International Center for Chemical Studies (SAUS)
ICCS......... International Center for Criminological Studies (BARN)
ICCS......... International Center of Criminological Studies (SAUO)
ICCS......... International Centre for Chemical Studies [*See also CIEC*] (EAIO)
ICCS......... International Centre of Criminological Studies (SAUS)
ICCS......... International Classification of Clinical Services (HCT)
ICCS......... International Commission of Control and Supervision [*Composed of representatives of Canada, Hungary, Indonesia, and Poland, and charged with supervising the ceasefire in Vietnam, 1973*]
ICCS......... International Commission on Civil Status [*See also CIEC*] [*Strasbourg, France*] (EAIO)
ICCS......... International Committee of Contamination Control Societies (SAUO)
ICCS......... International Committee of Creole Studies [*Aix-En-Provence, France*] (EAIO)
ICCS......... International Committee on Clinical Sociology [*See also CISC*] [*Later, International Group on Clinical Sociology*] (EAIO)
ICCS......... International Conference in Computer Science (SAUS)
ICCS......... International Conference of Catholic Scouting (SAUO)
ICCS......... International Conference on Composite Structures [*Paisley, Scotland*] (EAIO)
ICCS......... International Container and Chassis Services (SAUO)
ICCS......... International Convention on the Continental Shelf (NOAA)
ICCS......... International Cork Cutters' Society [*A union*]
ICCS......... International Council for Canadian Studies [*See also CIEC*]
ICCS......... International Council on Civil Status (SAUO)
ICCS......... International Council on Clinical Sociology (SAUO)
ICCS......... International Group on Clinical Sociology [*Formerly, International Committee on Clinical Sociology*] (EA)
ICCS......... Intersite Control and Communications System (SAUS)
ICCS......... IUKADGE Command & Control System (SAUS)
ICCS......... Senior Chief Interior Communications Electrician [*Navy rating*]
ICCSASW..... International Commission for/of the Coordination of Solidarity among Sugar Workers (SAUO)
ICCSASW..... International Commission for the Co-ordination of Solidarity among Sugar Workers [*Canada*]
ICCSHE......... Interagency Committee for Computer Support of Handicapped Employees [*General Services Administration*] (EGAO)
ICCSL......... International Commission of the Cape Spartel Light (SAUO)
ICCSP......... Chicago School of Professional Psychology, Chicago, IL [*Library symbol*] [*Library of Congress*] (LCLS)
ICCSR......... Interagency Committee on Climate Services and Research
ICCSSSAR.... International Coordinating Committee on Solid State Sensors and Actuators Research (SAUO)
ICCSTI......... Interdepartmental Coordinating Committee for Scientific and Technical Informatio (SAUS)
ICCSTI......... Interdepartmental Co-ordinating Committee for Scientific and Technical Information (SAUO)
ICCSTR......... International Coordinating Committee on Solid State Transducers Research (EA)
ICCT......... Consoer, Townsend & Associates, Chicago, IL [*Library symbol*] [*Library of Congress*] (LCLS)
ICCT......... Image Computer Compatible Tape (ACAE)
ICCT......... Initial Contact Control Time [*Aerospace*] (AAG)
ICCT......... International Community Circle (SAUO)
ICCT......... Intracavitary Chemotherapy [*Medicine*] (MELL)
ICCT......... Iowa Community College Telenetwork [*Marshalltown*] (TSSD)
ICCTA......... Illinois Community College Trustees Association (SAUO)
ICCTA......... International Committee for the Coordination of Terminological Activities (SAUO)
ICCTA......... International Consultative Council of Travel Agents
ICCTA......... International Consultative Council of Travel Agents, London (SAUO)
ICCTA......... International Coordination Committee for Terminological Activities (SAUO)
ICC Tch......... ICC Technologies, Inc. [*Associated Press*] (SAG)
ICCTE......... International Federation of Commercial, Clerical and Technical Employees (SAUO)
ICC-TM......... Interstate Commerce Commission Transport Mobilization [*Federal emergency order*]
ICCTR......... Intelligence Case Control and Time Reporting System [*IRS*]
ICC Transistor... Inverted Common Collector Transistor (SAUS)
ICCTT......... International Committee of Cooperation between Teachers Trade Unions (SAUO)
ICCTU......... International Confederation of Christian Trade Unions (SAUO)
ICCU......... Intensive Coronary Care Unit [*of a hospital*]
ICCU......... Inter-Channel Comparison Unit [*Nuclear energy*] (NRCH)
ICCU......... Intercomputer Communications Unit (SAUS)
ICCU......... Intercomputer Communication Unit (IAA)
ICCU......... Intercomputer Compatibility Unit [*Computer science*]
ICCU......... Inter-Computer Control Unit (VLIE)
ICCU......... Intermediate Coronary Care Unit [*Medicine*]
ICCU......... International Cross-Country Union (EA)
ICCUS......... International Claims Commission of the United States [*Abolished, 1954*] [*Department of State*]

ICCUSA........ Interagency Coordinating Committee on US-Soviet Affairs [*Department of State*]
ICCUSA........ International Child Care (USA) (EA)
ICCUSA........ Ireland Chamber of Commerce in the United States (NTPA)
ICCV............ International Credit Card Validation (SAUS)
ICC Valuation Rep... Interstate Commerce Commission Valuation Reports [*A publication*] (DLA)
ICCVAM....... Interagency Coordinating Committee on the Validation of Alternative Methods [*To amend for biological testing*]
ICCW........... In-Containment Chilled Water [*Nuclear energy*] (NRCH)
ICCW........... Indian Council for Child Welfare (SAUO)
ICCY............ International Cultural Center for Youth (SAUS)
ICCY............ International Cultural Center for Youth in Jerusalem (SAUO)
ICCY............ International Cultural Center of Youth (SAUO)
ICCY............ International Cultural Centers for Youth (EA)
ICCYM......... Central YMCA Community College, Chicago, IL [*Library symbol*] [*Library of Congress*] (LCLS)
ICCZ............ International Mineral [*Federal Railroad Administration identification code*]
ICD.............. College of Saint Francis, Joliet, IL [*OCLC symbol*] (OCLC)
ICD.............. De Paul University, Chicago, IL [*Library symbol*] [*Library of Congress*] (LCLS)
ICD.............. I-cell Disease [*Medicine*] (EDAA)
ICD.............. Idiopathic Cerebral Dysfunction [*Medicine*] (CPH)
ICD.............. Iesu Christo Duce [*With Jesus Christ as Leader*] [*Latin*]
ICD.............. Image Component Data (SAUS)
ICD.............. Imitative Communication Deception [*Military*]
ICD.............. Imitative Communications Deception (SAUS)
ICD.............. Immune Complex Disease
ICD.............. Implantable Cardioverter-Defibrillator [*Medical device for heart patients*]
ICD.............. Implanted Cardiac Defibrillator (SAUS)
ICD.............. Impulse Control Disorder (MELL)
ICD.............. Index to Class Directory (VLIE)
ICD.............. Induced Circular Dichroism [*Physics*]
ICD.............. Industrial Control Division (TIMI)
ICD.............. Industrial Cooperation Division [*Navy*]
ICD.............. Industry Cooperation Division (SAUO)
ICD.............. Informal Clearance Document [*Customs*]
ICD.............. Information Control Division (SAUO)
ICD.............. Inguinal Compressive Device (DB)
ICD.............. Initative Christo Duce (SAUS)
ICD.............. Initial Case Design (MCD)
ICD.............. Initial Claudication Distance (DB)
ICD.............. Initial Conceptual Design (SAUS)
ICD.............. Initiative Communications Deception (PDAA)
ICD.............. Injuries and Causes of Death (SAUO)
ICD.............. Inland Clearance Depot [*Shipping*]
ICD.............. Inland Container Depot (SAUO)
ICD.............. Input Control Device (SAUS)
ICD.............. Insert Character in Display (SAUS)
ICD.............. Installable Client Driver (SAUS)
ICD.............. Installation Completion Date (CET)
ICD.............. Installation Control Drawing [*DoD*]
ICD.............. Instantaneous Cardiac Death [*Cardiology*] (DAVI)
ICD.............. Institute, Center, Division (SAUS)
ICD.............. Institute for Crippled and Disabled (DAVI)
ICD.............. Institute for the Crippled and Disabled (SAUO)
ICD.............. Institute of Chemical Defense (SAUS)
ICD.............. Institute of Civil Defence [*British*] (EAIO)
ICD.............. Institute of Civil Defense (SAUS)
ICD.............. Institute of Community Development [*British*] (DBA)
ICD.............. Institute of Cooperative Directors (ODBW)
ICD.............. Instrumentation Control Document (KSC)
ICD.............. Integrated Circuit Design (SAUS)
ICD.............. Intelligent Call Distribution (SAUS)
ICD.............. Interactive Call Distribution (ROAS)
ICD.............. Interactive COBOL Debugger [*Computer science*] (HODG)
ICD.............. Inter Canadian Development [*Vancouver Stock Exchange symbol*]
ICD.............. Intercanthal Distance [*Anatomy*]
ICD.............. Interchangeability and Control Division (SAUO)
ICD.............. Interface Connecting Device [*Air Force*] (DOMA)
ICD.............. Interface Control Diagram (NRCH)
ICD.............. Interface Control Dimension (IAA)
ICD.............. Interface Control Document [*Apollo*] [*NASA*]
ICD.............. Interface Control Drawing (SAUS)
ICD.............. Interface Control Drawing or Documentation (SAUS)
ICD.............. Interface Control Drawings (NRCH)
ICD.............. Interim Checkout Device
ICD.............. Interim Conceptual Design (SAUS)
ICD.............. Interim Control Document (ACAE)
ICD.............. Internal Cardioverter Defibrillator [*Medicine*] (MELL)
ICD.............. International Candle
ICD.............. International Center for Development (SAUS)
ICD.............. International Center for the Disabled (EA)
ICD.............. International Center on Deafness (SAUO)
ICD.............. International Centre for Development (SAUO)
ICD.............. International Circulation Distributors, Inc.
ICD.............. International Classification of Diseases [*A publication*]
ICD.............. International Classification of Diseases, Injuries and Causes of Death (journ.) (SAUS)
ICD.............. International Climatic Decades
ICD.............. International Code Designator [*Telecommunications*] (OSI)
ICD.............. International College of Dentists (EA)
ICD.............. International Committee of Dermatology (SAUO)
ICD.............. International Communes Desk (SAUO)
ICD.............. International Congress for Data Processing
ICD.............. International Congress of Druggists (SAUO)
ICD.............. International Cooperation Department (SAUS)
ICD.............. International Cooperation for Development [*Commercial firm*] [*British*] (ECON)
ICD.............. International Cooperative Distributors (SAUO)
ICD.............. International Country Designator (AGLO)
ICD.............. Interoperability Control Document (SAUO)
ICD.............. Intracervical Device [*Medicine*] (DB)
ICD.............. Intracommunity Directive [*Meat-shipping plants*] [*European Community*]
ICD.............. Intrauterine Contraceptive Device [*Medicine*]
ICD.............. Inventory Control Department (SAUO)
ICD.............. Investment Certificate of Deposit (SAUS)
ICD.............. Investment Company Data, Inc. [*Database producer*] (IID)
ICD.............. Ion Controlled Diode (SAUS)
ICD.............. Ion-Controlled Diode [*Electronics*] (IAA)
ICD.............. Iran Center for Documentation (SAUO)
ICD.............. Ischemic Coronary Disease [*Medicine*]
ICD.............. Isocitrate Dehydrogenase [*Also, ICDH, IDH*] [*An enzyme*]
ICD.............. Iterative Coordinate Descent (SAUS)
ICD-9.......... International Classification of Diseases-9th revision (SAUO)
ICD-9.......... International Classification of Diseases. 9th Revision [*A publication*] (DHSM)
ICD-9-CM..... International Classification of Diseases-9th revision-Clinical Modification (SAUO)
ICD-9-CM..... International Classification of Diseases. 9th Revision. Clinical Modification [*A publication*] (DHSM)
ICD-10......... International Statistical Classification of Diseases and Related Health Problems, tenth revision (SAUO)
ICD-10-AM... International Classification of Diseases-10th revision-Australian Modification (SAUO)
ICD-10-CM... International Classification of Diseases-10th revision-Clinical Modification (SAUO)
ICD-10 DCR... ICD-10 Diagnostic Criteria for Research (SAUS)
ICD-10-DCR... International Classification of Disease-10th revision-Diagnostic Criteria for Research (SAUO)
ICD-10-PCS... International Classification of Disease-10th revision-Procedure Classification System (SAUO)
ICD-10 PCS... International Classification of Disease-10th revision-Procedure Coding System (SAUS)
ICDA........... Industrial Civil Defence Association [*British*] (BI)
ICDA........... Industrial Compressor Distributors Association (EA)
ICDA........... Infantry Combat Developments Agency [*Pronounced "ick-da"*] [*Army*]
ICDA........... Infrared Charge Coupled Detector Array (ACAE)
ICDA........... Institute for Community Design Analysis (EA)
ICDA........... Integrated Cached Disk-Arrays (SAUS)
ICdA........... International Cadmium Association (NTPA)
ICDA........... International Catholic Deaf Association (EA)
ICDA........... International Cheese and Deli Association [*Later, IDDA*] (EA)
ICDA........... International Circulation Directors Association (SAUO)
ICDA........... International Classification of Diseases, Adapted for Use in the United States (SAUO)
ICDA........... International Classification of Diseases Adopted (SAUS)
ICDA........... International Classification of Diseases, Adopted for Use in the United States
ICDA........... International Coalition for Development Action [*See also CIAD*] (EAIO)
ICDA........... International Committee of Dietetic Associations (SAUO)
ICDA........... International Compressor Distributors Association (SAUO)
ICDA........... International Congress of Dealers Associations (EA)
ICDA........... International Cooperative Development Association [*Later, ACDI*]
ICDA-8........ International Classification of Diseases, Adopted for Use in the United States. 8th Revision [*A publication*] (DHSM)
ICDAIT........ International Conference on Drug Abuse and Illicit Trafficing (SAUS)
ICDB........... Ice Core Data Bank (CARB)
ICDB........... Immunoclone Database (SAUO)
ICDB........... Inorganic Crystal Data Base (SAUS)
ICDB........... Integrated Communications Database (SAUS)
ICDB........... Integrated Corporate Database
ICDB........... Intercultural Data Bank (SAUS)
ICDBL......... International Committee for the Defence (or Defense) of the Breton Language (SAUO)
ICDBL......... International Committee for the Defense of the Breton Language [*See also CISLB*] [*Brussels, Belgium*] (EAIO)
ICDC........... Implantable Cardioverter Defibrillator Catheter [*Medicine*] (MELL)
ICDC........... Improved Control Display Console (SAUS)
ICDC........... Indian Cotton Development Council (SAUO)
ICDC........... Industrial and Commercial Development Corp. [*Kenya*]
ICDC........... Industrial and Commercial Development Corporation (SAUO)
ICDC........... Interim Career Development Course (SAUO)
ICDC........... International Cable Development Corporation (SAUO)
ICDC........... International Conference on Distributed Computing (SAUS)
ICDC........... National Dairy Council, Chicago, IL [*Library symbol*] [*Library of Congress*] (LCLS)
ICDCP......... Interface Control Drawing Change Proposal (SAUS)
ICDCP......... Interface Control Drawings Change Proposal (IAA)
ICDCS......... International Conference on Distributed Computing Systems (SAUS)
ICDCS......... Interstate Committee for Drought Control in the Sahel (SAUS)
ICDCS......... Interstate Permanent Committee for Drought Control in the Sahelian Zone (SAUO)
ICDD........... International Center for Diffraction Data (SAUS)
ICDD........... International Center for Dynamics of Development (EA)

ICDDB .... DDB Needham Worldwide, Inc. Information Center, Chicago, IL [*Library symbol*] [*Library of Congress*] (LCLS)
ICDDB .... Internal Control Description Data Base (SAUS)
ICDDB .... Internal Control Description Database
ICDDB .... International Control Description Database (SAUS)
ICDDR .... International Center for Diarrhoeal Diseases Research (PDAA)
ICDDR .... International Centre for Diarrhoeal Disease Research [*Bangladesh*]
ICDDRB .... International Center for Diarrhoeal Disease Research (SAUS)
ICDDRB .... International Centre for Diarrhoeal Disease Research, Bangladesh (ECON)
ICDDS .... Institute of Civil Defence and Disaster Studies [*British*] (EAIO)
ICDE .... International Council for Distance Education [*Australia*] (EAIO)
ICDECAA .... International Committee for the Development of Educational and Cultural Activities in Africa (SAUO)
ICDES .... Item Class Description (SAUS)
ICDF .... Inorganic Crystallographic Data File (SAUS)
ICDF .... Intermediate Coupling Dirac-Fock (SAUS)
ICDF .... International Christian Dance Fellowship (EAIO)
ICDFMS .... Industrial Controls Department Field Marketing Support (TIMI)
ICDFS .... Increased Capacity Drum Feed System (MCD)
ICD/FS .... Iterative Coordinate Descent using Functional Substitution (SAUS)
ICDH .... Isocitrate Dehydrogenase [*Also, ICD, IDH*] [*An enzyme*]
ICDI .... Imperial Court, Daughters of Isis (EA)
ICDIA .... International Compact Disc Interactive Association (NTPA)
ICD-L .... De Paul University, Law Library, Chicago, IL [*Library symbol*] [*Library of Congress*] (LCLS)
ICDL .... Integrated Circuit Description Language
ICDL .... Inter-Center Data Link (MCD)
ICDL .... Interface Control Documentation Log (KSC)
ICDL .... Internal Control Description Language
ICDL .... International Centre for Distance Learning [*United Nations University*] (DUND)
ICDL .... International Conference on Conduction and Breakdown in Dielectric Liquids (SAUO)
ICDLA .... Internal Control Description Language Analyzer [*Computer science*] (MHDI)
ICDLI .... International Committee for the Decorative Laminate Industry (SAUO)
ICDM .... IAMAP Commission on Dynamic Meteorology (SAUS)
ICDM .... Industrial Civil Defense Management
ICDM .... Institut Canadien pour la Deficience Mentale [*Canadian Institute on Mental Retardation*] [*Canada*]
ICDM .... International Commission on Dynamic Meteorology (SAUO)
ICDMA .... Independent Carbon-Dioxide Manufacturers Association (EA)
ICDN .... International College of Dentists Newsletter [*Medicine*] (EDAA)
ICDN .... International Diplomatic Computer (SAUS)
ICDNA .... Imidazole (Carbonic Acid) Dinitroanilide [*Organic chemistry*]
ICD/NR .... Iterative Coordinate Descent using Newton-Raphson root location (SAUS)
ICDO .... International Civil Defence (or Defense) Organization (SAUO)
ICDO .... International Civil Defence Organization [*Switzerland*]
ICD-O .... International Classification of Diseases - Oncology [*Medicine*] (EDAA)
ICD OMG .... Information Control Division of the Office of the Military Government (SAUO)
ICDP .... Integrated Circuits Demonstration Plant [*Taiwan*] (NITA)
ICDP .... Integrated Conservation and Development Project
ICDP .... Integrated Conservation/Development Project (SAUO)
ICDP .... Intelligence Career Development Program (AFM)
ICDP .... International Center for Development Policy (EA)
ICDP .... International Confederation for Disarmament and Peace [*British*]
ICDP .... International Conference on Population and Development (SAUO)
ICDP .... International Continental Drilling Program (SAUO)
ICDP .... International Continental Scientific Drilling Program [*Originated by the US, China, and Germany*]
ICDR .... Incremental Critical Design Review (NASA)
ICDR .... Initial Critical Design Review (SAUO)
ICDR .... Interagency Committee on Disability Research (SAUO)
ICDR .... Interim Conceptual Design Report (SAUS)
ICDR .... International Confederation of Drum Reconditioners (SAUO)
ICDR .... International Council for Dispute Resolution (EA)
ICDR .... Inward Call Detail Recording [*Telecommunications*] (TEL)
ICDR .... Ion Cyclotron Double Resonance
ICDRC .... International Contact Dermatitis Research Center [*Medicine*] (EDAA)
ICDRG .... International Contact Dermatitis Research Group (SAUO)
IC DRUM .... Intercommunication Drum (MSA)
ICDS .... Improved Conventional Dive System (DOMA)
ICDS .... Industrial Civil Defence Service (SAUO)
ICDS .... Industry Council for Development Services (SAUO)
ICDS .... Information Collection Dissemination System (SAUS)
ICDS .... Input Command Data Set [*Computer science*] (ELAL)
ICDS .... Institutional Cooperation and Development Services (SAUS)
ICDS .... Instrumentation Control and Data System (SAUS)
ICDS .... Integrated Chemical Defence System (SAUS)
ICDS .... Integrated Chemical Defense System (ACAE)
ICDS .... Integrated Child Development Scheme (DMAA)
ICDS .... Integrated Circuit Design System (CIST)
ICDS .... Integrated Cockpit Display System (SAUS)
ICDS .... Integrated Combat Direction System [*Military*]
ICDS .... Integrated Control and Display System (MCD)
ICDS .... Intelligence Communications Distribution System (ACAE)
ICDS .... Intelligent Content Distribution Service (GART)
ICDS .... Interim Contractor Depot Support [*DoD*]
ICDS .... International Cardiac Doppler Society (DMAA)
ICDS .... International Conference on Defects in Semiconductors (SAUS)
ICDS .... Intregrated Child Development Services (SAUO)
ICDSC .... International Conference on Digital Satellite Communications (SAUO)
ICDSI .... Independent Commission on Disarmament and Security Issues (ACAE)
ICDSP .... Interim Contractor Depot Support Plan [*DoD*]
ICDSRHP .... International Committee for the Defense of Salman Rushdie and His Publishers (EAIO)
ICDSSS .... Intelligence Communication & Defense Special Security System (SAUS)
ICDS/WA .... Interuniversity Consortium for Development Studies/WA (SAUO)
ICDT .... Chicago Daily Tribune, Chicago, IL [*Library symbol*] [*Library of Congress*] (LCLS)
ICDT .... Incident (AABC)
ICDT .... Inverse Discrete Cosine Transform [*Mathematics*]
ICDT .... Islamic Center for Development of Trade (SAUS)
ICDT .... Islamic Centre for Development of Trade [*See also CIDC*] [*Casablanca, Morocco*] (EAIO)
ICDU .... Inertial Coupling Data Unit (NASA)
ICDU .... Inertial Coupling Display Unit (KSC)
ICDU .... Integrated Control & Display Unit (SAUS)
ICDUP .... International Council for the Development of Underutilized Plants (SAUO)
ICD-USA .... International College of Dentists, United States of America Section (NTPA)
IC/DV .... Import Certificate and Delivery Verification (SAUO)
ICDV .... Import Certificate Delivery Verification [*Military*]
ICDWS .... Integrated Chemical Detection and Warning System (ACAE)
ICDxC .... International Club for Dxing and Communication (SAUO)
ICE .... Arctic Alaska Fisheries Corp. [*AMEX symbol*] (COMM)
ICE .... Concordia Teachers College, River Forest, IL [*OCLC symbol*] (OCLC)
ICE .... Economist Newspapers, Chicago, IL [*Library symbol*] [*Library of Congress*] (LCLS)
ICE .... Ice, Compression, Elevation (CPH)
ICE .... Ice Edge Ecosystem study (SAUO)
Ice .... Iceland (SHCU)
ICE .... Iceland
ICE .... Icelandair [*ICAO designator*] (FAAC)
Ice .... Icelandic (DIAR)
ice .... Icelandic [*MARC language code*] [*Library of Congress*] (LCCP)
ICE .... Ice Station Resources [*Vancouver Stock Exchange symbol*]
ICE .... Illinois Computing Educators
ICE .... Illness-Correctional Environments
ICE .... Immediate Cable Equalizer (IAA)
ICE .... Implicit Continuous-Fluid Eulerian
ICE .... Improved Combat Efficiency (ACAE)
ICE .... Improved Combat Engineering (SAUS)
ICE .... Improved Cost Estimate (RDA)
ICE .... Improving Career Education (OICC)
ICE .... In-Car Entertainment [*Automotive audio system*]
ICE .... Incidental Campaign Expense [*Ticket scalping*]
ICE .... In-Circuit Emulation (SAUS)
ICE .... In-Circuit Emulator [*A trademark*]
ICE .... Increased Combat Effectiveness (AFM)
ICE .... Independent Collection Equipment (SAUS)
ICE .... Independent Cost Estimate
ICE .... Index of Combat Effectiveness (CINC)
ICE .... Indiana Computer Educators (EDAC)
ICE .... Indicative Cost Estimate (SAUS)
ICE .... Indigenous Council for the Environment (SAUO)
ICE .... Individual Career Exploration [*Vocational guidance test*]
ICE .... Individual Commitment to Excellence [*DoD*]
ICE .... Individual Compass Error (IAA)
ICE .... Induction Certificate Examination [*British Institute of Innkeeping*]
ICE .... Industrial Combustion Emissions Model [*Environmental Protection Agency*] (GFGA)
ICE .... Industrial Computer Enclosure (IAA)
ICE .... Industrial Cost Exclusion [*Amendment to Federal Clean Water Act which limits use of federal money*]
ICE .... Information and Content Exchange
ICE .... Information Center for the Environment (SAUO)
ICE .... Information Center on Education [*New York State Education Department*] [*Albany*] [*Information service or system*] (IID)
ICE .... Information Centre Exchange [*Canada*] (EAIO)
ICE .... Information Collecting Equipment (SAUS)
ICE .... Information Collection and Exchange [*Peace Corps*]
ICE .... Information Content Exchange
ICE .... Infrared Countermeasures Equipment [*Military*] [*Electronics*] (CAAL)
ICE .... Initial Combat Employment [*of new munitions*]
ICE .... Initial Cooling Experiment [*Nuclear physics research*]
ICE .... Initial Cost Estimate (SAUO)
ICE .... Inner City Enterprises [*British*]
ICE .... Input Checking Equipment (SAUS)
ICE .... Input-Checking Equipment
ICE .... Input Control Electronics (SAUS)
ICE .... Input Control Element (MCD)
ICE .... Input Count Error (VLIE)
ICE .... Insertion Communications Equipment (SAUS)
ICE .... Instant Camouflage Envelope (SAUS)
ICE .... Institute for Chemical Education (EA)
ICE .... Institute for Christian Education [*Australia*]
ICE .... Institute for Community Economics (EA)
ICE .... Institute for Consumer Ergonomics [*British*] (IRUK)
ICE .... Institute for Continuing Education (AIE)
ICE .... Institute of Ceramic Engineers (NUCP)
ICE .... Institute of Chartered Engineers (SAUS)
ICE .... Institute of Christian Education (SAUO)

ICE.............. Institute of Consumer Ergonomics (SAUO)
ICE.............. Institute of Control Engineering (SAUS)
ICE.............. Institution of Chemical Engineers [*British*] (EAIO)
ICE.............. Institution of Civil Engineers [*British*]
ICE.............. Instruction Curriculum Environment (SAUS)
ICE.............. Instructor Course Evaluation (SAUS)
ICE.............. Instrumentation Communication Equipment (NASA)
ICE.............. Instrument Checkout Equipment [*NASA*] (KSC)
ICE.............. Instrument Communication
ICE.............. Instrument/Communication Equipment (SAUS)
ICE.............. Insulated Cable Engineer (SAUS)
ICE.............. Integral Contract Enhancement
ICE.............. Integrated Car Engineer
ICE.............. Integrated Car Engineering
ICE.............. Integrated Circuit Engineering (SAUS)
ICE.............. Integrated Circuits Engineering Corp.
ICE.............. Integrated Clinical Encounters
ICE.............. Integrated Coil Electronic [*Automotive engineering*]
ICE.............. Integrated Communications Architecture (SAUS)
ICE.............. Integrated Communications Environment [*Computer architecture*] (NITA)
ICE.............. Integrated Component Evaluator (SAUS)
ICE.............. Integrated Computer Environment (ABAC)
ICE.............. Integrated Computing Environment (SAUS)
ICE.............. Integrated Conceptual Environment [*Computer science*]
ICE.............. Integrated Conceptual Environments (SAUO)
ICE.............. Integrated Cooling Electronics (SAUS)
ICE.............. Integrated Cooling for Electronics
ICE.............. Integrated Curriculum Environment [*Army*]
ICE.............. Integration with Controlled Error (MCD)
ICE.............. Intelligence and Counterespionage [*Fictitious organization in the Matt Helm series of books and movies*]
ICE.............. Intelligent Concept Extraction [*Technology*] [*Computer science*]
ICE.............. Interactive Collaborative Environment (VLIE)
ICE.............. Interactive Concurrent Engineering [*Software*]
ICE.............. Interactive Cost Estimating (SAUS)
ICE.............. Intercity Experimental (SAUS)
ICE.............. Inter City Express [*Electric train*] [*Germany*]
ICE.............. InterCity Express (SAUS)
ICE.............. Inter-Client Exchange (SAUS)
ICE.............. Intercomparison Experiment (SAUS)
ICE.............. Intercomputer Electronics (IAA)
ICE.............. Inter-Computer Electronics, Incorporated (SAUO)
ICE.............. Interconnect Communication Element (SAUS)
ICE.............. Interconnection Equipment (VLIE)
ICE.............. Interface Cancellation Equipment [*Telecommunications*] (EECA)
ICE.............. Interface Configuration Experiment (SAUS)
ICE.............. Interfaith Coalition on Energy (EA)
ICE.............. Interference Cancellation Equipment [*Telecommunications*]
ICE.............. Interference Cancelling Equipment (SAUS)
ICE.............. Interleukin-Converting Enzyme [*Biochemistry*]
ICE.............. Intermediate Cable Equalizer (SAUS)
ICE.............. Intermediate Cable Equalizers (IEEE)
ICE.............. Internal Combustion Engine
ICE.............. Internal Communications Element (SAUO)
ICE.............. Internal Communications Exchange (SAUS)
ICE.............. International Center for the Environment
ICE.............. International Centre for Economics [*British*]
ICE.............. International Cirrus Experiment [*Funded by West Germany, Britain, France, Sweden, and the European Communities Commission*] [*Climatology*]
ICE.............. International Collaborative Effort on Injury Statistics (SAUO)
ICE.............. International Comatary Explorer (SAUS)
ICE.............. International Cometary Explorer [*Formerly, International Sun-Ea rth Explorer*] [*NASA*]
ICE.............. International Comet Explorer (SAUS)
ICE.............. International Commercial Exchange [*Defunct*] (EA)
ICE.............. International Committee of Experts (SAUO)
ICE.............. International Computer Component Exchange
ICE.............. International Congress of Ecology (SAUO)
ICE.............. International Congress of Entomology [*Later, CICE*] (EA)
ICE.............. International Construction Equipment Exhibition (ITD)
ICE.............. International Consulting Engineers Inc. (SAUO)
ICE.............. International Council on Electrocardiology [*Glasgow, Scotland*] (EAIO)
ICE.............. International Cultural Exchange [*An association*] (EA)
ICE.............. Internet Commerce Enabled (HODG)
ICE.............. Internet Commerce Exchange
ICE.............. Internet Connections for Engineering
ICE.............. Interstate Cost Estimate [*Federal Highway Administration*]
ICE.............. Interworking Public Key Certification Infrastructure for Europe (SAUO)
i ce.............. Intracerebral [*Medicine*] (EDAA)
ICE.............. Intracochlear Electrodes [*Medicine*] (MELL)
ICE.............. Intrusion Countermeasure Electronics (VLIE)
ICE.............. Intrusion Countermeasures Electronics
ICE.............. Inventory Control Effectiveness
ICE.............. IOMTR Committee for Europe (SAUO)
ICE.............. Ion Chromatography Exclusion
ICE.............. Ion Convection Electrodynamics (MCD)
ICE.............. Iridocorneal Endothelial syndrome (SAUS)
ICE.............. Irridescent Color Exchange [*Heat-sensitive clothing*]
ICE.............. Islamic Council of Europe
ICE.............. Isoprene Canopy Experiment (SAUS)
ICE.............. Isoprene Closure Experiment (SAUS)
ICE.............. Isothermal Controlled Electrophoresis
ICE.............. Italian Cultural Exchange in the United States (EA)
ICE.............. It's Close Enough
ICE.............. Icing [*Meteorology*] (ODA)
ICEA............ Institut Canadien d'Education des Adultes [*Canadian Institute of Adult Education*]
ICEA............ Institution of Chemical Engineers in Australia
ICEA............ Instrument Contracting and Engineering Association (EA)
ICEA............ Insulated Cable Engineers Association (EA)
ICEA............ International Childbirth Education Association (EA)
ICEA............ International Christian Education Association (EA)
ICEA............ International Christian Esperanto Association (EA)
ICEA............ International College of Executives and Administrators (SAUO)
ICEA............ International Commission for Environmental Assessment (GNE)
ICEA............ International Commission on Environmental Assessment (SAUS)
ICEA............ International Community Education Association (SAUO)
ICEA............ International Consulting Economists Association [*British*] (DBA)
ICEA............ International Consumer Electronics Association (SAUO)
Ice Abs........ Ice Abstracts (journ.) (SAUS)
ICEAM.......... Institute of Computer Aided Engineering and Management [*University of Dundee*] [*British*] (IRUK)
ICEAM.......... International Committee on Economic and Applied Microbiology [*ICSU*] (EAIO)
ICE Approach... Implicit Continuous Eulerian Approach (SAUS)
ICEAR.......... International Centre for Equatorial Atmospheric Research, Indonesia (SAUS)
ICEAS.......... Intermittent Cycle Extended Aeration System (SAUO)
ICEATCA...... Icelandic Air Traffic Controllers Association (SAUO)
ICEATT......... Index of Continuing Education Attitudes
ICEB............ Indonesian Commodity Exchange Board [*Badan Pelaksana Bursa Komoditi*] [*Indonesia*] (FEA)
ICEBAC........ International Council of Employers of Bricklayers and Allied Craftsmen (SAUO)
ICE/BAC....... International Council of Employers of Bricklayers and Allied Craftworkers (NTPA)
ICEBY........... International Conference for the Education of Blind Youth (SAUO)
ICEC............ Ice Center Environment Canada (SAUS)
ICEC............ Ice Centre (SAUS)
ICEC............ Illinois Citizens Education Council (SAUO)
ICEC............ Institute of Chartered Engineers of Canada (SAUS)
ICEC............ Interagency Career Education Committee (OICC)
ICEC............ Intercontinental Energy Corporation (SAUO)
ICEC............ International Coast Engineering Council (SAUO)
ICEC............ International Committee of Enamelling Creators (EAIO)
ICEC............ International Conference on Education in Chemistry
ICEC............ International Cost Engineering Council (EA)
ICEC............ International Council for Exceptional Children [*Later, CEC*]
ICEC............ International Cryogenic Engineering Committee (EAIO)
ICEC............ International Cryogenic Engineering Committee (or Conference) (SAUS)
ICEC............ Interuniversity Consortium for Educational Computing [*Database*]
IC/EC........... Ion Chromatography using Electroconductivity Detector (SAUS)
ICECA.......... Indochina Ethnic Chinese Association of Victoria [*Australia*]
ICECAN........ Iceland-Canada Cable (NITA)
ICECAN........ Iceland-Canada Submarine Cable (SAUS)
ICECAN........ Iceland-Canada Submarine Cable System [*Telecommunications*] (TEL)
ICECAN........ Iceland-Canada telephone cable (SAUO)
ICECAN Telephone Cable... Iceland Canada Telephone Cable (SAUS)
ICECAP........ Infrared Chemistry Experiments Coordinated Auroral Program [*Defense Nuclear Agency*] (PDAA)
ICECAP........ Infrared Chemistry Experiments-Coordinated Auroral Program (SAUS)
ICEC/ICMC... International Cryogenic Engineering Conference/International Cryogenic Materials Conference (SAUS)
ICECOLORS... Cold water component of Watercolors (SAUS)
ICECON........ Control of Sea Ice Information (NATG)
ICECOOP...... Chilean Institute for Cooperative Education (SAUO)
ICE Corporation... Integrated Circuit Engineering Corp. (SAUS)
ICE Corporation... Integrated Circuit Engineering Corporation (SAUO)
ICECS........... Integrated Closed-Loop Environmental Control System (PDAA)
ICED............ Industrial and Construction Equipment Division (EA)
ICED............ Institute for Community Education Development [*Ball State University*] [*Research center*] (RCD)
ICEd............ Institute of Craft Education (SAUO)
ICED............ Interface Control Envelope Drawings (KSC)
ICED............ Interface Control Environment Drawing (IAA)
ICED............ International Coalition for Energy Development (SAUS)
ICED............ International Coalition on Energy for Development
ICED............ International Conference on Engineering Design (SAUS)
ICED............ International Congress on the Education of the Deaf
ICED............ International Consortium of Educational Development (SAUO)
ICED............ International Council for Educational Development (EA)
ICED............ International Council on Environmental Design (SAUO)
ICED............ Interprofessional Commission on Environmental Design (SAUO)
ICED............ Interprofessional Council of Environmental Designers (SAUO)
ICED............ Interprofessional Council on Environmental Design (EA)
ICED............ Intraprofessional Council on Environmental Design (SAUO)
ICED............ Ionospheric Conductivity and Electron Density (SAUO)
ICED............ Packaged Ice, Inc. [*NASDAQ symbol*] (NASQ)
ICEDA.......... Intracranial Epidural Abscess [*Medicine*] (MELL)
ICEDEFOR.... Iceland Defense Force
ICEDF........... Ice Decontamination Factor (SAUS)
ICEDIS......... International Committee on EDI for Serials (SAUS)
ICEDIS......... International Committee on Electronic Data Interchange for Serials
ICEdit.......... EDITEC, Chicago, IL [*Library symbol*] [*Library of Congress*] (LCLS)

ICEDOC........ International Committee for Establishment and Development of Oncology Centers (ADWA)
ICEDS.......... Insurance Company Education Directors Society (EA)
ICEDS.......... International Co-Operation for Economic Development and Solidarity (SAUO)
ICEE............ Interafrican College of Electrical Engineering (SAUO)
ICEE............ Interafrican College of Eletrical Engineering (SAUS)
ICEE............ International Commission on Rules for Approval of Electrical Equipment (SAUO)
ICEE............ International Committee on Exhibition Exchange (SAUO)
ICEE............ International Control Engineering Expnsition (SAUS)
ICEE............ Iranian Conference on Electrical Engineering (SAUO)
ICEEC.......... International Congress of Electrical and Electronic Communications
ICEED.......... International Center for Energy and Economic Development
ICEED.......... International Research Center for Energy and Economic Development [*University of Colorado*] [*Research center*]
ICEEGL........ Index to Current [*Medicine*] (EDAA)
ICEF............ Institute for the Community as Extended Family (EA)
ICEF............ Interactive Composition and Editing Facility [*IBM Corp.*]
ICEF............ International Chemical and Energy Workers Federation
ICEF............ International Children's Emergency Fund [*United Nations*] (DLA)
ICEF............ International Committee for Ethnographic Films (SAUO)
ICEF............ International Committee for Research and Study of/on Environmental Factors (SAUO)
ICEF............ International Committee for Research and Study on Environmental Factors
ICEF............ International Conferences on Environmental Future (SAUS)
ICEF............ International Congress on Engineering and Food (SAUS)
ICEF............ International Cooperative Emulsion Flights (SAUO)
ICEF............ International Council for Educational Films [*Later, ICEM*]
ICEF............ International Federation of Chemical, Energy and General Workers Unions (SAUO)
ICEFs.......... International Conferences on Environmental Future (SAUO)
ICEG............ Insulated Conductors Export Group (SAUS)
ICEH............ International Centre for Eye Health (SAUO)
ICEI............. Independent Cold Extruders Institute
ICEI............. Institute of Civil Engineers of Ireland (SAUO)
ICEI............. Institution of Civil Engineers of Ireland (BI)
ICEI............. Internal Combustion Engine Institute [*Later, EMA*] (EA)
ICEI............. Internal Combustion Engine Institute, Inc.
ICEI............. International Combustion Engine Institute (SAUS)
ICEIDA......... Icelandic International Development Agency (SAUS)
Icel.............. Iceland (VRA)
ICEL............ Icelandic
ICEL............ Industry Committee for Emergency Lighting (SAUO)
ICEL............ Intercel, Inc. [*NASDAQ symbol*] (SAG)
ICEL............ International Commission on English in the Liturgy (SAUO)
ICEL............ International Committee for Ethnic Liberty [*See also IKEL*] (EAIO)
ICEL............ International Committee on English in the Liturgy (EA)
ICEL............ International Council for Environmental Law (SAUS)
ICEL............ International Council for/of Environmental Law (SAUO)
ICEL............ International Council of Environmental Law [*Bonn, Federal Republic of Germany*] (EA)
ICELA.......... International Computer Exposition for Latin America (SAUO)
ICEM............ Incremental Cost Effectiveness Model
ICEM............ Independent Cluster Emission Model [*Atomic physics*]
ICEM............ Induced Contamination Experimental Monitor (MCD)
ICEM............ Integrated Computer-aided Engineering and Manufactoring (SAUS)
ICEM............ Integrated Computer Engineering and Management (SAUS)
ICEM............ Integrated Computer Engineering and Manufacturing (SAUS)
ICEM............ Intergovernmental Committee for European Migration [*Later, ICM*]
ICEM............ International Commission for European Migration (SAUO)
ICEM............ International Confederation for Electroacoustic Music (EA)
ICEM............ International Conference on Electron Microscopy (SAUS)
ICEM............ International Conference on Emergency Medicine (SAUO)
ICEM............ International Congress on Experimental Mechanics (SAUS)
ICEM............ International Council for Educational Media [*Formerly, ICEF*]
ICEM............ International Federation of Chemical, Energy, Mine and General Workers Unions (SAUS)
ICEM............ Inverted Coaxial Magnetron (MCD)
ICEM............ Irish Council European Movement
ICEMES........ International Cooperation on Marine Engineering Systems (SAUO)
ICEM/IM....... International Migration. Quarterly review (journ.) (SAUS)
ICEM/IM....... International Migration Quarterly review of the Intergovernmental Committee for European Migration and the Research Group for European Migration Problems (SAUO)
ICEMO.......... Institute of Christian Education at Home and Overseas (SAUO)
ICE MODEL... Industrial Combustion Emissions Model (EAGT)
ICEMS.......... Infra-Company Electronic Mail System (SAUS)
ICEMS.......... Intra-Company Electronic Mail System (SAUO)
ICen............ Centralia Public Library, Centralia, IL [*Library symbol*] [*Library of Congress*] (LCLS)
ICEN............ [*The*] Israel Commercial Economic Newsletter [*A publication*] [*Also, an information service or system*] (IID)
ICEnB.......... Encyclopaedia Britannica, Inc., Chicago, IL [*Library symbol*] [*Library of Congress*] (LCLS)
ICenC.......... Centralia Correctional Center, Centralia, IL [*Library symbol*] [*Library of Congress*] (LCLS)
ICenHS........ Centralia District High School, District 200, Centralia, IL [*Library symbol*] [*Library of Congress*] (LCLS)
IC Ent.......... International Congress of Entomology (SAUO)
ICEO............ International Conference of Engineering Organization (SAUO)
ICEOB.......... Sea Ice Observation Code [*Marine science*] (MSC)
ICEOP.......... Inner-City Engineering Orientation Program (SAUS)
ICEP............ Iberoamerican Cultural Exchange Program [*An association*] (EA)
ICEP............ Institut Canadien d'Enseignement Personnalise Inc. (AC)
ICEP............ Institute for Cultural Exchange thru Photography (EA)
ICEP............ Instituto do Comercio Externo (Lisbon, Portugal) [*Institute of Commercial Exports*] (EY)
ICEP............ International Federation of Anti-Leprosy Associations (SAUO)
ICEP............ Intra-Corporate Entrepreneurial Programme (SAUO)
ICEPAK........ Intelligent Classifier Engineering Package (SAUS)
ICEPART...... Index of Continuing Education Participation
ICEPAT........ Iceland Patrol [*Navy*]
ICEPF.......... International Commission for the Eriksson Prize Fund (EAIO)
ICEPM.......... Internal Combustion Engine Powered Material (MCD)
ICEPM.......... Internal Combustion Engine Powered Materiel (SAUO)
ICEPS.......... Institute for International Economic Cooperation and Development (SAUO)
ICEPS.......... International Center for Economic Policy Studies (SAUO)
ICEPT.......... International Committee for Enteric Page Typing (SAUO)
ICEQ............ Individualized Classroom Environment Questionnaire (EDAC)
ICER............ Information Center of the European Railways (SAUO)
ICER............ Information Centre of the European Railways
ICER............ Infrared Cell, Electronically Refrigerated
ICER............ Institute for Central European Research (EA)
ICER............ Interdepartmental Committee of External Relations [*Canada*]
ICER............ Interdepartmental Committee on External Relations (SAUS)
ICER............ Interdisciplinary Committee for Environmental Research (SAUO)
ICER............ International Conference on Electromagnetic Relays (SAUO)
ICER............ Interstate Congress for Equal Rights and Responsibilities (SAUO)
I Ceram....... Institute of Ceramics (SAUO)
ICERA-VIC.... Indo-Chinese Elderly Refugee Association of Victoria [*Australia*]
ICERC.......... Interagency Country Exposure Review Committee (SAUS)
ICERC.......... International Cetacean Education Research Center (SAUO)
ICERD.......... International Centre for Economics & Related Disciplines (SAUO)
ICEROCC...... Iceland Regional Operational Control Center [*Aircraft surveillance*]
ICEROCC...... Iceland Regional Operations Control Center (SAUS)
ICERP.......... Internal Combustion Engine Repair Shop
ICERR.......... Interstate Congress for Equal Rights and Responsibilities (EA)
ICERUN........ Ice on the Runway (SAUS)
ICES............ Ice, Compression, Elevation, Support [*Medicine*] (MEDA)
ICES............ Import Cargo Electronic System
ICES............ Information Center for Energy Safety (SAUS)
ICES............ Information Collection and Evaluation System (DMAA)
ICES............ Information, Communication, Entertainment, Safety, and Security
ICES............ Information Communications, Entertainment, and Security
ICES............ Initial Graphics Exchange Specifications (SAUS)
ICES............ Institute for Clinical Evaluative Sciences (SAUO)
ICES............ Institute for Complex Engineered Systems (SAUO)
ICES............ Institution of Civil Engineering Surveyors [*British*] (DBA)
ICES............ Institution of Civil Engineers (SAUO)
ICES............ Institution of Surveyors in Civil Engineering [*British*]
ICES............ Instructor and Course Evaluation System (EDAC)
ICES............ Integrated Civil Engineering Software System (CIST)
ICES............ Integrated Civil Engineering System [*Programming language*] [*Computer science*]
ICES............ Integrated Combat Electronics System (SAUO)
ICES............ Integrated Community Energy System (SAUO)
ICES............ Interactive Cost Estimating System (TIMI)
IC/ES.......... Intercommunication/Emergency Station (SAUS)
IC/ES.......... Intercommunications/Emergency Station (MCD)
ICES............ Intercontinental Engine Service, Inc. (SAUO)
ICES............ Interference-Causing Equipment Standard (SAUS)
ICES............ Internal-Conversion Electron Spectroscopy (SAUS)
ICES............ International Carnival of Experimental Sound (SAUO)
ICES............ International Centre for Ethnic Studies (EA)
ICES............ International Commission on Erosion and Sedimentation (SAUO)
ICES............ International Commission on Erosion Sedimentation (NUCP)
ICES............ International Committee for Earth Sciences (SAUO)
ICES............ International Conference of Engineering Societies (SAUO)
ICES............ International Conference of Engineering Studies (SAUS)
ICES............ International Conference on Environmental Systems
ICES............ International Conference on Evolvable Systems (SAUS)
ICES............ International Convention for the Exploration of the Seas (SAUO)
ICES............ International Council for the Exploration of the Sea [*Denmark*]
ICES............ International Council of Electrophoresis Societies (HGEN)
ICES............ International Cultural Exchange Service
ICEs............ International Customs Examinations (SAUS)
ICES............ Intersociety Conference on Environmental Systems (ACAE)
ICES............ Interuniversity Centre for European Studies [*Canada*] (IRC)
ICES............ National Easter Seal Society for Crippled Children and Adults, Chicago, IL [*Library symbol*] [*Library of Congress*] (LCLS)
ICES............ University Centre for European Studies (SAUO)
ICES66........ International Covenant on Economic, Social, and Cultural Rights of 16 December 1966 (SAFN)
ICESA.......... International Conference on Environmental Sensing and Assessment
ICESA.......... Interstate Conference of Employment Security Agencies (EA)
ICESat......... Ice, Cloud and land Elevation Satellite (SAUS)
ICESAT......... Ice Processes Satellite (SAUS)
ICESC.......... Industry Crew Escape Systems Committee
ICESC.......... International Committee for European Security and Co-Operation [*See also CISCE*] (EAIO)
ICESC.......... International Council for Economic and Social Cooperation (SAUO)
ICESCR........ International covenant on economic, social and cultural rights (SAUO)
ICESD.......... Intergovernment Committee on Ecologically Sustainable Development (SAUO)
ICESS.......... Institute for Computational Earth System Science
ICESSP........ International Council for Elementary and Secondary School Philosophy (SAUO)

ICES-STRUDL... Integrated Civil Engineering System Structural Design Language (SAUO)
ICET............ Forty-Eight Item Counseling Evaluation Test [*Psychology*]
ICET............ Institute for Certification of Engineering Technicians (SAUS)
ICET............ Institute for Comparative and Environmental Toxicology [*Cornell University*] [*Research center*] (RCD)
ICET............ Institute for the Certification of Engineering Technicians [*Later, National Institute for Certification in Engineering Technologies*]
ICET............ Integrated Cumulus Ensemble Turbulence (SAUS)
ICET............ Interagency Committee on Excavation Technology [*Federal Council for Science and Technology*] [*Terminated, 1976*]
ICET............ International Center for Earth Tides (SAUS)
ICET............ International Center of Economy and Technology (SAUS)
ICET............ International Centre for Earth Tides [*See also CIMT*] [*Belgium*] (EAIO)
ICET............ International Centre for Economy and Technology (SAUO)
ICET............ International Centre of Economy and Technology (SAUS)
ICET............ International Council on Education for Teaching (EA)
IceTec.......... Technological Institute of Iceland (SAUS)
ICETK.......... International Committee of Electrochemical Thermodynamics and Kinetics (SAUO)
ICETK.......... International Council of Electrochemical Thermodynamics and Kinetics (SAUO)
ICETRAN...... Integrated Civil Engineering System FORTRAN (SAUO)
ICETT.......... Industrial Council for Educational and Training Technology (SAUO)
ICETT.......... Industrial Council for Educational Training Technology [*British*] (DS)
ICEU............ Improved Combat Efficiency Upgrade (SAUS)
ICEUM.......... International Conference on Energy Use Management
ICEV............ Initial Condition Evaluation [*Orbit identification*]
ICEV............ Internal Combustion Engine Vehicle
ICEVH.......... International Council for Education of the Visually Handicapped [*Bensheim, Federal Republic of Germany*] (EAIO)
ICEWATER... Inter-Agency Committee on Water Resources (SAUS)
ICEWG.......... Interim C and E Working Group (SAUS)
ICEWG.......... Interim Communications-Electronics Working Group (SAUO)
ICEX............ Ice and Climate Experiment (SAUO)
ICEX............ Integrated Civil Engineering Executive (MHDI)
ICEX............ Intelligence Coordination and Exploitation [*Joint CIA-MACV program*]
ICEYF.......... International Capital Equipment Ltd. [*NASDAQ symbol*] (COMM)
ICF.............. Field Museum of Natural History, Chicago, IL [*Library symbol*] [*Library of Congress*] (LCLS)
ICF.............. George Williams College, Downers Grove, IL [*OCLC symbol*] (OCLC)
ICF.............. Ice Cream Federation (SAUO)
ICF.............. Ice Cream Federation, Ltd. (SAUO)
ICF.............. ICF Kaiser International [*NYSE symbol*] (SPSG)
ICF.............. Immigration Card Facility (SAUS)
ICF.............. Incommunication Flip-Flop (SAUS)
ICF.............. Incremental Cost per Foot (SAUS)
ICF.............. Independent Cat Federation (SAUO)
ICF.............. Indirect Centrifugal Flotation
ICF.............. Industrial and Commercial Finance Corp. (SAUO)
ICF.............. Industrial Christian Fellowship [*British*] (DBA)
ICF.............. Inertial Confinement Fusion [*Nuclear physics*]
ICF.............. Inertial Confulement Fusion (SAUS)
ICF.............. Insert Character in Field (SAUS)
ICF.............. Inspection Check Fixture (MSA)
ICF.............. Inspection Checking Fixture (SAUS)
ICF.............. Installation Confinement Facility [*Army*] (AABC)
ICF.............. Institut Canadien du Film [*Canadian Film Institute - CFI*]
ICF.............. Institute for Canadian Futures
ICF.............. Institute of Chart Foresters [*British*] (DBA)
ICF.............. Instructional Computing Facility (SAUS)
ICF.............. Instrument Control Facility (EOSA)
ICF.............. Insulated Concrete Form
ICF.............. Integral Coach Factory [*Indian Railway*] [*Perambur*] (TIR)
ICF.............. Integrated Catalog Facility (HGAA)
ICF.............. Integrated Control Facility [*Sperry UNIVAC*]
ICF.............. Integrated Crystal Filter (IAA)
ICF.............. Intelligence Contingency Funds (CINC)
ICF.............. Intensive Care Facility [*Medicine*]
ICF.............. Interacting Correlated Fragment [*Physical chemistry*]
ICF.............. Interactive Command Facility (VLIE)
ICF.............. Interactive Communications Feature [*IBM Corp.*]
ICF.............. Interactive Computer Facility (NITA)
ICF.............. Inter-Bureau Citation of Funds [*Navy*]
ICF.............. Intercellular Fluorescence (DB)
ICF.............. Interciliary Fluid (STED)
ICF.............. Intercommunication Flip-Flop [*Computer science*]
ICF.............. Interconnect Facilities (SAUS)
ICF.............. Interconnect Facility
ICF.............. Interface Control Function (MCD)
ICF.............. Intermediate Care Facility [*Medicine*]
ICF.............. Intermediate Control Field (SAUS)
ICF.............. International Canoe Federation [*See also FIC*] [*Florence, Italy*] (EAIO)
ICF.............. International Cardiology Foundation (EA)
ICF.............. International Cardiovascular Foundation (SAUO)
ICF.............. International Carpet Fair
ICF.............. International Casting Federation (EAIO)
ICF.............. International Cheerleading Foundation (EA)
ICF.............. International Congregational Fellowship (EA)
ICF.............. International Congress on Fracture [*ICSU*] [*Sendai, Japan*] (EAIO)
ICF.............. International Consultants Foundation (EA)
ICF.............. International Cotton Federation (SAUO)
ICF.............. International Crane Foundation (EA)
ICF.............. International Craniofacial Foundations (EA)
ICF.............. International Cremation Federation (EAIO)
ICF.............. International Cryptographic Framework (SAUS)
ICF.............. International Curling Federation (EAIO)
ICF.............. International Federation of Chemical and General Workers (SAUO)
ICF.............. International Federation of Chemical and General Workers Union
ICF.............. Intern Classification Farrier [*Equine term*] (TED)
ICF.............. Internet Connection Firewall
ICF.............. Intracellular Fluid [*Physiology*]
ICF.............. Intravascular Coagulation and Fibrinolysis Syndrome [*Medicine*]
ICF.............. Intrinsic Coercive Force
ICF.............. Iota-Cam Fiberscope [*Also, ICFS*]
ICF.............. Iowa College Foundation (SAUO)
ICF.............. Italian Catholic Federation Central Council (EA)
ICF.............. Item Control File [*Computer science*] (VLIE)
ICF-A.......... Field Museum of Natural History, Edward E. Ayer Ornithological Library, Chicago,IL [*Library symbol*] [*Library of Congress*] (LCLS)
ICFA............ Fireman Apprentice, Interior Communications Electrician, Striker [*Navy rating*]
ICFA............ Incomplete Freund Adjuvant (STED)
ICFA............ Independent College Funds of America [*Later, FIHE*] (EA)
ICFA............ Induced Complement Fixing Antigen (SAUS)
ICFA............ Induced Complement-Fixing Antigen (STED)
ICFA............ Inland Commercial Fisheries Association (EA)
ICFA............ Institute of Chartered Financial Analysis (SAUO)
ICFA............ Institute of Chartered Financial Analysts [*Later, AIMR*] (EA)
ICFA............ Interior Communications Electrician Fireman Apprentice (SAUS)
ICFA............ International Cemetery and Funeral Association (NTPA)
ICFA............ International Chicken Flying Association (SAUO)
ICFA............ International Committee for Future (SAUS)
ICFA............ International Committee for Museums of Fine Arts (SAUO)
ICFA............ International Committee for/on Future Accelerators (SAUO)
ICFA............ International Committee on Future Accelerators [*International Union of Pure and Applied Physics*]
ICFA............ International Computer Facsimile Association (PS)
ICFA............ International Cystic Fibrosis Association (SAUO)
ICFAC.......... Inertial Confinement Fusion Advisory Committee [*Department of Energy*]
ICFAD.......... International Council of Fine Arts Deans (EA)
ICFAR.......... Federal Archives and Records Center, General Services Administration, Chicago, IL [*Library symbol*] [*Library of Congress*] (LCLS)
ICFAR.......... Indianapolis Center for Advanced Research [*Indiana University - Purdue University at Indianapolis*] [*Research center*] (RCD)
ICFAS.......... International Council of Fine Arts Deans (SAUO)
ICFATCM...... Individual Cleared for Access to Classified Material (AAG)
ICFATCMUTAI... Individual Cleared for Access to Classified Material Up to and Including
ICFAX.......... Integrated Circuit Failure Analysis Expert System
ICFB............ International Catholic Film Bureau (SAUO)
ICFC............ Felician College, Chicago, IL [*Library symbol*] [*Library of Congress*] (LCLS)
ICFC............ Industrial and Commercial Finance Corporation (SAUO)
IC/FC.......... Instrumentation Calibration Functional Check (SAUS)
ICFC............ International Center for Fairs and Congresses (SAUS)
ICFC............ International Centre of Films for Children
ICFC............ International Cold Forging Corporation, Monaco (SAUO)
ICFC............ International Council of Fan Clubs [*Defunct*] (EA)
ICFCB.......... Foote, Cone & Belding Advertising, Inc., Corporate Inforamtion Center, Chicago, IL [*Library symbol*] [*Library of Congress*] (LCLS)
ICFCM.......... International Convention of Faith, Churches, and Ministers (EA)
ICFCYP........ International Centre of Films for Children and Young People [*France*] (EY)
ICFD............ Institute for Computational Fluid Dynamics (SAUS)
ICFE............ Independent Colleges of Further Education [*British*]
ICFE............ Institute for Consumer Financial Education (EA)
ICFE............ International Contract Flooring Exhibition [*British*] (ITD)
ICFE............ Intra-Collisional Field Effect (IAA)
ICFET.......... Inhomogeneous Channel Field-Effect Transistor (PDAA)
ICFF............ International Contemporary Furniture Fair (ITD)
ICFFO.......... International Council of Folklore Festival Organizations and Folk Art (EA)
ICFG............ International Cold Forging Group (SAUO)
ICFG............ International Commission on Fungal Genetics [*International Council of Scientific Unions*]
ICFI............ International Cooperative Fracture Institute
ICFI............ Iota-Cam Fiberscope Instrument
ICFID.......... Inter-Church Fund for International Development (SAUO)
ICF Int........ ICF Kaiser International [*Associated Press*] (SAG)
ICFIU.......... International Confederation of Free Trade Unions (SAUO)
ICF Journal... Industrial Christian Fellowship Journal (journ.) (SAUS)
ICFK............ Friedman and Koven, Library, Chicago, IL [*Library symbol*] [*Library of Congress*] (LCLS)
ICF KH........ ICF Kaiser Hanford Co. (SAUS)
ICF KH........ ICF Kaiser Hanford Company (SAUO)
ICFL............ International Council of the French Language [*See also CILF*] [*Paris, France*] (EAIO)
ICFLC.......... International Curling Federation - Ladies Committee [*Defunct*] (EA)
ICFLPRMFS... Items Not Available through Cannibalization, Fabrication, or Local Procurement or Replacement from Maintenance Float Stock
ICFM............ I Confirm (SAUS)
ICFM............ In-Core Fuel Management (PDAA)
ICFM............ Inlet Cubic Feet per Minute (PDAA)
ICFM............ Institute of Charity Fundraising Managers [*British*] (DBA)

ICFM International Company for Finance and Investment [*Russian bank*]
ICFM International Convention of Faith Ministries (EA)
ICFMA International Cystic Fibrosis Mucoviscidosis Association (EA)
ICFMC FMC Corp., Chicago, IL [*Library symbol*] [*Library of Congress*] (LCLS)
ICFMH International Committee on Food Microbiology and Hygiene [*ICSU*] [*Frederiksberg, Denmark*] (EAIO)
ICF-MR Intensive-Care Facility for the Mentally Retarded [*Medicine*] (EDAA)
ICF-MR Intermediate-Care Facility for Mentally Retarded (STED)
ICFMR Intermediate Care Facility for the Mentally Retarded
ICF-MR/DD Intermediate Care Facility for the Mentally Retarded/Developmentally Disabled
ICFN Fireman, Interior Communications Electrician, Striker [*Navy rating*]
ICFN Interior Communications Electrician Fireman (SAUO)
ICFNB First National Bank of Chicago, Chicago, IL [*Library symbol*] [*Library of Congress*] (LCLS)
ICFNC Independent College Fund of North Carolina (SAUO)
ICFNDT International Committee for Non-Destructive Testing (SAUO)
ICFNJ Independent College Fund of New Jersey (SAUO)
ICFO International Catholic Film Office (SAUO)
ICFOST International Committee for Food Science Technology (SAUO)
ICFP Institute for/of Certified Financial Planners (SAUO)
ICFP Institute of Certified Financial Planners (EA)
ICFP International Conservation Financing Project (SAUO)
ICF-PADA International Christian Federation for/of the Prevention of Alcoholism and Drug Addiction (SAUO)
ICFPM International Centre for Fundamental Physics in Moscow
ICFPW International Confederation of Former Prisoners of War
ICFR Intercollegiate Conference of Faculty Representatives (EA)
ICFR Interdepartmental Committee of Futures Research (SAUS)
ICFR Inter-departmental Committee on Futures Research (SAUO)
ICFRB Federal Reserve Bank of Chicago, Chicago, IL [*Library symbol*] [*Library of Congress*] (LCLS)
ICFRM International Committee on Fusion Reactor Materials (SAUS)
ICFRM International Conference on Fusion Reactor Materials (SAUS)
ICFRU Idaho Cooperative Fishery Research Unit [*University of Idaho*] [*Research center*] (RCD)
ICFS Industry Coalition for Fire Safety [*Defunct*] (EA)
ICFS Installation Conus Forstat (SAUS)
ICFS Installation CONUS FORSTAT System [*Military*]
ICFS International Collective in Support of Fishworkers (SAUO)
ICFS International Conference on Fluid Sealing (SAUO)
ICFS Iota-Cam Fiberscope [*Also, ICF*]
ICFSHG International Committee of French-Speaking Historians and Geographers (EAIO)
ICFSRT International Council of French-Speaking Radio and Television (EAIO)
ICFT Interagency Commitee on Federal Technology Transfer (SAUS)
ICFT Inverse Chirp Fourier Transform (SAUS)
ICFTA International Committee of Foundry Technica1 Associations (SAUS)
ICFTA International Committee of Foundry Technical Associations (SAUO)
ICFTU Inter-American Regional Organization of Workers of the ICFTU (SAUO)
ICFTU International Confederation of Free Trade Unions [*Belgium*]
ICFTU International Council of Free Trade Unions
ICFTU-ARO International Confederation of Free Trade Unions-Asian Regional Organisation [*India*]
ICFTU-ARO International Confederation of Free Trade Unions-Asian Regional Organization (SAUO)
ICFTUE International Center of Free Trade Unionists in Exile [*France*] [*Defunct*]
ICFTUE International Center (or Centre) of Free Trade Unionists in Exile (SAUO)
ICFU International Council on the Future of the University [*Defunct*]
ICFW International Christian Federation of Food, Drink, Tobacco and Hotelworkers (SAUO)
IC fx Intracapsular Fracture [*Medicine*] (STED)
ICG Garden Centre International (SAUO)
ICG Icelandic Coast Guard [*ICAO designator*] (FAAC)
ICG ICG Communications [*AMEX symbol*] [*Formerly, IntelCom Group*] (SG)
ICG Icing [*Meteorology*] (BARN)
ICG Illinois Benedictine College, Lisle, IL [*OCLC symbol*] (OCLC)
ICG Illinois Central Gulf Railroad Co. [*AAR code*]
ICG Illinois Council for the Gifted (EDAC)
ICG Impedance Cardiogram [*Medicine*] (DMAA)
ICG Indian Conciliation Group (SAUO)
ICG Indicator Control Group (SAUO)
ICG Indochina Curriculum Group [*Defunct*] (EA)
ICG Indocyanine Green [*Liver function test*] [*Medicine*]
ICG Industrial Chemistry Group (SAUO)
ICG Industries Consultative Group (SAUO)
ICG In-Flight Coverall Garment [*Apollo*] [*NASA*]
ICG Installation and Configuration Guide (SAUS)
ICG Institute of Careers Guidance (COBU)
ICG Institute of Cytology and Genetics [*Akademgorodek, Russia*]
ICG Integrated Combat Group [*Air Force*]
ICG Interactive Computer Graphics (ELAL)
ICG Interactive Computerized Graphic (SAUS)
ICG Interagency Coordination Group (SAUO)
ICG Inter-City Gas Corp. (SAUO)
ICG Interface Control Group (ACAE)
ICG Interface Coordination Group (SAUS)
ICG International Commission on Glass [*See also CIV*] [*Prague, Czechoslovakia*] (EAIO)
ICG International Committee of Geophysics (SAUO)
ICG International Conference Group [*Commercial firm*] (EA)
ICG International Congress of Genetics
ICG International Congress on Glass (SAUS)
ICG International Consultative Group for Peace and Disarmament (SAUO)
ICG International Coordination Group (USDC)
ICG Internet Capital Group
ICG Inter-Union Commission on Geodynamics (SAUO)
ICG Interviewers Classification Guide (SAUS)
ICG IntlCom Group [*AMEX symbol*] (TTSB)
ICG IOC Committee on GOOS (SAUO)
ICG Iowa Corn Growers (SAUO)
ICG Isochromatid Gaps (SAUS)
ICG Isotope Cisternography (DMAA)
ICGA Directory of International and Corporate Giving in America and Abroad [*A publication*]
ICGA Illinois Corn Growers Association (SRA)
ICGA Imperial Continental Gas Association (SAUO)
ICGA International Carnival Glass Association (EA)
ICGA International Classic Guitar Association (SAUO)
ICGA International Conference on Genetic Algorithms
ICGA Iowa Corn Growers Association (SRA)
ICGB International Cargo Gear Bureau (EA)
ICGC Indocyanine-Green Clearance [*Medicine*] (EDAA)
ICGCD Gardner, Carton, and Douglas, Chicago, IL [*Library symbol*] [*Library of Congress*] (LCLS)
ICG Com ICG Communications, Inc. [*Associated Press*] (SAG)
ICGE International Center of Genetic Epistemology [*Geneva, Switzerland*]
ICGEB International Center for Genetic Engineering and Biotechnology (SAUS)
ICGEB International Centre for Genetic Engineering and Biotechnology [*United Nations Development Organization*] (EAIO)
ICGEC Interagency Collaborative Group on Environmental Carcinogenesis [*Bethesda , MD*] [*National Institutes of Health*] (EGAO)
ICGEL International Crushing and Grinding Equipment Limited (SAUO)
ICGGI Internationale Coronelli-Gesellschaft fuer Globen- und Instrumentkunde [*International Coronelli Society - ICS*] (EAIO)
ICG-GIPME International Co-ordination Group for the Global Investigation of Pollution in the Marine Environment (SAUO)
ICGH Greeley & Hansen Engineering Library, Chicago, IL [*Library symbol*] [*Library of Congress*] (LCLS)
ICGH International Confederation of Genealogy and Heraldry [*See also CIGH*] [*Paris, France*] (EAIO)
ICGI Integrated Computer Graphics, Incorporated (SAUO)
ICGI International Conference on Geoscience Information (SAUS)
ICGI International Council of Goodwill Industries (EA)
ICGIC Icing in Clouds [*NWS*] (FAAC)
ICGICIP Icing in Clouds and Precipitation [*NWS*] (FAAC)
ICGICIP Icing in Clouds in Precipitation (SAUS)
ICGIP Icing in Precipitation [*NWS*] (FAAC)
ICG-ITSU International Coordination Group for the Tsunami Warning System in the Pacific [*Marine science*] (OSRA)
ICG/ITSU Intrnational Coordination Group for the Tsunami Warning System in the Pacific (USDC)
ICGM Intercontinental Glide [*or Guided*] Missile (KSC)
ICGM Intercontinental Guided Missile (SAUO)
ICGM International Colloquium about Gas Marketing (EA)
ICGN ICC Technologies, Inc. [*NASDAQ symbol*] (SAG)
ICGN Immune Complex-Mediated Glomerulonephritis (STED)
ICGN International Cogeneration Corp. (SAUO)
ICGP Irish College of General Practitioners (SAUO)
ICGP Russian programme studying the influences of pollution on the Arctic environment (SAUO)
ICGR Gas Research Institute, Chicago, IL [*Library symbol*] [*Library of Congress*] (LCLS)
ICGR In-Core Gas Release (SAUS)
ICGR Ivory Coast - Ghana Ridge [*Geology*]
ICGRC International Connoisseurs of Green and Red Chile (EA)
ICGS Icelandic Coast Guard Service (SAUO)
ICGS Interactive Careers Guidance System (AIE)
ICGS International Catholic Girls' Society
ICGS Interreligious Committee of General Secretaries (EA)
ICGS Interactive Computer-Graphics System (ODA)
ICGSCA Infants', Children's, and Girls' Sportswear and Coat Association (EA)
ICGVAN International Committe on Gross Veterinary Anatomical Nomenclature (SAUO)
ICGVD International Consultative Group for Vaccine Development (SAUO)
ICGW International Commission on Ground Water (CARB)
ICGX ICG Communications [*NASDAQ symbol*] (SG)
ICh Chicago Heights Free Public Library, Chicago Heights, IL [*Library symbol*] [*Library of Congress*] (LCLS)
Ich Ichabod (SAUS)
ICH ICH Corp. [*Later, Southwestern Life*] [*AMEX symbol*] (SPSG)
ICH Ichthyology
ICH Idiopathic Cortical Hyperostosis [*Medicine*] (DMAA)
ICH Illinois College, Jacksonville, IL [*OCLC symbol*] (OCLC)
ICH IMPAC Commercial Holdings [*AMEX symbol*] [*Formerly, IMH Commercial Holdings*] (SG)
ICH In Calf Heifer (SAUS)
ICH Incumbent Come Home [*Political humor*] [*Pronounced "itch"*]
ICH Induction-Conduction Heating
ICH Infantile Cortical Hyperostosis [*Medicine*] (MELL)
ICH Infectious Canine Hepatitis [*Veterinary medicine*]
ICh Information Chain (SAUS)
ICh Information Channel (SAUS)

ICH............. Information Clearinghouse (SAUS)
ICH............. Information Clearing House, Inc.
ICH............. Inhalation Cycle Histogram [*Biometrics*]
ICH............. Institute of Child Health (SAUO)
ICH............. Instituto Cubao de Higrafia [*Cuba*] [*Marine science*] (OSRA)
ICH............. Instructor Contact Hours (MCD)
ICH............. Intelligent Connection Handling (SAUS)
ICH............. Interchange
ICH............. Interchanger (NASA)
ICH............. Intermediate Chain Home (IAA)
ICH............. Internal Communication Highway (SAUS)
ICH............. International Conference Harmonization
ICH............. International Countermeasures Handbook (CCCA)
ICH............. International Harmonization Conference (SAUS)
ICh............. Inter-Union Commission on the Lithosphere (SAUO)
ICH............. Intracerebral Hemorrhage [*Medicine*]
ICH............. Intracortical Hemorrhage [*Medicine*] (MELL)
ICH............. Intracranial Hemorrhage [*Medicine*]
ICH............. Intracranial Hypertension [*Medicine*] (MELL)
ICH............. I/O Controller Hub (SAUS)
ICH............. Ion Channeling (SAUS)
ICH............. Ion Cyclotron Heating (SAUS)
ICH............. Israel Chemical Ltd. [*NYSE symbol*] (SAG)
ICHA............. Intercellular Hartree Approximation (SAUS)
IChaAF......... United States Air Force, Chanute Air Force Base Library, Chanute Air Force Base, IL [*Library symbol*] [*Library of Congress*] (LCLS)
ICham.......... Champaign Public Library, Champaign, IL [*Library symbol*] [*Library of Congress*] (LCLS)
ICHAM......... Institute of Cooking and Heating Appliance Manufacturers (SAUO)
IChamBH..... Burnham City Hospital, Champaign, IL [*Library symbol*] [*Library of Congress*] (LCLS)
IChamCE...... United States Army Construction Engineering Research Laboratory, Champaign, IL [*Library symbol*] [*Library of Congress*] (LCLS)
IChamGS..... Church of Jesus Christ of Latter-Day Saints, Genealogical Society Library, Champaign Stake Branch, Champaign, IL [*Library symbol*] [*Library of Congress*] (LCLS)
IChamIG...... Illinois State Geological Survey, Champaign,IL [*Library symbol*] [*Library of Congress*] (LCLS)
IChamL........ Lincoln Trail Libraries, Champaign, IL [*Library symbol*] [*Library of Congress*] (LCLS)
IChamMH.... Illinois Department of Mental Health and Developmental Disabilities, Herman M. Adler Center Library, Champaign, IL [*Library symbol*] [*Library of Congress*] (LCLS)
IChamNG..... News-Gazette, Champaign, IL [*Library symbol*] [*Library of Congress*] (LCLS)
IChamP........ Parkland College, Champaign, IL [*Library symbol*] [*Library of Congress*] (LCLS)
I-Channel..... In-phase Channel (SAUS)
ICHAP.......... Improved Chaparral [*Military*] (MCD)
IChar........... Charleston Carnegie Public Library, Charleston, IL [*Library symbol*] [*Library of Congress*] (LCLS)
ICharE.......... Eastern Illinois University, Charleston, IL [*Library symbol*] [*Library of Congress*] (LCLS)
ICharF.......... Charleston Area Cooperative Film Library, Charleston, IL [*Library symbol*] [*Library of Congress*] (LCLS)
ICharH......... Charleston Community Memorial Hospital, Charleston, IL [*Library symbol*] [*Library of Congress*] (LCLS)
ICharSD....... Charleston Community Unit School District, Charleston, IL [*Library symbol*] [*Library of Congress*] (LCLS)
ICHBC.......... Institute of Certified Healthcare Business Consultants (SAUO)
ICHC........... International Commitee for Histochemistry and Cytochemistry (SAUO)
ICHC........... International Committee for Horticultural Congresses
ICHC........... International Congress of Heterocyclic Chemistry
ICHCA.......... International Cargo Handling and Coordination Association (SAUS)
ICHCA.......... International Cargo Handling Coordination Association [*London, England*] (EA)
ICHCA Journal... International Cargo Handling Coordination Association Journal (journ.) (SAUS)
ICH CIS........ Interstate Council on Hydrometeorology of the Countries of the Commonwealth of Independent States (SAUO)
ICHD........... Inter-Society Commission for Heart Disease Resources (EA)
ICHDA.......... International Cooperative Housing Development Association
ICHDR.......... Intersociety Commission for Heart Disease Resources [*American Heart Assoc iation - AHA*] [*Absorbed by*]
ICHE............ Infection Control and Hospital Epidemiology (SAUO)
ICHE............ Infection Control and Hospital Epidemiology (journ.) (SAUS)
I Ch E.......... Institution of Chemical Engineers [*British*]
ICHE............ International Commission on Human Ecology (EA)
ICHE............ International Councils on Higher Education [*Defunct*]
IChemE......... Institute of Chemical Engineers (SAUO)
I Chem E..... Institution of Chemical Engineers [*British*]
ICHENP........ International Conference on High Energy Nuclear Physics (SAUS)
ICHEO.......... Interuniversity Council for Higher Education Overseas [*British*] (DI)
ICherSD....... Cherry School District 92, Cherry, IL [*Library symbol*] [*Library of Congress*] (LCLS)
IChevE......... Cherry Valley Elementary School, Cherry Valley, IL [*Library symbol*] [*Library of Congress*] (LCLS)
ICHF............ Child Health Foundation [*Formerly, International Child Health Foundation*] (EA)
ICHF............ International Child Health Foundation (EA)
ICHFC.......... Household Finance Corp., Chicago, IL [*Library symbol*] [*Library of Congress*] (LCLS)
ICHFST........ International Council of Health Fitness and Sports Therapists [*British*]
ICHG............ International Conference on the Holocaust and Genocide (EAIO)
ICHG............ International Congress of Human Genetics (HGEN)
IChGS.......... Church of Jesus Christ of Latter-Day Saints, Genealogical Society Library, Chicago Heights Branch, Chicago Heights, IL [*Library symbol*] [*Library of Congress*] (LCLS)
ICHHS.......... International Council of Home-Help Services (SAUO)
IChi............. Chicago Historical Society, Chicago, IL [*Library symbol*] [*Library of Congress*] (LCLS)
ICHI............. International Conference on Hyperfine Interactions (SAUS)
ICHIB........... Information Center of the Hungarian Industry in Budapest (SAUS)
ICHID........... Harrington Institute of Interior Design, Chicago, IL [*Library symbol*] [*Library of Congress*] (LCLS)
IChil............ Chillicothe Township Free Public Library, Chillicothe, IL [*Library symbol*] [*Library of Congress*] (LCLS)
IChL............ Chicago Heights Free Public Library, Chicgo Heights, IL [*Library symbol*] [*Library of Congress*] (LCLS)
ICHL............ International Conference on Historical Linguistics (SAUO)
ICHLM......... International Conference of Historians of the Labour Movement [*Vienna, Austria*] (EAIO)
ICHM........... Institute of Care-Home Managers [*British*] (DBA)
ICHM........... International College of Hotel Management
ICHM........... International Committee for Historical Metrology (SAUO)
ICHM........... International Committee on Historical Metrology (SAUS)
ICHMAE....... International Conference on Heavy Metals in the Aquatic Environment (SAUS)
ICHMH......... Interstate Clearing House on Mental Health [*Defunct*]
ICHMMC...... International Society of Hotel and Motel Management Companies (SAUO)
ICHMT......... International Center for Heat and Mass Transfer (SAUS)
ICHMT......... International Centre for Heat and Mass Transfer (EAIO)
ICHNA.......... International Child Health Nursing Alliance (ADWA)
ichnol.......... ichnolite (SAUS)
ichnol.......... ichnologist (SAUS)
ichnol.......... ichnology (SAUS)
ICHNR......... International Committee of Horticultural Nomenclature and Registration (SAUS)
IChO............ International Chemistry Olympiad [*For high school students*]
ICHOHYP..... International Committee of Hard of Hearing Young People [*Frederiksberg, Denmark*] (EAIO)
ICHoLS........ International Conference on the History of Language Sciences (SAUO)
ICHOR.......... ICHOR Corp. [*Associated Press*] (SAG)
ICHP............ ICN Pharmaceuticals, Inc. (SAUO)
ICHP............ Illinois Council on Health System Pharmacists (SRA)
ICHP............ Institute for Child Health Policy (ADWA)
ICHP............ International Commission for/of Health Professionals for Health and Human Rights (SAUO)
ICHP............ International Commission of Health Professionals for Health and Human Rights (EA)
ICHP............ Investors Chronicle/Hillier Parker [*British*] [*A publication*]
IChP............ Prairie State College, Learning Center, Chicago Heights, IL [*Library symbol*] [*Library of Congress*] (LCLS)
ICHPER........ International Council for Health, Physical Education and Recreation (SAUS)
ICHPER........ International Council for/on Health, Physical Education, and Recreation (SAUO)
ICHPPC........ International Classification of Health Problems in Primary Care (ADWA)
ICHPR.......... International Council for Health, Physical Education, and Recreation (SAUO)
IChr............. Chrisman Public Library, Chrisman, IL [*Library symbol*] [*Library of Congress*] (LCLS)
ICHR............ ICHOR Corp. [*NASDAQ symbol*] (SAG)
ICHR............ Illinois Catholic Historical Review (journ.) (SAUS)
ICHR............ Indian Council for Historical Research (SAUO)
ICHR............ Indian Council of Historical Research
ICHR............ Inter-American Commission on Human Rights [*OAS*] (PD)
ICHR............ Interfaith Council for Human Rights (EA)
ICHR............ International Council for Human Rights (SAUO)
I Ch R.......... Irish Chancery Reports [*A publication*] (DLA)
ICHRI........... Islamic Committee for Human Rights in Iraq [*Later, IODHRI*] (EA)
ICHRPI......... International Commission for the History of Representative and Parliamentary Institutions [*Rome, Italy*] (EAIO)
ICHRT.......... International Committee for Human Rights in Taiwan (EA)
ICHS............ Information Center for Hearing, Speech and Human Communication (SAUS)
ICHS............ Inter-African Committee for Hydraulic Studies [*See also CIEH*] [*Ouagadougou, Burkina Faso*] (EAIO)
ICHS............ International Center for Holocaust Studies (EA)
ICHS............ International Committee for Historical Sciences [*Paris, France*] (EA)
ICHS............ International Committee for/of Historical Sciences (SAUO)
ICHS............ International Committee of Historical Sciences (SAUS)
ICHS............ International Council of Homehelp Services [*See also CISAF*] [*Driebergen-Rijsenburg, Netherlands*] (EAIO)
I/C Hs.......... Iran-Contra Hearings (SAUS)
ICHSCDM..... International Commission for a History of the Scientific and Cultural Development of Mankind (SAUO)
ICHSLTA...... International Council of Hides Skins and Leather Traders Associations (SAUO)
ICHSMSS..... International Commission for the History of Social Movements and Social Structures [*Paris, France*] (EAIO)
ICHSPP........ International Congress on High-Speed Photography and Photonics (EA)
ICHSRI......... International Clearinghouse of Health System Reform Initiatives (ADWA)
ICHSWW...... International Committee for/on the History of the Second World War (SAUO)

ICHSWW International Committee for the History of the Second World War (EAIO)
ICHT Harris Trust and Savings Bank, Chicago, IL [*Library symbol*] [*Library of Congress*] (LCLS)
ICHT International Committee on Haemostasis and Thrombosis (SAUO)
ICHT International Council of Holistic Therapists [*British*]
ICHTH Ichthyology
ichthyol Ichthyology (BARN)
ICHTHYS Jesous Christos, Theou Uios Soter [*Jesus Christ, Son of God, Savior*]
ICHTM International Congress on the Heat Treatment of Materials (SAUS)
ICHTSP International Conference on the Hydraulic Transport of Solids in Pipes (PDAA)
ICHW Ion-Cyclotron Harmonic Wave (SAUS)
ICHY International Council of Hindoo Youth (EAIO)
ICI Cicia [*Fiji*] [*Airport symbol*] (OAG)
ICI Ice Condenser Instrumentation [*Nuclear energy*] (NRCH)
ICI ICI Pharmaceuticals [*Great Britain*] [*Research code symbol*]
ICI Illinois Central Industries (SAUO)
ICI Illinois Institute of Technology, Chicago, IL [*Library symbol*] [*Library of Congress*] (LCLS)
ICI Image Component Information (SAUS)
ICI Imperial Chemical Industries
ICI Imperial Chemical Industries Ltd. [*NYSE symbol*] (SPSG)
ICI Imprial Chem Ind ADR [*NYSE symbol*] (TTSB)
ICI Incoming Call Identification [*Telecommunications*]
ICI In-Core Instrumentation (SAUO)
ICI Independent Commercial Importer [*Automotive retailing*]
ICI Independent Curators, Incorporated (SAUO)
ICI Individual/Collective Integration
ICI Industrial Computing Initiative (SAUS)
ICI Info Concepts, Incorporated (SAUO)
ICI Information & Communications, Inc.
ICI Information Centre International [*Telecommunications service*] (TSSD)
ICI Information Concepts, Incorporated (SAUO)
ICI Information Consultants, Inc. [*Information service or system*] (IID)
ICI Information Consultants, Incorporated (SAUO)
ICI Information Science Institute (SAUO)
ICI Initial Capabilities Inspection [*Military*] (AFM)
ICI Inspector of Catering in India (SAUO)
ICI Institut Canadien des Ingenieurs [*Engineering Institute of Canada*]
ICI Institute of Chemistry-Ireland (SAUS)
ICI Institute of Chemistry of Ireland (BI)
ICI Institution of Chemistry in Ireland (SAUS)
ICI Instruction Check Indicator (SAUS)
ICI Intelligent Communications Interface (IEEE)
ICI Interactive Communications Interface (SAUS)
ICI Interagency Committee on Intelligence
ICI Interagency Committee on Intermodal Cargo (SAUO)
ICI Interagency Cooperative Issuances (OICC)
ICI Inter-American Children's Institute [*OAS*]
ICI Inter-American Cooperative Institute
ICI Inter-American Copyright Institute (SAUO)
ICI Inter Carrier Interface (SAUS)
ICI Intercarrier Interface (ACRL)
ICI Interchannel Interference (SAUS)
ICI Interclick Interval [*Entomology*]
ICI Interexchange Carrier Interface [*Telecommunications*] (ACRL)
ICI Interface Control Information (SAUS)
ICI Interface Control Information Institute (SAUO)
ICI Interim Cargo Integrator (MCD)
ICI Internal Change Identifier (MCD)
ICI International Castles Institute (EA)
ICI International Colonial Institute (SAUO)
ICI International Commission on Illumination [*Since 1951, has been known exclusively as CIE, which see*]
ICI International Congress Institute (SAUO)
ICI International Copyright Information Centre (SAUO)
ICI International Correspondence Institute (SAUO)
ICI International Cotton Institute (SAUO)
ICI Interpersonal Communication Inventory [*Interpersonal skills and attitudes test*]
ICI Intracardiac Infection [*Medicine*] (DMAA)
ICI Intracavitary Irradiation [*Medicine*] (MELL)
ICI Intracervical Insemination (ADWA)
ICi Intracisternal (DMAA)
ICI Inuit Cultural Institute [*Canada*]
ICI Investment Casting Institute (EA)
ICI Investment Company Institute (EA)
ICI Investment Costing Institute (SAUO)
ICI Ion Composition Instrument [*Cometary physics*]
ICI Istituto Chemioterapico Italiano [*Italy*] [*Research code symbol*]
ICI Italian Cultural Institute (EA)
ICI MacMurray College, Jacksonville, IL [*OCLC symbol*] (OCLC)
ICI-A Illinois Institute of Technology, Armour Research Foundation, Chicago, IL [*Library symbol*] [*Library of Congress*] (LCLS)
ICIA Industrial, Commercial, and Institutional Accountant (DD)
ICIA Institute of Cultural Affairs International [*Information service or system*] (IID)
ICIA Interagency Committee on International Athletics (SAUO)
ICIA Intergovernmental Council for Information in Africa (SAUO)
ICIA International Center of Information on Antibiotics (EAIO)
ICIA International Centre of Information on Antibiotics (SAUS)
ICIA International Communications Industries Association (EA)
ICIA International Communications Industries Association, Inc. (SAUO)
ICIA International Communications Industry Association (SAUO)
ICIA International Conference Industry Association [*Defunct*] (EA)
ICIA International Credit Insurance Association [*Zurich, Switzerland*] (EAIO)
ICIA International Crop Improvement Association [*Later, AOSCA*] (EA)
ICIAgr International Commission of Illumination Agreement (SAUO)
ICIANZ Imperial Chemical Industries, Australia and New Zealand (SAUS)
ICIANZ Imperial Chemical Industries of Australia and New Zealand Ltd. (SAUO)
ICIAO International Association of Assessing Officers, Chicago, IL [*Library symbol*] [*Library of Congress*] (LCLS)
ICIAP Interagency Committee on International Aviation Policy [*Department of State*] (AFM)
ICIAQC International Conference on Indoor Air Quality and Climate (SAUS)
ICIASF International Conference on Instrumentation in Aerospace Simulation Facilities (SAUS)
ICIASF International Congress on Instrumentation in Aerospace Simulation Facilities (SAUO)
ICIB Indian Commercial Information Bureau (SAUO)
ICIB International Cargo Inspection Bureau (SAUS)
ICIB International Classification and Indexing Bibliography (SAUO)
ICIB International Copper Information Bulletin (journ.) (SAUS)
ICic Cicero Public Library, Cicero, IL [*Library symbol*] [*Library of Congress*] (LCLS)
ICIC Industrial Credit and Investment Corporation (SAUO)
ICIC Interagency Committee on Intermodal Cargo
ICIC Intercalibrations-Intercomparisons (SAUO)
ICIC Interdepartmental Commission on Interplanetary Communications (SAUO)
ICIC Interdisciplinary Committee on Institutes and Conferences
ICIC International Cancer Information Center [*Public Health Service*] [*Information service or system*] (IID)
ICIC International Commission on Irrigation and Canals (SAUO)
ICIC International Copyright Information Center (or Centre) (SAUO)
ICIC International Copyright Information Centre [*UNESCO*] (PDAA)
ICIC International Copyrights Information Center (WDAA)
ICIC Interstitial Cystitis Information Center (NRGU)
ICIC Iranian Centre for International Conferences (SAUO)
ICIC Islamic Committee of International Crescent (SAUO)
ICICI Industrial Credit & Investment Corp. of India Ltd.
ICICI Industrial Credit and Investment Corporation of India (SAUO)
ICICLE Integrated Cryogenic Isotope Cooling Equipment
ICicM Morton College, Cicero, IL [*Library symbol*] [*Library of Congress*] (LCLS)
ICICO Illinois College of Optometry, Chicago, IL [*Library symbol*] [*Library of Congress*] (LCLS)
IC/ICP Ion Chromatography/Inductively Coupled Plasma (SAUS)
ICICR International Center for Interdisciplinary Cycle Research (SAUO)
ICICS International College of Surgeons, Chicago, IL [*Library symbol*] [*Library of Congress*] (LCLS)
ICICX International Community Interconnected Computing Exchange (SAUS)
ICI-D Illinois Institute of Technology, Institute of Design, Chicago, IL [*Library symbol*] [*Library of Congress*] (LCLS)
ICID Information Center for Individuals with Disabilities (EA)
ICID Intensified Charge Injection Device [*For television camera used in astronomy*]
ICID International Commission on Irrigation and Drainage [*See also CIID*] [*ICSU*] [*New Delhi, India*] (EAIO)
ICID International Commission on/to Irrigation and Drainage (SAUO)
ICIDH International Classification of Impairments, Disabilities, and Handicaps [*Occupational therapy*]
ICIDH International Classification of Impairments, Disabilities and Handicaps (journ.) (SAUS)
ICIDH-2 International Classification of Impairments, Activities and Participation (SAUO)
ICIDI Independent Commission on International Development Issues [*Also known as the Brandt Commission*] [*Studies problems arising from the inequity between more developed Northern nations and less developed Southern countries*]
ICIDR International Centers for Infectious Diseases Research (SAUO)
ICIDR International Collaboration in Infectious Diseases Research [*Tulane University*] [*Research center*] (RCD)
ICIDS Integrated Commercial Intrusion Detection System [*Army*]
ICIDSS International Committee for Information and Documentation in Social Sciences (SAUS)
ICIE Infogrow Communications Information Exchange [*Database directory*] (NITA)
ICIE Information Center for Internal Exposure [*Department of Energy*] [*Defunct*] (IID)
ICIE International Center for Industry and the Environment (DCTA)
ICIE International Center for the Industry and the Environment (SAUS)
ICIE International Centre for Industry and the Environment (SAUO)
ICIE International Council for Innovation in Higher Education (SAUO)
ICIE International Council of Industrial Editors [*Later, IABC*]
ICIE International Council of Industrial Engineers
ICIECA Interagency Council on International Educational and Cultural Affairs (SAUO)
ICI Eng Plast ICI Engineering Plastics (journ.) (SAUS)
ICIEQ Illinois Institute for Environmental Quality, Chicago, IL [*Library symbol*] [*Library of Congress*] (LCLS)
ICIF Independent Colleges of Indiana Foundation (SRA)
ICIF International Commodities Investment Fund (SAUS)

ICIF............ International Cooperative Insurance Federation [*Manchester, England*] (EAIO)
ICIF............ International Council of Infant Food Industries (SAUO)
ICIFI............ International Council of Infant Food Industries
ICI-G............ Illinois Institute of Technology, Institute of Gas Technology, Chicago, IL [*Library symbol*] [*Library of Congress*] (LCLS)
ICIg............ Intracytoplasmic Immunoglobulin
ICIHI............ Independent Commission on International Humanitarian Issues (SAUO)
ICIHSOP....... International Convention Relating to Intervention on the High Seas in Cases of Oil Pollution Casualties of 1969 (COE)
ICII............ Imperial Credit [*NASDAQ symbol*] (TTSB)
ICII............ Imperial Credit Industries, Inc. [*NASDAQ symbol*] (SAG)
ICII............ International Controlled Investments, Incorporated (SAUO)
ICII............ International Culture Institute [*Japan*] (EAIO)
ICIJ............ Institute for Juvenile Research, Chicago, IL [*Library symbol*] [*Library of Congress*] (LCLS)
ICI-K............ Illinois Institute of Technology, Chicago-Kent College of Law, Chicago, IL [*Library symbol*] [*Library of Congress*] (LCLS)
ICIL............ IFIP [*International Federation for Information Processing*] Committee for International Liaison
ICILB............ Isham-Lincoln-Beale, Chicago, IL [*Library symbol*] [*Library of Congress*] (LCLS)
ICIM............ Institute for Computer Integrated Manufacturing [*Strathclyde University*] [*British*]
ICIM............ International Computers Indian Manufacture (SAUS)
ICI Mag........ ICI Magazine (journ.) (SAUS)
ICIMOD........ International Center for Integrated Mountain Development (SAUO)
ICIMOD........ International Centre for Integrated Mountain Development [*Kathmandu*] (ECON)
ICIMOD........ International Centre for Integrated Mountain Development for the Hindu-Kush Himalayan Region (SAUS)
ICIMP............ Interagency Committee for International Meteorological Programs (SAUO)
ICIMS-NOE... Intelligent Control and Integration of Manufacturing Systems Network of Excellence (SAUO)
ICIMSS........ International Centre for Information Management Systems and Services [*Poland*]
ICINR............ Institute of Natural Resources, Chicago, IL [*Library symbol*] [*Library of Congress*] (LCLS)
ICIntR............ Library of International Relations, Chicago, IL [*Library symbol*] [*Library of Congress*] (LCLS)
ICIO............ Interim Cargo Integration Operations (MCD)
icio............ Interim Cargo Integration Operations [*NASA*] (NAKS)
ICIP............ ICI Protocol (SAUS)
ICIP............ Indirect Component Improvement Program
ICIP............ Institute for Psychoanalysis, Chicago, IL [*Library symbol*] [*Library of Congress*] (LCLS)
ICIP............ International Confederation of Intellectual Professions (SAUO)
ICIP............ International Conference on Image Processing (SAUO)
ICIP............ International Conference on Information Processing [*Paris, 1959*]
ICIP............ Vespasian Warner Public Library, Clinton, IL [*Library symbol*] [*Library of Congress*] (LCLS)
ICIPE............ International Center for Insect Physiology and Ecology (SAUS)
ICIPE............ International Center of Insect Physiology and Ecology (SAUS)
ICIPE............ International Centre for Insect Pest Ecology (SAUS)
ICIPE............ International Centre for Insect Physiology and Ecology (SAUS)
ICIPE............ International Centre of Insect Physiology and Ecology [*ICSU*] [*Nairobi, Kenya*] (EAIO)
ICI Polyurethane Newsl... ICI Polyurethanes Newsletter (journ.) (SAUS)
ICIPP............ Infantry Company Intensive Pacification Program (SAUO)
ICipSD............ Cissna Park Community Unit School District, Cissna Park, IL [*Library symbol*] [*Library of Congress*] (LCLS)
ICIR............ In Commission, In Reserve [*Vessel status*] [*Navy*]
ICIREPAT..... International Committee in Information Retrieval among Examining Patent offices (SAUS)
ICIREPAT..... International Co-operation Information Retrieval among Examining PATent offices (SAUS)
ICIREPAT..... International Cooperation in Information Retrieval among Examining Patent Offices (SAUS)
ICIREPAT..... Paris Union Committee for International Cooperation in Information Retrieval Among Examining Patent Offices (SAUO)
ICIRN............ Interagency Council on Information Resources for Nursing (SAUO)
ICIRN............ International Council on Information Resources for Nursing (SAUO)
ICIRO............ Interim Commission of the International Refugee Organization
ICIS............ Current-Controlled Current Source (SAUS)
ICIS............ ICIS Management Group, Inc. [*NASDAQ symbol*] (SAG)
ICIS............ Independent Chemical Information Services (SAUS)
ICIS............ Independent Chemical Information Services Ltd. [*Information service or system*] (IID)
ICIS............ Information Control Intelligence Summary (SAUO)
ICIS............ Integrated Chemical Information System [*Information Consultants, Inc.*] [*Information service or system*] (IID)
ICIS............ Integrated Circuit Inspection System (SAUS)
ICIS............ Integrated Communication Identification System (ACAE)
ICIS............ Intelligent Configuration Identification System [*NASA*]
ICIS............ Interactive Construction Industry System [*NCR Ltd.*] [*Software package*] (NCC)
ICIS............ Inter-Campus Information System (SAUS)
ICIS............ Interdepartmental Committee on Internal Security [*Washington, DC*]
ICIS............ International Cargo Information System (SAUS)
ICIS............ International Center for Integrative Studies (SAUO)
ICIS............ International Centre for Industrial Studies [*United Nations*]
ICIS............ International Conference on Ion Sources (SAUO)
ICIS............ International Council for Infant Survival [*Later, NCGIS*] (EA)
ICIS............ IUD Claims Information Source (EA)
ICis............ Willow Branch Library, Cisco, IL [*Library symbol*] [*Library of Congress*] (LCLS)
ICISA............ International Conference on Information Systems Auditing (SAUS)
ICISE............ International Conference on Interface Science and Engineering (SAUS)
ICISI............ International Center for Interdisciplinary Studies of Immunology at Georgetown [*Georgetown University*] [*Research center*] (RCD)
ICIS Mgt...... ICIS Management Group, Inc. [*Associated Press*] (SAG)
ICISS............ Impact-Collision Ion Scattering Spectroscopy
ICIST............ Institut Canadien de l'Information Scientifique et Technique [*Canadian Institute for Scientific and Technical Information - CISTI*]
ICIT............ Information Center on Instructional Technology
ICIT............ Intensified Conventional Insulin Therapy [*Medicine*]
ICITA............ International Chain of Industrial and Technical Advertising Agencies (EA)
ICITA............ International Cooperative Investigations of the Tropical Atlantic [*Navy*]
ICITAP........ International Criminal Investigation and Training Assistance Program (SAUO)
ICITAP........ International Criminal Investigative Training Assistance Program [*Department of Justice*]
ICITO............ Interim Commission for/of the International Trade Organization (SAUO)
ICITO............ Interim Commission for the International Trade Organization
ICITO............ International Committee of the International Trade Organization (SAUS)
ICITP............ International Conference on Impact Treatment Processes (SAUS)
ICITV............ Institut de la Carte Internationale du Tapis Vegetal (SAUS)
ICIU............ University of Illinois at Chicago Circle, Chicago, IL [*Library symbol*] [*Library of Congress*] (LCLS)
ICIU-PM....... University of Illinois at Chicago Circle, Peoria School of Medicine, Peoria, IL [*Library symbol*] [*Library of Congress*] (LCLS)
ICIU-RM....... University of Illinois at Chicago Circle, Rockford School of Medicine, Rockford,IL [*Library symbol*] [*Library of Congress*] (LCLS)
ICIU-S............ University of Illinois at Chicago Circle, Science Library, Chicago, IL [*Library symbol*] [*Library of Congress*] (LCLS)
ICIW............ International Confederation of Intellectual Workers (SAUO)
ICIWWW...... International Congress of Industrial Waste Water and Wastes
ICIX............ Intermedia Communications [*NASDAQ symbol*] (TTSB)
ICIX............ Intermedia Communications, Inc. [*NASDAQ symbol*] (SAG)
ICJ............ Ileocecal Junction [*Anatomy*] (DAVI)
ICJ............ Ileocolonic Junction [*Anatomy*]
ICJ............ Incoming Junction [*Telecommunications*] (TEL)
ICJ............ Institute of Creative Judaism (SAUO)
ICJ............ Institute of Criminal Justice (SAUO)
ICJ............ International Commission of Jurists [*Switzerland*]
ICJ............ International Committee of Jurists (CARL)
ICJ............ International Court of Justice [*United Nations*]
ICJ............ Interstate Compact on Juveniles [*Public human service program*] (PHSD)
ICJ............ John Crerar Library, Chicago, IL [*Library symbol*] [*Library of Congress*] (LCLS)
ICJ............ McKendree College, Lebanon, IL [*OCLC symbol*] (OCLC)
ICJA............ Intelligence and Criminal Justice Academy [*Defunct*] (EA)
ICJA............ International Criminal Justice Association (EA)
ICJAS............ International Commission of Jurists Australian Section
ICJB............ Jenner and Block, Chicago, IL [*Library symbol*] [*Library of Congress*] (LCLS)
ICJC............ Immaculate Conception Junior College [*New Jersey*]
ICJC............ Institute of Criminal Justice and Criminology (SAUS)
ICJC............ International Council of Jews from Czechoslovakia [*British*] [*Defunct*] (EAIO)
ICJC............ International Criminal Justice Clearinghouse [*Law Enforcement Ass istance Administration*] [*Information service or system*]
ICJCM............ John T. and Catherine McArthur Foundation, Chicago, IL [*Library symbol*] [*Library of Congress*] (LCLS)
ICJCS............ International Conference of Jewish Communal Service [*Later, WCJCS*] (EA)
ICJIB............ International Coalition for Justice in Bhopal (SAUO)
ICJKM............ Jesuit-Krauss-McCormick Library, Chicago, IL [*Library symbol*] [*Library of Congress*] (LCLS)
ICJL............ Institute for Computer in Jewish Life (SAUS)
ICJL............ Institute for Computers in Jewish Life (EA)
ICJM............ John Marshall Law School, Chicago, IL [*Library symbol*] [*Library of Congress*] (LCLS)
ICJOB............ IBM-to-Cray Interactive Interface (SAUS)
ICJP............ Irish Commission for Justice and Peace [*An association*] (EAIO)
ICJR............ Institute for Criminal Justice, University of Richmond (DLA)
ICJ Reports... International Court of Justice Reports [*A publication*] (SAFN)
ICJS............ Independent Carpenters' and Joiners' Society [*A union*] [*British*]
ICJS............ Spertus College of Judaica, Chicago, IL [*Library symbol*] [*Library of Congress*] (LCLS)
ICJSh............ John G. Shedd Aquarium, Chicago, IL [*Library symbol*] [*Library of Congress*] (LCLS)
ICJST............ Jesuit School of Theology in Chicago, Chicago, IL [*Library symbol*] [*Library of Congress*] (LCLS)
ICJUB............ Intercontinental Jet Unmanned Bomber
ICJV............ Jewish Vocational Service Library, Chicago, IL [*Library symbol*] [*Library of Congress*] (LCLS)
ICJW............ International Council of Jewish Women (EA)
ICK............ Inscriptions Cuneiformes du Kultepe (BJA)
ICK............ Interdepartmental Committee on Nuclear Energy [*Netherlands*] (EY)
ICK............ Internacia Centra Komitato de la Esperanto-Movado (SAUO)

ICK............ International Cherokee [*Vancouver Stock Exchange symbol*]
ICK............ Metlakatla, AK [*Location identifier*] [*FAA*] (FAAL)
ICK............ Millikin University, Decatur, IL [*OCLC symbol*] (OCLC)
ICK............ Nieuw Nickerie [*Surinam*] [*Airport symbol*] (OAG)
ICKCMX....... Integrated Circuit Keyset Central Multiplexer (CAAL)
ICKE............ Kirkland & Ellis, Chicago, IL [*Library symbol*] [*Library of Congress*] (LCLS)
ICKK............ Kennedy-King College of the City College of Chicago, Chicago, IL [*Library symbol*] [*Library of Congress*] (LCLS)
ICKL............ International Council of Kinetography Laban (EA)
ICKMC........ Keck, Mahin, and Cate, Chicago, IL [*Library symbol*] [*Library of Congress*] (LCLS)
ICKMZ......... Katten, Munchin & Zavis, Pearl, Greenburger & Galler, Chicago, IL [*Library symbol*] [*Library of Congress*] (LCLS)
ICL............ Cavei Avir Lemitanim [*Israel*] [*ICAO designator*] (FAAC)
ICL............ Clarinda, IA [*Location identifier*] [*FAA*] (FAAL)
Icl............ Iceland (MILB)
ICL............ Income Contingent Loan
ICL............ Incoming Correspondence Log (AAG)
ICL............ Incoming Line
ICL............ Indal Ltd. [*Toronto Stock Exchange symbol*]
ICL............ Index to Chiropractic Literature (SAUO)
ICL............ Industrial Code and Logic
ICL............ Inflight Calibration Lamp [*Instrumentation*]
ICL............ Initial Contact Link (SAUS)
ICL............ Input Capacitorless (SAUS)
ICL............ Inrush Current Limiter (SAUS)
ICL............ Insert Character in/on Line (SAUS)
ICL............ Inserted Connection Loss [*Telecommunications*]
ICL............ Institute for Continued Learning (SAUS)
ICL............ Instructional Center Library
ICL............ Instrumentation Configuration Log (IAA)
ICL............ Instrument Calibration Laboratory
ICL............ Instrument Control Language [*Computer science*]
ICL............ Instrument Controlled Landing (SAUO)
ICL............ Instrument-Controlled Landing [*Aviation*] (IAA)
ICL............ Integrated Circuit Logic
ICL............ Integrated Cloud Liquid (CARB)
ICL............ Integrated Configuration List (NG)
ICL............ Intellicall, Inc. [*NYSE symbol*] (SPSG)
ICL............ Interactive Computer Learning
ICL............ Interagency Checklist [*United States Employment Service*] (OICC)
ICL............ Intercommunication Logic
ICL............ Intercomputer Communication Link (SAUS)
ICL............ Intercomputer Communication Logic (NITA)
ICL............ Inter-Computer Communications Logic (SAUS)
ICL............ Interconnection List (ACAE)
ICL............ Interdepartmental Committee on Land [*Canada*]
ICL............ Interest Checklist [*US Employment Service*] [*Department of Labor*]
ICL............ Interface Clear (SAUS)
ICL............ Interface Control Layer (SAUS)
ICL............ Internal Control Loop [*Chemical engineering*]
ICL............ International Cancer League [*Defunct*] (EA)
ICL............ International Catholic Library [*A publication*]
ICL............ International Christian Leadership (EA)
ICL............ International Clinical Laboratories, Inc.
ICL............ International Combustion Holding Limited (SAUO)
ICL............ International Combustion Limited (SAUO)
ICL............ International Commission on the Lithosphere (SAUO)
ICL............ International Communications Limited (SAUO)
ICL............ International Communications Ltd. [*Fayville, MA*] [*Telecommunications service*] (TSSD)
ICL............ International Communist League (SAUO)
ICL............ International Computers Limited (SAUO)
ICL............ International Computers Ltd. [*Great Britain*] [*Computer manufacturer*]
ICL............ International Congress of Linguists (SAUO)
ICL............ International Containers Ltd. (SAUS)
ICL............ International Cooperative Logistics (AFIT)
ICL............ International Council for Christian Leadership (EA)
ICL............ International Council of Languages (SAUO)
ICL............ International-Union Commission of/on the Lithosphere (SAUO)
ICL............ International-Union Commission on the Lithosphere (SAUS)
ICL............ Interpersonal Check List [*Psychology*]
ICL............ Interpretative Coding Language (SAUS)
ICL............ Interrupt Class List (SAUS)
ICL............ Inter-Union Commission on Lithosphere (SAUO)
ICL............ Inter-Union Commission on the Lithosphere [*NASA*]
ICL............ Iris-Clip Lens (DMAA)
ICL............ Irish Central Library (SAUS)
ICL............ Irish Central Library for Students (BI)
ICL............ Isentropic Condensation Level (SAUS)
ICL............ Isocitrate Lyase [*An enzyme*]
ICL............ Israel Chemicals Ltd. (SAUS)
ICL............ Loyola University, Chicago, IL [*Library symbol*] [*Library of Congress*] (LCLS)
ICL............ Monmouth College, Monmouth, IL [*OCLC symbol*] (OCLC)
ICl............ Vespasian Warner Public Library, Clinton, IL [*Library symbol*] [*Library of Congress*] (LCLS)
ICLA............ Indian College Library Association (SAUS)
ICLA............ Indian College LibraryAssociation (SAUO)
ICLA............ International Commission on Laboratory Animals (SAUO)
ICLA............ International Committee on Laboratory Animals
ICLA............ International Comparative Literature Association (EA)
ICLAA.......... International Council for Latin American Advancement (SAUO)
ICLA Bulletin... International Committee on Laboratory Animals Bulletin (journ.) (SAUS)
ICLAE.......... International Council of Library Association Executives (EA)
ICLAM.......... International Committee for Life Assurance Medicine [*Zurich, Switzerland*] (EAIO)
ICLARM....... International Center for Living Aquatic Resources Management [*Makati, Metro Manila, Philippines*] (EAIO)
ICLARM....... International Center (or Centre) for Living Aquatic Resources Management (SAUO)
ICLARM....... International Centre for Living Aquatic Research Management (SAUO)
ICLARM....... International Centre for Living Aquatic Resources Management (SAUS)
ICLAS.......... International Committee on Laser Atmospheric Studies (SAUO)
ICLAS.......... International Council for Laboratory Animal Science (GVA)
ICLAS.......... Intracavity LASER Absorption Spectroscopy
ICLASS........ International Conference on Liquid Atomization and Spray Systems
ICLaw.......... Chicago Law Institute, Chicago, IL [*Library symbol*] [*Library of Congress*] (LCLS)
ICL-B.......... Loyola University, Julia Deal Lewis Library, Chicago, IL [*Library symbol*] [*Library of Congress*] (LCLS)
IcLc............ Identity Correct, Location Correct [*Psychology*]
ICLC............ International Caucus of Labor Committees (SAUO)
ICLC............ International Centre for Local Credit [*The Hague, Netherlands*] (EAIO)
ICLC............ International Congress on Lightweight Concrete (PDAA)
ICLC............ International Contact Lens Clinic (SAUO)
ICLC............ International Criminal Law Commission (EA)
ICLCCM........ Inter-comparison of Land-Surface Codes in Climate Models (SAUS)
ICLCES........ International Computers Limited Computer Education for Schools (SAUS)
ICLCF.......... International Conference on Low-Cycle Fatigue (SAUS)
ICLCP.......... International Conference on Large Chemical Plants [*Antwerp, Belgium*] (EAIO)
ICLCUA........ ICL Computer Users Association (SAUS)
ICLD............ International Center for Law in Development (EA)
ICLD............ International Commission on Large Dams (SAUO)
ICL-D.......... Loyola University, Dental School, Chicago, IL [*Library symbol*] [*Library of Congress*] (LCLS)
ICLDS.......... ICL Data Services (SAUS)
ICLE............ Institute of Continuing Legal Education [*Research center*] (RCD)
ICLE............ Intacapsular Lens Extraction [*Ophthalmology*] (DAVI)
ICLEI........... International Council for Local Environmental Initiatives [*Marine science*] (OSRA)
ICLEP.......... Individualized Computer Literacy Education Plan (EDAC)
ICLES.......... International Common Law Exchange Society (EA)
ICLES.......... International Conference on Large Electrical Systems
ICLES.......... International Conference on Large Electric Systems (SAUO)
ICLGUA........ International Computers Limited Computer Users Association (SAUO)
IClh............ Clarendon Hills Public Library, Clarendon Hills, IL [*Library symbol*] [*Library of Congress*] (LCLS)
ICLH............ Imperial College - London Hospital [*British*] (DI)
IClH............ John Warner Hospital, Clinton, IL [*Library symbol*] [*Library of Congress*] (LCLS)
IClhP........... Clarendon Hills Public Library, Clarendon Hills, IL [*Library symbol*] [*Library of Congress*] (LCLS)
IcLi............ Identity Correct, Location Incorrect [*Psychology*]
ICLID........... Incoming Caller Identification [*Telecommunications*]
ICLID........... Incoming-Call Line Identification (SAUS)
ICLID........... Individual Calling Line ID (SAUS)
ICL-L........... Loyola University, Law Library, Chicago, IL [*Library symbol*] [*Library of Congress*] (LCLS)
ICLM............ Induced Course Load Matrix (PDAA)
ICLM............ Inter-California Line in Mexico (SAUS)
ICLM............ Inter-California Line in Mexico R. R. [*AAR code*]
ICLM............ International Christian Leprosy Mission (EA)
ICLM............ International Committee for Literary Museums (SAUO)
ICL-M........... Loyola University, School of Medicine, Maywood, IL [*Library symbol*] [*Library of Congress*] (LCLS)
ICLMC.......... Intersociety Council on Laboratory Medicine of Canada
Iclnd............ Iceland (SAUS)
ICLoop......... Loop College, Chicago, IL [*Library symbol*] [*Library of Congress*] (LCLS)
ICLP............ Institute of Criminal Law and Procedure (SAUO)
ICLP............ Internal Connectionless Protocol [*Telecommunications*]
ICLP............ International Conference on Lightning Control (SAUS)
ICLR............ Interdepartmental Committee on Labour Requirements [*British*] [*World War II*]
ICLR............ International Committee for Lift Regulations [*See also CIRA*] [*Saint-Yvelines, France*] (EAIO)
ICLR............ International Computerized Land Research Company (SAUO)
ICLR............ Irish Common Law Reports [*A publication*] (DLA)
ICLR Can..... Index to Current Legal Research in Canada [*A publication*] (DLA)
ICLR Company... International Computerized Land Research Company (SAUO)
ICLREW........ Incorporated Council of Law Reporting for England and Wales [*Established in 1866*]
ICLRN.......... Interagency Council on Library Resources for Nursing (EA)
ICLRSQ........ Incorporated Council of Law Reporting of the State of Queensland [*Australia*]
ICLS............ Inequality Constrained Least-Squares [*Statistics*]
ICLS............ Instrument Carrier Landing System [*Navy*] (DOMA)
ICLS............ Integrated Carrier Landing System [*Military*] (MCD)
ICLS............ International Courtly Literature Society (EA)
ICLS............ Irish Central Library for Students (TELE)

ICLSA.......... United States League of Savings Associations, Chicago, IL [*Library symbol*] [*Library of Congress*] (LCLS)
ICLT.......... International Committee of Lawyers for Tibet
ICLT.......... Lutheran School of Theology, Chicago, IL [*Library symbol*] [*Library of Congress*] (LCLS)
ICLTC.......... Illinois Council on Long Term Care (SRA)
ICL Tech J... ICL Technical Journal (journ.) (SAUS)
ICLU.......... Indiana Civil Liberties Union (SAUO)
ICLW.......... Latham & Watkins, Chicago, IL [*Library symbol*] [*Library of Congress*] (LCLS)
ICLX.......... Intercoastal Leasing [*Private rail car owner code*]
ICLY.......... International Council on Lethal Yellowing (SAUO)
ICM.......... ICM Property Investors, Inc. [*NYSE symbol*] (COMM)
ICM.......... Ignition Control Module (HAWK)
ICM.......... Image Color Management (MWOL)
ICM.......... Image Color Matching (SAUS)
ICM.......... Immune Combination Molecules (DB)
ICM.......... Improved Capability Minuteman (SAA)
ICM.......... Improved Capability Missile [*Air Force*]
ICM.......... Improved Cluster Munition (SAUS)
ICM.......... Improved Conventional Ammunition (SAUO)
ICM.......... Improved Conventional Munitions
ICM.......... In-Call Modification (SAUS)
ICM.......... In-Can Melter [*Nuclear energy*] (NUCP)
ICM.......... In-Can Melters (SAUS)
ICM.......... Incoming Message [*Telecommunications*]
ICM.......... Increased Capability Missile (SAUS)
ICM.......... Independent Citizens' Movement [*US Virgin Islands*] (PPW)
ICM.......... Independent Color Matching [*Computer science*]
ICM.......... Indian Campaign Medal
ICM.......... Individual Case Management (WYGK)
ICM.......... Individual Clutch Modulation [*Automotive engineering*]
ICM.......... Industrial and Construction Machines (SAUS)
ICM.......... Information and Communication Management (SAUS)
ICM.......... Infracostal Margin [*Anatomy*] (DAVI)
ICM.......... Initial Condition Mode (SAUS)
ICM.......... Initiator Command Module
ICM.......... Injection-Compression Molding [*Plastics*]
ICM.......... Inner Cell Mass [*Embryology*]
ICM.......... Installable Compression, Manager [*Computer science*]
ICM.......... Instantaneous Center of Motion
ICM.......... Institut Canadien de la Mediterranee [*Canadian Mediterranean Institute*]
ICM.......... Institut Canadien des Mines et de la Metallurgie [*Canadian Institute of Mining and Metallurgy*] (EAIO)
ICM.......... Institute for Complementary Medicine [*An association*] (EAIO)
ICM.......... Institute for Composite Materials [*Defunct*] (EA)
ICM.......... Institute for Court Management of the National Center for State Courts (EA)
ICM.......... Institute of Caster Manufacturers (EA)
ICM.......... Institute of Construction Management [*British*]
ICM.......... Institute of Credit Management [*British*]
ICM.......... Institution for Computeration Management (SAUS)
ICM.......... Instituto de Ciencias del Mar [*Barcelona, Spain*] [*Marine science*] (OSRA)
ICM.......... Instruction Control Memory
ICM.......... Instrumentation and Communications (SAUS)
ICM.......... Instrumentation and Communications Monitor
ICM.......... Instrumentation Comparison Monitor (SAUS)
ICM.......... Instrument Cluster Module [*Automotive electronics*]
ICM.......... Integral Charge-Control Model [*Electronics*] (OA)
ICM.......... Integrated Call Management
ICM.......... Integrated Catchment Management [*Water resources*]
ICM.......... Integrated Circuit Mask
ICM.......... Integrated Coastal Management (SAUO)
ICM.......... Integrated Compact Mill [*Steel manufacture*]
ICM.......... Integrated Controller Module [*Automotive engineering*]
ICM.......... Integrated Countermine system (SAUS)
ICM.......... Integrated Coverage Measurement [*Statistical technique*]
ICM.......... Integrated Crop Management [*Agriculture*]
ICM.......... Intelligence Correlation Module (SAUS)
ICM.......... Interbus Cache (SAUS)
ICM.......... Interchangeable Control Media (MCD)
ICM.......... Intercommunication (MSA)
ICM.......... Intercomp (EFIS)
ICM.......... Intercontinental Missile (IAA)
ICM.......... Intercostal Margin [*Anatomy*]
ICM.......... Intercostal Muscle [*Medicine*] (MELL)
ICM.......... Interface Civil/Military (SAUS)
ICM.......... Interface Communication Memorandum (ACAE)
ICM.......... Interface Co-ordination Meeting (SAUS)
ICM.......... Interface Coordination Memorandum (MCD)
ICM.......... Interference Control Monitor (AAG)
ICM.......... Intergovernmental Committee for Migration (EBF)
ICM.......... Interim Catalog Module [*MEDLARS*]
ICM.......... Interim Control Module (SAUS)
ICM.......... Interim Corrective Measure (SAUS)
ICM.......... Internacional De Ceramica ADS [*NYSE symbol*] (TTSB)
ICM.......... Internacional de Ceramica SA de CV [*NYSE symbol*] (SAG)
ICM.......... International Chaplain's Ministry (EA)
ICM.......... International Coating Materials N.V. (SAUO)
ICM.......... International Colour Management [*Commercial firm*] [*British*]
ICM.......... International Confederation of Midwives [*British*] (EAIO)
ICM.......... International Conference on Microlithography (SAUS)
ICM.......... International Conference on the Mechanical Behaviour of Metals (SAUO)
ICM.......... International Congress of Mathematicians
ICM.......... International Congress on Mechanical Behavior of Materials (SAUS)
ICM.......... International Connections Manager
ICM.......... International Control Mechanism
ICM.......... International Council for Music (SAUO)
ICM.......... International Council Meeting (SAUO)
ICM.......... International Creative Management [*Commercial firm*]
ICM.......... Internet Call Manager
ICM.......... Interoperability Configuration Manager
ICM.......... Intra-Cavity Modulation (ACAE)
ICM.......... Intracluster Medium [*Galactic science*]
ICM.......... Intracompany Memorandum
ICM.......... Intra-Contractor Correspondence Memorandum (ACAE)
ICM.......... Intracostal Margin (SAUS)
ICM.......... Inventory Control Manager (MCD)
ICM.......... Inverted Coaxial Magnetron (SAUS)
ICM.......... Investment Casting Mold (MCD)
ICM.......... Ion Chromatography Module
ICM.......... Ion Conductance Modulator [*Cytochemistry*]
ICM.......... Irish Church Missions
ICM.......... Ischemic Cardiomyopathy [*Also, IC*] [*Cardiology*]
ICM.......... Isolation, Control, and Monitoring [*Pollution control*]
ICM.......... Iterative Cell Majority (SAUS)
ICM.......... Iterative Construction Method (SAUS)
ICM.......... Missionary Sisters of the Immaculate Heart of Mary (TOCD)
ICM.......... Mundelein College, Chicago, IL [*OCLC symbol*] (OCLC)
ICM.......... Soeurs Missionnaires du Coeur Immacule de Marie [*Missionary Sisters of the Immaculate Heart of Mary*] [*Italy*] (EAIO)
ICM.......... Task Force on Integrated Coastal Management/GESAMP/ (SAUS)
ICMA.......... Imino(cyanomorpholinyl)deaminoadriamycin [*Antineoplastic drug*]
ICMA.......... Independent Cabinet Makers' Association [*A union*] [*British*]
ICMA.......... Independent Cable Makers Association (SAUO)
ICMA.......... Industrial Capacitor Manufacturers Association (SAUO)
ICMA.......... Initial Clothing Monetary Allowance [*Military*]
ICMA.......... Institute for Computational Mathematics and Applications [*University of Pittsburgh*] [*Research center*] (RCD)
ICMA.......... Institute of Certified Management Accountants [*Montvale, NJ*] (EA)
ICMA.......... Institute of Cost and Management Accountants [*British*]
ICMA.......... Intelligence Collection Management Architecture (ACAE)
ICMA.......... International Card Manufacturers Association (NTPA)
ICMA.......... International Center of Medieval Art (EA)
ICMA.......... International Christian Maritime Association [*Felixstone, Suffolk, England*] (EAIO)
ICMA.......... International Cigarette Makers' Association [*A union*]
ICMA.......... International Circulation Managers Association (EA)
ICMA.......... International City Management Association [*Later, ICMA-The Professional Local Government Management Association*] (EA)
ICMA.......... International City Managers Association (SAUO)
ICMA.......... International Congresses for Modern Architecture (SAUS)
ICMA.......... International Congress for Modern Architecture (SAUO)
ICMA.......... International Congress on Metalworking and Automation (SAUS)
ICMA.......... International County Managers Association (PA)
ICMA.......... Intracranial Microaneurysm [*Medicine*] (MELL)
ICMAD.......... Independent Cosmetic Manufacturers and Distributors (EA)
ICMAH.......... International Committee for Museums of Archeology and History (SAUO)
ICMARD.......... International Center for Marine Resources Development (ASF)
ICMAREP.......... Interagency Committee on Marine Environmental Prediction [*Marine science*] (OSRA)
ICMAS.......... International Conference on Modem Aspects of Superconductivity (SAUS)
ICMAS.......... International Conference on Multiagent Systems (SAUS)
ICMASA.......... Intersociety Committee on Methods for Air Sampling and Analysis (EA)
ICMay.......... Mayfair College, Chicago, IL [*Library symbol*] [*Library of Congress*] (LCLS)
ICMB.......... Illinois Corn Marketing Board (SAUS)
ICMB.......... International Center for Monetary and Banking Studies [*Switzerland*] (ECON)
ICMB.......... Moody Bible Institute, Chicago, IL [*Library symbol*] [*Library of Congress*] (LCLS)
ICM BB.......... Improved Conventional Munition, Base Bleed (SAUS)
ICMBE.......... International Conference on Medical and Biological Engineering (SAUO)
ICMBP.......... Mayer, Brown & Platt Law Library, Chicago, IL [*Library symbol*] [*Library of Congress*] (LCLS)
ICMC.......... Indian-Ocean Cable Management Committee (SAUS)
ICMC.......... Institute of Chemical Machine Construction (SAUS)
ICMC.......... Integrated Circuit Memory Card (SAUS)
ICMC.......... International Catholic Migration Commission [*See also CICM*] [*Geneva, Switzerland*] (EAIO)
ICMC.......... International Catholic Migration Congress (SAUO)
ICMC.......... International Christian Media Commission (EA)
ICMC.......... International Circulation Managers Commission (SAUO)
ICMC.......... International Committee on Medical Chemistry (SAUO)
ICMC.......... International Cryogenic Materials Conference (EA)
ICMCA.......... Museum of Contemporary Art, Chicago, IL [*Library symbol*] [*Library of Congress*] (LCLS)
ICMcC.......... McCormick Theological Seminary, Chicago, IL [*Library symbol*] [*Library of Congress*] (LCLS)
ICMcDW.......... McDermott, Will & Emory, Chicago, IL [*Library symbol*] [*Library of Congress*] (LCLS)
ICMCST.......... International Conference on Microelectronics (SAUS)

ICMCST........ International Conference on Microelectronics, Circuit and System Theory (SAUS)
ICMCST........ International Conference on Microelectronics, Circuits and System Theory (SAUO)
ICMCTF........ International Conference on Metallurgical Coatings and Thin Films (SAUS)
ICME........... Intergovernmental Committee for Migration from Europe (SAUO)
ICME........... International Clearinghouse on the Military and the Environment (EA)
ICME........... International Code of Medical Ethics
ICME........... International Commission for Medical Equipment (SAUO)
ICME........... International Committee for Museum of Ethnography (SAUO)
ICME........... International Conference on Mathematical Education (SAUS)
ICME........... International Conference on Medical Electronics
ICME........... International Congress on Mathematical Education [*International Council of Scientific Unions*]
ICME........... International Contemporary Music Exchange (EA)
ICME........... International Council on Metals and the Environment
ICMe........... Meadville Theological School, Chicago, IL [*Library symbol*] [*Library of Congress*] (LCLS)
ICMEDC....... International Council of Masonry Engineering for Developing Countries (SAUO)
ICMEDC....... International Council of Masonry Engineers for Developing Countries (SAUO)
ICMEE.......... Institution of Certificated (or Certified) Mechanical and Electrical Engineers (SAUS)
ICMEE.......... Institution of Certified Mechanical and Electrical Engineers (SAUO)
ICMen.......... Chicago Mercantile Exchange, Chicago, IL [*Library symbol*] [*Library of Congress*] (LCLS)
ICMEO......... Inter-University Council for Higher Education Overseas (SAUO)
ICMer.......... Charles E. Merriam Center for Public Administration, Merriam Center Library, Chicago, IL [*Library symbol*] [*Library of Congress*] (LCLS)
ICMES.......... International Conference on Marine Engineering Systems (SAUO)
ICMES.......... International Cooperation on Marine Engineering Systems (SAUO)
ICMF........... Indian Cotton Mills Federation (SAUO)
ICMF........... Intercontinental Missile Facility (ACAE)
ICMF........... International Colloquium on Magnetic Films (SAUO)
ICMF........... International Conference on Metal Forming Techniques (SAUS)
ICMFDS....... International Center of Methodology for Future and Development Studies (SAUO)
ICMG........... International Commission for Microbial Genetics [*International Council of Scientific Unions*]
ICMG........... International Commission on Microbial Genetics (SAUS)
ICMH........... Institut Canadien de Microreproductions Historiques [*Canadian Institute for Historical Microreproductions - CIHM*]
ICMH........... Institute for Child Mental Health [*Medicine*] (EDAA)
ICMH........... International Commission of Maritime History (SAUO)
ICMH........... International Commission of Military History
ICMH........... Interstate Compact on Mental Health [*Public human service program*] (PHSD)
ICMH........... Mercy Hospital and Medical Center, Chicago, IL [*Library symbol*] [*Library of Congress*] (LCLS)
ICMI............ Imperial Credit Comm'l Mtg. [*NASDAQ symbol*] (SG)
ICMI............ Index of Childhood Memory and Imagination
ICMI............ Indonesian Muslim Intellectuals Association [*Political party*] (EY)
ICMI............ International Commission for Mathematical Instruction (SAUS)
ICMI............ International Commission of Mathematical Instruction (SAUS)
ICMI............ International Commission on Mathematical Instruction [*British*]
ICMI............ Inventory of Childhood Memories and Imaginings [*Medicine*] (EDAA)
ICMICA........ Pax Romana, International Catholic Movement for Intellectual and Cultural Affairs [*See also MIIC*] [*Geneva, Switzerland*] (EAIO)
ICMID.......... International Committee for Microbiological and Immunological Documentation [*International Council of Scientific Unions*]
ICMIS........... Integrated Computerized Management Information System (PDAA)
ICMIS........... Interface CMIS (SAUS)
ICMIT........... International Consortium for Medical Imaging Technology (SAUO)
ICMJE.......... International Committee of Medical Journal Editors [*An association*]
ICML........... International Center for Medicine and Law (EA)
ICML........... International Congress on Medical Librarianship (ADWA)
ICMLF.......... International Catholic Migrant Loan Fund (SAUO)
ICMLT.......... International Congress of Medical Laboratory (SAUS)
ICMLT.......... International Congress of Medical Laboratory Technicians (SAUS)
ICMLT.......... International Congress of Medical Laboratory Technologists
ICMM........... Illinois Masonic Medical Center, Chicago, IL [*Library symbol*] [*Library of Congress*] (LCLS)
ICMM........... Incomplete Correlation Matrix Memory (PDAA)
ICMM........... International Committee of Military Medicine [*Belgium*] (EAIO)
ICMM........... International Congress of Maritime Museums (EA)
ICMMA......... Industrial Cleaning Machine Manufacturers Association [*British*] (DBA)
ICMMA......... International Council of the Museum of Modern Art (SAUO)
ICMMB......... International Conference on Mechanics in Medicine and Biology (EA)
ICMMHS...... Integrated Containerized Movement/Materials-Handling System (SAUO)
ICM/MIRV.... Intercontinental Missile/ Multiple Independently-guided Reentry Vehicle (SAUO)
ICMMM........ International Conference on Microcomputers Minicomputers Microprocessors (SAUS)
ICMMP......... Integrated CONUS [*Continental United States*] Medical Mobilization Pla n (DOMA)
ICMMP......... International Committee of Military Medicine and Pharmacy [*Belgium*]
ICMMP......... Standing Committee for International Congresses of Military Medicine and Pharmacy (SAUO)
ICMMs......... Incomplete Correlation Matrix Memories (SAUS)
ICMO........... Indirect Cost Monitoring Office (AAGC)
ICMO........... Integrated Configuration Management Office [*NASA*] (NASA)
ICMOD......... International Conference on Management of Data (SAUO)
IC-MOS........ Integrated Circuit-Metal Oxide Semiconductor (SAUS)
ICMP........... Intelligence Collection Management Process (SAUO)
ICMP........... Interchannel Master Pulse
ICMP........... International Confederation of Music Publishers [*British*] (EAIO)
ICMP........... International Conference on Marine Pollution (ILCA)
ICMP........... International Conference on Medical Physics (SAUO)
ICMP........... Internet Control and Message Protocol [*Telecommunications*]
ICMP........... Internet Control Message Protocol (SAUO)
ICMP........... Internet Control Messaging Protocol (ITCA)
ICMPC......... International Conference on Materials and Process Characterization (SAUS)
ICMPD......... International Centre for Migration Policy Development [*Austria*] (ECON)
ICMPH......... International Center of Medical and Psychological Hypnosis [*Milan, Italy*] (EA)
ICMPH......... International Center (or Centre) of Medical and Psychological Hypnosis (SAUO)
ICMPS......... Induction Compass
ICMPV6....... Internet Control Message Protocol Version 6 (SAUS)
ICMR........... Chicago Municipal Reference Library, Chicago, IL [*Library symbol*] [*Library of Congress*] (LCLS)
ICMR........... Indian Council of Medical Research
ICMR........... Instrument Calibration and Maintenance Record (MCD)
ICMR........... Interagency Committee on Medical Records (AAGC)
ICMR........... International Center for Medical Research (SAUO)
ICMRD......... International Center for Marine Resources Development [*University of Rhode Island*]
ICMREF........ Interagency Committee on Marine Science, Research, Engineering and Facilities (SAUO)
ICMRT......... International Center for Medical Research and Training (SAUO)
ICMS........... Inbucon Corporate Modelling System (SAUO)
icms............ Indirect Cost Management System (NAKS)
ICMS........... Indirect Cost Management System (NASA)
ICMS........... Information Center Management System [*Cullinet*] (NITA)
ICMS........... Institute of Club Managers and Secretaries [*Australia*]
ICMs........... Instructional Curriculum Maps (SAUS)
ICMS........... Instrument Calibration and Maintenance Schedule
ICMS........... Integrated Circuit and Message Switch
ICMS........... Integrated Circuit Measurement System (AAEL)
ICMS........... Integrated Configuration Management System (SAUS)
ICMS........... Integrated Countermeasures Suite (SAUS)
ICMS........... Integrated Countermeasures System (SAUS)
ICMS........... Integrated Crop Management Services (SAUS)
ICMS........... Intercom Master Station (SAUS)
ICMS........... Interdepartmental Committee for Meteorological Services [*National Weather Service*]
ICMS........... International Center for Medical Specialties (ADWA)
ICMS........... International Centre for Mathematical Sciences [*Heriot-Watt University*] (ECON)
ICMS........... International Commission on Mushroom Science [*Later, ISMS*] (EA)
ICMS........... International Committee on Museum Security (SAUO)
ICMS........... Intracortical Microstimulation [*For study of brain function*]
ICMSA......... Institute of Corporate Managers, Secretaries and Administrators [*Australia*]
ICMSA......... Irish Creamery Milk Suppliers' Association (BI)
ICMSD......... Institute for Comparative Music Studies and Documentation (SAUO)
ICMSE.......... Interagency Committee on Marine Science and Engineering [*Federal Council for Science and Technology*]
ICMSF.......... International Commission on Microbiological Specifications for Foods (EA)
ICMSSR....... Interagency Committee on Meteorological Services and Supporting Research (SAUO)
ICMSSR....... Interdepartmental Committee for Meteorological Services and Supporting Research (SAUO)
ICMST.......... International Conference on Machine Searching and Translation
ICMT........... Intercontract Material Transfer
ICMT........... International Commission on Mycotoxicology [*International Council of Scientific Unions*]
ICMTC......... Interdepartmental Commission on Military-Technical Co-operation (SAUS)
ICMTO......... Independent Carrier Military Traffic Office [*MTMC*] (TAG)
ICMU........... Isolation Configuration and Monitor Unit (MCD)
ICMUA......... IAMAS Commission on the Meteorology of the Upper Atmosphere (SAUS)
ICMUA......... International Commission on Meteorology in Upper Atmosphere (SAUS)
ICMUA......... International Commission on the Meteorology of the Upper Atmosphere (SAUS)
ICMund........ Mundelein College, Chicago, IL [*Library symbol*] [*Library of Congress*] (LCLS)
ICMUP......... Instruction Control Memory Update Processor (MHDB)
ICMV........... Input Common Mode Voltage (VLIE)
ICMV........... Integrated Circuit Multivibrator (SAUS)
ICMW........... Inherent Corrective Maintenance Workload
ICMWG........ Integrated Catchment Management Working Group (SAUO)
ICMX........... Malcolm X College of the City College of Chicago, Chicago, IL [*Library symbol*] [*Library of Congress*] (LCLS)
ICMZ........... International Mineral Chemical [*Federal Railroad Administration identification code*]
ICN............. Ice Condensation Nuclei (SAUS)
ICN............. ICN Pharmaceuticals [*NYSE symbol*] (TTSB)
ICN............. ICN Pharmaceuticals, Inc. [*Formerly, SPI Pharmaceuticals*] [*NYSE symbol*] (SPSG)

icn Icon (VRA)
ICN Idle Channel Noise (IAA)
ICN Immune Complex Nephritis [*Medicine*] (MELL)
ICN In Christi Nomine [*In the Name of Christ*] [*Latin*]
ICN Inclusion Conjunctivitis Neonate [*Ophthalmology*]
ICN Index of Community Noise
ICN Indicator Coupling Network (IAA)
ICN Infection Control Nurse (NUJO)
ICN Information Communication System (SAUS)
ICN Information Control Net (SAUS)
ICN Inocan Technologies Ltd. [*Vancouver Stock Exchange symbol*]
ICN Institute of Child Nutrition (SAUO)
ICN Instrumentation and Calibration Network (AAG)
ICN Instrument Communication Network (SAUS)
ICN Integrated Computer Network
ICN Intensive Care Nursery [*Medicine*]
ICN Inter-Canadian [*ICAO designator*] (FAAC)
ICN Intercity Night (SAUS)
ICN Interface Change Notice (MCD)
ICN Interim Change Notice (AFM)
ICN Internal Control Number (SAUS)
ICN International Chemical and Nuclear Corp. (SAUO)
ICN International Communes Network (EAIO)
ICN International Communications Network (SAUO)
ICN International Computer Negotiations, Inc. (SAUO)
ICN International Conference on Nutrition [*United Nations*]
ICN International Cooperating Network (VLIE)
ICN International Council of Nurses [*Switzerland*] (EY)
ICN Inter-University Computer Network (VLIE)
ICN Intromogenous Computer Network
ICN Inventory Change Notice (TIMI)
ICN Newberry Library, Chicago, IL [*Library symbol*] [*Library of Congress*] (LCLS)
ICN North Central College, Naperville, IL [*OCLC symbol*] (OCLC)
ICNA Infants' and Children's Novelties Association (EA)
ICNA Infection Control Nurses Association (SAUO)
ICNa Intracellular Concentration of Sodium [*Medicine*] (EDAA)
ICNAF International Commission for the Northwest Atlantic Fisheries [*Superseded by NAFO*]
ICNAF International Committee of North American Federation
ICNAF International Convention of the Northwest Atlantic Fisheries (SAUS)
IC NAS International Conference on Non-Aqueous Solutions (SAUO)
IC/NATAS International Council-National Academy of Television Arts and Sciences (SAUO)
ICNATAS International Council of the National Academy of Television Arts and Sciences (SAUO)
IC/NATVAS International Council of the National Academy of Television Arts and Sciences (EA)
ICNB International Code of Nomenclature of Bacteria (SAUO)
ICNB International Committee on Nomenclature of Bacteria
ICNBC International Committee on Nomenclature for Blood Coagulation [*Medicine*] (EDAA)
ICNC Intercerebral Nuclear Cell [*Medicine*] (EDAA)
ICNC International Chemical and Nuclear Corporation [*Medicine*] (EDAA)
ICNCP International Code of Nomenclature of Cultivated Plants (SAUO)
ICNCP International Commission for the Nomenclature of Cultivated Plants [*Wageningen, Netherlands*] (EA)
ICNCP International Committee for the Nomenclature of Cultivated Plants (SAUS)
ICND International Commission on Narcotic Drugs (SAUO)
ICND Irish Campaign for Nuclear Disarmament (EAIO)
ICNDAF Ivory Cross National Dental Aid Fund (SAUO)
ICNDT International Committee for/on Non-Destructive Testing (SAUO)
ICNDT International Committee on NDT [*Nondestructive Testing*] [*Brazil*] (EAIO)
ICNDT International Committee on Nondestructive Testing (SAUS)
ICNDT International Conference on Nondestructive Testing (SAUS)
ICNDT International Conference on Non-Destuctive Testing (PDAA)
ICNE Income Collected, Not Earned (EBF)
ICNE Institute for Christian-National Education (SAUO)
ICNE Northeastern Illinois University, Chicago, IL [*Library symbol*] [*Library of Congress*] (LCLS)
ICNEM Internacia Centra de la Neutrala Esperanto-Movado (SAUO)
ICNEM Internacia Centro de la Neutrala Esperanto-Movado [*International Center of the Neutral Esperanto Movement*] [*Defunct*] (EAIO)
ICNEM International Center of the Neutral Esperanto Movement (SAUO)
ICNEP Initiative Committee for National Economic Planning
ICNF Irredundant Conjunctive Normal Formula
ICNI Instruction Control Memory (SAUS)
ICNI Integrated Communication, Navigation, Identification [*System*]
ICNI Integrated Communications, Navigation, and Identification Study (SAUO)
ICNI Integrated Communications Network, Inc. [*NASDAQ symbol*] (SAG)
ICNI Integrated Commun Ntwk [*NASDAQ symbol*] (TTSB)
ICNI Integrated Cornmunication Navigation/ Identification (SAUS)
ICNIA Integrated Communication, Navigation, and Identification Avionics [*Air Force*]
ICNIA Integrated Communications Navigation Identification Avionics (SAUS)
ICNICP Integrated Communication/ Navigation/Identification Control Panel (SAUO)
ICNICP Integrated Communications/ Navigation Identification Control Panel (SAUS)
ICNICS Integrated Communication/ Navigation/Identification Control Set (SAUO)
ICNIRP International Commission on Non-Ionizing Radiation Protection (ADWA)
ICNL International Center for Not-For-Profit Law (SAUO)
ICNN International Conference on Neural Networks (SAUS)
ICNND Interdepartmental Committee on Nutrition for National Defense
I-CNOS International-Customer Network Optimization System [*Communications term*] (DCT)
ICNP International Classification of Nursing Practice (DMAA)
ICNP International Commission for National Parks (SAUO)
ICNP International Commission on National Parks [*Later, CNPAA*] (EA)
ICNP International Conference on Network Protocols (VLIE)
ICN Ph ICN Pharmaceuticals, Inc. [*Formerly, International Chemical & Nuclear Corp.*] [*Associated Press*] (SAG)
ICNPPA International Commission on National Parks and Protected Areas (SAUS)
ICNPT North Park College and Theological Seminary, Chicago, IL [*Library symbol*] [*Library of Congress*] (LCLS)
ICNS Information Center on Nuclear Standards [*American Nuclear Society*] [*Information service or system*]
ICNS Information Centre on Nuclear Standards (SAUS)
ICNS Integrated Command & Navigation System (SAUS)
ICNS Integrated Communications and Navigation System
ICNS Integrated Communications/ Navigation System (SAUS)
ICNS National Safety Council, Chicago, IL [*Library symbol*] [*Library of Congress*] (LCLS)
ICNSH Idiopathic Central Nervous System Hypersommia [*Medicine*] (MELL)
ICNT INCOMNET, Inc. [*Formerly, Intelligent Commercial Net*] [*NASDAQ symbol*] (NQ)
ICNT Informal Composite Negotiated Text (SAUS)
ICNT Informal Composite Negotiating Text [*United Nations Conference on the Law of the Sea*]
ICNT International Committee for Natural Therapeutics (SAUO)
ICNT International Conference on Non-destructive Testing (SAUO)
ICNT Northern Trust Co., Chicago, IL [*Library symbol*] [*Library of Congress*] (LCLS)
ICNTG Intracoronary Nitroglycerine [*Pharmacology*]
ICNU National College of Education, Urban Campus, Chicago, IL [*Library symbol*] [*Library of Congress*] (LCLS)
ICNV International Code of Nomenclature of Viruses (SAUS)
ICNV International Committee for the Nomenclature of Viruses (SAUO)
ICNV International Committee on Nomenclature of Viruses [*Later, ICTV*]
ICNY International Center in New York (EA)
ICNY Islamic Center of New York (EA)
ICO Conference of International Catholic Organizations (SAUO)
ICO ICO, Inc. [*Associated Press*] (SAG)
ico iconology (SAUS)
ICO Identified Camouflaged Objects [*Hunting*]
ICO Idiopathic Cyclic Oedema [*Medicine*] (DMAA)
ICO Illinois College of Optometry [*Chicago*]
ICO Illinois Wesleyan University, Bloomington, IL [*OCLC symbol*] (OCLC)
ICO Immediate Commanding Officer
ICO Impedance Cardiac Output [*Medicine*] (DMAA)
ICO InaCom Corp. [*NYSE symbol*] (SG)
ICO In Case Of
ICO In Case of Interagency Committee on Oceanography (SAUS)
ICO Incident Command Organization [*Environmental science*] (COE)
ICO Independent Conducting Officer
ICO Indian Commissioned Officer [*British military*] (DMA)
ICO Individual Commodity Organization (SAUO)
ICO Information for the Contracting Officer (MCD)
ICO Initial Operating Capability (SAUS)
ICO Input Current Offset [*Computer science*]
ICO Inspecting Chief Officer [*Military*] [*British*] (ROG)
I/CO Installation and Check-Out (ADWA)
ICO Institut Canadien des Oceans [*Oceans Institute of Canada*] (IRC)
ICO Institute of Careers Officers [*British*]
ICO Institute of Chemists-Opticians [*British*] (DAS)
ICO Instrumentation Control Officer (AAG)
ico Integrated Checkout (NAKS)
ICO Integrated Checkout (NASA)
ICO Integration and Checkout (SAUS)
ICO Integrator Cutoff
ICO Interagency Committee on Oceanography [*Later, ICMSE*]
ICO Intercristo [*An association*] (EA)
ICO Interface Control Officer (SAUS)
ICO Intergovernmental Commission on Oceanography (NUCP)
ICO Intergovernmental Committee on Oceanography (SAUS)
ICO Interim Care Order (WDAA)
ICO Interim Conservation Order
ICO Intermediate Circular Orbit (SAUS)
ICO International Carbohydrate Organization [*Aberdeen, Scotland*] (EAIO)
ICO International Cardero Resources [*Vancouver Stock Exchange symbol*]
ICO International Catholic Organizations
ICO International Catholic Organizations Center (SAUO)
ICO International Chemistry Office (SAUO)
ICO International Civil Aviation Organization [*ICAO designator*] (FAAC)
ICO International Coffee Organization (EAIO)
ICO International College of Officers [*Salvation Army*]
ICO International Commission for/on Optics (SAUO)
ICO International Commission for Optics [*See also CIO*] [*ICSU*] [*Delft, Netherlands*] (EAIO)
ICO International Commission on Oceanography (SAUO)
ICO International Commission on Optics (SAUS)
ICO International Communications Operations (SAUS)

ICO International Computer Orphanage (EA)
ICO International Congress of Ophthalmology (SAUS)
ICO International Congress of Orientalists (SAUO)
ICO International Congress of Otolaryngology (SAUO)
ICO International Consultancy Organization (SAUO)
ICO International Council of Ophthalmology (EA)
ICO Internet Connectivity Option [*Galacticomm, Inc.*] [*Telecommunications*]
ICO Intracartilaginous Ossification [*Medicine*] (MELL)
ICO Intracompany Objective (TIMI)
ICO Inventory Control Officer
ICO Islamic Conference Association (SAUO)
ICO Israel Chamber Orchestra (SAUO)
ICO Istallation & Check Out (SAUS)
ICO Le Iscrizioni Fenicie e Puniche delle Colonie in Occidente (BJA)
ICOA International Castor Oil Association (EA)
ICOA International CBX Owners Association (EA)
ICOBA International Confederation of Book Actors (EA)
ICOBLA International Committee for Breaking the Language Barrier (SAUO)
ICOC ICO, Inc. [*NASDAQ symbol*] (NQ)
ICOC Indian Central Oil Seeds Committee (SAUS)
ICOC Indian Central Oilseeds Committee (SAUO)
ICOC Instruction for Commodores of Convois (SAUO)
ICOC Instructions for Commodores of Convoys [*Navy*] [*Obsolete*]
ICOC International Commission for Orders of Chivalry (EA)
i-coch Intra-Cochlear [*Medicine*] (EDAA)
ICOCS Interim Circuit Order Control System [*Bell System*]
ICOCZ ICO Inc. 6.75% Cv Dep Pfd [*NASDAQ symbol*] (TTSB)
ICOD Intelligence Cutoff Date [*Military*] (MCD)
ICOD International Center for Ocean Development (SAUS)
ICOD International Centre for Ocean Development [*See also CIEO*] [*Canada*]
ICOD International Conference on Database (SAUS)
ICOD International Conference on Databases (SAUS)
ICOD International Council on Disability (EA)
I-Code Intermediate Code (SAUS)
ICODS Interagency Committee on Dam Safety [*Federal Emergency Management Agency*] [*Washington, DC*] (EGAO)
ICOE International Center for Orthopaedic Education
ICOEES Interagency Committee on Ocean Exploration and Environmental Services [*Terminated, 1971*] (NOAA)
ICOEES International Committee on Ocean Exploration and Environmental Services [*Defunct*] (USDC)
ICOEI Integral Components of End Items (MCD)
ICOF Industrial Common Ownership Finance [*An association*] [*British*]
ICOF Integrated Command Operations Facility (SAUO)
ICOFA International Scientific Commission on the Family (SAUO)
ICOFOM International Committee for Museology (SAUO)
I-COFT Institutional Conduct of Fire Trainer [*Army*]
ICOFTA Indian Council of Foreign Trade (SAUO)
ICOFUND International Commodity Share Fund (SAUO)
ICOG International Conference on Geochronology (SAUO)
ICOGRADA International Conference of Graphic Design Association (SAUO)
ICOGRADA International Council of Graphic Design Associations [*British*] (EA)
ICOH International Commission of Occupational Health (EA)
ICOH International Commission of/on Occupational Health (SAUO)
ICOH International Commission on Occupational Health (SAUS)
ICOH International Congress on Occupational Health (SAUO)
ICOH Olive-Harvey College Library, City Colleges of Chicago, Chicago, IL [*Library symbol*] [*Library of Congress*] (LCLS)
ICOHEPANS International Conference on High Energy Physics and Nuclear Structure
ICOHH International Concatenated Order of Hoo-Hoo [*Later, International Order of Hoo-Hoo*] (EA)
ICOHTEC International Committee for the History of Technology (EA)
ICOHTEC International Cooperation in/on History of Technology Committee (SAUO)
ICOI Information Council of the Optical Industry (SAUO)
ICOI International Congress of Oral Implantologists (EA)
ICoIaD International Commission on Irrigation and Drainage (SAUO)
ICOIN Inland Waters, Coastal and Ocean Information Network (SAUS)
ICO Inc ICO, Inc. [*Associated Press*] (SAG)
ICO Journal Institute of Chemist-Opticians Journal (journ.) (SAUS)
ICol Collinsville Public Library, Collinsville, IL [*Library symbol*] [*Library of Congress*] (LCLS)
ICOLC International Coalition of Library Consortia
IColCU Collinsville Community Unit 10, Collinsville, IL [*Library symbol*] [*Library of Congress*] (LCLS)
ICOLD International Commission on Large Dams [*See also CIGB*] [*ICSU*] [*Paris, France*] (EAIO)
ICOLD International Congress on Large Dams (SAUS)
ICOLE International Centre of Landscape Ecology within Geography (SAUS)
ICOLP Industry Cooperative for Ozone Layer Protection
IColu Columbia Public Library, Columbia, IL [*Library symbol*] [*Library of Congress*] (LCLS)
ICoIuD Columbia Unit District 4, Columbia, IL [*Library symbol*] [*Library of Congress*] (LCLS)
ICOM Challenger International [*NASDAQ symbol*] (SAG)
ICOM Improved Conventional Mine System [*Military*] (MCD)
ICOM Industrial Common Ownership Movement [*British*]
ICOM Input-Channel-Output-Mechanism (SAUS)
ICOM Input, Control, Output, Mechanism (VLIE)
ICOM Institute of Computational Mechanics [*University of Cincinnati*] [*Research center*] (RCD)
ICOM Integrated Communications Security (SAUS)
ICOM Integrated COMSEC SINCGARS (SAUS)
ICOM Intelect Communications Systems Ltd. [*NASDAQ symbol*] (SAG)
ICOM Intercommunications (NASA)
ICOM Interfaith Church of Metaphysics (EA)
ICOM International Church of Metaphysics (EA)
ICOM International Council of Museums [*France*]
IComA Institute of Company Accountants [*British*] (EAIO)
ICOMAT International Conference on Martensitic Transformation (SAUS)
ICOMC International Conference on Organometallic Chemistry
ICOMC International Conferences on Organometallic Chemistry (SAUS)
ICOM-CC ICOM [*International Council of Museums*] Committee for Conservation (EAIO)
ICOME International Commission on Microbial Ecology (SAUO)
ICOME International Committee on Microbial Ecology [*ICSU*] (EAIO)
ICOMF Intelect Communications [*NASDAQ symbol*] (TTSB)
ICOMIA International Council of Marine Industries (or Industry) Associations (SAUO)
ICOMIA International Council of Marine Industry Associations [*Weybridge, Surrey, England*] (EA)
ICOMIDC International Committee on Mathematics in Developing Countries (SAUO)
ICOM News International Council of Museums News (SAUO)
ICOM News International Council of Museums News (journ.) (SAUS)
ICOMOS International Committee on Monuments and Sites (SAUO)
ICOMOS International Council for Monuments and Sites (SAUS)
ICOMOS International Council for/of/on Monuments and Sites (SAUO)
ICOMOS International Council of Monuments and Sites [*France*] (EA)
ICOMOS International Council on Monuments and Sites (SAUS)
ICOMP Iceland Ocean Meeting Point [*Navy*]
iCOMP Intel Comparative Microprocessor Performance Index (PCM)
ICOMP International Committee on the Management of Population Programmes (SAUO)
ICOMP International Council on Management of Population Programmes [*Kuala Lumpur, Malaysia*] (EAIO)
ICOMS Improved Conventional Mine System (ACAE)
icon iconic (SAUS)
ICON Iconoclasm (ADA)
icon Iconographical (SAUS)
ICON Iconography
ICON Image Communications & Operations Node (SAUS)
ICON Image Converter (SAUS)
ICON Imagery Communications and Operations Node (DOMA)
ICON Indexed Currency Option Note [*Student Loan Marketing Association*]
ICON Indexed Currency Option Notes (EBF)
ICON Information Consortium (SAUS)
ICON Integrated Acoustic Console (ACAE)
ICON Integrated COMSEC [*Communications Security*] [*Army*] (DOMA)
ICON Integrated Control
ICON Integration Concept (ACAE)
ICON Integration Contract (SAUS)
ICON Interactive Creation of NASTRAN (SAUS)
ICON Inter Continental (SAUS)
ICON Inter-Institutional Committee on Nutrition
ICON International Communication of Orthodox Nations
ICONA Institute for the Conservation of Nature (SAUS)
ICONA National Institute for the Conservation of Nature (SAUO)
ICONCLASS Iconography Classification [*Netherlands*] (NITA)
ICONDA International Construction Database [*Information Centre for Regional Planning and Building Construction of the Fraunhofer-Society*] [*Database*]
ICONE Comparative Index of National and European Standards (SAUO)
ICONMIG International Conference on Numerical Methods in Geomechanics
iCONN Connecticut Digital Library
Iconog Iconography (DIAR)
Iconol Iconology (DIAR)
ICONS Information Center on Nuclear Standards [*American Nuclear Society*] [*La Grange Park, IL*] [*Information service or system*]
ICONS Information Center on Nuclear Systems (SAUO)
ICONS Inner Continental Shelf Sediments and Structure Program [*Army Corps of Engineers*] (GFGA)
ICONS Integrated Conservation Networking System (SAUO)
ICONS Interagency Conference on Nursing Statistics (SAUO)
ICONS International Communication and Negotiation Simulation
ICONS Isotopes of Carbon, Oxygen, Nitrogen, and Sulfur [*AEC project*]
IConsA Independent Consultants Association (COBU)
iconst Iconostasis (VRA)
ICON System Integrated Control System (SAUS)
ICONTEC Instituto Colbiano de Normas Tecnicas (AG)
ICONZ Internet Company of New Zealand (SAUO)
ICOO Iraqi Company for Oil Operations (SAUO)
ICOP Imported Crude Oil Processing
ICOP Intelligence Collect Program
ICOP Interagency Contingency Options Plan [*Military*]
ICOP Inventory Control Point
ICOPA International Conference of Police Associations (SAUO)
ICOPA International Congress on Parasitology (SAUO)
ICOPAMP Integrated Circuit Operational Amplifier [*Electronics*] (IAA)
ICOPAV International Congress of Parasitologists (SAUO)
IC-OPC Integrating Contractor-Official Point of Contact (SAUS)
ICOPRAPA International Conference of Peace Researchers and Peace Activities (SAUO)
ICOPS Institute for the Comparative Study of Political Systems
ICOR In Charge of Room [*Military*] (DNAB)
ICOR Incremental Capital Output Ratio
ICOR Incremental Capital Output Ratios (SAUO)

ICOR .... Interagency Commission on Ocean Resources (SAUO)
ICOR .... Intergovernment al Conference on Oceanic Research (SAUO)
ICOR .... Intergovernmental Conference on Oceanic Research
ICOR .... Meicor, Inc. (SAUO)
ICORC .... International Committee for the Reconstruction of Cambodia (SAUO)
ICORELS .... International Commission for the Reception of Large Ships (SAUO)
ICORRST .... Institution of Corrosion Science and Technology (PDAA)
ICORRT .... Institution of Corrosion Technology (PDAA)
ICORS .... International Committee of Radical Sociologists (SAUO)
ICORS .... International Conference of Raman Spectroscopy
ICOS .... ICOS Corp. [*NASDAQ symbol*] (SPSG)
icos .... Improved Crew Optical Sight [*NASA*] (NAKS)
ICOS .... Improved Crew Optical Sight (NASA)
ICOS .... Integrated Checkout System (KSC)
ICOS .... Integrated Control System (SAUO)
ICOS .... Integrated Cost Operation System (IAA)
ICOS .... Interactive COBOL Operating System
ICOS .... International Committee of Onomastic Sciences [*Belgium*]
ICOS .... International Committee on Onomastic Sciences (SAUS)
ICOS .... Interpretation Canada. Ontario Section [*A publication*]
ICOS .... Irish Cooperative Organisation Society, Inc (SAUO)
ICOS .... Irish Council for Overseas Students
ICOSA .... International Council of Seamen's Agencies (EA)
ICOSAI .... International Congress of Supreme Audit Institutions (SAUO)
ICOSI .... International Committee on Smoking Issues [*Brussels, Belgium*] (EAIO)
ICOSMOS .... International Council of Monuments and Sites (SAUO)
ICOSO .... International Committee for Outer Space Onomastics
ICOSO .... International Committee on Outer Space Onomastics (SAUS)
ICOSS .... Inertial-Command Off-Set System (MCD)
ICOT .... ICOT Corp. [*NASDAQ symbol*] (NQ)
Icot .... ICOT Corp. [*Associated Press*] (SAG)
ICOT .... Institute for Computer Technology (SAUS)
ICOT .... Institute for new generation Computer Technology (SAUO)
ICOT .... Institute of Coastal Oceanography and Tides [*British*]
ICOT .... Institute of New Generation Commputer Technology (SAUS)
ICOT .... Institute of New Generation Computer Technology [*Japan*]
ICOT .... Institute on Computer Technology (SAUO)
ICOT .... International Commission on Olfaction and Taste (SAUO)
ICOTAS .... International Committee on the Organisation of Traffic at Sea [*British*] (DS)
ICOTOM .... International Conference on Textures of Materials (SAUS)
ICOTS .... Interagency Committee on Transportation Security [*Department of Transportation*]
ICOTS .... International Conference on Teaching Statistics
ICOTT .... Industry Coalition on Technology Transfer (SAUS)
ICOTY .... Import Car of the Year [*Automotive promotion*]
icou .... Inertial Coupling Data Unit (NAKS)
ICOU .... International Consommateurs Organization des Unions [*International Organization of Consumers Unions*]
ICP .... ICS [*Interpretive Computer Simulator*] Control Program [*Army*]
ICP .... Idaho Chemical Program (SAUO)
ICP .... Ignition Control Programmer (MCD)
ICP .... Illinois Curriculum Program (SAUO)
ICP .... Image Coprocessor (SAUS)
ICP .... Immunocompromised Patient [*Medicine*] (MELL)
ICP .... Impact Copolymer Polypropylene [*Plastics*] [*Automotive engineering*]
ICP .... Imput Control Procedure (SAUS)
ICP .... Incentive Compensation Plan (MCD)
ICP .... Incident Command Post [*Environmental science*] (COE)
ICP .... Incident Control Point [*Environmental science*] (COE)
ICP .... INCOLSA [*Indiana Cooperative Library Services Authority*] Processing Center, Indianapolis, IN [*OCLC symbol*] (OCLC)
ICP .... Incoming [*Message*] Process [*Telecommunications*] (TEL)
ICP .... Incubation Period [*Medicine*] (DB)
ICP .... Independent Content Provider (SAUS)
ICP .... Indian Communications Project
ICP .... Indicator Control Panel
ICP .... Indo-Chinese Communist Party [*Vietnam*] [*Political party*] (VNW)
ICP .... Inducrively Coupled Plasma (SAUS)
ICP .... Induction Coupled Plasma (EDCT)
ICP .... Inductively Coupled Plasma [*Spectrometry*]
ICP .... Industrial Control Package (SAUO)
ICP .... Industrial Control Products (MCD)
ICP .... Industrial Cooperation Program (SAUS)
ICP .... Industrial Coupling Program [*Refers to university-industry interaction*]
ICP .... Industry Cooperation Programme (SAUO)
ICP .... Industry Cooperative Program [*United Nations*]
ICP .... Infection-Control Practitioner [*Medicine*]
ICP .... Infection-Control Procedure (SAUS)
ICP .... Infectious Cell Protein [*Genetics*]
ICP .... Information Controlled Printer (SAUS)
ICP .... Initial Connection Protocol [*Computer science*] [*Telecommunications*]
ICP .... Initial Contact Period (SAUS)
ICP .... Injection Control Pressure (HAWK)
ICP .... Inner City Partnership [*EEC and British program to regenerate blighted areas*]
ICP .... Innovative Concepts Program (SAUS)
ICP .... Input Control Procedure (SAUS)
ICP .... Insecticidal Crystal Protein [*Agrochemistry*]
ICP .... Installation Input Change Package (MCD)
ICP .... Instant Control Point [*British police*]
ICP .... Institute for Circadian Physiology [*Boston, MA*]
ICP .... Institute for Comprehensive Planning [*Defunct*] (EA)
ICP .... Institute of Cellular and Molecular Pathology (SAUS)
ICP .... Institutional Conservation Program (GNE)
ICP .... Instructor Control Panel
ICP .... Instrumentation Calibration Procedure (SAUS)
ICP .... Instrument Calibration Procedure
ICP .... Insurance Conference Planners (EA)
ICP .... Intake Control Panel (SAUS)
ICP .... Integral Circuit Package
ICP .... Integrated Channel Processor (SAUS)
ICP .... Integrated Chemists of the Philippines
ICP .... Integrated Circuit Package (SAUS)
ICP .... Integrated Commodity Program (SAUO)
ICP .... Integrated Communications Platform (SAUS)
ICP .... Intelligence Collection Plan [*Military*] (AFM)
ICP .... Intelligent Communications Processor
ICP .... Intelligent Computer Peripherals (SAUO)
IC-P .... Intelligent Copier-Printer [*Electrophotography*]
ICP .... Inter-Computer Processor (SAUS)
ICP .... Interconnect Controller Program (SAUS)
ICP .... Interconnected Processing (SAUS)
ICP .... Interconnection Partner (SAUS)
icp .... Inter-Contact-Partners AG, Business Relations & Promotions (SAUO)
ICP .... Intercontinental Candle Power (SAUS)
ICP .... Intercontinental Club for the Use of Plastics in Building and Construction (SAUO)
ICP .... Intercountry Program on Integrated Pest Control (SAUO)
ICP .... Interdisciplinary Care Plan [*Information service or system*] (HCT)
ICP .... Interdisciplinary Communications Program
ICP .... Interface Change Proposal
ICP .... Interface Control Panel (MCD)
ICP .... Interface Control Procedure (SAUS)
ICP .... Interim Compliance Panel (SAUS)
ICP .... Intermittent Catheterization or Inspiratory Capacity [*Therapy term*] (CTAA)
ICP .... Intermittent Catheterization Protocol [*Medicine*] (MELL)
ICP .... Internal Combustion Powered (ADA)
ICP .... Internal Connection Protocol [*Telecommunications*]
ICP .... International Candle Power (SAUS)
ICP .... International Center of Photography (EA)
ICP .... International Classification of Patents [*Council of Europe*] (PDAA)
ICP .... International Club for Plastics Use in Building and Construction (SAUO)
ICP .... International Comfort Products
ICP .... International Commerce Promoters (SAUO)
ICP .... International Commission for Palynology (SAUO)
ICP .... International Committee for Learning by Participation (SAUO)
ICP .... International Communication Planning (SAUS)
ICP .... International Computer Programs, Inc. [*Indianapolis, IN*] [*Information service or system*]
ICP .... International Congress of Plastics (SAUO)
ICP .... International Congress of Publishers (DIT)
ICP .... International Control Plan (MCD)
ICP .... International Cooperative Program (SAUO)
ICP .... International Council of Psychologists (EA)
ICP .... International Institute of Cellular and Molecular Pathology [*Belgium*] (IRC)
ICP .... Internet Cache Protocol [*Computer science*] (AGLO)
ICP .... Internet Caching Protocol (SAUS)
ICP .... Internet Content Provider [*Computer science*]
ICP .... Internet Control Protocol [*Telecommunications*] (PCM)
ICP .... Interoceanic Canal Project [*National Oceanic and Atmospheric Administration*] (NOAA)
ICP .... Interpreting Card Punch (SAUS)
ICP .... Intertheater COMSEC Package (SAUS)
ICP .... Inter-University Case Program
ICP .... Inter-University Cooperation Program [*EC*] (ECED)
ICP .... Interuniversity Cooperation Programme (SAUO)
ICP .... Intraanial Pressure (SAUS)
ICP .... Intracarcass Pressure [*Tire technology*]
ICP .... Intracranial Pressure [*Medicine*]
ICP .... Intracuff Pressure [*In mechanical ventilation*] [*Medicine*]
ICP .... Intracytoplasmic [*Medicine*] (DB)
ICP .... Intraperitoneal Cisplatinum [*Medicine*] (MELL)
ICP .... Intrinsically Conductive Plastic [*Organic chemistry*]
ICP .... Intrinsically Conductive Polymer (SAUS)
ICP .... Inventory Communications Processor (SAUS)
ICP .... Inventory Control Point
ICP .... Investment Corporation of Pakistan (SAUO)
ICP .... Ion-Carburizing Calculation Program (SAUS)
ICP .... Ion Coupled Plasma [*Oil analysis*]
ICP .... Iraqi Communist Party [*Political party*] (PPW)
ICP .... Irish Company Profiles [*Institute of Industrial Research and Standards - IIRS*] [*Dublin, Ireland*] [*Information service or system*] (IID)
ICP .... Ischemic Cardiac Pain [*Cardiology*]
ICP .... Islands of Cartilage Pattern [*Anatomy*]
ICP .... Italian Communist Party
ICP .... Item Control Point (AFM)
IC-PA .... Industrial Co-Partnership Association (SAUO)
ICPA .... Information Centre for Polish Affairs (EAIO)
ICPA .... Insurance Conference Planners Association (NTPA)
ICPA .... International Cast Polymer Association (NTPA)
ICPA .... International Chiropractic Pediatric Association (SAUO)
ICPA .... International Commission for the Prevention of Alcoholism [*Later, InternationalCommission for the Prevention of Alcoholism and Drug Dependency*]

ICPA............ International Commission on Penicillium and Aspergillus (SAUO)
ICPA............ International Conference of Police Associations [*Defunct*]
ICPA............ International Cooperative Petroleum Association (EA)
ICPA............ International Cruise Passengers Association (EA)
ICPA............ Public Administration Service, Joint Reference Library, Chicago, IL [*Library symbol*] [*Library of Congress*] (LCLS)
ICPAC.......... Instantaneous Compressor Performance Analysis Computer
ICPADD........ International Commission for the Prevention of Alcoholism and Drug Dependency (EA)
ICPADS........ International Conference on Parallel and Distributed Systems (SAUS)
ICPAE.......... Interagency Committee on Public Affairs in Emergencies (SAUO)
ICPAE.......... International Commission on Planetary Atmospheres and their Evolution (SAUO)
ICP-AES....... Inductively Coupled Plasma - Atomic Emission Spectrometry [*See also ICPES*]
ICP-AES....... Inductively-Coupled Plasma-Atomic Emission Spectroscopy (SAUS)
ICPAM.......... International Centre for Pure and Applied Mathematics [*United Nations*] (EA)
ICPAN.......... Interfaith Council for the Protection of Animals and Nature (EA)
ICPAS.......... Illinois Certified Public Accountants Society (SRA)
ICPAS.......... Indiana Certified Public Accountants Society (SRA)
ICPas.......... Passionist Academic Institute, Chicago, IL [*Library symbol*] [*Library of Congress*] (LCLS)
ICPB............ Inert Components Parts Building
ICPB............ Inert Components Processing Building (SAUS)
ICPB............ International Collection of Phytopathogenic Bacteria [*Medicine*] (EDAA)
ICPBC.......... Institute of Certified Professional Business Consultants [*Chicago, IL*] (EA)
ICPBR.......... International Commission for Plant-Bee Relationships (EAIO)
ICPC............ International Cable Protection Committee [*British*] (EAIO)
ICPC............ International Classification of Primary Care (SAUO)
ICPC............ International Cloud Physics Conference (SAUS)
ICPC............ International Commission of Catholic Prison Chaplains (EA)
ICPC............ International Confederation of Popular Credit [*See also CICP*] [*Paris, France*] (EAIO)
ICPC............ International Conference of Police Chaplains (EA)
ICPC............ International Criminal Police Commission [*Later, INTERPOL*]
ICPC............ Interrange Communications Planning Committee
ICPC............ Interstate Compact on the Placement of Children [*Public human service program*] (PHSD)
ICPC............ Intracranial Pressure Catheter [*Neurology*] (DAVI)
ICPCC.......... International Council for Pastoral Care and Counselling (EAIO)
ICPCCP........ Illinois Council of Public Community College Presidents (SAUO)
ICPCI........... International Conference on the Performance of Computer Installations (PDAA)
ICPCN.......... Intersite Command Post Communication Network (SAUO)
ICPCSH........ International Conference on Physics and Chemistry of Semiconductor Heterostructures (SAUS)
ICPD............ International Commission on Physics for Development (SAUO)
ICPDATA...... Commodity Production Statistics [*United Nations Statistical Office*] [*Information service or system*] (CRD)
ICPDATA...... International Commodity Production Data [*United Nations Statistical Office*] (NITA)
ICP/DCP....... Inductively-Coupled Plasma/Directly-Coupled Plasma (SAUS)
ICPDES......... International Cancer Patient Data Exchange System
ICPDP.......... International Committee for Pollution Damage to Plants (SAUO)
ICPDS.......... Interactive Continuous Process Dynamic Simulation (PDAA)
ICPE............ Internal Combustion Piston Engine (PDAA)
ICPE............ International Catholic Programme of Evangelisation (SAUO)
ICPE............ International Center for Public Enterprises in Developing Countries [*Ljubljana, Yugoslavia*] (EAIO)
ICPE............ International Commission on Physics Education [*See also CIEP*] (EA)
ICPE............ International Conference on Public Education [*International Bureau of Education*] [*Switzerland*]
ICPE............ Inventory Control Point Europe
ICPEAC........ International Conference on the Physics of Electronic and Atomic Collisions (SAUO)
ICPECA........ International Center for the Protection of European Culture in Africa (SAUS)
ICPEM.......... Independent Computer Peripheral Equipment Manufacturers
ICPEMC........ International Commission for/on Protection against Environmental Mutagens and Carcinogens (SAUO)
ICPEMC........ International Commission for Protection Against Environmental Mutagens and Carcinogens [*Rijswljk, Netherlands*] (EAIO)
ICPERS........ Instant Computer Public Employment Relations Search [*Database*] [*Labor Relations Press*] [*Information service or system*] (CRD)
ICPES.......... Inductively Coupled Plasma Emission Spectrometry [*See also ICP-AES*]
ICP-ES......... Inductively-Coupled Plasma-Emission Spectroscopy (SAUS)
ICPES.......... Intergovernmental Committee for Physical Education and Sport [*United Nations*] [*France*] (EY)
ICPF............ International Corrugated Packaging Foundation (NTPA)
ICPFF........... Incentive Cost plus Fixed Fee [*Contracts*]
ICP-Forest... Internationale Cooperative Programme on the Assessment and Monitoring of Air Pollution Effects on Forests (SAUS)
ICPFR.......... International Committee on Physical Fitness Research (SAUO)
ICPFR.......... International Council for Physical Fitness Research [*Research center*] [*Canada*] (IRC)
ICPG............ People Gas Light Co., Chicago, IL [*Library symbol*] [*Library of Congress*] (LCLS)
ICPHS.......... International Council for Philosophical (or Philosophy) and Humanistic Studies (SAUS)
ICPHS.......... International Council for Philosophy and Humanistic Studies [*Paris, France*]
ICPHS/D....... Diogenes. International Council for Philosophy and Humanistic Studies (SAUO)
ICPI............. Insurance Crime Prevention Institute [*Westport, CT*] (EA)
ICPI............. Interagency Committee on Product Information (EA)
ICPI............. Interlocking Concrete Pavement Institute
ICPI............. International Conference on Polyimides (SAUS)
ICPI............. Intersociety Committee on Pathology Information (EA)
ICPIC........... Internatioanl Council for Philosophical Inquiry with Children (SAUO)
ICPIC........... International Cleaner Production Information Clearinghouse (GNE)
ICPIC........... International Conference on Phenomena in Ionised Gases (PDAA)
ICPIC........... International Council for Philosophical Inquiry with Children [*Iceland*] (EAIO)
ICPIC........... International Criminal Police Commission (SAUS)
ICPICH......... International Commission for the Preservation of Islamic Cultural Heritage (EA)
ICPIG........... International Conference on Phenomena in Ionised (or Ionized) Gases (SAUO)
ICPIG........... International Conference on Phenomena in Ionized Gases (SAUS)
ICPIGP......... Internationale Chretienne Professionelle pour les Industries Graphiques et Papetieres [*International Federation of Christian Trade Unions of Graphical and Paper Industries*]
ICPIN........... International Crime Prevention Information Network (SAUO)
ICPIWC........ International Council for Philosophical Inquiry with Children (EA)
ICpKSD........ J. F. Kennedy Consolidated Community School District 129, Cedar Point, IL [*Library symbol*] [*Library of Congress*] (LCLS)
ICPL............. Initial Control Program Load [*Computer science*] (IAA)
ICPL............. Interactive Control and Programming Language (HODG)
ICPL............. International Centre on Protected Landscapes (SAUS)
ICPL............. International Committee of Passenger Lines (PDAA)
ICPL............. Iowa City Public Library [*Iowa*]
ICPLC........... International Commission for the Protection of Lake Constance (SAUO)
ICPLS........... International College of Podiatric Laser Surgery (EA)
ICPM............ Illinois College of Podiatric Medicine, Chicago, IL [*Library symbol*] [*Library of Congress*] (LCLS)
ICPM............ Institute of Certified Professional Managers [*Harrisonburg, VA*] (EA)
ICPM............ Interim Commission for Phytosanitary Measures (SAUO)
ICPM............ International Classification of Procedures in Medicine (SAUS)
ICPM............ International College of Psychosomatic Medicine (SAUO)
ICPM............ International Commission for Plant Raw Materials (SAUO)
ICPM............ International Conference on Polymers in Medicine (SAUS)
ICPM............ International Congress of Physical Medicine (PDAA)
ICPME.......... International Center for Peace in the Middle East (EA)
ICPMM......... Incisors, Canines, Premolars, Molars [*Dentistry*]
ICPMM......... Peat, Marwick, and Mitchell, Chicago, IL [*Library symbol*] [*Library of Congress*] (LCLS)
ICPMP.......... International Commission for the Protection of the Mosel Against Pollution (SAUO)
ICPMP.......... International Commission for the Protection of the Moselle against Pollution (SAUS)
ICPMS.......... Inductively-Coupled Plasma Mass Spectrometer (SAUS)
ICP-MS......... Inductively Coupled Plasma - Mass Spectrometry
ICPMS.......... Inductively Coupled Plasma Mass Spectrometry (SAUO)
ICPMS.......... International Council of Prison Medical Services [*Vancouver, BC*] (EAIO)
ICPN............ International Committee of Plant Nutrition (EA)
ICPN............ International Council of Plant Nutrition (SAUO)
ICPNET........ Inventory Control Point Network (SAUO)
ICPNS.......... International Conference on the Physics of Noncrystalline Solids (SAUS)
ICPO............ Institute for Certified Park Operators (EA)
ICPO............ International CLIVAR [*Climate Variability and Prediction*] Project Office [*Marine science*] (OSRA)
ICPO............ International Criminal Police Organization [*France*]
ICPO............ Investment Co-Operative Programme Office [*UNIDO*]
ICPOA.......... Intelligence Center, Pacific Ocean Areas [*Obsolete*]
ICP-OES....... Inductively Coupled Plasma - Optical Emission Spectrometry
ICP-OES....... Inductively-Coupled Plasma-Optical Emission Spectroscopy (SAUS)
ICPP............ Idaho Chemical Processing Plant [*AEC*]
ICPP............ Institutional Child Protection Project [*Ohio State University*] (EDAC)
ICPP............ Interactive Computer Presentation Panel [*To display computer-generated information for military use*]
ICPP............ International Commission on Plasma Physics (SAUO)
ICPP............ International Committee on Planned Parenthood (SAUO)
ICPP............ International Comparative Political Parties Project [*Northwestern University*] [*Inactive*] (IID)
ICPP............ International Conference on the Internal and External Protection of Pipes (SAUO)
ICPP............ Intubated Continuous Positive Pressure [*Medicine*] (DAVI)
ICPP............ Isochromic Color Perception Plates [*Ophthalmology*] (DAVI)
ICPPS.......... Interim Critical Parts Planning System (SAUS)
ICPR............ Incoming Capital Property Record
ICPR............ Indian Council of Peace Research (SAUO)
ICPR............ Industrial Cost and Performance Report (NG)
ICPR............ Integrated Circuit Parameter Retrieval [*Information Handling Services*] [*Database*]
ICPR............ International Conference on Pattern Recognition (SAUO)
ICPR............ International Conference on Production Research (SAUO)
ICPR............ Inter-University Consortium for Political Research [*Later, ICPSR*] (EA)
ICPRAP........ International Commission for the Protection of the Rhine Against Pollution [*See also ICPRP, IKSR*] [*Germany*] (EAIO)
ICPRB.......... Interstate Commission on Potomac River Basin (SAUO)

ICPRB Interstate Commission on the Potomac River Basin

ICPRCPCO Intergovernmental Committee for Promoting the Return of Cultural Property to its Country of Origin or its Restitution in Case of Illicit Appropriation (SAUO)

ICPRCU Polish Roman Catholic Union of America, Chicago, IL [*Library symbol*] [*Library of Congress*] (LCLS)

ICPrM Provident Medical Center, Chicago, IL [*Library symbol*] [*Library of Congress*] (LCLS)

ICPRP International Commission for the Protection of the Rhine against Pollution (SAUO)

ICPRP Inventory Control Points Resolicitation Project (SAUS)

ICPRS Inter-University Consortium for Political an Social Research (SAUO)

ICPRS Petersen, Ross, Schloerb & Seidel, Library, Chicago, IL [*Library symbol*] [*Library of Congress*] (LCLS)

ICPS ICBM [*Intercontinental Ballistic Missile*] Code Processing System (DWSG)

ICPS Image Collecting and Processing System (SAUS)

ICPS Inductively Coupled Plasma Spectroscopy (MEC)

ICPS Institute for Cultural Policy Studies [*Griffith University*] [*Australia*]

ICPS Institute of Cost and Production Surveyors (SAUO)

ICPS Integrated Command Post System (SAUS)

ICPS Interamerican College of Physicians and Surgeons (EA)

ICPS International Carnivorous Plant Society (EA)

ICPS International Cerebral Palsy Society [*British*] (EAIO)

ICPS International Conference on the Physics of Semiconductors (SAUS)

ICPS International Conference on the Properties of Steam

ICPS International Congress of Photographic Science

ICPS International Council of Perfusion Societies [*Defunct*] (EA)

ICPS International Credit Protection Services (SAUO)

ICPS Interpersonal Cognitive Problem Solving (STED)

ICPS Interpersonal Cognitive Problem-Solving Program (EDAC)

ICPS Trade Unions International of Chemical, Oil and Allied Workers (SAUO)

ICPSI International Conference on Plasma Surface Interactions (SAUS)

ICPSR Inter-University Consortium for Political and Social Research (EA)

ICPT InterCept Group [*NASDAQ symbol*] (SG)

ICPT Intracranial Pituitary [*Medicine*] (EDAA)

ICPTO International China Painting Teachers Organization [*Later, International Porcelain Artist Teachers*]

ICPTUR International Conference for Promoting Technical Uniformity on Railways [*Berne, Switzerland*] (EAIO)

ICPU International Catholic Press Union [*Later, UCIP*]

ICPUAE International Conference on the Peaceful Uses of Atomic Energy

ICPV International Committee on Polar Viruses

ICPVT International Council for Pressure Vessel Technology (EA)

ICPYY Institute of Clinical Pharmacology PLC (MHDW)

i-cq- Comoro Islands [*MARC geographic area code*] [*Library of Congress*] (LCCP)

ICQ Internal Control Questionnaire (ADA)

ICQ International Capri Resources [*Vancouver Stock Exchange symbol*]

ICQ International Career Quotient (SAUS)

ICQ Invested Capital Questionnaire (SAUS)

ICQ I Seek You [*Internet dialog*]

ICQA International Columbian Quincentenary Alliance (EA)

ICQC International Conference on Quality Control (PDAA)

ICQL International Council for the Quality of Working Life (SAUO)

ICQMS International Centre for Quality and Management Sciences (SAUO)

ICQSA International Conference on Quanititative Surface Analysis (SAUS)

ICr Chicago Ridge Public Library, Chicago Ridge, IL [*Library symbol*] [*Library of Congress*] (LCLS)

ICR Compuring Intelligent Character Recognition (SAUS)

ICR Eagle Aero, Inc. [*ICAO designator*] (FAAC)

ICR Identification and Compliance Record (MCD)

ICR Iliac Crest [*Anatomy*]

ICR Iliac Crests [*Distance between*] [*Medicine*] (EDAA)

ICR Illinois Central Railroad

ICR Illinois Central Railroad Co. (SAUO)

ICR Illustration Change Request

ICR Image Character Recognition (IDAI)

ICR Immunodeficiency Cancer Registry

ICR In-Circuit Reconfigurable (SAUS)

ICR In-Commission Rate

ICR Increment (SAUS)

ICR Indefinite Contract Review (SAUS)

ICR Independent Component Release [*Computer science*] (IBMDP)

ICR Independent Congo Republic (SAUO)

ICR Independent Contact Release (SAUS)

ICR Indirect Control Register [*Computer science*]

ICR Individual Census Report (GFGA)

ICR Individually Carried Records [*Military*]

ICR Inductance-Capacitance-Resistance

ICR Industrial Cases Reports [*Law reports*] [*British*] (DCTA)

ICR Industrial Clear Room (SAUS)

ICR Industrial Cost Recovery [*Environmental Protection Agency*]

ICR Industrial Court Reports [*England*] [*A publication*] (DLA)

ICR Inertial Confinement Fusion Reactor [*Nuclear energy*] (MCD)

ICR Information Collection Request [*Paperwork Reduction Act*] (GFGA)

ICR Information Collection Rule [*Environmental Protection Agency*]

ICR Initial Cell Rate (SAUS)

ICR Initial Concentrated Rubber (SAUS)

ICR Input and Compare Register

ICR Input Card Reader (SAUS)

ICR Input Control Register [*Computer science*]

ICR Insert, Controlled Release (SAUS)

ICR Instantaneous Center of Rotation

ICR Institute for Cancer Research (EA)

ICR Institute for Chemical Research (SAUS)

ICR Institute for Communications Research [*Texas Tech University*] [*Research center*] (RCD)

ICR Institute for Computer Research [*University of Waterloo*] [*Canada*] [*Research center*] (RCD)

ICR Institute for Constitutional Research (EA)

ICR Institute for Cooperative Research

ICR Institute for Creation Research (EA)

ICR Institute for Creative Research (SAUO)

ICR Institute for Cultural Research [*Research center*] [*British*] (IRC)

ICR Institute for/of Cancer Research (SAUO)

ICR Institute of Coal Research [*University of Newcastle*] [*Australia*]

ICR Institution for Creation Research (SAUO)

ICR Instruction Change Request (NASA)

ICR Instruction Counting Register (SAUS)

ICR Instrumentation Control Racks (AAG)

ICR Instrument Calibration Requirements (SAUS)

ICR Insulated Core Reactor

ICR Integral Cesium Reservoir

ICR Integrated Color Removal [*Printing technology*]

ICR Integrated Control Register (SAUS)

ICR Integrated Cueing Requirements (ACAE)

ICR Integration Cancellation Ratio (SAUS)

ICR Integration of Cellular Responses [*Research initiative*] [*bbswrc - Biotechnology and Biological Sciences Research Council*] [*British*]

ICR Intelligence Collection Requirement [*Army*] (RDA)

ICR Intelligent Character Reader (SAUO)

ICR Intelligent Character Recognition [*Computer science*]

ICR Intensive Care Room [*Medicine*] (DAVI)

ICR Interactive Conflict Resolution (PDAA)

ICR Interception Report (SAUS)

ICR Intercity Relay [*Broadcasting*] (NTCM)

ICR Intercolonial Railway [*1858-1923*] [*Canada*]

ICR Intercooled (SAUS)

ICR Intercooled Recuperated (SAUS)

ICR Intercooled Recuperative [*Engine*] (DOMA)

ICR Intercooled Regenerative engine (SAUS)

ICR Intercultural Relations (DNAB)

ICR Interest Coverage Ratio

ICR Interface Change Request (ACAE)

ICR Interface Compatibility Record (NASA)

ICR Interface Control Register (IAA)

ICR Intermediate Circulating Reflux [*Chemical engineering*]

ICR Intermediate Common Room (SAUO)

ICR Intermittent Catheter Routine [*Medicine*] (DMAA)

ICR Internal Control Region [*Genetics*]

ICR Internal Control Review [*DoD*]

ICR International Calibrated Ratio (STED)

ICR International Celebrity Register (EFIS)

ICR International Commission on Rheology (SAUS)

ICR International Committee for Regional Museums (SAUO)

ICR International Committee on Refugees [*World War II*]

ICR International Committee on Rheology (SAUO)

ICR International Communications Recorders (SAUS)

ICR International Computer Resources, Inc. [*Information service or system*] (IID)

ICR International Congress of/on Radiology (SAUO)

ICR International Consumer Reports [*Consumers' Association*] [*British*] [*Information service or system*] (IID)

ICR International Corona Resources Ltd. [*Vancouver Stock Exchange symbol*]

ICR International Corporate Rate (SAUO)

ICR International Council for Reprography

IC/R International Cruiser/Race Class [*Yachting*]

ICR Interrupt Code Register (SAUS)

ICR Interrupt Control Register [*Computer science*]

ICR Interrupt Control Routine (VLIE)

ICR Intracardiac Catheter Recording [*Medicine*] (DMAA)

ICR Intracavitary Radium [*Medicine*] (MELL)

ICR Intracranial Reinforcement

ICR Intuitive Character Recognition (SAUS)

ICR Inventory Change Report

ICR Ion Cyclotron Radiation

ICR Ion Cyclotron Resonance [*Spectrometry*]

ICR Irish Chancery Reports [*A publication*] (DLA)

ICR Irish Circuit Reports [*1841-43*] [*A publication*] (DLA)

ICR Irish Communication Review (SAUS)

ICR Iron-Core Reactor (MSA)

ICR Island Creek Coal Co. (SAUO)

ICR Item Change Request (AFIT)

ICR Item Control Record (VLIE)

ICR Nicaro [*Cuba*] [*Airport symbol*] [*Obsolete*] (OAG)

ICRA Indian Civil Rights Act [*1968*]

ICRA Indo-Chinese Refugee Association (SAUO)

ICRA Industrial Chemical Research Association (EA)

ICRA Industrial Copyright Reform Association [*British*] (DBA)

ICRA Interagency Committee on Radiological Assistance

ICRA Interagency Committee on Radiological Protection (SAUS)

ICRA International Cartridge Recycling Association (EA)

ICRA International Catholic Rural Association

ICRA International Centre for Research in Accounting [*University of Lancaster*] [*British*] (CB)

ICRA International Compressor Remanufacturers Association (NTPA)

ICRA International Conference on Robotics and Automation (VLIE)
ICRA International Content Rating Association
ICRA International Copper Research Association (SAUO)
ICRA Internet Content Rating Association (SAUO)
ICRA Iowa Court Reporters Association (SRA)
ICRA Irish Civil Rights Association (SAUO)
ICRA Islamic Correctional Reunion Association (EA)
ICRAD Interactive Color Radar Display (SAUS)
ICRAEE International Commission on Rules for the Approval of Electrical Equipment [*Later, CEE*]
ICRAF Institut Canadien de Recherches pour l'Avancement de la Femme [*Canadian Research Institute for the Advancement of Women*]
ICRAF International Center for Agroforestry (SAUS)
ICRAF International Center (or Centre) for Research in Agroforestry (SAUO)
ICRAF International Centre for Research in Agroforestry
ICRAF International Council for Research in Agroforestry [*See also ICRAF*] [*Kenya*] (EAIO)
ICRaH Ravenswood Hospital Medical Center, Chicago, IL [*Library symbol*] [*Library of Congress*] (LCLS)
ICRand Rand McNally & Co., Chicago, IL [*Library symbol*] [*Library of Congress*] (LCLS)
ICRAR Interfaith Center to Reverse the Arms Race (EA)
ICRAS International Committee for the Release of Anatoly Scharansky [*Defunct*] (EA)
ICRA(V) Indo-Chinese Refugee Association (Victoria) [*Australia*]
ICRB Indefinite Contract Review Board (SAUS)
ICRB Inscribe (VLIE)
ICRB International Center for Research on Bilingualism [*Universite Laval*] [*Canada*]
ICRB International Co-Operative Reinsurance Bureau [*Manchester, England*] (EAIO)
ICRC Imperial College Reactor Centre [*Imperial College of Science and Technology*] [*British*] (WND)
ICRC Indian Cancer Research Centre (SAUO)
ICRC Indian Cancer Research Institute (SAUS)
ICRC Infant Care Review Committee [*Medicine*] (DMAA)
ICRC Interagency Classification Review Committee [*Abolished, 1978*] [*DoD*]
ICRC International Committee of the Red Cross
ICRC International Committee to the Red Cross [*Geneva, Switzerland*] (EAIO)
ICRC International Conference on Robotics in Construction (SAUS)
ICRC International Cosmic Ray Conference (SAUS)
ICRC Roosevelt University, Chicago, IL [*Library symbol*] [*Library of Congress*] (LCLS)
ICRCCM Intercomparison of Radiation Codes for/in Climate Models (SAUS)
ICRCL Interdepartmental Committee on the Redevelopment of Contaminated Land (SAUO)
ICRCM International Centre for Recent Crustal Movement (SAUO)
ICRC-N Roosevelt University, North Campus, Arlington Heights, IL [*Library symbol*] [*Library of Congress*] (LCLS)
ICRCP International Centre for Relief to Civilian Population (SAUO)
ICRD Index of Codes for Research Drugs [*A publication*]
ICRD Input Collection Reports Data [*IRS*]
ICRD Intellicard International, Inc. (SAUO)
ICRD Interior Committee on Research and Development
ICRD International Cooperative Research and Development Program (SAUO)
ICRD Richard J. Daley College, Chicago, IL [*Library symbol*] [*Library of Congress*] (LCLS)
ICRDA Independent Cash Register Dealers Association (EA)
ICRDB International Cancer Research Data Bank [*National Cancer Institute*] [*Database producer*] (IID)
ICRDB International Cancer Research Databank Branch (SAUS)
ICRDD Institute for Community Resource Development [*Australia*]
ICRDG International Crust Research Drilling Group (SAUO)
ICre Crete Public Library, Crete, IL [*Library symbol*] [*Library of Congress*] (LCLS)
ICRE Ignitability Corrosivity, Reactivity, Extraction (GNE)
ICRE Ignitable, Corrosive, Reactive, and/or Effluent [*Environmental science*] (COE)
ICRE International Center (or Centre) for Remedial Education (SAUO)
ICRE International Commission on Radiological Education (DMAA)
ICRE International Council of Religious Education (SAUO)
ICREB International Champlain-Richelieu Engineering Board [*Canada*]
ICREF Institut Canadien de Recherches sur les Femmes (AC)
IC Rep Interstate Commerce Commission Reports [*A publication*] (DLA)
ICRETT International Cancer Research Technology Transfer [*Program*]
ICREW International Cancer Research Workshop
I-CRF Immunoreactive Corticotropin-Releasing Factor [*Medicine*] (STED)
ICRF Imperial Cancer Research Fund [*British*]
ICRF Intergrated Cryptographic Feature (SAUS)
ICRF International Cancer Research Foundation (SAUO)
ICRF Ion Cyclotron Radio Frequency
ICRF Ion Cyclotron Range of Frequencies (SAUS)
ICRF Ion Cyclotron Resonance Frequency [*Nuclear energy*]
ICRF 159 Imperial Cancer Research Fund 159 [*Razoxane*] [*Antineoplastic drug*]
ICRFL Imperial Cancer Research Fund Laboratories [*Medicine*] (EDAA)
ICRFSDD Independent Citizens Research Foundation for the Study of Degenerative Diseases (EA)
ICR-FT-MS Ion-Cyclotron Resonance Fourier Transform Mass Spectrometry (SAUS)
ICRGR International Consultative Research Group on Rape [*See also GCIRC*] (EAIO)
ICRH Information Center - Recreation for the Handicapped
ICRH Institute for Computer Research in the Humanities [*New York University*]
ICRH International Congress on Religious History (SAUO)
ICRH Ion Cyclotron Resonance Heating (MCD)
ICRH Michael Reese Hospital and Medical Center, Lillian W. Florsheim Memorial Library, Chicago, IL [*Library symbol*] [*Library of Congress*] (LCLS)
ICRHO Ross, Hardies, O'Keefe, Babcock, and Parsons, Chicago, IL [*Library symbol*] [*Library of Congress*] (LCLS)
ICRHS Illinois Central Railroad Historical Society (EA)
ICRI Illinois Committee for Responsible Investment (SAUS)
ICRI Industrial Chemistry Research Institute [*Plastics industry*]
ICRI International Child Resource Institute (EA)
ICRI International Coma Recovery Institute (EA)
ICRI International Communications Research Institute (SAUS)
ICRI International Concrete Repair Institute (NTPA)
ICRI International Coral Reef Initiative (SAUS)
ICRI International Interdisciplinary Cycle Research Institute (SAUO)
ICRI Iron Casting Research Institute (EA)
ICRI Rehabilitation Institute of Chicago, Chicago, IL [*Library symbol*] [*Library of Congress*] (LCLS)
ICRICE International Centre of Research and Information on Collective Economy
ICRIER Indian Council for Research on International Economic Relations (SAUO)
ICRIN Injury Control Resource Information Network (SAUO)
ICRIP International Circle for Research in Philosophy [*Research center*] (RCD)
ICRIS Integrated Customer Record Information System (SAUS)
ICRISAT International Centre for Research in the Semi-Arid Tropics (SAUS)
ICRISAT International Crops Research Institute for the Semi-Arid Tropics [*India*]
ICRK Indian Creek Railroad [*Federal Railroad Administration identification code*]
ICRL Center for Research Libraries, Chicago, IL [*Library symbol*] [*Library of Congress*] (LCLS)
ICRL Indirect Certificate Revocation List (DINT)
ICRL Individual Component Repair List [*DoD*]
ICRL Injury Control Research Laboratory [*HEW*]
ICRL(ARL) Foreign Newspaper Microfilm Project, Association of Research Libraries, Center for Research Libraries, Chicago, IL [*Library symbol*] [*Library of Congress*] (LCLS)
ICRL(CAMP) Cooperative Africana Microform Project, Archives-Libraries Committee, African Studies Association, Center for Research Libraries, Chicago, IL [*Library symbol*] [*Library of Congress*] (LCLS)
ICrlF Follett Library Book Co., Crystal Lake, IL [*Library symbol*] [*Library of Congress*] (LCLS)
ICRL-LA Latin America Microform Project, Center for Research Libraries, Chicago, IL [*Library symbol*] [*Library of Congress*] (LCLS)
ICRLP International Center for Research on Language Planning [*Laval University*] (IRC)
ICRL-RR Injury Control Research Laboratory Research Report [*HEW*]
ICRL(SAMP) South Asian Microform Project, South Asian Microform and Library Committee, Association for Asian Studies, Center for Research Libraries, Chicago, IL [*Library symbol*] [*Library of Congress*] (LCLS)
ICRL-SEA South East Asia Microform Project, Center for Research Libraries, Chicago, IL [*Library symbol*] [*Library of Congress*] (LCLS)
I CRM Ice Cream [*Freight*]
ICRM Institute of Certified Records Managers (NTPA)
ICRM Intercontinental Reconnaissance Missile (DNAB)
ICRM International Carpet and Rug Market (ITD)
ICRM International Cliff Richard Movement (EAIO)
ICRM International Committee for/on Radionuclide Metrology (SAUO)
ICRM Rush Medical College, Chicago, IL [*Library symbol*] [*Library of Congress*] (LCLS)
ICRMLCK Islamic Congolese Revolutionary Movement Lumumbist of Congo Kinshasa (SAUO)
ICRMS Integrated Computer-Reactor Monitoring System (PDAA)
ICRO Interallied Confederation of Reserve Officers [*See also CIOR*] (EAIO)
ICRO International Cell Research Organization [*ICSU*] [*Paris, France*] (EAIO)
ICROSS International Community for the Relief of Starvation and Suffering (EA)
ICRP Internal Control Review Program [*Air Force*] (DOMA)
ICRP International Climatic Research Program
ICRP International Commission on Radiation Protection (SAUO)
ICRP International Commission on Radiological Protection [*International Society of Radiology*] [*British*]
ICRP International Committee for Radiation Protection (SAUS)
ICRP International Council for Radiation Protection (SAUO)
ICRPDS Ion Cyclotron Resonance Photodissociation [*Spectrometry*]
ICRPG Interagency Chemical Rocket Propulsion Group
ICRPMA International Committee for Recording the Productivity of Milk Animals [*See also CICPLB*] [*Rome, Italy*] (EAIO)
ICRR Illinois Central Railroad System (SAUO)
ICRR International Congress of Radiation Research (SAUS)
ICRS Imagery Collection Requirements Subcommittee [*Military*]
ICRS Index Chemicals Registry System [*Databank*] (NITA)
ICRS Index Chemicus Registry System [*Information service or system*] [*A publication*]
ICRS Institute of Contemporary Russian Studies [*Fordham University*]
ICRS Instrument Calibration and Recall System [*Nuclear energy*] (NRCH)

ICRS .... Integrated Chemical Retrieval System [*Pergamon InfoLine*] [*Computer science*]
ICRS .... Intelligence Collection Reporting System [*Military*] (MCD)
ICRS .... International Commission on Radium Standards (SAUO)
ICRS .... International Conference on Residual Stresses (SAUS)
ICRSC .... International Council for Research in the Sociology of Cooperation (SAUO)
ICRSDT .... International Commission on Remote Sensing and Data Transmission (SAUS)
ICRSDT .... International Committee on Remote Sensing and Data Transmission [*Marine science*] (OSRA)
ICRS Medical Reports... Institute of Contemporary Russian Studies Medical Reports (SAUS)
ICRSs.......... Industrial X-Ray Systems (SAUS)
ICRT............ Incorrect (VLIE)
ICRT............ Individual Criterion-Referenced Test [*Education*]
ICRT............ Intelligent Content Recognition Technology [*Computer science*]
ICRT-MATH... Individualized Criterion Referenced Testing Mathematics [*Strotman and Steen*] (TES)
ICRT-READING... Individualized Criterion Referenced Testing-Reading (TES)
ICRU .... International Commission of/on Radiation Units and Measurements (SAUO)
ICRU .... International Commission on Radiation Units (SAUS)
ICRU .... International Commission on Radiation Units and Measurements (EA)
ICRU .... International Commission on Radiological Units (STED)
ICRU .... International Committee on Radiological Units (SAUO)
IcRU............ University of Icelands (Haskoli Islands), Reykjavik, Iceland [*Library symbol*] [*Library of Congress*] (LCLS)
ICRUM .... International Commission on Radiation Units and Measurements
ICRV .... Inns of Court Rifle Volunteers [*Military*] [*British*] (ROG)
ICRW .... International Center for Research on Women (EA)
ICRW .... International Center (or Centre) for Research on Women (SAUO)
ICRW .... International Convention for the Regulation of Whaling (ASF)
ICRW .... Rednik & Wolfe, Chicago, IL [*Library symbol*] [*Library of Congress*] (LCLS)
ICRX .... Iron Cliffs Railway [*Federal Railroad Administration identification code*]
ICRYVE .... International Centre of Research Youth, Violence, Environment (SAUO)
ICS.............. IBM Cabling System (SAUO)
ICS.............. Identification of Character Set (SAUS)
ICS.............. Identifying Criteria for Success [*Software package*] [*Development Dimensions Inc.*]
ICS.............. Idnetify Control Section (SAUS)
ICS.............. Ileocecal Sphincter [*Medicine*] (DMAA)
ICS.............. Illinois Chiropractic Society (SRA)
ICS.............. Image Correction System (ACAE)
ICS.............. Image Creation System (SAUS)
ICS.............. Immotile Cilia Syndrome [*Medicine*] (DMAA)
ICS.............. Immunochemistry System [*Medicine*]
ICS.............. Imperial College of Science [*British*]
ICS.............. Imperial College of Science and Technology (SAUO)
ICS.............. Implementation Conformance Statement (SAUS)
ICS.............. Improved Composite Sandwich (SAUS)
ICS.............. Improved Composite Structure (SAUS)
ICS.............. Impulse Conducting System [*Physiology*]
ICS.............. In-Can System [*Device that improves quality of beer and ale*] [*British*]
I/Cs............. In Cases (SAUS)
ICS.............. Incident Command System [*Regional emergency response system*] (DHSM)
ICS.............. Include Segment (VLIE)
ICS.............. Income & Capital Shares, Inc. (SAUO)
ICS.............. Incoming Call Screening (SAUS)
ICS.............. In-Core Shim (SAUS)
ICS.............. Index to the Contemporary Scene (SAUO)
ICS.............. Indian Civil Service [*British*]
ICS.............. Induction Communications System
ICS.............. Industrial Computing Society (DDC)
ICS.............. Industrial Control System
ICS.............. Industry and Custom Systems (SAUS)
ICS.............. Inertial Control System (SAUO)
ICS.............. Infinity Color-Corrected System [*Optics*]
ICS.............. Informatic Communication System (SAUS)
ICS.............. Information Calling Services [*Telecommunications*]
ICS.............. Information Carrier System (SAUS)
ICS.............. Information Centers Service [*United States Information Agency*] (IID)
ICS.............. Information Channel Selection (SAUS)
ICS.............. Information Collection System (MHDI)
ICS.............. Information Computer System (IAA)
ICS.............. Information Control Service (SAUO)
ICS.............. Information Control System [*Military*]
ICS.............. Infrared Calibration System
ICS.............. Infrared Camera System
ICS.............. Infrared Communications System
ICS.............. Infrared Countermeasures System [*Military*] [*Electronics*]
ICS.............. Injection Compression System
ICS.............. Inland Computer Service (IEEE)
ICS.............. Inner Continental Shelf (SAUS)
ICS.............. Innes Clan Society (EA)
ICs.............. Innovation Centres (SAUS)
ICS.............. Innovation, Communication Structures (SAUS)
ICS.............. Input Contactor Switch
ICS.............. Input Control Subsystem
ICS.............. Input Control System (SAUS)
ICS.............. Insert Card Section
ICS.............. Inspection Clean-Up Sheet (SAUS)
ICS.............. Installation Control Specification [*Computer science*] (ITCA)
ICS.............. Installment Credit Selling (SAUS)
ICS.............. Institute for Chemical Studies (GNE)
ICS.............. Institute for Christian Studies
ICS.............. Institute for Cognitive Science [*University of California, San Diego*] [*Research center*] (RCD)
ICS.............. Institute for Computer Sciences (HGAA)
ICS.............. Institute for Contemporary Studies (EA)
ICS.............. Institute for Cultural Studies [*Defunct*] (EA)
ICS.............. Institute for the Comparative Study of History, Philosophy, and the Sciences Ltd. [*British*] (BI)
ICS.............. Institute of Caribbean Studies (EA)
ICS.............. Institute of Chartered Shipbrokers [*British*]
ICS.............. Institute of Chartered Shipbuilders (SAUS)
ICS.............. Institute of Chartered Surveyors (SAUS)
ICS.............. Institute of Child Study [*University of Toronto*] [*Research center*] (RCD)
ICS.............. Institute of Cognitive Science [*University of Colorado, Boulder*] [*Research center*] (RCD)
ICS.............. Institute of Commonwealth Studies [*British*]
ICS.............. Institute of Complemental Systems (SAUO)
ICS.............. Institute of Complementary Sciences [*Defunct*] (EA)
ICS.............. Institute of Computer Science (SAUO)
ICS.............. Institute of Cornish Studies [*British*]
ICS.............. Institution of Computer Sciences [*British*] (DIT)
ICS.............. Instructional Communications Systems [*University of Wisconsin*] [*Telecommunications service*] (TSSD)
ICS.............. Instrumentation and Communication Subsystem [*NASA*] (KSC)
ICS.............. Instrumentation and Control Subsystem
ICS.............. Instrumentation Checkout Station (AAG)
ICS.............. Instrumentation Control Systems (SAUS)
ICS.............. Instrument Cooling System (SAUS)
ICS.............. Insurance Communication Service [*IBM Information Network*] [*Tampa, FL*] [*Telecommunications*] (TSSD)
ICS.............. Integrated Case Study [*Medicine*] (DMAA)
ICS.............. Integrated Checkout Station (SAUS)
ICS.............. Integrated Checkout System (KSC)
ICS.............. Integrated Circuit System (IMH)
ICS.............. Integrated Collection System [*IRS*]
ICS.............. Integrated Combat Ship
ICS.............. Integrated Combat System
ICS.............. Integrated Command System
ICS.............. Integrated Communication Services (SAUO)
ICS.............. Integrated Communications System [*Communications term*] (DCT)
ICS.............. Integrated Communication Systems, Inc. [*Roswell, GA*] [*Telecommunications*] (IEEE)
ICS.............. Integrated Composite Spinning (PDAA)
ICS.............. Integrated Computer Solutions
ICS.............. Integrated Computer Systems [*Culver City, CA*] [*Telecommunications service*] (TSSD)
ICS.............. Integrated Configuration Summary (AAG)
ICS.............. Integrated Conning System (PDAA)
ICS.............. Integrated Container Service (SAUO)
ICS.............. Integrated Controller Software (SAUS)
ICS.............. Integrated Control Storage [*Computer science*]
ICS.............. Integrated Control System (NRCH)
ICS.............. Integrated Countermeasures Set (SAUS)
ICS.............. Integration Control System (SAUS)
ICS.............. Intelligence Center and School [*Army*] (RDA)
ICS.............. Intelligence Community Staff [*Military*] (MCD)
ICS.............. Intensive Care Society [*British*] (EAIO)
ICS.............. Intensive Care, Surgical [*Medicine*]
ICS.............. Interactive Communications Software
ICS.............. Interactive Communications System (SAUS)
ICS.............. Interactive Compatibility Software [*Gateway Communications, Inc.*] [*Computer science*] (PCM)
ICS.............. Interactive Control Station (SAUS)
ICS.............. Interactive Control System (SAUS)
ICS.............. Interactive Counting System (IAA)
ICS.............. Interagency Communications System [*Military*]
ICS.............. InterCapital Ins Cal Muni Sec [*NYSE symbol*] (TTSB)
ICS.............. InterCapital Insured California Municipal Securities [*NYSE symbol*] (SAG)
ICS.............. Intercarrier Sound (IAA)
ICS.............. Intercellular Space (DMAA)
ICS.............. Inter-Celtic Society (EAIO)
ICS.............. Intercistronic Spacer [*Genetics*]
ICS.............. Intercockpit Communications System [*Navy*] (DOMA)
ICS.............. Intercommunication Control Set (SAUS)
ICS.............. Intercommunication Control Station (KSC)
ICS.............. Intercommunications System
ICS.............. Intercommunication System FFTF (SAUS)
ICS.............. Intercom System (SAUS)
ICS.............. Intercontinental Church Society [*British*] (EAIO)
ICS.............. Intercostal Space [*Medicine*]
ICS.............. Interdepartmental Commit. on Space (SAUS)
ICS.............. Interdigital Communications Subsystem [*Communications term*] (DCT)
ICS.............. Interdisciplinary Climate Systems (SAUS)
ICS.............. Interface Control Specification (MCD)
ICS.............. Interference Check Sample [*Spectroscopy*]
ICS.............. Interference Check Standard (SAUS)

ICS .... Interim Contractor Support (MCD)
ICS .... Interim Contract Support (SAUS)
ICS .... Interior Communications System (SAUS)
ICS .... Interior Contractor Support
ICS .... Interlinked Computerized Storage and Processing System of Food and Agricultural Data [*Databank*] [*United Nations*] [*Information service or system*] (IID)
ICS .... Interlinked Computerized System (SAUS)
ICS .... Intermittent Control Strategies (SAUO)
ICS .... Intermittent Control Strategy [*Environmental Protection Agency*] (GFGA)
ICS .... Intermittent Control System [*Environmental Protection Agency*]
ICS .... Internal Calibration Sources (ACAE)
ICS .... Internal Chemical Shift
ICS .... Internal Communication System [*Space Flight Operations Facility, NASA*]
ICS .... Internal Correction System (SAUS)
ICS .... Internal Countermeasures Set (MCD)
ICS .... Internal Countermeasure System (SAUO)
ICS .... International Camellia Society [*Worcester, England*] (EAIO)
ICS .... International Cardiovascular Society
ICS .... International Catacomb Society (EA)
ICS .... International Chamber of Shipping [*British*] (EAIO)
ICS .... International Chemical Society [*Proposed*]
ICS .... International Chemometrics Society [*Brussels, Belgium*] (EAIO)
ICS .... International Chili Society (EA)
ICS .... International Churchill Society (EA)
ICS .... International Clarinet Society [*Later, ICS/CI*] (EA)
ICS .... International Classification for Standards (SAUS)
ICS .... International Code of Signals (IAA)
ICS .... International Cogeneration Society (EA)
ICS .... International Cold Storage
ICS .... International College of Scientists [*See also ISK*] [*International Academy of Sciences*] [*Paderborn, Federal Republic of Germany*] (EAIO)
ICS .... International College of Surgeons (EA)
ICS .... International Commission on Stratigraphy (SAUO)
ICS .... International Committee of Slavists [*Sofia, Bulgaria*] (EAIO)
ICS .... International Committee on Sarcoidosis [*British*] (EAIO)
ICS .... International Communications Sciences
ICS .... International Communications System
ICS .... International Computer Symposium (SAUS)
ICS .... International Computer System (IAA)
ICS .... International Computing Symposium (SAUO)
ICS .... International Confederation of Students (SAUO)
ICS .... International Congress of Surgeons [*Association*] [*Medicine*] (MTAA)
ICS .... International Connecting Set (IAA)
ICS .... International Conrad Society (EA)
ICS .... International Consultancy Service (SAUO)
ICS .... International Container Service (SAUO)
ICS .... International Contract Specialists (SAUO)
ICS .... International Controlled Industry [*Vancouver Stock Exchange symbol*]
ICS .... International Coronelli Society [*See also ICGGI*] (EAIO)
ICS .... International Council for Science (SAUO)
ICS .... International Council of Scientific Unions (SAUO)
ICS .... International Craniopathic Society [*SORSI*] [*Absorbed by*] (EA)
ICS .... International Crocodilian Society [*Defunct*] (EA)
ICS .... Internet Caching Service [*Computer science*]
ICS .... Internet Connection Sharing
ICS .... Interphone Control Station
ICS .... Interphone Control System
ICS .... Interpretative Computer Simulation (SAUS)
ICS .... Interpreter Computer Simulator (SAUS)
ICS .... Interpretive Computer Simulation (or Simulator) (SAUS)
ICS .... Interpretive Computer System
ICS .... Interviewer Card Scheme [*Business term*]
ICS .... Interway Container Service (SAUO)
ICS .... Intracapillary Space [*In bioreactor*]
ICS .... Intracellular-Like Solution [*Cardioplegic solution*] [*Pharmacology*] (DAVI)
ICS .... Intracommunication System
ICS .... Intracostal Space (SAUS)
ICS .... Intracranial Self-Stimulation [*Also, ICSS*] [*Neurophysiology*]
ICS .... Intracranial Stimulation [*Neurophysiology*]
ICS .... Intuitive Command Structure (SAUS)
ICS .... Inventory Change Sheet (SAUS)
ICS .... Inventory Control System [*Computer science*]
ICS .... Inverse Conical Scan (DNAB)
ICS .... Inverse Conical Scanning (SAUS)
ICS .... Investors Compensation Scheme (SAUS)
ICS .... Ion-Channel Switch [*Biochemistry*]
ICS .... Ionization Current Source (PDAA)
ICS .... Iowa Chiropractic Society (SRA)
ICS .... Irish Computer Society
ICS .... Iron Castings Society (EA)
ICS .... Irritable Colon Syndrome [*Medicine*] (DMAA)
ICS .... Isolation Containment Spray [*Nuclear energy*] (IEEE)
ICS .... Israel Chemical Society (SAUO)
ICS .... Israel Crystallographic Society (SAUO)
ICS .... Issued Capital Stock
ICS .... Saint Xavier College, Chicago, IL [*OCLC symbol*] (OCLC)
ICS .... Society of Inter-Celtic Arts and Culture (EA)
ICS2 .... Intelligent Communication Subsystem Two Board [*Controls input from computer terminals to mainframe*] [*Prime Computer, Inc.*]
ICSA .... In-Core Shim Assembly [*Nuclear energy*] (NRCH)
ICSA .... Indian Council of South America [*See also CISA*] [*Lima, Peru*] (EAIO)
ICSA .... Information and Computing Services Association (ACII)
ICSA .... Infrared Charge Scanned Array (ACAE)
ICSA .... Institute of Chartered Secretaries and Administrators (AIE)
ICSA .... Intercollegiate Community Service Association (SAUO)
ICSA .... International Cemetery Supply Association (EA)
ICSA .... International Chain Salon Association (EA)
ICSA .... International Christian Studies Association (EA)
ICSA .... International Civil Service Agency (SAUO)
ICSA .... International Claims Settlement Act of 1949
ICSA .... International Committee Against Apartheid, Racism, and Colonialism in Southern Africa [*British*] [*Defunct*] (EAIO)
ICSA .... International Computer Security Association
ICSA .... International Cooperatives Services (SAUO)
ICSA .... International Correspondence Society of Allergists (EA)
ICSA .... International Correspondence Society of Allergists and Clinical Immunologists [*Formerly, International Correspondence Society of Allergists*] (EA)
ICSA .... International Council for Scientific Agriculture (SAUO)
ICSA .... International Council of Scientific Associations (SAUO)
ICSA .... International Council of Shopping Centers (SAUO)
ICSA .... International Customer Service Association [*Chicago, IL*] (EA)
ICSA .... Intracranial Self-Administration [*Neurophysiology*]
ICSA .... Islet Cell Surface Antibody [*Immunology*]
ICSA .... Sidley and Austin Library, Chicago, IL [*Library symbol*] [*Library of Congress*] (LCLS)
ICSAB .... International Civil Service Advisory Board
ICSAC .... Inter-American Catholic Social Action Confederation (SAUO)
ICSAC .... International Confederation of Societies of Authors and Composers
ICSAC .... International Council of Regional School Accrediting Commissions (NTPA)
ICSac .... Sachnoff Weaver & Rubenstein, Chicago, Il [*Library symbol*] [*Library of Congress*] (LCLS)
ICSAF .... International Commission for the Southeast Atlantic Fisheries [*See also CIPASE*] (EAIO)
ICSAL .... Integrated Communications System, Alaska [*Air Force, FAA*]
ICS&T .... Imperial College of Science and Technology (SAUO)
ICSAPI .... Internet Connection Services [*Computer science*] (PCM)
ICSAR .... Interagency Committee on Search and Rescue (COE)
ICSAR .... Interdepartment Committee on Search and Rescue (SAUS)
ICSB .... Intelligence Control Staff, Berlin (SAUO)
ICSB .... Interim Command Switchboard [*Navy*] (NVT)
ICSB .... International Center of School Building (SAUS)
ICSB .... International Commission on Systematic Bacteriology (SAUO)
ICSB .... International Committee on Systematic Bacteriology [*London, ON*] (EA)
ICSB .... International Council for Small Business (EA)
ICSBA .... International Committee for the Study of Bauxite, Alumina and Aluminium (SAUO)
ICSBA .... International Committee on the Study of Bauxite, Alumina and Aluminum (SAUS)
ICSBC .... Interstate Council of State Boards of Cosmetology [*Later, NIC*]
ICSBS .... International Chinese Snuff Bottle Society (EA)
ICSC .... Idiopathic Central Serous Chorioretinopathy (SAUS)
ICSC .... Independent Colleges of Southern California (SAUO)
ICSC .... Indian Central Sugarcane Committee (SAUO)
ICSC .... Industrial Council of Shopping Centers (SAUO)
ICSC .... Institute for Cardiovascular Studies [*University of Houston*] [*Research center*] (RCD)
ICSC .... Integrated Command Support Center [*Military*] (MCD)
ICSC .... Intelligent Channel/Storage Control (SAUS)
ICSC .... Interim Commission on Satellite Communication (NITA)
ICSC .... Interim Communications Satellite Commission (SAUO)
ICSC .... Interim Communications Satellite Commission (or Committee) (SAUS)
ICSC .... Interior Communication Switching Center (DNAB)
ICSC .... Inter LATA Customer Service Center (SAUS)
ICSC .... International Center for Safety Communication (SAUS)
ICSC .... International Chemical Safety Card
ICSC .... International Civil Service Commission (EA)
ICSC .... International Commission for Supervision and Control [*Composed of delegates from Canada, India and Poland established by the 1954 Geneva Accords*] (VNW)
ICSC .... International Committee for/of Silent Chess (SAUO)
ICSC .... International Committee of Solidarity with Cyprus (SAUO)
ICSC .... International Communications Satellite Consortium (MCD)
ICSC .... International Communications Systems Consultants [*British*] (NITA)
ICSC .... International Computer Science Conventions (SAUO)
ICSC .... International Conferences on Solution Chemistry (SAUO)
ICSC .... International Council of Shopping Centres [*Australia*]
ICSC .... Inter-Ocean Canal Study Commission (PDAA)
ICSC .... Interoceanic Canal Study Commission (SAUO)
ICSC .... Irish Christian Study Centre [*New University of Ulster*] [*British*] (CB)
ICSC .... Irvine Computer Sciences Corporation (NITA)
ICSC .... Italy and Colonies Study Circle (EA)
ICSC .... Swift & Company, Research Laboratory Library, Chicago, IL [*Library symbol*] [*Library of Congress*] (LCLS)
ICSCA .... Industry Committee on Standardisation and Conformity Assessment (SAUS)
ICSCA .... Institute for Computing Science and Computer Applications [*University of Texas at Austin*] [*Research center*] (RCD)
ICSCCF .... Joint Commission of the Socialist Countries on Cooperation in the Field of Fisheries (SAUO)
ICSch .... Schiff, Harden & Waite, Chicago, IL [*Library symbol*] [*Library of Congress*] (LCLS)

ICSCHM .... International Commission for a History of the Scientific and Cultural Development of Mankind (SAUS)
ICSCI .... International Center for Soil Conservation Information (SAUS)
ICSCI .... International Centre for Soil Conservation Information (SAUO)
ICS/CI .... International Clarinet Society/Clarinetwork International (EA)
ICSCN .... Sonnenschein, Carlin, Nath & Rosenthal, Chicago, IL [*Library symbol*] [*Library of Congress*] (LCLS)
ICSD .... Initial Care, Stabilization and Diagnosis (SAUS)
ICSD .... Inorganic Crystal Structure Database [*University of Bonn*] [*Germany*]
ICSD .... International Continental Scientific Drilling (SAUS)
ICSD .... Ionization Chamber Smoke Detector [*Nuclear energy*] (NRCH)
ICSD .... Metropolitan Sanitary District of Greater Chicago, Chicago, IL [*Library symbol*] [*Library of Congress*] (LCLS)
ICS/DMC ...... Institute for Continuing Studies in Design, Management and Communication [*University of Cincinnati*] [*Research center*] (RCD)
ICSDV .... Ice-Cutter Semi-Submersible Drilling Vessel (PDAA)
ICSDW .... International Council of Social Democratic Women [*Later, SIW*] (EA)
ICSE .... Interdepartmental Committee on Software Engineering [*British*]
ICSE .... Intermediate Current Stability Experiment (DEN)
ICSE .... International Committee for Sexual Equality (SAUO)
ICSE .... International Conference on Software Engineering (SAUO)
ICSE .... Item Change/Schedule Estimate (ACAE)
IC-SEA .... Impact Center-Southeast Asia (SAUS)
ICSEAF .... International Commission for the Southeast Atlantic Fisheries
ICSears .... Sears, Roebuck & Co., Chicago, IL [*Library symbol*] [*Library of Congress*] (LCLS)
ICSEB .... International Congress of/on Systematic and Evolutionary Biology (SAUO)
ICSEB .... International Congress of Systematic and Evolutionary Biology (SAUS)
ICSED .... Inter-American Centre for Sustainable Ecosystem Development (SAUS)
ICSEES .... International Committee for Soviet and East European Studies (EAIO)
ICSEES .... International Council for Soviet and East European Studies (SAUO)
ICSEM .... International Center of Studies on Early Music
ICSEM .... International Council for the Scientific Exploration of the Mediterranean (SAUS)
ICSEMS .... International Commission for the Scientific Exploration of the Mediterranean Sea (NOAA)
ICSEP .... International Center for the Solution of Environmental Problems (EA)
ICSEP .... International Council of Sex Education and Parenthood (EA)
ICSey .... Seyfarth, Shaw, Fairweather & Geraldson, Chicago, IL [*Library symbol*] [*Library of Congress*] (LCLS)
ICSF .... Integrated Care System France (SAUO)
ICSF .... International Collegiate Sports Foundation (EA)
ICSFS .... International Conference on Solid Films and Surfaces (SAUS)
ICSG .... International Center for Social Gerontology [*Later, TCSG*] [*Defunct*] (EA)
ICSH .... International Committee for Standardization in Haematology [*Louvain, Belgium*] [*Research center*] (EAIO)
ICSH .... International Congress Services Holland (SAUO)
ICSH .... International Council for Standardization in Haematology (SAUO)
ICSH .... Interstitial Cell Stimulating Hormone [*Also, LH, LSH*] [*Endocrinology*]
ICSHB .... International Committee for Standardization in Human Biology
ICSHM .... International Conference on the Science of Hard Materials (SAUS)
ICSHT .... International Center for Science and High Technology (SAUS)
ICSI .... Institut Canadien de la Sante Infantile [*Canadian Institute of Child Health*]
ICSI .... Institute for Clinical Systems Integration (DMAA)
ICSI .... International Commission of/on Snow and Ice (SAUO)
ICSI .... International Commission on Snow and Ice
ICSI .... International Computer Science Institute (SAUO)
ICSI .... International Conference on Scientific Information
ICSI .... International Container System (EFIS)
ICSI .... Intracytoplasmic Sperm Injection [*In vitro fertilization*]
ICSIC .... Integrated Communications System for Intensive Care (SAUO)
ICSIC .... International Conference on Shallow Impurity Centers (SAUS)
ICSID .... International Centre for Settlement of Investment Disputes (EA)
ICSID .... International Council of Societies of Industrial Design [*Helsinki, Finland*] (EA)
ICSISM .... Institute for Cooperative Study of International Seafood Markets (SAUS)
ICSISP .... International Center for Science Information Services in Phytovirology (SAUO)
ICS/JCCP ..... Journal of Commonwealth and Comparative Politics. University of London, Institute of Commonwealth Studies. London (journ.) (SAUS)
ICSK .... International Cultural Society of Korea [*Seoul, Republic of Korea*] (EAIO)
ICSK .... Intracoronary Streptokinase [*An enzyme*]
ICSL .... Inner-City Simulation Laboratory [*Teacher training game*]
ICSL .... Innovative Clinical Solutions [*NASDAQ symbol*] (SG)
ICSL .... Inns of Court School of Law [*British*] (DI)
ICSL .... Interactive Computer Systems Ltd. (NITA)
ICSL .... Interactive Continuous Simulation Language [*Computer science*] (PDAA)
ICSL .... Intercollegiate Swimming League (PSS)
ICSL .... International Committee of Slavists (SAUO)
ICSL .... International Computer Services, Limited (SAUO)
ICSL .... Presbyterian Saint Luke's Hospital, Chicago, IL [*Library symbol*] [*Library of Congress*] (LCLS)
ICSLS .... International Convention for Safety of Life at Sea (BARN)
ICSM .... Instant Corn-Soya-Milk
ICSM .... International Committee of Scientific Management (SAUO)
ICSM .... International Confederation of Societies of Music (EA)
ICSM .... International Conference on Structural Mechanics (SAUS)
ICSM .... International Conference on Synthetic Metals (SAUS)
ICSMA .... International Conference on Strength of Metals and Alloys (SAUO)
ICSMM .... International Conference on Superlattices, Microstructures and Microdevices (SAUO)
ICSMP .... Integrated Combat System Management Plan (SAUO)
ICSMP .... Integrated Command System Management Plan [*Military*] (DNAB)
ICSMP .... Interactive Continuous Systems Modeling Program
ICSMRT .... International Conference on Structural Mechanics in Reactor Technology (SAUS)
ICSMS .... Integrated Conventional Stores Management System [*DoD*] (DWSG)
ICSN .... Chicago Sun-Times and Chicago Daily News, Chicago, IL [*Library symbol*] [*Library of Congress*] (LCLS)
ICSO .... Intermittent Coronary Sinus Occlusion [*Medicine*] (EDAA)
ICSOBA .... International Congress on Bauxite-Alumina-Aluminium (PDAA)
ICSOG .... International Correspondence Society of Obstetricians and Gynecologists (SAUO)
ICSOM .... International Conference of Symphony and Opera Musicians (EA)
ICSon .... Sonicraft, Inc., Chicago, IL [*Library symbol*] [*Library of Congress*] (LCLS)
ICSOS .... Internal Conference on Structure of Surfaces (SAUS)
ICSOS .... International Conference on Structure of Surfaces (SAUS)
ICSP .... Illinois State Psychiatric Institute, Chicago, IL [*Library symbol*] [*Library of Congress*] (LCLS)
ICSP .... In Commission, Special [*Vessel status*] [*Navy*] (DNAB)
ICSP .... Interagency Council on Standards Policy (SAUO)
ICSP .... Interim Contractor Support Plan
ICSP .... International Committee for the Science of Photography (SAUO)
ICSP .... International Committee on Science Photography (SAUS)
ICSP .... International Committee on Sport Pedagogy (SAUO)
ICSP .... International Congress on Social Psychiatry [*Medicine*] (EDAA)
ICSP .... International Council of Societies of Pathology (EA)
ICSPAT .... International Conference on Signal Processing Applications and Technology (SAUS)
ICSPE .... International Council of Sport and Physical Education
ICSPFT .... International Committee on the Standardization of Physical Fitness Tests (SAUO)
ICSPHR .... International Center (or Centre) of Studies for the Protection of Human Rights (SAUO)
ICSPM .... Dr. William M. Scholl College of Podiatric Medicine, Chicago, IL [*Library symbol*] [*Library of Congress*] (LCLS)
ICSPP .... International Society of Crime Prevention Practitioners (SAUO)
ICSPP .... Interstate Compact for Supervision of Parolees and Probationers [*Public human service program*] (PHSD)
ICSPR .... International Council of Sport and Physical Recreation (SAUS)
ICSPRDC ...... International Committee on Social Psychological Research in Developing Countries (EA)
ICSPRO .... International Calcium Silicate Products Research Organization (SAUO)
ICSPRO .... Intersecretarial Committee on Scientic Problems Relating to Oceanography (SAUS)
ICSPRO .... Inter-Secretariat Committee on Scientific Problems Relating to Oceanography [*United Nations*]
ICSPS .... International Council for Science Policy Studies (SAUO)
ICSPTF .... International Conference on Structure and Properties of Thin Films (SAUS)
ICSQD .... International Conference on Superconducting Quantum Devices (SAUS)
IC SQUD .... International Conference on Superconducting Quantum Devices (SAUO)
ICS/R .... Individual Soldier's Computer/Radio [*Military*]
ICSR .... Inter-American Committee for Space Research (SAUO)
ICSR .... International Co-operation in Ship Research (SAUO)
ICSR .... Interuniversity Centre for the Study of Religion [*Canada*]
ICSR .... Scottish Rite of Freemasonry Library, Chicago, IL [*Library symbol*] [*Library of Congress*] (LCLS)
ICSRD .... Interdepartmental Committee on Scientific Research and Development (SAUO)
ICSRE .... International Centre for Studies in Religious Education [*Brussels, Belgium*] (EAIO)
ICSRI .... Intelligent Computer Systems Research Institute [*University of Miami*] [*Research center*] (RCD)
ICSRI .... Interfaith Committee on Social Responsibility in Investments [*Later, ICCR*] (EA)
ICSS .... Improved Computerized Sighting System (SAUS)
ICSS .... Improved Contact Support Set (TIMI)
ICSS .... Initial Conventional Support System (SAUO)
ICSS .... Instrumentation and Control Society of Singapore (SAUO)
ICSS .... Integrated Communications Switching System (SAUS)
ICSs .... Intercomputer Synchronizers (SAUS)
ICSS .... International Center for Strategic Studies (SAUO)
ICSS .... International Centre for Child Studies (SAUO)
ICSS .... International Commission on Signs and Symbols
ICSS .... International Committee for/of the Sociology of Sport (SAUO)
ICSS .... International Committee for Shell Structures (SAUO)
ICSS .... International Conference on Solid Surfaces
ICSS .... International Congress of Soil Science (SAUO)
ICSS .... International Council for the Social Studies (DIT)
ICSS .... Internet Connection Secure Server (SAUS)
ICSS .... Inter-University Committee on the Superior Student [*Defunct*] (EA)
ICSS .... Intracranial Self-Stimulation [*Also, ICS*] [*Neurophysiology*]
ICSSC .... Interagency Committee on Seismic Safety in Construction (SAUS)

ICSSD .... International Committee for Social Science Information and Documentation [*Information service or system*] (IID)
ICSSD .... International Committee for Social Sciences Documentation (SAUO)
ICSSEA .... Integrated Communications System South-East Asia [*Australia*]
ICSSID .... International Committee for Social Science Information and Documentation [*Paris, France*] [*Information service or system*] (IID)
ICSSPE .... International Council of Sport Science and Physical Education (EA)
ICSSR .... Indian Council for/of Social Science Research (SAUO)
ICSSS .... Inventory Control and Supervisory Support System (SAUS)
ICSST .... Institute of Child Study Security Test [*Psychology*]
ICSST .... International Conference on Solid State Transducers (EA)
ICSSVM .... International Commission for Small Scale Vegetation Maps [*Pondicherry, India*] (EAIO)
ICSSW .... International Committee of Schools for Social Work (SAUO)
ICS System... Intercarrier Sound System (SAUS)
ICST .... Imperial College of Science and Technology (PDAA)
ICST .... Industrial Complex Short-Term (SAUS)
ICST .... Institute for Chemical Science and Technology [*Canada*]
ICST .... Institute [*formerly, Center*] for Computer Sciences and Technology [*Gaithersburg, MD*] [*NIST*]
ICST .... Institution of Corrosion Science and Technology (PDAA)
ICST .... Integrated Circuit Systems [*NASDAQ symbol*] (SPSG)
ICST .... Integrated Combined System Test
ICST .... International Concept Study Team [*for bridges*] [*US, Great Britain, Germany*] (RDA)
ICST .... Intracranial Secondary Tumor [*Medicine*] (EDAA)
ICSTF .... Integrated Combat Systems Test Facility (NVT)
ICSTI .... International Center for Scientific and Technical Information [*Moscow, USSR*] (EAIO)
ICSTI .... International Council for Scientific and Technical Information [*Information service or system*] (IID)
ICStJ .... St. Joseph Hospital, Chicago, IL [*Library symbol*] [*Library of Congress*] (LCLS)
ICSTK .... Intracoronary Streptokinase [*An enzyme*]
ICSTM .... Imperial College of Science, Technology and Medicine (SAUS)
ICSTM .... International Conference on Scanning-Tunneling Microscopy (SAUS)
ICSTND .... Information Center of Science and Technology for National Defense [*Chinese library*]
ICSTO .... International Civil Service Training Organization
ICSTS .... Intermediate Combined System Test Stand (SAUS)
ICSU .... Chicago State University, Chicago, IL [*Library symbol*] [*Library of Congress*] (LCLS)
ICSU .... ICSU-UNESCO Coordinating Committee (SAUO)
ICSU .... Independent Canadian Steelworkers' Union
ICSU .... Integrated Container Services Unit (SAUS)
ICSU .... Intelligent Channel Service Unit (CIST)
ICSU .... International Christian Social Union (SAUO)
ICSU .... International Committee of Scientific Unions (SAUO)
ICSU .... International Council for Science (SAUS)
ICSU .... International Council of/on Scientific Unions (SAUO)
ICSU .... International Council of Scientific Unions [*Research center*] [*France*]
ICSU .... International Council of Space Union (SAUO)
ICSU AB .... International Council of Scientific Unions Abstracting Board [*Also, IAB*] [*Later, ICSTI*] (EA)
ICSU-ACE ..... ICSU Advisory Committee on the Environment (SAUS)
ICSU-ACE ..... International Council of Scientific Unions Advisory Committee on the Environment (SAUO)
ICSU-CODATA... International Council of Scientific Unions-Committee on Data for Science and (SAUS)
ICSU-CODATA... International Council of Scientific Unions-Committee on Data for Science and Technology (SAUO)
ICSU-CTS ..... Committee on the Teaching of Science of the International Council of Scientific Unions [*York, England*] (EAIO)
ICSU-CTS ..... International Council of Scientific Unions Committee on the Teaching of Science (SAUO)
ICSUP .... Intercept Control Supervisor (SAUO)
ICSW .... Interdepartmental Committee on the Status of Women [*Terminated, 1978*]
ICSW .... International Commission on Surface Water (SAUO)
ICSW .... International Committee on Seafarer's Welfare Office (EAIO)
ICSW .... International Conference of Social Work
ICSW .... International Council on Social Welfare (EA)
ICSW .... Sherwin Williams Chemicals, Chicago, IL [*Library symbol*] [*Library of Congress*] (LCLS)
ICSWBD .... Interior Communications Switchboard
ICSWOA .... International Center for Scientific Work Organization in Agriculture (SAUS)
ICSWOA .... International Centre for Scientific Work Organization in Agriculture (SAUO)
ICSWSA .... International Chain Saw Wood Sculptors Association (EA)
ICSX .... Saint Xavier College, Chicago, IL [*Library symbol*] [*Library of Congress*] (LCLS)
ICSZ .... ICS Industries [*Federal Railroad Administration identification code*]
ICT .... Chicago Theological Seminary, Chicago, IL [*Library symbol*] [*Library of Congress*] (LCLS)
Ict .... Icterus (AMHC)
ICT .... Icterus [*Jaundice*] [*Medicine*]
ICT .... Ideal Cycle Time (AAEL)
ict .... Identity Conversion Training (SAUS)
ICT .... Iesu Christo Tutore [*With Jesus Christ as Protector*] [*Latin*]
ICT .... Igniter Circuit Test (IAA)
IC/T .... Image Compression/Transmission
ICT .... Image Converter Tube
ICT .... Image Creation Terminal (NITA)
ict .... Immunoreactive Calcitonin [*Medicine*] (EDAA)
ICT .... Immunoreactive Calcitonin [*Endocrinology*]
ICT .... Impaired Glucose Tolerance [*Medicine*] (MELL)
ICT .... Imperial College of Technology (SAUO)
ICT .... In-Camp Training (SAUS)
ICT .... In Circuit Test [*Electronics*] (EECA)
ICT .... Incoming Trunk [*Telecommunications*] (BUR)
ICT .... Incremental Change Type (SAUS)
ICT .... Independent Crew Training (SAUS)
ICT .... Indirect Coombs' Test [*Immunochemistry*]
ICT .... Indirect Coulometric Titration [*Analytical chemistry*]
ICT .... Individual Collective Training [*Army*]
ICT .... Individual Combat Training (SAUS)
ICT .... Industrial Ceramics Technology (SAUS)
ICT .... Industrial Computed Tomography (SAUS)
ICT .... Inflammation of Connective Tissue [*Medicine*]
ICT .... Influence Coefficient Tests (MCD)
ICT .... Information and Communication Technology
ICT .... Infralateral Cartilage Tensor (SAUS)
ICT .... Initiation Control and Termination (SAUS)
ICT .... Insect Carrier Toxicant
ICT .... Inspection Check Template (MSA)
ICT .... Inspection Control Test (SAA)
ICT .... Institut Canadien des Textiles [*Canadian Textiles Institute*] (EAIO)
ICT .... Institute for Computer Typesetting (SAUS)
ICT .... Institute for Creative Technologies
ICT .... Institute of Circuit Technology [*Oxford, England*] [*Defunct*] (EAIO)
ICT .... Institute of Clay Technology [*British*]
ICT .... Institute of Computer Technology
ICT .... Institute of Concrete Technology [*British*]
ICT .... Institution of Corrosion Technology (PDAA)
ICT .... Insulated [*or Insulating*] Core Transformer
ICT .... Insulating Core Transformer (SAUS)
ICT .... Insulator Core Transformer (SAUS)
ICT .... Insulin Coma Therapy [*Medicine*]
ICT .... Insulin Convulsive Therapy [*Medicine*] (MAH)
ICT .... Integrated-Circuit Technology (SAUS)
ICT .... Integrated Circuit Tester
ICT .... Integrated Combat Training (SAUS)
ICT .... Integrated Composites Technology [*Plastics*]
ICT .... Integrated Computer Telemetry
ICT .... Integrated Computer Telephony (DCOM)
ICT .... Integrated Concept Team [*Army*] (INF)
ICT .... Intelligence Cycle Time (MCD)
ICT .... Intensified Confirmatory Test (SAUO)
ICT .... Intensive Conventional Therapy [*Medicine*] (DAVI)
ICT .... Interaction Control Table [*Computer science*] (OA)
ICT .... Interactive Command Test [*Computer science*]
ICT .... Interactive Consumer Terminal (SAUS)
ICT .... Inter Cable Communications, Inc. [*Toronto Stock Exchange symbol*]
ICT .... Intercept Controller Technician (SAUO)
ICT .... Interchangeability Control Tool (MCD)
ICT .... Interchangeability Test (MCD)
ICT .... Inter-City Train (SAUO)
ICT .... Intercontinental de Aviacion Ltd. [*Colombia*] [*ICAO designator*] (FAAC)
ICT .... Interface Control Technician (SAUS)
ICT .... Interface Control Tool (SAUS)
ICT .... Interface Control Tooling (NASA)
ICT .... Interference Compliance Test (SAA)
ICT .... Intermittent Cervical Traction [*Orthopedics*] (DAVI)
ICT .... Internal Cold Target (ADWA)
ICT .... Internal COMPOOL [*Communications Pool*] Table (SAA)
ICT .... International Cablecasting Technologies Inc. (SAUO)
ICT .... International Call for Tenders (NATG)
ICT .... International Campaign for Tibet (EA)
ICT .... International Circuit Technology [*Electronics*] (IAA)
ICT .... International CMOS Technology [*Computer science*]
ICT .... International Commercial Terms (SAUO)
ICT .... International Commission on Tracers (SAUS)
ICT .... International Commission on Trichinellosis (EA)
ICT .... International Computer and Tabulator (SAUS)
ICT .... International Computers and Tabulators Ltd. [*Later, ICL*]
ICT .... International Council of Tanners [*See also CIT*] [*Lewes, East Sussex, England*] (EAIO)
ICT .... International Critical Tables
ICT .... International Critical Tables of Numerical Data (SAUO)
ICT .... Interstitial Cell Tumor [*Medicine*] (MELL)
ICT .... Intracardiac Thrombus [*Medicine*] (DB)
ICT .... Intracranial Tumor [*Medicine*] (MELL)
ICT .... Intra-Cranial Tumour (SAUS)
ICT .... Intradermal Cancer Test [*Oncology*]
ICT .... Intramolecular Charge Transfer [*Physical chemistry*]
ICT .... Investors Capital Trust, Inc. (SAUO)
ICT .... Irrigated, Conventionally Tilled [*Agriculture*]
ICT .... Isometric Contraction Time [*Medicine*] (DAVI)
ICT .... Isovolumic Contraction Time [*Cardiology*]
ICT .... Trinity College, Deerfield, IL [*OCLC symbol*] (OCLC)
ICT .... Wichita [*Kansas*] [*Airport symbol*] (OAG)
ICT .... Wichita Weather Forecast Office (SAUS)
ICTA .... Chicago Transit Authority, Chicago, IL [*Library symbol*] [*Library of Congress*] (LCLS)
ICTA .... Imperial College of Tropical Agriculture (SAUO)
ICTA .... Income and Corporation Taxes Act (SAUO)
ICTA .... Industry Council for Tangible Assets [*Washington, DC*] (EA)

ICTA .... Institute of Certified Travel Agents (EA)
ICTA .... International Center for the Typographic Arts
ICTA .... International Center for Typographical Arts (SAUS)
ICTA .... International Centre for Technology Assessment
ICTA .... International College of Tropical Agriculture (SAUS)
ICTA .... International Commission on Technical Aids, Building and Transportation (SAUO)
ICTA .... International Commission on Technology and Accessibility (SAUO)
ICTA .... International Computer Training Association (PCM)
ICTA .... International Confederation for Thermal Analysis [*Jerusalem, Israel*] (EA)
ICTA .... International Confederation of Technical Agriculturists (SAUO)
ICTA .... International Co-operative Trading Agency (SAUO)
ICTA .... International Council of Travel Agents (SAUS)
ICTAA .... Imperial College of Tropical Agriculture Association [*British*] (BI)
ICTAB .... Institut Canadien de Tole d'Acier en Batiment [*Canadian Sheet Steel Building Institute*]
ICTAF .... Interdisciplinary Center (or Centre) for Technological Analysis and Forecasting (SAUS)
ICTAF .... Interdisciplinary Centre for Technological Analysis and Forecasting (SAUO)
ICTAM .... International Congress of Theoretical and Applied Mechanics (PDAA)
ICTASD .... International Convention on Transistors and Associated Semiconductor Devices (SAUO)
ICTASD .... International Convention on Transistors and Semiconductor Devices
ICTASD .... International Conversion on Transistors and Associated Semiconductor Devices (SAUS)
ICTB .... International Companies and Their Brands [*A publication*]
ICTB .... International Conference on Tall Buildings (SAUS)
ICTB .... International Customs Tariffs Bureau (DLA)
ICTBA .... Infants', Children's, and Teens' Wear Buyers Association (EA)
ICTC .... Impeller Clutch Torque Converter [*Automotive engineering*]
ICTC .... Inertial Components Temperature Controller (KSC)
ICTC .... Inferior Cornu of Thyroid Cartilage [*Medicine*] (MELL)
IC/TC .... Intelligent Color/Trash Coordinator (SAUS)
ICTC .... Interdepartmental Committee on Toxic Chemicals (SAUS)
ICTC .... International Capital & Technology Corporation (SAUO)
ICTC .... International Cooperative Training Center
ICTCD .... Insecticide (MSA)
ICTD .... Individual and Collective Training Development (MCD)
ICTD .... Inter-Channel Time Displacement
ICTDR .... International Centers for Tropical Disease Research (SAUO)
ICTDS .... International Centre for Trade and Sustainable Development (SAUO)
ICTE .... Inertial Component Test Equipment
ICTEC .... Identification of Critical Tasks and Equipment Items (SAUS)
ICTED .... International Cooperation in the Field of Transport Economics Documentation [*European Conference of Ministers of Transport*] [*Information service or system*] (IID)
ICTED .... International Cooperation in Transport Economics Documentation (SAUS)
ICTERCENTRE ... International Centre for the Terminology of the Social Sciences (SAUO)
ICTEX .... Icon Information Technology
ICTF .... Interagency Crisis Task Force
ICTF .... International Cocoa Trades Federation [*British*]
ICTF .... International Commission on the Taxonomy of Fungi
ICTF .... International Conference on Thin Films (PDAA)
ICTF .... Internet Content Task Force (SAUO)
ICTG .... ICT Group, Inc. [*NASDAQ symbol*] (SAG)
ICT Grp .... ICT Group, Inc. [*Associated Press*] (SAG)
ICTH .... International Commission for the Teaching of History [*Brussels, Belgium*] (EA)
ICTH .... International Committee on Thrombosis and Hemostasis
ICTI .... Interstate Cellular Telecommunications, Inc. (SAUS)
ICTI .... Interstate Cellular Telecommunications, Incorporated (SAUO)
ict ind .... Icterus Index [*Liver function test*] [*Medicine*] (AAMN)
ICTJ .... Industry Compatible Test Jig (SAUS)
ICTL .... Image Control Table (MCD)
ICTL .... Industrial Control (IAA)
ICTL .... Input Control (SAUS)
ICTL .... International Cabletel, Inc. [*NASDAQ symbol*] (SAG)
ICTL .... Intl Cabletel [*NASDAQ symbol*] (TTSB)
ICTM .... Integrated Circuits, Inc. [*NASDAQ symbol*] (COMM)
ICTM .... International Coal Trade Model [*Department of Energy*] (GFGA)
ICTM .... International Council for Traditional Music (EA)
ICTME .... International Conference on Tribo-Terotechnology and Maintenance Engineering (PDAA)
ICTMM .... International Congresses on Tropical Medicine and Malaria
ICTMM .... International Congress for/on Tropical Medicine and Malaria (SAUO)
ICTN .... Industry Center for Trade Negotiations [*Defunct*]
ICTO .... International Cooperative Trading Organization (SAUO)
ICTOC .... Independent Corps Tactical Operations Center
ICTP .... Individual/Collective Training Plan [*Army*]
ICTP .... Institute for Certification of Tax Professionals (EA)
ICTP .... Integrated Coordinated Test Program (SAUO)
ICTP .... Intensified Combat Training Program
ICTP .... International Center for Theoretical Physics [*Trieste, Italy*] (EA)
ICTP .... International Conference on the Technology of Plasticity (SAUS)
ICTPA .... International Conference on Titanium Products and Applications (SAUS)
ICTPDC .... Imperial College Thermophysical Properties Data Centre [*British*] (CB)
ICTP-IUPAP ... International Center for Theoretical Physics-International Union of Pure and Applied Physics (SAUO)
ICTR .... Institut Canadien de Recherches en Telecommunications (AC)
ICTR .... Institute of Commercial and Technical Representatives Ltd. [*British*] (BI)
ICTR .... International Center for Technical Research (SAUO)
ICTR .... International Center of Theatre Research (EA)
ICTR .... International Criminal Tribunal for Ruanda (or Rwanda) (SAUO)
ICTr .... Truman College, Chicago, IL [*Library symbol*] [*Library of Congress*] (LCLS)
ICTRF .... Ice Cream and Temperance Refreshment Federation (SAUO)
ICTRM .... Interagency Committee on the Transportation of Radioactive Materials
ICTRTQM ..... Institute for Control Theory, Reality Therapy and Quality Management (EA)
ICTS .... Idiopathic Carpal Tunnel Syndrome [*Medicine*] (DMAA)
ICTS .... In-Car Temperature Sensor [*Automotive engineering*]
ICTS .... Integrated Circuit Test Set
ICTS .... Integrated Composite Tooling System
ICTS .... Integrated Computerized Test Set
ICTS .... Intermediate Capacity Transit System
ICTS .... International Catholic Truth Society (EA)
ICTS .... International Center for Transportation Studies (SAUO)
ICTS .... International Congress of the Transplantation Society
ICTS .... International Congress on Transplantation (SAUS)
ICTS .... International Consultants on Targeted Security (SAUS)
ICTS .... Isothermal Capacitance Transient Spectroscopy (SAUS)
ICTSI .... International Container Terminal Services, Inc. [*Philippines*] [*Commercial firm*]
ICTT .... Intensified Confirmatory Troop Test (AABC)
ICTTC .... International Consultative Telegraph and Telephone Committee (SAUO)
ICT-TST .... Incoming Trunk Tester (SAUS)
ICTTT .... International Congress on Technology and Technology Transfer (SAUS)
ICTU .... Catholic Theological Union, Chicago, IL [*Library symbol*] [*Library of Congress*] (LCLS)
ICTU .... Independent Canadian Transit Union
ICTU .... Iraqi Confederation of Trade Unions
ICTU .... Irish Congress of Trade Unions
ICTUR .... International Center for Trade Union Rights (SAUO)
ICTV .... Integrated Circuit Television (SAUS)
ICTV .... Interactive Cable Television
ICTV .... International Committee on Taxonomy of Viruses [*ICSU*] [*Rennes, France*] (EAIO)
ICTV .... Intracerebroventricular [*Also, ic, ICV*] [*Brain anatomy*]
ICtvS .... Shawnee Library System, Carterville, IL [*Library symbol*] [*Library of Congress*] (LCLS)
ICTVTR .... Islamic Center for Technical and Vocational Training and Research (SAUS)
ICTVTR .... Islamic Centre for Technical and Vocational Training and Research (SAUO)
ICTX .... Intermittent Cervical Traction [*Medicine*] (DMAA)
ICTY .... International Criminal Tribunal for the Former Yugoslavia
ICTZ .... I Corps Tactical Zone [*Vietnamese designation for both a military zone and a political region*]
ICU .... ICG Utility Investments Ltd. [*Toronto Stock Exchange symbol*]
ICU .... Immunologic Contact Urticaria [*Medicine*] (DMAA)
ICU .... Indicator Console Unit (SAUS)
ICU .... Indicator Control Unit
ICU .... Industrial Consulting Unit (SAUS)
ICU .... Industrial Control Unit (IAA)
ICU .... Industry Capacity Utilization [*Engineering economics*]
ICU .... Infant Care Unit [*Medicine*] (DMAA)
ICU .... InfoColor Conversion Unit (DGA)
ICU .... Informatie en Communicatie Unie [*Information and Communication United*] [*Dutch publishing house*]
ICU .... Information and Coordination Unit (SAUS)
ICU .... Information Control Unit (SAUO)
ICU .... Information Coordination Unit (SAUO)
ICU .... Infrared Command Unit
ICU .... Institut d'Urbanisme du Canada [*Town Planning Institute of Canada*]
ICU .... Institute for University Cooperation (SAUO)
ICU .... Instruction Cache Unit [*Computer science*]
ICU .... Instruction Control Unit
ICU .... Instructors Computer Utility (SAUS)
ICU .... Instrument Control Unit [*Automotive electronics*]
ICU .... Integrated Control Unit [*Automotive electronics*]
ICU .... Intel Configuration Utility (SAUS)
ICU .... Intelligence Collecting Unit (SAUO)
ICU .... Intelligent Connector Unit [*Telecommunications*] (TSSD)
ICU .... Intensive-Care Unit [*of a hospital*]
ICU .... Intensive Caring Unlimited [*An association*] (EA)
ICU .... Interactive Chart Utility [*IBM Corp.*]
ICU .... Interconnection Unit [*Computer science*]
ICU .... Interconnect Unit (SAUS)
ICU .... Interface Connecting (or Connection) Unit (SAUS)
ICU .... Interface Control Unit [*Army*]
ICU .... Interface Conversion Unit (SAUS)
ICU .... Interface Converter Unit (SAUS)
ICU .... Interim Capacity Upgrade (ACAE)
ICU .... Intermediate Care Unit [*of a hospital*]
ICU .... Internal Communication Unit (SAUS)
ICU .... International Chemistry Union (SAUO)
ICU .... International Chick Unit (DB)
ICU .... International Christian University [*Tokyo*]
ICU .... International Christian University Library [*UTLAS symbol*]
ICU .... International Clearing Union (SAUO)

ICU............. International Code Use (BARN)
ICU............. International Code User (SAUO)
ICU............. International [*or Internal*] Communication Unit [*Telecommunications*] (TEL)
ICU............. International Cultural Understanding (SAUS)
ICU............. International Cultural University (SAUO)
ICU............. International Cycling Union (EA)
ICU............. Interrupt Control Unit [*Computer science*] (IAA)
ICU............. ISA Configuration Utility (SAUS)
ICU............. Texas Christian University, Fort Worth, TX [*OCLC symbol*] (OCLC)
ICU............. University of Chicago, Chicago, IL [*Library symbol*] [*Library of Congress*] (LCLS)
ICU2........... Interface Control Unit 2 (SAUS)
ICUA........... Institute for College and University Administrators [*Later, CPAA*] (EA)
ICUA........... Institute for/of College and University Administrators (SAUO)
ICUA........... Interdenominational Church Ushers Association
ICUAE......... International Congress of University Adult Education [*Fredericton, NB*] (EAIO)
ICUAER....... International Committee on Urgent Anthropological and Ethnological Research [*Vienna, Austria*] (EAIO)
ICUAER/B..... Bulletin of the International Committee on Urgent Anthropological and Ethnological Research. Vienna (SAUS)
ICUB........... International Integration, Inc. [*NASDAQ symbol*] (NASQ)
ICUC........... Union Carbide Corp., Film-Packaging Division, Chicago, IL [*Library symbol*] [*Library of Congress*] (LCLS)
ICUD........... Index to Current Urban Documents [*Information service or system*] (IID)
ICU-D.......... University of Chicago, Divinity School, Chicago, IL [*Library symbol*] [*Library of Congress*] (LCLS)
ICUE........... International Committee on the University Emergency (EA)
ICUE........... International Council on the University Emergency (SAUO)
ICUEPR....... International Conference on University Education for Public Relations (SAUO)
ICUF........... Independent Colleges and Universities of Florida (SAUO)
ICU-FE........ University of Chicago, Far Eastern Library, Chicago, IL [*Library symbol*] [*Library of Congress*] (LCLS)
ICUFON....... Intercontinental UFO Galactic Spacecraft Research and Analytic Network (EA)
ICUFON....... Intercontinental Ufo Research Analytic Network (SAUO)
ICUFR......... International Council on United Fund Raising (EA)
ICUG........... United States Gypsum Co., Chicago, IL [*Library symbol*] [*Library of Congress*] (LCLS)
ICUGA......... International Computer Users Groups Association [*Defunct*] (EA)
ICU-H.......... University of Chicago, Center for Health Administration Studies, Chicago, IL [*Library symbol*] [*Library of Congress*] (LCLS)
ICUI............ ICU Medical, Inc. [*NASDAQ symbol*] (SAG)
ICUI............ Independent Colleges and Universities of Indiana (SAUO)
ICUIS.......... Institute on the Church in Urban-Industrial Society [*Defunct*]
ICUIS Bibliog... Institute on the Church in Urban-Industrial Society. Bibliography Series (journ.) (SAUS)
ICU-L.......... University of Chicago, Law Library, Chicago, IL [*Library symbol*] [*Library of Congress*] (LCLS)
ICU-LS........ University of Chicago, Graduate Library School, Chicago, IL [*Library symbol*] [*Library of Congress*] (LCLS)
ICUM........... Independent Colleges and Universities of Missouri (SAUO)
ICU-M.......... University of Chicago, Bio-Medical Libraries, Chicago, IL [*Library symbol*] [*Library of Congress*] (LCLS)
ICU Med...... ICU Medical, Inc. [*Associated Press*] (SAG)
ICUMSA....... International Clearinghouse for Uniform Methods of Sugar Analysis (SAUO)
ICUMSA....... International Commission for Uniform Methods of Sugar Analysis [*Mackay, QLD, Australia*] (EAIO)
ICUMSA....... International Committee for Unified Methods of Sugar Analysis (SAUO)
ICUnC.......... University Club of Chicago, Chicago, IL [*Library symbol*] [*Library of Congress*] (LCLS)
IC unit......... Intensive-Care unit (SAUO)
ICUnW......... United Way of Metropolitan Chicago, Chicago, IL [*Library symbol*] [*Library of Congress*] (LCLS)
ICUP........... Individual Circuit Usage and Peg Count [*Telecommunications*] (TEL)
ICUP........... International Catholic Union of the Press (EA)
ICUPE......... International Conference on Undergraduate Physics Education (SAUS)
ICU/PLANIT... Instructors Computer Utility/Programming Language for Interactive Teaching (SAUS)
ICUPLANT.... Instructor's Computer Utility Programming Language for Interactive Teaching (IAA)
ICUR........... International Committee for UFO Research (SAUO)
ICURR......... Intergovernmental Committee on Urban and Regional Research [*Canada*]
ICUS........... Inside Continental United States [*Military*]
ICUS........... International Committee on Urgent Surgery [*Milan, Italy*] (EAIO)
ICUS........... International Conference on the Unity of Sciences (SAUO)
ICUS........... International Conference on the Unity of the Sciences
ICUSA......... International Christians for Unity in Social Action (EA)
ICUSQ......... United States Quartermaster Corps, Food and Container Institute [*for the Armed Forces*], Chicago, IL [*Library symbol*] [*Library of Congress*] (LCLS)
ICUT........... Independent Colleges and Universities of Texas (SRA)
ICUT........... Initial COHORT [*Cohesion, Operational Readiness Training*] Unit Training [*Military*] (GFGA)
ICUT........... International Cutlery Ltd. [*NASDAQ symbol*] (SAG)
ICUT........... Intl Cutlery [*NASDAQ symbol*] (TTSB)
ICUTN......... International Committee for Unification of Terminological Neologismes (SAUO)
ICUTO......... International Conference of University Teacher Organizations
ICUTW......... Intl Cutlery Wrrt'A' [*NASDAQ symbol*] (TTSB)
ICUTZ......... Intl Cutlery Wrrt'B' [*NASDAQ symbol*] (TTSB)
ICU-Y.......... University of Chicago, Yerkes Observatory, Williams Bay, WI [*Library symbol*] [*Library of Congress*] (LCLS)
ICUZ........... Installation Compatible Use Zone (SAUO)
ICUZ........... Integrated Compatible Use Zone [*Army*] (RDA)
ICV............. Elmhurst College, Elmhurst, IL [*OCLC symbol*] (OCLC)
ICV............. Ice-Cream Van [*Slang*] [*British*]
ICV............. Ileocecal Valve [*Medicine*] (MELL)
ICV............. Improved Capital Value [*Business term*] (ADA)
ICV............. Individual Cell Voltmeter (DNAB)
ICV............. Individually Controlled Ventilation
ICV............. Indoor Cricket Victoria [*Australia*] [*An association*]
ICV............. Infantry Combat Vehicle (MCD)
ICV............. Initial Calibration Verification
ICV............. Initial Capability Test (SAUS)
ICV............. Initial Chaining Value [*Computer science*]
ICV............. Integrity Check Value (SAUS)
ICV............. Inter-Center Vector (MCD)
ICV............. Interdecadal Climate Variability [*Marine science*] (OSRA)
ICV............. Interim Control Values (SAUS)
ICV............. Intermediate Calculation Variable [*Automotive emissions*]
ICV............. Internal Correction Voltage
ICV............. International Commission of Viticulture (SAUO)
ICV............. Interphase Chromosome Volume
ICV............. Intracellular Virus [*Medicine*] (PDAA)
ICV............. Intracellular Volume [*Medicine*] (MELL)
ICV............. Intracerebroventricular [*Also, ic, ICTV*] [*Brain anatomy*]
icv.............. Intracervical [*Medicine*] (EDAA)
ICV............. United States Veterans Administration, West Side Hospital, Chicago, IL [*Library symbol*] [*Library of Congress*] (LCLS)
ICVA........... International Council of Voluntary Agencies (GNE)
ICVA........... International Council of Volunteer Agencies (SAUO)
ICVAN......... International Committee on Veterinary Anatomical Nomenclature [*See also CINAV*] [*Zurich, Switzerland*] (EAIO)
ICVC........... VanderCook College of Music, Chicago, IL [*Library symbol*] [*Library of Congress*] (LCLS)
ICVD........... Inns of Court Volunteer Decoration [*Military*] [*British*] (ROG)
ICVD........... Isotopic Chemical Vapor Deposition (PDAA)
ICVEN......... International Committee on Veterinary Embryological Nomenclature (SAUO)
ICVF........... Inner-City Ventures Fund [*National Trust for Historical Preservation*]
ICVG........... International Council for the Study of Viruses and Virus Diseases of Grapevine (SAUO)
ICVGAN....... International Committee on Veterinary Gross Anatomical Nomenclature [*Cornell University*] [*Ithaca, NY*] (EY)
ICVGE......... International Conference on Vapor Growth Epitaxy (SAUS)
ICVGE......... International Conference on Vapour Growth and Epitaxy (SAUO)
ICVH........... Ischemic Cerebrovascular Headache [*Medicine*] (DAVI)
ICVHI.......... International Conference on Voluntary Health Insurance [*Medicine*] (EDAA)
ICVHN......... International Committee on Veterinary Histological Nomenclature (SAUO)
ICVI............ Isothermal Chemical Vapor Infiltration [*Materials science*]
ICVM........... International Conference on Vacuum Metallurgy (SAUS)
ICVNA......... Visiting Nurses Association, Chicago, IL [*Library symbol*] [*Library of Congress*] (LCLS)
ICvR........... River Bend Library System, Coal Valley, IL [*Library symbol*] [*Library of Congress*] (LCLS)
ICVS........... Current-Controlled Voltage Source (SAUS)
ICVS........... International Cardiovascular Society (EA)
ICVS........... International Society for Cardiovascular Surgery (EA)
ICVT........... Intracerebroventricular [*Medicine*] (DB)
ICVU........... International Carriage and Luggage-Van Union (SAUO)
ICw............ Crestwood Library District, Crestwood, IL [*Library symbol*] [*Library of Congress*] (LCLS)
ICW............ In Compliance With (MUGU)
ICW............ In Conjunction With (AAGC)
ICW............ In Connection With
ICW............ India-China Wing [*World War II*]
ICW............ Initial Condition Word [*Computer science*]
ICW............ Initialization Command Word (VLIE)
ICW............ Input Command Word
ICW............ Input Control Word [*Computer science*] (MCD)
ICW............ Institute of Child Welfare (SAUO)
ICW............ Institute of Clay Workers [*British*] (BI)
ICW............ Institute of Clayworkers (SAUO)
ICW............ Institute of Clerks of Work (PDAA)
ICW............ Institute of Clerks of Works of Great Britain (SAUO)
ICW............ Intake Cooling Water (IEEE)
ICW............ Interactive Courseware [*Air Force*]
ICW............ Inter-American Commission of Women [*OAS*]
ICW............ Interblock Communication Word (IAA)
ICW............ Intercoastal Waterway
ICW............ Interface Control Word [*Computer science*]
ICW............ Interface Word (SAUS)
ICW............ Intermittent Continuous Wave (SAUS)
ICW............ International Chemical Workers Union
ICW............ International Commission on Whaling (SAUO)
ICW............ International Council for/of Women (SAUO)
ICW............ International Council of Women [*France*]
ICW............ Internet Connection Wizard [*Computer science*]
ICW............ Interrupt Continuous Waves (SAUS)
ICW............ Interrupted Carrier Wave (SAUS)

icw.......... Interrupted Continuous Wave (NAKS)
ICW.......... Interrupted Continuous Wave [*Electronics*]
ICW.......... Intracellular Water [*Physiology*]
ICW.......... Intracoastal Waterway
ICW.......... Ion-Cyclotron Waves (SAUS)
ICW.......... Western Society of Engineers, Chicago, IL [*Library symbol*] [*Library of Congress*] (LCLS)
ICW.......... Wheaton College, Wheaton, IL [*OCLC symbol*] (OCLC)
ICWA.......... Indian Child Welfare Act [*1978*]
ICWA.......... Indian Council of World Affairs (SAUO)
ICWA.......... Institute of Cost and Works Accountants [*British*] (BI)
ICWA.......... Institute of Cost and Works Accounts (SAUS)
ICWA.......... Institute of Current World Affairs (EA)
ICWA.......... International Carwash Association
ICWA.......... International Coil Winding Association (EA)
ICWA.......... Israel Centre for Waterworks Appliances (SAUO)
ICWAI.......... Institute of Cost and Works Accountants of India (SAUO)
ICWAR.......... Improved Continuous-Wave Acquisition RADAR [*Army*] (AABC)
ICWB.......... Intermediate Cold-Wet Boot [*Military*] (INF)
ICWB.......... World Book-Childcraft International, Inc., Chicago, IL [*Library symbol*] [*Library of Congress*] (LCLS)
ICWC.......... Wilbur Wright Community College, Chicago, IL [*Library symbol*] [*Library of Congress*] (LCLS)
ICWD.......... Interface Control/Weapon Delivery
ICWDP.......... International Committee for World Day of Prayer (EA)
ICWeH.......... Louis A. Weiss Memorial Hospital, Chicago, IL [*Library symbol*] [*Library of Congress*] (LCLS)
ICWES.......... International Conference of Women Engineers and Scientists
ICWF.......... Interactive Computer Worded Forecast [*Marine science*] (OSRA)
ICWF.......... International Christian Women's Fellowship (EA)
ICWG.......... Ice Core Working Group (SAUO)
ICWG.......... Interface Control Working Group [*NASA*] (KSC)
ICWG.......... International Clubroot Working Group (EAIO)
ICWG.......... International Co-operative Women's Guild
ICWG.......... International Coordinating Working Group (SAUO)
ICWG.......... International Coordination Working Group [*Marine science*] (OSRA)
ICWGA.......... Interface Control Working Group Action [*NASA*] (KSC)
ICWG-EO.......... International Coordination Working Group for Earth Observation (SAUO)
ICWG-GR.......... Inter-Center Working Group on Genetic Resources (SAUO)
ICWH.......... International Conference on Women in Health [*Medicine*] (EDAA)
ICWHA.......... Wildman, Harrold, Allen & Dixon, Chicago, IL [*Library symbol*] [*Library of Congress*] (LCLS)
ICWI.......... International Car Wash Institute (EA)
ICwL.......... Crestwood Library District, Crestwood, IL [*Library symbol*] [*Library of Congress*] (LCLS)
ICWL.......... International Creative Writers League (EA)
ICWM.......... Institute for Chemical Waste Management (GNE)
ICWM.......... Interdepartmental Committee on Weather Modification [*Military*]
ICWM.......... International Committee on Weights and Measures
ICWM.......... International Congress on Women in Music [*Defunct*] (EA)
ICWMA.......... International Country and Western Music Association (EA)
ICWO.......... Indications Center Watch Officer [*Military*] (MCD)
ICWO.......... Intercomponent Work Order
ICWORR.......... International Conference on Waste Oil Recovery and Reuse
ICWP.......... International Council of Women Psychologists [*Later, ICP*]
ICWP.......... Interstate Conference on Water Policy (EA)
ICWP.......... Interstate Conference on Water Problems (SAUO)
ICWQ.......... International Commission on Water Quality (SAUO)
ICWR.......... Interagency Committee on Water Resources
ICWRS.......... International Commission on Water Resources Systems (SAUO)
ICWS.......... Improved Commander's Weapon Station
ICWS.......... Institute of Civil War Studies (EA)
ICWS.......... Intersection Collision Warning System [*Automotive safety*]
ICWS.......... Winston & Strawn, Chicago, IL [*Library symbol*] [*Library of Congress*] (LCLS)
ICWSG.......... Infants' and Children's Wear Salesmen's Guild (EA)
ICWT.......... Inter-Component Work Transmitted (MCD)
ICWT.......... Interrupted Continuous Wave Telegraphy (IAA)
ICWU.......... International Chemical Workers Union (EA)
ICWWP.......... Interagency Committee for World Weather Programs [*Department of Commerce*] (NOAA)
ICX.......... IC Industries, Inc. [*NYSE symbol*] (COMM)
ICx.......... Immune Complex [*Medicine*] (EDAA)
ICX.......... Immune Complex (STED)
ICX.......... Inferior Colliculus
ICX.......... Inter Cartridge Exchange (SAUS)
ICX.......... International Charter Xpress Limited Liability Co. [*ICAO designator*] (FAAC)
ICX.......... International Computer Exchange (IAA)
ICX.......... International Cultural Exchange
ICX.......... International Customer Executive (SAUS)
ICX.......... Internet College Exchange [*Database*] [*Computer science*]
ICX.......... Lewis University, Lockport, IL [*OCLC symbol*] (OCLC)
ICXM.......... Intercontinental Experimental Missile (SAUS)
ICXOM.......... International Congress on X-Ray Optics and Microanalysis (SAUS)
ICY.......... Augustana College, Rock Island, IL [*OCLC symbol*] (OCLC)
ICY.......... ICEE-USA [*AMEX symbol*] (COMM)
ICY.......... Instruction Cycle [*Computer science*] (IAA)
ICY.......... International Christian Youth (EA)
ICY.......... International Commission on Yeasts and Yeast-Like Microorganisms [*ICSU*] [*France*] (EAIO)
ICY.......... International Cooperation Year [*1965*] [*20th anniversary of UN*]
ICY.......... Packaged Ice [*AMEX symbol*]
I-cycle.......... Instruction Cycle (NITA)
ICYE.......... Federation of National Committees in the International Christian Youth Exchange (SAUO)
ICYE.......... International Christian Youth Exchange (EA)
ICYE.......... International Council for the International Christian Youth Exchange (SAUO)
ICYF.......... Institute for Children, Youth, and Families [*Michigan State University*] [*Research center*] (RCD)
ICYF.......... Inter-County Youth Federation (SAUO)
ICYF.......... International Catholic Youth Federation [*Later, WFCY*]
ICYO.......... International Committee of Youth Organizations (EAIO)
ICYP.......... Iodocyanopindolol [*Biochemistry*]
ICYRA.......... Inter-Collegiate Yacht Racing Association [*of North America*] [*Later, ICYRA/NA*]
ICYRA.......... International Collegiate Yacht Racing Association [*Association*] [*Nautical term*] (NTA)
ICYRA/NA.......... Inter-Collegiate Yacht Racing Association of North America (EA)
ICySIP.......... International Command and Control Systems Interoperability Project (SAUS)
ICYT.......... Instituto de Informacion y Documentacion en Ciencia y Tecnologia [*Institute for Information and Documentation in Science and Technology*] [*Database originator and host*] [*Information service or system*] [*Spain*] (IID)
ICYYLM.......... International Commission for/on Yeasts and Yeast-Like Microorganisms (SAUO)
ICYYLM.......... International Commission on Yeast and Yeast-Like Microorganisms (SAUS)
ICZ.......... International Climate Zone
ICZ.......... International Congress of Zoology (SAUO)
ICZ.......... Intertropical Convergence Zone [*Trade winds*] [*Meteorology*]
ICZ.......... Isthmian Canal Zone
ICZ.......... North Park College and Theological Seminary, Chicago, IL [*OCLC symbol*] (OCLC)
ICZM.......... Integrated Coastal Zone Management [*Marine science*] (OSRA)
ICZN.......... International Code of Zoological Nomenclature (QUAC)
ICZN.......... International Commission on Zoological Nomenclature [*British*] (EAIO)
ID.......... Apollo Airlines [*ICAO designator*] (AD)
ID.......... Democratic Left Party (Ecuador) [*Political party*] (PSAP)
ID.......... [*Official Decisions of the*] Department of Interior (AAGC)
Id.......... Idaho (SHCU)
ID.......... Idaho [*Postal code*]
ID.......... Idaho Operations Office [*Energy Research and Development Administration*]
ID.......... Idaho Reports [*A publication*] (DLA)
Id.......... Idaho State Library, Boise, ID [*Library symbol*] [*Library of Congress*] (LCLS)
ID.......... Iddin-Dagan (BJA)
ID.......... Idea [*Slang*]
ID.......... Ideal Toy Corporation (SAUO)
id.......... Idem (ELAL)
ID.......... Idem [*The Same*] [*Latin*]
ID.......... Identification [*Motor vehicle violation code used in state of Maryland*] (MVRD)
ID.......... Identification [*or Identichip*] (SPVS)
ID.......... Identification Card (SAUO)
ID.......... Identification Data
ID.......... Identification Date
ID.......... Identification Dissector (MCD)
ID.......... Identification Division
ID.......... Identification/image detector (SAUO)
ID.......... Identification Interface Device
ID.......... Identification Record Only [*Motor vehicle violation driver status code in state of North Dakota*] (MVRD)
id.......... Identifier (ELAL)
ID.......... Identifier [*Dialog*] [*Searchable field*] (NITA)
ID.......... Identifier Code (SAUO)
ID.......... Identify [*or Identification*] (DAVI)
ID.......... Identity
ID.......... [*The*] Ides
ID.......... Idiotype (MELL)
Id.......... Idiotype (QSUL)
ID.......... Iditol Dehydrogenase (MAE)
Id.......... Idylls [*of Theocritus*] [*Classical studies*] (OCD)
ID.......... Ifostamide, Doxorubicin [*Antineoplastic drug*] (CDI)
ID.......... Ill-Defined (STED)
id.......... Ill-defined [*Image*] [*Medicine*] (EDAA)
ID.......... Illegal Direct (VLIE)
ID.......... Image Digitization (SAUS)
ID.......... Image Digitizer [*Computer science*]
ID.......... Image Display (SAUS)
ID.......... Image Dissector (KSC)
ID.......... Immediate Delivery [*Shipping*]
ID.......... Immigration Department (SAUO)
ID.......... Immunodeficiency [*Immunology*]
ID.......... Immunodiffusion [*Immunology*]
ID.......... Immunoglobulin Deficiency [*Immunology*] (AAMN)
ID.......... Immunological Distance [*in primate phylogeny*]
ID.......... Implant Dentistry (SAUO)
ID.......... Implicit Declaration (SAUS)
ID.......... Import Declaration (SAUS)
ID.......... Import Duty [*Customs*] (DS)
ID.......... Improvement District (SAUS)
ID.......... Impulse Device (SAUS)
ID.......... Inanna's Descent (BJA)
ID.......... Inappropriate Disability (STED)

ID........ Inaugural Dissertation (BJA)
ID........ Incapacitation Dose
ID........ Inclusion Dependency (SAUS)
ID........ Inclusion Disease [*Medicine*]
ID........ Inclusive Depth [*Typography*] (DGA)
ID........ Income Debenture [*Type of bond*] [*Investment term*]
ID........ Income Duty (SAUS)
ID........ Incorporation Data (SAUO)
ID........ Increased Deployability [*Posture*] (DOMA)
ID........ Indefinite Delivery [*Shipping*]
ID........ Indentification [*Communications term*] (DCT)
ID........ Independence Day (SAUO)
ID........ Independence Dogs [*An association*] (EA)
ID........ Independent Dealer [*Automobile sales*]
ID........ Independent Development (SAUS)
ID........ Independent Distributor
ID........ Index of Discrimination
ID........ Index of Dissimilarity
ID........ Indicating Device
ID........ Indicator Driver (MSA)
ID........ Indirect Damage [*Insurance*]
ID........ Indirect Departmental (DGA)
ID........ Indirect Detection (SAUS)
I/D........ Indirect Labor (AAG)
ID........ Individual Development
ID........ Individual Dose [*Radioactivity calculations*]
ID........ Individualized Dialing [*Communications term*] (DCT)
ID........ Indonesia [*ANSI two-letter standard code*] (CNC)
ID........ Induced Draft (or Draught) (SAUS)
ID........ Inductance [*Electromagnetism*] (IAA)
ID........ Induction Delivery (STED)
ID........ Industrial Democracy
ID........ Industrial Design (WGA)
ID........ Industrial Designer (SAUS)
ID........ Industrial Development
ID........ Industrial Diamond (SAUS)
ID........ Industrial Digital (SAUS)
ID........ Industrial Drive (SAUS)
ID........ Industrial Drying (SAUS)
ID........ Industrial Dynamics [*Management analysis*]
ID........ Ineffective Dose (SAUS)
ID........ Inelastic Demand (MHDB)
ID........ Inertial Delay (SAUS)
ID........ Infant Death (MAE)
ID........ Infantry Division
ID........ Infectious Disease [*Medicine*]
ID........ Infective Dose
ID........ Inferior Division [*Medicine*] (DAVI)
ID........ Informal Decorative [*Horticulture*]
ID........ Informal Document (SAUS)
ID........ Information and Documentation [*Royal Tropical Institute*] [*Information service or system*] (IID)
ID........ Information Density (SAUS)
ID........ Information Department (SAUS)
ID........ Information Design, Inc. (SAUO)
ID........ Information Distribution (SAUS)
ID........ Information Distributor
Id........ Infradentale [*Medicine*] (EDAA)
ID........ Inhibitory Dose [*Medicine*]
ID........ Inhomogeneous Deposition (STED)
ID........ Initial Data (SAUS)
ID........ Initial Deflection (SAUS)
ID........ Initial Denial Authority (AAGC)
ID........ Initial Diagnosis [*Medicine*] (CPH)
ID........ Initial Distribution
ID........ Initial Dose [*Medicine*] (CPH)
ID........ Initial dyskinesia [*Medicine*] (DMAA)
ID........ Injected Dose
ID........ Inner Detector
id........ Inner Diameter (NTIO)
ID........ Inner Diameter
ID........ Inniskilling Dragoons [*Military*] [*British*]
ID........ Innovator's Digest [*The Infoteam, Inc.*] [*Information service or system*] (IID)
ID........ Inoculum Density
ID........ Input Data (SAUS)
ID........ Input Diode (SAUS)
ID........ Input Display [*Computer science*] (IAA)
ID........ Input Division (SAUS)
ID........ Insect Damage (ADWA)
ID........ Insertion Device [*Series of magnets*] [*Physics*]
ID........ Inside Diameter
ID........ Inside Dimension [*Construction term*] (MIST)
ID........ Installation Data
ID........ Installation Date (VLIE)
ID........ Institute of Dietitians (SAUO)
ID........ Institute of Directors (SAUO)
ID........ Institute of Distribution [*Defunct*] (EA)
ID........ Instructional Developer (MCD)
ID........ Instructional Development (SAUS)
ID........ Instructional Duties (SAUS)
I/D........ Instruction/Data (IEEE)
ID........ Instruction Decoder (VLIE)
ID........ Instructor Dependent (SAUO)
ID........ Instrumentation Directorate [*White Sands Missile Range*] [*Army*]
ID........ Insufficient Data (STED)
ID........ Insulation Displacement
ID........ Insurance Department (SAUS)
ID........ Integral Derivative (IAA)
ID........ Integral Dose (SAUS)
ID........ Integrated Data (SAUS)
ID........ Integrated Demonstration (AUEG)
ID........ Integrated Diagnostics (AAGC)
ID........ Integrated Display (SAUS)
ID........ Integrating Device (SAUS)
ID........ Integration Domain (VLIE)
ID........ Integrator-Decoupled (SAUS)
ID........ Intellectual Digest [*A publication*]
ID........ Intelligence Department [*Army*] (MCD)
ID........ Intelligence Detachment (SAUO)
ID........ Intelligence Division [*NATO*] (NATG)
ID........ Intelligence Duties
ID........ Intelligent Device [*Computer science*] (CIST)
ID........ Intelligent Digitizer
ID........ Intelligent Documentation [*Computer science*]
I-D........ Intensity Duration (Curve)
ID........ Interactive Debugging (IEEE)
ID........ Interactive Discrimination (ACAE)
ID........ Intercept Direction (SAA)
ID........ Intercept Director (SAUS)
ID........ Intercommunication Devices (MCD)
ID........ Interconnection Device (MCD)
ID........ Interconnection Diagram (IAA)
ID........ Interdendritic (SAUS)
Id........ Interdentale [*Medicine*] (EDAA)
ID........ Interdepartmental (SAUS)
ID........ Interdepartmental Group (SAUO)
ID........ Interdiction (SAUS)
ID........ Interdigital [*Telecommunications*] (IEEE)
ID........ Interdigitating Cells (STED)
ID........ Interdisciplinary
ID........ Interest Deductible [*Banking*] (ADA)
ID........ Interface Device (MCD)
ID........ Interface Document (NASA)
ID........ Interferometer and Doppler
ID........ Interim Dividend [*Investment term*]
ID........ Interior Department
ID........ Interior Department Decisions [*United States*] [*A publication*] (DLA)
ID........ Interior Designer (SAUS)
ID........ Interlocking Directorate [*Business term*]
ID........ Intermediate Description (IEEE)
ID........ Intermittent Duty (IAA)
ID........ Intermodulation Distortion
ID........ Internal Diameter (MSA)
ID........ International Daleco Technology [*Vancouver Stock Exchange symbol*]
ID........ International Department (SAUO)
ID........ International Division [*Army Service Forces*] [*World War II*]
ID........ Internet Draft (VLIE)
I-D........ Internet-Draft (DINT)
ID........ Interrectal Spike Discharge [*Neurophysiology*]
ID........ Interrupt Decoder (or Decoding) (SAUS)
ID........ Interstitial Disease (STED)
ID........ Intestinal Distress
id........ Intradermal [*Medicine*] (WDAA)
ID........ Intradermal [*Medicine*]
ID........ Intraductal [*Anatomy*]
ID........ Intraduodenal [*Medicine*] (MAE)
ID........ Intransit Depot (SAUS)
ID........ Intrinsicoid Deflection [*Cardiology*]
ID........ Introduction (WDMC)
ID........ Inventory Data (SAUS)
ID........ Inventory Difference [*Formerly, MUF*] [*NRC/ERDA*]
ID........ Inventory Discrepancy (SAUS)
ID........ Inverted (SAUS)
ID........ Investigation Department (SAUO)
ID........ Invoice Distribution
ID........ Iraqi Dinar [*Monetary unit*] (BJA)
ID........ Iris Diaphragm [*Photography*]
ID........ Irish Duke (ROG)
ID........ Irvine Dataflow (RALS)
ID........ Islamic Dinar [*Monetary unit*] (EY)
ID........ Island (ADA)
id........ islander (SAUS)
ID........ Isodynamic (SAUS)
ID........ Isosorbide Dinitrate (STED)
ID........ Isothermal Desorption (SAUS)
ID........ Isotope Dating (SAUS)
ID........ Isotope Dilution
ID........ Isotopic Dilution (SAUS)
ID........ Issue Date
ID........ Item Description
ID........ Item Descriptor [*Computer science*] (CIST)
ID........ Item Documentation (IEEE)
ID........ Izquierda Democratica [*Democratic Left*] [*Ecuador*] [*Political party*] (PPW)
ID........ Noncathode Ray Tube Indicators [*JETDS nomenclature*] [*Military*] (CET)
ID........ Sumitomo Chemical Co. [*Japan*] [*Research code symbol*]
ID_{50}........ Infective Dose, Median

ID-86 .... Infantry Division - 1986
IDA.............. Dallas Baptist College, Dallas, TX [*OCLC symbol*] (OCLC)
IDA.............. Idacorp, Inc. [*NYSE symbol*] (SG)
Ida .... Idaho (BEE)
IDA.............. Idaho
IDA.............. Idaho Array [*Idaho*] [*Seismograph station code, US Geological Survey*] [*Closed*] (SEIS)
IDA.............. Idaho Falls [*Idaho*] [*Airport symbol*] (OAG)
IDA.............. Idaho Power Co. [*NYSE symbol*] (SPSG)
Ida .... Idaho Reports [*A publication*] (DLA)
IDA.............. Identification Data Accessory (NTCM)
IDA.............. Illinois Department of Agriculture (SAUS)
IDA.............. Image Display and Analysis (MAE)
IDA.............. Iminodiacetic Acid [*Organic chemistry*]
IDA.............. Immediate Damage Assessment
IDA.............. Immortalis Dei Auspicio [*With the Help of God*] [*Latin*]
IDA.............. Import Duties Act (SAUO)
IDA.............. Import Duty Act [*British*] (DS)
IDA.............. In Defense of Animals (EA)
IDA.............. Independent Democratic Action (SAUS)
IDA.............. Independent Disk Array (SAUS)
IDA.............. Independent Distributors Association (NTPA)
IDA.............. Independent Drive Array (SAUS)
IDA.............. Indian Dairy Association (SAUO)
IDA.............. Indian Dental Association (SAUO)
IDA.............. Indicator Digest Average [*Stock exchange term*] (SPSG)
IDA.............. Indirect Data Addressing [*Computer science*] (VLIE)
IDA.............. Individual Development Account (SAUS)
IDA.............. Indonesia Air Transport PT [*ICAO designator*] (FAAC)
IDA.............. Industrial Design Award
IDA.............. Industrial Developers Association (SAUO)
IDA.............. Industrial Development Abstracts [*Database*] [*UNIDO*] (CRD)
IDA.............. Industrial Development Agency (SAUO)
IDA.............. Industrial Development Authority [*Ireland*]
IDA.............. Industrial Distribution Association (NTPA)
IDA.............. Industry Development Arrangement
IDA.............. Infant-Toddler Developmental Assessment [*Test*] (TMMY)
IDA.............. Information, Decision, Action
IDA.............. Information Dispersal Algorithm (SAUS)
IDA.............. Infrared Detection and Acquisition (ACAE)
IDA.............. Infrared Detection Array
IDA.............. Initial Data Analysis [*Statistics*]
IDA.............. Initial Denial Authority (AABC)
IDA.............. Initial Diversion Assessment (SAUS)
IDA.............. Inpatient Data Administration (PDAA)
IDA.............. Input Data Acknowledge (SAUS)
IDA.............. Input Data Assembler
IDA.............. Inspekteur der Artillerie [*Inspector of Artillery*] [*German military - World War II*]
IDA.............. Installation Design Authority (SAUS)
IDA.............. Institute for Agricultural Development (SAUO)
IDA.............. Institute for Defense Analyses (EA)
IDA.............. Institute for Design Analysis (SAUO)
IDA.............. Institute for Development Anthropology (EA)
IDA.............. Institute of Design Analyses (SAUS)
IDA.............. Institute of Directors in Australia (SAUO)
IDA.............. Institute of Domestic Arts (WDAA)
IDA.............. Integrated Data Access (NITA)
IDA.............. Integrated Data Analysis (SAUS)
IDA.............. Integrated Debugging Aid (IAA)
IDA.............. Integrated Digital Access [*Telecommunications*]
IDA.............. Integrated Digital Avionics (MCD)
IDA.............. Integrated Disbursing and Accounting (MCD)
IDA.............. Integrated Disk Adapter [*Sperry UNIVAC*]
IDA.............. Integro-Differential Analyzer
IDA.............. Intelligent Data Access
IDA.............. Intelligent Database Assistant
IDA.............. Intelligent Drive Array [*COMPAQ Computer Corp.*] [*Computer science*]
IDA.............. Interactive Data Analysis (SAUS)
IDA.............. Interactive Data on Accidents [*Engineering*]
IDA.............. Interactive Debugging Aid
IDA.............. Interactive Differential Analyzer
IDA.............. Interamerican Development Association (SAUO)
IDA.............. Intercept Distance Aid (SAA)
IDA.............. Interchange of Data between Administrations (SAUO)
IDA.............. Intercollegiate Dramatic Association [*Defunct*] (EA)
IDA.............. Intercommunication Data Areas (SAUS)
IDA.............. Interconnect Device Arrangement (HGAA)
IDA.............. Interdigitated Array [*Electronics*]
IDA.............. Inter-Divisional Agreement
IDA.............. Interdivisional Authorization (SAUS)
IDA.............. Interface Display Assembly [*NASA*] (NASA)
IDA.............. International Dance Alliance (EA)
IDA.............. International Dark-Sky Association
IDA.............. International Data and Analysis [*Bureau of Mines*]
IDA.............. International Database Association [*Defunct*] (EA)
IDA.............. International Defenders of Animals (EA)
IDA.............. International Deployment of Accelerometers [*Project*] [*Seismography*]
IDA.............. International Depository Authority (SAUO)
IDA.............. International Desalination Association (EA)
IDA.............. International Development Action (SAUO)
IDA.............. International Development Agency [*United Nations*] (NUCP)
IDA.............. International Development Association (EA)
IDA.............. International Diplomatic Academy (SAUO)
IDA.............. International Discotheque Association [*Defunct*] (EA)
IDA.............. International Dispensary Association [*Acronym is used as association name*] (EAIO)
IDA.............. International Distribution Association (SAUO)
IDA.............. International Documentary Association (EA)
IDA.............. International Doll Association [*Defunct*] (EA)
IDA.............. International Downtown Association (EA)
IDA.............. International Drapery Association (EA)
IDA.............. International Dredging Association
IDA.............. International Drummers Association (SAUO)
IDA.............. International Dyslexia Association (NRGU)
IDA.............. Intrusion Detection Alarm (CINC)
IDA.............. Investment Dealers Association of Canada
IDA.............. Ionospheric Dispersion Analysis [*Air Force*]
IDA.............. Iowa Dental Association (SAUO)
IDA.............. Irish Dental Association (BI)
IDA.............. Irish Development Authority (SAUS)
IDA.............. Irish Drug Association (BI)
IDA.............. Iron Deficiency Anemia [*Medicine*]
IDA.............. Islamic Democratic Alliance [*Pakistan*] [*Political party*]
IDA.............. Islamic Democratic Association (SAUO)
IDA.............. Isotope Dilution Analysis
IDA.............. Isotopic Dilution Analysis (or Analyzer) (SAUS)
IDA.............. Israeli Dental Association (SAUO)
IDA.............. Iterative Differential Analyzer (IAA)
IDA .... Industrial Diamond Association (ODA)
IDAA .... Industrial Diamond Association of America
IDAA .... International Diabetic Athletes Association (EA)
IDAA .... International Dictionary of Architects and Architecture [*A publication*]
IDAA .... International Doctors in Alcoholics Anonymous (EA)
IDAAS .... Integrated Data Acquisition & Analysis Station (SAUS)
IDAAS .... International Directory of Astronomical Associations and Societies [*A publication*]
IdAb .... Aberdeen Public Library, Aberdeen, ID [*Library symbol*] [*Library of Congress*] (LCLS)
IDAB .... Industrial Advisory Board (SAUO)
IDAB .... Industrial Development Advisory Board [*British*]
IDAB .... International Development Advisory Board (SAUO)
IDABEE .... Institute of Defense Analysis Compiler (SAA)
ID AC .... Idem Ac [*The Same As*] [*Latin*]
IDAC .... Industrial Data Acquisition Control (IAA)
IDAC .... Industrial Developers Association of Canada (SAUO)
IDAC .... Infobus Data Access Component (SAUS)
IDAC .... Instant Data Access Control [*National Design Center, Inc.*] [*Information service or system*] (IID)
IDAC .... Integrated Data Acquisition and Control [*Jet Propulsion Laboratory, NASA*]
IDAC .... Integrated Digital-Analog Converter (MCD)
IDAC .... Intelligent Data Acquisition and Control (SAUS)
IDAC .... Interim Data Acquisition (SAUS)
IDAC .... Interim Digital-Analog Converter
IDAC .... International Decorative Accessories Center (EA)
IDAC .... International Disaster Advisory Committee
IDAC .... Internet Directory of Advisors and Consultants (COBU)
IDACA .... Institute for the Development of Agricultural Co-operatives in Asia (SAUO)
IDACA .... International District Heating and Cooling Association (SAUO)
IDACE .... Association des Industries des Aliments Dietetiques de la CEE [*Association of Dietetic Foods Industries of the European Economic Community*]
ID-ACK .... Identification-Acknowledge (MCD)
IDACON .... Iterative Differential Analyzer Control
IDA-CRD .... Institute for Defense Analysis-Communications Research Division
IDACS .... Integrated Detection and Classification Station
IDACS .... Integrated Digital Audio Control System (SAUS)
IDAD .... Infrared Detector Array Development (ACAE)
IDAD .... Internal Defense and Development [*Army*] (AABC)
IDADS .... Information Displays Automatic Drafting System (SAUO)
IDADS .... Interactive Drafting and Digitizing System (MCD)
IDAF .... IGAC DEBITS Africa (SAUS)
IDAF .... International Defense and Aid Fund for Southern Africa, US Committee [*Defunct*] (EA)
IDAFIPS .... Integrated Disbursing and Accounting Financial Information Processing System [*DoD*]
IDAFMS .... Integrated Disbursing and Accounting Financial Management System (DNAB)
IDAFSA .... International Defense and Aid Fund for Southern Africa (SAUO)
IDAGAM .... Institute for Defense Analysis Gaming Model (MCD)
IDA-HEAL-NET... Idaho Health Libraries Network [*Library network*]
Idaho .... Idaho Supreme Court Reports [*A publication*] (DLA)
Idaho Adm Code... Idaho Administrative Code [*A publication*] (AAGC)
Idaho Dep Fish Game Wildl Bull... Idaho Department of Fish and Game Wildlife Bulletin (journ.) (SAUS)
Idaho LJ ...... Idaho Law Journal [*A publication*] (DLA)
Idaho NS ..... Idaho Reports, New Series [*A publication*] (DLA)
IdahoP.......... Idaho Power Co. [*Associated Press*] (SAG)
Idaho Sess Laws... Session Laws of Idaho [*A publication*] (DLA)
Idaho St U... Idaho State University (GAGS)
IDAI .... Industrial Development Authority of Ireland (SAUO)
Ida IAB .... Idaho Industrial Accident Board Reports [*A publication*] (DLA)
IDAID .... International Defense and Internal Development (SAUO)
IDA Ireland... Industrial Development Authority of Ireland (SAUO)
IdAl .... Albion Community Library, Albion, ID [*Library symbol*] [*Library of Congress*] (LCLS)
IDAL............ Illinois Digital Academic Library

IDAL .... Indirect Data Access List (SAUS)
IDAL .... Indirect Data Address List [*Computer science*] (ECII)
IDAL .... Integrated Defense Avionics Laboratory (SAUS)
IdAIN .... Albion State Normal School, Albion, ID [*Library symbol*] [*Library of Congress*] (LCLS)
Ida LR .... Idaho Law Review (journ.) (SAUS)
IdAIS .... Southern Idaho College of Education, Albion, ID [*Library symbol*] [*Library of Congress*] [*Obsolete*] (LCLS)
IdAm .... American Falls District Library, American Falls, ID [*Library symbol*] [*Library of Congress*] (LCLS)
IDAM .... Image Data Access Method (SAUS)
IDAM .... Indexed Direct Access Method
IDAM .... Infant of Drug-Abusing Mother (MELL)
IDAM .... Infant of Drug-Addicted Mother (MELL)
IDAM .... Interactive Data Access Method [*Computer science*] (TIMI)
IDAMF .... Interdenominational African Ministers Federation (SAUO)
IdAmHS .... American Falls High School, American Falls, ID [*Library symbol*] [*Library of Congress*] (LCLS)
IDAMIS .... Integrated Data Analysis and Management Information System (SAUS)
IDAMIS .... Integrated Drug Abuse Management Information Systems
IDAMS .... Image Display and Manipulation System [*NASA*]
IDAMS .... Integrated Data Analysis and Management (SAUS)
IDAMS .... Integrated Data Analysis and Management System (SAUS)
IDAMS .... Isotope Dilution Analysis Mass Spectrometry
IDAMST .... Integrated Digital Avionics for Medium STOL Transport (MCD)
IDAN .... Idan Software Industries ISI Ltd. [*NASDAQ symbol*] (NQ)
I/D & C .... Instrumentation/Displays and Controls [*Subsystem*] (MCD)
ID & CA .... Inverter Distribution and Control Assembly (MCD)
ID & PD .... Industrial Democracy and Personnel Development
IDANF .... Idan Software Ind ISI [*NASDAQ symbol*] (TTSB)
IdanSft .... Idan Software Industries ISI Ltd. [*Associated Press*] (SAG)
IDanvi .... Danville Public Library, Danville, IL [*Library symbol*] [*Library of Congress*] (LCLS)
IDanviC .... Danville Junior College, Danville, IL [*Library symbol*] [*Library of Congress*] (LCLS)
IDanviCS ...... Central Vermillion County Schools Cooperative, Danville, IL [*Library symbol*] [*Library of Congress*] (LCLS)
IDanviHS ..... Schlarman High School, Danville, IL [*Library symbol*] [*Library of Congress*] (LCLS)
IDanviL .... Lake View Memorial Hospital, Doctor's Library, Danville, IL [*Library symbol*] [*Library of Congress*] (LCLS)
IDanviSD ..... Danville Community Unit School District, Danville, IL [*Library symbol*] [*Library of Congress*] (LCLS)
IDanviSE ...... Saint Elizabeth Hospital, Danville, IL [*Library symbol*] [*Library of Congress*] (LCLS)
IDanviStE ..... Saint Elizabeth Hospital, Danville, IL [*Library symbol*] [*Library of Congress*] (LCLS)
IDanviVA ...... United States Veterans Administration Hospital, Danville, IL [*Library symbol*] [*Library of Congress*] (LCLS)
IDAP .... Industrial Design Assistance Program [*National Design Council, Canada*]
IDAP .... Integrated Defense Avionic Platform (SAUS)
IDAP .... Integrated Defensive Aids Program (SAUS)
IDAP .... Integrated Defensive Avionics Program [*Navy*] (DOMA)
IDAP .... Intelligence Data Acquisition and Processing (SAUS)
IDAP .... Interactive Data Access System (SAUS)
IDAP .... Internal Development and Assistance Program (AFM)
IDAP .... International Development and Assistance Program (KSC)
IDAP .... Isomorphously Doped Ammonium Perchlorate
IDAP .... Iterative Differential Analyzer Pinboard
IDAPA .... Idaho Administrative Code [*A publication*] (AAGC)
IDAPI .... Independent Database Application Program Interface (PCM)
IDAPI .... Integrated Database Application Programming Interface (GART)
IDAPR .... Individual DSS [*Direct Support System*] Activity Performance Report
IDAPS .... Image Data Processing System
IDAPS .... Inspection Diagnostic and Prognostic System (ACAE)
IdAr .... Lost River District Library, Arco, ID [*Library symbol*] [*Library of Congress*] (LCLS)
IDARP .... Integrated Drug Abuse Reporting Process [*National Institutes of Health*]
IDARS .... Integrated Document Archive and Retrieval System [*Computer science*] (GART)
IDART .... Individual Drill Attendance and Retirement Transaction [*Military*] (DNAB)
IdAs .... Ashton Public Library, Ashton, ID [*Library symbol*] [*Library of Congress*] (LCLS)
I-DAS .... Image Data Analysis System (SAUS)
IDAS .... Image Data Analysis Systems (SAUO)
IDAS .... Importers, Distributors, Adhesives and Sealants sector (SAUS)
IDAS .... Individual Data Acquisition System (SAUS)
IDAS .... Industrial Data Acquisition System (IAA)
IDAS .... Information Display Automatic System (SAUS)
IDAS .... Information Displays Automatic Drafting System (IEEE)
IDAS .... Instrument Data Acquisition System
IDAS .... Integrated Data Acquisition and Simulation System (SAUS)
IDAS .... Integrated Data Acquisition System (MCD)
IDAS .... Integrated Data Analysis System (SAUS)
IDAS .... Integrated Data-Processed Assembly System [*Computer science*] (TIMI)
IDAS .... Integrated Defense Avionics System [*Air Force*] (DOMA)
IDAS .... Integrated Defensive Aids System (SAUS)
IDAS .... Integrated Design Automation System (MCD)
IDAS .... Integrated Development Approval System (SAUO)
IDAS .... Integrated Dual Accounting System (SAUS)
IDAS .... Intelligent Data Acquisition System
IDAS .... Interchange Data Structure (SAUS)
IDAS .... International Danger & Disaster Assistance (SAUS)
IDAS .... International Database Access Service [*Bahrain Telecommunications Co.*] [*Information service or system*] (IID)
IDAS .... Intrusion Detection Alarm System
IDAS .... Isothermal Decompression Analysis System (SAUS)
IDAS .... Isotope Dilution Alpha Spectrometry
IDAS .... Iterative Differential Analyzer Slave
IDASA .... Institute for Democracy in South Africa
IDASAT .... Integrated Distance and Speed and Tilt (SAUS)
IDASP .... Infrared Detection and Acquisition Signal Processing (ACAE)
IDASS .... Integrated Data Assimilation and Sounding System (SAUO)
IDAST .... Interpolated Data and Speech Transmission [*Computer science*]
Ida Supp ...... Idaho Supplement [*A publication*] (DLA)
IDAT .... Initial Development Acceptance Tests (SAUS)
IDAT .... Interfacility Data (FAAC)
IDATS .... International Data Acquisition and Transmission System (SAUS)
IDATU .... Irish Distributive and Administrative Trade Union (EAIO)
IDA (USA) .... Indian Dental Association (USA) (EA)
IDAV .... Immune Deficiency Associated Virus
IDAW .... Indirect Data Address Word (SAUS)
IdB .... Boise Public Library, Boise, ID [*Library symbol*] [*Library of Congress*] (LCLS)
IDB .... Identification Supervisor (SAUS)
IDB .... Illicit Diamond Buyer [*or Buying*]
IDB .... Illinois Central College, East Peoria, IL [*OCLC symbol*] (OCLC)
IDB .... Image Data Base (SAUS)
IDB .... Immediate Direct Broadcast (SAUS)
IDB .... Incomplete Data Base [*Statistics*] (DAVI)
IDB .... Inductance Decade Box
IDB .... Industrial Data Bank Department [*Gulf Organization for Industrial Consulting*] [*Qatar*] [*Information service or system*] (IID)
IDB .... Industrial Development Bank [*Kenya*] (IMH)
IDB .... Industrial Development Bank [*Jordan*]
IDB .... Industrial Development Board [*Northern Ireland*] (GEA)
IDB .... Industrial Development Bond
IDB .... Industrial Development Bureau (SAUS)
IDB .... Inertial Data Box (KSC)
IDB .... Infantry Demonstration Battalion (SAUS)
IDB .... Infared Diving Binoculors (MCD)
IDB .... Information Database (SAUS)
IDB .... Information Descriptor Board (VLIE)
IDB .... Initial Dummy Block (SAUS)
IDB .... INPADOC [*International Patent Documentation Center*] Data Base [*Information service or system*] (CRD)
IDB .... Input Data Buffer
IDB .... Inspection Data Bulletin
IDB .... In-Suit Drink Bag [*Aerospace*] (MCD)
IDB .... Insurance Development Bureau [*Guelph, ON*] (EAIO)
IDB .... Integral Databank (SAUS)
IDB .... Integrated Data Base [*Computer science*]
IDB .... Integrating Double Buffer (SAUS)
IDB .... Intelligence Data Base (SAUO)
IDB .... Interaction Database
IDB .... Inter-American Defense Board (EA)
IDB .... Inter-American Development Bank [*Also, IADB*]
IDB .... Intercept During Boost [*Aerospace*]
IDB .... Intercept During Burning (SAUS)
IDB .... Inter-Dealer Broker [*British*]
IDB .... Interdepartmental Billing (SAUS)
IDB .... Inter-Dynamic Balance
IDB .... Interface Description Block [*Computer science*] (DINT)
IDB .... Intermediary Dealer Broker [*Investment term*] (NUMA)
IDB .... Internal Drainage Board (SAUS)
IDB .... International Data Base [*Bureau of Census*] [*Database*]
IDB .... Interoperable Data Base (VLIE)
IDB .... Interpreters Dictionary of the Bible (journ.) (SAUS)
IDB .... Interpretive Debugger [*Computer science*] (ECII)
IDB .... Inverni & Della Beffa [*Italy*] [*Research code symbol*]
IDB .... Inverted Data Base (VLIE)
IDB .... Islamic Development Bank [*Saudi Arabia*]
IDB .... Israel Diamond Building (SAUO)
IDB .... Israel Discount Bank
IDBA .... International Deli-Bakery Association [*Defunct*] (EA)
IDBA .... International Drag Bike Association (SAUO)
IdBB .... Boise State College, Boise, ID [*Library symbol*] [*Library of Congress*] (LCLS)
IdBBC .... Boise Bible College, Boise, ID [*Library symbol*] [*Library of Congress*] (LCLS)
IdBBC .... Boise Cascade Corp. Library, Boise, ID [*Library symbol*] [*Library of Congress*] (LCLS)
IDBBY .... IDB Bankholding Corporation Ltd. [*NASDAQ symbol*] (COMM)
IdBC .... Ada County District Library, Boise, ID [*Library symbol*] [*Library of Congress*] (LCLS)
IDBC .... Infiltrating Ductal Breast Cancer (MELL)
IDBC .... International Dictionary of Black Composers [*A publication*]
IdBCH .... CH2M Hill Library, Boise, ID [*Library symbol*] [*Library of Congress*] (LCLS)
IdBDB .... Diocese of Boise, Resource Center, Boise, ID [*Library symbol*] [*Library of Congress*] (LCLS)
IdBe .... Bellevue Public Library, Bellevue, ID [*Library symbol*] [*Library of Congress*] (LCLS)
IDBE .... ID Biomedical Corp. [*NASDAQ symbol*] (SAG)
IDBEF .... ID Biomedical [*NASDAQ symbol*] (TTSB)

IDBEF.......... Integrated DataBase Extract Format (SAUS)
IdBEH.......... Idaho Elks Rehabilitation Hospital, Medical Library, Boise, ID [*Library symbol*] [*Library of Congress*] (LCLS)
IdBf.......... Blackfoot Public Library, Blackfoot, ID [*Library symbol*] [*Library of Congress*] (LCLS)
IdBfBH.......... Bingham Memorial Hospital, Medical Library, Blackfoot, ID [*Library symbol*] [*Library of Congress*] (LCLS)
IdBFG.......... Fish & Game Library, Boise, ID [*Library symbol*] [*Library of Congress*] (LCLS)
IdBfGS.......... Church of Jesus Christ of Latter-Day Saints, Genealogical Society Library, Blackfoot West Branch, Stake Center, Blackfoot, ID [*Library symbol*] [*Library of Congress*] (LCLS)
IdBfH.......... State Hospital South, Medical Library, Blackfoot, ID [*Library symbol*] [*Library of Congress*] (LCLS)
IdBfS.......... Snake River School and Community Library, Blackfoot, ID [*Library symbol*] [*Library of Congress*] (LCLS)
IdBG.......... Genealogical Library, Boise, ID [*Library symbol*] [*Library of Congress*] (LCLS)
IdBHP.......... Hewett-Packard, Boise Site Library, Boise, ID [*Library symbol*] [*Library of Congress*] (LCLS)
IDBI.......... Industrial Development Bank of India (ECON)
IDBI.......... Industrial Development Bank of Israel (IMH)
IdBI.......... Information and Referral Service, Boise, ID [*Library symbol*] [*Library of Congress*] (LCLS)
ID Bio.......... ID Biomedical Corp. [*Associated Press*] (SAG)
ID Biom.......... ID Biomedical Corp. [*Associated Press*] (SAG)
IdBL.......... Idaho Legislative Council, Legislative Library, Boise, ID [*Library symbol*] [*Library of Congress*] (LCLS)
IdBLM-B.......... Bureau of Land Management, Boise, ID [*Library symbol*] [*Library of Congress*] (LCLS)
IDBM.......... Intelligent Data Base Machine (SAUS)
IDBMA.......... International Data Base Management Association (EA)
IdBMK.......... Morrison-Krudsen Co., Inc., Records and Micrographics Center, Boise, ID [*Library symbol*] [*Library of Congress*] (LCLS)
IDBMS.......... Image Database Management System (SAUS)
IDBMS.......... Integrated Database Management System
IDBMS.......... International Data Base Management Association (SAUO)
IDBMS/R.......... Integrated Data Base Management System/Relational (VLIE)
IDBN.......... Integrated Digital Backbone Network [*Telecommunications*]
IdBnf.......... Boundary County Library District, Bonners Ferry, ID [*Library symbol*] [*Library of Congress*] (LCLS)
IDBP.......... Industrial Development Bank of Pakistan (SAUO)
IDBP.......... Intel Data Base Processor (SAUS)
IDBPF.......... Interdigital Band-Pass Filter [*Electronics*] (IAA)
Id-BPH.......... Idaho State Library, Blind and Physically Handicapped Services, Boise, ID [*Library symbol*] [*Library of Congress*] (LCLS)
IdBr.......... Bruneau District Library, Bruneau, ID [*Library symbol*] [*Library of Congress*] (LCLS)
IDBR.......... Indirect Bilirubin [*Biochemistry*] (DAVI)
IDBR.......... Input Data Buffer Register [*Computer science*] (MHDB)
IDBRA.......... International Drivers' Behaviour Research Association [*Paris, France*] (EAIO)
IdBRC.......... Roman Catholic Diocese of Boise, Boise, ID [*Library symbol*] [*Library of Congress*] (LCLS)
IdBRE.......... Real Estate Comm. Library, Boise, ID [*Library symbol*] [*Library of Congress*] (LCLS)
IdBS.......... Idaho Statesman Library, Boise, ID [*Library symbol*] [*Library of Congress*] (LCLS)
IDBS.......... Imports Data Base (SAUS)
IDBS.......... Infantile Diffuse Brain Sclerosis [*Medicine*] (DB)
IDBS.......... Intelligent Data Base System (SAUS)
IdBSA.......... Saint Alphonsus Regional Medical Center, Medical Library, Boise, ID [*Library symbol*] [*Library of Congress*] (LCLS)
IdBSH.......... Boise Senior High School, Boise, ID [*Library symbol*] [*Library of Congress*] (LCLS)
IdBSL.......... Saint Luke's Regional Center Medical Library, Boise, ID [*Library symbol*] [*Library of Congress*] (LCLS)
IDBT.......... Immune Dot-Blot Test [*Medicine*] (MELL)
IDBT.......... Industrial Development Bank of Turkey (PDAA)
IDBTF.......... Integrated DataBase Transaction Format (SAUS)
IdBTI.......... Mountain State Tumor Institute Medical Library, Boise, ID [*Library symbol*] [*Library of Congress*] (LCLS)
IDBUG.......... Interagency Data Base Users Group (SAUO)
IdBuh.......... Buhl Public Library, Buhl, ID [*Library symbol*] [*Library of Congress*] (LCLS)
IdBur.......... Burley Public Library, Burley, ID [*Library symbol*] [*Library of Congress*] (LCLS)
IdBurGS.......... Church of Jesus Christ of Latter-Day Saints, Genealogical Society Library, Burley Branch, Burley, ID [*Library symbol*] [*Library of Congress*] (LCLS)
IdBV.......... United States Veterans Administration Medical Center, Medical Library, Boise, ID [*Library symbol*] [*Library of Congress*] (LCLS)
IDBX.......... IDB Communications Group, Inc. [*NASDAQ symbol*] (COMM)
IdC.......... Coeur D'Alene Public Library, Coeur D'Alene, ID [*Library symbol*] [*Library of Congress*] (LCLS)
IDC.......... Idiopathic Dilated Cardiomyopathy [*Cardiology*]
IDC.......... IIMBLMS Digital Computer (SAUS)
IDC.......... Image Dissector Camera
IDC.......... IMBLMS [*Integrated Medical Behavioral Measurement System*] Digital Computer (MCD)
IDC.......... Imperial Defence College [*British*]
IDC.......... Imperial Defence Committee (SAUO)
IDC.......... Improved Data Converter (SAUO)
IDC.......... Impulse-Driven Clock (SAUS)
IDC.......... Incentive Development Contract (SAUS)
IDC.......... Indirect Costs
IDC.......... Indirect Digital Control (VLIE)
IDC.......... Individual Defense Counsel
IDC.......... In Due Course (SAUS)
IDC.......... Industrial Democracy Commission
IDC.......... Industrial Design Certificate [*British*]
IDC.......... Industrial Development Certificate [*Department of Industry*] [*British*]
IDC.......... Industrial Development Commission (SAUO)
IDC.......... Industrial Development Corp.
IDC.......... Industrial Development Corporation of South Africa Ltd. (SAUO)
IDC.......... Industries Development Committee
IDC.......... Industry Development Commission (SAUO)
IDC.......... Infectious Diseases in Children (SAUO)
IDC.......... Information and Direction Center
IDC.......... Information and Documentation Center [*Royal Institute of Technology Library*] [*Information service or system*] (IID)
IDC.......... Information Design Change (NG)
IDC.......... Information Dissemination Committee (SAUO)
IDC.......... Information Dynamics Corp.
IDC.......... Infrared Detector Cryostat
IDC.......... Inner Dead-Center (DNAB)
IDC.......... Input Data Carrier (SAUS)
IDC.......... Input Display Console [*Computer science*]
IDC.......... Inspection Data Card (MCD)
IDC.......... Inspection Data Code (ACAE)
IDC.......... Installation Data (or Date) Confirmation (SAUS)
IDC.......... Installation Date Confirmation (VLIE)
IDC.......... Instantaneous Derivation Control (SAUS)
IDC.......... Instantaneous Deviation Control (SAUS)
IDC.......... Instruction Distribution Channel (SAUS)
IDC.......... Instrument Development Co. (SAUS)
IDC.......... Instrument Development Company (SAUO)
IDC.......... Insulating Displacement Connector (SAUS)
IDC.......... Insulation-Displacement Connection (SAUS)
IDC.......... Insulation Displacement Connector [*Electronics*]
IDC.......... Insulation Displacement Contact (SAUS)
IDC.......... Intangible Drilling and Development Costs (SAUS)
IDC.......... Intangible Drilling Cost (SAUO)
IDC.......... Intangible Drilling Costs [*Petroleum industry*]
IDC.......... Integrated Database Connector (SAUS)
IDC.......... Integrated Demonstration Coordinator (ABAC)
IDC.......... Integrated Desktop Connector (VLIE)
IDC.......... Integrated Device Controller
IDC.......... Integrated Digital Capability [*Communications term*] (DCT)
IDC.......... Integrated Disk Control [*NCR Corp.*]
IDC.......... Intelligence Documentation Center (SAUO)
IDC.......... Interactive Data Class [*Telecommunications*]
IDC.......... Interactive Data Corp. (SAUS)
IDC.......... Interactive Data Corporation (NITA)
IDC.......... Interagency Defector Committee (CARL)
IDC.......... Interceptor Distance Computer
IDC.......... Intercontinental Dynamics Corporation (SAUO)
IDC.......... Interdepartmental Communication
idc.......... interdepartmental cypher (SAUO)
IDC.......... Inter-Department Correspondence (SAUS)
IDC.......... Inter-Device Communication (SAUS)
IDC.......... Interdigital Communications [*AMEX symbol*] (SPSG)
IDC.......... Interdigitating Cell [*Medicine*] (DMAA)
IDC.......... Inter Documentation Co. AG, Zug, Switzerland [*Library symbol*] [*Library of Congress*] (LCLS)
IDC.......... Inter-Documentation Company (SAUO)
IDC.......... Interest During Construction
IDC.......... Interface Document Control (MCD)
IDC.......... Interior Designers of Canada [*See also DIC*]
IDC.......... Interior Design Society (SAUO)
IDC.......... Internal Data Channel
IDC.......... Internal Destination Code (TIMI)
IDC.......... Internal Document Control
IDC.......... International Dairy Committee
IDC.......... International Dairy Congress (SAUO)
IDC.......... International Dance Council [*See also CIDD*] (EAIO)
IDC.......... International Danube Commission (SAUO)
IDC.......... International Data Center (SAUO)
IDC.......... International Data Connector
IDC.......... International Data Consultants [*Market research organization*] (NITA)
IDC.......... International Data Corp. [*Information service or system*] (IID)
IDC.......... International Dermatological Committee (SAUO)
IDC.......... International Design Conference in Aspen (SAUS)
IDC.......... International Development Center (SAUS)
IDC.......... International Development Conference (EA)
IDC.......... International Development Corp. [*Proposed corporation to combine Alliance for Progress and Agency for International Development*]
IDC.......... International Diabetes Center (SAUO)
IDC.......... International Diamond Corporation (SAUO)
IDC.......... International Diamond Council [*Antwerp, Belgium*] (EAIO)
IDC.......... International Diastema Club (EA)
IDC.......... International Digital Communications (AGLO)
IDC.......... International Diode Corporation (SAUO)
IDC.......... International Display Corp. [*Vancouver Stock Exchange symbol*]
IDC.......... International Disposal Corporation (SAUO)
IDC.......... International Documentation Center
IDC.......... International Documentation in Chemistry (DIT)
IDC.......... International Donau Commission (SAUO)
IDC.......... International Drug Constituents (SAUO)
IDC.......... International Drug Convention (SAUO)

IDC International Drycleaners Congress (EA)
IDC Internationale Democrate Chretienne [*Christian Democrat International*] [*Belgium*] (EAIO)
IDC Internationale Dokumentationsgesellschaft fuer Chemie [*International Company for Documentation in Chemistry*] [*Frankfurt, West Germany*]
IDC Internet Database Connector [*Computer science*] (PCM)
IDC Intraductal Carcinoma [*Oncology*]
IDC Intransit Data Card (AFM)
IDC Inventor's Desktop Companion [*A publication*]
IDC Iowa Development Commission (SAUO)
IDC Iranian Democratic Committee (EA)
IDC Irrigated, Double Cropped [*Agriculture*]
IDC Item Description Code (SAUS)
IDC Item Design Change
IDC Item Detail Card [*Military*] (AABC)
IDC Iterated Deferred Correction (PDAA)
IDC Peoples Gas, Light & Coke Co., Chicago, IL [*OCLC symbol*] (OCLC)
IdCa Caldwell Public Library, Caldwell, ID [*Library symbol*] [*Library of Congress*] (LCLS)
IDCA Image Disector Camera Assembly (SAUS)
ID(C)A Indecent Displays (Control) Act [*British*]
IDCA Indian Diamond and Colorstone Association (EA)
IDCA Industrial Design Council of Australia (SAUO)
IDCA Integrated Detector/Cooler Assembly (SAUS)
IDCA International Design Conference in Aspen (EA)
IDCA International Development Cooperation Act of 1979
IDCA [*United States*] International Development Cooperation Agency (USGC)
IDCA International Development Corporation Agency (SAUO)
IDCA International Dolphin Conservation Act [*1993*]
IDCA International Dragon Class Association (EAIO)
IDCA Inverter Distribution and Control Assembly (NAKS)
IDCA United States International Development Cooperation Agency (SAUS)
IdCaC College of Idaho, Caldwell, ID [*Library symbol*] [*Library of Congress*] (LCLS)
IdCaH West Valley Medical Center, Medical Library, Caldwell, ID [*Library symbol*] [*Library of Congress*] (LCLS)
IDCAMS IDC Access Method Services (SAUS)
IdCar Little Wood River District Library, Carey, ID [*Library symbol*] [*Library of Congress*] (LCLS)
Id card Identification card (SAUO)
IDCARS Integrated Document Control And Retrieval System (SAUS)
IDCAS Industrial Development Center for Arab States [*Later, AIDO*]
IDCB Immediate Device Control Block [*Computer science*] (ELAL)
IdCC Consolidated Free Library District, Coeur d'Alene, ID [*Library symbol*] [*Library of Congress*] (LCLS)
IDCC Ideal Cement [*Federal Railroad Administration identification code*]
IDCC Industrial Development and Consulting Company (SAUO)
IDCC Integrated Data Communications Controller
IDCC Integrated Dual-Use Commercial Companies
IDCC INTEK Diversified [*NASDAQ symbol*] (TTSB)
IDCC INTEK Diversified Corp. [*NASDAQ symbol*] (NQ)
IDCC Interactive Display and Control Component (MCD)
IDCC Inter-Departmental Consultative Committee
IDCC International Data Communications Center (or Centre) (SAUS)
IDCC International Data Rescue Co-ordination Centre (SAUO)
IdCC-A Consolidated Free Library District, Athol Branch, Athol, ID [*Library symbol*] [*Library of Congress*] (LCLS)
IDCCC Interim Data Communications Collection Center
IDCCC Interior Department Cartographic Coordinating Committee (SAUO)
IDCCC Interior Digital Cartographic Coordination Committee (SAUO)
IDCCC International Dredging Conference Coordinating Committee (EAIO)
IdCCIN Cooperative Information Network, Coeur d'Alene, ID [*Library symbol*] [*Library of Congress*] (LCLS)
IdCC-R Consolidated Free Library District, Rathdrum Branch, Rathdrum, ID [*Library symbol*] [*Library of Congress*] (LCLS)
IdCC-SC Consolidated Free Library District, Service Center, Couer d'Alene, ID [*Library symbol*] [*Library of Congress*] (LCLS)
IdCC-SL Consolidated Free Library District, Spirit Lake Branch, Spirit Lake, ID [*Library symbol*] [*Library of Congress*] (LCLS)
IDCD Inter-Departmental Committee on Dentistry (SAUO)
IDCDA Independent Dealer Committee Dedicated to Action (EA)
IDCESTD Intergovernmental Committee of Experts on Science and Technology Development (SAUO)
IDCF Immunodiffusion Complement Fix [*Immunochemistry*] (DAVI)
IDCF Indirect Command File [*Computer science*] (WDAA)
IDCF Industrial Development Completion Form (SAUS)
IDCFC International David Cassidy Fan Club (EAIO)
IDCH International Directory of Company Histories [*A publication*]
IdCH Kootenai Medical Center, Medical Library, Couer d'Alene, ID [*Library symbol*] [*Library of Congress*] (LCLS)
IdCha Challis Public Library, Challis, ID [*Library symbol*] [*Library of Congress*] (LCLS)
IDCHE Intergovernmental Documentation Center on Housing and Environment (SAUS)
IDCHEC Intergovernmental Documentation Centre on Housing and Environment of the Countries of the United Nations Economic Commission for Europe (SAUO)
IdCHM Hecla Mining Co. Library, Couer d'Alene, ID [*Library symbol*] [*Library of Congress*] (LCLS)
IdChP Portneuf Library District, Chubbuck, ID [*Library symbol*] [*Library of Congress*] (LCLS)
IdCHS Couer d'Alene High School, Couer d'Alene, ID [*Library symbol*] [*Library of Congress*] (LCLS)
IDCI Intradiplochromatid Interchange (PDAA)
IDCJ International Development Center for/of Japan (SAUO)
IDCJ International Development Center, Japan (SAUS)
IdCl Clarkia District Library, Clarkia, ID [*Library symbol*] [*Library of Congress*] (LCLS)
IdCL Coeur d'Alene Public Library, Coeur d'Alene, ID [*Library symbol*] [*Library of Congress*] (LCLS)
IDCL Information Design Change List (MCD)
IDCL Installation Drawing Control List (SAUS)
IdCm Cambridge District Library, Cambridge, ID [*Library symbol*] [*Library of Congress*] (LCLS)
IDCM Interplant Debit and Credit Memo (ACAE)
IDCMA Independent Data Communications Manufacturers Association (EA)
IDCN Interchangeability Document Change Notice (KSC)
IDCN International Diplomatic Computer Network (SAUS)
IdCN North Idaho College, Coeur d'Alene, ID [*Library symbol*] [*Library of Congress*] (LCLS)
IDCNA Insulation Distributor Contractors National Association [*Later, NICA*] (EA)
IdCnL Council District Library, Council, ID [*Library symbol*] [*Library of Congress*] (LCLS)
IDCNS Interdivisional Committee on Nomenclature and Symbols (SAUS)
IDCNY International Design Center, New York
IDCOL Industrial Development Corporation of Orissa Limited (SAUO)
IDCOOP Industry Committee for the Development of Offsets to Offshore Procurement (SAUO)
IDCOP Integral Driver Coil on Plug
IDCOR Industry Degraded Core Rulemaking (SAUS)
IDCOR Industry Degraded Core Rulemaking Program [*Nuclear industry sponsored group*]
ID Corp International Data Corporation (SAUO)
IdCoStG College of Saint Gertrude, Library, Cottonwood, ID [*Library symbol*] [*Library of Congress*] (LCLS)
IDCP Infectious Diseases in Clinical Practice (SAUO)
IDCP Integrated Data Processing Circuit (SAUS)
IDCP International Data Collecting Platform (TEL)
IDCR Interchangeability Document Change Request (MCD)
IDCR International Decade of Cetacean Research
IdCs Cascade Public Library, Cascade, ID [*Library symbol*] [*Library of Congress*] (LCLS)
IDCS Image Data Calibration System (SAUS)
IDCS Image Dissector Camera System
IDCS Initial Defense Communications Satellite (MCD)
IDCS Instrumentation/Data Collection System
IDCS Integrated Data Coding System (NG)
IDCS Interdepartment Courier Service
IDCS International Data Collection System (SAUS)
IDCS International Digital Channel Service [*Federal Trade Commission*]
IDCSC Integrated Defense Communications System Control (SAUO)
IDCSP Initial Defense Communication Satellite Program (SAUO)
IDCSP Initial Defense Communications Satellite Program [*or Project*]
IDCSP Interim Defense Communication Satellite Program (SAUS)
IDCSP Interim Defense Communication Satellite Project (SAUO)
IDCSP-A Initial Defense Communications Satellite Program-Augmented (CET)
IDCSP-A Initial Defense Communications Satellite Project-Augmented (SAUO)
IDCSP/ADCSP Initial Defense Communications Satellite Program / Advanced Defense Communications Satellite Program (SAA)
IDCSS Initial Defense Communications Satellite System (NATG)
IDCSS Intermediate Defense Communications Satellite System (IAA)
IDCT Initial Detection & Classification Trainer (SAUS)
IDCT Integrated Daily Cycle Test (MCD)
IDCT Inverse Discrete Cosine Transform [*Electronics*] (ACRL)
IDCTR Inductor (MSA)
IDCU Improved Digital Computer Unit (SAUS)
I-D Curve Intensity-Duration Curve (SAUS)
IDCZ Industrial Development Co-Operative of Clinton County [*Federal Railroad Administration identification code*]
IDD Detroit Diesel Allison Division, General Motors Corp., Indianapolis, IN [*OCLC symbol*] (OCLC)
idd identified (SAUS)
IDD Illicit Diamond Dealing (ROG)
IDD Image Definition Device
IDD Imaging and Display Device (SAUS)
IDD Immunodeficiency Disease (SAUO)
IDD Indeed (SAUS)
IDD Indirect by Direct (MCD)
IDD Industrial Development Division [*Vietnam*]
IDD Industrial Diamond Drill (SAUS)
IDD Infant Development Distress Syndrome [*Medicine*] (ADA)
IDD Information and Data Dissemination (SAUO)
IDD Input and Designation Device (SAUS)
IDD Institute for Drafting and Design [*Australia*]
IDD Instrument Definition Document
IDD Insulin-Dependent Diabetes
IDD Integrated Data Dictionary
IDD Integrated Decision Document (SAUO)
IDD Intelligence Data Handling Division [*United States European Command*]
IDD Inter-Director Designation (NG)
IDD Interface Definition Document (MCD)
IDD Interface Designation Drawing
IDD Interface Design Document (CTAS)
IDD Interface Diagnostic Diagrams (SAUS)
IDD Interim Drydocking [*Navy*] (NVT)
IDD International Data and Development, Inc. (SAUO)

IDD .... International Data Development, Inc. (SAUO)
IDD .... International Defense Directory [*A publication*]
IDD .... International Direct Dialing [*Telecommunications*]
IDD .... International Dorado Resources [*Vancouver Stock Exchange symbol*]
IDD .... Internet Data Distribution (SAUS)
IDD .... Inventory to Diagnose Depression [*Psychology*]
IDD .... Investment Dealer's Digest
IDD .... Iodine Deficiency Disorders [*Medicine*]
IDD .... Iodotyrosine Deiodinase Deficiency [*Medicine*] (MELL)
IDD .... Island Development Department (SAUO)
IdD .... South Bannock District Library, Downey Branch, Downey, ID [*Library symbol*] [*Library of Congress*] (LCLS)
IDDA .... Interior Decorators and Designers Association [*British*] (EAIO)
IDDA .... International Dairy-Deli Association (EA)
IDDAS .... Intelligent Dummy Data Acquisition System [*Crash testing*] [*Automotive engineering*]
IDDBA .... International Dairy Deli-Bakery Association (SAUO)
IDDC .... International Demographic Data Center [*Bureau of the Census*] [*Database*] [*Information service or system*] (IID)
IDDC .... International Development Data Center [*Georgia Institute of Technology*]
IDDD .... Intercontinental Direct Distance Dialling (SAUS)
IDDD .... International Demographic Data Directory [*Agency for International Development*] (IID)
IDDD .... International Direct Distance Dialing [*AT & T*]
IDDE .... Integrated Development and Debugging Environment [*Symantec Corp.*] [*Computer science*] (PCM)
IDDE .... Interactive Development and Debugging Environment (PCM)
IDDF .... Intermediate Data Distribution Facility (COE)
IDDF .... Intermediate Digital Distribution Frame [*Telecommunications*] (TEL)
Iddings DRB... Iddings' Dayton Term Reports [*Ohio*] [*A publication*] (DLA)
Iddings TRD... Iddings' Dayton Term Reports [*Ohio*] [*A publication*] (DLA)
IDDIS .... IDD Information Services, Inc. (IID)
IDDJ .... Interim Decisions of the Department of Justice
IDDL .... Interactive Database Design Laboratory [*Computer science*] (MHDB)
IDDL .... Intermediate Data Description Language (SAUS)
IdD-L .... South Bannock District Library, Lava Hot Springs Branch, Lava Hot Springs, ID [*Library symbol*] [*Library of Congress*] (LCLS)
IDDM .... Insulin-Dependent Diabetes Mellitus
IDDN .... Integrated Digital Defense Network (SAUS)
IDDP .... Interface Design Definition Paper [*Military*] (CAAL)
IDDP .... Interface Device-Dependent Port (SAUS)
IDDP .... International Dairy Development Programme [*FAO/DANIDA Dairy Development P rogramme and International Scheme for the Coordination of Dairy Development*] [*Formed by a merger of*] [*United Nations*] (EAIO)
IDDP .... Isodecyl Diphenyl Phosphate [*Organic chemistry*]
IDDRG .... International Deep Drawing Research Group [*British*]
IdDrGS .... Church of Jesus Christ of Latter-Day Saints, Genealogical Society Library, Driggs Branch, Driggs, ID [*Library symbol*] [*Library of Congress*] (LCLS)
IDDS .... Implantable Drug Delivery System [*Pharmacology*] (DAVI)
IDDS .... Improved Data Display System
IDDS .... Information Distribution and Display System (SAUO)
IDDS .... Institute for Defense and Disarmament Studies (EA)
IDDS .... Instrumentation Data Distribution System (MUGU)
IDDS .... Integrated Data Display System
IDDS .... Integrated Display Development Station (MCD)
IDDS .... International Dairy Development Scheme
IDDS .... International Digital Data Service [*Western Union Corp.*] [*Data transmission service*]
IDDSAC .... Interim Data Documentation Standard for ARC/INFO Averages (SAUO)
IDD TR .... Iddings' Dayton Term Reports [*Ohio*] [*A publication*] (DLA)
IDE .... Idea. The Journal of Law and Technology (journ.) (SAUS)
IDE .... Imbedded Drive Electronics [*Computer science*]
IDE .... Independent Development Environment [*Computer science*] (PCM)
IDE .... Industrial Development Equipment (SAUS)
IDE .... Industrial Development Executive (SAUO)
IDE .... Industrial Dynamics Electronics (SAUS)
IDE .... Industry-Developed Equipment (AAG)
IDE .... Information, Documentation, Evaluation (SAUS)
IDE .... Infrared Decoy Evaluator
IDE .... Initial Design Evaluation (MCD)
IDE .... Inner Dental Epithelium (DB)
IDE .... Innovative Design Expertise (SAUO)
IDE .... Institute for Democratic Education [*Absorbed by Anti-Defamation League of B'nai B'rith*] (EA)
IDE .... Institute for Developing Economics (SAUS)
IDE .... Institute of Developing Economics, Tokyo [*UTLAS symbol*]
IDE .... Institute of Diesel Engineers (SAUO)
IDE .... Insulin-Degrading Enzyme [*Biochemistry*]
IDE .... Integrated Development Environment
IDE .... Integrated Device Electronics
IDE .... Integrated Drive Electronics [*Hard disk interface*] [*Computer science*] (PCM)
IDE .... Intelligent Distributed Editor (HGAA)
IDE .... Intelligent Drive Electronics
IDE .... Interactive Data Entry
IDE .... Interactive Design and Engineering (SAUO)
IDE .... Interactive Development Environments, Inc. (SAUS)
IDE .... Interchange Data Element [*Telecommunications*] (OSI)
IDE .... Interdisciplinary Enquiry [*Education*] (AIE)
IDE .... Interface Design Enhancement (SAUS)
IDE .... Interim Data Element [*Army*] (AABC)
IDE .... Interior Design Engineering (SPST)
IDE .... Internal Display Element (SAUS)
IDE .... International Development Enterprises (SAUS)
IDE .... Intrusion Detection Equipment
IDE .... Investigational Device Exemption [*Food and Drug Administration*]
IDE .... Isla Desecheo [*Puerto Rico*] [*Seismograph station code, US Geological Survey*] (SEIS)
IDE .... Israel Desalination Engineering Ltd. (SAUO)
IDEA .... Centre for International Development Education and Action (SAUO)
IdEa .... Eagle Public Library, Eagle, ID [*Library symbol*] [*Library of Congress*] (LCLS)
IDEA .... ESPRIT Project (SAUS)
IDEA .... Ideas Deserving Exploratory Analysis (SAUS)
IDEA .... IDEAssociates, Inc. [*Telecommunications*] (TSSD)
IDEA .... Identification, Distribution, and Exchange for Action [*Project*]
IDEA .... Identify, Design, Execute, Augment (BB)
IDEA .... Identify, Develop, Expose, Act (TIMI)
IDEA .... Identify, Develop, Expose and Action (SAUS)
IDEA .... Illinois Drug Education Alliance (SAUO)
IDEA .... Improved Data Effectiveness and Availability
IDEA .... Index for Design Engineering Applications [*Data retrieval service*] [*Product engineering*]
IDEA .... Individuals with Disabilities Education Act [*Formerly, The Education for All Handicapped Children Act*] (PAZ)
IDEA .... Inductive Data Exploration and Analysis [*Computer science*]
IDEA .... Industrial Designers Excellence Award (SAUS)
IDEA .... Industrial Design Excellence Award
IDEA .... Industrial Design Exploiting Automation (SAUS)
IDEA .... Information Display Evolution and Advances (SAUO)
IDEA .... Innovasive Devices, Inc. [*NASDAQ symbol*] (SAG)
IDEA .... Innovation Development for Employment Advancement (SAUS)
I/D/E/A .... Institute for Development of Educational Activities (EA)
IDEA .... Institute of Diesel Engineers of Australia (SAUO)
IDEA .... Instructional Development and Effectiveness Assessment (SAUS)
IDEA .... Integrated Database Environment for Assessment of Drought (SAUS)
IDEA .... Integrated Data for Enforcement Analysis System [*Environmental science*]
IDEA .... Integrated Design Engineering Aid [*Computer science*] (RDA)
IDEA .... Integrated Digital Electric Aircraft (PDAA)
IDEA .... Integrated Digital Electronic Automatic (PDAA)
IDEA .... Integrated Dose Environment Analysis
IDEA .... Intelligence Design Assistant (ACAE)
IDEA .... Interactive Data Entry Access [*Data General Corp.*]
IDEA .... Interactive Data Extraction and Analysis (SAUO)
IDEA .... Interactive Differential Equation Algorithm (SAUO)
IDEA .... Interactive Digital Electronic Appliance [*Computer science*]
IDEA .... Interface and Display Electronics Assembly
IDEA .... International Association of Fitness Professionals (EA)
IDEA .... International Dalkon Shield Victims Education Association (EA)
IDEA .... International Dance-Exercise Association (EA)
IDEA .... International Data Encryption Algorithm [*Telecommunications*]
IDEA .... International Defence Economics Association (SAUO)
IDEA .... International Defence Equipment & Aerospace Exhibition (SAUS)
IDEA .... International Defence Equipment & Avionics Exhibition (SAUS)
IDEA .... International Desalination and Environmental Association [*Later, IDA*] (EA)
IDEA .... International Development Ethics Association (SAUO)
IDEA .... International Disability Education and Awareness (SAUO)
IDEA .... International District Energy Association (NTPA)
IDEA .... International Diving Educators Association
IDEA .... International Downtown Executives Association [*Later, IDA*] (EA)
IDEA .... International Drug Enforcement Association (SAUO)
IDEA .... International Institute for Democracy and Electoral Assistance
IDEA .... Internet Design, Engineering and Analysis notes (SAUS)
IDEA .... Invention, Design, Engineering Association, Inc. (SAUO)
IDEA .... Inverted Duplication Exchange and Advocacy (SAUO)
IDEA .... Investment, Development and Economic Assistance (SAUO)
IDEA .... Isolation of Dimensions and Elimination of Alternatives
Idea .... Patent, Trademark, and Copyright Journal of Research and Education [*A publication*] (DLA)
IDEA .... United Towns Centre for International Promotion of Innovation and Applied Research (SAUO)
IDEAL .... Identify, Define, Explore, Action, Lookback (BB)
IDEAL .... Identify [*the problem*], Define [*and represent*], Explore [*possible strategies*], Act [*on the strategies*], Look back [*and evaluate the effects of your actions*] [*Training term*] [*Problem Solving*] (LPT)
IDEAL .... Initiating, Diagnosing, Establishing, Acting, Leveraging
IDEAL .... Institute for Democracy and Leadership (SAUS)
IDEAL .... Integrated Design and Engineering Analysis Languages (ACAE)
IDEAL .... Integrated Design Engineering and Logistics (PDAA)
IDEAL .... Interactive Database Editor and Linker (SAUS)
IDEAL .... Interdisciplinary Drug Engineering and Assessment Laboratory [*Medicine*] (DB)
IDEAL .... International Decade of East African Lakes (QUAC)
IDEAL .... International Digital Electronic Access Library
IDEALS .... Information Directory of European Automated Library Services (TELE)
IDEALS .... Institute for the Development of Emotional and Life Skills (EA)
IDEALS .... Integrated Design of Effective and Logical Systems (SAUO)
IDEALS .... Intelligent Direct European Access to Library Systems (SAUS)
IDEAS .... Information in Disability-Equipmemt Access Service (ADWA)
IDEAS .... Information on Disability-Equipment, Access Service (SAUO)
IDEAS .... Innovations Deserving Exploratory Analysis Program [*FHWA*] (TAG)
IDEAS .... Inquiry Data Entry Access System (IAA)

IDEAS .... Institutional Development and Economic Affairs Service [*Defunct*] (EA)
IDEAS .... Integrated Design Analysis System [*Space shuttle*] [*NASA*]
IDEAS .... Integrated Design and Engineering Automated System (IEEE)
I-DEAS .... Integrated Design Engineering Analysis Software (SAUS)
IDEAS .... Integrated Design/Engineering/ Architectural System (SAUS)
IDEAS .... Intelligence Data Element Authorization Standards [*Military*] (MCD)
IDEAS .... Interactive Database Easy Access System (SAUS)
IDEAS .... Interactive Design and Evaluation of Advanced Spacecraft (SAUS)
IDEAS .... Interactive Document Easy Accessing System (SAUS)
IDEAS .... Interest Determination and Assessment System [*Vocational guidance test*]
IDEAS .... Interest Determination, Exploration, and Assessment System [*Test*] [*Charles B. Johansson*] (TES)
IDEAS .... Interior Department Electronic Acquisition System (SAUS)
IDEAS .... International Data Exchange for Aviation Safety [*ICAO*] (DA)
IDEAS .... International Decade of Exploration and Assessment of the Seas [*Inactive*] [*Marine science*] (OSRA)
IDEAS .... International Development - Economics Awareness System
IDEAS .... Intregrated Design and Analysis System (SAUS)
IDEAS .... Inverted Duplication Exchange and Advocacy and Support [*Founded in 1994*] (NRGU)
IDEAS System... Information Dissemination, Editing and Switching System (SAUS)
IDEB............ Intermittent Dual-Fluid Exhaust Burner
IDec............ Decatur Public Library, Decatur, IL [*Library symbol*] [*Library of Congress*] (LCLS)
IDEC............ IDEC Pharmaceuticals Corp. [*Associated Press*] (SAG)
IDEC............ Indirect Evaporative Cooler
IDEC............ Industrial and Domestic Equipment Corp. (SAUS)
IDEC............ Integrated Dynamic Echo Chancellation (SAUS)
IDEC............ Interior Design Educators Council (EA)
IDEC............ International Defence Equipment Catalogue (SAUO)
IDEC............ International Disaster Emergencies Committee (SAUO)
IDEC............ International Drug Enforcement Conference
IDECC.......... Interstate Distributive Education Curriculum Consortium (EDAC)
IDecH.......... Decatur Memorial Hospital, Medical Staff and Nursing School Library, Decatur, IL [*Library symbol*] [*Library of Congress*] (LCLS)
IDecJ .... James Millikin University, Decatur, IL [*Library symbol*] [*Library of Congress*] (LCLS)
IdEcL .... Elk City School/Community Library, Elk City, ID [*Library symbol*] [*Library of Congress*] (LCLS)
IDecM.......... Adolph Meyer Mental Health Center, Decatur, IL [*Library symbol*] [*Library of Congress*] (LCLS)
IDECO .... International Development Education Committee of Ontario (SAUS)
IDecR.......... Rolling Prairie Libraries, Decatur, IL [*Library symbol*] [*Library of Congress*] (LCLS)
IDecS.......... A.E. Staley Manufacturing Co., Decatur, IL [*Library symbol*] [*Library of Congress*] (LCLS)
IDECS .... Image Discrimination, Enhancement, and Combination System [*Electronic optical system*]
IDECS .... Image Discrimination, Enhancement, Combination and Sampling (SAUS)
IDecStM....... Saint Mary's Hospital, Medical Staff and Nursing Library, Decatur, IL [*Library symbol*] [*Library of Congress*] (LCLS)
ID/ED .... Internal Diameter to External Diameter [*Ratio for cardiac valve replacement*] [*Cardiology*] (DAVI)
IDEDS .... International Development Education Documentation Service [*University of Pittsburgh*] (IID)
IdEdS .... Silver & Gold Senior Citizens Library, Eden, ID [*Library symbol*] [*Library of Congress*] (LCLS)
IDEE............ Institute for Democracy in Eastern Europe (EA)
IDEE............ International Defence Electronic Exposition (SAUS)
IDEEA.......... Information and Data Exchange Experimental Activities
IDEEA.......... Information Development Experimental Exchange Activities (SAUO)
IDEEA.......... Instantaneous Drilling Evaluation Log (PDAA)
IDEEA.......... International Defense Equipment Exhibitors Association (EA)
IDEEA.......... International Design for Extreme Environments Association (SAUO)
IDEEA ONE... First International Design for Extreme Environments Assembly (SAUS)
IDEEC.......... Improved Digital Electronic Engine Control (SAUS)
IDEF............ ICAM Definition (MCD)
IDEF............ Institut International de Droit d'Expression Francaise [*International Institute of Law of the French Speaking Countries - IILFSC*] [*Paris, France*] (EAIO)
IDEF............ Integrated computer aided manufactoring Definition (SAUS)
IDEF............ Integrated Data Engineering Facility (RALS)
IDEF............ Integrated Data Exchange Facility (SAUO)
IDEF............ Integrated Definition (SAUS)
IDEF............ Integrated Definition for Function (SAUS)
IDEF............ Integrated (or Integration) Definition (SAUS)
IDEF............ Integrated System Definition Language [*Computer science*] (IEEE)
IDEF............ Intercept During Exo-atmospheric Fall (SAUS)
IDEF............ International Defence Industry & Civil Aviation Fair (SAUS)
IDEF-1 .... ICAM Definition Method One (SAUO)
IDEFIX .... Integration Definition for Information Modeling (SAUS)
IDEFO .... Integration Definition for Function Modeling (SAUS)
IDeKN .... Northern Illinois University, De Kalb, IL [*Library symbol*] [*Library of Congress*] (LCLS)
IDeKN-L....... Northern Illinois University, College of Law, De Kalb, IL [*Library symbol*] [*Library of Congress*] (LCLS)
IDeKN-LS..... Northern Illinois University, Department of Library Sciences, De Kalb, IL [*Library symbol*] [*Library of Congress*] (LCLS)
IDEL............ Instantaneous drilling evaluation log (SAUO)
IDelan.......... Goose Creek Township Carnegie Library, De Land, IL [*Library symbol*] [*Library of Congress*] (LCLS)
IDelanSD..... Bond County Community Unit, School District 2, De Land, IL [*Library symbol*] [*Library of Congress*] (LCLS)
IDelav.......... Ayer Public Library, Delavan, IL [*Library symbol*] [*Library of Congress*] (LCLS)
IDELR .... Individuals with Disabilities Education Law Report
IdEm .... Emmett Public Library, Emmett, ID [*Library symbol*] [*Library of Congress*] (LCLS)
IDEM............ Interactive Data Exchange Module (SAUS)
IDEM............ Interdepartmental Electronic Mail (SAUS)
IDEM............ International Defence Market Show (SAUS)
Idem .... Italian Derivatives Market (NUMA)
IDEMA .... International Disk Drive Equipment and Materials Association (NTPA)
IDEMIS .... International Demographic Information System (SAUS)
IDEMS .... Integrated Diagnostic Engine Monitoring System (SAUS)
IDEN .... Identification module (SAUS)
iDEN .... Integrated Digital Enhanced Network [*Telecommunications*]
IDEN .... Interactive Data Entry Network [*Computer science*] (MHDB)
IDENT .... Identical (MSA)
IDENT .... Identification (AFM)
Ident .... Identification [*Business term*] (EBF)
IDENT .... Identify (ECII)
IDENTGEN.... Identification Generator (SAUS)
IDENTIFD..... Identified (ROG)
Identificat.... Identification Data [*Aerospace*] (NAKS)
Identix .... Identix, Inc. [*Associated Press*] (SAG)
Identra System... Identification Train System (SAUS)
Ideo .... Ideological
Ideol Lit....... Ideologies and Literature. Institute for the Study of Ideologies and Literature. Minneapolis (journ.) (SAUS)
Ideon .... Ideon Group, Inc. [*Associated Press*] (SAG)
IDEON.......... Science Park in Lund (SAUS)
IDEP............ African Institute for Economic Development and Planning (SAUO)
IDEP............ African Institute for Economic Planning of the United Nations (SAUO)
IDep............ DePue Public Library, DePue, IL [*Library symbol*] [*Library of Congress*] (LCLS)
IDEP............ Industry Data Exchange Program
IDEP............ Institut Africain de Developpement Economique et de Planification [*African Institute for Economic Development and Planning*] [*Dakar, Senegal*] (AF)
IDEP............ Institute for Economic Development and Planning (SAUS)
IDEP............ Interagency Data Exchange Program [*Later, GIDEP*] (RDA)
IDEP............ Interagency Data Exchange Program Policy Board (SAUO)
IDEP............ Inter-Departmental Data Exchange Program (SAUO)
IDEP............ Inter-Department Data Exchange Program [*Air Force*] (AFM)
IDEP............ International and Development Education Program (SAUO)
IDEP............ International Data Exchange Program (NITA)
IDEP............ Interservice Data Exchange Program (AFIT)
IDEP............ Ion Density Electronics Package
IDEPAZ .... Institute for Development, Democracy and Peace (SAUO)
IDEPC .... IEMATS Data Entry Personal Computer (SAUS)
IDEPSCA .... Instituto de Educacion Popular del Sur de California
IDepSD .... DePue Unit, School District 103, DePue, IL [*Library symbol*] [*Library of Congress*] (LCLS)
IDEPT........... Image Document Entry Processing Terminal [*Computer science*] (CIST)
IdEr............. Elk River School/Community Library, Elk River, ID [*Library symbol*] [*Library of Congress*] (LCLS)
IDERA........... International Development Education Resources Association
i derm .... Intradermal [*Medicine*] (AAMN)
IDES............. Image Detail Enhancement System (SAUS)
IDES............. Image Dissector Echelle Spectrograph [*Instrumentation*]
IDES............. Incoterm Data Entry Software [*Incoterm*] (NITA)
IDES............. Information and Data Exchange System (IAA)
IDES............. Information/Documentation/ Education/Suisse (SAUS)
IDES............. Institute for Demographic and Economic Studies [*Research center*] (RCD)
IDES............. Integrated Defense System
IDES............. Integrated Design and Engineering System (SAUS)
IDES............. Interactive Data Entry System [*Computer science*] (MHDI)
IDES............. Interactive Doppler Editing Software (SAUS)
IDES............. Interactive Drawing Editing Station (MCD)
IDES............. International Demonstration and Education System (SAUS)
IDES............. Intrusion Detection Expert System (SAUS)
IDES............. Ionospheric Data Entry System (SAUO)
IDesA........... American Foundrymen's Society, Des Plaines, IL [*Library symbol*] [*Library of Congress*] (LCLS)
IDesB........... Borg-Warner Corp., Ingersoll Research Center, Des Plaines, IL [*Library symbol*] [*Library of Congress*] (LCLS)
IDesD........... De Soto, Inc., Des Plaines, IL [*Library symbol*] [*Library of Congress*] (LCLS)
IDesN........... National Association of Independent Insurers, Des Plaines, IL [*Library symbol*] [*Library of Congress*] (LCLS)
IDesS........... Signal Research Center, Inc., Des Plaines, IL [*Library symbol*] [*Library of Congress*] (LCLS)
IDESSA .... Institut des Savanes (SAUO)
IDesSC.......... Sandoz Crop Protection Corp., Des Plaines, IL [*Library symbol*] [*Library of Congress*] (LCLS)
IDESTA .... Identification and Statistic Evaluation of Process Data (SAUS)
IDesU........... Universal Oil Products Co., Des Plaines, IL [*Library symbol*] [*Library of Congress*] (LCLS)
IDET............. Institute for Development, Employment and Training (SAUS)
IDETX........... IDEX II: Growth Ptfl. Cl.A [*Mutual fund ticker symbol*] (SG)
Idex .... IDEX Corp. [*Associated Press*] (SAG)
IDEX............. Imagery Digital Exploitation (ACAE)
IDEX............. Initial Defense Experiment (IEEE)

IDEX............ International Defence Exhibition (SAUS)
IDEX II......... Imagery Digital Exploitation System (SAUO)
IdexxLb........ IDEXX Laboratories, Inc. [*Associated Press*] (SAG)
IDEZ............ Independent Explosive [*Federal Railroad Administration identification code*]
IDF............. Belleville Area College, Belleville, IL [*OCLC symbol*] (OCLC)
IDf............. Deerfield Public Library, Deerfield, IL [*Library symbol*] [*Library of Congress*] (LCLS)
IDF............. Iceland Defense Force (SAUO)
IDF............. Identifier (IAA)
IDF............. Identify (SAUS)
IDF............. Idiopathic Diffuse Fibrosis [*Medicine*] (MELL)
IDF............. Image Description File
IDF............. Immune Deficiency Foundation (EA)
IDF............. Incident Dark-Field (SAUS)
IDF............. Incremental-input Describing Function (SAUS)
IDF............. Indicating Direction Finder (IAA)
IDF............. Indigeneous Defence (or Defense) Fighter (SAUS)
IDF............. Indigenous Defense Fighter [*Military*]
IDF............. Industrial Development Fund (SAUO)
IDF............. Industrial Diesel Fuel
IDF............. Infantile Digital Fibromatosis [*Medicine*] (DB)
IDF............. In-Flight Diverted Force (CINC)
IDF............. Infrared Decoy Flare [*Military*]
IDF............. Ink Donor Film (EDCT)
IDF............. Innovative Design Fund, Inc. (EA)
IDF............. Input Data Flow (SAUS)
IDF............. Inquiry and Development Facility (VLIE)
IDF............. Instantaneous Direction Finding (MCD)
IDF............. Instanteneous Direction Finder (SAUS)
IDF............. Instructional Dialogue Facility (IAA)
IDF............. Instrumentation Data File (SAUS)
IDF............. Instrument Day-Fighter (SAUS)
IDF............. Integrated Data File
IDF............. Integrated Development Facility (ACAE)
IDF............. Intel Developer Forum (SAUO)
IDF............. Interactive Data Facility [*Computer science*] (VLIE)
IDF............. Interactive Dialogue Facility [*Programming language*] (CSR)
IDF............. Interceptor Day Fighter (NATG)
IDF............. Interior Design Institute (SAUS)
IDF............. Intermediate Distributing Frame [*Telecommunications*]
IDF............. Internal Data Format (ACAE)
IDF............. Internal Delay Factor [*Computer science*]
IDF............. Internal Distribution Frame [*Television*] (IAA)
IDF............. International Dairy Federation [*See also FIL*] [*Brussels, Belgium*] (EAIO)
IDF............. International Democratic Fellowship
IDF............. International Dental Federation [*British*]
IDF............. International Development Foundation (EA)
IDF............. International Diabetes Federation [*See also FID*] (EAIO)
IDF............. International Distress Frequency (MUGU)
IDF............. International Domesticated Furs Ltd. [*Vancouver Stock Exchange symbol*]
IDF............. International Drilling Federation (EA)
IDF............. International Drilling Fluids [*Singapore*]
IDF............. Intestinal Disease Foundation (NRGU)
IDF............. Inverse Document Frequency (NITA)
IDF............. Iron Dragon-Fly Ltd. [*Russian Federation*] [*ICAO designator*] (FAAC)
IDF............. Isotropic Distribution Function
IDF............. Israel Defence Force (SAUS)
IDF............. Israeli Defense Forces
IDF............. Item Data File (MCD)
IdFa............ Camas County District Library, Fairfield, ID [*Library symbol*] [*Library of Congress*] (LCLS)
IDFA............ Infant and Dietetic Foods Association [*British*] (DBA)
IDFA............ International Dairy Foods Association (EA)
IDFA............ Irish Dryers and Finishers Association (SAUO)
IDF/AF.......... Israeli Defense Force/Air Force (SAUO)
IDFAIP.......... International Development Fund to Assist Indigenous Peoples of the Russian North (SAUO)
IDFB............ Internationales Daunen- und Federn-Bureau [*International Down and Feather Bure au*] (EAIO)
IDFC............ Identification Field Checking (SAUS)
IDFC............ Immature Dead Female Child [*Neonatology*] (DAVI)
IDFC............ Indo-Pacific Fisheries Council (SAUO)
IdFe............ Tri-Community Library, Fernwood, ID [*Library symbol*] [*Library of Congress*] (LCLS)
IDFF............ Internationale Demokratische Frauenfoederation [*Women's International Democratic Federation*]
IDFG............ Idaho Department of Fish and Game (SAUO)
IdFh............ Shoshone-Bannock Library, Fort Hall, ID [*Library symbol*] [*Library of Congress*] (LCLS)
IdFi............ Filer Public Library, Filer, ID [*Library symbol*] [*Library of Congress*] (LCLS)
IDFM............ Induced Directional FM
IDFN............ In Domino Fiducia Nostra [*In the Lord Is Our Trust*] [*Motto of August, Prince of Anhalt-Plotzkau (1575-1653)*] [*Latin*]
IDFOR........... Idle Waiting Convoy Forward [*Vessel status*] [*Navy*]
IdFr............ Franklin County District Library, Franklin, ID [*Library symbol*] [*Library of Congress*] (LCLS)
IDFR............ Identified Friendly [*Military*]
IDFS............ Interferometer Direction Finding System [*Military*] (CAAL)
IDFSS........... Infantry Direct-Fire Simulation System (MCD)
IDFSS........... Infantry Direct-Fire Simulator System (SAUO)
IDFT............ Inverse Discrete Fourier Transform [*Electronics*] (IEEE)
IDfT............ Trinity Evangelical Divinity School, Deerfield, IL [*Library symbol*] [*Library of Congress*] (LCLS)
IDFTA........... International Dwarf Fruit Trees Association (EA)
IDfTD........... Trinity Evangelical Divinity School, Deerfield, IL [*Library symbol*] [*Library of Congress*] (LCLS)
IDFUN........... International Dull Folks Unlimited [*Defunct*] (EA)
IDFV............ In Deo Faciemus Virtutem [*Through God We Shall Do Valiantly*] [*(Ps., IX. 12) Motto of August, Prince of Anhalt-Plotzkau (1575-1653)*] [*Latin*]
IDFW............ Institute for a Drug-Free Workplace (EA)
IDG............. Chicago Theological Seminary, Chicago, IL [*OCLC symbol*] (OCLC)
IDG............. Ida Grove, IA [*Location identifier*] [*FAA*] (FAAL)
IDG............. Immunodiffusion in Gel (PDAA)
IDG............. Indigo Technologies, Inc. [*Vancouver Stock Exchange symbol*]
IDG............. Individual Drop Glider
IDG............. Industrial Development Group (MCD)
IDG............. Industrial Distribution Grp. [*NYSE symbol*] (SG)
IDG............. Inniskilling Dragoon Guards [*British military*] (DMA)
IDG............. Inspector of Degaussing [*Navy*]
IDG............. Integrated Drive Generator (MCD)
IDG............. Inter-Dialog Gap (VLIE)
IDG............. Interdisciplinary Group (STED)
IDG............. Intermediate-Dose Group [*Medicine*] (STED)
IDG............. Internal Drive Generator
IDG............. International Data Group [*Publisher of computer magazines*] [*Framingham, MA*]
IdGa............ Garden Valley District Library, Garden Valley, ID [*Library symbol*] [*Library of Congress*] (LCLS)
IdGc............ Garden City Public Library, Garden City, ID [*Library symbol*] [*Library of Congress*] (LCLS)
IDG/CMG......... IDG Conference Management Group [*Framingham, MA*] (TSSD)
IDGE............ Isothermal Dendrite (or Dendritic) Growth Experiment (SAUS)
IdGf............ Glenns Ferry Public Library, Glenns Ferry, ID [*Library symbol*] [*Library of Congress*] (LCLS)
IdGg............ Grangeville Public Library, Grangeville, ID [*Library symbol*] [*Library of Congress*] (LCLS)
IdGi............ Gibbonsville Community Library, Gibbonsville, ID [*Library symbol*] [*Library of Congress*] (LCLS)
IDGI............ International Design Group, Inc. (SAUO)
IDGIT........... Integrated Data Generation Implementation Technique
IdGo............ Gooding Public Library, Gooding, ID [*Library symbol*] [*Library of Congress*] (LCLS)
IdGoPS.......... Gooding Public School District, Gooding, ID [*Library symbol*] [*Library of Congress*] (LCLS)
IdGoS........... Idaho State School for the Deaf and Blind, Gooding, ID [*Library symbol*] [*Library of Congress*] (LCLS)
IDGP............ Illawarra Division of General Practice (SAUO)
IDGPRT.......... Indigo Print (SAUS)
IdGr............ Grace District Library, Grace, ID [*Library symbol*] [*Library of Congress*] (LCLS)
ID Grinding..... Inner Diameter Grinding (SAUS)
ID Grinding..... Internal Grinding (SAUS)
IDGS............ Isotope-Dilution Gamma Spectrometry (SAUS)
IDGSS........... Integrated Digital Grid Switching System (SAUO)
IdGv............ Eastern Owyhee County District Library, Grand View, ID [*Library symbol*] [*Library of Congress*] (LCLS)
IDH............. Infectious Diseases Hospital (SAUO)
IDH............. IPI, Inc. [*AMEX symbol*] (SG)
IDH............. Isocitrate Dehydrogenase [*Also, ICD, ICDH*] [*An enzyme*]
IDH............. Isocitric Acid Dehydrogenase (STED)
IDH............. Meadville Theological School, Chicago, IL [*OCLC symbol*] (OCLC)
IDH1............ Isocitrate Dehydrogenase, Soluble (STED)
IDH2............ Isocitrate Dehydrogenase Mitochondrial (STED)
IDHA............ International District Heating Association [*Later, IDHCA*] (EA)
IdHamSD......... Hamer Elementary School, Hamer, ID [*Library symbol*] [*Library of Congress*] (LCLS)
IdHb............ Horseshoe Bend District Library, Horseshoe Bend, ID [*Library symbol*] [*Library of Congress*] (LCLS)
IDHC............ International District Heating Conference (SAUO)
IDHCA........... International District Heating and Cooling Association (EA)
ID HE........... Index Head (SAUS)
IDHE............ Institute of Domestic Heating Engineers (SAUO)
IDHEC........... Institut des Hautes Etudes Cinematographiques [*French institute for the study of the motion picture*]
IDHF............ International Dental Health Foundation (EA)
IdHg............ Hagerman Public Library, Hagerman, ID [*Library symbol*] [*Library of Congress*] (LCLS)
IDHHB........... Institute for the Development of the Harmonious Human Being (EA)
IdHi............ Idaho State Historical Society, Boise, ID [*Library symbol*] [*Library of Congress*] (LCLS)
IDHIDH.......... In dem Herrn Ist das Heil [*In the Lord Is Salvation*] [*Motto of Dorothee, Princess of Anhalt (1580-1618)*] [*German*]
IdHi-G.......... Idaho Genealogical Society, Boise, ID [*Library symbol*] [*Library of Congress*] (LCLS)
IdHl............ Hailey Public Library, Hailey, ID [*Library symbol*] [*Library of Congress*] (LCLS)
IdHlH........... Blaine County Medical Center, Medical Library, Hailey, ID [*Library symbol*] [*Library of Congress*] (LCLS)
IdHm............ Homedale Public Library, Homedale, ID [*Library symbol*] [*Library of Congress*] (LCLS)
IdHn............ Hansen Public Library, Hansen, ID [*Library symbol*] [*Library of Congress*] (LCLS)
IdHr............ Harrison Public Library, Harrison, ID [*Library symbol*] [*Library of Congress*] (LCLS)

IDH-RH .... Institute for Research, Documentation and Human Rights (Dominican Rep.) [*Political party*] (PSAP)
IDHS .... Information Data Handling System
IDHS .... Integrated Data Handling System
IDHS .... Intelligence Data Handling System (AFM)
IDH-S .... Isocitrate Dehydrogenase, Soluble (STED)
IDHSC .... Intelligence Data Handling System Communications (MCD)
IDHSS .... Intelligence Data Handling Support System (ACAE)
IDHT .... Instrument Data-Handling and Transmission (SAUS)
IDHT .... Instruments Data Handling and Transmission Subsystem (SAUS)
IDHTS .... Instrument Data Handling and Transmission System (ACAE)
IDHW .... Idaho Department of Health and Welfare (EEVL)
IdHyl .... Hayden Lake Library, Hayden Lake, ID [*Library symbol*] [*Library of Congress*] (LCLS)
IDI .... Bethany and Northern Baptist Theological Seminaries Library, Oak Brook, IL [*OCLC symbol*] (OCLC)
IDI .... Illegal Declaration of Independence (SAUO)
IDI .... Imaging Doppler Interferometer (SAUS)
IDI .... Immediate Data Input [*Computer science*] (VLIE)
IDI .... Immunologically Detectable Insulin [*Medicine*] (DMAA)
IDI .... Implantable Defibrillator Insertion [*Medicine*] (MELL)
IDI .... Improved Data Interchange
IDI .... Indiana, PA [*Location identifier*] [*FAA*] (FAAL)
IDI .... Indian Development Institute (SAUO)
IDI .... Indirect Injection Engine [*Engineering*]
IDI .... Induction-Delivery Interval [*Medicine*]
IDI .... Industrial Designers' Institute [*Later, IDSA*] (EA)
IDI .... Industrial Development Institute [*France*]
IDI .... Infor Development International (SAUO)
IDI .... Information Dimensions, Inc. [*Information service or system*] (IID)
IDI .... Information Dimensions, Incorporated (SAUO)
IDI .... Information Displays, Incorporated (SAUO)
IDI .... Initial Domain Identifier [*Computer science*] (TNIG)
IDI .... Initial Domain Part [*Telecommunications*] (OSI)
IDI .... Inspection Departmental Instruction (AAG)
IDI .... Instant Drug Index [*A publication*] (DAVI)
IDI .... Institut de Droit International [*Institute of International Law*]
IDI .... Instructional Dynamics, Inc. (AEBS)
IDI .... Instrumentation Data Items (NASA)
IDI .... Instrumentation Development and Intercomparisons (SAUS)
IDI .... Instrument Detection Limit (ABAC)
IDI .... Insurance Department and Inspectorate (SAUO)
IDI .... Integrated Design Inspection (NRCH)
IDI .... Integrated Direct Ignition [*Automotive engineering*]
IDI .... Intelligent Dual Interface
IDI .... Intercomp Design, Inc. [*Neshanic Station, NJ*] [*Telecommunications*] (TSSD)
IDI .... Inter-Dentale Inferius [*Medicine*] (DMAA)
IDI .... Interdivision Invoice (AAG)
IDI .... International Defense Intelligence (journ.) (SAUS)
IDI .... International Development and Investment Co. (SAUO)
IDI .... International Development Institute [*Agency for International Development program*]
IDI .... International Diabetes Institute [*Australia*] (IRC)
IDI .... International Dialect Institute
IDI .... International Disaster Institute [*British*]
IDI .... Interrupt Digital Inputs (ACAE)
IDI .... Intractable Diarrhea of Infancy [*Pediatrics*]
IDI .... Intradiskal Injection [*Medicine*] (MELL)
IDI .... Ion Dipole Interaction
IDI .... Iron Disorders Institute
IDI .... Omproved Data Interchange (SAUS)
IDIA .... Industrial Design Institute of Australia (SAUO)
IDIA .... Industrial Disputes Investigation Act [*Canada*]
IDIA .... Internal Defense Identification Area (SAA)
IDIA .... International Digital Imaging Association (NTPA)
IDIAD .... Internal Defense and Internal Development (SAUO)
IDiagE .... Institution of Diagnostic Engineers (COBU)
I-DIAS .... Improved Defensive Integrated Avionics System (SAUS)
IDIB .... Industrial Diamond Information Bureau [*British*] (BI)
IdIc .... Boise Basin District Library, Idaho City, ID [*Library symbol*] [*Library of Congress*] (LCLS)
IDIC .... Industrial Development and Investment Center (SAUS)
IDIC .... Infinite Diversity in Infinite Combinations (ADWA)
IDIC .... Institut de Developpement International et de Cooperation [*Institute for International Development and Cooperation IIDC*] [*University of Ottawa*] [*Canada*]
IDIC .... Intelligence Division Indications Center [*Military*] (MCD)
IDIC .... Internal Dose Information Center [*ORNL*]
IDIC .... International Drought Information Center
IDIC .... Islamic Documentation and Information Centre (SAUO)
IDIC .... Islamic Documentation Information Center (SAUS)
IDID .... Comparator Sys [*NASDAQ symbol*] (TTSB)
IDID .... Comparator Systems Corp. [*NASDAQ symbol*] (SAG)
IDID .... Induced Dipole-Induced Dipole (SAUS)
IDID .... Industrial Documentation and Information Department [*Industrial Development Center for Arab States*] [*Information service or system*] (IID)
IDID .... Internal Defense/Internal Development (SAUO)
IDIDAS .... Interactive Digital Image Display and Analysis System [*Marine science*] (OSRA)
IdIf .... Idaho Falls Public Library, Idaho Falls, ID [*Library symbol*] [*Library of Congress*] (LCLS)
IdIfA .... Aerojet Nuclear Co., Idaho Falls, ID [*Library symbol*] [*Library of Congress*] (LCLS)
IdIfAL .... Argonne National Laboratory, Argonne-West Technical Library, Idaho Falls, ID [*Library symbol*] [*Library of Congress*] (LCLS)
IdIfC .... Bonneville County District Library, Idaho Falls, ID [*Library symbol*] [*Library of Congress*] (LCLS)
IdIfE .... Energy Incorp., Idaho Falls, ID [*Library symbol*] [*Library of Congress*] (LCLS)
IdIfEG .... EG & G Idaho, Inc., INEL Technical Library, Idaho Falls, ID [*Library symbol*] [*Library of Congress*] (LCLS)
IdIfGS .... Church of Jesus Christ of Latter-Day Saints, Genealogical Society Library, IdahoFalls Branch, Idaho Falls, ID [*Library symbol*] [*Library of Congress*] (LCLS)
IdIfH .... Eastern Idaho Regional Medical Center, Medical Library, Idaho Falls, ID [*Library symbol*] [*Library of Congress*] (LCLS)
IDIIOM .... IDI Input Output Machine (SAUS)
IDIIOM .... Information Displays, Incorporated, Input-Output Machine
IDIL .... Institute for the Development of Indian Law (EA)
IDIM .... Integrated Departmental Instructions Manual
IDIMS .... Interactive Data Integration and Management System (SAUO)
IDIMS .... Interactive Digital Image Manipulation System [*Minicomputer*]
IDIN .... Iowa Drug Information Network (SAUO)
Idings TRD ... Iddings' Dayton Term Reports [*Ohio*] [*A publication*] (DLA)
idio .... idiograph (SAUS)
idio .... idiomatic (SAUS)
IDIOT .... Ice Depth Instrument Operator Transportable (SAUS)
IDIOT .... Instrumentation Digital On-Line Transcriber [*Computer science*]
IDIP .... Intelligence Data Input Package (MCD)
IDIP .... Intensified Drug Inspection Program [*FDA*]
IDIP .... International Directories in Print [*A publication*]
IDIPS .... Institute for Domestic and International Policy Studies (SAUO)
IDIQ .... Indefinite Delivery, Indefinite Quantity [*Type of contract*] (AAGC)
IDIS .... Idaho Drug Information Service [*Information service or system*] (IID)
IDIS .... Information Discovery System (HODG)
IDIS .... Institut fuer Dokumentation, Information, und Statistik [*Institute for Documentation, Information, and Statistics*] [*Information service or system*] (IID)
IDIS .... Institut fuer Dokumentation und Information ueber Sozialmedizin und Oeffentliches Gesundheitswesen [*Institute for Documentation and Information in Social Medicine and Public Health*] [*Information retrieval*] [*Germany*]
IDIS .... Integrated Dealer and Importer System (SAUS)
IDIS .... Integrated Driver Information System [*Automotive electronics*]
IDIS .... Interdisciplinary Studies (SAUS)
IDIS .... International Dairy Industry Society (SAUO)
IDIS .... International Directory Inquiry System (SAUS)
IDIS .... International Dismantling Information System [*Recycling*]
IDIS .... Intrusion Detection and Identification System (PDAA)
IDIS .... Iowa Drug Information Service [*University of Iowa*] [*Information service or system*] (IID)
IDISA .... Intraoperative Digital Subtraction Angiography [*Medicine*] (EDAA)
IDIS&RPCC ... Idaho Drug Information Service and Regional Poison Control Center (SAUO)
IDITEM .... Identifier Item (SAUS)
IDIU .... Interdepartmental Intelligence Unit (SAUO)
IDIU .... Interdivisional Information Unit [*Department of Justice intelligence unit*]
IDIU .... Interdivisional Intelligence Unit (SAUO)
IDIV .... Integer Divide (SAUS)
IDJ .... Catholic Theological Union, Chicago, IL [*OCLC symbol*] (OCLC)
IDJ .... I Dance Jazz [*Jazz music group*] (ECON)
IDJ .... Information Design Journal [*A publication*] (DGA)
IDJ .... International Dental Journal (SAUO)
IdJ .... Jerome Public Library, Jerome, ID [*Library symbol*] [*Library of Congress*] (LCLS)
IDJC .... India Docks Joint Committee (ROG)
IdJH .... Saint Benedict's Family Medical Center, Medical Library, Jerome, ID [*Library symbol*] [*Library of Congress*] (LCLS)
IdK .... Community Library Association, Inc., Ketchem, ID [*Library symbol*] [*Library of Congress*] (LCLS)
IDK .... Internal Derangement of Knee [*Medicine*] (DMAA)
IDK .... Internal Derangement of Knee Joint
IDK .... Jesuit-Krauss-McCormick Library, Chicago, IL [*OCLC symbol*] (OCLC)
IdKe .... Kellogg Public Library, Kellogg, ID [*Library symbol*] [*Library of Congress*] (LCLS)
IDKH .... I Don't Know How (VLIE)
IdKi .... Kimberly Public Library, Kimberly, ID [*Library symbol*] [*Library of Congress*] (LCLS)
IdKo .... Kooskia Public Library, Kooskia, ID [*Library symbol*] [*Library of Congress*] (LCLS)
IdKu .... Kuna School/Comm Library, Kuna, ID [*Library symbol*] [*Library of Congress*] (LCLS)
IDL .... Idaho Department of Lands (SAUO)
Id-L .... Idaho Supreme Court, Idaho State Law Library, Boise, ID [*Library symbol*] [*Library of Congress*] (LCLS)
IDL .... Ideal
IDL .... Ideal Basic Industries, Inc. (SAUO)
IDL .... Ideal Group of Companies, Inc. [*Toronto Stock Exchange symbol*]
idl .... Idle (ELAL)
IDL .... Idler
IDL .... Indentured Drawing List
IDL .... Index to Dental Literature (STED)
IDL .... Indianola, MS [*Location identifier*] [*FAA*] (FAAL)
IDL .... Industrial Design Laboratory (SAUO)
ID(L) .... Infantry Division (Light) [*Army*] (INF)
IDL .... Information Description Language

IDL....... Insertion-Deletion Loop-Type [*Genetics*]
IDL....... Instructional Development Laboratory [*University of Minnesota of Minneapolis Saint Paul*] [*Research center*] (RCD)
IDL....... Instruction Definition Language
IDL....... Instrumentation Development Laboratories (SAUS)
IDL....... Instrument Detection Level [*Analytical chemistry*]
IDL....... Instrument Detection Limit (SAUS)
IDL....... Instrument Development Laboratories
IDL....... Integrated Device Logic (SAUS)
IDL....... Intelligent Database Language (SAUS)
IDL....... Intensity Difference Limen (STED)
IDL....... Interactive Data Language [*Marine science*] (OSRA)
IDL....... Interactive Data Librarian (TIMI)
IDL....... Interactive Display Language (SAUS)
IDL....... Interdisciplinary Materials Laboratory [*Various universities*]
IDL....... Interdisciplinary Research Laboratory (SAUS)
IDL....... Interdiscrepancy Laboratory (SAUO)
IDL....... Interface Definition Language [*Computer science*]
IDL....... Interface Description Language (SAUS)
IDL....... Interfacility Data Link [*FAA*] (TAG)
IDL....... Intermediate Density Lipoprotein [*Biochemistry*]
IDL....... International Data Line (SAUS)
IDL....... International Data Link (SAUS)
IDL....... International Date Line (MCD)
IDL....... Internet Definition Language (SAUS)
IDL....... Isotope Development Limited (SAUO)
IDL....... Isotope Development Ltd.
IdL....... Lewiston City Library, Lewiston, ID [*Library symbol*] [*Library of Congress*] (LCLS)
IDL....... Rush University, Chicago, IL [*OCLC symbol*] (OCLC)
IDL & RS....... International Data Library and Reference Service
IDLC....... Integrated Digital Logic Circuit
IDLC....... Integrated Digital Loop Carrier [*Telecommunications*] (ACRL)
IDLE....... Idaho Department of Law Enforcement (SAUO)
IDLE....... International Date Line East (SAUS)
IdLe....... Leadore Community Library, Leadore, ID [*Library symbol*] [*Library of Congress*] (LCLS)
IdLES....... Lewiston Elementary Schools, Lewiston, ID [*Library symbol*] [*Library of Congress*] (LCLS)
IdLES-CM....... Lewiston Elementary Schools, Camelot Elementary School, Lewiston, ID [*Library symbol*] [*Library of Congress*] (LCLS)
IdLES-CN....... Lewiston Elementary Schools, Centennial Elementary School, Lewiston, ID [*Library symbol*] [*Library of Congress*] (LCLS)
IdLES-MG....... Lewiston Elementary Schools, McGhee Elementary School, Lewiston, ID [*Library symbol*] [*Library of Congress*] (LCLS)
IdLES-MS....... Lewiston Elementary Schools, McSorley Elementary School, Lewiston, ID [*Library symbol*] [*Library of Congress*] (LCLS)
IdLES-OR....... Lewiston Elementary Schools, Orchards Elementary School, Lewiston, ID [*Library symbol*] [*Library of Congress*] (LCLS)
IdLES-WB....... Lewiston Elementary Schools, Webster Elementary School, Lewiston, ID [*Library symbol*] [*Library of Congress*] (LCLS)
IdLES-WH....... Lewiston Elementary Schools, Whitman Elementary School, Lewiston, ID [*Library symbol*] [*Library of Congress*] (LCLS)
IdLGS....... Church of Jesus Christ of Latter-Day Saints, Genealogical Society Library, Lewiston Branch, Stake Center, Lewiston, ID [*Library symbol*] [*Library of Congress*] (LCLS)
IDLH....... Immediate Danger to Life and Health (SAUS)
IDLH....... Immediately Dangerous to Life and/or Health (SAUS)
IDLHC....... Immediately Dangerous to Life or Health Concentration [*Toxicology*]
IdLHS....... Lewiston High School, Lewiston, ID [*Library symbol*] [*Library of Congress*] (LCLS)
IdLI....... Independent School District No. 1, Lewiston, ID [*Library symbol*] [*Library of Congress*] (LCLS)
IDLIB....... Item Description Library (SAUS)
IdLI-C....... Independent School District No. 1, Curriculum Resource Center, Lewiston, ID [*Library symbol*] [*Library of Congress*] (LCLS)
IDLIS....... International Desert Locust Information Service
ID LJ....... Idaho Law Journal [*A publication*] (DLA)
IdLN....... Lewis-Clark State College, Lewiston, ID [*Library symbol*] [*Library of Congress*] (LCLS)
IdLNP....... Nez Perce County Free Library District, Lewiston, ID [*Library symbol*] [*Library of Congress*] (LCLS)
IdLNP-Cu....... Nez Perce County District Library, Culdesac Branch, Culdesac, ID [*Library symbol*] [*Library of Congress*] (LCLS)
IdLNP-L....... Nez Perce County District Library, Lapwai Branch, Lapwai, ID [*Library symbol*] [*Library of Congress*] (LCLS)
IdLNP-N....... Nez Perce County District Library, Nez Perce Branch, Nez Perce, ID [*Library symbol*] [*Library of Congress*] (LCLS)
IdLNP-P....... Nez Perce County District Library, Peck Branch, Peck, ID [*Library symbol*] [*Library of Congress*] (LCLS)
IdLNP-W....... Nez Perce County District Library, Winchester Branch, Winchester, ID [*Library symbol*] [*Library of Congress*] (LCLS)
IDLOD....... Idle Waiting to Load [*Shipping*]
IDLR....... Instrumentation Development Laboratory Report (MCD)
IDLS....... Integrated Decoy Launching System [*Navy*] (CAAL)
IDLSG....... International Drycleaners and Launderers Study Group (SAUO)
IdLSJH....... Saint Joseph's Hospital, Medical Library, Lewiston, ID [*Library symbol*] [*Library of Congress*] (LCLS)
IDLT....... Identification Light
IDLT....... Increment-Decrement Life Table [*Statistics*]
IDLW....... International Date Line West (SAUS)
IDLWD....... Idlewild, OH [*American Association of Railroads railroad junction routing code*]
IDM....... Idiopathic Disease of the Myocardium [*Cardiology*] (MAE)
IDM....... IDM Environmental Corp. [*Associated Press*] (SAG)
IDM....... Ignition Diagnostic Monitor [*Automotive engineering*]
IDM....... Illicit Diamond Mining (SAUS)
IDM....... Illinois Valley Library System, Pekin, IL [*OCLC symbol*] (OCLC)
IDM....... Image Data Manager (SAUS)
IDM....... Immune Defense Mechanism [*Medicine*] (DMAA)
IDM....... Impact Delay Module (SAUS)
IDM....... Improved Data Modem [*Air Force*] (DOMA)
IDM....... Indirect Method
IDM....... Induced Dipole Moment
IDM....... Inductive Debris Monitor (SAUS)
IDM....... Industrial Data Management (SAUS)
IDM....... Infant of Diabetic Mother [*Medicine*]
IDM....... Information and Data Management (SSD)
IDM....... Information Distribution Manager (SAUS)
IDM....... Information Document Matching Program [*IRS*]
IDM....... Initial Draft Manuscript (SAUO)
IDM....... Injector Driver Module [*Automotive term*] (HAWK)
IDM....... Instant Dimmer Memory (IAA)
IDM....... Institute of Defense Management (SAUS)
IDM....... Instructional Diagram Manual (SAUS)
IDM....... Integral and Differential Monitoring [*Telecommunications*] (OA)
IDM....... Integrated Data Management (TIMI)
IDM....... Integrated Defense Model (ACAE)
IDM....... Integrated Delta Modulation (IAA)
IDM....... Integrated Design Methodology [*Electrical engineering*]
IDM....... Integrated Diagnostic Model (ACAE)
IDM....... Integrated Direct Metering (SAUS)
IDM....... Integrated Document Management (SAUS)
IDM....... Integrating Delta Modulation (SAUS)
IDM....... Integrative Decision Making (MCD)
IDM....... Intelligent Database Machine [*Computer science*]
IDM....... Intelligent Data Management (ACAE)
IDM....... Intelligent Data Mapper (SAUS)
IDM....... Intelligent Document Management [*Computer science*]
IDM....... Interactive Data Machines [*British*] (NITA)
IDM....... Interactive Decision Making (SAUS)
IDM....... Interdepartmental Meeting (SAUO)
IDM....... Interdiction Mission [*Air Force*]
IDM....... Intermediate-Dose Methotrexate [*Medicine*] (DMAA)
IDM....... International Development and Management (SAUO)
IDM....... International Direct Mail [*British*]
IDM....... Interpolating Delta Modulator
IDM....... Ion Drift Meter [*Instrumentation*]
IDM....... Issue Definition Memorandum [*Jimmy Carter Administration*]
IDMA....... Insurance Data Management Association
IDMA....... International Dancing Masters Association (BARN)
IDMA....... International Destination Management Association (EAIO)
IDMA....... International Diamond Manufacturers Association (SAUO)
IDMA....... International Doll Makers Association (EA)
IDMA....... Isaac Delgado Museum of Art (SAUO)
IdMa....... Oneida County District Library, Malad City, ID [*Library symbol*] [*Library of Congress*] (LCLS)
IdMac....... Mackay District Library, Mackay, ID [*Library symbol*] [*Library of Congress*] (LCLS)
IdMaGS....... Church of Jesus Christ of Latter-Day Saints, Genealogical Society Library, MaladStake Branch, Malad City, ID [*Library symbol*] [*Library of Congress*] (LCLS)
IDMA-Internationals... International Doll Makers Association-Internationals (SAUO)
IDMAPL....... Integrated Developers and Managers Associates Pvt. Ltd. (SAUO)
IdMar....... Lizard Butte District Library, Marsing, ID [*Library symbol*] [*Library of Congress*] (LCLS)
IDMAS....... Interactive Database Manipulator and Summarizer
IDMB....... International Dictionary of Medicine and Biology [*A publication*]
IDMC....... IDM Environmental [*NASDAQ symbol*] (TTSB)
IDMC....... IDM Environmental Corp. [*NASDAQ symbol*] (SAG)
IDMC....... Immature Dead Male Child [*Neonatology*] (DAVI)
IDMC....... Immune Defence Mechanism [*Medicine*] (EDAA)
IDMC....... Interdigestive Motility Complex [*Gastroenterology*]
IDMC....... International Dull Men's Club (EA)
IdMC....... Moscow-Latah County Library System, Moscow, ID [*Library symbol*] [*Library of Congress*] (LCLS)
IdMC-D....... Moscow-Latah County District Library, Deary Branch, Deary, ID [*Library symbol*] [*Library of Congress*] (LCLS)
IdMC-G....... Moscow-Latah County District Library, Genesee Branch, Genesee, ID [*Library symbol*] [*Library of Congress*] (LCLS)
IdMC-J....... Moscow-Latah County District Library, Juliaetta Branch, Juliaetta, ID [*Library symbol*] [*Library of Congress*] (LCLS)
IDM Conference... International Datacenter Management Conference (SAUS)
IdMcP....... McCall Public Library, McCall, ID [*Library symbol*] [*Library of Congress*] (LCLS)
IdMC-P....... Moscow-Latah County District Library, Potlatch Branch, Potlatch, ID [*Library symbol*] [*Library of Congress*] (LCLS)
IdMC-T....... Moscow-Latah County District Library, Troy Branch, Troy, ID [*Library symbol*] [*Library of Congress*] (LCLS)
IDMCW....... IDM Environmental Wrrt'A' [*NASDAQ symbol*] (TTSB)
IDMD....... Idiopathic Dystonia Musculorum Deformans [*Medicine*] (EDAA)
IdMe....... Meridian Library District, Meridian, ID [*Library symbol*] [*Library of Congress*] (LCLS)
IdMen....... Jefferson County District Library, Menan Branch, Menan, ID [*Library symbol*] [*Library of Congress*] (LCLS)
IdMen-H....... Jefferson County District Library, Hamer Branch, Hamer, ID [*Library symbol*] [*Library of Congress*] (LCLS)
IdMen-HV....... Jefferson County District Library, Heart of the Valley Branch, Terreton, ID [*Library symbol*] [*Library of Congress*] (LCLS)

IdMenSD...... School District No. 251, Menan, ID [*Library symbol*] [*Library of Congress*] (LCLS)
IDM Env...... IDM Environmental Corp. [*Associated Press*] (SAG)
IdMGH........ Gritman Memorial Hospital, Medical Library, Moscow, ID [*Library symbol*] [*Library of Congress*] (LCLS)
IDMH.......... Input Destination Message Handler
IdMh.......... Mountain Home Public Library, Mountain Home, ID [*Library symbol*] [*Library of Congress*] (LCLS)
IdMhAF........ United States Air Force, Mountain Home Air Force Base Library, Mountain Home, ID [*Library symbol*] [*Library of Congress*] (LCLS)
IdMhH......... Elmore Memorial Hospital, Medical Library, Mountain Home, ID [*Library symbol*] [*Library of Congress*] (LCLS)
IdMhP......... Prairie District Library, Mountain Home, ID [*Library symbol*] [*Library of Congress*] (LCLS)
IdMHS......... Moscow High School, Moscow, ID [*Library symbol*] [*Library of Congress*] (LCLS)
IDMI.......... Interface Document Master Index (DNAB)
IDMI.......... International Dun's Market Identifiers [*Dun & Bradstreet International*] [*Information service or system*] (IID)
IdMi.......... Middleton Public Library, Middleton, ID [*Library symbol*] [*Library of Congress*] (LCLS)
IdMid......... Midvale District Library, Midvale, ID [*Library symbol*] [*Library of Congress*] (LCLS)
IdMin......... Minidoka-Acequia District Library, Minidoka, ID [*Library symbol*] [*Library of Congress*] (LCLS)
IdMJH......... Moscow Junior High School, Moscow, ID [*Library symbol*] [*Library of Congress*] (LCLS)
IDML.......... Interactive Data Manipulation Language (SAUS)
IDML.......... Internal Data Manipulation Language [*Computer science*] (PDAA)
IDMM.......... Intermediate and Depot Maintenance Manual (NASA)
IDMMS......... Integrated Dynamic Modeling and Management System (SAUS)
IdMoGS........ Church of Jesus Christ of Latter-Day Saints, Genealogical Society Library, MooreBranch, Lost River Stake Center, Moore, ID [*Library symbol*] [*Library of Congress*] (LCLS)
IdMonB........ Bear Lake County District Library, Montpelier, ID [*Library symbol*] [*Library of Congress*] (LCLS)
IdMonB-P.... Bear Lake County District Paris Branch, Paris, ID [*Library symbol*] [*Library of Congress*] (LCLS)
IdMonGS...... Church of Jesus Christ of Latter-Day Saints, Genealogical Society Library, Bear Lake Branch, Montpelier, ID [*Library symbol*] [*Library of Congress*] (LCLS)
IDMP.......... Integrated Diagnostic Master Plan (ACAE)
IDMP.......... International Conference on Medical Physics (SAUS)
IDMP.......... Intraductal Mammary Pressure
IDMS.......... Image and Document Management System [*Aquidneck Data Corp.*] (NITA)
IDMS.......... Improved Data Modem System (SAUS)
IDMS.......... Improved Deep Moored Sweep [*Military*] (MCD)
IDMS.......... Information and Data Management System (SSD)
IDMS.......... Information for Decision-Makers System (MCD)
IDMS.......... Integrated Database Management System
IDMS.......... Integrated Data Management Network (SAUS)
IDMS.......... Integrated Data Management System (SAUS)
IDMS.......... Integrated Disposal Management System [*DoD*]
IDMS.......... Integrated DWPF Melter System (SAUS)
IDMS.......... Integrated Missile Defence System (SAUS)
IDMS.......... Interim Deployable Maintenance System (SAUO)
IDMS.......... International Directory of Marine Scientists [*Marine science*] (OSRA)
IDMS.......... Isotope Dilution Mass Spectrometry
IDMS/R........ Integrated Data Management System/Relation (SAUS)
IDMT.......... Inverse Definite Minimum Time (SAUS)
IDMT Relay.. Inverse Definite Minimum Time Relay (SAUS)
IdMu.......... Mullan Public Library, Mullan, ID [*Library symbol*] [*Library of Congress*] (LCLS)
I-DMV......... Internet Department of Motor Vehicles
IDMY.......... International Daylight Measurement Year (SAUS)
IDN........... Chicago, IL [*Location identifier*] [*FAA*] (FAAL)
IDN........... Identify (SAUS)
IDN........... Inanna's Descent to the Netherworld (BJA)
IDN........... Indagen [*Papua New Guinea*] [*Airport symbol*] (OAG)
IDN........... In Dei Nomine [*In God's Name*] [*Latin*]
IDN........... Indonesia [*ANSI three-letter standard code*] (CNC)
IDN........... Industrial Development Organization (SAUS)
IDN........... Inspection Due Notice [*Military*]
IDN........... Integrated Data Network (ACAE)
IDN........... Integrated Digital Network [*Telecommunications*]
IDN........... Integrated Healthcare Network [*Health care provider*]
IDN........... Intelligent Data Network
IDN........... International Destron Technologies, Inc. [*Vancouver Stock Exchange symbol*]
IDN........... International Directory Network (USDC)
IDN........... Internet Daily News (SAUS)
IdN........... Nampa Public Library, Nampa, ID [*Library symbol*] [*Library of Congress*] (LCLS)
IDN........... National Democratic Initiative (Andorra) [*Political party*] (PSAP)
IDN........... United Way of Metropolitan Chicago, Chicago, IL [*OCLC symbol*] (OCLC)
iDNA.......... Intercalary Dexoyribonucleic Acid [*Medicine*] (EDAA)
IDNAC......... International Databank for the Non-Aligned Countries (SAUS)
IDNB.......... Association of Registered Interior Designers of New Brunswick [*Association des Designers d'Interieur Immatricules du Nouveau-Brunswick*] (AC)
IDNC.......... Integrated Direct Numerical Control [*Burroughs Machines Ltd.*] [*Software package*] (NCC)
IDNDR......... International Decade for Natural Disaster Reduction [*1990's*] [*United Nations*]
IDNE.......... Indictione [*In the Indiction*] [*Latin*] (ROG)
IDNE.......... Inertial Doppler Navigation Equipment (DNAB)
IDNF.......... Irredundant Disjunctive Normal Formula
IDNHR......... International Decade of Natural Hazard Reduction (SAUS)
IdNI.......... Idaho State School & Hospital, Medical Library, Nampa, ID [*Library symbol*] [*Library of Congress*] (LCLS)
IDNID......... Immediate Diversion Network Invalid Dialing [*Communications term*] (DCT)
IDNIYRA...... International DN [*Detroit News*] Ice Yacht Racing Association (EA)
IDNL.......... Indiana Dunes National Lakeshore (SAUO)
IdNm.......... Meadows Valley Community Library, New Meadows, ID [*Library symbol*] [*Library of Congress*] (LCLS)
IdNMH......... Mercy Medical Center, Medical Library, Nampa, ID [*Library symbol*] [*Library of Congress*] (LCLS)
IdNN.......... Northwest Nazarene College, Nampa, ID [*Library symbol*] [*Library of Congress*] (LCLS)
ID NO......... Identification Number (DNAB)
IdNo.......... Notus Public Library, Notus, ID [*Library symbol*] [*Library of Congress*] (LCLS)
IdNP.......... Lewis County Free District Library, Nez Perce, ID [*Library symbol*] [*Library of Congress*] (LCLS)
IdNp-K........ Lewis County District Library, Kamiah Branch, Kamiah, ID [*Library symbol*] [*Library of Congress*] (LCLS)
IdNpm......... Armoral Tutle Public Library, New Plymouth, ID [*Library symbol*] [*Library of Congress*] (LCLS)
IDNR.......... Illinois Department of Natural Resources (SAUS)
IDNS.......... Illinois Department of Nuclear Safety
IDNS.......... Intelligence Digest News Service (SAUO)
IDNSS......... International Directory of Non-Official Statistical Sources [*A publication*]
IdNTS......... National Reactor Testing Station, Technical Library, Phillips Petroleum Co., Idaho Falls, ID [*Library symbol*] [*Library of Congress*] (LCLS)
ID NUMB..... Identification Number (SAUS)
IDNX.......... Integrated Digital Network Exchange [*Telecommunications*] (ACRL)
IDNX.......... Intelligent Direct European Access to Library Systems (SAUS)
IDO........... Idaho Operations Office [*Energy Research and Development Administration*] (MCD)
IDO........... Identification Officer [*Military*]
IDO........... Immediate Data Output (SAUS)
IDO........... Indoleamine-Dioxygenase [*An enzyme*]
IDO........... Industrial Development Office (SAUO)
IDO........... Industrial Development Organization [*United Nations*]
IDO........... Industrial Diesel Oil (ADA)
IDO........... Infrared Drying Oven
IDO........... Inspection Drawing Office (SAUO)
IDO........... Inspekteur der Ordnungspolizei [*Inspector of Uniformed Police*] [*German military - World War II*]
IDO........... Intelligence Division Office (SAUO)
IDO........... Intelligence Duty Officer
IDO........... Interdivisional Operations [*NASA*] (NASA)
IDO........... Interdivisional Order
IDO........... Interface Definition Object [*Computer science*]
IDO........... Interim Development Order (ADA)
IDO........... Interim Development Ordinance (PA)
IDO........... Internal Distribution Only (SAA)
IDO........... International Dental Organization (SAUO)
IDO........... International Development Office (SAUS)
IDO........... International Disarmament Organization
IDO........... International District Office
IDO........... Isolated Digital Output (SAUS)
IDO........... Iterative Discrete On-Axis (SAUS)
IdO........... Osburn Public Library, Osburn, ID [*Library symbol*] [*Library of Congress*] (LCLS)
IDO........... Santa Isabel Do Morro [*Brazil*] [*Airport symbol*] (OAG)
IDOA.......... Illinois Department of Agriculture (SAUS)
IdOa.......... Oakley District Library, Oakley, ID [*Library symbol*] [*Library of Congress*] (LCLS)
IDOC.......... Illinois Department of Corrections (SAUO)
IDOC.......... Inner Diameter of Outer Conductor (SAUS)
IDOC.......... Inside Diameter of Outer Conductor
IDOC.......... Intermediate Document (SAUS)
IDOC.......... Internal Dynamic Overload Control (SAUS)
IDOC.......... International Documentation and Communication Center [*Formerly, Council for Development of Religious Information and Documentation - IDOC International*] [*Rome, Italy*] (SLS)
IDOC.......... International Documentation and Communication Centre (SAUO)
IDOC.......... International Documentation on the Contemporary Church [*Later, International Documentation and Communication Center*] (EA)
IDOC.......... International Documentation on the Contemporary Church (journ.) (SAUS)
IDOC.......... Intrusion Detection Optical Cable (ACAE)
IDOC.......... Intrusion Detection Optical Communication (SAUS)
IDOCS......... Intrusion Detection Optical Communications System [*Computer system security*]
IDOD.......... Immediate Dissolved Oxygen Demand (EEVL)
ID/OD......... Inside Diameter/Outside Diameter
IDOD.......... International Directory of Directories [*A publication*]
IDOE.......... International Decade of Ocean Exploration [*1970's*]
IDOFOR........ Improving the Definition of the Objective Force [*Military*]
IDol.......... Dolton Public Library District, Dolton, IL [*Library symbol*] [*Library of Congress*] (LCLS)
IDOL.......... Improved Disk-time Overlap (SAUS)

IdOl............ Ola District Library, Ola, ID [*Library symbol*] [*Library of Congress*] (LCLS)
IDOMENEUS... Information and Data on Open Media for Networks of Users (SAUO)
IDON............ Idongus [*Proper*] [*Pharmacy*] (ROG)
IDON VEHIC... Idoneo-Vehiculo [*In a Suitable Vehicle*] [*Pharmacy*]
IdOr............ Clearwater Memorial Public Library, Orofino, ID [*Library symbol*] [*Library of Congress*] (LCLS)
IdOrHS........ Orofino High School Library, Orofino, ID [*Library symbol*] [*Library of Congress*] (LCLS)
IDOR System... Inhouse Document Online Retrieval System (SAUS)
IDOS............ Interactive Disk Operating System [*Computer Associates, Inc.*]
IDOS............ Interrupt Disk Operating System
IDOSARCS... Institute of Development of Southern African Red Cross Societies (SAUO)
IDOT............ Illinois Department of Transportation (SAUS)
IDOT............ Instrumentation Online Transcriber (IDOE)
IDoV............ United States Veterans Administration Hospital, Downey, IL [*Library symbol*] [*Library of Congress*] (LCLS)
IDow............ Downers Grove Public Library, Downers Grove, IL [*Library symbol*] [*Library of Congress*] (LCLS)
IDowG.......... George Williams College, Downers Grove, IL [*Library symbol*] [*Library of Congress*] (LCLS)
IDOX............ Lockheed Idaho Technologies [*Private rail car owner code*]
IDOX............ Maxson [*Federal Railroad Administration identification code*]
IDP............ Idiopathic Pulmonary Hemosiderosis [*Medicine*] (MELL)
IDP............ Image Data Processor
IDP............ Image Difference Processor (SAUS)
IDP............ Immediate Decision Plan (SAUS)
IDP............ Immunodiffusion Procedure [*Immunochemistry*]
IDP............ Improvement Data Plan (MCD)
IDP............ Incremental Dividend Preferred [*Share*] [*Investment term*]
IDP............ Indenture Part List (KSC)
IDP............ Independence [*Kansas*] [*Airport symbol*] (AD)
IDP............ Independence, KS [*Location identifier*] [*FAA*] (FAAL)
IDP............ Independence Petroleums [*Vancouver Stock Exchange symbol*]
IDP............ Independent Democratic Party [*Liberia*] [*Political party*] (EY)
IDP............ Independent Democratic Party [*Gibraltar*] [*Political party*]
IDP............ Independent Development Program (SAUS)
IDP............ Independent Development Project (SAUS)
IDP............ Individual Development Plan (RDA)
IDP............ Individual Development Program [*Civil Service Commission*]
IDP............ Industrial Data Processing
IDP............ Information and Data Base Publishing Report [*A publication*]
IDP............ Information and Data Processing (SAUS)
IDP............ Information Data Processing
IDP............ Information Display Planner (SAUS)
IDP............ Initial Delay Position [*Military*] (AABC)
IDP............ Initial Delivery Period (SAUO)
IDP............ Initial Domain Part [*Telecommunications*] (OSI)
IDP............ Initial Dose Period [*Medicine*] (MAE)
IDP............ Inosine Diphosphate [*Biochemistry*]
IDP............ Input Data Processing (or Processor) (SAUS)
IDP............ Input Data Processor (CET)
IDP............ Instantaneous Diastolic Pressure (MAE)
IDP............ Institute for Defence Policy (SAUS)
IDP............ Institute of Data Processing [*Later, IDPM*]
IDP............ Instructor Display Panel
IDP............ Instrumentation Development Plan (MCD)
IDP............ Instrument Departure Procedure (SAUO)
IDP............ Instrument Development Program (SAUO)
IDP............ Integrated Data Presentation (MCD)
IDP............ Integrated Data Processing
IDP............ Integrated Data Processor (NAKS)
IDP............ Integrated Diagnostic Plan (ACAE)
IDP............ Integrated Digital Processor (ACAE)
IDP............ Intelligence Data Processing (MCD)
IDP............ Intelligence Data Processing Module (SAUS)
IDP............ Interactive Database Processor [*Xerox Corp.*] (MCD)
IDP............ Interactive Display Panel (MCD)
IDP............ Interagency Drainage Program (SAUO)
IDP............ Intercept Deployment Plan [*National Security Agency*]
IDP............ Interchange Document Profile (SAUS)
IDP............ Interdigit Pause [*Telecommunications*] (TEL)
IDP............ Interface Design Plan [*Air Force*]
IDP............ Interface Development Plan (SAUO)
IDP............ Interim Digital Processor (SAUS)
IDP............ Intermodulation Distortion Percentage
IDP............ Internal Data Processing (IAA)
IDP............ Internal Defense Plans (CINC)
IDP............ Internal Design Pressure (PDAA)
IDP............ Internal Distribution Publication [*Navy*] (MCD)
IDP............ Internally Displaced People (SAUO)
IDP............ Internally Displaced Person (SAUS)
IDP............ Intern-Architect Development Program (DICI)
IDP............ International Data Post (SAUO)
IDP............ International Data Processing (SAUS)
IDP............ International Driving Permit
IDP............ Internet Datagram Protocol [*Computer science*] (ACRL)
IDP............ Inter-network Datagram Protocol (SAUS)
IDP............ Interpersonal Diagnosis of Personality [*Psychology*]
IDP............ Interplanetary Dust Particle
IDP............ Intraductal Papilloma [*Medicine*] (MELL)
IDP............ Investment Dollar Premium (ADA)
IDP............ Island Drilling Programme (SAUS)
IDP............ Isotope Development Program [*AEC*] (MCD)
IdP............ Pocatello Public Library, Pocatello, ID [*Library symbol*] [*Library of Congress*] (LCLS)
IDPA............ Inland Daily Press Association
IDPAI............ International Directory of Professional Astronomical Institutions [*A publication*]
IDPAR............ Institute of Donations and Public Affairs Research [*Former name of Canadian Centre for Business in the Community*] (NFD)
IdPar............ Parma Public Library, Parma, ID [*Library symbol*] [*Library of Congress*] (LCLS)
IDPase............ Inosine Diphosphatase [*Medicine*] (EDAA)
IdPay............ Payette Public Library, Payette, ID [*Library symbol*] [*Library of Congress*] (LCLS)
IdPBH............ Bannock Regional Medical Center, Medical Library [*Library symbol*] [*Library of Congress*] (LCLS)
IDPC............ Integrated Data Processing Center
IDPE............ Incorporated Data Processing Executives (SAUO)
IDPF............ Integrated Digital Photogrammetric Facility [*National Oceanic and Atmospheric Administration*]
IdPf............ Post Falls Public Library, Post Falls, ID [*Library symbol*] [*Library of Congress*] (LCLS)
IDPG............ Impact Data Pulse Generator (IAA)
IDPGF............ Institutional Data Products Generation Facility (SAUS)
IdPGS............ Church of Jesus Christ of Latter-Day Saints, Genealogical Society Library, Pocatello Branch, Pocatello, ID [*Library symbol*] [*Library of Congress*] (LCLS)
IDPH............ IDEC Pharmaceuticals [*NASDAQ symbol*] (TTSB)
IDPH............ IDEC Pharmaceuticals Corp. [*NASDAQ symbol*] (SPSG)
IDPH............ Idiopathic Pulmonary Hemosiderosis [*Medicine*]
IDPH............ Illinois Department of Public Health (SAUO)
IDPH............ Iowa Department of Public Health (SAUO)
IdPH............ Pocatello Regional Medical Center, Medical Library, Pocatello, ID [*Library symbol*] [*Library of Congress*] (LCLS)
IdPI............ Idaho State University, Pocatello, ID [*Library symbol*] [*Library of Congress*] (LCLS)
IDPI............ International Data Processing Institute (MCD)
IdPi............ Pierce District Library, Pierce, ID [*Library symbol*] [*Library of Congress*] (LCLS)
IdPiES............ Pierce Elementary School, Pierce, ID [*Library symbol*] [*Library of Congress*] (LCLS)
IdPin............ Pinehurst-Kingston Library, Pinehurst, ID [*Library symbol*] [*Library of Congress*] (LCLS)
ID PL............ Identification Plate (SAUS)
IDPL............ Indian Drugs and Pharmaceuticals Limited (SAUO)
IdPlu............ Plummer Public Library, Plummer, ID [*Library symbol*] [*Library of Congress*] (LCLS)
IDPM............ Industry Direct Purchase Manufacturer (AFIT)
IDPM............ Initial Draft (SAUS)
IDPM............ Initial Draft Presidential Memorandum
IDPM............ Institute for Development Policy and Management [*University of Manchester*] [*British*] (ECON)
IDPM............ Institute of Data Processing Management [*DPMA and Institute of Data Proce ssing - IDP*] [*Formed by a merger of*] (EAIO)
IdPM............ Pocatello Regional Medical Center, Pocatello, ID [*Library symbol*] [*Library of Congress*] (LCLS)
IDPMA............ International Data Processing Management Association (SAUO)
IDPM Inf Manage... IDPM Information Management (journ.) (SAUS)
IDPMN............ Initial Draft Proposed Materiel Need (SAUO)
IDPMX............ Interim Digital SAR Processor with Multiple Execution (SAUS)
IDPN............ B-Iminodiproprionitrile (SAUS)
IDPN............ Iminodipropionitrile [*Biochemistry*]
IDPP............ Integrated Diagnostics Program Plan (ACAE)
IDPR............ Inmate Development Pre-release (WDAA)
IdPr............ Priest River Library, Priest River, ID [*Library symbol*] [*Library of Congress*] (LCLS)
IdPre............ Preston Carnegie Library, Preston, ID [*Library symbol*] [*Library of Congress*] (LCLS)
IdPrP............ Priest Lake Community Library, Priest River, ID [*Library symbol*] [*Library of Congress*] (LCLS)
IDPRS............ Interactive Data Processing and Research System (SAUS)
IDPS............ Improvement Data Plan Sheet (MCD)
IDPS............ Incremental Differential Pressure System (AAG)
IDPS............ Initial Deployable Processing Station (ACAE)
IDPS............ Instrument Data Processing System
IDPS............ Integrated Data Processing System
IDPS............ Interactive Direct Processing System [*NCR Corp.*]
IDPS............ Interface Digital Processor (MCD)
IDPS............ Interim Deployable Process Station (SAUO)
IDPs............ Internally Displaced Persons (SAUO)
IDPS............ IRRI Discussion Paper Series (SAUO)
IDPS/LF............ Interactive Direct Processing System/Large File (SAUS)
IDP System... Industrial Data Processing System (SAUS)
IDPT............ Image Dissector Photomultiplier Tube
IDPT............ International Donkey Protection Trust (EAIO)
IDPTF............ Indirect Productive Time Factors (MCD)
IDPU............ Information, Documentation and Publication Unit (SAUS)
IdQ............ Identification Qualification
IDQ............ Individualized Dementia Questionnaire [*Medicine*] (DMAA)
IDQ............ Industrial Development Quotient
IDQ............ International Dairy Queen, Inc. (EFIS)
IDQ............ International Delta Resources [*Vancouver Stock Exchange symbol*]
IDQ............ Quincy Public Library, Quincy, IL [*OCLC symbol*] (OCLC)
IDQA............ Individual Documented Quality Assurance
IDQAR............ Interdivisional Quality Assurance Requirements (SAUS)
IDR............ Greeley & Hansen, Chicago, IL [*OCLC symbol*] (OCLC)
IDR............ Identification Record [*Computer science*] (MCD)

IDR .... Image Data Resampler (SAUS)
IDR .... Im Deutschen Reich. Zeitschrift des Central-Vereins Deutscher Staatsbuerger Juedischen Glaubens [*Berlin*] [*A publication*] (BJA)
IDR .... Iminodaunorubicin [*Antineoplastic drug*]
IDR .... Implementation Delay Report [*Social Security Administration*]
IDR .... Incremental Design Review (CTAS)
IDR .... Incremental Digital Recorder
IDR .... Independent Design Review (NRCH)
IDR .... Indian Defense Rules
IDR .... Indicator Co. [*Hungary*] [*FAA designator*] (FAAC)
IDR .... Individual Data Record
IDR .... Indonesian Rupiah (SAUS)
IDR .... Indore [*India*] [*Airport symbol*] (AD)
IDR .... Induction Dependent Resistor (SAUS)
IDR .... Industrial Damage Reports [*Formerly, ITR*] [*British*] [*World War II*]
IDR .... Industrial Data Reduction (MUGU)
IDR .... Industrial Development Revenue (SAUS)
IDR .... Industrial Development Revenue Bond [*Investment term*]
IDR .... Infantry Drill Regulations
IDR .... Infinite-Duration Impulse (IAA)
IDR .... Information Descriptor Record (MHDB)
IDR .... Information Dissemination and Retrieval [*System*] [*Reuters Ltd.*]
IDR .... Initial Design Review
IDR .... Initial Dummy Record (SAUS)
IDR .... Input Data Request
IDR .... Inspection Discrepancy Report (MCD)
IDR .... Installation Data Record
IDR .... Institute for Delphine Research (SAUO)
IDR .... Institute for Delphinid Research (EA)
IDR .... Institute for Desert Research (SAUO)
IDR .... Institute for Dream Research (SAUO)
IDR .... Institute of Dental Research [*Medicine*] (EDAA)
IDR .... Instrumentation Development Request (MCD)
IDR .... Integral Dryway Route [*Nuclear energy*] (NUCP)
IDR .... Integrated Dry Route (PDAA)
IDR .... Intelligent Disaster Recovery [*Computer science*]
IDR .... Intelligent Document Recognition (SAUS)
IDR .... Intercept During Reentry [*Aerospace*] (IAA)
IDR .... Interface Data Report (NRCH)
IDR .... Interface Drawing (SAUS)
IDR .... Intergalactic Digital Research (SAUS)
IDR .... Interim Depot Repair
IDR .... Interim Design Review (MCD)
IDR .... Interim Development Report
IDR .... Interim Discrepancy Report
IDR .... Intermediate Data Rate (SAUS)
IDR .... Intermediate Design Review (NASA)
IDR .... Intermittent-Duty Rating
IDR .... Internal Design Review (ACAE)
IDR .... Internal Development Report
IDR .... International Damascus Resources [*Vancouver Stock Exchange symbol*]
IDR .... International Defence Review (SAUS)
IDR .... International Defense Review [*Interavia Publications*] [*Information service or system*] [*A publication*] (CRD)
IDR .... International Dental Relief (SAUO)
IDR .... International Depositary Receipt [*Investment term*]
IDR .... International Development & Resources Inc. (SAUO)
IDR .... International Drawing Rights
IDR .... Internet Domain Registrars
IDR .... Intradermal Reaction [*Medicine*] (MAE)
idr .... Intradermaly(ly) [*Medicine*] (EDAA)
IDR .... Intrawest Corp. [*NYSE symbol*] (SG)
IDR .... Invoice Discrepancy Report [*Business term*]
IdR .... Madison County Library District, Rexburg, ID [*Library symbol*] [*Library of Congress*] (LCLS)
IDR .... Winder, GA [*Location identifier*] [*FAA*] (FAAL)
IDRA .... Insanity Defense Reform Act of 1984
IDRA .... Intercultural Development Research Association (EA)
IDRA .... International Desert Racing Association [*Automobile racing*]
IDRA .... International Disaster Recovery Association (EA)
IDRA .... Irish Dinghy Racing Association (BI)
IDR&DS .... International Dictionary of Research & Development Scientists (SAUO)
IDR & DS .... International Directory of Research and Development Scientists [*A publication*]
IDRAS .... Interactive Data Reduction Analysis Station (ACAE)
IDRB .... Industrial Design Registration Bureau (SAUO)
IDRB .... Industrial-Development Revenue Bond [*Issued by a state or local government to finance construction by a private company, which then becomes responsible for repaying the debt*] [*Investment term*]
IDRC .... Identification Redundancy Check (SAUS)
IDRC .... Improved Data Recovery Capability (SAUS)
IDRC .... Industrial Development Research Council (EA)
IDRC .... Interdigitating Dendritic Reticulum Cell (SAUS)
IDRC .... Interim Depot Repair Capability (ACAE)
IDRC .... International Development and Research Center (SAUS)
IDRC .... International Development Research Center (or Centre) (SAUO)
IDRC .... International Development Research Centre [*ICSU*] [*Research center*] [*Canada*]
IDRC .... International Development Research Centre of Canada (SAUS)
IDRC .... International Development Research Council (SAUO)
IDRCC .... International Data Rescue Coordination Centre (SAUS)
IDRC/ID .... Industrial Development and Manufacturers Record. The Industrial Development Research Council (SAUO)
IDRC/ID .... Industrial Development and Manufacturers Record. The Industrial Development Research Council. Atlanta (SAUS)
IDRD .... Increment Definition Requirements Document (SPST)
IDRD .... Information Definition Requirements Document (NASA)
IDRD .... Internal Data Requirement Description (MCD)
IDREA .... Idle Other Reasons [*Vessel status*] [*Navy*]
IDREF .... Implant Dentistry Research and Education Foundation (SAUO)
IDRES .... Institute for the Development of Riverine and Estuarine Systems (SAUO)
IDRF .... International Development and Refugee Foundation
IDRF .... International Disaster Relief Force (SAUO)
IdRg .... Salmon River Public Library, Riggins, ID [*Library symbol*] [*Library of Congress*] (LCLS)
IDRH .... Madison Memorial Hospital, Medical Library, Rexburg, ID [*Library symbol*] [*Library of Congress*] (LCLS)
IDRI .... International Development Research Institute (SAUO)
IdRi .... Richfield District Library, Richfield, ID [*Library symbol*] [*Library of Congress*] (LCLS)
IDRI .... Thailand Development Research Institute (SAUO)
IdRig .... Rigby Public Library, Rigby, ID [*Library symbol*] [*Library of Congress*] (LCLS)
IdRir .... Ririe Public Library, Ririe, ID [*Library symbol*] [*Library of Congress*] (LCLS)
IDRIS .... Intelligent Drive for Shop Floor Systems (SAUO)
IDRL .... Intercompany Data Requirements List (MCD)
IDRL .... Intradivision Requirements Lst (SAUS)
IdRMH .... Madison Memorial Hospital, Rexburg, ID [*Library symbol*] [*Library of Congress*] (LCLS)
IDRN .... Intradivisional Review Notice (SAUS)
IDRO .... Industrial Development and Renovation Organization (ACAE)
IDRO .... Industrial Development and Renovation Organization of Iran (SAUO)
IdRo .... Roberts Public Library, Roberts, ID [*Library symbol*] [*Library of Congress*] (LCLS)
IdRoc .... Rockland School/Community Library, Rockland, ID [*Library symbol*] [*Library of Congress*] (LCLS)
IDRON .... International Rainfed Lowland Rice Observational Nursery (SAUO)
IDRP .... Intellectual Disability Review Panel
IDRP .... Interdomain Routing Protocol [*Computer science*] (TNIG)
IDRP .... International Relief/Development Project (SAUO)
IdRR .... Ricks College, Rexburg, ID [*Library symbol*] [*Library of Congress*] (LCLS)
IDRS .... Integrated Data Retrieval System [*Department of the Treasury*]
IDRS .... Intellectual Disability Rights Service
IDRS .... International Double Reed Society (EA)
IDRTY .... Indirectly
IdRu .... DeMary Memorial Public Library, Rupert, ID [*Library symbol*] [*Library of Congress*] (LCLS)
IDRU .... Tropical Disease Research Units (SAUS)
IdRuH .... Minidoka Memorial Hospital, Medical Library, Rupert, ID [*Library symbol*] [*Library of Congress*] (LCLS)
IDRV .... Ionic Drive
IDRYN .... International Deepwater Rice Yield Nursery (SAUO)
IDS .... Identification Section
IDS .... Identification Supervisor [*Military*]
IDS .... I-Distinguishing Sequence (SAUS)
IDS .... Idle Signal Unit (SAUS)
IDS .... IDS Aircraft Lt. [*British*] [*FAA designator*] (FAAC)
IDS .... Iduronate Sulfatase [*An enzyme*]
IDS .... Illegal Declaration of Strikes (SAUO)
IDS .... Illicit Diamond Smuggling (SAUS)
IDS .... Image Display System
IDS .... Image Dissector Scanner [*Instrumentation*]
IDS .... Image Distribution System (SAUS)
IDS .... Immune Deficiency State
IDS .... Improved Data Set (SAUS)
IDS .... Improvement Data System (MCD)
IDS .... Impulse Duplexer Study
IDS .... Inadvertent Destruct [*Aerospace*] (AAG)
IDS .... Inclined Drive Shaft (DA)
IDS .... Income Data Service [*Research firm*] [*British*]
IDS .... Income Distribution Survey
IDS .... Incremented Dynamic Scanning (DAVI)
IDS .... India Development Service (EA)
IDS .... Indicator Drive Screw
IDS .... Individual Detail Specifications (SAUS)
IDS .... Industrial Data Systems [*AMEX symbol*] (SG)
IDS .... Industrial Design Section (SAUS)
IDS .... Industrial Development (journ.) (SAUS)
IDS .... Industries Development Strategy
IDS .... Industry Data Sources [*Information Access Co.*] [*Information service or system*] (CRD)
IDS .... Industry Department for Scotland (SAUS)
IDS .... Inertial Data System
IDS .... Inertial Doppler System
IDS .... Infectious Disease Service (DAVI)
IDS .... Information and Documentation Service (SAUS)
IDS .... Information and Documentation System (SAUS)
IDS .... Information Data Search, Inc. [*Information service or system*] (IID)
IDS .... Information Decision Systems (SAUS)
IDS .... Information Delivery Service [*Telecommunications*]
IDS .... Information Delivery Serviceor Information Dissemination Services (SAUS)
IDS .... Information Delivery System (SAUO)

IDS.......... Information Display System
IDS.......... Information Dissemination Service (SAUS)
IDS.......... Information Dissemination System (OICC)
IDS.......... Information Distribution & Switching system (SAUS)
IDS.......... Infrared Detection Set
IDS.......... Infrared Discrimination System
IDS.......... Inhibitor of DNA Synthesis [*Immunochemistry*]
IDS.......... Input Data Strobe
IDS.......... Institute for Democratic Socialism (EA)
IDS.......... Institute of Development Studies [*University of Sussex*] [*British*]
IDS.......... Institut fuer Deutsche Sprache [*Institute for German Language*] [*Information service or system*] (IID)
IDs.......... Instructional Designers [*Training term*] (LPT)
IDS.......... Instructional Dimensions Study (SAUS)
IDS.......... Instruction Set Process (ECII)
IDs.......... Instructural Designs (SAUS)
IDS.......... Instrument Data System
IDS.......... Instrument Development Section
IDS.......... Instrument Development Set
IDS.......... Integral Direct Station Selection (PDAA)
IDS.......... Integrated Database (COE)
IDS.......... Integrated Data Storage (NITA)
IDS.......... Integrated Data Store [*or System*] [*Honeywell, Inc.*] [*Computer science*]
IDS.......... Integrated Data System (SAUO)
IDS.......... Integrated Defensive System
IDS.......... Integrated Delivery System (IDYL)
IDS.......... Integrated Design Support (ACAE)
IDS.......... Integrated Dictionary Search (SAUO)
IDS.......... Integrated Display Set
IDS.......... Integrated Display Situation
IDS.......... Integrated Display System (SAUS)
IDS.......... Integrated Driver Support
IDS.......... Integrated Dynamic System (SAUS)
IDS.......... Intellectual Disability Services [*Australian Capital Territory, Queensland*]
IDS.......... Intelligence Data System
IDS.......... Intelligent Decision Server (SAUS)
IDS.......... Intelligent Disk Subsystem [*Northgate Computer Systems*] [*Computer science*] (PCM)
IDS.......... Intelligent Display System [*Computer science*]
IDS.......... Interactive Data System [*Computer science*]
IDS.......... Interactive Debugging System (SAUS)
IDS.......... Interactive Design Software (NITA)
IDS.......... Interactive Design System (SAUS)
IDS.......... Interactive Diagnostic System (AAEL)
IDS.......... Interactive Display System
IDS.......... Interagency Dialing System [*Telephones*]
IDS.......... Intercept Data Storage (SAUS)
IDS.......... Interceptor Defence Strike (SAUS)
IDS.......... Inter Data Systems (SAUS)
IDS.......... Inter Data Systems GmbH (SAUO)
IDS.......... Interdepartmental Dial Service [*or System*] [*Telephones*]
ID/S.......... Interdiction/Strike (SAUS)
IDS.......... Interdictor (SAUS)
IDS.......... Interdictor Strike
IDS.......... Interdictor/Strike (SAUS)
IDS.......... Interdisciplinary Science (EOSA)
IDS.......... Inter-Disciplinary Studies [*Education*] (AIE)
IDS.......... Interdisciplinary Study (SAUS)
IDS.......... Interface Data Sheet (NASA)
IDS.......... Interface Design Specification (CAAL)
IDS.......... Interface Design Standards (COE)
IDS.......... Interim Decay Storage [*Nuclear energy*] (NRCH)
IDS.......... Interim Development Status Report (SAUO)
IDS.......... Interior Designers Society (SAUO)
IDS.......... Interior Design Society (EA)
IDS.......... Interlibrary Delivery Service of Pennsylvania [*Library network*]
IDS.......... Intermediate Decay Storage [*Nuclear energy*] (NRCH)
IDS.......... Intermediate Direct Support [*DoD*]
IDS.......... Intermediate Drum Storage (CET)
IDS.......... Internal Directory System (SAUS)
IDS.......... Internal Distribution System [*Television*]
IDS.......... International Data Sciences, Inc. (SAUS)
IDS.......... International Data Services Corp. [*Vancouver Stock Exchange symbol*]
IDS.......... International Data Systems, Inc. (SAUO)
IDS.......... International Defence Systems (SAUS)
IDS.......... International Development Services
IDS.......... International Development Staff (SAUO)
IDS.......... International Development Strategy [*United Nations*]
IDS.......... International Diabetes Federation (SAUO)
IDS.......... International Digitization Strategy (SAUS)
IDS.......... International Doctor's Society (EA)
IDS.......... International Documents Service [*Defunct*] (EA)
IDS.......... International Dostoevsky Society (EA)
IDS.......... International Dove Society [*Defunct*] (EA)
IDS.......... Internet Database Service [*Cambridge Scientific Abstracts*]
IDS.......... Internet Dermatology Society (SAUO)
IDS.......... Interstate Dept. Stores, Inc. (EFIS)
IDS.......... Intrusion Detection System (MCD)
IDS.......... Inventory of Drinking Situations [*Test*] (TMMY)
IDS.......... Investigative Dermatological Society (DAVI)
IDS.......... Investors Diversified Services, Inc. [*Mutual funds*]
IDS.......... Ion Dip Spectroscopy
IDS.......... Ion Drift Semiconductor
IDS.......... Ionization Detector System (ACAE)
IDS.......... Isotope Detection System [*Nuclear energy*] (NRCH)
IDS.......... Istrian Democratic Assembly (Croatia) [*Political party*] (PSAP)
IDS.......... Item Description Sheet (NASA)
Id-S.......... Office of the Secretary of State, Boise, ID [*Library symbol*] [*Library of Congress*] (LCLS)
IdS.......... Shelley Public Library, Shelley, ID [*Library symbol*] [*Library of Congress*] (LCLS)
IDS.......... Spoon River College, Canton, IL [*OCLC symbol*] (OCLC)
IDSA.......... Indian Daily Sciences Association (SAUO)
IDSA.......... Industrial Designers' Society of America (EA)
IDSA.......... Industrial Development Subsidiary Agreement (SAUS)
IDSA.......... Industrial Services of America, Inc. [*NASDAQ symbol*] (SAG)
IDSA.......... Infectious Diseases Society of America (EA)
IDSA.......... Institute for Defence Studies and Analysis (SAUO)
IDSA.......... Interactive Digital Software Association (NTPA)
IDSA.......... International Dark-Sky Association (EA)
IDSA.......... International Development Service of America (SAUO)
IDSA.......... International Diving Schools Association (EA)
IdSa.......... St. Anthony Public Library, St. Anthony, ID [*Library symbol*] [*Library of Congress*] (LCLS)
IdSaF.......... Fremont County District Library, St. Anthony, ID [*Library symbol*] [*Library of Congress*] (LCLS)
IdSal.......... Salmon Public Library, Salmon, ID [*Library symbol*] [*Library of Congress*] (LCLS)
IdSalH.......... Steel Memorial Hospital, Salmon, ID [*Library symbol*] [*Library of Congress*] (LCLS)
IdSan.......... East Bonner County Free Public Library District, Sandpoint, ID [*Library symbol*] [*Library of Congress*] (LCLS)
IdSan-C.......... East Bonner County District Library, Clark Fork Branch, Clark Fork, ID [*Library symbol*] [*Library of Congress*] (LCLS)
IdSanH.......... Bonner General Hospital, Medical Library, Sandpoint, ID [*Library symbol*] [*Library of Congress*] (LCLS)
IDSB.......... Independent Double Sideband
IDSC.......... Information and Decision Support Center (SAUO)
IDSC.......... Information Dissemination Service Center (SAUO)
IDSC.......... International Demographic Statistics Center (SAUO)
IDSC.......... International Die Sinkers' Conference (EA)
IDSC.......... International Distributed Systems Center (or Centre) (SAUS)
IDSC.......... Interstate Defense and Security Committee (SAUS)
IdSc.......... Sugar Salem School/Community Library, Sugar City, ID [*Library symbol*] [*Library of Congress*] (LCLS)
IDSCM.......... Initial Defense Satellite Communication (KSC)
IDSCP.......... Initial Defense Satellite Communications Project [*Telecommunications*] (TEL)
IDSCS.......... Initial Defense Satellite Communication System (KSC)
IDSD.......... Individual Data Storage Device (SAUS)
IDSD.......... Institutional Data System Division [*Johnson Space Center*] [*NASA*] (NASA)
IDSE.......... International Data Switching Exchange (SAUS)
IdSEA.......... Idaho Society of Enrolled Agents (SAUO)
IDSEG.......... International Development Studies Group
IDSF.......... Intelligence Defector Source File [*Military*] (MCD)
IDSF.......... Inter-Agency Data Systems Facility [*General Services Administration*] (MCD)
IDSF.......... Interim Data Switching Facility (ADA)
IdSh.......... Shoshone Public Library, Shoshone, ID [*Library symbol*] [*Library of Congress*] (LCLS)
IDSI.......... Interactive Data Services, Inc. [*Database producer*] [*Information service or system*] (IID)
IDSIA.......... Immune Deficiency Syndrome "Innocently" Acquired (ADA)
IDS/IGS.......... Intermediate Direct Support/Intermediate General Support [*Army*]
IDSIPS.......... Interactive Digital Satellite Image Processing System (SAUS)
IDSL.......... Integrated Digital Subscriber Line
IDSL.......... Intrusion Detection and Sensor Laboratory [*Army*] (RDA)
IDS-LSC.......... Interdisciplinary Sciences-Land Surface Climatology (SAUS)
IDSM.......... Indian Distinguished Service Medal [*British*]
IDSM.......... Inertial Dampened Servomotor
IDSM.......... Integrated Direct Support Maintenance (MCD)
IDSM.......... Intermediate Direct Support Maintenance (MCD)
IdSm.......... St. Maries Public Library, St. Maries, ID [*Library symbol*] [*Library of Congress*] (LCLS)
IdSmB.......... Benewah County Library District, St. Maries, ID [*Library symbol*] [*Library of Congress*] (LCLS)
IDSMT.......... Institutional Intermediate Support Maintenance Trainer (SAUO)
iDSN.......... international Domain Name System (SAUO)
IDSO.......... Instructor Defensive Systems Operator (ACAE)
IDSO.......... Interdivisional Sales Order [*NASA*] (NASA)
IDSO.......... International Diamond Security Organization (BARN)
IDSOT.......... Interim Daily System Operational Test [*Navy*] (NG)
IDSP.......... Intercept Data Storage Position (SAUS)
IDSRD.......... Investigation Description anad Science Requirements Document (ACAE)
IDSRS.......... Ionization-Detected Stimulated Raman Spectroscopy
IDSS.......... Image Data System Simulation [*NASA*]
IDSS.......... Information Decision Support System (MCD)
IDSS.......... Instrumented Drill-String Sub (SAUS)
IDSS.......... Integral Direct Station Selection (SAUO)
IDSS.......... Integrated Data Sounding System (SAUO)
IDSS.......... Integrated Decision Support System (SAUO)
IDSS.......... Integrated Design Support System (SAUO)
IDSS.......... Integrated Diagnostic Support System (ACAE)
IDSS.......... Integrated Documentation Support System (SAUS)
IDSS.......... Interlingua Division of Science Service (SAUO)

IDSS International Development Support Services Pty. Ltd. [*Australia*] (ECON)
IDSS Interoperability Decision Support System (COE)
IdSs Soda Springs Public Library, Soda Springs, ID [*Library symbol*] [*Library of Congress*] (LCLS)
IDSSMS Isotope Dilution Spark Source Mass Spectroscope (or Spectroscopy) (SAUS)
IDST Information and Documentation on Science and Technology (NITA)
IDST Intradermal skin testing (SAUS)
IdSt Stanley City Library, Stanley, ID [*Library symbol*] [*Library of Congress*] (LCLS)
IDSTN Integrated Digital Switching and Transmission Network [*Computer science*] (ELAL)
IDSTO Idle Used for Storage [*Shipping*]
IdSuIGS Church of Jesus Christ of Latter-Day Saints, Genealogical Society Library, Salmon Branch, Salmon River Stake Center, Salmon, ID [*Library symbol*] [*Library of Congress*] (LCLS)
IdSvH Moritz Community Hospital, Medical Library, Sun Valley, ID [*Library symbol*] [*Library of Congress*] (LCLS)
IDT Identification & Tracking (SAUS)
IDT Identification Table (SAUS)
IDT I-Load Data Tape (NASA)
IDT Image Dissector Tube
IDT Immune Diffusion Test [*Medicine*] (DMAA)
IDT Immunodiffusion Test [*Medicine*] (DB)
IDT Implantation Doping Technique
IDT Improved Definition Television (NTCM)
IDT Inactive Duty Training [*Military*] (AABC)
IDT Independent Development Trust (SAUO)
IDT Independent Duty Medical Technician (SAUO)
IDT Indicator Dilution Technique [*Medicine*] (MELL)
IDT Industrial Data Terminal
IDT Industrial Data Terminals Corporation (NITA)
IDT Industrial Detergents Trade (SAUO)
IDT Industrial Diesel Tune [*Automotive service equipment*]
IDT Industrial Disputers Tribunal [*British*]
IDT Information Display Technology (EFIS)
IDT Input Data Translator (SAUS)
IDT Inspection Discrepancy Tag (KSC)
IDT Instillation Delivery Time [*Medicine*] (DMAA)
IDT Instrument Definition Team
IDT Instrument Development Team (ACAE)
IDT Instrumented Drop Tube (SAUS)
IDT Integrated Development Team (SAUS)
IDT Integrated Device Technology, Inc. (PS)
IDT Integrated Digital Terminal [*Communications term*] (DCT)
IDT Integrated Display Terminal [*Communications term*] (DCT)
IDT Integrated Document Traceability (ACAE)
IDT Integrated Dynamic Tester
IDT Intelligent Data Terminal
IDT Interactive Data Terminal (SAUS)
IDT Interactive Display Terminal (MCD)
IDT Interdigital-electrode Transducer (SAUS)
IDT Interdigital Transducer [*Physics*]
IDT Interdisciplinary Dentofacial Therapy (SAUO)
IDT Interdisciplinary Team [*Education*]
IDT Interdivision Time [*Cytology*]
IDT Interdivision Transfer (AAG)
IDT Interface Design Tool (SAUS)
IDT International Data Telephone Corp. (SAUO)
IDT International Diagnostic Technology [*Medicine*]
IDT International Discount Telecommunications (ECON)
IDT International Domain Team (SAUS)
IDT Interrupt Description (or Descriptor) Table (SAUS)
IDT Interrupt-Descriptor Table [*Computer science*]
IDT Intradermal Typhoid [*Medicine*] (DMAA)
IDT Investigation Definition Team (SAUS)
IDT Ion Doping Technique
IDT Isodensitracer
IDT Peoria Heights Public Library, Peoria Heights, IL [*OCLC symbol*] (OCLC)
IDTA Institute of Drug Technology Australia
IDTA Interdivisional Technical Agreement [*NASA*] (NASA)
IDTA International Dance Teachers Association (SAUO)
IDTA International Differential Treatment Association
IDTC IDT Corp. [*NASDAQ symbol*] (TTSB)
IDTC Indefinite Delivery Type Contract [*DoD*]
IDTCorp IDT Corp. [*Associated Press*] (SAG)
IDTE ID Table Entry [*Galaxy*] [*Computer science*]
ID TER Idaho Territory
IdTerSD West Jefferson School District No. 253, Terreton, ID [*Library symbol*] [*Library of Congress*] (LCLS)
IDTF Interactive Display Text Facility [*Computer science*] (VLIE)
IDTF International Documents Task Force [*Government Documents Round Table*] [*American Library Association*]
IdTf Twin Falls Public Library, Twin Falls, ID [*Library symbol*] [*Library of Congress*] (LCLS)
IdTfGS Church of Jesus Christ of Latter-Day Saints, Genealogical Society Library, Twin Falls Branch, Twin Falls, ID [*Library symbol*] [*Library of Congress*] (LCLS)
IdTfH Magic Valley Regional Medical Center, Medical Library, Twin Falls, ID [*Library symbol*] [*Library of Congress*] (LCLS)
IdTfSI College of Southern Idaho, Twin Falls, ID [*Library symbol*] [*Library of Congress*] (LCLS)
IDTI Integrated Device Tech [*NASDAQ symbol*] (TTSB)
IDTI Integrated Device Technology [*NASDAQ symbol*] (SAG)
IDTI Integrated Device Technology, Inc. (NQ)
IDTIMS Isotope Dilution Thermal Ionization Mass Spectrometry
IDTM Integrated Development Test Matrix [*Army*]
IDTN Interim Data Transmission Network (SAUO)
IDTOC Independent Division Tactical Operations Center [*Army*] (AABC)
IDTP Integrated Data Transmittal Package
IDTR Institute for Demographic Training and Research (SAUO)
IDTR Interdivisional Transfer Register
IDTR Interrupt Descriptor Table Register
IDTRC Interrupt Descriptor Table Register Cache (SAUS)
IDTS Improved Doppler Tracking System
IDTS Instrumentation Data Test Station
IDTS Instrumentation Data Transmission System
IDTS Instrument Data Telemetry System (SAUS)
IDTS Instrumented Data Telemetry System (SAUS)
IDTS Integrated Data Test Station (SAUS)
IDTS Integrated Data Transport System (SAUS)
IDTS Integrated Demonstration Tracking System (SAUS)
IDTS Integrated Development Test Schedule
IDTS Integrated Digital Telecommunications System (SAUS)
IDTS Interactive Data Transfer System (TIMI)
IDTS Interim Data Transmission System [*Communications term*] (DCT)
IDTS Iron Dressers Trade Society [*A union*] [*British*]
IDTSC Instrumentation Data Transmission System Controller
IDTU Intoxicated Driver Testing Unit [*Criminology*] (LAIN)
IDTV Improved Definition Television
IDTV Interactive Digital Television
IDTW International Union of Doll and Toy Workers of the US and Canada [*Later, IUANPW*] (EA)
IDTX Indiana Dinner Train [*Federal Railroad Administration identification code*]
IDTY Intermittent Duty (MSA)
IDU De Pauw University, Greencastle, IN [*OCLC symbol*] (OCLC)
idu Idaho [*MARC country of publication code*] [*Library of Congress*] (LCCP)
IDU Idle Signal Unit [*Electronics*] (EECA)
IDU Idoxuridine [*or Iododeoxyuridine*] [*Also, IDUR, IdUrd, IUDR*] [*Pharmacology*]
IDU Immunological Distance Unit [*Genetics*]
IDU Independent Distinct Units (SAUO)
IDU Indicator Drive Unit (IAA)
IDU Industrial Development Unit (IEEE)
IDU Industrial Documentation Unit (SAUS)
IDU Industry, TX [*Location identifier*] [*FAA*] (FAAL)
IDU Infrared Detection Unit
IDU Injection Drug User (SHCU)
IDU Instruction Decoding Unit (RALS)
IDU Instrumentation Data Unit (ACAE)
IDU Interactive Database Utilities (SAUS)
IDU Interactive Database Utility [*Computer science*] (VLIE)
IDU Interactive Display Unit (SAUO)
IDU Interface Data Unit [*Computer science*] (VLIE)
IDU Interface Demonstration Unit (NASA)
IDU Intermittent Drive Unit
IDU International Democratic Union (SAUO)
IDU International Democrat Union (EA)
IDU International Dendrology Union
IDU International Development Unit (SAUS)
IDU Iododeoxyuridine (DB)
IdU University of Idaho, Moscow, ID [*Library symbol*] [*Library of Congress*] (LCLS)
IdUA Iduronic Acid
IDUD Independent Deployable Unit Detachment (MCD)
IDUF Interactive Display and Update Facility (SSD)
IdU-L University of Idaho, Law Library, Moscow, ID [*Library symbol*] [*Library of Congress*] (LCLS)
IDun Dunlap Public Library District, Dunlap, IL [*Library symbol*] [*Library of Congress*] (LCLS)
IDup A. C. Dougherty Memorial Township Library, Dupo, IL [*Library symbol*] [*Library of Congress*] (LCLS)
IDUPGSSAPI Independent Data Unit Protection Generic Security Service API (SAUS)
IDupHS Dupo Junior-Senior High School, Dupo, IL [*Library symbol*] [*Library of Congress*] (LCLS)
IDUR Idoxuridine [*or Iododeoxyuridine*] [*Also, IDU, IdUrd, IUDR*]
IDUR Intercept During Unpowered Rise [*Aerospace*] (IAA)
IdUrd Iododeoxyuridine [*Also, IDU, IDUR, IUDR*] [*Pharmacology*]
IDV Dunlap Public Library District, Dunlap, IL [*OCLC symbol*] (OCLC)
IDV Indinavir [*An antiviral drug*]
IDV Indirect View (SAUS)
idv Individuals
IDV Initial Development Ltd. [*Vancouver Stock Exchange symbol*]
IDV Integrating Digital Voltmeter
IDV Interlibrational Derived Vehicle (SAUS)
IDV Intermittent Demand Ventilation [*Medicine*]
IDV International Distillers & Vintners [*British*]
IDV Internationaler Deutschlehrerverband [*International Association of Teachers of German - IATG*] [*Copenhagen, Denmark*] (EAIO)
IdV Valley of Tetons District Library, Victor, ID [*Library symbol*] [*Library of Congress*] (LCLS)
IDVC Indwelling Venous Catheter [*Medicine*]
IDVC Integrated Data/Voice Channel (VLIE)
IDVHS Idaho Virtual High School
IDVID Immersed Deflection Vidicon Device (IAA)

IDVLS .... Integrally-Ducted Vertical Launch System (SAUS)
IDVM .... Integrated Digital Voltammeter (VLIE)
IDVM .... Integrating Digital Voltmeter
IDVP .... Independent Design Verification Program (NRCH)
IDW .... Indian Deep Water (SAUS)
IDW .... Individual Defence Weapon (SAUS)
IDW .... Input Data Word
IDW .... Institut fuer Dokumentationswesen [*Germany*]
IDW .... Integrated Depth Wheel (SAUS)
IDW .... International Dolphin Watch (SAUO)
IDW .... Investigation-Derived Waste (BCP)
IdW .... Wallace Public Library, Wallace, ID [*Library symbol*] [*Library of Congress*] (LCLS)
IDW .... Washington Township Library, Washington, IL [*OCLC symbol*] (OCLC)
IDWA .... Interdivisional Work Authorization
IDWA .... Intra-Divisional Work Authorization (SAUO)
IDWD .... Input Data Word (MCD)
IdWe .... Weippe Public Library, Weippe, ID [*Library symbol*] [*Library of Congress*] (LCLS)
IdWeES .... Weippe Elementary School, Weippe, ID [*Library symbol*] [*Library of Congress*] (LCLS)
IdWei .... Weiser Public Library, Weiser, ID [*Library symbol*] [*Library of Congress*] (LCLS)
IdWen .... Wendell Public Library, Wendell, ID [*Library symbol*] [*Library of Congress*] (LCLS)
IdWenSD .... Wendell School District, Wendell, ID [*Library symbol*] [*Library of Congress*] (LCLS)
IDWF .... Individual Drinking Water Flavors [*Developed by Natick Research and Development Center to encourage soldiers to drink more fluids to prevent dehydration*] (INF)
IDWG .... Interdepartmental Working Group (SAUO)
IDWI .... Imperial Direct West India Mail Service Co. (ROG)
IdWi .... Wilder District Library, Wilder, ID [*Library symbol*] [*Library of Congress*] (LCLS)
IDWO .... Intelligence Division, War Office (SAUO)
IDWO .... Inter-Division Work Order
IDWR .... Idaho Department of Water Resources (SAUO)
IDWR .... Interim Design and Workmanship Rules (PDAA)
IDWT .... Inverse Discrete Walsh Transform (SAUS)
IDX .... Caterpillar Tractor Co., Peoria, IL [*OCLC symbol*] (OCLC)
IDX .... Identix, Inc. [*AMEX symbol*] (SPSG)
IDX .... Index (MSA)
IDX .... Individual Index File [*Computer science*] (PCM)
IDX .... Integrated Digital Exchange (SAUS)
IDX .... Intelligent Digital Exchange (NITA)
IDXC .... IDX Systems Corp. [*NASDAQ symbol*] (SAG)
IDXC .... IDX Systmes [*NASDAQ symbol*] (TTSB)
IDXO .... International DX Organization (SAUS)
IDXSys .... IDX Systems Corp. [*Associated Press*] (SAG)
IDXX .... Identix, Inc. [*NASDAQ symbol*] (COMM)
IDXX .... IDEXX Laboratories [*NASDAQ symbol*] (SPSG)
IDY .... Fondulac Public Library District, East Peoria, IL [*OCLC symbol*] (OCLC)
IDYN .... Innerdyne, Inc. [*NASDAQ symbol*] (SAG)
IDZ .... Bank Marketing Association, Chicago, IL [*OCLC symbol*] (OCLC)
IDZ .... Inner Defense Zone
IE .... Assistant Secretary for International Affairs and Energy Emergencies (SAUO)
IE .... Evanston Public Library, Evanston, IL [*Library symbol*] [*Library of Congress*] (LCLS)
IE .... Ice Edge (ACAE)
IE .... Idees pour l'Europe [*Paris, France*] (EAIO)
IE .... Id Est [*That Is*] [*Latin*]
IE .... Image Enhancement (SAUS)
IE .... Imbedded Error [*Factor analysis*]
IE .... Immediate-Early [*Genetics*]
IE .... Immobilized Enzyme [*Physiology*]
IE .... Immunitaetseinheit [*Immunizing Unit*] [*Medicine*]
IE .... Immunoelectrophoresis [*Analytical biochemistry*]
IE .... Impacted Embolism [*Medicine*] (MELL)
IE .... Import Executive [*British*]
IE .... Independent Estimate [*Army*]
IE .... Independent Evaluation (MCD)
IE .... Independent Expenditure [*Campaign-finance law provision*]
IE .... Index Error [*Navigation*]
IE .... Index of Enrichment
IE .... Indian Empire (SAUS)
IE .... Indicator Equipment (IAA)
IE .... Individual Education (DIPS)
IE .... Indo-European
IE .... Industrial Electronics (MCD)
IE .... Industrial Energy (EFIS)
IE .... Industrial Engine
IE .... Industrial Engineer [*or Engineering*]
IE .... Industrial Ergonomics (SAUS)
IE .... Industrial Espionage (SAUS)
IE .... Industrial Exhauster (SAUS)
IE .... Industry and Environment Office (SAUO)
IE .... In Excess
IE .... Infection Efficiency [*Pathology*]
IE .... Infective Endocarditis [*Cardiology*]
IE .... Inflammatory Exudate [*Medicine*] (MELL)
IE .... Information and Education (AAGC)
IE .... Information Electronics Ltd. (SAUS)
IE .... Information Element (ACRL)
IE .... Information Engineering (HODG)
IE .... Information Enterprises [*Chesterfield, MO*] [*Telecommunications service*] (TSSD)
IE .... Information Environment
IE .... Information Exchange (SAUS)
IE .... Infrared Emission
I/E .... Ingress/Egress
i/e .... ingresslegress (SAUS)
IE .... Initial Equipment [*Navy aircraft*]
IE .... Initial Establishment [*British military*] (DMA)
IE .... Initiating Event (NRCH)
IE .... Inner Ear (MELL)
I/E .... Input Electronics (SAUS)
IE .... Insert Exon [*Genetics*]
IE .... Insert Extract (IAA)
I-E .... Insert-Extract (SAUS)
IE .... Inside Edge
IE .... Inside English (SAUS)
IE .... Inspection and Enforcement (NRCH)
I/E .... Inspection and Evaluation [*Environmental science*] (COE)
IE .... Inspection Equipment
IE .... Inspection Error (KSC)
I/E .... Inspiratory-Expiratory (Ratio) [*Physiology*]
IE .... Installation Engineer (SAUO)
IE .... Installation Equipment [*Army*] (AABC)
IE .... Institute of Education (SAUO)
IE .... Institute of Energy [*An association*] (EAIO)
IE .... Institute of Engineers (SAUS)
IE .... Institute of Engineers and Technicians [*British*]
IE .... Institute of Entomology (SAUS)
IE .... Institute of Expertology (EA)
IE .... Institute of Export [*British*]
IE .... Institution of Electronics (SAUO)
IE .... Institution of Engineers (SAUO)
IE .... Instruction Element (VLIE)
IE .... Instruction Execution (IAA)
IE .... Instrument Engineer (SAUS)
IE .... Instrument Engineering
IE .... Intake (of a Unit of Food) Energy [*Nutrition*]
IE .... Integral Electronics (SAUO)
I/E .... Integrated Electronics (SAUO)
IE .... Intelligence Estimate (SAUO)
IE .... Intensive Electrification (SAUS)
IE .... Interconnection Equipment
IE .... Inter Ethernet (SAUS)
IE .... Interface Electronics (ACAE)
IE .... Interface Equipment (ACAE)
IE .... Intermediate Early [*Genetics*]
IE .... Intermediate Electrode (SAUS)
IE .... Intermediate Erection
IE .... Internal Elastica [*Artery anatomy*]
IE .... Internal Environment
i-e .... internal-external (SAUS)
I-E .... Internal-External Scale (SAUS)
IE .... International Education Committee (SAUS)
IE .... International Exhibition (IMH)
IE .... Internet Enabled
IE .... Internet Explorer [*Microsoft Corp.*]
I/E .... Intern/Extern (SAUS)
IE .... Interrogation Entry Register (IAA)
IE .... Interrupt Enable [*Computer science*]
I/E .... Introversion/Extroversion [*Psychology*] (AEE)
IE .... Inverted Elevation (SAUS)
IE .... Ion Ejection (SAUS)
IE .... Ion Exchange (WDAA)
IE .... Ionization Energy [*Chemistry*]
IE .... Ionospheric Explorer [*NASA/National Bureau of Standards*]
IE .... Ireland [*ANSI two-letter standard code*] (CNC)
ie .... Ireland [*MARC country of publication code*] [*Library of Congress*] (LCCP)
IE .... Ireland [*Internet country code*]
IE .... Irish Earl (ROG)
IE .... Irradiation Effects (NRCH)
IE .... Isoelectric (SAUS)
IE .... Isoetharine [*Medicine*]
IE .... Isothermal Expansion (SAUS)
IE .... Solomon Islands Airways [*ICAO designator*] (AD)
ie .... That Is [*Id est*] [*Latin*] (WDMC)
IE3 .... Institute of Electrical and Electronic Engineers (SAUO)
IEA .... American Hospital Supply Corp., Evanston, IL [*Library symbol*] [*Library of Congress*] (LCLS)
IEa .... East Alton Public Library, East Alton, IL [*Library symbol*] [*Library of Congress*] (LCLS)
IEA .... East Texas State University, Commerce, TX [*OCLC symbol*] (OCLC)
IEA .... Idaho Education Association (SRA)
IEA .... Illinois Education Association (SRA)
IEA .... Immediate Early Antigen (DB)
IEA .... Immuno-Electroadsorption [*Medicine*] (DMAA)
IEA .... Immunoelectro Adsorption (SAUS)
IEA .... Immunoelectrophoretic Analysis (STED)
IEA .... Immunoenzyme Assay [*Biochemistry*] (DAVI)
IEA .... Import Entitlement Agreement [*United Arab Republic*]
IEA .... Index of Economic Activity (ADA)
IEA .... Indian Economic Association (SAUO)

IEA .... Indian Education Act (SAUS)
IEA .... Indian Engineering Association (SAUO)
IEA .... Indian-Eskimo Association of Canada [*Later, CASNP*] (EA)
IEA .... Indian Evidence Act (ROG)
IEA .... Indoleethanol [*Organic chemistry*]
IEA .... Industrial Editors Association
IEA .... Industrial Engineering Activity [*Army*] (AAGC)
IEA .... Industrial Environmental Association (SAUO)
IEA .... Infectious Equine Anemia [*Veterinary medicine*] (DMAA)
IEA .... Information Engineering Association (SAUO)
IEA .... Information Exchange Agreement (SAUO)
IEA .... Initial Environmental Assessment (SAUO)
IEA .... Institute for Economic Analysis (EA)
IEA .... Institute for Educational Affairs (EA)
IEA .... Institute for Energy Analysis (SAUS)
IEA .... Institute for Environmental Awareness (EA)
IEA .... Institute for Expressive Analysis (EA)
IEA .... Institute for/of Energy Analysis (SAUO)
IEA .... Institute of Applied Economics [*University of Montreal*] [*Canada*] (IRC)
IEA .... Institute of Economic Affairs [*British*]
IEA .... Institute of Energy Analysis (SAUS)
IEA .... Institute of Environmental Action (EA)
IEA .... Institute of Environmnental Action (SAUS)
IEA .... Institution of Engineers, Australia (SAUO)
IEA .... Instruments, Electronics, and Automation [*Exhibit*]
IEA .... Insurance Educational Association
IEA .... Integral Error Squared (PDAA)
IEA .... Integrated Electronic Assembly (NAKS)
IEA .... Intereuropean Airways Ltd. [*British*] [*ICAO designator*] (FAAC)
IEA .... Inter-Exchanges Assistance (SAUS)
IEA .... Interface Electronics Assembly
IEA .... Interment Exchange of America
IEA .... Intermountain Electrical Association (SRA)
IEA .... International Association for the Evaluation of Educational Achievement [*See also AIERS*] [*University of Stockholm*] [*Sweden*] (EAIO)
IEA .... International Economic Association [*See also AISE*] [*Paris, France*] (EAIO)
IEA .... International Education Act
IEA .... International Education Assembly [*World War II*]
IEA .... International Education Association
IEA .... International Electrical Association (SAUO)
IEA .... International Emergency Action [*See also AUI*] [*Paris, France*] (EAIO)
IEA .... International Endometriosis Association (SAUO)
IEA .... International Energy Agency [*OECD*] [*Research center*] [*France*] (IRC)
IEA .... International Entomological Association (SAUO)
IEA .... International Entrepreneurs Association [*Later, AEA*] (EA)
IEA .... International Environment Assistance (SAUO)
IEA .... International Epidemiological Association (EA)
IEA .... International Ergonomics Association (EA)
IEA .... International Evaluation of Education (SAUS)
IEA .... International Exchange Association (EA)
IEA .... International Executives Association (EA)
IEA .... International Exhibitors Association (EA)
IEA .... International Instruments (SAUS)
IEA .... International Instruments, Electronics and Automation Exhibition (SAUS)
IEA .... International Study of Educational Achievement (SAUS)
IEA .... Intravascular Erythrocyte Aggregation [*Hematology*]
IEA .... Ion Energy Analysis (or Analyzer) (SAUS)
IEA .... Irish Exporters Association (EAIO)
IEAAIE .... Industrial and Engineering Applications of Artificial Intelligence and Expert systems (SAUS)
IEAB .... Internacia Esperanto-Asocio de Bibliotekistoj [*International Association of Esperanto-Speaking Librarians*] [*Later, IAEL*] (EA)
IEAC .... IEEE [*Institute of Electrical and Electronics Engineers*] Automatic Control (IAA)
IEACC .... International Instruments, Electronics, Automation, Control Equipment and Communication (SAUS)
IEACS .... Institut Europeen des Armes de Chasse et de Sport [*European Institute of Hunting and Sporting Weapons - EIHSW*] (EAIO)
IEAEMM .... International Energy Agency Emergency Management Manual [*A publication*] (COE)
IEAF .... Imperial Ethiopian Air Force
IEAH .... American Hospital Supply Corp., Evanston, IL [*Library symbol*] [*Library of Congress*] (LCLS)
IEAHC .... Institute of Early American History and Culture (EA)
IEAJ .... Internacia Esperanto - Asocio de Juristoj [*International Esperanto - Association of Jurists*] [*Graz, Austria*] (EAIO)
IEAJ .... International Esperanto-Association of Jurists (SAUO)
IEAK .... Internet Explorer Administration Kit
IEAL .... International Energy Associates Limited (SAUO)
IEAL .... International Energy Associates Ltd. (SAUS)
IE & ID .... Interiors Engineering and Industrial Design (MCD)
IE&S .... Institutional, Environmental and Safety (SAUS)
IEA News .... Instruments, Electronics, Automation News (journ.) (SAUS)
IEA/ORAU .... Institute of Energy Analysis/ Oak Ridge Associated Universities (SAUO)
IEA/ORAU .... Institute of Energy Analysis/Oak Ridge Associated Universities (SAUS)
IEAP .... Institut Europeen d'Administration Publique [*European Institute of Public Administration - EIPA*] (EAIO)
IEar .... Earl Township Public Library, Earlville, IL [*Library symbol*] [*Library of Congress*] (LCLS)
IEAR .... Internacia Esperanto-Amikaro de Rotarianoj [*International Esperanto Fellowship of Rotarians*] [*British*] (EAIO)
I/EAR .... International Electronic & Aerospace Report (SAUO)
IEAR .... International Electronic and Aerospace Report (journ.) (SAUS)
IEarFSD .... Freedom Community Unit, School District 245, Earlville, IL [*Library symbol*] [*Library of Congress*] (LCLS)
IEARN .... International Education and Resource Network [*Information service or system*] (IID)
IEarSD .... Earlville Community Unit, School District 9, Earlville, IL [*Library symbol*] [*Library of Congress*] (LCLS)
IEAS .... Ice Elevation Altimeter System (SAUS)
IEAS .... Institute of East Asian Studies [*University of California, Berkeley*] [*Research center*] (RCD)
IEAS .... International Economic Appraisal Service [*The Economist Publications Ltd.*] [*British*] [*Information service or system*]
IEASMA .... International Electronic Article Surveillance Manufacturers Association (NTPA)
IEATP .... Information Engineering Advanced Technology Programme [*British*]
IE Aust .... Institution of Engineers, Australia (SAUO)
IEB .... Elkhart Public Library, Elkhart, IN [*OCLC symbol*] (OCLC)
IEB .... Improved Electronics Box (SAUS)
IEB .... Industrial Evaluation Board [*BDSA*]
IEB .... Infanterie-Ersatzbataillon [*Infantry Replacement Training Battalion*] [*German military - World War II*]
IEB .... Institute of Economic Botany [*New York Botanical Garden*]
IEB .... Institute of Electronic Business (SAUO)
IE-B .... Institute of Engineers-Bangladesh (SAUS)
IEB .... Institution of Engineers, Bangladesh (SAUS)
IEB .... Interdiction Executive Board (MCD)
IEB .... Interdivisional Engineering Bulletin (SAUS)
IEB .... International Education Board (SAUO)
IEB .... International Energy Bank Ltd. [*British*]
IEB .... International Environmental Bureau for the Non-Ferrous Metals Industry
IEB .... International Environment Bureau (SAUS)
IEB .... International Executive Board [*UAW*]
IEB .... International Exhibitions Bureau
IEB .... Irish Evangelistic Band
IEB .... Irish Export Board
IEB .... Office of Inspection and Enforcement. Bulletin [*A publication*] (NRCH)
IEBL .... Inter-Entity Boundary Line [*Military*] (INF)
IEBM .... Institute of Epidemiology and Behavioral Medicine [*Medical Research Institute of San Francisco*] [*Research center*] (RCD)
IEBM .... Interplay of Engineering with Biology and Medicine (SAUO)
IEBR .... Institute for Economic and Business Research [*University of Kansas*] [*Research center*] (RCD)
IEC .... Earlham College, Richmond, IN [*OCLC symbol*] (OCLC)
IEC .... Experimental Cardiology [*Russian*]
IEC .... Illinois Environmental Council (SRA)
IEC .... Imaginative Educational Cooperation Project (EDAC)
IEC .... Implementation and Effectiveness of International Environmental Commitments (SAUO)
IEC .... Incremental Engineering Change (SAUS)
IEC .... Independent Electoral Commission (South Africa) [*Political party*] (PSAP)
IEC .... Independent Electrical Contractors (EA)
IEC .... Indicative Estimate of Cost (SAUS)
IEC .... Individual Employment Contract (SAUS)
I/EC .... Industrial and Engineering Chemistry (journ.) (SAUS)
IEC .... Industrial & Engineering Consulting Co. (SAUO)
IEC .... Industrial Electrification Council [*Later, TEC*] (EA)
IEC .... Industrial Energy Conservation (ODBW)
IEC .... Industry-Education Council (SAUO)
IEC .... Infectious Endocarditis [*Medicine*] (MELL)
IEC .... Infective Endocarditis [*Medicine*] (MELL)
IEC .... Inflatable Exit Cone (MCD)
IEC .... Information, Education and Communication programs (SAUO)
IEC .... Information, Education and Communications (SAUO)
IEC .... Information Exchange Center
IEC .... Infused Emitter Coupling
IEC .... Inherent Explosion Clause [*Insurance*]
IEC .... Injection Electrode Catheter
IEC .... Inpatient Exercise Center [*Rehabilitation*] (DAVI)
IEC .... Institut d'Etudes Congolaises [*Congolese Institute of Studies*]
IEC .... Institute of Early Childhood [*Macquarie University*] [*Australia*]
IEC .... Institute of Educational Cinematography [*British*]
IEC .... Institute of Employment Consultants Ltd. [*British*]
IEC .... Institute of Engineers of Chile
IEC .... Institut Europeen de la Communication [*European Institute for the Media - EIM*] (EAIO)
IEC .... Integrated Electronic Central (SAUS)
IEC .... Integrated Electronic Circuit (SAUS)
IEC .... Integrated Electronic Components (BUR)
IEC .... Integrated Electronic Control
IEC .... Integrated Electronics Components (SAUO)
IEC .... Integrated Engine Control
IEC .... Integrated Environmental Control (AAG)
IEC .... Intelligence Evaluation Committee [*Department of Justice*]
IEC .... Intercontinental Energy Corporation (SAUO)
IEC .... Interexchange Carrier [*Telecommunications*]
IEC .... Interface Efficiency Council [*Computer science*]
IEC .... Intergraph Education Center (SAUS)
IEC .... Intermittent Electrical Contact (IAA)

IEC.......... International Economic Conference (SAUO)
IEC.......... International Economic Review (journ.) (SAUS)
IEC.......... International Edsel Club (EA)
IEC.......... International Educational and Cultural Exchange
IEC.......... International Education Center (or Centre) (SAUO)
IEC.......... International Egg Commission [*British*] (EAIO)
IEC.......... International Electrical Commission (SAUS)
IEC.......... International Electric Company (SAUO)
IEC.......... International Electrochemical Commission (SAUO)
IEC.......... International Electronical Commission (or Conference) (SAUS)
IEC.......... International Electronics Corporation (SAUO)
IEC.......... International Electrotechnical Commission [*See also CEI*] [*Standards body*] [*Geneva, Switzerland*] (EAIO)
IEC.......... International Electrotechnical Committee (SAUO)
IEC.......... International Emergency Committee (SAUO)
IEC.......... International Energy Commission (WDAA)
IEC.......... International Energy Cooperative Inc. (SAUO)
IEC.......... International Engineering Consortium (NTPA)
IEC.......... International Environmental Commitments
IEC.......... International Equipment Company (SAUO)
IEC.......... International Ethological Committee (SAUO)
IEC.......... International Exchange Committee (SAUO)
IEC.......... International Extension College (SAUO)
IEC.......... Interstate Economic Committee (SAUS)
IEC.......... Interstate Electronics Corporation (SAUO)
IEC.......... Intraepithelial Carcinoma [*Medicine*]
IEC.......... Intrinsic Electron Conduction (IAA)
IEC.......... Inverse Electrode Current
IEC.......... Ion Exchange Chromatography
IEC.......... Ion-Exchange Conference (SAUS)
IEC.......... Iowa Egg Council (SRA)
IEC.......... Iris Epithelium Cell [*Cytology*]
IEC.......... Iso-Echo Contour
IEC.......... Isotropic Elastic Constant (SAUS)
IEC.......... Israel Economic Conference
IEC.......... Israel Electric Corporation (SAUO)
IEC.......... Item Entry Control (AFM)
IEC.......... Office of Inspection and Enforcement. Circular [*A publication*] (NRCH)
IEC.......... PEC Israel Economic [*NYSE symbol*] (TTSB)
IEC.......... PEC Israel Economic Corp. Ltd. [*NYSE symbol*] (SAG)
IECA.......... Independent Educational Consultants Association (EA)
IECA.......... Independent Educational Counselors Association (SAUO)
IECA.......... Independent Election Corp. of America (WDMC)
IECA.......... Industry, Education Councils of America (OICC)
IECA.......... International Erosion Control Association (EA)
IECa.......... Intraepithelial Carcinoma [*Medicine*] (EDAA)
IE Ca cx.......... Intraepithelial Carcinoma of Cervix [*Medicine*] (STED)
IECBSHM.......... International Editoral Committee for Book Series on Hydraulic Machinery (SAUO)
IEC Bus.......... International Electrotechnical Commission Bus (SAUS)
IECC.......... Informix Enterprise Command Center (SAUO)
IECC.......... Inspection Equipment Coordination Committee (SAUS)
IECC.......... Integrated Electronic Control Centre (HEAS)
IECC.......... Intercultural E-mail Classroom Connections (SAUO)
IECC.......... International Economic Conversion Campaign [*Defunct*] (EA)
IECC.......... International Electronic Components Committee (SAUS)
IECC.......... International Email Chess Club
IECCA.......... Inter-Establishment Committee for Computer Applications (SAUO)
IECD.......... Ignition Energetics Characterization Device (MCD)
IECDF.......... International Economic Cooperation Development Fund (SAUS)
IECE.......... IEC Electronics [*NASDAQ symbol*] (TTSB)
IECE.......... IEC Electronics Corp. [*NASDAQ symbol*] (NQ)
IECE.......... Institute of Electronic and Communication Engineers (SAUS)
IECE.......... Institute of Electronic Communications Engineers (SAUS)
IECE.......... Institute on East Central Europe [*Columbia University*] [*Research center*] (RCD)
IECEC.......... Intersociety Energy Conversion Engineering Conference
IECEE.......... IEC System for Conformity Testing and Certification of Electrical Equipment (SAUS)
IECEE.......... IEC System for Conformity Testing to Standards for Safety of Electrical Equipment (SAUO)
IECEE.......... International Electrotechnical Commission System for Conformity Testing to Standards for Safety of Electrical Equipment [*Switzerland*] (EA)
IECEJ.......... Institute of Electrical Communication Engineers of Japan (SAUS)
IECEJ.......... Institute of Electronic and Commission Engineers of Japan (SAUS)
IECEJ.......... Institute of Electronic Communications Engineers of Japan
IECEJ.......... Interreligious Emergency Campaign for Economic Justice (EA)
IEC Elc.......... IEC Electronics Corp. [*Associated Press*] (SAG)
IECF.......... International European Construction Federation (SAUO)
IECG.......... Independent Energy Consultants Group [*British*]
IECG.......... Interagency Emergency Coordinating Group [*Federal disaster planning*]
IECG.......... International Email Chess Group
IECI.......... Independent Electrical Contractors, Inc. [*An association*]
IECI.......... Industrial Electronics and Control Instrumentation (journ.) (SAUS)
IECI.......... Institute for Esperanto in Commerce and Industry (EA)
IECIC.......... International Engineering and Construction Industries Council (PDAA)
IECIRTS.......... Improved Electrical Circuit Test Set (ACAE)
IECL.......... Instrumentation Equipment Configuration Log (SAA)
IECL.......... International Esperantist Chess League [*See also ESLI*] (EAIO)
IECM.......... Induced Environmental Contamination Monitor (MCD)
IECM.......... Internal Electronic Countermeasure
IECMS.......... Inflight Engine Condition Monitoring System [*Military*] (CAAL)
IECO.......... Inboard Engine Cutoff
IECO.......... Institute of Experimental and Chemical Oncology [*Medicine*] (EDAA)
IECO.......... International Engineering Company (SAUO)
IECOK.......... International Economic Consultative Organization for Korea [*Ten-nation consortium*]
IECP.......... Injected Electric Current Perturbation
IECP.......... Interface Engineering Change Procedure
IECP.......... Intermediate Engineering Change Proposal (SAUS)
IEC Process Des Dev... Industrial and Engineering Chemistry, Process Design and Development (journ.) (SAUS)
IECPS.......... International Electronic Circuit Packaging Symposium (SAUO)
IECPS.......... International Electronic Packaging Symposium (MCD)
IECQ.......... IEC Quality Assessment System for Electronic Components (SAUO)
IECQ.......... International Electronic Component Qualification
IECQ.......... International Electronic Component Qualification system (SAUS)
IECQA.......... International Electrotechnical Commission Qualification Assessment (SAUS)
IECQA.......... International Electrotechnical Commission Quality Assessment (SAUO)
IECQU.......... International Electrotechnical Commission Quality Assessment (PDAA)
IECR.......... Institute of Engineering Cybernetics and Robotics (SAUS)
IECRM.......... Intrinsic Excitation Coupled to Rotator Model (SAUS)
IECS.......... Igloo Environment Control Subsystem (MCD)
IECS.......... Intelligence Evaluation Center [*Saigon*] [*Obsolete*] (CINC)
IECS.......... Internal-External Control Scale [*Psychology*] (DHP)
IECT.......... IEEE [*Institute of Electrical and Electronics Engineers*] Circuit Theory (IAA)
IECT.......... Impulsive Ergodic Collision Theory [*Mathematics*]
IEC/TC.......... International Electrotechnical Commission, Technical Committee (SAUS)
IECU.......... Improved Environmental Control Unit [*Army*] (STAH)
IEd.......... Edwardsville Free Public Library, Edwardsville, IL [*Library symbol*] [*Library of Congress*] (LCLS)
IED.......... Illuminating Engineering Design (SAUS)
IED.......... Imitative Electronic Deception
IED.......... Impact Energy Density
IED.......... Improved Explosive Device
IED.......... Improvised Explosive Device
IED.......... Improvised Explosive Device Disposal (PDAA)
IED.......... Incident Energy Density
IED.......... Income Eligibility Determination [*Food and Nutrition Service*] [*Department of Agriculture*] (GFGA)
IED.......... Income Equalization Deposit (ADA)
IED.......... Independent Exploratory Development [*Navy*] (NG)
IED.......... Individual Effective Dose (IEEE)
I ED.......... Industrial Education Building (SAUS)
IED.......... Inherited Epidermal Dysplasia [*Medicine*] (DMAA)
IED.......... Initial Effective Data (IAA)
IED.......... Initial Engine Development [*Air Force*]
IED.......... Initiative Electronic Deception (ADDR)
IED.......... Insertion/Extraction Device [*Aviation*]
IED.......... Inspection Equipment Drawing
IED.......... Institute for Educational Development [*Defunct*]
IED.......... Institution of Electrical Designers (COBU)
IED.......... Institution of Engineering Designers [*British*] (BI)
IED.......... Instrumental Engineering Division [*National Weather Service*]
IED.......... Instrument Electrical Diagram (SAUO)
IED.......... Integrated Electric Drive [*Navy*] (DOMA)
IED.......... Integrated Electronics Division (SAUO)
IED.......... Integrated Engineering Design Service (PDAA)
IED.......... Integrated Environmental Design (PDAA)
IED.......... Interacting Equipment Documents (MCD)
IED.......... Interactive Electronic Display (SAUS)
IED.......... Intermediate Educational District (SAUS)
IED.......... Intermittent Explosive Disorder
IED.......... International Education Development (SAUO)
IED.......... International Electron Devices Meeting (PDAA)
IED.......... Intraepithelial Dysplasia [*Medicine*] (MELL)
IED.......... Intrinsic Event Discrimination (SAUS)
IED.......... Ion Exchange Desalination
IED.......... Ionospheric Electron Density
IED.......... Suburban Library System, Burr Ridge, IL [*OCLC symbol*] (OCLC)
IEDA.......... Intercontinental Electronic Data Systems et Aviation (SAUO)
IEDC.......... International Energy Development Corp. (SAUS)
IEDD.......... Improvised Explosive Device Disposal (SAUS)
IEDD.......... Institution of Engineering Draftsmen and Designers (SAUS)
IEDD.......... Institution of Engineering Draughtsmen and Designers (SAUO)
IEDD.......... Investigative Explosive Device Detonation (SAUS)
IEDF.......... Ion Energy Distribution Function (AAEL)
IeDL.......... Lembaga Ilmu Pengetahuan Indonesia, Pusat Dokumentasi Ilmiah Nasional, Jakarta, Indonesia [*Library symbol*] [*Library of Congress*] (LCLS)
IEdL.......... Lewis and Clark Library System, Edwardsville, IL [*Library symbol*] [*Library of Congress*] (LCLS)
IEdL-A.......... Lewis and Clark Library System, Alhambra, Alhambra, IL [*Library symbol*] [*Library of Congress*] (LCLS)
IEdL-C.......... Lewis and Clark Library System, Chesterfield, Chesterfield, IL [*Library symbol*] [*Library of Congress*] (LCLS)
IEdL-H.......... Lewis and Clark Library System, Hamel, Hamel, IL [*Library symbol*] [*Library of Congress*] (LCLS)
IEdL-HP.......... Lewis and Clark Library System, Hillsboro Prison, Edwardsville, IL [*Library symbol*] [*Library of Congress*] (LCLS)
IeDLIP.......... Lembaga Ilmu Pengetahuan Indonesia, Pusat Dokumentasi Ilmiah Nasional, Jakarta, Indonesia [*Library symbol*] [*Library of Congress*] (LCLS)

IEdL-L .... Lewis and Clark Library System, Livingston, Livingston, IL [*Library symbol*] [*Library of Congress*] (LCLS)
IEdL-M .... Lewis and Clark Library System, Marine, Marine, IL [*Library symbol*] [*Library of Congress*] (LCLS)
IEdL-Mg .... Lewis and Clark Library System, Mulberry Grove, Mulberry Grove, IL [*Library symbol*] [*Library of Congress*] (LCLS)
IEdL-P .... Lewis and Clark Library System, Palmyra, Palmyra, IL [*Library symbol*] [*Library of Congress*] (LCLS)
IEdL-Sh .... Lewis and Clark Library System, Shipman, Shipman, IL [*Library symbol*] [*Library of Congress*] (LCLS)
IEdL-StJ .... Lewis and Clark Library System, St. Jacob, St. Jacob, IL [*Library symbol*] [*Library of Congress*] (LCLS)
IEDM .... International Electron Devices Meeting (SAUO)
IEdMC .... Pere Marquette Youth Center, Edwardsville, IL [*Library symbol*] [*Library of Congress*] (LCLS)
IEDMS .... International Electron Devices & Materials Symposium (SAUS)
IEDO .... Institution of Economic Development Officers [*British*] (DBA)
IeDP .... Perpustakaan Museum Pusat, Jakarta, Indonesia [*Library symbol*] [*Library of Congress*] (LCLS)
IEDR .... Institute of Economic Development and Research (SAUO)
IEDR .... Integrated Electric-Drive Propulsion (SAUS)
IEDS .... Electronic Information Delivery Service (SAUS)
IEDS .... Income Equalization Deposits Scheme
IEDS .... Integrated Engineering Design Service (SAUO)
IEDS .... International Environmental Data Service [*European Commodities Exchange*] [*United Nations*] (DUND)
IEDS .... international Environment and Development Service (GNE)
IEdS .... Southern Illinois University, Edwardsville Campus, Edwardsville, IL [*Library symbol*] [*Library of Congress*] (LCLS)
IEdSD .... Edwardsville Community Unit, School District 7, Edwardsville, IL [*Library symbol*] [*Library of Congress*] (LCLS)
IEdS-D .... Southern Illinois University, School of Dental Medicine, Biomedical Library, Edwardsville, IL [*Library symbol*] [*Library of Congress*] (LCLS)
IEDSS .... Institute of European Defence and Strategic Studies [*British*] (DBA)
IEE .... Independent Educational Evaluation
IEE .... Induced Electrical Effect
IEE .... Induced Electron Emission
IEE .... Industrial Electronic Engineer (IAA)
IEE .... Industrial Electronics Engineers (SAUS)
IEE .... Information Expert Environment [*Software*] [*Market research organization*] (NITA)
IEE .... Inner Enamel Epithelium [*Dentistry*]
IEE .... Institute for Earth Education (EA)
IEE .... Institute for Ecological Economics (SAUS)
IEE .... Institute for Environmental Education (EA)
IEE .... Institute of Electrical Engineering [*Hitchin, Herts., England*] (NATG)
IEE .... Institute of Electrology Educators (EA)
IEE .... Institute of Electronic Engineering (SAUO)
IEE .... Institute of Energy Economics (SAUS)
IEE .... Institute of Environmental Education (SAUS)
IEE .... Institute of Environmental Engineers [*Later, IES*]
IEE .... Institute of Explosives Engineers (SAUO)
IEE .... Institution of Electrical Engineers [*London, England*] [*Database producer*]
IEE .... Institution of Electronical Engineers (SAUS)
IEE .... Institution of Environmental Engineers (SAUO)
IEE .... Integrated Electrical Svcs. [*NYSE symbol*] (SG)
IEE .... Intelligent Electronics Europa (NITA)
IEE .... Interim Expendable Emitter (NVT)
IEE .... International Electrology Education (SAUO)
IEE .... International Electrology Educators (NTPA)
IEE .... International Employment Exchange (SAUO)
IEE .... International Institute for Hydraulic and Environmental Engineering [*Netherlands*] (IRC)
IEE .... National College of Education, Evanston, IL [*Library symbol*] [*Library of Congress*] (LCLS)
IEE .... North Suburban Library System, Wheeling, IL [*OCLC symbol*] (OCLC)
IEEA .... Industrial Energy and Environmental Analysis (SAUS)
IEEA .... Integrated Environmental and Economic Accounting (SAUS)
IEEA .... Integrated System of Environmental and Economic Accounting (SAUO)
IEEC .... IEEE [*Institute of Electrical and Electronics Engineers*] Electronic Computer (IAA)
IEEC .... Industrial Electrical Equipment Council (SAUO)
IEEC .... Integrated Electronics Engineering Center [*State University of New York, Binghamton*] [*Research center*] (RCD)
IEEC .... Interafrican Electrical Engineering College (SAUO)
IEEC .... International Electrical Engineering College (SAUO)
IEEE .... Institute of Electrical and Electronics Engineering (NITA)
IEEE .... Institute of Electrical and Electronics Engineers (IGQR)
IEEE .... International Electrical and Electronics Exhibition (SAUO)
IEEE .... Trans Inform. Theory (SAUS)
IEEE-CS .... Institute of Electrical and Electronic Engineers-Computer Society (SAUS)
IEEE Exp ...... IEEE Expert: Intelligent Systems and Their Applications [*A publication*] (BRI)
IEEE-PES ...... Institute of Electrical and Electronics Engineers-Power Engineering Society (SAUS)
IEEE/PES ...... Power Engineering Society of the Institute of Electrical and Electronic Engineers (ITD)
IEEE Proceedings... Institute of Electrical and Electronic Engineers Proceedings (journ.) (SAUS)
IEEF .... Ion Exchange Evaporation Filter (PDAA)
IEEI .... Institute of Electrical Engineers of Japan (SAUS)
IEEI .... International Electronics Engineering, Inc. (AAG)
IEEI .... University of Illinois Hospital Eye and Ear Infirmary [*University of Illnois at Chicago*] [*Research center*] (RCD)
IEEIE .... Institution of Electrical and Electronics Inc. Engineers (DS)
IEEJ .... Institute of Electrical Engineers of Japan (SAUO)
IEEJ .... International Electrical Engineers of Japan (SAUS)
IEELG .... International Education Exchange Liaison Group (EA)
IEEMA .... Indian Electrical and Electronics Manufacturers Association (SAUO)
IEE News ..... Institution of Electrical Engineers News (journ.) (SAUS)
IEENSW .... Institution of Electrical Engineers New South Wales [*Australia*]
IEEP .... Incapacitated Emergency Egress Practice [*NASA*] (KSC)
IEEP .... Institute for European Environmental Policy [*Germany*] (EAIO)
IEEP .... Interagency Energy/Environment Program [*Environmental Protection Agency*]
IEEP .... International Environment Education Program (SAUS)
IEEPA .... International Emergency Economic Powers Act [*1977*]
IEER .... Institute for Energy & Environmental Research
IEES .... Imaging Electron Energy Spectrometer (SAUS)
IEES .... International Education Exchange Service [*Department of State*]
IEETE .... Institution of Electrical and Electronics Technician Engineers (MCD)
IEEU .... Instituto de Estudios de Estados Unidos [*Studies Mexico/US relations, US domestic politics, US economy, and US foreign policy*] [*Mexico*] (CROSS)
IEEV .... Institution of Electrical Engineers Victoria [*Australia*]
IE-Ex .... Evanston Public Library, Extension (Bookmobile), Evanston, IL [*Library symbol*] [*Library of Congress*] (LCLS)
IEF .... Imaging Energy Filter (AAEL)
IEF .... Indian Educators Federation (NTPA)
IEF .... Indian Expeditionary Force [*British military*] (DMA)
IEF .... Information Engineering Facility (CDE)
IEF .... Institute of European Finance (SAUO)
IEF .... Instruction Execution Function (NITA)
IEF .... INTACT [*Infants Need to Avoid Circumcision Trauma*] Educational Foundation [*Later, NO-CIRC*] (EA)
IEF .... Integral Equation Formulation (PDAA)
IEF .... Integrated Expansion Force (SAUS)
IEF .... International Ecumenical Fellowship (SAUS)
IEF .... International Environment Facility (SAUO)
IEF .... International Environment Forum (SAUO)
IEF .... International Equestrian Federation (EAIO)
IEF .... International Exhibitions Foundation (EA)
IEF .... International Eye Foundation (EA)
IEF .... Interrupt Flip-Flop (SAUS)
IEF .... Inventory Exchange Format (SAUO)
IEF .... Isoelectric Focusing [*Analytical chemistry*]
IEF .... Isoelectric Focusing Experiment (SAUS)
IEF .... Israel Education Fund
IEF .... Itala Esperanto-Federacio (SAUO)
IEF .... Italian Expeditionary Force
IEF .... Starved Rock Library System, Ottawa, IL [*OCLC symbol*] (OCLC)
IEFC .... International Emergency Food Committee (SAUO)
IEFC .... International Emergency Food Council [*Post-World War II*]
IEFCC .... Israels Enhanced Fire Control Computer (SAUS)
IEFD .... Instrument and Electrical Flow Diagram (SAUS)
IEFD .... Instrument and Equipment Flow Diagram (SAUS)
IEFD .... Instrument Electrical Flow Diagram (SAUS)
IEFP .... International Exposition for Food Packagers (SAUS)
IEFP .... International Exposition for Food Processors (ITD)
IEFR .... International Esperanto Fellowship of Rotarians [*See also IEAR*] (EAIO)
IEFS .... Integrated Electronic Filing System [*Computer science*] (DGA)
IEFUA .... International Electronic Facsimile Users Association (EA)
IEG .... Garrett-Evangelical Theological Seminary, Evanston, IL [*Library symbol*] [*Library of Congress*] (LCLS)
IEG .... Harry S Truman College, Chicago, IL [*OCLC symbol*] (OCLC)
IEG .... Imagery Exploitation Group
IEG .... Immediately Early Gene [*Genetics*]
IEG .... Immunopathology Exchange Group (SAUO)
IEG .... Imperial Ethiopian Government (CINC)
IEG .... Independent Evaluation Group (SDI)
IEG .... Industrial Electronics Group [*of General Motors Corp.*]
IEG .... Information Exchange Group [*National Institutes of Health*]
IEG .... Institute of Economic Growth-Research Center on Social and Economic Development in Asia (SAUO)
IEG .... Integral Engine Governor
IEG .... Interdivisional Engineering Guide (SAUS)
IEG .... Internal Engine Generator (PDAA)
IEG .... Internet Entertainment Group, Inc.
IEG .... Zielona Gora [*Poland*] [*Airport symbol*] (OAG)
IEGE .... IEEE [*Institute of Electrical and Electronics Engineers*] Geoscience Electronics (IAA)
IEGP .... Information Exchange Group Program (SAUO)
IEGP .... Interagency Economic Growth Project [*Department of Transportation*]
IEGS .... Integral Engine Governing System
IEH .... American Library Association, Chicago, IL [*OCLC symbol*] (OCLC)
IEH .... Industrial Electric Heating (SAUS)
IEH .... Institute for Environment and Health (ADWA)
IEH-3 .... International Extrem Ultraviolet Hitchhiker (SAUS)
IEHA .... International Economic History Association [*Paris, France*] (EA)
IEHA .... International Executive Housekeepers Association (NTPA)
IEHC .... Industrial Electronic Hardware Corp. (SAUS)
IEHC .... Industrial Electronics Hardware Corp. (SAUS)
IEHD .... Institute for the Editing of Historical Documents

IEHIURM....... Institute for Encyclopedia of Human Ideas on Ultimate Reality and Meaning (SAUO)
IEHMO......... Iterative Extended Hueckel Molecular Orbital (DB)
IEHO........... Institute of Environmental Health Officers [*British*]
IEHO........... Institution of Environmental Health Officers (SAUS)
IEHS........... Evanston Township High School, Evanston, IL [*Library symbol*] [*Library of Congress*] (LCLS)
IEI............... Immunocytochemistry, ELISA [*Enzyme-Linked Immunosorbent Assay*], and Immunoblotting
IEI............... Implantation-Enhanced Interdiffusion (SAUS)
IEI............... Indeterminate Engineering Items
IEI............... Indiana Energy [*NYSE symbol*] (TTSB)
IEI............... Indiana Energy, Inc. [*NYSE symbol*] (SPSG)
IEI............... Indiana Energy, Incorporated (SAUO)
IEI............... Industrial Education Institute
IEI............... Industrial Education International, Ltd. (SAUO)
IEI............... Industrial Engineering Institute
IEI............... Institute for Educational Innovation [*Later, Education Development Center*]
IEI............... Institute of Electrical Inspectors (SAUO)
IEI............... Institute of Engineering Inspection (SAUO)
IEI............... Institution of Engineering Inspection [*British*] (BI)
IEI............... Institution of Engineers of India (SAUS)
IEI............... Institution of Engineers of Ireland (ACII)
IEI............... International Educator's Institute (EA)
IEI............... International Electronics Industries (SAUO)
IEI............... International Enamellers Institute [*Derby, England*] (EAIO)
IEI............... International Environmental Institute (SAUS)
IEI............... International Epitek, Inc. [*Toronto Stock Exchange symbol*]
IEI............... International Evaluations, Inc.
IEI............... Interrupt Enable In (SAUS)
IEI............... Investment Education Institute (EA)
IEI............... Iran Electronics Industries
IEI............... Isoelectric Interval (DMAA)
IEIA............. Installation Environmental Impact Assessment (PDAA)
IEIA............. Insurance Employers' Industrial Association [*Australia*]
IEIA............. Integrated Educational Information Agency (SAUS)
IEIA............. Integrated Educational Information System (PDAA)
IEIA............. International Export Import Association (SAUO)
IEIAS........... Institut Europeen Interuniversitaire de l'Action Sociale [*Inter-University European Institute on Social Welfare - IEISW*] (EAIO)
IEIB............. International Electronics, Inc. [*NASDAQ symbol*] (NQ)
IEIC............. Independent Engineering Insurers' Committee (HEAS)
IEIC............. Institution of Engineers-in-Charge [*British*] (BI)
IEIC............. International Education Information Center (SAUS)
IEIC............. Iowa Educational Information Center (SAUO)
IEICE........... Institute of Electronics, Information and Communication Engineers (SAUS)
IEICEJ.......... Institute of Electronics, Information and Communication Engineers of Japan (SAUS)
IEIDATA....... International Economic Indicators Database [*Columbia Business School*] [*Information service or system*] (CRD)
IEIE............. International Electrs [*NASDAQ symbol*] (TTSB)
IEII.............. Institution of Engineering Inspection Incorporated (SAUO)
IEIJ.............. Illuminating Engineering Institute of Japan (SAUS)
IEIM............. IEEE [*Institute of Electrical and Electronics Engineers*] Instrumentation and Measurement Society (IAA)
IEIP............. Institut Europeen des Industries de la Pectine [*European Institute of the Pectin Industries*]
IEIP............. International Education Information Program
IEIS............. Integrated Educational Information System (SAUO)
IEIS............. Integrated Engine Instrument System (MCD)
IEISW.......... Inter-University European Institute on Social Welfare (EA)
IEIT............. IEEE [*Institute of Electrical and Electronics Engineers*] Information Theory Society (IAA)
IEJ............... Deere & Co., Moline, IL [*OCLC symbol*] (OCLC)
IEJ............... Infite Ltd. [*British*] [*ICAO designator*] (FAAC)
IEJ............... Institut Europeen du Jouet [*European Toy Institute - ETI*] (EAIO)
IEJ............... Israel Exploration Journal [*A publication*] (ABAR)
IEJE............. Institut d'Etudes Juridiques Europeennes [*Benelux*]
IEK............... Kendall College, Evanston, IL [*Library symbol*] [*Library of Congress*] (LCLS)
IEKA............. Internacia Esperanto Klubo Automobilista [*International Automobile Esperanto Club*] (EAIO)
IEKKK........... Invisible Empire Knights of the Ku Klux Klan (EA)
IEKV............. Internationale Eisenbahn-Kongress-Vereinigung [*International Railway Congress Association*]
IEL............... IE Industries, Inc. (MHDW)
IEL............... Illustrative Evaluation Scenario [*Environmental science*] (COE)
IEL............... Improved Efficiency of Learning [*Project*] (AIE)
IEL............... Improved Erector-Launcher (SAA)
IEL............... Indian Explosives Limited (SAUO)
IEL............... Industrial Engineering Ltd. (SAUS)
IEL............... Industrial Equity Limited (SAUO)
IEL............... Industrial Exhibitions Limited (SAUO)
IEL............... Information Exchange List [*Military*] (AABC)
IEL............... Inspection Equipment List (ACAE)
IEL............... Institute for Educational Leadership (EA)
IEL............... Interdivisional Engineering List (SAUS)
IEL............... Internacia Esperanto-Ligo (SAUO)
IEL............... Internal Elastic Lamina [*Medicine*] (DMAA)
IEL............... International Electrochemical Commission
IEL............... Intimal Elastic Lamina [*Medicine*] (STED)
IEL............... Intraepithelial Lymphocyte [*Hematology*]
IEL............... Iota Exploration Ltd. [*Vancouver Stock Exchange symbol*]
IEL............... Iowa Electric Light & Power Co. (SAUO)
IEL............... Parlin Public Library, Canton, IL [*OCLC symbol*] (OCLC)
IELA............. International English Language Association (SAUO)
IELA............. International Exhibition Logistics Associates [*Geneva, Switzerland*] (EAIO)
IELE............. Institute for Language Education (SAUO)
IElg............. Gail Borden Public Library, Elgin, IL [*Library symbol*] [*Library of Congress*] (LCLS)
IELG............. International Esperantist League for Go (EA)
IElgB........... Brethren Historical Library and Archives, Elgin, IL [*Library symbol*] [*Library of Congress*] (LCLS)
IElgC........... Elgin Community College, Elgin, IL [*Library symbol*] [*Library of Congress*] (LCLS)
IELI............. Intensive English Language Institute (SAUS)
IElm............ Elmhurst Public Library, Elmhurst, IL [*Library symbol*] [*Library of Congress*] (LCLS)
IElmC.......... Elmhurst College, Elmhurst, IL [*Library symbol*] [*Library of Congress*] (LCLS)
IELP............. Iowa Electric Light & Power Co. (SAUO)
IELS............. Isotope Exciter Light Source
IElsP........... Principia College, Elsah, IL [*Library symbol*] [*Library of Congress*] (LCLS)
IELTS........... International English Language Testing System
IELV............. Intermediate Expendable Launch Satellite (SAUS)
IELV............. Intermediate Expendable Launch Vehicle (SAUS)
IElw............. Morrison and Mary Wiley Public Library, Elmwood, IL [*Library symbol*] [*Library of Congress*] (LCLS)
IElwp........... Elmwood Park Public Library, Elmwood Park, IL [*Library symbol*] [*Library of Congress*] (LCLS)
IEM............... East Texas State University, Metroplex Center, Commerce, TX [*OCLC symbol*] (OCLC)
IEM............... Ideal Effort Multiplier
IEM............... Immune Electron Microscopy
IEM............... Immuno-Electron Microscopy [*Medicine*] (EDAA)
IEM............... Inactive Equipment Maintenance (DNAB)
IEM............... Inborn Error of Metabolism [*Medicine*]
IEM............... Individual Engagement Model (MCD)
IEM............... Industrial Engineer for Management
IEM............... Information Engineering Methodology (TIMI)
IEM............... Informations Engineering Methode (SAUS)
IEM............... Infrared Projector Energy Monitor (MCD)
IEM............... Institute of Environmental Managers (COBU)
IEM............... Institute of Experimental Meteorology [*Former USSR*]
IEM............... Interim Examination and Maintenance [*Nuclear energy*] (NRCH)
IEM............... Interim Examination/Maintenance (SAUO)
IEM............... Internal Environment Monitoring
IEM............... Intromission and Ejaculatory Mechanism [*Physiology*]
IEM............... Isocyanatoethylmethacrylate (SAUS)
IEMA............. Immunoenzymometric Assay [*Clinical chemistry*]
IEMA............. Independent Electrical Manufacturers Association (EA)
IEMA............. International Eight Meter Association (SAUS)
IEMA............. International Explosive Metalworkers Association (SAUO)
IEMA............. Iowa Educational Media Association
IEMAE........... Institute of Evolutionary Morphology and Animal Ecology [*Commonwealth of Independent States*]
IEMATS......... Improved Emergency Message Automatic Transmission System (MCD)
IEMBA........... International Executive Masters of Business Administration (PGP)
IEMC............. IEEE [*Institute of Electrical and Electronics Engineers*] Electromagnetic Compatibility Society (IAA)
IEMC............. Independent Electronic Music Center [*Defunct*]
IEMC............. Industrial Equipment Manufacturers Council [*Later, ICED*] (EA)
IEMC............. International Electronics Manufacturing Co. (AAG)
IEMCAP......... Intrasystem Electromagnetic Compatibility Analysis Program [*Computer science*] [*Air Force*]
IEM CELL...... Interim Examination and Maintenance Cell (SAUS)
IEMCS........... Industrial Estates Management Corporation for Scotland (SAUO)
IEMD............. Integrated Environmental Management Division [*Environmental Protection Agency*] (EPA)
IEME............. Corps of Indian Electrical and Mechanical Engineers [*British military*] (DMA)
IEME............. Inspectorate of Electrical and Mechanical Engineering [*Military*] (IAA)
IEME............. Inspectorate of Electrical and Mechanical Equipment (SAUO)
IEMEMC........ Instrument, Electrical, and Miscellaneous Equipment Modification Committee (SAUO)
IEMEMC........ Instrument, Electrical and Miscellaneous Modification Committee (SAUS)
IEMG............. Integrated Electromyogram [*Medicine*]
IEMGI........... Imperial Ethiopian Mapping and Geography Institute (SAUO)
IEMIS........... Integrated Emergency Management Information System [*Federal Emergency Management Agency*] (GFGA)
IEMMC.......... Internet Electronic Mail Marketing Council (SAUO)
IEMN............. Insufficient Evidence of Medical Necessity (AMHC)
IEMO............. Installation Equipment Management Office [*Military*] (AFIT)
IEMP............. Induced Electromagnetic Pulse (RDA)
IEMP............. Institute of Environmental Medicine and Physiology
IEMP............. Integrated Environmental Management Project [*Environmental Protection Agency*] (GFGA)
IEMP............. Interior Electromagnetic Pulse (MCD)
IEMP............. Internal Electromagnetic Pulse
IEMP............. International Executive Masters Programme [*London Business School*]
IEMS............. Installation Equipment Management System
IEMS............. Institute of Experimental Medicine and Surgery (SAUO)
IEMS............. Integrated Emergency Management System (SAUO)

I/EMS .... Intergraph Corp./Engineering Modeling System
IEMS .... Interim Electronic Maintenance Support (AFIT)
IEMS .... International Electronic Mail System (SAUS)
IEMSA .... Institution of Engineering and Mining Surveyors Australia Inc. (SAUO)
IEMSA .... Iowa Emergency Medical Services Association (SRA)
IEMSI .... Interactive Electronic Mail Standard Identification (SAUO)
IEMSL .... Instantaneous Electromagnetic Mean Sea Level (ACAE)
IEMT .... Intermediate Emergency Medical Technician [*Also, EMT-I*] (DHSM)
IEMT .... International Electronic Manufacturing Technology (SAUS)
IEMTF .... Interim Examination and Maintenance Training Facility [*Nuclear energy*] (NRCH)
IEMU .... Integrated Extravehicular Mobility Unit (SSD)
IEMVT .... Institut d'Elevage et de Medecine Veterinaire des Pays Tropicaux [*Institute of Stockraising and Veterinary Medicine in Tropical Countries*] [*France*]
IEMW .... Internacia Esperanto-Muzeo en Wien (SAUO)
IEN .... Die Israelitischen Eigennamen [*A publication*] (BJA)
IE-N .... Evanston Public Library, North Branch, Evanston, IL [*Library symbol*] [*Library of Congress*] (LCLS)
IEN .... Imperial Ethiopian Navy (SAUO)
IEN .... Individualized Electronic Newspaper (VLIE)
IEN .... Industrial Equipment News (journ.) (SAUS)
IEN .... Information Exchange Network (SAUS)
IEN .... Integrated Enterprise Network (SAUS)
IEN .... Interactive Employment Network (SAUS)
IEN .... Internet Engineering Note (VLIE)
IEN .... Internet Engineering Notes (SAUS)
IEN .... Internet Experimental Note
IEN .... Internet Experiment Notebook (SAUS)
IEN .... Interpenetrating Elastomeric Networks [*Organic chemistry*]
IEN .... Northwestern University, Evanston, IL [*Library symbol*] [*Library of Congress*] (LCLS)
IENA .... Irish Emergency Nurses Association (SAUO)
IENC .... Income Earned, Not Collected (EBF)
IEN-C .... Northwestern University, Joseph Schaffner Library of Commerce, Chicago, IL [*Library symbol*] [*Library of Congress*] (LCLS)
IEN-D .... Northwestern University, Dental School, Chicago, IL [*Library symbol*] [*Library of Congress*] (LCLS)
IENDA .... International Education Center for New Technologies and their Industrial Applications (SAUO)
IEng .... Incorporated Engineer (SAUO)
IEng .... Incorporate Engineer (ACII)
IEN-L .... Northwestern University, Law Library, Chicago, IL [*Library symbol*] [*Library of Congress*] (LCLS)
IEN-M .... Northwestern University, Medical School, Chicago, IL [*Library symbol*] [*Library of Congress*] (LCLS)
IEN-Mu .... Northwestern University, Music Library, Evanston, IL [*Library symbol*] [*Library of Congress*] (LCLS)
IENS .... Indian and Eastern Newspapers Society (SAUO)
IEN-T .... Northwestern University, Technological Institute, Evanston, IL [*Library symbol*] [*Library of Congress*] (LCLS)
IEN-Tr .... Northwestern University, Transportation Library, Evanston, IL [*Library symbol*] [*Library of Congress*] (LCLS)
IEnvSc .... Institution of Environmental Sciences [*British*] (DBA)
IEO .... Incoherent Electronic Oscillator
IEO .... Industry and Environment Office (GNE)
IEO .... Installation Engineers Office (SAA)
I/EO .... Instructor/Equipment Operator
IEO .... Integrated Electronic Office (NITA)
IEO .... Interim Engineering Order (AAG)
IEO .... Intermediate Earth Orbit (SSD)
IEO .... International Education Office [*World War II*]
IEO .... International Exchange Office (AFM)
IEO .... Interrupt Enable Out (SAUS)
IEO .... Union of International Engineering Organizations (SAUO)
IEOAM .... Inborn Errors of Organic Acid Metabolism [*Medicine*] (MELL)
IEOCS .... Interim Equipment Order Control System [*Bell System*]
IEOE .... Integrated Enterprise Operation Environment (VLIE)
IEOM .... Institute of Environment and Offshore Medicine (SAUO)
IEON .... International Esperantist Organization of Naturists [*See also INOE*] [*Frankfurt, Federal Republic of Germany*] (EAIO)
IEOP .... Immunoelectroosmophoresis [*Analytical biochemistry*]
IEOR .... Department of Industrial Engineering and Operations Research (SAUO)
IEOS .... Institute of Elemental-Organic Compounds (SAUO)
IEOS .... Integrated Electronical Office System (SAUS)
IEOS .... Integrated Electronic Office System (IAA)
IEOS .... International component of EOS (SAUS)
IEOS .... International Earth Observation (or Observing) System (SAUO)
IEOSM .... International Earth Observation Satellite Missions (SAUO)
IEOTSG .... Integral Economizer Once-Through Steam Generator (NRCH)
IEP .... Evansville Public Library and Vanderburgh County Public Library, Evansville, IN [*OCLC symbol*] (OCLC)
IEp .... Fondulac District Library, East Peoria, IL [*Library symbol*] [*Library of Congress*] (LCLS)
IEP .... Image Edge Profile [*Photography*] (OA)
IEP .... Immunoelectrophoresis [*Analytical biochemistry*]
IEP .... Independent Electric Plant (SAUS)
IEP .... Independent European Program Group (JAGO)
IEP .... Independent Evaluation Plan
IEP .... Independent Exchange Plan
IEP .... Indicateur Electronique de Pilotage [*Electronic Pilotage Indicator*] [*Aviation*]
IEP .... Individual Educational Program (SAUS)
IEP .... Individual Education Plan
IEP .... Individual Evaluation Plan [*Army*]
IEP .... Individualized Education Plan [*Special education*] (PAZ)
IEP .... Individualized Education Program [*For the education of a handicapped person*]
IEP .... Industry and Environment Office (SAUO)
IEP .... Information Economics and Policy (journ.) (SAUS)
IEP .... Information Exchange Program [*or Project*] [*Military*]
IEP .... Information Exchange Project (SAUO)
IEP .... Ingestion Exposure Pathway [*Nuclear emergency planning*]
IEP .... Initial Engineering Phase (ACAE)
IEP .... Initial Enrollment Period [*Insurance*]
IEP .... Instantaneous Effective Photo Cathodes (NAKS)
IEP .... Instantaneously Effective Photocathode (SAUS)
IEP .... Institute for Ecological Policies [*Defunct*] (EA)
IEP .... Institute for Experimental Psychiatry
IEP .... Institute of Earth Physics (SAUS)
IEP .... Institute of European Politics (SAUO)
IEP .... Institute of Experimental Psychology (SAUO)
IEP .... Institut Europeen pour la Promotion des Entreprises
IEP .... Institut fuer Europaeische Politik [*Institute of European Politics*] (EAIO)
IEP .... Instrumentation for the Evaluation of Pictures (SAUS)
IEP .... Instrument for Evaluation of Photographs
IEP .... Integrated Engineering Program
IEP .... Intelligence Estimate for Planning
IEP .... Interdivisional Engineering Practices (SAUS)
IEP .... Internal Economic Problems [*British*]
IEP .... International Economic Policy
IEP .... International Economic Publishers (SAUO)
IEP .... International Education Project [*American Council on Education*] (PDAA)
IEP .... International Energy Program
IEP .... International Exchange Program (SAUS)
IEP .... International Potential [*Vancouver Stock Exchange symbol*]
IEP .... Intext Educational Publishers
IEP .... Inverted Energy Population
IEP .... Inverted Engineer Population (SAUO)
IEP .... Isoelectric Point [*Also, IP, PH_1, pI*] [*Chemistry*]
IEPA .... Illinois Environmental Protection Agency (DOGT)
IEPA .... Independent Electron Pair Approximation [*Physics*]
IEPA .... International Early Psychosis Association (ADWA)
IEPA .... International Economic Policy Act of 1972
IEPA .... International Economic Policy Association (EA)
IEPA .... International Environment Protection Act of 1983
IEPA .... Intra-European Payments Agreement
IE/PAC .... Industry and Environment Program Activity Centre (SAUO)
IEPALA .... Instituto de Estudios Politicos para America Latina y Africa [*Spain*]
IEPB .... Interagency Emergency Planning Board [*Federal disaster planning*]
IEPC .... Instantaneous Effective Photocathodes (MCD)
IEPC .... Interagency Emergency Planning Committee
IEPD .... Industrial and Extractive Processes Division [*Environmental Protection Agency*] (EPA)
IEpE .... East Peoria Elementary School District, East Peoria, IL [*Library symbol*] [*Library of Congress*] (LCLS)
IEPE .... Integrated Electronics Piezo-Electric [*Electronics*]
IEPES .... Institute of Political, Economic and Social Studies (Mexico) [*Political party*] (PSAP)
IEPFCHK .... International Elvis Presley Fan Club, Hong Kong (EAIO)
IEPG .... Independent European Program Group [*NATO*]
IEPG .... Internet Engineering Planning Group
IEpI .... Illinois Central College, East Peoria, IL [*Library symbol*] [*Library of Congress*] (LCLS)
IEPP .... Institute of Earth and Planetary Physics [*University of Alberta*] [*Research center*] (RCD)
IEPP .... International Energy Policy Perspectives (journal) [*Medicine*] (EDAA)
IEPPA .... International Encyclopedia of Public Policy and Administration [*A publication*]
IEPPL .... Integrated Engineering Planning Parts List
IE/P/R .... Independent Evaluation/Plan/Report (ACAE)
IEPR .... Initial Exercise Press Release (SAUO)
IEPR .... Integrated Engine Pressure Ratio (GAVI)
IEPR .... International Economic Policy and Research [*Medicine*] (EDAA)
IEPRC .... International Electronic Publishing Research Centre [*British*] (IRC)
IEPS .... Incentives and Earned Privileges Scheme (WDAA)
IEPs .... Individualized Education Programs (SAUS)
IEPS .... Institute for Ecological Problems of the North, Russia (SAUO)
IEPS .... International Electronics Packaging Society (EA)
IEPT .... Intermediate End Point of Therapy (MELL)
IEPW .... Interim Earth Penetrator Weapon (SAUS)
IEQ .... Illinois Prairie District Public Library, Metamora, IL [*OCLC symbol*] (OCLC)
IEQ .... Index of Environmental Quality (WDAA)
IEQE .... IEEE [*Institute of Electrical and Electronics Engineers*] Quantum Electronics (IAA)
I Eq R .... Irish Equity Reports [*A publication*] (DLA)
IER .... Independent Evaluation Report
IER .... Individual Clothing and Equipment Record (SAUO)
IER .... Individual Education Record
IER .... Individual Equipment Reliability (SAUS)
IER .... Individual Evaluation Report
IER .... Industrial Equipment Reserve
IER .... Infanterie-Ersatzregiment [*Infantry Replacement Training Regiment*] [*German military - World War II*]
IER .... Inherent Equipment Reliability
IER .... Initial Engagement Range (MCD)

IER............. Installation Enhancement Release [*Computer science*]
IER............. Institute for Econometric Research (EA)
IER............. Institute for Economic Research (SAUO)
IER............. Institute for Ecumencial Research (SAUO)
IER............. Institute for Education by Radio [*Defunct*] (NTCM)
IER............. Institute for Environmental Research [*Environmental Science Services Administration*]
IER............. Institute for Exploratory Research (SAUO)
IER............. Institute of Educational Research [*Defunct*] (EA)
IER............. Institute of Engineering Research [*Research center*] [*British*] (IRC)
IER............. Institute of Engineering Research [*University of California*] [*Research center*] (MCD)
IER............. Institute of Environmental Research (SAUS)
IER............. Institute of Exploratory Research [*Army*]
IER............. Instruction Execution Rate (SAUS)
IER............. Interface Evaluation Report (KSC)
IER............. Interim Engineering Report
IER............. Internal Economic Rate of Return
IER............. Inventory Equipment Requirement
IER............. Investigative Engineering Request (SAUO)
IER............. Ion Exchange Resin
IER............. Irish Ecclesiastical Record (journ.) (SAUS)
IER............. Irish Equity Reports [*A publication*] (DLA)
IER............. Mackinaw Township Library, Mackinaw, IL [*OCLC symbol*] (OCLC)
IER............. Natchitoches, LA [*Location identifier*] [*FAA*] (FAAL)
IER............. Organization for International Economic Relations [*Vienna, Austria*] (EAIO)
IERB............ Islamic Economics Research Bureau (SAUO)
IERC............ Independent Evaluation Review Committee (SAUO)
IERC............ Indian Education Resources Center (SAUO)
IERC............ Industrial Equipment Reserve Committee (SAA)
IERC............ International Electronic Research Corp. (MCD)
IERC............ International Enuresis Research Center (ADWA)
IERD............ Industry Energy Research and Development (SAUS)
IERD............ Industry Energy Research and Development Program [*Canada*]
IERD............ International Exposition of Rural Development (SAUO)
IERE............ Institute of Electrical and Radio Engineers (SAUO)
IERE............ Institute of Electronics and Radio Engineers [*British*]
IERE............ Institution of Electronic and Radio Engineers (SAUS)
IERE............ Institution of Electronics and Radio Engineers (SAUO)
IERESM........ Institut Europeen de Recherches et d'Etudes Superieures en Management [*European Institute for Advanced Studies in Management - EIASM*] [*Brussels, Belgium*] (EA)
IERF............ Industrial Educational and Research Foundation (SAUO)
IERF............ International Education and Research Foundation (SAUS)
IERF............ International Education Research Foundation (EA)
IERFC.......... Integral Error Function Complement (SAUS)
IERFC.......... Integrated Error Function Complement (SAUS)
IERI............ Illuminating Engineering Research Institute (EA)
IERI............ Interagency Education Research Initiative
IERI............ International Electronics Reliability Institute within Electronic and Electrical Engineering (SAUS)
IERL............ Industrial Environmental Research Laboratory [*Environmental Protection Agency*]
IERM........... Individual Employment Rights Manual [*A publication*]
IERN............ Internal-External Recurrent Neural Network (AAEL)
IERO............ Institute for Engineering Research in the Oceans [*Marine science*] (MSC)
IERQ............ Institute of Electrical Research of Quebec (SAUS)
IERS............ International Earth Reference System (SAUO)
IERS............ International Earth Rotation Service (SAUO)
IERS............ International Educational Reporting Service [*International Bureau of Education*] [*United Nations*] (EY)
IERS............ International Ellipsoid Reference System (SAUO)
IERS............ Inventory Equipment Requirement Specification
IERT............ Indiana Eastern Railroad & Transportation [*Federal Railroad Administration identification code*]
IERT............ Institute for Education by Radio-Television (NTCM)
IERTM.......... Institute for Environmental Research Technical Memorandum
IERW........... Initial Entry Rotary Wing [*Student*] (MCD)
IERW........... Ion Exchange Regeneration Waste (SAUS)
IERW ITS..... Initial Entry Rotary Wing Integrated Training System (SAUS)
IEs.............. East St. Louis Public Library, East St. Louis, IL [*Library symbol*] [*Library of Congress*] (LCLS)
IES.............. Eli Lilly & Co., Indianapolis, IN [*OCLC symbol*] (OCLC)
IE-S............ Evanston Public Library, South Branch, Evanston, IL [*Library symbol*] [*Library of Congress*] (LCLS)
IES.............. Id, Ego, Superego [*Test*] [*Psychology*]
IES.............. Identify External Symbol (SAUS)
IES.............. IEEE Industrial Electronics Society (EA)
IES.............. IES Industries [*NYSE symbol*] (SPSG)
IES.............. Illuminating Engineering Society
IES.............. Illuminating Engineers Society (SAUO)
IES.............. Illustrative Evaluation Scenario (DOMA)
IES.............. Image Enhancement System (SAUS)
IES.............. Image Exploitation System (SAUS)
IES.............. Imagery Exploitation System (DOMA)
IES.............. Implemented External Schemata (VLIE)
IES.............. Income and Expense Statement (MHDW)
IES.............. Incoming Echo Suppressor [*Telecommunications*] (TEL)
IES.............. Independent Educational Services (EA)
IES.............. Indian Educational Service [*British*]
I-ES............ Induction-Electric Survey (SAUS)
IES.............. Inductive Energy Storage
IES.............. Industrial Electronics Society (SAUO)
IES.............. Industrial Electronic System
IES.............. Industrial Engineering Services
IES.............. Industrial Engineering Standard (MCD)
IES.............. Ineffective Erythropoiesis Syndrome [*Medicine*] (MELL)
IES.............. Inferior Esophageal Sphincter [*Medicine*] (MELL)
IES.............. Information Exchange Service (SAUO)
IES.............. Information Exchange System (SAUO)
IES.............. Information Exchange Systems [*British*]
IES.............. Institute for Earth Sciences [*Environmental Science Services Administration*]
IES.............. Institute for Employment Studies (COBU)
IES.............. Institute for Environmental Sciences (SAUO)
IES.............. Institute of Ecosystem Studies
IES.............. Institute of Employment Studies (HEAS)
IES.............. Institute of English Studies (DBA)
IES.............. Institute of Environmental Sciences (EA)
IES.............. Institute of Environmental Studies (SAUS)
IES.............. Institute of European Studies (EA)
IES.............. Institution of Electrical Engineers, Singapur (SAUO)
IES.............. Institution of Engineers and Shipbuilders [*Scotland*] (DI)
IES.............. Institution of Engineers and Shipbuilders in Scotland (SAUO)
IE-S............ Institution of Engineers-Singapore (SAUO)
IES.............. Institution of Environmental Sciences (EAIO)
IES.............. Integral Error Squared (IEEE)
IES.............. Integrated Electronic System
IES.............. Integrated Energy System (SAUS)
IES.............. Intelligence Evaluation Staff
IES.............. Intelligence Expert System (SAUS)
IES.............. Intelligence Exploitation Squadron [*Air Force*]
IES.............. Intelligent Emulation Switching (SAUS)
IES.............. Intensive Employability Services [*Work Incentive Program*]
IES.............. Intensive Employment Services (SAUS)
IES.............. Interactive Estimating System (SAUS)
IES.............. Interface Editor System (SAUS)
IES.............. Inter-Island Air Services Ltd. [*Grenada*] [*ICAO designator*] (FAAC)
IES.............. Internal Environment Simulator
IES.............. International Ecology Society (EA)
IES.............. International Education Exchange Service [*Department of State*]
IES.............. International Education Series [*A publication*]
IES.............. International Employment Service (SAUO)
IES.............. International Exchange Service [*For publications*] [*Smithsonian Institution*]
IES.............. International Explorers Society
IES.............. Intrinsic Electric Strength (IEEE)
IES.............. Invariant-Ellipticity States (PDAA)
IES.............. Inventory Equipment Sheet
IES.............. Inverness Petroleum Ltd. [*Toronto Stock Exchange symbol*]
IES.............. Inverted Echo Sounder
IES.............. Ion Energy Selector
IES.............. Ion Engine Simulator
IES.............. Ion Engine System
IES.............. Iowa Engineering Society (SAUO)
IES.............. Iran Economic Service (SAUO)
IES.............. Irish Emigrant Society (EA)
IES.............. Irradiation Effects Simulation (NRCH)
IES.............. Israel Exploration Society (SAUO)
IESA............ Illuminating Engineering Society of Australia (SAUO)
IESA............ Indiana Electronic Service Association (SAUO)
IESA............ Instituto de Estudios Superiores de Administracion [*Institute of Higher Studies of Administration*] [*Venezuela*]
IESA............ Insurance Economics Society of America [*Defunct*] (EA)
IESABA........ Institute for the Economic and Social Advancement of Black Africa (SAUS)
IEsAHS........ Assumption High School, East St. Louis, IL [*Library symbol*] [*Library of Congress*] (LCLS)
IESAM.......... Institute of Environmental Science and Management (SAUO)
IESB............ Ireland Electricity Supply Board (SAUO)
IESC............ Information Exchange Steering Committee (SAUO)
IESC............ International Executive Service Corps [*Stamford, CT*] (EA)
IEsCH.......... Christian Welfare Hospital, East St. Louis, IL [*Library symbol*] [*Library of Congress*] (LCLS)
IEsCTH........ Centreville Township Hospital, East St. Louis, IL [*Library symbol*] [*Library of Congress*] (LCLS)
IESD............ Instrumentation and Electronic Systems Division [*NASA*] (MCD)
IES-DC........ IES [*Information Exchange System*] Data Collections [*Commission of the European Communities*] [*Information service or system*] (CRD)
IES-DC........ Information Exchange System-Data Collections (SAUO)
IESG............ Internet Engineering Steering Group [*Computer science*] (ACRL)
IESL............ Institute of Electronic Structure and Laser (SAUS)
IESL............ Institution of Engineers of Sri Lanka (SAUS)
IESL............ Istitution of Engineers, Sri Lanka (SAUS)
IESM............ Inductive Energy Storage Modulator
IESM............ Irradiation Effects on Structural Materials (SAUS)
IESMA.......... Illinois Emergency Services Management Association (SAUO)
IESMP.......... Information Exchange System for Minority Personnel (SAUS)
IESNA.......... Illuminating Engineering Society of North America (EA)
IESP............ Installation Engineer Supply Point (SAUO)
IESP............ Integrated Electronic Signal Processor
IEsP............ Parks College of Aeronautical Technology, East St. Louis, IL [*Library symbol*] [*Library of Congress*] (LCLS)
IEsPC.......... Project Choice, East St. Louis, IL [*Library symbol*] [*Library of Congress*] (LCLS)
IESq............ Intelligence Exploitation Squadron [*Air Force*]
IESq............ Intelligence Exploration Squadron (SAUS)

IESR .... Institute of Economic and Social Research (SAUS)
IESR .... International English Shepherd Registry (EA)
IESRA .... Interim Employment Services Regulatory Authority
IESS .... Institution of Engineers and Shipbuilders in/of Scotland (SAUS)
IESS .... Institution of Engineers and Shipbuilders in Scotland (SAUO)
IESS .... Integrated Electromagnetic System Simulator (ADWA)
IESS .... Intergroup Ewing Sarcoma Study [*Medicine*] (DMAA)
IESS .... International Encyclopedia of the Social Sciences [*A publication*]
IESS .... Ion Engine System Section
IESSA .... Institute of Economic Studies and Social Action (SAUO)
IESSC .... Irish El Salvador Support Committee (EAIO)
IEsSC .... State Community College of East St. Louis, Learning Resources Center, East St. Louis, IL [*Library symbol*] [*Library of Congress*] (LCLS)
IEsSD .... East Saint Louis Public School District 189, East St. Louis, IL [*Library symbol*] [*Library of Congress*] (LCLS)
IEsSMH .... Saint Mary's Hospital, East St. Louis, IL [*Library symbol*] [*Library of Congress*] (LCLS)
IEST .... Implanted Electrode Stimulation Therapy [*Medicine*] (MELL)
IEST .... Impulses, Ego, and Superego Test [*Psychology*] (AEBS)
IEST .... Taiwan Provincial Institute for Elementary School Teachers In-Service Education
IES Test ...... Id, Ego, Superego Test (SAUS)
IESU .... IEEE [*Institute of Electrical and Electronics Engineers*] Sonics and Ultrasonics (IAA)
IESU .... Installation Engineer Supply Unit (SAUO)
IES Ut25 ..... IES Utilities [*Associated Press*] (SAG)
IESV .... Institute for Epidemiologic Studies of Violence (EA)
IESX .... IES Utilities [*Private rail car owner code*]
IET .... East Texas State University, Texarkana, Texarkana, TX [*OCLC symbol*] (OCLC)
IET .... Image Enhancement Technology (SAUO)
IET .... Impact Excited Transmitter
IET .... Implanted Electrode Technique
IET .... Independent Evaluation Teams [*Army Systems Acquisitions Review Council*] (MCD)
IET .... Indo-European Telegraph (SAUO)
IET .... Inelastic Electron Tunneling (SAUS)
IET .... Initial Engine Test
IET .... Initial Entry Training
IET .... Installed Equipment Test (SAUS)
IET .... Institute for Environmental Toxicology (SAUO)
IET .... Institute of Educational Technology [*British*]
IET .... Institute of Engineers and Technicians [*British*] (EAIO)
IET .... Instrument and Electrical Technician (MCD)
IET .... Instrumentation Engineering Technician (SAUS)
IET .... Instrumentation Engineering Technologist (SAUS)
IET .... Instrumentation Engineering Technology (SAUS)
IET .... Integrated Equipment Test [*Nuclear energy*]
IET .... Integrated Equipment Test Facility (SAUO)
IET .... Inter-Entity Transfer (SAUS)
IET .... Interest Equalization Tax
IET .... Intermolecular Energy Transfer [*Chemistry*]
IET .... International Embryo Transfer Society (GVA)
IET .... Interval Embossed Tube
IETA .... International Electrical Testing Association (EAIO)
IETAS .... Interim Escort Towed Array System (MCD)
IETC .... Initial Education and Training Committee (ACII)
IETC .... Interagency Emergency Transportation Committee
IETC .... International Environmental Technology Centre [*United Nations*] (ECON)
IETCA .... International E-22 Class Association (EA)
IETE .... Institution of Electronics and Telecommunications Engineers [*Information service or system*] (TSSD)
IETEJ .... Institute of Electronics & Telecommunications Engineers of Japan (NITA)
IETF .... Initial Engine Test Facility
IETF .... Initial Engine Test Firing (IAA)
IETF .... Integrated Equipment Test Facility [*Department of Energy*]
IETF .... International Engineering Task Force [*Computer science*]
IETF .... Internet Engineering Task Force
IETFWG .... Internet Engineering Task Force-Working Group (SAUO)
IETG .... International Energy Technology Group (SAUO)
IETM .... Informal European Theatre Meeting (EURO)
IETM .... Interactive Electronic Technical Manual [*Military*] (RDA)
IETM .... Intradural Extramedullary Thoracic Meningioma [*Medicine*] (EDAA)
IETO .... Interagency Environmental Technologies Office (BCP)
IETO .... Interagency Office of Environmental Technology (SAUS)
IETP .... Individualized Education and Training Plan (OICC)
IETRA .... Interhuman Embryonic Transfer and Restabilization Agency (SAUS)
IETS .... Individual Extension Training System (ACAE)
IETS .... Industrial Energy Thrift Scheme (SAUO)
IETS .... Inelastic Electron Tunneling Spectroscopy
IETS .... Inelastic Electron Tunneling Spectrum (SAUS)
IETS .... Interim European Telecommunications Standards (SAUO)
I-ETS .... Interim European Telecommunication Standard (OSI)
IETS .... Intermediate Examiner Training School [*Federal Home Loan Bank Board*]
IETS .... International Embryo Transfer Society (EA)
IETTAB .... International Environmental Technology Transfer Advisory Board [*Environmental Protection Agency*] (EGAO)
IEU .... Forum International: International Ecosystems University (EA)
IEU .... IES Util 7.875%JrSubDebs [*NYSE symbol*] (TTSB)
IEU .... IES Utilities [*NYSE symbol*] (SAG)
IEU .... Improved Electronics Unit (SAUS)
IEU .... Independent Education Union [*Australia*]
IEU .... Individual Education Unit [*Medicine*] (EDAA)
IEU .... Industry & Education Unit (SAUO)
IEU .... Input Expansion Unit
IEU .... Instruction Execution Unit [*Computer science*] (IAA)
IEU .... Integer Execution Unit (VLIE)
IEU .... Integrated Electronics Unit (MCD)
IEU .... Interface Electronics Unit [*NASA*]
IEU .... Intermediate Education Unit
IEU .... Ion Exchange Unit
IEU .... Lewis and Clark Library System, Edwardsville, IL [*OCLC symbol*] (OCLC)
IEUBK .... Integrated Exposure Uptake Biokinetic Model (SARE)
IEuC .... Eureka College, Eureka, IL [*Library symbol*] [*Library of Congress*] (LCLS)
IEUP .... Institut fuer Europaeische Umweltpolitik [*Institute for European Environmental Policy - IEEP*] (EAIO)
IEV .... Initial Entry Vehicle (ABAC)
IEV .... Integrated Experimental Version (SAUS)
IEV .... International Electrotechnical Vocabulary (IEEE)
IEV .... Intracellular Enveloped Virus
IEV .... Kewanee Public Library, Kewanee, IL [*OCLC symbol*] (OCLC)
IEV .... Kiev [*Former USSR*] [*Airport symbol*] (OAG)
IEVD .... Integrated Electronic Vertical Display
IEvp .... Evergreen Park Public Library, Evergreen Park, IL [*Library symbol*] [*Library of Congress*] (LCLS)
IEVS .... Income Eligibility Verification Systems (BARN)
IE-W .... Evanston Public Library, West Branch, Evanston, IL [*Library symbol*] [*Library of Congress*] (LCLS)
IEW .... Information Engineering Workbench (CDE)
IEW .... Integrated Electronic Warfare (SAUS)
IEW .... Intelligence and Electronic Warfare [*System*] [*Military*] (RDA)
I/EW .... Intelligence/Electronic Warfare (SAUS)
IEW .... International Energy Workshop (SAUO)
IEW .... Pekin Public Library, Pekin, IL [*OCLC symbol*] (OCLC)
IEW .... Winters, TX [*Location identifier*] [*FAA*] (FAAL)
IEW&S .... Intelligence, Electronic Warfare & Sensors [*Army*]
IEWCS .... Intelligent Electronic Warfare Common Sensor (DWSG)
I/EW FOSS ... Intelligence/Electronic Warfare Family of Systems Study [*Military*] (MCD)
IEWG .... International Elbow Working Group (GVA)
IEWI .... Indirect Environmental Warming Impact
IEWNI .... Washington National Insurance Co., Evanston, IL [*Library symbol*] [*Library of Congress*] (LCLS)
IEWS .... Integrated Electronic Warfare System
IEWS .... Integrated EW Suite (SAUS)
IEWS .... International Electronic Warfare System (SAUO)
IEWSE .... Intelligence Electronic Warfare Support Element (ADDR)
IEWT .... National Woman's Christian Temperance Union, Evanston, IL [*Library symbol*] [*Library of Congress*] (LCLS)
IEWTD .... Improved Electronic Warfare Training Device (SAUS)
IEWTD .... Intelligence/Electronic Warfare Test Directorate (SAUS)
IEW UAV ...... IEW Unmanned Aerial Vehicle (SAUS)
IEW-UAV ...... Intelligence/Electronic Warfare Unmanned Aerial Vehicle [*Army*]
IEX .... Harrington Institute of Interior Design, Design Library, Chicago, IL [*OCLC symbol*] (OCLC)
IEX .... IDEX Corp. [*NYSE symbol*] (SPSG)
IEX .... Imaging Extensions for XWS (SAUS)
IEX .... Indirect Exempt (TIMI)
IEX .... Institute of Export (SAUO)
IEX .... Instruction Execution [*Computer science*] (IAA)
IEX .... Ion Exchanger
IEX .... Issue Exception Code [*Air Force*] (AFIT)
IEXAS .... Institute of Experimental Animal Sciences [*Osaka University*] (GVA)
IEXPE .... Institute of Explosive Engineers (PDAA)
IExpE .... Institute of Explosives Engineers (SAUS)
IEXS .... Integrated Expert System [*Computer science*]
IEXTRU .... International Conference on Extrusion (SAUS)
IEY .... Barrow, AK [*Location identifier*] [*FAA*] (FAAL)
IEY .... Chicago Board of Trade, Chicago, IL [*OCLC symbol*] (OCLC)
IEY .... International Education Year [*UN designation*]
IEZ .... Cumberland Trail Library System, Flora, IL [*OCLC symbol*] (OCLC)
IEZ .... Institut Europeen du Zinc [*European Zinc Institute - EZI*] (EA)
IF .... Frame Identification (SAUS)
IF .... Ice Fog
IF .... Ictal Fear [*Medicine*] (MELL)
IF .... Ideational Fluency [*Research test*]
IF .... Identification Field (SAUS)
IF .... Identifier Field (SAUS)
IF .... Idiopathic Fibroplasia [*Medicine*] (DMAA)
IF .... Idiopathic Flushing [*Medicine*] (DMAA)
IF .... Idirect Fluorescence [*Medicine*] (DMAA)
IF .... Ifosfamid (SAUS)
IF .... Image Frequency (IAA)
I/F .... Image-to-Frame Ratio (MUGU)
IF .... Immersion Fixation [*Microbiology*]
IF .... Immersion Foot [*Medicine*] (DMAA)
IF .... Immunofixation [*Medicine*] (MELL)
IF .... Immunofluorescence [*Immunochemistry*]
IF .... Immunofluorescent (SAUS)
IF .... Impact Form (SAUS)
IF .... Imperial Father [*of the Chapel*] [*Unions*] [*British*] (DGA)
IF .... Imperial Forces (SAUO)
IF .... Implant Failure [*Medicine*] (MELL)
IF .... Implementers Forum (MWOL)

IF .... Importance Factor [*Statistics*]
IF .... Imprest Fund (MCD)
IF .... Incentive Fee (ACAE)
IF .... Incompressible Flow (SAUS)
IF .... Independent Force [*British military*] (DMA)
IF .... Independent Foundation
IF .... Indexed File (VLIE)
IF .... Indexing Feature (SAUS)
IF .... Indian Financial Questions [*British*]
IF .... Indirect Fire (SAUS)
IF .... Indirect Fluorescent
IF .... Indonesia Fund [*NYSE symbol*] (SPSG)
IF .... Industrial Appointment Full Time [*Chiropody*] [*British*]
IF .... Industrial Fund (AFM)
IF .... Industrial Furnace (SAUS)
IF .... Inertial Fusion (SAUS)
IF .... Inferior Facet [*Medicine*] (MELL)
IF .... Infertility (SAUS)
IF .... Infield [*Baseball term*] (NDBD)
IF .... Infielder [*Position in baseball*]
IF .... Infield Fly [*Baseball term*] (NDBD)
IF .... In-Flight (AAG)
IF .... Information Collector (SAA)
IF .... Information Feedback
IF .... Information Flow (SAUS)
IF .... Information Format (SAUS)
IF .... Information Function (SAUS)
IF .... Infrapatellar Fat [*Medicine*] (MELL)
IF .... Infrared (MCD)
IF .... Infrared Filter
IF .... In Full
IF .... Inhibiting Factor
IF .... Inhibitory Factor (SAUS)
IF .... Iniriation Factor (SAUS)
IF .... Initiation Factor [*Protein biosynthesis*]
IF .... Inner Flame (SAUS)
IF .... Inner Forme [*Imposition*] (DGA)
IF .... Inside Face (DAC)
IF .... Inside Frosted
IF .... Installation Fixtures (MCD)
IF .... Instantaneous Flow [*Medicine*] (DMAA)
IF .... Institute for the Future (SAUO)
IF .... Institute of Fuel [*British*]
IF .... Instructional Television, Fixed [*FCC*] (NTCM)
IF .... Instruction Field
IF .... Instruction Folder (MSA)
IF .... Instruction Format (SAUS)
IF .... Instrument Flight (IAA)
IF .... Instrument Flying [*Aviation*]
IF .... Insufficient Funds
IF .... Insular Force
IF .... Integration Facility (MCD)
IF .... Intellectual Framework
IF .... Intellectual Freedom
IF .... Intelligence Fusion [*Army*] (RDA)
IF .... Intensification Factor (SAUS)
IF .... Intensity Factor
IF .... Intensive Flying (SAUS)
I/F .... Interface [*Computer science*] (KSC)
IF .... Interference Filter
IF .... Interferon [*Also, IFN*] [*Biochemistry*]
IF .... Interferon Foundation [*Defunct*] (EA)
IF .... Interflug [*ICAO designator*] (AD)
IF .... Interfuture (EA)
IF .... Interior Facet [*Medicine*] (DMAA)
IF .... Intermediate Facility (ARMP)
IF .... Intermediate Factor (SAUS)
IF .... Intermediate Filament [*Anatomy*]
IF .... Intermediate Fix [*FAA*] (TAG)
IF .... Intermediate Forward [*Army*]
if .... Intermediate Frequency (ABAC)
IF .... Intermediate Frequency [*Electronics*]
IF .... Intermittent Frequency (ACAE)
IF .... Internal Fixation [*Orthopedics*] (DAVI)
IF .... Internal Focusing (SAUS)
IF .... Internal Friction (SAUS)
IF .... Internal Function [*Electronics*] (ECII)
IF .... Internally Flawless [*Diamond clarity grade*]
if .... International Federation for Hydrocephalus and Spina Bifida (SAUO)
IF .... International Federation of American Homing Pigeon Fanciers (EA)
IF .... International Fellowship (SAUO)
IF .... International Forum (EA)
IF .... International Foundation (EAIO)
IF .... International Foundation fo Employee Benefit Plans (NTPA)
IF .... Interrupt Flag [*Computer science*]
IF .... Interstitial Fluid [*Physiology*]
IF .... Interstitial-Free [*Metallurgical engineering*]
IF .... Interventional Fluoroscopy [*Medicine*] (DMAA)
IF .... Intrinsic Factor [*Biochemistry*]
IF .... Inventory File (SAUS)
IF .... Inventrepreneurs' Forum (EA)
IF .... Inverted File (NITA)
IF .... Inviscid Flow (SAUS)
IF .... Involved Field [*Medicine*]
IF .... Ion Focusing (SAUS)
IF .... Ionization Front (SAUS)
IF .... Ipse Fecit [*He Did It Himself*] [*Latin*]
IF .... Ipso Facto [*By the Fact Itself*] [*Latin*]
IF .... Ireland Fund (EA)
IF .... Irish Fusiliers [*British military*] (DMA)
IF .... Irregular Force [*Military*] (CINC)
IF .... Isothermal Flow (SAUS)
IF .... Isotta-Fraschini [*Italian luxury auto maker*]
IF .... Royal Inniskilling Fusiliers (SAUO)
IFA .... Association Internationale de l'Industrie des Engrais [*International Fertilizer Industry Association - IFA*] (EAIO)
IFA .... FAI Airservice, Nurnberg [*Germany*] [*FAA designator*] (FAAC)
IFA .... Fort Worth Public Library, Fort Worth, TX [*OCLC symbol*] (OCLC)
IFA .... Idiopathic Fibrosing Alveolitis [*Medicine*] (DMAA)
IFA .... Igniter-Fuel Assembly
IFA .... Illegal File Access [*Computer science*] (VLIE)
IFA .... Imero Fiorentino Associates, Inc. [*New York, NY*] [*Telecommunications*] (TSSD)
IFA .... Immunofluorescence Analysis (SAUS)
IFA .... Immunofluorescence [*or Immunofluorometric*] Assay [*Also, IFMA*] [*Analytical biochemistry*]
IFA .... Immunofluorescent Antibody [*Immunochemistry*]
IFA .... Incomplete Freund's Adjuvant
IFA .... Independent Fee Appraiser, Member [*National Association of Independent Fe e Appraisers, Inc.*] [*Designation awarded by*]
IFA .... Independent Financial Adviser [*British*] (ECON)
IFA .... Independent Financial Analysis (ADA)
IFA .... Indian Football Association (SAUO)
IFA .... Indirect Fluorescence Assay (DB)
IFA .... Indirect Fluorescent Antibody [*Immunochemistry*]
IFA .... Indirect Immunofluorescence Assay [*Medicine*] (MELL)
IFA .... Individualized Functional Assessment [*Social Security Administration*]
IFA .... Industrial Forestry Association [*Later, NFA*] (EA)
IFA .... Industry Film Association (SAUO)
IFA .... In-Flight Abort (MCD)
IFA .... In-Flight Alignment (PDAA)
IFA .... In-Flight Analysis
IFA .... Information Flow Analysis (MHDB)
IFA .... Inslee Family Association (EA)
IFA .... Institute and Faculty of Actuaries (SAUO)
IFA .... Institute for Astronomy (SAUS)
IFA .... Institute for Atomic Energy (SAUS)
IFA .... Institute of Field Archaeologists [*British*] (DBA)
IFA .... Institute of Financial Accountants (EAIO)
IFA .... Institute of Foreign Affairs (SAUO)
IFA .... Institute of Foresters of Australia (SAUO)
IFA .... Institut Fiziki Atmosfery (SAUS)
IFA .... Instrumental Fuel Assembly (SAUS)
IFA .... Instrumented Fuel Assembly (PDAA)
IFA .... Insulation Fabricators Association [*Defunct*] (EA)
IFA .... Integrated Feed Aerial (or Antenna) (SAUS)
IFA .... Integrated Feed Antenna
IFA .... Integrated File Adapter [*Computer science*] (BUR)
IFA .... Intensive Flux Array [*Marine science*] (OSRA)
IFA .... Intercessors for America (EA)
IFA .... Intercollegiate Fencing Association (EA)
IFA .... Interface Adapter (or Adaptor) (SAUS)
IFA .... Interface Forematter Assembly (ACAE)
IFA .... Interface Functional Analysis (NASA)
IFA .... Inter-Financial Association (EA)
IFA .... Inter Fraternal Association (SAUO)
IFA .... Interim Functional Alternate
IFA .... Intermediate Frequency Amplifier [*or Attenuator*]
IFA .... Intermediate Frequency Attenuator (SAUS)
IFA .... International Federation of Accountants (ADA)
IFA .... International Federation of Actors
IFA .... International Federation of Airworthiness [*Middlesex, England*] (EAIO)
IFA .... International Federation of Aromatherapists (SAUO)
IFA .... International Federation on Aging (SAUO)
IFA .... International Ferret Association (EA)
IFA .... International Fertility Association [*Defunct*]
IFA .... International Fertilizer Industry Association [*Paris, France*] (EAIO)
IFA .... International Festivals Association (EA)
IFA .... International Fiction Association (EAIO)
IFA .... International Fighter Aircraft
IFA .... International Filariasis Association (EA)
IFA .... International Finance Alert [*Financial Times Business Information*] [*British*] [*Information service or system*] (CRD)
IFA .... International Financial Accountants (SAUS)
IFA .... International Finn Association [*Madrid, Spain*] (EAIO)
IFA .... International Fiscal Association [*Rotterdam, Netherlands*] (EAIO)
IFA .... International Florists Association [*Later, National Florists Association*] (EA)
IFA .... International Footprint Association (EA)
IFA .... International Footwear Association (EA)
IFA .... International Formalwear Association (NTPA)
IFA .... International Franchise Association (EA)
IFA .... International Freight Apron
IFA .... International Friendships Association (SAUO)
IFA .... International Frisbee Association [*Later, IFDA*]
IFA .... International Fructase Association (SAUO)
IFA .... International Fructose Association (SAUO)
IFA .... Interracial Family Alliance (EA)
IFA .... Inverse-Function Amplifier (SAUS)
IFA .... Ionization Front Accelerator [*Physics*]

IFA............ Iowa Falls, IA [*Location identifier*] [*FAA*] (FAAL)
IFA............ Iraq Football Association (SAUO)
IFA............ Irish Features Agency [*News agency*]
IFA............ Irish Football Association (BI)
IFA............ Israel Folktale Archive (BJA)
IFA............ Israel Futurologists Association (SAUO)
IFA............ Issue for Approval (SAUS)
IFA............ Istituto di Fisica dell'Atmosfera [*Institute of Atmospheric Physics*] [*Italy*]
IFA............ Majma'a al-Fiqh al-Islami [*Islamic Jurisprudence Academy - IJA*] (EAIO)
IFA............ Incorporated Faculty of Arts (ODA)
IFAA............ Institute For African Alternatives (SAUS)
IFAA............ International Federation of Advertising Agencies [*Sarasota, FL*] (EA)
IFAA............ International Federation of Associations of Anatomists (EA)
IFAA............ International Flight Attendants Association (EA)
IFAA............ International Flow Aids Association (EA)
IFAA............ International Furniture Accessory Association (SAUS)
IFAA............ International Furniture and Accessory Association (EA)
IFAAB............ International Fiscal Association, Australian Branch
IFAAD............ Intermediate Field Army Air Defense (SAUO)
IFAB............ Integrated Fire Direction System for the Artillery Battery [*German*]
IFAB............ International Football Association Board (SAUO)
IFABC............ International Federation of Audit Bureaus of Circulations (SAUO)
IFABC............ International Federation of Audit Bureaux of Circulations (EAIO)
IFABSM............ Incorporated Federated Association of Boot and Shoe Manufacturers (SAUO)
IFAC............ Independent Fee Appraiser/Counselor [*National Association of Independent Fee Appraisers, Inc.*] [*Designation awarded by*]
IFAC............ Instrumented Fast Reactor Accelerated Component (SAUS)
IFAC............ Integrated Flexible Automation Center (SAUS)
IFAC............ Interamerican Federation of Advertising Colleges (SAUO)
IFAC............ Interfirm Accounting Project (IAA)
IFAC............ International Family Association of Canada (SAUO)
IFAC............ International Federation for/of Automatic Control (SAUO)
IFAC............ International Federation of Accountants [*New York, NY*] (EA)
IFAC............ International Federation of Advertising Clubs (SAUO)
IFAC............ International Federation of Automatic Control [*Laxenburg, Austria*]
IFAC............ International Fellowship in Arts and Crafts (SAUO)
IFAC............ International Food Additives Council (EA)
IFAC............ International Industrial Finishing and Anti-Corrosion Exhibition (SAUO)
IFACE............ Interface Element (NITA)
IFAC/IFIP SOCOCO... IFAC/IFIP Symposium on Software for Computer Control (SAUS)
IFAC-SI............ Instrumented Fast Reactor Accelerated Component-Sheath Insulator (SAUS)
IFAD............ Institute of Applied Computer Science (SAUO)
IFAD............ Interactive Finite Element Analysis and Design [*Software*] [*Automotive engineering*]
IFAD............ International Foundation for Agricultural Development [*Defunct*] (EA)
IFAD............ International Fund for Agricultural Development [*United Nations*]
IF-ADD ICMA... Insular Force - Additional Initial Clothing Monetary Allowance [*Military*] (DNAB)
IF-ADD ICMA... Insular Force-Additional Initial Clothing Monetary Allowance (SAUS)
IFAE............ Interamerican Federation for Adult Education (SAUO)
IFAE............ International Farmers Association for Education [*Defunct*] (EA)
IFaf............ Fairfield Public Library, Fairfield, IL [*Library symbol*] [*Library of Congress*] (LCLS)
IFAF............ International Football Association Federation (SAUO)
IFAFA............ Italian Folk Art Federation of America (EA)
IFAFP............ International Federation of Associations of Film Producers (SAUO)
IFAHC............ International Foundation for Alternating Hemiplegia of Childhood (NRGU)
IFAHPF............ International Federation of American Homing Pigeon Fanciers (EA)
IFAI............ Industrial Fabrics Association International (EA)
IFAI............ International Fire Administration Institute
IFai............ Vance Township Library, Fairmount, IL [*Library symbol*] [*Library of Congress*] (LCLS)
IFALP............ International Federation of Air Line Pilots (SAUO)
IFALPA............ International Airline Pilots Association (SAUS)
IFALPA............ International Federation of Airline Pilot Associations (SAUS)
IFALPA............ International Federation of Air Line Pilots Associations [*Egham, England*] (EAIO)
IFALS............ International Federation of Arts, Letters, and Sciences (SAUO)
IFAM............ Information Systems for Associative Memories (SAUO)
IFAM............ Initial-Final Address Message [*Telecommunications*] (TEL)
IFAM............ Inverted File Access Method
IFAMP............ If Approach Missed Proceed [*Aviation*] (FAAC)
IFAMS............ Integrated Force Administration System [*Bell System*]
IFAN............ Fundamental Institute of Black Africa (SAUS)
IFAN............ Institut Francais d'Afrique Noire [*French Institute of Black Africa*]
IFAN............ Intellectual Freedom Action Network
IFAN............ Internationale Foderation der Ausschusse Normenpraxis [*International Federation for the Application of Standards*] (EAIO)
IFAN............ International Federation for the Application of Standards (SAUO)
IFANC............ International Free Academy of New Cosmology (EA)
IF&DBD............ Inspector of Fortification and Director of Bomb Disposal (SAUS)
IF&DBD............ Inspector of Fortifications and Director of Bomb Disposal (SAUO)
IF & F............ Intermediate Flush and Fill (AAG)
IFANS............ Institute of Foreign Affairs & National Security (SAUS)
IFAO Bibl d'Et... Institut Francais d'Archeologie Orientale du Caire. Bibliotheque d'Etude [*A publication*] (BJA)
IFAORS............ Institute for Atmospheric Optics and Remote Sensing (SAUS)
IFAP............ Industrial Foundation for Accident Prevention (ADWA)
IFAP............ International Federation of Agricultural Producers (BARN)
IFAP............ International Federation of Airline Pilots (SAUO)
IFAP............ International Federation of the Agricultural Press (SAUO)
IFAP............ International Foundation for Airline Passengers (EAIO)
IFAPA............ International Federation of Airline Pilots Association (SAUO)
IFAPA............ International Foundation of Airline Passengers Associations (EAIO)
IFAPAO............ International Federation of Asian and Pacific Associations of Optometrists [*Australia*] (EAIO)
IF APL............ If Applicable (SAUS)
IFAPP............ International Federation of Associations of Pharmaceutical Physicians [*Italy*] (EAIO)
IFAPP............ International Federation of the Associations of Pharmaceutical Physicians (SAUO)
IFAPWE............ Institute of Ferro-Alloy Producers in Western Europe [*Defunct*] (EA)
IFAR............ Injector Face Acoustic Resonator (MCD)
IFAR............ Interferometric Angle Resolver (ACAE)
IFAR............ International Forum for AIDS Research [*Institute of Medicine*]
IFAR............ International Foundation for Art Research (EA)
IFAR............ International Fund for Avian Research (GVA)
IFARD............ International Federation for Agricultural Research and Development (SAUO)
IFARD............ International Federation of Agricultural Research Systems for Development [*Netherlands*]
IFarE............ Farmington East Unit District No. 324, Farmington, IL [*Library symbol*] [*Library of Congress*] (LCLS)
IFARS............ Individual Flight Activity Reporting System [*Navy*]
IFAS............ Independent Fee Appraiser, Senior [*National Association of Independent Fe e Appraisers, Inc.*] [*Designation awarded by*]
IFAS............ Institute for American Strategy (SAUS)
IFAS............ Institute for First Amendment Studies
IFAS............ Institute of Food and Agricultural Sciences (SAUS)
IFAS............ International Federation for the Application of Standards (PDAA)
IFAS............ International Federation of Aquarium Societies
IFAS............ International Financial Advisory Service (SAUO)
IFAS............ International Fund for the Aral Sea (SAUS)
IFASC............ Integrated Functions Assessment Steering Committee [*NASA*] (NASA)
IFaSD............ Farina-LaGrove Community Unit, School District 206, Farina, IL [*Library symbol*] [*Library of Congress*] (LCLS)
IFASS............ Integrated Fire and Air Support System (SAUS)
IFAST............ Integrated Facility for Avionics Simulation and Testing (ACAE)
IFAST............ Integrated Facility for Avionics System Test [*Air Force*]
IFAT............ Indirect Fluorescent Antibody Technique (SAUS)
IFAT............ Indirect Fluorescent Antibody Test [*Immunology*]
IFAT............ Indirect Immunofluorescent Antibody Test [*Clinical chemistry*]
IFATCA............ International Federation of Air Traffic Controllers' Associations [*Dublin, Republic of Ireland*] (EAIO)
IFATE............ International Federation of Aerospace Technology and Engineering (SAUO)
IFATE............ International Federation of Airworthiness Technology and Engineering (SAUO)
IFATSEA............ International Federation of Air Traffic Safety Electronic Associations [*British*] (EAIO)
IFATU............ International Federation of Arab Trade Unions (SAUO)
IFAVWU............ International Federation of Audio-Visual Workers Unions [*See also FISTA*] (EAIO)
IFAW............ International Fund for Animal Welfare (EA)
IFAWPCA............ International Federation of Asian and Western Pacific Contractors' Associations [*Pasig, Metro Manila, Philippines*] (EAIO)
IFAX............ International Facsimile Service [*Telecommunications*] (TEL)
IFAXA............ International Facsimile Association (EA)
IFB............ Fort Wayne Bible College, Fort Wayne, IN [*OCLC symbol*] (OCLC)
IFB............ Incendiary Fragmentation Bomb
IFB............ Independent Forward Bloc [*Mauritian political party*]
IFB............ Information for Business (SAUS)
IFB............ Initiation for Bid
IFB............ Institute of Foreign Bankers [*New York, NY*] (EA)
IFB............ Interdivisional Facilities Bulletin (SAUS)
IFB............ Internationales Federn-Bureau [*International Feather Bureau - IFB*] (EAIO)
IfB............ International Feather Bureau (SAUO)
IFB............ International Federation of the Blind [*Later, WBU*]
IfB............ International Film Bureau (SAUO)
IFB............ International Film Bureau Invitation for Bids (SAUS)
IfB............ International Forum for Biophilosophy (SAUO)
IFB............ Interrupted Feedback [*Wireless earphone*] (NTCM)
IFB............ Interrupt Feedback Line [*Computer science*] (IAA)
IFB............ Investment Finance Bank Ltd. [*Malta*]
IFB............ Invitation for Bid [*Marine science*] (OSRA)
IFBA............ International Fire Buff Associates (EA)
IFBA............ International Fire Buff Associates (or Association) (SAUS)
IFBA............ International Foodservice Brokers Association (NTPA)
IFBB............ International Federation of Bodybuilders [*Montreal, PQ*] (EA)
IFBBF............ Imported Fibre Building Board Federation (SAUO)
IFBC............ International Federation of the Blue Cross (EA)
IFBD............ International Foundation for Bowel Dysfunction (SAUO)
IFBDO............ International Federation of Blood Donor Organizations [*See also FIODS*] [*Dole, France*] (EAIO)
IFBE............ International Federation for Business Education (NTPA)
IFBH............ Intermediate Force Beachhead [*Military*] (DNAB)
IFB Line............ Interrupted Feedback Line (SAUS)
IFBM............ Improved Fleet Ballistic Missile
IFBPW............ International Federation of Business and Professional Women (EA)
IFBS............ Individual Flexible Barrier System (SAUS)
IFBS............ International Fashion and Boutique Show (ITD)

IFBS........ Interrupted Feedback System (SAUS)
IFBSO........ International Federation of Boat Show Organisers (EA)
IFBSS........ Individual Flexible Barrier Shelter Systems (MCD)
IFBW........ Intermediate Frequency Band Width
IFBWW........ International Federation of Building and Wood Workers [*Sweden*]
IFC........ Cefi Aviation SRL [*Italy*] [*ICAO designator*] (FAAC)
I/FC........ Current to Frequency Converter (SAUS)
IFC........ Franklin College of Indiana, Franklin, IN [*OCLC symbol*] (OCLC)
IFC........ Idiots Fools and Clowns (MUSM)
IFC........ If Clause
IFC........ IGOSS Flexible Code (SAUS)
IFC........ Illegal Frontier Crosser (SAUO)
IFC........ Image Flow Computer (SAUS)
IFC........ Imasco Financial Corp. [*Vancouver Stock Exchange symbol*] [*Toronto Stock Exchange symbol*]
IFC........ Imasco Financial Corporation (SAUO)
IFC........ Improved Flotation Chamber
IFC........ Incremental Frequency Control
IFC........ Incrementally Funded Contract (ACAE)
IFC........ Independent Film Channel
IFC........ Independent Fire Control [*Area*] (NATG)
IFC........ Indicated Final Cost (SAA)
IFC........ Industrial Finance Corp. (SAUS)
IFC........ Industrial Finance Corporation (SAUO)
IFC........ Industrial Frequency Changer
IFC........ Infant Formula Council (EA)
IFC........ Inflight Black Body Calibrator (SAUS)
IFC........ In-Flight Calibration (or Calibrator) (SAUS)
IFC........ In-Flight Collision (SAUS)
IFC........ Information Collector (SAUS)
IFC........ Infrared Fire Control
IFC........ Initial Fleet Capability (SAUS)
IFC........ Initial Flight Clearance (SAUS)
IFC........ Initial Floristic Composition [*Theory of plant succession*]
IFC........ Inland Fisheries Commission (SAUO)
IFC........ Inner Front Cover (SAUS)
IFC........ Inside Front Cover [*Publishing*] (NTCM)
ifc........ Inside Front Cover [*Publishing*] (WDAA)
IFC........ Inspiratory Flow Cartridge (STED)
IFC........ Installed First Cost (ACRL)
IFC........ Instantaneous Frequency Correlation
IFC........ Institute Freight Clause (MARI)
IFC........ Institute of Forest Conservation (SAUO)
IFC........ Institut Forestier du Canada [*Formerly, Canadian Society of Forest Engineers*] (AC)
IFC........ Instruction Flow Chart (SAUS)
IFC........ Instrument Flight Center [*Air Force*]
IFC........ Insulated Food Container [*Military*] (INF)
IFC........ Integrated Factory Control (SAUS)
IFC........ Integrated Fire Control [*RADAR*]
IFC........ Integrated Forcing Contribution [*Environmental science*]
IFC........ Intellectual Freedom Committee [*American Library Association*]
IFC........ Intensive Field Campaign (SAUS)
IFC........ Interface Circuit (SAUS)
IFC........ Interface Clear (IAA)
IFC........ Interfaculty Council (SAUO)
IFC........ Inter-Faith Compassionists (EA)
IFC........ Interfirm Comparison (ADA)
IFC........ InterFirst Corporation (SAUO)
IFC........ Interfruitlet Corking [*of pineapple*]
IFC........ Intermittent Flow Centrifugation (STED)
IFC........ Internal Fission Counter [*Environmental science*] (COE)
IFC........ International Facilitating Committee [*World Resources Institute*]
IFC........ International Fashion Council (SAUO)
IFC........ International Federation of Master-Craftsmen [*See also IFH*] (EAIO)
IFC........ International Film Chamber (SAUO)
IFC........ International Film Completion Corp.
IFC........ International Finance Cooperation (SAUO)
IFC........ International Finance Corp. [*Affiliate of International Bank for Reconstruction and Development*]
IFC........ International Finance Corporation (SAUO)
IFC........ International Financial Corporation (EBF)
IFC........ International Firestop Council (NTPA)
IFC........ International Fisheries Commission [*Later, IPHC*] [*US and Canada*]
IFC........ International Forging Congress (SAUS)
IFC........ International Formulation Committee (SAUO)
IFC........ International Foundry Congress (SAUO)
IFC........ International Freighting Corp. (SAUS)
IFC........ International Friendship Club (SAUO)
IFC........ International Fuel Cells
IFC........ Internet Foundation Classes [*Netscape*] (IGQR)
IFC........ Interracial Family Circle [*An association*]
IFC........ Interstate and Foreign Commerce (DLA)
IFC........ Intrinsic Factor Concentrate [*Biochemistry*]
IFC........ Investment Finance Co. (SAUS)
IFC........ Investment Finance Company (SAUO)
IFC........ Istituto di Fisica Cosmica [*Italy*]
IFCA........ Independent Fundamental Churches of America (EA)
IFCA........ Instrumentation to Follow the Course of an Accident [*Nuclear energy*] (NRCH)
IFCA........ Integrated Fire Control Area (SAUS)
IFCA........ International Fan Club Association [*Formerly, FCA*] (EA)
IFCA........ International Federation of Catholic Alumnae (EA)
IFCAA........ International Fire Chiefs' Association of Asia (EAIO)
IFC-ALA........ Intellectual Freedom Committee-American Library Association (SAUO)
IFCAM........ Industrial Fuel Choice Analysis Model [*Environmental Protection Agency*] (GFGA)
IF Canceler... Intermediate Frequency Canceler (SAUS)
IFCAS........ Indirect Fire Casualty Assessment/Suppression System [*Military*] (MCD)
IFCAS........ Integrated Flight Control and Augmentation System (SAUO)
IFCAT........ Institute for Field Communication and Agricultural Training (SAUO)
IFCATI........ International Federation of Cotton and Allied Textile Industries [*Later, ITMF*]
IFCB........ International Federation of Cell Biology [*Toronto, ON*] (EAIO)
IFCB........ International Friendly Circle of the Blind (EA)
IFCB........ Interrupt Fan Control Block [*Computer science*] (ELAL)
IFCbl........ Intrinsic Factor Cobalamin (Complex) [*Biochemistry*]
IFCC........ Iconized Flowchart Compilers [*Software*] [*Computer science*]
IFCC........ Initial Fleet Command Center [*Navy*] (CAAL)
IFCC........ Intergovernmental Follow-up and Coordination Committee of the Group of 77 in ECDC (SAUO)
IFCC........ Interim Fleet Command Center [*Navy*] (MCD)
IFCC........ International Federation of Camping and Caravanning
IFCC........ International Federation of Children's Communities [*Later, FICE*]
IFCC........ International Federation of Clinical Chemistry [*Vienna, Austria*] (EA)
IFCC........ International Federation of Culture Collections of Microorganisms (SAUO)
IFCC........ International Fibreboard Case Code (SAUS)
IFCCA........ International Federation of Community Centre Associations
IFCCPTE........ International Federation of Commercial, Clerical, Professional and Technical Employees (SAUO)
IFCCTE........ International Federation of Commercial (SAUS)
IFCCTE........ International Federation of Commercial, Clerical, and Technical Employees
IFCDG........ Injection of Fuel Containing Dissolved Gas [*Diesel engines*]
IFCE........ Integral Fire Control Equipment (AAG)
IFCE........ International Federation of Consulting Engineers (NUCP)
IFCEB........ International Foundation for Computerbased Education in Banking (SAUO)
IFCF........ Integrated Fuel Cycle Facilities [*Nuclear energy*] (NRCH)
IFCF........ Integrated Fuel Cycle Facility (SAUS)
IFCF........ Intermediate Frequency Crystal Filter
IFCF........ International Frederic Chopin Foundation [*Poland*] (EAIO)
IFCGWU........ International Federation of Chemical and General Workers Union
IFCHHRC........ International Friends of the Chilean Human Rights Commission (SAUO)
IFCI........ Industrial Finance Corporation of India (SAUO)
IFCI........ International Fibercom, Inc. [*NASDAQ symbol*] (SAG)
IFCI........ Intl Fibercom Inc. [*NASDAQ symbol*] (TTSB)
IFCID........ Instrumentation Facility Component Identifier (SAUS)
IFCIW........ International Fibercom Wrrt [*NASDAQ symbol*] (TTSB)
IFCJ........ International Federation of Catholic Journalists
IFC KAISER... IFC Kaiser Hanford Co. (SAUO)
IFCL........ Inter-Facility Communication Link (SAUO)
IFCL........ Intermittent Flow Centrifugation Leukapheresis (STED)
IFCL........ International Faculty of Comparative Law (SAUO)
IFCM........ Independent Flow Control Messages (SAUS)
IFCM........ International Federation for Choral Music (EA)
IFCM........ International Federation of Christian Metalworkers (SAUS)
IFCMI........ International Federation of Children of Mary Immaculate [*Paris, France*] (EAIO)
IFCMU........ International Federation of Christian Miners' Unions
IFCN........ INFICON ADS [*NASDAQ symbol*]
IFCN........ Interfacility Communication Network
IFCN........ Inter-Facility Flow Control Network [*FAA*] (TAG)
IFCN........ International Federation of Clinical Neurophysiology (EAIO)
IFCO........ IFCO Systems, NV [*NASDAQ symbol*] (SG)
IFCO........ International Fan Club Organization (EA)
IFCO........ International Fisheries Cooperative Organization (BARN)
IFCO........ Interreligious Foundation for Community Organization (EA)
IFCO........ Interstate Financial Corporation (SAUO)
IFCOL........ Integrated Fiber Optics Communication Link (SAUS)
IFCP........ Institute for Financial Crime Prevention [*Later, NACFE*] (EA)
IFCP........ International Federation of Catholic Pharmacists
IFCP........ International Federation of the Cinematographic Press [*See also FIPRESCI*] (EAIO)
IFCP........ International Fund for Concerned Photography [*Later, ICP*]
IFCPC........ International Federation of Cervical Pathology and Colposcopy [*Dundee, Scotland*] (EAIO)
IFCR........ Interface Control Register (IAA)
IFCR........ International Foundation for Cancer Research (EA)
IFCRA........ International Floor Covering Representatives Association (NTPA)
IFCRM........ International Federation of Catholic Rural Movements (EAIO)
IFCS........ Improved Fire Control System [*Military*] (MCD)
IFCS........ Inactivated Fetal Calf Serum [*Medicine*] (DMAA)
IFCS........ In-Flight Checkout System (IEEE)
IFCS........ Infrared Fire Control System
IFCS........ Institute for Family and Child Study [*Michigan State University*] [*Research center*] (RCD)
IFCS........ Integrated Fire Control System (SAUO)
IFCS........ Integrated Flight Control System
IFCS........ Intergovernmental Forum on Chemical Safety
IFCS........ Interim Fire Control System (SAUS)
IFCS........ International Federation for/of Computer Sciences (SAUO)
IFCS........ International Federation of Classification Societies (SAUO)
IFCS........ International Federation of Computer Sciences
IFCS........ International Forum on Chemical Safety (EPAT)

IFCSC........... Intercollegiate Fencing Conference of Southern California (PSS)
IFCSS........... Independent Federation of Chinese Students and Scholars (EA)
IFCST........... Institutional Fire Control System Trainer (SAUS)
IFCT............. Industrial Finance Corporation of Thailand (SAUO)
IFCT............. Institute of Fine Chemical Technology (SAUS)
IFCTIO......... International Federation of Commercial Travelers Insurance Organizations [*Later, CTIF*] (EA)
IFCTU........... International Federation of Christian Trade Unions [*Often uses initialism CISC, based on name in French, to avoid confusion with ICFTU*]
IFCTUBWW... International Federation of Christian Trade Unions of Building and Wood Workers
IFCTUGP...... International Federation of Christian Trade Unions of Graphical and Paper Industries
IFCTUGPI..... International Federation of Christian Trade Unions of Graphical and Paper Industries (SAUO)
IFCTUSETMSCT... International Federation of Christian Trade Unions of Salaried Employees, Technicians, Managerial Staff and Commercial Travellers (SAUO)
IFCTUTCW... International Federation of Christian Trade Unions of Textile and Clothing Workers (SAUO)
IFCTUTGW... International Federation of Christian Trade Unions of Textile and Garment Workers (SAUO)
IFCU............. Interface Control Unit [*Army*] (IAA)
IFCU............. International Federation of Catholic Universities [*See also FIUC*] [*Paris, France*] (EAIO)
IFCUAW........ International Federation of Christian Unions of Agricultural Workers
IFCWU.......... International Federation of Chemical Workers' Unions
IFCY............. International Federation of Catholic Youth (SAUO)
IFCYP........... International Centre of Films for Children and Young People (SAUO)
IFD............... Idealization to Frustration to Demoralization
IFD............... Image File Directory [*Computer science*]
IFD............... Incipient Fire Detection (or Detector) (SAUS)
IFD............... Indentation Force Deflection [*Automotive seat testing*]
IFD............... Indirect Flare Detector (SAUS)
IFD............... Industrial Facilities Discharge (AUEG)
IFD............... Industrial Facilities Discharge [*File*] [*Environment term*] (EGA)
IFD............... In Flagrante Delicto [*Caught in the Act*] [*Latin*]
IFD............... In-Flight Deployment
IFD............... In-Flight Display (SAUS)
IFD............... Information Flow Diagram (SAUS)
IFD............... Infrared Detector
IFD............... Initial Fill Date [*Army*] (AABC)
IFD............... In-Line Filter Degasser
IFD............... Instantaneous Frequency Discriminator (IEEE)
IFD............... Institute of Food Distribution (SAUO)
IFD............... Instrument Flow Diagram (ABAC)
IFD............... Integrated Flight Director [*Aviation*]
IFD............... Intelligent Field Device (ACII)
IFD............... Interfiber Distance
IFD............... Inter-Fighter Director
IFD............... Internal Friction Damping (PDAA)
IFD............... International Bureau of Fiscal Documentation (SAUO)
IFD............... Internationale Foderation des Dachdeckerhandwerks [*International Federation of Roofing Contractors*] (EAIO)
IFD............... International Federation for Documentation [*Also, FID*] [*Later, IFID*]
IFD............... International Federation for/of Documentation (SAUO)
IFD............... International Foundation Directory [*A publication*]
IFDA............. Illinois Farming Development Authority (SAUS)
IFDA............. Independent Film Distributors' Association [*British*]
IFDA............. Institutional Food Distributors of America [*Later, NAWGA*] (EA)
IFDA............. International Federation for Data Processing Associations (SAUS)
IFDA............. International Federation for/of Data Processing Associations (SAUO)
IFDA............. International Foodservice Distributors Association (EA)
IFDA............. International Foundation for Development Alternatives [*See also FIPAD*] [*Nyon, Switzerland*] (EAIO)
IFDA............. International Franchised Dealers Association [*Later, SFDA*] (EA)
IFDA............. International Frisbee Disc Association [*Formerly, IFA*] (EA)
IFDA............. International Furnishings and Design Association (EA)
IFDAPS......... Integrated Flight Data Processing System [*Air Force*]
IFDAS........... International Federation of Dental Anesthesiology Societies [*British*] (EAIO)
IFDC............. Industrial Funding Corp. [*NASDAQ symbol*] (NQ)
IFDC............. Integrated Facilities Design Criteria (SAA)
IFDC............. Interim Full Operating Capability (CCCA)
IFDC............. International Fertilizer Development Center (EA)
IFDC............. Intraductal and Infiltrating Duct Carcinoma [*Oncology*]
IFDCAUS....... International Flying Dutchman Class Association of the US (EA)
IFDCO........... International Flying Dutchmen Class Organization [*Berlin, Federal Republic of Germany*] (EAIO)
IFDE............. Intermittent Fault Detection Experiment (SAUS)
IFDFA........... International Freeze-Dry Floral Association (EA)
IFDI............... International Fibre Drum Institute (NTPA)
IFDI............... Israel Folk Dance Institute (EA)
IFDIB............ International Festivals Documentation and Information Bureau (SAUO)
IFDM............. Integrated Finite-Difference Method (SAUS)
IFDM............. International Foundation of Doll Makers (EA)
IFDO............. International Federation of Dalit Organizations (EA)
IFDO............. International Federation of Data Organizations (SAUS)
IFDO............. International Federation of Data Organizations for the Social Sciences [*Amsterdam, Netherlands*] (EAIO)
IFDOS........... Interactive Floppy Disk Operating System (SAUO)
IFDP............. Institute for Food and Development Policy (EA)
IFDR............. Interface Data Register (IAA)
IFDS............. Inertial Flight Data System (KSC)
IFDS............. Integrated Flagship Data System [*Navy*] (NG)
IFDS............. Interlocking Full-Depth Sipe [*Tire design*]
IFDS............. Isolated Follicle-Deficiency Syndrome [*Medicine*] (STED)
IF-DSU-DIV... Intermediate Forward Direct Support at Division (SAUS)
IFDVS........... Indian Field Depot Veterinary Stores [*British military*] (DMA)
IFE............... Federal Electoral Institute [*Mexico City, Mexico*]
IFE............... Image Feature Extraction [*Air Force*]
IFE............... Immunofixation Electrophoresis [*Clinical chemistry*]
IFE............... Incipient Failure Everywhere [*Hypothesis descending forces in a sand-pile*]
IFE............... Industrial Foundation on Education (SAUO)
IFE............... Industrially Furnished Equipment (ACAE)
IFE............... In-Flight Emergency (MCD)
IFE............... In-Flight Entertainment
IFE............... Inner Front End (MSA)
IFE............... Institute for Energy Technology (SAUO)
IFE............... Institute for Fluitronics Education (EA)
IFE............... Institute of Federal Elections [*Mexico City, Mexico*]
IFE............... Institute of Financial Education [*Chicago, IL*] (EA)
IFE............... Institute of Fire Engineers
IFE............... Institut Francais de l'Energie [*French Institute of Energy*] [*Paris*] [*Information service or system*] (IID)
IFE............... Institution of Fire Engineers (SAUO)
IFE............... Intelligent Front End (NITA)
IFE............... Intelligent Functional Unit (SAUS)
IFE............... Interfollicular Epidermis [*Medicine*] (STED)
IFE............... Internal Field Emission
IFE............... International Family Entertainment
IFE............... International Fasteners Exposition (ITD)
IFE............... International Food and Drink Exhibition [*British*] (ITD)
IFE............... Internet Forum Europe (SAUO)
IFE............... Intl Flavors/Fragr [*NYSE symbol*] (TTSB)
IFE............... Italian Films Export (SAUO)
IFEA............. In-Flight Emergency Assistance [*FAA*] (TAG)
IFEA............. Institute of Fire Engineers in Australia
IFEA............. Integrated Furnace Experiment Assembly (SAUO)
IFEA............. International Federation of Endodontic Associations (SAUO)
IFEA............. International Federation of National Engineering Associations (SAUO)
IFEA............. Internet Free Expression Alliance (RALS)
IFEAT........... International Federation of Essential Oils and Aroma Trades [*British*] (EAIO)
IFEB............. International Federation of Engine Reconditioners (SAUO)
IFEB............. International Federation of Railway Advertising Companies (SAUO)
IFEBP........... International Foundation of Employee Benefit Plans (EA)
IFEBS........... Integrated Foreign Exchange and Banking System (PDAA)
IFEC............. International Food Emergency Committee (SAUO)
IFEC............. International Foodservice Editorial Council (EA)
IFEC............. International Foundation for Earth Construction (SAUO)
IFECYE......... International Federation for Educative Children and Youth Exchanges (SAUO)
IFED............. Integrated Fuel/Engine Display (MCD)
IFED............. Inter Federal Savings Bank (SAUS)
IFED............. International Federation of Esthetic Dentistry (SAUO)
IFED............. Iraqi Fund for External Development (SAUO)
IFEE............. Institute for Free Enterprise Education (SAUO)
IFEES........... International Federation of Electro-Encephalographical Societies (SAUO)
IFEEX........... International Fishing Equipment Exposition [*Canada*] (ITD)
IFEF............. Internacia Federacio Esperantista Fervojista (SAUO)
IFEF............. Internacia Fervojista Esperanto Federacio [*International Federation of Esperantist Railwaymen*] (EAIO)
IFEG............. Information for Energy Group (SAUO)
IFEH............. International Federation of Environmental Health (SAUO)
IFEH............. International Federation of Europe Houses [*See also FIME*] (EAIO)
IFEI............... Imagine Films Entertainment, Incorporated (SAUO)
IFEI............... Integrated Fuel/Engine Instrument (MCD)
IFEL............. Induction Free-Electron Laser (SAUS)
IFEL............. Inverse Free Electron LASER [*Plasma physics*]
IFELP........... International Federation for Family Life Promotion (SAUO)
IFEM............. In-Flight Engine Monitor (MCD)
IFEM............. Institute of Fireplace Equipment Manufacturers (EA)
IFEMA........... Industrial Finishing Equipment Manufacturers Association (EA)
IFEMA........... International Fund for Equipment and Mutual Aid (SAUO)
IFEMS........... International Federation of Electron Microscope Societies
IFEN............. French Institute for the Environment (SAUS)
IFEN............. Institut Francais de l'Environnement [*Marine science*] [*France*] (OSRA)
IFEN............. Intercompany File Exchange Network (TELE)
IFenE............ Institute of Fence Engineers [*British*] (DBA)
IFEO............. International Federation of Eugenic Organizations (SAUO)
IFEOS........... International Forum for Earth Observations from Space (SAUS)
IFEOS........... International Forum on Earth Observations Using Space Station Elements (SAUO)
IFEP............. Inflation from an Energy Perspective [*Economic theory*]
IFEP............. In-Flight Experiments Panel
IFEP............. Integrated Front-End Processor (SAUS)
IFEPFC......... International Federation of Elvis Presley Fan Clubs [*Defunct*] (EA)
IFEPT........... International Federation for Enteric Phage Typing [*International Council of Scientific Unions*]
IFER............. Internationale Foederation der Eisenbahn-Reklame-Gesellschaften [*International Federation of Railway Advertising Companies*] [*British*] (EA)
IFER............. International Federation of Engine Reconditioners [*See also FIRM*] [*Paris, France*] (EAIO)

IFER............ International Foundation for Ethical Research (EA)
IFERS........... International Flat Earth Research Society (EA)
IFES............ Image Feature Extraction System [*Air Force*]
IFES............ Integrated Front-End System [*Automotive engineering*]
IFES............ International Federation of Evangelical Students (SAUO)
IFES............ International Fellowship of Evangelical Students (EA)
IFES............ International Field Emission Symposium (SAUS)
IFES............ International Foundation for Election Systems [*Political party*] (PSAP)
IFES............ International Foundation for Electoral Systems (EA)
IFESLG.......... International Fellowship of Evangelical Students Link Group (EA)
IFET............ International Federation of Employers and Technicians (SAUO)
IFeT............ Intestinal Iron (Ferrum) Transport [*Physiology*]
IFEVA........... International Federation for the Defence of Fundamental Human Values (SAUO)
IFEW............ Inter-American Federation of Entertainment Workers
IFf............. Frankfort Public Library District, Frankfort, IL [*Library symbol*] [*Library of Congress*] (LCLS)
IFF............. Icelandic Film Fund (SAUO)
IFF............. Identification, Friend or Foe [*Military*]
IFF............. If and Only If (IEEE)
iff............. If and Only If (SHCU)
IFF............. Iffley [*Australia*] [*Airport symbol*] [*Obsolete*] (OAG)
IFF............. Image File Format (SAUS)
IFF............. Individual Freedom Federation (EA)
IFF............. Induced Fluid Flow
IFF............. Industrial Funding Fee (AAGC)
IFF............. Inert Fluid Fill (AAG)
IFF............. Information, Friend for Foe (SAUO)
IFF............. Inner Fracture Face [*Medicine*] (DB)
IFF............. Institute for the Future
IFF............. Institute of Freight Forwarders [*British*]
IFF............. Institute of Natural Resources, Springfield, IL [*OCLC symbol*] (OCLC)
IFF............. Intensity Fluctuation Factor [*Telecommunications*] (TEL)
IFF............. Interchangeable File Format (SAUS)
IFF............. Interchange File Format [*Computer science*] (DCOM)
IFF............. Interchange Format File (SAUS)
IFF............. Interfreight Forwarding Ltd. [*Sudan*] [*ICAO designator*] (FAAC)
IFF............. Intergovernmental Forum on Forests (SAUS)
IFF............. Intermediate Financing Facility (SAUO)
IFF............. International Federal Film [*Fictitious organization of agents in TV series "Scarecrow and Mrs. King"*]
IFF............. International Federation of Falerists (EA)
IFF............. International Fencing Federation [*Paris, France*] (EA)
IFF............. International Film Foundation
IFF............. International Flavors & Fragrances, Inc. [*NYSE symbol*] (SPSG)
IFF............. International Flying Farmers (EA)
IFF............. International Forum Foundation
IFF............. International Forum on Forests (SAUO)
IFF............. International Freedom Foundation (EA)
IFF............. Internet Fast Forward (SAUS)
IFF............. Interrogate Friend or Foe (CCCA)
IFF............. Interrogation Friend or Foe (SAUS)
IFF............. Ionized Flow Field
IFF............. Iran Freedom Foundation (EA)
IFF............. Isoelectric Focusing Facility
IFF............. Item Intelligence File [*DoD*]
IFF............. Iterative Function Fractal (SAUS)
IFFA............ Independent Federation of Flight Attendants (EA)
IFFA............ Indigenous Flora and Fauna Association (SAUO)
IFFA............ Interactive Flash Flood Analyzer
IFFA............ International Federation of Film (SAUO)
IFFA............ International Federation of Film Archives
IFFA............ International Fly Fishing Association (EAIO)
IFFA............ International Frozen Food Association (EA)
IFFAA........... Inland Fish Farming Association of Australia
IFF/ATCRBS...... Identification Friend or Foe/Air-Traffic Control RADAR Beacon System [*Military*]
IFFC............ Integrated Flight Fire Control (SAUS)
IFFC............ Integrated Flight and Fire Control
IFFC............ Integrated Flight Fire Control (SAUS)
IFFCO........... Indian Farmers Fertilizer Cooperative Ltd. (SAUO)
IF/FCS.......... Integrated Fire/Flight Control System (SAUS)
IFFCS........... International Fancy Food and Confection Show (ITD)
IFFEC........... International Federation of Free Evangelical Churches (EA)
IFFEX........... International Frozen Food Exhibition and Congress
IFFF............ Internationale Frauenliga fuer Frieden und Freiheit [*Women's International League for Peace and Freedom*]
IFFGD........... International Foundation for Functional Gastrointestinal Disorders (NRGU)
IFFH............ International Federation for Family Health [*Bandung, Indonesia*] (EA)
IFFIT........... International Facility for Food Irradiation Technology [*Netherlands*] (WND)
IFF IU.......... IFF Interface Unit (SAUS)
IFFJ............ International Federation of Free Journalists [*British*]
IFFJP........... International Federation of Fruit Juice Producers [*See also FIJU*] [*Paris, France*] (EAIO)
IFFL............ International Institute of Foods and Family Living (SAUO)
IFFLP........... International Federation for Family Life Promotion (EA)
IFFN............ Identification as Friend, Foe, or Neutral (SAUO)
IFFN............ Identification Friend or Foe Network (SAUS)
IFFN............ Identification, Friend or Foe or Neutral (MCD)
IFF/NCTR........ Identification Friend or Foe/Non-Cooperative Target Recognition (SAUS)
IFFN JTF........ Identification Friend or Foe, or Neutral Joint Test Force (SAUS)
IFFPA........... International Federation of Film Producers' Associations
IFFPS........... Fauna and Flora Preservation Society (SAUO)
IFFS............ Identification, Friend or Foe, Switching Circuit [*Military*] (MSA)
IFFS............ Intermediate Future Forecasting System [*Department of Energy*] (GFGA)
IFFS............ International Federation of Fertility Societies (EAIO)
IFFS............ International Federation of Film Scienes (SAUO)
IFFS............ International Federation of Film Societies
IFFS............ International Fellowship of Former Scouts and Guides (SAUO)
IFFSA........... Inflight Food Service Association (EA)
IFFSAH.......... Instrument Formation Flight System for Army Helicopter (SAUO)
IFFSG........... International Fellowship of Former Scouts and Guides (SAUO)
IFF/SIF......... Identification, Friend or Foe/Selective Identification Feature [*Military*]
IFF Structure... Internal Fan-out Free Structure (SAUS)
IFFT............ International Federation of Forensic Toxicologists [*Medicine*] (WDAA)
IFFTU........... International Federation of Free Teachers' Unions [*See also SPIE*] [*Amsterdam, Netherlands*] (EAIO)
IFFU............ Identification, Friend or Foe Unit (MCD)
IFF-UK.......... International Freedom Foundation - United Kingdom Branch (EAIO)
IFFWS........... Inland Fisheries, Forestry and Wildlife Sectors of SADC (SAUS)
IFFWS........... Inland Fisheries, Forestry and Wildlife Sectors of the SADC (SAUO)
IFG............. Incoming Fax Gateway (SAUS)
IFG............. Indian Feld Gun (SAUS)
IFG............. Individual and Family Grant (SAUO)
IFG............. Inferior Frontal Gyrus [*Brain anatomy*]
IFG............. Information File Generator (SAUS)
IFG............. Inland Fisher Guide [*General Motors Corp.*]
IFG............. Institute for Research on Educational Finance and Governance [*Department of Education*] (GRD)
IFG............. Instream Flow Service Group [*United States Fish and Wildlife Service*]
IFG............. Instrument Flight Guide (SAUS)
IFG............. Interference-Free Gate (SAUS)
IFG............. Inter Frame Gap (SAUS)
IFG............. International Fashion Group [*Later, Fashion Group International*] (EA)
IFG............. International Federation of/on Glucose Industries (SAUO)
IFG............. International Foundation for the Conservation of Game (SAUO)
IFG............. Inter-Regional Financial Group, Inc. [*NYSE symbol*] (SPSG)
IFG............. Inter-Regional Fin. Gr. [*NYSE symbol*] (TTSB)
IFG............. Kaskaskia Library System, Smithton, IL [*OCLC symbol*] (OCLC)
IFGA............ International Fancy Guppy Association (EA)
IFGA............ International Federation of Grocers' Associations [*See also IVLD*] [*Bern, Switzerland*] (EAIO)
IFGAE........... International Federation for Gerda Alexander Eutony [*Belgium*] (EAIO)
IFGB............ Institute of Chartered Foresters [*British*]
IFGB............ Institute of Foresters of Great Britain (SAUO)
IFGE............ International Federation of Gynecologic Endoscopists (ADWA)
IFGE............ International Foundation for Gender Education (EA)
IFGI............ International Federation for/of the Graphical Industries (SAUO)
IFGI............ International Federation of Graphical Industries (SAUS)
IFGL............ Initial File Generation Language
IFGMA........... International Federation of Grocery Manufacturers Associations (EA)
IFGN............ InFerGene Co. [*NASDAQ symbol*] (COMM)
IFGO............ International Federation of Gynecology and Obstetrics
IFGOJ........... International Federation of Gynecology and Obstetrics Journal [*Medicine*] (EDAA)
IFGR............ International Foundation for Genetic Research (ADWA)
IFGS............ International Fantasy Gaming Society (EA)
IFGS............ Interstitial Fluids and Ground Substance (STED)
IFGVP........... International Federation of Gastronomical and Vinicultural Press
IFH............. Industrial Facilities Handbook [*A publication*] (AAGC)
IFH............. In-Flight Helium
IFH............. Interferon, Human (SAUS)
IFH............. Internationale Foderation des Handwerks [*International Federation of Master-Craftsmen - IFMC*] [*Vienna, Austria*] (EAIO)
IFH............. International Foundation for Homeopathy (EA)
IFH............. International Hospital Federation (SAUO)
IFH............. Judson College Library, Elgin, IL [*OCLC symbol*] (OCLC)
IFHBT........... International Federation of Health and Beauty Therapists
IFHE............ International Federation for Home Economics [*See also FIEF*] [*Paris, France*] (EAIO)
IFHE............ International Federation of Hospital Engineering (PDAA)
IFHG............ Institute of Family History and Genealogy (EA)
IFhGS........... Grant-Illini School 110, Fairview Heights, IL [*Library symbol*] [*Library of Congress*] (LCLS)
IFhGSD.......... Grant Community Consolidated School District 110, Fairview Heights, IL [*Library symbol*] [*Library of Congress*] (LCLS)
IFHOH........... International Federation of Hard of Hearing People (SAUO)
IFHOH........... International Federation of the Hard of Hearing [*Kampen, Netherlands*] (EAIO)
IFHOL........... If Holding [*Aviation*] (FAAC)
IFHP............ International Federation for Housing and Planning [*Netherlands*]
IFHP............ International Federation of Health Professionals (EA)
IFHP............ International Federation of Housing and Planning (SAUS)
IFHPM........... International Federation of Hydraulic Platform Manufacturers [*Later, IPAF*] (EAIO)
IFHPMSM......... International Foundation for Hygiene, Preventative Medicine, Social Medicine (BABM)
IFhPSD.......... Pontiac-William Holliday School District 105, Fairview Heights, IL [*Library symbol*] [*Library of Congress*] (LCLS)
IFHPSM.......... International Federation for Hygiene, Preventive, and Social Medicine [*France*] (EAIO)
IFHRO........... International Federation of Health Records Organizations [*Munich, Federal Republic of Germany*] (EAIO)

IFHS .... Irish Family History Society (EA)
ifHSB .... International Federation for Hydrocephalus and Spina Bifida (SAUS)
IFHTM .... International Federation for the Heat Treatment of Materials (PDAA)
IFHTP .... International Federation for Housing and Town Planning
IFHV .... In Flight Homing View (ACAE)
IFI .... Immune Interferon (DMAA)
IFI .... Imperial Forestry Institute [*British*] (BI)
IFI .... Industrial Fasteners Institute (EA)
IFI .... Infisy Systems, Inc. [*Vancouver Stock Exchange symbol*]
IFI .... In-Flight Insertion (NG)
IFI .... Information for Industry (SAUS)
IFI .... Information for Industry Inc. (NITA)
IFI .... Information for Industry Ltd. (SAUO)
IFI .... In-Line Fuel Injection [*Automotive engineering*]
IFI .... Inspector Followup Items [*Environmental science*] (COE)
IFI .... Institutional Functioning Inventory [*Psychology*] (DHP)
IFI .... Instrumentation Facility Interface (SAUS)
IFI .... Instruments for Industry Inc. (SAUO)
IFI .... Interfault Interval (SAUS)
IFI .... Inter-Freight International [*Steamship*] (MHDB)
IFI .... International Fabricare Institute (EA)
IFI .... International Fastener Institute (SAUS)
IFI .... International Federation of Interior Architects/Interior Designers [*Amsterdam, Netherlands*] (EAIO)
IFI .... International Federation of Interior Designers (SAUO)
IFI .... International Feedstuffs Institute [*Utah State University*] [*Research center*] [*Defunct*] (RCD)
IFI .... International Film Institute
IFI .... International Financial Institution
IFI .... International Foundation for Independence (EA)
IFI .... International Fund for Ireland [*United States, Canada, and New Zealand*]
IFI .... ISPRA Fibroptic Industries (SAUS)
IFI .... Israel Furniture Industry (SAUO)
IFI .... Italian for Idiots [*Facetious travel terminology*]
IFI .... Iterated Fission Expectation (SAUS)
IFI .... Kingfisher, OK [*Location identifier*] [*FAA*] (FAAL)
IFI .... Sidley & Austin, Chicago, IL [*OCLC symbol*] (OCLC)
IFIA .... Intermountain Forest Industry Association (EA)
IFIA .... International Federation of Inventors' Associations [*Stockholm, Sweden*] (EAIO)
IFIA .... International Federation of Ironmongers and Iron Merchants Associations [*See also FIDAQ*] [*Zurich, Switzerland*] (EAIO)
IFIA .... International Fence Industry Association (EA)
IFIA .... International Fertilizer Industry Association (SAUO)
IFIA .... International Financial Institutions Act [*1977*]
IFIA NAC .... International Federation of Inspection Agencies - North American Committee (NTPA)
IFIAS .... International Federation of Institutes for Advanced Study [*ICSU*] [*Toronto, ON*] (EAIO)
IFIAS .... International Federation of Institutes for/of Advanced Studies (or Study) (SAUO)
IFIAT .... International Federation of Independent Air Transport
IFIC .... Institute for International Cooperation (SAUS)
IFIC .... International Ferrocement Information Center [*Asian Institute of Technology*] (IID)
IFIC .... International Food Information Council (EA)
IFIC .... Investment Funds Institute of Canada (SAUS)
IFICB .... International Finance Investment and Commerce Bank Ltd. [*Bangladesh*] (EY)
IFICO .... Industrial Finance and Investment Corp. [*British*]
IFICS .... In-Flight Interceptor Communications System [*Military*]
IFID .... International Federation for Information and Documentation [*See also FIID*] (EAIO)
IFID .... International Forum on Information and Documentation (SAUS)
IFIDA .... Independent Film Importers and Distributors of America [*Defunct*] (EA)
IFIE .... International Federation of Industrial Employers (SAUO)
IFIEC .... International Federation of Industrial Energy Consumers [*Geneva, Switzerland*] (EA)
IFIEC-Europe ... International Federation of Industrial Energy Consumers, Europe (SAUO)
I (field) .... Information Field (NITA)
IFIESR .... International Foundation for Industrial Ergonomics and Safety Research (SAUO)
IFIF .... International Federation for Inner Freedom (SAUO)
IFIF .... International Federation for Internal Freedom [*Later, Castalia Foundation*] (EA)
IFIF .... International Federation of Industrial Organizations and General Workers' Unions
IFIF .... International Federation of Interior Designers (SAUO)
IFIF .... International Feed Industry Federation (SAUO)
IFIF .... International Forum for Internal Freedom (WDAA)
IFIF .... International Foundation for Individual Freedom (SAUO)
IFIF .... International Foundation for Internal Freedom (SAUO)
IFIFR .... International Federation of International Furniture Removers [*See also FIDI*] [*Brussels, Belgium*] (EAIO)
IFII .... Indiana Financial Investors, Incorporated (SAUO)
IFIJG .... International Federation of Infantile and Juvenile Gynecology [*See also FIGIJ*] [*Sierre, Switzerland*] (EAIO)
IFILE .... Interface File (NITA)
IFIM .... Instream Flow Incremental Methodology (SAUO)
IFIM .... International Flight Information Manual
ifimp .... If Impossible (SAUS)
IFIN .... Investors Financial Services Corp. [*NASDAQ symbol*] (SAG)
IFIN .... Investors Finl Svcs [*NASDAQ symbol*] (TTSB)
IFINS .... If Instrument Conditions Encountered [*Aviation*] (FAAC)
IFIO .... Information for Industry Office [*Air Force*] (MCD)
IFIOM .... Intelligent FDDI Input Output Module (SAUS)
IFIP .... Iguazu Falls International Park (SAUO)
IFIP .... Instream Flow Information Paper (SAUO)
IFIP .... Integrated Flight Instrument Panel (SAUS)
IFIP .... International Federation for Information Processing [*Formerly, IFIPS*] (EA)
IFIP .... International Federation of Information Processing Societies (SAUO)
IFIP .... International Food Irradiation Project [*Food and Agricultural Organization*] (PDAA)
IFIP/ICC .... International Federation for/of Information Processing/International Computation Center (SAUO)
IFIP/ICC .... International Federation of Information Processing/International Computation Center (SAUS)
IFIPS .... International Federation of Information Processing Societies [*Later, IFIP*]
IFIRA .... Information Facility for Indigenous Resources for Australia
I Fire E .... Institution of Fire Engineers (SAUO)
IFIS .... Independent Flight Inspection System (SAUO)
IFIS .... Industry File Index System [*Chemical Information Systems, Inc.*] [*Information service or system*] (CRD)
IFIS .... Industry File Information System (SAUO)
IFIS .... Infrared Flight Inspection System (IAA)
IFIS .... Instrument Flight Instructors School [*Navy*]
ifis .... Integrated flight instrument system (SAUO)
IFIS .... International Financial Intelligence Service (NITA)
IFIS .... International Food Information Service [*Database producer*] [*Germany*]
IFIS .... International Food Information System (SAUS)
IFISH .... Integrated Fisheries Information System (SAUS)
IFISRR .... International Federation of Institutes for Socio-Religious Research [*Louvain, Belgium*] (EA)
IFIT .... International Forest Investigation Team (SAUS)
IFITU .... Indian Federation of Independent Trade Unions (SAUO)
IFIWA .... International Federation of Importers and Wholesale Grocers Associations [*The Hague, Netherlands*] (EAIO)
IFIX .... Immunofixation (STED)
IFJ .... Franklin-Johnson County Public Library, Franklin, IN [*OCLC symbol*] (OCLC)
IFJ .... International Federation of Journalists [*See also FIJ*] [*Brussels, Belgium*] (EAIO)
IFJ .... Isafjordur [*Iceland*] [*Airport symbol*] (OAG)
IFJ .... Winnfield, LA [*Location identifier*] [*FAA*] (FAAL)
IFJAFC .... International Federation of Journalists of Allied or Free Countries (SAUO)
IFJG .... International Federation of Infantile and Juvenile Gynecology (SAUO)
IFJU .... International Federation of Friut Juice Producers (SAUO)
IFK .... Indirect Free Kick [*Soccer*]
IFK .... Installations Fragenkommission [*Later, International Commission on Rules for the Approval of Electrical Equipment*] [*CEE*]
IFK .... Integral equation of the First Kind (SAUS)
IFK .... Interfunk & Co. [*Yugoslavia*] [*ICAO designator*] (FAAC)
IFK .... Internal Flow Kinematics (SAUS)
IFK .... River Bend Library System, Coal Valley, IL [*OCLC symbol*] (OCLC)
IFKC .... International Federation of Kennel Clubs (EA)
IFKM .... Internationale Foederation fuer Kurzschrift und Maschinenschreiben [*International Federation of Shorthand and Typewriting*]
IFKT .... International Federation of Knitting Technologists [*See also FITB*] [*Frauenfeld, Switzerland*] (EAIO)
IFL .... Flora Carnegie Library, Flora, IL [*Library symbol*] [*Library of Congress*] (LCLS)
IFL .... Icelandic Federation of Labor
IFL .... Immunofluorescence (DB)
IFL .... Imperial Fascist League [*British*]
IFL .... Indian Federation of Labour (SAUO)
IFL .... Induction Field Locator (IAA)
IFL .... Inflatable (MSA)
IFL .... Initial Flight Level
IFL .... Innisfail [*Australia*] [*Airport symbol*]
IFL .... Inside Face of Liner (SAUS)
IFL .... Integer Function Language [*Computer science*] (PDAA)
IFL .... Integrated Fuse Logic (NITA)
IFL .... Intelligent Fault Locator [*McDonnell Douglas Helicopter Co.*] [*Army*]
IFL .... Intelligent Forms Language [*Delrina Corp.*] [*Computer science*] (PCM)
IFL .... Interdivisional Facilities List (SAUS)
IFL .... Interfacility Link (LAIN)
IFL .... Interfacility List (SAUS)
IFL .... Interfacility optical Fiber communications Link (SAUS)
IFL .... International Federation of Labor (SAUO)
IFL .... International Federation of Lithographers, Process Workers and Kindred Trades (SAUO)
IFL .... International Frequency List (NATG)
IFL .... International Friendship League [*Defunct*] (EA)
IFL .... Internet For Learning (SAUS)
IFL .... Intra Facility Link (SAUS)
IFLA .... International Federation of Landscape Architects [*Versailles, France*] (EAIO)
IFLA .... International Federation of Library Associations and Institutions
IFLA .... International Finance and Leasing Association (MHDB)
IFLANET .... Computer Network of IFLA (SAUS)
IFLASC .... International Federation of Latin American Study Centers [*Mexico City, Mexico*] (EAIO)

IFLB .... Islamic Front for the Liberation of Bahrain [*Political party*] (PD)
IFLBP .... International Federation of the Little Brothers of the Poor [*See also FIPFP*] (EAIO)
IFL Bulletin ... Indian Federation of Labour Bulletin (journ.) (SAUS)
IFLC .... International Frequency List Committee
IFLCC .... Inital Force Level Control Capability (SAUS)
IFICL .... Cumberland Trail Library System, Flora, IL [*Library symbol*] [*Library of Congress*] (LCLS)
IFLCS .... Interim Force Level Control System (SAUO)
IFL-DFL .... Inflating-Deflating
IFLET .... Interim Focal-Length Optical Tracker (SAUS)
IFLG .... International Federation of Leather Guilds (EA)
IFLIPS .... Integrated Flight Prediction System [*Aviation*] (DA)
IFLIR .... Integrated Forward Looking Infrared (ACAE)
IFLM .... International Fund Land Management (SAUO)
IFLN .... Interstate Freeze Lobbying Network (EA)
IFlo .... Flossmoor Public Library, Flossmoor, IL [*Library symbol*] [*Library of Congress*] (LCLS)
IFLO .... IFlow Corp. [*NASDAQ symbol*] (SAG)
IFLO .... Islamic Front for Liberation of Oromo [*Ethiopia*] [*Political party*] (EY)
IF/LOAL .... Indirect Fire/Lock-On-After-Launch (SAUS)
IFLOT .... Intermediate Focal Length Optical Tracer (SAUS)
IFLOT .... Intermediate Focal Length Optical Tracker
I-Flow .... IFlow Corp. [*Associated Press*] (SAG)
IFLOWS .... Integrated Flood Observing and Warning System [*National Oceanic and Atmospheric Administration*]
IFLrA .... Recombinant Human Leukocyte Interferon A [*Pharmacology*] (DAVI)
IFL Rev .... International Financial Law Review [*A publication*] (DLA)
IFLRY .... International Federation of Liberal and Radical Youth (EAIO)
IFLS .... International Federation of Law Students (DLA)
IFLS .... International Federation of Little Singers (EAIO)
IFLTT .... Intermediate Focal Length Tracking Telescope (MUGU)
IFLWU .... International Fur and Leather Workers Union (MHDB)
IFM .... Improved Frequency Modulation (MCD)
IFM .... Induction Flowmeter (SAUS)
IFM .... Industrial Facility Manager (SAUO)
IFM .... Infantry Field Manual (SAUO)
IFM .... In-Flight Maintenance
IFM .... In-Right Monitor (SAUS)
IFM .... Instantaneous Frequency Measurement
IFM .... Instantaneous Frequency Meter (SAUS)
IFM .... Instanteneous Frequency Monitoring (SAUS)
IFM .... Institute for Forensic Medicine (SAUO)
IFM .... Institute of Fisheries Management [*British*]
IFM .... Instrument Flag Motor
IFM .... Integrating Fluctuation Meter
IFM .... Integrating Frequency Meter (SAUS)
IFM .... Intelligent Flow Management (SAUS)
IFM .... Interactive File Manager [*Computer science*]
IFM .... Interface Machine (SAUS)
IFM .... Interface Measurements (SAUS)
IFM .... Interfacial-Force Microscope
IFM .... Intermediate Frame Memory [*Computer science*]
IFM .... Internal Fetal Monitor [*Medicine*] (DMAA)
IFM .... International Falcon Movement
IFM .... International Federation of Musicians (SAUO)
IFM .... International Finance Managers Study [*Database*] [*Research Services Ltd.*] [*Information service or system*] (CRD)
IFM .... International Financial Markets Trading Ltd.
IFM .... International Fund for Monuments
IFM .... Intrafusal Muscle [*Anatomy*]
IFM .... Intrapulse Frequency Modulation (SAUS)
IFM .... Ionospheric Forecast Model (SAUO)
IFM .... Iowa Farm-to-Market Carriers Tariff Bureau, Ottumwa IA [*STAC*]
IFM .... Tifton, GA [*Location identifier*] [*FAA*] (FAAL)
IFMA .... Immunofluorescence [*or Immunofluorometric*] Assay [*Also, IFA*] [*Analytical biochemistry*]
IFMA .... Immunofluorometric Assay [*Analytical biochemistry*]
IFMA .... Independent Furniture Manufacturers' Associaiton [*British*] (DBA)
IFMA .... Industrial Furnace Manufacturers Association (SAUO)
IFMA .... In-Flight Mission Abort (SAUS)
IFMA .... Information Resources Management Association
IFMA .... Interdenominational Foreign Mission Association of North America (EA)
IFMA .... International Facility Management Association (EA)
IFMA .... International Farm Management Association [*Reading, Berkshire, England*] (EAIO)
IFMA .... International Federation of Margarine Associations [*Brussels, Belgium*] (EAIO)
IFMA .... International Food Service Manufacturers Association (SAUS)
IFMA .... Irish Flour Millers Association (BI)
IFMAP .... Irish Federation of Musicians and Associated Professions (SAUO)
IFMBE .... International Federation for Medical and Biological Engineering [*ICSU*] [*Ottawa, ON*] (EA)
IFMC .... Illinois Foundation for Medical Care [*Medicine*] (EDAA)
IFMC .... International Federation of Master-Craftsmen (EA)
IFMC .... International Federation of Motorhome Clubs [*Belgium*] (EAIO)
IFMC .... International Folk Music Centre (SAUO)
IFMC .... International Folk Music Council [*Later, ICTM*]
IFMC/J .... Journal of the International Folk Music Council. Cambridge (journ.) (SAUS)
IFMCS .... Integrated Fire and Manoeuvre Control System (SAUS)
IFMD .... Informal Maintainability Demonstration (SAUS)
IFME .... International Federation for Medical Electronics
IFME .... International Federation of Municipal Engineers [*See also FIIM*] [*British*] (EAIO)
IFMEBE .... International Federation for Medical Electronics and Biological Engineering [*Medicine*] (EDAA)
IFMEO .... International Fish Meal Exporters Organization (SAUO)
IF/MF .... Intermediate Frequency/Medium Frequency (NATG)
IFMI .... Irish Federation of Marine Industries (SAUO)
IFMIF .... International Fusion Materials Irradiation Facility (COE)
IFMIS .... Implementation Field Microfilm/Micrographics Information System
IFMIS .... Industrial Facilities and Material Information System
IFMIS .... Integrated Facilities Management Information System
IFMIS .... Integrated Force Management Information System (SAUO)
IFMIS .... Intelligent Fire Management Information System (SAUS)
IFML .... International Film Management Ltd. [*Australia*]
IFMM .... International Federation of Manual Medicine (EA)
IFMMS .... International Federation of Mining and Metallurgical Students (SAUO)
IFMO .... Imperial and Foreign Money Orders
IFMOD .... Interactive Forecasting Model (GFGA)
IFMP .... International Federation for Medical Psychotherapy [*See also IGAP*] [*Oslo, Norway*] (EAIO)
IFMP .... International Federation of Maritime Philately [*Livorno, Italy*] (EAIO)
IFMP .... International Federation of Married Priests (EAIO)
IFMP .... International Federation of Medical Psychotherapy (SAUO)
IFMP .... Ipsilon Flow Management Protocol (SAUS)
IFMPO .... Integrated Farm Management Program Option [*Department of Agriculture*]
IFMR .... Instantaneous Frequency Measurement Receiver (SAUS)
IFMS .... Impact Force Measuring System
IFMS .... In-Flight Management System
IFMS .... Integrated Farm Management System
IFMS .... Integrated Financial Management System (AABC)
IFMS .... Interactive File Management System (ACAE)
IFMS .... Interagency Fleet Management System [*GSA*] (TAG)
IFMS .... International Federation of Magical Societies [*See also FISM*] (EAIO)
IFMSA .... International Federation of Medical Students Associations [*See also FIAEM*] [*Vienna, Austria*] (EAIO)
IFMSAN .... International Federation of Medical Student Associations News [*Medicine*] (EDAA)
IFM-SEI .... International Falcon Movement - Socialist Educational International
IFM/SHR .... IFM Superheterodyne Receiver (SAUS)
IFMSS .... International Federation of Multiple Sclerosis Societies [*British*] (EAIO)
IFMU .... Integrated Flight Management Unit (SAUS)
IFMW .... International Federation of Mazdaznan Women (SAUO)
IFMX .... Informix Corp. [*NASDAQ symbol*] (NQ)
IFN .... Ice-Freezing Nuclei (SAUS)
IFN .... India Fund, Inc. [*NYSE symbol*] (SAG)
IFN .... Information [*Computer science*] (MDG)
IFN .... Interferon [*Also, IF*] [*Biochemistry*]
IFN .... International Feminist Network
IFN .... International Friends of Nature [*See also NFI*] [*Zurich, Switzerland*] (EAIO)
IFN .... Isfahan [*Iran*] [*Airport symbol*] (OAG)
IFN .... Items for Negotiation
IFN-A .... Alpha-Interferon [*Medicine*] (TAD)
IFNA .... Interferon Alpha (SAUS)
IFNA .... International Federation of Netball Associations [*Glasgow, Scotland*] (EAIO)
IFNA .... International Federation of Nurse Anesthetists (SAUO)
IFNA .... International FidoNet Association [*Defunct*] (EA)
IFNA .... International Flying Nurses Association (EA)
IFNAES .... International Federation of the National Associations of Engineering Students (SAUO)
IFNAFSS .... International Feminist Network Against Female Sexual Slavery (SAUS)
IFNB .... Idaho First National Bank (SAUO)
IFNB .... Interferon Beta (SAUS)
IFNC .... Integrated Flight Control/Navigation Computer (MCD)
IFND .... Interfund Corp. [*NASDAQ symbol*] (COMM)
IFNE .... International Federation for Narcotic Education
if nec .... if necessary (SAUS)
IFNG .... Interferon Gamma [*Medicine*] (DMAA)
IFNGO .... International Federation of Non-Governmental Organizations for the Prevention for Drug and Substance Abuse (SAUO)
IFNP .... International Federation of Newspaper Publishers (NTCM)
IFNP .... International Food and Nutrition Programme (SAUO)
IFNs .... Interferons [*Biology*] (DOG)
IFNS .... Irish Family Names Society (EA)
IFNSA .... International Federation of the National Standardization (or Standardizing) Associations (SAUS)
IFNSA .... International Federation of the National Standardizing (or Standardization) Associations (SAUO)
IFNY .... Infinity, Inc. [*NASDAQ symbol*] (SAG)
IFO .... Identified Flying Object [*Air Force*]
IFO .... Improved Fiber Optics
ifo .... in favor of (SAUS)
IFO .... Information for Offerers (SAUO)
IFO .... Information Systems Office [*NASA*] (NASA)
IFO .... Info-Stop Communications [*Vancouver Stock Exchange symbol*]
IFO .... In Front Of (WDAA)
IFO .... Institute for Fermentation (SAUO)
IFO .... Intensive Field Observations (ACAE)
IFO .... Intermediate Fuel Oil (RIMS)
IFO .... International Farmers Organization (SAUO)
IFO .... International Field Office (SAUO)

IFO.......... International Fortran Organization (NITA)
IFO.......... Interplanetary Flying Object (SAUS)
I/FOA.......... Installation/Field Operating Activities (SAUO)
IFOA.......... Isotta Fraschini Owner's Association [*Defunct*] (EA)
IFOAD.......... International Federation of Original Art Diffusors [*France*] (EAIO)
IFOAM.......... International Federation of Organic Agriculture Movements [*Witzenhausen, Federal Republic of Germany*] (EA)
IFOB.......... Improved Fiber Optics Bundle
IFOBL.......... In-Flight Operable Bomb Lock (SAUS)
IFOBRL.......... In-Flight Operable Bomb Rack Lock (MCD)
IFOBS.......... International Federation for Open Bibliographic Systems (TELE)
IFOC.......... Integrated Fibre Optic Communication (SAUO)
IFOC.......... Intermountain Field Operations Center [*Bureau of Mines*] [*Denver, CO*] (GRD)
IFOCUS.......... Interprofessional Fostering of Ophthalmic Care for Underserved Sectors [*An association*] (EA)
IFOFSAG.......... International Fellowship of Former Scouts and Guides [*Brussels, Belgium*]
IFOG.......... Interferometric Fiber Optic Gyroscope
IFOG.......... International Federation of Olive Growers (SAUO)
IFOMA.......... Independent Fuel Oil Marketers of America [*Defunct*] (EA)
IFOMA.......... Instructions for Mailers [*A publication*]
IFop.......... Forest Park Public Library, Forest Park, IL [*Library symbol*] [*Library of Congress*] (LCLS)
IFOP.......... Institut Francais d'Opinion Publique [*French Institute of Public Opinion*]
IFOP.......... International Federation of the Oriental Press (SAUO)
IFOPA.......... International Fibrodysplasia Ossificans Progressiva Association (EA)
IFOR.......... Implementation Force (VLIE)
Ifor.......... Implementation Force [*Bosnia*] (WDAA)
IFOR.......... Intelligent Forces [*Army*] (RDA)
IFOR.......... Interactive FORTRAN [*Formula Translating System*] [*Computer science*] (IAA)
IFOR.......... Internal Format Object Report (MCD)
IFOR.......... International Federation of Operation Research Societies (BARN)
IFOR.......... International Fellowship of Reconciliation [*Alkmaar, Netherlands*] (EA)
IFOR.......... International Fellowship of Reconstruction (SAUO)
IFORD.......... Institut de Formation et de Recherche Demographiques [*Institute for Training and Demographic Research - ITDR*] (EAIO)
IFORG.......... Integrated Fiber Optics Resonator Gyro (ACAE)
IFORL.......... International Federation of Oto-Rhino-Laryngology [*Medicine*] (EDAA)
IFORO.......... Interphone (Service F) Resumed Operation [*Aviation*] (FAAC)
IFORS.......... International Federation of Operational Research Science (SAUO)
IFORS.......... International Federation of Operational Research Societies [*ICSU*] [*Lyngby, Denmark*] (EAIO)
IFORS.......... International Federation of Operations Research Science (SAUO)
IFORS.......... International Federation of Operations Research Societies (SAUO)
IFORVU.......... International Federation of Recreational Vehicle Users [*Later, FOR*] (EA)
IFOS.......... Integrated Fibre Optical System (SAUS)
IFOS.......... International Federation of Ophthalmological Societies [*Nijmegen, Netherlands*] (EA)
IFOS.......... International Federation of Oto-Rhino-Laryngological Societies [*Berchem, Belgium*] (EAIO)
IFOS.......... Ion Formation from Organic Solids [*International conference*]
IFOSA.......... International Federation of Scoliosis Associations (EA)
IFOSA.......... International Federation of Stationers Association (SAUO)
IFOSCE.......... International Federation of Organizations for School Correspondence and Exchange (SAUO)
IFOSS.......... Intelligence Family of Systems Study [*Military*] (MCD)
IFOT.......... In-Flight Operations and Training (MCD)
IFOTES.......... International Federation of Telephonic Emergency Services [*Jorn, Sweden*] (EA)
IFOTES.......... International Federation of Telephony Emergency Services (SAUO)
IFoTMM.......... International Federation of Theory of Machines and Mechanism (SAUO)
IFOV.......... Individual Field of View
IFOV.......... Instantaneous Field of View
IFOV.......... Instrument Field of View
IFOX.......... Irish Futures and Options Exchange (NUMA)
IFP.......... Glycerol [*Medicine*] (EDAA)
IFP.......... Illinois Functional Programming Language [*Computer science*]
IFP.......... Imperial and Foreign Post (IAA)
IFP.......... IMS/VS fast path (SAUS)
IFP.......... Independent Feature Project (EA)
IFP.......... Indexes of Firepower Potential
IFP.......... Indian Famine Relief (SAUO)
IFP.......... Indigenous Forest Policy (SAUS)
IFP.......... Inflammatory Fibroid Polyp [*Gastroenterology*]
IFP.......... In-Flight Performance
IFP.......... Inflight Printer (SAUS)
IFP.......... In Forma Pauperis [*As a Pauper*] [*Latin*]
IFP.......... Inkatha Freedom Party [*Afrikaans*] [*Political party*] (ECON)
IFP.......... Institute of Fluid Power
IFP.......... Institute of Physical Problems [*Former USSR*] (MCD)
IFP.......... Institut Francais du Petroles [*French Institute of Petroleum*] [*Paris*]
IFP.......... Instruction Fetch Phase (SAUS)
IFP.......... Instruction Fetch Pipeline [*Computer science*]
IFP.......... Insulin, Compound F (hydrocortisone) Prolactin [*Medicine*] (EDAA)
IFP.......... Integrated File Processor
IFP.......... Interactive Forecast Preparation (SAUS)
IFP.......... Interface Processor (RALS)
IFP.......... Interfacial Polymerization (SAUS)
IFP.......... Intermediate Filament Protein [*Biochemistry*] (DB)
IFP.......... Intermediate Frequency Patch (SAUS)
IFP.......... International Federation of Pedestrians (EA)
IFP.......... International Federation of Prestressing (SAUO)
IFP.......... International Federation of Purchasing
IFP.......... International Fixed Public
IFP.......... International Forest Products Ltd. [*Toronto Stock Exchange symbol*] [*Vancouver Stock Exchange symbol*]
IFP.......... Interns for Peace (EA)
IFP.......... Interplant Finished Parts (SAUS)
IFP.......... Intrapatellar Fat Pad (DMAA)
IFP.......... Invitation for Proposal (NOAA)
IFPA.......... Independent Film Producers of America (NTCM)
IFPA.......... Independent Fluorspar Producers Association (EA)
IFPA.......... Independent Forest Products Association (NTPA)
IFPA.......... Independent Free Papers of America (EA)
IFPA.......... Industrial Film Producers Association (SAUO)
IFPA.......... Industrial Fire Protection Association of Great Britain
IFPA.......... Information Film Producers of America [*Later, Association of Visual Communicators*] (EA)
IFPA.......... Institute for Foreign Policy Analysis, Inc. [*Tufts University*] [*Research center*] (RCD)
IFPA.......... Inter-American Federation of Personnel Administration (SAUO)
IFPA.......... International Federation of Agricultural Producers (SAUO)
IFPA.......... International Federation of Photographic Art
IFPA.......... International Federation of Psoriasis Associations [*Stockholm, Sweden*] (EAIO)
IFPA.......... International Fighter Pilots Academy [*Slovak Air Force*]
IFPA.......... International Fire Photographers Association (EA)
IFPA.......... International Flipper Pinball Association (EA)
IFPA.......... International Fresh-Cut Produce Association (NTPA)
IFPA.......... Isoelectric Focusing in Polyacrylamide [*Gel*] [*Analytical chemistry*]
IFPAAW.......... International Federation of Plantation, Agricultural, and Allied Workers [*Switzerland*]
IFPAG.......... Isoelectric Focusing on Polyacrylamide Gel (SAUS)
IFP Broadcast Band... International Fixed Public Broadcast Band (SAUS)
IFPC.......... Integrated Flight and Propulsion Control (MCD)
IFPC.......... Integration of Flight & Propulsion Control (SAUS)
IFPC.......... International Fair Play Committee (SAUO)
IFPCA.......... International Federation of Press Cutting Agencies (EA)
IFPCS.......... International Federation of Unions of Employees in Public and Civil Services
IFPCW.......... International Federation of Petroleum and Chemical Workers (CARL)
IFPD.......... International Federation of Postcard Dealers (EA)
IFPDA.......... International Fine Print Dealers Association
IFPE.......... Institute for Fluid Power Education (SAUS)
IFPE.......... Institute of Fiscal and Political Education [*Defunct*] (EA)
IFPE.......... International Federation for Parent Education [*See also FIEP*] [*Sevres, France*] (EAIO)
IFPEB.......... International Federation of Physical Education Bulletin [*Medicine*] (EDAA)
IFPEC.......... Improved Floating-Point Engineering Change (VLIE)
IFPEC.......... Independent Film Producers Export Corp. [*Defunct*]
IFPF.......... Idaho Fuels Processing Facility (SAUO)
IFPFP.......... Individual Flight Plans from This Point [*Aviation*] (FAAC)
IFPG.......... Intermediate Frequency Pulse Generator (SAUS)
IFPG.......... International Frequency Planning Group (SAUO)
IFPI.......... Identified Friendly Prior to Interception (SAUS)
IFPI.......... Imaging Fabry-Perot Interferometer (SAUS)
IFPI.......... International Federation of the Phonographic Industry (EAIO)
IFPI.......... International Federation of the Photographic Industry
IFPIA.......... Independent Film Producers International Association (SAUO)
IFPITB.......... Inorganic Feed Phosphates International Technical Bureau (SAUO)
IFPL.......... In-Flight Power Loss (MCD)
IFPL.......... Initial Flight Plan (SAUS)
IFPL/SD.......... In-Flight Power Loss/Shutdown (MCD)
IFPM.......... In-Flight Performance Monitor
IFPM.......... In-Flight Performance Monitoring (SAUS)
IFPM.......... Intelligent Flight Path Monitor (SAUS)
IFPM.......... International Federation of Physical Medicine
IFPMA.......... International Federation of Pharmaceutical Manufacturers Associations [*See also FIIM*] [*Geneva, Switzerland*] (EAIO)
IFPMM.......... International Federation of Purchasing and Materials Management [*Aarau, Switzerland*] (EAIO)
IFPMNI.......... International Federation of Purchasing and Materials Management (SAUO)
IFPMO.......... International Federation of Psychological-Medical Organizations [*See also FIOPM*] [*Lausanne, Switzerland*] (EAIO)
IFPMR.......... International Federation of Physical Medicine and Rehabilitation (EA)
IFPNT.......... International Federation of Practitioners of Natural Therapeutics [*British*]
IFPO.......... Institute of Fire Prevention Officers [*British*] (DBA)
IFPO.......... International Foundation for Protection Officers (EA)
IFPO.......... International Freelance Photographers Organization
IFPO.......... Interplant Finished Parts Order (SAUS)
IFPOS.......... International Federation of Pediatric Orthopaedic Societies (ADWA)
IFPP.......... Imperial and Foreign Parcel Post (IAA)
IFPP.......... Industrial Facilities Protection Program [*DoD*]
IFPP.......... Industrial Fugitive Process Particulate (GNE)
IFPP.......... Information for Proposal Preparation (ACAE)
IFPP.......... Instructions for Proposal Preparation (SAUO)
IFPP.......... International Federation of the Periodicals Press (SAUS)
IFPP.......... Irradiated Fuel Processing Plant (DEN)
IFPPE.......... Interregional Fund for Programme Preparation, Promotion and Evaluation (SAUO)
IFPRA.......... Interamerican Federation of Public Relations Associations

IFPRA .... International Family Planning Research Association [*Later, ISRM*] (EA)
IFPRA .... International Federation of Park and Recreation Administration [*Reading, England*] (EAIO)
IFPRA .... International Federation of Public Relations Association (SAUO)
IFPRI .... International Fine Particle Research Institute
IFPRI .... International Food Policy Research Institute (EA)
IFPRO .... European Association of Importers of Finished Products (SAUO)
IFPS .... In-Flight Performance Signal [*Aviation*] (IAA)
IFPS .... Initial Flight Plan Processing (SAUS)
IFPS .... Initial Flightplan Processing System of Eurocontrol (SAUO)
IFPS .... Institute for Foreign Policy Studies (SAUS)
IFPS .... Integrated Flight Plan Processing (SAUS)
IFPS .... Integrated Flight Plan Processing System (SAUS)
IFPS .... Integrated Initial Flight Plan Processing System [*Aviation*] (DA)
IFPS .... Interactive Financial Planning System [*Harris Systems Ltd.*] [*Software package*] (NCC)
IFPS .... International Federation of Palynological Societies (EAIO)
IFPS .... International Federation of Philosophical Societies [*See also FISP*] [*Fribourg, Switzerland*] (EAIO)
IFPS .... International Federation of Popular Sports [*See also IVV*] (EAIO)
IFPS .... International Federation of Psychoanalytic Societies (EA)
IFPS .... International Fluid Power Symposium (SAUO)
IFPS .... Interplant-File Processing System (SAUS)
IFPS .... Intra-Formation Positioning System (SAUS)
IFPSM .... International Federation for Preventive and Social Medicine (EAIO)
IFPTE .... International Federation of Professional and Technical Engineers (EA)
IFPTO .... International Federation of Popular Travel Organisations [*Paris, France*] (EAIO)
IFPTS .... Intertype Fototronic Photographic System (DIT)
IFPTS .... Intertype Fototronic Photographic Typesetting System (SAUS)
IFPUG .... International Function Point Users Group (NTPA)
IFPV .... International Federation of Pelota Vasca (EA)
IFPVP .... International Federation of Phonogram and Videogram Producers (EA)
IFPVS .... International Federation of Phonogram and Videogram Societies (SAUO)
IFPW .... International Federation of Petroleum Workers
IFPW .... International Federation of Pharmaceutical Wholesalers (NTPA)
IFPWA .... International Federation of Protestant Workers' Associations
IFPWA .... International Federation of Public Warehousing Associations [*Formerly, IFPWKA*] (EAIO)
IFPWKA .... International Federation of Public Warehouse Keepers Associations [*Later, IFPWA*] (EAIO)
IFQ .... Individual Fishing Quota (SAUS)
IFQ .... Invitation for Quote (MCD)
IFQT .... Incremental Formal Qualification Test (SAUO)
IFR .... I Follow Railroad (SAUS)
IFR .... Ifrane [*Morocco*] [*Seismograph station code, US Geological Survey*] (SEIS)
IFR .... IFR Systems, Inc. [*Associated Press*] (SAG)
IFR .... Image-to-Frame Ratio
IFR .... Immediate Free Recall (PDAA)
IFR .... Imported Food Regulations [*British*]
IFR .... Impulse Fast Reactor [*Former USSR*]
IFR .... Impulse Frequency Rate (VLIE)
IFR .... Income Fund Reimbursable (SAUS)
IFR .... Increased Frequency Reporting (SAUS)
IFR .... Increasing Failure Rate
IFR .... Incremental Financial Rate of Return
IFR .... Indian Foodgrain Requirements [*British*]
IFR .... Industrial Fuels & Resources, Inc. (EFIS)
IFR .... In-Flight Refueling
IFR .... Information Flow Rate (SAUS)
IFR .... In-Frame Response [*Automotive engineering*] [*Electronics*]
IFR .... Infrared
IFR .... Infrared Filter Radiometer
IFR .... Inspiratory Flow Rate [*Physiology*]
IFR .... Instantaneous Frequency [*Indicating*] Receivers (IEEE)
IFR .... Instant Failure Report (ACAE)
IFR .... Institute of Fisheries Research [*University of North Carolina*]
IFR .... Institute of Food Research [*British*]
IFR .... Institut Federatif de Recherche [*Federal Research Institute*] [*France*]
IFR .... Instituts Federatifs de Recherche [*France*]
IFR .... Instrument Fighter Rules (SAUS)
IFR .... Instrument Flight Recovery [*NASA*]
IFR .... Instrument Flight Regulation (SAUS)
IFR .... Instrument Flight Research (SAUO)
IFR .... Instrument Flight Rules [*Aviation*]
IFR .... Instrument Flying Regulations (SAUS)
IFR .... Insufficient Data For Reporting (WDMC)
IFR .... Integral Fast Reactor [*Nuclear energy*]
IFR .... Interface Register
IFR .... Interim Final Rule [*RSPA*] (TAG)
IFR .... Interleaved Frame Recording (SAUS)
IFR .... Intermediate Free Recall (SAUO)
IFR .... Intermediate Frequency Range (MCD)
IFR .... Internal Function Register
IFR .... Internationaler Frauenrat [*International Council of Women*]
IFR .... International Federation of Radio Officers (SAUO)
IFR .... International Federation of Radio-Telegraphists (SAUO)
IFR .... International Federation of Religions (SAUO)
IFR .... International Fellowship of Reconciliation (SAUO)
IFR .... International Fiction Review [*A publication*] (ANEX)
IFR .... International Fighter RADAR
IFR .... International Film Representatives [*Division of International Film Completion Corp.*]
IFR .... International Financing Review [*A publication*]
IFR .... International Flyer Resources Ltd. [*Vancouver Stock Exchange symbol*]
IFR .... Interrupt Flag Register [*Computer science*] (IAA)
IFR .... Intrinsic Failure Rate (VLIE)
IFR .... Isolated Flow Responder [*Physiology*]
IFRA .... INCA [*International Newspaper Color Association*]-FIEJ Research Association [*Federation Internationale des Editeurs de Journaux*] [*Research center*] [*Germany*] (IRC)
IFRA .... INCA-FIEJ Research Association-International Association for Newspaper and Media Technology (SAUO)
IFRA .... Increasing Failure Rate Average [*Statistics*]
IFRA .... Independent Fabric Retailers Association [*Defunct*] (EA)
IFRA .... Independent Footwear Retailers Association [*British*] (DBA)
IFRA .... Indirect Fluorescent Rabies Antibody Test [*Immunology*] (MAE)
IFRA .... Infrasonics, Inc. [*NASDAQ symbol*] (NQ)
IFRA .... International Family Recreation Association (EA)
IFRA .... International Foundation for Research in the Field of Advertising
IFRA .... International Fragrance Association [*Geneva, Switzerland*] (EAIO)
IFRA .... International Fund-Raising Association (EA)
IFRAA .... Interfaith Forum on Religion, Art, and Architecture (EA)
IFRAC .... Imported Food Risks Advisory Committee [*Australia*]
IFRAC .... International Federation of Railway Advertising Companies [*British*] (EA)
IFRA Spec Rep ... IFRA Special Report (journ.) (SAUS)
IFRB .... International Frequency Registration Board [*ITU*] [*United Nations*]
IFRB .... International Frequency Regulation Board (SAUO)
IFRB List ..... International Frequency Registration Bureau List (SAUS)
IFRC .... Inland Forest Resource Council (EA)
IFRC .... Instantaneous Frequency Correlation (NG)
IFRC .... International Federation of Roofing Contractors [*See also IFD*] (EAIO)
IFRC .... International Federation of the Red Cross (SAUS)
IFRC .... International Ford Retractable Club (EA)
IFRC .... International Futures Research Conference (PDAA)
IFRCC .... International Fight'n Rooster Cutlery Club (EA)
IFRD .... International Federation of Retail Distributors (EAIO)
IFRE .... Institute for Family Research and Education [*Defunct*] (EA)
IFREMER ..... French Marine Research Institute (SAUS)
IFREMER ..... Institut Francais de Recherche pour l'Exploitation de la Mer [*French Research Institute for Ocean Utilization*] [*Research center*] (IID)
IFREO .... Industrial Forecast Requirements (SAUS)
IFREQ .... Industrial Forecast Requirements (DNAB)
IFRF .... International Federation of Resistance Fighters (BJA)
IFRG .... International Genealogy and Heraldry Fellowship of Rotarians (EA)
IFRHO .... International Federation of Health Records Organizations (SAUO)
IFrHS .... Freeburg Community High School 77, Freeburg, IL [*Library symbol*] [*Library of Congress*] (LCLS)
IFRI .... Inland Fisheries Research Institute (SAUO)
IFRI .... International Fund-Raising Institute [*Later, IFRA*]
IFRIP .... Institut Francais de Recherche et de Technologie Polaires [*Public interest group*] [*French Southern and Antarctic Territories*] (EY)
IFRIS .... Intelligence Finished Reports Information Subsystem [*Computer science*]
IFRM .... International Federation of Resistance Movements [*Vienna, Austria*] (EA)
IFRM .... International Federation of the Rights of Man (EA)
IFRNA .... Inhibited Fuming Red Nitric Acid (ACAE)
IFRO .... Internal Feed Rate Override
IFROLS .... Integrated Fresnel Rainbow Optical Landing System (SAUO)
IFRON .... International Floating Rice Observational Nursery (SAUO)
IFRP .... International Fertility Research Program [*Later, FHI*]
IFRPD .... Institute of Food Research and Product Development (SAUO)
IFRPS .... Intercity Facility Relief Planning System (SAUS)
IFRRO .... International Federation of Reproductive Rights Organisations (AIE)
IFRS .... IFR Systems, Inc. [*NASDAQ symbol*] (NQ)
IFRS .... Individuals for a Rational Society [*Defunct*] (EA)
IFRS .... Interface Roughness Scattering (SAUS)
IFRT .... Institute for Fitness Research and Training (SAUO)
IFRT .... Intellectual Freedom Round Table [*American Library Association*]
IFRT .... Internal Floating Roof Tank [*Engineering*]
IFRT .... Involved Field Radiotherapy [*Medicine*] (DMAA)
IFRTA .... International Federation of Railwaymen's Travel Associations (EA)
IFRTP .... Institute for Polar Research and Technology (SAUO)
IFRU .... In-Flight Replaceable Unit (KSC)
IFRU .... In-Flight Replacement Unit (SAUS)
IFRU .... Interference Frequency Rejection Unit [*Military*]
IFRU .... Interference Rejection Unit (SAUS)
IFRW .... International Federation of Resistance Workers (SAUO)
IFR Weather ... Instrument Flight Rules Weather (SAUS)
i-fs- .... French Southern and Antarctic Lands [*MARC geographic area code*] [*Library of Congress*] (LCCP)
IFS .... ICOT Free Software (SAUS)
IFS .... Identification, Friend or Foe, Switching Circuit [*Military*]
IFS .... Inactivated Fetal-Calf Serum [*Immunology*]
IFS .... In-Band Framing System [*Simulation Laboratories, Inc.*]
IFS .... Increased Forward Stocking [*Military*] (DNAB)
IFS .... Independent Front Suspension [*Automotive engineering*]
Ifs .... Independent Front Suspension
IFS .... Indian Forest Service [*British*]
IFS .... Indirect Fire Simulator (SAUS)
IFS .... Inertia Fuel Shutoff (HAWK)

IFS.............. In-Flight Safety
IFS.............. Inflight Survey [*USTTA*] (TAG)
IFS.............. Information Fatigue Symdrome (WDAA)
IFS.............. Information Flow Standards (KSC)
IFS.............. Information Flow System (SAUS)
IFS.............. Infrared Frequency Synthesis
IFS.............. Input Factor Storage (SAUS)
IFS.............. Inshore Fire Support Ship [*Later, LFR*]
IFS.............. Insignia Financial Group [*NYSE symbol*] (SAG)
IFS.............. Inspectorate of Flight Safety (SAUS)
IFS.............. Installable File System [*Computer science*]
IFS.............. Institute for Fiscal Studies [*British*]
IFS.............. Institute of Financial Services [*Australia*]
IFS.............. Institute of Flight Structures [*Columbia University*]
IFS.............. Institute of Fusion Studies (SAUS)
IFS.............. Instructions for Service
IFS.............. Instrumentation Field Station (SAUO)
IFS.............. Instrument Fact Sheets (SAUO)
IFS.............. Instrument Flight Simulator (MCD)
IFS.............. Instrument Flight System (SAUS)
IFS.............. Instrument Right Simulator (SAUS)
IFS.............. Integrated Facilities System [*Army*]
IFS.............. Integrated File System (SAUS)
IFS.............. Integrated Financial System (SAUS)
IFS.............. Integrated Flight System
IFS.............. Integrated Forest Study on the Effects of Atmospheric Deposition (SAUO)
IFS.............. Intelligent Fax System (SAUS)
IFS.............. Intelligent File Store [*British*]
IFS.............. Intelligent Fixturing System (VLIE)
IFS.............. Interactive File Sharing
IFS.............. Interactive Flow Simulator (TEL)
IFS.............. Interchange File Separator [*Computer science*] (BUR)
IFS.............. Interdivisional Facilities Standard (SAUS)
IFS.............. Interface Specification
IFS.............. Inter Frame Space (SAUS)
IFS.............. Interframe Space (SAUS)
IFS.............. Intermediate Frequency Stage (SAUS)
IFS.............. Intermediate Frequency Strip
IFS.............. Internal Field Separator (SAUO)
IFS.............. Internal File System [*Computer science*] (VLIE)
IFS.............. Internal Focus Sensor (PDAA)
IFS.............. International Faculty of Sciences (SAUO)
IFS.............. International Federation of Settlements and Neighbourhood Centers (EAIO)
IFS.............. International Federation of Ski (SAUO)
IFS.............. International Federation of Surveyors [*See also FIG*] (EAIO)
IFS.............. International Fertilizer Supply Scheme (SAUO)
IFS.............. International Film Seminars (EA)
IFS.............. International Flower Service (SAUO)
IFS.............. International Fluidics Services (SAUS)
IFS.............. International Flying Services SRL [*Italy*] [*ICAO designator*] (FAAC)
IFS.............. International Focus Resources, Inc. [*Vancouver Stock Exchange symbol*]
IFS.............. International Foodservice Systems, Inc. (EFIS)
IFS.............. International Foundation for/of Science (SAUO)
IFS.............. International Foundation for Science [*See also FIS*] [*ICSU*] [*Stockholm, Sweden*] (EAIO)
IFS.............. International Foundation for Stutterers (EA)
IFS.............. International Frankenstein Society (EA)
IFS.............. International Freephone Service (SAUS)
IFS.............. International Freight Services (SAUO)
IFS.............. Internationella Forsurningssekretariatet [*International Secretariat on Acid Rain*] [*Sweden*] (EAIO)
IFS.............. Interrelated Flow Simulation
IFS.............. Interstitial Fluid Space [*Medicine*] (DMAA)
IFS.............. Investment Feasibility Studies (TEL)
IFS.............. Ionospheric Forward Scatter (TEL)
IFS.............. Irish Free State [*Later, Republic of Ireland*]
IFS.............. Iron Fortified Common Salt [*Nutrition*]
IFS.............. Iterated Function System [*Computer science*] (BYTE)
IFSA............ Inflight Food Service Association (SAUO)
IFSA............ Institute of Fundamental Studies Association (SAUO)
IFSA............ Instock Footwear Suppliers Association [*British*] (DBA)
IFSA............ International Federation of Scoliosis Associations (EA)
IFSA............ International Federation of Sound Archives (SAUO)
IFSA............ International Federation of Sports Acrobatics [*Sofia, Bulgaria*] (EAIO)
IFSA............ International Fuzzy Systems Association (EA)
IFSA............ International Inflight Food Service Association (NTPA)
IFSA............ Intumescent Fire Seals Association [*British*] (DBA)
IFSAL.......... Integral Frequency Scan Approach and Landing
IFS&M......... Inactive Facilities Surveillance and Maintenance (SAUS)
IFSAR.......... Interferometric Synthetic Aperture RADAR (RDA)
IFSARE........ Inter-Ferometric Synthetic Aperture Radar for Elevation (SAUS)
IFSAS.......... Interim Fire Support Automated System (SAUS)
IFSAS.......... Interim Fire Support Automation System [*Army*] (DOMA)
IFSAT.......... International Financial Services and Technology Exhibition [*British*]
IFSB............ Independence Federal Savings Bank [*NASDAQ symbol*] (NQ)
IFSB............ Independence Fed Svgs Bk [*NASDAQ symbol*] (TTSB)
IFSB............ International Flying Saucer Bureau [*Defunct*]
IFSBAC........ Institute for Folklore Studies in Britain and Canada
IFSC............ Information Field Separator Character (VLIE)
IFSC............ Interferon Sciences, Inc. [*NASDAQ symbol*] (NQ)
IFSC............ International Federation of Surgical Colleges [*Dublin, Republic of Ireland*] (EAIO)
IFSC............ International Federation of Surgical Congresses (SAUO)
IFSC............ International Forest Science Consultancy (SAUO)
IFSC............ International Fuel Service Centers (SAUS)
IFSC............ Introduction to the Federal Supply Catalog System
IFSCC.......... International Federation of Societies of Cosmetic Chemists [*Luton, England*] (EAIO)
IFSCS.......... International Federation of the Societies of Classical Studies (EA)
IFSD............ Inflight Shutdown (MCD)
IFSD............ In-Flight Shutdown Data (SAUS)
IFSD............ International Fund Sports Disabled (SAUO)
IFSDA.......... International Federation of Stamp Dealers' Associations (EA)
IFSDP.......... International Federation of the Socialist and Democratic Press [*Milan, Italy*] (EAIO)
IFSE............ Internal Fetal Scalp Electrode [*Medicine*] (MELL)
IFSEA.......... International Federation of Scientific Editors' Associations (EA)
IFSEA.......... International Food Service Executives Association (SAUO)
IFSEC.......... International Fire and Security Exhibition and Conference [*British*] (ITD)
IFSECN........ International Federation of Societies for Electroencephalography and Clinical Neurophysiology [*Amsterdam, Netherlands*] (EA)
IFSED.......... Initial Full-Scale Engineering Development
IFSED.......... Integrated Full Scale Engineering Development (ACAE)
IFSEEGCN.... International Federation of Societies for Electroencephalography and Clinical Neurophysiology [*Medicine*] (EDAA)
IFSEM.......... International Federation of Scienties for Electron Microscopy (SAUS)
IFSEM.......... International Federation of Societies for Electron Microscopy (EA)
IFSF............ Independent Fuel Storage Facility (SAUO)
IFSF............ Investment Feasibility Study Facility [*United Nations Development Programme*] [*Ghana*]
IFSF............ Irradiated Fuels Storage Facility [*National Reactor Testing Station*]
IFSH............ International Federation of Sound Hunters (EA)
IFSHC.......... International Federation of Societies for Histochemistry and Cytochemistry (EAIO)
IFSHJ.......... International Federation for Secular Humanistic Judaism (EA)
IFSHJ.......... International Federation of Secular Humanistic Jews (EA)
IFSHT.......... International Federation of Societies of Hand Therapists (SAUO)
IFSI............ Interface Flooring Systems, Incorporated (SAUO)
IFSI............ Interface, Inc. [*NASDAQ symbol*] (NQ)
IFSI............ Interiace, Inc. (SAUO)
IFSIA.......... Interface Inc.'A' [*NASDAQ symbol*] (TTSB)
IF-SICMA..... Insular Force - Special Initial Clothing Monetary Allowance [*Military*] (DNAB)
IFSIS........... Iterated Function System-Image Synthesizer [*Computer science*] (BYTE)
IFSIT........... In-Flight Safety Inhibit Test
IFSL............ Indiana Federal Corp. [*NASDAQ symbol*] (NQ)
IFSL............ Indiana Federal Savings and Loan Association (SAUO)
IFSL............ Industrial Fire Safety Library [*National Fire Protection Association*]
IF-SICMA..... Insular Force-Special Initial Clothing Monetary Allowance (SAUS)
IFSM............ Information Systems Management (VLIE)
IFSM............ Integrated Fuel System Module
IFSM............ Inter-Fuel Substitution Model (SAUS)
IFSM............ International Federation of Sports Medicine (EA)
IFSMA.......... International Federation of Shipmasters Associations [*See also FIAPN*] (EAIO)
IFSMC.......... International Federation of Small and Medium-Sized Commercial Enterprises (SAUO)
IFSMGR........ Installable File System Manager [*Computer science*] (MWOL)
IFSMI........... International Federation of Smail and Medium-Sized Industrial Enterprises (SAUO)
IFSMTF........ International Fusion Superconducting Magnet Test Facility [*Oak Ridge National Laboratory*]
IFSMU.......... Irish Free State Medical Union (SAUO)
IFSN............ Iterative Full-Switch Network (SAUS)
IFSNC.......... International Federation of Settlements and Neighbourhood Centres [*Defunct*]
IFSNC/CD..... International Review of Community Development. International Federation of Settlements and Neighbourhood Centres (SAUO)
IFSNC/CD..... International Review of Community Development. International Federation of Settlements and Neighbourhood Centres (journ.) (SAUS)
IFSO............ In-Flight Safety Officer (SAUO)
IFSO............ International Federation of Sanitarians Organizations [*Defunct*] (EA)
IFSOT.......... Irradiated Fused Silica Open Tubular [*Column for chromatography*]
IFSP............ Individualized Family Service Plan [*Required under the Individuals with Disabilities Education Act (IDEA)*] (PAZ)
IFSP............ International Federation of Societies of Philosophy
IF Spec........ Interface Specification (SAUS)
IFSPLM........ Internet Freeware Shareware Programming Languages for the Macintosh (SAUS)
IFSPO.......... International Federation of Senior Police Officers (EA)
IFSPS.......... International Federation of Students in Political Sciences
IFSR............ International Federation for Systems Research (EAIO)
IFSR............ International Flight Service Receiver (SAUS)
IFSR............ International Flight Service Receiver Site (SAUO)
IFSRC.......... Independent Family Schools Resource Center (EA)
IFSRC.......... International Financial Services Research Center [*Massachusetts Institute of Technology*] [*Research center*] (RCD)
IFSS............ If Signal Source (MCD)
IFSS............ Index of Federal Specifications and Standards
IFSS............ Inertia Fuel Shutoff Switch [*Automotive engineering*]
IFSS............ Infinite Solution Set (SAUS)
IFSS............ Instrumentation Flight Safety System (SAUS)
IFSS............ Instrument Flight Safety System (MUGU)
IFSS............ Instrument Flight Service Station (LDOE)

IFSS............ International Federation of Sleddog Sports (EA)
IFSS............ International Fertilizer Supply Scheme [*FAO*] [*United Nations*]
IFSS............ International Flight Service Station [*FAA*]
IFSSEC......... International Fire (SAUS)
IFSSEC......... International Fire, Security and Safety Exhibition and Conference (PDAA)
IFSSH.......... International Federation of Societies for Surgery of the Hand (EA)
IFS Ship...... Inshore Fire Support Ship (SAUS)
IFSSO.......... International Federation of Social Science Organizations [*See also FIOSS*] [*Copenhagen, Denmark*] (EAIO)
IFSSPC........ International Fatigue Syndromes Share and Prayer Chain (EA)
IFST............ Institute of Food Science and Technology (ADWA)
IFST............ Institute of Food Science and Technology of the United Kingdom
IFST............ International Federation of Seed Trade (SAUO)
IFST............ International Federation of Shorthand and Typewriting
IFST............ International Flight Service Transmitter (SAUS)
IFST............ International Flight Service Transmitter Site (SAUO)
IFSTA.......... International Fire Service Training Association (EA)
IFSTAD........ Islamic Foundation for Science, Technology, and Development (BARN)
IFSTD.......... Interim Fund for Science and Technology for Development [*International Council of Scientific Unions*]
IFSTD.......... Islamic Foundation for Science, Technology and Development [*Saudi Arabia*] (PDAA)
IFSTM.......... International Federation of Sewing Thread Manufacturers (EA)
IFSTS.......... International Flight Service Transmitter Site (SAUS)
IFSW........... International Federation of Social Workers [*Switzerland*]
IFSWA.......... International Figure Skating Writers Association [*Defunct*]
IFT.............. Immediate Forecasting Technique (SAUS)
IFT.............. Immunofluorescence Test [*Immunology*]
IFT.............. Income Opportunities Fund 2000 [*NYSE symbol*] (SPSG)
IFT.............. Indexed, Folioed, and Titled [*Publishing*] (DGA)
IFT.............. Indiana Federation of Teachers (SAUO)
IFT.............. Indirect Fire Trainer (SAUS)
IFT.............. Industrial Field Trip (DOMA)
IFT.............. In-Flight Test [*Air Force*]
IFT.............. Inflight Text (SAUS)
IFT.............. In Flight Training (ACAE)
IFT.............. Inland Fisheries Trust, Inc. [*Republic of Ireland*] (BI)
IFT.............. Innovative Feasibility Test
IFT.............. Input Frequency Tolerance [*Computer science*]
IFT.............. Instantaneous Field Tube [*Astrophysics*]
IFT.............. Instantaneous Fourier Transform [*Computer science*]
IFT.............. Institute for Food Technologists (SAUS)
IfT.............. Institute for Tropospheric Research (SAUS)
IFT.............. Institute of Family Therapy [*British*] (DBA)
IFT.............. Institute of Food Technologists (EA)
IFT.............. Institute of Food Technology (SAUS)
IFT.............. Instructor-Flown Advisory Target
IFT.............. Instructor Flown Target (SAUS)
IFT.............. Instrument Flight Trainer (MCD)
IFT.............. Interface Tool (MCD)
IFT.............. Interfacial Tension [*Physical chemistry*]
IFT.............. Interfacial Test
IFT.............. Interflight [*British*] [*ICAO designator*] (FAAC)
IFT.............. Intermediate Frequency Transformation (or Transformer) (SAUS)
IFT.............. Intermediate Frequency Transformer
IFT.............. Internal Function Test (SAUS)
IFT.............. International Federation of Translators [*See also FIT*] [*Ghent, Belgium*] (EAIO)
IFT.............. International Flight Test (SAUS)
IFT.............. International Foundation for Telemetering (EA)
IFT.............. International Foundation for Timesharing (EA)
IFT.............. International Frequency Tables
IFT.............. Io Flux Tube [*Cosmology*]
IFT.............. Ion Focusing Technique
IFT.............. Isolation Functional Testing (PDAA)
IFTA............ In-Flight Thrust Augmentation
IFTA............ In-Flight Training Aid
IFTA............ Insect Farming and Trading Agency (SAUO)
IFTA............ International Fair for Film, Television and Audiovision (SAUS)
IFTA............ International Federation of Teachers' Associations [*Later, WCOTP*] (EAIO)
IFTA............ International Federation of Television Archives [*See also FIAT*] [*Madrid, Spain*] (EAIO)
IFTA............ International Federation of Thanatologists Associations [*Saint-Ouen, France*] (EA)
IFTA............ International Federation of Thanatopractic Associations (SAUO)
IFTA............ International Fine Technics Association (SAUO)
IFTA............ International Free Trade Area
IFTA............ International Fuel Tax Agreement [*FHWA*] (TAG)
IFTAA.......... International Forum of Travel and Tourism Advocates (TRID)
IFTAC.......... Inter-American Federation of Touring and Automobile Clubs [*See also FITAC*] (EAIO)
IF TACCA..... Intermediate Frequency Time Averaged Clutter Coherent Airborne [*RADAR*] (DNAB)
IF TACCAR... Intermediate Frequency Time Averaged Clutter Coherent Airborne RADAR (NG)
IFTAD.......... Initial and Final Terminal Arrival Date [*Army*] (AABC)
IFTBCS........ International Federation of the Temperance Blue Cross Societies [*Later, IBC*] (EA)
IFTC............ International Council for Film Television and Audiovisual Communication (SAUO)
IFTC............ International Federation of Thermalism and Climatism [*Bad Ragaz, Switzerland*] (EA)
IFTC............ International Film and Television Council [*Rome, Italy*]
IFTC............ International Fox-Tango Club [*Defunct*] (EA)
IFTCD.......... In-Flight Thrust-Calculation Deck (SAUS)
IFTDO.......... International Federation of Training and Development Organizations (EA)
IFTE............ Integrated Family of Test Equipment [*Army*] (RDA)
IFTE............ Intermediate Field Test Equipment (ACAE)
IFTE............ Intermediate Forward Test Equipment
IFTEX.......... International Flower Trades Exhibition [*British*] (ITD)
IFTF............ Institute for the Future [*Research center*] [*Telecommunications*] (RCD)
IFTF............ Inter-Faith Task Force (EA)
IFTF............ International Federation of Teachers of French [*See also FIPF*] [*Sevres, France*] (EAIO)
IFTF............ International Fur Trade Federation [*British*] (EAIO)
IFTI............. Ionic Fuel Technology [*NASDAQ symbol*] (TTSB)
IFTI............. Ionic Fuel Technology, Inc. [*NASDAQ symbol*] (SAG)
IFTIW.......... Ionic Fuel Technology Wrrt'A' [*NASDAQ symbol*] (TTSB)
IFTIZ........... Ionic Fuel Technology Wrrt'B' [*NASDAQ symbol*] (TTSB)
IFTL............ Institute for Friendship through Learning (EA)
IFTM............ In-Flight Test and Maintenance (KSC)
IFTM............ Inverse Fourier Transform Module [*An enzyme*] (MCD)
IFTO............ International Federation of Tour Operators [*Lewes, East Sussex, England*] (EAIO)
IFTOA.......... Independent Fuel Terminal Operators' Association
IFToM.......... International Federation of Theory of Machines and Mechanics (SAUO)
IFToMM....... International Federation for the Theory of Machines and Mechanisms [*Warsaw, Poland*] (EAIO)
IFTPA.......... International Forest Product Transport Association (SAUO)
IFTPNDC...... Institute on the Federal Theatre Project and New Deal Culture [*George Mason University*] [*Research center*] (RCD)
IFTPP.......... International Federation of the Technical and Periodical Press (DIT)
IFTR............ In-Flight Thrust Reverser (SAUS)
IFTR............ International Federation for Theatre Research [*British*] (EAIO)
IFTR............ International Federation of Teachers of Rhythmics (EA)
IFTR............ International Foundation for Theatrical Research (EA)
IFTRS.......... Individual Flying Time Report System [*Military*] (DNAB)
IFTS............ Imaging Fourier Transform Spectrometer (SAUS)
IFTS............ Individual Functional Test Summary (SAUS)
IFTS............ In-Flight Test System
IFTS............ International Federation of Teratology Societies (EA)
IFTS............ Irradiated Fuel Transfer System [*Nuclear energy*] (NRCH)
IFTSSS........ In-Flight Test System Scan Select (IAA)
IFTTA.......... International Forum of Travel and Tourism Advocates (TVEL)
IFTU............ In Flight Targeting Updates (ACAE)
IFTU............ Intensive Flying Trials Unit (SAUO)
IFTU............ International Federation of Teachers' Unions
IFTU............ International Federation of Trade Unions
IFTU............ Iraq Federation of Trade Unions
IFTUTW....... International Federation of Trade Unions of Transport Workers [*See also FIOST*] [*Brussels, Belgium*] (EAIO)
IFTW............ International Federation of Tobacco Workers
IFTWA.......... International Federation of Textile Workers' Associations
IFTwA.......... International Federation of Tiddlywinks Associations (EA)
IFU.............. Fraunhofer Institute for Atmospheric Environmental Research (SAUO)
IFU.............. Inflatable Ward Unit (SAA)
IFU.............. Infusion-Forming Units [*Medicine*]
IFU.............. Instruction Fetch Unit [*Computer science*]
IFU.............. Integrated Fluorescence Unit [*Image formation*]
IFU.............. Intelligence Field Unit [*Navy*]
I/FU............ Interface Unit [*Computer science*] (NASA)
IFU.............. Interferon Unit [*Medicine*] (DMAA)
IFUEPCS...... International Federation of Unions of Employees in Public and Civil Services (SAUO)
IFUN............ If Unable [*Aviation*] (FAAC)
IFUNO.......... Indian Federation of United Nations Association (SAUO)
IF/USA......... Interfurnishings USA (TSPED)
IFUT............ Irish Federation of University Teachers (SAUO)
IFUW........... International Federation of University Women (EA)
IFV.............. Igniter-Fuel Valve (KSC)
IFV.............. Infantry Fighting Vehicle
IFV.............. Instantaneous Field of View (DNAB)
IFV.............. Interface Verification (ACAE)
IFV.............. Internationaler Faustball-Verband (EAIO)
IFV.............. Interstitial [*Medicine*] (EDAA)
IFV.............. Intracellular Fluid Volume [*Physiology*]
IFVA............ Independent Film and Video Makers' Association [*British*]
IFVA............ International Federation of Variety Artists (SAUO)
IFVC............ Instantaneous Force-Velocity Curve (SAUS)
IFVC............ International Federation for Victory over Communism
IF-VCA......... Immunofluorescence-Viral Capsid Antigen [*Clinical chemistry*]
IFVCGE........ Infantry Fighting Vehicle Command Guidance Equipment (ACAE)
IFVH............ Indian Field Veterinary Hospital [*British military*] (DMA)
IFVHSF........ Federation of Health Funds - International [*International Federation of Voluntary Health Service Funds*] [*Later, FHF*] [*Acronym is based on former name,*] (EAIO)
IFVHSF........ International Federation of Voluntary Health Service Funds (SAUO)
IFVLS.......... If Flight Visibility Becomes Less Than [*Aviation*] (FAAC)
IFVM............ Intermediate Frequency Video Microwave (MCD)
IFVME.......... Inspectorate of Fighting Vehicles and Mechanical Equipment [*Military*]
IFVPA.......... Independent Film, Video, and Photographers Association [*British*] (DBA)
IFVR............ If Visibility Remains [*Aviation*] (FAAC)

IFVTCC......... Internationale Foderation der Vereine der Textilchemiker und Coloristen [*International Federation of Associations of Textile Chemists and Colorists*] (EAIO)
IFVTCC......... International Federation of Associations of Textile Chemists and Colourists (SAUO)
IFVwCM....... Infantry Fighting Vehicle with Integrated Countermeasures (SAUS)
IFW............. Inland Fisheries and Wildlife
IFW............. International Federation of Wargaming [*Defunct*] (EA)
IFW............. Interrupt Flag Word (SAUS)
IFWA............ International Federation for Works of Art (SAUO)
IFWC............ Integrated Flight/Weapons Controls (MCD)
IFWEA.......... International Federation of Workers' Educational Associations [*See also IVB*] [*Tel Aviv, Israel*] (EAIO)
IFWES.......... Indirect Fire Weapon Effect Simulation (SAUS)
IfWfW........... ISDN for Windows for Workgroups (SAUO)
IFWG............ Interface Working Group [*NASA*] (SSD)
IFWHA.......... International Federation of Women's Hockey Associations
IFWJ............ Indian Federation of Working Journalists
IFWJ............ International Federation of Working Journalists (SAUO)
IFWL............ International Federation of Women Lawyers (EA)
IFWRI........... Institute of the Furniture Warehousing and Removing Industry (EAIO)
IFWS............ International Federation of Wines and Spirits [*See also FIVS*] (EAIO)
IFWSTI......... International Federation of Wines and Spirits, Trade, and Industry (EA)
IFWTO.......... International Federation of Women's Travel Organizations (EA)
IFWTWA....... International Food, Wine, and Travel Writers Association (EAIO)
IFWVO.......... International Federation of War Veterans Organizations (SAUO)
IFX.............. Immunofixation [*Clinical chemistry*]
IFX.............. Infineon Technologies ADS [*NYSE symbol*] (SG)
IFX.............. Interactive Financial Exchange (GART)
IFY.............. Independent Fission Yield
IFYC............ International Federation of Young Cooperators
IFYE............ International Farm Youth Exchange
IFYGL.......... International Field Year for the Great Lakes
IFYHA.......... International Federation of Youth Hostels Association (SAUO)
IFZ.............. Industrial Free Zone (SAUS)
IG................ Alisarda [*ICAO designator*] (AD)
IG................ ALISARDA SpA [*Italy*] [*ICAO designator*] (ICDA)
IG................ Galesburg Public Library, Galesburg, IL [*Library symbol*] [*Library of Congress*] (LCLS)
IG................ IGI, Inc. [*AMEX symbol*] (SPSG)
IG................ Igloo [*Spacelab Pallet Missions*]
ig................ igneous (SAUS)
IG................ Ignitor [*Electron device*] (MSA)
IG................ Illawarra Greens [*Political party*] [*Australia*]
IG................ Illustrators Guild [*Later, GA*] (EA)
IG................ Image Generator (MCD)
IG................ Immature Granule (DMAA)
IG................ Immune Globulin
Ig................ Immunoglobulin [*Immunology*]
IG................ Immunology [*Medical specialty*] (DHSM)
iG................ Immunoreactive Gastrin [*Medicine*] (MEDA)
IG................ Imperial Gallon
IG................ Impulse Generator (IAA)
IG................ Index of Gravity [*Engineering*]
IG................ Indicating (SAUS)
IG................ Indicator Group (MCD)
I/G.............. Individual/Group (ACRL)
IG................ Indo-Germanic [*Language, etc.*]
IG................ Induction Generator (SAUS)
IG................ Inductor Generator (SAUS)
IG................ Industrial Grade
IG................ Industrial Group (SAUO)
IG................ Industriegewerkschaft [*Industrial Trade Union*] [*Germany*]
IG................ Industry Group (HEAS)
IG................ Inertial Guidance
IG................ Inertial Gyroscope
IG................ Infantile Glaucoma (MELL)
IG................ Inflammatory Glaucoma (MELL)
IG................ Information Group (SAUO)
IG................ Ingot (DNAB)
IG................ In-Ground (ADA)
i/g.............. in ground (SAUS)
IG................ Inner Gimbal
IG................ Inner Guard [*Freemasonry*]
IG................ Input Gate (SAUS)
IG................ Input Generator (ACAE)
IG................ Inscriptiones Graecae [*Epigraphic notation*]
IG................ Inside Guardian [*Freemasonry*] (ROG)
IG................ Inspection Gauge (MCD)
IG................ Inspector General [*Air Force, Army, Marine Corps*]
IG................ Instantaneous Grid (IAA)
IG................ Institute of Geography (SAUO)
IG................ Institute of Geophysics [*Later, IGPP*] [*University of California*] (MCD)
IG................ Institute of Groundsmanship (EA)
IG................ Institution of Geologists (EAIO)
IG................ Instruction [*or Instructor*] Guide
IG................ Instructor in Gunnery [*Military*] [*British*]
IG................ Instructor of Gunnery (SAUO)
IG................ Instructors Guide (SAUS)
IG................ Instrumentation Group
IG................ Instrument Ground (NASA)
IG................ Insulated Gate (DEN)
IG................ Insulin and Glucose [*Medicine*] (DMAA)
IG................ Integrated Genetics
IG................ Intelligence Generator
IG................ IntelliGenetics (HGEN)
IG................ Intendant-General
IG................ Interagency Group [*Federal government*]
IG................ Interblock Gap (SAUS)
IG................ Interconnect Group (CAAL)
IG................ Interdepartmental Group [*DoD*]
IG................ Interest Group
IG................ Interframe Gap [*Communications term*] (DCT)
IG................ Inter-Gas System
IG................ Inter-Governmental (SAUO)
IG................ Intergranular [*Metallurgy*]
IG................ Internal Guidance (NASA)
IG................ Internationale Kunstgilde [*International Art Guild - IAG*] (EAIO)
IG................ International Gateway (SAUS)
IG................ International General (EA)
IG................ International Graphics [*Formerly, IGI*] (EA)
IG................ International Guides' Club (EAIO)
IG................ Intestinal Gas (MELL)
IG................ Intestinal Groove
IG................ Intragastric
ig................ Intragastrically [*Medicine*] (DB)
IG................ Inverse Gain (NVT)
IG................ Inverse Gate (SAUS)
IG................ Inverse Gaussian [*Statistics*]
IG................ Investigative Operations (SAUS)
IG................ Investment Grant [*British*]
IG................ Involute Gear (SAUS)
IG................ Ion Gun (SAUS)
IG................ Ionization Gauge (SAUS)
IG................ Iris Guide (PDAA)
IG................ Irish Guards [*Military unit*]
IG................ Iron Guard (SAUO)
IG................ Irritable Gut [*Medicine*] (DMAA)
IG................ Irvine Group [*An association*] (EA)
IG................ Islamic Group [*Government term*] (GA)
IG................ Isotope Geology (SAUS)
IG................ Izmenyaemaya Geometriya [*Variable Geometry*] [*Suffix letters on Soviet combat aircraft*]
IGA.............. Dallas Public Library, Dallas, TX [*OCLC symbol*] (OCLC)
IGA.............. Great Inagua Island [*Bahamas*] [*Airport symbol*] (AD)
IgA.............. Human Immunoglobulin A (DOG)
IGA.............. Illinois General Assembly (SAUO)
IgA.............. Immunoglobulin A [*Immunology*]
IGA.............. Inagua [*Bahamas*] [*Airport symbol*] (OAG)
IGA.............. Increased Groove Area (SAUS)
IGA.............. Independent Grocers Alliance Distributing Co. [*Facetious translation: "I Get Attention"*] (EA)
IGA.............. Industry and General Applications (MCD)
IGA.............. Infantile Genetic Agranulocytosis [*Medicine*] (DMAA)
IGA.............. Inhaled Gas Analyzer
IGA.............. Inherited Genetic Abnormalities [*Medicine*] (EDAA)
IGA.............. Inner Gimbal Angle (NASA)
IGA.............. Inner Gimbal Assembly
IGA.............. Inner Gimbal Axis
IGA.............. Inscriptiones Graecae Antiquissimae (BJA)
IGA.............. Institute of Group Analysis (COBU)
IGA.............. Insulation Glazing Association (SAUO)
IGA.............. Integrated Grant Administration
IGA.............. Integrated Graphics Adaptor (SAUS)
IGA.............. Integrated Graphics Array (ADWA)
IGA.............. Integrating Gyro Accelerometer
IGA.............. Intergovernmental Agreement (COE)
IGA.............. Intergranular Attack [*Nuclear energy*] (NRCH)
IGA.............. Internacia Geografa Asocio (SAUO)
IGA.............. International Galdos Association (EA)
IGA.............. International Gamers Association (EA)
IGA.............. International Gay Association - International Association of Lesbians/Gay Women and Gay Men (EAIO)
IGA.............. International General Aviation
IGA.............. International Geneva Association (EA)
IGA.............. International Geographical Association [*Esperantist*]
IGA.............. International Glaucoma Association (EAIO)
IGA.............. International Goat Association (SAUO)
IGA.............. International Gold Association (SAUO)
IGA.............. International Golf Association (EA)
IGA.............. International Graduate Achievement [*Defunct*] (EA)
IGA.............. International Grains Arrangement
IGA.............. International Green Alliance (EA)
IGA.............. International Grenfell Association (SAUO)
IGA.............. International Journal of Government Auditing (journ.) (SAUS)
IGA.............. Interstate Gambling Activities
IGA.............. Ion Gun Assembly
IGA.............. Irish Gas Association (BI)
IGA.............. Irish Gas Board (SAUO)
IGAA............ Intermountain Graphic Arts Association (DGA)
IGAAS.......... Integrated Ground/Airborne Avionics System (MCD)
IGAB............ Interagency Group on Agricultural Biometeorology (SAUO)
IGAB............ International Group of Agents and Bureaus (EA)
IGAC............ Illinois Guardian Advocacy Commission (SAUO)
IGAC............ International Geosphere-Biosphere Programme (SAUO)
IGAC............ International Global Atmospheric Chemistry [*Project*] (USDC)
IGAC............ International Global Atmospheric Chemistry Program [*Marine science*] (OSRA)
IGAC............ Israeli General Avionics Computer (SAUS)

IGACLS .... Integrated Guidance and Control System (SAUO)
IGACP .... International Global Atmospheric Chemistry Program (SAUS)
IGACS .... Integrated Guidance and Control System [*Aerospace*]
IGACSM .... Intergovernmental Advisory Committee on Surveying and Mapping (SAUO)
IGAC-SSC .... IGAC Scientific Steering Committee (SAUO)
IGAD .... International Authority on Drought and Development (SAUO)
IGaDC .... Illinois State Department of Conservation, Division of Parks and Memorials, Galena, IL [*Library symbol*] [*Library of Congress*] (LCLS)
IGADD .... Intergovernmental Authority on Drought and Development [*Djibouti*] (EY)
IGADD .... Inter-Government Authority on Drought and Development (SAUS)
IGAE .... Intergovernmental Agreement on the Environment [*Australia*]
IGAEA .... International Graphic Arts Education Association (EA)
IGAeM .... Internationale Gesellschaft fuer Aerosole in der Medizin [*International Society for Aerosols in Medicine - ISAeM*] (EAIO)
IGAF .... Intergovernmental Affairs Fellowship Program [*Military*] (MCD)
IGAF .... International Group of Accounting Firms (SAUO)
IgAIC .... Immunoglobulin A Immune Complex [*Immunochemistry*]
IGA-ICIC-REL... International Gay Association-International Coordination and Information Centre on Religion (SAUO)
IGal .... Galva Township Library, Galva, IL [*Library symbol*] [*Library of Congress*] (LCLS)
IGALL .... Imperial Gallon (SAUS)
IGAM .... Internationale Gesellschaft fuer Allgemeinmedizin [*International Society of General Medicine*]
IGAM .... International Game Technology (MHDW)
IgAN .... Immunoglobulin A Nephropathy [*Nephrology*]
IG & GA .... International Grooving and Grinding Association (EA)
IGAP .... Illinois Goal Assessment Program
IGAP .... Institute for Grassland and Animal Production [*Research center*] [*British*] (IRC)
IGAP .... Internationale Gesellschaft fuer Arztliche Psychotherapie [*International Federation for Medical Psychotherapy - IFMP*] [*Oslo, Norway*] (EAIO)
IGAP .... International Get Acquainted Program (SAUO)
IGAP .... International Global Aerosol Program (EOSA)
IGAP .... International Global Atmosphere Programme (SAUO)
IGARSS .... International Geoscience and Remote Sensing Society (SAUO)
IGARSS .... International Geoscience and Remote Sensing Symposium (MCD)
IGAS .... Inspection Generale des Affaires Sociales [*General Inspection of Social Affairs*] [*France*]
IGAS .... Integrated Ground/Air System (SAUO)
IGAS .... Interactive General Accounting System (MHDB)
IGAS .... International General Assembly of Spiritualists [*Later, LDTF*] (EA)
IGAS .... International General Aviation Society (SAUO)
IGAS .... International Graphic Arts Society (EA)
IGAS .... International Graphoanalysis Society (EA)
IGasE .... Institution of Gas Engineers (COBU)
IGAT .... Iranian Gas Truck Pipeline (SAUS)
IGAU .... Indira Gandhi Agricultural University (SAUO)
IGAUP .... Interceptor Generation and Umpiring Program (SAA)
IGAX .... Inner Gimbal Axis (NASA)
IGB .... Columbus, MS [*Location identifier*] [*FAA*] (FAAL)
IGB .... Illicit Gold Buyer [*or Buying*]
IGB .... Inlet Gear Box (MCD)
IGB .... Intercontinental Glide Bomber [*Unmanned*]
IGB .... Interference Guard Bands
IGB .... Inter-German Border (MCD)
IGB .... Intermediate Gearbox (DA)
IGB .... Internationaler Genossenschaftsbund [*International Cooperative Alliance*]
IGB .... Internationales Gewerkschafts Buro [*International Trades Union Office*]
IGB .... International Geophysical Bulletin (SAUS)
IGB .... International Geophysics Bulletin (SAUO)
IGB .... International Geophysics Bulletin (journ.) (SAUS)
IGB .... International Gravimetric Bureau [*Toulouse, France*] (EAIO)
IGB .... Ischiogluteal Bursa [*Medicine*] (MELL)
IGB .... Ischiogluteal Bursitis [*Medicine*] (MELL)
IGB .... Israelitisches Gemeindeblatt [*Muelheim/Koeln*] [*A publication*] (BJA)
IGB .... National College of Education, Evanston, IL [*OCLC symbol*] (OCLC)
IGBC .... Interagency Grizzly Bear Committee [*Forest Service*] [*Missoula, MT*] (EGAO)
IGBD .... Impotent Grain Boundary Dislocation
IGBE .... International Gold Bullion Exchange [*Bankrupt investment firm*]
IGBM .... International Group on Breastfeeding Monitoring (WDAA)
IGBP .... Immunoglobulin-Binding Protein
IGBP .... International Geosphere-Biosphere Program [*ICSU*] [*Proposed for 1992*]
IGBP .... International Geosphere-Biosphere Programme [*Australia*]
IGBP .... International Global Change Program (SAUS)
IGBP-DIS ...... Data and Information System [*Marine science*] (OSRA)
IGBP-DIS ...... IGBP Data and Information System (SAUS)
IGBP-DIS ...... International Geosphere-Biosphere Programme Data and Information System (SAUS)
IGBP-SAC .... International Geosphere-Biosphere (or Global Change) Programme Scientific Advisory Committee (SAUS)
IGBP-SAC .... International Geosphere-Biosphere Programme Scientific Advisory Committee (SAUO)
IGBP/START... International Geosphere-Biosphere Programme/Global Change System for Analysis, Research and Training (SAUO)
IGBP-START... International Geosphere-Biosphere Programme System for Analysis, Research and Training (SAUO)
IGBS .... International Gas Bearings Symposium (PDAA)
IGBST .... Interagency Grizzly Bear Study Team [*Montana State University*] [*Bozeman, MT*] (EGAO)
IGBT .... Insulated Gate Bipolar Transistor [*Electronics*] (AAEL)
IGBT .... Insulator Gate Bipolar Transistor (SAUS)
IGBT .... Isolated Gate Bipolar Transistor [*Electronics*]
IGC .... Goshen College, Goshen, IN [*OCLC symbol*] (OCLC)
IGC .... Illinois Groundwater Consortium (SAUS)
IGC .... Indiana Gaming Commission (SAUS)
IGC .... Indiana Gas Corporation (SAUO)
IGC .... Informative Graphics Corporation (SAUO)
IGC .... Inspectorate General of Customs (SAUS)
IGC .... Inspector General of Communications (SAUO)
IGC .... Inspector-General of Communications [*British military*] (DMA)
IGC .... Institute for Galactic Communications (SAUO)
IGC .... Institute for Global Communications [*Internet*]
IGC .... Institute for Graphic Communication [*Defunct*] (EA)
IGC .... Institute for/of Graphical Communications (SAUO)
IGC .... Institute of Graphic Communication (SAUS)
IGC .... Institutional Grants Committee (SAUO)
IGC .... Integrated Geophysics Corporation (SAUO)
IGC .... Integrated Graphics Controller (SAUS)
IGC .... Intellectually Gifted Children
IGC .... Intelligence Graphics Controller [*Computer science*]
IGC .... Intelligent Graphics Controller (SAUS)
IGC .... Interactive Gaming & Communications Corp.
IGC .... Interactive Graphics Controller (SAUS)
IGC .... Intergovernmental Committee (SAUO)
IGC .... Inter-Governmental Committee of the Universal Copyright Convention (SAUO)
IGC .... Intergovernmental Committee on Refugees [*Post-World War II*] (DLA)
IGC .... Inter-Governmental Conference [*European Union*] (ECON)
IGC .... Inter-Governmental Conferences [*European Community*]
IGC .... Intergovernmental Copyright Committee [*See also CIDA*] [*Paris, France*] (EAIO)
IGC .... Intergranular Corrosion (PDAA)
IGC .... Interim Gunnery Computer (SAUS)
IGC .... Intermagnetics General Corp.
IGC .... Internal Gain Control (IAA)
IGC .... International Garden Centres (SAUO)
IGC .... International Garden Club (EA)
IGC .... International Geochemical Congress (SAUS)
IGC .... International Geological Congress
IGC .... International Geophysical Committee [*Also, CIG*]
IGC .... International Geophysical Cooperation [*World Meteorological Organization*]
IGC .... International Geotechnical Classification (SAUS)
IGC .... International Gift Corporation (SAUO)
IGC .... International Glaucoma Congress (EA)
IGC .... International Gold Corporation (SAUO)
IGC .... International Government Conference (SAUS)
IGC .... International Grassland Congress
IGC .... International Guides' Club (EAIO)
IGC .... Interstate General Ltd. [*AMEX symbol*] (SPSG)
IGC .... Interstate Genl L.P. [*AMEX symbol*] (TTSB)
IGC .... Inter-Union Geodynamics Commission [*Also, ICG*] (MSC)
IGC .... Intragastric Cannula (STED)
IGC .... Inverse Gas Chromatography
IGC .... Ion Gun Collector
IGC .... Irish Goods Council (ACII)
IGC .... Isothermal Gas Chromatography
IGCA .... Industrial Gas Cleaning Association (SAUO)
IGCA .... Innovative Gaming Corp. [*NASDAQ symbol*] (SAG)
IGCA .... Innovative Gaming Corp. Amer [*NASDAQ symbol*] (TTSB)
IGCA .... International Garden Centre Association (SAUO)
IGCA .... International Guild of Candle Artisans (EA)
IGCA .... Israel Government Corporation Authority (SAUO)
IGCA .... Italian Greyhound Club of America (EA)
IGCAR .... Indira Gandhi Center for Atomic Research (SAUS)
IGCBT .... Interagency Group for Computer-Based Training [*Later, IGITT*] (EA)
IGCC .... Institute on Global Conflict and Cooperation [*University of California, Berkeley*]
IGCC .... Insulating Glass Certification Council (EA)
IGCC .... Integrated Coal Gasification Combined Cycle (SAUS)
IGCC .... Integrated Gasification-Combined Cycle [*Chemical engineering*]
IGCC .... Interagency Geothermal Coordinating Council
IGCC .... Intergovernmental Coordinating Committee for Population and Family Planning in Southeast Asia (SAUO)
IGCC .... Intergovernmental Copyright Committee [*See also CIDA*]
IGCC .... Intergovernmental Panel on Climate Change [*World Meteorological Organization*]
IGCCBD .... Inter-Governmental Committee on the Convention on Biological Diversity (SAUO)
IGCE .... Independent Government Cost Estimate [*Army*]
IGCE .... Institute of Global Climate and Ecology (SAUO)
IGCG .... Inertial Guidance and Calibration Group [*Air Force*]
IGCI .... Industrial Gas Cleaning Institute (EA)
IGCJAP .... International Guild of Craft Journalists, Authors, and Photographers [*Inactive*] (EA)
IGCM .... Imperial Guild of Church Musicians (SAUO)
IGCM .... Incorporated Guild of Church Musicians (SAUO)
IGCMI .... International Global Centre on Marine Information (SAUS)
IGCN .... Irish Guild of Catholic Nurses [*Medicine*] (EDAA)
IGCO .... International Genealogy Consumer Organization (EA)

IGCP............ Intelligence Guidance for COMINT [*Communications Intelligence*] Programming (MCD)
IGCP............ International Geological Correlation Programme [*See also PICG*] [*ICSU*] [*Paris, France*] (EAIO)
IGCP............ International Global Change Program (SAUO)
IGCPES........ Intergovernmental Committee for Physical Education and Sport (SAUO)
IGCPK.......... Industrie Gewerkschaft Chemie, Papier, und Keramik [*West German union*]
IGCP Projcet 174... International Geological Correlation Programme Geological Events at the Eocene-Oligocene Boundary (SAUS)
IGCP Project 24... International Geological Correlation Programme Quaternary Glaciations in the Northern Hemisphere (SAUS)
IGCP Project 27... International Geological Correlation Programme Caledonide Orogen (SAUS)
IGCP Project 58... International Geological Correlation Programme Events of the Mid-Cretaceous (SAUS)
IGCP Project 60... International Geological Correlation Programme Correlation of Caledonian Stratabound Sulphides (SAUS)
IGCP Project 61... International Geological Correlation Programme Sea-levels of the Last 15,000 years (SAUS)
IGCP Project 92... International Geological Correlation Programme Origin and Evolution of the Archaean Continental Crust (SAUS)
IGCP Project 114... International Geological Correlation Programme Pacific Neogene (SAUS)
IGCP Project 158... International Geological Correlation Programme Palaeohydrology of the Temperate Zone During the Last 15,000 Years (SAUS)
IGCP Project 158A... International Geological Correlation Programme Fluvial Environments (SAUS)
IGCP Project 158B... International Geological Correlation Programme Mire Environments (SAUS)
IGCP Project 169... International Geological Correlation Programme Geotectonic Evolution and Metallogeny in the Eastern Mediterranean and Western Asia (SAUS)
IGCP Project 171... International Geological Correlation Programme Circum-Pacific Jurassic (SAUS)
IGCP Project 200... International Geological Correlation Programme Late Quaternary Sea-Level Changes: Measurements, Correlations and Future Applications (SAUS)
IGCP Project 216... International Geological Correlation Programme Global Biological Events in Earth History (SAUS)
IGCP Project 235... International Geological Correlation Programme Metamorphism and Geodynamics (SAUS)
IGCP Project 242... International Geological Correlation Programme Cretaceous of Latin America (SAUS)
IGCP Project 252... International Geological Correlation Programme Past and Future Evolution of Deserts (SAUS)
IGCP Project 253... International Geological Correlation Programme Termination of the Pleistocene (SAUS)
IGCP Project 259... International Geological Correlation Programme International Geochemical Mapping (SAUS)
IGCP Project 274... International Geological Correlation Programme Coastal Evolution in the Quaternary (SAUS)
IGCP Project 288... International Geological Correlation Programme Gondwanaland Sutures and Fold Belts (SAUS)
IGCP Project 290... International Geological Correlation Programme Origin of Anorthosite and Related Rocks (SAUS)
IGCP Project 293... International Geological Correlation Programme Geochemical Event Markers in the Phanerozoic (SAUS)
IGCP Project 296... International Geological Correlation Programme Quaternary Stratigraphy of Asia and the Pacific (SAUS)
IGCP Project 299... International Geological Correlation Programme Geology, Climate, Hydrology and Karst Formation (SAUS)
IGCP Project 301... International Geological Correlation Programme Palaeogene of South America (SAUS)
IGCP Project 302... International Geological Correlation Programme The Structure and Metallogenesis of Central African Late Proterozoic Belts (SAUS)
IGCP Project 304... International Geological Correlation Programme Lower Crustal Processes (SAUS)
IGCP Project 306... International Geological Correlation Programme Stratigraphic Correlation in South-East Asia (SAUS)
IGCP Project 314... International Geological Correlation Programme Alkaline and Carbonatitic Magmatism (SAUS)
IGCP Project 315... International Geological Correlation Programme Rapakivi Granites and Related Rocks (SAUS)
IGCP Project 317... International Geological Correlation Programme Palaeoweathering Records and Paleosurfaces (SAUS)
IGCP Project 318... International Geological Correlation Programme Genesis and Correlation of Marine Polymetallic Oxides (SAUS)
IGCP Project 319... International Geological Correlation Programme Global Paleogeography of the Late Precambrian and Early Paleozoic (SAUS)
IGCP Project 320... International Geological Correlation Programme Neoproterozoic Events and Resources (SAUS)
IGCP Project 321... International Geological Correlation Programme Gondwana Dispersion and Asian Accretion (SAUS)
IGCP Project 322... International Geological Correlation Programme Jurassic Events in South America (SAUS)
IGCP Project 324... International Geological Correlation Programme Global Limnology (SAUS)
IGCP Project 326... International Geological Correlation Programme Oligocene-Miocene Transition in the Northern Hemisphere (SAUS)
IGCP Project 328... International Geological Correlation Programme Paleozoic Microvertebrates (SAUS)
IGCP Project 329... International Geological Correlation Programme Neogene of the Paratethys (SAUS)
IGCP Project 335... International Geological Correlation Programme Biotic Recoveries from Mass Extinctions (SAUS)
IGCP Project 336... International Geological Correlation Programme Intraplate Magmatism and Metallogeny (SAUS)
IGCP Project 341... International Geological Correlation Programme Southern Hemisphere Paleo- and Neoclimates (SAUS)
IGCP Project 342... International Geological Correlation Programme Age and Isotopes of South American Ores (SAUS)
IGCP Project 343... International Geological Correlation Programme Stratigraphic Analysis of Peritethyan Basins (SAUS)
IGCP Project 345... International Geological Correlation Programme Andean Lithospheric Evolution (SAUS)
IGCP Project 346... International Geological Correlation Programme Neogeodynamica Baltica (SAUS)
IGCP Project 347... International Geological Correlation Programme Correlation of Ganges-Brahmaputra Sediments (SAUS)
IGCP Project 348... International Geological Correlation Programme The Mozambique and Related Belts (SAUS)
IGCP Project 349... International Geological Correlation Programme Quaternary Deserts and Climatic Change/Desert Margins and Paleomonsoons in the Old World/Desert Margins (SAUS)
IGCP Project 350... International Geological Correlation Programme Cretaceous Environmental Change in East and Southeast Asia (SAUS)
IGCP Project 351... International Geological Correlation Programme Early Paleozoic Evolution in NW Gondwana (SAUS)
IGCP Project 354... International Geological Correlation Programme Economic Superaccumulations of Metals in Lithosphere (SAUS)
IGCP Project 356... International Geological Correlation Programme Carpatho-Balkan Plate Tectonics and Metallogeny (SAUS)
IGCP Project 357... International Geological Correlation Programme Organics and Mineral Deposits (SAUS)
IGCP Project 359... International Geological Correlation Programme Correlation of Tethyan, Circum-Pacific and Marginal Gondwanan Permo-Triassic (SAUS)
IGCP Project 360... International Geological Correlation Programme Global Geochemical Baselines (SAUS)
IGCP Project 361... International Geological Correlation Programme East Asia Activated Zones (SAUS)
IGCP Project 362... International Geological Correlation Programme Tethyan and Boreal Cretaceous (SAUS)
IGCP Project 363... International Geological Correlation Programme Lower Proterozoic of the Sub-Equatorial Africa (SAUS)
IGCP Project 364... International Geological Correlation Programme Caribbean Volcanic Arcs and Ophiolites (SAUS)
IGCP Project 366... International Geological Correlation Programme Ecological Aspects of the Cambrian Radiation (SAUS)
IGCP Project 367... International Geological Correlation Programme Late Quaternary Coastal Records of Rapid Change: Application to Present and Future Conditions (SAUS)
IGCP Project 368... International Geological Correlation Programme Proterozoic Events in East Gondwana Deposits (SAUS)
IGCP Project 369... International Geological Correlation Programme Peritethyan Rift Basins (SAUS)
IGCP Project 371... International Geological Correlation Programme North Atlantic Precambrian (SAUS)
IGCP Project 374... International Geological Correlation Programme Paleoclimatology and Palaeoceanography from Laminated Sediments (SAUS)
IGCP Project 376... International Geological Correlation Programme Laurentian-Gondwanan Connections (SAUS)
IGCP Project 378... International Geological Correlation Programme Circumalpine Quaternary Correlations (SAUS)
IGCP Project 379... International Geological Correlation Programme Karst Processes and the Carbon Cycle (SAUS)
IGCP Project 380... International Geological Correlation Programme Biosedimentology of Microbial Buildups (SAUS)
IGCP Project 381... International Geological Correlation Programme South Atlantic Mesozoic Correlations (SAUS)
IGCP Project 382... International Geological Correlation Programme Seismotectonics and Seismic Hazard Assessment of the Mediterranean Basin (SAUS)
IGCP Project 383... International Geological Correlation Programme Palaeostress, Neotectonics, Geodynamics and Natural Hazards in West Pacific/Asia (SAUS)
IGCP Project 384... International Geological Correlation Programme Impact and Extraterrestrial Spherules (SAUS)
IGCP Project 386... International Geological Correlation Programme Response of the Ocean/Atmosphere System to Past Global Changes (SAUS)
IGCP Project 389... International Geological Correlation Programme Geoenvironmental Evaluation of Coastal Belts in Arab Countries (SAUS)
IGCP Project 391... International Geological Correlation Programme Sand Accumulations and Groundwater in the Sahara (SAUS)
IGCP Project 393... International Geological Correlation Programme Neritic Middle-Upper Eocene (SAUS)
IGCP Project 396... International Geological Correlation Programme Continental Shelves in the Quaternary (SAUS)
IGCP Project 400... International Geological Correlation Programme Geodynamics of Continental Rifting (SAUS)
IGCP Project 404... International Geological Correlation Programme Terrestrial Carbon in the Past 125 ka (SAUS)

IGCP Project 405... International Geological Correlation Programme Anthropogenic Impact on Weathering Processes (SAUS)
IGCP Project 406... International Geological Correlation Programme Circum-Arctic Palaeozoic Vertebrates (SAUS)
IGCR .... Inter-Governmental Committee for Refugees (SAUO)
IGCR .... Intergovernmental Committee on Refugees [*Post-World War II*]
IGCS .... Imperial Glass Collectors Society (EA)
IGCS .... Integrated Guidance and Control System [*Aerospace*] (AAG)
IGCS .... International Group on Clinical Sociology (SAUO)
IGCSE .... International General Certificate of Secondary Education (AIE)
IGCSTD .... Inter-Governmental Committee on Science and Technology for Development (SAUO)
IG-CUFMG ... Instituto de Geociencias Universidade Federal de Minas Gerais
IGCX .... Industrial Generating [*Federal Railroad Administration identification code*]
IGCZ............ Indiana Grain [*Federal Railroad Administration identification code*]
IGD .... Illicit Gold Dealer
IgD.............. Immunoglobulin D [*Immunology*]
IGD .... Indian Gold Resources Ltd. [*Vancouver Stock Exchange symbol*]
IGD .... Inspector General Division [*Environmental Protection Agency*] (GFGA)
IGD .... Inspector General's Department
IGD .... Institute of Grocery Distribution Ltd. [*British*]
IGD .... Interaction Graphics Display
IGD .... Interactive Grafics Digitizer [*Computer science*]
IGD .... Interglobal Distance (STED)
IGD .... Interior Guard Duty (SAUO)
IGD .... Inverse Gated Decoupling (SAUS)
IGD .... Irma Graphics for DOS [*Digital Operation System*] [*DCA, Inc.*]
IGD .... Isolated Gonadotropin Deficiency (STED)
IGDA .... International Game Developers Association
IGDC .... Interagency Geographic Data Committee (SAUO)
IGDC .... Interior Geographic Data Committee (SAUS)
IGDE .... Idiopathic Gait Disorders of Elderly [*Medicine*] (STED)
IGDM .... Infant of Gestational Diabetic Mother [*Obstetrics*]
IGDM .... Infant of Mother With Gestational Diabetes Mellitus [*Medicine*] (STED)
IGDMR......... Initial Gross Depot Maintenance Requirement [*Military*]
IGDO .... International Guild of Dispensing Opticians (SAUO)
IGDO .... International Guild of Opticians [*International Guild of Dispensing Optic ians*] [*Acronym is based on former name,*] (EAIO)
IGDOD .... Inspector General, Department of Defense (USGC)
IGDR .... Interim Geophysical Data Record [*From spacecraft data*]
IGDS .... Integrated Graduate Development Scheme [*British*]
IGDS .... Integrated Graphics Design System (SAUS)
IGDS .... Interactive Graphics Design Software (SAUS)
IGDS .... Interactive Graphics Design System (MCD)
IGDS .... Interactive Graphics Display Systems [*Computer monitor*] [*Military*]
IGDS .... Intergraph Design Software (SAUS)
IGDS .... Iodine Generating and Dispensing System (NASA)
IGds............ Irish Guards (SAUO)
IGE.............. Iguela [*Gabon*] [*Airport symbol*] [*Obsolete*] (OAG)
IgE .... Immunoglobin E (SAUS)
IgE .... Immunoglobulin E [*Immunology*]
IGE.............. Impaired Gas Exchange (DMAA)
IGE.............. Independent Government Estimate (MCD)
IGE.............. Individually Guided Education [*for upgrading students' skills*]
IGE.............. In-Ground Effect [*Aviation*] (NG)
IGE.............. Innovative Growth Firm (FOTI)
IGE.............. Institution of Gas Engineers [*British*] (DAS)
IGE.............. Instrumentation Graphics Environment (SAUS)
IGE.............. Instrumentation Ground Equipment (MCD)
IGE.............. International Geographics [*Vancouver Stock Exchange symbol*]
IGE.............. International Geophysical Extension
IGE.............. International Greenland Expedition
IGE.............. International Group Elements (SAUO)
IGE.............. International Guiding Eyes (EA)
IGE.............. Isopropyl Glycidyl Ether (SAUS)
IGEA............ International Group of Funding Agencies for Global Change Research (SAUO)
IgEAR.......... Immunoglobulin E Antiragweed [*Medicine*] (EDAA)
IGEB............ Intergency Global Positioning System Executive Board
IGEB............ International Society for the Promotion and Investigation of Band Music (SAUO)
IGEC............ International General Electric Company (SAUO)
IGEI............. International Genetic Engineering, Incorporated (SAUO)
IGEIEPSI ...... International Group for the Exchange of Information and Experience Among Postal Savings Institutions [*Geneva, Switzerland*] (EAIO)
IGEMS .... Interactive Generalized Modeling System (PDAA)
IGEN .... Current Source (MSA)
IGEN .... IGEN, Inc. [*NASDAQ symbol*] (SAG)
IGenD .... DuPage Library System, Geneva, IL [*Library symbol*] [*Library of Congress*] (LCLS)
IgE ND .... Immunoglobulin E ND [*Medicine*] (EDAA)
IGeo............ Georgetown Public Library, Georgetown, IL [*Library symbol*] [*Library of Congress*] (LCLS)
IGEOSA........ International General Electric Operations (SAUS)
IGEOSA........ International General Electric Operation SA (SAUO)
IGeoSD .... Georgetown Community Unit School District, Georgetown, IL [*Library symbol*] [*Library of Congress*] (LCLS)
IGER .... Institute of Grassland and Environmental Research [*British*]
IGERT .... Integrating Graduate Education and Research Training [*National Science Foundation*]
IGES............ Initial Graphic Exchange Standard [*Computer science*] (ELAL)
IGES............ Initial Graphics Exchange Software (SAUS)
IGES............ Initial Graphics Exchange Specification [*or System*] [*National Standards Institute*]
IGES............ Initial Graphics Exchange Standard (SAUS)
IGES............ Institute of Global Environment and Society (SAUO)
IGES............ Integrated Graphics Exchange System (AAEL)
IGES............ International Genetics Epidemiology Societies (HGEN)
IGES............ International Geochemical Exploration Symposium (SAUO)
IGES............ International Graphics Exchange Specification [*Computer science*]
IGES............ International Graphics Exchange Standard (NITA)
IGES............ International Graphics Exchange System (SAUS)
IGES/DXF...... Initial Graphics Exchange Specification/Data Exchange Format (SAUS)
IGESM .... IGOSS Group of Experts on Scientific Matters (SAUO)
IGES/PDES... Initial Graphics Exchange Specification/Product Design Exchange Specification (SAUS)
IGESUCO...... Infrastructure Ground Environment Sub-Committee (SAUO)
IGESUCO...... International Ground Environment Interrupted Continuous Wave (SAUS)
IGESUCO...... International Ground Environment Subcommittee [*NATO*]
IGETC.......... Intersegmental General Education Transfer Curriculum
IG-EV .... Interagency Group on Energy Vulnerability (COE)
IGEX............ International Germanium Experiment (SAUS)
IGF.............. Fondation Internationale pour la Sauvegarde du Gibier [*International Foundation for the Conservation of Game*] (EAIO)
IGF.............. IGF Metals, Inc. [*Vancouver Stock Exchange symbol*]
IGF.............. Image Generation Facility (MCD)
IGF.............. India Growth Fund, Inc. [*NYSE symbol*] (CTT)
IGF.............. Inert Gas Fusion (SAUS)
IGF.............. Inner German Frontier (SAUS)
IGF.............. Inset Graphics Format (SAUS)
IGF.............. Inspector General of Fortifications (SAUO)
IGF.............. Inspector-General of Fortifications [*British*]
IGF.............. Insulin Gene Family
IGF.............. Insulin-Like Growth Factor
IGF.............. Intergranular Fracture (SAUS)
IGF.............. International Foundation for the Conservation of Game (SAUO)
IGF.............. International Genetics Federation [*See also FIG*] [*England*] (EA)
IGF.............. International Graphical Federation [*See also FGI*] [*Berne, Switzerland*] (EAIO)
IGF.............. International Grieg Festival (SAUO)
IGF.............. International Growth Funds (SAUO)
IGF.............. International Gymnastic Federation [*See also FIG*] (EAIO)
IGF.............. Irish Genealogical Foundation (EA)
IGF.............. Island Games Foundation [*Canada*] (EAIO)
IGF.............. Israel Ground Forces (SAUO)
IGF-1 .... Insulin-Like Growth Factor-1
IGFA............ Inspector General, Foreign Assistance [*Department of State*]
IGFA............ Interessen Gemeinschaft der Farbenindustrie Aktiengesellschaft [*A dye trust*] [*Germany*]
IGFA............ Inter-Governmental Funding Agencies (SAUO)
IGFA............ Inter-Governmental Funding Agency (SAUS)
IGFA............ International Game Fish Association (EA)
IGFA............ International Group of Funding Agencies for Global Change Research (QUAC)
IGFA............ Isaac Garrison Family Association (EA)
IGFBP .... Insulin-Like Growth Factor Binding Protein [*Biochemistry*]
IGFES.......... Interactive Graphics Finite Element System (RDA)
IGFET.......... Insulated-Gate Field-Effect Transistor [*Electronics*]
IGFET.......... Isolated-Gate Field-Effect Transistor [*Electronics*]
IGFL............ Integral Green Fluorescence (DMAA)
IGFM........... Internal Gamma Flux Monitor
IGFM........... Internationale Gesellschaft fuer Menschenrechte [*International Society for Human Rights - ISHR*] (EA)
IGFO .... Inspector General Field Office [*Military*]
IGFOV .... Instantaneous Geometric Field of View
IGFPIL .... International Grotius Foundation for the Propagation of International Law
IGFR .... Insulin-Like Growth Factor Receptor (DMAA)
IGFR .... International Genealogical Fellowship of Rotarians (EA)
IGFS............ International Gem Finders Society
IGFVP .... Interservice Group for Flight Vehicle Power [*Military*]
IGG .... Igiugig [*Alaska*] [*Airport symbol*] (OAG)
igg .... ill-gotten gains (SAUS)
IgG.............. Immunoglobulin G [*Immunology*]
IGG .... Inert Gas Generator
IGG .... Inhibit Gate Generator (SAUS)
IGG .... Institut for Geography and Geoecology (SAUO)
IGG .... Internationale Gesellschaft fuer Geschichtsdidaktik [*International Society for History Didactics*] (EAIO)
IGGA .... International Grooving and Grinding Association (NTPA)
IG-GCI......... International Geological-Geophysical Cruise Inventory [*Marine science*] (OSRA)
IGGDA......... International G. G. Drayton Association (EA)
IgG Frac ...... Immunoglobulin G Fraction of Antiserum (SAUS)
IGGI .... Inter-Governmental Group for Indonesia [*Defunct*]
IGGI .... Inter-Governmental Group for/of Indonesia (SAUO)
IgGIC .... Immunoglobulin G Immune Complex [*Immunochemistry*]
IGGNU .... Intratubular Germ Cell Neoplasia of the Unclassified Type [*Medicine*] (PALA)
IGGS .... Interactive Geo-facilities Graphic Support (SAUS)
IGGT .... Institute for Guided Ground Transport [*Canada*] (PDAA)
IGG Theory... Improved Greuling Goertzel Theory (SAUS)
IGH .... Icy Grain Halo [*Model of comet structure*]
IGH .... Idiopathic Growth Hormone [*Medicine*] (MAE)
IgH.............. Immunoglobulin Heavy Chain [*Biochemistry*]

IGH .... Immunoreactive Growth Hormone [*Immunology*] (MAE)
IGH .... Indian General Hospital (SAUO)
IGH .... Ingham [*Australia*] [*Airport symbol*]
IGH .... International Guild of Hypnotists (EA)
IGHA .... Independent Group for Health in Africa (SAUO)
IGHAT .... Integrated Gasification Humid Air Turbine [*Chemical engineering*]
IGHD .... Isolated Growth Hormone Deficiency [*Medicine*]
IGHIA .... International Garden Horticultural Industry Association (EA)
IGHMHS .... Inventory of General Hospital Mental Health Services [*Department of Health and Human Services*] (GFGA)
IGHP .... Illinois Governor Home Page (SAUO)
IGHP .... Innovative Guided Hypervelocity Projectile (SAUS)
IGHP .... Isentropic Gas Horsepower (SAUS)
IGHS .... Inert Gas Handling System (SAUS)
IGI .... IGI, Inc. [*Associated Press*] (SAG)
IGI .... Imperial Gazetteer of India (SAUO)
IGI .... Index of General Icons (SAUO)
IGI .... Industrial Graphics International [*Later, IG*] [*An association*] (EA)
IGI .... Industrial Guest Investigation (SAUS)
IGI .... Industrial Guest Investigator [*NASA*]
IGI .... Information Gatekeepers, Inc. [*Telecommunications*] [*Information service or system*] (IID)
IGI .... Information General, Inc. [*Information service or system*] (IID)
IGI .... Information General, Incorporated (SAUO)
IGI .... Inner Grid Injection
IGI .... Institutional Goals Inventory [*Test*]
IGI .... Interactive Geographical Index (SAUO)
IGI .... Interlocked Grain Index [*Botany*]
IGI .... Intermountain Gas Industries, Inc. (EFIS)
IGI .... International Gallery Invitational (ITD)
IGI .... International Genealogical Index [*A publication*] [*Australia*]
IGI .... International Graphics, Inc. [*Defunct*] (EA)
IGI .... International Wallcovering Manufacturers Association [*Belgium*] (EAIO)
IGI .... International Wallpaper Manufacturers Association (SAUO)
IGI .... Investigative Group International
IGI .... Investors Group, Inc. [*Toronto Stock Exchange symbol*]
IGIA .... Interagency Group for International Aviation (SAUS)
IGIA .... Interagency Group on International Aviation
IGib .... Moyer Library, Gibson City, IL [*Library symbol*] [*Library of Congress*] (LCLS)
IGibH .... Gibson Community Hospital, Gibson City, IL [*Library symbol*] [*Library of Congress*] (LCLS)
IGibSD .... Gibson City Community Unit School District, Gibson City, IL [*Library symbol*] [*Library of Congress*] (LCLS)
IGIC .... Global Interdependence Center (SAUO)
IGIC .... International Gay Information Center [*Defunct*] (EA)
IGIC .... Isoconductive Gradient Ion Chromatography (SAUS)
IGlcB .... Chicago Botanic Gardens, Glencoe, IL [*Library symbol*] [*Library of Congress*] (LCLS)
IGIER .... Innocenzo Gasparini Institute for Economic Research
IGIF .... Interferon Gamma-Inducing Factor [*Biochemistry*]
IGIF .... International Geographic Information Foundation
IGII .... Intermark Gaming International, Incorporated (SAUO)
IGil .... Douglas Township Library, Gilman, IL [*Library symbol*] [*Library of Congress*] (LCLS)
IGill .... Gillespie Public Library, Gillespie, IL [*Library symbol*] [*Library of Congress*] (LCLS)
IGillMCD .... Macoupin Community District 7, Gillespie, IL [*Library symbol*] [*Library of Congress*] (LCLS)
IGIM .... Immune Globulin Intramuscular (SAUS)
IGinseng .... Imprial Ginseng Products Ltd. [*Associated Press*] (SAG)
IGIP .... Institute of Geophysics and Interplanetary Physics (SAUO)
IGIP .... Internationale Gesellschaft fuer Ingenieurpaedagogik [*International Society for Engineering Education*] (EAIO)
IGIPAS .... Interagency Group on International Programs in Atmospheric Science
IGir .... Girard Township Library, Girard, IL [*Library symbol*] [*Library of Congress*] (LCLS)
IGirMCD .... Macoupin Community District 3, Girard, IL [*Library symbol*] [*Library of Congress*] (LCLS)
IGIS .... Illinois Geographic Information System (SAUO)
IGIS .... Integrated Geographical Information System (SAUS)
IGIS .... Intelligent Geographic Information System (SAUO)
IGIS .... Intelligent Geographic System [*Computer science*]
IGIS .... Interactive Geological Interpretation System (SAUO)
IGIS .... International Group of users of Information Systems (SAUO)
IGIS .... International Guild for Infant Survival (SAUO)
IGISE .... Institute for GIS in Education (SAUO)
IGITT .... Interagency Group for Interactive Training Technologies (EA)
IGIV .... Immune Globulin, Intravenous (CPH)
IGIW .... Indices of General Industrial Worth
IGJ .... International Society for Jazz Research (SAUO)
IGJAS .... Industrie Group JAS (SAUO)
IGK .... Infanteriegeschuetz - Kompanie [*Infantry Howitzer Co.*] [*German military - World War II*]
IGK .... Knox College, Galesburg, IL [*Library symbol*] [*Library of Congress*] (LCLS)
IGKB .... Internationale Gewasserschutz Kommission fur den Bodensee [*International Commission for the Protection of Lake Constance*] (EA)
IGKG .... Internationale Gesellschaft fuer Kiefer- und Gesichtschirurgie [*International Association for Maxillo-Facial Surgery*] (EAIO)
IGKT .... International Guild of Knot-Tyers (SAUO)
IGL .... Ideal Gas Law
IGL .... Igloolik [*Northwest Territories*] [*Seismograph station code, US Geological Survey*] (SEIS)
IGL .... IMC Global [*NYSE symbol*] (TTSB)
IGL .... IMC Global, Inc. [*Formerly, IMC Fertilizer Group*] [*NYSE symbol*] (SAG)
IGL .... Index Guided LASER (IAA)
IGL .... Information Grouping Logic [*Computer science*]
IGL .... Infrared Gunfire Locator
IGL .... Installation Group List (SAUO)
IGL .... Integrated Graphics Library (SAUO)
IGL .... Interactive Graphics Language
IGL .... Interactive Graphics Library (SAUS)
IGL .... Intergeniculate Leaflet [*Anatomy*]
IGL .... Intermediate Graphics Language (TIMI)
IGL .... Internal Granule Layer [*Cytology*]
IGL .... Internationale Gesellschaft fuer Lymphologie [*International Society of Lymphology*] (EAIO)
IGL .... International Minerals & Chemical Corp. (SAUO)
IGL .... Ionized Gas LASER
IGL .... Izmir [*Turkey*] Cigli Airport [*Airport symbol*] (OAG)
IGlc .... Glencoe Public Library, Glencoe, IL [*Library symbol*] [*Library of Congress*] (LCLS)
IGLC .... International Group for Lean Construction (SAUO)
IGlca .... Glen Carbon Library, Glen Carbon, IL [*Library symbol*] [*Library of Congress*] (LCLS)
IGLD .... International Great Lakes Datum
IGle .... Glen Ellyn Public Library, Glen Ellyn, IL [*Library symbol*] [*Library of Congress*] (LCLS)
IGleD .... College of Du Page, Glen Ellyn, IL [*Library symbol*] [*Library of Congress*] (LCLS)
IGleM .... Maryknoll Seminary, Glen Ellyn, IL [*Library symbol*] [*Library of Congress*] (LCLS)
IGLF .... Irish Grand Lodge of Freemasons (SAUO)
IGLF .... Issa Gurgura Liberation Front [*Ethiopia*]
IGLFA .... International Gay and Lesbian Franchise Association (NTPA)
IGLHRC .... International Gay and Lesbian Human Rights Commission (EA)
IGLIC .... International Grain Legume Information Centre (SAUO)
IGLM .... Limnos [*Greece*] [*ICAO location identifier*] (ICLI)
IGIN .... United States Naval Training Center, Great Lakes, IL [*Library symbol*] [*Library of Congress*] (LCLS)
IGLOSS .... Integrated Global Ocean Station System [*Surrey, England*] [*See also IGOSS*] [*UNESCO*]
IGLSF .... Insituform Group Ltd. [*NASDAQ symbol*] (COMM)
IGLU .... Institute of University Management and Leadership (SAUO)
IGlvK .... Kraftco Corp., Research and Development Library, Glenview, IL [*Library symbol*] [*Library of Congress*] (LCLS)
IGlvK-L .... Kraft, Inc., Law Library, Glenview, IL [*Library symbol*] [*Library of Congress*] (LCLS)
IGlw .... Glenwood Public Library District, Glenwood, IL [*Library symbol*] [*Library of Congress*] (LCLS)
IGM .... I Got Mine [*Slang describing attitude of some nouveaux riches*]
IgM .... Immunoglobulin M [*Immunology*]
IgM .... Immunoglobulin Macro [*Also known as RF*] [*Immunology*]
IGM .... Index to Geologic Maps (SAUO)
IGM .... Inertial Guidance Mode
IGM .... Interactive Guidance Mode (NASA)
IGM .... Intergalactic Medium
IGM .... Internationale Gesellschaft fuer Menschenrechte [*International Society for Human Rights - ISHR*] (EAIO)
IGM .... International Geophysical Month (SAUS)
IGM .... International Grail Movement (EA)
IGM .... Internet Grateful Med [*Program for assisted searching of MEDLINE*] (MELL)
IGM .... Interplanetary Global Model [*Marine science*] (OSRA)
IGM .... Irma Graphics for Macintosh [*DCA, Inc.*]
IGM .... ISDN [*Integrated Services Digital Network*] Gateway Module [*Telecommunications*]
IGM .... Iterative Guidance Mode [*NASA*]
IGM .... Kingman [*Arizona*] [*Airport symbol*] (OAG)
IGMA .... International Guild of Miniature Artisans (EA)
IGMAA .... International Gas Model Airplane Association (SAUO)
IGMAC .... Illinois Geologic Mapping Advisory Committee (SAUO)
IGMAP .... Illinois Geological Mapping Advisory Committee (SAUO)
IGMC .... Independent Gasoline Marketers Council [*Defunct*] (EA)
IGMDP .... Integrated Guided Missile Development Program (SAUS)
IGMDP .... Integrated Guided Missile Development Programme (SAUS)
IGME .... Institute of Geologic Mining Exploration (SAUO)
IGME .... Institute of Geology and Mineral Exploration (SAUS)
IGME .... Institutr of Geology and Mineral Exploration (SAUO)
IGMF .... Inertial Guidance Maintenance Facility (IAA)
IGMF .... Intergalactic Magnetic Fields
IGMG .... Institute of Geriatric Medicine and Gerontology [*British*]
IGMG .... Internationale Gustav Mahler Gesellschaft [*International Gustav Mahler Society*] (EA)
IgMIC .... Immunoglobulin M Immune Complex [*Immunochemistry*]
IGMIRS .... Inspector General Management Information and Reporting (SAUO)
IgMN .... Immunoglobulin M Nephropathy [*Medicine*] (EDAA)
IGMOSFET .... Insulated Gate Metal Oxide Semiconductor Field Effect Transistor (SAUS)
IGMP .... Integrated Ground Management Plan (SAUS)
IGMP .... Internet Group Management Protocol [*Computer science*]
IGMP .... Internet Group Membership Protocol (SAUO)
IGMP .... Internet Group Message Protocol (SAUO)
IGMP .... Internet Group Multicast Protocol (SAUO)
IgM-RF .... Immunoglobulin M - Rheumatoid Factor [*Medicine*]

IGMT........... Impingement [*Engineering*]
IGMW.......... International Musicological Society (SAUO)
IGM-WCP..... Intergovernmental Meeting on the World Climate Programme (SAUS)
IGM/WCP..... Intergovernmental Negotiating Committee for Framework Convention on Climate Change (SAUO)
IGN............. IBM Global Network (SAUO)
IGN............. Ignite (SAUS)
ign.............. Ignition (ADWA)
IGN............. Ignition (KSC)
IGN............. Ignitron [*Electronics*]
IGN............. Ignorant
IGN............. Ignore (TVEL)
IGN............. Ignotus [*Unknown*] [*Latin*]
IGN............. Iligan [*Philippines*] [*Airport symbol*] (OAG)
IGN............. International Geographic Institute (SAUS)
IGN............. International-Great Northern [*AAR code*]
IGN............. Internet Group Names (MWOL)
IGN............. Kingston, NY [*Location identifier*] [*FAA*] (FAAL)
IGNC........... International Good Neighbor Council [*See also CIBV*] [*Monterrey, Mexico*] (EAIO)
IgND........... Immunoglobulin ND [*Immunology, provisional class*]
IGNDET........ Ignition Detector
IGNE........... IGENE Biotechnology, Inc. [*NASDAQ symbol*] (COMM)
IGNET.......... Inspector General Network [*Military*] (GFGA)
IGNITOR...... Ignition Torus (SAUS)
IGNOU......... Indira Gandhi National Open University (SAUO)
IGNR........... Igniter
IGNRR......... International Great Northern Railroad (SAUO)
IGNS........... Interactive Graphics Network System (MCD)
IGNSEL........ Ignition Selector (SAUS)
IGNTR......... Igniter (MSA)
IGNTR......... Ignitor (SAUS)
IGNU........... Interim Government of National Unity (Liberia) [*Political party*] (PSAP)
IGO............. Chigorodo [*Colombia*] [*Airport symbol*] (OAG)
IGO............. Impulse-Governed (SAUS)
IGO............. Impulse-Governed Oscillator (SAUS)
IGO............. Independent Garage Owners (SAUO)
IGO............. Inspecting General Officer (SAUS)
IGO............. Inspector General Officer (SAUO)
IGO............. Inspector General's Office [*Air Force*]
IGO............. Intergovernmental Organization [*Generic term*]
IGO............. Investment Grant Office [*British*]
IGO............. Irish Genealogical Office (SAUO)
IGOA........... Independent Garage Owners of America [*Later, Automotive Service Councils*] (EA)
IGoL............ Lewis and Clark Community College, Godfrey, IL [*Library symbol*] [*Library of Congress*] (LCLS)
IGOM........... Integrated Global Ocean Monitoring [*Marine science*] (OSRA)
IGoM........... Monticello College, Godfrey, IL [*Library symbol*] [*Library of Congress*] (LCLS)
I-GOOS........ IOC Committee for Global Ocean Observing System (SAUO)
I-GOOS........ IOC-WMO-UNEP Committee for the Global Ocean Observing System (SAUS)
I-GOOS........ IOC-WMO-UNEP Intergovernmental Committee for GOOS (SAUO)
IGOR........... Instrument Ground-based Optical Recording (SAUO)
IGOR........... Instrument Ground Optical Recording
IGOR........... Interactive Guidance on Routes [*FHWA*] (TAG)
IGOR........... Intercept Ground Optical Recorder [*NASA*]
IGORTT........ Intercept Ground Optical Recorder Tracking Telescope [*NASA*]
IGOS........... Image Guided Orthopaedic Surgery (EURO)
IGOS........... Integrated Global Observing Strategy (SAUO)
IGOS........... Inward Grade of Service (DNAB)
IGOSS......... Industry/Government Open Systems Specification (ACRL)
IGOSS......... Integrated Global Ocean Services System [*Marine science*] (OSRA)
IGOSS......... Integrated Global Ocean Station System [*See also IGLOSS*] [*UNESCO*] [*British*]
IGOSS......... International Global Ocean Services System (SAUO)
IGOSS......... International Global Ocean Station System (SAUS)
IGOSS......... International Group on Soil Sampling
IGOSS-CP.... IGOSS Group of Experts on Communications and Products (SAUO)
IGP............. Gary Public Library, Gary, IN [*OCLC symbol*] (OCLC)
IGP............. Igap [*Former USSR*] [*FAA designator*] (FAAC)
IGP............. Igneous & Geothermal Processes [*Marine science*] (OSRA)
IGP............. Imidazole Glycerol Phosphate [*Biochemistry*]
IGP............. Imitation Greaseproof Parchment (DGA)
IGP............. Industrial Gas Platoon (SAUO)
IGP............. Industrial Government Party (SAUO)
IGP............. Inertial Guidance Package
IGP............. Inertial Guidance Platform
IGP............. Information Generation and Publishing (SAUS)
IGP............. Inside Gravel Pack (SAUS)
IGP............. Inspection Gauges Production (MCD)
IGP............. Inspector General of Police (SAUO)
IGP............. Institute of Geology and Palaeontology (SAUO)
IGP............. Institute of the Great Plains (EA)
IGP............. Instituto Geofisico del Peru [*Marine science*] (OSRA)
IGP............. Integrated Graphics Processor
IGP............. Intelligent Gateway Processor [*Computer science*]
IGP............. Intelligent Graphics Processor [*Computer science*] (PCM)
IGP............. Interim Ground Processor (SAUS)
IGP............. Interior Gateway Protocol [*Computer science*] (TNIG)
IGP............. International Garment Processors
IGP............. International Geodynamics Project
IGP............. International Green Party (EA)
IGP............. International Green Party - Ecologism USA (EA)
IGP............. International Guild of Prestidigitators [*Defunct*] (EA)
IGP............. Internet Gateway Protocol (SAUS)
IGP............. Intestinal Glycoprotein [*Biochemistry*] (MAE)
IGP............. Inverted Groundplane (PDAA)
IGP............. Investment Guaranty Program [*AID*]
IGP............. Ion-Getter-Pumping [*Electron microscopy*]
IGPA........... Igor-Patrick Air Force Base (KSC)
IGPA........... Illinois Groundwater Protection Act (SAUO)
IGPA........... International General Produce Association (SAUO)
IGPAC......... Intergovernmental Policy Advisory Committee on Trade
IGPB........... Special Committee for the International Geosphere-Biosphere Programme: A Study of Global Change (SAUO)
IGPC........... Impregnated Gas-Pressure Cable (SAUS)
IGPC........... Inter-Governmental Philatelic Corp. (EA)
IGPCE......... International Great Plains Conference of Entomologists (SAUO)
IGPD........... Imidazoleglycerol-phosphate Dehydratase [*An enzyme*]
IGPE........... International Guild of Professional Electrologists (EA)
IGPF........... Canadian Imperial Ginseng Products Ltd. [*NASDAQ symbol*] (SAG)
IGPF........... Imperial Ginseng Products Ltd. [*NASDAQ symbol*] (SAG)
IGPFF......... Imperial Ginseng Prod [*NASDAQ symbol*] (TTSB)
IGP-GIPME... Joint IOC-UNEP Intergovernmental Panel for the Global Investigation of Pollution in the Marine Environment (SAUS)
igpm........... imperial gallons per mile (SAUS)
IGPM........... Imperial Gallons per Minute
IGPO........... International GEWEX Program Office (SAUS)
IGPO........... International GEWEX Project Office (SAUO)
IGPP........... Institute of Geophysics and Planetary Physics [*Livermore, CA*] [*Department of Energy*] (MCD)
IGPP........... Interactive Graphics Packaging Program [*Computer science*]
IGPPS......... Institute of Geophysics and Planetary Physics at Scripps (SAUO)
IGPRAD....... Intergovernmental Panel of Experts on Radioactive Waste Disposal at Sea (SAUS)
IGPRAD....... Intergovernmental Panel on Radioactive Waste (SAUO)
IGPRAD....... Intergovernmental Panel on Radioactive Waste (SAUS)
I-GPRF........ Isothermal General Purpose Rocket Furnace (SAUS)
IGQ............. Illinois Geologic Quadrangle (SAUO)
IGR............. Grace College, Winona Lake, IN [*OCLC symbol*] (OCLC)
IGR............. Iceland-Greenland Ridge (SAUS)
IGR............. Igitur [*Therefore*] [*Latin*] (ADA)
IGR............. Iguazu [*Argentina*] [*Airport symbol*] (OAG)
IGR............. Immediate Generalized Reaction (DB)
IGR............. Improved Ground Rent (SAUO)
IGR............. Improved Ground Rents (ROG)
IGR............. Improved Guard Rail
IGR............. Increased Growth Response [*Botany*]
IGR............. Indian Government Railways (SAUO)
IGR............. Infanteriegranate [*Infantry Howitzer Shell*] [*German military - World War II*]
IGR............. Inscriptiones Graecae ad Res Romanas Pertinentes [*A publication*] (BJA)
IGR............. Insect Growth Regulator
IGR............. Institute of Geomantic Research (EAIO)
IGR............. Integra, Inc. [*AMEX symbol*] [*Formerly, A pogee, Inc.*]
IGR............. Inter-Globe Resources Ltd. [*Vancouver Stock Exchange symbol*]
IGR............. Intergovernmental Review System (OICC)
IGR............. Intrauterine Growth Retardation [*Neonatology*] (DAVI)
IGRA........... Indian Gaming Regulatory Act
IGrac.......... Granite City Public Library, Granite City, IL [*Library symbol*] [*Library of Congress*] (LCLS)
IGracCU....... Granite City Community Unit 12, Granite City, IL [*Library symbol*] [*Library of Congress*] (LCLS)
IGRAF......... Inspector-General of the Royal Air Force [*British*]
IGrafPM....... Pere Marquette Residential Center, Grafton, IL [*Library symbol*] [*Library of Congress*] (LCLS)
IGralC......... College of Lake County, Grayslake, IL [*Library symbol*] [*Library of Congress*] (LCLS)
IGR & P....... Inert Gas Receiving and Processing (NRCH)
IGranHS....... Hopkins Elementary School, Granville, IL [*Library symbol*] [*Library of Congress*] (LCLS)
IGranPSD..... Putnam County Community Unit, School District 535, Granville, IL [*Library symbol*] [*Library of Congress*] (LCLS)
IGRAP......... Inert Gas Receiving and Processing (IAA)
IGRC........... International Gas Research Conference (SAUS)
IGRDC......... Institute for Genome Research for Developing Countries [*Tunisia*] [*Proposed for 1996*]
IGRE........... Improved Ground Reconnaissance Equipment [*Military*] (MCD)
IGref........... Greenfield Public Library, Greenfield, IL [*Library symbol*] [*Library of Congress*] (LCLS)
IGrefCU....... Greenfield Community Unit, District 10, Greenfield, IL [*Library symbol*] [*Library of Congress*] (LCLS)
IGrevi.......... Greenville Public Library, Greenville, IL [*Library symbol*] [*Library of Congress*] (LCLS)
IGreviC........ Greenville College, Greenville, IL [*Library symbol*] [*Library of Congress*] (LCLS)
IGRF........... International Geomagnetic Reference Field
IGRL........... Industrial Group Risley Lancashire (SAUO)
IGRL........... Inter-Globe Resources Limited (SAUO)
IG Rom....... Inscriptiones Graecae ad Res Romanas Pertinentes [*A publication*] (OCD)
IGROUP....... Inspection Group (SAUO)
IGRP........... Indus Group [*NASDAQ symbol*] (TTSB)
IGRP........... Indus Group, Inc. (The) [*NASDAQ symbol*] (SAG)
IGRP........... Interior Gateway Routing Protocol [*Cisco Systems, Inc.*]
IGRP........... International Genetic Resources Programme [*Later, RAFI-USA*] (EA)
IGRP........... Internet Gateway Resolution Protocol (CIST)

IGRP Internet Gateway Routing Protocol (SAUS)
IGRP Isophthalic Glass Reinforced Plastic [*Materials science*]
IGRPS Inert Gas Receiving and Processing System (NRCH)
IGRS Irish Genealogical Research Society (EAIO)
IGrSD Grand Ridge Consolidated Community School District 95, Grand Ridge, IL [*Library symbol*] [*Library of Congress*] (LCLS)
IGRSS International Geoscience and Remote Sensing Society (CARB)
IGRV Improved Guard Rail V [*Army*] (DOMA)
IGRV Improved Guardrail V Software (SAUS)
IGRV Integrated GUARDRAIL V
IGS Carl Sandburg Birthplace Association, Galesburg, IL [*Library symbol*] [*Library of Congress*] (LCLS)
IGS Gary Community School Corp., Gary, IN [*OCLC symbol*] (OCLC)
IGS Geological Survey of Israel (SAUS)
IGS Idaho Geological Survey (SAUO)
IGS Identify Graphic Subrepertoire (SAUS)
IGS Illinois Geological Survey (SAUO)
IGS Illinois Grandstand Stage (SAUO)
IGS Image Guided Surgery
IGS Immigrant Genealogical Society (EA)
Igs Immunoglobulins [*Chemistry*] (MEC)
IGS Immunogold Stain [*Cytochemistry*]
IGS Immunogold Staining (SAUS)
IGS Imperial General Staff
IGS Improved Gray Scale
IGS Inappropriate Gonadotrophin Secretion [*Endocrinology*]
IGS Independent Grammar School (SAUS)
IGS Indiana Geological Survey (SAUO)
IGS Indian Geographical Society (SAUO)
IGS Indicator Group Speed
IGS Inert Gas-Shielded Welding (SAUS)
IGS Inert Gas Storage
IGS Inert Gas Supply (SAUS)
IGS Inert Gas System [*Engineering*]
IGS Inertial Guidance System [*NASA*]
IGS Infogram Service (SAUS)
IGS Information & Graphics Systems Inc. (SAUO)
IGS Information Generator System (SAUS)
IGS Information Group Separator
IGS Information Group System (SAUO)
IGS Inner Glide Slope [*Aviation*] (NASA)
IGS Inner Glideslope (SAUS)
IGS Inner Gulf Shelf [*Marine science*] (OSRA)
IGs Inspector Generals (SAUO)
IGS Institute of General Semantics (EA)
IGS Institute of Geological Sciences [*British*] [*Marine science*] (OSRA)
IGS Institute of Geological Studies (SAUO)
IGS Institute of Government Studies [*University of California at Berkeley*]
IGS Instrumentation Ground System
IGS Instrument Guidance System [*Aviation*] (DA)
IGS Integrated Gas Spacer (SAUS)
IGS Integrated Geophysical System (SAUS)
IGS Integrated Graphics System [*Computer science*] (BUR)
IGS Interactive Graphics System (TIMI)
IGS Intercapillary Glomerulosclerosis (PDAA)
IGS Interchange Group Separator [*Computer science*] (BUR)
IGS Interchromatin Granular Cluster [*Cytology*]
IGS Interconnected Ground Segment (SAUS)
IGS Intergenic Spacer [*Genetics*]
IGS Interior Guard Station (SAUS)
IGS Intermediate General Support [*Army*]
IGS Internal German Service (SAUS)
IGS Internal Guide Sequence [*Genetics*]
IGS Internal Gun System (SAUS)
IGS International Gadget Service (SAUO)
IGS International Geranium Society (EA)
IGS International Glaciological Society [*Cambridge, England*]
IGS International Glaciospeleological Society (QUAC)
IGS International Global Positioning System Geodynamic Service (SAUS)
IGS International GPS Service (SAUS)
IGS International Graduate School (SAUO)
IGS International Graphoanalysis Society (SAUO)
IGS International Graphological Society (EA)
IGS International Graphonomics Society (SAUO)
IGS Internet Go Server (SAUS)
IGS IONDS Global Satellite (SAUO)
IGS Iowa Geological Survey (SAUO)
IGS Irish Genealogical Society (EA)
IGS Irish Georgian Society (EA)
IGS Irish Graphical Society (BI)
IGS Isla Grande Flying School [*Puerto Rico*] [*ICAO designator*] (FAAC)
IGS Morgan StanGp 6.50% IGT'PERQS' [*AMEX symbol*] (TTSB)
IGS Morgan Stanley Group, Inc. [*AMEX symbol*] (SAG)
IGSA Indoor Gardening Society of America (EA)
IGSA International Golf Sponsors' Association [*Later, AGS*]
IGS&E Institute of Glass Science and Engineering (SAUS)
IGSB Iowa Geological Survey Bureau (SAUO)
IGSC Carl Sandburg College, Galesburg, IL [*Library symbol*] [*Library of Congress*] (LCLS)
IgSC Immunoglobulin-Secreting Cell (DB)
IGSC Inspector General, Supply Corps
IGSC International Gold and Silver Conference (SAUS)
IGSCC Intergranular Stress-Corrosion Cracking [*Plant engineering*]
IGSD International Ground Systems Division (SAUO)
IGSE In-Space Ground Support Equipment [*NASA*] (NASA)
IGSE Instrument Ground Support Equipment (MCD)
IGSE Integrated Ground Support Equipment (SAUS)
IGSE Interim Ground-Support Equipment (SAUS)
IGSEAP Inertial Guidance System Error Analysis Program (SAUS)
IGSESS International Graduate School for English-Speaking Students (SAUO)
IgSF Immunoglobulin Superfamily [*Immunology*]
IGSHPA International Ground Source Heat Pump Association (EA)
IGSI Insituform Gulf South, Inc. [*NASDAQ symbol*] (COMM)
IG SI Wg Inspector General Special Investigation Wing (SAUS)
IGSL Institute of Governmental Studies (SAUS)
IGSL Interactive Gaming Simulation Language (SAUS)
IGSM Indian General Service Medal [*British*]
IGSM Interim Ground Station Module [*Joint Surveillance/Target Attack RADAR Syste m*] (DOMA)
IGSM International Graduate School of Management
IGSMA Inertial Guidance System Maintenance Area [*Aerospace*] (AAG)
IGSN International Gravity Standardization Net (PDAA)
IGSOBM International Guild of Symphony, Opera, and Ballet Musicians (EA)
IGSP Institute for Gravitational Strain Pathology (EA)
IGSP Internationale Gesellschaft der Schriftpsychologie [*International Society for the Psychology of Writing*]
IGSP International Greenland Sea Project (USDC)
IGSP Interntional Greenland Sea Project [*Marine science*] (OSRA)
IGSPS International Gold and Silver Plate Society (EA)
IGSS Immunogold Silver Staining [*Cytochemistry*]
IGSS Inertial Guidance System Simulator [*NASA*] (IAA)
IGSS International Graduate Summer School in Librarianship and Information Service (SAUO)
IGST Intergovernmental Committee on Science and Technology (BARN)
IGSU Improved Gunner's Sight Unit [*Military*] (MCD)
IGSWS Iowa Geological Survey Web Server (SAUO)
IGT Impaired Glucose Tolerance [*Physiology*]
IGT Improved Gas Turbine (MCD)
IGT Ingot (MSA)
IGT Ingot Resources Ltd. [*Vancouver Stock Exchange symbol*]
IGT Inspector-General of Transportation [*British military*] (DMA)
IGT Inspector-General to the Forces for Training [*British military*]
IGT Institute of Gas Technology (EA)
IGT Instrument Guide Tube [*Nuclear energy*] (NRCH)
IGT Insulated Gate Tetrode (SAUS)
IGT Insulated-Gate Tetrode (IAA)
IGT Insulated Gate Transistor (SAUS)
IGT Insulating-Gate Transistor (SAUS)
IGT Integrated Government Testing (SAUO)
IGT Integrated GPS Technologies Inc. (SAUO)
IGT Integrated Ground Test
IgT Integrated Telecom Technology (SAUS)
IGT Intelligent Graphics Terminal [*Tektronix*] (NITA)
IGT Interactive Graphics Terminal [*Computer science*]
IGT Intercontinental General Trading Establishment (SAUO)
IGT Internally Generated Transaction (SAUS)
IGT International Game Technology [*NYSE symbol*] (SPSG)
IGT Intl Game Technology [*NYSE symbol*] (TTSB)
IGT Intragastric Titration [*Gastroenterology*]
IGT Ionization Gauge Tube
IGT Nightmute, AK [*Location identifier*] [*FAA*] (FAAL)
IGTA International Gay Travel Association (EA)
IGTC Inertial Guidance Test Center [*Aerospace*] (IAA)
IGTC International Gas Turbine Center (SAUS)
IGTC International Glutamate Technical Committee (EA)
IGTCP International Global Tropospheric Chemistry Programme (SAUO)
IGTD Inertial Guidance Technology Demonstration (ACAE)
IGTDS Interactive Graphic Transit Design System (PDAA)
IGTEX IDEX II: Tax Exempt Ptfl. Cl.A [*Mutual fund ticker symbol*] (SG)
IGTI Image Guided Technologies, Inc. [*NASDAQ symbol*] (SAG)
IGTI International Gas Turbine Institute [*Later, ASMEIGTI*] (EA)
IGTM Inertial Guided Tactical Missile (SAUO)
IGTN Ingrown Toenail (MELL)
IGT News Letter Institute of Gas Technology News Letter (journ.) (SAUS)
IGTO India Government Tourist Office (SAUO)
IGTO Israel Government Tourist Office (SAUO)
IGTO Italian Government Tourist Office (SAUO)
IGTS Interactive Graphic Transit Simulator (PDAA)
IGTT Intravenous Glucose Tolerance Test [*Clinical medicine*]
IGTYF International Good Templar Youth Federation [*Oslo, Norway*] (EAIO)
IGU Iguassu Falls [*Brazil*] [*Airport symbol*] (OAG)
IGU Iminoglycinuria [*Medicine*] (MELL)
IGU Infantile Gastroenteritis Virus [*Medicine*] (PDAA)
IGU Internationale Gewerbeunion [*International Association of Crafts and Small and Medium Sized Enterprises - IACME*] [*Berne, Switzerland*] (EAIO)
IGU International Gas Union [*See also UIIG*] (EAIO)
IGU International Geographical Union [*ICSU*] [*Edmonton, AB*] (EA)
IGU International Geophysical Union
IGUA International Guards Union of America (EA)
IGUAT Indira Gandhi University of Agriculture and Technology (SAUO)
IGUC Information Gained per Unit Cost [*Computer science*]
IGUCC International Geographical Union Commission on Climatology [*Switzerland*] (EAIO)
IGUG Intergraph Graph Users Group (SAUO)
IGU Newsletter International Geographical Union Newsletter (journ.) (SAUS)
IGV Incremental Growth Vehicle (MCD)
IGV Inlet Guide Valve (MCD)
IGV Inlet Guide Vane
IGV Intake Guide Vane (SAUS)

IGV International Gravis Computer Technology, Inc. [*Formerly, Gravis Computer Peripherals, Inc.*] [*Vancouver Stock Exchange symbol*]
IGV Intrathoracic Gas Volume [*Medicine*] (MAE)
IGVP International Guild of Vatican Philatelists [*Defunct*] (EA)
IGW Image West Entertainment Corp. [*Vancouver Stock Exchange symbol*]
IGW Indiana Gear Works, Inc. (SAUO)
IGW Information Group West Corp., Calgary, Alberta [*National Library of Canad a*] [*Library symbol*] (IID)
IGW Internal Gravity Wave [*in the atmosphere*]
IGW Irma Graphics for Windows [*DCA, Inc.*]
IGWA Inter Group Work Authorization (ACAE)
IGWAP CPA [*Canadian Psychological Association*] Interest Group on Women and Psychology
IGWES Inert Gas Wire Enamel Stripper (PDAA)
IGWF International Garment Workers' Federation
IGWIS Integrated Ground Water Information System
IGWMC International Ground Water Modeling Center [*Butler University*]
IGWO Integrated and Guided Wave Optics (ACAE)
IGWP International Group of Women Pilots (EA)
IGWT In God We Trust (SAUS)
IGWT Internationale Gesellschaft fuer Warenkunde und Technologie [*International Association for Commodity Science and Technology*] (EA)
IGWU International Garment Workers Union (SAUO)
IGWU International Glove Workers' Union of America [*Later, ACTWU*]
IGWUA International Glove Workers Union of America (MHDB)
IGWUA International Grove Workers Union of America (SAUO)
IGY International Geophysical Year [*1958-1959*] [*ICSU*]
IGYN Imagyn Medical [*NASDAQ symbol*] (TTSB)
IGYN Imagyn Medical, Inc. [*NASDAQ symbol*] (SAG)
IGY-WDC International Geophysical Year, World Data Center
IGZ Iguatu [*Brazil*] [*Airport symbol*] (AD)
IGZ Internet Gaming Zone (SAUS)
IH Channel Flying [*ICAO designator*] (AD)
IH Hinsdale Public Library, Hinsdale, IL [*Library symbol*] [*Library of Congress*] (LCLS)
IH Iacet Hic [*Here Lies*] [*Latin*]
IH Ice Haulage
IH ICH Corp. [*AMEX symbol*] (SG)
IH Idiopathic Hemachromatosis [*Medicine*]
IH Idiopathic Hirsutism [*Medicine*] (MELL)
IH Idiopathic Hypercalciuria [*Medicine*]
IH Idiopathic Hypersomnia [*Medicine*]
IH Immediate Hypersensitivity [*Immunology*]
IH Immediate-type Hypersensitivity (SAUS)
IH Immersion Heater (SAUS)
IH Immobilized Histamine [*Biochemistry*]
IH Impact on Hunger (EA)
IH Imperforate Hymen [*Medicine*] (MELL)
IH Incipient Heavies [*Slang for rising young bureaucrats in the foreign policy field*]
IH Incisional Hernia [*Medicine*] (MELL)
IH Incompletely Healed [*Medicine*] (MELL)
IH Indent Hanging [*Graphic arts*] (DGA)
IH Index of Homogeneity [*Botany*]
IH Indirect Heating (SAUS)
IH Indirect Hemagglutination [*Hematology*] (DAVI)
IH Indirectly Heated (DEN)
IH Indo-Hittite (BJA)
IH Induction Heating (SAUS)
I/H Industria del Hierro [*Part of a large Mexican industrial complex*]
IH Industrial Handling (SAUO)
IH Industrial House (ROG)
IH Industrial Hygiene (LDOE)
IH Industrial Hygienist [*Occupational Safety and Health Administration*]
IH Industrialized Housing (SAUS)
IH Infantile Hydrocephalus [*Medicine*] (EDAA)
IH Infectious Hepatitis [*Medicine*]
IH Infective Hepatitis [*Medicine*] (EDAA)
IH Informed Homebirth [*Later, IH/IBP*] (EA)
IH Inguinal Hernia [*Gastroenterology*] (DAVI)
IH Inhibit
IH Inhibiting Hormone
IH Inhibitory Hormone (SAUS)
IH In Home [*Men's lacrosse position*]
IH In-House
IH In-House Application (SAUS)
IH Initial Heading
IH Innateness Hypothesis [*Linguistics*]
IH Inner Half (MAE)
IH Inner Housing (COE)
IH Inpatient, Hospital
IH Inside Height
IH Inside Home [*Baseball*]
IH Inspector-General of Hospitals and Fleets [*Navy*] [*British*] (ROG)
IH Inspired Humidity [*Anesthesiology*]
IH Installation Handbook
IH Institute of Housing [*British*]
IH Institute of Hydrology [*Research center*] [*British*]
IH Institute of Hygiene (SAUO)
IH Instrument Head
IH Interaction Handler [*Computer science*] (OA)
IH Interior Height (SAUS)
IH Internationale Horngesellschaft [*International Horn Society*] (EAIO)
IH International Harvester (SAUS)
IH International Harvester Co.
IH International Holdings Corp. (SAUO)
ih International House (SAUO)
IH International Humanism (SAUS)
IH Internet Hub (SAUS)
IH Interrupt Handler [*Computer science*] (IAA)
IH Interval History (SAUS)
IH Intracerebral Haematoma (SAUS)
IH Intracranial Hematome [*Medicine*] (MELL)
IH Inverted Hour (SAUS)
IH Irish Horse [*British military*] (DMA)
IH Iron Hematoxylin [*A dye*]
IH Isme-Dagan Hymn (BJA)
IH Israel's Herald [*A publication*] (BJA)
IH Itavia [*ICAO designator*] (AD)
IH3PA International Home and Private Poker Players Association (EA)
IHa Harvey Public Library, Harvey, IL [*Library symbol*] [*Library of Congress*] (LCLS)
IHA Hydrographic Institute of the Chilean Army (SAUS)
IHA Idaho Hospital Association (SRA)
IHA Idiopathic Hyperaldosteronism [*Medicine*] (DMAA)
IHA Idiopathic Hyperplastic Aldosteronism [*Endocrinology*]
IHA Illinois Hospital and Health Systems Association (SRA)
IHA Immune Hemolytic Anemia [*Medicine*]
IHA Imperial Highway Authority (SAUO)
IHA Independent Hospitals Association [*British*] (DBA)
IHA Indian Housing Authorities (USGC)
IHA Indian Housing Authority [*Department of Housing and Urban Development*] (GFGA)
IHA Indirect Hemagglutination [*Clinical chemistry*]
IHA Indirect Hemagglutination Antibody [*Medicine*] (DMAA)
IHA Individual Housing Account
IHA Infusion Hepatic Angiography [*Medicine*]
IHA Institute of Hospital Administrators [*British*] (BI)
IHA Institute of Hospital Almoners (SAUO)
IHA Integrated Hazards Assessments [*Environmental science*] (COE)
IHA Integrated Healthcare Association (SAUO)
IHA Intel Hub Architecture
IHA Intercept Hydrophone Array (SAUS)
IHA Interfaith Hunger Appeal (EA)
IHA Interim Housing Allowance [*Military*] (AFM)
IHA International Hahnemannian Association [*Defunct*]
IHA International H-Boat Association (SAUO)
IHA International Herb Association (NTPA)
IHA International Hopkins Association
IHA International Horse Association (SAUO)
IHA International Hospitals Association (SAUO)
IHA International Hotel Association [*Paris, France*] (EA)
IHA International House Association [*Defunct*]
IHA International Huntington Association (NRGU)
IHA Iowa Hospitality Association (SRA)
IHA Issuing Houses Association [*British*] [*Defunct*] (DI)
IHA Reese Hospital and Medical Center, Chicago, IL [*OCLC symbol*] (OCLC)
IHAA International Hard Anodizing Association (NTPA)
IHAAS Integrated Helicopter Avionics System (SAUO)
IHAB International Horticultural Advisory Board
IHAB International Horticultural Advisory Bureau (SAUO)
IHAC I Haven't A Clue (VLIE)
IHAC Industrial Health Advisory Council [*British*]
IHACE International Heating and Air-Conditioning Exposition (SAUS)
IHAD I Have a Dream Foundation (EA)
IHADS Integrated Helmet and Display Sight System (SAUO)
IHADSS Integrated Helmet and Display Sight System
IHAF Institut d'Histoire de l'Amerique Francaise [*Institute of French America History*] [*Canada*]
IHAG Integrated Healthcare Advisory Group (SAUO)
IHAH Illustrated Handbooks of Art History [*A publication*]
IHal Ingalls Memorial Hospital, Harvey, IL [*Library symbol*] [*Library of Congress*] (LCLS)
IHAI Institute of Heating and Air-Conditioning Industries
IHAIO International Historical Association of the Indian Ocean (SAUO)
IH&HM Industrial Hygiene and Hazardous Material (SAUS)
IH & HU Industrial Health and Hazards Update [*Merton Allen Associates*] [*Information service or system*] (CRD)
IH & MEE International Hotel and Motel Educational Exposition [*Later, IHM & RS*] (EA)
IH&S Industrial Health and Safety (SAUS)
IH&S Industrial Hygiene and Safety (ABAC)
IH-ANES Inhalation Anesthesia
IHAP Image Handling and Processing (ACAE)
IHAP International Human Assistance Programs (EA)
IHAR Institute for Human-Animal Relationships (SAUS)
IHar Mitchell Carnegie Public Library, Harrisburg, IL [*Library symbol*] [*Library of Congress*] (LCLS)
IHardCSD Calhoun Community Unit, School District 40, Hardin, IL [*Library symbol*] [*Library of Congress*] (LCLS)
IHardR Hardin Reading Center, Hardin, IL [*Library symbol*] [*Library of Congress*] (LCLS)
IHARDS Improved High-Altitude Radiation Detection System (SAUS)
IHart Hartford Public Library, Hartford, IL [*Library symbol*] [*Library of Congress*] (LCLS)
IHAS Icelandic Horse Adventure Society (EA)
IHAS Idiopathic Hypertrophic Aortic Stenosis [*Cardiology*] (DAVI)

IHAS .... Illinois Hearing Aid Society (SRA)
IHAs .... Indian Housing Authorities (SAUS)
IHAS .... Integrated Helicopter Attack System (SAUS)
IHAS .... Integrated Helicopter Avionics System [*Navy*] (NG)
IHAS .... International High Altitude Station (SAUO)
IHAS .... Iowa Hearing Aid Society (SRA)
IHASA .... International Hotel Association South Asia (SAUO)
IHASFC .... International Hearts Air Supply Fan Club [*Defunct*] (EA)
IHAS/ILAAS ... Integrated Helicopter Avionics System / Integrated Light Attack Avionics System [*Navy*] (SAA)
IHAT .... Indirect Haemagglutination Test (SAUS)
IHATIS .... International Hide and Allied Trades Improvement Society
IHAWK .... Improved Homing All the Way Killer [*Missile*]
IHB .... Barnes, Hickam, Pantzer & Boyd, Indianapolis, IN [*OCLC symbol*] (OCLC)
IHB .... Incomplete Heart Block [*Cardiology*] (DAVI)
IHB .... Indiana Harbor Belt Railroad Co. [*AAR code*]
IHB .... Indiana History Bulletin (journ.) (SAUS)
IHB .... Industrial Home for the Blind [*Medicine*] (EDAA)
IHB .... Inhibin [*Biochemistry*]
IHB .... In-House Bid (SAUS)
IHB .... Intermittent Heartburn (MELL)
IHB .... Internationale Hoptrenbaubuero [*International Hop Growers Convention*]
IHB .... International Health Board (SAUO)
IHB .... International Hockey Board (SAUO)
IHB .... International Hydrographic Bureau [*Later, IHO*] [*Monaco*]
IHBC .... International Health and Beauty Council [*British*]
IHBCA .... International H Boat Class Association (EA)
IHBI .... Indian Head Banks, Incorporated (SAUO)
IHBPA .... International Hepato-Biliary-Pancreatic Association (EA)
IHBR .... Indiana Harbor Belt Railroad (SAUO)
IHBS .... International Hajji Baba Society (EA)
IHBT .... Incompatible Hemolytic Blood Transfusion
IHBTD .... Incompatible Haemolytic Blood Transfusion Disease (SAUS)
IHBTD .... Incompatible Hemolytic Blood Transfusion Disease (MAE)
IHC .... Hanover College, Hanover, IN [*OCLC symbol*] (OCLC)
IHC .... Identified Hair Cell (DB)
IHC .... Idiopathic Hemochromatosis [*Medicine*] (CPH)
IHC .... Idiopathic Hypercalcemia [*Medicine*]
IHC .... Idiopathic Hypercalciuria (STED)
IHC .... Immaculate Heart College [*California*]
IHC .... Immobilization Hypercalcemia [*Medicine*] (DAVI)
IHC .... Immunohistochemical
IHC .... Immunohistochemistry
IHC .... Indian Heritage Council (EA)
IHC .... Indian Hospital Corps [*British military*] (DMA)
IHC .... Indirectly Heated Cathode
IHC .... Individuality Hospitality, Courtesy (SAUO)
IHC .... Industrial Hygiene Conference (SAUS)
IHC .... Infant Hypercalcemia [*Medicine*]
IHC .... Inner Hair Cells [*of cochlea*] [*Anatomy*]
IHC .... Institute of Hospital Catering [*Australia*]
IHC .... Intellectually Handicapped Child (SAUS)
IHC .... Intelligence Handling Committee [*Military*]
IHC .... Interactive Health Communication (SAUO)
IHC .... Intercontinental Hotels Corp. (SAUS)
IHC .... Interdepartmental Hurricane Conference (SAUO)
IHC .... Intergranular Hot Cracking (SAUS)
IHC .... Interim Hazard Classification (SAUS)
IHC .... International Harvester Co.
IHC .... International Health Center
IHC .... International Health Conference (SAUO)
IHC .... International Health Consultants (EA)
IHC .... International Health Council (EA)
IHC .... International Help for Children
IHC .... International Hotel Code (SAUO)
IHC .... International Housing Committee (SAUO)
IHC .... International Hug Center [*Defunct*] (EA)
IHC .... International Hunting Council (SAUO)
IHC .... International Joint Commission on Boundary Waters (SAUO)
IHC .... Internet Healthcare Coalition (SAUO)
IHC .... Interstate Highway Capability (SAUO)
IHC .... Intrahepatic Cholestasis (STED)
IHC .... Ionic Heated Cathode
IHCA .... Individual Health Care Account (HCT)
IHCA .... In Hands of Civil Authorities [*Military*]
IHCA .... International Hebrew Christian Alliance [*Ramsgate, Kent, England*] (EA)
IHCA .... International Hobie Class Association (EA)
IHCA .... Isocapnic Hyperventilation with Cold Air [*Medicine*] (DMAA)
IHCC .... Illinois Home Care Council (SRA)
IHCC .... Intensiva HealthCare Corp. [*NASDAQ symbol*] (SAG)
IHCC .... International Harvester Credit Co. (SAUS)
IHCC .... International Harvester Credit Corp. (ADA)
IHCD .... International Holocaust Commemoration Day (SAUS)
IHCF .... Inherited High Cholesterol Foundation (NRGU)
IHCF .... International Healthy Cities Foundation (SAUO)
IHCM .... Idiopathic Hypertrophic Cardiomyopathy [*Cardiology*]
IHCMCB .... International Hazard Control Manager Certification Board (SAUS)
IHCNE .... Institute for Hospital Clinical Nursing Education (EA)
IHCOS .... Isotope-Heated Catalytic Oxidizer System (KSC)
IHCP .... Increment Hazard Control Plan (SPST)
IHCP .... Induction Hardened Chrome Plating (SAUS)
IHCP .... Institute of Health and Consumer Protection (EURO)
IHCP .... Institute on Hospital and Community Psychiatry (EA)
IHCP .... International Handbook on Coal Petrology (SAUS)
IHCPV .... Initial Hydrocarbon Pore Volume [*Petroleum technology*]
IHCS .... Integrated Helicopter Control System (SAUO)
IHCS .... Interactive Health Care System (SAUS)
IHCSERS .... International Health Centre of Socio-Economics Researches and Studies [*See also CIERSES*] [*Lailly En Val, France*] (EAIO)
IHD .... American Hospital Association Library, Chicago, IL [*OCLC symbol*] (OCLC)
IHD .... In-Center Hemodialysis [*Medicine*] (DMAA)
IHD .... Indian Head, Inc. (SAUO)
IHD .... Indian Head, PA [*Location identifier*] [*FAA*] (FAAL)
IHD .... Institute of Human Development [*University of California, Berkeley*] [*Research center*] (RCD)
IHD .... Institut Henry-Dunant [*Henry Dunant Institute*] [*Geneva, Switzerland*] (EAIO)
IHD .... Integrated Help Desk (SAUS)
IHD .... Integration a Haut Degre (SAUS)
IHD .... International Hard Suits [*Vancouver Stock Exchange symbol*]
IHD .... International Health Division (SAUO)
IHD .... International Hydrological Decade [*UNESCO*] [*Later, IHP*]
IHD .... Intrahepatic Duct [*or Ductule*] [*Gastroenterology*] (DAVI)
IHD .... Ischemic Heart Disease
IHDA .... Illinois Housing and Development Authority (SAUO)
IHDA .... International Hardware Distributors Association (NTPA)
IH Day .... Incredible Heating Day (SAUS)
IHDI .... International Hearing Dog, Inc. (EA)
IHDP .... Independent Hungarian Democratic Party [*Political party*] [*Hungary*] (EAIO)
IHDP .... Infant Health and Development Program
IHDP .... International Human Dimensions of Global Change Programme
IHDP .... International Human Dimensions Program on Global Environmental Change (QUAC)
IHDRT .... Interim High-Data Rate Terminal (CAAL)
IHDS .... Institute for Higher Defense Studies [*National Defense University*]
IHDS .... Integrated Health Delivery System (SAUO)
IHDS .... Integrated Helmet Display System
IHDS .... Interstate Highway and Defense System (SAUS)
IHDT .... Integrated Helicopter Design Tool
IHE .... Evanston Public Library, Evanston, IL [*OCLC symbol*] (OCLC)
IHE .... Improved High Explosive (SAUS)
IHE .... Improved High Explosivemainly (SAUS)
IHE .... Induction Heating Equipment (SAUS)
IHE .... Industry, Human Settlements and Environment Division (SAUO)
IHE .... Insensitive High Explosive (MCD)
IHE .... Institute for the Human Environment (EA)
IHE .... Institute of Higher Education
IHE .... Institute of Highway Engineers [*British*]
IHE .... Institute of Home Economics [*of ARS, Department of Agriculture*]
IHE .... Institute of Hospital Engineering (EAIO)
IHE .... Institutes of Higher Education (SAUS)
IHE .... Institution of Highway Engineers (SAUO)
IHE .... Institutions of Higher Education (SAUS)
IHE .... Intergranular Hydrogen Embrittlement [*Metallurgy*]
IHE .... Intermediate Heat Exchanger [*Nuclear energy*]
IHE .... Internal Hydrogen Embrittlement (SAUS)
IHE .... International Historic Enterprises
IHE .... International Institute for Hydraulic and Environmental Engineering [*Netherlands Universities Foundation for International Cooperation*] [*Research center*]
IHE .... International Institute for Hydrologic and Environmental Engineering (SAUO)
IHE .... International Institute for Infrastructure, Hydraulic and Environmental Engineering (SAUS)
IHE .... Interservice Home Exchange [*Commercial firm*] (EA)
IHEA .... Industrial Health Engineering Association (SAUO)
IHEA .... Industrial Heating Equipment Association (EA)
IHEA .... International Health Economics Association (SAUO)
IHEA .... International Health Evaluation Association (EA)
IHEAL .... Interactive Health Ecology Access Links (SAUO)
IHEB .... International Heat Economy Bureau (SAUO)
IHEC .... American Indian Higher Education Consortium (SAUO)
IHEc .... Institute of Home Economics [*British*] (DBA)
IHEEM .... Institute of Healthcare Engineering & Estate Management (WDAA)
IHEI .... Interhome Energy (SAUS)
IHEI .... Interhome Energy, Inc. (SAUO)
IHEIF .... Interhome Energy, Inc. [*NASDAQ symbol*] (COMM)
IHEIP .... International Human Rights Internship Programme (SAUO)
IHEM .... In-House Energy Management (SAUS)
IHEMI .... International Health Economics and Management Institute (EA)
IHen .... Henry Public Library, Henry, IL [*Library symbol*] [*Library of Congress*] (LCLS)
IHenn .... Putnam County Library, Hennepin, IL [*Library symbol*] [*Library of Congress*] (LCLS)
IHennC .... Hennepin Attendance Center, Hennepin, IL [*Library symbol*] [*Library of Congress*] (LCLS)
IHenn-G .... Putnam County Library, Granville Branch, Granville, IL [*Library symbol*] [*Library of Congress*] (LCLS)
IHenn-H .... Putnam County Library, Hennepin Branch, Hennepin, IL [*Library symbol*] [*Library of Congress*] (LCLS)
IHenn-M .... Putnam County Library, Magnolia Branch, Magnolia, IL [*Library symbol*] [*Library of Congress*] (LCLS)
IHenn-Mc .... Putnam County Library, McNabb Branch, McNabb, IL [*Library symbol*] [*Library of Congress*] (LCLS)

IHenn-P .... Putnam County Library, Condit Branch, Putnam, IL [*Library symbol*] [*Library of Congress*] (LCLS)
IHenn-S .... Putnam County Library, Standard Branch, Standard, IL [*Library symbol*] [*Library of Congress*] (LCLS)
IHEP .... Improved Head-End Processing (SAUS)
IHEP .... Insensitive High Explosives and Propellants [*DoD/DOE program*] (RDA)
IHEP .... Institute for High-Energy Physics [*China*]
IHEP .... Institute for Higher Education Policy
IHEP .... Institute of High Energy Physics [*Former USSR*]
IHERC .... Inter-Hemispheric Education Resource Center (EA)
IHERC .... Inter-Hemispheric Resource Center (EA)
IHERS .... Institute of Higher Education Research and Services [*University of Alabama*] [*Research center*] (RCD)
IHES .... Idiopathic Hypereosinophilic Syndrome [*Medicine*] (DMAA)
IHES .... Illinois Horticultural Experiment Station (SAUO)
IHET .... Industrial Heat Exchanger Technology (SAUS)
IHETA .... Institute of Health Economics and Technology Assessment (SAUS)
IHETS .... Indiana Higher Education Telecommunication System [*Indianapolis*] [*Telecommunications*] (TSSD)
IHEU .... In-House Equipment Utilization (SAUO)
IHEU .... International Humanist and Ethical Union [*Utrecht, Netherlands*] (EA)
IHEWS .... Integrated Helicopter EWS Suite (SAUS)
IHF .... Improved High Explosive [*Military*] (MUSM)
IHF .... Independent Health Food (SAUS)
IHF .... Independent High Frequency (IAA)
IHF .... Industrial Health Foundation (EA)
IHF .... Industrial Hygiene Foundation of America
IHF .... Inhibit Halt Flip-Flop [*Computer science*]
IHF .... Inspection Holding Fixture (MCD)
IHF .... Institute of Gas Technology, Chicago, IL [*OCLC symbol*] (OCLC)
IHF .... Institute of High Fidelity [*Formerly, IHFM*] [*Later, EIA*] (EA)
IHF .... Institute of High Fidelity Inc. (SAUO)
IHF .... Integrated Hazard Function
IHF .... Integration Host Factor [*Genetics*]
IHF .... Interesting Historic Figure (SAUS)
IHF .... Intermediate High Frequency (IIA)
IHF .... International Handball Federation [*Basel, Switzerland*] (EA)
IHF .... International Harvester France (SAUO)
IHF .... International Health Foundation [*Brussels, Belgium*] (EAIO)
IHF .... International Helicopter Foundation [*Later, HFI*] (EA)
IHF .... International Helsinki Federation for Human Rights (ECON)
IHF .... International Hockey Federation (BARN)
IHF .... International Home Foods [*NYSE symbol*] (SG)
IHF .... International Hospital Federation (EA)
IHF .... International Lawn Hockey Federation
IHF .... Inverse Hyperbolic Function
IHF .... Irish Heritage Foundation (EA)
IHF .... Irish Hotels Federation (EAIO)
IHF .... Isothermal (SAUS)
IHF .... Isothermal Heating Furnace
IHF .... Israel Histadrut Foundation (EA)
IHFA .... Industrial Hygiene Foundation of America (SAUS)
IHFA .... Industrial Hygiene Foundation of America, Inc. (SAUO)
IHFAS .... Integrated High-Frequency Antenna System
IHFBC .... International High Frequency Broadcasting Conference (SAUO)
IHFF .... Inhibit Halt Flip-Flop [*Computer science*] (MSA)
IHFHR .... International Helsinki Federation for Human Rights (EA)
IHFIAW .... International Association of Heat and Frost Insulators and Asbestos Workers (SAUO)
IHFM .... Institute of High Fidelity Manufacturers [*Later, IHF*]
IHFMA .... International Home Furnishings Marketing Association (EA)
IHFR .... Improved High-Frequency Radio (INF)
IHFR .... Institute of Health Food Retailing [*British*] (DBA)
IHFRA .... International Home Furnishings Representatives Association (EA)
IHG .... Ichthyosis Hystrix Gravior (STED)
IHG .... Immunoreactive Human Gastrin [*Medicine*] (EDAA)
IHG .... Independent Honeywell Group (SAUO)
IHG .... Internationale Hegel Gesellschaft (EA)
IHG .... Skokie Public Library, Skokie, IL [*OCLC symbol*] (OCLC)
IHGA .... International Hop Growers Association (SAUO)
IHGC .... International Hop Growers Convention [*See also CICH*] [*Zalec, Yugoslavia*] (EAIO)
IHGD .... Isolateral Human Growth Deficiency [*Medicine*] (DMAA)
IHGF .... Immobilized pH Gradient Isoelectric Focusing (SAUS)
IHGMA .... International Herb Growers and Marketers Association [*Defunct*] (EA)
IHGP .... International Human Genome Project (SAUO)
IHGS .... Institute of Heraldic and Genealogical Studies [*British*]
IHGT .... Institute for Human Gene Therapy (SAUO)
IHh .... Eisenhower Public Library District, Harwood Heights, IL [*Library symbol*] [*Library of Congress*] (LCLS)
IHH .... Huntington College, Huntington, IN [*OCLC symbol*] (OCLC)
IHH .... Idiopathic Hypogonadotropic Hypogonadism [*Endocrinology*]
IHH .... Illinois Happy Hollow (SAUO)
IHH .... Infectious Human Hepatitis [*Medicine*] (DMAA)
IHHA .... Indiana Hospital and Health Association (SRA)
IHHA .... International Halfway House Association (EA)
IHHI .... In Home Health, Inc. [*NASDAQ symbol*] (NQ)
IHHNV .... Infectious Hypodermal and Hematopoietic Necrosis Virus [*Aquaculture*]
IHHO .... Institute of Home Help Organisers [*British*]
IHHRR .... International Health Human Resources Registry (SAUO)
IHHS .... Idiopathic Hyperkinetic Heart Syndrome [*Medicine*] (DMAA)
IHHS .... Improved Hawk Hardware Simulation (ACAE)
IHHSF .... International Habitat and Human Settlement Foundation (SAUO)
IHi .... Illinois State Historical Library, Springfield, IL [*Library symbol*] [*Library of Congress*] (LCLS)
IHI .... Impact of Hypertension Information Study [*Department of Health and Human Services*] (GFGA)
IHI .... Improved Holographic Image
IHI .... Index to Health Information (ADWA)
IHI .... Information Holdings [*NYSE symbol*] (SG)
IHI .... Institute for Healthcare Improvement (DMAA)
IHI .... Integrated Hit Indicator
IHI .... Internet Health Information [*Medicine*] (EDAA)
IHI .... Ishikawajima-Harima Heavy Industries Co. Ltd. [*Japan*]
IHI .... Lincoln Trail Libraries System, Champaign, IL [*OCLC symbol*] (OCLC)
IHIA .... Include This Headquarters Information Addressee [*Army*] (AABC)
IHIA .... International Health Industries Association (EA)
IH/IBP .... Informed Homebirth/Informed Birth and Parenting (EA)
IHI Bull .... IHI Bulletin (journ.) (SAUS)
Ihic .... International Holding and Investment Company S.A., Luxembourg (SAUO)
IHIC .... International Hydrocarbon Intercomparison Committee (QUAC)
IHIE .... Institute of Highway Incorporated Engineers [*British*] (EAIO)
IHI Eng Rev ... IHI Engineering Review (journ.) (SAUS)
IHig .... Louis Latzer Memorial Library, Highland, IL [*Library symbol*] [*Library of Congress*] (LCLS)
IHigp .... Highland Park Public Library, Highland Park, IL [*Library symbol*] [*Library of Congress*] (LCLS)
IHigSD .... Highland Community Unit, School District 5, Highland, IL [*Library symbol*] [*Library of Congress*] (LCLS)
IHII .... Independent Health Insurance Institute [*Inactive*] (EA)
IHII .... Industrial Holdings [*NASDAQ symbol*] (TTSB)
IHII .... Industrial Holdings, Inc. [*NASDAQ symbol*] (SAG)
IHIIW .... Industrial Holdgs Wrrt'A' [*NASDAQ symbol*] (TTSB)
IHIIZ .... Industrial Hldgs Wrrt'B' [*NASDAQ symbol*] (TTSB)
IHil .... Hillside Public Library, Hillside, IL [*Library symbol*] [*Library of Congress*] (LCLS)
IHilb .... Hillsboro Public Library, Hillsboro, IL [*Library symbol*] [*Library of Congress*] (LCLS)
IHilbGC .... John A. Graham Correctional Center, Hillsboro, IL [*Library symbol*] [*Library of Congress*] (LCLS)
IHilbSD .... Hillsboro Community Unit, School District 3, Hillsboro, IL [*Library symbol*] [*Library of Congress*] (LCLS)
IHineJ .... John J. Madden Mental Health Center, Training Staff Development Library, Hines, IL [*Library symbol*] [*Library of Congress*] (LCLS)
IHineV .... United States Veterans Administration Hospital, Hines, IL [*Library symbol*] [*Library of Congress*] (LCLS)
IHIPIR .... Improved High-Power Illuminator RADAR [*IHAWK Missile*] (MCD)
IHIS .... Integrated Hit Indicator System
IHIS .... Integrated Hospital Information System (DMAA)
IHIS .... Interactive Healthcare Information System (SAUS)
IHISS .... Improved Helicopter Icing Spray System (SAUS)
IHIT .... Industrial Hygienist in Training (SARE)
IHIYX .... IDEX II: Income Plus Cl.A [*Mutual fund ticker symbol*] (SG)
IHJ .... International Heroines of Jericho [*Later, General Conference of Grand Courts Heroines of Jericho, Prince Hall Affiliation, USA*] (EA)
IHK .... Imperial Holly Corp. [*AMEX symbol*] (SPSG)
IHK .... Imperial Sugar [*AMEX symbol*] (SG)
IHK .... International Homestock Resources Ltd. [*Vancouver Stock Exchange symbol*]
IHK .... Ionic Heated Kathode
IHKSV .... Imperial Holly Corp. [*NYSE symbol*] (COMM)
IHL .... Illinois Health Libraries Consortium [*Library network*]
IHL .... Imperial Light Horse [*Military*] [*British*] (ROG)
IHL .... Imprisonment with Hard Labor (SAUS)
Ihl .... Inhalation [*Medicine*] (EDAA)
IHL .... International Hockey League (EA)
IHL .... International Homeopathic League
IHL .... International Humanitarian Law (SAUO)
IHL .... Internet Header Length [*Computer science*] (ACRL)
IHLC .... International Humanitarian Law Commission (SAUO)
IHLCADS .... Interim High-Level Container Airdrop System
IHLS .... International Herring Larvae Survey
IHLZY .... Ichud Habonim Labor Zionist Youth (EA)
IHM .... Brothers of the Immaculate Heart of Mary (TOCD)
ihm .... Brothers of the Immaculate Heart of Mary (TOCD)
IHM .... [*The*] California Institute of the Sisters of the Most Holy and Immaculate Heart of the Blessed Virgin Mary (TOCD)
IHM .... Daughters of the Immaculate Heart of Mary [*Roman Catholic religious order*]
i-hm- .... Heard and McDonald Islands [*MARC geographic area code*] [*Library of Congress*] (LCCP)
IHM .... Images from the History of Medicine (SAUO)
IHM .... Imitation Handmade Paper (DGA)
IHM .... Institute of Hotel Marketing (SAUO)
IHM .... Institute of Housing Managers [*British*] (BI)
IHM .... Interactive Hydrographic Map (SAUO)
IHM .... Interface Home Machine (SAUS)
IHM .... Mansfield, MA [*Location identifier*] [*FAA*] (FAAL)
IHM .... Sister Servants of the Immaculate Heart of Mary of Scranton (SAUO)
IHM .... Sisters of the Immaculate Heart of Mary [*California Institute of the Most Holy and Immaculate Heart of the BVM*] [*Roman Catholic religious order*]
IHM .... Sisters of the Most Holy and Immaculate Heart of Blessed Virgin Mary (Wichita Foundation) (TOCD)

IHM .... Sisters, Servants of the Immaculate Heart of Mary [*Roman Catholic religious order*]
IHMA .... Indiana Hotel and Motel Association (SRA)
IHMA .... Industrial Housing Manufacturers Association (SAUS)
IHMA .... Industrialized Housing Manufacturers Association (SAUS)
IHMA .... International Hazardous Materials Association (NTPA)
IHM & RS .... International Hotel/Motel and Restaurant Show (EA)
IHMDE .... Imitation Handmade Deckle Edges Paper (DGA)
IHMEE .... International Hotel and Motel Educational Exposition (SAUO)
IHMF .... International Herpes Management Forum
IHMI .... Institute for Housing Management Innovations (EA)
IHMM .... Institute of Hazardous Materials Management (NTPA)
IHMSA .... International Handgun Metallic Silhouette Association (EA)
IHM-SBF .... Insan Haklari Merkezi, Siyasal Bilgiler Fakueltesi [*Turkey*]
IHMZ .... Indian Head Mining [*Federal Railroad Administration identification code*]
IHN .... Iliohypogastric Nerve [*Medicine*] (MELL)
IHN .... Infectious Hematopoietic Necrosis [*Fish pathology*]
IHN .... In His Name
IHN .... Integrated Delivery Networks [*Health care provider*]
IHN .... International Handicappers' Net (EA)
IHN .... Iron Horse Resources, Inc. [*Vancouver Stock Exchange symbol*]
IHNI .... Iatros Health Network [*NASDAQ symbol*] (TTSB)
IHNI .... Iatros Health Network, Inc. [*NASDAQ symbol*] (SAG)
IHNIW .... Iatros Health Network Wrrt [*NASDAQ symbol*] (TTSB)
IHo .... Hoopestown Public Library, Hoopestown, IL [*Library symbol*] [*Library of Congress*] (LCLS)
IHO .... Idiopathic Hypertrophic Osteoarthropathy [*Medicine*]
IHO .... Impartial Hearing Officer
IHO .... Impeded Harmonic Operation
IHO .... In Honor Of
IHO .... In-House Operation (SAUS)
IHO .... Inorganic Halogen Oxidizer
IHO .... Inspection Hold Order (SAUS)
IHO .... Institute of Human Origins (EA)
IHO .... Integrated Healthcare Organization (ADWA)
IHO .... International Health Organization (SAUO)
IHO .... International Hydrographic Association (SAUS)
IHO .... International Hydrographic Organization [*See also BHI*] [*Monaco*]
IHOC .... Incoherent light Hybrid Optical Correlator (SAUS)
IHOC .... International Healthcare Opportunities Clearinghouse (SAUO)
IHod .... Hodgkins Public Library District, Hodgkins, IL [*Library symbol*] [*Library of Congress*] (LCLS)
IHoF .... Vermilion County Elementary Film Library, Hoopeston, IL [*Library symbol*] [*Library of Congress*] (LCLS)
IHoH .... Hoopestown Community Memorial Hospital, Hoopestown, IL [*Library symbol*] [*Library of Congress*] (LCLS)
IHom .... Homer Community Library, Homer, IL [*Library symbol*] [*Library of Congress*] (LCLS)
IHOP .... IHOP Corp. [*NASDAQ symbol*] (SAG)
IHOP .... International House of Pancakes [*Restaurant chain*] [*Pronounced "eye-hop"*]
IHOP .... Isophosphamide, Hydroxydaunomycin [*Adriamycn*], Oncovin , Prednisone [*Vincristine*] [*Antineoplastic drug regimen*] (DAVI)
IHOPCp .... IHOP Corp. [*Associated Press*] (SAG)
IHospE .... Institute of Hospital Engineering (COBU)
IHOSPE .... Institute of Hospital Engineering (PDAA)
IHot .... Hometown Public Library, Hometown, IL [*Library symbol*] [*Library of Congress*] (LCLS)
IHOU .... Institute of Home Office Underwriters [*Louisville, KY*] (EA)
IHow .... Homewood Public Library, Homewood, IL [*Library symbol*] [*Library of Congress*] (LCLS)
IHP .... Hammond Public Library, Hammond, IN [*OCLC symbol*] (OCLC)
IHP .... Idiopathic Hypoparathyroidism [*Medicine*]
IHP .... Idiopathic Hypopituitarism [*Medicine*] (AAMN)
IHP .... IHOP Corp [*NYSE symbol*]
IHP .... Illinois Home Page (SAUO)
ihp .... Indicated Horsepower (ADWA)
IHP .... Indicated Horsepower
IHP .... Individualized Habilitation Plan
IHP .... Information Handling Panel (SAUS)
IHP .... Information Handling Project (DIT)
IHP .... Inner Helmholtz Plane (IAA)
IHP .... Inositol Hexaphosphate [*Biochemistry*]
IHP .... Institute for Human Progress [*Defunct*]
IHP .... Institutional Hearing Program (SAUS)
IHP .... Instrumentation Habitability Power (MCD)
IHP .... Integral Horsepower (SAUS)
IHP .... Integrated Humanities Program (SAUS)
IHP .... Intergovernmental Council for the International Hydrological Programme (EA)
IHP .... International Hydrographic Program
IHP .... International Hydrological Program [*UNESCO*] [*France*]
IHP .... Interrupt Handling Process (SAUS)
IHP .... Inverted Hand Position [*Neuropsychology*]
IHP .... Isostatic Hot Pressing (PDAA)
IHPA .... Illinois Historic Preservation Agency (SAUO)
IHPA .... Imported Hardwood Plywood Association (SAUO)
IHPA .... International Hand Protection Association (NTPA)
IHPA .... International Hardwood Products Association (EA)
IHPBA .... International Hepato-Pancreato-Biliary Association (EA)
IHPC .... International Hydrolyzed Protein Council (EA)
IHPC .... Intrahepatic Cholestasis [*Medicine*] (DMAA)
IHPD .... International Health Physics Data Base [*Creative Information Systems, Inc.*] [*Information service or system*] (CRD)
IHPF .... Ideal High-Pass Filter (SAUS)
IHPH .... Indicated Horsepower-Hour
IHPH .... Intrahepatic Portal Hypertension [*Medicine*] (MAE)
IHP-HR .... Indicated Horsepower-Hour
IHPI .... IHS [*Information Handling Services*] Product/Subject Index [*Information service or system*] (CRD)
IHPI .... Improved High Power Illumination (SAUS)
IHPI .... Improved High-Power Illuminator (CAAL)
IHPM .... Institute for Health and Productivity Management (SAUO)
IHPMI .... International Health Policy and Management Institute (EAIO)
IHP Motor .... Integral Horsepower Motor (SAUS)
IHPO .... International Health Program Office [*Atlanta, GA*] [*Department of Health and Human Services*] (GRD)
IHP/OHP .... International Hydrological Program/Operation Hydrological Program (SAUS)
IHPP .... Intergovernmental Health Policy Project (EA)
IHPP .... International Health Policy Program (SAUO)
IHPR .... Institute of Health Promotion Research (ADWA)
IH Pr .... International Hydro-Electrical System (SAUS)
IHPRPT .... Integrated High Payoff Rocket Propulsion Technology
IHPRS .... International Husserl and Phenomenological Research Society (EA)
IHPS .... Infantile Hypertrophic Pyloric Stenosis [*Medicine*]
IHPS .... Intelligence Host Processing System (SAUS)
IHPST .... Institute for the History and Philosophy of Science and Technology [*University of Toronto*] [*Canada*] (IRC)
IHPTEP .... Integrated High-Performance Turbine Engine Program (SAUS)
IHPTET .... Integrated High-Performance Turbine Engine Technology Initiative [*NASA and DOD*]
IHPTET .... Intermediate High Performance Turbine Engine Technology (SAUS)
IHPVA .... International Human Powered Vehicle Association (EA)
IHQ .... Indian History Quarterly (journ.) (SAUS)
IHQ .... International Headquarters (DNAB)
IHQ .... Rolling Prairie Libraries, Decatur, IL [*OCLC symbol*] (OCLC)
IH/QAS .... Indian Head [*Maryland*] - Quality Assurance Department [*Naval ordnance station*]
IHR .... Carl Sandburg College, LRC, Galesburg, IL [*OCLC symbol*] (OCLC)
IHR .... Cocoa, FL [*Location identifier*] [*FAA*] (FAAL)
IHR .... Increased Hazard Rate
IHR .... Infrared Heterodyne Radiometer
IHR .... Institute for Historical Research
IHR .... Institute for Historical Review (EA)
IHR .... Institute of Horticultural Research [*Research center*] [*British*] (IRC)
IHR .... International Heart Relief (SAUO)
IHR .... Internet Health Resources (SAUO)
IHR .... Intrahepatic Resistance [*Medicine*] (MAE)
IHR .... Intrinsic Heart Rate [*Cardiology*]
IHR .... Ishihara [*Japan*] [*Seismograph station code, US Geological Survey*] [*Closed*] (SEIS)
IHRA .... Increasing Hazard Rate Average
IHRA .... Independent Human Rights Association (SAUO)
IHRA .... International Harm Reduction Association (SAUO)
IHRA .... International Hot Rod Association (EA)
IHRB .... Industrial Health Research Board [*British*]
IHRB .... Institute of Historical Research, Bulletin (journ.) (SAUS)
IHRB .... International Hockey Rules Board (SAUO)
IHRBI .... Hotot Rabbit Breeders International (SAUO)
IHRBLR .... International Human Resources, Business, and Legal Research Association (EA)
IHRC .... Illinois Human Rights Commission (SAUO)
IHRC .... Immigration History Research Center [*University of Minnesota*] [*Research center*] (RCD)
IHRC .... Indiana Hi-Rail [*Federal Railroad Administration identification code*]
IHRC .... In-Home Respite Care
IH/RE .... Indian Head Research and Development Department [*Naval Ordnance Station*] [*Maryland*]
IHRG .... Interdisciplinary Health Research Group [*See also GRIS*] [*Universite de Montreal*] [*Canada*] [*Research center*]
IHRIM .... International Association for Human Resource Information Management (NTPA)
IHRIP .... International Human Rights Internship Programme (SAUO)
IHRLA .... International Human Rights Law Group (SAUO)
IHRLG .... International Human Rights Law Group (EA)
IHRMA .... Irish Hotel and Restaurant Managers' Association (BI)
IHRN .... International Health Research Network (SAUO)
IHRR .... Institute for Human Rights (EA)
IHRR .... Institute for Human Rights Research (EA)
IHRSA .... International Health Racquet, and Sportsclub Association (NTPA)
IHRWG .... Iranian Human Rights Working Group (EA)
IHS .... Fort Carson, CO [*Location identifier*] [*FAA*] (FAAL)
IHS .... Idiopathic Headache Score [*Neurology*] (DAVI)
IHS .... Iesous Hemeteros Soter [*Jesus, Our Savior*] [*Greek*]
IHS .... Iesus Heiland Seligmacher [*Jesus, Savior, Sanctifier*] [*German*]
IHS .... Iesus Hominum Salvator [*Jesus, Savior of Mankind*] [*Latin*] (ADA)
IHS .... Immigration Historical Society (SAUO)
IHS .... Immigration History Society (EA)
IHS .... Improved HAWK Simulator [*Military*]
IHS .... Inactivated Horse Serum [*Immunology*]
IHS .... Inclined Heterolithic Stratification [*Geology*]
IHS .... Independent Hemopathic Syndrome (SAUS)
IHS .... Indescor Hydrodynamics, Inc. [*Vancouver Stock Exchange symbol*]
IHS .... Indiana Horticultural Society (SAUO)
IHS .... Indian Health Service
IHS .... Industrial Health and Safety Committee (SAUO)
IHS .... Information Handling Services [*Englewood, CO*]
IHS .... Information Handling System (SAUO)

IHS.............. Information Highway Secretariat (FOTI)
IHS.............. Infrared Homing System (AAG)
IHS.............. Infrared Horizon Sensor
IHS.............. In Hoc Signo (Vinces) [*In This Sign (You Will Conquer)*] [*Latin*]
IHS.............. Institute for Housing Studies (SAUO)
IHS.............. Institute for Housing Urban Development Studies [*Netherlands*]
IHS.............. Institute for Humane Studies, Inc. [*Research center*] (RCD)
IHS.............. Institute for Hydrogen Studies (SAUS)
IHS.............. Institute for Hydrogen Systems [*UTLAS symbol*]
IHS.............. Institute of Health Sciences (SAUO)
IHS.............. Institute of Home Safety [*British*] (DBA)
IHS.............. Institute of Human Sciences (SAUO)
IHS.............. Institute of Hypertension Studies (SAUO)
IHS.............. Institute of Hypertension Studies - Institute of Hypertension School of Research[*Later, NIHS*] (EA)
IHS.............. Integrated Headgear Subsystem [*Army*] (RDA)
IHS.............. Integrated Health Services, Inc. [*NYSE symbol*] (SPSG)
IHS.............. Integrated Heat Sink (PDAA)
IHS.............. Integrated Home Systems (EURO)
IHS.............. Integrated Hospital Support (SAUS)
IHS.............. Integrated Hospital System (SAUS)
IHS.............. Intellectually Handicapped Society (SAUS)
IHS.............. Intensity, Hue, Saturation (SAUS)
IHS.............. Interactive Home System (PDAA)
IHS.............. International Haemophilia Society (SAUO)
IHS.............. International Headache Society (SAUO)
IHS.............. International Health Society (EA)
IHS.............. International Hearing Society (PAZ)
IHS.............. International Heliospheric Study (CARB)
IHS.............. International Heritage Site [*UNESCO*]
IHS.............. International Hibernation Society (EA)
IHS.............. International Horn Society (EA)
IHS.............. International Hurling Society
IHS.............. International Hydrofoil Society (EAIO)
IHS.............. Interrupt Handling System (SAUS)
IHS.............. Interstate Highway System (SAUS)
IHS.............. Intrahepatic Arteriovenous Shunt [*Medicine*]
IHS.............. Ipco Hospital Supply Corp. (SAUO)
IHs.............. Iris Hamartoma [*Oncology*] (DAVI)
IHS.............. Irish Historical Studies (SAUO)
IHS.............. Irish Historical Studies (journ.) (SAUS)
IHS.............. Irish Hospitals Sweepstakes (SAUS)
IHS.............. Isotope Heat Source
IHS.............. Italian Historical Society of America (EA)
IHS.............. Ivory Hunters Society (SAUO)
IHS.............. Suburban Library System, Hinsdale, IL [*Library symbol*] [*Library of Congress*] (LCLS)
IHS.............. University of Texas, Health Science Center at Dallas, Dallas, TX [*OCLC symbol*] (OCLC)
IHSA............ Institute of Health Service Administrators (SAUO)
IHSA............ Intercollegiate Horse Show Association (EA)
IHSA............ International Headquarters of the Salvation Army (EA)
IHSA............ Intervention on the High Seas Act (COE)
IHSA............ Iodinated Human Serum Albumin
IHSA............ Italian Historical Society of America (SAUO)
IHSB............ Industrial Health and Safety Branch (SAUS)
IHSB............ In-Flight Helmet Stowage Bag (KSC)
IHSBR.......... Improved High-Speed Bombing RADAR
IHSC............ Immunoreactive Human Skin Collagenase [*Medicine*] (DB)
IHSC............ InSight Health Services Corp. [*NASDAQ symbol*] (SAG)
IHSC............ International Headquarters & Support Command (SAUS)
IHSD............ Inertial Height Sensing Device
IHSD............ In-House Systems Developer [*Personal computer*] (PCM)
IHSDC.......... Irish Health Services Development Corp.
IHSEC.......... Illinois Hunters Safety Education Course (SAUO)
IHSG............ Internationale Heinrich Schutz-Gesellschaft [*International Heinrich Schutz Society*] (EAIO)
IHSGB.......... Icelandic Horse Society [*British*] (DBA)
IHSI............ Induction Heating Stress Improvement [*Nuclear energy*] (NUCP)
IHSM............ Institute for High Speed Mechanics (SAUS)
IHSM............ Institute of Health Services Management (DBA)
IHSPCB........ International Healthcare Safety Professional Certification Board (EA)
IHSPRG........ International Herbage Seed Production Research Group (SAUO)
IHSR............ Improved High Speed Rail (PDAA)
IHSR............ Institute for Health Services Research [*Tulane University*] [*Research center*] (RCD)
IH/SR.......... Integration Hardware and Software Review (MCD)
IHSRC.......... International Heat Stress Research Center [*Sudan*] (IRC)
IHSS............ Idiopathic Hypertrophic Subaortic Stenosis [*Medicine*]
IHSS............ In-Home Supportive Services (SAUS)
IHSS............ In-Home Support Services [*Medicine*] (MEDA)
IHSS............ Institute of Human Science and Services [*University of Rhode Island*] [*Research center*] (RCD)
IHSS............ Integrated Hydrographic Survey System (PDAA)
IHSS............ International Heinrich Schutz Society [*See also IHSG*] [*Germany*] (EA)
IHSS............ International Humic Substances Society
IHST............ Institute for Halieutic Sciences and Techniques (SAUS)
IHT.............. Icelandic Horse Trekkers (EA)
IHT.............. Ideal Handler Time (AAEL)
IHT.............. Impact Hand Tool
IHT.............. Indirect Hemagglutination Test (SAUS)
IHT.............. Inheritance Tax [*British*]
IHT.............. Innsuites Hospitality SBI [*Formerly, Realty Refund SBI*] [*NYSE symbol*]
IHT.............. Inspection Hold Tag
IHT.............. Institute of Handicraft Teachers (SAUO)
IHT.............. Institute of Heat Technology
IHT.............. Institution of Highways and Transportation [*British*] (DBA)
IHT.............. Insulin Hypoglycemia Test [*Endocrinology*] (DAVI)
IHT.............. Integrated Hydrostatic Transmission [*Automotive engineering*]
IHT.............. Intermittent Hormone Therapy [*Medicine*]
IHT.............. International Association of Health and Therapy Instruments [*Japan*] (EAIO)
IHT.............. International Herald Tribune [*A publication*]
IHT.............. Intravenous Histamine Test [*Clinical Medicine*] (MAE)
IHT.............. Ipsilateral Head Turning [*Medicine*] (EDAA)
IHT.............. Trinity Evangelical Divinity School, Rolfing Memorial Library, Deerfield, IL [*OCLC symbol*] (OCLC)
IHTA............ International Health and Temperance Association (EA)
IH-TAS.......... Improved HAWK-Tracking Adjunct System [*Military*] (MCD)
IHTC............ International Heat Transfer Conference (SAUO)
IHTD............ Improved HAWK Training Detachment
IHTS............ Integrated Hybrid Transistor Switch (PDAA)
IHTS............ Intermediate Heat Transport System [*Nuclear energy*] (NRCH)
IHTTA.......... International High-Technology Training Association (EA)
IHTU............ Interservice Hovercraft Trials Unit [*Military*]
IHTV............ Interim Hypersonics Test Vehicle [*NASA*] (NASA)
IHU.............. Chicago Mercantile Exchange, Chicago, IL [*OCLC symbol*] (OCLC)
IHU.............. Ihu [*Papua New Guinea*] [*Airport symbol*] (OAG)
IHU.............. Impaired Hepatic Uptake [*Medicine*] (MELL)
IHU.............. Instantaneous Unit Hydrograph (PDAA)
IHU.............. Integrated Helmet Unit (SAUS)
IHU.............. Interferon Reference Unit (SAUS)
IHU.............. Interservice Hovercraft Unit [*Military*]
IHU.............. Irish Hockey Union (SAUO)
IHUMS.......... Integrated Health & Usage Monitoring System (SAUS)
IHumSD........ Shiloh Community Unit School District, Hume, IL [*Library symbol*] [*Library of Congress*] (LCLS)
IHuSD.......... Hutsonville Community Unit, School District 1, Hutsonville, IL [*Library symbol*] [*Library of Congress*] (LCLS)
IHV.............. Highland Park Public Library, Highland Park, IL [*OCLC symbol*] (OCLC)
IHV.............. Independent Hardware Vendor [*Computer science*] (CDE)
IHV.............. Institute of Human Values [*See also IMH*] [*Canada*]
IHV.............. Institute of Human Virology [*University of Maryland*]
IHV.............. Internationale Hegel-Vereinigung [*Munich, Federal Republic of Germany*] (EAIO)
IHV.............. Intravenous Hyperalimentation (SAUS)
IHVE............ Institute of Heating and Ventilating Engineers (SAUS)
IHVE............ Institution of Heating and Ventilating Engineers [*Later, CIBSE*]
IHVE Guide... Institution of Heating and Ventilating Engineers Guide (journ.) (SAUS)
IHVE Journal... Institution of Heating and Ventilating Engineers Journal (journ.) (SAUS)
IHVS............ Intelligent Vehicle Highway Systems
IHW.............. Industrial and Hazardous Waste (SAUS)
IHW.............. In House Warranty (SAUS)
IHW.............. Inner Heel Wedge [*Orthopedics*] (DAVI)
IHW.............. International Halley Watch [*Defunct*] (EA)
IHW.............. Internet Health Watch (ADWA)
IHW.............. John G. Shedd Aquarium, Chicago, IL [*OCLC symbol*] (OCLC)
IHWG............ Internationale Hugo Wolf Gesellschaft [*Vienna, Austria*] (EAIO)
IHWRIC........ Illinois Hazardous Waste Research and Information Center (SAUO)
IHWU............ Independent Hospital Workers Union (EA)
I-Hwy............ Interstate Highway (TBD)
IHX.............. Interim Hypersonics Test Vehicle
IHX.............. Interloop Heat Exchanger [*NASA*] (NASA)
IHX.............. Intermediate Heat Exchanger [*Nuclear energy*]
IHX.............. Western Illinois Library System, Monmouth, IL [*OCLC symbol*] (OCLC)
IHXGV.......... Intermediate Heat Exchanger Guard Vessel [*Nuclear energy*] (NRCH)
IHXX............ Iron Highway [*Federal Railroad Administration identification code*]
IHY.............. Ela Area Public Library District, Lake Zurich, IL [*OCLC symbol*] (OCLC)
IHY.............. I Heard You (MHDI)
IHY.............. International Historical Year (SAUS)
IHY.............. Interservice Hovercraft Unit (SAUO)
IHYC............ Indian Harbour Yacht Club (SAUO)
IHY MAT...... Isarco Hydro-Electric Co. (SAUO)
IHYP............ Iodohydroxybenzylpindolol [*Organic chemistry*]
IHZ.............. Warren-Newport Public Library District, Gurnee, IL [*OCLC symbol*] (OCLC)
II................ Aer Arann Teoranta [*Ireland*] [*ICAO designator*] (ICDA)
ii................ Bid in Die [*Twice a Day*] [*Symbol*] [*Pharmacology*] (DAVI)
II................ Committee Information for Industry (SAUO)
II................ Committee on Information and Industry (SAUS)
I/I................ Current to Current [*Converter*] (NRCH)
II................ Identifying Information (SAUS)
II................ Igniter Initiator
II................ Ignore Instruction (SAUS)
II................ Ikebana International [*Japan*]
II................ Illegal Immigrant
II................ Illegal Instruction (SAUS)
II................ Illinium [*or Promethium*] [*Cardiology*] (DAVI)
II................ Image Intensifier
II................ Image Interpretation (SAUS)
II................ Imagery Interpretation
II................ Imaging Intensifier (SAUS)
II................ Immigrant Inspector [*Immigration and Naturalization Service*]

II ..... Impact Ionization (SAUS)
II ..... Impaired Intellect (MELL)
II ..... Imperative Instruction (SAUS)
II ..... Imperial Airlines [*ICAO designator*] (AD)
II ..... Imperial Institute [*British*] (DAS)
II ..... Implementation Instructions (MCD)
II ..... Incapacitating Illness (MELL)
II ..... Incapacitating Injury (MELL)
II ..... Incarcerated Innocent
ii ..... Incision Inferius [*Medicine*] (EDAA)
II ..... Incoming Inspection (SAUS)
II ..... Independent Inspector (AIE)
II ..... Indexing Instruction (SAUS)
ii ..... India [*MARC country of publication code*] [*Library of Congress*] (LCCP)
II ..... Indicator Instruction (SAUS)
II ..... Individualized Instruction
II ..... Indochina Institute (EA)
I/I ..... Indorsement Irregular [*Banking*]
I/I ..... Industrial and Institutional [*Waste*] (GAAI)
II ..... Industrial Imaging (SAUS)
II ..... Industrial Investigator (SAUO)
II ..... Information Index [*LIMRA*]
II ..... Information Indicator (ACRL)
II ..... Information Input (SAUS)
II ..... Infrared Industries (SAUS)
II ..... Ingot Iron
II ..... Inhalation Injury (MELL)
II ..... Inheritance International (SAUO)
II ..... Initial Instruction (SAUS)
II ..... Initial Issue
II ..... Injectivity Index (SAUS)
II ..... Innovators International [*Defunct*] (EA)
II ..... Input Impedance
II ..... Input Information (SAUS)
II ..... Input Instruction (SAUS)
II ..... Insol International (EA)
I-I ..... Inspector-Instructor [*Marine Corps*]
II ..... Installation Instruction
II ..... Installation Instructions (SAUO)
II ..... Institute of Inventors [*British*] (BI)
II ..... Institutional Investor [*Business term*]
II ..... Instituto Interamericano (EA)
II ..... Instruction and Inspection (IAA)
II ..... Insulated Inverter (SAUS)
II ..... Intellectual Impairment (MELL)
II ..... Intentional Injury (MELL)
II ..... Interactive Interface (SAUS)
II ..... Interamerican Institute (SAUO)
II ..... Interdisciplinary Investigator (EOSA)
II ..... Interest Included (SAUS)
I/I ..... Interfaith Impact for Justice and Peace [*An association*] (EA)
II ..... Interlingua Institute (EA)
II ..... Interrupt Inhibit
II ..... Intersystems, Inc. [*Formerly, Bamberger Polymers, Inc.*] [*AMEX symbol*] (SPSG)
II ..... Interval International (EA)
II ..... Intestional Ischemia [*Medicine*] (MELL)
II ..... Intransit Inventory (AFM)
II ..... Inventions and Inventors [*A publication*]
II ..... Inventory and Inspection Report [*Army*]
II ..... Inverse Integrator (SAUS)
II ..... Ion Implant (AAEL)
II ..... Ion Implantation (SAUS)
II ..... Irish Independent (SAUO)
II ..... Irish Institute (EA)
II ..... Irradiated Iodine (SAUS)
I/I ..... Irregular Indorsement (SAUS)
II ..... Islamic Institute (SAUS)
II ..... Item Identification (MSA)
II ..... London City Airways [*ICAO designator*] (AD)
II ..... Requires Medical Supplies [*Search and rescue symbol that can be stamped in sand or snow*]
IIA ..... Aerline Eireann (SAUS)
IIA ..... Carnegie Public Library, Angola, IN [*OCLC symbol*] (OCLC)
IIA ..... If Incorrect Advise [*Aviation*]
IIA ..... ILA [*Instruction Look Ahead*] Interrupt Address [*Computer science*]
IIA ..... Image Intensifier Assembly
IIA ..... Importation Impact Assessment (SAUS)
IIA ..... Impotence Institute of America (EA)
IIA ..... Incinerator Institute of America [*Later, NSWMA*] (EA)
IIA ..... Independent Innkeepers Association (EA)
IIA ..... Independent Inspection Agency [*RSPA*] (TAG)
IIA ..... Indirect Immunofluorescence Assay [*AIDS confirmation test*] (CPH)
IIA ..... Industrial Injuries Act (SAUO)
IIA ..... Inertial Instrument Assembly
IIA ..... Inflationary Impact Assessment (SAUO)
IIA ..... Information Industry Association (EA)
IIA ..... Information Interchange Architecture [*IBM Corp.*]
IIA ..... Informatlon Industry Association (SAUS)
IIA ..... Inner Inch Adjustment (SAUS)
IIA ..... Inspector under the Inebriates Act (SAUO)
IIA ..... Institute of Industrial Arts (SAUO)
IIA ..... Institute of Inter-American Affairs [*Washington, DC*]
IIA ..... Institute of Internal Affairs
IIA ..... Institute of Internal Auditors [*Altamonte Springs, FL*] (EA)
IIA ..... Institute of International Affairs
IIA ..... Institut International d'Anthropologie [*International Institute of Anthropology*] (EAIO)
IIA ..... Instrument Integration Agreement (SAUS)
IIA ..... Instrument Interface Agreements (SAUS)
IIA ..... Insurance Institute of America (EA)
IIA ..... Integrated Irradiance Analyzer (SAUS)
IIA ..... Intelligence Industries Association (EA)
IIA ..... Interamericana de Aviacion Ltda. [*Colombia*] [*ICAO designator*] (FAAC)
IIA ..... Interim ASOC Automation (SAUO)
IIA ..... Internal Iliac Artery [*Medicine*] (EDAA)
IIA ..... Internatioal Internet Association
IIA ..... International Illawarra Association [*Defunct*] (EA)
IIA ..... International Imagery Association (EA)
IIA ..... International Information Administration [*Transferred to U SIS, 1953*] [*Department of State*]
IIA ..... International Information Agency (SAUO)
IIA ..... International Institute for Africa (SAUO)
IIA ..... International Institute of Agriculture
IIA ..... International Institute of Andragogy [*See also INSTIA*] (EAIO)
IIA ..... International Inventor's Association [*Defunct*] (EA)
IIA ..... International Investors Association (EA)
IIA ..... Invention Industry Association of America
IIA ..... Invert Indicator from Accumulator (SAA)
IIA ..... Invert Indicators from Accumulator (SAUS)
IIA ..... Irish International Airlines (SAUO)
IIAA ..... Independent Insurance Agents Association (SAUO)
IIAA ..... Independent Insurance Agents of America [*New York, NY*] (EA)
IIAA ..... Institute of Inter-American Affairs [*United Nations*]
IIAA ..... International Institute for Africa (SAUO)
IIAA ..... Invention Industry Association of America (SAUO)
IIAANY ..... Independent Insurance Agents Association of New York (SRA)
IIAAR ..... International Institute for Arab-American Relations [*Defunct*] (EA)
IIABC ..... Independent Insurance Agents and Brokers of California
IIAC ..... Impulse International Auto Club [*Defunct*] (EA)
IIAC ..... Independent Insurance Agents of Connecticut (SRA)
IIAC ..... Industrial Injuries Advisory Council [*British*] (DCTA)
IIAC ..... Infrared Information and Analysis Center [*University of Michigan*] (MCD)
IIAC ..... Inter-Image Amplifying Chemistry [*Color film technology*]
IIAC ..... International Institute of Archaeo-civilization (SAUO)
IIAC ..... International Insurance Advisory Council [*Later, IIC*] (EA)
IIAC ..... Iowa Intercollegiate Athletic Conference (PSS)
IIAD ..... Independent Insurance Agents of Delaware (SRA)
IIAF ..... Idaho Image Analysis Facility (SAUO)
IIAF ..... Imperial Iranian Air Force
IIAF ..... Iranian Imperial Air Force (SAUO)
IIAFC ..... International Irwin Allen Fan Club (EA)
IIAG ..... Interbureau Insurance Advisory Group
IIAH ..... Interim Improved Armed Helicopter (ACAE)
IIAI ..... International Institute of American Ideals (EA)
IIAILS ..... Interim Integrated Aircraft Instrumentation and Letdown System
IIAL ..... International Institute of African Languages and Culture (BARN)
IIAL ..... International Institute of Arts and Letters
IIALC ..... International Institute of African Languages and Cultures (SAUS)
IIALM ..... International Institute for Adult Literacy Methods [*Tehran, Iran*] (EAIO)
IIANC ..... Independent Insurance Agents of North Carolina (SRA)
II & W ..... Intelligence Interface and Warning [*Military*] (MCD)
IIANH ..... Independent Insurance Agents of New Hampshire (SRA)
IIANJ ..... Independent Insurance Agents of New Jersey (SRA)
IIANM ..... Independent Insurance Agents of New Mexico (SRA)
IIAO ..... Independent Insurance Agents of Oregon (SRA)
IIAP ..... Independent Insurance Agents of Pennsylvania (SRA)
IIAP ..... Innovation Information and Analysis Project [*Medicine*] (EDAA)
IIAP ..... Institut International d'Aluminium Primaire [*International Primary Aluminum Institute*] (EAIO)
IIAP ..... Insurance Institute for Asia and the Pacific (DS)
IIAP ..... International Institute of Artists and Photographers (SAUO)
IIAPCO ..... Independent Indonesian-American Petroleum Co. (SAUS)
IIAPCO ..... Independent Indonesian-American Petroleum Company (SAUO)
IIAR ..... Incurably Ill for Animal Research (EA)
IIAR ..... International Institute of Ammonia Refrigeration (EA)
IIARI ..... Independent Insurance Agents of Rhode Island (SRA)
IIAS ..... Institute of Interamerican Studies [*University of Miami*] [*Research center*] (RCD)
IIAS ..... Interactive Image Analysis System (SAUS)
IIAS ..... Interactive Instructional Answering System (SAUS)
IIAS ..... International Image Analysis System (SAUO)
IIAS ..... International Institute for Administrative Sciences (SAUS)
IIAS ..... International Institute for Advanced Studies (EA)
IIAS ..... International Institute of Administrative Services (SAUS)
IIASA ..... Institute of Islamic and Arabic Sciences in America (EA)
IIASA ..... International Institute for Advanced Systems Applications (SAUS)
IIASA ..... International Institute for Applied Systems Analysis
IIASC ..... Independent Insurance Agents of South Carolina (SRA)
IIASES ..... Inernational Institute for Aerospace Survey and Earth Sciences (SAUO)
IIASES ..... International Institute for Aerial Survey and Earth Sciences (SAUS)
IIASH ..... International Institute for the Advancement of the Science of Hypnology (SAUO)
IIASR ..... Israel Institute of Applied Social Research (SAUS)
IIAU ..... Independent Insurance Agents of Utah (SRA)

IIAV .... Independent Insurance Agents of Vermont (SRA)
IIAZ .... International Institute of the Arid Zone (SAUO)
IIB .... Butler University, Indianapolis, IN [*OCLC symbol*] (OCLC)
IIB .... Illinois Intrastate Motor Carrier Rate & Tariff Bureau, Springfield IL [*STAC*]
IIB .... Illinois Investment Board (SAUO)
IIB .... Independence, IA [*Location identifier*] [*FAA*] (FAAL)
IIB .... Independent Infantry Battalion
IIB .... Industrial Information Bulletin [*A publication*]
IIB .... Information Industry Bulletin [*Digital Information Group*] [*Information service or system*] (IID)
IIB .... Institute for Independent Business (EA)
IIB .... Institute of International Bankers (SAUS)
IIB .... Institut International de Bibliographie
IIB .... Institut International des Brevets [*International Patent Institute*]
IIB .... Intelligence Interpretation Branch (SAUS)
IIB .... Intense Ion Beam
IIB .... International Institute of Bankers Buildings Association (SAUO)
IIB .... International Institute of Bibliography (SAUO)
IIB .... International Institute of Biotechnology [*University of Kent at Canterbury*] [*British*] (IRC)
IIB .... International Investment Bank [*Moscow, USSR*]
IIB .... Internordic Investment Bank [*Scandinavia*]
IIB .... Iowa Independent Bankers (TBD)
IIB .... Irish Intercontinental Bank Ltd.
IIB .... Italian International Bank
IIBA .... International Institute for Bioenergetic Analysis (EA)
IIBA .... International Intelligent Buildings Association [*Washington, DC*] (EA)
IIBA .... International Intelligent Educational Planning (SAUS)
II Bar .... II Baruch [*Pseudepigrapha*] (BJA)
IIBBR .... International Institute for Biological and Botanical Research (SAUS)
IIBC .... Insurance Institute of British Columbia (FOTI)
IIBC .... International Institute of Biological Control [*CAB International*] [*British*] (IRC)
IIBD .... Incorporated Institute of British Decorators (DAS)
IIBDID .... Incorporated Institute of British Decorators and Interior Designers (BI)
IIB/EIB .... Essays in International Business. Published by the Institute of International Business in cooperation with Georgia State College, School of Business Administration (SAUS)
IIBEM .... Indian Institute of Biochemistry and Experimental Medicine (SAUO)
IIBH .... International Institute of Biological Husbandry [*Ipswich, Suffolk, England*] [*Defunct*] (EAIO)
II Bn .... Independent Infantry Battalion (SAUO)
IIBQ .... Illinois Institute for Environmental Quality (SAUS)
IIBS .... Interactive International Banking System [*NCR Corp.*]
IIBTT .... Ion-Implanted Base Transistor Technology (IAA)
IIC .... AMIGOS [*Access Method for Indexed Data Generalized for Operating System*] Bibliographic Council, Dallas, TX [*OCLC symbol*] (OCLC)
IIC .... Igniter Initiater Container (SAUS)
IIC .... Igniter Initiator Cartridge [*or Container*]
IIC .... Illinois Industrial Commission (SAUO)
IIC .... Image Interpretation Cell
IIC .... Imagery Interpretation Center
IIC .... Impact Insulation Class (SAUS)
IIC .... Impact Isolation Class [*Noise rating of insulation*]
IIC .... Independent Insurance Conference
IIC .... Independent Investment Co. [*British*]
IIC .... India International Center (SAUS)
IIC .... Indian Investment Centre (SAUO)
IIC .... Industrial Information Centre (SAUS)
IIC .... Industrial Intelligence Centre [*British*] [*World War II*]
IIC .... Inflation-Indexed Charge [*Medicare*] (GFGA)
IIC .... Information Industries Committee [*Information service or system*] (IID)
IIC .... Information Institute of Canada (SAUS)
IIC .... Information Integration Center
IIC .... Innovation Information Center [*George Washington University*] (PDAA)
IIC .... Insearch Institute of Commerce [*University of Technology, Sydney, Australia*]
IIC .... Institute for Instrumentation and Control (SAUS)
IIC .... Institute of Insurance Consultants [*British*] (DBA)
IIC .... Institut International des Communications [*International Institute of Communications*] (EA)
IIC .... Instructional Improvement Committee [*Individually-guided education*] (AEE)
IIC .... Insurance Institute of Canada
IIC .... Integrated Information Center (SAUS)
IIC .... Integrated Interface Circuit (IAA)
IIC .... Intelligence Information Center [*Military*] (MCD)
IIC .... InterCapital California Insurance Municipal Income Fund [*NYSE symbol*] (SPSG)
IIC .... InterCapital Cal Ins Muni Inc. [*NYSE symbol*] (TTSB)
IIC .... Interceptor Identification Capability
IIC .... Intercraft Industries Corp. (EFIS)
IIC .... Interdepartmental Intelligence Conference [*Interagency conference of the National Security Council*] (EGAO)
IIC .... Inter-IC (SAUS)
IIC .... Inter-Institutional Commission (SAUO)
IIC .... Inter-Integrated Circuit (SAUS)
IIC .... Inter-Integrated Circuits (SAUS)
IIC .... International Ice Patrol [*Coast Guard*]
IIC .... International Imaging Center
IIC .... International Import Certificate (SAUS)
IIC .... International Information Committee (SAUO)
IIC .... International Institute for Conservation of Historic and Artistic Work (SAUS)
IIC .... International Institute for Cotton [*Belgium*] (FEA)
IIC .... International Institute for Pure and Applied Chemistry (SAUS)
IIC .... International Institute for the Conservation of Historic and Artistic Works (SAUS)
IIC .... International Institute for the Conservation of Museum Objects
IIC .... International Institute of Commerce (SAUO)
IIC .... International Institute of Communications [*Formerly, IBI*] (EA)
IIC .... International Institute of Conservation (SAUS)
IIC .... International Insurance Council (EA)
IIC .... International Interchange Committee (SAUO)
IIC .... International Investment Corp. (SAUS)
IIC .... International Investment Corporation (SAUO)
IIC .... International Ionarc, Inc. [*Vancouver Stock Exchange symbol*]
IIC .... International Irrigation Center (SAUO)
IIC .... Ion-Ion Collision
IIC .... Iron Information Center [*Battelle Memorial Institute*] [*Information service or system*] (IID)
IIC .... Islamic Investment Co. (SAUS)
IIC .... Isotopes Information Center [*ORNL*]
IIC .... Item Identification Code
IIC .... Rita Coyotepec [*Mexico*] [*Seismograph station code, US Geological Survey*] (SEIS)
IICA .... Indians into Communications Association (EA)
IICA .... Institute of Instrumentation and Control Australia (SAUS)
IICA .... Instituto Internacional de Ciencias Administrativas [*International Institute of Administrative Sciences*]
IICA .... Interamerican Institute for Cooperation on Agriculture [*Formerly, IAIAS*] (EA)
IICA .... International Ice Cream Association (EA)
IICA .... Intracranial Internal Carotid Artery [*Medicine*] (MELL)
IICA .... Islamic Information Center of America (EA)
IICAB .... Institute for International Cooperation in Animal Biologics (GVA)
IICAF .... Institute for International Collaboration in Agriculture and Forestry (SAUO)
IICB .... International Import Custom Brokers (SAUS)
I-ICB .... Isolation-Interface Control Board (SAUS)
IICBM .... Intermediate Intercontinental Ballistic Missile
IICC .... Institute for Inter-Continental Cooperation (SAUO)
IICC .... Institut International d'Etude et de Documentation en Matiere de Concurrence Commerciale [*International Institute for Commercial Competition*] [*Belgium*] (EA)
IICC .... Insurance Information Centre of Canada (FOTI)
IICC .... International Institute for Commercial Competition (SAUO)
IICC .... International Institute for Study and Research in the Field of Commercial Competition
IICCB .... Informal International Conference of Christian Broadcasting (SAUO)
IICCB .... Informal International Conference on Christian Broadcasting (SAUS)
IICCG .... International Institute of Conservation-Canadian Group (SAUO)
IICCI .... International Information Center of Cosmetic Industries (SAUO)
IICCSE .... International Information Centre for Computers in Secondary Education (SAUO)
IICE .... Institute for Internal Combustion Engines (MCD)
IICE .... Institut International des Caisses d'Epargne [*International Savings Banks Institute - ISBI*] [*Geneva, Switzerland*] (EAIO)
IICF .... Insurance Industry Charitable Foundation
IICF .... Interdisciplinary Investigator Computing Facilities (ACAE)
IICG .... ICSU [*International Council of Scientific Unions*] Inter-Union Commission for Geodynamics [*Marine science*] (MSC)
IICG .... International Institute of Comparative Government (SAUO)
IICH .... International Information Clearing House (SAUS)
IICHAW .... International Institute for Conservation of Historic and Artistic Works
IICheE .... Indian Institute of Chemical Engineers (SAUO)
IICHG .... Institute of the International Conference on the Holocaust and Genocide (SAUO)
IICI .... Image Industry Council International (NTPA)
IIC Ind .... IIC Industries, Inc. [*Associated Press*] (SAG)
IICIT .... International Institute of Connector and Interconnection Technology (NTPA)
IICL .... Institute of International Container Lessors (EA)
IICLRR .... International Institute for Children's Literature and Reading Research [*Vienna, Austria*] (EA)
IICM .... Institute for Information processing and Computer supported new Media (SAUO)
IICM .... International Institute of Convention Management (NTPA)
IICMFA .... Integrated Information Centre of the Ministry of Foreign Affairs [*Saudi Arabia*] (NITA)
IICMSD .... International Institute for Comparative Music Studies and Documentation [*Berlin, Federal Republic of Germany*] (EA)
IiCN .... National Library of India, Calcutta, India [*Library symbol*] [*Library of Congress*] (LCLS)
IICNTR .... International Institute of Children's Nature and Their Rights (EA)
IICP .... Increased Intracranial Pressure (CPH)
IICP .... International Intersociety Committee on Pathology
IICR .... IIC Industries [*NASDAQ symbol*] (TTSB)
IICR .... IIC Industries, Inc. [*NASDAQ symbol*] (SAG)
IICR .... Inspection Item Change Request (MCD)
IICR .... Israel Investors Corp. [*NASDAQ symbol*] (COMM)
IICS .... Intelligent Image Caching Software [*Courtland Group, Inc.*] (PCM)
IICS .... International Interactive Communications Society [*San Francisco, CA*] [*Telecommunications service*] (TSSD)
IICU .... Infant Intensive Care Unit [*of a hospital*]

IICU .... Intermediate Intensive Care Unit [*Medicine*]
IICUC .... Institute of Inspection Cleaning and Restoration (NTPA)
IICUC .... International Institute of Carpet and Upholstery Certification (EA)
IICWG .... Interprogram Interface Control Working Group (ACAE)
IICY .... International Independent Christian Youth [*See also JICI*] [*Paris, France*] (EAIO)
IICY .... International Investment Corporation for Yugoslavia (SAUO)
IID .... Identically Independently Distributed (SAUS)
IID .... Iida [*Japan*] [*Seismograph station code, US Geological Survey*] (SEIS)
IID .... Image Intensifier Device
IID .... Impact Ionization Diode
IID .... Independent and Identically Distributed (SAUS)
IID .... Independent Identically Distributed [*Statistics*] (IEEE)
IID .... Indicator (SAUS)
IID .... Infectious Intestinal Disease (SAUS)
IID .... Information Industry Directory [*A publication*]
IID .... Infrared Intrusion Detection (NVT)
IID .... Infrared Intrusion Detector (SAUO)
IID .... Institute for Integral Development (EA)
IID .... Insulin-Dependent Diabetes [*Mellitus*] [*Endocrinology*] (DAVI)
IID .... Insulin-Independent Diabetes (SAUS)
IID .... Insulin-Independent Diabetes Mellitus (MAE)
IID .... Insurgent Incident Data
IID .... Integrated Information Display (MCD)
IID .... Integrated Instrument Development
IID .... Interaural Intensity Differences
IID .... Interaural Intensity Disparity [*Audiology*]
IID .... Interface Identifier (SAUS)
IID .... Interior Intrusion Device (SAUS)
IID .... Intermittent-Integrated Doppler (OA)
IID .... Internal Investigation Division (SAUO)
IID .... International Information Department (SAUS)
IID .... International Institute of Documentation (SAUO)
IID .... Intrinsic Infrared Detector
IID .... Investment in Default [*Business term*]
IID .... Ion Implantation Doping
IID .... Ionospheric Ion Density
iid .... Once a Day (SPVS)
IIDA .... Individualized Instruction for Data Access (SAUS)
IIDA .... Indivisualized Instruction for Data Access [*Drexel University and Franklin Institute*] [*Education package*] (NITA)
IIDA .... Instituto Interamericano de Direito de Autor [*Interamerican Copyright Institute*] (EAIO)
IIDA .... International Interior Design Association (NTPA)
IIDA .... Irish Industrial Development Authority (SAUO)
IIDA-FACT .... Individualized Instruction for Data Access to Factual Data Bank (SAUS)
IIDARA .... Instituto Iberoamericano de Derecho Agrario y Reforma Agraria [*Ibero-American Institute of Agrarian Law and Agrarian Reform - IAIALAR*] (EAIO)
IiDaU .... University of North Bengal, Darjeeling District, West Bengal, India [*Library symbol*] [*Library of Congress*] (LCLS)
IIDB .... Integrated Intelligence Data Base (SAUO)
IIDC .... Institute for International Development and Cooperation [*University of Ottawa*] [*See also IDIC*] [*Canada*]
IIDC .... Institut for International Development and Cooperation (SAUO)
IIDC/C .... Civilisations. International Institute of Differing Civilizations. Bruxelles (SAUS)
IIDD .... Interface Identification Data Document (DNAB)
IIDET .... International Institute of Dental Ergonomics and Technology [*Germany*] (EAIO)
IIDH .... Institut International de Droit Humanitaire [*International Institute of Humanitarian Law - IIHL*] (EAIO)
IIDH .... Instituto Interamericano de Derechos Humanos [*Inter-American Institute of Human Rights - IIHR*] (EA)
IIDH .... Inter-American Institute for Human Rights (SAUO)
IIDLC .... Institut International de Droit Linguistique Compare [*International Institute of Comparative Linguistic Law*] (EAIO)
IIDM .... Iberoamerican Institute of Maritime Law (SAUO)
IIDM .... Insulin-Independent Diabetes Mellitus [*Medicine*] (MELL)
I-IDNS .... In-Garrison IDNS (SAUS)
IIDP .... Integrated Instrument Development Program
IIDP .... Integrated Intelligence Development Plan (MCD)
IIDQ .... Isobut,yl 1,2-Dihydro-2-Isobutoxyl-1-Quinoline Carboxylate (SAUS)
IIDR .... International Institute for Development Research (SAUO)
IIDS .... Institute for Integrated Development Studies (SAUS)
IIDS .... Integrated Information Display System (MCD)
IIDS .... Integrated Instrumentation Display System
IIDS .... Interior Intruder Detection System (SAUS)
IIDT .... Ion Implantation Doping Technique
IIE .... Idiopathic Ineffective Erythropoiesis [*Hematology*] (AAMN)
IIE .... Imperial Institute of Entomology [*British*]
IIE .... Initial Ion Event
IIE .... Installation Identification Element (MCD)
IIE .... Institute for Independent Education (EA)
IIE .... Institute for International Economics
IIE .... Institute of Industrial Economics [*University of Newcastle*] [*Australia*]
IIE .... Institute of Industrial Engineers (EA)
IIE .... Institute of Industrial Exhibitions (SAUO)
IIE .... Institute of International Education (EA)
IIE .... Institut International de l'Epargne
IIE .... Instituto Interamericano de Estadistica [*Inter-American Statistical Institute - IASI*] [*Washington, DC*]
IIE .... Integrated Instrumentation Environment (SAUS)
IIE .... Inter-American Institute of Ecology [*Ecological Society of America*]
IIE .... International Institute of Embryology [*Later, ISDB*]
IIE .... International Institute of Islamic Economics (SAUO)
IIE .... Invalid Instruction Exception (SAUS)
IIEA .... Immediate Identifiable Emergency Action [*Red Cross*]
IIEA .... International Institute for Environmental Affairs [*Later, IIED*]
IIEC .... Inter-Industry Emission Control [*Program*] (EA)
IIEC .... International Institute for Energy Conservation (EA)
IIEC Program ... Inter-Industry Emission Control Program (SAUS)
IIED .... International Institute for Environmental and Development (SAUS)
IIED .... International Institute for Environment and Development [*Research center*] [*British*] (IRC)
iied .... International Institute for Environment and Development [*British*]
IIEE .... Institut International d'Etudes sur l'Education [*International Institute for Education Studies*]
IIEE .... Ion-Induced Electron Emission (SAUS)
IIEG .... Interest Inventory for Elementary Grades [*Psychology*]
IIE GR .... Institute of Industrial Exhibitions (SAUS)
IIEIC .... International Institute Examinations Inquiry Committee (SAUO)
IIEL .... Institut International d'Etudes Ligures [*International Institute for Ligurian Studies - IILS*] (EAIO)
IIEM .... International Impotence Education Month (SAUO)
IIEM .... International Institute for Earth, Environmental and Marine Sciences and Technologies (SAUS)
IIEP .... Illionois Inventory of Educational Progress (EDAC)
IIEP .... International Institute for Educational Planning [*Paris, France*] [*United Nations*] (EA)
IIEQ .... Illinois Institute for Environmental Quality (PDAA)
IIER .... International Institute for Economic Research (EA)
IIES .... Industrial Innovation Extension Service (SAUS)
IIES .... International Institute for Environmental Studies (ASF)
IIES .... International Institute for Environment and Society (SAUO)
IIES .... International Institute of the Environment Society (SAUO)
IIETF .... Information Industries Education and Training Foundation [*Australia*]
IIExE .... Institution of Incorporated Executive Engineers [*British*] (DBA)
IIF .... IBM [*International Business Machines Corp.*] IGES Format [*Initial Graphics Exchange Specification*]
IIF .... Image Interchange Facility (SAUS)
IIF .... Image Interpretation Facility (ACAE)
IIF .... Imagery Interpretation Facility (SAUO)
IIF .... Immediate IF (SAUS)
IIF .... Immediate Interface (SAUS)
IIF .... Immune Interferon [*Cell biology*]
IIF .... Imprint Immuno-Fixation [*Immunochemistry*]
IIF .... Independent Investors Forum [*Information service or system*] (IID)
IIF .... Indirect Immunofluorescence [*Immunochemistry*]
IIF .... Information Item File (SAUS)
IIF .... Institute of International Finance [*Washington, DC*] (EA)
IIF .... Institut International du Froid [*International Institute of Refrigeration*]
IIF .... Intelligent Influence Fuze (SAUS)
IIF .... Intense Irregular Field
IIF .... Internals Indexing Fixture (NRCH)
IIF .... International Institute of Forecasters [*See also IIM*] (EA)
IIF .... Morgan Stanley India Investment Fund [*NYSE symbol*] (SAG)
IIF .... Morgan Stanley India Inv Fd [*NYSE symbol*] (TTSB)
IIFA .... International Institute of Films on Art
IIFAR .... Incurably Ill for Animal Research (EA)
IIFAS .... Integration of Intelligence from All Sources (MCD)
IIFET .... International Institute of Fisheries Economics and Trade (EA)
IIFFL .... International Institute of Foods and Family Living (EA)
IIfIA .... International Institute for Inhalant Abuse (SAUS)
IIFP .... Institut International de Finances Publiques [*International Institute of Public Finance*] (EAIO)
IIFS .... Integrated Individual Fighting System [*US Army Natick Research, Development, and Engineering Center*] (INF)
IIFS .... Intelligent Information Fusion System (ACAE)
IIFS .... International Institute of Forensic Science (SAUO)
IIFSO .... International Islamic Federation of Student Organizations [*Salimiyan, Kuwait*] (EAIO)
IIFSP .... Integrated Individual Fighting System Program [*Army*] (INF)
IIFT .... Indirect Immunofluorescence Technique [*Immunochemistry*]
IIFV .... Interim Infantry Fighting Vehicle [*Military*] (MCD)
IIG .... Illuminated Internal Graticule
IIG .... Imagery Intelligence Group [*Military*] (MCD)
IIG .... Indian Institute of Geomagnetism (CARB)
IIG .... Industrial Interface Group (SAUO)
IIG .... Instantaneous Inverse Gain
IIG .... Intercast Industry Group (SAUO)
IIG .... International Institute of Geophysics (SAUO)
IIG .... International Investors Group (SAUO)
IIG .... Investors Ins Group [*AMEX symbol*] (TTSB)
IIG .... Investors Insurance Group [*Formerly, Gemco National, Inc.*] [*AMEX symbol*] (SPSG)
IIG .... Ion Implant Gettering (SAUS)
IIG .... Item Identification Guide
IIGA .... IEEE [*Institute of Electrical and Electronics Engineers*] Industry and General Applications (IAA)
IIGB .... International Institute of Genetics and Biophysics [*Italy*]
IIGE .... Iowa Illinois Gas & Electric (SAUS)
IIGE .... Iowa Illinois Gas & Electric Company (SAUO)
IIGF .... Imperial Iranian Ground Forces
IIGR .... Ipsilateral Instinctive Grasp Reaction [*Medicine*] (DMAA)
IIGS .... Initial Image Generating Subsystem [*ERTS*] (MCD)
IIGS .... Initial Image Generating System (SAUS)
IIH .... Institute of International Health (GVA)

IIH............... Internet Infrastruct Holdrs. Tr. [*AMEX symbol*] (SG)
IIH............... Isoimmune Hydrops [*Medicine*]
IIHA............. Intercollegiate Ice Hockey Association [*Later, ECHA*] (EA)
IIHCEHV....... International Institute of Health Care, Ethics and Human Values (SAUO)
IIHD............. Institute for International Health and Development (EA)
IIHF............. International Ice Hockey Federation (EAIO)
IIHHT........... International Institute of Health and Holistic Therapies [*British*]
IIHL............. International Institute for Home Literature [*See also MIKK*] [*Belgrade, Yugoslavia*] (EAIO)
IIHL............. International Institute of Humanitarian Law [*See also IIDH*] [*San Remo, Italy*] (EAIO)
IIHR............. Indian Institute for Horticultural Research (SAUO)
IIHR............. Institute for International Human Resources (NTPA)
IIHR............. Inter-American Institute of Human Rights [*See also IIDS*] [*San Jose, Costa Rica*] (EAIO)
IIHR............. International Institute of Human Rights (EA)
IIHR............. Iowa Institute of Hydraulic Research [*University of Iowa*] [*Research center*] (MCD)
IIHS............. Insurance Institute for Highway Safety (EA)
IIHSC........... Inter-Industry Highway Safety Committee [*Later, DSMC*] (EA)
III............... Idealist International, Inc. (EA)
III............... Illinois, Indiana, Iowa (IIA)
III............... Illumination Industries, Inc.
III............... Incapacitating Illness (SAUS)
III............... Incapacitating Injury (SAUS)
III............... Incapacity, Illness, or Injury [*Environmental science*] (COE)
III............... Indiana Central University, Indianapolis, IN [*OCLC symbol*] (OCLC)
III............... Information Intelligence, Inc. [*Information service or system*] (IID)
III............... Information International, Inc. [*Phoenix, AZ*] [*Information broker*] (MCD)
III............... Innovative Interfaces, Inc. [*Information service or system*] (IID)
III............... Innovative Interfaces, Incorporated (SAUO)
III............... Insteel Industries [*NYSE symbol*] (SAG)
III............... Insteel Industries Inc. [*NYSE symbol*] (TTSB)
III............... Institute for Information Industry [*Information service or system*] (IID)
III............... Institute of the Ironworking Industry (EA)
III............... Insurance Information Institute [*New York, NY*] (EA)
III............... Integrated Imaging Irradiance (ACAE)
III............... Inter-American Indian Institute [*OAS*]
III............... International Industrial Information Ltd. [*Information service or system*] (IID)
III............... International Institute of Interpreters [*United Nations*] (BARN)
III............... International Institute of Intrapreneurs (SAUO)
III............... International Insurance Intelligence
III............... International Intertrade Index [*No longer available online*] [*Information service or system*] (IID)
III............... International Isostatic Institute (SAUO)
III............... Interstate Identification Index [*NCIC*]
III............... Investors in Industry [*British*]
III............... Sturgeon Bay, WI [*Location identifier*] [*FAA*] (FAAL)
iii................ Ter in Die [*Three Times a Day*] [*Symbol*] [*Pharmacology*] (DAVI)
IIIA............. International Investment Insurance Agency [*Of IBRID*] (EBF)
IIIA............. Israeli Institute of International Affairs (SAUO)
III Bar......... III Baruch [*Pseudepigrapha*] (BJA)
IIIC............. Immediate Imagery Interpretation Center (SAUS)
IIIC............. International Irrigation Information Center (IID)
III/C........... Interoperability, Integration, Immunity, Continuity (ACAE)
IIIC (LN)...... International Institute of Intellectual Cooperation of the League of Nations [*Obsolete*]
IIICR........... International Institute of Interdisciplinary Cycle Research (SAUS)
IIID............. International Institute of Information Design (CARB)
IIIDB........... International Interchangeability Interface Data Base (ACAE)
IIIE............. International Institute of Islamic Economics (SAUO)
IIIF............. Impurity-Induced Intergranular Fracture (SAUS)
III-FA.......... Ad hoc Study Group on Implications and Implementation of IOC Functional Autonomy (SAUO)
IIIHS........... International Institute of Integral Human Sciences [*See also IISHI*] (EAIO)
IIII............. Innotech Inc. [*NASDAQ symbol*] (TTSB)
IIIL............. International Institute of Iberoamerican Literature (EA)
IIIL............. International Interchangeability Interface List (ACAE)
IIIL............. Isoplanar Integrated Injection Logic (MCD)
IIIMB........... International Institute of Investment and Merchant Banking [*Washington, DC*] (EA)
IIIP............. Institute for International Information Programs [*University of Maryland*] (NITA)
IIIR............. Integrated Instructional Information Resource [*Educational Products Information Exchange Institute*] [*Information service or system*] (CRD)
IIIR............. Integration of Internet Information Ressources (SAUO)
IIIS............. Interactive Image Interpretation System (SAUS)
IIIS............. Interim International Information Service [*World War II*]
IIIS............. International Institute of Informatics and Systemics (SAUO)
IIIT............. International Institute of Instructional Technology [*British*]
IIIT............. International Institute of Islamic Thought (EA)
IIIVC........... Infrahepatic Interruption of the Inferior Vena Cava [*Medicine*] (AAMN)
IIJ............... Indo-Iranian Journal (journ.) (SAUS)
IIJ............... Internet Initiative Japan
IIJ............... Internet Initiative Japan, Inc.
IIJM............. Institut International Jacques Maritain [*International Jacques Maritain Institute - IJMI*] (EAIO)
IIJR............. Illinois Institute of Juvenile Research (SAUO)
IIK............... Imagery Interpretation Key
IIK............... Internacia Instruista Kunlaborado (SAUO)
IIK............... Kipnuk, AK [*Location identifier*] [*FAA*] (FAAL)
IIL............... India International Airways (P) Ltd. [*ICAO designator*] (FAAC)
IIL............... Indianapolis Law Catalog Consortium, Indiana University School of Law Library, Indianapolis, IN [*OCLC symbol*] (OCLC)
IIL............... Induction Ion LASER
IIL............... Institute of Industrial Launderers (EA)
IIL............... Institute of International Law [*Geneva, Switzerland*] (EA)
IIL............... Insurance Institute of London (SAUO)
IIL............... Integrated Injection Logic [*Microprocessing*] (BUR)
IIL............... Intelligence International Limited (SAUO)
IIL............... Intelligence International Ltd. (SAUS)
IIL............... Invert Indicator of the Left Half (IAA)
IILA............. Institute for the Integration of Latin America
IILA............. Instituto Italo Latino Americano [*Italo-Latin American Institute*] (EAIO)
IILA............. Istituto Italo-Latino-Americano [*Italian-Latin American Institute*] [*Rome, Italy*]
IiLc............. Identity Incorrect, Location Correct [*Psychology*]
IILE............. Ion-Induced Light Emission (MCD)
IILFSC......... International Institute of Law of the French Speaking Countries [*See also IDEF*] [*Paris, France*] (EAIO)
IiLi.............. Identity Incorrect, Location Incorrect [*Psychology*]
IILI.............. Instituto Internacional de Literatura Iberoamericana [*International Institute of Iberoamerican Literature*] (EA)
IILP............. Index to Indian Legal Periodicals [*A publication*] (DLA)
IILP............. Institute of International Licensing Practitioners (EAIO)
IILP............. International Institute for Lath and Plaster (EA)
IILR............. Institute of International Labor Research (EA)
IILS............. Image Interpretation Light Station (ACAE)
IILS............. International Institute for Labor Studies [*Switzerland*]
IILS............. International Institute for Ligurian Studies (EA)
IIM.............. Children's Museum of Indianapolis, Indianapolis, IN [*OCLC symbol*] (OCLC)
IIM.............. India Independence Medal (SAUO)
IIM.............. Indian Institute of Management (SAUO)
IIM.............. Indian Institute of Metals (SAUO)
IIM.............. Individual Indian Money
IIM.............. Institute for Information Management (EA)
IIM.............. Institut International des Meteorologists [*International Institute of Forecasters*] (EAIO)
IIM.............. Institut International du Manganese [*International Insitute of Manganese*] [*France*] (EAIO)
IIM.............. Institution of Industrial Managers [*British*]
IIM.............. Insurance Institute of Manitoba [*Canada*] (FOTI)
IIM.............. Interagency Intelligence Memorandum (MCD)
IIM.............. InterCapital Ins Muni Income [*NYSE symbol*] (TTSB)
IIM.............. InterCapital Insurance Municipal Income Fund [*NYSE symbol*] (SPSG)
IIM.............. International Investment Monitor [*Global Analysis Systems*] [*Information service or system*] (CRD)
IIM.............. Inventory in Motion
IIM.............. Item Intelligence Maintenance [*DoD*]
IIMA............ Industrial Instruments Manufacturing Association (SAUO)
IIMA............ Insurance Industry Meetings Association [*St. Louis, MO*] (EA)
II MAF......... Second Marine Amphibious Force (SAUO)
IIMAI........... Information, Intention, Method, Administration, Intercommunication (SAUS)
II Maloy....... Treaties, Conventions, International Acts, Protocols, and Agreements between the United States of America and other Powers, 1776-1909, Compiled under the Direction of the U.S. Senate by William M. Malloy (SAFN)
IIMAPS........ Incremental IMAPS (SAUS)
IIMC............ International Industrial Marketing Club [*Formerly, MMEC*] [*Defunct*] (EA)
IIMC............ International Information Management Congress (SAUS)
IIMC............ International Institute of Maritime Culture (EA)
IIMC............ International Institute of Municipal Clerks (EA)
IIMC............ International Institute of the Middle Classes (SAUO)
IIMC............ International Materials Conference (SAUS)
IIMD............ International Institute for Management Development (SAUS)
IIME............ Institute of International Medical Education
IIME............ Interuniversity Institute for Missiological and Ecumenical Research (SAUO)
IIMEBE........ International Institute for Medical Electronics and Biological Engineering (SAUO)
II MEF......... II Marine Expeditionary Force (SAUS)
IIMI............. International Irrigation Management Institute [*Sri Lanka*] [*Research center*] (IRC)
IIMIPX......... International Microelectronic Products, Inc. (SAUO)
IIMOS.......... Iona Implanted Metal Oxide Semiconductor (SAUS)
I-IMP.......... I-Labeled Iodoamphetamine
IIMR............ Institute of Industrial Market Research (COBU)
IIMR............ Institute of Investment Managers and Research (COBU)
IIMRD.......... Imperial Institute Mineral Resources Department (SAUO)
IIMS............ Intensive Item Management System (AABC)
IIMS............ International Institute of Marine Surveyors (SAUO)
IIMS............ Ion Implantation Manufacturing System
IIMS............ Ion implementation manufacturing system (SAUO)
IIMSD.......... International Institute for Music Studies and Documentation (SAUO)
IIMT............ International Institute for the Management of Technology [*Defunct*] (EA)
IIMT............ International Institute of Milling Technology (SAUO)
IIN.............. IBM [*International Business Machines Corp.*] Information Network (HGAA)
IIN.............. Idiopathic Inflammatory Neuropathy [*Medicine*] (EDAA)

IIN............... Instituto Interamericano del Nino [*Inter-American Children's Institute*] [*Uruguay*] (EA)
IIN............... Insurance Institute of Newfoundland [*Canada*] (FOTI)
IIN............... Integrated Information Network (SAUO)
IIN............... INX Insearch Group of Companies Ltd. [*Vancouver Stock Exchange symbol*]
IIN............... Item Identification Number (AFM)
IIN............... ITT Industries [*NYSE symbol*] (TTSB)
IIN............... ITT Industries, Inc. Indiana [*NYSE symbol*] (SAG)
IINA............ Insurance Institute of Northern Alberta [*Canada*] (FOTI)
IINA............ International Islamic News Agency [*Jeddah, Saudi Arabia*] (EAIO)
IINA............ Islamic International News Agency (SAUO)
IiNaU........... University of Nagpur, Nagpur, India [*Library symbol*] [*Library of Congress*] (LCLS)
IINB............ Insurance Institute of New Brunswick [*Canada*] (FOTI)
I-in-C.......... Inspector-in-Chief (SAUO)
IINC............ International Institute of Novel Computing [*Japan*]
IINCE........... International Institute for Noise Control Engineering (SAUS)
IINCOMNET... Intra-Theater Communications Network (ACAE)
IINCOM NET... Intratheater Intelligence Communication Network (SAUS)
IINDR........... International Information Network on Development Research (SAUS)
IINERT......... In-Place Inactivation and Natural Restoration Technologies (SAUO)
I Inf Sc....... Institute of Information Scientists [*British*] (DLA)
IiNI.............. Indian National Scientific Documentation Center, Hillside Road, New Delhi, India [*Library symbol*] [*Library of Congress*] (LCLS)
IiNI.............. Indian National Scientific Documentation Centre, New Delhi, India [*Library symbol*] [*Library of Congress*]
IiNN............ Nehru Memorial Museum and Library, New Delhi, India [*Library symbol*] [*Library of Congress*] (LCLS)
IINREN......... Interagency Interim National Research and Education Network (TNIG)
IINS............ Image Intensifier Night Sight
I/Ins............ Inactive Insurance (DLA)
IINS............ Incoherent Inelastic Neutron Scattering [*Physics*]
IINS............ Inelastic Incoherent Neutron Scattering [*Spectrometry*]
IINS............ Insurance Institute of Nova Scotia [*Canada*] (FOTI)
IINS............ Integrated Inertial Navigation System (MCD)
IINS............ Interuniversity Institute of Nuclear Sciences (SAUO)
IINSE........... International Institute of Nuclear Science and Engineering
IINT............ Information International, Inc. [*NASDAQ symbol*] (NQ)
IINTE........... Institute for Scientific, Technical and Economic Information (SAUO)
IINTE........... Instytut Informacji Naukowej, Technicznej, i Ekonomicznej [*Institute of Scientific, Technical, and Economic Information*] [*Information service or system*] (IID)
IINZ............ Insurance Institute of New Zealand (SAUO)
IIO.............. Image Intensifier Orthicon
IIO.............. Immigration Information Officer (SAUS)
IIO.............. Industrial In/Out (SAUS)
IIO.............. Information Item Only
IIO.............. Institute for International Order [*Later, IWO*]
IIO.............. Insurance Institute of Ontario [*Canada*] (FOTI)
IIO.............. Inter-Allied Insurance Organization [*NATO*] (NATG)
IIO.............. International Industrial Organization (SAUS)
IIOC............ Independent International Organisation for Certification (SAUS)
IIOC............ Intelligent Input Output Channel (NITA)
IIOC............ Intelligent I/O Controller (SAUS)
IIODRFES..... International Information Office of the Democratic Revolutionary Front of El Salvador [*See also OIIFDRES*] [*San Jose, Costa Rica*] (EAIO)
IIOE............ International Indian Ocean Expedition [*Navy*]
IIOIC........... International Intra-Ocular Implant Club (EAIO)
IIOOF.......... International Independent Order of Odd Fellows (SAUO)
IIOP............ Integrated Input/Output Processor
IIOP............ Intelligent Input/Output Processor [*Disk Controller*]
IIOP............ Internet Interface Operating Procedures (TELE)
IIOP............ Internet Inter-Object Request Broker Protocol [*Computer science*] (IGQR)
IIOP............ Internet Inter-Operability Protocol (SAUS)
IIOP............ Internet Inter-ORB Protocol (SAUS)
IIOP............ Internet Inter-ORG [*Object Request Broker*] Protocol [*Computer science*]
IIOS............ International Indian Ocean Survey (SAUS)
IIP.............. El Pinto [*Mexico*] [*Seismograph station code, US Geological Survey*] (SEIS)
IIP.............. Idiopathic Interstitial Pneumonia [*Medicine*] (STED)
IIP.............. Idiopathic Interstitial Pneumonitis [*Medicine*] (MELL)
IIP.............. Idiopathic Intestinal Pseudo-Obstruction [*Medicine*] (STED)
IIP.............. Immediate Impact Point (SAA)
IIP.............. Immigrant Investor Program (SAUS)
IIP.............. Implantable Insulin Pump
IIP.............. Implementation and Installation Plan (SAUO)
IIP.............. Implementation and Integration Plan (CCCA)
IIP.............. Implementation/Installation Plan [*Telecommunications*] (TEL)
IIP.............. Inadvertent Ignition Panel
IIP.............. Increasing Intracranial Pressure [*Medicine*]
IIP.............. Index of Industrial Production
IIP.............. Indian Imperial Police (SAUS)
IIP.............. Individual Implementation Plan [*For the education of a handicapped person*]
IIP.............. Individualized Instructional Planning (SAUS)
IIP.............. Industrial Incentive Plan [*NAVFAC*] (DNAB)
IIP.............. Initial Issue Provisioning [*Marine Corps*] (DOMA)
IIP.............. Inorganic Insulative Plastic
I/IP............ Installation/Implementation Plan (SAUS)
IIP.............. Instantaneous Impact Plots (SAUO)
IIP.............. Instantaneous Impact Points (KSC)
IIP.............. Instantaneous Impact Predictor
IIP.............. Institute of Incorporated Photographers [*British*]
IIP.............. Institut International de la Potasse [*International Potash Institute*] (EAIO)
IIP.............. Institut International de la Presse [*International Press Institute*]
IIP.............. Institut International de Philosophie [*International Institute of Philosophy*] (EAIO)
IIP.............. Integrated Image Processing (MELL)
IIP.............. Integrated Information Presentation (ACAE)
IIP.............. Integrated Infrastructure Planning (SAUS)
IIP.............. Interceptor Improvement Program
IIP.............. Interface Implementation Plan (SAUO)
IIP.............. Intergovernmental Informatics Programme [*UNESCO*]
IIP.............. Interim Impact Predictor (AAG)
IIP.............. Intermediate Interceptor Program (SAUS)
IIP.............. International Ice Patrol [*Coast Guard*]
IIP.............. International Income Property, Inc. [*AMEX symbol*] (COMM)
IIP.............. International Institute for Peace [*Vienna, Austria*] (EA)
IIP.............. International Institute of Parasitology (SAUO)
IIP.............. International Institute of Peace (SAUS)
IIP.............. International Institute of Philosophy (AEBS)
IIP.............. International Institute of the Press (SAUS)
IIP.............. International Inter-Visitation Program in Educational Administration [*UniverstiyCouncil for Educational Administration*] (AEE)
IIP.............. Internet Imaging Protocol (SAUS)
IIP.............. Interoperability Improvement Panel (SAUS)
IiP.............. Investors in People (HEAS)
IIP.............. Irish Independence Party [*Political party*] (PPW)
IIP.............. ISDN Intermediate Interworking Profile (SAUS)
IIP.............. Israel Institute of Petroleum (SAUO)
IIP.............. Italian Institute for Plastic Materials (SAUO)
IIPA............ Indian Institute of Public Administration (SAUO)
IIPA............ Institute of Incorporated Practitioners in Advertising [*British*] (BI)
IIPA............ International Icelandic Pony Association (EA)
IIPA............ International Index to the Performing Arts [*Website*]
IIPA............ International Intellectual Property Association (EA)
IIPACS......... Integrated Information Presentation and Control System [*Aviation*]
IIPBM.......... Index of Individually Planned Bills of Material (SAUS)
IIPC............ Image Intensifier Plumbicon Camera
IIPCS.......... International Programme on Chemical Safety (SAUO)
IIPE............ Institute of International Politics and Economics, Beograd (SAUO)
IIPE............ Institut International de Planification de l'Education [*International Institute for Educational Planning*]
IIPE............ Institution of Incorporated Plant Engineers (SAUO)
IIPE............ International Institute for Educational Planning (SAUO)
IIPE............ International Institute on Peace Education (SAUO)
IIPEC.......... Institute for Interconnecting and Packaging Electronic Circuits (EA)
IIPER.......... International Institute for Production Engineering Research (EAIO)
IIPF............ International Institute of Public Finance [*Saarbrucken, Federal Republic of Germany*] (EAIO)
IIPG............ International Institute of Practical Geomancy [*Formerly, Society for Symbolic Studies*] (EA)
IIPI............. International Income Property, Incorporated (SAUO)
IIPIP........... International Union for the Protection of Industrial Property (SAUO)
IIPL............ Independent Investor Protective League (EA)
IIPL............ Interactive Image Processing Laboratory (SAUO)
IIPM........... Input Image Processing Method (SAUS)
IIPM........... Irish International Peace Movement (EAIO)
IIPO............ Illinois Inventory of Parent Opinion
IIPOA.......... International Institute for the Promotion of Outdoor Activities (SAUO)
IIPP............ Injury and Illness Prevention Program [*California*] (SARE)
IIPP............ Interactive Input Processing Program (SAUO)
IIPP............ International Institute for Promotion and Prestige [*Geneva, Switzerland*] (EAIO)
IIPR............ Installation Inspection Procedure Report
IIPR............ Istituto Internazionale di Psicologia della Reliosita' [*International Institute for the Psychology of Religion*] [*Italy*] (IRC)
IIPS............ Instantaneous Impact Prediction System (DNAB)
IIPS............ Institute of International Peace Studies (SAUO)
IIPS............ Interactive Image Processing Software (SAUS)
IIPS............ Interactive Information Processing Systems (SAUS)
IIPS............ Interactive Instructional Presentation System [*IBM*] (NITA)
IIPS............ International Conference on Interactive Information and Processing Systems (SAUS)
IIPS............ Irrevocably Interruptible Power Supply (SAUS)
IIPSF.......... Independent Interim Plutonium Oxide Storage Facility (SAUO)
IIQ.............. Initial Issue Quantities [*Military*]
IIR.............. Illinois Internet Resources (SAUO)
IIR.............. Image Interpreter Response
IIR.............. Imagery Interpretation Report (SAUS)
IIR.............. Imaging Infrared [*Air Force*] (MCD)
IIR.............. Imaging Infrared Sensor (SAUS)
IIR.............. Immediate Impulse Response (SAUO)
IIR.............. Infinite-Duration Impulse-Response (IEEE)
IIR.............. Infinite Impulse Response [*Electronics*]
IIR.............. Infra-red Imaging Radar (SAUS)
IIR.............. Initial Integration Review (SAUO)
IIR.............. Institute of Industrial Relations [*Loyola University of Chicago*] [*Research center*] (RCD)
IIR.............. Institute of Interdisciplinary Research (SAUS)
IIR.............. Institute of Intergovernmental Relations (SAUS)
IIR.............. Institute of Intermodal Repairers (EA)
IIR.............. Institute of International Relations (SAUO)
IIR.............. Institute of International Research (SAUS)

IIR Institut International du Froid [*International Institute of Refrigeration*] [*France*] (EA)
IIR Integrated Instrumentation RADAR
IIR Intelligence Information Report (NVT)
IIR Interactive Image Regeneration (VLIE)
IIR Intercom Information Resources, Inc. [*Information service or system*] (IID)
IIR Intermediate Infrared
IIR International Impala Resources [*Vancouver Stock Exchange symbol*]
IIR International Insitute of Refrigeration (SAUO)
IIR International Institute for Robotics (EA)
IIR International Institute of Rehabilitation [*Defunct*] (EA)
IIR International Institute of Reprography (SAUO)
IIR International Inventors Registry (NITA)
IIR Inventory and Inspection Report [*Army*] (MUGU)
IIR Invert Indicator of the Right Half (SAA)
IIR IRI International [*NYSE symbol*] (SG)
IIR Isobutene-Isoprene Rubber
IIR Isotactic Isoprene Rubber (SAUS)
IIR Resistance Heating (SAUS)
IIRA Integrated Inertial Reference Assembly (PDAA)
IIRA International Ice Racing Association
IIRA International Industrial Relations Association [*Geneva, Switzerland*] (EA)
IIRB Institut International de Recherches Betteravieres [*International Institute for Sugar Beet Research*] [*Brussels, Belgium*] (EA)
IIRB International Institute for Sugar Beet Research (SAUO)
IIRC If I Recall Correctly (SAUS)
IIRC If I Remember Correctly (VLIE)
IIRC Inactive Item Review Card [*Military*] (AFIT)
IIRC Incident Investigation Review Committee [*Nuclear Regulatory Commission*] (NRCH)
IIRC Indiana Interstate Railroad Co., Inc. [*AAR code*]
IIRC Indiana Interstate Railroad Company (SAUO)
IIRC Interrogation and Information Reception Circuit [*Telecommunications*] (OA)
IIRCAID If I Recall Correctly and I Do (ADWA)
IIRD International Interdependent Research and Development (AABC)
IIRE International Institute for Resource Economics [*Defunct*] (EA)
IIRES Imagery Reporting/Exploitation System (SAUO)
IIRES Imagery Reporting/Exploit System (SAUS)
IIRF Intergalactic Infrared Radiation Field
IIRFD Infinite-Impulse Response Filter Design (SAUS)
IIRFilter Infinite Impulse Response Filter (SAUS)
IIRG Institut International de Recherches Graphologiques
IIRGU Imaging Infrared Guidance Unit (ACAE)
IIRI International Industrial Relations Institute (SAUO)
IIRI International Institute for Land Reclamation and Improvement (SAUO)
IIRM Improved Infrared Missile
IIRM International Institute of Reconstructive Microsurgery (NRGU)
IIRM Irish Immigration Reform Movement (EA)
IIRMP Interim Indoor Radon Measurement Protocol [*Environmental science*] (COE)
IIRMS Industrial Information's Record Management System [*Computer science*]
IIRN Inactive Item Review Notification (ACAE)
IIRP Integrated Installation Requirement Plan (MCD)
IIRR Institute of Industrial Race Relations
IIRR International Institute for Rice Research (SAUO)
IIRR International Institute of Rural Reconstruction (EA)
IIRS Imaging Infrared System (ACAE)
IIRS Indian Institute of Remote Sensing (SAUO)
IIRS Institute of Industrial Research and Standards [*Ireland*] [*Research center*] [*Database producer*] (IID)
IIRS Instrumentation Inertial Reference Set [*Aviation*]
IIRS International Information Retrieval Service (SAUS)
IIRSM International Institute for/of Risk and Safety Management (SAUO)
IIRV Improved Inter-Range Vector (MCD)
IIs Iberial Inquisitions in Spain and Portugal (SAUS)
IIS IBM [*International Business Machines Corp.*] Information Services (HGAA)
IIS IIS Intelligent Information Systems [*Associated Press*] (SAG)
IIS Image Intensified System
IIS Imagery Interpretation Segment (SAUS)
IIS Imagery Interpretation System (MCD)
IIS Imaging Infrared System (SAUS)
IIS Immediate Image System (SAUS)
IIs Immigration Inspectors (SAUS)
IIS Improved Infrared Source
IIS INA Investment Sec [*NYSE symbol*] (TTSB)
IIS INA Investment Securities, Inc. [*NYSE symbol*] (SPSG)
IIS Increasing Index Sequence (SAUS)
IIS Indexation Information Statement [*Accounting*]
IIS Index to International Statistics [*A publication*]
IIS Indian Information Service (SAUO)
IIS Indian Institute of Science (SAUO)
IIS Indirect Identification System [*Military*] (MCD)
IIS Individual Information System (VLIE)
IIS Industrial Information Services [*Southern Methodist University*] [*Dallas, TX*]
IIS Industrial Inquiry Service (SAUO)
IIS Inflationary Impact Statement [*Economics*]
IIS Informational Intelligence Summary (SAUO)
IIS Information Improvement Support Program (SAUO)
IIS Information Input Signal (SAUS)
IIS Infrared Imaging System
IIS Infrared Instrumentation System
IIS Inmate Information System [*Bureau of Prisons*] (GFGA)
IIS Innovative Information Systems (ACAE)
IIS Inquiry into Science Program (SAUS)
IIS Inspection Instruction Sheet
IIS Inspection Item Sheet (MCD)
iis Inspection Item Sheet (NAKS)
IIS Inspections and Investigations Staff [*Vietnam*]
IIS Installation Information System (VLIE)
IIS Institute for Information Studies [*Inactive*] [*Research center*] (RCD)
IIS Institute for Intercultural Studies (EA)
IIS Institute of Industrial Sciences (ACAE)
IIS Institute of Industrial Supervisors (SAUO)
IIS Institute of Informatics Systems [*Russia*] (DDC)
IIS Institute of Information Scientists [*British*] (EAIO)
IIS Institute of International Studies (EA)
IIS Institut International de la Soudure [*International Institute of Welding - IIW*] (EAIO)
IIS Institut International de Statistique [*International Statistical Institute*]
IIS Instrumentation Integration System (SAUS)
IIS Insurance Institute of Singapore (SAUO)
IIS Integral Information System (SAUO)
IIS Integrated Information System
IIS Integrated Instrument Sheet (MCD)
IIS Integrated Instruments System
IIS Integrated Insulation System
IIS Intelligence Information System [*Military*] (DNAB)
IIS Intensive Immunosuppression [*Medicine*] (DMAA)
IIS Interactive Instructional System [*IBM Corp.*]
IIS Interface Instruction Sheet (SAUS)
IIS Intermediate Interceptor System (SAUS)
IIS Intermittent Infusion Sets (STED)
IIS Internationales Institut der Sparkassen [*International Savings Banks Institute*]
IIS International Information Service Ltd. [*Information service or system*] (IID)
IIS International Institute of Seismology and Earthquake Engineering [*Japan*] [*Seismograph station code, US Geological Survey*] (SEIS)
IIS International Institute of Sociology
IIS International Institute of Stress (EA)
IIS International Institutional Services (EA)
IIS International Insurance Seminars [*University, AL*] (EA)
IIS International Insurance Society (EAIO)
IIS International Isotope Society (EA)
IIS International Medical Imagery [*Vancouver Stock Exchange symbol*]
IIS Internet Information Server [*Computer science*] (PCM)
IIS Internet Integrated Services (SAUO)
IIS Internetted Information System (SAUO)
IIS Intrinsic Instruction Set (SAUS)
IIS Invert Indicator From Storage (SAA)
IIS Investment Income Surcharge [*Finance*] (MHDW)
IIS Ion Implantation Study
IIS Irish Institute of Secretaries Ltd. (BI)
IIS Nissan Island [*Papua New Guinea*] [*Airport symbol*] (OAG)
IISA Institut International des Sciences Administratives [*International Institute for Administrative Sciences*]
IISA Integrated Inertial Sensor Assembly (MCD)
IISA Integrated Information System Architecture (ACAE)
IISA Interservice/Interagency Support Agreement (MCD)
IISBR International Institute for Sugar Beet Research (EA)
IISC Integrated Iron and Steel Commission (SAUS)
IISC Intelligence Information Systems Committee (SAUO)
IISCC Intersociety Color Council (SAUO)
IISD If Incorrect Service Direct (FAAC)
IISD International Institute for Sustainable Development (QUAC)
IISD International Institute for the Study of Death (EA)
IISDI International Institute for the Study of Death and Immortality [*Later, IISD*] (EA)
IISE Insure Integrated Survivability Experiments (SAUS)
IISE Intelligence Information Services Enhancement programme (SAUS)
IISE International Institute of Social Economics [*Hull, England*] (EAIO)
IISEA Illinois Society of Enrolled Agents (SAUO)
II SEGMENT Imagery Interpretation Segment (SAUO)
IISF Intermediate Level Sample Flow (SAUS)
IISG Internationaal Instituut voor Sociale Geschiedenis [*International Institute for Social History*] (EA)
IISG International Institute of Social History (SAUO)
IISGP Illinois-Indiana Sea Grant Program (SAUS)
IISHI Institut International des Sciences Humaines Integrales [*International Institute of Integral Human Sciences - IIIHS*] (EAIO)
IISI International Iron and Steel Institute [*Brussels, Belgium*] [*Research center*] (EA)
IISIA Israeli Institute for the Study of International Affairs (SAUO)
IISJ Institute for Independent Social Journalism (EA)
IISL IIS [*Intelligent Information Systems*] Ltd. [*NASDAQ symbol*]
IISL International Institute of Space Law [*Baarn, Netherlands*] (EAIO)
IISL Istituto Internazionale di Studi Liguri [*International Institute for Ligurian Studies*]
IISLF I.I.S. Intellig't Info [*NASDAQ symbol*] (TTSB)
IISLS Improved Interrogator Sidelobe Suppression (SAUS)
IISLT Internal Information Systems Leadership Team (TIMI)
IISO If Incorrect Service Originator (SAUS)
IISO Institution of Industrial Safety Officers (SAUO)

IISP .... Improved Industrial Standard Process (MCD)
IISP .... Information Infrastructure Standards Panel (ITD)
IISP .... Interim Inter Signalling Protocol (SAUS)
IISP .... Interim Inter Switch Protocol (SAUS)
IISP .... Interim Interswitch Signaling Protocol [*Telecommunications*] (ACRL)
IISP .... International Institute of Site Planning (EA)
IISPA .... Interactive Instructional Systems-Presentation and Authoring Special Interest Group [*Association for the Development of Computer-Based Instructional Systems*] (EDAC)
IISPB .... Image and Information Standards Policy Board (SAUS)
IISPS .... International Institute of Social and Political Sciences (SAUO)
IISR .... International Institute for Submarine Research (SAUS)
IISRP .... Instrument Landing System Reference Point (SAUS)
IISRP .... International Institute of Synthetic Rubber Producers (EA)
IISS .... Image Inventory Search & Summary (SAUS)
IISS .... Integrated Information Support System [*Computer science*]
IISS .... Intelligence Information Subsystem [*Military*] (MCD)
IISS .... International Institute for Strategic Studies (EA)
IISS .... International Institute for the Science of Sintering [*Belgrade, Yugoslavia*] (EAIO)
IISS Comment... IISS Commentary (journ.) (SAUS)
IISSM .... Istituto Internazionale Suore di Santa Marcellina [*Milan, Italy*] (EAIO)
IISST .... Instrumental Interrogation System and Supporting Techniques (SAUO)
IIST .... Initial Interface Systems Test (ACAE)
IIST .... Institute for Information Storage Technology [*University of Santa Clara*] [*Research center*] (RCD)
IIST .... Institute for International Studies and Training (SAUO)
IIST .... Institution of Instrumentation Scientists and Technologists (SAUS)
IIST .... Integrated Interface Systems Test (ACAE)
IIST .... Intense Islet Stimulation Test [*Endocrinology*]
IIST .... International Institute for Safety in Transportation [*Formerly, IST*] (EA)
IIST .... International Institute of Sports Therapy [*British*]
IISTR .... International Institute of Scientific Travel Research (SAUO)
IISWM .... Institute of Iron and Steel Wire Manufacturers (MHDB)
IISWM .... International Institute of Iron and Steel Wire Manufacturers (SAUS)
IISX .... Integrated Information Sy. [*NASDAQ symbol*] (SG)
IIT .... Iligan Institute of Technology (SAUS)
IIT .... Illinois Institute of Technology (IID)
IIT .... Image Intensifier Tube
IIT .... Inclinable Indexing Table
IIT .... Independent Inclusive Tour (SAUS)
IIT .... Indiana Institute of Technology (SAUS)
IIT .... Individual Inclusive Tour [*Air fare plan*]
IIT .... Indonesian Satellite Corp. [*NYSE symbol*] (SAG)
IIT .... Industrial Information Transfer (NITA)
IIT .... Ineffective Iron Turnover (DMAA)
IIT .... Information Input Terminal (SAUS)
IIT .... Institut des Ingenieurs des Transports [*Institute of Transportation Engineers*] [*Canada*]
IIT .... Institute of Industrial Technicians (SAUO)
IIT .... Institut Interafricain du Travail
IIT .... Institut Internationale du Theatre [*International Theatre Institute - ITI*] (EAIO)
IIT .... Integrated Information Technology (SAUO)
IIT .... Integrated Information Transport (ACRL)
IIT .... Integrated Isometric Tension (STED)
IIT .... Internal Information Transfer (SAUO)
IIT .... International Investment Trust
IIT .... Intra-Industry Trade
IIT .... Islet-Infiltrating T
IIT .... Israel Institute of Technology (KSC)
IIT .... Perusahaan PT IndoSatADS [*NYSE symbol*] (TTSB)
IITA .... Info Infrastructure Technology and Applications (SAUS)
IITA .... Information Infrastructure Technology Applications [*Marine science*] (OSRA)
IITA .... Inland International Trade Association [*Sacramento, CA*] (EA)
IITA .... International Institute of Tropical Agriculture [*Ibadan, Nigeria*] [*Research center*] (EAIO)
IITB .... Indian Institute of Technology, Bombay (SAUS)
IITB .... Indian Institute of Technology-Bombay (SAUO)
IITC .... IITC Holdings Ltd. [*NASDAQ symbol*] (SAG)
IITC .... Inspector of Infantry Training Centers (SAUS)
IITC .... Insurance Industry Training Council (PDAA)
IITC .... Interactive Instructional Television Center (ACAE)
IITC .... Intera Information Technologies Corp. [*NASDAQ symbol*] (SAG)
IITC .... International Indian Treaty Council (EA)
IITCF .... IITC Holdings [*NASDAQ symbol*] (TTSB)
IITCHld .... IITC Holdings Ltd. [*Associated Press*] (SAG)
IITCS .... Igloo Internal Thermal Control Section [*Aerospace*] (MCD)
IITD .... Indian Institute of Technology, Delhi (SAUS)
IITD .... Institute of International Trade and Development (EA)
IITE .... Information Infrastructure Task Force [*Marine science*] (OSRA)
I/ITEC .... Interservice/Industry Training Equipment Conference [*Military*]
IITF .... In-Core Instrument Test Facility [*Nuclear energy*] (IAA)
IITF .... Information Infrastructure Task Force (USDC)
IITI .... International Information Technology Institute (CIST)
IITJ .... International Institute for Training of Journalists (SAUO)
IITK .... Indian Institute of Technology, Kanpur (SAUS)
IITK .... Indian Institute of Technology, Kharagpur (SAUS)
IITM .... Indian Institute for Tropical Meteorology (CARB)
IITM .... Indian Institute of Technology, Madras (SAUS)
IITM .... International Institute for High Technologies and New Materials (SAUS)
IITM .... International Institute for Traditional Music [*Germany*] (EAIO)
IITPW .... Inertial Interchange True Polar Wander [*Geophysics*]
IITR .... Illinois Institute of Technology Research (SAUO)
IITRAN .... Illinois Institute of Technology Translator (SAUO)
IITRAN .... Illinois Institute Training Council (SAUO)
IIT RES IN ... Illinois Institute of Technology Research Institute (MCD)
IITRI .... IIT Research Institute (SAUS)
IITRI .... Illinois Institute of Technology Research Institute [*Information service or system*] (IID)
IITRI-CSC ..... Illinois Institute of Technology Research Institutes Computer Search Center (SAUS)
IITS .... Igniter Initiator Test Set
IITS .... International Institute of Theoretical Sciences (SAUO)
IITS .... International Institute of Tourism Studies (SAUO)
IITS .... International Intradiscal Therapy Society (SAUO)
IITS .... Intratheater Imagery Transmission System [*Air Force*]
I/ITSC .... Interservice/Industry Training Systems Conference [*Military*]
I/ITSEC .... Interservice/Industry Training Systems and Education Conference (SAUS)
IITT-IITW ..... Institut International du Travail Temporaire - International Institute for Temporary Work (EAIO)
IITV .... Image-Intensified Television (MCD)
IITV .... Interactive Instructional Television (ACAE)
IITYWYBMAD... If I Tell You, Will You Buy Me a Drink [*Tavern sign*]
IIU .... Input Interface Unit [*Computer science*]
IIU .... Instruction Input Unit
IIU .... International Islamic University (SAUO)
IIUBS .... International Union of Biological Sciences (SAUO)
IIUPL .... International Institute for the Unification of Public Law (SAUO)
IIV .... Image Intensifier Viewer
IIV .... International Institute of Valuers (EA)
IIV&V .... Independent Integration, Verification, and Validation (SAUS)
IIVD .... Image Intensifier Viewing Device
IIVI .... II-VI, Inc. [*NASDAQ symbol*] (NQ)
IIVI 0-7 .... International Institute for Visually Impaired, Zero-7 (EA)
IIVRS .... International Institute for Vital Registration and Statistics (SAUO)
IIVS .... Intransit Item Visibility System (MCD)
IIVT .... Intensive Intravenous Treatment [*Medicine*]
IIVTG .... Industrial in Vitro Toxicology Group (GVA)
IIVW .... Internationales Institut fuer Verwaltungswissenschaften [*International Institute of Administrative Sciences*]
IIW .... International Inner Wheel (SAUO)
IIW .... International Institute of Welding [*See also IIS*] [*British*] (EAIO)
IIWG .... IEMATS Implementation Working Group (SAUO)
IIWG .... International Industry Working Group [*of the Air Transport Association of America*] (EAIO)
IIWG .... International Investigator Working Group (SAUO)
IIWI .... Interior Insulating Window Institute [*Defunct*] (EA)
IIWP .... Institute for Individual and World Peace (EA)
IIWPA .... International Information/Word Processing Association [*Formerly, IWPA*] [*Later, IWP*] (EA)
IIWPL .... International Institute for Women's Political Leadership [*Defunct*] (EA)
IIWS .... Intersystems Inc. Wrrt [*AMEX symbol*] (TTSB)
IIX .... Ion-Induced X-Rays (SAUS)
IIXC .... IXC Communications [*NASDAQ symbol*] (SG)
IIXL .... iXL Enterprises [*NASDAQ symbol*] (SG)
IIY .... International Institute of Youth (SAUO)
IIYA .... Institute for International Youth Affairs
IIZ .... Issaquah Industries [*Federal Railroad Administration identification code*]
IJ .... Ilejejunal [*Gastroenterology*] (DAVI)
IJ .... Im Jahre [*In the Year*] [*German*]
IJ .... Immigration Judge (SAUS)
IJ .... Incoming Junctor (SAUS)
IJ .... Indian Jurist, Old Series [*A publication*] (DLA)
IJ .... Indirect to Job Costs (DGA)
IJ .... Institute of Journalists [*British*] (NTCM)
IJ .... Instructor's Journal [*Air Force*]
IJ .... Internal Jugular [*Anatomy*]
IJ .... Internal Junctor [*Electronics*] (IAA)
IJ .... Intrajejunal (STED)
IJ .... Irish Jurist (SAUO)
IJ .... Irish Jurist (journ.) (SAUS)
IJ .... Jacksonville Public Library, Jacksonville, IL [*Library symbol*] [*Library of Congress*] (LCLS)
IJ .... Sisters of the Holy Infant Jesus [*Roman Catholic religious order*]
IJ .... Sisters of the Infant Jesus (TOCD)
IJ .... Touraine Air Transport [*ICAO designator*] (AD)
IJA .... Imperial Japanese Army [*World War II*]
IJA .... Institute of Jewish Affairs (EA)
IJA .... Institute of Judicial Administration (EA)
IJA .... International Journal of the Addictions (journ.) (SAUS)
IJA .... International Judiciary Association (SAUO)
IJA .... International Jugglers Association (EA)
IJA .... Inventory of Job Attitudes [*LIMRA*]
IJA .... Irving Independent School District, Irving, TX [*OCLC symbol*] (OCLC)
IJA .... Islamic Jurisprudence Academy [*See also IFA*] (EAIO)
IJAB .... Internationaler Jugendaustausch und Besucherdienst der Bundesrepublik Deutschland [*International Youth Exchange and Visitor Service of the Federal Republic of Germany*]
IJAB .... International Youth Exchange and Visitors Service of the Federal Republic of Germany (SAUO)
IJABC .... Iwo Jima Air Base Command (SAUO)
IJAHS .... International Journal of African Historical Studies [*A publication*]

IJAJ .... Intentional Jitter Antijam [*Military*]
IJAJ .... International Jitter Antijam (SAUS)
IJAL .... International Journal of American Folklore (journ.) (SAUS)
IJAL .... International Journal of American Linguistics (journ.) (SAUS)
IJAPA .... Internet Journal of Academic Physician Assistants (SAUS)
IJB .... Industrial Bank of Japan Ltd. (SAUO)
IJB .... Internationale Jugendbibliothek [*International Youth Library - IYL*] [*Munich, Federal Republic of Germany*] (EAIO)
IJB .... Interstate Job Bank
IJBBA .... International Junior Brangus Breeders Association (EA)
IJBC .... International Journal of Bio-Medical Computing [*Medicine*] (EDAA)
IJBE .... International Journal of Biomedical Engineering [*Medicine*] (EDAA)
IJBF .... International Jacques Brel Foundation (EA)
IJBFC .... International Jack Benny Fan Club (EA)
IJBS .... Integrated Joint Broadband System [*Army*] (AABC)
IJC .... Individual Job Card (SAUS)
IJC .... Interjob Communications (MHDB)
IJC .... International Joint Commission (EA)
IJC .... International Joint Conference (SAUS)
IJC .... International Journal of Cancer (journ.) (SAUS)
IJC .... Irvine's Justiciary Cases [*England*] [*A publication*] (DLA)
IJC .... Irving Public Library System, Irving, TX [*OCLC symbol*] (OCLC)
IJC .... Itasca Junior College [*Later, Itasca Community College*] [*Minnesota*]
IJC .... Itawamba Junior College [*Fulton, MS*]
IJCAA .... Iowa Junior College Athletic Association (PSS)
IJCAI .... International Joint Conference on Artificial Intelligence
IJCAII .... International Joint Conferences on Artificial Intelligence, Incorporated (SAUO)
IJ Cas .... Irvine's Justiciary Cases [*England*] [*A publication*] (DLA)
IJCEH .... International Journal of Clinical & Experimental Hypnosis (SAUS)
IJCI .... Junior Chamber International (SAUO)
IJCIC .... International Jewish Committee on Interreligious Consultations (EA)
IJCIS .... International Journal of Computer and Information Sciences (journ.) (SAUS)
IJCIS .... International Journal of Computers and Information Sciences (journ.) (SAUS)
IJCNN .... International Joint Conference on Neural Networks
IJCR .... Institute for Jewish-Christian Relations (EA)
IJCRAB .... International Joint Commission Research Advisory Board (SAUS)
IJCS .... Integrated Joint Communication System [*Military*] (AABC)
IJCS .... International Journal of Comparative Sociology. Karnatak University, Department of Social Anthropology (SAUO)
IJCS .... INT Journal of Comparative Sociology (journ.) (SAUS)
IJCS-PAC .... Integrated Joint Communication System - Pacific [*Military*]
IJCT .... International Journal of the Classical Tradition (journ.) (SAUS)
IJD .... Inflammatory Joint Disease [*Medicine*] (DMAA)
IJD .... Institutum Judaicum Delitzschianum (BJA)
IJD .... Interim JOPES Dictionary (SAUS)
IJD .... International Journal of Dermatology (journ.) (SAUS)
IJDA .... International Joseph Diseases Association (EA)
IJDA .... International Journal of Dental Anthropology (SAUS)
IJDF .... International Joseph Diseases Foundation (EA)
IJDL .... International Journal of Dravidian Linguistics (journ.) (SAUS)
IJDM .... Israel Journal of Dental Medicine [*Medicine*] (EDAA)
IJDS .... Indian Journal of Dairy Science (SAUO)
IJDS .... Indian Journal of Dairy Science (journ.) (SAUS)
IJDW .... Im Jahre der Welt [*In the Year of the World*] [*German*]
IJE .... Avijet SA de CV [*Mexico*] [*ICAO designator*] (FAAC)
IJE .... Indian Journal of Economics (journ.) (SAUS)
IJE .... Institute for Journalism Education (SAUS)
IJE .... Institute of Jewish Education [*British*] (DBA)
IJE .... International Journal of Ethics (SAUO)
IJE .... Inverse Joule Effect
IJe .... Jerseyville Free Library, Jerseyville, IL [*Library symbol*] [*Library of Congress*] (LCLS)
IJEA .... Interim Joint Engineering Agency (SAUO)
IJeH .... Jersey Community Hospital, Jerseyville, IL [*Library symbol*] [*Library of Congress*] (LCLS)
IJEHR .... International Journal of Environmental Health Research (SAUS)
IJES .... Indian Journal of English Studies (journ.) (SAUS)
IJeSD .... Jersey Community Unit, School District 100, Jerseyville, IL [*Library symbol*] [*Library of Congress*] (LCLS)
IJF .... Image Journal File (SAUS)
IJF .... Internationale Judo Foederation [*International Judo Federation*] [*Germany*] (EA)
IJF .... International Jazz Federation (EA)
IJF .... Robinson Crusoe Island [*Juan Fernandez Archipelago*] [*Seismograph station code, US Geological Survey*] (SEIS)
I-J FC .... Iselin-Jefferson Financial Co. (SAUS)
I-J FC .... Iselin-Jefferson Financial Company (SAUO)
IJFD .... International Journal of Forensic Dentistry [*UK*] [*Medicine*] (EDAA)
IJFRS .... Irish Joint Fiction Reserve Scheme (AIE)
IJGIS .... International Journal of Geographical Information Systems (journ.) (SAUS)
IJH .... Iowa Journal of History (journ.) (SAUS)
IJHP .... Internet Journal of Health Promotion (SAUS)
IJHP .... Iowa Journal of History and Politics (journ.) (SAUS)
IJI .... Illegal Jewish Immigrant [*British occupation of Palestine, 1945-48*] (DI)
IJI .... Illinois College, Jacksonville, IL [*Library symbol*] [*Library of Congress*] (LCLS)
IJI .... Internationaal Juridisch Instituut [*International Juridical Institute*] [*BENELUX*]
IJI .... International Journalism Institute (SAUO)
IJI .... International Juridical Institute (SAUO)
IJI .... Islamic Jamhoori Ittedad [*Islamic Democratic Alliance*] [*Pakistan*] [*Political party*]
IJIAP .... International Juridical Institute for Animal Protection (SAUO)
IJIC .... International Journal of Intelligence and Counterintelligence (CARL)
IJIN .... International Jensen, Inc. [*NASDAQ symbol*] (SAG)
IJIN .... IntlJensen [*NASDAQ symbol*] (TTSB)
IJIR .... International Journal of Impotence Research [*A publication*]
IJIR .... International Journal of Intercultural Relations [*A publication*] (DHP)
IJISID .... Imperial Japanese Institute for the Study of Infectious Diseases (SAUO)
IJISID .... Imperial Sapanese Institute for the Study of Infectious Diseases (SAUS)
IJ/JJ .... Jamaica Journal. Institute of Jamaica. Kingston (journ.) (SAUS)
IJJU .... Intentional Jitter Jamming Unit [*Military*]
IJK .... Internationale Juristen-Kommission [*International Commission of Jurists*]
IJL .... Indian Journal of Linguistics/Praci-Bhasha-Vijnan (journ.) (SAUS)
IJL .... Institute for Jewish Life (SAUO)
IJL .... Institute of Jewish Life Media Project [*Later, JMS*]
IJL .... International Journal of Leprosy [*A publication*]
IJL .... Interstate/Johnson Lane [*NYSE symbol*] (TTSB)
IJL .... Interstate Johnson Lane, Inc. [*NYSE symbol*] (SAG)
IJLB .... Infantry Junior Leaders Battalion (SAUS)
IJLB .... International Jewish Labor Bund (EA)
IJLOMD .... International Journal of Leprosy and Other Mycobacterial Disease [*Medicine*] (EDAA)
IJLP .... Islamic Jihad for the Liberation of Palestine (SAUS)
IJMA .... Indian Jute Millers Association (SAUO)
IJMA .... Infant and Juvenile Manufacturers Association (EA)
IJMA .... International Jewish Media Association (NTPA)
IJMac .... MacMurray College, Jacksonville, IL [*Library symbol*] [*Library of Congress*] (LCLS)
IJMARI .... Indian Jute Millers Association Research Institute (SAUS)
IJMARI .... Indian Jute Mills Association Research Institute (SAUO)
IJMES .... International Journal for Middle East Studies [*A publication*] (ABAR)
IJMH .... International Journal of Mental Health [*Medicine*] (EDAA)
IJMI .... International Jacques Maritain Institute [*See also IIJM*] (EAIO)
IJMMS .... International Journal of Man-Machine Studies (SAUO)
IJMS .... Interim Joint Message System (SAUS)
IJMS .... Interim JTDS Message Standard (SAUS)
IJMS .... Interim JTIDS [*Joint Tactical Information Distribution System*] Message Standard
IJMS .... Israel Journal of Medical Sciences (journ.) (SAUS)
IJMVT .... International Journal of Micrographics and Video Technology [*A publication*]
IJN .... Imperial Japanese Navy [*World War II*]
IJN .... International Justice Network [*Defunct*] (EA)
IJNA .... International Journal of Nautical Archaeology and Underwater Exploration [*A publication*] (ABAR)
IJNMB .... International Journal of Nuclear Medicine and Biology [*Medicine*] (EDAA)
IJNME .... International Journal for Numerical Methods in Engineering (journ.) (SAUS)
IJNP .... International Journal of Nursing Practice (journ.) (SAUS)
IJO .... Idiopathic Juvenille Osteoporosis [*Medicine*] (MELL)
IJO .... Independent Jewelers Organization (EA)
IJO .... Individual Job Order
IJO .... International Journal of Oral and maxillofacial surgery (SAUS)
IJO .... International Journal of Osteoarchaeology [*A publication*]
IJO .... International Juridical Organization [*Later, IJOED*] (EAIO)
IJO .... International Juridical Organization for Developing Countries (SAUO)
IJO .... International Juridical Organization for Environment and Development (SAUO)
IJO .... Internet Journal of Ophthalmology (SAUS)
IJO .... Inventory of Job Openings [*State Employee Security Agency*] (OICC)
IJOA .... International Juvenile Officers' Association (EA)
IJOAR .... International Journal of Opinion and Attitude Research (journ.) (SAUS)
IJOED .... International Juridical Organization for Environment and Development (EAIO)
IJoI .... Joliet Public Library, Joliet, IL [*Library symbol*] [*Library of Congress*] (LCLS)
IJoIStF .... College of Saint Francis, Joliet, IL [*Library symbol*] [*Library of Congress*] (LCLS)
IJOPM .... International Journal of Operations and Production Management (journ.) (SAUS)
IJOSC .... International Junior Officers Course (SAUS)
IJP .... Idiopathic Juvenile Periodontitis [*Dentistry*] (PDAA)
IJP .... Inhibitory Junction Potential [*Neurophysiology*]
IJP .... Ink Jet Printer (SAUS)
IJP .... Ink Jet Printing
IJP .... Internal Job Processing (IAA)
IJP .... Internal Job Processor (SAUS)
IJP .... Internal Jugular Pressure [*Medicine*] (MAE)
IJP .... International Journal of Parapsychology (journ.) (SAUS)
IJP .... International Journal of Physical Distribution and Materials Management (journ.) (SAUS)
IJP .... International Juvenile Publications
IJP .... Israel Jewish Press (BJA)
IJPA .... International Jelly and Preserve Association (EA)
IJPA .... International Journal of Psychoanalysis (SAUS)
IJPC .... International Journal of Pharmaceutical Compounding (journ.) (SAUS)
IJPhys .... Indian Journal of Physics and Proceedings of the Indian Association for the Cultivation of Science (SAUO)
IJPM .... International Journal of Psychiatry in Medicine (journ.) (SAUS)

IJPN International Journal of Palliative Nursing (SAUS)
IJPPP International Journal of Psychopathology, Psychopharmacology, and Psychotherapy (SAUS)
IJPPR Institute for Jewish Policy Planning and Research [*Defunct*] (EA)
IJPR International Journal of Production Research (journ.) (SAUS)
IJPR Israel Journal of Psychiatry and Related Sciences (journ.) (SAUS)
IJPsa International Journal of Psychoanalysis (journ.) (SAUS)
IJPSMHI Industrial Jacks Product Section of the Material Handling Institute [*Defunct*] (EA)
IJPT Integrated Job Performance Training (SAUS)
IJR Institute for Justice Research [*American University*] [*Research center*] (RCD)
IJR Institute for Juvenile Research [*Illinois Department of Mental Health-University of Illinois at Chicago*] [*Research center*] (RCD)
IJR International Journal of Research in Marketing (journ.) (SAUS)
IJRCS International Joint Rules Committee on Softball [*Later, ASA*] (EA)
IJROBP International Journal of Radiation Oncology Biology Physics (journ.) (SAUS)
IJS Inferior Joint Space (SAUS)
IJS Input Job Stream (SAUS)
IJS Institute of Jazz Studies [*Rutgers University, University of New Jersey*] [*Research center*] (EA)
IJS Institute of Jesuit Sources (SAUO)
IJS Institute of Jewish Studies (SAUO)
IJS Interactive Job Submission [*Computer science*]
IJS International Journal of Sexology (journ.) (SAUS)
IJS International Journal of Social Economics (journ.) (SAUS)
IJS Interrupt Jet Sensor
IJS Rutgers-[*The*] State University, Institute of Jazz Studies, Newark, NJ [*OCLC symbol*] (OCLC)
IJS Silvair, Inc. [*ICAO designator*] (FAAC)
IJSBA International Jet Ski Boating Association (EA)
IJSHOF International Jewish Sports Hall of Fame
IJSLP International Journal of Slavic Linguistics and Poetics (journ.) (SAUS)
IJSP International Journal of Social Psychiatry (SAUS)
IJSS International John Steinbeck Society (EA)
IJT Interflight (Learjet) Ltd. [*British*] [*ICAO designator*] (FAAC)
IJTC Incoming Junctor Test Circuit (SAUS)
IJTN International Journal of Trauma Nursing (SAUS)
IJU Ijui [*Brazil*] [*Airport symbol*] (OAG)
IJV Internal Jugular Vein [*Medicine*] (DMAA)
IJV Jeffersonville Township Public Library, Jeffersonville, IN [*OCLC symbol*] (OCLC)
IJVA International Journal of Verbal Aggression (journ.) (SAUS)
IJVC International Joint Venture Co. (SAUS)
IJVC International Joint Venture Company (SAUO)
IJWU International Jewelry Workers Union [*Later, Service Employees International Union*] (EA)
IJX Equidyne Corp. [*AMEX symbol*]
IJX Jacksonville, IL [*Location identifier*] [*FAA*] (FAAL)
IJZ Summersville, WV [*Location identifier*] [*FAA*] (FAAL)
IK Eureka Aero Industries [*ICAO designator*] (AD)
Ik Ichabod (SAUS)
IK Ihud ha-Kibbutsim (BJA)
IK I Know (SAUS)
IK Imitation Kraft [*Paper*] (DGA)
IK Immobilized Knee [*Orthopedics*]
IK Immunekoerper [*Immune Bodies*] [*Medicine*]
IK Immunoconglutinin (MAE)
IK Index Kewensis (SAUS)
IK Indicator Kit
IK Infanteriekolonne [*Infantry Supply Column*] [*German military - World War II*]
IK Infusoria Killing [*Unit*] [*Medicine*]
IK Inner Keel
I/K Inspector/Killer
IK Installation Kit (SAUS)
IK Interbank (ADA)
IK Interchange Key (SAUS)
IK Intercollegiate Knights [*An association*] (EA)
IK Interkinase Domain [*Genetics*]
IK Interlake Corp. [*NYSE symbol*] (TTSB)
IK Interlake, Inc. (SAUO)
IK Interstitial Keratitis [*Ophthalmology*]
IK Inverse Kinematics [*Computer science*]
IKA International Kitefliers Association [*Defunct*] (EA)
IKampR Kampsville Reading Center, Kampsville, IL [*Library symbol*] [*Library of Congress*] (LCLS)
IKan Kansas Community Memorial Library, Kansas, IL [*Library symbol*] [*Library of Congress*] (LCLS)
IKanSD Kansas Community Unit School District, Kansas, IL [*Library symbol*] [*Library of Congress*] (LCLS)
IKAR Internationale Kommission fuer Alpines Rettungswesen [*International Commission for Alpine Rescue*] [*Birchwil, Switzerland*] (EAIO)
IKAROS Intelligence and Knowledge Aided Recognition of Speech (EURO)
IKAT Interactive Keyboard and Terminal [*Computer science*] (MCD)
IKB Intelligent Keyboard (SAUS)
IKB Internationale Kommunistenbond [*International Communist League*] [*Netherlands*] (PPW)
IKB International Klein Blue [*Color named after French painter Yves Klein*]
IKB Isambard Kingdom Brunei (SAUS)
IKB Wilkesboro, NC [*Location identifier*] [*FAA*] (FAAL)
IKBD Intelligent Keyboard Device
IKBM Integrated Knowledge Based Modelling (NITA)
IKBS Intelligent Knowledge-Based System [*Artificial intelligence*]
IKC In-Kind Contribution (COE)
IKC Inquiry Keyboard Control (SAUS)
IKC Interkernal Communication (NITA)
IKC International Kennel Club of Chicago (EA)
IKC Kankakee Community College, Kankakee, IL [*Library symbol*] [*Library of Congress*] (LCLS)
IK-CAPE Industriekooperation Computer Aided Process Engineering (SAUS)
IKCs International Keratorefractive Centers (SAUS)
IKE IBM Kiosk for Education (SAUS)
ike Iconoscope [*A television camera tube*] (WDMC)
ike ikebana (SAUS)
ike ikebanism (SAUS)
IKE Imperial Klingon Embassy/Star Trek [*An association*] (EA)
IKE Internet Key Exchange (SAUS)
IKE Ion Kinetic Energy
IKe Kewanee Public Library, Kewanee, IL [*Library symbol*] [*Library of Congress*] (LCLS)
IKEA Ingvar Kamprad, Elmtaryd, Agunnaryd [*Initialism is company name derived from the names of its founder, the farm on which he grew up, and a Swedish village*]
IKeB Black Hawk College, East Campus, Kewanee, IL [*Library symbol*] [*Library of Congress*] (LCLS)
IKEC Indiana-Kentucky Electric Corporation (SAUO)
IKEC InterAction Media Corp. [*NASDAQ symbol*] (SAG)
IKECA International Kitchen Exhaust Cleaning Association (NTPA)
IKEL Internacia Komitato por Etnaj Liberecoj [*International Committee for Ethnic Liberty - ICEL*] [*Eschweiler, Federal Republic of Germany*] (EAIO)
IKES Internacia Komisiono Esperanto kaj Sociologio (SAUO)
IKES Ion Kinetic Energy Spectrometry
IKET Individual Knowledge Evaluation Test (AFM)
IKF International Kart Federation (EA)
IKF International Kneeboarding Federation (SAUO)
IKF International Korfball Federation (EA)
IKF International Kraft Federation (EA)
IKFC International Knife and Fork Clubs (EA)
IKFS International Kids Fashion Show (ITD)
IKG Champaign Public Library, Champaign, IL [*OCLC symbol*] (OCLC)
IKG Internationale Kommission fuer Glas [*International Commission on Glass*]
IKG International Gift Commission (SAUO)
IKG Israelitische Kultusgemeinde [*Vienna*] [*A publication*] (BJA)
IKGS Indiana-Kentucky Geological Society (SAUO)
IKH Ihre Koenigliche Hoheit [*His (or Her) Royal Highness*] [*German*]
IKHS International Kodak Historical Society (EA)
IKI Iki [*Japan*] [*Airport symbol*] (OAG)
IKI Incendiary Kit, Improved (SAUO)
IKI Institute of Space Research [*Former USSR*] [*Acronym is based on foreign phrase*]
IKI Internacional Kongreso di Ido (SAUO)
IKIF Individual Name and Address Key Index File [*IRS*]
IKIHS I-Know-It's-Here-Somewhere [*Keyboarding technique*]
IKIM Institute of Islamic Understanding [*Think-tank*] [*Malaysia*] (ECON)
IKJ Ikusaka [*Japan*] [*Seismograph station code, US Geological Survey*] (SEIS)
IKJ Internationales Kuratorium fuer das Jugendbuch [*International Board on Books for Young People*]
IKK Kankakee, IL [*Location identifier*] [*FAA*] (FAAL)
IKL Ikela [*Zaire*] [*Airport symbol*] (AD)
IKL Intersecting Kikuchi Lines (SAUS)
IKL Isaenmaallinen Kansanliike [*Patriotic People's Movement*] [*Finland*] [*Political party*] (PPE)
IKM In Kind Matching (OICC)
IKM Institut Kimia Malaysia
IKM Texas State Library and Historical Commission, Austin, TX [*OCLC symbol*] (OCLC)
IKMB Internationale Katholische Mittelstandsbewegung [*International Catholic Union of the Middle Class*]
IKMP Internet Key Management Protocol (SAUS)
IKN Delco Electronics Division, General Motors Corp., Technical Library, Kokomo, IN [*OCLC symbol*] (OCLC)
IKN Ikon Office Solutions [*NYSE symbol*] (SG)
IKN Inmont Corp. (SAUO)
IKN Interchemical Corp. (SAUO)
IKN Internationale Kommission fuer Numismatik [*International Numismatic Commission*]
IKO International Kiwifruit Organization (SAUO)
IKO Nikolski [*Alaska*] [*Airport symbol*] (OAG)
IKON Olivet Nazarene College, Kankakee, IL [*Library symbol*] [*Library of Congress*] (LCLS)
IKOR Immediate Knowledge of Results
IKOR Instant Knowledge of Results (SAUS)
IKOS IKOS Systems [*NASDAQ symbol*] (TTSB)
IKOS Ikos Systems, Inc. [*NASDAQ symbol*] (SAG)
IKP Indiai Kommunista Part [*Communist Party of India*] [*Political party*]
IKP Indian Communist Party [*Political party*]
IKP Indonesian Communist Party [*Political party*]
IKP Inkopah [*California*] [*Seismograph station code, US Geological Survey*] (SEIS)
IKP Instructor and Key Personnel
IKP Internet Keyed Payments (SAUS)
IKP Irakskaia Kommunisticheskaia Partiia [*Iraqi Communist Party*] [*Political party*]
IKP Iranian Communist Party [*Political party*]

IKP .... Iraqi Communist Party [*Political party*]
IKP .... Irish Communist Party [*Political party*]
IKP .... Israeli Communist Party [*Political party*]
IKP .... Italian Communist Party [*Political party*]
IKP .... Kokomo Public Library, Kokomo, IN [*OCLC symbol*] (OCLC)
IKPO .... Internationale Kriminalpolizeiliche Organisation [*International Criminal Police Organization*]
IKPT .... Instructor and Key Personnel Training
IKr .... Icelandic Krona (SAUS)
IKR .... Ikaros DK [*Denmark*] [*ICAO designator*] (FAAC)
IKRA .... International Kirlian Research Association (EA)
I/KRC .... Information/Knowledge Research Centre (SAUS)
IKRD .... Inverse Kinetics Rod Drop [*Nuclear energy*] (NRCH)
IKRK .... Internationales Komittee vom Roten Kreuz [*International Committee of the Red Cross*]
IKS .... Imaging Kernel System [*Computer science*] (BTTJ)
IKS .... Integrated Key Set [*Computer science*]
IKS .... International Kodaly Society (EAIO)
IKS .... International Kolping Society [*See also IKW*] [*Cologne, Federal Republic of Germany*] (EAIO)
IKS .... Intraspect Knowledge Server (HODG)
IKS .... Inverse Kinetics Simulator
IKSR .... Internationale Kommission zum Schutze des Rheins Gegen Verunreinigung [*International Commission for the Protection of the Rhine Against Pollution - ICPRAP*] (EAIO)
IKT .... Iakutaviatrans [*Russian Federation*] [*ICAO designator*] (FAAC)
IKT .... INTRUST Capital Trust [*AMEX symbol*] (NASQ)
IKT .... Irkutsk [*Former USSR*] [*Airport symbol*] (OAG)
IKTS .... International Klaus Tennstedt Society [*Defunct*] (EA)
IKU .... Infusoria-Killing Unit (DB)
IKU .... Interface Keying Unit [*Computer science*] (KSC)
IKUE .... Internacia Katolica Unuigo Esperantista [*International Catholic Esperanto Association*] (EA)
IK Unit .... Infusoria Killing Unit (SAUS)
IKV .... Internationaler Kranckenhausverbaund [*International Hospital Federation*]
IKVSA .... Internationale Katholische Vereinigung fuer Soziale Arbeit [*Catholic International Union for Social Service*]
IKW .... Indicated Kilowatts per Hour [*Engine emissions testing*]
IKW .... Intercept & Kill Weapon (SAUS)
IKW .... Internationales Kolpingwerk [*International Kolping Society - IKS*] [*Cologne, Federal Republic of Germany*] (EAIO)
IKX .... Windsor Locks, CT [*Location identifier*] [*FAA*] (FAAL)
IL .... Bomber [*Russian aircraft symbol*]
IL .... Iceland [*IYRU nationality code*]
IL .... Identification Letter (SAUS)
IL .... Identification List
IL .... Identifying Label (SAUS)
IL .... Ideologies and Literature. Institute for the Study of Ideologies and Literature. Minneapolis (journ.) (SAUS)
IL .... Idle (BUR)
IL .... Ileum (DB)
Il .... Iliad [*of Homer*] [*Classical studies*] (OCD)
IL .... Ilinium (SAUS)
IL .... Ilio-Lumbar (SAUS)
IL .... Illinium (MAE)
IL .... Illinois [*Postal code*]
IL .... Illinois Central Industries, Inc. (SAUO)
IL .... Illinois Supreme Court Reports [*A publication*] (DLA)
IL .... Illite [*A mineral*]
IL .... Illium [*Anatomy*] (IAA)
IL .... Illogical Logic (SAUS)
il .... Illustrated [*or Illustrator*]
IL .... Illustration
il .... Ilmenite [*Also, ILM*] [*CIPW classification*] [*Geology*]
IL .... Ilyushin [*Former USSR*] [*ICAO aircraft manufacturer identifier*] (ICAO)
Il .... Ilyushin Design Bureau (SAUO)
IL .... Imaging Language (SAUS)
IL .... Imaging Library (SAUS)
IL .... I'm Leavin' Elvis Photos, Exclusive (EA)
IL .... Impact Level (ABAC)
IL .... Imperial Life Assurance Company of Canada (SAUO)
IL .... Imperial Life Assurance Co. of Canada [*Toronto Stock Exchange symbol*]
I/L .... Import Licence (SAUO)
IL .... Impulse Laser (SAUS)
IL .... Incandescent Light (SAUS)
IL .... Incisolingual [*Dentistry*]
IL .... Inclined Ladder (AAG)
IL .... Including Loading
IL .... Incoming Letter
IL .... Incorrect Length (SAUS)
IL .... Incres Line (SAUS)
IL .... Indent Left [*Typography*] (DGA)
il .... Indent Left (WDMC)
IL .... Independence League (SAUO)
IL .... Independent Laboratory (SAUO)
IL .... Independent Living [*An association*] [*Defunct*] (EA)
IL .... Index Linked [*Government bonds*] [*British*]
IL .... Index Lists [*DoD*]
IL .... Indicating Lamp (SAUS)
IL .... Indicating Light
IL .... Indication Lamp (SAUS)
IL .... Indicator Location (SAUS)
IL .... Individualized Learning (OICC)
IL .... Individual Line (IAA)
IL .... Inertial Laboratory [*NASA*] (KSC)
IL .... Information Labeling
IL .... Information Language (VLIE)
IL .... Information Loss (SAUS)
IL .... Informative Language (SAUS)
IL .... Inhibit Line (SAUS)
IL .... Initial Library (VLIE)
IL .... Initial Line (SAUS)
IL .... Injection Long Wheelbase [*Automotive engineering*]
IL .... Injection Luminescence (SAUS)
IL .... In Ladestreifen [*Loaded in Clips*] [*German military - World War II*]
I-L .... In-Law
IL .... In-Lock
IL .... Input Language (SAUS)
IL .... Insensible Weight Loss (MEDA)
IL .... Insertion Loss
IL .... Insert Line (SAUS)
IL .... Inside Layer [*Technical drawings*]
IL .... Inside Left [*Soccer position*]
IL .... Inside Leg (ADA)
IL .... Inside Length [*Technical drawings*]
IL .... Institute of Linguists [*British*] (BI)
IL .... Instruction Label (SAUS)
IL .... Instruction Leader (SAUS)
IL .... Instruction Leaflet (MSA)
IL .... Instruction List
IL .... Instructor-Lieutenant [*Navy*] [*British*]
IL .... Instrumental Landing (SAUS)
IL .... Instrumentation Laboratory (MCD)
IL .... Instrument Landing (IAA)
IL .... Insulation Level (IAA)
IL .... Insulators [*JETDS nomenclature*] [*Military*] (CET)
IL .... Intelligence Liaison [*Program*] [*Department of State*]
IL .... Intensity Level [*Physics*] (IAA)
IL .... Intercommunication Link (SAUS)
IL .... Intereact Ltd. [*British*]
IL .... Interface Loop (SAUS)
IL .... Interior Landscape (SAUO)
IL .... Interior Length
IL .... Interior Lighting [*Automotive engineering*]
IL .... Interleaver (ACAE)
IL .... Interleukin [*Biochemistry*]
IL .... Interline
il .... interlinear (SAUS)
il .... interlinearly (SAUS)
IL .... Intermediary Letter
IL .... Intermediate Land (DNAB)
IL .... Intermediate Language [*Computer science*] (BUR)
I/L .... Intermediate Layover (SAUS)
IL .... Intermediate Level (MCD)
IL .... Intermediate Loop
IL .... Internal Label (VLIE)
IL .... Internal Logic (SAUS)
IL .... International Baseball League (SAUO)
IL .... International League [*Baseball*]
IL .... International Library [*A publication*]
IL .... International Linguistics Corp. (SAUO)
IL .... International List
IL .... International Logistics (AABC)
IL .... Interocean Line (SAUS)
IL .... Interpolated Learning [*Psychology*]
IL .... Interpretative Language (SAUS)
IL .... Interpretive Language (PDAA)
IL .... Interrupt Level (SAUS)
IL .... Interrupt List (VLIE)
IL .... Intervention Level (SAUO)
il .... Intralesional (DB)
IL .... Intralipid [*Pharmacology*] (DAVI)
IL .... Intralumbal (SAUS)
IL .... Intraocular Lens [*Ophthalmology*] (DAVI)
IL .... Investigation Level (SAUS)
IL .... Ionization (Energy) Loss [*Physical chemistry*] (ODA)
IL .... Ionoluminescence (SAUS)
IL .... Irish Land Reports (Fitzgibbon) [*A publication*] (DLA)
IL .... Iron Loss (SAUS)
IL .... Island Air [*ICAO designator*] (AD)
IL .... Isolation League (SAUO)
IL .... Israel [*ANSI two-letter standard code*] (CNC)
Il .... Israel (MILB)
IL .... Israel Lira (BJA)
IL .... Italiana Luce (EFIS)
Il .... Italian Line (SAUS)
IL .... Italian Lira [*Monetary unit*]
IL .... Item List (AFIT)
IL .... Ives Laboratories [*Research code symbol*]
IL .... Ivy League (EA)
IL .... L'Internationale Liberale
IL .... Lisle Library District, Lisle, IL [*Library symbol*] [*Library of Congress*] (LCLS)
IL 1 .... Implementation Language 1 (SAUS)
IL1 .... Interleukin I (LDT)
IL1RAcM ...... Interleukin-1-Receptor Accessory Molecule (SAUS)
IL2 .... Interleukin II (LDT)

IL 2d .... Illinois Supreme Court Reports, Second Series [*A publication*] (DLA)
ILA .... All India Library Association (SAUO)
ILA .... Ilan [*Giran*] [*Republic of China*] [*Seismograph station code, US Geological Survey*] (SEIS)
ILA .... Illaga [*Indonesia*] [*Airport symbol*] (OAG)
IL A .... Illinois Appellate Court Reports [*A publication*] (DLA)
ILA .... Illinois Library Association (SAUO)
ILA .... Image Light Amplifier (SAUS)
ILa .... Incisolabial [*Dentistry*]
ILA .... Independent Label Association (EA)
ILA .... Independent Literary Agent (SAUS)
ILA .... Indiana Library Association (SAUO)
ILA .... Indian Limitation Act [*British*] (ROG)
ILA .... Indonesian Library Association (SAUO)
ILA .... Induction Linear Accelerator (SAUS)
ILA .... Informationsstelle Lateinamerika [*Germany*]
ILA .... Initial Load Address (SAUS)
ILA .... Injection Locked Amplifier (PDAA)
ILA .... Institute of Landscape Architects [*British*]
ILA .... Institute of Latin America of the Academy of Sciences of the USSR (SAUO)
ILA .... Instruction Look-Ahead [*Unit*] [*Computer science*]
ILA .... Instrument Landing Aid
ILA .... Instrument Landing Approach
ILA .... Instrument Low Approach [*Aircraft landing method*]
ILA .... Insulin-Like Activity
ILA .... Insurance Logistics Automated (PDAA)
ILA .... Integrated Laboratory Automation
ILA .... Intelligent Line Adapter
ILA .... Interim Legislative Assembly (SAUS)
ILA .... Inter-Laboratory Agreement (SAUS)
ILA .... Intermediate Level Amplifier (MHDB)
ILA .... International Labelling Association (SAUO)
ILA .... International Language for Aviation
ILA .... International Laundry Association
ILA .... International Law Association [*British*] (EA)
ILA .... International Law Association, Sezione Italiana (SAUO)
ILA .... International Leading Association (SAUO)
ILA .... International Leprosy Association [*India*]
ILA .... International Linguistic Association (SAUO)
ILA .... International Listening Association (EA)
ILA .... International Llama Association (EA)
ILA .... International Longshoremen's Association (EA)
ILA .... Internet Learning Agent (IDAI)
ILA .... Internet Library Association (TELE)
iLA .... Intralaminar [*Medicine*] (EDAA)
ILA .... Iowa Library Association (SAUO)
ILA .... Iranian Library Association (SAUO)
ILA .... Iraq Library Association (SAUO)
ILA .... Iterative Linear Algebra (SAUS)
ILA .... Iterative Logic Array (MCD)
ILA .... Lafayette School Corp., Lafayette, IN [*OCLC symbol*] (OCLC)
ILa .... Lansing Public Library, Lansing, IL [*Library symbol*] [*Library of Congress*] (LCLS)
ILA .... Williams, CA [*Location identifier*] [*FAA*] (FAAL)
IL A 2d .... Illinois Appellate Court Reports, Second Series [*A publication*] (DLA)
IL A 3d .... Illinois Appellate Court Reports, Third Series [*A publication*] (DLA)
ILAA .... Independent Literary Agents Association (EA)
ILAA .... International Lawyers in Alcoholics Anonymous (EA)
ILAA .... International Legal Aid Association [*Defunct*]
ILAA .... International Literary and Artistic Association (SAUO)
ILAAB .... International Law Association, American Branch (SAUO)
ILAADS .... Interim Low-Altitude Air Defense System
ILAAS .... Integrated Light Attack Aircraft [*or Attack Avionics*] System
ILAAS .... Integrated Low Altitude Attack Subsystem (SAUS)
ILAAS .... International League Against Anti-Semitism (SAUO)
ILAAT .... Interlaboratory Air-to-Air Missile Technology (MCD)
ILAB .... Bureau of International Labor Affairs [*Department of Labor*]
ILAB .... Instrumental Laboratory SpA [*NASDAQ symbol*] (SAG)
I-LAB .... Instrumentation Laboratory (SAUS)
ILAB .... International League of Antiquarian Booksellers [*See also LILA*] [*Bonn, Federal Republic of Germany*] (EAIO)
ILAB .... Irish Laboratory Accreditation Board [*Now the Irish National Accreditation Board*] (ACII)
ILABC .... Inter-Laboratory Committee (SAA)
ILABS .... Image Library and Browse System (SAUO)
I-Lac .... Imidazolelactic Acid [*Medicine*] (MEDA)
ILAC .... International Laboratory Accreditation Conference [*Gaithersburg, MD*] [*National Institute of Standards and Technology*] (EGAO)
ILAC .... International Laboratory Accreditation Co-operation (SAUO)
ILACD .... Ibero Latin American College of Dermatology (EA)
ILACDE .... Instituto Latinoamericano de Cooperacion y Desarrollo [*Latin American Institute for Cooperation and Development*] (EAIO)
ILACIF .... Latin American Institute of Auditing Sciences (SAUO)
ILACO .... International Land Development Consultants Ltd.
ILACS .... Integrated Library Administration and Cataloguing System (PDAA)
ILAD .... Inner Layer Air Defence system (SAUS)
ILad .... Ladd Public Library, Ladd, IL [*Library symbol*] [*Library of Congress*] (LCLS)
ILADES .... Instituto Latinoamericano de Doctrina y Estudios Sociales [*Latin American Institute of Social Doctrine and Social Studies*] [*Chile*] (EAIO)
ILadSD .... Ladd Consolidated Community School District 94, Ladd, IL [*Library symbol*] [*Library of Congress*] (LCLS)
ILADT .... Instituto Latinoamericano de Derecho Tributario [*Latin American Tax Law Institute*] (EAIO)
ILAE .... International League Against Epilepsy (EA)
ILAEDS .... Illinois Association for Educational Data Systems (EDAC)
ILAF .... Identical Location of Accelerometer and Force [*NASA*]
ILAFA .... Instituto Latinoamericano del Fierro y el Acero [*Latin American Iron and Steel Institute*] (EAIO)
ILAFA .... Latin American Institute of Iron and Steel (SAUS)
ILAG .... INLOGOV [*Institute of Local Government*] Local Authority Game
ILag .... La Grange Public Library, La Grange, IL [*Library symbol*] [*Library of Congress*] (LCLS)
ILagp .... La Grange Park Library District, La Grange Park, IL [*Library symbol*] [*Library of Congress*] (LCLS)
ILagpS .... Suburban Audio-Visual Service, La Grange Park, IL (LCLS)
ILAI .... Italian-Latin American Institute (SAUO)
ILAI .... Italo-Latin American Institute (EA)
ILAIS .... Institute for Latin American and Iberian Studies [*Columbia University*] [*Research center*] (RCD)
ILAM .... Institute of Leisure and Amenity Management (EAIO)
ILam .... LaMoille-Clarion District Library, LaMoille, IL [*Library symbol*] [*Library of Congress*] (LCLS)
ILAMA .... International Life-Saving Appliance Manufacturers Association (PDAA)
ILAMS .... Infrared LASER Atmospheric Monitoring System
ILamSD .... LaMoille Community Unit, School District 303, LaMoille, IL [*Library symbol*] [*Library of Congress*] (LCLS)
ILAN .... Implementation of Local Area Networks (SAUO)
ILAN .... Industrial Local Area Network [*Telecommunications*] (OSI)
ILAN .... Input Language [*Computer science*] (VLIE)
ILAN .... [*The*] Israeli Academic Network [*Computer science*] (TNIG)
ILAN .... Israel Network
IL & FM .... Assistant Secretary of the Army for Installations, Logistics, and Financial Management (MCD)
IL&FM .... Installations (SAUS)
IL&FM .... Installations, Logistics, and Financial Management (ACAE)
IL & M .... Ichthyological Laboratory and Museum [*University of Miami*]
IL&P .... Insolvency Law and Practice (SAFN)
ILANG .... Illinois Air National Guard (MUSM)
ILAO .... International Law and Accounting Office (SAUO)
ILAP .... Individualized Language Arts Program (SAUS)
ILAP .... Industry and Labour Adjustment Program (SAUS)
ILAP .... Integrated Local Area Planning
ILAR .... Institute for Laboratory Animal Research (SAUO)
ILAR .... Institute of Laboratory Animal Resources (EA)
ILAR .... International League Against Rheumatism (EA)
ILAR .... International League for Animal Rights (EA)
ILAR .... Interrupt List Address Register [*Computer science*] (VLIE)
ILARCO .... Illinois Arms Co. (SAUS)
ILARCO .... Illinois Arms Company (SAUO)
ILA Record .... Illinois Library Association Record (journ.) (SAUS)
ILARTS .... Integrated Launch and Recovery Television System (MCD)
ILAS .... Improved Limb Atmospheric Spectrometer [*Matsushita Electronics*]
ILAS .... Institute of Latin American Studies [*China*] (IRC)
ILAS .... Instrument Landing Approach System [*Aviation*] (IAA)
ILAS .... Instrument Low-Approach System [*Aircraft landing method*]
ILAS .... International Laser Acupuncture Society (EA)
ILAS .... International Linear Algebra Society (SAUO)
ILAS .... Interrelated Logic Accumulating Scanner
ILAS .... Isotrace Laboratory for Analytical Services (SAUS)
ILas .... LaSalle Public Library, LaSalle, IL [*Library symbol*] [*Library of Congress*] (LCLS)
ILasC .... Carus Chemical Co., Inc., LaSalle, IL [*Library symbol*] [*Library of Congress*] (LCLS)
ILASE .... Internacia Ligo de Agrikulturaj Specialistoj-Esperantistoj [*International League of Agricultural Specialists-Esperantists - ILASE*] (EAIO)
ILASE .... International League of Agricultural Specialists-Esperantists (SAUO)
ILasH .... Hygiene Institute, Medical Library, LaSalle, IL [*Library symbol*] [*Library of Congress*] (LCLS)
ILasJ .... Jefferson Elementary School, LaSalle, IL [*Library symbol*] [*Library of Congress*] (LCLS)
ILasL .... Lincoln Junior High School, LaSalle, IL [*Library symbol*] [*Library of Congress*] (LCLS)
ILasN .... Northwest Elementary School, LaSalle, IL [*Library symbol*] [*Library of Congress*] (LCLS)
ILASS .... Integrated Light Attack Avionics System [*Navy*] (NVT)
ILASS .... Intermediate Level Avionics Support System (MCD)
ILASSA .... Institute of Latin American Studies Students Association (SAUO)
ILasSD .... LaSalle-Peru Township High School, LaSalle, IL [*Library symbol*] [*Library of Congress*] (LCLS)
ILA Unit .... Instruction Look-Ahead Unit (SAUS)
I-LAW .... Improved Light Antiarmor [*or Antitank*] Weapon (RDA)
ILAW .... Improved Light Antitank Weapon (ACAE)
ILAW .... Improved Light Assault Weapon (SAUS)
ILaw .... Lawrence Township Library, Lawrenceville, IL [*Library symbol*] [*Library of Congress*] (LCLS)
ILB .... Eli Lilly & Co., Business Library, Indianapolis, IN [*OCLC symbol*] (OCLC)
ILB .... Illinois Business Review (journ.) (SAUS)
ILB .... Import Licensing Branch (SAUO)
ILB .... Independent Lateral Band (IAA)
ILB .... Industry Lead Body (HEAS)
ILB .... Infant, Low Birth Weight [*Medicine*] (DMAA)
ILB .... Infant Lung Burden [*Medicine*] (EDAA)
ILB .... Initial Load Block
ILB .... Initial Lung Burden [*Medicine*] (DMAA)

ILB .... Inner Lead Bond [*Integrated circuit technology*]
ILB .... Inshore Life Boat (PDAA)
ILB .... Inside Line-Backer (SAUS)
ILB .... Insurance Law Bulletin [*Australia*] [*A publication*]
ILB .... International Labour Branch (SAUO)
ILB .... International Liaison Bureau (SAUO)
ILB .... Involvement Limited to Bone [*Oncology*]
ILBA .... International League for Bolivarian Action (EA)
ILBB .... Improved Life Blower Bearing
ILBBB .... Incomplete Left Bundle Branch Block [*Medicine*] (EDAA)
ILBC .... Independent Living Behavior Checklist (TES)
ILBC .... International Livestock Brand Conference (EA)
ILBE .... International League of Blind Esperantists [*See also LIBE*] [*Belgrade, Yugoslavia*] (EAIO)
ILBFRLP .... International Lelio Basso Foundation for the Rights and Liberation of Peoples (EA)
ILBM .... Interleave Bit Map (SAUS)
ILBM .... Interleaved Bitmap (SAUS)
ILBT .... Indonesian Low Speed Windtunnel (SAUS)
ILBT .... Interrupt Level Branch Table [*Computer science*] (ELAL)
ILBTC .... International Livestock Brand and Theft Conference (EA)
ILBW .... Infant, Low Birth Weight
ILC .... Ichthyosis Linearis Circumflex [*Medicine*] (DMAA)
ILC .... Idiopathic CD4-Lymphocytopenia [*Medicine*]
ILC .... Idle Load Compensator [*Automotive engineering*]
ILC .... Improved Life Core (SAUS)
ILC .... Improved Line Charge (DOMA)
ILC .... Incipient Lethal Concentration
ILC .... Independent Labor Congress [*Nigeria*]
ILC .... Independent Learning Center (SAUO)
ILC .... Independent Living Center
ILC .... Individualized Learning Center (SAUO)
ILC .... Industrial Liaison Centre [*British*]
ILC .... Industry-Labor Council (EA)
ILC .... Infantry Leader Course [*Army*] (INF)
ILC .... Infiltrating Lobular Carcinoma [*Medicine*] (PALA)
ILC .... Initial Launch Capability [*Aerospace*]
ILC .... Initial Launch Complex (SAUO)
ILC .... Initiate Logical Connection (SAUS)
ILC .... In-Line Code (SAUS)
ILC .... Input Language Converter [*Computer science*] (IAA)
ILC .... Inrevocable Letter of Credit (SAUS)
ILC .... Institute for Liberty and Community (EA)
ILC .... Institute of Land Combat [*Army*]
ILC .... Instruction Length Code [*Computer science*] (BUR)
ILC .... Instruction Length Converter (SAUS)
ILC .... Instruction Length Counter [*Computer science*] (IAA)
ILC .... Instruction Location Counter
ILC .... Instructor Lieutenant-Commander [*Navy*] [*British*]
ILC .... Integrated Laminating Center (SAUS)
ILC .... Integrated Launch Complex (MCD)
ILC .... Integrated Logic Circuit
ILC .... Interim Library Catalog (SAUO)
ILC .... Interlanguage Communication (SAUS)
ILC .... Intermediate Language Code (SAUS)
ILC .... Intermediate-Level Cell [*Nuclear energy*] (NRCH)
ILC .... Intermediate Loads Cycle (SAUS)
ILC .... Intermediate Longitudinal Crease [*Medicine*] (MELL)
ILC .... Internal Locus of Control [*Psychology*]
ILC .... International Labelling Centre [*Defunct*] (EA)
ILC .... International Labor Conference [*A section of the International Labor Organization*] [*United Nations*]
ILC .... International Language Centre (SAUO)
ILC .... International Latex Corp.
ILC .... International Law Commission [*United Nations*]
ILC .... International Leadership Center [*Defunct*] (EA)
ILC .... International Legal Center [*Formerly, SAILER*] [*Later, International Center for Law and Development*] (EA)
ILC .... International Licensed Carrier [*Telecommunications*]
ILC .... International Lifeboat Conference (SAUO)
ILC .... International Linear Collider
ILC .... International Lines of Communication (MCD)
ILC .... International Logistics Center [*Army*]
ILC .... Ion/Liquid Chrommatography (SAUS)
ILC .... Iron/Liquid Chromatography (SAUS)
ILC .... Irrevocable Letter of Credit [*Business term*]
ILC .... ISDN [*Integrated Services Digital Network*] Link Controller [*Telecommunications*]
ILC .... Lake County Public Library, Merrillville, IN [*OCLC symbol*] (OCLC)
ILC .... Wilson Creek, NV [*Location identifier*] [*FAA*] (FAAL)
ILCA .... Belgique Judiciaire [*A publication*] (ILCA)
ILCA .... Indian Land Consolidation Act [*1983*]
ILCA .... Insurance Loss Control Association [*Indianapolis, IN*] (EA)
ILCA .... International Labor Communications Association (EA)
ILCA .... International Lactation Consultant Association (EA)
ILCA .... International Launching Class Association (SAUO)
ILCA .... International Lightning Class Association (EA)
ILCA .... International Livestock Centre for Africa [*Addis Ababa, Ethiopia*]
ILCA .... Inverter Light Control Assembly (MCD)
ILCC .... Initial Launch Capability Complex [*Aerospace*]
ILCC .... Integrated Launch Control and Checkout (KSC)
ILCC .... Integrated Living Communities, Inc. [*NASDAQ symbol*] (SAG)
ILCC .... Italian Language and Culture Center [*Australia*]
ILCCD .... Interest/Late Charge Code (SAUS)
ILCCG .... International Laity and Christian Community Group [*See also LAEEC*] [*Sion, Switzerland*] [*Defunct*] (EAIO)
IIC Cl .... Illinois Court of Claims Reports [*A publication*] (DLA)
ILCCS .... Integrated Launch Control and Checkout System
ILCCTC .... International Liaison Committee on Co-Operative Thrift and Credit [*Paris, France*] (EA)
ILCEP .... Inter-Laboratory Committee on Editing and Publishing [*Navy*] (MCD)
ILCF .... Inter-Laboratory Committee on Facilities [*Navy*] (MCD)
ILCI .... International Loss Control Institute (SARE)
ILCK .... Inductosyn Linearity Checkout Kit
ILCM .... Individual Level Cost Method [*Insurance*]
ILCMP .... International Liaison Committee on Medical Physics (SAUO)
ILC Newl .... International Legal Center. Newsletter [*A publication*] (DLA)
ILCNY .... I Love a Clean New York (SAUO)
ILCO .... Infrastructural, Logistics, Council Operations [*NATO*]
ILCO .... Instantaneous Launch Control Officer [*Aerospace*] (AAG)
ILCO .... Intercontinental Life Corp. [*NASDAQ symbol*] (NQ)
ILCO .... Intercontl Life [*NASDAQ symbol*] (TTSB)
ILCO .... International Logistics Control Office (AAGC)
ILCOP .... International Liaison Committee of Organizations for Peace
ILCORK .... International Liaison Committee for Research on Korea
ILCOS .... Instantaneous Lead Computing Optical Sight [*Gunsight*] [*Navy*] (DOMA)
ILCP .... Internal Light Control Panel (SAUS)
ILCR .... Incremental Lifetime Cancer Rate (SAUS)
ILCRPK .... International Liaison Committee for Reunification and Peace in Korea (EAIO)
ILCS .... Improved Low-Cost Sonobuoy (SAUS)
ILCS .... Induction Loop Communications System
ILCS .... Institute of Land Combat Studies (SAUO)
ILCT .... ILC Technology [*NASDAQ symbol*] (TTSB)
ILCT .... ILC Technology, Inc. [*NASDAQ symbol*] (NQ)
ILCTA .... International League of Commercial Travelers and Agents (EA)
ILC Tc .... ILC Technology, Inc. [*Associated Press*] (SAG)
ILC (UN) .... International Law Commission of the United Nations
ILCV .... Inscriptiones Latinae Christianae Veteres
ILCW .... Inter-Lutheran Commission on Worship (SAUO)
ILCX .... International Latex [*Private rail car owner code*]
ILD .... Deep Induction Resistivity (SAUS)
ILD .... Eli Lilly & Co., Agricultural Library, Greenfield, IN [*OCLC symbol*] (OCLC)
ILD .... Identation Load Deflection (SAUS)
ILD .... I Love Dance [*Competition in US and Canada*]
ILD .... Import Licensing Department (SAUO)
ILD .... Indentation Load Deflection (SAUS)
ILD .... Indent Load Deflection [*Measure of hardness*]
ILD .... Individual Lift Device (SAUO)
ILD .... Inductive Loop Detector
ILD .... Inflammatory Lung Disease (MELL)
ILD .... Information Lead Distance
ILD .... Initial Load (SAUS)
ILD .... Initial Lung Deposit (PDAA)
ILD .... Injection LASER Diode (TEL)
ILD .... Injection Luminescence Device
ILD .... Inland Recovery Group [*Vancouver Stock Exchange symbol*]
ILD .... In-Lock Detector
ILD .... Instructional Logic Diagram (IAA)
ILD .... Instrument Loop Diagram (ACII)
ILD .... Integrated LAN Driver (SAUS)
ILD .... Integrated Logistics Data (SAUO)
ILD .... Integrating Light Detector (PDAA)
ILD .... Interlayer Dielectric (AAEL)
ILD .... Interlevel Dielectric (AAEL)
ILD .... Intermediate-Level Diagram (IAA)
ILD .... Intermediate Level Diagramming (SAUS)
ILD .... Intermediate Logic Diagram (SAUS)
ILD .... Internal Load Deflection [*Automotive seating*]
ILD .... International Labor Defense [*An association*]
ILD .... International Labour Documentation (SAUO)
ILD .... Intersection Loop Detection (MHDI)
ILD .... Interstitial Lung Disease
ILD .... Intraoperative Localization Device [*Medicine*] (DMAA)
ILD .... Ischemic Leg Disease [*Medicine*]
ILD .... Ischemic Limb Disease [*Medicine*]
ILD .... Isolated Lactase Deficiency [*Medicine*] (DMAA)
ILDA .... Independent Laboratory Distributors Association (NTPA)
ILDA .... Industrial Lands Development Authority [*Australia*]
ILDA .... Industrial Lighting Distributors of America (EA)
ILDA .... Inter Laboratory Data Acceptance (PDAA)
ILDA .... Inter-Laboratory Data Acceptance (SAUS)
ILDA .... International LASER Display Association (EA)
ILDA .... International Lutheran Deaf Association (EA)
ILDC .... International Legal Defense Counsel (EA)
ILDC .... Israel Land & Development Co. [*NASDAQ symbol*] (SAG)
ILDCO .... International Land Development Consultants, Ltd. (SAUO)
ILDCSI .... Individual Learning Disabilities Classroom Screening Instruments
ILDCY .... Israel Ld Dev Ltd [*NASDAQ symbol*] (TTSB)
I L de Gaule .... Inscriptions Latines des Trois Gaules [*A publication*] (OCD)
ILDF .... Integrated Logistic Data File (ACAE)
ILDIS .... International Legume Database and Information Service
ILDIS .... International Legume Database and Information System (SAUO)
ILDM .... Institute of Logistics and Distribution Management [*British*] (DBA)
ILDP .... In-Line Data Processing (SAUS)
ILDP .... Interlook Dormant Period (NVT)
ILDR .... Indexes of Limited Distribution Reports (SAUS)

ILDR .... Index of Limited Distribution Reports [*A publication*]
ILDR .... Item Logistics Data Record (ACAE)
ILDS .... Integrated Logistics Data System
ILDS .... International League of Dermatological Societies [*Vancouver, BC*] (EAIO)
ILDSC .... Industrial Land Development Subcommittee [*New South Wales, Australia*]
ILDT .... Item Logistics Data Transmittal
ILDTF .... Item Logistics Data Transmittal Form (NATG)
ILDX .... General Electric [*Private rail car owner code*]
ILDX .... Incandescent Lamp Division of General Electric Co. (SAUO)
ILE .... Ileum [*Anatomy*]
ILE .... Impact Level Evaluation (SAUS)
ILE .... Indiana Law Encyclopedia [*A publication*] (DLA)
ILE .... Individual Learning Expectations (SAUS)
ILE .... Inel Resources Ltd. [*Vancouver Stock Exchange symbol*]
ILE .... Infantile Lobar Emphysema [*Medicine*] (MELL)
ILE .... Inline Engine
ILE .... Installations, Logistics & Environment (SAUS)
ILE .... Institute of Legal Executives [*Australia*]
ILE .... Institute of Locomotive Engineers (SAUS)
ILE .... Institution of Lighting Engineers (EAIO)
ILE .... Institution of Locomotive Engineers (SAUO)
ILE .... Integral Linear Error (IAA)
ILE .... Integrated Language Environment (SAUS)
ILE .... Intelligent Life Elsewhere
ILE .... Interface Latching Element
ILE .... Interfacing Latching Element (SAUS)
ILE .... International Language Engineering (SAUS)
ILE .... International Lubrication Exhibition (SAUO)
ile .... Isoleucine [*An amino acid*] (DOG)
Ile .... Isoleucine [*or iLeu, Ileu*] [*Also, I*] [*An amino acid*]
Ile .... Isoleucyl (SAUS)
ILE .... Isotopic Lead Experiment (EURO)
ILE .... Killeen [*Texas*] [*Airport symbol*] (OAG)
ILE .... Killeen, TX [*Location identifier*] [*FAA*] (FAAL)
ILE .... Lincolnwood Public Library District, Lincolnwood, IL [*OCLC symbol*] (OCLC)
ILEA .... Inner London Education Authority [*British*]
ILEA .... International League of Electrical Associations (EA)
ILeb .... Lebanon Public Library, Lebanon, IL [*Library symbol*] [*Library of Congress*] (LCLS)
ILebHS .... Lebanon High School, Lebanon, IL [*Library symbol*] [*Library of Congress*] (LCLS)
ILebM .... McKendree College, Lebanon, IL [*Library symbol*] [*Library of Congress*] (LCLS)
ILEC .... Incumbent Local Exchange Carrier [*Telecommunications*] (DINT)
ILEC .... Independent Local Exchange Carrier (SAUO)
ILEC .... Inner London Education Committee (SAUS)
ILEC .... International Lake Environmental Preservation Committee (SAUO)
ILEC .... International Lake Environment Committee (SAUO)
ILECS .... Incumbent Local Exchange Carriers
ILeD .... De Andreis Seminary, Lemont, IL [*Library symbol*] [*Library of Congress*] (LCLS)
ILEED .... Inelastic Low-Energy Electron Diffraction (IAA)
ILEF .... Internacia Ligo de Esperantistaj Foto-Kino-Magnetofon-Amatoroj [*International League of Esperantist Amateur Photographers, Cinephotographers, and Tape-Recording*] (EAIO)
ILEI .... Index of Leading Economic Indicators (SAUS)
ILEI .... Internacia Ligo de Esperantistaj Instruistoj [*International League of Esperantist Teachers*] (EAIO)
ILEI .... International League of Esperanto Instructors (SAUS)
ILEJ .... Internet Library of Early Journals (TELE)
ILeISD .... Leland Community Unit, School District 1, Leland, IL [*Library symbol*] [*Library of Congress*] (LCLS)
ILEM .... Inter-Library Electronic Mail (NITA)
ILEMP .... Immigration Law Enforcement Monitoring Project [*American Friends Service Committee*] (CROSS)
ILENP .... Institute of Low-Energy Nuclear Physics (SAUS)
ILEOA .... International Law Enforcement Officers Association (EA)
ILEP .... Federation Internationale des Associations Contre la Lepre [*International Federation of Anti-Leprosy Associations - ILEP*] (EAIO)
ILEP .... International Federation of Anti-Leprosy Associations (SAUO)
ILEPTO .... Internacia Ligo de Esperantista Post-kaj Telegraf-Oficistaro (SAUO)
ILERA .... International League of Esperantist Radio Amateurs (EA)
ILERT .... Independent Librarians Exchange Round Table [*American Library Association*]
ILES .... Indian Landsat Earth Station (SAUO)
ILESA .... International Law Enforcement Stress Association (EA)
i-lesion .... Intralesional [*Medicine*] (MEDA)
ILET .... Instituto Latinoamericano de Estudios Transnacionales [*Latin American Institute for Transnational Studies - LAITS*] (EAIO)
ILETS .... International Law Enforcement Telecommunications Seminar
Ileu .... Isoleucine [*or iLeu, Ile*] [*Also, I*] [*An amino acid*]
ILEV .... Inherently Low-Emissions Vehicle
ILE(V) .... Institute of Legal Executives (Victoria) [*Australia*]
I LEVEL .... Intermediate Level of Maintenance (SAUS)
ILEX .... ILX, Inc. [*NASDAQ symbol*] (SAG)
ILEX .... Institute of Legal Executives [*British*] (DBA)
ILEX .... Interactive Landsat Executive (SAUO)
ILEX .... International Leisure Enterprises, Inc. (SAUO)
ILF .... Idaho Laboratory Facility [*Later, IRC*] [*Idaho Falls, ID*] [*Department of Energy*] (GRD)
IL/F .... Imaging Library/FORTRAN (SAUS)
ILF .... Immigrants in the Labour Force [*British*]
ILF .... Indian Local Forces [*Military*] [*British*]
ILF .... Indicated Low Forceps [*Medicine*] (MELL)
ILF .... Inductive Loss Factor (IEEE)
ILF .... Industrial Leathers Federation [*British*] (BI)
ILF .... Infra Low Frequencies (or Frequency) (SAUS)
ILF .... Infra Low-Frequency [*Telecommunications*] (TEL)
ILF .... Input Loading Factor (SAUS)
ILF .... Integral Lift Fan [*Aviation*]
ILF .... Integrated Lift fan (SAUS)
ILF .... Integrity Loss Factor
ILF .... Interdepartmental Liaison Forum (SAUS)
ILF .... Interlaminar Failure (SAUS)
ILF .... International Falcon Resources Ltd. [*Vancouver Stock Exchange symbol*]
ILF .... International Lacrosse Federation (EA)
ILF .... International Landworkers' Federation [*Later, IFPAAW*]
ILF .... International Liaison Forum of Peace Forces [*See also FILFP*] [*Moscow, USSR*] (EAIO)
ILF .... International Lifeboat Federation [*England*] (EAIO)
ILF .... International Loan Fund /for Health and Family Projects (SAUO)
ILF .... International Lotto Fund
ILF .... International Luge Federation [*Austria*]
ILF .... Intralow Frequency (SAUS)
ILf .... Lake Forest Library, Lake Forest, IL [*Library symbol*] [*Library of Congress*] (LCLS)
ILF .... Milford Haven [*Wales*] [*Airport symbol*] (AD)
ILfB .... Barat College of the Sacred Heart, Lake Forest, IL [*Library symbol*] [*Library of Congress*] (LCLS)
ILFC .... Immature Living Female Child [*Neonatology*] (DAVI)
ILFC .... International Lease Finance Corp. (SAUS)
ILFC .... International Lease Finance Corporation (ACAE)
ILfC .... Lake Forest College, Lake Forest, IL [*Library symbol*] [*Library of Congress*] (LCLS)
ILFCG .... International Logistics Functional Coordinating Group (MCD)
ILFI .... International Labour Film Institute [*Defunct*]
ILFO .... International Logistics Field Office [*Army*] (AABC)
ILFP .... Forum International de Liaison des Forces de la Paix [*International Liaison Forum of Peace Forces - ILF*] (EA)
ILFRO .... International Labour Force Registration Orders (SAUO)
ILFZ .... Ivanhoe Lake Fault Zone [*Geology*] [*Canada*]
ILG .... Consolidated Inland Recovery [*Vancouver Stock Exchange symbol*]
ILG .... Information Liaison Group (SAUO)
ILG .... Inge Lehmann [*Greenland*] [*Seismograph station code, US Geological Survey*] [*Closed*] (SEIS)
ILG .... Instrument Landing Guidance
ILG .... Interagency Literacy Group (SAUO)
ILG .... International Leisure Group [*Commercial firm*] [*British*]
ILG .... International Logistics Group (SAUO)
ILG .... Irish Linen Guild [*Defunct*] (EA)
ILG .... University of Illinois, Graduate School of Library Science, Urbana, IL [*OCLC symbol*] (OCLC)
ILG .... Wilmington [*Delaware*] [*Airport symbol*] (OAG)
ILGA .... Immiscible Lattice-Gas Automata [*Fluid mechanics*]
ILGA .... Institute of Local Government Administration [*British*]
ILGA .... International Lesbian and Gay Association [*Formerly, International Gay Association*] (EA)
ILGB .... International Laboratory of Genetics and Biophysics
ILGF .... Insulin-Like Growth Factor
ILGO .... Irish Local Government Officials Union (SAUO)
ILGPNWU .... International Leather Goods, Plastic, and Novelty Workers' Union (EA)
ILGSA .... Indoor Light Gardening Society of America (EA)
ILGWU .... International Ladies' Garment Workers' Union (EA)
ILGYO .... International Lesbian and Gay Youth Organization (SAUO)
ILH .... Del Rio, TX [*Location identifier*] [*FAA*] (FAAL)
ILH .... Immunoreactive Luteinizing Hormone (DMAA)
ILH .... Imperial Light Horse [*Military*] [*British*] (ROG)
ILH .... International League of Honolulu (SAUO)
ILH .... Interscholastic League of Honolulu (SAUO)
ILH .... Jus Liberorum Habens [*Possessing the Right of Children*] [*Latin*]
ILH .... Northern Illinois University, Department of Library Science, De Kalb, IL [*OCLC symbol*] (OCLC)
ILHA .... International Labor History Association
ILHL .... International Leisure Hosts Ltd. [*NASDAQ symbol*] (NQ)
ILHL .... Intl Leisure Hosts [*NASDAQ symbol*] (TTSB)
ILHMFLT .... International Laboratory for High Magnetic Fields and Low Temperatures (SAUS)
ILHP .... Illinois Journal of Health, Physical Education and Recreation (journ.) (SAUS)
ILHR .... International League for Human Rights (EA)
ILI .... Ili [*Former USSR*] [*Seismograph station code, US Geological Survey*] [*Closed*] (SEIS)
ILI .... Iliamna [*Alaska*] [*Airport symbol*] (OAG)
ILI .... Iliamna, AK [*Location identifier*] [*FAA*] (FAAL)
IL/I .... Implementation Language/I (SAUS)
ILI .... Indiana Lime Institute (SAUS)
ILI .... Indiana Limestone Institute of America (EA)
ILI .... Indiana University, School of Law Library, Indianapolis, IN [*OCLC symbol*] (OCLC)
ILI .... Influenza-Like Illness [*Medicine*]
ILI .... Injection LASER Illuminator
ILI .... Instant Lunar Ionosphere
ILI .... Institute for Land Information [*Research center*] [*Information service or system*] (RCD)

ILI .... Institute of Life Insurance [*Later, ACLI*] (EA)
ILI .... Instrumentation and Laboratory Improvement (SAUS)
ILI .... Intamar Logistics Inc. (SAUO)
ILI .... Inter-African Labour Institute
ILI .... Interamerican Labour Institute
ILI .... Intercan Leasing, Inc. [*Toronto Stock Exchange symbol*]
ILI .... Interlott Technologies [*AMEX symbol*] [*Formerly, International Lottery*] (SG)
ILI .... International Language Institute (SAUO)
ILI .... International Law Institute (EA)
ILI .... International Legal Institute (SAUO)
ILI .... International Library and Institutes (SAUO)
ILI .... International Life Insurance Company S.A. (SAUO)
ILI .... International Lottery, Inc. [*AMEX symbol*] (SAG)
ILIA .... Indiana Limestone Institute of America
ILIA .... International Livestock Investigators Association (EA)
ILIAD .... IDEA Local Implementation by Local Administrators Partnership
ILIAD .... International Lookout for Infectious Animal Disease (SAUO)
ILIADA .... Spanish National Library automation project (SAUS)
ILIAS .... Inforonics Library Automation Services (SAUO)
ILib .... Cook Memorial Public Library District, Libertyville, IL [*Library symbol*] [*Library of Congress*] (LCLS)
ILIC .... In-Line Integrated Circuit
ILIC .... In-Loop Integration Control (SAUS)
ILIC .... International Library Information Center (EA)
IL-IC-IM .... It's Life, I Can't, I Must [*Element of psychotherapist Joseph Bird's self-help theory*]
I-LIDS .... Indian Legal Information Development Service (EA)
ILIERS .... Integrated Library Information Education and Retrieval System (TELE)
ILIF .... International Logistics Information File (MCD)
ILIL .... Input Longitudinal Interference Loss (SAUS)
ILIM .... Institute for Land Information Management (SAUO)
ILIMA .... International Licensing Industry and Merchandisers' Association (EA)
ILIMS .... Integrated Logistical Informations Management System (SAUO)
ILINC .... Interactive Learning International Corp.
i-line .... Identification Line [*Photojournalism*] (WDMC)
ILINET .... Interlibrary Loan and Information Network (SAUS)
ILINET Model... Interlibrary Loan and Information Network Model (SAUS)
ILinL .... Lincoln Christian College, Lincoln, IL [*Library symbol*] [*Library of Congress*] (LCLS)
ILinw .... Lincolnwood Public Library, Lincolnwood, IL [*Library symbol*] [*Library of Congress*] (LCLS)
ILIOS .... In-Line Infinity Optical System
ILIP .... In-Line Instrument Package [*Nuclear energy*] (NRCH)
ILIR .... In-House Laboratories Independent Research Program [*Army*] (RDA)
ILIR .... In-House Laboratory Independent Research (SAUO)
ILIR .... Institute of Labor and Industrial Relations [*University of Michigan*] [*Research center*] (RCD)
ILIR .... Institute of Labor and Industrial Relations [*University of Illinois*] [*Research center*] (RCD)
ILIS .... Inner Layer Inspection System (ACAE)
ILIS .... Integrated Logistics Information Support System (SAUS)
ILIS .... Intelligent Landscape Integrated System (SAUS)
I-listed PRPQ... IBM-listed PRPQ (SAUS)
ILit .... Litchfield Carnegie Public Library, Litchfield, IL [*Library symbol*] [*Library of Congress*] (LCLS)
I-LITE .... Iowa Library Information Teletype Exchange [*Des Moines, IA*] [*Telecommunications*] [*Library network*]
ILitSD .... Litchfield Community Unit, School District 12, Litchfield, IL [*Library symbol*] [*Library of Congress*] (LCLS)
ILivSD .... Livingston Community Consolidated School District, Livingston, IL [*Library symbol*] [*Library of Congress*] (LCLS)
ILJ .... Springfield, MO [*Location identifier*] [*FAA*] (FAAL)
ILK .... IIT Chicago-Kent College of Law, Chicago, IL [*OCLC symbol*] (OCLC)
ILK .... Integrin-Linked Kinase [*An enzyme*]
ILK .... Interlock [*Technical drawings*]
ILKE .... Internacia Libro-Klubo Esperantista (EA)
ILL .... Iliolumbar Ligament [*Medicine*] (MELL)
ILL .... Illinois (AFM)
Ill .... Illinois (BEE)
Ill .... Illinois Reports [*A publication*] (AAGC)
ILL .... Illuminated (NTCM)
ill .... Illuminated (WDMC)
ILL .... Illuminating [*Ammunition*] (NATG)
ILL .... Illuminator (SAUS)
ILL .... Illuminite (SAUS)
Ill .... Illusion [*Medicine*] (EDAA)
ILL .... Illusion
ill .... illusionary (SAUS)
ill .... illusionist (SAUS)
ill .... Illustrated (BJA)
ill .... Illustration (WDMC)
ILL .... Illustration
ill .... Illustrator [*MARC relator code*] [*Library of Congress*] (LCCP)
ILL .... Illustrissimus [*Most Illustrious*] [*Latin*]
ILL .... Impact Limit Lines (MUGU)
ILL .... Incipient Lethal Level (SAUS)
ILL .... Individual Learning Laboratory (OICC)
ILL .... Input Logic Level
ILL .... Institute of Languages and Linguistics (DIT)
ILL .... Institute of Lifetime Learning (EA)
ILL .... Institut Laue-Langevin [*Grenoble, France*] (ECON)
ILL .... Interlibrary Loan
ILL .... Intermediate Lymphocytic Lymphoma [*Medicine*]
ILL .... International Larder Minerals, Inc. [*Toronto Stock Exchange symbol*]
ILL .... International Lunar Laboratory (SAUO)
ILL .... Interstate Loan Library [*Council of State Governments*] (IID)
ILL .... Interstitial Liquid Level (SAUS)
ILL .... Intl Lottery [*AMEX symbol*] (TTSB)
ILL .... Irving Langmuir Laboratory [*New Mexico Institute of Mining and Technology*] [*Research center*] (RCD)
ILL .... Ontario Library Service - Escarpment, Hamilton [*UTLAS symbol*]
ILL .... Willmar, MN [*Location identifier*] [*FAA*] (FAAL)
Ill 2d .... Illinois Reports, Second Series [*A publication*] (DLA)
Ill A .... Illinois Appellate Court Reports [*A publication*] (DLA)
ILLA .... Irish Ladies Lacrosse Association (SAUO)
Ill Adm Code... Illinois Administrative Code [*A publication*] (AAGC)
Ill Admin Code... Illinois Administrative Code [*A publication*] (AAGC)
Ill Admin Reg... Illinois Register [*A publication*] (DLA)
Ill Ann Stat... Smith-Hurd Illinois Annotated Statutes [*A publication*] (AAGC)
Ill Ann Stat... Smith-Hurd's Illinois Annotated Statutes [*A publication*] (DLA)
Ill Ap .... Illinois Appellate Court Reports [*A publication*] (DLA)
Ill App .... Illinois Appellate Court Reports [*A publication*] (DLA)
Ill App 2d ..... Illinois Appellate Court Reports, Second Series [*A publication*] (DLA)
Ill App 3d ..... Illinois Appellate Court Reports, Third Series [*A publication*] (DLA)
Ill App Ct Rep... Illinois Appellate Court Reports [*A publication*] (DLA)
Ill App Illinois... Appellate Court Reports [*A publication*] (AAGC)
Ill Apps .... Illinois Appellate Court Reports [*A publication*] (DLA)
ILLB .... Insurance and Liability Law Bulletin [*A publication*]
Ill BA Bull.... Illinois State Bar Association. Quarterly Bulletin [*A publication*] (DLA)
ILLC .... Inner London Library Committee (SAUO)
Ill CC .... Illinois Commerce Commission Opinions and Orders [*A publication*] (DLA)
Ill CC .... Matthew and Bangs' Illinois Circuit Court Reports [*A publication*] (DLA)
Ill Cir .... Illinois Circuit Court (DLA)
Ill Cir Ct ...... Illinois Circuit Court Reports [*A publication*] (DLA)
Ill Cont L Ed... Illinois Continuing Legal Education [*A publication*] (DLA)
ILLCS .... Intralaunch Facility and Launch Control Facility Cabling Subsystem (IAA)
Ill Ct Cl .... Illinois Court of Claims (AAGC)
ILLD .... Illustrated (ROG)
Ill Dec .... Illinois Decisions [*A publication*] (DLA)
ILLEGIT .... Illegitimate (WDAA)
IL LF .... Illinois Law Forum (DLA)
ILLIAC .... Illinois Advanced Computer (SAUO)
ILLIAC .... Illinois Algorithmic Decoder [*Southern Illinois University*] (SAA)
ILLIAC .... Illinois Automatic Computer (SAUS)
ILLIAC .... Illinois Institute for Advanced Computing
ILLIAC .... Illinois Integrator and Automatic Computer [*University of Illinois*] (BUR)
ILLIAD .... Illinois Algorithmic Decoder (SAUO)
illic lag obturat... Illico Lagena Obturatur [*Let the Bottle be Closed at Once*] [*Latin*] (STED)
ILLIC LAG OBTURAT... Illico Lagena Obturatur [*Stopper the Bottle at Once*] [*Pharmacy*]
IlliCtr .... Illinois Central Corp. [*Associated Press*] (SAG)
ILLIGAL .... Illinois Genetic Algorithm Laboratory (SAUO)
ILLIN .... Illinantur [*Anoint*] [*Pharmacy*] (ROG)
ILLINEND ...... Illinendus [*To Be Smeared*] [*Pharmacy*]
ILLINET .... Illinois Library and Information Network [*Library network*]
IlliniSup .... Illinois Superconductor Corp. [*Associated Press*] (SAG)
Illinois Miner Notes... Illinois Mineral Notes (journ.) (SAUS)
Illinois Rep... Illinois Reports [*A publication*] (DLA)
Illinova .... Illinova Corp Holding Co. [*Formerly, Illinois Power*] [*Associated Press*] (SAG)
Ill Inst Tech... Illinois Institute of Technology (GAGS)
ILLIP .... Illinois Integer Programming (SAUS)
Illit .... Illiteracy (SAUS)
Illit .... Illiterate (BEE)
ILLIT .... Illiterate
Ill J Math..... Illinois Journal of Mathematics (journ.) (SAUS)
ILLL .... International Lutheran Laymen's League (EA)
Ill Laws .... Laws of Illinois [*A publication*] (DLA)
Ill LB .... Illinois Law Bulletin [*A publication*] (DLA)
Ill Legis Serv... Illinois Legislative Service (West) [*A publication*] (DLA)
Ill Leg N .... Illustrated Legal News [*India*] [*A publication*] (DLA)
Ill Libr .... Illinois Libraries (journ.) (SAUS)
Ill LQ .... Illinois Law Quarterly [*A publication*] (DLA)
Ill L Rec .... Illinois Law Record [*A publication*] (DLA)
IllLRev .... Illinois Law Review (SAUO)
ILLLTV .... Integrated Low-Light-Level Television
Ill Med J....... Illinois Medical Journal (journ.) (SAUS)
ILLMO .... Illmo, MO [*American Association of Railroads railroad junction routing code*]
ILLMO .... Illustrissimo [*Most Illustrious*] [*Latin*]
ILLODIE-AIF... Illinois University Logical Design by Implicit Enumeration Using the All-Interconnection Inequality Formulation (PDAA)
illog .... Antilog [*Mathematics*] (BARN)
Ill Op Att'y Gen... Illinois Attorney General's Opinion [*A publication*] (DLA)
IllP .... Illinois Power Co. [*Associated Press*] (SAG)
ILLPC .... Illinois Power Capital Ltd. [*Associated Press*] (SAG)
IllPF .... Illinois Power Financing I [*Associated Press*] (SAG)
ILL PHU .... Illawarra Public Health Unit (SAUO)
Ill PUC Ops... Illinois Public Utilities Commission Opinions and Orders [*A publication*] (DLA)
Ill R .... Illinois Reports [*A publication*] (DLA)

Ill R & WC... Illinois Railroad and Warehouse Commission Reports [*A publication*] (DLA)
Ill R & WCD... Illinois Railroad and Warehouse Commission Decisions [*A publication*] (DLA)
ILL rate........ Illiteracy Rate
Ill Reg......... Illinois Register [*A publication*] (AAGC)
Ill Rep......... Illinois Reports [*A publication*] (DLA)
Ill Res......... Illinois Research (journ.) (SAUS)
Ill Rev Stat... Illinois Revised Statutes [*A publication*] (AAGC)
ILLRI........... Industrial Lift and Loading Ramp Institute [*Defunct*] (EA)
ILLRP........... Inscriptiones Latinae Liberae Rei Publicae [*A publication*] (OCD)
ILLS............ Illinois (ROG)
Ills............ Illinois Reports [*A publication*] (DLA)
ILLS............ Interlibrary Loan System (SAUS)
Ills App........ Illinois Appellate Court Reports [*A publication*] (DLA)
Ill SBA.......... Illinois State Bar Association. Reports [*A publication*] (DLA)
Ill SBAQB....... Illinois State Bar Association. Quarterly Bulletin [*A publication*] (DLA)
Ills R........... Illinois Reports [*A publication*] (DLA)
Ills Rep........ Illinois Reports [*A publication*] (DLA)
Ill St Hist Lib... Illinois State Historical Library (SAUO)
Ill St Hist Soc... Illinois State Historical Society (SAUO)
ILLSTN.......... Illustration
Ill St U......... Illinois State University (GAGS)
ILLT............ Illinois Terminal Railroad Co.
illum........... illuminant (SAUS)
ILLUM........... Illuminate (KSC)
illum........... Illuminated (VRA)
IllumES......... Illuminating Engineering Society (SAUO)
Ill Univ......... University of Illinois (SAUO)
ILLUS........... Illustrate [*or Illustration*] (AABC)
illus............ Illustrated (WDMC)
illus............ Illustration (WDMC)
illus............ Illustrator (WDMC)
Illus Archaeol... Illustrated Archaeologist (journ.) (SAUS)
IllusLondN...... Illustrated London News (journ.) (SAUS)
illus mat....... Illustrative Material (VRA)
ILLUSTN......... Illustration
ILLUSTR......... Illustrator (ROG)
ILLW............ Intermediate Level Liquid Waste (SAUS)
Ill WCC......... Illinois Workmen's Compensation Cases [*A publication*] (DLA)
ILM............. Iliamna [*Alaska*] [*Seismograph station code, US Geological Survey*] (SEIS)
ILM............. Ilmenite [*Also, il*] [*Geology*]
ILM............. Immobilized-Liquid Membrane [*Chemical engineering*]
ILM............. Independent Landing Monitor [*RADAR-TV landing guidance*] [*NASA*]
ILM............. Independent Learning Modules (ACII)
ILM............. Index-Linked Mortgage (FOTI)
ILM............. Induced Longitudinal Magnetism (SAUS)
ILM............. Industrial Learning Modules (ACII)
ILM............. Industrial Light & Magic [*Special effects company owned by George Lucas*]
ILM............. Industrial Light Magic [*Electronics*] [*Commercial firm*]
ILM............. Information Logic Machine (IEEE)
ILM............. Insertion Loss Measurement (SAUS)
ILM............. Instant Laser Meeting (SAUS)
ILM............. Institute of Labour Management
ILM............. Instrumental Landing System (SAUS)
ILM............. Insulin-Like Material
ILM............. Integrated LASER Modulator (AAEL)
ILM............. Integrated Logistic Management (DNAB)
ILM............. Intelligent Library Manager [*Computer science*] (CIST)
ILM............. Interceptor Launch Module [*Military*]
ILM............. Intermediate Language Machine [*Computer science*]
ILM............. Intermediate Level Maintenance (ACAE)
ILM............. Internal Limiting Membrane [*Medicine*] (DMAA)
ILM............. Lincoln Library, Springfield, IL [*OCLC symbol*] (OCLC)
ILM............. Wilmington [*North Carolina*] [*Airport symbol*] (OAG)
ILM............. Wilmington, NC [*Location identifier*] [*FAA*] (FAAL)
ILMA............ Immunochemiluminometric Assay [*Analytical biochemistry*]
ILMA............ Incandescent Lamp Manufacturers Association [*Defunct*] (EA)
ILMA............ Independent Lubricant Manufacturers Association (EA)
ILMA............ International Licensing and Merchandisers' Association [*Later, ILIMA*] (EA)
ILMA............ Intraocular Lens Manufacturers Association [*Defunct*] (EA)
ILMA............ Morton Arboretum, Lisle, IL [*Library symbol*] [*Library of Congress*] (LCLS)
ILMAC........... International Congress and Fair for Laboratory (SAUS)
ILMAC........... International Congress and Fair for Laboratory, Measuring and Automation Techniques in Chemistry (SAUS)
ILMAC........... Israel-Lebanon Mixed Armistice Commission (SAUO)
ILMC............ Immature Living Male Child [*Neonatology*] (DAVI)
ILMC............ Indiana Labor Management Council (SAUO)
ILMC............ International Light Metal Congress (SAUS)
ILMD............ Item Logistics Management Data [*DoD*]
ILMF............ Intermediate Level Maintenance Facility (ACAE)
ILMH............ Institute for Labor and Mental Health (EA)
ILMI............ Index-Linked Mortgage and Investment (DI)
ILMI............ Inferolateral Myocardial Infarct [*or Infarction*] [*Cardiology*] (DAVI)
ILMI............ Interim Link Management Interface (SAUS)
ILMI............ Interim Local Management Interface
ILMM............ Security Output Main Module (SAUO)
ILMN............ Incomplete Lower Motor Neuron [*Lesion*] [*Neurology*] (DAVI)
ILMO............ Illustrissimo [*Most Illustrious*] [*Latin*] (WGA)
ILMO............ International Legal Metrology Organization (SAUO)
ILMP............ Integrated Logistic Management Program (NG)
ILMP............ International Literary Market Place [*A publication*]
ILMR............ Independent Landing Monitor Radar (ACAE)
ILMR............ International Laboratory for Marine Radioactivity (SAUO)
ILMS............ Improved Launcher Mechanical System [*Military*]
ILMS............ Inner Layer Missile System [*Military*]
ILMT............ Innovative Large Mining Truck
ILMT............ Integrated Logistics Management Team
ILMT............ Intermediate Level Maintenance Training (SAUS)
ILMT............ Intermediate-Level Maintenance Training
ILMT............ International Institute of Milling Technology (SAUS)
ILMT............ International Liquid Mirror Telescope (SAUS)
ILMWSC.......... International Lifesaving Museum and Water Safety Center [*Defunct*] (EA)
ILN............. East Peoria Elementary Schools, East Peoria, IL [*OCLC symbol*] (OCLC)
ILN............. Idle Line Network
ILN............. Illinois League for Nursing (SRA)
ILN............. Illinova Corp. [*NYSE symbol*] (TTSB)
ILN............. Illinova Corp. Holding Co. [*Formerly, Illinois Power*] [*NYSE symbol*] (SAG)
ILN............. Illustrated London News [*A publication*] (BRI)
ILN............. Inferior Laryngeal Nerve [*Medicine*] (EDAA)
ILN............. Inguinal Lymph Node [*Medicine*] (MELL)
ILN............. Instruction List Name (SAUS)
ILN............. Intermediolateral Nucleus (SAUS)
ILN............. Internal Line Number (SAUS)
ILN............. International Law News [*A publication*]
ILN............. International Logistics Negotiations [*Military export sales*]
ILN............. Island Lagoon [*Australia*] [*Seismograph station code, US Geological Survey*] [*Closed*] (SEIS)
ILN............. Wilmington, OH [*Location identifier*] [*FAA*] (FAAL)
ILNC............ International Long Navigation Course (SAUO)
ILNR............ Intralobar Nephrogenic Rest [*Medicine*] (EDAA)
ILNY............ International League of New York
ILo............. Helen M. Plum Memorial Library, Lombard, IL [*Library symbol*] [*Library of Congress*] (LCLS)
ilo............. Ilocano [*MARC language code*] [*Library of Congress*] (LCCP)
ILO............. Iloilo [*Philippines*] [*Airport symbol*] (OAG)
ILO............. Iloilo [*Philippines*] [*Seismograph station code, US Geological Survey*] [*Closed*] (SEIS)
ILO............. Individual Load Operation
ILO............. Individual Operation (SAUS)
ILO............. Industrial Labour Organization (SAUS)
ILO............. Industrial Liaison Officer (SAUO)
ILO............. Industrial Liaison Organization [*MIT*]
ILO............. Injection-Locked Oscillator (IEEE)
ILO............. In Lieu Of
ILO............. Integrated Logistics Overhaul (SAUO)
ILO............. Integrated Logistics Overhead (SAUS)
ILO............. Interlayer Oxide (SAUS)
ILO............. Interlevel Oxide (SAUS)
ILO............. Interlockend Operation (SAUS)
ILO............. Internally Linked Operation
ILO............. International Labor Office [*A section of the International Labor Organization*] [*United Nations*]
ILO............. International Labor Organization [*United Nations*] (LDOE)
ILO............. International Labour Organisation [*Geneva, Switzerland*] [*United Nations*] (EA)
ILO............. International Latitude Observatory (SAUO)
ILO............. Interservice Liaison Office [*Military*] (CAAL)
ILo............. Iodine Lotion [*Medicine*]
ILO............. Islamic Liberation Organization
ILO............. School of the Art Institute of Chicago Library, Chicago, IL [*OCLC symbol*] (OCLC)
ILOA............ Industrial Life Offices Association [*British*] (BI)
ILOAD........... Initialization Load (MCD)
I-load.......... Initial-Load (NAKS)
ILOAT........... Administrative Tribunal of the International Labour Organization (SAUS)
ILOC............ Internal Location (SAUS)
ILOC............ International Lunar Occulation Centre (SAUO)
ILOC............ Irrevocable Letter of Credit [*Business term*] (DS)
ILoc............ Lockport Township Public Library, Lockport, IL [*Library symbol*] [*Library of Congress*] (LCLS)
ILoC............ National College of Chiropractic, Lombard, IL [*Library symbol*] [*Library of Congress*] (LCLS)
ILoCC........... National College of Chiropractic, Lombard, IL [*Library symbol*] [*Library of Congress*] (LCLS)
ILocL........... Lewis University, Lockport, IL [*Library symbol*] [*Library of Congress*] (LCLS)
ILocL-L......... Lewis University, College of Law, Glen Ellyn, IL [*Library symbol*] [*Library of Congress*] (LCLS)
ILOCO........... International Land Development Consultants (SAUO)
ILod............ Loda Public Library, Loda, IL [*Library symbol*] [*Library of Congress*] (LCLS)
ILoE............ National College of Education, Lombard, IL [*Library symbol*] [*Library of Congress*] (LCLS)
ILOG............ Institute of Logistics (COBU)
ILOGS........... Integrated Logistics System [*Army*] (RDA)
ILoM............ MidCon Corp., Lombard, IL [*Library symbol*] [*Library of Congress*] (LCLS)
ILOP............ Initial Light Off Procedure (MCD)
ILO/R........... International Labour Review. International Labour Office. GenSve (SAUS)
ILORSRS......... Independent Line-Of-Sight Reference System (SAUS)

I-LOS .... Initial Data Load (SAUS)
ILos .... Lostant Community Library, Lostant, IL [*Library symbol*] [*Library of Congress*] (LCLS)
ILosHSD ...... Lostant Consolidated High School District 400, Lostant, IL [*Library symbol*] [*Library of Congress*] (LCLS)
ILOSS .... Integrated LASER Optical Sight Set
ILosSD .... Lostant Consolidated Community School District 25, Lostant, IL [*Library symbol*] [*Library of Congress*] (LCLS)
ILOST .... International Liaison Center of Schools of Cinema and Television
ILOSU .... International Labor Organization Staff Union [*Geneva, Switzerland*] (EAIO)
ILOUE .... In Lieu of Until Exhausted [*Military*]
ILovjD .... Lovejoy Unit, District 188, Lovejoy, IL [*Library symbol*] [*Library of Congress*] (LCLS)
ILOWB .... International Labor Office, Washington Branch (SAUO)
ILP .... Clausen, Miller, Gorman, Caffrey & Witous, Chicago, IL [*OCLC symbol*] (OCLC)
ILP .... Ile Des Pins [*New Caledonia*] [*Airport symbol*] (OAG)
ILP .... Illinois Law and Practice [*A publication*] (DLA)
ILP .... Ilpo Aruba Cargo NV [*ICAO designator*] (FAAC)
ILP .... Inadequate Luteal Phase (STED)
ILP .... Independent Labour Party [*British*]
ILP .... Independent Liberal Party [*Israel*] [*Political party*] (BJA)
ILP .... Index to Legal Periodicals (journ.) (SAUS)
ILP .... Individual Learning Package (OICC)
ILP .... Individual Learning Programme (AIE)
ILP .... Inductive Logic Programming (IDAI)
ILP .... Industrial Liaison Program [*Refers to university-industry interaction*]
ILP .... In-Line Printer
ILP .... In-Line Processing (SAUS)
ILP .... Instant Linear Programming (SAUS)
ILP .... Instruction-Level Parallelism [*Computer science*]
ILP .... Integer Linear Programming Model [*Statistics*]
ILP .... Integrated Logistics Panel (NASA)
ILP .... Intermediate Language Processor [*Computer science*] (BUR)
ILP .... Intermediate Language Program [*Computer science*]
ILP .... Intermediate Level Program (ACAE)
ILP .... International Legal Practitioner (SAFN)
ILP .... International Links Program [*Overseas aid*] [*Australia*]
ILP .... International Logistics Program
ILP .... Interstitial Lymphocytic Pneumonia [*Medicine*] (STED)
ILP .... Inventory of Learning Processes [*Psychology*] (DHP)
ILP .... Irish Labour Party [*Political party*] (ROG)
ILP .... Islamic Liberation Party [*Tunisia*] [*Political party*] (MENA)
ILP .... Isle des Pins [*New Caledonia*] [*Airport symbol*] (AD)
ILP .... Israel Labor Party [*Political party*]
ILPA .... Independent Labor Press Association (SAUO)
ILPA .... Institute of Life and Pension Advisers (SAFN)
ILPA .... International Labor Press Association (EA)
ILPA .... Iowa Limestone Producers Association (SRA)
ILpB .... Barber Colman Co., Technical Library, Loves Park, IL [*Library symbol*] [*Library of Congress*] (LCLS)
ILPBC .... International League of Professional Baseball Clubs (EA)
ILPC .... International League for the Protection of Cetaceans (SAUO)
ILPC .... International Linen Promotion Commission (EA)
ILPD .... Intergranular Liquid Phase Distribution (SAUS)
ILPES .... Instituto Latinoamericano de Planificacion Economica y Social [*Latin American Institute for Economic and Social Planning*] [*Santiago, Chile*] [*United Nations*]
ILPF .... Ideal Low Pass Filter
ILPH .... International League for the Protection of Horses (DI)
ILPL .... Index to Legal Periodical Literature [*1887-1937*] [*A publication*] (DLA)
ILPIH .... International League for the Protection of Horses (SAUS)
ILPNET .... Inductive Logic Programming Pan-European Scientific Network (SAUO)
ILPNET .... Inductive Logic Programming scientific Network (SAUO)
IlPow .... Illinois Power Co. [*Associated Press*] (SAG)
ILPPSM .... International Library of Philosophy, Psychology, and Scientific Method [*Book publishing*] [*British*]
ILPS .... Industrial Location Planning System [*Department of Commerce*] (GFGA)
ILPS .... Interactive Linear Programming System (SAUS)
ILPS .... International Lecithin and Phospholipid Society
ILPZ .... Illinois Power [*Federal Railroad Administration identification code*]
ILQ .... Chadwell, Kayser, Ruggles, McGee & Hastings, Chicago, IL [*OCLC symbol*] (OCLC)
ILQ .... Indian Law Quarterly [*A publication*] (DLA)
ILQ .... International Law Quarterly [*A publication*] (AAGC)
ILQR .... Indian Law Quarterly Review [*A publication*] (DLA)
ILQTS .... Idiopathic Long QT Syndrome [*Medicine*] (EDAA)
ILR .... Air Iliria [*Yugoslovia*] [*ICAO designator*] (FAAC)
ILR .... Burns, OR [*Location identifier*] [*FAA*] (FAAL)
ILR .... Ilorin [*Nigeria*] [*Airport symbol*] (OAG)
ILR .... Incurred Loss Ratio [*Insurance*]
ILR .... Independent Law Reports (SAUS)
ILR .... Independent Local Radio [*British*]
ILR .... Indian Law Reports [*A publication*] (DLA)
ILR .... Indicating Light Relay
ILR .... Industrial and Labor Relations
ILR .... Industrial Law Review [*A publication*] (ILCA)
ILR .... Industrial Rayon Corp. (SAUS)
ILR .... Infanterie-Lehrregiment [*Infantry Demonstration Regiment*] [*German military - World War II*]
ILR .... In-Line Reciprocator
ILR .... Inner Lindblad Resonance [*Galactic science*]
ILR .... Institute of Library Research [*University of California*] (DIT)
ILR .... Institute of Logistics Research [*Army*] (RDA)
ILR .... Instruction Location Register (NITA)
ILR .... Insurance Law Reporter [*A publication*] (DLA)
ILR .... Integrated Logistics Report (SAUO)
ILR .... Interleukin Receptor [*Medicine*] (DMAA)
ILR .... International Labour Review [*A publication*] (BRI)
ILR .... International Laco Resources [*Vancouver Stock Exchange symbol*]
ILR .... International Law Reports [*A publication*]
ILR .... International League of Reform (SAUO)
ILR .... International Luggage Registry [*Computer system for recovery of airline luggage*]
ILR .... Irish Law Reports [*A publication*] (DLA)
ILR .... Irreversible Loss Rate (DB)
ILRA .... Inbred Livestock Registry Association (EA)
ILRA .... International Laboratory for Marine Radioactivity (SAUS)
ILRA .... International Lactic Acid Research Association (SAUO)
ILRA .... International Log Rolling Association
ILRA .... International Roleo Association (SAUO)
ILRAD .... International Laboratory for Research on Animal Diseases [*Nairobi, Kenya*]
ILRAD .... International Laboratory Research Animal Diseases (SAUS)
ILR All .... Indian Law Reports, Allahabad Series [*A publication*] (DLA)
ILR And .... Indian Law Reports, Andhra Series [*A publication*] (DLA)
ILR Assam ... Indian Law Reports, Assam Series [*A publication*] (DLA)
ILR Bom .... Indian Law Reports, Bombay Series [*A publication*] (DLA)
ILRC .... Indian Law Reports, Calcutta Series [*A publication*] (DLA)
ILRC .... Indian Law Resource Center (EA)
ILRC .... Integral Launch and Reentry Vehicle (SAUO)
ILRC .... International LASER RADAR Conference (PDAA)
ILR Cal .... Indian Law Reports, Calcutta Series [*A publication*] (DLA)
ILR Calc .... Indian Law Reports, Calcutta Series [*A publication*] (DLA)
ILR Cut .... Indian Law Reports, Orissa Series [*A publication*] (DLA)
ILREC .... International League for the Rational Education of Children (SAUS)
ILRERF .... International Labor Rights Education and Research Fund (EA)
ILRF .... International Labor Rights Fund (EA)
ILR Hyderabad ... Indian Law Reports, Hyderabad Series [*A publication*] (DLA)
ILRI .... Indian Lac Research Institute (SAUO)
ILRI .... International Livestock Research Institute
ILRIG .... International Labour Research and Information Group (SAUO)
ILRIS .... Intermediate Long-Range Interceptor System
ILR Kar .... Indian Law Reports, Karachi Series [*A publication*] (DLA)
ILR Ker .... Indian Law Reports, Kerala Series [*A publication*] (DLA)
ILR Lah .... Indian Law Reports, Lahore Series [*A publication*] (DLA)
ILRLP .... International League for the Rights and Liberation of Peoples [*Rome, Italy*] (EAIO)
ILR Luck .... Indian Law Reports, Lucknow Series [*A publication*] (DLA)
ILRM .... International League for the Rights of Man [*Later, ILHR*]
ILR Mad .... Indian Law Reports, Madras Series [*A publication*] (DLA)
ILR Madhya Bharat ... Indian Law Reports, Madhya Bharat Series [*A publication*] (DLA)
ILR Mysore ... Indian Law Reports, Mysore Series [*A publication*] (DLA)
ILRN .... International Livedo Reticularis Network (EA)
ILR Nag .... Indian Law Reports, Nagpur Series [*A publication*] (DLA)
ILRO .... Industrial Labor Relations Office [*DoD*]
ILR Or .... Indian Law Reports, Orissa Series [*A publication*] (DLA)
ILRP .... Indian Law Reports, Patna Series [*A publication*] (DLA)
ILR Pat .... Indian Law Reports, Patna Series [*A publication*] (DLA)
ILR Patiala ... Indian Law Reports, Patiala Series [*A publication*] (DLA)
ILR Pun .... Indian Law Reports, Punjab Series [*A publication*] (DLA)
ILRR .... Industrial and Labor Relations Review [*A publication*] (BRI)
ILRR .... Interlaboratory Reaction Rate (SAUS)
ILR Rajasthan ... Indian Law Reports, Rajasthan Series [*A publication*] (DLA)
ILR Ran .... Indian Law Reports, Rangoon Series [*A publication*] (DLA)
ILR Rev .... Industrial and Labor Relations Review [*A publication*] (DLA)
ILRRJ .... International League for the Repatriation of Russian Jews (EA)
ILRRP .... International Long-Range Reconnaissance Patrol
ILRRPS .... International Long-Range Reconnaissance Patrol School (SAUO)
ILRS .... Integrated Logistic Reporting System (SAUO)
ILRS .... International League of Religious Socialists [*Aerdenhout, Netherlands*] (EAIO)
ILRSS .... International Labour Review. Statistical Supplement (journ.) (SAUS)
ILRT .... Integrated Leak Rate Test [*Nuclear energy*] (NRCH)
ILRT .... Intermediate Level Reactor Test (IEEE)
ILR Trav-Cochin ... Indian Law Reports, Kerala Series [*A publication*] (DLA)
ILRU .... Independent Living Research Utilization Program (PAZ)
ILRV .... In-Line Relief Valve
ILRV .... Integral [*or Integrated*] Launch and Recovery Vehicle [*or Reentry*] [*NASA*]
ILRV .... Integral (or Integrated) Launch and Reentry Vehicle (SAUO)
ILRVS .... Integral [*or Integrated*] Launch and Recovery Vehicle System [*or Reentry*] [*NASA*]
ILRWG .... International Labor Rights Working Group (EA)
ILS .... Ideal Liquidus Structures (IEEE)
ILS .... Identification List
ILS .... Idiopathic Leucine Sensitivity (STED)
ILS .... Idiopathic Lymphadenopathy Syndrome (STED)
ILS .... Idle Line State (SAUS)
ILS .... Illinois Benedictine College, Lisle, IL [*Library symbol*] [*Library of Congress*] (LCLS)
ILS .... Incoherent-Light System (SAUS)
ILS .... Incorporated Law Society [*British*]
ILS .... Increase in Life-Span
ILS .... Incremental Life Support (DB)
ILS .... Independent Line-of-Sight (SAUS)

ILS .... Independent Living Skills [*Needed by the handicapped*]
ILS .... Indiana Union List of Serials, Indianapolis, IN [*OCLC symbol*] (OCLC)
ILS .... Industrial Law Society (HEAS)
ILS .... Industrial Liaison Scheme (SAUS)
ILS .... Industrial Locomotive Society [*British*]
ILS .... Inertial Latching Switch (SAUS)
ILS .... Infared Liver Scan [*Medicine*] (MELL)
ILS .... Information & Library Services [*Information service or system*] (IID)
ILS .... Infrared Live Scanner [*Medicine*] (DMAA)
ILS .... Inland Library System [*Library network*]
ILS .... In-Line Subroutine (SAUS)
ILS .... Input Laser System (ACAE)
ILS .... Inscriptiones Latinae Selectae [*A publication*] (ODCC)
ILS .... Inspection Lot Size
ILS .... Institute for Learning Systems (SAUO)
ILS .... Institute of Life Sciences [*British*] (DBA)
ILS .... Institute of Lithuanian Studies (EA)
ILS .... Instrument Landing System [*Aviation*]
ILS .... Instrument Line Shape (SAUS)
ILS .... Integrated Laboratory Sequence [*A system of teaching chemistry devised by Mary L. Good at Louisiana State University in New Orleans*]
ILS .... Integrated Large Screen display (SAUS)
ILS .... Integrated LASER System [*Salford Engineering*]
ILS .... Integrated LASER Systems [*Software*] [*British*]
ILS .... Integrated Learning System (AIE)
ILS .... Integrated Library System [*National Library of Medicine*] [*Information service or system*] (IID)
ILS .... Integrated Logistics Support [*DoD*]
ILS .... Integrated Logistics System
ILS .... Intelligent Library System (SAUO)
ILS .... Intensifier Lens System
ILS .... Interactive Laboratory System (NITA)
ILS .... Interactive Learning System (SAUO)
ILS .... Interferometric LASER Source
ILS .... Intergovernmental Liaison Staff [*Environmental Protection Agency*] (GFGA)
ILS .... Interlaminar Shear (SAUS)
ILS .... Interlibrary Services (SAUS)
ILS .... Intermediate Level School
ILS .... International Institute for Labour Studies (SAUO)
ILS .... International Language Support (SAUO)
ILS .... International Latitude Service
ILS .... International Laughter Society [*Commercial firm*] (EA)
ILS .... International Launch Services (ISAK)
ILS .... International Learning Systems
ILS .... International Lilac Society (EA)
ILS .... International Limnological Society [*See also SIL*] (ASF)
ILS .... International Line Selector
ILS .... International Lunar Society [*Spain*]
ILS .... International Lyrics Server (SAUS)
ILS .... International Salt Company (SAUO)
ILS .... Internet Locator Service (GART)
ILS .... Interrupt Level Subroutine (CMD)
ILS .... Interstate Land Sales [*HUD*]
ILS .... Intracavity LASER Spectroscopy (AAEL)
ILS .... Intralobar Sequestration (DB)
ILS .... Intralobular Sequestration (STED)
ILS .... Inventory Locator Service [*Database*] [*Inventory Locator Service, Inc.*] [*Information service or system*] (CRD)
ILS .... Inverse Least-Squares (SAUS)
ILS .... Ionization Loss Spectroscopy (SAUS)
ILS .... Irish Literary Supplement [*A publication*] (BRI)
ILSA .... Improvement of Live Stock Act (SAUO)
ILSA .... Industry Large Structures Assembly (SSD)
ILSA .... Insured Locksmiths and Safemen of America [*Defunct*] (EA)
ILSA .... Integrated Logistic Support Analysis Paper (MCD)
ILSA .... Inter-American Legal Services Association (EA)
ILSA .... International Law Students Association (EAIO)
ILSA .... International Lending Supervision Act of 1983
ILSA .... International Lung Sounds Association (EA)
ILSA .... Interstate Land Sales Full Disclosure Act (COE)
ILSA .... Italian Longitudinal Study of Aging
ILSAA .... Improved Lighting System for Army Aircraft (RDA)
ILSAC .... International Legal Services Advisory Committee
ILSAC .... International Lubricant Standardization and Approval Committee [*Automotive engine oils*]
ILSAM .... International Language for Servicing and Maintenance (PDAA)
ILSAP .... Instrument Landing System Approach [*Aviation*]
ILS(C) .... Industry Launch Service (Cryogenic) (SSD)
ILSC .... Integrated Logistics Support Cadre (AFIT)
ILSC .... International Learning Systems Corporation (SAUO)
ILSCAE .... International League for/of Social Commitment in Adult Education (SAUO)
ILSCM .... Integrated Logistics Support Control Manual (MCD)
ILSCM .... Integrated Logistics Support Coordination Meeting (MCD)
ILSD .... Integrated Logistics Support Division (ACAE)
ILSDB .... Indiana Libraries Serials Data Bank (SAUS)
ILSDF .... Integrated Logistics Support Data File
ILSDP .... International Logistics Supply Delivery Plan (MCD)
ILS-DS .... Integrated Logistic Support - Detail Specification
ILSE .... Integrated Logistics Support Evaluation (SAUS)
ILSE .... Interagency Life Sciences Supporting Space Research and Technology Exchange
ILSE .... Interagency of Life Sciences Support Research and Technology Exchange (SAUS)
ILSE .... Intermediate-Level Support Equipment (MCD)
ILSES .... Integrated Library and Survey-Data Extraction Service (TELE)
ILSF .... Incandescent Liquid Spheroidal Formation [*Combustion technology*]
ILSF .... Integrated Logistics Support Facility (SAUO)
ILSF .... Intermediate Level Sample Flow (IEEE)
ILSF .... Iterative Least-Squares Fitting [*Mathematics*]
ILSG .... Integrated Logistics Subgroup [*Military*] (MCD)
ILSG .... Interim Logistics Support Guide (NVT)
ILSGB .... International Language Society of Great Britain
ILSI .... International Life Science Institute, Europe (SAUO)
ILSI .... International Life Sciences Institute [*Later, ILSI-NF*] (EA)
ILSI .... International Life Services, Inc. (EA)
ILSINA .... International Life Sciences Institute-North America (EA)
ILSI-NF .... International Life Sciences Institute - Nutrition Foundation (EA)
ILS/IS/D .... Integrated Logistics Support/Information System/Dictionary
ILSL .... Initial Logistics Support Letter (SAUO)
ILS/LAR .... Integrated Logistics System and Logistics Assessment Review (MCD)
ILSM .... Integrated Logistics Support Manager [*Military*] (MCD)
ILSM .... Integrated Logistics Support Model [*Military*] (MCD)
ILSMH .... International League of Societies for Persons with Mental Handicap [*Brussels, Belgium*] (EA)
ILSMIS .... Industrial Logistics Management Information System (SAUO)
ILSMIS .... Industrial Logistics MIS (SAUS)
ILSMP .... Integrated Logistic Support Maintenance [*or Management*] Plan (MCD)
ILSMP .... Integrated Logistic Support Management Plan (SAUO)
ILSMRS .... Integrated Logistics Support Milestone Reporting System [*Military*] (MCD)
ILSMR/T .... Integrated Logistics Support Management Review/Team (SAUO)
ILSMRT .... Integrated Logistic Support Management Review Team
ILSMT .... Integrated Logistic Support Management Team
ILS/MT/P .... Integrated Logistics Support/Management Team/Plan (ACAE)
ILSNI .... Incorporated Land Society of Northern Ireland
ILSO .... Incremental Life Support Operation (SAUS)
ILSO .... Incremental Life Support Operations
ILSO .... Integrated Logistic Support Office [*DoD*]
ILSOM .... Improved Light-Scattering Dust Monitor (PDAA)
ILSP .... Integrated Logistics Support Plan
ILSP .... Integrated Logistic Support Plan [*or Program*]
ILSP .... Integrated Logistic Support Program (SAUO)
ILSP .... Integration Logistics Support Plan (SAUS)
ILSP .... International Library of Sports and Pastimes [*A publication*]
ILSPER .... Integrated Logistics Support Performance Evaluation Report [*Military*] (MCD)
ILSPIP .... International Logistics Supply Performance Improvement Program (NG)
ILSR .... Institute for Law and Social Research (SAUO)
ILSR .... Institute for Local Self-Reliance (EA)
ILSR .... Integrated Logistics Support Review [*Military*] (MCD)
ILSREM .... Instrument Landing System Radio Environmental Monitor (SAUS)
ILSRO .... Interstate Land Sales Registration Office [*HUD*] (IAA)
ILSS .... Industry Launch Services - Storable (SSD)
ILS-S .... Instrument Landing System-Solidstate (SAUS)
ILSS .... Integrated Life Support System [*NASA*]
ILSS .... Integrated Logistics Support System (SSD)
ILSS .... Integrated Logistic Support System (SAUO)
ILSS .... Interlaminar Shear Strength (MCD)
ILSSE .... Integrated Life Science Shuttle Experiments (MCD)
ILST .... Integrated Logistics Support Team (ACAE)
ILST .... Integrated Logistic Support and Training (SAUS)
ILST .... Iterative Least Squares Technique (SAUS)
ILSTAC .... Indian Library Services Technical Assistance Center (SAUS)
ILSTAC .... Instrument Landing System and TACAN
ILST&E .... Integrated Logistics Support Test & Evaluation (SAUO)
ILSTM .... Incorporated Liverpool School of Tropical Medicine (SAUO)
ILSUS .... Integrated Library System Users Society [*Defunct*] (EA)
ILS/VOR .... Instrument Landing System / VHF [*Very-High-Frequency*] Omnidirectional Range [*Aviation*] (SAA)
ILSW .... Interrupt Level Status Word
ILSWG .... Integrated Logistics Support Working Group (SSD)
ILSX .... Independent Locomotive Service [*Private rail car owner code*]
ILT .... Albuquerque, NM [*Location identifier*] [*FAA*] (FAAL)
ILT .... Iliotibial Tract [*Medicine*] (DMAA)
ILT .... Illinois Terminal (SAUO)
ILT .... Imaging Laser Technology (SAUS)
ILT .... Imprecisely Located Target (ACAE)
ILT .... Incapacidad Laboral Transitoria (SAUS)
ILT .... Industrial Language Training (HEAS)
ILT .... Infantry Liaison Team (INF)
ILT .... Infectious Laryngo-Tracheitis [*Medicine*] (ADA)
ILT .... Inferolateral Trunk [*Neuroanatomy*]
ILT .... In Lieu Thereof [*Military*]
ILT .... Insect Lighting Trap (SAUS)
ILT .... Installation Lead Time
ILT .... Institute for Learning and Teaching (SAUO)
ILT .... Instructor Led Training (SAUO)
ILT .... Interferometric Landmark Tracker (PDAA)
ILT .... Interlayer Tunneling [*Model for superconductivity*]
ILT .... Inter-Line Transfer (SAUS)
ILT .... Intermediate Lay-Up Tool [*Plastics technology*]
ILT .... International Logistics Training
ILT .... Ion Laser Technology [*AMEX symbol*] (TTSB)
ILT .... Ion Laser Technology, Inc. [*AMEX symbol*] (SAG)

ILT .... Irish Law Times [*A publication*]
ILT .... Iultin [*Former USSR*] [*Seismograph station code, US Geological Survey*] (SEIS)
ILT .... Keck, Mahin & Cate, Chicago, IL [*OCLC symbol*] (OCLC)
ILTA .... Independent Liquid Terminals Association (EA)
ILTA .... Indiana Library Trustee Association (SAUO)
ILTA .... International Learning and Teaching Aids Foundation (SAUO)
ILTAM .... Institute for Literature and Mass Artistic Techniques (SAUO)
ILTC .... International Leadership Training Conference
ILTCP .... Inventory of Long-Term Care Places [*Department of Health and Human Services*] (GFGA)
ILTDF .... Item Logistics Data Transmittal Form (SAUO)
ILTEB .... Inner London Tertiary Education Board [*British*] (AIE)
ILTER .... International Long Term Ecological Research (SAUS)
ILTER .... International Long-Term Ecological Research Network (SAUS)
ILTF .... International Lawn Tennis Federation [*Later, ITF*]
ILTIA .... International Livestock Theft Investigators Association (NTPA)
ILT Jo .... Irish Law Times Journal [*A publication*] (DLA)
ILTMS .... International Leased Telegraph Line Switching Service (SAUS)
ILTMS .... International Leased Telegraph Message Switching (SAUS)
ILTMS .... International Leased Telegraph Message Switching Service [*British Telecom*] [*Telecommunications*] (TEL)
ILTMS Service... International Leased Telegraph Message Switching Service (SAUS)
ILTO .... Industrial Liaison Technical Officer [*British*] (DI)
ILTO .... Integrated Logistic Technology Office (ACAE)
ILTR .... Irish Law Times Reports [*A publication*] (DLA)
ILTS .... Industrial Language Training Service [*British*]
ILTS .... Integration Level Test Series [*Psychology*]
ILTS .... Intermediate Level Test Station (MCD)
ILTS .... International Liver Transplantation Society (NTPA)
ILT Sensor... Inter-Line Transfer Sensor (SAUS)
ILTSF .... Intermediate-Level Transuranic Storage Facility (SAUO)
ILTTA .... International Light Tackle Tournament Association (EA)
ILTV .... Association of Local Television Stations (NTPA)
ILTW .... Intermediate Level Transuranic Waste (SAUS)
ilu .... Illinois [*MARC country of publication code*] [*Library of Congress*] (LCCP)
ILU .... Illinois University (IEEE)
ilu .... Illuminator [*MARC relator code*] [*Library of Congress*] (LCCP)
ILU .... Institute of Life Insurance (SAUO)
ILU .... Institute of London Underwriters (ECON)
ILU .... International Legal Union (SAUO)
ILU .... Inventory of Land Use (BARN)
ILU .... Texas Tech University, Lubbock, TX [*OCLC symbol*] (OCLC)
ILU .... University of Illinois, Physics Astronomy Library (SAUO)
ILUMS .... Innovations in Land Use Management Symposium
ILUVM .... I Love You Very Much [*Correspondence*] (DSUE)
ILV .... Impatiens Latent Virus [*Plant pathology*]
ILV .... Indicative Limit Value (HEAS)
ILV .... Industrial Launch Vehicle
ILV .... International Laser Tech, Inc. [*Vancouver Stock Exchange symbol*]
ILv .... Lake Villa District Library, Lake Villa, IL [*Library symbol*] [*Library of Congress*] (LCLS)
ILV .... Sonnenschein, Carlin, Nath & Rosenthal, Chicago, IL [*OCLC symbol*] (OCLC)
ILVBIDT .... In Liebe Vereint bis in dem Tod [*United in Love until Death*] [*German*]
ILVD .... Inductive Loop Vehicle Detector (SAUS)
ILVS .... In-Line Vehicle Sequencing [*Automotive manufacturing*]
ILVSI .... Instant Lead Vertical Speed Indicator (MCD)
ILW .... Illinois Western Railroad [*Federal Railroad Administration identification code*]
ILW .... Industrial Liquid Waste (SAUS)
ILW .... Institute of Land Warfare [*Association of the US Army*] (DOMA)
ILW .... Integrated Liquid Water (ARMP)
ILW .... Intermediate Level radioactive Waste (SAUO)
ILW .... Intermediate-Level Wastes (IEEE)
ILW .... International Association of Assessing Officers, Chicago, IL [*OCLC symbol*] (OCLC)
ILW .... International Low Water
ILW .... Investment Laws of the World [*A publication*] (DLA)
ILWAS .... Integrated Lake-Watershed Acidification Study
ILWC .... Intermediate-Level Waste Concentrate [*Nuclear energy*] (NRCH)
ILWC .... International League of Women Composers (EA)
ILWCHSG .... International Labor and Working Class History Study Group (EA)
ILWD .... Intermediate-Level Waste Distillate [*Nuclear energy*] (NRCH)
ILWF .... Intermediate-Level Waste Feed [*Nuclear energy*] (NRCH)
ILWM .... In-Line Wear Monitor (SAUS)
ILWML .... International Lutheran Women's Missionary League (EA)
ILWS .... Intermediate-Level Waste Storage [*Nuclear energy*] (GFGA)
ILWSS .... Institute of Labor, Welfare and Social Security (SAUS)
ILWU .... International Longshoremen's and Warehousemen's Union (EA)
ILWW .... International Letter Writing Week (SAUO)
ILX .... ILX Resorts [*AMEX symbol*] (SG)
ILX .... Inland Molasses Co. (SAUO)
ILX .... Visiting Nurse Association of Chicago, Chicago, IL [*OCLC symbol*] (OCLC)
ILX Inc .... ILX, Inc. [*Associated Press*] (SAG)
ILY .... I Love You (VLIE)
ILY .... International Literacy Year
ILY .... Islay [*Scotland*] [*Airport symbol*] (OAG)
ILY .... Italian Liberal Youth [*Political party*] (EAIO)
ILy .... Lyons Public Library, Lyons, IL [*Library symbol*] [*Library of Congress*] (LCLS)
ILY .... Northern Illinois University, Law Library, Glen Ellyn, IL [*OCLC symbol*] (OCLC)
ILYA .... Incompletely Launched Young Adult (ADWA)
ILYA .... Inland Lake Yachting Association (EA)
I-LYA .... Inter-Lake Yachting Association (EA)
ILz .... Ela Area Public Library, Lake Zurich, IL [*Library symbol*] [*Library of Congress*] (LCLS)
ILZ .... Illinois Zinc Co. (SAUO)
ILZ .... Intensive Landuse Zone (SAUO)
ILZ .... International Lead and Zinc (SAUS)
ILZ .... Isham, Lincoln & Beale, Chicago, IL [*OCLC symbol*] (OCLC)
ILZ .... Newport, RI [*Location identifier*] [*FAA*] (FAAL)
ILZRO .... International Lead Zinc Research Organization (EA)
ILZSG .... International Lead and Zinc Study Group [*British*] (EA)
IM .... Ideal Modulation (IAA)
IM .... Idle Money [*Business term*] (MHDB)
IM .... Image Memory (SAUS)
Im .... Imaginary [*Mathematics*]
Im .... Imaginary part of (SAUS)
IM .... Imaging Model (VLIE)
IM .... Imago Mundi. A review of early cartography (journ.) (SAUS)
IM .... Immature
IM .... Im Mittel [*On an Average*] [*German*]
IM .... Immunoassay [*Marine science*] (OSRA)
IM .... Immuno-Suppression Method [*For increasing fertility*]
IM .... Impact Memorandum (MCD)
Im .... Imperial (SAUS)
IM .... Imperial Measure
IM .... Implementation Monitoring (HCT)
IM .... Import Monthly Data [*Department of Commerce*] (GFGA)
IM .... Impulse Modulation
IM .... Income Maintenance (OICC)
IM .... Independent Maintenance (SAUS)
IM .... Index Marker (MHDB)
IM .... Indian Marines (ODA)
IM .... Indicator Module (SAUS)
IM .... Individual Medley [*Swimming*]
IM .... Indomethacin [*An analgesic*]
IM .... Indonesia Minas [*Crude oil*]
IM .... Induced Magnetization
IM .... Induction Meter (SAUS)
IM .... Induction Motor (SAUS)
IM .... Industrial Manager
IM .... Industrial Mathematics (SAUS)
IM .... Industrial Medicine (DAVI)
IM .... Industry Motion Picture [*FCC*] (MCD)
IM .... Inerceptor Missile (SAUS)
IM .... Infantile Myofibromatosus [*Medicine*]
IM .... Infant Mortality (ROG)
IM .... Infectious Mononucleosis [*Medicine*]
IM .... Inferior Mediastinum [*Medicine*] (MELL)
IM .... Inferior Mesenteric (SAUS)
IM .... Informal Memo (SAUS)
IM .... Informal Memorandum (MCD)
IM .... Information Management (AAGC)
IM .... Information Manager [*A publication*]
IM .... Information Market [*Commission of the European Communities*] [*Information service or system*] (IID)
IM .... Information Memory (MCD)
IM .... Information Modeling (SAUO)
IM .... Ingot Metallurgy
IM .... Ingram Micro, Inc. [*NYSE symbol*] (SAG)
IM .... Inherent Moisture [*Coal industry*]
IM .... Initialization Mode (SAUS)
IM .... Initial Makeup (SAUS)
IM .... Initial Mass [*Agronomy*]
IM .... Injection Module (ACAE)
IM .... Injection Mold (MCD)
IM .... Injection Molding (SAUS)
IM .... Inland Marine [*Insurance*]
IM .... In Maintenance
im .... In Margine [*On the Margin*] [*Latin*]
IM .... Inner Marker [*Part of an instrument landing system*] [*Aviation*]
IM .... Inner Membrane (DB)
IM .... Inner Modulator (ACAE)
IM .... Innocent Murmur [*Medicine*] (MELL)
IM .... Inoffizielle Mitarbeiter [*Unofficial Collaborators*] [*German*]
IM .... Input Machine (SAUS)
IM .... Input Memory (SAUS)
IM .... Input Message (SAUS)
IM .... Insensitive Munitions (MCD)
IM .... Insertion Mark (SAUS)
IM .... Inside Macintosh (VLIE)
I/M .... Inside of Metal (MSA)
I/M .... Inspection and Maintenance (ERG)
IM .... Inspection Manual (MCD)
IM .... Inspection Memorandum
IM .... Inspector of Machinery
IM .... Installation Maintenance (SAUS)
IM .... Installation Manual (VLIE)
IM .... Installation Material (AAGC)
IM .... Installment Mortgage (WDAA)
IM .... Instant Message [*Computer science*]
IM .... Instant Messaging [*Computer science*]
IM .... Institute for Metals (SAUS)

IM .... Institute for Metals Research (SAUO)
IM .... Institute of Management (COBU)
IM .... Institute of Marketing (EAIO)
IM .... Institute of Marketing and Sales Management (SAUO)
IM .... Institute of Medicine [*National Academy of Sciences*]
IM .... Institute of Metallurgists (SAUO)
IM .... Institute of Metallurgy (SAUS)
IM .... Institute of Meteorology (SAUS)
IM .... Institute of Metrology (SAUS)
IM .... Institution of Metallurgists [*British*]
IM .... Instruction Manual
IM .... Instruction Memory
IM .... Instruction Motor (SAUS)
IM .... Instrumentation (MDG)
IM .... Instrumentation and Measurement (MCD)
IM .... Instrumentation Manager [*NASA*] (KSC)
IM .... Instrumentation of Measurement (SAUS)
IM .... Instrument Man (SAUS)
IM .... Instrumentman [*Navy rating*]
IM .... Instrument Measurement (SAUS)
IM .... Instrument Module (SAUS)
IM .... Instrument Myopia (PDAA)
IM .... Insulation Material (SAUS)
IM .... Integrated Manufacturing (SAUS)
IM .... Integrated Master (NRCH)
IM .... Integrated Model (AAEL)
IM .... Integrated MODEM
IM .... Integrating Meter (SAUS)
IM .... Integration Modified
IM .... Intelligence Memorandum
IM .... Intelligent Measurement [*Function*] (ACII)
IM .... Intelligent Messaging (VLIE)
IM .... Intelligent Modularity [*Computer science*] (ELAL)
IM .... Intensity Measuring Devices [*JETDS nomenclature*] [*Military*] (CET)
IM .... Intensity Modulation
IM .... Interactive Marketing (GART)
IM .... Interactive Mode (IAA)
IM .... Interact Ministries [*An association*] (EA)
IM .... Intercept Missile (SAUS)
IM .... Interceptor Missile
IM .... Interdepartmental Memorandum (AAG)
IM .... Interface Measurements (SAUS)
IM .... Interface Module (MCD)
IM .... Interfaith Movement [*Defunct*] (EA)
IM .... Interference Microscopy (SAUS)
IM .... Interim Measures
IM .... Interim Memorandum
IM .... Interim Mission (SAUS)
IM .... Intermedia (SAUS)
IM .... Intermediate Maintenance (MCD)
IM .... Intermediate Megaloblast (DB)
IM .... Intermediate Missile (MSA)
IM .... Intermediate Modeling [*Marine science*] (OSRA)
IM .... Intermediate Modulation
IM .... Intermediate Modulus (SAUS)
IM .... Intermediate Moisture (KSC)
IM .... Intermetatarsal [*Anatomy*] (DAVI)
IM .... Inter Mirifica [*Decree on the Instruments of Social Communication*] [*Vatican II document*]
IM .... Intermodal (SAUS)
IM .... Intermodulation
IM .... Intermodulation Distortion (NTCM)
IM .... Intermuscular [*Anatomy*] (DAVI)
IM .... Internal Medicine
IM .... Internal Memorandum
IM .... Internal Memory (SAUS)
IM .... Internal Monitor [*Medicine*] (MELL)
IM .... International Management (journ.) (SAUS)
IM .... International Master [*Chess*] (ODA)
IM .... International Microfilm (SAUS)
IM .... International Mining Corp. (SAUO)
IM .... International Missions [*An association*] (EA)
IM .... International Musician (journ.) (SAUS)
IM .... Internet Medicine (SAUO)
IM .... Interrupt Mask
IM .... Interrupt Mode (SAUS)
IM .... Interview Measure (SAUS)
IM .... Intestinal Metaplasia [*Medicine*]
IM .... Intramedullary [*Medicine*]
IM .... Intramural
IM .... Intramuscular [*Injection*] [*Medicine*]
IM .... Intra-Muscularly (SAUS)
IM .... In-Use Maintenance Test
IM .... Invasive Mole
I/M .... Inventory Management [*Business term*]
IM .... Inventory Manager [*Military*]
IM .... Inventory Master (VLIE)
IM .... Inverse Matrix (SAUS)
IM .... Inverted Microscope [*Instrumentation*]
IM .... Invisible Ministry (EA)
IM .... Ion Micrnscope (SAUS)
IM .... Iowa Mountaineers (EA)
IM .... Irish Marquis (ROG)
IM .... Isle of Man [*England*]
IM .... Isomagnetic (SAUS)
IM .... Isometric (SAUS)
IM .... Isotropic Mixing (SAUS)
IM .... Istanbuler Mitteilungen [*A publication*] (BJA)
IM .... Item Management
IM .... Item Manager (AAGC)
IM .... Item Mark (BUR)
IM .... Jamaire [*ICAO designator*] (AD)
IM .... Sisters of Charity of the Infant Mary (TOCD)
IM1 .... Instrumentman, First Class [*Navy rating*]
IM2 .... Instrumentman, Second Class [*Navy rating*]
IM2 .... Integrated Materiel Management [*Military*]
IM3 .... Instrumentman, Third Class [*Navy rating*]
IMA .... Iamalele [*Papua New Guinea*] [*Airport symbol*] (OAG)
IMA .... Ice Motion Algorithm (SAUS)
IMA .... Idaho Medical Association (SRA)
IMA .... Idaho Mining Association (SRA)
IMA .... Ideal Mechanical Advantage (SAUS)
IMA .... Ignition Manufacturers Institute (SAUO)
IMA .... Illinois Manufacturers Association (SRA)
IMA .... Immobilized Metal Affinity [*Protein chromatography*]
IMA .... Impedance Matching Attenuator
IMA .... Important Materiel Actions (SAUO)
IMA .... Independent Management Activity (SAUS)
IMA .... Independent Manufacturing Assessment (MCD)
IMA .... Independent Midwives Association [*British*] (DBA)
IMA .... Independent Music Association (EA)
IMA .... Indiana Manufacturers Association (SRA)
IMA .... Indian Medical Academy (SAUO)
IMA .... Indian Medical Association (SAUO)
IMA .... Indian Military Academy
IMA .... Indian Mountain [*Alaska*] [*Seismograph station code, US Geological Survey*] (SEIS)
IMA .... Individuai Mobilization Augmentation (SAUS)
IMA .... Individual Medical Account (SAUS)
IMA .... Individual Mobilization Augmentation [*or Augmentees*] [*DoD*]
IMA .... Individual Mobilization Augmentee (AAGC)
IMA .... Indonesian Mining Association (SAUO)
IMA .... Industrial Marketing Associates (EA)
IMA .... Industrial Marketing Association (SAUO)
IMA .... Industrial Medical Association [*Later, AOMA*] (EA)
IMA .... Inferior Mesenteric Artery [*Anatomy*]
IMA .... Information Management Architecture (SAUO)
IMA .... Information Management Area (SAUO)
IMA .... Information Management Associates (SAUS)
IMA .... Information Medicale Automatisee [*Automated Medical Information*] [*INSERM*] [*Information service or system*] (IID)
IMA .... Information Mission Area
IMA .... Inherent Mobile Availability [*Military*]
IMA .... Initial Military Assistance (CINC)
IMA .... Input Message Acknowledgment [*Computer science*]
IMA .... Input Message Area (SAUS)
IMA .... Installation Maintenance Activity (MCD)
IMA .... Institute for Manufacturing Automation (SAUS)
IMA .... Institute for Mathematics and Its Applications [*University of Minnesota*] [*Research center*] (RCD)
IMA .... Institute for Media Analysis (EA)
IMA .... Institute for Mediterranean Affairs (EA)
IMA .... Institute for Military Assistance [*Army*]
IMA .... Institute of Management Accountants (EBF)
IMA .... Institute of Management Accounting (EA)
IMA .... Institute of Mathematics and Its Applications [*South-End-On-Sea, England*] (CSR)
IMA .... Institute of Municipal Administration (SAUO)
IMA .... Instituto Magdelena Aulina [*Magdalena Aulina Institute*] [*Barcelona, Spain*] (EAIO)
IMA .... Integer Multiplication Algorithm (SAUS)
IMA .... Integrated Mission Avionics (SAUS)
IMA .... Integrated Modular Avionics [*Honeywell, Inc.*]
IMA .... Intelligent Media Adapter (VLIE)
IMA .... Interactive Multimedia Association [*Database producer*] (IID)
IMA .... Interbank Marketing Association (SAUO)
IMA .... Interbank Merchants Association [*Pigeon Forge, TN*] (EA)
IMA .... Interchurch Medical Assistance (EA)
IMA .... Interdisciplinary Master of Arts (PGP)
IMA .... Interface Management Agent (MCD)
IMA .... Interim Measures Agreement (SAUO)
IMA .... Interior Mesenteric Artery (SAUS)
IMA .... Intermap Analytic (SAUO)
IMA .... Intermediate Maintenance Activity
IMA .... Intermodal Marketing Association (SAUO)
IMA .... Intermodulation Analyzer (SAUS)
IMA .... Inter-Mountain Airways [*ICAO designator*] (FAAC)
IMA .... Internal Mammary Artery (SAUS)
IMA .... Internal Mammary Artery (Implant) [*Medicine*]
IMA .... International Magnesium Association (EA)
IMA .... International Maintenance Agency
ima .... International Management Associates (SAUO)
IMA .... International Management Association [*Later, AMA/I*] (EA)
IMA .... International Maritime Academy (SAUS)
IMA .... International Massage Association (EA)
IMA .... International Medical Assistance [*Society*]
IMA .... International Message Centre [*Vancouver Stock Exchange symbol*]
IMA .... International Messaging Associates [*Commercial firm*]
IMA .... International Metaphysical Association [*Defunct*] (EA)

IMA International MIDI [*Musical Instrument Digital Interface*] Association (EA)
IMA International Military Archives (EA)
IMA International Milling Association [*See also AIM*] [*Brussels, Belgium*] (EAIO)
IMA International Mineralogical Association [*ICSU*] [*Marburg, Federal Republic of Germany*] (EA)
IMA International Minilab Association (EA)
IMA International Mobjack Association (EA)
IMA International Mohair Association (EAIO)
IMA International Monovision Association (SAUO)
IMA International Multimedia Association (AGLO)
IMA International Music Association
IMA International Mycological Association [*See also AIM*] [*England*] (EAIO)
IMA International Mycophagist Association (EA)
IMA Invalid Memory Address [*Computer science*]
IMA Inventory Management Activity
IMA Inventory of Marine Activities (SAUS)
IMA Ion Mass Analyzer (SAUS)
IMA Ion Microprobe Analyzer
IMA Ion Microspectroscope Analysis (SAUS)
IMA Iowa Manufacturers Association (SAUO)
IMA Irish Medical Association
IMA Iron Mining Association of Minnesota (SRA)
IMA Islamic Medical Association (EA)
IMA Islamic Mission of America (EA)
IMA Israel Medical Association (SAUO)
IMA Issues Management Association (EA)
IMA Item Manager [*DoD*]
IM-A1 Inorganic Monomeric Aluminum (CARB)
IMAA Imidazoleacetic Acid [*Biochemistry*]
IMAA Indochinese Mutual Assistance Association (SAUO)
IMAA Industrial Medical Administrators' Association [*Later, OMAA*] (EA)
IMAA Information Management Associates, Inc. [*NASDAQ symbol*] (NASQ)
IMAA Institute for Mediterranean Art and Archaeology [*Defunct*] (EA)
IMAA Intelligence Mission Area Analysis [*Military*] (MCD)
IMAA International Marketing Audit Association (EA)
IMAA Iodinated Macroaggregated Albumin [*Medicine*] (MAE)
IMAAWS Infantry Manportable Antiarmor Weapon System
IMAAWS Infantry Man-portable Anti-armour/Assault Weapon System (SAUO)
IMAB Internal Mammary Artery Bypass [*Medicine*] (DMAA)
IMAB International Medical Advisory [*Medicine*] (EDAA)
IMAC Ifosfamide, Mesna, Adriamycin, Cisplatin [*Antineoplastic drug*] (CDI)
IMAC Illinois Microfilm Automated Cataloging [*Illinois State Library*] (NITA)
IMAC Illinois State Library Microfilm Automated Catalog (PDAA)
IMAC Immobilized Metal Affinity Chromatography
IMAC Information Management, Archiving, and Communication (DMAA)
IMAC Installations, Moves, Adds, and Changes [*Computer science*] (GART)
IMAC Integrated Material Accountability Control (ACAE)
IMAC Integrated Microwave Amplifier Converter
IMAC Interim Message Automated Capability (SAUO)
IMAC International Management Advisory Council (SAUO)
IMAC International Metals Acquisition Corp. [*NASDAQ symbol*] (SAG)
IMAC International Metals and Commodities (SAUO)
IMAC International Mobile Air Conditioning Association, Inc.
IMAC International Movement of Apostolate of Children [*Paris, France*] (EA)
iMAC Internet Macintosh (SAUO)
IMAC Inventory Management and Control (TIMI)
I-MAC Isochronous MAC (SAUO)
IMAC Isochronous Media Access Control (SAUO)
IMAC 90 Immigration Act of 1990 (WYGK)
IMACA International Mobile Air Conditioning Association (EA)
IMACE Association des Industries Margarinieres des Pays de la CEE [*Association of Margarine Industries of the EEC Countries*] [*Belgium*]
IMACE Association of the Margarine Industry of the EEC Countries (SAUO)
IMACHA Intermountain Automated Clearing House Association (MHDW)
IMACON Image Converting Camera (SAUS)
IMacoW Western Illinois University, Macomb, IL [*Library symbol*] [*Library of Congress*] (LCLS)
IMACS Image Management and Communication System (SAUO)
IMACS Integrity Monitoring and Control Software (SAUS)
IMACS International Association for Mathematics and Computers in Simulation (EA)
IMACS International Association for Mathematics and Science (SAUO)
IMACUAC Information Management and Computer Utilization Advisory Committee (SAUO)
IMAD Integral Model of Aerosol Dynamics (SAUS)
IMAD Integrated Multisensor Airborne Display
IMad Madison Public Library, Madison, IL [*Library symbol*] [*Library of Congress*] (LCLS)
IMadCU Madison Community, Unit 12, Madison, IL [*Library symbol*] [*Library of Congress*] (LCLS)
IMADE International Military and Defense Encyclopedia [*A publication*]
IMADS Integrated Machinery Analysis and Diagnostic System (SAUS)
IMAEM International Maritime Association of the East Mediterranean (SAUO)
IMAF International Martial Arts Federation (EAIO)
IMAG IEEE [*Institute of Electrical and Electronics Engineers*] Magnetics (IAA)
IMAG Image Industries [*NASDAQ symbol*] (SAG)
IMAG Image Retailing Group, Inc. (SAUO)
IMAG Imagination (SAUS)
IMAG Imagine [*or Imaginary*] (MSA)
Imag Imagines [*of Philostratus*] [*Classical studies*] (OCD)
IMAG Information Management Advisory Group (SAUO)
IMAG Institute of Agricultural Engineering (SAUO)
IMAG Instituut voor Mechanistie Arbeid en Gebouwen [*Netherlands*] (NITA)
IMAG Internal Mammary Artery Graft [*Cardiology*] (DAVI)
IMAG International Mail-Art Group (SAUO)
IMAGE Imager for Magnetopause-to-Aurora Global Exploration (SAUS)
Im Age Imagination Age (journ.) (SAUS)
IMAGE Information Management by Application Generation (IAA)
IMAGE Innovative Management Achieves Greater Effectiveness (SAUO)
IMAGE Institute for Molecular and Agricultural Genetic Engineering [*University of Idaho*] [*Research center*]
IMAGE Instruction in Motivation Achievement and General Education [*YMCA program*]
IMAGE Integrated Mapping and Geographic Encoding System (SAUO)
IMAGE Integrated Model for Assessment of the Greenhouse Effect (SAUO)
IMAGE Integrated Molecular Analysis of Gene Expression (HGEN)
IMAGE Interactive Menu-Assisted Graphics Environment (SAUS)
IMAGE Interactive Meteorological Information Access in a Graphic Environment (SAUS)
IMAGE International Monitor for Auroral Geomagnetic Effects
IMAGE International Multicenter Angina Exercise (DMAA)
IMAGE International Multi-Channel Action Group for Education (SAUO)
IMAGE Intruder Monitoring and Guidance Equipment (MCD)
IMAGE Involvement of Mexican-Americans in Gainful Endeavors (SAUO)
IMAGE 100 Interactive Multispectral Image Analysis System (SAUS)
IMAGED Image-Based Analysis of Geographic Data (SAUS)
Image Dyn Sci Med Image Dynamics in Science and Medicine (journ.) (SAUS)
ImageInd Image Industries [*Associated Press*] (SAG)
Image J Nurs Sch Image. Journal of Nursing Scholarship (journ.) (SAUS)
ImagEn Image Entertainment, Inc. [*Associated Press*] (SAG)
Image Process Image Processing (journ.) (SAUS)
IMAGER Imaging Middle-Atmosphere Geophysical Radar (SAUS)
IMAGERY Multispectral Scanner and Photographic Imagery (SAUO)
IMAGES Image Analysis and Graphic Facility for Ecological Studies (SAUO)
ImageS Image Sensing Systems, Inc. [*Associated Press*] (SAG)
IMAGES Improving Morale And Giving Excellent Service (SAUS)
IMAGES Instructional Material Adequacy Guide and Evaluation Standard (RDA)
IMAGES Instrumental Manual Adequacy Guide and Evaluation Standard
IMAGES Interactive Modal Analysis and Gain Estimation for Eigensystem [*NASA digital computer program*]
IMAGES Intermediate Model for the Annual and Global Evolution of Interactive Systems (SAUO)
IMAGES Intermediate Model for the Annual and Global Evolution of Species (SAUS)
IMAGES Intermediate Model of Global Evaluation of Species (SAUO)
IMAGES International Marine Global Change Study [*Research programs*]
ImageSft Image Software, Inc. [*Associated Press*] (SAG)
IMAGE Software Interactive Multi-Activity Graphics Environment Software (SAUS)
Image Vis Comput Image and Vision Computing (journ.) (SAUS)
IMAGI Index Measuring Accurate Growth of Inflation (SAUS)
Imagyn Imagyn Medical, Inc. [*Associated Press*] (SAG)
IMah Mahomet Township Public Library, Mahomet, IL [*Library symbol*] [*Library of Congress*] (LCLS)
IMAI Imaging Management Associates [*NASDAQ symbol*] (SAG)
IMAI Imaging Mgmt Assoc [*NASDAQ symbol*] (TTSB)
IMAI Internal Mammary Artery Implant [*Medicine*] (DMAA)
IMAID Image Analysis and Image Data-base (SAUS)
IMAID Integrated Image Analysis and Image Data-Base Management System (SAUS)
IMAIL Intelligent MAIL (SAUO)
IMAIS Integrated Magnetic & Acoustic Influence Sweep (SAUS)
IMAJ Initiative d'Un Mouvement d'Animation Jeunesse pour l'Annee Internationale de laJeunesse en 1985 [*Canada*]
IMA J Appl Math IMA Journal of Applied Mathematics (journ.) (SAUS)
IMA J Math Appl Med Biol IMA Journal of Mathematics Applied in Medicine and Biology (journ.) (SAUS)
IMA J Math Control Inf IMA Journal of Mathematical Control and Information (journ.) (SAUS)
IMA J Numer Anal IMA Journal of Numerical Analysis (journ.) (SAUS)
IMAK International Imaging Materials, Inc. [*NASDAQ symbol*] (SAG)
IMAK Intl Imaging Materials [*NASDAQ symbol*] (TTSB)
IMAL i-Mall, Inc. [*NASDAQ symbol*] (SG)
IM-AI Inorganic Monomeric Aluminum (SAUS)
IMAL Integrated Media Architecture Laboratory (SAUO)
I Malloy Treaties, Conventions, International Acts, Protocols, and Agreements between the United States of America and other Powers, 1776-1909, Compiled under the Direction of the U.S. Senate by William M. Malloy (SAFN)
IMAM International Meeting on Advanced Materials (SAUS)
IMA MOD Information Mission Area Modernization [*Army*] (RDA)
IMan Blue Ridge Township Public Library, Mansfield, IL [*Library symbol*] [*Library of Congress*] (LCLS)
IMAN Image Analysis (SAUS)
IMAN Intermap Analytic Nucleus (SAUS)
IMAN International Mail Art Network (EA)
IMAN NEIC Image Analysis System (SAUO)
IMANCO Image Analysing Computers, Inc.
IM & AWU International Molders' and Allied Workers' Union [*AFL-CIO*] (EA)
IM & D Image Mapping and Display (NOAA)
IM&T Information Management and Technology (SAUO)
IM&T Inspector of Mechanized Troops (SAUO)
IM&T Institute of the Motor Trade (SAUO)

IM & TPR.... Information Management and Telecommunications Pentagon Renovation (RDA)
IMANF........ Institute of Manufacturing [*Royal Leamington Spa, Warwickshire, England*] (EAIO)
IMAO........ In My Arrogant Opinion [*Computer hacker terminology*] (NHD)
IMAO........ International Military Assistance Office
IMAP........ Immediately After Passing [*Aviation*] (FAAC)
IMAP........ Indian Middle Atmosphere Programme (SAUO)
IMAP........ Initial Manufacturing Assignment Program (ACAE)
IMAP........ Input, Management, Analysis, and Presentation (SAUS)
IMAP........ Institute of Materials and Advanced Processes [*University of Idaho*] [*Research center*] (RCD)
IMAP........ Integrated Mechanical Analysis Project (SAUS)
IMAP........ Interactive Mail Access Protocol (SAUS)
IMAP........ Interactive Manpower Alternatives Processor (DNAB)
IMAP........ Intergrated Mission Analysis Planning (SAUS)
IMAP........ International Merger and Acquisition Professionals (NTPA)
IMAP........ Internet Mail Access Protocol [*Computer science*]
IMAP........ Internet Managed Application Provider (SAUO)
IMAP........ Internet Message Access Protocol [*Computer science*]
IMAP........ Internet Messaging Access Protocol [*Computer science*] (IGQR)
IMAP3........ Interactive Mail Access Protocol Version 3 (SAUS)
IMAP4........ Internet Mail Access Protocol Version 4 (SAUS)
IMAP4........ Internet Message Access Protocol [*Computer science*]
IMAP4........ Internet Message Access Protocol 4 [*Electronic mail*]
IMAPPA........ International Martial Arts Pen Pal Association [*Defunct*] (EA)
IMAPS........ Intake Manifold Absolute Pressure Sensor [*Automotive engineering*]
IMAPS........ Integrated Military Airlift Planning System (CCCA)
IMAPS........ Interactive Microcomputer Array Processing System (SAUO)
IMAPS........ International Microelectronics and Packaging Society (NTPA)
IMAR........ Inner Mongolia Autonomous Region (SAUO)
IMar........ Markham Public Library, Markham, IL [*Library symbol*] [*Library of Congress*] (LCLS)
IMarE........ Institute of Marine Engineers [*British*] [*Database producer*]
IMARE........ Institution of Marine Engineers (SAUS)
Imari........ Marion Carnegie Library, Marion, IL [*Library symbol*] [*Library of Congress*] (LCLS)
IMARPE........ Instituto del Mar de Peru [*Marine science*] (OSRA)
IMARS........ Institutional Management for Accountability and Renewal System (SAUS)
IMars........ Marshall Public Library, Marshall, IL [*Library symbol*] [*Library of Congress*] (LCLS)
IMarse........ Marseilles Public Library, Marseilles, IL [*Library symbol*] [*Library of Congress*] (LCLS)
IMarseHS.... Marseilles High School, Marseilles, IL [*Library symbol*] [*Library of Congress*] (LCLS)
IMarseMSD... Miller Township Consolidated Community, School District 210, Marseilles, IL [*Library symbol*] [*Library of Congress*] (LCLS)
IMART........ International Medical Association for Radio and Television [*Brussels, Belgium*] (EAIO)
IMart........ Martinsville Township Library, Martinsville, IL [*Library symbol*] [*Library of Congress*] (LCLS)
IMartSD........ Martinsville Community Unit Schools District, Martinsville, IL [*Library symbol*] [*Library of Congress*] (LCLS)
IMaryR........ Maryville Reading Center, Maryville, IL [*Library symbol*] [*Library of Congress*] (LCLS)
IMAS........ Impurity Monitoring and Analysis System [*Nuclear energy*] (NRCH)
IMAS........ Industrial Management Assistance Survey [*Air Force*]
IMAS........ Integrated Management Accounting System (SAUS)
IMAS........ Integrated Mass Announcement System (SAUS)
IMAS........ Integrated Mulit-sensor Airborne Survey (SAUS)
IMAS........ International Marine and Shipping Conference (NOAA)
IMas........ Mascoutah Public Library, Mascoutah, IL [*Library symbol*] [*Library of Congress*] (LCLS)
IMASA........ International Medico-Athletic and Scientific Association (SAUO)
IMASD........ Index of Mission Area Source Documentation (SAUS)
I-MASF........ Interim Maintenance and Storage Facility (SAUO)
IMasHS........ Mascoutah High School, Mascoutah, IL [*Library symbol*] [*Library of Congress*] (LCLS)
IMAT........ Imatron, Inc. [*NASDAQ symbol*] (NQ)
IMAT........ Integrated, Modification and Trial
IMAT........ Interactive Multimedia Arts and Technologies Association [*Canada*] (DDC)
IMAT........ Interim Maintenance Assistance Team (MCD)
IMAT........ Intermodal Automated Transfer (PDAA)
IMAT........ International Masonry Apprenticeship Trust (SAUS)
IMAT........ International Mechanism for Appropriate Technology
IMat........ Mattoon Public Library, Mattoon, IL [*Library symbol*] [*Library of Congress*] (LCLS)
IMATA........ Independent Military Air Transport Association [*Later, Independent Airlines Association*]
IMATA........ International Marine Animal Trainers Association (SAUO)
IMATCE........ Information Mission Area Training Center of Excellence [*Army*] (RDA)
IMATDFW.... International Movement ATD Fourth World [*France*] (EAIO)
Imatec........ Imatec Ltd. [*Associated Press*] (SAG)
IMatH........ Memorial Hospital District Library, Mattoon, IL [*Library symbol*] [*Library of Congress*] (LCLS)
IMatL........ Sara Bush Lincoln Health Center, Mattoon, IL [*Library symbol*] [*Library of Congress*] (LCLS)
ImatLC........ Lake Land College, Mattoon, IL [*Library symbol*] [*Library of Congress*] (LCLS)
Imatrn........ Imatron, Inc. [*Associated Press*] (SAG)
IMATS........ Issue Management (SAUO)
IMATS........ Issue Management and Tracking System (SAUS)
IMatt........ Matteson Public Library, Matteson, IL [*Library symbol*] [*Library of Congress*] (LCLS)
IMAU........ Institute for Marine and Atmospheric Resesarch (SAUO)
IMAU........ International Movement for Atlantic Union (EA)
IMAURO........ Integrated Model for the Analysis of Urban Route Optimization (SAUO)
IMAV........ Intermediate Maintenance Availability
IMAW........ International Molders' and Allied Workers' Union [*AFL-CIO*]
IMAWS........ Integrated Multiple Aimpoint Weapon Selector (SAUO)
IMAWU........ International Molders and Allied Workers Union (SAUS)
IMAX........ Image-Maximum [*Photography*]
IMAX........ Imax Corp. [*NASDAQ symbol*] (SG)
IMAX........ Isotope Matter Antimatter Experiment
IMAX........ Shuttle Cabin Camera (SAUO)
Imax Cp........ Imax Corp. [*Associated Press*] (SAG)
IMAXF........ Imax Corp. [*NASDAQ symbol*] (SAG)
IMay........ Maywood Public Library, Maywood, IL [*Library symbol*] [*Library of Congress*] (LCLS)
IMAZ........ IMC Agrico [*Federal Railroad Administration identification code*]
IMAZON........ Institute of Man and the Amazon Environment (SAUO)
IMB........ Imbaimadai [*Guyana*] [*Airport symbol*] (OAG)
IMB........ Independent Mixed Brigade [*Military*]
IMB........ Independent Mortar Battery [*British military*] (DMA)
IMB........ Indian Mountain Battery [*British military*] (DMA)
IMB........ Information Management Branch (AUEG)
IMB........ Input Memory Buffer [*Computer science*]
IMB........ Institute for Marine Biochemistry [*British*]
IMB........ Institute of Marine Biology (SAUO)
IMB........ Institute of Microbiology
IMB........ Institute of Molecular Biophysics [*Florida State University*] [*Research center*] (RCD)
IMB........ Institute of Molecular Biotechnology [*Germany*]
IMB........ Instrument Material Bulletin (MCD)
IMB........ Integration Management Board (ACAE)
IMB........ Intel Media Bench (SAUS)
IMB........ Interaction of Man and the Biosphere (SAUS)
IMB........ InterCapital Ins Muni Bd Fd [*NYSE symbol*] (TTSB)
IMB........ InterCapital Insurance Municipal Bond Fund [*NYSE symbol*] (SPSG)
IMB........ Intercontinental Medical Book Corp.
IMB........ Intermenstrual Bleeding [*Medicine*]
IMB........ Intermode Bus (SAUS)
IMB........ Inter-Module Bus (NITA)
IMB........ Intermountain Tariff Bureau Inc. (SAUO)
IMB........ Intermountain Tariff Bureau, Inc., Salt Lake City UT [*STAC*]
IMB........ Internationaler Metalarbeiterbund [*International Metalworkers' Federation*]
IMB........ International Maritime Bureau [*Research center*] [*British*] (IRC)
IMB........ International Mission Board (EA)
IMB........ Investigator of Micro-Biosphere (EOSA)
IMB........ Irish Meat Board (SAUO)
IMB........ Irish Medicines Board (GVA)
IMB........ Irvine/Michigan/Brookhaven [*Experiment on proton decay*]
IMB........ Kimberly, OR [*Location identifier*] [*FAA*] (FAAL)
IMBA........ Insurope-Multinational Benefits Association (SAUO)
IMBA........ Integrative Master of Business Administration (PGP)
IMBA........ International Master of Busness Administration [*University of South Carolina*]
IMBA........ International Media Buyers Association [*Defunct*] (EA)
IMBA........ International Morab Breeders Association (EA)
IMBA........ International Mountain Bicycling Association (EA)
IMBB........ Institute of Molecular Biology and Biochemistry [*Simon Fraser University*] [*Canada*]
IMBB........ Institute of Molecular Biology and Biotechnology [*Greece*]
IMBC........ Independent and Multicultural Broadcasting Corporation (SAUO)
IMBC........ Indirect Maximum Breathing Capacity [*Medicine*]
IMBC........ Institute of Marine Biology of Crete (SAUO)
IMBC........ International Marine Biotechnology Conference
IMBDC........ International Marine Biodiversity Development Corp. (SAUS)
IMBDC........ International Marine Biodiversity Development Corporation (SAUO)
IMBE........ Improved Multi-Band Encoding [*Telecommunications*] (ACRL)
IMBE........ Improved Multi-Band Excitation (SAUS)
IMBE........ Institute for Minority Business Education [*Defunct*] (EA)
IM Beacon... Inner Marker Beacon (SAUS)
IMBEX........ International Men's and Boys' Wear Exhibition
IMBI........ Institute of Medical and Biological Illustration [*British*]
IMBISA........ Interregional Meeting of the Bishops of Southern Africa (SAUS)
IMBL........ Independent Meat Buyers Ltd. [*British*] (BI)
IMBLM........ Integrated Medical and Behavioral Laboratory Management (DNAB)
IMBLMS........ Integrated Medical and Behavioral Laboratory Measurement System
IMBM........ Institute of Maintenance and Building Management [*British*] (DBA)
IMBM........ Institute of Municipal Building Management [*British*]
IMBN........ International Molecular Biology Network
IMBO........ Indian and Metis Brotherhood Organization
IMB-project... Irvine-Michigan-Brookhaven project (SAUO)
IMBR........ Institute of Marine Biomedical Research [*University of North Carolina at Wilmington*] [*Research center*] (RCD)
IMBS........ Individual Motor Behavior Survey [*Test*]
IMBT........ Iron Masters Board of Trade
IMC........ Chief Instrumentman [*Navy rating*]
IMC........ Consolata Missionaries (TOCD)
imc........ Consolata Missionaries (TOCD)
IMC........ Ice Mass Content (CARB)
IMC........ Image Motion Compensation [*or Compensator*]
IMC........ Image Motion Compensator (SAUS)
IMC........ Image Motion Configuration

IMC .... Imco Resources Ltd. [*Vancouver Stock Exchange symbol*]
IMC .... Immunohistochemical [*Medicine*] (PALA)
IMC .... Improved Meteorological Conditions (MCD)
IMC .... Incident Management Center [*Nuclear Regulatory Commission*] (NRCH)
IMC .... Indigent Medical Care (HCT)
IMC .... Industrial Management Center (SAUO)
IMC .... Industrial Marketing Council (SAUO)
IMC .... Industrial Metal Containers Section of the Material Handling Institute (EA)
IMC .... Industrial Microcomputer
ImC .... Industrial Microfilm Co., Detroit, MI [*Library symbol*] [*Library of Congress*] (LCLS)
IMC .... Infant Mortality Commission (SAUS)
IMC .... Informational Media Center (SAUS)
IMC .... Information Management Center (ACAE)
IMC .... Information Management Committee (SAUO)
IMC .... Information Management Concepts (SAUS)
IMC .... Information Management Consultants [*Database producer*] (IID)
IMC .... Information Memory Cell (SAUS)
IMC .... Information-Memory-Concentration (DMAA)
IMC .... Initial Marks [*Held*] Constant [*Psychology*]
IMC .... Initial Microcode Load (SAUS)
IMC .... Initial Moisture Content (IAA)
IMC .... In-Mold Coating [*Organic chemistry*]
IMC .... In-Mold Compounding
IMC .... Inspection Method Control
IMC .... Institute of Management Consultants [*New York, NY*] (EA)
IMC .... Institute of Measurement and Control [*British*]
IMC .... Institute of Measurement Control (SAUS)
IMC .... Institute of Medicine of Chicago (SAUO)
IMC .... Institute of Motorcycling [*British*] (DBA)
IMC .... Instructional Materials Center
IMC .... Instructional Media Center (SAUO)
IMC .... Instrument [*Flight*] Meteorological Conditions [*Aviation*]
IMC .... Instrument Meteorological Control (SAUS)
IMC .... Integrated Maintenance Chart [*or Concept*]
IMC .... Integrated Maintenance Concept (SAUS)
IMC .... Integrated Management Control (ACAE)
IMC .... Integrated Marketing Communications [*Advertising*] [*Public relations*] (WDMC)
IMC .... Integrated Medical Curriculum (SAUO)
IMC .... Integrated Meteo-Database in Cala (SAUO)
IMC .... Integrated Microcircuit (SAUS)
IMC .... Integrated Microcircuits, Inc. (EFIS)
IMC .... Integrated Microelectronic Circuitry (AAG)
IMC .... Integrated Microwave Circuit
IMC .... Integrated Monolithic Circuit
IMC .... Integrated Multiplexer Channel
IMC .... Intelligent Matrix Control [*T-Bar, Inc.*]
IMC .... Intensity Millicurie [*Nucleonics*] (IAA)
IMC .... Interactive Medical Communications (SAUS)
IMC .... Interactive Module Controller
IMC .... Interagency Management Council (SAUO)
IMC .... Interceptor Monitor and Controller
IMC .... Intercollegiate Men's Chorus, a National Association of Male Choruses (EA)
IMC .... Intercollegiate Musical Council (SAUO)
IMC .... Intercontinental Monetary Corporation (SAUO)
IMC .... Interdigestive Migrating Contractions [*Medicine*] (DMAA)
IMC .... Interdigestive Myoelectric Complex [*Gastroenterology*]
IMC .... Interface Military Civil (SAUS)
IMC .... Interface Module Cabinet (SAUS)
IMC .... Interim Message Change
IMC .... INTERMARC [*International Machine-Readable Cataloging*] [*French National Library*] [*Source file*] [*UTLAS symbol*]
IMC .... Intermediate Care Unit (NUJO)
IMC .... Intermediate Maintenance Costs (MCD)
IMC .... Intermediate Message Change (AAGC)
IMC .... Intermediate Metal Conduit
IMC .... Intermediate Moisture Content (SAUS)
IMC .... Intermetallic Compound [*Materials science*]
IMC .... Intermetallic Matrix Composite [*Materials science*]
IMC .... Intermittent Catheterization [*Medicine*] (MELL)
IMC .... Intermodal Marketing Company [*A third-party shipping broker*] (ECON)
IMC .... Intermodule Connector (SSD)
IMC .... Internal Mammary Chain [*Medicine*] (DAVI)
IMC .... Internal Management Control (DOMA)
IMC .... Internal Model Control [*Chemical engineering*] [*Computer science*]
IMC .... International Conference Management, Inc. [*Telecommunications service*] (TSSD)
IMC .... International Information Management Congress (EA)
IMC .... International Machine Contact (SAUS)
IMC .... International Machine Corporation (SAUO)
IMC .... International Magazine Collection [*JA Micropublishing, Inc.*] [*Eastchester, NY*] [*Information service or system*] (IID)
IMC .... International Mailbag Club (EA)
IMC .... International Maintenance Center (or Centre) (SAUS)
IMC .... International Maintenance Control [*Telecommunications*]
IMC .... International Management Center [*Hungary*] (ECON)
IMC .... International Management Communications, Inc. [*Database producer*]
IMC .... International Management Consultants, Ltd.
IMC .... International Management Council (EA)
IMC .... International Map Committee (SAUS)
IMC .... International Maritime Committee
IMC .... International Marketing Commission [*See also CIM*] [*Brixham, Devonshire, England*] (EAIO)
IMC .... International Match Corporation (SAUO)
IMC .... International Material Conference (SAUO)
IMC .... International Materials Conference (DCTA)
IMC .... International Meat Council (SAUO)
IMC .... International Medical Centers
IMC .... International Medical Commission for Health and Human Rights [*Switzerland*]
IMC .... International Medical Corps (EA)
IMC .... International Meeting Center [*Germany*] (EAIO)
IMC .... International Meteorological Center (or Centre) (SAUO)
IMC .... International Meteorological Committee
IMC .... International Microfilm Congress (SAUO)
IMC .... International Micrographic Congress (EA)
IMC .... International Microwave Corporation (SAUO)
IMC .... International Midshipman Course (SAUS)
IMC .... International Minerals & Chemical Corp.
IMC .... International Mining Corporation (SAUO)
IMC .... International Missionary Council [*Later, CWME*]
IMC .... International Monetary Conference (ECON)
IMC .... International Morse Code (ADDR)
IMC .... International Multifoods Corp. [*NYSE symbol*] (SPSG)
IMC .... International Multifoods Corporation (SAUO)
IMC .... International Music Conference (AEBS)
IMC .... International Music Council [*Paris, France*] (EA)
IMC .... International Musselwatch Committee (SAUS)
IMC .... Internet Mail Consortium (SAUO)
IMC .... Internet Message Center
IMC .... Interstitial Myocarditis [*Medicine*] (MELL)
IMC .... Intestinal Mast Cells [*Anatomy*]
IMC .... Intl Multifoods [*NYSE symbol*] (TTSB)
IMC .... Intramedullary Catheter [*Medicine*] (EDAA)
IMC .... Inventory Management Center (MCD)
IMC .... Inventory of Marital Conflicts [*Psychology*] (DHP)
IMC .... Iran Meat Corporation (SAUO)
IMC .... Irish Manuscripts Commission (SAUO)
IMC .... Isochronous Maintenance Channel [*Electronics*]
IMC .... Israel Materials Conference (SAUS)
IMC .... Issues Management Council (SAUO)
IMC .... Item Management Coding [*Military*] (AABC)
IMC .... Item Management Concept
IMC .... Item Master Card [*Military*] (AABC)
IMC .... Marion College, Marion, IN [*OCLC symbol*] (OCLC)
IMC .... Preparatory Committee for the International Medical Commission for Health and Human Rights (EAIO)
IMC .... Society of Professional Management Consultants (SAUO)
IMCA .... Indian Major Crimes Act [*1909*]
IMCA .... Indian Motorcycle Club of America (EA)
IMCA .... Information Management and Consulting Association [*Information service or system*] (IID)
IMCA .... Insurance Marketing Communications Association (EA)
IMCA .... Internal Model Control Approach (SAUS)
IMCA .... International Mistral Class Association (EA)
IMCA .... International Motor Contest Association (EA)
IMCA .... Investment Management Consultants Association (EA)
IMCAB .... Internal Mammary Coronary Artery Bypass [*Cardiology*]
IMCAC .... Intermountain Collegiate Athletic Conference (PSS)
IMCAM .... Integrated Marine and Coastal Area Management (SAUO)
IMCAR .... International Movement of Catholic Agricultural and Rural Youth G2 [*See also MIJARC*]
IMCARY .... International Movement of Catholic Agricultural and Rural Youth [*See also MIJARC*] [*Louvain, Belgium*] (EAIO)
IMCAS .... Interactive Man/Computer Augmentation System
IMCAST .... Instructor Model Characteristics for Automated Speech Technology (MCD)
IMCA-US .... International Moth Class Association - US (EA)
IMCB .... Institute of Molecular & Cell Biology [*Singapore*]
IMCB .... Institute of Scientific Business (SAUO)
IMCB .... International Management Centre of Birmingham (SAUO)
IMCB .... International Mine Clearance Board (SAUO)
IMCC .... Image Motion Compensation and Calibration
IMCC .... IMC Mortgage Co. [*NASDAQ symbol*] (SAG)
IMCC .... Initial Mobile Command Center (SAUO)
IMCC .... Institute of Management Consultants of Canada (SAUS)
IMCC .... Integrated Mission Control Center [*NASA*]
IMCC .... International Minerals Chemical [*Federal Railroad Administration identification code*]
IMCC .... Interstate Mining Compact Commission (EA)
IMCC .... Item Management Control Code (AABC)
IMcc .... McCook Public Library District, McCook, IL [*Library symbol*] [*Library of Congress*] (LCLS)
IMccA .... Armak Co., McCook, IL [*Library symbol*] [*Library of Congress*] (LCLS)
IMCCSRA .... International MC Class Sailboat Racing Association (EA)
IMCD .... Information Management and Compliance Division [*Department of Education*] (GFGA)
IMCD .... Inner Medullary Collecting Ducts [*Kidney anatomy*]
IMCD .... Input Marginal Checking and Distribution
IMCDO .... in My Conceited Dogmatic Opinion (SAUS)
IMCE .... Image Motion Compensation Electronics (SAUS)
IMCE .... Institute for Molecular and Cellular Evolution [*University of Miami*] [*Research center*] (RCD)
IMCE .... Inter-Ministerial Committee for Environment (SAUO)

IMCE International Meeting of Cataloging Experts
IMCEA International Military Club Executives Association (EA)
IMCEA International Military Community Executives Association (NTPA)
IMC Glob IMC Global, Inc. [*Formerly, IMC Fertilizer Group*] [*Associated Press*] (SAG)
Imchem Immunochemistry [*Publication*] [*Medicine*] (EDAA)
IMchF Follett Software Co., McHenry, IL [*Library symbol*] [*Library of Congress*] (LCLS)
IMCI Individual and Marriage Counseling Inventory [*Psychology*]
IMCI Induced Myocardial Ischemia [*Medicine*] (MELL)
IMCI Infinite Machines [*NASDAQ symbol*] (TTSB)
IMCI Infinite Machines Corp. [*NASDAQ symbol*] (SAG)
IMCI Interracial Music Council, Inc. (SAUS)
IMCI Interracial Music Council, Incorporated (SAUO)
IMC-IFR Instrument [*Flight*] Meteorological Conditions - Instrument Flight Rules [*Aviation*] (DNAB)
IMC-IFR Instrument Meteorological Conditions-Instrument Flight Rules (SAUS)
IMCIS Identify, Manage, Change, Improve, Show (BB)
IMCIW Infinite Machines Wrrt [*NASDAQ symbol*] (TTSB)
IMCJ International Movement of Catholic Jurists (EAIO)
IMCL ImClone Systems [*NASDAQ symbol*] (TTSB)
IMCL ImClone Systems, Inc. [*NASDAQ symbol*] (SPSG)
IMCL International Movement of Catholic Lawyers [*France*]
Imclne ImClone Systems, Inc. [*Associated Press*] (SAG)
IMCM In Medio Currere Metuo [*I Fear to Go in the Middle*] [*Motto of Julius, Duke of Braunschweig-Wolfenbuttel (1529-89)*] [*Latin*]
IMCM Master Chief Instrumentman [*Navy rating*]
IMC Mt IMC Mortgage Co. [*Associated Press*] (SAG)
IMCO IMCO Recycling, Inc. [*Associated Press*] (SAG)
IMCO IMPCO Technologies [*NASDAQ symbol*] [*Formerly, AirSensors, Inc.*] (SG)
IMCO Improved Combustion
IMCO In My Considered Opinion (SAUO)
IMCO Institute of Management Consultants of Ontario (SAUS)
IMCO Intercontinental Manufacturing Company (ACAE)
IMCO Intergovernmental Marine Consultative Organization (SAUO)
IMCO Inter-government Maritime Consultative Organization (SAUS)
IMCO International Maritime Consultive Organization
IMCO International Maritime Countries Organization (SAUS)
IMCO International Metered Communications
IMCO Interwest Medical Corporation (SAUO)
IMCOA Insulation Materials Corp. of America
IMCoS International Map Collectors' Society (EAIO)
IMCOS International Meteorological Consultants Service (SAUO)
IMCOV Iron Mines Company of Venezuela (SAUO)
IMCP Intake Manual Control Panel (SAUS)
IMCP Integrated Monitor and Control Panel (MCD)
IMCP Item Management Coding Program [*Military*] (AFM)
IMCPM Improved Capability Missile [*Air Force*] (IAA)
IMCR Institute for Mediation and Conflict Resolution (EA)
IMCR Internal Management Control Review (SAUS)
IMCRA Interim Marine Regionalisation of Australia (SAUO)
IMC/RMC Instructional Materials Centers/Regional Media Centers
IMCS Individual Microclimate Cooling System [*Army*] (INF)
IMCS Integrated Machining Control System (SAUS)
IMCS Integrated Management Control System (ACAE)
IMCS Integrated Monitoring and Control System (SAUS)
IMCS Intelligent Motion Control System (PDAA)
IMCS Interactive Manufacturing Control System [*NCR Ltd.*] [*Software package*] (NCC)
IMCS Interactive Multimedia Computing Systems (TELE)
IMCS International Meeting in Community Service [*Germany*] (EAIO)
IMCS International Metal Container Section (SAUS)
IMCS International Movement of Catholic Students [*France*]
IMCS Pax Romana, International Movement of Catholic Students [*See also MIEC*] [*Fribourg, Switzerland*] [*Paris, France*] (EAIO)
IMCS Senior Chief Instrumentman [*Navy rating*]
IMCSAC International Movement of Catholic Students - African Secretariat [*An association*] (EAIO)
IMcSC John Swaney Attendance Center, McNabb, IL [*Library symbol*] [*Library of Congress*] (LCLS)
IMCSMHI Industrial Metal Containers Section of the Material Handling Institute (EA)
IMCSRS Installation Materiel Condition Status Reporting System [*Army*]
IMCT Information-Memory-Concentration [*Medicine*] (EDAA)
IMCTS Intake Manifold Charge Temperature Sensor [*Automotive engineering*]
IMCU Intensity Millicurie [*Nucleonics*] (IAA)
IMCU Intermediate [*Medicine*] (EDAA)
IMCV Input Media Conversion (SAUS)
IMCWR International Movement of Conscientious War Resisters [*Tel Aviv, Israel*] (EAIO)
IMCX ImageMatrix Corp. [*NASDAQ symbol*] (SAG)
IMCZ IMC Industries [*Federal Railroad Administration identification code*]
IMD Immunologically Mediated Disease [*Medicine*]
IMD Imo Delaval, Inc. [*NYSE symbol*] (COMM)
IMD Imo Industries [*NYSE symbol*] (TTSB)
IMD Imo Industries, Inc. [*NYSE symbol*] (SPSG)
IMD Imonda [*Papua New Guinea*] [*Airport symbol*] (OAG)
IMD Implementation Management Document (SAUO)
IMD Incremental Multiple Development (PDAA)
IMD Independent Module Development (PDAA)
IMD India Meteorological Department (SAUO)
IMD Indianapolis-Marion County Public Library, Indianapolis, IN [*OCLC symbol*] (OCLC)
IMD Indian Medical Department [*British military*] (DMA)
IMD Indian Meteorological Department (SAUO)
IMD Indian Meteorology Department (SAUO)
IMD Industrial Machinery Division (SAUO)
IMD Industry Marketing Development (SAUS)
IMD Inertia-Measuring Device [*Mechanical engineering*]
IMD Information Management Division [*Environmental Protection Agency*] (GFGA)
IMD Information Marketing Development (SAUS)
IMD Information Marketing Division (SAUS)
IMD Information Media Department (SAUO)
IMD Inhibit Momentum Dump
IMD In-Mold Decoration (SAUS)
IMD Institute for Marine Dynamics [*Canada*] (PDAA)
IMD Institute for Muscle Disease [*Defunct*] (EA)
IMD Institute of Metals Division (SAUO)
IMD Institut fur Maschinelle Dokumentation (NITA)
IMD Institutions for Mental Diseases [*Department of Health and Human Services*] (GFGA)
IMD Integrated Missile Defence Patrol (SAUS)
IMD Intelligent Missile Defense (ACAE)
IMD Interactive Map Definition (IAA)
IMD Interactive Minefield Display (ACAE)
IMD Interactive Multimedia Document (SAUS)
IMD Intercept Monitoring Display
IMD Interim Management Directive (SAUO)
IMD Intermediate (NASA)
IMD Intermetal Dielectric (AAEL)
IMD Intermittent Motion Driver
IMD Intermodulation Distortion (MSA)
IMD International Institute for Management Development
IMD International Institute for Management Development, Lausanne (SAUS)
IMD International Market Development Program [*Department of Energy*]
IMD International MTM [*Methods-Time-Measurement*] Directorate (EA)
IMD Invasive Meningococcal Disease
IMD Inventory Management Division (SAUO)
IMD Ion Mobility Detector [*Instrumentation*]
IMD Isove's Modified Dulbecco's Medium [*Oncology*]
IMDA Independent Medical Distributors Association (EA)
IMDA Indian Mineral Development Act of 1982
IMDA Indirect Missile Damage Assessment (SAUS)
IMDA International Magic Dealers Association (EA)
IMDA International Mail Dealers Association (EA)
IMDA International Map Dealers Association (EA)
IMDAA Institute of Management Development Alumni Associates (COBU)
IMDACS Integrated Multivariate Data Analysis and Classification System (SAUO)
IMDB In-Memory Database (RALS)
IMDB Integrated Maintenance Database (MCD)
IMDB Internet Movie Database (SAUO)
IMDB Issues Management Database (SAUS)
IMDC Inamed Corp. [*NASDAQ symbol*] (NQ)
IMDC Instructional Media Distribution Center [*University of Wisconsin - Madison*] [*Research center*] (RCD)
IMDC Integrated Mission/Display Computer (SAUS)
IMDC Interceptor Missile Direction Center
IMDC Internal Message Distribution Center (NATG)
IMDC Intramedullary Metatarsal Decompression [*Medicine*] (DMAA)
IMDD Idiopathic Midline Destructive Disease [*Dentistry*]
IM-DD Intensity Modulation with Direct Detection (SAUS)
IMDEG Insurance Management Decision Game
IMDES Interdepartmental Meteorological Data Exchange System (SAUO)
IMDES Item Management Data Element Standardization [*or System*] [*Military*]
IM Device Intensity Measuring Device (SAUS)
IMDEX International Maritime Defence Exhibition (SAUO)
IMDFNA Inhibited Maximum Density Fuming Nitric Acid (MCD)
IMDG International Maritime Dangerous Goods
IMDGC International Maritime Dangerous Goods Code (MCD)
IMDI International Management and Development Institute
IMDL Inter-Laboratory Method Detection Limit [*Environmental Protection Agency*]
IM/DM Information Management / Data Management (HGAA)
IMDM Iscove's Modified Dulbecco's Medium [*For nematode culture*]
IMDN International Mitochondrial Disease Network (SAUO)
IMDO Installation and Materiel District Office [*FAA*]
IMDO Intelligence Material Development Office [*Military*] (MCD)
IMDP Integrated Management Development Program [*Australia*]
IMDP Integrated Missile Development Programme (SAUS)
IMDP International Management Development Program (SAUO)
IMDQ Injected Minimum Detectable Quantity [*Analytical chemistry*]
IMDR Intelligent Mark Document Reader (MHDI)
IMDR Item Management Data Reply (MCD)
IMDS Image Data Stream (SAUS)
IMDS International Meat Development Scheme [*United Nations*] [*Defunct*] (EAIO)
IMDS International Microform Distribution Service (NITA)
IMDSO Intelligence Materiel Development and Support Office [*Army*] (RDA)
imdt Immediately (BARN)
IMDT International Institute for Music, Dance, and Theatre in the Audio-Visual Media [*Later, Mediacult International Institute for Audio-Visual Communication and Cultural Development*]
IMDTC International Multiple Destination Television Connection (SAUS)
IMDTLY Immediately (WGA)

IMDur .... Inscriptiones Mithriacae Duranae (BJA)
IME .... Immobilized Enzyme
IME .... Incendiary Munitions Evaluation
IME .... Independent Medical Evaluation
IME .... Independent Medical Examination [*British*]
IME .... Independent Medical Examiner (HGAA)
IME .... Indiana & Michigan Electric Co. (SAUO)
IME .... Indiana & Michigan Power [*NYSE symbol*] (SAG)
IME .... Indirect Manufacturing Expense
IME .... Indirect Medical Education [*Department of Health and Human Services*] (GFGA)
IME .... Indo-Malaysian Engineering (SAUO)
IME .... Industrial Measuring Equipment (SAUS)
IME .... Industria Machine Electroniche [*Computer manufacturer*] [*Italy*] (NITA)
IME .... Information Management & Engineering (SAUS)
IME .... Information Management & Engineering Ltd. [*Information service or system*] (IID)
IME .... In My Experience [*Internet dialog*]
IME .... Input Method Editor (SAUS)
IME .... Institute for Municipal Engineering
IME .... Institute of International Material Evaluation (SAUS)
IME .... Institute of Makers of Explosives (EA)
IME .... Institute of Marine Engineers [*British*]
IME .... Institute of Mathematics Education [*La Trobe University*] [*Australia*]
IME .... Institute of Mechanical Engineers [*British*]
IME .... Institute of Mining Engineers [*British*]
IME .... Institute of Municipal Engineering (SAUS)
IME .... Institute on the Military and the Economy (EA)
IME .... Institution of Mechanical Engineers (SAUO)
IME .... Institution of Military Engineers (SAUO)
IME .... Institution of Mining Engineers (SAUO)
IME .... Institution of Municipal Engineers (SAUO)
IME .... Integrated Modelling Environment (SAUS)
IME .... Intercontinental Metals Export Co. (SAUO)
IME .... International Magnetospheric Explorer [*NASA/ESRO*]
IME .... International Materiel Evaluation Program [*Army*] (RDA)
IME .... International Medical Exchange [*Defunct*] (EA)
IME .... International Microcomputer Exhibition (NITA)
IME .... International Microcomputer Exposition
IME .... International Mirtone, Inc. [*Toronto Stock Exchange symbol*]
IME .... Interplanetary Meteoroid Experiment [*NASA*]
IME .... Mennonite Biblical Seminary Library, Elkhart, IN [*OCLC symbol*] (OCLC)
IMEA .... Incorporated Municipal Electrical Association (SAUO)
IMEA .... Indiana Music Educators Association (SAUO)
IMEA .... Indirect Medical Education Adjustment
IMEA .... International Middle East Association (EA)
IMEA .... Iowa Music Educators Association (SAUO)
IME(AB) .... Institution of Mechanical Engineers (Australian Branch)
IMEAC .... Interagency Motor Equipment Advisory Committee (SAUO)
IMEAC .... Northeast Interagency Motor Equipment Advisory Committee [*Terminated, 1981*] [*General Services Administration*] (EGAO)
IMEASY .... Integrated Management and Economic Analysis Model [*Federal Emergency Management Agency*] (GFGA)
IMEB .... International Movement of Esperantist Bicyclists [*See also BEMI*] [*The Hague, Netherlands*] (EAIO)
IMEC .... Imatec Ltd. [*NASDAQ symbol*] (SAG)
IMEC .... Institut Mondial d'Ecologie et de Cancerologie [*World Institute of Ecology and Cancer - WIEC*] (EAIO)
IMEC .... Interstate Migrant Education Council (EA)
IMEC .... Interuniversity Micro-Electronics Center (or Centre) (SAUO)
IMEC .... Item Mission Essentially Code (MCD)
IMECC .... Independent Metallurgical Engineering Consultants of California (SAUS)
IMechE .... Institute of Mechanical Engineers (SAUO)
I Mech E .... Institution of Mechanical Engineers [*British*]
IMECHIE .... Institution of Mechanical Incorporated Engineers [*British*] (EAIO)
IMECO .... International Measurement Confederation (SAUO)
IMECO .... International Measurement Confederation (or Congress) (SAUS)
IMED .... Informedics, Inc. [*NASDAQ symbol*] (SAG)
IME-D .... Interplanetary Monitoring Explorer-Daughter (SAUS)
IMEG .... Innovations in Medical Education Grant (DMAA)
IMEG .... International Management and Engineering Group [*British*]
IMEI .... Institute of Marine Engineers, Inc. (SAUS)
IMEI .... International Mobile Equipment Identifier (SAUO)
IMEI .... International Mobile Equipment Identifier (or Identity) (SAUS)
IMEI .... International Mobile Equipment Identity (SAUO)
IMEKO .... Internationale Messtechnische Konfoderation [*International Measurement Confederation*] [*ICSU*] [*Budapest, Hungary*] (EAIO)
IMEL .... IAEA [*International Atomic Energy Agency*] Marine Environment Laboratory [*Marine science*] (OSRA)
IMel .... Melvin Public Library, Melvin, IL [*Library symbol*] [*Library of Congress*] (LCLS)
IMelF .... Ford County Film Cooperative, Melvin, IL [*Library symbol*] [*Library of Congress*] (LCLS)
IMelp .... Melrose Park Public Library, Melrose Park, IL [*Library symbol*] [*Library of Congress*] (LCLS)
IMelpA .... Alberto-Culver Co., Melrose Park, IL [*Library symbol*] [*Library of Congress*] (LCLS)
IMelSD .... Melvin-Sibley Community Unit School District, Melvin, IL [*Library symbol*] [*Library of Congress*] (LCLS)
IMEM .... Improved Minimum Essential Medium [*Microbiology*]
IMEM .... International Mass Education Movement (EA)
IMEM-HS .... Improved Minimal Essential Medium, Hormone Supplemented (DB)
IMEMME .... Institution of Mining Electrical and Mining Mechanical Engineers (EAIO)
IMEMO .... Institute of World Economics and International Affairs [*Russian*] (BARN)
IMEMO .... Institute of World Economy and International Relations, Moscow (SAUS)
IMen .... Graves Public Library, Mendota, IL [*Library symbol*] [*Library of Congress*] (LCLS)
IMEN .... International Mother-tongue Education Network (SAUO)
IMenHS .... Mendota High School, Mendota, IL [*Library symbol*] [*Library of Congress*] (LCLS)
IMenN .... Northbrook Elementary School, Mendota, IL [*Library symbol*] [*Library of Congress*] (LCLS)
IMEO .... Initial Mass in Earth Orbit [*NASA*]
IMEO .... In My Educated Opinion [*Internet dialog*]
IMEO .... Interim Maintenance Engineering Order (AAG)
IMEP .... Indicated Mean Effective Pressure [*Aerospace*]
IMEP .... International Materiel Evaluation Program [*Army*] (RDA)
IMEP .... International Meteorological Educational Program (SAUO)
IMER .... Immobilized-Enzyme Reactor
IMER .... Institute for Marine Environmental Research [*British*] (ARC)
IMerD .... Meredosia-Chambersburg River Valley Public Library District, Meredosia, IL [*Library symbol*] [*Library of Congress*] (LCLS)
IMERSE .... Indonesian Marine Environment Remote Sensing Experiments (SAUO)
IMES .... Integrated Missile Electronics Set
IMES .... Internacia Ministа Esperanto-Societo (SAUO)
IMet .... Institute of Metals (SAUO)
IMET .... Intermetrics, Inc. (SAUO)
IMET .... International Military Education and Training [*Program of grant military training in the United States for foreign military and civilian personnel*]
IMET .... Isometric Endurance Time (STED)
I METH .... Independent Methodist (WDAA)
IMeth .... Independent Methodists (SAUO)
IMETP .... International Military Education and Training Program [*DoD*]
IMETS .... Integrated Meteorological System [*Army*] (RDA)
IMEWS .... Integrated Missile Early Warning Satellite (SAUS)
IMEWS .... Integrated Missile Early Warning System (ACAE)
IMEWS .... International Mobile Early Warning System for Volcanic Eruptions and Related Seismic Activities (SAUS)
IMEX .... Image Modelling Expert (SAUS)
IMEX .... Imex Medical Systems [*NASDAQ symbol*] (TTSB)
IMEX .... Imex Medical Systems, Inc. [*NASDAQ symbol*] (NQ)
IMEX .... Import/Export (TIMI)
IMEX .... Inner Magnetosphere Explorer [*NASA*]
IMEX .... Integrated Manufacturing Exposition [*Penton/IPC*] (TSPED)
IMEX .... International Mail Exchange (SAUO)
IMEX .... International Marine Exhibition (SAUO)
IMF .... Allen County Public Library, Fort Wayne, IN [*OCLC symbol*] (OCLC)
IMF .... Ice Mass Flux (CARB)
IMF .... Idiopathic Myelofibrosis (STED)
IMF .... Ifosfamide, Mesna Uroprotection, Methotrexate, and Fluorouracil (STED)
IMF .... Ifosfamide, Methotrexate, Fluorouracil (CDI)
IMF .... IFRA Message Format (SAUS)
IMF .... Image Furnace (SAUS)
IMF .... Image-Matched Filter (IAA)
IMF .... Immunofixation [*Analytical biochemistry*]
IMF .... Immunofluorescent [*Immunology*]
IMF .... Impact Mechanical Fuse (MCD)
IMF .... Imphal [*India*] [*Airport symbol*] (OAG)
IMF .... Impossible Mission Force [*Fictitious group of undercover agents in TV series, "Mission: Impossible"*]
IMF .... Indian Multipurpose Food (SAUS)
IMF .... Individual Master File
IMF .... Industrial Metal Finishes (SAUS)
IMF .... [*The*] Inefficient-Market Fund [*AMEX symbol*] (SPSG)
IMF .... Initial Mass Function [*Galactic science*]
IMF .... Installation Master File (MCD)
IMF .... Instanteneous Frequency Measuring (SAUS)
IMF .... Institut de Mecanique des Fluides [*Originator and database on fluid mechanics*] [*France*] (NITA)
IMF .... Institute for Metal Forming [*Lehigh University*] [*Research center*] (RCD)
IMF .... Institute for Monetary Freedom (EA)
IMF .... [*The*] Institute of Metal Finishing [*British*]
IMF .... Integrated Maintenance Facility
IMF .... Intelligent Minefield [*Army*] (MUSM)
IMF .... Intense Magnetic Field
IMF .... Interactive Mainframe Facility (HGAA)
IMF .... Interface Modal Fitering (SAUS)
IMF .... Interim Minesweeping Force [*Military*]
IMF .... Intermaxillary Fixation (MAE)
IMF .... Intermediate Filament (STED)
IMF .... Intermediate Fuel (SAUS)
IMF .... Intermediate Maintenance Facility
IMF .... Intermediate Moisture Food
IMF .... Internal Magnetic Focus
IMF .... International Marketing Federation [*Paris, France*] (EAIO)
IMF .... International Metalworkers Federation [*See also FIOM*] [*Geneva, Switzerland*] (EAIO)
IMF .... International Ministerial Federation [*Defunct*] (EA)
IMF .... International Miracle Fellowshop (SAUO)
IMF .... International Monetary Fund [*United Nations*] (EA)

IMF International Monetary Funel (SAUS)
IMF International Motorcycle Federation (SAUO)
IMF International Music Fund (SAUO)
IMF International Myeloma Foundation (SAUO)
IMF International Myomassethics Federation (EA)
IMF Interplanetary Magnetic Field
IMF Interstate Motor Freight (SAUS)
IMF Inventory Master File (NASA)
IMF Iowa Medical Foundation
IMF Israel Music Foundation (EA)
IMF Item Master File (MCD)
IMF Iuliu Maniu American Romanian Relief Foundation (EA)
i-mf- Mauritius [*MARC geographic area code*] [*Library of Congress*] (LCCP)
IMFA Immigration Marriage Fraud Amendments (SAUS)
IMFA Immigration Marriage Fraud Amendments Act of 1986
IMF/APWA Institute of Municipal Engineering/ American Public Works Association (SAUS)
IMF/APWA Institute of Municipal Engineering/American Public Works Association (SAUO)
IMFC Immaculate Mary Fan Club (EA)
IMFC Investment and Merchant Finance Corp. (SAUS)
IMFC Investment and Merchant Finance Corporation (SAUO)
IMFC Iron Maiden Fan Club [*British*] (EAIO)
IMFET Internally Matched FETs [*Field Effect Transistor*] [*Avantek*] (NITA)
IMfgE Institution of Manufacturing Engineers (SAUO)
IMFHS Isle of Man Family History Society [*British*] (EAIO)
IMFI Industrial Mineral Fiber Institute (SAUO)
IMFI International Mineral Fiber Institute (SAUS)
IMF/IBRD International Monetary Fund and International Bank for Reconstruction and Development
IMFJC International Metalworkers Federation Japan Council (SAUO)
IMFK Integrated Multifunction Keyboard (MCD)
IMFL Inventory of Marriage and Family Literature [*Sage Publications, Inc.*] (IID)
IM/FM Intensity Modulated / Frequency Modulated (WDAA)
IMFP Inelastic Mean Free [*or Face*] Path [*Surface analysis*]
IMFP Interaction Mean Free Path [*Astrophysics*]
IMFR Institute of Marriage and Family Relations (EA)
IMFRAD Integrated Multifrequency RADAR (MCD)
IMFRAD Integrated Multiple Frequency Radar (SAUS)
IMF/SDR International Monetary Fund-Special Drawing Rights (SAUS)
IMF/SP Staff Papers. International Monetary Fund. Washington (SAUS)
IMFSS Integrated Missile Flight Safety System
IMFT Insensitive Munition Fuze Technology (SAUS)
IMFT Inter-Multics File Transfer Facility [*Computer science*] (HODG)
IMF Tube Internal Magnetic Focus Tube (SAUS)
IMFU Imperial Military Foul-Up [*Bowdlerized version*] (DSUE)
IMFURP International Movement for Fraternal Union among Races and Peoples (SAUO)
IMFWUNA International Molders' and Foundry Workers' Union of North America [*Later, IM &AWU*]
IMG GEM Paint image format (SAUS)
IMG Image
IMG Immigration
ImG Immunogenetics
IMG Imperial Cargo Airlines Ltd. [*Ghana*] [*ICAO designator*] (FAAC)
IMG Implementation Guide (SAUS)
IMG Improved Measurement Group (SAUO)
IMG Individual Mobility Grants (EURO)
IMG Inertial Measurement Group (KSC)
IMG Inferior Mesenteric Ganglia [*Anatomy*]
IMG Inferior Mesenteric Ganglion [*Medicine*] (STED)
IMG Informational Media Guarantee (SAUS)
IMG Informational Media Guaranty
IMG Information Management Group (SAUO)
IMG Installation and Maintenance Guide
IMG Integrated Matching Gate (SAUS)
IMG Interactive Media Group
IMG Interference-free Monolithic Gate (SAUS)
IMG Interferometric Monitor of Greenhouse Gases (EOSA)
IMG Interim Management Guidelines (SAUO)
IMG Intermagnetics General Corp. [*AMEX symbol*] (SPSG)
IMG Internal Medicine Group [*Group practice*] (DAVI)
IMG International Mail Gram (MHDB)
IMG International Mailgram (SAUS)
IMG International Maintenance Group [*FAA*] (TAG)
IMG International Management Group
IMG International Marxist Group [*British*] (PPW)
IMG International Medical Graduate
IMG International Modular Group (SAUO)
IMG International Music Guide [*A publication*]
IMG Intertheater Movement Generator (SAUO)
IMG Islamic Missionaries Guild of the Caribbean and South America (SAUO)
IMG Mead Johnson & Co., Research Library, Evansville, IN [*OCLC symbol*] (OCLC)
IMg Morton Grove Public Library, Morton Grove, IL [*Library symbol*] [*Library of Congress*] (LCLS)
IMGCN Integrated Missile Ground Control Network
IMGCSA Islamic Missionaries Guild of the Caribbean and South America (EAIO)
ImgeGud Image Guided Technologies, Inc. [*Associated Press*] (SAG)
ImgeM ImageMatrix Corp. [*Associated Press*] (SAG)
ImgeMat ImageMatrix Corp. [*Associated Press*] (SAG)
IMGF International Minigolf Federation (SAUO)
IMGG Institute of Marine Geology and Geophysics [*Russian Federation*] [*Marine science*] (OSRA)
IMGG Intramuscular Gammaglobulin [*Medicine*] (DMAA)
IMGI Improved Maintenance Guidance Information
ImgMgt Imaging Management Associates [*Associated Press*] (SAG)
IMGN Immuncogen, Inc. [*NASDAQ symbol*] (SAG)
IMGN ImmunoGen, Inc. [*NASDAQ symbol*] (NQ)
IMGNG Imaging
IMGNTN Imagination
IMgO Oakton Community College, Morton Grove, IL [*Library symbol*] [*Library of Congress*] (LCLS)
IMgO-Dp Oakton Community Colleges, Learning Resources Center, Des Plaines, IL [*Library symbol*] [*Library of Congress*] (LCLS)
IMGP Internal Medicine Group Practice (SAUO)
IMGRASS Inner Mongolia Grasland-Atmosphere Surface Study (SAUO)
IMGRASS Inner Mongolia Semi-Arid Grassland Soil-Vegetation Atmosphere Interaction (SAUO)
IMGRID Information Manipulation System for Grid Cell Data Structures (SAUO)
IMGS International Mammalian Genome Society (HGEN)
IMGS Irrigation Management Grants Scheme (SAUO)
IMGT Immunogenetics database (SAUO)
IMGT Interim Missile Guidance Test (MCD)
IMgT Travenol Laboratories, Morton Grove, IL [*Library symbol*] [*Library of Congress*] (LCLS)
IMGTE Institution of Mechanical and General Technician Engineers (SAUO)
IMGTechE Institution of Mechanical and General Technician Engineers [*British*]
IMGX Network Imaging Corp. [*NASDAQ symbol*] (SAG)
IMGXP Network Imaging $2.00 Cv Pfd [*NASDAQ symbol*] (TTSB)
IMGXW Network Imaging Wrrt [*NASDAQ symbol*] (TTSB)
IMH Idiopathic Myocardial Hypertrophy [*Cardiology*]
IMH IMPAC Mortgage Holdings [*AMEX symbol*] [*Formerly, Imperial Credit Mortgage Holdings*] (SG)
IMH Imperial Credit Mortagage Holdings, Inc. [*AMEX symbol*] (SAG)
IMH Imperial Credit Mtge Hldgs [*AMEX symbol*] (TTSB)
IMH Indiana Magazine of History (journ.) (SAUS)
IMH Indirect Microhemagglutination Test [*Medicine*] (DMAA)
IMH Individual Machine History (SAUS)
IMH Inlet Manhole [*Technical drawings*]
IMH Inspectorate of the Ministry of Health (SAUO)
IMH Institut des Moeurs Humaines [*Institute of Human Values - IHV*] [*Canada*]
IMH Institute of Materials Handling [*British*] (BI)
IMH Interactive Message Handling (SAUO)
IMH International Majestic Holdings Ltd. [*Formerly, Majestic Resources Corp.*] [*Vancouver Stock Exchange symbol*]
IMH International Marketing Handbook [*A publication*]
IMH International Military Headquarters (SAUO)
IMH Mennonite Historical Library, Goshen College, Goshen, IN [*OCLC symbol*] (OCLC)
IMHA Interamerican Medical and Health Association (EA)
IMHE Industrial Materials Handling Equipment
IMHE Institutional Management in Higher Education (AIE)
IMHE International Management in Higher Education (SAUS)
IMHEP Ideal Man Helicopter Engineering Project
IMHEPFC Idol of My Heart Elvis Presley Fan Club (EA)
IMHI Infomed Holdings, Inc. [*NASDAQ symbol*] (SAG)
IMHI Institute for Mental Health Initiatives (EA)
IMHO In My Honest Opinion
IMHO In My Humble Opinion [*Internet language*] [*Computer science*]
IMHO Inventory of Mental Health Organizations [*Department of Health and Human Services*] (GFGA)
IMHOF International Motor Sports Hall of Fame [*Automotive racing history*]
IMHO/GHMHS Inventory of Mental Health Organizations and General Hospital Mental Health Services [*Department of Health and Human Services*] (GFGA)
IMHP Iodomercuri-Hydroxypropane [*Chemistry*] (DAVI)
IMHP Isopropyl Methyl Pyrimidinone [*Organic chemistry*]
IMHQ International Military Headquarters (CINC)
IMHR International Miniature Horse Registry (EA)
IMHRN International Mental Health Research [*Medicine*] (EDAA)
IMHSSACE Inventory of Mental Health Services in State Adult Correctional Facilites [*Department of Health and Human Services*] (GFGA)
IMHT Institute for Material Handling Teachers (SAUO)
IMHT Institute of Materials Handling Teachers (SAUS)
IMHU Incoming Message Holding Unit (SAUS)
IMHV Intermediate and Medial Part of the Hyperstriatum Ventrale [*Bird brain anatomy*]
IMHZ Intermodal Hub [*Federal Railroad Administration identification code*]
IMI ICAN Minerals Ltd. [*Toronto Stock Exchange symbol*]
IMI Ignition Manufacturers Institute [*Later, TMI*] (EA)
IMI I Mean It (SAUS)
ImI IMI of Philadelphia, Camp Hill, PA [*Library symbol*] [*Library of Congress*] (LCLS)
IMI Imipramine [*Antidepressant*]
IMI Immunologically Measurable Insulin [*Medicine*] (AAMN)
IMI Impact Message Inventory (EDAC)
IMI Impenal Metal Industries (SAUS)
IMI Impending Myocardial Infarction [*Medicine*] (MELL)
IMI Imperative Macro-Instruction (SAUS)
IMI Imperial Metal Industries (SAUS)
IMI Imperial Metal Industries, Limited (SAUO)
IMI Imperial Metal Industries Ltd. [*British*]
IMI Imperial Mycological Institute (SAUO)

IMI .... Implantable Micro-Identification Device [*for laboratory animals*]
IMI .... Improved Manned Interceptor [*Proposed plane*] [*Air Force*]
IMI .... Improved Massed Intercept (MCD)
IMI .... Improved Mass Intercept (SAUS)
IMI .... Incentives Management Index [*Test*]
IMI .... Individualized Mathematics Instruction (SAUS)
IMI .... Individual Marketing Initiative (ACAE)
IMI .... Ine [*Marshall Islands*] [*Airport symbol*] (OAG)
IMI .... Inferior Myocardial Infarction [*Cardiology*]
IMI .... Information Management, Inc. (SAUS)
IMI .... Information Management, Incorporated (SAUO)
IMI .... Information Marketing International [*Information service or system*] (IID)
IMI .... Infrared Measurement Instrument
IMI .... Innovative Management, Inc. (SAUS)
IMI .... Innovative Manufacturing Initiative (SAUS)
IMI .... Installation and Maintenance Instruction
IMI .... Installation Modification Instruction (SAUS)
IMI .... Institute for Marine Information [*Defunct*] (EA)
IMI .... Institute of the Motor Industry, Inc. [*British*] (BI)
IMI .... Institute on Money and Inflation (EA)
IMI .... Institut Metapsychique International [*International Metaphysics Institute*] [*France*] (EAIO)
IMI .... Instructor-Managed Instruction (SAUS)
IMI .... Instrumentman (Instrument Repair) [*U.S. Navy enlisted rating*] (AUER)
IMI .... Integrally Molded Insulation
IMI .... Intensive Management Items (MCD)
IMI .... Interactive Menu Interface (SAUS)
IMI .... Interactive Multimedia Instruction [*Training term*] (LPT)
IMI .... Interim Manned Interceptor (PDAA)
IMI .... Intermark, Inc. [*AMEX symbol*] (COMM)
IMI .... Intermediate Machine Instruction
IMI .... Intermediate Maintenance Instruction (SAUS)
IMI .... Intermediate Manned Interceptor (MUGU)
IMI .... International Maintenance Institute (EA)
IMI .... International Management Institute [*Switzerland*]
IMI .... International Manganese Institute [*France*] (EAIO)
IMI .... International Maple Institute
IMI .... International Marina Institute (NTPA)
IMI .... International Maritimes Industries Forum (SAUS)
IMI .... International Market Index (NUMA)
IMI .... International Marketing Information (JAGO)
IMI .... International Marketing Institute (EA)
IMI .... International Market Intelligence [*Databank originator*] [*Norway*] (NITA)
IMI .... International Masonry Institute (EA)
IMI .... International Medical Implant (SAUO)
IMI .... International Medical Informatics Association (SAUO)
IMI .... International Memories, Inc. (SAUS)
IMI .... International Metaphysical Institute (SAUO)
IMI .... International Meteorological Institute [*Marine science*] (OSRA)
IMI .... International Ministries to Israel (EA)
IMI .... International Missions (EA)
IMI .... International Mycological Institute (SAUO)
IMI .... Internet MSS Interface (SAUS)
IMI .... Intramuscular Injection [*Medicine*] (MAE)
IMI .... Intraoperative Myocardial Ischemia [*Cardiology*]
IMI .... Invention Marketing, Inc. [*Information service or system*] (IID)
IMI .... Invention Marketing, Incorporated (SAUO)
IMI .... Invention Marketing Institute (EA)
IMI .... Investment Management Institute [*Information service or system*] (IID)
IMI .... Ion Microwelding Instrument
IMI .... Irish Management Institute (EAIO)
IMI .... Isolated Meconium Ileus [*Medicine*] (MELL)
IMI .... Israeli Military Intelligence (SAUO)
IMI .... Israel Military Industries (SAUS)
IMI .... Israel Military Industries Ltd. (SAUO)
IMI .... Israel Music Institute (SAUO)
IMI .... Istituto Bancario Ital ADS [*NYSE symbol*] (SG)
IMI .... Istituto Mobiliare Italiano [*NYSE symbol*] (SAG)
IMI .... Istituto Mobiliare Ital ADS [*NYSE symbol*] (TTSB)
IMI .... Istituto Mobiliare Italiana [*Italian state-owned bank*] (ECON)
IMI .... Marian College, Indianapolis, IN [*OCLC symbol*] (OCLC)
IMIA .... Institute of Mathematics and Its Applications [*South-End-On-Sea, England*]
IMIA .... International Machinery Insurers Association [*Munich, Federal Republic of Germany*] (EAIO)
IMIA .... International Medical Informatics Association [*IFIP special interest group*] [*Richmond Hill, ON*] (EAIO)
IMIA .... International Metal Industries, Ltd. (SAUO)
IMIA-LAC ..... Regional Federation of Health Informatics Societies in Latin America and the Caribbean (SAUO)
IMIAT .... International Masonry Institute Apprenticeship and Training (EA)
IMIB .... Inland Marine Insurance Bureau [*Later, ISO*] (EA)
IMIC .... Independent Medical Insurance Consultants Ltd. [*British*]
IMIC .... Industir-Matematik International Corp. [*NASDAQ symbol*] (SAG)
IMIC .... Industrial Minerals International Congress (SAUS)
IMIC .... Infrastructure Modernization Implementing Council (SAUO)
IMIC .... Inhibitor of Mevalonate Incorporation to Cholesterol [*Food science*]
IMIC .... Integrated Management Information Computer (SAUS)
IMIC .... Internal Modulation Information Coding (SAUS)
IMIC .... International Medical Information Center (SAUS)
IMIC .... International Medical Information Center, Inc. [*Tokyo, Japan*]
IMIC .... International Music Industry Conference
IMIC .... Interval Modulation Information Coding (PDAA)
IMICS .... Integrated Mine-hunting Combat System (SAUS)
IMID .... Inadvertent Missile Ignition Detection
IMID .... Indiana Midland Railway [*Federal Railroad Administration identification code*]
IMID .... Infrared Miniaturized Intrusion Detector (PDAA)
IMid .... Midlothian Public Library, Midlothian, IL [*Library symbol*] [*Library of Congress*] (LCLS)
IMIDCA .... Interim Motorized Infantry Division Capability Analysis [*Military*]
IMIE .... Institution of Mining Engineers [*British*]
IMIF .... International Maritime Industries Forum [*British*] (EAIO)
IMIG .... Intramuscular Immunoglobulin [*Immunology*] (DAVI)
IMIg .... Itramuscular Immunoglobulin [*Medicine*] (EDAA)
IMII .... Intelligent Medical Imaging, Inc. [*NASDAQ symbol*] (SAG)
IMII .... Intelligent Med'l Imaging [*NASDAQ symbol*] (TTSB)
IMil .... Milford Township Public Library, Milford, IL [*Library symbol*] [*Library of Congress*] (LCLS)
IMilsSD .... Millstadt Community Consolidated School District 160, Millstadt, IL [*Library symbol*] [*Library of Congress*] (LCLS)
IMiM .... Inner Mitochondrial Membrane [*Cytology*]
IMIMG .... ISDN Memorandum of Understanding Implementation Management Group (SAUO)
IMIMI .... Industrial Mineral Insulation Manufacturers Institute [*Later, TIMA*]
IMINCO .... Iran Marine International Oil Co. (SAUS)
IMINCO .... Iran Marine International Oil Company (SAUO)
IMinE .... Institution of Mining Engineers [*British*]
IMINICO .... Iranian Marine International Oil Co.
IMINOCO .... Iranian Marine International Oil Co. (SAUS)
IMINT .... Imagery Intelligence
IMINT .... Imaginary Intelligence (COE)
IMINT .... Imaging Intelligence [*RADAR, photos, etc.*]
IMIP .... Industrial Management Improvement Program (NG)
IMIP .... Industrial Modernization Improvement Plan [*DoD*] (RDA)
IMIP .... Industrial Modernization Incentive Program [*DoD*]
IMIP .... International Microforms in Print (SAUS)
IM/IPF .... Information Management / Information Processing Family (HGAA)
IMIR .... Interceptor Missile Interrogation RADAR
IM/IRA .... Interim Measure/Interim Remedial Action (SAUS)
IMIRS .... Improved Modular Infra-Red Sensor (SAUS)
IMIS .... IERL-RTP Management Information System (SAUO)
IMIS .... Installation Management Information System [*Army*]
IMIS .... Institute of Medical Illustrators in Scotland (SAUO)
IMIS .... Instructional Materials Information System [*Database*]
IMIS .... Integrated Maintenance Information System (ACAE)
IMIS .... Integrated Management Information System [*Air Force*]
IMIS .... Integrated Manufacturing Information System
IMIS .... Integrated Motorists' Information System [*Computerized guidance system to speed traffic and avoid tie-ups*]
IMIS .... Integrated Municipal Information System (IAA)
IMIS .... Intelligence Management Information System [*Military*] (MCD)
IMIS .... Interim Maneuver Identification System (IAA)
IMIS .... International Management Information System
IMISO .... Intersectoral Meeting of International Students Organizations (SAUO)
imit .... imitanon (SAUS)
imit .... imitarive (SAUS)
IMIT .... Imitate [*or Imitative*] (WDAA)
IMIT .... Imitation (MSA)
imit .... Imitative (BEE)
Imit .... Imitator (SAUS)
IMIT .... IMT, Inc. [*NASDAQ symbol*] (COMM)
IMIT .... Institute of Musical Instrument Technicians (SAUO)
IMIT .... Institute of Musical Instrument Technology [*British*] (BI)
IM-IT .... Insured Municipals-Income Trust [*Investment term*]
IMITAC .... Image Input to Automatic Computers
Imit Lea .... Imitation Leather (SAUS)
IMITS .... Interim Mobile Independent Target System [*Military*] (INF)
IMIU .... International Marine Insurance Union (MARI)
IMIX .... Imaging Workstation in X-Ray Microanalysis
IMJ .... Indiana & Michigan Power [*NYSE symbol*] (SAG)
IMJ .... Indiana Mich Pwr 8%JrSubDebs [*NYSE symbol*] (TTSB)
IMJ .... Infrared Miniaturized Jammer
IMJ .... International Medical Journal (SAUO)
IMJ .... Israel Museum News (journ.) (SAUS)
IMJ .... RCA [*Radio Corp. of America*] Consumer Electronics Library, Indianapolis, IN [*OCLC symbol*] (OCLC)
IMJHCA .... International Messianic Jewish Hebrew Christian Alliance [*British*] (EAIO)
IMK .... Identification Mark (IAA)
IMK .... Income Monitoring Kit
IMK .... Increased Maneuverability Kit
IMK .... Injection Molding Kit
IMK .... Instrument Marking Kit
IMK .... International Makaoo [*Vancouver Stock Exchange symbol*]
IMK .... Simikot [*Nepal*] [*Airport symbol*] (OAG)
IMK .... Union Carbide Corp., Library, Indianapolis, IN [*OCLC symbol*] (OCLC)
IMKA .... Initiative for Managing Knowledge Assets (TIMI)
IMKE .... Inmark Enterprises, Inc. [*NASDAQ symbol*] (SAG)
IMKR .... Inner Marker [*Part of an instrument landing system*] [*Aviation*]
IMKT .... Ingles Markets, Inc. [*NASDAQ symbol*] (NQ)
IMKTA .... Ingles Markets'A' [*NASDAQ symbol*] (TTSB)
IML .... Impedance-Modified Lamp (SAUS)
IML .... Imperial, NE [*Location identifier*] [*FAA*] (FAAL)
IML .... Incoming Matching Loss [*Telecommunications*] (TEL)

IML.......... Indusmin Ltd. [*Toronto Stock Exchange symbol*]
IML.......... Information Manipulation Language
IML.......... Initial Machine Load [*Computer science*] (IBMDP)
IML.......... Initial Measurement List (KSC)
IML.......... Initial Memory Load (SAUS)
IML.......... Initial Microcode Load (SAUS)
IML.......... Initial Microprogram Load [*Also, IMPL*] [*Computer science*] (IBMDP)
IML.......... In My Life [*Internet dialog*]
IML.......... Inside Mold Layer (SAUS)
IML.......... Inside Mold Line [*Technical drawings*]
IML.......... Institute for Medical Literature (SAUO)
IML.......... Institute of Modern Languages
IML.......... Instructional Media Laboratory
IML.......... Interactive Maintenance Language [*Denelcor*] (NITA)
IML.......... Interdivisional Manufacturing List (SAUS)
IML.......... Intermediary Musical Language (PDAA)
IML.......... Intermediary Music Language (NITA)
IML.......... Intermediate Language [*Computer science*] (TEL)
IML.......... Intermediate Machine Language (SAUS)
IML.......... Intermediate Maintenance Level
IML.......... Internal Medullary Lamina [*Neuroanatomy*]
IML.......... International Machine Language (SAUS)
IML.......... International Media Law (SAFN)
IML.......... International Medical Libraries Ring (SAUO)
IML.......... International Microgravity Laboratory
IML.......... International Music League (SAUO)
IML.......... Introspective Multistrategy Learning (SAUS)
ImL.......... Irish Microforms Ltd., Dublin, Ireland [*Library symbol*] [*Library of Congress*] (LCLS)
IML.......... Irradiated Materials Laboratory
IML.......... Island Air Ltd. [*Fiji*] [*ICAO designator*] (FAAC)
IML.......... Island Merchants Limited (SAUO)
IML.......... Island Merchants Ltd. (SAUS)
IML.......... Merrill Lynch & Co. [*NYSE symbol*] (SAG)
IML.......... Miles Laboratories, Inc., Library Resources and Services, Elkhart, IN [*OCLC symbol*] (OCLC)
IML-1.......... First International Microgravity Laboratory (SAUS)
IMLA.......... International Maritime Law Association (SAUO)
IMLA.......... International Maritime Lecturers Association (SAUO)
IMLA.......... Intramural Left Anterior Artery [*Medicine*] (DMAA)
IMLC.......... Indexed Monthly License Charge (GART)
IMLC.......... Infantry Mortar Leader's Course [*Army*] (INF)
IMLI.......... International Maritime Law Institute (SAUO)
IMLN.......... Internal Mammary Lymph Node [*Medicine*] (MELL)
IMLS.......... Institute of Medical Laboratory Sciences [*British*]
IMLS.......... Institute of Museum and Library Science
IMLS.......... Institute of Museum and Library Services
I-MLS.......... Interim Microwave Landing System (SAUS)
IMLSG.......... Interim Mobile Logistic Support Group [*Military*] (CAAL)
IMLSS.......... Integrated Maneuvering and Life Support System [*NASA*]
IMLT.......... Institute of Medical Laboratory Technology [*British*] (DI)
IMLT.......... Integrated Mechanized Loop Testing [*Communications term*] (DCT)
IMLUT.......... Inspection-Maintenance Look-Up Table [*Automotive emissions*]
ImLy.......... Immune Lysis [*Medicine*] (DMAA)
IMM.......... Immaculata College, Immaculata, PA [*OCLC symbol*] (OCLC)
IMM.......... Immediate
IMM.......... Immersion (ECII)
Imm.......... Immission (SAUS)
IMM.......... Immobilize (SAUS)
IMM.......... Immokalee, FL [*Location identifier*] [*FAA*] (FAAL)
imm.......... Immovable (SAUS)
IMM.......... Immune [*or Immunization*] (AFM)
IMM.......... Immunization Area (SAUO)
IMM.......... Immunize (SAUS)
IMM.......... Impairing a Minors Morals (SAUS)
IMM.......... Impairing the Morals of a Minor [*Police terminology*] (IIA)
IMM.......... Independent Manned Manipulator [*NASA*] (KSC)
IMM.......... Inhibitor-Containing Minimal Medium [*Microbiology*]
IMM.......... Inner Mitochondrial Membrane [*Cytology*]
IMM.......... Input Message Manual (SAUS)
IMM.......... Institute for Manpower Management (EA)
IMM.......... Institute for Molecular Manufacturing
IMM.......... Institute of Clinical Molecular Biology [*British*] (DBA)
IMM.......... Institute of Male Masseurs [*British*] (DBA)
IMM.......... Institute of Marketing and Management (SAUO)
IMM.......... Institute of Marketing Management (SAUO)
IMM.......... Institute of Materials Handling (SAUO)
IMM.......... Institute of Materials Management [*British*] (DBA)
IMM.......... Institute of Mathematics Machines (SAUS)
IMM.......... Institute of Molecular Medicine (SAUO)
IMM.......... Institute of Molecular Medicine for the Prevention of Human Diseases (SAUS)
IMM.......... Institution of Mining and Metallurgy [*London, England*]
IMM.......... Integrated Magnetic Memory (IAA)
IMM.......... Integrated Maintenance Management
IMM.......... Integrated Maintenance Manual
IMM.......... Integrated Material Manager (SAUO)
IMM.......... Integrated Materiel Management [*or Manager*]
IMM.......... Intelligent Memory Manager [*Computer science*]
IMM.......... Intel Mobile Module [*Computer science*]
IMM.......... Interactive Multimedia
IMM.......... Intergovernmental Meeting on Monitoring (SAUS)
IMM.......... Intermediate Maintenance Manual [*Military*] (CAAL)
IMM.......... Intermediate Mode (SAUS)
IMM.......... Intermittent Mixing Model (SAUS)
IMM.......... Internal Medial Malleolus [*Medicine*] (DMAA)
IMM.......... International Maggie Mines Ltd. [*Vancouver Stock Exchange symbol*]
IMM.......... International Mail Manual
IMM.......... International Maritime Mobile [*Telecommunications*]
IMM.......... International Media Ministries (SAUO)
IMM.......... International Mercantile Marine (SAUO)
IMM.......... International Merchant Marine (SAUO)
IMM.......... International Monetary Market [*Chicago Mercantile Exchange*]
IMM.......... International Money Management [*Business term*]
IMM.......... International-Money-Management-System (SAUO)
IMM.......... International Money Market (SAUO)
IMM.......... Intersection Midblock Model [*Environmental Protection Agency*] (GFGA)
IMM.......... Inventory Management Module (TIMI)
IMM.......... Isotope Measurement Laboratory (SAUO)
IMMA.......... Institute of Muslim Minority Affairs (EAIO)
IMMA.......... International Marine Mammal Association Inc. (SAUO)
IMMA.......... International Model Managers Association (EA)
IMMA.......... Ion Microprobe Mass Analyzer
IMM Abstracts... Institution of Mining and Metallurgy Abstracts (journ.) (SAUS)
IMMAC.......... Immaculate
IMMAC.......... Inventory Management and Material Control (IAA)
IMMAC System... Inventory Management and Material Control System (SAUS)
IMMACT.......... Immigration Act (SAUS)
IMMAGE.......... Information on Mining, Metallurgy and Geological Exploration (SAUS)
IMMAPI.......... International Meeting of Medical Advisers in the Pharmaceutical Industry (SAUO)
Imm AR.......... Immigration Appeal Reports [*A publication*] (DLA)
Immarsat.......... International Maritime Satellite Organization (WA)
IMMAT.......... Immaterial (AABC)
IMMAT.......... Immature
Immat.......... Immaturity (SAUS)
IMMBC.......... International Mass Media Research Center (SAUS)
IMMC.......... Integrated Materiel Management Center [*Army*]
IMMC.......... Intelligence Materiel Management Center (SAUO)
IMMC.......... Interdigestive Migrating Motor Complex [*Medicine*] (DMAA)
IMMC.......... International Mobile Machines Corporation (SAUO)
IMMCL.......... Integrated Master Measurement and Command List (SPST)
IMMCLT.......... Immaculate
IMMCo.......... International Mercantile Marine Company (SAUO)
IMMD.......... Intensity-Maximizing Multidither (PDAA)
IMMDELREO... Immediate Delivery Required (SAUS)
IMMDELREQ... Immediate Delivery Required (DNAB)
IMMDT.......... Immediate
IMME.......... Institute of Mining and Metallurgical Engineers (SAUS)
IMME.......... Institute of Municipal Maintenance Engineers [*British*] (BI)
IMME.......... Isobaric Multiplet Mass Equation
IMMED.......... Immediate (AFM)
Immens.......... Immensurabel (SAUS)
IMMER.......... Institute for Marine Environmental Research (SAUS)
IMMEX.......... Interactive Multi-Media Exercises [*A Windows-based program*]
IMMGRTN.......... Immigration
IMMH.......... Indirect Maintenance Man-Hour
IMMI.......... Index of Medieval Medical Images in North America (SAUO)
IMMI.......... Inphynet Medical Management [*NASDAQ symbol*] (SAG)
IMMI.......... International Irrigation Management Institute (GNE)
IMMI.......... International Mass Media Institute (EA)
IMMIG.......... Immigration
Immig & Naturalization Serv Mo Rev... United States Immigration and Naturalization Service, Monthly Review [*A publication*] (DLA)
Immig B Bull... Immigration Bar Bulletin [*A publication*] (DLA)
Immig Newsl... Immigration Newsletter [*A publication*] (DLA)
IMMIRS.......... Integrated Maintenance Management Information Retrieval System [*DoD*]
IMMITTANCE... Impedance and Admittance (IAA)
IMMLC.......... Improved Medium Mobility Load Carrier (SAUS)
IMMLC.......... Improved Medium Mobility Load Class (SAUS)
IMMLEP.......... Immunization Against Leprosy Program [*World Health Organization*]
IMMLS.......... Interim Military Microwave Landing System (RDA)
IMMM.......... Institute of Nuclear Materials Management (SAUS)
IMMM.......... Internal Monthly Management Meeting (ACAE)
IMMM.......... International Microcomputer Minicomputers Microprocessors (SAUS)
IMMO.......... Installation Maintenance Management Officer (SAUO)
IMMO.......... Intermediate Main Meteorological Office (SAUO)
IMMOA.......... International Mercantile Marine Officers Associations (SAUS)
Immob.......... Immobilization (SAUS)
IMMOB.......... Immobilize [*Medicine*]
IMMOBIL.......... Immobilize (BABM)
IMMP.......... Information Management Master Plan [*DoD*]
IMMP.......... Information Mission Management Plan
IMMP.......... Integrated Maintenance and Modernization Planning (SAUS)
IMMP.......... Integrated Maintenance Management Plan
IMMPC.......... International Maritime Meteorological Punch Card (SAUS)
IMMR.......... Initial Manpower and Materiel Requirements (SAUO)
IMMR.......... Installation, Modification, Maintenance, and Repair (AAG)
IMMR.......... Institute for Mining and Mineral Research [*University of Kentucky*] [*Research center*] (RCD)
IMMRAN.......... International Meeting of Marine Radio Aids to Navigation (SAUO)
IMMRC.......... International Mass Media Research Center (SAUO)
IMMRL.......... Individual Maintenance Material Readiness List (MCD)
IMMRN.......... International Multimedia Research Network (SAUO)
IMMRRI.......... Idaho Mining and Minerals Resources Research Institute [*University of Idaho*] [*Research center*] (RCD)
IMMS.......... Indore Mill Mazdoor Sangh [*Indore Textile Labour Association*] [*India*]

IMMS.......... Installation Maintenance Management System (MCD)
IMMS.......... Integrated Maintenance Management System [*Army*]
IMMS.......... Interactive Multimedia System (MCD)
IMMS.......... Interim Manpower Maintenance System
IMMS.......... Intermediate Maintenance Management System (SAUS)
IMMS.......... International Marine Minerals Society (SAUO)
IMMS.......... International Material Management Society (EA)
IMMS.......... Ion Microprobe Mass Spectrometer (SAUS)
IMMS-RD..... Interim Maintenance Activity Management System (SAUO)
IMMT.......... Integrated Maintenance Management Team
IMMT.......... International Maritime Meteorological Tape (SAUS)
IMMTS......... Indian Mercantile Marine Training Ship [*British*]
ImmU.......... Immunizing Unit [*Medicine*] (MEDA)
IMMU.......... Immunomedics, Inc. [*NASDAQ symbol*] (NQ)
IMMU.......... Independent Munitions Maintenance Unit
IMMU.......... InPhyNet Medical Mgmt [*NASDAQ symbol*] (TTSB)
IMMU.......... Instruction Memory Management Unit [*Computer science*] (VLIE)
ImmuCell..... ImmuCell Corp. [*Associated Press*] (SAG)
IMMUN........ Immunity
IMMUN........ Immunization (WDAA)
IMMUN........ Immunological (SAUS)
IMMUN........ Immunology (ADA)
Immun.......... Immunology (journ.) (SAUS)
Immun Bull... Immunity Bulletin (journ.) (SAUS)
IMMUNHMTLGY... Immunohematology
IMMUNO...... Immunoglobulin [*Immunology*] (DAVI)
Immunobiol Suppl... Immunobiology. Supplement (journ.) (SAUS)
Immunodefic Rev... Immunodeficiency Reviews (journ.) (SAUS)
immunol...... Immunology (SHCU)
IMMUNOL.... Immunology
Immunol Cell Biol... Immunology and Cell Biology (journ.) (SAUS)
Immunol Infect Diseases... Immunology and Infectious Diseases (journ.) (SAUS)
Immunol Lett... Immunology Letters (journ.) (SAUS)
Immunol Rev... Immunological Reviews (journ.) (SAUS)
Immunol Ser... Immunology Series (journ.) (SAUS)
Immunol Serol Transplant... Immunology, Serology and Transplantation (journ.) (SAUS)
Immunol Suppl... Immunology. Supplement (journ.) (SAUS)
Immunomicrobiol... Immunomicrobiology (SAUS)
Immunopathol... Immunopathology (SAUS)
Immunopharmacol Immunotoxicol... Immunopharmacology and Immunotoxicology (journ.) (SAUS)
Immut.......... Quod Deus Sit Immutabilis [*Philo*] (BJA)
IMMV.......... Individual Mileage May Vary
IMMV.......... Iris Mild Mosaic Virus
IMMY.......... Immediately
IMMY.......... Information Marketing Achievement Award [*Information Industry Association*]
IMN............. Imation Corp. [*NYSE symbol*] (SG)
IMN............. Indicated Mach Number (AFM)
IMN............. Infectious Mononucleosis [*Medicine*] (MELL)
IMN............. Initial Malignant Neoplasm [*Medicine*] (MELL)
IMN............. Inmet Mining Toronto Stock Exchange symbol (SG)
IMN............. Intermediate Node (SAUS)
IMN............. Internal Mammary [*Lymph*] Node [*Medicine*] (DAVI)
IMN............. Internal Mix Nozzle (SAUS)
IMN............. Internal-Mix Nozzle
IMN............. Israel Museum News [*A publication*] (ABAR)
IMN............. Manchester College, North Manchester, IN [*OCLC symbol*] (OCLC)
IMNB........... Isopropyl(methyl)nitrobenzene [*Organic chemistry*]
IMNDN......... Internal Medicine News & Diagnosis [*Medicine*] (EDAA)
Imnet.......... Imnet Systems, Inc. [*Associated Press*] (SAG)
IMNET......... International MarketNet [*System of broker work stations created by IBM Corp. and Merrill Lynch & Co.*] [*New York, NY*]
IMNH........... Idaho Museum of Natural History [*Idaho State University*] [*Research center*] (RCD)
IMNO........... Immuno Therapeutics, Inc. (SAUO)
IMNO........... ImmunoTherapeutics, Inc. (SAUS)
IMNO........... In My Noble Opinion [*Online dialog*]
IMNR........... Immune Response Corp. [*NASDAQ symbol*] (SAG)
IMNS........... Imperial Military Nursing Service [*British*]
IMNS........... Indian Military Nursing Service (SAUO)
IMNSCO....... In My Not So Considered Opinion (SAUO)
IMNSHO....... In My Not So Humble Opinion (SAUO)
IMNSHO....... In My Not-So-Humble Opinion [*Computer hacker terminology*] (NHD)
IMNT........... IMNET Systems [*NASDAQ symbol*] (TTSB)
IMNT........... Imnet Systems, Inc. [*NASDAQ symbol*] (SAG)
IMNX........... Immunex Corp. [*NASDAQ symbol*] (NQ)
IMNX........... Immunex Corporation (SAUO)
IMO............. Asheville, NC [*Location identifier*] [*FAA*] (FAAL)
IMO............. Icelandic Meteorological Office (SAUO)
Imo............. Imitation (SAUS)
IMO............. Immobilized (NVT)
IMO............. Imperial Oil Ltd. [*AMEX symbol*] [*Toronto Stock Exchange symbol*] [*Vancouver Stock Exchange symbol*] (SPSG)
IMO............. Improper Order
IMO............. Indianapolis Museum of Art, Indianapolis, IN [*OCLC symbol*] (OCLC)
IMO............. Information Market Observatory (TELE)
IMO............. Information Monitor
IMO............. In My Opinion [*Internet language*] [*Computer science*]
IMO............. Installation Maintenance Officer [*Military*] (AABC)
IMO............. Installation Mobility Officer (SAUO)
IMO............. Institute of Market Officers [*British*]
IMO............. Instrumentman (Office Machine Repairman) [*U.S. Navy enlisted rating*] (AUER)
IMO............. Integrated Marketing Organization (SAUO)
IMO............. Integrated Multiple Option
IMO............. Inter-American Municipal Organization
IMO............. Interband Magneto-Optic [*Effect*] (DEN)
IMO............. Interface Management Office
IMO............. Inter-Governmental Maritime Organisation (SAUO)
IMO............. Interim Management Office (SAUO)
IMO............. Interim Management Organization (SAUS)
IMO............. Intermetal Oxide (SAUS)
IMO............. International Insurance Monitor (journ.) (SAUS)
IMO............. International Management Organization (SAUO)
IMO............. International MARC Office (SAUO)
IMO............. International Maritime Organization [*Nautical term*] (NTA)
IMO............. International Materials Organization (NATG)
IMO............. International Mathematical Olympiad (RDA)
IMO............. International Messianic Outreach (EA)
IMO............. International Meteorological Organization [*Later, World Meteorological Organization*]
IMO............. International Meteor Organization
IMO............. International Miners Organization (ODA)
IMO............. International Money Order [*Business term*] (DS)
IMO............. Isla Mona [*Puerto Rico*] [*Seismograph station code, US Geological Survey*] (SEIS)
IMOA........... International Mercury Owners Association (EA)
IMOAS......... Information Management and Office Automation System (SAUO)
IMOC........... Integrated Mission Operations Center (SAUS)
IMOC........... Inventory Management Order Control (VLIE)
Imodco........ International Marine and Oil Development Corporation (SAUO)
IMOG........... Interagency Mechanical Operations Group [*Lawrence Livermore Laboratory*]
IMoH........... John and Mary Kirby Hospital, Monticello, IL [*Library symbol*] [*Library of Congress*] (LCLS)
ImoInd......... Imo Industries, Inc. [*Associated Press*] (SAG)
IMoI............ Moline Public Library, Moline, IL [*Library symbol*] [*Library of Congress*] (LCLS)
IMoIB.......... Black Hawk College, Moline, IL [*Library symbol*] [*Library of Congress*] (LCLS)
IMoID.......... Deere & Co., Moline, IL [*Library symbol*] [*Library of Congress*] (LCLS)
IMOM........... Improved Many-on-Many [*Computer science*]
IMON........... ImaginOn, Inc. [*NASDAQ symbol*] (SG)
IMonC.......... Monmouth College, Monmouth, IL [*Library symbol*] [*Library of Congress*] (LCLS)
IMont.......... Allerton Public Library, Monticello, IL [*Library symbol*] [*Library of Congress*] (LCLS)
IMontF......... Piatt County Schools Film Library, Monticello, IL [*Library symbol*] [*Library of Congress*] (LCLS)
IMontSD...... Monticello Community Unit School District, Monticello, IL [*Library symbol*] [*Library of Congress*] (LCLS)
IMonW......... Western Illinois Library System, Monmouth, IL [*Library symbol*] [*Library of Congress*] (LCLS)
IMOP........... Infantry Mortar Program (MCD)
IMOP........... Instruments and Methods of Observation Programme (SAUO)
IMOP........... Intelligence Master Objectives Program (SAUO)
IMORL......... Infrared Mobile Optical Radiation Laboratory [*Navy*] (PDAA)
IMort........... Morton Public Library, Morton, IL [*Library symbol*] [*Library of Congress*] (LCLS)
IMOS........... Federal Interagency Task Force on Inadvertent Modification of the Statosphere (SAUS)
IMOS........... Inadvertent Modification of the Stratosphere [*Interagency government task force*]
IMOS........... Interactive Multiprogramming Operating System [*NCR Corp.*]
IMOS........... Ion-Implanted Metal-Oxide Semiconductor
IMOSAR....... IMO Search and Rescue Manual (SAUO)
IMOT........... Installed Maximum Operating Time
IMOT........... Interim Maximum Operating Time
IMOX........... Implanted Micro-Oxide (SAUS)
IMOX-S....... Ion Implantation, Oxide Isolation with Scaling (NITA)
IMP............. Cargo Information Message Procedures [*IATA*] (DS)
IMP............. Ice Mass Path (CARB)
IMP............. Ice Motion Package (SAUS)
IMP............. ICL Micromation Pack (SAUS)
IMP............. Ideas Marketing Pool Ltd. (SAUO)
IMP............. Idiopathic Myeloid Proliferation [*Medicine*] (DMAA)
IMP............. Illustrated Melbourne Post [*A publication*]
IMP............. Image Processing Program [*Computer program*]
IMP............. Image Projection (SAUS)
IMP............. Imager for Mars Pathfinder [*Instrumentation*]
IMP............. Immunoperoxidase [*An enzyme*]
IMP............. Impact (KSC)
IMP............. Impacted (SAUS)
IMP............. Impaction [*or Impacted*] [*Medicine*] (DAVI)
imp............. Impaction [*Medicine*] (DMAA)
IMP............. Impact Predictor [*NASA*] (MUGU)
imp............. Impaired [*Medicine*] (EDAA)
IMP............. Impaired
imp............. Impasse (DD)
IMP............. Impedance (KSC)
IMP............. Impeller
IMP............. Impenal (SAUS)
imp............. Imperative (WDMC)
IMP............. Imperative
IMP............. Imperator [*or Imperatrix*] [*Emperor or Empress*] [*Latin*]
IMP............. Imperatriz [*Brazil*] [*Airport symbol*] (OAG)
imp............. Imperfect (WDMC)

IMP Imperfect
IMP Imperial (AFM)
Imp Imperial [*Record label*]
IMP Imperial Air [*Peru*] [*ICAO designator*] (FAAC)
IMP Imperial Bancorp [*NYSE symbol*] (SG)
IMP Imperious [*Grammar*] (ROG)
IMP Imperium [*Empire*] [*Latin*]
IMP Impersonal
IMP Impersonating [*FBI standardized term*]
Imp Impetus [*A publication*]
IMP IMP, Inc. [*Associated Press*] (SAG)
IMP Implant (SAUS)
IMP Implantation (SAUS)
imp Implant(ed) [*Medicine*] (EDAA)
IMP Implement (AFM)
IMP Implementation (COE)
IMP Implementation Language [*Edinburgh multiaccess system*] (CSR)
IMP Implementation Management Plan (SAUO)
IMP Implementation Milestone Plan (SAUS)
Imp Import (EBF)
IMP Import (GOBB)
imp Import (WDMC)
imp Important (WDMC)
IMP Important
imp Importation (GEAB)
imp Imported (SHCU)
IMP Imported
IMP Importer (WDAA)
imp Importer (WDAA)
IMP Impracticable (FAAC)
Imp Impression (AMHC)
imp Impression (WDAA)
IMP Impression
imp Imprimatur [*Latin for let it be printed*] (WDMC)
IMP Imprimatur [*Let It Be Printed*] [*Latin*]
Imp Imprime [*Printed*] [*French*] (ILCA)
Imp Imprimeur [*Printer*] [*French*] (ILCA)
IMP Imprimis [*In the First Place*] [*Latin*] (WGA)
IMP Imprint
IMP Improper [*Motor vehicle violation code used in state of Maryland*] (MVRD)
Imp Improper (SAUS)
IMP Impropriator (ROG)
imp improve (SAUS)
imp Improved (MILB)
IMP Improved
IMP Improved Maintenance Program [*Air Force*] (AFM)
IMP Improved Manoeuvrability Package (SAUS)
IMP Improved Manufacturing Procedure [*Computer science*] (PDAA)
IMP Improved Manufacturing Procedures computer programme (SAUO)
IMP Improved Manufracturing Procedure (SAUS)
IMP Improved Mobility Package [*Wheelchair system*]
IMP Improved Multi-Processor (VLIE)
Imp Improvement [*Business term*] (EBF)
IMP Improvement [*Real estate*]
IMP Improvement Maintenance Program (MCD)
Imp Improver (SAUS)
IMP Impulse (KSC)
IMP Impulse Generator
IMP Incomplete Male Pseudohermaphroditism [*Medicine*] (AAMN)
IMP Independence for Malaya Party (SAUO)
IMP Independent Malay Party (SAUO)
IMP Independent Motion Picture Co.
IMP Indeterminate Mass Particle
IMP Index to Maritime Publications [*A publication*]
IMP Indication of Microwave Propagation (SAUS)
IMP Indicative Market Price (SAUO)
IMP Indicator Maintenance Panel (VLIE)
IMP Individual Merit Promotion
IMP Individual Modular Program (SAUS)
IMP Industrial Management Plan (SAUS)
IMP Industrial Management Program
IMP Industrial Membrane Processing [*Chemical engineering*]
IMP Industrial Mobilization Planning
IMP Industrial Models and Patterns [*A publication*] (EAAP)
IMP Industry Market Potential [*Business term*] (MHDW)
IMP Inertial Measuring Platform (SAUS)
IMP Infantry Mine Project (SAUS)
IMP Infantry Mortar Plan (MCD)
IMP Inflatable Micrometeroid Paraglide
IMP Information/Interface Message Processor (SAUS)
IMP Information Management Package (SAUS)
IMP Information Management Plan [*DoD*]
IMP Information Management Processor (NITA)
IMP Information Management Program [*Army*]
IMP Infrastructure Modernization Program (SAUO)
IMP Initial Material Management (SAUS)
IMP Initial Memory Protection (MCD)
IMP Initial Military Program (NATG)
IMP Injection into Microwave Plasma (SAUS)
IMP Injection into Microwave Products (SAUS)
IMP Injection Microwave Plasma [*Oak Ridge National Laboratory*]
IMP Inosine Monophosphate [*Biochemistry*]
IMP Inosinic Acid [*Biochemistry*] (DAVI)
IMP Inpatient Multidimensional Psychiatric Scale
IMP Input Message Processor
IMP Insoluble Metaphosphate [*Inorganic chemistry*]
IMP Installation Management Planning (SAUS)
IMP Installation Master Planning [*Military*]
IMP Instant Management Power (SAUS)
IMP Institute of Modern Procedures [*Defunct*] (EA)
IMP Institute of Molecular Pathology [*Austria*]
IMP Instrumental Match Prediction (SAUS)
IMP Instrumented Mobile Platform (SAUS)
IMP Instrumented Monkey Pod
IMP Instrument Maintenance Procedure [*Nuclear energy*] (NRCH)
IMP Instrument Monkey Pod (SAUS)
IMP Instrument Mounting Platform (ADWA)
IMP Intatable Micrometeroid Paraglide (SAUS)
IMP Integral Membrane Protein [*Cytology*]
IMP Integrated Macro Package (SAUS)
IMP Integrated Maintenance Package (SAUS)
IMP Integrated Maintenance Plan [*or Procedure*]
IMP Integrated Manufacturing Plan (IAA)
IMP Integrated Master Plan [*Business term*] (RDA)
IMP Integrated Mathematics Project (AIE)
IMP Integrated Memory Processor
IMP Integrated Message Processor (NITA)
IMP Integrated Microprocessor [*National Semiconductor*]
IMP Integrated Micro Products [*British*] (NITA)
IMP Integrated Microwave Package (IAA)
IMP Integrated Microwave Products (IEEE)
IMP Integrated MIDI [*Musical Instrument Digital Interface*] Processor
IMP Integrated Mission Processor (ACAE)
IMP Integrated Modular Personnel Software [*Percom*] (NITA)
IMP Integrated Monitoring Panel
IMP Integrated Multi-Protocol Processor (SAUS)
IMP Integrating Monitoring Panel (SAUS)
IMP Integrating Motor Pneumotachograph
IMP Intelligent Machine Prognosticator (SAUS)
IMP Intelligent Message Processor [*Delta Data Systems*] (NITA)
IMP Intelligent Multiport Cards [*Computer hardware*] (PCM)
IMP Intensity Measurement Program (ACAE)
IMP Interactive Machine-Language Programming (SAUS)
IMP Interactive Mathematics Program [*High school curriculum*]
IMP Interactive Microprogrammable Control (MCD)
IMP Interactive Minicomputer Programming (SAUS)
IMP Interagency Integrated Pest Management Coordinating Committee [*Terminated, 1980*] [*Council on Environmental Quality*] (EGAO)
IMP Interchurch Media Programme (SAUO)
IMP Interconnection Manual Procedure (SAUS)
IMP Interdivisional Manufacturing Practice (SAUS)
IMP Interface Management Plan [*Air Force*]
IMP Interface Management Processor (SAUS)
IMP Interface Message Processor [*Computer science*]
IMP Interface Message Protocol (SAUS)
IMP Interim Monitoring Program
IMP Inter-Industry Management Program (IAA)
IMP Intermeccanica-Puch [*Italian-Austrian specialty car maker*]
IMP Intermenstrual Pain (MELL)
IMP Intermessage Processor (IAA)
IMP Intermodulation Product
IMP International Maple Leaf Resource Corp. [*Vancouver Stock Exchange symbol*]
IMP International Match Point [*Game of bridge*]
IMP International Microelectronic Products, Inc. [*Associated Press*] (SAG)
IMP International Micro-Print Preservation, Inc.
IMP International Mimes and Pantomimists [*Defunct*]
IMP International Missile Proliferation (SAUO)
IMP International Monitoring Probe (SAUS)
IMP Internet Mercantile Protocol (SAUS)
IMP Interplanetary Magnetometer Probe
IMP Interplanetary Measurement Probe
IMP Interplanetary Monitoring Platform [*A spacecraft*]
IMP Interplanetary Monitoring Probe [*A spacecraft*]
IMP Interplanetaty Monitoring Platform (SAUS)
IMP Intra-Industry Management Program [*Small Business Administration*]
IMP Intramembranous Particle [*Cytology*]
IMP Intramuscular Compartment Pressure [*Medicine*] (DMAA)
IMP Intrinsic Multiprocessing (IEEE)
IMP Inventory Management Package (SAUS)
IMP Inventory Management Plan [*Military*] (AFIT)
IMP Ion Microprobe [*Surface analysis*]
IMP Ion Moderated Partition [*Chromatography*]
IMP Ischemic Muscle Pain (MELL)
IMP Israeli Music Publications (SAUO)
IMP Item Management Plan (AAGC)
IMP Marathon, TX [*Location identifier*] [*FAA*] (FAAL)
IMP Mishawaka Public Library, Mishawaka, IN [*OCLC symbol*] (OCLC)
Imp 8 Imperial Octavo (SAUS)
IMP-8 Interplanetary Monitoring Platform 8 (SAUS)
IMPA Incisal Mandibular Plane Angle [*Dentistry*]
IMPA Independent Media Producers Association [*Later, IMPC*] (EA)
IMPA Information Management and Processing Association [*Defunct*] (EA)
IMPA Information Management Professional Association (SAUO)
IMPA Initialized Moore Probabilistic Automation (IAA)
IMPA International Management Professional Association (SAUO)
IMPA International Marine Purchasing Association (SAUO)
IMPA International Maritime Pilots Association (EAIO)

IMPA............ International Marketing Public Relations and Advertising Consultants (SAUO)
IMPA............ International Master Printers Association [*Brussels, Belgium*]
IMPA............ International Meat Processors Association (EA)
IMPA............ International Motor Press Association (EA)
IMPA............ International Movement for Peace Action (SAUO)
IMPA............ International Museum Photographers Association (EA)
IMPA............ International Myopia Prevention Association (EA)
IMPA............ Ion Microprobe Analysis
IMPAC......... Image Analysis Computer Package (SAUS)
IMPAC......... Image Analysis Package for Microcomputers (SAUS)
IMPAC......... Immediate Psychiatric Aid and Referral Center
IMPAC......... Industrial Multilevel Process Analysis and Control (IAA)
IMPAC......... Information for Management Planning Analysis and Coordination (PDAA)
IMPAC......... Instrument Meters Packaged as Components (SAUS)
IMPAC......... Integrated Message Processing and Communications system (SAUS)
IMPAC......... Interagency Map and Publications Acquisitions Committee [*Department of State*] [*Washington, DC*]
IMPAC......... International Merchant Purchase Authority (or Authorization) Card (SAUS)
IMPAC......... International Merchant Purchases Authorization Care [*Visa*] (RDA)
IMPAC......... International Microfiche Parts Access Catalogue [*Auto parts*] [*A publication*]
IMPACC....... Intestinal Multiple Polyposis and Colorectal Cancer (MELL)
IMPACS....... Integrated Manufacturing Planning and Control System (SAUO)
IMPACS....... International Packet-Switching Service [*MCI International, Inc.*] [*Rye Brook, NY*] [*Telecommunications*] (TSSD)
IMPACT........ An International Initiative against Avoidable Disablement (SAUO)
IMPACT........ Illinois Microarchitecture Project Utilizing Advanced Compiler Technology
IMPACT........ Image Processing and Color Transmission [*Time, Inc. photograph transmission center*]
IMPACT........ Immunization Monitoring Program, Active (SAUS)
IMPACT........ Implanted Advanced Composed Technology [*Texas Instruments, Inc.*]
IMPACT........ Implementation Aspects concerning Planning and Legislation (SAUO)
IMPACT........ Implementation of Micropublishing (SAUS)
IMPACT........ Implementation of Micropublishing, Army Concept and Technology (SAUS)
IMPACT........ Implementation Planning and Control Technique [*Computer science*]
IMPACT........ Implementing Agency for Cooperation and Training (SAUO)
IMPACT........ Improved Management Procurement and Contracting Technique (AABC)
IMPACT........ Improved Manpower Production and Controller Technique [*Navy*]
IMPACT........ Improved Manufracturing Planning and Assembly Control Technique (SAUS)
IMPACT........ Improved Modern Pricing and Costing Techniques [*Air Force*] (MCD)
IMPACT........ Improved Multi-mission Payload Aerial Combat (SAUS)
IMPACT........ Improving Public Awareness of Concepts of Telecommunications (SAUS)
IMPACT........ Information Market Action Program (TELE)
IMPACT........ Information Market Policy Actions (SAUO)
IMPACT........ Instructional Model Prototypes Attainable in Computerized Training (SAUO)
IMPACT........ Integrated Management Planning and Control Technique [*British*]
IMPACT........ Integrated Management, Project Analysis and Control Technique (SAUS)
IMPACT........ Integrated Managerial Programming Analysis Control Technique [*Air Force*]
IMPACT........ Integrated Manufacturing Planning and Control Technique (SAUS)
IMPACT........ Integrated Manufacturing Precision Assembled Cellular Technology [*Communications*]
IMPACT........ Integrated Material Programming Analysis Control Technique (SAUS)
IMPACT........ Integrated Materials Handling Production and Control Technology
IMPACT........ Integrated Microform Parts Cataloging (PDAA)
IMPACT........ Integrated Missile Procedure and Control Trainer (SAUS)
IMPACT........ Integrated Model of Plumes and Atmosphere in Complex Terrain [*Environmental Protection Agency*] (GFGA)
IMPACT........ Integrated Module Packaging Technology (SAUS)
IMPACT........ Intensive Matched Probation and After-Care Treatment (PDAA)
IMPACT........ Interdisciplinary Model Programs in the Arts for Children and Teachers
IMPACT........ International Initiative Against Avoidable Disablement (SAUO)
IMPACT........ International Marketing Program for Agricultural Commodities and Trade Center [*Washington State University*] [*Research center*] (RCD)
IMPACT........ Intervention Moves Parents and Children Together [*Drug abuse treatment program sponsored by Phoenix House Foundation*]
IMPACT........ Inventory Management Product and Control Technique (SAUS)
IMPACT........ Inventory Management Program and Control Technique [*IBM Corp.*] [*Computer science*]
IMPACTS..... Instant Media Planning and Analysis by Computer Time Sharing (SAUS)
Impacts Aust Econ... Impacts on the Australian Economy [*A publication*]
Impact Sci Soc... Impact of Science on Society. UNESCO (SAUO)
Impact Sci Soc... Impact of Science on Society. UNESCO. Paris (journ.) (SAUS)
IMPALA........ International Motion Picture and Lecturers Association (EA)
Imp&Trac RB... Implement and Tractor Red Book (journ.) (SAUS)
IMPAS-WG... Improved Military Parts Availability and Selection Working Group [*Army*] (RDA)
IMP-ATACMS... Improved Army Tactical Missile System (RDA)
Impath......... Impath, Inc. [*Associated Press*] (SAG)
IMPATT........ Impact Avalanche and Transit Time (ACAE)
IMPATT........ Impact Avalanche Transit Time (AEBE)
IMPATT........ Impact Ionization Avalanche Transit Time [*Solid state diodes*] [*Transistor technology*]
IMPAV......... Inter-Urban Microwave-Powered Air-Cushion Vehicle (PDAA)
IMPBA......... International Model Power Boat Association (EA)
IMPC............ Independent Media Producers Council (EA)
IMPC............ Infantry Mortar Platoon Course (INF)
IMPC............ Institutional and Municipal Parking Congress (EA)
IMPC............ International Mineral Processing Congress (SAUO)
IMPC............ International Municipal Parking Congress (SAUO)
IMPC............ International Myopia Prevention Centre (DAVI)
IMPCA......... International Methanol Producers and Consumers Association [*British*]
IMP CDU...... Interactive Microprogrammable Control Display Unit (SAUS)
IMPCE.......... Importance
impce........... impotance (SAUS)
ImpCM......... Imperial Credit Mortgage Holdings, Inc. [*Associated Press*] (SAG)
IMPCM......... Improved Capability Missile [*Air Force*] (MCD)
ImpCMtg....... Imperial Credit Mortgage Holdings, Inc. [*Associated Press*] (SAG)
IMPCON....... Inventory Management and Production Control [*ISTEL*] [*Software package*] (NCC)
ImpCrd......... Imperial Credit Industries, Inc. [*Associated Press*] (SAG)
ImpctSy....... Impact Systems, Inc. [*Associated Press*] (SAG)
IMP CYL....... Impression Cylinder [*Publishing*] (DGA)
IMPD............ Impedance [*Electricity*]
IMPD............ Improved [*Real estate*] (ROG)
IMPD............ Interactive Multipurpose Display (SAUS)
IMPDAA....... Independent Motion Picture Distributors Association of America
IMPDH......... Inosine Monophosphate Dehydrogenase [*An enzyme*]
IMP DICT...... Imperial Dictionary [*A publication*] (ROG)
IMPDMNT..... Impediment
IMPDS......... Improved Missile Point Defence System (SAUS)
IM-PDU........ InterMediate Protocol Data Unit (SAUS)
impe............. Imperative (ELAL)
IMPE............ Impregnate (IAA)
IMPE............ International Meeting on Petroleum Engineering (SAUS)
Impedaverter... Impedance Converter (SAUS)
IMPEL.......... Insurance Management Performance Evaluation Life (MHDB)
IMPEND....... Improved Effectiveness Nuclear Depth Bomb
IMPEND Bomb... Improved Effectiveness Nuclear Depth Bomb (SAUS)
Imper........... Imperative [*Medicine*] (EDAA)
IMPER......... Imperative
IMPER......... Imperfect
Imper........... Imperial [*Medicine*] (EDAA)
IMPER......... Impersonal (ROG)
Imperf.......... Imperfect (STED)
IMPERF........ Imperfect
imperf........... Imperforate (STED)
IMPERF........ Imperforate [*Philately*]
Imperial........ Imperial Savings Association (SAUO)
Imperial institute bulletins... Bulletin of the Imperial institute. London (SAUS)
IMPERS....... Impersonal
IMPES.......... Implicit Pressure, Explicit Saturation [*Petroleum reservoir simulation*]
IMPEX.......... Immediate Postexercise (STED)
Imp-Exp....... Import-Export (SAUS)
IMPF............ Imperfect (MSA)
IMPFT.......... Imperfect (ADA)
IMPG............ Imperial Group Ltd.
impg............. importing (SAUS)
IMPG............ Impregnate (KSC)
IMPG............ Instructional Materiel Plan and Guide (SAUO)
IMPGAC....... Improved Guidance and Control (MCD)
IMP GAL....... Imperial Gallon (SAUS)
imp gal......... Imperial Gallon
IMPGEN....... Impulse Generator (IAA)
IMPH............ Impath Inc. [*NASDAQ symbol*] (TTSB)
ImpHly.......... Imperial Holly Corp. [*Associated Press*] (SAG)
IMPI.............. Internal Microprogramming Instruction (SAUS)
IMPI.............. Internal Microprogramming Interface (SAUS)
IMPI.............. International Microwave Power Institute (EA)
IMPICS......... Integrated Manufacturing Program Information and Control System (PDAA)
impig............ impignorating (SAUS)
impig............ impignoration (SAUS)
IMPIS........... Indirect Material Purchasing Information Standards
IMPIS........... Integrated Management Planning Information Systems [*Computer science*]
IMPIS........... Integrated Manufacturing Process Information System (ACAE)
IMPL............. Illustrated Maintenance Parts List
Impl............... Imperial [*British military*] (DMA)
IMPL............. Implement (AABC)
IMPL............. Implementation Language (NITA)
IMPL............. Impulse (FAAC)
IMPL............. Initial Microprogram Load [*Also, IML*] [*Computer science*]
IMPL............. Initital Microprogram Load (SAUS)
IMPL............. International Microwave Power Institute (PDAA)
IMP LFT TRN... Improperly Executing a Left Turn [*Conviction term used in state of Oregon*] (MVRD)
IMPLNTN..... Implementation
IMP LOG LD... Improperly Securing a Log Load [*Conviction term used in state of Oregon*] (MVRD)
IMPLR......... Impeller [*Mechanical engineering*]
IMPLS......... Impulse (MSA)
IMP LT ATV... Operating an All-Terrain Vehicle without Proper Lighting Equipment [*Conviction term used in state of Oregon*] (MVRD)
Imp Man...... Impey's Law and Practice of Mandamus [*1826*] [*A publication*] (DLA)

IMP/MON..... Implementation and Monitoring (SAUO)
IMPN.......... Importation
IMPN.......... Integrated Microprocessors Network (SAUS)
IMPO.......... Imposition (DSUE)
ImpOil........ Imperial Oil Ltd. [*Associated Press*] (SAG)
I M POOL..... Intramural Building (SAUS)
IMPOP........ Integrated Maintenance Program Operation (MCD)
IMPOS........ Interactive Multi-Programming Operating System (PDAA)
IMPOSN....... Imposition (ROG)
IMPOSS....... Impossible (ADA)
IMPOT........ Imposition (DSUE)
IMPOV........ In My Point Of View (SAUS)
IMPP.......... Industrial Mobilization Production Planning [*DoD*]
IMPP.......... Interchangeable Multisource Pharmaceutical Products (SAUS)
IMPPA........ Independent Motion Picture Producers Association [*Defunct*] (EA)
IMPPACT..... Integrated Modelling of Products and Processes Using Advanced Computer Technologies (SAUO)
IMP PINT/HPHR... Imperial Pint per Horse-Power-Hour (SAUS)
Imp Pl........ Impey's Modern Pleader [*2nd ed.*] [*1814*] [*A publication*] (DLA)
Imp Pr CP.... Impey's Practice, Common Pleas [*A publication*] (DLA)
Imp Pr KB.... Impey's Practice, King's Bench [*A publication*] (DLA)
IMP PS........ Improved Plow Steel (SAUS)
IMP PT........ Imperial Pint (SAUS)
IMP QT........ Imperial Quart (SAUS)
IMPR.......... Impedor
IMPR.......... Impractical (AABC)
IMPR.......... Impression (ROG)
Impr........... Impressionism (VRA)
IMPR.......... Imprint [*Online database field identifier*]
IMPR.......... Imprint Records, Inc. [*NASDAQ symbol*] (SAG)
IMPR.......... Improved
Impr........... Improving (SAUS)
Impr........... Improvisator (SAUS)
Impr........... Improvised (SAUS)
IMPR.......... Instrument Malfunction Problem Report (SAUS)
IMPRAC....... Impracticable (DSUE)
impracl....... impracticable (SAUS)
ImprAr........ Imperial Aramaic (BJA)
ImprBc........ Imperial Bancorp [*Associated Press*] (SAG)
IMPRD........ Impaired
IMPREG....... Impregnable (ADA)
IMPREG....... Impregnated (TEL)
Impr era...... Improvement Era. Mutual Funds, Inc. (SAUO)
IMPRESS..... Implementation Maintenance and Promotion of the EDILIBE/ EDITEUR Standards Sets (SAUS)
IMPRESS..... Impression
IMPRESS..... Integrated Multi-Train Passenger Reservation System [*Indian Railway*] (TIR)
IMPRESS..... Interdisciplinary Machine Processing for Research and Education in Social Sciences [*Dartmouth College, Hanover, NH*] [*Data processing system*]
IMPREST..... IMPREST System (SAUS)
IMPRG........ Impregnate (AABC)
IMPRIGA..... Imprimerie Centrale d'Afrique [*Publisher*] [*Gabon*] (EY)
IMPRINT..... Image Processing Identification of Non-Cooperative Targets (ACAE)
IMPRINT..... Imbricated Program for Information Transfer [*Computer science*]
Imprint....... Imprint Records, Inc. [*Associated Press*] (SAG)
IMPRINT..... Improved Medical Programs and Readiness Immediately, Not Tomorrow [*TROA*]
IMPRINT..... Improved Performance Research Integration Tool [*Army*]
IMPRINT..... Inbricated Program for Information Transfer (SAUS)
ImprintR..... Imprint Records, Inc. [*Associated Press*] (SAG)
IMPRL........ Imperial (MSA)
imprm........ Imprimatura (VRA)
IMPROP...... Improper (ADA)
improp....... improperly (SAUS)
IMPROV...... Improvement (MSA)
IMPROVE..... Immediate Production Verification (ACAE)
IMPROVE..... Interagency Monitoring of Protected Visual Emissions (COE)
IMPROVE..... Interagency Monitoring of Protected Visual Environments [*Marine science*] (OSRA)
IMPROVE..... Inventory Management, Product Replenishment and Order Validity Evaluation (MHDB)
IMPRS........ Information Management Process Reporting System (HGAA)
IMPRSN...... Impression (MSA)
IMPRT........ Import
IMPRTD...... Imported
IMPRTNG.... Importing
IMPRTR...... Importer
IMPRV........ Improvement (AABC)
IMPRVMNT... Improvement
IMPRVMT.... Improvement
Imps........... Imperial Tobacco Co. (SAUO)
IMPS.......... Imperial Tobacco Co. Shares [*Stock exchange term*] [*British*] (DSUE)
IMPS.......... Imports (SAUS)
IMPS.......... Impose (MSA)
IMPS.......... Individual Multipurpose Shelter [*Army*] (INF)
IMPS.......... Industry Media Publishing System [*Omni Industry Corp.*] [*Information service or system*] (IID)
IMPS.......... Inpatient Multidimensional Psychiatric Scale
IMPS.......... Institute of Management Public Speaking (SAUO)
IMPS.......... Institutional Meat Purchase Specification [*Department of Agriculture*]
IMPS.......... Intact Months of Patient Survival [*Medicine*] (DMAA)
IMPS.......... Integrated Mail Preparation System
IMPS.......... Integrated Master Programming and Scheduling
IMPS.......... Integrated Microcomputer Processing System [*Bureau of the Census*] (GFGA)
IMPS.......... Integrated Mission Planning Station (ACAE)
IMPS.......... Integrated Modular Panel System
IMPS.......... Integrated Modular Pushbutton Switch (SAUS)
IMPS.......... Intelligent Management Programming System (SAUS)
IMPS.......... Intelligent Mission Planning System (SAUS)
IMPS.......... Interaction Measurements Payload for Shuttle (SAUO)
IMPS.......... Interface Message Processors [*Computer science*] (NITA)
IMPS.......... Intermediate Minimum Property Standards [*Department of Housing and Urban Development*] (GFGA)
IMPS.......... International Mensan Philatelists Society (EA)
IMPS.......... International Micro Programmers Society (SAUS)
IMPS.......... International Microprogrammers' Society
IMPS.......... International M [*formerly, Mensa*] Philatelists Society (EA)
Imp Sav....... Imperial Savings (SAUS)
Imp/sec....... Impulse per second (SAUS)
Imp Sh........ Impey's Office of Sheriff [*6th ed.*] [*1835*] [*A publication*] (DLA)
IMPS System... Integrated Master Programming and Scheduling System (SAUS)
impst.......... Impasto (VRA)
IMPT.......... Implement Important (SAUS)
impt........... Important (BARN)
Impt........... Imprisonment [*British military*] (DMA)
IMPT.......... Improvement [*Real estate*] (ROG)
IMPT.......... IMPSAT Fiber Networks [*NASDAQ symbol*] (SG)
IMPT.......... Integrated Micro Products [*NASDAQ symbol*] (SAG)
IM-PT......... Portuguese national Meteorological Institute (SAUS)
ImpThft....... Imperial Thrift & Loan Association [*Associated Press*] (SAG)
IMPTN........ Imputation
IMPTR........ Importer (ADA)
IMPTS........ Improved Programmer Test Station (IEEE)
Imptypco..... Imperial Typewriter Co. (SAUS)
Imptypco..... Imperial Typewriter Company (SAUO)
IMPU.......... Information Management Projects Unit (SAUS)
Imp Univ of Japan Coll of S... Imperial University of Japan. College of Science, Journal (SAUO)
Imp Univ of Japan Coll of S... Imperial University of Japan. College of Science, Journal (journ.) (SAUS)
Imp Univ of Japan Fac of S... Imperial University of Japan. Faculty of Science, Journal (SAUO)
Imp Univ of Japan Fac of S... Imperial University of Japan. Faculty of Science, Journal (journ.) (SAUS)
IMPUTN....... Imputation
IMPV.......... Imperative
impv........... Impervious (SAUS)
IMPVD........ Improved [*Real estate*] (ROG)
IMPVE........ Improve [*Real estate*] (ROG)
Impvt.......... Improvement (STED)
Impx........... Impacted [*Medicine*] (DMAA)
IMPX.......... Impaction [*Dentistry*]
IMPX.......... Imperatrix [*Empress*] [*Latin*]
IMPX.......... IMP, Inc. [*NASDAQ symbol*] (SAG)
IMPX.......... International Microelectronics Products, Inc. (SAUO)
IMPZ.......... Imperial [*Federal Railroad Administration identification code*]
IMQ........... Industrial Management Qualification
IMQ........... La Porte County Library, La Porte, IN [*OCLC symbol*] (OCLC)
IMQC.......... Imported Merchandise Quantity Control (SAUS)
IMQT.......... Initial Mission Qualification Training (SAUO)
IMR........... Ice Mixing Ratio (ARMP)
IMR........... Image Microwave Radiometer (SAUO)
IMR........... Imaging Microwave Radiometer (SAUS)
IMR........... IMCO Recycling [*NYSE symbol*] (TTSB)
IMR........... IMCO Recycling, Inc. [*NYSE symbol*] (NQ)
IMR........... Impala Resources [*Vancouver Stock Exchange symbol*]
IMR........... Imperial Military Railways [*British military*] (DMA)
IMR........... Improved Military Rifle (PDAA)
IMR........... Impulse-Aero [*Russian Federation*] [*ICAO designator*] (FAAC)
IMR........... Independent Modification Review [*Military*] (AFIT)
IMR........... Indian Midland Railway [*Indian Railway*] (TIR)
IMR........... Individual Medical Record
IMR........... Individual Medical Report (SAUS)
IMR........... Infant Mortality Rate
IMR........... Infant Mortality Risk [*Medicine*] (DMAA)
IMR........... Infectious Mononucleosis Receptor [*Biochemistry*] (AAMN)
IMR........... Informal Memorandum Report
IMR........... Information Management Representitive (SAUO)
IMR........... Information Management Review [*A publication*] (NITA)
IMR........... Initial Missile Report (CINC)
IMR........... Initial Mortality Rate
IMR........... Inmate Medical Record (WDAA)
IMR........... Inner Metropolitan Region (ADA)
IMR........... Input Message Report (SAUO)
IMR........... Insensitive Munition Requirements (SAUS)
IMR........... Institute for Marine Resources (SAUS)
IMR........... Institute for Masonry Research (SAUS)
IMR........... Institute for Materials Research [*Later, NSL*] [*National Institute of Standards and Technology*]
IMR........... Institute for Medical Research [*Camden, New Jersey*]
IMR........... Institute for Mortuary Research (SAUO)
IMR........... Institute for Motivational Research (SAUO)
IMR........... Institute for Muscle Research (SAUO)
IMR........... Institute of Man and Resources
IMR........... Institute of Marine Resources [*University of California*] [*Research center*] (RCD)
IMR........... Institute of Masonry Research [*Defunct*] (EA)

IMR............. Institute of Materials Research (SAUO)
IMR............. Institute of Metal Repair (EA)
IMR............. Institute of Mineral Research (SAUS)
IMR............. Institute of Mortuary Research (SAUO)
IMR............. Institute of Muscle Research (SAUO)
IMR............. Institution for Mentally Retarded [*Generic term*] (DHSM)
IMR............. Integrated Microscopy Resource (SAUS)
IMR............. Integrated Model Repository (SAUS)
IMR............. Integrated Model Respository (AAEL)
IMR............. Integrated Multiport Repeater [*Computer science*] (PCM)
IMR............. Intelligent Machine Research (NITA)
IMR............. Intelligent Mark Reader (SAUS)
IMR............. Interim Material Release
IMR............. Intermodulation Ratio (SAUS)
IMR............. Internal Mold Release [*Plastics technology*]
IMR............. International Marine Radio (SAUS)
IMR............. International Market Research Report (JAGO)
IMR............. International Medical Research
IMR............. Internet Monthly Report
IMR............. Interruption Mask Register (SAUS)
IMR............. Interrupt-Mask Register [*Computer science*]
IMR............. Inventory Management Record [*Military*] (AFM)
IMR............. Inventory Management Review
IMR............. Inventory Measurement Report (SAUS)
IMR............. Inventory Modified Round
IMR............. Irreducible Matrix Representation (SAUS)
IMR............. Isla Mona [*Puerto Rico*] [*Seismograph station code, US Geological Survey*] [*Closed*] (SEIS)
IMR............. Isolation Mode Rejection (IAA)
IMR............. Monroe County Public Library, Bloomington, IN [*OCLC symbol*] (OCLC)
IMRA.......... Incentive Manufacturers Representatives Association [*Naperville, IL*] (EA)
IMRA.......... Independent Motorcycle Retailers of America [*Defunct*] (EA)
IMRA.......... Independent Music Retailers Association (NTPA)
IMRA.......... Industrial Management Research Association (SAUO)
IMRA.......... Industrial Marketing Research Association [*British*]
IMRA.......... Infrared Monochromatic Radiation
IMRA.......... Insurance Market Risk Assessment
IMRA.......... International Manufacturers Representatives Association [*Tulsa, OK*] (EA)
IMRA.......... International Marine Radio Association (SAUO)
IMRA.......... International Market Research Association (SAUO)
IMRA.......... International Mass Retail Association (NTPA)
IMRA.......... International Military Recreation Association [*Defunct*] (EA)
IMRA.......... International Mission Radio Association (EA)
IMRAD........ Introduction, Methodology, Results, and Discussion (WDMC)
IMRAD........ Introduction, Methods, Results, and Discussion [*Scientific writing*]
IMRADS...... Information, Management, Retrieval, and Data System (ACAE)
IMRADS...... Information Management, Retrieval, and Dissemination System (DIT)
IMRAMN...... International Meeting on Radio Aids to Marine Navigation (SAUS)
IMRAMN...... International Meeting on Radio-Aids to Marine Navigation (SAUO)
IMRAN........ International Marine Radio Aids to Navigation
IMRB.......... Improved Main Rotor Blade (RDA)
IMRC.......... Indian Muslim Relief Committee (EA)
IMRC.......... Indigenous Minorities Research Council [*British*]
IMRC.......... Instructional Materials Reference Center [*American Printing House for the Blind - APH*] [*Absorbed by*] (EA)
IMRC.......... Intake Manifold Runner Control [*Automotive term*] (HAWK)
IMRC.......... International Management & Research Corporation (SAUO)
IMRC.......... International Marine Radio Co. (SAUS)
IMRC.......... International Marine Radio Committee (SAUO)
IMRC.......... International Marine Radio Company (SAUO)
IMRC.......... International Metropolitan Railway Committee (SAUO)
IMRC.......... Inventory [*or Item*] Management Responsibility Code
IMRC.......... Item Management Responsibility Code (ACAE)
IMRCT........ Interim Medium-Range Communications Terminals (SAUS)
IMRE.......... IMRE Corp. [*NASDAQ symbol*] (NQ)
IMRE.......... Institute for Medical Record Economics (EA)
IMREC........ Interior Ministerial Real Estate Committee [*Vietnam*]
IMREP........ Immediately Report
IMREP........ Immediate Report (SAUS)
IMRETES..... Immunization Readiness Training Exercises [*Army*]
IMRF.......... Independent Manufacturers Representatives Forum (EA)
IMRF.......... International Medical and Research Foundation [*Later, AMREF*] (EA)
IMRF/SMRF... International Medical Relief Fund/Salvadoran Medical Relief Fund (EA)
IMRGA........ Imreg, Inc. (Class A) [*NASDAQ symbol*] (COMM)
IMRHS........ Inactive Materiel Request History and Status File [*Army*]
IMRI........... Industrial Materials Research Institute (SAUS)
IMRI........... Integrated Medical Resources, Inc. [*NASDAQ symbol*] (SAG)
IMRI........... International Marian Research Institute [*University of Dayton*] [*Research center*] (RCD)
IMRL........... I & M Rail Link [*Federal Railroad Administration identification code*]
IMRL........... Immediate Material Requirement List
IMRL........... Individual Maintenance Readiness List
IMRL........... Individual Material Readiness List [*DoD*]
IMRL........... Integrated Materials Research Laboratory [*Sandia National Laboratories*]
IMRL........... Intermediate Maintenance Repair Level (MCD)
IMRL........... Intermediate Maintenance Requirements List
IMRMPS...... Institute for Medical Research and Medicinal Plants Studies (SAUS)
IMRMS........ Ion Molecular Reaction Mass Spectroscopy
IMRO.......... Inspection Minor Rework Order (SAUS)
IMRO.......... Internal Macedonian Revolutionary Organization [*Bulgaria*] [*Political party*] (PPE)
IMRO.......... Interplant Material Requisition Order
IMRO.......... Investment Management Regulatory Organization (SAUS)
IMRO.......... Investment Managers Regulatory Organisation [*British*] (ECON)
IMROC........ Inner Metropolitan Regional Organisation of Councils (SAUO)
IMRO-DPMNU... Internal Macedonian Revolutionary Organization - Democratic Party for Macedonian[*Bulgaria*] National Unity [*Political party*] (EY)
IMRP.......... Integrated Maintenance Requirements Plan (SAUO)
IMRP.......... International Meeting on Radiation Processing (EA)
IMRR.......... Illinois & Midland Railroad [*Federal Railroad Administration identification code*]
IMRR.......... Isolation Mode Rejection Rate (SAUS)
IMRR.......... Isolation Mode Rejection Ratio (IAA)
IMR Reserve Fund... Infant Mortality Reduction Reserve Fund (SAUO)
IMRRS........ Installation Materiel Readiness Reporting System [*Army*]
IMRRS........ Institute of Market and Reward Regional Surveys [*British*]
IMRS.......... Immersion (MSA)
IMRS.......... Improved Munitions Requirements System (SAUO)
IMRS.......... IMRglobal Corp. [*Formerly, Information Management Resources*] [*NASDAQ symbol*]
IMRS.......... Information Management Resources, Inc. [*NASDAQ symbol*] (SAG)
IMRS.......... Inpatient Multidimensional Rating Scale (SAUS)
IMRS.......... International Mutual Response System (SAUO)
IMRSA........ International Medical Regulatory and Shipping Association (GVA)
IM-RSI........ International Military Rationalization, Standardization, and Interoperability (RDA)
IMRT.......... Infant Mortality Review Team [*Department of Health and Human Services*] (GFGA)
IMRT.......... Intensity Modulated Radiation Therapy [*Medicine*]
IMRU.......... Industrial Materials Research Unit (SAUO)
IMRU.......... Institute of Microbiology, Rutgers University [*New Jersey*]
IMS............. Air Images [*British*] [*FAA designator*] (FAAC)
IMS............. Division of Inorganic and Metallic Structure (SAUS)
IMS............. Idle Matrix Search [*Computer science*]
IMS............. IEEE Instrumentation and Measurement Society (EA)
IMS............. Ignition Module Signal [*Automotive engineering*]
IMS............. Image Management Solutions (SAUS)
IMS............. Image Management System [*Filenet*] (NITA)
IMS............. Image Manipulation System (SAUS)
IMS............. Image Motion Simulator
IMS............. Imasco Ltd. [*Toronto Stock Exchange symbol*] [*Vancouver Stock Exchange symbol*]
IMS............. Immersed Midship Section (SAUS)
ImS............. Immune Serum [*Also, IS*]
IMS............. Impulse Manoeuvering System (SAUS)
IMS............. IMS Management Services Group (SAUO)
IMS............. I Must Say (SAUS)
IMS............. Income Matching System
IMS............. In-Core Monitoring System [*Nuclear energy*] (NRCH)
IMS............. Incurred in Military Service [*Medicine*] (MAE)
IMS............. Independent Milk Supplies, Ltd. (SAUO)
IMS............. Index Management System (PDAA)
IMS............. Indianapolis Motor Speedway [*Auto racing venue*]
IMS............. Indian Medical Service [*British*]
IMS............. Indirect Measuring System
IMS............. Individualized Mathematics System [*Education*]
IMS............. Individual Mobility System (SAUO)
IMS............. Inductive Magnetic Saturation [*Electronic sensors*]
IMS............. Industrial Management Service Group (SAUO)
IMS............. Industrial Management Society (EA)
IMS............. Industrial Management System (SAUS)
IMS............. Industrial Manpower Section (SAUS)
IMS............. Industrial Mathematical Society (SAUO)
IMS............. Industrial Mathematics Society (EA)
IMS............. Industrial Measurement Systems/ Institute of Manpower Studies [*British*]
IMS............. Industrial Medical Service (SAUO)
IMS............. Industrial Medicine and Surgery (journ.) (SAUS)
IMS............. Industrial Methylated Spirit
IMS............. Industrial Modular System (SAUS)
IMS............. Industry Marketing Segment (SAUS)
IMS............. Inertial Measuring Set [*or System*] (NVT)
IMS............. Infertile Male Syndrome (MELL)
IMS............. In-Flight Management System
IMS............. Information Maintenance System (SAUS)
IMS............. Information Management Specialists, Inc. [*Denver, CO*] [*Information service or system*] (IID)
IMS............. Information Management Staff [*Environmental Protection Agency*] (GFGA)
IMS............. Information Management System [*Communications term*] (DCT)
IMS............. Information Management System [*IBM Corp.*] [*Computer science*]
IMS............. Information Marketing Segment (SAUS)
IMS............. Infrared Measuring System
IMS............. Initial Measurement System [*Nuclear missiles*]
IMS............. Ink Management System (SAUS)
IMS............. In-Mold Surfacing [*Plastics technology*]
IMS............. Inshore Minesweeper [*Navy*] [*British*]
IMS............. Inspector of Medical Services (SAUO)
IMS............. Installation Measurement System (SAUS)
IMS............. Instant Mobility System [*Automotive tires*]
IMS............. Institute for Mathematical Statistics (SAUS)
IMS............. Institute for Mesoamerican Studies [*State University of New York, Albany*] [*Research center*] (RCD)

IMS .... [*The*] Institute of Management Sciences
IMS .... Institute of Management Services [*British*]
IMS .... Institute of Management Specialists [*Royal Leamington Spa, Warwickshire, England*] (EAIO)
IMS .... Institute of Manpower Studies [*Department of Employment*] [*British*]
IMS .... Institute of Marine Science [*University of Alaska*] [*Research center*]
IMS .... Institute of Materials Science (KSC)
IMS .... Institute of Mathematical Sciences (SAUS)
IMS .... Institute of Mathematical Statistics (EA)
IMS .... Institute of Mental Subnormality [*British*]
IMS .... Institute of Mine Sweepers (SAUO)
IMS .... Institute of Museum Services [*National Foundation of the Arts and the Humanities*] (GRD)
IMS .... Institute on Man and Science [*Formerly, Council on World Tensions*]
IMS .... Institutional Management Support (SAUO)
IMS .... Instructional Management System (IEEE)
IMS .... Instructional Management Systems
IMS .... Instrumentation and Measurement Society (SAUO)
IMS .... Instrumented Measuring System
IMS .... Insulated Metal Substrate [*Automotive emissions control*]
IMS .... Integrated Maintenance Schedule
IMS .... Integrated Maintenance System
IMS .... Integrated Management System (SAUO)
IMS .... Integrated Manufacturing System (MHDI)
IMS .... Integrated Mapping System
IMS .... Integrated Master Schedule [*Business term*] (RDA)
IMS .... Integrated Measurement System (ACAE)
IMS .... Integrated Mechanical System (SAUS)
IMS .... Integrated Media Service (SAUO)
IMS .... Integrated Medical Services
IMS .... Integrated Meteorological System [*Army*] (IEEE)
IMS .... Integrated Microcomputer Systems, Inc.
IMS .... Integrated Mission System (SAUS)
IMS .... Integrated Multiplexing System (SAUS)
IMS .... Integrated Multiplex System (SAUS)
IMS .... Intelligent Manufacturing Systems [*Japan*] [*Agreement for conducting cooperative global research*]
IMS .... Intensive Manpower Services (OICC)
IMS .... Interactive data integration and Management System (SAUS)
IMS .... Interactive Market Systems [*New York, NY*] [*Information service or system*] (IID)
IMS .... Interactive Media Systems [*Information service or system*] (IID)
IMS .... InterCapital Ins Muni Sec [*NYSE symbol*] (TTSB)
IMS .... InterCapital Insured Municipal Securities [*NYSE symbol*] (SAG)
IMS .... Interceptor Missile (IAA)
IMS .... Interceptor Missile Subsystem (ACAE)
IMS .... Interceptor Mission Sheet (SAA)
IMS .... Intercontinental Medical Statistics (SAUS)
IMS .... Intercontinental Medical Statistics Ltd. (SAUO)
IMS .... Interdivisional Manufacturing Standard (SAUS)
IMS .... Interim Meteorological Satellite
IMS .... Intermagnetic Shield (SAUS)
IMS .... Intermediate Maintenance Squadron (MCD)
IMS .... Intermediate Maintenance Standards (VLIE)
IMS .... Intermediate Map Scale (SAUS)
IMS .... Intermediate Multiprocessing System (SAUS)
IMS .... Intermembrane Space [*Biochemistry*]
IMS .... Inter-Message Separation [*Communications*]
IMS .... Intermodal Management System [*VDOT*] (TAG)
IMS .... Internal Management System [*Military*] (AFIT)
IMS .... Internal Measurement System
IMS .... International Magnetosphere Study (SAUO)
IMS .... International Magnetospheric Studies (or Study) (SAUS)
IMS .... International Magnetospheric Study [*1976-78*] [*National Science Foundation*]
IMS .... International Maledicta Society (EA)
IMS .... International Male Studio (SAUO)
IMS .... International Management Services, Inc. [*Framingham, MA*] [*Information service or system*] (IID)
IMS .... International Management System (SAUO)
IMS .... International Management System Corp. (SAUO)
IMS .... International Marine Science Newsletter (journ.) (SAUS)
IMS .... International Marketing Services
IMS .... International Marketing Services Ltd. (SAUO)
IMS .... International Market Search Report (JAGO)
IMS .... International Measurement System [*Nautical term*] (NTA)
IMS .... International Medication Systems [*Pharmacology*] (DAVI)
IMS .... International Meditation Society
IMS .... International Metallographic Society (EA)
IMS .... International Meta Systems (SAUO)
IMS .... International Metric System
IMS .... International Micropatrological Society (SAUO)
IMS .... International Micro Systems (EFIS)
IMS .... International Migration Service (SAUO)
IMS .... International Military Sales Ltd. (SAUS)
IMS .... International Military Services Ltd. [*Ministry of Defence*] [*British*]
IMS .... International Military Staff [*NATO*]
IMS .... International Module System (SAUS)
IMS .... International Monitoring System [*For nuclear tests*]
IMS .... International Montessori Society
IMS .... International Mountain Association (SAUO)
IMS .... International Mountain Society (EA)
IMS .... International Moving Service Inc. (SAUO)
IMS .... International Multihull Society [*Formerly, International Hydrofoil and Multihull Society*] [*Defunct*] (EA)
IMS .... International Musical Society (SAUO)
IMS .... International Musicians Seminar (SAUO)
IMS .... International Musicological Society [*Basel, Switzerland*] (EA)
IMS .... Internet Map Server (SAUS)
IMS .... Internet Multicasting Service [*Non-profit information service*]
IMS .... Interpersonal Messaging Service (SAUS)
IMS .... Interplanetary Measurement Satellite (IAA)
IMS .... Interplanetary Mission Support
IMS .... Interplanetary Monitor Satellite (IAA)
IMS .... Interpretive Microinstruction Simulator (ACAE)
IMS .... Inter-service Incident Management Service (SAUO)
IMs .... Intranmuscular Injections (SAUS)
IMS .... Intrinsic Monomer Stress [*Physical chemistry*]
IMS .... Inventory Management and Simulator
IMS .... Inventory Management Specialist (ACAE)
IMS .... Inventory Management System (NASA)
IMS .... Inviscid Melt Spinning (EDCT)
IMS .... Ionization and Momentum Sensor
IMS .... Ion Mass Spectrometer
IMS .... Ion Mobility Spectrometry
IMS .... Ion Mobility Spectroscopy (SAUS)
IMS .... Ionospheric Measuring System (SAUO)
IMS .... Irish Mathematics Society
IMS .... Irradiance Measuring System
IMS .... Irrigation Management Strategy (SAUO)
IMS .... Island Missionary Society (EA)
IMS .... Issues Monitoring System (SAUS)
IMS .... Madison, IN [*Location identifier*] [*FAA*] (FAAL)
IMS .... St. Mary-Of-The-Woods College, Library, St. Mary-Of-The-Woods, IN [*OCLC symbol*] (OCLC)
IMSA .... Illinois Mathematics and Science Academy
IMSA .... Instrumentman Seaman Apprentice (SAUS)
IMSA .... International Management Systems Association [*Later, Internet-International Management Systems Association*] (EA)
IMSA .... International Memorialization Supply Association (NTPA)
IMSA .... International Metallic Silhouette Association (DICI)
IMSA .... International Motor Sports Association (EA)
IMSA .... International Municipal Signal Association (EA)
IMSA .... Seaman Apprentice, Instrumentman, Striker [*Navy rating*]
IMSAM .... Interceptor Missile, Surface-to-Air-Missile (MCD)
IMSAP .... International Marine Sciences Affairs Panel [*Defunct*] (USDC)
IMS Bull .... Institute of Mathematical Statistics Bulletin (journ.) (SAUS)
IMSC .... Industry Missile and Space Conference
IMSC .... Information Management Steering Committee (SAUO)
IMSC .... Integrated Measurement Sys [*NASDAQ symbol*] (TTSB)
IMSC .... Integrated Measurement Systems [*NASDAQ symbol*] (SAG)
IMSC .... International Maritime Satellite Corp. (SAUS)
IMSC .... International Military Sports Council (SAUO)
IMSC & D .... Inventory Manager Stock Control and Distribution [*Military*] (AFM)
IMSC & DS .... Inventory Manager Stock Control and Distribution System [*Military*]
IMSCO .... Initial Maritime Satellite Consortium [*Six United States and two British oil companies and tanker operators*] (PDAA)
IMSCOM .... International Military Staff Communication [*NATO*] (NATG)
IMSD .... Information Management and Services Division [*Environmental Protection Agency*] (GFGA)
IMS-DB .... IMS-Database (NITA)
IMS-DC .... IMS-Data Communications (NITA)
IMSDP .... Innovator Multiple Source Drug Product
IMSE .... Improved Mobile Subscriber Equipment (SAUS)
IMSE .... Industrial and Manufacturing Systems Engineering (SAUS)
IMSE .... Institute for Materials Science and Engineering (SAUS)
IMSE .... Integrated Mean Square Error [*Statistics*]
IMSE .... Interagency Materials Sciences Exchange
IMSE .... Intermediate Maintenance Support Equipment [*Army*]
IMSEP .... Improved Modular Scientific Experiments Package (SAUS)
IMS/ESA .... Information Management System/Enterprise Systems Architecture (SAUS)
IMSF .... Indian Marine Special Force (SAUO)
IMSF .... International Microcomputer Software, Inc. (SAUO)
IMSG .... Imperial Merchant Service Guild [*A union*] [*British*]
IMSG .... Information Management Steering Group (SAUO)
IMSG .... International Medical School Graduate (MELL)
IMS/HEW .... Institute of Museum Services-Health, Education and Welfare (SAUO)
IMS/HEW .... Institute of Museum Services-HEW (SAUS)
IMSI .... Information Management System Interface
IMSI .... International Maple Syrup Institute (EA)
IMSI .... International Microcomputer Software, Inc. [*NASDAQ symbol*] (SAG)
IMSI .... International Mobile Station Identity (SAUO)
IMSI .... International Mobile Subscriber Identity (SAUO)
IMSI .... International Mobile System Identifier (DINT)
IMSI .... Intl Microcomputer Software [*NASDAQ symbol*] (TTSB)
IMSIM .... Information Management Simulation (KSC)
IMS INC .... International Management Services, Inc. [*Franklyn, MA*] (TSSD)
IMS/INQ .... Information Management System Inquiry
IMS Journal ... International Musicological Society Journal (SAUO)
IMS Journal ... International Musicological Society Journal (journ.) (SAUS)
IMSL .... Independent Measurement Standards Laboratory (SAUO)
IMSL .... Integrated Mathematics and Statistics Library (ACAE)
IMSL .... Intermediate Seal (SAUS)
IMSL .... International Mathematical and Statistical Libraries, Inc.
IMSL .... International Mathematical Subroutine Library (SAUO)
IMSL .... International Mathematics and Statistics Library [*Marine science*] (OSRA)
IMSM .... Institute of Marketing and Sales Management [*British*] (BI)
IMSM .... International Military Staff Memorandum [*NATO*] (NATG)

IMS/METU ... Institute of Marine Sciences, Middle East Technical University (SAUO)
IMSN .... Instrumentman Seaman (SAUS)
IMSN .... Internal-Mix Spray Nozzle
IMSN .... Seaman, Instrumentman, Striker [*Navy rating*]
IMSO .... Initial Materiel Support Office [*Army*] (AABC)
IMSO .... Integrated Micro Systems Operation (SAUO)
IMSO .... International Maritime Safety Organization (SAUO)
IMSO .... International Maritime Satellite Organization (SAUO)
IMSOC .... Interceptor Missile Squadron (SAUS)
IMSOC .... Interceptor Missile Squadron Operations Center [*Air Force*]
IMSP .... Independent Manufacturer Support Program (SAUS)
IMSP .... Integrated Mass Storage Processor
IMSP .... International Magnetosphere Study Programme (SAUS)
IMSP .... International Meteorological Service Program (SAUO)
IMSP .... Internet Message Support Protocol (SAUS)
IMSR .... Improved Missile Site Radar (SAUS)
IMSR .... Institute for Marine Scientific Research (SAUO)
IMSR .... Interplanetary Mission Support Requirements
IMSR .... Isle of Man Steam Railway (SAUO)
IMSS .... In-Flight Medical Support System [*Skylab*] [*NASA*]
IMSS .... Institute for Mathematical Studies in the Social Sciences (SAUO)
IMSS .... Integrated Mission Support System (SAUS)
IMSS .... Integrated Multi-Sensor System (SAUS)
IMSS .... International Micro-Surgical Society (SAUO)
IMSS .... International Museum of Surgical Science (SAUO)
IMSS .... Item Management Statistical Series
IMSSCE .... Interceptor Missile Squadron and Supervisory Control Equipment
IMSSOC .... Institute of Manpower Studies System of Occupational Classification (SAUO)
IMSSS .... Institute for Mathematical Studies in the Social Sciences [*Stanford University*] [*Research center*] (RCD)
IMSSS .... Interceptor Missile Squadron Supervisory Station
IMS/SSC .... International Magnetospheric Study / Satellite Situation Committee [*NASA*] (PDAA)
IMST .... Institute of Marine Sciences and Technology
IMST .... Institute of Media Sciences and Techniques (SAUS)
IMST .... Insulated-Metal-Substrate-Technology (SAUS)
IMST .... International Mushroom Society for the Tropics (EAIO)
IMSTech .... Institution of Metallurgists Senior Technician (SAUO)
IMSTI .... Institute of Marine Scientific and Technological Information [*China*] [*Marine science*] (OSRA)
IMSU .... Integrated Mass-Storage Unit (SAUS)
IMSU .... Intermediate Maintenance Support Unit (SAUS)
IMSU .... International Muslim Students Union (EA)
IMSUM .... International Military Staff Summary [*NATO*] (NATG)
IMS/VS .... Information Management System/Virtual Storage (MCD)
IMSW .... Institute of Medical Social Workers [*British*] (BI)
IMSWE .... Investigations of Marine Shallow Water Ecosystems (NOAA)
IMSWEP .... Investigations of Marine Shallow-Water Ecosystems Program [*Smithsonian Institution*] (GFGA)
IMS-WG .... Working Group on Intelligent Manufacturing Systems (SAUO)
IMSWM .... IMS Working Memorandum (SAUS)
IMSWM .... International Military Staff Working Memorandum [*NATO*] (NATG)
IMT .... Idaho Motor Tariff Bureau, Boise ID [*STAC*]
IMT .... Image Management Terminal (SAUS)
IMT .... Immediate
IMT .... Immediately (FOTI)
IMT .... Immediate Money Transfer (DCTA)
IMT .... Immersion Testing (SAUS)
IMT .... Impulse-Modulated Telemetering (SAUS)
IMT .... Impulse Modulated Telemetry (SAUS)
IMT .... Impulse-Modulated Telemetry (IAA)
IMT .... Independent Model Triangulation (PDAA)
IMT .... Individual Movement Technique [*Military*] (INF)
IMT .... Induced Muscular Tension [*Physiology*]
IMT .... Industrial & Materials Technologies (ACII)
IMT .... Industrial Management (journ.) (SAUS)
IMT .... Industrial Materials Technologist (SAUS)
IMT .... Industrial Materials Technology (SAUS)
IMT .... Infantry Military Training (SAUS)
IMT .... Inflammatory Myofibroblastic Tumor [*Medicine*] (PALA)
IMT .... Inflight Maintenance Technician (SAUS)
IMT .... Information and Manufacturing Technologies Division [*British*]
IMT .... Information Management Team (SAUO)
IMT .... Information Management Technologies (SAUO)
IMT .... Insert Mounting Technology (SAUS)
IMT .... Inspector of Mechanized Troops (SAUS)
IMT .... Inspiratory Muscle Training [*Medicine*] (DMAA)
IMT .... Institute of Metal and Technology (SAUS)
IMT .... Institute of Metallurgical Technicians (SAUO)
IMT .... Institute of Municipal Transport [*British*] (DBA)
IMT .... Institute of the Motor Trade (SAUS)
IMT .... Institutional Maintenance Trainer (SAUS)
IMT .... Integrated Management Team (SAUO)
IMT .... Integrated Microimage Terminal [*Kodak*] (NITA)
IMT .... Intelligent Microfilm Terminal (SAUS)
IMT .... Intelligent Microimage Retrieval Terminal (SAUS)
IMT .... Intelligent Microimage Terminal [*Kodak*]
IMT .... Interactive Multimedia Terminal (SAUS)
IMT .... InterCapital Ins Muni Tr [*NYSE symbol*] (TTSB)
IMT .... InterCapital Insured Municipal Trust [*NYSE symbol*] (SAG)
IMT .... Intermachine Trunk [*Telecommunications*] (TEL)
IMT .... Intermediate Maintenance Trainer [*Army*]
IMT .... Intermediate Tape [*Telecommunications*] (TEL)
IMT .... International Markatech [*Vancouver Stock Exchange symbol*]
IMT .... International Military Trainer (SAUS)
IMT .... International Military Tribunal [*Post-World War II*]
IMT .... International Mobile Telecommunications (SAUO)
IMT .... International Mobile Telephony (SAUO)
IMT .... Internet Media Type (SAUS)
IMT .... Intestinal Mutagenicity Test [*Clinical chemistry*]
IMT .... Ion Microtomography [*High-resolution imaging technique*]
IMT .... Iron Mountain [*Michigan*] [*Airport symbol*] (OAG)
IMT .... Iron Mountain/Kingsford, MI [*Location identifier*] [*FAA*] (FAAL)
IMT .... Morton Grove Public Library, Morton Grove, IL [*OCLC symbol*] (OCLC)
IMT-2000 ...... International Mobile Telecommunications for the Year 2000
IMTA .... Indiana Motor Truck Association (SAUO)
IMTA .... Institut de la Medecine du Travail et des Ambiances [*Institute of Occupational and Environmental Health*] [*Canada*]
IMTA .... Institute of Municipal Treasurers and Accountants [*Later, CIPFA*] [*British*]
IMTA .... Intensive Military Training Area (DA)
IMTA .... International Map Trade Association (NTPA)
IMTA .... International Marine Transit Association (EA)
IMTA .... International Marine Transport Association (SAUO)
IMTA .... International Maritime Transport Academy (SAUO)
IMTA .... International Mass Transit Association (EA)
IMTA .... International Mobile Telecommunications Association (CGWS)
IMTAC .... Information Management Technology [*NASDAQ symbol*] (SAG)
IMTAL .... International Museum Theater Alliance (NTPA)
IMTB .... Isle Of Man Tourist Board (DCTA)
IMTC .... Imtec, Inc. [*NASDAQ symbol*] (NQ)
IMTC .... Infantry Moving Target Carrier [*Army*]
IMTC .... Instrumentation/Measurement Technology Conference (SAUS)
IMTC .... International Multimedia Teleconferencing Consortium
IMtca .... Mount Carmel Public Library, Mt. Carmel, IL [*Library symbol*] [*Library of Congress*] (LCLS)
IMtcaSD .... Mount Carmel Community Unit School District No. 348, Mt. Carmel, IL [*Library symbol*] [*Library of Congress*] (LCLS)
IMTD .... Inspector of the Military Training Directorate (SAUS)
IMTD .... Inspectors of the Military Training Directorate (SAUO)
IMTD .... Institute of Master Tutors of Driving [*British*] (BI)
IMTD .... Intake Manifold Temperature Differential [*Automotive engineering*]
IMTE .... Institut de la Medecine du Travail et de l'Environnement [*Institute of Occupational and Environmental Health*] [*Canada*]
IMTE .... International Machine Tool Exhibition (SAUO)
IMTE .... International Military Tribunal for Europe [*Post-World War II*]
Imtec .... Imtec, Inc. [*Associated Press*] (SAG)
IMTEC .... Information Management and Technology (CIST)
IMTEC .... Institute of Marine and Terrestrial Ecology [*Research center*] (RCD)
IMTEC .... International Manpower Training for Educational Change (SAUO)
IMTEC .... International Marine Trades Exhibit and Convention [*National Marine Manufacturers Association*]
IMTEC .... International Movements toward Educational Change [*Later, IMTEC-The International Learning Cooperative*] (EAIO)
IM Tech .... Institute of Metallurgists Technician (SAUS)
IMTED .... Information Management and Technology Division (AAGC)
IMTEL .... Institute for Microwave Technique & Electronics (SAUO)
IMTF .... Improved Materials Test Facility (SAUO)
IMTFC .... International Movement for Therapeutic Free Choice [*France*] (EAIO)
IMTFE .... International Military Tribunal for the Far East (SAUO)
IMTFJ .... International Military Tribunal for Japan [*Post-World War II*]
IMTG .... Internationale Moor und Torf-Gesellschaft [*International Peat Society - IPS*] (EAIO)
IMTI .... International Mirtone, Inc. (SAUS)
IMTI .... International Mirtone, Incorporated (SAUO)
IMTK .... Information Management Technologies Corp. (SAUS)
IMTK .... Information Management Technology [*NASDAQ symbol*] (SAG)
IMTKA .... Information Mgmt Tech'A' [*NASDAQ symbol*] (TTSB)
IMTKW .... Information Mgmt Tech Wrrt'A' [*NASDAQ symbol*] (TTSB)
IMTL .... Integrated Manufacturing Technologies Laboratory (SAUO)
IMTLYM .... Immature Lymphocytes [*Hematology*] (DAVI)
IMTN .... Iron Mountain [*NASDAQ symbol*] (TTSB)
IMTN .... Iron Mountain, Inc. [*NASDAQ symbol*] (SAG)
IMTNE .... International Meteorological Teletype Network Europe (NATG)
IMto .... Mount Olive Public Library, Mount Olive, IL [*Library symbol*] [*Library of Congress*] (LCLS)
IMtoMCD .... Macoupin Community, District 5, Mount Olive, IL [*Library symbol*] [*Library of Congress*] (LCLS)
IMTP .... Industrial Mobilization Training Program
IMTP .... Injection-Molded Thermoplastic [*Materials science*]
IMTP .... Integrated Maintenance Test Plan
IMTP .... International Musa Testing Program [*United Nations*] (ECON)
IMTP .... Itim Mizrah News Agency. Teleprinter Service (BJA)
IMTR .... International Musculoskeletal Tumor Registry (SAUO)
IMTRAN .... Implicit Transport (PDAA)
IMTRO .... Integrated Maintenance Test Requirement Outline
IMTS .... Improved Mobile Telephone Service [*Telecommunications*]
IMTS .... Improved Mobile Telephone System (SAUS)
IMTS .... Improved Moving Target Simulator (SAUS)
IMTS .... Individualized Manpower Training System (OICC)
IMTS .... Intelligent Multi-Mode Transit System [*Public transportation*]
IMTS .... Interactive Modular Training System (SAUS)
IMTS .... International Machine Tool Show (ITD)
IMT System ... Impulse-Modulated Telemetering System (SAUS)
IMTV .... Interactive Multimedia Television (SAUO)
IMtv .... Mount Vernon Public Library, Mt. Vernon, IL [*Library symbol*] [*Library of Congress*] (LCLS)

IMtvSD......... Summersville School District 79, Mount Vernon, IL [*Library symbol*] [*Library of Congress*] (LCLS)
IMTWC......... Information Management Technology [*NASDAQ symbol*] (SAG)
IMTX.......... Ag Processing [*Private rail car owner code*]
IMTX.......... Interactive Media Technologies, Inc. (NQ)
IMU.......... Immudyne, Inc. [*Vancouver Stock Exchange symbol*]
IMU.......... Impedance Matching Unit (MCD)
IMU.......... Income Maintenance Unit [*Work Incentive Program*] [*Department of Labor*]
IMU.......... Increment Memory Unit
IMU.......... Index of Medical Underservice (DMAA)
IMU.......... Inertial Measurement Unit
IMU.......... Inertial Measuring Unit (SAUS)
IMU.......... Information Management Unit (NITA)
IMU.......... Information Message Unit (SAUS)
IMU.......... Instruction Memory Unit
IMU.......... Interference Mockup (IAA)
imu.......... Internal Measurement Unit (NAKS)
IMU.......... Internal Measurement Unit (NASA)
IMU.......... Internationale Metall Union [*International Metal Union*] (EA)
IMU.......... International Mailers Union [*Later, International Typographical Union*] (EA)
IMU.......... International Maritime Union (SAUO)
IMU.......... International Mathematical Union [*See also UMI*] [*ICSU*] [*Helsinki, Finland*] (EAIO)
IMU.......... International Metal Union (SAUO)
IMU.......... International Milliunit
ImU.......... International Milliunit(s) [*Medicine*] (EDAA)
IMU.......... Irish Missionary Union (EAIO)
IMU.......... Islamic Movement of Uzbekistan
IMU.......... Muncie Public Library, Muncie, IN [*OCLC symbol*] (OCLC)
IMUA.......... Inland Marine Underwriters Association [*New York, NY*] (EA)
IMUA.......... International Management University of Asia (SAUO)
IMUA.......... Interservice Materiel Utilization Agency [*Military*] (AABC)
Imucor.......... Immucor, Inc. [*Associated Press*] (SAG)
IMUDS.......... Illustration Makeup Data Sheet
IMUGSE.......... Inertial Measurement Unit Ground Support Equipment (SAA)
IMUL.......... ImmuLogic Pharmaceutical [*NASDAQ symbol*] (TTSB)
IMUL.......... ImmuLogic Pharmaceutical Corp. [*NASDAQ symbol*] (SPSG)
IMUL.......... Integer Multiply [*Computer science*]
IMulgSD.......... Mulberry Grove Community Unit, School District 1, Mulberry Grove, IL [*Library symbol*] [*Library of Congress*] (LCLS)
ImuLog.......... ImmuLogic Pharmaceutical Corp. [*Associated Press*] (SAG)
IMunE.......... Institution of Municipal Engineers [*British*]
Imunex.......... Immunex Corp. [*Associated Press*] (SAG)
Imungn.......... Immuncogen, Inc. [*Associated Press*] (SAG)
Imunmd.......... Immunomedics, Inc. [*Associated Press*] (SAG)
ImunRsp.......... Immune Response Corp. [*Associated Press*] (SAG)
IMunS.......... Saint Mary of the Lake Seminary, Mundelein, IL [*Library symbol*] [*Library of Congress*] (LCLS)
IMUR.......... Interactive Multiple Regression System (MCD)
IMUS.......... Internal Measuring Unit System (MCD)
IMUS.......... Inventario Musical [*Database*] [*Ministerio de Cultura*] [*Spanish*] [*Information service or system*] (CRD)
IMUT.......... Imutec Corp. [*NASDAQ symbol*] (SAG)
Imutec.......... Imutec Corp. [*Associated Press*] (SAG)
IMUTF.......... IMUTEC Corp. [*NASDAQ symbol*] (TTSB)
IMUX.......... Intelligent Multiplexer [*Telecommunications*] (ACRL)
IMUX.......... Inverse Multiplexer (SAUS)
IMV.......... Cornell College, Mount Vernon, IA [*OCLC symbol*] (OCLC)
IMV.......... Improve (SAUS)
IMV.......... Industrija Motornih Vozil [*Yugoslav automaker*]
IMV.......... Infantry Mobility Vehicles (SAUS)
IMV.......... Inferior Mesenteric Vein [*Anatomy*]
IMV.......... Inoue-Melnick Virus (SAUS)
IMV.......... Instruction Memory Unit [*Computer science*] (ELAL)
IMV.......... Instrumented Measurement Vehicle (ACAE)
IMV.......... Intermittent Mandatory Ventilation [*Respiratory therapy*] [*Medicine*]
IMV.......... Intermittent Mechanical Ventilation [*Respiratory therapy*] [*Medicine*] (DAVI)
IMV.......... Inter-Module Ventilation (SAUS)
IMV.......... Internal Motor Vehicle [*Type of tugboat*] (DS)
IMV.......... Internationaler Metzgermeisterverband [*International Federation of Meat Traders' Associations*] (EAIO)
IMV.......... Internationaler Milchwirtschaftverband [*International Dairy Federation*]
IMV.......... International Meteorological Vocabulary (SAUS)
IMV.......... International Movie Group, Inc. [*Vancouver Stock Exchange symbol*]
IMV.......... Intracellular Mature Virus
IMV.......... Intravehicular Ventilation (SAUS)
IMV.......... Isophosphamide, Methotrexate, and Vincristine [*Medicine*] (DMAA)
IMVA.......... International Medical Volunteers Association (SAUO)
IMVCi.......... Indole, Methyl-Red, Voges-Proskauer, Citrate Test [*Bacteriology*]
IMVDS.......... Item Management Vehicle Data System (SAUO)
IM/VE.......... Information Management / Virtual Environment (HGAA)
IMVEC.......... International Military Vehicle Engineering Consultants (SAUS)
IMVH.......... Indian Military Veterinary Hospital [*British military*] (DMA)
IMVHO.......... In My Very Humble Opinion [*Computer hacker terminology*]
IMVIC.......... Indole, Methyl Red, Voges-Proskauer and Citrate Test (SAUS)
IMViC.......... Indole, Methyl Red, Voges-Proskauer, Citrate [*Reaction and test*] [*Biochemistry*] (DAVI)
IMViC.......... Indol, Methyl Red, Voges-Proskauer, Citrate Reactions [*Bacteriology*] [*Medicine*] (BABM)
IMVIC.......... International Motor Vehicle Inspection Committee [*Belgium*] (EAIO)
IMVP.......... Idiopathic Mitral Valve Prolapse [*Medicine*] (EDAA)
IMVP.......... Ifostamide, Methotrexate, VePesid (CDI)
IMVP.......... International Motor Vehicle Program [*MIT*]
IMVP-16.......... Isophosphamide, Methotrexate, Vesposide [*Antineoplastic drug regimen*] (DAVI)
IMVS.......... Indian Mobile Veterinary Stores [*British military*] (DMA)
IMVTS.......... Industrial Model Vocational Training Systems (EDAC)
IMW.......... In My World [*Internet dialog*]
IMW.......... Institute of Masters of Wine (BARN)
IMW.......... Instrument Man, Watch (SAUS)
IMW.......... Instrumentman (Watch and Clock Repairman) [*U.S. Navy enlisted rating*] (AUER)
IMW.......... Intelligent Machining Workstation (TIMI)
IMW.......... Intermediate Molecular Weight (SAUS)
IMW.......... International Map of the World
IMW.......... International Musselwatch Programme (SAUS)
IMW.......... Knox County Public Library, Vincennes, IN [*OCLC symbol*] (OCLC)
IMWA.......... International Mine Water Association [*Madrid, Spain*] (EAIO)
IMWA.......... International Ministers' and Widows' Association (EA)
IMWIC.......... International Maize and Wheat Improvement Centre (SAUO)
IMWIR.......... Interim Mixed Waste Inventory Report (SAUS)
IMWoodT.......... Institute of Machine Woodworking Technology [*British*] (BI)
IMWRP.......... Item Manager Wholesale Requisitions Process (SAUO)
IMWXPRT.......... Imitation Wax Prints (SAUS)
IMX.......... Indiana Institute of Technology, McMillen Library, Fort Wayne, IN [*OCLC symbol*] (OCLC)
IMX.......... Inquiry Message Exchange
IMX.......... Instruction Memory Exchange (SAUS)
IMX.......... Island Mining [*Vancouver Stock Exchange symbol*]
IMX.......... Zimex Aviation Ltd. [*Switzerland*] [*ICAO designator*] (FAAC)
IMXP.......... Introspective Meta-Explanation Pattern (SAUS)
IMY.......... Groupo Imsa Sa de CV [*NYSE symbol*] (SAG)
IMY.......... Ida-May Resources Ltd. [*Vancouver Stock Exchange symbol*]
IMY.......... International Mahogany Corp. [*Toronto Stock Exchange symbol*] [*Vancouver Stock Exchange symbol*]
IMY.......... Michigan City Public Library, Michigan City, IN [*OCLC symbol*] (OCLC)
IMYCW.......... International Movement of Young Christian Workers (SAUO)
Im Yem.......... Imamate of Yemen (SAUO)
IMZ.......... Binghamton, NY [*Location identifier*] [*FAA*] (FAAL)
IMZ.......... Internationales Musikzentrum [*International Music Center*] [*Vienna, Austria*] (EAIO)
IM/ZEUS.......... Information Management / Zero Effort User System (HGAA)
IN.......... East Hampton Air [*ICAO designator*] (AD)
IN.......... Ice (Deposition) Nuclei [*Atmospheric science*]
IN.......... Ice Nuclei (SAUS)
IN.......... Icterus Neonatorum [*Medicine*]
IN.......... Idaho Nuclear (MCD)
IN.......... Identification Number (SAUS)
IN.......... Ilioinguinal Nerve [*Anatomy*]
IN.......... Illinois Northern Railway [*AAR code*]
IN.......... Impetigo Neonatorum [*Medicine*] (DMAA)
IN.......... Improvement Notice (HEAS)
IN.......... Inch (EY)
In.......... Inch (SAUS)
in.......... Inch
in.......... Inches (VRA)
In.......... Income
in.......... Increase (ELAL)
IN.......... Index Number (ELAL)
IN.......... India [*ANSI two-letter standard code*] (CNC)
IN.......... Indian (WDAA)
IN.......... Indiana [*Postal code*]
IN.......... Indiana Northeastern Railroad [*Federal Railroad Administration identification code*]
In.......... Indiana State Library, Indianapolis, IN [*Library symbol*] [*Library of Congress*] (LCLS)
IN.......... Indian Navy
In.......... Indian Reports [*A publication*] (DLA)
In.......... Indium [*Chemical element*]
IN.......... Individual Network (SAUO)
IN.......... Inductor (SAUS)
IN.......... Industrial Nucleonics (SAUS)
IN.......... Industrial Nurse (MELL)
IN.......... Inertial (MCD)
IN.......... Inertial Navigation (IAA)
IN.......... Inertial Navigator (SAUS)
IN.......... Infant (TVEL)
IN.......... Infantry [*Army*]
IN.......... Inferonasal (SAUS)
IN.......... Inflammatory Response (SAUS)
IN.......... Information Network (ELAL)
IN.......... Information Systems Directorate [*Kennedy Space Center*] [*NASA*] (NASA)
IN.......... Infundibular Nucleus (DB)
IN.......... Ingress Node (ACRL)
IN.......... Initial Dose [*Medicine*]
IN.......... Inlet [*Maps and charts*]
in.......... Input (IDOE)
IN.......... Input (MDG)
IN.......... INS Insurance [*Vancouver Stock Exchange symbol*]
IN.......... Insoluble Nitrogen (SAUS)
IN.......... Inspection
IN.......... Institute of Navigation [*US and British*]
IN.......... Institute of Neurobiology (SAUS)
IN.......... Institution [*Online database field identifier*]
In.......... Instructor [*Navy*] [*British*]

IN.......... Instructor Navigator (AFM)
IN.......... Instrumentation Notice (AAG)
IN.......... Instrument Note
IN.......... Insulated [*Shipping*] (DCTA)
In.......... Insulin
IN.......... Insulin Neuritis [*Medicine*] (MELL)
IN.......... Insurance
IN.......... Intake
IN.......... Integon Corp. [*NYSE symbol*] (SAG)
IN.......... Integrating Network (SAUS)
IN.......... Intelligence
IN.......... Intelligence Corps [*Army*] (RDA)
IN.......... Intelligent Network [*Telecommunications*]
IN.......... Intensity
IN.......... Interaction Notes (SAUS)
IN.......... Interactive Network
IN.......... Interception [*Football*]
I/N.......... Interchangeability Code Number (SAUS)
IN.......... Interchangeability Number (SAUS)
IN.......... Interconnecting Network (MHDI)
IN.......... Interest [*Finance, Law*] (ADA)
IN.......... Interference-to-Noise (SAUS)
IN.......... Interference-to-Noise Ratio (IEEE)
IN.......... Intermittent Noise
IN.......... Internal Node (SAUS)
IN.......... Internal Note
IN.......... International (TRID)
IN.......... International House - World Trade Center [*Later, WTC*] (EA)
IN.......... Internegative [*Photography*] (WDMC)
IN.......... Interneuron [*Neurology*] (DAVI)
IN.......... Internist (MELL)
IN.......... Interstitial Nephritis [*Medicine*] (DMAA)
IN.......... Interstitium (SAUS)
IN.......... Intertechnique
IN.......... Intraductal [*Medicine*]
IN.......... Intranasal
In.......... Inulin [*Biochemistry*] (DAVI)
IN.......... Inundic [*Soil biology*] (QSUL)
IN.......... Inventors [*Pergamon-Infoline*] (NITA)
IN.......... Inventory Nonrecurring (MCD)
In.......... Inversion (QSUL)
IN.......... Investigator
IN.......... Investigator Name [*Dialog*] [*Searchable field*] (NITA)
IN.......... Irish Nationalist (ROG)
IN.......... Irritation of Nociceptors [*Medicine*] (DMAA)
IN.......... Italian Navy (NATG)
IN.......... Item Name [*Military*]
IN.......... Item Number (IAA)
IN.......... Neisler Laboratories, Inc. [*Research code symbol*]
IN.......... Office of Inspection and Enforcement Information Notice [*Nuclear energy*] (NRCH)
IN^2.......... Square Inch
IN^3.......... Cubic Inch
in3/lb.......... Cubic Inch per Pound (SAUS)
INA.......... Anderson College, Anderson, IN [*OCLC symbol*] (OCLC)
INA.......... Department of Indian and Northern Affairs Library [*UTLAS symbol*]
INA.......... Icana [*Brazil*] [*Airport symbol*] (AD)
INA.......... Ice Nucleating Activity [*Biology*] [*Physics*]
INA.......... Iinan [*Japan*] [*Seismograph station code, US Geological Survey*] (SEIS)
INA.......... Illinois Nurses Association (SAUO)
INA.......... Immigration and Nationality Act (GFGA)
INA.......... Immunonephelometric Assay [*Clinical chemistry*]
INA.......... Inaccessible [*Automotive emissions*]
INA.......... INA Corp. (SAUO)
INA.......... Inactivator (SAUS)
INA.......... Inactivator Accelerator [*Immunology*]
INA.......... Independent Newsletter Association
InA.......... Indiana Appellate Court Reports [*A publication*] (DLA)
INA.......... Indian and Northern Affairs Department [*Canada*]
INA.......... Indian National Airways
INA.......... Indian National Army [*World War II*]
INA.......... Indian Naval Aviation (SAUS)
INA.......... Individual Nonrecurrence Action (KSC)
INA.......... Industrija Nafta [*State-owned company*] [*Yugoslavia*]
INA.......... Infectious Nucleic Acid (DMAA)
INA.......... Inferior Nasal Artery [*Medicine*] (DMAA)
INA.......... Information Networking Alliance [*British*] (TELE)
INA.......... Information Networking Architecture (SAUS)
INA.......... Information Not Available (OICC)
INA.......... Innopac, Inc. [*Toronto Stock Exchange symbol*]
INA.......... Inspector Naval Aircraft (SAUS)
INA.......... Inspector of Naval Aircraft
INA.......... Institute for Anthropology [*State University of New York at Albany*] [*Research center*] (RCD)
INA.......... Institute for New Antibiotics [*Former USSR*]
INA.......... Institute of National Affairs (SAUO)
INA.......... Institute of Nautical Archaeology (EA)
INA.......... Institute of Naval Architects (SAUO)
INA.......... Institution of Naval Architects [*British*]
INA.......... Institut National de la Communication Audiovisuelle [*France*] (NITA)
INA.......... Insurance Company of North America (SAUO)
INA.......... Integrated Network Architecture
INA.......... Intelligent Network Architecture (SAUS)
INA.......... Interair Aviation Ltd. [*British*] [*ICAO designator*] (FAAC)
INA.......... International Nannoplankton Association (QUAC)
INA.......... International Nanny Association (EA)
INA.......... International Naturopathic Association [*Later, IAHHP*] (EA)
INA.......... International Neurological Association (DAVI)
INA.......... International Neurotoxicology Association
INA.......... International Newsreel and News Film Association [*Later, INANEWS*] (EAIO)
INA.......... International Newsreel Association (SAUO)
INA.......... International Noaval Atmosphere (SAUS)
INA.......... International Normal Atmosphere
INA.......... International Nurses Anonymous (EA)
INA.......... Iodonaphthyl Azide [*Organic chemistry*]
INA.......... Iowa Nurses Association (SAUO)
INA.......... Iraqi News Agency
INA.......... Irish Naturist Association, Dublin (SAUO)
INA.......... Irish News Agency (SAUO)
INA.......... Irish Northern Aid
INA.......... Iron Nickel Alloy
INA.......... Isonicotinic Acid [*Organic chemistry*]
INA.......... Israeli News Agency (SAUO)
INA.......... Israel News Agency
INA.......... Jena Nomina Anatomic a [*Also, INA*] [*Anatomy*] (DAVI)
INAA.......... Instrumental Neutron Activation Analysis
INAA.......... Irish National Association of Australasia
INAAP.......... Indiana Army Ammunition Plant (AABC)
INAB.......... [*The*] Irish National Accreditation Board (ACII)
inabi.......... inability (SAUS)
INABU.......... Imprimerie Nationale du Burundi [*Government publishing house*] [*Burundi*] (EY)
Inac.......... Inaccuracy (SAUS)
Inac.......... Inaccurate (SAUS)
INAC.......... Inacom Corp. [*NASDAQ symbol*] (SAG)
INAC.......... Inacomp Computer Centers, Inc. (SAUO)
inac.......... Inactive
InAcdC-T.......... Anderson College, Graduate School of Theology, Anderson, IN [*Library symbol*] [*Library of Congress*] (LCLS)
INACDUTRA... Inactive Duty Training [*Air Force*] (AFM)
Inacom.......... Inacom Corp. [*Associated Press*] (SAG)
InAcous.......... Industrial Acoustics Co., Inc. [*Associated Press*] (SAG)
INACP.......... Institute of Nutrition of Central America and Panama (SAUO)
INACS.......... Interstate Airways Communications Station (IAA)
INACT.......... Inactive (AABC)
INACTFLTLANT... Inactive Fleet, Atlantic Fleet (DNAB)
INACTFLTPAC... Inactive Fleet, Pacific Fleet
INACTLANT... Inactive Fleet, Atlantic Fleet
INACTNOTERM... Inactive Duty Are Not Terminated (SAUS)
INACTPAC.... Inactive Fleet, Pacific Fleet
INACTSERVCRAFAC... Inactive Service Craft Facility [*Military*] (DNAB)
INACTSHIPDET... Inactive Ship Maintenance Detachment (SAUS)
INACTSHIPFAC... Inactive Ship Maintenance Facility [*Navy*]
INACTSHIPSTORFAC... Inactive Ship Storage Facility (SAUS)
Inactv.......... Inactivate (SAUS)
INACTV.......... Inactivate [*or Inactive*] (MSA) (MSA)
Inactv.......... Inactivation (SAUS)
INAD.......... Inadequate (AFM)
INAD.......... Inadequated (SAUS)
INAD.......... Inadmissible Passenger [*Travel industry*] (TRID)
INAD.......... Inadvertent
INAD.......... Infantile Neuroaxonal Dystrophy [*Medicine*] (DMAA)
INAD.......... In No Apparent Distress [*Medicine*] (MELL)
INAD.......... Investigational New Animal Drug [*Food and Drug Administration*]
INADA.......... Investigational New Animal Drug Application
IN-ADDR.......... Inverse Addressing
INADEQUATE... Incredible Natural Abundance Double Quantum Transfer Experiment (SAUS)
INADQT.......... Inadequate (FAAC)
INADS.......... Initialization and Administration System (SAUS)
INADS.......... Initialization and Administrative System (SAUO)
INAE.......... International Newspaper Advertising Executives [*Later, INAME*] (EA)
INAEA.......... International Newspaper Advertising Executives Association (SAUO)
INAEC.......... Iloilo-Negros Air Express Company (SAUO)
INAETP.......... Indian and Native American Employment and Training Program [*Department of Labor*]
InAF.......... Indian Air Force
INAF.......... Individual Name and Address File [*IRS*]
INAF.......... International Name Authority File (SAUS)
INAFA.......... Nordic Anthropological Film Association (SAUO)
INAFBO.......... International Association for Business Organizations [*Baltimore, MD*] (EA)
INAH.......... Interstitial Nuclei of the Anterior Hypothalamus [*Brain anatomy*]
INAH.......... Isonicotinic Acid Hydrazide [*See also INH, ISONIAZID*] [*Antituberculous agent*]
INAHTA.......... International Network of Agencies for Health Technology Assessment (SAUO)
INAI.......... IntelliCorp, Inc. [*NASDAQ symbol*] (NQ)
INAI.......... Iowa Natural Areas Inventory [*Iowa State Conservation Commission*] [*Des Moines*] [*Information service or system*] (IID)
INA/IC.......... Inactive - In Commission, In Reserve [*Vessel status*] [*Navy*]
INAIIS.......... Inactive-In Service (SAUS)
INAIn.......... INA Investment Securities, Inc. [*Associated Press*] (SAG)
IN/AIN.......... Intelligent Network/Advanced Intelligent Network (DINT)
INA/IS.......... Inactive - In Service, In Reserve [*Vessel status*] [*Navy*]
InAk.......... Akron Carnegie Public Library, Akron, IN [*Library symbol*] [*Library of Congress*] (LCLS)
IN AL.......... Inter Alia [*Among Other Things*] [*Latin*] (WDAA)

InAlb .... Noble County Public Library, Albion, IN [*Library symbol*] [*Library of Congress*] (LCLS)
InAle .... Alexandria Public Library, Alexandria, IN [*Library symbol*] [*Library of Congress*] (LCLS)
InAleN .... Alexandria News, Alexandria, IN [*Library symbol*] [*Library of Congress*] (LCLS)
InAleTT .... Alexandria Times-Tribune, Alexandria, IN [*Library symbol*] [*Library of Congress*] (LCLS)
InAlGaP .... Indium Aluminum Gallium Phophide [*Organic chemistry*]
Inalwa .... International Airlift West Africa (SAUO)
INAME .... International Newspaper Advertising and Marketing Executives (EA)
Inamed .... Inamed Corp. [*Associated Press*] (SAG)
INAMI .... InfoBank Advertising and Marketing Intelligence (SAUS)
InAnd .... Anderson Carnegie Public Library, Anderson, IN [*Library symbol*] [*Library of Congress*] (LCLS)
InAndB .... Anderson Daily Bulletin, Anderson, IN [*Library symbol*] [*Library of Congress*] (LCLS)
InAndC .... Anderson College, Anderson, IN [*Library symbol*] [*Library of Congress*] (LCLS)
InAndC-T .... Anderson College, Graduate School of Theology, Anderson, IN [*Library symbol*] [*Library of Congress*] (LCLS)
IN & EA .... International Nuclear and Energy Association [*Defunct*] (EA)
InAndH .... Anderson Herald, Anderson, IN [*Library symbol*] [*Library of Congress*] (LCLS)
INA-NEWS .... International Newsreel and News Film Association (SAUO)
INANEWS .... International Newsreel Association (EAIO)
INA Newsl ... INA Newsletter. Institute of Nautical Archaeology. College Station (journ.) (SAUS)
InAng .... Carnegie Public Library, Angola, IN [*Library symbol*] [*Library of Congress*] (LCLS)
InAngT .... Tri-State University, Angola, IN [*Library symbol*] [*Library of Congress*] (LCLS)
inanim .... inanimate (SAUS)
INANIM .... Inanimative (SAUS)
InAnw .... Andrews-Dallas Township Public Library, Andrews, IN [*Library symbol*] [*Library of Congress*] (LCLS)
INAO .... Institut National des Appellations d'Origine [*Semigovernmental organization that fixes the appellations on all French wines*]
INA/OC .... Inactive - Out of Commission, In Reserve [*Vessel status*] [*Navy*]
INA/OS .... Inactive - Out of Service, In Reserve [*Vessel status*] [*Navy*]
INAP .... Infogram Network Access Protocol (SAUS)
INAP .... Integrated Neutron Activation Prediction [*Code system*]
INAP .... Intelligent Network Application Part [*Computer science*] (DINT)
INAP .... Intelligent Network Application Protocol (SAUS)
INap .... Nichols Library, Naperville, IL [*Library symbol*] [*Library of Congress*] (LCLS)
INapC .... College & Seminary Library, Inc., Naperville, IL [*Library symbol*] [*Library of Congress*] [*Obsolete*] (LCLS)
INAPEM .... National Institute for Small and Medium Enterprises (SAUO)
INAPEN .... International AIDS Prospective Epidemiology Network (EA)
INapGS .... Church of Jesus Christ of Latter-Day Saints, Genealogical Society Library, Naperville Branch, Naperville, IL [*Library symbol*] [*Library of Congress*] (LCLS)
INapN .... North Central College, Naperville, IL [*Library symbol*] [*Library of Congress*] (LCLS)
inappbl .... inapplicable (SAUS)
INapS .... Standard Oil Research Center, Naperville, IL [*Library symbol*] [*Library of Congress*] (LCLS)
InAr .... Argos Public Library, Argos, IN [*Library symbol*] [*Library of Congress*] (LCLS)
INAR .... Institute of Northen Agricultural Research (SAUS)
INAR .... Institute of Northern Agricultural Research (SAUO)
IN ARCH .... Inland Architect [*A publication*] (ROG)
INARCO .... International Artware Corp. (EFIS)
InArcT .... Tri Town Topics, Arcadia, IN [*Library symbol*] [*Library of Congress*] (LCLS)
INAROEO .... National Institute for the Removal of Obstacles and Explosive Ordnance (SAUO)
InARP .... Inverse Address Resolution Protocol [*Telecommunications*] (ACRL)
InArT .... Argos Tribune, Argos, IN [*Library symbol*] [*Library of Congress*] (LCLS)
INAS .... Indexing and Abstracting Services
InAs .... Indium Arsenide (MED)
INAS .... Industrial Naval Air Stations (NG)
INAS .... Inertial Navigation and Attack System (MCD)
INAS .... Inpatient Non-Availability Statement [*DoD*]
INAS .... Integrated Navigation/Attack System (SAUO)
INAS .... Integrated Night Attack Sensor (ACAE)
INAS .... Interbank National Authorization System
INas .... Nashville Public Library, Nashville, IL [*Library symbol*] [*Library of Congress*] (LCLS)
INASEN .... International Assembly of Non-Governmental Organizations concerned with the Environment (SAUO)
INasHS .... Nashville High School, Nashville, IL [*Library symbol*] [*Library of Congress*] (LCLS)
INAsicrz .... Istituto Nazionale Delle Assicoraziono SPA [*Associated Press*] (SAG)
INASP .... International Network for the Availability of Scientific Publications
INasSD .... Nashville Community High School District 99, Nashville, IL [*Library symbol*] [*Library of Congress*] (LCLS)
INat .... New Athens Public Library, New Athens, IL [*Library symbol*] [*Library of Congress*] (LCLS)
INATAPROBU ... International Association of Professional Bureaucrats (EA)
INatCD .... New Athens Community Consolidated District 60, New Athens, IL [*Library symbol*] [*Library of Congress*] (LCLS)
InATMARP ... Inverse ATMARP (SAUS)
INATS .... International New Age Trade Show
INATS .... Interruption of Air Traffic Service (SAUO)
INATS .... Interruption of Air Traffic Services (FAAC)
InAtt .... Attica Public Library, Attica, IN [*Library symbol*] [*Library of Congress*] (LCLS)
InAttCF .... Covington Friend, Attica, IN [*Library symbol*] [*Library of Congress*] (LCLS)
InAttFO .... Attica Friendly Oracle, Attica, IN [*Library symbol*] [*Library of Congress*] (LCLS)
InAttLT .... Attica Daily Ledger Tribune, Attica, IN [*Library symbol*] [*Library of Congress*] (LCLS)
InAub .... Eckhart Public Library, Auburn, IN [*Library symbol*] [*Library of Congress*] (LCLS)
InAubS .... Auburn Evening Star, Auburn, IN [*Library symbol*] [*Library of Congress*] (LCLS)
inaud .... inaudible (SAUS)
inaug .... inaguration (SAUS)
Inaug .... Inaugural (SAUS)
INAUG .... Inaugurated (ADA)
inaug diss ... inaugural dissertation (SAUS)
InAur .... Aurora Public Library, Aurora, IN [*Library symbol*] [*Library of Congress*] (LCLS)
IN AUR .... In Auri [*To the Ear*] [*Pharmacy*]
InAurHi .... Hillforest Historical Foundation, Inc., Aurora, IN [*Library symbol*] [*Library of Congress*] (LCLS)
InAusN .... Austin-Crothersville News, Austin, IN [*Library symbol*] [*Library of Congress*] (LCLS)
INAV .... Integrated Navigation (TIMI)
INAW .... Institute of the Northamerican West (EA)
INAZ .... Intalco Aluminum [*Federal Railroad Administration identification code*]
INAZ .... Interference Accommodation Zone [*Geology*]
INB .... Bartholomew County Library, Columbus, IN [*OCLC symbol*] (OCLC)
InB .... Bedford Public Library, Bedford, IN [*Library symbol*] [*Library of Congress*] (LCLS)
INB .... Community Independent Bank [*AMEX symbol*] (SG)
IN B .... In Bonis [*In the Goods Of*] [*Latin*] (ADA)
INB .... In Bono [*In Good Order*]
INB .... Independence [*Belize*] [*Airport symbol*] (OAG)
INB .... Indiana Motor Rate and Tariff Bureau Inc., Indianapolis IN [*STAC*]
INB .... Industrial National Corporation (SAUO)
INB .... Instalbud [*Poland*] [*ICAO designator*] (FAAC)
INB .... Install Busy [*Telecommunications*] (DINT)
INB .... Interbev Packaging Corp. [*Vancouver Stock Exchange symbol*]
INB .... International Sodium Breeder Reactor Construction Co. (SAUO)
INB .... Internuclear Bridging (DMAA)
INB .... Intl Thunderbird Gaming [*Exchange symbol*] (TTSB)
INB .... Ischemic Necrosis of Bone [*Medicine*] (EDAA)
INb .... Northbrook Public Library, Northbrook, IL [*Library symbol*] [*Library of Congress*] (LCLS)
INB .... Oakland, CA [*Location identifier*] [*FAA*] (FAAL)
INBA .... InBancshares [*NASDAQ symbol*] (COMM)
INBA .... International Nubian Breeders Association (EA)
INBACS .... Infantry Battalion as a Combat System [*Study*] (MCD)
InBaHT .... Batesville Herald Tribune, Batesville, IN [*Library symbol*] [*Library of Congress*] (LCLS)
in bal .... in ballast (SAUS)
INBAP .... International Network for the Improvement of Banana and Plantain (SAUO)
INbAS .... Allstate Insurance, Inc., Corporate Library, Northbrook, IL [*Library symbol*] [*Library of Congress*] (LCLS)
INBATIM .... Integrated Battlefield Interactive Model (SAUO)
INBC .... InnoPet Brands Corp. [*NASDAQ symbol*] (SAG)
INBC .... Interlibrary Network of Baltimore County [*Library network*]
INBC .... International Nestle Boycott Committee (SAUO)
InBCR .... Lawrence County Recorder's Office, Bedford, IN [*Library symbol*] [*Library of Congress*] (LCLS)
INbD .... Dart & Kraft, Inc., Northbrook, IL [*Library symbol*] [*Library of Congress*] (LCLS)
INBD .... Inboard (KSC)
INBD .... Inbound
InBer .... Berne Public Library, Berne, IN [*Library symbol*] [*Library of Congress*] (LCLS)
INBH .... Brokaw Hospital Medical Center, Normal, IL [*Library symbol*] [*Library of Congress*] (LCLS)
INBI .... Industrial Bancorp [*NASDAQ symbol*] (TTSB)
INBI .... Industrial Bancorp, Inc. [*NASDAQ symbol*] (SAG)
InBiKN .... Knox County Daily News, Bicknell, IN [*Library symbol*] [*Library of Congress*] (LCLS)
INBio .... Biodiversity Institute [*Center established to inventory wildlife*] (PS)
INBIT .... Input BIT [*Binary Digit*] [*Computer science*] (NASA)
INBK .... Indiana Bancshares, Inc. (SAUO)
InBl .... Bloomfield Public Library, Bloomfield, IN [*Library symbol*] [*Library of Congress*] (LCLS)
InBlCR .... Greene County Recorder's Office, Bloomfield, IN [*Library symbol*] [*Library of Congress*] (LCLS)
InBLHi .... Lawrence County Historical Society, Bedford, IN [*Library symbol*] [*Library of Congress*] (LCLS)
InBlo .... Monroe County Public Library, Bloomington, IN [*Library symbol*] [*Library of Congress*] (LCLS)
InBloHT .... Bloomington Herald-Telephone, Bloomington, IN [*Library symbol*] [*Library of Congress*] (LCLS)
InBloKi .... Alfred C. Kinsey Institute for Sex Research, Bloomington, IN [*Library symbol*] [*Library of Congress*] (LCLS)
InBlu .... Bluffton-Wells County Public Library, Bluffton, IN [*Library symbol*] [*Library of Congress*] (LCLS)

InBlWN .... Bloomfield Evening World and News, Bloomfield, IN [*Library symbol*] [*Library of Congress*] (LCLS)
INBNX .... IDS Bond Cl.A [*Mutual fund ticker symbol*] (SG)
InBoM .... Borden Museum, Borden, IN [*Library symbol*] [*Library of Congress*] [*Obsolete*] (LCLS)
InBoo .... Boonville Warrick County Public Library, Boonville, IN [*Library symbol*] [*Library of Congress*] (LCLS)
InBooE .... Warrick Enquirer, Boonville, IN [*Library symbol*] [*Library of Congress*] (LCLS)
InBooS .... Boonville Standard, Boonville, IN [*Library symbol*] [*Library of Congress*] (LCLS)
InBosE .... Boswell Enterprise, Boswell, IN [*Library symbol*] [*Library of Congress*] (LCLS)
InBou .... Bourbon Public Library, Bourbon, IN [*Library symbol*] [*Library of Congress*] (LCLS)
In-BPH .... Indiana State Library, Blind and Physically Handicapped Division, Indianapolis, IN [*Library symbol*] [*Library of Congress*] (LCLS)
INBR .... Inbrand Corp. [*NASDAQ symbol*] (SAG)
inbr .... Inbreeding [*Medicine*] (EDAA)
InBra .... Brazil Public Library, Brazil, IN [*Library symbol*] [*Library of Congress*] (LCLS)
InBraCHi ...... Clay County Historical Society, Brazil, IN [*Library symbol*] [*Library of Congress*] (LCLS)
Inbrand .... Inbrand Corp. [*Associated Press*] (SAG)
InBraT .... Brazil Times, Brazil, IN [*Library symbol*] [*Library of Congress*] (LCLS)
InBrb .... Brownsburg Public Library, Brownsburg, IN [*Library symbol*] [*Library of Congress*] (LCLS)
InBrbG .... Brownsburg Guide, Brownsburg, IN [*Library symbol*] [*Library of Congress*] (LCLS)
INBRD .... Inboard (ADA)
InBre .... W. E. Walter Memorial Library (Bremen Public Library), Bremen, IN [*Library symbol*] [*Library of Congress*] (LCLS)
InBreE .... Bremen Enquirer, Bremen, IN [*Library symbol*] [*Library of Congress*] (LCLS)
InBri .... Bristol-Washington Township Public Library (Bristol Public Library), Bristol, IN [*Library symbol*] [*Library of Congress*] (LCLS)
InBriEHi ...... Elkhart County Historical Society, Bristol, IN [*Library symbol*] [*Library of Congress*] (LCLS)
InBrkvA .... Brookville American, Brookville, IN [*Library symbol*] [*Library of Congress*] (LCLS)
InBrkvCR ...... Franklin County Recorder's Office, Brookville, IN [*Library symbol*] [*Library of Congress*] (LCLS)
InBrkvD .... Brookville Democrat, Brookville, IN [*Library symbol*] [*Library of Congress*] (LCLS)
InBro .... Brook-Iroquois Public Library, Brook, IN [*Library symbol*] [*Library of Congress*] (LCLS)
InBroA .... George Ade Hazeldon Home, Brook, IN [*Library symbol*] [*Library of Congress*] (LCLS)
InBrt .... Brownstown Public Library, Brownstown, IN [*Library symbol*] [*Library of Congress*] (LCLS)
InBrtB .... Brownstown Banner, Brownstown, IN [*Library symbol*] [*Library of Congress*] (LCLS)
InBrtHi .... Jackson County Historical Society, Brownstown, IN [*Library symbol*] [*Library of Congress*] (LCLS)
INBS .... Iowa National Bankshares Corp. (SAUO)
INBSV .... Interim Narrow-Band Secure Voice (NVT)
InBTM .... Bedford Times-Mail, Bedford, IN [*Library symbol*] [*Library of Congress*] (LCLS)
InBu .... Butler Carnegie Library, Butler, IN [*Library symbol*] [*Library of Congress*] (LCLS)
INBU .... Internal Navigation Battery Unit (SAUS)
InBuB .... Butler Bulletin, Butler, IN [*Library symbol*] [*Library of Congress*] (LCLS)
INBUCON .... International Business Consultants (SAUO)
INbW .... Wiss, Janney, Elstner, & Associates, Northbrook, IL [*Library symbol*] [*Library of Congress*] (LCLS)
InC .... Crawfordsville District Public Library, Crawfordsville, IN [*Library symbol*] [*Library of Congress*] (LCLS)
INC .... Ice Navigation Center [*Marine science*] (MSC)
INC .... Idaho Nuclear Corp.
INC .... Ideal Non-Linear Capacitance (SAUS)
INC .... Iglesia Ni Cristo [*Religious organization*]
INC .... Igniter Nozzle Closure
INC .... Illinois Nature Conservancy (SAUS)
INC .... Improved Navigation Computer (SAUS)
INC .... Incendiary
INC .... In Chain (SAUO)
INC .... Inchon [*Tyosen, Zinsen*] [*South Korea*] [*Seismograph station code, US Geological Survey*] [*Closed*] (SEIS)
INC .... Incidit [*Engraved*] [*Latin*] (ROG)
INC .... Incinerator
INC .... Incisal (STED)
inc .... Incised (VRA)
INC .... Incision (STED)
inc .... Incision
Inc .... Incisional (STED)
INC .... Incisus [*Being Cut*] [*Pharmacy*] (ROG)
INC .... Inclinable (SAUS)
INC .... Inclosure
INC .... In Cloud (SAUS)
INC .... In Clouds [*ICAO*] (FAAC)
inc .... Included (MIST)
Inc .... Including (STED)
INC .... Including
INC .... Inclusive
Inc .... Income (EBF)
inc .... Income (WDMC)
INC .... Income (ROG)
INC .... Incoming [*Telecommunications*] (KSC)
INC .... Incoming Trunk [*Telecommunications*] (TEL)
Inc .... Incompatibility (STED)
inc .... Incomplete (WDMC)
INC .... Incomplete
Inc .... Inconclusive (STED)
INC .... Inconclusive
inc .... Incontinent [*Therapy term*] (CTAA)
Inc .... Incontinent (STED)
INC .... Incontinent [*Medicine*]
INC .... Incorporated (EY)
inc .... Incorporated (WDMC)
Inc .... Incorporated (STED)
INC .... Incorporated Place (SAUO)
INC .... Incorporation (SAUO)
INC .... Increase (AABC)
inc .... Increase (WDMC)
Inc .... Increment (STED)
INC .... Increment
INC .... Incrementally Funded Contract (SAUS)
INC .... Incumbent (ROG)
inc .... Incurred
INC .... Indiana Cooperative Library Services Authority, Indianapolis, IN [*OCLC symbol*] (OCLC)
INC .... Indian National Congress
inc .... Indic [*MARC language code*] [*Library of Congress*] (LCCP)
INC .... Industrial National Corp. (SAUS)
INC .... Inertial Navigation Computer (MCD)
INC .... Information and Censorship [*Allied Forces*] [*World War II*]
INC .... In Nomine Christi [*In the Name of Christ*] [*Latin*]
INC .... Input Control (SAUS)
INC .... Input Control System [*Military*]
INC .... Insectivorous Cyprinids [*Pisciculture*]
INC .... Insertable Nuclear Components (MCD)
INC .... Inside-the-Needle Catheter [*Cardiology*] (DAVI)
INC .... Installation Notice Card (KSC)
INC .... Installation Notification Certification (MCD)
INC .... Institute of Nature Conservation (SAUO)
In C .... Instructor Captain (SAUS)
INC .... Integrated Network Corp. (PCM)
INC .... Intelligence Coordination [*Program*] [*Department of State*]
INC .... Intelligent Numerical Control [*Machine tools*]
INC .... Interface Network Controller (SAUS)
INC .... Intergovernmental Negotiating Committee (SAUS)
INC .... Internal Communication (SAUO)
INC .... International Carrier (SAUS)
INC .... International Controls Corporation (SAUO)
INC .... International Narcotics Control (SAUO)
INC .... International Negotiating Committee [*World Resources Institute*]
INC .... International Negotiating Convention (SAUO)
INC .... International Nickel Company (SAUO)
INC .... International Numismatic Commission
INC .... International Nut Council (EAIO)
INC .... Internet Computer (SAUS)
INC .... Internodular Cortex [*Medicine*] (EDAA)
INC .... Interstitial Nucleus of Cajal [*Brain anatomy*]
INC .... Invermay Resources [*Vancouver Stock Exchange symbol*]
INC .... Iraqi National Congress [*Political party*] (ECON)
INC .... Irish National Caucus (EA)
INC .... Ironfounders' National Confederation [*British*] (BI)
INC .... Ishikawajima Noise Control Co. Ltd. (SAUO)
INC .... Island Navigation Co. (SAUS)
INC .... Island Navigation Company (SAUO)
INC .... Isotope and Nuclear Chemistry Division (SAUO)
INC .... Item Name Code [*Military*] (AFM)
INC .... Jet Air Internacional Charters CA [*Venezuela*] [*ICAO designator*] (FAAC)
INC .... National Institute of Culture
INC .... Yinchuan [*China*] [*Airport symbol*] (OAG)
INC. .... Nutrition Education Association (EA)
INcA .... Abbott Laboratories, North Chicago, IL [*Library symbol*] [*Library of Congress*] (LCLS)
InCa .... Carlisle Public Library, Carlisle, IN [*Library symbol*] [*Library of Congress*] (LCLS)
INCA .... Idaho Nuclear Code Automation [*AEC*]
INCA .... Implementation of New Carrier Arrangements [*Telecommunications*]
INCA .... In-Car Acquisition [*Testing*]
INCA .... In-Core Analysis [*Nuclear energy*] (NRCH)
INCA .... Information Council of the Americas (EA)
INCA .... Innovation through Creative Analysis (PDAA)
INCA .... Institute for Numerical Computation and Analysis (MCD)
INCA .... Integrated Catalog Algorithm (MCD)
INCA .... Integrated Communications Agency [*Air Force*]
INCA .... Integrated Navigation and Communications, Automatic
INCA .... Integrated Network Architecture for Office Communications (SAUO)
INCA .... Integrated Network Communication Architecture (OSI)
INCA .... Integrated Nuclear and Chemical Analysis
INCA .... Integrated Nuclear Communications Assessment
INCA .... Integrated Numerical Control Approach
INCA .... Intelligence Communications Architecture
INCA .... Interactive Controls Analysis [*NASA*] (CIST)
INCA .... Interleaved Native Compiled Architecture (SAUS)

INCA .... International Narcotics Control Act
INCA .... International Newspaper and Colour Association [*Later, IFRA*] (EA)
INCA .... International Newspaper Colour Association (SAUO)
Inca .... International Notification and Compensation Agreement (SAUO)
INCA .... Inventory Control and Analysis (MHDB)
Inc Ab .... Incomplete Abortion [*Obstetrics*] (DAVI)
INCAD .... Incapacitated Passengers' Handling Advice [*British*]
INCAE .... Instituto Centroamericano de Administracion de Empresas [*Central American Institute of Business Administration*] [*Nicaragua*]
INCAIR .... Including Air
InCaL .... Carlisle Public Library, Carlisle, IN [*Library symbol*] [*Library of Congress*] (LCLS)
Incalz .... Incalzando [*Music*]
InCam .... Camden-Jackson Township Public Library, Camden, IN [*Library symbol*] [*Library of Congress*] (LCLS)
INCAM .... Inducible Cell Adhesion Molecule [*Immunochemistry*]
INCAMS .... Individual Cassette Manufacturing System (AAEL)
InCan .... Cannelton Public Library, Cannelton, IN [*Library symbol*] [*Library of Congress*] (LCLS)
incan .... Incandescent (WDMC)
InCanCR .... Perry County Recorder's Office, Cannelton, IN [*Library symbol*] [*Library of Congress*] (LCLS)
INCAND .... Incandescent (MSA)
incap .... incapacitant (SAUS)
incap .... incapacitating (SAUS)
INCAP .... Incapacitating Chemical Agent (SAUS)
INCAP .... Instituto de Nutricion de Centro America y Panama [*Institute of Nutrition of Central America and Panama*] [*Guatemala, Guatemala*] (EAIO)
InCar .... Carmel Public Library, Carmel, IN [*Library symbol*] [*Library of Congress*] (LCLS)
INCAR .... International Committee Against Racism (EA)
Incarnate Word C ... Incarnate Word College (GAGS)
InCarNJ .... Carmel News Journal, Carmel, IN [*Library symbol*] [*Library of Congress*] (LCLS)
InCarS .... Carmel Clay Schools, Carmel IN [*Library symbol*] [*Library of Congress*] (LCLS)
INCAS .... Integrated Navigation and Collision Avoidance System (PDAA)
INCAS .... International Center for Advanced Studies [*Russia*]
InCayHN .... Cayuga Herald News, Cayuga, IN [*Library symbol*] [*Library of Congress*] (LCLS)
IncB .... Inclusion Body [*Cytology*]
INCB .... Indiana Cmnty Bk SB [*NASDAQ symbol*] (TTSB)
INCB .... Indiana Community Bank A Savings Bank [*NASDAQ symbol*] (SAG)
INCB .... International Narcotics Control Board (DMAA)
INCB .... International Nuclear Credit Bank (NRCH)
INCBE .... Israel National Committee on the Biosphere and Environment
INC BOMB .... Incendiary Bomb (SAUS)
INCBR .... Incubator (MSA)
InCc .... Cambridge City Public Library, Cambridge City, IN [*Library symbol*] [*Library of Congress*] (LCLS)
INCC .... Inspiration Consolidated Copper [*Federal Railroad Administration identification code*]
INCC .... Institut National du Cancer du Canada [*National Cancer Institute of Canada*] (EAIO)
INCC .... Interim National Coordinating Committee [*Ghana*] (PPW)
INCC .... International Network Controlling Center [*Telecommunications*] (TEL)
INCC .... International Newspaper Collector's Club (EA)
INCC .... International Nippon Collectors Club (EA)
INCC .... International Nuclear Credit Co. (SAUS)
INCC .... Internet Communications [*NASDAQ symbol*] (SAG)
INCCA .... International Network of Centres for Computer Applications (SAUO)
InCcNR .... National Road Traveler, Cambridge City, IN [*Library symbol*] [*Library of Congress*] (LCLS)
INCCT .... Incorrect (SAUS)
inccty .... incorrectly (SAUS)
INCD .... Incandescent
INCD .... Incendiary (AABC)
INCD .... Incorporated [*Legal term*] (EY)
INCD .... Infantile Nuclear Cerebral Degeneration [*Medicine*] (DMAA)
INCD .... Intergovernmental Negotiating Committee for a Convention to Combat Desertification (SAUO)
INCD .... International Convention to Combat Decertification (SAUO)
INCDG .... Including (SAUS)
INCDT .... Incident (MSA)
INCDU .... Inertial Navigator Control and Display Unit (SAUS)
InCe .... Centerville and Center Township Library, Centerville, IN [*Library symbol*] [*Library of Congress*] (LCLS)
INCE .... Central European Initiative [*Government term*] (GA)
INCE .... Institute of Noise Control Engineering (EA)
INCE .... Insurance
INCE .... International Network for Chemical Education [*Samoa*] (EAIO)
INCEP .... Interceptor
INCEPT .... Inception (ROG)
INCERFA .... Uncertainty Phase Code (Alerting Service) [*Aviation*] (FAAC)
IncFB .... Increase Feedback
INC/FCCC .... Intergovernmental Negotiating Committee for a Framework Convention on Climate Change (SAUO)
INCFMY .... Inconformity (SAUS)
INCFO .... Institute of Newspaper Controllers and Finance Officers [*Later, INFE*] (EA)
INCH .... Inchoative (WGA)
INCH .... Independent Channel (SAUS)
INCH .... Independent Channel Handler (IAA)
INCH .... Indirectly-Bonded Carbon-Hydrogen (SAUS)
INCH .... Integrated Chopper
INCH .... Interaction Checklist for Augmentative Communication, Revised Edition [*Test*] (TMMY)
INCH .... Interim Charging [*Electric vehicle technology*]
INCH .... International Center for High Quality Scrap [*Scrap salvage*]
InCha .... Charlestown Township Public Library, Charlestown, IN [*Library symbol*] [*Library of Congress*] (LCLS)
InChe .... Westchester Public Library, Chesterton, IN [*Library symbol*] [*Library of Congress*] (LCLS)
InCheT .... Chesterton Tribune, Chesterton, IN [*Library symbol*] [*Library of Congress*] (LCLS)
INCH Handler ... Independent Channel Handler (SAUS)
INCHO .... Inchoate (ADA)
incho .... Inchoative (ADWA)
IN CH Q .... Indian Church Quarterly Review [*A publication*] (ROG)
INCIAWPBC ... Indian National Committee of the International Association on Water Pollution and Control (SAUO)
incid .... Incide [*Cut*] [*Latin*] (STED)
INCID .... Incide [*Cut*] [*Pharmacy*]
incid .... incidence (SAUS)
INCID .... Incident (SAUS)
incid .... Incidental (GROV)
Incidences/Ottawa ... Incidences. University of Ottawa. Ottawa (SAUS)
INCIDI .... Institut International des Civilisations Differentes [*International Institute of Differing Civilizations*]
Incid Mus .... Incidental Music (SAUS)
INCIDR .... Intramural NIAID Center for International Disease Research (SAUS)
INC-IEC .... Indian National Committee of the International Electrotechnical Commission (SAUO)
INCIID .... International Council on Infertility Information Dissemination
INCIN .... Incinerator (MSA)
InCINC .... International Chemometrics Internet Conference
INCINC .... International Copyright Information Center (EA)
INCING .... International Copyrights Information Center (SAUO)
INCIPIT .... CD-ROM of incunabula (SAUS)
INCIRS .... International Communication Information Retrieval System [*University of Florida*] (PDAA)
INCIS .... Incisus [*Being Cut*] [*Pharmacy*] (ROG)
INCITE .... Instructional Notation for Computer-controlled Inspection and Test Equipment (SAUS)
INCJHS .... International Network of Children of Jewish Holocaust Survivors (EA)
InCJR .... Crawfordsville Journal and Review, Crawfordsville, IN [*Library symbol*] [*Library of Congress*] (LCLS)
INCL .... Inclination [*Angular distance from equator in degrees*]
incl .... incline (SAUS)
INCL .... Inclosure (AFM)
INCL .... Include [*or Including*] (EY)
incl .... Include
Incl .... Include (TBD)
incl .... Included (REAL)
INCL .... Included (VLIE)
incl .... Including (WDMC)
incl .... Inclusive (WDMC)
INCL .... Inclusive
INCL .... Incoming Line (IAA)
INCL .... Inconclusive
INCL .... In Control, Inc. [*NASDAQ symbol*] (SAG)
INCL .... Infantile Neuronal Ceroid Lipofuscinoses [*Medicine*]
INCL .... Intellicall, Inc. (SAUO)
InClcN .... Clay City News, Clay City, IN [*Library symbol*] [*Library of Congress*] (LCLS)
INCLD .... Including [*Freight*]
incldg .... Including
InCli .... Clinton Public Library, Clinton, IN [*Library symbol*] [*Library of Congress*] (LCLS)
InCliC .... Daily Clintonian, Clinton, IN [*Library symbol*] [*Library of Congress*] (LCLS)
INCLN .... Incline (SAUS)
INCLN .... Inclined (MSA)
INCLN .... Inclusion
inclntr .... inclinator (SAUS)
INCLR .... Intercooler
INCLS .... Inclosure (MSA)
incls .... Includes
INCLU .... Inclusive (ROG)
INCLUDE .... Implementing New Concepts of the Library for Urban Disadvantaged Ethnics [*Cleveland Public Library*] (NITA)
INCLV .... Inclusive (FAAC)
InCLW .... General Lew Wallace Studio, Crawfordsville, IN [*Library symbol*] [*Library of Congress*] (LCLS)
INCM .... Income
INCM .... Incoming (MSA)
INCM .... Intelligent Network Conceptual Model (SAUO)
INCMD .... Indianapolis Contract Management District (SAUS)
INCMG .... Incoming
INCND .... Incendiary (MSA)
INCNIA .... Integrated Communications-Navigation-Identification Avionics (MUSM)
INCNR .... Increment Number (DOMA)
IncnW Mkt ... Incentive Marketing (journ.) (SAUS)
InCo .... Connersville Public Library, Connersville, IN [*Library symbol*] [*Library of Congress*] (LCLS)
INCO .... INCO Ltd. [*Formerly, International Nickel Co. of Canada*] [*Associated Press*] (SAG)
INCO .... Inconel (SAUS)
INCO .... Information and Control (SAUS)

INCO .... Installation and Checkout [*Military*] (CAAL)
INCO .... Instrumentation and Communications Officer [*NASA*]
INCO .... Integrated Communications Officer (SAUO)
INCO .... Intelligence Noncommissioned Officer (SAUS)
INCO .... International Chamber of Commerce (IEEE)
INCO .... International Cooperation (SAUO)
INCo .... International Navigation Company (SAUO)
INCO .... International Nickel Co.
Inco .... International Nickel Company of Canada (SAUO)
INCO .... International Nickel Corporation (SAUO)
INCO .... Iranian National Centre for Oceanography (SAUS)
INCO .... Specific Research, Technological Development and Demonstration Programme in the Field of Cooperation with Tird Countries and International Organization (SAUO)
INCO 2 .... Programme for Research, Technological Development and Demonstration on Confirming the International Role of Community Research (SAUO)
InCoa .... Coatesville Public Library, Coatesville, IN [*Library symbol*] [*Library of Congress*] (LCLS)
Inco Alloys Int... Inco Alloys International (journ.) (SAUS)
INCO-COPERNICUS... Specific Research, Technological Development and Demonstration Programme in the Field of Cooperation with Third Countries and International Organization-Specific and Technological Cooperation with the Countries of Central and Eastern Europe and the New I (SAUO)
InCODA .... International Congress of Dealers Associations (EA)
INCO-DC ...... Specific Research, Technological Development and Demonstration Programme in the Field of Cooperation with Third Countries and International Organization-Specific and Technological Cooperation with Developing Countries (SAUO)
INCODEL ...... Interstate Commission on the Delaware River Basin
INCOFILT ..... International Consortium of Filtration Research Group (SAUO)
INCOFT .... Intelligent Conduct of Fire Trainer [*Military*] (ACAE)
INCOG .... Incognito (GOBB)
incog .... Incognito [*Unknown*] [*Latin*]
INCOG .... Indian Nations Council of Governments
INCOH .... Incoherent (MSA)
IncoHm .... Inco Homes Corp. [*Associated Press*] (SAG)
InColc .... Peabody Library, Columbia City, IN [*Library symbol*] [*Library of Congress*] (LCLS)
InColcCR ...... Whitley County Recorder's Office, Columbia City, IN [*Library symbol*] [*Library of Congress*] (LCLS)
InColf .... Colfax Public Library, Colfax, IN [*Library symbol*] [*Library of Congress*] (LCLS)
InColo .... Bartholomew County Library, Columbus, IN [*Library symbol*] [*Library of Congress*] (LCLS)
INCOLR .... Intercooler
INCOLSA ...... Indiana Cooperative Library Services Authority [*Indianapolis, IN*] [*Library network*]
InColu .... Bartholomew County Library, Columbus, IN [*Library symbol*] [*Library of Congress*] (LCLS)
InColuHi ...... Bartholomew County Historical Society, Columbus, IN [*Library symbol*] [*Library of Congress*] (LCLS)
InColuR .... Columbus Republic, Columbus, IN [*Library symbol*] [*Library of Congress*] (LCLS)
INCOM .... Incomplete (AABC)
INCOM .... Indicator Compiler (IAA)
INCOM .... Input Compiler (IAA)
INCOM .... International Symposium on Manufacturing Technology (SAUS)
INCOMAG .... International Communication Agency (SAUO)
INCOMAS ..... International Conference on Marketing Systems for Developing Countries (SAUO)
INCOMEX ..... International Computer Exhibition
INCOMINDIOS... International Committee for the Indians of the Americas [*Kaiseraugst, Switzerland*] (EAIO)
Incomnt .... INCOMNET, Inc. [*Associated Press*] (SAG)
INCOMP .... Incomplete (MSA)
Incompat ..... Incompatibility (SAUS)
INCOMPAT... Incompatible [*Medicine*]
incompl .... Incomplete (WDMC)
INCOMPL ..... Incomplete
InCon .... Converse Jackson Township Public Library, Converse, IN [*Library symbol*] [*Library of Congress*] (LCLS)
INCON .... Installation Console (MCD)
INCONCBYO... International Congress on Cryogenics (SAUS)
INCONCRYO... International Conference on Cryogenics (SAUO)
INCONCRYO-ISC... International Conference on Cryogenics - International Steering Committee (EAIO)
InCoNE .... Connersville News-Examiner, Connersville, IN [*Library symbol*] [*Library of Congress*] (LCLS)
INCONREP ... Intra-CONUS Movement Reports (SAUO)
incont .... Incontinent [*Medicine*] (DAVI)
InControl ...... InControl, Inc. [*Associated Press*] (SAG)
INCONUS ..... Intra-Continental United States (SAUO)
IncOp2 .... Income Opportunities Fund II, Inc. [*Associated Press*] (SAG)
IncOp2000 .... Income Opportunities Fund 2000 [*Associated Press*] (SAG)
INCOPAC ...... International Consumer Policy Advisory Committee (SAUS)
IncOpRT .... Income Opportunity Realty Trust [*Associated Press*] (SAG)
InCor .... Corydon Public Library, Corydon, IN [*Library symbol*] [*Library of Congress*] (LCLS)
INCOR .... Incorporated [*Legal term*]
INCOR .... Incorrect (MSA)
INCOR .... Institutional Collaborative Research-Nuclear Science Fund (SAUO)
INCOR .... Intergovernmental Conference on Oceanographic Research (MCD)
INCOR .... Intergovernmental Conference on Oceanography (SAUS)
INCORACO ... International Commercial Radio Corp. (SAUS)
INCORACO ... International Commercial Radio Corporation (SAUO)
InCorCP .... Harrison County Press, Corydon, IN [*Library symbol*] [*Library of Congress*] (LCLS)
InCorCR .... Harrison County Recorder's Office, Corydon, IN [*Library symbol*] [*Library of Congress*] (LCLS)
InCorD .... Corydon Democrat, Corydon, IN [*Library symbol*] [*Library of Congress*] (LCLS)
INCORE .... Initiative on Conflict Resolution and Ethnicity
INCORE .... International Programme on Conflict Resolution and Ethnicity
INCORE .... Internet Content Rating for Europe (SAUO)
INCORP .... Incorporated [*Legal term*] (EY)
Incorp .... Incorporation (DIAR)
INCORPN ..... Incorporation [*Legal term*] (ROG)
INCORR .... Incorrect (ADA)
INCOS .... Institute of Computer Science (SAUS)
INCOS .... Integrated Control System [*Navy*] (NVT)
INCOSADA ... Integrated Corporate Spatial and Attribute Database (SAUO)
INCOSAI .... International Congress of Supreme Audit Institutions (PDAA)
INCOSE .... International Council on Systems Engineering (NTPA)
INCOT .... In-Core Instrument Test (SAUS)
INCOT .... In-Core Test Facility [*Nuclear energy*] (NRCH)
INCOTEC ...... International Committee for Training and Education of Co-Operators (EAIO)
INCOTEC ...... International Co-operative Training and Education Committee (SAUO)
INCOTERM... International Commerce Term [*International Chamber of Commerce*]
INCOTERMS... International Commercial Terms (SAUO)
INCOTERMS... International Contracting Terms (AAGC)
INCOTERMS... International Terms of Sale (GART)
InCov .... Covington Public Library, Covington, IN [*Library symbol*] [*Library of Congress*] (LCLS)
InCovFS .... Fountain County Star, Covington, IN [*Library symbol*] [*Library of Congress*] (LCLS)
INCP .... Inertial Navigation Control Panel (SAUS)
INCPD ACCT... Incorporated Accountant [*British*] (ROG)
INCPEC .... Indonesian National Committee for Pacific Economic Cooperation
INCPEN .... Industry Committee for Packaging and the Environment [*British*] (DI)
INCPLT .... Incomplete (VLIE)
INCPT .... Intercept
INCPT .... Intercepting (SAUS)
INCPT .... Interceptor (SAUS)
INCR .... Increase (AFM)
incr .... Increase (WDMC)
inc(r) .... Increase (Relative) (AAMN)
INCR .... Increasingly (SAUS)
INCR .... Increment (AFM)
incr .... Increment (ELAL)
INCR .... Incremental (SAUS)
incr .... incressed (SAUS)
INCR .... Institute for Childhood Resources (SAUO)
INCR .... Institute of Nature Conservation and Resources (SAUO)
In Cr .... Instructor Commander (SAUS)
INCR .... Interrupt Control Register [*Computer science*] (MSA)
INCRA .... International Copper Research Association [*Research center*] [*British*] (IRC)
INCRA .... National Institute for Colonization and Agrarian Reform (Brazil) [*Political party*] (PSAP)
INCRAPLAN... Integrated Crew and Aircraft Planning (PDAA)
INCRB .... Inscribe (VLIE)
INCRE .... Increment
INCREF .... International Childrens Rescue Fund (SAUS)
INCREM .... Incremental
INCREP .... Incident Report [*Military*] (CINC)
INCRF .... Inca Resources, Inc. [*NASDAQ symbol*] (COMM)
incrim .... incriminate (SAUS)
incrim .... incrimination (SAUS)
incrim .... incriminatory (SAUS)
INCRNTN ..... Incarnation
InCrp .... Crown Point Center Public Library, Crown Point, IN [*Library symbol*] [*Library of Congress*] (LCLS)
INCRP .... Intelligent Network Call Routing Protocol (DINT)
InCrpCS .... Crown Point Community Schools, Crown Point, IN [*Library symbol*] [*Library of Congress*] (LCLS)
InCrpLS .... Lake County Star, Crown Point, IN [*Library symbol*] [*Library of Congress*] (LCLS)
INCS .... Incomplete Resolution, Scan to Follow [*Radiology*] (DAVI)
INCS .... Integrated Battlefield Control System (MCD)
INCS .... International Netsuke Collectors Society [*Commercial firm*] (EA)
INCSEA .... Incident at Sea [*Navy*] (NVT)
INCSEA .... Incidents on and Over the High Seas (SAUS)
inc sed .... Incertae Sedis [*Uncertain Position*] [*Biology, taxonomy*]
INCSR .... International Narcotics Control Strategy Report [*Department of State*]
INCST .... Invoice Cost (SAUS)
Incstar .... Incstar Corp. [*Associated Press*] (SAG)
INC System... Input Control System (SAUS)
INCT .... Incumbent (ROG)
Inc Tax Cas... Reports of Cases Relating to Income Tax [*A publication*] (DLA)
Inc Tax LJ ... Income Tax Law Journal [*India*] [*A publication*] (DLA)
Inc Tax R ..... Income Tax Reports [*India*] [*A publication*] (DLA)
INCTN .... Incorporation
InCtPd .... Inter-City Products Corp. [*Associated Press*] (SAG)
INCTRL .... Installation Control [*Computer science*] (PCM)
InCu .... Culver Public Library, Culver, IN [*Library symbol*] [*Library of Congress*] (LCLS)
INCUM .... Indiana Computer Users Meeting (SAUO)

INCUMB Incumbent
INCUMBCE Incumbrance (ROG)
INCUMBD Incumbered (ROG)
INCUN Incunabula (ADA)
INCUR Incurable [*Medicine*]
INCV Inclusive (MSA)
InCW Wabash College, Crawfordsville, IN [*Library symbol*] [*Library of Congress*] (LCLS)
INCWAR Inbound Control Word Address Register [*Computer science*] (VLIE)
INCWF Indian National Cement Workers' Federation
INCX INFOCURE Corp. [*NASDAQ symbol*] (SG)
INCY Incendiary Bomb (DSUE)
INCY INCYTE Pharmaceuticals [*NASDAQ symbol*] (TTSB)
InCyA Cynthiana Argus, Cynthiana, IN [*Library symbol*] [*Library of Congress*] (LCLS)
Incyte Incyte Pharmaceuticals, Inc. [*Associated Press*] (SAG)
Ind Adversus Indoctum [*of Lucian*] [*Classical studies*] (OCD)
IND American Industrial Properties [*Formerly, Trammell Crow Real Estate Investment*] [*NYSE symbol*] (SPSG)
IND Amer Industrial Prop [*NYSE symbol*] (TTSB)
IND Immigration and Nationality Directorate
IND Improvised Nuclear Device
IND Indecent [*FBI standardized term*]
ind Indefinite [*Medicine*] (EDAA)
IND Indefinite [*Motor vehicle violation code used in state of Maryland*] (MVRD)
IND Indent Number (SAUS)
ind Independence (IDYL)
ind Independent (WDMC)
IND Independent
Ind Independents [*Pakistan*] [*Political party*]
ind Index (WDMC)
IND Index
Ind India (MILB)
IND India [*IYRU nationality code*] [*ANSI three-letter standard code*] (CNC)
IND Indian (AABC)
Ind Indian (SHCU)
Ind Indiana (BEE)
IND Indiana
IND Indianapolis [*Indiana*] [*Airport symbol*] (OAG)
Ind Indianapolis Colts [*National Football League*] [*1984-present*] (NFLA)
Ind Indiana Supreme Court Reports [*A publication*] (DLA)
Ind Indianian (SAUS)
Ind Indian Ocean (SAUS)
Ind Indians (GEAB)
IND Indicate [*or Indicator*] (KSC)
IND Indicative (ROG)
ind Indicator (IDOE)
IN D In Dies [*Daily*] [*Pharmacy*]
IND Indies
ind Indigo (WDMC)
IND Indigo
ind Indirect [*Medicine*] (EDAA)
IND Indirect
ind indirectly (SAUS)
Ind Indo- (SAUS)
IND Indomethacin [*An analgesic*]
IND Indonesia (SAUO)
ind Indonesian [*MARC language code*] [*Library of Congress*] (LCCP)
IND Indoors (ROG)
IND Indorse [*Legal term*] (AABC)
IND Induced Nuclear Disintegration
ind Inductance (IDOE)
IND Inductance
IND Induction (MSA)
IND Inductive (SAUS)
ind Inductor (IDOE)
Ind Indurated (SAUS)
Ind Indus [*Constellation*]
Ind Industrial (AL)
ind Industrial (WDMC)
IND Industrial
IND Industrial Distribution (journ.) (SAUS)
ind industrially (SAUS)
IND Industrial Medicine (DMAA)
IND Industrial Metabolism Project (SAUO)
Ind Industries (SAUS)
IND Industry (AFM)
Ind Industry (AL)
IND Industry Division [*Census*] (OICC)
IND In Nomine Dei [*In the Name of God*] [*Latin*]
IND Intercept Director [*Military*]
IND Interceptor Director (SAUS)
IND Inter Mountain Development, Inc. [*Vancouver Stock Exchange symbol*]
IND International Nomenclature of Diseases (SAUO)
IND International Number Dialing [*Telecommunications*] (TEL)
IND Investigational New Device [*U.S. Food and Drug Administration*]
IND Investigational New Drug [*Application*] [*FDA*]
IND Investigative New Drug (SAUS)
IND Iona National Airways Ltd. [*Republic of Ireland*] [*ICAO designator*] (FAAC)
IND University of Notre Dame, Notre Dame, IN [*OCLC symbol*] (OCLC)
INDA INDA, Association of the Nonwoven Fabrics Industry [*Formerly, International Nonwovens and Disposables Association*]
INDA Indexible Address (SAUS)
INDA International Nonwoven and Disposables Association (SAUO)
INDA Investigational New Drug Application (MELL)
INDA IVSN Data Base (SAUS)
INDAC Industrial Data Acquisition and Control [*Computer science*] (MHDI)
INDAC Integral Nuclear Data Center (SAUS)
Ind Acc Com Decisions of the Industrial Accident Commission of California [*A publication*] (DLA)
INDAC Language Industrial Data Acquisition and Control Language (SAUS)
INDACS Indexing by the Atlas Computer System (SAUS)
INDAC System Industrial Data Acquisition and Control System (SAUS)
Ind Acts Acts of Indiana [*A publication*] (DLA)
Ind A Dig United States Indian Affairs Office, Digest of Decisions [*A publication*] (DLA)
IndAdmin Industrial Administration (DD)
Ind Admin R Burns' Indiana Administrative Rules and Regulations [*A publication*] (DLA)
InDaDN Dale News, Dale, IN [*Library symbol*] [*Library of Congress*] (LCLS)
Ind Advocate Indian Advocate [*A publication*] (DLA)
Ind Aeron Index Aeronauticus (journ.) (SAUS)
INDAIR Identification of Aircraft
InDair International Dairy Queen, Inc. [*Associated Press*] (SAG)
InDairA International Dairy Queen [*Associated Press*] (SAG)
InDairB International Dairy Queen [*Associated Press*] (SAG)
InDaN Dale News, Dale, IN [*Library symbol*] [*Library of Congress*] (LCLS)
InDan Danville Public Library, Danville, IN [*Library symbol*] [*Library of Congress*] (LCLS)
InDanCR Hendricks County Recorder's Office, Danville, IN [*Library symbol*] [*Library of Congress*] (LCLS)
Ind & Intell Prop Aust Industrial and Intellectual Property in Australia [*A publication*] (DLA)
InDanN Central Normal College, Danville, IN [*Library symbol*] [*Library of Congress*] [*Obsolete*] (LCLS)
InDanR Danville Republican, Danville, IN [*Library symbol*] [*Library of Congress*] (LCLS)
INDAP Indianapolis, IN [*American Association of Railroads railroad junction routing code*]
Ind App Indiana Court of Appeals Reports [*A publication*] (DLA)
Ind App Law Reports, Indian Appeals [*A publication*] (DLA)
Ind App Ct Indiana Appellate Court Reports [*A publication*] (DLA)
Ind App Supp Supplemental Indian Appeals, Law Reports [*A publication*] (DLA)
INDAPS Integrated Navigation, Data Acquisition and Processing System (SAUS)
InDar Darlington Public Library, Darlington, IN [*Library symbol*] [*Library of Congress*] (LCLS)
Ind Arch Industrial Architecture (journ.) (SAUS)
Ind Arts Index Industrial Arts Index (journ.) (SAUS)
IndArts M Industrial Arts Magazine (journ.) (SAUS)
INDAS Integrated Navigation and Data Acquisition System (SAUO)
INDASAT Indian Scientific Satellite
INDAT Incoming Data (MCD)
INDAT Industrial Data Technologies (SAUS)
INDAT Intermediate Data Technologies (SAUS)
INDATA Service Industrial Data Service (SAUS)
Ind Aub J India Rubber Journal (journ.) (SAUS)
Ind Awards Industrial Awards Recommendations [*New Zealand*] [*A publication*] (DLA)
INDAX Interactive Data Exchange (SAUS)
INDB Independent Bank Corp. [*NASDAQ symbol*] (NQ)
INDB Independent Bank(MA) [*NASDAQ symbol*] (TTSB)
IndBc Independence Bancorp, Inc. [*Associated Press*] (SAG)
IndBkMA Independent Bank Corp. Massachusetts [*Associated Press*] (SAG)
IndBkMI Independent Bank Corp. Michigan [*Associated Press*] (SAG)
IndBnk Independent Bankshares, Inc. [*Associated Press*] (SAG)
INDC Indian National Democratic Congress (BARN)
INDC Indicate (FAAC)
INDC Industrial Chemicals [*Federal Railroad Administration identification code*]
INDC International Nuclear Data Committee [*of International Atomic Energy Agency*]
Ind Can L P Lit Index to Canadian Legal Periodical Literature [*A publication*] (DLA)
Ind Cas Indian Cases [*India*] [*A publication*] (DLA)
Ind C Aw Industrial Court Awards [*England*] [*A publication*] (DLA)
IndCCF Independent Cooperative Commonwealth Federation (SAUO)
INDCD Industry Code (VLIE)
Ind Ceram Industrial Ceramics (journ.) (SAUS)
Ind Chem Eng Industrial Engineering Chemical Research (MEC)
Ind Code Ann Burns' Indiana Statutes, Annotated Code Edition [*A publication*] (DLA)
Ind Com Law Indermaur and Thwaites' Principles of the Common Law [*12th ed.*] [*1914*] [*A publication*] (DLA)
Ind Comm Dev Industry, Commerce, Development (journ.) (SAUS)
Ind Commer Train Industrial and Commercial Training (journ.) (SAUS)
Ind Comput Industrial Computing (journ.) (SAUS)
INDCONS Industrial Conditions (SAUS)
Ind Corp Change Industrial and Corporate Change [*A publication*] (JLIT)
Ind Corros Industrial Corrosion (journ.) (SAUS)
Ind Court Aw Industrial Court Awards [*England*] [*A publication*] (DLA)
INDCT Inducted (SAUS)
Ind Ct Awards Industrial Court Awards [*England*] [*A publication*] (DLA)
Indctd Inducted [*Army*]
INDCTR Indicator

Ind Daf Chron... Industrial Safety Chronicle (SAUS)
Ind Day........ Independence Day (SAUS)
Ind Dec........ Indiana Decisions [*A publication*] (DLA)
Ind Dec........ Indiana Decisions and Law Reporter [*A publication*] (DLA)
Ind Dem...... Independent Democrat (SAUO)
Ind Diamond Rev... Industrial Diamond Review (journ.) (SAUS)
Ind Dig........ All India Reporter, Indian Digest [*1946-52*] [*A publication*] (DLA)
Ind Div........ Inderwick's Divorce and Matrimonial Causes Acts [*1862*] [*A publication*] (DLA)
INDE........... IndeNet Inc. [*NASDAQ symbol*] (TTSB)
INDE........... Independence National Historical Park
INDE........... Independent TeleMedia Group [*NASDAQ symbol*] (SAG)
Ind E........... Industrial Engineer
INDE........... Integrated Nondestructive Evaluation (MCD)
Indebt.......... Indebtedness [*Legal term*] (DLA)
InDec.......... Decatur Public Library, Decatur, IN [*Library symbol*] [*Library of Congress*] (LCLS)
indec........... Indeclinable (BJA)
INDEC.......... Independent Nuclear Disarmament Election Committee [*British*] (DI)
INDEC.......... Interdepartmental Committee
InDecD........ Decatur Daily Democrat, Decatur, IN [*Library symbol*] [*Library of Congress*] (LCLS)
INDECL........ Indeclinable [*Grammar*]
INDECO....... Industrial Development Company (SAUO)
INDECO....... Industrial Development Corp. (SAUS)
INDECO....... International Development and Construction Corp. (SAUO)
INDECS....... Immigration and Nationality Department Electronic Computer System (BARN)
INDECS....... Interactive Design of Control Systems (DI)
Ind Ed News... Industrial Education Council. Newsletter (journ.) (SAUS)
IndEducM.... Industrial Education Magazine (journ.) (SAUS)
INDEF.......... Indefinite (AABC)
indef........... Indefinite [*Medicine*] (EDAA)
INDEFART.... Indefinite Article (SAUS)
INDEFOPS.... Indefinite Operations (NVT)
InDel........... Delphi Public Library, Delphi, IN [*Library symbol*] [*Library of Congress*] (LCLS)
INDEL.......... Industry Education Liaison (AIE)
InDelCC....... Carroll County Comet, Delphi, IN [*Library symbol*] [*Library of Congress*] (LCLS)
InDelCHi...... Carroll County Historical Museum, Delphi, IN [*Library symbol*] [*Library of Congress*] (LCLS)
InDelCR....... Carroll County Recorder's Office, Delphi, IN [*Library symbol*] [*Library of Congress*] (LCLS)
INDELISA..... Indirect Enzyme-Linked Immunosorbent Assay
INDELSEC.... Industrial Electronic Security (AABC)
indem.......... indemnify (SAUS)
Indem.......... Indemnity [*Legal term*] (DLA)
INDEMFY..... Indemnify [*Legal shorthand*] (LWAP)
INDEMTY..... Indemnity [*Legal shorthand*] (LWAP)
INDEMY...... Indemnity (ROG)
Inden.......... Indention (SAUS)
Inden.......... Indenture (SAUS)
Inden.......... Indentured (SAUS)
Inden.......... Indenturing (SAUS)
IndeNet....... IndeNet, Inc. [*Associated Press*] (SAG)
IndEng......... Industrial Engineering (DD)
Ind Eng 1922-1931 (NY)... Industrial Engineering 1922-1931 (New York) [*A publication*]
Ind Engng.... Industrial Engineering (journ.) (SAUS)
Indent.......... Indenture (EBF)
INDENT........ Indenture (ROG)
Indeo........... Intel Video (ODA)
INDEP.......... Independent (AFM)
Indep........... Independent (DIAR)
IndepBc....... Independence Bancorp, Inc. [*Associated Press*] (SAG)
INDEP CONTR... Independent Contractor (DLA)
Independent Rev... Independent Review [*A publication*] (JLIT)
IndepHld...... Independence Holding Co. [*Associated Press*] (SAG)
Indep J Philos... Independent Journal of Philosophy (journ.) (SAUS)
Indep Power... Independent Power (journ.) (SAUS)
INDEP R...... Independent Review [*London*] [*A publication*] (ROG)
INDEPTH...... International Deep Profiling of Tibet and the Himalaya [*Geology*] [*China*]
INDEPTY...... Independently (ROG)
INDESYS...... Information Delivery System Inc. [*Information service or system*] (NITA)
INDET.......... Indeterminate (MSA)
Indet........... Indetermination (SAUS)
indeterm..... Indeterminative (BJA)
Ind-Eur........ Indo-European
IN-DEV-IL.... Institute for the Development of Indian Law (EA)
INDEX.......... Index NASA Data Exchange (SAUS)
INDEX.......... Indiana Exchange, Inc.
INDEX.......... Indian Ocean Experiment
INDEX.......... Intelligence System for Decision-making Executives (SAUS)
INDEX.......... Inter-NASA Data Exchange (IEEE)
Index FBIS Dly Rep /CD-ROM... Index FBIS Daily Report. NewsBank/Readex. New Canadian (journ.) (SAUS)
Index Foreign Leg Period... Index to Foreign Legal Periodicals. American Association of Law Libraries. Berkeley (SAUO)
Index Foreign Leg Period... Index to Foreign Legal Periodicals. American Association of Law Libraries. Berkeley (journ.) (SAUS)
Index JBMPE... Index of Transactions and Journal. Society of Motion Picture Engineers (journ.) (SAUS)
Ind Exp Tech... Industrial and Experimental Techniques (journ.) (SAUS)
IndFdg......... Industrial Funding Corp. [*Associated Press*] (SAG)
IndFdl.......... Independence Federal Savings Bank [*Associated Press*] (SAG)
Ind Finish.... Industrial Finishing (journ.) (SAUS)
IND FN REG... Indirect Function Register (SAUS)
Indft........... Indefinite (SAUS)
INDG........... Indigo N.V. [*NASDAQ symbol*] (SG)
IndGebiet..... Industriegebiet (SAUS)
INDGF......... Indigo NV [*NASDAQ symbol*] (SAG)
INDH........... Independent Insurance Group, Inc. [*NASDAQ symbol*] (NQ)
INDH........... Indirect Hire [*Military*]
IndH........... Industrial Holdings, Inc. [*Associated Press*] (SAG)
IndHealth..... Industrial Health (DD)
Ind Health... Industrial Health (journ.) (SAUS)
Ind Heat...... Industrial Heating (journ.) (SAUS)
INDHK......... Independent Insurance Group, Inc. [*NASDAQ symbol*] (COMM)
INDHR......... Indiana Harbor, IN [*American Association of Railroads railroad junction routing code*]
INDI............ Indepth Data, Inc. (SAUO)
ind i............ India Ink (VRA)
INDI............ Indiana
INDI............ Indiana Interstate [*Federal Railroad Administration identification code*]
INDI............ Indicate
INDI............ Individual Investor Group [*NASDAQ symbol*] (SAG)
Indi............ Indus [*Constellation*]
INDI............ International Neutron Doismetry Intercomparsion (SAUS)
INDI............ Irish Nutrition and Dietetic Institute (SAUS)
INDI............ Irish Nutrition and Dietetics Institute (EAIO)
India AIR Manual... AIR [*All India Law Reporter*] Manual: Unrepealed Central Acts [*2nd ed.*] [*India*] [*A publication*] (DLA)
India Cen Acts... Central Acts, India [*A publication*] (DLA)
India Code Civ P... Code of Civil Procedure [*India*] [*A publication*] (DLA)
India Code Crim P... Code of Criminal Procedure [*India*] [*A publication*] (DLA)
India Crim LJR... Criminal Law Journal Reports [*India*] [*A publication*] (DLA)
IndiaFd....... India Fund, Inc. [*Associated Press*] (SAG)
IndiaG......... India Growth Fund, Inc. [*Associated Press*] (SAG)
India Gen R & O... General Rules and Orders, India [*A publication*] (DLA)
INDIAMA...... Angolan Diamond Co. (SAUO)
INDIAMA...... Angolan Diamond Company (SAUS)
INDIAN........ Interplanar Distances and Angles (SAUS)
Indiana........ Indiana Reports [*A publication*] (DLA)
Indiana Bus A... Indiana Business Review (journ.) (SAUS)
Indiana Bus Rev... Indiana Business Review [*A publication*] (JLIT)
Indian Agric... Indian Agriculturist [*A publication*] (PABS)
Indiana Mag Hist... Indiana Magazine of History (journ.) (SAUS)
Indiana Med... Indiana Medicine (journ.) (SAUS)
Indian App... Law Reports, Privy Council, Indian Appeals [*India*] [*A publication*] (DLA)
Indiana Sup Ct Rep... Indiana Reports [*A publication*] (DLA)
Indian Cas... Indiana Cases [*A publication*] (DLA)
Indian Ceram... Indian Ceramics (journ.) (SAUS)
Indian Chem Eng... Indian Chemical Engineer (journ.) (SAUS)
Indian Chem J... Indian Chemical Journal (journ.) (SAUS)
Indian Chem Mfr... Indian Chemical Manufacturer (journ.) (SAUS)
Indian East Eng... Indian and Eastern Engineer (journ.) (SAUS)
Indian Econ R... Indian Economic Review (journ.) (SAUS)
Indian Eng... Indian Engineer (journ.) (SAUS)
Indian For.... Indian Forester [*A publication*] (PABS)
Indian Foundry J... Indian Foundry Journal (journ.) (SAUS)
Indian Heart J... Indian Heart Journal (journ.) (SAUS)
Indian J Agric Chem... Indian Journal of Agricultural Chemistry (journ.) (SAUS)
Indian J Agric Econ... Indian Journal of Agricultural Economics [*A publication*] (PABS)
Indian J Agric Res... Indian Journal of Agricultural Research [*A publication*] (PABS)
Indian J Agric Sci... Indian Journal of Agricultural Science (journ.) (SAUS)
Indian J Appl Chem... Indian Journal of Applied Chemistry (journ.) (SAUS)
Indian J Biochem... Indian Journal of Biochemistry (journ.) (SAUS)
Indian J Biochem Biophys... Indian Journal of Biochemistry and Biophysics (journ.) (SAUS)
Indian J Cancer... Indian Journal of Cancer (journ.) (SAUS)
Indian J Chem... Indian Journal of Chemistry (journ.) (SAUS)
Indian J Chem A... Indian Journal of Chemistry, Section A (journ.) (SAUS)
Indian J Chest Dis Allied Sci... Indian Journal of Chest Diseases and Allied Sciences (journ.) (SAUS)
Indian J Exp Biol... Indian Journal of Experimental Biology (journ.) (SAUS)
Indian J Gastroenterol... Indian Journal of Gastroenterology (journ.) (SAUS)
Indian J Genet Plant Breed... Indian Journal of Genetics and Plant Breeding (journ.) (SAUS)
Indian J Hort... Indian Journal of Horticulture (journ.) (SAUS)
Indian J Lepr... Indian Journal of Leprosy (journ.) (SAUS)
Indian J Malariol... Indian Journal of Malariology (journ.) (SAUS)
Indian J Med Res... Indian Journal of Medical Research (journ.) (SAUS)
Indian J Med Sci... Indian Journal of Medical Sciences (journ.) (SAUS)
Indian J Meteorol Geophys... Indian Journal of Meteorology and Geophysics (journ.) (SAUS)
Indian J Ophthalmol... Indian Journal of Ophthalmology (journ.) (SAUS)
Indian J Pathol Bacteriol... Indian Journal of Pathology and Bacteriology (journ.) (SAUS)
Indian J Pathol Microbiol... Indian Journal of Pathology and Microbiology (journ.) (SAUS)
Indian J Pediatr... Indian Journal of Pediatrics (journ.) (SAUS)
Indian J Pharm Educ... Indian Journal of Pharmaceutical Education (journ.) (SAUS)
Indian J Physiol Pharmacol... Indian Journal of Physiology and Pharmacology (journ.) (SAUS)
Indian J Public Health... Indian Journal of Public Health (journ.) (SAUS)

Indian J Pure Appl Phys... Indian Journal of Pure and Applied Physics (journ.) (SAUS)
Indian J Radiol... Indian Journal of Radiology (journ.) (SAUS)
Indian J Radio Space Phys... Indian Journal of Radio and Space Physics (journ.) (SAUS)
Indian J Theor Phys... Indian Journal of Theoretical Physics (journ.) (SAUS)
Indian Librn... Indian Librarian (journ.) (SAUS)
Indian LJ..... Indian Law Journal [*A publication*] (DLA)
Indian LR..... Indian Law Reports [*A publication*] (DLA)
Indian L R Calc... Indian Law Reports, Calcutta Series [*A publication*] (DLA)
Indian LR Mad... Indian Law Reports, Madras Series [*A publication*] (DLA)
Indian Min Eng J... Indian Mining and Engineering Journal (journ.) (SAUS)
Indian Pediatr... Indian Pediatrics (journ.) (SAUS)
Indian Potato J... Indian Potato Journal (journ.) (SAUS)
Indian Rul ... Indian Rulings [*A publication*] (DLA)
Indian Terr... Indian Territory Reports [*A publication*] (DLA)
Indian Weld J... Indian Welding Journal (journ.) (SAUS)
India Pen Code... Indian Penal Code [*A publication*] (DLA)
India S Ct.... India Supreme Court Reports [*A publication*] (DLA)
India Subs Leg... Subsidiary Legislation [*India*] [*A publication*] (DLA)
INDIC.......... Indicate (AABC)
INDIC.......... Indicating (SAUS)
INDIC.......... Indication Report (MCD)
indic.......... Indicative (SHCU)
INDIC.......... Indicative [*Grammar*]
INDIC.......... Indicator (WDAA)
IndiCBk........ Indiana Community Bank a Savings Bank [*Associated Press*] (SAG)
INDICI......... International Institute of Different Civilization (SAUO)
INDICN......... Indication
INDICOM...... Indications Communications (MCD)
INDICOM...... Indications Intelligence Communications Network (SAUO)
indie.......... Independent [*Filmmaking*] [*Slang*] (WDMC)
INDIE.......... Integrated Network of Disability Information and Education (SAUO)
Indie.......... The Independent [*A publication*] (WDAA)
IndiEngy...... Indiana Energy, Inc. [*Associated Press*] (SAG)
Indies......... East Indies (SAUS)
IndiFdl........ Indiana Federal Corp. [*Associated Press*] (SAG)
IndiFedl....... Indiana Federal Corp. [*Associated Press*] (SAG)
INDIG.......... Indigenous (AABC)
Indig.......... Indigenous (DIAR)
indig.......... Indigestion [*Medicine*] (EDAA)
INDIGO........ Indian Ocean Geochemistry [*France*] [*Marine science*] (OSRA)
INDIGO........ Intelligence Division Gaming Operations
IndigoNV...... Indigo NV [*Associated Press*] (SAG)
IndiM.......... Indiana & Michigan Power [*Associated Press*] (SAG)
IND IMP....... Indiae Imperator [*Emperor of India*] [*Latin*]
Ind Ind LP ... Index to Indian Legal Periodicals [*A publication*] (DLA)
Ind Information Bul... Industrial Information Bulletin (journ.) (SAUS)
IndInsr......... Independent Insurance Group, Inc. [*Associated Press*] (SAG)
INDIPEX....... India International Philatelic Exhibition
INDIR.......... Indirect Coombs Test [*Hematology*] (DAVI)
INDIRS......... Indiana Information Retrieval System [*Library network*]
INDIS.......... Industrial Information and Advisory Services [*UNIDO*] (IID)
INDIS.......... Industrial Information Service (SAUS)
INDIS.......... Industrial Information System [*UN Industrial Development Organization*] (NITA)
INDIS.......... Information Dissemination in European Research and Technological Development (SAUO)
INDIS.......... Interbourse Data Information Service (SAUO)
INDIS-IC...... Information Dissemination in European RTD (SAUO)
INDIV.......... Individual (AFM)
individ........ Individual (ADWA)
Individul...... Individual, Inc. [*Associated Press*] (SAG)
INDIVL......... Individual [*Freight*]
INDIV PSYCHOL... Individual Psychology (SAUS)
INDIX.......... International Network for Development Information Exchange (SAUO)
Ind J Int'l L... Indiana Journal of International Law [*A publication*] (DLA)
Ind Jud Pr... Indermaur's Practice of the Supreme Court of Judicature [*12th ed.*] [*1919*] [*A publication*] (DLA)
Ind Jur......... Indian Jurist [*Calcutta or Madras*] [*A publication*] (DLA)
Ind Jur NS.... Indian Jurist, New Series [*A publication*] (DLA)
Ind Jur OS.... Indian Jurist, Old Series [*A publication*] (DLA)
Ind Jur Pr.... Indermaur's Practice of the Supreme Court of Judicature [*12th ed.*] [*1919*] [*A publication*] (DLA)
IND L.......... Independent Liberal (WDAA)
INDL.......... Industrial (MSA)
Ind Lab........ Industrial Laboratory (journ.) (SAUS)
Ind Lab........ Industry and Labour. International Labour Office. Geneva (SAUS)
Ind Labor Relat Rev... Industrial and Labor Relations Review. New York State School of Industrial and Labor Relations (journ.) (SAUS)
Ind LC Com Law... Indermaur's Leading Cases in Common Law [*10th ed.*] [*1921*] [*A publication*] (DLA)
Ind LC Eq..... Indermaur's Leading Cases in Conveyancing and Equity [*A publication*] (DLA)
Indl Designr... Industrial Designer (SAUS)
Ind Led........ Individual Ledger [*Business term*] (MHDW)
Indl Engr...... Industrial Engineer (SAUS)
Ind LH.......... Indian Law Herald [*A publication*] (DLA)
Ind LJ.......... Industrial Law Journal [*A publication*]
Ind L Mag.... Indian Law Magazine [*A publication*] (DLA)
IND LP......... Indicating Lamp (SAUS)
Indl Planner... Industrial Planner (SAUS)
Ind LQ.......... Indian Law Quarterly [*A publication*] (DLA)
Ind LQ Rev... Indian Law Quarterly Review [*A publication*] (DLA)
Ind LR.......... Indiana Law Reporter [*1881*] [*A publication*] (DLA)
Ind LR.......... Indiana Legal Register [*A publication*] (DLA)
Ind LR.......... Indian Law Reports (East) [*A publication*] (DLA)
Ind LR.......... Industrial Law Review [*A publication*] (ILCA)
Ind LR All.... Indian Law Reports, Allahabad Series [*A publication*] (DLA)
Ind LR Alla... Indian Law Reports, Allahabad Series [*A publication*] (DLA)
Ind LR And... Indian Law Reports, Andhra Series [*A publication*] (DLA)
Ind LR Assam... Indian Law Reports, Assam Series [*A publication*] (DLA)
Ind LR Bomb... Indian Law Reports, Bombay Series [*A publication*] (DLA)
Ind LR Calc... Indian Law Reports, Calcutta Series [*A publication*] (DLA)
Ind L Reg.... Indiana Legal Register [*A publication*] (DLA)
Ind L Rep.... Indiana Law Reporter [*1881*] [*A publication*] (DLA)
Ind L Rep.... Indian Law Reporter [*A publication*] (DLA)
Ind LR Hyderabad... Indian Law Reports, Hyderabad Series [*A publication*] (DLA)
Ind LR Kar... Indian Law Reports, Karachi Series [*A publication*] (DLA)
Ind LR Ker... Indian Law Reports, Kerala Series [*A publication*] (DLA)
Ind LR Lah... Indian Law Reports, Lahore Series [*A publication*] (DLA)
Ind LR Luck... Indian Law Reports, Lucknow Series [*A publication*] (DLA)
Ind LR Mad... Indian Law Reports, Madras Series [*A publication*] (DLA)
Ind LR Madhya Bharat... Indian Law Reports, Madhya Bharat Series [*A publication*] (DLA)
Ind LR Mysore... Indian Law Reports, Mysore Series [*A publication*] (DLA)
Ind LR Nag... Indian Law Reports, Nagpur Series [*A publication*] (DLA)
Ind LR Or..... Indian Law Reports, Orissa Series [*A publication*] (DLA)
Ind LR Pat... Indian Law Reports, Patna Series [*A publication*] (DLA)
Ind LR Patiala... Indian Law Reports, Patiala Series [*A publication*] (DLA)
Ind LR Pun... Indian Law Reports, Punjab Series [*A publication*] (DLA)
Ind LR Rajasthan... Indian Law Reports, Rajasthan Series [*A publication*] (DLA)
Ind LR Ran... Indian Law Reports, Rangoon Series [*A publication*] (DLA)
Ind LS.......... Indiana Law Student [*A publication*] (DLA)
Ind L Stud... Indiana Law Student [*A publication*] (DLA)
Ind LT.......... Indian Law Times [*A publication*] (DLA)
Ind Lubr Tribol... Industrial Lubrication and Tribology (journ.) (SAUS)
Indm........... Indemnity (EBF)
INDM........... Indemnity [*Legal term*]
Ind M........... Independent Monthly [*A publication*]
INDM........... Infant of Nondiabetic Mother [*Obstetrics*]
INDMAN....... Industrial Manager
Ind Management... Industrial Management (journ.) (SAUS)
Ind Market Dig... Industrial Marketing Digest (journ.) (SAUS)
IndMed......... Index Medicus (SAUS)
Ind Med Gaz... Indian Medical Gazette (journ.) (SAUS)
Ind Med Rec... Indian Medical Record (journ.) (SAUS)
Ind Med Surg... Industrial Medicine and Surgery (journ.) (SAUS)
IND METH.... Independent Methodist (WDAA)
INDMGR....... Industrial Manager
Ind Mining Stand... Industrial and Mining Standard [*A publication*]
Ind Mktng.... Industrial Marketing (journ.) (SAUS)
INDMNTY..... Indemnity
INDN........... Indian
indn........... Indication (ADWA)
INDN........... Indication (WGA)
INDN........... Induction
IndNatuz...... Industrie Natuzzi SA [*Associated Press*] (SAG)
INDN CY...... Indication Cycle (SAUS)
Ind News..... Industry News [*A publication*]
IndO........... Indian Ocean
INDO........... Indomethacin [*An analgesic*]
Indo........... Indonesia (MILB)
INDO........... Indonesia
INDO........... Intermediate Neglect of Differential Overlap [*Quantum mechanics*]
INDOAFR..... Indo-African (SAUS)
INDO-AMER... Indo-American (SAUS)
INDOC......... Indochina [*or Indochinese*] (WDAA)
Indoc.......... Indochinese (SAUS)
INDOC......... Indoctrinate (AABC)
INDOC......... Indoctrination (SAUS)
INDOC......... Indonesian Documentation and Information Centre [*Leiden, Netherlands*] (EAIO)
INDOC......... Information-Documentation and Communication (PDAA)
INDOC......... International Documentation in Chemistry (SAUS)
INDOCHEM... Indian Ocean GEOSECS Program (MSC)
Indo-Chi....... Indo-China (SAUS)
Indo-Chi....... Indo-Chinese (SAUS)
indocin........ indomethacine (SAUS)
INDOCNREGREPCEN... Indoctrination Naval Regional Reporting Center (DNAB)
INDO-EUR.... Indo-European (ROG)
INDOEX........ Indian Ocean Experiment [*National Science Foundation project*]
INDO-GER.... Indo-Germanic [*Language, etc.*] (ROG)
Indo-Germ Forsch... Indogermanische Forschungen [*A publication*] (OCD)
Indol........... Indology (DIAR)
Indo-Mal....... Indo-Malayan (SAUS)
Indon........... Indonesia (BARN)
Indones........ Indonesia Fund [*Associated Press*] (SAG)
Indo-Pak....... India-Pakistan (SAUS)
INDOR.......... Internuclear Double Resonance
Ind Organ Rev... Industrial Organization Review [*A publication*] (JLIT)
Ind Org Hlth... Industrial Organisation and Health (journ.) (SAUS)
IndoSatel..... Indonesian Satellite Corp. [*Associated Press*] (SAG)
IndoTel........ Indonesian Telekomunikas [*Associated Press*] (SAG)
Indp........... Independent (AL)
Ind P........... Pharmacopoeia of India [*A publication*]
INDPD.......... Independence, KS [*American Association of Railroads railroad junction routing code*]
INDPDNC..... Independence
IND PENS.... Indian Pension [*Army*] [*British*] (ROG)

IND PH .... Indian Pharmacopoeia (ROG)
Ind Pharm ... Indian Pharmacist (journ.) (SAUS)
Indpls .... Indianapolis (BEE)
INDPNDNT ... Independent
INDPOL .... Industrial Pollutant (or Pollution) (SAUS)
Ind Prod Mag... Industrial Products Magazine (journ.) (SAUS)
Ind Prog Dev... Industrial Progress and Development [*A publication*]
Ind Prop ...... Industrial Property [*Legal term*] (DLA)
Ind Prop Q.... Industrial Property Quarterly [*A publication*] (DLA)
INDQ............ International Dairy Queen, Inc. [*NASDAQ symbol*] (NQ)
INDQA.......... Intl Dairy Queen 'A' [*NASDAQ symbol*] (TTSB)
INDQB.......... Intl Dairy Queen 'B' [*NASDAQ symbol*] (TTSB)
Ind R .... Indiana Reports [*A publication*] (DLA)
INDR............ Indicator (IAA)
Ind Radiogr... Industrial Radiography and Non-Destructive Testing (journ.) (SAUS)
INDRA Project... Internet Display and Remote Access Project (SAUS)
INDRB.......... Inactive Nondisability Retirement Branch [*BUPERS*]
INDR Device... Indicator Device (SAUS)
INDRE.......... Indenture
Ind Recovery... Industrial Recovery (journ.) (SAUS)
Ind Ref Serv... Industrial Reference Service. United States Bureau of Foreign and Domestic Commerce. Department of Commerce. Washington (SAUS)
INDREG........ Inductance Regulator (IEEE)
INDREG........ Induction Regulator (SAUS)
IndRelat....... Industrial Relations (journ.) (SAUS)
Ind Rel J Econ & Soc... Industrial Relations: Journal of Economy and Society [*A publication*] (DLA)
Ind Rep........ Independent Republican (SAUS)
Ind Rep........ Indiana Reports [*A publication*] (DLA)
IndRes .... Industrial Research (journ.) (SAUS)
Ind Res Dev... Industrial Research and Development (journ.) (SAUS)
Ind Review Jap... Industrial Review of Japan (journ.) (SAUS)
Ind Robot...... Industrial Robot (journ.) (SAUS)
INDS .... In-Core Nuclear Detection System [*Nuclear energy*] (IEEE)
INDS .... Investigational New Drug Submission [*Medicine*] (DB)
Ind Safety Survey... Industrial Safety Survey. International Labour Office. Geneva, Switzerland and Montreal (SAUS)
Ind SBA .... Indiana State Bar Association Reports [*A publication*] (DLA)
IndsBc .... Industrial Bancorp, Inc. [*Associated Press*] (SAG)
INDSCAL...... Individual Differences Scaling (PDAA)
IndSci.......... Industrial Scientific Corp. [*Associated Press*] (SAG)
Ind Sci Instrum... Industrial and Scientific Instruments (journ.) (SAUS)
Ind Sci Technol... Industrial Science and Technology (journ.) (SAUS)
INDSL .... Industrial (WGA)
Ind Soc B..... Indian Sociological Bulletin (journ.) (SAUS)
IndSqS......... Independence Square Income Securities [*Associated Press*] (SAG)
IndSqS......... Independence Square Income Securities, Inc. [*Associated Press*] (SAG)
Ind standard... Industrial standardization and commercial standards monthly. New York City (SAUS)
Ind St U........ Indiana State University (GAGS)
Ind Super..... Wilson's Indiana Superior Court Reports [*A publication*] (DLA)
Ind Sym........ Indianapolis Symphony (SAUS)
INDT .... Indent (MSA)
IND T.......... Indian Territory (ROG)
INDT .... Induction (DNAB)
INDT .... Institute for Non-Destructive Testing [*Milwaukee School of Engineering*] (PDAA)
INDT .... Interceptor Director Technician (SAA)
INDT .... Interdisciplinary Technology (SAUS)
Ind T Ann St... Indian Territory Annotated Statutes [*A publication*] (DLA)
IndTc .... Industrial Technologies, Inc. [*Associated Press*] (SAG)
IndTech........ Industrial Technologies, Inc. [*Associated Press*] (SAG)
INDTEL .... Industry and Teacher Education Liaison (AIE)
IND TER....... Indian Territory
Ind Ter......... Indian Territory Reports [*A publication*] (DLA)
Ind Terr .... Indian Territory (DLA)
INDTNG........ Individual Training [*Navy*] (NVT)
Indtr............ Indentor (SAUS)
INDTR .... Indicator-Transmitter
IndTrn.......... Industrial Training Corp. [*Associated Press*] (SAG)
Indty .... Indemnity [*Legal term*] (DLA)
Ind U .... Indiana University (GAGS)
IndUAP .... Independent United Australia Party [*Political party*]
INDUC.......... Induction (AABC)
Ind UCD .... Indiana Unemployment Compensation Division, Selected Appeal Tribunal Decisions [*A publication*] (DLA)
Induced EMF... Induced Electromotive Force (SAUS)
Ind Un Art B... Indiana University. Art Museum. Bulletin (journ.) (SAUS)
Ind univ publ anthrop ling... Indiana University Publications in Anthropology and Linguistics. Memoir 4 and 5 of the International Journal of American Linguistics. Supplement to V. (SAUO)
Ind U Penn... Indiana University of Pennsylvania (GAGS)
IND U PR..... Indiana University Press (DGA)
indus .... Industrial (NTIO)
Indus .... Industrialist
indus .... Industry (NTIO)
INDUS.......... Industry
Indus .... Industry
INDUS.......... Interactive Duct Sizing [*Facet Ltd.*] [*Software package*] (NCC)
Indus & Lab Rel Rev... Industrial and Labor Relations Review [*A publication*] (AAGC)
Indus Cas R... Industrial Cases Reports [*Law reports*] [*British*] (DLA)
IndusG .... Indus Group, Inc. (The) [*Associated Press*] (SAG)
IndusHld ...... Industrial Holdings, Inc. [*Associated Press*] (SAG)
Indus L Rev... Industrial Law Review [*A publication*] (DLA)
INDUSMIN ... Industrial Mineral Service [*Midland, ON*]
IndusMt .... Industir-Matematik International Corp. [*Associated Press*] (SAG)
Indus Rel Guide... Industrial Relations Guide [*A publication*] (DLA)
INDUSSIM ... Industry Simulation (SAUS)
INDUSSIM ... Total Industry Simulation [*Game*]
Indust .... Industrial (TBD)
INDUST......... Industrial [*or Industry*]
indust .... industrialization (SAUS)
indust .... industrious (SAUS)
INDUST........ Industry
Indust Acc Com... Decisions of the Industrial Accident Commission of California [*A publication*] (DLA)
Indust Austn & Mining Std... Industrial Australian and Mining Standard [*A publication*]
Indust Bull... Industrial Bulletin [*A publication*] (DLA)
Indust C Aw... Industrial Court Awards [*England*] [*A publication*] (DLA)
Indust Ct Aw... Industrial Court Awards [*England*] [*A publication*] (DLA)
INDUSTL...... Industrial
Indust Law Rev... Industrial Law Review [*A publication*] (DLA)
Indust L Rev... Industrial Law Review [*A publication*] (DLA)
Indust L Soc Bull... Bulletin. Industrial Law Society [*A publication*] (DLA)
Indust Prop... Industrial Property [*Legal term*] (DLA)
Indust Prop Q... Industrial Property Quarterly [*A publication*] (DLA)
Indust Prop'y Yb... Industrial Property Yearbook [*A publication*] (DLA)
INDUSTR ..... Industrial (ROG)
Industrial Phot... Industrial Photography (journ.) (SAUS)
Industr Prop'y Q... Industrial Property Quarterly [*A publication*] (DLA)
Industry Devel... Industry and Development [*A publication*] (JLIT)
IndUtd.......... Indiana United Bancorp [*Associated Press*] (SAG)
Indv .... Individual (TBD)
INDV .... Individual Inc. [*NASDAQ symbol*] (TTSB)
INDV .... Individually (MSA)
Ind Veg Turf Pest Manage... Industrial Vegetation Turf and Pest Management (journ.) (SAUS)
Indvl .... Individual Investor Group [*Associated Press*] (SAG)
IndvInv......... Individual Investor Group [*Associated Press*] (SAG)
Ind Week..... Industry Week (journ.) (SAUS)
Ind Wills...... Inderwick on Wills [*1866*] [*A publication*] (DLA)
INDX .... Enforcement Document Retrieval System (SAUS)
INDX .... Index Technology Corp. (SAUO)
INDX .... Industrial Propane Supply [*Private rail car owner code*]
Indy .... Indianapolis Speedway (SAUS)
INDY .... Industry (SAUS)
Ind YB Int'l Aff... Indian Yearbook of International Affairs [*A publication*] (DLA)
IndyCar .... Championship Auto Racing Teams [*An association*] (EA)
INDZ .... Industrial Park [*Federal Railroad Administration identification code*]
INE.............. East Chicago Public Library, East Chicago, IN [*OCLC symbol*] (OCLC)
InE .... Evansville Public Library and Vanderburgh County Public Library, Evansville, IN [*Library symbol*] [*Library of Congress*] (LCLS)
INE.............. Incorrect Negative Expectancy [*Psychometrics*]
ine .... Indo-European [*MARC language code*] [*Library of Congress*] (LCCP)
INE.............. Inertial Navigation Element (SAUS)
INE.............. Inertial Navigation Equipment (MCD)
INE.............. Infantile Necrotizing Encephalomyelopathy [*Medicine*] (MAE)
INE.............. Initiatives for Not-for-Profit Entrepreneurship [*Research center*] (RCD)
INE.............. Inline Network Encryptors (SAUS)
INE.............. Institution of Naval Engineers (SAUO)
INE.............. Institution of Nuclear Engineers (PDAA)
INE.............. International Kenergy Resource Corp. [*Vancouver Stock Exchange symbol*]
INE.............. Interoperable Network Event (SAUS)
INE.............. Missoula, MT [*Location identifier*] [*FAA*] (FAAL)
INEA............ Ethnobiological Institute of Australia (SAUO)
INEA............ International Electronics Association (SAUO)
INEA............ Internationaler Elektronik-Arbeitskreis [*International Electronics Association*]
INEAC .... Institut National pour l'Etude Agronomique du Congo [*National Institute for the Study of Agronomy in the Congo*]
InEaP .... Earl Park Public Library, Earl Park, IN [*Library symbol*] [*Library of Congress*] (LCLS)
InEc .... East Chicago Public Library, East Chicago, IN [*Library symbol*] [*Library of Congress*] (LCLS)
INEC............ European Institute of Ecology and Cancer (SAUS)
INEC............ IndTech Corp. (SAUO)
INEC............ Institut Europeen d'Ecologie et de Cancerologie [*European Institute of Ecology and Cancer - EIEC*] (EA)
INEC............ Institut Europeen des Industries de la Gomme de Caroube [*European Institute of Carob Gum Industries*] [*EC*] (ECED)
INEC............ Inverted Emulsifiable Concentrate (SAUS)
INECA .... Industrial Energy Conservation Abstracts [*UNIDO*] [*United Nations*] (DUND)
InEcIP .... Indiana City Press, Indiana City, IN [*Library symbol*] [*Library of Congress*] (LCLS)
InEd .... Edinburg Public Library, Edinburg, IN [*Library symbol*] [*Library of Congress*] (LCLS)
INED .... Inedible
INED .... Inedites [*Unpublished*] [*French*] (ROG)
INED .... Ineditus [*Not Made Known*] [*Latin*]
INED .... Institute for New Enterprise Development (EA)
INED .... International Network for Educational Information (EAIO)
INEEL.......... Idaho National Engineering and Environmental Laboratory

INEEL URC... Idaho National Engineering and Environmental Laboratory University Research Consortium
INEF............ International Excellence Exchange Foundation (SAUO)
INEFCO........ Insurance Export Finance Company (SAUO)
INEFFCY...... Inefficiency
INEFFY......... Inefficiency (AABC)
InefMkt........ [*The*] Inefficient-Market Fund [*Associated Press*] (SAG)
inefvy........... ineffectively (SAUS)
INeg............. Index to Periodicals by and about Blacks
INEGI........... Instituto Nacional de Estadistica, Geografia e Informatica [*Main government clearinghouse for statistical information*] [*Mexico*] (CROSS)
INEI............. Insituform East [*NASDAQ symbol*] (TTSB)
INEI............. Insituform East, Inc. [*NASDAQ symbol*] (NQ)
INEI............. International Exhibition of Industrial Electronics (MCD)
INEI............. International Network for Educational Information (SAUS)
INEL............. Idaho National Engineering Laboratory [*Idaho Falls, ID*] [*Department of Energy*]
INEL............. Idaho Nuclear Engineering Laboratory (SAUS)
inel.............. inelastic (SAUS)
INEL............. Inelasticity (SAUS)
INEL............. Intelligent Electroncs [*NASDAQ symbol*] (TTSB)
INEL............. Intelligent Electronics, Inc. [*NASDAQ symbol*] (SAG)
INEL............. International Exhibition of Industrial Electronics (SAUS)
InElk........... Elkhart Public Library, Elkhart, IN [*Library symbol*] [*Library of Congress*] (LCLS)
InElkB......... Mennonite Biblical Seminary, Elkhart, IN [*Library symbol*] [*Library of Congress*] (LCLS)
InElkM......... Miles Laboratories, Inc., Elkhart, IN [*Library symbol*] [*Library of Congress*] (LCLS)
InElkT......... Elkhart Truth, Elkhart, IN [*Library symbol*] [*Library of Congress*] (LCLS)
InEllJ.......... Ellettsville Journal, Ellettsville, IN [*Library symbol*] [*Library of Congress*] (LCLS)
INELTEC...... Exhibition of Industrial Electronics, Electrical Engineering, and Technical Installation (TSPED)
InElw.......... Elwood Public Library, Elwood, IN [*Library symbol*] [*Library of Congress*] (LCLS)
InElwCL....... Elwood Call-Leader, Elwood, IN [*Library symbol*] [*Library of Congress*] (LCLS)
InEM........... Mead Johnson Research Center, Evansville, IN [*Library symbol*] [*Library of Congress*] (LCLS)
INEN........... Andean Community-Colombia, Bolivia, Ecuador, Venezuela and Peru (SAUO)
INEN........... Ecuadorian Institute of Standardization (SAUS)
INENCO....... Center for International Environmental Cooperation (SAUO)
INENCO....... International Environmental Cooperation (SAUS)
InEng.......... Crawford County Public Library, English, IN [*Library symbol*] [*Library of Congress*] (LCLS)
InEngD........ Crawford County Democrat, English, IN [*Library symbol*] [*Library of Congress*] (LCLS)
InENR......... Northside Reporter, Evansville, IN [*Library symbol*] [*Library of Congress*] (LCLS)
InEnt.......... Inmark Enterprises, Inc. [*Associated Press*] (SAG)
INEOA......... International Narcotic Enforcement Officers Association (EA)
INEOS......... Integrated National Environmental Observing System (FOTI)
InEP........... Evansville Press and Courier, Evansville, IN [*Library symbol*] [*Library of Congress*] (LCLS)
INEP........... Institute of North Industrial Ecology Problems (SAUO)
INEP........... International Nurse Education Program
INep........... Neponset Public Library, Neponset, IL [*Library symbol*] [*Library of Congress*] (LCLS)
INEPA......... Institute of Entomology and Parasitology of Africa (SAUO)
INepL......... Neponset Public Library, Neponset, IL [*Library symbol*] [*Library of Congress*] (LCLS)
INEPT......... EN Engineering Panel Telemail (SAUS)
INEPT......... Insensitive Nuclear (or Nuclei) Enhanced by Polarization Transfer (SAUS)
INEPT......... Insensitive Nuclei Enhanced by Polarization Transfer [*Spectroscopy*]
INEPT......... Insensitive Nucleus Enhancement by Polarization Transfer (SAUS)
INEPT CR.... Insensitive Nuclear (or Nuclei) Enhanced by Polarization under Composite Refocusing (SAUS)
ineq........... inequality (SAUS)
INER.......... Inertial (KSC)
INER.......... Institute of Nuclear Energy Research (SAUS)
INERT......... Index of National Enervation and Related Trends [*Department of Commerce*]
Inertial Gu... Inertial Guidance [*Aerospace*] (NAKS)
InES........... Indiana State University, Evansville Campus, Evansville, IN [*Library symbol*] [*Library of Congress*] (LCLS)
INES........... Information Editing System (SAUS)
INES........... International Nuclear Event Scale
InESC......... Evansville-Vanderburgh School Corp., Library Services Center, Evansville, IN [*Library symbol*] [*Library of Congress*] (LCLS)
INESKA....... Information Exchange Scheme Kingston Area (SAUS)
INET........... Image Network (DMAA)
INet........... Indiana Network
INET........... Inertial Navigation Equipment Tester (SAUS)
INET........... Instinet Corp. [*NASDAQ symbol*] (COMM)
INET........... Institute of Nuclear Energy Technology (SAUS)
I-Net.......... Institutional Network (SAUS)
INET........... Intelligent Network [*Telecom Canada*] [*Database*]
INET........... Intelligent Network Simulator (SAUS)
INET........... Interbank Network Electronic, Inc. (SAUO)
INET........... Interbank Network for Electronic Transfer
INET........... International Networking Conference (SAUO)
INET........... International Networks in Education and Development (SAUO)
I-Net.......... Intranet (SAUS)
INET........... Intrenet, Inc. [*NASDAQ symbol*] (SAG)
inetiv.......... ineffective (SAUS)
INETS......... Integrated Effects Tests for Survivability (SAUS)
InEU........... University of Evansville, Evansville, IN [*Library symbol*] [*Library of Congress*] (LCLS)
In Evang Iohan... Tractatus in Evangelium Iohannis [*of Augustine*] [*Classical studies*] (OCD)
INew........... Newman Township Library, Newman, IL [*Library symbol*] [*Library of Congress*] (LCLS)
InEW........... Willard Library, Evansville, IN [*Library symbol*] [*Library of Congress*] (LCLS)
INEWAM...... Integrated Electronic Warfare Analysis and Model (ACAE)
INEWF........ Indian National Electricity Workers' Federation
INewm........ Newman Township Library, Newman, IL [*Library symbol*] [*Library of Congress*] (LCLS)
INEWS........ Integrated Electronic Warfare System
InEWS........ West Side Story, Evansville, IN [*Library symbol*] [*Library of Congress*] (LCLS)
INEWSS...... Integrated Electronic Warfare System Simulation (ACAE)
INewt.......... Newton Public Library, Newton, IL [*Library symbol*] [*Library of Congress*] (LCLS)
INEX........... Indirect Nonexempt (TIMI)
INEX........... Inexperienced (DAVI)
IN EX.......... In Extenso [*At Full Length*] [*Latin*] (ROG)
INEX........... International Emergency Preparedness Exercise (SAUO)
INF............ Infamous [*FBI standardized term*]
inf............. Infant (GEAB)
INF............ Infant
Inf............. Infantible (SAUS)
INF............ Infantile (CPH)
inf............. Infantile (DMAA)
INF............ Infantry (AFM)
inf............. Infantry (MILB)
inf............. Infarction [*Medicine*] (EDAA)
INF............ Infarction [*Medicine*] (MELL)
inf............. Infected (CPH)
INF............ Infected (SAUS)
INF............ Infection [*Medicine*]
inf............. Inferior (WDMC)
INF............ Inferior
INF............ Infield (WGA)
IN F........... In Fine [*Finally*] [*Latin*]
INF............ Infinite (MSA)
INF............ Infinite Resources, Inc. [*Vancouver Stock Exchange symbol*]
inf............. Infinitive (WDMC)
INF............ Infinitive
INF............ Infinity
INF............ Infinity Broadcasting'A' [*NYSE symbol*] (TTSB)
INF............ Infinity Broadcasting Corp. [*NYSE symbol*] (SAG)
INF............ Infirmary
inf............. Inflamed [*Medicine*] (EDAA)
INF............ Influence (WDAA)
INF............ Influenza [*Medicine*]
INF............ In Folio (DGA)
INF............ Inform
INF............ Informaatiopalvelulaitos [*Information Service*] [*Technical Research Center of Finland*] [*Espoo*] [*Information service or system*] (IID)
INF............ Informal
INF............ Informant (WGA)
Inf............. Information (AL)
INF............ Information [*Computer science*]
inf............. Information (WDMC)
INF............ Information Paper (SAUO)
INF............ Informationszentrum und Bibliotheken [*Information retrieval*]
Inf............. Informative (SAUS)
INF............ Informed
Inf............. Infortiatum [*A publication*] (DSA)
INF............ Infra [*Beneath or Below*] [*Latin*]
INF............ Infunde [*Pour In*] [*Pharmacy*]
INF............ Infundibulum of Neurohypophysis [*Pituitary stalk*] [*Medicine*] (DB)
INF............ Infusion [*Medicine*]
INF............ Infusum [*Infusion*] [*Pharmacy*] (ROG)
INF............ Inland Navigation Facility
INF............ Intemediate Nuclear Forces (SAUO)
INF............ Interactive Network Facility (SAUO)
INF............ Interceptor Night Fighter (NATG)
INF............ Interface (KSC)
INF............ Interface. Data Processing Management (journ.) (SAUS)
INF............ Interference (KSC)
INF............ Interferon [*Medicine*] (MELL)
INF............ Intermediate Nuclear Forces Negotiations (SAUO)
INF............ Intermediate-Range Nuclear Forces
INF............ International Nature Friends (SAUO)
INF............ International Naturist Federation [*Antwerp, Belgium*] (EA)
INF............ International Nuclear Forces (NATG)
INF............ International Nudist Federation (SAUO)
INF............ Intervertebral Foramina (SAUS)
INF............ Intravenous Nutritional Feeding (MELL)
INF............ Iranian National Front (PPW)
INF............ Irredundant Normal Formula
INF............ ISDN [*Integrated Services Digital Network*] Numbering Forum (OSI)
INF............ National Front of Iran [*Political party*] (PSAP)

INF............ Parke, Davis & Co. [*Great Britain*] [*Research code symbol*]
infa-............ Faroe Islands [*MARC geographic area code*] [*Library of Congress*] (LCCP)
INFA............ Informatica Corp. [*NASDAQ symbol*] (NASQ)
INFA............ International Federation of Aestheticians [*Brussels, Belgium*] (EAIO)
INFa............ International Fiscal Association (SAUO)
INFA............ International Nuclear Fuel Authority
INFAC......... Instrumented Factory (SAUS)
INFAC......... Instrumented Factory for Gears [*Illinois Institute of Technology Research Institute*] [*Research center*] (RCD)
INFACON...... International Ferro-Alloys Congress
INFACT....... Infant Formula Action Coalition (EA)
InFACT....... Integrated Flexible Assembly Cell Technology (SAUS)
Inf Age........ Information Age (journ.) (SAUS)
InFai........... Fairmount Public Library, Fairmount, IN [*Library symbol*] [*Library of Congress*] (LCLS)
InFaiN.......... Fairmount News, Fairmount, IN [*Library symbol*] [*Library of Congress*] (LCLS)
Infalum Bull... Infalum Bulletin (journ.) (SAUS)
INFAMA....... International Fair Promotion and Marketing (SAUS)
INFANT....... Infants Need to Find Adequate Nourishment Today [*An association*]
INFANT....... Interactive Networks Functioning on Adaptive Neural Topographies [*Robot*]
INFANT....... Iroquois Night Fighter and Night Tracker [*Military*] (MCD)
Infantry....... Infantry Magazine (journ.) (SAUS)
Infantry J..... Infantry Journal (SAUS)
INFANTS...... Interested Future Attorneys Negotiating for Tot Safety [*Student legal action organization*]
INFANTS...... Iroquois Night Fighter And Night Tracker System (SAUS)
infarc.......... infarction (SAUS)
InFarl........... Farmland Public Library, Farmland, IN [*Library symbol*] [*Library of Congress*] (LCLS)
InFb............ Fort Branch Public Library, Fort Branch, IN [*Library symbol*] [*Library of Congress*] (LCLS)
INFBAT........ Infantry Battalion [*Army*]
Inf Bde.......... Infantry Brigade
Inf Bn........... Infantry Battalion (SAUO)
Inf Brig......... Infantry Brigade (SAUO)
InFbT........... Fort Branch Times, Fort Branch, IN [*Library symbol*] [*Library of Congress*] (LCLS)
INFBTA........ Incorporated National Federation of Boot Trades Associations (SAUO)
INF-C........... Influenza-C [*Medicine*]
INFCE........... Influence (ROG)
INFCE........... International Fuel Cycle Evaluations (SAUS)
INFCE........... International Nuclear Fuel Cycle Evaluation
INFCEP........ International Fuel-Cycle Evaluation Program (SAUS)
INFCEP........ International Nuclear Fuel Cycle Evaluation Porgram (SAUO)
Inf Circ South Pac Comm... Information Circular. South Pacific Commission (journ.) (SAUS)
INFCO.......... Committee on Scientific and Technical Information on Standardization (SAUO)
INFCO.......... Information Committee [*International Organization for Standardization*] (IEEE)
INFCO.......... Information Committee of the International Standards Organization (NITA)
INFCO.......... Working Group on Scientific and Technical Information on Standardization (SAUO)
Inf Comput... Information and Computation (journ.) (SAUS)
InfContr....... Information and Control (journ.) (SAUS)
INFCY.......... Infancy (ROG)
INFD............ Infodata Systems [*NASDAQ symbol*] (TTSB)
INFD............ Infodata Systems, Inc. [*NASDAQ symbol*] (NQ)
INFD............ Informed (ROG)
Inf Decis Technol... Information and Decision Technologies (journ.) (SAUS)
Inf Dev......... Information Development (journ.) (SAUS)
inf dis.......... Infectious Disease (MEDA)
Inf Disp......... Information Display (journ.) (SAUS)
Inf Div.......... Infantry Division (SAUO)
INFDS.......... Information Data Structure (SAUS)
INFE............ Instituto Nacional de Fomento de la Exportacion [*National Institute of Export Development*] [*Spain*] (EY)
INFE............ International Newspaper Financial Executives (EA)
infec dis....... Infectious Disease [*Medicine*] (CPH)
Inf Econ Policy... Information Economics and Policy (journ.) (SAUS)
infect........... Infected (STED)
infect........... Infection [*or Infectious*] (DAVI)
Infect Control Hosp Epidemiol... Infection Control and Hospital Epidemiology (journ.) (SAUS)
Infect dis..... Infectious Disease [*Medicine*] (EDAA)
Infect Dis Clin North Am... Infectious Disease Clinics of North America (journ.) (SAUS)
Infect Immun... Infection and Immunity (journ.) (SAUS)
INFEDOP...... International Federation of Employees in Public Service [*Brussels, Belgium*] (EAIO)
infer............ Inferior (STED)
InFerC.......... Sisters of St. Benedict, Convent and Academy of the Immaculate Conception, Ferdinand, IN [*Library symbol*] [*Library of Congress*] (LCLS)
INFEREX...... Inference Execution Language
INFEREX Language... Interference Execution Language (SAUS)
InFerN......... Ferdinand News, Ferdinand, IN [*Library symbol*] [*Library of Congress*] (LCLS)
Infernce....... Inference Corp. [*Associated Press*] (SAG)
INF file........ Information File [*Computer science*] (IGQR)
InfFincl......... Infinity Financial Technology, Inc. [*Associated Press*] (SAG)
INFG........... Infinite Graphics, Inc. [*NASDAQ symbol*] (COMM)
INFH............ Incorporated National Federation of Hairdressers (SAUO)
INFH............ Ischemic Necrosis of Femoral Head [*Orthopedics*] (DAVI)
InfHA........... Influenza Virus Hemagglutinin [*Immunology*]
infib............ infibulate (SAUS)
infib............ infibulation (SAUS)
INFIC........... International Network of Feed Information Centers (EA)
infil............ Infiltrate [*or Infiltrated*] (DAVI)
INFIL/EXFIL... Infiltration and Exfiltration (DOMA)
INFIN........... Infinitive [*Grammar*]
InfinBr......... Infinity Broadcasting Corp. [*Associated Press*] (SAG)
InfinBrd........ Infinity Broadcasting Corp. [*Associated Press*] (SAG)
INFINET....... International Financial Networks
Infinity......... Infinity, Inc. [*Associated Press*] (SAG)
InFinSv........ Interchange Financial Services Corp. [*Associated Press*] (SAG)
INFINT......... Infinite
INFIRM........ Infirmary
INFIRM........ Integrated File of Information for Resources Management (SAUS)
INFIRS......... Invented-File-Search System (DICI)
INFIRS......... Inverted File Information Retrieval System [*UK Chemical Information Service*] (NITA)
INFIS........... Indonesian Aquatic Sciences Fisheries Information System [*Marine science*] (OSRA)
INFIS........... Inertial Navigation Flight Inspection System (SAUS)
INFIS........... International Federation of Information Services (SAUO)
INFIWEB....... Internet Professionnel des InfirmiSres Francophones (SAUS)
InFl............. Flora-Monroe Public Library, Flora, IN [*Library symbol*] [*Library of Congress*] (LCLS)
INFL............ Inflammability (SAUS)
INFL............ Inflammable
infl.............. Inflammation (STED)
INFL............ Inflated (ADA)
infl.............. inflect (SAUS)
In-Fl............ In-Flight (SAUS)
infl.............. Inflorescence [*Botany*]
infl.............. Influence (STED)
INFL............ Influence
infl.............. Influenced (BEE)
infl.............. Influx (STED)
INFL............ Influx
In Flacc....... In Flaccum [*of Philo Judaeus*] [*Classical studies*] (OCD)
INFLAM........ Inflammable
inflam.......... Inflammation [*or Inflammatory*] (DAVI)
Inflamm....... Inflammation (STED)
Inflamm....... Inflammatory (SAUS)
Inflammation... Inflammation (SAUS)
infln............ infulitive (SAUS)
INFLO.......... Integrated Flight Optimization (PDAA)
INFLO.......... Integrated Flight Optimization System (SAUO)
INFLO System... Integrated Flight Optimization System (SAUS)
infl proc....... Inflammatory Process (STED)
InFlt............ Interactive Flight Technologies, Inc. Cl.A [*Associated Press*] (SAG)
INFLTREP.... Inflight Report (SAUS)
influ............ influential (SAUS)
INFM............ Infectious Mononucleosis [*Medicine*] (DAVI)
INFM............ Infinium Software, Inc. [*NASDAQ symbol*] (NASQ)
INFM............ Inform (ROG)
InfMach........ Infinite Machines Corp. [*Associated Press*] (SAG)
Inf Manage... Information and Management (journ.) (SAUS)
InfMch.......... Infinite Machines Corp. [*Associated Press*] (SAG)
Inf Media Technol... Information Media and Technology (journ.) (SAUS)
INF Message... Information Message (SAUS)
InfMgeR........ Information Management Resources, Inc. [*Associated Press*] (SAG)
InfMgt.......... Information Management Technology [*Associated Press*] (SAG)
Inf MI............ Inferior Myocardial Infarction [*Cardiology*]
inf mono...... Infectious Mononucleosis [*Medicine*] (MAE)
INFMRY....... Infirmary
INFMTL........ Informational
INFN............ Infinity Financial Technology, Inc. [*NASDAQ symbol*] (SAG)
INFN............ Information (ROG)
INFN............ Infotron Systems Corp. [*NASDAQ symbol*] (COMM)
INFN............ Italian National Institute for Nuclear Physics
InFnDM........ International Finance Corp. [*Associated Press*] (SAG)
InFnDY......... International Finance Corp. [*Associated Press*] (SAG)
INFNET........ Istituto Nazionale Fisica Nucleare Network [*National Institute for Nuclear Physics Network*] [*Italian*] [*Computer science*] (TNIG)
Inf Nitrate Corp Chile Chil Nitrate Agric Serv... Information. Nitrate Corporation of Chile. Chilean Nitrate Agricultural Service (journ.) (SAUS)
INFNT.......... Infant
INFNT.......... Iroquois Night Fighter and Night Tracker [*Military*] (DNAB)
InFnYB......... International Finance Corp. [*Associated Press*] (SAG)
InFo............. Benton County Public Library, Fowler, IN [*Library symbol*] [*Library of Congress*] (LCLS)
INFO............ Infonautics, Inc. [*NASDAQ symbol*] (SAG)
INFO............ Infonautics Inc.'A' [*NASDAQ symbol*] (TTSB)
INFO............ Information (AFM)
info............. Information (DD)
Info............. Information (TBD)
INFO............ Information Network and File Organization [*Computer science*] (BUR)
INFO............ Information Network for Ontario [*Canada*]
INFO............ Information Network for Operations [*Computer science*]
INFO............ Integrated Fleet Operations
INFO............ Integrated Network Fiber Optics (MCD)
INFO............ International Forestry Consultants, Inc., Seattle (SAUS)

INFO .... International Fortean Organization (EA)
INFO .... International Information Management Exposition and Conference (SAUO)
INFO .... International Referral System (SAUO)
Info and Record Managem... Information and Records Management (journ.) (SAUS)
INFOBANK ... Information Bank (SAUS)
infobit .... Information Bit [*Computer science*] (BARN)
InfoCan .... Information Canada
INFOCEN...... Information Center (MCD)
INFOCEN...... Information Central (SAUO)
INFOCLIMA... Climate Data Referral System (SAUS)
INFOCLIMA... World Climate Data Information Referral Service [*World Meteorological Organization*] [*Information service or system*] (IID)
INFOCOMM... Information and Communications Technology Exposition (ITD)
InFoCR......... Benton County Recorder's Office, Fowler, IN [*Library symbol*] [*Library of Congress*] (LCLS)
InFocu .... In Focus System, Inc. [*Associated Press*] (SAG)
InFOCUS ...... Interprofessional Fostering of Opthalmic Care for Underserved Sectors (EA)
Infodat .... Infodata Systems, Inc. [*Associated Press*] (SAG)
INFODATA.... Database Information Science and Practice [*Database*]
info-dense ... Informationally Dense (ADWA)
InfoDev .... Information for Development Program (SAUO)
INFODOC ..... Information Documentation (SAUS)
INFO/DOC .... Information/Documentation [*Information service or system*] (IID)
Info Econ Pol... Information Economics and Policy [*A publication*] (JLIT)
INFOES .... In-Flight Operational Evaluation of a Space System
INFOEX .... Information Exchange, Inc. [*Telecommunications service*] (TSSD)
INFOFISH..... Intergovernmental Organization for Marketing Information and Technical Advisory Services for Fishery Products in the Asia-Pacific (SAUO)
INFOHOST ... Database Guide to German Host Operators [*Database*]
INFOHOST ... Information on Hosts (NITA)
INFOHYDRO... Hydrological Information Referral Service (SAUO)
InfoIntl .... Information International, Inc. [*Associated Press*] (SAG)
INFOL .... Information Oriented Language [*Information retrieval*]
INFOLAC ...... Information for Latin American Countries Project (NITA)
IN FOL ARG VOLVEND... In Folio Argenti Volvendae [*To Be Silvered*] [*Pharmacy*]
INFOMAG..... Information Magnetics Corp. (EFIS)
Info Manager... Information Manager (journ.) (SAUS)
INFOMARK... Information Market News [*Database*] [*EC*] (ECED)
INFOMART... Information Market [*Exhibition and conference centre*] [*Dallas*] (NITA)
INFOMAT ..... Information on Materials and Coatings (SAUS)
Infomed .... Infomed Holdings, Inc. [*Associated Press*] (SAG)
INFONAC...... Instituto de Fomento Nacional [*Industrial promotion agency*] [*Nicaragua*]
Infonau .... Infonautics, Inc. [*Associated Press*] (SAG)
INFONET ...... Information Network [*A federally registered trademark and service mark of Infonet Services Corporation, El Segundo, California*] (TEL)
Info O .... Information Officer (SAUO)
INFOODS ..... International Network of Food Data Systems [*Massachusets Institute of Technology*] [*Cambridge*] [*Information service or system*] (IID)
INFOPAC...... Pacific Bell Information System (SAUS)
INFOPAL ...... Latin American Population Information Storage, Retrieval and Processing Programme (SAUO)
INFO PASS... Central Mississippi Library Council [*Library network*]
INFOR .... Information (DSUE)
INFOR .... Information Network and File Organization (MHDB)
INFOR .... Information-processing and Operational Research (SAUS)
INFOR .... Interactive FORTRAN [*Formula Translating System*] [*Computer science*] (IAA)
INFORBW .... Information on Research in Baden-Wurttemberg [*Fachinformationszentrum Karlsruhe GmbH*] [*Germany*] [*Information service or system*] (CRD)
INFOREM..... Inventory Forecasting and Replenishment Modules [*IBM Corp.*]
INFOREP...... Information Report (CINC)
Info Rep M-X Mar For Res Cent... Information Report M-X. Maritimes Forest Research Centre. Canadian Forestry Service (journ.) (SAUS)
INFOREQ...... Information Requested [*or Required*]
INFOREQ...... Information Required as to (SAUS)
InfoRes .... Information Resources, Inc. [*Associated Press*] (SAG)
INFOREUROP... Press Information and Public Relations Service of Common Market Enterprises (SAUO)
INFORFILM... International Information Film Service (SAUO)
INFORM....... Information
INFORM....... Information for Minnesota (SAUO)
INFORM....... Information for Optimum Resource Management (MCD)
INFORM....... Information Management and Decision Support in High Dependency Environments (SAUO)
INFORM....... Information Management System (SAUO)
INFORM....... Information Network for Freight Overhead Billing, Rating, and Message Switching
INFORM....... Information Network for Online Retrieval Maintenance (SAUS)
INFORM....... Information Network for Operational Resources Management (SAUO)
INFORM....... Institute for Operations Research and Management (SAUS)
INFORM....... International Reference Organization in Forensic Medicine and Sciences (EA)
INFORMAC... Immediate Information for Merchant and Customer (PDAA)
INFORMAC... Information for Merchant and Customer (SAUS)
INFORMAL... Information for Avionics Laboratory
INFORMALUX... Information Luxembourg (NITA)
INFORMAP... Information Necessary for Optimum Resource Management and Protection (PDAA)
INFORMAP... Information Necessary for Optimum Resources Management Planning (SAUS)
Informbureau... Information Bureau (SAUS)
Inform Contr... Information Control (SAUS)
Informed...... Informedics, Inc. [*Associated Press*] (SAG)
Informercial... Information Commercial (ADWA)
INFORMN ..... Information
INFORM-R ... Management Information System for Agricultural Research (SAUO)
INFORMS..... Information Organization Reporting and Management System (IAA)
INFORMS..... Institute for Operations Research and the Management Sciences (NTPA)
INFORMS..... Iowa Network for Obtaining Resource Materials for Schools (SAUS)
Inform Sci and Syst... Information Science and Systems (journ.) (SAUS)
Inform Tech Ser... Information Technology Series (journ.) (SAUS)
Informx .... Informix Corp. [*Associated Press*] (SAG)
INFORS .... International Federation of Engineers (SAUO)
INFORTERM... International Information Center for Terminology (SAUO)
INFOS .... Information Network for Official Statistics [*Department of Statistics*] [*Information service or system*] (IID)
INFOS .... Informationszentrum fuer Schnittwerte [*Cutting Data Information Center*] [*Germany*] [*Information service or system*] (IID)
INFOSAFE.... Information System fo Roaduser Safety and Traffic Performance (SAUO)
Infosafe .... Infosafe Systems, Inc. [*Associated Press*] (SAG)
INFOSAMAK... Fish Marketing Information, Promotion and Technical Advisory Services for Arab Countries (SAUO)
INFOSEC ...... Information Security (COE)
INFOSEC ...... Information Systems Security (AAGC)
Infoseek........ Infoseek Corp. [*Associated Press*] (SAG)
Infosf .... Infosafe Systems, Inc. [*Associated Press*] (SAG)
Infosfe .... Infosafe Systems, Inc. [*Associated Press*] (SAG)
INFOSOCEE... Information Society and Industrial Development in Central and Eastern Europe (SAUO)
INFOSOR ..... Information Sources [*Information service or system*] (IID)
INFO-SOUTH/Online... INFO-SOUTH Latin American Information System. North-South Center, University of Miami (SAUS)
Infospecs..... Information Specialists Ltd. [*Information service or system*] (IID)
INFOSTOR ... Information Storage (SAUS)
InfoStor........ Information Storage Devices, Inc. [*Associated Press*] (SAG)
INFOSTOR ... Information Store (SAUS)
INFOTAB ...... International Tobacco Information Center (SAUO)
INFOTERM ... International Information Centre for Technology (SAUO)
INFOTERM ... International Information Centre for Terminology [*UNESCO*] (IID)
INFOTERRA... International Environmental Information System (SAUO)
INFOTERRA... International Environmental Research and Referral Service of UNEP (SAUO)
INFOTERRA... International Referral System for Sources of Environmental Information [*Formerly, IRS*] [*United Nations Environment Program*] (ASF)
INFOTERRA... International Register for Sources of Environmental Information (SAUO)
INFOTEX ...... Information via Telex [*Telecommunications*] (TEL)
Info Theory... Information Theory (SAUS)
INFOWAR .... Information Warfare
Info Wash.... Information Washington (journ.) (SAUS)
INFP............. Introverted, Intuitive, a Feeler, and Perceiver [*Keirsey Temperament Test Result*] [*Psychology*]
Inf Pap Aust AEC... Information Paper. Australian Atomic Energy Commission (journ.) (SAUS)
Inf Power..... Information Power (journ.) (SAUS)
Inf Prcht Regt... Infantry Parachute Regiment (SAUO)
Inf Process Lett... Information Processing Letters (journ.) (SAUS)
Inf Process Manage... Information Processing and Management (journ.) (SAUS)
Inf Process Soc Jpn... Information Processing Society of Japan (journ.) (SAUS)
INFQ .... International Information Management Exposition and Conference (SAUS)
INFR .... Inference Corp. [*NASDAQ symbol*] (SAG)
INFR .... Inference Corp.'A' [*NASDAQ symbol*] (TTSB)
INFR .... Inferior (ROG)
INFRA .... Information Research Analysts [*Database producer*] (IID)
infra .... Infrared (VRA)
INFRA .... Infrastructure (SAUS)
INFRA .... International Freedom Academy (SAUO)
INFRA DIG... Infra Dignitatem [*Undignified*] [*Latin*]
INFRAL .... Information Retrieval Automatic Language [*Computer science*]
INFRAPTUM... Infrascriptum [*Written Below*] [*Latin*] (ROG)
Infrasnc .... Infrasonics, Inc. [*Associated Press*] (SAG)
Inf RC .... Infantry Reserve Corps (SAUO)
InFrem .... Fremont Public Library, Fremont, IN [*Library symbol*] [*Library of Congress*] (LCLS)
InFren .... Melton Public Library, French Lick, IN [*Library symbol*] [*Library of Congress*] (LCLS)
InFrenSH ..... Springs Valley Herald, French Lick, IN [*Library symbol*] [*Library of Congress*] (LCLS)
Inf Rep North For Res Cent... Information Report Northern Forest Research Centre (SAUO)
Inf-Res......... Infantry Reserve (SAUO)
Inf Resour Manage J... Information Resources Management International Journal (journ.) (SAUS)
InFrf............. Frankfort Community Public Library, Frankfort, IL [*Library symbol*] [*Library of Congress*] (LCLS)
INF RHEI...... Infusum Rhei [*Infusion of Rhubarb*] [*Pharmacy*] (ROG)
INFRIC .... Infricetur [*Let It Be Rubbed In*] [*Pharmacy*]
InFrl............. Franklin Public Library, Franklin, IN [*Library symbol*] [*Library of Congress*] (LCLS)

InFrlC.......... Franklin College of Indiana, Franklin, IN [*Library symbol*] [*Library of Congress*] (LCLS)
InFrlCR........ Johnson County Recorder's Office, Franklin, IN [*Library symbol*] [*Library of Congress*] (LCLS)
InFrlJ.......... Franklin Daily Journal, Franklin, IN [*Library symbol*] [*Library of Congress*] (LCLS)
InFrlJM........ Johnson County Museum, Franklin, IN [*Library symbol*] [*Library of Congress*] (LCLS)
INFRM......... Infirm
INFRMRY..... Infirmary
INFRN.......... Inference (MSA)
INFROSS...... Information Requirements of the Social Sciences [*British*] (DIT)
INFROSS...... Investigation into Information Requirements of Social Sciences [*1970s study*] [*British*] (NITA)
INFROSS...... Investigation into Information Requirements of the Social Sciences (SAUS)
InfRsc.......... Information Resource Engineering, Inc. [*Associated Press*] (SAG)
InFrv............ Francesville-Salem Township Public Library, Francesville, IN [*Library symbol*] [*Library of Congress*] (LCLS)
InFrvT.......... Francesville Tribune, Francesville, IN [*Library symbol*] [*Library of Congress*] (LCLS)
INFS............. In Focus System, Inc. [*NASDAQ symbol*] (SAG)
INFS............. In Focus Systems [*NASDAQ symbol*] (TTSB)
INFS............. Internet Network File System (SAUS)
Inf Sch.......... Infantry School (SAUO)
Inf Sci.......... Information Sciences (journ.) (SAUS)
Inf Serv Use... Information Service and Use (journ.) (SAUS)
Inf Soc.......... Information Society (journ.) (SAUS)
Inf Softw Technol... Information and Software Technology (journ.) (SAUS)
InfStrRetr..... Information Storage & Retrieval (journ.) (SAUS)
Inf Syst........ Information Systems (journ.) (SAUS)
INFT............. Infant (ROG)
INFT............. Informal Training (NASA)
INFT............. Inforte Corp. [*NASDAQ symbol*] (SG)
Inf TAI.......... Information TAI (journ.) (SAUS)
InFtbh.......... United States Army, Post Library, Fort Benjamin Harrison, IN [*Library symbol*] [*Library of Congress*] (LCLS)
InFtbhP........ United States Army, Post Library, Fort Benjamin Harrison, IN [*Library symbol*] [*Library of Congress*] (LCLS)
Inf Technol Dev... Information Technology for Development (journ.) (SAUS)
Inf Technol Learn... Information Technology and Learning (journ.) (SAUS)
Inf Technol Public Policy... Information Technology and Public Policy (journ.) (SAUS)
Inf Technol Res and Dev... Information Technology. Research and Development (journ.) (SAUS)
Inf Tech People... Information Technology and People (journ.) (SAUS)
Inf Today..... Information Today (journ.) (SAUS)
Inf Today..... Information Today. Learned Information, Inc. (SAUO)
Inf Today..... Information Today. Learned Information, Inc., Medford (SAUS)
INfTr............ Info Trac
INF Treaty... Intermediate-Range Nuclear Forces Treaty (MUSM)
InFtv............ Carnegie Public Library District, Fortville, IN [*Library symbol*] [*Library of Congress*] (LCLS)
InFtvT.......... Fortville Tribune, Fortville, IN [*Library symbol*] [*Library of Congress*] (LCLS)
Infty............. Infantry [*British military*] (DMA)
INFU............. Infu-Tech, Inc. [*NASDAQ symbol*] (SAG)
InFu............. Phyllis Meyer Library, Fulton, IN [*Library symbol*] [*Library of Congress*] (LCLS)
INFUND........ Infunde [*Pour In*] [*Pharmacy*]
Infus............ Infusible (SAUS)
Infus............ Infusion [*Medicine*] (EDAA)
INFUS........... Infusum [*Infusion*] [*Pharmacy*] (ROG)
INFUSA........ International Network for a UN Second Assembly (SAUO)
INFUT.......... Information Utility (SAUS)
InfuTech...... Infu-Tech, Inc. [*Associated Press*] (SAG)
InFw............. Public Library of Fort Wayne and Allen County, Fort Wayne, IN [*Library symbol*] [*Library of Congress*] (LCLS)
InFwAHi...... Allen County-Fort Wayne Historical Society Library, Fort Wayne, IN [*Library symbol*] [*Library of Congress*] (LCLS)
InFwB.......... Fort Wayne Bible College, Fort Wayne, IN [*Library symbol*] [*Library of Congress*] (LCLS)
InFwC.......... Concordia Senior College, Fort Wayne, IN [*Library symbol*] [*Library of Congress*] (LCLS)
InFwCS........ Fort Wayne Community Schools, Fort Wayne, IN [*Library symbol*] [*Library of Congress*] (LCLS)
InFwCT........ Concordia Theological Seminary, Fort Wayne, IN [*Library symbol*] [*Library of Congress*] (LCLS)
InFwGS........ Church of Jesus Christ of Latter-Day Saints, Genealogical Society Library, Fort Wayne Branch, Fort Wayne, IN [*Library symbol*] [*Library of Congress*] (LCLS)
InFwI........... Indiana Institute of Technology, Fort Wayne, IN [*Library symbol*] [*Library of Congress*] (LCLS)
InFwIP......... Indiana-Purdue University, Fort Wayne, IN [*Library symbol*] [*Library of Congress*] (LCLS)
InFwJG........ Fort Wayne Journal-Gazette, Fort Wayne, IN [*Library symbol*] [*Library of Congress*] (LCLS)
InFwL.......... Lincoln National Life Foundation, Fort Wayne, IN [*Library symbol*] [*Library of Congress*] (LCLS)
InFwI-F........ National Life Insurance Co., Lincoln National Life Foundation, Louis A. Warren Lincoln Library and Museum, Fort Wayne, IN [*Library symbol*] [*Library of Congress*] (LCLS)
InFwLW....... Louis A. Warren Lincoln Library and Museum, Fort Wayne, IN [*Library symbol*] [*Library of Congress*] (LCLS)
InFwM......... Magnavox Co., Fort Wayne, IN [*Library symbol*] [*Library of Congress*] (LCLS)
InFwSF........ Saint Francis College, Fort Wayne, IN [*Library symbol*] [*Library of Congress*] (LCLS)
INFX............. Information Exchange (SAUO)
INFX............. Inspection Fixture
INFY............. Infancy [*Legal shorthand*] (LWAP)
Infy............. Infantry [*British military*] (DMA)
INFY............. Infosys Technologies ADS [*NASDAQ symbol*] (SG)
INFY............. Infosys Technologies, Ltd. [*NASDAQ symbol*] (NASQ)
ING.............. Ambler, PA [*Location identifier*] [*FAA*] (FAAL)
InG.............. Gary Public Library, Gary, IN [*Library symbol*] [*Library of Congress*] (LCLS)
ING.............. Inactive National Guard
ING.............. Index Nominum Genericorum (SAUO)
ING.............. Inertial Navigation and Guidance [*Aerospace*] (AAG)
ING.............. Inertial Navigation Gyro
ING.............. Inertial Neutron Generator (SAUS)
ING.............. Ingalls Shipbuilding Corp. (SAUO)
ing.............. Ingenieur (DD)
ING.............. Ingenieur [*Engineer*] [*French*] (EY)
ING.............. Inglis Ltd. [*Toronto Stock Exchange symbol*]
ING.............. Ingram Ranch [*California*] [*Seismograph station code, US Geological Survey*] (SEIS)
Ing.............. Inguina [*Medicine*] (AMHC)
ing.............. Inguinal [*Medicine*] (EDAA)
ING.............. Inguinal [*Anatomy*]
ING.............. Inside Nazi Germany [*A publication*]
ING.............. Integrated Ground (SAUS)
ING.............. Integrated News Gathering
ING.............. Intense Graphic Generator (SAUS)
ING.............. Intense Neutron Generator
ING.............. Internationale Nederlanden Groep [*Netherlands*] (ECON)
ING.............. International Newspaper Group (EA)
ING.............. Isotope Nephrogram (DMAA)
ING.............. Lago Argentino [*Argentina*] [*Airport symbol*] (OAG)
INGA............ Indium Gallium Arsenide
INGA............ Inspection Gauge
INGA............ Interactive Graphics Analysis
INGA............ Interstate Natural Gas Association (SAUO)
INGAA.......... Independent Natural Gas Association of America (SAUO)
INGAA.......... Interstate Natural Gas Association of America (EA)
INGAALP...... Indium-Gallium-Aluminum Phosphide [*Light-emitting diode construction*]
InGaAs......... Alloy Semiconductor (SAUS)
InGaAs......... Indiumgalliumarsenid (SAUS)
InGaAs......... Indium Gallium Arsenide (AAEL)
InGaAs APD... Indium Gallium Arsenide Avalanche Photodiode
InGaAsP....... Indium Gallium Arsenide Phosphide (AAEL)
InGaN.......... Indium Gallium Nitride (AAEL)
InGaP.......... Alloy Semiconductor (SAUS)
INGAP.......... Indian Gap, Pennsylvania (SAUO)
InGar.......... Garrett Public Library, Garrett, IN [*Library symbol*] [*Library of Congress*] (LCLS)
InGarC........ Garrett Clipper, Garrett, IN [*Library symbol*] [*Library of Congress*] (LCLS)
INGAT.......... Ingatestone [*Village in England*]
Ing B............ Ingenium Baccalaureus [*Bachelor of Engineering*]
INGB............ Nordic Gene Bank for Agricultural and Horticultural Plants (SAUO)
InGc............ Gas City-Mill Township Public Library, Gas City, IN [*Library symbol*] [*Library of Congress*] (LCLS)
INGC............ International Nutrition and Genetics Corp. (SAUO)
Ing Comp..... Ingram's Compensation for Interest in Lands [*2nd ed.*] [*1869*] [*A publication*] (DLA)
Ing D............ Ingenium Doctor [*Doctor of Engineering*]
Ing Dig........ Ingersoll's Digest of the Laws of the United States [*A publication*] (DLA)
InGe............ Geneva Public Library, Geneva, IN [*Library symbol*] [*Library of Congress*] (LCLS)
INGEBA........ International Cooperative Bank Co. (SAUO)
INGEE.......... Internally Generated Electronic Environment (SAUO)
InGeL.......... Limberlost State Memorial, Geneva, IN [*Library symbol*] [*Library of Congress*] (LCLS)
INGENINST... Office of the Inspector General Instructions [*Navy*]
INGER.......... Ingersoll, ON [*American Association of Railroads railroad junction routing code*]
INGER.......... International Network on Genetic Evaluation in Rice (ECON)
IngerRd........ Ingersoll Rand [*Associated Press*] (SAG)
Ingg............ Inggeris (SAUS)
Ing Hab Corp... Ingersoll on Habeas Corpus [*A publication*] (DLA)
InGHi.......... Gary Historical and Cultural Society, Gary, IN [*Library symbol*] [*Library of Congress*] (LCLS)
INGIFPI........ Irish National Group of International Federation of the Phonographic Industry (EAIO)
Ing Insolv.... Ingraham on Insolvency [*Pennsylvania*] [*A publication*] (DLA)
ING LINAC... Intense Neutron Generator Linear Accelerator (SAUS)
InglMkt........ Ingles Markets, Inc. [*Associated Press*] (SAG)
Ing M............ Ingenium Magister [*Master of Engineering*]
INGN............ Integrated Genetics, Inc. (SAUO)
InGo............ Goshen College, Goshen, IN [*Library symbol*] [*Library of Congress*] (LCLS)
INGO............ International Non-Governmental Organization
INGO/DPI Executive Committee... Executive Committee of Non-Governmental Organizations associated with the United Nations Division of Public Information (SAUO)

InGoM Mennonite Historical Library, Goshen College, Goshen, IN [*Library symbol*] [*Library of Congress*] (LCLS)
INGOMESA International Non-Governmental Organization Management Network for East and Southern Africa (SAUO)
InGoN Goshen News, Goshen, IN [*Library symbol*] [*Library of Congress*] (LCLS)
InGoo Goodland Public Library (Mitten Memorial Library), Goodland, IN [*Library symbol*] [*Library of Congress*] (LCLS)
InGoP Goshen Public Library, Goshen, IN [*Library symbol*] [*Library of Congress*] (LCLS)
InGP Indol Glycerophosphate [*Biochemistry*]
InGPS Indoleglycerolphosphate Synthase [*Biochemistry*]
InGPS Indoleglycerolphosphate Synthetasee (SAUS)
InGPT Gary Post-Tribune, Gary, IN [*Library symbol*] [*Library of Congress*] (LCLS)
InGr Greencastle-Putnam County Library, Greencastle, IN [*Library symbol*] [*Library of Congress*] (LCLS)
Ingr Ingredients (SAUS)
Ingr Ingress (SAUO)
ingr ingresso (SAUS)
INGR Intergraph Corp. [*NASDAQ symbol*] (NQ)
INGR Isophthalic Neopentyl Glycol Resin [*Plastics*]
InGrBG Greencastle Banner-Graphic, Greencastle, IN [*Library symbol*] [*Library of Congress*] (LCLS)
InGrD De Pauw University, Greencastle, IN [*Library symbol*] [*Library of Congress*] (LCLS)
INGRD Ingredient
InGrD-Ar De Pauw University, Archives, Greencastle, IN [*Library symbol*] [*Library of Congress*] (LCLS)
INGRDNT Ingredient
InGreb Greensburg Public Library, Greensburg, IN [*Library symbol*] [*Library of Congress*] (LCLS)
InGrebCR Decatur County Recorder's Office, Greensburg, IN [*Library symbol*] [*Library of Congress*] (LCLS)
InGrebDHi Decatur County Historical Society, Greensburg, IN [*Library symbol*] [*Library of Congress*] (LCLS)
InGrebHi Decatur County Historical Society, Greensburg, IN [*Library symbol*] [*Library of Congress*] (LCLS)
InGref Greenfield Public Library, Greenfield, IN [*Library symbol*] [*Library of Congress*] (LCLS)
InGrefL Eli Lilly & Co., Library Agricultural Services, Greenfield, IN [*Library symbol*] [*Library of Congress*] (LCLS)
InGrefR Greenfield Daily Reporter, Greenfield, IN [*Library symbol*] [*Library of Congress*] (LCLS)
INGRES Interactive Graphic and Retrieval System
InGretN Howard County News, Greentown, IN [*Library symbol*] [*Library of Congress*] (LCLS)
InGrew Greenwood Public Library, Greenwood, IN [*Library symbol*] [*Library of Congress*] (LCLS)
Ingria Ingermanland (SAUS)
IngrmM Ingram Micro, Inc. [*Associated Press*] (SAG)
Ing Roc Ingersoll's Edition of Roccus' Maritime Law [*A publication*] (DLA)
InGS Gary School System, Gary, IN [*Library symbol*] [*Library of Congress*] (LCLS)
INGS Inland Gold and Silver Corp. (SAUO)
INGSOC English Socialism [*From George Orwell's novel, "1984"*]
Ing Ves Vesey, Junior's, English Chancery Reports, Edited by Ingraham [*A publication*] (ILCA)
INGYO International Nongovernmental Youth Organization (PDAA)
INH Improved Nike Hercules [*Missile*]
IN/H Inches per Hour
INH Infectious Necrotic Hepatitis (SAUS)
inh Inhalation [*Medicine*] (EDAA)
INH Inhalation
INH Inhambane [*Mozambique*] [*Airport symbol*] (AD)
INH Inheritance [*Legal shorthand*] (LWAP)
inh Inherited (GEAB)
INH Inhibit (NASA)
inh Inhibiting [*Medicine*] (EDAA)
INH Intelligent Networking Hub (SAUS)
INH Isangel [*New Hebrides*] [*Seismograph station code, US Geological Survey*] (SEIS)
INH Isoniazid (DMAA)
INH Isonicotinic Acid Hydrazide [*or Isonicotinylhydrazine*] [*See also INAH, ISONIAZID*] [*Antituberculous agent*]
INH Isonicotinic Hydrazide (SAUS)
inH2O Conventional Inch of Water (SAUS)
INHA Inhibin Alpha (DMAA)
inhab Inhabitant (GEAB)
INHAB Inhabitant
INHABD Inhabited (ROG)
InHag Hagerstown Public Library, Hagerstown, IN [*Library symbol*] [*Library of Congress*] (LCLS)
InHagE Hagerstown Exponent, Hagerstown, IN [*Library symbol*] [*Library of Congress*] (LCLS)
INHAL Inhalatio [*Inhalation*] [*Pharmacy*]
InhalTh Inhale Therapeutic Systems [*Associated Press*] (SAG)
InHam Hammond Public Library, Hammond, IN [*Library symbol*] [*Library of Congress*] (LCLS)
InHamP Purdue University, Calumet Campus, Hammond, IN [*Library symbol*] [*Library of Congress*] (LCLS)
InHamT Hammond Times, Hammond, IN [*Library symbol*] [*Library of Congress*] (LCLS)
InHan Hanover College, Hanover, IN [*Library symbol*] [*Library of Congress*] (LCLS)
InHar Hartford City Public Library, Hartford City, IN [*Library symbol*] [*Library of Congress*] (LCLS)
InHarBHi Blackford County Historical Society, Hartford City, IN [*Library symbol*] [*Library of Congress*] (LCLS)
InHazN White River News, Hazelton, IN [*Library symbol*] [*Library of Congress*] (LCLS)
INHB Inhibin Beta (DMAA)
INHB Inhibit (MSA)
INHBD Inhibited
INHCE Inheritance [*Legal term*] (ROG)
InHeb Hebron Public Library, Hebron, IN [*Library symbol*] [*Library of Congress*] (LCLS)
InHebPH Porter County Herald, Hebron, IN [*Library symbol*] [*Library of Congress*] (LCLS)
Inher Inheritance [*Legal term*] (DLA)
Inher Est & Gift Tax Rep (CCH) Inheritance, Estate, and Gift Tax Reports (Commerce Clearing House) [*A publication*] (DLA)
in Hg inch of mercury (SAUS)
InHhW Workingmen's Institute, New Harmony, IN [*Library symbol*] [*Library of Congress*] (LCLS)
InHi Indiana Historical Society, Indianapolis, IN [*Library symbol*] [*Library of Congress*] (LCLS)
INHIB Inhibition
Inhib Inhibitory (SAUS)
INHIGEO International Commission on the History of the Geological Sciences [*ICSU*] [*Paris, France*] (EAIO)
INHIGEO International Committee on the History of the Geological Sciences (SAUO)
INHL Inhale Therapeutic Sys [*NASDAQ symbol*] (TTSB)
INHL Inhale Therapeutic Systems [*NASDAQ symbol*] (SAG)
InHld Industrial Holdings, Inc. [*Associated Press*] (SAG)
INHM Inco Homes [*NASDAQ symbol*] (TTSB)
INHM Inco Homes Corp. [*NASDAQ symbol*] (SAG)
INH Missile Improved Nike Hercules Missile (SAUS)
INHO Independence Hldg [*NASDAQ symbol*] (TTSB)
INHO Independence Holding Co. [*NASDAQ symbol*] (NQ)
InHobG Hobart Gazette, Hobart, IN [*Library symbol*] [*Library of Congress*] (LCLS)
InHobHi Pleak Memorial Library/Hobart Historical Society, Hobart, IN [*Library symbol*] [*Library of Congress*] (LCLS)
InHoG Hobart Gazette, Hobart, IN [*Library symbol*] [*Library of Congress*] (LCLS)
InHoHi Pleak Memorial Library/Hobart Historical Society, Hobart, IN [*Library symbol*] [*Library of Congress*] (LCLS)
InHome In Home Health, inc. [*Associated Press*] (SAG)
INHP Independence National Historical Park (SAUO)
INHS Illinois Natural History Survey [*Illinois Institute of Natural Resources*] [*Research center*] (RCD)
INHS Indian Naval Hospital Ship (SAUO)
INHS Irish National Hunt Steeplechase (ROG)
Inh Sw 1 B Inhibit Switch 1 Bit (SAUS)
Inh Sw 2 B Inhibit Switch 2 Bit (SAUS)
Inh Sw 4 B Inhibit Switch 4 Bit (SAUS)
Inh Sw 8 B Inhibit Switch 8 Bit (SAUS)
Inh Sw A Inhibit Switch A (SAUS)
Inh Sw Wd Mk Inhibit Switch Word Mark (SAUS)
Inh Sw Y B Inhibit Switch Y Bit (SAUS)
InHu Huntington Public Library, Huntington, IN [*Library symbol*] [*Library of Congress*] (LCLS)
InHub Huntingburg Public Library, Huntingburg, IN [*Library symbol*] [*Library of Congress*] (LCLS)
InHuCR Huntington County Recorder's Office, Huntington, IN [*Library symbol*] [*Library of Congress*] (LCLS)
InHuH Huntington College, Huntington, IN [*Library symbol*] [*Library of Congress*] (LCLS)
InHuHi Huntington County Historical Society, Huntington, IN [*Library symbol*] [*Library of Congress*] (LCLS)
InHuHP Huntington Herald-Press, Huntington, IN [*Library symbol*] [*Library of Congress*] (LCLS)
INHYX IDS High Yield Tax Exempt Cl.A [*Mutual fund ticker symbol*] (SG)
INI Incipient Nonequilibrium Index
InI Indianapolis-Marion County Public Library, Indianapolis, IN [*Library symbol*] [*Library of Congress*] (LCLS)
INI Indianapolis Newspapers Incorporated (SAUO)
INI Industrial Networking, Inc. [*Joint venture of Ungermann-Bass, Inc. and General Electric Corp.*]
INI Industrial Nurses Institute (SAUO)
ini Initialize (VLIE)
ini Initiator (SAUS)
INI Inner Integument [*Botany*]
INI In Nomine Iesu [*In the Name of Jesus*] [*Latin*]
INI Inspectorate of Nuclear Installations (SAUO)
INI Instituto Nacional de Industria [*National Institute for Industry*] [*Spain*]
INI Interface Noise Inverter
INI International Nonviolent Initiatives (EA)
INI International Nursing Index (ADWA)
INI Intervideo Network, Inc. [*Beverly Hills, CA*] [*Telecommunications*] (TSSD)
INI Intervideo Network, Incorporated (SAUO)
INI Intranuclear Inclusion
INI National Indigenous Institute
InIA Indiana Academy of Science, Indianapolis, IN [*Library symbol*] [*Library of Congress*] (LCLS)
InIAL American Legion, National Headquarters Library, Indianapolis, IN. [*Library symbol*] [*Library of Congress*] (LCLS)

INIAP .... Instituto de Investigacion y Autoformacion Politica [*Guatemala, Guatemala, C.P.*]
InIB .... Butler University, Indianapolis, IN [*Library symbol*] [*Library of Congress*] (LCLS)
INIBAP .... International Network for the Improvement of Banana and Plantain [*Affilia ted with the Consultative Group on International Agricultural Research*] [*France*]
InIBHM .... President Benjamin Harrison Memorial Home, Indianapolis, IN [*Library symbol*] [*Library of Congress*] (LCLS)
InIBHP .... Barnes, Hickam, Pantzer & Boyd, Law Library, Indianapolis, IN [*Library symbol*] [*Library of Congress*] (LCLS)
InIBio .... Bio-Dynamics, Inc., BMC Library, Indianapolis, IN [*Library symbol*] [*Library of Congress*] (LCLS)
InIB-P .... Butler University, College of Pharmacy, Indianapolis, IN [*Library symbol*] [*Library of Congress*] (LCLS)
InIBr .... Everett I. Brown Co., Indianapolis, IN [*Library symbol*] [*Library of Congress*] (LCLS)
INIC .... Current Negative Immittance Converter (SAUS)
INIC .... Ideal Current Negative Immittance Converter
InIC .... Indianapolis Commercial, Indianapolis, IN [*Library symbol*] [*Library of Congress*] (LCLS)
INIC .... Inverse Negative Impedance Converter (IAA)
INICAE .... International Information, Communication and Education (journ.) (SAUS)
InICC .... Indiana Central University, Indianapolis, IN [*Library symbol*] [*Library of Congress*] (LCLS)
INICE .... Inexpensive In-Circuit Emulator (NITA)
InICM .... Children's Museum of Indianapolis, Indianapolis, IN [*Library symbol*] [*Library of Congress*] (LCLS)
INICR .... Institute for Childhood Resources (EA)
InID .... General Motors Corp., Detroit Diesel Allison Division, Plant 8 Library, Indianapolis, IN [*Library symbol*] [*Library of Congress*] (LCLS)
INID .... Institutul National de Informare si Documentare [*National Institute for Information and Documentation*] [*National Council for Science and Technology*] [*Information service or system*] (IID)
INID/NOD .... Immediate Network-In Dial/Network-Out Dial (DNAB)
InIDow .... DOWELANCO, Indianapolis, IN [*Library symbol*] [*Library of Congress*] (LCLS)
INIDX .... IDS Growth Cl.A [*Mutual fund ticker symbol*] (SG)
InIFHi .... Franklin Township Historical Society, Indianapolis, IN [*Library symbol*] [*Library of Congress*] (LCLS)
INIFOM .... Institute for the Promotion of Municipalities (SAUO)
INIG .... International Nutritional Immunology Group (EA)
InIGS .... Church of Jesus Christ of Latter-Day Saints, Genealogical Society Library, Indianapolis Branch, Indianapolis, IN [*Library symbol*] [*Library of Congress*] (LCLS)
InIH .... Hudson Institute, Indiannapolis, IN [*Library symbol*] [*Library of Congress*] (LCLS)
InII .... Indiana Cooperative Library Service Authority (INCOLSA), Indianapolis, IN [*Library symbol*] [*Library of Congress*] (LCLS)
InIIY .... Indiana Youth Institute, Indianapolis, IN [*Library symbol*] [*Library of Congress*] (LCLS)
InIJ .... Herron School of Art, Indianapolis, IN [*Library symbol*] [*Library of Congress*] (LCLS)
InIL .... Eli Lilly & Co., Scientific Library, Indianapolis, IN [*Library symbol*] [*Library of Congress*] (LCLS)
InILB .... Eli Lilly & Co., Business Library, Indianapolis, IN [*Library symbol*] [*Library of Congress*] (LCLS)
InILL .... Eli Lilly & Co., Law Library, Indianapolis, IN [*Library symbol*] [*Library of Congress*] (LCLS)
InILS .... Indianapolis Law School, Indianapolis, IN [*Library symbol*] [*Library of Congress*] (LCLS)
InIM .... Marian College, Indianapolis, IN [*Library symbol*] [*Library of Congress*] (LCLS)
InIMa .... Indiana Masonic Library and Museum, Indianapolis, IN [*Library symbol*] [*Library of Congress*] (LCLS)
INIMPACT .... Initial Impact [*National Highway Traffic Safety Administration Fatal Accident Recording System code*]
InIMu .... Indianapolis Museum of Art, Reference Library, Indianapolis, IN [*Library symbol*] [*Library of Congress*] (LCLS)
in/in .... inch per inch (SAUS)
ININ .... InStent Inc. [*NASDAQ symbol*] (TTSB)
ININ .... Mexican Nuclear Institute (SAUO)
IN INIT .... In Initio [*In the Beginning*] [*Latin*]
INIP .... Institute of Non-Numerical Information Processing [*Switzerland*] [*Information service or system*] (IID)
InIPE .... Indiana University - Purdue University at Indianapolis, School of Physical Education, Indianapolis, IN [*Library symbol*] [*Library of Congress*] (LCLS)
InIR .... James Whitcomb Riley Home, Indianapolis, IN [*Library symbol*] [*Library of Congress*] (LCLS)
InIRCA .... RCA, Selectavision Video Disc Operations Library, Indianapolis, IN [*Library symbol*] [*Library of Congress*] (LCLS)
INIS .... Information System Internetted (SAUO)
INIS .... International Nuclear Information System [*International Atomic Energy Agency*] (IID)
INIS .... Internation Nuclear Information Service [*International Atomic Energy Authority*] (NITA)
INIS ATOMINDEX... International Nuclear Information System [*International Atomic Energy Agency*] [*Vienna, Austria*] [*Bibliographic database*]
InISC .... Indiana Supreme Court Law Library, Indianapolis, IN [*Library symbol*] [*Library of Congress*] (LCLS)
InISIN .... Sigma Theta Tau International Nursing Library, Indianapolis, IN [*Library symbol*] [*Library of Congress*] (LCLS)
INIST .... Institute de l'Information Scientifique et Technique [*Institute of Scientific and Technical Information*] [*Information service or system*] (IID)
INISWF .... Indian National Iron and Steel Workers' Federation
InIT .... Christian Theological Seminary, Indianapolis, IN [*Library symbol*] [*Library of Congress*] (LCLS)
INIT .... Initial (AFM)
INIT .... Initialization (KSC)
INIT .... Initialization Resource [*Communications term*] (DCT)
init .... Initialize (ELAL)
INIT .... Initialize (VLIE)
init .... initially (SAUS)
INIT .... Initial Training [*Aviation*] (FAAC)
INIT .... Initiate (NASA)
INIT .... Initiation (MSA)
INIT .... Initilize (SAUS)
INIT .... Initio [*In the Beginning*] [*Latin*] (ROG)
INIT .... Interliant, Inc. [*NASDAQ symbol*] (SG)
INIT & REF... Initiative and Referendum [*Legal term*] (DLA)
INITCCA .... Initial Cash Clothing Allowance [*Military*] (DNAB)
INITCCCA..... Initial Civilian Cash Clothing Allowance [*Military*] (DNAB)
Initio .... Initio, Inc. [*Associated Press*] (SAG)
INITUNIFALW... Initial Uniform Allowance [*Military*]
InIU .... Indiana University - Purdue University at Indianapolis, Downtown Campus, Indianapolis, IN [*Library symbol*] [*Library of Congress*] (LCLS)
INIU .... Interim Network Interface Unit (SAUO)
InIU-L .... Indiana University - Purdue University at Indianapolis, School of Law, Indianapolis, IN [*Library symbol*] [*Library of Congress*] (LCLS)
iniv .... initiative (SAUS)
INIVX .... Van Eck Funds: Intl. Investors [*Mutual fund ticker symbol*] (SG)
InIWis .... Wishard Memorial Hospital, Indianapolis, IN [*Library symbol*] [*Library of Congress*] (LCLS)
InIZ .... Indianapolis, Zoological Society, Inc., Indianapolis, IN [*Library symbol*] [*Library of Congress*] (LCLS)
INJ .... Inject
INJ .... Injectio [*An Injection*] [*Pharmacy*]
inj .... Injection (IDYL)
INJ .... Injection (SAUS)
INJ .... Injector (KSC)
inj .... Injunction (ELAL)
Inj .... Injunction [*Legal term*]
INJ .... Injure (AABC)
Inj .... Injurious (SAUS)
INJ .... Injury (CPH)
INJ .... In Nomine Jesu [*In the Name of Jesus*] [*Latin*]
INJ .... Interjet [*Greece*] [*FAA designator*] (FAAC)
INJ .... International North American Resources, Inc. [*Vancouver Stock Exchange symbol*]
INJ .... Ion Beam Injector (SAUS)
INJ .... Israel Numismatic Journal [*A publication*] (ABAR)
InJ .... Jasper Public Library, Jasper, IN [*Library symbol*] [*Library of Congress*] (LCLS)
InJa .... Jasonville Public Library, Jasonville, IN [*Library symbol*] [*Library of Congress*] (LCLS)
InJaL .... Jasonville Leader, Jasonville, IN [*Library symbol*] [*Library of Congress*] (LCLS)
InJamP .... Jamestown Press, Jamestown, IN [*Library symbol*] [*Library of Congress*] (LCLS)
INJCT .... Injunction [*Legal term*]
INJCTN .... Injection
InJDHi .... Dubois County Historical Society, Jasper, IN [*Library symbol*] [*Library of Congress*] (LCLS)
InJe .... Jeffersonville Township Public Library, Jeffersonville, IN [*Library symbol*] [*Library of Congress*] (LCLS)
INJECT .... Injection [*Medicine*]
INJ ENEM .... Injiciatur Enema [*Let an Enema Be Injected*] [*Pharmacy*]
INJFACS .... Injection Facilities (DNAB)
InJH .... Jasper Herald, Jasper, IN [*Library symbol*] [*Library of Congress*] (LCLS)
INJ HYP .... Injectio Hypodermica [*Hypodermic Injection*] [*Pharmacy*]
INJIC .... Injiciatur [*Let It Be Given*] [*Pharmacy*] (ROG)
INJICIAT .... Injiciatur [*Let It Be Given*] [*Pharmacy*] (ROG)
Inj Mldg .... Injection Moulding (SAUS)
INJN .... Injunction [*Legal term*] (ROG)
InJo .... Jonesboro Public Library, Jonesboro, IN [*Library symbol*] [*Library of Congress*] (LCLS)
INJON .... Injunction [*Legal term*] (ROG)
Inj site .... Injection Site [*Medicine*] (AMHC)
INK .... Injury Not Known (SAUS)
INK .... International Coast Minerals Corp. [*Vancouver Stock Exchange symbol*]
INK .... Inuvik [*Northwest Territories*] [*Seismograph station code, US Geological Survey*] (SEIS)
INK .... Kentair (International) Ltd. [*British*] [*ICAO designator*] (FAAC)
INK .... Wink, TX [*Location identifier*] [*FAA*] (FAAL)
INKA .... Individual Network Region Karlsruhe (SAUO)
INKA .... Informationssystem Karlsruhe [*Karlsruhe Information System*] [*Information service or system*] [*Germany*]
INKA .... Information System Karlsruhe (SAUS)
INKA-CONF... Informationssystem Karlsruhe - Conference [*Database*]
INKA-CONF... Information System Karlsruhe-Conference Announcements (SAUS)
INKA-CORP... Informationssystem Karlsruhe - Corporates in Energy [*Database*] [*Defunct*]

INKA-DATACOMP... Informationssystem Karlsruhe - Data Compilations in Energy and Physics [*Database*]
INKA-MATH... Informationssystem Karlsruhe - Mathematics [*Database*]
INKA-MATHDI... Informationssystem Karlsruhe - Mathematical Education [*Database*]
INKA-NUCLEAR... Information System Karlsruhe-Database on Nuclear Science and Technology (SAUS)
INKA-NUCLEAR... INKA Nuclear Science and Technology [*Database*] (NITA)
INKA-NUCLEAR PART INIS... Informationssystem Karlsruhe - Nuclear Database Part: International Nuclear Information System [*Database*]
INKA-NUCLEAR PART KKK... Informationssystem Karlsruhe - Nuclear Database Part: Conference Papers: NuclearResearch, Nuclear Technology [*Database*]
INKA-NUCLEAR PART NSA... Informationssystem Karlsruhe - Nuclear Database Part: Nuclear Science Abstracts [*Database*]
INKA-PHYS... Informationssystem Karlsruhe - Physics [*Database*]
InKend........ Kendallville Public Library, Kendallville, IN [*Library symbol*] [*Library of Congress*] (LCLS)
InKendNS.... Kendallville News-Sun, Kendallville, IN [*Library symbol*] [*Library of Congress*] (LCLS)
InKent......... Kentland Public Library, Kentland, IN [*Library symbol*] [*Library of Congress*] (LCLS)
InKentCR..... Newton County Recorder's Office, Kentland, IN [*Library symbol*] [*Library of Congress*] (LCLS)
InKentE........ Newton County Enterprise, Kentland, IN [*Library symbol*] [*Library of Congress*] (LCLS)
InKew.......... Kewanna Public Library, Kewanna, IN [*Library symbol*] [*Library of Congress*] (LCLS)
InKewO........ Kewanna Observer, Kewanna, IN [*Library symbol*] [*Library of Congress*] (LCLS)
InKir............ Kirklin Public Library, Kirklin, IN [*Library symbol*] [*Library of Congress*] (LCLS)
InKni............ Knightstown Public Library, Knightstown, IN [*Library symbol*] [*Library of Congress*] (LCLS)
InKniB.......... Knightstown Banner, Knightstown, IN [*Library symbol*] [*Library of Congress*] (LCLS)
InKno........... Henry F. Schricker Library, Knox, IN [*Library symbol*] [*Library of Congress*] (LCLS)
InKnoCHi..... Starke County Historical Museum, Knox, IN [*Library symbol*] [*Library of Congress*] (LCLS)
InKnoCR...... Starke County Recorder's Office, Knox, IN [*Library symbol*] [*Library of Congress*] (LCLS)
InKo............. Kokomo Public Library, Kokomo, IN [*Library symbol*] [*Library of Congress*] (LCLS)
InKoC........... Cabot Corp., Stellite Division, Kokomo, IN [*Library symbol*] [*Library of Congress*] (LCLS)
InKoT........... Kokomo Tribune, Kokomo, IN [*Library symbol*] [*Library of Congress*] (LCLS)
InKouT......... Kouts Times, Kouts, IN [*Library symbol*] [*Library of Congress*] (LCLS)
INKP............ InKine Pharmaceutical
Ink Print...... Ink and Print (journ.) (SAUS)
INKT............ Inktomi [*Software provider*]
INKT............ Inktomi Corp. [*NASDAQ symbol*] (SG)
INL.............. Independent Newspapers Ltd. (SAUS)
InL.............. Indian Literature (journ.) (SAUS)
INL.............. Initial (SAUS)
Inl............... Inland (SAUS)
INL.............. Inland Natural Gas Co. Ltd. [*Toronto Stock Exchange symbol*] [*Vancouver Stock Exchange symbol*]
Inl............... Inlaut (SAUS)
inl............... Inlay (MAE)
INL.............. Inlet (KSC)
INL.............. Inner Nuclear Layer
INL.............. Inspection Log (SAUO)
In L............. Instructor Lieutenant (SAUS)
InL.............. Instructor-Lieutenant (SAUO)
INL.............. Internal Noise Level (IEEE)
INL.............. International Falls [*Minnesota*] [*Airport symbol*] (OAG)
INL.............. International Falls, MN [*Location identifier*] [*FAA*] (FAAL)
INL.............. International Narcotics and Law Enforcement (SAUO)
INL.............. Internodal Link (ACRL)
INL.............. Inter Node Link (SAUS)
INL.............. Morgan Intertrades Ltd. [*Nigeria*] [*FAA designator*] (FAAC)
InL.............. tippecanoe County Public Library, Lafayette, IN [*Library symbol*] [*Library of Congress*] (LCLS)
InL.............. Wells Memorial Library, Lafayette, IN [*Library symbol*] [*Library of Congress*] (LCLS)
INLA............ International Nuclear Law Association [*See also AIDN*] [*Brussels, Belgium*] (EAIO)
INLA............ Iowa Nursery and Landscape Association (SRA)
INLA............ Irish National Liberation Army
InLacN........ Lacrosse Regional News, La Crosse, IN [*Library symbol*] [*Library of Congress*] (LCLS)
InLad.......... Ladoga-Clark Township Public Library, Ladoga, IN [*Library symbol*] [*Library of Congress*] (LCLS)
InLag.......... LaGrange County Library, LaGrange, IN [*Library symbol*] [*Library of Congress*] (LCLS)
InLagHi....... LaGrange County Historical Society, LaGrange, IN [*Library symbol*] [*Library of Congress*] (LCLS)
InLagNS...... LaGrange News and Standard, LaGrange, IN [*Library symbol*] [*Library of Congress*] (LCLS)
INLAN......... Instant Language [*Trademark*] [*Computer science*]
INLAND....... Informal Natural Language Access to Navy Data (SAUS)
Inland P...... Inland Printer/American Lithographer (journ.) (SAUS)
InLap.......... La Porte Public Library, La Porte, IN [*Library symbol*] [*Library of Congress*] (LCLS)
InLapHA...... LaPorte Herald-Argus, LaPorte, IN [*Library symbol*] [*Library of Congress*] (LCLS)
InLapHi....... LaPorte County Historical Society, LaPorte, IN [*Library symbol*] [*Library of Congress*] (LCLS)
InLaR.......... Lapel Review, Lapel, IN [*Library symbol*] [*Library of Congress*] (LCLS)
InLasH........ Hygiene Institute, La Salle, IN [*Library symbol*] [*Library of Congress*] (LCLS)
INLAW........ Infantry LASER Weapon (MCD)
InLaw.......... Lawrenceburg Public Library, Lawrenceburg, IN [*Library symbol*] [*Library of Congress*] (LCLS)
InLawCR...... Dearborn County Recorder's Office, Lawrenceburg, IN [*Library symbol*] [*Library of Congress*] (LCLS)
IN/LB.......... Inches per Pound
IN-LB.......... Inch-Pound
in-lb........... inch pound (SAUS)
In-LB.......... Indiana Legislative Council, State House, Indianapolis, IN [*Library symbol*] [*Library of Congress*] (LCLS)
in-lbf.......... inch-pound -force (SAUS)
INLC........... Initial Launch Capability (IEEE)
InLcLM........ Lincoln Boyhood National Memorial, Lincoln City, IN [*Library symbol*] [*Library of Congress*] (LCLS)
InLCr.......... Instructor Lieutenant-Commander (SAUO)
INLD........... Inland Casino [*NASDAQ symbol*] (TTSB)
INLD........... Inland Casino Corp. [*NASDAQ symbol*] (SAG)
INLD........... Inland Entertainment Corp. [*NASDAQ symbol*] (NASQ)
InldCas....... Inland Casino Corp. [*Associated Press*] (SAG)
InldRs......... Inland Resources [*Associated Press*] (SAG)
InldStl......... Inland Steel Industries, Inc. [*Associated Press*] (SAG)
INLE........... Instituto Nacional del Libro Espanol
InLeb.......... Lebanon Public Library, Lebanon, IN [*Library symbol*] [*Library of Congress*] (LCLS)
InLebCR...... Boone County Recorder's Office, Lebanon, IN [*Library symbol*] [*Library of Congress*] (LCLS)
InLebR........ Lebanon Reporter, Lebanon, IN [*Library symbol*] [*Library of Congress*] (LCLS)
INLET......... Inlet [*Commonly used*] (OPSA)
INLETS....... In-Line Execution Tests (SAUS)
INLF........... Investors Heritage Life Insurance of Kentucky [*NASDAQ symbol*] (COMM)
InLib.......... Union County Public Library, Liberty, IN [*Library symbol*] [*Library of Congress*] (LCLS)
InLibCN....... College Corner News, Liberty, IN [*Library symbol*] [*Library of Congress*] (LCLS)
InLibH........ Liberty Herald, Liberty, IN [*Library symbol*] [*Library of Congress*] (LCLS)
INLICA........ Indiana Land Improvement Contractors Association (SRA)
InLigAL....... Ligonier Advance-Leader, Ligonier, IN [*Library symbol*] [*Library of Congress*] (LCLS)
IN LIM........ In Limine [*At the Outset*] [*Latin*]
InLind......... Linden Public Library, Linden, IN [*Library symbol*] [*Library of Congress*] (LCLS)
INLINON...... Interlineation (ROG)
InLint.......... Linton Public Library, Linton, IN [*Library symbol*] [*Library of Congress*] (LCLS)
InLintC........ Linton Daily Citizen, Linton, IN [*Library symbol*] [*Library of Congress*] (LCLS)
in litt.......... In Litteris [*In Correspondence*] [*Latin*] (EES)
IN LITT........ In Litteris [*In Correspondence*] [*Latin*]
InLJC.......... Lafayette Journal and Courier, Lafayette, IN [*Library symbol*] [*Library of Congress*] (LCLS)
INLK........... Interlock (VLIE)
INLN........... Inland Resources [*NASDAQ symbol*] (SAG)
INLND......... Inland
INLO........... In Lieu Of
IN LOC........ In Loco [*In the Place Of*] [*Latin*]
IN LOC CIT... In Loco Citato [*In the Place Mentioned*] [*Latin*] (ROG)
InLog.......... Logansport-Cass County Public Library, Logansport, IN [*Library symbol*] [*Library of Congress*] (LCLS)
InLogCHi...... Cass County Historical Society Museum Library, Logansport, IN [*Library symbol*] [*Library of Congress*] (LCLS)
INLOGOV..... Institute of Local Government [*University of Birmingham*] [*British*] (AIE)
INLOGOV..... Institute of Local Government Studies [*British*]
InLogPT....... Pharos-Tribune, Logansport, IN [*Library symbol*] [*Library of Congress*] (LCLS)
InLoo.......... Frances L. Folks Memorial Library (Loogootee Public Library), Loogootee, IN [*Library symbol*] [*Library of Congress*] (LCLS)
InLooT........ Loogootee Tribune, Loogootee, IN [*Library symbol*] [*Library of Congress*] (LCLS)
InLow.......... Lowell Public Library, Lowell, IN [*Library symbol*] [*Library of Congress*] (LCLS)
InLowT........ Lowell Tribune, Lowell, IN [*Library symbol*] [*Library of Congress*] (LCLS)
INLP........... Integer Non-Linear Programming [*Computer science*] (PDAA)
InLP........... Purdue University, Lafayette, IN [*Library symbol*] [*Library of Congress*] (LCLS)
InLP-Ham.... Purdue University, Calumet Campus, Hammond, IN [*Library symbol*] [*Library of Congress*] [*Obsolete*] (LCLS)
INLPRMAX... Inlet Pressure Test Maximum Pressure [*Automotive emissions*]
INLPRMIN.... Inlet Pressure Test Minimum Pressure [*Automotive emissions*]
INLPTA........ International Neuro-Linguistic Programming Trainers Association (SAUO)

INLQ .... INTERLING Software Corp. [*NASDAQ symbol*] (SAG)
INLQ .... Interlinq Software [*NASDAQ symbol*] (SAG)
INLR .... Item No Longer Required
INLS .... Individualized Learning System (DNAB)
INLS .... International Network of Language Services (SAUO)
InLS .... Lafayette Schools System, Lafayette, IN [*Library symbol*] [*Library of Congress*] (LCLS)
INLS-code .... International Noxious Liquid Substances (SAUO)
INLS-code .... International Noxious Liquid Substances code (SAUS)
InLSEH .... St. Elizabeth Hospital Medical Center, Bannon Health Science Library, Lafayette, IN [*Library symbol*] [*Library of Congress*] (LCLS)
In-L-Skt .... In-Line Socket (SAUS)
INLT .... Inlet [*Board on Geographic Names*] (MCD)
InLTHi .... Tippecanoe County Historical Association, Lafayette, IN [*Library symbol*] [*Library of Congress*] (LCLS)
InLv .... Independent Living
INLV .... Interleave (VLIE)
InLv .... Lake Village Library, Lake Village, IN [*Library symbol*] [*Library of Congress*] (LCLS)
INLX .... INCOAL [*Private rail car owner code*]
inly .... initially (SAUS)
InLy .... Washington Township Public Library, Lynn, IN [*Library symbol*] [*Library of Congress*] (LCLS)
INM .... Imbokodvo National Movement [*Swaziland*] [*Political party*] (PPW)
INM .... Informed Notaries of Maine (SRA)
INM .... Innamincka [*South Australia*] [*Airport symbol*] (AD)
INM .... Inspector of Naval Machinery
INM .... Inspector of Naval Material
INM .... Institute for New Media (SAUS)
INM .... Institute of Naval Medicine [*British*] (DMA)
INM .... Integrated Network Management [*for Companies*]
INM .... Integrated Noise Model (LDOE)
INM .... Interception Mission [*Air Force*]
INM .... International Migration. Quarterly review (journ.) (SAUS)
INM .... International Narcotics Matters [*Department of State*]
INM .... International Nautical Mile
INM .... International Nuclear Model [*Department of Energy*] (GFGA)
INM .... Irish National Museum (SAUO)
INM .... Istel Network Monitoring System (NITA)
INMA .... International Newspaper Marketing Association (EA)
Inmac .... Inmac Corp. [*Associated Press*] (SAG)
INMAC .... Instant Mini/Micro Computer Accessories and Cables [*Manufacturer/distributor*] [*British*] (NITA)
INMAC .... International Minicomputer Accessories Corp. (SAUO)
InMad .... Madison-Jefferson County Public Library, Madison, IN [*Library symbol*] [*Library of Congress*] (LCLS)
InMadC .... Madison Daily Courier, Madison, IN [*Library symbol*] [*Library of Congress*] (LCLS)
INMAP .... Independent Microelectronics Applications [*British*] (NITA)
InMar .... Marion Public Library, Marion, IN [*Library symbol*] [*Library of Congress*] (LCLS)
InMarC .... Marion College, Marion, IN [*Library symbol*] [*Library of Congress*] (LCLS)
InMarCT .... Marion Chronicle Tribune, Marion, IN [*Library symbol*] [*Library of Congress*] (LCLS)
InMarGHi ..... Grant County Historical Society, Marion, IN [*Library symbol*] [*Library of Congress*] (LCLS)
INMARSAT ... International Maritime Organization [*Nautical term*] (NTA)
INMARSAT ... International Maritime Satellite [*Satellite communications organization*] (NITA)
IN-MARSAT ... International Maritime Satellite Communications Organisation (SAUS)
INMARSAT ... International Maritime Satellite Organization
INMARSAT ... International Mobile Satellite Organization (SAUO)
INMARSATORG ... International Maritime Satellite Organization (SAUO)
INMARSAT System ... International Maritime Satellite System (SAUS)
InMart .... Morgan County Public Library, Martinsville, IN [*Library symbol*] [*Library of Congress*] (LCLS)
InMarV .... United States Veterans Administration Hospital, Marion, IN [*Library symbol*] [*Library of Congress*] (LCLS)
INMAS .... Institute of Nuclear Medicine and Allied Sciences (SAUO)
InMat .... Matthews Public Library, Matthews, IN [*Library symbol*] [*Library of Congress*] (LCLS)
INMC .... Inmac Corp. [*NASDAQ symbol*] (NQ)
INMC .... International Network Management Center [*Telecommunications*] (TEL)
INMC .... International Network Management Center (or Centre) (SAUS)
INMD .... IntegraMed America, Inc. [*NASDAQ symbol*] (SAG)
InMe .... Bell Memorial Public Library, Mentone, IN [*Library symbol*] [*Library of Congress*] (LCLS)
INMED .... Indians into Medicine (EA)
INMED .... International Medical Services for Health (EA)
InMelRP ...... Richland Press, Mellott, IN [*Library symbol*] [*Library of Congress*] (LCLS)
IN MEM .... In Memoriam [*In Memory Of*] [*Latin*] (ROG)
INMEP .... Institute for a New Middle East Policy (EA)
InMerL .... Lake County Public Library, Merrillville, IN [*Library symbol*] [*Library of Congress*] (LCLS)
INM-ES .... Spanish National Meteorological Institute (SAUS)
INMETCO ..... International Metals Reclamation Company (SAUO)
INMETRO ..... Instituto Nacional de Metrologia, Normalizacao e Qualidade Industrial [*Government advisory body*] [*Brazil*] (EY)
INMHC .... International Network for Mutual Help Centers (EA)
INMHO .... In My Humble Opinion (BARN)
INMI .... Institute of Microbiology (of the Academy of Sciences, USSR)
InMic .... Michigan City Public Library, Michigan City, IN [*Library symbol*] [*Library of Congress*] (LCLS)
InMicLM ...... Old Lighthouse Museum, Michigan City, IN [*Library symbol*] [*Library of Congress*] (LCLS)
InMicND ...... Michigan City News-Dispatch, Michigan City, IN [*Library symbol*] [*Library of Congress*] (LCLS)
INMID .... Infantry Mid-Range Concepts and Force Design Study (SAUO)
InMid .... Middletown Public Library, Middletown, IN [*Library symbol*] [*Library of Congress*] (LCLS)
InMidb .... Middlebury Public Library, Middlebury, IN [*Library symbol*] [*Library of Congress*] (LCLS)
InMidbI .... Middlebury Independent, Middlebury, IN [*Library symbol*] [*Library of Congress*] (LCLS)
InMidN .... Middletown News, Middletown, IN [*Library symbol*] [*Library of Congress*] (LCLS)
InMil .... Milford Public Library, Milford, IN [*Library symbol*] [*Library of Congress*] (LCLS)
InMilMJ ...... Milford Mail-Journal, Millford, IN [*Library symbol*] [*Library of Congress*] (LCLS)
in/min .... inches per minute (SAUS)
InMis .... Mishawaka Public Library, Mishawaka, IN [*Library symbol*] [*Library of Congress*] (LCLS)
InMisB .... Bethel College, Mishawaka, IN [*Library symbol*] [*Library of Congress*] (LCLS)
InMisER .... Mishawaka Enterprise-Record, Mishawaka, IN [*Library symbol*] [*Library of Congress*] (LCLS)
InMit .... Mitchell Community Public Library, Mitchell, IN [*Library symbol*] [*Library of Congress*] (LCLS)
InmkEnt .... Inmark Enterprises, Inc. [*Associated Press*] (SAG)
INMM .... Institute of Nuclear Materials Management (EA)
InMon .... Monon Town and Township Library, Monon, IN [*Library symbol*] [*Library of Congress*] (LCLS)
InMonN .... Monon News, Monon, IN [*Library symbol*] [*Library of Congress*] (LCLS)
InMont .... Monterrey-Tippecanoe Township Public Library Monterrey, IN [*Library symbol*] [*Library of Congress*] (LCLS)
InMoo .... Mooresville Public Library, Mooresville, IN [*Library symbol*] [*Library of Congress*] (LCLS)
InMop .... Montpelier Public Library, Montpelier, IN [*Library symbol*] [*Library of Congress*] (LCLS)
InMopH .... Montpelier Herald, Montpelier, IN [*Library symbol*] [*Library of Congress*] (LCLS)
InMotc .... Monticello Union Township Public Library, Monticello, IN [*Library symbol*] [*Library of Congress*] (LCLS)
InMotz .... Montezuma Public Library, Montezuma, IN [*Library symbol*] [*Library of Congress*] (LCLS)
INMR .... Insider Network Market Report [*Information service or system*] (IID)
INMR .... Instrumentarium Corp. [*NASDAQ symbol*] (NQ)
INMR .... Invese Magnetic Resonance (SAUS)
INMRY .... Instrumentarium 'B' ADR [*NASDAQ symbol*] (TTSB)
INMS .... Helmet Mounted Sight (SAUS)
INMS .... Integrated Network Management System [*Telecommunications*] (ACRL)
INMS .... International Network Management System (SAUO)
IN/MSX .... Intellimac Multi-System Executive (SAUS)
INMT .... Intermet Corp. [*NASDAQ symbol*] (NQ)
INMTS .... International Nuclear Materials Tracking System (SAUO)
InMtv .... Alexandrian Free Public Library, Mount Vernon, IN [*Library symbol*] [*Library of Congress*] (LCLS)
INMU .... Inertial Navigation Measurement Unit (MCD)
InMu .... Muncie Public Library, Muncie, IN [*Library symbol*] [*Library of Congress*] (LCLS)
InMuB .... Ball State University, Muncie, IN [*Library symbol*] [*Library of Congress*] (LCLS)
InMuMC .... Minnetrista Cultural Center, Muncie, IN [*Library symbol*] [*Library of Congress*] (LCLS)
InMuP .... Muncie Evening Press, Muncie, IN [*Library symbol*] [*Library of Congress*] (LCLS)
InMuSP .... Muncie Morning Star-Evening Press, Muncie, IN [*Library symbol*] [*Library of Congress*] (LCLS)
INMUX .... IDS Mutual Cl.A [*Mutual fund ticker symbol*] (SG)
INMWF .... Indian National Mine Workers' Federation
INMX .... InforMax, Inc. [*NASDAQ symbol*]
INMZ .... Inglehand Minerals & Chemicals [*Federal Railroad Administration identification code*]
INN .... ImagiNation Network [*Entertainment*]
INN .... Independent Network News [*Television*]
InN .... Indian Navy (SAUO)
INN .... Initial Nodal Network (SAUS)
INN .... Inning (WGA)
INN .... Innsbruck [*Austria*] [*Airport symbol*] (OAG)
INN .... Innsbruck [*Austria*] [*Seismograph station code, US Geological Survey*] [*Closed*] (SEIS)
INN .... Integrated Network Node [*Communications term*] (DCT)
INN .... Intermediate Network Node (IAA)
INN .... Intermediate Routing Node [*Communications term*] (DCT)
INN .... International Negotiation Network (SAUO)
INN .... International Nonproprietary Name (SAUS)
INN .... International Nonproprietary Names [*World Health Organization*]
INN .... Internet News (SAUO)
INN .... Inter Node Network (SAUO)
INN .... Minneapolis, MN [*Location identifier*] [*FAA*] (FAAL)
INN .... New Albany-Floyd County Public Library, New Albany, IN [*OCLC symbol*] (OCLC)
INNA .... International Newsreel and News Film Association [*Belgium*] (EAIO)

InNap .... Nappanee Public Library, Nappanee, IN [*Library symbol*] [*Library of Congress*] (LCLS)
InNapAN ...... Nappanee Advance News, Nappanee, IN [*Library symbol*] [*Library of Congress*] (LCLS)
InNas .... Brown County Public Library, Nashville, IN [*Library symbol*] [*Library of Congress*] (LCLS)
InNasBHi ..... Brown County Historical Society, Nashville, IN [*Library symbol*] [*Library of Congress*] (LCLS)
InNasCR ...... Brown County Recorder's Office, Nashville, IN [*Library symbol*] [*Library of Congress*] (LCLS)
InNasD .... Brown County Democrat, Nashville, IN [*Library symbol*] [*Library of Congress*] (LCLS)
INNC .... International Neural Network Conference (SAUO)
InNcar .... New Carlisle and Olive Township Public Library, New Carlisle, IN [*Library symbol*] [*Library of Congress*] (LCLS)
InNcas .... New Castle - Henry County Public Library, New Castle, IN [*Library symbol*] [*Library of Congress*] (LCLS)
InNcasCT ..... New Castle Courier Times, New Castle, IN [*Library symbol*] [*Library of Congress*] (LCLS)
InNcasHi ...... Henry County Historical Society, Reference Room, New Castle, IN [*Library symbol*] [*Library of Congress*] (LCLS)
InNcasNR ..... Henry County News-Republican, New Castle, IN [*Library symbol*] [*Library of Congress*] (LCLS)
INNCNT .... Innocent
INND .... Internet News Daemon (SAUO)
InNd .... University of Notre Dame, Notre Dame, IN [*Library symbol*] [*Library of Congress*] (LCLS)
InNd-L .... University of Notre Dame, Law School, Notre Dame, IN [*Library symbol*] [*Library of Congress*] (LCLS)
InNd-LS .... University of Notre Dame, Life Sciences Research Library, Notre Dame, IN [*Library symbol*] [*Library of Congress*] (LCLS)
InNdS .... Saint Mary's College, Notre Dame, IN [*Library symbol*] [*Library of Congress*] (LCLS)
INNDX .... IDS New Dimensions Cl.A [*Mutual fund ticker symbol*] (SG)
InNea .... New Albany-Floyd County Public Library, New Albany, IN [*Library symbol*] [*Library of Congress*] (LCLS)
Inn Eas .... Innes on Easements [*8th ed.*] [*1911*] [*A publication*] (DLA)
Inn Ease ...... Innes on Easements [*8th ed.*] [*1911*] [*A publication*] (DLA)
InNeaTL ...... New Albany Tribune and Ledger-Tribune, New Albany, IN [*Library symbol*] [*Library of Congress*] (LCLS)
InNeb .... Newburgh-Ohio Township Public Library, Newburgh, IN [*Library symbol*] [*Library of Congress*] (LCLS)
InNep .... Newport-Vermillion County Library, Newport, IN [*Library symbol*] [*Library of Congress*] (LCLS)
Innerdyn ...... Innerdyne, Inc. [*Associated Press*] (SAG)
Inner Gimba... Inner Gimbal [*Aerospace*] (NAKS)
Inner Glide... Inner Glideslope [*Aerospace*] (NAKS)
INNERTAP.... Information Network on New and Renewable Energy Resources and Technologies for Asia and the Pacific [*UNESCO*] (DUND)
INNERV .... Innervation [*Medicine*]
Innes .... Innes' Registration of Title [*A publication*] (ILCA)
INNF .... Intermediate Naval Nuclear Forces (DOMA)
InNhvAT ...... Allen County Times, New Haven, IN [*Library symbol*] [*Library of Congress*] (LCLS)
InNhW .... Workingmen's Institute, New Harmony, IN [*Library symbol*] [*Library of Congress*] (LCLS)
Innis .... Inniskilling (SAUS)
Innis .... Royal Inniskilling Fusiliers (SAUO)
Innis DG ...... Royal Inniskilling Dragoon Guards (SAUO)
Innisfail Canegr... Innisfail Canegrower [*A publication*]
Innkeepr ...... Innkeepers USA Trust [*Associated Press*] (SAG)
INNKPR .... Innkeeper
INNL .... Improved Nonnuclear LANCE
INNO .... Innocente [*Innocently*] [*Music*] (ROG)
Inno .... Innovations [*Record label*]
INNO .... Innovo Group [*NASDAQ symbol*] (TTSB)
INNO .... Innovo Group, Inc. [*NASDAQ symbol*] (SAG)
InNob .... Noblesville Public Library, Noblesville, IN [*Library symbol*] [*Library of Congress*] (LCLS)
InNobL .... Noblesville Daily Ledger, Noblesville, IN [*Library symbol*] [*Library of Congress*] (LCLS)
Innodata ...... Innodata Corp. [*Associated Press*] (SAG)
InnoDev .... Innovasive Devices, Inc. [*Associated Press*] (SAG)
InNoj .... North Judson-Wayne Township Public Library, North Judson, IN [*Library symbol*] [*Library of Congress*] (LCLS)
INNOLOG ..... Innovative Logistics Techniques (SAUS)
InnoM .... Innovative Medical Services [*Associated Press*] (SAG)
InNom .... North Manchester Public Library, North Manchester, IN [*Library symbol*] [*Library of Congress*] (LCLS)
InNoman ...... North Manchester Public Library, North Manchester, IN [*Library symbol*] [*Library of Congress*] (LCLS)
InNomanC.... Manchester College, North Manchester, IN [*Library symbol*] [*Library of Congress*] (LCLS)
InNomanNJ... North Manchester News-Journal, North Manchester, IN [*Library symbol*] [*Library of Congress*] (LCLS)
InnoMed ...... Innovative Medical Services [*Associated Press*] (SAG)
InNomMC .... Manchester College, North Manchester, IN [*Library symbol*] [*Library of Congress*] (LCLS)
InnoPet .... InnoPet Brands Corp. [*Associated Press*] (SAG)
InnoServe .... InnoServe Technologies, Inc. [*Associated Press*] (SAG)
Innotech ...... Innotech, Inc. [*Associated Press*] (SAG)
INNOTECH ... Institute for Educational Innovation and Technology (SAUO)
INNOTECH ... Regional Centre for Educational Innovation and Technology (SAUS)
INNOTECH ... SEAEMO Regional Centre for Educational Innovation and Technology (SAUS)
Innovex .... Innovex, Inc. [*Associated Press*] (SAG)
Innov High Educ... Innovative Higher Education (journ.) (SAUS)
InnovirL .... Innovir Laboratories, Inc. [*Associated Press*] (SAG)
InNovJ .... Jennings County Public Library, North Vernon, IN [*Library symbol*] [*Library of Congress*] (LCLS)
Innovo .... Innovo Group, Inc. [*Associated Press*] (SAG)
InNovSP .... North Vernon Sun-Plain Dealer, North Vernon, IN [*Library symbol*] [*Library of Congress*] (LCLS)
InnovT .... Innovative Tech Systems, Inc. [*Associated Press*] (SAG)
InnoVTch ..... Innovative Tech Systems, Inc. [*Associated Press*] (SAG)
Innovus .... Innovus Corp. [*Associated Press*] (SAG)
INNR .... Inner
INNS .... International Neural Network Society (EA)
INNS .... Krisch American Inns, Inc. [*NASDAQ symbol*] (COMM)
Inn Sc Leg Ant... Innes' Scotch Legal Antiquities [*A publication*] (DLA)
INNTAB .... Interpret Table [*Communications term*] (DCT)
Innvr .... Innovir Laboratories, Inc. [*Associated Press*] (SAG)
INNVTN .... Innovation
INNVTV .... Innovative
INO .... In Nomine Domini (SAUS)
INO .... Inongo [*Zaire*] [*Airport symbol*] (OAG)
INO .... Inosine (DMAA)
Ino .... Inosine [*Also, I*] [*A nucleoside*]
INO .... Inspector of Naval Ordnance [*British*]
INO .... Institute for Naval Oceanography [*Bay St. Louis, MS*] [*Navy*]
InO .... Intelligence Officer (SAUO)
INO .... International NOTAM Office (SAUO)
INO .... Internuclear Ophthalmoplegia
INO .... Inter-Oceanic Resources Ltd. [*Formerly, Inter-Oceanic Oil & Gas*] [*Vancouver Stock Exchange symbol*]
INO .... Intranuclear Ophthalmolplegia [*Ophthalmology*] (DAVI)
INO .... Irish Nurses Organisation (BI)
INO .... Issue Necessary Orders
INO .... Item Number
INO .... Iterative Natural Orbital [*Atomic physics*]
INO .... Northbrook Public Library, Northbrook, IL [*OCLC symbol*] (OCLC)
INOA .... Intelligence Operations Division (SAUO)
INOA .... International Norton Owners' Association (EA)
INOAVNOT... If Not Available Notify (SAUS)
INOAVNOT... If Not Available Notify This Office at Once
INOBA .... Intelligent Node for Basic Access (SAUS)
INOC .... Innotrac Corp. [*NASDAQ symbol*] (NASQ)
Inoc .... Inoculate (SAUS)
INOC .... Inoculation (AABC)
INOC .... Inter-Islamic Network on Oceanography (SAUS)
INOC .... International Navigating Officers Course (SAUO)
INOC .... Internet Network Operations Center (SAUO)
INOC .... Iraqi National Oil Co. [*Government company*]
INOC .... Isonicotinoyloxycarbonyl [*Medicine*] (DMAA)
INOCA .... International Network of Centres for Computer Applications (SAUO)
InOcC .... Oakland City College, Oakland City, IN [*Library symbol*] [*Library of Congress*] (LCLS)
INOCO .... Indonesian Nippon Oil Corp. (SAUS)
INOCO .... Indonesian Nippon Oil Corporation (SAUO)
INOD .... Improved Night/Day Observation Device
INOD .... Innodata Corp. [*NASDAQ symbol*] (SAG)
InOd .... Odon Winkelpeck Memorial Library, Odon, IN [*Library symbol*] [*Library of Congress*] (LCLS)
INODC .... Indian National Oceanographic Data Centre [*Information service or system*] (IID)
INODEP .... Institut Oecumenique pour le Developpement des Peuples [*Ecumenical Institute for the Development of Peoples*] [*Paris, France*] (EAIO)
InOdJ .... Odon Journal, Odon, IN [*Library symbol*] [*Library of Congress*] (LCLS)
Inodta .... Innodata Corp. [*Associated Press*] (SAG)
INODW .... Innodata Corp.Wrrt [*NASDAQ symbol*] (TTSB)
INOE .... Internacia Naturista Organizo Esperantista [*International Esperantist Organization of Naturists - IEON*] (EAIO)
IN OEDIB ..... In Oedibus [*In the House Of*] [*Latin*] (ROG)
INOEX .... Indian Ocean Experiment (SAUS)
INOF .... If Not Off (FAAC)
INOGATE ...... Interstate Oil and Gas Transport to Europe (EURO)
INOH .... Indiana & Ohio Railroad [*Federal Railroad Administration identification code*]
INOHYC .... Integrated Optical Hybrid Circuit (SAUS)
INok .... Nokomis Public Library, Nokomis, IL [*Library symbol*] [*Library of Congress*] (LCLS)
INokSD .... Nokomis Community Unit, School District 22, Nokomis, IL [*Library symbol*] [*Library of Congress*] (LCLS)
INol .... Northlake Public Library District, Northlake, IL [*Library symbol*] [*Library of Congress*] (LCLS)
INOMACOS... Institut for Operational Research Marketing and Computersystems (SAUS)
INOP .... Inoperative
INOPBL .... Inoperable (SAUS)
InOr .... Orleans Public Library, Orleans, IN [*Library symbol*] [*Library of Congress*] (LCLS)
INORAC .... Inquiry, Ordering and Accounting (SAUS)
INORG .... Inorganic
Inorg Chem... Inorganic Chemistry (MEC)
Inorg Chim Acta... Inorganica Chimica Acta (journ.) (SAUS)
Inorg Mater... Inorganic Materials (journ.) (SAUS)
Inorg Nucl Chem Lett... Inorganic and Nuclear Chemistry Letters (journ.) (SAUS)
Inorg phos... Inorganic Phosphorus [*Medicine*] (MEDA)

InOrPE .... Orleans Progress-Examiner, Orleans, IN [*Library symbol*] [*Library of Congress*] (LCLS)
inor phos ..... Inorganic Phosphorus [*Biochemistry*] (DAVI)
iNOS .... Inducible Nitric Oxide Synthase [*An enzyme*]
INOS .... Isoform of Nitric Oxide Synthase [*An enzyme*]
INOSHAC ..... Indian Ocean and Southern Hemisphere Analysis Center (BARN)
InOsJ .... Osgood Journal, Osgood, IN [*Library symbol*] [*Library of Congress*] (LCLS)
InOssJ .... Ossian Journal, Ossian, IN [*Library symbol*] [*Library of Congress*] (LCLS)
InoStT .... Saint Thomas High School, Rockford (SAUS)
Inotek .... Inotek Technologies, Inc. [*Associated Press*] (SAG)
INOUIRE ...... Issues Needing Qualification Using Intensive Real-Time Experimentation (SAUS)
INOV .... Association Internationale du Nouvel Objet Visuel [*International Association for New Visual Objects*] [*Paris, France*] (EAIO)
InovGme ...... Innovative Gaming Corp. [*Associated Press*] (SAG)
InOw .... Owensville Public Library, Owensville, IN [*Library symbol*] [*Library of Congress*] (LCLS)
InOwSE .... Owensville Star-Echo, Owensville, IN [*Library symbol*] [*Library of Congress*] (LCLS)
InOx .... Oxford Public Library, Oxford, IN [*Library symbol*] [*Library of Congress*] (LCLS)
InOxG .... Oxford Gazette, Oxford, IN [*Library symbol*] [*Library of Congress*] (LCLS)
IN-OZ .... Inch-Ounce
in oz .... inch ounce (SAUS)
INOZ .... Indications and Warning Center (SAUO)
INP .... FA Naval del Peru [*ICAO designator*] (FAAC)
INP .... If Not Possible (FAAC)
INP .... Independent Network Processor [*Computer science*] (CIST)
INP .... Indiana, PA [*Location identifier*] [*FAA*] (FAAL)
InP .... Indium Phosphide (AAEL)
INP .... Indium Phosphide [*Inorganic chemistry*] (IAA)
INP .... Inert Nitrogen Protection (IEEE)
INP .... Information-Need-Product [*Sales technique*]
INP .... Inhibit Presentation (SAUS)
INP .... Initial Program Load [*Computer science*]
INP .... In Pace [*In Peace*] [*Latin*]
inp .... Input (ELAL)
INP .... Input (MSA)
INP .... Insulator Nose Projection [*Automotive spark plugs*]
INP .... Integrated Network Planning (SAUS)
INP .... Integrated Network Processor
INP .... Intelligence Processor (SAUS)
INP .... Intelligent Network Processor
INP .... International News Photo
INP .... International Pipe & Ceramics Corp. (SAUO)
INP .... Internet Nodal Processor [*Computer science*] (ACRL)
INP .... Inter-Net Predicts (MCD)
INP .... Interpace Corporation (SAUO)
INP .... Inyanga National Park (SAUO)
INPA .... Instituto Nacional de Pesquisas de Amazonia [*Brazil*] (EOSA)
INPA .... International Newspaper Promotion Association (EA)
InPa .... Paoli Public Library, Paoli, IN [*Library symbol*] [*Library of Congress*] (LCLS)
INPACON ..... Input Activity Control (SAUS)
INPACON ..... Input Audit and Control (SAUS)
INPACS .... International Packet-Switching Service (SAUO)
INPADOC ..... INKA Patent Documentation (NITA)
INPADOC ..... International Patent Documentation Center [*Information service or system*] (IID)
InPaN .... Paoli News, Paoli, IN [*Library symbol*] [*Library of Congress*] (LCLS)
InPaR .... Paoli Republican, Paoli, IN [*Library symbol*] [*Library of Congress*] (LCLS)
INPARQUES ... Institute of National Parks of the Ministry of Environment and Renewable Natural Resources of the Republic of Venezuela (SAUO)
INPB .... Irish National Pipe Band
INPBM .... Information Not Provided by Manufacturer
INPC .... Impulse Noise Performance Curve (SAUS)
INPC .... Irish National Petroleum Corp.
INPC .... Irish National Productivity Committee (BI)
INPC .... Isopropyl Phenylcarbamate [*Also, IPC, IPPC*] [*Herbicide*]
INPC .... O-Isopropyl N-Phenylcarbamate (SAUS)
INPDN .... Nordic Public Data Network (SAUO)
INPE .... Brazilian Institute for Space Research (SAUS)
INPE .... Brazilian Space Agency (SAUS)
INPE .... Instituto Nacional de Pesquisas Espaciais [*Brazil*] (EOSA)
INPE .... National Space Research Institute (SAUS)
INPEN .... Independence, OR [*American Association of Railroads railroad junction routing code*]
InPen .... Pendleton and Fall Creek Township Public Library, Pendleton, IN [*Library symbol*] [*Library of Congress*] (LCLS)
InPenT .... Pendleton Times, Pendleton, IN [*Library symbol*] [*Library of Congress*] (LCLS)
InPer .... Peru and Miami County Public Library, Peru, IN [*Library symbol*] [*Library of Congress*] (LCLS)
InPerM .... Miami County Historical Museum, Peru, IN [*Library symbol*] [*Library of Congress*] (LCLS)
InPerT .... Peru Tribune, Peru, IN [*Library symbol*] [*Library of Congress*] (LCLS)
InPet .... Barrett Memorial Library, Petersburg, IN [*Library symbol*] [*Library of Congress*] (LCLS)
InPetPD .... Petersburg Press-Dispatch, Petersburg, IN [*Library symbol*] [*Library of Congress*] (LCLS)
INPEX .... International Postage Stamp Exhibition
INPFC .... International North Pacific Fisheries Commission (EA)
INPFC-US ..... International North Pacific Fisheries Commission, United States Section
INPFL .... Independent National Patriotic Front of Liberia [*Political party*] (EY)
IN PH .... Indian Pharmacopoeia [*A publication*] (ROG)
INPH .... Interphase Corp. [*NASDAQ symbol*] (SAG)
INPH .... Interphone
INPH .... Iproniazid Phosphate [*Organic chemistry*]
INPHO .... Information Network for Public Health Officials [*CDC*]
InPHO .... International Photographic Historical Organization (EA)
Inphynet ...... Inphynet Medical Management [*Associated Press*] (SAG)
INPI .... Institut National de la Propriete Industrielle [*National Institute for Industrial Property*] [*France*] [*Information service or system*] (IID)
InPi .... Pierceton and Washington Township Library, Pierceton, IN [*Library symbol*] [*Library of Congress*] (LCLS)
INPI 1 .... INPI Database 1 [*Database on French patents*] (NITA)
INPI 2 .... INPI Database 2 [*Database on European patents*] (NITA)
InPla .... Plainfield Public Library, Plainfield, IN [*Library symbol*] [*Library of Congress*] (LCLS)
InPla-Hi .... Plainfield Public Library, Guilford Township and Hendricks County Historical Collection, Plainfield, IN [*Library symbol*] [*Library of Congress*] (LCLS)
INPLAY .... Random Access Microfilm Information Retrieval Display System (SAUO)
InPly .... Plymouth Public Library, Plymouth, IN [*Library symbol*] [*Library of Congress*] (LCLS)
InPlyHi .... Marshall County Historical Society Library, Plymouth, IN [*Library symbol*] [*Library of Congress*] (LCLS)
INPM .... Integrated Network and Premise Management [*MUX Lab*]
INPO .... In No Particular Order (ADWA)
INPO .... Institute for Nonprofit Organizations
INPO .... Institute of Nuclear Power Operations (EA)
INPOLSE ...... International Police Services
InPorP .... Portage Press, Portage, IN [*Library symbol*] [*Library of Congress*] (LCLS)
InPorS .... Portage Township Schools, Portage, IN [*Library symbol*] [*Library of Congress*] (LCLS)
InPosN .... Posey County News, Poseyville, IN [*Library symbol*] [*Library of Congress*] (LCLS)
INPOWER .... Independent Power Generation Conference and Exhibition [*British*] (ITD)
INPP .... Ignalina Nuclear Power Plant (SAUO)
INPR .... Idaho Northern & Pacific Railroad [*Federal Railroad Administration identification code*]
IN PR .... In Principio [*In the Beginning*] [*Latin*] (ROG)
INPR .... Inprise Corp. [*NASDAQ symbol*] [*Formerly, Borland International*]
INPR .... In Progress
INPR .... Institute for Natural Products Research [*University of Georgia*] [*Research center*] (RCD)
INPr .... Integon Cp $3.875 Cv Pfd [*NYSE symbol*] (TTSB)
INPR .... International Network on Personal Relationships (SAUO)
InPr .... Princeton Public Library, Princeton, IN [*Library symbol*] [*Library of Congress*] (LCLS)
INPRA .... International Public Relations Association
INPRC .... Item Name Policy Review Committee [*DoD*] [*Washington, DC*] (EGAO)
InPrC .... Princeton Daily Clarion, Princeton, IN [*Library symbol*] [*Library of Congress*] (LCLS)
Inprecorr ...... International Press Correspondence (SAUS)
in prep .... in Preparation (SAUS)
INPRESSA .... Indonesian Press Agency (SAUO)
INPRIS .... Investment Promotion Information System [*UNIDO*] [*United Nations*] (DUND)
in pro .... in proportion (SAUS)
INPROCNS ... Information Processing in the Central Nervous System (SAUS)
INPRODE ..... Instituto Profesional para el Desarrollo [*Professional Development Institute*] [*Colombia*]
INPRONS ..... Information Processing in the Central Nervous System
Inprop .... Investment Properties International, Montreal (SAUO)
inps .... if not previously sold (SAUS)
INPS .... Istituto Nazionale della Previdenza Sociale [*Italy*] (ECON)
IN-PT .... Inpatient [*Medicine*] (DAVI)
INPT .... In Port [*Navy*] (NVT)
INPT .... Input [*Amateur radio shorthand*] (WDAA)
INPT .... Input Software, Inc. [*NASDAQ symbol*] (NASQ)
InPtlC .... Jay County Commercial Review, Portland, IN [*Library symbol*] [*Library of Congress*] (LCLS)
InPtlCR .... Jay County Recorder's Office, Portland, IN [*Library symbol*] [*Library of Congress*] (LCLS)
INPUFF .... Gaussian Puff Dispersion Model (COE)
IN PULM ..... In Pulmento [*In Gruel*] [*Pharmacy*]
INPUT .... Annual international screening conference for the exchange of program ideas (SAUO)
INPUT .... Induced Pulse Transient (PDAA)
INPUT .... International Public Television [*An association*] (NTCM)
InputOut ...... Input Output, Inc. [*Associated Press*] (SAG)
INPV .... Intermittent Negative-Pressure Ventilation [*Medicine*]
INPZ .... Industrial Paper [*Federal Railroad Administration identification code*]
INQ .... Index of Nutritional Quality
INQ .... Inferior Nasal Quadrant [*Medicine*] (STED)
INQ .... Inquire (ECII)
INQ .... Inquiry (AFM)
Inq .... Inquiry (DIAR)
inq .... Inquiry (WDMC)

Inq .... Inquisition (SAUS)
INQ .... Intercontinental Venture [*Vancouver Stock Exchange symbol*]
INQ .... Interior Nasal Quadrant [*Medicine*] (DMAA)
inq .... Query (WDMC)
inq .... Question (WDMC)
INQD .... Inquired (ROG)
INQ PM .... Inquisitio Post-Mortem [*Latin*] (ROG)
IN QRS .... In Quires [*Publishing*] (DGA)
INQSTV .... Inquisitive
INQT .... Inquest (ROG)
INQUA .... Commission of Formation and Properties of Glacial Deposits (SAUS)
INQUA .... Commission on Applied Quaternary Studies (SAUS)
INQUA .... Commission on Carbon (SAUO)
INQUA .... Commission on Glaciation (SAUO)
INQUA .... Commission on Global Continental (SAUO)
INQUA .... Commission on Human Evolution and Palaeoecology (SAUO)
INQUA .... Commission on Land Carbon (SAUS)
INQUA .... Commission on Loess (SAUO)
INQUA .... Commission on Neotectonics (SAUO)
INQUA .... Commission on Palaeoclimate (SAUO)
INQUA .... Commission on Paleopedology (SAUO)
INQUA .... Commission on Quaternary Shorelines (SAUS)
INQUA .... Commission on Sea Level Changes and Coastal Evolution (SAUO)
INQUA .... Commission on Stratigraphy (SAUO)
INQUA .... Commission on Tephrochronology (SAUS)
INQUA .... Commission on Tephrochronology and Volcanism (SAUO)
INQUA .... Commission on the Holocene (SAUO)
INQUA .... Commission on the Paleoecology of Early Man (SAUS)
INQUA .... Commission on the Paleogeographic Atlas of the Quaternary (SAUS)
INQUA .... Commission on the Quaternary of South America (SAUS)
INQUA .... Commission on the Study of the Holocene (SAUS)
INQUA .... Committee on Quaternary Economic Deposits (SAUO)
INQUA .... International Association on Quaternary Research (SAUO)
INQUA .... International Quaternary Research Association (SAUO)
INQUA .... International Union for/of Quaternary Research (SAUO)
INQUA .... International Union for Quaternary Research [*Research center*] [*France*] (IRC)
INQUA .... Working Group on the Paleogeographic Atlases of the Quaternary (SAUO)
INQUA/C .... Commission on Carbon (SAUO)
INQUA/G .... Commission on Glaciation (SAUO)
INQUA/GLOCOPH... Commission on Global Continental Palaeohydrology (SAUO)
INQUA/H .... Commission on the Holocene (SAUO)
INQUA/HEP... Commission on Human Evolution and Palaeoecology (SAUO)
INQUA/L .... Commission on Loess (SAUO)
INQUA/N .... Commission on Neotectonics (SAUO)
INQUA/PAQWG... Working Group on the Paleogeographic Atlases of the Quaternary (SAUO)
INQUA/PC .... Commission on Palaeoclimate (SAUO)
INQUA/PP .... Commission on Paleopedology (SAUO)
INQUA/QED... Committee on Quaternary Economic Deposits (SAUO)
INQUA/S .... Commission on Stratigraphy (SAUO)
INQUA/SLCCE... Commission on Sea Level Changes and Coastal Evolution (SAUO)
INQUA/TV .... Commission on Tephrochronology and Volcanism (SAUO)
INQUEST .... Interim Query System (SAUO)
INQY .... Inquiry (ROG)
INR .... Bureau of Intelligence and Research [*Department of State*]
INR .... Image Navigation and Registration (GAVI)
INR .... Impact Noise Rating [*of insulation*]
INR .... Impact Noise Ratio (SAUS)
INR .... Impact Noise Reduction (SAUS)
INR .... Independent National Radio (SAUS)
INR .... Index of Nursing Research (SAUS)
INR .... Indian Rupee (SAUS)
INR .... Inertial Reference (MCD)
INR .... Initial Negotiating Right (JAGO)
INR .... Initial Nuclear Radiation (SAUO)
INR .... Inner (MSA)
INR .... Insilco Corp. (SAUO)
INR .... Institute of Natural Resources [*Montana State University*] [*Research center*] (RCD)
INR .... Institute of Natural Resources [*University of Georgia*] [*Research center*] (RCD)
INR .... Institute of Nuclear Research [*Poland*]
INR .... Institut National de Radiodiffusion [*Belgium*]
INR .... Intelligence and Research (DNAB)
INR .... Interaction Resources Ltd. [*Toronto Stock Exchange symbol*]
INR .... Inter Air AB [*Sweden*] [*ICAO designator*] (FAAC)
INR .... Interference-to-Noise Ratio
INR .... International Narcotic Report (journal) [*Medicine*] (EDAA)
INR .... International Normalized Ratio [*Hematology*]
INR .... International Silver Co. (SAUO)
INR .... Morrisson-Reeves Public Library, Richmond, IN [*OCLC symbol*] (OCLC)
INRA .... Immigration Nursing Relief Act (SAUS)
INRA .... Individual Nonrecurrence Action (SAA)
INRA .... Information Research Analysts (SAUS)
INRA .... Inland Navigational Rules Act of 1980
INRA .... Institut National de la Recherche Agronomique (NITA)
INRA .... International Network for Religion and Animals (EA)
INRA .... International Research Associates of Sweden (SAUS)
INRAC .... Immigration Nursing Relief Advisory Committee [*Department of Labor*] (EGAO)
INRAD .... Interactive Radiation (SAUS)
INRAD .... Interactive Real-Time Advanced Display
INRC .... Identity, Negation, Reciprocal, and Correlative Transformations [*Developed by J. Piaget*] (DIPS)
INRC .... Indian Nation Restoration Committee
INRC .... Innovative Naval Reserve Concept (DOMA)
InRCS .... Richmond Community School, Richmond, IN [*Library symbol*] [*Library of Congress*] (LCLS)
INRCTN .... Interaction
INRD .... Indiana Rail Road [*Federal Railroad Administration identification code*]
INRDM .... Interdisciplinary Natural Resources Development and Management Program (SAUO)
InRE .... Earlham College, Richmond, IN [*Library symbol*] [*Library of Congress*] (LCLS)
IN RE .... In Regard To
IN REF .... In Reference To
INREM .... Internal REM [*Roentgen-Equivalent-Man*] [*Radiation dose*]
InRem .... Remington Carpenter Township Public Library, Remington, IN [*Library symbol*] [*Library of Congress*] (LCLS)
InRen .... Jasper County Public Library, Rensselaer, IN [*Library symbol*] [*Library of Congress*] (LCLS)
INRENARE ... Institute for the Management of Renewable Natural Resources (SAUO)
InRenS .... Saint Joseph's College, Rensselaer, IN [*Library symbol*] [*Library of Congress*] (LCLS)
INREP .... Installation Damage Report [*Air Force*]
INREPL .... Incoming Replacement [*Army*] (AABC)
INREQ .... Information on Request (MCD)
INREQ .... Information Request (COE)
INREQ .... Information Requested
INREQS .... Information Requests [*Army*] (AABC)
INRES .... Independent Reservation System [*Hotels and motels*]
INRESA .... Integrated Rural Energy Systems Association (SAUO)
Inrest Geotherm Potential UK Br Geol Surv... Investigation of the Geothermal Potential of the UK. British Geological Survey (journ.) (SAUS)
in/rev .... inches per revolution (SAUS)
INREX .... Investors Research [*Mutual fund ticker symbol*] (SG)
INRF .... International Nutrition Research Foundation (EA)
INRG .... Inrange Technologies "B" [*NASDAQ symbol*]
INRH .... Institut National de Recherches en Hydrologie [*National Hydrology Research Institute*] [*Canada*]
INRI .... Iesus Nazarenus Rex Iudaeorum [*Jesus of Nazareth, King of the Jews*] [*Latin*]
INRI .... Imperator Napoleon Rex Italiae [*Emperor Napoleon, King of Italy*] [*Latin*]
INRI .... Inter-National Research Institute Inc. (SAUO)
INRIA .... French National Institute for Research in Computer Science and Control (SAUS)
INRIA .... Institut National de Recherche en Informatique et en Automatique [*National Institute for Research in Informatics and Automation*] [*Research center and database originator*] [*France*] [*Information service or system*] (IID)
INRIC .... International Network of Resource Information Centers (SAUO)
INRIC .... International Network of Resource Information Centres (SAUS)
InRid .... Ridgeville Public Library, Ridgeville, IN [*Library symbol*] [*Library of Congress*] (LCLS)
InRis .... Ohio County Public Library, Rising Sun, IN [*Library symbol*] [*Library of Congress*] (LCLS)
InRisCN .... Ohio County News, Rising Sun, IN [*Library symbol*] [*Library of Congress*] (LCLS)
InRisCR .... Ohio County Recorder's Office, Rising Sun, IN [*Library symbol*] [*Library of Congress*] (LCLS)
InRisHi .... Ohio County Historical Society, Rising Sun, IN [*Library symbol*] [*Library of Congress*] (LCLS)
InRisR .... Rising Sun Recorder, Rising Sun, IN [*Library symbol*] [*Library of Congress*] (LCLS)
InRM .... Morrison-Reeves Public Library, Richmond, IN [*Library symbol*] [*Library of Congress*] (LCLS)
InRM .... Wayne Township Library, Richmond, IN [*Library symbol*] [*Library of Congress*] (LCLS)
INRNE .... Institute of Nuclear Research and Nuclear Energy (SAUS)
INRO .... International Natural Rubber Organization [*Kuala Lumpur, Malaysia*] (EAIO)
INRO .... International Naval Research Organization (EA)
InRo .... Roachdale Public Library, Roachdale, IN [*Library symbol*] [*Library of Congress*] (LCLS)
InRoa .... Roanoke Public Library, Roanoke, IN [*Library symbol*] [*Library of Congress*] (LCLS)
InRoc .... Fulton County Public Library, Rochester, IN [*Library symbol*] [*Library of Congress*] (LCLS)
InRocCR .... Fulton County Recorder's Office, Rochester, IN [*Library symbol*] [*Library of Congress*] (LCLS)
InRocFHi .... Fulton County Historical Society, Rochester, IN [*Library symbol*] [*Library of Congress*] (LCLS)
InRocS .... Rochester Sentinel, Rochester, IN [*Library symbol*] [*Library of Congress*] (LCLS)
InRomS .... Gene Stratton-Porter Memorial, Rome City, IN [*Library symbol*] [*Library of Congress*] (LCLS)
INROWASP... In Rotating Water Spinning Process (SAUS)
InRoyR .... Royal Center Record, Royal Center, IN [*Library symbol*] [*Library of Congress*] (LCLS)
InRPI .... Richmond Palladium-Item, Richmond, IN [*Library symbol*] [*Library of Congress*] (LCLS)
InRpt .... Rockport-Ohio Township Public Library, Rockport, IN [*Library symbol*] [*Library of Congress*] (LCLS)

InRptD .... Rockport Democrat, Rockport, IN [*Library symbol*] [*Library of Congress*] (LCLS)
InRptJ .... Rockport Journal, Rockport, IN [*Library symbol*] [*Library of Congress*] (LCLS)
INRS .... Institut National de la Recherche Scientifique [*National Institute for Scientific Research*] [*Canada*] [*Research center*]
INRS .... Intranet Solutions, Inc. [*NASDAQ symbol*] (SAG)
INRT .... Inertia (KSC)
INRTFLR .... Inert Filler
INRTG .... Inert Gas
INRTL .... Inertial (MSA)
INRTLVEL .... Inertial Velocity (MCD)
INRUD .... International Network for the Rational Use of Drugs (SAUO)
InRusCR .... Rush County Recorder's Office, Rushville, IN [*Library symbol*] [*Library of Congress*] (LCLS)
InRusR .... Rushville Republican, Rushville, IN [*Library symbol*] [*Library of Congress*] (LCLS)
InRv .... Rockville Public Library, Rockville, IN [*Library symbol*] [*Library of Congress*] (LCLS)
InRvCR .... Parke County Recorder's Office, Rockville, IN [*Library symbol*] [*Library of Congress*] (LCLS)
INS .... Idiopathic Nephrotic Syndrome
INS .... Idiopathic Neurologic Syndrome [*Medicine*] (MELL)
INS .... Illinois State University, Normal, IL [*Library symbol*] [*Library of Congress*] (LCLS)
INS .... Illuminated Nasal Speculum [*Medicine*] (MELL)
INS .... Immigration and Naturalization Service [*Department of Justice*]
INS .... Improved Navigational Satellite
INS .... Improved Night Sight
INS .... Impulse Noise Simulator
INS .... Inches (EY)
ins .... Inches (ODBW)
IN/S .... Inches per Second
INS .... Independent News Service [*In TV series "The Night Stalker"*]
INS .... Indian Naval Ship (SAUO)
INS .... Indian Navy Ship (SAUS)
INS .... Indian News Service (SAUO)
INS .... Indian Springs, NV [*Location identifier*] [*FAA*] (FAAL)
INS .... Indiopahtic Nephrotic Syndrome [*Nephrology*] (DAVI)
INS .... Indirect NICS Subscriber (SAUS)
INS .... Inelastic Neutron Scattering
INS .... Inertial Navigation Sensor (IAA)
INS .... Inertial Navigation Set (SAUS)
INS .... Inertial Navigation System [*Aviation*]
INS .... Information Network System [*Japan*]
INS .... Information Systems (KSC)
INS .... Initial Navigation System (AABC)
INS .... Inland Steel [*Federal Railroad Administration identification code*]
INS .... Inlet Resources Ltd. [*Vancouver Stock Exchange symbol*]
Ins .... Inositol [*Biochemistry*]
INS .... Input String (SAUS)
INS .... Input String, Instance Object (SAUS)
INS .... Input String Integrated Network Server (SAUS)
INS .... Inrealistic Neutron Scattering [*Physics*]
INS .... Insane (ROG)
INS .... Inscribed
ins .... Inscriber [*MARC relator code*] [*Library of Congress*] (LCCP)
INS .... Inscription (ADA)
INS .... Insect
Ins .... Insecta (SAUS)
INS .... Insert (NVT)
ins .... Insertion (STED)
INS .... Insertion Burn [*Orbital Maneuvering Subsystem 1*] [*NASA*] (NASA)
INS .... Insertion Mutation [*Genetics*]
Ins .... Insert Key (ADWA)
INS .... Insert Shot [*Film production*] (NTCM)
ins .... Inshell
INS .... Inside (MSA)
INS .... In Situ [*In Place*] [*Latin*] (ADA)
INS .... Insolubilization (SAUS)
Ins .... Insolvency [*Legal term*] (DLA)
INS .... Inspection Checklist (SAUO)
INS .... Inspection Division [*Coast Guard*]
INS .... Inspector
INS .... Installation Noise Standard (SAUS)
INS .... Installation Squadron
INS .... Instance Object (SAUS)
ins .... Instant (VRA)
INS .... Institute for Naval Studies
INS .... Institute for Nuclear Study [*Japan*]
INS .... Institute of Neurological Science [*University of Pennsylvania*]
INS .... Institute of Nuclear Studies [*Oak Ridge, TN*]
INS .... Institute of Nucler Sciences (SAUS)
INS .... Institute of Nutritional Sciences (SAUO)
INS .... Institute Scholars (SAUO)
INS .... Institutional Net Settlements (NUMA)
INS .... Instrucion (SAUS)
INS .... Insufficient Sample (SAUS)
INS .... Insular
Ins .... Insulate (MIST)
INS .... Insulate
Ins .... Insulin [*Endocrinology*] (DAVI)
INS .... Insulin (STED)
INS .... Insurance (AFM)
Ins .... Insurance (EBF)
ins .... Insurance (WDAA)
INS .... Insure
Ins .... Insured (EBF)
ins .... Insured (STED)
INS .... Integrated Navigation System
INS .... Integrated Network Server (SAUO)
INS .... Integrated Network Systems, Inc.
INS .... Integrated Nitrogen System (SSD)
INS .... Integration Navigation System (SAUS)
INS .... Intelligent Systems Corp. [*AMEX symbol*] (SPSG)
INS .... Interceptor Simulator (SAA)
INS .... Interchangeable-Substitute Items (AAG)
INS .... Internal Navigation System
INS .... International Navigation System
INS .... International Network for Self-Reliance (EA)
INS .... International Network Service [*Mercury*] [*British*] (TELE)
INS .... International Network Services (SAUO)
INS .... International Neuropsychological Society (NTPA)
INS .... International News Service [*Later, UPI*]
INS .... International Numismatic Society (EAIO)
INS .... International Seaway Trading Corp. (MHDW)
INS .... Internet Naming Service (RALS)
INS .... Interstate Nuclear Services (SAUO)
INS .... Interstation Noise Suppression
INS .... Intravenous Nurses Society (EA)
INS .... Investors News Service (SAUS)
INS .... Involuntary Nervous System (DIPS)
INS .... Ion Neutralization Spectroscope (SAUS)
INS .... Ion Neutralization Spectroscopy (SAUS)
INS .... Ion-Neutralization Spectroscopy
INS .... Iron Nickel System
INS .... Iron Soldering
INS .... Isolated Neutron Star [*Astrophysics*]
INS .... Israel Naval Ship (BJA)
INS .... Israel News Service (BJA)
INS .... Northern Illinois Library System, Rockford, IL [*OCLC symbol*] (OCLC)
InS .... South Bend Public Library, South Bend, IN [*Library symbol*] [*Library of Congress*] (LCLS)
INSA .... Indonesian Shipowners Association (SAUO)
INSA .... Institut National des Sciences Appliques [*France*] (EOSA)
INSA .... Institut National de Systematique Appliquee [*Canada*]
INSA .... International Naples Sabot Association (EA)
INSA .... International Service Association for Health (SAUO)
INSA .... International Shipowners' Association [*See also MAS*] [*Gdynia, Poland*] (EAIO)
INSA .... National Institute of Agricultural Sciences (SAUO)
INSA .... National Tire Industry Corporation (SAUO)
InSa .... Salem Public Library, Salem, IN [*Library symbol*] [*Library of Congress*] (LCLS)
INS AB .... Insulin Antibody [*Endocrinology*] (DAVI)
INS Ab .... Insulin Antibody [*Medicine*] (STED)
INSAB .... International Numismatic Society Authentication Bureau (EA)
INSAC .... Integrated National Surveillance and Control (ACAE)
INSAC .... Interstate Airways Communications (IAA)
InSaCR .... Washington County Recorder's Office, Salem, IN [*Library symbol*] [*Library of Congress*] (LCLS)
INSACS .... Interstate Airways Communications Station
INSACS .... Interstate Airways Communications System (SAUS)
INSAET .... Institute of Agricultural Engineering and Technology (SAUO)
INSAF .... Interim Name Source Authority File (SAUS)
INSAG .... International Nuclear Safety Advisory Group [*United Nations*] (EY)
Ins Agt .... Insurance Agent (SAUO)
INSAIR .... Inspector of Aircraft (SAUS)
INSAIR .... Inspector of Naval Aircraft
InSaLD .... Salem Leader/Democrat, Salem, IN [*Library symbol*] [*Library of Congress*] (LCLS)
INSALUD .... National Institute of Health (SAUS)
INS&E .... Institute of Nuclear Science and Engineering (SAUO)
INSAP .... Inspiration of Astronomical Phenomena
INSAR .... Instruction Address Register [*Computer science*]
InSAR .... Interferometric Synthetic Aperture RADAR [*Imaging system*]
INSAS .... Indian Small Arms System (SAUS)
INSAT .... Indian Geostationary Meteorological Satellite (SAUO)
INSAT .... Indian Geostationary Satellite [*Marine science*] (OSRA)
INSAT .... Indian National Satellite System [*Bangalore, India*] [*Telecommunications*]
INSAT .... Indian Satellite (USDC)
INSAT .... India Satellite [*Telecommunications*] (NITA)
INSAT .... Instrumented Subassembly Test (SAUS)
INSATRAC .... Interception by Satellite Tracking (SAUS)
InsAut .... Insurance Auto Auctions [*Associated Press*] (SAG)
INSAV .... Interim Shipboard Availability (MCD)
InSaWHi .... Washington County Historical Society, Salem, IN [*Library symbol*] [*Library of Congress*] (LCLS)
InSb .... Indium Antimonide (AAEL)
INSB .... Intelligence and Security Board [*Army*] (RDA)
INSB .... Internet Services for the Blind (SAUO)
In-SC .... Indiana State Supreme Court, Law Library, Indianapolis, IN [*Library symbol*] [*Library of Congress*] (LCLS)
INSC .... Inscribed [*or Inscription*] (MSA)
INSC .... Insulating Concrete [*Technical drawings*]
Ins C .... Insurance Code [*A publication*] (DLA)
INSC .... Internal Shape Components (CINC)
InSc .... Scott County Public Library, Scottsburg, IN [*Library symbol*] [*Library of Congress*] (LCLS)

INSCA International Natural Sausage Casing Association (EA)
INSCAIRS Instrumentation Calibration Incident Repair Service
INSCE Insurance
INS CHAR Insert Character (SAUS)
in sched In Schedula [*On a Herbarium Sheet*] [*Latin*] (EES)
Inschr Inschrift (BJA)
INSCI Information Science, Inc. [*Information service or system*] (IID)
Insci Insci Corp. [*Associated Press*] (SAG)
INSCO Intercontinental Shipping Corp. (MHDW)
INSCOM Intelligence and Security Command [*Army*] (RDA)
INSCOM International Satellite Communication, Limited (ACAE)
INSCOM US Army Intelligence and Security Command (SAUS)
INSCOPE Information System for Coffee and Other Product Economics [*International Coffee Organization*] (NITA)
Ins Couns J Insurance Counsel Journal [*A publication*] (DLA)
Inscr Inscription (DIAR)
INSCR Inscription
INSCR Insecure
INSCRPTN Inscription
INSCRUIT Inspector of Navy Recruiting and Naval Officer Procurement
INSD Insured
INS Data Base United States International Air Travel Statistics Data Base [*I. P. Sharp Associates*] [*Canada*] (NITA)
INSDC Indian National Scientific Documentation Centre [*New Delhi*]
INSDEN Inspector of Dental Activities
INSDOC Indian National Scientific Documentation Centre [*Council of Scientific and Industrial Research*]
INSDOC List Indian National Scientific Documentation Centre List (SAUS)
Insd Val Insured Value [*Business term*] (MHDB)
InSEA Indiana Society of Enrolled Agents (SAUO)
INSEA International Society for Education through Art [*Corsham, England*]
INSEAD Institut Europeen d'Administration des Affaires [*European Business Management Institute*] [*France*] (PDAA)
IN/SEC Inches per Second (WDAA)
INSEC Informal Sector Service Centre (SAUO)
INSEC Internal Security
INSECT Institute for Social, Economic and Civic Training (SAUS)
INSECTI Insecticide(s) [*Freight*]
Insectic Insecticide (SAUS)
Insect Mol Biol Insect Molecular Biology (SAUS)
INSEE Institut National de la Statistique et des Etudes Economiques [*National Institute of Statistics and Economic Research*] [*Paris, France*]
INSEL International Nickel Southern Exploration Limited (SAUO)
INSEL International Nickel Southern Exploration Ltd. (SAUS)
InSelS Sellersburg Star, Sellersburg, IN [*Library symbol*] [*Library of Congress*] (LCLS)
insem Insemination [*Medicine*] (STED)
INSEM Insemination
INSEM Inter-Institutional Service of Electronic Mail (EURO)
INSENG Inspector of Engineering (SAUS)
INSENG Inspector of Naval Engineering
INSEP Inseparable (MSA)
INSERM Institut National de la Sante et de la Recherche Medicale [*National Institute for Health and Medical Research*] [*France*] [*Information service or system*] (IID)
INSERT Insert Code (SAUO)
Insertion B Insertion Burn [*Aerospace*] (NAKS)
INSERV In Service [*Military*] (CAAL)
INSET In-Service Education and Training [*British*] (DET)
INSET In-service Education for Teachers [*Australia*]
INSET In-Service Training (PDAA)
INSEX IDS Selective Cl.A [*Mutual fund ticker symbol*] (SG)
InSey Seymour Public Library, Seymour, IN [*Library symbol*] [*Library of Congress*] (LCLS)
InSeyT Seymour Daily Tribune, Seymour, IN [*Library symbol*] [*Library of Congress*] (LCLS)
INSF Insulating Fill [*Technical drawings*]
INS Factor Iodine Number and Saponification Factor (SAUS)
INSFFER International Network on Soil Fertility and Fertilizer Evaluation for Rice (SAUO)
INSG Insignia Solutions, plc [*NASDAQ symbol*] (NASQ)
INSGCY Insurgency (AABC)
INSGEN Inspector General [*Navy*]
INSGENLANTFLT Inspector General, Atlantic Fleet [*Navy*]
INSGENPAC Inspector General, Pacific Fleet and Pacific Ocean Areas [*Navy*]
InsgFn Insignia Financial Group [*Associated Press*] (SAG)
InSghtH InSight Health Services Corp. [*Associated Press*] (SAG)
InsgSol Insignia Solutions [*Associated Press*] (SAG)
InsgtEnt Insight Entertainment Corp. [*Associated Press*] (SAG)
INSGY Insignia Solutions [*NASDAQ symbol*] (SAG)
INSGY Insignia Solutions ADS [*NASDAQ symbol*] (TTSB)
INSH Inspection Shell
InShe Shelbyville-Shelby County Public Library, Shelbyville, IN [*Library symbol*] [*Library of Congress*] (LCLS)
InSheCR Shelby County Recorder's Office, Shelbyville, IN [*Library symbol*] [*Library of Congress*] (LCLS)
InSheN Shelbyville News, Shelbyville, IN [*Library symbol*] [*Library of Congress*] (LCLS)
InSherN Sheridan News, Sheridan, IN [*Library symbol*] [*Library of Congress*] (LCLS)
InSho Shoals Public Library, Shoals, IN [*Library symbol*] [*Library of Congress*] (LCLS)
InShoD Martin County Democrat, Shoals, IN [*Library symbol*] [*Library of Congress*] (LCLS)
InShoHi Martin County Historical Society, Shoals, IN [*Library symbol*] [*Library of Congress*] (LCLS)
InShoN Shoals News, Shoals, IN [*Library symbol*] [*Library of Congress*] (LCLS)
INSHOREPAT Inshore Patrol
INSHOREUNSEAWARDIV Inshore Undersea Warfare Division (SAUS)
INSHOREUNSEAWARGRU Inshore Undersea Warfare Group (SAUO)
INSHORUNSEAWARGRU Inshore Undersea Warfare Group [*Navy*]
ins/hr inches per hour (SAUS)
INSI Information Sciences, Incorporated (SAUO)
INSI INSCI Corp. [*NASDAQ symbol*] (TTSB)
insid Insidious (STED)
Inside Diam Inside Diameter (NAKS)
INSIDE Jupiter Interior Structure and Internal Dynamical Evolution of Jupiter (SAUS)
INSIGHT Information System Integrated by Using Global Hypermedia Technology (SAUO)
Insight Insight Enterprises, Inc. [*Associated Press*] (SAG)
INSIGHT Instructional Systems Investigation Graphic Tool (SAUS)
INSIGHT Interactive System for Investigation by Graphics of Hydrological Trends (SAUO)
Insignia Insignia Systems, Inc. [*Associated Press*] (SAG)
Insilco Insilco Corp. [*Associated Press*] (SAG)
INSILCO International Silver Co. [*Acronym now used as firm's name*]
INSIM Interactive Simulation (SAUS)
InSIN Indianapolis Star and News, Indianapolis, IN [*Library symbol*] [*Library of Congress*] (LCLS)
INSINSTR Inspector-Instructor, Naval Reserve
INSIPID Inadequate Sensitivity Improvement by Proton Indirect (SAUS)
INSIS Inter-Institutional Integrated Services Information System
IN SIT Initial Situation (SAUS)
INSIT Intelligence Situation Report (SAUO)
INSITE Independent Services for Instruction Testing and Evaluations (SAUO)
INSITE Information on Nuclear Site Data System [*Nuclear Regulatory Commission*] (GFGA)
InsitE Insituform East, Inc. [*Associated Press*] (SAG)
INSITE Institutional Space Inventory Technique [*Computer science*]
INSITE Integral Sensor Interpretation Techniques (SAUS)
INSITE Integrated Sensor Interpretation Techniques
INSITE Intel Software Index and Technology Exchange (SAUS)
INSITE International Network of Somewhere in Time Enthusiasts (EA)
INSITE System Institutional Space Inventory Technique System (SAUS)
InSiteVis InSite Vision, Inc. [*Associated Press*] (SAG)
INSITS International Symposium on IT Standardization (SAUO)
InsitTc Insituform Technology [*Associated Press*] (SAG)
in situ In Place (DOG)
INSIU Insci Corp. [*NASDAQ symbol*] (SAG)
INSIW INSCI Corp.Wrrt [*NASDAQ symbol*] (TTSB)
INSJ Institute of Nuclear Study, Japan (SAUS)
INS J PL Insulated Jack Plug (SAUS)
Ins key Insert Key [*Computer science*]
INSL Insulate
InSL South Bend Public Library, South Bend, IN [*Library symbol*] [*Library of Congress*] (LCLS)
InsL&P Insurance Law and Practice (SAFN)
INSLAW Institute for Law and Social Research (IID)
ins/lb inches per pound (SAUS)
Ins Liability Rep Insurance Liability Reports [*A publication*] (DLA)
Ins LJ Insurance Law Journal (SAUO)
Ins LJ Insurance Law Journal (journ.) (SAUS)
Ins LR Insurance Law Reporter [*A publication*] (DLA)
Ins L Rep Insurance Law Reporter [*A publication*] (DLA)
INSLTD Insulated
INSLTN Insulation
INSLUG Insulating
INSM Insituform Mid-America, Inc. [*NASDAQ symbol*] (NQ)
INSM Integrated Network and Systems Management [*Computer science*] (GART)
INSMAB Inspector of Materiel Board (SAUS)
INSMACH Inspector of Naval Machinery
INSMARSAT International Maritime Satellite [*Organization*] (DOMA)
INSMAT Inspector of Materiel (SAUO)
INSMAT Inspector of Naval Material
INSMAT Material Inspection Service [*Navy*] (AAGC)
INSMAT PET Inspector of Naval Material, Petroleum
INSMATPETMIDEASTAREA Inspector of Naval Material Petroleum products, Middle East Area (SAUO)
INSMATS Inspectors of Naval Material (AAGC)
INSMETLS International Shielding Metals (SAUO)
Ins Mon Insurance Monitor [*A publication*] (DLA)
InsMuni Insured Municipal Income Fund [*Associated Press*] (SAG)
InSn Indium Antimonide (SAUS)
INSN InSilicon Corp. [*NASDAQ symbol*] (SG)
INSNA International Network for Social Network Analysis [*University of Toronto*] [*Toronto, ON*] (EAIO)
INSNAVMAT Inspector of Navigational Material
INSNCTR Instruction Counter (SAUS)
InSNHi Northern Indiana State Historical Society, South Bend, IN [*Library symbol*] [*Library of Congress*] (LCLS)
Insn Rg Instruction Ring (SAUS)
Insn T Instruction Time (SAUS)
INSO InfoSoft International, Inc. [*NASDAQ symbol*] (SAG)
INSO Innovative Software, Inc. (SAUO)
INSO INSO Corp. [*Associated Press*] (SAG)
INSOL Insoluble (MSA)

insol........ Insoluble (STED)
INSOLT........ I've Never Seen One Like That [*Antiques market*]
Insolv........ Insolvency [*Legal term*] (DLA)
INSOLV........ Insolvent [*Legal term*] (ADA)
Insolv LJ........ Insolvency Law Journal (journ.) (SAUS)
INSOLVT........ Insolvent (ROG)
INSONA........ International Society of Naturalists (SAUO)
INSORD........ Inspector of Ordnance
INSORDINC... Inspector of Ordnance in Charge
InSow........ South Whitley Cleveland Township Public Library, South Whitley, IN [*Library symbol*] [*Library of Congress*] (LCLS)
InSowTN........ South Whitley Tribune-News, South Whitley, IN [*Library symbol*] [*Library of Congress*] (LCLS)
INSP........ InfoSpace.com, Inc. [*NASDAQ symbol*] (NASQ)
INSP........ Inspect [*or Inspector*] (AFM)
Insp........ Inspected (SAUS)
Insp........ Inspection (STED)
Insp........ Inspector (TBD)
Insp........ Inspiration (STED)
INSP........ Inspiration
INSP........ International Nuclear Safety Program (SAUO)
INSP........ Internet Name Server Protocol (TNIG)
InSp........ Speedway Public Library, Speedway, IN [*Library symbol*] [*Library of Congress*] (LCLS)
Insp Adr........ Inspection and Advice (journ.) (SAUS)
INSPASS........ INS Passenger Accelerated Service System (SAUS)
INSPAT........ Inshore Patrol
INSPCTN........ Inspection
INSPCTR........ Inspector
InSpe........ Spencer Public-Owen County Contractual Library, Spencer, IN [*Library symbol*] [*Library of Congress*] (LCLS)
INSPEC........ Information Service for/in Physics, Electrotechnology, Computers, and Control (SAUO)
INSPEC........ Information Service for Physics, Electrotechnology and Control (SAUS)
INSPEC........ Information Service for the Physics and Engineering Communities (SAUS)
INSPEC........ Information Service: Physics, Electrical and Electronics, and Computers and Con trol [*Information service*] [*British*] (NITA)
INSPEC........ Information Services in Physics, Electronics, and Computers [*Information service or system*]
INSPEC........ Information Services: Physics (SAUS)
INSPEC........ Initial Specialty [*Military*] (INF)
INSPEC........ Inspection
INSPEC........ Institution of Electrical Engineers Information Service (SAUS)
INSPEC........ International Information Services for the Physics and Engineering Communities
INSPECC........ Information Service for Physics, Electrotechnology, Computers and Control (SAUS)
INSPECC........ Information Services in Physics, Electrotechnology, Computers and Control (SAUS)
INSPECT........ Infrared System for Printed Circuit Testing (SAUS)
INSPECT........ Inquiry into Pollution and Environmental Conservation (SAUS)
Inspector Gen Rep... Inspector General Reports (AAGC)
INSPEL........ International Journal of Special Libraries (journ.) (SAUS)
INSPEL........ International Newsletter of Special Libraries [*A publication*]
INSPETRES... Inspector of Petroleum Reserves
INSPETRES... Inspector of Petroleum Resources (SAUS)
InSpeW........ Spencer Evening World, Spencer, IN [*Library symbol*] [*Library of Congress*] (LCLS)
INSPEX........ Engineering Inspection and Quality Control Conference and Exhibition (SAUO)
INSPEX........ Indonesia Space Experiment (SAUO)
INSPEX........ International Measurement and Inspection Technology Exposition
Insp Gen........ Inspector General (WGA)
InspGen of Hosp... Inspector General of Hospitals (SAUS)
Insp-Gen of Hosp... Inspector-General of Hospitals (SAUO)
INSPI........ Innovative Nuclear Space Power Institute (SAUS)
INSPINSTF... Inspector-Instructor Staff [*Military*] (DNAB)
INSP-INSTR... Inspector-Instruction [*Marine Corps*]
inspir........ Inspiration [*or Inspiratory*] (CPH)
Inspir........ Inspiration/tory [*Medicine*] (EDAA)
INSPIR........ Inspiretur [*Let It Be Inspired*] [*Pharmacy*]
INSPIRAPLEX... Respiratory Health Network of Centres of Excellence (SAUO)
INSPIRE........ Indiana Spectrum of Information Resources
INSPIRE........ Institute for Public Interest Representation [*Later, CCCIPR*] [*Georgetown University*]
INSP L........ Inspection Laws (DLA)
INSPN........ Inspection (SAUS)
INSPNAVMAT... Inspector of Naval Material (SAUS)
InspNavMedActy... Inspector, Naval Medical Activity (SAUS)
InspOff........ Inspecting Officer (SAUS)
Insp of R Eng... Inspector of Royal Engineers (SAUS)
Insp of RF Arty... Inspector of Royal Field Artillery (SAUS)
INSPON........ Inspection (ROG)
INSPR........ Inspector
INSPR........ Intelligence Systems Program Review [*Military*] (MCD)
InspST........ Inspector of Supply and Transport (SAUS)
INSP W & M... Inspector of Weights and Measures [*British*] (ROG)
INSR........ Insert (MSA)
INSR........ Insulin Receptor [*Medicine*] (DMAA)
INSRADMAT... Inspector of Radio Material
Ins Rep........ Insurance Reporter [*A publication*] (DLA)
Insrnc........ Insurance (SAUS)
INSRP........ Inter-Agency Network Safety Review Panel [*NASA*] (NASA)
INSRP........ Interagency Nuclear Safety Review Panel
InSrvAm........ Industrial Services of America, Inc. [*Associated Press*] (SAG)
INSS........ Information Network Satellite System (ACAE)
INSS........ Integrated Navigation Sensor System
INSS........ International Network Services [*NASDAQ symbol*] (SAG)
INSS........ International Neuroblastoma Staging System [*Medicine*] (DMAA)
INSSCC........ Interim National Space Surveillance Control Center
Inst........ Coke's Institutes [*England*] [*A publication*] (DLA)
INST........ Customs and Excise Institutions List [*Database*] (IID)
INST........ Indian National Satellite System (SAUS)
INST........ Indian Studies (SAUS)
INST........ Information Standards and Technology Standardization (SAUO)
INST........ In Nomine Sanctae Trinitatis [*In the Name of the Holy Trinity*] [*Latin*]
INST........ Insert Screw Thread
inst........ Installation (MIST)
INST........ Installed
Inst........ Installment (EBF)
INST........ Installment [*Business term*]
INST........ Instance (GOBB)
INST........ Instans [*The Current Month*] [*Latin*]
Inst........ Instant [*Of the present month*] [*Business term*] (EBF)
inst........ Instant (ELAL)
INST........ Instant
INST........ Instantaneous (MSA)
INST........ Institute [*or Institution*] (AFM)
inst........ Institute (BEE)
Inst........ Institutes of England, in Two Parts, or A Commentary upon Littleton by Sir Edward Coke [*A publication*] (DLA)
Inst........ Institution (AL)
inst........ Institution (VRA)
Inst........ Institutional (AL)
Inst........ Institutio Oratoria [*of Quintilian*] [*Classical studies*] (OCD)
INST........ Instruction [*or Instructor*] (AFM)
inst........ Instructional Manual
Inst........ Instructor [*A publication*] (BRI)
INST........ Instrument (AAG)
Inst........ Instrument (EBF)
inst........ Instrument (ELAL)
INST........ Instrumental (MELL)
INST........ Instrumental Delivery [*Obstetrics*] (DAVI)
INST........ International Numbering System for Tides (MSC)
INST........ IPI, Inc. [*NASDAQ symbol*] (SAG)
Inst........ Justinian's Institutes [*A publication*] (DLA)
INST........ Revenue Canada - Customs and Excise Institutions List [*Revenue Canada - Customs and Excise*] [*Information service or system*] (CRD)
InST........ South Bend Tribune, South Bend, IN [*Library symbol*] [*Library of Congress*] (LCLS)
INSTA........ Instruments Authorized (FAAC)
INSTA........ Interstate (FAAC)
INSTAAR........ Institute of Arctic and Alpine Research [*University of Colorado*]
INSTAB........ Information Service on Toxicity and Biodegradability [*Water Pollution Research Laboratory*] [*British*] (IID)
instab........ Instability [*Medicine*] (EDAA)
INSTAB........ Instability (SAUS)
INSTA-CAM... Instant Camera (SAUS)
InstAct........ Institute of Actuaries [*British*]
INSTAD........ Institute for Training and Development
Inst Ad Legal Stud Ann... Institute of Advanced Legal Studies. Annals [*A publication*] (DLA)
INSTAL........ Installation
INSTALL........ Installment [*Motor vehicle violation code used in state of Maryland*] (MVRD)
Installatio........ Installation Notification Certificate (NAKS)
Install Engr... Installation Engineer (SAUS)
INSTALLN.... Installation
Inst&Maint Engr... Installation and Maintenance Engineer (SAUS)
INSTAR........ Inertialess Scanning, Tracking, and Ranging
INSTARR........ Institute for Arctic and Alpine Research (SAUO)
INSTARS........ Information Storage and Retrieval System [*Computer science*]
in stat pup... In Statu Pupillari [*Subject to the Rule of the Institution*] [*Latin*] (BARN)
Inst BE........ Institution of British Engineers
InstBks........ Institute of Bankers (SAUO)
INSTBY........ Instability (FAAC)
InstCE........ Institution of Civil Engineers (SAUO)
Inst Ceram... Institution of Ceramics (SAUO)
InstCES........ Institution of Civil Engineering Surveyors (DAC)
InstCh........ Institute of Charity (SAUO)
Inst Chem Eng Symp Ser... Institution of Chemical Engineers Symposium Series (journ.) (SAUS)
Inst Civil Eng Proc... Institute of Civil Engineers Proceedings (SAUS)
Inst Cler........ Instructor Clericalis (DLA)
Inst Com Com... Interstate Commerce Commission Reports [*A publication*] (DLA)
INST/COMM... Instrumentation and Communication (MCD)
Inst Comput Res... Institute of Computer Research (SAUS)
INSTCTL........ Instrumentation and Control [*Aerospace*] (IAA)
INSTD........ Instead (ROG)
InstD........ Institute of Directors [*British*]
Inst Dirs........ Institute of Directors (SAUO)
InstDokAB.... Institutionendokumentation zur Arbeitsmarkt- und Berufsforschung [*Database*] [*Institut fuer Arbeitsmarkt- und Berufsforschung der Bundesanstalt fuer Arbeit*] [*German*] [*Information service or system*] (CRD)

INSTE International Network for Information in Science and Technology Education (SAUO)
INSTEAD Information Service on Technological Alternatives for Development [*ILO*] [*United Nations*] (DUND)
INSTEAD International Student, Trade, Environment and Development Program (CROSS)
INSTEE Institution of Electrical Engineers (IAA)
Insteel Insteel Industries, Inc. [*Associated Press*] (SAG)
Inst E E Proc Institution of Electronical Engineers. Proceedings (journ.) (SAUS)
Inst Elec Eng Conf Publ Institution of Electrical Engineers. Conference Publication (journ.) (SAUS)
Inst Elec Eng J Institution Of Electrical Engineers. Journal (SAUS)
Inst Eng Aust Mech and Chem Eng Trans Institution of Engineers, Australia. Mechanical and Chemical Engineering Transactions (journ.) (SAUS)
InStent Instent, Inc. [*Associated Press*] (SAG)
Inst Environ Sci Tech Meet Proc Institute of Environmental Sciences. Technical Meeting. Proceedings (journ.) (SAUS)
INSTEP Indian Steel Training and Education Program [*India*]
INSTEP Indonesian Seas Flow Through Experiment (SAUO)
INSTEP In-Service Training and Education Panel (AIE)
Inst Epil Epilogue to (a Designated Part or Volume of) Coke's Institutes [*A publication*] (DLA)
InstF Institute of Fuel [*British*]
Inst Fed Tax Institute on Federal Taxation (DLA)
INSTFLTNG Instrument Flight Training (NVT)
Inst Forum Institute Forum (journ.) (SAUS)
INSTFURASPERS Instruction and Further Assignment by Commander, Naval Military Personnel Command (DNAB)
Inst Gas Eng Institute of Gas Engineers (SAUS)
InstGasEng Institution of Gas Engineers (SAUS)
Inst Gen Sem Institute of General Semantics (SAUO)
Inst Geol Sci Rep Institute of Geological Science Report (journ.) (SAUS)
Inst HE Institute of Highway Engineers (SAUO)
Insti Institutes of Justinian [*Roman law*] [*A publication*] (DSA)
INSTIA Instituto Internacional de Andragogia [*International Institute of Andragogy - IIA*] (EAIO)
INSTILL Instillandus [*To Be Dropped In*] [*Pharmacy*]
instill Instillation [*Medicine*] (EDAA)
INSTINET Institutional Networks Corp.
Inst Int Educ Institute of International Education (SAUO)
InstIntRelProc Institute of International Relations, Proceedings (journ.) (SAUS)
Institutes Institutes of Justinian [*Roman law*] [*A publication*] (DLA)
Inst Iust Institutiones Iustiniani [*Classical studies*] (OCD)
InStjN Saint Joe News, Saint Joe, IN [*Library symbol*] [*Library of Congress*] (LCLS)
Inst Jur Angl Institutiones Juris Anglicani, by Cowell [*A publication*] (DLA)
Instl Install (SAUS)
INSTL Installation (AFM)
instl Installation (VRA)
Instl Installment [*Banking*] (TBD)
INSTL Installment
INSTL Instalment (SAUS)
instl institutional (SAUS)
Inst Lab Rel Bull Institute for Labor Relations. Bulletin [*A publication*] (DLA)
INSTL & C/O Installation and Checkout (NASA)
Instl LO Installment Loan Officer [*Banking*] (TBD)
INSTLLR Installer
INSTLN Installation
INSTLR Installer
INSTLTN Installation
INSTM Instrumentation (MSA)
InStmaS St. Mary-Of-The-Woods College, St. Mary-Of-The-Woods, IN [*Library symbol*] [*Library of Congress*] (LCLS)
INSTMC Institute of Measurement and Control [*British*] (EAIO)
INST ME Institute of Mechanical Engineers [*British*] (WDAA)
Inst M E Institute of Media Executives [*British*]
InstME Institute of Mining Engineers (SAUS)
Inst ME Institution of Mechanical Engineers (SAUO)
InStme St. Meinrad College and Seminary, St. Meinrad, IN [*Library symbol*] [*Library of Congress*] (LCLS)
Inst Mech E Institution of Mechanical Engineers (SAUS)
Inst Mediaeval Mus Institute of Mediaeval Music (SAUO)
InstMet Institute of Metals [*British*]
Inst MM Institution of Mining and Metallurgy (BARN)
INSTMN Instrumentation
INSTMNS Instrumentation Squadron [*Military*]
Inst Mod Lang Institute of Modern Languages (SAUO)
INSTMT Instrument (WGA)
Instn Institution [*Medicine*] (EDAA)
INSTN Institution
instn institutional (SAUS)
INSTN Instruction [*Computer science*] (TEL)
INSTN Instrumentation (MUGU)
InSTN Tri-County News, South Bend, IN [*Library symbol*] [*Library of Congress*] (LCLS)
InstNA Institute of Naval Architects (SAUS)
Inst NA Institution of Naval Architects (BARN)
INSTNL Institutional
INSTNS Institutions (ROG)
INSTNS Instructions
INSTNT Instant
INSTOC Institute for the Study of the Continents (SAUS)
Inst on Plan Zoning & Eminent Domain Institute on Planning, Zoning, and Eminent Domain. Proceedings [*Southwestern Legal Foundation*] (DLA)
Inst on Priv Inv & Inv Abroad Institute on Private Investments and Investors Abroad. Proceedings [*A publication*] (DLA)
INSTOP Instrument or on-Top-of-Clouds Authorized
INSTOR Inventory and Storage (ACAE)
INST P Institute of Physics [*British*] (WDAA)
Inst Pat Institute of Patentees (SAUO)
Inst Pckg Institute of Packing (SAUO)
Inst Pet Institute of Petroleum (SAUO)
InstPet Institute of Petroleum Engineers (SAUS)
Inst Plan & Zoning Institute on Planning, Zoning, and Eminent Domain. Proceedings [*A publication*] (DLA)
Inst Plan Zoning & ED Institute on Planning, Zoning, and Eminent Domain. Proceedings [*A publication*] (DLA)
INSTPN Instrument Panel
Inst Proem Proeme [*Introduction to Coke's Institutes*] [*A publication*] (DLA)
InstPS Institute of Purchasing and Supply [*British*]
InstPubl [*The*] Instant Publishers, Inc. [*Associated Press*] (SAG)
INSTR Instruct [*or Instructor*] (AABC)
Instr Instruction (AL)
instr Instruction (SAFN)
INSTR Instruction
Instr Instructional (AL)
instr Instructions (SHCU)
Instr Instructor (AL)
instr Instructor (SHCU)
Instr Instrument (DIAR)
INSTR Instrument
instr Instrumental [*Grammar*]
INSTR Instrumentation (NAKS)
Inst Radio Electron Eng Aus Institution of Radio and Electronics Engineers, Australia, Proceedings (journ.) (SAUS)
INSTRAT Investment Strategy [*Game*]
INST RATE Instrument Rating (SAUS)
INSTRAW International Research and Training Institute for the Advancement of Women [*Dominican Republic*] [*United Nations*] [*Research center*] (IRC)
Instr Cler Instructor Clericalis (DLA)
INSTRCTR Instructor
INSTRD Instructed (ROG)
INSTRE Institute of Radio Engineers [*Later, IEEE*] (IAA)
INSTREF Instrument Reference (IAA)
Instr Engr Instrumentation Engineer (SAUS)
Instr Engr Instrument Engineer (SAUS)
INSTRL Instructional
InstrLab Instrumentation Laboratory SpA [*Associated Press*] (SAG)
INST RLY Instantaneous Relay (SAUS)
INSTRM Instrumented
INSTRMNTN Instrumentation
INSTRMT Instrument
INSTRN Instruction
INSTRNL Instructional
InstRNVR Instructor of Royal Naval Volunteer Reserve (SAUO)
Instron Instron Corp. [*Associated Press*] (SAG)
INSTRONS Instructions (ROG)
INSTRPI Instrument Pilot Instructor [*Air Force*]
INSTRPIT Instructor Pilot [*Air Force*]
INSTRU Instrumentation
INSTRUC Instruction
InstruCp Instrumentarium Corp. [*Associated Press*] (SAG)
INSTRUCTA Intelligent Naval Structures Assistant
INSTRUM Instrumentation Subsystem [*NASA*] (NASA)
Instrum Control Eng Instrumentation and Control Engineering (journ.) (SAUS)
Instrum Contr Syst Instruments and Control Systems (journ.) (SAUS)
Instrumenta Instrumentation and Communication (NAKS)
Instrumenta Instrumentation Group (NAKS)
Instrum India Instruments India (journ.) (SAUS)
Instrum Pract Instrument Practice, Control Systems, Electronics, Automation (journ.) (SAUS)
Instrum Technol Instrumentation Technology (journ.) (SAUS)
Instru Soc Am Instrument Society of America (SAUO)
Inst Sci & Indust Bull Australia. Institute of Science and Industry. Bulletin [*A publication*]
Inst Sec Reg Institute on Securities Regulation [*A publication*] (DLA)
Inst SMM Institute of Sales and Marketing Management [*British*]
Inst Socioeconomic Studies J Institute for Socioeconomic Studies. Journal (journ.) (SAUS)
INSTSYS Instrumentation System (MCD)
Inst Tech Instrumentation Technology (journ.) (SAUS)
Inst WE Institution of Water Engineers (SAUO)
INSTX IDS Stock Cl.A [*Mutual fund ticker symbol*] (SG)
INSU (French) National Institute for Sciences of the Universe (SAUS)
InSU Indiana University at South Bend, South Bend, IN [*Library symbol*] [*Library of Congress*] (LCLS)
INSU Insituform Technology [*NASDAQ symbol*] (SPSG)
INSU Intensive Neurosurgery Unit (DAVI)
INSU National Institute for Sciences of the Universe (SAUO)
InSu Sullivan County Public Library, Sullivan, IN [*Library symbol*] [*Library of Congress*] (LCLS)
INSUA Insituform Technol'A' [*NASDAQ symbol*] (TTSB)
InSuC Sullivan County Public Library, Sullivan, IN [*Library symbol*] [*Library of Congress*] (LCLS)

InSuCR .... Sullivan County Recorder's Office, Sullivan, IN [*Library symbol*] [*Library of Congress*] (LCLS)
insuf .... Insufficiency/ient [*Medicine*] (EDAA)
INSUF .... Insufficient (AABC)
INSUF .... Insufficient Scheduled Time Available [*Aviation*] (FAAC)
insuf .... Insufflation [*Medicine*] (EDAA)
INSUFF .... Insufflatio [*An Insufflation*] [*Pharmacy*]
InSuHi .... Sullivan County Historical Society, Sullivan, IN [*Library symbol*] [*Library of Congress*] (LCLS)
INSUL .... Insulated [*or Insulation*]
insul .... Insulation (MIST)
INSUL .... Insulator (VLIE)
Insulation J... Insulation Journal (journ.) (SAUS)
INSULR .... Insulator
INSUPGENCRUIT... Inspect, Supervise, Generally Superintend Recruitment Methods
Insur .... Insurance
Insurance F... Insurance Facts (journ.) (SAUS)
INSURE .... Industry Network for Social, Urban, and Rural Efforts
INSURF .... International Network on Soil Fertility and Sustainable Rice Farming (SAUO)
Insur L Rep... Insurance Law Reporter [*A publication*] (DLA)
INSURPAC ... Independent Insurance Agents of America, Inc. Political Action Committee
INSURR .... Insurrection (DLA)
Insur Rec Aust NZ... Insurance Record of Australia and New Zealand [*A publication*]
INSURV .... Board of Inspection and Survey [*Navy*]
INSURV .... Inspection and Survey (SAUS)
INSURVINST... Board of Inspection and Survey, Instructions [*Navy*]
InSuT .... Sullivan Daily Times, Sullivan, IN [*Library symbol*] [*Library of Congress*] (LCLS)
INSUWG ...... Inshore Undersea Warfare Group [*Navy*]
INSV .... InSite Vision [*NASDAQ symbol*] (TTSB)
INSV .... InSite Vision, Inc. [*NASDAQ symbol*] (SAG)
INSW .... In Status Word (SAUS)
INSW .... InsWeb Corp. [*NASDAQ symbol*] (SG)
InSw .... Swayzee Public Library, Swayzee, IN [*Library symbol*] [*Library of Congress*] (LCLS)
Ins Wkr .... Insurance Worker (journ.) (SAUS)
INSY .... Interim Systems Corp. (SAUO)
InSy .... Syracuse Public Library, Syracuse, IN [*Library symbol*] [*Library of Congress*] (LCLS)
INSYD .... Instantaneous Systems Display [*Computer science*] (MHDB)
in sync .... in synchronization (SAUS)
Insz .... Inszenierung (SAUS)
INT .... Ad Interim Specification [*Navy*]
INT .... Air Inter (SAUS)
Int .... De Interpretatione [*of Aristotle*] [*Classical studies*] (OCD)
INT .... Department of the Interior (SAUO)
INT .... Greensboro/High Point/West Salem [*North Carolina*] Reynolds [*Airport symbol*] (OAG)
INT .... Image 'N Transfer [*Developed by 3M Co.*] (WDMC)
INT .... Individual Needs Test (DNAB)
INT .... Induction Neutralizing Transformer [*Computer science*]
INT .... Infrared Nondestructive Testing [*Electrical technique*]
INT .... Initial (IAA)
INT .... Institute for Nuclear Theory (SAUS)
INT .... Intair, Inc. [*Canada*] [*ICAO designator*] (FAAC)
int .... Intake (MIST)
INT .... Intake
INT .... Integer
INT .... Integer Internal Interrupt (SAUS)
INT .... Integral (MSA)
INT .... Integrase [*Biochemistry*]
INT .... Integrated (MCD)
INT .... Integrated Test (NASA)
INT .... Integrated Testing (NASA)
int .... Intelligence (WDAA)
INT .... Intelligence
INT .... Intelligence and Law Enforcement Division [*Coast Guard*]
INT .... Intelligence Point (SAUS)
int .... Intense [*Philately*]
INT .... Intensifier [*Linguistics*]
INT .... Intensity
INT .... Intent [*FBI standardized term*]
Int .... Interaction (SAUS)
INT .... Intercept [*or Interceptor*] (CINC)
INT .... Intercepting (SAUS)
INT .... Interception [*Football*] (GOBB)
INT .... Interchange
Int .... Interchange: Papers on Biblical and Current Questions [*A publication*] (APTA)
INT .... Interest [*Finance, Law*] (AFM)
int .... Interest (WDMC)
Int .... Interest (EBF)
INT .... Interface
INT .... Interim (MSA)
INT .... Interior (KSC)
int .... Interior (VRA)
Int .... Interior
INT .... Interjection
INT .... Interleaved (WGA)
int .... Interlingua [*MARC language code*] [*Library of Congress*] (LCCP)
INT .... INTERMARC [*International Machine-Readable Cataloging*] [*French National Library*] [*UTLAS symbol*]
INT .... Intermediate (MCD)
INT .... Intermetco Ltd. [*Toronto Stock Exchange symbol*]
INT .... Intermittent
INT .... Intern (GOBB)
INT .... Internal (AAG)
Int .... Internal (TBD)
int .... Internal (WDMC)
Int .... International (DIAR)
INT .... International (EY)
int .... International (WDMC)
INT .... International Recovery Corp. [*AMEX symbol*] (COMM)
INT .... Interne [*Medicine*] [*British*]
INT .... Interned (AABC)
INT .... Internist [*Medicine*]
INT .... Internship (DAVI)
int .... Internus [*Internal*] [*Latin*]
INT .... Interphone (MDG)
INT .... Interpreter
int .... Interred (GEAB)
INT .... Interrogate (MDG)
INT .... Interrogation [*British naval signaling*]
INT .... Interrupt
INT .... Interrupter (MSA)
INT .... Intersect (SAUS)
INT .... Intersection (VLIE)
INT .... Interstate [*Railroad*] (MHDW)
INT .... Interstate Railroad Co. [*AAR code*]
int .... Interval (WDMC)
INT .... Interval
INT .... Interview
int .... Interviewer
Int .... Intestinal (AAMN)
INT .... Intransitive
Int .... Introduction (DLA)
int .... Introit (WDAA)
INT .... Introit
INT .... Iodonitrotetrazolium Violet
INT .... Irrigated, No Tillage [*Agriculture*]
INT .... Isaac Newton Optical Telescope
INT .... Isaac Newton Telescope (SAUS)
INT .... Iterative Numerical Technique (SAUS)
INT .... National Institute of Technology (SAUO)
INT .... North Texas State University, Denton, TX [*OCLC symbol*] (OCLC)
INT .... P-Iodonitrotetrazolium (SAUS)
INT .... Winston-Salem [*North Carolina*] [*Airport symbol*] (AD)
INT .... Winston-Salem, NC [*Location identifier*] [*FAA*] (FAAL)
INT .... World Fuel Services [*NYSE symbol*] (TTSB)
INT .... World Fuel Services Corp. [*NYSE symbol*] (SAG)
INTA .... Intasys Corp. [*NASDAQ symbol*] (SAG)
INTA .... Interaction (journ.) (SAUS)
INTA .... International Association for the Development and Management of Existing and NewTowns (EAIO)
INTA .... International Newspaper and Trade Advertising (SAUO)
INTA .... International New Thought Alliance (EA)
INTA .... International New Towns Association (SAUO)
INTA .... International Trademark Association (NTPA)
INTA .... Interrupt Acknowledge [*Computer science*]
INTAAS .... Integrated Aircraft Armament System (MCD)
INTAAW .... Integrated Air-to-Air Weapons (SAUS)
in-tab .... In-Tabulation [*Broadcasting*] (WDMC)
IntAbs .... International Absorbents [*Associated Press*] (SAG)
INTABS .... International Terminal Accounting and Banking Service [*Computer science*] (MHDB)
INTAC .... Individual Terrorism Awareness Course (COE)
INTAC .... Intercept Tracking and Control Group
INTACK .... Interrupt-Acknowledge [*Intel Corp.*] (CIST)
IntACom .... InterAmericas Communications Corp. [*Associated Press*] (SAG)
INTACS .... Integrated Tactical Communications Study [*or System*] [*Army*] (AABC)
INTACS .... Integrated Tactical Communications System (SAUO)
INTACT .... Infants Need to Avoid Circumcision Trauma (SAUS)
INTACT .... Interactive Netherlands Tactical Trainer (SAUS)
INTACVAL .... Intelligence Aid For Plan Evaluation (SAUO)
Int Advances Econ Res... International Advances in Economic Research [*A publication*] (JLIT)
INTAF .... Internal Affairs (SAUO)
INTAF .... Internal Affairs Ministry (SAUS)
INTAF .... Special Assistant to SACEUR for International Affairs (SAUS)
Int Aff /London... International Affairs. Royal Institute of International Affairs. Oxford Univ. Press. London (journ.) (SAUS)
Int Aff /Moscow... International Affairs. Moscow (journ.) (SAUS)
INTAG .... Intaglio [*Engraving*] (ROG)
INTAG .... International Advisory Group on Technology Management [*Information broker and consultancy*] (NITA)
INTAG .... International Technology Management Advisory Group (SAUO)
INTAGCY ...... Interagency
INTAL .... Institute for Latin American Integration (SAUS)
INTAL .... Instituto para la Integracion de America Latina [*Institute for Latin American Integration*] (EAIO)
INT AL .... Inter Alia [*Among Other Things*] [*Latin*]
IntAlu .... International Aluminum Corp. [*Associated Press*] (SAG)
INTAMCL ..... International Association of Metropolitan City Libraries (SAUO)

INTAMEL...... International Association of Metropolitan City Libraries [*The Hague, Netherlands*] (EA)
INTAMEL Study... International Association of Metropolitan-City Libraries Study (SAUO)
Int Amer Bibliog Rev... Inter-American Bibliographical Review. Washington (journ.) (SAUS)
Int amer intel interchange... Proceedings of the Inter American Conference on Intellectual Interchange. University of Texas. Institute of Latin American Studies. Austin (SAUO)
Int Amer Monthly... Inter-American Monthly. Washington (journ.) (SAUS)
Int Amer Quart... Inter-American Quarterly (journ.) (SAUS)
INTAMIC...... International Association for Microcircuit Cards (SAUO)
INTAMIC...... International Microcircuit Card Association [*Paris, France*] [*Defunct*] (EAIO)
INTAMP....... Intermediate Amplifier (IAA)
Int Anesthesiol Clin... International Anesthesiology Clinics (journ.) (SAUS)
Int Angiol..... International Angiology (journ.) (SAUS)
INTAP.......... Interoperatbility Technology Association for Information Technology (OSI)
INTAPUC...... International Association of Public Cleansing [*Later, ISWA*]
INTAR.......... International Arts Relations
Int Arb J....... International Arbitration Journal [*A publication*] (DLA)
Int Arch Allergy Appl Immunol... International Archives of Allergy and Applied Immunology (Basel) (SAUS)
Int Arch Occup Environ Health... International Archives of Occupational and Environmental Health (journ.) (SAUS)
INTAS.......... International Association for the Promotion of Cooperation with Scientists from the Independent States of the Former Soviet Union (SAUO)
INTASAFCON... International Tanker Safety Conference (DS)
INTASAT...... Instituto Nacional de Tecnica Aeroespacial Satellite [*Spain*]
INTASGRO... Interallied Tactical Study Group [*NATO*] (NATG)
Int Assoc Engng Geol Bull... International Association of Engineering Geology. Bulletin (journ.) (SAUS)
Intasys......... Intasys Corp. [*Associated Press*] (SAG)
Int At Energy Agency Bull... International Atomic Energy Agency Bulletin (journ.) (SAUS)
INTAV.......... Interim Availability (DNAB)
INTAVA........ International Aviation Association
INTAX.......... IDS Tax Exempt Bond Cl.A [*Mutual fund ticker symbol*] (SG)
INT BAL....... Intensity Balance (SAUS)
Int Bar J...... International Bar Journal [*A publication*] (DLA)
IntBas.......... International Basic Resources, Inc. [*Associated Press*] (SAG)
Int Biodeterior... International Biodeterioration (journ.) (SAUS)
Int Biodeterioration Biodegrad... International Biodeterioration and Biodegradation (journ.) (SAUS)
Int Broadcast... International Broadcasting (journ.) (SAUS)
Int Broadcast Eng... International Broadcast Engineer (journ.) (SAUS)
INTBUL........ Intelligence Bulletin (CINC)
Int Bull Indust Prop... International Bulletin of Industrial Property [*A publication*] (DLA)
Int Bull Int Refrig... International Bulletin on Information on Refrigeration (journ.) (SAUS)
Int Bus Equip... International Business Equipment (journ.) (SAUS)
Int Bus Lawy... International Business Lawyer [*A publication*] (DLA)
IntBusSch.... International Business Schools [*Associated Press*] (SAG)
INTC............ Industrial Nuclear Technology Conference (SAUS)
INTC............ Intel Corp. [*NASDAQ symbol*] (NQ)
INTC............ Intelligence Committee (SAUO)
INTC............ Intelligence Corps [*Army*]
INTC............ Intercept (GAVI)
INTC............ International Nick Tate Club (EAIO)
InTc............ Tell City-Perry County Public Library, Tell City, IN [*Library symbol*] [*Library of Congress*] (LCLS)
INTCA.......... Immigration and Nationality Technical Corrections Act (SAUS)
IntCabl......... International Cablecasting Technologies, Inc. [*Associated Press*] (SAG)
Intcapln....... Intercapital Insurance Municipal Bond Fund [*Associated Press*] (SAG)
Intcaplns...... InterCapital Insured Municipal Securities [*Associated Press*] (SAG)
IntCAQI........ Intercapital California Quality Municipal Security Trust [*Associated Press*] (SAG)
Intcardia...... Intercardia, Inc. [*Associated Press*] (SAG)
Int Cas......... Rowe's Interesting Cases [*England and Ireland*] [*A publication*] (DLA)
Int Case....... Rowe's Interesting Cases [*England and Ireland*] [*A publication*] (DLA)
Int Cast Met J... International Cast Metals Journal (journ.) (SAUS)
Int Cav......... Internal Cavity (SAUS)
IntCble......... International Cabletel, Inc. [*Associated Press*] (SAG)
INTCH.......... Interchange (VLIE)
INTCHC........ Interchanger (NAKS)
INTCHG........ Interchange (NAKS)
INTCHG........ Interchangeability (SAUS)
INTCHG........ Interchangeable (MSA)
INTCHGR..... Interchanger (NASA)
int cib.......... Between Meals [*Latin*] [*Inter Cibos*] [*Medicine*] (EDAA)
INT CIB........ Inter Cibos [*Between Meals*] [*Pharmacy*]
INTCL.......... Intercoastal (SAUS)
IntCl............ International Classification of Patents for Invention (SAUO)
Int Classif.... International Classification (journ.) (SAUS)
IntCm.......... Interdigital Communications Corp. [*Associated Press*] (SAG)
InTcN........... Tell City News, Tell City, IN [*Library symbol*] [*Library of Congress*] (LCLS)
INTCNTL...... Intercontinental
INTC/O........ Integrated Checkout (NASA)
INTCO.......... International Code of Signals
INTCOL........ Intelligence Collection [*Military*] (NVT)
IntColng....... International Colin Energy [*Associated Press*] (SAG)
INTCOM....... International Liaison Committee (SAUS)
INTCOMBATSYSTESTFAC... Integrated Combat Systems Test Facility (SAUS)
Int Com Com... Interstate Commerce Commission. Reports [*A publication*] (DLA)
Int Com Commn... Interstate Commerce Commission [*Independent government agency*] (DLA)
Int Com Illum... International Commission on Illumination (SAUO)
Int Commun Heat Mass Transf... International Communications in Heat and Mass Transfer (journ.) (SAUS)
Int Comput Law Advis... International Computer Law Adviser (journ.) (SAUS)
Int Com Rep... Interstate Commerce Commission Reports [*A publication*] (DLA)
INTCON........ Interconnection (MSA)
Int Con......... Internal Connection (SAUS)
Int Constr..... International Construction (journ.) (SAUS)
Int Contrib to Lab Stud... International Contributions to Labour Studies [*A publication*] (JLIT)
Int Copper Inf Bull... International Copper Information Bulletin (journ.) (SAUS)
Int Cor......... Intelligence Corps (SAUO)
INT CORPS... Intelligence Corps (SAUO)
INTCP.......... Intercept (AFM)
INTCP.......... Interceptor (SAUS)
IntcpIM........ Intercapital Insured Municipal Income Trust [*Associated Press*] (SAG)
INTCP RNG... Intercept Range
intcp station... Intercept Station (SAUS)
IntCpt.......... Intersciences Computer Corp. [*Associated Press*] (SAG)
INTCPTS...... Intercepts (ACAE)
INTCR.......... Input Tape Cartridge Reader (VLIE)
InTCS.......... Commercial Solvents Corp., Terre Haute, IN [*Library symbol*] [*Library of Congress*] [*Obsolete*] (LCLS)
IntctlBk........ Intercontinental Bank [*Associated Press*] (SAG)
INTCW......... Intel Corp.Wrrt [*NASDAQ symbol*] (TTSB)
INTCYL........ Intercylinder
InTD............ Eugene V. Debs Foundation, Terre Haute, IN [*Library symbol*] [*Library of Congress*] (LCLS)
INTD............ Institut National des Techniques de la Documentation [*National Institute for Information Science*] [*France*] [*Information service or system*] (IID)
INTD............ InteliData Technologies Corp. [*NASDAQ symbol*] (SAG)
INTD............ Intend (FAAC)
INTD............ International Nuclear Target Development (SAUO)
INTDD.......... Intended
INT DEC....... Interior Decorator (SAUS)
Int Def Rev... International Defense Review (journ.) (SAUS)
Int Dent J.... International Dental Journal (journ.) (SAUS)
Int Dep........ Intermediate Depot (SAUS)
INTDEPT...... Interdepartmental
INTDISP....... Interdisciplinary
INT DIV........ Intelligence Division (SAUO)
Int Doc Serv... International Documents Service (SAUO)
INTE............ Industrial Technology (SAUS)
INTE............ Interactive Group, Inc. [*NASDAQ symbol*] (SAG)
INTE............ Interrupt Enable [*Computer science*]
INTEBCOMP... Intercompany (SAUO)
INTEBCOOP... International Association of Consumer Cooperatives (SAUO)
INTEBRID..... Integrated and Hybrid Circuitry (SAUS)
INTEC.......... Information Network Technologies, Inc. (SAUS)
INTEC.......... Interface Technology [*British*] (NITA)
INTEC.......... Interference [*Telecommunications*] (MDG)
INTEC.......... International Naval Technology Expo and Conference (SAUS)
INTEC.......... International Technology Underwriters [*Consortium, Washington*] (NITA)
INTECH........ Institute for New Technologies (SAUO)
INTECH........ Instrument Technology-Journal of ISA (ACII)
INTECH........ Integrated Information Technology Conference and Exposition [*National Trade Productions*] (TSPED)
INTECOL...... International Association for Ecology [*University of Georgia*] [*Athens, GA*] (EAIO)
INTECOL...... International Organization for Ecology (SAUO)
Int Econ Insights... International Economic Insights [*A publication*] (JLIT)
Int Econ J..... International Economic Journal [*A publication*] (JLIT)
Int Economy... International Economy [*A publication*] (JLIT)
Int Econ Rev... International Economic Review [*A publication*] (JLIT)
Integ........... Integ Inc. [*Associated Press*] (SAG)
INTEG.......... Integrate [*or Integrating*] (MSA)
INTEG.......... Integument [*Dermatology*] (DAVI)
IntegCirc...... Integrated Circuit Systems [*Associated Press*] (SAG)
Integ Ed Assoc... Integrated Education Associates (SAUO)
IntegFn........ Integra Financial Corp. [*Associated Press*] (SAG)
IntegMed..... IntegraMed America, Inc. [*Associated Press*] (SAG)
Integn.......... Integon Corp. [*Associated Press*] (SAG)
Integon........ Integon Corp. [*Associated Press*] (SAG)
INTEGR........ Integrate [*or Integration*] (NASA)
INTEGR........ Integration (SAUO)
Integral........ Integral Systems, Inc. [*Associated Press*] (SAG)
INTEGRAL.... International Gamma-Ray Astrophysics Laboratory [*Sponsored by European Space Agency*]
Integrity....... Integrity, Inc. [*Associated Press*] (SAG)
Integr Physiol Behav Sci... Integrative Physiological and Behavioral Science (journ.) (SAUS)
Integr VLSI J... Integration, The VLSI Journal (journ.) (SAUS)
IntegSrg....... Integrated Surgical Systems, Inc. [*Associated Press*] (SAG)
IntegTc........ Integrated Technology USA, Inc. [*Associated Press*] (SAG)
Intek........... INTEK Diversified Corp. [*Associated Press*] (SAG)
INTEL.......... Idaho National Engineering Laboratory (SAUO)

INTEL.......... Integrated Electronics (VLIE)
INTEL.......... Integrated Electronics Intelligence (SAUS)
Intel.......... Intel Corp. [*Associated Press*] (SAG)
INTEL.......... Intelligence (AABC)
intel.......... Intelligent (ADWA)
Intel Anal..... Intelligence Analyst (SAUS)
Intelcal....... Intellicall, Inc. [*Associated Press*] (SAG)
INTELCAST...... Intelligence Broadcast (DOMA)
INTELCEN.... Intelligence Center
INTELCENPAC... Intelligence Center, Pacific Ocean Areas [*Obsolete*]
Intelcm........ Intelcom Group [*Associated Press*] (SAG)
INTELCOM... Intelligence Command (SAUS)
INTELCOM... Worldwide Intelligence Communication (MCD)
INTELCOM Exposition... International Telecommunications Exposition (SAUS)
INTEL DIV.... Intelligence Division (SAUO)
IN-TELE........ Internet-Based Teaching and Learning (EURO)
INTELEC........ International Telecommunications Energy Conference (SAUO)
Intelect....... Intelect Communications Systems Ltd. [*Associated Press*] (SAG)
INTELECT...... Interceptor Electronics (ACAE)
INTEL-ED..... International Tele-Education (SAUO)
IntelEl.......... Intellignet Electronics, Inc. [*Associated Press*] (SAG)
Intel Est....... Intelligence Estimate (SAUS)
INTELEVENT... International Televent (EA)
InteliDta...... InteliData Technologies Corp. [*Associated Press*] (SAG)
Intell........... Intelligence (DIAR)
INTELL......... Intelligence (ROG)
Intellect....... Intellectual (SAUS)
Intellect trends Lat Amer... Intellectual Trends in Latin America. Austin, Texas. University of Texas. (SAUO)
Intellect trends Lat Amer... Intellectual Trends in Latin America. Austin, Texas. University of Texas (journ.) (SAUS)
Intellectual Property L Rev... Intellectual Property Law Review [*A publication*] (DLA)
Intellgrp....... Intelligroup, Inc. [*Associated Press*] (SAG)
Intelli.......... Intelli Corp., Inc. [*Associated Press*] (SAG)
Intell Instrum Comput... Intelligent Instruments and Computers (journ.) (SAUS)
INTELLIVISION... Intelligent Television [*Home video game*] [*Mattel, Inc.*]
Intell Syst Eng... Intelligent Systems Engineering [*A publication*] (CABS)
INTELNET.... Intelligence Network (DOMA)
INTELNET.... Service provided by the INTELSAT Network (SAUS)
INTELO........ Intelligence Officer [*Military*]
INTELPOST... International Electronic Post [*Postal Service*]
INTELPOST... International Telecommunications Post [*Facsimile transmission service*] (NITA)
INTELSA...... International Telecommunications Satellite Consortium [*Later, International Telecommunications Satellite Organization*] (IAA)
INTELSAT.... Intelligence Satellite (SAUS)
INTELSAT.... International Telcommunications Satellite Consortium (SAUS)
Intelsat....... International Telecommunications Satellite (SAUO)
INTELSAT.... International Telecommunications Satellite Consortium (NITA)
INTELSAT.... International Telecommunications Satellite Organization (EA)
Intelsat........ International Telecommunications Satellite Organization [*Washington, D.C.*] (WDMC)
INTELTNG.... Intelligence Training [*Military*] (NVT)
inten........... Intensity (ELAL)
INTEN.......... Intensity (MSA)
Int Enc Comp Law... International Encyclopedia of Comparative Law [*A publication*] (DLA)
Int Endontic J... International Endodontic Journal (journ.) (SAUS)
INTENS........ Intensify (SAUS)
intens.......... Intensive (BEE)
INTENS........ Intensive
Intensif........ Intensification (SAUS)
Intensva....... Intensiva Healthcare Corp. [*Associated Press*] (SAG)
INTENT........ Initial Teacher Education and New Technology [*Project*] (AIE)
INTENTN...... Intention (ROG)
inter............ interborough (SAUS)
inter............ intercalation (SAUS)
INTER.......... Interception [*Football*]
INTER.......... Interdenominational
INTER.......... Interest [*Motor vehicle violation code used in state of Maryland*] (MVRD)
Inter............ Interior (DIAR)
Inter............ Interiors, Inc. [*Associated Press*] (SAG)
INTER.......... Interleave (DGA)
INTER.......... Intermediate (AAG)
inter............ Intermediate (WDMC)
INTER.......... Intermittent
INTER.......... Internal (KSC)
INTER.......... Interphone (MCD)
INTER.......... Interpolated Schedule of Reinforcement (DIPS)
INTER.......... Interrogation (ADA)
Inter............ Interrogation Mark (SAUS)
INTER.......... Interrogative
INTER.......... Interrupt
INTER.......... Intertype (DGA)
Intera........... Intera Information Technologies Corp. [*Associated Press*] (SAG)
INTERACT.... Integrated Research Aircraft Control Technology (MCD)
InterAct........ InterAction Media Corp. [*Associated Press*] (SAG)
Interact........ Interactive Group, Inc. [*Associated Press*] (SAG)
InteracT........ Interactive Technologies Corp., Inc. [*Associated Press*] (SAG)
INTERACT.... Interactive Television Network [*Dartmouth-Hitchcock Medical Center*] [*Hanover, NH*] [*Telecommunications*] (TSSD)
INTERACT.... International Education and Research for Applications in Computer Technology (SAUS)
INTERACTA... Associazione Italiana della Communicazione Interattiva [*Organization for multimedia professionals*] [*Italy*] (DDC)
InterAction Council... InterAction Council of Former Heads of Government (SAUO)
Interact Learn Int... Interactive Learning International (journ.) (SAUS)
INTERAISE... International Environmental and Natural Resource Assessment Information Service (SAUS)
INTERALIS... International Advanced Life Information System (BUR)
INTERALP.... Intercultural Action Learning Program
Interam........ Interamerican (SAUS)
Inter American U... Inter American University (GAGS)
Inter-Am Law Rev... Inter-American Law Review. Univ. of Miami, School of Law. Coral Gables (journ.) (SAUS)
Inter-Am Music Rev... Inter-American Music Review (journ.) (SAUS)
INTERAMPOL... Inter-American Police (SAUO)
INTERAN...... International Conference on the Analysis of Geological Materials (SAUO)
Interarmco... International Armament Corp. (SAUS)
Interarmco... International Armament Corporation (SAUO)
Interarms.... International Armament Corporation (SAUO)
INTER ARTS... Intermediate of Arts [*British*] (ROG)
INTERASMA... International Association for the Study of Asthma (SAUS)
INTERASMA... International Association of Asthmology [*Lisbon, Portugal*] (EAIO)
INTERASMA... International Asthmological Medical Association (SAUO)
INTERATOM... Internationale Atomreactorbau [*German*]
Interatominstrument... International Company for Nuclear Instruments (SAUO)
INTERATOMINSTRUMENT... International Economic Association for Nuclear Instrument Building (SAUO)
Interavia Aerosp Rev... Interavia Aerospace Review (journ.) (SAUS)
Interb.......... Interbedded (SAUS)
INTER BA...... Intermediate Bachelor of Arts [*British*] (ROG)
Interbank..... International Bank for Reconstruction and Development (SAUO)
INTERBEV.... International Beverage Industry Exhibition and Congress [*National Soft Drink Association*]
INTERBOR... Union Internationale des Techniciens Orthopedistes [*International Association of Orthotists and Prosthetists*] (EA)
INTERBRIGHT... International Literary and Information Centre in Science Extension (IID)
Interbuild..... International Building and Construction Exhibition (SAUO)
Intercargo.... International Association for Dry Cargo Shipowners (SAUO)
INTERCARGO... International Association of Dry Cargo Shipowners (EAIO)
INTERCEDE... International Coalition to End Domestics' Exploitation
Intercel........ Intercel, Inc. [*Associated Press*] (SAG)
INTERCENTRE... International Centre for the Terminology of the Social Sciences [*Grand-Saconnex, Switzerland*] (EA)
INTERCH...... Interchangeable (SAUS)
Interchange... Interchangeability and Replacement (NAKS)
Interchem.... Interchemical (SAUS)
Interchem.... Interchemical Corp. (SAUS)
Interchem.... Interchemical Corporation (SAUO)
INTERCHIM... International Organization for Co-operation in Small-Tonnage (SAUO)
Interchim..... International Organization for Cooperation in Small Volume Chemicals Production (SAUO)
Interco......... Interco, Inc. [*Formerly, International Shoe Co.*] [*Associated Press*] (SAG)
INTERCO...... International Code of Signals (PDAA)
INTERCO...... International Council on Jewish Social and Welfare Services [*Geneva, Switzerland*] (EAIO)
INTERCO...... International Shoe Co. (EFIS)
Interco......... International Shoe Company (SAUO)
INTERCODE... International CODEN Service [*Chemical Abstracts Service*] [*Information service or system*] (IID)
INTERCOL.... Intercolonial (ADA)
Intercollege... International College of Management and Communication Studies (SAUO)
INTERCOLOR... International Commission for Fashion and Textile Colors (SAUS)
INTERCOM... Intercommunicating System (SAUS)
INTERCOM... Intercommunication System
INTERCOM... Intercom. World Affairs Center for the United States. Foreign Policy Association (SAUO)
INTERCOM... Internal Communications (SAUS)
INTERCOM... International Committee on Management (SAUO)
INTERCOM... Interslave Communication (SAUS)
INTERCOM... Intertribal Christian Communications
Intercommun... Intercommunications (NAKS)
Intercommun... Intercommunication System (NAKS)
Intercomponent... International Organization for Electronics (SAUO)
INTERCOM System... Intercommunication System (SAUS)
INTERCON... Interconnection (KSC)
INTERCON... Intercontinental
INTERCON... Intercontinental Church Society (SAUO)
INTERCON... Intermediate-Size Cargo Container
INTERCON... International Convention
INTERCON... International Convention and Exposition (SAUO)
Interconnect Technol... Interconnection Technology [*A publication*] (CABS)
INTERCONTAINER... International Company for the Transport by Transcontainers (SAUO)
INTERCOOP... International Agricultural Cooperative Society (SAUO)
INTERCOOP... International Organisation (or Organization) for Consumer Co-operative Distributive Trade (SAUO)
INTERCOOP... International Organization for Consumer Co-Operative Distributive Trade (EAIO)
INTERCOSMOS... Council for International Cooperation for the Exploitation of the Cosmos (SAUO)

INTERCOSMOS... Council on International Cooperation in the Study and Utilization of Outer Spac e
Intercry........ Intercrystalline (SAUS)
interd........... interested (SAUS)
INTERDACO... Intercontinental Data Control Corp. Ltd. [*Ottawa, ON*] [*Telecommunications*] (TSSD)
INTERDATA... Interdata Computers (SAUS)
INTERDEPT... Interdepartmental (KSC)
INTERDICT... Interference Detection and Interdiction Countermeasures Team [*Electromagnetic compatibility programs*]
INTERDICT-2... Intelligence Detection and Interdiction Countermeasures (SAUS)
InterDig....... Interdigital Communications Corp. [*Associated Press*] (SAG)
Interdiscip Sci Rev... Interdisciplinary Science Reviews (journ.) (SAUS)
Interdisip..... Interdisciplinary (DIAR)
INTERDOC... Integrated Terminology Document Management System (IAA)
INTERDOK... International Documentation and Information Centre
Interecon..... Intereconomics (journ.) (SAUS)
INTEREG...... Internationales Institut fuer Nationalitatenrecht und Regionalismus [*International Institute for Ethnic Group Rights and Regionalism*] (EA)
INTEREGEN... Internal Regenerative (KSC)
INTERELEKTRO... International Organization for Co-operation in the Electrical (SAUS)
Interenergoremont... Coordination Center for Repair Work in Power Stations (SAUO)
INTEREST.... Interactive Estimating [*Camic Ltd.*] [*Software package*] (NCC)
INTEREX...... International Exchangors Association (EA)
INTER-EXPERT... International Association of Experts (SAUO)
INTEREXPO... Committee of Organizers of National Participations in International Economic Displays (SAUO)
INTEREXPO... International Expositions (SAUS)
Interf........... Interface Systems, Inc. [*Associated Press*] (SAG)
INTERF........ Interference (IAA)
INTERF........ Interferometer
INTERFACE... Internationally recognized format for automatic commercial exchange (SAUO)
Interface C... Interface Compatibility Record (NAKS)
Interface C... Interface Control Drawing (NAKS)
Interface C... Interface Control Specification (NAKS)
Interface C... Interface Control Unit (NAKS)
Interface D... Interface Document (NAKS)
Interface F... Interface Functional Analysis (NAKS)
Interfaces Comput... Interfaces in Computing (SAUS)
INTERFAIS... International Food Aid Information System [*World Food Program*] [*United Nations*] (DUND)
INTERFAST... International Industrial Fastener Engineering Exhibition and Conference (SAUO)
INTERFC...... Integral of Error Function Complement (SAUS)
Interfc.......... Interface Systems, Inc. [*Associated Press*] (SAG)
INTERFER.... Interference
INTERFILM... International Church Film Center (SAUS)
INTERFILM... International Inter-Church Film Center [*Hilversum, Netherlands*] (EAIO)
INTERFINISH... International Union for Electrodeposition and Surface Finishing (SAUO)
INTERFOOD... International Exhibition of Foodstuffs, Fast Food, and Traditional and Mass Catering
INTERFORST... International Exposition of the Technology of Forestry and Forest Industries (SAUO)
INTERFRIGO... International Railway-Owned Company for Refrigerated Transport (EAIO)
Interfund...... International Monetary Fund (SAUO)
interg........... interesting (SAUS)
INTERGALVA... International Galvanizing Conference (MCD)
Intergeotechnika... International Organization for Technical Cooperation in Geology (SAUO)
INTERGOVT... Intergovernmental
INTERGU...... International Copyright Society (SAUO)
INTERGU...... Internationale Gesellschaft fuer Urheberrecht [*International Copyright Society*] (EAIO)
INTERHYBRID... Association Intercontinentale du Mais Hybride
INTERHYBRID... Intra-Continental Association for Hybrid Maize (SAUO)
Interim......... Interim Services, Inc. [*Associated Press*] (SAG)
Interior Dec... Decisions of the Department of the Interior [*A publication*] (DLA)
Interiors....... Interiors, Inc. [*Associated Press*] (SAG)
interj............ Interjection (WDMC)
INTERJ......... Interjection
INTERKAMA... International Congress and Exhibition for Instrumentation and Automation (SAUO)
Inter-L......... Interlibrary (AL)
INTERLAINE... Comite des Industries Lainieres de la CEE [*Committee of the Wool Textile Industry in the EEC*] (EAIO)
INTERLAINE... Committee for the Wool Industries of the EEC (SAUO)
INTERLIB..... Interdepartmental Committee for Computer Processing in Departmental Libraries (SAUS)
Interlink....... Interlink Electronics, Inc. [*Associated Press*] (SAG)
Interlinq....... INTERLINQ Software Corp. [*Associated Press*] (SAG)
INTERLOCK... Ignition Interlock Device [*Motor vehicle violation code used in state of Maryland*] (MVRD)
INTERMAC... International Association of Merger and Acquisition Consultants (EA)
INTERMAG... International Association of Television Political Magazines (SAUO)
INTERMAG... International Conference on Magnetics (MCD)
INTERMAG... International Magnetics Conference (SAUO)
INTERMAMA... International Congress for Measurement and Automation (IEEE)
INTERMAPS... Interactive Multimedia Access Publishing Services (SAUO)
INTERMARC... French internal MARC format (SAUS)
INTERMEC... Interface Mechanism (SAUS)
INTERMED... Intermediate (ADA)
Intermed...... Intermediate (EBF)
INTERMED SH... Intermediate Shield (SAUS)
INTERMET... International Association for Metropolitan Research and Development (SAUO)
INTERMETAL... International Organization for Co-operation in the Iron & Steel Industry (SAUO)
Intermex...... International Mexican Bank (SAUS)
Intermex...... International Mexican Bank Ltd. [*British*] (EY)
INTER/MICRO... International Conference on Microscopy (SAUO)
INTERMILPOL... International Military Police [*NATO*]
INTERMIN.... International Terminological Information Network (SAUS)
INTERMOL... Intermolecular (SAUS)
Intermorgeo... Internatioinal Organization for Marine Geology (SAUO)
INTERMORGEO... International Organization for Marine Geology [*Council for Mutual Economic Assistance*] [*Riga, Union of Soviet Socialist Republics*] Defunct] (EAIO)
Intermountain Econ Rev... Intermountain Economic Review [*A publication*] (JLIT)
INTERMSTA... Intermediate Station
INTERMTRA... Intermediate Training [*Naval Air*]
intern........... Internal [*Medicine*] (EDAA)
INTERN........ Internal
INTERN........ International
Internal EMF... Internal Electromotive Force (SAUS)
Interna LN... International Law Notes [*London*] [*A publication*] (DLA)
INTERNAT.... International
Internat........ Internationalism (SAUS)
Internat........ Internationalist (SAUS)
Internat Bar Assoc... International Bar Association (DLA)
International/INCE... International Institute of Noise Control Engineering (SAUO)
Internat J Mental Health... International Journal of Mental Health (journ.) (SAUS)
Internat J of Leg Res... International Journal of Legal Research [*A publication*] (DLA)
Internat J Physical Distribution and Materials Mgt... International Journal of Physical Distribution and Materials Management (journ.) (SAUS)
Internat J Sociol... International Journal of Sociology (journ.) (SAUS)
INTERNATL... International
Internatl Goat Sheep Res... International Goat and Sheep Research (journ.) (SAUS)
Internat LN... International Law Notes [*A publication*] (DLA)
Internat Org... International Organization (journ.) (SAUS)
Internat Problems... International Problems (journ.) (SAUS)
Internat Security... International Security (journ.) (SAUS)
Internat Ser Appl Systems Anal... International Series on Applied Systems Analysis (journ.) (SAUS)
INTER NAVEX... International and National Audio-Visual Exhibition (SAUO)
INTERNAVEX... International Audio-Visual Aids Exhibition (SAUS)
INTERNEG.... Intermediate Negative (SAUS)
INTER/NEPCON... International Electronic Packaging Conference (SAUO)
INTERNEPCON... International Electronics Production Conference (SAUO)
INTERNET.... Interactive Network (SAUS)
INTERNET.... International Congress for Project Planning by Network Analysis (SAUO)
internet........ Internetwork (DINT)
INTERNET Analysis... Interactive Network Analysis (SAUS)
Interneur...... Interneuron Pharmaceuticals, Inc. [*Associated Press*] (SAG)
INTER-NIC... International Network Information Center (SAUS)
InterNIC....... Internet Network Information Center [*Computer science*]
Internic........ Internet Network Information Center
INTERNL...... Internal
INTER NOCT... Inter Noctem [*During the Night*] [*Pharmacy*]
INTERNOISE... International Conference on Noise Control Engineering (SAUO)
INTERNST.... Intenist
Internt.......... Internet Communications [*Associated Press*] (SAG)
INTEROBS.... International Observations (DNAB)
INTEROCEAN... International Conference and Exhibition for Marine Technology (SAUO)
INTEROG...... Interrogate (NASA)
INTEROP...... External Systems Interoperations (SAUS)
INTEROP...... Interoperability
INTERP........ Interpolation (SAUS)
interp........... Interpreter (ELAL)
INTERP........ Interpreter
Interpace..... International Pipe and Ceramics (SAUS)
Interpace..... International Pipe & Ceramics Corporation (SAUO)
INTERPACK... International Fair for Packaging Machinery, Packaging Materials and Confectionery Machinery (SAUS)
INTERPAR.... International Partnerships Group Inc. (SAUO)
Interpen/IAB... Intercontinental Penetration Force/International Anti-communist Brigade (SAUO)
INTERPET.... International Petroleum Co.
INTERPEX.... International Philatelic Exhibition [*American Stamp Dealers Association*]
INTERPHES... International Pharmaceutical Cosmetics, Toiletry, and Allied Industries Exhibition [*England*]
INTERPHIL... International Conference for the Study of Promotion of Philantropy (SAUO)
INTERPHIL... International Standing Conference on Philanthropy [*Yalding, Kent, England*] (EAIO)
INTERPHOTO... International Federation of Photograph and Cinema Merchants (SAUO)
INTERPIPE... International Pipeline Technology Commission (SAUO)
INTERPIPE... International Pipeline Technology Convention (SAUS)

INTERPIPE... International Pipeline Technology Conventionion (SAUS)
INTERPIPE... International Pipeline Technology Convertion (SAUS)
INTERPL...... Interplead [*Legal shorthand*] (LWAP)
INTERPLAN... International Group for Studies in National Planning
Interplanet... Interplanetary (SAUS)
INTERPLAS... International Plastics and Rubber Exhibition [*British Plastics Federation*] (TSPED)
Interpol........ International Criminal Police Commission (SAUO)
INTERPOL.... International Criminal Police Organization
Interpol........ International Police Organisation (WDAA)
Interpol........ Interpool, Inc. [*Associated Press*] (SAG)
INTERPOLL... Interchange of Pollutants between the Atmosphere and the Oceans (SAUS)
Interp Op..... Interpretative Opinion [*Legal term*] (DLA)
INTERPORT... International Organization for Seaports (SAUO)
INTERPOS.... Intermediate Positive (SAUS)
INTERPR...... Interpreter (WGA)
INTERPRESSFOTO... International Press Photography Exhibition (SAUO)
INTERPRO... International Probation Organization (EA)
INTERPRON... Interpretation Squadron (SAUS)
INTERPRON... Photointerpretation Squadron [*Military*]
INTERQUANT... International Commission for the Application of Quantitative Methods in History (SAUO)
interr.......... Interrogative (BJA)
INTERRAD... International Association of Radiolarian Palaeontologists (SAUO)
Interrelat..... Interrelation (SAUS)
INTERRIDGE... International RIDGE-Programme (SAUO)
INTERROG... Interrogation
interrog........ Interrogative (SHCU)
INTERROGS... Interrogatories (ROG)
INTERROGY... Interrogatory (ROG)
Inters Com Rep... Interstate Commerce Commission Reports [*A publication*] (DLA)
INTERSEARCH... International Productions and Safety Research [*Auto accident reconstruction*]
INTERSEC.... Intermediate Section
INTERSECT... International Security Technics [*Organization in TV series "The Gemini Man"*]
INTERSHIPNIK... International Organization for Co-operation of Bearings Industry (SAUO)
INTERSHOE... International Federation of the Independent Shoe Trade (SAUO)
Interslv.... Intersolv, Inc. [*Associated Press*] (SAG)
INTERSOL.... International Solutions (SAUO)
INTERSPACE... Interactive System for Pattern Analysis, Classification, and Enhancement (PDAA)
INTERSPUTNIK... International Organization of Space Communications [*Moscow, USSR*] (EAIO)
INTERST...... Interstate [*Legal shorthand*] (LWAP)
Interstate..... Forecast. First interstate Bank. Annual Report (journ.) (SAUS)
Interstate Com R... Interstate Commerce Reports [*A publication*] (DLA)
Interst Com R... Interstate Commerce Commission Reports [*A publication*] (DLA)
INTERSTENO... Federation Internationale de Stenographie et de Dactylographie [*International Federation of Shorthand and Typewriting*] [*Bonn, Federal Republic of Germany*] (EAIO)
INTERSTOL... Inter-City Short Takeoff and Landing [*Aviation*]
INTERSUGAR... International Sugar Council (SAUO)
Intersure..... Intersure of International Insurance Agents (SAUO)
INTERTANKO... International Association of Independent Tanker Owners [*Oslo, Norway*] (EAIO)
INTERTEL.... International Intelligence, Inc.
INTERTEL.... International Legion of Intelligence [*Acronym is used as official name of association*] (EA)
INTERTEL.... International Television (SAUS)
INTERTEL.... International Television Federation (SAUS)
INTERTELL... International Intelligence Legion (SAUS)
INTERTEST... Interactive Test (SAUS)
INTERTEST... Interactive Test Controller (MHDI)
INTERTEX.... International Textile and Fabrics Trade Fair
Intertextilmash... International Production Amalgamation for Manufacturing Textile Technological Equipment (SAUO)
INTERV........ Interval
INTERV........ Interview
INTERV........ Interviewer
INTERVAC.... Intervac International Holiday Service (SAUO)
INTERVENTION... International Convention relating to Intervention on the High Seas in Cases of Oil Pollution Casualties (SAUO)
INTERVERSITAS... World Association of Experiments in Post-Secondary Education (SAUO)
INTERVICO... Inter-American Organization of Cooperative Housing Technical Service Organizations (SAUO)
INTERVISION... International Television (IAA)
INTER/W...... Intersection With (WDAA)
INTERWOOLABS... International Association of Wool and Textile Laboratories (EAIO)
INTERWOOLLABS... International Association of Wool Textile Laboratories (SAUO)
intes........... Intestinal/ne [*Medicine*] (EDAA)
INTESCA...... Internacional de Ingenieria y Estudios Tecnicos SA [*Spain*] (PDAA)
INTEST......... Intestinal
Intest........... intestine (SAUS)
Intevac......... Intevac, Inc. [*Associated Press*] (SAG)
INTEX........... Integer Extraction (PDAA)
INTEX........... International Exploration, Inc. (EFIS)
INTEX........... International Fallout Warning Exercise (NATG)
INTEXT......... International Textbook Co.
INTF............. Interface (NASA)
INTF............. Interface Systems, Inc. [*NASDAQ symbol*] (NQ)
INTF............. Interim National Test Facility (ACAE)
INTF............. Internal Frosted (IAA)
IntF............. International Finance Corp. [*Associated Press*] (SAG)
INTFA........... International Falls, MN [*American Association of Railroads railroad junction routing code*]
IntFam......... International Family Entertainment [*Associated Press*] (SAG)
IntFast......... International Fast Food Corp. [*Associated Press*] (SAG)
INTFC........... Interface (MSA)
INTFC........... Interference (FAAC)
INTFER......... Interference (AABC)
Int FHR........ Internatl Fetal Heart Rate [*Medicine*] (MEDA)
IntFib........... International Fibercom, Inc. [*Associated Press*] (SAG)
IntFibcm...... International Fibercom, Inc. [*Associated Press*] (SAG)
IntFlav......... International Flavors & Fragrances, Inc. [*Associated Press*] (SAG)
Int For Fire News... International Forest Fire News (SAUO)
Int Forum Inf Doc... International Forum on Information and Documentation (journ.) (SAUS)
INTFR........... Interference (KSC)
Intfrn........... Interferon Sciences, Inc. [*Associated Press*] (SAG)
INTFU........... Interface Unit [*Computer science*]
intg............... Intaglio (VRA)
INTG............. Integrated (SAUS)
INTG............. Integration (NASA)
INTG............. Intergroup Corp. [*NASDAQ symbol*] (TTSB)
INTG............. Interim National Transition Government (SAUS)
INTG............. Interpreting (SAUS)
INTG............. Interrogate (AABC)
IntGame....... International Game Technology [*Associated Press*] (SAG)
IntgDv......... Integrated Device Technology, Inc. [*Associated Press*] (SAG)
INTGEN......... Interpreter Generator
Int Geol Rev... International Geology Review (journ.) (SAUS)
IntgHS......... Integrated Health Services, Inc. [*Associated Press*] (SAG)
INTGL........... Integral (KSC)
IntgMed....... Integrated Medical Resources, Inc. [*Associated Press*] (SAG)
IntgMic........ Integrated Micro Products [*Associated Press*] (SAG)
IntgMus....... Integrity Music, Inc. [*Associated Press*] (SAG)
Intgph......... Intergraph Corp. [*Associated Press*] (SAG)
INTGR......... Integrate (AABC)
IntgrBr........ Integrated Brands [*Associated Press*] (SAG)
INTGRD....... Integrated
Intgrp......... [*The*] Inner Group Corp. [*Associated Press*] (SAG)
INTGRTD...... Integrated
IntgSc......... Integrated Security Systems [*Associated Press*] (SAG)
IntgSec....... Integrated Security Systems [*Associated Press*] (SAG)
IntgSrg....... Integrated Surgical Systems, Inc. [*Associated Press*] (SAG)
IntgTec....... Ingredient Technology Corp. (SAUO)
INTGTR........ Integrator (SAUS)
IntgWst....... Integrated Waste Services, Inc. [*Associated Press*] (SAG)
Inth............. Intrathecal [*Medicine*] (EDAA)
INTH............. Intrathecal [*Medicine*]
Int Harv....... International Harvester (SAUO)
INTHERM..... International Oil and Gas Firing Trade Fair (SAUO)
InTho........... Thorntown Public Library, Thorntown, IN [*Library symbol*] [*Library of Congress*] (LCLS)
InThr........... International Thoroughbred Breeders, Inc. [*Associated Press*] (SAG)
InTI............. Indiana State University, Terre Haute, IN [*Library symbol*] [*Library of Congress*] (LCLS)
INTI............. Industrial and Technological Information (SAUS)
INTI............. Industrial Technologies, Inc. [*NASDAQ symbol*] (SAG)
INTI............. Inet Technologies [*NASDAQ symbol*] (SG)
INTI............. Inti. University of Connecticut, Department of Romance Languages (SAUS)
InTi............. Tipton County Public Library, Tipton, IN [*Library symbol*] [*Library of Congress*] (LCLS)
INTIB........... Industrial and Technological Information Bank [*UNIDO*] (IID)
INTIM........... Interrupt and Timing [*Telecommunications*] (TEL)
IntImag....... International Imaging Materials, Inc. [*Associated Press*] (SAG)
InTIMC........ IMC Chemical Group, Inc., Technical Library, Terre Haute, IN [*Library symbol*] [*Library of Congress*] (LCLS)
Intime.......... Information on Technology in Manufacturing Engineering [*Society of Manufacturing Engineers*] [*Dearborn, MI*]
INTIME........ Interactive Textual Information Management Experiment (PDAA)
Intime.......... Intime Systems International, Inc. [*Associated Press*] (SAG)
IntIMT......... Intercapital Insured Municipal Trust [*Associated Press*] (SAG)
Intimte........ Intimate Brands, Inc. [*Associated Press*] (SAG)
IntInd......... International Index (SAUS)
IntInd......... International Index to Periodicals (SAUO)
Int Inf Commun Educ... International Information, Communication and Education (journ.) (SAUS)
IntIns CA...... InterCapital Insured California Municipal Securities [*Associated Press*] (SAG)
INTIP........... Integrated Information Processing
InTip........... Tipton County Public Library, Tipton, IN [*Library symbol*] [*Library of Congress*] (LCLS)
INTIPS......... Integrated Information Processing System [*Air Development Center, Rome, NY*]
INTIPS......... Intelligence Information Processing System (SAUO)
Int Iron Steel Inst Bull... International Iron and Steel Institute Bulletin (journ.) (SAUS)
INTIST......... International Institute for Science and Technology (SAUS)
INTIW......... Industrial Technol Wrrt'A' [*NASDAQ symbol*] (TTSB)
INTIZ........... Industrial Technol Wrrt'B' [*NASDAQ symbol*] (TTSB)
Int J Adapt Control Signal Process... International Journal of Adaptive Control and Signal Process (journ.) (SAUS)
Int J Addict... International Journal of the Addictions (journ.) (SAUS)

Int J Adhes Adhes... International Journal of Adhesion and Adhesives (journ.) (SAUS)
Int J Adv Couns... International Journal for the Advancement of Counselling (journ.) (SAUS)
Int J Adv Manuf Technol... International Journal of Advanced Manufacturing Technology (journ.) (SAUS)
Int J Aging Hum Dev... International Journal of Aging and Human Development (journ.) (SAUS)
Int J Ambient Energy... International Journal of Ambient Energy (journ.) (SAUS)
Int J Am Linguist... International Journal of American Linguistics. Chicago (journ.) (SAUS)
Int J Androl... International Journal of Andrology (journ.) (SAUS)
Int J Antimicro Ag... International Journal of Antimicrobial Agents (journ.) (SAUS)
Int J Appl Electromag Mater... International Journal of Applied Electromagnetics in Materials (journ.) (SAUS)
Int J Appl Eng Educ... International Journal of Applied Engineering Education (journ.) (SAUS)
Int J Appl Radiat Isot... International Journal of Applied Radiation and Isotopes (journ.) (SAUS)
Int J Artif Organs... International Journal of Artificial Organs (journ.) (SAUS)
Int J Biochem... International Journal of Biochemistry (journ.) (SAUS)
Int J Biochem Cell Biol... International Journal of Biochemistry and Cell Biology (journ.) (SAUS)
Int J Biol Markers... International Journal of Biological Markers (journ.) (SAUS)
Int J Bio-Med Comput... International Journal of Bio-Medical Computing (journ.) (SAUS)
Int J Biometeorol... International Journal of Biometeorologie (SAUO)
Int J Biometeorol... International Journal of Biometeorology (journ.) (SAUS)
Int J Bulk Solids... International Journal of Bulk Solids (journ.) (SAUS)
Int J Bulk Solids Storage Silos... International Journal of Bulk Solids, Storage in Silos (journ.) (SAUS)
Int J Bus...... International Journal of Business [*A publication*] (JLIT)
Int J Cancer... International Journal of Cancer (journ.) (SAUS)
Int J Cancer Suppl... International Journal of Cancer. Supplement (journ.) (SAUS)
Int J Card Imaging... International Journal of Cardiac Imaging (journ.) (SAUS)
Int J Cardiol... International Journal of Cardiology (journ.) (SAUS)
Int J Cell Cloning... International Journal of Cell Cloning (journ.) (SAUS)
Int J Cem Compos Lightweight Concr... International Journal of Cement Composites and Lightweight Concrete (journ.) (SAUS)
Int J Circuit Theory Appl... International Journal of Circuit Theory and Applications (journ.) (SAUS)
Int J Climatol... International Journal of Climatology (SAUO)
Int J Climatol... International Journal of Climatology (journ.) (SAUS)
Int J Clin Exp Hypn... International Journal of Clinical and Experimental Hypnosis (journ.) (SAUS)
Int J Clin Lab Res... International Journal of Clinical and Laboratory Research (journ.) (SAUS)
Int J Clin Monit Comput... International Journal of Clinical Monitoring and Computing (journ.) (SAUS)
Int J Clin Pharmacol Ther... International Journal of Clinical Pharmacology and Therapeutics (journ.) (SAUS)
Int J Clin Pharmacol Ther Toxicol... International Journal of Clinical Pharmacology, Therapy and Toxicology (journ.) (SAUS)
Int J Colorectal Dis... International Journal of Colorectal Disease (journ.) (SAUS)
Int J Comp Sociol... International Journal of Comparative Sociology. York University, Department of Sociology and Anthropology. Toronto (journ.) (SAUS)
Int J Comput Adult Educ Train... International Journal of Computers in Adult Education and Training (journ.) (SAUS)
Int J Comput Appl Technol... International Journal of Computer Applications in Technology (journ.) (SAUS)
Int J Comput Integr Manuf... International Journal of Computer Integrated Manufacturing (journ.) (SAUS)
Int J Comput Math... International Journal of Computer Mathematics (journ.) (SAUS)
Int J Comput Vis... International Journal of Computer Vision (journ.) (SAUS)
Int J Comput Vision... International Journal of Computer Vision [*A publication*] (CABS)
Int J Criminol... International Journal of Criminology and Penology [*A publication*] (DLA)
Int J Dermatol... International Journal of Dermatology (journ.) (SAUS)
Int J Dev Biol... International Journal of Developmental Biology (journ.) (SAUS)
Int J Dev Neurosci... International Journal of Developmental Neuroscience (journ.) (SAUS)
Int J Digit Analog Cabled Syst... International Journal of Digital and Analog Cabled Systems (journ.) (SAUS)
Int J Earthquake Eng Struct Dyn... International Journal of Earthquake and Structural Dynamics (journ.) (SAUS)
Int J Eat Disord... International Journal of Eating Disorders (journ.) (SAUS)
Int J Econ Bus... International Journal of the Economics of Business [*A publication*] (JLIT)
Int J Electr Eng Educ... International Journal of Electrical Engineering Education (journ.) (SAUS)
Int J Electron... International Journal of Electronics (journ.) (SAUS)
IntJen.......... International Jensen, Inc. [*Associated Press*] (SAG)
Int J Energy Res... International Journal of Energy Research (journ.) (SAUS)
Int J Energy Syst... International Journal of Energy Systems (journ.) (SAUS)
Int J Eng Fluid Mech... International Journal of Engineering Fluid Mechanics (journ.) (SAUS)
Int J Eng Intell Syst... International Journal of Engineering Intellectual Systems [*A publication*] (CABS)
Int J Eng Sci... International Journal of Engineering Science (journ.) (SAUS)
Int J Environ Stud... International Journal of Environmental Studies (journ.) (SAUS)
Int J Epidemiol... International Journal of Epidemiology (journ.) (SAUS)
Int J Expert Syst Res Appl... International Journal of Expert Systems Research and Applications (journ.) (SAUS)
Int J Fatigue... International Journal of Fatigue (journ.) (SAUS)
Int J Fertil Menopausal Stud... International Journal of Fertility and Menopausal Studies (journ.) (SAUS)
Int J Food Sci Nutr... International Journal of Food Sciences and Nutrition (journ.) (SAUS)
Int J Food Sci Technol... International Journal of Food Science and Technology (journ.) (SAUS)
Int J Forecast... International Journal of Forecasting (journ.) (SAUS)
Int J Forecasting... International Journal of Forecasting [*A publication*] (JLIT)
Int J Fract.... International Journal of Fracture (journ.) (SAUS)
Int J Game Theory... International Journal of Game Theory (journ.) (SAUS)
Int J Gen Syst... International Journal of General Systems (journ.) (SAUS)
Int J Geogr Inf Syst... International Journal of Geographical Information Systems (SAUO)
Int J Geogr Int Syst... International Journal of Geographical Information Systems (journ.) (SAUS)
Int J Glob Energy Issues... International Journal of Global Energy Issues (journ.) (SAUS)
Int J Group Psychother... International Journal of Group Psychotherapy (journ.) (SAUS)
Int J Gynaecol Obstet... International Journal of Gynaecology and Obstetrics (journ.) (SAUS)
Int J Gynecol Cancer... International Journal of Gynecological Cancer (journ.) (SAUS)
Int J Gynecol Pathol... International Journal of Gynecological Pathology (journ.) (SAUS)
Int J Health Serv... International Journal of Health Services (journ.) (SAUS)
Int J Heat Fluid Flow... International Journal of Heat and Fluid Flow (journ.) (SAUS)
Int J Hematol... International Journal of Hematology (journ.) (SAUS)
Int J High Technol Ceram... International Journal of High Technology Ceramics (journ.) (SAUS)
Int J High Temp Ceram... International Journal of High Temperature Ceramics (journ.) (SAUS)
IntJhn.......... Interstate/Johnson Lane, Inc. [*Formerly, Interstate Securities, Inc.*] [*Associated Press*] (SAG)
Int J Hydrog Energy... International Journal of Hydrogen Energy (journ.) (SAUS)
Int J Hyperthermia... International Journal of Hyperthermia (journ.) (SAUS)
Int J Immunopharmacol... International Journal of Immunopharmacology (journ.) (SAUS)
Int J Impact Eng... International Journal of Impact Engineering (journ.) (SAUS)
Int J Ind Organ... International Journal of Industrial Organization [*A publication*] (JLIT)
Int J Inf Manage... International Journal of Information Management (journ.) (SAUS)
Int J Infrared Millim Waves... International Journal of Infrared and Millimeter Waves (journ.) (SAUS)
Int J Insect Morphol Embryol... International Journal of Insect Morphology and Embryology (journ.) (SAUS)
Int J Inst Mangt in Higher Educ... International Journal of Institutional Management in Higher Education (journ.) (SAUS)
Int J Intell Syst... International Journal of Intelligent Systems (journ.) (SAUS)
Int J Intercult Relat... International Journal of Intercultural Relations. Society for Intercultural Education, Training and Research (journ.) (SAUS)
Int J Intercult Relat... International Journal of Intercultural Relations. Society for Intercultural Education, Training, and Research; Pergamon Press. New York (SAUO)
Int J Invertebr Repr Dev... International Journal of Invertebrate Reproduction and Development (journ.) (SAUS)
Int J Joining Mater... International Journal for the Joining of Materials (journ.) (SAUS)
Int J Law Psychiatry... International Journal of Law and Psychiatry (journ.) (SAUS)
Int J Legal Med... International Journal of Legal Medicine (journ.) (SAUS)
Int J Lepr..... International Journal of Leprosy (journ.) (SAUS)
Int J Lepr Other Mycobact Dis... International Journal of Leprosy and Other Mycobacterial Diseases (journ.) (SAUS)
Int J Life Educ... International Journal of Lifelong Education (journ.) (SAUS)
Int J Mach Tools Manuf... International Journal of Machine Tools and Manufacture (journ.) (SAUS)
Int J Man-Mach Stud... International Journal of Man-Machine Studies (journ.) (SAUS)
Int J Manpower... International Journal of Manpower [*A publication*] (JLIT)
Int J Manuf Technol... International Journal of Manufacturing Technology (journ.) (SAUS)
Int J Mass Spectrom Ion Process... International Journal of Mass Spectrometry and Ion Processes (journ.) (SAUS)
Int J Mater Eng Appl... International Journal of Materials in Engineering Applications (journ.) (SAUS)
Int J Mater Prod Technol... International Journal of Materials and Product Technology (journ.) (SAUS)
Int J Math Educ Sci Technol... International Journal of Mathematical Education in Science and Technology (journ.) (SAUS)
Int J Mech Sci... International Journal of Mechanical Sciences (journ.) (SAUS)
Int J Med Microbiol... International Journal of Medical Microbiology (journ.) (SAUS)
Int J Med Microbiol Virol Parasitol Infect Dis... International Journal of Medical Microbiology, Virology, Parasitology and Infectious Diseases (journ.) (SAUS)
Int J Microcirc Clin Exp... International Journal of Microcirculation: Clinical and Experimental (journ.) (SAUS)
Int J Microgr Video Technol... International Journal of Micrographics and Video Technology (journ.) (SAUS)
Int J Min Eng... International Journal of Mining Engineering (journ.) (SAUS)
Int J Miner Process... International Journal of Mineral Processing (journ.) (SAUS)

Int J Mini Microcomput... International Journal of Mini and Microcomputers (journ.) (SAUS)
Int J Model Simul... International Journal of Modelling and Simulation (journ.) (SAUS)
Int J Mod Phys A... International Journal of Modern Physics A (journ.) (SAUS)
Int J Mod Phys B... International Journal of Modern Physics B (journ.) (SAUS)
Int J Multiphase Flow... International Journal of Multiphase Flow [*A publication*] (CABS)
Int J Multiph Flow... International Journal of Multiphase Flow (journ.) (SAUS)
Int J Naut Archaeol... International Journal of Nautical Archaeology. Nautical Archaeology Society. San Diego (SAUO)
Int J Naut Archaeol... International Journal of Nautical Archaeology. Nautical Archaeology Society. San Diego (journ.) (SAUS)
Int J Network Manage... International Journal of Network Management [*A publication*] (CABS)
Int J Neural Syst... International Journal of Neural Systems (journ.) (SAUS)
Int J Neurol... International Journal of Neurology (journ.) (SAUS)
Int J Neuroradiol... International Journal of Neuroradiology (journ.) (SAUS)
Int J Neurosci... International Journal of Neuroscience (journ.) (SAUS)
Int J Nondestr Test... International Journal of Nondestructive Testing (journ.) (SAUS)
Int J Nucl Med Biol... International Journal of Nuclear Medicine and Biology (journ.) (SAUS)
Int J Numer Anal Methods Geomech... International Journal for Numerical and Analytical Methods in Geomechanics (journ.) (SAUS)
Int J Numer Methods Eng... International Journal for Numerical Methods in Engineering (journ.) (SAUS)
Int J Numer Methods Fluids... International Journal for Numerical Methods in Fluids (journ.) (SAUS)
Int J Nurs Pract... International Journal of Nursing Practice (journ.) (SAUS)
Int J Nurs Stud... International Journal of Nursing Studies (journ.) (SAUS)
Int J Obes.... International Journal of Obesity (journ.) (SAUS)
Int J Obes Relat Metab Disord... International Journal of Obesity and Related Metabolic Disorders (journ.) (SAUS)
Int J Occup Med Environ Health... International Journal of Occupational Medicine and Environmental Health (journ.) (SAUS)
Int J Oper Prod Manage... International Journal of Operations and Production Management (journ.) (SAUS)
Int J Optoelectron... International Journal of Optoelectronics (journ.) (SAUS)
Int J Oral Maxillofac Implants... International Journal of Oral and Maxillofacial Implants (journ.) (SAUS)
Int J Oral Maxillofac Surg... International Journal of Oral and Maxillofacial Surgery (journ.) (SAUS)
Int J Orthod... International Journal of Orthodontics (journ.) (SAUS)
Int jour amer ling... International Journal of American Linguistics. Indiana University. Bloomington (SAUO)
Int J Paediat Dent... International Journal of Paediatric Dentistry (journ.) (SAUS)
Int J Pancreatol... International Journal of Pancreatology (journ.) (SAUS)
Int J Parallel Program... International Journal of Parallel Programming (journ.) (SAUS)
Int J Parasitol... International Journal for Parasitology (journ.) (SAUS)
Int J Parasitol... International Journal of Parasitology (journ.) (SAUS)
Int J Pattern Recognit Artif Intell... International Journal of Pattern Recognition and Artificial Intelligence (journ.) (SAUS)
Int J Pediatr Otorhinolaryngol... International Journal of Pediatric Otorhinolaryngology (journ.) (SAUS)
Int J Pept Protein Res... International Journal of Peptide and Protein Research (journ.) (SAUS)
Int J Pharm... International Journal of Phamaceutics (journ.) (SAUS)
Int J Pharm... International Journal of Pharmaceutics (journ.) (SAUS)
Int J Phys Distrib Mater Manage... International Journal of Physical Distribution and Materials Management (journ.) (SAUS)
Int J Plast.... International Journal of Plasticity (journ.) (SAUS)
Int J Pol ...... International Journal of Politics [*A publication*] (DLA)
Int J Policy Inf... International Journal on Policy and Information (journ.) (SAUS)
Int J Polym Mater... International Journal of Polymeric Materials (journ.) (SAUS)
Int J Powder Metall... International Journal of Powder Metallurgy (journ.) (SAUS)
Int J Pressure Vessels Piping... International Journal of Pressure Vessels and Piping (journ.) (SAUS)
Int J Prod Res... International Journal of Production Research (journ.) (SAUS)
Int J Proj Manage... International Journal of Project Management (journ.) (SAUS)
Int J Psychiatry Med... International Journal of Psychiatry in Medicine (journ.) (SAUS)
Int J Psychoanal... International Journal of Psychoanalysis (journ.) (SAUS)
Int J Psychophysiol... International Journal of Psychophysiology (journ.) (SAUS)
Int J Psychosom... International Journal of Psychosomatics (journ.) (SAUS)
Int J Qual Health Care... International Journal for Quality in Health Care (journ.) (SAUS)
Int J Quant Chem Symp... International Journal of Quantum Chemistry, Symposium (journ.) (SAUS)
Int J Quantum Chem... International Journal of Quantum Chemistry (MEC)
Int J Quantum Chem Symp... International Journal of Quantum Chemistry Symposium (MEC)
Int J Radiat Biol... International Journal of Radiation Biology (journ.) (SAUS)
Int J Radiat Oncol Biol Phys... International Journal of Radiation Oncology Biology Physics (journ.) (SAUS)
Int J Radiat Phys Chem... International Journal for Radiation Physics and Chemistry (journ.) (SAUS)
Int J Rapid Solidif... International Journal of Rapid Solidification (journ.) (SAUS)
Int J Refract Hard Mater... International Journal of Refractory Metals and Hard Materials (journ.) (SAUS)
Int J Remote Sens... International Journal of Remote Sensing (journ.) (SAUS)
Int J Robot Autom... International Journal of Robotics and Automation (journ.) (SAUS)
Int J Robot Res... International Journal of Robotics Research (journ.) (SAUS)
Int J Rock Mech Min Sci... International Journal of Rock Mechanics and Mining Sciences (journ.) (SAUS)
Int J Rock Mech Min Sci Geomech Abstr... International Journal of Rock Mechanics and Mining Sciences and Geomechanics Abstracts (journ.) (SAUS)
Int J Satell Commun... International Journal of Satellite Communications (journ.) (SAUS)
Int J Sci Educ... International Journal of Science Education (journ.) (SAUS)
Int J Soc Econ... International Journal of Social Economics [*A publication*] (JLIT)
Int J Space Struct... International Journal of Space Structures [*A publication*] (CABS)
Int J Sport Nutr... International Journal of Sport Nutrition (journ.) (SAUS)
Int J Sports Med... International Journal of Sports Medicine (journ.) (SAUS)
Int J STD AIDS... International Journal of STD and AIDS (journ.) (SAUS)
Int J Supercomput Appl... International Journal of Supercomputer Applications (journ.) (SAUS)
Int J Syst Sci... International Journal of Systems Science (journ.) (SAUS)
Int J Technol Assess Health Care... International Journal of Technology Assessment in Health Care (journ.) (SAUS)
Int J Technol Manage... International Journal of Technology Management (journ.) (SAUS)
Int J Theoretical Appl Finance... International Journal of Theoretical and Applied Finance [*A publication*] (JLIT)
Int J Thermophys... International Journal of Thermophysics (journ.) (SAUS)
Int J Tissue React... International Journal of Tissue Reactions (journ.) (SAUS)
Int J/Toronto... International Journal. Canadian Institute of International Affairs. Toronto (journ.) (SAUS)
Int J Transport Econ... International Journal of Transport Economics [*A publication*] (JLIT)
Int J Turbo Jet-Engines... International Journal of Turbo and Jet-Engines (journ.) (SAUS)
Int J Urban Reg Res... International Journal of Urban and Regional Research. E. Arnold. London (journ.) (SAUS)
Int Jurid Assn Bull... International Juridical Association. Bulletin [*A publication*] (DLA)
Int J Urol ..... International Journal of Urology (journ.) (SAUS)
Int J Veh Des... International Journal of Vehicle Design (journ.) (SAUS)
INTK............ Inotek Technologies [*NASDAQ symbol*] (TTSB)
INTK............ Inotek Technologies, Inc. [*NASDAQ symbol*] (SAG)
INTK............ Intake (MSA)
INTK............ Intertank (KSC)
INTL............ Internal
INTL............ International (AFM)
intl............ International (VRA)
INTL............ International Movement of Catholic Students [*France*]
INTL............ International Studies (SAUS)
INTL............ Inter-Tel Inc. [*NASDAQ symbol*] (TTSB)
INTLA.......... Inter-Tel, Inc. (Class A) [*NASDAQ symbol*] (COMM)
Int Lab......... International Laboratory (journ.) (SAUS)
Int Labor Work Class Hist... International Labor and Working Class History. Study Group on International Labor and Working Class History. New Haven (SAUO)
Int Labor Work Class Hist... International Labor and Working Class History. Study Group on International Labor and Working Class History. New Haven (journ.) (SAUS)
Int Labour R... International Labour Review (journ.) (SAUS)
Int Lab Rev... International Labour Review [*A publication*] (JLIT)
IntlAffairs .... International Affairs (DD)
IntlAllSv....... International Alliance Services, Inc. [*Associated Press*] (SAG)
Int'l & Comp L Bull... International and Comparative Law Bulletin [*A publication*] (DLA)
Int'l Arb Awards... Reports of International Arbitral Awards [*A publication*] (DLA)
Int'l Arb J.... International Arbitration Journal [*A publication*] (DLA)
Int'l Assoc L Lib Bull... International Association of Law Libraries. Bulletin [*A publication*] (DLA)
IntlAsst........ International Assets Holding Corp. [*Associated Press*] (SAG)
IntlAst......... International Assets Holding Corp. [*Associated Press*] (SAG)
Int Law Tr.... International Law Tracts [*A publication*] (DLA)
Int'l BA Bull... International Bar Association. Bulletin [*A publication*] (DLA)
Int'l Bar J.... International Bar Journal [*A publication*] (DLA)
Int'l BJ......... International Bar Journal [*A publication*] (DLA)
Int L Bull..... International Law Bulletin [*A publication*] (DLA)
IntlBus........ International Business Schools, Inc. [*Associated Press*] (SAG)
Intl Bus Law... International Business Lawyer (journ.) (SAUS)
Int'l Bus Lawyer... International Business Lawyer [*London, England*] [*A publication*] (DLA)
Int'l Bus Ser... International Business Series [*A publication*] (DLA)
IntlCable....... International Cabletel, Inc. [*Associated Press*] (SAG)
IntlCer....... Internacional de Ceramica SA de CV [*Associated Press*] (SAG)
Intl Colloq ... International Colloquium on Luso-Brazilian Studies, Washington (SAUS)
INTL COMB... Internal Combustion [*Freight*]
Intl Comm Jurists Rev... International Commission of Jurists. Review (journ.) (SAUS)
Int'l Crim Pol Rev... International Criminal Police Review [*A publication*] (DLA)
IntlCt........... International Cutlery Ltd. [*Associated Press*] (SAG)
Intl Ctr Envir... International Center for Environmental Research (SAUO)
IntlCut.......... International Cutlery Ltd. [*Associated Press*] (SAG)
Int'l Dig Health Leg... International Digest of Health Legislation [*A publication*] (DLA)
Int Legal Materials... International Legal Materials [*A publication*] (DLA)
IntlLeisr........ International Leisure Hosts Ltd. [*Associated Press*] (SAG)
IntlElec........ International Electronics, Inc. [*Associated Press*] (SAG)
Int I Electr Power Energy Syst... International Journal of Electrical Power and Energy Systems (journ.) (SAUS)

Int'l Encycl Comp L... International Encyclopedia of Comparative Law [*A publication*] (DLA)
IntLfe.......... Intercontinental Life Corp. [*Associated Press*] (SAG)
Intl Film Bur... International Film Bureau (SAUO)
Int'l Fin L Rev... International Financial Law Review [*A publication*] (DLA)
Intl Fin Stat... International Financial Statistics. International Monetary Fund. Washington (SAUS)
IntlgC.......... Intelligent Controls, Inc. [*Associated Press*] (SAG)
IntlgSys....... Intelligent Systems Corp. [*Associated Press*] (SAG)
Int Lib.......... Intrationum Liber [*A publication*] (DSA)
IntLibrRev.... International Library Review (journ.) (SAUS)
Int Lichenol Newsl... International Lichenological Newsletter (SAUO)
INTLINE....... International Online Data Base [*The WEFA Group*] [*Information service or system*]
IntLivC......... Integrated Living Communities, Inc. [*Associated Press*] (SAG)
Intl J Am Ling... International Journal of American Linguistics. Indiana University. Bloomington (SAUO)
Int'l J Crim & Pen... International Journal of Criminology and Penology [*A publication*] (DLA)
Int'l J Crimin & Penol... International Journal of Criminology and Penology [*A publication*] (DLA)
Int'l J Legal Res... International Journal of Legal Research [*A publication*] (DLA)
Intl JL Lib.... International Journal of Law Libraries (journ.) (SAUS)
Int'l J Off Ther & Comp Crim... International Journal of Offender Therapy and Comparative Criminology [*A publication*] (DLA)
Intl J Op Att Research... International Journal of Opinion and Attitude Research (journ.) (SAUS)
Int'l Jurid Ass'n Bull... International Juridical Association. Bulletin [*A publication*] (DLA)
INTLK.......... Interlock (MSA)
INTLK.......... Interlocking (SAUS)
Int'l Lab Reports... International Labour Reports [*A publication*] (DLA)
Int'l L Ass'n... Reports of the International Law Association [*A publication*] (DLA)
Int'l L Ass'n Bull... Bulletin. International Law Association [*1936-38*] [*A publication*] (DLA)
Int'l Law...... International Law [*A publication*] (DLA)
Intl Law....... International Lawyer (journ.) (SAUS)
Intl Law Reps... International Law Reports (journ.) (SAUS)
Intllcll......... Intellicell Corp. [*Associated Press*] (SAG)
Int'l L Comm'n... International Law Commission [*United Nations*] (DLA)
Int'l L Doc... International Law Documents [*A publication*] (DLA)
Int'l Legal Ed Newsl... International Legal Education Newsletter [*A publication*] (DLA)
Intl Legal Mats... International Legal Materials (SAUS)
INTLLGNC.... Intelligence
Int'l LLL...... International Lutheran Laymen's League (EA)
Int'l L Persp... International Law Perspective [*A publication*] (DLA)
Int'l LR........ International Law Reports [*A publication*]
Int'l L Rep... International Law Reports [*A publication*] (DLA)
Int'l L Stud... International Law Studies [*Naval War College*] [*A publication*] (DLA)
Int LN.......... International Law Notes [*A publication*] (DLA)
Int L Notes... International Law Notes [*England*] [*A publication*] (DLA)
IntlNtwk....... International Network Services [*Associated Press*] (SAG)
IntlNurs........ International Nursing Services, Inc. [*Associated Press*] (SAG)
INTLOC......... Interdiction of Lines of Communication (PDAA)
Intl Org......... International Organization. Boston (SAUS)
IntLotry........ International Lottery, Inc. [*Associated Press*] (SAG)
IntLotTot...... International Lottery & Totalizator Systems [*Associated Press*] (SAG)
IntlPizza....... International Pizza Co. [*Associated Press*] (SAG)
IntlPlatin...... International Platinum Corp. [*Associated Press*] (SAG)
IntlPost........ International Post Ltd. [*Associated Press*] (SAG)
IntlPrec........ International Precious Metals [*Associated Press*] (SAG)
IntlPrecM...... International Precious Metals [*Associated Press*] (SAG)
Int'l Prop Inv J... International Property Investment Journal [*A publication*] (DLA)
Int LQ.......... International Law Quarterly (journ.) (SAUS)
IntLR........... International Law Reports [*A publication*] (DI)
Int'l Rev Ad Sci... International Review of Administrative Sciences [*A publication*] (DLA)
Int'l Rev Crim Policy... International Review of Criminal Policy [*United Nations*] (DLA)
Intl Review... International Review Service (SAUS)
Intl Soc Sci B... International Social Science Bulletin (journ.) (SAUS)
Int'l Soc'y of Barr Q... International Society of Barristers. Quarterly [*A publication*] (DLA)
IntlSpdw...... International Speedway Corp. [*Associated Press*] (SAG)
IntlSpr......... International Sports Wagering, Inc. [*Associated Press*] (SAG)
IntlSrgL........ Intelligent Surgical LASERs, Inc. [*Associated Press*] (SAG)
Int'l Surv LDLL... International Survey of Legal Decisions on Labour Law [*1925-38*] [*A publication*] (DLA)
Int'l Sym Comp L... International Symposium on Comparative Law [*A publication*] (DLA)
Int'l Tax & Bus Law... International Tax and Business Lawyer [*A publication*] (DLA)
Intl Tax J..... International Tax Journal (journ.) (SAUS)
IntlTDS........ International Telecommunication Data Systems, Inc. [*Associated Press*] (SAG)
Intl Trade Am States... International Trade of the American States (journ.) (SAUS)
Intl Trade Am States... International Trade of the American States. Pan American Union. Inter-American Economic and Social Council. Washington (SAUO)
Intl Univs Pr... International Universities Press (SAUO)
IntlVit.......... International Vitamin Corp. [*Associated Press*] (SAG)
INTLVR........ Interleaver (MCD)
Int'l Woman Law... International Woman Lawyer [*A publication*] (DLA)
INTM.......... Interim Services [*NASDAQ symbol*] (TTSB)
INTM.......... Intermediate (KSC)
INTMA......... International Mail [*A publication*]
Int Manage... International Management (journ.) (SAUS)
Intmd.......... Intermediate [*Medicine*] (EDAA)
INTMD......... Intermediate (MSA)
INTMED....... Intermediate (AFM)
INTMED....... Internal Medicine (AABC)
Int Med........ Internal Medicine [*Medicine*] (EDAA)
IntMedI........ Intelligent Medical Imaging, Inc. [*Associated Press*] (SAG)
IntMet......... International Metals Acquisition Corp. [*Associated Press*] (SAG)
IntmetC........ Intermet Corp. [*Associated Press*] (SAG)
Int Mgmt...... International Management (journ.) (SAUS)
IntMicr........ International Microcomputer Software, Inc. [*Associated Press*] (SAG)
Int Microwave Symp Dig... International Microwave Symposium Digest (journ.) (SAUS)
Int Migr....... International Migration. Intergovernmental Committee for European Migration; Research Group for European Migration Problems (SAUO)
Int Migr....... International Migration. Quarterly review (journ.) (SAUS)
Int Min......... International Mining (journ.) (SAUS)
Int Miner Scene... International Minerals Scene (journ.) (SAUS)
IntMJ........... International Microfilm Journal of Legal Medicine, New York, NY [*Library symbol*] [*Library of Congress*] (LCLS)
Int Mod Foundry... International Modern Foundry (journ.) (SAUS)
INT MOD FREQ... Internal Modulation Frequency (SAUS)
Int mon........ Internal Monitor [*Medicine*] (EDAA)
Int Monet Fund Staff Pap... International Monetary Fund Staff Papers [*A publication*] (JLIT)
IntMP.......... International Micro-Print Preservation, Inc., New York, NY [*Library symbol*] [*Library of Congress*] (LCLS)
INTMS......... Internal Messenger Service [*Hotels*]
INTMT......... Intermittent (MSA)
IntMult......... International Multifoods Corp. [*Associated Press*] (SAG)
IntMur......... International Murex Technologies [*Associated Press*] (SAG)
IN/TN.......... Insoluble Nitrogen to Total Nitrogen (SAUS)
INTN........... InStent, Inc. [*NASDAQ symbol*] (SAG)
INTN........... Intention
IntNDS......... Interstate National Dealer Services, Inc. [*Associated Press*] (SAG)
INTNET........ Integration Network (SAUS)
INTNET........ Intelligence Network (SAUO)
IntnetS......... Intranet Solutions, Inc. [*Associated Press*] (SAG)
IntnetSol...... Intranet Solutions, Inc. [*Associated Press*] (SAG)
INTNEW....... International News [*Database*] (IT)
intnl........... International (ADWA)
INTN'L......... International
Intnl Demo... International Demographics (journ.) (SAUS)
INT NOCT..... Inter Noctem [*During the Night*] [*Pharmacy*]
Int North Pac Fish Comm Bull... International North Pacific Fisheries Commission Bulletin (SAUO)
Int North Pac Fish Comm Bull... International North Pacific Fisheries Commission Bulletin (journ.) (SAUS)
INTNS......... Intentions (FAAC)
INTNS......... In Transit
intns........... intransit (SAUS)
INTNTNL...... Intentional
IntNur.......... International Nursing Services, Inc. [*Associated Press*] (SAG)
IntNur.......... Interntional Nursing Services, Inc. [*Associated Press*] (SAG)
IntNYQ......... Intercapital New York Quality Municipal Security Trust [*Associated Press*] (SAG)
INTO........... Industrial Training Opportunities Exhibition (ITD)
INTO........... Inhibited Nitrogen Tetroxide
INTO........... Initio, Inc. [*NASDAQ symbol*] (SAG)
INTO........... Intelligence Officer [*Army*]
INTO........... Interrupt if Overflow occurs (SAUS)
INTO........... Interrupt on Overflow (SAUS)
INTO........... Intuitive Network Total Office [*Benchmark Associates*] [*Computer science*]
INTO........... Iran National Tourist Organization
INTO........... Irish National Teachers' Organisation
int obst........ Intestinal Obstruction [*Medicine*] (MAE)
intol............ Intolerance [*Medicine*] (EDAA)
INTOP......... International Operations Simulation (IEEE)
INTOPS....... Interdiction Operations [*Navy*] (NVT)
INTOP Simulation... International Operations Simulation (SAUS)
INTOR......... International TOKAMAK Reactor [*Thermonuclear-fusion system*]
INTOR......... International Torus (SAUS)
INTOR......... International Torus Design [*Nuclear energy*] (NUCP)
Int Organ..... International Organization [*A publication*] (JLIT)
Int Organ..... International Organization. World Peace Foundation; Univ. of Wisconsin Press. Madison (SAUO)
INTOSAI....... International Organization of Supreme Audit Institutions [*Vienna, Austria*] (EA)
IN TOUCH..... In Touch Trust [*British*] (NRGU)
InTour......... International Tourist Entertainment Corp. [*Associated Press*] (SAG)
Intourist....... Soviet Tourist Office (SAUO)
INTOX......... Intoxicant (SAUS)
INTOX......... Intoxicated (SAUS)
INTOX......... Intoxication
INTOX L....... Intoxicating Liquor [*Legal term*] (DLA)
Int P............ International Pharmacopoeia [*A publication*]
INTP............ Interpoint [*NASDAQ symbol*] (SAG)
INTP............ Interpoint Corp. [*NASDAQ symbol*] (TTSB)
INTP............ Interport Trucking [*MTMC*] (TAG)
IntPack........ Integrated Packaging Assembly Corp. [*Associated Press*] (SAG)
Int Pap......... International Paper (SAUS)
IntPap.......... International Paper Co. [*Associated Press*] (SAG)

Int Pbd Ind... International Paperboard Industry (journ.) (SAUS)
IntpbGp........ [*The*] Interpublic Group of Companies, Inc. [*Associated Press*] (SAG)
Int Perspect... International Perspectives (journ.) (SAUS)
INTPH.......... Interphone
INTPHIBRFT... Interim Amphibious Refresher Training [*Navy*] (NVT)
Intphse........ Interphase Corp. [*Associated Press*] (SAG)
INTPHTR....... Interphase Transformer [*Electronics*]
INTPLDR...... Interpleader [*Legal*] [*British*] (ROG)
IntPly.......... Intertape Polymer Group [*Associated Press*] (SAG)
INTPN.......... Interpretation (AFM)
Intpnt.......... Interpoint Corp. [*Associated Press*] (SAG)
INTPO.......... Interpole [*Electromagnetics*]
INTPOL........ Interpolation (SAUS)
Int Pol Rev... International Policy Review [*A publication*] (JLIT)
IntPoly......... Intertape Polymer Group [*Associated Press*] (SAG)
Int Polym Process... International Polymer Processing (journ.) (SAUS)
Intpore......... Interpore International [*Associated Press*] (SAG)
Int Power Gener... International Power Generation (journ.) (SAUS)
INTPR.......... Interpret (AFM)
Intpr............ Interpretation: A Journal of Bible and Theology [*A publication*] (BRI)
Int Private Law... Private International Law [*A publication*] (DLA)
INTPS.......... Integrated Navigation & Tactical Plotting System (SAUS)
INTPSC......... International Program Service Center (SAUS)
Int Psychogeriatr... International Psychogeriatrics (journ.) (SAUS)
IntPtr........... International Petroleum Corp. [*Associated Press*] (SAG)
Int QC Forum... International QC Forum (journ.) (SAUS)
Int Qk........... Interrupted Quick [*Flashing*] Light [*Navigation signal*]
INTQKFL....... Interrupted Quick Flashing Light [*Navigation signal*]
Int Qk Fl Lt... Interrupted Quick Flashing Light (SAUS)
IntQuest....... IntelliQuest Information Group, Inc. [*Associated Press*] (SAG)
intr.............. Intarsia (VRA)
intr.............. Interested (ADWA)
INTR............ Interior (KSC)
INTR............ INTERMEC Corp. [*NASDAQ symbol*] (COMM)
INTR............ Intermittent (AFM)
INTR............ Internal (KSC)
intr.............. Interrupt (ELAL)
INTR............ Interrupt [*Computer science*] [*Telecommunications*]
INTR............ Interrupt Register [*Computer science*] (CIST)
INTR............ Interrupt Request [*Computer science*] (CIST)
INTR............ Intersciences Computer Corp. [*NASDAQ symbol*] (SAG)
intr.............. Intransitive (SHCU)
INTR............ Intransitive
intr.............. Introduction (WDAA)
INTR............ Introduction
Intr.............. Introitus (SAUS)
INTR............ Intruder
INTR............ Intrusion (SAUS)
InTR............ Rose Polytechnic Institute, Terre Haute, IN [*Library symbol*] [*Library of Congress*] (LCLS)
INTRA.......... International Travel (MCD)
INTRA.......... Interrupt Program for Transmitter (SAUS)
Intra............ Intramural (DLA)
intra............ intrastate (SAUS)
INTRACO...... International Trading Co. (SAUS)
INTRACO...... International Trading Company (SAUO)
INTRACONS... In-Transit Control System (PDAA)
IntrAct.......... InterAction Media Corp. [*Associated Press*] (SAG)
Int Rad Conf Rec... International Radar Conference Record (SAUS)
INTRAFAX.... Facsimile System [*Western Union trade name*]
INTRAFILM... International Travel-Adventure Film Guild [*Defunct*] (EA)
INTRAH........ International Training in Health (ADWA)
INTRAINTEXSA... INEXPORT Textile Factory Workers Union (SAUO)
INTRALAB.... Information Transfer Laboratory (SAUO)
Intra LR....... Intramural Law Review of New York University (SAUO)
Intra L Rev (St LU)... Intramural Law Review (St. Louis University) [*A publication*] (DLA)
Intramol....... Intramolecular (SAUS)
Intramural LJ... Intramural Law Journal [*A publication*] (DLA)
Intramural L Rev... Intramural Law Review [*A publication*] (DLA)
INTRAN........ Information Transfer (SAUS)
INTRAN........ Infrared Transmitting
INTRAN........ Input Translator [*IBM Corp.*] [*Computer science*]
In trans........ In Transit (EBF)
intrans......... Intransitive (NTIO)
INTRANS...... Intransitive (ROG)
IN TRANS.... In Transitu [*In Transit*] [*Latin*] (ROG)
INTRANST.... International Transportation Tracking System [*Department of Transportation*]
INTRAOP...... Intraoperability (SAUO)
INTRAST...... Intrastate [*Legal shorthand*] (LWAP)
INTRASTAT... International Transport Statistics Working Group (SAUO)
INTRATA...... International Trading and Credit Company of Tanzania (SAUO)
Intrav........... Intrav, Inc. [*Associated Press*] (SAG)
Intravasc...... Intravascular (SAUS)
INTRC.......... Intricate (MSA)
IntrCal......... Intercapital California Insured Municipal Income Trust [*Associated Press*] (SAG)
INTRCHNG... Interchange
IntrCm......... Intermedia Communications of Florida, Inc. [*Associated Press*] (SAG)
Intrcrgo........ Intercargo Corp. [*Associated Press*] (SAG)
INTRCTV...... Interactive
INTRD.......... Interned (SAUS)
INTRDR........ Internal Reader (SAUS)
INTRE.......... Interrupt Program for Receiver (SAUS)
IntRect......... International Rectifier Corp. [*Associated Press*] (SAG)
INTREDIS..... International Tree Disease Register [*US Forest Service*] (NITA)
INTREDIS..... International Tree Disease Register System for Literature Retrieval in Forest Pathology [*National Agricultural Library*]
Int Ref Serv... International Reference Service (SAUS)
Int Reg Sci Rev... International Regional Science Review [*A publication*] (JLIT)
Int Reinf Plast Ind... International Reinforced Plastics Industry (journ.) (SAUS)
INTREP......... Intelligence Report (NATG)
Int Rep Bibliogr... Information Reports and Bibliographies (journ.) (SAUS)
INTREPT...... Intelligence Report
INT REV....... Internal Revenue (ROG)
Int Rev......... International Review (journ.) (SAUS)
Int Rev Adm Sci... International Review of Administrative Sciences (journ.) (SAUS)
Int Rev Appl Econ... International Review of Applied Economics [*A publication*] (JLIT)
Int Rev Appl Linguist Lang Teach... International Review of Applied Linguistics in Language Teaching (journ.) (SAUS)
Int Rev Bull... Internal Revenue Bulletin [*A publication*] (DLA)
Int Rev Chiro... International Review of Chiropractic (journ.) (SAUS)
Int Rev Connect Tissue Res... International Review of Connective Tissue Research (journ.) (SAUS)
Int Rev Crim Pol... International Review of Criminal Policy [*United Nations*] (DLA)
Int Rev Cytol... International Review of Cytology (journ.) (SAUS)
Int Rev Cytol... International Reviews in Cytology (journ.) (SAUS)
Int Rev Econ Finance... International Review of Economics and Finance [*A publication*] (JLIT)
Int Rev Educ... International Review of Education (journ.) (SAUS)
Int Rev Exp Pathol... International Review of Experimental Pathology (journ.) (SAUS)
Int Rev Finan Anal... International Review of Financial Analysis [*A publication*] (JLIT)
Int Rev Immunol... International Reviews of Immunology (journ.) (SAUS)
Int Rev Law Econ... International Review of Law and Economics [*A publication*] (JLIT)
Int Rev Missions... International Review of Missions (journ.) (SAUS)
Int Rev Neurobiol... International Review Neurobiology (journ.) (SAUS)
Int Rev Neurobiol... International Review of Neurobiology (journ.) (SAUS)
Int Rev Phys Chem... International Reviews in Physical Chemistry (journ.) (SAUS)
Int Rev Sport Soc... International Review of Sport Sociology (journ.) (SAUS)
INTREX........ Information Transfer Complex (SAUS)
INTREX........ Information Transfer Exchange [*Library science*]
INTREX........ Information Transfer Experiment [*Massachusetts Institute of Technology*] (DIT)
INTRF.......... Interference [*Telecommunications*] (MSA)
INTRFAIS..... International Food Aid Information System (SAUO)
Intrfcln......... Interface, Inc. [*Associated Press*] (SAG)
IntrFlt.......... Interactive Flight Technologies, Inc. [*Associated Press*] (SAG)
IntrFlt.......... Interactive Flight Technologies, Inc. Cl.A [*Associated Press*] (SAG)
INTRFT........ Interim Refresher Training [*Navy*]
INTRFTH...... Interfaith
INTRG.......... Integrate (AFIT)
INTRG.......... Interrogate (MSA)
Intrirs.......... Interiors, Inc. [*Associated Press*] (SAG)
INTRISCA..... Integrated Resource Inventory for South-Central Alaska (SAUO)
INTRLCD...... Interlaced
Intrleaf......... Interleaf, Inc. [*Associated Press*] (SAG)
Intrlk........... Interlink Electronics, Inc. [*Associated Press*] (SAG)
INTRLKD...... Interlocked
Intrlke.......... [*The*] Interlake Corp. [*Associated Press*] (SAG)
Intrlne.......... Interline Resources Corp. [*Associated Press*] (SAG)
INTRLVR...... Interleaver (NASA)
INTRM.......... Intermittent (VLIE)
Intrmagn....... Intermagnetics General Corp. [*Associated Press*] (SAG)
intr-md......... Inter-media (VRA)
INTRMT........ Interment (AABC)
INTRMTRGN... Inter-Mountain Region (FAAC)
Intrn............ Interneuron Pharmaceuticals, Inc. [*Associated Press*] (SAG)
INTRN.......... Intravenous [*Medicine*]
Intrnt........... Intrenet, Inc. [*Associated Press*] (SAG)
INTRNTL...... International
Intrnu........... Interneuron Pharmaceuticals, Inc. [*Associated Press*] (SAG)
INTRO.......... Introduction (MSA)
intro............ Introduction (WDMC)
intro............ Introductory (WDMC)
intro............ introversion (SAUS)
Intro............ Introvert (SAUS)
Int Road Safety Traffic Rev... International Road Safety Traffic Revue (journ.) (SAUS)
INTROD........ Introduction
INTROD........ Introduzione [*Introductory Movement*] [*Music*] (ROG)
INTROP........ Information Centre of Tropical Plant Protection (SAUO)
INTROPTA.... Introscripta [*Written Within*] [*Latin*] (ROG)
int rot.......... Internal Rotation [*Orthopedics*] (DAVI)
Int Rot......... Internal Rotation [*Medicine*] (EDAA)
Intrp............ Interpretation (SAUS)
INTRP.......... Interrupt
INTRPL........ Interpolation (MSA)
INTRPLRY.... Interpupillary
Intrpol.......... Interpool, Inc. [*Associated Press*] (SAG)
Intrpt........... Interpretation (SAUS)
INTRPT........ Interrupt (MSA)
INTRQ.......... Interrupt Request [*Computer science*] (MHDI)
IntRR........... International Rules of the Road [*Nautical term*] (NTA)
INTRST........ Interest
INTRSTG...... Interstage (KSC)

Intrsy .... Intersystems, Inc. [*Associated Press*] (SAG)
Intrsystm ..... Intersystems, Inc. [*Associated Press*] (SAG)
Intrtan .... Intertan, Inc. [*Associated Press*] (SAG)
IntrTel .... Inter-Tel, Inc. [*Associated Press*] (SAG)
INTRVN .... Intervention (VLIE)
INTRW .... Interscience Computer Wrrt [*NASDAQ symbol*] (TTSB)
IntrWBcp ...... InterWest Bancorp [*Associated Press*] (SAG)
INTS .... Integrated National Telecommunications System (SAUS)
INTS .... Integrated Systems, Inc. [*NASDAQ symbol*] (SAG)
INTS .... Intense
INTS .... Interlake Steel [*Federal Railroad Administration identification code*]
INTS .... International Switch (SAUS)
INTS .... International Telephone System (SAUS)
InTS .... Terre Haute Spectator, Terre Haute, IN [*Library symbol*] [*Library of Congress*] (LCLS)
IntscCpt .... Intersciences Computer Corp. [*Associated Press*] (SAG)
INTSCT .... Intersect (MSA)
Intsf .... Intensification (SAUS)
INTSF .... Intensify
IntShip .... International Shipholding Corp. [*Associated Press*] (SAG)
INTSHP .... Intership
INT SIG .... Interval Signal (SAUS)
IntSilSy .... Integrated Silicon Systems [*Associated Press*] (SAG)
INTSIM .... Integrated Simulator (TIMI)
Int Soc Sci J... International Social Science Journal [*A publication*] (JLIT)
Int Soc Sci Rev/New York... International Social Science Review. United Nations. New York (journ.) (SAUS)
Int Soc Sec Rev/Geneva... International Social Security Review. International Security Association. Geneva (SAUO)
Int Soc Sec Rev/Geneva... International Social Security Review. International Security Association. Geneva (journ.) (SAUS)
INTSORMIL... International Sorghum and Millet Research
INTSOY .... International Soybean Program
IntSpclty ...... International Specialty Products [*Associated Press*] (SAG)
Int Spectr ...... International Spectrum (journ.) (SAUS)
INT SPKR ..... Internal Speaker (SAUS)
IntSr .... Intelligent Surgical Lasers, Inc. [*Associated Press*] (SAG)
INTST .... Intensity
INTST .... Interest [*Finance, Law*] (ROG)
IntStand .... International Standards Group Ltd. [*Associated Press*] (SAG)
IntstBak .... Interstate Bakeries Corp. [*Formerly, Interstate Brands Corp.*] [*Associated Press*] (SAG)
INTSTDTHD... International Standard Thread (MCD)
INTSTE .... Interstate
INTSTG .... Interstage
IntstGC .... Interstate General Ltd. [*Associated Press*] (SAG)
IntstNDS .... Interstate National Dealer Services, Inc. [*Associated Press*] (SAG)
IntstPw .... Interstate Power Co. [*Associated Press*] (SAG)
Int Stud /Delhi... International Studies. Indian School of International Studies. Delhi (journ.) (SAUS)
Int Stud Q.... International Studies Quarterly (journ.) (SAUS)
INTSTY .... Intestacy [*Legal shorthand*] (LWAP)
Int Sugar J... International Sugar Journal (journ.) (SAUS)
INTSUM .... Intelligence Summary
INTSUMs ..... Intelligence Summaries (SAUO)
INTSV .... Intensive (WGA)
INTSY .... Intensify (DNAB)
Int Symp Princess Takamatsu Cancer Res Fund... International Symposium of the Princess Takamatsu Cancer Research Fund (SAUS)
IntSysC .... Integrated Systems Consulting Group, Inc. [*Associated Press*] (SAG)
INTT .... Interest [*Finance, Law*] (ROG)
INTT .... inTest Corp. [*NASDAQ symbol*] (NASQ)
Int Tax Jour... International Tax Journal [*A publication*] (DLA)
Int Tax Public Finance... International Tax and Public Finance [*A publication*] (JLIT)
Int Tech Transf Bus... International Tech Transfer Business (journ.) (SAUS)
IntTest .... International Testing Services Inc. [*Associated Press*] (SAG)
IntThr .... International Thoroughbred Breeders, Inc. [*Associated Press*] (SAG)
IntThrgh .... International Throughbred Breeders, Inc. [*Associated Press*] (SAG)
IntTourE .... International Tourist Entertainment Corp. [*Associated Press*] (SAG)
Int Trade J... International Trade Journal [*A publication*] (JLIT)
Int Trade LJ... International Trade Law Journal [*A publication*] (DLA)
Int Tree Crops J... International Tree Crops Journal (SAUO)
INT TRIG ...... Internal Triggering (SAUS)
Int trx .... Intermittent Traction [*Medicine*] (EDAA)
InTTS .... Terre Haute Tribune-Star, Terre Haute, IN [*Library symbol*] [*Library of Congress*] (LCLS)
INTU .... Indian National Trade Union Congress [*Political party*] (PSAP)
INTU .... Intuit, Inc. [*NASDAQ symbol*] (SAG)
intub .... Intubation [*Medicine*] (EDAA)
INTUC .... Indian National Trades Union Congress
INTUG .... International Telecommunications Users Group [*Telecommunications*] [*Information service or system*] (IID)
Intuit .... Intuit, Inc. [*Associated Press*] (SAG)
INTURISMO... Instituto Nicaraguense de Turismo (EY)
INTV .... Association of Independent Television Stations (EA)
INTV .... Instrumentation Television (AFM)
INTV .... Interim Hypersonics Test Article (SAUS)
INTV .... Interval (VLIE)
INTV .... Interview (CINC)
INTV .... InterVoice, Inc. [*NASDAQ symbol*] (NQ)
InTV .... Vigo County Public Library, Terre Haute, IN [*Library symbol*] [*Library of Congress*] (LCLS)
IntVer .... International Verifact, Inc. [*Associated Press*] (SAG)
IntVerif .... International Verifact, Inc. [*Associated Press*] (SAG)
IntvisB .... Intervisual Books, Inc. [*Associated Press*] (SAG)
INTVL .... Interval (MSA)
INTVLM .... Intervalometer [*Military ordnance*]
INTVN .... Intervention (VLIE)
Intvoice .... InterVoice, Inc. [*Associated Press*] (SAG)
InTVS .... Vigo County School Corp., Instructional Materials Center, Terre Haute, IN [*Library symbol*] [*Library of Congress*] (LCLS)
INTVW .... Interview (AFM)
Int Water Power Dam Constr... International Water Power and Dam Construction (journ.) (SAUS)
INTWF .... Indian National Textile Workers' Federation
InTWHi .... Wabash Valley Historical Society, Terre Haute, IN [*Library symbol*] [*Library of Congress*] (LCLS)
Int Woman L... International Woman Lawyer [*A publication*] (DLA)
INTWORLSA... International Third World Legal Studies Association (EA)
INT WT .... Intaken Weight (SAUS)
INTX .... International Terminals [*Federal Railroad Administration identification code*]
INTXA .... Interiors, Inc. [*NASDAQ symbol*] (SAG)
INTXA .... Interiors Inc.'A' [*NASDAQ symbol*] (TTSB)
INTXL .... Interiors Inc. Wrrt [*NASDAQ symbol*] (TTSB)
INTXP .... Interiors Inc.Cv'A'Pfd [*NASDAQ symbol*] (TTSB)
INTXW .... Interiors Inc. Wrrt'A' [*NASDAQ symbol*] (TTSB)
INTXZ .... Interiors Inc.Wrrt'B' [*NASDAQ symbol*] (TTSB)
INTY .... Intestacy [*Legal*] (ROG)
IntYog .... International Yogurt Co. [*Associated Press*] (SAG)
INTZ .... Integrated Ingredients [*Federal Railroad Administration identification code*]
inu .... Indiana [*MARC country of publication code*] [*Library of Congress*] (LCCP)
InU .... Indiana University, Bloomington, IN [*Library symbol*] [*Library of Congress*] (LCLS)
INU .... Inertial Navigation Unit
INU .... Integration Unit
INU .... Internal Navigation Unit (SAUS)
INU .... International Nutrition & Genetics Corp. [*Vancouver Stock Exchange symbol*]
InU .... International Unit [*Medicine*] (EDAA)
INU .... Inuyama [*Japan*] [*Seismograph station code, US Geological Survey*] (SEIS)
INU .... Nauru [*Nauru*] [*Airport symbol*] (OAG)
InU .... Swain Hall Library, Indiana University, Bloomington (SAUO)
InU-A .... Indiana University, Anatomy-Physiology Laboratory, Bloomington, IN [*Library symbol*] [*Library of Congress*] (LCLS)
InU-AT .... Indiana University, Archive of Traditional Music, Bloomington, IN [*Library symbol*] [*Library of Congress*] (LCLS)
InU-B .... Indiana University, Biology Library, Bloomington, IN [*Library symbol*] [*Library of Congress*] (LCLS)
InU-BA .... Indiana University, School of Business Administration, Bloomington, IN [*Library symbol*] [*Library of Congress*] (LCLS)
InUc .... Union City Public Library, Union City, IN [*Library symbol*] [*Library of Congress*] (LCLS)
INucE .... Institute of Nuclear Engineering (SAUS)
INUCE .... Institute of Nuclear Engineers (SAUS)
INucE .... Institution of Nuclear Engineers [*British*]
InU-D .... Indiana University, School of Dentistry, Indianapolis, IN [*Library symbol*] [*Library of Congress*] (LCLS)
InU-Fw .... Indiana University, Fort Wayne Regional Campus, Fort Wayne, IN [*Library symbol*] [*Library of Congress*] (LCLS)
InU-I .... Indiana University, Indianapolis Regional Campus, Indianapolis, IN [*Library symbol*] [*Library of Congress*] (LCLS)
InU-ISR .... Indiana University, Institute for Sex Research, Bloomington, IN [*Library symbol*] [*Library of Congress*] (LCLS)
InU-K .... Indiana University, Kokomo Regional Campus, Kokomo, IN [*Library symbol*] [*Library of Congress*] (LCLS)
InU-L .... Indiana University, Law Library, Indianapolis, IN [*Library symbol*] [*Library of Congress*] (LCLS)
InU-Li .... Indiana University, Lilly Library, Bloomington, IN [*Library symbol*] [*Library of Congress*] (LCLS)
InU-M .... Indiana University, School of Medicine, Indianapolis, IN [*Library symbol*] [*Library of Congress*] (LCLS)
INUMRC .... Northwest Indiana Health Science Library Consortium [*Library network*]
InU-Mu .... Indiana University at Bloomington, Music Library, Bloomington, IN [*Library symbol*] [*Library of Congress*] (LCLS)
InU-N .... Indiana University, Northwest Regional Campus, Gary, IN [*Library symbol*] [*Library of Congress*] (LCLS)
InU-Nea .... Indiana University Southeast, New Albany, IN [*Library symbol*] [*Library of Congress*] (LCLS)
InU-O .... Indiana University, Optometry Library, Bloomington, IN [*Library symbol*] [*Library of Congress*] (LCLS)
InUpT .... Taylor University, Upland, IN [*Library symbol*] [*Library of Congress*] (LCLS)
InU-R .... Indiana University at Bloomington, Lilly Rare Books, Bloomington, IN [*Library symbol*] [*Library of Congress*] (LCLS)
INUR .... Inventory Update Rule (SARE)
inurn .... inurnment (SAUS)
INUS .... Innovus Corp. [*NASDAQ symbol*] (SAG)
INUS .... Inside Continental Limits of the United States (SAUS)
INUS .... Inside the United States
InU-Sb .... Indiana University, South Bend Regional Campus, South Bend, IN [*Library symbol*] [*Library of Congress*] (LCLS)
InU-Se .... Indiana University, Southeastern Regional Campus, Jeffersonville, IN [*Library symbol*] [*Library of Congress*] (LCLS)
in utero .... Within the Uterus [*Medicine*] (EDAA)

INUW.......... Irish National Union of Woodworkers (BI)
INV.......... Amer Residential Inv Trust [*NYSE symbol*] (SG)
INV.......... Inductive Null Voltage
INV.......... Inferior Nasal Vein [*Medicine*] (EDAA)
Inv.......... Informative (SAUS)
INV.......... In-Line Needle Valve
INV.......... Invalid (IAA)
INV.......... Invasion
INV.......... Invective
INV.......... Invenit [*He, or She, Designed It*] [*Latin*]
inv.......... Invennon (SAUS)
INV.......... Invent (AABC)
Inv.......... Invention (SAUS)
INV.......... Inventor (GOBB)
INV.......... Inventories (SAUS)
INV.......... Inventory (AFM)
inv.......... Inventory (DIAR)
Inv.......... Inventory (SAUS)
INV.......... Inveralochy [*Australia*] [*Seismograph station code, US Geological Survey*] (SEIS)
INV.......... Inverness [*Scotland*] [*Airport symbol*] (OAG)
inv.......... Inverse (IDOE)
INV.......... Inverse [*or Invert*]
INV.......... Inversia [*Latvia*] [*ICAO designator*] (FAAC)
inv.......... Inversion (DAVI)
INV.......... Inverted (SAUS)
INV.......... Inverter (KSC)
INV.......... Investigation
Inv.......... Investing (EBF)
Inv.......... Investment (EBF)
INV.......... Investment
INV.......... Invitation
INV.......... Invitational Race [*Harness racing*]
INV.......... Invoice [*Billing*] (AFM)
Inv.......... Invoice (EBF)
inv.......... Invoice [*Billing*] (ODBW)
INV.......... Involuntary
INV.......... Iris Neovascularization [*Opthalmology*]
INVAC.......... Investment Account [*Postal Service*] [*British*]
INVADJ.......... Inventory Adjustment (MCD)
INVAID.......... Integration of Computer Vision Techniques for Automatic Incident Detection (SAUO)
INVAL.......... Invalid (IAA)
inval.......... invalidate (SAUS)
InVal.......... Valparaiso-Porter County Public Library System, Valparaiso, IN [*Library symbol*] [*Library of Congress*] (LCLS)
InValCR.......... Porter County Recorder's Office, Valparaiso, IN [*Library symbol*] [*Library of Congress*] (LCLS)
InValHi.......... Historical Society of Porter County, Valparaiso, IN [*Library symbol*] [*Library of Congress*] (LCLS)
InValU.......... Valparaiso University, Valparaiso, IN [*Library symbol*] [*Library of Congress*] (LCLS)
InValVM.......... Valparaiso Vidette-Messenger, Valparaiso, IN [*Library symbol*] [*Library of Congress*] (LCLS)
INVAM.......... Invoice Amount (SAUS)
INVAR.......... Invariant
Invasion Metastasis... Invasion and Metastasis (SAUS)
INV AUTO CHANGE... Inverter Automatic Changeover (SAUS)
InVb.......... Van Buren Public Library, Van Buren, IN [*Library symbol*] [*Library of Congress*] (LCLS)
InvBank.......... Investors Bank Corp. [*Associated Press*] (SAG)
Invcare.......... Invacare Corp. [*Associated Press*] (SAG)
invcd.......... invoiced (SAUS)
INVCE.......... Invoice [*Billing*] (ROG)
INVCURR.......... Inverse Current [*Electronics*] (IAA)
INVD.......... Invalidate Data [*Cache*] [*Computer instruction*] (PCM)
Inv Dd.......... Investment Dealers Digest (journ.) (SAUS)
INV DOC ATTACH... Invoice with Documents Attached [*Billing*] (ROG)
INVDT.......... Invoice Date (SAUS)
InVe.......... Switzerland County Public Library, Vevay, IN [*Library symbol*] [*Library of Congress*] (LCLS)
InVeCR.......... Switzerland County Recorder's Office, Vevay, IN [*Library symbol*] [*Library of Congress*] (LCLS)
INVECS.......... Innovative Vehicle Electronic Control System [*Motor vehicles*]
INVECS.......... Intelligent and Innovative Vehicle Electronic Control System
Inven.......... Invention (DIAR)
INVENT.......... Institute for Ventures in New Technology
Inventory C... Inventory Control Point (NAKS)
inver.......... Inversion (DAVI)
InVeRE.......... Vevay Reville-Enterprise, Vevay, IN [*Library symbol*] [*Library of Congress*] (LCLS)
INVERN.......... Inverness [*County in Scotland*]
InVerR.......... Versailles Republican, Versailles, IN [*Library symbol*] [*Library of Congress*] (LCLS)
InVerRHi.......... Ripley County Historical Society, Versailles, IN [*Library symbol*] [*Library of Congress*] (LCLS)
INVERT.......... Invertebrate (WGA)
INVERTEB.......... Invertebrate
Invertebr Repr Dev... Invertebrate Reproduction and Development (SAUS)
Inverter As... Inverter Assembly [*Aerospace*] (NAKS)
INVES.......... Investigate [*or Investigation*] (AFM)
Invesco.......... Invesco PLC [*Associated Press*] (SAG)
InvescoF.......... Invesco Funding [*Associated Press*] (SAG)
InVeSD.......... Switzerland Democrat, Vevay, IN [*Library symbol*] [*Library of Congress*] (LCLS)
INVEST.......... Integrated Vehicle System Technology (MCD)
invest.......... Investigate [*Medicine*] (EDAA)
Invest.......... Investigation (STED)
INVEST.......... Investigation
invest.......... Investment (DD)
INVEST.......... Investment
INVESTIG.......... Investigation
Invest Ophthalmol... Investigative Ophthalmology (journ.) (SAUS)
Invest Ophthalmol Vis Sci... Investigative Ophthalmology and Visual Science (journ.) (SAUS)
Invest Pol.......... Investment Policy [*A publication*] (JLIT)
Invest Radiol... Investigative Radiology (journ.) (SAUS)
Invet.......... Inveterate (STED)
Inv/Ev.......... Inversion/Eversion [*Medicine*] (EDAA)
INVEX.......... International Exhibition of Inventions and Novel Features (TSPED)
INV Facility... Invalid Facility (SAUS)
InvFnSv.......... Investors Financial Services Corp. [*Associated Press*] (SAG)
INVG.......... Investigate (ADWA)
INVG.......... INVG Mortgage Securities Corp. [*NASDAQ symbol*] (COMM)
InvGrMu.......... Investment Grade Municipal Income Fund [*Associated Press*] (SAG)
INVH.......... Integrated Night Vision Helmet (SAUS)
INVI.......... Integral Vision [*NASDAQ symbol*] (SG)
INVI.......... Invitro International [*Formerly, Ropak Laboratories*] [*NASDAQ symbol*] (SPSG)
InVi.......... Vincennes and Knox County Public Libraries, Vincennes, IN [*Library symbol*] [*Library of Congress*] (LCLS)
inv ins.......... Inverted Insertion (STED)
InvIns.......... Investors Insurance Group [*Associated Press*] (SAG)
INVIS.......... Integrated Night Vision System (SAUS)
Invis.......... Invisible (SAUS)
InViSC.......... Vincennes Sun Commercial, Vincennes, IN [*Library symbol*] [*Library of Congress*] (LCLS)
InVision.......... InVision Technologies, Inc. [*Associated Press*] (SAG)
INVIT.......... Invitation (KSC)
Invitr.......... Invitro International [*Associated Press*] (SAG)
INVITRO.......... HERL-RTP In Vitro System (SAUS)
In Vitro Toxicol... In Vitro Toxicology [*A publication*] (PABS)
InViU.......... Vincennes University, Vincennes, IN [*Library symbol*] [*Library of Congress*] (LCLS)
InViU-Hi.......... Vincennes University, Byron R. Lewis Historical Collections Library, Vincennes, IN [*Library symbol*] [*Library of Congress*] (LCLS)
Invivo.......... Invivo Corp. [*Associated Press*] (SAG)
INVL.......... Involute (VLIE)
INVLT.......... Involute
INVLV.......... Inventory Level (SAUS)
INV MAN CHANGE... Inverter Manual Changeover (SAUS)
INV MGT.......... Inventory Management (MCD)
INVN.......... Intervention (VLIE)
INVN.......... Inventory (MSA)
INVN.......... InVision Technologies, Inc. [*NASDAQ symbol*] (SAG)
INVN.......... Invitron Corp. (SAUO)
InVnCR.......... Jennings County Recorder's Office, Vernon, IN [*Library symbol*] [*Library of Congress*] (LCLS)
INVNR.......... Invoice Number (SAUS)
INV OBJ.......... Investment Objective (SAUS)
INVOF.......... in the Vicinity of (SAUS)
INVOG.......... Information Officers Working in Voluntary Organisations (AIE)
invol.......... Involuntary (STED)
INVOL.......... Involuntary
invol.......... involute (SAUS)
INVOLEX.......... Involuntary Extension
INVOLV.......... Involve [*Coat*] [*Pharmacy*]
involv.......... Involvement (STED)
INVOS.......... In Vivo Optical Spectroscopy (SAUS)
INVPX.......... IDS Equity Select Cl.A [*Mutual fund ticker symbol*] (SG)
INVR.......... Innovir Laboratories [*NASDAQ symbol*] (TTSB)
INVR.......... Innovir Laboratories, Inc. [*NASDAQ symbol*] (SAG)
INVREC.......... Inventory Record (MCD)
Inv Reg Cas... Notes of Decisions of Appeal Court of Registration at Inverness [*1835-53*] [*Scotland*] [*A publication*] (DLA)
Inv Rhet.......... De Inventione Rhetorica [*of Cicero*] [*Classical studies*] (OCD)
INVRN.......... Inversion [*NWS*] (FAAC)
INVRW.......... Innovir Laboratories Wrrt'A' [*NASDAQ symbol*] (TTSB)
INVRZ.......... Innovir Laboratories Wrrt'B' [*NASDAQ symbol*] (TTSB)
InVS.......... Institut de Veille Sanitaire. National Institute for Public Health Surveillance (SAUO)
INVS.......... Inverse (MSA)
INVS.......... Investors Savings Corp. (Minnesota) [*NASDAQ symbol*] (COMM)
INVSL.......... Indian National Veterinary Science (SAUO)
INVST.......... Invest
INVSTAR.......... Investigate and Report (FAAC)
INVSTD.......... Invested
INVSTGN.......... Investigation (SAUS)
INVSTGTN.......... Investigation
INVSTGTV.......... Investigative
INVSTMNT.......... Investment
INVSTR.......... Investigator
INVT.......... Incorp, Inc. (SAUO)
INVT.......... Invenit [*He, or She, Designed It*] [*Latin*] (ROG)
INVT.......... Inventory (AABC)
INVT.......... Invert (MSA)
INVT.......... Investext [*Business Research Corp.*]
Invt.......... Investment (SAUS)
InvTech.......... Investment Technology Group [*Associated Press*] (SAG)
InvTitl.......... Investors Title Insurance Co. [*Associated Press*] (SAG)

Invtn .... Invitation (SAUS)
INVTNL .... Invitational
INVTR .... Inverter
invtrx .... inventrix (SAUS)
INVTY .... Inventory
INVV .... Inverse Voltage [*Electronics*] (IAA)
INV V .... Inverted Vee antenna (SAUS)
INVX .... Innovex, Inc. [*NASDAQ symbol*] (NQ)
INVY .... Inventory (ROG)
INW .... Internet World
INW .... Isotropic Nuclear Weapon (ACAE)
INW .... Winslow [*Arizona*] [*Airport symbol*] (OAG)
INW .... Winslow, AZ [*Location identifier*] [*FAA*] (FAAL)
InWab .... Wabash Carnegie Public Library, Wabash, IN [*Library symbol*] [*Library of Congress*] (LCLS)
InWabHi .... Wabash County Historical Museum, Wabash, IN [*Library symbol*] [*Library of Congress*] (LCLS)
InWabPD .... Wabash Plain Dealer, Wabash, IN [*Library symbol*] [*Library of Congress*] (LCLS)
InWak .... Wakarusa Public Library, Wakarusa, IN [*Library symbol*] [*Library of Congress*] (LCLS)
InWal .... Walkerton-Lincoln Township Public Library, Walkerton, IN [*Library symbol*] [*Library of Congress*] (LCLS)
InWalIN .... Walkerton Independent-News, Walkerton, IN [*Library symbol*] [*Library of Congress*] (LCLS)
InWan .... Wanatah Public Library, Wanatah, IN [*Library symbol*] [*Library of Congress*] (LCLS)
INWARDAM .... Islamic Network of Water Resources Development and Mangement (SAUO)
InWars .... Warsaw Public Library, Warsaw, IN [*Library symbol*] [*Library of Congress*] (LCLS)
InWarsR .... Kosciusko County Recorder's Office, Warsaw, IN [*Library symbol*] [*Library of Congress*] (LCLS)
InWarsTU .... Warsaw Times-Union, Warsaw, IN [*Library symbol*] [*Library of Congress*] (LCLS)
InWas .... Carnegie Public Library, Washington, IN [*Library symbol*] [*Library of Congress*] (LCLS)
INWAS .... Inertial Navigation and Weapons Attack System (MCD)
InWasTH .... Washington Times-Herald, Washington, IN [*Library symbol*] [*Library of Congress*] (LCLS)
InWat .... Waterloo-Grant Township Public Library, Waterloo, IN [*Library symbol*] [*Library of Congress*] (LCLS)
INWATE .... Integrating Waveguide Technology (PDAA)
IN-WATS .... Incoming Wide-Area Telephone Service
INWATS .... Inward Wide Area Telecommunications Service (CIST)
INWATS .... Inward Wide Area Telephone Service [*Bell System*]
InWav .... Waveland Public Library, Waveland, IN [*Library symbol*] [*Library of Congress*] (LCLS)
INWD .... Inward (MSA)
InWebaC .... West Baden College, West Baden Springs, IN [*Library symbol*] [*Library of Congress*] (LCLS)
InWefG .... GTE North, Inc., Westfield, IN [*Library symbol*] [*Library of Congress*] (LCLS)
InWele .... West Lebanon Pike Township Public Library, West Lebanon, IN [*Library symbol*] [*Library of Congress*] (LCLS)
InWevP .... Purdue University, North Central Campus, Westville, IN [*Library symbol*] [*Library of Congress*] (LCLS)
INWG .... International Network Working Group [*International Federation for Information Processing*]
INWG .... Internet Working Group (SAUS)
InWh .... Whiting Public Library, Whiting, IN [*Library symbol*] [*Library of Congress*] (LCLS)
InWhC .... Calumet College, Whiting, IN [*Library symbol*] [*Library of Congress*] (LCLS)
InWhHi .... Whiting-Robertsdale Historical Society, Whiting, IN [*Library symbol*] [*Library of Congress*] (LCLS)
InWil .... Williamsport-Washington Township Public Library, Williamsport, IN [*Library symbol*] [*Library of Congress*] (LCLS)
InWilCR .... Warren County Recorder's Office, Williamsport, IN [*Library symbol*] [*Library of Congress*] (LCLS)
InWilR .... Williamsport Review-Republican, Williamsport, IN [*Library symbol*] [*Library of Congress*] (LCLS)
InWina .... Pulaski County Public Library, Winamac, IN [*Library symbol*] [*Library of Congress*] (LCLS)
InWincCR .... Randolph County Recorder's Office, Winchester, IN [*Library symbol*] [*Library of Congress*] (LCLS)
InWinFM .... Free Methodist Historical Center, Winona Lake, IN [*Library symbol*] [*Library of Congress*] (LCLS)
InWinG .... Grace College, Winona Lake, IN [*Library symbol*] [*Library of Congress*] (LCLS)
INWL .... International Network of Women Liberals (EAIO)
INWN .... International Systems & Technology (SAUS)
INWO .... International Association for a Natural Economic Order (SAUO)
InWo .... Worthington Jefferson Township Public Library, Worthington, IN [*Library symbol*] [*Library of Congress*] (LCLS)
InWol .... Wolcott Public Library, Wolcott, IN [*Library symbol*] [*Library of Congress*] (LCLS)
InWolE .... New Wolcott Enterprise, Wolcott, IN [*Library symbol*] [*Library of Congress*] (LCLS)
InWoT .... Worthington Times, Worthington, IN [*Library symbol*] [*Library of Congress*] (LCLS)
INWR .... Imperial National Wildlife Refuge (SAUO)
INWR .... Iroquois National Wildlife Refuge (SAUO)
INWS .... Inertial Navigation and Weapon System (SAUS)
INWS .... Interservice Nuclear Weapons School (SAUO)
INX .... Illinois Northern Railway [*Federal Railroad Administration identification code*]
INX .... Inanwatan [*West Irian, Indonesia*] [*Airport symbol*] (AD)
INX .... Index Character [*Computer science*]
INX .... Inexco Oil Co. [*Toronto Stock Exchange symbol*]
INX .... Information Exchange (SAUO)
INX .... Ion Exchange (NRCH)
INXLTR .... Input Translator [*IBM Corp.*] [*Computer science*] (MSA)
INXS .... Internet Exchange Service (SAUO)
INXS .... Internet Exchange System (SAUO)
INY .... Batesville, AR [*Location identifier*] [*FAA*] (FAAL)
INY .... Ithaca [*New York*] [*Seismograph station code, US Geological Survey*] (SEIS)
iny .... square inch (SAUS)
iny/trgr .... square inch per troy grain (SAUS)
INZ .... In Salah [*Algeria*] [*Airport symbol*] (OAG)
INZ .... Istituto Nazionale ADS [*NYSE symbol*] (TTSB)
INZ .... Istituto Nazionale Delle Assicorazione SPA [*NYSE symbol*] (SAG)
INZP .... Index to New Zealand Periodicals (SAUS)
InZSM .... Sullivan Museum, Zionsville, IN [*Library symbol*] [*Library of Congress*] (LCLS)
IO .... Air Paris [*ICAO designator*] (AD)
IO .... British Indian Ocean Territory [*ANSI two-letter standard code*] (CNC)
IO .... Chagos Islands (SAUS)
IO .... Icendiary Oil (SAUS)
IO .... Ice Plow (SAUS)
IO .... Identification Officer (SAUO)
IO .... Illegal Operation (SAUS)
IO .... Illuminator Operator (SAUS)
IO .... Image Orthicon
IO .... Immediate Office (COE)
IO .... Immediate Order (VLIE)
IO .... Imperial Oil (SAUO)
i/o .... in and/or over (SAUS)
I/O .... In and Out (STED)
I/O .... Inboard-Outboard [*Boating*]
IO .... Incendiary Oil (SAUS)
IO .... Incisal Opening [*Medicine*] (MAE)
IO .... Incoming Orders
IO .... Indexing Operation (SAUS)
IO .... Index Operator (SAUS)
IO .... Indian Ocean
IO .... Indian Ocean Region [*Communications term*] (DCT)
IO .... India Office [*British*]
io .... Indonesia [*pt (Portuguese Timor) used in records cataloged before January 1978*] [*MARC country of publication code*] [*Library of Congress*] (LCCP)
IO .... Industrial Operations (MCD)
I/O .... Industry/Occupation (OICC)
IO .... Industry Outstanding (SAUO)
IO .... Infant Orphan [*British*] (ROG)
IO .... Infantry Officer [*British military*] (DMA)
IO .... Inferior Oblique [*Muscle*] [*Anatomy*]
IO .... Inferior Olive [*Neuroanatomy*]
IO .... Information Objectives (COE)
IO .... Information Officer
IO .... Information Operation [*Military*] (RDA)
IO .... Information Organization (SAUS)
IO .... Information Overload
IO .... Initial Only (CARL)
IO .... Initial Opening [*Pressure*] [*Measurement*] (DAVI)
IO .... Initial Order (SAUS)
IO .... Injection Opportunity (ACAE)
IO .... Injector Orifice
i/o .... in/or (SAUS)
IO .... In Order
I/O .... In/Out (SAUS)
I/O .... In-Port Operations [*USCG*] (TAG)
I/O .... Input/Output [*Computer science*]
IO .... Input/Output Inc. [*NYSE symbol*] (TTSB)
IO .... Insh Office (SAUS)
IO .... Inside-Out [*Vesicle*] (DB)
I/O .... Inspecting Order (SAUS)
IO .... Inspection Opening (ADA)
IO .... Inspection Order (NATG)
IO .... Inspection Outline
i/o .... instead of (SAUS)
IO .... Institute for Oceanography [*Environmental Science Services Administration*]
IO .... Institute of Ophthalmic Opticians (SAUO)
I/O .... Instructor/Operator
I/O .... Intake and Output (STED)
IO .... Intake Opens [*Valve position*]
IO .... Integrated Optics (SAUS)
IO .... Intelligence Office [*or Officer*]
IO .... Intelligence Oversight (DOMA)
IO .... Intensive Observation (STED)
IO .... Interest Only [*Finance*]
IO .... Interest Only Strip [*Mortgage security*]
IO .... Interior Orientation (SAUS)
IO .... Intermediary Organization [*Physiology*]
IO .... Internal Os [*or Orifice*] [*Medicine*] (DAVI)
IO .... International Octal (IAA)
IO .... International Organizations [*A publication*]
IO .... Interpersonal Orientation (BARN)

IO ... Interpreter Officer [*Military*] [*British*]
IO ... Interpretive Operation
IO ... Intestinal Obstruction [*Medicine*]
IO ... Intraocular
IO ... Inventory Objective
IO ... Inverted Original (SAUS)
IO ... Investigating Officer
IO ... Inward Operator (VLIE)
io ... Iodo [*As substituent on nucleoside*] [*Biochemistry*]
IO ... Ion Engine (AAG)
Io ... Ionium [*Th^{230}, radioactive isotope of thorium*]
IO ... Iowa
IO ... Irish Office
IO ... Iron Overload [*Medicine*]
IO ... Issue Order (SAUO)
IO ... Issuing Office
IO ... Iterative Operation
IO ... Inspecting Officer (ODA)
IO3C ... International Ozone Commission (SAUO)
IOA ... Illinois Optometric Association (SRA)
IOA ... Imaging Optics Assembly (MCD)
IOA ... Independent Operational Assessment (SAUO)
IOA ... Indiana Optometric Association (SRA)
IOA ... Indian Ocean Area (MCD)
IOA ... Indian Ocean Arts Association [*Australia*]
IOA ... Indian Overseas Airways
IOA ... Inflammatory Osteoarthritis [*Medicine*]
IOA ... Initial Outfitting Allowance [*Navy*]
IOA ... Inner Optic Anlage (STED)
IOA ... Input-Output Adapter [*Computer science*] (NASA)
IOA ... Input-Output Address [*Computer science*] (KSC)
IOA ... Input-Output Analysis [*Economics*]
IOA ... Input/Output Area (SAUS)
IOA ... Input-Output Assembly [*Computer science*] (MCD)
IOA ... Input/Output Attachment (SAUS)
IOA ... Input/Output or Assembly [*Aerospace*] (NAKS)
IOA ... Institute of Acoustics [*British*] (DBA)
IOA ... Institute of Actuaries (SAUO)
IoA ... Institute of Administration [*University of New South Wales*] [*Australia*]
IOA ... Institute of Arbitrators (SAUO)
IoA ... Institute of Astronomy (SAUO)
IOA ... Institute of Outdoor Advertising [*New York, NY*] (EA)
IOA ... Institute on Aging [*Portland State University*] [*Research center*] (RCD)
IOA ... Institute on Aging [*University of Wisconsin - Madison*] [*Research center*] (RCD)
IOA ... Institutional Overlay zone (SAUS)
IOA ... Instrument Operating Assembly
IOA ... Intelligence Oversight Act (SAUS)
IOA ... Interfaith Office on Accompaniment (EA)
IOA ... International Office for Audiophonology (EA)
IOA ... International Olympic Academy
IOA ... International Omega Association (EA)
IOA ... International Order of the Armadillo (EA)
IOA ... International Orthoptic Association [*British*] (EAIO)
IOA ... International Osteopathic Association (EA)
IOA ... International Ostomy Association (SAUO)
IOA ... International Ozone Association (EA)
IOA ... International Police Association (SAUO)
IOA ... Interocular Asynchrony [*Ophthalmology*]
IOA ... Intraoperative Autotransfusion [*Medicine*]
IOA ... I/O Adapter (SAUS)
IOA ... Ioannina [*Greece*] [*Airport symbol*] (OAG)
IOA ... Iona Industries, Inc. [*Vancouver Stock Exchange symbol*]
IOA ... Iowa Airways, Inc. [*ICAO designator*] (FAAC)
IOA ... Irish Orienteering Association (EAIO)
IOa ... Oak Park Public Library, Oak Park, IL [*Library symbol*] [*Library of Congress*] (LCLS)
IOAA ... Immediate Office of Assistant Administrator (COE)
IOAA ... Independent Offices Appropriation Act of 1952 (COE)
IOAA ... International Operating Authority Agreement (SAUO)
IOAC ... Infantry Officer Advanced Course [*Army*] (INF)
IOAC/RC ... Infantry Officer Advanced Correspondence Course/Reserve Component (INF)
IOa-D ... Oak Park Public Library, Dole Branch, Oak Park, IL [*Library symbol*] [*Library of Congress*] (LCLS)
IOAE ... Institution of Automobile Engineers (SAUO)
IOaHS ... Oak Park-River Forest High School, Oak Park, IL [*Library symbol*] [*Library of Congress*] (LCLS)
IOakSD ... Oakland Unit School District, Oakland, IL [*Library symbol*] [*Library of Congress*] (LCLS)
IOAL ... Intraoperative Abdominal Lavage [*Medicine*] (MELL)
IOA Line ... Input/Output Address Line (SAUS)
IOAM ... Institute of Appliance Manufacturers (SAUO)
IOa-M ... Oak Park Public Library, Maze Branch, Oak Park, IL [*Library symbol*] [*Library of Congress*] (LCLS)
IOAN ... Inspect [*and Repair*] Only as Needed [*MTMC*] (TAG)
IOAN ... P.P. Shirshov Institute of Oceanology, Academy of Sciences, Moscow (SAUS)
IO&SHA ... Interim Operating & Support Hazard Analysis (SAUO)
IOAP ... Internally-Oxidized Alloy Powder (SAUS)
IOAP ... International Office for Audiophonology (SAUO)
IOA-PAGB ... International Ozone Association-Pan American Group Branch (NTPA)
IOAR ... International Organization for Aid to Revolutionaries (SAUO)
IOAS ... Input/Output Attachment Services (SAUS)
IOAS ... International Organic Accreditation Service (SAUO)
IOAT ... International Organization Against Trachoma [*Creteil, France*] (EA)
IOAU ... Input/Output Access Unit [*Computer science*]
IOAU ... Input/Output Arithmetic Unit [*Computer science*] (IAA)
IOaWH ... West Suburban Hospital, Oak Park, IL [*Library symbol*] [*Library of Congress*] (LCLS)
IOB ... Briar Cliff College, Sioux City, IA [*OCLC symbol*] (OCLC)
IOB ... Implantation of Blastocyst [*Medicine*] (MELL)
IOB ... Industrial Order of Battle (MCD)
IOB ... Information Officer, Basic [*DoD Information School*] (DNAB)
IOB ... Input/Output Block [*Computer science*] (CMD)
IOB ... Input/Output Board (SAUS)
IOB ... Input-Output Box [*Computer science*] (MCD)
IOB ... Input-Output Buffer [*Computer science*]
I/OB ... Input/Output Bus [*Computer science*] (NASA)
IOB ... Installation Operation Budget (AABC)
IOB ... Institute of Bankers [*Later, CIB*] [*British*] (EAIO)
IOB ... Institute of Biology (GVA)
IOB ... Institute of Brewing [*Also, IB*] [*British*]
IOB ... Institute of Builders (SAUO)
IOB ... Institute of Building [*or Builders*] [*British*]
IOB ... Insurance Ombudsman Bureau (PDAA)
IOB ... Intelligence Oversight Board [*Federal government*]
IOB ... Internal Operating Budget
IOB ... Interorganization Board (SAUS)
IOB ... Inter-Organization Board for Information Systems [*United Nations*] (IID)
IOB ... Inter-Organization Board for Information Systems and Related Activities (NITA)
IOB ... Iron Ore Beneficiation (COE)
IOB ... Institute of Bookkeepers (ODA)
IOBB ... Independent Order of B'nai B'rith [*Later, BBI*]
IOBB ... International Organization of Biotechnology and Bioengineering [*Guatemala, Guatemala*]
IObC ... Chicago Bridge & Iron Co., Oak Brook, IL [*Library symbol*] [*Library of Congress*] (LCLS)
IOBC ... Indian Ocean Biological Center (or Centre) (SAUS)
IOBC ... Infantry Officer Basic Course [*Army*]
IOBC ... International Organization for Biological Control of Noxious Animals and Plants [*See also OILB*] [*ICSU*] [*Montpellier, France*] [*Research center*] (EAIO)
IOBC-RC ... Infantry Officer Basic Course-Reserve Component (INF)
IOBFR ... Input/Output Buffer (NITA)
IOBI ... Institute of Bankers in Ireland (SAUO)
IOBK ... Institute of Book-Keepers (SAUO)
IOBM ... In Ocean By Mistake (SAUS)
IOBP ... International Organization of PLant Biosystematists (SAUO)
IOBPS ... Input-Output Box and Peripheral Simulator [*Computer science*] (MCD)
IOBS ... Input/Output Buffering System [*Computer science*]
IOBS ... Input/Output Buffer Store (SAUS)
IOBS ... Institute of Bankers in Scotland (DI)
IObSE ... Swift-Eckrich, Research and Development Information Center Library, Oak Brook, IL [*Library symbol*] [*Library of Congress*] (LCLS)
IObT ... Bethany and Northern Baptist Theological Seminaries Library, Oak Brook, IL [*Library symbol*] [*Library of Congress*] (LCLS)
IOBUS ... Input/Output Bus (SAUS)
IOBYTE ... Input/output Byte (SAUS)
IOC ... Clarke College, Dubuque, IA [*OCLC symbol*] (OCLC)
IOC ... Identity of Carrier (SAUS)
IOC ... Illegal Operation Code (SAUS)
IOC ... Image Orthicon Camera
IOC ... Image Orthicon Control
IOC ... Immediate-or-Cancel Order [*Stock exchange term*]
IOC ... Imperial Opera Company (SAUO)
IOC ... Imperial Owners Club, International (EA)
IOC ... Improved Operational Capability (SAUS)
IOC ... Inception of Contract (SAUS)
IOC ... Inclusive OR Circuit (SAUS)
IOC ... Index of Components (SAUS)
IOC ... Index of Cooperation
IOC ... Indian Ocean Commission [*Port Louis, Mauritius*] (EAIO)
IOC ... Indian Oil Corporation (SAUO)
ioc ... Indirect Operating Costs (NAKS)
IOC ... Indirect Operating Costs
IOC ... Industrial Operations Command [*Army*]
IOC ... Initial Operating Capability
ioc ... Initial Operational Capability (NAKS)
IOC ... Initial Operational Capability [*Military*]
IOC ... Initial Operational Capable [*Military*]
IOC ... Initial Operational Capacity
IOC ... Initial Operational Clearance (SAUS)
IOC ... Initial Operation Capability (SAUO)
IOC ... Initial Orbital Configuration (MCD)
IOC ... Initial Orbiting Capability (SAUS)
IOC ... Initial Order Condition (MCD)
IOC ... In-Orbit Checkout and Calibration (SAUS)
IOC ... Inorganic Chemical [*Environmental science*]
IOC ... In Our Culture
IOC ... In-Out Converter
IOC ... Input Offset Current
IOC ... Input/Output Cell (SAUS)
IOC ... Input-Output Channel [*Computer science*] (DIT)
IOC ... Input/Output Cluster (SAUS)
IOC ... Input/Output Code (SAUS)

IOC.......... Input-Output Comparator [*Computer science*]
IOC.......... Input/Output Computer (SAUS)
IOC.......... Input/Output Connector (NITA)
I/OC.......... Input/Output Console [*Computer science*] (CAAL)
IOC.......... Input/Output Control (NITA)
IOC.......... Input-Output Controller [*Computer science*]
ioc.......... Input/Output Controller (NAKS)
IOC.......... Input/Output Controlling (SAUS)
IOC.......... Input-Output Converter [*Computer science*]
IOC.......... Installation and Operational Checkout
IOC.......... Instant Oil Change
IOC.......... Institute of Carpenters [*British*] (DBA)
IOC.......... Institute of Chemistry [*British*] (DAS)
IOC.......... Institute of Commerce [*British*] (DBA)
IOC.......... Institutes for Oceanography [*Marine science*] (MSC)
IOC.......... Integrated Operating Capability (SAUS)
IOC.......... Integrated Optical Circuit [*or Component*]
IOC.......... Integrated Optimization Control [*Engineering*]
IOC.......... Integrated Optoelectronic Circuit
IOC.......... Intelligence Operations Center [*Air Force*] (DOMA)
IOC.......... INTELSAT Operations Center
IOC.......... Interactive Operator Control (SAUS)
IOC.......... Intercept Operations Center (SAUS)
IOC.......... Interceptor Operations Centre (SAUS)
IOC.......... Intergovernmental Oceanographic Commission [*See also COI*] [*ICSU*] [*Paris, France*] (EAIO)
IOC.......... Intergovernmental Oceanographic Council (SAUO)
IOC.......... Interim Operational Capability
IOC.......... Internationaal Ontmoetings Centrum [*International Network for Self-Reliance - INS*] (EA)
IOC.......... International Oceanographic Commission [*NASA*]
IOC.......... International Oceanographic Committee (SAUS)
IOC.......... International Office of Chemistry (SAUO)
IOC.......... International Officers Club (SAUO)
IOC.......... International Oil Company (SAUO)
IOC.......... International Olympic Committee
IOC.......... International Operating Center (SAUO)
IOC.......... International Operating (or Operation) Center (SAUS)
IOC.......... International Opium Commission (SAUO)
IOC.......... International Opthalmology Clinics [*Journal*] [*Medicine*] (EDAA)
IOC.......... International Organization Committee (SAUS)
IOC.......... International Organizing Committee of World Mining Conferences (SAUO)
IOC.......... International Ornithological Congress [*New Zealand*]
IOC.......... International Ozone Commission [*IAMAP*] (NOAA)
IOC.......... Intern on Call (HGAA)
IOC.......... Inter-Office Channel [*Telecommunications*] (TSSD)
IOC.......... Inter-Office Communication (SAUS)
IOC.......... Interoffice Correspondence
IOC.......... Interpretive Object Code (ACAE)
IOC.......... Interstate Oil Compact
IOC.......... Intraoperative Cholangiogram [*Radiology*] (DAVI)
IOC.......... Iron Ore Co. of Canada Ltd.
IOC.......... ISDN [*Integrated Services Digital Network*] Ordering Code (PCM)
IOC.......... Item on Change (SAUS)
IOC.......... Iterative Orbit Calculator
IOC.......... Kiowa, CO [*Location identifier*] [*FAA*] (FAAL)
IOC.......... Medical Commission of the International Olympic Committee (SAUO)
IOCA.......... Image Object Content Architecture (CDE)
IOCA.......... Independent Oil Compounders Association [*Later, ILMA*] (EA)
IOCA.......... Intercollegiate Outing Club Association (EA)
IOCA.......... International Organization for Civil Aviation (SAUO)
IOCA.......... Interstate Oil Compounders Association (SAUO)
IOCARIBE..... Intergovernmental Oceanographic Commission Sub-commission for the Caribbean and Adjacent Regions (SAUO)
IOCARIBE..... IOC [*Intergovernmental Oceanographic Commission*] Sub-commission for the Caribbean and Adjacent Region [*Marine science*] (OSRA)
IOCARIBE IOC... Sub-Commission for the Caribbean and Adjacent Regions (SAUS)
IOC/B & CC... Intergovernmental Oceanographic Commission - Bureau and Consultative Council [*UNESCO*]
IOC/B&CC.... Intergovernmental Oceanographic Commission-Bureau and Consultative Council (SAUO)
IOC-BSRC.... IOC Black Sea Regional Committee (SAUS)
IOCC.......... Infantry Officer Career Course [*Army*]
IOCC.......... Input/Output Channel Converter (SAUS)
IOCC.......... Input/Output Code Converter (SAUS)
IOCC.......... Input/Output Command Control (SAUS)
IOCC.......... Input-Output Control Center [*or Command*] [*Computer science*]
IOCC.......... Input/Output Control Center (or Centre) (SAUS)
IOCC.......... Input/Output Control Command (SAUS)
I/OCC.......... Input/Output Control Console [*Computer science*] (CAAL)
IOCC.......... Input/Output Controller Chip (SAUS)
IOCC.......... International Office of Cocoa and Chocolate [*Later, IOCCSC*] (EAIO)
IOCC.......... International Optical Computer Conference (SAUS)
IOCC.......... International Overseas Completion Center (SAUS)
IOCC.......... Inter-Organization Coordinating Committee (SAUO)
IOCC.......... Interstate Oil Compact Commission (EA)
IOCC Bull..... Interstate Oil Compact Commission. Bulletin [*A publication*] (DLA)
IOCCC.......... International Obfuscated C Code Contest (SAUO)
IOCCC.......... International Office of Cocoa, Chocolate, and Sugar Confectionary [*Belgium*] (EAIO)
IOCCG.......... International Ocean Color Coordination Group (SAUO)
IOC Clause... Identity of Carrier Clause (SAUS)
IOCCSC.......... International Office of Cocoa, Chocolate and Sugar Confectionary (SAUO)
IOCD.......... Initial Operation Capability Date [*Military*] (AABC)
IOCD.......... Input Output under Count Control and Disconnect [*Computer science*] (SAA)
IOCD.......... International Organization for Chemical Sciences in Development [*Brussels, Belgium*] (EA)
IOCDS.......... Input/Output Configuration Data Set (SAUS)
I/OCE.......... Input/Output Control Element [*Computer science*] (MCD)
IOCEA.......... Intergovernmental Oceanographic Commission Regional Committee for the Central Eastern Atlantic (SAUO)
IOCEA.......... IOC Regional Committee for the Central Eastern Atlantic (SAUS)
IOC/EC.......... Intergovernmental Oceanographic Commission/Executive Council (MSC)
IOCF.......... International Oil Compensation Fund
IOC-FDTE..... Initial Operational Capability - Force Development Testing and Experimentation
IOCG.......... Industrial Oil Consumers Group (EA)
IOCG.......... International Organization of Crystal Growth (SAUO)
IOCG.......... Intraoperative Cholecystogram [*Radiology*] (DAVI)
IOCHC.......... International Organization for Cooperation in Health Care [*See also MMI*] [*Nijmegen, Netherlands*] (EAIO)
IOCHS.......... International Organization for Cultivating Human Spirit [*Later, OISCA*]
IOCI.......... Imperial Order of the Crown of India [*British*] (ROG)
IOCI.......... Interstate Organized Crime Index [*Computer databank*]
IOCINCWIO... IOC Regional Committee for the Cooperative Investigation in the North and Central Western Indian Ocean (SAUS)
IOCINDIO..... Intergovernmental Oceanographic Commission Regional Committee for the Central Indian Ocean (SAUO)
IOCINDIO..... IOC Regional Committee for the Central Indian Ocean (SAUS)
IOC-IODE..... IOC Committee on International Oceanographic Data and Information Exchange (SAUS)
IOC-LOS....... Intersessional Working Group on IOCs Possible Role in Relation to the United Nations Convention on the Law of the Sea (SAUS)
IOCLP.......... International Organization for Consultation-Liaison Psychiatry (SAUO)
IOCM.......... Input/Output Control Module (SAUS)
IOCM.......... Interim Operational Contamination Monitor (SAUS)
IOC-MRI....... Office of the Intergovernmental Oceanographic Commission and Marine Science Related Issues (SAUS)
IOCO.......... Industry-Owned Contractor Operator (SAUS)
IOCOM.......... India-Malaysia Submarine Cable (SAUS)
IOC-OPC....... IOC Committee on Ocean Processes and Climate (SAUS)
IOCP.......... Indian Overseas Communication Project
IOCP.......... Input/Output Configuration Program [*Computer science*] (ITCA)
IOCP.......... Input/Output Connection Panel (SAUS)
IOCP.......... Input/Output Control Procedure (SAUS)
IOCP.......... Input/Output Control Processor [*Computer science*]
IOCP.......... Input/Output Control Program [*Computer science*]
IOCP.......... Input/Output under Count Control and Proceed [*Computer science*] (IAA)
IOCR.......... Indiana & Ohio Central Railroad [*Federal Railroad Administration identification code*]
IOCR.......... Input/Output Control Routine [*Computer science*] (IAA)
IOCR.......... Intelligent Optical Character Recognition (SAUS)
IOC-RFS....... IOC Research Fellowship Scheme (SAUS)
IOCS.......... Input/Output Computer Service (IAA)
IOCS.......... Input/Output Control Service (SAUS)
IOCS.......... Input/Output Control Subroutine (SAUS)
IOCS.......... Input-Output Control System [*Computer science*]
IOCS.......... Instant Ocean Culture System
IOCS.......... Interoffice Comment Sheet (NATG)
IOCSOC....... IOC Regional Committee for the Southern Ocean (SAUS)
IOC-TEMA.... Intergovernmental Oceanographic Commission Committee for Training, Education, and Mutual Assistance in the Marine Sciences (SAUO)
IOC-TEMA.... IOC Committee for Training, Education and Mutual Assistance in the Marine Sciences (SAUO)
IOC-TF.......... IOC Trust Fund (SAUS)
IOCTL.......... Indian Ocean Conventional Target List (MCD)
IOCTL.......... Input/Output Control (SAUO)
IOCTR.......... Input/Output Controller (NITA)
IOCU.......... Input-Output Control Unit [*Computer science*]
iocu.......... Input/Output Control Unit (NAKS)
IOCU.......... International Office of Consumers Unions (SAUS)
IOCU.......... International Organization of Consumers Unions [*The Hague, Netherlands*] (EA)
IOCV.......... International Organization of Citrus Virologists (EA)
IOC/VAP....... Intergovernmental Oceanographic Commission/Voluntary Assistance Program (MSC)
IOC-VCP....... Intergovernmental Geographic Commission Voluntary Cooperation Program [*Marine science*] (OSRA)
IOCW.......... Input/Output Control Words (ACAE)
IOCWMC....... International Organizing Committee of the World Mining Congress (SAUS)
IOCyW.......... Intelligence Operation/Command and Control Warfare (SAUS)
IOD.......... Drake University, Des Moines, IA [*OCLC symbol*] (OCLC)
IOD.......... Identified Outward Dialing [*Telecommunications*] (TEL)
IOD.......... Immediate Oxygen Demand [*Marine science*] (MSC)
IOD.......... Imperial Order of the Dragon (EA)
IOD.......... Industrial Operations Division (SAUS)
IOD.......... Information Object Definition (SAUO)
IOD.......... Information on Demand, Inc. [*Information service or system*] (IID)
IOD.......... Initial Operational Date (SAUO)
IOD.......... Initial Operational Demonstration (SAUS)
IOD.......... Injured on Duty

IOD .... Input/Output Device [*Telecommunications*] (TEL)
IOD .... Input/Output Dump Program [*Computer science*] (IAA)
IOD .... Insertion of Data (SAUS)
IOD .... Institute of Directors [*British*] (DCTA)
IoD .... Institute of Directors [*British*] (ODBW)
IOD .... Institute of Diving (EA)
IOD .... Institute of Outdoor Drama (EA)
IOD .... Integrated Observation Device (MCD)
IOD .... Integrated Optical Density [*Instrumentation*]
IOD .... Intercept Opportunities Determination (ACAE)
IOD .... International Operations Division (SAUS)
IOD .... Interorbital Distance [*Ophthalmology*] (DAVI)
IOD .... Iron Overload Diseases Association (EA)
IOD .... Issue of Data
IODA .... Iron Overload Diseases Association (EA)
IODAM .... Infant of Drug-Addicted Mother (MELL)
IOD&D .... Institution of Designers and Draughtsmen (SAUO)
IODB .... Input/Output Data Buffer (SAUS)
IODBE .... Imperial Order Daughters of the British Empire (SAUO)
IODC .... In-Out Delay Counter (SAUS)
IODC .... Input-Output Data Channel [*Computer science*]
IODC .... Input/Output Define Card (SAUS)
IODC .... Input-Output Delay Counter [*Computer science*]
IODC .... Integrated Optical Disk Controller (SAUS)
IODD .... Ideal One-Dimensional Device (IAA)
IODD .... Input-Output Data Document [*Computer science*] (MCD)
IODE .... Imperial of Daughters of the Empire (SAUO)
IODE .... Imperial Order of Daughters of the Empire [*Canada*]
IODE .... Independent Order of Daughters of the Empire (SAUO)
IODE .... International Ocean Data Exchange (SAUO)
IODE .... International Oceanographic Data and Information Exchange [*Marine science*] (OSRA)
IODE .... International Oceanographic Data Exchange Working Group (SAUO)
IODHRI .... International Organization for the Defense of Human Rights in Iraq (EA)
IODM .... Infant of Diabetic Mother [*Neonatology*] (DAVI)
IODMM .... International Office of Documentation on Military Medicine (EA)
IODP .... Input/Output Digital Processor (SAUS)
IODS .... Institute of Dermatology, Singapore (SAUO)
IODS .... International Ocean Disposal Symposium (EA)
IODSTR .... Input and Output Driven Selt-Timing Repeater (PDAA)
IODT .... Input/Output Data Transfer (SAUS)
IOE .... Buena Vista College, Storm Lake, IA [*OCLC symbol*] (OCLC)
IOE .... Indian Ocean Expedition (SAUO)
IOE .... Initial Operating Experience (PIPO)
IOE .... Initial Operational Evaluation (SAUS)
IOE .... Inlet Over Exhaust [*Automotive engineering*]
IOE .... Input/Output Engine (SAUS)
IOE .... Input/Output Error (SAUS)
IOE .... Input-Output Error Log Table [*Computer science*] (MCD)
IOE .... Inspectorate of Explosives (SAUO)
IOE .... Institute for the Officialization of Esperanto
IOE .... Institute of Ecology [*Research center*] (RCD)
IOE .... Institute of Education (SAUO)
IOE .... Institute of Energy (SAUS)
IOE .... Institute of Offshore Engineering [*Heriot-Watt University*] [*Information service or system*] (IID)
IOE .... Institution of Electronics (SAUO)
IOE .... Instituto por Oficialigo de Esperanto (SAUO)
IOE .... Instrumentation Operations Engineer (MCD)
IOE .... Intake Opposite Exhaust (IAA)
IOE .... Intensity of Operational Employment [*Army*] (RDA)
IOE .... International Office of Epizootics
IOE .... International Operations Europe (SAUS)
IOE .... International Organization of Employers [*Geneva, Switzerland*]
IOE .... International Organization of Experts (EAIO)
IOE .... Irregular Outer Edge [*Army*] (ADDR)
IOEBT .... Intraoperative Electron Beam Therapy [*Medicine*] (DAVI)
IOEC .... Integrated Opto-Electronic Circuit (SAUS)
IOEC .... International Order for Ethics and Culture (SAUO)
IOEC .... International Order tor Ethics and Culture (SAUS)
IOED .... International Office of Epizootic Diseases (SAUO)
IOEH .... Institute of Occupational and Environmental Health [*See also IMTA, IMTE*]
IOEHI .... International Organization for the Education of the Hearing Impaired (SAUO)
IOEM .... Invert Oil Emulsion Mud (SAUS)
IOEMTFS .... Independent Order of Engineers and Machinists Trade and Friendly Society [*A union*] [*British*]
IO Engine ..... Ion Engine (SAUS)
IOER .... Indiana & Ohio Eastern Railroad [*Federal Railroad Administration identification code*]
IOf .... Acorn Library District, Oak Forest, IL [*Library symbol*] [*Library of Congress*] (LCLS)
IOF .... Graceland College, Lamoni, IA [*OCLC symbol*] (OCLC)
IOF .... Income Opportunities Fd 1999 [*NYSE symbol*] (TTSB)
IOF .... Income Opportunities Fund [*NYSE symbol*] (SPSG)
IOF .... Independent Order of Foresters (SAUO)
IOF .... Independent Order of Foresters International Oceanographic Foundation (SAUS)
IOF .... Indian Ordnance Factories (SAUS)
IOF .... Infraorbital Foramen [*Medicine*] (MELL)
IOF .... Infrared Optical Film
IOF .... Initial Operational Flight (MCD)
IOF .... Input/Output Front End [*Computer science*]
IOF .... Input/Output Function (SAUS)
IOF .... Institute of Fuel [*British*] (BI)
IOF .... Interactive Operations Facility [*Honeywell, Inc.*]
IOF .... Internationale Orientierungslauf Foderation [*International Orienteering Federation*] (EA)
IOF .... International Oceanographic Foundation (EA)
IOF .... International Olympic Federation (SAUO)
IOF .... International Olympic Foundation (SAUO)
IOF .... International Orienteering Federation (SAUO)
IOF .... Intraocular Fluid [*Ophthalomology*] (DAVI)
IOF .... Intraorbital Foramen [*Medicine*] (MELL)
IofA .... Inspector of Anatomy (SAUS)
IofA .... Inspector of Artillery (SAUS)
I of A .... Instructor of Artillery [*British*]
IOfa .... O'Fallon Public Library, O'Fallon, IL [*Library symbol*] [*Library of Congress*] (LCLS)
IOfaCD .... O'Fallon Community Consolidated District 90, O'Fallon, IL [*Library symbol*] [*Library of Congress*] (LCLS)
I of Arb .... Institute of Arbitrators (SAUO)
IOfaSD .... O'Fallon Township High School District 203, O'Fallon, IL [*Library symbol*] [*Library of Congress*] (LCLS)
I of B .... Institute of Bankers (SAUO)
I of B .... Institute of Biology (SAUO)
IOFB .... Intraocular Foreign Body [*Ophthalmology*]
IOFB I .... Intraocular Foreign Body (SAUS)
IOFC .... Income Over Feed Cost [*Livestock*] (OA)
IOFC .... Indian Ocean Fishery Commission [*FAO*] [*Italy*] [*United Nations*]
I of CA .... Institute of Chartered Accountants (SAUO)
IofE .... Information of Enemy (SAUS)
IOFE .... Inside-Out Flow Element [*Automotive engineering*]
IofE .... Inspectorate of Establishments (SAUS)
IofE .... Institute of Electrolysis [*British*] (DBA)
IOFEXT .... Input/Output Far End Crosstalk (SAUS)
IOfH .... Oak Forest Hospital, Oak Forest, IL [*Library symbol*] [*Library of Congress*] (LCLS)
IOFI .... International Organization of the Flavor Industry [*Geneva, Switzerland*] (EAIO)
I of L .... Institute of Linguists (SAUO)
I of M .... Institute of Medicine (SAUO)
I of M .... Instructor of Musketry [*British*]
I of M .... Isle of Man [*England*]
I of N .... Institute of Navigation (SAUO)
IOFOS .... International Organization for Forensic Odonto-Stomatology [*Formerly, International Society of Forensic Odonto-Stomatology*] (EA)
I of Q .... Institute of Quarrying (SAUO)
IofR .... Inspector of Recruiting (SAUS)
IOFS .... International Organ Festival Society (EA)
IofSA .... Inspector of Small Arms (SAUS)
IOFSG .... International Orienteering Federation, Scientific Group [*See also IOFWA*] (EAIO)
IOFSI .... Independent Order of the Free Sons of Israel [*Freemasonry*] (ROG)
IOFT .... Institution on Farm Training
IOFU .... Instruction and Operand Fetch Unit (SAUS)
I of W .... Isle of Wight
IOFWA .... Internationale Orientierungslauf Foderation, Wissenschaftliche Arbeitsgruppe [*International Orienteering Federation, Scientific Group - IOFSG*] (EAIO)
I of WR .... Isle of Wight Railway (SAUO)
IOG .... Grinnell College, Grinnell, IA [*OCLC symbol*] (OCLC)
IOG .... Innogy Hldgs. plc ADS NYSE symbol
IOG .... Input-Output Gate [*Computer science*]
IOG .... Inside Out Gimble (SAUS)
IOG .... Institute of Groundsmanship [*British*] (ITD)
IOG .... Intercollegiate Opera Group [*Defunct*] (EA)
IOg .... Oglesby Public Library, Oglesby, IL [*Library symbol*] [*Library of Congress*] (LCLS)
IOGA .... Industry-Organized Government-Approved
IOGAWV .... Independent Oil and Gas Association of West Virginia (SRA)
IOGCC .... Interstate Oil and Gas Compact Commission (NTPA)
IOgd .... Rose Library, Ogden, IL [*Library symbol*] [*Library of Congress*] (LCLS)
IOGE .... Integrated Operational Ground Equipment
IOGEN .... Input-Output Generation [*Computer science*]
IOgIV .... Illinois Valley Community College, Oglesby, IL [*Library symbol*] [*Library of Congress*] (LCLS)
IOGP .... Independent Oil and Gas Producers (COE)
IOGP .... International Outboard Grand Prix
IOgPS .... Oglesby Public Schools, Oglesby, IL [*Library symbol*] [*Library of Congress*] (LCLS)
IOGR .... International Order of the Golden Rule [*Springfield, IL*] (EA)
IOGS .... Input/Output Group Switch (SAUO)
IOGT .... Independent Order of Good Templars (SAUO)
IOGT .... International Organisation (or Organization) of Good Templars (SAUO)
IOGT .... International Organization of Good Templars [*Oslo, Norway*] (EAIO)
IOH .... Idiopathic Orthostatic Hypotension [*Medicine*]
IOH .... Indication of Hostilities [*Military*]
IOH .... Infundibulum of Hypophysis [*Medicine*] (MELL)
IOH .... Input/Output Handler (SAUS)
IOH .... Inside-Out Helmholtz
IOH .... [*The*] Institute of Heraldry [*Military*]
IOH .... Institute of Housing [*British*] (DBA)
IOH .... Intermediate Overhaul [*Indian Railway*] (TIR)
IOH .... Inventory on Hand

IOH .... Item [*or Items*] on Hand
IOH .... Luther College, Decorah, IA [*OCLC symbol*] (OCLC)
IOh .... Ohio Township Library, Ohio, IL [*Library symbol*] [*Library of Congress*] (LCLS)
IOHA .... International Occupational Health Association (LDOE)
IOHA .... International Occupational Hygiene Association [*Industrial hygiene term*] (OHS)
IOHC .... Institute of Occupational Hazard Control (SAUO)
IOHE .... Inter-American Organization for Higher Education [*See also OUI*]
IOHE .... International Organization for Human Ecology (EAIO)
IOHFI .... International Organization for Housing Finance Institutions (EA)
IOHH .... International Order of Hoo-Hoo (EA)
IOHMD .... Interim Operational Helmet Mounted Display (ACAE)
IOHO .... Improving Our Health Odds (SAUO)
IOHS .... Integrated Operational Hydrological System [*Marine science*] (MSC)
IOHS .... International Occupational Hygiene Society (SARE)
IOI .... Indication of Interest [*Business term*] (MHDW)
IOI .... Industrial Oxygen Incorporated (SAUO)
IOI .... Integrated Orthopaedics [*AMEX symbol*] (SG)
IOI .... Interest on Investment (AFIT)
IOI .... Interim Operating Instructions
IOI .... Internal Operating Instruction
IOI .... International Ocean Institute [*Valetta, Malta*] (EAIO)
IOI .... International Ombudsman Institute [*University of Alberta*] [*Edmonton, AB*] [*Research center*] (EAIO)
IOI .... International Orphans, Inc. (EA)
IOI .... International Ozone Institute [*Later, IOA*] (EA)
IOI .... Intraocular Implant [*Medicine*] (MELL)
IOI .... Intraosseous Infusion [*Medicine*] (EDAA)
IOI .... Iori Enterprises, Inc. [*Vancouver Stock Exchange symbol*]
IOI .... Iowa Wesleyan College, Mount Pleasant, IA [*OCLC symbol*] (OCLC)
IOI .... Israel Office of Information (SAUO)
IOI .... Item of Importance (SAUS)
IOI .... Item of Inspection (SAUO)
IOI .... Item of Interest (FOTI)
IOIC .... Integrated Operational Intelligence Center
IOICC .... Illinois Occupational Information Coordinating Committee (SAUS)
IOICS .... Integrated Operational Intelligence Center System [*Military*] (DNAB)
IOIE .... International Organization of Industrial Employers (SAUO)
IOIH .... Input/Output Interrupt Handler [*Computer science*]
IOIM .... Input/Output Interrupt Message (SAUS)
IOIRS .... International Online Information Retrieval Service [*Institute of Scientific and Technical Information of China*] [*Beijing*] [*Information service or system*] (IID)
IOIS .... Input/Output Interface Subsystem (SAUS)
IOIS .... Integrated Operational Intelligence System (MCD)
IOIT .... Institute of Information Technology (SAUO)
IOIUBC .... Institute of Oceanography, University of British Columbia (SAUO)
IOJ .... Institute of Journalists [*British*]
IOJ .... International Organization of Journalists [*See also OIJ*] [*Prague, Czechoslovakia*] (EAIO)
IOJ .... St. Ambrose College, Davenport, IA [*OCLC symbol*] (OCLC)
IOJD .... International Order of Job's Daughters (EA)
IOJD .... International Organization for Justice and Development (EAIO)
IOK .... Industrial and Occupational Knowledge (AIE)
IOK .... International Order of Kabbalists (EA)
IOK .... Iokea [*Papua New Guinea*] [*Airport symbol*] (OAG)
IOK .... Simpson College, Indianola, IA [*OCLC symbol*] (OCLC)
IOkCD .... West Washington County Community District 10, Okawville, IL [*Library symbol*] [*Library of Congress*] (LCLS)
IOKDS .... International Order of the King's Daughters and Sons (EA)
IOKh .... Institute of Organic Chemistry, Academy of Sciences (SAUO)
IOL .... Independent Opposition Legislators (SAUS)
IOL .... India Office Library (SAUO)
IOL .... India Office Library and Records [*British*]
IOL .... Induction of Labor [*Obstetrics*] (DMAA)
IOL .... Initial Outfitting List [*for advanced naval bases*]
IOL .... Input/Output List (SAUS)
IOL .... Input/Output Logic (SAUS)
IOL .... Instantaneous Overload
I o L .... Institute of Librarians (SAUO)
IoL .... Institute of Linguists (SAUO)
IOL .... Intermediate Objective Lens
IOL .... International Old Lacers (EA)
IOL .... Interoffice Letter (SAUS)
IOL .... Interoperability Laboratory (SAUO)
IOL .... Inter-Orbit Link (SAUS)
IOL .... Intraocular Lens [*Ophthalmology*]
IOL .... Intraocular Lens Implant (SAUS)
IOL .... Iron Overload [*Medicine*] (MELL)
IOL .... Islet of Langerhans [*Medicine*] (MELL)
IOL .... Loras College, Dubuque, IA [*OCLC symbol*] (OCLC)
IOl .... Oak Lawn Public Library, Oak Lawn, IL [*Library symbol*] [*Library of Congress*] (LCLS)
IOLA .... Input/Output Link Adapter [*Computer science*]
IOLA .... Iota, KS [*American Association of Railroads railroad junction routing code*]
IOlC .... Christ Hospital, Oak Lawn, IL [*Library symbol*] [*Library of Congress*] (LCLS)
IOLC .... Inoperable Lung Cancer (MELL)
IOLC .... Input/Output Link Control [*Computer science*]
IOLC .... Input/Output Link Controller (NITA)
IOLC .... Integrated Optical Logic Circuit
IOL/CR .... Initial Outfitting List / Complete Repair, Parts, and Tools (SAA)
IOlE .... Evangelical School of Nursing, Oak Lawn, IL [*Library symbol*] [*Library of Congress*] (LCLS)
IOLI .... International Old Lacers, Inc. (EA)
IOLI .... Intraocular Lens Implantation [*Medicine*] (MELL)
IOLIM .... International Online Information Meeting
IOLM .... International Organization for Legal Metrology
IOln .... Olney Carnegie Public Library, Olney, IL [*Library symbol*] [*Library of Congress*] (LCLS)
IOLS .... Input/Output Label System [*Computer science*] (OA)
IOLS .... Integrated Online Library Systems
IOLS .... Iterated Ordinary Least Squares [*Statistics*]
IOLS .... Vision Technologies International, Inc. (SAUO)
IOLT .... Institute of Logistics and Transport (SAUO)
IOLTA .... Interest on Lawyers' Trust Accounts
IO Ltd .... Imperial Oil Limited (SAUO)
IO Ltd .... Imperial Oil Ltd. (SAUS)
IOLV .... Independent Order Ladies of Vikings (EA)
IOM .... Illegal Operation Mode (SAUS)
IOM .... Including Other Minerals (SAUS)
IOM .... Index and Options Market (NUMA)
IOM .... Indian Order of Merit
IOM .... Inert Operational Missile (NG)
IOM .... Inferior Orbitomeatal Line [*Brain anatomy*]
IOM .... Innovator of the Month
IOM .... Input/Output Manager (SAUS)
IOM .... Input/Output-Modulation (SAUS)
IOM .... Input-Output Module [*Computer science*] (MCD)
I/OM .... Input-Output Multiplexer [*Computer science*]
I/OM .... Input/Output Multiplexor (SAUS)
IOM .... Inside Office Memo (SAUS)
IOM .... Insoluble Organic Material [*or Matter*] [*Analytical chemistry*]
IOM .... Inspector of Ordnance Machinery [*British military*] (DMA)
IOM .... Installation, Operation, and Maintenance (COE)
IOM .... Institute for Organization Management (SAUO)
IOM .... Institute of Marketing and Sales Management (SAUO)
IOM .... Institute of Materials [*British*] (EAIO)
IOM .... Institute of Meat [*British*] (DBA)
IOM .... Institute of Medicine [*National Academy of Sciences*] (EA)
IoM .... Institute of Medicine
IOM .... Institute of Metallurgists (SAUO)
IOM .... Institute of Metals [*Institution of Metallurgists - IM and Metals Society - MS*] [*Formed by a merger of*] (EAIO)
IOM .... Institute of Occupational Medicine [*British*] (IRUK)
IOM .... Institute of Office Management [*British*] (BI)
IOM .... Institute of Organization Management (SAUS)
IOM .... Institution of Metallurgists (SAUO)
IOM .... International Office for Migration (SAUO)
IOM .... International Options Market [*Australian Options Market, European Options Exchange in Amsterdam, Montreal Exchange, and Vancouver Stock Exchange*]
IOM .... International Organization for Migration (EAIO)
IOM .... International Organization for Mycoplasmology (EA)
IOM .... International Organization of Movement (SAUO)
IOM .... Interoffice Memorandum
IOM .... Iomega Corp. [*NYSE symbol*] (SG)
IOM .... Island Aviation & Travel Ltd. [*British*] [*ICAO designator*] (FAAC)
IOM .... Isle of Man [*England*] [*Airport symbol*] (OAG)
IOM .... Morningside College, Sioux City, IA [*OCLC symbol*] (OCLC)
IOM .... National Academy of Sciences Institute of Medicine (SAUO)
IOM2 .... Extended IOM (SAUS)
IOMA .... Idaho Oil Marketers Association (SRA)
IOMA .... Independent Oil Marketer's Association of New England (SRA)
IOMA .... Independent Oxygen Manufacturers Association (SAUO)
IOMA .... International Oxidative Medicine Association (SAUO)
IOMA .... International Oxygen Manufacturers Association (EA)
IOMAC .... Indian Ocean Marine Affairs Cooperation (SAUS)
IOMAC .... Organization for Indian Ocean Marine Affairs Cooperation (SAUS)
IOMACI .... Indian Ocean Marine Affairs Cooperation Conference
IOMC .... IGOSS Operations Management Committee (SAUS)
IOMC .... International Organization for Medical Cooperation
IOMCSA .... Isle of Man Civil Service Association (SAUO)
IOME .... Irgun Olej Merkas Europa (BJA)
I/O Media .... Input/Output Media (SAUS)
IOMEF .... Isle of Man Employment Federation (SAUO)
Iomega .... Iomega Corp. [*Associated Press*] (SAG)
IOMF .... Inactive-Officer Master File (DNAB)
IOMG .... Iomega Corp. [*NASDAQ symbol*] (NQ)
IOMI .... Independent Company [*Communications term*] (DCT)
I/OMI .... Integration/Operations and Maintenance Instruction [*NASA*] (NASA)
IOML .... Infraorbitomeatal Line [*Anatomy*] (DAVI)
IOMM&P .... International Organization of Masters, Mates, and Pilots
IOMMD .... International Office of Military Medicine Documentation (SAUO)
IOMMP .... International Organization of Masters, Mates, and Pilots
IOMMU .... Input/Output Memory Management Unit (SAUS)
IOMO .... Invitation of Member Only
IOMP .... Input/Output Message Processor [*Computer science*] (IAA)
IOMP .... Input/Output Microprocessor (NITA)
IOMP .... Institute of Management in Printing (SAUS)
IOMP .... International Organisation for Medical Physics (SAUS)
IOMP .... International Organization for Medical Physics (DAVI)
IOMQ .... Input/Output Manager Queue (SAUS)
IOMR .... International Offshore Multihull Rule (SAUS)
IOMR .... Isle of Man Railways (SAUO)
IOMS .... Input-Output Management System [*Computer science*] (MHDI)
IOMS .... Interim Operation Meteorological System

IOMS .... International Organization for Masoretic Studies
IOMSA .... International Oil Mill Superintendents Association (NTPA)
IOMSG .... Input/Output Message (SAUS)
IOM SPC ...... Isle of Man Steam Packet Co. (SAUS)
IOM SPC ...... Isle of Man Steam Packet Company (SAUO)
IOMSPCo ..... Isle of Man Steam Packet Company (SAUO)
IOMT .... Isomet Corp. [*NASDAQ symbol*] (NQ)
IOMTR .... International Office for Motor Trades and Repairs (SAUO)
IOMTR .... International Organization for Motor Trades and Repairs [*Rijswljk, Netherlands*] (EAIO)
IOMUX .... Input/Output Multiplexer (SAUS)
IOMVM .... International Organization of Motor Vehicle Manufacturers (EAIO)
ION .... Bionaire, Inc. [*Toronto Stock Exchange symbol*]
ION .... Biotech Electronics Ltd. [*Toronto Stock Exchange symbol*]
ION .... Coe College, Cedar Rapids, IA [*OCLC symbol*] (OCLC)
ION .... Impfondo [*Congo*] [*Airport symbol*] (OAG)
ION .... Indian Ocean Newsletter [*A publication*]
ION .... Inferior Olivary Nucleus [*Neuroanatomy*]
ION .... Infraorbital Nerve [*Medicine*] (MELL)
ION .... Input/Output Node (SAUS)
ION .... Insthmo-Optic Nucleus (SAUS)
ION .... Institute for Optimum Nutrition [*British*]
ION .... Institute of Navigation (EA)
ION .... Institute of Neuroscience [*University of Oregon*] [*Research center*] (RCD)
ION .... Institute of Neurotoxicology [*Yeshiva University*] [*Research center*] (RCD)
ION .... Institute of Nutrition (ADWA)
ION .... Integrated On-Demand Network [*Sprint program*] (GART)
ION .... Interlending OSI Network (SAUS)
ION .... International Organization of Nerds (EA)
ION .... Internetworking Over NBMA (SAUO)
ION .... Interoperability Open Network (SAUS)
ION .... Ione, WA [*Location identifier*] [*FAA*] (FAAL)
ION .... Ionic
ION .... Ionics, Inc. [*NYSE symbol*] (SPSG)
ION .... Ionosphere and Aural Phenomena Advisory Committee [*European Space Research Organization*] (IEEE)
ION .... Ischemic Optic Neuropathy [*Medicine*]
ION .... Isthmo-Optic Nucleus [*or Nuclei*] [*In midbrain of chick*]
Iona .... De Iona [*Philo*] (BJA)
IONA .... International Organization New Acropolis (SAUO)
IONA .... IONA Technologies ADR [*NASDAQ symbol*] (SG)
IOna .... Onarga Public Library, Onarga, IL [*Library symbol*] [*Library of Congress*] (LCLS)
IonaApp ...... Iona Appliances, Inc. [*Associated Press*] (SAG)
Iona C .... Iona College (GAGS)
IONCAP ...... Ionospheric Communications Analysis and Predictions Program (SAUS)
Ion Channels... Ion Channels (SAUS)
IONDDS ...... Integrated Operational Nuclear Detonation Detection System (ACAE)
IONDS .... Initial Operational Nuclear Detection System
IONDS .... Integrated Onboard Nuclear Detection System (SAUS)
IONDS .... Integrated Operational Nuclear Detonation Detection System
IONDS .... Integrated Operational NUDETS Detecting (or Detection) System (SAUS)
IONDT .... Ischemic Optic Neuropathy Decompression Trial
IONE .... Ione, CA [*American Association of Railroads railroad junction routing code*]
Ion Exch and Membranes... Ion Exchange and Membranes (journ.) (SAUS)
IONIA .... Ionia, MI [*American Association of Railroads railroad junction routing code*]
Ionic .... Ionic Fuel Technology, Inc. [*Associated Press*] (SAG)
IonicFuel ..... Ionic Fuel Technology, Inc. [*Associated Press*] (SAG)
Ionics .... Ionics, Inc. [*Associated Press*] (SAG)
Ioniz .... Ionization (SAUS)
IONKhAN ...... Institute of General and Inorganic Chemistry, Academy of Sciences (SAUO)
IONL .... Internal Organization of the Network Layer (SAUO)
IONL .... International Organization of the Network Layer (ITCA)
IonLaser ...... Ion Laser Technology [*Associated Press*] (SAG)
IonLsr .... Ion Laser Technology, Inc. [*Associated Press*] (SAG)
ION-M .... Integrated On-Line Non-Stop Manufacturing [*Safe Computing Ltd.*] [*Software package*] (NCC)
IONO .... Ionosphere (MSA)
IONPRINTEX... Cooperative Activity Ion Printing Technology (SAUO)
IONS .... Heavy Nucleii (SAUS)
IONS .... Institute of Noetic Sciences (EA)
IONS .... Institute of Oceanography Nova Scotia [*Canada*] [*Marine science*] (OSRA)
IONS .... Intraoperative Neurosonography [*Radiology*]
IONS .... Studies of the Ionization States of Solar and Galactic Cosmic Ray (SAUS)
IONT .... In Order Not to (SAUS)
ionto .... Iontophoresis [*Medicine*] (EDAA)
IOO .... ICOR Oil & Gas Co. Ltd. [*Toronto Stock Exchange symbol*]
IOO .... Idaho Operations Office [*Energy Research and Development Administration*]
IOO .... Input/Output Operation (HGAA)
IOO .... Inspecting Ordnance Officer
IOO .... Institute of Ophthalmic Opticians (SAUO)
IOO .... Northwestern College, Orange City, IA [*OCLC symbol*] (OCLC)
IOOC .... Integrated Optics and Optical Fiber Communications (MCD)
IOOC .... International Conference on Integrated Optics and Optical Fibre Communication (SAUS)
IOOC .... International Olive Oil Council [*See also COI*] [*Madrid, Spain*] (EAIO)
IOOC .... Iranian Oil Operating Companies
IOOC .... Irish Organization of Celts (SAUO)
IOOF .... Independent Order of Odd Fellows (EA)
IOOF .... International Order of Odd Fellows (SAUO)
IOOL .... International Optometric and Optical League [*British*] (EAIO)
IOOP .... Input/Output Operation [*Computer science*]
IOOSF .... Integrated Orbital Operations Simulation Facility
IOOTS .... International Organization of Old Testament Scholars
IOOW .... In Our Own Way (EA)
IOP .... Caliop [*France*] [*ICAO designator*] (FAAC)
IOP .... Central College, Pella, IA [*OCLC symbol*] (OCLC)
IOP .... Ibero-American Organization of Pilots [*See also OIP*] [*Mexico City, Mexico*] (EAIO)
IOP .... Improving Organizational Performance (IDYL)
I/OP .... Inboard/Outboard Profile (NASA)
IOP .... Increment Operations Plan (SPST)
IOP .... Indian Ocean Panel (SAUS)
IOP .... Industrial Opportunities Program (SAUS)
IOP .... Infraventral Odentophore Protractor (SAUS)
IOP .... Initial Operating Production (MCD)
IOP .... Initial Operational Period (SAUS)
IOP .... Innovation-Oriented Research Programmes (SAUS)
IOP .... In-Orbit Plane (KSC)
IOP .... In/Out Process (SAUS)
I/OP .... Input/Outboard Profile (SAUS)
IOP .... Input-Output Package [*IBM Corp.*] [*Computer science*]
IOP .... Input/Output Pool (SAUS)
IOP .... Input-Output Port [*Computer science*] (MCD)
IOP .... Input-Output Processor [*Computer science*]
IOP .... Input-Output Pulse [*Computer science*]
IOP .... Inspection Operation Procedure (MCD)
IOP .... Inspection Operations Pictorials (SAUS)
IOP .... Installation Operating Program (AABC)
IOP .... Institute of Packaging [*British*] (BI)
IOP .... Institute of Painters in Oil Colours [*British*]
IOP .... Institute of Patentees (SAUS)
IOP .... Institute of Patentees, Inc. (SAUO)
IOP .... Institute of Petroleum [*British*] (BI)
IOP .... Institute of Physics [*British*] (EAIO)
IOP .... Institute of Physisists (SAUO)
IOP .... Institute of Plumbing (EAIO)
IoP .... Institute of Plumbing (WDAA)
IoP .... Institute of Poverty (SAUO)
IoP .... Institute of Printing (SAUS)
IOP .... Institute of Printing [*British*]
IOP .... Institute of Pyramidology [*Harpenden, Hertfordshire, England*] (EA)
IOP .... Institut of Physics (SAUS)
IOP .... Integrated Obstacle Plan [*Military*]
IOP .... Integrated Operation Plan [*NASA*] (NASA)
IOP .... Integrated Optics Processor (SAUS)
IOP .... Integrated Ordnance Package (MCD)
IOP .... Intensive Observation Period [*Marine science*] (OSRA)
IOP .... Intensive Observing Period (USDC)
IOP .... Intensive Office Procedures (SAUO)
IOP .... Intensive Operational Period (ARMP)
IOP .... Intensive Operations Period (SAUS)
IOP .... Interface Operating Procedures (TELE)
IOP .... Interim Operating Procedure (NVT)
IOP .... Internal Operating Plan (SAUO)
IOP .... Internal Operating Procedure
IOP .... International Organization of Palaeobotany [*British*]
IOP .... International Organization of Psychophysiology [*See also IPO*] [*Montreal, PQ*] (EAIO)
IOP .... International Potter Distilling Corp. [*Toronto Stock Exchange symbol*] [*Vancouver Stock Exchange symbol*]
IOP .... Interoperability (SAUS)
IOP .... Inter-ORB Protocol (SAUS)
IOP .... Intraocular Power (SAUS)
IOP .... Intraocular Pressure [*Ophthalmology*]
IOP .... Ioma [*Papua New Guinea*] [*Airport symbol*] (OAG)
IOP .... I/O Processor (SAUS)
IOP .... Iranian Oil Participants Ltd.
IOP .... Irish Organization of Papists (SAUO)
iop .... Irrespective of Percentage (MARI)
IOp .... Orland Park Public Library, Orland Park, IL [*Library symbol*] [*Library of Congress*] (LCLS)
IOPA .... Independent Organ Procurement Agency [*Medicine*] (MELL)
IOPA .... International Organizations Procurement Act of 1947
IOPAB .... International Organization for Pure and Applied Biophysics
IOP&LOA ...... Independent Oil Producers and Land Owners Association (SAUO)
IOPB .... Input/Output Parameter Block (SAUS)
IOPB .... International Organization of Plant Biosystematics (SAUO)
IOPB .... International Organization of Plant Biosystematists [*St. Anne De Bellevue, PQ*] (EA)
IOPC .... Institute of Paper Conservation (EA)
IOPC .... Interagency Oil Policy Committee
IOPC .... International Oil Pollution Compensation [*In association name IOPC Fund*] [*See also FIPOL*]
IOPC Fund ... International Oil Pollution Compensation Fund (SAUO)
IOPE .... Input/Output Parity Error (SAUS)
IOPEC .... International Oil Pollution Exhibition and Conference (PDAA)
IO/PG .... Indian Ocean/Persian Gulf
IOPG .... Indian Ocean Planning Group (SAUO)
IOPG .... Input/Output Processor Group (NITA)

IOPH International Office of Public Health (SAUO)
IOPH International Office of Public Hygiene (SAUO)
IOPI International Organization for Plant Information
IOPIDDS International Organization for Plant Data Standards Group (SAUO)
IOPIISC International Organization for Plant Information Information Systems Committee (SAUO)
IOPK Independent Order of Panamanian Kangaroos (SAUO)
IOPKG Input/Output Package [*IBM Corp.*] [*Computer science*]
IOPL Instructional Objectives Preference List (AEBS)
IOPL Integrated Open Problem List (NASA)
IOPL Intermittent Operating Life (IAA)
IOPL Internal Optical Path Length (SAUS)
IOPL I/O [*Input/Output*] Privilege Level [*Computer science*]
IOP-MP Input/Output Processor for Message Buffer (SAUS)
IOPN In Operation (IAA)
IOPN International Office for the Protection of Nature (SAUO)
IOPNSG Institute of Physics Neutron Scattering Group [*Medicine*] (EDAA)
IOPO Interest-Only/Principal-Only [*Stock exchange term*]
IOPO Internal Optical Parametric Oscillator (SAUS)
IoPP Institute of Packaging Professionals (EA)
IoPP Institute of Physics Publishing (TELE)
IOPP International Oil Pollution Prevention
IOPPEC International Oil Pollution Prevention Exhibition and Conference (SAUO)
IOPS Input/Output Processing System (SAUS)
IOPS Input-Output Programming System [*Computer science*]
IOPWE International Organization of Pakistani Women Engineers (SAUS)
IOPX IOP Extension Card (SAUS)
IOPX Iowa Power & Light [*Federal Railroad Administration identification code*]
IOPX Mid-American Energy [*Private rail car owner code*]
IOPZ Indian Ocean Zone of Peace (SAUS)
IOPZ Iowa Public Service [*Federal Railroad Administration identification code*]
IOQ Input-Output Queue [*Computer science*] (IBMDP)
IOQ Installational and Operational Qualifications [*Manufacturing*]
IOQ Institute of Quarrying [*British*]
IOQ Iowa State Historical Society, Iowa City, IA [*OCLC symbol*] (OCLC)
IOQE Input-Output Queue Element [*Computer science*] (MCD)
IOR Immature Oocyte Retrieval [*Medicine*]
IOR Immediate Operational Requirement (MCD)
IOR Independent Order of Rechabites
IOR Index of Refraction (MCD)
IOR Index of Response [*Medicine*] (DMAA)
IOR Indian Ocean Rank (SAUS)
IOR Indian Ocean Region [*INTELSAT*]
IOR Indian Other Rank [*British military*] (DMA)
IOR Industrially Oriented Research (SAUS)
IOR Input/Output Read (SAUS)
IOR Input-Output Register [*SAGE*]
IOR Input/Output Routine (SAUS)
IOR Institute for Operational Research (SAUS)
IOR Institute of Operational Research (SAUO)
IOR Institute of Religion (HGEN)
IoR Institute of Roofing [*British*] (DBA)
IOR Instituto per le Opere di Religione [*Institute for Religious Works*] [*The Vatican bank*]
IOR International Ocean Racing (SAUO)
IOR International Ocean Rule (SAUS)
IOR International Offshore Rule [*Nautical term*] (NTA)
IOR International Order of Runeberg (EA)
IOR International Rectifier Co. (SAUO)
IOR Interoperability Requirement (SAUS)
IOR Interoperable Object Reference (SAUS)
IoR Investigator of Record (HVTR)
IOR Iowa Resources, Inc. (EFIS)
IOR Issue on Request [*or Requisition*]
IOR Item on Request (SAUS)
IOR Marycrest College, Davenport, IA [*OCLC symbol*] (OCLC)
IORA Intelligence Officer, Royal Artillery (SAUS)
IORB Input/Output Record Block [*Computer science*]
IORC Input-Output Read Control [*Computer science*] (MHDI)
IORCB Input/Output Record Block [*Computer science*] (VLIE)
IORD International Organization for Rural Development
IORD I/O Read Strobe pin (SAUS)
IOREG Input/Output Register (IAA)
IOREQ Input/Output Request [*Computer science*]
IORL Input Output Requirements Language [*Teledyne Braun Engineering*] (NITA)
IORLS Interactive Otorhinolaryngological Sciences (SAUO)
IORM Improved Order of Red Men
IORP Input/Output of a Record and Proceed (SAUS)
IORP Interface Operational and Recording Program (ACAE)
IORS Inflatable Occupant Restraint System
IORS Input-Output Request Subroutine [*Computer science*] (MHDI)
IORS International Orders Research Society (SAUO)
IORS Irish Operations Research Society (SAUO)
IORT Incremental Oil Revenue Tax (SAUS)
IORT Input Output of a Record and Transfer [*Computer science*] (SAA)
IORT Input-Output Remote Terminal [*Computer science*] (MHDI)
IORT Intraoperative Radiation Therapy [*Medicine*]
IORT Intraoperative Ratio (ADWA)
IOR-TOCC Technical and Operational Control Centre in the Indian Ocean Region (SAUO)
IORV Inadvertently Opened Relief Valve [*Environmental science*] (COE)
IORV Inadvertent Opening of a Safety Relief Valve [*Nuclear energy*] (NRCH)
IORX Indiana & Ohio Rail Passenger [*Federal Railroad Administration identification code*]
IORY Indiana & Ohio Railway [*Federal Railroad Administration identification code*]
IOS Davenport Public Library, Davenport, IA [*OCLC symbol*] (OCLC)
Ios De Iosepho [*Philo*] (BJA)
IOS IGOSS [*Integrated Global Ocean Station System*] Observing System [*Marine science*] (MSC)
IOS Ilheus [*Brazil*] [*Airport symbol*] (OAG)
IOS Illinois Orthopaedic Society (SAUO)
IOS Image Optical Scanner
IOS Image Orthicon System
IOS Inbound Operation Signal (SAUS)
IOS Independent Order of Svithiod (EA)
IOS Indian Ocean Ship
IOS Indian Ocean Site (SAUS)
IOS Indian Ocean Station (MCD)
IOS Initial Operational System (SAUO)
IOS Initial Operations System (ACAE)
I/O/S Inlet/Orifice/Shield (SAUS)
IOS Input-Output Selector [*Computer science*] (IEEE)
IOS Input-Output Sense [*Computer science*] (KSC)
IOS Input-Output Skip [*Computer science*]
IOS Input/Output Statement (SAUS)
IOS Input/Output Strobe (VLIE)
IOS Input/Output Subsystem (NITA)
IOS Input-Output Supervision [*Computer science*] (NASA)
IOS Input/Output Supervisor (SAUS)
IOS Input-Output Switch [*Computer science*]
IOS Input/Output Synchronizer (SAUS)
IOS Input/Output System [*General Automation*] [*Computer science*]
IOS Inspection Operation Sheet (AAG)
IOS Inspection Operation System (AAG)
IOS Inspector of Schools [*British*] (DAS)
IOS Instant On Switch (SAUS)
IOS Institute for Objectivist Studies (EA)
IOS Institute of Oceanographic Sciences [*British*] [*Research center*] (IRC)
IOS Institute of Oceanographic Services (SAUO)
IOS Institute of Ocean Sciences [*Canadian Department of Fisheries and Oceans*] [*Research center*] (RCD)
IOS Institute of Optimization and Systems Theory [*Stockholm*]
IOS Institute of Sociology (SAUO)
IOS Institute of Statisticians [*British*] (DBA)
IOS Instructor Operation Station [*Army*] (NASA)
IOS Instructor Operator Station (SAUS)
IOS Instrumentation Operation Station
IOS Instrument Operating System
IOS Insurance Officials Society (SAUO)
IOS Integrated Observation System (MCD)
IOS Integrated Office System [*JSB Computer Systems/Olivetti*] (NITA)
IOS Integrated Operation System (SAUS)
IOS Integrated Operator System [*Telecommunications*]
IOS Intelligence Operations Specialist [*Military*] (MCD)
IOS Intelligence Oversight
IOS Intelligent Optical Sensor (SAUS)
IOS Interactive Operating System [*Computer science*]
IOS Interceptor Operator Simulator (IAA)
IOS Interim Operational System
IOS Internationale Organisation fuer Sukkulentenforschung [*International Organization for Succulent Plant Study - IOS*] (EAIO)
IOS International Oculoplastic Society (NTPA)
IOS International Officer School [*Military*]
IOS International Offshore Services Ltd. (SAUO)
IOS International Oleander Society (EA)
IOS International Organization for Standardization [*Official initialism is ISO*]
IOS International Organization for Succulent Plant Study (SAUO)
IOS International Orthokeratology Society (EA)
IOS Internet Ophthalmology Society (SAUO)
IOS Internetworking Operating System (SAUS)
IOS Internetwork Operating System [*Computer science*] (IGQR)
IOS Inter-Operability Specifications (SAUO)
IOS Interorganizational Systems (SAUO)
IOS Interplanetary Scintillation (SAUS)
IOS Interplant Order Status (SAUS)
IOS Intraoperative Sonography [*Radiology*] (DAVI)
IOS Investors Overseas Services Ltd. [*Firm which sells mutual funds in foreign countries*]
IOS I/O Subsystem (SAUS)
IOS Iraqi Organization for Standardization (SAUO)
IOS Iraqui Organization for Standardization (SAUO)
IOS Isle Of Skye [*Scotland*]
IOS Isles of Scilly Skybus Ltd. [*British*] [*ICAO designator*] (FAAC)
IOS Israel Oriental Society (SAUO)
IOS Israel Oriental Studies (journ.) (SAUS)
IOs Oswego Township Library, Oswego, IL [*Library symbol*] [*Library of Congress*] (LCLS)
IOSA Input/Output Systems Association [*Defunct*] (EA)
IOSA Integrated Optical Spectrum Analyzer (CAAL)
IOSA International Oil Scouts Association (EA)
IOSA Irish Offshore Services Association (EAIO)
IOSAP Input/Output Subordinate Application Program [*Computer science*] (VLIE)

iosc .... Integrated Operations Support Center [*NASA*] (NAKS)
IOSC .... Integrated Operations Support Center [*NASA*] (NASA)
IOSC .... International Oxygen Steelmaking Congress (SAUS)
IOSCD .... International Organization for Scientific Cooperation and Development (SAUO)
IOSCO .... International Organization of Securities Commissions (SAUO)
IOSCS .... International Organization for Septuagint and Cognate Studies (EA)
IOSD .... Information and Office Systems Division [*Exxon Research and Engineering Co.*] [*Information service or system*] (IID)
IOSD .... Initial Operational Support Date (MCD)
IOSD .... International Organization Sport for Disabled (SAUS)
IOS Data Report... Institute of Oceanographic Sciences. Data Report (journ.) (SAUS)
IOSDL .... Institute of Oceanographic Sciences Deacon Laboratory [*Natural Environment Research Council*] [*British*] (IRC)
IOSEWR .... International Organization for the Study of the Endurance of Wire Ropes [*Paris, France*] (EAIO)
IOSG .... International Oncology Study Group (SAUO)
IOSGA .... Input/Output Support Gate Array [*Computer science*] (VLIE)
IOSGT .... International Organization for the Study of Group Tensions (EA)
IOSH .... Independent Order Sons of Hermann
IOSH .... Institute of Occupational Safety and Health (SAUO)
IOSH .... Institution of Occupational Safety and Health [*British*] (DBA)
IOSHD .... International Organization for the Study of Human Development [*Defunct*] (EA)
IOSI .... Independent Order Sons of Italy (SAUO)
IOSI .... International Oculoplastic Society, Inc. (EA)
IOSIM .... Input/Output Simulator [*Computer science*] (VLIE)
IOSL .... Independent Order of St. Luke [*Defunct*] (EA)
IOSM .... Independent Order of Sons of Malta
IOSN .... Indian Ocean Standard Net
IOS/OSI .... International Organization for Standardization Open Systems Interconnection Model
IOSOT .... International Organization for the Study of the Old Testament [*British*]
IOSP .... Input/Output under Signal and Proceed [*Computer science*] (IAA)
IOSR .... Input/Output Service Routine (SAUS)
IOSR .... Input/Output Support Routine (SAUS)
IOSR .... Interim Operational Safety Requirements (SAUS)
IOSS .... Indian Ocean Station Support
IOSS .... Input/Output Subsystem [*NCR Corp.*]
IOSS .... Integrated Ocean Surveillance System [*Navy*] (NG)
IOSS .... Integrated Operational Support Study (MCD)
IOSS .... Integrated Orbital Service System (SAUO)
IOSS .... Intelligence Organization Stationing Study [*Army*] (MCD)
IOSS .... Intraoperative Spinal Sonography [*Radiology*]
IOSSP .... Inter-Organization Study Section on Salaries and Prices (SAUS)
IOST .... Input/Output under Signal and Transfer [*Computer science*] (IAA)
IOST .... International Organization of Study Tours for Teachers (SAUO)
IOSTA .... Comission Internationale de l'Organisation Scientifique du Travail [*International Committee of Work Study and Labour Management in Agriculture*] (EAIO)
IOSTA .... International Committee of Work Study and Labour Management in Agriculture (SAUO)
IOSTE .... International Organisation for Science and Technology Education (AIE)
IOSTE .... International Organization of Science, Technology and Education (SAUS)
IOSTT .... International Organization of Scenographers and Theatre Technicians (SAUO)
IOSV .... Interorbital Space Vehicle (MCD)
IOSX .... Indiana & Ohio Scenic Rail [*Federal Railroad Administration identification code*]
IOSYS .... Input/Output System [*Computer science*] (VLIE)
IOT .... British Indian Ocean Territory [*ANSI three-letter standard code*] (CNC)
IOT .... Dordt College, Sioux Center, IA [*OCLC symbol*] (OCLC)
IOT .... Image Output Terminal [*Computer science*] (HGAA)
IOT .... Income Opportunity Realty [*AMEX symbol*] (SPSG)
IOT .... Income Opportunity Rlty [*AMEX symbol*] (TTSB)
IOT .... Indian Ocean Territory (SAUO)
IOT .... Individual Operation Test
IOT .... Induction Output Tube
IOT .... Information Origination/Termination Equipment [*Telecommunications*] (OTD)
IOT .... Initial Operational Test [*Army*]
IOT .... Initial Operational Training (SAUS)
IOT .... Initial Orbit Time [*Aerospace*]
IOT .... In-Orbit Test Antenna (SAUS)
IOT .... Input-Output Termination [*Computer science*]
I/OT .... Input/Output Test [*Computer science*] (NASA)
IOT .... Input-Output Transfer [*Computer science*]
IOT .... Input-Output Trap [*Computer science*] (MHDI)
IOT .... Input/Output Trunk (NITA)
IOT .... Input/Output Typewriter (SAUS)
IOT .... Inspection Operation Tag
IOT .... Institute of Operating Theatre Technicians [*British*]
IOT .... Institute of Taxation (SAUO)
IOT .... Institute of Transport (SAUO)
IOT .... Institutional Operator Training (SAUO)
IOT .... Integral Operator Trainer (SAUS)
IOT .... International Optical Telecommunications, Inc. [*Information service or system*] (IID)
IOT .... Interocular Transfer [*Ophthalmology*]
IOT .... Interoffice Trunk (IAA)
IOT .... Interoperability Test (SAUS)
IOT .... Interorganizational Transfer (AAGC)
IOT .... Intraocular Tension [*Ophthalmology*] (DAVI)
IOT .... Intraocular Transfer [*Ophthalmology*] (DAVI)
IOT .... Intraocular Tumor [*Medicine*] (MELL)
IOT .... Ipsilateral Optic Tectum [*Medicine*]
IOT .... Iron Ore Transport [*Steamship*] (MHDW)
IOt .... Reddick's Library, Ottawa, IL [*Library symbol*] [*Library of Congress*] (LCLS)
IOTA .... Inbound/Outbound Traffic Analysis [*Military*] (AABC)
IOTA .... Inbound Tourism Organisation of Australia
IOTA .... Incremental Operational Tape Adapter (SAUS)
IOTA .... Index of Technical Articles (SAUS)
IOTA .... Information Overload Testing Aid [*or Apparatus*]
IOTA .... Infrared Observer Television Analysis (SAUS)
IOTA .... Infrared-Optical Telescope Array
IOTA .... Instant Oxide Thickness Analyzer (IAA)
IOTA .... Institute of the Americas (SAUS)
IOTA .... Institute of Theoretical Astronomy [*University of Cambridge*]
IOTA .... Institute of Transport Administration [*British*] (DCTA)
IOTA .... Integrated On-Line Text Arrangement
IOTA .... Interest on Trust Accounts Program
IOTA .... International Occultation Timing Association (EA)
IOTA .... International Organization against Trachoma (SAUO)
IOTA .... Islands on the Air (SAUO)
IOTAE .... Initial Operating Test and Evaluation (IAA)
IOTA/ES .... International Occultation Timing Association-European Section (SAUO)
IOT & E .... Independent Operational Test and Evaluation [*Military*]
IOT & E .... Initial Operating Test and Evaluation (MCD)
IOT & E .... Initial Operational Test and Evaluation [*Army*] (DOMA)
IOT&E .... Initial Operation Test and Evaluation (SAUS)
IOT&E .... Initital Operating Test and Evaluation (SAUS)
IOT&E .... Installation Operational Test and Evaluation (SAUO)
IOtBD .... LaSalle County Board for Developmentally Disabled, Ottawa, IL [*Library symbol*] [*Library of Congress*] (LCLS)
IOTC .... Infantry Officers Training Camp
IOTC .... Input/Output Test Console (ACAE)
IOTC .... International Originating Toll Center [*Bell System*]
IOtCE .... LaSalle County Cooperative Extension, Ottawa, IL [*Library symbol*] [*Library of Congress*] (LCLS)
IOTCG .... International Organization for Technical Cooperation in Geology (EAIO)
IOtCH .... Community Hospital of Ottawa, Ottawa, IL [*Library symbol*] [*Library of Congress*] (LCLS)
IOtDSD .... Deer Park Consolidated Community School District 82, Ottawa, IL [*Library symbol*] [*Library of Congress*] (LCLS)
IOTE .... Individual Operator Training Equipment (MCD)
IOTE .... Initial Operational Test and Evaluation [*Army*]
IOTE .... Initial Outfitting Technical Evaluation (MCD)
IOTE .... Instant Oxide Thickness Evaluation (SAUS)
IOTECH .... Iotech Incorporated (SAUO)
IOTEP .... Initial Operating Test and Evaluation Period [*Navy*]
IOtES .... LaSalle County Educational Service Region, Ottawa, IL [*Library symbol*] [*Library of Congress*] (LCLS)
IOT/ESVA .... In-Orbit Test and Earth Station Verification and Assistance (ACAE)
IOtF .... Friendship Facilities, Ottawa, IL [*Library symbol*] [*Library of Congress*] (LCLS)
IOTF .... International Obesity Task Force
IOTG .... Input/Output Task Group [*CODASYL*]
IOTG .... Isooctyl Thioglycolate [*Organic chemistry*]
IOtGH .... Ottawa General Hospital, Ottawa, IL [*Library symbol*] [*Library of Congress*] (LCLS)
IOTHAL .... Iothalamate Sodium (SAUS)
IOTHAL MEG... Iothalamate Meglumine (SAUS)
IOtHS .... Ottawa Township High School District 140, Ottawa, IL [*Library symbol*] [*Library of Congress*] (LCLS)
IOTLV .... Inter Orbit Transfer and Logistics Vehicle (SAUS)
IOtM .... Marquette High School, Ottawa, IL [*Library symbol*] [*Library of Congress*] (LCLS)
IOTP .... International Ozone Trends Panel (SAUO)
IOTPD .... International Organization for the Transition of Professionals Dancers [*Switzerland*]
IOTR .... Intra-Ocular Tension Recorder (SAUS)
IOTR .... Intratrabecular Osteoclastic Tunneling Resorption [*Medicine*]
IOTR .... Item Operation Trouble Report (AAG)
IOtRP .... LaSalle County Regional Planning Commission, Ottawa, IL [*Library symbol*] [*Library of Congress*] (LCLS)
IOtRSD .... Rutland Consolidated Community School District 230, Ottawa, IL [*Library symbol*] [*Library of Congress*] (LCLS)
IOTs .... Indian Ocean Territories (SAUO)
IOtS .... Starved Rock Library System, Ottawa, IL [*Library symbol*] [*Library of Congress*] (LCLS)
IOTT .... Institute of Operating Theatre Technicians (SAUO)
IOTT&E .... Improved Operational Test (SAUS)
IOTT & E .... Improved Operational Test, Training, and Evaluation [*Military*]
IOTTSG .... International Oil Tanker Terminal Safety Group (PDAA)
IOTV .... Interoffice Transfer Voucher (SAUO)
IOtWSD .... Wallace Consolidated Community School District 195, Ottawa, IL [*Library symbol*] [*Library of Congress*] (LCLS)
IOU .... Industrial Operations Unit (SAUS)
IOU .... Input-Output Unit [*Computer chip*]
IOU .... Input-Output Utility [*Computer science*]
IOU .... Integrated Ornstein-Uhlenbeck motion model (SAUS)
IOU .... Intensive Care Observation Unit [*Medicine*] (DMAA)
IOU .... Intensive Therapy Observation Unit (MAE)

IOU .... Interim OPCON Update (SAUS)
IOU .... International Opacity Unit (DB)
IOU .... Investor-Owned Utilities (BARN)
IOU .... I Owe You [*Slang*]
IOU .... Public Library of Des Moines, Des Moines, IA [*OCLC symbol*] (OCLC)
IOUBC .... Institute of Oceanography, University of British Columbia
IOUBC .... International Office for Universal Bibliographic Control (TELE)
IOUG .... International Oracle Users Group (SAUO)
IOU Routine ... Input/Output Utilizer Routine (SAUS)
IOUS .... Input/Output Utility Subsystem (SAUS)
IOUs .... Investor-Owned Utilities (SAUS)
IOV .... Independent Order of Vikings [*Des Plaines, IL*] (EA)
IOV .... Initial Office Visit [*Medicine*] (DAVI)
IOV .... Initial Operating Version [*Automotive emissions*]
IOV .... Input Offset Voltage
IOV .... Inside-Out Vesicle [*Biochemistry*]
IOV .... Institute of Virology [*British*] (ARC)
IOV .... University of Dubuque, Dubuque, IA [*OCLC symbol*] (OCLC)
IOVC .... In the Overcast [*Aviation*]
IOV-CFEIS .... Initial Operating Version-Certification and Fuel Economy Information System [*Automotive emissions*]
IOVS .... Investigative Ophthalmology and Visual Science (SAUO)
IOVS .... Investigative Ophthalmology and Visual Science (journ.) (SAUS)
IOVST .... International Organization for Vacuum Science and Technology
IOV/VAP .... Intergovernmental Oceanographic Commission/Voluntary Assistance Program (SAUS)
IOW .... Inert Ordnance Warehouse
IOW .... Infected Open Wound (MELL)
IOW .... In Other Words
IOW .... Input-Output Write [*Computer science*] (MHDI)
IOW .... Inspector of Works [*Indian Railway*] (TIR)
IOW .... Iowa City, IA [*Location identifier*] [*FAA*] (FAAL)
Iow .... Iowa Reports [*A publication*] (DLA)
IOW .... Isle Of Wight
IOW .... Wartburg College, Waverly, IA [*OCLC symbol*] (OCLC)
IOWA .... Interorganizational Work Authorization (KSC)
IOWA .... Iowa Bancorporation, Inc. [*NASDAQ symbol*] (SAG)
Iowa .... Iowa Supreme Court Reports [*A publication*] (DLA)
Iowa Acts ..... Acts and Joint Resolutions of the State of Iowa [*A publication*] (DLA)
Iowa Admin Bull ... Iowa Administrative Bulletin [*A publication*] (DLA)
Iowa Admin Code ... Iowa Administrative Code [*A publication*] (DLA)
IOWA Agric Exp Stn Res Bull ... IOWA Agricultural Experiment Station Research Bulletin (SAUO)
Iowa Agric Home Econ Exp Stn Soil Surv Rep ... Iowa. Agriculture and Home Economics Experiment Station. Soil Survey Reports (journ.) (SAUS)
Iowa Bar Rev ... Iowa Bar Review [*A publication*] (DLA)
IowaBcp .... Iowa Bancorporation, Inc. [*Associated Press*] (SAG)
Iowa B Rev ... Iowa Bar Review [*A publication*] (DLA)
IOWAC .... Iowa City, IA [*American Association of Railroads railroad junction routing code*]
Iowa Code ... Code of Iowa [*A publication*] (AAGC)
IOWAF .... Iowa Falls, IA [*American Association of Railroads railroad junction routing code*]
IOWAJ .... Iowa Junction, LA [*American Association of Railroads railroad junction routing code*]
Iowa Law R ... Iowa Law Review (journ.) (SAUS)
Iowa LB .... Iowa Law Bulletin [*A publication*] (DLA)
Iowa L Bull ... Iowa Law Bulletin [*A publication*] (DLA)
Iowa Legis Serv ... Iowa Legislative Service (West) [*A publication*] (DLA)
Iowa Med .... Iowa Medicine (journ.) (SAUS)
Iowa Orthop J ... Iowa Orthopaedic Journal (journ.) (SAUS)
Iowa RC .... Iowa Railroad Commissioners Reports [*A publication*] (DLA)
Iowa SBA ..... Iowa State Bar Association. Proceedings [*A publication*] (DLA)
Iowa State Univ Vet ... Iowa State University Veterinarian (journ.) (SAUS)
Iowa St BAQ ... Iowa State Bar Association. Quarterly [*A publication*] (DLA)
Iowa St U .... Iowa State University of Science and Technology (GAGS)
Iowa Univ L Bull ... Iowa University. Law Bulletin [*A publication*] (DLA)
IOWC .... International One World Crusade (SAUO)
IOWE .... International Office for Water Education [*Utah State University*]
IOWE .... International Organization of Women Executives [*Defunct*] (EA)
IOWIT .... International Organization of Women in Telecommunications [*Defunct*] (TSSD)
IOWMC .... International Organization of Wooden Money Collectors (EA)
IOWQ .... Input-Output Wait Queue [*Computer science*] (MHDI)
IOWR .... I/O write strobe pin (SAUS)
IOWT .... International Organization of Women in Telecommunications [*Defunct*] (EA)
IOX .... Input-Output Executive [*Computer science*] (MHDI)
IOX .... Input/Output Transfer Unit (SAUS)
IOX .... Instructional Objectives Exchange (SAUS)
IOX .... Iomed, Inc. [*AMEX symbol*] (SG)
IOX .... William Penn College, Oskaloosa, IA [*OCLC symbol*] (OCLC)
IOXAG .... Ioxaglate Sodium (SAUS)
IOXAG MEG ... Ioxaglate Meglumine (SAUS)
IOY .... Iron Ore Year (SAUS)
IOY .... Upper Iowa University, Fayette, IA [*OCLC symbol*] (OCLC)
IOZ .... Internal Oxidation Zone (SAUS)
IOZ .... State Library Commission of Iowa, Des Moines, IA [*OCLC symbol*] (OCLC)
IOZP .... Indian Ocean Zone of Peace
IP .... Airlines of Tasmania [*ICAO designator*] (AD)
IP .... Cathode-Ray Tube Indicators [*JETDS nomenclature*] [*Military*] (CET)
I/P .... Current/Pneumatic [*Nuclear energy*] (NRCH)
I/P .... Current to Pressure [*Electropneumatic*] (ACII)
IP .... Defense Industrial Plant Equipment Center (SAUO)
IP .... Empresa AVIAIMPORT [*Cuba*] [*ICAO designator*] (ICDA)
IP .... Ice Particle (SAUS)
IP .... Ice Pellets (SAUS)
IP .... Ice Plow [*Coast Guard*] (DNAB)
IP .... Ice Point
IP .... Icterus Precox [*Medicine*]
IP .... Identification of Position
IP .... Identification Peculiarity
IP .... Identification Point
IP .... Identified Patient [*Medicine*] (DHP)
IP .... Identifying Perforation (SAUS)
IP .... Identity Preserved [*Wheat*] [*Department of Agriculture*]
IP .... Idiopathic Parkinsonism [*Medicine*] (MELL)
IP .... Idle Period (SAUS)
IP .... Idler Pulley
IP .... Igloo Pallet [*Spacelab*] [*NASA*] (NASA)
IP .... Igneous Petrology (SAUS)
IP .... Ignition Point [*Chemistry*] (IAA)
IP .... Iliopsoas [*Muscle*] [*Anatomy*] (DAVI)
IP .... Image Point (SAUS)
IP .... Image Previewer (DGA)
IP .... Image Process
IP .... Image Processing (SAUS)
IP .... Image Processor (ADWA)
IP .... Imagery Analysis Paper
IP .... Imaginary Part [*of a complex number*] (DEN)
IP .... Imipramine (SAUS)
IP .... Immediate Past Office
IP .... Immediate Permanent Incapacitation [*Radiation casualty criterion*] [*Army*]
IP .... Immersible Pump
IP .... Immune Precipitate [*Immunology*]
IP .... Immunoblastic Plasma [*Medicine*] (EDAA)
IP .... Immunoperoxidase (Technique) [*Clinical chemistry*]
IP .... Immunoprecipitation
IP .... Impact Point (AFM)
IP .... Impact Prediction (SAUS)
IP .... Impact Predictor [*NASA*]
IP .... Impact Printer [*Computer science*]
IP .... Impact Prognosticator [*Aerospace*] (AAG)
IP .... Impedance Probe
IP .... Imperial Preference (ADA)
IP .... Impingement Point
IP .... Implementation of Plan
IP .... Implementation Period
IP .... Implementation Procedures (SAUO)
IP .... Import Penetration
IP .... Impostor Phenomenon [*Subject of book "If I'm So Successful, Why Do I Feel Like a Fake - The Impostor Phenomenon" by Joan C. Harvey*] [*Psychology*]
IP .... Improved Performance
IP .... Improved Product (SAUS)
IP .... Improvement Program (AFM)
IP .... Improvement Purchase (ADA)
iP .... Impulse P Wave [*Earthquakes*] [*Exclamation point signifies a very sharp earthquake*]
IP .... Inactivated Pepsin [*Medicine*] (MELL)
IP .... Inbound Prepaid (SAUS)
IP .... Inca Pacific Resources [*VS, exchange symbol*] (TTSB)
IP .... Incentive Pay
IP .... Incisoproximal [*Dentistry*]
IP .... Incisopulpal [*Dentistry*]
IP .... Income Protection
IP .... Incompetent Patient (MELL)
IP .... Incontinentia Pigmenti (DB)
IP .... Incubation Period [*Medicine*]
IP .... Independence Party
IP .... Independent Pixel (CARB)
ip .... Indexed and Paged (ODA)
IP .... Index of Performance
IP .... Index of Preprogramming [*Computer science*] (PDAA)
IP .... Index of Programming (SAUS)
IP .... Index Point (SAUS)
IP .... Index Pointer (ACAE)
IP .... Index Pulse (ACAE)
IP .... Indiana Pacers
I-P .... Indian-Pacific (SAUS)
IP .... Indian Paper (SAUS)
IP .... Indian Pattern [*British military*] (DMA)
IP .... Indian Pharmacopoea
IP .... Indian Police (SAUO)
IP .... Indian Preference [*Civil Service*]
IP .... India Paper
IP .... Indicator Panel
IP .... Indigenous Peoples (SAUO)
IP .... Indirect Proof [*Method in logic*]
IP .... Indium Phosphide [*Materials science*]
IP .... Individualized Plan [*Medicine*] (EDAA)
IP .... Individual Protection (ACAE)
IP .... Indochina Project [*An association*] (EA)
IP .... Indoor Pollution (SAUS)
IP .... Induced Polarization [*Geophysical prospecting*]
IP .... Induced Protein [*Biochemistry*] (DAVI)

IP................ Induction Period [*Medicine*]
IP................ Industrial Packages (SAUS)
IP................ Industrial Park (SAUS)
IP................ Industrial Participation [*Civil Defense*]
IP................ Industrial Partnership Programs (SAUO)
IP................ Industrial Photographer (SAUS)
IP................ Industrial Photography (SAUS)
IP................ Industrial Plan (SAUO)
IP................ Industrial Planning
IP................ Industrial Plus (SARE)
IP................ Industrial Police
IP................ Industrial Policy
IP................ Industrial Production
IP................ Industrial Products (SAUS)
IP................ Industry Program [*Defense Systems Management College*] (DOMA)
IP................ Industry Protection (SAUS)
IP................ Inertial Platform
IP................ Inertial Processing (MCD)
IP................ Infection Prevention
IP................ Information Packets [*or Packages*] (GNE)
IP................ Information Paper
IP................ Information Parameter (SAUS)
IP................ Information Pool (IAA)
IP................ Information Processing (BUR)
IP................ Information Processor (SAUS)
IP................ Information Professional (SAUS)
IP................ Information Provider
IP................ Information Publication [*HUD*]
IP................ Information Publications [*Singapore, Hong Kong, Australia*]
IP................ Information Publishing
IP................ Information Pulse (SAUS)
IP................ Informations Processing (SAUS)
IP................ Infundibular Process [*Medicine*] (DMAA)
IP................ Infundibulopelvic [*Ligament*] [*Anatomy*] (DAVI)
IP................ Inhalable Particles (EEVL)
IP................ Inhalable Particulates [*Environmental science*] (COE)
IP................ Inhaled Particles [*or Particulates*] [*Environmental chemistry*]
IP................ Inhibit Pulse (SAUS)
IP................ Inhouse Publishing (IAA)
IP................ Initialization Phase (SAUS)
IP................ Initial Parameter (SAUS)
IP................ Initial Permutation (SAUS)
IP................ Initial Phase (IEEE)
IP................ Initial Phrase (SAUS)
IP................ Initial Point [*Military*]
IP................ Initial Position
IP................ Initial Post [*Military*]
IP................ Initial Pressure [*On lumbar puncture*] [*Neurosurgery*] (DAVI)
IP................ Initial Production
IP................ Initial Program (SAUS)
IP................ Initial Provisioning (MCD)
IP................ Injured Person (SAUS)
IP................ Inland Postage (IAA)
IP................ Innings Pitched [*Baseball*]
Ip................ Innings Played [*Baseball*]
IP................ Innovation Potential (SAUS)
IP................ Innovative Project
IP................ Inorganic Phosphorus (OA)
IP................ Inosine Phosphate (SAUS)
IP................ Inosine Phosphorylase [*An enzyme*] (MAE)
IP................ Inositol Phosphate (SAUS)
IP................ In Patient (SAUO)
IP................ Inpatient [*Medicine*]
IP................ In-Phase [*Gynecology*]
IP................ In Place [*Dancing*]
IP................ In Plaster [*Medicine*] (DAVI)
i p................ in primary (SAUS)
IP................ In Process
I/P................ In Progress (MCD)
I/P................ Input [*Computer science*]
IP................ Input Parameter (SAUS)
IP................ Input Port (CCCA)
IP................ Input Power [*Computer science*]
IP................ Input Primary (SAUS)
IP................ Input Procedure (SAUS)
IP................ Input Processor [*Computer science*]
IP................ Insolated Platform
IP................ Inspection Pit [*Motor garage*] (ROG)
IP................ Inspection Plan (SAUO)
IP................ Inspection Procedure [*Nuclear energy*] (NRCH)
IP................ Installation Procedure
IP................ Installment Paid [*Business term*]
IP................ Instantaneous Pressure [*Medicine*] (MAE)
IP................ Institute for Psychohistory (EA)
IP................ Institute of Packaging (SAUO)
IP................ Institute of Petroleum [*British*]
IP................ Institute of Physics [*British*] (EAIO)
IP................ Institute of Plumbing (SAUO)
IP................ Institute of Printing [*British*]
IP................ Institutional Plan (SAUO)
IP................ Instructional Psychologist (MCD)
IP................ Instruction Package (SAUS)
IP................ Instruction Pamphlet
I/P................ Instruction Permit [*Motor vehicle term used in state of Washington*] (MVRD)
IP................ Instruction Plate (MSA)
IP................ Instruction Pointer [*Computer science*]
IP................ Instruction Processor [*Computer science*]
IP................ Instructor-Patient [*Medicine*]
IP................ Instructor Pilot [*Air Force*] (AFM)
IP................ Instrumentation and Piping (SAUS)
IP................ Instrumentation Paper (SAUS)
IP................ Instrumentation Papers [*Air Force*] (MCD)
IP................ Instrumentation Payload (NASA)
IP................ Instrumentation PCM [*Power Control Mission*] [*NASA*]
IP................ Instrumentation PCM data bus (SAUS)
IP................ Instrumentation Plan (MUGU)
IP................ Instrumentation Power (MCD)
IP................ Instrumentation/Pulse Code Modulation Master Unit Data Bus (NAKS)
IP................ Instrument Panel [*Automotive engineering*]
IP................ Insular Police (SAUO)
IP................ Insulated Platform (MCD)
IP................ Insurance Patient [*Medicine*]
IP................ Insurance Payment (SAUS)
IP................ Integer Part (SAUS)
IP................ Integer Programming (SAUS)
IP................ Integrated Processor [*Computer science*]
IP................ Integrated Program (ABAC)
IP................ Intellectual Properties (or Property) (SAUS)
IP................ Intelligence Police (SAUO)
IP................ Intelligence Publications (MCD)
IP................ Intelligent Peripheral [*Computer science*] (ACRL)
IP................ Interactive Processing (IAA)
IP................ Intercept Point [*Air Force*]
IP................ Intercept Post (CARL)
IP................ Interchangeable Solid and Screen Panels [*Technical drawings*]
IP................ Interdigital Pause [*Telecommunications*] (TEL)
IP................ Interelement Protection (IAA)
IP................ Interface Principle [*Medicine*] (EDAA)
IP................ Interface Process (SAUS)
IP................ Interface Processor [*Computer science*]
IP................ Interface Program [*Computer science*] (IAA)
IP................ Interference Pattern (CAAL)
IP................ Interlocks Package [*Space launch term*] (ISAK)
IP................ Intermediate Pallet (NASA)
IP................ Intermediate Point (VLIE)
IP................ Intermediate Pressure
IP................ Intermediate Processor (SSD)
IP................ Internal Phloem [*Botany*]
IP................ Internal Pressure (SAUS)
IP................ Internal Production
IP................ Internal Protocol (SSD)
IP................ Internal Publication (SAUO)
IP................ International Ice Patrol (SAUO)
IP................ International Paper Co. [*NYSE symbol*] (SPSG)
IP................ International Partner (SAUS)
IP................ International Patrol (SAUO)
IP................ International Pharmacopoeia
IP................ International Pictures (SAUS)
IP................ International Priority (SAUO)
IP................ International Program (SAUS)
IP................ International Programming (IAA)
IP................ International Programming Ltd. (SAUS)
IP................ Internet Protocol [*Computer science*] (PCM)
IP................ Interpersonal (SAUS)
IP................ Interphalangeal [*Anatomy*]
IP................ Interplanetary
IP................ Interpool (SAUS)
IP................ Interpositive [*Photography*] (WDMC)
IP................ Inter Provider (SAUS)
IP................ Interpupillary (DB)
IP................ Interscience Publishers
IP................ Intervention Point (SAUS)
IP................ Intl Paper [*NYSE symbol*] (TTSB)
IP................ Intraperitoneal [*Medicine*] (EDAA)
IP................ Invalid Pension
IP................ Inverse Photoemission [*Spectroscopy*]
IP................ Ionic Polymer (SAUS)
IP................ Ionic Product (SAUS)
IP................ Ionization Potential
IP................ Ion-Pair [*Physical chemistry*]
IP................ Ion Plating (SAUS)
IP................ Ion Projection (SAUS)
IP................ Ion Pump (SAUS)
IP................ Ipatropium [*Pharmacology*]
IP................ Irate Parent (ADA)
IP................ Irish Party (ROG)
IP................ Iron Pipe
I/P................ Irregular Input Process [*Telecommunications*] (TEL)
IP................ Isidis Planitia [*A filamentary mark on Mars*]
IP................ Isoelectric Point [*Also, IEP, PH_1, pI*] [*Chemistry*]
IP................ Isolation Pulse
IP................ Isoproterenol [*An adrenergic*]
IP................ Israeli Pound (BJA)
IP................ Issue Paper
IP................ Issue Price [*Business term*]
IP................ Issuing Point
IP................ Italian Patent (IAA)
IP................ Item Peculiarity (SAUO)
IP................ Item Processing

IP .... Izquierda de los Pueblos [*Spain*] [*Political party*] (ECED)
IP .... Office of International Programs [*Nuclear energy*] [*National Science Foundation*] (NRCH)
IP .... Office of Technology Development Integrated Program (SAUO)
IP .... Peer of Ireland (ROG)
IP .... Peoria Public Library, Peoria, IL [*Library symbol*] [*Library of Congress*] (LCLS)
IP .... Positive Identification (ECII)
IP .... Powder Injection (SAUS)
ip .... Identification Points (ODA)
IP3 .... Intercept Point of third order (SAUS)
IPA .... Allied Agencies Center, Peoria, IL [*Library symbol*] [*Library of Congress*] (LCLS)
IPA .... Illinois Pharmaceutical Association (SAUO)
IPA .... Illinois Principals Association (SAUO)
IPA .... Image Pac Attribute (SAUS)
IPA .... Image Power Amplifier (IAA)
IPA .... Image Processing Applications [*Computer graphics*]
IPA .... Imagery Product Archive (SAUO)
IPA .... Immediate Power Amplifier (VLIE)
IPA .... Immunoperoxidase Antibody Assay [*Clinical chemistry*]
IPA .... Imperial Pale Ale
IPA .... Incapacidad Permanente Absoluta (SAUS)
IPA .... Including Particular Average [*Insurance*]
IPA .... Income Properties of America Investment Management Co. Ltd. (SAUO)
IPA .... Incontienentia Pigmenti Achromians (STED)
IPA .... Incorporeal Personal Agency [*Parapsychology*]
IPA .... Independent Petroleum Association (SAUO)
IPA .... Independent Pilots Association
IPA .... Independent Pixel Approximation (ARMP)
IPA .... Independent-Practice Association [*Medical insurance*]
IPA .... Independent Press Association
IPA .... Independent Product Assurance (SSD)
IPA .... Independent Provider Association (SAUO)
IPA .... Independent Public Accountant
IPA .... Independent Publishers' Association [*Canada*]
IPA .... Indiana Pharmaceutical Association (SAUO)
IPA .... Indian Pale Ale (SAUO)
IPA .... Indian Pharmaceutical Association (SAUO)
IPA .... India Pale Ale
IPA .... India Press Agency
IPA .... Indicated Pressure Altitude
IPA .... Individual, Partnership, and Corporation [*Deposits*] (EBF)
IPA .... Individual Practice Association [*Medicine*]
IPA .... Indolepyruvic Acid [*Biochemistry*] (DB)
IPA .... Industrial Participation Association [*British*]
IPA .... Industrial Perforators Association (EA)
IPA .... Industrial Property Administration
IPA .... Industrial Publicity Association (EA)
IPA .... Industries Perforators Association, Inc.
IPA .... Information for Public Affairs, Inc. [*Information service or system*] (IID)
IPA .... Information Planning Associates, Inc. (SAUO)
IPA .... Information Please Almanac (SAUS)
IPA .... Information Process Analysis (BUR)
IPA .... Information Processing Architecture (IAA)
IPA .... Information Processing Association [*Israel*]
IPA .... Information Processing promotion Agency (SAUO)
IPA .... Information-technology Promotion Agency [*Japan*] (NITA)
IPA .... Initial Perceptual Alphabet (SAUS)
IPA .... In-Principle Agreement
IPA .... Insolvency Practitioners Association [*British*] (EAIO)
IPA .... Institute for Physics of the Atmosphere
IPA .... Institute for Policy Analysis [*University of Toronto*] [*Canada*] (IRC)
IPA .... Institute for Polyacrylate Absorbents (EA)
IPA .... Institute of Park Administration (ODA)
IPA .... Institute of Physics of the Atmosphere (SAUO)
IPA .... Institute of Practitioners in Advertising
IPA .... Institute of Propaganda Analysis (SAUO)
IPA .... Institute of Public Administration (EA)
IPA .... Institute of Public Affairs [*Dalhousie University*] [*Canada*] [*Research center*]
IPA .... Institutional Patent Agreements [*General Services Administration*]
IPA .... Instrument Performance Assessment
IPA .... Integrated Peripheral Adapter
IPA .... Integrated Photodetection Assemblies (or Assembly) (SAUS)
IPA .... Integrated Plan of Action (MCD)
IPA .... Integrated Printer Adapter
IPA .... Integrated Publishing Architecture (GART)
IPA .... Intelligence Production Activity [*Military*] (MCD)
IPA .... Intelligence Production Agency (COE)
IPA .... Interaction-Process Analysis (DIPS)
IPA .... Interamerican Press Association
IPA .... Intergovernmental Personnel Act [*1970*]
IPA .... Intergovernmental Personnel Action (SAUO)
IPA .... Intergovernmental Personnel Agreement (COE)
IPA .... Interior Plantscape Association [*Later, ALCA/IPD*] (EA)
IPA .... Intermediate Power Amplifier [*Electronics*]
IPA .... Internal Power Amplifier (SAUS)
IPA .... International Association for the Child's Right to Play [*International Pl ayground Association*] [*Acronym is based on former name,*] (EA)
IPA .... International Journal of Public Administration (journ.) (SAUS)
IPA .... International Paddleball Association [*Later, AARA*] (EA)
IPA .... International Paediatric Association (SAUO)
IPA .... International Palaeontological Association (EA)
IPA .... International Patent Agreement
IPA .... International Peace Academy (EA)
IPA .... International Peach Academy (BUAC)
IPA .... International Pediatric Association [*See also AIP*] [*Paris, France*] (EAIO)
IPA .... International Permafrost Association (QUAC)
IPA .... International Petroleum Annual [*Department of Energy*] [*Database*]
IPA .... International Phonetic Alphabet
IPA .... International Phonetic Association [*University College*] [*Leeds, England*] (EA)
IPA .... International Photographers Association (BUAC)
IPA .... International Phototherapy Association (EA)
IPA .... International Pietenpol Association (EA)
IPA .... International Pinball Association (EA)
IPA .... International Pipe Association [*Later, TPF*] (EA)
IPA .... International Platform Association (EA)
IPA .... International Playground Association (SAUO)
IPA .... International Poetry Archives (ODA)
IPA .... International Police Academy [*Formerly, Inter-American Police Academy*]
IPA .... International Police Association [*Maidstone, Kent, England*] (EAIO)
IPA .... International Polka Association (EA)
IPA .... International Porcelain Artist (EA)
IPA .... International Porcelain Artists (SAUO)
IPA .... International Prepress Association (EA)
IPA .... International Press Association [*Defunct*] (EA)
IPA .... International Priority Airmail (SAUO)
IPA .... International Processing Association (SAUO)
IPA .... International Psycho-Analytical Association [*British*] (EAIO)
IPA .... International Psychoanalytic Association
IPA .... International Psychogeriatric Association (EA)
IPA .... International Psychohistorical Association (EA)
IPA .... International Publishers Association [*See also UIE*] [*Geneva, Switzerland*] (EAIO)
IPA .... International Publishers Audio-Visual Association (BUAC)
IPA .... International Pumpkin Association (EA)
IPA .... Internation Police Association (SAUO)
IPA .... Inter-Pacific Resource Corp. [*Vancouver Stock Exchange symbol*]
IPA .... Interstate Pollution Abatement Notice (COE)
IPA .... Intrapulmonary Artery (STED)
IPA .... Invasion Plasmid Antigens [*Medicine*] (MELL)
IPA .... Invasive Pulmonary Aspergillosis [*Medicine*] (DAVI)
IPA .... Investment Partnership Association (EA)
IPA .... Investment Program Association (NTPA)
IPA .... Involvement & Participation Association (BUAC)
IPA .... Involvement Participation Association (SAUO)
IPA .... Iowa Pharmaceutical Association (SAUO)
IPA .... Ipec Aviation Pty Ltd. [*Australia*] [*ICAO designator*] (FAAC)
IPA .... Ipota [*Vanuatu*] [*Airport symbol*] (OAG)
IPA .... Isopentenyl Adenosine (SAUS)
IPA .... Isopentenyladenosine [*Biochemistry*]
IPA .... Isophthalic Acid [*Organic chemistry*]
IPA .... Isopropane [*Organic chemistry*]
IPA .... Isopropyl Alcohol [*Organic chemistry*]
IPA .... Isopropyl Amine (SAUS)
IPA .... Issue-Position-Argument [*Computer science*] (BYTE)
IPAA .... Ileal Pouch-Anal Anastomosis [*Medicine*] (PALA)
IPAA .... Ileumpouch-Anale Anastomose (SAUS)
IPAA .... Independent Petroleum Association of America (EA)
IPAA .... Industrial Photographers Association of America [*Later, Industrial Photographers of New Jersey*] (EA)
IPAA .... Instrumental Photon Activation Analysis [*National Institute of Standards and Technology*]
IPAA .... International Patient Advocacy Association (SAUO)
IPAA .... International Pesticide Applicators Association (EA)
IPAA .... International Plan of Action on Aging (SAUS)
IPAA .... International Prisoners Aid Association (EA)
IPAA .... International Psycho-Analytical Association (SAUO)
IPAA .... Interstate Professional Applicators Association (SAUO)
IPAA .... Inventario del Patrimonio Arquitectonico [*Database*] [*Ministerio de Cultura*] [*Spanish*] [*Information service or system*] (CRD)
IPAAACS .... Image Process Auto Acquisition and Aimpoint Control System (ACAE)
IPAB .... International Program for Antarctic Buoys [*Marine science*] (OSRA)
IPABS .... Integrated Planning and Budgeting System (SAUO)
IPAC .... American Regional Interprofessional Advisory Committee of World Federation for Mental Health (SAUO)
IPAC .... Illinois Public Aid Commission (SAUO)
IPAC .... Independent Petroleum Association of Canada
IPAC .... Industrial and Professional Advisory Council (SAUO)
IPAC .... Information Processing and Control [*Systems Laboratory*] [*Northwestern University*]
IPAC .... Infrared Processing & Analysis Center (SAUO)
IPAC .... Institute of Public Administration of Canada
IPAC .... Integral Perturbed Angular Correlation (SAUS)
IPAC .... Integrated Packaging Assembly [*NASDAQ symbol*] (TTSB)
IPAC .... Integrated Packaging Assembly Corp. [*NASDAQ symbol*] (SAG)
IPAC .... Intelligence Center, Pacific [*Military*] (MCD)
IPAC .... Intelligence Pacific (SAUO)
IPAC .... Intelligence, Pacific Area Command (MCD)
IPAC .... International Peace Academy Committee (BUAC)
IPAC .... International Pharmaceutical Aerosol Consortium (SAUO)
IPAC .... Iranian Pan-American Oil Co. (SAUS)

IPAC............ Iran Pan-American Oil Co. (SAUS)
IPACE........... Intelligence Plan Allied Command Europe (SAUO)
IPACE........... Interprovincial Advisory Council on Energy [*Canada*]
IPACK........... International Packaging Material Suppliers (DGA)
IPACK........... International Packaging Material Suppliers Association (PDAA)
IPACS........... Conrad Grebel College Institute for Peace and Conflict Studies (SAUO)
IPACS........... Institute of Peace and Conflict Studies (SAUO)
IPACS........... Integrated Power and Attitude-Control System [*NASA*]
IPACS........... Interactive Pattern Analysis and Classification System (PDAA)
IPAD............ Incoming Procurement Authorization Document [*Air Force*] (AFM)
IPAD............ Integrated Program Aircraft Design
IPAD............ Integrated Programs for Aerospace-Vehicle Design
IPAD............ International Plastics Association Directors
IPAD............ Intra-Government Procurement Advisory Council on Drugs (SAUO)
IPADAE.......... Integrated Passive Action Detection Acquisition Equipment
IPADD........... Intra-Governmental Professional Advisory Council on Drugs and Devices [*Inactive*] [*FDA*] (EGAO)
IP address...... Internet Protocol Address [*Computer science*] (IGQR)
IPADE........... Instituto Panamericano de Alta Direccion de Empresa [*Panamerican Institute for Business Management*] [*Mexico*] (PDAA)
IPADI........... Integrated Database Application Programmjng Interface [*Computer science*] (HODG)
IPADS........... Improved Processing And Display System (SAUS)
IPADS........... Integrated Passive Air Defense System (ACAE)
IPADS........... Interactive Processing and Display System (MCD)
IPAE............ IP Address Encapsulation (SAUO)
IPAE............ (Isopropylamino)ethanol [*Organic chemistry*]
IPAF............ International Powered Access Federation (EAIO)
IPAFUG.......... International PAF User's Group (EA)
IPAG............ Information Planning and Analysis Group (SAUO)
IPAG............ International Products and Goods (SAUO)
IPAHGEIS........ Inter-Professional Ad Hoc Group for Environmental Information Sharing (SAUO)
IPAI............ Information Processing Association of Israel (SAUO)
IPAI............ International Primary Aluminium Institute [*British*] (EAIO)
I-PAL........... Improved PAL (SAUS)
IPAL............ Index to Periodical Articles Related to Law [*A publication*] (DLA)
IP/AL........... Inland Printer / American Lithographer [*A publication*] (DGA)
IPAL............ Integrated Program on Arid Lands (BUAC)
IPal............ Palatine Public Library District, Palatine, IL [*Library symbol*] [*Library of Congress*] (LCLS)
IPALAC.......... International Programme for Arid Land Crops (SAUS)
Ipalco.......... IPALCO Enterprises, Inc. [*Associated Press*] (SAG)
IPale........... La Motte Township Library, Palestine, IL [*Library symbol*] [*Library of Congress*] (LCLS)
IPalH........... William Rainey Harper College, Palatine, IL [*Library symbol*] [*Library of Congress*] (LCLS)
IPalmSD......... Northwestern Community Unit, School District 2, Palmyra, IL [*Library symbol*] [*Library of Congress*] (LCLS)
IPALS........... Integrated Pathology Audio-Visual Learning System (PDAA)
IPALSS.......... Information Processing Adinistrators of Large School Systems (NTPA)
IPAM............ Improved Point Analysis Model (ACAE)
IPAM............ Intellectual Property Asset Management (GART)
IPAM............ Inter-Partition Access Method (SAUS)
IPAM............ Isopropylaclylamide (SAUS)
IPAMS........... Independent Petroleum Association of Mountain States
IPANA........... Indian People's Association in North America (EA)
IP & BE......... Initial Program and Budget Estimate [*Army*]
IP & C.......... Instrumentation Program and Component (KSC)
IP&PA........... Instrument Panel and Panel Assembly (SAUS)
IP & T.......... Intellectual Property and Technology
IPANY........... Individual Psychology Association of New York
IPAO............ Insulin-Induced Peak Acid Output (STED)
IPAP............ Inspiratory Positive Airway Pressure [*Medicine*] (DMAA)
IPAP............ Interagency Placement Assistance Program [*Office of Personnel Management*]
IPAP............ Investment Promotion Action Plan [*Bangkok*]
IPAP............ Iodophenyl(piperidinoacetyl)piperazine [*Biochemistry*]
IPAPS........... Institute for Pure and Applied Physical Sciences (SAUO)
IPAR............ Improved Pulse Acquisition RADAR (AABC)
IPAR............ Incident Photosynthetically Active Radiation (SAUS)
IPAR............ Initial Product Assessment Report (SAUS)
IPAR............ Innovative Photovoltaics Applications for Residences
IPAR............ Institute of Personality Assessment and Research [*University of California*] [*Research center*]
IPAR............ Institute of Policy Analysis and Research [*Nairobi, Kenya*] [*Research center*] (ECON)
IPAR............ Intercepted Photosynthetically Active Radiation [*Photosynthesis*]
IPAR............ Inter Parfums [*NASDAQ symbol*] (SG)
IPAR............ Intra-Pulse Analysis Receiver (SAUS)
IPar............ Paris Carnegie Public Library, Paris, IL [*Library symbol*] [*Library of Congress*] (LCLS)
IPAR............ United States Department of Agriculture, Agricultural Research Service, NorthernResearch Center Library, Peoria, IL [*Library symbol*] [*Library of Congress*] (LCLS)
IPARA........... International Publishers Advertising Representatives Association
I-Para.......... Primipara [*Obstetrics*] (DAVI)
I-para.......... Primipara (STED)
IPARC........... International Permanent Association of Road Congresses (SAUO)
IPARC........... International Pesticide Application Research Centre [*Imperial College at Silwood Park*] [*British*] (CB)
IPARCOM......... Interim Paris Commission [*British*]
IPA Review...... Institute of Public Affairs Review (journ.) (SAUS)
IparF........... Edgar County Film Library, Paris, IL [*Library symbol*] [*Library of Congress*] (LCLS)
IParH........... Paris Community Hospital, Paris, IL [*Library symbol*] [*Library of Congress*] (LCLS)
Ipark........... Park Ridge Public Library, Park Ridge, IL [*Library symbol*] [*Library of Congress*] (LCLS)
IParkA.......... American Society of Anesthesiologists, Park Ridge, IL [*Library symbol*] [*Library of Congress*] (LCLS)
IParkD.......... Dames and Moore Chicago Branch Library, Park Ridge, IL [*Library symbol*] [*Library of Congress*] (LCLS)
IParkL.......... Lutheran General Hospital, Park Ridge, IL [*Library symbol*] [*Library of Congress*] (LCLS)
IParP........... Paris Carnegie Public Library, Paris, IL [*Library symbol*] [*Library of Congress*] (LCLS)
IPARS........... International Passenger Airline Reservation System (SAUO)
IPARS........... International Passenger Programmed Airlines Reservation System (SAUS)
IPARS........... International Programmed Airline Reservations System (SAUO)
IPARS........... International Programmed Airline Reservation System (SAUO)
IParSD.......... Paris Union School District, Paris, IL [*Library symbol*] [*Library of Congress*] (LCLS)
IPART........... Institute of Photographic Apparatus Repair Technicians (BUAC)
IPAS............ Independants et Paysans d'Action Sociale [*Independents and Peasants of Social Action*] [*French*] (PPE)
IPAS............ Institute of Psychology, Academia Sinica (BUAC)
IPAS............ Integrated Pneumatic Air System (MCD)
IPAS............ Integrated Problem Assessment (SAUS)
IPAS............ International Projects Assistance Services
IPAS............ Interplatform Alignment System (MCD)
IPASS........... Interactive Policy Analysis Simulation System [*Department of Agriculture*]
IPAST........... IGOSS [*Integrated Global Ocean Services System*] Pilot Project on AlimetricSea-Surface Topography Data [*Marine science*] (OSRA)
IPA/STM......... International Group of Scientific (SAUO)
IPAT............ European Confernce on Ion Plating and Allied Techniques (SAUS)
IPAT............ Inertial Pointing Aided Tracking (SAUS)
IPAT............ Institute for Personality and Ability Testing [*Champaign, IL*]
IPAT............ International Conference on Ion Plating and Allied Techniques (BUAC)
IPAT............ International Porcelain Artist Teachers (BUAC)
IPAT............ International Porcelain Art Teachers [*Later, IPA*] (EA)
IPAT............ Inventario del Patrimonio Historico Artistico Espanol [*Ministerio de Cultura*] [*Spain*] [*Information service or system*] (CRD)
IPAT............ Ion & Plasma Assisted Techniques-International Conference (SAUO)
IPAT............ Iowa Pressure Articulation Test (DMAA)
IPat............ Patoka Public Library, Patoka, IL [*Library symbol*] [*Library of Congress*] (LCLS)
IPATA........... Independent Pet and Animal Transportation Association (EA)
IPAT CPQ........ Institute for Personality and Ability Testing, Children's Personality Questionnaire [*Psychology*] (AEBS)
IPAT NPFT....... Institute for Personality and Ability Testing, Neurotic Personality Factor Test [*Psychology*] (AEBS)
IPAV............ Institute of Professional Auctioneers and Valuers [*Ireland*] (BUAC)
IPAVS........... International Project of the Association for Voluntary Sterilization
IPax............ Paxton Carnegie Library, Paxton, IL [*Library symbol*] [*Library of Congress*] (LCLS)
IPaxH........... Paxton Community Hospital, Paxton, IL [*Library symbol*] [*Library of Congress*] (LCLS)
IPB............. Bogor Agriculture Institute, Indonesia (SAUS)
IPB............. Bradley University, Peoria, IL [*Library symbol*] [*Library of Congress*] (LCLS)
IPB............. Ice-Penetrating Communications Buoy (DWSG)
IPB............. IGOSS Products Bulletin (SAUS)
IPB............. Illuminated Push Button (NASA)
IPB............. Illustrated Parts Book (IAA)
IPB............. Illustrated Parts Breakdown (AFIT)
IPB............. Illustrated Parts Brochure (ACAE)
IPB............. Impact Predictor Building (ACAE)
IPB............. Inert Processing Building
IPB............. Information Parts Breakdown (MCD)
IPB............. Information Policy Board (SAUO)
IPB............. Infrapopliteal Bypass (STED)
IPB............. Initial Plan of Battle (SAUO)
IPB............. Injury-Prone Behavior [*Medicine*] (DMAA)
IPB............. Installation Parts Breakdown (SAUO)
IPB............. Installation Property Book [*Military*] (AABC)
IPB............. Institute of Plant Breeding (SAUO)
IPB............. Institute of Practitioners in Beauty (BUAC)
IPB............. Institute of Professional Businesswomen (EA)
IPB............. Instruction Prefetch Buffer [*IBM Corp.*] (CIST)
IPB............. Instrumentation Pull Box (SAUS)
IPB............. Integrated Processor Board
IPB............. Intelligence Preparation of the Battlefield [*Army*] (RDA)
IPB............. Intelligence Preparatory Brief [*Army*] (DOMA)
IPB............. Intelligence Property Book [*Army*] (ADDR)
IPB............. Interactive Processing Branch (SAUO)
IPB............. Intercept Priorities Board [*Armed Forces Security Agency*]
IPB............. Interconnection and Program Bay (IAA)
IPB............. Interconnection and Programming Bay (SAUO)
IPB............. Interdivisional Programming Bulletin (SAUS)
IPB............. International Pathfinder, Inc. [*Toronto Stock Exchange symbol*]
IPB............. International Peace Bureau [*Geneva, Switzerland*] (EA)
IPB............. International Pigeon Board (SAUO)
IPB............. Interprocessor Buffer
IPB............. Inter Processor Bus (SAUS)

IPB.......... Interprocessor Bus (ACAE)
IPB.......... Inventions Promotion Board (SAUO)
IPB.......... Irish Peat Board (EAIO)
IPB.......... Isopropyl Benzene (SAUS)
IPB.......... Jenner & Block, Chicago, IL [*OCLC symbol*] (OCLC)
IPBA.......... India, Pakistan, and Bangladesh Association (PDAA)
IPBA.......... Irish Paper Box Association (BI)
IPBAM.......... International Permanent Bureau of Automobile Manufacturers (SAUO)
IPBAM.......... International Permanent Bureau of Automotive Manufacturers (SAUS)
IPBC.......... India, Pakistan, Bangladesh Conference (DS)
IPBC.......... International Panel on Biodiversity Conservation (SAUO)
IPBC.......... International Power Beam Conference (SAUS)
IPBC.......... Iodopropynyl Butyl Carbamate [*Wood preservative*]
IPBF.......... Installed Peripheral Base Flexibility (SAUS)
IPBF.......... International Pony Breeders Federation (SAUO)
IPBF.......... International Professional Bodyboarding Federation (SAUO)
IPBF.......... International Professional Bodysurfing Federation (SAUO)
IPBM.......... Illustrated Parts Breakdown Manual (SAUS)
IPBM.......... Integrated Planning Bill of Material (SAUS)
IPBM.......... Integrated Program, Budget, Manpower [*System*] [*Defense Supply Agency*]
IPBM.......... International Permanent Bureau of Motor Manufacturers (SAUO)
IPBM.......... Interplanetary Ballistic Missile [*Air Force*]
IPBMM.......... International Permanent Bureau of Motor Manufacturers (BARN)
IPBNet.......... International Plant Biotech Network (EA)
IPBS.......... Israel Plate Block Society (EA)
IPBSF.......... International Professional Boat Surfing Federation (SAUO)
IPBX.......... International Private Branch Exchange (SAUS)
IPC.......... Easter Island [*Chile*] [*Airport symbol*] (OAG)
IPC.......... Icelandic Prime Contractor (SAUO)
IPC.......... Iceland Prime Contractor (SAUS)
IPC.......... Idaho Potato Commission (EA)
IPC.......... Illinois Power Co. [*NYSE symbol*] (SPSG)
IPC.......... Illinois Power Company (SAUO)
IPC.......... Illinois Power Financing I [*NYSE symbol*] (SAG)
IPC.......... Image Processing Center [*Drexel University*] [*Research center*] (RCD)
IPC.......... Image Processing Computer (SAUS)
IPC.......... Image Products Co.
IPC.......... Imaging Proportional Counter [*Astronomy*]
IPC.......... Impact Predictor Computer (SAUS)
IPC.......... Impact Program Committee (TELE)
IPC.......... Impact Programme Committee (SAUO)
IPC.......... Impurity Photoconductivity (PDAA)
IPC.......... Independent Control Point (SAUS)
IPC.......... Independently Programmed Computer (SAUS)
IPC.......... Index of Personality Characteristics [*Test*] [*Brown and Coleman*] (TES)
IPC.......... Indicative Planning Council (BUAC)
IPC.......... Indirect Photometric Chromatography
IPC.......... Indirect Platelet Count [*Medicine*] (MELL)
IPC.......... Indirect Pulp Capping [*Dentistry*]
IPC.......... Individual Plan of Care
IPC.......... Industrial Partnership Center (SAUO)
IPC.......... Industrial Personal Computer (NITA)
IPC.......... Industrial Planning Committee [*NATO*] (NATG)
IPC.......... Industrial Policy Committee (SAUS)
IPC.......... Industrial Policy Council [*Washington, DC*] (EA)
IPC.......... Industrial Pollution Control (EFIS)
IPC.......... Industrial Process Control [*by computers*]
IPC.......... Industrial Production Corp. [*Sudan*] (BUAC)
IPC.......... Industrial Programmable Controller (IAA)
IPC.......... Industrial Property Committee [*US Military Government, Germany*]
IPC.......... Industrial Publishing Co.
IPC.......... Industry Planning Council (EA)
IPC.......... Industry Policy Council (SAUO)
IPC.......... Information Processing Center [*of General Motors Corp.*]
IPC.......... Information Processing Code (DIT)
IPC.......... Information Processing Computer (SAUS)
IPC.......... Information Publishing Corp. [*Telecommunications service*] (TSSD)
IPC.......... Initial Planning Conference [*Military*] (INF)
IPC.......... Innings Pitched Corrector (SAUS)
IPC.......... Inspector of Pioneer Corps (SAUO)
IPC.......... Institute for Interconnecting and Packaging Electronic Circuits [*Formerly, Institute of Printed Circuits*] (EA)
IPC.......... Institute for interconnecting and Packaging ICs (SAUO)
IPC.......... Institute for Interconnection and Packaging Electric Circuits (SAUO)
IPC.......... Institute for Personal Computing (EA)
IPC.......... Institute for Printed Circuits (SAUS)
IPC.......... Institute of Paper Chemistry [*Lawrence University*] [*Research center*] (EA)
IPC.......... Institute of Paper Conservation [*Formerly, International Institute for Conservation of Historic and Artistic Works Paper Group*] (EA)
IPC.......... Institute of Pastoral Care (EA)
IPC.......... Institute of Philippine Culture (BUAC)
IPC.......... Institute of Printed Circuits (MCD)
IPC.......... Institute of Production Control [*British*]
IPC.......... Institute of Public Cleansing (SAUO)
IPC.......... Institute of Pure Chiropractic [*British*] (DBA)
IPC.......... Institutional Population Component [*National Medical Expenditure Survey*] [*Department of Health and Human Services*] (GFGA)
IPC.......... Instructions Per Clock (SAUO)
IPC.......... Instrumentation Package Container
IPC.......... Instrument Panel Cluster [*Automotive engineering*]
IPC.......... Instrument Processing Center (SAUO)
IPC.......... Integral Plate Chamber
IPC.......... Integrated Passive Component (SAUS)
IPC.......... Integrated Peripheral Channel
IPC.......... Integrated Peripheral Controller [*Computer chip*]
IPC.......... Integrated Personal Computer (SAUS)
IPC.......... Integrated Pest Control
IPC.......... Integrated Pollution Control
IPC.......... Integrated Procedures Control
IPC.......... Integrated Process Control (IAA)
IPC.......... Integrated Program Coordinator (ABAC)
IPC.......... Integrated Programme for Commodities [*UNCTAD*] (EY)
IPC.......... Integrated Protocol Converter (SAUS)
IPC.......... Intelligence Priorities Committee [*British*] [*World War II*]
IPC.......... Intelligent Peripheral Controller [*Computer science*]
IPC.......... Inter-African Phytosanitary Commission
IPC.......... Interagency Programming Committee (SAUO)
IPC.......... Intercalated Polymer-Derived Carbon [*Chemistry*]
IPC.......... Interconnections Packaging Circuitry (MCD)
IPC.......... Interim Procedure Change (SAUS)
IPC.......... Intermediate Pressure Compressor (SAUS)
IPC.......... Intermediate Processing Center (SAUS)
IPC.......... Intermittent Positive Control [*Aviation*]
IPC.......... Internal Positive Control [*Genetics*]
IPC.......... International Pacific Corp. (SAUS)
IPC.......... International Pacific Cypress Minerals Ltd. [*Vancouver Stock Exchange symbol*]
IPC.......... International Packings Corp. (SAUS)
IPC.......... International Palynological Congress (QUAC)
IPC.......... International Paper Chemists (SAUO)
IPC.......... International Paralympic Committee (BUAC)
IPC.......... International Patent Classification
IPC.......... International PBX [*Private Branch Exchange*]/Telecommunicators (EA)
IPC.......... International Peace Campaign
IPC.......... International Penpal Club (EAIO)
IPC.......... International Pensions Consultants GmbH (SAUO)
IPC.......... International Pepper Community [*Indonesia*] [*Research center*] (IRC)
IPC.......... International Petroleum Cartel
IPC.......... International Petroleum Co. (SAUS)
IPC.......... International Petroleum Company (SAUO)
IPC.......... International Photographic Council (BUAC)
IPC.......... International Photosynthesis Committee [*Stockholm, Sweden*] (EAIO)
IPC.......... International Phytosanitary Commission (SAUO)
IPC.......... International Planning Corp.
IPC.......... International Plasma Corp.
IPC.......... International Police Conference (SAUO)
IPC.......... International Poliomyelitis Congress
IPC.......... International Political Committee (CARL)
IPC.......... International Poplar Commission [*FAO*] [*Rome, Italy*] [*United Nations*] (EA)
IPC.......... International Potato Centre [*Peru*] (BUAC)
IPC.......... International Press Center (or Centre) (SAUO)
IPC.......... International Pressure Conference (SAUS)
IPC.......... International Prison Commission (BUAC)
IPC.......... International Procurement Committee [*ABA*] (AAGC)
IPC.......... International Program Classifier (SAUO)
IPC.......... International Programme Committee (SAUO)
IPC.......... International Psychological Congress (SAUO)
IPC.......... International Publishing Corp. [*England*]
IPC.......... International Publishing Corporation (SAUO)
IPC.......... International Pyrheliometer Comparison (SAUO)
IPC.......... Internet Privacy Coalition (SAUO)
IPC.......... Internet Proxy Cache (SAUS)
IPC.......... Interpenduncular Cistern [*Medicine*] (DAVI)
IPC.......... Inter-Personal Communication (SAUS)
IPC.......... Inter Personal Computer (SAUS)
IPC.......... Interplanetary Communications (AAG)
IPC.......... Interpressor Communication (SAUS)
IPC.......... Inter Process Communication (CTAS)
IPC.......... Inter-Process Control (SAUS)
IPC.......... Inter-Process Coupler (NITA)
IPC.......... Interprocessor Channel (IAA)
IPC.......... Inter Processor Communications (SAUS)
IPC.......... Interstate Pollution Control (EFIS)
IPC.......... Interstate Processing Center [*Department of Labor*]
IPC.......... Intraductal Papillary Carcinoma [*Medicine*] (PALA)
IPC.......... Intraperitoneal Chemotherapy [*Medicine*] (MELL)
IPC.......... Inventory Process Control (SAUS)
IPC.......... Investment Promotion Centre [*Tanzania*]
IPC.......... Investors Planning Corp.
IPC.......... Ion Pair Chromatography [*Medicine*] (MELL)
IPC.......... Ion-Pair Comonomers [*Organic chemistry*]
IPC.......... Irish Peace Council (EAIO)
IPC.......... Irish Presbyterian Church (ROG)
IPC.......... Irish Productivity Centre (BUAC)
IPC.......... Irish Productivity Council (ACII)
IPC.......... Iron Phosphate Coating
IPC.......... Ischemic Preconditioning [*Medicine*] (MELL)
IPC.......... Islamic Peace Committee (BUAC)
IPC.......... Isolation-Physiological Characterization [*Microbiology*]
IPC.......... Isopinocampheyl (SAUS)
IPC.......... Isopropyl Carbanilate [*Also, INPC, IPPC*] [*Herbicide*]
IPC.......... Isopropyl Chlorophenyl [*Medicine*] (MAE)
IPC.......... Isopropyl Cresol (SAUS)
IPC.......... Isoproyl Carbinol (SAUS)

IPC.............. Item Processing Card
IPC.............. Purdue University, Calumet Campus, Hammond, IN [*OCLC symbol*] (OCLC)
IPC .... Iraq Petroleum Company (ODA)
IPCA............. Independent Parametric Cost Analysis (MCD)
IPCA............. Independent Police Complaints Authority [*British*]
IPCA............. Industrial Pest Control Association [*British*] (BI)
IPCA............. International Passengers Consumer Association (SAUO)
IPCA............. International Petroleum Co-Operative Alliance (BUAC)
IPCA............. International Petroleum Credit Association (NTPA)
IPCA............. International Postcard Collectors Association (EA)
IPCAIL .... International Pacific Corporation Australian Investments Ltd. (SAUS)
IPCAPR........ International Peace Conference on the Pacific and Asian Regions (SAUO)
IPC-ASA....... Intermittent Positive Control - Automatic Seperation [*Aviation*] (PDAA)
IPCC............. Infantry Precommand Course [*Army*] (INF)
IPCC............. Information Processing in Command and Control [*Air Force*]
IPCC............. Infrantry Precommend Cource (SAUS)
IPCC............. Institute of Political Campaign Consultants (NTPA)
IPCC............. Interdepartmental Packaging Co-ordinating Committee (SAUO)
IPCC............. Intergovernmental Panel on Climate Change [*World Meteorological Organization*]
IPCC............. International Peace Communication and Coordination Center (SAUO)
IPCC............. International Pin Collectors Club (EA)
IPCC............. International Professional Communication Conference (SAUO)
IPCC............. Irish Peatland Conservation Council (BUAC)
IPCC............. Irradiation Program Coordination Committee (SAUO)
IPCCB .... Inter-Parliamentary Consultative Council of Benelux (EA)
IPCCC .... International Peace, Communication, and Coordination Center [*The Hague, Netherlands*] (EAIO)
IPCC-EIS...... IPCC-Energy and Industry Subgroup (SAUO)
IPCCIOS....... Indo-Pacific Council of the International Committee of Scientific Mangement (SAUS)
IPCCIOS....... Indo-Pacific Regional Council of the International Committee of Scientific Management (SAUO)
IPCC/RSWG/EIS... IPCC/Response Strategies Working Group/Energy and Industry Subgroup (SAUO)
IPCCS .... Information Processing in Command and Control Systems [*Air Force*]
IPCC Sg .... Intergovernmental Panel on Climate Change/Subgroup (SAUO)
IPCC WG...... Intergovernmental Panel on Climate Change/Working Group (SAUO)
IPCD .... Infantile Polycistic Disease (DAVI)
IPCDA .... International Penguin Class Dinghy Association (EA)
IPCDN.......... IP Over Cable Data Network working group of the IETF (SAUO)
IPCE............. Independent Parametric Cost Estimate (AABC)
IPCE............. Interprocess Communication Environment (SAUO)
IPCEA........... Insulated Power Cable Engineers Association [*Later, ICEA*] (EA)
IPCF............. Interactive Program Checkout Facility [*Computer science*] (HODG)
IPCF............. Interprocess Communication Facility [*Digital Equipment Corp.*]
IPCF............. Interprogram Communication Facility [*Prime Computer, Inc.*]
IPCG .... International Plate Collectors Guild (EA)
IPCH .... Institute of Paper Chemistry (SAUO)
IPCHold .... IPC Holdings Ltd. [*Associated Press*] (SAG)
IPCI.............. Industrial PCI (SAUS)
IPCI.............. International Potato Chip Institute (SAUO)
IPCI.............. IPC Information Systems, Inc. [*NASDAQ symbol*] (SAG)
IPCI.............. Islamic Propagation Centre International (BUAC)
IPCID .... International Programme for the Control of Iodine Deficiency Disorders (SAUO)
IPC Info .... IPC Information Systems, Inc. [*Associated Press*] (SAG)
IPCIS .... Integrated Plant Control and Information System [*Nuclear energy*] (NUCP)
IPCL............. Central Illinois Light Co., Resource Center, Peoria, IL [*Library symbol*] [*Library of Congress*] (LCLS)
IPCL............. Indian Petrochemical Corporation Ltd. (SAUS)
IPCL............. India Petrochemicals Ltd. (BUAC)
IPCL............. Instrumentation Program and Component List (NASA)
IPCL............. International Postal Collectors League [*Commercial firm*] (EA)
IPC Module... Inter-Process Communication Module (SAUS)
IPCO .... Idaho Power Co.
IPCO .... In-Place Cleanable Oilfilter
IPCO .... International Paper Co. (WDMC)
IPCO .... International Paper Company (SAUO)
IPCOG.......... Informal Policy Committee for Germany
IPCOG.......... Interdepartmental Planning Committee on Germany [*US*]
IP Control.... Interplant Control (SAUS)
IPCP............. Improved Platoon Command Post (SAUS)
IPCP............. Integrated Printing Collating Processing (DGA)
IPCP............. Interdisciplinary Patient Care Plan (HCT)
IPCP............. Internet Protocol Control Protocol (SAUS)
IPCPA .... Institute of Povate Clinical Psychologists of Australia (SAUS)
IPCPA .... Institute of Private Clinical Psychologists of Australia
IPCPP .... International Physicians Commission for the Protection of Prisoners (SAUO)
IPCPrA......... Illinois Pwr 4.08% Pfd [*NYSE symbol*] (TTSB)
IPCPrB......... Illinois Pwr 4.20% Pfd [*NYSE symbol*] (TTSB)
IPCPrC......... Illinois Pwr 4.26% Pfd [*NYSE symbol*] (TTSB)
IPCPrD......... Illinois Pwr 4.42% Pfd [*NYSE symbol*] (TTSB)
IPCPrE .... Illinois Pwr 4.70% Pfd [*NYSE symbol*] (TTSB)
IPCPrL .... Illinois Pwr Adj Rt A Pfd [*NYSE symbol*] (TTSB)
IPCPrM........ Illinois Pwr Cap 9.45%'MIPS' [*NYSE symbol*] (TTSB)
IPC Process... Inco Pressure Carbonyl Process (SAUS)
IPCPrT .... Illinois Pwr Fin I 8%'TOPrS' [*NYSE symbol*] (TTSB)
IPCR .... Institute for Physical and Chemical Research [*Japan*] (BUAC)
IPCR .... International Conference on Pattern Recognition (SAUO)
IPCR .... Inverse Polymerase Chain Reaction [*Genetics*]
IPCR .... IPC Holdings Ltd. [*NASDAQ symbol*] (SAG)
IPCR .... Israel Palestine Center for Research and Information (SAUO)
IPCRA.......... Irish Professional Conservators and Restorers Association (BUAC)
IPC Rept...... International Procurement Committee Report [*ABA*] [*A publication*] (AAGC)
IPCRESS...... Induction of Psychoneuroses by Conditioned Reflex under Stress [*In book and film "The Ipcress File"*]
IPCRF .... IPC Holdings [*NASDAQ symbol*] (TTSB)
IPCRI .... Israel Palestine Center for Research and Information (SAUO)
IPCRI .... Israel Palestine Center for Research Information (SAUS)
IPCS............. Image Photon Counting System [*Instrumentation*]
IPCS............. Image Production Control System (SAUO)
IPCS............. Infrapatellar Contracture Syndrome [*Sports medicine*]
IPCS............. Institute of Professional Civil Servants [*British*]
IPCS............. Institution of Professional Civil Servants [*British*] (BI)
IPCS............. Integrated PC Server (SAUS)
IPCS............. Integrated Personnel Communication System (ACAE)
IPCS............. Integrated Powertrain Control System [*Automotive engineering*]
IPCS............. Integrated Propulsion Control System [*Air Force*]
IPCS............. Intelligent Process-Control System (SAUS)
IPCS............. Interactive Problem-Control System [*IBM Corp.*]
IPCS............. International Peace Corps Secretariat (SAUO)
IPCS............. International Petula Clark Society (EAIO)
IPCS............. International Playing-Card Society (EA)
IPCS............. International Programme on Chemical Safety (EA)
IPCS............. International Program on Chemical Safety (GNE)
IPCS............. Interproject Control Station (IAA)
IPCS............. Intrauterine Progesterone Contraceptive System [*Gynecology*]
IPCS HQ ...... Institution of Professional Civil Servants Headquarter (SAUS)
IPCT............. Caterpillar Tractor Co., Business Library, Peoria, IL [*Library symbol*] [*Library of Congress*] (LCLS)
IPCT............. Industrial Process Cooling Towers
IPCT............. Intraperitoneal Chemotherapy [*Medicine*] (MELL)
IPCT-T .... Caterpillar Tractor Co., Technical Information Center, Peoria, IL [*Library symbol*] [*Library of Congress*] (LCLS)
IPCU .... Intensive Psychiatric Care Unit (SAUS)
IPC Union.... Union for the International Patent Classification (SAUO)
IPCV............. Indian Peanut Clump Virus [*Plant pathology*]
IPCWN......... Irish Permaculture Worknet (BUAC)
IPCX............. International Paper [*Private rail car owner code*]
IP Cyl........... Intermediate Pressure Cylinder (SAUS)
IPCZ............. International Paper [*Federal Railroad Administration identification code*]
IPD............... Idiopathic Parkinson's Disease [*Medicine*] (CPH)
IPD............... Illustrated Provisioning Document (MCD)
IPD............... Imaging Photon Detector (QUAC)
IPD............... Immediate Pigment Darkening [*Dermatology*]
IPD............... Impact Patient Data (SAUS)
IPD............... Impact Prediction Data (AFM)
IPD............... Implicit Price Deflator
IPD............... Impounded Parcels Department (SAUO)
IPD............... Improved Point Defense
IPD............... Impulse to Progress and Democracy (Benin) [*Political party*] (PSAP)
IPD............... Incident Power Density (SAUS)
IPD............... Increase in Pupillary Diameter (SAUS)
IPD............... Incurable Problem Drinker (MELL)
IPD............... Individual Package Delivery [*Shipping*]
IPD............... Individual Protective Device [*Toxicology*]
IPD............... Industrial Porperty Departments (SAUO)
IPD............... Industrial Products Division (ACAE)
IPD............... Infantile Polycystic Disease [*Medicine*] (MELL)
IPD............... Inflammatory Pelvic Disease [*Medicine*] (MAE)
IPD............... Information Processing Department (SAUS)
IPD............... Information Processing Division [*NASA*] (NASA)
IPD............... Information Protection and Destruction Plan (GART)
IPD............... Information-Psychological activity Directorate (SAUS)
IPD............... Initial Patient Data (SAUS)
IPD............... Initial Performance Data
IPD............... Initial Production Delivery (SAUS)
IPD............... In Praesentia Dominorum [*In the Presence of the Lords of Session*] [*Latin*]
IPD............... Insertion Phase Delay
IPD............... Insertion Phase Difference (SAUS)
IPD............... Inspection Planning Document [*Military*] (MCD)
IPD............... Institute for Professional Development (EA)
IPD............... Institute of Personnel Development (WDAA)
IPD............... Institute of Professional Designers
IPD............... Instructional Program Development (NVT)
IPD............... Integrated Pin Diode
IPD............... Integrated Process Demonstration [*Nuclear energy*]
IPD............... Integrated Product Development [*Business term*] (RDA)
IPD............... Intelligence Planning Document [*Military*] (MCD)
IPD............... Intelligent Power Device (CIST)
IPD............... Intelligent Printer Data (SAUS)
IPD............... Intelligent Protection Device [*American Solenoid Co.*] [*Somerset, NJ*]
IPD............... Interaural Phase Disparity [*Audiology*]
IPD............... Intermediate Peritoneal Dialysis [*Medicine*] (BARN)
IPD............... Intermittent Peritoneal Dialysis [*Medicine*]
IPD............... International Journal of Physics Distribution and Materials Management (journ.) (SAUS)
IPD............... International Police Dogs (EA)
IPD............... Interplanetary Dust [*Science*]
IPD............... Inter-Provincial Diversified Holding Ltd. [*Toronto Stock Exchange symbol*]
IPD............... Interpupillary Distance

IPD.............. Intra-Penile Device [*Contraceptive*] (DI)
IPD.............. Inventory of Psychosocial Development
IPD.............. Investment Property Databank [*London, England*]
IPD.............. Isophorone Diamine [*Organic chemistry*]
IPD.............. Isophoronediamine (SAUS)
IPD.............. Isotope-Powered Device
IPD.............. Issue Priority Designation (or Designator) (SAUS)
IPD.............. Iterated Prisoner's Dilemma [*Psychology*]
IPDA............ International Periodical Distributors Association (EA)
IPDA............ Intrapulse Demodulation Analysis
IPD/AC......... Institut Panafricain pour le Developpement, Afrique Centrale [*Pan African Institute for Development, Central Africa*] [*Cameroun*] (PDAA)
IPDAS.......... Intestinal Protective Drug Absorption System [*Medicine*] (MELL)
IPDB............ Intelligence Production Database [*Military*] (MCD)
IPDC............ International Program for the Development of Communications [*UNESCO*]
IPDD............ Initial Project Design Description (NRCH)
IPDE............ Identify, Predict, Decide, Execute (SAUS)
IPDE............ Integrated Product Data Environment
IPDES.......... Integrated Product Design System (EURO)
IPDF............ Input Data Funnel (SAUS)
IPDF............ Intensity Probability Density Function (PDAA)
IPDH............ In-Service Planned Derated Hours [*Electronics*] (IEEE)
IPDI............ Implicit Price Deflator Index [*Economics*]
IPDI............ Isophorone Diisocyanate [*Organic chemistry*]
IPDL............ Indentured Parts and Document List (ACAE)
IPDL............ Isotopes Process Development Laboratory [*AEC*]
IPDM............ Institute of Physical Distribution Management [*British*]
IPDMS.......... Integrated Point Defense Missile System [*Military*] (CAAL)
IPDMUG....... International Product Data Management (SAUS)
IPDMUG....... International Product Data Management Users Group (SAUO)
IPDN............ International Paleoclimatic Data Network
IPDN............ International Public Data Network (SAUS)
IPDNY.......... Information Processing and Delivery, New York (SAUS)
IPDP............ Industrial Programmed Data Processor (SAUS)
IPDP............ Intervals of Pulsations of Diminishing Period
IPDP............ Isopropylphenyl(diphenyl)phosphate [*Fire-resistant hydraulic fluid*]
IPDR............ Incremental Preliminary Design Review (MCD)
IPDR............ Incremental Reliminary Design Review (SAUS)
IPDR............ Initial Program Design Review (SAUO)
IPDR............ In Process Design Review (SAUS)
IPDR............ Inter-Plan Data Reporting System [*Health insurance*] (GHCT)
IPDS............ IBM Personal Dication System [*Computer science*]
IPDS............ Imagery Processing and Dissemination System (DOMA)
IPDS............ Improved Point Defense Missile System [*Navy*] (DOMA)
IPDS............ Inland Petroleum Distribution System (COE)
IPDS............ Instrument Pool Data System (SAUS)
IPDS............ Integrated Personnel Data System (SAUS)
IPDS............ Integrated Product Development System [*FAA*] (TAG)
IPDS............ Integrated Program Development Support System [*Allen Bradley*] (NITA)
IPDS............ Intelligent Printer Data Stream [*IBM Corp.*] (CIST)
IPDSMS....... Improved Point Defense Surface Missile System
IPDT............ Inventory of Piaget's Developmental Tasks (DB)
IPD/TAC....... Improved Point Defense/Target Acquisition (SAUS)
IPDTAS........ Improved Point Defense Target Acquisition System (SAUO)
IPDTAS........ Interim Point Defense Target Acquisition System [*Military*] (IAA)
IPDU............ Instantaneous Panoramic Display Unit
IPDU............ Internet Protocol Data Unit (SAUS)
IPDU............ Inter-network Protocol Data Unit (SAUS)
IPDVMRP..... IP Distance Vector Multicast Routing Protocol (SAUS)
IPDWS.......... Interim Primary Drinking Water Standard (EEVL)
IPE.............. Idle Industrial Plant Equipment (ACAE)
IPE.............. Image Pac Extension (SAUS)
IPE.............. Image Processing Engine (SAUS)
IPE.............. Image Processing Equipment (SAUS)
IPE.............. Improved Performance Engine (SAUS)
IPE.............. Inband Parameter Exchange (SAUS)
IPE.............. Incentive PERT [*Program Evaluation and Review Technique*] Events
IPE.............. Incorporated Plant Engineers (BUAC)
IPE.............. Increased Performance Engine (ACAE)
IPE.............. Individual Plant Evaluation (SAUS)
IPE.............. Individual Plant Examination [*Environmental science*] (COE)
IPE.............. Individual Protective Equipment
IPE.............. Industrial Plant [*or Production*] Equipment
IPE.............. Industrial Plant Requirement (SAUS)
IPE.............. Industrial Production Equipment (SAUO)
IPE.............. Infectious Porcine Encephalomyelitis [*Medicine*] (DMAA)
IPE.............. Information Processing Equipment
IPE.............. Infrared Parameter Exchange (SAUS)
IPE.............. Initial Portable Equipment
IPE.............. Initial Psychiatric Evaluation (DAVI)
IPE.............. Inscriptiones Orae Septentrionalis Ponti Euxini [*A publication*] (OCD)
IPE.............. Installation Performance Evaluation (SAUS)
IPE.............. Institute for Program Evaluation (AAGC)
IPE.............. Institute of Petroleum Engineers (BUAC)
IPE.............. Institute of Physics of the Earth (SAUO)
IPE.............. Institute of Power Engineers (SAUS)
IPE.............. Institute of Production Engineers [*British*]
IPE.............. Institute of Public Enterprise [*India*] (BUAC)
IPE.............. Institution of Plant Engineers [*British*]
IPE.............. Institution of Plant Equipment (SAUS)
IPE.............. Institution of Production Engineering (SAUS)
IPE.............. Institution of Production Engineers (SAUO)
IPE.............. Institution of Professional Engineers (SAUS)
IPE.............. Integral Protective Entrances (SAUS)
IPE.............. Integrated Programming Environment (SAUS)
IPE.............. Intelligent Peripheral Equipment [*Telecommunications*] (ITD)
IPE.............. Intelligent Program Editor (PDAA)
IPE.............. International Institute on Peace Education (SAUO)
IPE.............. International Partners Facility
IPE.............. International Petroleum Encyclopedia (SAUO)
IPE.............. International Petroleum Exchange [*British*]
IPE.............. International Petroleum Exposition (SAUO)
IPE.............. International Political Economy (SAUS)
IPE.............. International Prism Exploration Ltd. [*Vancouver Stock Exchange symbol*]
IPE.............. Interpret Parity Error
IPE.............. Interstitial Pulmonary Emphysema [*Medicine*] (AAMN)
IPE.............. Inverse Photoelectric Effect
IPE.............. Inverse Photoemission Experiment (SAUS)
IPE.............. Inverted Print Edit (SAUS)
IPE.............. Iris Pigmentepithelium
IPE.............. Isopropoxyethanol (SAUS)
IPE.............. Isopropyl Ether [*Organic chemistry*]
IPe.............. Peotone Township Library, Peotone, IL [*Library symbol*] [*Library of Congress*] (LCLS)
IPEA............ Independent Poster Exchanges of America (EA)
IPEA............ Ireland-Poland Economic Association (BUAC)
IPEAA.......... Industrial Packaging Engineers Association of America (SAUO)
IPEC............ Integrated Process Equipment [*NASDAQ symbol*] (SAG)
IPEC............ International Patient Education Council (EAIO)
IPEC............ International Petroleum Exploration Co. (SAUS)
IPEC............ International Pharmaceutical Excipients Council (EA)
IPEC............ International Police Exhibition and Conference [*British*] (ITD)
IPEC............ International Power and Engineering Consultants
IPEC............ International Programme on the Elimination of Child Labour
IPEC............ International Program on Ecosystem Change (SAUO)
IPEC............ Interstate Parcel Express Co. (SAUS)
IPECAC........ Ipecacuanha [*Pharmacy*] (ROG)
IPECS.......... Integrated Power and Environmental Control System (MCD)
IPEDS.......... Integrated Postsecondary Education Data System [*National Center for Education Statistics*] (OICC)
IPEE............ Inclination of a Plane to the Plane of the Earth's Equator [*Aerospace*]
IPEE............ Institute of Problems of Evolutionary Ecology (SAUO)
IPEE............ International Peace, Economy, and Ecology (EA)
IPEE............ International Pollution Engineering Exposition & Congress (SAUS)
IPEE............ International Programme on Environmental Education [*UNESCO*] (BUAC)
IPEG............ International Pharmaco-EEG Group (SAUO)
IPEH............ International Physicians for Equitable Healthcare (SAUO)
IPEH............ Intravascular Papillary Endothelial Hyperplasia [*Medicine*]
IPEI............ Ionospheric Plasma and Electrodynamics Instrument (CARB)
IPEI............ Ionospheric Plasma and Eletrodynamics Instruments (ACAE)
IPE Int Ind Prod Eng... IPE International Industrial and Production Engineering (journ.) (SAUS)
IPek............ Pekin Public Library, Pekin, IL [*Library symbol*] [*Library of Congress*] (LCLS)
IPekC.......... Pekin Community High School District No. 30, Pekin, IL [*Library symbol*] [*Library of Congress*] (LCLS)
IPekH.......... Pekin Memorial Hospital, Pekin, IL [*Library symbol*] [*Library of Congress*] (LCLS)
IPEL............ International Pipeline Engineering Limited (SAUO)
IPEL............ International Pipeline Engineering Ltd. [*Canada*] (BUAC)
IPEMB.......... Institution of Physics and Engineering in Medicine and Biology (ADWA)
IPEME.......... International Program in Environmental Management Education
IPEN............ Pan American Institute of Naval Engineering (EAIO)
IPENEB........ International PEN [*Poets, Playwrights, Editors, Essayists, Novelists*]-Estonian Center (EAIO)
IPENHKE...... International PEN - Hong Kong English (EAIO)
IPENI.......... International PEN - Ireland (EAIO)
IPENS.......... International PEN - Scotland (EAIO)
IPENUS........ International PEN - United States [*Later, PCUSAW*] (EA)
IPENWIE...... International PEN [*Poets, Playwrights, Editors, Essayists, Novelists*]-Writers inExile [*British*] (EAIO)
IPENY.......... International PEN - Yiddish (EA)
IPENZ.......... Institution of Professional Engineers of New Zealand (SAUS)
IPEP............ Integrated Performance Evaluation Program
IPEP............ International Permanent Exhibition of Publications (SAUO)
IPER............ Industrial Production Equipment Reserve (NG)
IPer............ Peru Public Library, Peru, IL [*Library symbol*] [*Library of Congress*] (LCLS)
IPerIH.......... Illinois Valley Community Hospital, Peru, IL [*Library symbol*] [*Library of Congress*] (LCLS)
i-periton...... Intraperitoneal [*Medicine*] (MEDA)
IPERS.......... Industrial Plant Equipment Reutilization System [*DoD*]
IPerSD........ Peru Consolidated Community School District 124, Peru, IL [*Library symbol*] [*Library of Congress*] (LCLS)
IPerStB........ Saint Bede Academy, Peru, IL [*Library symbol*] [*Library of Congress*] (LCLS)
IPES............ Improved Proposed Encryption Standard (SAUO)
IPES............ Institute of Permanent Energy Sources (SAUO)
IPES............ Inverse Photoemission Spectroscopy
IPE/T.......... Improved Protective Entrance/Tent [*Army*]
IPET............ Independent Professional Electronic Technicians
IPET............ Pets.com, Inc. [*NASDAQ symbol*] (SG)
IPETE.......... International Petroleum Equipment and Technology Exhibition (SAUS)

IPETE.......... International Petrolium Equipment and Technology Exhibition (SAUS)
IPETEX......... Institute of Petroleum Working Group on Petroleum Exploration Training (SAUO)
IPetM.......... Edgar Lee Masters Memorial Museum, Petersburg, IL [*Library symbol*] [*Library of Congress*] (LCLS)
IPEU.......... International Photo-Engravers Union [*Later, GAIU*] (EA)
IPEX.......... Indeck Power Equipment [*Private rail car owner code*]
IPEX.......... Instant Purchase Excursion Fares [*Aviation*]
IPEX.......... International Printing Exhibition
IPEX.......... Organization for International Professional Exchanges, Inc. (EA)
IPF.......... Idiopathic Pulmonary Fibrosis [*Medicine*]
IPF.......... Image Processing Facility (ACAE)
IPF.......... Inches per Foot (IAA)
IPF.......... Indicative Planning Figure
IPF.......... Individual Project Fellowships
IPF.......... Infection Potentiating Factor (AAMN)
IPF.......... Information Presentation Facility (SAUO)
IPF.......... Information Processing Facility (MHDI)
IPF.......... Inherent Power Factor (SAUS)
IPF.......... Initial Production Facilities (or Facility) (SAUS)
IPF.......... Initial Production Funds (SAUO)
IPF.......... Initial Protective Force
IPF.......... In-Process Factor
IPF.......... In Process File (SAUS)
IPF.......... Input Filter (SAUS)
IPF.......... Inspector of Physical Fitness (SAUO)
IPF.......... Institute of Public Finance [*British*] (ECON)
IPF.......... Insulin Promoter Factor [*Biochemistry*]
IPF.......... Intaken Piled Fathom [*Shipping*] (DS)
IPF.......... Integral Pulse Frequency (SAUS)
IPF.......... Integrated Processing Facility [*DoD*]
IPF.......... Integration and Processing Facility (ISAK)
IPF.......... Intellectual Property Forum [*A publication*]
IPF.......... Interactive Processing Facility (SAUO)
IPF.......... Interactive Productivity Facility (HGAA)
IPF.......... Intergovernmental Panel on Forests (SAUO)
IPF.......... Intermediate Plot File
IPF.......... International Paddleboarding Federation (SAUO)
IPF.......... International Pain Foundation (EA)
IPF.......... International Peace Force (SAUO)
IPF.......... International Pen Friends (EA)
IPF.......... International Pharmaceutical Federation [*Netherlands*] (EAIO)
IPF.......... International Pigeon Federation [*See also FCI*] (EAIO)
IPF.......... International Podrabinek Fund [*Defunct*] (EA)
IPF.......... International Poetry Forum (EA)
IPF.......... International Police Federation (SAUO)
IPF.......... International Police Force (SAUS)
IPF.......... International Powerlifting Federation [*Hagersten, Sweden*] (EAIO)
IPF.......... International Prayer Fellowship (EA)
IPF.......... Interstitial Pulmonary Fibrosis [*Medicine*] (DMAA)
IPF.......... Iodine Protection Factor [*Nuclear energy*] (GFGA)
IPF.......... Irish Printing Federation (BI)
IPF.......... Isotope Production Facility
IPF.......... IUS Processing Facility [*NASA*] (NASA)
IPf.......... Park Forest Public Library, Park Forest, IL [*Library symbol*] [*Library of Congress*] (LCLS)
IPFA.......... Information Project for Africa [*Washington, D.C.*] (EA)
IPFA.......... Institute for Psychiatry and Foreign Affairs [*Defunct*] (EA)
IPFA.......... Institute of Public Finance Accountants (SAUS)
IPFA.......... Institute of Public Finance and Accountancy (SAUS)
IPFA.......... Insurance Premium Finance Association (EA)
IPFA.......... International Physical Fitness Association (EA)
IPFA.......... International Population and Family Association (EA)
IPFA.......... International Professional Security Association (SAUO)
IPFA.......... Member of the Chartered Institute of Public Finance and Accountancy [*British*]
IPFAA.......... International Police and Fire Athletic Association [*Defunct*] (EA)
IPF Bulletin... Infantile Paralysis Fellowship Bulletin (journ.) (SAUS)
iPFC.......... Indirect Plaque-Forming Cell [*Immunology*]
IPFC.......... Indo-Pacific Fisheries Commission [*or Council*] [*FAO*] [*ICSU*] [*Bangkok, Thailand*] [*United Nations*] (ASF)
IPFC.......... Indo-Pacific Fisheries Council (SAUO)
IPFC.......... Indo-Pacific Fishery Commission (EAIO)
IPFC.......... Industrial Promotion and Productivity Center (SAUS)
IPFC.......... Information Presentation Facility Compiler (SAUS)
IPFC.......... Integrated Flight and Propulsion Control (SAUS)
IPFD.......... Incident Power Flux Density (NITA)
IPFD.......... Input Power Flux Density (SAUS)
IPFD.......... Intrapartum Fetal Distress [*Obstetrics*] (DAVI)
IPFEO.......... Institut des Producteurs de Ferro-Alliages d'Europe Occidentale [*Institute of Ferro-Alloy Producers in Western Europe - IFAPWE*] [*Defunct*] (EA)
IPFF.......... International Planned Parenthood Federation (SAUO)
IPFM.......... Impact Form (SAUS)
IPFM.......... Inlet Plenum Feature Model (SAUS)
IPFM.......... Integral Pulse Frequency Modulation (IEEE)
IPFM.......... Integral-type Pulse Frequency Modulation (SAUS)
IPFP.......... Institut Professionnel de la Fonction Publique du Canada [*Professional Institute of the Public Service of Canada - PIPS*]
IPFP.......... Iterated Proportional Fitting Procedure [*Statistics*]
IPFR.......... Institute of Plasma and Fusion Research [*University of California, Los Angeles*] [*Research center*] (RCD)
IPFR.......... Institute on Plasma and Fusion Research (SAUS)
IPFS.......... Integrated Polygenerator Fertilizer System
IPFS.......... International Pen Friend Service (EA)
IPfs.......... Park Forest South Public Library, Park Forest South, IL [*Library symbol*] [*Library of Congress*] (LCLS)
IPFSC.......... International Pacific Salmon Fisheries Commission [*Marine science*] (OSRA)
IPfsG.......... Governors State University, Park Forest South, IL [*Library symbol*] [*Library of Congress*] (LCLS)
IPfsI.......... Inolex Pharmaceutical Co., Park Forest South, IL [*Library symbol*] [*Library of Congress*] (LCLS)
IPFV.......... Intake Pseudo-Flow Velocity
IPFW.......... Indiana University - Purdue University at Fort Wayne
IPF/X.......... Interactive Productivity Facility for X-Windows (SAUS)
IPG.......... Immediate Participation Guarantee (SAUS)
IPG.......... Immediate Participation Guarantee Plan [*Insurance*]
IPG.......... Immobilized pH Gradients [*Chemistry*]
IPG.......... Impedance Plethysmography [*Medicine*]
IPG.......... Implantable Pulse Generator (SAUS)
IPG.......... In-Circuit Program Generator [*Computer science*] (PDAA)
IPG.......... Income Property Group (SAUO)
IPG.......... Independent Publishers Group
IPG.......... Independent Publishers' Guild [*British*]
IPG.......... Index Pulse Generator (ACAE)
IPG.......... Individually Polymerized Grass [*Organic chemistry*] (DAVI)
IPG.......... Induction Plasma Gun
IPG.......... Industrial Painters Group [*British*] (BI)
IPG.......... Industrial Physics Group [*University of Essex*] [*British*] (IRUK)
IPG.......... Industrial Policy Group (SAUO)
IPG.......... Information Planning Group (SSD)
IPG.......... Information Policy Group (NITA)
IPG.......... Information Publishing Group [*The Thomson Corp.*]
IPG.......... Inositol-Phosphoglycan [*Biochemistry*]
IPG.......... INPADOC Patent Gazette (NITA)
IPG.......... In Plane Gate Transistor (SAUS)
IPG.......... Inspiration-Phase Gas (DMAA)
IPG.......... Institut de Physique du Globe [*France*]
IPG.......... Institute of Professional Goldsmiths [*British*] (DBA)
IPG.......... Integrative Policy Group (GART)
IPG.......... Interactive Presentation Graphics [*IBM Corp.*]
IPG.......... Internal Problem Generator (IAA)
IPG.......... International Pagurian Corp. Ltd. [*Toronto Stock Exchange symbol*] [*Vancouver Stock Exchange symbol*]
IPG.......... International Parliamentary Group for Human Rights in the Soviet Union (EA)
IPG.......... International Payments Group (NATG)
IPG.......... International Piano Guild (EA)
IPG.......... International Planning Group [*Belgium, Germany, Netherlands*] (AABC)
IPG.......... International Portrait Gallery
IPG.......... International Preparatory Group (SAUO)
IPG.......... International Professional Groomers (NTPA)
IPG.......... International Programmers Guild (SAUO)
IPG.......... Inter Packet Gap (SAUS)
IPG.......... Inter-Professional Group (GVA)
IPG.......... Interproject Group
IPG.......... [*The*] Interpublic Group of Companies, Inc. [*NYSE symbol*] (SPSG)
IPG.......... Interpublic Grp Cos. [*NYSE symbol*] (TTSB)
IPG.......... Isopropylidene Glycerol [*Biochemistry*]
IPG.......... Isopropylthiogalactoside [*Also, IPTG*] [*Organic chemistry*]
IPG.......... Isotope Power Generator
IPG.......... Issue Priority Group [*Army*]
IPG.......... Phoolbagh [*India*] [*Airport symbol*] (AD)
IPGA.......... Illinois Personnel and Guidance Association (SAUO)
IPGA.......... Illinois Propane Gas Association (SRA)
IPGA.......... Indiana Propane Gas Association (SRA)
IPGA.......... Iowa Personnel and Guidance Association (SAUO)
IPGA.......... Island Park Geothermal Area
IPGCU.......... International Printing and Graphic Communications Union
iPGE.......... Prostaglandin E, immunoreactive [*Biochemistry*]
IPGEN.......... Intersection Point Generator (PDAA)
IPGF.......... Immobilized pH Gradient Isoelectric Focusing [*Analytical biochemistry*]
IPGH.......... Instituto Panamericano de Geografia e Historia [*Panamerican Institute of Geography and History*] [*Peru*]
IPGI.......... Institute on Pluralism and Group Identity (EA)
IPGIT.......... International Planning Group Implementation Team (SAUO)
IPGP.......... Illegal Possession of Government Property
IPGRI.......... International Plant Genetic Resources Institute [*Italy*]
IPGS.......... Industrial Postgraduate Scholarship (SAUS)
IPGS.......... Intercollegiate Program of Graduate Studies
IPGS.......... Internationale Paracelsus-Gesellschaft zu Salzburg (EAIO)
IPGS.......... International Percy Grainger Society (EA)
IPH.......... Idiopathic Portal Hypertension [*Medicine*]
IPH.......... Idiopathic Pulmonary Hemosiderosis [*Medicine*]
iph.......... Impressions per Hour (WDAA)
IPH.......... Impressions per Hour [*Printing*]
IPH.......... Inches per Hour (TEL)
IPH.......... Industrial and Pastoral Holdings (ADA)
IPH.......... Inflammatory Papillary Hyperplasia [*Dentistry*]
IPH.......... Interdisciplinary Programs in Health [*Harvard University*]
IPH.......... International Association of Paper Historians (EA)
IPH.......... International Pharmadyne Ltd. [*Vancouver Stock Exchange symbol*]
IPH.......... International Publishing House (SAUO)
IPh.......... Interphalangeal [*Medicine*] (EDAA)
IPH.......... Interphalangeal [*Anatomy*]
IPH.......... Intraparenchymal Hemorrhage [*Medicine*]
IPH.......... Ipoh [*Malaysia*] [*Airport symbol*] (OAG)

IPh .... Peoria Heights Public Library, Peoria Heights, IL [*Library symbol*] [*Library of Congress*] (LCLS)
IPH .... Industrial Process Heat(ing) (ODA)
IphA .... Illinois Pharmacists Association (SRA)
IPHA .... Illinois Public Health Association (SRA)
IPHAB .... Intergovernmental Panel on Harmful Algal Blooms (SAUS)
IPHC .... International Pacific Halibut Commission (EA)
IPHCSP .... International Pacific Halibut Commission. Scientific Report (journ.) (SAUS)
IPHCTR .... International Pacific Halibut Commission. Technical Report (journ.) (SAUS)
IPHE .... Individual Personal Hygiene Equipment (KSC)
IPHE .... Institute of Public Health Engineers [*British*]
IPHE .... Institution of Public Health Engineers (SAUO)
IPHE .... International Personal Hygiene Equipment (SAUS)
IPhe .... Palos Heights Public Library, Palos Heights, IL [*Library symbol*] [*Library of Congress*] (LCLS)
IPHF .... Illinois Poultry and Hatchery Federation (SAUO)
IP/HHCL .... Initial Point/H-Hour Control Line [*Aviation*]
IPhi .... Green Hills Public Library District, Palos Hills, IL [*Library symbol*] [*Library of Congress*] (LCLS)
IPHi .... Peoria Historical Society, Peoria, IL [*Library symbol*] [*Library of Congress*] (LCLS)
IPhil .... Philo Township Public Library, Philo, IL [*Library symbol*] [*Library of Congress*] (LCLS)
IPhiM .... Moraine Valley Community College, Palos Hills, IL [*Library symbol*] [*Library of Congress*] (LCLS)
IPhiP .... Green Hills Public Library District, Palos Hills, IL [*Library symbol*] [*Library of Congress*] (LCLS)
IPHIR .... Interplanetary Helioseismology with Irradiance Observations (ADWA)
IPHM .... Individual Personal Hygiene Module (KSC)
IPHO .... International Public Health Office (SAUO)
IPHP .... Intraperitoneal Hyperthermic Perfusion [*Medicine*] (MELL)
IP-HPLC .... Ion-Pair High-Performance Liquid Chromatography [*Medicine*]
IPhQ .... International Philosophical Quarterly (SAUO)
IPHR .... Inverted Polypoid Hamartoma of the Rectum [*Medicine*] (DMAA)
IPHRD .... International Program for Human Resource Development [*Defunct*] (EA)
IPHT .... Institute of Physical High Technology [*Germany*]
IPhys .... Institute of Physics (COBU)
IPI .... Identified Friendly Prior to Interception [*Military*]
IPI .... Image Processing and Interchange (SAUS)
IPI .... Image Processing Interface [*Computer science*] (PCM)
IPI .... Imagined Process Inventory (STED)
IPI .... Immigration Patrol Inspector [*Immigration and Naturalization Service*]
IPI .... Implicit Price Index (MHDW)
ipi .... Impregnated Paper Insulated (SAUS)
IPI .... Improved Processing Inspection [*Food Safety and Inspection Service*] [*Department of Agriculture*]
IPI .... Incipient Paranoia Index (SAUS)
IPI .... Income and Price Index (DICI)
IPI .... INCYTE Pharmaceuticals, Inc. [*AMEX symbol*] (SPSG)
IPI .... Index of Production Industries [*Department of Employment*] [*British*]
IPI .... Indian Political Intelligence (SAUO)
IPI .... Individually Planned [*or Prescribed*] Instruction [*Education*]
IPI .... Individually Presented Instruction (NITA)
IPI .... Individual Process Instructional (SAUS)
IPI .... Individual Progress Instructional (SAUS)
IPI .... Industrial Product Information (SAUS)
IPI .... Industrial Production Index (PDAA)
IPI .... Industrial Programming, Inc. (SAUS)
IPI .... Industrial Programming, Incorporated (SAUO)
IPI .... Infinite Position Indicator (PDAA)
IPI .... Inflation Protected Income (DICI)
IPI .... Information Professionals Institute (IID)
IPI .... Information Publications International [*Publisher*] [*British*]
IPI .... Initial Position Indicator (SAUS)
IPI .... Initial Product Inspection
IPI .... Initial Protocol Identifier [*Computer science*] (TNIG)
Ipl .... Inosylylinosine (SAUS)
IPI .... In Partibus Infidelium [*In the Countries, Lands, or Regions of Unbelievers*] [*Latin*]
IPI .... In Process Inventory (SAUS)
IPI .... Inspection Planning for Installation (SAUO)
IPI .... Institute for Practical Idealism (EA)
IPI .... Institute for Public Information
IPI .... Institute of Patentees and Inventors [*British*] (ILCA)
IPI .... Institute of Physical Medicine and Rehabilitation, Peoria, IL [*Library symbol*] [*Library of Congress*] (LCLS)
IPI .... Institute of Polymer Industry (SAUS)
IPI .... Institute of Poultry Industries
IPI .... Institute of Professional Investigators (EA)
IPI .... Instrument Principal Investigator (SAUS)
IPI .... Insurance Periodicals Index [*Nils Publishing Co.*] [*Chatsworth, CA*] [*Information service or system*] (IID)
IPI .... Integrated Permits and Inspections (SAUS)
IPI .... Integrated Position Indicator
IPI .... Intelligence Publications Index [*Published January, 1953, through February, 1968, by the Defense Intelligence Agency*]
IPI .... Intelligent Peripheral Interface [*Computer science*]
IPI .... Intelligent Peripherals Interface (SAUO)
IPI .... Intelligent Printer Interface
IPI .... Intense Product Inspection
IPI .... Intercept Pattern for Identification (SAUS)
IPI .... Interchemical Printing Inks
IPI .... Interested Party Information
IPI .... Interior Point Intermodal (SAUS)
IPI .... Internal Procedures Instruction
IPI .... International Patent Institute [*Later, EPO*]
IPI .... International Patents Institute (SAUS)
IPI .... International Pesticide Institute
IPI .... International Petroleum Institute (SAUO)
IPI .... International Phototherapy Institute [*Defunct*] (EA)
IPI .... International Police Information (SAUO)
IPI .... International Population Institute [*Defunct*] (EA)
IPI .... International Potash Institute [*See also IIP*] (EAIO)
IPI .... International Press Institute [*Switzerland*] (PDAA)
IPI .... International Press Institute, American Committee (EA)
IPI .... International Psychosomatics Institute (EA)
IPI .... Interphonemic Interval (STED)
IPI .... Interpositional Implant (SAUS)
IPI .... Interpulse Interval
IPI .... Intrapair Interval
IPI .... Inventory, Print, and Index [*System*]
IPI .... Investment-Properties International Ltd. (SAUO)
IPI .... Inwald Personality Inventory [*Test*] (TES)
IPI .... Iolani Place Irregulars (EA)
IPI .... IPC Information Systems, Inc. [*AMEX symbol*] (NASQ)
IPI .... Ipiales [*Colombia*] [*Airport symbol*] (OAG)
IPI .... Isophorone Diisocyanate (SAUS)
IPIA .... Immunoperoxidase Infectivity Assay (DB)
IPIA .... Independent Primary Inspection Agency [*Department of Housing and Urban Development*] (GFGA)
IPIA .... Induced Psycho-Intellectual Activity (PDAA)
IPIACFA .... International Private Investment Advisory Council on Foreign Aid [*Agency for International Development*] (EGAO)
IPiaMCD .... Macoupin Community Unit, District 9, Piasa, IL [*Library symbol*] [*Library of Congress*] (LCLS)
IPiaSD .... Southwestern Community Unit, School District 9, Piasa, IL [*Library symbol*] [*Library of Congress*] (LCLS)
IPIB .... Israel Produce Information Bureau (SAUO)
IPIC .... Initial Production and Inventory Control (SAUS)
IPIC .... In Process Inventory Control (SAUS)
IPIC .... Institute of Personal Image Consultants (EA)
IPIC .... Intelligent Power Integrated Circuit [*Electronics*]
IPIC .... Interneuron Pharmaceuticals [*NASDAQ symbol*] (TTSB)
IPIC .... Interneuron Pharmaceuticals, Inc. [*NASDAQ symbol*] (SAG)
IPICS .... Initial Production and Information Control System [*Computer science*] (PDAA)
IPICS .... Initial Production Inventory Control System (SAUS)
IPICS .... Initial Produdion and Inventory Control System (SAUS)
IPID .... International Project in Dendroclimatology (SAUO)
IPIE .... Institute of Profit Improvement Executives [*British*] (DBA)
IPIE .... Intrapulmonary Interstitial Emphysema [*Medicine*] (MELL)
IPIECA .... International Petroleum Industry Environmental Conservation Association [*British*] (EAIO)
IPIECA .... International Petroleum Manufacturers of Internal Combustion Engines (SAUO)
IPIF .... Institute of Pacific Islands Forestry [*Honolulu, HI*] [*Department of Agriculture*] (GRD)
IPIG .... ILL-Protocol Implementors Group (SAUO)
IPI/IMPC .... International Parking Institute (NTPA)
IPI Inc .... IPI, Inc. [*Associated Press*] (SAG)
IPIL .... Integrated Primary Inspection Line (FOTI)
IPILL .... Individualized Programmed Learning Laboratory (SAUO)
IPI/MIS .... Individually Planned Instruction/Management and Information System
IPI/MIS .... International Press Institute/Management and Information System [*Switzerland*]
IPIN .... Instituto Panamericano de Ingenieria Naval [*Pan American Institute of Naval Engineering*] (EAIO)
IPIN .... Integrated Photogrammetric Instrument Network (PDAA)
IP/IN .... Interpositive/Internegative [*Photography*] (WDMC)
IPIP .... Implantable Programmable Infusion Pump [*Medicine*]
IPIP .... Information Processing Improvement Program
IPIP .... Input Intercept-Point (SAUS)
IPIP .... International Personhood of Illiterate Programmers (SAUO)
IPIP .... Internet Protocol within Internet Protocol (SAUS)
IPip .... Piper City Public Library, Piper City, IL [*Library symbol*] [*Library of Congress*] (LCLS)
IPIPS .... Interactive Planetary Image Processing System
IPipSD .... Ford Central Community Unit Shool District, Piper City, IL [*Library symbol*] [*Library of Congress*] (LCLS)
IPIR .... Immediate Photographic Interpretation Report (SAUO)
IPIR .... Immediate Photograph Intelligence Report [*Military*] (AFM)
IPIR .... Initial Photographic Interpretation Report [*Air Force*]
IPIR .... Initial Programmed Interpretation Report (SAUO)
IPIR .... Institute for Public Interest Representation [*Later, CCCIPR*] [*Georgetown University*]
IPIR .... Integrated Personnel Information Report (AAG)
IPI Report .... International Press Institute Report (journ.) (SAUS)
IPIS .... Incomplete Pulmonary Infarction [*Medicine*] (MELL)
IPIS .... Individually Prescribed Instructional Systems (OICC)
IPIS .... Institute for Peace and International Security (EA)
IPIS .... Instrument Pilot Instructor School [*Air Force*]
IPIS .... International Peace Information Service [*Belgium*]
IPISD .... Interservice Procedures for Instructional Systems Development
IPI System .... Inventory, Print and Index System (SAUS)
IPIT .... International Property Investment Trust, Luxembourg (SAUO)
IPit .... Pittsfield Public Library, Pittsfield, IL [*Library symbol*] [*Library of Congress*] (LCLS)

IPIU .... Instrument Power Interface Unit (ACAE)
IPIV .... Illinois Valley Library System, Peoria, IL [*Library symbol*] [*Library of Congress*] (LCLS)
IPIX .... Interface Processor for Imagery Exchange (SAUS)
IPIx .... International Plant Index (SAUO)
IPJ .... Institute for Peace and Justice (EA)
IPJ .... Intellectual Property Journal [*A publication*]
IPJ .... International Pursuit Corp. [*Toronto Stock Exchange symbol*]
IPJ .... Interphalangeal Joint [*Anatomy*] (DAVI)
IPJP .... Interpost Junction Panel
IPJT .... Interplant Job Ticket
IPK .... Imperial Parking Corp. [*AMEX symbol*] (SG)
IPK .... Individual Protection Kit (SAUS)
IPK .... Interactive Press Kit [*Public relations*] (WDMC)
IPK .... International Packers, Ltd. (SAUO)
IPK .... International Prototype Kilogram
IPK .... Interphalangeal Keratosis [*Orthopedics*] (DAVI)
IPK .... Intractable Plantar Keratosis [*Orthopedics*] (DAVI)
IPK .... Painter Creek, AK [*Location identifier*] [*FAA*] (FAAL)
IPK .... Peoria Kindergarten Primary Training School, Peoria, IL [*Library symbol*] [*Library of Congress*] (LCLS)
IPKC .... International Pot and Kettle Clubs (EA)
IPKD .... Infantile Polycystic Kidney Disease [*Medicine*] (STED)
IPKF .... Indian Peace-Keeping Force [*Army*]
IPKF .... International Professional Kneeboarding Federation (SAUO)
IPKO .... International Information Centre on Peace-Keeping Operations (SAUO)
IPKO .... International Information on Peace-Keeping Operations
IPL .... Air Charter Services (Pty) Ltd. South Africa [*ICAO designator*] (FAAC)
IPL .... El Centro/Imperial [*California*] [*Airport symbol*] (OAG)
IPL .... Identified Parts List
IPL .... Illustrated Parts List (NATG)
IPL .... Illustrated Pocket Library [*A publication*]
IPL .... Image Processing Laboratory [*University of Houston*] [*Research center*] (RCD)
IPL .... Imperial, CA [*Location identifier*] [*FAA*] (FAAL)
IPL .... Improved Position Locator (PDAA)
IPL .... Indentured Parts List
IPL .... Independent Publishers League [*Defunct*] (EA)
IPL .... Indianapolis Power and Light (SAUS)
IPL .... Indianapolis Power and Light Company (SAUO)
IPL .... Individual Protection Laboratory [*Natick, MA*] [*Army*] (RDA)
IPL .... Industrial Programming Language (SAUO)
IPL .... Inferior Parietal Lobule [*Anatomy*]
IPL .... Information Processing Language [*Computer science*]
IPL .... Information Processing Letters (journ.) (SAUS)
IPL .... Information Processing Ltd. (SAUO)
IPL .... Information Program Loading (SAUS)
IPL .... Information Programming Language (SAUO)
IPL .... Initialize Program Load (SAUS)
IPL .... Initial Program Load [*Computer science*]
IPL .... Initial Program Loader [*Computer science*] (ELAL)
IPL .... Initial Program Loading [*Computer science*] (ELAL)
IPL .... Initial Provisioning List (MCD)
IPL .... Inner Plexiform Layer [*Retina*]
IPL .... In-Pile Loop (SAUS)
IPL .... Input Parameter List (SAUS)
IPL .... Installation Parts List (AAG)
IPL .... Institute of Professional Librarians [*Canada*]
IPL .... Instro Precision Ltd. (SAUO)
IPL .... Instrumentation Program List
IPL .... Instrument Panel Lighting (MCD)
IPL .... Instrument Pool Laboratory (IAA)
IPL .... Instrumet Panel Lighting (SAUS)
IPL .... Integrated Parts List (SAUS)
IPL .... Integrated Payload [*NASA*]
IPL .... Integrated Perceived Level [*Acoustics*]
IPL .... Integrated Priority List [*DoD*]
IPL .... Interconnected Porosity (SAUS)
IPL .... Interconnected Porosity Level
IPL .... Interdivisional Programming List (SAUS)
IPL .... Interested Parties List
IPL .... Interim Parts List [*Navy*]
IPL .... Interim Policy Letter [*Air Force*] (AAGC)
IPL .... International Packers Limited (SAUO)
IPL .... Internet Public Library [*Established by the University of Michigan in 1995*]
IPL .... Interplanetary Physics Laboratory (SAUO)
IPL .... Interprovincial Pipe Line Ltd. [*Toronto Stock Exchange symbol*]
IPL .... Interpupillary Line (STED)
IPL .... Interrupt Priority Level
ipl .... Intrapleural [*Medicine*] (EDAA)
IPL .... Intrapleural
IPL .... Ion Projection Lithography (AAEL)
IPL .... Iota Phi Lambda Sorority (AEBS)
IPL .... IPALCO Enterprises [*NYSE symbol*] (TTSB)
IPL .... IPALCO Enterprises, Inc. [*NYSE symbol*] (SPSG)
IPL .... Isolated Perfused Lung [*Medicine*] (MELL)
IPL .... Isotope Products Laboratory (SAUS)
IPL .... Italian Pacific Line (SAUO)
IPL .... Purdue University, Lafayette, IN [*OCLC symbol*] (OCLC)
IPLA .... Institute of Public Loss Assessors [*British*] (DBA)
IPLA .... Instituto Pastoral Latinoamericano
IPLA .... Interstate Producers Livestock Association (EA)
IPLAN .... Integrated Planning and Analysis (SAUS)
IPLAN .... Joint IOC/WMO Planning Group for IGOSS [*Marine science*] (MSC)
IPlantE .... Institution of Plant Engineers [*British*] (EAIO)
I Plant Eng ... Institution of Plant Engineers (SAUS)
IPLC .... Interferometer Position Location Concept (ACAE)
IPLC .... International Private Leased Circuit (SAUO)
IPLC .... International Private Leased Circuits [*British Telecom International*] (NITA)
IPLCA .... International Pipe Line Contractors Association [*Later, IPOCA*] (EA)
IPLCA .... International Pipeline Contractors Association (SAUO)
IPLDC .... International Private Leased Data Circuit (SAUS)
IPLE .... Index Pulse Leading Edge (ACAE)
IPLE .... Institute for Political/Legal Education (SAUO)
IPLE .... Institute of Public Lighting Engineers (SAUS)
IPLE .... Institution of Public Lighting Engineers [*British*]
IPL En .... IPL Energy, Inc. [*Associated Press*] (SAG)
IPLF .... Isogrid Payload Fairing (MCD)
IPLGY .... Institute for the Protection of Lesbian and Gay Youth (EA)
IPLI .... Internet Private Line Interface (ACAE)
IPLIB .... Image Processing Library (SAUS)
IPLL .... Illinois Publications in Language and Literature (journ.) (SAUS)
IPLL .... InterPharm Laboratories Limited (SAUO)
IPLLF .... InterPharm Laboratories Ltd. [*NASDAQ symbol*] (COMM)
IPLO .... Institute of Professional Librarians of Ontario (SAUO)
IPLO .... Iranian Palestine Liberation Organization (CARL)
IPLOCA .... International Pipe Line and Offshore Contractors Association [*Belgium*] (EAIO)
IPLO Quart ... Institute of Professional Librarians of Ontario Quarterly (SAUO)
IPLO Quart ... Institute of Professional Librarians of Ontario Quarterly (journ.) (SAUS)
IPLP .... Initial Program Load Program (SAUS)
IPLS .... IPL Systems Cl'A' [*NASDAQ symbol*] (TTSB)
IPLS .... IPL Systems, Inc. [*NASDAQ symbol*] (NQ)
IPLSA .... Illinois Professional Land Surveyors Association (SAUO)
IPLSA .... IPL Systems, Inc. (Class A) [*NASDAQ symbol*] (COMM)
IPL Sy .... IPL Systems, Inc. [*Associated Press*] (SAG)
IPLV .... Indicated Part-Load Value
IPLV .... Information Processing Language Five
IPL-V .... Information Processing Language-V (DIPS)
IPLV .... Intermediate Payload Launch Vehicle
IPLWG .... Industrial Partnership Laboratory Working Group (SAUO)
IPLX .... Illinois Power [*Private rail car owner code*]
IPlx .... International Plant Index [*A publication*]
IPLY .... Interplay Entertainment Corp. [*NASDAQ symbol*] (NASQ)
ipm .... Iches Per Month (SAUS)
IPM .... Illumination per Minute
IPM .... Illuminations per Minute (SAUS)
IPM .... Images Per Minute (SAUS)
IPM .... Immediate Past Master [*Freemasonry*]
IPM .... Immediate Pigment Darkening [*Medicine*] (MELL)
IPM .... Immigration Program Manager (FOTI)
IPM .... Imperial Metals Corp. [*Toronto Stock Exchange symbol*] [*Vancouver Stock Exchange symbol*]
IPM .... Implementation Program Manager (SAUO)
IPM .... Impulses per Minute [*Telecommunications*]
IPM .... Inches Penetration per Month (IAA)
ipm .... Inches per Minute (IDOE)
IPM .... Inches per Minute
IPM .... Incidental Phase [*or Pulse*] Modulation
IPM .... Incident Popwer Monitor (SAUS)
IPM .... Incident Power Meter (SAUS)
IPM .... Incident Power Monitor [*Military*] (CAAL)
IPM .... Incremental Phase Modulation (CIST)
IPM .... Incremental Phase Modulator (SAUS)
IPM .... Independent Particle Model (SAUS)
IPM .... Indomethacin-Treated Platelet Microsomes
IPM .... Industrial Preparedness Measures
IPM .... Industrial Productivity Monitoring (SAUS)
IPM .... Industry Preparedness Measures (SAUS)
IPM .... Infant Passive Mitt (STED)
IPM .... Infectious Polymyositis [*Medicine*] (MELL)
IPM .... Informal Planning Meeting (SAUS)
IPM .... Information Processing Machine (SAUS)
IPM .... Infusible Platelet Membrane [*Substitute for blood tranfusion*]
IPM .... Inhalable Particulate Matter (GNE)
IPM .... Initial Pretreatment Module (ABAC)
IPM .... Inner Peace Movement (EA)
IPM .... Innter Peace Movement (SAUO)
IPM .... Input Pins of Module (SAUS)
IPM .... Input Position Map [*Computer science*] (OA)
IPM .... Input Position Mapper (SAUS)
IPM .... Insect Populations Management Research Unit [*Department of Agriculture*] (GRD)
IPM .... Inspirable Particulate Mass (LDOE)
IPM .... Install Permanent Mitigation pump (SAUS)
IPM .... Institute for Police Management (SAUS)
IPM .... Institute for Practical Mathematics (SAUS)
IPM .... Institute of Personnel Management [*British*] (DCTA)
IPM .... Institute of Police Management (SAUO)
IPM .... Institute of Practical Mathematics [*Germany*]
IPM .... Institute of Precious Metals [*China*]
IPM .... Institute of Printing Management [*British*]
IPM .... Institute of Project Management (COBU)
IPM .... Instructional Programming Model [*Individually-guided education*] (AEE)

IPM............ Instrument Performance Model (ARMP)
IPM............ Integrated Past Management (SAUO)
IPM............ Integrated Pest Management [*Agronomy*]
IPM............ Integrated Post Management (SAUS)
IPM............ Integrated Power Management
IPM............ Integrated Program Manager (ABAC)
IPM............ Integrated Propulsion Module (SAUS)
IPM............ Intelligent Power Management [*Laptop computers*] (BYTE)
IPM............ Intelligent Power Mode (SAUO)
IPM............ Intelligent Power Module (CIST)
IPM............ Intelligent Power MOS (SAUS)
IPM............ Intelligent Processing of Materials [*Computer science*]
IPM............ Intel Power Monitor (PCM)
IPM............ Interaction Place Map (EDAC)
IPM............ Interactive Performance Monitor (SAUS)
IPM............ Interaural Phase Modulation [*Audiology*]
IPM............ Interference Prediction Model
IPM............ Intermediate Past Master (SAUO)
IPM............ Internal Polarization Modulation (IEEE)
IPM............ International Prison Ministry (EA)
IPM............ International Program Manager (SAUS)
IPM............ International Prototype Meter
IPM............ Internet Protection Module [*Computer science*]
IPM............ Interpersonal Mail System [*Computer science*] (TNIG)
IPM............ Interpersonal Message (SAUO)
IPM............ Interpersonal Messaging [*Telecommunications*] (OSI)
IPM............ Interpersonal Messaging Service
IPM............ Interpersonal Perception Method [*Psychology*]
IPM............ Interphotoreceptor Matrix [*Ophthalmology*]
IPM............ Interplanetary Medium
IPM............ Inter-Processor/Multiplexer (MCD)
IPM............ Interruptions per Minute
IPM............ Inventory Policy Model (MHDI)
IPM............ Inventory Project Management (SAUO)
IPM............ Investment Performance Measurement (SAUS)
IPM............ IPM Technology, Inc. (SAUO)
IPM............ Isolated Pacing Message (SAUS)
IPM............ Isopropylmalate (SAUS)
IPM............ Isopropyl Myristate [*Pharmacology*]
IPM............ Morrison and Mary Wiley Public Library, Elmwood, IL [*OCLC symbol*] (OCLC)
IPM............ Peoria Masonic Temple, Peoria, IL [*Library symbol*] [*Library of Congress*] (LCLS)
IPMA............ In-Plant Management Association (EA)
IPMA............ In-Plant Printing Management Association
IPMA............ Interlocking Paving Manufacturers Association [*Defunct*] (EA)
IPMA............ International Personnel Management Association (EA)
IPMA............ International Planned Music Association (EA)
IPMA............ International Primary Market Association (EAIO)
IPMA............ International Publishing Management Association (NTPA)
IPMANA....... Interstate Postgraduate Medical Association of North America (EA)
IPMAR........ Portuguese Institute of Marine Research (SAUS)
IPMC.......... International Police Motor Corporation (SAUO)
IPmc........... IP Multicast [*Communications term*] (DCT)
IPMCF......... International Precious Metals [*NASDAQ symbol*] (SAG)
IPMDH......... Isopropylmalate Dehydrogenase [*An enzyme*]
IPMER......... Institute of Post-Graduate Medical Education and Research (SAUO)
IP Method.... Induced Polarization Method (SAUS)
IPMF........... In Process Material File (SAUS)
IPMH........... Methodist Hospital of Central Illinois, Peoria, IL [*Library symbol*] [*Library of Congress*] (LCLS)
IPMH-M....... Methodist Medical Center of Illinois, Medical Library, Peoria, IL [*Library symbol*] [*Library of Congress*] (LCLS)
IPMI............ Inferoposterior Myocardial Infarct [*or Infarction*] [*Cardiology*] (DAVI)
IPMI............ Intelligent Platform Management Interface [*Computer science*]
IPMI............ International Photographers of the Motion Picture Industries (SAUO)
IPMI............ International Powder Metallurgy Institute (SAUS)
IPMI............ International Precious Metals Institute (EA)
IPMI............ Internet Provider Multicast Initiative (SAUS)
IPMIS.......... Integrated Procurement Management Information System (SAUO)
IPMIS.......... Interim Project Management Information System (SAUO)
IPMLF.......... Intl Precious Metals [*NASDAQ symbol*] (TTSB)
IP-MMP....... Info Process-Mask Management Package (SAUS)
IPMN........... Inhalable Particulate Network (SAUS)
IPMN........... Integrated Pest Management Network (SAUO)
IPMO........... Implementation Program Management Office (SAUO)
IPMO........... International Program Management Office (SAUS)
IPMO........... International Project Management Office (ACAE)
IPMP........... IEEE [*Institute of Electrical and Electronics Engineers*] Parts, Materials and Packaging (IAA)
IPMP........... Industrial Plant Modernization Program [*Air Force*]
IPMP........... Industrial Plant Modernization Program set (SAUS)
IP/MP.......... Inphase/Midphase (MHDI)
IPMP........... Integrated Pest Management Programs (SAUO)
IPMP........... Intellectual Property Management Program (SAUS)
IPMP........... Isopropyl(methoxy)pyrazine [*Organic chemistry*]
IPMPCS....... Integrated Pest Management and Program Coordination Staff [*Environmental Protection Agency*] (GFGA)
IPMPI.......... International Photographers of the Motion Picture Industries (SAUO)
IPMR........... Institute of Physical Medicine and Rehabilitation (SAUO)
IPMRN......... Integrated Pest Management Research Network (SAUO)
IPMS........... Impact Predictor Monitor Set [*NASA*] (AAG)
IPMS........... Impact Predictor Monitor System (SAUS)
IPMS........... Infinite Periodic Minimal Surface
IPMS........... Information Processing Management System (SAUO)
IPMS........... Institute for Problems of Materials Science [*Ukraine*]
IPMS........... Institute of Physical Scientists in Medicine (WDAA)
IPMS........... Institution of Professionals, Managers, and Specialists [*British*]
IPMS........... Integrated Pest Managment and Program Coordination Staff (SAUS)
IPMS........... Integrated Platform Management System (SAUS)
IPMS........... Integrated Program Management System [*Navy*]
IPMS........... Intergrated Program Management System (SAUS)
IPMS........... International Plastic Modelers Society (EA)
IPMS........... International Plastic Modellers Society (SAUO)
IPMS........... International Polar Motion Service
IPMS........... International Primitive Money Society (EA)
IPMS........... Interpersonal Message (or Messaging) Services (SAUO)
IPMS........... Inter-Personal Messaging Service (SAUS)
IPM/S.......... Interruption per Minute/Second (SAUS)
IPM/S.......... Interruptions per Minute/Second (DEN)
IPMS........... Investment Performance Monitoring Service [*British*]
IPMS........... Isopropylmethane Sulphonate (SAUS)
IPMS/USA.... International Plastic Modelers Society/US Branch (EA)
IPMT........... Interim Programme Management Team (SAUS)
IPM TLVs..... Inhalable Particulate Mass TLVs [*Industrial hygiene term*] (OHS)
IPMV95....... Integrated Packet Trunk Module V.95 Interface (SAUS)
IPMZ........... Interstate Paper Mill [*Federal Railroad Administration identification code*]
IPN............. Impulse Noise
IPN............. Indigenous People's Network (EA)
IPN............. Industri Pesawat Terbang Nusantara PT [*Indonesia*] [*ICAO designator*] (FAAC)
IPN............. Infantile Periarteritis Nodosa [*Cardiology*] (DAVI)
IPN............. Infectious Pancreatic Necrosis [*Medicine*]
IPN............. Info Pool Network (SAUO)
IPN............. Information Processing Network
IPN............. Initial Priority Number [*Computer science*] (OA)
IPN............. Initial Processing Number (NITA)
IPN............. Inspection Progress Notification
IPN............. Instant Private Network
IPN............. Instrumentation Plan Number (MUGU)
IPN............. Instrument Plan Number (SAUS)
IPN............. Integrated Packet Network [*Hughes Network Systems, Inc.*]
IPN............. Integrated Priority Number (SAUS)
IPN............. Integrated Project Network (SAUO)
IPN............. Integrated Provider Network (ADWA)
IPN............. Intellectual Property Network, Ltd. [*Information service or system*] (IID)
IPN............. Interim Progress Note (STED)
IPN............. Internal Priority Number (SAUS)
IPN............. International Platinum Corp. [*Toronto Stock Exchange symbol*]
IPN............. International Polio Network (EA)
IPN............. International Publishing Newsletter (NITA)
IPN............. Internet Protocol Number (SAUS)
IPN............. Intern's Progress Note [*Medical records*] (DAVI)
IPN............. Interpeduncular Nucleus [*Cytology*]
IPN............. Interpenetrating Network (SAUS)
IPN............. Interpenetrating Polymer Network [*Organic chemistry*]
IPN............. Interplanetary Network [*Astronomy*]
IPn............. Interstitial Pneumonitis [*Medicine*] (STED)
IPN............. Ipatinga [*Brazil*] [*Airport symbol*] (OAG)
IPN............. Isophthalonitrile [*Organic chemistry*]
IPN............. Isopropyl Nitrate (SAUS)
IPN............. Purdue University, North Central Campus, Westville, IN [*OCLC symbol*] (OCLC)
IPNA........... International Pediatric Nephrology (EA)
IPNA........... Isopropylnoradrenaline [*Isoproterenol*] (STED)
IPNC........... Independence Plan for Neighborhood Councils (EA)
IPNC........... International Council of Plant Nutrition [*Australia*] (EAIO)
IPNFC......... International Peter Noone Fan Club (EA)
IPNG........... Internet Protocol New (or Next) Generation (SAUS)
IPng............ Internet Protocol Next Generation (CDE)
IPNG........... Internet Protocol-Next Generation (SAUS)
IPng............ IP Next Generation (SAUS)
IPNI............ International Plant Names Index (SAUO)
IPNJ............ Industrial Photographers of New Jersey (EA)
I/PNL.......... Instrument Panel [*Automotive engineering*]
IPNL........... Integrated Perceived Noise Level [*Acoustics*]
IPN MILE..... Integrated Project Network Milestone (SAUS)
IPNNI.......... Integrated Private Network to Network Interface [*Communications term*] (DCT)
IPNS........... Intense Pulsating (or Pulsed) Neutron Source (SAUS)
IPNS........... Intense Pulsed Neutron Source
IPNS........... Internet Patent News Service (SAUO)
IPNS........... Interpenetrating Networks of Samples [*Statistics*]
IPNS........... Isopenicillin N Synthase [*An enzyme*]
IP-Number... Internet Protocol Number (SAUS)
IPNV........... Infectious Pancreatic Necrosis Virus
IPO............. Crown Point Community Schools, Crown Point, IN [*OCLC symbol*] (OCLC)
IPO............. Improved Pregnancy Outcome [*Medicine*] (DMAA)
IPO............. Independent Practitioner Organization [*Medicine*] (MTAA)
IPO............. Indigenous Peoples' Organization (FOTI)
IPO............. Indirect Program Office (SAUO)
IPO............. Indolephenoloxidase (SAUS)
IPO............. Indophenol Oxidase [*An enzyme*]
IPO............. Industrial Partnership Office (SAUO)
IPO............. Industrial Planning Office (SAUS)
IPO............. Information Program Officer [*Foreign service*]
IPO............. Initial Planning Option [*Medicine*] (DAVI)

IPO.............. Initial Public Offering [*Business term*]
IPO.............. Input, Process, and Output (MHDB)
IPO.............. Input Processing Output (SAUS)
IPO.............. Inquiry Programmed Operations (SAUS)
IPO.............. Inspection Planning Order
IPO.............. Installation Planning Order
IPO.............. Installation Planning Organization (SAUS)
IPO.............. Installation Production Order
IPO.............. Installation Productivity Option [*IBM Corp.*]
IPO.............. Instantaneous Power Output
IPO.............. Institutional Program Office (SAUO)
IPO.............. Integrated Program Office (SAUO)
IPO.............. Integrated Provider Organization
IPO.............. Intellectual Property Owners (EA)
IPO.............. Interim Protection Order (SAUS)
IPO.............. International Pact Organization
IPO.............. International Parents' Organization [*Later, PS*] (EA)
IPO.............. International Payment Order (DCTA)
IPO.............. International Post Organization (SAUO)
IPO.............. International Procurement Office (SAUS)
IPO.............. International Programme Office (SAUO)
IPO.............. International Program Office (SAUS)
IPO.............. International Programs Office (SAUO)
IPO.............. International Progress Organization [*Vienna, Austria*] (EAIO)
IPO.............. Ipora [*Brazil*] [*Airport symbol*] (AD)
IPO.............. Iranian Plan Organization (SAUO)
IPO.............. Isotope Program Office (SAUO)
IPO.............. Israel Philharmonic Orchestra (SAUO)
IPO.............. Iterative Planning Optimization (SAUO)
IPO.............. WOCE International Planning Office (SAUO)
IPOC............ Iberian Peninsula Operating Committee [*World War II*]
IPOC............ Incoming Parts Order Control (SAUS)
IPOC............ Interim Policy Oversight Committee (SAUO)
IPOC............ International Partner Operations Center (EOSA)
IPOCA.......... International Pipe Line and Offshore Contractors Association [*Belgium*] (EAIO)
IPOD............ Initial Phase of Ocean Drilling (SAUS)
IPOD............ International Program of Ocean Drilling [*Formerly, DSDP*] [*National Science Foundation*]
IPOD............ Interstate Project on Dissemination (SAUS)
IPO/E........... Installation Productivity Option/Extended [*IBM Corp.*]
IPOEE.......... Institute of Post Office Electrical Engineers [*British*]
IPOF............ Immediate Postoperative Fitting [*Medicine*] (EDAA)
IPOFA.......... Integrated Programmed Operational and Functional Appraisals
IPoH............ Saint James Hospital, Pontiac, IL [*Library symbol*] [*Library of Congress*] (LCLS)
IpOHA.......... Isopropyl Oxalyl Hydroxamate [*Organic chemistry*]
IPOL............ Institute of Polarology [*British*]
IPOM........... Installation Planning Operation Manual (VLIE)
IPOM........... Intelligent Plant Operating Manual [*Combustion Engineering Simcon, Inc.*]
IPOMS......... International Polar Orbiting Meteorological Satellite (SAUS)
IPOMS......... International Polar-Orbiting Meteorological Satellite
IPOMS......... International Polar-Orbiting Meteorological Satellite Group (SAUO)
IPON........... Intelligent Passive Optical Network (SAUO)
IPOP........... Immediate Postoperative Prosthesis [*Medicine*] (EDAA)
IP/OP.......... Input/Output Interface (SAUS)
IP/OP.......... Input/Output Interface Element [*Computer science*] (NITA)
IPOP........... Installer Point of Purchase
IPOPI.......... International Patient Organization for Primary Immunodeficiencies (NRGU)
IPOR........... International Population Research Center [*University of California*] [*Defunct*]
IPOR........... International Public Opinion Research Inc. (SAUO)
IPOS........... Insulation by Oxidized Porous Silicon (SAUS)
IPOS........... Intellectual Property Owners (SAUS)
IPOs........... Interim Protection Orders (SAUO)
IPOS........... International Psycho-Oncology Society (SAUO)
IPOSA......... International Photo Optical Show Association [*Defunct*] (EA)
IPOSS......... Interim Pacific Oceanographic Support System (DNAB)
IPOT............ Imperial Philharmonic Orchestra of Tokyo (SAUO)
IPOT............ Inductive Potential (SAUS)
IPOT............ Inductive Potential Divider [*Electronics*] (ECII)
IPOT............ Inductive Potentiometer (MDG)
IPot............. Potomac Public Library, Potomac, IL [*Library symbol*] [*Library of Congress*] (LCLS)
IPOTMS....... Isopropenyloxytrimethylsilane [*Organic chemistry*]
IPOTP......... Integrated Payload Operations Training Plan (SAUS)
IPOX........... A and R Leasing [*Private rail car owner code*]
IPP.............. British Institute of Practical Psychology
IPP.............. Imaging Photo-Polarimeter (SAUS)
IPP.............. Imaging Polarimeter [*or Photopolarimetry*] [*NASA*]
IPP.............. Immediate Past President (ADA)
IPP.............. Imminent Peril to the Public (MHDB)
IPP.............. Imnpact Point Prediction (SAUS)
IPP.............. Impact Point Prediction (SAUO)
IPP.............. Impact Prediction Point [*NASA*]
IPP.............. Impaired Physician Program (EA)
IPP.............. Implementation Planning Program [*Environmental Protection Agency*] (GFGA)
IPP.............. Import Parity Pricing (ADA)
IPP.............. Inanities per Page [*Facetious criterion for determining insignificance of Supreme Court Justices*] [*Proposed by University of Chicago professor David P. Currie*]
IPP.............. Independent People's Party [*Political party*] [*Germany*] (EAIO)
IPP.............. Independent Power Producer
IPP.............. Independent Power Production (EEVL)
IPP.............. Independent Power Projects (AAGC)
IPP.............. Independent Practice Plan [*Medicine*] (EDAA)
IPP.............. Independent Progressive Party (SAUO)
IPP.............. Index of Prices Paid [*Economics*]
IPP.............. Indianapolis Public Schools, Indianapolis, IN [*OCLC symbol*] (OCLC)
IPP.............. Indian Print and Paper [*A publication*] (DGA)
IPP.............. India Paper Proofs
IPP.............. Individual Parameter Perturbation
IPP.............. Individual Physician Profile [*Medicine*] (EDAA)
IPP.............. Individual Practice Program [*Health care*] (MHCS)
IPP.............. Individual Program Plan
IPP.............. Industrial Partnering Program [*Department of Energy*]
IPP.............. Industrial Partnership Programs Office (SAUO)
IPP.............. Industrial Preparedness Planning [*DoD*]
IPP.............. Industrial Preparedness Program [*Environmental science*] (COE)
IPP.............. Inferior Point [*of the*] Pubic [*Bone*] [*Anatomy*] (DAVI)
IPP.............. Inflatable Penile Prosthesis [*Urology*] (DAVI)
IPP.............. Information Privacy Principle
IPP.............. Information Processing Professional
IPP.............. Infrared Pointer Package
IPP.............. Initial Production Phase (SAUS)
IPP.............. Injury Prevention Program
IPP.............. Inosine, Pyruvate, and (inorganic) Phosphate [*Medicine*] (EDAA)
IPP.............. In-Plant Plus Program (SAUS)
IPP.............. In-Plant Printing (VLIE)
IPP.............. In Propria Persona [*In Person*] [*Latin*] [*Legal term*] (DLA)
IPP.............. Input Processor Programs [*Computer science*]
IPP.............. Insert Present Position (SAUS)
IPP.............. Inspired Partial Pressure [*Physiology*]
IPP.............. Institute for Plasma (SAUS)
IPP.............. Institute for Public Policy (SAUO)
IPP.............. Institute of Print Purchasing (DGA)
IPP.............. Integrated Payload Package (ACAE)
IPP.............. Integrated Planning Process (SAUO)
IPP.............. Integrated Plotting Package (NRCH)
IPP.............. Integrated Program Plan (ABAC)
IPP.............. Integrated Project Plan (SAUS)
IPP.............. Integrated Project Planning (SAUO)
IPP.............. Interactive Post Processor (ACAE)
IPP.............. Intercept Planning and Prelaunch (ACAE)
IPP.............. Interdivisional Programming Practice (SAUS)
IPP.............. Interface Package Process (SAUS)
IPP.............. Interface Program Plan (MCD)
IPP.............. Intermedia Priority Pollutant (GNE)
IPP.............. Intermittent Positive Pressure [*Medicine*]
IPP.............. Internal Packet Protocol [*Telecommunications*]
IPP.............. Internationally Protected Person (ADA)
IPP.............. International Partners in Prayer (EA)
IPP.............. International Phototelegraph Position [*Telecommunications*] (TEL)
IPP.............. International Precision Products (SAUO)
IPP.............. International Price Program [*Bureau of Labor Statistics*] (GFGA)
IPP.............. International Priority Paid (ADA)
IPP.............. Internet Presence Provider (AGLO)
IPP.............. Internet Printing Protocol (SAUS)
IPP.............. Interplant Parts Planning (SAUS)
IPP.............. Interplant Purchase (SAUS)
IPP.............. Interprocessor Process [*Telecommunications*] (TEL)
IPP.............. Inter-Pulse Period
IPP.............. Intractable Pelvic Pain [*Medicine*] (MELL)
IPP.............. Intrapleural Pressure [*Biology*]
IPP.............. Inventory Preparation Plan (SAUS)
IPP.............. Inverse Polarity Protection
IPP.............. Investment Promotion Program
IPP.............. Ionospheric Propagation Path
IPP.............. Ipplepen [*England*]
IPP.............. Islamic Peoples Party (SAUS)
IPP.............. Isopentenyl Pyrophosphate [*Organic chemistry*]
IPP.............. Isopropyl Percarbonate [*or Diisopropyl Peroxydicarbonate*] [*Organic chemistry*]
IPP.............. Isotactic Polypropylene [*Organic chemistry*]
IPP.............. Isotentenyl Pyrophosphate (SAUS)
IPP.............. Isothermal Pressure Profile
IPP.............. Itek Positive Plate [*Publishing*] (DGA)
IPp.............. Paw Paw Public Library, Paw Paw, IL [*Library symbol*] [*Library of Congress*] (LCLS)
IPPA............ Illinois Pork Producers Association (SAUO)
IPPA............ Independent Professional Painting Contractors Association (SAUO)
IPPA............ Independent Professional Painting Contractors Association of America (NTPA)
IPPA............ Independent Programme Producers' Association [*British*]
IPPA............ Inspection, Palpation, Percussion, Auscultation [*Medicine*]
IPPA............ Inspection, Palpitation, Percussion, Auscultation (SAUS)
IPPA............ Instant Potato Products Association [*Defunct*] (EA)
IPPA............ Institute for Public Policy and Administration [*Later, CPPUI*] (EA)
IPPA............ Intensive Pig Producers of Australia
IPPA............ Intercontinental Press Publishing Association [*Defunct*] (EA)
IPPA............ International Paintball Players Association (EA)
IPPA............ International Pectin Producers Association [*Switzerland*] (EAIO)
IPPA............ International Pentecostal Press Association (EA)
IPPA............ International Planned Parenthood Association (SAUO)
IPPA............ International Press Publishing Association (SAUO)
IPPA............ International Printing Pressmen and Assistants Union (SAUO)

IPPA International Printing Pressmen and Assistants' Union of North America [*Later, IPGCU*]
IPPA International Program for Population Analysis
IPPA Isopropylphenyl Acetate [*Organic chemistry*]
IPpa Palos Park Public Library, Palos Park, IL [*Library symbol*] [*Library of Congress*] (LCLS)
IPP & A Inspection, Percussion, Palpation and Auscultation (SAUS)
IPPase Inosine Pyrophosphate Phosphoribosyltransferase [*Medicine*] (EDAA)
IPPAU International Printing Pressmen and Assistants' Union of North America [*Later, IPGCU*] (EA)
IPPB Incremental Provisioning Parts Breakdown (SAA)
IPPB Intermittent Positive Pressure Breathing [*Medicine*]
IPPBA Intermittent Positive-Pressure Breathing Apparatus [*Medicine*] (MEDA)
IPPB/I Intermittent Positive Pressure Breathing/Inspiratory
IPPBS Integrated Personnel Planning and Budgeting System
IP/PBX Internet Protocol Private Branch Exchange (GART)
IPPC Industrial Promotion and Productivity Centre (SAUO)
IPPC Infrastructure Payments and Progress Committee [*NATO*] (NATG)
IPPC Integrated Pollution Prevention and Control [*Environmental science*]
IPPC International Penal and Penitentiary Commission (SAUO)
IPPC International Philatelic Press Club (EA)
IPPC International Plant Protection Center [*Oregon State University*] [*Research center*] (RCD)
IPPC Isopropyl N-phenylcarbamate [*Also, INPC, IPC*] [*Herbicide*]
IPPC Isopropyl-N-Phenylcarbamate (SAUS)
IPPCA Independent Professional Painting Contractors Association of America (EA)
IPPD Integrated Product and Process Development [*Business term*] (RDA)
IPPD Intermittent Positive Pressure Dialysis [*Medicine*] (DB)
IPPD Isopropyl(phenyl)para-phenylene Diamine [*Organic chemistry*]
IPPDSEU International Plate Printers, Die Stampers, and Engravers' Union of North America (EA)
IPPDT Integrated Product and Process Development Team [*Military*] (RDA)
IPPF Instruction Preprocessing Function
IPPF International Penal and Penitentiary Foundation [*See also FIPP*] [*Bonn, Federal Republic of Germany*] (EAIO)
IPPF International Planned Parenthood Federation (EA)
IPPF International Planned Parenthood Foundation (SAUO)
IPPF International Professional Paddleboarding Federation (SAUO)
IPPF/WHR International Planned Parenthood Federation, Western Hemisphere Region (SAUO)
IPPH Proctor Community Hospital, Peoria, IL [*Library symbol*] [*Library of Congress*] (LCLS)
IPPHA International Peruvian Paso Horse Association (EA)
IPPI Instructional Procedures Preference Inventory
IPPI International Public Policy Institute
IPPI Interruption of Pregnancy for Psychiatric Indication
IPPIA International Plasma Products Industry Association (NTPA)
IPPIF IPL Energy [*NASDAQ symbol*] (TTSB)
IPPIF IPL Energy, Inc. [*NASDAQ symbol*] (SAG)
IPPJ Institute of Plasma Physics, Japan
IPPL Indentured Parts Price List (MCD)
IPPL Independent Progressive Party of Liberia (SAUO)
IPPL Industrial Preparedness Planning List
IPPL Integrated Planning Parts List (MCD)
IPPL International Primate Protection League (EA)
IPPL Inter PNO Physical Link (SAUS)
IPPM Integrated Product and Process Management [*Military*]
IPPM Ionospheric Propagation Prediction Method (SAUS)
IPPMA In-Plant Powder Metallurgy Association (EA)
IPPMA In-Plant Printing Management Association
IPPMHN International Post-Partum Mental Health Network (EA)
IPPN Interplant Part Number (SAUS)
IPPNO International Philosophers for the Prevention Network (SAUS)
IPPNO International Philosophers for the Prevention of Nuclear Omnicide (EA)
IPPNW International Physicians for the Prevention of Nuclear War (EA)
IPPO Intermittent Positive-Pressure inflation with Oxygen (SAUS)
IPPO Intermittent Positive Pressure with Oxygen [*Medicine*]
IPPP Industrial Preparedness Planning Program (SAUS)
IPPP Industrial Preparedness Production Planning [*DOD*] (AAGC)
IPPP Industrial Property Policy Program [*Insurance*]
IPPP Institute for Philosophy and Public Policy (EA)
IPPP Institute of Private Practicing Psychologists [*Australia*]
IPPPE Institute on Public Policy and Private Enterprise (SAUO)
IPPR Industrial Production Performance Reporting
IPPR Institute for Public Policy Research [*British*] (ECON)
IPPR Integrated Pancreatic Polypeptide Response [*Medicine*] (DMAA)
IPPR Intermittent Positive Pressure Respiration
IPPRI International Peace Policy Research Institute (SAUO)
IPPS Improved Processing System (MCD)
IPPS Infiniti Personalized Protection System
IPPS Institute of Physics and the Physical Society [*British*] (DI)
IPPS Integrated Personal Protection System (SAUS)
IPPS Integrated Power Protection System (RALS)
IPPS International Philippine Philatelic Society (EAIO)
IPPS International Plant Propagators Society, Eastern Region (EA)
IPpS Paw Paw School System, Paw Paw, IL [*Library symbol*] [*Library of Congress*] (LCLS)
IPPSA Israel-Palestine Philatelic Society of America [*Later, SIP*]
IPPSF Isolated Perfused Porcine Skip Flap [*Clinical chemistry*]
IPPT Individual Proficiency Test (SAUS)
IPPT Inter-Person Perception Test [*Personality development test*] [*Psychology*]
IPPTT International Postal, Telegraph, and Telephone Personnel (SAUO)
IPPUAD Immediate Postprandial Upper Abdominal Distress
IPPV Intermittent Positive Pressure Ventilation
IPQ Information Processing Quotient (SAUS)
IPQ Intellectual Property Quarterly [*A publication*]
IPQ International Philosophical Quarterly [*A publication*] (BRI)
IPQ International Praxis Resources [*Vancouver Stock Exchange symbol*]
IPQ Intimacy Potential Quotient
IPQ Invitation to Pre-Qualify (FOTI)
IPQC In-Process Quality Control
IPQI Intermediate Personality Questionnaire for Indian Pupils [*Personality development test*] [*Psychology*]
IPR Icar Airlines [*Ukraine*] [*FAA designator*] (FAAC)
IPR Imposter Pass Rate (MHDI)
IPR Inches per Rack (SAUS)
IPR Inches per Revolution
IPR Independent Product Review (SAUS)
IPR Independent Professional Review [*Medicaid*] (DHSM)
IPR Index of Prices Received [*Economics*]
IPR Individual Pay Record [*Military*]
IPR Individual Performance Review (WDAA)
IPR Indochina Postwar Reconstruction
IPR Industrial Property Rights (SAUS)
IPR Industrial Public Relations (SAUS)
IPR Industry Planning Representative [*DoD*]
IPR Inflation Pressure Retention [*Tire technology*]
IPR Inflow Performance Relationship (SAUS)
IPR Informal Progress Report
IPR Ingestion Pathway Receptor (SAUS)
IPR Initial Pressure Regulator [*Nuclear energy*] (NRCH)
IPR Injector Pressure Regulator [*Automotive term*] (HAWK)
IPR In-Place Repair
IPR In-Processor Reviews (SAUS)
IPR In-Process Report
IPR In-Process Review
IPR In Progress Review (SAUS)
IPR In-Progress Review (DOMA)
IPR In Pulse to Register [*Telecommunications*] (TEL)
IPR In-Pulse to Register (SAUS)
IPR Inspection Planning and Reliability (SAA)
IPR Installation Planning Review (VLIE)
IPR Institute for Peace Research (SAUO)
IPR Institute for Philosophical Research (SAUS)
IPR Institute for Plasma Research (SAUO)
IPR Institute for Policy Research [*University of Wyoming*] [*Research center*] (RCD)
IPR Institute for Policy Research [*University of Cincinnati*] [*Research center*] (RCD)
IPR Institute for Polymer Research (SAUS)
IPR Institute for Public Representation (SAUO)
IPR Institute for Public Research (AAGC)
IPR Institute for Puerto Rican Policy, Inc. [*Research center*] (RCD)
IPR Institute of Pacific Relations
IPR Institute of Peace Research [*La Trobe University*] [*Australia*]
IPR Institute of Philosophical Research (SAUO)
IPR Institute of Population Registration [*British*]
IPR Institute of Population Research [*Beijing University*]
IPR Institute of Psychophysical Research [*British*]
IPR Institute of Public Relations [*British*]
IPR Insulin Production Rate [*Medicine*] (DMAA)
IPR Intellectual Property Reports (journ.) (SAUS)
IPR Intellectual Property Rights
IPR Intelligence Periodic Report (SAUO)
IPR Intelligence Production Requests
IPR Intelligence Production Requirement (AFIT)
IPR Intelligence Production Requirements (SAUS)
IPR Interactive Photorealistic Rendering [*Computer-assisted design*]
IPR Inter-City Products [*AMEX symbol*] (TTSB)
IPR Inter-City Products Corp. [*AMEX symbol*] (SPSG)
IPR Interdepartmental Procurement Request
IPR Interdepartmental Purchase Request [*DoD*] (AFIT)
IPR Interim Problem Report (NASA)
IPR Interim Program Review (SAUS)
IPR Interim Progress Report
IPR Interior Procurement Regulations [*Department of the Interior*]
IPR Internal Progress Report
IPR International Public Relations (journ.) (SAUS)
IPR Interpersonal Process Recall [*Psychology*]
IPR Interplant Parts Requirements (SAUS)
ipr Intraperitoneal [*Medicine*] (EDAA)
IPR Inventory Project Report (SAUO)
IPR Inward Processing Relief (DCTA)
IPR Ion Production Rate
IPR Irish Publishing Record (TELE)
IPR Isolated Pacing Response [*Computer science*] (ELAL)
IPR Isolated Pentagon Rule [*Physical chemistry*]
iPr Isopropyl (DB)
IPR Isoproterenol [*An adrenergic*]
IPR Item Performance Report (SAUO)
IPRA Illinois Park and Recreation Association (SRA)
IPRA Imaging Products Remanufacturing Association (NTPA)
IPRA Indian Paint Research Association (SAUO)
IPRA Indigenious Peoples Rights Act [*Philippines*]
IPRA In-Place Repairable Assembly (MCD)
IPRA Institute of Park and Recreation Administration [*British*] (BI)

IPRA .... International Paddle Racket Association [*Later, AARA*]
IPRA .... International Peace Research Association (EA)
IPRA .... International Professional Rodeo Association (EA)
IPRA .... International Public Relations Association [*London, England*] (WDMC)
IPRA .... International Public Relations Association, US Section (EA)
IPRA .... Iowa Park and Recreation Association (SRA)
IPra .... Vernon Area Library District, Prairie View, IL [*Library symbol*] [*Library of Congress*] (LCLS)
IPRAF .... International Plastic, Reconstructive, and Aesthetic Foundation (ADWA)
IPRA Newsletter ... International Peace Research Newsletter (SAUO)
IPRA Newsletter ... INT Peace Research Newsletter (journ.) (SAUS)
IPRAS .... International Confederation for Plastic, Reconstructive, and Aesthetic Surgery (ADWA)
IPRB .... Installations Planning and Review Board [*DoD*]
IPRB .... Intellectual Property Review Board (SAUO)
IPRB .... Inter-Allied Postwar Requirements Bureau [*World War II*]
IPRC .... Indiana Prevention Resource Center (SAUO)
IPRC .... Information Privacy Research Center [*Purdue University*] (PDAA)
IPRC .... Institute of Puerto Rican Culture (SAUO)
IPRC .... Institute Port Risk Clause (MARI)
IPRC .... Interrupt Processor Control (SAUS)
IPRD .... In Process Review Document (ACAE)
IPRD .... Integrated Payload Requirements Document (SAUS)
IPRE .... Incorporated Practical Radio Engineers (SAUO)
IPRE .... Incorporated Practitioners in Radio and Electronics (SAUO)
IPRE .... Incorporated Practitioners in Radio and Electronics Ltd. [*British*] (BI)
IPRE .... Institute of Practical Radio Engineers (SAUO)
IPRE .... International Professional Association for/of Environmental Affairs (SAUO)
IPREA .... International Professional Association for Environmental Affairs (SAUO)
IP Review .... Institute of Petroleum Review (journ.) (SAUS)
IPRF .... International Pediatric Research Foundation [*Medicine*] (EDAA)
IPRF .... International Planned Parenthood Federation (SAUO)
IPRG .... International Procurement Research Group (SAUS)
IPRGOC .... International Public Relations Group of Companies (SAUO)
IPRI .... International Plant Research Institute (PDAA)
IPri .... Matson Public Library, Princeton, IL [*Library symbol*] [*Library of Congress*] (LCLS)
IPriBSD .... Bureau Township Consolidated School District 250, Princeton, IL [*Library symbol*] [*Library of Congress*] (LCLS)
I-PRIDE .... Interracial-Intercultural Pride (EA)
IPriDS .... Douglas Elementary School, Princeton, IL [*Library symbol*] [*Library of Congress*] (LCLS)
IPriHi .... Bureau County Historical Society, Princeton, IL [*Library symbol*] [*Library of Congress*] (LCLS)
IPriJS .... Jefferson Elementary School, Princeton, IL [*Library symbol*] [*Library of Congress*] (LCLS)
IPriLH .... Logan Junior High School, Princeton, IL [*Library symbol*] [*Library of Congress*] (LCLS)
IPriPH .... Perry Memorial Hospital, Princeton, IL [*Library symbol*] [*Library of Congress*] (LCLS)
IPriv .... Lillie M. Evans Memorial Library, Princeville, IL [*Library symbol*] [*Library of Congress*] (LCLS)
IPriWS .... Washington Middle School, Princeton, IL [*Library symbol*] [*Library of Congress*] (LCLS)
IPRL .... Interceptor Pilot Research Laboratory (SAA)
IPRL .... Isolated Perfused Rabbit Lung (STED)
IPRL .... Isolated Perfused Rat Liver (DB)
IPRM .... Indium Phosphide Related Materials (AAEL)
IPRM .... Integrated Performance and Risk Management
IPR Memoranda ... Institute of Pacific Relations Memoranda (journ.) (SAUS)
I-PRO .... Independent Professional Representatives Organization (EA)
IPRO .... Input Processing (SAUS)
I/Pro .... Interactive Profiles [*Computer science*]
IPRO .... International Pallet Recycling Organisation (SAUS)
IPRO .... International Pallet Recycling Organization (PDAA)
IPRO .... International Patent Research Office (IAA)
I/PRO .... Internet Profiles Corp.
IProD .... Prospect Heights Public Library District, Prospect Heights, IL [*Library symbol*] [*Library of Congress*] (LCLS)
IProdE .... Institute of Production Engineers [*British*] (DI)
I Prod E .... Institution of Production Engineers [*British*]
I Prod Eng .... Institute of Production Engineers (SAUS)
IProdEng .... Institution of Production Engineers (SAUS)
IPROP .... Ionic Propulsion (IAA)
IPROS .... Integrated Proposal System (TIMI)
IPRP .... Implementation Plan for Recovery of Plutonium (SAUS)
IPRP .... Implementation Plan for the Recovery of Plutonium (SAUO)
IPRP .... Institute for Puerto Rican Policy (EA)
IP-RPLC .... Ion-Pair-Reversed-Phase Liquid Chromatography
IPRR .... Initial Production Readiness Review (SAUS)
IPRR .... Integrated Payload Requirements Review (SAUS)
IPRR .... Integrated Personnel Requirement Report (AAG)
IPRS .... Inmate Personal Record System (WDAA)
IPRs .... Intellectual Property Rights (SAUO)
IPRS .... International Confederation for Plastic and Reconstructive Surgery [*Montreal, PQ*] (EAIO)
IPRSF .... Interim Protocol for Radon Screening and Followup [*Environmental science*] (COE)
iPrSGal .... Isopropylthiogalactoside (ADWA)
IPRSO .... Illinois Professional Review Standards Organization [*Medicine*] (EDAA)
IPRT .... Industrial Platinum Resistance Thermometer (PDAA)
IPRT .... Institute for Physical Research and Technology (SAUS)
IPRT .... Internal Processing Response Time (SAUS)
IPRT .... Interpersonal Reaction Test [*Medicine*] (MAE)
IPS .... American Income Properties L.P. [*AMEX symbol*] (COMM)
IPS .... Arctic Indigenous Peoples Secretariat (SAUO)
IPS .... Arctic Interplanetary Scintillation Experiment (or Project) (SAUO)
IPS .... East African Industrial Promotion Services (SAUO)
IPS .... Ibero-American Philosophical Society [*Madrid, Spain*] (EAIO)
IPS .... Idiopathic Pain Syndrome [*Medicine*] (DMAA)
IPS .... Idiopathic Postprandial Syndrome [*Medicine*] (DMAA)
IPS .... Ignition Pressure Switch [*Automotive engineering*]
IPS .... Illinois Psychiatric Society (SRA)
IPS .... Illustrative Planning Scenario [*DoD*]
IPS .... Image Processing System (MCD)
IPS .... Impact Polystyrene (EDCT)
IPS .... Impact Predictor System [*NASA*]
IPS .... Imperial Parliament Series [*A publication*]
IPS .... Improved Plow Steel (PDAA)
IPS .... Improved Processing System
IPS .... Impulses per Second [*Telecommunications*] (TEL)
ips .... Inches per Second (DOM)
IPS .... Inches per Second
IPS .... Income per Share (GOBB)
IPS .... Incorporated Phonographic Society [*British*] (BI)
IPS .... Incorporated Poetry Society (SAUO)
IPS .... Increased Processing Speed (SAUS)
IPS .... Incremental Purchasing System (SAA)
IPS .... Independent Particle Shell Modul (SAUS)
IPS .... Independent Preparer Services, Inc. (SAUS)
IPS .... Independent Preparer Services Incorporated (SAUO)
IPS .... Independent Progressive Socialist (SAUO)
IPS .... Index Participation (SAUS)
IPS .... Index Preparation System [*Foxon-Maddocks Associates*] [*Information service or system*] (IID)
IPS .... Indian Phytopathological Society (SAUO)
IPS .... Indian Point Station [*Nuclear energy*] (NRCH)
IPS .... Indian Police Service [*British*]
IPS .... Indian Political Service [*British*]
IPS .... Indigenous Peoples Secretariat (SAUS)
IPS .... Industrial Planning Specification
IPS .... Industrial Promotion Service (SAUO)
IPS .... Industrial Promotion Services (SAUO)
IPS .... Inertial Pointing System
IPS .... Inertial Positioning System (PDAA)
IPS .... Informal Priority-Setting (SAUS)
IPS .... Information Processing Standard (SAUO)
IPS .... Information Processing Site (SAUS)
IPS .... Information Processing Society (SAUO)
IPS .... Information Processing Standards (SAUO)
IPS .... Information Processing Subsystem (SAUO)
IPS .... Information Processing System
IPS .... Information Provider System (SAUS)
IPS .... Infundibular Pulmonic Stenosis [*Medicine*] (DAVI)
IPS .... Initial Processing Sites (SAUS)
IPS .... Initial Prognostic Score [*Medicine*] (MAE)
IPS .... Initial Program Specification (SAA)
IPS .... Inlet Particle Separator (MCD)
IPS .... Inlet Pressure Survey (SAUS)
IPS .... Inner Polar Site [*Cytology*]
IPS .... In-Pavement System
IPS .... In Plane Switching (SAUS)
IPS .... In Plant Stores (SAUS)
IPS .... In-Plant Support (MCD)
IPS .... In Pulse to Sender [*Telecommunications*] (TEL)
IPS .... In-Pulse to Sender (SAUS)
IPS .... Inside Pipe Size (DAC)
IPS .... Installation Performance Specification [*Computer science*] (IBMDP)
IPS .... Institute for Palestine Studies (EA)
IPS .... Institute for Policy Studies (EA)
IPS .... Institute of Plant Science [*Australia*]
IPS .... Institute of Polar Studies [*Ohio State University*] [*Later, BPRC*]
IPS .... Institute of Polymer Science (SAUO)
IPS .... Institute of Population Studies (BARN)
IPS .... Institute of Private Secretaries (SAUO)
IPS .... Institute of Public Safety (SAUO)
IPS .... Institute of Public Service (SAUS)
IPS .... Institute of Public Supplies (SAUO)
IPS .... Institute of Purchasing and Supply [*British*]
IPS .... Institutional Payment Summary [*Pell Grant Program*] [*Department of Education*] (GFGA)
IPS .... Instruction Prescription System (SAUS)
IPS .... Instructions per Second [*Computer science*]
IPS .... Instructor Power Supply (SAUS)
IPS .... Instrument and Property Services (SAUO)
IPS .... Instrumentation Power Subsystem (SAUS)
IPS .... Instrumentation Power Supply
IPS .... Instrumentation Power System [*or Subsystem*] [*NASA*] (NASA)
IPS .... Instrument Penetration Subassembly (SAUS)
IPS .... Instrument Pointing Subsystem (SAUS)
IPS .... Instrument Pointing System (MCD)
IPS .... Instrument Power Supply (SAUS)
IPS .... Instrument Power System (SAUS)
IPS .... Integral Propulsion Subsystem (SAUS)
IPS .... Integrated Payload System (SAUS)
IPS .... Integrated Photosector (SAUS)

IPS ... Integrated Planning Summary (MCD)
IPS ... Integrated Plant Systems (GART)
IPS ... Integrated Power Semiconductors Ltd. [*British*] (NITA)
IPS ... Integrated Power System
IPS ... Integrated Process System (SAUS)
IPS ... Integrated Procurement System [*Army*]
IPS ... Integrated Product Support (SAUS)
IPS ... Integrated Program Study (MCD)
IPS ... Integrated Program Summary [*Military*] (CAAL)
IPS ... Integrated Project Schedule (SAUS)
IPS ... Integrated Project Support (IAA)
IPS ... Integrated Propulsion System (MCD)
IPS ... Integrated Protection System (SAUS)
IPS ... Integrated Publishing System (SAUS)
IPS ... Integrated System for Procurement (SAUS)
IPS ... Intellectual Property Services (SAUO)
IPS ... Intelligence Processing Subsystem (ACAE)
IPS ... Intelligence Production Support (SAUO)
IPS ... Intelligence Production System (SAUO)
IPS ... Intelligent Power Management System [*Laptop computers*] (BYTE)
IPS ... Intelligent Power Switch [*Electronics*]
IPS ... Intelligent Printing System [*Dataroyal, Inc.*]
IPS ... Intelligent Programming System (SAUS)
IPS ... Intensive Probation Supervision (SAUS)
IPS ... Interactive Pictures Systems [*In IPS Dance, a computer program for choreographers*]
IPS ... Interactive Processing System (SAUS)
IPS ... Interceptor Pilot Simulator [*SSTM*]
IPS ... Intercept Passive Sonar (SAUS)
IPS ... Intercept Pilot Simulator (SAUS)
IPS ... Interconnected Power Systems (SAUS)
IPS ... Interconnects Per Second (SAUS)
IPS ... Interdivisional Programming Standard (SAUS)
IPS ... Interface and Processing Subsystem (SAUS)
IPS ... Interface Problem Sheet (NASA)
IPS ... Interim Policy Statement (NRCH)
IPS ... Interim POMSEE [*Performance, Operating, and Maintenance Standards for Electronic Equipment*] Sheet
IPS ... Interior Pipe Size (SAUS)
IPS ... Interlink Press Service (EA)
IPS ... Intermediate Primary Section (SAUS)
IPS ... Intermittent Photic Stimulation [*Electroencephalography*] (STED)
IPS ... Intermolecular Pair Potential Surface [*Physical chemistry*]
IPS ... Intermolecular Potential (Energy) Surface [*Spectroscopy*]
IPS ... Internal Pipe Size (SAUS)
IPS ... Internal Plate Screen (IAA)
IPS ... Internal Power Supply [*Computer science*]
IPS ... International Confederation for Plastic Surgery
IPS ... Internationale Paracelsus-Gesellschaft zu Salzburg [*International Paracelsus Society*] (EA)
IPS ... International Packing Services (SAUO)
IPS ... International Palm Society (EA)
IPS ... International Paracelsus Society [*Salzburg, Austria*] (EA)
IPS ... International Peace Society (SAUO)
IPS ... International Peat Society [*See also IMTG*] [*Helsinki, Finland*] (EAIO)
IPS ... International Perimetric Society (EA)
IPS ... International Phenomenological Society (EA)
IPS ... International Phycological Society (EA)
IPS ... International Physical Society (SAUO)
IPS ... International Pipe Standard
IPS ... International Planetarium Society (EA)
IPS ... International Planning Staff (SAUO)
IPS ... International Plastics Selector, Inc. [*Information service or system*] (IID)
IPS ... International Plastic Surgery (SAUO)
IPS ... International Polaris Energy Corp. [*Toronto Stock Exchange symbol*]
IPS ... International Press Service (SAUO)
IPS ... International Pressure Society (SAUO)
IPS ... International Preview Society (EA)
IPS ... International Primatological Society (EA)
IPS ... International Processes Simulation [*Game*]
IPS ... International Psycho Service (SAUO)
IPS ... International Pyrheliometric Scale (SAUS)
IPS ... Internet Printing System [*Computer science*]
IPS ... Interpersonal Perception Scale (STED)
IPS ... Interplanetary Scintillation
IPS ... Interplanetary Scintillation Experiment (SAUO)
IPS ... Inter Press Service (SAUS)
IPS ... Inter-Press Service (SAUO)
IPS ... Inter/Press Service - Third World News Agency (EA)
IPS ... Interpretive Programming System
IPS ... Interruptions per Second
IPS ... Intractable Pain Society of Great Britain and Ireland
IPS ... Intrapartum Stillbirth [*Medicine*] (DMAA)
IPS ... Intraperitoneal Shock [*Psychology*]
IPS ... Introductory Physical Science [*Project*] [*Education*]
IPS ... Invariant Plane Strain (SAUS)
IPS ... Inventing and Patenting Sourcebook [*A publication*]
IPS ... Inventory of Perceptual Skills [*Visual and auditory test*]
IPS ... Inverse Photoemission Spectroscopy
IPS ... Inverter Power Supply (NASA)
IPS ... Investors Protection Scheme (DCTA)
IPS ... Iodophenylsulfonyl [*Pipsyl*] (STED)
IPS ... Ionospheric Prediction Service [*Telecommunications*] (TEL)
IPS ... Ion Plating Supply
IPS ... Ion Projection System (SAUS)
IPS ... Iowa Public Service Corporation (SAUO)
IPS ... Iron Pipe Size (WGA)
IPS ... Iron Pipe Standard (SARE)
IPS ... Ischiopubic Synchondrosis (STED)
IPS ... Iso-insulation Power Satellite (SAUS)
IPS ... Isopenicillin N-Synthetase (DB)
I-PS ... Isotactic Polystyrene (SAUS)
IPS ... Israel Prison Service (SAUO)
IP's ... Issue Priority Designators (AFIT)
IPS ... Item Processing System (BUR)
IPS ... Office of Information Programmes and Services [*UNESCO*] (IID)
IPSA ... Incremental Microwave Power Spectrum Analyzer [*Air Force*]
IPSA ... Independent Passenger Steamship Association (SAUO)
IPSA ... Independent Pool Service Association (SAUO)
IPSA ... Independent Postal System of America [*Alternative to US Postal Service*]
IPSA ... Industrial Police and Security Association [*British*] (BI)
IPSA ... Institute for Psychological Study of the Arts [*University of Florida*] [*Research center*] (RCD)
IPSA ... International Passenger Ship Association [*Merger of Atlantic Passenger St eamship Conference, Trans-Atlantic Passenger Steamship Conference, Caribbean Cruise Association*] [*Defunct*]
IPSA ... International Police and Security Association (SAUO)
IPSA ... International Political Science Abstracts (SAUO)
IPSA ... International Political Science Association (EA)
IPSA ... International Professional Security Association [*Paignton, Devonshire, England*] (EAIO)
IPSA ... International Professional Surrogates Association (EA)
IPSALO ... Integrated Power Supply and Line Output (SAUS)
IPSAM ... International Presort Airmail [*US Postal Service*]
IPSANET ... Sharp [*I. P.*] Communications Network [*I.P. Sharp Associates Ltd.*] [*Toronto, ON*] (TSSD)
IPSAR ... Integrated Plant Safety Assessment Report [*Nuclear energy*] (NRCH)
IPSB ... Institute of Psycho-Structural Balancing (SAUO)
IPSB ... Interprocessor Signal Bus
IPSB ... Intrapartum Stillbirth (STED)
IPSC ... Informating Processing Standards for Computers (SAUS)
IPSC ... Information Processing Standards for Computers
IPSC ... Information Processing Supplies Council [*Defunct*] (EA)
IPSC ... Inhibitory Postsynaptic Current [*Neurophysiology*]
iPSC ... Intel Personal Supercomputer (SAUO)
IPSC ... Interagency Primate Steering Committee [*National Institutes of Health*]
IPSC ... International Paper Selection Committee (SAUO)
IPSC ... International Practical Shooting Confederation
IPSC ... Inventory of Psychic and Somatic Complaints [*Medicine*] (DB)
IPSC ... Ipsco, Inc. [*NASDAQ symbol*] (SAG)
IPSCE ... Inventory of Psychic and Somatic Complaints in the Elderly (SAUS)
IPSCF ... IPSCO Inc. [*NASDAQ symbol*] (TTSB)
Ipsco ... Ipsco, Inc. [*Associated Press*] (SAG)
IPSD ... Interservice Procedures for Systems Development [*Military*]
IPSE ... Implementing Primary Science Education (AIE)
IPSE ... INSAT Payload Specialist (SAUS)
IPSE ... Integrated Programming Support Environment [*BIS Applied Systems*] [*British*]
IPSE ... Integrated Project Software Environment (SAUS)
IPSE ... Integrated Project Support Environment (NITA)
IPSE ... Intelligent Program Support Environment (TELE)
IPSEC ... Internet Protocol Security (SAUO)
IPSEP ... International Project for Soft Energy Paths [*Defunct*] (EA)
IPSF ... Immediate Postsurgical Fitting of Prosthesis (STED)
IPSF ... Intermediate Postsurgical Fitting [*Medicine*]
IPSF ... International Pharmaceutical Students' Federation [*Jerusalem, Israel*] (EAIO)
IPSF ... International Pharmacy Students Federation (SAUO)
IPSF ... International Piano Symphony Foundation (SAUO)
IPSF ... International Professional Sailsurfing Federation (SAUO)
IPSF ... International Professional Surfboating Federation (SAUO)
IPSF ... International Professional Surfthion Federation (SAUO)
IPSFC ... International Pacific Salmon Fisheries Commission [*Canada*] (EA)
IPSG ... International Programs Steering Group [*DoD*]
IPS Game ... International Process Simulation Game (SAUO)
IPSI ... International Political Science Institute (SAUO)
IPSICM ... International PSI Committee of Magicians [*See also CIEPP*] (EAIO)
IPSID ... Immunoproliferative Small Intestinal Disease (MAE)
IPSIG ... Independent Private Sector Inspector General (LDOE)
IPSJ ... Information Processing Society of Japan (NITA)
IPSL ... Interface Problem Status Log (NASA)
IPSLN ... Indo-Pacific Sea Level Network [*Marine science*] (OSRA)
IPSM ... Improved Performance Space Motor (MCD)
IPSM ... Institute of Physical Sciences in Medicine [*British*] (DBA)
IPSMCB ... International Product Safety Management Certification Board (SAUS)
IPSN ... Institute for Protection and Nuclear Safety (NUCP)
IPSN ... International Packet Switching Network (SAUS)
IPSNI ... Integration of People with Special Needs by IBC (SAUO)
IPSO ... Initiating Production by Sales Order (PDAA)
IPSO ... Interface Peripheral Standard Olivetti (NITA)
IPSO ... International Programs and Studies Office [*Later, DIA*] (EA)
IPSO ... International Program Support Office (SAUS)
IPSOC ... Information Processing Society of Canada
IPSP ... Industrial Personnel Security Program (SAUS)
IPSP ... Inhibitory Postsynaptic Potential [*Neurophysiology*]
IPSP ... Intelligence Priorities for Strategic Planning [*Military*]
IPSP ... Internet Protocol Security Protocol [*Computer science*]

IPS Project... Introductory Physical Science Project (SAUO)
IPSR... Institute of Plant Science Research [*Research center*] [*British*] (IRC)
IPSR... International Political Science Review (SAUO)
IPSR... INT Political Science Review (journ.) (SAUS)
IPSRA... International Professional Ski Racers Association (EA)
IPSS... Ice Penetrating Sensor System (SAUS)
IPSS... Information Processing System Simulator [*Computer science*] (MHDI)
IPSS... Initial Pre-planned Supply Support (DOMA)
IPSS... Institute of Planetary and Space Science (MCD)
IPSS... Interactive Population Statistical System [*Computer science*]
IPSS... Interactive Programming Support System (SAUO)
IPSS... Intermediate Plutonium Storage System [*Nuclear energy*] (NUCP)
IPSS... International Packet Switched Service [*Telecommunications system*] (NITA)
IPSS... International Packet-Switched Service (SAUS)
IPSS... International Packet Switching Service [*British Telecom International, Inc.*] [*Telecommunications service*] (TSSD)
IPSS... International Packet-Switching Service (SAUO)
IPSS... International Packet Switching Stream (SAUS)
IPSS... International Packet Switching System (SAUS)
IPSS... International Packet Switch Stream [*Computer science*]
IPSS... International Pilot Study of Schizophrenia [*WHO*]
IPSS... International Power Sources Symposium (SAUS)
I-PSS... International Prostate Symptoms Score [*Medicine*] (WDAA)
IPSS... Interprocessor Signaling System [*Telecommunications*] (TEL)
IPSSB... Information Processing Systems Standards Board [*Later, Board of Standards Review of ANSI*] [*American Standards Association*]
IPSSB... International Processing Systems Standards Board (SAUS)
IPSSD... Integrated Program Scheduling Standard Document (SPST)
IPSSF... International Professional Standup Surfing Federation (SAUO)
IPSSG... International Printers Supply Salesmen's Guild (EA)
IPSSS... Philosophical Society for the Study of Sport (SAUO)
IPST... In-Process Self Test (MCD)
IPST... Institute for Physical Science and Technology [*University of Maryland*] [*Research center*] (RCD)
IPST... Institute of Paper Science and Technology (NTPA)
IPST... International Practical Scale of Temperature (PDAA)
IPST... Israel Program for Scientific Translations [*An agency of the Government of Israel*]
IPStF... Saint Francis Hospital, Peoria, IL [*Library symbol*] [*Library of Congress*] (LCLS)
IPS/UIS... International Programmes and Services/UNESCO Information Services (SAUS)
IPSW... Ipswich [*City in England*] (ROG)
IPSW... Ipswich Savings Bank [*NASDAQ symbol*] (SAG)
IPSW... Ipswich Svgs Bk Mass [*NASDAQ symbol*] (TTSB)
IpswchSv... Ipswich Savings Bank [*Associated Press*] (SAG)
IpswichSv... Ipswich Savings Bank [*Associated Press*] (SAG)
IPSX... Interprocessor Switch Matrix (SAUS)
IPSX... Mid-American Energy [*Private rail car owner code*]
IPSY... Interactive Planning System (MHDI)
I Psy L... Institute of Psycholinguists (SAUO)
IPSZ... Indiana Public Service Commission [*Federal Railroad Administration identification code*]
IPT... Icelandic Pony Trekkers [*Later, IHT*] (EA)
IPT... Ideal Process Time (AAEL)
IPT... Image Processing Technology [*Computer graphics*]
IPT... Immersive Projection Technology (SAUS)
IPT... Immunoprecipitation Technique [*Clinical chemistry*]
IPT... Improved (SAUS)
IPT... Improved Productivity Techniques (TIMI)
IPT... Improved Programming Technologies (BUR)
IPT... Incapacidad Permanente Total (SAUS)
IPT... Inches per Tooth (IAA)
IPT... Incremental Proof Testing
IPT... Indexed, Paged, and Titled (ADA)
IPT... Individual Perception Threshold (PDAA)
IPT... Induction Plasma Torch
IPT... Industrial and Performance Technology [*Human performance analysis*]
IPT... Industrial Power Tube
IPT... Information Presentation Technologies, Inc.
IPT... Information Presentation Technology (SAUS)
IPT... Information Processing Technology
IPT... Information Processing Theory (SAUS)
IPT... Information Programming Technologies (SAUS)
IPT... Infrared Plume Target
IPT... Initial Production Test [*Army*] (AABC)
IPT... In-Pile Tube (SAUS)
IPT... In-Plant Test (KSC)
IPT... In-Plant Training
IPT... In-Plant Transporter (MCD)
IPT... In Port [*Navy*] (NVT)
IPT... In-Process Testing
IPT... Input Punched Tape (SAUS)
IPT... Inspector of Physical Training (SAUO)
IPT... Installation Preflight Test
IPT... Institute for Paralegal Training [*Later, Philadelphia Institute*] [*Commercial firm*] (EA)
IPT... Institute of Petroleum Technologists
IPT... Institute of Petroleum Technology (SAUO)
IPT... Institute of Photographic Technology (SAUO)
IPT... Institute of Property Taxation (EA)
IPT... Instituto de Promocao Turistica [*Portugal*] (EY)
IPT... Integrated Process Team [*Business term*]
IPT... Integrated Product Team [*Business term*] (RDA)
IPT... Integrated Project Team (SAUS)
IPT... Intellectual Property Transfer
IPT... Intelligent Procedure Trainer (SAUS)
IPT... Interagency Planning Teams (SAUO)
IPT... Intermediate Phase Training (DOMA)
IPT... Intermediate Pressure Turbine (SAUS)
IPT... Intermittent Pelvic Traction (DAVI)
IPT... Internal Pipe Thread
IPT... International Pipe Thread (NASA)
IPT... International Planning Team [*NATO*] (NATG)
IPT... International Production Technology (IAA)
IPT... International Project Team (SAUO)
IPT... Internet Protocol Telephony (SAUO)
IPT... Interpersonal Psychotherapy (DIPS)
IPT... Interpersonal Therapy [*Mental health treatment technique*]
IPT... Interphase Transformer [*Electronics*] (IAA)
IPT... Interplanetary Travel (AAG)
IPT... Interport Corp. [*ICAO designator*] (FAAC)
IPT... Inverse Path Table (SAUS)
IPT... Io Plasma Torus [*Cosmology*]
IPT... iParty Corp. [*AMEX symbol*] (SG)
IPT... IP Timberlands Cl'A' [*NYSE symbol*] (TTSB)
IPT... IP Timberlands Ltd. [*NYSE symbol*] (SAG)
IPT... Iron Pipe Thread (MSA)
IPT... Isopentenyl Transferase [*An enzyme*]
IPT... Isopropyl Toluene (SAUS)
IPT... MAP International, Wheaton, IL [*OCLC symbol*] (OCLC)
IPT... Williamsport [*Pennsylvania*] [*Airport symbol*] (OAG)
IPT... Williamsport, PA [*Location identifier*] [*FAA*] (FAAL)
IPT 1... Idea Oral Language Proficiency Test (TES)
IPTA... International Patent and Trademark Association [*Later, IIPA*] (EA)
IPTA... International Piano Teachers Association [*Defunct*]
IPTAR... Institute for Psychoanalytic Training and Research
IPTC... Industrial Products Trading Corporation (SAUO)
IPTC... International Polar Transportation Conference
IPTC... International Press Telecommunication Center (SAUS)
IPTC... International Press Telecommunication Committee (SAUO)
IPTC... International Press Telecommunications Council [*See also CIPT*] [*Telecommunications*] [*An association*] [*Defunct*] (EA)
IPTCCS... Integrated Pipeline Transportation and Coal-Cleaning System (SAUS)
IPTCS... Igloo Passive Thermal Control Section [*Aerospace*] (MCD)
IPTD... Internet Platform and Tools Division (SAUO)
IPTEA... Internacia Postista kaj Telekomunikista Esperanto-Asocio [*International Esperanto Association of Post and Telecommunication Workers*] (EAIO)
IPTEC... Division of Inter-institutional Cooperation in Science and Technology (SAUO)
iptel... Internet Protocol Telephony (SAUO)
IP Terminal... Input Terminal (SAUS)
IPTF... Indo-Pacific Theosophical Federation (EAIO)
IPTF... Infrastructure Protection Task Force (FOTI)
IPTG... Isopropylthingalactopyranoside (SAUS)
IPTG... Isopropyl-Thio-a-D-Galactoside (SAUS)
IPTG... Isopropylthiogalactoside [*Also, IPG*] [*Organic chemistry*]
IPTH... Immunoreactive Parathyroid [*Medicine*] (EDAA)
IPTH... Immunoreactive Parathyroid Hormone [*Endocrinology*]
IPTIC... International Pulse Trade and Industry Confederation [*FAO*]
IP Timb... IP Timberlands Ltd. [*Associated Press*] (SAG)
IPTLF... International Phasor Telecom (SAUS)
IPTM... Interval Pulse Time Modulation
IPTME... Institute of Polymer Technology and Materials Engineering (SAUS)
IPTN... Independent Professional Typists Network (EA)
IPTO... Independent Power Take-Off (SAUS)
IPTO... Information Processing Techniques Office (SAUO)
IPTO... Information Processing Technologies Office (SAUS)
IPTO... Information Processing Technology Office (SAUO)
IPTO... International Pet Trade Organization [*Defunct*] (EAIO)
IPTP... In-Plant Test Program (IAA)
IPTPA... International Professional Tennis Players Association (BARN)
IPTRID... International Program for Technology Research in Irrigation and Drainage (SAUO)
IPTS... Improved Programmer Test Section (SAUS)
IPTS... Inplant Terminal System (SAUS)
IPTS... Integrated Powertrain Test System
IPTS... International Pharmaceutical Technology Symposium (SAUO)
IPTS... International Pistol Target System (SAUO)
IPTS... International Practical Temperature Scale [*National Institute of Standards and Technology*]
IPTS... Interplant Terminal System (SAUS)
IPTS... Interplant Transmission System (SAUS)
IPTSF... International Professional Tandem Surfing Federation (SAUO)
IPTS/PS... Improved Programmer Test Station / Power Station (SAA)
IPTT... Internationale du Personnel des Postes, Telegraphes, et Telephones [*Postal, Telegraph, and Telephone International - PTTI*] [*Geneva, Switzerland*] (EAIO)
IPTV... Initial Propulsion Test Vehicle
IPTX... Intermittent Pelvic Traction [*Medicine*] (DMAA)
IPU... Eastern New Mexico University, Portales, NM [*OCLC symbol*] (OCLC)
IPU... Ibadan Progressive Union (SAUO)
IPU... Image Processing Unit (SAUS)
IPU... Immediate Pick-Up (DNAB)
IPU... Imposition Processing Unit (SAUS)
IPU... Individual Patient Usage

IPU .... Information Processing Utility
IPU .... Information Provider Unit (SAUO)
IPU .... Initial Production Unit
IpU .... Inosylyluridine (SAUS)
IPU .... Inpatient Unit [*Medicine*]
IPU .... Input Preparation Unit [*Computer science*] (WDAA)
IPU .... Institute for Public Understanding (EA)
IPU .... Institute of Public Utilities (EA)
IPU .... Instruction Processing Unit (BUR)
IPU .... Instruction Processor Unit (SAUS)
IPU .... Instrument Processor Unit (SAUS)
IPU .... Integrated Physiological Unit
IPU .... Integrated Power Unit (ADWA)
IPU .... Integrated Processor Unit (VLIE)
IPU .... Integrating Processor Unit (SAUS)
IPU .... Intellient Processing Unit (SAUS)
IPU .... Intelligent Processing Unit [*Canon, Inc.*] [*Computer science*] (PCM)
IPU .... Interface and Priority Unit
IPU .... Interface Processor Unit (SAUS)
IPU .... Internal Power Up (SAUS)
IPU .... Internal Processing Unit (VLIE)
IPU .... International Paleontological Union
IPU .... International Peace University (SAUO)
IPU .... International Peasant Union
IPU .... Inter-Parliamentary Union [*See also UI*] [*Switzerland*]
IPU .... Interphase Unit
IPU .... Inter-Processor Unit (VLIE)
IPU .... Irish Postal Union
IPU .... Irish Print Union (DGA)
IPU .... Islamic Press Union (SAUO)
IPU .... Isotope Power Unit
IPUI .... International Portable User Identity (SAUO)
IPU/IPB .... Inter-Parliamentary Bulletin. Official publication of the Inter-Parliamentary Union. Geneva (SAUO)
IPU/IPB .... Inter-Parliamentary Bulletin. Official publication of the Inter-Parliamentary Union. Geneva (journ.) (SAUS)
IPUI R .... International Portable User Identity for public/GSM (SAUO)
IPV .... Imperative (WGA)
IPV .... Improve (SAUS)
IPV .... Improvement (SAUS)
IPV .... Inaccessible Pore Volume [*Petroleum technology*]
IPV .... Inactivated Poliomyelitis Vaccine (SAUS)
IPV .... Inactivated Polio Vaccine [*Also, Salk vaccine*] (PAZ)
IPV .... Inactivated Poliovirus Vaccine
IPV .... Infectious Peritonitis Virus [*Medicine*] (MELL)
IPV .... Infectious Pustular Vaginitis [*Medicine*]
IPV .... Infectious Pustular Vulvovaginitis [*Veterinary medicine*]
IPV .... Injectable Poliovirus Vaccine (ADWA)
IPV .... Inner Pilot Valve
IPV .... In-Place Value (GART)
IPV .... In-Plant Verification (AFIT)
IPV .... In-Process Verification [*Manufacturing*]
IPV .... Inshore Patrol Vessel (SAUS)
IPV .... Internal Podalic Version [*Obstetrics*]
IPV .... International Prime Tech [*Vancouver Stock Exchange symbol*]
IPV .... Inter-Prison Visit (WDAA)
IPV .... Intrinsic Payload Value
IPV .... Inverse Peak Voltage (CIST)
IPV .... Isentropic Potential Vorticity (SAUS)
IPV .... Isopycnic Potential Vorticity [*Oceanography*]
IPV .... Italian Polydor Variable Microgroove [*Record label*]
Ipv6 .... Internet Protocol
IPVC .... Interpolated Premature Ventricular Contraction [*Medicine*] (EDAA)
IPVC .... Irradiated Polyvinyl Chloride (SAUS)
IPVG .... Isopycnic Potential Vorticity Gradient [*Oceanography*]
IPVO .... International Private Voluntary Organizations (SAUO)
IP VPN .... Internet Protocol Virtul Private Network (SAUO)
IPVRA .... International Professional Vinyl Repair Association (EA)
IPVS .... International Pig Veterinary Society [*Amer, Spain*] (EAIO)
IPVS .... Ion Pump Vacuum System
IPW .... Incremental Packet Writing (SAUS)
IPW .... Injury Prevention Web (SAUO)
IPW .... International Peace Walk [*An association*] (EA)
IPW .... International Powertech Systems, Inc. [*Vancouver Stock Exchange symbol*]
IPW .... Interphalangeal Width [*Medicine*] (EDAA)
IPW .... Interpole Winding [*Wiring*] (DNAB)
IPW .... Interrogation of Prisoners of War (SAUO)
IPW .... Interrogation Prisoner of War
IPW .... Interstate Power [*NYSE symbol*] (TTSB)
IPW .... Interstate Power Co. [*NYSE symbol*] (SPSG)
IPW .... Interstate Power Company (SAUO)
IPW .... Ipswich [*England*] [*Airport symbol*] (AD)
IPWA .... Invisible Panel Warming Association [*British*] (BI)
IPWAF .... Initial Postwar Air Force (SAUO)
IPWC .... Inspector of Prisoner of War Camps (SAUO)
IPW Company ... Interstate Power Co. (SAUS)
IPW Company ... Interstate Power Company (SAUO)
IPWD .... India Public Works Department (SAUO)
IPWE .... Institution of Permanent Way Engineers [*Indian Railway*] (TIR)
IPWF .... International Public Works Federation (EA)
IPWG .... In-Plant Working Group (SAUO)
IPWI .... Infrared Proximity Warning Indicator
IPWO .... Interplant Work Order (MCD)
IPWR .... Integrated Pressurized Water Reactor (PDAA)
IPWS .... Iron Plate Workers' Society [*A union*] [*British*]
IPWSO .... International Prader-Willi Syndrome Organisation (SAUO)
IPWSOM .... Institute of Practitioners in Work Study, Organisation, and Management (AIE)
IPWSOM .... Institute of Practitioners in Work Study, Organization and Methods (SAUO)
IPX .... International Phasor Telecom [*Vancouver Stock Exchange symbol*]
IPX .... Internet Package Exchange [*Computer science*] (DDC)
IPX .... Internet Packet Exchange (SAUS)
IPX .... Internet Packet Exchanged (SAUS)
IPX .... Internetwork Packet Exchange
IPX .... Internetwork Protocol Exchange [*Novell, Inc.*] [*Computer science*] (PCM)
IPX .... Interpool, Inc. [*NYSE symbol*] (SPSG)
IPX Acid .... Isopropylxanthic Acid (SAUS)
IPXCP .... Internet Packet Exchange Control Protocol (SAUS)
IPXCP .... Internetwork Packet Exchange Control Protocol (SAUS)
IPXI .... Intrinsic Peroxidase Inhibition Solution [*Clinical chemistry*]
IPXODI .... IPX Open Datalink Interface (SAUS)
IPXPrA .... Interpool Inc. 5.75% Cv Pfd [*NYSE symbol*] (TTSB)
IPX/SPX .... Internet Packet Exchange / Sequenced Packet [*Computer science*] (PCM)
IPX/SPX .... Internetwork Packet Exchange/Sequenced Packet Exchange (SAUS)
IPXSPX .... IPX/Sequenced Packet Exchange (SAUS)
IPXWAN .... Internet Packet eXchange over various WAN media (SAUS)
IPY .... Inches per Year
IPY .... International Phoenix Energy [*Vancouver Stock Exchange symbol*]
IPY .... International Polar Year
IPY .... Ion Pair Yield
IPZ .... George A. Zeller Zone Center, Professional Library, Peoria, IL [*Library symbol*] [*Library of Congress*] (LCLS)
IPZ .... Insulin Protamine Zinc (DMAA)
IPZ .... Insulin-Protamine-Zinc (SAUS)
IPZ .... Intalco Plant [*Federal Railroad Administration identification code*]
IPZ .... Investment Promotion Zone
IPZ .... IPC International Prospector [*Vancouver Stock Exchange symbol*]
IPZ .... World Book - Childcraft International, Inc., Research Library, Chicago, IL [*OCLC symbol*] (OCLC)
IPZP .... Iranian Peace Zebra Program [*Military*] (MCD)
IQ .... Caribbean Airways [*ICAO designator*] (AD)
IQ .... Ideal Quota [*Vitamin supplement*] [*British*]
IQ .... Idem Quod [*The Same As*] [*Latin*]
IQ .... Ideon Group, Inc. [*NYSE symbol*] (SAG)
IQ .... Import Quota (SAUS)
IQ .... Inclined Quartz (SAUS)
IQ .... Indefinite Quantity (AFM)
IQ .... Inflation Quotient
IQ .... Information Quantity (SAUS)
IQ .... Information Quick (PDAA)
I/Q .... In-phase and Quadrature (SAUS)
I/Q .... In Phase/Quadrature (MCD)
IQ .... Input Queue (SAUS)
IQ .... Inquix Consulting Ltd. [*Information service or system*] (IID)
IQ .... Installation Qualification (ACII)
IQ .... Institute of Quarrying [*British*]
IQ .... Instruction-fetch Queue (SAUS)
IQ .... Instrument Quality (IAA)
IQ .... Insured Quality (SAUS)
IQ .... Intelligence Quotient [*Psychological and educational testing*]
IQ .... Intelligent Quattro (SAUO)
IQ .... Intelligent Query
IQ .... Intelligent Quisine [*Campbell Soup Co.*]
IQ .... Interactive Query (SAUO)
IQ .... Internal Quality
IQ .... International Quorum of Film and Video Producers (EA)
IQ .... International Quorum of Motion Picture Producers (SAUO)
IQ .... International Quota (SAUS)
IQ .... Interrupted Quick [*Flashing*] Light [*Navigation signal*]
IQ .... Investment Quotient
IQ .... Iowa Quality [*of pigs*]
IQ .... I Quit [*Smoking*]
IQ .... Iraq [*ANSI two-letter standard code*] (CNC)
iq .... Iraq [*MARC country of publication code*] [*Library of Congress*] (LCCP)
IQ .... Quincy Free Public Library, Quincy, IL [*Library symbol*] [*Library of Congress*] (LCLS)
IQA .... Indians of Quebec Association (SAUO)
IQA .... Inertial Quality Attitude
IQA .... Inspection Quality Assurance
IQA .... Institute of Quality Assurance [*British*]
IQA .... Integrated Quality Assurance (SAUS)
IQA .... International Quality Award [*LIMRA*]
IQA .... Irish Quality Association (ACII)
IqAF .... Iraqi Air Force
IQ & S .... Iron, Quinine, and Strychnine [*Elixir*]
IQB .... Individual Quick Blanching (DICI)
IQC .... Incoming Quality Control (TIMI)
IQC .... Indefinite Quantity Contract (SAUO)
IQC .... Indefinite-Quantity Contract (AAGC)
IQC .... Industrial Quality Control
IQC .... Institutional Quality Control [*Department of Education*] (GFGA)
IQC .... Integrated Quality Control [*Department of Health and Human Services*] (GFGA)
IQC .... InterCapital California Quality Municipal Securities [*NYSE symbol*] (SPSG)

IQC.............. InterCapital Cal Qual Muni Sec [*NYSE symbol*] (TTSB)
IQC.............. International Quality Center (or Centre) (SAUS)
IQC.............. Quincy College, Quincy, IL [*Library symbol*] [*Library of Congress*] (LCLS)
IQCA........... Irish Quality Control Association (SAUO)
IQCDPS........ Integrated Quality Control Data Processing System [*Department of Health and Human Services*] (GFGA)
IQCODE........ Informant Questionnaire on Cognitive Decline in the Elderly
IQCPP.......... Institutional Quality Control Pilot Project [*Department of Education*] (GFGA)
IQCS............ Inservice Quality Control System (SAUO)
IQCT............ Institute for Quality Control Training (SAUO)
IQE.............. Interruption Queue Element [*Computer science*] (MHDI)
IQEC............ International Quantum Electronics Conference (CIST)
IQED........... Id Quod Erat Demonstrandum [*That Which Was to Be Proved*] [*Latin*]
IQF.............. Individually Quick Frozen (SAUS)
IQF.............. Individually Quick-Frozen [*Food technology*]
IQF.............. Individual Quick Freezing (SAUS)
IQF.............. Instant Quick Frozen (SAUS)
IQF.............. Interactive Query Facility [*Computer science*]
IQF.............. International Quail Foundation [*Defunct*] (EA)
IQG.............. Great River Library System, Quincy, IL [*Library symbol*] [*Library of Congress*] (LCLS)
IQHE........... Integer Quantum Hall Effect [*Solid state physics*]
IQHE........... Integral Quantum Hall Effect [*Solid-state physics*]
IQHL........... Institute for Quality in Human Life (SAUO)
IQI............... Image Quality Indicator
IQI............... Industrial Quality, Inc.
IQI............... Industrial Quality Index (SAUO)
IQI............... Inlage Quality Indicator (SAUS)
IQI............... Instructional Quality Inventory
IQI............... InterCapital Quality Municipal Income [*NYSE symbol*] (SPSG)
IQI............... InterCapital Qual Muni Income [*NYSE symbol*] (TTSB)
IQIQ............. Applied Intelligence Group, Inc. [*NASDAQ symbol*] (SAG)
IQISA........... Interest Questionnaire for Indian South Africans [*Vocational guidance test*]
IQIT............. Issue Quality Improvement Team (TIMI)
IQK.............. Interrupted Quick (SAUS)
I Qk.............. Interrupted Quick [*Flashing*] Light [*Navigation signal*]
I Qk Fl......... Interrupted Quick Flashing Light [*Navigation signal*]
IQkFl Lighting... Interrupted Quick Flashing Lighting (SAUS)
IQk Lighting... Interrupted Quick Lighting (SAUS)
IQL.............. Incoming Quality Level [*Computer science*] (ELAL)
IQL.............. Information Query Language (NITA)
IQL.............. Interactive Query Language [*Digital Equipment Corp.*] [*Computer science*]
IQL.............. Intermediate Query Language [*Computer science*]
IQM.............. Input Queue Manager (NITA)
IQM.............. InterCapital Quality Municipal Securities [*NYSE symbol*] (SPSG)
IQM.............. InterCapital Qual Muni Sec [*NYSE symbol*] (TTSB)
IQM.............. Qiemo [*China*] [*Airport symbol*] (OAG)
IQMF............ Image Quality Merit Function [*Color image*]
IQMH........... Input Queue Message Handler [*Computer science*]
IQMInc......... Intercapital Quality Municipal Income Trust [*Associated Press*] (SAG)
IQMInv......... Intercapital Quality Municipal Investment Trust [*Associated Press*] (SAG)
IQMS........... Industrial Quality Management Science [*Quality control*]
IQMSec........ InterCapital Quality Municipal Securities [*Associated Press*] (SAG)
IQN.............. Inner Quantum Number
IQN.............. Intercapital New York Quality Municipal Securities [*NYSE symbol*] (SAG)
IQN.............. InterCapital N.Y.Qual Muni Sec [*NYSE symbol*] (TTSB)
IQN.............. Qingyang [*China*] [*Airport symbol*] (OAG)
IQNet........... International Certification Network (SAUO)
IQO.............. Initial Quantity Order (NG)
IQ of Pigs.... Iowa Quality of Pigs (SAUS)
IQP.............. Incoming Quality Plan (TIMI)
IQP.............. Institute for Quality and Productivity (SAUS)
IQPC............ Incoming Quality Plan Control (TIMI)
IQPF............ International Quick Printing Foundation [*Defunct*] (EA)
IQPP............ Interactive Query Pre-Processor (NITA)
IQPS............ Institute of Qualified Private Secretaries Ltd. [*British*] (BI)
IQQ.............. Caribbean Airways [*Barbados*] [*ICAO designator*] (FAAC)
IQQ.............. Iquique [*Chile*] [*Airport symbol*] (OAG)
IQQ.............. Iquique [*Chile*] [*Seismograph station code, US Geological Survey*] (SEIS)
IQR.............. Inquiry (SAUS)
IQR.............. Instruction Queue Register (SAUS)
IQR.............. Interquartile Range
IQRC............ Institut Quebecois de la Recherche sur la Culture [*Database producer*]
IQRP............ Interactive Query and Report Processing (or Processor) (SAUS)
IQRP............ Interactive Query and Report Processor [*IBM Corp.*] [*Computer science*]
IQS.............. Initial Quality Survey
IQS.............. Institute of Quality Surveyors (SAUO)
IQS.............. Institute of Quality Surveyors, London (SAUO)
IQS.............. Institute of Quantity Surveyors [*Later, RICS*]
IQS.............. Institute of Quantity Surveyors, London (SAUO)
IQS.............. Interactive Query System [*Computer science*] (IAA)
IQS.............. International "Q" Signal
IQS.............. International Quality Study (SAUS)
IQS.............. Internet Quality of Service (GART)
IQSA............ Institute of Quantity Surveyors of Australia (SAUO)
IQ Smoking... I Quit Smoking (SAUS)
IQSoft.......... IQ Software Corp. [*Associated Press*] (SAG)
IQST............ IntelliQuest Information Group, Inc. [*NASDAQ symbol*] (SAG)
IQST............ ItelliQuest Info Group [*NASDAQ symbol*] (TTSB)
IQSU............ International Quiet Sun Year [*1964-65*] [*Also, IQSY, IYQS*] (IAA)
IQSW........... IQ Software [*NASDAQ symbol*] (TTSB)
IQSW........... IQ Software Corp. [*NASDAQ symbol*] (SAG)
IQSY............ International Quiet Solar Year (SAUO)
IQSY............ International Quiet Sun Year [*1964-65*] [*Also, IYQS*]
IQSY............ International Quiet Sun Years (SAUO)
IQSY/EX....... International Quiet Years of the Sun Experiments (SAUO)
IQT.............. Initial Qualification Training
IQT.............. Intercapital Quality Municipal Investment Trust [*NYSE symbol*] (SPSG)
IQT.............. InterCapital Qual Muni Inv [*NYSE symbol*] (TTSB)
IQT.............. Interquest Resources Corp. [*Toronto Stock Exchange symbol*]
IQT.............. Iquitos [*Peru*] [*Airport symbol*] (OAG)
IQTOC.......... Indefinite Quantity Task Order Contract (SAUS)
IQU.............. University of New Mexico, Albuquerque, NM [*OCLC symbol*] (OCLC)
IQUA............ Irish Association for Quaternary Studies (SAUO)
IQUE............ In-Plant Quality Evaluation Program (AAGC)
IQV.............. Illinois Veterans Home, Quincy, IL [*Library symbol*] [*Library of Congress*] (LCLS)
IQV.............. Pekin Community High School, Pekin, IL [*OCLC symbol*] (OCLC)
IQW............. Individuelle Quantitative Wert [*Mean Total Ridge Count*] [*Anatomy*]
IQW............. John Wood Community College, Quincy, IL [*Library symbol*] [*Library of Congress*] (LCLS)
IQW............. Western New Mexico University, Silver City, NM [*OCLC symbol*] (OCLC)
IQX.............. Bradford Public Library, Bradford, IL [*OCLC symbol*] (OCLC)
IQY.............. Internet Query [*Computer science*]
IQY.............. Limestone High School, Bartonville, IL [*OCLC symbol*] (OCLC)
IQZ.............. Farmington East High School, Farmington, IL [*OCLC symbol*] (OCLC)
IR................ Current, Reverse (SAUS)
IR................ Ice on Runway [*NWS*] (FAAC)
IR................ Ice Rinks [*Public-performance tariff class*] [*British*]
IR................ Ileal Resection [*Medicine*] (EDAA)
IR................ Illinois Railnet [*Federal Railroad Administration identification code*]
IR................ Illumentation Rate (SAUS)
IR................ Illumination Rate (CAAL)
IR................ Illuminator RADAR (NATG)
IR................ Illustration Request
IR................ Image Readout [*Computer graphics*]
IR................ Image Reconstruction (SAUS)
IR................ Image Register (TIMI)
IR................ Image Rejection
IR................ Imaging RADAR (MCD)
IR................ Imaging Radiometer (SAUS)
IR................ Imitation Russia [*Bookbinding*] (DGA)
IR................ Immediate Relative (SAUS)
IR................ Immediate Reserve [*Air Force*] [*British*]
IR................ Immune Response [*Also, Ir*] [*Genetics*]
IR................ Immunization Rate (AFM)
ir................. Immunoreactive [*Medicine*] (EDAA)
IR................ Immunoreactive
IR................ Immunoreagent (DB)
IR................ Improved Retrofit (CAAL)
IR................ Impurity Removal Subsystem (MCD)
IR................ Incidence Rate (WDAA)
IR................ Incident Report
IR................ Inclination of the Ascending Return [*Aviation*] (NASA)
IR................ Indent Right [*Typography*] (DGA)
ir................. Indent Right (WDMC)
IR................ Independent Release (SAUS)
IR................ Independent Research (NG)
IR................ Indexing Register (SAUS)
IR................ Index of Response [*Medicine*] (MAE)
IR................ Index Record (SAUS)
IR................ Index Register (WDAA)
IR................ Index Return [*Computer science*] (DCDG)
IR................ In-dial Register (SAUS)
IR................ Indiana Railroad System
IR................ Indiana Register [*A publication*] (AAGC)
IR................ Indian Railways (SAUO)
IR................ Indian Reservation (SAUS)
IR................ Indian Reserve (SAUS)
IR................ Indian Rulings [*A publication*] (DLA)
IR................ India Rubber (SAUS)
IR................ India-Rubber (DEN)
IR................ Indicating Recorder [*Electronics*] (ECII)
IR................ Indicator Reading (IAA)
IR................ Indicator Ready (SAUS)
IR................ Indicator Register (IAA)
IR................ Individual Recorder [*Sports*]
IR................ Individual Referral (OICC)
IR................ Individual Reinforcement (SAUS)
IR................ Inductive Resistor (SAUS)
IR................ Industrial Kelations (SAUS)
IR................ Industrial Registry [*New South Wales, Australia*]
IR................ Industrial Relations
IR................ Industrial Reports [*Australia*] [*A publication*]
I-R............... Industrial Research
IR................ Industrial Robot (ELAL)
IR................ Industry Remarketer (CDE)
IR................ Infantry Regiment (SAUO)

IR................ Inferior Rectus [*Muscle*] [*Anatomy*]
IR................ Inflation Rate (SAUS)
IR................ Inflight Report (SAUS)
IR................ Informal Report
IR................ Information and Technology [*Educational Resources Information Center (ERIC) Clearinghouse*] [*Syracuse University*] (PAZ)
IR................ Information Rate (SAUS)
IR................ Information Reading (SAUS)
IR................ Information Region (SAUS)
IR................ Information Release (DLA)
IR................ Information Report
IR................ Information Representation (SAUS)
IR................ Information Request (AAG)
IR................ Information Requirement [*Military intelligence*] (INF)
IR................ Information Resource (SAUS)
IR................ Information Restoring (SAUS)
IR................ Information Retrieval [*Computer science*]
IR................ Information Retrieval, Infrared (SAUS)
ir................ Infrared (CARB)
IR................ Infrared
IR................ Infrared Diffraction (SAUS)
IR................ Infrared Radiation
IR................ Infrared Radiometer
IR................ Infrared Reconnaissance
IR................ Infrared Reflectance (IAA)
IR................ Infra-Red Spectroscopy (EDCT)
Ir................ Ingenieur [*Engineer*] [*French*]
IR................ Ingersoll-Rand [*NYSE symbol*] (TTSB)
IR................ Ingersoll-Rand Co. [*NYSE symbol*] (SPSG)
IR................ Ingram-Rude Information Researchers [*Information service or system*] (IID)
IR................ Ingreee Router (ACRL)
IR................ Initialized Routine (SAUS)
IR................ Initializer Routine (SAUS)
IR................ Initial Reactive Results
IR................ Initial Release (MCD)
IR................ Initial Reports of the Proceedings of ODP (journ.) (SAUS)
IR................ Initial Reserve
IR................ Initiation Region [*Genetics*]
IR................ Ink Receptivity
IR................ Inland Revenue [*British*]
IR................ Inner Roll Gimbal (NASA)
IR................ Innovations Representation (SAUS)
IR................ Input Reader (SAUS)
IR................ Input Register (SAUS)
IR................ Input Request (SAUS)
IR................ Input Routine (SAUS)
I/R................ Inquiry/Response [*Automotive engineering*] [*Electronics*]
IR................ Inside Radius [*Technical drawings*]
IR................ Inside Right [*Soccer position*]
IR................ Insoluble Residue
IR................ Inspection Record (MCD)
IR................ Inspection Rejection
IR................ Inspection Release
IR................ Inspection [*or Inspector's*] Report
IR................ Inspection Request (IAA)
IR................ Inspectors Report (SAUS)
IR................ Installation Report
IR................ Installation Restoration (MCD)
IR................ Instantaneous Relay
IR................ Instantaneous Release (IAA)
IR................ Instant Release [*Typography*] (DGA)
IR................ Institute of Refrigeration [*British*]
IR................ Institutional Research (SAUS)
IR................ Instruction Register [*Computer science*]
IR................ Instruction Ring (SAUS)
IR................ Instrumentation Report
IR................ Instrumentation Requirement (SAUS)
IR................ Instrumentation Requirements (MUGU)
IR................ Instrumentations Requirements (SAUS)
IR................ Instrument Rating [*Aviation*] (PIAV)
IR................ Instrument Reading (AFM)
IR................ Instrument Register (IAA)
IR................ Instrument Restricted Controlled Airspace (DA)
IR................ Instrument Route (ACAE)
IR................ Insulation Resistance
IR................ Intake Restriction [*Automotive engineering*]
IR................ Intelligence Ratio
IR................ Intelligence Report
IR................ Intelligence Request (DOMA)
IR................ Intelligence Requirement [*Military*] (INF)
IR................ Intelligence Review
IR................ Intensive Reading
IR................ Interaction Resistance [*Plant pathology*]
IR................ Interagency Report (PDAA)
IR................ Interface Repository (SAUS)
IR................ Interference Refractometer (SAUS)
IR................ Intergovernmental Relations (OICC)
IR................ Interim Report
IR................ Intermediate Range (MCD)
IR................ Intermediate Register [*Telecommunications*] (OA)
IR................ Intermediate Representation (VLIE)
IR................ Intermediate Resonance (SAUS)
IR................ Intermediate Results (SAUO)
IR................ Intermediate Review (NATG)
IR................ Internal Range (SAUS)
IR................ Internal Register (IAA)
IR................ Internal Reliability
IR................ Internal Repeat [*Genetics*]
IR................ Internal Report
IR................ Internal Request (SAUS)
IR................ Internal Resistance
IR................ Internal Revenue
IR................ Internal Revenue Decisions [*Department of the Treasury*] [*A publication*] (DLA)
IR................ Internal Review [*Army*] (AABC)
IR................ Internal Rotation [*Myology*]
IR................ Internationale de la Resistance [*Resistance International - RI*] (EAIO)
IR................ International Randonneurs [*An association*] (EA)
IR................ International Rectifier Corp. (EFIS)
IR................ International Registration (BARN)
IR................ International Rendezvous (MCD)
IR................ International Representative (SAUS)
IR................ International Rice (IIA)
IR................ Internet Registry
IR................ Internetwork Router (SAUS)
IR................ Interpretation Report
IR................ Interpreter Releases (SAUS)
IR................ Interpreting Routine (SAUS)
IR................ Interpretive Routine (SAUS)
IR................ Interregio (SAUS)
IR................ InterRent [*Car rental group*]
IR................ Interrogation Report
I-R................ Interrogator-Responder (VLIE)
IR................ Interrupt Register (IAA)
IR................ Interrupt Request [*Computer science*] (MHDB)
IR................ Interrupt Routine (SAUS)
IR................ Interval Rate [*Army*] (AABC)
IR................ Intrarachidian (SAUS)
ir................ Intrarectal [*Medicine*] (DB)
ir................ Intrarenal [*Medicine*] (DB)
IR................ Invention Report
IR................ Inventory Record (SAUS)
IR................ Inventory Report (SAUS)
IR................ Inversion Recovery [*NMR imaging*]
IR................ Inverted Repeat [*Genetics*]
IR................ Investigation Record
IR................ Investigation Report (SAUS)
IR................ Investigation Request (SAUS)
IR................ Investment Recurring (MCD)
IR................ Investor Relations
IR................ Ionizing Radiation (SAUS)
IR................ Iran [*ANSI two-letter standard code*] (CNC)
ir................ Iran [*MARC country of publication code*] [*Library of Congress*] (LCCP)
Ir................ Iran (MILB)
IR................ Iran Air [*ICAO designator*] (AD)
IR................ Iran National Airlines [*ICAO designator*] (AD)
IR................ Iran National Airlines Corp. (SAUO)
Ir................ Iredell's North Carolina Equity Reports [*A publication*] (DLA)
Ir................ Iredell's North Carolina Law Reports [*A publication*] (DLA)
IR................ Ireland [*IYRU nationality code*] (ROG)
Ir................ Iridium [*Chemical element*]
Ir................ Irish (BEE)
IR................ Irish
IR................ Irish Law Reports [*A publication*] (DLA)
IR................ Irish Rails (SAUO)
IR................ Irish Reports [*A publication*]
Ir................ Irnerius [*Flourished, 1113-18*] [*Authority cited in pre-1607 legal work*] (DSA)
ir................ Iron [*CIPW classification*] [*Geology*]
IR................ Iron Roughneck (SAUS)
IR................ Irradiance [*Electromagnetism*] (IAA)
IR................ Irrelevancy [*Used in correcting manuscripts, etc.*]
IR................ Irrigated Rice Research Program (SAUO)
IR................ Isophthalic Resin [*Plastics*]
IR................ Isoprene Rubber
IR................ Isotope Ratio (DB)
IR................ Isotope Reactor [*Former USSR*]
IR................ Isotype Radiograph (SAUS)
IR................ Israel Railways (SAUO)
IR................ Item Record (AFIT)
IR................ Iterative Realization (SAUS)
I-R................ Ito-Reenstierna [*Reaction*] [*Medicine*]
IR................ Izquierda Republicana [*Republican Left*] [*Spain*] [*Political party*] (PPE)
IR................ Rock Island Public Library, Rock Island, IL [*Library symbol*] [*Library of Congress*] (LCLS)
IR1................ Iran Long-Period Array [*Iran*] [*Seismograph station code, US Geological Survey*] (SEIS)
IR2................ Iran Long-Period Array [*Iran*] [*Seismograph station code, US Geological Survey*] (SEIS)
IR3................ Iran Long-Period Array [*Iran*] [*Seismograph station code, US Geological Survey*] (SEIS)
IR4................ Iran Long-Period Array [*Iran*] [*Seismograph station code, US Geological Survey*] (SEIS)
IR5................ Iran Long-Period Array [*Iran*] [*Seismograph station code, US Geological Survey*] (SEIS)
IR6................ Iran Long-Period Array [*Iran*] [*Seismograph station code, US Geological Survey*] (SEIS)

IR7.............. Iran Long-Period Array [*Iran*] [*Seismograph station code, US Geological Survey*] (SEIS)
IRA.............. Augustana College, Rock Island, IL [*Library symbol*] [*Library of Congress*] (LCLS)
IRA.............. Ileorectal Anastomosis [*Medicine*]
IRA.............. Immunoradioassay [*Medicine*] (MELL)
IRA.............. Immunoregulatory alpha-Globulin [*Immunology*]
IRA.............. Impact Ratio (AAGC)
IRA.............. Implant Resection Arthroplasty [*Medicine*] (MELL)
IRA.............. Impulse-Radiating Antenna (SAUS)
IRA.............. Inactive Renin Activity [*Medicine*] (DMAA)
IRA.............. Independent Regulatory Agency [*US Government*]
IRA.............. Independent Retirement Account (SAUS)
IRA.............. Indian Registration Act [*British*] (ROG)
IRA.............. Indian Reorganization Act (OICC)
IRA.............. Indian Rights Association (EA)
IRA.............. Individual Retirement Account
IRA.............. Individual Retirement Annuity [*Insurance*]
IRA.............. Individual Retirement Arrangement (SAUS)
IRA.............. Industrial Recreation Association (SAUO)
IRA.............. Industrial Relations Act [*1971*] [*British*] (DCTA)
IRA.............. Industrial Risk Insurers (SAUO)
IRA.............. Inertial Reference Assembly (SAUS)
IRA.............. Information Release Administration (SAUO)
IRA.............. Information Resource Administration
IRA.............. Infrared Atmospheric Band Airglow Radiometer (SAUS)
IRA.............. Initial Rate of Absorption (EEVL)
IRA.............. Input Reference Axis (IEEE)
IRA.............. Inspector of the Royal Artillery [*British*]
IRA.............. Inspector's Report Addendum (AAG)
IRA.............. Institute of Agronomic Research (SAUO)
IRA.............. Institute of Registered Architects [*British*]
IRA.............. Instruction Register, Address Portion [*Computer science*] (MHDI)
IRA.............. Instruction Register, Address-portion (SAUS)
IRA.............. Instrument Representatives Association (SAUO)
IRA.............. Integrated RADOME [*RADAR Dome*] Antenna
IRA.............. Intelligence Related Activities [*Military*] (MCD)
IRA.............. Intercollegiate Rowing Association (EA)
IRA.............. Interface Requirement Agreement (SAUO)
IRA.............. Interim Remedial Action (BCP)
IRA.............. Interim Repair Activity (ACAE)
IRA.............. Interim Response Action (SAUS)
IRA.............. Interim Response Actions [*Army*] (DOMA)
IRA.............. Intermediate Range Aircraft (SAUS)
IRA.............. Internacia Radio-Asocio (SAUO)
IRA.............. Internal Reflection Attachment (SAUS)
IRA.............. Internal Release Agent
IRA.............. Internal Revenue Act
IRA.............. International Racquetball Association [*Later, AARA*] (EA)
IRA.............. International Reading Association (EA)
IRA.............. International Recreation Association [*Later, WLRA*]
IRA.............. International Reference Alphabet (SAUO)
IRA.............. International Registration Authority [*Botany*] (PDAA)
IRA.............. International Reprographics Association (EA)
IRA.............. International Research Associates (SAUO)
IRA.............. International Rodeo Association (EA)
IRA.............. International Roleo Association [*Later, International Log Rolling Association*] (EA)
IRA.............. International Rubber Association [*Kuala Lumpur, Malaysia*] (EAIO)
IRA.............. International Ruhr Authority (SAUO)
IRA.............. Interprocedural Register Allocation (VLIE)
IRA.............. Interstate Racing Association (AGLO)
IRA.............. Investment Recovery Association (EA)
IRA.............. Investment Return Assumption (SAUS)
IRA.............. Investment-Return Assumption [*Finance*] (PDAA)
ira.............. Iranian [*MARC language code*] [*Library of Congress*] (LCCP)
IRA.............. Iranian Airways (SAUS)
IRA.............. Iranian Airways Co.
IRA.............. Iran National Airlines Corp. [*ICAO designator*] (FAAC)
IRA.............. Irish Republican Army [*Government term*] (GA)
IRA.............. Islamic Research Association (SAUO)
IRA.............. Israel Railway Administration (SAUO)
IRA.............. Ithaca Railroad Association [*Defunct*] (EA)
IRA.............. Kira Kira [*Solomon Islands*] [*Airport symbol*] (OAG)
IRA.............. Rutland, VT [*Location identifier*] [*FAA*] (FAAL)
IRAA.............. Independent Refiners Association of America [*Later, AIRA*] (EA)
IRAA.............. Indoor Radon Abatement Act (AUEG)
IRAA & A..... Increase and Replacement of Armor, Armament, and Ammunition [*Naval budget appropriation title*]
IRAAM.......... Improved Remote Area Anti-Armor Mine (SAUS)
IRAAM.......... Improved Remote-Area Armor Mine (MCD)
IRAAM.......... Intermediate Range Air-to-Air Missile (SAUS)
IRAB.............. Index to Reviews of Australian Books [*A publication*]
IRAB.............. Institute for Research in Animal Behavior (SAUO)
IRAC.............. Indochina Refugee Assistance Program (SAUS)
IRAC.............. Indochina Resource Action Center (EA)
IRAC.............. Indpendent Review Advisory Committee (SAUO)
IRAC.............. Industrial Relations Advisory Committee (SAUO)
IRAC.............. Industrial Relations Advisory Council [*Australia*]
IRAC.............. Industrial Research Advisory Council (SAUO)
IRAC.............. Information Resource and Analysis Center (SAUS)
IRAC.............. Information Resources Administration Council (SAUO)
IRAC.............. Information Resources Administration Councils [*General Services Administration*] [*Washington, DC*] (EGAO)
IRAC.............. Information Resources and Analysis Center (SAUS)
IRAC.............. Infrared Advisory Center
IRAC.............. Infrared Analysis Center (ACAE)
IRAC.............. Infrared Array Camera
IRAC.............. Institut Royal d'Architecture du Canada [*Royal Architectural Institute of Canada*] (EAIO)
IRAC.............. Integrated Random Access Channel (PDAA)
IRAC.............. Intelligence Resources Advisory Committee [*To supervise US intelligence budget*]
IRAC.............. Interagency Records Administration Conference (SAUO)
IRAC.............. Interagency Research Animal Committee [*Department of Health and Human Services*] (GFGA)
IRAC.............. Interdepartmental Radio Advisory Committee (SAUO)
IRAC.............. Interdepartment Radio Advisory Committee [*Department of Commerce*] (EGAO)
IRAC.............. Interfraternity Research and Administrative Council (SAUO)
IRAC.............. Interfraternity Research and Advisory Council [*Defunct*] (EA)
IRAC.............. Interim Rapid Action Change (MCD)
IRAC.............. International Records Administration Conference (SAUO)
IRAC.............. Issue, Rule, Application, Conclusions (AAGC)
IRA-CA......... Inebriates Reformation and After-Care Association (SAUO)
IRACCR......... Initial Release and Change Control Record (SAUS)
IRACOR......... Infrared Acquisition RADAR (MSA)
IRACQ.......... Infrared Acquisition (SAUS)
IRACQ.......... Infrared Acquisition RADAR
IRACQ.......... Instrumentation RADAR and Acquisition
IRACQ.......... Instrumented Range Acquisition (KSC)
IRACQ Panel... Instrumentation Radar and Acquisition Panel (SAUS)
IRACQ Radar... Infrared Acquisition Radar (SAUS)
IRACS.......... Intermediate Reactor Auxiliary Cooling System (SAUS)
IRACT.......... Incident Response Action Coordination Team [*Nuclear energy*] (NRCH)
IR-ACTH....... Immunoreactive Adrenocorticotropic Hormone [*Medicine*] (DMAA)
IRAD.............. Inbound Radial (SAUS)
IRAD.............. Independent Research and Development
IRAD.............. Infrared Adaptive Discrimination (ACAE)
IRAD.............. Infrared Ambush Device
IRAD.............. Institute for Research on Animal Diseases [*British*]
IRAD.............. Institutional Research and Development Office [*Kirksville College of Osteopathic Medicine*] [*Research center*] (RCD)
IRAD.............. International Research & Development Corp. (EFIS)
IRAD.............. Internet Rapid Application Development (ITCA)
IRAD.............. IRAD Manufacturing Company (SAUO)
IRADDS......... Infrared Air Defense Detection System
IRADS.......... Infrared Acquisition and Designation System (DOMA)
IRADS.......... Infra-Red Acquisition and Detection System (SAUO)
IRADS.......... Infra-Red Acquisition Designation System (SAUS)
IRA-EEA....... Ileorectal Anastomosis with End-to-End Anastomosis (STED)
IRAEN.......... International Rice Agro-Economic Network (SAUO)
IRAF.............. Image Reduction and Analysis Facility
IRAF.............. Indexed Random Access File (SAUS)
IRAF.............. Individual Retirement Account File [*IRS*]
IRAF.............. Interferogram Requirements and Analysis Funnel (SAUS)
IrAF.............. Iraqi Air Force (SAUO)
IRAFV.......... Corona Corp. (Class A) [*NASDAQ symbol*] (COMM)
Ir Age Int..... Iron Age Metalworking International (journ.) (SAUS)
IRAH.............. Infrared Active Homing (MCD)
IRAH.............. Infrared Alternate Head
IRAL.............. International Review of Applied Linguistics in Language Teaching (journ.) (SAUS)
IR All.............. Indian Rulings, Allahabad Series [*A publication*] (DLA)
IRALON......... International Rice Acid Lowland Soils Observational Nursery (SAUO)
IRALSN......... International Rice Acid Lowland Soil Nursery (SAUO)
IRAM.............. Improved Random Access Memory [*Computer science*]
IRAM.............. Improved Reliability and Maintainability
IRAM.............. Improved Repairables Asset Management (DNAB)
IRAM.............. Indexed Random Access Memory (NITA)
IRAM.............. Indexed Random Access Method (SAUS)
IRAM.............. Institut de Recherches et d'Applications des Methodes de Developpement [*Institute of Research and Application of Development Methods - IRAM*] (EAIO)
IRAM.............. Institute for Radio Astronomy in the Millimeter-wavelengths (SAUS)
IRAM.............. Institute of Millimeteric Radioastronomy
IRAM.............. Institute of Research and Application of Development Methods (SAUO)
IRAM.............. Integrated Random-Access Memory [*Computer science*]
IRAM.............. Integrated Random Access Method (SAUS)
IRAM.............. International Reformed Agency for Migration (SAUO)
IRAMMP........ Infrared Analysis, Measurement, and Modeling Program
IRAMMP........ Infra-Red Analysis Measurements & Modeling Program (SAUS)
IRAMS.......... Infrared Automatic Mass Screening [*Electronics*]
I-RAMS......... Integrated Retractable Aircraft Munition System (SAUS)
IRAN.............. Individual Retirement Annuity (ADWA)
IRAN.............. Inspect and Repair as Necessary [*Aviation*]
IRAN.............. Inspection and Repair as Necessary (SAUS)
IRAN.............. Inspection and Repairs as Necessary (SAUO)
Iran.............. Iranian (BEE)
IRAN.............. Iranian [*Language, etc.*] (ROG)
Iran.............. Iran. Journal of the British Institute of Persian Studies [*A publication*] (ABAR)
IRANAIR....... Iran National Airlines (SAUS)
IRANAIR....... Iran National Airlines Corp. (SAUO)
Iran Air......... Iran National Airlines Corporation, Teheran (SAUO)
IRanASD....... Allen Township Consolidated Community School District 65, Ransom, IL [*Library symbol*] [*Library of Congress*] (LCLS)
IR&A.............. Independent Review and Assessment (SAUS)

IR & A......... Information Research and Analysis [*Oak Ridge National Laboratory*] [*Oak Ridge, TN*] [*Department of Energy*] (GRD)
IR & AC....... Internal Review and Audit Compliance [*Army*]
IR&D........... Independent Research and Development (AAGC)
IR & D......... Independent Research and Development
IR & D......... Industrial Research and Development
IR & D......... Internal Research and Development [*Army*]
IR&D........... Internal Revenue Department (SAUO)
IR & D/B & P... Independent Research and Development/Bid and Proposal
IR&D/B&P.... Independent Research and Development/Bidding and Proposal (SAUO)
IR&DG......... Industrial Research and Development Grants (SAUS)
IR&G........... International Relations and Government (SAUO)
IRANDOC..... Iranian Documentation Centre [*Ministry of Culture and Higher Education*] [*Tehran*]
IR and T...... International Research and Technology Corporation (SAUO)
IRANF.......... Immunoreactive Atrial Natriuretic Factor
IrANP.......... Immunoreactive Artrial Natriuretic Peptide [*Medicine*] (EDAA)
IRANSAT...... Iranian Government Communications Satellite [*NASA*] (NASA)
IRant.......... Rantoul Public Library, Rantoul, IL [*Library symbol*] [*Library of Congress*] (LCLS)
Iranvest....... Iran Overseas Investment Bank Ltd. (SAUO)
IRAOH......... International Registration Authority for Orchid Hybrids (SAUO)
IRAOS......... Interview for the Retrospective Assessment of the Onset of Schizophrenia (SAUS)
IRAP........... Indochinese Refugees Assistance Program (SAUS)
IRAP........... Industrial Research Assistance and Promotion (SAUO)
IRAP........... Industrial Research Assistance Program [*Canada*]
IRAP........... Industrial Research Assistance Programme (SAUO)
I-RAP.......... Infra-Red Augmented Projectile (SAUS)
IRAP........... Integrated Risk Assessment Project (SAUS)
IRAP........... Interagency Radiological Assistance Plan (SAUO)
IRAP........... Interagency Radiological Assistance Program [*Nuclear Regulatory Commission*] (NRCH)
IRAP........... Interdisciplinary Panel on Climate Change (SAUO)
IRAP........... Interleukin Receptor Antagonist Protein [*Biochemistry*]
Iraqi J Sci... Iraqi Journal of Science (journ.) (SAUS)
IRAR........... Impulse Response Area Ratio
IRAR........... Individual Retirement Account Register [*IRS*]
IRAR........... Infrared Airborne RADAR (PDAA)
IRAR........... Infrared Augmentation Reliability (MCD)
IRAR........... Integrated Random Access Reservation [*Computer science*] (CIST)
IRAR........... Integrator Register Address Register (PDAA)
IRAR........... Internal Variable (SAUS)
IRA Relay..... In-dial Register Access Relay (SAUS)
IRAS........... Indian Railway Accounts Services [*Indian Railway*] (TIR)
IRAS........... Infared Astronomical Satellite [*Launched in January 1983*]
IRAS........... Information Resources Access System (SAUS)
IRAS........... Information Retrieval Advisory Services Limited [*British*] (NITA)
IRAS........... Information Retrieval Advisory Services Ltd. (SAUS)
IRAS........... Infrared Absorption Spectroscopy (SAUS)
IRAS........... Infrared Acquisition Sensor (ACAE)
IRAS........... Infrared Astronomical Satellite [*NASA*] (MCD)
IRAS........... Infrared Attack System
IRAS........... Infrared Automatic System (DNAB)
IRAS........... Infra-Red Measuring Astronomical Satellite (SAUS)
IRAS........... Infrared-measuring Astronomical Satellite (SAUS)
IRAS........... Infrared Reflection Absorption Spectroscopy [*Also, IRRAS, RAIR, RAIRS, RAIS*]
IRAS........... Infra-Rod Astronomical Satellite (SAUS)
IRAS........... Institute on Religion in an Age of Science (EA)
IRAS........... Integrated RADOME [*RADAR Dome*] Antenna Structure
IRAS........... Intelligent Runway Attack Submunition (SAUS)
IRAS........... Interdiction Reconnaissance Attack System (PDAA)
IRAS........... Internet Routing and Access Service [*Computer science*] (ACRL)
IRASA......... International Radio Air Safety Association
IRASE......... Institute of Refrigeration and Air Conditioning Service Engineers (SAUO)
IRASER....... Infrared Amplification by Stimulated Emission of Radiation
IRASER....... Infrared MASER (CET)
IRASI.......... Internal Review and System Improvement [*Army*]
IRASP......... Infrared Advanced Seeker Program (ACAE)
IRAT........... Infrared Angle Track (ACAE)
IRAT........... Institut de Recherche Appliquee sur le Travail [*Canada*]
IRAT........... Institut de Recherches Agronomiques Tropicales et des Cultures Vivrieres [*Food and agricultural research foundation supported by France and several African states*]
IRATA......... Industrial Rope Access Trade Association [*British*] (DBA)
IRATA......... Irata, Inc. [*NASDAQ symbol*] (SAG)
IRATA......... Irata Inc.'A' [*NASDAQ symbol*] (TTSB)
IRATE......... Inertial Range Atmospheric Turbulence Entrainment (PDAA)
IRATE......... Intelligence Review and Assessment Task Element [*Study of the effectiveness of the air war in Southeast Asia*]
IRATE......... Interactive Retrieval and Text Editor [*Computer science*] (PDAA)
IRATE......... Interim Remote Air Terminal Equipment (SAUS)
IRATE......... Interim Remote Area Terminal Equipment [*Air Force*]
IRATS......... Infrared Algorithm Test Simulator (ACAE)
IRATW......... Irata Inc.Wrrt [*NASDAQ symbol*] (TTSB)
IRAUSN....... International Rice Acid Upland Soil Nursery (SAUO)
IR-AVP........ Immunoreactive Arginine Vaso-Pressin [*Medicine*] (EDAA)
IRAWS......... Infrared Attack Weapon System
IRayL.......... Lincolnwood Community Reading Center, Raymond, IL [*Library symbol*] [*Library of Congress*] (LCLS)
IRaySD....... Panhandle Community Unit, School District 2, Raymond IL [*Library symbol*] [*Library of Congress*] (LCLS)
IRB............. Improved Ribbon Bridge (SAUS)
IRB............. Improved Ribbon-Type Bridge [*Military*] (RDA)
IRB............. Improved Rotor Blade [*Rotorcraft*]
IRB............. Impulse Resistance Bridge
IRB............. Indiana Rating Bureau (SAUO)
IRB............. Individual Records Brief [*Military*] (AABC)
IRB............. Individual Retirement Bond (SAUS)
IRB............. Inducto-Ratio Bridge
IRB............. Inductor Ratio Bridge (SAUS)
IRB............. Industrial and Regional Benefits (FOTI)
IRB............. Industrial Readjustment Branch
IRB............. Industrial Reference Black (SAUS)
IRB............. Industrial Relations Board [*Navy*]
IRB............. Industrial Relations Bulletin [*A publication*] (AAG)
IRB............. Industrial Revenue Bond
IRB............. Industrial Revenue Bonds (SAUO)
IRB............. Industrial Review Board (SAUO)
IRB............. Infinitely Rigid Beam [*Engineering*] (OA)
IRB............. Infinitely Rigid Bear (SAUS)
IRB............. Inflatable Rescue Boat
IRB............. Information and Records Branch (SAUO)
IRB............. Informationsverbundzentrum Raum und Bau [*Germany*] (NITA)
IRB............. Informationszentrum Raum und Bau [*Information Center for Regional Planning and Building Construction*] [*Germany*] [*Information service or system*] (IID)
IRB............. Infrared Binocular [*Military*] (VNW)
IRB............. Infrared Binoculars (SAUS)
IRB............. Infrared Brazing
IRB............. Inland Revenue Business (SAUO)
IRB............. Inner Radiation Belt
IRB............. In-shore Rescue Boat (SAUS)
IRB............. Inside Reactor Building (NRCH)
IRB............. Inspection Requirements Branch (SAUO)
IRB............. Inspection Review Board (KSC)
IRB............. Institute of Radiation Breeding (SAUO)
IRB............. Institutional Review Board
IRB............. Institution Review Board (SAUO)
IRB............. Instruction Recoder Buffer (SAUS)
IRB............. Instrumentation Request Broker (SAUO)
IRB............. Insurance Rating Board [*Later, ISO*]
IRB............. Interdivisional Records Bulletin (SAUS)
IRB............. Internal Revenue Bulletin
IRB............. Internal Revenue Bureau (SAUO)
IRB............. Internal Review Board (SAUO)
IRB............. Internal Review Budget (SAUO)
IRB............. International Register on Biosafety (SAUO)
IRB............. International Resources Bank
IRB............. International Rice Bran Industries Ltd. [*Vancouver Stock Exchange symbol*]
IRB............. International Rugby Board [*Australia*]
IRB............. Interruption Request Block (SAUS)
IRB............. Interrupt Request Block (CMD)
IRB............. Iranair Tours Co. [*Iran*] [*ICAO designator*] (FAAC)
IRB............. Irish Republican Brotherhood
IRB............. Iron Rotating Band
IRB............. Irregular Route Motor Carriers Bureau, Oklahoma City OK [*STAC*]
IRb............. Red Bud Public Library, Red Bud, IL [*Library symbol*] [*Library of Congress*] (LCLS)
IRBA........... International Rhythm and Blues Association (EA)
IRBAA......... Institute of Rural Business Administration of Australasia
IRBBB......... Incomplete Right Bundle Branch Block [*Cardiology*]
IRBBN......... International Rice Bacterial Blight Nursery (SAUO)
IRBC........... Immature Red Blood Cell (STED)
IRBC........... Infected Red Blood Cell (STED)
IRBC........... Intermediate Rate Battery Charge (ACAE)
IRBDC......... Insurance Rating Bureau of the District of Columbia (SAUO)
IRBEL......... Indexed References to Biomedical Engineering Literature [*A publication*] (IID)
IRBFV......... Corona Corp. (Class B) [*NASDAQ symbol*] (COMM)
IRBIA.......... I'd Rather Be In Ambridge (BB)
IRBIC.......... Infrared Beam Induced Contrast (SAUS)
IRBIC.......... Infrared Beam Induced Current (SAUS)
IRBM........... Intelligent Repeater Bridge Module (SAUS)
IRBM........... Intermediate Range Ballistic Missile (SAUS)
IRBM........... Intermediate-Range Ballistic Missile
IRBN........... International Rice Blast Nursery (SAUO)
IRBN-L........ International Rice Blast Nursery-Lowland (SAUO)
IRBN-U........ International Rice Blast Nursery-Upland (SAUO)
IRBO........... Infrared Bomb (ACAE)
IRBO........... Infrared Homing Bomb (IEEE)
IR Bom........ Indian Rulings, Bombay Series [*A publication*] (DLA)
IRBON......... International Rice Boro Observational Nursery (SAUO)
IRBOSS....... Infrared Beacon Offset Strike System (ACAE)
IRBP........... Interphotoreceptor Retinoid-Binding Protein [*Biochemistry*]
IRBP........... Interstitial Retinol-Binding Protein [*Biochemistry*]
IRBPHN....... International Rice Brown Planthopper Nursery (SAUO)
IRBS........... Infrared Background Sensor (ACAE)
IRBS........... Intermediate Range Booster System (ACAE)
IRBS........... Interns and Residents Business Session [*Medicine*] (EDAA)
IRbSCH....... Saint Clement Hospital, Red Bud, IL [*Library symbol*] [*Library of Congress*] (LCLS)
IRBT........... Infrared Brightness Temperature
IRBT........... Intelligent Remote Batch Terminal [*Computer science*] (IAA)
IRC............. Circle [*Alaska*] [*Airport symbol*] (OAG)
IRC............. Immediate Reaction Company [*Military*] (INF)

IRC.............. Immigration Restriction Council (SAUO)
IRC.............. Immunology Researching Centre, Inc. (SAUO)
IRC.............. Improper Routing Character (SAUS)
IRC.............. Incident Response Center [*Nuclear Regulatory Commission*] (NRCH)
IRC.............. Incrementally Related Carriers [*Telecommunications*] (OTD)
IRC.............. Incremental Related Carrier (SAUS)
IRC.............. Independent Record Charts (EA)
IRC.............. Indian Railways Corporation [*Indian Railway*] (TIR)
IRC.............. Indian Relief Committee (SAUO)
IRC.............. Indicating Recording Controller [*Electronics*] (ECII)
IRC.............. Indications Review Committee [*Military*] (CINC)
IRC.............. Indirect Radionuclide Cystography [*Medicine*] (EDAA)
IRC.............. Individual Request for Classification (SAUS)
IRC.............. Indonesian Red Cross (SAUO)
IRC.............. Inductance, Resistance, Capacitance [*Electronics*] (BARN)
IRC.............. Industrial Reconstruction Corporation (SAUO)
IRC.............. Industrial Recreation Council (SAUO)
IRC.............. Industrial Relations Center [*University of Minnesota*] [*Research center*] (RCD)
IRC.............. Industrial Relations Committee (SAUO)
IRC.............. Industrial Relations Councelors (or Counselors) (SAUO)
IRC.............. Industrial Relations Council (SAUS)
IRC.............. Industrial Relations Council for the Plumbing and Pipe Fitting Industry [*Chicago, IL*] (EA)
IRC.............. Industrial Relations Counselors [*New York, NY*] (EA)
IRC.............. Industrial Reorganizanon Corp. (SAUS)
IRC.............. Industrial Reorganizanon Corporation (SAUO)
IRC.............. Industrial Reorganization Corp. (SAUS)
IRC.............. Inebriate Reception Center (SAUS)
IRC.............. INEL [*Idaho National Engineering Laboratory*] Research Center [*Idaho Falls, ID*] [*Department of Energy*] (GRD)
IRC.............. Infantry Reserve Corps (WDAA)
IRC.............. Information Recovery Capsule
IRC.............. Information Research Center (DIT)
IRC.............. Information Resource Center (SAUS)
IRC.............. Information Resource Consultants [*Information service or system*] (IID)
IRC.............. Information Resources Center [*of Mental Health Materials Center*]
IRC.............. Information Retrieval Center [*BBDO International*] [*Information service or system*] (IID)
IRC.............. Informations Ressource Controlling (SAUS)
IRC.............. Informations Ressourcen Controlling (SAUO)
IRC.............. Infrared Camera (SAUS)
IRC.............. Infrared Coagulator [*Hematology*] (DAVI)
IRC.............. Infrared Countermeasures [*Military electronics*]
IRC.............. Initial Rate of Climb (SAUS)
IRC.............. Initiative Resource Center [*Defunct*] (EA)
IRC.............. Inland Revenue Commissioner (SAUS)
IRC.............. Inland Revenue Commissioners [*British*]
IRC.............. Inspection Record Card [*Navy*] (NG)
IRC.............. Inspiration Resources (EFIS)
IRC.............. Inspiration Resources Corporation (SAUO)
IRC.............. Inspiratory Reserve Capacity [*Physiology*] (MAE)
IRC.............. Instant Response Chromatography (SAUS)
IRC.............. Institute for Research in Construction [*National Research Council of Canada*] [*Database producer*] (IID)
IRC.............. Institute of Naval Studies Research Contribution (SAUO)
IRC.............. Institutional Research Council [*Defunct*] (EA)
IRC.............. Institutional Review Committee [*Generic term*]
IRC.............. Instructional Resources Center (SAUO)
IRC.............. Instrument Remote Controller (PIPO)
IRC.............. Insurance Research Council (EA)
IRC.............. Integrated Radio Control (NVT)
IRC.............. Integrator Register Counter (PDAA)
IRC.............. Interchange Resource Center (EA)
IRC.............. Interdisciplinary Research Centre [*British*]
IRC.............. Intergovernmental Refugee Committee [*London*] [*World War II*]
IRC.............. Intergraph Registered Consultant (SAUO)
IRC.............. Interline Resources Corp. [*AMEX symbol*] (SAG)
IRC.............. Intermediate Routing Center (SAUS)
IRC.............. Internal Reflected Component (SAUS)
IRC.............. Internal Response Coupon (SAUS)
IRC.............. Internal Revenue Code
IRC.............. Internal Revenue Code of 1986 (COE)
IRC.............. Internal Review Committee (SAUO)
IRC.............. International Radio Carrier (NTCM)
IRC.............. International Railways of Central America (SAUO)
IRC.............. International Rainwear Council
IRC.............. International Rating Class [*Yachting*]
IRC.............. International Record Carrier [*Telecommunication companies providing international service*] (TSSD)
IRC.............. International Record Carrier, Inc. (SAUO)
IRC.............. International Rectifier Corp. (SAUS)
IRC.............. International Rectifier Corporation (SAUO)
IRC.............. International Recycling Congress (SAUO)
IRC.............. International Red Cross and Red Crescent Movement (EAIO)
IRC.............. International Reference Centre [*Community water supply and sanitation*] (NITA)
IRC.............. International Refugee Committee (SAUO)
IRC.............. International Relations Committee [*Library Association of Australia*]
IRC.............. International Relations Committee [*American Library Association*]
IRC.............. International Relief Committee (SAUO)
IRC.............. International Reply Coupon
IRC.............. International Rescue Commission (SAUS)
IRC.............. International Rescue Committee (EA)
IRC.............. International Research Council [*Later, ICSU*]
IRC.............. International Research Group on Wear of Engineering Materials (SAUO)
IRC.............. International Reservation Corporation (SAUO)
IRC.............. International Resistance Co. (AAG)
IRC.............. International Resistance Company (SAUO)
IRC.............. International Resistor Center
IRC.............. International Resource Committee (SAUS)
IRC.............. International Revenue Code (WDAA)
IRC.............. International Rice Commission [*See also CIR*] (EAIO)
IRC.............. International Route Charge [*Travel industry*] (TRID)
IRC.............. International Rubber Conference (SAUO)
IRC.............. Internet Relay Chat [*Computer science*]
IRC.............. Inter-Regional Capital Account [*Inter-American Development Bank*]
IRC.............. Inter Relay Chat (SAUS)
IRC.............. Interrow Cultivation (SAUO)
IRC.............. Interservice Recruiting Committee [*Military*] (DNAB)
IRC.............. Intrinsic Reaction Coordinate [*Physical chemistry*]
IRC.............. Inuvialuit Regional Corporation (SAUO)
IRC.............. Investor Responsibility Center Inc. (SAUO)
IRC.............. Ionosphere Research Committee (MCD)
IRC.............. Ion Recombination Chamber
IRC.............. Iran Asseman Airline [*ICAO designator*] (FAAC)
IRC.............. Iraqi Communist Party [*Also, ICP*] [*Political party*] (MENA)
IRC.............. IRC International Water and Sanitation Centre [*International Reference Ce ntre for Community Water Supply and Sanitation*] [*Acronym is based on former name,*] (EAIO)
IRC.............. Iron Canyon [*California*] [*Seismograph station code, US Geological Survey*] (SEIS)
IRC.............. Ironclad
IRC.............. Iron Ring Compressor (SAUS)
IRC.............. Irregular Route Carrier
IRC.............. Issue Restriction Code (MCD)
IRC.............. Italian Red Cross (SAUO)
IRC.............. Item Responsibility Code
IRC.............. SCI International Resource Center (or Centre) (SAUO)
IRC.EC......... Interline Resources [*Exchange symbol*] (TTSB)
IRCA............ [*The*] Immigration Reform and Control Act [*1986*] (ECON)
IRCA............ Immigration Reform and Control Act of 1986
IRCA............ Indiana Resource Center for Autism
IRCA............ Indian Railway Conference Association [*Indian Railway*] (TIR)
IRCA............ International Radio Club of America (EA)
IRCA............ International Ragdoll Cat Association (EA)
IRCA............ International Railway Congress Association [*Belgium*]
IRCA............ International Register of Certificated Auditors (SAUO)
IRCA............ International Remodeling Contractors Association (EA)
IRCA............ Intravascular Red Cell Aggregation [*Medicine*] (DMAA)
IR Cal.......... Indian Rulings, Calcutta Series [*A publication*] (DLA)
IRCAM......... Institute for Research and Coordination into Acoustics and Musiç (SAUS)
IRCAN......... Iran Canada Oil Company (SAUO)
IRC&LINK.... Interdisciplinary Research Centres and Link Initiative (SAUS)
IRC & M....... Increase and Replacement of Construction and Machinery [*Naval budget appropriation title*]
IRCAR.......... International Reference Center for Abortion Research (IID)
IRCAR.......... International Reference Centre for Abortion Research (SAUO)
IRCAS.......... Information Requirements Control Automated System [*Defense Supply Service/Pentagon*] (AABC)
IRCAT.......... Infrared Clear Air Turbulence (SAUS)
IRCAT.......... Infrared Radiometer Clear Air Turbulence [*Instrument*]
IRCAT Instrument... Infrared Radiometer Clear Air Turbulence Instrument (SAUS)
IRCB............ Inter-Residence and Campus Businesses (SAUS)
IRCC............ Instruction and Research Computer Center [*Ohio State University*] [*Research center*] (RCD)
IRCC............ Instrument Repair and Calibration Center (SAUS)
IRCC............ Instrument Repair and Calibration Centre (SAUO)
IRCC............ International Radio Consultative Committee
IRCC............ International Record Collectors' Club [*Record label*]
IRCC............ International Red Cross Committee [*World War II*]
IRCCCOB...... Inter Research Council Coordinating Committee on Biotechnology (NITA)
IRCCD.......... Infrared Charge-Coupled Device
IRCCD.......... Infrared-sensitive Charge Coupled Device (SAUS)
IRCCM.......... Infrared Counter-Counter Measures (SAUO)
IRCCM.......... Infrared Counter-Countermeasures [*Military electronics*]
IRCCM.......... Infra-Red Counter-Countermeasures System (SAUS)
IRCCOPR..... Inter-Research Council Committee on Pollution Research [*British*]
IRCCS.......... Intrusion Resistant Communications Cable System (DNAB)
IRCD............ Information Retrieval Center on the Disadvantaged [*ERIC*]
IRCD............ Infrared Circular Dichroism (SAUS)
IRCD............ Integrated Radar Communications Development (SAUS)
IRCD............ International Research Centers Directory [*A publication*]
IRCD Bulletin... Information Retrieval Center on the Disadvantaged Bulletin (journ.) (SAUS)
IRCDP.......... International Research Career Development Program [*Public Health Service*]
IRCert.......... Industrial Relations Certificate (ODBW)
IRCFE........... Infrared Communication Flight Experiment (SAUS)
IRCFPA........ International Reference Center for Fertility-Promoting Agents [*Medicine*] (EDAA)
IRCG............ Incident Report Code Guide (SAUS)
Ir Ch............ Irish Chancery Reports [*A publication*] (DLA)
IR CH........... Iron Chimney (SAUS)
I-R Charts.... Infrared Correlation Charts (SAUS)
IRCHMB....... International Research Centre of/on Hydraulic Machinery (SAUO)

Ir Ch Rep..... Irish Chancery Reports [*A publication*] (DLA)
IR CHSA...... Iron Chimney with Spark Arrestor (SAUS)
IRCICA......... Research Centre for Islamic History, Art, and Culture [*of the Organization of the Islamic Conference*] (EAIO)
IRCIHE......... International Referral Center for Information Handling Equipment [*Former Yugoslavia*] [*UNESCO*] (IID)
Ir Cir........... Irish Circuit Reports [*1841-43*] [*A publication*] (DLA)
Ir Cir Cas..... Crawford and Dix's Irish Circuit Court Cases [*A publication*] (DLA)
Ir Circ Cas... Irish Circuit Cases [*A publication*] (DLA)
Ir Circ Rep... Irish Circuit Reports [*1841-43*] [*A publication*] (DLA)
Ir Cir Rep.... Reports of Irish Circuit Cases [*A publication*] (DLA)
IRCISAT....... International Crops Research Institute for Semi-Arid Tropics (SAUO)
IRCL............ International Research Center on Lindane (SAUS)
IRCL............ International Research Centre on Lindane [*See also CIEL*] [*Brussels, Belgium*] (EAIO)
Ir CL........... Irish Common Law Reports [*A publication*] (DLA)
IRCL............ Irish Reports, Common Law Series [*A publication*] (DLA)
IRCM........... Infrared Counter Measures (SAUO)
IRCM........... Infrared Countermeasures [*Military electronics*] (NVT)
IRCM........... Integrated Relay Controller Module [*Ford Motor Co.*] [*Automotive engineering*]
IRCM........... Intermediate Range Cruise Missile [*Military*] (CAAL)
IRCMHFLE... Information Resources Center for Mental Health and Family Life Education [*Medicine*] (EDAA)
IRCMIS........ Initial Requirements Computation and Management Information System (SAUO)
IRCMS......... International Radio-Controlled Models Society (SAUO)
IRCN........... Interagency Report Control Number
IRCND.......... International Research Council of Neuromuscular Disorders (EA)
IRCNSW....... Industrial Relations Commission of New South Wales [*Australia*]
IRCO........... Industrial Rustproof Co. (SAUS)
IRCO........... Industrial Rustproof Company (SAUO)
IRCO........... International Rubber Conference Organization (EAIO)
Irco............. Irish Continental Tourist Development Association Ltd. (SAUO)
IRCOB.......... International Research Council on the Biokinetics of Impacts (SAUO)
IRCOBI......... International Research Committee on the Biokinetics of Impact (SAUO)
IRCOBI......... International Research Committee on the Biokinetics of Impacts [*Later, International Research Council on the Biokinetics of Impacts*] (EAIO)
IRCOBI......... International Research Council on the Biokenetics of Impacts (SAUO)
IRCOL.......... Institute for Information Retrieval and Computational Linguistics [*Bar Ilam University*] [*Israel*] (NITA)
IRCOM......... Infra-Red Communications (SAUS)
Ir Com Law Rep... Irish Common Law Reports [*A publication*] (DLA)
Ir Com L Rep... Irish Common Law Reports [*A publication*] (DLA)
Ir Comput.... Irish Computer (journ.) (SAUS)
IR Comrs...... Inland Revenue Commissioners [*England*] (DLA)
IRCON......... Indian Railways Construction Company [*Indian Railway*] (TIR)
IRCON......... International Ltd [*Indian Railway*] (TIR)
IRCOPPS...... Interprofessional Research Commission on Pupil Personnel Services [*Defunct*]
IR-COSY...... Inversion Recovery-Correlation Spectroscopy (SAUS)
IRCOT.......... Indian Railways Central Organization for Telecom [*Indian Railway*] (TIR)
IRCP........... Intermediate Range Construction Program [*Military*]
IRCPAL........ International Research Council on Pure and Applied Linguistics (EA)
IRCPG.......... Inter-Range and Global Planning Group (SAUO)
IRCPPFI....... Industrial Relations Council for the Plumbing and Pipe Fitting Industry (SAUO)
IRCPUBS...... Publications of the Institute for Research in Construction [*National Research Council of Canada*] [*Information service or system*] (IID)
IRCQ........... Industrial Relations Commission of Queensland [*Australia*]
IRCR........... Integratoregister Control Register (SAUS)
IRCR........... Integrator Register Control Register (PDAA)
IRCs............ Inebriate Reception Centers (SAUS)
IRCS........... Inertial Reference and Control System [*Aerospace*] (AAG)
IRCS........... Infrared Communications System
IRCS........... Inspector of the Royal Corps of Signals (SAUO)
IRCS........... Institute for Research in Cognitive Science (SAUO)
IRCS........... Integrated Radar and Communications Subsystem (ACAE)
IRCS........... Integrated Radiocommunication Systems (SAUO)
IRCS........... Interceptor Reaction Control System
IRCS........... Intercomplex Radio Communications System (IAA)
IRCS........... Interdisciplinary Research Center on Suicide [*Italy*] (EAIO)
IRCS........... International Radio Call Sign
IRCS........... International Research Communications System [*Electronic journal publisher*] [*British*]
IRCS........... Intersite Radio Communications System (MCD)
IRCS........... Intersite Radio Communication System (SAUS)
IRCS........... Intrusion-Resistant Communications System (SAUS)
IRCS........... Inuit Regional Conservation Strategy (SAUO)
IRCS........... Italian Red Cross Society
IRCSA......... International Reference Collection of Soybean Arthropods [*INTSOY*]
IRCSI.......... International Rabbinic Committee for the Safety of Israel (EA)
IRCS-JMS.... International Research Communications System Journal of Medical Science [*Medicine*] (EDAA)
IRCS-MS...... International Research Communications System Medical Science [*UK*] [*Series of journals*] [*Medicine*] (EDAA)
IRCT........... International Research on Communist Techniques
IRCTC.......... Indian Railways Catering and Tourism Corp. [*Indian Railway*] (TIR)
IRCTN.......... International Rice Cold Tolerance Nursery (SAUO)
IRCTR.......... International Research Centre for Telecommunication-transmission and Radar (SAUO)
IRCU........... Intensive Respiratory Care Unit [*Medicine*] (EDAA)
IRCV........... Industrial Relations Commission of Victoria [*Australia*]
IRCWD......... International Reference Center for Water Disposal (SAUS)
IRCWD......... International Reference Centre for Water Disposal (SAUO)
IRCX........... Morrison Plan [*Private rail car owner code*]
IRCZ........... Itel Rail [*Federal Railroad Administration identification code*]
IRD............ Iceberg-Rafted Detritus (SAUS)
IRD............ Ice Rafted Debris (SAUS)
IRD............ Ice-Rafted Debris [*Oceanography*]
IRD............ Ice-Rafted Detritus (SAUS)
IRD............ Immune Renal Disease [*Medicine*]
IRD............ Incidental Radiation Device (SAUS)
IRD............ Income in Respect of a Decedent [*Banking*]
IRD............ Independent Research and Development (TIMI)
IRD............ Industrial Relations Department (SAUO)
IRD............ Industrial Research and Development (SAUS)
IRD............ Infantile Refsum's Syndrome [*Medicine*] (MELL)
IRD............ Information Network on Integrated Rural Development (SAUO)
IRD............ Information Records Division (SAUS)
IRD............ Information Requirements Description [*or Document*] (KSC)
IRD............ Information Requirements Document (SAUO)
IRD............ Information Resource Dictionary (SAUO)
IRD............ Information Resources Directory (SAUO)
IRD............ Information Resources Division (SAUO)
IRD............ Infrared Detector
IRD............ Infrared Display
IRD............ Initiating Reference Document (MCD)
IRD............ Inland Rail Depot (DCTA)
IRD............ Inspection of Research and Development (SAUS)
IRD............ Installation Requirement Documents (SAUS)
IRD............ Institute of Reading Development (SAUO)
IRD............ Institute on Religion and Democracy (EA)
I/RD........... Institutes and Research Divisions [*National Institutes of Health*]
IRD............ Instrumentation Requirements Document (SAUS)
IRD............ Instrument Requirement Document (SAUS)
IRD............ Instruments and Regulators Division (SAUO)
IRD............ Integrated Radio Decoder (SAUS)
IRD............ Integrated Receiver Decoder [*Telecommunications*]
IRD............ Integrated Receiver/Descrambler (SAUS)
IRD............ Integrated Record Data System (SAUO)
IRD............ Integrated Rural Development (SAUO)
IRD............ Integration Requirements Document (SAUS)
IRD............ Interactive Report Definition (SAUO)
IRD............ Interface Requirements Document
IRD............ Intermediate Reduction Drive [*Mechanical transmissions*]
IRD............ Internal Assearch and Development (SAUS)
IRD............ Internal Revenue Department
IRD............ International Radiation Detectors [*Marine science*] (OSRA)
IRD............ International Research and Development
IRD............ International Research and Development Co. (SAUO)
IRD............ International Research & Development Co. Ltd. [*Northern Engineering Industries*] [*British*] (IRUK)
IRD............ International Research and Development Corp. (SAUO)
IRD............ International Research Development (SAUO)
IRD............ International Resource Development, Inc. [*Norwalk, CT*] [*Telecommunications*] [*Information service or system*] (IID)
IRD............ Internet Resource Directory (SAUO)
IRD............ Interoperability Requirements Documents (SAUO)
IRD............ Investment Recovery Department (SAUS)
IRD............ Investment Research and Development (SAUS)
IRD............ Iron Lady Resources [*Vancouver Stock Exchange symbol*]
IRD............ Ishurdi [*Bangladesh*] [*Airport symbol*] (OAG)
IRD............ Isotopes and Radiation Division [*American Nuclear Society*]
IRD............ Itinerant Recruiting Detail
IRDA........... Improved Respiratory Device for Air Crewmen (SAUO)
IRDA........... Independent Reinol Distributors Association [*British*] (DBA)
IRDA........... Industrial Research and Development Assistance (SAUS)
IRDA........... Industrial Research & Development Authority (WDAA)
IrDA............ Infrared Data Association (PCM)
IRDA........... Infrared Detection & Acquisition (SAUS)
IRDA........... Infrared Detection and Acquisition System (ACAE)
IRDA........... Infrared Detection Array
IRDA........... Infrared Developers Association (PCM)
IRDA........... Infrared Interface Committee (SAUO)
IRDA........... Innovative Research and Development Announcement (ACAE)
IRDA........... Integrated Reliability Design Assessment (ACAE)
IRDA........... Interactive Route Development and Analysis (CAAL)
IRDA........... Inter-Church Relief and Development Agency (SAUO)
IrDA............ PSA Infrared
IRDAC......... Industrial Research and Development Advisory Committee [*European Union*]
IRD & S....... International Research, Development, and Standardization [*Division*] [*Army*] (RDA)
IRDAR......... Infra-Red Detection and Ranging (SAUS)
IRDATA........ Industrial Robot Data (SAUS)
IRDATS........ Infrared Data Seeker (ACAE)
IRDB........... Image Reference Data Base (SAUS)
IRDB........... Information Retrieval Databank (IEEE)
IRDB........... Information Retrieval Data Base (SAUS)
IRDB........... Integrated Regional Data Base (SAUO)
IRDBMS....... Installation Restoration Data Base Management System (SAUO)
IRDC........... Improved RADAR Data Correlator (DWSG)
IRDC........... Industrial Research and Development Center [*University of Virginia*] (PDAA)
IRDC........... Industry Research and Development Committee (SAUO)

IRDC .... Intelligence Research and Development Council (MCD)
IRDC .... International Development Research Centre (GNE)
IRDC .... International Research Development Center (or Centre) (SAUS)
IRDC .... International Road Documentation Center
IRDC .... International Rubber Development Committee
IRDD .... Infrared Distraction Decoy
IRDDS .... Infrared Decoy Discrimination System (ACAE)
IRDF .... Indentation Residual Deflection Force (SAUS)
IRDF .... Infrared Direction Finding (SAUS)
IRDF .... Interactive Report Definition Facility (MCD)
IRDG .... Inter-Range Documentation Group [*White Sands Missile Range*]
IRDHC .... Institute for Research and Development in Health Care [*Medicine*] (EDAA)
IRDHS .... Imagery Related Data Handling System (MCD)
IRDI .... Indian Resources Development and Internship (SAUO)
IRDIA .... Industrial Research and Development Incentives Act (SAUO)
IRDIA .... Industrial Research and Development Investment Assistance [*Department of Industry*] [*Canada*] (PDAA)
IRDISP .... International Research Institute for Disarmament, Development and Peace (SAUO)
IR Divergence... Infrared Divergence (SAUS)
IRDL .... Information Retrieval and Display Language [*Computer science*] (AABC)
IRDLO .... Infantry Research and Development Liaison Office [*Army*] (RDA)
IRDM .... Illuminated Runway Distance Marker (PDAA)
IRDM .... Illuminated Runway Marker (SAUS)
IRDM .... International Rendezvous and Docking Mission [*Aerospace*]
IRDMS .... Installation Restoration Data Management System (SAUO)
IRDN .... Illinois Resource and Dissemination Network [*Illinois State Board of Education*] [*No longer in operation*] [*Information service or system*] (IID)
IRDN .... Important Risk Data Notice [*Insurance*]
IRDO .... Infrared Drying Oven
IRDO .... Intermediate Retention of Differential Overlap [*Physics*]
IRDOE .... Institute for Research and Development in Occupational Education [*City University of New York*] [*Research center*] (RCD)
irdome .... Infrared Dome (MED)
IRDome .... Infrared Dome (SAUS)
IRDP .... Icelandic Research Drilling Project
IRDP .... Industrial and Regional Development Program (SAUS)
IRDP .... Industrial Regional Development Program [*Canada*]
IRDP .... Industrial Research Development Program (SAUS)
IRDP .... Information Retrieval Data Bank (SAUS)
IRDP .... Integrated Regional Development Planning (GNE)
IRDS .... Hanford Site Information Resource Dictionary System (SAUS)
IRDS .... Idiopathic Respiratory Distress Syndrome [*Pediatrics*]
IRDS .... Independent Rear-Drive Suspension [*Automotive engineering*]
IRDS .... Infant Respiratory Distress Syndrome [*Medicine*]
IRDS .... Information Resource Dictionary Standard (SAUO)
IRDS .... Information Resource Dictionary System (SAUS)
IRDS .... Information Resources Dictionary System (SSD)
IRDS .... Infra-Read Detection System (SAUS)
IRDS .... Infrared Detecting Set [*or System*] (MCD)
IRDS .... Integrated Reliability Data System (AAG)
IRDS .... International Road Documentation Scheme (NITA)
IRDSN .... International Rice Drought Screening Nursery (SAUO)
IRDSS .... Infrared Defeating Smoke System
IRDTN .... International Rice Drought Tolerance Nursery (SAUO)
IRDU .... Infrared Detection Unit
IRDV .... International Research & Development Corp. [*NASDAQ symbol*] (COMM)
IRDWON .... International Rice Deep Water Observational Nursery (SAUO)
IRDWYN .... International Rice Deep Water Yield Nursery (SAUO)
IRE .... Bank of Ireland Governor & Co ADS [*NYSE symbol*] (SG)
IRE .... Governor & Co. of the Bank of Ireland [*NYSE symbol*] (SAG)
IRE .... IFF Reply Evaluator
IRE .... Immediate Ready Element [*Military*] (AABC)
IRE .... Infrared Electronics (ACAE)
IRE .... Infrared Emission
IRE .... Infrared Engineering (SAUS)
IRE .... Institute for Responsive Education (EA)
IRE .... Institute of Radio Engineers [*Later, IEEE*]
IRE .... Institute of Refractories Engineers [*British*] (DBA)
IRE .... Institute of Refrigerating Engineers (SAUO)
IRE .... Instruction Register for Execution (SAUS)
IRE .... Instrument Rating Examiner [*Aviation*] (DA)
IRE .... Integrated Resources, Inc. (SAUO)
IRE .... Intelligence Resources [*Program*] [*Department of State*]
IRE .... Interferon Regulatory Element [*Biochemistry*]
IRE .... Internal Reflection Element [*Spectroscopy*]
IRE .... Internal Rotation in Extension [*Orthopedics*] (DAVI)
IRE .... International Association of Railway Employees
IRE .... International Relations Exercise (DNAB)
IRE .... International Research and Evaluation [*Research Center*] [*Also, an information service or system*] (IID)
IRE .... International Retail Systems, Inc. [*Toronto Stock Exchange symbol*] [*Vancouver Stock Exchange symbol*]
IRE .... International Royal Enterprises (EA)
IRE .... Investigative Reporters and Editors (EA)
Ire .... Ireland (VRA)
IRE .... Ireland
IRE .... Iron Replacement Element [*Biosynthesis*]
IRE .... Iron-Respondive Element (SAUS)
IRE .... Iron-Responsive Element [*Genetics*]
IRE .... Iron-Ring Experiment (SAUS)
i-re- .... Reunion [*MARC geographic area code*] [*Library of Congress*] (LCCP)
IREA .... Institute of Chemical Reagents (SAUO)
IREA .... Institute of Radio Engineers, Australia (SAUO)
IREA .... Institute of Radio Engineers-Australia (SAUS)
IREA .... Institution of Radio Engineers, Australia (SAUS)
IREA .... Intermountain Rural Electrical Association
IREA .... Japanese Railway Engineering Association (SAUO)
IREB .... Indian Railways Executive Board [*Indian Railway*] (TIR)
IREB .... Intense Relativistic Electron Beams [*Physics*]
IRE-BP .... Iron-Responsive Element - Binding Protein
IREC .... Increase and Replacement of Emergency Construction [*Ships*] [*Naval budget appropriation title*]
IREC .... International Real Estate Corp. (SAUS)
IREC .... International Real Estate Corporation (SAUO)
IREC .... International Registry of Early Corvettes (EA)
IREC .... International Rotary Engine Club [*Later, RX-7 Club of America*] (EA)
IREC .... Irrigation Research and Extension Advisory Committee (SAUO)
IREC .... Irrigation Research and Extension Commission (SAUS)
IRECA .... International Rescue and Emergency Care Association (EA)
Ir Eccl .... Irish Ecclesiastical Reports, by Milward [*1819-43*] [*A publication*] (DLA)
IRECUS .... Sherbrooke University Institut de Recherche et d'Enseignement pour les Cooperatives [*Canada*] [*Research center*] (RCD)
IRED .... Infrared (SAUS)
IRED .... Infrared Emitting Diode (SAUS)
IRED .... Infrared-Emitting Diode (IEEE)
IRED .... Innovations et Reseaux pour le Developpement [*Development Innovations and Networks*] [*Geneva, Switzerland*] (EAIO)
IRED .... Internal Review and Evaluation Division (SAUO)
IRED .... International Real Estate Directory [*Real estate computer site*]
Ired .... Iredell's North Carolina Equity Reports [*36-43 North Carolina*] [*A publication*] (DLA)
IREDA .... International Radio and Electrical Distributors Association (MHDB)
IREDA .... International Radio Electrical Distributors Association (SAUS)
Ired Dig .... Iredell's North Carolina Digest [*A publication*] (DLA)
Ired Eq .... Iredell's North Carolina Equity Reports [*36-43 North Carolina*] [*A publication*] (DLA)
Ired Eq (NC)... Iredell's North Carolina Equity Reports [*36-43 North Carolina*] [*A publication*] (DLA)
Ired L .... Iredell's North Carolina Equity Reports [*36-43 North Carolina*] [*A publication*] (DLA)
Ired L (NC)... Iredell's North Carolina Law Reports [*A publication*] (DLA)
IreDNCA .... National College of Art and Design, Dublin, Ireland [*Library symbol*] [*Library of Congress*] (LCLS)
IreDNL .... National Library of Ireland, Dublin, Ireland [*Library symbol*] [*Library of Congress*] (LCLS)
IreDR .... Royal Dublin Society, Ballsbridge, Dublin, Ireland [*Library symbol*] [*Library of Congress*] (LCLS)
IreDT .... Trinity College, University of Dublin, Dublin, Ireland [*Library symbol*] [*Library of Congress*] (LCLS)
IREE .... Institut de Recherches et d'Etudes Europeennes [*Institute of European Research and Studies*] (EAIO)
IREE .... Institute of Radio and Electric Engineers (SAUS)
IREE .... Institution of Radio and Electronics Engineers (SAUS)
IREEA .... Institute of Radio Engineering, Electronics and Automation (SAUS)
IREEA .... Institution of Radio and Electronic Engineers of Australia (SAUS)
IREEA .... Institution of Radio and Electronic Engineers of Australia, Sidney (SAUO)
IREECON .... Institute of Radio and Electronics Engineers Conference (ACAE)
IREECON .... Institution of Radio and Electronics Engineers Convention (SAUS)
IREF .... International Real Estate Federation
IREF .... Ischemia Research and Education Foundation
IREFAC .... International Real Estate Federation Australian Chapter
IREG .... Industriradets Industriregister [*Federation of Danish Industries' Register of Industries*] (EY)
IREG .... Information Res Engineering [*NASDAQ symbol*] (TTSB)
IREG .... Information Resource Engineering, Inc. [*NASDAQ symbol*] (SAG)
IREG .... Infrared Environment Generator (ACAE)
IREG .... ITU-T Recommendation Experiment Group (SAUO)
IREH .... Institute for Rural Environmental Health [*Colorado State University*] [*Research center*] (RCD)
IREHR .... Institute for Research and Education on Human Rights [*Defunct*] (EA)
IREI .... International Real Estate Institute (EA)
IRE-ITTD .... International Research and Evaluation - Information and Technology Transfer Database [*International Research and Evaluation*] [*Information service or system*] (CRD)
Ireld Yrbk .... Ireland Administration. Yearbook and Diary (journ.) (SAUS)
IREM .... Incorporation of Readiness into Effectivenss Modeling (MCD)
IREM .... Inspector of Royal Engineers (SAUO)
IREM .... Inspector of Royal Engineers Machinery (SAUS)
IREM .... Institut de Recherche en Exploration Minerale [*Mineral Exploration Research Institute*] [*Canada*] [*Research center*] (RCD)
IREM .... Institute of Real Estate Management [*Chicago, IL*] (EA)
IREM .... Institute of Real Estate Managers (SAUO)
IREM .... Integrated Regional Environmental Management (SAUS)
IREM .... Integrated Regional Environmental Management Project (EA)
IREMAM .... Institut de Recherches et d'Etudes sur le Monde Arabe et Musulman [*Institute for Research and Studies on the Arab and Muslim World*] [*France*] [*Information service or system*] (IID)
I-REMBASS... Improved REMBASS (SAUS)
IREM-BASS... Improved Remotely Monitored Battlefield Sensor System
IR/EME .... Infrared/Eletromagnetic Environment (ACAE)
IREM Project... Integrated Regional Environmental Management Project (SAUS)

IRENATH...... Interational Institute for Research and Development on Natural and Holistic Therapies (SAUO)
IRENE.......... Indicating Random Electronic Numbering Equipment (SAUO)
IRENE.......... Industrial Restructuring and Education Network Europe
IRENE.......... Integrated Modelling of Renewable Natural Resources (SAUO)
IRENE.......... International Restructuring Education Network Europe (SAUO)
IR/EO.......... Infra-Red/Electro-Optical (SAUS)
IREP............ Industrial Resource Enhancement Program (SAUS)
IREP............ Integrated Reliability Evaluation Program [*Nuclear energy*] (NRCH)
IREP............ Interdisciplinary Research Equipment Program
IREP............ Interim Reliability Evaluation Program [*Nuclear energy*]
IREP............ Internal Representation (MHDB)
IREP............ International Recruitment Programme (SAUS)
IREPS.......... Integrated Refraction Effects Prediction System (SAUS)
IREPS.......... Integrated Refractive Effect Prediction System (SAUO)
IREPS.......... Integrated Refractive Effects Prediction System [*Military*] (CAAL)
IREQ............ Institut de Recherche d'Hydro-Quebec [*Canada*]
IREQ............ Institute of Research Quebec (SAUS)
IR Eq........... Irish Reports, Equity Series [*A publication*] (DLA)
Ir Eq Rep..... Irish Equity Reports [*A publication*] (DLA)
IRER............ Infrared Extra Rapid (ADA)
IRES............ Imagery Reporting and Exploitation Station (SAUO)
IRES............ Infrared Emission Spectroscopy (SAUS)
IRES............ Institute for Resource and Environmental Studies [*Dalhousie University*] [*Canada*] [*Research center*] (RCD)
IRES............ Intercultural and Etnic Studies (SAUO)
IRES............ Internal Ribosomal Entry Site [*Genetics*]
IRES............ Internal Ribosome Entry Sequence [*To 21st site sequence*]
IRES............ IOC [*Intergovernmental Oceanographic Commission*] Group of Experts on Oceanographic Research as It Relates to IGOSS [*Marine science*] (MSC)
IRESOC........ Institute for International Sociological Research (SAUO)
IRET............ Institute for Rational-Emotive Therapy (EA)
IRET............ Institute for Research on the Economics of Taxation [*Research center*] (RCD)
IRET............ Intercontinental Real Estate Trust (SAUO)
IRET............ Interrupt Return [*PC instruction*] (PCM)
IRETA.......... Institute for Research, Extension and Training in Agriculture (SAUO)
IRETIJ.......... Institut de Recherches et d'Etudes pour le Traitement de l'Information Juridique [*Institute of Research and Study for the Treatment of Legal Information*] [*University of Montpellier*] [*Information service or system*] (IID)
IRETP.......... Innovative Rural Education and Training Program
IRE Trans Inform Theory... Institute of Radio Engineers. Transactions on Information Theory (journ.) (SAUS)
IRETS.......... Infantry Remoted Target System [*Military*] (ACAE)
IRETS.......... Infantry Remote Targeting System [*Army*] (RDA)
IRETS.......... Infantry Remote Target System (SAUS)
IREW............ Infraed Electronic Warefare (SAUS)
IREW............ Infrared Electronic Warfare
IREWS.......... Infrared Early Warning System
IREWS.......... Infra-Red Electronic Warfare System (SAUS)
IREX............ Ideas, Resources, Exchange [*Computer*] [*British*]
IrEx............. Industrial Training Exhibition and Symposium (SAUS)
IREX............ International Research and Exchanges Board (EA)
IRF.............. Idiopathic Retroperitoneal Fibrosis [*Medicine*] (DMAA)
IRF.............. Immediate Reaction Force [*Military*] (AABC)
IRF.............. Immediate Ready Force (SAUO)
IRF.............. Immunology Research Foundation (SAUO)
IRF.............. Impact Release Fraction (SAUS)
IRF.............. Impedance Reduction Factor (SAUS)
IRF.............. Impedance-Reduction Factor (IAA)
IRF.............. Induced Radiation Flux
IRF.............. Inducing Resistance Factor [*Plant pathology*]
IRF.............. Industrial Relations Forum (SAUO)
IRF.............. Industrial Research Fellowship (SAUS)
IRF.............. Information Retrieval Facility (TIMI)
IRF.............. Inheritance (or Inherited) Rights Filter (SAUS)
IRF.............. Inherited Rights Filter [*Computer science*]
IRF.............. Input Register Full
IRF.............. Instantaneous Radiative Flux (ARMP)
IRF.............. Instantaneous Radiative Transfer (CARB)
IRF.............. Instrument Reliability Factor (PDAA)
IRF.............. Instrument Response Function
IRF.............. Interferon Regulatory Factor [*Biochemistry*]
IRF.............. Interger Register File (SAUS)
IRF.............. Interim Repair Facility (ACAE)
IRF.............. Intermediate Routing Function (SAUS)
IRF.............. Intermittent Reinforcement [*Psychology*]
IRF.............. Internal Raster File (SAUS)
IRF.............. Internal Raster Format (SAUS)
IRF.............. Internal Rotation in Flexion [*Orthopedics*] (DAVI)
IRF.............. International Racquetball Federation (EAIO)
IRF.............. International Rectifier Corp. [*NYSE symbol*] (SPSG)
IRF.............. International Rectifier Corporation (SAUO)
IRF.............. International Reform Federation (EA)
IRF.............. International Religious Fellowship (EA)
IRF.............. International Religious Foundation (SAUO)
IRF.............. International Research Fellowship Program [*Department of Health and Human Services*] (GFGA)
IRF.............. International Road Federation (EA)
IRF.............. International Rowing Federation
IRF.............. Interrogation Recurrence Frequency (SAUS)
IRF.............. Interrogation Repetition Frequency [*RADAR beacon*]
IRF.............. Intl Rectifier [*NYSE symbol*] (TTSB)
IRF.............. Intrinsic Rectifying Factor [*Biochemistry*]
IRF.............. Islamic Research Foundation (EA)
IRF.............. Island Resources Foundation (EA)
IRF.............. Islands Research Foundation [*Inactive*] (EA)
IRFA............ Initial Regulatory Flexibility Analysis (AAGC)
IRFA............ Institut de Recherches sur les Fruits et Agrumes [*Institute of Research on Fruits and Citrus Fruits*] [*International Cooperation Center of Agricultural Research for Development*] [*Database producer*]
IRFAA.......... International Rescue and First Aid Association [*Later, IRECA*] (EA)
IRFAON........ International Rice Finegrain Aromatic Observational Nursery (SAUO)
IRFAP.......... International Religious Fine Art Program (EA)
IRFB............ International Radio Frequencies (or Frequency) Board (SAUS)
IRFC............ Indian Railways Finance Corp. [*Indian Railway*] (TIR)
IRFC............ Ingersoll-Rand Finance Corp. (SAUS)
IRFC............ Ingersoll-Rand Finance Corporation (SAUO)
IRFC............ Intermediate-Range Function Test (IAA)
IRFCS.......... Infrared Fire Control System (ACAE)
IR Fed Ct..... Indian Rulings, Federal Court [*A publication*] (DLA)
IRFF............ International Relief Friendship Foundation (EA)
IRFIS.......... Inertial Referenced Flight Inspection System [*Aviation*] (PDAA)
IRFIS.......... Inertial Vehicle Referenced Flight Inspection System (SAUS)
IRFIS.......... International Research Forum in Information Science (SAUO)
Ir Fish Invest Ser A Freshwater... Irish Fisheries Investigations. Series A. Freshwater (journ.) (SAUS)
Ir Fish Invest Ser B Mar... Irish Fisheries Investigations. Series B. Marine (journ.) (SAUS)
IRFITS......... Infrared Fault Isolation Test System
IRFL............ Integral Red Fluorescence (DMAA)
IRFM............ Integral Reactor Flow Model [*Nuclear energy*] (NRCH)
IRFMS.......... Interservice Radio Frequency Management School (DOMA)
IRFNA.......... Inhibited Red Fuming Nitric Acid [*Rocket fuel*]
IRFN/UDMH... Inhibited Red Fuming Nitric Acid and Unsymmetrical Dimethylhydrazine [*Rocket fuel*]
IRFO............ International Road Freight Office (WDAA)
IRFOA4........ Irish Forestry (journ.) (SAUS)
IRFP............ International Relations and Foreign Policy [*Army*] [*British*]
IRFPA.......... Infrared Focal Plane Array [*DoD*]
IRFPA.......... Infra-Red Focal Plane Assembly (SAUS)
IRFRH.......... Institut de Recherche et de Formation aux Relations Humaines [*Institute for Research and Training in Human Relations*] [*Research center*] [*France*] (IRC)
IRFT............ Interim Refresher Training [*Navy*] (NVT)
IRFT............ Intermediate Range Function Test (SAUS)
IRFT............ Invesion-Recovery Fourier Transform (SAUS)
IRFU............ Irish Rugby Football Union (EAIO)
IRG.............. Immediate Replenishment Group (SAUO)
IRG.............. Immunoreactive Gastrin [*Medicine*] (DMAA)
IRG.............. Immunoreactive Glucagon [*Immunochemistry*]
IRG.............. Implicit Regeneration (SAUS)
IRG.............. Independant Regulators Group (SAUO)
IRG.............. Indian Resources Group (WDAA)
IRG.............. Industrial Reprocessing Group (SAA)
IRG.............. Inertial Rate Gyro (KSC)
IRG.............. Information Research Group (SAUO)
IRG.............. Information Resource Group [*Information service or system*] (IID)
IRG.............. Information Retrieval Group (SAUO)
IRG.............. Infrared Generator
IRG.............. Initial Review Group [*National Institutes of Health*]
IRG.............. Inner Roll Gimbal (MCD)
IRG.............. Institut de Reescompte et de Garantie [*Development bank*] [*Belgium*] (EY)
IRG.............. Integrated Rate Gyro (SAUS)
IRG.............. Interagency Regulatory Group
IRG.............. Interagency Review Group [*Nuclear Regulatory Commission*] (NRCH)
IRG.............. Interagency Review Group on Nuclear Waste Management (SAUS)
IRG.............. Intercommittee Recruitment Group (SAUO)
IRG.............. Interdepartmental Regional Group [*Army*] (AABC)
IRG.............. Interest Rate Guarantee (NUMA)
IRG.............. Internationale des Resistants a la Guerre [*War Resisters International - WRI*] [*British*] (EA)
IRG.............. International Register (IAA)
IRG.............. International Research Group (SAUO)
IRG.............. International Research Group on Wear of Engineering Materials (PDAA)
IRG.............. International Research Group on Wood Preservation [*Stockholm, Sweden*] (EAIO)
IRG.............. Interrange Instrumentation Group (SAUO)
IRG.............. Inter-Record Gap [*Computer science*] [*Telecommunications*] (MCD)
IRG.............. Interrelationship Graph (PDAA)
IRG.............. Iron Range [*Queensland*] [*Airport symbol*] (AD)
IRG.............. Issues in Bank Regulation (journ.) (SAUS)
IRG.............. Lockhart Rivers [*Australia*] [*Airport symbol*] (OAG)
IRG.............. Naft Air Lines [*Iran*] [*FAA designator*] (FAAC)
IRGA............ Infrared Gas Analyser (or Analyzer) (SAUS)
IRgA............ International Reprographics Association (EA)
Ir Gael......... Irish Gaelic (SAUS)
IRGAR.......... Infrared Gas Radiation
IRGB............ Infrared Guided Bomb [*DoD*]
IRGBA.......... International Repro Graphic Blueprint Association [*Later, IRA*] (EA)
IRGBA.......... International Reprographic Blueprint Association (SAUO)
IRGC............ International Rice Germplasm Center (SAUO)
IRGC............ Iran's Islamic Revolutionary Guard Corps [*Government term*] (GA)
IRGCP.......... International Research Group for Carcino-Embryonic Proteins (SAUO)

IRGCVD........ International Research Group on Colour Vision Deficiencies [*Ghent, Belgium*] (EAIO)
IRGD........... Infrared Guidance Demo (ACAE)
IRGD........... Irrigated Village Dummy (SAUO)
IRGDLP........ International Research Group on Drug Legislation and Programs (SAUO)
IRGDLP........ International Research Group on Drug Registration and Programs (SAUS)
Ir Gene........ Immune Response Gene (SAUS)
Ir Geogr B... Irish Geographical Bulletin (journ.) (SAUS)
IRGH........... Immunoreactive Growth Hormone [*Immunology*]
IR-GIP.......... Immunoreactive Gastric Inhibitory Peptide [*Biochemistry*]
IRGI............ Immunoreactive Glucagon [*Immunochemistry*]
IRGL............ Indentation Residual Gauge Level [*Automotive engineering*]
IRGL............ Infrared Gunfire Locator
IRGM........... Infrared Guidance Module (ACAE)
IRGMA......... Information Retrieval Group of the Museums Association [*British*] (NITA)
IRGMN......... International Rice Gall Midge Nursery (SAUO)
IRG-OECD.... International Research Group on Wear of Engineering Materials under the sponsorship of OECD (SAUO)
IRGOM......... International Research Group on Management (SAUO)
IRGP........... Infrared Guided Projectile (MCD)
IRGPG.......... Inter-Range and Global Planning Group [*White Sands Missile Range*] (MUGU)
IRGRD......... International Research Group on Refuse Disposal [*Later, ISWA*]
IRGT............ Institut Royal pour la Gestion durable des ressources naturelles et la promotion des Technologies propres (SAUO)
IRGT............ Insulin-Regulatable Glucose Transporter [*Biochemistry*]
IRGWP......... International Research Group on Wood Preservation (SAUO)
IRH............. Inductive Recording Head
IRH............. Infrared Heater
IRH............. Infrared Hygrometer (SAUS)
IRH............. Inspection Requirements Handbook [*Navy*] (NG)
IRH............. Institute for Reproductive Health (EA)
IRH............. Institute for Research in History
IRH............. Institute for Research in Hypnosis [*Later, IRHP*] (EA)
IRH............. Institutes of Religion and Health (EA)
IRH............. Integrated Recording Heads (SAUS)
IRH............. International Rhodes Resources [*Vancouver Stock Exchange symbol*]
irha............. Independent Retail Hardwaremen of America (SAUO)
IRHA........... Injured as Result of Hostile Action [*Military*] (NVT)
IRHA........... Injury Received by Hostile Action (SAUO)
IRHA........... Interchurch Response for the Horn of Africa (EA)
IRHA........... Interior Regional Housing Authority (SAUO)
IRHC........... Isolated Rat Hepatocyte Complex
IRHCG......... Immunoreactive Human Chorionic Gonadotropin [*Medicine*] (EDAA)
IRHCS......... Immunoradioassayable Human Chorionic Somatomammotropin [*Medicine*] (MAE)
IRHD........... Internationaler Rat der Hauspflegedienste [*International Council of Home-Help Services*]
IRHD........... International Rubber Hardness Degree
IRHF........... Integral Radiative Heat Flux
IRHGH......... Immunoreactive Human Growth Hormone [*Immunology*] (AAMN)
IRhGH......... Immunoreactive Human Growth Hormone [*Medicine*] (EDAA)
IRHIS.......... Intelligent Adaptive Information Retrieval system on Hospital Information System Front End (SAUO)
IRHON......... International Rice Hybrid Observational Nursery (SAUO)
IRHP........... Institute for Research in Hypnosis and Psychotherapy (EA)
IRHP........... Institute for Responsible Housing Preservation (NTPA)
IRHPL.......... Immunoreactive Human Placental Lactogen [*Medicine*] (EDAA)
IRhPL.......... Immunoreactive Human Placental Lactogen [*Medicine*] (EDAA)
IRHR........... Institute for Research in Human Relations (MCD)
IRHS........... Intact Reentry Heat Source (OA)
IRHS........... Intraoral Recurrent Herpes (SAUS)
IRHS........... Intraoral Recurrent Herpes Simplex [*Medicine*]
IRHVTA........ Infra-Red High Value Target Acqtsisition (SAUS)
IRHVTA........ Infrared High Value Target Acquisition (ACAE)
IR-HVTA....... Infrared-High Value Target Acquisition (SAUS)
IRHX........... Iron Horse Railroad [*Federal Railroad Administration identification code*]
IRI............... Image Resources, Inc. [*Winter Park, FL*] [*Telecommunications*] (TSSD)
IRI............... Image Resources, Incorporated (SAUO)
IRI............... Imagery Reconnaissance and Interpretation (SAUS)
IRI............... Imagery Release Interface (SAUS)
IRI............... Immunobiology Research Institute [*Annandale, NJ*]
IRI............... Immunoreactive Insulin
IRI............... Inca Resources, Inc. [*Toronto Stock Exchange symbol*] [*Vancouver Stock Exchange symbol*]
IRI............... Inca Resources, Incorporated (SAUO)
IRI............... Industrial Reconstruction Institute (SAUO)
IRI............... Industrial Reseach Institute Interreference Interval (SAUS)
IRI............... Industrial Research Institute [*Canada*] [*Research center*] (RCD)
IRI............... Industrial Risk Insurance (EEVL)
IRI............... Industrial Risk Insurers (EA)
IRI............... Informal Reading Inventory [*Education*]
IRI............... Information Researchers, Inc. [*Information service or system*] (IID)
IRI............... Information Researches, Incorporated (SAUO)
IRI............... Information Resources, Inc. [*Information service or system*] (IID)
IRI............... Information Resources, Incorporated (SAUO)
IRI............... Information Retrieval, Inc.
IRI............... Information Retrieval, Incorporated (SAUO)
IRI............... Infrared Image (SAUS)
IRI............... Infrared Imagery
IRI............... Infrared Industries, Inc. (SAUS)
IRI............... Infrared Industries, Incorporated (SAUO)
IRI............... Infrared Instrumentation
IRI............... Innovative Resources, Inc.
IRI............... Innovative Resources Incorporated (SAUO)
IRI............... Input Reader Interpreter (SAUS)
IRI............... Institute for Industrial Reconstruction (SAUO)
IRI............... Institute of the Rubber Industry (SAUO)
IRI............... Institute Research Institute (SAUS)
IRI............... Institution of the Rubber Industry [*British*]
IRI............... Insulin Radioimmunoassay
IRI............... Insulin Resistance Index [*Medicine*] (DMAA)
IRI............... Integrated Range Instrumentation
IRI............... Interagency Research Internet (SAUO)
IRI............... Interfaculty Reactor Institute [*Netherlands*]
IRI............... International Industrial Relations Institute
IRI............... International Reference Ionosphere
IRI............... International Relay, Inc. [*New York, NY*] [*Telecommunications*] (TSSD)
IRI............... International Relay, Incorporated (SAUO)
IRI............... International Remote Imaging Systems, Inc. [*AMEX symbol*] (SPSG)
IRI............... International Republican Institute (ECON)
IRI............... International Research Institute (SAUS)
IRI............... International Research Institute for Climate Prediction
IRI............... International Research Institute for Seasonal to Interannual Prediction (SAUS)
IRI............... International Robotmotion Intelligence (NITA)
IRI............... International Roughness Index [*BTS*] [*FHWA*] (TAG)
IRI............... Interreference Interval (SAUS)
IRI............... Intl Remote Imaging [*AMEX symbol*] (TTSB)
IRI............... Intravehicular Referenced Information [*NASA*]
IRI............... Inveresk Research International Ltd. [*British*] (IRUK)
IRI............... Ionospheric Research Instrument (ADWA)
IRI............... Iringa [*Tanzania*] [*Airport symbol*] (OAG)
IRI............... IRI Research Institute (SAUO)
iri............... Irish [*MARC language code*] [*Library of Congress*] (LCCP)
IRI............... Islamic Republic of Iran (SAUO)
IRI............... Islamic Research Institute (SAUO)
IRI............... Istituto per la Ricostruzione Industriale [*Institute for Industrial Reconstruction*] [*Government holding company*] [*Italy*]
IRIA............ Indirect Radioimmunoassay (DB)
IRIA............ Infrared Information Analysis Agency (SAUS)
IRIA............ Infrared Information and Analysis (SAUS)
IRIA............ Infrared Information and Analysis Center [*University of Michigan*]
IRIA............ Institut de Recherche d'Informatique et d'Automatique [*French*] [*Research center*]
IRIAC.......... Infrared Information and Analysis Center [*University of Michigan*]
IRIAF.......... Islamic Republic of Iran Air Force (SAUO)
IRIA Group... Infrared Information and Analysis Group (SAUO)
IRIAM.......... International Institute of Robotics and Artificial Intelligence (SAUO)
IRIATT......... Indian Railways Institute of Advanced Track Technology [*Indian Railway*] (TIR)
IRIBS.......... Inclination Removal Ionospheric Beacon Satellite (PDAA)
IRIC............ Information Resources [*NASDAQ symbol*] (TTSB)
IRIC............ Information Resources, Inc. [*NASDAQ symbol*] (NQ)
IRIC............ Infrared Image Converter
IRIC............ Inter-Regional Insurance Conference [*Later, ISO*]
IRICA.......... Industrial Research Institute for Central America (SAUO)
IRICBM........ Intermediate-Range Intercontinental Ballistic Missile
IRICC.......... Interagency Resource Information Coordination Council (SAUO)
IRICE.......... Integrated Remote Interface Control Element (SAUS)
IRICEN........ Indian Railways Institute of Civil Engineering [*Pune*] [*Indian Railway*] (TIR)
IRICON........ Infrared Iconoscope (SAUS)
IRICON........ Infrared Vidicon Tube
IRICON........ International Information Service via a Computer-Oriented Network (TSSD)
IRICP.......... International Research Institute for Climate Prediction [*Marine science*] (OSRA)
IRICS.......... Interim Reciprocal Information & Consultation System (SAUO)
IRICU.......... Intermountain Respiratory Intensive Care Unit [*Medicine*] (BABM)
IRicv........... Richview Township Public Library, Richview, IL [*Library symbol*] [*Library of Congress*] (LCLS)
IRid............. Elwood Township Carnegie Library, Ridge Farm, IL [*Library symbol*] [*Library of Congress*] (LCLS)
IRID............ Infrared Identification (ACAE)
Irid............. Iridectomy [*Medicine*] (EDAA)
irid............. Iridescent (ADWA)
IRID............ Iridescent (WGA)
IRID............ Iridium World Communications'A' [*NASDAQ symbol*] (SG)
Iridex.......... Iridex Corp. [*Associated Press*] (SAG)
IRIDS.......... Infrared Identification System (ACAE)
IRidSD......... Ridge Farm Community Unit School District, Ridge Farm, IL [*Library symbol*] [*Library of Congress*] (LCLS)
IRIE............ Infrared Information Exchange
IRIE............ Infrared Interference Envelope (SAUS)
IR/IED......... Independent Research/Independent Exploratory Development
IRIEEN........ Indian Railways Institute of Electrical Engineering [*Nasik*] [*Indian Railway*] (TIR)
IRIG............ Inertial Reference Integrating Gyro [*NASA*] (NASA)
IRIg............ Insulin-Reactive Immunoglobulin [*Endocrinology*] (DAVI)
IRIG............ Inter-Range Instrumentation Graph (SAUS)
IRIG............ Inter-Range Instrumentation Group [*White Sands Missile Range*]
IRI/G.......... Ratio of Immunoreactive Insulin to Serum or Plasma Glucose [*Medicine*] (STED)

IRIG-B.......... Inter-Range Instrumentation Group B [*NASA*] (GFGA)
IRIG-MWG... Inter-Range Instrumentation Group - Meteorological Working Group [*White Sands Missile Range*]
IRIG/TM....... Inter-Range Instrumentation Group Telemetry (ACAE)
IRII............... Industrial Research Institute of Ishikawa (SAUS)
IRIMEE......... Indian Railways Institute of Mechanical and Electrical Engineering [*Jamalpur*] [*Indian Railway*] (TIR)
IRIMO.......... Islamic Republic of Iran Meteorological Organization (SAUS)
IRIN............ Integrated Regional Information Network (SAUO)
IRI News...... Institution of the Rubber Industry News (journ.) (SAUS)
IR/IOD.......... Independent Research/Independent Objective Document (SAUO)
IR/IOD.......... Independent Research/Independent Objectives Document [*Military*] (DNAB)
IRIP............ Industrial Research Institute Program (SAUO)
IRIP............ Industrial Research Institutes Program (SAUS)
IRIPS.......... Infrared Industrial Process Supervision (SAUS)
IRIR............ Interchangeability Replaceability Information Report (SAUS)
IRIRC.......... International Refugee Integration Resource Centre [*Later, CDR*] (EAIO)
Irirs............ Riverside Public Library (SAUS)
IRIS............ Center for Institutional Reform and the Informal Sector [*University of Maryland*] (ECON)
IRIS............ Database searching/document ordering service for libraries and business users in Ireland (SAUS)
IRIS............ Division of Information, Robotics and Intelligent Systems (SAUO)
IRIS............ European Network of Training Schemes for Women (SAUO)
IRIS............ IBM [*International Business Machines Corp.*] Recruitment Information System
IRIS............ Illinois Researcher Information Service (SAUS)
IRIS............ Illinois Resource Information System (SAUS)
IRIS............ Imaging of Radicals Interacting with Surfaces [*Electronics*] (AAEL)
IRIS............ Inarihan River Irrigation System (SAUO)
IRIS............ Incident Resource and Information System [*Police*] [*British*] (NITA)
IRIS............ Incorporated Research Institutions for Seismology
IRIS............ Increased Readiness Information System
IRIS............ Index of References in Information Science (SAUS)
IRIS............ Industrial Relations Information Service [*Labour Canada*]
IRIS............ Industrial Research and Information Service (SAUO)
IRIS............ Inertial Reactor with Internal Separation [*Coal furnace*] [*Tecogen, Inc.*]
IRIS............ Inertia Resonance Induction Service (SAUS)
IRIS............ Inertia Resonance Induction System [*Automotive engineering*]
IRIS............ Infared Intruder System (SAUS)
IRIS............ Inferential Retrieval Indexing System (SAUO)
IRIS............ Information Relayed Instantly from the Source [*Project*]
IRIS............ Information Resources Information System [*Library of Congress*]
IRIS............ Information Retrieval by Interactive Search (SAUS)
IRIS............ Infrared Image Scanner
IRIS............ Infrared Imaging Seeker
IRIS............ Infra-Red Imaging Subsystem (SAUS)
IRIS............ Infrared Imaging System
IRIS............ Infrared Information Symposia (or Symposium) (SAUS)
IRIS............ Infrared Information System [*Sadtler Research Laboratories, Inc.*] [*Philadelphia, PA*] [*Database*]
IRIS............ Infrared Interference Spectrometer (SAUS)
IRIS............ Infrared Interferometer Spectrometer
IRIS............ Infrared Intruder Seeker (SAUS)
IRIS............ Infrared Intruder System
IRIS............ Infrared Radiation Interferometer Spectrometer
IRIS............ Infrared Research Information Symposium (AAG)
IRIS............ Infrared Research Information System (SAUS)
IRIS............ Instantaneous Retrieval Information System [*Computer science*] (ELAL)
IRIS............ Instant Response Information System (IEEE)
IRIS............ Instant Retrieval Information System (SAUS)
IRIS............ Institute for Regional and International Studies (EA)
IRIS............ Institute for Research in Information and Scholarship [*Brown University*] [*Research center*] (RCD)
IRIS............ Institute for Research on Interactive Systems [*Research center*] (TSSD)
IRIS............ Institute for Robotics and Intelligence Systems (SAUS)
IRIS............ Institute for Robotics and Intelligent Systems [*Research center*] (RCD)
IRIS............ Institutes Retrieval of Information Study (SAUS)
IRIS............ Instructional Resources Information System [*Ohio State University*] [*Information service or system*]
IRIS............ Instruction and Research Information Systems [*Computer science*]
IRIS............ Insurance Regulatory Information System [*National Association of Insurance Commissioners*]
IRIS............ Integrated Radar Imaging System (SAUS)
IRIS............ Integrated Radio and Intercommunications System [*Canada*]
IRIS............ Integrated Radio Information System (SAUO)
IRIS............ Integrated Reactor Information System (SAUO)
IRIS............ Integrated Reconnaissance Intelligence System (IEEE)
IRIS............ Integrated Regional Impact Studies (SAUO)
IRIS............ Integrated Requirement Implementation System (ACAE)
IRIS............ Integrated Reservation and Information System (SAUS)
IRIS............ Integrated Resonator Induction System
IRIS............ Integrated Risk Information System [*Environmental Protection Agency*]
IRIS............ Integrated Road Safety Information and Navigation System (SAUO)
IRIS............ Intelligence Report Index Summary
IRIS............ Intelligence Reports Information Subsystem [*Computer science*]
IRIS............ Intelligent Remote Input Stand [*Computer science*]
IRIS............ Interactive Real-Time Information System [*Marine science*] (MSC)
IRIS............ Interactive Recorded Information Service [*British*] [*Telecommunications*] (TEL)
IRIS............ Interactive Retrieval of Information System (SAUS)
IRIS............ Interim Research and Intelligence Service (SAUO)
IRIS............ Interleukin Regulation of Immune System [*Medicine*] (DMAA)
IRIS............ International Radiation Investigation Satellite [*NASA*]
IRIS............ International Radio Interferometric Surveying [*International Association of Geodesy*]
IRIS............ International Recruitment Investigation in the Subarctic [*Marine science*] (OSRA)
IRIS............ International Recruitment Investigations in the Subarctic (USDC)
IRIS............ International Relations Information System [*Forschungsinstitut fuer Internationale Politik und Sicherheit*] [*Germany*] (IID)
IRIS............ International Remote Imaging Systems, Inc. [*Associated Press*] (SAG)
IRIS............ International Reporting and Information Services [*International Private Intelligence Service*] [*Terminated, 1983*]
Iris.............. International Reporting and Informations System (SAUO)
IRIS............ International Reporting Information Systems
IRIS............ International Research and Information Service (SAUS)
IRIS............ International Research Information Service [*American Foundation for the Blind*]
IRIS............ International Research on the Interior of the Sun
IRIS............ International REST [*Restricted Environmental Stimulation Techniques*] Investigators Society (EA)
IRIS............ International Rights Information Service
IRIS............ International Rotary Inspection System (SAUO)
IRIS............ Internet Reach and Involvement Scale [*Advertising value of an Internet site*]
IRIS............ Inter-Range Instrumentation System (SAUS)
IRIS............ Interregional Information Society Initiative (SAUO)
IRIS............ Interrogation Requirements Information System [*DoD*] (AFIT)
IRIS............ Iran Radar Intercept System (ACAE)
IRIS............ Italian Research Interim Stage (NASA)
IRISA.......... Integrated Risk Information System (SAUO)
IRISET......... Indian Railways Institute of Signal Engineering and Telecommunications [*Secunderabad*] [*Indian Railway*] (TIR)
IRISH.......... Infrared Image Seeker Head (SAUS)
IRISH.......... Infrared Imaging Seeker Hardware (ACAE)
IRISH.......... Infrared Imaging Seeker Head (MCD)
Irish Agr Creamery Rev... Irish Agricultural and Creamery Review (journ.) (SAUS)
Irish Banking R... Irish Banking Review (journ.) (SAUS)
Irish Bcasting R... Irish Broadcasting Review (journ.) (SAUS)
Irish Beekpr... Irish Beekeeper (journ.) (SAUS)
Irish Bldr&Engineer... Irish Builder and Engineer (journ.) (SAUS)
Irish Bus...... Business and Finance (journ.) (SAUS)
Irish Econ...... Irish Economist (journ.) (SAUS)
Irish Folk M Stud... Irish Folk Music Studies (journ.) (SAUS)
Irish FP........ Irish Fishing Port (SAUS)
Irish Georgian Soc Qly Bull... Irish Georgian Society. Quarterly Bulletin (journ.) (SAUS)
Irish Georgisn Soc Bull... Irish Georgian Society. Bulletin (journ.) (SAUS)
IrishIn.......... Irish Investment Fund [*Associated Press*] (SAG)
Irish J Agric Econ and Rural Sociol... Irish Journal of Agricultural Economics and Rural Sociology (journ.) (SAUS)
Irish J Ed..... Irish Journal of Education (journ.) (SAUS)
Irish J Med... Irish Journal of Medical Science (journ.) (SAUS)
Irish J Psy... Irish Journal of Psychology (journ.) (SAUS)
Irish Lib Bul... Irish Library Bulletin (journ.) (SAUS)
Irish Lit S.... Irish Literary Studies (journ.) (SAUS)
Irish Med Times... Irish Medical Times (journ.) (SAUS)
Irish Mo....... Irish Monthly (journ.) (SAUS)
Irish Num.... Irish Numismatics (journ.) (SAUS)
Irish Q......... Irish Quarterly Review (journ.) (SAUS)
Irish S.......... Irish Sword (journ.) (SAUS)
Irish Sword... Irish Sword. Military History Society of Ireland. Dublin (SAUO)
IrishThQ....... Irish Theological Quarterly (journ.) (SAUS)
Irish U Rev... Irish University Review (journ.) (SAUS)
Irish VR....... Irish Vehicle Registration (SAUS)
Irish Wildfowl Comm Publ... Irish Wildfowl Committee. Publication (journ.) (SAUS)
IRIS-M......... Infrared Interferometer Spectrometer - Michelson
IRIS/OPS...... Illinois Researcher Information Service/Online Periodical Service (SAUS)
IRIS R&A..... Interim Research and Intelligence Service, Research and Analysis Branch (SAUO)
IRIS R&A..... Research and Analysis Branch, Interim Research and Intelligence Service (SAUS)
IRISS.......... Infrared Radiometric Imager/Surrogate Seeker (ACAE)
IRISS.......... Institute for Research in the Social Sciences [*University of York*] [*British*] (IRC)
IRI System... Integrated Range Instrumentation System (SAUS)
IRIV............ Immunopotentiating Reconstituted Influenza Virosome [*Immunochemistry*]
IRIV............ Immunostimulating Reconstituted Influenza Virosome [*Immunochemistry*]
IRivd........... Riverdale Library District, Riverdale, IL [*Library symbol*] [*Library of Congress*] (LCLS)
IRivf........... River Forest Public Library, River Forest, IL [*Library symbol*] [*Library of Congress*] (LCLS)
IRivfR......... Rosary College, River Forest, IL [*Library symbol*] [*Library of Congress*] (LCLS)
IRivfT.......... Concordia Teachers College, River Forest, IL [*Library symbol*] [*Library of Congress*] (LCLS)
IRivg........... River Grove Public Library, River Grove, IL [*Library symbol*] [*Library of Congress*] (LCLS)

IRivgT.......... Triton College, River Grove, IL [*Library symbol*] [*Library of Congress*] (LCLS)
IRivs............ Riverside Public Library, Riverside, IL [*Library symbol*] [*Library of Congress*] (LCLS)
IRIX............ IRIDEX Corp. [*NASDAQ symbol*] (TTSB)
IRJ............. European Rubber Journal (journ.) (SAUS)
IRJ............. Industrial Relations Journal (journ.) (SAUS)
IRJ............. Industrial Relations Law Journal (journ.) (SAUS)
IRJ............. Infrared Jammer
IRJ............. International Railway Journal (SAUO)
IRJ............. La Rioja [*Argentina*] [*Airport symbol*] (OAG)
IRJADJ......... Iranian Journal of Agricultural Sciences (journ.) (SAUS)
IRJC............ Indian River Junior College (SAUO)
IRJE............ Infrared Jammer Equipment
IRJE............ Interactive Remote Job Entry
IRJE............ Internet Remote Job Entry (SAUS)
Ir J Environ Sci... Irish Journal of Environmental Science (journ.) (SAUS)
Ir J Med Sci... Irish Journal of Medical Science (journ.) (SAUS)
IR Jour........ Indian Rulings, Journal Section [*A publication*] (DLA)
IR Jour........ Indian Rulings, Journal Section (journ.) (SAUS)
IRJPAR........ Irish Journal of Psychology (journ.) (SAUS)
IRJPDU........ Irish Journal of Psychotherapy (journ.) (SAUS)
Ir J Psychol... Irish Journal of Psychology (journ.) (SAUS)
Ir J Psychol Med... Irish Journal of Psychological Medicine (journ.) (SAUS)
Ir J Psychother... Irish Journal of Psychotherapy (journ.) (SAUS)
Ir J Psychother Psychosom Med... Irish Journal of Psychotherapy and Psychosomatic Medicine (journ.) (SAUS)
IRJSD5........ Iraqi Journal of Science (journ.) (SAUS)
Ir Jur.......... Irish Jurist Reports [*1849-66*] [*A publication*] (DLA)
Ir Jur NS...... Irish Jurist. New Series (journ.) (SAUS)
Ir Jur Rep.... Irish Jurist Reports [*1849-66*] [*A publication*] (DLA)
IRK............. Infrared Kit
IRK............. Insulin Receptor Kinase [*An enzyme*]
IRK............. Interlake Development [*Vancouver Stock Exchange symbol*]
IRK............. Irkutsk [*Former USSR*] [*Seismograph station code, US Geological Survey*] (SEIS)
IRK............. Kirksville [*Missouri*] [*Airport symbol*] (OAG)
IRK............. Kirksville, MO [*Location identifier*] [*FAA*] (FAAL)
IRK............. Kish Air [*Iran*] [*ICAO designator*] (FAAC)
IRL............. Illustrations Requirements List (SAUS)
IRL............. Immigration Restriction League
IRL............. Indexed Repayment Loan
IRL............. Index Retrieval Language [*Computer science*] (PDAA)
IRL............. Industrial Reactor Laboratories [*New Jersey*]
IRL............. Industrial Relations Law Journal (journ.) (SAUS)
IRL............. Industrial Research Laboratories [*A publication*]
IRL............. Industrial Research Laboratory (SAUO)
IRL............. Industrial Research Labotatories (journ.) (SAUS)
IRL............. Indy Racing League [*Automobile racing*]
IRL............. Information Request Letter [*Automotive safety*]
IRL............. Information Requirements List (KSC)
IRL............. Information Research Limited (SAUO)
IRL............. Information Research Ltd. [*Information service or system*] (IID)
IRL............. Information Retrieval Language [*Computer science*]
IRL............. Information Retrieval Limited (SAUO)
IRL............. Information Retrieval Ltd. [*Database originator*] [*British*] [*Information service or system*]
IRL............. Infrared Lamp [*or Light*]
IRL............. Infrared Lens
IRL............. Infrared Light (SAUS)
IRL............. Initiating Reference Letter (MCD)
IRL............. In Real Life [*Computer hacker terminology*]
IRL............. Institute for Rational Living [*Absorbed by IRET*]
IRL............. Institute of Rural Life at Home and Overseas [*British*] (BI)
IRL............. Institute on Religious Life (EA)
IRL............. Interactive Reader Language [*Computer science*]
IRL............. Interactive Root Locus (PDAA)
IRL............. Interagency Review Letter (SAUO)
IRL............. Interface Requirement List (NASA)
IRL............. Internationaler Ring fuer Landarbeit [*International Committee of Scientific Management in Agriculture*]
IRL............. International Meridian Resources [*Vancouver Stock Exchange symbol*]
IRL............. Inter-Repeater Link (SAUS)
IRL............. Interrogation and Locating (or Location) (SAUS)
IRL............. Intersection of Range Legs
IRL............. Intuitive Robot Language (VLIE)
IRL............. Ionosphere Research Laboratory [*Pennsylvania State University*] (PDAA)
IRL............. Ireland [*ANSI three-letter standard code*] (CNC)
Irl............... Ireland (MILB)
IRL............. Irish Air Corps [*ICAO designator*] (FAAC)
IRL............. Irish Investment Fund [*NYSE symbol*] (SAG)
IrL.............. Irish Law Reports [*A publication*] (DLA)
IRLA........... Independent Research Libraries (or Library) Association (SAUO)
IRLA........... Information Retrieval & Library Automation [*A publication*] (BRI)
IRLA........... Information Retrieval and Library Automation (journ.) (SAUS)
IRLA........... International Religious Liberty Association (EA)
IRLA........... Item Repair Level Analysis [*DoD*]
IR Lah......... Indian Rulings, Lahore Series [*A publication*] (DLA)
IRLah.......... Indian Rulings, Lahore Series (journ.) (SAUS)
IrL & Eq...... Irish Law and Equity Reports [*1838-50*] [*A publication*] (DLA)
IRLAP......... Infrared Link Access Protocol (SAUS)
IRLAS......... Infrared LASER
IRLAS......... Infrared Tracker and Laser Rangefinder (ACAE)
Ir Law & Ch... Irish Common Law and Chancery Reports, New Series [*1850-53*] [*A publication*] (DLA)
Ir Law&Ch... Irish Common Law and Chancery Reports, New Series (journ.) (SAUS)
Ir Law & Eq... Irish Law and Equity Reports [*1838-50*] [*A publication*] (DLA)
Ir Law Rec... Irish Law Recorder [*1827-38*] [*A publication*] (DLA)
Ir Law Rec... Irish Law Recorder (journ.) (SAUS)
Ir Law Rec NS... Irish Law Recorder, New Series [*1833-38*] [*A publication*] (DLA)
Ir Law Rec NS... Irish Law Recorder, New Series (journ.) (SAUS)
Ir Law Rep... Irish Law Reports [*A publication*] (DLA)
Ir Law Rep... Irish Law Reports (journ.) (SAUS)
Ir Law Rep NS... Irish Common Law Reports, New Series [*A publication*] (DLA)
Ir Law T...... Irish Law Times (journ.) (SAUS)
IRLC........... Illinois Regional Library Council [*Library network*]
IRLCO......... International Red Locust Control Organization (SAUS)
IRLCO-CSA... International Red Locust Control Organisation (or Organization) for Central and Southern Africa (SAUO)
IRLCO-CSA... International Red Locust Control Organization for Central and Southern Africa (EAIO)
IRLCS......... International Red Locust Control Service
IRLD........... Institute for Research on Learning Disabilities [*University of Minnesota*] [*Research center*] (RCD)
IRLDA......... Independent Retail Lumber Dealers Association
IRLED......... Infrared Light Emitting Diode (PDAA)
IRLG........... Interagency Regulatory Liaison Group [*Comprising several federal agencies*] [*Terminated, 1981*]
IRLI............ Immigration Reform Law Institute (SAUS)
IRLIB.......... Industrial Relations Legal Information Bulletin (journ.) (SAUS)
IRLJ............ Infraction Rules for Courts of Limited Jurisdiction (SAUO)
Ir LJ........... Irish Law Journal [*1895-1902*] [*A publication*] (DLA)
IRLM.......... Internal Resource Lock Manager (SAUS)
Ir L NS........ Irish Common Law Reports, New Series (journ.) (SAUS)
IRLON......... International Rainfed Lowland Rice Observational Nursery (SAUO)
IRLR........... Industrial Relations Law Reports (journ.) (SAUS)
IRLR........... Infrared LASER Ranger (MCD)
Ir LR........... Irish Law Reports [*A publication*] (DLA)
Ir L Rec....... Irish Law Recorder, First Series [*1827-31*] [*A publication*] (DLA)
Ir L Rec 1st Ser... Law Recorder, First Series [*Ireland*] [*A publication*] (DLA)
Ir L Rec NS... Law Recorder, New Series [*Ireland*] [*A publication*] (DLA)
IRLS........... Information, Retrieval, and Location System (ACAE)
IRLS........... Infrared Laser Scanner (SAUS)
IRLS........... Infrared LASER Spectrometer
IRLS........... Infrared Line Scanner (MCD)
IRLS........... Infrared Linescan System (SAUS)
IRLS........... Integrated Rural Locum Service (SAUO)
IRLS........... Interrogation & Reading Location System (SAUS)
IRLS........... Interrogation Recording (SAUS)
IRLS........... Interrogation, Recording, and Locating System [*Naval Oceanographic Office*]
IRLS........... Interrogation, Recording and Location Subsystem (SAUS)
IRLS........... Interrogation, Recording and Location System (SAUO)
IRLS........... Iteratively Reweighted Least Squares
IRLSA......... Illinois Registered Land Surveyors Association (SAUO)
IRLSC......... Industrial Relations and Labor Studies Center [*University of Maryland*] [*Research center*] (RCD)
Ir L Times and Solicitors J... Irish Law Times and Solicitors Journal. A Weekly Gazette of Legal News and Information (journ.) (SAUS)
Ir LTJ.......... Irish Law Times Journal [*A publication*] (DLA)
Ir LT Jour.... Irish Law Times Journal [*A publication*] (DLA)
Ir LTR......... Irish Law Times Reports [*A publication*] (DLA)
Ir LT Rep..... Irish Law Times Reports [*A publication*] (DLA)
IRLWR........ Institute for Research on Land and Water Resources [*Pennsylvania State University*] (PDAA)
IRLYN......... International Rainfed Lowland Rice Yield Nursery (SAUO)
IRLYN-E...... International Rainfed Lowland Rice Yield Nursery-Early (SAUO)
IRLYN-M...... International Rainfed Lowland Rice Yield Nursery-Medium (SAUO)
IRM............ HCFAs Information Resources Management Plan (SAUS)
IRM............ Illinois Railway Museum (EA)
IRM............ Image Rejection Mixer [*Electronics*] (OA)
IRM............ Image Repetition Memory (SAUS)
IRM............ Image Risk Mixer (SAUS)
IRM............ Immune Response Modifier [*Medicine*] (MELL)
IRM............ Improved Risk Mutuals (EA)
IRM............ Indiana Railway Museum [*Federal Railroad Administration identification code*]
IRM............ Induced Remanent Magnetization
IRM............ Industrial Raw Materials (SAUO)
IRM............ Information and Records Management (journ.) (SAUS)
IRM............ Information Management (journ.) (SAUS)
IRM............ Information Records Management (SAUO)
IRM............ Information Request Message (SAUS)
IRM............ Information Research Management (MCD)
IRM............ Information Resource Management [*Computer science*]
IRM............ Information Resource Manager (SAUO)
IRM............ Information Resource Monitor Subsystem (SAUO)
IRM............ Information Resources Management [*Marine science*] (OSRA)
IRM............ Information Resources Management Plan (SAUO)
IRM............ Information Resources Manager (SAUO)
IRM............ Infrared Mapper
IRM............ Infrared Measurement
IRM............ Infrastructure Resource Management (GART)
IRM............ Inherent Rights Mask (SAUS)
IRM............ Inherited Releasing Mechanism [*Psychiatry*]
IRM............ Inherited Rights Mask (VLIE)
IRM............ Initial Release Memorandum

IRM Innate Release Mechanism [*Endocrinology*]
IRM Innate Releasing Mechanism (STED)
IRM Inorganic Reaction Mechanism (SAUS)
IRM Inside Rearview Mirror [*Automotive engineering*]
IRM Inspection, Repair, and Maintenance (VLIE)
IRM Inspection Requirements Manual (AAG)
IRM Institute for Resource Management (EA)
IRM Institute of Rehabilitation Medicine (DAVI)
IRM Institute of Religion and Medicine [*British*] (DBA)
IRM Institute of Respiratory Medicine
IRM Institute of Risk Management (EAIO)
IRM Integrated Range Missile (MCD)
IRM Integrated Range Mission [*Military*]
IRM Integrated Resource Management (SAUO)
IRM Integrated Review Model
IRM Intelligent Remote Multiplexer [*Computer science*] (MHDI)
IRM Intelligent Repeater Module (VLIE)
IRM Interactive Request Modification (IAA)
IRM Interference Reflection Microscopy
IRM Interim Remedial Measure (EPA)
IRM Interim Research Memo
IRM Interim Research Memorandum (SAUO)
IRM Intermediate Range Monitor (NRCH)
IRM Intermediate Remedial Measures (GNE)
IRM Intermediate Restorative Material [*Dentistry*]
IRM Internal Revenue (Service) Manual [*A publication*] (AAGC)
IRM International Research Monitoring (SAUS)
IRM International Resource Management (SAUS)
IRM International Review of Missions (journ.) (SAUS)
IRM International Roaming MIN (SAUO)
IRM International Royalon Minerals, Inc. [*Vancouver Stock Exchange symbol*]
IRM International Royalty Minerals, Inc. (SAUO)
IRM Iodine Radiation Monitor (IEEE)
IRM Ion Rate Monitoring (AAEL)
IRM Ion Release Module [*Spacecraft*] [*Germany*]
IRM Iron Mountain [*NYSE symbol*] (SG)
IRM Isothermal Remanence (SAUS)
IRM Isothermal Remanent Magnetization
IRMA European Industrial Research Management Association (SAUO)
IRMA Illinois Reliable Multicast Architecture (VLIE)
IRMA Immunoradiometric Assay [*Immunology*]
IRMA Indian Refractory Makers Association (SAUO)
IRMA Individual Retirement Mortgage Account
IRMA Individual Reverse Mortgage Account [*American Homestead, Inc.*]
IRMA Information and Referral Manual (SAUS)
IRMA Information Referral Manual
IRMA Information Revision and Manuscript Assembly
IRMA Infrared Milk Analyser (or Analyzer) (SAUS)
IRMA Infrared Miss-Distance Approximator
IRMA Infrared Miss-distance Approximator (or Approximeter) (SAUS)
IRMA Integrated Resource Management Architecture (VLIE)
IRMA Integrated Revenue and Marketing Applications (SAUS)
IRMA Interactive Real-Time Music Assembler (PDAA)
IRMA International Rail Makers Association (SAUS)
IRMA International Rail Markers Association (SAUO)
IRMA International Regional Magazine Association (NTPA)
IRMA International Rehabilitation Medicine Association (EA)
IRMA International Road Management Agency (SAUO)
IRMA International Rock 'n' Roll Music Association (EA)
Irma International Rollmakers Association (SAUO)
IRMA Intraretinal Microangiopathy [*Ophthalmology*]
IRMA Intraretinal Microvascular Abnormality [*Ophthalmology*]
IRMA Inverted Roof Membrane Assembly [*Construction*]
IRMAC Information Resource Management Association of Canada (EAIO)
IR Mad Indian Rulings, Madras Series [*A publication*] (DLA)
IRMAE Ius Romanum Medii Aevi [*Latin*]
IRMAS International Review of Music, Aesthetics and Sociology (journ.) (SAUS)
IRMB Joint Resources Management Board (SAUS)
IRMC Information Resource Management Council [*DoD*]
IRMC Information Resources Management College (USGC)
IRMC Institute of Risk Management Consultants [*Later, SRMC*] (EA)
IRMC Interagency Risk Management Council [*Environmental Protection Agency*] (EPA)
IRMC International Radio-Maritime Committee (SAUO)
IRMC International Records Management Council (SAUO)
IRMC Inter-Regulatory Risk Management Council [*Environmental science*] (EPAT)
IRMCO Iranian Rolling Mills Company (SAUO)
IRME Initiator Resistance Measuring Equipment (NASA)
IRMEA Inland Revenue Minor Establishment Association (SAUO)
IRMF International Records Management Federation (SAUO)
IRMFI I Reply Merely for Information (ADWA)
IRMFSG Inter-Range Missile Flight Safety Group [*White Sands Missile Range*]
IRMGARD Information Resources Management Group and Regulatory Directorate (SAUO)
IRMGPC International Record of Medicine and General Practice Clinics [*Journal*] [*Medicine*] (EDAA)
IRMGSG Inter-Range Missile Ground Safety Group [*White Sands Missile Range*] (KSC)
IRMI Indirect Reading Measuring Instruments (DICI)
IRMI Industrial Research Materials Institute (SAUS)
IRMI International Risk Management Institute [*Dallas, TX*] (EA)
IR Mim Internal Revenue Service Mimeographed Ruling (AAGC)
IR-MIM Published Internal Revenue Mimeograph [*A publication*] (DLA)
IRMIS Integrated Resource Management Information System (SAUS)
IRMJ Infrared Miniaturized Jammer
IRML Isotope Research Material Laboratory (SAUO)
IRMM Institute for Reference Materials and Measurement [*Belgium*]
IRMM Institute of Reference Materials and Measurement (SAUO)
IRMMH Institute for Research into Mental and Multiple Handicap [*British*]
IRMNA2 Institute for Research into Mental Retardation. Monograph (journ.) (SAUS)
IRMO Information Resources Management Office [*Army Corps of Engineers*]
IRMP Industrial Readiness and Mobilization Production Planning [*Military*]
IRMP Information Resource Management Plan (SAUO)
IRMP Infrared Measurement Program
IRMP Infrared Multiple-Photon [*Physics*]
IRMP Integrated Resource Management Plan (SAUO)
IRMP Intermountain Regional Medical Program (BABM)
IRMP Interoperability Requirements Management Plan (SAUO)
IRMP Interservice Radiation Measurement Program
IRMP Iron-Regulated Membrane Protein [*Biochemistry*]
IRMPC Industrial Raw Materials Planning Committee [*NATO*] (NATG)
IRMPD Infrared Multiple-Photon Dissociation [*Physics*]
IRMR Infra-Red Micro Radiometry (VLIE)
IRMR Infrared Micro-Radiometry (or Radiometer) (SAUS)
IRMR Institute for Research into Mental Retardation
IRMRA Infrared Monochromatic Radiation (MSA)
IR/MRBM Intermediate-Range/Medium Range Ballistic Missile (SAUO)
IR/MRBM Intermediate-Range/Medium-Range Ballistic Missile (NG)
IRMS Imperial Russian Musical Society (SAUO)
IRMS Indian Railway Medical Services [*Indian Railway*] (TIR)
IRMS Information Resource Management Service [*Veterans Administration Medical Center*] [*Information service or system*] (IID)
IRMS Information Resource Management System (ACAE)
IRMS Information Resources Management Service (SAUO)
IRMS Information Retrieval and Management System (IAA)
IRMS Infrared Mapping System
IRMS Infrared Mass Spectroscopy (SAUS)
IRMS Integrated Radio Management System (MCD)
IRMS International Robert Musil Society [*See also SIRM*] [*Saarbrucken, Federal Republic of Germany*] (EAIO)
IRMS Isotope Ratio Mass Spectrometer (SAUS)
IRMS Isotope Ratio Mass Spectrometry
IRMS Isotopic-Ratio Mass Spectrometry (SAUS)
IR-MSS Infrared Multispectral (SAUS)
IR-MSS Infrared Multispectral Scanner (SAUS)
IRMT International Register of Manipulative Therapists
IRMU IR Mode Upgrade (SAUS)
IRMVS Institute for Reparative Medicine and Vascular Surgery (ADWA)
IRMWS Infra-Red Missile Warning Subsystem programme (SAUS)
IRMZ Integrated Resource Management Zone (SAUO)
IRN Illinois Resource Network [*University of Illinois*] [*Urbana*] [*Information service or system*] (IID)
IRN Import Release Note (DS)
IRN Input Reconfiguration Network (SAUS)
IRN Interface Revision Notice [*NASA*] (KSC)
IRN Interim Revision Notice (SAA)
IRN Intermediate Routing Node (SAUS)
IRN Internal Recurrent Neural Network (AAEL)
IRN Internal Reference Number
IRN Internal Routing Network
IRN International Rivers Network (EA)
irn Intrarenal [*Medicine*] (EDAA)
IRN Invoice Register Number [*Business term*] (MCD)
IRN Iran [*ANSI three-letter standard code*] (CNC)
IRN Iron [*Chemical element*] (DAVI)
IRN Iron or Steel [*Freight*]
IRN Iron River Resources [*Vancouver Stock Exchange symbol*]
IRN [*The*] Ironton Railroad Co. [*Absorbed into Consolidated Rail Corp.*] [*AAR code*]
IRN Item Removal Notice [*Nuclear energy*] (NRCH)
iRNA Immune/Informational ribonucleic acid [*Medicine*] (EDAA)
IRNA Immune Ribonucleic Acid (STED)
IRNA Informational Ribonucleic Acid (STED)
iRNA Information Ribonucleic Acid [*Biochemistry*] (DB)
IRNA Iranian [*or Islamic Republic*] News Agency
IRNA Islamic Republic News Agency
I-RNA Ribonucleic Acid, Immune [*Biochemistry, genetics*]
IR Nag Indian Rulings, Nagpur Series [*A publication*] (DLA)
IR Nag Indian Rulings, Nagpur Series (journ.) (SAUS)
Ir Nat J Irish Naturalists Journal (journ.) (SAUS)
IRND Interand Corp. (SAUO)
IRNDT Infrared Nondestructive Tester (SAUS)
IRNDT Infrared Nondestructive Testing [*Electrical technique*]
IRNES Institut de Recherches et de Normalisation Economiques en Scientifiques [*Canada*]
IRNMO Iron Mountain, MI [*American Association of Railroads railroad junction routing code*]
IRNP Identifying Research Needs Program (SAUS)
IRNP Isle Royale National Park (SAUO)
IRNP Isle Royal National Park (SAUS)
IRNRAJ Iraq Natural History Museum. Report (journ.) (SAUS)
IRNS Inertial Reference and Navigation System (SAUS)
IRNS Inertial Reference Navigational System
IRNTN Ironton, MN [*American Association of Railroads railroad junction routing code*]

IRNU........... Institut de Recherche des Nations Unies pour le Developpement Social [*United Nations Research Institute for Social Development*]
Ir Nurse J.... Irish Nurses Journal (journ.) (SAUS)
Ir Nurs News... Irish Nursing News (journ.) (SAUS)
IRNV........... Increase and Replacement of Naval Vessels [*Naval budget appropriation title*]
IRNWRK...... Ironwork
IRO............. Birao [*Central African Republic*] [*Airport symbol*] (AD)
IRO............. CSA Air, Inc. [*ICAO designator*] (FAAC)
IRO............. Immediate Response Option (SAUO)
IRO............. Independent Retailer Organisation (EAIO)
IRO............. Industrial Recycling Organization (SAUO)
IRO............. Industrial Relations Office [*Army*]
IRO............. Inflight Refueling Operator
IRO............. Infrared Oven
IRO............. Inland Revenue Office [*or Officer*] [*British*]
IRO............. Inland Revenue Officer (SAUO)
iro............... in rear of (SAUS)
IRO............. Institute for Research on Onchocerosis (SAUS)
IRO............. Institute of Rent Officers [*British*] (DBA)
IRO............. Interim Range Operations (MUGU)
IRO............. Internal Revenue Office [*or Officer*]
IRO............. International Reception Operators [*Defunct*] (EA)
IRO............. International Refugee Organization [*Later, UNHCR*]
IRO............. International Relations Office [*American Library Association*]
IRO............. International Relief Organization [*Post-World War II*]
IRO............. International Revenue Officer (SAUS)
IRO............. Inventory Research Office [*Army*]
iro............... Iroquoian [*MARC language code*] [*Library of Congress*] (LCCP)
IRo.............. Rockford Public Library, Rockford, IL [*Library symbol*] [*Library of Congress*] (LCLS)
IROA........... Independent Rabbinate of America
IRoAH.......... Auburn High School, Rockford, IL [*Library symbol*] [*Library of Congress*] (LCLS)
IROALA........ International Relations Office-American Library Association (SAUS)
IROAN......... Initial Repair Only As Necessary (ACAE)
IROAN......... Inspect and Repair Only as Necessary [*or Needed*] [*Military*]
IROAN......... Inspect and Repair Only as Needed (SAUO)
IRob............ Robinson Public Library, Robinson, IL [*Library symbol*] [*Library of Congress*] (LCLS)
IRoBaE........ Barbour Elementary School, Rockford, IL [*Library symbol*] [*Library of Congress*] (LCLS)
IRobb........... Robbins Public Library District, Robbins, IL [*Library symbol*] [*Library of Congress*] (LCLS)
IRoBeE........ Beyer Elementary School, Rockford, IL [*Library symbol*] [*Library of Congress*] (LCLS)
IRoBlE......... Bloom Elementary School, Rockford, IL [*Library symbol*] [*Library of Congress*] (LCLS)
IRoBrE......... Brookview Elementary School, Rockford, IL [*Library symbol*] [*Library of Congress*] (LCLS)
IRobSD........ Robinson Community School District 2, Robinson, IL [*Library symbol*] [*Library of Congress*] (LCLS)
IROC........... International Race of Champion (SAUO)
IROC........... International Race of Champions [*Auto racing*]
IROC........... International Rose O'Neill Club (EA)
IROC........... International Royalty & Oil Co. (SAUS)
IROC........... International Royalty & Oil Company (SAUO)
IROC........... Intrusion Resistant Optical Communications (SAUO)
IROC........... Intrusion Resistant Optic Communications (ACAE)
IRoC............ Rockford College, Rockford, IL [*Library symbol*] [*Library of Congress*] (LCLS)
IRoCaE........ Carlson Elementary School, Rockford, IL [*Library symbol*] [*Library of Congress*] (LCLS)
IRoChE........ Church Elementary School, Rockford, IL [*Library symbol*] [*Library of Congress*] (LCLS)
IRockt.......... Talcott Free Public Library, Rockton, IL [*Library symbol*] [*Library of Congress*] (LCLS)
IRocL........... Flagg Township Library, Rochelle, IL [*Library symbol*] [*Library of Congress*] (LCLS)
IRocN.......... Rochelle News, Rochelle, IL [*Library symbol*] [*Library of Congress*] (LCLS)
IRoCoE........ Conklin Elementary School, Rockford, IL [*Library symbol*] [*Library of Congress*] (LCLS)
IROD........... Instantaneous Readout Detector [*Satellite instrument*]
IRoDE.......... Dennis Elementary School, Rockford, IL [*Library symbol*] [*Library of Congress*] (LCLS)
IRODP......... International Registry of Organization Development Professionals (EA)
IRODS......... Inertial Rate of Descent Sensor (MCD)
IROE........... Intelligent Robot Operating Environment (SAUO)
IRoEE.......... Ellis Elementary School, Rockford, IL [*Library symbol*] [*Library of Congress*] (LCLS)
IRoEH.......... East High School, Rockford, IL [*Library symbol*] [*Library of Congress*] (LCLS)
IRoEM......... Einsehower Middle School, Rockford, IL [*Library symbol*] [*Library of Congress*] (LCLS)
IROF........... Imagery Requirement Objectives File (MCD)
IROF........... Improved Rate of Fire (SAUS)
IRoFE.......... Froberg Elementary School, Rockford, IL [*Library symbol*] [*Library of Congress*] (LCLS)
Ir Offshore Rev... Irish Offshore Review (journ.) (SAUS)
IRO-FIET...... Interamerican Regional Organization of the International Federation of Commercial, Clerical, Professional, and Technical Employees [*Willemstad, Netherlands Antilles*] (EAIO)
IRoFM.......... B. W. Flinn Middle School, Rockford, IL [*Library symbol*] [*Library of Congress*] (LCLS)
IROFMS....... International Reference Organization in Forensic Medicine and Sciences [*Medicine*] (EDAA)
IRoFP........... Fairview Preschool, Rockford, IL [*Library symbol*] [*Library of Congress*] (LCLS)
IRoGaE........ Garrison Elementary School, Rockford, IL [*Library symbol*] [*Library of Congress*] (LCLS)
IRoGH.......... Guilford High School, Rockford, IL [*Library symbol*] [*Library of Congress*] (LCLS)
IRoGrE......... Gregory Elementary School, Rockford, IL [*Library symbol*] [*Library of Congress*] (LCLS)
IROH........... Interest Rate of Return (SAUS)
IRoHaE........ Haskell Elementary School, Rockford, IL [*Library symbol*] [*Library of Congress*] (LCLS)
IRoHgE........ Haight Elementary School, Rockford, IL [*Library symbol*] [*Library of Congress*] (LCLS)
IRoHiE......... Hillman Elementary School, Rockford, IL [*Library symbol*] [*Library of Congress*] (LCLS)
IRoHlE......... Hallstrom Elementary School, Rockford, IL [*Library symbol*] [*Library of Congress*] (LCLS)
IRoJaE......... Jackson Elementary School, Rockford, IL [*Library symbol*] [*Library of Congress*] (LCLS)
IRoJH........... Jefferson High School, Rockford, IL [*Library symbol*] [*Library of Congress*] (LCLS)
IRoJoE......... Johnson Elementary School, Rockford, IL [*Library symbol*] [*Library of Congress*] (LCLS)
IRoKE........... King Elementary School, Rockford, IL [*Library symbol*] [*Library of Congress*] (LCLS)
IRoKiE......... Kishwaukee Elementary School, Rockford, IL [*Library symbol*] [*Library of Congress*] (LCLS)
IRoKM.......... John F. Kennedy Middle School, Rockford, IL [*Library symbol*] [*Library of Congress*] (LCLS)
IROL............ Imagery Requirements Objective Listing (SAUO)
IROL............ Imagery Requirements Objectives List (MCD)
IROL............ Instruments R&D Laboratory (SAUS)
IRoLE........... Lathrop Elementary School, Rockford, IL [*Library symbol*] [*Library of Congress*] (LCLS)
IRoLM.......... Lincoln Middle School, Rockford, IL [*Library symbol*] [*Library of Congress*] (LCLS)
IROM........... Ion-implanted Read-Only Memory (SAUS)
IRoMcE........ McIntosh Elementary School, Rockford,IL [*Library symbol*] [*Library of Congress*] (LCLS)
IRoMH.......... Rockford Memorial Hospital, Rockford, IL [*Library symbol*] [*Library of Congress*] (LCLS)
IROMM........ International Register of Microform Masters (TELE)
IRoMuE........ Muhl Center Elementary School, Rockford, IL [*Library symbol*] [*Library of Congress*] (LCLS)
IRON........... Infrared Optical Noise (IAA)
IRON........... International Rice Observational Nursery (SAUO)
IRON........... Inter-Range Operation Number (SAUS)
Iron............. Ironical (ROG)
IRON........... Ironstone Group, Inc. (SAUO)
IRON........... Ironton, OH [*American Association of Railroads railroad junction routing code*]
Iron............. Ironwood (journ.) (SAUS)
IRoN............ Northern Illinois Library for Mental Health, Rockford, IL [*Library symbol*] [*Library of Congress*] (LCLS)
IRoNaE........ Nashold Elementary School, Rockford, IL [*Library symbol*] [*Library of Congress*] (LCLS)
Iron Age...... Iron Age. Metal Producing Management Edition (journ.) (SAUS)
Iron Age Metalwork Int... Iron Age Metalworking International (journ.) (SAUS)
Iron Age Met Prod... Iron Age Metals Producer (journ.) (SAUS)
Iron Coal Trades Rev... Iron and Coal Trades Review (journ.) (SAUS)
IROND......... Irondale, IL [*American Association of Railroads railroad junction routing code*]
IRON-E........ International Rice Observational Nursery-Early (SAUO)
IRoNeE........ Nelson Elementary School, Rockford, IL [*Library symbol*] [*Library of Congress*] (LCLS)
IRoNL.......... Rockford Northern Illinois Library System, Rockford, IL [*Library symbol*] [*Library of Congress*] (LCLS)
IRON-M....... International Rice Observational Nursery-Medium (SAUO)
Ironmaking Proe AIME... Ironmaking Proceedings. Metallurgical Society of AIME. Iron and Steel Division (journ.) (SAUS)
IRONMAN.... Improving Reliability of New Machines at Night (AAEL)
IRoNmE....... New Milford Elementary School, Rockford, IL [*Library symbol*] [*Library of Congress*] (LCLS)
Ironmkg Steelmkg... Ironmaking and Steelmaking (journ.) (SAUS)
IronMnt......... Iron Mountain, Inc. [*Associated Press*] (SAG)
IRONS......... Iron and Total Iron Binding Capacity [*Hematology*] (DAVI)
Irons Pol Law... Irons on Police Law [*A publication*] (DLA)
Irons Pol Law... Irons on Police Law (journ.) (SAUS)
Irons Pub H... Irons on Public Houses [*A publication*] (DLA)
Irons Pub H... Irons on Public Houses (journ.) (SAUS)
Iron Steel Ind... Iron and Steel Industry (journ.) (SAUS)
Iron Steel Inst Carnegie Scholarship Mem... Iron and Steel Institute. Carnegie Scholarship Memoirs (journ.) (SAUS)
Iron Tr R...... Iron Trade Review (journ.) (SAUS)
IRON-VE...... International Rice Observational Nursery-Very Early (SAUO)
IRoo............ Roodhouse Public Library, Roodhouse, IL [*Library symbol*] [*Library of Congress*] (LCLS)
IROP........... Imagery Requirements Objectives Plan (MCD)
IROP........... Infrared Optical Intelligence (MCD)
IROPC......... Inter-Range Operations Planning Group (SAUO)
IROPCO....... Iranian Offshore Petroleum Co. (SAUS)

IROPG......... Inter-Range Operations Planning Group [*White Sands Missile Range*]
IRoPpE......... Page Park Center Elementary School, Rockford, IL [*Library symbol*] [*Library of Congress*] (LCLS)
IROQ........... Iroquois Bancorp [*NASDAQ symbol*] (TTSB)
IROQ........... Iroquois Bancorp, Inc. [*NASDAQ symbol*] (SAG)
IROQBRD..... Iroquois Brands Ltd. (SAUO)
Iroquoi......... Iroquois Bancorp, Inc. [*Associated Press*] (SAG)
IroquoisB..... Iroquios Bancorp [*Associated Press*] (SAG)
IROR........... Improppved Range-Only Radar (SAUS)
IROR........... Improved Range-Only RADAR (MCD)
IROR........... Incremental Rate of Return (SAUS)
IROR........... Inspection, Repair, Overhaul, and Rebuild
IROR........... Interest Rate of Return [*Finance*]
IROR........... Internal Rate of Return [*Telecommunications*] (TEL)
IRoR........... Rockford Newspapers, Inc., Rockford, IL [*Library symbol*] [*Library of Congress*] (LCLS)
IRoRC......... Teacher Resource Center, Rockford, IL [*Library symbol*] [*Library of Congress*] (LCLS)
IRoRgE........ Rolling Green Elementary School, Rockford, IL [*Library symbol*] [*Library of Congress*] (LCLS)
IRoRrE......... Rock River Elementary School, Rockford, IL [*Library symbol*] [*Library of Congress*] (LCLS)
IRoRvE......... Riverdahl Elementary School, Rockford, IL [*Library symbol*] [*Library of Congress*] (LCLS)
IROS........... Improved Reliability Operational System (MCD)
IROS........... Increased Reliability Operational System (SAUS)
IROS........... Increase Reliability of Operational Systems (AFM)
IROS........... Infra-Red Omnidirectional Sensor (SAUS)
IROS........... Infrared Operational Satellite (NOAA)
IROS........... Instant Response Ordering System [*Teleordering system*] [*Information service or system*] (IID)
IROS........... Ipsilateral Routing of Signal
Iros............ Iranian Oil Service (SAUO)
IRoSA.......... Sundstrand Aviation, Engineering Library, Rockford, IL [*Library symbol*] [*Library of Congress*] (LCLS)
IROSB.......... Inactive Reserve Officer Status Branch [*BUPERS*]
IRoScE......... Spring Creek Elementary School, Rockford, IL [*Library symbol*] [*Library of Congress*] (LCLS)
IRoSH......... Swedish-American Hospital, Rockford, IL [*Library symbol*] [*Library of Congress*] (LCLS)
IroStA.......... Saint Anthony Hospital, Rockford (SAUS)
IRoStA......... Saint Anthony Hospital, Rockford, IL [*Library symbol*] [*Library of Congress*] (LCLS)
IRoStE......... Stiles Elementary School, Rockford, Il [*Library symbol*] [*Library of Congress*] (LCLS)
IRoStT......... Saint Thomas High School, Rockford, IL [*Library symbol*] [*Library of Congress*] (LCLS)
IRoSuE......... Summerdale Elementary School, Rockford, IL [*Library symbol*] [*Library of Congress*] (LCLS)
IRoSvE......... Sky View Center Elementary School, Rockford, IL [*Library symbol*] [*Library of Congress*] (LCLS)
IROT........... Information Read-Out Time (SAUS)
IROT........... Infrared on Target
IRoTE.......... Thompson Elementary School, Rockford, IL [*Library symbol*] [*Library of Congress*] (LCLS)
IR Oudh....... Indian Rulings, Oudh Series [*A publication*] (DLA)
IR Oudh....... Indian Rulings, Oudh Series (journ.) (SAUS)
IRoVC.......... Rockford Area Vocational Center, Rockford, IL [*Library symbol*] [*Library of Congress*] (LCLS)
IRoVE........... Vandercook Elementary School, Rockford, IL [*Library symbol*] [*Library of Congress*] (LCLS)
IRoWaE........ Walker Elementary School, Rockford, IL [*Library symbol*] [*Library of Congress*] (LCLS)
IRoWC......... Washington Center, Rockford, IL [*Library symbol*] [*Library of Congress*] (LCLS)
IRoWeE........ Welsh Elementary School, Rockford, IL [*Library symbol*] [*Library of Congress*] (LCLS)
IRoWH......... West High School, Rockford, IL [*Library symbol*] [*Library of Congress*] (LCLS)
IRoWhE........ Whitehead Elementary School, Rockford, IL [*Library symbol*] [*Library of Congress*] (LCLS)
IRoWM......... Winnebago County Medical Society, Rockford, IL [*Library symbol*] [*Library of Congress*] (LCLS)
IRoWMS....... Wilson Middle School, Rockford, IL [*Library symbol*] [*Library of Congress*] (LCLS)
IRoWsE........ White Swan Elementary School, Rockford, IL [*Library symbol*] [*Library of Congress*] (LCLS)
IRoWvE........ West View Elementary School, Rockford, IL [*Library symbol*] [*Library of Congress*] (LCLS)
Irox............. Roxana Public Library (SAUS)
IRox............ Roxana Public Library, Roxana, IL [*Library symbol*] [*Library of Congress*] (LCLS)
IRoxCU........ Roxana Community Unit 1, Roxana, IL [*Library symbol*] [*Library of Congress*] (LCLS)
IR-P............ Ice on Runway-Patch (SAUS)
IRP............. Ice on Runway - Patchy [*Aviation*]
IRP............. Iceon Runway-Patchy (SAUS)
IRP............. Image Retaining Panel (SAUS)
IRP............. Immunoglobulin Reference Preparation [*Clinical chemistry*]
IRP............. Immunoreactive Peptides [*Biochemistry*]
IRP............. Immunoreactive Plasma [*Immunochemistry*] (DMAA)
IRP............. Immunoreactive Proinsulin [*Immunochemistry*]
IRP............. Improved Radar Program (ACAE)
IRP............. Improved Replenishment-at-Sea Program (MCD)
IRP............. Improved Replenishment Program (SAUO)
IRP............. Income Recovery Program (SAUO)
IRP............. Incus Replacement Prosthesis [*Medicine*] (DMAA)
IRP............. Independent Routing Processor [*Telecommunications*] (ACRL)
IRP............. Indianapolis Raceway Park [*Auto racing venue*]
IRP............. Individualized Reading Program [*Education*]
IRP............. Individual Reinforcement Plan (SAUS)
IRP............. Individual Responsibility Program [*Medicine*] (DHSM)
IRP............. Individual Retention Plan
IRP............. Indrail Pass [*Indian Railway*] (TIR)
IRP............. Industrial Readiness Planning [*Military*] (NG)
IRP............. Industry Recognition Program (MCD)
IRP............. Industry Resource Protection (SAUO)
IRP............. Inertial Reference Package (MCD)
IRP............. Information Reporting Program [*IRS*] (EGAO)
IRP............. Information Resources Press [*Washington, DC*]
IRP............. Information Return Program [*IRS*]
IRP............. Information Returns Processing [*Computer science*]
IRP............. Infrared Photography (SAUS)
IRP............. Infrared Preamplifier
IRP............. Infrared Probe (ACAE)
IRP............. Infrared Projector (MCD)
IRP............. Infrared Radiation Profile
IRP............. Infrared Responsive Phosphor
IRP............. Inhibitor of Radical Processes (STED)
IRP............. Initial Receiving Point
IRP............. Installation Restoration Program [*Army*] (RDA)
IRP............. Institute for Research on Poverty [*University of Wisconsin - Madison*] [*Research center*] (RCD)
IRP............. Institute for Retired Professionals (EA)
IRP............. Institute of Psychological Research (SAUO)
IRP............. Institutional Revolutionary Party [*Mexico*] [*Political party*]
IRP............. Instructional Resource Package (ACII)
IRP............. Insulin-Releasing Polypeptide [*Medicine*] (DMAA)
IRP............. Integrated Reference Package (SAUS)
IRP............. Integrated Resource Planning (ADWA)
IRP............. Intelligence Report Plan (NATG)
IRP............. Intelligence Research Paper (SAUO)
IRP............. Interdivisional Record Practice (SAUS)
IRP............. Interest Rate Parity
IRP............. Interference Reporting Point (NATG)
IRP............. Interference Reporting Points (SAUO)
IRP............. Intermediary Relending Program
IRP............. Intermediate Rated Power (MCD)
IRP............. Intermediate Related Power
IRP............. Intermediate Rotating Plug (NRCH)
IRP............. Internal Reflection Plate
IRP............. Internal Renection Plate (SAUS)
IRP............. International Petroleum Corp. [*Vancouver Stock Exchange symbol*] [*Toronto Stock Exchange symbol*]
IRP............. International Reference Preparation [*World Health Organization*]
IRP............. International Registered Profile (TELE)
IRP............. International Research Program (SAUS)
IRP............. International Rostrum of Young Performers [*See also TIJE*] (EAIO)
IRP............. International Routing Plan [*Telecommunications*] (TEL)
IRP............. Interrupt Processor (IAA)
IRP............. Interstitial Radiation Pneumonitis [*Medicine*] (DMAA)
IRP............. Inventory and Requirements Planning (MHDI)
IRP............. Irish Pound (SAUS)
IRP............. Iron Regulatory Protein [*Biochemistry*]
IRP............. Islahat Refah Partisi [*Reformation and Welfare Party*] [*Turkish Cypriot*] (PPE)
IRP............. Islamic Renaissance Party [*Commonwealth of Independent States*] (ECON)
IRP............. Islamic Republican Party [*Iran*] [*Political party*] (PPW)
IRP............. Payam (Air Center Service) [*Iran*] [*FAA designator*] (FAAC)
IRp............. Richton Park Library District, Richton Park, IL [*Library symbol*] [*Library of Congress*] (LCLS)
IRPA........... Institut de Recherche sur le Profil d'Apprentissage [*Canada*]
IRPA........... International Racing Press Association (SAUO)
IRPA........... International Radiation Protection Association [*Vienna, Austria*] (EAIO)
IRPA........... International Retinitis Pigmentosa Association (SAUO)
IRPA........... Irrigation Pump Administration (SAUO)
IRPAS......... Infrared Photoacoustic Spectroscopy (SAUS)
IR Pat.......... Indian Rulings, Patna Series [*A publication*] (DLA)
IR Pat.......... Indian Rulings, Patna Series (journ.) (SAUS)
IRPBDS........ Infrared Photothermal Beam Deflection Spectroscopy (SAUS)
IRPC........... Indian Rulings, Privy Council [*1929-47*] [*A publication*] (DLA)
IRPC........... Indirect Reading Pocket Chamber
IRPC........... Industrial Relations Policy Committee [*General Council of British Shipping*] (DS)
IRPC........... Integrated Resource Planning Committee (SAUO)
IRPCS......... International Regulations for Preventing Collisions at Sea [*Nautical term*] (NTA)
IRPD........... Industrial Relations and Personnel Development [*A publication*]
IR-PERS-REC... Industrial Relations Personnel Record [*Military*] (DNAB)
IR-PERS-REC... Industrial Relations Personnel Records (SAUO)
IR Pesh........ Indian Rulings, Peshawar Series [*1933-47*] [*A publication*] (DLA)
IR Peshawar... Indian Rulings, Peshawar Series [*1933-47*] [*A publication*] (DLA)
Ir Pet SJ...... Irish Petty Sessions Journal [*A publication*] (DLA)
Ir Pet SJ...... Irish Petty Sessions Journal (journ.) (SAUS)
IRPF........... Independent Racing Pigeon Federation [*Australia*]
IRPFC......... International Ray Price Fan Club (EA)
IRPG........... Interactive Report Generator (SAUS)
IRPG........... Iranian Research and Publication Group

IRPGN......... Idiopathic Rapidly Progressive Glomerulonephritis [*Medicine*] (MELL)
IRPHD......... International Review of Physiology (journ.) (SAUS)
IRPI............ Icelandic Radiation Protection Institute (SAUO)
IRPI............ Individual Rod Position Indicator [*Nuclear energy*] (NRCH)
IRPIA.......... Intelligence Information Report Photo Index [*Military*] (MCD)
IRPIMS........ IRP Information Management System (SAUO)
IRPL............ Index to Religious Periodical Literature [*Database*]
IRPL............ Industrial Robot Programming Language (SAUS)
IRPL............ Interim Repair Parts List
IRPL............ Interservice Radio Propagation Laboratory (MCD)
IRPM........... Individual Risk Premium Modification [*Insurance*]
IRPM........... Infrared Physical Measurement
IRPM........... Infrared Physical Measurement Research (SAUS)
IRPMR......... Information Resources Procurement and Management Review (AAGC)
IRPOD......... Individual Repair Parts Ordering Data [*Program*] [*DoD*]
IRPOS.......... Interdisciplinary Research Relevant to Problems of Our Society [*Later, RANN*] [*National Science Foundation*]
IRPP............ Industrial Readiness Planning Program
IRPP............ Infrared Pointer Package
IRPP............ Institute for Research on Public Policy [*Canada*]
IRPP............ International Petroleum Corp. [*NASDAQ symbol*] (SAG)
IRPPF.......... Intl Petroleum [*NASDAQ symbol*] (TTSB)
IRPPS.......... Information Resource Planning and Projection System Survey (SAUO)
IR Pr C........ Indian Rulings, Privy Council [*1929-47*] [*A publication*] (DLA)
IRPRD......... In-Plant Reproductions (journ.) (SAUS)
IRPRI........... International Relations and Peace Research Institute [*Guatemala*] (EAIO)
IRPRL.......... Initial Repair Parts Requirements List (MCD)
IRPS............ Indian Railway Personnel Services [*Indian Railway*] (TIR)
IRPS............ Individual Resource Protection Sensor
IRPS............ Individual Resource Protection System (SAUS)
IRPS............ Institute for Research in Public Safety [*Indiana University*] [*Research center*] (RCD)
IRPS............ Institute of Reconstructive Plastic Surgery [*New York University*] [*Research center*] (RCD)
IRPS............ International Relations and Pacific Studies (SAUS)
IRPS............ International Reliability Physics Symposium (SAUS)
IRPS............ International Religious Press Service (SAUO)
IRPS............ International Review of Publications in Sociology [*Sociological Abstracts, Inc.*] [*Information service or system*] (CRD)
IRPSL.......... Interim Repair Parts Support List (ACAE)
IRPT............ Inland Rivers, Ports and Terminals (SAUS)
IRPT............ International Rice Testing Program (SAUO)
IRPT............ Islamic Renaissance Party of Tajikistan [*Political party*] (PSAP)
IRPTC.......... International Register of Potentially Toxic Chemicals [*United Nations Environment Program*] [*Geneva, Switzerland*]
IRPTC.......... International Registry for Potentially Toxic Chemicals (SAUS)
IRPWA......... Irrigation and Power (journ.) (SAUS)
IRQ............. Faraz Qeshm Airlines [*Iran*] [*FAA designator*] (FAAC)
IRQ............. Institute of Research Quebec (SAUO)
IRQ............. Intermediate Review Questionnaire (SAUO)
IRQ............. Interpersonal Relations Questionnaire [*Personality development test*] [*Psychology*]
IRQ............. Interrupt Request [*Computer science*]
IRQ............. Interrupt Request Line [*Computer science*]
IRQ............. Interrupt-Request Line (SAUS)
IRQ............. Interrupt Request Query (SAUS)
IRQ............. Intimate Relationship Questionnaire
IRQ............. Iraq [*ANSI three-letter standard code*] (CNC)
Irq.............. Iraq (MILB)
IRQ............. Rose-Hulman Institute of Technology Library, Terre Haute, IN [*OCLC symbol*] (OCLC)
IRQC........... Infrared Quantum Counter
IRQPC......... International Rubber Quality and Packing Conferences (SAUO)
IRQR........... Information Requirement [*Military*]
IRR............. Immediate Ready Reserve [*Army*]
IRR............. Improved Rearming Rates [*Military*] (NG)
IRR............. Incidence Rate Ratio [*Mathematics*]
IRR............. Indian Reservation Roads System [*Bureau of Indian Affairs*]
IRR............. Indian River Resources, Inc. [*Vancouver Stock Exchange symbol*]
IRR............. Individual Ready Reserve [*Army*]
IRR............. Individual Ready Reservist (SAUS)
IRR............. Individual Retirement Record [*Air Force*] (AFM)
IRR............. Industrial Retaining Ring Co.
IRR............. Information Reduction Research [*Information service or system*] (IID)
IRR............. Information Release Record (SAUO)
IRR............. Information Release Request (SAUO)
IRR............. Information Resource Repository
IRR............. Infrared Radiometer
IRR............. Infrared Rays (SAUS)
IRR............. Infrared Receiver
IRR............. Initial Rate of Return [*Finance*] (MCD)
IRR............. Initial Reliability Review
IRR............. Initial Requirements Review (ACAE)
IRR............. Initial Response Resources (SAUO)
IRR............. Inspection Rejection Report [*NASA*] (KSC)
IRR............. Installation and Removal Record [*NASA*] (KSC)
IRR............. Institute for Reactor Research [*Switzerland*]
IRR............. Institute for Rehabilitation and Research [*Baylor College of Medicine*] [*Research center*] (RCD)
IRR............. Institute for Risk Research [*University of Waterloo*] [*Canada*] [*Research center*] (RCD)
IRR............. Institute of Race Relations [*British*] (EAIO)
IRR............. Institute of Resource Recovery (GNE)
IRR............. Institute of Rubber Research (MCD)
IRR............. Instrumentation Revision Record (IAA)
IRR............. Integral Rocket Ramjet [*Navy*]
IRR............. Integrated Radio Room (MCD)
IRR............. Integrated Readiness Report (COE)
IRR............. Integrated Reed Relay (SAUS)
IRR............. Integrated Requirements Review (SAUS)
IRR............. Integration Readiness Review (SAUS)
IRR............. Intelligence and Radar Reporting Line (SAUO)
IRR............. Intelligence RADAR Reporting
IRR............. Interest Rate Return (SAUS)
IRR............. Interest Rate Risk
IRR............. Interface Requirements Review (SSD)
IRR............. Interimpurity Radiative Recombination (SAUS)
IRR............. Interim Release Request (MCD)
IRR............. Interim Requirements Review (ACAE)
IRR............. Internal Rate of Return [*Finance*]
IRR............. Internal Revenue Looseleaf Regulations System
IRR............. International Rate of Return [*Finance*]
IRR............. International Revenue Record [*New York City*] [*A publication*] (DLA)
IRR............. Interrupt Request Register (SAUS)
IRR............. Interrupt Return Register
IRR............. Intrarenal Reflux [*Medicine*] (AAMN)
IRR............. Inventory Reporting Requirement System (SAUO)
Ir R............. Irish Law Reports [*A publication*] (DLA)
Ir R............. Irish Review (journ.) (SAUS)
IRR............. Irish Royal Rifles [*Military*] [*British*] (ROG)
IRR............. Iron Range Research Center, Chisholm, MN [*OCLC symbol*] (OCLC)
Irr.............. Irradiation [*Medicine*] (EDAA)
irr............... Irradiation
IRR............. Irredeemable [*Banking*]
IRR............. Irregular (WGA)
IRR............. Irreversible (SAUS)
irr............... Irrigate [*or Irrigated*] (DAVI)
IRR............. Irrigation [*Type of water project*]
IRR............. Irritant
IRR............. Irritation (DAVI)
Irr.............. Irritation [*Medicine*] (EDAA)
IRR............. Israeli Research Reactor
IRR............. Israel Research Reactor (SAUO)
IRR............. Tara Air Line [*Iran*] [*FAA designator*] (FAAC)
IRRA........... Indian Railways Regulatory Authority [*Indian Railway*] (TIR)
IRRA........... Industrial Relations Reform Act [*Australia*]
IRRA........... Industrial Relations Research Association (EA)
IRRA........... Institute for Rubber Research in Africa (SAUS)
IRRA........... International Routing and Reporting Activity (DNAB)
IRRA........... International Routing Reporting Authority (SAUO)
IRRA........... International Rubber Regulation Agreement (SAUS)
IR-RAD........ Infrared Radiometer (SAUS)
IRRAD......... Infrared Range and Detection
IRRAD......... Infrared Ranging and Detecting (or Detection) (SAUS)
IRRADN....... Irradiation
IR Ran......... Indian Rulings, Rangoon Series [*A publication*] (DLA)
IR Ran......... Indian Rulings, Rangoon Series (journ.) (SAUS)
IRR & L........ Irish Reports, Registry and Land Cases [*A publication*] (DLA)
IR-RAP......... Infra-Red/Radar Augmented Projectile (SAUS)
IRRAPST....... Individual Ready Reserve - Alternative Preassignment System Test (MCD)
IRRAS.......... Infrared Reflection Absorption Spectroscopy [*Also, IRAS, RAIR, RAIRS, RAIS*]
IRRB........... Infrastructure Requirements Review Board (SAUS)
IRRB........... Infrastructure Requirements Revue Board (SAUS)
IRRB........... International Rubber Research Board
IRRC........... Illinois Research and Reference Center (SAUO)
IRRC........... International Relief and Rescue Committee [*Post-World War II*]
IRRC........... International Rescue and Relief Committee (SAUO)
IRRC........... International Rubber Regulation Committee [*World War II*]
IRRC........... Interstate Revenue Research Center (SAUO)
IRRC........... Investor Responsibility Research Center (EA)
IRRC........... Iowa Railroad [*Federal Railroad Administration identification code*]
Ir RC........... Irish Regiment of Canada (SAUO)
Ir R Ch......... Irish Chancery Reports [*A publication*] (DLA)
Ir RCL.......... Irish Reports, Common Law Series [*A publication*] (DLA)
IRRCS.......... Institute for Regional, Rural, and Community Studies [*Western Illinois University*] [*Research center*] (RCD)
IRRD........... Institute for Research of Rheumatic Diseases [*Defunct*] (EA)
IRRD........... International Raod Research Documentation (NITA)
IRRDB......... International Rubber Research and Development Board [*Brickendonbury, Hertford, England*] (EAIO)
IRRDB......... International Rubber Research and Development Bureau (SAUO)
IRRD System... International Road Research Documentation System (SAUS)
Irred........... Irredeemable (EBF)
IRRED......... Irredeemable (ROG)
IRREG......... Irregular (KSC)
irreg........... Irregular (WDMC)
Irreg........... Irregular Light [*Navigation signal*]
irreg........... Irregularly (WDMC)
IR Rep......... Reports of Inland Revenue Commissioners [*A publication*] (DLA)
Ir Rep Ch...... Irish Chancery Reports [*A publication*] (DLA)
Ir Rep CL...... Irish Reports, Common Law Series [*A publication*] (DLA)
Ir Rep Eq...... Irish Reports, Equity Series [*A publication*] (DLA)
Ir Rep NS...... Irish Common Law Reports, New Series [*A publication*] (DLA)
Irreprod....... Irreproducible (SAUS)
Ir Rep VR..... Irish Reports, Verbatim Reprint [*A publication*] (DLA)

Ir R Eq......... Irish Reports, Equity Series [*A publication*] (DLA)
irres.......... irrespective (SAUS)
IR Research Repts... IR Research Reports (journ.) (SAUS)
Irrev............ Irrevocable (EBF)
IRREV.......... Irrevocable
IRRF........... Institut pour la Repression des Ravageurs Forestiers [*Forest Pest Management Institute*] [*Canada*]
irrg.............. Irrigate [*Medicine*] (EDAA)
IRRG........... Irrigation
IRRGTN........ Irrigation
irrgty........... irregularity (SAUS)
irrgy............ irregularly (SAUS)
IRRI............ Industrial Relations Research Institute [*University of Wisconsin - Madison*] [*Research center*] (RCD)
IRRI............ Interagency Rehabilitation Research Information System [*National Institute on Disability and Rehabilitation Research*] [*Washington, DC*] [*Information service or system*] (IID)
IRRI............ International Rice Research Institute [*Philippines*]
IRRI-BN....... International Rice Research Institute-Blast Nursery (SAUO)
IRRIC........... International Rice Research Information Center (SAUS)
IRRICAB....... Current Annotated Bibliography of Irrigation [*Bet Dagan, Israel*] [*A publication*]
irrig............ Irrigate [*Medicine*] (EDAA)
IRRIG.......... Irrigate
Irrig............ Irrigation [*Medicine*] (AMHC)
Irrig Age....... Irrigation Age (journ.) (SAUS)
Irrig&Power Abstr... Irrigation and Power Abstracts (journ.) (SAUS)
Irrig Eng Maint... Irrigation Engineering and Maintenance (journ.) (SAUS)
Irrig Farmer... Irrigation Farmer (journ.) (SAUS)
Irrig Fmr...... Irrigation Farmer (journ.) (SAUS)
Irrig J......... Irrigation Journal (journ.) (SAUS)
Irrig Power... Irrigation and Power (journ.) (SAUS)
Irrig Sci....... Irrigation Science (journ.) (SAUS)
Irrig Winter Wheat Tech Publ... Irrigated Winter Wheat. Technical Publication (journ.) (SAUS)
IRRIS........... International Rehabilitation Research Information System [*National Institute of Handicapped Research*] [*Database*]
IRRL............ Information Retrieval Research Laboratory [*University of Illinois*] [*Urbana*] [*Information service or system*] (IID)
IRRM........... Information Requested in Above Referenced Message [*Army*] (AABC)
IRRMA......... Institut Romand de Recherche Numerique en Physique des Materiaux
IRRMP......... Information Reports Requirement Management Program (SAUO)
IRRMP......... Infrared RADAR Measurement Program
IRRN............ Illinois Research and Reference Center Libraries
IRRN............ Illinois Research and Reference Network (SAUS)
IRRN............ International Rice Research Notes (SAUO)
IRR/N........... Newsletter. The Institute of Race Relations. London (SAUS)
Irr N............ Tasmanian Irregular Notes [*A publication*]
IRR News.... Individual Rights and Responsibilities Newsletter (journ.) (SAUS)
IRR Newsl... Individual Rights and Responsibilities Newsletter [*A publication*] (DLA)
IRRO........... Indian Reprographics Rights Organization
IRRO........... Information Resource for the Release of Organisms into the Environment (SAUO)
IRROLA........ Inflatable Radar-Reflective Optical Location Aid (SAUS)
IRRP........... Icefield Ranges Research Project
IRRP........... Improved Rearming Rate Plan (SAUO)
IRRP........... Improved Rearming Rate Program [*Military*] (NVT)
IRRP........... Improved Rearming Rate Project (SAUO)
IRRP........... Improved Rearming Rates Project (SAUS)
IRRP........... Inter-domain Routing Protocol (SAUS)
IRRPOS........ Interdisciplinary Research Relevant to Problems of Our Society [*Later, RANN*] [*National Science Foundation*]
IRRR........... Industrial Relations Review and Report [*A publication*]
IRRR........... Interest Rate Reduction Refinancing [*Veterans Administration*]
Ir R Reg & L... Irish Reports, Registry and Land Cases [*A publication*] (DLA)
Ir R Reg App... Irish Reports, Registration Appeals [*1868-76*] [*A publication*] (DLA)
IRRS........... Individual Ready Reserve System [*Military*]
IRRS........... Infrared Reconnaissance Set
IRRS........... Infrared Reconnaissance System (MCD)
IRRS........... Infrared Reflection Spectroscopy
IRRS........... International Rail Road Systems [*Federal Railroad Administration identification code*]
IRRS........... Irish Railway Record Society
IRRSA8........ Indian Council of Agricultural Research. Review Series (journ.) (SAUS)
IRRSAM....... Integral Rocket Ramjet Surface-to-Air Missile (MCD)
IRRSSM....... Integral Rocket Ramjet Surface-to-Surface Missile (MCD)
IRRSWON.... International Rainfed Rice Shallow Water Observational Nursery (SAUO)
IRRSWON-E... International Rainfed Rice Shallow Water Observational Nursery-Early (SAUO)
IRRSWON-M... International Rainfed Rice Shallow Water Observational Nursery-Medium (SAUO)
IRRSWYN-E... International Rainfed Rice Shallow Water Yield Nursery-Early (SAUO)
IRRSWYN-M... International Rainfed Rice Shallow Water Yield Nursery-Medium (SAUO)
IRRT........... Institution of Rail and Rapid Transit (SAUS)
IRRT........... International Radio and Television Society (SAUO)
IRRT........... International Relations Round Table [*American Library Association*]
IRRTI.......... Infrared Reconnaissance Target Imagery (ACAE)
IRRTI.......... Infrared Reconnaissance Target Imagery System (SAUO)
IRRTS.......... Infrared Resolution Target System (MCD)
IRRTTM....... Integral Rocket Ramjet Torpedo Tube Missile (MCD)
IRRU........... Industrial Relations Research Unit (SAUO)
IRRV........... Institute of Revenues, Rating, and Valuation [*British*]
IRS............. Identification and Reference Sheets (MCD)
IRS............. Illinois Radiological Society (SAUO)
IRS............. Immunoreactive Secretin [*Endocrinology*]
IRS............. Immunoreactive Somatostatin [*Endocrinology*]
IRS............. Improved RADAR Simulation (DWSG)
IRS............. Improved Radar Simulator (SAUS)
IRS............. Impurity Removal System
IRS............. Inactive Reserve Section [*Military*]
IRS............. Inboard Rotating Shield
IRS............. Incident Reporting System [*IAEA*] (NUCP)
IRS............. Income Reduction Service (SAUO)
IRS............. Incremental Range Summary
IRS............. Independent Rear Suspension [*Automotive engineering*]
Irs............. Independent Rear Suspension
IRS............. Independent Research Service [*Defunct*]
IRS............. Indian earth Research Satellite (SAUS)
IRS............. Indian Railway Standards (SAUO)
IRS............. Indian Remote-Sensing Satellite
IRS............. Indian Resources Satellite (SAUS)
IRS............. Indirect Representative Supplement [*British*]
IRS............. Induction and Recruiting Station [*Marine Corps*]
IRS............. Industrial Relations Section [*Princeton University*] [*Research center*] (RCD)
IRS............. Industrial Relations Services [*Eclipse Group Ltd.*] [*British*] (ECON)
IRS............. Industrial Rubber Sales (SAUS)
IRS............. Industry-Research-Services (SAUO)
IRS............. Ineligible Reserve Section
IRS............. Inertial Reference Sensor
IRS............. Inertial Reference System [*Aviation*]
IRS............. Inertial Retical System
IRS............. Infant Rating Scale [*Child development test*]
IRS............. Infinitely Rigid System [*Engineering*] (OA)
IRS............. Inflatable Restraint System [*Automotive engineering*]
IRS............. Informal Routing Slip
IRS............. Information Receiving Station (SAUS)
IRS............. Information Recovery [*or Retrieval*] System [*or Subsystem*]
IRS............. Information Referral Service (SAUS)
IRS............. Information Research Services [*Information service or system*] (IID)
IRS............. Information Resources Specialists [*Information service or system*] (IID)
IRS............. Information Retrieval Service [*European Space Agency*] (IID)
IRS............. Information Retrieval Service [*Memphis State University Libraries*] (OLDSS)
IRS............. Information Retrieval Subsystem (SAUS)
IRS............. Information Retrieval System (OICC)
IRS............. Infrared RADAR Suppressor (MCD)
IRS............. Infrared Reconnaissance Set (MCD)
IRS............. Infrared Reflective Spectra
IRS............. Infrared Reflow-Solderable (SAUS)
IRS............. Infra-Red Scanner (SAUS)
IRS............. Infra Red Soldering (SAUS)
IRS............. Infrared Soldering
IRS............. Infrared Source
IRS............. Infrared Spectrometer [*or Spectroscopy*]
IRS............. Infrared Spectrophotometry (PALA)
IRS............. Infrared Spectrum (SAUS)
IRS............. Infrared Star (BARN)
IRS............. Initial Readiness Site (SAUS)
IRS............. Inorganic Resin System [*Fire-resistant cement*]
IRS............. Input Read Submodule
IRS............. Inquiry and Reporting System
IRS............. Insertion Reference signal (SAUS)
IRS............. Inspection Record Sheet
IRS............. Inspection Report Sheets (SAUO)
IRS............. Inspector of Radio Services [*Military*] (IAA)
IRS............. Installation Readiness System [*Army*]
IRS............. Instantaneous Response Spectra (SAUS)
IRS............. Institute for Industrial Research and Standards (SAUO)
IRS............. Institute of Religious Studies [*Australia*]
IRS............. Instructional Review System
IRS............. Instrumentation RADAR Set
IRS............. Instrumentation Radar System (SAUO)
IRS............. Instrument Removal System (SAUS)
IRS............. Instrument Retrieval System [*Containers*] [*Medicine*] (DAVI)
IRS............. Insulated Return System (SAUS)
IRS............. Insulin Receptor Species [*Medicine*] (DMAA)
IRS............. Insulin Receptor Substrate [*Biochemistry*]
IRS............. Insurance Sales (journ.) (SAUS)
IRS............. Intact Rock Strength [*Mining*]
IRS............. Integrated Radiator System (SAUS)
IRS............. Integrated Rate System
IRS............. Integrated Recovery Scheduling (SAUS)
IRS............. Integrated Reporting System (SAUO)
IRS............. Integrated Retrieval System (SAUS)
IRS............. Integrated Review Schedule [*Department of Health and Human Services*] (GFGA)
IRS............. Integration Review Section [*Social Security Administration*]
IRS............. Intelligence Research Specialist [*Military*] (MCD)
IRS............. Intelligible Reserve Section (SAUO)
IRS............. Interactive Retrieval Software (SAUO)
IRS............. Interchange Record Separator [*Computer science*] (BUR)

IRS Interdivisional Records Standard (SAUS)
IRS Interface Requirements Document [*DoD*]
IRS Interface Requirements Specification (MCD)
IRS Interferon Response Sequence [*Genetics*]
IRS Interformation Retrieval System (SAUS)
IRS Intergovernmental Relations Staff (SAUO)
IRS Intergroup Rhabdomyosarcoma Study [*Oncology*]
IRS Intermedia Ranking Staff (COE)
IRS Intermediate Reference Structure
IRS Intermediate Reference System (SAUO)
IRS Internal Reflection Spectroscopy
IRS Internal Revenue Service [*Department of the Treasury*] [*Washington, DC*]
IRS Internal Revenue Service Library, Washington, DC [*OCLC symbol*] (OCLC)
IRS Internationally Recruited Staff (SAUO)
IRS International Radio Science (SAUS)
IRS International Radio Silence
IRS International Records Syndicate, Inc.
IRS International Recruiting Service (SAUO)
IRS International Reference Unit (SAUS)
IRS International Referral Service (SAUO)
IRS International Referral System [*United Nations Environment Programme*]
IRS International Repeater Station [*Telecommunications*] (TEL)
IRS International Research Service (SAUO)
IRS International Reservation Switzerland (SAUO)
IRS International Rhinologic Society (EA)
IRS International Rorschach Society [*Strasbourg, France*] (EA)
IRS Internetwork Routing Service [*Telecommunications*] (OSI)
IRS Interpersonal Relationship Scale (EDAC)
IRS Interrecord Separator (SAUS)
IRS Interspersed Repetitive Sequence [*Genetics*]
IRS Inverse Raman Scattering [*Spectroscopy*]
IRS Investment Removal Salt (SAUS)
IRS Investor Relations Society (COBU)
IRS Iodine Removal System [*Nuclear energy*] (NRCH)
IRS Ionospheric Radio Signal
IRS Iran Service (journ.) (SAUS)
IRS Irish Standard (IAA)
IRS Irish Standards Institute (SAUO)
IRS Irrigation Research Station (SAUO)
IRS IRSA Inversiones y Rep GDS [*NYSE symbol*] (TTSB)
IRS IRSA Inversions y Representaciones SA [*NYSE symbol*] (SAG)
IRS Isentification and Reference Sheets (SAUS)
IRS Isoleucyl-tRNA Synthetase [*An enzyme*]
IRS Isotope Radiography System
IRS Isotope Removal Service (IEEE)
IRS Isotope Removal System (SAUS)
IRS Item Reduction Studies (MSA)
IRS Sturgis, MI [*Location identifier*] [*FAA*] (FAAL)
IRS Transavia Ltd. [*Romania*] [*FAA designator*] (FAAC)
IRSA Idiopathic Refractory Sideroblastic Anemia [*Medicine*] (MAE)
IRSA Immigration and Refugee Services of America (EA)
IRSA Improved Radiator Standards Association (EA)
IRSA Independent Road Service Association (EA)
IRSA Industrial Radiographic Service Association (SAUO)
IRSA International Racquet Sports Association [*Later, IRSAAQC*] (EA)
IRSA International Radiator Standards Association (SAUO)
IRSA International Rett Syndrome Association (EA)
IRSA International Rural Sociological Association (SAUO)
IRSA International Rural Sociology Association (EA)
IRSA Iodinated Rat Serum Albumin (DMAA)
IRSA Irish Research Scientists Association
IRSA IRSA Inversiones y Representaciones SA [*Associated Press*] (SAG)
IRSAAQC IRSA [*International Racquet Sports Association*], the Association of Quality Clubs (EA)
IRSAC Institut pour la Recherche Scientifique en Afrique Centrale [*Brussels*]
IRS Alcohl Alcohol, Tobacco and Firearms Summary Statistics. US Internal Revenue Service (journ.) (SAUS)
IRS&GHL Infrared Systems and Guidance Heads laboratory (ACAE)
IRSATON International Rice Salinity and Alkalinity Tolerance Observational Nursery (SAUO)
IRSB Institute for Research in Social Behavior [*Research center*] (RCD)
IRSB Interim Retention Storage Basins (SAUS)
IRSBN International Rice Stem Borer Nursery (SAUO)
IRSC Indy Rail Car Service [*Federal Railroad Administration identification code*]
IRSC Institut de Recherches Scientifiques au Congo
IRSC Internal Revenue Service Centers
IRSC International Radium Standard Commission (SAUO)
IRSC Internet Resources for Special Children (SAUO)
IRSC Inter-Regional Subject Coverage (SAUS)
IRSC Inter-Regional Subject Coverage Scheme [*Libraries cooperative scheme*] [*British*] (NITA)
IRSCAN Infrared Scanner
IRSCC International Relief Service of Caritas Catholica [*Belgium*] (EAIO)
IRSCD2 Irrigation Science (journ.) (SAUS)
IRSCL International Research Society for Children's Literature [*Cadaujac, France*] (EA)
IRSCOT Infrared Structural Correlation Tables [*A publication*]
IRSCS Inter-Regional Subject Coverage Scheme (SAUS)
IRSD Information and Regulatory Systems Division [*Environmental Protection Agency*] (GFGA)
IRSD Information Retrieval, Storage and Dissemination (SAUS)
IRSD Infra-Red Detection System (SAUS)
IRSDA Inland Revenue Stamping Department Association (SAUO)
IRSDL Information Resource Specification and Design Language (SAUS)
IRSE Indian Railway Service of Engineers [*Indian Railway*] (TIR)
IRSE Infrared System Engineering (SAUS)
IRSE Infrared Systems Engineering
IRSE Institution of Railway Signal Engineers [*British*]
IRSE International Reactor Safety Evaluation (SAUS)
IRSEE Indian Railway Service of Electrical Engineers [*Indian Railway*] (TIR)
IRSEM Institute for Social Re-integration of Ex-Combatants (SAUO)
IRSEN International Rehabilitation - Special Education Network (SAUO)
IRSF Infrared Simulation Facility (ACAE)
IRSF Inland Revenue Staff Federation [*A union*] [*British*] (DCTA)
IRSF International Roller Skating Federation (EA)
IRSFC International Rayon and Synthetic Fibres Committee [*See also CIRFS*] [*Paris, France*] (EAIO)
IRSG Information Retrieval Specialist Group [*British Computer Society*] (NITA)
IRSG Infra-Red Scene Generator (SAUS)
IRSG Internationale Richard Strauss Gesellschaft [*An association*] (EAIO)
IRSG International Rubber Study Group [*London, England*] (EAIO)
IRSG Internet Research Steering Group [*Computer science*] (ACRL)
IRSGHL Infrared Systems and Guidance Heads Laboratory
IRSGON International Rice Slender Grain Observational Nursery (SAUO)
IRSH Infrared Spectral Hygrometer (PDAA)
IRSH International Review of Social History. Amsterdam (SAUO)
IRSH International Review of Social History (journ.) (SAUS)
IRSI Industrial Research and Service Institute
IRSI Infra-Red Space Interferometry Mission (SAUS)
IRSI International Radar Symposium (SAUO)
IRSI International Remote Sensing Institute (MCD)
IRSIGS Infrared Signatures (SAUO)
IR Sind Indian Rulings, Sind Series [*A publication*] (DLA)
IRSIO International Rationalization, Standardization, and Interoperability Office (SAUO)
IRSL Infra-Red Stimulated Luminscence (SAUS)
IRSL International Review of Slavic Linguistics (journ.) (SAUS)
IRSLL Image Recording System, Low Light
IRSM Immunoreactive Somatomedin [*Endocrinology*]
IRSM Incubator Refrigerator Storage Module (SAUS)
IRSM Infra-Red Surveillance Measures (SAUS)
IRSM Infrared System Manufacturing (SAUS)
IRSM Infrared Systems Manufacturing
IRSME Indian Railway Service of Mechanical Engineers [*Indian Railway*] (TIR)
IRSN Irvine Sensors [*NASDAQ symbol*] (TTSB)
IRSN Irvine Sensors Corp. [*NASDAQ symbol*] (NQ)
IRSO Information Resources Security Officer (SAUS)
IRSO Infrared Solder Oven
IRSO Institute of Road Safety Officers [*British*]
IRSO International Rope Skipping Organization
IRSP Infrared Spectrometer [*or Spectroscopy*]
IRSP Irish Republican Socialist Party [*Pairti Poblachtach Soisialach na h-Eireann*] (PPW)
IRSPECT Infrared Spectrometer [*or Spectroscopy*] (MCD)
IrSpelaeol Irish Spelaeology (journ.) (SAUS)
IRSQ Internet Reference Services Quarterly (SAUO)
IRSR Immediate Replacement Support Requirement (MCD)
IRSS Indian Railway Standard Specification (SAUO)
IRSS Indian Railway Stores Services [*Indian Railway*] (TIR)
IRSS Indian Remote Sensing Satellite (CARB)
IRSS Inertial Reference Stabilization System
IRSS Infra-Red Search & Surveillance (SAUS)
IRSS Infrared Search Sensor (ACAE)
IRSS Infrared Search Set
IRSS Infrared Search System [*Institut za Nuklearne Nauke Boris Kidric*] [*Former Yugoslavia*] [*Information service or system*] (CRD)
IRSS Infrared Search System [*Database*] [*Environmental Protection Agency*] [*Information service or system*] (CRD)
IRSS Infrared Sensor System
IRSS Infra-Red Signature Suppression (SAUS)
IRSS Infrared Smoke Simulator (MCD)
IRSS Infra-Red Suppression System (SAUS)
IRSS Infrared Surveillance Subsystem
IRSS Instant Recall Signal Storage (SAUS)
IRSS Institute for Religious and Social Studies (EA)
IRSS Institute for Research in Social Science [*University of North Carolina at Chapel Hill*] [*Research center*] (RCD)
IRSS Institute for Resource and Security Studies (EA)
IRSS Instrumentation and Range Safety Program (SAUS)
IRSS Instrumentation and Range Safety System [*NASA*] (KSC)
IRSS Integrated Range Safety System (IAA)
IRSS Intelligent Remote Station Support [*Computer science*] (ELAL)
IRSS International Rough Set Society (SAUO)
IRSSE Indian Railway Service of Signal Engineers [*Indian Railway*] (TIR)
IRSSO Infrared Search Set Operator
IRSSP Interactive Remote Sensing Software Package (SAUO)
IRSSTN International Rice Soil Stress Nursery (SAUO)
IRST Infrared Search and Track
IRST Infrared Search and Track Sensor (SAUS)
IRST Infra-Red Sensor Technology (SAUS)
IRSTA International Roller Skating Trainer Association (SAUO)
Ir Stat Irish Statutes [*A publication*] (DLA)
IrStat Irish Statutes (journ.) (SAUS)
IRSTD Infra-Red Search and Target Designation (SAUS)

IRSTD .... Infrared Search and Target Designation System (SAUS)
IRSTD .... Infrared Search and Target Destination System (SAUS)
IRSTDS .... Infrared Surveillance and Target Designation System (PDAA)
IRSTE .... Indian Railway Signal and Telecom Engineering [*Indian Railway*] (TIR)
IRSTG .... International Rubber Study Group (SAUO)
IRSTON .... International Rice Salinity Tolerance Observational Nursery (SAUO)
IRSTS .... Infrared Search and Tracking System (SAUO)
IRSTS .... Infrared Search and Track Set (ACAE)
IRSTS .... Infrared Search and Track System
IRSTS .... Infrared Search-Track System (SAUS)
Ir St Tr .... Irish State Trials (journ.) (SAUS)
Ir St Tr .... Irish State Trials (Ridgeway's) [*A publication*] (DLA)
IRSU .... International Radio Scientific Union (DEN)
IRSU .... International Religious Studies Unit [*American Topical Association*] (EA)
IRSU .... ISDN [*Integrated Services Digital Network*] Remote Subscriber Unit [*Telecommunications*]
Ir Sword ...... Irish Sword (journ.) (SAUS)
IRT .... Icing Research Tunnel [*Built at Lewis Research Center in 1944 by the National Advisory Committee for Aeronautics*]
IRT .... Image Rejection Technology [*RADAR detection*]
IRT .... Imaging Radar Technology (SAUS)
IRT .... Immunoreactive Trypsin
IRT .... Independent Receiver Tuning (SAUS)
IRT .... Independent Receive/Transmit (SAUS)
IRT .... Independent Review Team (ACAE)
IRT .... Index Return Character [*Computer science*]
IRT .... Indicating Round Technique [*British*]
IRT .... Individual Reliability Test
IRT .... Industrial Reading Test
IRT .... Infinite-Resolution Trimmer
IRT .... Information Retrieval Technique (AAG)
IRT .... Infrared Radiation Thermometer (NOAA)
IRT .... Infrared Technologies GmbH (SAUO)
IRT .... Infrared Telescope
IRT .... Infrared Temperature
IRT .... Infrared Thermography
IRT .... Infrared Thermometer
IRT .... Infrared Tracker
IRT .... Infrared Tube
IRT .... Initialize Reset Tape
IRT .... Initial Response Team (SAUO)
IRT .... Input Revision Typewriter
IRT .... In-Reactor Thimble (IEEE)
IRT .... In Reference To (NVT)
IRT .... In Regard To (MCD)
IRT .... In Reply To (NVT)
IRT .... In Response To (NVT)
IRT .... [*The*] Inscriptions of Roman Tripolitania (BJA)
IRT .... Installation Restoration Program (SAUO)
IRT .... Institute for Radiological Technologists
IRT .... Institute for Rapid Transit [*Later, APTA*] (EA)
IRT .... Institute for Reality Therapy (EA)
IRT .... Institute for Research on Teaching [*East Lansing, MI*] [*Department of Education*] (GRD)
IRT .... Institute of Reprographic Technology
IRT .... Institution of Rubber Technologist (SAUS)
IRT .... Institution of Rubber Technologists (SAUO)
IRT .... Instrumentation/Research/Technology Corp. (SAUO)
IRT .... Instrument Retrieval Containers [*Medicine*] (DAVI)
IRT .... Integrated Readiness Testing
IRT .... Integrated Rendezvous Target (SAUS)
IRT .... Intelcom Radiation Technology, Inc.
IRT .... Interboro Rapid Transit [*A New York City subway line*]
IRT .... Interborough Rapid Transit (SAUS)
IRT .... Interface Response Teams (SAUO)
IRT .... Interim Remote Terminals (MCD)
IRT .... Intermediate Range Technology (SAUS)
IRT .... Intermediate-Range Technology
IRT .... Intermediate Rated Thrust [*Military*] (CAAL)
IRT .... Internal Reflection Technique
IRT .... International Radio Telegraph (SAUO)
IRT .... International Research and Technology, Inc.
IRT .... Interot Air Service [*Germany*] [*ICAO designator*] (FAAC)
IRT .... Interresponse Time [*Psychometrics*]
IRT .... Interrogator-Responder-Transducer
IRT .... Interrogator-Responder-Transponder (SAUS)
IRT .... Interrupted Real Time (SAUS)
IRT .... Interrupted Ring Tone [*Telecommunications*] (TEL)
IRT .... Interrupt Ring Tone (SAUS)
IRT .... Interstitial Radiotherapy (DMAA)
IRT .... Intrared Thermography (SAUS)
IRT .... Inverse Reflex Tetrode [*Physics*]
IRT .... Irish Times (journ.) (SAUS)
IRT .... IRT Properities [*Formerly, Investors Realty Trust*] [*Associated Press*] (SAG)
IRT .... IRT Property [*NYSE symbol*] (TTSB)
IRT .... IRT Property Co. [*Formerly, Investors Realty Trust*] [*NYSE symbol*] (SPSG)
IRT .... Isometric Relaxation Time [*Medicine*] (DAVI)
IRT .... Isotope Ratio Tracer (PDAA)
IRT .... Isovolumic Relaxation Time [*Cardiology*]
IRT .... Item Response Theory (GFGA)
IRT .... Richmond Community Schools, Richmond, IN [*OCLC symbol*] (OCLC)
IRTA .... Illinois Retired Teachers Association (SAUO)
IRTA .... Independent Retail Tobacconists Association of America [*Defunct*] (EA)
IRTA .... In-Reactor Thimble Assembly (SAUS)
IRTA .... International Reciprocal Trade Association (EA)
IRTA .... International Road Racing Teams Association (SAUO)
IRTA .... Intramural Research Training Award [*National Institutes of Health*]
IRTAC .... International Round Table for the Advancement of Counseling [*British*]
IRTAFS .... International Ready-to-Assemble Furniture Show (ITD)
IRTAS .... Infrared Target Simulator (ACAE)
IRTC .... Infantry Replacement Training Center
IRTC .... Infrared Thermocouple (SAUS)
IRTC .... International Radio and Television Corp. (SAUS)
IRTC .... International Radio and Television Corporation S.A. (SAUO)
IRTC .... International Railway Transport Committee (SAUO)
IRTC .... International Road Tar Conference (SAUO)
IRTC .... International Road Transport Committee (SAUO)
IRTC .... International Round Table Conference (SAUS)
IRTC-1 .... Interconnect Reliability Test Chip-1 (AAEL)
IRTCA4 .... Instrumentation Technology (journ.) (SAUS)
IRTCC .... Installation Restoration Technology Coordinating Committee (SAUO)
IRTCES .... International Research and Training Center on Erosion and Sedimentation [*China*] (EAIO)
IRTCES .... International Research and Training Centre on Erosion and Sedimentation (SAUO)
IRTCES .... International Research Training Center for Erosion and Sedimentation (SAUS)
IRTCG .... Installation Restoration Technology Coordinating Group [*Army*] (RDA)
IRTCM .... Integrated Reaal Time Contermination (SAUS)
IRTCM .... Integrated Real-Time Contamination Monitor [*Module*]
IRTCM Module... Integrated Real-Time Contamination Monitor Module (SAUS)
IRTCP .... IRT Corp. (SAUO)
IRTD .... Infantry Reinforcement Training Depot [*British military*] (DMA)
IRTD .... Infrared Target Detector
IrTD .... Iranian Documentation Centre, Tehran, Iran [*Library symbol*] [*Library of Congress*] (LCLS)
IRTE .... Institut de Radio-Telediffusion pour Enfants [*Children's Broadcast Institute*] [*Canada*]
IRTE .... Institute of Road Transport Engineers (EAIO)
IRTE Journal... Institute of Road Transport Engineers Journal (journ.) (SAUS)
Ir Term Rep... Irish Term Reports, by Ridgeway, Lapp, and Schoales [*A publication*] (DLA)
Ir Term Rep... Irish Term Reports (journ.) (SAUS)
Ir Text J .... Irish Textile Journal (journ.) (SAUS)
IRTF .... Industry Restructuring Task Force
IRTF .... Infrared Telescope Facility
IRTF .... Intermediate-Range Task Force
IRTF .... International Radio and Television Foundation, Inc. [*International Radio and Television Society*] (NTCM)
IRTF .... Internet Research Task Force
IRTF .... Inter-Religious Task Force on Central America [*Defunct*] (EA)
IRTGSM .... Infra-Red Terminally Guided Submunition (SAUS)
IRTGSM .... Infrared Terminally-Guided Submunition
IRTH .... Infra-Red Terminal Simulator (SAUS)
IRTI .... Islamic Research & Training Institute [*Saudi Arabia*]
IRTI .... Islamic Research and Training Institute of the IDB (SAUO)
IRTIP .... International Rice Testing and Improvement Program (SAUO)
IRTIS .... Inter Regional Training Information System (SAUO)
IRTIS .... Inter-Regional Training Information System [*International Labor Organization*] [*United Nations*] (DUND)
IRTL .... Intelecom Radiation Technology Laboratory (SAUO)
IRTM .... Infrared Thermal Mapper [*NASA*]
IRTM .... Infrared Thermal Mapper Subsystem (SAUS)
IRTN .... International Rice Tungro Nursery (SAUO)
IRTO .... International Radio and Television Organisation (or Organization) (SAUS)
IRTO .... International Radio and Television Organization (SAUO)
IRTON .... International Rice Temperate Observational Nursery (SAUO)
IRTOS .... I2O Real-Time Operating System (SAUS)
IRTP .... Initial Recruiting and Training Plan [*Military*]
IRTP .... International Rice Testing Program (SAUO)
IRTP .... Internet Reliable Transaction Protocol (SAUS)
IRTPA .... Ijebu-Remo Taxpayers Association (SAUO)
IRTR .... Impaired Renal Tubular Reabsorption [*Medicine*] (MELL)
Ir TR .... Irish Term Reports, by Ridgeway, Lapp, and Schoales [*A publication*] (DLA)
IRTR .... IRT Realty Services, Inc. (SAUO)
IRTRAN .... Infrared Transmitting
IRTRAN .... Inter-Range Telemetry Working Group (SAUO)
IRTRN .... Infrared Transmission
IRTS .... Indian Railway Traffic Services [*Indian Railway*] (TIR)
IRTS .... Infrared Target Seeker (MSA)
IRTS .... Infrared Target Simulator (ACAE)
IRTS .... Infrared Telescope in Space (SAUS)
IRTS .... Infrared Temperature Sounder (PDAA)
IRTS .... Infrared Test System (SAUS)
IRTS .... Interim Recovery Technical Specification (IEEE)
IRTS .... International Radio and Television Society (EA)
IRTS .... Irish Radio Transmitters Society (SAUO)
IRTTD .... Infrared Transmission through the Diffusion (PDAA)
IRTU .... Integrating Regulatory Transcription Units [*Genetics*]
IRTU .... Intelligent Remote Terminal Unit

IRTU .... International Railway Temperance Union
IRTU .... International Road Transport Union (SAUO)
IRT Unit .... Interrogator-Responder-Transponder Unit (SAUS)
IRTV .... Information Retrieval Television [*Tele-education project*] (NITA)
IRTVSU .... Infrared Television Sight Unit (ACAE)
IRTW .... Infrared Surveillance and Threat Warning System (ACAE)
IRTWG .... Inter-Range Telemetering (or Telemetry) Working Group (SAUO)
IRTWG .... Interrange Telemetry Working Group
IRTWS .... Infrared Tail Warning Set (MCD)
IRU .... General Individual Reinforcement Unit (SAUS)
IRU .... Immediate Response Unit [*Police*] [*British*] (DI)
IRU .... Indefeasible Right of User [*Telecommunications*] (TEL)
IRU .... Individual Reinforcement Unit (SAUO)
IRU .... Industrial Rehabilitation Units [*British*]
IRU .... Industrial Research Unit (SAUS)
IRU .... Informarion Resources Unit (SAUS)
IRU .... Information Retrieval Unit (NITA)
IRU .... Infrared Unit (SAUS)
IRU .... Integrated Recovery Utility (SAUO)
IRU .... Interferon Reference Unit
IRU .... Intergenic Repeat Unit [*Genetics*]
IRU .... Internationale Raiffeisen-Union [*International Raiffeisen Union*] (EAIO)
IRU .... International Radium Unit
IRU .... International Raiffeisen Union (EA)
IRU .... International Railway Union (SAUO)
IRU .... International Relief Union
IRU .... International Road Transport Union [*Geneva, Switzerland*] (EAIO)
IRU .... International Romani Union (EA)
IRU .... Irvine Research Unit [*University of California, Irvine*]
IRU .... IVA [*Intravehicular Activity*] Replacement Unit (SSD)
IRU .... New Mexico State University, Las Cruces, NM [*OCLC symbol*] (OCLC)
IRUC .... Information and Research Utilization Center in Physical Education and Recreation for the Handicapped (SAUO)
IRUC .... Information and Research Utilization Center in Physical Education and Recreationfor the Handicapped [*American Association for Health, Physical Education, and Recreation*]
IRUC .... Intermediate Resource Usage Condition (MHDI)
IRUG .... Intel Real-time Users Group (SAUS)
IRUN .... International Rice Ufra Nursery (SAUO)
iruptd .... interrupted (SAUS)
IRUPTN .... Interruption (SAUS)
IRUPTNG .... Interrupting (SAUS)
IRUS .... Infantry Rifle Unit Study [*Army*]
IRUSS .... International Rice Ufra Screening Set (SAUO)
IRut .... Rutland Community Library, Rutland, IL [*Library symbol*] [*Library of Congress*] (LCLS)
IR/UV-LS .... Infrared/Ultraviolet Line Scanner (PDAA)
IRV .... Improved Recovery Vehicle [*Army*] (RDA)
IRV .... Inglewood [*Forest*] Rifle Volunteers [*British military*] (DMA)
IRV .... Inspiratory Reserve Volume [*Physiology*]
IRV .... Instant Runoff Voting (AGLO)
IRV .... Institute for Rehabilitation Research (SAUO)
IRV .... Internationale Rat fuer Vogelschutz [*International Council for Bird Preservation*]
IRV .... International Reference Version (OSI)
IRV .... International Rex Ventures, Inc. [*Vancouver Stock Exchange symbol*]
IRV .... Inter-Range Vector [*NASA*] (KSC)
IRV .... Interrupt Request Vector
IRV .... Inversed Ratio of Ventilation
Irv .... Irvine's Scotch Justiciary Reports [*1851-68*] [*A publication*] (DLA)
Irv .... Irvines Scotch Justiciary Reports (journ.) (SAUS)
IRV .... Isotope Reentry Value (SAUS)
IRV .... Isotope Reentry Vehicle [*NASA*] (NASA)
IRV .... Item Rating Value (DNAB)
IR Valve .... Inverting Relay Valve (SAUS)
IRVAT .... Infrared Video Automatic Tracking (PDAA)
IRVAT .... Infrared Video-Auto Tracker (DWSG)
IRVB .... India Rubber Vulcanized, Braided (SAUS)
IRVB .... India-Rubber Vulcanized, Braided [*Wire insulation*] (IAA)
IRVC .... Indian Remount and Veterinary Corps [*British military*] (DMA)
Irv Civ Law ... Irving's Civil Law [*A publication*] (DLA)
Ir Vet J .... Irish Veterinary Journal (journ.) (SAUS)
IRVH .... Integrated Reactor Vessel Head [*Nuclear energy*] (NRCH)
Irvine .... Irvine Sensors Corp. [*Associated Press*] (SAG)
IrvineApt .... Irvine Apartment Communities [*Associated Press*] (SAG)
Irvine Just Cas ... Irvine's Justiciary Cases [*England*] [*A publication*] (DLA)
Irving .... Irving Trust Co. (SAUS)
Irving .... Irving Trust Company (SAUO)
Irving Civ Law ... Irving's Civil Law [*A publication*] (DLA)
Irving View ... Irving Trust Company. Economic View from One Wall Street (journ.) (SAUS)
Irv Just .... Irvine's Justiciary Cases [*England*] [*A publication*] (DLA)
IRVNG .... Irving, TX [*American Association of Railroads railroad junction routing code*]
IRVR .... Instrumented Runway Visual Range [*Aviation*] (DA)
IRVS .... Interactive Voice Response System [*Indian Railway*] (TIR)
IRVSS .... Infrared Vertical Sounding System [*Oceanography*] (MSC)
IRVW .... Integrated Research Volkswagen [*Automotive engineering*]
IRW .... Impulse Response Width (SAUS)
IRW .... Index of Relative Worth (MCD)
IRW .... Indirect Reference Word (BUR)
IRW .... Infrared Window
IRW .... Institute for Rural Water (EA)
IRW .... Institute of Rural Water (SAUS)
IRW .... International Rehabilitation Week [*Trade show*]
IRW .... International Rocket Week
IRW .... Inverted Rib Waveguide (NITA)
IRW .... Iowa Reformatory for Women (SAUO)
IRWA .... International Right of Way Association (EA)
IRWA .... International Rodeo Writers Association [*Later, RMA*] (EA)
IRWBPHN .... International Rice Whitebacked Planthopper Nursery (SAUO)
IRWC .... Institute of Roofing and Waterproofing Consultants International (NTPA)
IRWC .... International Registry of World Citizens
Ir WCC .... Irish Workmen's Compensation Cases [*A publication*] (DLA)
Ir WCC .... Irish Workmens Compensation Cases (journ.) (SAUS)
IRWD .... Irvine Ranch Water District (SAUO)
IRWEP .... International Register for the White Eared Pheasant (EAIO)
IRWG .... Interface Requirements Working Group (SSD)
IrwinFin .... Irwin Financial Corp. [*Associated Press*] (SAG)
Irwin's Code ... Clark, Cobb, and Irwin's Code [*Georgia*] [*A publication*] (DLA)
Irwins Code ... Clark, Cobb and Irwins Code (journ.) (SAUS)
IRWIT .... International Rice-Wheat Integrated Trial (SAUO)
IRWJF .... Irwin Toy Ltd. Vtg (SAUO)
IRWKF .... Irwin Toy Ltd. Non Vtg (SAUO)
IRWL .... Interchangeability and Reliability Working List (ACAE)
IRWL .... Interchangeability and Replaceability Wording List (SAUS)
Ir WLR .... Irish Weekly Law Reports [*1895-1902*] [*A publication*] (DLA)
IRWN .... Irwin Financial Corp. [*NASDAQ symbol*] (SAG)
IRWN .... Irwin Magnetic Systems, Inc. (SAUO)
IrwnFn .... Irwin Financial Corp. [*Associated Press*] (SAG)
IRWR .... Infrared Warning Receiver [*Aviation*] (MCD)
IRWSS .... Infrared Weapon System Simulation (ACAE)
IRX .... Information Retrieval Experiment (SAUO)
IRX .... Infrared Telescope System (ACAE)
IRX .... Interactive Resource Executive [*NCR Corp.*]
IRY .... Intertype Corporation (SAUO)
IRY .... Iron Bay Trust [*Toronto Stock Exchange symbol*]
IRYM .... Illinois Railway Museum [*Federal Railroad Administration identification code*]
IRYN .... International Rice Yield Nursery (SAUO)
IRYN-E .... International Rice Yield Nursery-Early (SAUO)
IRYN-M .... International Rice Yield Nursery-Medium (SAUO)
IRYN-VE .... International Rice Yield Nursery-Very Early (SAUO)
IRZ .... Inner Radiation Zone
IRZ .... International Reference Zero [*Level for pure-tone audiometers*]
IS .... Air Survey Co. of India Ltd. (SAUO)
IS .... Defense Industrial Supply Center (SAUO)
IS .... Eagle Air [*ICAO designator*] (AD)
IS .... Ibbi-Sin (BJA)
IS .... Iceland [*ANSI two-letter standard code*] (CNC)
IS .... Ice Screamers (EA)
IS .... Ichthyosis Simplex [*Medicine*] (MELL)
IS .... Ideological Survey [*Psychology*]
IS .... IDS Aircraft Ltd. [*British*] [*ICAO designator*] (ICDA)
IS .... If Statement (SAUS)
IS .... Ignition and Separation (IAA)
IS .... Image Stabilization [*Technology from Canon*]
IS .... Image Stabilizer [*Canon's technology for binoculars*]
IS .... Image Subtraction (SAUS)
IS .... Imaging Spectrometer (SSD)
IS .... Immediate Sensitivity [*Medicine*] (DB)
IS .... Immediate Support (SAUS)
IS .... Immittance Spectroscopy (EDCT)
IS .... Immortalist Society (EA)
IS .... Immune Serum [*Also, ImS*]
IS .... Immunological Similarity
IS .... Immunology Status [*Medicine*] (DB)
IS .... Immunosuppressive [*Immunochemistry*]
IS .... Impact Strength (SAUS)
IS .... Impact Switch (SAA)
IS .... Imperative Sentence (SAUS)
IS .... Imperative Statement (SAUS)
IS .... Improved Suspension (MCD)
IS .... Incentive Spirometer [*or Spirometry*] [*Medicine*] (DMAA)
IS .... Include Statement (SAUS)
IS .... Including Sheeting
IS .... Incoherent Scatter
IS .... Income Statement [*Business term*]
IS .... Incomplete Sequence (MSA)
IS .... Independent School (BARN)
IS .... Independent Sector (EA)
IS .... Independent Seminar (SAUS)
IS .... Independent Shoemen of America [*Defunct*] (EA)
IS .... Independent Spherical Aluminum Tank [*on a ship*] (DS)
IS .... Independent Study (SAUS)
IS .... Independent Suspension
IS .... Indexed Sequential [*Computer science*]
IS .... Indexing in Source
IS .... Index of Sexuality (SAUS)
IS .... Index Sequential (SAUS)
IS .... Indian Show
IS .... Indian Standard (IAA)
IS .... Indian Summer (SAUS)
IS .... India Society (SAUO)
IS .... Indicating Switch (NRCH)
IS .... Indicator Score (SAUS)
IS .... Induced Sputum [*Otorhinolaryngology*] (DAVI)

IS .... Induction Soldering
IS .... Industrial Safety (SAUS)
IS .... Industrial School [*British*] (ROG)
IS .... Industrial Service [*Equipment specifications*]
IS .... Industrial Society (AIE)
IS .... Industrial Source (GNE)
IS .... Industrial Specialist
IS .... Industrial Systems (DS)
IS .... Industry Standard (BCP)
IS .... Inertial Systems (AFIT)
IS .... [*The*] Infantry School [*Army*] (MCD)
IS .... Infant Size (DB)
IS .... Infection Structure [*Plant pathology*]
IS .... Infectious Spondylitis [*Medicine*] (MELL)
IS .... Information Science (IEEE)
IS .... Information Seekers
IS .... Information Selection (SAUS)
IS .... Information Separation (NITA)
IS .... Information Separator [*Control character*] [*Computer science*]
IS .... Information Series (SAUS)
IS .... Information Service
IS .... Information Services [*Portion of InterNIC General Atomics Corporation*]
IS .... Information Signal (SAUS)
IS .... Information Source (SAUS)
IS .... Information Storage (SAUS)
IS .... Information Stream (SAUS)
IS .... Information Supply (SAUS)
IS .... Information System
IS .... Information Systems [*Ori, Inc.*] [*Information service or system*] (IID)
IS .... Infrared Spectrometer [*or Spectroscopy*] (IAA)
IS .... Infrared Spectroscopy (SAUS)
IS .... Ingglish Speling 3soesiaesh3n [*An organization to reform spelling*] [*See also IS3*] (EA)
IS .... Ingot Sheet (SAUS)
IS .... Inguinal Syndrome [*Medicine*] (MELL)
IS .... Inhibiting Signal (SAUS)
IS .... Initializing Sequence (SAUS)
IS .... Initial Shortage (AFM)
IS .... Initial State (SAUS)
IS .... Initiate Statement (SAUS)
IS .... Initiation Supervisor
IS .... Inner Sheath [*Botany*]
IS .... Inorganic Semiconductor [*Materials science*]
IS .... Input Secondary [*Electronics*]
IS .... Input Section (SAUS)
IS .... Input Signal (ACAE)
IS .... Input Simulator
IS .... Input Source (SAUS)
IS .... Input Stream (SAUS)
IS .... Input System (SAUS)
IS .... In Secondary (SAUS)
IS .... Insect Screen (AAG)
IS .... Insenion Sequences (SAUS)
Is .... Insertion (QSUL)
IS .... Insertion Sequence [*Genetics*]
IS .... In Service [*Telecommunications*] (TEL)
IS .... In Shop (MCD)
I/S .... Inside [*Automotive engineering*]
IS .... Inside Sentinel [*Freemasonry*]
IS .... In Situ [*In Place*] [*Latin*]
IS .... Insoluble (SAUS)
IS .... Inspection Services, Inc. (EA)
IS .... Installation of Systems (IAA)
IS .... Installation Squadron (SAUO)
IS .... Installation Start [*Telecommunications*] (TEL)
IS .... Installation Support (KSC)
is .... Installation Support [*Aerospace*] (NAKS)
I/S .... Instate (SAUS)
IS .... Institute of Science (SAUS)
IS .... Institute of Statisticians [*British*]
IS .... Institute Sponsors (SAUO)
IS .... Instructional System (SAUS)
IS .... Instruction Section [*Association of College and Research Libraries*] [*American Library Association*]
IS .... Instruction Sequence (SAUS)
IS .... Instruction Set (SAUS)
IS .... Instruction Sheet
IS .... Instructions to Ship (AAG)
IS .... Instruction System (SAUS)
IS .... Instructor Squadron
IS .... Instructor Station [*Training term*] (LPT)
IS .... Instrument (IAA)
IS .... Instrumentation Ships Project [*Navy*]
IS .... Instrumentation Summary (MUGU)
IS .... Instrumentation System (KSC)
IS .... Insufficiently Stamped [*Post office*] [*British*] (ROG)
IS .... Insufficient Signal (PALA)
IS .... Insulated System (SAUS)
IS .... Insulating Sleeve
IS .... Insurance Salesman (journ.) (SAUS)
IS .... Integrally Stiffened
IS .... Integrated Satellite [*Military spacecraft*]
IS .... Integrated Service (SAUO)
IS .... Integrated Systems (SAUS)
IS .... Integrating Support
IS .... Integration Software (SAUS)
IS .... Intelligence in the Sky [*An extraterrestrial intelligence with whom Dr. Andrija Puharich and psychic Uri Geller claim to have communicated*]
IS .... Intelligence Service (IAA)
IS .... Intelligence Signal (SAUS)
IS .... Intelligence Specialist [*Navy*]
IS .... Intelligence Support [*Program*] [*Department of State*]
IS .... Intelligence System (SAUO)
IS .... Intelligence Systems [*Military*] (MCD)
IS .... Intensity Stereo (SAUS)
IS .... Intent Share (SAUS)
IS .... Interactive Service (SAUO)
IS .... Interblock Space (SAUS)
IS .... Intercellular Space (DB)
IS .... Interchangeability and Substitution
IS .... Intercoastal Space (SAUS)
IS .... Interconnecting Station (MCD)
IS .... Intercostal Space [*Medicine*]
IS .... Interdepartmental Settlement (FOTI)
IS .... Interface Specifications (AAEL)
IS .... Interface Structure (ACAE)
IS .... Interface Summary (SAUS)
IS .... Interference Spectroscope (SAUS)
IS .... Interference Suppression (SAUS)
IS .... Interference Suppressor (IEEE)
IS .... Interim Services [*NYSE symbol*]
IS .... Interim Status (GNE)
IS .... Interim Storage (SAUS)
IS .... Interim Study (SAUS)
IS .... Interior Surface
IS .... Intermediate School
IS .... Intermediate Suppression (MCD)
IS .... Intermediate System [*Computer science*] (TNIG)
IS .... Internal Security [*Military*] [*British*]
IS .... Internal Shield [*Electronics*]
IS .... Internal Standard [*Chemistry*]
IS .... Internal Standards (SAUO)
IS .... Internal Surface (AAG)
IS .... Internationaler Suchdienst [*International Tracing Service*] (EAIO)
IS .... Internationale Schutzenunion [*International Shooting Union*] (EAIO)
IS .... International Sales (SAUO)
IS .... International Services [*Red Cross*]
IS .... International Socialist (journ.) (SAUS)
IS .... International Socialists
IS .... International Society of Sculptors, Painters, and Gravers
IS .... International Staff (NATG)
IS .... International Standard
IS .... International Status (SAUS)
IS .... International Stock [*Business term*]
IS .... International Studies (journ.) (SAUS)
IS .... International Supplement (SAUO)
IS .... International Symposium (SAUS)
IS .... Internet Standard [*Communications term*] (DCT)
IS .... Interrupt Set (SAUS)
IS .... Interrupt Signal (SAUS)
IS .... Interrupt State (SAUS)
IS .... Interrupt Status (SAUO)
IS .... Intersegmental
IS .... Interservice
IS .... Intership [*Freight forwarding company*] [*British*]
IS .... Interspace
I/S .... Interstage
IS .... Interstage Section (SAUS)
IS .... Interstage Shielding (SAUS)
IS .... Interstate
IS .... Interstate/Johnson Lane [*Formerly, Interstate Securities, Inc.*] [*NYSE symbol*] (SPSG)
IS .... Interstate Securities, Inc. (SAUO)
IS .... Interval Signal
IS .... Intestinal Stenosis [*Medicine*] (MELL)
IS .... Intracardial Shunt [*Medicine*] (DB)
IS .... Intraspinal [*Injection*]
IS .... Intrasplenic (DB)
IS .... Intrastriatal (DB)
IS .... Intraventricular Septum [*Cardiology*] (AAMN)
IS .... Intrinsic Safety (SAUS)
IS .... Invalided from Service [*Medicine*] [*Navy*]
IS .... Invalid Semantics (SAUS)
IS .... Inventory Schedule
IS .... Inventory Store (SAUS)
IS .... Inventory System (SAUS)
I/S .... Inventory to Sales Ratio [*Business term*]
IS .... Inverted Stepanov (SAUS)
IS .... Investment-Savings [*Economics*]
I-S .... Investment-Savings Curve [*Economics*]
IS .... Investors Group (SAUO)
I-S .... Ionescu-Shiley [*Artificial cardiac valve*] [*Medicine*] (STED)
IS .... Ion Source [*Spectroscopy*]
IS .... Ion Spectroscopy (SAUS)
IS .... Ion Spectrum (SAUS)
IS .... Iowa State University of Sciences and Technology (SAUS)
IS .... Irish Society
IS .... Irish Standard (IAA)

IS .... Irish Statesman (journ.) (SAUS)
IS .... Irrational Screening (SAUS)
Is .... Isaiah [*Old Testament book*]
Is .... Isidore [*Authority cited in pre-1607 legal work*] (DSA)
Is .... Isis (journ.) (SAUS)
Is .... Islam (BJA)
Is .... Islamic (SAUS)
IS .... Island (DA)
is .... Island (STED)
Is .... Islands [*Maps and charts*]
IS .... Isle (EY)
I/S .... Isle Of Skye [*Scotland*] (ROG)
is .... Islet (STED)
IS .... Isolated Step
is .... Isolation (STED)
IS .... Isolation
IS .... Isomeric Shift (OA)
IS .... Isomer Shut (SAUS)
IS .... Isometric Strength [*Medicine*] (MELL)
IS .... Isotonic Strength [*Medicine*] (MELL)
IS .... Isotopic Separation [*Subsystem*] (MCD)
Is .... Israel [*IYRU nationality code*] (BJA)
is .... Israel [*MARC country of publication code*] [*Library of Congress*] (LCCP)
IS .... Israeli Shekel (SAUS)
IS .... ISSN [*International Standard Serial Number*] [*Online database field identifier*]
IS .... Issue Code [*Online database field identifier*]
IS .... Issue Number [*Dialog*] [*Searchable field*] (NITA)
IS .... Istituto Superiore di Sanita [*Italy*] [*Research code symbol*]
IS .... Office of Intelligence and National Security (SAUS)
IS .... Terminal in Service (SAUO)
IS1 .... Intelligence Specialist, First Class [*Navy*] (DNAB)
IS1B .... Inhibit Switch 1 Bit (SAUS)
IS2 .... Information System Integration Support (SAUO)
IS2 .... Intelligence Specialist, Second Class [*Navy*] (DNAB)
IS2B .... Inhibit Switch 2 Bit (SAUS)
IS3 .... Ingglish Speling 3soesiaesh3n [*English Spelling Association*] (EA)
IS3 .... Intelligence Specialist, Third Class [*Navy*] (DNAB)
IS4B .... Inhibit Switch 4 Bit (SAUS)
IS5 .... Interstellar Scattering (SAUS)
IS8B .... Inhibit Switch 8 Bit (SAUS)
IS 10S .... 10% Invert Sugar in Saline [*Medicine*] (EDAA)
IS-41 .... Interim Standard 41 for North American Inter-Switch Signaling (CGWS)
IS-54 .... Interim Standard 54 for the First North American Dual-Mode Time Division Multiple Access Cellular System (CGWS)
IS-88 .... Interim Standard 88 for the Narrowband Advanced Mobile Phone System Cellular System (CGWS)
IS92 .... IPCC Scenarios, 1992 (SAUO)
IS-95 .... Interim STandard for Code Division Multiple Access Cellular Service (CGWS)
IS-136 .... Interim Standard 136 for North American Time Division Multiple Access Cellular Access (CGWS)
IS 499 .... Polindine Methylsulfate [*Medicine*] (EDAA)
ISA .... English Spelling Association (SAUO)
ISA .... Ibsen Society of America (EA)
ISA .... ICAO Standard Atmosphere (SAUS)
ISA .... Idle Speed Actuator [*Automotive engineering*]
ISA .... Ignition and Separation Assembly
ISA .... IGOSS Scientific Adviser (SAUO)
ISA .... Illinois Sheriffs Association (SRA)
ISA .... Illinois Sign Association (SRA)
ISA .... Illinois Soybean Association (SRA)
ISA .... Illinois Studies in Anthropology (journ.) (SAUS)
ISA .... Image Sequence Analysis (SAUS)
ISA .... Imaging Sensor Autoprocessor (ACAE)
ISA .... Incest Survivors Anonymous (SAUS)
ISA .... Incest Survivors' Association [*Australia*]
ISA .... Incorporated Society of Authors, Playwrights and Composers (SAUO)
ISA .... Independent Scholars of Asia (EA)
ISA .... Independent Schools Association [*British*] (AEBS)
ISA .... Independent Shoemen of America [*Defunct*]
ISA .... Independent Signcrafters of America (EA)
ISA .... Independent Stores Association Ltd. [*British*] (BI)
ISA .... Indexed Sequential Access (SAUS)
ISA .... Index of Spouse Abuse
ISA .... Indiana Sheriffs' Association (SRA)
ISA .... Indian Science Abstracts (journ.) (SAUS)
ISA .... Individual Savings Account [*Proposed*]
ISA .... Inductee Special Assignment
ISA .... Industrial Security Acquisition (MCD)
ISA .... Industrial Standard Architecture (SAUS)
ISA .... Industrial Standards Architecture (SAUO)
ISA .... Industry Standard Architecture [*Computer hardware*] (PCM)
ISA .... Industry Standards Association (SAUO)
ISA .... Inertial Sensor Assemblies (SAUS)
ISA .... Inertial Sensor Assembly [*Military*] (CAAL)
ISA .... Infantry Sailing Association [*British*]
ISA .... Infinite Storage Architecture (SAUS)
ISA .... Information Science Abstracts (journ.) (SAUS)
ISA .... Information Services Assistance (TIMI)
ISA .... Information Services Association (SAUO)
ISA .... Information System Access (SAUS)
ISA .... Information Systems and Automation (SAUS)
ISA .... Information Systems Architecture [*AT & T*]
ISA .... Information Systems Association (EA)
ISA .... Infrared spectrometric Sulfur Analyzer (SAUS)
ISA .... Initiative for Southern Africa (SAUO)
ISA .... Innkeepers Society of America [*Defunct*] (EA)
ISA .... Inorganic Sampling and Analysis
ISA .... Insecta Research [*Vancouver Stock Exchange symbol*]
ISA .... Inspection Summary Analysis (SAUS)
ISA .... Installation and Services Agency (SAUS)
ISA .... Installations and Services Agency [*Army Materiel Command*]
ISA .... Installation Supply Accounting
ISA .... Installation Supply Activity
ISA .... Institute for Scientific Analysis (EA)
ISA .... Institute for Sustainable Agriculture [*Australia*]
ISA .... Institute of Strategic Affairs (SAUO)
ISA .... Institute of Surveyors of Australia (SAUO)
ISA .... Institute of Systems Analysis [*Army*]
ISA .... Institution of Surveyors-Australia (SAUS)
ISA .... Institut Superieur des Affaires [*Chamber de Commerce et d'Industrie de Paris*] (ECON)
ISA .... Instructional Systems Association (EA)
ISA .... Instruction Set Architecture [*Computer science*] [*Army*] (RDA)
ISA .... Instructor of Small Arms (SAUO)
ISA .... Instrumentation Society of America (AAEL)
ISA .... Instrument Society for Measurement and Control (SAUO)
ISA .... Instrument Society of America [*Medicine*] (EDAA)
ISA .... Instruments, Systems and Automation (ACII)
ISA .... Instrument Subassembly (IEEE)
ISA .... Insulating Siding Association [*Defunct*] (EA)
ISA .... Insurance Service Associates [*Later, Assurex International*]
ISA .... Integrated Sequence Analysis (SAUO)
ISA .... Integrated Services Architecture (SAUO)
ISA .... Integrated Software Architecture (HODG)
ISA .... Integrated Support Area (NVT)
ISA .... Integrated Systems Architecture (SAUS)
ISA .... Integrator Shaft Assembly (ACAE)
ISA .... Intelligence Support Activity [*Military*]
ISA .... Intelligent Speed Adaptation
ISA .... Interactive Services Association (NTPA)
ISA .... Interactive Survey Analysis (IAA)
ISA .... Intercoastal Steamship Freight Association, New York NY [*STAC*]
ISA .... Interconexion Electrica, Sociedad Anonima
ISA .... Interface Standard Architecture (SAUS)
ISA .... Interface Switching Assembly
ISA .... Intergalactic SYSOP [*System Operator*] Alliance (EA)
ISA .... Interim Standard Atmosphere (SAUS)
ISA .... Interim Stowage Assembly
ISA .... Interlaced Storage Assignment (SAUS)
ISA .... Intermediate Service Agency (SAUO)
ISA .... Intermediate Specific Activity [*Radioisotope*]
ISA .... Intermediate Supply Activity [*Marine Corps*] (DOMA)
ISA .... Internal Security Act
ISA .... Internal Storage Area [*Computer science*] (BYTE)
ISA .... International Federation of National Standardizing Associations (SAUO)
ISA .... International Safety Academy
ISA .... International Schools Association [*Geneva, Switzerland*] (EA)
ISA .... International Seabed Authority
ISA .... International Security Act [*Malaysia*] [*Government term*] (GA)
ISA .... International Security Affairs [*DoD*]
ISA .... International Security Agency
ISA .... International Security Assistance (SAUS)
ISA .... International Service Agencies
ISA .... International Shakespeare Association (EA)
ISA .... International Shipmasters Association of the Great Lakes (EA)
ISA .... International Shuffleboard Association (EA)
ISA .... International Sign Association [*NESA*] [*Absorbed by*] (EA)
ISA .... International Silk Association - USA (EA)
ISA .... International Silo Association (EA)
ISA .... International Skateboard Association (EA)
ISA .... International Skating Association (SAUO)
ISA .... International Skeeter Association
ISA .... International Society for Measurement and Control (NTPA)
ISA .... International Society of Aboriculture (SAUS)
ISA .... International Society of Acupuncture (SAUO)
ISA .... International Society of Appraisers [*Hoffman Estates, IL*] (EA)
ISA .... International Society of Arboriculture (EA)
ISA .... International Society of Women Airline Pilots (EA)
ISA .... International Sociological Association [*Research center*] [*Spain*] (IRC)
ISA .... International Soling Association [*Bordon, Hampshire, England*] (EAIO)
ISA .... International Songwriters' Association (EAIO)
ISA .... International Standard Atmosphere [*ICAO*] (FAAC)
ISA .... International Standardization Association (SAUO)
ISA .... International Standards Association
ISA .... International Stiltwalkers Association (EA)
ISA .... International Strabismological Association (EAIO)
ISA .... International Studies Association (EA)
ISA .... International Submariners Association (SAUO)
ISA .... International Sugar Agreement [*1958*]
ISA .... International Surfing Association [*Swansea, England*] (EAIO)
ISA .... International Swift Association (EA)
ISA .... International Symbol of Access [*Department of Transportation*] (EGAO)

ISA Internet Starter Applications (SAUS)
ISA Interplant Shipping Authority
ISA Interrupt Storage Area
ISA Intersecting Storage Accelerator [*In name of atomic reactor, Isabelle*]
ISA Intersecting Storage and Acceleration (SAUS)
ISA Inter-Series Adapter (SAUS)
IS/A Interservice/Agency (SAUO)
ISA Interservice Agreement [*DoD*]
ISA Interservice Support Agreement [*Military*]
ISA Intersubstrate Alignment (SAUS)
ISA Intracarotid Sodium Amytal [*Medicine*] (EDAA)
ISA Intrinsic Stimulating Activity (DB)
ISA Intrinsic Sympathomimetic Activity [*Biochemistry*]
ISA Invalid Storage Address (SAUS)
ISA Investment Savings Account (ADA)
ISA Iodinated Serum Albumin [*Medicine*]
ISA Ion Scattering Analysis
ISA Iowa Soybean Association (SRA)
ISA Iranian Students Association (SAUO)
ISA Irish Stammering Association (SAUO)
ISA Irregular Serials and Annuals [*A publication*]
ISA Irregular Spiking Activity [*Electrophysiology*]
ISA Isabella [*California*] [*Seismograph station code, US Geological Survey*] (SEIS)
Isa Isaiah [*Old Testament book*]
Isa Isaiah, The Book of the Prophet (SAUS)
ISA Isaias [*Old Testament book*] [*Douay version*]
ISA Islamic Shipowners Association (SAUO)
ISA Island Airlines, Inc. [*ICAO designator*] (FAAC)
ISA Israel Society of Anesthesiologists (SAUO)
ISA Israel Space Agency [*Israel*]
ISA Italian Space Agency (CARB)
ISA Mount Isa [*Australia*] [*Airport symbol*] (OAG)
ISA Pacific Island Airways (SAUS)
ISA Santa Isabel ADS [*NYSE symbol*] (TTSB)
ISA Santa Isabel SA [*NYSE symbol*] (SAG)
ISA WWW Implementation Support Activity (SAUS)
ISA_5 Internal Surface Area of Lung at Volume of 5 Liters [*Medicine*] (MAE)
ISA + 21 International Social Affiliation of Women Airline Pilots [*Later, ISWAP*] (EA)
ISA 21 International Society of Women Airline Pilots (SAUO)
ISAA Institute of Shops Acts Administration [*British*] (BI)
ISAA Insurance Service Association of America [*Later, Assurex International*] (EA)
ISAA Intercollegiate Soccer Association of America (EA)
ISAA International Society of Performing Arts Administrators (SAUO)
ISAA Israel Society of Aeronautics and Astronautics (SAUO)
ISAAA International Service for the Acquisition of Agri-Biotech Applications
ISAAA International Service for the Acquisition of Agricultural Biotechnology (SAUO)
ISAAC Information System for Advanced Academic Computing (IID)
ISAAC Integrated System for Automated Acquisition and Control
ISAAC International Society for Alternative and Augmentative Communication (EA)
ISAAC International Society for Augmentative and Alternative Communication (SAUS)
ISAAI Illinois Society of Allergy, Asthma, and Immunology (SRA)
IS/A AMPE Inter-Service Agency Automated Message Processing Exchange
I-S/A AMPE Inter-Service/Agency Automated Message Processing Exchange (SAUO)
ISAARE Information System for Adaptive, Assistive and Recreational Equipment (SAUS)
ISAARE Information System for Adaptive, Assistive, and Rehabilitation Equipment [*For the handicapped*]
ISAAS Indian Society for Afro-Asian Studies (SAUO)
ISAB Institute for the Study of Animal Behavior (BARN)
ISAB International Scholastic Advisory Bureau, London (SAUO)
ISAB International Scientific Advisory Board [*Medicine*] (EDAA)
ISABC International Society Against Breast Cancer (EAIO)
ISABE International Symposium on Air Breathing Engines (ACAE)
ISABGR International Society for Animal Blood Group Research (SAUO)
ISABP International South Atlantic Buoy Program [*Marine science*] (OSRA)
ISABPS Integrated Submarine Automated Broadcasting Processing System (MCD)
ISABPS Integrated Submarine Automated Broadcast Processing System (SAUO)
ISABR International Society for Animal Blood Group Research [*Australia*] (EAIO)
ISABR International Society for Animal Genetics [*Australia*] (EAIO)
ISABS Integrated Submarine Automated Broadcast Processing System [*Navy*] (CAAL)
ISA BUS Industry Standard Architecture Bus
ISAC Icelandic Board for Technical Accreditation (SAUO)
ISAC I.C. Isaacs & Company, Inc. [*NASDAQ symbol*] (NASQ)
ISAC Indian Satellite Applications Center (SAUO)
ISAC Industrial Safety Advisory Council [*British*]
ISAC Industrial Sector Advisory Committee (SAUS)
ISAC Industrial Security Association of Canada
ISAC Industry Sector Advisory Committee [*Established by Trade Reform Act for industry-to-government advice*]
ISAC Industry Sector Advisory Council [*Department of Commerce*] (WPI)
ISAC Information Systems Advisory Committee
ISAC Information Systems Advisory Council (SAUO)
ISAC In Service, Active [*Vessel status*] [*Navy*] (DNAB)
ISAC Institute for the Study of American Cultures (EA)
ISAC Instrumentation System Assessment Center (MCD)
ISAC Intelestat Solar Array Coupon (SAUS)
ISAC Interior Scaling Advisory Committee (SAUO)
ISAC International Scientific Agricultural Council (SAUO)
ISAC International Security Affairs Committee
ISAC International Society for Analytical Cytology (EAIO)
ISAC International Society for Autistic Children [*Defunct*] (EA)
ISAC Interuniversity Southeast Asia Committee [*of the Association for Asia*]
ISACA Information Systems Audit and Control Association (NTPA)
ISACAR Inter Service and Civil Air Rally (SAUO)
ISACC Initial Satellite Command and Control Center (MCD)
ISACCC Initial Military Satellite Command and Control Center (ACAE)
ISACCC Initial Satellite Communications Control Center (MCD)
ISACCC Interim Satellite Communications Control Center (SAUO)
ISACCD International Society of Adult Congential Cardiac Disease (ADWA)
ISACMETU International Secretariat of Arts, Communications Media, and Entertainment TradeUnions (EAIO)
ISACP Italian Society of Authors, Composers and Publishers (SAUO)
ISACS Independent Schools Association of the Central States (AEBS)
ISAC Structure Ion-implanted and Self-Aligned Contact Structure (SAUS)
ISA/CUR Comparative Urban Research. International Sociological Association, Committe for Community Research. College Park (SAUO)
ISAD Information Science and Automation Division [*Later, LITA*] [*American Library Association*]
ISAD Information Systems, Authorization Directory (SAUO)
ISAD Integrated Starter-Alternator-Damper [*Automotive engineering*]
ISAD Integrate Sample and Dump [*Telecommunications*] (IAA)
ISAD International Society of Abortion Doctors (ADWA)
ISAD Introduction to ADP Systems Analysis and Design (SAUO)
ISADC Interim Standard Airborne Digital Computer (MCD)
ISADH Inappropriate Secretion of Antidiuretic Hormone [*Endocrinology*] (MAE)
ISADN International Standard Authority Data Number (SAUS)
ISADPM International Society for the Abolition of Data Processing Machines (SAUO)
ISADPM International Society for the Abolition of Data-Processing Machines (SAUS)
ISADS Innovative Strategic Aircraft Design Studies (or Study) (SAUS)
ISADS Integrated Strapdown Air Data System (SAUS)
ISADS International Symposium on Autonomous Decentralized Systems (SAUO)
ISAE Indian Society of Agricultural Economics (SAUO)
ISAE Indian Society of Agricultural Engineers (SAUO)
ISAE Internacia Scienca Asocio Esperantista [*International Association of Esperanto-Speaking Scientists*] [*Oslo, Norway*] (EA)
ISAE International Esperantist Scientific Association (SAUO)
ISAE International Society for AIDS Education (EA)
ISAE International Society of Association Executives (SAUO)
Isae Isaeus [*Fourth century BC*] [*Classical studies*] (OCD)
ISAeM International Society for Aerosols in Medicine [*See also IGAeM*] (EAIO)
ISAF Indexed Sequential Access File (SAUS)
ISAF Intelligent Sensor Assessment Facility (ACAE)
ISAF Intermediate Super Abrasion Furnace (SAUS)
ISAF Intermediate Super-Abrasion Furnace
ISAF International Security Assistance Force
ISAF Isotopic Source Adjustable Fissometer [*Nuclear energy*] (NRCH)
IsAF Israeli Air Force
ISAFA Industrial Safety (journ.) (SAUS)
ISAF Black Intermediate Super Abrasion Furnace Black (SAUS)
ISAF Black Intermediate Super Abrasive Furnace Black (SAUS)
ISAF-HM Intermediate Super Abrasion Furnace-High Modulus (SAUS)
ISAFIS Indonesian Students Association for International Studies (SAUO)
ISAF-LM Intermediate Super Abrasion Furnace-Low Modulus (SAUS)
ISAF-LS Intermediate Super Abrasion Furnace-Low Structure (SAUS)
ISAFP Intelligence Service at the Philippine Armed Forces (SAUS)
ISAG IGOSS [*Integrated Global Ocean Services System*] Scientific Advisory Group [*Marine science*] (OSRA)
ISAG International Society for Animal Genetics (HGEN)
ISAG Internet Security Advisors Group
ISAG Office of the Auditor General, Springfield, IL [*Library symbol*] [*Library of Congress*] (LCLS)
ISAGA International Simulation and Gaming Association (EA)
ISAGAT Industry Standard Architecture-Guaranteed Access Time (SAUO)
ISAGE International Symposium on Antarctic Glaciological Exploration
ISAGEX International Satellite Geodesy Experiment
ISAGEX International Satellite Geodesy Experiments (SAUO)
ISAGL International Shipmasters Association of the Great Lakes
ISAGUG International Software AG Users Group (EA)
ISAH Integrated System for Automated Hydrography (SAUS)
ISAH International Symposium on Acoustical Holography (SAUO)
ISAHM International Society for Animal and Human Mycology (SAUO)
ISAI Independent Schools Association [*British*]
ISAI Independent Schools Association Inc. (AIE)
ISAI ISA [*Instruments, Systems and Automation*] International (ACII)
ISAIAH Israel Space Agency Investigation About Hornets (SAUO)
ISAID Institute for the Study and Application of International Development (SAUO)
ISAIS Indian Society for Automation and Information Sciences (SAUO)
ISA Journal Instrument Society of America Journal (SAUO)
ISA Journal Instrument Society of America Journal (journ.) (SAUS)
ISAKE Internacia Societo de Arkitektoj kaj Konstruistoj Esperantistoj (SAUO)
ISAKMP Internet Security Association Key Management Protocol (SAUS)
ISAKOS International Society of Arthroscopy, Knee Surgery and Orthopaedic Sports Medicine (SAUO)

ISal............ Bryan-Bennett Public Library, Salem, IL [*Library symbol*] [*Library of Congress*] (LCLS)
ISAL............ Icelandic Aluminium Co. Limited (SAUO)
ISAL............ Information Service Access Lines (SAUO)
ISAL............ Information System Access Lines [*Computer science*]
ISAL............ International Society of African Lawyers (SAUO)
ISAL............ International Surface Air Lift (SAUS)
ISALC........... International Society of Animal License Collectors (EA)
ISalCD......... Selmaville Community Consolidated District 10, Salem, IL [*Library symbol*] [*Library of Congress*] (LCLS)
ISALPA........ Incorporated Society of Auctioneers and Landed Property Agents [*British*] (ILCA)
ISAM............ Independent School Association of Massachusetts (SAUO)
ISAM............ Indexed Sequential Access Management (SAUO)
ISAM............ Indexed Sequential-Access Management (SAUS)
ISAM............ Indexed Sequential Access Method [*Pronounced "i-sam"*] [*Computer science*]
ISAM............ Indexed Sequential File Access Method (SAUS)
ISAM............ Index Sequential Access Method [*Telecommunications*] (ACRL)
ISAM............ Infant of Substance-Abusing Mother [*Pediatrics*]
ISAM............ Information System Acquisition Methods (ACAE)
ISAM............ Institute for Studies in American Music (EA)
ISAM............ Integrated Switching and Multiplexing [*IBM Corp.*]
ISAM............ International Society for Aerosols in Medicine (EAIO)
ISAM............ Intravenous Streptokinase in Acute Myocardial Infarction [*Cardiology study*]
Isam............ Iran System Analysis and Management Corporation (SAUO)
ISAM............ Israeli Society for the Application of Mathematics (MCD)
ISAMS.......... Improved Stratospheric and Mesospheric Sounder (MCD)
ISAM System... Integrated Switching and Multiplexing System (SAUS)
ISAM-VLR.... Indexed Sequential Access Method-Variable Length Record (SAUS)
ISAN............ Isentropic Analysis (SAUS)
ISan............ Sandwich Township Public Library, Sandwich, IL [*Library symbol*] [*Library of Congress*] (LCLS)
I/S Anal....... I/S Analyzer (journ.) (SAUS)
ISanCH........ Sandwich Community Hospital, Sandwich, IL [*Library symbol*] [*Library of Congress*] (LCLS)
IS&C............ International Systems and Controls (SAUS)
IS & CG....... Information Systems and Communications Group (HGAA)
IS&D............ Integrate Sample and Dump (SAUS)
IS&DN......... Illustrated Sporting & Dramatic News [*A publication*] (WDAA)
IS&E............ Industrial Science and Engineering (SAUO)
IS&EU.......... International Stereotypers and Electrotypers Union (SAUO)
IS&FP.......... Industrial Safety and Fire Protection (SAUO)
IS&H............ Industrial Safety and Health (SAUO)
IS&MD......... Instructional Standards and Materials Division (SAUO)
IS&RP.......... Initial Spares and Repair Parts (SAUO)
IS&R System... Information Storage and Retrieval System (SAUS)
ISandSD....... Sandoval Community Unit School District 50 (SAUS)
ISandSD....... Sandoval Community Unit School District 501, Sandoval, IL [*Library symbol*] [*Library of Congress*] (LCLS)
IS & T.......... Industry, Science, and Technology
IS&T............ Information Systems and Technology (SAUO)
IS & T.......... Innovative Science and Technology (DOMA)
IS&T............ International Science and Technology (journ.) (SAUS)
IS&T............ Society for Imaging Science and Technology (NTPA)
ISanH.......... Lynn G. Haskin School, Sandwich, IL [*Library symbol*] [*Library of Congress*] (LCLS)
ISanHS........ Sandwich Community High School, Sandwich, IL [*Library symbol*] [*Library of Congress*] (LCLS)
ISanJS......... Sandwich Junior High School, Sandwich, IL [*Library symbol*] [*Library of Congress*] (LCLS)
ISanP........... Prairie View School, Sandwich, IL [*Library symbol*] [*Library of Congress*] (LCLS)
I-SANTA....... Industrial Stapling and Nailing Technical Association (EA)
ISANTA........ International Staple, Nail, and Tool Association (EA)
ISanW.......... W. W. Woodbury School, Sandwich, IL [*Library symbol*] [*Library of Congress*] (LCLS)
ISAO............ International Society for/of Artificial Organs (SAUO)
ISAP............ Individual System Automation Plans [*Military*]
ISAP............ Information Sort and Predict
ISAP............ Institute for the Study of Animal Problems [*Defunct*] (EA)
ISAP............ Instituto Sudamericano del Petroleo [*South American Petroleum Institute*]
ISAP............ Integrated Safety Assessment Program [*Nuclear energy*] (NRCH)
ISAP............ Interactive Survey Analysis Package (IAA)
ISAP............ International School Art Program [*Defunct*]
ISAP............ International Society for Adolescent Psychiatry (NTPA)
ISAP............ International Society for Asphalt Pavements (SAUO)
ISAP............ International Society of Art and Psychopathology [*Paris, France*] (EA)
ISAP............ Internet Self-Assessment in Pharmacology (SAUO)
ISAP............ South American Petroleum Institute (SAUS)
ISAPA.......... International Screen Advertising Producer's Association [*Defunct*] (EA)
ISAPC.......... Incorporated Society of Authors, Playwrights, and Composers (BARN)
ISAPI........... Internet Server API [*All-Purpose Interface*] [*Microsoft and Process Software Corp.*] [*Computer science*]
ISAPI........... Internet Server Application Program Interface [*Computer science*] (IGQR)
ISAPI........... Internet Services API [*Computer science*]
ISAPI........... Internet Servier API (SAUS)
ISAPM......... International Shipowners Association of Peninsular Malaysia (SAUO)
ISAPS.......... International Society of Aesthetic Plastic Surgery (SAUO)
ISAR............ Indirect Scratchpad Address Register (SAUS)
ISAR............ Indirect Scratehpad Address (SAUS)
ISAR............ Information Storage and Retrieval [*Computer science*] (DIT)
ISAR............ Institute for/on Soviet-American Relations (SAUO)
ISAR............ Intelligent Synthetic Aperture Radar (SAUS)
ISAR............ Interim Storage and Retrieval (SAUS)
ISAR............ International Safety for Astrological Research (SAUO)
ISAR............ International Society for Animal Rights (EA)
ISAR............ International Society for Astrological Research (EA)
ISAR............ Inter-Seamount Acoustic Range
ISAR............ Inverse Synthetic Aperture Laser (ACAE)
ISAR............ Inverse Synthetic Aperture RADAR [*Navy*] (ANA)
ISAR............ Science and Agricultural Institute of Rwanda (SAUO)
ISAR Base... Information Storage and Retrieval Base (SAUS)
ISARC.......... Installation Shipping and Receiving Capability [*Army*] (AABC)
ISARD.......... International School for Agriculture and Resource Development (SAUO)
ISARL.......... Indirect Scratchpad Address Register Lower (SAUS)
ISARN Bulletin... Iowa State Association for Registered Nurses Bulletin (journ.) (SAUS)
ISARU.......... Indirect Scratchpad Address Register Upper (SAUS)
ISAS............ Illinois State Academy of Science (PDAA)
ISAS............ Industrial Sales and Service (SAUO)
ISAS............ Information Science and Automation Section (SAUS)
ISAS............ Infrared Small Astronomical Spacecraft
ISAS............ Institute for Space and Aeronautical Science (SAUO)
ISAS............ Institute for Space and Astronautical Science
ISAS............ Institute for Spectrochemistry and Applied Spectroscopy (SAUS)
ISAS............ Institute of Social and Administrative Studies (SAUO)
ISAS............ Institute of Southern African Studies (SAUO)
ISAS............ Institute of Space and Aeronautical Science [*Japan*]
ISAS............ Institute of Space and Atmospheric Science (SAUS)
ISAS............ Institute of Space and Atmospheric Studies (SAUO)
ISAS............ Integrated Smart Artillery Synthesis (RDA)
ISAS............ Integrated Spacecraft Avionics System (IAA)
ISAS............ Integrated Strike Avionics System (ACAE)
ISAS............ Intelligent Shelter Attack Submunition (SAUS)
ISAS............ International School for Advanced Studies (SAUO)
ISAS............ International Schools Association (SAUO)
ISAS............ International Screen Advertising Association (SAUS)
ISAS............ International Society of African Scientists (EA)
ISAS............ International Society of Air Safety Investigators (SAUO)
ISAS............ Isotopic Source Assay System
ISAS............ Iterative Single Wavelength Anomalous Scattering [*Crystallography*]
ISASC.......... International Society of Antique Scale Collectors (EA)
ISASD.......... International Symposium on Aeroelastics and Structural Dynamics (SAUS)
ISASI........... International Society for/of Air Safety Investigators (SAUO)
ISASM.......... Intelligent Shelter Attack Submunition (ACAE)
ISASNP........ International Symposium on Aerospace Nuclear Propulsion (MCD)
ISAST.......... International Society for the Arts, Sciences, and Technology (EA)
ISAS/T......... Transactions of the Illinois State Academy of Science. Chicago (SAUO)
ISAT............ Initial Surface Absorption Test
ISAT............ Integrated Science and Technology Program [*Military*]
ISAT............ Integration of Safety Analysis Techniques for Process Control Systems (SAUO)
ISAT............ International Society for/of Analytical Trilogy (SAUO)
ISAT............ International Society of Analytical Trilogy [*See also SITA*] [*Sao Paulo, Brazil*] (EAIO)
ISAT............ Interrupt Storage Area Table [*Computer science*] (OA)
ISAT............ Invite, Show, and Test [*Military*] (SDI)
ISATA.......... International Symposium on Automotive Technology and Automation (SAUS)
ISATA.......... International Symposium on Automotive Technology and Automation (SAUO)
ISATATU...... International Society of Air Travellers and Air Transport Users (SAUO)
ISATT.......... International Study Association on Teacher Thinking (SAUO)
ISAU............ International Staff Association of UNESCO (SAUO)
ISAUS.......... Indonesian Students Association in the United States (EA)
ISAUS.......... Iranian Students Association in the United States
IS Aust........ Institute of Surveyors, Australia (SAUO)
ISAV............ Institute of Sound and Vibration (MCD)
ISAV............ Instituto de Sistemas Audio-Visuales [*Institute of Audio-Visual Media*] [*Colombia*]
ISAVVT........ International Symposium on the Aerodynamics and Ventilation of Vehicle Tunnels (PDAA)
ISAW............ International Society of Aviation Writers
ISAZ............ International Society for Anthrozoology (GVA)
ISAZ............ Isolation Accommodation Zone [*Geology*]
ISB.............. Illinois Baptist Historical Library, Springfield, IL [*Library symbol*] [*Library of Congress*] (LCLS)
ISB.............. Incentive Spirometry Breathing [*Medicine*] (DAVI)
ISB.............. Incident Shadow Boundary (SAUS)
ISB.............. Incomplete Sentences Blank [*Psychology*] (DIPS)
ISB.............. Independent School Bulletin (journ.) (SAUS)
ISB.............. Independent Side Band (SAUS)
ISB.............. Independent Sideband
ISB.............. Independent Society of Bricklayers [*A union*] [*British*]
ISB.............. Industrial Security Bulletin (ACAE)
ISB.............. Industry Service Bureaus
ISB.............. Information Sciences Building (SAUO)
ISB.............. Information Service Branch (SAUS)

ISB .... Information Services Branch [*Chalk River Nuclear Laboratories*] [*Atomic Energy of Canada Ltd.*] [*Information service or system*] (IID)
ISB .... Information Services Branch [*SHAPE Technical Center*] [*The Hague, Netherlands*]
ISB .... Information System Branch (SAUS)
ISB .... Information Systems Branch [*National Institutes of Health*] (IID)
ISB .... Information Systems Building (SAUS)
ISB .... Infrared Security Barrier (SAUS)
ISB .... Initial Staging Base [*Army*] (DOMA)
ISB .... Initial Status Byte (SAUS)
ISB .... Institute of Scientific Business [*British*]
ISB .... Institute of Small Business [*British*]
ISB .... Integrated System Bus (GART)
ISB .... Intelligence and Security Board [*Military*] (MCD)
ISB .... Intelligence Support Branch (SAUO)
ISB .... Intelligence Systems Branch [*Military*] (IAA)
ISB .... Interchangeability Survey Board
ISB .... Interchange Financial Services Corp. [*Formerly, Interchange State Bank*] [*AMEX symbol*] (SPSG)
ISB .... Interchange Finl Svcs [*AMEX symbol*] (TTSB)
ISB .... Interlanguage Studies Bulletin (SAUO)
ISB .... Intermediate Sideband (NATG)
ISB .... Intermediate Staging Base
ISB .... Intermediate Support Base [*Military*] (NVT)
ISB .... Internationaler Studentenbund [*International Union of Students*]
ISB .... International Sanitary Bureau (SAUO)
ISB .... International School of Brussels (SAUO)
ISB .... International Sinabarb [*Vancouver Stock Exchange symbol*]
ISB .... International Society of Bassists. Newsletter (journ.) (SAUS)
ISB .... International Society of Biometeorology [*See also SIB*] [*Zurich, Switzerland*] (EAIO)
ISB .... International Society of Biorheology [*Germany*] (EAIO)
ISB .... International Symposium on Bioceramics (SAUS)
ISB .... International Symposium on Biomembranes
ISB .... Internet3D Space Builder
ISB .... Interstate Tariff Bureau, Inc., Lakewood OH [*STAC*]
ISB .... Investors Service Bureau [*Investment term*]
ISB .... Islamabad/Rawalpindi [*Pakistan*] [*Airport symbol*] (OAG)
ISB .... Issues Screening Board [*NASA*] (SPST)
ISB .... Nisab [*South Arabia*] [*Airport symbol*] (AD)
ISB .... Southern Methodist University, Bridwell Library, Dallas, TX [*OCLC symbol*] (OCLC)
ISBA .... Imperial Services Boxing Association (SAUO)
ISBA .... Incorporated Society of British Advertisers [*British*]
ISBA .... Independent Safety Board Act (SAUS)
ISBA .... Independent Safety Board Act of 1974
ISBA .... Independent Schools Bursars' Association [*British*]
ISBA .... Indiana School Boards Association (SAUO)
ISBA .... Inflatable Seat Belt Assembly [*Automotive safety*]
ISBA .... International Safety Belt Association (SAUO)
ISBA .... International Sea-Bed Area (SAUO)
ISBA .... International Sea-Bed Authority [*Marine science*] [*United Nations*] (OSRA)
ISBA .... International Ships-in-Bottles Association (EA)
ISBA .... International Society of British Advertisers (SAUO)
ISBACLUB .... International Shipbrokers & Agents Protect & Indemnity Club Ltd. (SAUO)
ISBB .... Inhibit Switch B Bit (SAUS)
ISBB .... International Society for/of Bioclimatology and Biometeorology (SAUO)
ISBB .... International Society of Bioclimatology and Biometeorology (IEEE)
ISBB .... International Society of Biometeorology and Bioclimatology (SAUS)
ISBC .... Infantry Squad Battle Course [*Army*]
ISBC .... Institute of Certified Business Counselors (EA)
ISBC .... Intel Single Board Computer (SAUS)
ISBC .... Interdepartmental Savings Bond Committee [*Military*] (AABC)
ISBC .... International Small Business Congress (SAUS)
ISBC .... International Society of Bible Collecíors (SAUO)
ISBC .... International Society of Bible Collectors (EA)
ISBCFH .... International Society for British Genealogy and Family History (SAUO)
ISBD .... Information Services Business Division (SAUO)
ISBD .... International Bibliographic Description (SAUO)
ISBD .... International Soap Box Derby, Inc. (EA)
ISBD .... International Standard Bibliographic Description [*Library of Congress*]
ISBD .... International Standard Book Description (SAUS)
ISBD(A) .... International Standard Bibliographic Description - Antiquarian
ISBD(CM) .... International Standard Bibliographic Description for Cartographic Materials [*Library of Congress*]
ISBD(CP) ..... International Standard Bibliographic Description (Component Parts)
ISBD(G) .... International Standard Bibliographic Description - General
ISBDG .... International Standard Bibliographic Description-General (SAUS)
ISBDM .... International Standard Bibliographic Description for Monographic Publications (SAUS)
ISBD(M) .... International Standard Bibliographic Description for Monographs [*Library of Congress*]
ISBD(NBM)... International Standard Bibliographic Description for Non-Book Materials
ISBD(PM) .... International Standard Bibliographic Description for Printed Music
ISBDS .... International Standard Bibliographic Description for Serial Publications (SAUS)
ISBD(S) .... International Standard Bibliographic Description for Serials [*Library of Congress*]
ISBE .... Independent Small Business Employers of America (EA)
ISBE .... International Society for Boundary Elements (EAIO)
ISBE .... International Society for Business Education (SAUO)
ISBE .... International Society for Business Education, US Chapter [*Reston, VA*] (EA)
ISBE .... International Standard Bible Encyclopaedia [*A publication*] (BJA)
ISBEA .... Independent Small Business Employers of America [*Later, ISBE*] (EA)
ISBF .... Interactive Search of Bibliographic Files
ISBF .... ISB Financial [*NASDAQ symbol*] (TTSB)
ISBF .... ISB Financial Corp. [*NASDAQ symbol*] (SAG)
ISBFA .... International Sphynx Breeders and Fanciers' Association (EA)
ISB Fn .... ISB Financial Corp. [*Associated Press*] (SAG)
ISBGA .... Irish Sugar Beet Growers Association (SAUO)
ISBGFH .... International Society for British Genealogy and Family History (EA)
ISBI .... International Savings Banks Institute [*See also IICE*] [*Geneva, Switzerland*] (EAIO)
ISBI .... International Society for Burn Injuries (EAIO)
ISBIC .... Inter Service Balkan Intelligence Committee (SAUO)
ISBIC .... Interservice Balkan Intelligence Committee [*World War II*]
ISBJ .... Interchange Financial Services Corp. (New Jersey) [*NASDAQ symbol*] (COMM)
ISBL .... Information System Base Language
ISBL .... Inside Battery Limits [*Chemical engineering*]
ISBM .... Institute for the Study of Business Markets [*Pennsylvania State University*] [*Research center*] (RCD)
ISBM .... International Schools of Business Management (SAUO)
ISBM .... International Society of Behavioural Medicine (SAUO)
ISBM .... International Society of Biophysical Medicine [*British*] (IRUK)
ISbM .... Motorola Communications Sector Library, Schaumburg, IL [*Library symbol*] [*Library of Congress*] (LCLS)
ISB Modulation... Independent Sideband Modulation (SAUS)
ISBN .... Integrated Satellite Business Network (ACAE)
ISBN .... International Scientific Book Number (SAUS)
ISBN .... International Standard Book Number [*Library of Congress*]
ISBN 0-03.... Harcourt Brace (SAUO)
ISBN 0-06.... Harper Collins (SAUO)
ISBN 0-07.... McGraw-Hill (SAUO)
ISBN 0-08.... Pergamon (SAUO)
ISBN 0-12.... Acadernic Press (SAUO)
ISBN 0-19.... Clarendon (SAUO)
ISBN 0-201... Addison-Wesley (SAUO)
ISBN 0-226... University of Chicago Press (SAUO)
ISBN 0-256... Irwin (SAUO)
ISBN 0-262... MIT Press (SAUO)
ISBN 0-306... Plenum (SAUO)
ISBN 0-316... Little, Brown (SAUO)
ISBN 0-385... Doubleday (SAUO)
ISBN 0-387... Springer-Verlag New York (SAUO)
ISBN 0-393... W. W. Norton (SAUO)
ISBN 0-395... Houghton-Mifflin (SAUO)
ISBN 0-412... Chapman & Hall (SAUO)
ISBN 0-415... Routledge (SAUO)
ISBN 0-440... Dell (SAUO)
ISBN 0-442... Van Nostrand Reinhold (SAUO)
ISBN 0-471... Wiley (SAUO)
ISBN 0-486... Dover (SAUO)
ISBN 0-521... Cambridge University Press (SAUO)
ISBN 0-536... Xerox (SAUO)
ISBN 0-553... Bantam (SAUO)
ISBN 0-670... Penguin (SAUO)
ISBN 0-671... Simon and Schuster (SAUO)
ISBN 0-672... Adobe Press (SAUO)
ISBN 0-674... Harvard University Press (SAUO)
ISBN 0-679... Vintage and other Random Houseimprints (SAUO)
ISBN 0-688... William Morrow (SAUO)
ISBN 0-691... Princeton University Press (SAUO)
ISBN 0-887... William Morrow & Co. (SAUO)
ISBN 0-7503... Adam Hilger (SAUO)
ISBN 0-7645... IDG (SAUO)
ISBN 0-7821... Sybex (SAUO)
ISBN 0-8014... Cornell University Press (SAUO)
ISBN 0-8018... Johns Hopkins University Press (SAUO)
ISBN 0-8020... University of Toronto Press (SAUO)
ISBN 0-8052... Schocken Books (SAUO)
ISBN 0-8053... Benjamin/Cumnings (SAUO)
ISBN 0-8162... Holden-Day (SAUO)
ISBN 0-8186... IEEE (SAUO)
ISBN 0-8194... SPIE (SAUO)
ISBN 0-8306... TAB Books (SAUO)
ISBN 0-85274... IOP as well (SAUO)
ISBN 0-88029... Barnes and Noble (SAUO)
ISBN 981-02... World Scientific (SAUO)
ISBN 1-57444... St. Luice Press CRC Press LLC (SAUO)
ISBN 0-911014... NEO Press (SAUO)
ISBN 0-912675... Ardsley House Publ., Inc. (SAUO)
ISBNA .... International Standard Book Numbering Agency (SAUO)
ISBO .... Islamic States Broadcasting Organisation (or Organization) (SAUO)
ISBO .... Islamic States Broadcasting Organization [*Jeddah, Saudi Arabia*] (EAIO)
ISBOA .... Idaho School Business Officials Association (SAUO)
ISBOR .... International Society of Breath Odor Research (SAUO)
ISBP .... International Society for Biochemical Pharmacology
I-SBR .... Innovative Space Based Radar (ACAE)
ISBR .... Interior Salt Basin Region (SAUS)
ISBRA .... International Society Biomedical Research on Alcoholism (EAIO)

ISBS............ Icelandic State Broadcasting Service (SAUO)
ISBS............ Integrated Small Business Software (NITA)
ISBS............ International Scholarly Book Services (SAUO)
ISBS............ International Society of Biomechanics in Sports (SAUO)
ISBS............ International Specialized Books Services [*Book distributor*]
ISBT............ International Society of Beverage Technologists (NTPA)
ISBT............ International Society of Blood Transfusion (EA)
ISBX............ Integrated Services Branch Exchange [*Telecommunications*] (OSI)
ISC.............. Chief Intelligence Specialist (SAUS)
ISC.............. Concordia Theological Seminary, Springfield, IL [*Library symbol*] [*Library of Congress*] [*Obsolete*] (LCLS)
ISC.............. Duneland School Corp., Chesterton, IN [*OCLC symbol*] (OCLC)
ISC.............. Duneland School Corporation (SAUO)
ISC.............. Freemasonry International Supreme Council (SAUO)
ISC.............. Icelandic Steamship Co. (SAUS)
ISc.............. Iconic Store, Central [*Psychophysiology*]
ISC.............. Idaho State College [*Later, Idaho State University*] (AEBS)
ISC.............. Ideal Standard Cost (VLIE)
ISC.............. Idle Speed Control [*Automotive engineering*]
I-SC............ Illinois Supreme Court, Springfield, IL [*Library symbol*] [*Library of Congress*] (LCLS)
ISC.............. Image Stabilization Compensation (ACAE)
ISC.............. Immune Spleen (SAUS)
ISC.............. Immune Spleen Cell
ISC.............. Immunoglobulin-Secreting Cell [*Medicine*] (DB)
ISC.............. Imperial Service College [*British*]
ISC.............. Imperial Smelting Corporation (SAUO)
ISC.............. Imperial Staff College (ODA)
ISC.............. Implicit Subroutine Call (SAUS)
ISC.............. Implied Subroutine Call (SAUS)
ISC.............. Improved Submarine Communication (MCD)
ISC.............. Incorporated Society of Chiropodists (SAUO)
ISC.............. Incorporated Staff Sight-Singing College [*London*]
ISC.............. Incremental Support Capability (ACAE)
ISC.............. Independent Search Consultants [*An association*] (EA)
ISC.............. Independent Search Consultants, Inc. (SAUO)
ISC.............. Index of Status Characteristics
ISC.............. Indiana State College (SAUO)
ISC.............. Indian School Certificate (SAUO)
ISC.............. Indian Space Commission (SAUO)
ISC.............. Indian Staff Corporation (SAUO)
ISC.............. Indian Staff Corps [*British*] (ROG)
ISC.............. Indirect Semiconductor (SAUS)
ISC.............. Indirect Strike Control
ISC.............. Individual Soldier's Computer [*Army*] (RDA)
ISC.............. Indoor Sports Club (EA)
ISC.............. Industrial Security Commission (SAUO)
ISC.............. Industrial Security Committee (SAUO)
ISC.............. Industrial Source Complex [*Environmental science*] (GFGA)
ISC.............. Industrials Source Complex (SAUO)
ISC.............. Industrial Support Contactor (SAUS)
ISC.............. Industrial Support Contractor (KSC)
ISC.............. Industry Steering Council (AAEL)
ISC.............. Inertial Start Command
ISC.............. Infantry Section Carrier (SAUS)
ISC.............. Infiltration Surveillance Center (CINC)
ISC.............. Information Science Center (MCD)
ISC.............. Information Science Corp. (SAUS)
ISC.............. Information Science Corporation (NITA)
ISC.............. Information Security Contact (SAUO)
ISC.............. Information Separator Character (VLIE)
ISC.............. Information Services Center (VLIE)
ISC.............. Information Services Center (or Centre) (SAUO)
ISC.............. Information Services Control Branch [*Control Commission for Germany*] [*World War II*]
ISC.............. Information Services of Cranston [*Information service or system*] (IID)
ISC.............. Information Society of Canada (MCD)
ISC.............. Information Specialties Corp. (IID)
ISC.............. Information Store Cell (SAUS)
ISC.............. Information System Coordinator (SAUS)
ISC.............. Information Systems Center (SAUO)
ISC.............. Information Systems Co. (SAUS)
ISC.............. Information Systems Command [*DoD*]
ISC.............. Information Systems Committee [*Universities Funding Council*] (AIE)
ISC.............. Information Systems Company (SAUO)
ISC.............. Information Systems Council (SAUO)
ISC.............. Infrared Sightline Control
ISC.............. Infrastructure Special Committee [*NATO*] (NATG)
ISC.............. Initial Slope Circuit [*Telecommunications*] (OA)
ISC.............. Initial Software Configuration Map (MCD)
isc.............. Initial Software Configuration Map (NAKS)
ISC.............. Initial Student Characteristics
ISC.............. Input Signal Conditioner (SAUS)
ISC.............. In Situ Combustion [*Engineering*]
ISC.............. Insoluble Collagen [*Biochemistry*]
ISC.............. Inspection and Safety Center [*Military*]
ISC.............. Inspectorate of Stores and Clothing (SAUO)
ISC.............. Installation Support Center (VLIE)
ISC.............. Institute for the Study of Conflict [*British*]
ISC.............. Instruction Set Computer (VLIE)
ISC.............. Instruction Staticizing Control (IEEE)
ISC.............. Instrumentation System Corp. (MCD)
ISC.............. Instrumentation System Corporation (SAUO)
ISC.............. Instrumentation Systems Center [*University of Wisconsin - Madison*] [*Research center*] (RCD)
isc.............. in such case (SAUS)
ISC.............. Insulated Signal Coupler (IAA)
ISC.............. Integrated Semiconductor Circuit (VLIE)
ISC.............. Integrated Ship Control
ISC.............. Integrated Stage Concept (MCD)
ISC.............. Intelligence Subject Code
ISC.............. Intelligence Support Cells (SAUO)
ISC.............. Intelligence Support Center
ISC.............. Intelligence Support Command (CARL)
ISC.............. Intelligent Screen Cognition (SAUS)
ISC.............. Intelligent Subject Code (SAUS)
ISC.............. Intelligent Synchronous Controller [*Computer science*] (NITA)
ISC.............. Intelligent System Corp. (SAUO)
ISC.............. Intelligent Systems Corp.
ISC.............. Intelligent Systems Corporated (SAUS)
ISC.............. Intelligent Systems Corporation (SAUO)
ISC.............. Intensive Supportive Care (STED)
ISC.............. Interactive Sciences Corp. [*Information service or system*] (IID)
ISC.............. Interactive Systems Corporation (SAUO)
ISC.............. Interagency Staff Committee (SAUS)
ISC.............. Interagency Staff Committee on Public Law 480 [*Department of Agriculture*] (EGAO)
ISC.............. Inter-American Society of Cardiology [*Mexico City, Mexico*] (EAIO)
ISC.............. Interceptor Subsystem Controller
ISC.............. Intercommunications Set Control (SAUO)
ISC.............. Intercompany Services Coordination [*Telecommunications*] (TEL)
ISC.............. Intercomponent Subcontractor (MCD)
ISC.............. Interdisciplinary Scientific Commission [*COSPAR*]
ISC.............. Interface Signal Chart
ISC.............. Intermediate Slack Compensation (SAUS)
ISC.............. Intermediate Switching Center (SAUO)
ISC.............. Intermittent Self-Catherization [*Medicine*] (ODA)
ISC.............. Internal State Code (SAUS)
ISC.............. International Cruiseships [*Vancouver Stock Exchange symbol*]
ISC.............. International Salmonella Center
ISC.............. International Salon of Cartoons (EA)
ISC.............. International Salt Co. (SAUS)
ISC.............. International Salt Company (SAUO)
ISC.............. International School Correspondence (SAUO)
ISC.............. International Science Center (or Centre) (SAUS)
ISC.............. International Scientific Commission (SAUO)
ISC.............. International Scientific Publications [*Tel Aviv, Israel*]
ISC.............. International Security Conference and Exposition (ITD)
ISC.............. International Security Council (EA)
ISC.............. International Seismic Centre (SAUO)
ISC.............. International Seismological Centre [*ICSU*] [*Newbury, Berkshire, England*] (EAIO)
ISC.............. International Serials Catalogue [*A publication*]
ISC.............. International Sericultural Commission [*See also CSI*] [*La Mulatiere, France*] (EAIO)
ISC.............. International Service Carrier (SAUS)
ISC.............. International Signal and Control [*Army*]
ISC.............. International Signal Code (SAUS)
ISC.............. International Society for Chemotherapy (SAUO)
ISC.............. International Society for Chronobiology (EA)
ISC.............. International Society of Cardiology [*Later, ISFC*]
ISC.............. International Society of Chemotherapy [*Bad Heilbrunn, Federal Republic of Germany*] (EAIO)
ISC.............. International Society of Citriculture (EA)
ISC.............. International Society of Copoclephologists [*British*] (EAIO)
ISC.............. International Society of Cryosurgery [*Turin, Italy*] (EAIO)
ISC.............. International Society of Cryptozoology (EA)
ISC.............. International Softball Congress (EA)
ISC.............. International Softswitch Consortium (SAUO)
ISC.............. International Space Congress
ISC.............. International Space Corp.
ISC.............. International Space Corporation (SAUO)
ISC.............. International Sports Company (SAUO)
ISC.............. International Standard Electric Corporation (SAUO)
ISC.............. International Standard Electronic Corp. (SAUS)
ISC.............. International Standard Electronic Corporation (SAUO)
ISC.............. International Standards Committee (SAUO)
ISC.............. International Standards Council (SAUO)
ISC.............. International Statistical Classification
ISC.............. International Student Committee (SAUO)
ISC.............. International Student Conference
ISC.............. International Student Council (SAUO)
ISC.............. International Sugar Council [*London*] [*Later, ISO*]
ISC.............. International Supply Committee [*World War II*]
ISC.............. International Supreme Council (SAUS)
ISC.............. International Supreme Council of World Masons (EA)
ISC.............. International Surfing Committee (SAUO)
ISC.............. International Switching Center [*Communications*]
ISC.............. International Symposium on Chemiluminescence
ISC.............. Internet Service Center (SAUO)
ISC.............. Internet Software Consortium (SAUO)
ISC.............. Interseas Shipping Corp. (SAUS)
ISC.............. Interseas Shipping Corporation (SAUO)
ISC.............. Inter-Service Communication [*British*] [*World War II*]
ISC.............. Inter-Service Sports Council [*Military*]
ISC.............. Interservice Support Code [*Military*]
ISC.............. Interservice Support Coordinator (SAUO)
ISC.............. Inter-Shift Coordination [*Medicine*] (DMAA)

ISC ...... Intersociety Committee on Methods for Air Sampling and Analysis
ISC ...... Interstage Section Container
ISC ...... Interstate Commerce
ISC ...... Interstate Sanitation Commission (SAUO)
ISC ...... Interstellar Communications (AAG)
ISC ...... Interstitial Cells [*Histology*]
ISC ...... Inter-System Communication (NITA)
ISC ...... Inter-System Crossing [*Chemical Kinetics*]
ISC ...... Inter-Systems Communication (SAUO)
ISC ...... Intersystems Communications (SAUS)
ISC ...... Interval Selection Circuit
ISC ...... Interview Schedule for Children
ISC ...... Intrasite Cabling (CET)
ISC ...... Intrinsic Stimulating Activity (STED)
ISC ...... Introduction to the Federal Supply Catalog (SAUO)
ISC ...... Intuit Services Corp.
ISC ...... Invention Submission Corp. [*Information service or system*] (IID)
ISC ...... Invention Submission Corporation (SAUO)
ISC ...... Inverse Symbolic Calculator (SAUS)
ISC ...... Iowa Safety Council (SRA)
ISC ...... Iowa State College of Agriculture and Mechanic Arts [*Later, Iowa State University*] (MCD)
ISC ...... Iron and Steel Corporation of South Africa (SAUO)
ISC ...... Irreversibly Sickled Cell [*Hematology*]
ISC ...... Island Air Charters, Inc. [*ICAO designator*] (FAAC)
ISC ...... Isles Of Scilly [*England*] [*Airport symbol*] (OAG)
ISC ...... ISOLDE Committee (SAUS)
ISC ...... Isolette Servo Control [*Medicine*] (EDAA)
ISC ...... Italian Space Commission
ISC ...... Item Standardization Code (SAUO)
ISC ...... Item Status Code (NATG)
ISC2 ...... International Information Systems Security Certification Consortium (GART)
ISCA ...... Idle Speed Control Actuator [*Automotive engineering*]
ISCA ...... Independent Safety Consultants Association (DBA)
ISCA ...... Independent Schools Classical Association (SAUO)
ISCA ...... Industrial Specialty Chemical Association (EA)
ISCA ...... Information Systems Consultants Association (NTPA)
ISCA ...... Integrated Systems Control Architecture (SAUO)
ISCA ...... Intelligent Synchronous Communication Adapter (SAUS)
ISCA ...... Interest Standby Credit Arrangement
ISCA ...... Interlake Sailing Class Association (EA)
ISCA ...... International Sailing Craft Association [*Exeter, Devonshire, England*] (EAIO)
ISCA ...... International Scientific Collectors Association (EA)
ISCA ...... International Secretariat of Christian Artists (SAUO)
ISCA ...... International Senior Citizens Association (EA)
ISCA ...... International Shooting Coaches Association (EA)
ISCA ...... International Show Car Association (EA)
ISCA ...... International Society of Copier Artists (EA)
ISCA ...... International Specialty Car Association (EA)
ISCA ...... International Speedway Corp. [*NASDAQ symbol*] (SAG)
ISCA ...... International Stamp Collectors Association (SAUO)
ISCA ...... International Standards Coordination Association (SAUO)
ISCA ...... International Standards Steering Committee for Consumer Affairs (SAUO)
ISCA ...... International Stewards and Caterers Association (SAUO)
ISCA ...... International Sunfish Class Association (EA)
ISCA ...... International Symposium on Computer Architecture (SAUS)
ISCA ...... International Symposium on Computer Arithmetic (SAUS)
ISCA ...... Inter-Society Committee on Methods for Ambient Air Sampling and Analysis (SAUO)
ISCA ...... Ionization Spectroscopy for Chemical Analysis (DB)
ISCA ...... Iowa Student Computer Association (SAUO)
ISCA ...... Irish Setter Club of America (EA)
ISCAC ...... International Superconductor Applications Convention (SAUS)
ISCAC ...... Interstate Collegiate Athletic Conference (PSS)
ISCAD ...... International Suez Canal Advertising (SAUO)
IScAF ...... United States Air Force, Base Library, Scott AFB, IL [*Library symbol*] [*Library of Congress*] (LCLS)
IScAF-A ...... United States Air Force, Airlift Operations School, Scott Air Force Base, IL [*Library symbol*] [*Library of Congress*] (LCLS)
IScAF-E ...... United States Air Force, Environmental Technical Applications Center, Air Weather Service Technical Library, Scott Air Force Base, IL [*Library symbol*] [*Library of Congress*] (LCLS)
ISCAIC ...... International Symposium on Computing in Anesthesia and Intensive Care (SAUO)
ISCAIP ...... International Society for Child and Adolescent Injury Prevention (SAUO)
ISCAMPME ... Iodosuccinyl CAMP Tyrosine Methyl Ester [*Biochemistry*]
ISCAMS ...... Installation Standard Command Automated Data Processing Management System [*Army*]
ISCAMS ...... Installation Standard Command Automatic Data Processing Management System (SAUO)
ISCAN ...... Inertialess Steerable Communications Antenna
ISCAN ...... International Sanitary Convention for Air Navigation
IScan ...... I Scanner (SAUS)
ISCAR ...... Interdlsciplinary Science Committee on Antarctic Research (SAUO)
ISCAS ...... Integrated Submarine Communications Antenna System [*Navy*] (CAAL)
ISCAS ...... International Symposium on Circuits and Systems [*IEEE*] (MCD)
ISCAT ...... Integration of Systems in the Combined Arms Team (SAUO)
ISCAT ...... International Symposium on Computer-Assisted Tomography [*Medicine*] (EDAA)
ISCAY ...... International Solidarity Committee with Algerian Youth
ISCB ...... Inhibit Switch C Bit (SAUS)
ISCB ...... Interallied Staff Communications Board [*World War II*]
ISCB ...... International Society for Cell Biology [*Later, IFCB*] (ASF)
ISCB ...... International Society for Classical Bibliography [*Paris, France*] (EAIO)
ISCB ...... International Society for Clinical Biostatistics (EAIO)
ISCB ...... International Society for/of Cell Biology (SAUO)
ISCB ...... International Society of Cardiology Bulletin [*Medicine*] (EDAA)
ISCBA ...... Insulating Siding Core Board Association [*Defunct*] (EA)
ISCBL ...... Interrupt System Control Block List (SAUS)
ISCBMC ...... International Single Comb Black Minorca Club (EA)
ISCC ...... Interdepartmental Sub-committee for Component Co-ordination (SAUO)
ISCC ...... Internal Service Coordination Center (SAUO)
ISCC ...... International Semiconductor Conference (SAUS)
ISCC ...... International Service Coordination Center [*Communications*]
ISCC ...... International Society Corrosion Commission (SAUO)
ISCC ...... International Somali Cat Club
ISCC ...... International Standard Commodity Classification of All Goods and Services
ISCC ...... International Strata Control Conference (SAUS)
ISCC ...... Inter-Service Components Technical Committee (SAUO)
ISCC ...... Inter-Society Color Council (EA)
ISCC ...... Inter-Society Committee on Corrosion (SAUO)
ISCC ...... Inter-Society Cytology Council [*Later, American Society of Cytology - ASC*]
ISCC ...... Interstate Solar Coordination Council (EA)
ISCC ...... Iranian Students Counseling Center (EA)
ISCC ...... Iron and Steel Consumer Council (SAUO)
ISCCED ...... Independent Sector Coordinating Committee on Environment and Development (GNE)
ISCCF ...... International Study Center for Children and Families (SAUO)
ISCCP ...... International Cloud Climatology Project (SAUO)
ISCCP ...... International Satellite Cloud Climate (or Climatology) Project (SAUO)
ISCCP ...... International Satellite Cloud Climate Program (SAUS)
ISCCP ...... International Satellite Cloud Climatology Program (SAUO)
ISCD ...... Interface Specification Control Document (KSC)
ISCD ...... International Society for Clinical Densitometry (SAUO)
ISCD ...... International Society for Community Development (EA)
ISCD ...... International Society for Computerized Dentistry (SAUO)
ISCDD ...... International Scheme for the Coordination of Dairy Development (EAIO)
ISCDP ...... International Standing Committee on Distribution Problems [*International Water Supply Association*]
ISCDS ...... International Stop Continental Drift Society [*Defunct*] (EA)
ISCE ...... Institute for the Study of Conscious Evolution [*Defunct*] (EA)
ISCE ...... International Society for a Complete Earth (EA)
ISCE ...... International Society for Clinical Enzymology [*Hanover, Federal Republic of Germany*] (EAIO)
ISCE ...... International Society of Chemical Ecology (EA)
ISCE ...... Interstate Substitute Cost Estimate [*Federal Highway Administration*]
ISCEBS ...... International Society of Certified Employee Benefit Specialists [*Brookfield, WI*] (EA)
ISCED ...... International Society of Continuing Education in Dentistry [*See also SIECD*] [*Brussels, Belgium*] (EAIO)
ISCED ...... International Standard Classification of Education (MCD)
ISCEH ...... International Society for Clinical and Experimental Hypnosis [*Charles University*] (EA)
ISCERC ...... International Society for Clinical Electroretinography (SAUO)
ISCERG ...... International Society for Clinical Electroretinography
ISCES ...... International Society of Complex Environmental Studies (SAUO)
ISCES ...... International Symposium on Condensation and Evaporation of Solids (SAUS)
ISCET ...... International Society of Certified Electronics Technicians (EA)
ISCEV ...... International Society and/for Clinical Electrophysiology of Vision (SAUO)
ISCEV ...... International Society for Clinical Electrophysiology and/of Vision (SAUS)
ISCF ...... Industrial Sentence Completion Form [*Psychology*]
ISCF ...... Inter-School Christian Fellowship [*British*] (BI)
ISCF ...... Interstitial Cell Fluid (DMAA)
ISCF ...... Inter-System Control Facility (SAUS)
ISCFLG ...... Idle Speed Control Flag [*Automotive emissions*]
ISCG ...... Institute of School and College Governors [*British*] (EAIO)
ISCG ...... Institutional and Socioeconomic Coordinating Group (SAUO)
ISCG ...... Integrated Sys Consulting Gp [*NASDAQ symbol*] (TTSB)
ISCG ...... Integrated Systems Consulting Group, Inc. [*NASDAQ symbol*] (SAG)
ISCGM ...... International Steering Committee on Global Mapping (SAUO)
ISCGNBS ...... Inter-Society Color Council-National Bureau of Standards (SAUO)
ISCh ...... Incorporated Society of Chiropodists [*British*] (DI)
ISch ...... Steger-South Chicago Heights Library District, South Chicago Heights, IL [*Library symbol*] [*Library of Congress*] (LCLS)
ISCHDR ...... Inter-Society Commission for Heart Disease Resources
ISCHE ...... International Standing Committee for History of Education (SAUO)
ISCHE ...... International Standing Conference for the History of Education (AIE)
ISCHME ...... International Society for Computational Methodes in Engineering (SAUO)
ISCh Year Book ... Incorporated Society of Chiropodists Year Book (SAUO)
ISCh Year Book ... Incorporated Society of Chiropodists Year Book (journ.) (SAUS)
IScI ...... Information Science, Inc. (SAUS)
IScI ...... Information Science, Incorporated (SAUO)
ISCI ...... Information Service Civil International (SAUO)
ISCI ...... Information Systems Consultants, Inc. [*Information service or system*] (IID)
ISCI ...... Information Systems Consultants, Incorporated (SAUO)
ISCIE ...... Institute of Systems, Control and Information Engineers (SAUS)

ISCIG.......... Interservice Coordinating and Integrating Group (SAUO)
ISCII.......... International Standard Code for Information Interchange (NATG)
ISCJ.......... International Ski Club of Journalists (EAIO)
ISCL.......... Interim Status Compliance Letter [*Environmental Protection Agency*] (GFGA)
ISCLC.......... International Symposium of Column Liquid Chromatography (SAUS)
ISCLC.......... International Symposium on Column Liquid Chromatography [*1986*] [*San Francisco, CA*]
ISCLT.......... Industrial Source Complex Long-Term Model [*Environmental Protection Agency*] (GFGA)
ISCLT.......... International Society for Clinical Laboratory Technology (EA)
ISCLT.......... International Society of Clinical Laboratory Technologists (SAUO)
ISCM.......... International Society for/of Contemporary Music (SAUO)
ISCM.......... International Society of Cybernetic Medicine (EA)
ISCMA.......... International Superphosphate and Compound Manufacturers Association (SAUO)
ISCME.......... International Society for Computational Methods in Engineering (EAIO)
ISCMMS.......... Integrated Ship Control, Management & Monitoring System (SAUS)
ISCMMS.......... Integrated Ship Control Monitoring and Management System (SAUS)
ISCN.......... International Standard Cartographic Number (SAUS)
ISCN.......... International System for Human Cytogenetic Nomenclature
ISCNET.......... Inter-System Communications Sub-Network (SAUO)
ISCNI.......... Institute for the Study of Contract with Non-Human Intelligence
ISCO.......... Illinois Superconductor [*NASDAQ symbol*] (TTSB)
ISCO.......... Illinois Superconductor Corp. [*NASDAQ symbol*] (SAG)
ISCO.......... Independent Schools Careers Organisation (or Organization) (SAUS)
ISCO.......... Indicated Specific Carbon Monoxide
ISCO.......... Initial Systems Checkout
ISCO.......... Instrumentation Specialties Co.
ISCO.......... Instrumentation Specialties Company (SAUO)
ISCO.......... Interactive Systems Corporation (SAUO)
ISCO.......... International Scientific Council (SAUO)
ISCO.......... International Society of Corvette Owners
ISCO.......... International Standard Classification of Occupations (WDAA)
Isco.......... Isco, Inc. [*Associated Press*] (SAG)
ISCO.......... Istituto Nazionale per lo Studio della Congiuntura [*Data Resources, Inc.*] [*Database*]
ISCOL.......... International Systems Corporation of Lancaster (SAUO)
ISCOM.......... Immunostimulatory Complex [*Immunochemistry*]
ISCOM.......... Indian Satellite for Communication Technology (SAUS)
ISCOM.......... International Symposium on Communications (SAUS)
ISCOM.......... Island Commander
ISCOM.......... Israel Composites Institute [*Plastics research*]
ISCOMADEIRA... Island Commander Madeira (AABC)
ISCOMAZORES... Island Commander Azores
ISCOMBERMUDA... Island Commander Bermuda
ISCOMFAR... Island Commander, The Faroes (SAUO)
ISCOMFAROES... Island Commander Faroes
ISCOMGREENLAND... Island Commander Greenland
ISCOMICE.... Island Commander, Iceland (SAUO)
ISCOMICELAND... Island Commander Iceland
ISCOMS.......... Immunity-Stimulating Complexes (DB)
ISCON.......... Indian Steelworks Construction Company (SAUO)
ISCONG.......... International Society of Computers in Obstetrics, Neonatology, Gynecology (SAUO)
ISCOR.......... Iron and Steel Industrial Corp. (SAUS)
ISCOR.......... Iron and Steel Industrial Corporation (SAUO)
ISCOR.......... South African Iron & Steel Corp.
ISCORE.......... Intelligence Score (MCD)
ISCOS.......... Institute for Security and Cooperation in Outer Space (EA)
ISCOSS.......... International Symposium on the Chemistry of the Organic Solid State (SAUO)
ISCP.......... India Study Circle for Philately (EA)
ISCP.......... Infection Surveillance and Control Program [*Medicine*] (DMAA)
ISCP.......... Installation Spill Contingency Plan [*DoD*] (AFIT)
ISCP.......... Integrated Subsystem Calibration Plan (SAA)
ISCP.......... Intermediate Sodium Characterization Package [*Nuclear energy*] (NRCH)
ISCP.......... International Society for Chinese Philosophy (EA)
ISCP.......... International Society for/of Clinical Pathology (SAUO)
ISCP.......... International Society for/of Comparative Psychology (SAUO)
ISCP.......... International Society of Clinical Pathology [*Later, WASP*]
ISCP.......... Iowa State College Press (SAUO)
ISCPES.......... International Society on Comparative Physical Education and Sport (SAUO)
ISCPET.......... Illinois Statewide Curriculum Study Center in the Preparation of Secondary School English Teachers
ISCPLN.......... International Society of Psychiatric Consultation Liaison Nurses (NTPA)
ISCPP.......... International Society of Crime Preventation Practitioners (SAUO)
ISCPP.......... International Society of Crime Prevention Practitioners (EAIO)
ISC Process... Internal Surface Cooling Process (SAUS)
ISC Process... Intersystem Crossing Process (SAUS)
ISCPVS.......... Istituto Sindacale per la Cooperazione con i Paesi in Via di Sviluppo [*Trade Union Institute for Cooperation with Developing Countries*] [*Italy*] (EAIO)
ISC/R.......... Individual Soldier's Computer/Radio [*Army*] (INF)
ISCR.......... Intrastromal Corneal Ring [*Medicine*] (MELL)
ISCRE.......... International Symposium on Chemical Reaction Engineering
ISCRI.......... International Special Committee on Radio Interface (SAUO)
IS Crim.......... International Society of Criminology (SAUO)
ISCRO.......... Industrial Security Clearance Review Office [*DoD*]
ISCRP.......... International Society of City and Regional Planners [*See also AIU*]
ISCS.......... Inferred Self-Concept Scale [*Psychology*] (DHP)
ISCS.......... Information Service Computer System (DIT)
ISCS.......... Information Services Computer System (SAUS)
ISCS.......... Information Services Control Section (SAUO)
ISCS.......... Integrated Sensor Control System (ACAE)
ISCS.......... Integrated Ship Control System
ISCS.......... Integrated Submarine Combat System (SAUS)
ISCS.......... Integrated Submarine Communications System (MCD)
ISCS.......... Interim Sea Control Ship (MCD)
ISCS.......... Intermediate Science Curriculum Study
ISCS.......... International Sand Collectors Society (EA)
ISCS.......... International Scientific Cooperative Service (SAUO)
ISCS.......... International Services Computer System (SAUS)
ISCS.......... International Society for Cardiovascular Surgery (DAVI)
ISCS.......... International Society of Communications Specialists (EA)
ISCS.......... International Stamp Collectors Society (EA)
ISCS.......... International Symposium on Cooling Systems (PDAA)
ISCS.......... Interservice/Cross Service [*Support*]
ISCS.......... ISC Systems Corp. (SAUO)
ISCSA.......... Industrial Sports Clubs Secretaries' Association [*British*] (BI)
ISCSC.......... International Society for the Comparative Study of Civilizations (EA)
ISCSH.......... Independent Scientific Committee on Smoking and Health [*British*]
ISCSP2.......... Integrated Submarine Cornmunications System Polaris/Poseidon (SAUS)
ISCST.......... Industrial Source Complex Short-Term Model [*Environmental Protection Agency*] (GFGA)
ISCST2.......... Industrial Source Complex Short-Term Model Version 2
ISCSTM.......... Industrial Source Complex Short-Term Model (COE)
ISCT.......... Inner Seal Collar Tool [*Nuclear energy*] (NRCH)
IScT.......... Institute of Science Technology (SAUO)
ISCT.......... International Society for Cleaning Technicians (NTPA)
ISCT.......... International Society for the Classical Tradition (SAUO)
ISCT.......... Ito System Color Television [*Japan*]
ISCTC.......... Inter-Services Components Technical Committee (SAUO)
ISCTechC.......... Inter-Services Components Technical Committee (SAUO)
ISCTF.......... Interservice Committee on Technical Facilities [*Aerospace*] (AAG)
ISCTF.......... Inter-Services Committee on Technical Facilities (SAUO)
ISCTP.......... International Study Commission for Traffic Police
ISCTR.......... International Scientific Committee for Trypanosomiasis Research [*Medicine*] (EDAA)
ISCU.......... International Scientific Corporation Union (SAUO)
ISCUS.......... Indian-Soviet Cultural Unity Society (SAUO)
ISC/USO.......... Inter-Company Service Coordination/Universal Service Order (SAUS)
ISC/USO.......... Intercompany Services Coordination/Universal Service Order [*Telecommunications*] (TEL)
ISCV.......... Idle Speed Control Valve [*Exhaust emissions*] [*Automotive engineering*]
ISCVS.......... International Society for Cardiovascular Surgery (EA)
ISCVS.......... International Society of Cardiovascular Surgeons
ISCVS-NA.......... International Society for Cardiovascular Surgery - North American Chapter (NTPA)
ISCWFD.......... Intergovernmental Steering Committee on World Food Day (EA)
ISCWQT.......... International Standing Committee on Water Quality and Treatment [*International Water Supply Association*]
ISCX.......... Industrial Scientific [*NASDAQ symbol*] (TTSB)
ISCX.......... Industrial Scientific Corp. [*NASDAQ symbol*] (SAG)
ISCX.......... Integrated Software Systems Corporation (SAUO)
ISCX.......... Interlake Steel [*Private rail car owner code*]
ISCYRA.......... International Star Class Yacht Racing Association (EA)
ISD.......... Cabot Corp., Stellite Division, Kokomo, IN [*OCLC symbol*] (OCLC)
ISD.......... IBM [*International Business Machines Corp.*] Standard Data (IAA)
ISD.......... Image Section Descriptor (SAUO)
ISD.......... Image Stabilization Device (SAUO)
ISD.......... Immune-Suppression Drug (MELL)
ISD.......... Immune System Disease [*Medicine*] (EDAA)
ISD.......... Immunosuppressive Drug [*Medicine*] (DMAA)
ISD.......... Impact Sound Duty (SAUS)
ISD.......... Impulse Storing Device (SAUS)
ISD.......... Independent School District (SAUS)
ISD.......... Independent Sealing Distributors (NTPA)
ISD.......... Indian Store Department (SAUO)
ISD.......... Indian Stores Depot [*British military*] (DMA)
ISD.......... Indicators of Sustainable Development (SAUO)
ISD.......... Induction System Deposit
ISD.......... Industrial Supplies Department (SAUO)
ISD.......... Industrial Survey Division (SAUO)
ISD.......... Industrial Systems Division (TIMI)
ISD.......... Infection Sanitary Department (SAUO)
ISD.......... Information Services Department [*Ohio State University Libraries*] [*Columbus*] [*Information service or system*] (IID)
ISD.......... Information Services Division [*Mississippi State Research and Development Center*] [*Information service or system*] (IID)
ISD.......... Information Services Division [*Scottish Health Service*] [*Research center*]
ISD.......... Informations Systems Division (SAUS)
ISD.......... Information Storage Density (SAUS)
ISD.......... Information Storage Device (SAUS)
ISD.......... Information Structure Design
ISD.......... Information System Definition (SAUO)
ISD.......... Information System Design, Incorporated (ACAE)
ISD.......... Information System Development [*Telecommunications*] (TEL)
ISD.......... Information System Division (SAUS)
ISD.......... Information Systems Department [*Franklin Research Center, Inc.*] [*Information service or system*] (IID)
ISD.......... Information Systems Design (SAUS)
ISD.......... Information Systems Development (SAUS)

ISD .... Information Systems Directive (SAUO)
ISD .... Information Systems Division [*Ori, Inc.*] [*Bethesda, MD*]
ISD .... Infrared Suppression Device
ISD .... Inhibited Sexual Desire [*Sex therapy*]
ISD .... Initial Search Depth
ISD .... Initial Selection Done
ISD .... Initial Service Date (SAUS)
ISD .... Initial Ship Design
ISD .... Initial Sleep Disturbance [*Medicine*] (EDAA)
ISD .... Initial System Description (SAUO)
ISD .... Initial System Design (SAUO)
ISD .... Innovative Software Design [*South Africa*] [*ICAO designator*] (FAAC)
ISD .... Insert Subcaliber Device [*Weaponry*] (INF)
ISD .... In Service Date (SAUO)
ISD .... In-Service Date (SAUS)
ISD .... In-Service Deployment (SAUS)
ISD .... Inspector of Submarine Defences (SAUO)
ISD .... Installation Specification Drawing (MCD)
ISD .... Installation Start Date (CET)
ISD .... Installation Supply Division [*Military*] (AABC)
ISD .... Institute for Security Design (EA)
ISD .... Institute for the Study of Diplomacy (SAUS)
ISD .... Institute of Single Dynamics (EA)
ISD .... Institute of Surplus Dealers (EA)
ISD .... Institute of Sustainable Development (SAUO)
ISD .... Instructional System Design (SAUS)
ISD .... Instructional System Design Model
ISD .... Instructional Systems Design (DOM)
ISD .... Instructional Systems Development (AFM)
ISD .... Integrated Strategic Defense (SAUO)
ISD .... Integrated Symbolic Debugger [*Computer science*] (IID)
ISD .... Integrated System Dictionary (SAUO)
ISD .... Integrated Systems Demonstrator (MCD)
ISD .... Intensity, Severity, and Discharge [*Medicine*] (DHSM)
ISD .... Interactive Screen Definition (IAA)
ISD .... Interface State Density (AAEL)
ISD .... Interface Summary Design (SAUS)
ISD .... Interim Simulation Display [*FAA*] (TAG)
ISD .... Interim Status Document [*Environmental Protection Agency*] (GFGA)
ISD .... Intermediate School District (AEE)
ISD .... Intermediate Storage Device
ISD .... Internal Security Division [*Abolished 1973; functions transferred to Criminal Division*] [*Department of Justice*]
ISD .... Internal Symbol Dictionary [*Computer science*] (OA)
ISD .... International Security Detachment (SAUO)
ISD .... International Society for Differentiation (SAUO)
ISD .... International Society of Dermatology: Tropical, Geographic and Ecologic (SAUS)
ISD .... International Society of Differentiation (EA)
ISD .... International Society of Dramatists (EA)
ISD .... International Standard Data Network (SAUO)
ISD .... International Standards Development (SAUO)
ISD .... International Subscriber Dialing [*Later, IDD*] [*Telecommunications*]
ISD .... International Subscriber Dialling (SAUO)
ISD .... International Symbol Dictionary (SAUS)
ISD .... International Systems Design, Inc. (SAUS)
ISD .... International Systems Design, Incorporated (SAUO)
ISD .... Interstate Stores, Inc. (SAUO)
ISD .... Intersystem Designation (CAAL)
ISD .... Interventricular Septal Defect [*Medicine*] (MELL)
ISD .... Intractable Seizure Disorder [*Medicine*] (MELL)
ISD .... Intrinsic Sleep Disorder [*Medicine*] (MELL)
ISD .... Investors Services and Discounts Proprietary Ltd. (SAUO)
ISD .... Invoice Shipping Documentation [*Business term*]
ISD .... Iron-Storage Disease [*Medicine*] (MELL)
ISD .... Isosorbide Dinitrite [*Coronary vasodilator*]
ISD .... MENU - the International Software Database [*Menu the International Software Database Corp.*] [*Information service or system*] (CRD)
ISD .... Winner, SD [*Location identifier*] [*FAA*] (FAAL)
ISD .... International Standard Depth (ODA)
ISDA .... Indian Self-Determination Act [*1975*]
ISDA .... Institute for the Study of Drug Addiction [*Later, ISDM*] (EA)
ISDA .... Institutional Summary Data Service
ISDA .... International Sculpteurs et Designers Associes [*Paris, France*] (EAIO)
ISDA .... International Security and Detective Alliance (EA)
ISDA .... International Swap Dealers' Association
ISDA .... International Swaps and Derivatives Association (ECON)
ISDA .... International Systems Dealers Association (SAUO)
ISDAIC .... International Staff Disaster Assistance Information Coordinator [*NATO*] (NATG)
ISDARS .... Instrumentation Sensor Data Acquisition and Reduction System
ISDB .... Indirect Self-Destructive Behavior (DIPS)
ISDB .... Industry Studies Data Base (SAUO)
ISDB .... Information System and Data Bank (SAUS)
ISDB .... Initial Subordinate Dominates Bystander [*Sociology*]
ISDB .... Integrated Satellite Communications Database (COE)
ISDB .... Integrated Satellite Data Base (SAUO)
ISDB .... International Society of Developmental Biologists (SAUS)
ISDB .... International Society of Development Biologists [*Formerly, IIE*] [*Nogent-Sur-Marne, France*]
ISDC .... Indiana State Data Center [*Indiana State Library*] [*Indianapolis*] [*Information service or system*] (IID)
ISDC .... Intense Sample Data Collection System (MCD)
ISDC .... Iraqi Scientific Documentation Centre (SAUS)
ISDCC .... Illinois State Data Center Cooperative [*Illinois State Bureau of the Budget*] [*Springfield*] [*Information service or system*] (IID)
ISDCP .... Integrated Strategic Defense Concept Plan (SAUO)
ISDD .... Information Systems Development Division (SAA)
ISDD .... Institute for the Study of Drug Dependence [*London*]
ISDD .... Instructional Systems Development Department (SAUS)
ISDD .... Integrated Spatial Data Dictionary (SAUO)
ISDD .... Integrated Systems Development Department (SAUS)
ISDE .... Integral Square Delay Error (IAA)
ISDE .... International Seismic Data Exchange [*Geology*]
ISDE .... International Six Days Enduro [*Motorcycle racing*]
ISDE .... International Society for Diseases of the Esophagus [*Tokyo, Japan*] (EAIO)
ISDEF .... International Soil Data Exchange File (SAUO)
ISDF .... Impact Short Delay Fuze (MCD)
ISDF .... Indexed Sequential Data File (SAUS)
ISDF .... Intercrystalline Structure Distribution Function (SAUS)
ISDF .... Intermediate Sodium Disposal Facility [*Nuclear energy*] (NRCH)
ISDF .... International Shooter Development Fund [*National Rifle Association*]
ISDG .... Information Science Discussion Group [*British*] (NITA)
ISDH .... Indiana State Department of Health (SAUO)
ISDI .... Information Storage Devices [*NASDAQ symbol*] (TTSB)
ISDI .... Information Storage Devices, Inc. [*NASDAQ symbol*] (SAG)
ISDI .... Insulated Steel Door Institute (NTPA)
ISDI .... International Social Development Institute
ISDI .... International Society of Dietetic Including All Infant and Young Children Food Industries (EAIO)
ISDI .... International Special Dietary Foods Industries [*France*] (EAIO)
ISDIN .... Isosorbide Dinitrate [*Also, ISDN*] [*Coronary vasodilator*]
ISD/IS .... Information Services Department/Division (SAUO)
ISDM .... Indian Self-Determination Memorandum [*Indian Health Service*] [*Department of Health and Human Services*] (GFGA)
ISDM .... Institute for the Study of Drug Misuse [*Formerly, ISDA*] (EA)
ISDM .... International Society for/of Disaster Medicine (SAUO)
ISDN .... Information Service Data Network [*Telecommunications*]
ISDN .... Institute for the Study of Developing Nations (EA)
ISDN .... Integer Services Digital Network (SAUO)
ISDN .... Integrated Services Digital Network [*Telecommunications*]
ISDN .... Integrated Systems Digital Network (RALS)
ISDN .... Intergrated Services Digital Network (SAUS)
ISDN .... International Society for Developmental Neuroscience (EA)
ISDN .... International Society for Development of Neuroscience (SAUO)
ISDN .... International Standard Data Network (NITA)
ISDN .... Isosorbide Dinitrate [*Also, ISDIN*] [*Coronary vasodilator*]
ISDN .... It Still Does Nothing [*Facetious translation for ISDN - Integrated Services Digital Network*]
ISDNA .... Inverse Standard Deviation of Nucleolar Area [*Oncology*]
ISDN-BRI .... Integrated Standard Digital Network-Basic Rate Interface (CGWS)
ISDN-PBX .... Integrated Services Digital Network-Private Branch Exchange (SAUS)
ISDN-PRI .... Integrated Services Digital Network-Primary Rate Interface (CGWS)
ISDN-UP .... Integrated Services Digital Network-User Part (CGWS)
ISDO .... Institute for Systems Design and Optimization
ISDO .... International Staff Duty Officer [*NATO*] (NATG)
ISDOS .... Information System Design and/by Optimization System (SAUS)
ISDOS .... Information Systems Design Optimisation System (SAUS)
ISDOS .... Information Systems Design Optimization System
ISDP .... Ice Shelf Drilling Projects (SAUO)
ISDP .... Income Survey Development Program [*Department of Health and Human Services*] (GFGA)
ISDP .... Infantry Scout Dog Platoon (SAUO)
ISDP .... Integrated Ship Design and Production (SAUS)
ISDP .... Interagency Staff Development Project (SAUO)
ISDP .... International Society for Developmental Psychobiology (EA)
ISDP .... Interregional Sales Development Programme (SAUO)
ISDPG .... Independent Social Democratic Party of Germany [*Political party*] (EAIO)
ISDR .... Information Services Division Request (SAUO)
ISDRA .... International Sled Dog Racing Association (EA)
ISDRP .... Interface Simulation and Data Reduction Program (ACAE)
ISDS .... Illinois State Dental Association (SAUO)
ISDS .... Image Switching & Distribution System (SAUS)
ISDS .... Improved Self-Defense System (SAUS)
ISDS .... Inadvertent Separation and Destruct System [*Aerospace*]
ISDS .... Inadvertent Separation Destruct Subsystem (SAUS)
ISDS .... Indexed Sequential Data Set (SAUS)
ISDS .... Infantry Self-Defense System (SAUS)
ISDS .... Institute for Social Dance Studies [*Defunct*] (EA)
ISDS .... Institute for the Study of Defects in Solids [*State University of New York at Albany*] [*Research center*] (RCD)
ISDS .... Instructional Systems Development Squadron
ISDS .... Instruction Set Design System (PDAA)
ISDS .... Integrated Ship Design System (IEEE)
ISDS .... Integrated Software Development System
ISDS .... Integrated Switched Data Service [*Telecommunications*] (TEL)
ISDS .... Intelligence Support Display System [*Military*] (MCD)
ISDS .... Interagency Subcommittee on Disability Statistics (SAUO)
ISDS .... International Security & Defense Systems Ltd. (SAUO)
ISDS .... International Serials Data System [*Database*] (EA)
ISDS .... International Sheep Dog Society [*Bedford, England*] (EAIO)
ISDS .... International Society for/of Dermatologic Surgery (SAUO)
ISDS .... IRCM Self-Defence System (SAUS)
ISD/SAT .... Instructional Systems Development/Systems Approach to Training [*Training term*] (LPT)
ISDSI .... Insulated Steel Door Systems Institute (EA)
ISDS/IC .... International Center of the International Senes Data System (SAUS)

ISDS/IC........ International Center of the International Serials Data System [*UNESCO*] (PDAA)
ISDS/IC........ International Centre of the International Serials Data System (SAUS)
ISDS/IC........ International Serials Data System/International Centre (SAUS)
ISDSMS....... Improved Self Defense Surface Missile System (ACAE)
ISDSN.......... Integrated Services Digital Satellite Network (SAUS)
ISDT............ Institute of Shaft Drilling Technicians (SAUS)
ISDT............ Instructional Systems Development Team [*Air Force*]
ISDT............ Integrated Services Digital Terminal (SAUS)
ISDT............ Integrated Systems Development Tool (SAUO)
ISDT............ International Six Days Trial [*Motorcycling*]
ISDT............ International Symposium on Dredging Technology (PDAA)
ISDTS.......... Iron and Sleel Dressers Trade Society (SAUO)
ISDTS.......... Iron and Steel Dressers Trade Society [*A union*] [*British*]
ISDU............ Indonesian Social Democratic Union (SAUO)
ISDU............ Inertial System Display Unit (HLLA)
ISDU............ Interim Secure Data Unit (ACAE)
ISDU............ International Standard Density Unit (DGA)
ISDV............ Integrated Software Development and Verification (SAUS)
ISDWG......... Information Systems Development Working Group (SAUO)
ISDX............ Integrated Services Digital Exchange [*British*]
ISE.............. Ibadan Studies in English (journ.) (SAUS)
ISE.............. Idaho Society of Engineers (SAUO)
ISE.............. Ideas in Science and Electronics, Inc. (SAUO)
ISE.............. Illogical Sequence Error (IAA)
ISE.............. Independent Safety Evaluation (SAUO)
ISE.............. Independent Scheduled Exercises
ISE.............. Independent Ship Exercise [*Navy*]
ISE.............. Indiana State University, Evansville Campus, Evansville, IN [*OCLC symbol*] (OCLC)
ISE.............. Indian Service of Engineers [*British*]
ISE.............. India Society of Engineers (SAUO)
ISE.............. Individial Ship (SAUS)
ISE.............. Individual Ship Exercises [*Navy*]
ISE.............. Individual Soldier Energy [*Military*] (RDA)
ISE.............. Induced Secondary Electron (SAUS)
ISE.............. Induced Surface Effect
ISE.............. Inertia Simulation Error [*Automotive emissions*]
ISE.............. Influence Strategies Exercise [*Test*] (TMMY)
ISE.............. Information in Science Extension [*INTERBRIGHT database*] [*Budapest, Hungary*] [*Information service or system*] (IID)
ISE.............. Information Science Education (SAUS)
ISE.............. Information Services to Education [*American Society for Information Science*]
ISE.............. Information Systems Engineering (SAUO)
ISE.............. Inhibited Sexual Excitement [*Medicine*] (DMAA)
ISE.............. Initial Support Element (MCD)
ISE.............. In-Service Education (ADA)
ISE.............. In-Service Engineering [*Navy*]
ISE.............. Installation Support and Evaluation (AAG)
ISE.............. Institute for Sex Education (SAUO)
ISE.............. Institute for Software Engineering (EA)
ISE.............. Institute for Solid Wastes (SAUS)
ISE.............. Institute of Sanitary Engineers [*British*] (DAS)
ISE.............. Institute of Social Engineering (SAUO)
ISE.............. Institute of Social Ethics (EA)
ISE.............. Institute of Space Engineering (SAUO)
ISE.............. Institute of Space Engineers (SAUO)
ISE.............. Institution of Sales Engineers [*British*] (BI)
ISE.............. Institution of Sanitary Engineers (SAUO)
ISE.............. Institution of Structural Engineers [*British*] (EAIO)
ISE.............. Institution of Stuctural Engineers (SAUS)
ISE.............. Instrumentation Suitability Evaluation (MCD)
ISE.............. Insystem Emulator (SAUS)
ISE.............. In System Evaluator [*National Semiconductor Company*] (NITA)
ISE.............. In-System Evaluator (SAUS)
ISE.............. Integral Squared Error
ISE.............. Integrated Safeguards Experiment
ISE.............. Integrated Solid Effect (AAEL)
ISE.............. Integrated Space Experiment (MCD)
ISE.............. Integrated Storage Element [*Computer science*]
ISE.............. Integrated Switching Element (SAUS)
ISE.............. Intelligence Support Element [*Military*] (MCD)
ISE.............. Intelligent Synthesis Environment
ISE.............. Interactive Software Engineering
ISE.............. Intercept System Environment [*Army*] (AABC)
ISE.............. Interface Science and Engineering (SAUS)
ISE.............. Intergovernmental Meeting of Scientific Experts on Biological Diversity (SAUO)
ISE.............. Intermountain Stock Exchange [*Salt Lake City, UT*]
ISE.............. Internal Sales Engineer (TIMI)
ISE.............. International Journal of Social Economics (journ.) (SAUS)
ISE.............. International Semi-Tech Microelectronics, Inc. [*Toronto Stock Exchange symbol*]
ISE.............. International Society for/of Electrostimulation (SAUO)
ISE.............. International Society of Electrochemistry [*Graz, Austria*] (EA)
ISE.............. International Society of Endocrinology (EA)
ISE.............. International Society of Endoscopy
ISE.............. International Sports Exchange (EA)
ISE.............. International Standard Electric Corporation (SAUO)
ISE.............. International Stock Exchange
ISE.............. International Stock Exchange of the United Kingdom and the Republic of Ireland (DFIT)
ISE.............. International Submarine Engineering (SAUS)
ISE.............. International Submarine Engineering Ltd. (SAUO)
ISE.............. Interpret Sign Error
ISE.............. Interrupt System Enable
ISE.............. Inter System Emulator (NITA)
ISE.............. Intersystem Emulator (SAUS)
ISE.............. Ion Selective Electrode (SAUS)
ISE.............. Ion-Selective Electrode [*Instrumentation*]
ISE.............. Ion Sensitive Electrode (SAUS)
ISE.............. Ion-Sensitive Electrode [*Instrumentation*] (IAA)
ISE.............. Ion Specific Electrode (SAUS)
ISE.............. Ion-Specific Electrode (COE)
ISE.............. Irish School of Ecumenics
ISE.............. Ise [*Japan*] [*Seismograph station code, US Geological Survey*] (SEIS)
ISE.............. Italien-Skandinavien Express (SAUO)
i-se-............ Seychelles [*MARC geographic area code*] [*Library of Congress*] (LCCP)
ISEA............ Industrial Safety Equipment Association [*Arlington, VA*] (EA)
ISEA............ Industrial Safety Equipment Association, Inc.
ISEA............ Inland Seas Education Association
ISEA............ In-Service Engineering Activity (SAUO)
ISEA............ Inservice Engineering Agent [*Military*] (CAAL)
ISEA............ Institute for Spiritual and Environmental Awareness (EA)
ISEA............ International Society of Exposure Analysis (SAUO)
ISEA............ International Stamp Exchange Association
ISEA............ Iowa State Education Association (SAUO)
ISEAM.......... Interactive System for Experimental Applied Mathematics (SAUS)
ISEANSW..... Institute of Senior Educational Administrators of New South Wales [*Australia*]
ISEAR.......... International Standard Entry for Authority and Reference (SAUS)
ISEARCH...... Information Services Electronic Archives (SAUS)
ISEARCH...... Information Services Electronic Archiving (SAUO)
ISEAS.......... Institute of Southeast Asian Studies
ISEATRA...... International Symposium on Ecological Aspects of Tree-Ring Analysis (SAUO)
ISEB............ Independent Schools Education Board [*Later, National Association of IndependentSchools*] (AEBS)
ISEB............ Interim Support Equipment Bulletin (MCD)
ISEB............ International Symposium on Environmental Biogeochemistry (SAUO)
ISEBD4........ International Series on Biomechanics (journ.) (SAUS)
ISEC............ Industrial Safety Equipment & Clothing, London (SAUO)
ISEC............ Information System Electronic Command [*Army*]
ISEC............ Information Systems Engineering Command (SSD)
ISEC............ Insituform Southeast Corporation (SAUO)
ISEC............ Institute for Social Economic Change
ISEC............ Institute of Social and Economic Change, Bangalore (SAUS)
I Sec........... Intelligence Section (SAUO)
ISEC............ International Securities and Exchange Commission (SAUO)
ISEC............ International Solvent Extraction Conference [*Toronto, ON, 1977*] [*Canada*]
ISEC............ International Standard Electric Corp. (NATG)
ISEC............ International Standard Electric Corporation (SAUO)
ISEC............ International Statistical Education Centre [*India*]
ISEC............ International Statistics Educational Center (or Centre) (SAUS)
ISEC............ International Symposium on Engineering Ceramics (SAUS)
ISECCo......... International Space Exploration and Colonization Company [*An association*] (EA)
I Sec NCO.... Intelligence Section Non-Commissioned Officer (SAUO)
ISECS........... International Society for Eighteenth-Century Studies [*See also SIEDS*] [*Oxford, England*] (EAIO)
ISECSI......... International Society for Educational, Cultural and Scientific Interchanges (SAUO)
I sect.......... Intelligence section (SAUO)
ISECW......... Incorporated Society of Estate Clerks of Works (SAUO)
ISED............ Information Systems Equipment Division (SAUO)
ISED............ Institute for Social Evaluation and Design
ISEE............ Incident-Shock Equilibrium Expansion
ISEE............ Information System Engineering Environment (SAUO)
ISEE............ Initial System Evaluation Experiment [*Photovoltaic energy systems*]
ISEE............ Institute for Study of Economics and the Environment
ISEE............ Integrated Software Engineering Environment (SAUO)
ISEE............ International Society for Ecological Economics (SAUO)
ISEE............ International Society for Engineering Education [*Austria*] (EAIO)
ISEE............ International Society for Enterprise Engineering (SAUO)
ISEE............ International Society for Environmental Education (SAUO)
ISEE............ International Society for Environmental Epidemiology (SAUO)
ISEE............ International Society for the Enhancement of Eyesight (SAUO)
ISEE............ International Society of Electrostimulation (SAUO)
ISEE............ International Society of Explosives Engineers (NTPA)
ISEE............ International Sun-Earth Explorer [*NASA/ESRO satellite*]
ISEE............ Sterling Vision [*NASDAQ symbol*] (TTSB)
ISEE............ Sterling Vision, Inc. [*NASDAQ symbol*] (SAG)
ISEE 1-3...... International Sun-Earth Explorer 1-3 (SAUO)
ISEEM.......... International Society for Economic Evaluation of Medicines
ISEEP........... Infrared Sensitive Element Evaluation Program
ISEERB......... Inter-Service Environmental Education Review Board (BCP)
ISEES........... Institute of Soviet and East European Studies (SAUO)
ISEE Satellite... International Sun-Earth Explorer Satellite (SAUS)
ISEF............ International Science and Engineering Fair
ISEG............ Independent Safety Engineering Group [*Nuclear energy*] (NRCH)
ISEGR.......... Institute of Social, Economic, and Governmental Research [*Later, ISER*] [*University of Alaska*]
ISEGRN........ Institute of Social, Economic and Government Research. University of Alaska. Research Notes (journ.) (SAUS)
ISEGROP...... Institute of Social, Economic and Government Research. University of Alaska Occasional Papers (journ.) (SAUS)

ISEGRR........ Institute of Social, Economic and Government Research. University of Alaska. Report (journ.) (SAUS)
ISEGRS........ Institute of Social, Economic and Government Research. University of Alaska. Research Summary (journ.) (SAUS)
ISEH............ International Society for Ecosystem Health
ISEH............ International Society for Experimental Hematology (SAUO)
ISEH............ International Society of Experimental Hematology (NTPA)
ISEI............ Institute for Systems Engineering and Informatics (EURO)
ISEI............ International Standard Engineering, Inc. (NATG)
ISEI............ International Standard Engineering, Incorporated (SAUO)
ISEIC........... Information Systems Engineering and Integration Center (SAUO)
ISEIG........... Inter-Services Electronic Identification Group (SAUO)
ISEIU........... International Society of Ergonomics for Information Users (SAUO)
ISEK............ International Society of Electromyographic Kinesiology (EA)
ISEK............ International Society of Electrophysiological Kinesiology [*Montreal, PQ*] (EA)
ISEL............ Institute of Shipping Economics and Logistics [*See also ISL*] [*Bremen, Federal Republic of Germany*] (EAIO)
IS-ELEMENT... Insertion Sequence Element (DB)
ISELS........... Institute of Society, Ethics, and Life Sciences [*Later, HC*] (EA)
ISELS........... Institute of Society, Ethics and Life Sciences, Inc. (SAUO)
ISEM............ Immunosorbent Electron Microscopy
ISEM............ Improved Standard Electronic Module (MHDB)
ISEM............ Inspection/Review Specific Equipment Model (AAEL)
ISEM............ Institute for the Study of Earth and Man [*Southern Methodist University*] [*Research center*] (RCD)
ISEM............ Integrated Simulation Evaluation Model
ISEM............ International Society for Ecological Modelling [*Vaerloese, Denmark*] (EAIO)
ISEMS........... International Society of Emergency Medical Services (EA)
ISEN............ Interactive Satellite Education Network [*IBM Corp.*] [*New York, NY*] (TSSD)
Isen............ Seneca Public Library (SAUS)
ISen............ Seneca Public Library, Seneca, IL [*Library symbol*] [*Library of Congress*] (LCLS)
ISenMS........ Miller Township Consolidated Community, School District 210, Seneca, IL [*Library symbol*] [*Library of Congress*] (LCLS)
ISEO............ Institute of Shortening and Edible Oils (EA)
ISEP............ Innovative Special Education Project (SAUO)
ISEP............ Installation Strategic Energy Planning
ISEP............ Instructional Scientific Equipment Program [*National Science Foundation*]
ISEP............ Integrated Safety Evaluation Program (SAUO)
ISEP............ Integrated System Engineering Plan (ACAE)
ISEP............ International Society for Educational Planners (or Planning) (SAUO)
ISEP............ International Society for Evolutionary Protistology (EA)
ISEP............ International Society of Esperantist-Philologists [*See also IUEFI*] (EAIO)
ISEP............ International Standard Equipment Practice (MHDB)
ISEP............ International Standard of Engineering Practice (SAUS)
ISEP............ International Student Exchange Program [*United States Information Agency*]
ISEP............ International Student Exchange Programme (SAUO)
ISEP............ International Summer Education Project (SAUS)
ISEP............ International Symposium on Environmental Pollution (SAUS)
ISEP............ International Telegraph and Telephone Standard Equipment Practice (SAUO)
ISEP............ International Telephone and Telegraph Standard Equipment Practice (SAUS)
ISEP............ Interservice Experiments Program
ISEP............ Isolated/Stabilized Exercise Platform (SAUS)
isepc........... Installation Specification (SAUS)
ISEPDC........ International Series in Experimental Psychology (journ.) (SAUS)
ISEPP........... International Sun-Earth Physics Program (SAUS)
ISEPS........... International Sun-Earth Physics Satellite
I-SEQ........... Indexed Sequential (SAUS)
ISEQ............ Irish Stock Exchange Equity index (SAUO)
ISER............ InnoServe Technologies, Inc. [*NASDAQ symbol*] (SAG)
ISER............ InnoServ Technologies [*NASDAQ symbol*] (TTSB)
ISER............ Institute for Sex Education and Research (SAUO)
ISER............ Institute of Sex Education and Research [*British*] (DBA)
ISER............ Institute of Social and Economic Research [*Memorial University of Newfoundland*] [*Research center*] [*Canada*] (RCD)
ISER............ Institute of Social and Economic Research [*Formerly, ISEGR*] [*University of Alaska*]
ISER............ Integral Systems Experimental Requirements (NRCH)
ISER............ International Society for Eye Research (SAUO)
ISER............ Intrinsically Safe and Economical Reactor (SAUO)
ISerSD......... Serena Consolidated High School District 390, Serena, IL [*Library symbol*] [*Library of Congress*] (LCLS)
ISerSD......... Serena Consolidated High School District 390 (SAUS)
ISES............ Independent Space Experiment Systems (SAUO)
ISES............ Information Systems Enhancement & Stability (SAUO)
ISES............ In Silentio et Spe [*In Silence and in Hope*] [*Motto of Bernhard, Prince of Anhalt (1572-96)*] [*Latin*]
ISES............ Institute for Socioeconomic Studies (EA)
ISES............ International Electric Service Association (SAUO)
ISES............ International Schools Examination Syndicate (SAUO)
ISES............ International Ship Electric Service Association [*British*] (EAIO)
ISES............ International Society of Explosives Specialists (EA)
ISES............ International Solar Energy Society [*Australia*] (EAIO)
ISES............ International Special Events Society (EA)
ISES............ Iron Safe Engineers' Society [*A union*] [*British*]
ISESA........... Information Systems Engineering Support Activity (SAUO)
ISESCO........ Islamic Educational, Cultural and Scientific Organisation (or Organization) (SAUO)
ISESCO........ Islamic Educational, Scientific, and Cultural Organization [*United Nations*]
ISESCO........ Islamic Organization for Education, the Sciences and Culture (SAUS)
ISES-SI........ International Solar Energy Society, Sezione Italiana (SAUO)
ISET............ Independent Software Evaluation Test (SAUO)
ISET............ Institute for Solar Energy Technology (SAUS)
ISET............ Intercenter Systems Engineering Team (SAUO)
ISETAP........ Intergovernmental Science, Engineering, and Technology Advisory Panel [*National Science Foundation*]
ISETC........... International Society for Environmental Toxicology and Cancer (EAIO)
ISETI............ In-Service Teacher Training Institute (SAUO)
ISETU........... International Secretariat of Entertainment Trade Unions [*Geneva, Switzerland*]
ISEU............ International Socio-Ecological Union (SAUO)
ISEU............ International Stereotypers and Electrotypers Union [*Later, IPGCU*]
ISEU............ International Stereotypers and Electrotypers Union of North America (SAUO)
ISEUNA........ International Stereotypers and Electrotypers Union of North America (SAUO)
ISEW............ Index of Sustainable Economic Welfare (PS)
ISEW............ Intelligence, Security, and Electronic Warfare [*DoD*]
ISEY............ International Student Exchange Program (SAUS)
ISF.............. Alpha Park Public Library District, Pekin, IL [*OCLC symbol*] (OCLC)
ISF.............. Identification Sequence Field (SAUS)
ISF.............. Imagination Science Fiction (journ.) (SAUS)
ISF.............. Imperial Smelting Furnace [*Zinc and lead*]
ISF.............. Improved Support Facility (SAUO)
ISF.............. Incremental Stretch Forming
ISF.............. Indian States Force [*British military*] (DMA)
ISF.............. Indian States Forces (SAUS)
ISF.............. Individual Store and Forward
ISF.............. Industrial Space Facility [*Space Industries, Inc.*]
ISF.............. Infant Soy Formula
ISF.............. Information Systems Factory (NITA)
ISF.............. Information Systems Flight [*Military*]
ISF.............. Infrasonic Frequency
ISF.............. Infrastructure Support Facilities (SAUO)
ISF.............. Instrument Standards Foundation (ACII)
ISF.............. Insurance, Surety, and Fidelity (MHDB)
ISF.............. Insured Savings Fund (SAUS)
ISF.............. Integrated Subject File
ISF.............. Integrated Support Facility (DWSG)
ISF.............. Intelligence Support Facility (SAUO)
ISF.............. Interdistrict Settlement Fund [*Banking*]
ISF.............. Interim Security Facility (SAUO)
ISF.............. Intermediate Scale Facilities (SAUO)
ISF.............. Intermediate-Scale Facilities (or Facility) (SAUS)
ISF.............. Intermediate Scale Facility [*Department of Energy*]
ISF.............. Intermediate Scale File (SAUS)
ISF.............. Intermediate Support Facility (SAUS)
ISF.............. Internationale Schulsport Foderation [*International School Sport Federation*] (EAIO)
ISF.............. International Sailsurfing Federation (SAUO)
ISF.............. International Schools Foundation (SAUO)
ISF.............. International School Sport Federation (EAIO)
ISF.............. International Science Fair (SAUO)
ISF.............. International Science Foundation (EA)
ISF.............. International Scleroderma Federation [*Later, SF*] (EA)
ISF.............. International Sensitivity Forum (SAUO)
ISF.............. International Shipping Federation [*British*] (EAIO)
ISF.............. International Ski Federation
ISF.............. International Snowshoe Federation (EA)
ISF.............. International Socialist Forum (SAUO)
ISF.............. International Society for/of Fat Research (SAUO)
ISF.............. International Society of Financiers (EA)
ISF.............. International Softball Federation (EA)
ISF.............. International Solidarity Fund (SAUO)
ISF.............. International Spiritualist Federation [*British*]
ISF.............. International Sporting Federations (SAUO)
ISF.............. International Spring Fair [*British*] (ITD)
ISF.............. International Students Federation (SAUO)
ISF.............. International Surfing Foundation (SAUO)
ISF.............. International Surfskiing Federation (SAUO)
ISF.............. International Surfthion Federation (SAUO)
ISF.............. International Symposium on Forecasting (SAUO)
ISF.............. Interrecord Sequence Field (SAUS)
ISF.............. Intersection of the Shifted Fringes (SAUS)
ISF.............. Intersection of the Shift Fringes (PDAA)
ISF.............. Interstitial Fluid [*Physiology*]
ISF.............. Investment Support Facility (SAUO)
ISF.............. Ionizer, Slab Fabrication
ISF.............. Isfjord [*Norway*] [*Seismograph station code, US Geological Survey*] [*Closed*] (SEIS)
ISF.............. Isotope Separation Factor (MCD)
ISF.............. Isotope Seperation Factor (SAUS)
ISFA............ Industrial Support Functional Area (SAUO)
ISFA............ Inspector of Supply and Fleet Accounting (SAUS)
ISFA............ Intercoastal Steamship Freight Association (EA)
ISFA............ International Scientific Film Association
ISFA............ International Society of Financial Analysts (SAUO)
ISFA............ International Society of Friends of Albania (SAUO)
ISFA............ Isaac Garrison Family Association (EA)

ISFAA.......... Intercollegiate Soccer-Football Association of America [*Later, ISAA*] (EA)
ISFAA.......... International Society of Fine Arts Appraisers (EA)
IS-FACT....... Irwin Stone Foundation for Ascorbate Capability and Therapy
ISFADPM..... International Society for the Abolition of Data Processing Machines (SAUO)
ISFAHSIG..... International Society for the Advancement of Humanistic Studies in Gynecology (EA)
ISFC............ Indicated Specific Fuel Consumption
ISFC............ International Short Film Conference (EAIO)
ISFC............ International Society and Federation of Cardiology [*International Cardiol ogy Federation and International Society of Cardiology - ISC*] [*Formed by a merger of*] (EAIO)
ISFC............ International Symposium on Fluorine Chemistry
ISFD............ Integrated Software Functional Design
ISFD............ Integrated Software Functional Device (SAUS)
ISFDB.......... Internet Speculative Fiction DataBase
ISFE............ Igniter Safety Fuze, Electric (SAUS)
ISFE............ Incident-Shock Frozen Expansion
ISFE............ Integrated Site Facilities and Equipment (MCD)
ISFE............ International Societies of Flying Engineers (SAUS)
ISFE............ International Society of Facilities Executives (NTPA)
ISFE............ International Society of Flying Engineers [*Defunct*] (EA)
ISFEA.......... Infosafe Systems'A' [*NASDAQ symbol*] (TTSB)
ISFEA.......... Infosafe Systems, Inc. [*NASDAQ symbol*] (SAG)
ISFEIP......... International Soil Fertility Evaluation and Improvement Program (SAUO)
ISFET.......... Ion-Selective Field Effect Transistor
ISFET.......... Ion-Selective Field-Effect Transistor (SAUS)
ISFEU.......... Infosafe Sys Units'99 [*NASDAQ symbol*] (TTSB)
ISFEW.......... Infosafe Sys Wrrt'A' [*NASDAQ symbol*] (TTSB)
ISFEZ.......... Infosafe Sys Wrrt'B [*NASDAQ symbol*] (TTSB)
ISFF............ Integrated Surface Flux Facilities (SAUS)
ISFFSR........ Institute for the Study of Fatigue Fracture and Structural Reliability [*George Washington University*]
ISFGW......... International Society of Friendship and Good Will (EA)
ISFHC.......... International Society of Folk Harpers and Craftsmen (EA)
ISFIS........... Selective Fisheries Information Service (IID)
ISFJ............ Introversion Sensing Feeling Judging (ADWA)
ISFL............ International Scientific Film Library
ISFL............ International Society of Family Law [*Cambridge, England*] (EAIO)
ISFL............ International Society of/on Family Law (SAUO)
ISFM............ Indexed Sequential File Manager [*Computer science*]
ISFMP.......... Interstate Fisheries Management Program (GNE)
ISFMS.......... Indexed Sequential File Management System [*Computer science*] (BUR)
ISFMS.......... Index Sequential File Management System (SAUS)
ISFNR.......... International Society for Folk-Narrative Research [*Turku, Finland*] (EA)
ISFNT.......... International Symposium on Fusion Nuclear Technology (SAUS)
ISFO............ Information Systems and Finance Office (SAUO)
IS Foam....... Integral Skin Foam (SAUS)
ISFP............ Igniter Safety Fuze, Percussion (SAUS)
ISFP............ Introversion Sensing Feeling Perception (ADWA)
ISFPP.......... International Symposium on Fine Particles Processing (SAUS)
ISFR............ Institute for the Study of Fatigue and Reliability (SAUO)
ISFR............ International Society for Fluoride Research
ISFSC.......... International Society of Food Service Consultants [*Later, FCSI*] (EA)
ISFSC.......... International Society of Free Space Colonizers [*Superseded by Political Action Caucus*] (EA)
ISFSF.......... Independent Spent Fuel Storage Facility [*Department of Energy*] [*Nuclear energy*]
ISFSI........... Independent Spent Fuel Storage Installation [*Nuclear energy*] (NRCH)
ISFSI........... International Society of Fire Service Instructors (EA)
ISFSM.......... Incompletely Specified Finite State Machine (SAUS)
ISFSM.......... Incompletely-Specified Finite State Machine (MHDB)
ISfT............. International Society for Telemedicine (SAUO)
ISFUG.......... Integrated Software Federal User Group (SAUS)
ISFV............ Interstitial Fluid Volume [*Medicine*] (DMAA)
ISG.............. Ayer Public Library, Delavan, IL [*OCLC symbol*] (OCLC)
ISG.............. Idaho State Grange (SRA)
ISG.............. Immersion Sensing Group (SAUO)
ISG.............. Immune Serum Globulin
ISG.............. Imperial Standard Gallon
ISG.............. Independent Zimbabwe Group (SAUO)
ISG.............. Indiana State Grange (SRA)
ISG.............. Industrial Savings Groups (SAUO)
ISG.............. Industrial Support Group (SAUO)
ISG.............. Information Services Group (SAUO)
ISG.............. Information Strategies Group (SAUO)
ISG.............. Information Systems Group (SAUO)
ISG.............. Inland Shipping Group [*British*]
ISG.............. Institute for the Study of Genocide (EA)
ISG.............. Instrumentation Selection Guide (SAUS)
ISG.............. Instrumentation Support Group (SAUO)
ISG.............. Insurance Services Group
ISG.............. Integrated Survey Grid
ISG.............. Intelligence Support Group (SAUO)
ISG.............. Interchangeable and Substitute Group [*Military*] (AFIT)
ISG.............. Interconnected Systems Group
ISG.............. Interdivisional Standards Group (SAUO)
ISG.............. Interfacial Surface Generation [*Instrumentation*]
ISG.............. Internal Shutter Grid
ISG.............. Internal Steering Group (EURO)
ISG.............. International Stratigraphic Guide (SAUS)
ISG.............. International SYSOP [*System Operator*] Guild
ISG.............. Interoperability Study Group (SAUO)
ISG.............. Interservice Group [*Military*]
ISG.............. Intersite Gateway (ACAE)
ISG.............. Intersite Gateway Processor (SAUS)
ISG.............. Intersubblock Gap
ISG.............. Ishigaki [*Japan*] [*Airport symbol*] (OAG)
ISG.............. Isolated Ground (SAUS)
ISG.............. ISS International Service Systems AS [*NYSE symbol*] (SAG)
ISG.............. ISS-Intl Service Sys ADS [*NYSE symbol*] (TTSB)
ISGA............ Idaho Sugarbeet Growers Association (SRA)
ISGA............ Illinois Specialty Growers' Association (SRA)
ISGA............ Indiana Soybean Growers Association (SRA)
ISGA............ International Sprout Growers Association
ISGA............ International Stained Glass Association (EA)
ISGA............ International Study Group for Aerogrammes
ISGBBC........ Israel. Geological Survey. Bulletin (journ.) (SAUS)
ISGC............ International Society of Guatemala Collectors (EA)
ISGC............ International Steel Guitar Convention (EA)
ISGD............ International Study Group of Diabetes in Children and Adolescents [*Linkoping, Sweden*] (EAIO)
ISGE............ International Society for Geothermal Engineering [*Defunct*] (EA)
ISGE............ International Society of Gastroenterology
ISGEUR........ Intelligence and Security Group, Europe (SAUO)
ISGF............ Interferon-Stimulated Gene Factor [*Biochemistry*]
ISGG............ International Society for Geometry and Graphics (SAUO)
ISGI............ International Sheep and Goat Institute [*Utah State University*] [*Research center*] (RCD)
ISGI............ International Standards Group Ltd. [*NASDAQ symbol*] (SAG)
ISGI............ Intl Standards Group Ltd [*NASDAQ symbol*] (TTSB)
ISG Intl........ ISG International Software Group [*Associated Press*] (SAG)
ISGM............ Isabella Stewart Gardner Museum (SAUO)
ISGML.......... International Study Group for Mathematics Learning [*British*]
ISGN............ Insignia (MSA)
ISGO............ International Society of Geographic Ophthalmology [*Montreal, PQ*] (EAIO)
ISGP............ International Society of General Practice [*Germany*] (PDAA)
ISGP............ International Society of Geographical Pathology [*Australia*] (EY)
ISGP............ International Society of Gynaecological Pathologists (SAUO)
ISGPA.......... Information System for Government and Public Authorities (SAUS)
ISGRA.......... International Study Group on Risk Analysis
ISGS............ Illinois State Geological Survey [*Champaign*] [*Information service or system*] (IID)
ISGS............ International Society for General Semantics (EA)
ISGSH.......... International Study Group for Steroid Hormones [*Rome, Italy*] (EAIO)
ISGSH.......... International Study Group on Steroid Hormones (SAUS)
ISGT............ ISG Technologies, Inc. [*NASDAQ symbol*] (SAG)
ISG Tech...... ISG Technologies, Inc. [*Associated Press*] (SAG)
ISGTF.......... I.S.G. Technologies [*NASDAQ symbol*] (TTSB)
ISGW............ International Society of Girl Watchers (SAUO)
ISgW............ Waubonsee Community College, Sugar Grove, IL [*Library symbol*] [*Library of Congress*] (LCLS)
ISGWR.......... Inter-secretariat Group on Water Resources (SAUO)
ISGWRCA..... International Study Group for Waterworks in the Rhine Catchment Area [*See also IAWR*] (EAIO)
ISH.............. Caterpillar Tractor Co., Technical Information Center, Peoria, IL [*OCLC symbol*] (OCLC)
ISH.............. Icteric Serum Hepatitis [*Medicine*]
ISH.............. Industrial Safety & Health Program Services (SAUO)
ISH.............. Information Super Highway (SAUS)
ISH.............. Information Superhighway [*Telecommunications*] (PCM)
ISH.............. Inner Self-Helper [*Mulitple personality*] [*Psychology*]
ISH.............. In Situ Heating (ABAC)
ISH.............. In Situ Hybridization [*Biology*]
ISH.............. Institute for Scientific Humanism [*Later, WISH*]
ISH.............. Institute for Storm Research (SAUS)
ISH.............. Interim Scout Helicopter (MCD)
ISH.............. Intermediate System Hello [*Computer science*] (TNIG)
ISH.............. International Seamen and Harbour Workers (SAUO)
ISH.............. International Shipholding Corp. [*NYSE symbol*] (NQ)
ISH.............. International Society for Homeric Studies (SAUO)
ISH.............. International Society of Hematology (DAVI)
ISH.............. International Society of Hypertension (EA)
ISH.............. International Sterling [*Vancouver Stock Exchange symbol*]
ISH.............. International Trade Fair: Sanitation-Heating-Air Conditioning (SAUS)
ISH.............. Intl Shipholding [*NYSE symbol*] (TTSB)
ISH.............. Inventory Shortage (SAUS)
ISH.............. Ishtion [*Former USSR*] [*Seismograph station code, US Geological Survey*] (SEIS)
ISH.............. Isolated Systolic Hypertension [*Cardiology*] (DAVI)
ISHA............ Islamic Shipowners Association (SAUO)
ISHA............ National Subacute Care Association (NTPA)
ISHAE.......... International Society of Hotel Association Executives (EA)
ISHAM.......... International Society for Human and Animal Mycology [*London School of Hygiene and Tropical Medicine*] [*British*]
ISHAM.......... International Society of Human and Animal Mycology (SAUS)
ISHBPR........ International Society of Hepato-Biliary Pancreatic Radiology (SAUO)
ISHBR.......... International Society of Hepato-Biliary Radiology (SAUO)
ISHBSS........ International Society for the History of Behavioral and Social Sciences (NTPA)
ISHC............ Indicated Specific Hydrocarbon [*Automotive exhaust emission testing*]
ISHC............ International Siberian Husky Club
ISHC............ International Symposium on Homogeneous Catalysis

ISHC .... Intersociety Safety and Health Committee (SAUO)
IShCoH .... Shelby County Memorial Hospital, Shelbyville, IL [*Library symbol*] [*Library of Congress*] (LCLS)
ISHD .... International Society of Hydatid [*Medicine*] (EDAA)
ISHE .... International Safety and Health Exhibition [*British*] (ITD)
ISHE .... International Society for Human Ethology (EA)
ISHE .... International Society of Healthcare Executives (EA)
IShe .... Sheldon Township Public Library, Sheldon, IL [*Library symbol*] [*Library of Congress*] (LCLS)
ISherESD ..... Sheridan Elementary School District 272, Sheridan, IL [*Library symbol*] [*Library of Congress*] (LCLS)
ISHG .... Indian Society of Human Genetics
ISHH .... In Situ Hybridization Histochemistry
ISHI .... Institute for the Study of Human Issues (EA)
ISHI .... International Society for the History of Ideas (EA)
Ishikawajima-Harima Eng Rev... Ishikawajima-Harima Engineering Review (journ.) (SAUS)
ISHK .... Institute for the Study of Human Knowledge (EA)
ISHL .... Illinois Social Hygiene League (SAUO)
ISHL .... International Society for Historical Linguistics (EAIO)
ISHLT .... International Society for Heart and Lung Transplantation (EAIO)
ISHM .... International Society for Hybrid Microelectronics (EA)
ISHN .... Industrial Safety & Hygiene News (SAUO)
ISho .... South Holland Public Library, South Holland, IL [*Library symbol*] [*Library of Congress*] (LCLS)
ISHOBSS ...... International Society for the History of the Behavior and Social Sciences (SAUO)
ISHOF .... International Swimming Hall of Fame (EA)
IShoSHi .... South Suburban Genealogical and Historical Society, South Holland, IL [*Library symbol*] [*Library of Congress*] (LCLS)
IShoT .... Thornton Community College, South Holland, IL [*Library symbol*] [*Library of Congress*] (LCLS)
ISHOW .... Information System for Hazardous Organics in Water [*Database*] [*Environmental Protection Agency*] [*Information service or system*] (CRD)
(I)SHP .... (Intermediate) Shaft Horsepower
ISHP .... Intershop Communic. ADS [*NASDAQ symbol*]
ISHPC .... International Symposium on High Performance Computing (SAUS)
ISHPES .... International Society for the History of Physical Education and Sport [*Belgium*] (EAIO)
ISHPG .... Ishpeming, MI [*American Association of Railroads railroad junction routing code*]
ISHR .... Intermediate Scale Homogeneous Reactor
ISHR .... International Society for Heart Research [*Winnipeg, MB*] (EA)
ISHR .... International Society for Human Rights [*See also IGM*] [*Frankfurt, Federal Republic of Germany*] (EAIO)
ISHR .... International Society for the History of Rhetoric (EA)
ISHRA .... Iron and Steel Holding and Realization Agency (SAUO)
ISHRA .... Iron and Steel Holdings and Realisation Agency [*British*]
ISHS .... Illinois State Historical Society. Journal (journ.) (SAUS)
ISHS .... Improved Spartan Homing Sensor [*Missiles*]
ISHS .... International Society for Horticultural Science [*See also SISH*] [*ICSU*] [*Wageningen, Netherlands*] (EAIO)
ISHS .... International Society for Humor Studies (EA)
ISHS .... International Society of Horticultural Science (SAUS)
ISHT .... International Society for Heart Transplantation (EA)
ISHTAR .... Implementing Secure Health Telematics Applications in Europe (SAUO)
ISHTAR .... Inner Shelf Transfer and Recycling [*Marine science*] (OSRA)
ISHTCP .... Inventory of Sources for History of Twentieth Century Physics [*University of California, Berkeley*] [*Information service or system*] (IID)
ISHTE .... In-Situ Heat Transfer Experiment [*Nuclear energy*] (NUCP)
ISHU .... International Student Hitch-Hiking Union (SAUO)
ISHU .... Inter-Service Hovercraft Unit (SAUO)
ISHVBS .... International Society for Hildegard Von Bingen Studies (EA)
ISI .... Chillicothe Township Free Public Library, Chillicothe, IL [*OCLC symbol*] (OCLC)
ISI .... EPA Information Systems Inventory (SAUS)
ISI .... Image Subsystem Interface (SAUO)
ISI .... Image Systems, Inc. (SAUS)
ISI .... Image Systems Incorporated (SAUO)
ISI .... Indian Standards Institute (or Institution) (SAUS)
ISI .... Indian Statistical Institute
ISI .... Indian Statistical Institution (SAUS)
ISI .... Induced Spatial Incoherence [*Physics*]
ISI .... Industrial Safety Instructions (SAUO)
ISI .... Industrial Security International
ISI .... Industrial Standard Item (SAUS)
ISI .... Industrial Static Inverter
ISI .... Industry Standard Item (AAG)
ISI .... Infarct Size Index [*Cardiology*]
ISI .... Infodata Systems, Inc. [*Information service or system*] (IID)
ISI .... Infodata Systems, Incorporated (SAUO)
ISI .... Informal Spelling Inventory [*Education*]
ISI .... Information Science, Inc.
ISI .... Information Science, Incorporated (SAUO)
ISI .... Information Science Institute (SAUS)
ISI .... Information Sciences Institute [*University of Southern California, Marina Del Rey*]
ISI .... Information Service of India
ISI .... Information Services, Inc. [*Information service or system*] (IID)
ISI .... Information Services, Incorporated (SAUO)
ISI .... Information Services International [*Information service or system*] (IID)
ISI .... Information Society Initiative (SAUO)
ISI .... Information Storage, Inc.
ISI .... Information Storage, Incorporated (SAUO)
ISI .... Information Structure Implementation (SAUS)
ISI .... Information Systems Interoperability (SAUO)
ISI .... Information Systems Inventory (AEPA)
ISI .... Inhibited Sporozoite Invasion [*Immunology*]
ISI .... Initial Shipping Instructions (MCD)
ISI .... Initial Slope Index (STED)
ISI .... Initial Spread Index (SAUS)
ISI .... Initial Support Increments [*Army*] (AABC)
ISI .... Initial Support Item
ISI .... Initial System Integration (SAUS)
ISI .... Initial Systems Installation (NASA)
ISI .... Injury Severity Index (MCD)
ISI .... In-Service Incentive (SAUO)
ISI .... In-Service Institute [*National Science Foundation*]
ISI .... Institute for Science Information (SAUS)
ISI .... Institute for Scientific Information [*Philadelphia, PA*] [*Database producer*]
ISI .... Institute for Signal and Information Processing (SAUS)
ISI .... Institute for Social Inquiry [*University of Connecticut*] [*Storrs*] [*Information service or system*] (IID)
ISI .... Institute of Scientific Information (SAUS)
ISI .... Institute of Scientific Information at Bath (SAUO)
ISI .... Instructional Styles Inventory [*Test*] [*Canfield and Canfield*] (TES)
ISI .... Instrumentation Support Instruction (KSC)
isi .... Instrumentation Support Instruction [*NASA*] (NAKS)
ISI .... Instrument/Spacecraft Interface (ADWA)
ISI .... Instrument Systems Installation (SAUS)
ISI .... Insurance Selection Inventory [*Test*] [*London House, Inc.*] (TES)
ISI .... Integral Systems, Inc. (SAUS)
ISI .... Integral Systems Incorporated (SAUO)
ISI .... Integra Systems, Inc. [*Toronto Stock Exchange symbol*] [*Vancouver Stock Exchange symbol*]
ISI .... Integration Sensor Intelligence (SAUS)
ISI .... Intelligence Source Identification (SAUO)
ISI .... Intelligent Serial Interface [*Computer science*]
ISI .... Intelligent Standard Interface [*Computer science*] (ELAL)
ISI .... Intercollegiate Society of Individualists (SAUO)
ISI .... Intercollegiate Studies Institute (EA)
ISI .... Interim Support Item (MCD)
ISI .... Interior Space International (SAUS)
ISI .... International Safety Institute [*Defunct*] (EA)
ISI .... International Sales Indicator (TVEL)
ISI .... International Sales Institute (SAUO)
ISI .... International Satellite for Ionospheric Studies [*NASA-Canada*] (NOAA)
ISI .... International Satellite, Inc. [*Telecommunications*]
ISI .... International Satellite, Incorporated (SAUO)
ISI .... International Scientific Instruments (SAUS)
ISI .... International Scientific Instruments Inc. (SAUO)
ISI .... International Sensitivity Index [*Hematology*]
ISI .... International Services, Inc. (SAUS)
ISI .... International Services, Incorporated (SAUO)
ISI .... International Services International (SAUS)
ISI .... International Services of Information Foundation (SAUO)
ISI .... International Slope Index (STED)
ISI .... International Standards Institute (SAUS)
ISI .... International Statistical Institute [*ICSU*] [*Voorburg, Netherlands*] (EA)
ISI .... International Students, Inc. (EA)
ISI .... International Students, Incorporated (SAUO)
ISI .... Interpersonal Style Inventory [*Personality development test*] [*Psychology*]
ISI .... Interpretation System, Inc. (SAUS)
ISI .... Interpretation Systems, Incorporated (SAUO)
ISI .... Inter-Service Intelligence directorate (SAUO)
ISI .... Inter-Sound Interval (EDAC)
ISI .... Interspike Interval [*Neurophysiology*]
ISI .... Interstimulus Interval
ISI .... Inter-Symbol Interference (AEBE)
ISI .... Ion Signal for Imaging (SAUS)
ISI .... Ion Source Injector
ISI .... Iron and Steel Institute (MCD)
ISI .... Ishigakijima [*Ryukyu Islands*] [*Seismograph station code, US Geological Survey*] (SEIS)
ISI .... Isisford [*Australia*] [*Airport symbol*] (OAG)
ISI .... Israel Standards Institute (SAUO)
ISI .... ISS-International Service System, Inc. (SAUS)
ISI .... ISS-International Service System, Incorporated (SAUO)
ISI .... Italic Studies Institute (EA)
ISI .... Item Station and Indenture (AAG)
ISI .... USC Information Sciences Institute (SAUS)
ISIA .... Ice Skating Institute of America (EA)
ISIA .... Institute of Sustainable Agriculture (SAUO)
ISIA .... International Ski Instructors' Association (ECON)
ISIA .... International Snowmobile Industry Association (EA)
ISIA .... Italo Svevo International Association [*Defunct*] (EA)
ISIADL .... Insect Science and Its Application (journ.) (SAUS)
ISIAL .... Incorporated Society of Irish/American Lawyers (EA)
ISIAME .... International Symposium on the Industrial Applications of the Mossbauer Effect
ISIAN .... International Society for Immuno-Allergology of the Nasal Sinuses (SAUO)

ISIAQ .... International Society of Indoor Air Quality and Climate [*Industrial hygiene term*] (OHS)
ISIB .... Institute for the Study of Intellectual Behavior [*University of Colorado*] (PDAA)
ISIB .... Inter-Service Ionosphere Bureau [*Military*]
ISIB .... Interservice Ionospheric Bureau (SAUS)
ISIB .... Inter-Services Ionosphere Bureau (SAUO)
ISI/BIOMED... Institute for Scientific Information/Biomedical Online (SAUS)
ISI Bulletin... Indian Standards Institution Bulletin (journ.) (SAUS)
ISIC .... Immediate Senior in Command (SAUS)
ISIC .... Immediate Superior in Command [*Military*]
ISIC .... Information and Software Integration Contractor (SAUO)
ISIC .... Intelligence Support and Indications Center [*Military*] (MCD)
ISIC .... Interceptor System Integration Contractor (ACAE)
ISIC .... International Service Identity Card (SAUS)
ISIC .... International Solvay Institute of Chemistry (SAUO)
ISIC .... International Standard Industrial Classification (EY)
ISIC .... Intersymbol Interference Corrector
ISICC .... International SAP IBM Competence Center (SAUS)
ISICCE .... International Society of India Chemists and Chemical Engineers (EA)
ISI/CID .... Institute for Scientific Information/ Chemical Information Division (SAUS)
ISICR .... International Society for Interferon and Cytokine Research (SAUO)
ISICS .... Indian Self-Identified Certified Staff (EDAC)
ISID .... Improved Standard Information Display (ACAE)
ISID .... International Society for Infectious Diseases (NTPA)
ISID .... International Society of Interior Designers (EA)
ISID .... Isolated-Section Inductive Divider (SAUS)
ISid .... Sidell District Library, Sidell, IL [*Library symbol*] [*Library of Congress*] (LCLS)
ISIDHI .... International Society on Infectious Diseases and Human Infertility (EA)
ISidn .... Sidney Community Library, Sidney, IL [*Library symbol*] [*Library of Congress*] (LCLS)
ISIDPP .... Initial Shut-In Drill Pipe Pressure
ISidSD .... Jamaica Community Unit School District, Sidell, IL [*Library symbol*] [*Library of Congress*] (LCLS)
ISIE .... Integral Square Ideal Error (IAA)
ISIF .... Intermediate Standard Transfer Format (SAUO)
ISIF .... International Symposium on Integrated Ferroelectrics (SAUS)
ISIFM .... International Society of Industrial Fabric Manufacturers (EA)
ISIG .... Implementation Special Interest Group [*Association for the Development of Computer-Based Instructional Systems*] (EDAC)
ISIG .... Industrial Standards Institute of Ghana (SAUO)
ISIG .... Insignia Sys [*NASDAQ symbol*] (TTSB)
ISIG .... Insignia Systems, Inc. [*NASDAQ symbol*] (SAG)
ISIG .... Institute of International Sociology, Gorizia (SAUO)
ISIG .... Irish Special Interest Group of American Mensa (EA)
ISIH .... Interspike Interval Histogram [*Neurophysiology*]
ISII .... Integra Systems, Incorporated (SAUO)
ISII .... International Society for Individualized Instruction (AIE)
ISI/IST .... In-Service Inspections and In-Service Testing
ISI/ISTP&B... Institute for Scientific Information/Index to Scientific and Technical Proceedings and Books (SAUS)
ISI/ISTP & B... ISI/Index to Scientific and Technical Proceedings and Books [*Institute for Scientific Information*] [*Philadelphia, PA*] [*Bibliographic database*]
ISIJ .... Iron and Steel Institute of Japan
ISIJU .... Indian Statistical Institute and Jadaipur University (SAUO)
ISIJU .... Inian Statistical Institute and Jadaipur University (SAUS)
ISIJU Computer... Indian Statistical Institute and Jadaipur University Computer (SAUO)
ISIL .... Interim Support Items List (NASA)
ISIL .... International Society for Individual Liberty (EAIO)
ISIL .... Intersil Holdings 'A' [*NASDAQ symbol*] (SG)
ISILT .... Information Science Index Language Text (NITA)
ISIM .... Inhibit Simultaneity (IAA)
ISIM .... [*The*] International School of Information Management, Inc. [*Denver, CO*] (ECON)
ISIM .... International Society of Internal Medicine [*Langenthal, Switzerland*] (EA)
ISIM .... Inventory Simulation (IAA)
ISIMC .... International Study Institution of the Middle Classes [*Brussels, Belgium*] (EAIO)
ISIMEP .... International Symposium on Identification and Measurement of Environmental Pollutants (PDAA)
ISIMM .... International Society for the Interaction of Mechanics and Mathematics (EA)
ISIN .... Indiana Seminar on Information Network (SAUS)
ISIN .... Information Systems Internetting (SAUO)
ISINC .... Immediate Superior in Command [*Military*]
IS Ind Soc Mag... IS Industrial Society Magazine (journ.) (SAUS)
IS Injection... Intra-Spinal Injection (SAUS)
ISIO .... Institute for the Study of International Organizations (SAUO)
ISIO .... Intelligent Serial In-/Output (SAUS)
ISIP .... Indexed Security Investment Plan [*Canada*]
ISIP .... Inertial System Indication Position (SAUS)
ISIP .... Information Systems Improvement Program (SAUO)
ISIP .... Information Systems Planning Services (SAUO)
ISIP .... Instantaneous Shut-In Pressure (SAUS)
ISIP .... Intelligence Support Interface Program
ISIP .... Iron and Steel Industry Profile Services (SAUO)
ISIP .... Iron and Steel Industry Profiles (journ.) (SAUS)
ISIP .... Isis Pharmaceuticals [*NASDAQ symbol*] (SPSG)
ISIPBMP .... International Symposium on Interfacial Phenomena in Biotechnology and Materials Processing (SAUS)
ISIPO .... International Systems Integration Project Office (SAUS)
ISIPP .... Information System for Improved Plant Protection [*FAO*] [*United Nations*] (DUND)
ISIPS .... Information Services Integrated Publishing System (SAUO)
ISIR .... Initial Sample Inspection Report
ISIR .... In Service, In Reserve [*Vessel status*] [*Navy*]
ISIR .... Institute of Scientific and Industrial Research (SAUS)
ISIR .... Institute of Standards and Industrial Research (SAUS)
ISIR .... Interactive Single Isomorphous Replacement [*Crystallographic procedure*]
ISIR .... International Satellite for Ionospheric Research [*NASA Canada*] (IAA)
ISIR .... International Society for Interferon Research (SAUO)
ISIR .... International Society for Invertebrate Reproduction (SAUS)
ISIR .... International Society for/of Invertebrate Reproduction (SAUO)
ISIR .... International Society for the Immunology of Reproduction (EA)
ISIR .... International Symposium on Industrial Robots (PDAA)
ISIR .... Iterative Single Isomorphous Replacement [*Crystallography*]
ISIRC .... International Statistical Institute Research Center [*Research center*] [*Netherlands*] (IRC)
ISIRS .... International Sorption Information Retrieval System [*Nuclear Energy Agency*] (EY)
ISIRTA .... I'm Sorry, I'll Read That Again [*BBC radio comedy program*]
ISIS .... Image and Scanner Interface Specification (MWOL)
ISIS .... Image and Scanner Interface Standard (RALS)
ISIS .... Image-Selected in Vivo Spectroscopy
ISIS .... Impact Shock Isolation System [*Tennis-racket technology*] [*Dunlop Slazenger Corp.*]
ISIS .... Improved Speech Intelligibility System (SAUS)
ISIS .... Independence Square Income Securities [*NASDAQ symbol*] (SAG)
ISIS .... Independence Square Income Securities, Inc. [*NASDAQ symbol*] (NQ)
ISIS .... Independent Schools Information Service [*British*]
ISIS .... Indian School of International Studies [*Delhi*]
ISIS .... Indian Society for Information Science (SAUO)
ISIS .... Individualized Science Instructional System [*National Science Foundation project*]
ISIS .... Individual Service Information System (SAUS)
ISIS .... Industry File Indexing System (SAUO)
ISIS .... Information System Indexing System [*Federal Judicial Center*] [*Database*]
ISIS .... Infratest Software Information Service (SAUS)
ISIS .... Infratest Software Informations-Service (SAUO)
ISIS .... Infratest Software Information System (SAUS)
ISIS .... Infratest System Language (SAUS)
ISIS .... Instant Sales Indicator System (IAA)
ISIS .... Institute for Self Improvement (SAUO)
ISIS .... Institute for the Study of Inquiring Systems
ISIS .... Institute of Science in Society (SAUO)
ISIS .... Institute of Scrap Iron and Steel [*Later, ISRI*] (EA)
ISIS .... Institute of Strategic and International Studies [*Malaysia*] (ECON)
ISIS .... Institutional Sector Investment Services [*Chase Manhattan Securities*] [*British*]
ISIS .... Integral Service Information System (IAA)
ISIS .... Integral Spare Inspection System (SAUS)
ISIS .... Integral Spar Inspection System
ISIS .... Integrated Safeguard Information System (NRCH)
ISIS .... Integrated Satellite Information Service (ACAE)
ISIS .... Integrated Scientific Information Service (SAUO)
ISIS .... Integrated Scientific Information System
ISIS .... Integrated Set of Information Systems (IAA)
ISIS .... Integrated Shape Imaging System (MELL)
ISIS .... Integrated Shipboard Information System [*Nautical term*] (NTA)
ISIS .... Integrated Ship Instrumentation System (IAA)
ISIS .... Integrated Side-Impact System [*Automotive safety*]
ISIS .... Integrated Signals Intelligence System (SAUO)
ISIS .... Integrated Silviculture Information System (SAUO)
ISIS .... Integrated Software Invocation System [*Computer science*] (MHDI)
ISIS .... Integrated Staff Information System (SAUS)
ISIS .... Integrated Standardization Information System (SAUS)
ISIS .... Integrated Statistical Information Service (WDAA)
ISIS .... Integrated Statistical Information System (SAUS)
ISIS .... Integrated Strike and Interception (or Interceptor) System (SAUS)
ISIS .... Integrated Strike and Interceptor System
ISIS .... Integrated Student Information System (SAUS)
ISIS .... Integrated Supply Chain Information System (HODG)
ISIS .... Integrated Surface Irradiance Study [*Marine science*] (OSRA)
ISIS .... Integrated System for Improved Separations [*Membrane filtration*]
ISIS .... Integrated Systems and Information Services (SAUO)
ISIS .... Integriertes Statistisches Informationssystem [*Integrated Statistical Information System*] [*Central Statistical Office*] [*Vienna, Austria*] [*Information service or system*] (IID)
ISIS .... Intelligentes Satellitendaten-Informationssystem (SAUS)
ISIS .... Intelligent Satellite Data Information System (SAUO)
ISIS .... Intelligent Scheduling and Information System (AGLO)
ISIS .... Intel System Implementation Supervisor (SAUS)
ISIS .... Interactive Sound Information System (SAUS)
ISIS .... Interchangeability and Substitutability Item Subgroup (MCD)
ISIS .... Interdisciplinary Studies of Intelligent Systems (SAUS)
ISIS .... Intermarket Surveillance Information System (DFIT)
IS-IS .... Intermediate System-Intermediate System (SAUS)
IS-IS .... Intermediate System-to-Intermediate System [*Telecommunications*]
IS-IS .... Intermediate System to Intermediate System Protocol (SAUO)
ISIS .... Internally Switched Interface System [*Tymnet, Inc.*]

ISIS .... Internal Scientific Information System (SAUS)
ISIS .... Internal Systems Information System (SAUS)
ISIS .... Internationale de Services Industriels and Scientifiques
ISIS .... Internationally Syndicated Information Services [*Information service or system*] [*Defunct*] (IID)
ISIS .... International Satellite for Ionospheric Studies [*NASA-Canada*]
ISIS .... International Science Information Services [*Earth sciences data center*] [*Dallas, TX*]
ISIS .... International Scientific Information Service (SAUO)
ISIS .... International Shipping Information Service (DS)
ISIS .... International Society for Intelligent Systems (NTPA)
ISIS .... International Society of Introduction Services (EA)
ISIS .... International Society on Infant Studies (SAUO)
ISIS .... International Space Information System [*United Nations*] (DUND)
ISIS .... International Specialized Information System (SAUS)
ISIS .... International Species Identification System (SAUS)
ISIS .... International Species Information System (IID)
ISIS .... International Species Inventory System [*Data processing for animal mating*] [*Minnesota Zoological Gardens*] [*Apple Valley, MN*]
ISIS .... International Spinal Injection Society (SAUO)
ISIS .... International Student Information Service
ISIS .... International Student Information System (SAUS)
ISIS .... International Student Insurance Scheme (SAUO)
ISIS .... International Study of Infarct Survival [*Medicine*]
ISIS .... International Superconductivity Industry Summit [*Conference*]
ISIS .... International Switching Interface System (SAUS)
ISIS .... International Symposium on Isotope Separation (SAUO)
ISIS .... Interstate Settlement Information System [*AT & T*]
ISIS .... Intratest Software Information Service (SAUS)
ISIS .... Investigative Support Information System [*Federal Bureau of Investigation*]
ISIS .... Ion-Beam Synthesis in Semiconductors (SAUS)
Isis .... Isis (SAUS)
Isis .... Isis Pharmaceuticals, Inc. [*Associated Press*] (SAG)
ISIS .... Item Standardization Information System [*DoD*]
ISIS .... Rutherford Laboratory Neutron Facility (SAUO)
ISIS .... Serials management package marketed by B.H.Blackwell Ltd. (SAUO)
ISIS .... Women's International Information and Communication Service [*Italy and Switzerland*]
ISISA .... Individual Scale for Indian South Africans [*Intelligence test*]
ISISC .... Istituto Superiore Internazionale di Scienze Criminali [*Italy*]
IS/ISD .... Instructional Systems/Instructional Systems Division (SAUO)
ISISS .... International Summer Institute in Surface Science (SAUS)
ISISSAPORCI ... International Section of ISSA [*International Social Security Association*] on the Prevention of Occupational Risks in the Construction Industry [*Boulogne-Billancourt, France*] (EAIO)
ISIS-WICCE ... ISIS [*Women's International Information Communication Service*] - Women's International Cross-Cultural Exchange (EAIO)
ISIS-X .... International Satellites for Ionosphere Studies - Experimental [*NASA/Canada*] (SAA)
ISiT .... Fraunhofer Institut of Silicon Technology (SAUS)
ISIT .... Initial System Integrated Test (ACAE)
ISIT .... Institute for Studies in International Terrorism (SAUO)
ISiT .... Institute of Silicon Technology (SAUS)
ISiT .... Institut of Silicon Technology (SAUO)
ISIT .... Intensified Silicon Intensified (or Intensifier) Target (SAUS)
ISIT .... Intensifier Silicon Intensifier Target (SAUS)
ISIT .... International Symposium on Information Theory (SAUS)
ISITB .... Iron and Steel Industry Training Board [*British*] (BI)
I-SITE .... Intelligent Screening of Imagery for Teleophthalmology (SAUS)
ISIUP .... Islamic Society for International Unity and Peace [*Pakistan*] (EAIO)
ISIWM .... Incorporated Society of Inspectors of Weights and Measures (SAUO)
ISIYM .... International Society of Industrial Yarn Manufacturers [*Later, ISIFM*] (EA)
ISJ .... Infrared Society of Japan (SAUO)
ISJ .... Institute for Social Justice (EA)
ISJ .... Internet Science Journal (SAUO)
ISJ .... Israel Export and Trade Journal (journ.) (SAUS)
ISJ .... Saint Josephs College, Rensselaer (SAUS)
ISJ .... Saint Joseph's College, Rensselaer, IN [*OCLC symbol*] (OCLC)
ISJAC .... Independent Schools Joint Action Committee (AIE)
ISJB .... Interim System Junction Box (SAUS)
ISJC .... Independent Schools Joint Committee (SAUO)
ISJC .... Independent Schools Joint Council [*British*]
ISJCAT .... Israel Journal of Chemistry (journ.) (SAUS)
ISJCT .... International Symposium on Jet Cutting Technology (PDAA)
ISJIS .... Infrared Solder Joint Integrity System (ACAE)
IsJJNL .... Jewish National and University Library, Hebrew University, Jerusalem, Israel [*Library symbol*] [*Library of Congress*] (LCLS)
ISJL .... International Society of Jewish Librarians (EA)
ISJM .... Israeli Journal of Mathematics (journ.) (SAUS)
ISJP .... International Society for Japanese Philately (EA)
ISJRA9 .... Iowa State Journal of Science (journ.) (SAUS)
ISJTA .... Intensive Student Jet Training Area
ISJTAC .... Israel Journal of Technology (journ.) (SAUS)
ISK .... Galva Township Public Library, Galva, IL [*OCLC symbol*] (OCLC)
ISK .... Icelandic Krona (SAUS)
ISK .... Insert Storage Key (IEEE)
ISK .... Instruction Space Key
ISK .... Intercept Sonar (SAUS)
ISK .... Internacia Scienca Kolegio [*International College of Scientists - ICS*] [*Paderborn, Federal Republic of Germany*] (EAIO)
ISK .... Internationale Seidenbau Kommission [*International Sericultural Commission*]
ISK .... International Society of the Knee (EA)
ISK .... Ion Source Kit
ISK .... Iskenderon [*Turkey*] [*Airport symbol*] (AD)
ISK .... Iskut Gold Corp. [*Vancouver Stock Exchange symbol*]
ISK .... Istanbul-Kandilli [*Turkey*] [*Seismograph station code, US Geological Survey*] (SEIS)
ISK .... Nasik [*India*] [*Airport symbol*] (OAG)
ISk .... Skokie Public Library, Skokie, IL [*Library symbol*] [*Library of Congress*] (LCLS)
ISKA .... International Saw and Knife Association (EA)
ISKC .... International Society for Krishna Consciousness (SAUO)
ISKCON .... International Society for Krishna Consciousness (EA)
ISKDC .... International Study of Kidney Disease in Children
ISkH .... Hebrew Theological College, Skokie, IL [*Library symbol*] [*Library of Congress*] (LCLS)
ISKI .... International Secretariat of the Knitting Industries [*Paris, France*] (EAIO)
ISKM .... Internet Starter Kit for the Macintosh (SAUS)
ISKO .... International Society for Knowledge Organisation (SAUO)
ISKO .... International Society for Knowledge Organization [*Germany*] (EAIO)
ISKO .... Isco, Inc. [*NASDAQ symbol*] (NQ)
ISKR .... Identification, Station Keeping and Rendezvous (SAUS)
ISkS .... G. D. Searle & Co., Inc., Skokie, IL [*Library symbol*] [*Library of Congress*] (LCLS)
IskS .... O. D. Searle & Co., Inc. (SAUO)
ISkT .... Triodyne, Skokie, IL [*Library symbol*] [*Library of Congress*] (LCLS)
ISL .... Eagle Air Ltd. [*Iceland*] [*ICAO designator*] (FAAC)
ISL .... First Israel Fund [*NYSE symbol*] (TTSB)
ISL .... Iceland [*ANSI three-letter standard code*] (CNC)
ISL .... Iceland Steamship Co. (SAUS)
ISL .... Iceland Steamship Company (SAUO)
ISL .... Illinois State Library (SAUO)
ISL .... Immunodeficiency-Virus-Suppressing Lymphokine [*Virology*]
ISL .... Inactive Status List (MUGU)
ISL .... Indiana State Library, Indianapolis, IN [*OCLC symbol*] (OCLC)
ISL .... Industrial Security Letter [*DoD*]
ISL .... Inertial Systems Laboratory [*NASA*] (GFGA)
ISL .... Informatics Services [*Oakville, ON*] [*Telecommunications service*] (TSSD)
ISL .... Information Science Librarian (SAUS)
ISL .... Information Search Language
ISL .... Information Services Ltd. [*Publisher*] [*British*]
ISL .... Information Studies Ltd. (SAUS)
ISL .... Information System Language [*Computer science*] (IEEE)
ISL .... Information System Leasing (SAUS)
ISL .... Information Systems Laboratories, Inc.
ISL .... Information Systems Laboratory (SAUS)
ISL .... Initial Spare Parts List (IAA)
ISL .... Initial Stocks List
ISL .... Initial System Loader (SAUS)
ISL .... Initial System Loading
ISL .... Injection Coupled Synchronous Logic (IAA)
ISL .... Injection-coupled Synchronous Logic (SAUS)
ISL .... Inner Scapular Line [*Medicine*] (DMAA)
ISL .... Inner Structured Layer (SAUS)
ISL .... In Situ Leaching (GAAI)
ISL .... Institute of Space Law
ISL .... Institut fuer Seeverkehrwirtschaft und Logistik [*Institute of Shipping Economics and Logistics - ISEL*] [*Bremen, Federal Republic of Germany*] (EAIO)
ISL .... Instructional Systems Language [*Computer science*] (IEEE)
I S-L .... Instructor Sub-Lieutenant (SAUO)
ISL .... Instrument Standards Laboratory [*Space Flight Operations Facility, NASA*]
ISL .... Integrated Schottky Logic (IEEE)
ISL .... Integrated Services Layer (GART)
ISL .... Integrated Simulation Logic (SAUS)
ISL .... Integrated Stock List (SAUO)
ISL .... Integrated Stock Listing
ISL .... Integrated Synthesis Logic [*Computer science*]
ISL .... Intelligence Service, Levant (SAUO)
ISL .... Intelligent Systems Laboratory (SAUS)
ISL .... Interactive Simulation Language [*Computer science*] (IEEE)
ISL .... Interactive System Language (SAUO)
ISL .... Interdivisional Systems List (SAUS)
ISL .... Interface Socket Listing (SAUS)
ISL .... Intermediate Stage Letter (SAUS)
ISL .... Intermountain Swim League (PSS)
ISL .... Internally-Silvered Lamp [*Light bulb*] (DI)
ISL .... Internal Standard Line
ISL .... International Shipping Legislation (SAUS)
ISL .... International Soccer League
ISL .... International Society of Literature [*Ilkley, Yorkshire, England*] (EAIO)
ISL .... International Society of Lymphology (EA)
ISL .... International Subcommittee on Lactobacilli and Closely Related Organisms (SAUS)
ISL .... International Subcommittee on Lactobacilli and Closely Related Organismus (SAUO)
ISL .... International Surfing League (SAUO)
ISL .... Intersatellite Link
ISL .... Interscapular Line (STED)
ISL .... Interseas Shipping Lines (SAUS)
ISL .... Interspinous Ligament [*Medicine*] (DMAA)
ISL .... Intersystem Link
ISL .... Inventory Systems Language (SAUS)

ISL.............. Iranian Shipping Lines (SAUO)
ISL.............. Irish Shipping Limited (SAUO)
ISL.............. Irish Shipping Ltd. (SAUS)
ISL.............. Irish Sign Language (SAUS)
Isl.............. Island (NTIO)
ISL.............. Island [*Board on Geographic Names*]
ISL.............. Isle
ISL.............. Islington (ROG)
ISL.............. Isolated Signal Line (IAA)
ISL.............. Item Selection List
ISL.............. Item Survey List (DNAB)
ISL.............. Lincoln Library, Springfield, IL [*Library symbol*] [*Library of Congress*] (LCLS)
ISLA............ Idaho State Library Association (SAUO)
ISLA............ Information Services on Latin America (EA)
ISLA............ Information System for the Leicester Area (SAUS)
ISLA............ International Survey Libraries Association [*University of Connecticut*] (NITA)
ISLA............ International Survey Library Association (EA)
ISLA............ Investors Savings Bank (Virginia) [*NASDAQ symbol*] (COMM)
ISLADE........ Interactive Structural Layout and Design [*Module*]
Islam.......... Islamic (DIAR)
Islamabad J Sci... Islamabad Journal of Sciences. Journal of Mathematics Sciences (journ.) (SAUS)
Islam Cult.... Islamic Culture (journ.) (SAUS)
Islam Mod Age... Islam and the Modern Age (journ.) (SAUS)
Islam Stud... Islamic Studies (journ.) (SAUS)
ISLAN.......... Integrated Services Local Area Network [*Telecommunications*] (ACRL)
ISLAND........ Island [*Commonly used*] (OPSA)
ISLANDS....... Islands [*Commonly used*] (OPSA)
ISLAR.......... International Symposium on Laboratory Automation and Robotics
ISLAS........... Institute for Study of the Liberal Arts and Sciences (SAUS)
ISLB............ Initial Search Lower Bound (SAUS)
ISLC............ International Sporting and Leisure Club
ISLC............ Lincoln Land Community College, Springfield, IL [*Library symbol*] [*Library of Congress*] (LCLS)
ISLCBS........ International Seal, Label, and Cigar Band Society (EA)
ISLD............ Digital Island [*NASDAQ symbol*] (SG)
ISLD............ Institute for the Study of Learning Difficulties [*Flinders University*] [*Australia*]
ISLD............ International Society for Lasers in Dentistry (SAUO)
ISLD............ International Special Librarians Day
ISLD............ Inter-Services Liaison Department [*World War II*]
ISLE............ Institute of Sociology of Law for Europe (SAUO)
ISLE............ Integral Square Linear Error (IAA)
ISLE............ Integrated Simulation Language Environment [*Computer science*]
ISLE............ Intensely Supportive Learning Environment (SAUS)
ISLE............ Isle [*Postal Service standard*] (OPSA)
ISLE............ Isle Resources, Inc. (SAUO)
ISLEC.......... Institute for the Study of Labor and Economic Crisis (EA)
ISLER.......... Islander
ISLES.......... Isle [*Commonly used*] (OPSA)
ISLF............ Improved Saturn Launch Facility
ISLFD.......... Incorporated Society of London Fashion Designers
ISLH............ International Holding Capital Corp. (SAUO)
ISLI............. INTERSOLV [*NASDAQ symbol*] (TTSB)
ISLI............. Intersolv, Inc. [*NASDAQ symbol*] (SAG)
ISLIC........... Indian Association of Special Libraries and Information Centres (SAUO)
ISLIC........... Islamic Library Information Centre (SAUS)
ISLIC........... Israel Society of Special Libraries and Information Centers
ISLIC Bull.... Israel Society of Special Libraries and Information Centers. Bulletin (journ.) (SAUS)
ISLISL......... International Society for Labor Law and Social Legislation (SAUO)
ISLISS......... International Society for Labor Law and Social Security (SAUO)
Is Lit........... Islamic Literature (journ.) (SAUS)
ISLL............ Illinois Studies in Language and Literature (journ.) (SAUS)
ISLL............ International Survey of Legal Decisions on Labour Law [*1925-38*] [*A publication*] (DLA)
ISL/LAR....... Integrated Logistics System and Logistics Assessment Review
ISLLSL......... International Society for Labor Law and Social Legislation [*Later, International Society for Labor Law and Social Security United States National Branch*] (EA)
ISLLSS......... International Society for Labor Law and Social Security [*International Co ngresses of Labour Law and International Society for Social Law*] [*Formed by a merger of*] (EAIO)
ISLM........... Integrated Services Line Module (SAUS)
ISLM........... Integration Shop/Laboratory Manager (MCD)
IS/LM.......... Investment-Saving, Money Demand-Money Supply (SAUO)
ISLM........... Investment-Savings, Liquidity-Money [*Economics*] (ODBW)
ISLMA......... Illinois School Library Media Association (SRA)
ISLMC......... Internet School Library Media Center
Islm Rep Pak... Islamic Republic of Pakistan (SAUS)
Islm Wld D... Islamic World Defence (journ.) (SAUS)
ISLN........... Integrated Services Local Network (SAUO)
ISLN........... Isolation (MSA)
ISLND......... Island [*Commonly used*] (OPSA)
ISLNDS....... Islands [*Commonly used*] (OPSA)
ISLO........... International Solidarity Labour Organization (SAUO)
ISLP........... IGOSS Sea-Level Programme (SAUS)
ISLP........... IGOSS [*Integrated Global Ocean Services System*] Sea Level Project [*Marine science*] (OSRA)
ISLPP......... IGOSS Sea-Level Pilot Project (SAUS)
ISLPP......... IGOSS Sea-Level Pilot Project in the Pacific Ocean (SAUO)
ISLP-Pac...... GOSS [*Integrated Global Ocean Station System*] Sea Level Project in the Pacific (USDC)
ISLP-PAC..... IGOSS Sea-Level Programme in the Pacific (SAUS)
ISLP-Pac...... IGOSS [*Integrated Global Ocean Services System*] Sea Level Project in the Pacific [*Marine science*] (OSRA)
ISLPP-NTA... IGOSS Sea-Level Pilot Project in the North and Tropical Atlantic (SAUS)
ISLR............ Initial Sample Laboratory Report
ISLR............ Integrated Side-Lobe Ratio
ISLR............ International Symposium on Laboratory Robotics
ISLR............ Isolator (MSA)
ISLRS.......... Inactive Status List Reserve Section
ISLS............ Improved Sidelobe Suppression (SAUS)
ISLS............ Improved Side-Lobe Supression (PDAA)
ISLS............ Information System Language Studies (journ.) (SAUS)
ISLS............ Intelligent Surgical Lasers, Inc. [*NASDAQ symbol*] (SAG)
ISLS............ Interrogation Side-Lobe Suppression
ISLS............ Interrogator Side Lobe Suppression (SAUO)
ISLS............ Islands [*Board on Geographic Names*]
ISLSA.......... Integrated Sensor for Large-Scale Applications (SAUS)
ISLSCP........ International Land Surface Climatology Project (SAUS)
ISLSCP........ International Satellite Land Surface Climatology Program (SAUS)
ISLSCP........ International Satellite Land Surface Climatology Project [*Federal government*]
ISLSCP........ International Satellite Land-Surface Climatology Project (SAUO)
Isl St........... Islamic Studies (journ.) (SAUS)
ISLT............ International Snow Leopard Trust (EA)
ISLTC.......... International Society of Leather Trades Chemists (SAUO)
ISLTS.......... Incorporated Society of Licensed Trade Stocktakers [*British*] (DBA)
ISLU............ Integrated Services Line Unit (SAUS)
ISLVW......... Island View [*Travel industry*] (TRID)
ISLW........... Indian Spring Low Water [*Tides and currents*]
ISLWF......... International Shoe and Leather Workers' Federation
ISLWG........ International Shipping Legislation Working Group (SAUO)
ISLWG........ Working Group on International Shipping Legislation [*UNCTAD*] (DS)
ISLW Time... Indian Spring Low Water Time (SAUS)
ISLY........... Isaly Co., Inc. (SAUO)
ISM............ Iesus Salvator Mundi [*Jesus, Savior of the World*] [*Latin*]
ISM............ Igniter Safety Mechanism (ACAE)
ISM............ Illinois State Museum (QUAC)
ISM............ Image Compression and Multiplexing (SAUS)
ISM............ Immited Sander Machine (SAUS)
ISM............ Imperial Service Medal [*British*]
ISM............ Improved Sensing Munitions (RDA)
ISM............ Imtegrated Skills Method (SAUS)
ISM............ Incorporated Society of Musicians [*British*]
ISM............ Independent Subcarrier Method (PDAA)
ISM............ Indian Supply Mission [*World War II*]
ISM............ Inductor Super Magnetron [*Electronics*] (AAEL)
ISM............ Industrial, Scientific and Medical [*Communications term*] (DCT)
ISM............ Industrial, Scientific and Medical Applications
ISM............ Industrial, Scientific, Medical (SAUS)
ISM............ Industrial Security Manual (MCD)
ISM............ Industrials Scientific-Medical (SAUO)
ISM............ Industrial Staff Member (SAUO)
ISM............ Industrial Sugar Mills (SAUO)
ISM............ Information System for Management (SAUS)
ISM............ Information System Manager (NATG)
ISM............ Information System Medical (SAUO)
ISM............ Information Systems for Management (IEEE)
ISM............ Information Systems Manual (SAUS)
ISM............ Information Systems Marketing, Inc. [*Information service or system*] (IID)
ISM............ Infrared Systems Manufacturing
ISM............ Initial Segment Membrane
ISM............ In-Service Monitoring (SAUS)
ISM............ Inside of Metal
ISM............ In Situ Measurements (SAUS)
ISM............ In Space Maintenance (SAUS)
ISM............ Installation Support Module (SAUS)
ISM............ Institute for the Study of Man (EA)
ISM............ Institute of Sales and Marketing (SAUO)
ISM............ Institute of Sales Management (SAUO)
ISM............ Institute of Sanitation Management [*Later, EMA*] (EA)
ISM............ Institute of Service Management (SAUO)
ISM............ Institute of Spiritualist Mediums [*British*] (DBA)
ISM............ Institute of Sports Medicine [*British*]
ISM............ Institute of Statistical Mathematics (SAUO)
ISM............ Institute of Supervisory Management [*British*]
ISM............ Instructional System in Mathematics Program (EDAC)
ISM............ Insulation System Module [*Engineering*] (OA)
ISM............ Integrated Safety Management (SAUO)
ISM............ Integrated Sander Machine [*Disk controller*] [*Apple Computer, Inc.*] (BYTE)
ISM............ Integrated Services Model (SAUS)
ISM............ Integrated Skills Method [*Education*]
ISM............ Integrated Sustainment Maintenance
ISM............ Integrated System Management Framework (SAUS)
ISM............ Intelligent Synchronous Multiplexer (SAUS)
ISM............ Interactive Siting Method (PDAA)
ISM............ Interavia Space Markets [*Interavia Publications*] [*Information service or system*] (CRD)
ISM............ Interim Surface Missile (PDAA)
ISM............ International Camero Resources [*Vancouver Stock Exchange symbol*]

ISM............ International School of Management (SAUS)
ISM............ International Sea Mapping (SAUS)
ISM............ International Ship Management Code (SAUO)
ISM............ International Society for Metaphysics (EA)
ISM............ International Society of Microbiologists (DAVI)
ISM............ International Software Marketing (HGAA)
ISM............ International Soil Museum
ISM............ International Staff Memoranda (SAUO)
ISM............ International Standards Method (IAA)
ISM............ International Studies of Management and Organization (journ.) (SAUS)
ISM............ International Sweets Market [*Trade fair*] [*Cologne, West Germany*] [*1982*]
ISM............ International Symposium on Microchemistry
ISM............ International Symposium on Microtechniques
ISM............ International Systems Meeting [*Computer science*]
ISM............ Internet Service Manager (SAUO)
ISM............ Internetwork Status Monitor (DINT)
ISM............ Interpretive Structural Modeling [*A computer-assisted learning process for structuring information*]
ISM............ Intersegmental Muscles [*Anatomy*] (DAVI)
ISM............ Interstellar Matter (SAUS)
ISM............ Interstellar Medium [*Planetary science*]
ISM............ Inverse-Speed Motor (SAUS)
ISM............ Ion-Selective Material [*Chemistry*]
ISM............ Ion Selective Microelectrodes [*Instrumentation*]
ISM............ Ion-Selective Microelectrodes (SAUS)
ISM............ Irish School of Music (ROG)
ISM............ ISDN [*Integrated Services Digital Network*] Subscriber Module [*Telecommunications*]
ISM............ Istituto Internazionale Suore di Santa Marcellina [*Also, Instituto Marcelline*] [*Italy*] (EAIO)
ISM............ Kissimmee, FL [*Location identifier*] [*FAA*] (FAAL)
ISM............ Southern Methodist University, Central Library, Dallas, TX [*OCLC symbol*] (OCLC)
ISMA........... Indiana School Music Association (SAUO)
ISMA........... Indiana State Medical Association (SRA)
ISMA........... Industrial Silencer Manufacturers Association (EA)
ISMA........... Infantile Spinal Muscular Atrophy [*Medicine*] (DAVI)
ISMA........... Information Systems Management Activity (SAUS)
ISMA........... Information Systems Management Architecture (VLIE)
ISMA........... Institute of Sisters of Mercy of Australia
ISMA........... International Satellite Monitoring Agency (ACAE)
ISMA........... International Securities Market Association (NUMA)
ISMA........... International Security Management Association [*Boston, MA*] (EA)
ISMA........... International Snowmobile Manufacturers Association (NTPA)
ISMA........... International Stress Management Association (NTPA)
ISMA........... International Superphosphate Manufacturers' Association [*Later, IFA*]
ISMA........... International Symposium on Mining in the Arctic (SAUS)
ISMA........... International Symposium on Mining with Backfill (SAUS)
ISMA........... Inter-State Manufacturers Association (SAUO)
ISMaC.......... Industrial Safety Management Centre (SAUO)
ISMAG.......... Indian School of Mines and Applied Geology (SAUS)
Is Mag......... Island Magazine [*A publication*]
Is Mag......... Island Magazine (journ.) (SAUS)
ISMAP.......... Indirect Source Model for Air Pollution [*Environmental Protection Agency*] (GFGA)
ISMAP.......... Instrumentation System Margin Analysis Programme (SAUO)
ISMAP.......... Integrated System for the Management of Agricultural Production (SAUO)
ISM Apparatus... Industrial Scientific and Medical Apparatus (SAUS)
ISMAR.......... International Society of Magnetic Resonance
ISMARC......... Irrigation System Management Research Committee (SAUO)
ISMARE......... Irish Marine Data Centre (SAUS)
ISMASS......... Ice Sheet Mass Balance and Sea-level Contributions (SAUO)
ISMATS......... Integrated Supply, Maintenance, and Transportation Study (SAUO)
ISMB........... Information System Management Board [*NATO*] (NATG)
ISMB........... Intelligent Systems for Molecular Biology (HGEN)
ISMB........... International Society of Mathematical Biology [*See also SIBM*] [*Antony, France*] (EAIO)
ISMC........... EFMC International Symposium on Medicinal Chemistry (SAUS)
ISMC........... Independent Schools Microelectronics Centre [*British*]
ISMC........... Information Systems Management Committee (TIMI)
ISMC........... International Switching Maintenance Center [*Communications*]
ISMC........... International Symposium on Medicinal Chemistry (SAUO)
ISMCEE......... International Series of Monographs on Chemistry (journ.) (SAUS)
ISM Code....... International Safety Management Code (SAUO)
ISMD........... Indian Subordinate Medical Department [*British military*] (DMA)
ISMD........... International Medical Society for Motor Disturbances (SAUO)
ISMDA.......... Independent Sewing Machine Dealers Association (EA)
ISMDA.......... Independent Sewing Machine Dealers of America (SAUO)
ISMDKTS........ Iron, Steel, Metal Dressers, and Kindred Trades Society [*A union*] [*British*]
ISMDTS......... Iron, Steel, and Metal Dressers Trade Society (SAUO)
ISME........... Institute of Sheet Metal Engineering [*British*]
ISME........... International Society for Music Education (EA)
ISME........... International Society of Marine Engineers
ISME........... International Society of Mechanical Engineers
ISME........... International Survey of Management Education (SAUO)
ISME........... International Sysmposium on Marine Engineering (PDAA)
ISMEC.......... Information Service in Mechanical Engineering [*Cambridge Scientific Abstracts*] [*British*] [*Information service or system*] (IID)
ISMED.......... International Society on Metabolic Eye Disease (EA)
ISMED.......... International Society or Metabolic Eye Disease (SAUS)
ISMED.......... International Symposium on Molecular Electronic Devices (SAUS)
ISMES.......... Experimental Institute for Models and Structures [*Italy*]
ISMET.......... Inter-Service Metallurgical Research Council [*British*] (MCD)
ISMEX.......... International Shoe Machinery Exhibition (SAUS)
ISMEX.......... International Show Machinery Exhibition (SAUO)
ISMF........... Inactive Ship Maintenance Facility
ISMF........... Interactive Storage Management Facility [*Computer science*] (VLIE)
ISMF........... International Sports Massage Federation (EA)
ISMFE.......... International Society for Soil Mechanics and Foundation Engineering (SAUO)
ISM frequencies... Industrial, Scientific and Medical frequencies (SAUO)
ISMG........... Interim Scientific and Management Group (SAUO)
ISMG........... International Scientific Management Group [*GARP*] (NOAA)
ISMGC.......... International Stoke Mandeville Games Committee (SAUO)
ISMGF.......... International Stoke Mandeville Games Federation [*Aylesbury, Buckinghamshire, England*] (EA)
ISMGR.......... Island Manager (FAAC)
ISMH........... Illinois Society for Mental Hygiene (SAUO)
ISMH........... Input Source Message Handler
ISMH........... International Society of Medical Hydrology (SAUS)
ISMH........... International Society of Medical Hydrology and Climatology
ISMHC.......... International Society of Medical Hydrology and Climatology (EA)
ISMH Newsletter... Illinois Society for Mental Hygiene Newsletter (journ.) (SAUS)
ISMI........... Improved Space Manned Interceptor (IAA)
ISMIII......... International Symposium on Medical Imaging and Image Interpretation (SAUS)
ISMIS.......... Interservice Depot Maintenance Interrogation Systems
ISMIT.......... International Society for Mental Imagery Techniques [*France*] (EAIO)
ISMJAV......... Israel Medical Journal (journ.) (SAUS)
ISmK........... Kaskaska Library System, Smithton, IL [*Library symbol*] [*Library of Congress*] (LCLS)
ISML........... Institute for the Study of Matrimonial Laws (EA)
ISML........... Intermediate System Mock-Up Loop (IEEE)
ISML........... Inter-Shop Markup Language [*Computer science*] (VLIE)
ISMLS.......... Interim Standard Microwave Landing System [*Aviation*]
ISMM........... Institute of Sales and Marketing Management (COBU)
ISMM........... International Society for Music in Medicine (EAIO)
ISMM........... International Society of Mini- and Micro-Computers [*Calgary, AB*] (EAIO)
ISMMP.......... International Standard Methods for Measuring Performances (SAUO)
ISMMP.......... International Standards Methods for Measuring Performances (SAUS)
ISMMRRI........ Iowa State Mining and Mineral Resources Research Institute [*Iowa State University*] [*Research center*] (RCD)
ISMMS.......... Integrated Stores Monitor and Management System [*Later, Armament Control Panel*] (MCD)
ISMMS.......... Intrinsically Safe Mine Monitoring System (SAUS)
ISMN........... Isosorbide Mononitrate [*Coronary vasodilator*]
ISMN........... Isosorbit-Mononitrat (SAUS)
ISMO........... Information System Management Office (SAUS)
ISMO........... Ion-Sieve-Type Manganese Oxide [*Inorganic chemistry*]
ISMO........... Isosorbide-5-Mononitrate (DB)
ISMOD.......... Index Sequential Module (IAA)
ISMP........... In-Situ Measurements Project (SAUO)
ISMP........... Institute for Safe Medication Practices (ADWA)
ISMP........... International Society of Meeting Planners (TVEL)
ISMPH.......... International Society for Medical and Psychological Hypnosis (EA)
ISMPMI......... International Society for Molecular Plant Microbe Interactions (NTPA)
ISM Purposes... Industrial, Scientific and Medical Purposes (SAUS)
ISMR........... Independent Snowmobile Medical Research [*An association*] (EA)
ISMRC.......... Inter-Services Metallurgical Research Council [*British*]
ISMRM.......... Integrated Soil Moisture Retrieval Models (SAUO)
ISMRM.......... International Society for Magnetic Resonance in Medicine (NTPA)
ISMRRD......... Institute for the Study of Mental Retardation and Related Disabilities [*Medicine*] (EDAA)
ISMS........... Illinois State Medical Society (SRA)
ISMS........... Image Store Management System
ISMS........... Improved SPRINT [*Solid-Propellant Rocket Intercept*] Missile Subsystem [*Army*]
ISMS........... Independent Stationary Maintenance Section (SAUO)
ISMS........... Indian Society for Medical Statistics (SAUO)
ISMS........... Industrial Standards and Military Specifications [*Information Handling Services*] [*Information service or system*] (CRD)
ISMS........... Information Systems and Media Services [*Eastern Illinois University*] [*Information service or system*] (IID)
ISMS........... Information Systems Maintenance Squadron (SAUO)
ISMS........... Infrared Spectral Measurement System (MCD)
ISMS........... Inherently Safe Mining Systems (PDAA)
ISMS........... Integrated Environmental, Safety and Health Management System (SAUO)
ISMS........... Integrated Safety Management System (SAUO)
ISMS........... Integrated Software Maintenance System
ISMS........... Integrated Stores Management Subsystem (SAUO)
ISMS........... Integrity and Schedule Management Subsystem (SAUS)
ISMS........... Interactive Solids Modeling System [*Gould Electronics Ltd. Computer Systems*] [*Software package*] (NCC)
ISMS........... Interim Stores Management System (SAUS)
ISMS........... International Society for Mushroom Science [*Braunschweig, Federal Republic of Germany*] (EA)
ISMS........... Iowa State Medical Society (SAUO)
ISMS-D......... Improved SPRINT [*Solid-Propellant Rocket Intercept*] Missile Subsystem - Derated [*Army*]
ISMSD.......... Istituto delle Suore Maestre di Santa Dorotea [*Rome, Italy*] (EAIO)
IsmSD.......... Smithton Community Consolidated School District 130 (SAUS)
ISmSD.......... Smithton Community Consolidated School District 130, Smithton, IL [*Library symbol*] [*Library of Congress*] (LCLS)
ISMT........... Indoor Simulated Marksmanship Trainer [*Military*]

ISMT........... Information System Management Team (SAUS)
ISMT........... Integrated System Maintenance Trainer (MCD)
ISMTR........... Instrumentalist (journ.) (SAUS)
ISMUN........... International Student Movement for the United Nations (SAUS)
ISMUN........... International Youth and Student Movement for the United Nations [*Geneva, Switzerland*] (EA)
ISMV........... Iris Severe Mosaic Virus
ISMVL........... International Symposium on Multiple-Valued Logic (SAUS)
ISM Wavelengths... Industrial, Scientific and Medical Wavelengths (SAUS)
ISM Wavelengths... Industrial, Scientific, Medical Wavelengths (SAUS)
ISMWSF........... International Stoke Mandeville Wheelchair Sports Federation (SAUO)
ISMX........... Integrated Subrate Data Multiplexer (TEL)
ISMX........... Isomedix, Inc. (SAUO)
ISN........... Information System & Networks Corp. (SAUS)
ISN........... Information Systems Network [*AT & T*] [*Telecommunications*]
ISN........... Initial Segment Number (SAUS)
ISN........... Initial Sequence Number (IAA)
ISN........... Input Sequence Number (SAUS)
ISN........... Instron Corp. [*AMEX symbol*] (SPSG)
ISN........... Integrated Service Network (AMHC)
ISN........... Integrated Systems Network (VLIE)
ISN........... Intelligent Storage Network [*Sun Microsystems*] (AGLO)
ISN........... Internal Sequence Number (SAUS)
ISN........... Internal Statement Number (IAA)
ISN........... International Society for Neurochemistry [*Kjeller, Norway*] (EA)
ISN........... International Society of Nephrology
ISN........... International Society of Neurochemistry (SAUO)
ISN........... International Standard Nomenclature (SAUS)
ISN........... International Suneva Resources [*Vancouver Stock Exchange symbol*]
ISN........... Internet School Networking (SAUO)
ISN........... Internment Serial Number
ISN........... Interplant Shipping Notice
ISN........... Interrogation Serial Number (SAUO)
ISN........... Inter-Systems Network (TIMI)
ISN........... Ishinomaki [*Japan*] [*Seismograph station code, US Geological Survey*] (SEIS)
ISN........... Item Sequence Number (MCD)
ISN........... Saint Mary's College, Notre Dame, IN [*OCLC symbol*] (OCLC)
ISN........... Williston [*North Dakota*] [*Airport symbol*] (OAG)
ISN........... Williston, ND [*Location identifier*] [*FAA*] (FAAL)
ISNA........... International Society for New Atlantis (EA)
ISNA........... International Space: 1999 Alliance (EA)
ISNA........... International Symposium on Novel Aromatic Compounds
ISNA........... Intersex Society of North America (SAUO)
ISNA Bulletin... Iowa State Nurses Association Bulletin (journ.) (SAUS)
ISNAC........... Inactive Ships in Naval Custody (SAUO)
ISNAC........... Inactive Ships Navy Custody (NVT)
ISNAR........... International Service for National Agricultural Research [*The Hague, Netherlands*]
ISND........... International Solidarity Network Desk (SAUO)
ISNE........... International Scale of Nuclear Events
ISNET........... Inter-Islamic Network in Space Sciences and Technology (SAUS)
ISNG........... International Society of Nurses in Genetics (SAUO)
ISNI........... Idependent Service Network, International (NTPA)
ISNIM........... International Society for Neuroimmunomodulation (SAUO)
ISNO........... International Society for Neuro-Ophthalmology (SAUO)
ISNOT........... Is Not Equal To (VLIE)
ISNOX........... Indicated Specific Oxides of Nitrogen [*Automotive exhaust emission testing*]
ISNP........... Independent Scholarship National Program [*Defunct*] (EA)
ISNP........... International Society of Naturopathic Physicians
ISNQR........... International Symposium of Nuclear Quadruple Resonance Spectroscopy (SAUS)
ISNR........... Institute of Natural Resources, Energy Information Library, Springfield (SAUS)
ISNR........... State of Illinois, Institute of Natural Resources, Energy Information Library, Springfield, IL [*Library symbol*] [*Library of Congress*] (LCLS)
ISNR-E........... Institute of Natural Resources, Division of Environmental Management, Chicago (SAUS)
ISNR-E........... State of Illinois, Institute of Natural Resources, Division of Environmental Management, Chicago, IL [*Library symbol*] [*Library of Congress*] (LCLS)
ISNS........... Image Sensing Systems [*NASDAQ symbol*] (TTSB)
ISNS........... Image Sensing Systems, Inc. [*NASDAQ symbol*] (SAG)
ISNS........... Institute for the Study of Natural Systems (EA)
ISNS........... International Society for Neoplatonic Studies (EA)
ISNSA........... Independent Software Nuclear Safety Analysis (SAUO)
ISNSE........... International School for Nuclear Science and Engineering
ISNSL........... Incremental Stock Number Sequence List [*Military*] (CAAL)
ISNSPM........... International Standard Numbering System for Printed Music (TELE)
ISNT........... Informal Single Negotiating Text [*Marine science*] (MSC)
ISNTA........... International Staple, Nail and Tool Association (SAUO)
ISNTANV........... Indian Society for Nuclear Techniques in Agriculture and Biology. Newsletter (journ.) (SAUS)
ISNU........... Illinois State Normal University
ISNV........... Institute for the Study of Nonviolence [*Defunct*] (EA)
ISNVP........... International Society for Non Verbal Psychotherapy (SAUO)
ISNY........... Insurance Society of New York [*New York, NY*] (EA)
ISO........... Illegal Support Officer [*CIA*] (LAIN)
ISO........... Imaging Spectrometer Observatory (SAUO)
ISO........... Imaging Spectrometric Observatory (MCD)
ISO........... Imaging Spectroscopic Observatory (SAUS)
ISO........... Imperial Service Order [*British*]
ISO........... I'm So Optimistic [*Dance company*]
ISO........... Incentive Stock Option
ISO........... Independent Sales Organization (HGAA)
ISO........... Independent System Operator
ISO........... Indianapolis Symphony Orchestra (SAUO)
ISO........... Individual System Operation
ISO........... Industrial Safety Office
ISO........... Information Services Officer
ISO........... Information Society (journ.) (SAUS)
ISO........... Information-Structure-Oriented (SAUS)
ISO........... Information Systems Office [*Library of Congress*]
ISO........... Infrared Space Observatory [*Astronomy term*]
ISO........... Initial Spares Order (SAUS)
ISO........... In Search Of [*Classified advertising*]
ISO........... Inside-Out [*Biochemistry*]
iso........... in spite of (SAUS)
ISO........... Installation Supply Officer [*Military*]
ISO........... Insurance Services Office [*An association*] (EA)
IS(O)........... Intelligence Section, Operations [*Control Commission for Germany*] [*World War II*]
ISO........... Intelligence Support Office (SAUO)
ISO........... Intergalactic Sysop Alliance (SAUS)
ISO........... Interior Systems Optimization [*Automotive engineering*]
ISO........... Intermediate Station Operation (IAA)
ISO........... Internal Standard Organization Code (CMD)
ISO........... Internal System Organization (ECII)
ISO........... International Organisation (or Organization) for Standardisation (or Standardization) (SAUO)
ISO........... International Organization for Standardization [*Geneva, Switzerland*] [*United Nations*]
ISO........... International Organization of Standards (SAUS)
ISO........... International Science Organization
ISO........... International Self-Service Organization
ISO........... International Services Organization (SAUO)
ISO........... International Ship Operators (SAUS)
ISO........... International Shopfitting Organization [*Zurich, Switzerland*] (EAIO)
ISO........... International Sikh Organization (EA)
ISO........... International Socialist Organization (EA)
ISO........... International Society of Organbuilders [*Levallois-Perret, France*] (EAIO)
ISO........... International Space Observatory (SAUS)
ISO........... International Standardisation Organisation (SAUS)
ISO........... International Standardization Organisation (or Organization) (SAUS)
iso........... International Standardization Organizations (NAKS)
ISO........... International Standard Organisation (or Organization) (SAUS)
ISO........... International Standards Association (SAUO)
ISO........... International Standards Institute (WPI)
ISO........... International Standards of Operation (SAUS)
ISO........... International Standards Organisation (SAUS)
ISO........... International Standards Organization [*Communications term*] (DCT)
ISO........... International Stevedore Organization (SAUO)
ISO........... International Sugar Organization [*See also OIA*] [*British*] (EAIO)
ISO........... Interplant Shipping Order
ISO........... Intraseasonal Atmospheric Oscillation (USDC)
ISO........... Intra Seasonal Oscillations (SAUS)
ISO........... Irish Symphony Orchestra (SAUO)
ISO........... ISG Technologies, Inc. [*Toronto Stock Exchange symbol*]
ISO........... Isochromatic (ROG)
ISO........... Isoflurane [*An anesthetic*]
ISO........... Isola [*France*] [*Seismograph station code, US Geological Survey*] (SEIS)
iso........... Isolated [*Slang*] (WDMC)
ISO........... Isolated Camera (NTCM)
ISO........... Isolation
ISO........... Isolette (MELL)
ISO........... Isomedix Inc. [*NYSE symbol*] (TTSB)
ISO........... Isometric (MSA)
iso........... Isometric (VRA)
Iso........... Isophase
Iso........... Isophase Light [*Nautical term*] (NTA)
Iso........... Isoproterenol (STED)
ISO........... Isoproterenol [*An adrenergic*]
iso........... isotonic (SAUS)
ISO........... Isotope
Iso........... Isotopic (SAUS)
ISO........... Isotropic (KSC)
Iso........... Isotropic (STED)
ISO........... Isotype
ISO........... Israel Students Organization
ISO........... Kinston [*North Carolina*] [*Airport symbol*] (OAG)
ISO........... Kinston, NC [*Location identifier*] [*FAA*] (FAAL)
ISO........... South Bend Public Library, South Bend, IN [*OCLC symbol*] (OCLC)
ISO-30........... Inventory of Suicide Orientation-30 [*Test*] (TMMY)
ISO9736........... UN/EDIFACT Syntax Rules (AG)
ISO 8859-2... Eastern Europe (SAUS)
ISOA........... Improved State-of-the-Art (PDAA)
ISOA........... Indian Society of Oriental Art (SAUO)
ISO-ALPHABET... International Standards Organization-Authorized Alphabetic Characters (MCD)
ISO/ASA........... International Standards Organization/American Standards Association (SAUO)
ISOB........... Incorporated Society of Organ Builders [*British*] (BI)
ISOB........... International Society of Barristers (EA)
ISOB........... International Society of Biotelemetry (SAUS)
ISOB........... International Society of/on Biotelemetry (SAUO)

ISOBM .... International Society for/of Oncodevelopmental Biology and Medicine (SAUO)
iso-BTX .... Isobatrachotoxin [*Toxicology*] (LDT)
Isobu .... Isobutyl (SAUS)
Isoc .... De Isocrate [*of Dionysius Halicarnassensis*] [*Classical studies*] (OCD)
ISOC .... Individual System/Organization Cost (MHDB)
ISOC .... Institutional Safety Office Contact (SAUO)
ISOC .... Instituto de Informacion y Documentacion en Ciencias Sociales y Humanidades [*Institute for Information and Documentation in the Social Sciences and Humanities*] [*Higher Council for Scientific Research*] [*Information service or system*] (IID)
ISOC .... Integrated Science Operations Center (SAUO)
ISOC .... Internal Security Operation Command (SAUS)
ISOC .... Internal Security Operations Command
ISOC .... Internet Society
ISOC .... Internet Society International (AG)
Isoc .... Isocrates [*436-338BC*] [*Classical studies*] (OCD)
ISoCaRP ...... International Society of City and Regional Planners [*See also AIU*] [*The Hague, Netherlands*] (EAIO)
ISoCaRP ...... International Society of City and Regional Planning (SAUO)
ISOCC .... Input System for Operator Connected Calls (PDAA)
isochr .... isochronal (SAUS)
ISO-CMOS ... Isolated Fully Recessed Complementary Metal-Oxide Semiconductor (TEL)
ISOCRAF-A... International Standard Optical Character Recognition, Alphanumeric Font Type A (SAUS)
ISOD .... International Society for Orbital Disorders (EAIO)
ISOD .... International Sports Organization for the Disabled [*Farstn, Sweden*] (EA)
ISOD .... Interplanetary Satellite Orbit Determination (ACAE)
ISODARCO ... International School of Disarmament and Research of Conflicts (SAUO)
ISODARCO ... International School of Disarmament and Research on Conflicts
ISODATA ...... Interactive Self-Organizing Data Analysis Technique (RALS)
ISODATA ...... Iterative Self-Organizing Data Analysis Technique A [*Computer science*]
ISODE .... International Organization for Standardization Development Environment (SAUS)
ISODE .... International Standards Organization Development Environment (SAUO)
ISODIS .... International Organization for Standardization Draft International Standard (IAA)
ISODOC .... International Information Centre for Standards in Information and Documentation (ADA)
ISO/DR .... International Standardization Organization/Draft (SAUS)
ISOD/RCO .... International School of Disarmament and Research on Conflicts (SAUS)
ISOE .... International Society for Optical Engineering (EA)
ISOE .... ISOETEC Communications, Inc. (SAUO)
IsoENET .... Isochronous Ethernet [*Computer science*] (CDE)
isoenz .... Isoenzyme (AAMN)
ISOF .... International Society for Ocular Fluorophotometry (EAIO)
ISOF .... International Society for/of Ocular Fluorophotometry (SAUO)
ISOF .... International Society of Ocular Fluorophotometry (SAUS)
Is of Lang .... Islets of Langerhans (STED)
IS of LANG ... Islets of Langerhans [*Anatomy*]
ISOFO .... International Symposium on Operational Fisheries Oceanography (SAUS)
isogone .... isogonal line (SAUS)
isogons .... isogonic lines (SAUS)
ISOHP .... International Society for Organ History and Preservation (EA)
ISOHYC .... Isotopes in the Hydrological Cycle (SAUO)
ISOL .... IMAGE Software [*NASDAQ symbol*] (TTSB)
ISOL .... Image Software, Inc. [*NASDAQ symbol*] (SAG)
ISOL .... Information Solutions, Inc. (SAUO)
isol .... Isolate [*or Isolated*] (DAVI)
ISOL .... Isolate (NAKS)
ISOL .... Isolated (SAUS)
ISOL .... Isolation (KSC)
isol .... Isolation (STED)
Isol .... Isolette (STED)
ISOL CAP ..... Isolating Capacitor (SAUS)
ISOLDE .... Isotope Separator On-line Detector (SAUS)
ISOLDE .... Isotope Separator On-Line Development (SAUO)
ISOLDE .... Isotopic Low-Weight Device (IAA)
ISOLDE .... Isotype On-Line Separator
ISOL Method... Isotope Separator On-Line Method (SAUS)
ISOLN .... Isolation
ISOLR .... Isolationer
Isol Tr .... Isolating Transformer (SAUS)
Isolyser .... Isolyser Co., Inc. [*Associated Press*] (SAG)
ISOM .... International Society for Orthomolecular Medicine (SAUO)
ISOM .... International Standard Orthopaedic Measurements [*Medicine*]
ISOM .... Isometric (KSC)
isom .... Isometric (STED)
isom .... Isometrophic (STED)
ISom .... Somonauk Public Library, Somonauk, IL [*Library symbol*] [*Library of Congress*] (LCLS)
ISOMAP .... Isotope Mapping (SAUO)
ISOMATA ..... Idlewild School of Music and the Arts (SAUS)
ISOMATA ..... Idyllwild School of Music and the Arts [*California*]
ISOMB .... International Society of Oncodevelopmental Biology and Medicine (SAUO)
Isomdx .... Isomedix, Inc. [*Associated Press*] (SAG)
ISOMED .... International Society of Mediterranean Ecology (SAUO)
Isomet .... Isomet, Corp. [*Associated Press*] (SAG)
ISOMITE ...... Isotope Miniature Thermionic Electric (IAA)
Isomorph ..... Isomorphism (SAUS)
ISomSD .... Somonauk Community Unit, School District 432, Somonauk, IL [*Library symbol*] [*Library of Congress*] (LCLS)
ISON .... Isolation Network (PDAA)
ISONE .... International Standard of Nuclear Electronics (SAUO)
ISONET .... International Organization for Standardization Information Network [*United Nations*] [*Geneva, Switzerland*] (IID)
ISONET .... International Standardization Organization Network (SAUS)
ISONET .... International Standards Organisation Information Network (SAUS)
ISONET .... International Standards Organization Network (SAUO)
ISONET .... International Standards Organization Network Committee (SAUS)
ISONG .... International Society of Nurses in Genetics (HGEN)
ISONIAZID ... Isonicotinic Acid Hydrazide [*See also INAH, INH*] [*Antituberculous agent*]
ISOO .... Information Security Oversight Office [*National Archives and Records Service*]
ISOO .... International Society of Online Ophthalmologists (SAUO)
ISO OCR ...... International Standards Organization-Standards on Optical Character Recognition (SAUS)
ISO OSI .... International Standards Organisation Open Standards Interconnect [*Computer science*]
ISO-OSI .... International Standards Organisation Open System Interconnection (SAUS)
ISO/OSI .... International Standards Organization/ Open System Interface (SAUS)
ISO/OSI .... International Standards Organization/Open System Interface [*Motorola, Inc.*]
ISOP .... Incentive Stock Option Plan (SAUS)
ISOP .... Integrated Spacecraft Operations Plan [*NASA*]
ISOP .... Internal Standard Operating Procedure [*Military*] (MCD)
ISOPA .... European Isocyanate Producers Association (SAUO)
ISOPADS ...... Individual Soldier Operational Personnel Acoustic Detection System (SAUS)
ISOPAR .... Improved Symbolic Optimizing Assembly Routine
ISOPE .... International Offshore and Polar Engineering Conference (SAUO)
ISOPE .... International Society of Offshore and Polar Engineers
ISOPEDAC .... Integrated System of Pipework Estimating, Detailing, and Control (PDAA)
ISOPEP .... Isometric Piping Efficiency Program
ISOPGU .... International Security Officer's Police and Guard Union (EA)
ISOPLANAR... Isolation Oxide Planar (SAUS)
IsoPPC .... Isopropylphenylcarbamate (DB)
IS(Ops) .... Intelligence Section, Operations [*Joint Intelligence Subcommittee of Chiefs of Staff*] [*World War II*]
ISOR .... Initial Statement of Requirement (SAUS)
Iso-RAS .... Isorenin-Angiotensin System (DB)
ISORDIL .... Isorbide Dinitrate (SAUS)
ISO/REMCO... International Organisation for Standardisation/Reference Materials Committee (SAUO)
ISO/REMCO... ISO/Reference Materials Committee (SAUS)
ISORID .... International Information System on Research in Documentation [*International Federation for Documentation*] [*UNESCO*] (IID)
ISORT .... Interdisciplinary Student-Originated Research Training [*National Science Foundation*]
ISOS .... Information Systems Operations Squadron (SAUO)
ISOS .... International Ship Operating Services (SAUS)
ISOS .... International Society of Shropshires (SAUO)
ISOS .... International Southern Ocean Studies (or Study) (SAUO)
ISOS .... International Southern Ocean Study [*National Science Foundation*]
ISOS .... Interplanetare Sonnensonde
isos .... isoceles (SAUS)
ISOS .... Isosceles [*Triangle*]
ISOSC .... International Society for Soilless Culture [*Wageningen, Netherlands*] (EAIO)
ISOSJ .... Institute of Social Order of the Society of Jesus [*Later, JCSS*] (EA)
ISOSS .... Immobile Suspension Feeders on Soft Substrata [*Oceanography*]
ISOST .... Internet Society of Orthopaedic Surgery and Trauma (SAUO)
ISOT .... International School of Offshore Technology (SAUS)
ISOT .... International Symposium on Olfaction and Taste
ISOTAP .... Interservice Occupational Task Analysis Program [*Military*] (NVT)
ISO/TC 154... ISO Technical Committee 154 [*Documents and data elements in administration, commerce and industry*] (AG)
ISO TC211 ... International Standards Organisation-Technical Committee 211 (SAUO)
ISOTEC .... Isotope Thermoelectric Converter
ISO-TEX .... ISO-TEX Diagnostics Inc. (SAUO)
Isot Geosci... Isotope Geoscience (journ.) (SAUS)
ISOTH .... Isothermal (KSC)
Isot News .... Isotope News (journ.) (SAUS)
Isotopes Radiat... Isotopes Radiation (journ.) (SAUS)
Isot Radiat... Isotopes and Radiation (journ.) (SAUS)
Isot Radiat Res... Isotope and Radiation Research (journ.) (SAUS)
Isot Radiat Res... Isotopes and Radiation Research (journ.) (SAUS)
Isot Radiat Res Anim Dis Vec... Isotope and Radiation Research on Animal Diseases and Their Vectors. Proceedings (journ.) (SAUS)
ISOU .... International Society for Ophthalmic Ultrasound (EA)
ISOW .... Iceland-Scotland Overflow Water [*Oceanography*]
ISOWD .... Isolation Ward (SAUS)
Isoworg .... International Society for World Government (WDAA)
Isozymes Curr Top Biol Med Res... Isozymes. Current Topics in Biological and Medical Research (journ.) (SAUS)
ISP .... Distance between Iliac Spines [*Anatomy*] (DAVI)
ISP .... Henry Public Library, Henry, IL [*OCLC symbol*] (OCLC)
ISp .... Iconic Store, Peripheral [*Psychophysiology*]

ISP.............. Idaho State Penitentiary (SAUO)
ISP.............. Ideal Splash Point (SAUS)
ISP.............. Image Stabilization Program [*Photography*]
ISP.............. Image Storage Panel [*Computer science*] (PDAA)
ISP.............. Image Store Panel (SAUS)
ISP.............. Image Store Processor [*Computer science*]
ISP.............. Image Synthesis Processor [*Computer science*]
ISP.............. Imaging Spectro-Photometer (SAUS)
ISP.............. Immunoreactive Substance P [*Immunology*]
ISP.............. Imperial Smelting Process
ISP.............. Implementation Support Package [*Army*]
ISP.............. Implementation Support Plan (SAUO)
ISP.............. Impulse, Specific (KSC)
ISP.............. Income Supplement Program (SAUO)
ISP.............. Independent Service Provider [*Telecommunications*]
ISP.............. Independent Smallholders' Party [*Hungary*] [*Political party*] (EY)
ISP.............. Independent Studies Project [*Navy*]
ISP.............. Independent Study Program [*IBM Corp.*]
ISP.............. Indexed Sequential Processor
ISP.............. Index of Social Position [*Advertising*] (DOAD)
ISP.............. Index Sequential Processor (SAUO)
ISP.............. Indiana State Police (SAUO)
ISP.............. Individual Seal Packaging [*Food technology*]
ISP.............. Individual Service Plan
ISP.............. Industrial Security Plan [*Nuclear energy*] (NRCH)
ISP.............. Industrial Security Program [*Air Force, Army*]
ISP.............. Industrial Services Program (SAUO)
ISP.............. Industry Service Package
ISP.............. Infirmiers de Secteur Psychiatrique (SAUO)
ISP.............. Information Search and Processing [*Database search service*] (OLDSS)
ISP.............. Information Security Program (SAUO)
ISP.............. Informations Strategy Planning (SAUS)
ISP.............. Information Strategy Plan (SAUO)
ISP.............. Information System Plan (MCD)
ISP.............. Information Systems Office (SAUO)
ISP.............. Information Systems Plan [*USAID*] (ECON)
ISP.............. Information Systems Professional (DD)
ISP.............. Information Systems Professional of Canada (ASC)
ISP.............. Information Systems Program [*University of Oklahoma*] [*Norman, OK*]
ISP.............. Infrared Spectrophotometer
ISP.............. Initial Specific Impulse (MCD)
ISP.............. Initial Status Presentation (SAUS)
ISP.............. Initial Support Package (MCD)
ISP.............. Instantaneous Sound Pressure
ISP.............. Instant Set Polymer (SAUO)
ISP.............. Instant-Set Polymer (PDAA)
ISP.............. Institute for Studies in Pragmaticism [*Texas Tech University*] [*Research center*] (RCD)
ISP.............. Institute of Sales Promotion [*ICSU*] [*British*]
ISP.............. Institute of Social Psychiatry (SAUO)
ISP.............. Institute of Store Planners (EA)
ISP.............. Instituto de Seguros de Portugal [*Insurance regulatory agency*] [*Portugal*] (EY)
ISP.............. Institut pour une Synthese Planetaire [*Institute for Planetary Synthesis - IPS*] [*Geneva, Switzerland*] (EAIO)
ISP.............. In-Store Processor [*Computer science*] (CIST)
ISP.............. In-Store Promotions [*Marketing events for US goods held by retail establishments in foreign countries*] [*Department of Commerce*]
ISP.............. Instructional System Package (MCD)
ISP.............. Instruction Set Processor [*1971*] [*Computer science*]
ISP.............. Instrumentation Signal Processor (ACAE)
ISP.............. Instrumentation Support Plan (MCD)
ISP.............. In-System Programmable (SAUS)
ISP.............. Integrated Scientific Processor [*Sperry*] (NITA)
ISP.............. Integrated Shear Plate
ISP.............. Integrated Steel Plant (SAUS)
ISP.............. Integrated Steel Plants (SAUS)
ISP.............. Integrated Support Plan (MCD)
ISP.............. Integrated System Peripheral [*Computer science*]
ISP.............. Integrated Systems Planning, Inc. [*Baltimore, MD*] (TSSD)
ISP.............. Intelligence Software Package (SAUS)
ISP.............. Intensively Supervised Probation [*Legal term*] (BARN)
ISP.............. Interactive Session Protocol (SAUS)
ISP.............. Interactive String Processor (SAUS)
ISP.............. Interamerican Society of Psychology (EA)
ISP.............. Interception System Processor (SAUS)
ISP.............. Interdivisional Systems Practice (SAUS)
ISP.............. Interface Strain Parameter (AAEL)
ISP.............. Interferometer Software Package (SAUS)
ISP.............. Intergovernmental Science Programs
ISP.............. Interim Support Period
ISP.............. Interim Support Plan (MCD)
ISP.............. Interim System Production (SAUS)
ISP.............. Internally Stored Program (AAG)
ISP.............. Internal Security Plan (CINC)
ISP.............. Internationale des Services Publics [*Public Service International - PSI*] [*Ferney Voltaire, France*] (EAIO)
ISP.............. Internationally Standardized Profile (SAUS)
ISP.............. International Security Policy (SAUS)
ISP.............. International Shadow Project (EA)
ISP.............. International Signalling Point (SAUS)
ISP.............. International Society for Photogrammetry [*Later, ISPRS*]
ISP.............. International Society for Plastination (EA)
ISP.............. International Society of Postmasters [*Montreal, PQ*] (EAIO)
ISP.............. International Society of Psychophysics (SAUS)
ISP.............. International Solar Polar [*Mission*] [*NASA*]
ISP.............. International Specialty Products [*NYSE symbol*] (SPSG)
ISP.............. International Standardised Profile (SAUS)
ISP.............. International Standardized Profile (SAUS)
ISP.............. International Streptomyces Project
ISP.............. International Stretch Products, Inc. (EFIS)
ISP.............. International Student Pugwash [*Formerly, USSPC*] [*Later, Student Pugwash (USA)*] (EA)
ISP.............. International Study Program
ISP.............. International Study Programme (SAUS)
ISP.............. International Swappers Paradise (SAUO)
ISP.............. Internet Service Provider
ISP.............. Internet Service Providers [*Telecommunications*]
ISP.............. Interoperable System Project (SAUS)
ISP.............. Interoperable Systems Project [*Computer science*]
ISP.............. Interpretive Scanner and Processor (SAUS)
ISP.............. Interrupt Stack Pointer (SAUO)
ISP.............. Interrupt Status Port (SAUO)
ISP.............. Inter-Sensor Prediction (SAUS)
ISP.............. Interspace (MAE)
ISP.............. Interspinal [*Anatomy*] (DAVI)
ISP.............. Interstage Punching (SAUS)
ISP.............. Interstation Prediction (SAUS)
ISP.............. Interstellar Probe (SAUS)
ISP.............. Intersystem Spool Processor (SAUS)
ISP.............. Intl Specialty Products [*NYSE symbol*] (TTSB)
ISP.............. Intraspinal
ISP.............. Inverse Sampling Procedure
ISP.............. Ipsco, Inc. [*Toronto Stock Exchange symbol*]
ISP.............. Irish Society of Periodontology (SAUO)
ISP.............. Irrigation Support Project for Asia and the Near East (SAUS)
ISP.............. Islip, NY [*Location identifier*] [*FAA*] (FAAL)
ISP.............. Isolated Safflower Protein [*Food technology*]
ISP.............. Isolated Soy Protein [*Food technology*]
ISP.............. Isoproterenol (DMAA)
ISP.............. Isotope Separation Power
ISP.............. Italian Society of Physics
ISP.............. Long Island [*New York*] MacArthur [*Airport symbol*] (OAG)
ISp.............. Schiller Park Public Library, Schiller Park, IL [*Library symbol*] [*Library of Congress*] (LCLS)
ISP.............. Specific Impulse (MCD)
ISPA............ Idaho State Pharmaceutical Association (SAUO)
ISPA............ International Screen Publicity Association
ISPA............ International Skat Players Association (SAUO)
ISPA............ International Sleep Products Association (NTPA)
ISPA............ International Small Printers Association (SAUS)
ISPA............ International Society for the Performing Arts (NTPA)
ISPA............ International Society for the Protection of Animals [*Later, WSPA*] [*British*] (EA)
ISPA............ International Society of Parametric Analysts (EA)
ISPA............ International Software Products Association (SAUO)
I/SPA.......... International Spa and Fitness Association
ISPA............ International Sporting Press Association
ISPA............ International Squash Players Association [*Cardiff, Wales*] (EAIO)
ISPA............ Internet Service Provider Association
ISPA............ Internet Service Provider Austria (SAUO)
ISPA............ Inverted Socket Process Architecture [*Computer science*]
ISPAA.......... International Society of Performing Arts Administrators (EA)
ISPAA.......... International Society of Plastic and Audio-Visual Art
ISPABX........ Integrated Services Private Automatic Branch Exchange (SAUS)
ISPAC.......... International Society for Polycyclic Aromatic Compounds (SAUO)
ISPAE.......... Institute of Statistics, Planning and Applied Economics (SAUS)
ISPAF.......... Intelligence Service of the Philippine Armed Forces (SAUO)
ISPAN.......... Information Stream Project for AWIPS and NOAAport (SAUO)
ISPAN.......... Information Stream Project for AWIPS/NOAAPORT (SAUS)
ISP&D.......... Information Systems Planning & Development (SAUO)
ISPANET...... Sharp Communications Network (SAUS)
ISPAS.......... International Society of Professional Ambulance Services (SAUO)
ISPAS.......... Swedish Peace and Arbitration Society (SAUO)
ISPA-uk....... Internet Services Provider Association of the United Kingdom (SAUO)
ISPBX.......... Integrated Services PBX [*Telecommunications*] (NITA)
ISPBX.......... Integrated Services Private Branch Exchange (SAUS)
ISPBX.......... ISDN Private Branche Exchange (SAUO)
ISPC............ International Signalling Point Code (SAUS)
ISPC............ International Society for the Philosophy of Chemistry
ISPC............ International Sound Programming Center [*Telecommunications*]
ISPC............ International Spotted Pony Club [*Defunct*] (EA)
ISPC............ International Statistical Program Center (SAUO)
ISPC............ International Statistical Programs Center [*Department of Commerce*] (IID)
ISPC............ International Storage Product Center (SAUS)
ISPC............ International Symposium on Plasma Chemistry (SAUO)
ISPC............ Interspec, Inc. (SAUO)
ISPCA.......... Irish Society for the Prevention of Cruelty to Animals (DBA)
ISPCAN........ International Society for Prevention of Child Abuse and Neglect (EA)
ISPCC.......... International Ship Painting and Corrosion Conference (SAUO)
ISPCC.......... Irish Society for the Prevention of Cruelty to Children (DI)
ISPCON........ Internet Service Provider Convention [*Annual trade show*] (IGQR)
ISPD............ International Society for Peritoneal Dialysis (EA)
ISPE............ Illinois Society of Professional Engineers (SAUO)
ISPE............ Improved SONAR Processing Equipment [*Military*] (CAAL)
ISPE............ Information Systems Processing Equipment (ACAE)
ISPE............ Institute and Society of Practicioners in Electrolysis Ltd. [*British*] (BI)

ISPE .... Institute and Society of Practitioners in Electrolysis (SAUO)
ISPE .... Institute of Swimming Pool Engineers [*British*] (DBA)
ISPE .... Interim Software Progress Emulation (SAUO)
ISPE .... International Society for Pharmacoepidemiology (SAUO)
ISPE .... International Society for Philosophical Enquiry (EA)
ISPE .... International Society for Productivity Enhancements (SAUO)
ISPE .... International Society of Pharmaceutical Engineers (EA)
ISPE .... International Society of Planetarium Educators (SAUO)
ISPEC .... Independent Schools Physical Education Conference (AIE)
ISPEC .... Insulation Specification (MSA)
ISPEC .... Interagency Scientific Products Evaluation Committee (SAUO)
ISPELL .... Interactive SPELL-checker (SAUS)
ISPEMA .... Industrial Safety Personal (or Personnel) Equipment Manufacturers Association (SAUS)
ISPER .... IPAC [*Intelligence, Pacific Area Command*] Special Report
ISPERN .... Illinois State Police Emergency Radio Network (SAUS)
ISPES .... Inner-Shell Photoelectron Spectroscopy
ISPF .... Integral Skinned Polyurethane Foam (PDAA)
ISPF .... Interactive Structured Programming Facility (SAUO)
ISPF .... Interactive System Productivity Facility [*Computer science*]
ISPF .... Interactive System Programming Facility (SAUO)
ISPF .... International Save the Pun Foundation (EA)
ISPF .... International Science Policy Foundation (EAIO)
ISPF/PDF .... Interactive System Productivity Facility/Program Development Facility [*Computer science*]
ISPF/PDF .... ISPF Program Development Facility (SAUS)
ISPG .... Institute of Sedimentary and Petroleum Geology [*Geological Survey of Canada*] [*Research center*] (RCD)
ISPG .... Institutional Support Planning Group [*NASA*] (NASA)
ISPH .... International Society for Professional Hypnosis (EA)
ISPH .... International Society for the Protection of Horses (DI)
ISPH .... International Society of Psychology of Handwriting [*Milan, Italy*] (EA)
ISPHS .... International Society for Phenomenology and Human Sciences (EA)
ISPhS .... International Society for Phonetic Sciences (SAUO)
ISPhS .... International Society of Phonetic Sciences (EA)
ISPI .... Illinois State Psychiatric Institute
ISPI .... Information Systems Processing Installation (SAUO)
ISPI .... Intermediate-scale Product Inventory (SAUS)
ISPI .... International Society for Performance Improvement
ISPI .... International Society for Prevention of Infertility (EAIO)
ISPIC .... International Society for the Prevention of Iatrogenic Complications (SAUO)
ISPICE .... Interactive Simulation Program with Integrated Circuit Emphasis [*Computer science*] (MHDI)
I-Spin .... Isotopic Spin (SAUS)
ISPK .... Insulin-Stimulated Protein Kinase [*An enzyme*]
ISPK .... Isolated Spontaneous Psychokinesis [*Parapsychology*]
ISPL .... Illustrated Spare Parts List (SAUO)
ISPL .... Incremental System Programming Language [*Computer science*]
ISPL .... Initial Spare Parts List (IAA)
ISPL .... Instruction Set Processor Language [*Computer science*]
ISPL .... Interim Spare Parts List (AAG)
ISPL .... International Society for Phenomenology and Literature (EA)
ISPLS .... Indiana Society of Professional Land Surveyors (SAUO)
ISPLS .... International Society of Podiatric Laser Surgery (EA)
ISPM .... In Situ Particle Monitor (AAEL)
ISPM .... International Society of Plant Morphologists [*Delhi, India*] (EAIO)
ISPM .... International Solar Polar Mission [*NASA*]
ISPM .... International Solar Probe Mission (SAUO)
ISPM .... International Staff Planners Memorandum (SAUO)
ISPM .... International Staff Planners Message [*NATO*] (NATG)
ISPM .... Interplanetary Shock Propagation Model (USDC)
ISPMB .... International Society for Plant Molecular Biology (SAUS)
ISPMB .... International Society for the Protection of Mustangs and Burros (EA)
ISPMB .... International Society of Plant Molecular Biology (EA)
ISPMEMO .... International Staff Planners Memo [*NATO*] (NATG)
ISPMM .... International Symposium on Purine Metabolism in Man
ISPMs .... International Standards for Phytosanitary Measures (SAUO)
ISPN .... Integrated Surveys Processing Network [*Bureau of the Census*] (GFGA)
ISPN .... International Society for Pediatric Neurosurgery (EA)
ISPN .... International Society of Parenteral Nutrition (SAUO)
ISPN .... International Standard Program Number [*Numbering system for software*]
ISPN .... International Students Peace Network (EA)
ISPO .... Industrial Staffing Plan Occupations (MCD)
ISPO .... Information Society Project Office (DDC)
ISPO .... Instrumentation Ships Project Office [*Navy*]
ISPO .... International Society for Preventive Oncology (EA)
ISPO .... International Society for Prosthetics and Orthotics - US National Member Society (EA)
ISPO .... International Sports Equipment Fair [*Germany*]
ISPO .... International Statistical Programs Office [*Department of Commerce*] (IEEE)
ISPO .... Irradiation Special Purchase Order (SAA)
ISPOB .... Illinois Soybean Program Operating Board (SAUS)
ISPOG .... International Society of Psychosomatic Obstetrics and Gynaecology (PDAA)
ISPOR .... International Society for Pharmacoeconomics and Outcomes Research (SAUO)
ISPOUSC .... International Society for Prosthetics and Orthotics - US Committee [*Later, ISPO*] (EA)
ISPP .... Illinois State Physics Project (SAUO)
ISPP .... Indian Society for Plant Physiology (SAUO)
ISPP .... Information System for Policy Planning (SAUS)
ISPP .... Information Systems Program Plan (SAUO)
ISPP .... In-Service Professional Program (SAUS)
ISPP .... In-Situ Propellant Production
ISPP .... Internationale Studiengemeinschaft fuer Pranatale Psychologie [*International Society for the Study of Prenatal Psychology - ISPP*] (EAIO)
ISPP .... International Society for/of Plant Pathology (SAUO)
ISPP .... International Society for Plant Pathology (EAIO)
ISPP .... International Society for Portuguese Philately (EA)
ISPP .... International Society for Preretirement Planning (SAUO)
ISPP .... International Society for Retirement Planning [*Later, ISRP*] (EA)
ISPP .... International Society for the Study of Prenatal Psychology (EAIO)
ISPP .... International Society of Political Psychology (EA)
ISPP .... International Society of Prenatal and Perinatal Psychology and Medicine (EAIO)
ISPP .... International Society of Preretirement Planners (SAUO)
ISPP .... Inter-Services Plastic Panel (SAUO)
ISPPD .... Integrated Schedule Planning Process Document (SAUS)
ISPPP .... International Symposium on HLtd. of Proteins, Peptides, and Polynucleotides
ISPPP .... International Symposium on HPLC of Proteins, Peptides and Polynucleotides (SAUS)
ISPPS .... Item Support Plan Policies Statement (AFIT)
ISPR .... Infantry Systems Program Review [*Army*] (AABC)
ISPR .... Information Security Program Regulation (MCD)
ISPR .... Integrated Support Parts Requirement (KSC)
ISPR .... Intelligence Systems Program Review (SAUO)
ISPR .... International Special Commission on Radio Interference (MCD)
ISPR .... International Standard Payload Rack (SAUS)
ISPRA .... Israel Product Research Co. Ltd. (SAUO)
ISPRAD .... International Symposium on the Planning of Radiological Departments [*Medicine*] (EDAA)
ISPRB .... Information Systems Planning Review Board (SAUO)
ISPRS .... International Society for Photogrammetry and Remote Sensing [*Royal Institute of Technology*] [*Research center*] [*Sweden*] (IRC)
ISPRS .... International Society of Photogrammetry and Remote Sensing (SAUS)
ISprv .... Spring Valley Public Library, Spring Valley, IL [*Library symbol*] [*Library of Congress*] (LCLS)
ISprvHSD .... Hall Township High School District 502, Spring Valley, IL [*Library symbol*] [*Library of Congress*] (LCLS)
ISprvSD .... Spring Valley Consolidated Community School District 99, Spring Valley, IL [*Library symbol*] [*Library of Congress*] (LCLS)
ISPS .... Instruction Set Processor Specification [*1977*] [*Computer science*] (CSR)
ISPS .... Integrated Secondary Power System (ACAE)
ISPS .... Integrated Secondary Propulsion System (MCD)
ISPs .... Integrated Steel Plants (SAUO)
ISPS .... Integrated Strike Planning System (SAUS)
ISPS .... International Society of Phonetic Sciences (EA)
ISPS .... International Society of Plastic Surgeons (SAUO)
ISPS .... International Society of Police Surgeons (SAUO)
ISPS .... International Standard Paper Sizes
ISPS .... Item Support Policy Statement (ACAE)
ISPT .... Division of Intergovernment Science and Public Technology (SAUS)
ISPT .... Industry Superannuation Property Trust
ISPT .... Initial Satisfactory Performance Test (AAG)
ISPT .... Institute for Studies in Psychological Testing
ISPT .... Intergovernmental Science and Public Technology [*of ASRA*] [*National Science Foundation*]
ISPT .... Interspecies Ovum Penetration Test [*Medicine*] (BABM)
ISPTC .... Information Systems Performance Technical Center (SAUO)
ISPT/IP .... Intergovernmental Science and Technology/Industrial Programs (SAUS)
ISPV .... In Situ Plasma Vitrification
ISPW .... International Society for the Psychology of Writing (EA)
ISPWP .... International Society for the Prevention of Water Pollution [*Alton, Hampshire, England*] (EAIO)
ISPX .... Secular Institute of Pius X (EA)
ISPZ .... ISU Power Plant [*Federal Railroad Administration identification code*]
ISQ .... In Status Quo
ISQ .... Lillie M. Evans Memorial Library, Princeville, IL [*OCLC symbol*] (OCLC)
ISQ .... Manistique, MI [*Location identifier*] [*FAA*] (FAAL)
ISQA .... International Association for Quality Assurance in Health Care (SAUO)
ISQA .... Israeli Society for Quality Assurance (SAUS)
ISQA .... Israel Society for Quality Assurance (SAUS)
ISQC .... Indian Society for Quality Control (SAUO)
ISQD .... Identification System for Questioned Documents [*Book title*]
ISQIT .... Information Systems Quality Improvement Team (SAUO)
ISQL .... Interactive SQL [*Computer science*]
ISQL .... Interactive Standard Query Language (HGEN)
ISQL .... Interactive Structured Query Language (SAUS)
ISQOLS .... International Society for Quality-of-Life Studies (NTPA)
ISR .... Ice Sounding RADAR
ISR .... Identification Safety Range [*Military*] (NVT)
ISR .... Image Storage Retrieval
ISR .... Impulse Sequencing Relay
ISR .... Incoherent Scatter RADAR [*Instrumentation*]
ISR .... Incstar Corp. [*AMEX symbol*] (SPSG)
ISR .... Indian State Railway (ROG)
ISR .... Indian State Railways (SAUO)
ISR .... Indirect Source Review [*Environmental Protection Agency*] (FFDE)
ISR .... Individual Schedule Request (SAUS)

ISR............. Individual Soldier Radio [*Military*] (INF)
ISR............. Individual Soldier's Report
ISR............. Induction Skull Remelting (SAUS)
ISR............. Inductive Source Resistivity (SAUS)
ISR............. Industrial Security Regulations [*DoD*]
ISR............. Information Processing and Management (journ.) (SAUS)
ISR............. Information Research and Retrieval (SAUO)
ISR............. Information Service Representative [*Veterans Administration*]
ISR............. Information Storage and Retrieval [*Computer science*]
ISR............. Information Systems Research (SAUO)
ISR............. Infrared Scanning Radiometer (KSC)
ISR............. Infrared Spectral Radiometer (SAUS)
ISR............. Initial Sample Report
ISR............. Initial Selection Routine (SAUS)
ISR............. Initial Spares (SAUS)
ISR............. Initial System Release (MCD)
ISR............. Innovative Systems Research (NITA)
ISR............. Input Select and Reset (IAA)
ISR............. Input Selection Routine (SAUS)
ISR............. Input Shift Register
ISR............. Input Status Register (SAUS)
ISR............. In-Service Recruiter [*Army*]
ISR............. In-Service Repair (SAUS)
ISR............. In Situ Remediation (ABAC)
ISR............. In Situ Rinse (AAEL)
ISR............. Inspection/Surveillance Report (SAUO)
ISR............. Institute for Sex Research, Inc. [*National Institute of Mental Health*] (IID)
ISR............. Institute for Social Research [*University of Michigan*] (EA)
ISR............. Institute for Social Research [*York University*] [*Information service or system*] (IID)
ISR............. Institute for Space Research (SAUS)
ISR............. Institute for Standards Research (SAUS)
ISR............. Institute for Storm Research (MCD)
ISR............. Institute for Study of Regulation [*Defunct*] (EA)
ISR............. Institute of Seaweed Research [*British*]
ISR............. Institute of Semiconductor Research [*Former USSR*]
ISR............. Institute of Sex Research (SAUS)
ISR............. Institute of Snow Research (SAUO)
ISR............. Institute of Social Research [*Indiana University*] [*Information service or system*] (IID)
ISR............. Institute of Surgical Research [*San Antonio, TX*] [*Army*]
ISR............. Institutional Supporting Research (SAUO)
ISR............. Instructional System Review
ISR............. Instrumentation Status Report (MUGU)
ISR............. Insulin Secretion Rate [*Medicine*] (DMAA)
ISR............. Integral Superheat Reactor
ISR............. Integrated Safety Review (ACAE)
ISR............. Integrated Secretory Response [*Biochemistry*] (DAVI)
ISR............. Integrated Support Requirements (AAG)
ISR............. Intelligence Systems-Rear (SAUS)
ISR............. Interagency Source Register [*Intelligence*] (MCD)
ISR............. Interdisciplinary Science Reviews (journ.) (SAUS)
ISR............. Interim Scientific Report
ISR............. Interim System Review (SSD)
ISR............. Interim Systems Review (SAUS)
ISR............. Intermediate Session Routing (ACRL)
ISR............. Intermediate Sodium Removal [*Nuclear energy*] (NRCH)
ISR............. Internal Scientific Report
ISR............. International Sacred Recordings, Christian Artists' Record Corp. [*Record label*]
ISR............. International Sanitary Regulations [*World Health Organization*]
ISR............. International Shasta Resources [*Vancouver Stock Exchange symbol*]
ISR............. International Society for Radiology (SAUS)
ISR............. International Society of Radiobiology (SAUO)
ISR............. International Society of Radiology [*Berne, Switzerland*] (EA)
ISR............. International Sourdough Reunion (EA)
ISR............. International Star Registry
ISR............. International Student Relief [*Later, WUS*]
ISR............. International Submarine Race
ISR............. International Survey Research [*London consultancy firm*]
ISR............. International Synthetic Rubber Co. [*United Kingdom*]
ISR............. Interrupt Service Register (SAUS)
ISR............. Interrupt Service Routine (IEEE)
ISR............. Interrupt Status Register (IAA)
ISR............. Interrupt Status Report (SAUS)
ISR............. Intersecting Storage Ring [*High-energy physics*]
ISR............. Intersecting Storage Routine (SAUS)
ISR............. Inventory Status Report
ISR............. Iowa Southern Railroad [*Federal Railroad Administration identification code*]
ISR............. Iraq Syrian Railroad (SAUO)
ISR............. Israel [*ANSI three-letter standard code*] (CNC)
Isr............. Israel (VRA)
Isr............. Israeli (DIAR)
ISR............. Istra Air [*Slovakia*] [*ICAO designator*] (FAAC)
ISR............. Methodist Medical Center of Illinois, Peoria, IL [*OCLC symbol*] (OCLC)
ISRA........... Installment Sales Revision Act (SAUS)
ISRA........... Installment Sales Revision Act of 1980
ISRA........... Intercollegiate Squash-Racquet Association (PSS)
ISRA........... International Seabed Research Authority
ISRA........... International Service Robot Association (NTPA)
ISRA........... International Ski Racers Association [*Later, WPS-RA*]
ISRA........... International Society for Research on Aggression (EA)
ISRA........... Irish Squash Rackets Association (EAIO)
ISRAC......... Information Storage and Retrieval with Automatic Control (SAUS)
ISRAC......... Israel Laboratory Accreditation Authority (SAUO)
ISRAC......... ITT [*International Telephone & Telegraph Corp.*] Secure Ranging and Communications System
ISRAD......... Information Storage, Retrieval and Dissemination (SAUS)
ISRAD......... Institute for Social Research and Development [*University of New Mexico*]
ISRAD......... Integrated Software Research and Development (SAUS)
ISRAD......... Integrated Software Research and Development Program (MCD)
Isr AEC IA Rep... Israel. Atomic Energy Commission. IA Report (journ.) (SAUS)
Isr AEC IS Rep... Israel. Atomic Energy Commission. IS Report (journ.) (SAUS)
Israel Ann Psychiat... Israel Annals of Psychiatry (journ.) (SAUS)
Israel Bus.... Israel Business (journ.) (SAUS)
Israel Ch...... Israel Chemical Ltd. [*Associated Press*] (SAG)
Israel E........ Israel Economist (journ.) (SAUS)
Israel Inv..... Israel Business and Investors Report (journ.) (SAUS)
Israel J Ent... Israel Journal of Entomology (journ.) (SAUS)
Israel Stud Criminol... Israel Studies in Criminology [*Jerusalem, Israel*] [*A publication*] (DLA)
Israel Yb on Human Rights... Israel Yearbook on Human Rights (journ.) (SAUS)
Isr Agric Res Organ Spec Publ... Israel. Agricultural Research Organization. Special Publication (journ.) (SAUS)
Isr Agric Res Org Div For Trienn Rep Res... Israel. Agricultural Research Organization. Division of Forestry. Triennial Report of Research (journ.) (SAUS)
Isramc......... Isramco, Inc. [*Associated Press*] (SAG)
ISR and D..... Information Storage, Retrieval and Dissemination (SAUS)
Isr Aquacult Bamidgeh... Israeli Journal of Aquaculture Bamidgeh (journ.) (SAUS)
ISRB........... Idaho Surveying and Rating Bureau (SAUO)
ISRB........... Individual Serve Review Board (SAUS)
ISRB........... Information Systems Requirements Board (SAUO)
ISRB........... Inter-Service Research Bureau [*British*]
ISRC........... Information Services Readiness Center (SAUO)
ISRC........... International Service Robot Congress
ISRC........... International Society of Radiology Congress
ISRC........... International Standard Recording Code (TELE)
ISRC........... International Student Research Center (SAUS)
ISRC........... International Survey Research Corp.
ISRC........... International Synthetic Rubber Co. (SAUS)
ISRCDVS...... International Society for Research on Civilization Diseases and Vital Substances (PDAA)
ISRCSC........ Inter-Services Radio Components Standardization Committee (SAUO)
ISRD........... Information Storage Retrieval and Dissemination (NITA)
ISRD........... Information Systems Requirements Document (SAUO)
ISRD........... In-Service Reliability Demonstration (SAUS)
ISRD........... Institutional Supporting Research and Development (SAUO)
ISRD........... International Society for Rehabilitation of the Disabled [*Later, RehabilitationInternational*]
ISRDB......... Incoherent Scatter Radar Data Base (SAUS)
ISRDS......... Istituto di Studi sulla Ricerca e Documentazione Scientifica [*Institute for Study of Scientific Research and Documentation*] [*National Research Council*] [*Information service or system*] (IID)
ISRE........... Interferon-Stimulated Response Element [*Medicine*]
ISREC......... Swiss Institute of Experimental Research into Cancer [*Medicine*] (EDAA)
IS Relay...... Incomplete Sequence Relay (SAUS)
ISR-ERS-1... Coordinated Proposal Ice-Sheet Research with ERS-1 (SAUS)
ISRERS-1.... Ice-Sheet Research with ERS-1 (SAUO)
IS Revw...... International Socialist Review (journ.) (SAUS)
ISRF........... International Squash Rackets Federation [*Cardiff, Wales*] (EAIO)
ISRF........... International Sugar Research Foundation [*Later, WSRO*] (EA)
ISRF........... Internet Screenphone Forum (SAUO)
ISRFCTC..... Inter-Services Radio Frequency Cables Technical Committee (SAUS)
ISRFCTC..... Inter-Services Radio-Frequency Cables Technical Committee (SAUO)
ISRG........... Independent Safety Review Group (SAUO)
ISRG........... Independent Space Research Group (EA)
ISRG........... International Space Research Group (SAUO)
ISRG........... International Standard Recording Group (SAUO)
Isr Geol Soc Annu Meet... Israel Geological Society. Annual Meeting (journ.) (SAUS)
Isr Geol Surv Bull... Israel. Geological Survey. Bulletin (journ.) (SAUS)
Isr Geol Surv Geol Data Process Unit Rep... Israel. Geological Survey. Geological Data Processing Unit. Report (journ.) (SAUS)
Isr Geol Surv Rep... Israel. Geological Survey. Report (journ.) (SAUS)
ISRGLU........ Independent Ship, Riverside, and General Labourers' Union [*British*]
ISRHAI......... International Secretariat for Research on the History of Agricultural Implements [*Lyngby, Denmark*] (EAIO)
Isr Hydrol Serv Rep... Israel. Hydrological Service. Report (journ.) (SAUS)
ISRI............ Institute of Scrap Recycling Industries (NTPA)
ISRI............ Israeli Shipping Research Institute (SAUS)
ISRI............ Israel Shipping Research Institute (SAUO)
ISRIC.......... International Soil Reference and Information Centre [*Research center*] [*Netherlands*] (IRC)
Isr Inst Agric Eng Sci Act... Israel. Institute of Agricultural Engineering. Scientific Activities (journ.) (SAUS)
Isr Inst Field Gard Crops Sci Act... Israel. Institute of Field and Garden Crops. Scientific Activities (journ.) (SAUS)
Isr Inst Hortic Sci Act... Israel. Institute of Horticulture. Scientific Activities (journ.) (SAUS)
Isr Inst Plant Prot Sci Act... Israel. Institute of Plant Protection. Scientific Activities (journ.) (SAUS)
Isr Inst Soils Water Sci Act... Israel. Institute of Soils and Water. Scientific Activities (journ.) (SAUS)

Isr Inst Technol Storage Agric Prod Sci Act... Israel. Institute for Technology and Storage of Agricultural Products. Scientific Activities (journ.) (SAUS)
ISRIP.......... In Situ Redox Integrated Program (SAUS)
Isr J Dent Med... Israel Journal of Dental Medicine (journ.) (SAUS)
Isr J Earth Sci... Israel Journal of Earth Sciences [*A publication*] (STAH)
Isr J Entomol... Israel Journal of Entomology (journ.) (SAUS)
Isr J Exp Med... Israel Journal Experimental Medicine (journ.) (SAUS)
Isr J Exp Med... Israel Journal of Experimental Medicine (journ.) (SAUS)
Isr J Plant Sci... Israel Journal of Plant Science (journ.) (SAUS)
Isr J Psychiatry... Israel Journal of Psychiatry (SAUS)
Isr J Vet Med... Israel Journal of Veterinary Medicine (journ.) (SAUS)
ISRL........... Isramco, Inc. [*NASDAQ symbol*] (NQ)
IsrlLd.......... Israel Land & Development Co. [*Associated Press*] (SAG)
IsrLLetters... Israel Life and Letters (journ.) (SAUS)
ISRLW......... Isramco Inc.Wrrt'A' [*NASDAQ symbol*] (TTSB)
ISRLZ.......... Isramco Inc.Wrrt'B' [*NASDAQ symbol*] (TTSB)
ISRM.......... Index of Stability of Relative Magnitudes [*Statistics*]
ISRM.......... Information System Resource Manager (SAUS)
ISRM.......... Information Systems Resource Manager
ISRM.......... Initial Service Request Message (SAUS)
ISRM.......... International Society for/of Rock Mechanics (SAUO)
ISRM.......... International Society for Range Management (EA)
ISRM.......... International Society for Rock Mechanics [*Lisbon, Portugal*] (EA)
ISRM.......... International Society of Reproductive Medicine (EA)
ISRM.......... Inter-Service Radio Measurements [*British*] [*World War II*]
Isrm........... Isramco, Inc. [*Associated Press*] (SAG)
Isr Med J..... Israel Medical Journal (journ.) (SAUS)
Isr Min Agr Water Comm Hydrol Serv Hydrol Paper... Israel. Ministry of Agriculture. Water Commission. Hydrological Service. Hydrological Paper (journ.) (SAUS)
Isr Mus N.... Israel Museum News (journ.) (SAUS)
ISRN.......... Incorporated Society of Registered Naturopaths [*British*]
ISRN.......... International Standard Recording Number (SAUO)
Isr Natl Counc Res Dev Rep... Israel. National Council for Research and Development. Report (journ.) (SAUS)
Isr Natl Counc Res Dev Rep NCRD... Israel. National Council for Research and Development. Report NCRD (journ.) (SAUS)
ISRNI.......... Incest Survivors Resource Network, International (EA)
Isr Num J.... Israel Numismatic Journal (journ.) (SAUS)
ISRO.......... Indian Space Research Organisation (or Organization) (SAUO)
ISRO.......... India Space Research Organisation (SAUS)
ISRO.......... International Securities Regulatory Organisation [*London, England*] [*Business term*]
ISRO.......... International Society of Radiation Oncology (SAUO)
ISRO.......... Isle Royale National Park
Isr Oceanogr Limnol Res Annu Rep... Israel Oceanographic and Limnological Research. Annual Report (journ.) (SAUS)
ISROP.......... Israel European Company (SAUO)
Isr Orient Stud... Israel Oriental Studies (journ.) (SAUS)
ISRP.......... Improved Stabilization References Package (SAUS)
ISRP.......... Indirect Source Review Program (COE)
ISRP.......... Initial Spares and Repair Parts
ISRP.......... Internal Surface Reverse Phase [*Chromatography column*]
ISRP.......... International Society for Respiratory Protection (EA)
ISRP.......... International Society for Retirement Planning (EA)
ISRP.......... International Society of Respiratory Protection (SAUS)
Isr Pharm J... Israel Pharmaceutical Journal (journ.) (SAUS)
ISRR.......... Indiana Southern Railroad [*Federal Railroad Administration identification code*]
ISRR.......... Institute of Social and Religious Research (SAUO)
ISRR.......... International Society for Rorschach Research (SAUO)
ISRR.......... International Soundex Reunion Registry (EA)
ISRR.......... International Symposium on Roofs and Roofing (SAUO)
ISRRA.......... International Standard Rex Rabbit Association (SAUO)
ISRREC.......... Institute for Sex Research Library Records [*Database*] [*Kinsey Institute for Research in Sex, Gender, and Reproduction*] [*Information service or system*] (CRD)
ISRRS.......... International Symposium on Research Reactor Safety (SAUS)
ISRRT.......... International Society of Radiographers and Radiological Technicians [*Don Mills, ON*] (EA)
ISRS.......... Impulsive Stimulated Raman Scattering [*Physics*]
ISRS.......... Indian Steam Railway Society [*Indian Railway*] (TIR)
ISRS.......... Information Search and Recording System [*of UMREL*]
ISRS.......... Integrated Status Reporting System (MCD)
ISRS.......... International Safety Rating System (SAUS)
ISRS.......... International Society for Reef Studies
ISRS.......... International Society of Refractive Surgery (NTPA)
ISRS.......... International Symposium on the Reactivity of Solids (SAUS)
ISRSA.......... International Synthetic Rubber Safety Association (SAUO)
ISRSM.......... International Symposium on Rocket and Satellite Meteorology
Isr Soc Spec Libr Inf Cent Bull... Israel Society of Special Libraries and Information Centers. Bulletin (journ.) (SAUS)
ISRT.......... In-School Resources Teacher (SAUS)
ISRT.......... International Spinal Research Trust [*British*]
ISRT.......... Invisible Soft Return (SAUS)
ISRT.......... Iowa Silent Reading Tests [*Education*]
ISRT.......... Iowa Society of Radiologic Technologists (SAUO)
ISRT.......... Isotopes and Radiation Technology [*A publication*]
ISRTP.......... International Society of Regulatory Toxicology and Pharmacology
ISRU.......... Information Search and Retrieval Unit (SAUS)
ISRU.......... Intergovernmental Science and Research Utilization [*National Science Foundation*]
ISRU.......... International Scientific Radio Union [*Also, URSI*]
IsRW.......... Weizmann Institute of Science, Rehovot, Israel [*Library symbol*] [*Library of Congress*] (LCLS)
ISS.......... Ideal Solidus Structures (IEEE)
ISS.......... Idiopathic Short Stature [*Medicine*] (DMAA)
ISS.......... Ignition Shielding (SAUS)
ISS.......... Ignition Shielding System
ISS.......... Ilon Scattering Spectroscopy (SAUS)
ISS.......... Image Sensor System
ISS.......... Image Sharpness Scale [*Photography*] (OA)
ISS.......... Image Store System (SAUS)
ISS.......... Imaging Science Subsystem
ISS.......... Immune System Suspected (SAUS)
ISS.......... Impact Surface Science (ACAE)
ISS.......... Imperfect Single Stamp [*Philately*]
ISS.......... Imperial Service Sappers [*British military*] (DMA)
ISS.......... Independent Schools Section [*American Association of School Libraries*] [*American Library Association*]
ISS.......... Independent Sweep System
ISS.......... Index of Specifications and Standards (MCD)
ISS.......... Index Sequential Storage (SAUS)
ISS.......... Indiana Slavic Studies (journ.) (SAUS)
ISS.......... Indirect Sighting System (ACAE)
ISS.......... Indirect Sub-System (SAUS)
ISS.......... Individual Studies School (SAUO)
ISS.......... Individual Style Survey [*Test*] (TMMY)
ISS.......... Inductive Storage Switch
ISS.......... Industrial Security Section [*NATO*] (NATG)
ISS.......... Industrial Systems Service (EFIS)
ISS.......... Industry Sole Source (AFIT)
ISS.......... Industry Standard Specifications (AAG)
ISS.......... Inertial Sensor System (KSC)
ISS.......... Inertial Subsystem (MCD)
iss.......... Inertial Subsystem (NAKS)
ISS.......... Inertial Survey System (SAUS)
ISS.......... Inferior Sagittal Sinus [*Medicine*] (MELL)
ISS.......... Information & Scientific Systems (SAUO)
ISS.......... Information Sampling System (SAUS)
ISS.......... Information Search Services (SAUS)
ISS.......... Information Security Specialist (SAUO)
ISS.......... Information Sending Station (SAUS)
ISS.......... Information Service Specialist (SAUO)
ISS.......... Information Services Seminar (SAUS)
ISS.......... Information Sharing System (NITA)
ISS.......... Information Storage System (IEEE)
ISS.......... Information Support Services (SAUO)
ISS.......... Information Support System [*Nondestructive Testing Information Analysis Center - NTIAC*] [*Southwest Research Institute*] [*Information service or system*] (CRD)
ISS.......... Information System Services (SAUS)
ISS.......... Information Systems Section [*Battelle Memorial Institute*] [*Information service or system*] (IID)
ISS.......... Information Systems Security
ISS.......... Information Systems Services [*Brigham Young University*] [*Research center*] (RCD)
ISS.......... Information Systems Specialists (SAUO)
ISS.......... Information Systems Specialists Office [*Library of Congress*] (NITA)
ISS.......... Information Systems Squadron (SAUO)
ISS.......... Information Systems Staff (SAUO)
ISS.......... Information Systems Subdivision (MCD)
ISS.......... Infrared Sensor System
ISS.......... Infrared Surveillance Sensor (ACAE)
ISS.......... Infrared Surveillance Set
ISS.......... Inherent Shutdown System (SAUS)
iss.......... Inhibit/Override Summary Snapshot (NAKS)
ISS.......... Inhibit/Override Summary Snapshot Display (NASA)
ISS.......... Initial Selection Sequence (SAUS)
ISS.......... Initial Space Station (KSC)
ISS.......... Injury Severity Score [*Auto safety research*]
ISS.......... Input Shaft Speed [*Automotive term*] (HAWK)
ISS.......... Input Subsystem
ISS.......... In-School Suspension (SAUO)
ISS.......... In-Service Support (SAUS)
ISS.......... Inside Skin (MCD)
ISS.......... Inside Surface (MCD)
ISS.......... In Situ Sampling (ABAC)
ISS.......... Inspection Surveillance Sheet (SAUS)
ISS.......... Installation Site Survey (MCD)
ISS.......... Installation Support School [*Army*]
iss.......... Installation Support Services (NAKS)
ISS.......... Installation Support Services (NASA)
ISS.......... Institute for Socioeconomic Studies (EA)
ISS.......... Institute for Southern Studies (EA)
ISS.......... Institute for Space Studies [*NASA*]
ISS.......... Institute for Strategic Studies [*Later, IISS*] [*Obsolete*]
ISS.......... Institute of Salesian Studies
ISS.......... Institute of Social Studies [*Netherlands*]
ISS.......... Institute of Somatic Sciences
ISS.......... Institute of Space Studies (SAUS)
ISS.......... Institute of Special Studies [*Army*]
ISS.......... Institute of Sports Sponsorship [*British*] (DBA)
ISS.......... Institute of Systems Science [*Singapore*] (DDC)
ISS.......... Institutional Shareholder Services
ISS.......... Institutional Staff Services (SAUO)
iss.......... Instruction Summary Sheet (NAKS)
ISS.......... Instruction Summary Sheet (NASA)

ISS............. In-Structure Shock [*Army*] (RDA)
ISS............. Instrumentation Support Service
ISS............. Instrument Servo System
ISS............. Instrument Society of Sweden (SAUO)
ISS............. Instrument Summary Sheet (SAUS)
ISS............. Integrated Safety System [*Automotive safety*]
ISS............. Integrated Satellite System
ISS............. Integrated Sealift Study [*Army*] (AABC)
ISS............. Integrated Separation Systems [*Electrophoresis*]
ISS............. Integrated Sounding System [*Marine science*] (OSRA)
ISS............. Integrated Source Sensor (ACAE)
ISS............. Integrated Start System (AAG)
ISS............. Integrated Storage System (NITA)
ISS............. Integrated Structural Seat [*Automotive engineering*]
ISS............. Integrated Support Stand (SAUS)
ISS............. Integrated Support System (SAUS)
ISS............. Integrated Switching System (SAUS)
ISS............. Integrated Switch Stick (IAA)
iss............. Integrated System Schematic (NAKS)
ISS............. Integrated System Schematic (NASA)
ISS............. Integrated WWW System Study (SAUS)
ISS............. Integration Support Service
ISS............. Intelligence Sensor System (SAUS)
ISS............. Intelligence Support Staff (SAUO)
ISS............. Intelligence Support System
ISS............. Intelligence System Simulation (SAUO)
ISS............. Intelligent Support System
ISS............. Intelligent Support Systems (SAUO)
ISS............. Interactive Selling System (GART)
ISS............. Intercept Surveillance Station (ACAE)
ISS............. INTERCO, Inc. [*Formerly, International Shoe Co.*] [*NYSE symbol*] (SPSG)
ISS............. Intercommunication Service System Inc. [*Information service or system*] (IID)
ISS............. Interdivisional Systems Standard (SAUS)
ISS............. Interface Shipset (SAUS)
ISS............. Interface Signal Simulator (SAA)
ISS............. Interface Simulation System (CAAL)
ISS............. Interface Supply Support (SAA)
ISS............. Interim Standard Set
ISS............. Interim Status Standards (GNE)
ISS............. Interim Stowage Shelf (KSC)
ISS............. Intermediate Secondary Section (SAUS)
ISS............. Intermediate Service School [*Military*] (AFM)
ISS............. Internal Switching System
ISS............. Internationale Gesellschaft fuer Stereologie [*International Society for Stereology*] (EAIO)
ISS............. International Savant Society (EA)
ISS............. International School of Sailing
ISS............. International School Service (SAUS)
ISS............. International Schools Services (EA)
ISS............. International Scientific Series [*A publication*]
ISS............. International Scotist Society [*See also SIS*] [*Rome, Italy*] (EAIO)
ISS............. International Seaweed Association (EAIO)
ISS............. International Seaweed Symposium [*Trondheim, Norway*] (MSC)
ISS............. International Security Services Ltd. (SAUO)
ISS............. International Seismological Summary (SAUO)
ISS............. International Self-Service Organization [*Cologne, Federal Republic of Germany*] (EAIO)
ISS............. International Service System A/S (SAUO)
ISS............. International Shoe Company (SAUO)
ISS............. International Sinatra Society (EA)
ISS............. International Skeletal Society (EA)
ISS............. International Social Service [*See also SSI*] [*Geneva, Switzerland*] (EAIO)
ISS............. International Society for Stereology. (EA)
ISS............. International Society of Shropshires (EA)
ISS............. International Society of Social Defence (SAUO)
ISS............. International Society of Surgery (DAVI)
ISS............. International Softbill Society (EA)
ISS............. International Space Station
ISS............. International Staging System [*Medicine*] (MELL)
ISS............. International Steamboat Society (EA)
ISS............. International Student Service (SAUO)
ISS............. International Students Society [*Defunct*] (EA)
ISS............. International Summer School (SAUS)
ISS............. International Sunshine Society (EA)
ISS............. Internet Security Systems (GART)
ISS............. Interrupt Safety System (SAUS)
ISS............. Interrupt Service Subroutine (CMD)
ISS............. Interservice Supply Support [*Military*] (AABC)
ISS............. Interstage Section Shell
ISS............. Interstellar Scattering [*of radio waves in the galaxy*]
ISS............. Interstellar [*Phase*] Scintillation [*Galactic science*]
ISS............. Intra-List Stimulus Similarity (PDAA)
ISS............. Inventory Service System (AFIT)
ISS............. Inventory Status System (ACAE)
ISS............. Involuntary Servitude and Slavery
ISS............. Ionespheric Sounding Satellite (SAUS)
ISS............. Ionosphere Sounding Satellite (SAUS)
ISS............. Ionospheric Sounding Satellite [*Japan*]
ISS............. Ion-Scattering Spectrometer [*or Spectrometry*]
ISS............. Ion Scattering Spectrometry (SAUS)
ISS............. Ion Scattering Spectroscope (SAUS)
ISS............. Ion Scattering Spectroscopy (SAUS)
ISS............. Ion-Scattering Spectroscopy (EDCT)
ISS............. Ion-Scattering Spectrum (SAUS)
ISS............. Ion Silicon System (IAA)
ISS............. Ion Source Spectrometer (SAUS)
ISS............. Ion Source Spectrometry (SAUS)
ISS............. Ion Spectroscopy Scattering [*Surface analysis*]
ISS............. Ion Surface Scattering (DB)
ISS............. Iraqi Intelligence Service
ISS............. Iris Spinning Stage (SAUS)
ISS............. Iron and Steel Society - of AIME (EA)
ISS............. Irritable Stomach Syndrome [*Medicine*] (MELL)
ISS............. Islands [*Postal Service standard*] (OPSA)
ISS............. Isotope Separation System (SAUS)
ISS............. Isotopic Separation Subsystem
ISS............. Israeli Secret Service (SAUO)
ISS............. ISS-International Service System, Inc. (SAUO)
ISS............. Issue (AABC)
ISS............. Issued (SAUS)
ISS............. Issy-Les Moulineaux Airport [*France*]
ISS............. Meridiana SpA [*Italy*] [*ICAO designator*] (FAAC)
ISS............. Sangamon State University, Springfield, IL [*Library symbol*] [*Library of Congress*] (LCLS)
ISS............. St. Meinrad College, St. Meinrad, IN [*OCLC symbol*] (OCLC)
ISS............. Wiscasset, ME [*Location identifier*] [*FAA*] (FAAL)
ISS............. YMCA [*Young Men's Christian Association*] International Student Service (EA)
ISSA............ Association Internationale des Ecoles de Voile [*International Sailing Schools Association*] [*France*] (EAIO)
ISSA............ Iberian Social Studies Association (SAUO)
ISSA............ Independent Software Safety Assessor (SAUS)
ISSA............ Information & Scientific Systems Administration (SAUO)
ISSA............ Information Systems Security Association (EA)
ISSA............ Installation Supply Support Activity (ACAE)
ISSA............ Installation Support Site Activity (ACAE)
ISSA............ Institute for Systems Studies and Analyses (SAUS)
ISSA............ Institute for the Study of Sexual Assault [*Defunct*] (EA)
ISSA............ Institute of Social Services Alternatives [*Defunct*] (EA)
ISSA............ Intelligence Specialist, Seaman Apprentice [*Navy*] (DNAB)
ISSA............ International Sailing Schools Association (EA)
ISSA............ International Sanitary Supply Association (EA)
ISSA............ International Sanitary Supply Association, Inc. (SAUO)
ISSA............ International Ship Suppliers Association [*Wimbledon, England*] (EA)
ISSA............ International Slurry Seal Association (EA)
ISSA............ International Slurry Surfacing Association (EAIO)
ISSA............ International Socialists of South Africa (SAUS)
ISSA............ International Social Security Association [*Geneva, Switzerland*] (EA)
ISSA............ International Society of Scientists-Artists (SAUO)
ISSA............ International Society of Stress Analysis (SAUO)
ISSA............ International Society of Stress Analysts (EA)
ISSA............ International Space Station Alpha (SAUS)
ISSA............ International Strategic Studies Association (EA)
ISSA............ International Swimming Statisticians Association (SAUO)
ISSA............ Interservice Supply Support Agreements [*Military*]
ISSA............ Inter-Service Support Agreement (COE)
ISSA............ Intra-Service Support Agreement (SAUS)
ISSA............ Irish Schools Swimming Association (EAIO)
ISSAA.......... Information Systems Selection & Acquisition Activity office (SAUS)
ISSAA.......... Information Systems Selection and Acquisition Agency (AAGC)
ISSA/B......... Bulletin of the International Social Security Association. Geneva (SAUO)
ISS/AB......... International Social Service, American Branch (EA)
ISSAB.......... International Social Service, Australian Branch [*An association*]
ISSAC.......... Integrated Surface Search and Attack Coordinate
ISSAC.......... International Symposium on Symbolic and Algebraic Computation (SAUO)
ISS-AIME..... Iron and Steel Society of the American Institute of Mining, Metallurgical and Petroleum Engineers (SAUO)
ISSAPD........ International Spanish Speaking Association of Physicians and Dentists (SAUO)
ISSAS.......... Interactive Structural Sizing and Analysis System [*Computer science*]
ISSB............ Information Systems Standards Board [*American National Standards Institute*] [*Telecommunications*]
ISSB............ International Symposium on Small Business (SAUO)
ISSB............ Interservice Security Board [*World War II*]
ISSBB.......... Inertial Sensor System Breadboard
ISSBD.......... International Society for the Study of Behavioural Development [*Nijmegen, Netherlands*] (EAIO)
ISSBN.......... Improved Fleet Ballistic Missile Submarine (SAUS)
ISSC............ Information Systems Software Center [*Fort Belvoir, VA*] [*Army*] (RDA)
ISSC............ Information Systems Steering Committee (SAUO)
ISSC............ Institute for the Study of Social Conflict (SAUO)
ISSC............ Integrated Systems Solutions Corp. (HODG)
ISSC............ Interdisciplinary Surface Science Conference (SAUS)
ISSC............ International Ship Structures Committee (SAUO)
ISSC............ International Ship Structures Conference (or Congress) (SAUS)
ISSC............ International Smart Shoppers Club (EA)
ISSC............ International Snowshoe Council [*Defunct*] (EA)
ISSC............ International Social Science Council [*See also CISS*] [*Paris, France*] [*Research center*] (EAIO)
ISSC............ International Social Sciences Council (SAUS)
ISSC............ International Subcommision on Stratigraphic Classification (SAUO)
ISSC............ Interservice Sports Council [*Later, ISC*]
ISSC............ Inter-Services Staff College (SAUO)

ISSC .... Interservice Supply Support Committee [*or Coordinator*] [*Military*] (AABC)
ISSC .... Interservice Supply Support Coordinator (SAUS)
ISSC .... Inter-Service Support Coordinator (SAUO)
ISSC .... Interstate Shellfish Sanitation Conference
ISSC .... ISSC Industries Solid State (SAUS)
ISSCA .... Institute of Steel Setvice Centres of Australia (SAUS)
ISSCA .... International Swizzle Stick Collectors Association (EA)
ISSCAAP .... International Standard Statistical Classification of Aquatic Animals and Plants
ISSCB .... International Society for Sandwich Construction and Bonding
ISSCC .... International Small Ships Command Course (SAUO)
ISSCC .... International Solid State Circuits Conference (MCD)
ISSCC .... International Solid-State Circuits Conference (SAUS)
ISSCG .... International Summer School on Crystal Growth (SAUS)
ISSCM .... International Society for the Study of Church Monuments [*Later, CMS*] (EA)
ISSCO .... Integrated Software Systems Corp.
ISSCO .... Integrated Software Systems Corporation (SAUO)
ISSCORP .... Integrated Software Systems Corporation (SAUO)
ISSC/SSI .... International Social Science Council/Social Sciences Information (SAUO)
ISSCT .... International Society for/of Sugar Cane Technologists (SAUO)
ISSCT .... International Society of Sugar Cane Technologists [*Piracicaoa, Brazil*] (EA)
ISSCT .... International Society of Sugar Cane Technology (SAUO)
ISSD .... Information System for Sustainable Development (SAUO)
ISSD .... Information Systems and Services Division [*Department of Commerce*] (IID)
ISSD .... International Shipping and Shipbuilding Directory (SAUO)
ISSD .... International Society for/of Social Defence (SAUO)
ISSD .... International Society for Social Defence [*See also SIDS*] [*Paris, France*] (EAIO)
ISSD .... International Society for the Study of Dissociation (NTPA)
ISSDF .... International Society for the Study of Dendrobatid Frogs (EA)
ISSDN .... Integrated Services Satellite Digital Network (MCD)
ISSE .... Imaging Science Subsystem Electronics (ACAE)
ISSE .... Information Security Solutions Europe (SAUO)
ISSE .... Information Systems Security Engineering (SAUS)
ISSE .... In Situ Spectroscopic Ellipsometry (AAEL)
ISSE .... International School-to-School Experience (SAUO)
ISSE .... International Sight and Sound Exploration (SAUS)
ISSE .... International Sight and Sound Exposition
ISSE .... International Society for the Study of Expressionism [*Formerly, ETMS*] (EA)
ISSE .... Internet Streaming SIMD Extension (SAUS)
ISSE .... Inter-Sun-Earth Explorer (SAUS)
ISSEC .... Internal Spectral Shifter and Energy Converter (MCD)
ISSE-ETMS ... International Society for the Study of Expressionism - Ernst Toller Memorial Society (EA)
ISSEL .... University of Illinois Solid State Electronics Laboratory [*Research center*] (RCD)
ISSEM .... Information System Security Evaluation Method (IAA)
ISSEM .... Information System Security Evaluation Methodology (SAUS)
ISSEP .... Integrated System Safety Engineering Plan
ISSEP .... International Soros Science Education Program [*Privately-funded program for former Soviet Republics*]
ISSER .... Institute of Statistical, Social and Economic Research (SAUO)
ISSES .... International Stationary Steam Engine Society (EAIO)
ISSET .... International Symposium on Space Electronics (MCD)
ISSF .... Industry Satellite Services Facility (SSD)
ISSF .... International Service of the Society of Friends (SAUO)
ISSF .... International Standup Surfing Federation (SAUO)
ISSF .... International Student Solidarity Fund (SAUO)
ISSG .... Illustrated Shipboard Shopping Guide [*Navy*]
ISSG .... Information Systems Support Group (AAGC)
ISSG .... Internet Services Study Group (SAUO)
ISSGA .... International Society for the Study of Ghosts and Apparitions
ISSHCAB .... International Society for the Study of the Human-Companion Animal Bond [*Later, IAHAIO*] (EA)
ISSHP .... Index to Social Sciences and Humanities Proceedings (SAUS)
ISSI .... Information Security Systems Inc. (SAUO)
ISSI .... Integrated Silicon Solution [*NASDAQ symbol*] (TTSB)
ISSI .... Integrated Silicon Solution, Inc. [*NASDAQ symbol*] (SAG)
ISSI .... International Social Science Institute [*Later, International Academy at Santa Barbara*] (EA)
ISSI .... International Society for Scientometrics and Informetrics
ISSI .... Interswitching System Interface [*Telecommunications*] (ACRL)
ISSID .... International Society for the Study of Individual Differences (EAIO)
ISS Int .... ISS International Service Systems AS [*Associated Press*] (SAG)
ISSIP .... Interswitching System Interface Protocol [*Telecommunications*] (ACRL)
ISS/ISG/ISW ... Information Systems Squadron/Group/Wing (SAUO)
ISSJ .... International Social Science Journal (journ.) (SAUS)
ISSK .... International Society for the Sociology of Knowledge [*St. John's, NF*] [*Defunct*] (EAIO)
ISSL .... Initial Spares Support List (AFM)
ISSL .... Initial Supplies Support List (SAUO)
ISSL .... Integrated Systems Simulation Laboratory (SAUS)
ISSL .... International Speed Skating League (SAUO)
ISSLIC .... Israel Societies of Special Libraries and Information Centers (SAUS)
ISSLIC .... Israel Societies (or Society) of Special Libraries and Information Centers (SAUO)
ISSLL .... Integrated Services over Specific Link Layers (GART)
ISSLS .... International Symposium on Subscriber Loops and Services (SAUO)
ISSLS .... International Symposium on Subscribers' Loops and Services [*Telecommunications*] (TEL)
ISSM .... Incompletely Specified Sequential Machine (PDAA)
ISSM .... Independent Society of Stick Makers [*A union*] [*British*]
ISSM .... Information System Security Manager (SAUO)
ISSM .... Initialized Stochastic Sequential Machine (IAA)
ISSM .... Institute of Safety and Systems Management (SAUS)
ISSM .... Institute of Sterile Services Management [*British*] (DBA)
ISSM .... Interim Surface-to-Surface Missile [*Military*] (CAAL)
ISSM .... Sangamon County Medical Society, Springfield, IL [*Library symbol*] [*Library of Congress*] (LCLS)
ISSM .... Secular Institute of Schoenstatt Sisters of Mary (TOCD)
ISSMB .... Information Systems Standards Management Board
ISSMC .... Institute for Social Studies and Medical Care (SAUO)
ISSMC .... Interim Surface-to-Surface Missile Capability [*Military*] (CAAL)
ISSMD .... Imaging Seeker Surface-to-Surface Missile Demonstration (SAUS)
ISS/MD .... ISS Microsystems Development (SAUO)
ISSMFE .... International Society for Soil Mechanics and Foundation Engineering [*See also SIMSTF*] (EA)
ISSMFE .... International Society of Soil Mechanics and Foundation Engineering (SAUS)
ISSMIS .... Integrated Support Services Management Information System (AABC)
ISSMPD .... International Society for the Study of Multiple Personality and Dissociation (EA)
ISSMS .... Integrated Support Services Management System (SAUO)
ISSMS .... Interim Surface-to-Surface Missile System [*Military*] (NVT)
ISSN .... Integrated Special Services Network (SAUO)
ISSN .... Intelligence Specialist, Seaman [*Navy*] (DNAB)
ISSN .... International Standard Serial Number [*Library of Congress*]
ISSN .... International Subcommission on Stratigraphic Nomenclature (SAUS)
ISSO .... Information System Security Officer (SAUS)
ISSO .... Information Systems Security Officer (SAUS)
ISSO .... Information Systems Security Organization (VLIE)
ISSO .... Information Systems Services Office (SAUO)
ISSO .... Information Systems Staff Officer (SAUO)
ISSO .... Institute of Strategic and Stability Operations [*Army*]
ISSO .... International Side-Saddle Organization (EA)
ISSO .... International Small Satellite Organization (NTPA)
ISSOA .... International Symposium on Ship Operation Automation (SAUO)
ISSOE .... Instructional Support System for Occupational Education (SAUS)
ISSOL .... International Society for the Study of the Origin of Life (EA)
ISSOP .... Intra-Fleet Supply Support Operations Program [*Navy*] (DNAB)
ISSOT .... Inactive Ship Supply Overhaul Team
ISSOT .... Intra-Fleet Supply Support Operations Team [*Navy*] (DNAB)
ISSP .... ICSU Solar System Panel (SAUO)
ISSP .... Indian Scientific Satellite Project (SAUS)
ISSP .... Individual Service Strategy Portfolio [*Test*] (TMMY)
ISSP .... Information Sciences and Systems Planning (SAA)
ISSP .... Information Society Service Providers
ISSP .... Information Systems Standardization Program (SAUO)
ISSP .... Information System Strategic Plan (SAUO)
ISSP .... Installation Specified Selection Parameters (VLIE)
ISSP .... Institute for Solid State Physics (SAUO)
ISSP .... Institute of Solid State Physics (SAUS)
ISSP .... Integrated Ship Systems Project (SAUS)
ISSP .... International Society of Sports Psychology (EA)
ISSP .... International Summer School of Physics (SAUS)
ISSP .... Internet Satellite Service Provider (SAUO)
ISSP .... Interservice Supply Source Program (SAUS)
ISSP .... Interservice Supply Support Program [*Military*] (AABC)
ISSP .... Inter-Switch Signalling Protocol (SAUS)
ISSP .... Irish Society for Surveying and Photogrammetry (SAUO)
ISSP .... ISS Program (SAUS)
ISSPA .... International Sport Show Producers Association (EA)
ISSPIC .... International Symposium on Small Particles and Inorganic Clusters (SAUS)
ISSPP .... Integrated System Safety Program Plan [*DoD*]
ISSPR .... International Society for the Study of Personal Relationships (SAUO)
ISSP-S .... Interim Single Source Processor-Signals Intelligence (SAUO)
ISSR .... Independent Secondary Surveillance Radar (SAUS)
ISSR .... Information Storage, Selection, and Retrieval [*Computer science*]
ISSR .... Information System Service Request (DNAB)
ISSR .... Institute for Social Science Research [*Research center*] (RCD)
ISSR .... International Society for the Sociology of Religion [*Italy*] (EAIO)
ISSR .... International Society for the Sociology of Religions (SAUO)
ISSR .... International Society of Root Research (SAUO)
ISSR .... ISS Rail [*Federal Railroad Administration identification code*]
ISSRA .... Individual Social Security Retirement Account
ISSRE .... International Symposium on Software Reliability Engineering (SAUO)
ISSRI .... Institute for Sustainable Rural Development Foundation (SAUO)
ISSRO .... Information Systems Support and Review Office (SAUO)
ISSRO .... International Securities Self Regulatory Organization (SAUO)
ISSRO .... Interservice Supply Support Records Office [*Military*] (AABC)
ISSRP .... Army INFOSEC Resource Program (SAUS)
ISSRT .... Illinois State Society of Radiologic Technologists (SRA)
ISSRT .... International Society of Radiographers and Radiological Technicians (SAUO)
ISSRU .... Information Science and Scientometrics Research Unit [*Hungarian Academy of Sciences Library*] [*Budapest*] [*Information service or system*] (IID)
ISSS .... IBM Speech Server Series
ISSS .... Information Selection and Sampling System (VLIE)
ISSS .... Information Society Standardization System (GART)
ISSS .... Information Systems Support Squadron (SAUO)

ISSS............ Inherent Secondary Shutdown System (PDAA)
ISSS............ Initial Sector Suite System (CTAS)
ISSS............ Installation Service Supply Support
ISSS............ Institute for Space and Security Studies (EA)
ISSS............ Institute for the Study of Sport and Society
ISSS............ Integrated Silicon Systems [*NASDAQ symbol*] (SAG)
ISSS............ Integrated Support Software System (ACAE)
ISSS............ Integrated Support System Sort [*Computer science*] (MHDB)
ISSS............ International Seebeck Study Society (EA)
ISSS............ International Seminars Support Scheme
ISSS............ International Society for Socialist Studies
ISSS............ International Society for Soil Science (SAUO)
ISSS............ International Society for the Study of Symbols
ISSS............ International Society for the Systems Sciences (NTPA)
ISSS............ International Society of Soil Science [*See also AISS*] [*ICSU*] [*Wageningen, Netherlands*] (EAIO)
ISSS............ International Society of Sport Sponsors (EA)
IS-SS.......... International Society of Statistical Science (NTPA)
ISSS............ International Soil Science Society (SAUO)
ISSS............ International Student and Scholar Services (SAUS)
ISSS............ International Symposium on Surface Science (SAUS)
ISSS............ Schoenstatt Institute of Secular Priests (TOCD)
ISSSA......... International Society for/of Strategic Studies/Africa (SAUO)
ISSSA......... International Society for Strategic Studies (Africa) [*Formerly, Africa Society forStrategic Studies*] (EA)
ISSSB......... International Symposium on Separation Science and Biotechnology (SAUS)
ISSSC......... International Society for the Suppression of Savage Customs (SAUO)
ISSSC......... International Summer School on Solidification and Casting (SAUS)
ISSSC......... International Symposium on Solid State Chemistry (SAUS)
ISSSC......... Interservice Supply Support Subcommittee [*Military*] (CINC)
ISSSE......... International Society of Statistical Science in Economics (EA)
ISSSEEM...... International Society for the Study of Subtile Energies and Energy Medicine (SAUS)
ISSSEEM...... International Society for the Study of Subtle Energies and Energy Medicine (NTPA)
ISSS/ISSG.... Information Systems Support Squadron/Group (SAUO)
ISSSM......... Imaging Seeker Surface-to-Surface Missile (PDAA)
ISSSMD....... Imaging Seeker Surface-to-Surface Missile Demonstration (SAUO)
ISSSP......... Information System Security Support Plan (ACAE)
ISSSP......... International Sacerdotal Society Saint Pius X (EA)
ISSSS......... Integrated SONAR System for Surface Ships (SAA)
ISSST......... Integrated Submarine SONAR System Technician
Iss Stud....... Issues and Studies (journ.) (SAUS)
ISST............ ICBM SHF Satellite Terminal (SAUO)
ISST............ ICBM Silo Superhardening Technology (SAUS)
ISST............ Infrared Surveillance of Surface Targets [*Military*] (CAAL)
ISST............ Institute for Space Science and Technology, Inc. [*Research center*] (RCD)
ISST............ Institute of Surface Science and Technology within Physics (SAUS)
ISST............ Integrated Solid State Transistor (TIMI)
ISST............ International Society for the Study of Time (EA)
ISST............ International Society of Skilled Trades (SAUO)
ISST............ Involuntary Second SEA [*Southeast Asia*] Tour [*Air Force*]
ISSTA.......... Israel Student Tourist Association
IS Standards... International Safety Standards (SAUS)
ISSTD......... International Society for the Study of Trophoblastic Disease (SAUO)
ISSTDR....... International Society for STD [*Sexually Transmitted Diseases*] Research (EA)
ISStH.......... Saint John's Hospital, Science Library, Springfield, IL [*Library symbol*] [*Library of Congress*] (LCLS)
ISSTI........... International System of Scientific and Technical Information (SAUS)
ISSTIS......... International Sectoral Scientific and Technical Information System (SAUS)
ISSTO......... Instructions for Superintending Sea Transport Officers (SAUO)
ISSTO......... Integrated Security Systems in a Theater of Operations (SAUO)
ISSU........... Inter-Services Signals Unit [*British military*] (DMA)
ISSUE......... Information System Software Update Environment
Issue Briefing Pap USDA Off Gov Pub Aff... Issue Briefing Paper. United States Department of Agriculture. Office of Governmental and Public Affairs (journ.) (SAUS)
Issues Account Educ... Issues in Accounting Education (journ.) (SAUS)
Issues Bank Regul... Issues in Bank Regulation (journ.) (SAUS)
Issues Compr Pediatr Nurs... Issues in Comprehensive Pediatric Nursing (journ.) (SAUS)
Issues Crim... Issues in Criminology (journ.) (SAUS)
Issues Eng... Issues in Engineering (journ.) (SAUS)
Issues Engng J Prof Activities Proc ASCE... Issues in Engineering. Journal Professional Activities. Proceedings of the American Society of Civil Engineers (journ.) (SAUS)
Issues Health Care Women... Issues in Health Care of Women (journ.) (SAUS)
Issues Law Med... Issues in Law and Medicine (journ.) (SAUS)
Issues Ment Health Nurs... Issues in Mental Health Nursing (journ.) (SAUS)
Issues Policy Summ... Issues and Policy Summaries (journ.) (SAUS)
Issues Rev Teratol... Issues and Reviews in Teratology (journ.) (SAUS)
Issues Sci Technol... Issues in Science and Technology (journ.) (SAUS)
Issuing Age... Issuing Agency (NAKS)
ISSUP......... Institute for Strategic Studies, University of Pretoria (SAUO)
ISSVD......... International Society for the Study of Vulvar Disease (DAVI)
ISSX........... Interchange Specialty Service [*Federal Railroad Administration identification code*]
ISSX........... International Society for the Study of Xenobiotics
ISSX........... ISS Group [*NASDAQ symbol*] (SG)
IST............. Division of Information Science and Technology (SAUS)
IST............. Imagery Support Terminal (SAUO)
IST............. Immerse System Technology (SAUO)
IST............. Immunosuppressive Therapy [*Medicine*] (MELL)
IST............. Impact Surface Treatment (SAUS)
IST............. Implementation Systems Test (SAUO)
IST............. Improved Surface Treatment (SAUS)
IST............. Improved System Technology (NITA)
IST............. Inappropriate Sinus Tachycardia [*Medicine*] (EDAA)
IST............. Incident Support Team (SAUO)
IST............. Incident Tracking System (SAUS)
IST............. Incompatible Simultaneous Transfer (IAA)
IST............. Incredibly Small Transistor (IAA)
IST............. Incremental System Test
IST............. Indexing Slide Table
IST............. Indiana State Teachers College (SAUO)
IST............. Indian Standard Time (IAA)
IST............. Indian Summer Time (SAUO)
IST............. Individualized Study by Telecommunications [*Alaska*] (EDAC)
IST............. Individual Sales Transaction
IST............. Indonesian Speaking Test [*Center for Applied Linguistics*] (TES)
IST............. Industrielle-Services Techniques Inc. [*Industrial Life-Technical Services Inc.*] [*Information service or system*] (IID)
IST............. Industry (SAUS)
IST............. Industry, Science and Technology (SAUS)
IST............. Information Science and Technology (BUR)
IST............. Information Sciences Technology (SAUO)
IST............. Information Society Technologies (or Technology) (SAUO)
IST............. Information Society Technology (TELE)
IST............. Information Systems and Technology (SAUS)
IST............. Initial Sea Training (SAUS)
IST............. Initial Service Test (AABC)
IST............. Initial Support Team [*Military*] (AFM)
IST............. Initial System Test (VLIE)
IST............. Innovative Science and Technology [*DoD*]
IST............. Input Stack Tape (IAA)
IST............. In-Service Testing (SAUO)
IST............. In-Service Training (SAUO)
IST............. Inside Trim (DAC)
IST............. In Situ Transcription (DB)
IST............. In Situ Treatment (COE)
IST............. Inspection Status Tag (ACAE)
IST............. Instantaneous Spatial Transference
IST............. Institute for Science and Technology (SAUO)
IST............. Institute for Simulation and Training [*University of Central Florida*] [*Research center*] (RCD)
IST............. Institute for the Study of Terrorism (SAUS)
IST............. Institute of Science and Technology [*University of Michigan*] [*Research center*] (RCD)
IST............. Institute of Science Technology (SAUO)
IST............. Institute on Strategic Trade (SAUO)
IST............. Institutional Skill Training (OICC)
IST............. Instraspinal Tumor [*Medicine*] (EDAA)
IST............. Instruction-Set Translator [*IBM Corp.*]
IST............. Instrumentation Support Team (KSC)
IST............. Instrumented Sensor Technologies
IST............. Instrument Support Terminal (EOSA)
IST............. Insulin Sensitivity Test
IST............. Insulin Shock Therapy [*Psychiatry*]
IST............. Integral Simulation Test [*Nuclear energy*] (NRCH)
IST............. Integrated Services Telephone (SAUS)
IST............. Integrated Status Tag (ACAE)
IST............. Integrated Switching and Transmission [*Telecommunications*] (TEL)
IST............. Integrated Switching Technique (SAUS)
IST............. Integrated System (NITA)
IST............. Integrated Systems Technology (IAA)
IST............. Integrated Systems Test [*NASA*] (KSC)
IST............. Integrated System Team (SAUS)
IST............. Integrated System Trainer (MCD)
IST............. Integrated System Transformer (IEEE)
IST............. Integrated Training System (SAUO)
IST............. Intelligence Structure Test (SAUO)
IST............. Intelligent Sports Technology Ltd.
IST............. Interagency Testing Committee Tracking System (SAUO)
IST............. International Institute for Safety in Transportation [*Later, IIST*] (EA)
IST............. International Skelton Tables (SAUO)
IST............. International Society of Toxicology (SAUS)
IST............. International Society on Toxicology (EA)
IST............. International Software Team (SAUO)
IST............. International Standard [*Vancouver Stock Exchange symbol*]
IST............. International Standard Thread (MSA)
IST............. International Steam Table (SAUS)
IST............. International Telecommunications Services Inc. (SAUO)
IST............. International Telecommunications Society (SAUO)
IST............. Interrupt Service Task [*Computer science*] (ELAL)
IST............. Interstation Transmission (KSC)
IST............. Interstellar Travel (AAG)
IST............. Inter Switch Trunk (SAUO)
IST............. Interswitch Trunk (SAUS)
IST............. Intraspecific Antigenic Typing (PDAA)
IST............. Inversion Stress Test [*Medicine*] (MELL)
IST............. Invite (SAUS)
IST............. Invite, Show & Test (SAUS)
IST............. Iron, Steel and Heavy Transporters Association, Cleveland OH [*STAC*]
IST............. Isometric Systolic Tension (SAUS)
IST............. Isothermal Storage Test [*For hazardous chemicals*]

IST.............. ISPAT Intl'A' [*NYSE symbol*] (SG)
IST.............. Istanbul [*Turkey*] [*Airport symbol*] (OAG)
IST.............. Istanbul [*Turkey*] [*Seismograph station code, US Geological Survey*] (SEIS)
IST.............. Istanbul Airlines [*Turkey*] [*ICAO designator*] (FAAC)
IST.............. Missouri Airlines, Inc. (SAUO)
IST.............. Morton Public Library, Morton, IL [*OCLC symbol*] (OCLC)
ISt.............. Stickney-Forest View Library District, Stickney, IL [*Library symbol*] [*Library of Congress*] (LCLS)
ISTA.............. Illinois School Transportation Association (SRA)
ISTA.............. Illinois Seed Trade Association (SRA)
IST-A.............. Incident Support Team-Advance Element (SAUO)
ISTA.............. Independent Secretarial Training Association [*British*]
ISTA.............. Independent Software Testing Association (SAUO)
ISTA.............. Indiana State Teachers Association (SAUO)
ISTA.............. Indian Scientific Translators Association (SAUO)
ISTA.............. Industrial Science and Technology Agency (SAUO)
ISTA.............. Information Science, Technologies and Activities (SAUS)
ISTA.............. Intelligence, Surveillance, and Target Acquisition [*Military*]
ISTA.............. International Safe Transit Association (NTPA)
ISTA.............. International Schools Theatre Association (SAUO)
ISTA.............. International Seed Testing Association [*Switzerland*]
ISTA.............. International Shipping and Transport Agencies N.V. (SAUO)
ISTA.............. International Sightseeing and Tours Association [*Defunct*] (EA)
ISTA.............. International Society for Technology Assessment (CIST)
ISTA.............. International Special Tooling Association [*Frankfurt, Federal Republic of Germany*] (EA)
ISTA.............. International Steel Trades Association (SAUO)
ISTA.............. Intertank Structural Test Assembly [*NASA*] (NASA)
ISTAB.............. Information Systems Technical Advisory Board (SAUS)
ISTAC.............. Interim Scientific and Technical Advisory Committee (SAUS)
ISTAC.............. International Science and Technology Advisory Committee [*Australia*]
ISTAC.............. International Skilled Trades Advisory Committee [*UAW*]
I Staff.............. Intelligence Staff (SAUO)
ISTAG.............. IST Advisory Group (SAUO)
ISTAHC.............. International Society of Technology Assessment in Health Care (ADWA)
ISTAIA.............. Institute for the Study of Traditional American Indian Arts (EA)
Istanbul Contrib Clin Sci... Istanbul Contribution to Clinical Science (journ.) (SAUS)
Istanbul Med Fac Med Bull Istanbul Univ... Istanbul Medical Faculty Medical Bulletin. Istanbul University (journ.) (SAUS)
Istanbul Univ Med Bull... Istanbul University. Medical Bulletin (journ.) (SAUS)
Istanbul Univ Med Fac Med Bull... Istanbul University. Medical Faculty. Medical Bulletin (journ.) (SAUS)
Istanbul Univ Rev Geog Inst Internat Ed... Istanbul University. Review of the Geographical Institute. International Edition (journ.) (SAUS)
ISTAP.............. Information Systems Technology Application Program (SAUO)
ISTAP.............. International Space Technology Assessment Program (SAUO)
ISTAR.............. Image Storage Translation and Reproduction
ISTAR.............. Information Science Technology Assessment for Research [*Army*]
ISTAR.............. Information Storage Translation and Reproduction (SAUS)
ISTAR.............. Institute for Stuttering Treatment and Research (SAUO)
ISTARS.............. Integrated System Target Acquisition Reconnaissance Surveillance (SAUO)
ISTARTLE.... Integrated Surveillance Target Acquisition Radar for Tank (SAUS)
ISTAT.............. International Society of Transport Aircraft Traders (or Trading) (SAUS)
ISTAT.............. International Society of Transport Aircraft Trading (EA)
I-STAT.............. I-STAT Corp. [*Associated Press*] (SAG)
Istau.............. Staunton Public Library (SAUS)
IStau.............. Staunton Public Library, Staunton, IL [*Library symbol*] [*Library of Congress*] (LCLS)
IStauMCD.... Macoupin Community District 6, Staunton, IL [*Library symbol*] [*Library of Congress*] (LCLS)
ISTB.............. Integrated Subsystem Test Bed (NASA)
ISTB.............. International Student Travel Bureau (SAUO)
ISTB.............. Interstate Tariff Bureau, Inc.
ISTB.............. Introductory Science Text-Books [*A publication*]
IstBnbul Unir Tip Fak Mecm... Istanbul Universitesi Tip Fakultesi Mecmuas (journ.) (SAUS)
ISTC.............. Incunable Short Title Catalogue [*British Library*] [*Information service or system*] (IID)
ISTC.............. Incunabula Short Title Catalogue (SAUO)
ISTC.............. Indiana State Teachers College (SAUO)
ISTC.............. Industry, Science, and Technology Canada [*Government agency*]
ISTC.............. Inland Society of Tax Consultants (SAUO)
ISTC.............. Institute for Scientific and Technological Cooperation (SAUO)
ISTC.............. Institute of Science and Technical Communicators (SAUS)
ISTC.............. Institute of Scientific and Technical Communication (SAUS)
ISTC.............. Institute of Scientific and Technical Communicators [*British*]
ISTC.............. Institute of Scientific and Technical Communicators Ltd. (SAUO)
ISTC.............. Instructivision, Inc. (SAUO)
ISTC.............. Integrated System Test Complex (SAUS)
ISTC.............. Interdepartmental Screw Thread Committee [*Departments of Commerce and Defense*]
ISTC.............. International Science & Technology Center
ISTC.............. International Shade Tree Conference [*Later, ISA*] (EA)
ISTC.............. International Society for Training and Culture
ISTC.............. International Spa and Tub Council [*Defunct*] (EA)
ISTC.............. International Steam Tables Conference (SAUO)
ISTC.............. International Stress and Tension Control Association (EA)
ISTC.............. International Students Identity Card (SAUO)
ISTC.............. International Student Travel Confederation [*Switzerland*] (EAIO)
ISTC.............. International Student Travel Conference (SAUO)
ISTC.............. International Switching and Testing Center [*Communications*]
ISTC.............. Iowa State Teachers College (SAUO)
ISTC.............. Iron and Steel Trades Confederation [*British*]
IStc.............. Saint Charles Public Library District, Saint Charles, IL [*Library symbol*] [*Library of Congress*] (LCLS)
ISTCL.............. International Scientific and Technical Committee and/on Laundering (SAUO)
ISTCL.............. International Scientific and Technical Committee on Laudering (SAUS)
ISTD.............. Imperial Society of Teachers of Dancing
ISTD.............. Institute for the Scientific Treatment of Delinquency (SAUO)
ISTD.............. Institute for the Study and Treatment of Delinquency [*British*]
IStd.............. Insulin/International Standard [*Medicine*] (EDAA)
ISTD.............. International Society of Tropical Dermatology [*Later, International Society of Dermatology: Tropical, Geographic, and Ecologic - ISD*]
ISTD.............. Inter-Service Topographical Department [*British*]
ISTDA.............. Institutional and Service Textile Distributors Association (EA)
ISTDF.............. Istec-Industries Technologies [*NASDAQ symbol*] (SAG)
ISTE.............. Information Scientifique (SAUS)
ISTE.............. International Society for Technology in Education (EAIO)
ISTE.............. International Society for Tropical Ecology (EA)
ISTE.............. Istec Industries and Technologies Ltd. (SAUO)
ISte.............. Saint Elmo Public Library, St. Elmo, IL [*Library symbol*] [*Library of Congress*] (LCLS)
ISTEA.............. Initial Screening Training Effectiveness Analysis
ISTEA.............. Intermodal Surface Transportation Efficiency Act [*1990*]
ISTEA.............. Iron and Steel Trades Employers' Association [*British*] (BI)
ISTEC.............. International Superconductivity Technology Center [*Japan*]
ISTECH.............. Information Systems Technology (SAUO)
Istecln.............. Istec-Industries Technologies [*Associated Press*] (SAG)
ISTEF.............. Istec Industry & Technology Ltd. [*NASDAQ symbol*] (COMM)
ISTEH.............. International Society of Theoretical and Experimental Hypnosis (SAUO)
ISTEI.............. Institute for Scientific (SAUS)
ISTEI.............. Institute for Scientific, Technical and Economic Information (SAUS)
ISTEM.............. Inter-Seminary Theological Education for Ministry (SAUS)
ISTEP.............. Indiana Statewide Testing for Educational Progress
ISter.............. Sterling Public Library, Sterling IL [*Library symbol*] [*Library of Congress*] (LCLS)
ISTERH.............. International Society for/of Trace Element Research in Humans (SAUO)
ISTERH.............. International Society of Trace Element Research in Humans (SAUS)
ISteSD.............. Saint Elmo Community Unit, School District 202, Saint Elmo, IL [*Library symbol*] [*Library of Congress*] (LCLS)
ISTES TEMP... Istesso Tempo [*Same Time*] [*Music*] (ROG)
ISTESU.............. International Secretariat for Teaching Educational Sciences in Universities (SAUO)
ISTF.............. Integrated Services and Test Facility (SAUO)
ISTF.............. Integrated Servicing and Test Facilities [*Canada*]
ISTF.............. Integrated System Test Flow (NASA)
ISTF.............. International Social Travel Federation [*See also FITS*] [*Brussels, Belgium*] (EAIO)
ISTF.............. International Society for/of Tropical Foresters (SAUO)
ISTF.............. International Society of Tropical Foresters [*See also SIIFT*] (EA)
ISTFA.............. International Society for Testing and Failure Analysis (MCD)
ISTFA.............. International Symposium for Testing and Failure Analysis [*Annual electronics symposium*] (NITA)
Ist Fil Zhur AN Armian... Istoriko-Filologiceskij Zhurnal. Akademia Nauk Armianskoi (journ.) (SAUS)
ISTG.............. Information Systems and Technology Group (SAUO)
ISTH.............. International Society on Thrombosis and Hemostasis (EA)
isth.............. Isthmus (SHCU)
ISTH.............. Isthmus [*Board on Geographic Names*]
ISTHM.............. Isthmian (ROG)
Isthm.............. Isthmian Odes [*of Pindar*] [*Classical studies*] (OCD)
ISTI.............. Institute of Scientific and Technical Information (SAUS)
ISTI.............. International Sciences and Technology Institute (SAUO)
ISTI.............. International Spa and Tub Institute (EA)
ISTI.............. Iowa State Technical Institute (SAUO)
ISTIC.............. Institute of Scientific and Technical Information of China [*INFOTERM*] [*Beijing*]
ISTIC.............. Institute of Scientific and Technical Information of/on China (SAUS)
ISTIG.............. Intercooled Steam-Injected Gas Turbine
ISTIM.............. Interchange of Scientific and Technical Information in Machine Language [*Office of Science and Technology*]
ISTIP.............. Information Systems Technical Integration Panel (SSD)
ISTIS.............. Institute of Scientific and Technical Information of Shanghai (SAUS)
ISTIS.............. International Science and Technology Information Service (SAUS)
ISTIS.............. International Scientific and Technical Information System (EAIO)
ISTJ.............. Introversion Sensing Thinking Judging (ADWA)
IST/J.............. Journal of the Institute of Science and Technology (journ.) (SAUS)
IStjo.............. Saint Joseph Township Library (Swearingen Memorial Library), St. Joseph, IL [*Library symbol*] [*Library of Congress*] (LCLS)
IStJSD.............. Tiraid Community Unit, School District 2, St. Jacob, IL [*Library symbol*] [*Library of Congress*] (LCLS)
ISTM.............. Incorporated Society of Trained Masseurs (SAUO)
ISTM.............. Institute of Strata Title Management [*Australia*]
ISTM.............. International Society for Testing Materials
ISTM.............. International Society of Travel Medicine (SAUO)
ISTM.............. Irish Society of Travel Medicine (SAUO)
ISTM.............. It Seems to Me (VLIE)
ISTMC.............. Instrumentation Section Test and Monitor Console (SAA)
ISTMH.............. Indefinite Substitute Temporary Mail Handler [*US Postal Service employee classification*]
IstMobl.............. Istituto Mobilaire Italiano [*Associated Press*] (SAG)

ISTN............ Integrated Switching and Transmission Network [*Telecommunications*] (TEL)
ISTN............ Interstate National Dealer Services, Inc. [*NASDAQ symbol*] (SAG)
ISTN............ Interstate Natl Dealer Svcs [*NASDAQ symbol*] (TTSB)
ISTNW......... Interstate Natl Dealer Wrrt [*NASDAQ symbol*] (TTSB)
ISTO............ Industry Standards and Technology Organization (SAUO)
ISTO............ Information Science and Technology Office [*Arlington, VA*] [*DoD*] (TSSD)
ISTO............ International Semiconductor Trade Operations (TIMI)
ISTO............ Italian State Tourist Office (SAUO)
ISTP............ IGOSS Sub-surface Thermal Structure Programme (SAUS)
ISTP............ Index of Scientific and Technical Publications (TELE)
ISTP............ Index to Scientific & Technical Proceedings (SAUO)
ISTP............ Index to Technical Proceedings (SAUS)
ISTP............ Information Systems Tasking Plan (SAUO)
ISTP............ Information System Theory Project (IAA)
ISTP............ Integrated Systems Test Procedure (SAUS)
ISTP............ Interagency Solar Terrestrial Programme [*European Space Agency*]
ISTP............ International Society of Tropical Pediatrics [*Philippines*] (EAIO)
ISTP............ International Solar Terrestrial Physics [*Proposed NASA mission*]
ISTP............ International Solar-Terrestrial Physics (SAUO)
ISTP............ International Solar Terrestrial Physics Program (SAUS)
ISTP............ International Solar-Terrestrial Programme (SAUS)
ISTP............ International Solar Terrestrial Project (SAUO)
ISTP............ International Stretch Products, Inc. (SAUO)
ISTP............ Isotope
ISTP & B..... Index to Scientific and Technical Proceedings and Books [*Institute for Scientific Information*] [*Database*]
ISTP/STEP... International Solar-Terrestrial Physics/Solar-Terrestial Energy Programme (SAUO)
ISTPW......... Impact Signature Training Practice Warhead [*Army*]
ISTR............ Incstar Corp. [*NASDAQ symbol*] (TTSB)
ISTR............ Indexed Sequential Table Retrieval
ISTR............ Institute for Science Training and Research (HGEN)
ISTR............ International Seed Trade Rules (SAUO)
ISTR............ International Society for Third-Sector Research (NFD)
ISTR............ International Standard Resources Ltd. (SAUO)
ISTR............ I Seem to Recall (ADWA)
IStr............. Streator Public Library, Streator, IL [*Library symbol*] [*Library of Congress*] (LCLS)
ISTRA.......... Interplanetary Space Travel Research Association
ISTRACK...... Indian Space Tracking Network (SAUS)
ISTRACON... Interstation Supersonic Trac Conference (SAUS)
ISTRACON... Interstation Supersonic Track Conferences (MCD)
ISTRC.......... International Society for/of Tropical Root Crops (SAUO)
ISTRC.......... International Society of Tropical Root Crops (SAUS)
IStrESD........ Eagle Elementary Consolidated School District 43, Streator, IL [*Library symbol*] [*Library of Congress*] (LCLS)
IStrHSD........ Streator Township High School District 40, Streator, IL [*Library symbol*] [*Library of Congress*] (LCLS)
ISTRO.......... International Soil Tillage Research Organization [*Netherlands*] (EAIO)
IStrOSD........ Otter Creek Elementary School District 56, Streator, IL [*Library symbol*] [*Library of Congress*] (LCLS)
ISTRS.......... Index of Submarine Technical Repair Standards [*Military*] (DNAB)
IStrSD.......... Streator Elementary School District 45, Streator, IL [*Library symbol*] [*Library of Congress*] (LCLS)
IStrSMH....... Saint Mary's Hospital, Henegen Medical Library, Streator, IL [*Library symbol*] [*Library of Congress*] (LCLS)
I Struct E..... Institute of Structural Engineers (SAUS)
IStructE........ Institution of Structural Engineers (COBU)
ISTRUCTE.... Institution of Structural Engineers [*British*]
ISTS............ Infrared Search & Track System (SAUS)
ISTS............ Institute for Space and Terrestrial Science [*Research center*] [*Canada*] (RCD)
ISTS............ International Shock Tube Symposium (SAUS)
ISTS............ International Simultaneous Translation Service
ISTS............ International Society for Twin Studies [*Rome, Italy*] (EA)
ISTS............ International Symposium on Space Technology and Science (MCD)
ISTS............ Intersite Transmission Subsystem [*Ground Communications Facility, NASA*]
ISTS............ Intradermal Skin Test Score [*Immunology*]
ISTSE.......... Integral Square Time Square Error (SAUS)
ISTSP.......... Independent Schools Talent Search Program [*Later, A Better Chance*] (EA)
ISTSR.......... International Society for Third-Sector Research (EA)
ISTSS.......... International Society for Traumatic Stress Studies (NTPA)
ISTT............ In-Service Training of Teachers [*Scottish National Committee*]
ISTT............ International Society for Trenchless Technology (EAIO)
ISTT............ Intersegmental Travel Time [*Zoology*]
ISTTE.......... International Society of Travel and Tourism Educators (TVEL)
ISTU............ Isometric Strength Testing Unit [*Medicine*] (DMAA)
IsTU............ Tel Aviv University, Tel Aviv, Israel [*Library symbol*] [*Library of Congress*] (LCLS)
ISTV............ Insight Entertainment Corp. [*NASDAQ symbol*] (SAG)
ISTVC.......... Inter-Service Technical Valve Committee (SAUO)
ISTVS.......... International Society for Terrain-Vehicle Systems (EA)
IStw............ Popular Creek Public Library District, Streamwood, IL [*Library symbol*] [*Library of Congress*] (LCLS)
ISU.............. Idaho State University (SAUO)
ISU.............. Ignition Safety Unit (SAUS)
ISU.............. In-Arm Suspension Unit [*Tank Technology*]
ISU.............. Independent Signal Unit [*Telecommunications*] (TEL)
ISU.............. Indiana State University, Terre Haute, IN [*OCLC symbol*] (OCLC)
ISU.............. Industry Solution Unit (SAUO)
ISU.............. Inertial Sensing Unit
ISU.............. Inertial Sensor Unit (SAUS)
ISU.............. Information Services and Use (journ.) (SAUS)
ISU.............. Information Service Unit [*International Potato Center*] [*Information service or system*] (IID)
ISU.............. Information Systems Unit (SAUS)
ISU.............. Initial Signal Unit [*Telecommunications*] (TEL)
ISU.............. Instruction Storage Unit
ISU.............. Instructor Scoring Unit (ACAE)
ISU.............. Instrument Signalling Unit (SAUS)
ISU.............. Instrument Switching Unit (SAUS)
ISU.............. Integrated Service Unit (GART)
ISU.............. Integrated Sight Unit [*Weaponry*] (INF)
ISU.............. Interface Sharing Unit
ISU.............. Interface Surveillance Unit (SAA)
ISU.............. Interface Switching Unit (BUR)
ISU.............. Interference Suppression Unit (IAA)
ISU.............. Intermediate Selection Unit (SAUS)
ISU.............. Intermediate Storage Unit (SAUS)
ISU.............. Internacia Somera Universitato (SAUO)
ISU.............. Internal Airlift/Helicopter Slingable Container Unit [*MTMC*] (TAG)
ISU.............. Internal Stability Unit (SAFN)
ISU.............. International Salvage Union (PDAA)
ISU.............. International Scientific Union
ISU.............. International Seaman's Union
ISU.............. International Seamens Union (SAUS)
ISU.............. International Shooting Union
ISU.............. International Sigma Security, Inc. [*Vancouver Stock Exchange symbol*]
ISU.............. International Skating Union [*See also UIP*] [*Davos-Platz, Switzerland*] (EAIO)
ISU.............. International Society of Urology [*See also SIU*] [*Lille, France*] (EAIO)
ISU.............. International Space University [*Strasbourg, France*]
ISU.............. International Stereoscopic Union (PDAA)
ISU.............. International Students Union (SAUO)
ISU.............. International System of Units
ISU.............. Iowa Southern Utilities [*Southern Industrial Railroad, Inc.*] [*AAR code*]
ISU.............. Iowa State University [*Ames*]
ISU.............. Italian Service Unit [*Italian prisoners of war who became volunteers in the Allied war effort*]
ISU.............. Southern Iowa Railway (SAUS)
ISu.............. Summit-Argo Public Library, Summit, IL [*Library symbol*] [*Library of Congress*] (LCLS)
ISUA........... Iowa State University at Ankeny (SAUO)
ISUAIC........ Intelligence School, United States Army Intelligence Center (SAUO)
I-Sub.......... Inhibitor Substance [*Medicine*] (DMAA)
ISU/CCL...... Iowa State University / Cyclone Computer Laboratory (PDAA)
ISU C-FAR... Illinois State University internal C-FAR funds (SAUO)
ISUDO......... International Society on Ultrasonic Diagnostics in Ophthalmology (SAUO)
ISUDO......... International Symposium on Ultrasonic Diagnostics in Ophthalmology [*Later, ISO U*] (EA)
ISUDS......... Iterative Scheme Using a Direct Solution
ISU-ERI....... Iowa State University - Engineering Research Institute (PDAA)
ISUH........... Institute for the Study of Universal History through Arts and Artifacts [*Defunct*] (EA)
ISUM........... Intelligence Summary
ISUM........... Southern Illinois University, School of Medicine, Springfield, IL [*Library symbol*] [*Library of Congress*] (LCLS)
ISumSD....... Red Hill Community Unit, School District 10, Sumner, IL [*Library symbol*] [*Library of Congress*] (LCLS)
ISUP........... Integrated Services User Part
ISUP........... Iowa State University Press (DGA)
ISUP........... ISDN [*Integrated Services Digital Network*] User Part [*Telecommunications*]
ISU/PS........ Politics & Society. Gerald A. Dorfman, publisher. Iowa State Univ. Ames (SAUS)
ISU/PS........ Politics & Society. Iowa State University. Ames (SAUO)
ISUPTTS...... International Sports Union of Post, Telephone, and Telecommunications Service (EA)
ISURL.......... Indiana State University Remote Sensing Laboratory (SAUS)
ISURSL........ Indiana State University Remote Sensing Laboratory [*Research center*] (RCD)
ISUS........... Information Services and User Support (SAUO)
ISUS........... Integrated Sensor Underwater System (SAUS)
ISUS........... International Society for Utilitarian Studies [*British*] (EAIO)
ISUSAIC...... Intelligence School, United States Army Intelligence Center
ISUSE......... International Secretariat for the University Study of Education
ISUSS......... Integrated Surface and Upper-air Sounding System (SAUS)
ISUST......... Iowa State University of Science and Technology (SAUO)
ISUZ........... Iowa Southern Utilities [*Federal Railroad Administration identification code*]
ISV............. Independent Software Vendor [*Computer science*]
ISV............. Independent Solution Vendor (SAUO)
ISV............. Information Service Vendor (SAUO)
ISV............. Inlet Swirl Vane (SAUS)
ISV............. Input Signal Voltage
ISV............. InSite Vision [*AMEX symbol*] (SG)
ISV............. In Situ Vitrification [*Radioactive waste cleanup*]
ISV............. Instantaneous Speed Variation [*Tape recorders*]
ISV............. Institute for the Study of Violence (SAUO)
ISV............. Intelligence Secure Voice (SAUO)
ISV............. Intensified Silicon Vidicon (SAUS)
ISV............. Internal Security Vehicle (SAUS)
ISV............. Internal Service Value (SAUS)

ISV International Scientific Vocabulary
ISV International Society for Vaccines [*Gaithersburg, MD*]
ISV International Society of Videographers (EA)
ISV International Software Vision (SAUO)
ISV Interorbital Space Vehicle
ISV Interval Service Value (BUR)
ISV Iron-Solution Value (PDAA)
ISV Irradiated Silicon Vidicon
ISV Islena de Inversiones SA [*Honduras*] [*ICAO designator*] (FAAC)
ISV Iso Ventures, Inc. [*Vancouver Stock Exchange symbol*]
ISV Neponset Public Library, Neponset, IL [*OCLC symbol*] (OCLC)
ISv Sauk Village Library District, Sauk Village, IL [*Library symbol*] [*Library of Congress*] (LCLS)
ISVA Incorporated Society of Valuers and Auctioneers (EAIO)
ISVA International Satellite Verification Agency
ISVA International Society for Vibroacoustics (EAIO)
ISVAS Interactive System for Visual Analysis (SAUS)
ISVBM International Society of Violin and Bow Makers [*Basel, Switzerland*] (EAIO)
ISVC Incoming Switched Virtual Circuit (SAUS)
ISVCS Improved Secure Voice Conferencing System [*Military*] (MCD)
ISVD Information System for Vocational Decisions (SAUS)
ISVD Information System for Vocational Decisions Program
ISVE Istituto di Studi per lo Sviluppo Economico [*Institute for the Study of Economic Development*] [*Italy*]
ISVESTA Individual Survival Vest for Aircrew [*Army*] (RDA)
ISVL Vachel Lindsay Association, Springfield, IL [*Library symbol*] [*Library of Congress*] (LCLS)
ISVMA Illinois State Veterinary Medical Association (GVA)
ISVN Interim Secure Voice Network (SAUO)
ISVO Interdisciplinary Research and Training Center for Development Cooperation (SAUO)
ISVP Interim Secure Voice Project (SAUS)
ISVP International Society for Vehicle Preservation (EA)
ISVP International Society of Veterinary Perinatology (GVA)
ISVR Institute of Sound and Vibration Research [*Southampton University, England*]
ISVR Intel Smart Video Recorder (SAUS)
ISVR3 Intel Smart Video Recorder III
ISVs Independent Software Vendors (SAUO)
ISVS In Situ Vapor Sampling (ABAC)
ISVS In Situ Vapro Stripping [*Environmental science*]
ISVS Integrated Secure Voice System
ISVS International Secretariat for Volunteer Service [*Defunct*]
ISVS International Society for Vegetation Science (SAUO)
ISVS International Switched Voice Service (SAUO)
ISVS International Switched-Voice Services (AGLO)
ISVSK Internationaler Staendiger Verband fuer Schiffahrt-Kongresse [*Permanent International Association of Navigation Congresses*]
ISVT Integrated Secure Voice Terminal (SAUS)
ISVTNA International Symposium on Vacuum Technology and Nuclear Applications (SAUS)
ISV Words International Scientific Vocabulary Words (SAUS)
ISW Ice Shelf Water [*Oceanography*]
ISW Ice Station Weddell (SAUO)
ISW Indian Standard Wagon Works [*Indian Railway*] [*Satna*] (TIR)
ISW Industrial Solid Waste (SAUS)
ISW Information Services of Warwick [*Rhode Island*] [*Information retrieval*] (IID)
ISW Information Systems Wing (SAUO)
ISW Initial Status Word (IAA)
ISW Institute for Solid Wastes
ISW Institute of Social Welfare [*British*] (BI)
ISW Institute of Solid Waste (SAUO)
ISW Institute of Solid Wastes (SAUS)
ISW Integrated Sachs-Wolfe [*Effect in cosmic microwave background*]
ISW Integrated Software
ISW Integrated Strike Warfare (SAUS)
ISW Intermediate Scale Warfare
ISW Internal Status Word (IAA)
ISW Interrupt Status Word (SAUS)
ISW Interstitial Water [*Physiology*]
ISW Ion Switch (IAA)
ISW Isolated Constant Wattage (SAUS)
ISW Serib Wings [*Italy*] [*ICAO designator*] (FAAC)
ISW Toulon Public Library, Toulon, IL [*OCLC symbol*] (OCLC)
ISW Wisconsin Rapids [*Wisconsin*] [*Airport symbol*] (OAG)
ISW Wisconsin Rapids, WI [*Location identifier*] [*FAA*] (FAAL)
ISWA Association Internationale pour les Residus Solides et le Nettoiement des Vil les [*International Solid Wastes and Public Cleansing Association*] [*INTAPUC and IRGRD*] [*Formed by a merger of*] [*Denmark*] (EAIO)
ISWA Insect Screening Weavers Association (EA)
ISWA Insect Screening Weavers Institute (SAUS)
ISWA International Science Writers Association
ISWA International Ski Writers Association [*Riehen, Switzerland*] (EA)
ISWA International Solid Waste and Public Cleansing Association (SAUO)
ISWA International Solid Wastes and Public Cleaning Association (SAUO)
ISWAP International Society of Women Airline Pilots (EA)
ISWBBHA Iron, Steel, and Wood Barge Builders' and Helpers' Association [*A union*] [*British*]
ISWC Industrial Social Welfare Center [*Columbia University*] [*Research center*] (RCD)
ISWC International Secretariat of World Citizens (SAUO)
ISWC International Short Wave Club (SAUO)
ISWC International Society for the Welfare of Cripples [*Later, Rehabilitation International*]
ISWC International Standard Work Code
ISWG Imperial Standard Wire Gauge
ISWG Independent Schools Working Group (AIE)
ISWG Information Systems Working Group (SAUO)
ISWG Integrated Support Working Group (SDI)
ISWG Interoperability Sub-Working Group (SAUO)
ISWG Item Selection Working Group [*NATO*] (NATG)
ISWI Incisional Surgical Wound Infection [*Medicine*] (DMAA)
ISWI International Sports Wagering, Inc. [*NASDAQ symbol*] (SAG)
ISWIM If You See What I Mean (PDAA)
ISWL International Short Wave League (SAUO)
ISWL Isolated Single Wheel Load (AIA)
ISWM Inhibit Switch Word Mark (SAUS)
ISWM Institute of Solid Waste Management [*British*] (DCTA)
ISWM International Society of Weighing and Measurement (EA)
ISWM International Society of Weigthing and Measurement (SAUO)
ISWNE International Society of Weekly Newspaper Editors (EA)
ISWO International Sponsorship of War Orphans (SAUO)
ISWRN International Spring Wheat Rust Nursery (SAUO)
ISWRRI Iowa State Water Resources Research Institute [*Iowa State University*] [*Department of the Interior*] [*Research center*] (RCD)
ISWS Illinois State Water Survey [*Illinois Department of Energy and Natural Resources*] [*Research center*] (RCD)
ISWS Bull Ill Water Surv ISWS Bulletin. Illinois Water Survey (journ.) (SAUS)
ISWSC International Society of Worldwide Stamp Collectors [*Formerly, Worldwide Collectors' Club - WCC*]
ISWT International Society of Wine Tasters [*Defunct*] (EA)
ISWU Iron and Steel Workers' Union [*India*]
ISWWG International Special Weapon Working Group (SAUO)
ISWYM I See What You Mean (ADWA)
ISX Impurity Study Experiment [*Oak Ridge National Laboratory*]
ISX Information Switching Exchange (IAA)
ISX Inherently Self-X (SAUS)
ISX Integrated Switching Exchange (SAUS)
ISX Wyoming Public Library, Wyoming, IL [*OCLC symbol*] (OCLC)
ISY Black Hawk College, East Campus, Gustav E. Lundberg Learning Center, Kewanee, I L [*OCLC symbol*] (OCLC)
ISY City Air Ltd. [*British*] [*ICAO designator*] (FAAC)
ISY Instrument Systems Corp. [*NYSE symbol*] (SAG)
ISY International Space Year [*1992*]
ISY Intrasynovial [*Medicine*]
ISy Sycamore Public Library, Sycamore, IL [*Library symbol*] [*Library of Congress*] (LCLS)
IsYAEC Israel Atomic Energy Commission, Soreq Nuclear Research Centre, Yavne (SAUS)
IsYAEC Israel Atomic Energy Commission, Soreq Nuclear Research Centre, Yavne, Israel [*Library symbol*] [*Library of Congress*] (LCLS)
ISYB Inhibit Switch Y Bit (SAUS)
ISYH Instrument Systems Corp. (SAUO)
ISYN Inductosyn
I-SYNC Intelligent Synchronous [*General Data-Comm, Inc.*] [*Communications term*] (DCT)
ISYS Integral Sys MD [*NASDAQ symbol*] (TTSB)
ISYS Integral Systems, Inc. [*NASDAQ symbol*] (SAG)
ISYSCON Integrated System Control [*Military*]
ISYSCON Integrated Systems Control (SAUS)
ISYVC International Sivananda Yoga Vedanta Center (EAIO)
ISYVO International Sivananda Yoga Vedanta Organization [*Val Morin, PQ*] (EAIO)
ISZ Increment and Skip on Zero [*Computer science*]
ISZ Increment Skip to Zero (SAUS)
ISZ Interplate Shear Zone [*Geology*]
ISZ Iskustvennyi Sputnik Zemil [*Former USSR*]
IT Air Inter [*ICAO designator*] (AD)
IT Air Inter, Societe [*France*] [*ICAO designator*] (ICDA)
It Biblioteca Nazionale Centrale, Rome, Italy [*Library symbol*] [*Library of Congress*] (LCLS)
IT Gartner Group "A" [*NYSE symbol*]
IT Idaho Territory [*Obsolete*] (ROG)
IT Identification and Traceability (IAA)
IT Identification Transponder (MCD)
IT Idle Time (SAUS)
IT Ignition Temperature (SAUS)
IT Iliotibial [*Anatomy*] (DAVI)
IT Illite (SAUS)
IT Illusion Theater (EA)
IT Image Tube (SAUS)
IT Imitation Tiles
IT Immediate Transient Incapacitation [*Radiation casualty criterion*] [*Army*]
IT Immediate Transportation
IT Immunity Test
IT Immunology Today (SAUO)
IT Immunoreactive Tag [*Clinical chemistry*]
IT Immunotherapy [*Medicine*]
IT Immunotoxin
IT Immunoturbidimetry [*Analytical biochemistry*]
IT Impacted Tooth [*Medicine*] (MELL)
IT Impact Test (SAUS)
IT Imperial Territory (SAUO)
IT Imperial Typewriter (SAUS)
IT Implantation Test [*Medicine*] (MAE)
IT Implosive Therapy [*Type of behavior therapy*]

IT .... Improved Tartar
IT .... Improved Touring [*Class of racing cars*]
IT .... Impulse Telegraphy (SAUS)
IT .... Impulse Turbine (SAUS)
IT .... Inactivity Test (SAUS)
IT .... Incentive Travel [*Travel industry*]
IT .... Inclusive Tour (MCD)
IT .... Income Tax
IT .... Income Tax Unit Rulings [*US Internal Revenue Service*]
IT .... Incomplete Translation [*Telecommunications*] (TEL)
IT .... Indent Tab Character [*Computer science*]
IT .... Independent Tank (DS)
IT .... Index Table (SAUS)
IT .... Index Term [*Computer science*]
IT .... Index Track (SAUS)
IT .... Index Translationum [*UNESCO*]
IT .... Indian Territory [*in United States*]
IT .... Indian Troops (SAUO)
IT .... Individual Task (SAUO)
IT .... Individual Therapy
IT .... Individual Training [*Army*]
IT .... Individual Transportation [*Urban planning*]
I-T .... Inductive Tuner (SAUS)
IT .... Industrial Technician (SAUS)
IT .... Industrial Technologist (SAUS)
IT .... Industrial Technology
IT .... Industrial Therapy (SAUS)
IT .... Industrial Training
IT .... Industrial Transformation and Global Environmental Change (SAUO)
IT .... Industrial Tribunal [*British*] (DCTA)
IT .... Industry Telephone (SAUS)
IT .... Industry Telephone Maintenance [*FCC*] (IEEE)
IT .... Industry Transistor [*Electronics*] (IAA)
IT .... Infantry Tank (SAUS)
IT .... Infantry Training (SAUS)
IT .... Infection Type [*Pathology*]
IT .... Infective Thrombosis [*Medicine*] (MELL)
IT .... Infective Thrombus [*Medicine*] (MELL)
IT .... Inferior Temporal [*Anatomy*]
IT .... Inferior Turbinate [*Otorhinolaryngology*] (DAVI)
IT .... Inferotemperal (SAUS)
IT .... Information Technique (SAUS)
IT .... Information Technologies (SAUS)
IT .... Information Technologist (SAUS)
IT .... Information Technology [*Computer science*] (ECON)
IT .... Information Technology and Computer Science (SAUS)
IT .... Information Technology Building (SAUS)
IT .... Information Technology Division (SAUS)
IT .... Information Terminals Corp. (SAUO)
IT .... Information Theory (MCD)
IT .... Information Today (journ.) (SAUS)
IT .... Information Track (SAUS)
IT .... Information Transform [*Information service or system*] (IID)
IT .... Information Transport (SAUO)
IT .... Information Type (ACRL)
IT .... Infrared Transmitter (SAUS)
IT .... Infrastructure Test (SAUS)
IT .... Inhalation Test [*Clinical medicine*] (MAE)
IT .... Inhalation Therapy [*or Therapist*] [*Medicine*]
IT .... Initial Tension (SAUS)
I/T .... Initial Track (MCD)
IT .... Initial Turn (SAUS)
IT .... Initiation Technician (SAA)
IT .... Inner Targets (COE)
IT .... Inner Temple
IT .... Innovative Technology (SAUO)
IT .... Innovative Test
IT .... Input Tape (SAUS)
IT .... Input Terminal
IT .... Input Time (SAUS)
IT .... Input Translator [*IBM Corp.*] [*Computer science*]
IT .... Inspection and Test (IAA)
I-T .... Inspection and Testing (SAUO)
IT .... Inspection Tag
IT .... Inspection Time (DIPS)
IT .... Inspiratory Time [*Medicine*] (DAVI)
IT .... Installation Test (NASA)
IT .... Instant Transaction (IAA)
IT .... Instant Transactions (SAUS)
IT .... Institut du Textile [*Textile Institute*] (EAIO)
IT .... Institute of Taxation (SAUO)
IT .... Institute of Technology [*Air Force*]
IT .... Institute of Tribology (SAUS)
IT .... Institute of Trichologists (EAIO)
IT .... Institutional Training (OICC)
IT .... Instructional Technique (SAUO)
IT .... Instructional Technologist (EDAC)
IT .... Instructional Technology
IT .... Instruction Tag (MSA)
IT .... Instruction Termination (SAUS)
IT .... Instruction Type (SAUS)
IT .... Instructor Trainer [*Red Cross*]
IT .... Instrumentation Tape (SAUS)
IT .... Instrumentation Technician (SAUS)
IT .... Instrumentation Technologist (SAUS)
IT .... Instrumentation Technology (journ.) (SAUS)
IT .... Instrumented Laboratory Training
IT .... Instrument Team (ARMP)
IT .... Instrument Technician
IT .... Instrument Test [*or Tree*] [*Nuclear energy*] (NRCH)
IT .... Instrument Trainer (SAUS)
IT .... Instrument Transformer
IT .... Instrument Tree (SAUS)
IT .... Insulated Tank Container [*Shipping*] (DCTA)
IT .... Insulating Transformer (KSC)
IT .... Insulin Therapy [*Medicine*] (MELL)
IT .... Intact (DAVI)
IT .... Intdian Territory (SAUS)
IT .... Integral Time (SAUS)
IT .... Integrated Technology (ACAE)
IT .... Integrated Telecommunications (SAUS)
IT .... Integration (SAUS)
I/T .... Integration and Test (ACAE)
IT .... Integration Technologies Inc. (SAUO)
IT .... Integration Testing (SAUO)
IT .... Intelligent Terminal [*Computer science*]
IT .... Intelligent Transaction Router [*Telecommunications*]
IT .... Intelligent Transmitter (ACII)
IT .... Intelogic Trace, Inc. (SAUO)
IT .... Intensity of Telephone Interference (IAA)
I/T .... Intensity/Time [*Duration of contractions*] [*Medicine*] (STED)
IT .... Intensive Therapy [*Medicine*] (MAE)
IT .... Intention Tremor [*Medicine*] (DB)
IT .... Interactive Television
IT .... Intercepting Trap (SAUS)
IT .... Interceptor Trap
IT .... Intercircuit Tester (SAUS)
IT .... Interesting Transcript [*genetics*]
it .... Interface (ELAL)
IT .... Interface Tape (SAUS)
IT .... Interfacial Tension [*Physical chemistry*] (IAA)
IT .... Interfering Transmitter (IAA)
IT .... Interior Temporal (SAUS)
IT .... Interlogic Trace, Inc. [*NYSE symbol*] (COMM)
IT .... Intermediate Technology [*An association*] (EA)
IT .... Intermediate Terminal (ACAE)
IT .... Intermediate Trainer (SAUS)
IT .... Intermediate Treatment [*Special provision of British law for juvenile offenders*]
IT .... Intermittent Traction [*Medicine*] (MELL)
IT .... Internal Tank (SAUS)
IT .... Internal Thread
IT .... Internal Translator [*Carnegie Institute*] [*IBM Corp.*]
IT .... International Steam Table Calorie (IIA)
IT .... International Table (SAUS)
IT .... International Taekwondo (SAUO)
IT .... International Technology (SAUS)
IT .... International Technology Corp. [*Associated Press*] (SAG)
IT .... International Technology Division (SAUO)
IT .... International Tolerance
IT .... International Traders Association (EA)
IT .... International Travellers [*YWCA*]
IT .... Interrogating Typewriter (SAUS)
IT .... Interrogator-Transponder (KSC)
IT .... Interstate Theft
I/T .... Intertank (NASA)
IT .... Intertoll [*Trunk*] [*Telecommunications*] (TEL)
IT .... Intertuberous [*Diameter*] [*Medicine*]
IT .... Interval Timer [*Computer science*]
IT .... Interval Training [*Physical fitness program*]
IT .... Intestinal Type [*of epithelium*]
IT .... Intimal Thickening [*Medicine*] (MEDA)
IT .... Intradermal Test [*Medicine*] (MAE)
IT .... In Transit (SAUS)
IT .... In Transitu [*In Transit*] [*Latin*]
IT .... Intrathecal [*Medicine*]
IT .... Intrathoracic [*Medicine*]
IT .... Intratracheal [*Medicine*]
IT .... Intratracheal Tube [*Medicine*]
IT .... Intratumoral [*Medicine*] (MAE)
IT .... Inventory Transfer
I/T .... Inverted T (SAUS)
IT .... Ion Trap [*Instrumentation*]
IT .... Iphigenia Taurica [*of Euripides*] [*Classical studies*] (OCD)
IT .... Iran Time (SAUO)
IT .... Irradiation Time (SAUS)
IT .... Irrelevant Talk [*Slang*]
IT .... Ischial Tuberosity [*Medicine*]
IT .... Island Telephone Co. Ltd. [*Toronto Stock Exchange symbol*]
It .... Islet [*Maps and charts*]
IT .... Isomeric Transition [*Radioactivity*]
IT .... Isometric Transition (SAUS)
IT .... Isothermal (SAUS)
IT .... Isothermal Transformation [*Metallurgy*]
IT .... Isotocin [*Endocrinology*]
It .... Italian (GROV)
It .... Italian (SAFN)
IT .... Italian
IT .... Italic (IAA)
IT .... Italic Type (SAUS)

IT .... Italy [*ANSI two-letter standard code*] (CNC)
it .... Italy [*MARC country of publication code*] [*Library of Congress*] (LCCP)
It .... Italy (MILB)
IT .... Item (MCD)
IT .... Item Transfer
IT .... National Organization of Industrial Trade Unions
IT .... Tour-Based Fare [*Airline fare code*]
it .... transposed inversion (SAUS)
it .... Vetus Itala (BJA)
IT3 .... Interactive Tactical Team Trainer (SAUO)
IT-95 .... Information Technology 1995 [*Marine science*] (OSRA)
IT-290 .... Indole Analog of Amphetamine [*Medicine*] (EDAA)
ITA .... Great River Library System, Quincy, IL [*OCLC symbol*] (OCLC)
ITA .... IGOSS Telecommunication Arrangements (SAUS)
ITA .... Illinois Motor Truck Operators Association, Chicago IL [*STAC*]
ITA .... Imagining Technologies Association (NTPA)
IT-A .... Immunotoxin with A-Chain
ITA .... Income Tax Act Regulations [*Commerce Clearing House Canadian Ltd.*] [*Information service or system*] (CRD)
ITA .... Independent Teachers Association (SAUO)
ITA .... Independent Telecommunications Analysts [*Boulder, CO*] (TSSD)
ITA .... Independent Telephone Association (SAUO)
ITA .... Independent Television Association [*British*] (DBA)
ITA .... Independent Television Authority [*Later, IBA*] [*British*]
ITA .... Independent Truckers Association (SAUO)
ITA .... Indiana Telecommunications Association (CGWS)
ITA .... Individual Task Authorization
ITA .... Individual Treatment Assessment [*Medicine*] (STED)
ITA .... Indoor Tennis Association [*Later, NTA*] (EA)
ITA .... Industrial and Technical Assistance (SAUS)
ITA .... Industrial Technical Adviser (SAUS)
ITA .... Industrial Technological Associates, Inc. [*Information service or system*]
ITA .... Industrial Technology Adviser (SAUS)
ITA .... Industrial Telecommunications Association (NTPA)
ITA .... Industrial Training Act (SAUO)
ITA .... Industrial Truck Association [*Washington, DC*] (EA)
ITA .... Industry and Trade Administration [*Later, International Trade Administration*] [*Department of Commerce*]
ITA .... Inferior Temporal Artery [*Medicine*] (DMAA)
ITA .... Inferior Tympanic Artery [*Anatomy*]
ITA .... Influenza Type A [*Medicine*] (MELL)
ITA .... Information Technologies Association (SAUO)
ITA .... Initial Teaching Alphabet (ADWA)
i/t/a .... Initial Teaching Alphabet [*A 44-symbol alphabet planned to simplify beginning reading by representing sounds more precisely*]
ITA .... Inner Transport Area
ITA .... Inside Wheel Turning Angle [*Automotive engineering*]
ITA .... Inspection Test Assembly (MCD)
ITA .... Institut du Transport Aerien [*Institute of Air Transport*] [*Research center*] [*France*] (IRC)
ITA .... Institute for Telecommunications and Aeronomy [*ESSA*] (MCD)
ITA .... Institute for Transnational Arbitration (SAUO)
ITA .... Institute of the Arts [*Australian National University*]
ITA .... Institute of Theoretical Astronomy [*Leningrad, USSR*]
ITA .... Institute of Traffic Administration [*British*]
ITA .... Institute of Transactional Analysis [*British*] (DBA)
ITA .... Institute of Transport Administration [*Later, IoTA*] (EAIO)
ITA .... Institute of Transport Aviation (KSC)
ITA .... Institute of Travel Agents [*British*] (BI)
ITA .... Instrumentation Technology Associates, Inc.
ITA .... Instrument Time (Actual)
ITA .... Integrated Test Area (MCD)
ITA .... Integrated Test Article (NAKS)
ITA .... Integrated Thruster Assembly (KSC)
ITA .... Integrated Truss Assembly [*NASA*] (SPST)
ITA .... Intelligence Task Automation (SAUS)
ITA .... Intelligent Task Authority (SAUO)
ITA .... Intelligent Task Automation (ACAE)
ITA .... Interactive Television Association
ITA .... Inter-Air, Inc. [*ICAO designator*] (FAAC)
ITA .... Intercollegiate Tennis Association (NTPA)
ITA .... Interface Test Adapters (MCD)
ITA .... Interim Type Approval (SAUO)
ITA .... Interior Tympanic Artery (SAUS)
ITA .... Intermediate Teachers Association
ITA .... Intermediate Thrust Arc
ITA .... Intermediate Training Assessment (DOMA)
ITA .... Intermodal Transportation Association (EA)
ITA .... Internal Thoracic Artery [*Medicine*] (MELL)
ITA .... International 210 Association (EA)
ITA .... International Alphabet
ITA .... International Tap Association (EA)
ITA .... International Tape Association (NITA)
ITA .... International Tape/Disc Association (EA)
ITA .... International Taxicab Association (EA)
ITA .... International Teaching Alphabet (SAUS)
ITA .... International Teleconferencing Association (SAUO)
ITA .... International Telegraph Alphabet (NATG)
ITA .... International Telegraph Association (SAUO)
ITA .... International Telegraphy Alphabet (SAUS)
ITA .... International Telenurses Association (SAUO)
ITA .... International Television Academy (SAUO)
ITA .... International Television Almanac (journ.) (SAUS)
ITA .... International Temperance Association [*Later, IHTA*] (EA)
ITA .... International Texcan Tech [*Vancouver Stock Exchange symbol*]
ITA .... International Thermographers Association (EA)
ITA .... International Tin Agreement
ITA .... International Tin Association (SAUO)
ITA .... International Tire Association (EA)
ITA .... International Titanium Association (NTPA)
ITA .... International Tornado Association [*Germany*] (EAIO)
ITA .... International Touring Alliance [*Belgium*] (EAIO)
ITA .... International Track Association [*Defunct*]
ITA .... International Trade Administration [*Washington, DC*] [*Department of Commerce*]
ITA .... International Trade Administration Report (journ.) (SAUS)
ITA .... International Trade Association [*BTS*] (TAG)
ITA .... International Traders Association (SAUO)
ITA .... International Trainers Association (SAUO)
ITA .... International Transpersonal Association (SAUO)
ITA .... International Trombone Association (EA)
ITA .... International Tube Association [*Leamington Spa, Warwickshire, England*] (EAIO)
ITA .... International Tuberculosis Association (DAVI)
ITA .... International Tunneling Association (SAUS)
ITA .... International Tunnelling Association (EA)
ITA .... International Turquoise Association (EA)
ITA .... International Twins Association [*Defunct*] (EA)
ITA .... International Typographic Association (MCD)
ITA .... Internmediate Teachers Association (SAUO)
ITA .... Interstate Towing Association (SAUO)
ITA .... Interstate Towing Auxiliary (EA)
ITA .... Interstate Truckers Association
ITA .... In Total Agreement [*Online dialog*]
ITA .... Ionization Test Apparatus
ITA .... Irish Temperance Alliance (SAUO)
ITA .... Irish Tourist Association (SAUO)
ITA .... Itacoatiara [*Brazil*] [*Airport symbol*] (AD)
ITA .... Itaconic Acid [*Organic chemistry*]
ita .... Italian [*MARC language code*] [*Library of Congress*] (LCCP)
ITA .... Italy [*ANSI three-letter standard code*] (CNC)
ITA .... Italy Fund [*NYSE symbol*] (TTSB)
ITA .... Italy Fund, Inc. [*NYSE symbol*] (SPSG)
ITA .... Itapemirim Transportes Aereos SA [*Brazil*] [*ICAO designator*] (FAAC)
ITA .... I Totally Agree [*Online dialog*]
ITA .... Industrial Transport Association (ODA)
ITA1 .... International Telegraph Alphabet No. 1 (SAUS)
ITA2 .... International Telegraph Alphabet No. 2 (SAUS)
ITA3 .... International Telegraph Alphabet No. 3 (SAUS)
ITA4 .... International Telegraph Alphabet No. 4 (SAUS)
ITAA .... Independent Travel Agencies of America Association (EA)
ITAA .... Information Technology Association of America [*Arlington, VA*] (CDE)
ITAA .... International Textile and Apparel Association (NTPA)
ITAA .... International Theatrical Agencies Association (EA)
ITAA .... International Transactional Analysis Association (EA)
ITAAB .... ISDN Technical Advisory Ad hoc Board (SAUO)
ITAADS .... Installation the Army Authorization Document Systems (SAUS)
ITAADS .... Installation the Army Authorization Document System
ITAADS .... Interim Target Acquisition and Designation System
ITAADS .... Interim Target Acquisition and Designation Systems (SAUS)
ITAAG .... ISDN Technical Advisory Ad hoc Group (SAUO)
ITAAP .... Inspection Test and Analysis Plan (IAA)
ITAAS .... Integrated Aircraft Armament System (SAUO)
ITAB .... Industry Technical Advisory Board (SAUO)
ITAB .... Industry Training Advisory Board (SAUS)
ITAB .... Information Technology Advisory Board [*British*]
ITAB .... Intermodal Transportation Advisory Board (SAUO)
ITAB .... International Technical Assistance Bulletin (SAUS)
ITAB .... International Transportation Advisory Board [*BTS*] (TAG)
ITABC .... Independent Telephone Association of British Columbia (SAUO)
ITAC .... Imperial Three Arts Club (SAUO)
ITAC .... Independent Technical Advisory Committee (SAUO)
ITAC .... Industrial Training Atlantic Convention (SAUO)
ITAC .... Information Technology Acquisition Center [*Navy*] (CIST)
ITAC .... Information Technology Advisory Committee [*Office of Management and Budget*] (GFGA)
ITAC .... Information Technology Association of Canada (SAUO)
ITAC .... Integrated Tactical Aircraft Control [*Air Force*] (DOMA)
ITAC .... Intelligence and Threat Analysis Center [*Air Force*] (DOMA)
ITAC .... Intelligence Threat Analysis Center (SAUO)
ITAC .... Intelligence Tracking Analysis and Correlation (MCD)
ITAC .... Interagency Textile Administrative Committee
ITAC .... Interconnect Association of Canada (SAUO)
ITAC .... International Target Audience Code [*International Federation of Library Associations*]
ITAC .... International Trade Affairs Committee (SAUS)
ITAC .... International Transfer Ot Aircraft Comminee (SAUS)
ITAC .... Interprocessor Tasking And Communications (SAUS)
ITAC .... Intestinal Type Adenocarcinoma [*Oncology*]
ITAC .... ITU-T Advisory Committee (SAUO)
ITACA .... European Society of Professionals working with drug dependences (SAUS)
ITACC .... Incremental Tactical Communications Capability (SAUO)
ITACC .... Incremental Tactical Communications Capability Study [*Military*] (MCD)
ITACCS .... International Trauma Anesthesia and Critical Care Society (EA)
ITACIES .... Interim Tactical Imagery Exploitation System (SAUO)
ITACO .... Integration Trade and Analysis-Cycle O (SSD)

ITACS........... Integrated Tactical Air Control System
ITACS........... Integrated Tactical Command System (SAUO)
ITAC-T......... International Telecommunication Advisory Committee-Telecommunications (ACRL)
ITAC-T......... International Telecommunications Advisory Committee-Telecommunications (SAUO)
ITAD............ Individual Training Analysis and Design (MCD)
ITAD............ Information, Training and Agricultural Development [*British consultancy and training service*] (ECON)
ITAD............ Institute for Trauma and Addictive Disorders (SEAT)
ITAD............ Integrated Thermal Avionics Design (ACAE)
ITAD............ Intelligence Threat Analysis Detachment [*Army*] (RDA)
ITAD............ Internal Tank Access Device (SAUS)
ITAE............ Integral of Time-weighted Absolute value of Error (SAUS)
ITAE............ Integrated Time and Absolute Error
ITAEG.......... Information Technology Ad-hoc Expert Group (SAUO)
ITAEGM........ Information Technology Ad-hoc Expert Group for Advanced Manufacturing Technologies (SAUO)
ITAEGS........ Information Technology Ad-hoc Expert Group for OSI Functional Standardisation (SAUO)
ITAEGT........ Information Technology Ad-hoc Expert Group for Telecommunications (SAUO)
ITAffi2.......... Internationality Alphabet ffi2 (MCD)
I-Tag............ Identification Tag (SAUS)
ITAG............ Intelligence Threat Analysis Group [*Military*] (DNAB)
ITAG............ Internal Thoracic Artery (STED)
ITAG............ International Travel Agent Guild (TRID)
ITAG............ Invalid Tricycle Action Group [*British*] (DI)
ITAI............. Institute of Technical Authors and Illustrators (SAUS)
ITAI............. Institution of Technical Authors and Illustrators (SAUO)
ITAI............. Interceptor Technology Analysis and Integration (ACAE)
ITAIS........... Initial Task Analysis Information Sheet (SAUO)
ITAJ............. International Trombone Association. Journal (journ.) (SAUS)
ITAK............. Illankai Tamil Arasu Kadchi [*Federal Party*] [*Sri Lanka*] [*Political party*] (PPW)
ITAL............. Information Technologies and Libraries (SAUS)
ITAL............. Information Technology for Libraries [*Formerly, JOLA*] [*A publication*] (NITA)
ITAL............. Initial Task Assignment List
ITAL............. Initial Trial Allowance List (SAUS)
ITAL............. Introductory Trials Allowance List [*Military*] (AFIT)
ITAL............. Inventory Trial Allowance List Introductory Trials Allowance List (SAUS)
Ital............... Italian (ODCC)
ITAL............. Italian
Ital............... Italic (SHCU)
ITAL............. Italic [*or Italics*]
ital............... Italicize (NTIO)
Italamer....... Italamerican (journ.) (SAUS)
Ital Aust Bul Conmmerce... Italian-Australian Bulletin of Commerce (journ.) (SAUS)
ITALD........... Improved Tactical Air-Launched Decoy (DWSG)
Ital Dial........ Italic Dialects [*A publication*] (OCD)
Ital Gen Rev Oto-Rhino-Laryng... Italian General Review of Oto-Rhino-Laryngology (journ.) (SAUS)
Italian Am Bus... Italian American Business (journ.) (SAUS)
Italian Yb of Int'l L... Italian Yearbook of International Law [*A publication*] (DLA)
Ital J Chest Dis... Italian Journal of Chest Diseases (journ.) (SAUS)
Ital J Gastroenterol... Italian Journal of Gastroenterology (journ.) (SAUS)
Ital J Med.... Italian Journal of Medicine (journ.) (SAUS)
Ital J Neurol Sci... Italian Journal of Neurological Sciences (journ.) (SAUS)
Ital J Orthop Traumatol... Italian Journal of Orthopaedics and Traumatology (journ.) (SAUS)
Ital J Orthop Traumatol Suppl... Italian Journal of Orthopaedics and Traumatology. Supplementum (journ.) (SAUS)
Ital J Sports Traumatol... Italian Journal of Sports Traumatology (journ.) (SAUS)
Ital J Surg Sci... Italian Journal of Surgical Sciences (journ.) (SAUS)
Ital J Zool.... Italian Journal of Zoology (journ.) (SAUS)
Ital L............ Italian Linguistics (journ.) (SAUS)
Ital Rev Orthop Traumatol... Italian Review of Orthopaedics and Traumatology (journ.) (SAUS)
Italsat.......... Italy International Communications Satellite (SAUS)
ITALSS......... Integrated Test and Logistic Support System (ACAE)
Italy............. Italy Fund, Inc. [*Associated Press*] (SAG)
ITALY........... I Trust and Love You [*Correspondence*] (DSUE)
ITALZ........... Italian Web on Alzheimer Diseases (SAUO)
ITAM............ Immunoreceptor Tyrosine Activation Motif [*Biochemistry*]
ITAM............ Immunoreceptor Tyrosine-Based Activation Motif [*Immunology*]
ITAM............ Instituto Tecnologico Autonomo de Mexico [*Economic research*] [*Mexico*] (CROSS)
ITAM............ Integrated Training Area Management [*Military*] (INF)
ITAM............ Interactive Med Tech Ltd [*NASDAQ symbol*] (TTSB)
ITAM............ Interdata Telecommunications Access Method [*Computer science*] (MHDB)
ITAMA.......... Information Technology Acquisition and Marketing Association [*Defunct*] (EA)
ITAM VETS... Italian American War Veterans of the United States [*Defunct*] (EA)
ITA N........... International Trombone Association. Newsletter (journ.) (SAUS)
ITAN............ InterTAN, Inc. (SAUO)
IT & AP........ Inspection Test and Analysis Plan (NRCH)
IT&BL.......... Island Tug & Barge, Ltd. (SAUO)
IT&C............ Industry Trade and Commerce (SAUO)
IT&D............ Information Technology and Disabilities (SAUO)
IT & ME....... Incentive Travel and Meeting Executives Show [*Trade show*]
IT&T............ Information Technology and Telecommunications (SAUO)
IT and T....... International Telephone & Telegraph Corp. [*New York, NY*] [*Facetious translation: International Travel and Talk*]
IT&T............ International Telephone and Telegraph Corp. (SAUO)
IT&TEL........ Initial Tools and Test Equipment List (ACAE)
IT & TS........ International Turtle and Tortoise Society (EA)
I/T Antenna... Inverted T Antenna (SAUS)
ITANZ.......... Information Technology Association of New Zealand (SAUO)
ITAP............ Inexpensive Turbine Avionics Platform (SAUS)
ITAP............ Information Technology Advisory Panel [*British*]
ITAP............ Integrated Technical Assessment Panel [*NASA*] (NASA)
ITAP............ Interim Track Analysis Program (SAUS)
ITAP............ International Technology Advisory Panel (SAUO)
ITAQUA........ Information Technology Applied to Quality (SAUO)
ITAR............ Integrated Terrain Access and Retrieval (ACAE)
ITAR............ International Trade and Arms Regulations
ITAR............ International Traffic in Arms Regulation [*US*]
ITAR............ Interstate and foreign Travel (or transportation) in Aid of Racketeering enterprises (SAUS)
ITAR............ Interstate Transportation in Aid of Racketeering
ITARDA........ Institute for Traffic Accident Research and Data Analysis [*Highway safety*]
ITARFD........ Institute of Tropical Agronomic Research and Food Crops (SAUS)
ITARS.......... Integrated Terrain Access and Retrieval System [*Hughes Aircraft*] [*Digital mapping project*] (NITA)
ITARS.......... Integrated Terrain Retrieval System (MCD)
ITAS............ Improved Tactical Attack System
ITAS............ Improved Target Acquisition System [*Army*]
ITAS............ Improved TOW Acquisition Sight (SAUS)
ITAS............ Improved Tracking Adjunct System (SAUS)
ITAS............ Indicated True Air Speed [*Aviation*] (AFM)
ITAS............ Instantaneous Telephone Alerting System (SAUO)
ITAS............ Institute for Technology Assessment and Systems Analysis (SAUS)
ITAS............ Integrated Tactical Attack System (MCD)
ITAS............ Integrated Tactical Avionics System (SAUO)
ITAS............ Integrated Target Acquisition System (SAUS)
ITAS............ Integrated Test and Alignment System
ITAS............ Integrated Transport Accounting System (SAUS)
ITAS............ Inter-American Travel Agents Society (EA)
ITAS............ International Technology Analytical Services (SAUO)
ITAS-ATB..... European Institute of Transpersonal and Advanced Human Studies-Belgian Transpersonal Association (SAUO)
ITASC.......... Interim Theater ADP Service Center (SAUO)
ITASC.......... Itasca, WI [*American Association of Railroads railroad junction routing code*]
ITASE.......... International Trans-Antarctic Scientific Expedition (QUAC)
ITASS.......... Interim Towed Array Surveillance System [*Military*] (NVT)
ITAT............ International Telegraph and Telephone (SAUS)
ITAT............ International Trade and Transport Group (New Zealand) (AG)
ITATLIS....... Indian Association of Teachers of Library Science (BUAC)
ITAV............ Individual Tactical Air Vehicle
Itavia.......... Italian Aviation (SAUS)
ITAVS.......... Integrated Testing (SAUS)
ITAVS.......... Integrated Testing, Analysis, and Verification System
ITAWDS....... Integrated Tactical Amphibious Warfare Data System [*Navy*] (NVT)
ITAX............ Intermountain Aviation, Inc. [*Air carrier designation symbol*]
ITAX............ Italics
ITB.............. Abbott Laboratories, North Chicago, IL [*OCLC symbol*] (OCLC)
ITB.............. Bandung Institute of Technology, Indonesia (SAUS)
ITB.............. Iceland Tourist Bureau (SAUO)
ITB.............. Iliotibial Band [*Anatomy*]
ITB.............. Incoming Trunk Busy (SAUS)
ITB.............. Independent Tank Brigade (SAUS)
ITB.............. Individual Tour Basing [*Fares*]
ITB.............. Industrial Test Battery (TES)
ITB.............. Industrial Training Board [*British*]
ITB.............. Industry Training Board (SAUO)
ITB.............. Information Technology Branch (SAUO)
ITB.............. Information Technology Budget (SAUS)
ITB.............. Information Technology for Business (SAUO)
ITB.............. Inland Tug and Barge (SAUO)
ITB.............. Instantaneous Trip Block [*Computer science*] (IAA)
ITB.............. Institute of Technology at Bandung [*Indonesia*]
ITB.............. Institut Technique du Batiment [*Technical Institute for Building*] [*France*] [*Information service or system*] (IID)
ITB.............. Insurance Technical Bureau (SAUO)
ITB.............. Integral Terminal Block
ITB.............. Integrated Test Bed (ACAE)
ITB.............. Integrated Test Block
ITB.............. Integrated Training Brigade [*Navy*]
ITB.............. Integrated Tug Barge (DS)
ITB.............. Interbrasil Star, SA [*Brazil*] [*FAA designator*] (FAAC)
ITB.............. Intergovernmental TOGA Board (SAUO)
ITB.............. Intergrowth Tungsten Bronze (SAUS)
ITB.............. Intermediate Block [*Computer science*] (AGLO)
ITB.............. Intermediate Test Block (SAUS)
ITB.............. Intermediate Text Block
ITB.............. Intermediate Transmission Block [*Computer science*] (BUR)
ITB.............. Intermountain Tariff Bureau, Inc.
ITB.............. Internal Test Bus (SAUS)
ITB.............. Internal Transfer Bus
ITB.............. Internationaler Turnerbund [*International Gymnastic Federation*]
ITB.............. International Theft Bureau (SAUO)
ITB.............. International Thomson Books
ITB.............. International Thoroughbred Breeders, Inc. [*AMEX symbol*] (SPSG)
ITB.............. International Time Bureau

ITB .... International Tourist Bureau [*Indian Railway*] (TIR)
ITB .... International Training Branch [*Office of Education*]
ITB .... Internet Transaction Broker [*Computer science*]
ITB .... In the Business [*Refers to television and film industries*]
ITB .... Intl ThoroughBred [*AMEX symbol*] (TTSB)
ITB .... Invisible Trade Balance [*Business term*] (MHDW)
ITB .... Invitation to Bid
ITB .... Ion Thruster Beam
ITB .... Irish Tourist Board (EA)
ITB .... Irish Tourist Bureau (SAUO)
ITB .... Island Tug & Barge [*AAR code*]
ItB .... It Beaken (journ.) (SAUS)
ItBa .... Biblioteca Comunale "Angelillo", Servizio Prestito, Bari, Italy [*Library symbol*] [*Library of Congress*] (LCLS)
ITBA .... Idaho Thoroughbred Breeders Association (SRA)
ITBA .... International Toy Buff's Association (EA)
ITBA .... Irish Ten Pin Bowling Association (EAIO)
ItBar .... Biblioteca Comunale di Barletta, Barletta, Italy [*Library symbol*] [*Library of Congress*] (LCLS)
ItBaU .... Universita degli Studi di Bari, Bari, Italy [*Library symbol*] [*Library of Congress*] (LCLS)
ITBC .... Instructional Television Funding Cooperative (NTCM)
ITB Character ... Intermediate Transmission Block Character (SAUS)
ITB Check .... Intermediate Transmission Block Check (SAUS)
ITBE .... Interchannel Time Base Error (IAA)
ITBH .... Internal Broach (SAUS)
ITB-ID .... International Thomson Books - International Division
ITBL .... Incompressible Turbulent Boundary Layer
ITBL .... Integrated Transportation Bill of Lading (SAUS)
ITBOF .... Illinois Thoroughbred Breeders and Owners Foundation (SRA)
ITBP .... Indo-Tibetan Border Police (SAUS)
ITBP .... International Thomson Business Press, Inc. [*Publisher*]
ITBPrA .... Intl ThoroughBred A Pfd [*AMEX symbol*] (TTSB)
ITB Relay .... Instantaneous Trip Block Relay (SAUS)
ITBS .... Iliotibial Band Syndrome [*Medicine*]
ITBS .... Iowa Tests of Basic Skills
ITBTP .... Institut Technique du Batiment et des Travaux Publics [*Technical Institute for Building and Public Works*] [*Information service or system*] (IID)
ITC .... Concordia Theological Seminary, Fort Wayne, IN [*OCLC symbol*] (OCLC)
ITC .... Ice Technology Conference (ACAE)
ITC .... Ideal Toy Corp. (EFIS)
ITC .... Igloo Thermal Control [*Aerospace*] (MCD)
ITC .... Illinois Terminal Railroad Co. [*AAR code*]
ITC .... Imidazolyl-Thioguanine Chemotherapy [*Medicine*] (MAE)
ITC .... Immediate Track Control [*Automotive engineering*]
ITC .... Immense Technology Commitment (SAUS)
ITC .... Imperial Tobacco Co. [*of Great Britain and Ireland*] Ltd.
ITC .... Imperial Tobacco Company of Great Britain and Ireland Ltd. (SAUO)
ITC .... Inclusive Tour Charter
ITC .... Income Tax Case (SAFN)
ITC .... Incontinence Treatment Center [*Medicine*] (STED)
ITC .... Indent Tab Character [*Computer science*] (ELAL)
ITC .... Independent Tank Center [*of a ship*] (DS)
ITC .... Independent Telephone Co. (SAUS)
ITC .... Independent Telephone Company (SAUO)
ITC .... Independent Television Commission [*British*] (ECON)
ITC .... Independent Television Committee (SAUO)
ITC .... Independent Television Corp. (SAUS)
ITC .... Independent Television Corporation (SAUO)
ITC .... Indiana Technical College (SAUO)
ITC .... Individual Table of Contents (VLIE)
ITC .... Industrial Technology Centre [*Manitoba Research Council*] [*Canada*] [*Research center*] (RCD)
ITC .... Industrial Training Council
ITC .... Infantry Training Center [*Army*]
ITC .... Infantry Training Centre (SAUO)
ITC .... Information Technology Center (SAUO)
ITC .... Information Technology Committee (SAUO)
ITC .... Information Technology Council (SAUO)
ITC .... Information Technology Ltd. [*British*] (NITA)
ITC .... Information Terminals Corporation (SAUO)
ITC .... Information Transfer Center (SAUS)
ITC .... Ingredient Technology Corp. (SAUS)
ITC .... Ingredient Technology Corporation (SAUO)
ITC .... Inland Transport Committee of the United Nations Economic Commission for Europe (SAUO)
ITC .... Inner Tracking Chamber (SAUS)
ITC .... Innovative Technology Council (EPAT)
ITC .... Inovative Technology Council (SAUO)
ITC .... Input Transaction Card (SAUS)
ITC .... Installation Time and Cost (VLIE)
ITC .... Institute of Tax Consultants (EA)
ITC .... Institute Technical Group (SAUO)
ITC .... Instructional Telecommunications Consortium (EA)
ITC .... Instructional Telecommunications Council (SAUO)
ITC .... Instructor Training Course
ITC .... Instrumentation Tracking Controller
ITC .... Integral Tube Component (IAA)
ITC .... Integrated Technology Consultants, Norway (SAUS)
ITC .... Integrated Telemetry and Command (ACAE)
ITC .... Integrated Telemetry Complex
ITC .... Integrated Temperature Control (SAUS)
ITC .... Integrated Terminal Controller (NITA)
ITC .... Integrated Thermionic Circuit (SAUS)
ITC .... Integrated Tool Carrier
ITC .... Integrated Trajectory Computations
ITC .... Integrated Transaction Controller (SAUS)
ITC .... Intelligence Training Consolidation (SAUO)
ITC .... Intelligent Controls, Inc. [*AMEX symbol*] (SAG)
ITC .... Intelligent Tape Controller (PDAA)
ITC .... Intelligent Telecommunication Controller (IAA)
ITC .... Intelligent Telecommunications Controller (SAUS)
ITC .... Intelligent Transaction Controller (MHDB)
ITC .... Intense Training Course (SAUS)
ITC .... Intent to Change
ITC .... Interagency Testing Committee [*Toxicology*]
ITC .... Inter-American Telecommunications Network (SAUS)
ITC .... Inter-American Travel Congresses
ITC .... Intercept [*Telecommunications*] (TEL)
ITC .... Intercepted (SAUS)
ITC .... Interchurch Transportation Council [*Defunct*] (EA)
ITC .... Intercontinental Trailsea Corp.
ITC .... Intercontinental Trailsea Corporation (SAUO)
ITC .... Interdata Transaction Controller [*Perkin-Elmer*]
ITC .... Intermediate Toll Center [*Telecommunications*] (TEL)
ITC .... Intermediate Toll Centre (SAUS)
ITC .... Internationaal Instituut voor Lucht-en Ruimtekaartering an Aardkunde [*International Institute for Aerospace Survey and Earth Sciences*] [*Netherlands*] (EAIO)
ITC .... International Air Carrier Association [*ICAO designator*] (FAAC)
ITC .... International Chemalloy Corp. [*Toronto Stock Exchange symbol*]
ITC .... International Chemalloy Corporation (SAUO)
ITC .... International Committee on Tracer (SAUO)
ITC .... International Institute for Aerial Survey and Earth Sciences (SAUO)
ITc .... International Table Calorie [*Dietetics*] (DAVI)
ITC .... International Tar Conference [*See also CIG*] [*Paris, France*] (EAIO)
ITC .... International Tea Committee (EAIO)
ITC .... International Technology Corporation (SAUO)
ITC .... International Technology Council [*Defunct*] (EA)
ITC .... International Telemetering Conference
ITC .... International Telepresence Corp. (ECON)
ITC .... International Teletraffic Co. (SAUS)
ITC .... International Teletraffic Company (SAUO)
ITC .... International Teletraffic Conference (SAUO)
ITC .... International Teletraffic Congress [*Telecommunications*]
ITC .... International Teletype Code (SAUS)
ITC .... International Television Center [*Communications*]
ITC .... International Test Conference (AEBE)
ITC .... International Textbook Company Ltd. (SAUO)
ITC .... International Thunderbird Club (EA)
ITC .... International Timber Committee (SAUO)
ITC .... International Tin Convention (SAUO)
ITC .... International Tin Council [*See also CIE*] [*Defunct*] (EAIO)
ITC .... International Toastmistress Clubs (EA)
ITC .... International Touring Championship (SAUS)
ITC .... International Towing Conference (SAUO)
ITC .... International Trade Center (or Centre) (SAUO)
ITC .... International Trade Centre [*Switzerland*] [*United Nations*] (MCD)
ITC .... International Trade Club of Chicago [*Later, IBCM*] (EA)
ITC .... International Trade Commission [*Databank originator*]
ITC .... International Trade Council (EA)
ITC .... International Traders Club (EA)
ITC .... International Trading Certificate (DS)
ITC .... International Trading Co. (SAUS)
ITC .... International Training Cell (SAUO)
ITC .... International Training Center (or Centre) (SAUS)
ITC .... International Training Centre for Aerial Survey (SAUO)
ITC .... International Training Centre for Post-Graduate Soil Scientists (SAUO)
ITC .... International Training College [*Salvation Army*]
ITC .... International Training in Communication (EA)
ITC .... International Trans Asia [*Vancouver Stock Exchange symbol*]
ITC .... International Transducer Corp. (SAUS)
ITC .... International Transducer Corporation (SAUO)
ITC .... International Transit Centre (SAUS)
ITC .... International Translations Centre [*Formerly, ETC*] (EA)
ITC .... International Translators Center (SAUS)
ITC .... International Transport Commission (COE)
ITC .... International Transport Committee (SAUO)
ITC .... International Travel Catering (journ.) (SAUS)
ITC .... International Tree Crops Institute (SAUO)
ITC .... International Tribology Council (SAUO)
ITC .... International Tropical Confluence
ITC .... International Trypanotolerance Centre [*Gambia*]
ITC .... International Tuberculosis Campaign
ITC .... International Typeface Corp.
ITC .... International Typeface Corporation (SAUO)
ITC .... Intern Training Center [*DARCOM*]
ITC .... Inter-Task Communication (VLIE)
ITC .... Intertechnology Solar Corporation (SAUO)
ITC .... Intertropical Confluence (SAUS)
ITC .... Intertropical Convergence [*Trade winds*] [*Meteorology*]
ITC .... Interval Time Control [*Computer science*] (OA)
ITC .... In-Track Contiguous
ITC .... Intratropical Convergence (SAUS)
ITC .... Investment and Trust Companies (SAUO)
ITC .... Investment Tax Credit
ITC .... Ionic Thermoconductivity [*or Thermocurrent*]

ITC .... Ionic Thermocurrent (SAUS)
ITC .... Island Trading Co. (SAUS)
ITC .... Island Trading Company (SAUO)
ITC .... Isothermal Titration Calorimetry [*Analytical chemistry*]
ITC .... Israel Trade Commission
ITC .... Italian Civilization (SAUS)
ItC .... Italian Culture (journ.) (SAUS)
ITC .... Italian Tile Center (EA)
ITC .... Italian Trade Commission (EA)
ITC .... Srinivasan's Reports of Income Tax Cases [*India*] [*1886-*] [*A publication*] (ILCA)
ITC4 .... Interim Transportable Command and Control Computer Center (SAUO)
ITCA .... Independent Television Companies Association [*British*]
ITCA .... Independent Television Contractors Association (COBU)
ITCA .... Indian Transcontinental Airways
ITCA .... Inspector of Training Corps and Cadets [*Military*] [*British*]
ITCA .... Instituto Tecnologico Centroamericano [*El Salvador*]
ITCA .... Interamerican Technical Council of Archives (SAUS)
ITCA .... Inter-American Technical Council of/on Archives (SAUO)
ITCA .... Inter-American Technical Council on Archives (DIT)
ITCA .... Intercollegiate Tennis Coaches Association (EA)
ITCA .... International Technical Caramel Association (EA)
IT/CA .... International Tele/Conferencing Association (EA)
ITCA .... International Thunderbird Class Association (EA)
ITCA .... International Typographic Composition Association [*Later, TIA*] (EA)
ITCA .... Invest to Compete Alliance [*Washington, DC*] (EA)
ITCA .... Irish Terrier Club of America (EA)
ITCA .... Isothiocyanic Acid (SAUS)
ITCABIC .... Inter-Territorial Catholic Bishops' Conference (EAIO)
IT Cal .... International Steam Table Calorie (SAUS)
ITCAL .... International Table Calorie
ITCAN .... Inspect, Test, and Correct as Necessary (MCD)
ITCAS .... International Training Center for Aerial Survey (SAUS)
ITCAS .... International Training Centre for Aerial Survey (SAUO)
ItCaU .... Universita di Cagliari, Sardinia, Italy [*Library symbol*] [*Library of Congress*] (LCLS)
ITCC .... Industrial Training [*NASDAQ symbol*] (TTSB)
ITCC .... Industrial Training Corp. [*NASDAQ symbol*] (NQ)
ITCC .... Industrial Training Corporation (SAUO)
ITCC .... Intelligence Technical Coordinating Committee (SAUO)
ITCC .... International Technical Communications Conference [*Society for Technical Communication*]
ITCC .... International Technical Control Center (SAUS)
ITCC .... International Technical Cooperation Centre (SAUO)
ITCC .... International Telephone Consultative Committee (SAUO)
ITCC .... Interstate Truckload Carriers Conference
ITCCU .... Information Technology Centre Consultancy Unit [*British*] (AIE)
ITCD .... Integrated Test Concept Document (SAUS)
ITCD .... International Testbed for CSCW and DDH (SAUS)
ITCD .... ITC DeltaCom [*NASDAQ symbol*] (SG)
ITCDA .... International Telephone-Cable Development Association (SAUO)
ITCG .... Illegal Traffic of Cultural Goods (EURO)
ITCG .... Information Technology Co-Ordinating Group [*International Electrotechnical Commission*] [*ISO*] (DS)
ITCG .... International Trade Communications Group (SAUO)
ITCH .... Information Technology for Children in Hospital (WDAA)
ITCH .... Information Technology in Community Health (SAUS)
ITCH .... Infotechnology (SAUS)
ITCH .... Infotechnology, Inc. (SAUO)
ITCI .... International CMOS Technology, Inc. (SAUO)
ITCI .... International Tree Crops Institute (SAUO)
ITCI .... International Tree Crops Institute USA (EA)
ITCILO .... International Training Center of the International Labour Organization (SAUO)
IT-CIM .... Integration Testing for Computer-Integrated Manufacturing (SAUO)
ITCIS .... Integrated Telephone Customer Information System [*Telecommunications*] (IAA)
ITCK .... Issue Time Check [*Aviation*] (FAAC)
ITCL .... Indian Trade Commissioner in London (SAUO)
ITCL .... Item Class (SAUS)
ITCLC .... Item Class Code (VLIE)
ITCM .... Integrated Tactical Countermeasures [*Army*]
ITCM .... Integrated Telephony Cable Modem (DINT)
ITCM .... INTERCIM Corp. (SAUO)
ITCO .... International Trade Co-operation Organization (SAUO)
ITCOM .... Information Technology and Communications Bureau [*United Nations*] (ECON)
IT Corp .... International Technology Corp. [*Associated Press*] (SAG)
ITCP .... Idiopathic Thrombocytopenic Purpura [*Hematology*] (DAVI)
ITCP .... Integrated Test and Checkout Procedures (MCD)
ITCPGR .... International Technical Conference on Plant Genetic Resources (SAUO)
ITCP/IP .... Intercomputer Protocol, Transmission Control Protocol/Internal Protocol (SAUS)
ITCPN .... International Technical Conference on Protection of Nature (SAUO)
ITCPN .... International Technical Conference on the Protection of Nature (SAUS)
ItcpSe .... Intercapital Income Securities, Inc. [*Associated Press*] (SAG)
ItCr .... Biblioteca Statale di Cremona, Cremona, Italy [*Library symbol*] [*Library of Congress*] (LCLS)
ITC/REE .... Industry, Trade and Commerce and Regional Economic Expansion (SAUS)
ITC/REE .... Industy Trade and Commerce and Regional Economic Expansion (SAUS)
ITCRM .... Infantry Training Center-Royal Marines (SAUO)
IT Crp .... International Technology Corp. (SAUO)
ITCS .... Industrial Trade and Consumer Show (SAUS)
ITCS .... Installation Training/Coordination Section [*Social Security Administration*]
ITCS .... Institute for 21st Century Studies [*Defunct*] (EA)
ITCS .... Integrated Target Central System [*Military*] (CAAL)
ITCS .... Integrated Target Command [*or Control*] System (IAA)
ITCS .... Integrated Target Control System (MCD)
ITCS .... Integrated Temperature Control System (SAUS)
ITCS .... Integrated Test Control System (SAUS)
ITCSA .... Institute of Technical Communicators of Southern Africa (EAIO)
ITCSA .... In Vitro. Journal of the Tissue Culture Association (journ.) (SAUS)
ITCU .... Information Technology Consultancy Unit (NITA)
ITCU .... Intensive Thoracic Cardiovascular Unit [*Medicine*] (STED)
ITCU .... International Technological Collaboration Unit (SAUO)
ITCUA .... Information Technologies Credit Union Association (NTPA)
ITCUA .... International Telephone Credit Union Association (EA)
ITCVD .... Ischemic Thrombotic Cerebrovascular [*Medicine*] (EDAA)
ITCWRM .... International Training Center (or Centre) for Water Resources Management (SAUO)
ITCZ .... Intercontinental Terminals [*Federal Railroad Administration identification code*]
ITCZ .... Intertropical Convergence Zone [*Trade winds*] [*Meteorology*]
ITD .... Idiopathic Torsion Dytonia [*Medicine*]
ITD .... Inception-to-Date
ITD .... Individual'naya Trudovaya Deyatel'nost' [*Individual Labor Activity*] [*Government program designed to foster private enterprise*] [*Russian*]
ITD .... Industrial Technology Division [*Environmental Protection Agency*] (GFGA)
ITD .... Information and Technology for the Disabled
ITD .... Information Technology Development [*Project*] [*DoD*] (RDA)
ITD .... Information Technology Directorate [*British*]
ITD .... Information Technology Division [*Naval Research Laboratory*]
ITD .... Information Trade Directory [*Gale Research Co.*] (NITA)
ITD .... Infrared Target Detector
ITD .... Inhalation Toxicology Division [*Environmental Protection Agency*] (GFGA)
ITD .... Initial Temperature Difference (IAA)
ITD .... Input Transaction accepted for Delivery (SAUS)
ITD .... Inspection Test Data (SAUO)
ITD .... Institute of Training and Development (EAIO)
ITD .... Integral Trap Door [*Technical drawings*]
ITD .... Integrated Technology Demonstration (or Demonstrator) (SAUS)
ITD .... Integrated Test Document (MCD)
ITD .... Integration Test and Demonstration (SDI)
ITD .... Intensely Transfused Dialysis [*Medicine*] (DMAA)
ITD .... Intent to Deny
ITD .... Interactive Terminal Display [*Computer science*] (DGA)
ITD .... Interactive Typographic Display [*Computer science*] (DGA)
ITD .... Interaural Time Difference [*Andiology*]
ITD .... Interchannel Time Displacement [*Magnetic recording*]
ITD .... Intercontinental Data [*Vancouver Stock Exchange symbol*]
ITD .... Interface Timing Diagram
ITD .... Interim Technical Directive (MCD)
ITD .... Interim Terrain Data (SAUO)
ITD .... Intermediate Block Character [*Communications term*] (DCT)
ITD .... Intermittent Transistory Detachment (SAUS)
ITD .... Internal Test Directive (KSC)
ITD .... International Telephone Directory (SAUS)
ITD .... Intertropical Discontinuity [*Meteorology*]
ITD .... Ion Trap Detector [*Spectroscopy*]
ITD .... Isothermal Desorption Spectrometry (AAEL)
ITD .... University of Texas at Dallas, Richardson, TX [*OCLC symbol*] (OCLC)
ITDA .... Income Tax Decisions of Australasia (journ.) (SAUS)
ITDA .... Independent Truck Drivers Association (SAUS)
ITDA .... Independent Truckers and Drivers Association (EA)
ITDA .... Indirect Target Damage Assessment (AAG)
ITDA .... Integrated Tunnel Diode Amplifier
ITDA .... International Tape/Disc (or Disk) Association (SAUS)
ITDA .... International Theatre Design Archive
ITDA .... International Tire Dealers Association
ITDAC .... Interagency Trade Data Advisory Committee [*Department of Commerce*] (EGAO)
ITDB .... International Trade Data Bank (SAUS)
ITDC .... Indian Tourist Development Corporation (SAUO)
ITDC .... International Trade Development Center (or Centre) (SAUS)
ITDC .... International Trade Development Committee (SAUO)
ITDD .... Integrated Tunnel Diode Device (IAA)
ITDE .... Interchannel Time Displacement Error [*Magnetic recording*]
ITDE .... Intertrack Time Displacement Error (IAA)
ITDF .... Interactive Transaction Dump Facility [*Computer science*] (MHDB)
ITDG .... Intermediate Technology Development Group [*Rugby, Warwickshire, England*] (EAIO)
ITDG/NA .... Intermediate Technology Development Group of North America (EA)
ITDM .... Intelligent Time Division Multiplexer [*Communications term*] (DCT)
ITDN .... Integrated Tactical-Strategic Data Network (DOMA)
ITDN .... Integrated Telephone and Data Network (SAUS)
ITDNS .... Integrated Tour Operating Digital Network Service (MHDI)
ITDNS .... Integrated Tow Operating Digital Network Service (SAUO)
ITDP .... Individual Training and Development Plan (COE)
ITDP .... Institute for Transportation and Development Policy (EA)
ITDP .... Integrated Technology Demonstration Plan (ACAE)

ITDP .... Integrated Technology Development Plan (SAUS)
ITDP .... Integration Test and Diagnosis Program (SAUS)
ITDR .... Institute for Training and Demographic Research (EA)
ITDR .... Integrated Technology Design Review (ACAE)
ITDS .... Improved Technical Data System (ACAE)
ITDS .... Integrated Technical Data System (PDAA)
ITDS .... Integrated Technical Data Systems (SAUO)
ITDS .... International Telecommunication Data Systems, Inc. [*NASDAQ symbol*] (SAG)
ITDSC .... Item Description (SAUS)
ITDSS .... Intelligent Target Development Support System (SAUO)
ITDT .... Improved Technical Documentation and Training (ACAE)
ITDT .... Integrated Technical Documentation and Training
ITDU .... Infantry Trials and Development Unit [*British military*] (DMA)
ITDU .... Infrared Tracking Display Unit
ITE .... Incident Transverse Electric (SAUS)
ITE .... Indicated Terminal Efficiency (DNAB)
ITE .... Indicated Thermal Efficiency [*Automotive engineering*]
ITE .... Individual Training Evaluation (MCD)
ITE .... Information Technology Equipment (SAUO)
ITE .... Information Technology in Engineering [*British*]
ITE .... Information Transfer Efficiency (SAUS)
ITE .... Input Test Equipment
ITE .... Institute for Terrestrial Ecology (SAUO)
ITE .... Institute of Telecommunications Engineers
ITE .... Institute of Television Engineers (SAUO)
ITE .... Institute of Terrestrial Ecology [*Research center*] [*British*] (IRC)
ITE .... Institute of Tool Engineering (ACAE)
ITE .... Institute of Traffic Engineers (EA)
ITE .... Institute of Transportation Engineers (EA)
ITE .... Institution of Telecommunication Engineers (SAUO)
ITE .... Instrumentation Test Equipment (KSC)
ITE .... Instrument Test Equipment (SAUS)
ITE .... Insufficient Therapeutic Effect [*Medicine*] (DAVI)
ITE .... Integrated Test Equipment (SAUS)
ITE .... Integration Test Equipment (MCD)
ITE .... Intercity Transportation Efficiency (OA)
ITE .... Intercity Transport Effectiveness (SAUS)
ITE .... Interestatal de Aviacion SA de CV [*Mexico*] [*ICAO designator*] (FAAC)
ITE .... Interim Test Equipment (ACAE)
ITE .... Internal Terminal Emulator (SAUS)
ITE .... International Technology Exchange (SAUO)
ITE .... International Telephone Exchange [*Telecommunications*] (TEL)
ITE .... International Tests for Enamels Committee (SAUO)
ITE .... International Townplanning Exhibition (SAUO)
ITE .... Intersite Transportation Equipment [*NASA*] (NASA)
ITE .... Interstrat Resources, Inc. [*Vancouver Stock Exchange symbol*]
ITE .... In the Ear [*Hearing aid*]
ITE .... Intrapulmonary Interstitial Emphysema [*Medicine*] (DMAA)
ITE .... Inverse Time Element (MUGU)
ITE .... Involute Throat and Exit (SAUS)
ITEA .... Information Technology European Awards (EURO)
ITEA .... Infraestructura Teatral [*Ministerio de Cultura*] [*Spain*] [*Information service or system*] (CRD)
ITEA .... International Technology Education Association (EA)
ITEA .... International Test and Evaluation Association (EA)
ITEA .... International Theatre Equipment Association (NTPA)
ITEA-CS .... International Technology Education Association-Council for Supervisors (SAUO)
ITEC .... Information Technology Centre [*Training centres*] [*British*] (NITA)
ITEC .... Information Technology Electronics and Computers [*A publication*]
ITEC .... Infrared for Test, Evaluation and Control (SAUS)
ITEC .... Infrared Techniques for Electronics Committee (SAUO)
ITEC .... Integral Throat/Exit Cone (MCD)
ITEC .... International Telephone Energy Conference (SAUO)
ITEC .... International Thoroughbred Exposition and Conference [*Kentucky Thoroughbred Association, Inc.*] (TSPED)
ITEC .... International Tourist Entertainment Corp. [*NASDAQ symbol*] (SAG)
ITEC .... International Transport Exhibition
ITEC .... International Turbine Engine Corp. (EFIS)
ITECA .... International Temperance Educational and Cultural Association (SAUO)
ITECH .... Joint IOC/WMO Group of Experts on IGOSS Technical Systems Design and Developmentand Service Requirements [*Marine science*] (MSC)
ITECO .... Industrial Test Equipment Company (SAUO)
ITED .... Integrated Trajectory Error Display [*Aviation*]
ITED .... Iowa Tests of Educational Development
ITEDC .... Information Technology Economic Development Committee (SAUS)
ITEE .... International Transistor Electronics Establishment (SAUS)
ITEF .... Institute of Thermo- and Electrophysics, Estonian Academy of Sciences (SAUS)
ITEF .... Integrated Test Equipment Facility (MCD)
I-TEF .... International Toxicity Equivalency Factor [*Toxicology*]
ITEF .... International Trade Exhibitions in France (EA)
ITEG .... Individual Training Evaluation Group (MCD)
ITEG .... Isotope-Powered Thermoelectric Generator (PDAA)
ITEJ .... Institute of Television Engineers of Japan (SAUS)
ITEL .... Joint WMO/IOC Group of Experts on Telecommunications (MSC)
ITEL .... Wavetech Inc. [*NASDAQ symbol*] (TTSB)
IT Element... Integral Time-Delay Element (SAUS)
ITELIS .... Irish Times Eurolex Legal Information Service [*Database*] (NITA)
ITELO .... Itel Corp. [*NASDAQ symbol*] (COMM)
ITEM .... Integrated Test and Maintenance (PDAA)
ITEM .... Integrated Theater Engagement Model
ITEM .... Intelligence Threat Evaluation Model [*Military*] (MCD)
ITEM .... Interactive Tactical Engagement Model (SAUS)
ITEM .... Interactive Technique for Effective Management (SAUS)
ITEM .... Interference Technology Engineer's Master (IEEE)
ITEM .... Internal Thermal Environment Management (SAUS)
ITEM .... International Technology Environmental Management (SAUO)
ITEME .... Institution of Technical Engineers in Mechanical Engineering (SAUO)
ITEME .... Institution of Technician Engineers in Mechanical Engineering [*British*]
ITeMS .... Ideas in the Teaching of Mathematics and Science (AIE)
ITEMS .... Imaging Technologies and Evolving Management Systems (SAUS)
ITEMS .... INCOTERM [*International Commerce Term*] Transaction Entry Management System
ITEMS .... In-Service Inspection, Testing, Evaluation and Monitoring Service (SAUS)
ITEMS .... Integrated Turbine Engine Monitoring System (SAUS)
ITEMS .... Interactive Tactical Environment Management System (SAUS)
ITEMS .... Interactive Transaction Entry Management System (SAUS)
ITEMS .... Items. Social Science Research Council (SAUO)
ITEM System... Integrated Test and Maintenance System (SAUS)
ITEO .... International Trade and Employment Organization (SAUO)
ITEP .... Indian Teacher Education Project (SAUS)
ITEP .... Individual Training and Evaluation Program [*Army*] (INF)
ITEP .... Institute of Theoretical and Experimental Physics [*Moscow*]
ITEP .... Integrated Test/Evaluation Program (AABC)
ITEP .... Interim Tactical ELINT [*Electronic Intelligence*] Processor
ITEP .... International Technology Exchange Program (SAUO)
ITEP .... International Trade Enhancement Program
ITE-Plan .... Italian Tourist Economic Plan (SAUO)
ITER .... International Thermonuclear Engineering Reactor (SAUS)
ITER .... International Thermonuclear Experimental Reactor
ITER .... International Tokamak Engineering Reactor (SAUO)
ITER .... International Toxicity Estimates for Risk (SAUO)
ITER .... Interstrat Resources, Inc. (SAUO)
iter .... iteration (SAUS)
iter .... iterative (SAUS)
Iterative G... Iterative Guidance Mode [*Aerospace*] (NAKS)
ITERF .... Interstrat Resources, Inc. [*NASDAQ symbol*] (COMM)
ITES .... Inelastic Tunnelling Electron Spectroscopy
ITESC .... International Tanker Equipment Standing Committee (SAUO)
ITESM .... Instituto Tecnologico de Estudios Superiores de Monterrey [*Research institute onMexico/US relations*] [*Mexico*] (CROSS)
ITESO .... International Tanker Equipment Standing Committee (SAUS)
ITEST .... Institute for Theological Encounter with Science and Technology (EA)
ITET .... Isotonic Endurance Test [*Medicine*] (EDAA)
ITeuS .... Saint Joseph Seminary, Teutopolis, IL [*Library symbol*] [*Library of Congress*] (LCLS)
ITeuSD .... Teutopolis Community Unit, School District 50, Teutopolis, IL [*Library symbol*] [*Library of Congress*] (LCLS)
ITEWS .... Improved Tactical Electronic Warfare System (SAUO)
ITEWS .... Integrated Tactical Electronic Warfare System
ITEX .... Industrial Training Exhibition and Symposium (SAUO)
ITEX .... Information Technology Exchange Exhibition [*British*] (ITD)
ITEX .... Internal Tide Experiment [*Marine science*] (MSC)
ITEX .... International Tundra Experiment (QUAC)
ITEX .... Itex Corp. [*NASDAQ symbol*] (SAG)
ItexCp .... Itex Corp. [*Associated Press*] (SAG)
ITF .... Air Inter, Societe [*France*] [*ICAO designator*] (FAAC)
ITF .... Impulse Transfer Function (KSC)
ITF .... Indian Territorial Force [*British military*] (DMA)
ITF .... Industrial and Trade Fairs Ltd. [*Solihull, West Midlands, England*] (TSSD)
ITF .... Industrial Technology Fund [*British*]
ITF .... Information Technology Fund (AAGC)
ITF .... Inian Territorial Force (SAUS)
ITF .... Inland Transit Floater (SAUS)
ITF .... Instant Transference
ITF .... Institute of Tropical Forestry [*Rio Piedras, PR*] [*Department of Agriculture*] [*Research center*]
ITF .... Institut Textile de France [*French Textile Institute*] [*Boulogne-Billancourt*] [*Information service or system*] (IID)
ITF .... Integrated Test Facility [*Computer science*]
ITF .... Integrated Thermal Flux (AAG)
ITF .... Integration & Test Facility (SAUS)
ITF .... Integration Task Force (SAUO)
ITF .... Integration Test Folders (ACAE)
ITF .... Intelligence Task Force (DOMA)
ITF .... Intelligence Terminal Family [*Military*] (MCD)
ITF .... Intensity Transfer Function (ACAE)
ITF .... Interactive Terminal Facility
ITF .... Interagency Task Force (AAGC)
ITF .... Interface File (SAUS)
ITF .... Interferon (DMAA)
ITF .... Interim [*Contact*] File (MCD)
ITF .... Intermediate Terminal Facility (SAUS)
ITF .... Intermediate Test Facility (MCD)
ITF .... International Television Federation (SAUO)
ITF .... International Tennis Federation [*Formerly, ILTF*] (EA)
ITF .... International Toll Free [*Telecommunications*]
ITF .... International Trade Fair [*New Zealand*]
ITF .... International Trade Forum (journ.) (SAUS)
ITF .... International Trampolining Federation (SAUO)
ITF .... International Transfer Format (SAUO)

ITF International Transport Federation (SAUO)
ITF International Transport Workers' Federation [*London, England*] (EAIO)
ITF International Tremor Foundation (EA)
ITF Internet Trade Finance Exchange
ITF Interstate Transportation of Fireworks
ITF Interstitial Transfer Facility [*Nuclear energy*] (NRCH)
ITF Intertropical Front [*Meteorology*] (BARN)
ITF Intestinal Trefoil Factor [*Biochemistry*]
ITF Intra Task Forcs (SAUS)
ITF In Trust For [*Banking*]
ITF Inverse Trigonometric Function
ITF Isochronous Transfer (SAUS)
ITF Isochron Transfer (SAUS)
ITF Italfarmaco [*Italy*] [*Research code symbol*]
ITF Italy. Documents and Notes (journ.) (SAUS)
ITFA Installation, Testing, and Firing Apparatus [*Military*] (INF)
ITFA In the Final Analysis (SAUS)
IT fare Inclusive Tour Fare [*Travel industry*] (TRID)
ItFB Biblioteca Berenson, Florence, Italy [*Library symbol*] [*Library of Congress*] (LCLS)
ItFBM Biblioteca Marucelliana di Firenze, Servizio Prestito, Florence, Italy [*Library symbol*] [*Library of Congress*] (LCLS)
ITFCA International Track and Field Coaches Association [*Athens, Greece*] (EAIO)
ITFCC Initial Tactical Flag Command Center (SAUS)
ITFCC Interim Tactical Flag Command Center (SAUS)
ITFCS Institute for Twenty-First Century Studies (EA)
ITFE Inductive Terrain Feature Extraction (SAUS)
ITFF Inter-agency Task Force on Forests (SAUO)
ITFF Intertrochanteric Femoral Fracture [*Medicine*] (MEDA)
ITFH Industrial and Trade Fairs Holdings Ltd. (SAUO)
ITFL International Task Force on Literacy (SAUO)
ITFMC Indian Territorial Force Medical Corps [*British military*] (DMA)
ITFMSG Interscience Technological Forecasting Methodology Study Group
ITFO International Trade Fairs Office [*Department of Commerce*]
ITFS Iliotibial Tract Friction Syndrome [*Medicine*] (EDAA)
ITFS Incomplete Testicular Feminization Syndrome [*Medicine*] (AAMN)
ITFS Instructional Television Field Service (ACAE)
ITFS Instructional Television Fixed Service [*Educational TV*]
ITFS International Tropical Fern Society [*Defunct*] (EA)
ITF System Interactive Terminal Facility System (SAUS)
ITFTRIA Instrument Tree Flow and Temperature Removal Instrument Assembly [*Nuclear energy*] (NRCH)
ITFW Industry Training Fund for Women [*Australia*]
ITG Australian Income Tax Guide [*A publication*]
ITG Industrial Tachometer Generator
ITG Industry Technology Group [*Air Force*] (MCD)
ITG Industry Test Group [*Air Force*]
ITG Information and Telecommunications Technologies Group [*Electronic Industries Association*] [*Washington, DC*] (TSSD)
ITG Information Technology Group (TIMI)
ITG Information Theory Group (SAUO)
ITG Informnation and Telecommunications Technologies Group (SAUO)
ITG Innovationstechnik GmbH & Co. [*Database producer*] (IID)
ITG Institute Technical Group
ITG Integra Financial Corp. [*NYSE symbol*] (SPSG)
ITG Integrated Terminal Guidance
ITG Integrin (DMAA)
ITG Interactive Test Generator (SAUS)
ITG Interagency Task Group (SAUO)
ITG Inter-Continental Energy [*Vancouver Stock Exchange symbol*]
ITG Interdiction Target Graphic (MCD)
ITG Interlace Airlines Ltd. [*Gambia*] [*FAA designator*] (FAAC)
ITG International Trumpet Guild (EA)
ITG Inventory Type Group (SAUO)
ITG Investment Tech Group [*NYSE symbol*] (SG)
ITG Ion Temperature Gradient [*Physics*]
ITG Iterative Test Generator (SAUS)
ITGA Integrin Alpha (DMAA)
ITGA Isothermogravimetric Analysis
ITGB Institute of Transport of Great Britain
ITGB Integrin Beta (DMAA)
ITGBL International through Government Bill of Lading
ItgCom Integrated Communications Network, Inc. [*Associated Press*] (SAG)
ITGD Interstate Transportation of Gambling Devices
ITGD Interstate Transport of Gambling Devices (SAUO)
ITGEN Input Tape Generator (SAUS)
ITGI International Gas Turbine Institute (SAUO)
ITGI Investment Tech Group [*NASDAQ symbol*] (TTSB)
ITGI Investment Technology Group [*NASDAQ symbol*] (SAG)
ITG J International Trumpet Guild. Journal (journ.) (SAUS)
ItgLfSci Integra LifeSciences Corp. [*Associated Press*] (SAG)
ITGLWF International Textile, Garment, and Leather Workers' Federation [*See also FITTHC*] [*Brussels, Belgium*] (EAIO)
ITGN Integon Corp. (SAUO)
ITG N International Trumpet Guild. Newsletter (journ.) (SAUS)
ItgPrc Integrated Process Equipment [*Associated Press*] (SAG)
ITGR Integra Financial Corp. (SAUO)
ITGR Integrity, Inc. [*NASDAQ symbol*] (SAG)
ITGR Integrity Music'A' [*NASDAQ symbol*] (TTSB)
ITGR Integrity Music, Inc. [*NASDAQ symbol*] (SAG)
ITGS Integrated Track Guidance System (SAUS)
ItgSys Integrated Systems, Inc. [*Associated Press*] (SAG)
ITGV Intrathoracic Gas Volume [*Medicine*] (EDAA)
ITGWF International Textile and Garment Workers' Federation [*Later, ITGLWF*]
ITGWF International Textile, Garment Workers Federation (SAUO)
ITGWU Irish Transport and General Workers' Union (DCTA)
ITH Integrated Technology USA, Inc. [*AMEX symbol*] (SAG)
ITH International Conference of Historians of the Labour Movement (SAUO)
ITH Interstitial Hyperthermia [*Medicine*] (DMAA)
ITh Interthecal [*Anesthesiology*]
ITH Interturbine Holland (SAUO)
ITH In-the-Hole Drilling (SAUS)
Ith Intrathecal [*Medicine*] (CPH)
ITh Intrathoracic [*Anatomy*]
ITH Island Technologies Corp. [*Vancouver Stock Exchange symbol*]
ITH Ithaca [*New York*] [*Airport symbol*] (OAG)
ITH Ithaca [*New York*] [*Seismograph station code, US Geological Survey*] [*Closed*] (SEIS)
ITH Ithaca, NY [*Location identifier*] [*FAA*] (FAAL)
ITh Thornton Public Library, Thornton, IL [*Library symbol*] [*Library of Congress*] (LCLS)
ITHA International Tourist Health Association (SAUO)
ITHACA In-Depth Accident Data Collection and Analysis (SAUO)
Ithaca C Ithaca College (GAGS)
ITHB International Thoroughbred Breeders, Inc. (SAUO)
ITHE International Travel Host Exchange
i thec Intrathecal [*Medicine*] (AAMN)
ITHI International Thomson Holdings, Inc.
ITHI International Thomson Holdings, Incorporated (SAUO)
ITHI International Travelers Health Institute (EA)
ITHL Internal Triangular Hinge Ligament [*of scallops*]
ITHM Intenherm, Inc. (SAUO)
ITHOF International Tennis Hall of Fame (EA)
ITHP Increased Take-Home Pay
IThP Intrathyroidal Parathyroid [*Medicine*] (EDAA)
ITI Iceberg Transport International Ltd. [*Saudi Arabia*] (PDAA)
ITI Ideal Transformer Interconnection (SAUS)
ITI Immediate Transient Incapacitation [*Radiation casualty criterion*] [*Army*] (AABC)
ITI Inagua Transports, Inc. (SAUS)
ITI Inagua Transports Incorporated (SAUO)
ITI Indian Telephone Industries, Ltd. (SAUS)
ITI Industrial Technology Institute [*Research center*] (RCD)
ITI Industrial Tectonics Inc. (SAUS)
ITI Industrial Tectonics Incorporated (SAUO)
ITI Industrial Training Institute (SAUO)
ITI Industrial Turbines International (SAUO)
ITI Industrial Turnkey International (SAUO)
ITI Industries Technical Institute (SAUS)
ITI Industries Technical Institute Inc. (SAUO)
ITI Industry and Trade Information (SAUO)
ITI Infaunal Trophic Index [*Marine pollution*]
ITI Information Technologies Industries
ITI Information Technology Industry Council [*Formerly, Computer and Business Equipment Manufacturers Association*] (IGQR)
ITI Information Technology Infrastructure (FOTI)
ITI Information Technology Intelligence (SAUS)
ITI Information Transform, Inc. [*Information service or system*] (IID)
ITI Information Transform, Incorporated (SAUO)
ITI Initial Task Index (AAG)
ITI Inspection and Test Instruction (NASA)
ITI Inspection/Test Instruction (SAUS)
ITI Institute for Technical Interchange (SAUO)
ITI Institute of Translation and Interpreting [*British*] (DBA)
ITI Institut TNO voor Toegepaste Informatica [*TNO Institute of Applied Computer Science*] [*Information service or system*] (IID)
ITI Instrument Technology, Incorporated (ACAE)
ITI Insurance Testing Institute [*Malvern, PA*] (EA)
ITI Integrated Task Index (AAG)
ITI Integrated Task Indices (SAUS)
ITI Intelligent Transportation Infrastructure
ITI Interactive Terminal Interface [*Computer science*] (IEEE)
ITI Inter-Alpha-Trypsin Inhibitor (DB)
ITI Interceptor Technology Integration
ITI Intermittent Trouble Indication [*Telecommunications*] (TEL)
ITI International Tax Institute (EA)
ITI International Technical Institute of Flight Engineers
ITI International Technology Institute (EA)
ITI International Telecharge, Inc. (SAUS)
ITI International Telecharge, Incorporated (SAUO)
ITI International Telesis Industries Corp. [*Vancouver Stock Exchange symbol*]
ITI International Theatre Institute [*Paris, France*] (EAIO)
ITI International Thrift Institute
ITI International Trachoma Initiative
ITI International Trade-Invest Institute (SAUO)
ITI International Training Institute
ITI Intertial Interval (SAUS)
ITI Intertrial Interval [*Psychology*]
ITI Irish Timber Industries Ltd. (SAUO)
ITI Itapetinga [*Brazil*] [*Airport symbol*] (AD)
ITIA Industrial Tungsten Industry Association (SAUO)
ITIA International Trade and Investment Act [*1984*]
ITIA International Tungsten Industry Association (EAIO)
ITIAI Items Troop Installed or Authorized List (SAUS)
ITIAL Items Troop Installed or Authorized List (MCD)

ITIB .... Iceland Tourist Information Bureau (SAUO)
ITIC .... Information Technology Industry Council (AAGC)
ITIC .... Interior Tree Improvement Council (SAUO)
ITIC .... International Tactical Instructor Course (SAUO)
ITIC .... International Tsunami Information Center (EA)
ITIC .... Inter-Tribal Indian Ceremonial Association (EA)
ITIC .... Investors Title Co. [*NASDAQ symbol*] (TTSB)
ITIC .... Investors Title Company (SAUO)
ITIC .... Investors Title Insurance Co. [*NASDAQ symbol*] (SAG)
ITIC-PAC ...... INSCOM Theater Intelligence Center-Pacific (SAUO)
ITIES .... Interfaced between Two Immiscible Electrolyte Solutions [*Physical chemistry*]
ITIES .... Interservice Technical Information Exchange System [*Military*] (AFIT)
ITIF .... Individual Taxpayer Information File [*IRS*]
ITIG .... Intelligroup, Inc. [*NASDAQ symbol*] (SAG)
ITII .... Internal-to-Internal Interface (MCD)
ITII .... International Technology Institute, Inc. (SAUS)
ITII .... International Technology Institute, Incorporated (SAUO)
ITII .... International Thomson Information, Inc. [*Later, ITLS*]
ITII .... International Thomson Information, Incorporated (SAUO)
ITII .... ITI Technologies [*NASDAQ symbol*] (TTSB)
ITII .... ITI Technologies, Inc. [*NASDAQ symbol*] (SAG)
ITIL .... Information Technology Infrastructure Library (GART)
ITIM .... Immunoreceptor Tyrosine-Based Inhibitory Motif [*Immunology*]
ITIM .... Interchurch Trade and Industry Mission (SAUO)
ITIM .... Itonut Yisrael Meugedet [*ITIM News Agency of the Associated Israel Press Ltd.*]
I-time .... Inspiratory Time (STED)
I-time .... Instruction Time (VLIE)
ITIN .... Individual Taxpayer Identification Number
ITIN .... Information Technology in Nursing (SAUO)
ITIN .... Investors Trust, Inc. (SAUS)
ITIN .... Investors Trust, Incorporated (SAUO)
ITIN .... Itinerary (AFM)
itin .... Itinerary (ELAL)
ITIN .... Itinerating (ROG)
IT Info .... Income Tax Information Release (DLA)
ITIP .... Improved Transtage Injector Program (MCD)
ITIP .... International Technical Integration Panel
ITIP .... International Technology Integration Panel (SAUO)
ITIP .... International Thomson Industrial Press
ITIPAT .... Institute for the Technology and Industrialization of Tropical Agricultural Products [*Ivory Coast*]
ITIPI .... Interim Tactical Information Processing and Interpretation
ITIR .... Imaging Thermal Infrared (SAUO)
ITIR .... Infrared Thermal Imaging Radiometer (EOSA)
ITIR .... Intermediate and Thermal Infrared Radiometer (SAUS)
ITIR .... Intermediate Thermal Infrared Radiometer (SSD)
ITIRC .... IBM Technical Information Retrieval Center [*International Business Machines Corp.*] [*Armonk, NY*]
ITIRC .... International Business Machines Technical Information Retrieval Center (SAUS)
ITIRC .... International Technical Information and Retrieval Center (SAUS)
ITIS .... Industrial Technical Information Service [*Singapore*] (IID)
ITIS .... Insect Toxicologists Information Service (SAUO)
ITIS .... Integrated Tank Insulation System
ITIS .... Integrated Technical Information Services (SAUO)
ITIS .... Integrated Technical Information System [*Department of Energy*] [*Information service or system*] (IID)
ITIS .... Intelligent Target Imaging System (ACAE)
ITIS .... Interactive Terminal Interface System [*Computer science*] (VLIE)
ITIS .... Interagency Taxonomy Information System [*A database of all the flora and fauna in North America*] [*Created by the EPA and other agencies*]
ITIS .... Interim Test Item Stimulator (SAUO)
IT-IS .... Intermediate Technology Industrial Services [*ITDG*] [*British*]
ITIS .... Internal Translation Information Subsystem [*Computer science*]
ITIS .... International Trade Information Service
ITIS .... Intertial Translation Information Subsystem (SAUS)
ITIS .... Intra-Theater Imagery Transmission System (SAUO)
ITIS .... Italians in Service of the US [*World War II*]
ITis .... Tiskilwa Township Library, Tiskilwa, IL [*Library symbol*] [*Library of Congress*] (LCLS)
ITISN .... Information Technology Information Services Network [*British*] (NITA)
ITisP .... Plow Creek Commune Library, Tiskilwa, IL [*Library symbol*] [*Library of Congress*] (LCLS)
ITISS .... Integrated Tactical Intelligence Support System (MCD)
ITisSD .... Tiskilwa Community Unit, School District 300, Tiskilwa, IL [*Library symbol*] [*Library of Congress*] (LCLS)
ITI Tech .... ITI Technologies, Inc. [*Associated Press*] (SAG)
ITIU .... Inventory Temporarily in Use [*Army*] (AABC)
ITI/US .... International Theatre Institute of the United States (EA)
ITIWG .... International Test Integration Working Grop (SAUS)
ITJ .... Indian Tax Journal [*A publication*] (DLA)
ITJ .... Institute of Technical Journalists (SAUS)
ITJ .... International Tax Journal (journ.) (SAUS)
ITJ .... International Trojan Development Corp. [*Vancouver Stock Exchange symbol*]
ITJ .... Itajai [*Brazil*] [*Airport symbol*] (AD)
ITJ .... Societa' Italjet [*Italy*] [*ICAO designator*] (FAAC)
ITK .... Itokama [*Papua New Guinea*] [*Airport symbol*] (OAG)
ITKF .... International Traditional Karate Federation (EA)
ITL .... American Inter-Island, Inc. (SAUO)
ITL .... Ignition Transmission Line
ITL .... Incoming Transaction Listing (AFM)
ITL .... Incomplete Task Log (AAG)
ITL .... Independent Test Laboratory (SAUO)
ITL .... Individual Test Lane [*Automotive emissions*]
ITL .... Industrial Test Laboratory [*Philadelphia Navy Yard*] [*Navy*]
ITL .... Information Technology Laboratory [*Army Corps of Engineers*]
ITL .... Information Technology Ltd. [*British*] (NITA)
ITL .... Input Transformerless (SAUS)
ITL .... Institute of Tape Learning [*British*] (DBA)
ITL .... Instrumented Team Learning (ADA)
ITL .... Instrument Technology Laboratories (SAUO)
ITL .... Integrated Transfer Launch (SAUS)
ITL .... Integrate-Transfer-Launch [*Complex*] [*NASA*]
ITL .... Integration, Test and Launch (SAUS)
ITL .... Intent to Launch (NG)
ITL .... Interactive Technology Laboratory [*New York Institute of Technology*] [*Research center*] (RCD)
ITL .... Interceptor/Transporter/Loader
ITL .... Interdivisional Technical Liaison (SAUS)
ITL .... Intermediate Text Language (NITA)
ITL .... Intermediate Transfer Language
ITL .... International Theological Library [*A publication*]
ITL .... Inverse Taper Lens
ITL .... Inverse Time Limit (MSA)
ITL .... Irish Trade List (SAUO)
ITL .... Isolated Transmission Line (SAUS)
ITL .... Isolated Transmission Link (SAUS)
ITL .... Isomeric Transition Level [*Radioactivity*]
ITL .... Isothermal Luminescence (PDAA)
Itl .... Italian (BARN)
ITL .... Italian Lira (SAUS)
ITL .... ITEL Corp. (SAUO)
ITL .... ITL Industries Ltd. [*Toronto Stock Exchange symbol*]
ITL .... I Transmit Later (SAUS)
ITL .... Mikma Ltd. [*Moldova*] [*FAA designator*] (FAAC)
ITLA .... Imperial Thrift & Loan [*NASDAQ symbol*] (TTSB)
ITLA .... Imperial Thrift & Loan Association [*NASDAQ symbol*] (SAG)
ITLA .... International Taxicab and Livery Association (NTPA)
ITLA .... ITLA Capital [*NASDAQ symbol*] (SG)
ITLB .... Instruction Tanslation Look-aside Buffer (SAUS)
ITLB .... Instruction TLB (SAUO)
ITLB .... Instruction Translation Lookaside Buffer [*Computer science*] (PCM)
ITLB .... International Trade Law Branch [*United Nations*] (DUND)
ITLBV .... Individual Tactical Load Bearing Vest [*Army*] (INF)
ITLC .... Instant Thin-Layer Chromatography
ITLC .... Integrated Transfer Launch Complex (IAA)
ITLC/SA .... Polysilicic-Acid-Impregnated Glass Filter Paper [*Medicine*] (EDAA)
ITLC/SG .... Silica Gel Impregnated Glass Fibers [*Medicine*] (EDAA)
ITLD .... Individual Tube Leak Detector (SAUS)
ITLD .... International Top Level Domain (SAUS)
ITLGSWF ...... Interamerican Textile, Leather, Garment and Shoe Workers Federation (SAUO)
ITLJ .... Income Tax Law Journal [*India*] [*A publication*] (DLA)
ITLMCF .... Instrument Technicians Labor-Management Cooperation Fund (EA)
ITL/OTL .... Input Transformerless/Output Transformerless (SAUS)
ItlOven .... [*The*] Italian Oven, Inc. [*Associated Press*] (SAG)
ITLS .... International Thomson Library Services
ITLSA .... Integrated Torso Limb Suit Assembly [*NASA*] (KSC)
ITLT .... Interstate Transportation of Lottery Tickets
itlx .... italics (SAUS)
ITM .... Improved Thayer-Martin [*Medium*] (DMAA)
ITM .... Incentive Travel and Meetings Association (COBU)
ITM .... Inch Trim Moment [*Nautical*]
ITM .... Incident Transverse Magnetic (SAUS)
ITM .... Index of Technical Manuals [*Military*] (DNAB)
ITM .... Indirect Tag Memory
ITM .... Induction Tube Modulation
ITM .... Industrial Technology & Machinery (SAUS)
ITM .... Industrial Technology & Machines AG (SAUO)
ITM .... Infantry Target Mechanism [*Army*]
ITM .... Informatics for the Third World (SAUO)
ITM .... Information Technology Management (SAUO)
ITM .... Information Transfer Module [*Telecommunications*] (NITA)
ITM .... Insecticide-Treated Materials
ITM .... Inspector of Torpedoes and Mines [*Navy*]
ITM .... Institute of Thread Machiners [*Defunct*]
ITM .... Institute of Thread Machines (SAUO)
ITM .... Institute of Tropical Medicine (SAUS)
ITM .... Institute of Tropical Meteorology (SAUO)
ITM .... Instruction Trace Monitor (SAUS)
ITM .... Integral Telemetry
ITM .... Integrated Test and Maintenance (ACAE)
ITM .... Integrated Text Management (TIMI)
ITM .... Intelligent Tutoring Media [*Artificial intelligence*]
ITM .... Interceptor Tactical Missile [*Air Force*]
ITM .... Intercommunication Teleprocessing Monitor (IAA)
ITM .... Interim Technical Memorandum
ITM .... Intermedics, Inc. (SAUO)
ITM .... Internal Technical Memorandum
ITM .... Internal Tympaniform Membrane [*Zoology*]
ITM .... International Telecomputer Network Corp. (SAUO)
ITM .... International Tourism Management [*Australia*]
ITM .... Internet Transaction Mix (SAUS)
ITM .... In the Money [*Options*] [*Investment term*] (NUMA)
ITM .... Investment Trust Funds under Management
ITM .... Ionosphere-Thermosphere-Mesosphere (SAUS)

ITM ISDN [*Integrated Services Digital Network*] Trunk Module [*Telecommunications*]
ITM Israel Turkey Meningoencephalitis [*Medicine*] (DB)
ITM ITA [*Itapemirim Transportes Aereos SA*] [*Brazil*] [*ICAO designator*] (FAAC)
ITM Item [*Online database field identifier*]
ITM Ithomi [*Greece*] [*Seismograph station code, US Geological Survey*] (SEIS)
ITMA Income Tax Management Act (SAUO)
ITMA Information Technology Management Association (SAUO)
ITMA Institute for Training in Municipal Administration (EA)
ITMA Institute of Trade Mark Agents [*British*] (DI)
ITMA Institute of Trademark Agents (SAUO)
ITMA International Tanning Manufacturers Association [*Defunct*] (EA)
ITMA International Transmission Maintenance Centre (SAUO)
ITMA Investigation on Teaching Using Microcomputers as an Aid
ITMA Irradiation Test Management Activity (NRCH)
ITMA It's That Man Again [*Long-running English radio comedy, 1939-1949*]
ITMAR Information Technology Marketing Association (SAUO)
ITMARC Italian MARC (SAUS)
ITMC Interface/Time Mission Critical (SAUS)
ITMC International Multimedia Teleconferencing Consortium (SAUO)
ITMC International Transmission Maintenance Center [*Communications*]
ITMD Interim Theater Missile Defense (ACAE)
IT/ME Incentive Travel and Meeting Executives Show [*Trade show*] (ITD)
ITMEB International Tea Market Expansion Board (SAUO)
ITMF International Textile Manufacturers Federation [*Zurich, Switzerland*] (EA)
ITMG Integrated Thermal Micrometeoroid Garment [*Spacesuit*]
ITMG Intra-Theater Movement Generator (SAUO)
ItMGM Italian MGM [*Record label*]
ITMI Industrial Technology and Machine Intelligence (NITA)
ITMI International Talent Management, Inc. (SAUS)
ITMI International Talent Management Incorporated (SAUO)
ITMID Item Identification File
ITMIS Integrated Transportation Management Information System [*Army*]
ITMJ Incoming Trunk Message Junction [*Telecommunications*] (OA)
ITMN Installation Test Manual (SAUS)
ITMN InterMune Pharmaceuticals [*NASDAQ symbol*] (SG)
ITMRA Information Technology Management Reform Act (SAUS)
ITMRA Information Technology Management Reform Act of 1996 (AAGC)
ITMRC International Travel Market Research Council
ITMS Immediate check Truth Maintenance System (SAUS)
ITMS In-Core Temperature Monitoring System [*Nuclear energy*] (NRCH)
ITMS Ingestible Thermal Monitoring System
ITMS Integrated Thermal Monitoring System (SAUS)
ITMS Integrated Training Management System [*DoD*]
ITMS Interactive Tsunami Modeling System [*Marine science*] (OSRA)
ITMS International Tax Management System [*Price Waterhouse & Co.*]
ITMS Ion Trap Mass Spectrometer
ITMT Intermediate Thermomechanical Treatment (MCD)
ITMTX Intrathecal Methotrexate [*Medicine*] (EDAA)
ITMZ Indiana Transportation Museum [*Federal Railroad Administration identification code*]
ITN Identification Tasking and Networking (SAUO)
ITN Image Transmission Network [*Computer science*] (CIST)
ITN Independent Telecommunication Network (ACRL)
ITN Independent Transportation Network
ITN Indiana Teletype Network (SAUS)
ITN Industrias Titan SA [*Spain*] [*ICAO designator*] (FAAC)
ITN Information Transfer Node (SAUO)
ITN Insecticide Treated Nets (SAUO)
ITN Institute for TransPacific Networking [*Oakland, CA*] [*Telecommunications service*] (TSSD)
ITN Integrated Telecommunications Network (CIST)
ITN Integrated Teleprocessing Network
ITN Interim Technical Note
ITN International Telecomputer Network (SAUS)
ITN International Television Network (SAUO)
ITN International Television News [*A publication*] (EAAP)
ITN International Turbine Tech [*Vancouver Stock Exchange symbol*]
ITN Internegative [*Photography*] (NTCM)
ITN Internet Travel Network (SAUO)
ITN Inter-Service Telephone Network (SAUS)
ITN InterTan, Inc. [*NYSE symbol*] (CTT)
ITN In Touch Networks (EA)
ITN Itabuna [*Brazil*] [*Airport symbol*] (OAG)
ITN Independent Television News (ODA)
ITNA Independent Television News Association [*News service*]
ITNBR Item Number (SAUS)
ITNC In-Track Noncontiguous
ITND International Trade Names Dictionary [*Later, IBTC*] [*A publication*]
ITNFSA International Tanker Nominal Freight Scale Association
ITNL Interactive Tech [*NASDAQ symbol*] (TTSB)
ITNL Interactive Technologies Corp. [*NASDAQ symbol*] (SAG)
ITNL Internal (ECII)
ITNOTGAOTU In the Name of the Great Architect of the Universe [*Freemasonry*] (ROG)
ITNRNT Itinerant (FAAC)
ITNS Integrated Tactical Navigation System [*Navy*]
ITNS International Tactical Navigation System (SAUO)
ITNS International Transplant Nurses Society (EA)
ITNS Italian Naval Ship (SAUS)
ITNSA Item Net Sales Amount (SAUS)
ITNS/D-AHRS Integrated Tactical Navigation System/Doppler-Altitude Heading Reference System (SAUS)
ItNU Universita di Napoli, Naples, Italy [*Library symbol*] [*Library of Congress*] (LCLS)
ItNU-IC Universita di Napoli, Istituto Chimico, Naples, Italy [*Library symbol*] [*Library of Congress*] (LCLS)
ITO Hilo [*Hawaii*] [*Airport symbol*] (OAG)
ITO Hilo, HI [*Location identifier*] [*FAA*] (FAAL)
ITO Idiopathic Transient Osteoporosis [*Medicine*]
ITO Immunology Today Online (SAUO)
ITO Impulse Transfer Orbit
ITO Income Tax Office (DAS)
ITO Income Tax Order
ITO Independent Television Organization (NTCM)
ITO Independent Test Organization (ACAE)
ITO Indian Tourist Office (SAUO)
ITO Indian Tribal Organization (GFGA)
ITO India Tourist Office (SAUO)
ITO Indium Tin Oxide
ITO Individual Travel Order [*Military*] (CINC)
ITO Industrial Therapy Organisation [*British*]
ITO Industrial Therapy Organization (SAUO)
ITO Inspecting Torpedo Officer [*Navy*]
ITO Inspection, Test & Operation (SAUO)
ITO Installation Transportation Office [*or Officer*] [*Air Force*] (AFM)
ITO Institution of Training Officers [*British*]
ITO Instrument Takeoff
ITO Integration and Test Order (MCD)
ITO Interim Technical Order (AFM)
ITO Intermediate Training Objective [*Army*] (INF)
ITO Internal Test Organization (SAUO)
ITO International Technology Office (SAUO)
ITO International Terminal Operators (SAUO)
ITO International Thomson Organisation [*Later, The Thomson Corp.*]
ITO International Thomson Organization Ltd. (SAUO)
ITO International Trade Offices (JAGO)
ITO International Trade Organisation (or Organization) (SAUO)
ITO International Training Organization (SAUO)
ITO International Travel Orders
ITO Intertrochanteric [*Medicine*] (MELL)
ITO In Theory Only (journ.) (SAUS)
ITO Invitational Travel Order [*Army*] (AABC)
ITO Irish Tourist Office (BI)
ITO Ito [*Japan*] [*Seismograph station code, US Geological Survey*] [*Closed*] (SEIS)
ITOA Inbound Tourism Organisation of Australia
ITOA Independent Tanker Owners Association (DS)
ITOA Independent Taxi Owners Association (SAUO)
ITOA Independent Terminal Operators Association (EA)
ITOC Independent Telephone Operating Company (SAUO)
ITODA Independent Turf and Ornamental Distributors Association (NTPA)
ITOF Ion Time of Flight
ITOFCA Industrial Trailer-On Flatcar Associates (SAUS)
ITOFCA Industrial Trailer-on-Flatcar Associates (SAUO)
ITOFCN Interim Technical Order Field Change Notice [*Air Force*] (MCD)
ITOH Idiopathic Transient Osteoporosis of the Hip [*Medicine*]
ITOI International Thomson Organisation, Inc.
ITOI International Thomson Organization, Incorporated (SAUO)
ITOL International Thomson Organisation Ltd. [*Later, TTC*]
ITOL International Thomson Organization Limited (SAUO)
ITol Toluca City Library, Toluca, IL [*Library symbol*] [*Library of Congress*] (LCLS)
ITolo Tolono Township Library, Tolono, IL [*Library symbol*] [*Library of Congress*] (LCLS)
ITolSD Toluca Community Unit, School District 2306, Toluca, IL [*Library symbol*] [*Library of Congress*] (LCLS)
ITOM Interstate Transportation of Obscene Matter
ITONA Iveco Trucks of North America, Inc.
ITonSD Tonica Consolidated Community School District 79 and Consolidated High School District 360, Tonica, IL [*Library symbol*] [*Library of Congress*] (LCLS)
I-TOO Independent Truck Owner/Operator Association (EA)
ITOO Independent Truck Owner-Operators Association
I-TOOA Independent Truck Owner/Operator Association (SAUS)
ITOP Integrated Test Operate Panel
ITOP International Testing Operations Procedurse (SAUS)
ITOP International Test Operations Procedure [*DoD*]
ITOPF International Tanker Owners Pollution Federation
ITOPF International Tanker Owners Pollution Federation Ltd. (SAUO)
ITOPLC International Thomson Organisation (or Organization) Public Limited Company (SAUO)
ITOPLC International Thomson Organisation Public Limited Co.
ITOPLC International Thomson Organisation Public Ltd. Co. (SAUS)
ITOPS Interim Terminal Overseas Processing System (SAUO)
ITOPS Interim Transportation Overseas Processing System (SAUO)
ITOR Intercept Target Optical Reader
ITOS Improved TIROS [*Television Infrared Observation Satellite*] Operational Satellite [*or System*] [*National Oceanic and Atmospheric Administration*]
ITOS Improved TIROS Operational System (SAUO)
ITOS Interactive Terminal Operating System (NITA)
ITOS Interactive Terminal-Oriented Software (SAUS)
ITOS International Theosophical Order of Service (SAUO)
ITOS Iterative Time Optimal System

ITOSS .... Integrated Toolkit for Operating System Security [*Computer security system*]
ITOT .... ISO Transport service on TCP/IP (SAUS)
ITOU .... Intensive Therapy Observation Unit [*Medicine*] (DMAA)
ITou .... Toulon Public Library, Toulon, IL [*Library symbol*] [*Library of Congress*] (LCLS)
ITOVS .... International TOVS working group (SAUO)
ITOW .... Improved Tube-Launched, Optically Tracked, Wire-Guided [*Weapon*] (RDA)
ITOY .... International Tropospheric Ozone Year (CARB)
ITOY .... International Truck of the Year
ITOYO .... International Truck of the Year Organization
ItoYokd .... Ito-Yokado Co. Ltd. [*Associated Press*] (SAG)
ITP .... Idiopathic Thrombocytopenic Purpura [*Medicine*] (MTAA)
ITP .... Immune Thrombocytopenic Purpura [*Medicine*]
ITP .... Impact Time Prediction (SAUO)
ITP .... Incidental Take Permit
ITP .... Income Tax Professional (ADA)
ITP .... Independent Television Publications [*British*] (ECON)
ITP .... Index of Technical Publications [*Military*] (DNAB)
ITP .... Index to Proceedings [*Information service or system*] [*United Nations*] (DUND)
ITP .... Individual Training Plan [*Army*]
ITP .... Individual Training Program (MCD)
ITP .... Individual Treatment Plan [*For the medical care and the education of a handicapped person*]
ITP .... Inferior Thalamic Peduncle [*Anatomy*]
ITP .... Initial Trial Phase (NG)
ITP .... Innovative Training Project
ITP .... Inosine Triphosphate [*Biochemistry*]
ITP .... Input Translator Program [*Computer science*]
ITP .... Inspection Test Procedure
ITP .... Installation Test Program
ITP .... Installation Transition Processing (SAUS)
ITP .... Institute for Theoretical Physics (SAUS)
ITP .... Instruction to Proceed (NATG)
ITP .... Instruction-To-Proceed (SAUS)
ITP .... Instruction to Process (SAUO)
ITP .... Integral Thermal Process (SAUS)
ITP .... Integrated Technology Plan (SAUS)
ITP .... Integrated Test Package (CAAL)
ITP .... Integrated Test Plan (AAGC)
ITP .... Integrated Test Program
ITP .... Integrated Training Plan (SAUO)
ITP .... Integrated Transaction Processor (MHDI)
ITP .... Integration Test Plan (SAUS)
ITP .... Intelligence Town Plan
ITP .... Intensive Training Program
ITP .... Intention To Proceed (SAUS)
ITP .... Intent to Purchase (SAUO)
ITP .... Interactive Terminal Protocol [*Computer science*]
ITP .... Interactive Testing in Psychiatry (SAUO)
ITP .... Interceptor Technology Program
ITP .... Intercon Petroleum, Inc. [*Vancouver Stock Exchange symbol*]
ITP .... Interim Test Procedure (MCD)
ITP .... Interim Training Program [*Army*] (INF)
ITP .... Interior Thalamic Peduncle (SAUS)
ITP .... Intermin Treatment Plan [*Medicine*] (DAVI)
ITP .... International Television Program (SAUO)
ITP .... International Test Pilot School [*British*] [*ICAO designator*] (FAAC)
ITP .... International Thompson Publishing (SAUS)
ITP .... International Thomson Publishing [*Also, ITPI*]
ITP .... Internet Transport Protocol (SAUS)
ITP .... Interrupted Task Paradigm [*Psychometrics*]
ITP .... Interstitial Thickening Process (SAUS)
ITP .... Intertape Polymer Group [*AMEX symbol*] (SAG)
ITP .... Intrathoracic Pressure [*Medicine*]
ITP .... Islet-Cell Tumor of Pancreas [*Medicine*] (MELL)
ITP .... Isotachophoresis [*Analytical biochemistry*]
ITP .... Italian Patent (IAA)
It P .... Italian Pharmacopoeia [*A publication*]
It P .... Italian Pharmacopoeia (journ.) (SAUS)
ITp .... Tinley Park Public Library, Tinley Park, IL [*Library symbol*] [*Library of Congress*] (LCLS)
ITPA .... Illinois Test of Psycholinguistic Abilities
ITPA .... Independent Telephone Pioneer Association (EA)
ITPA .... International Tea Promotion Association [*Defunct*] (EAIO)
ITPA .... International Trotting and Pacing Association (EA)
ITPA .... International Truck Parts Association (EA)
ITPA .... Irish Trade Protection Association (DBA)
ITPAC .... Imported Tobacco Products Advisory Council [*British*] (DBA)
ITPAIS .... Image Technology Patent Information System [*Printing technology*] [*Rochester Institute of Technology*] [*Rochester, NY*]
ItPavU .... Universita degli Studi, Pavia, Italy [*Library symbol*] [*Library of Congress*] (LCLS)
ITPB .... Integrated Test Program Board
ITPC .... International Television Program Center [*Telecommunications*] (TEL)
ITPC .... International Tree Project Clearinghouse (SAUO)
ITPFF .... Interstate Transportation of Prize Fight Films
ITPI .... Integrated Transactional Processing Interface (SAUS)
ITPI .... International Thomson Publishing, Inc. [*Also, ITP*]
ITPI .... International Thomson Publishing, Incorporated (SAUO)
ITPI .... International Transfer Printing Institute (EA)
ITPIAL .... Infrared Target Pointer/Illuminator/Aiming Laser [*Military*] (INF)
ITP-ID .... International Thomson Publishing - International Division
ITpM .... Tinley Park Mental Health Center, Tinley Park, IL [*Library symbol*] [*Library of Congress*] (LCLS)
ITPMG .... Interstate Transportation of Prison-Made Goods
ITP-NSS .... Innovative Training Projects - National Skills Shortage
ITPO .... International TOGA Planning Office (SAUO)
ITPO .... International TOGA [*Tropical Ocean Global Atmosphere*] Project Office [*Geneva, Switzerland*] (EAIO)
ITPP .... Individual Training Plan Proposal [*Army*]
ITPP .... Institute of Technical Publicity and Publications [*British*] (BI)
ITPP .... International Thomson Professional Publishing
ITPP .... International TOVS Processing Package (SAUO)
ITPR .... Individual Training and Performance Research (SAUS)
ITPR .... Infrared Temperature Profile Radiometer
ITPR .... Inuit Tapirisat of Canada. Press Release (journ.) (SAUS)
ITPRL .... Individual Training and Performance Research Laboratory [*Army*] (RDA)
ITPRON .... International Tide-Prone Rice Observational Nursery (SAUO)
ITPS .... Income Tax Payers' Society [*British*] (BI)
ITPS .... Institute for Theological and Philosophical Studies (EA)
ITPS .... Integrated Technical Processing System (NITA)
ITPS .... Integrated Teleprocessing System (IEEE)
ITPS .... Interactive Teleprocessing System (NITA)
ITPS .... Interactive Test Preparation System [*Computer science*] (MHDI)
ITPS .... Interactive Text Preparation System (SAUS)
ITPS .... Interactive Text Processing System (NITA)
ITPS .... Internal Teleprocessing System (CMD)
ITPS .... International Test Pilots School (SAUO)
ITPS .... International Thomson Publishing Services
ITPTBG .... Interpretation (journ.) (SAUS)
ITPX .... Inteleplex Corp. (SAUO)
ITQ .... Individual Transferable Quota
ITQ .... Infant Temperament Questionnaire
ITQ .... Inferior Temporal Quadrant [*Medicine*] (DMAA)
ITQ .... Inspection Test Quantity (SAUS)
ITQ .... International Thesaurus of Quotations [*A publication*]
ITQ .... Invitation to Quote (MCD)
ItQ .... Irish Theological Quarterly (SAUO)
ITQ .... Itaqui [*Brazil*] [*Airport symbol*] (AD)
ITQS .... Information Technology Quality System (SAUS)
ITQS .... Information Technology Quality Systems (SAUO)
itqs .... in-text questions (SAUS)
ITR .... Australian Income Tax Reports [*A publication*] (DLA)
ITR .... Department of Industry (SAUS)
ITR .... Ignition Test Reactor (MCD)
IT-R .... Immunotoxin with Ricin
ITR .... Improved Tanar Retrofit (SAUS)
ITR .... Improved Tartar Retrofit [*Missile*] (MCD)
ITR .... Income Tax Regulations (FOTI)
ITR .... Income Tax Reports [*India*] [*A publication*] (DLA)
ITR .... In-Core Thermionic Reactor [*Nuclear energy*]
ITR .... In-Core Thermionic Record (SAUS)
ITR .... Incremental Tape Recorder
ITR .... Independent Tank Regiment (SAUS)
ITR .... Independent Technical Review (SAUO)
ITR .... Indiana Toll Road (SAUS)
ITR .... Indian Tax Reports [*A publication*] (ILCA)
ITR .... Individual Training Record [*Military*] (INF)
ITR .... Indoor Testing Range [*Golf*] (PS)
ITR .... Industrial Target Report [*Later, IDR*] [*British*] [*World War II*]
ITR .... Industrial Tribunal Reports (DCTA)
ITR .... Infantry Training Regiment (SAUO)
ITR .... Infantry Training Replacement
ITR .... Informal Training Review (SAUO)
ITR .... Information Technology Research [*Waltham, MA*] [*Telecommunications*] (TSSD)
ITR .... Information Technology Resources (SAUO)
ITR .... Initial Training Requirement
ITR .... Initial Trouble Report (IAA)
ITR .... Inlet Temperature Rise
ITR .... Inspection Test Report
ITR .... Institute Technical Reports (SAUO)
ITR .... Instrumentation Tape Recorder
ITR .... Instrumented Test Range [*Fort Huachuca, AZ*] [*United States Army Electronic Proving Ground*] (GRD)
ITR .... Instrument Test Rig [*Liquid Metal Engineering Center*] [*Energy Research and Development Administration*] (IEEE)
ITR .... Integrated Technology Rotor
ITR .... Integrated Telephone Recorder [*Telecommunications*] (TEL)
ITR .... Integrated Test Range (SAUS)
ITR .... Integrated Test Requirements
ITR .... Integrated Thyristor Rectifier (IAA)
ITR .... Integrated Tourism Resort
ITR .... Integrated Trans Ntwk Grp. [*AMEX symbol*] (SG)
ITR .... Intelcom Group [*AMEX symbol*] (SPSG)
ITR .... Intense Thermal Radiation
ITR .... Interactive Teleprocessing System (SAUS)
ITR .... Interactive Text Processing System (SAUS)
ITR .... Intergrated Test Requirements (SAUS)
ITR .... Interim Technical Report
ITR .... Interim Test Report
ITR .... Internal Technical Report
ITR .... Internal Throughput Rate (SAUS)
ITR .... International Trade Reporter (journ.) (SAUS)
ITR .... Internet Talk Radio (SAUO)
ITR .... Interstate Transport Region

ITR............ In-Transit Rendezvous
ITR............ Intraocular Tension Recorder
ITR............ Intra-Team Radio (SAUS)
ITR............ Intratracheal [*Medicine*]
IT/R............ Inventory Transfer Receipt
ITR............ Inverse Time Relay (KSC)
ITR............ Inverted Terminal Repeat [*Genetics*]
ITR............ Invitation to Register (ADA)
ITR............ Ion Transfer Reaction (SAUS)
ITR............ Iowa Terminal Railroad [*Federal Railroad Administration identification code*]
ITR............ Irish Term Reports, by Ridgeway, Lapp, and Schoales [*A publication*] (DLA)
ITR............ Isolation Test Routine (IAA)
Itr............ Iterationszahl (SAUS)
ITR............ ITR Airlines, Inc. (SAUO)
ITRA............ Integrated Test Requirements Analysis (CAAL)
ITRA............ Intercomparison of Transmittance and Radiance Algorithms (SAUS)
ITRA............ International Tenant Representative Alliance (SAUS)
ITRA............ International Tire and Rubber Association (NTPA)
ITRA............ International Truck Restorers Association (EA)
ITRAC............ Interdata Transaction Controller (SAUO)
i trach............ Intratracheal [*Medicine*] (AAMN)
ITRAM............ International [*Passenger*] Traffic Management System [*MTMC*] (TAG)
ITRAM............ International Traffic Passenger Management System (SAUO)
ITRB............ Initial Test Review Board (SAUO)
ITRB............ Internal Throughput Rate Ratio (SAUS)
ITRB............ Interservice Training Review Board (MCD)
ItRC............ Consiglio Nazionale delle Ricerche, Rome, Italy [*Library symbol*] [*Library of Congress*] (LCLS)
ITRC............ Industrial and Technical Referral Center (or Centre) (SAUS)
ITRC............ Industrial Testing and Research Centre (SAUO)
ITRC............ Industrial Toxicology Research Centre (SAUO)
ITRC............ Information Technology Requirements Council (CIST)
ITRC............ Information Technology Research Centre (SAUO)
ITRC............ Intercardia Inc. [*NASDAQ symbol*] (TTSB)
ITRC............ International Technology Resources, Inc. (SAUO)
ITRC............ International Terrorist Research Center (SAUO)
ITRC............ International Tin Research Council [*Middlesex, England*] (EAIO)
ITRC............ Interstate Technology Regulatory Coordination (SAUO)
ITRC............ Interstate Transport Region Commission
ITRC............ Iowa Terminal Railroad-Charles City [*Federal Railroad Administration identification code*]
ITRC............ Iowa Transfer Railway [*Federal Railroad Administration identification code*]
ITRC............ Irrigation Training and Research Center (SAUO)
ITRD............ Innovative Treatment Remediation Demostration (SAUO)
ITRD............ Integrated Test Requirements Documents (MCD)
ITRDB............ International Tree-Ring Data Bank [*University of Arizona*] (IID)
ITRDC............ Inland Transport Research and Development Council (SAUO)
ITRDS............ Integrated Test Requirements Documents (MCD)
ITRE............ Institute for Transportation Research and Education [*University of North Carolina*] [*Research center*] (RCD)
Itre............ Trenton Public Library (SAUS)
ITre............ Trenton Public Library, Trenton, IL [*Library symbol*] [*Library of Congress*] (LCLS)
ITreWHS............ Weslin Junior-Senior High School, Trenton, IL [*Library symbol*] [*Library of Congress*] (LCLS)
ITR/FRR............ Integrated Technology Rotor/Flight Research Rotor (SAUS)
ITRI............ Industrial Technology Research Institute [*Integrated Circuit Design Centre*] [*Taiwan*] (NITA)
ITRI............ Inhalation Toxicology Research Institute [*Albuquerque, NM*] [*Department of Energy*]
ItRI............ Institute Centrale Catalogo Unico delle Bibliotheche Italiane e per le Informazioni Bibliografiche, Rome, Italy [*Library symbol*] [*Library of Congress*] (LCLS)
ITRI............ Interconnection Technology Research Institute (AAEL)
ITRI............ International Tin Research Institute (EAIO)
ITRI............ International Travel Research Institute (SAUO)
ITRI............ Invitation to Register Interest
ITRI............ Itron, Inc. [*NASDAQ symbol*] (SAG)
ITRIA............ Instrument Tree Removable Instrument Assembly [*Nuclear energy*] (NRCH)
ITRIC............ International Root-crop Information Centre (SAUO)
ITRIS............ Integrated Tsunami Research and Information System (SAUO)
ITRIS............ Integrated Tsunami Research Information System [*Marine science*] (OSRA)
ITRIS............ International Trade and Resource Information System [*University of Alaska at Anchorage*] [*Information service or system*] (CRD)
ITRJDW............ International Tree Crops Journal (journ.) (SAUS)
ITRL............ Inhalation Toxicology Research Institute (SAUO)
ITRL............ Instrument Test Repair Laboratory (AAG)
ITRM............ Information Technology Resouces Management (SAUO)
ITRM............ Inverse Thermoremanent Magnetization
ITRM............ Iowa Terminal Railroad-Mason City [*Federal Railroad Administration identification code*]
ITRMS............ Information Technology Resource Management System (SAUO)
ITRN............ Intenrans Corp. (SAUO)
ITRO............ Installation Test Requirements Outline (MCD)
ITRO............ Integrated Test Requirements Outline
ITRO............ Interservice Training Requirements Organization (SAUO)
ITRO............ Interservice Training Review Organization [*Military*] (NVT)
ITro............ Tri-Township Library, Troy, IL [*Library symbol*] [*Library of Congress*] (LCLS)
ITROD............ Incendiary Torch Remote Opening Device (MCD)
ITRON............ Industrial TRON (NITA)
ITRON............ International Tidal Wetland Rice Observational Nursery (SAUO)
Itron............ Itron, Inc. [*Associated Press*] (SAG)
ITRP............ Institute of Transportation and Regional Planning (EA)
ITRP............ Interservice Training Program (SAUS)
ITRPF............ International Tire, Rubber and Plastics Federation (SAUS)
ITRR............ Integrated Technology Requirements Review (ACAE)
ITRS............ Income Tax Refund Service (SAUS)
ITRS............ International Terrestrial Reference System (SAUO)
ITRT............ Independent Technical Review Team (SAUO)
ITRU............ Industrial Training and Research Unit (ACII)
ITRU............ Industrial Training Research Unit (SAUO)
ItRU............ Universita degli Studi, Biblioteca Alessandrina, Rome, Italy [*Library symbol*] [*Library of Congress*] (LCLS)
IT Rulings............ Income Tax Rulings [*A publication*]
IT Rulings............ Income Tax Rulings (journ.) (SAUS)
ItRUN............ Centro di Documentazione Umberto Nobile, Museo Storico, Rome, Italy [*Library symbol*] [*Library of Congress*] (LCLS)
ITRY............ Itinerary (FAAC)
ITS............ Aeronautica Interespacial SA de CV [*Mexico*] [*ICAO designator*] (FAAC)
ITS............ AmericaIntelligent Transportation Society of America [*Formerly, IVHS America*]
ITS............ Idaho Test Station [*Nuclear energy*] (NRCH)
ITS............ Idle Tracking Switch [*Automotive engineering*]
ITS............ Ignition Test Simulator
ITS............ Imagery Transmission System (SAUS)
ITS............ Imaginary Transition Structure [*Organic chemistry*]
ITS............ Import Tabulation System [*United Nations*] (PDAA)
ITS............ Improved Third Stage [*of Minuteman rocket*]
ITS............ I'm Tired Syndrome
ITS............ Incident Tracking System
ITS............ Inclusive Tour Service (ADA)
ITS............ Incompatible Time-sharing System (NHD)
ITS............ Independent Triggering System
ITS............ Index to Speeches [*Information service or system*] [*United Nations*] (DUND)
ITS............ Individual Training Standard (ACAE)
ITS............ Industrial Technology Securities [*Investment firm*] [*British*]
ITS............ Industrial Television Society [*Later, ITVA*] (EA)
ITS............ Industrial TEMPEST Scheme Institute for Transportation Studies (SAUS)
ITS............ Industrial Trade Show (SAUS)
ITS............ Industrial Training Service (AIE)
ITS............ Industrial Translation System (SAUS)
ITS............ Industry Training Support
ITS............ Indus Tsangpo Suture [*Paleogeography*]
ITS............ Inertial Timing Switch (IAA)
ITS............ Infective Toxic Shock [*Medicine*] (DMAA)
ITS............ Infinite Time Span
ITS............ Inflatable Tubular Structure
ITS............ Informatics Teaching System (SAUS)
ITS............ Information Technology Security (FOTI)
ITS............ Information Technology Services [*Stanford University*] [*Information service or system*] (IID)
ITS............ Information Technology Services [*California State University, Long Beach*] [*Research center*] (RCD)
ITS............ Information Technology Services [*National Library of Canada*] (TSSD)
ITS............ Information Technology Systems
ITS............ Information Theory Society (SAUO)
ITS............ Information through Speech (SAUS)
ITS............ Information Transfer Satellite (KSC)
ITS............ Information Transfer [*or Transmission*] System
ITS............ Infrared Tracking System
ITS............ Inhaled Tobacco Smoke (MELL)
ITS............ Initial Training School [*British military*] (DMA)
ITS............ Initial Training Squadron (SAUO)
ITS............ Insertion Test Signal [*Telecommunications*] (TEL)
ITS............ Institute for Telecommunication Sciences [*Formerly, ITSA*] [*Boulder, CO*] [*Department of Commerce*]
ITS............ Institute for Telecommunication Service (SAUO)
ITS............ Institute for Transportation Studies [*University of Calgary*] [*Canada*] [*Research center*] (RCD)
ITS............ Institute of Telecommunications Services (MSC)
ITS............ Institute of Temporary Services [*Later, National Association of Temporary Services*] (EA)
ITS............ Institute of Theoretical Science [*University of Oregon*] [*Research center*] (RCD)
ITS............ Institute of Trading Standards (SAUO)
ITS............ Institute of Transportation Studies [*University of California*] [*Research center*] (RCD)
ITS............ Institute of Turkish Studies (EA)
ITS............ Instrument and Telemetry System (SAUS)
ITS............ Instrumentation and Telemetry System (SAUS)
ITS............ Instrumentation Telemetry Station [*NASA*] (NASA)
ITS............ Instrumentation Telemetry System [*NASA*] (IAA)
ITS............ Instrument Time (Simulated)
ITS............ Insulation Test Specification (MSA)
ITS............ In-Tank Solidification
ITS............ Integrated Target System
ITS............ Integrated Termination System (IAA)
ITS............ Integrated Test Schedule [*Army*]
ITS............ Integrated Test Software (CAAL)

ITS .... Integrated Test System (SAUS)
ITS .... Integrated Tracking System [*ARTRAC*] [*Obsolete*] (MCD)
ITS .... Integrated Trading System (SAUS)
ITS .... Integrated Training System (ACAE)
ITS .... Integrated Trajectory System
ITS .... Intelligent Terminal Service (SAUS)
ITS .... Intelligent Terminal Support (SAUS)
ITS .... Intelligent Terminal System [*IBM Corp.*]
ITS .... Intelligent Test System (SAUS)
ITS .... Intelligent Transportation Society [*formerly, IVHS, Intelligent Vehicle-Highway Society*]
ITS .... Intelligent Transportation System [*FTA*] [*NHTSA*] (TAG)
ITS .... Intelligent Transportation Systems (SAUS)
ITS .... Intelligent Transport System [*Traffic management*] (ECON)
ITS .... Intelligent Tutorial Systems (SAUS)
ITS .... Intelligent Tutoring System (RDA)
ITS .... Interactive Terminal Service (NITA)
ITS .... Interactive Terminal Support [*Computer science*]
ITS .... Interactive Terminal System (SAUO)
ITS .... Interactive Training System (SAUS)
ITS .... Interactive Translation System (SAUO)
ITS .... Interagency Testing Committee Tracking System (SAUO)
ITS .... Interconnection Test Set (SAUS)
ITS .... Interface Test Set (SAUS)
ITS .... Interim Table Simulation (SAA)
ITS .... Interim Teleprinter System
ITS .... Intermarket Trading System (IEEE)
ITS .... Intermediate Tape Store (CET)
ITS .... Intermediate-Term Standby [*Business term*] (EMRF)
ITS .... Internal Time Sharing (IAA)
ITS .... Internal Transcribed Spacer [*Genetics*]
ITS .... International Tanker Services (SAUO)
ITS .... International Technogeographical Society
ITS .... International Technologies & Systems [*Computer science*]
ITS .... International Telecommunications Service (SAUS)
ITS .... International Telecommunications Services Inc. (SAUO)
ITS .... International Telecommunications Society (EA)
ITS .... International Telecom Systems, Inc. [*Madison, WI*] [*Telecommunications*] (TSSD)
ITS .... International Telephone Service (SAUO)
ITS .... International Teleproduction Society (EA)
ITS .... International Television Service [*Turner Teleport, Inc.*] [*Atlanta, GA*] [*Telecommunications service*] (TSSD)
ITS .... International Temperature Scale (MUGU)
ITS .... International Tesla Society (EA)
ITS .... International Thermal Sight (SAUS)
ITS .... International Thespian Society (EA)
ITS .... International Time Sharing Corp. (SAUS)
ITS .... International Time-Sharing Corporation [*Telecommunications*] (NITA)
ITS .... International Totalizator Systems, Inc. (EFIS)
ITS .... International Tracing Service [*Arolsen, Germany*] (EAIO)
ITS .... International Trade Secretariats [*ICFTU*]
ITS .... International Trade Show (SAUS)
ITS .... International Trade Specialist (JAGO)
ITS .... International Training School
ITS .... International Transportation Service (SAUO)
ITS .... International Travel Show (ITD)
ITS .... International Trucking Show (ITD)
ITS .... International Turfgrass Society (EA)
ITS .... International Twin Study [*University of Southern California*] [*Research center*] (RCD)
ITS .... Internet Technology Series
ITS .... Internet Telephony Server (SAUO)
ITS .... Inter-plan Teleprocessing System (SAUO)
ITS .... Intersectional Transportation Service
ITS .... Interstate Energy [*Vancouver Stock Exchange symbol*]
ITS .... Intertime Switch [*Connection or Call*] [*Telecommunications*] (TEL)
ITS .... Interval Test Signal (SAUS)
ITS .... Interval Test System (SAUS)
ITS .... Invitation to Send [*Western Union*] [*Data communications*]
ITS .... Ion Thrust System
ITS .... Ion Trap System
ITS .... Iowa Transfer System
ITS .... Irish Texts Society (EAIO)
ITS .... Islamic Texts Society [*British*] (DBA)
ITS .... Tri-State University, Angola, IN [*OCLC symbol*] (OCLC)
ITSA .... Information Technology Skills Agency (NITA)
ITSA .... Information Technology Strategic Alliances Database (IID)
ITSA .... Insider Trading Sanctions Act (SAUS)
ITSA .... Insider Trading Sanctions Act of 1984
ITSA .... Installation and Test Support Associate Contractor [*Air Force*]
ITSA .... Institute for Telecommunication Sciences and Aeronomy [*Later, ITS*] [*National Oceanic and Atmospheric Administration*]
ITSA .... Institute of Trading Standards Administration [*British*]
ITSA .... Intelligent Transportation Society of America (SAUO)
ITSA .... International Technology SA (SAUO)
ITSA .... International Thermal Spray Association (SAUO)
ITSA .... Interstate Transportation of Stolen Aircraft
ITSAADCOTFOIK... International Twelve-Star Admiral and Deputy Custodian of the Fountain of Inexhaustible Knowledge [*Rank in Junior Woodchucks organization mentioned in Donald Duck comic by Carl Barks*]
ITSAC .... International Thermal Storage Advisory Council (EAIO)
ITSAEM .... Integrated Telematics System for Administrations Environmental Management (EURO)
ITSB .... Image Technology Standards Board (SAUO)
ITSB .... Interstate Transportation of Strikebreakers
ITSC .... Industrial Training Systems Corp. (SAUS)
ITSC .... Industrial Training Systems Corporation (SAUO)
ITSC .... International Technical Support Center (SAUS)
ITSC .... International Telecommunications Satellite Consortium [*Superseded by International Telecommunications Satellite Organization*]
ITSC .... International Telecommunications Services Complex (SAUS)
ITSC .... International Telephone Service Centre (SAUS)
ITSC .... International Telephone Service Centres (SAUO)
ITSC .... International Telephone Services Center [*Telecommunications*] (TEL)
ITSC .... International TOVS Study Conference (SAUO)
ITSC .... International Transit Switching Centre (SAUS)
ITSC .... International Tyre Specialists Congress (SAUO)
ITSC .... Interstate Transportation of Stolen Cattle
ITSC .... Item Type Storage Code (SAUS)
ITSC .... It Scale for Children [*Psychology*]
ITSCD .... Interagency Toxic Substances Data Committee (SAUS)
ITSDC .... Interagency Toxic Substances Data Committee [*Washington, DC*] [*Environmental Protection Agency*] (EGAO)
ITSDN .... Integrated Tactical/Strategic Data Network (SAUO)
ITSE .... Integral of Time Squared Error [*Statistics*] (PDAA)
ITSE .... Integral Time Square Error (SAUS)
ITSEC .... Information Technical Security Evaluation Criteria (SAUO)
ITSEC .... Information Technology Security Evaluation Certification (SAUO)
ITSEC .... Information Technology Security Evaluation Criteria (SAUO)
ITSEC .... Information Technology Standards Unit [*British*]
ITSEM .... Information Technology Security Evaluation Manual (SAUO)
ITSEM .... Information Technology Security Evaluation Methodology (SAUO)
ITSF .... International Tandem Surfing Federation (SAUO)
ITSG .... Interallied Technical Study Group (SAUO)
ITSH .... Internal Transport, Storage and Handling (SAUS)
ITSHD .... Isolated Thyroid Stimulating Hormone Deficiency [*Medicine*] (STED)
ITSI .... International Lottery & Totalizator Systems [*NASDAQ symbol*] (SAG)
ITSI .... International Totalizator Systems, Inc. [*NASDAQ symbol*] (NQ)
ITSI .... International Totalizator Systems, Incorporated (SAUO)
ITSI .... Intl Lottery & Totalizator [*NASDAQ symbol*] (TTSB)
ITSIE .... Intelligent Training Systems in Industrial Environment (SAUS)
ITSIPIST ...... Index to Standard Interrest Profiles in Science and Technology (SAUS)
ITSL .... Integrated Two-Step Liquefaction [*Chemical engineering*]
ITSL .... International Translator (IAA)
ITSM .... Institute for Technical and Scientific Marketing (SAUS)
ITSMV .... Interstate Transportation of Stolen Motor Vehicle
ITSO .... Incoming Trunk Service Observation (VLIE)
ITSO .... Instrument Technician Service Organization
ITSO .... International Technical Support Organization (SAUS)
ITSO .... International Telecommunication Satellite Organisation (SAUS)
ITSO .... International Telecommunications Satellite Organization (SAUO)
ITSO .... International Telegraphy Society Organization (ACAE)
ITSOP .... Integrated Telecommunications Systems Operational Planning (SAUO)
ITS/OT .... Institute for Telecommunications (SAUS)
ITS/OT .... Institute for Telecommunications USDC/Boulder Laboratories (SAUO)
ITSP .... Information Technology and System Planning (VLIE)
IT/SP .... Instrument Tree/Spool Piece [*Nuclear energy*] (NRCH)
IT/SP .... Instrument Tree/Spool Pierce (SAUS)
ITSP .... Integrated Training System Plan [*Army*]
ITSP .... Integrated Training System Planning (SAUS)
ITSP .... Internet Telephony Service Provider (VLIE)
ITSP .... Interstate Transportation of Stolen Property
ITSPA .... Interstate Transportation of Stolen Property Act (SAUO)
ITSPO .... Information Technology Standards Program Office (SAUO)
ITSS .... Integrated Tactical Surveillance System
ITSS .... Integrated Target Sensor Suite (MCD)
ITSS .... Integrated Technical Support Services System (SAUO)
ITSS .... Integrated Total Security System (TIMI)
ITSS .... Interim Time Sharing System (VLIE)
ITSS .... International Team for Studying Sintering (SAUS)
ITSS .... Investment Trust Savings Scheme [*British*]
ITSTC .... Information Technology Steering Committee (SAUO)
ITSTC .... International Telecommunictaions Standards Technical Council (OSI)
ITSTEC .... Integrated Transmission Switching & Technical Control (SAUO)
ITSU .... Information Technology Standards Unit (NITA)
ITSU .... International Co-ordination for the Tsunami Warning System in the Pacific (SAUS)
ITSU .... International Coordination Group for the Tsunami Warning System in the Pacific [*Marine science*] (OSRA)
ITSW .... International Total Services, Inc. [*NASDAQ symbol*] (NASQ)
ITSY .... Innovative Tech Systems, Inc. [*NASDAQ symbol*] (SAG)
ITSYLF .... Interactive Synthesizer of Letterforms
ITSYW .... Innovative Tech Sys Wrrt'A' [*NASDAQ symbol*] (TTSB)
ITSZ .... ITS Maersk [*Federal Railroad Administration identification code*]
ITT .... Federal Reserve Bank of Chicago Library (SAUS)
ITT .... Federal Reserve Bank of Chicago Library, Chicago, IL [*OCLC symbol*] (OCLC)
ITT .... Identical Twins Raised Together (STED)
ITT .... Iliotibial Tract [*Orthopedics*] (DAVI)
ITT .... Image Intensification Tube (MCD)
ITT .... Impact Transition Temperature (MCD)
ITT .... Import Transit Time (VLIE)
ITT .... Incoming Teletype
ITT .... Incoming Trunk Terminal [*Telecommunications*] (IAA)
ITT .... Indicator Time Test [*Chemistry*]
ITT .... Individual Technical Training [*Military*]

ITT .... Infrared Tympanic Thermometer [*Medicine*]
ITT .... Initial Teacher Training (AIE)
ITT .... Initial Training Test (SAUO)
ITT .... Inside Trim Template (MSA)
ITT .... Instant Touch Tuning (SAUS)
ITT .... Institute of Textile Technology (EA)
ITT .... Institute of Travel and Tourism [*British*] (DBA)
ITT .... Insulin Tolerance Test [*Physiology*]
ITT .... Integrated Test Team (SAUO)
ITT .... Internal Tibial Torsion [*Orthopedics*] (DAVI)
ITT .... International Interagency Telecommunications (SAUO)
ITT .... International Telegraph and Telephone (SAUO)
ITT .... International Telephone and Telegraph Corp. (SAUO)
ITT .... International Telephone and Telegraphs (SAUS)
ITT .... International Trade in Textiles [*Textile trade agreement*]
ITT .... Interpretative Trace and Trap Program (SAA)
ITT .... Interrogation-Translation Team [*Military*] (CINC)
ITT .... Interrogator-Translator Team (SAUO)
ITT .... Inter-Tandem Trunk (SAUS)
ITT .... Inter-Test Time (AAEL)
ITT .... Inter-Theater Transfer [*Army*] (AABC)
ITT .... Intertoll Trunk [*Telecommunications*]
ITT .... Inter-Turbine Temperature (ADA)
ITT .... Intertype Training [*Navy*] (NVT)
ITT .... In These Times (journ.) (SAUS)
ITT .... Inventaire des Tablettes de Tello. Mission Francaise en Chaldee [*Paris*] [*A publication*] (BJA)
ITT .... Invest Tracker Tecnologia
ITT .... Invitation To Tender (SAUO)
ITT .... Invitation to Transmit (SAUS)
ITT .... Iron Tolerance Test (STED)
ITT .... Islamic Institute of Technology (SAUO)
ITT .... ITT Canada Ltd. [*Toronto Stock Exchange symbol*]
ITT .... ITT Corp. [*Formerly, International Telephone & Telegraph Corp.*] [*Wall Street slang name: "It Girl," the sobriquet for early movie star Clara Bow*] [*NYSE symbol*] (SPSG)
ITT .... Wittenoom Gorge [*Western Australia*] [*Airport symbol*] (AD)
ITTA .... Independent Taxation with Transferable Allowance [*British*] (DI)
ITTA .... Independent Travel Technology Association (TVEL)
ITTA .... Indianapolis Television Technicians Association (SAUS)
ITTA .... Information Technology Training Association, Inc. (SAUO)
ITTA .... International Table Tennis Association (SAUO)
ITTA .... International Telegraph and Telephone Agency (SAUO)
ITTA .... International Tropical Timber Agreement (ECON)
ITTA .... International Tropical Timbers Agreement (SAUS)
ITTA .... ITT [*Institute of Textile Technology*] Austria (NITA)
ITTAC .... Information Technology Training Accredition Council [*British*] (NITA)
ITTAC .... International Telegraph and Telephone Advisory Committee (SAUS)
ITTAC .... International Telegraph and Telephonic Advisory Committee (AABC)
ITTA-C .... ITTA-C Corporation (SAUO)
ITTAP .... ITT [*Institute of Textile Technology*] Testability Analysis Program (NITA)
ITTB .... Idle Time to Boil [*Automotive engineering*]
ITTC .... Instrumentation Technology and Training Center (SAUO)
ITTC .... Inter-American Tropical Tuna Commission [*Scripps Institution of Oceanography*]
ITTC .... International Telegraph and Telephone Corporation (SAUO)
ITTC .... International Telephone and Telegraph Corporation (SAUO)
ITTC .... International Television Trading Corp. (SAUS)
ITTC .... International Television Trading Corporation (SAUO)
ITTC .... International Towing Tank Conference (SAUO)
ITTC .... International Travel and Trailer Club (EA)
ITTC .... International Tropical Timber Council [*Australia*]
ITTCCS .... ITT Corporate Communications Services, Inc.
ITTCCS .... ITT Corporative Communication Service, Inc. (SAUO)
ITTCOINS .... ITT [*Institute of Textile Technology*] Communications and Information Services Inc. (NITA)
ITTCOM .... International Telephone and Telegraph Communications, Inc. (SAUS)
ITTCOM .... International Telephone & Telegraph World Communications, Inc.
ITT Corp .... ITT Corp. [*Associated Press*] (SAG)
ITT Corporation ... International Telephone and Telegraph Corporation (SAUO)
ITT Cp .... ITT Corp. [*Formerly, International Telephone & Telegraph Corp.*] [*Wall Street slang name: "It Girl," the sobriquet for early movie star Clara Bow*] [*Associated Press*] (SAG)
ITTCS .... International Telegraph and Telephone Communications Systems (SAUS)
ITTCS .... International Telephone and Telegraph Communication System
ITTD .... Information and Technology Transfer Database [*International Research and Evaluation*]
ITT-DTS .... ITT Domestic Transmission Systems Inc. (SAUO)
ITTE .... Institute for the Transfer of Technology to Education (EA)
ITTE .... Institute of Transportation and Traffic Engineering [*UCLA*]
ITTE .... Interim Terminal Test Environment [*FAA*]
ITTE .... International Telegraph and Telephone, Europe (SAUO)
ITTE .... International Telephone and Telegraph, Europe (SAUS)
ITT Ed .... ITT Educational Services, Inc. [*Associated Press*] (SAG)
ITTETS .... ITT Employment & Training Systems, Inc. [*Telecommunications service*] (TSSD)
ITTF .... International Table Tennis Federation [*British*]
ITTF .... International Telephone and Telegraph, Federal (SAUO)
ITTF .... International Telephone and Telegraph Federal Laboratories
ITTFA .... Iterative Target Transformation Factor Analysis [*Computer science*]
ITTFL .... International Telephone and Telegraph Federal Laboratories
ITT/FSS .... International Telephone and Telegraph Federal Support System (SAUO)
ITT/FSS .... International Telephone and Telegraph/FTS Federal Support Services (SAUO)
ITTG .... Interdisciplinary Team Training in Geriatrics [*Veterans Administration*] (GFGA)
ITTGATC .... ITT [*Institute of Textile Technology*] Gallium Arsenide Technology Cen ter (NITA)
ITTI .... Information Technology Training Initiative (SAUO)
ITT Inds .... ITT Industries, Inc. Indiana [*Associated Press*] (SAG)
ITTL .... International Table Tennis League (EA)
ITTL .... International Telephone and Telegraph Laboratories (SAA)
ITTM .... Institute of Telecommunications and Information Technology (SAUS)
ITTM .... Institute of Telecommunications and Information Technology Malaysia (SAUO)
ITTO .... International Tropical Timber Organization [*Yokohama, Japan*] [*United Nations*]
ITTO .... International Tropical Timbers Organization (SAUS)
ITTP .... Indian Teacher Training Program (SAUS)
ITTP .... Informational Technology and Telecommunication Policy (SAUS)
ITTP .... Instrument Technician Training Program (ACII)
ITT/PMD .... Interpretative Trace and Trap Program Plus Modifications (SAA)
ITTR .... Inflatable Tubular Torso Restraint
ITTR .... ITT Rayonier Railroad [*Federal Railroad Administration identification code*]
ITTRI .... International Telegraph and Telephone Research Institute (SAUS)
ITTS .... Instrumentation, Target, and Threat Simulator [*Army*] (RDA)
ITTT .... Individual Tactical Technical Training [*Military*] (MCD)
ITTT .... Institute of Transportation, Travel, and Tourism
ITTTA .... International Technical Tropical Timber Association
ItTU .... Biblioteca Nazional Universitaria di Torino, Servizio Prestito, Turin, Italy [*Library symbol*] [*Library of Congress*] (LCLS)
ITTUCC .... International Teachers Trade Union Cooperation Committee (SAUO)
ITT-USTS .... ITT United States Transmission Systems, Inc. [*Telecommunications service*] (TSSD)
ITT-WC .... International Telephone and Telegraph World Communications, Inc. (SAUS)
ITT-WC .... International Telephone and Telegraph-World Communications, Inc. (SAUO)
ITTWORLDCOM ... International Telephone and Telegraph World Communications, Inc. (SAUO)
ITTZ .... ITT Grinnell [*Federal Railroad Administration identification code*]
ITU .... Ikutoku Technical University (SAUO)
ITU .... Image Transfer Unit (SAUS)
ITU .... Income Tax Unit
ITU .... Information Transport Utility (SAUO)
ITU .... Input Terminal Unit (SSD)
ITU .... Instructional Technologist Unit
ITU .... Integrated Terrain Unit (CARB)
ITU .... Intelligent Thermal Update (SAUS)
ITU .... Intensive Therapy Unit [*Medicine*] (MAE)
ITU .... Interamerican Telecommunications Unions (SAUO)
ITU .... Interface Transformation Unit (SAA)
ITU .... Interface Translation Unit (SAUS)
ITU .... International Comunication Union (SAUS)
ITU .... International Taurus Resources [*Vancouver Stock Exchange symbol*]
ITU .... International Technical University (SAUO)
ITU .... International Technological University (SAUO)
ITU .... International Telecommunications Unit (SAUS)
ITU .... International Telecommunication Union [*Formerly, International Telegraphic Union*] [*A specialized agency of the United Nations*] [*Switzerland*] [*Research center*]
ITU .... International Telephone Union (SAUO)
ITU .... International Temperance Union
ITU .... International Toxic Units (SAUO)
ITU .... International Triathlon Union (EAIO)
ITU .... International Typographical Union (EA)
ITU .... Inventory Temporarily in Use [*Army*] (AFIT)
ITU .... Investment Trust Unit [*British*]
ITU .... Istanbul Technical University (SAUO)
ITU .... Taylor University, Upland, IN [*OCLC symbol*] (OCLC)
ITu .... Tuscola Public Library (SAUS)
ITu .... Tuscola Public Library, Tuscola, IL [*Library symbol*] [*Library of Congress*] (LCLS)
ITUA .... Independent Trade Union Association [*Turkey*]
ITUA .... Industrial Trades Union of America (SAUO)
ITUC .... Irish Trade Union Congress
ITuCoH .... Douglas County Jarman Memorial Hospital, Tuscola, IL [*Library symbol*] [*Library of Congress*] (LCLS)
ITUCSTL .... International Trade Unions Committee of Social Tourism and Leisure [*See also CSITSL*] [*Prague, Czechoslovakia*] (EAIO)
ITU-D .... International Telecommunication Union-Telecommunication Development Sector (SAUO)
ITUE .... Integrated Technology Uplink Experiment (ACAE)
ITUG .... Information Technology Users Group [*Exxon Corp.*]
ITUG .... International Tandem Users' Group (EA)
ITUG .... International Telecommunications Users Group (SAUO)
ITUG .... International Telecommunication Users Group (SAUS)
ITUM .... International Trade Union Movement (SAUO)
i-tum .... Intratumoral [*Medicine*] (EDAA)
i-Tumor .... Intratumoral (STED)
ITU-Newsletter ... Newsletter of the International Telecommunication Union (SAUO)
ITU-R .... International Telecommunications Union-Radio Sector (CGWS)
ITUR .... International Telecommunications Union-Radiosector (SAUO)
ITU-R .... International Telecommunication Union-Radio Communication Sector (ACRL)

ITU-R .... International Telecommunication Union-Radiocommunication sector (SAUS)
ITUR .... Interstate Transportation of Unsafe Refrigerators
ITURM .... International Typographical Union Ruling Machine
ITURMI .... International Typographical Union Ruling Machine (SAUO)
ITUS .... Institute of Totally Useless Skills [*An association*] (EA)
ITUS .... Integrated Thermal Utility System (SAUS)
ITUSA .... Information Technology Users Association (SAUS)
ITUSA .... Information Technology Users' Standards Association [*British*]
ITUSA .... IT Users Standards Association (SAUS)
ITUSAF .... Institute of Technology, United States Air Force [*Wright-Patterson Air Force Base, Dayton, OH*] (AAG)
ITUSFP .... Interreligious Taskforce on US Food Policy (EA)
ITU-T .... International Telecommunications Union-Telecommunications Standards (or Standardization) Sector (SAUO)
ITUT .... ITU Technical Standards Group (SAUO)
ITU-TIES .... International Telecommunications Union-Telecom Information Exchange Services (SAUO)
ITU-TIES .... ITU-Telecom Information Exchange Services (SAUS)
ITU-TS .... International Telecommunications Union-Telecommunications Standardization (SAUS)
ITU-TS .... International Telecommunications Union-Telecommunications Standardization Sector (SAUO)
ITU-TS .... International Telecommunication Union-Telecommunication Standardization sector (SAUS)
ITU-TSB .... International Telecommunications Union-Telecommunications Board (SAUO)
ITUTSS .... International Telecommunications Standards Sector (SAUS)
ITU-TSS .... International Telecommunications Union - Telecommunications Switching System (PCM)
ITUTSS .... International Telecommunications Union Telecommunication Standards Sector (SAUS)
ITU-TSS .... ITU-Telecommunication Standards Section (SAUS)
ITV .... IMO Television Service (SAUS)
ITV .... Improved TOW [*Tube-Launched, Optically Tracked, Wire-Guided (Weapon)*] Vehicle
ITV .... Independently Targeted Vehicle [*Military*] (DA)
ITV .... Independent Television
ITV .... Independent Television Co. (SAUS)
ITV .... Industrial Television
ITV .... Inferior Temporal Vein [*Medicine*] (DMAA)
ITV .... Instructional Television
ITV .... Instrumental Test Vehicle
ITV .... Instrumented Target Vehicle (SAUS)
ITV .... Instrumented Test Vehicle (SAUO)
ITV .... Integrated Technology Validation
iTV .... Interactive Digital Television
ITV .... Interactive Television
ITV .... Intercept Test Vehicle (ACAE)
ITV .... Intermediate Test Vessel (NRCH)
ITV .... Internal Television (SAUS)
ITV .... Internal Transfer Voucher (SAUS)
ITV .... Intervuelo SA [*Mexico*] [*ICAO designator*] (FAAC)
ITV .... Intranet Visability [*Army*]
ITV .... In-Transit Visibility (COE)
ITV .... Israel Television (BJA)
ItV .... Italian RCA [*Victor*] [*Record label*]
ITVA .... Independent Television Association
ITVA .... Instructional Television Authority (SAUO)
ITVA .... International Industrial Television Association (NTCM)
ITVA .... International Television Association (EA)
ITVAC .... Industrial Transistor Value Automatic Computer
ITVAD .... Indwelling Transcutaneous Vascular Access Device [*Pharmacology*] (DAVI)
ITV&V .... Independent Technology and System Verification and Validation (ACAE)
ITVB .... International Television Broadcasting
ITVE .... Integrated Technology Validation Experiment (ACAE)
ITVETS .... Improved TOW [*Tube-Launched, Optically Tracked, Wire-Guided (Weapon)*] Vehicle Evasive Target Simulator [*Military*] (MCD)
ITVF .... Integration, Test, and Verification Facility (SAUO)
ITVFTT .... Improved TOW Vehicle Field Tactical Trainer (SAUS)
ITVM .... Integration, Test, and Verification Model (SAUS)
ItVox .... Italian Vox [*Record label*]
ITVS .... Ignition Timing Vacuum Switch [*Automotive engineering*]
ITVS .... Independent Television Service
ITVS .... International Television Symposium (SAUO)
ITVSDA .... Independent Television Service Dealers' Association
ITVTP .... Internationale Tieraerztliche Vereinigung fuer Tierproduktion [*International Veterinary Association for Animal Production*]
ITVU .... InterVU, Inc. [*NASDAQ symbol*] (SG)
ITW .... Illinois Tool Works [*NYSE symbol*] (TTSB)
ITW .... Illinois Tool Works, Inc. [*NYSE symbol*] (SPSG)
ITW .... Independent Tank Wing [*of a ship*] (DS)
ITW .... Independent True Whig Party [*Liberia*] [*Political party*]
ITW .... Inertia Test Weight [*Exhaust emissions*] [*Automotive engineering*]
ITW .... Initial Training Wing [*British military*] (DMA)
ITW .... International Technology Week (SAUS)
ITW .... Intertrack Wagering [*Equine term*] (TED)
ITW .... Introducing the World [*An association*] [*Canada*]
ITWA .... International Tug-of-War Association (EA)
ITWAA .... Integrated Tactical Warning and Attack (SAUS)
ITW/AA .... Integrated Tactical Warning/Attack Assessment (COE)
ITW&A .... Integrated Tactical Warning and Assessment (SAUO)
ITWC .... Inland Transport War Council [*World War II*]
ITWEA .... International Travel Writers and Editors Association (NTPA)
ITWF .... International Transport Workers' Federation
ITWG .... Information Transfer Working Group (SAUO)
ITWG .... Interface Technical Working Group
ITWG .... Intergovernmental Technical Working Group (SAUO)
ITWG .... Interim Working Group (SAUO)
ITWG-AnGR ... Intergovernmental Technical Working Group on Animal Genetic Resources for Food and Agriculture (SAUO)
ITWG-PGR ... Intergovernmental Technical Working Group on Plant Genetic Resources for Food and Agriculture (SAUO)
ITWI .... Interstate Transmission of Wagering Information
ITWIS .... Integrated Terminal Weather Information System (SAUS)
ITWO .... i2 Technologies [*NASDAQ symbol*] (TTSB)
ITWO .... Inspection Test Work Order (SAA)
ITWP .... Information Technology Working Party (SAUO)
ITWP .... Interstate Transportation of Wagering Paraphernalia
ITWS .... Integrated Target Weather System (CTAS)
ITWS .... Integrated Terminal Weather System [*Marine science*] (OSRA)
ITWS .... International Tsunami Warning System (SAUO)
ITX .... Iberiotoxin [*Biochemistry*]
ITX .... Imair [*Azerbaijan*] [*FAA designator*] (FAAC)
ITX .... Inclusive Tour Excursion [*Airline fare*]
ITX .... Independent Tank Common [*of a ship*] (DS)
ITX .... Information Transfer Exchange (PDAA)
ITX .... Interactive Transaction
ITX .... Intermediate Text Block (SAUS)
ITX .... International Technology Corp. [*NYSE symbol*] (SPSG)
ITX .... International Tillex Enterprises Ltd. [*Vancouver Stock Exchange symbol*]
ITX .... Intertriginous Xanthoma [*Medicine*] (AAMN)
ITX .... Intl Technology [*NYSE symbol*] (TTSB)
ITX .... IT Group [*NYSE symbol*] (SG)
ITXI .... Interactive Technologies, Inc. (SAUS)
ITXT .... Institute of Textile Technology (SAUO)
ITY .... Fort Riley (SAUS)
ITY .... Fort Riley, KS [*Location identifier*] [*FAA*] (FAAL)
ITY .... Imperial Tobacco Grp ADS [*NYSE symbol*] (SG)
ITY .... Information Technology Year [*1982*]
ITY .... Intensity Resources Ltd. [*Toronto Stock Exchange symbol*]
Ity .... Interchangeability
ITY .... International Tourist Year
ITYM .... I Think You Mean (SAUS)
ITyr .... Monoiodotyrosine (STED)
ITZ .... Inshore Traffic Zone [*Nautical term*] (HRNC)
ITZ .... Inter-Tropical Convergence Zone
ITZN .... International Trust for Zoological Nomenclature (EES)
IU .... Identification Unit (MSA)
IU .... If Used (RIMS)
IU .... Immunizing Unit [*Medicine*]
IU .... Impedance Unit (MCD)
IU .... Independent User (SAUO)
IU .... Indianapolis Union [*AAR code*]
IU .... Indiana University
IU .... Indicating Unit (SAUS)
IU .... Indicator Unit (SAUS)
IU .... Industrial Union (SAUO)
IU .... Industrial User (ERG)
iu .... Infectious Unit [*Medicine*] (EDAA)
IU .... Infectious Unit
IU .... Inflight-Update (SAUS)
IU .... Information Unit
IU .... Information Unlimited [*Information service or system*] (IID)
IU .... Initial User (SAUO)
IU .... Input Unit
IU .... Instant Update [*Professional Farmers of America*] [*Information service or system*] (TSSD)
IU .... Instructional Unit (SAUO)
IU .... Instruction Unit [*Computer science*]
IU .... Instrumentation Unit (SAUS)
iu .... Instrument Unit (NAKS)
IU .... Instrument Unit [*NASA*]
IU .... Integer Unit [*Computer science*]
IU .... Interaction Unit (SAUS)
IU .... Intercommunication Unit (SAUS)
IU .... Interface Unit [*Computer science*] (MCD)
iu .... Interface Unit (NAKS)
IU .... Interference Unit [*Military*]
IU .... Interlingue Union
IU .... Internal Upset (SAUS)
IU .... International Caribbean Tourist, Inc. (SAUO)
IU .... International Environmental Protection Union (SAUO)
IU .... International Undertaking (SAUO)
IU .... International Union (SAUO)
IU .... International Unit
IU .... International Utilities (SAUO)
IU .... International Utilities Corp. (SAUO)
IU .... Internet University [*Computer science*]
IU .... Interval of Uncertainty [*Psychology*]
IU .... Intrauterine [*Medicine*]
IU .... Inubaraki University (SAUO)
IU .... In Utero [*Gynecology*]
iu .... Israel-Syria Demilitarized Zones [*is (Israel) used in records cataloged after January 1978*] [*MARC country of publication code*] [*Library of Congress*] (LCCP)
IU .... IU International Corp. (SAUO)

IU .... Iwate University (SAUO)
IU .... Izquierda Unida [*United Left*] [*Spain*] [*Political party*] (ECED)
IU .... Izquierda Unida [*United Left*] [*Bolivia*] [*Political party*] (EY)
IU .... Izquierda Unida [*United Left*] [*Peru*] [*Political party*]
IU .... Midstate Airlines [*ICAO designator*] (AD)
IU .... United Left [*Political party*] (PSAP)
IU .... University of Idaho (SAUO)
IU .... University of Illinois, Urbana, IL [*Library symbol*] [*Library of Congress*] (LCLS)
IUA .... Image Understanding Architecture [*Computer science*]
IUA .... Individual Unit Action Model
IUA .... Inertial Unit Assembly
IUA .... Information User Association (NTPA)
IUA .... Inter-American University Association
IUA .... Interface Unit Adapter [*Computer science*] (MCD)
IUA .... Interlibrary Users Association [*University of Maryland*] [*College Park, MD*] [*Library network*]
IUA .... International Underwriting Association (SAUO)
IUA .... International Union against Alcoholism (SAUO)
IUA .... International Union of Academies (EA)
IUA .... International Union of Advertising (SAUO)
IUA .... International Union of Architects
IUA .... International University of America [*San Francisco, CA*] (ECON)
IUA .... Intrauterine Adhesion [*Medicine*] (DMAA)
IUA .... IOMEC Users Association [*Formerly, DUA*] [*Defunct*] (EA)
IUA .... Irish Unionist Alliance (SAUO)
IUA .... University of Texas at Arlington, Arlington, TX [*OCLC symbol*] (OCLC)
IUAA .... International Union of Advertisers Associations [*Later, WFA*] (EAIO)
IUAA .... International Union of Alpine Associations
IUAC .... International Union Against Cancer [*An association*] (CDI)
IUACE .... Indian University Association for Continuing Education
IUADM .... International Union of Associations of Doctor-Motorists
IUAES .... International Union of Anthropological and Ethnological Sciences [*See also UISAE*] [*ICSU*] [*Gwynedd, Wales*] (EAIO)
IUAI .... International Union of Aviation Insurers [*British*] (EAIO)
IUAIWA .... International Union of Allied Industrial Workers of America (SAUO)
IUAJ .... International Union of Agricultural Journalists
IU/AL .... Anthropological Linguistics, a Publication of the Archives of the Languages of the World. Indiana University. Anthropology Department. Bloomington (journ.) (SAUS)
IUAM .... Islamic Unity of Afghan Mujahadeen [*Afghanistan*] [*Political party*]
IUANPW .... International Union of Allied Novelty and Production Workers (EA)
IUAO .... Internationalen Union fuer Angewandte Ornithologie [*International Union for Applied Ornithology*] (EAIO)
IUAO .... International Union for Applied Ornithology (SAUS)
IUAO .... International Union of Applied Ornithology (SAUS)
IUAP .... Internet User Account Provider (SAUO)
IUAPPA .... International Union of Air Pollution Prevention Associations [*See also UIAPPA*] [*England*] (EAIO)
IUAR .... Institute for Urban Affairs and Research [*Howard University*] [*Research center*] (RCD)
IU-Ar .... University of Illinois, Archives, Urbana, IL [*Library symbol*] [*Library of Congress*] (LCLS)
IUAS .... International Union in Agricultural Sciences (SAUS)
IUAS .... International Union in/of Agricultural Sciences (SAUO)
IUAT .... International Union Against Tuberculosis [*Later, IUATLD*] (EAIO)
IUATLD .... International Union Against Tuberculosis and Lung Disease [*See also UICTMR*] (EAIO)
IUATM .... International Union of Applied and Theoretical Mechanics (SAUO)
IUAVDT .... International Union against Venereal Diseases and Treponematoses [*Medicine*] (EDAA)
IUB .... Baltimore, MD [*Location identifier*] [*FAA*] (FAAL)
IUB .... Indiana University Bookman (journ.) (SAUS)
IUB .... Indiana University, School of Law Library, Bloomington, IN [*OCLC symbol*] (OCLC)
IUB .... Instruction Used BIT [*Binary Digit*] [*Computer science*] (MHDI)
IUB .... Insurance Unemployment Board (SAUO)
IUB .... International Union of Biochemistry (EA)
IUB .... International Union of Biochemistry International Universities Bureau (SAUS)
IUB .... International Universities Bureau
IUB .... International University Booksellers Limited (SAUO)
IUB .... Interstate Underwriters Board (SAUO)
IU-B .... University of Illinois, Biology Library, Urbana, IL [*Library symbol*] [*Library of Congress*] (LCLS)
IUBC .... Indiana United Bancorp [*NASDAQ symbol*] (SAG)
IUBCTW .... International Union of Bakery, Confectionery, and Tobacco Workers (BARN)
IUBMB .... International Union for Biochemistry and Molecular Biology (SAUS)
IUBMB .... International Union of Biochemistry and Molecular Biology (HGEN)
IUBP .... International Union of Scientific Psychology (SAUO)
IUBS .... International Union of Biological Sciences [*Paris, France*]
IUBS .... International Union of Building Societies (SAUO)
IUBS-CBE .... IUBS Commission on Biological Education (AIE)
IUBSSA .... International Union of Building Societies and Savings Associations [*Later, IOHFI*] [*Chicago, IL*] (EA)
IUBSSA .... International Union of Housing Finance Institutions (SAUO)
IUBTP .... Inter-University Biology Teaching Project (SAUO)
IUC .... Association for Higher Education, Dallas, TX [*OCLC symbol*] (OCLC)
IUC .... Idiopathic Ulcerative Colitis [*Medicine*]
IUC .... Immediate Unit Commander [*Navy*] (NVT)
IUC .... Incurred but Unreported Claims [*Health insurance*] (GHCT)
IUC .... Independent User Center (SAUO)
IUC .... Information Unit for Conventions (SAUO)
IUC .... Initial User Capability (SSD)
IUC .... Instructor Utilization Course (MCD)
IUC .... International Education Centre (SAUO)
IUC .... International Underwater Contractors, Inc.
IUC .... International Unicode Conference (SAUS)
IUC .... International Union against Cancer (SAUO)
IUC .... International Union of Cartography (SAUO)
IUC .... International Union of Chemistry (MEC)
IUC .... International Union of Colleges Working for World Understanding (SAUO)
IUC .... International Union of Crystallography
IUC .... International University Consortium (SAUS)
IUC .... International University Consortium for Telecommunications in Learning (SAUS)
IUC .... International University Contact for Management Education
IUC .... International University of Communication [*Washington, DC*]
IUC .... Inter-University Centre of Post-Graduate Studies (SAUO)
IUC .... Inter-University Committee for Debate on Foreign Policy [*Defunct*]
IUC .... Inter-University-Contact (SAUO)
IUC .... Inter-University Council
IUC .... Inter-University Council for East Africa (SAUO)
IUC .... Inter-University Council for Higher Education Overseas (SAUO)
IUC .... Interuniversity Council of the North Texas Area (SAUS)
IUC .... Irish Underwater Council (SAUO)
IUCAA .... Inter-University Center for Astronomy and Astrophysic [*India*]
IUCAA .... Inter University Center for Astronomy and Astrophysics, Pune (SAUO)
IUCAB .... International Union of Commercial Agents and Brokers [*EC*] (ECED)
IUCADC .... Inter-Union Commission of Advice to Developing Countries [*of the International Union of Geodesy and Geophysics*] [*Mississauga, ON*] (EAIO)
IUCADC .... Inter-Union Commission of/on Advice to Developing Countries (SAUO)
IUCAF .... Inter-Union Commission on Allocation of Frequencies for Radio Astronomy and Space Science (SAUO)
IUCAF .... Inter-Union Commission on Frequency Allocations for Radio Astronomy and Space Science (EA)
IUCAT .... International Union of Cooperative and Associated Tourism (SAUO)
IUCC .... Information Unit on Climate Change (SAUO)
IUCc .... International Union of Crystallography (SAUO)
IUCD .... Intrauterine Contraceptive Device [*Medicine*]
IUCE .... International Union of Cinematograph Exhibitors (SAUO)
IUCED .... Inter-Union Commission of European Dehydrators [*See also CIDE*] [*Paris, France*] (EAIO)
IUCESD .... Inter-American University Council for Economic and Social Development (SAUO)
IUCEu .... Inter-Union Commission of European Dehydrators (SAUO)
IUCF .... Indiana University Cyclotron Facility [*Research center*] (RCD)
IUCI .... Inter-University Committee on Israel [*Later, America-Israel Cultural Foundation*] (EA)
IUCL .... Istanbul University Central Library (SAUO)
IUCLID .... International Uniform Chemicals Information Data base (SAUS)
IUCM .... Coordination of Maya Unity and Consensus (SAUO)
IUCM .... Inter-Union Commission for Studies of the Moon (SAUO)
IUCME .... International University Contact for Management Education
IUCN .... International Union for Conservation of Nature [*World Conservation Union*] (USDC)
IUCN .... International Union for Conservation of Nature and Natural Resources [*Research Center*] [*ICSU*] [*Switzerland*] (EA)
IUCN .... International Union for Conservation of Nature and Natural Resources. Technical Meeting (journ.) (SAUS)
IUCN .... World Conservation Union
IUCN/CERO ... International Union for the Conservation of Nature/Office for Central Europe (SAUO)
IUCN/CIS .... International Union for the Conservation of Nature/Office for the Commonwealth of Independent States (SAUO)
IUCN/ELC .... International Union for the Conservation of Nature/Environmental Law Centre (SAUO)
IUCN/ERO .... International Union for the Conservation of Nature/European Regional Office (SAUO)
IUCNGA .... International Union for the Conservation of Nature General Assembly (SAUO)
IUCNNR .... International Union for Conservation of Nature and Natural Resources [*ICS U*] [*Research center*] [*Switzerland*]
IUCNPSG .... International Union for Nature and Natural Resources-Primate Specialists Group (SAUS)
IUCNPSG .... International Union for the Conservation of Natures Primate Specialist Group (SAUO)
IUCO .... Irwin Union Corp. (SAUS)
IUCO .... Irwin Union Corporation (SAUO)
IUCOG .... Inter-Union Commission on Geodynamics (SAUO)
IU Cr .... International Union of Crystallography [*See also UIC*] (EA)
IUCRC .... Industry/University Cooperation Research Center [*National Science Foundation*]
I/UCRC .... Industry/University Cooperative Research Center (ADWA)
IUCRCB .... Inter-University Committee for Research on Consumer Behavior (EA)
IUCRM .... Inter-Union Commission on Radio Meteorology [*International Council of Scientific Unions*] [*Research center*]
IUCS .... Instruction Update Command System
IUCS .... Instrumentation Unit Update Command System [*NASA*] (NASA)
IUCS .... Inter-Union Commission on Spectroscopy [*International Council of Scientific Unions*]
IUCSTA .... Interational Union For Vacuum Science Technicues and Applications (SAUO)
IUCSTP .... Inter-Union Commission on Solar-Terrestrial Physics (MCD)

IUCT .... In-Use Confirmatory Testing [*Automotive emissions*]
IUCTG .... Inter-University Committee on Travel Grants
IUCW .... International Union for Child Welfare [*Geneva, Switzerland*] [*Defunct*]
IUD .... Incoordinate Uterine Dsyfunction [*Medicine*] (MELL)
IUD .... Independent, Uniformly Distributed (SAUS)
IUD .... Indiana University, School of Dentistry, Indianapolis, IN [*OCLC symbol*] (OCLC)
IUD .... Industrial Union Department [*of AFL-CIO*] (EA)
IUD .... Institute for Urban Design (EA)
IUD .... Institute for Urban Development
IUD .... Internal Unstable Damper (MCD)
IUD .... Intrauterine Death [*Medicine*]
iud .... Intrauterine Device (SAUS)
IUD .... Intrauterine Device [*A contraceptive*] [*Medicine*]
IUD .... Intrauterinpessar (SAUS)
IUDD .... Infrastructure and Urban Development Department (SAUO)
IUDH .... In-Service Unplanned Derated Hours [*Electronics*] (IEEE)
IUDH1 .... In-Service Unplanned Derated Hours, Class 1 (SAUS)
IUDR .... Idoxuridine [*Medicine*] (EDAA)
IUDR .... Iododexyuridine [*Medicine*] (PALA)
IUdR .... Iodouracildeoxyriboside [*Biochemistry*]
IUDTPNAPUSCAN ... International Union of Dolls, Toys, Playthings, Novelties and Allied Products of the United States and Canada (SAUO)
IUDWC .... Irish Union of Distributive Workers and Clerks (BI)
IUDZG .... International Union of Directors of Zoological Gardens [*Canada*] (EAIO)
IUDZG .... World Zoo Organization (SAUO)
IU/E .... Ethnohistory. Indiana University. Bloomington (SAUO)
IUE .... Instruction Unit Execution (SAUS)
IUE .... Interface Unit Error Count Table (MCD)
IUE .... International Thunderwood Explorations Ltd. [*Vancouver Stock Exchange symbol*] [*Toronto Stock Exchange symbol*]
IUE .... International Ultraviolet Experiment (ACAE)
IUE .... International Ultraviolet Explorer [*NASA*]
IUE .... International Unio Esperanto (SAUO)
IUE .... International Union for Electroheat [*Also, IUE-H*]
IUE .... International Union of Electrical, Radio, and Machine Workers
IUE .... International Union of Electrical, Technical, Salaried, Machine and Furniture Workers (SAUS)
IUE .... International Union of Electrical Workers
IUE .... International Union of Electronic [*Electrical, technical, salaried and machine workers*] (NITA)
IUE .... International Union of Electronic, Electrical, Technical, Salaried, Machine and Furniture Workers (SAUS)
IUE .... Iron Use Efficiency [*Metabolism*]
IUE .... Niue Island [*Niue*] [*Airport symbol*] (OAG)
IUE .... University of Evansville, Evansville, IN [*OCLC symbol*] (OCLC)
IUEC .... International Union Elevator Constructors (SAUS)
IUEC .... International Union of Elevator Constructors (EA)
IUED .... Institute of Development Studies, Geneva (SAUO)
IUEF .... Internacia Unuigo de la Esperantistoj-Filologoj [*International Union of Esperantist-Philologists - IUEP*] [*Sofia, Bulgaria*] (EAIO)
IUEFI .... Internacia Unuigo de la Esperantistoj-Filologoj [*International Union of Esperantist-Philologists - IUEP*] [*Sofia, Bulgaria*] (EA)
IUEGS .... International Union of European Guides and Scouts [*See also UIGSE*] [*Chateau Landon, France*] (EAIO)
IUE-H .... International Union for Electroheat [*Also, IUE*]
IUEP .... International Union of Esperantist-Philologists [*Sofia, Bulgaria*] (EAIO)
IUERMW .... International Union of Electrical, Radio, and Machine Workers (IAA)
IUEW .... Industrial Union of Engineering Workers (SAUO)
IUEW .... International Union of Electrical Workers
IUF .... Inquiry Unit File (SAUS)
IUF .... Interamerican Underwater Festival
IUF .... International Underwater Foundation (EA)
IUF .... International Unicycling Federation (EA)
IUF .... International Union of Food, Agricultural, Hotel, Restaurant (SAUO)
IUF .... International Union of Food and Allied Workers' Associations [*See also IUL*] [*Petit-Lancy, Switzerland*] (EAIO)
IUF .... International Union of Foodworkers (SAUO)
IUF .... International University Federation for the League of Nations (SAUO)
IUF .... International University Foundation (EA)
IUF .... Isolated Ultrafiltration [*Organic chemistry*] (DAVI)
IUF .... Southern Methodist University, Law Library, Dallas, TX [*OCLC symbol*] (OCLC)
IUFA .... Independent Union of Flight Attendants (SAUO)
IUFA .... Indiana University Fine Arts (SAUO)
IUFA .... International Union of Family Organizations (SAUO)
IUFB .... Intrauterine Foreign Body [*Gynecology*]
IUFD .... International Union of Food and Drink Workers Associations (SAUO)
IUFD .... Intrauterine Fetal Death [*or Demise*] [*Obstetrics*] (DAVI)
IUFDT .... International Union of Food, Drink and Tobacco Workers Associations (SAUO)
IUFED .... In-Use Vehicle Fuel Economy Data (SAUO)
IUFGR .... Intrauterine Fetal Growth Retardation [*Obstetrics*] (DAVI)
IUFLJP .... International Union of French-Language Journalists and Press [*See also UIJPLF*] [*Paris, France*] (EAIO)
IUFLN .... International University Federation for the League of Nations (SAUO)
IUFO .... International Union of Family Organisations (or Organizations) (SAUO)
IUFO .... International Union of Family Organizations [*Paris, France*]
IUFoST .... International Union of Food Science and Technology [*ICSU*] [*Dublin, Republic of Ireland*] (EAIO)
IUFoST .... International Union on Food Science and Technology (SAUO)
IUFRO .... International Union of Forestry Research Organizations [*Vienna, Austria*] [*Research center*] (EAIO)
IUFS .... Indiana University Folklore Series (SAUO)
IUFS .... Indiana University. Folklore Series (journ.) (SAUS)
Iug .... Bellum Iugurthinum [*of Sallust*] [*Classical studies*] (OCD)
IUG .... ICES [*Integrated Civil Engineering System*] Users Group [*Defunct*] (EA)
IUG .... Informix User Group (SAUO)
IUG .... Infusion Urogram [*Medicine*] (DMAA)
IUG .... Intelligence Users' Guide (MCD)
IUG .... Intercomm User Group (SAUS)
IUG .... Intercomm Users' Group (EA)
IUG .... Intercom Users Group (SAUO)
IU/g .... International Units Per Gram [*Medicine*] (EDAA)
IUG .... Intrauterine Gestation [*Obstetrics*] (DAVI)
IUGB .... International Union of Game Biologists [*Canada*] (EAIO)
IUGG .... International Union for/of Geodesy and Geophysics (SAUO)
IUGG .... International Union of Geodesy and Geophysics [*Brussels, Belgium*]
IUGG Newsl ... International Union of Geodesy and Geophysics. Newsletter (journ.) (SAUS)
IUGGTC .... International Union of Geodesy and Geophysics Tsunami Commission [*Marine science*] (OSRA)
IUGG/TC .... IUGG Tsunami Commission (USDC)
IUGM .... International Union of Gospel Missions (EA)
IUGR .... Intrauterine Growth Rate [*Medicine*] (MAE)
IUGR .... Intrauterine Growth Retardation [*Medicine*]
IUGRI .... International Union of Graphic Reproduction Industries [*Later, IUI*] (EAIO)
IUGS .... International Union of Geological Sciences [*ICSU*] [*Trondheim, Norway*] (EA)
IUGS .... International Union of Geophysical Sciences (SAUO)
IU-GS .... University of Illinois, Illinois State Geological Survey, Urbana, IL [*Library symbol*] [*Library of Congress*] (LCLS)
IUGS/CGM ... International Union of Geological Sciences Commission for Marine Geology (SAUO)
IUGS/CGM ... IUGS Commission for Marine Geology (SAUS)
IUGS/COGEODATA ... Commission on Storage, Automatic Processing and Retrieval of Geological Data (SAUS)
IUGS/COGEODATA ... International Union of Geological Sciences Commission on Storage, Automatic Processing and Retrieval of Geological Data (SAUO)
IUGS/COGEODOC ... International Union of Geological Sciences Commission on Geological Documentation (SAUO)
IUGS/COGEODOC ... IUGS Commission on Geological Documentation (SAUS)
IUGS/COMTEC ... Commission on Tectonics (SAUS)
IUGS/COMTEC ... International Union of Geological Sciences Commission on Tectonics (SAUO)
IUH .... Indiana University, School of Medicine, Health Library Cooperative, Indianapolis, IN [*OCLC symbol*] (OCLC)
IUH .... Instantaneous Unit Hydrograph
IU-H .... University of Illinois, School of Basic Medical Sciences, Library of Public Health Sciences, Urbana, IL [*Library symbol*] [*Library of Congress*] (LCLS)
IUHA .... Industrial Unit Heater Association (SAUO)
IUHE .... International Union for Health Education (SAUO)
IUHE .... International Union of Health Education [*See also UIES*] [*Paris, France*] (EAIO)
IUHFI .... International Union of Housing Finance Institutions (EAIO)
IUHPS .... International Union for History and Philosophy of Science (SAUS)
IUHPS .... International Union of the History and Philosophy of Science [*ICSU*] [*Uppsala, Sweden*] (EAIO)
IUHR .... International Union of Hotel, Restaurant, and Bar Workers
IU-HS .... Illinois Historical Survey, University of Illinois, Urbana, IL [*Library symbol*] [*Library of Congress*] (LCLS)
IUHS .... Indiana University. Humanities Series (journ.) (SAUS)
IUHS .... International Union of History of Science (SAUS)
IUHS .... International Union of the History of Science (SAUS)
IUHTAUTC .... If Used, Half Time Actually to Count (RIMS)
IUI .... Industrial Institute for Economic & Social Research (SAUO)
IUI .... Intelligent User Interface (SAUS)
IUI .... Interim Use Item (MCD)
IUI .... International Union of Interpreters (SAUO)
IUI .... Intrauterine Infection [*Medicine*] (EDAA)
IUI .... Intrauterine Insemination [*Medicine*] (DMAA)
IUI .... Shawnee Library System, Carterville, IL [*OCLC symbol*] (OCLC)
IUID .... Internal Unit Identification (SAUO)
IUIEC .... Inter-University Institute of Engineering Control (PDAA)
IU/IJAL .... International Journal of American Linguistics. Indiana Univ. Baltimore (journ.) (SAUS)
IUIN .... International Union for Inland Navigation [*Strasbourg, France*] (EA)
IUIRO .... International Union of Forest Research Organizations (SAUO)
IUIS .... Institute of Urban Information Systems (SAUS)
IUIS .... International Union of Immunological Societies (EA)
IUISTHE .... International Union of Industrial Service Transport Health Employees (NTPA)
IUJ .... International University of Japan (ECON)
IUJ .... John Marshall Law School, Chicago, IL [*OCLC symbol*] (OCLC)
IUJCD .... Internationale Union Junger Christlicher Demokraten [*International Union of Young Christian Democrats*]
IU/JFI .... Journal of the Folklore Institute. Indiana University Bloomington (journ.) (SAUS)
IUJH .... International Union of Journeyman Horseshoers
IUJHUSC .... International Union of Journeymen Horseshoers of the United States and Canada (SAUO)
IUKADGE .... Improved United Kingdom Air Defence Ground Environment (SAUO)
IUKADGE .... Improved United Kingdom Air Defense Ground Environment
Iul .... Divus Iulius [*of Suetonius*] [*Classical studies*] (OCD)

IUL .... Ibadan University Library (SAUO)
IUL .... Indiana University, Bloomington, IN [*OCLC symbol*] (OCLC)
IUL .... Indiana University Library (SAUO)
IUL .... Indian Unattached List [*British military*] (DMA)
IUL .... Information Utilization Laboratories (or Laboratory) (SAUS)
IUL .... Information Utilization Laboratory [*University of Pittsburgh*] (NITA)
IUL .... Institute of Urban Life (EA)
IUL .... Internationale Union der Lebens- und Genussmittelarbeiter-Gewerkschaften [*International Union of Food and Allied Workers Associations - IUF*] [*Petit-Lancy, Switzerland*] (EAIO)
IU/L .... International Units per Liter
IU-L .... University of Illinois, Lincoln Room, Urbana, IL [*Library symbol*] [*Library of Congress*] (LCLS)
IULA .... International Union of Local Authorities [*The Hague, Netherlands*] (EA)
IULC .... Committee on Instruction in the Use of Libraries [*Later, CUILL*] (EA)
IULC .... Independent United Labor Congress [*Nigeria*]
IULC .... Inter-University Library Council (SAUO)
IULCC .... Inter-University Large-scale Computer Center (SAUO)
IULC-RAILS .... Interuniversity Library Council: Reference and Interlibrary Loan Service [*Library network*]
IULC-RAILS .... IULC Reference and Interlibrary Loan Service (SAUS)
IULCS .... International Union of Leather Chemists Societies
IULCW .... International Union of Liberal Christian Women
IULD .... International Union of Lorry Drivers [*See also UICR*] [*Munich, Germany*] (EAIO)
IULEC .... Inter-University Labor Education Committee
IULIA .... International Union of Life Insurance Agents [*Milwaukee, WI*] (EA)
IULS .... Indiana Union List of Serials
IU-LS .... University of Illinois, Graduate School of Library Science, Urbana, IL [*Library symbol*] [*Library of Congress*] (LCLS)
IULVTFT .... International Union for Land Value Taxation and Free Trade [*British*] (EAIO)
IUM .... Honolulu, HI [*Location identifier*] [*FAA*] (FAAL)
IUM .... Indiana University, School of Medicine, Indianapolis, IN [*OCLC symbol*] (OCLC)
IUM .... Interim Use Manual (SPST)
IUM .... Interim Use Material (MCD)
IUM .... Intermediate Unit Marker (SAUS)
IUM .... Internal Urethral Meatus [*Medicine*] (EDAA)
IUM .... Intrauterine Fetally Malnourished [*Medicine*] (MAE)
IUM .... Intrauterine Membrane [*Medicine*] (DB)
IU-M .... University of Illinois at the Medical Center, Chicago, IL [*Library symbol*] [*Library of Congress*] (LCLS)
IUMA .... Interim Use Material Authorization (MCD)
IUMA .... International Union of Mountaineering Associations (SAUO)
IUMA .... Internet Underground Music Archive (WDAA)
IUMAC .... International Union of Medical Automobile Clubs (SAUO)
IUMC .... Indiana University Medical Center (SAUO)
IUMDA .... Information Unit on Militarization and Demilitarization in Asia (SAUO)
IU-MG .... University of Illinois, Map and Geography Library, Urbana, IL [*Library symbol*] [*Library of Congress*] (LCLS)
IUMI .... International Union of Marine Insurance [*Basel, Switzerland*]
IU/min .... International Units Per Minute [*Medicine*] (EDAA)
IUMMS .... Integrated Utilization Supply Movement/Materials Handling System (SAUO)
IUMMSW .... International Union of Mine, Mill, and Smelter Workers [*Later, USWA*]
IUMP .... International Union of Master Painters [*See also UNIEP*] [*Brussels, Belgium*] (EAIO)
IUMP .... International Union of the Medical Press (DIT)
IUMP .... International Upper Mantle Project (SAUO)
IUMRS .... International Union of Materials Research Societies (SAUO)
IUMS .... International Union for Moral and Social Action
IUMS .... International Union of Microbiological Societies [*University of Newcastle*] (EA)
IUMSA .... International Union for Moral and Social Action (SAUO)
IUMSBD .... International Union of Microbiological Societies-Bacteriological (or Bacteriology) Division (SAUO)
IUMSBD .... International Union of Microbiological Societies Bacteriology Division [*B eckenham, Kent, England*] (EAIO)
IUMSWA .... Industrial Union of Marine and Shipbuilding Workers of America (EA)
IUMSWA .... International Union of Marine and Shipbuilding Workers of America (SAUO)
IU-Mu .... University of Illinois, Music Library, Urbana, IL [*Library symbol*] [*Library of Congress*] (LCLS)
IUNA .... Irish United Nations Association (EAIO)
IUNDH .... In-Service Unit Derated Hours [*Electronics*] (IEEE)
IU-Ne .... University of Illinois at Urbana-Champaign, University of Illinois Newspaper Library, Urbana-Champaign, IL [*Library symbol*] [*Library of Congress*] (LCLS)
IU-NH .... University of Illinois, Illinois Natural History Survey, Urbana, IL [*Library symbol*] [*Library of Congress*] (LCLS)
IUNM .... International University of New Medicine (SAUO)
IUNS .... International Union of Nutritional Sciences [*Wageningen, Netherlands*]
IUNT .... Interservice Undergraduate Navigator Training
IUO .... ICG Utilities (Ontario) Ltd. [*Toronto Stock Exchange symbol*]
IUOB .... International Union of Biochemistry (SAUO)
IUOE .... International Union of Operating Engineers (EA)
IUoFST .... International Union of Food Science & Technology (SAUO)
IUOMWH .... Independent United Order of Mechanics - Western Hemisphere (EA)
IUOP .... Independent User Operations (SAUO)
IUOPA .... International Union of Practitioners in Advertising (SAUO)
IUOPAB .... International Union of Pure and Applied Biophysics (SAUO)
IUOT .... Indiana University Opera Theater (SAUO)
IUOTO .... International Union of Official Travel Organisations [*Later, WTO*]
IUOW .... Industrial Union of Oil Workers (SAUO)
IUP .... Indiana University of Pennsylvania
IUP .... Indiana University Press
IUP .... Indiana University - Purdue University at Indianapolis, Indianapolis, IN [*OCLC symbol*] (OCLC)
IUP .... Industrial Union Party (EA)
IUP .... Installed User Procedure [*Computer science*] (ELAL)
IUP .... Installed User Program [*Computer science*]
IUP .... Intended Use Plan [*Environmental science*] (EPAT)
IUP .... Interim Update Package (SAUS)
IUP .... International Union of Phlebology [*Paris, France*] (EA)
IUP .... International Union of Physiology (SAUO)
IUP .... International University Press (SAUO)
IUP .... Intrauterine Pregnancy (CPH)
IUP .... Intrauterine Pressure [*Gynecology*]
IUP .... Intrauterinpessar (SAUS)
IUP .... Irish University Press
IUP .... ISDN User Part [*Communications term*] (DCT)
IUP .... Israel Universities Press
IUPA .... International Union of Police Association (SAUO)
IUPA .... International Union of Police Associations (EA)
IUPA .... International Union of Practitioners in Advertising
IUPAB .... International Union for/of Pure and Applied Biology (SAUO)
IUPAB .... International Union for Pure and Applied Biophysics (SAUS)
IUPAB .... International Union of Pure and Applied Biophysics [*ICSU*] [*Pecs, Hungary*] [*Research center*] (EA)
IUPAC .... International Union for Pure and Applied Chemistry (SAUS)
IUPAC .... International Union of Pure and Applied Chemistry [*Research center*] [*British*] (IRC)
IUPAC Inf Bull .... International Union of Pure and Applied Chemistry. Information Bulletin (journ.) (SAUS)
IUPAC Inf Bull Append Provis Nomencl Symb Terminol Conv .... International Union of Pure and Applied Chemistry. Information Bulletin. Appendices on Provisional, Nomenclature, Symbols, Terminology and Convention (SAUO)
IUPAC Inf Bull Append Provis Nomencl Symb Terminol Conv .... International Union of Pure and Applied Chemistry. Information Bulletin. Appendices on Provisional, Nomenclature, Symbols, Terminology and Convention (journ.) (SAUS)
IUPAC Inf Bull Append Tentative Nomencl Symb Units Stand .... International Union of Pure and Applied Chemistry. Information Bulletin. Appendices on Tentative Nomenclature, Symbols, Units and Standards (journ.) (SAUS)
IUPAL .... Indiana University Publications. Anthropology and Linguistics (journ.) (SAUS)
IUPAL .... Indiana University Publications in Anthropology and Linguistics (SAUO)
IUPAL .... Indiana University Publications in Anthropology and Linguistics (journ.) (SAUS)
IUPAP .... International Conference on Few-Body Problems in Physics
IUPAP .... International Union for Pure and Applied Physics (SAUS)
IUPAP .... International Union of Pure and Applied Physics [*ICSU*] [*Goteborg, Sweden*] (EA)
IUPC .... Intrauterine Pressure Catheter [*Medicine*] (EDAA)
IUPD .... Intrauterne Pregnancy, Delivered [*Obstetrics*] (DAVI)
IUPDEP .... International Union of Producers and Distributors of Electric Power (SAUO)
IUPESM .... International Union for Physical and Engineering Sciences in Medicine [*ICSU*] [*Ottawa, ON*] (EAIO)
IUPFS .... Indiana University Publications, Folklore Series (SAUO)
IUPFS .... Indiana University Publications, Folklore Series (journ.) (SAUS)
IUPGR .... International Undertaking on Plant Genetic Resources (SAUS)
IUPGWA .... International Union of United Plant Guard Workers of America (SAUO)
IUPHAR .... International Union of Pharmacology [*ICSU*] [*Buckingham, England*] (MSC)
IUP/HJ .... Hispanic Journal. Indiana University of Pennsylvania, Department of Foreign Languages. Indiana (journ.) (SAUS)
IUPHS .... Indiana University Publications. Humanistic Series (journ.) (SAUS)
IUPHS .... Indiana University Publications, Humanistic Series (SAUO)
IUPISM .... Indiana University Publications. Language Science Monographs (journ.) (SAUS)
IUPIW .... International Union of Petroleum and Industrial Workers (EA)
IUPIW .... International Union of Petroleum Industrial Workers (SAUS)
IUPLAW .... International Union for the Protection of Literary and Artistic Works (SAUO)
IUPM .... International Union for Protecting Public Morality [*Later, International Union for Moral and Social Action*]
IUPN .... International Union for the Protection of Nature [*Later, IUCN*]
IUPOV .... International Union for the Protection of New Varieties of Plants (GNE)
IUPPE .... Independent Union of Plant Protection Employees (EA)
IUPPM .... International Union for Protecting Public Morality (SAUO)
IUPPR .... Institute for Urban and Public Policy Research [*University of Colorado - Denver*] [*Research center*] (RCD)
IUPPS .... International Union of Prehistoric and Protohistoric Sciences [*Ghent, Belgium*] (EAIO)
Iupp Trag .... Iuppiter Tragoedus [*of Lucian*] [*Classical studies*] (OCD)
IUPS .... International Union of Physiological Sciences [*ICSU*] [*Gif-sur-Yvette, France*] (ASF)
IUPS .... International Union of Psychological Science (EA)
IUPSEES .... Indiana University Publications, Slavic and East European Series (SAUO)

IUPSEES...... Indiana University Publications. Slavic and East European Series (journ.) (SAUS)
IUPsyS......... International Union for Psychological Sciences (SAUS)
IUPsyS......... International Union of Psychological Science (EA)
IUPT............ International Union of Public Transportation
IUPTB.......... Intrauterine Pregnancy, term birth, cesarean section [*Medicine*] (EDAA)
IUP,TBCS..... Intrauterine Pregnancy, Term Birth, living child [*Medicine*] (EDAA)
IUPUAS........ Indiana University Publications, Uralic and Altaic Series (SAUO)
IUPUAS........ Indiana University Publications. Uralic and Altaic Series (journ.) (SAUS)
IUPUI........... Indiana University - Purdue University at Indianapolis
IUPW........... Independent Union of Petroleum Workers (SAUO)
IUPW........... International Union of Petroleum Workers [*Later, IUPIW*] (EA)
IUQ.............. Interrupted Ultraquick [*Flashing*] Light [*Navigation signal*]
IUQ.............. Quaker Oats Co., Research Library, Barrington, IL [*OCLC symbol*] (OCLC)
IUQR............ International Union of Quarternary Research (SAUO)
IUR.............. Insured Unemployment Rate (OICC)
IUR.............. Integrated Voice Response Unit [*Communications term*] (DCT)
IUR.............. International Union of Radioecologists (EA)
IUR.............. International Union of Railways [*Paris*]
IUR.............. International Union Resources, Inc. [*Vancouver Stock Exchange symbol*]
IUR.............. International University of Radiophonics and Television (SAUO)
IUR.............. International User Requirements (SAUO)
IUR.............. Inter-User Reliability
IUR.............. In-Use Reserve (SAUS)
IUR.............. Inventory Update Rule [*Environmental Protection Agency*]
IUR.............. Irish University Review (journ.) (SAUS)
IU-R............. University of Illinois, Rare Book Room, Urbana, IL [*Library symbol*] [*Library of Congress*] (LCLS)
IUr............... Urbana Free Library, Urbana, IL [*Library symbol*] [*Library of Congress*] (LCLS)
IURA............ International Union of Radio Amateurs (SAUO)
IURAP.......... International Users Resource Allocation Panel
IURC............ International Underwater Research Corp.
IURC............ International Underwater Research Corporation (SAUO)
IURC............ International Union for Research of Communication [*Berne, Switzerland*] (EAIO)
IURCAFL...... Indiana University. Research Center in Anthropology, Folklore and Linguistics (journ.) (SAUS)
IUrCD.......... Clark Dietz Engineers, Urbana, IL [*Library symbol*] [*Library of Congress*] (LCLS)
IUrCH.......... Carle Foundation Hospital, Urbana, IL [*Library symbol*] [*Library of Congress*] (LCLS)
IURD............ Institute of Urban and Regional Development [*University of California, Berkeley*] [*Research center*] (RCD)
IUrE-E.......... Educational Resources Information Center, Elementary and Early Childhood Education (ERIC/ECE), Urbana, IL [*Library symbol*] [*Library of Congress*] (LCLS)
IUrE-NC........ Educational Resources Information Center, National Council of Teachers of English, Urbana, IL [*Library symbol*] [*Library of Congress*] (LCLS)
IUREP.......... International Uranium Resources Evaluation Project
IURES.......... International Union of Reticuloendothelial Societies (EA)
I U Res Ctr... Indiana University Research Center (SAUO)
IURFS.......... International Union of Reticuloendothelial Societies (SAUO)
IUrG............ Illinois State Geological Survey, Urbana, IL [*Library symbol*] [*Library of Congress*] (LCLS)
IURGRQR..... Item Urgently Required [*Army*] (AFIT)
IUrH............ Mercy Hospital, Urbana, IL [*Library symbol*] [*Library of Congress*] (LCLS)
IURMS.......... International Union of Railway Medical Services (SAUO)
IURMS.......... International Union of Railway Medical Services (EA)
IURON.......... International Upland Rice Observational Nursery (SAUO)
IURON-E...... International Upland Rice Observational Nursery-Early (SAUO)
IURON-M..... International Upland Rice Observational Nursery-Medium (SAUO)
IURP............ Integrated Unit Record Processor
IURP............ International Union of Radio Sciences (SAUO)
IURP............ International Union of Roofing and Plumbing (EAIO)
IURS............ Institute of Urban and Regional Studies [*Washington University*] [*Research center*] (RCD)
IURS............ International Union of Radio Science (MSC)
IUrSD.......... Urbana Community Unit School District, Urbana, IL [*Library symbol*] [*Library of Congress*] (LCLS)
IUrW............ Illinois State Water Survey, Urbana, IL [*Library symbol*] [*Library of Congress*] (LCLS)
IURW........... International Union of Revolutionary Writers (SAUO)
IURYN.......... International Upland Rice Yield Nursery (SAUO)
IURYN-E...... International Upland Rice Yield Nursery-Early (SAUO)
IURYN-M..... International Upland Rice Yield Nursery-Medium (SAUO)
IUS.............. Inertial [*formerly, Interim*] Upper Stage [*Air Force*]
ius............... Inertial Upper Stage [*NASA*] (NAKS)
IUS.............. Information Unit Separator [*Computer science*]
IUS.............. Information Unit Set (SAUS)
IUS.............. Information Unlimites Software (SAUS)
IUS.............. Initial Upper Stage [*NASA*]
IUS.............. Initial Upper State (IEEE)
IUS.............. Installed Users System (SAUS)
IUS.............. Installed User System [*Computer science*] (IAA)
IUS.............. Institute of Urban Studies (SAUO)
IUS.............. Institute of Urban Studies, University of Winnipeg [*UTLAS symbol*]
IUS.............. Interchange Unit Selector (NITA)
IUS.............. Interchange Unit Separator [*Computer science*] (BUR)
IUS.............. Interchange Unit Seperator (SAUS)
IUS.............. Interface Vertification Equipment (SAUS)
ius............... Interim/Intermediate Upper State [*NASA*] (NAKS)
IUS.............. Interim Upper Stage [*Missile*]
IUS.............. Interim Upper State (SAUS)
ius............... Interim Use Sheet (NAKS)
IUS.............. Interim Use Sheet (NASA)
IUS.............. Interior Upper Stage (NASA)
IUS.............. Intermediate Upper State (SAUS)
IUS.............. International Union of Speleology [*See also UIS*] [*Vienna, Austria*] (EAIO)
IUS.............. International Union of Students [*See also UIE*] [*Prague, Czechoslovakia*] (EAIO)
IUS.............. International Unlimited Services (SAUO)
IUS.............. International Urban Society (SAUO)
IUS.............. International Urban Studies (SAUS)
IUS.............. Inter-University Seminar (SAUS)
IUS.............. Inter-University Seminar on Armed Forces and Society (EA)
IUS.............. Intrauterine System [*Contraceptive device*] (ODA)
IUSA............ infoUSA, Inc. [*NASDAQ symbol*] (NASQ)
IUSA............ Institute of the United States of America (SAUO)
IUSA............ Institute of the USA (SAUS)
IUSA............ International Underwater Spearfishing Association (EA)
IUSA............ Interserve/USA [*An association*] (EA)
IUSAMH....... International Union of Societies for the Aid of Mental Health [*Bordeaux, France*] (EAIO)
IUSB............ Indiana University at South Bend
IUSB............ Indiana University South Bend (SAUS)
IUSB............ International Universities' Sports Board [*Defunct*] (EA)
IUSC............ Integrated Universal Serial Controller (SAUS)
IUSC............ Inter-University Software Committee [*Inter-University Committee on Computing*] (AIE)
IUSDT.......... International Union of Socialist Democratic Teachers (EAIO)
IUSF............ Industries of the United States Fund (SAUO)
IUSF............ International Union for Surface Finishing (EAIO)
IUSF............ International Union of Societies of Foresters [*See also UISIF*] [*Ottawa, ON*] (EAIO)
IUSF............ International Union Surface Finishing (SAUS)
IUSHTL........ Indiana University Studies in the History and Theory of Linguistics (journ.) (SAUS)
IUSIN........... Inter-University Science Information Network (SAUO)
IUS/ITB........ Interchange Unit Separator/Intermediate Transmission Block (SAUS)
IUSM........... Indiana University School of Music (SAUO)
IUSM........... Integrated Utilities System Management (SAUS)
IUSM........... International Union for/of Surveying (or Surveys) and Mapping (SAUO)
IUSM........... International Union of Surveys and Mapping (SAUS)
IUSO........... Institute of University Safety Officers [*British*] (DBA)
IUSO........... International Union of Security Officers (EA)
IUSP........... International Union of Scientific Psychology (SAUO)
IUSR........... International Union of Scientific Radio (SAUO)
IUSRAV........ Iowa State University. Statistical Laboratory. Annual Report (journ.) (SAUS)
IUSS........... Institute of United States Studies (SAUO)
IUSS........... Integrated Undersea-Surveillance System [*Oceanography*] (ECON)
IUSS........... Integrated Underwater Surveillance System [*Navy*] [*Marine science*] (OSRA)
IUSS........... International Union for Social Studies (SAUO)
IUSSI.......... International Union for the Study of Social Insects [*Utrecht, Netherlands*]
IUSSP.......... International Union for the Scientific Study of Population [*Liege, Belgium*]
IUSTD.......... International Union of Socialist Democratic Teachers (SAUO)
IUSTFI......... Institute on United States Taxation of Foreign Income [*Later, ITI*] (EA)
IUSTI........... International Union against Sexually Transmitted Infections (SAUO)
IUSTOC........ Independent US Tanker Owners Committee [*Defunct*] (EA)
IUSUHM....... International Union of School and University Health and Medicine [*See also UIHMSU*] [*Brussels, Belgium*] (EAIO)
IUSY........... International Union of Socialist Youth
IUT.............. Implementation Under Test [*Telecommunications*] (OSI)
IUT.............. Industrial Unit of Tribology [*University of Leeds*] [*An association*] [*Research center*] [*British*] (EA)
IUT.............. Instructor Under Training [*Navy*] (NVT)
IUT.............. International Union against Tuberculosis (SAUO)
IUT.............. International Union of Telecommunications (SAUO)
IUT.............. International Union of Tenants [*Stockholm, Sweden*] (EAIO)
IUT.............. Intrauterine Transfusion [*Gynecology*]
IUT.............. Item Under Test (SAUS)
IUt............... Utica Public Library, Utica, IL [*Library symbol*] [*Library of Congress*] (LCLS)
IUTA............ In-Use Technology Assessment (SAUO)
IUTAM......... International Union of Theoretical and Applied Mechanics [*Germany*]
IUTAO......... International Union of Technical Associations and Organizations [*France*] (EAIO)
IUTCA.......... International Union of Technical Cinematograph Associations [*See also UNIATEC*] [*Paris, France*] (EAIO)
IUTCT.......... International Union for Thermal Medicine and Climatothalassotherapy (SAUO)
IUTD............ Ann Arbor In-Use Test Data System (SAUS)
IUTD............ In-Use Test Data System (SAUO)
IUTDM......... International Union of Tool, Die, and Mold Makers (EA)
IUTDMM....... International Union of Tool, Die, and Mold Makers (EA)
IUTE............ Interface Unit Test Equipment (SAUS)
IUTL............ Iowa Southern, Inc. (SAUO)

IUTM........... International Union against Tuberculosis Mycobacterium [*Medicine*] (EDAA)
IUTMCT........ International Union for Thermal Medicine and Climatothalassotherapy (SAUO)
IUTO........... International Union of Official Travel Organizations (SAUO)
IUTOX.......... International Union for Toxicology
IUTOX.......... Inter-University Transit System (SAUO)
IUTRLMS..... International Union of Testing and Research Laboratories for Materials and Structures (SAUO)
IUTS............ Inter-University Transit System [*Interlibrary loan service*] [*Canada*] (NITA)
IUTSUT........ Implementation Under Test-System Under Test (SAUS)
IUUAAAIWA... International Union of United Automobile, Aerospace and Agricultural Implement Workers of America (SAUO)
IUUCLG........ International Union, United Cement, Lime & Gypsum Workers (SAUS)
IUUCLGW.... International Union, United Cement, Lime and Gypsum Workers (MHDB)
IU-UPGWA... International Union, United Plant Guard Workers of America (NTPA)
IUUU........... Industrial Unit, University of Ulster [*British*] (IRUK)
IUUW........... International Union, United Welders [*Later, IUOE*]
IUV.............. IATA [*International Air Transport Association*] Unit of Value [*International airline currency*]
IUV.............. Interlibrational Utility Vehicle (SAUS)
IU-V............ University of Illinois, Veterinary Medicine Library (SAUO)
IU-V............ University of Illinois, Veterinary Medicine Library, Urbana, IL [*Library symbol*] [*Library of Congress*] (LCLS)
IUVDT.......... International Union Against Venereal Diseases and Treponematoses (EAIO)
IUVP........... In-Use Verification Program [*Automotive emissions*]
IUVSTA........ International Union for Vacuum Science, Technique, and Applications [*See also UISTAV*] (EAIO)
IUW............ Industrial Union of Workers (SAUO)
IUW............ Inshore Undersea Warfare [*Navy*]
IUW............ Inshore Underwater Warfare (SAUS)
IUWA.......... International Union of Women Architects [*See also UIFA*] [*Paris, France*] (EAIO)
IUWC.......... Inshore Undersea Warfare Craft [*Navy*]
IUWCC........ Inshore Undersea Warfare Control Center [*Navy*] (NVT)
IUWD.......... Inshore Undersea Warfare Division (SAUO)
IUWDS........ International URSI [*Union Radio Scientifique Internationale*]-gram and World Day Service
IUWG.......... Inshore Undersea Warfare Group [*Navy*]
IUWPM........ Independent University, Washington-Paris-Moscow (SAUO)
IU-WS.......... University of Illinois, Illinois State Water Survey, Champaign, IL [*Library symbol*] [*Library of Congress*] (LCLS)
IUWSU......... Inshore Undersea Warfare Surveillance Unit [*Navy*] (DNAB)
IUWWML..... International Union of Wood, Wire, and Metal Lathers (MHDB)
IUYCD......... International Union of Young Christian Democrats [*Rome, Italy*]
iv................ Air Gambia [*Airline flight code*] (ODBW)
IV................ British Island Airways [*ICAO designator*] (AD)
IV................ Current Voltage (SAUS)
IV................ Evans Public Library, Vandalia, IL [*Library symbol*] [*Library of Congress*] (LCLS)
IV................ Iceland Veterans [*Defunct*] (EA)
IV................ Ichthyosis Vulgaris (STED)
IV................ Identity Verification (SAUS)
IV................ Immigrant Visa (SAUS)
IV................ Imperial Valley (SAUS)
IV................ Improved Value (ADA)
IV................ Inaccessible Value (SAUS)
IV................ Increased Value
IV................ Incremented Value (SAUS)
IV................ Independent Validation (SAUS)
IV................ Independent Variable (IAA)
IV................ Index Value (SAUS)
IV................ Indine Value (SAUS)
IV................ Induct Vent
IV................ Industrial Ventilation (LDOE)
IV................ Influenza Vaccination [*Medicine*] (MELL)
IV................ Information Victoria [*Australia*] [*An association*]
IV................ Information Volume (SAUS)
IV................ Information World (journ.) (SAUS)
IV................ Ingenieurvereinigung (SAUO)
IV................ Initialisation Vector (SAUS)
IV................ Initialization Value (DINT)
IV................ Initialization Vector (SAUO)
IV................ Initial Value
IV................ Initial Velocity [*Ballistics*]
IV................ Initial Visit [*Medicine*] (MELL)
I/V............... Inlet Valve (MCD)
IV................ Input Voltage
IV................ Instrumental Variable (SAUS)
I/V............... Instrument/Visual (SAUS)
I/V............... Instrument/Visual Controlled Airspace (DA)
IV................ Insurance Value (IAA)
IV................ Integrated Vehicle (MCD)
iv................ Integrated Vehicle [*NASA*] (NAKS)
IV................ Intelligent Vehicle (SAUS)
IV................ Intensifier Vidicon
IV................ Interactive Video (PDAA)
IV................ Interceptor Vehicle
IV................ Interface Vector (SAUS)
IV................ Interface Volume (MCD)
iv................ Interface Volume (NAKS)
iv................ Interior Upper Stage [*NASA*] (NAKS)
IV................ Intermediate Vacuum (SAUS)
IV................ Intermediate Valency (SAUS)
IV................ Intermediate Voltage (MSA)
IV................ Internal Velocity
IV................ Interval (IAA)
IV................ Intervening Variable (DIPS)
IV................ Interventricular [*Medicine*]
IV................ Intervertebral [*or Intravertebral*] [*Medicine*]
IV................ Interview [*Medicine*] (MELL)
IV................ Intravascular [*Medicine*]
IV................ Intravehicular (MCD)
iv................ Intravehicular (NAKS)
IV................ Intravenebral (SAUS)
IV................ Intravenous [*Medicine*]
IV................ Intravenously (ADWA)
IV................ Intraventricular [*Cardiology*]
IV................ Intravertebral [*Anatomy*] (DAVI)
IV................ Intrinsic Viscosity (SAUS)
IV................ In Vapour (ROG)
IV................ Invasive (MAE)
IV................ In Verbo [*Under the Word*] [*Latin*]
I/V............... Inverted V (SAUS)
IV................ Inverted Vertical [*Aircraft engine*]
IV................ Inverter
IV................ Investigation [*Dialog*] [*Searchable field*] [*Information service or system*] (NITA)
IV................ Investigator [*Military*] (POLM)
IV................ In View
IV................ In Vitro [*Medicine*] (MAE)
IV................ In Vivo [*Medicine*] (MAE)
iv................ Invoice Value (ODBW)
IV................ Invoice Value [*Business term*]
iv................ Iodine Value (STED)
IV................ Iodine Value [*Analytical biochemistry*]
IV................ Irish Viscount (ROG)
IV................ Irish Volunteers [*British military*] (DMA)
IV................ Island Airways (SAUS)
IV................ Isovalerianic Acid (SAUS)
IV................ Issue Voucher (SAUS)
iv................ Ivory (VRA)
iv................ Ivory Coast [*MARC country of publication code*] [*Library of Congress*] (LCCP)
IV................ Mark IV Industries [*NYSE symbol*] (TTSB)
IV................ Mark IV Industries, Inc. [*NYSE symbol*] (SPSG)
IVA.............. Ambanja [*Madagascar*] [*Airport symbol*] (OAG)
IVA.............. Evansville-Vanderburgh School Corp., Evansville, IN [*OCLC symbol*] (OCLC)
IVA.............. Illinois Vocational Association (SRA)
IVA.............. Imposta sul Valore Aggiunto [*Value-Added Tax*] [*Italian*]
IVA.............. Independent Voters Association [*Political organization in North Dakota, 1918-1932*]
IVA.............. Indiana Veal Association (SRA)
IVA.............. Individual Voluntary Arrangement (SAUS)
IVA.............. Industrial Veterinarians' Association [*Later, AAIV*] (EA)
IVA.............. Inlet Vane Actuator
IVA.............. Innotech Aviation Ltd. [*Canada*] [*ICAO designator*] (FAAC)
IVA.............. Inspection Visual Aid (AAG)
IVA.............. Integrated Vulnerability Assessment [*Military*]
IVA.............. Interactive Video Association (EA)
IVA.............. Intermediate Volatility Agent (SAUO)
IVA.............. Intermediate Volitility Agents (MCD)
IVA.............. Internationaler Verband fuer Arbeiterbildung [*International Federation of Workers' Educational Associations - IFWEA*] (EAIO)
IVA.............. Internationale Vereinigung der Anschlussgeleise-Benuetzer [*International Association of Users of Private Sidings*]
IVA.............. International Voice Association (SAUO)
IVA.............. International Volleyball Association [*Defunct*] (EA)
IVA.............. International Voyage Alliance (EA)
IVA.............. Inter-Vehicular Activities (SAUS)
IVA.............. Intervehicular Activity (SAUS)
IVA.............. Intraoperative Vascular Angiography [*Cardiology*]
IVA.............. Intra Vehicular Activities (SAUS)
IVA.............. Intravehicular Activities (or Activity) (SAUS)
IVA.............. Intravehicular Activity
IVA.............. Intravenous Angiogram/raphy [*Medicine*] (EDAA)
IVA.............. Invalidity Allowance (SAUS)
IVA.............. Inventory Valuation Adjustment [*Business term*]
IVA.............. Irish Veterinary Association (GVA)
IVA.............. Isovaleric Acid (DMAA)
IVA.............. Ivac [*Intravenous monitor*] [*Medicine*] (DHSM)
IVA.............. Ivaco, Inc. [*Toronto Stock Exchange symbol*]
IVA.............. Jugobanka. Economic News (journ.) (SAUS)
IVAAP.......... International Veterinary Association for Animal Production [*See also AIVPA*] [*Brussels, Belgium*] [*Research center*] (EAIO)
IVAC............ Inland Vacuum Industries, Inc. (SAUO)
IVAC............ International Video and Communications Exhibition [*British*] (ITD)
IVAC............ International Visual Aid Center (SAUS)
IVAC............ Intevac, Inc. [*NASDAQ symbol*] (SAG)
IVAC............ Intravenous Accurate Control [*Pharmacology*] (DAVI)
IVACG.......... International Vitamin A Consultative Group (EA)
IVAD............ Implantable Vascular Access Device [*Medicine*] (STED)
IVAES.......... International Union of Anthropological and Ethnological Sciences (SAUO)

IVAG .... Institutionenverzeichnis Auslaendischer Gesellschaften [*NOMOS Database*] [*Information service or system*]
IVag .... Intravaginal [*Medicine*] (MAE)
IVAK .... Igloo Vertical Access Kit [*Aerospace*] (NASA)
IVALA .... Integrated Visual Approach and Landing Aid [*System*] [*RADAR*]
IVALA System ... Integrated Visual Approach and Landing Aid System (SAUS)
IValSD .... Valmeyer Community Unit School District 3, Valmeyer, IL [*Library symbol*] [*Library of Congress*] (LCLS)
IVAM .... Interorbital Vehicle Assembly Mode
IVAML .... Instrumental Variable-Approximate Maximum Likelihood (PDAA)
IV & T .... Independent Verification and Test
IV & V .... Independent Validation and Verification (CAAL)
IV&V .... Independent Validation and Verification
IV&V .... Independent Vertification and Validation (SAUS)
IV-ANES .... Intravenous Anesthetic [*Medicine*]
IV-ANFS .... Intravenous Anesthetic (SAUS)
IVANK .... International Committee on Veterinary Anatomical Nomenclature (SAUO)
IVANS .... Insurance Value-Added Network Services [*Insurance Institute for Research*] (TSSD)
I/V Antenna ... Inverted V Antenna (SAUS)
IVAO .... International Union for Applied Ornithology (SAUO)
IVAP .... Implant Vascular Access Device [*Medicine*] (EDAA)
IVAP .... In Vivo Adhesive Platelet [*Medicine*] (MAE)
IVAR .... Insertion Velocity Adjust Routine [*NASA*]
IVAR .... Insulin Variable [*Medicine*] (STED)
IVAR .... Internal Variable (NASA)
IVAR .... International Voluntary Action and Voluntary Association Research Organization [*Defunct*] (EA)
I Variometer ... Inclination Variometer (SAUS)
IVAS .... Image Viewing and Analysis Station (SAUS)
IVAS .... International Veterinary Acupuncture Society (EA)
IVAS .... Internet Value-Added Service (PCM)
IvaxCp .... Ivaco Industries [*Associated Press*] (SAG)
IVAXCP .... IVAX Corp. (SAUO)
IvB .... Innenstadt von Babylon [*A publication*] (BJA)
IVB .... Intermediate Vector Beacon (SAUS)
IVB .... Intermediate Vector Boson [*Physics*]
IVB .... Internationaler Verband fuer Arbeiterbildung [*International Federation of Workers' Educational Associations - IFWEA*] (EAIO)
IVB .... Intraventricular Block [*Medicine*] (DMAA)
IVB .... Intravitreal Blood (STED)
IVB .... Invalidity Benefit (SAUS)
IVB .... Mason Memorial Public Library, Buda, IL [*OCLC symbol*] (OCLC)
IVBA .... International Veteran Boxers Association (EA)
IVBA .... International Volleyball Association [*Defunct*]
IVBAT .... Intravascular Bronchoalveolar Tumor [*Oncology*]
IVBC .... Integrated Vehicle Baseline Configuration (MCD)
IVBC .... Intravascular Blood Coagulation [*Medicine*] (DMAA)
IVBF .... International Volleyball Federation (EA)
IVBH .... Internationale Vereinigung fuer Brueckenbau und Hochbau [*International Association for Bridge and Structural Engineering*]
IVBK .... Intervisual Books'A' [*NASDAQ symbol*] (TTSB)
IVBK .... Intervisual Books, Inc. [*NASDAQ symbol*] (SAG)
IVBT .... Intravascular Brachytherapy [*Medicine*]
IVC .... Imperial Valley College [*California*]
IVC .... Independent Viewing Console
IVC .... Individual Viable Cells [*Metabolic studies*]
IVC .... Industrial View Camera
IVC .... Inferior Vena Cava [*Anatomy*]
IVC .... Inferior Venacavogram [*Cardiology*] (DAVI)
IVC .... Inner Van Connector (SAUS)
IVC .... Inspection Validation Center [*Nuclear energy*] (NUCP)
IVC .... Inspired Vital Capacity (AAMN)
IVC .... Installation Volunteer Coordinator
IVC .... Instant Video Confidence (SAUS)
IVC .... Intake Valve Closing [*Automotive engineering*]
IVC .... Integral Vapor Canister [*Automotive emissions*]
IVC .... Integrated Vacuum Circuit
IVC .... Integrated Vector Control [*Medicine*] (EDAA)
IVC .... Integrated Visual Computing [*Computer science*]
IVC .... Interactive Videodisc Consortium [*Defunct*] (EA)
IVC .... Interior Vena Cava (SAUS)
IVC .... Intermediate Velocity Cloud [*Astronomy*] (OA)
IVC .... Intermittent Vertical Chambers (SAUS)
IVC .... International Verilog HDL Conference (SAUS)
IVC .... International Veterinary Congress (SAUO)
IVC .... International Video Corp. (SAUS)
IVC .... International Video Corporation (SAUO)
IVC .... Internet Voice Chat (VLIE)
IVC .... Intervehicular Communication (KSC)
ivc .... Intervehicular Communications [*NASA*] (NAKS)
IVC .... Intravaginal Culture [*Alternative to traditional in-vitro fertilization (IVF)*] (PAZ)
IVC .... Intravascular Catheter [*Medicine*] (MELL)
IVC .... Intravascular Coagulation [*Medicine*] (DB)
IVC .... Intravenous Cholangiography [*Medicine*]
IVC .... Intraventricular Cannula [*Medicine*]
IVC .... Intraventricular Catheter [*Cardiology*] (DAVI)
IVC .... Invacare Corp. [*NYSE symbol*] (SG)
IVC .... Invercargill [*New Zealand*] [*Airport symbol*] (OAG)
IVC .... Invesco PLC [*NYSE symbol*] (SAG)
IVC .... INVESCO PLC ADS [*NYSE symbol*] (TTSB)
IVC .... Isovolumic Confraction [*Cardiology*]
IVC .... Isovolumic Contraction (SAUS)
IVC .... Permanent Committee for the International Veterinary Congresses
IVC .... Vandalia Correctional Center, Vandalia, IL [*Library symbol*] [*Library of Congress*] (LCLS)
IVC .... Vigo County Public Library, Terre Haute, IN [*OCLC symbol*] (OCLC)
IVCA .... International Visual Communication Association (SAUO)
IVCAP .... International Video Contest for Amateurs and Professionals [*British*]
IVCC .... Illinois Vocational Curriculum Center (EDAC)
IVCC .... Intravascular Consumption Coagulopathy [*Medicine*]
IVCC .... In-Vehicle Communication Computer
IVCC .... Isolation-merged Vertical Capacitor Cell (SAUS)
IVCD .... Indian Veterinary Convalescent Depot [*British military*] (DMA)
IVCD .... Initial Voice Channel Designation (CGWS)
IVCD .... Intraventricular Conduction Defect [*Cardiology*]
IVCD .... Intraventricular Conduction Delay [*Cardiology*] (AAMN)
IVCD .... In-Vehicle Communications Device [*Highway safety research*]
IVCD .... Undien Veterinary Convalescent Depot (SAUS)
IVCE .... Internal Voice Communications Equipment (SAUO)
IVCE .... International Video and Communications Exhibition (NITA)
IVCF .... International Varsity Christian Fellowship (SAUO)
IVCF .... Intervarsity Christian Fellowship (SAUS)
IVCF .... Inter-Varsity Christian Fellowship of the United States of America (EA)
IVCh .... Intravenous Cholangiography [*or Cholangiogram*] [*Medicine*] (DAVI)
IVCH .... Intravenous Cholangiography [*Medicine*] (DMAA)
IVCI .... International Venture Capital Institute (EA)
IVCI .... Intravenous Contrast Injection [*Medicine*] (EDAA)
IVCI .... IVCI Corp. (SAUO)
IVC/ICSS .... International Vacuum Congress/International Conference on Solid Surfaces (SAUS)
IVCL .... Intravehicular Cover Layer (SAUS)
IVCN .... International Network of Consumer Unions (SAUO)
IVCN .... Issue Voucher and Convoy Note (SAUS)
IVCO .... International Visits Control Office (SAUS)
IVCO .... International Vitamin Corp. [*NASDAQ symbol*] (SAG)
IVCO .... IVC Industries [*NASDAQ symbol*] [*Formerly, International Vitamin*] (SG)
Iv Co .... Ivory Coast (VRA)
IVCOD .... IVC Industries (New) [*NASDAQ symbol*] (SG)
IVCOW .... I V C Industries Wrrt [*NASDAQ symbol*] (TTSB)
IVCP .... Inferior Vena Cava Pressure [*Medicine*]
IVCP .... International Venture Capital Partners (SAUO)
IVCP .... Interoperable Virtual Connection Protocol (VLIE)
IVCR .... Inferior Vena Cava Reconstruction [*Medicine*] (DMAA)
IVCR .... Invacare Corp. [*NASDAQ symbol*] (NQ)
IVCS .... Integrated Vehicle Communications System (SAUO)
IVCS .... Integrated Vehicle Control System
IVCS .... Integrated Vehicular Communication System (MCD)
IVCS .... Integrated [*or Interior*] Voice Communications System (MCD)
IVCS .... Integrated Voice Communication System (SAUO)
IVCS .... Interior Voice Communications System (SAUO)
IVCS .... Intrasite Voice Communication Subsystem (ACAE)
Iv Cst .... Ivory Coast
IVCT .... Inferior Vena Cava Thrombosis [*Medicine*] (DMAA)
IVCT .... Intervalence Charge-Transfer [*Phyical chemistry*]
IVCT .... Isovolumic Contraction Time (DB)
IVCU .... Isotope-Voiding Cystourethrogram [*Urology*] (DAVI)
I-V Curve .... Current-Voltage Curve (SAUS)
IVCV .... Inferior Venacavography [*Medicine*]
IVCV .... Intake Valve Closing Volume
IVCV .... Interior Venacavography (SAUS)
IVCV .... Ivy Vein Clearing Virus [*Plant pathology*]
IVD .... Image Velocity Detector
IVD .... Indirect Video Display (MCD)
IVD .... Indirect View Display (SAUS)
IVD .... Induced Vestibular Dysfunction [*Medicine*] (MELL)
IVD .... Inductive Voltage Divider [*Electromagnetism*] (IAA)
IVD .... Information Viewing Device
IVD .... Innovative Vehicle Design (SAUS)
IVD .... Inside Vapor Deposition (SAUS)
IVD .... Intake Valve Detergent [*Automotive fuels*]
IVD .... Integrated Voice and Data (VLIE)
IVD .... Integrated Voice Data (SAUS)
IVD .... Intelligent Video Digitzer (SAUS)
IVD .... Interactive Videodisc (INF)
IVD .... Internal Vapor Deposition (ACRL)
IVD .... International Vending Technologies Corp. [*Vancouver Stock Exchange symbol*]
IVD .... Interpolated Voice Data (IAA)
IVD .... Intervertebral Disc [*Medicine*]
IVD .... Intravenous Drip [*Pharmacology*] (DAVI)
IVD .... Intraventricular Delay [*Medicine*] (MELL)
IVD .... Invalid Decimal (IAA)
IVD .... In Vitro Diagnostics [*Clinical chemistry*]
IVD .... Ionized Vacuum Deposit (MCD)
IVD .... Ion Vapor Deposition [*Coating technology*]
IVD .... Ischemic Vascular Disease [*Medicine*] (MELL)
IVD .... University of Dallas, Irving, TX [*OCLC symbol*] (OCLC)
IVDA .... Intravenous Digital Angiogram/raph [*Medicine*] (EDAA)
IVDA .... Intravenous Drug Abuser
IVDA .... Investors Daily [*JA Micropublishing, Inc.*]
IVDA/IVDU ... Intravenous Drug Abuser(r)/Intravenous Drug User(r) [*Medicine*] (EDAA)
IVDBA .... Imperial Valley Dune Buggy Association
IVDCD .... Interactive Video Disc Coursewear Development (ACAE)
IVDD .... Intervertebral Disk Disease [*Medicine*] (MELL)

iv Dei.......... Institut Voluntas Dei (EA)
IVDG.......... Innovative Vehicle Desgin Group (SAUO)
IVDG.......... Innovative Vehicle Design Group (SAUS)
IVD-IR/-MR... In-Vitro Dissolution-Immediate Release, or Modified Release [*Drug evalution*]
IVDLAN........ Integrated Voice and Data Local Area Network (SAUO)
IVDM.......... Integrated Voice Data Multiplexer [*Telecommunications*] (ACRL)
IVDMD.......... In Vitro Dry Matter Digestibility (SAUS)
IVDMS.......... Integrated Voice and Data Multiplexers (VLIE)
IVDN.......... Integrated Voice & Data Networking (SAUO)
IVDP.......... Identification, Validation and Dissemination Process (SAUS)
IVDP.......... Initial Vector Display Point (IAA)
IVDS.......... Independent Variable Depth Sonar (SAUS)
IVDS.......... Integrated Voice and Data Systems (SAUS)
IVDS.......... Interactive Video and Data Service
IVDS.......... Interactive Video Data Service (SAUS)
IVDS.......... Interactive Video Delivery System (SAUS)
IVDSA.......... Intravenous Digital Subtraction Angiography
IVDT.......... Integrated [*or Interactive*] Voice Data Terminal [*Telecommunications*]
IVDT.......... Interactive Voice Data Terminal (SAUS)
IVDTE.......... Integrated Voice/Data Terminal Equipment (VLIE)
IVDTS.......... Integrated Voice and Data Telecommunications System (AAGC)
IVDTS.......... Integrated Voice/Data Terminal System (VLIE)
IVDU.......... Intelligent Visual Display Unit (SAUS)
IVDU.......... Intravenous Drug User
IVDW.......... Integrated Voice/Data Workstations (SAUO)
IVDW.......... Intelligent Voice/Data Workstation (GART)
IVE.......... Image of Vocational Education [*ERIC*]
IVE.......... Institute of Vitreous Enamellers [*British*]
IVE.......... Integrated Visualization Environment [*Computer science*] (BTTJ)
IVE.......... Interactive Video Enterprises [*US West, Inc.*] (PCM)
IVE.......... Interface Verification Equipment (NASA)
IVE.......... Internationale Vereinigung der Eisenwaren- und Eisenhaendlerverbaende [*International Federation of Ironmongers and Iron Merchants Association*]
IVE.......... Internationale Vereinigung von Einkaufsverbanden [*International Association of Buying Groups - IABG*] (EAIO)
IVE.......... International Video Entertainment
IVE.......... Investment Equipment (MCD)
IVE.......... Isobutyl Vinyl Ether [*Organic chemistry*]
IVE.......... Isocyanate Vinyl Ester (SAUS)
IVE.......... University of Chicago, Graduate Library School, Chicago, IL [*OCLC symbol*] (OCLC)
IVEC.......... In Vitro Expression Cloning [*Analytical biochemistry*]
IVECO.......... Industrial Vehicles Corp. (SAUS)
IVECO.......... Industrial Vehicles Corporation (SAUO)
IVEN.......... Interactive Video Extension Network (ACAE)
IVen.......... Venice Public Library, Venice, IL [*Library symbol*] [*Library of Congress*] (LCLS)
IVenCU........ Venice Community Unit 3, Venice, IL [*Library symbol*] [*Library of Congress*] (LCLS)
IV Engine..... Inverted Vertical Engine (SAUS)
Iv Ersk.......... Ivory. Notes on Erskine's Institutes [*A publication*] (ILCA)
Iverson........ Iverson Technology Corp. (SAUO)
IVES.......... Information Vending Encryption System [*An AT&T security system*]
IVES.......... Internationaler Verband fuer Erziehung zu Suchtmittelfreiem Leben [*International Association for Education to a Life without Drugs*] (EAIO)
IVES.......... International Teachers Temperance Association [*Denmark*] (EAIO)
IVES.......... International Union for Alcohol-Free Life (SAUO)
IVES.......... Investment Technologies, Inc. [*NASDAQ symbol*] (COMM)
Ives Mil Law... Ives on Military Law [*A publication*] (DLA)
IVESS.......... Interactive Vehicle Scheduling System (MHDI)
IVET.......... In Vivo Expression Technology [*Genetics*]
IVETA.......... International Vocational Education and Training Association (EA)
IvexPkg........ Ivex Packaging Corp. [*Associated Press*] (SAG)
IVF.......... Idiopathic Ventricular Fibrillation [*Cardiology*]
IVF.......... Innocent Victims Fund (SAUO)
IVF.......... Internationale Viola Forschunggesellschaft [*International Viola Society*] [*Germany*] (EAIO)
IVF.......... International Varsity Fellowship (SAUO)
IVF.......... International Volunteers Force (SAUO)
IVF.......... Inter-Varsity Fellowship of Evangelical Unions [*British*] (BI)
IVF.......... Inter-Varsity Fellowship of Evangelic Unions (SAUO)
IVF.......... Interventricular Foramen [*Medicine*] (DMAA)
IVF.......... Intervertebral Foramen [*Medicine*] (MELL)
IVF.......... Intravascular Fluid [*Medicine*]
IVF.......... Intravenous Feeding [*Medicine*] (MELL)
IVF.......... Intravenous Fluid [*Pharmacology*] (DAVI)
IVF.......... In Vitro Fertilization [*Gynecology*]
IVF.......... IVF America, Inc. [*Associated Press*] (SAG)
IVF.......... Triodyne, Inc., Information Center, Skokie, IL [*OCLC symbol*] (OCLC)
IVFA.......... Intravenous Fluorescein Angiogram [*Medicine*] (MELL)
IVFA.......... Intravenous Fluoresce in Angiography (SAUS)
IVFA.......... IVF America [*NASDAQ symbol*] (TTSB)
IVFA.......... IVF America, Inc. [*NASDAQ symbol*] (SAG)
IVF Am........ IVF America, Inc. [*Associated Press*] (SAG)
IVFC.......... In Vitro Fertilization Clinic [*Medicine*] (EDAA)
IVFE.......... Intravenous Fat Emulsion [*Pharmacology*] (DAVI)
IVFET.......... In Vitro Fertilization with Embryo Transfer [*Gynecology*]
IVfgR.......... International Association for the Protection of Industrial Property (SAUO)
IVFGR.......... Internationale Vereinigung fuer Gewerblichen Rechtsschultz [*International Association for the Protection of Industrial Property*]
IVFRC.......... In Visual Flight Rules Conditions (SAUS)
IVFT.......... Intravenous Fluid Therapy [*Medicine*] (MELL)
IVFZ.......... International Veterinary Federation of Zootechnics [*Later, IVAAP*]
IVg.......... Camargo Township Library, Villa Grove, IL [*Library symbol*] [*Library of Congress*] (LCLS)
IVG.......... Immediate Visual Gratification (VLIE)
IVG.......... Internationale Vereinigung fuer Germanische Sprach - und Literaturwissenschaft [*International Association of Germanic Studies - IAGS*] [*Tokyo, Japan*] (EAIO)
IVG.......... Interrupt Vector Generator
IVG.......... Interrupt Vectur Generator (SAUS)
IVG.......... Isotopic Ventriculogram [*Cardiology*] (DAVI)
IVGA.......... Israel Vegetable Growers Association (SAUO)
IVGG.......... Institute of Volcanic Geology and Geochemistry [*Commonwealth of Independent States*]
IVGG.......... Intravenous Gamma Globulin [*Medicine*] (MELL)
IVGGD.......... Internationale Vereinigung fuer Geschichte und Gegenwart der Druckkunst [*International Association for Past and Present History of the Art of Printing*] (EAIO)
IVGMA.......... International Violin and Guitar Makers Association (EA)
IVGMMA...... International Violin, Guitar Makers and Musicians Association (SAUO)
IVGT.......... Intravenous Glucose Tolerance [*Medicine*] (DB)
IVGTT.......... Intravenous Glucose Tolerance Test [*Clinical medicine*]
IVGWP.......... Internationaler Verband der Gastronomie- und Weinbuau-Presse [*International Federation of Gastronomical and Vinicultural Press*]
IVH.......... Independent Variable Hull [*Statistics*]
IVH.......... Indian Veterinary Hospital [*British military*] (DMA)
IVH.......... Intravenous Hyperalimentation [*Medicine*] (EDAA)
IVH.......... Intraventricular Hemorrhage [*Cardiology*]
IVH.......... In vitro Hyperploidy [*Medicine*] (EDAA)
IVH.......... Ivishak, AK [*Location identifier*] [*FAA*] (FAAL)
IVHESM....... International Voluntary Historical Enlightenment Society Memorial (EAIO)
IVHH.......... Intravenous Gamma-Globulin [*Medicine*] (DB)
IVHM.......... In-Vessel Handling Machine [*Nuclear energy*] (NRCH)
IVHM-EM..... In-Vessel Handling Machine-Engineering Model [*Nuclear energy*] (NRCH)
IVHP.......... Intraventricular Hemorrhage Parents (EA)
IVHS.......... Intelligent Vehicle and Highway Society (SAUO)
IVHS.......... Intelligent Vehicle Highway System (USGC)
IVHSA.......... Intelligent Vehicle Highway Society of America (SAUO)
IVHU.......... In-Vessel Handling Unit (SAUS)
IVHW.......... Internationaler Verband fuer Hauswirtschaft [*International Federation for Home Economics*]
IVHX.......... In-Vessel Heat Exchanger [*Nuclear energy*] (NRCH)
IVI.......... American Conservatory of Music, Chicago, IL [*OCLC symbol*] (OCLC)
IVI.......... Ice-Core Volcanic Index
IVI.......... Incremental Velocity Indicator [*NASA*]
IVI.......... Indeo Video Interactive [*Computer science*]
IVI.......... Independent Voters of Illinois (SAUO)
IVI.......... Initial Ventricular Impulse
IVI.......... Initial Voluntary Indefinite [*Status*] [*Army*] (INF)
IVI.......... Instant Visual Index
IVI.......... Intelligent Vehicle Initiative
IVI.......... Interactive Videodisk Instruction (AGLO)
IVI.......... Interactive Visual Interface (SAUS)
IVI.......... Internal Vibration Isolator
IVI.......... International Vaccine Institute [*Korea*]
IVI.......... International Verifact, Inc. [*Toronto Stock Exchange symbol*]
IVI.......... International Verifact, Incorporated (SAUO)
IVI.......... Inventory Index (MCD)
IVI.......... In Vitro International, Inc. (DB)
IVI.......... Ivigtut [*Greenland*] [*Seismograph station code, US Geological Survey*] [*Closed*] (SEIS)
IVI.......... Tucson, AZ [*Location identifier*] [*FAA*] (FAAL)
IVIA.......... Interactive Video Industry Association (EA)
IVIA.......... International Videotex Industry Association
IVIA.......... International Videotext Industry Association (SAUS)
IVIAF.......... International Verifact, Inc. [*NASDAQ symbol*] (SAG)
IVIAF.......... Intl Verifact [*NASDAQ symbol*] (TTSB)
IVIAW.......... International Verifact Wrrt [*NASDAQ symbol*] (TTSB)
IVIC.......... International Videocassette and Videodisk Information Centre (SAUS)
IVIC.......... International Video Information Centre (SAUO)
IVICO.......... Integrated Video Codec (SAUO)
IVICS.......... Integrated Vehicle Information and Communicationss System (SAUS)
IVIDS.......... Intelligent Video Information Display System (SAUS)
IVIE.......... Independent Visually Impaired Enterprisers (EA)
IVIE.......... Interactive Video in Education [*National Interactive Video Centre*] (AIE)
IVIG.......... Intravenous Immunoglobulin [*Medicine*] (CPH)
IVIg.......... Intravenous Immunoglobulin [*Medicine*] (EDAA)
IVIL.......... iVillage, Inc. [*NASDAQ symbol*] (SG)
IVIM.......... Intravoxel Incoherent Motion [*Imaging technique*]
IVING.......... Ivinghoe [*England*]
IVINX.......... Ivy International Cl.A [*Mutual fund ticker symbol*] (SG)
IVIP.......... Internationale Vereinigung fuer Individualpsychologie [*International Association of Individual Psychology*]
IVIP.......... IVI Publishing [*NASDAQ symbol*] (TTSB)
IVIP.......... IVI Publishing, Inc. [*NASDAQ symbol*] (SAG)
IVIPA.......... International Videotex Information Providers' Association [*British*] [*Information service or system*] (IID)
IVIPA.......... International Videotext Information Providers Association (SAUS)
IVI Pub........ IVI Publishing, Inc. [*Associated Press*] (SAG)
IVird.......... Virden Public Library, Virden, IL [*Library symbol*] [*Library of Congress*] (LCLS)

IVirdMCD..... Macoupin Community District 4, Virden, IL [*Library symbol*] [*Library of Congress*] (LCLS)
IVIS............ Integrated Vacuum Instrumentation System (SAUO)
IVIS............ Integrated Vehicular Information System [*Army*] (RDA)
IVIS............ Interactive Video Information System (VLIE)
IVIS............ International Visitors Information Service (EA)
IVIS............ Intervehicle Information System (SAUS)
IVIS............ Intervehicle Intelligence System (SAUS)
IVIS............ Intervehicular Information System [*Army*] (RDA)
IViS............ Shawnee Correctional Center, Vienna, IL [*Library symbol*] [*Library of Congress*] (LCLS)
IV/IVC......... In-Vitro/In-Vivo Correlation [*Drug evaluation*]
IVIZ............ Institutionenverzeichnis fuer Internationale Zusammenarbeit [*Institutions for International Cooperation*] [*NOMOS Datapool*] [*Database*] (IID)
IVJ............ Oak Lawn Public Library, Oak Lawn, IL [*OCLC symbol*] (OCLC)
IVJC............ Intervertebral Joint Complex [*Medicine*]
IVJH............ Internationale Vereinigung fuer Jugendhilfe [*International Union for Child Welfare*]
IVJS............ International Jewish Vegetarian Society [*Formerly, Jewish Vegetarian Society*] (EA)
IVKMH......... Internationale Vereinigung der Klein- und Mittelbetriebe des Handels [*International Federation of Small and Medium-Sized Commercial Enterprises*]
IVL............ Independent Vendor League (SAUO)
IVL............ Intel Verification Laboratory (SAUO)
IVL............ Internationale Vereinigung der Lehrerverbaende [*International Federation of Teachers' Associations*]
IVL............ Internationale Vereinigung fuer Theoretische und Angewandte Limnologie [*International Association of Theoretical and Applied Limnology*]
IVL............ Intervalometer (KSC)
IVL............ Intravenous Leiomyomatosis [*Medicine*] (PALA)
IVL............ Intravenous Lock (STED)
IVL............ Invader Resources Ltd. [*Vancouver Stock Exchange symbol*]
IVL............ Inventory Validation Listing [*Computer science*]
IVL............ In Virtual Life (VLIE)
IVL............ Involucrin (DMAA)
IVL............ Ivalo [*Finland*] [*Airport symbol*] (OAG)
IVL............ Ivaran Lines (SAUS)
IVL............ Swedish Environmental Research Institute (SAUO)
IVLA............ International Visual Literacy Association (EA)
IVLBW......... Infant of Very Low Birth Weight [*Neonatology*] (DAVI)
IVLD............ Internationale Vereinigung der Organisationen von Lebensmittel-Detail-Listen [*International Federation of Grocers' Associations - IFGA*] (EAIO)
IVLS............ Illinois Valley Library System [*Library network*]
IVM............ Immediate Visual Memory (STED)
IVM............ Improved Visible Marker
IVM............ Induced Vertical Magnetism (SAUS)
IVM............ Initial Virtual Memory (VLIE)
IVM............ Institute of Value Management [*British*]
IVM............ Integrated Vector Management [*Insect control*]
IVM............ Interactive Volume Modelling (SAUS)
IVM............ Interface Virtual Machine [*Computer science*]
IVM............ Intervertebral Muscle [*Medicine*] (MELL)
IVM............ Intravascular Mass (MAE)
IVM............ Inventory Verification Manual
IVM............ In Vivo Metric [*System*] [*Medicine*] (EDAA)
IVM............ Involuntary Muscle [*Medicine*] (MELL)
IVMA............ Idaho Veterinary Medical Association (SRA)
IVMA............ Indiana Veterinary Medical Association (SRA)
IVMA............ Industrial Vegetation Management Association [*Defunct*] (EA)
IVMA............ Integrated Vegetation Management Association of BC (SAUO)
IVMA............ Intermountain Veterinary Medical Association (EA)
IVMA............ Iodovinylmethoprenol Analog [*Organic chemistry*]
IVMA............ Iowa Veterinary Medical Association (SRA)
IVMB............ Internationale Vereinigung der Musikbibliotheken, Musikarchive, und Dokumentationszentren [*International Association of Music Libraries, Archives, and Documentation Centers*]
IVMC............ International Vacuum Microelectronics Conference (SAUS)
IVMF............ Inter-Varsity Missions Fellowship (EA)
IVMI............ Ivy Medical, Incorporated (SAUO)
IVML............ In Vivo Measurements Laboratory (SAUO)
IVMMD......... Interim Vehicle Mounted Mine Detection System [*Military*]
IVMP............ Intravenous Methylprednisolone [*Medicine*]
IVMS............ Instrumented Vibration Measuring System
IVMS............ Integrated Vehicle Management Subsystem (MCD)
IVMS............ Integrated Vehicle Management System (SAUS)
IVMS............ Integrated Voice Messaging System [*Commterm, Inc.*] [*Atlanta, GA*] (TSSD)
IVMU............ Inertial Velocity Measurement Unit (IEEE)
IVN............ Inferior Vertebral Notch [*Medicine*] (MELL)
IVN............ Intercity Voice Network [*FTS*] (DNAB)
IVN............ Internationale Vereniging voor Neerlandistiek [*International Association of Dutch Studies*] (EAIO)
IVN............ Intervening Network (SAUO)
IVN............ Intervening Node (SAUS)
IVN............ Intervoice Communication System (SAUS)
IVN............ Intravenous Nutrition [*Medicine*]
IVNAA......... In Vivo Neutron Activation Analysis [*Analytical chemistry*]
IVNF............ Intravitreal Neovascular Frond (STED)
IVNTA......... International Veterinary Nurses and Technicians Association (GVA)
IVNTG......... Intravenous Nitroglycerin [*Medication order*] (CPH)
IVO............ Improved Virtual Orbitals [*Atomic physics*]
IVO............ Inova Optics, Inc. [*Vancouver Stock Exchange symbol*]
IVO............ Input Voltage Offset
IVO............ Intake Valve Open [*Automotive engineering*]
IVOD............ Interactive Video On Demand (SAUS)
IVOJC......... Ivorydale Junction, OH [*American Association of Railroads railroad junction routing code*]
IVOM............ Isolated Yolitional Oral Movements(s) [*Medicine*] (EDAA)
IVOQ............ Internet Vehicle Owner's Questionnaire [*Automotive safety*]
IVORY......... Ivorydale, OH [*American Association of Railroads railroad junction routing code*]
IVOS............ Investigative Opthalmology and Visual Science (ADWA)
IVOTTS......... Irvine Viable Organ [*Medicine*] (EDAA)
IVOX............ Intravascular Oxygenator [*Artificial lung*] [*Medicine*]
IVP............ Imitation Vegetable Parchment [*Paper*] (DGA)
IVP............ Implied Valve Position (ACII)
IVP............ Initial Value Problem (SAUS)
IVP............ Initial Vapor Pressure
IVP............ Insecticidal Viral Product [*Agricultural chemistry*]
IVP............ Inspected Variety Purity [*Agriculture*]
IVP............ Installation Verification Image (SAUO)
IVP............ Installation Verification Procedure (MCD)
IVP............ Installation Verification Program (SAUS)
IVP............ Institutional Venture Partners
IVP............ Insurance Verification Program Case [*Motor vehicle violation code used in state of Maryland*] (MVRD)
IVP............ Integrated Vacuum Processing (AAEL)
IVP............ Interactive Voice Response (TELE)
IVP............ Interface Verification Procedure [*NASA*] (IAA)
IVP............ Internationaler Verband der Pektinproduzenten [*International Pectin Producers Association*] [*Switzerland*] (EAIO)
IVP............ Inter-Varsity Press [*British*]
IVP............ Intravenous Pitocin [*Pharmacology*] (DAVI)
IVP............ Intravenous Polygram [*Medicine*] (IDYL)
IVp............ Intravenous Push [*Dose*] [*Medicine*] (STED)
IVP............ Intravenous Push [*Medicine*]
IVP............ Intravenous Pyelogram [*Radiology*]
IVP............ Intravenous Pyelography (SAUS)
IVP............ Intraventricular Pressure [*Cardiology*] (AAMN)
IVP............ Intravesical Pressure (STED)
IVP............ Ion Vacuum Pump
IVPA............ Independent Video Programmers Association [*Defunct*] (EA)
IVPAC......... International Union of Pure and Applied Chemistry (SAUO)
IVPB............ Intravenous Piggyback [*Method of drug administration*] [*Pharmacology*]
IVPC............ Internationaler Verband der Petroleum- und Chemiearbeiter [*International Federation of Petroleum and Chemical Workers*]
IV-PCA......... Intravenous-Patient-Controlled-Analgesia
IVPD............ In Vitro Protein Digestibility [*Nutrition*]
IVPDL......... Inter-Vehicle Positioning and Data Link (SAUS)
IVPF............ Isovolume Pressure Flow (SAUS)
IVPF............ Isovolume Pressure Flow Curve [*Cardiology*] (MAE)
IVPN............ International Virtual Private Network (SAUS)
IVPO............ Inside Vapor Phase Oxidation [*Glass technology*]
IVPP............ Institute of Vertebrate Palaeontology and Palaeoanthropology [*China*]
IVPT............ Inter-Vehicle Power Transfer (MCD)
IVPU............ Intravenous Push [*Medicine*] (EDAA)
IV push......... Introvenous Medication by Push [*Therapy term*] (CTAA)
IVQ............ Individual Vessel Quota [*Fisheries management*]
IVQ............ Interrupted Very Quick [*Flashing*] Light [*Navigation signal*]
IVR............ Idioventricular Rhythm [*Cardiology*] (DMAA)
IVR............ Illinois Veterinary Reports (journ.) (SAUS)
IVR............ Induction Voltage Regulator (SAUS)
IVR............ Inner Vertical Resonance [*Physics*]
IVR............ Instant Video Receiver [*Electronics*]
IVR............ Instrumental Visual Range (SAUS)
IVR............ Instrumented Visual Range (IAA)
IVR............ Instrument Visual Range (SAUS)
IVR............ Instrument Voltage Regulator [*Automotive engineering*]
IVR............ Integrated Voltage Regulator (IEEE)
IVR............ Interactive Voice Response (FOTI)
IVR............ Internal Visual Reference [*Motion sickness*]
IVR............ International Association for the Rhine Vessels Register [*Netherlands*] (EY)
IVR............ Internationale Vereinigung fuer Rechts- und Sozialphilosophie [*International Association for Philosophy of Law and Social Philosophy*] (EAIO)
IVR............ International Vehicle Registration (SAUS)
IVR............ Interventional Radiography [*Medicine*]
IVR............ Intramolecular Vibrational Redistribution [*Chemistry*]
IVR............ Intramolecular Vibrational Relaxation [*Organic chemistry*]
IVR............ Intravaginal Ring [*Medicine*] (DB)
IVR............ Inverell [*Australia*] [*Airport symbol*] (OAG)
IVR............ Irvco Resources [*Vancouver Stock Exchange symbol*]
IVR............ Isolated Volume Responders [*Physiology*]
IVR............ Isovolumic Relaxation [*Time*] [*Cardiology*] (DAVI)
IVRD............ In Vitro Rumen Digestibility [*Nutrition*]
IVRET......... Intramolecular Vibration-Rotation Energy Transfer [*Chemistry*]
IVRG............ International Verticillium Research Group (EAIO)
IVRG............ In-Vehicle Route Guidance System [*FHWA*] (TAG)
IVRR............ Integrated Voice and Radar Recorder Committee (SAUS)
IVRRF......... In Vivo Radioassay and Research Facility (SAUS)
IVRS............ Interactive Voice Response System [*Military*] (INF)
IVRS............ Interim Voice Response System (PIPO)
IVRT............ Isovolumic Relaxation Time (DMAA)
IVS............ Air Evasion [*France*] [*ICAO designator*] (FAAC)

IVS .... Idle Validation Switch [*Automotive electronics*]
IVS .... Inappropriate Vasopressin Secretion (DB)
IVS .... Independent Vertical System
IVS .... Index of Veterinary Specialities (journ.) (SAUS)
IVS .... Indian Vacuum Society (SAUO)
IVS .... Indian Veterinary Service (SAUO)
IVS .... Indirect Viewing Substitution (ACAE)
IVS .... Infrared Viewing Set
IVS .... Input Voltage Supply
IVS .... Insect Visual System
IVS .... Intact Ventricular System [*Cardiology*]
IVS .... Integrated Versaplot Software (PDAA)
IVS .... Intelligent Vehicle System (SAUS)
IVS .... Interactive Videodisk System (SAUO)
IVS .... Interactive Video Service (LAIN)
IVS .... Interactive Video Solutions (SAUS)
IVS .... Interactive Visualization Systems (SAUO)
IVS .... Interactive Voice System [*Electronics*]
IVS .... Interchange Units Separation (ECII)
IVS .... Intermittent Voice Service (SAUS)
IVS .... International Vestor Resources [*Vancouver Stock Exchange symbol*]
IVS .... International Voluntary Services (EA)
IVS .... Intervalley Scattering (SAUS)
IVS .... Intervening Sequence [*Genetics*]
IVS .... Interventricular Septum [*Cardiology*]
IVS .... Intervoice Communication System (SAUS)
IVS .... In-Vessel Storage [*Nuclear energy*] (NRCH)
IVS .... Vigo County School Corp., Terre Haute, IN [*OCLC symbol*] (OCLC)
IVSA .... International Veterinary Students Association [*Utrecht, Netherlands*] (EAIO)
IVSAN .... Initial Voice Switching Network (SAUO)
IVSAWS .... In-Vehicle Safety Advisory and Warning System [*FHWA*] (TAG)
IVSC .... Integrated Vehicle Speed Control [*Automotive term*] (HAWK)
IVSD .... Interventricular Septal Defect [*Cardiology*]
IVSD .... Vandalia Community Unit, School District 203, Vandalia, IL [*Library symbol*] [*Library of Congress*] (LCLS)
IVSE .... Interventricular Septal Excursion [*Medicine*] (EDAA)
IVSET .... Interactive Videodisc for Special Education Technology (EDAC)
IVSI .... Inertial Lead Vertical Speed Indicator (IAA)
IVSI .... Inertial Vertical Speed Indicator (PIPO)
ivsi .... Instantaneous Vertical Speed Indicator (NAKS)
IVSI .... Instantaneous Vertical Speed Indicator [*NASA*]
IVSK .... Intravenous Streptokinase [*An enzyme*]
IVSM .... In-Vessel Storage Module [*Nuclear energy*] (NRCH)
IVSN .... Initial Voice Switched Network [*NATO integrated communications system*] (NATG)
IVSN .... Initial Voice Switch Network (SAUO)
IVSP .... International Voluntary Service for Peace (SAUO)
IVSP .... In Vitro Synthesized Protein [*Biochemistry*]
IVSR .... Indus Valley State Railway [*Indian Railway*] (TIR)
IVSS .... Internationale Vereinigung fuer Soziale Sicherheit [*International Social Security Association*]
IVSS .... International Varna Sociological School (SAUO)
IVSS .... Intravenous Solu-Set [*Medicine*] (MEDA)
IVSU .... International Veterinary Students Union [*Later, IVSA*]
I vs V .... Current versus Voltage (SAUS)
IVSY .... International Union of Socialist Youth (SAUO)
IVT .... Independent Verification Team (SAUS)
IVT .... Index of Vertical Transmission [*Cultural evolution*]
IVT .... Inferential Value Testing (KSC)
IVT .... Infinitely Variable Transmission [*Automotive engineering*] (PS)
IVT .... Initial Vaporization Temperature (SAUS)
IVT .... Input Value Table [*Computer science*] (ECII)
IVT .... Inspection Verification Tag
IVT .... Institute for Victims of Trauma (EA)
IVT .... Intake Valve Throttling (SAUS)
IVT .... Integrated Video Terminal
IVT .... Interactive Video Technology [*Database*] [*Heartland Communications*] [*Information service or system*] (CRD)
IVT .... Interface Vacuum Test (ACAE)
IVT .... Interface Verification Test (ACAE)
IVT .... Internationale Vereinigung der Textileinkaufsverbande [*International Association of Textile Purchasing Societies*]
IVT .... International Visual Theatre Research Community (SAUO)
IVT .... Interrupt Vector Table (SAUS)
IVT .... Intervalve Transformer (IAA)
IVT .... Intervehicular Transfer (KSC)
IVT .... Intra-Vehicular Transfer (SAUS)
IVT .... Intravenous Transfusion [*Medicine*]
IVT .... Intraventricular [*Cardiology*]
IVT .... Investment Values of Today (SAUO)
IVT .... Isovolumetric Time (DB)
IVT .... Iventronics Ltd. [*Toronto Stock Exchange symbol*]
IVT .... Iverson Technology (ACAE)
IVT .... Iverson Technology Corp. (SAUO)
IVt .... Vigo County Public Library, Terre Haute (SAUS)
IVTC .... International Visitors and Travel Coordinator (COE)
IVTC .... Iverson Technology Corporation (SAUO)
IVTD .... Integrated Visual Testing Device
IVTE .... Integration and Verification Test Environment (SAUS)
IVTLAP .... International Association of Theoretical and Applied Limnology. Proceedings (journ.) (SAUS)
IVTM .... In-Vessel Transfer Machine [*Nuclear energy*] (NRCH)
IVTMAS .... Communications. International Association of Theoretical and Applied Limnology (journ.) (SAUS)
IVTS .... Interactive Video Training System (SAUO)
IVTS .... International Video Teleconferencing Service (SAUO)
IVTTT .... Intravenous Tolbutamide Tolerance Test [*Clinical medicine*] (MAE)
IVU .... International Vegetarian Union [*Stockport, Cheshire, England*]
IVU .... International Volunteers in Urology (SAUO)
IVU .... Intravehicular Umbilical [*NASA*] (KSC)
IVU .... Intravenous Urogram [*or Urography*] [*Medicine*]
IVU .... Intravenous Urography (SAUS)
IVU .... In-Vehicle Unit [*Electronic system for charging for road usage*] [*Singapore*] (ECON)
IVU .... Irish Veterinary Union (GVA)
IVU .... Valparaiso University, Valparaiso, IN [*OCLC symbol*] (OCLC)
IVUL .... IVSN User List (SAUS)
IVUN .... International Ventilator Users Network (NRGU)
IVUS .... Interventional Ultrasonography [*Medicine*] (MELL)
IVUS .... Intravascular Ultrasound [*Medicine*]
IVV .... Idle Vacuum Valve [*Exhaust emissions*] [*Automotive engineering*]
IVV .... Independent Validation and Verification (ACAE)
IVV .... Independent Verification and Validation (SAUO)
IVV .... Influenza Virus Vaccine [*Medicine*] (MELL)
IVV .... Instantaneous Vertical Velocity
IVV .... International Association for Vegetation Science (SAUO)
IVV .... Internationaler Volkssportverband [*International Federation of Popular Sports - IFPS*] (EAIO)
IVV .... Internationale Vereinigung fuer Vegetationskunde [*International Association for Vegetation Science - IAVS*] (EAIO)
IVV .... Intravenous Vasopressin [*Endocrinology*]
IVV .... Lebanon, NH [*Location identifier*] [*FAA*] (FAAL)
IVV .... Vincennes University, Vincennes, IN [*OCLC symbol*] (OCLC)
IVVC .... Instantaneous Vertical Velocity Computer (SAUO)
IVVI .... Instantaneous Vertical Velocity Indicator
IV vol .... Intravenous Volume [*Pharmacology*] (DAVI)
IVVS .... Instantaneous Vertical Velocity Sensor (NATG)
IVVS .... Interactive Verification and Visualization System (SAUO)
IVW .... International Vintage Wines (EFIS)
IVWA .... Indian Village Welfare Association (SAUO)
IVWCO .... International Voluntary Work Camp Organization (SAUO)
IVWL .... Intracapsular Volar Wrist Ligament [*Medicine*] (MELL)
IVWO .... International Vine and Wine Office
IVWSR .... Internationaler Verband fuer Wohnungswesen, Staedtebau und Raumordnung [*International Federation for Housing and Planning*]
IVX .... Columbus, OH [*Location identifier*] [*FAA*] (FAAL)
IVX .... Imperial Valley College, Imperial, CA [*OCLC symbol*] (OCLC)
IVX .... IVAX Corp. [*AMEX symbol*] (SAG)
IVY .... Ivory Oil & Minerals [*Vancouver Stock Exchange symbol*]
IVYBR .... Ivybridge [*England*]
IVYFX .... Ivy Growth Cl.A [*Mutual fund ticker symbol*] (SG)
IVYIX .... Ivy Growth with Income Cl.A [*Mutual fund ticker symbol*] (SG)
IVYLD .... Ivyland, PA [*American Association of Railroads railroad junction routing code*]
IVYRO .... Ivy Rock, PA [*American Association of Railroads railroad junction routing code*]
IVZ .... Valparaiso University, Law Library, Valparaiso, IN [*OCLC symbol*] (OCLC)
IW .... Impulse Weight (IAA)
IW .... Index Word [*Online database field identifier*]
IW .... Indications and Warning [*Subsystems*] [*Military*] (MCD)
IW .... Indicator Word (SAUS)
IW .... Indirect Waste
IW .... Individually Wrapped (SAUS)
IW .... Individual Weapon (MCD)
IW .... Induction Welding
IW .... Industrial Waste (SAUS)
IW .... Industrial Welfare (SAUO)
IW .... Inertia Weight [*Exhaust emissions*] [*Automotive engineering*]
IW .... Infectious Waste (EEVL)
IW .... Information Warfare
IW .... Information Window (SAUS)
IW .... Information Word (SAUS)
IW .... Information World [*A publication*]
IW .... Inland Waterways [*Organization that administered British canals during World War II*] [*Facetious translation: "Idle Women," due to high female workforce*]
IW .... Inner Wall [*Medicine*] (DMAA)
IW .... Inpatient Ward [*Medicine*] (DMAA)
IW .... Inside Width
IW .... Inside Wire [*Telecommunications*] (TEL)
IW .... Inspector of Works
IW .... Instruction Word [*Computer science*] (IAA)
IW .... Intentional Walk [*Baseball term*] (NDBD)
I/W .... Interchangeable With (AAG)
IW .... Interdiction Weapon (SAUS)
IW .... Interior Width (IAA)
IW .... International Air Bahama [*ICAO designator*] (AD)
IW .... International Wattier [*Process*] [*A method of making transparencies for rotogravure plates*]
IW .... International Workshop (SAUO)
I/W .... Interway Corp. (EFIS)
IW .... In Warranty (TIMI)
i/w .... in work (SAUS)
IW .... Irish Waters (SAUS)
IW .... Iron-Wustite [*Geology*]
IW .... Isle of Wight
IW .... Isotopic Weight

IW .... Isotropic Weight (SAUS)
iw .... Israel-Jordan Demilitarized Zones [*is (Israel) used in records cataloged after January 1978*] [*MARC country of publication code*] [*Library of Congress*] (LCCP)
IW .... Ivory Woodpecker (SAUS)
IW .... Wheaton Public Library, Wheaton, IL [*Library symbol*] [*Library of Congress*] (LCLS)
IWA .... Independent Watchmen's Association (EA)
IWA .... Individual Work Authorization (ACAE)
IWA .... Industrial Workers of Africa (SAUO)
IWA .... Inland Waterways Association [*British*] (DCTA)
IWA .... Inland Waterways Authority (WDAA)
IWA .... Institute of World Affairs [*Later, UFSI-IWA*] (EA)
IWA .... Insurance Workers of America (SAUO)
IWA .... Interdivisional Work Authorization (AAGC)
IWA .... International Water Association (SAUO)
IWA .... International Waterproofing Association [*See also AIE*] [*Brussels, Belgium*] (EAIO)
IWA .... International Webmasters Association (SAUO)
IWA .... International Wheat Agreement [*London*]
IWA .... International Wheelchair Aviators (EA)
IWA .... International Women's Auxiliary to the Veterinary Profession
IWA .... International Womens Auxiliary to the Vetetinary Profession (SAUS)
IWA .... International Woodworkers of America (EA)
IWA .... Interpreter Work Area (SAUS)
IWA .... Interrupt Work Area (SAUS)
IWA .... Iowa State University of Science and Technology, Ames, IA [*OCLC symbol*] (OCLC)
IWA .... Iwakuni [*Japan*] [*Airport symbol*] (AD)
IWAAC .... Inland Waterways Amenity Advisory Council [*British*] (DCTA)
IWAC .... Integrated Weapon Aiming Computer (SAUS)
I/WAC .... Interface/Weapon Aiming Computer (MCD)
IWAC .... International Women's Anthropology Conference (EA)
IWA-Canada ... Industrial, Wood & Allied Workers of Canada (SAUO)
IWAHMA .... Industrial Warm Air Heater Manufacturers
IWAHMA .... Industrial Warm Air Heater Manufacturers Association (SAUO)
IWaiHSD .... Walnut Consolidated High School District 508 (SAUS)
IWAIU .... Industrial Workers of America International Union (SAUO)
IWAK .... Improved Water Analysis Kit
IWal .... Walnut Township Library, Walnut, IL [*Library symbol*] [*Library of Congress*] (LCLS)
IWalHSD .... Walnut Consolidated High School District 508, Walnut, IL [*Library symbol*] [*Library of Congress*] (LCLS)
IWALS .... Integrated Weapon and Loading Subsystem (SAUS)
IWalSD .... Walnut Consolidated Community School District 285, Walnut, IL [*Library symbol*] [*Library of Congress*] (LCLS)
IWaltSD .... Waltonville Community Unit, School District 1, Waltonville, IL [*Library symbol*] [*Library of Congress*] (LCLS)
IWAN .... Integrated Wide Area Network (SAUS)
IWAP .... Interior Watershed Assessment Procedure (SAUO)
IWAP .... International Watershed Advocacy Project (SAUS)
IWARDS .... Iowa Water Resources Data System [*Iowa State Geological Survey*] [*Iowa City*] [*Information service or system*] (IID)
IWARS .... Installation Worldwide Ammunition Reporting System [*Army*]
IWARS .... Installation Worldwide Ammunitions Reporting System (SAUO)
IWas .... Washington Township Library, Washington, IL [*Library symbol*] [*Library of Congress*] (LCLS)
IWas-Su .... Washington Township Library, Sunnyland Branch, Sunnyland, IL [*Library symbol*] [*Library of Congress*] (LCLS)
IWat .... Watseka Public Library, Watseka, IL [*Library symbol*] [*Library of Congress*] (LCLS)
Iwate Univ Technol Rep ... Iwate University. Faculty of Engineering. Technology Reports (journ.) (SAUS)
Iwate Univ Technol Rep ... wate University. Faculty of Engineering. Technology Reports (SAUO)
IWatF .... Iroquois County Film Library, Watseka, IL [*Library symbol*] [*Library of Congress*] (LCLS)
IWatH .... Iroquois Memorial Hospital, Watseka, IL [*Library symbol*] [*Library of Congress*] (LCLS)
IWatl .... Morrison-Talbott Library, Waterloo, IL [*Library symbol*] [*Library of Congress*] (LCLS)
IWatlGHS .... Gibault High School, Waterloo, IL [*Library symbol*] [*Library of Congress*] (LCLS)
IWatlSD .... Waterloo Community School District 3, Waterloo, IL [*Library symbol*] [*Library of Congress*] (LCLS)
IWATSU Tech Rep ... IWATSU Technical Report (journ.) (SAUS)
IWau .... Waukegan Public Library, Waukegan, IL [*Library symbol*] [*Library of Congress*] (LCLS)
IWAV .... interWAVE Communic. Intl. [*NASDAQ symbol*] (SG)
I-WAY .... Information Highway (SAUO)
i-way .... Information Superhighway (CDE)
IWAY .... World Assembly of Youth (SAUO)
IWayc .... Wayne City Public Library, Wayne City, IL [*Library symbol*] [*Library of Congress*] (LCLS)
IWaycCD .... Wayne City Community Unit, District 100, Wayne City, IL [*Library symbol*] [*Library of Congress*] (LCLS)
IWB .... C. Berger & Co., Wheaton, IL [*Library symbol*] [*Library of Congress*] (LCLS)
IWB .... Council Bluffs Free Public Library, Council Bluffs, IA [*OCLC symbol*] (OCLC)
IWB .... Industry-Wide Bargaining (MHDB)
IWB .... Instruction Word Buffer (NITA)
IWB .... Intergalactic World Brain [*Underground press service*] (IIA)
IWB .... International Waterpolo Board (SAUO)
IWB .... International Women in Boating [*Nautical term*] (NTA)
IWBC .... Interim Wideband Communications (MCD)
IWBK .... InterWest Bancorp [*NASDAQ symbol*] (TTSB)
IWBK .... InterWest Savings Bank [*NASDAQ symbol*] (SAG)
IWBNI .... It Would Be Nice If [*Computer hacker terminology*] (NHD)
IWBP .... Integration with Britain Party [*Gibraltar*] (PPE)
IWBP .... Integration with British Party (SAUS)
IWBS .... Congregation of the Incarnate Word and Blessed Sacrament (SAUO)
IWBS .... Congregation of the Incarnate Word and the Blessed Sacrament [*Roman Catholic women's religious order*]
IWBS .... Indirect Work Breakdown Structure (NASA)
IWBS .... Integral Weight and Balance System [*Aviation*]
IWBS .... Integrated Weight & Balance System (SAUS)
IWC .... Ice Water Content
IWC .... Imperial War Cabinet [*British military*] (DMA)
IWC .... Implementation Working Group (SAUO)
IWC .... Incarnate Word College [*Texas*]
IWC .... Individual Weapons Captured
IWC .... Inertia Weight Class [*Automotive emissions*]
IWC .... Inland Waterways Corp. [*Later, Federal Barge Lines, Inc.; liquidated, 1963*]
IWC .... Inland Waterways Corporation (SAUO)
IWC .... Inside Wire Cable (SAUS)
IWC .... Institute for Workers' Control
IWC .... In-Stream Waste Concentration [*Environmental science*] (GFGA)
IWC .... Integrated Weapon Complex (SAUS)
IWC .... Integrated Weapon Control (SAUS)
IWC .... Interim Wilderness Committee [*Australia*]
IWC .... Internatioinal Wheat Council (SAUO)
IWC .... International Watch Co.
IWC .... International Watch Company (SAUO)
IWC .... International Welcome Club
IWC .... International Welding Conference (SAUS)
IWC .... International Whaling Commission [*Cambridge, England*]
IWC .... International Whaling Convention (SAUS)
IWC .... International Wheat Council [*See also CIB*] [*British*] (EAIO)
IWC .... International Wildcat Resources [*Vancouver Stock Exchange symbol*]
IWC .... International Wildlife Coalition (EA)
IWC .... International Willow Collectors [*An association*] (EA)
IWC .... Interwest Corporation (SAUO)
IWC .... In Which Case (SAUS)
IWC .... Iowa Wesleyan College
IWC .... IWC Resources Corp. [*Associated Press*] (SAG)
IWC .... Wabash College, Crawfordsville, IN [*OCLC symbol*] (OCLC)
IWCA .... Inside Wiring Cable [*Telecommunications*] (TEL)
IWCA .... International Window Cleaning Association (NTPA)
IWCA .... International Windsurfer Class Association (EA)
IWCA .... International World Calendar Association (EA)
IWCA .... Irish Wolfhound Club of America (EA)
IWCAC .... International Wireless Communications Advisory Committee (SAUO)
IWCB .... Internal Web Channel Bus (IAA)
IWCB .... Internal-Web Channel Bus (SAUS)
IWCC .... International Winter Cities Committee (SAUO)
IWCC .... International Women's Cricket Council [*Australia*] (EAIO)
IWCC .... International Workshop on Critical Currrents (SAUO)
IWCC .... International Wrought Copper Council [*British*] (EAIO)
IWCCA .... Inland Waterways Common Carriers Association [*Defunct*] (EA)
IWCD .... Integrated Wavefront Control Demonstration (SAUS)
IWCE .... International Workshop on Computational Electronics (SAUO)
IWCHL .... Illinois-Wisconsin Collegiate Hockey League (PSS)
IWCI .... Industrial Water Conditioning Institute (EA)
IWCI .... Industrial Wire Cloth Institute [*Later, AWCI*] (EA)
IWCLANA .... International Whaling Commission (SAUO)
IWCO .... Independent World Commission on the Oceans (SAUS)
IWCP .... Integrated Work Control Program (COE)
IWCP .... Interim Weapon Control Panel (SAUS)
IWCR .... International Whaling Commission. Reports (journ.) (SAUS)
IWCR .... Isle of Wight Central Railway Co. (SAUO)
IWCR .... IWC Resources Corp. [*NASDAQ symbol*] (NQ)
IWCRSI .... International Whaling Commission. Reports. Special Issue (journ.) (SAUS)
IWCS .... Integrated Weapons Control System
IWCS .... Integrated Wideband Communications System [*Military*]
IWCS .... Integrated Wideband Communication System (SAUO)
IWCS .... Interceptor Weapon Control System
IWCS .... International Wood Collectors Society (EA)
IWCS/SEA .... Integrated Wideband Communications System/Southeast Asia (IEEE)
IWCT .... International War Crimes Tribunal
IWCTF .... Interdepartmental Workers' Compensation Task Force [*Department of Labor*] [*Terminated, 1976*] (EGAO)
IW/CW .... Infectious Waste / Chemotherapeutic Waste
IWD .... Drake University, Law Library, Des Moines, IA [*OCLC symbol*] (OCLC)
IWD .... Industrial Works Department (SAUS)
IWD .... Information Warfare Division (SAUO)
IWD .... Inland Waters Directorate [*Canada*]
IWD .... Inland Waterways Directorate (SAUO)
IWD .... Integrated Weapon Display (SAUS)
IWD .... Integrated Weapons Display
IWD .... Interactive Weapon Display (SAUS)
IWD .... Intermediate Water Depth (MCD)
IWD .... International Waterways and Docks (SAUO)
IWD .... International Women's Day
IWD .... International Women's Decade
IWD .... Iron or Wood [*Freight*]
IWD .... Ironwood [*Michigan*] [*Airport symbol*] (OAG)

IWD .... Ironwood, MI [*Location identifier*] [*FAA*] (FAAL)
IWDA .... Independent Wire Drawers Association [*Later, AWPA*]
IWDCC .... Inter-Industry Wood Dust Coordinating Committee (WPI)
IWDCU .... Interim Wire Data Communication Unit (SAUS)
IWDGA .... Independent Wholesale Dry Goods Association (SAUO)
IWDM .... Intermediate Water Depth Mine (MCD)
IWDS .... Improved Weapon Delivery System (ACAE)
IWDS .... Integrated Warning and Display System (SAUO)
IWDS .... Integrated Weapons Delivery System (SAUS)
IWDS .... Interactive Wholesale Distribution System (MHDI)
IWDS .... International World Day Service
IWDS .... International World Days Service (SAUO)
IWE .... Camden, AL [*Location identifier*] [*FAA*] (FAAL)
IWE .... Illustrated World Encyclopedia [*A publication*]
IWE .... Instantaneous Word Encoder (IAA)
IWE .... Institute for Wholistic Education [*Later, SCIWE*] (EA)
IWE .... Institute of Water Engineers [*British*]
IWE .... Institution of Water Engineers [*British*] (BI)
IWE .... International World Executive (SAUO)
IWE .... Internet World Exhibition (SAUS)
IWE .... Interpolated Water Elevation (PDAA)
IWe .... Westchester Public Library, Westchester, IL [*Library symbol*] [*Library of Congress*] (LCLS)
IWE .... Winnetka Public Library, Winnetka, IL [*OCLC symbol*] (OCLC)
IWEC .... International Wildlife Education & Conservation (GVA)
IWedSD .... Wedron Consolidated Community School District 201, Wedron, IL [*Library symbol*] [*Library of Congress*] (LCLS)
IWEEA .... Industry Week (journ.) (SAUS)
IWEM .... Institution of Water and Environmental Management (EAIO)
IWEM .... Institution of Water Engineers and Scientists (SAUO)
IWem .... Westmont Public Library, Westmont, IL [*Library symbol*] [*Library of Congress*] (LCLS)
IWen .... Bond Public Library, Wenona, IL [*Library symbol*] [*Library of Congress*] (LCLS)
IWenSD .... Wenona Community Unit, School District 1, Wenona, IL [*Library symbol*] [*Library of Congress*] (LCLS)
IWer .... Westville Public Library (SAUS)
IWERC .... Industrial Waste Elimination Research Center [*Illinois Institute of Technology*] [*Research center*] (RCD)
Iwerks .... Iwerks Entertainment, Inc. [*Associated Press*] (SAG)
IWERRI .... Idaho Water and Energy Resources Research Institute [*University of Idaho*] [*Research center*] (RCD)
IWES .... Inhibited White Fuming Nitric Acid (PDAA)
IWES .... International Waste Energy System (SAUS)
IWES .... International Waste Energy Systems (EFIS)
IWes .... West Salem Public Library, West Salem, IL [*Library symbol*] [*Library of Congress*] (LCLS)
IWesp .... Thomas Ford Memorial Library, Western Springs, IL [*Library symbol*] [*Library of Congress*] (LCLS)
IWESS .... Infantry Weapons Effects Simulation System (SAUS)
IWETO .... Inventory of Scientific and Technological Research (SAUO)
IWev .... Westville Public Library, Westville, IL [*Library symbol*] [*Library of Congress*] (LCLS)
IWEWSULOTATDTO... I Wish Everyone Would Stop Using Letters of the Alphabet to Designate Their Organizations [*Originated by Bea von Boeselager in "Line o' Type," Chicago Tribune*]
IWEX .... Internal Wave Experiment (NOAA)
IWF .... Iliac Wing Fracture [*Medicine*] (MELL)
IWF .... IndustryWorkers Federation (SAUS)
IWF .... Information Word Format (SAUS)
IWF .... International Weightlifting Federation [*See also FHI*] [*Budapest, Hungary*] (EAIO)
IWF .... International Woodworking Machinery and Furniture Supply Fair (ITD)
IWF .... Internetworking Function [*Computer science*] (ACRL)
IWF .... Inter-Working Function (MLOA)
IWFA .... Inhibited White Fuming Nitric Acid [*Rocket fuel*] (SAA)
IWFA .... Intercollegiate Women's Fencing Association [*Later, NIWFA*]
IWFA .... International Wholesale Furniture Association (NTPA)
IWFA .... International Window Film Association (EA)
IWFA .... International Women's Fishing Association (EA)
IWFAI .... International Watch Fob Association, Inc. (EA)
IWFI .... Italian Wine and Food Institute (EA)
IWFNA .... Inhibited White Fuming Nitric Acid [*Rocket fuel*] (IAA)
IWFP .... International Women's Film Project (EA)
IWFS .... Industrial Waste Filter System (IEEE)
IWFS .... Integrated Waste Fluid System (SSD)
IWFS .... International Wine and Food Society [*British*] (EAIO)
IWG .... Grand View College, Des Moines, IA [*OCLC symbol*] (OCLC)
IWG .... Group/Intersystem Working Group (SAUO)
IWG .... Impacts Working Group (SAUO)
IWG .... Imperial Wire Gauge (ROG)
IWG .... Implementation Work Group [*DoD*]
IWG .... Implementation Work Group on Justice Information and Statistics [*See also GMO*] [*Canada*]
IWG .... Implementation Working Group (SAUO)
IWG .... Industry Working Group
IWG .... Integration Working Group (SAUO)
IWG .... Intelligence Working Group [*Military*] (CINC)
IWG .... Interagency Working Group (SAUO)
IWG .... Interface Working Group [*NASA*] (NASA)
IWG .... Intergovernmental Working Group [*United Nations*]
IWG .... Interim Working Group (SAUO)
IWG .... Internal Working Group (SAUO)
IWG .... International Working Group [*NATO*] (NATG)
IWG .... International Writers Guild
IWG .... Interprogram Working Group (ACAE)
IWG .... Investigator's Working Group [*Spacelab mission*]
IWG .... Iowa-Illinois Gas & Electric Co. (SAUO)
IWG .... Iron Wire Gauge
IWGA .... International Wheat Gluten Association (EA)
IWGA .... International World Games Association (EA)
IWG Bonn .... Bonn Institute for Economic and Social Research (SAUO)
IWGC .... Imperial War Graves Commission [*British*]
IWGCS .... International Working Group in Clinical Sociology (EAIO)
IWGCSFIPERM... Inter-Service Working Group for Cooperation and Standardization of Foto Interpretation Procedures, Equipment and Related Matters (SAUS)
IWGCSFIPERM... Inter-Service Working Group for Cooperation and Standardization of Photo Interpretation Procedures, Equipment and Related Matters (SAUO)
IWGDE .... Interlaboratory Working Group for Data Exchange [*Computer science*] (MHDI)
IWGDMGC ... Interagency Working Group on Data Management for Global Change (EOSA)
IWGDMGC ... International Working Group on Data Management for Global Change (SAUO)
IWGFR .... International Working Group on Fast Reactors (NRCH)
IWGGCDM ... International Working Group on Global Change and Data Management (SAUO)
IWGGDM ...... International Working Group on Graminaceous Downy Mildews [*Defunct*] (EAIO)
IWGGE .... Interdepartmental Working Group on the Greenhouse Effect (SAUO)
IWGIA .... International Work Group for Indigenous Affairs [*Copenhagen, Denmark*] (EAIO)
IWGLV .... International Working Group of Legume Virologists (SAUO)
IWGM .... Intergovernmental Working Group on Monitoring or Surveillance [*United Nations*] (ASF)
IWGMFS ...... International Working Group on Magnetic Field Satellites (SAUO)
IWGMP .... Intergovernmental Working Group on Marine Pollution [*Inter-Governmental Maritime Consultative Organization*]
IWGMS .... Intergovernmental Working Group on Monitoring or Surveillance [*United Nations*] (MSC)
IWGMT .... International Working Group on Mycobacterial Taxonomy [*Medicine*] (EDAA)
IWGN .... Intermediate Station Wagon (TVEL)
IWGNSRD .... International Working Group on Nuclear Structural (or Structure) and Reaction Data (SAUO)
IWGNSRD .... International Working Group on Nuclear Structure and Reaction Data (SAUS)
IWGP .... International Work Group for Palaeoethnobotany (SAUO)
IWGYC .... International Working Group Youth and Cooperation (SAUO)
IWH .... Institute for Work & Health (SAUO)
IWH .... Wabash, IN [*Location identifier*] [*FAA*] (FAAL)
IWHC .... International Women's Health Coalition (EA)
IWhh .... White Hall Township Library, White Hall, IL [*Library symbol*] [*Library of Congress*] (LCLS)
IWhhB .... Beecham Laboratories, White Hall, IL [*Library symbol*] [*Library of Congress*] (LCLS)
IWhhSD .... North Greene Community Unit, School District 3, White Hall, IL [*Library symbol*] [*Library of Congress*] (LCLS)
IWhI .... Indian Trails Public Library District, Wheeling, IL [*Library symbol*] [*Library of Congress*] (LCLS)
IWHM .... Institution of Works and Highways Management [*British*] (DBA)
IWHM .... Interwest Home Medical [*NASDAQ symbol*] (TTSB)
IWHM .... Interwest Home Medical, Inc. [*NASDAQ symbol*] (SAG)
IWhN .... North Suburban Library System, Wheeling, IL [*Library symbol*] [*Library of Congress*] (LCLS)
IWHS .... Institute of Works and Highways Superintendents [*British*]
IWHSD .... Irish War Hospital Supply Depot [*British military*] (DMA)
IWHTE .... Institution of Works and Highways Technician Engineers (SAUO)
IWI .... Inferior Wall Infarct [*Medicine*] (MELL)
IWI .... International Werner Tech [*Vancouver Stock Exchange symbol*]
IWI .... Interwave Interval [*Medicine*] (EDAA)
IWI .... Inventors' Workshop International [*Later, IWIEF*] (EA)
IWI .... Irreversible Warmup Indicator [*To detect whether frozen foods have risen above an acceptable temperature level*] [*Pronounced "ee-wee"*]
IWI .... Wishard Memorial Hospital, Indianapolis, IN [*OCLC symbol*] (OCLC)
IWi .... Witt Memorial Library, Witt, IL [*Library symbol*] [*Library of Congress*] (LCLS)
IWIEF .... Inventors Workshop International Education Foundation (EA)
IWIFR .... Integrated Wildlife-Intensive Forestry Research (SAUO)
IWI Hold ...... IWI Holding Ltd. [*Associated Press*] (SAG)
IWilB .... National Baha'i Museum, Wilmette, IL [*Library symbol*] [*Library of Congress*] (LCLS)
IWilGS .... Church of Jesus Christ of Latter-Day Saints, Genealogical Society Library, Wilmette Branch, Wilmette, IL [*Library symbol*] [*Library of Congress*] (LCLS)
IWIM .... Idealized Worker Idealized Manager (RALS)
IWin .... Winnetka Public Library, Winnetka, IL [*Library symbol*] [*Library of Congress*] (LCLS)
IWinfC .... Central DuPage Hospital, Medical Library, Winfield, IL [*Library symbol*] [*Library of Congress*] (LCLS)
IWin-N .... Winnetka Public Library District, Northfield Branch, Northfield, IL [*Library symbol*] [*Library of Congress*] (LCLS)
IWIPC .... Interim Wool Industry Policy Council [*Australia*]
IWIS .... Interceptor Weapons Instructor School [*Air Force*]
IWiSD .... Witt Community Unit, School District 66, Witt, IL [*Library symbol*] [*Library of Congress*] (LCLS)

IWISTK .... Issue While in Stock
IWIU .... Insurance Workers International Union
IWJG .... International Watch and Jewelry Guild
IWKB .... Inverse Wentzel-Kramers-Brillouin (SAUS)
IWL .... Infant Water Loss [*Medicine*] (CPH)
IWL .... Insensible Water Loss [*Medicine*]
IWL .... Institute of World Leadership (SAUO)
IWL .... Institute Warranties (or Warranty) Limits (SAUS)
IWL .... Institute Warranty Limits [*Shipping*] (DS)
IWL .... International Walther League (EA)
IWL .... Italian Welfare League (EA)
IWL .... Willard Library, Evansville, IN [*OCLC symbol*] (OCLC)
IWLA .... Izaak Walton League of America (EA)
IWLAE .... Izaak Walton League of America Endowment (EA)
IWLE .... Individual Whole of Life and Endowment [*Insurance*] (ADA)
IWLF .... International Wilderness Leadership Foundation
IWLP .... International Wild Life Protection (SAUO)
IWLRAA .... Indian Forest Records. Wild Life and Recreation (journ.) (SAUS)
IWLS .... International Water Lily Society (NTPA)
IWLS .... Iteractive Weighted Least Squares (SAUS)
IWLS .... Iterative Weighted Least Squares [*Statistics*]
IWM .... Bluffton-Wells County Public Library, Bluffton, IN [*OCLC symbol*] (OCLC)
IWM .... Imperial War Museum [*England*]
IWM .... Industrial Waste Management (MCD)
IWM .... Institute of Wastes Management [*British*]
IWM .... Institute of Works Managers (SAUS)
IWM .... Institution of Work Managers (SAUO)
IWM .... Institution of Works Managers [*British*]
IWM .... Integrated Woz Machine [*Apple Computer, Inc.*]
IWM .... Internal Waste Manifest [*Stanford University*]
IWM .... MAP International, Wheaton, IL [*Library symbol*] [*Library of Congress*] (LCLS)
IWMA .... Institute of Weights and Measures Administration [*Wales*]
IWMA .... International Wire and Machinery Association [*Leamington Spa, Warwickshire, England*] (EAIO)
IWMA .... International Working Men's Association (WDAA)
IWMF .... International Waldenstrom's Macroglobulinemia Foundation (NRGU)
IWMI .... Inferior Wall Myocardial Infarction [*Cardiology*]
IWMI .... International Water Management Institute
IWMIS .... Industrial Waste Management Information System (SAUO)
IWML .... Idiopathic White Matter Lesion [*Medicine*] (EDAA)
IWML .... Imperial War Museum Library (SAUO)
IWMP .... Integrated Watershed Management Plan (SAUO)
IWMP .... International Women's Media Project [*Defunct*] (EA)
IWMS .... Integrated Weed Management System [*Agriculture*]
IWN .... Indigenous Women's Network (EA)
IWN .... North Iowa Area Community College, Mason City, IA [*OCLC symbol*] (OCLC)
IWNFC .... International Willie Nelson Fan Club (EA)
IWO .... Indirect Word Order (TIMI)
IWO .... Institute for World Order (EA)
IWO .... Institute of Welfare Officers (SAUS)
IWO .... Institute of World Order (SAUS)
IWO .... Intelligence Watch Officer [*Military*] (MCD)
IWO .... Interdivisional Work Order (AAGC)
IWO .... International Vine and Wine Office (SAUO)
IWO .... International Workers Order (SAUO)
IWo .... Worth Public Library District, Worth, IL [*Library symbol*] [*Library of Congress*] (LCLS)
IWOC .... International Wizard of Oz Club (EA)
IWor .... Wood River Public Library, Wood River, IL [*Library symbol*] [*Library of Congress*] (LCLS)
IWordR .... Worden Reading Center, Worden, IL [*Library symbol*] [*Library of Congress*] (LCLS)
IWordSD .... Worden Community Unit, School District 16, Worden, IL [*Library symbol*] [*Library of Congress*] (LCLS)
IWorH .... Wood River Township Hospital, Medical Library, Wood River, IL [*Library symbol*] [*Library of Congress*] (LCLS)
IWorHS .... East Alton-Wood River Community High School 14, Wood River, IL [*Library symbol*] [*Library of Congress*] (LCLS)
IWori .... Woodridge Public Library, Woodridge, IL [*Library symbol*] [*Library of Congress*] (LCLS)
IWOSC .... International Working-Group of Soilless Culture
IWP .... Ice Water Path (ARMP)
IWP .... Idaho White Pine [*Lumber*]
IWP .... Illawarra Workers Party [*Political party*] [*Australia*]
IWP .... Indicative World Plan for Agricultural Development [*United Nations*]
IWP .... Indo-West Pacific [*Biogeographic region*]
IWP .... In-Service Work Plan (SAUO)
IWP .... Intelligent Work in Process (SAUS)
IWP .... Intelligent Work in Process Interim Working Party (SAUO)
IWP .... Intergovernmental WOCE Panel (SAUO)
IWP .... Interim Working Party (SAUO)
IWP .... Internal Working Paper
IWP .... Internationale Weltfriedens Partei [*International World Peace Party*] [*Germany*] [*Political party*] (PPW)
IWP .... International Information/Word Processing Association [*Formerly, IWPA*] (EA)
IWP .... International Waterpolo Board (SAUO)
IWP .... International Word Processing Association (NITA)
IWP .... International Working Party
IWP .... Intramyocardial Wall Pressure [*Medicine*] (EDAA)
IWP .... Inverse Wulff Plot (PDAA)
IWP .... IOC-WMO Intergovernmental WOCE Panel (SAUS)
IWP .... Irish Workers' Party [*Political party*] (PPW)
IWP .... Sioux City Public Library, Sioux City, IA [*OCLC symbol*] (OCLC)
IWPA .... Independent Wire Producers Association [*Later, AWPA*] (EA)
IWPA .... International Word Processing Association [*Later, IIWPA, IWP*]
IWPA .... International Work Platform Association (SAUO)
IWPA .... Irish Water Polo Association (EAIO)
IWPC .... Institute of Water Pollution Control [*Later, IWEM*] (EAIO)
IWPCA .... Inland Water Petroleum Carriers Association (SAUO)
IWPCD .... International Water Power and Dam Construction (journ.) (SAUS)
IWPF .... Idaho Waste Processing Facility (SAUO)
IWPM/2 .... IBM SAA ImagePlus Workstation Program/2 (SAUS)
IWPO .... International Word Processing Organization (SAUO)
IWPO .... International Word Processing Organizations (SAUS)
IWPPA .... Independent Waste Paper Processors Association [*British*] (DBA)
IWPS .... Institute of War and Peace Studies (SAUO)
IWPTB .... Integrated Weather Product Test Bed (ACAE)
IWPU .... Interim Weapon Programming Unit (SAUS)
IWPZ .... Iowa Power Service [*Federal Railroad Administration identification code*]
IWQ .... Index of Wilderness Quality (SAUO)
IWQ .... Individual Weapons Qualification [*Military*]
IWQ .... Input Work Queue (SAUS)
IWR .... Cedar Rapids Public Library, Cedar Rapids, IA [*OCLC symbol*] (OCLC)
IWR .... Connecticut Institute of Water Resources [*Storrs, CT*] [*Department of the Interior*] (GRD)
IWR .... Improved Weather Reconnaissance
IWR .... Information World Review [*A publication*] [*Information service or system*] (IID)
IWR .... Infrared Warning Receiver [*Aviation*] (DNAB)
IWR .... Institute for Water Resources [*Fort Belvoir, VA*] [*Army*] (MSC)
IWR .... Institute for Wildlife Research [*Defunct*] (EA)
IWR .... Institute of Water Research [*Michigan State University*]
IWR .... Interceptor Warning Receiver (ACAE)
IWR .... Interdivisional Work Requisition (SAUS)
IWR .... Internet Weather Report (SAUS)
IWR .... Islamic World Review (journ.) (SAUS)
IWR .... Isle Of Wight Railway [*British*]
IWR .... Isle Of Wight Rifles [*British military*] (DMA)
IWR .... Isolated Word Recognition (MCD)
IWRA .... International Water Resources Association (EA)
IWRA .... International Wild Rice Association (EA)
IWRAW .... International Women's Rights Action Watch (EAIO)
IWRB .... International Waterfowl and Wetlands Research Bureau (EAIO)
IWRB .... International Waterfowl Research Bureau (SAUS)
IWRB .... International Wildfowl Research Bureau (SAUO)
IWRBBR .... Iowa. Agriculture and Home Economics Experiment Station. Research Bulletin (journ.) (SAUS)
IWRC .... Illinois Water Reserves Center (SAUS)
IWRC .... Independent Wire Rope Center [*or Core*]
IWRC .... Independent Wire Rope Core (SAUS)
IWRC .... International Wildlife Rehabilitation Council (EA)
IWRC .... Iron Wire Rope Core [*Nuclear energy*] (NRCH)
IWRI .... Informal World Recognition Inventory [*Education*] (EDAC)
IWRI .... International Waterfowl Research Institute (SAUS)
IWRI .... International Wildfowl Research Institute (SAUO)
IWRK .... Iwerks Entertainment [*NASDAQ symbol*] (TTSB)
IWRK .... Iwerks Entertainment, Inc. [*NASDAQ symbol*] (SAG)
IWRM .... Integrated Warfare Requirements Methodology
IWRMA .... Independent Wire Rope Manufacturers Association (EA)
IWRMA .... Irish Wholesale Ryegrass Machiners Association (BI)
IWRO .... Interdepartmental Work Release Order
IWRP .... Individualized Written Rehabilitation Program [*Department of Education*]
IWRP .... Industrial Waste Reduction Program [*Environmental science*]
IWRP .... Industry Waste Reduction Plans (SAUS)
IWRPC .... Improved Weather Reconnaissance System Program Council (SAUO)
IWRR .... Intermountain Western Railroad [*Federal Railroad Administration identification code*]
IWRRC .... International Wheelchair Road Racers Club (EA)
IWRS .... Improved Weather Reconnaissance System (SAUO)
IWRS .... International Weed Research Society (SAUO)
IWRS .... International Wood Research Society (SAUO)
IWRT .... Information Warfare Red Team (SAUS)
IWRUAR .... Institute for Water Resources. University of Alaska. Report (journ.) (SAUS)
IWS .... Impact Warning System
IWS .... Improved Weapon System (SAUS)
IWS .... Incapacitating Weapons System (SAUO)
IWS .... Independent Workstation (SAUS)
IWS .... Index of Work Satisfaction [*Medicine*] (EDAA)
IWS .... Individual Weapon Scope (SAUO)
IWS .... Individual Weapon Sight (SAUS)
IWS .... Industrial Water Society [*British*] (DBA)
IWS .... Industrial Water Supply
IWS .... Industrial Water System (KSC)
IWS .... Industrial Welfare Society [*British*] (ILCA)
IWS .... Industrial Workstation (SAUS)
IWS .... Information Warfare Squadron [*Air Force*]
IWS .... Information Word Structure (SAUS)
IWS .... Infrared Laser Spectrometer (SAUS)
IWS .... Infra-red Weapon Sight (SAUS)
IWS .... Inland Waterway Service
IWS .... Inner Wall Space (SAUS)
IWS .... Institute of Water Study (SAUO)

IWS .... Institute of Wood Science [*British*] (BI)
IWS .... Institute of Wood Science, London (SAUO)
IWS .... Institute of Work Studies (SAUS)
IWS .... Institute of Work Study (SAUO)
IWS .... Instruction Word Stack (SAUS)
IWS .... Instruction Work Stack (MHDB)
IWS .... Instrument Workshop (SAUO)
IWS .... Instrument Work Station (ADWA)
IWS .... Integrated Water System (SSD)
IWS .... Integrated Weapon System
IWS .... Integrated Work Sequence (SAUS)
IWS .... Integrated Work Statement (MCD)
IWS .... Integrated Workstation (SAUS)
IWS .... Intelligence Work Station (SAUO)
IWS .... Intelligent Work Station (ACAE)
IWS .... Intelligent Workstation Support (SAUS)
IWS .... Interactive Work Station (MHDB)
IWS .... International Wildrose Resources, Inc. [*Vancouver Stock Exchange symbol*]
IWS .... International Wine Society (EA)
IWS .... International Wool Secretariat [*British*]
IWS .... Interworking Service (SAUS)
IWS .... In-Vessel Vehicle System (SAUS)
IWS .... Ionizing Wet Scrubber [*Environmental science*] (GFGA)
IWS .... Western Iowa Technical Community College, Sioux City, IA [*OCLC symbol*] (OCLC)
IWSA .... Integrated Waste Services Association (NTPA)
IWSA .... Intelligent Warning System (SAUS)
IWSA .... International Water Supply Association [*British*] (EAIO)
IWSA .... International Workers Sport Association
IWSAW .... Institute for Women's Studies in the Arab World [*Beirut, Lebanon*] (EAIO)
IWSB .... Insect Wire Screening Bureau [*Later, Insect Screening Weavers Association*] (EA)
IWSc .... Institute of Wood Science (SAUO)
IWSc .... Institute of Wood Science Ltd. [*British*]
IWSC .... International Weed Science Council (SAUO)
IWSC .... Internet & Web Services Corp.
IWSC .... Irrigation and Water Supply Commission (SAUO)
IWSCA .... Irish Water Spaniel Club of America (EA)
IWSD .... Integrated Weapon System Display (SAUO)
IWSDB .... Integrated Weapon System Data Base (SAUS)
IWSF .... Irish Waterski Federation (EAIO)
IWSG .... International Wool Study Group [*British*] [*Defunct*] (EAIO)
IWSI .... Integrated Waste Services, Inc. [*NASDAQ symbol*] (SAG)
IWSI .... Integrated Waste Svcs [*NASDAQ symbol*] (TTSB)
IWSI .... Irish Work Study Institute (SAUO)
IWSI .... Irish Work Study Institute Ltd. (BI)
IWS/IT .... Integrated Work Sequence/Inspection Traveler (NRCH)
IWS/LAN .... Intelligent Workstation/Local Area Network (SAUO)
IWSM .... Integrated Weapon Support Management (AFM)
IWSM .... Integrated Weapon System Management (SAUS)
IWSO .... Instructor Weapons System Officer [*Military*]
IWSO .... Instructor Weapon Systems Officer (SAUO)
IWSOE .... International Weddell Sea Oceanographic Expedition
IWSOM .... Institute of Practitioners in Work Study, Organization and Methods (SAUO)
IWSP .... Institute of Work Study Practitioners [*British*] (BI)
IWSP .... Integrated Weapon Secret Panel (MCD)
IWSR .... Integrated Weapon System Representative [*or Review*] (MCD)
IWSR .... Integrated Weapon System Review (SAUS)
IWSR .... International Wine and Spirit Record
IWSRA .... Irish Women's Squash Rackets Association (EAIO)
IWSRBC .... Iowa. Agriculture and Home Economics Experiment Station. Special Report (journ.) (SAUS)
IWSS .... Interim Weapon Support System (SAUS)
IWSS .... International Weed Science Society (EA)
IWSSA .... Interservice Warehousing Support Services Agreement
IWST .... Individual Weapon System Training (SAUO)
IWST .... Integrated Weapon System Training [*Air Force*]
IwstHM .... Interwest Home Medical, Inc. [*Associated Press*] (SAG)
IWT .... Impacted Wisdom Tooth (MELL)
IWT .... Indian Writing Today (journ.) (SAUS)
IWT .... Industrial Waste Treatment Management (MCD)
IWT .... Indus Water Treaty (SAUS)
IWT .... Inhibit Word Trigger (VLIE)
IWT .... Inland Water Transport [*British*]
IWT .... Inland Waterways Transport (LDOE)
IWT .... Institute of Wireless Technology (SAUO)
IWT .... Institute of Women Today (EA)
IWT .... Integrated Waste Water Treatment
IWT .... Internal Warm Target (ADWA)
IWT .... Internationaal Watertribunaal [*International Water Tribunal*] [*Netherlands*] (EAIO)
IWT .... International Water Tribunal (SAUO)
IWT .... International Working Team [*NATO*] (NATG)
IWT .... International Workshop on Telematics (SAUO)
IWT .... Irwin Toy Ltd. [*Toronto Stock Exchange symbol*]
IWT .... I Was There
IWT .... Schools of Theology in Dubuque, Dubuque, IA [*OCLC symbol*] (OCLC)
IWTA .... Interdivisional Work Transfer Agreement (SAUO)
IWTC .... Inland Water Transport Corp. (SAUS)
IWtC .... International Wheat Council (SAUO)
IWTC .... International Womens Tribune Centre (SAUS)
IWTD .... Inland Water Transport Department (SAUO)
IWTDS .... Inland Water Transport Department Section (SAUO)
IWTF .... Inland Waterways Trust Fund (COE)
IWTF .... International Water Tribunal Foundation [*Netherlands*] (EAIO)
IWTF .... Intractable Wastes Task Force (SAUO)
IWT/MIL .... Working Group on Inland Water Transport, Military Sub-Group (SAUO)
IWTO .... International Wool and Textile Organization (SAUS)
IWTO .... International Wool Testing Organisation [*Australia*]
IWTO .... International Wool Textile Organization [*See also FLI*] [*Brussels, Belgium*] (EAIO)
IWTP .... Industrial Waste Treatment Plant (BCP)
IWTR .... Indianapolis Water (SAUS)
IWTRC .... International Wool Textile Research Conference (SAUS)
IWTS .... Indications and Warning Training System [*Military*] (MCD)
IWTS .... Individual Weapon Thermal Sight [*Army*] (INF)
IWTS .... Industrial Waste Treatment System (NRCH)
IWTS .... Infantry Weapons Training Simulator (SAUS)
IWTS .... Infantry Weapon Training System (SAUS)
IWTS .... Integrated Wire Termination System (IAA)
IWTS .... Integrated Worldwide Topographic System (PDAA)
IWTS .... International Water Treatment and Shipping Consulting Engineers GmbH (SAUO)
I Wts .... International Weights (SAUS)
IWTT .... Industrial Wastewater Treatment Plant
IWT-WG .... Inland Waterways Working Group (SAUO)
IWU .... Illegal Wearing of Uniform
IWU .... Illinois Wesleyan University [*Bloomington*]
IWU .... Insurance Workers Union (SAUO)
IWU .... Intermediate Working Unit (VLIE)
IWU .... Inter Working Unit (SAUS)
IWU .... Interworking Unit [*Computer science*] (TNIG)
IWU .... Isolation Working Unit [*Telecommunications*] (TEL)
IWU .... Texas Woman's University, Denton, TX [*OCLC symbol*] (OCLC)
IWUL .... Irrigators and Water Users' League [*Australia*]
IW Univ .... Illinois Weslayan University (SAUO)
IWV .... Integrated Water Vapor (ARMP)
IWV .... Internationale Warenhaus-Vereinigung [*International Association of Department Stores*]
IWV .... Waterloo Public Library, Waterloo, IA [*OCLC symbol*] (OCLC)
IWVA .... International War Veterans' Alliance (EA)
IWVMTS .... Interim Water Velocity Meter Test Set
IWW .... Industrial Workers of the World (EA)
IWW .... Inland Waterway (AABC)
IWW .... International Westward Development Corp. [*Vancouver Stock Exchange symbol*]
IWW .... International Who's Who [*A publication*]
IWW .... International Woodworkers of America (SAUO)
IWW .... Internet Wired World (SAUO)
IWW .... Intracoastal Waterway
IWW .... Kenai, AK [*Location identifier*] [*FAA*] (FAAL)
IWW .... Westmar College, Le Mars, IA [*OCLC symbol*] (OCLC)
IWW .... Wheaton College, Wheaton, IL [*Library symbol*] [*Library of Congress*] (LCLS)
IWWA .... International Water Works Association (SAUO)
IWWA .... International Wild Waterfowl Association (EA)
IWWA .... International Woodworkers of America (SAUO)
IWWCS .... International Who's Who in Community Service [*A publication*]
IWWDD .... Information World (journ.) (SAUS)
IWWDF .... International Westward Development Corp. (SAUO)
IWWG .... International Women's Writing Guild (EA)
IWW-G .... Wheaton College, Billy Graham Center, Wheaton, IL [*Library symbol*] [*Library of Congress*] (LCLS)
IWWM .... International Who's Who in Music and Musicians Directory [*A publication*]
IWWP .... International Who's Who in Poetry [*A publication*]
IWWR .... Institute for Wetland and Waterfowl Research (SAUO)
IWWRB .... International Waterfowl and Wetlands Research Bureau (EAIO)
IWWRD .... Inland Waterways Reconnaissance Device (SAUO)
IWY .... International Women's Year [*1975*]
IWY .... New York, NY [*Location identifier*] [*FAA*] (FAAL)
IWya .... Raymond A. Sapp Memorial Library, Wyanet, IL [*Library symbol*] [*Library of Congress*] (LCLS)
IWyaSD .... Wyanet Consolidated High School District 510, Wyanet, IL [*Library symbol*] [*Library of Congress*] (LCLS)
IWYF .... International World Youth Friendship (SAUO)
IWyo .... Wymoning Public Library, Wymoning, IL [*Library symbol*] [*Library of Congress*] (LCLS)
IX .... Flandre Air [*ICAO designator*] (AD)
IX .... Iesus Christus [*Jesus Christ*] [*Latin*]
IX .... In Christo [*In Christ*] [*Latin*]
IX .... Index [*Computer science*] (BUR)
IX .... Industry Manufacturers [*FCC*] (MCD)
IX .... In Exchange (SAUO)
IX .... Information Exchange [*Advanced photo system*]
IX .... Intent Exclusive (SAUS)
ix .... Interactive Executive (HGAA)
IX .... Inter-Exchange [*Telecommunications*] (NITA)
IX .... Intersystem Crossing (SAUS)
IX .... Invalid Syntax (SAUS)
IX .... Inverted Index (NITA)
IX .... Ion Exchange (SAUS)
IX .... Ion Exchanger (NRCH)
IX .... IRT Corp. (SAUO)
IX .... Unclassified Auxiliary (SAUS)

IX ... Unclassified Miscellaneous [*Navy ship symbol*]
IX ... Unclassified Miscellaneous ship (SAUS)
IX ... Unclassified Vessel (SAUS)
IXA ... Agartala [*India*] [*Airport symbol*] (OAG)
i-xa- ... Christmas Island [*Indian Ocean*] [*MARC geographic area code*] [*Library of Congress*] (LCCP)
IXA ... Ion-Excited X-Ray Analysis
IXA ... University of Texas at Austin, Austin, TX [*OCLC symbol*] (OCLC)
IXAE ... International X-Ray Astrophysics Explorer
IXAS ... Indian X-ray Astronomy Satellite (SAUS)
IXB ... Bagdogra [*India*] [*Airport symbol*] (OAG)
i-xb- ... Cocos [*Keeling*] Islands [*MARC geographic area code*] [*Library of Congress*] (LCCP)
IXC ... Chandigarh [*India*] [*Airport symbol*] (OAG)
IXC ... Interchange Carrier (SAUS)
ixc ... interexchange (SAUS)
IXC ... Inter-Exchange Carrier [*Telecommunications*] (DINT)
IXC ... Interexchange Channel [*Telecommunications*]
IXC ... Interexchange Circuit [*Telecommunications*] (TSSD)
IXC ... Inter-Exchange Control (NITA)
IXC ... Interexchange Mileage (CET)
IXC ... Ixora Communications System [*Vancouver Stock Exchange symbol*]
i-xc- ... Maldives [*MARC geographic area code*] [*Library of Congress*] (LCCP)
IXCU ... Integrated Transmission Control Unit (VLIE)
IXD ... Allahabad [*India*] [*Airport symbol*] (OAG)
IXD ... Olathe, KS [*Location identifier*] [*FAA*] (FAAL)
IXE ... Mangalore [*India*] [*Airport symbol*] (OAG)
IXEE ... International X-Ray and Extreme Ultraviolet Explorer
IXES ... Information Exchange System [*or Subsystem*] [*Military*] (DNAB)
IXF ... Industrial X-Ray Film
IXF ... Integrated Crystal Filter (SAUS)
IXF ... Integrated Exchange Format (SAUO)
IXG ... Belgaum [*India*] [*Airport symbol*] (OAG)
IXH ... Infantile X-linked Hypogammaglobulinemia (SAUS)
IXH ... Kailashahar [*India*] [*Airport symbol*] (AD)
IXI ... International Interconnect (SAUS)
IXI ... International X.25 Infrastructure (SAUS)
IXI ... International X.25 Interconnect (SAUO)
IXI ... Lilabari [*India*] [*Airport symbol*] (OAG)
IXJ ... Jammu [*India*] [*Airport symbol*] (OAG)
IXK ... Keshod [*India*] [*Airport symbol*] (OAG)
IXL ... Leh [*India*] [*Airport symbol*] (OAG)
IXM ... Index Manager (MHDI)
IXM ... Interexchange Mileage (SAUS)
IXM ... Madurai [*India*] [*Airport symbol*] (OAG)
IXN ... Khowai [*India*] [*Airport symbol*] (AD)
IXO ... Inlet and Outlet
i-xo- ... Socotra Island [*MARC geographic area code*] [*Library of Congress*] (LCCP)
IXOH ... Inlet and Outlet Head
IXP ... Information Exchange Protocol [*Telecommunications*] (NTCM)
IXP ... Intelligent Polymers, Ltd. [*AMEX symbol*] (NASQ)
IXP ... Ivex Packaging Corp. [*AMEX symbol*] (SAG)
IXP ... Pathankot [*India*] [*Airport symbol*] (AD)
IXQ ... Kamalpur [*India*] [*Airport symbol*] (AD)
I(Xq) ... Long Arm Isochromosome [*Medicine*] (EDAA)
IXR ... Index Register (VLIE)
IXR ... Integrated X-Ray Reflection
IXR ... Intelligent Transparent Restore [*Computer science*] (CIST)
IXR ... Intersection of Runways [*Aviation*]
IXR ... Ranchi [*India*] [*Airport symbol*] (OAG)
IXRALM ... Imaging Soft X-Ray LASER Microscope
IXRDA ... Independent X-Ray Dealers Association (SAUO)
IXS ... Inelastic X-Ray Scattering [*Physics*]
IXS ... Information Exchange System [*or Subsystem*] [*Military*] (CAAL)
IXS ... International XAFS Society (SAUO)
IXS ... Silchar [*India*] [*Airport symbol*] (OAG)
IXSAAZ ... International Council for the Exploration of the Sea. Cooperative Research Report. Series A (journ.) (SAUS)
IXSBBS ... International Council for the Exploration of the Sea. Cooperative Research Report. Series B (journ.) (SAUS)
IXSD ... International Telex Subscriber Dialing (SAUS)
IXSD ... International Telex Subscriber Dialling (NITA)
IXSS ... Unclassified Auxiliary Submarine (SAUS)
IXSS ... Unclassified Miscellaneous Submarine [*Navy symbol*] (NVT)
IXT ... Christian Theological Seminary, Indianapolis, IN [*OCLC symbol*] (OCLC)
IXT ... Interaction Cross Talk [*Telecommunications*] (TEL)
IXT ... Interexchange Channel [*Computer science*] (TNIG)
IXT ... Ixtapalapa [*Mexico*] [*Seismograph station code, US Geological Survey*] [*Closed*] (SEIS)
IXT ... Lineas Aereas de Ixtlan SA de CV [*Mexico*] [*ICAO designator*] (FAAC)
IXT ... Pasighat [*India*] [*Airport symbol*] (AD)
Ixta ... Ixtaccihuatl (SAUS)
IXTR ... Intelligible Crosstalk Ratio
IXU ... Aurangabad [*India*] [*Airport symbol*] (OAG)
IXU ... Index Translation Unit [*Computer science*] (MHDB)
IXV ... Along [*India*] [*Airport symbol*] (AD)
IXW ... Jamshedpur [*India*] [*Airport symbol*] (AD)
IXX ... Dolphin Express Airlines, Inc. [*FAA designator*] (FAAC)
IXX ... Ivex Packaging [*NYSE symbol*] (SG)
IXY ... Kandla [*India*] [*Airport symbol*] (AD)
IXZ ... Port Blair [*Andaman Islands*] [*Airport symbol*] (OAG)
IY ... Imperial Yeomanry [*British*]
Iy ... International Interchangeability (SAUS)
IY ... International Petroleum (SAUS)
Iy ... Ion Implantation (SAUS)
IY ... Ionized Yeast
iy ... Iraq-Saudi Arabia Neutral Zone [*MARC country of publication code*] [*Library of Congress*] (LCCP)
IY ... Yemen Airlines [*Airline flight code*] (ODBW)
IY ... Yemen Airways [*ICAO designator*] (AD)
IYA ... Indian Youth of America (EA)
IYA ... Interlake Yachting Association (SAUO)
IYA ... Irish Yachting Association (EAIO)
IYAP ... Improve Your Army Program (SAUO)
IYAS ... International Yearbook of Agricultural Statistics (SAUO)
IYB ... Imperial Yeomanry Bearer Corps [*British military*] (DMA)
IYB ... International Year Book (SAUS)
IYB ... Israel Year Book (journ.) (SAUS)
IYC ... Individual Yield Coverage Program [*Department of Agriculture*]
IYC ... Inland Yacht Club (SAUO)
IYC ... Institute Yacht Clause (MARI)
IyC ... Inter-IC (SAUS)
IyC ... Inter IC Bus (SAUS)
IyC ... Inter-Integrated Circuits (SAUS)
IYC ... International Year of the Child [*United Nations*] (AEE)
IYC ... International Youth Congress
IYC ... International Youth Council (EA)
IYCM ... International Year of Canadian Music [*1986*]
IYCO ... Ito-Yokado Co. Ltd. [*NASDAQ symbol*] (NQ)
IYCO ... Ito-Yokado Company Ltd. (SAUO)
IYCOY ... Ito Yokado Ltd ADR [*NASDAQ symbol*] (TTSB)
IYCS ... International Young Christian Students (SAUO)
IYCW ... International Young Christian Workers [*See also JOCI*] (EAIO)
IYDP ... International Year of Disabled People (SAUO)
IYDP ... International Year of Disabled Persons (SAUO)
IYDP ... International Year of the Disabled Person [*1981*]
IYDU ... International Young Democratic Union [*Defunct*] (EAIO)
IYE ... Intrest Yield Equivalent (EBF)
IYE ... Yemenia, Yemen Airways [*ICAO designator*] (FAAC)
IYEO ... Institute of Youth Employment Officers (SAUO)
IyF ... Intelligent Influence Fuze (SAUS)
IYF ... International Year of the Family
IYF ... International Youth Federation for Environmental Studies and Conservation (EAIO)
IYF ... International Youth Federation for the Study and Conservation of Nature (SAUO)
IYF ... International Youth Foundation (EA)
IYFP ... Iowa Youth and Families Project
IYFS ... International Young Fish Survey [*Denmark, Great Britain, Norway, West Germany*] [*1987-88*] [*Oceanography*]
IYFS ... International Young Friends Society [*Pakistan*] (EAIO)
IYH ... Imperial Yeomanry Hospitals [*Military*] [*British*] (ROG)
IY'H ... Im Yirtseh Hashem (BJA)
IYH ... Israel Youth Horizon (journ.) (SAUS)
IYHA ... Irish Youth Hostel Association (EAIO)
IYHF ... International Youth Hostel Federation [*See also FAIJ*] [*Welwyn Garden City, Hertfordshire, England*] (EAIO)
IYHR ... Israel Yearbook on Human Rights (journ.) (SAUS)
IYIA ... Indian Yearbook of International Affairs (journ.) (SAUS)
IYIL ... Italian Yearbook of International Law [*A publication*] (SAFN)
IYJGDH ... Italian Journal of Gastroenterology (journ.) (SAUS)
IYK ... Inyokern [*California*] [*Airport symbol*] (OAG)
IYK ... Inyokern, CA [*Location identifier*] [*FAA*] (FAAL)
IyL ... Integrated + Injection Logic (SAUS)
IyL ... Integrated Injection Logic (SAUS)
IyL ... Integrated Injector Logic (SAUS)
IYL ... International Youth Library [*See also IJB*] [*Munich, Federal Republic of Germany*] (EAIO)
IyL ... Ion Implantation Logic (SAUS)
IyL-NPN-Transistor ... Integrated Injection Logic Negative-Positive-Negative Transistor (SAUS)
IyLyAS ... Infantry Issues and Lessons Learned Analysis System (SAUS)
Iy-MOS ... Ion Implantation Metal Oxide Semiconductor (SAUS)
Iy-MOS ... Ion Implanted Metal Oxide Semiconductor (SAUS)
IyO ... Intelligent Input/Output (SAUS)
IYO ... International Year of the Ocean [*1998*] (QUAC)
IYOP ... International Year of Older Persons (SAUO)
IYOR ... International Year of the Reef (SAUS)
IYP ... Instant Yellow Pages [*Information service or system*]
IYPD ... International Year for the Preparation of Disarmament [*Pugwash Conference*]
IYQS ... International Year of the Quiet Sun [*1964-65*] [*Also, IQSY*] (KSC)
IYQS Notes ... International Years of the Quiet Sun Notes (journ.) (SAUS)
IyR ... Resistance Heating (SAUS)
IYRA ... Intercollegiate Yacht Racing Association (PSS)
IYRU ... International Yacht Racing Union [*British*]
IyS ... Integrated Information System (SAUS)
IYS ... Inverted Y-Suspensor [*Medicine*]
IYSH ... International Year of Shelter for the Homeless [*1987*]
IYSWIM ... If You See What I Mean (ADWA)
IySy ... Intelligence Information Subsystem (SAUS)
IYTA ... International Yoga Teachers Association (ADA)
IyTy ... Intelligence Interactive Test Terminal (SAUS)
IYU ... Baylor University, Waco, TX [*OCLC symbol*] (OCLC)
IyV ... Intensifier Squared Vidicon (SAUS)
IYWIP ... International Year of the World's Indigenous People

IYY .... International Youth Year [*1985*] (AIE)
IYYC .... International Youth Year Commission [*Defunct*] (EA)
IZ .... Arkia-Israel Inland Airlines [*ICAO designator*] (AD)
IZ .... Infarction Zone [*Medicine*] (MELL)
IZ .... Informationszentrum Sozialwissenschaften [*Social Sciences Information Center*] [*Information service or system*] (IID)
IZ .... Inspection Zone
IZ .... Institute of Zoology (SAUS)
IZ .... Interfacial Zone
IZ .... Intermediate Zone
IZ .... Intervention Zone (SAUS)
IZ .... Ischemic (DB)
IZ .... Isolation Zone [*Nuclear energy*] (NRCH)
iz .... izzard (SAUS)
IZ .... Spofa Ltd. [*Czechoslovakia*] [*Research code symbol*]
IZ .... Zion-Benton Public Library District, Zion, IL [*Library symbol*] [*Library of Congress*] (LCLS)
IZA .... Independent Zinc Alloyers Association (SAUO)
IZA .... International Zen Association [*Formerly, European Zen Association*] (EA)
IZA .... International Zeolite Association
IZAA .... Independent Zinc Alloyers Association (EA)
IZAA .... Isotope-Shift, Zeeman-Effect Atomic Absorption
IZBA .... International Zebu Breeders Association (EA)
IZBB .... Interagency Zero-Based Budgeting [*Federal government*]
IZC .... International Zetcentrum [*International Typesetting Center, The Netherlands*]
IZC .... International Zoological Congress (SAUO)
IZCA .... International Zuma Class Association (EA)
IZD .... Implanted Zener Diode (MCD)
IZD .... Internationaler Zivildienst [*International Voluntary Service*]
IZE .... Elizabeth City, NC [*Location identifier*] [*FAA*] (FAAL)
IZE .... International Association of Zoo Educators (EA)
IZEPF .... Infarct Zone Subendocardial Purkinje Fiber [*Medicine*] (EDAA)
IZG .... Independent Zimbabwe Group [*Political party*] (PSAP)
IZK .... Iizuka [*Japan*] [*Seismograph station code, US Geological Survey*] [*Closed*] (SEIS)
IZK .... Wilkes-Barre/Scranton, PA [*Location identifier*] [*FAA*] (FAAL)
IZL .... Irgun Zeva'i Le'umi (BJA)
IZM .... Izmir [*Turkey*] [*Airport symbol*] (OAG)
IZM .... Izmir [*Turkey*] [*Seismograph station code, US Geological Survey*] (SEIS)
IZMIRAN ...... Institute of Terrestrial Magnetism, Radio Research and the Ionosphere (SAUO)
IZN .... International Trust for Zoological Nomenclature
IZN .... Izone International Ltd. [*Vancouver Stock Exchange symbol*]
IZO .... Izumo [*Japan*] [*Airport symbol*] (OAG)
iZQC .... Intermolecular Zero-Quantum Coherence [*Physics*]
IZR .... San Antonio, TX [*Location identifier*] [*FAA*] (FAAL)
IZS .... Insulin Zinc Suspension
IZS .... International Zoological Station (SAUO)
IZT .... Integrated Zero-Turn Transaxle [*Automotive engineering*]
IZT .... Ixtepec [*Mexico*] [*Airport symbol*] (AD)
IZTO .... Interzonal Trade Office [*NATO*] (NATG)
IZU .... Izuhara [*Japan*] [*Seismograph station code, US Geological Survey*] (SEIS)
IZUM .... Institute of Information Science (SAUO)
IZWO .... Sea Fisheries Research Station (SAUO)
IZY .... Intermediate Zone Yaw
IZY .... International Zoo Yearbook [*A publication*]
IZZI .... Integrated Security Sys [*NASDAQ symbol*] (TTSB)
IZZI .... Integrated Security Systems [*NASDAQ symbol*] (SAG)
IZZIW .... Integrated Sec Sys Wrrt [*NASDAQ symbol*] (TTSB)